2010-2011 LAW ENFORCEMENT HANDBOOK
QUICK REFERENCE GUIDE

Georgia
Law Enforcement Handbook

Criminal Law & Procedure

2010-2011 Edition

Prepared by
The Editorial Staff
of the Publisher

WEST®
A Thomson Reuters business

For Customer Assistance Call 1-800-328-4880

Mat #40843697

IMPORTANT NOTICE

The statutes and Constitution are current through the 2010 Regular Session of the Georgia General Assembly.

The statutes are subject to changes provided by the Georgia Code Commission. The Georgia Code Commission is authorized by section 28-9-5 of West's Code of Georgia Annotated to correct the spelling of words; change capitalization for the purpose of uniformity; correct manifest typographical and grammatical errors; substitute the proper Code section number, chapter number, or other number or designation for the terms "this Act," "the preceding Code section," and similar words or phrases; renumber, redesignate, and rearrange chapters, articles, parts, subparts, Code sections, or any combination or portion thereof; change cross-reference numbers to agree with renumbered chapters, Code sections, or portions of the Code; substitute the proper calendar date for "the effective date of this chapter" and other phrases of similar import; strike out figures if they are merely a repetition of written words or vice versa, or substitute figures for written words or vice versa for the purpose of uniformity; correct manifest errors in references to laws; correct inaccurate references to the titles of officers, the names of departments or other agencies of the state, local governments, or the federal government, and the short titles of other laws and make such other name changes as are necessary to be consistent with the laws currently in effect; rearrange definitions in alphabetical order; insert or delete hyphens in words so as to follow correct grammatical usage; change numerals or symbols to words or vice versa for purposes of uniformity and style; change nouns from the singular to the plural or vice versa for purposes of style and grammar; and change punctuation for purposes of uniformity and consistency of style.

THE GEORGIA PUBLIC SAFETY MEMORIAL

"WITH HONOR THEY SERVED"

This publication is dedicated to The State of Georgia's law enforcement officers, firefighters, correction officers and emergency medical technicians and their families for their valor, loyalty and commitment to preserving law and order in Georgia and these United States.

Artistic Rendering courtesy of Celeste Edge, Forsyth, GA

2010 LEGISLATIVE CHANGES

Listing sections of the Georgia Constitution and sections of the Code of Georgia Annotated affected by Acts of the 2010 Regular Session of the Georgia General Assembly.

	Effect	Act	Section	Bill/Resolution Number
Ga Const.				
Art. 3, § 6, ¶IV	Amended	—	1	HR 178
Art. 3, § 9, ¶VI	Amended	—	1	SR 277
Art. 7, § 4, ¶XII	Added	—	1	SR 821
	Added	—	1	SR 1231
Art. 11, § 1, ¶IV	Amended	—	1	HR 136
Code Section				
2–1–4	Amended	615	10	SB 388
2–1–5	Amended	360	1-1	HB 1055
2–2–8.1	Amended	360	1-2	HB 1055
2–5–8	Amended	615	10	SB 388
2–7–55	Amended	360	1-3	HB 1055
2–7–57	Amended	360	1-4	HB 1055
2–7–66	Repealed	360	1-4.1	HB 1055
	Reserved	360	1-4.1	HR 1055
2–7–71	Amended	360	1-4.2	HB 1055
2–7–99	Amended	360	1-5	HB 1055
2–9–33	Amended	360	1-6	HB 1055
2–9–42.1	Amended	615	10	SB 388
2–10–53	Amended	615	10	SB 388
2–11–25	Amended	615	10	SB 388
2–11–26	Amended	360	1-7	HB 1055
2–12–4	Amended	360	1-8	HB 1055
2–12–8	Amended	360	1-9	HB 1055
2–12–43	Amended	360	1-10	HB 1055
2–12–73	Amended	360	1-11	HB 1055
2–13–6	Amended	360	1-12	HB 1055
2–14–40	Amended	621	2	SB 296
2–14–102	Amended	360	1-13	HB 1055
2–15–12	Amended	615	10	SB 388
2–21–4	Amended	360	1-14	HB 1055
3–2–2	Amended	615	10	SB 388
3–2–10	Amended	621	2	SB 296
4–4–60	Amended	615	10	SB 388
4–4–82	Amended	360	1-15	HB 1055
4–10–5	Amended	360	1-16	HB 1055
4–11–3	Amended	360	1-17	HB 1055
4–11–5.1	Amended	386	1	HB 788
4–11–5.2	Added	556	1	HB 1106
5–6–35	Amended	389	1	HB 571
7–1–43	Amended	621	2	SB 296
7–1–74	Amended	615	10	SB 388
7–1–242	Amended	506	2	SB 131
7–1–243	Amended	624	7	HB 1387
7–1–285	Amended	346	1	HB 926
7–1–437	Amended	624	7	HB 1387
7–1–653	Amended	624	7	HB 1387
7–1–660	Amended	624	7	HB 1387
7–1–669	Amended	624	7	HB 1387
7–1–683	Amended	624	7	HB 1387
7–1–684.1	Amended	624	7	HB 1387

	Effect	Act	Section	Bill/Resolution Number
Code Section—continued				
7–1–692	Amended	624	7	HB 1387
7–1–700	Amended	624	7	HB 1387
7–1–704	Amended	624	7	HB 1387
7–1–707.2	Amended	624	7	HB 1387
7–1–1001	Amended	624	7	HB 1387
7–1–1002	Amended	624	7	HB 1387
7–1–1003.5	Amended	621	2	SB 296
7–1–1003.7	Amended	624	7	HB 1387
7–1–1004	Amended	624	7	HB 1387
7–1–1009	Amended	624	7	HB 1387
7–1–1011	Amended	360	1-18	HB 1055
7–4–12.1	Amended	624	7	HB 1387
8–2–3	Amended	542	8	SB 370
		634	1	HB 244
8–2–4	Added	461	1	HB 1196
8–2–23	Amended	542	9	SB 370
		634	1	HB 244
8–2–111	Amended	427	1	HB 516
			2	HB 516
8–2–112	Amended	427	3	HB 516
8–2–135	Amended	360	1-19	HB 1055
8–2–135.1	Amended	360	1-20	HB 1055
8–2–161	Amended	360	1-21	HB 1055
		615	10	SB 388
8–2–164	Amended	360	1-22	HB 1055
8–2–170	Added	420	1	SB 384
8–2–171	Added	420	1	SB 384
8–3–30	Amended	445	1	SB 369
8–3–206	Amended	615	10	SB 388
8–3–303	Amended	621	3	SB 296
8–3–304	Amended	621	3	SB 296
8–3–305	Amended	621	2	SB 296
8–3–309	Amended	621	3	SB 296
9–2–8	Added	543	2	SB 138
9–10–91	Amended	611	1	SB 491
9–10–152	Amended	418	9	SB 244
9–11–4	Amended	611	2	SB 491
			3	SB 491
			4	SB 491
9–11–4.1	Added	611	5	SB 491
9–11–133	Amended	624	9	HB 1387
10–1–157	Amended	360	1-23	HB 1055
10–1–159	Amended	360	1-24	HB 1055
10–1–161	Repealed	360	1-25	HB 1055
	Reserved	360	1-25	HR 1055
10–1–187	Amended	615	10	SB 388
10–1–203	Amended	360	1-26	HB 1055
10–1–206	Amended	615	10	SB 388
10–1–392	Amended	372	3	HB 1345
10–1–393	Amended	419	1	SB 368
10–1–393.4	Amended	402	1	SB 237
10–1–393.5	Amended	643	2-1	SB 308
10–1–393.11	Added	372	4	HB 1345
10–1–397	Amended	372	5	HB 1345
		419	2	SB 368
10–1–594	Amended	621	2	SB 296
10–1–622	Amended	645	2	HB 1072
10–1–623	Amended	645	3	HB 1072
10–1–624	Amended	645	4	HB 1072
10–1–627	Amended	645	5	HB 1072
10–1–641	Amended	645	6	HB 1072

	Effect	Act	Section	Bill/Resolution Number
Code Section—continued				
10-1-651	Amended	645	7	HB 1072
10-1-661	Amended	645	8	HB 1072
10-1-662	Amended	645	9	HB 1072
10-2-42	Amended	360	1-27	HB 1055
10-4-12	Amended	360	1-28	HB 1055
10-4-17	Amended	360	1-29	HB 1055
10-4-31	Amended	615	10	SB 388
10-4-101	Amended	360	1-30	HB 1055
10-4-115	Amended	360	1-31	HB 1055
10-4-142	Amended	360	1-32	HB 1055
10-5-25	Amended	615	10	SB 388
10-5-71	Amended	615	10	SB 388
10-5A-20	Amended	615	10	SB 388
10-6-142	Amended	506	3	SB 131
10-10-7	Amended	615	10	SB 388
10-14-6	Amended	506	4	SB 131
11-1-201	Amended	470	2-1	HB 451
11-2-103	Amended	470	2-2	HB 451
11-2-104	Amended	470	2-3	HB 451
11-2-310	Amended	470	2-4	HB 451
11-2-323	Amended	470	2-5	HB 451
11-2-401	Amended	470	2-6	HB 451
11-2-503	Amended	470	2-7	HB 451
11-2-505	Amended	470	2-8	HB 451
11-2-506	Amended	470	2-9	HB 451
11-2-509	Amended	470	2-10	HB 451
11-2-605	Amended	470	2-11	HB 451
11-2-705	Amended	470	2-12	HB 451
11-2A-103	Amended	470	2-13	HB 451
11-2A-514	Amended	470	2-14	HB 451
11-2A-526	Amended	470	2-15	HB 451
11-4-104	Amended	470	2-16	HB 451
11-4-210	Amended	470	2-17	HB 451
11-7-101	Amended	470	1-1	HB 451
11-7-102	Amended	470	1-1	HB 451
11-7-103	Amended	470	1-1	HB 451
11-7-104	Amended	470	1-1	HB 451
11-7-105	Amended	470	1-1	HB 451
11-7-106	Added	470	1-1	HB 451
11-7-201	Amended	470	1-1	HB 451
11-7-202	Amended	470	1-1	HB 451
11-7-203	Amended	470	1-1	HB 451
11-7-204	Amended	470	1-1	HB 451
11-7-205	Amended	470	1-1	HB 451
11-7-206	Amended	470	1-1	HB 451
11-7-207	Amended	470	1-1	HB 451
11-7-208	Amended	470	1-1	HB 451
11-7-209	Amended	470	1-1	HB 451
11-7-210	Amended	470	1-1	HB 451
11-7-301	Amended	470	1-1	HB 451
11-7-302	Amended	470	1-1	HB 451
11-7-303	Amended	470	1-1	HB 451
11-7-304	Amended	470	1-1	HB 451
11-7-305	Amended	470	1-1	HB 451
11-7-306	Amended	470	1-1	HB 451
11-7-307	Amended	470	1-1	HB 451
11-7-308	Amended	470	1-1	HB 451
11-7-309	Amended	470	1-1	HB 451
11-7-401	Amended	470	1-1	HB 451
11-7-402	Amended	470	1-1	HB 451
11-7-403	Amended	470	1-1	HB 451

	Effect	Act	Section	Bill/Resolution Number
Code Section—continued				
11–7–404	Amended	470	1-1	HB 451
11–7–501	Amended	470	1-1	HB 451
11–7–502	Amended	470	1-1	HB 451
11–7–503	Amended	470	1-1	HB 451
11–7–504	Amended	470	1-1	HB 451
11–7–505	Amended	470	1-1	HB 451
11–7–506	Amended	470	1-1	HB 451
11–7–507	Amended	470	1-1	HB 451
11–7–508	Amended	470	1-1	HB 451
11–7–509	Amended	470	1-1	HB 451
11–7–601	Amended	470	1-1	HB 451
11–7–602	Amended	470	1-1	HB 451
11–7–603	Amended	470	1-1	HB 451
11–8–103	Amended	470	2-18	HB 451
11–8–602	Repealed	506	5	SB 131
11–9–102	Amended	470	2-19	HB 451
11–9–203	Amended	470	2-20	HB 451
11–9–207	Amended	470	2-21	HB 451
11–9–208	Amended	470	2-22	HB 451
11–9–301	Amended	470	2-23	HB 451
11–9–310	Amended	470	2-24	HB 451
11–9–312	Amended	470	2-25	HB 451
11–9–313	Amended	470	2-26	HB 451
11–9–314	Amended	470	2-27	HB 451
11–9–317	Amended	470	2-28	HB 451
11–9–338	Amended	470	2-29	HB 451
11–9–406	Amended	506	6	SB 131
11–9–408	Amended	506	7	SB 131
11–9–526	Amended	615	10	SB 388
12–2–3	Amended	615	11	SB 388
12–2–4	Amended	615	11	SB 388
12–2–6	Amended	369	1	HB 1199
12–3–10	Amended	643	2-2	SB 308
12–3–34	Amended	373	1	SB 99
12–3–53	Amended	615	11	SB 388
12–3–93	Amended	615	10	SB 388
12–3–241	Amended	621	2	SB 296
12–3–522.1	Added	431	2	SB 523
12–3–550	Amended	431	3	SB 523
12–3–551	Amended	431	3	SB 523
12–3–552	Amended	431	3	SB 523
12–3–553	Amended	431	3	SB 523
12–3–554	Amended	431	3	SB 523
12–3–562	Amended	431	1	SB 523
12–3–562.1	Added	431	1	SB 523
12–3–580	Repealed	547	1	SB 449
12–3–581	Repealed	547	1	SB 449
12–3–582	Repealed	547	1	SB 449
12–3–583	Repealed	547	1	SB 449
12–3–584	Repealed	547	1	SB 449
12–3–585	Repealed	547	1	SB 449
12–3–586	Repealed	547	1	SB 449
12–3–587	Repealed	547	1	SB 449
12–3–588	Repealed	547	1	SB 449
12–3–589	Repealed	547	1	SB 449
12–3–590	Repealed	547	1	SB 449
12–3–591	Repealed	547	1	SB 449
12–3–592	Repealed	547	1	SB 449
12–3–651	Amended	378	1	HB 1090
12–3–662	Added	378	2	HB 1090
12–4–1	Amended	615	10	SB 388

Code Section	Effect	Act	Section	Bill/Resolution Number
Code Section—continued				
12–4–73	Amended	615	10	SB 388
12–4–101	Amended	621	2	SB 296
12–5–1	Amended	615	10	SB 388
12–5–4	Added	542	2	SB 370
12–5–4.1	Added	542	3	SB 370
12–5–7	Amended	542	4	SB 370
12–5–9	Added	364	1	HB 169
12–5–31	Amended	542	5	SB 370
12–5–38.1	Amended	634	1	HB 244
12–5–105	Amended	542	6	SB 370
12–5–122	Amended	411	1	HB 1206
12–5–125	Amended	411	2	HB 1206
12–5–134	Amended	411	3	HB 1206
12–5–135	Amended	624	12	HB 1387
12–5–180.1	Amended	542	7	SB 370
12–5–200	Added	397	2	SB 380
12–5–201	Added	397	2	SB 380
12–5–202	Added	397	2	SB 380
12–5–203	Added	397	2	SB 380
12–5–204	Added	397	2	SB 380
12–5–211	Amended	615	10	SB 388
12–5–471	Amended	634	1	HB 244
12–5–482	Amended	621	3	SB 296
12–5–524	Amended	634	1	HB 244
12–5–542	Amended	634	1	HB 244
12–5–580	Amended	634	1	HB 244
12–5–582	Amended	615	10	SB 388
12–5–583	Amended	615	10	SB 388
12–5–584	Amended	615	10	SB 388
12–6–5	Amended	615	10	SB 388
12–6–93	Amended	360	1-33	HB 1055
12–6A–2	Amended	634	1	HB 244
		668	1	SB 402
12–7–6	Amended	481	1	HB 1359
12–8–23.1	Amended	634	1	HB 244
12–8–24	Amended	407	1	HB 1059
12–8–31	Amended	634	1	HB 244
12–8–62	Amended	488	4	SB 78
		612	1	SB 490
12–8–92	Amended	488	5	SB 78
		612	2	SB 490
12–8–97	Amended	615	10	SB 388
12–8–102	Amended	624	12	HB 1387
12–8–104	Amended	488	1	SB 78
12–8–104.1	Added	488	2	SB 78
12–8–107	Amended	488	3	SB 78
12–8–108	Amended	488	3	SB 78
		624	12	HB 1387
12–11–4	Amended	428	1	HB 493
12–11–5	Amended	428	2	HB 493
12–11–7	Amended	428	2A	HB 493
12–11–8	Amended	428	3	HB 493
13–1–11	Amended	624	13	HB 1387
13–2–2	Amended	624	13	HB 1387
13–10–3	Added	421	1	SB 447
13–10–90	Amended	421	2	SB 447
13–10–91	Amended	421	2.A	SB 447
14–2–122	Amended	360	1-34	HB 1055
14–2–1109	Amended	506	8	SB 131
14–2–1110	Amended	506	9	SB 131
14–2–1408	Amended	621	2	SB 296

	Effect	Act	Section	Bill/Resolution Number
Code Section—continued				
14–2–1433	Amended	621	2	SB 296
14–2–1440	Amended	621	2	SB 296
14–3–1108	Amended	506	10	SB 131
14–3–1409	Amended	621	2	SB 296
14–3–1409.1	Amended	624	14	HB 1387
14–3–1433	Amended	621	2	SB 296
14–3–1440	Amended	621	2	SB 296
14–9–1101	Amended	360	1-35	HB 1055
14–10–4	Amended	360	1-36	HB 1055
14–11–1101	Amended	360	1-37	HB 1055
15–2–43	Amended	621	2	SB 296
15–5–21	Amended	624	15	HB 1387
15–5–24	Amended	615	10	SB 388
15–6–77	Amended	360	1-38	HB 1055
15–6–77.3	Amended	506	11	SB 131
15–9–30.8	Added	365	2-1	HB 207
15–9–60	Amended	360	1-39	HB 1055
		643	2-3	SB 308
15–9–127	Amended	506	12	SB 131
15–10–80	Amended	360	1-40	HB 1055
15–10–81	Amended	360	1-41	HB 1055
15–10–82	Amended	360	1-42	HB 1055
15–11–19	Amended	615	10	SB 388
15–11–30.3	Amended	674	1	HB 1104
15–11–40.1	Added	674	2	HB 1104
15–11–55	Amended	418	10	SB 244
15–11–58	Amended	469	1	HB 1085
			2	HB 1085
			3	HB 1085
15–11–63	Amended	465	1	SB 299
		674	3	HB 1104
			4	HB 1104
15–11–64.2	Amended	403	1	HB 567
15–11–66	Amended	674	5	HB 1104
15–11–78	Amended	403	2	HB 567
15–11–84	Amended	624	15	HB 1387
15–11–103	Amended	418	11	SB 244
15–11–154	Amended	624	15	HB 1387
15–11–155	Amended	403	3	HB 567
15–12–68	Amended	620	1	SB 313
15–16–21	Amended	360	1-43	HB 1055
15–21–74	Amended	621	2	SB 296
15–21–147	Amended	464	1	HB 1310
		621	3	SB 296
15–21–148	Amended	621	3	SB 296
15–21–180	Amended	621	2	SB 296
15–21–181	Amended	621	2	SB 296
15–21A–6	Amended	360	1-43.1	HB 1055
15–21A–6.1	Added	360	1-44	HB 1055
15–21A–6.2	Added	360	1-44	HB 1055
15–21A–7	Amended	624	15	HB 1387
16–5–21	Amended	646	1	HB 1002
16–6–5.1	Amended	389	2	HB 571
16–6–22	Amended	389	3	HB 571
16–7–2	Added	674	6	HB 1104
16–7–29	Amended	389	4	HB 571
16–8–104	Amended	678	1	SB 371
16–9–121	Amended	501	1	HB 1016
16–9–128	Amended	501	2	HB 1016
16–9–151	Amended	422	1	SB 470
16–9–154	Amended	422	2	SB 470

	Effect	Act	Section	Bill/Resolution Number
Code Section—continued				
16–10–4	Amended	680	24	SB 17
16–10–5	Amended	680	25	SB 17
16–10–6	Amended	405	1	HB 1007
16–10–51	Amended	643	2-4	SB 308
16–10–97	Amended	646	2	HB 1002
16–11–34.1	Amended	643	2-5	SB 308
16–11–37	Amended	646	3	HB 1002
16–11–37.1	Amended	646	4	HB 1002
16–11–101.1	Amended	643	2-6	SB 308
16–11–125.1	Added	643	1-1	SB 308
16–11–126	Amended	643	1-2	SB 308
16–11–127	Amended	643	1-3	SB 308
16–11–127.1	Amended	465	2	SB 299
		643	1-4	SB 308
16–11–127.2	Amended	643	1-5	SB 308
16–11–128	Amended	643	1-6	SB 308
16–11–129	Amended	643	1-7	SB 308
16–11–130	Amended	643	2-7	SB 308
16–11–132	Amended	643	1-8	SB 308
16–11–135	Amended	643	1-9	SB 308
16–12–1	Amended	674	7	HB 1104
16–12–120	Amended	624	16	HB 1387
16–12–123	Amended	643	2-8	SB 308
16–12–127	Amended	643	2-9	SB 308
16–13–25	Amended	433	1	HB 1309
		619	1	SB 353
16–13–26	Amended	619	2	SB 353
16–13–28	Amended	619	3	SB 353
16–13–29	Amended	619	4	SB 353
16–13–71	Amended	619	5	SB 353
			6	SB 353
			7	SB 353
		629	1	HB 1021
16–13–72	Amended	629	2	HB 1021
16–14–3	Amended	674	8	HB 1104
16–15–2	Amended	406	1	HB 1015
16–15–3	Amended	406	2	HB 1015
16–15–4	Amended	406	3	HB 1015
16–15–7	Amended	406	4	HB 1015
16–15–9	Amended	406	5	HB 1015
16–15–10	Amended	406	6	HB 1015
16–15–11	Added	406	7	HB 1015
17–4–40	Amended	423	1	HB 199
17–5–51	Amended	643	2-10	SB 308
17–6–1	Amended	404	1	HB 889
		406	8	HB 1015
			9	HB 1015
17–6–12	Amended	404	2	HB 889
17–7–23	Amended	643	2-11	SB 308
17–7–130	Amended	418	12	SB 244
17–8–30	Amended	418	13	SB 244
17–10–1	Amended	406	10	HB 1015
17–10–1.2	Amended	403	4	HB 567
17–10–7	Amended	498	1	HB 901
17–10–11	Amended	674	9	HB 1104
17–10–35.1	Amended	452	1	HB 323
17–10–37	Amended	452	2	HB 323
17–12–6	Amended	615	10	SB 388
17–12–22	Amended	404	2A	HB 889
17–14–3	Amended	403	5	HB 567
17–17–1	Amended	403	6	HB 567

	Effect	Act	Section	Bill/Resolution Number
Code Section—continued				
17–17–3	Amended	403	7	HB 567
17–17–5	Amended	403	8	HB 567
17–17–5.1	Added	403	9	HB 567
17–17–8	Amended	403	10	HB 567
17–17–8.1	Added	403	11	HB 567
17–17–9	Amended	403	12	HB 567
17–17–9.1	Added	403	13	HB 567
17–17–12	Amended	403	14	HB 567
17–17–12.1	Added	403	15	HB 567
19–3–30	Amended	439	1	SB 238
19–3–39	Amended	439	2	SB 238
19–3–42	Amended	439	3	SB 238
19–3–46	Amended	439	4	SB 238
19–3–48	Amended	439	5	SB 238
19–6–15	Amended	624	19	HB 1387
19–6–51	Amended	624	19	HB 1387
19–6–53	Amended	615	10	SB 388
19–7–1	Amended	624	19	HB 1387
19–9–127	Amended	624	19	HB 1387
19–9–129	Amended	624	19	HB 1387
19–11–3	Amended	410	1	HB 1118
19–11–9	Amended	621	2	SB 296
19–11–12	Amended	410	2	HB 1118
19–11–26	Amended	410	3	HB 1118
19–11–27	Amended	410	4	HB 1118
19–11–28	Amended	410	5	HB 1118
19–11–29	Amended	410	6	HB 1118
19–11–31	Reserved	624	19	HB 1387
19–13–17	Amended	621	2	SB 296
19–14–21	Amended	621	3	SB 296
19–14–22	Amended	621	3	SB 296
19–15–2	Amended	418	14	SB 244
20–1–10	Added	447	1	SB 392
20–1A–4	Amended	360	1-45	HB 1055
20–1A–10	Amended	360	1-46	HB 1055
		615	10	SB 388
20–1A–12	Amended	360	1-46.1	HB 1055
20–2–14.1	Added	448	1	SB 427
20–2–49	Added	463	1	SB 84
20–2–51	Amended	463	2	SB 84
20–2–52	Amended	463	3	SB 84
20–2–55	Amended	463	4	SB 84
20–2–57	Amended	463	5	SB 84
20–2–61	Amended	463	6	SB 84
20–2–63	Amended	463	7	SB 84
20–2–64	Amended	506	13	SB 131
20–2–72	Added	463	8	SB 84
		626	1	HB 1200
20–2–73	Added	463	8	SB 84
20–2–82	Amended	408	1C	HB 1079
20–2–101	Amended	463	9	SB 84
20–2–133	Amended	418	15	SB 244
20–2–142	Amended	449	1	SB 518
20–2–157	Amended	441	1	SB 340
20–2–161	Amended	615	10	SB 388
20–2–167	Amended	384	1	HB 908
20–2–182	Amended	384	3	HB 908
20–2–184.1	Amended	384	4	HB 908
20–2–188	Amended	647	1	HB 936
20–2–200	Amended	408	1	HB 1079
			1D	HB 1079

Code Section	Effect	Act	Section	Bill/Resolution Number
Code Section—continued				
20–2–200	Amended	413	1	HB 1307
20–2–211	Amended	349	1	HB 906
		408	1A	HB 1079
20–2–211.1	Added	408	1B	HB 1079
20–2–212	Amended	456	1	HB 923
20–2–212.6	Added	367	1	HB 977
20–2–230	Amended	463	10	SB 84
20–2–244	Amended	384	5	HB 908
		408	1E	HB 1079
20–2–250	Amended	418	16	SB 244
20–2–257	Amended	624	20	HB 1387
20–2–260	Amended	385	1	HB 905
			2	HB 905
20–2–262	Amended	385	3	HB 905
20–2–281	Amended	390	2	HB 400
20–2–315	Amended	383	1	HB 910
20–2–325	Added	390	1	HB 400
20–2–326	Added	390	1	HB 400
20–2–327	Added	390	1	HB 400
20–2–328	Added	390	1	HB 400
20–2–329	Added	390	1	HB 400
20–2–329.1	Added	390	1	HB 400
20–2–500	Amended	421	3	SB 447
20–2–520	Amended	544	0.5	HB 703
20–2–552	Amended	647	2	HB 936
20–2–553	Amended	647	3	HB 936
20–2–555	Amended	647	4	HB 936
20–2–556	Amended	647	5	HB 936
20–2–559	Amended	647	6	HB 936
20–2–560	Amended	647	7	HB 936
20–2–564	Amended	621	2	SB 296
		647	8	HB 936
20–2–567	Amended	647	9	HB 936
20–2–568	Amended	647	10	HB 936
20–2–569	Amended	647	11	HB 936
20–2–570	Amended	647	12	HB 936
20–2–571	Amended	647	13	HB 936
20–2–572	Amended	647	14	HB 936
20–2–577	Amended	647	15	HB 936
20–2–751.4	Amended	471	2	SB 250
20–2–881	Amended	615	10	SB 388
20–2–891	Amended	621	2	SB 296
			3	SB 296
20–2–911	Amended	615	10	SB 388
20–2–919	Amended	621	2	SB 296
			3	SB 296
20–2–982.1	Amended	408	1F	HB 1079
20–2–1010	Amended	490	1	SB 319
20–2–1181	Amended	471	3	SB 250
20–2–1184	Amended	643	2-12	SB 308
20–2–2064	Amended	492	1	SB 457
20–2–2065	Amended	408	1G	HB 1079
20–3–55	Amended	621	2	SB 296
20–3–63	Amended	621	2	SB 296
20–3–86	Amended	505	2-1	HB 1128
20–3–241	Amended	615	10	SB 388
20–3–242	Added	446	1	SB 387
20–3–250.27	Amended	621	3	SB 296
20–3–294	Amended	615	10	SB 388
20–3–328	Amended	615	10	SB 388
20–3–423	Amended	615	10	SB 388

	Effect	Act	Section	Bill/Resolution Number
Code Section—continued				
20–3–513	Amended	418	17	SB 244
20–3–519.6	Amended	442	1	SB 341
20–3–632	Amended	621	5	SB 296
20–3–633	Amended	621	3	SB 296
20–3–635	Amended	621	2	SB 296
			4	SB 296
20–3–637	Amended	621	4	SB 296
20–4–3	Amended	621	2	SB 296
20–4–17	Amended	624	20	HB 1387
20–4–21.1	Amended	505	2-2	HB 1128
21–2–2	Amended	632	1	HB 540
21–2–13	Amended	621	3	SB 296
21–2–31	Amended	615	10	SB 388
21–2–90	Amended	632	2	HB 540
21–2–92	Amended	632	3	HB 540
21–2–98	Amended	632	4	HB 540
21–2–101	Amended	632	5	HB 540
21–2–171	Amended	632	6	HB 540
21–2–212	Amended	632	7	HB 540
21–2–219	Amended	502	1	HB 1073
		632	8	HB 540
21–2–223	Amended	632	9	HB 540
21–2–224	Amended	632	10	HB 540
21–2–225	Amended	632	11	HB 540
21–2–230	Amended	632	12	HB 540
21–2–235	Amended	632	13	HB 540
21–2–284	Amended	632	14	HB 540
21–2–291	Amended	632	15	HB 540
21–2–379.8	Amended	632	16	HB 540
21–2–380	Amended	632	17	HB 540
21–2–381	Amended	502	2	HB 1073
		632	18	HB 540
21–2–381.1	Amended	502	3	HB 1073
21–2–382	Amended	632	19	HB 540
21–2–383	Amended	632	20	HB 540
21–2–384	Amended	502	4	HB 1073
			5	HB 1073
21–2–385	Amended	632	21	HB 540
21–2–387	Amended	557	1	HB 665
21–2–414	Amended	632	22	HB 540
21–2–419	Amended	632	23	HB 540
21–2–501	Amended	632	24	HB 540
21–2–540	Amended	632	25	HB 540
21–2–562	Amended	632	26	HB 540
21–2–568	Amended	632	27	HB 540
21–2–574	Amended	632	28	HB 540
21–2–575	Amended	632	29	HB 540
21–2–576	Amended	632	30	HB 540
21–2–578	Amended	632	31	HB 540
21–2–579	Amended	632	32	HB 540
21–2–587	Amended	632	33	HB 540
21–2–588	Amended	632	34	HB 540
21–2–594	Amended	632	35	HB 540
21–5–3	Amended	680	2	SB 17
21–5–4	Amended	680	3	SB 17
21–5–5	Amended	680	4	SB 17
21–5–6	Amended	615	10	SB 388
		680	5	SB 17
21–5–7.1	Amended	680	6	SB 17
21–5–11	Amended	680	7	SB 17
21–5–13	Amended	680	8	SB 17

	Effect	Act	Section	Bill/Resolution Number
Code Section—continued				
21–5–14	Added	680	9	SB 17
21–5–30	Amended	621	3	SB 296
		680	10	SB 17
21–5–34	Amended	360	1-47	HB 1055
		680	11	SB 17
21–5–34.1	Amended	680	12	SB 17
21–5–36	Amended	680	13	SB 17
21–5–40	Amended	680	14	SB 17
21–5–41	Amended	680	15	SB 17
21–5–50	Amended	360	1-48	HB 1055
		680	16	SB 17
21–5–51	Amended	680	17	SB 17
21–5–52	Repealed	680	18	SB 17
21–5–53	Repealed	680	19	SB 17
21–5–70	Amended	680	20	SB 17
21–5–71	Amended	360	1-49	HB 1055
		615	10	SB 388
		680	21	SB 17
21–5–73	Amended	680	22	SB 17
21–5–76	Amended	680	23	SB 17
24–4–23.1	Amended	624	24	HB 1387
24–9–61.1	Amended	403	16	HB 567
24–9–100	Amended	624	24	HB 1387
24–10–27.1	Amended	624	24	HB 1387
24–10–97	Amended	624	24	HB 1387
25–2–4.1	Amended	360	1-50	HB 1055
25–2–20	Amended	360	1-50.1	HB 1055
25–4–6	Amended	624	25	HB 1387
25–10–5	Amended	360	1-51	HB 1055
25–11–4	Amended	360	1-52	HB 1055
25–11–5	Amended	360	1-53	HB 1055
25–11–6	Amended	360	1-54	HB 1055
25–11–7	Amended	360	1-55	HB 1055
25–12–8	Amended	360	1-56	HB 1055
25–14–4	Amended	624	25	HB 1387
26–2–25	Amended	360	1-57	HB 1055
26–2–27.1	Amended	466	2	HB 883
			3	HB 883
			4	HB 883
26–2–232	Amended	615	10	SB 388
26–2–312	Amended	360	1-58	HB 1055
26–2–411	Amended	360	1-59	HB 1055
26–4–5	Amended	417	1	SB 195
26–4–29	Amended	615	10	SB 388
26–4–41	Amended	417	2	SB 195
26–4–42	Amended	417	3	SB 195
26–4–46	Amended	417	4	SB 195
26–4–81	Amended	417	5	SB 195
		494	1	HB 194
26–4–210	Added	392	1	HB 361
26–4–211	Added	392	1	HB 361
26–4–212	Added	392	1	HB 361
26–4–213	Added	392	1	HB 361
26–4–214	Added	392	1	HB 361
27–1–2	Amended	635	1	SB 474
27–1–6	Amended	615	10	SB 388
27–1–39	Amended	635	2	SB 474
27–2–3.1	Amended	624	27	HB 1387
27–2–7	Amended	624	27	HB 1387
27–2–30	Amended	621	3	SB 296
27–2–41	Amended	615	10	SB 388

	Effect	Act	Section	Bill/Resolution Number
Code Section—continued				
27–3–1.1	Amended	643	2-13	SB 308
27–3–4	Amended	635	3	SB 474
27–3–6	Amended	643	2-14	SB 308
27–3–15	Amended	635	4	SB 474
27–3–19.1	Added	635	5	SB 474
27–3–26	Amended	635	6	SB 474
27–3–28	Added	635	7	SB 474
27–3–47	Repealed and Reserved	635	8	SB 474
27–3–180	Added	635	9	SB 474
27–3–181	Added	635	9	SB 474
27–3–182	Added	635	9	SB 474
27–3–183	Added	635	9	SB 474
27–3–184	Added	635	9	SB 474
27–3–185	Added	635	9	SB 474
27–4–11.1	Amended	643	2-15	SB 308
27–4–130.1	Amended	635	10	SB 474
27–4–262	Amended	615	10	SB 388
28–4–3	Amended	615	1	SB 388
28–5–122	Amended	615	10	SB 388
28–12–1	Added	541	1	HB 1405
28–12–2	Added	541	1	HB 1405
28–12–3	Added	541	1	HB 1405
28–12–4	Added	541	1	HB 1405
29–3–32	Amended	506	14	SB 131
29–4–18	Added	616	2	SB 367
29–5–32	Amended	506	15	SB 131
30–5–8	Amended	624	30	HB 1387
31–1–11	Added	548	1	SB 411
31–2–4	Amended	650	1	HB 994
31–2–14	Amended	624	31	HB 1387
31–2–17.1	Added	491	1-3	SB 435
31–7–18	Amended	486	1	HB 1179
31–8–35	Amended	621	3	SB 296
31–8–133	Amended	624	31	HB 1387
31–8–152	Amended	621	3	SB 296
31–8–157	Amended	621	3	SB 296
31–8–158	Amended	621	3	SB 296
31–8–179	Added	360	2-1	HB 1055
31–8–179.1	Added	360	2-1	HB 1055
31–8–179.2	Added	360	2-1	HB 1055
31–8–179.3	Added	360	2-1	HB 1055
31–8–179.4	Added	360	2-1	HB 1055
31–8–179.5	Added	360	2-1	HB 1055
31–8–179.6	Added	360	2-1	HB 1055
31–8–179.7	Added	360	2-1	HB 1055
31–8–179.8	Added	360	2-1	HB 1055
31–8–195.1	Amended	399	1	SB 344
31–9–2	Amended	616	1	SB 367
31–10–1	Amended	615	11	SB 388
31–10–5	Amended	615	10	SB 388
31–10–15	Amended	546	1	SB 493
		624	31	HB 1387
		632	36	HB 540
31–12A–9	Amended	615	11	SB 388
31–21–7	Amended	398	1	SB 355
31–22–2	Amended	615	10	SB 388
31–33–4	Amended	418	18	SB 244
31–33–8	Amended	418	19	SB 244
31–34–1	Amended	429	1	HB 866
31–34–2	Amended	429	1	HB 866
31–34–3	Amended	429	1	HB 866

	Effect	Act	Section	Bill/Resolution Number
Code Section—continued				
31-34-4	Amended	429	1	HB 866
31-34-4.1	Added	429	1	HB 866
31-34-5	Amended	429	1	HB 866
31-34-6	Amended	429	1	HB 866
31-34-7	Amended	429	1	HB 866
31-34-8	Amended	429	1	HB 866
31-34-9	Amended	429	1	HB 866
31-38-4.1	Added	491	2-1	SB 435
31-38-8	Amended	491	2-2	SB 435
31-41-1	Amended	488	6	SB 78
31-41-2	Amended	488	6	SB 78
31-41-3	Amended	488	6	SB 78
31-41-4	Amended	488	6	SB 78
31-41-5	Amended	488	6	SB 78
31-47-1	Added	673	4	HB 1119
31-47-2	Added	673	4	HB 1119
31-47-3	Added	673	4	HB 1119
32-2-2	Amended	621	3	SB 296
32-2-20	Amended	610	1	SB 520
32-2-41	Amended	440	1	SB 305
		554	1.1	HB 277
		610	2	SB 520
32-2-41.2	Amended	615	10	SB 388
32-2-43	Amended	554	2	HB 277
32-2-66	Amended	615	10	SB 388
32-2-81	Amended	440	1	SB 305
32-5-1	Amended	621	3	SB 296
32-5-2	Amended	621	3	SB 296
32-6-24	Amended	460	1	HB 1174
32-6-27	Amended	460	2	HB 1174
32-6-28	Amended	460	3	HB 1174
32-6-75.2	Amended	360	1-60	HB 1055
32-7-2	Amended	443	1	SB 354
32-9-4	Amended	360	1-61	HB 1055
32-9-8	Amended	360	1-62	HB 1055
32-9-13	Added	554	3	HB 277
32-9-14	Added	554	3	HB 277
32-12-1	Added	554	4	HB 277
32-12-2	Added	554	4	HB 277
32-12-3	Added	554	4	HB 277
32-12-4	Added	554	4	HB 277
32-12-5	Added	554	4	HB 277
32-12-6	Added	554	4	HB 277
33-2-24	Amended	360	1-63	HB 1055
33-2-29	Amended	621	2	SB 296
33-5-32	Amended	621	2	SB 296
33-21-17	Amended	621	2	SB 296
33-21A-4	Amended	615	10	SB 388
33-24-21.1	Amended	362	1	HB 1268
33-24-59.13	Added	548	2	SB 411
33-34-5.1	Amended	366	1	HB 656
33-35-15	Amended	621	2	SB 296
33-36-11	Amended	666	1	HB 1364
33-36-14	Amended	666	2	HB 1364
33-36-20	Added	666	3	HB 1364
33-41-20.1	Amended	666	4	HB 1364
33-43-3	Amended	374	1	SB 316
33-50-3	Amended	549	2	SB 310
33-50-5	Amended	549	3	SB 310
33-50-6	Amended	549	4	SB 310
33-50-7	Amended	549	5	SB 310

	Effect	Act	Section	Bill/Resolution Number
Code Section—continued				
33-50-14	Added	549	6	SB 310
33-59-2	Amended	624	33	HB 1387
33-64-1	Added	549	1	SB 310
33-64-2	Added	549	1	SB 310
33-64-3	Added	549	1	SB 310
33-64-4	Added	549	1	SB 310
33-64-5	Added	549	1	SB 310
33-64-6	Added	549	1	SB 310
33-64-7	Added	549	1	SB 310
34-2-6	Amended	615	10	SB 388
34-8-76	Amended	615	10	SB 388
34-8-177	Amended	621	2	SB 296
34-8-197	Amended	624	34	HB 1387
34-9-12	Amended	377	1	HB 1101
34-9-40	Amended	621	2	SB 296
34-9-61	Amended	615	10	SB 388
34-9-106	Amended	377	2	HB 1101
34-9-127	Amended	377	3	HB 1101
34-9-129	Amended	621	2	SB 296
34-9-205	Amended	615	10	SB 388
34-9-352	Amended	621	3	SB 296
34-9-380	Amended	377	4	HB 1101
34-9-381	Amended	377	4	HB 1101
34-9-382	Amended	377	4	HB 1101
34-9-383	Amended	377	4	HB 1101
34-9-384	Amended	377	4	HB 1101
34-9-385	Amended	377	4	HB 1101
34-9-386	Amended	377	4	HB 1101
34-9-387	Amended	377	4	HB 1101
34-9-388	Amended	377	4	HB 1101
34-9-389	Amended	377	4	HB 1101
34-11-8	Amended	615	10	SB 388
34-14-1	Added	361	1	HB 1195
34-14-2	Added	361	1	HB 1195
34-14-3	Added	361	1	HB 1195
34-14-4	Added	361	1	HB 1195
34-15-7	Amended	621	2	SB 296
34-15-16	Amended	621	2	SB 296
35-2-120	Added	379	1	HB 1074
35-2-121	Added	379	1	HB 1074
35-2-122	Added	379	1	HB 1074
35-2-123	Added	379	1	HB 1074
35-2-124	Added	379	1	HB 1074
35-3-4	Amended	678	2	SB 371
35-3-4.2	Added	678	3	SB 371
35-3-33	Amended	615	10	SB 388
35-3-191	Added	473	1	SB 397
35-6A-5	Amended	622	1	SB 173
35-6A-7	Amended	615	10	SB 388
		622	2	SB 173
35-6A-9	Amended	622	3	SB 173
35-8-7	Amended	401	1	SB 324
36-9-3	Amended	544	1	HB 703
		663	1	SB 390
36-15-7	Amended	495	1	HB 858
36-15-11	Amended	495	2	HB 858
36-17-2	Amended	621	2	SB 296
			3	SB 296
36-17-3	Amended	621	2	SB 296
36-31-11.1	Added	353	1	HB 203
36-37-6	Amended	663	2	SB 390

	Effect	Act	Section	Bill/Resolution Number
Code Section—continued				
36–40–22	Amended	621	2	SB 296
36–40–24	Amended	621	2	SB 296
36–40–42	Amended	621	2	SB 296
36–40–44	Amended	621	2	SB 296
36–40–45	Amended	621	2	SB 296
36–40–46	Amended	621	2	SB 296
36–42–3	Amended	415	1	HB 1388
36–44–3	Amended	624	36	HB 1387
36–60–17.1	Amended	634	1	HB 244
36–61–19	Amended	613	1	SB 456
36–62–2	Amended	415	2	HB 1388
36–62–5	Amended	613	2	SB 456
36–62A–1	Amended	613	3	SB 456
36–66B–1	Added	430	1	SB 432
36–66B–2	Added	430	1	SB 432
36–66B–3	Added	430	1	SB 432
36–66B–4	Added	430	1	SB 432
36–70–27	Amended	667	1	HB 406
36–75–11	Amended	353	2	HB 203
36–80–15	Amended	621	3	SB 296
			4	SB 296
36–80–21	Added	472	1	HB 122
36–82–7	Amended	445	2	SB 369
36–83–7	Amended	621	3	SB 296
36–83–8	Amended	621	3	SB 296
			4	SB 296
36–89–3	Amended	624	36	HB 1387
37–1–6	Added	418	1	SB 244
37–1–21	Amended	418	2	SB 244
37–1–28	Amended	418	3	SB 244
37–1–50	Amended	418	4	SB 244
37–1–70	Amended	418	5	SB 244
37–2–4	Amended	418	6	SB 244
37–2–5.2	Amended	418	7	SB 244
		624	37	HB 1387
37–2–6	Amended	624	37	HB 1387
37–2–6.1	Amended	624	37	HB 1387
37–2–6.5	Amended	624	37	HB 1387
37–2–7	Amended	615	10	SB 388
37–2–10	Amended	624	37	HB 1387
37–3–1	Amended	418	8	SB 244
37–4–21	Amended	624	37	HB 1387
37–5–2	Amended	624	37	HB 1387
37–5–6	Amended	615	10	SB 388
37–7–3	Amended	624	37	HB 1387
37–9–8	Amended	506	16	SB 131
39–2–11	Amended	624	39	HB 1387
40–1–1	Amended	381	1	HB 1005
		460	4	HB 1174
40–2–8	Amended	381	2	HB 1005
40–2–9	Amended	360	1-64	HB 1055
		381	2.1	HB 1005
40–2–20	Amended	381	3	HB 1005
40–2–22	Amended	360	1-65	HB 1055
40–2–26	Amended	381	3.1	HB 1005
40–2–29	Amended	381	4	HB 1005
40–2–30	Amended	360	1-66	HB 1055
40–2–31	Amended	360	1-67	HB 1055
40–2–32	Reserved	360	1-74	HB 1055
40–2–32.1	Repealed	360	1-75	HB 1055
40–2–33	Amended	360	1-68	HB 1055

	Effect	Act	Section	Bill/Resolution Number
Code Section—continued				
40–2–49.2	Repealed	360	1-75	HB 1055
40–2–49.3	Repealed	360	1-75	HB 1055
40–2–60	Amended	360	1-69	HB 1055
40–2–60.1	Amended	360	1-70	HB 1055
40–2–61	Amended	360	1-71	HB 1055
40–2–62	Amended	360	1-72	HB 1055
40–2–64.1	Amended	360	1-73	HB 1055
40–2–75	Reserved	360	1-74	HB 1055
40–2–76	Reserved	360	1-74	HB 1055
40–2–77	Reserved	360	1-74	HB 1055
40–2–78	Reserved	360	1-74	HB 1055
40–2–85.3	Redesignated from 40–2–86.18	360	1-76	HB 1055
40–2–86	Redesignated from 40–2–86.21	360	1-77	HB 1055
40–2–86.1	Repealed	360	1-75	HB 1055
	Redesignated from 40–2–86.22	360	1-77	HB 1055
40–2–86.2	Repealed	360	1-75	HB 1055
40–2–86.4	Repealed	360	1-75	HB 1055
40–2–86.5	Repealed	360	1-75	HB 1055
40–2–86.7	Repealed	360	1-75	HB 1055
40–2–86.8	Repealed	360	1-75	HB 1055
40–2–86.9	Repealed	360	1-75	HB 1055
40–2–86.10	Repealed	360	1-75	HB 1055
40–2–86.11	Repealed	360	1-75	HB 1055
40–2–86.12	Repealed	360	1-75	HB 1055
40–2–86.14	Repealed	360	1-75	HB 1055
40–2–86.18	Redesignated as 40–2–85.3	360	1-76	HB 1055
	Amended	380	1	HB 1012
40–2–86.19	Repealed	360	1-75	HB 1055
40–2–86.20	Repealed	360	1-75	HB 1055
40–2–86.21	Redesignated as 40–2–86	360	1-77	HB 1055
	Amended	381	4.1	HB 1005
40–2–86.22	Redesignated as 40–2–86.1	360	1-77	HB 1055
40–2–131	Amended	621	3	SB 296
40–2–137	Amended	381	5	HB 1005
40–2–168	Added	381	6	HB 1005
40–3–26	Amended	381	7	HB 1005
40–5–1	Amended	360	1-78	HB 1055
		633	1	HB 396
40–5–2	Amended	633	1.1	HB 396
40–5–21.1	Amended	633	2	HB 396
40–5–21.2	Amended	633	3	HB 396
40–5–22	Amended	394	1	HB 258
40–5–23	Amended	633	5	HB 396
40–5–24	Amended	394	2	HB 258
		633	6	HB 396
40–5–25	Amended	360	1-79	HB 1055
		633	7	HB 396
40–5–28	Amended	633	8	HB 396
40–5–30	Amended	623	1	SB 6
		625	1	HB 1224
40–5–32	Amended	633	9	HB 396
40–5–38	Added	649	1	SB 419
40–5–52	Amended	633	4	HB 396
40–5–53	Amended	633	10	HB 396
40–5–56	Amended	633	12	HB 396
40–5–57	Amended	676	1	HB 23
		677	2	SB 360
40–5–63	Amended	633	13	HB 396
40–5–64	Amended	394	3	HB 258
		633	14	HB 396
40–5–67.1	Amended	360	1-80	HB 1055

	Effect	Act	Section	Bill/Resolution Number
Code Section—continued				
40-5-71	Repealed	381	8	HB 1005
40-5-72	Amended	381	9	HB 1005
40-5-75	Amended	633	15	HB 396
40-5-82	Amended	633	16	HB 396
40-5-83	Amended	633	17	HB 396
40-5-100	Amended	633	18	HB 396
40-5-103	Amended	360	1-81	HB 1055
		633	19	HB 396
40-5-120	Amended	633	20	HB 396
40-5-171	Amended	633	21	HB 396
40-5-173	Amended	633	22	HB 396
40-5-174	Amended	633	23	HB 396
40-5-175	Amended	633	24	HB 396
40-6-10	Amended	381	10	HB 1005
40-6-70	Amended	460	5	HB 1174
40-6-120	Amended	412	1	HB 1231
40-6-228	Amended	482	1	HB 1338
		643	2-16	SB 308
40-6-241	Amended	676	2	HB 23
		677	3	SB 360
40-6-241.1	Added	676	3	HB 23
		677	4	SB 360
40-6-250	Amended	677	5	SB 360
40-6-315	Amended	615	10	SB 388
40-6-352	Amended	615	10	SB 388
40-6-391	Amended	454	1	HB 898
40-6-395	Amended	412	2	HB 1231
40-7-3	Amended	365	1-1	HB 207
40-7-4	Amended	365	1-2	HB 207
40-7-6	Amended	365	1-3	HB 207
40-8-76.1	Amended	609	1	SB 458
40-8-78	Amended	615	10	SB 388
40-8-90	Amended	360	1-82	HB 1055
40-8-91	Amended	368	1-1	HB 981
40-8-92	Amended	363	1	SB 410
40-9-39	Amended	621	3	SB 296
40-13-2.1	Amended	633	25	HB 396
40-14-9	Amended	460	6	HB 1174
40-16-4	Amended	633	26	HB 396
40-16-5	Amended	615	10	SB 388
41-1-10	Added	635	11	SB 474
42-1-11.1	Added	416	2	SB 136
42-1-12	Amended	388	1	HB 651
		389	5	HB 571
			6	HB 571
			7	HB 571
			8	HB 571
			9	HB 571
			10	HB 571
			11	HB 571
42-1-14	Amended	389	12	HB 571
		624	42	HB 1387
42-1-15	Amended	389	13	HB 571
42-1-16	Added	389	14	HB 571
42-1-17	Added	389	14	HB 571
42-1-18	Added	389	14	HB 571
42-1-19	Added	389	15	HB 571
42-2-8	Amended	615	10	SB 388
42-5-50	Amended	403	17	HB 567
42-8-34.1	Amended	426	1	HB 329
42-8-36	Amended	496	1	HB 859

Code Section—continued	Effect	Act	Section	Bill/Resolution Number
42–8–151	Amended	624	42	HB 1387
42–9–43.1	Amended	416	3	SB 136
43–1–2	Amended	417	6	SB 195
			7	SB 195
43–1–3	Amended	621	3	SB 296
43–1–5	Amended	417	8	SB 195
		643	2-17	SB 308
43–1–9	Amended	417	9	SB 195
43–1–10	Amended	417	10	SB 195
43–1–11	Amended	417	11	SB 195
43–1A–1	Amended	437	1	SB 149
43–1A–2	Amended	437	1	SB 149
43–1A–3	Amended	437	1	SB 149
43–1A–4	Amended	437	1	SB 149
43–1A–5	Amended	437	1	SB 149
43–1A–6	Amended	437	1	SB 149
43–1A–7	Amended	437	1	SB 149
43–1A–8	Amended	437	1	SB 149
43–1A–9	Amended	437	1	SB 149
43–4–1	Amended	545	1	HB 231
43–4–9	Amended	417	12	SB 195
43–4–14	Amended	545	2	HB 231
43–4–30	Amended	545	3	HB 231
43–4–33	Amended	545	4	HB 231
43–4A–1	Amended	437	2	SB 149
43–4A–2	Amended	437	2	SB 149
43–4A–3	Repealed	437	2	SB 149
	Redesignated from 43–4A–4	437	2	SB 149
43–4A–4	Redesignated as 43–4A–3	437	2	SB 149
	Redesignated from 43–4A–4.1	437	2	SB 149
43–4A–4.1	Redesignated as 43–4A–4	437	2	SB 149
43–4A–5	Amended	437	2	SB 149
43–4A–6	Repealed	437	2	SB 149
	Redesignated from 43–4A–7	437	2	SB 149
43–4A–7	Redesignated as 43–4A–6	437	2	SB 149
	Redesignated from 43–4A–8	437	2	SB 149
43–4A–8	Redesignated as 43–4A–7	437	2	SB 149
	Redesignated from 43–4A–9	437	2	SB 149
43–4A–9	Redesignated as 43–4A–8	437	2	SB 149
	Redesignated from 43–4A–10	437	2	SB 149
43–4A–10	Redesignated as 43–4A–9	437	2	SB 149
	Redesignated from 43–4A–11	437	2	SB 149
43–4A–11	Redesignated as 43–4A–10	437	2	SB 149
	Redesignated from 43–4A–12	437	2	SB 149
43–4A–12	Redesignated as 43–4A–11	437	2	SB 149
	Redesignated from 43–4A–13	437	2	SB 149
43–4A–13	Redesignated as 43–4A–12	437	2	SB 149
	Redesignated from 43–4A–14	437	2	SB 149
43–4A–14	Redesignated as 43–4A–13	437	2	SB 149
	Redesignated from 43–4A–16	437	2	SB 149
43–4A–15	Redesignated from 43–4A–16.1	437	2	SB 149
	Redesignated as 43–4A–17	437	2	SB 149
43–4A–16	Redesignated as 43–4A–14	437	2	SB 149
	Redesignated from 43–4A–17	437	2	SB 149
43–4A–16.1	Redesignated as 43–4A–15	437	2	SB 149
43–4A–17	Redesignated as 43–4A–16	437	2	SB 149
	Redesignated from 43–4A–15	437	2	SB 149
43–4A–18	Redesignated from 43–4A–20	437	2	SB 149
	Redesignated as 43–4A–19	437	2	SB 149
43–4A–19	Redesignated from 43–4A–18	437	2	SB 149

	Effect	Act	Section	Bill/Resolution Number
Code Section—continued				
43-4A-19	Redesignated as 43-4A-20	437	2	SB 149
43-4A-20	Redesignated as 43-4A-18	437	2	SB 149
	Redesignated from 43-4A-19	437	2	SB 149
43-6-13	Amended	417	13	SB 195
43-7-7	Amended	417	14	SB 195
43-7-12	Amended	417	15	SB 195
43-7-16	Amended	417	16	SB 195
43-9-7	Amended	417	17	SB 195
43-9-14	Amended	417	18	SB 195
43-10-6	Amended	417	19	SB 195
43-11A-7	Amended	615	10	SB 388
43-12-3	Amended	395	1	HB 128
43-12A-6	Amended	633	27	HB 396
43-13-4	Amended	633	28	HB 396
43-13-5	Amended	633	29	HB 396
43-13-6.1	Amended	633	30	HB 396
43-13-9	Amended	621	2	SB 296
43-14-8.1	Amended	417	20	SB 195
43-14-13	Amended	400	1	SB 339
43-15-12	Amended	417	21	SB 195
43-16-4	Amended	438	1	SB 162
43-17-2	Amended	497	1	HB 863
			2	HB 863
43-17-3	Amended	497	3	HB 863
43-17-8	Amended	497	4	HB 863
43-17-8.1	Added	497	5	HB 863
43-17-11	Amended	615	10	SB 388
43-18-41	Amended	417	22	SB 195
43-18-42	Amended	417	23	SB 195
43-19-13	Amended	417	24	SB 195
43-20-5	Amended	417	25	SB 195
43-20-6	Amended	417	26	SB 195
43-20-8	Amended	417	27	SB 195
43-20-9	Amended	417	28	SB 195
43-20-12	Amended	417	29	SB 195
43-23-8	Amended	417	30	SB 195
43-24A-3	Amended	444	1	SB 364
43-24A-7	Amended	444	2	SB 364
43-24A-15	Amended	444	3	SB 364
43-24A-17	Amended	444	4	SB 364
43-24A-22	Amended	444	5	SB 364
43-24A-24	Amended	444	6	SB 364
43-25-3	Amended	360	1-83	HB 1055
43-26-8	Amended	624	43	HB 1387
43-26-12	Amended	675	1	HB 1040
43-28-9	Amended	417	31	SB 195
43-29-7	Amended	417	32	SB 195
43-29-8	Amended	417	33	SB 195
43-29-11	Amended	417	34	SB 195
43-30-7	Amended	417	35	SB 195
43-33-9	Amended	417	36	SB 195
43-33-10	Amended	615	10	SB 388
43-34-2	Amended	489	1	SB 252
43-34-5.1	Added	489	2	SB 252
43-34-6	Amended	643	2-18	SB 308
43-34-8	Amended	489	3	SB 252
		624	43	HB 1387
43-34-26	Amended	624	43	HB 1387
43-34-26.1	Amended	487	1	HB 1154
		624	43	HB 1387
43-34-30	Amended	624	43	HB 1387

	Effect	Act	Section	Bill/Resolution Number
Code Section—continued				
43-34-37	Amended	624	43	HB 1387
43-34-103	Amended	624	43	HB 1387
43-34-244	Amended	624	43	HB 1387
43-34-248	Amended	624	43	HB 1387
43-35-12	Amended	417	37	SB 195
43-35-14	Amended	417	38	SB 195
43-38-6	Amended	417	39	SB 195
43-38-7	Amended	417	40	SB 195
		438	2	SB 162
43-38-10	Amended	643	2-19	SB 308
43-39-9	Amended	417	41	SB 195
43-39A-1	Amended	552	1	HB 1050
43-39A-2	Amended	552	2	HB 1050
43-39A-6	Amended	552	3	HB 1050
43-39A-7	Amended	552	4	HB 1050
43-39A-11	Amended	552	5	HB 1050
43-39A-13	Amended	552	6	HB 1050
43-39A-14.1	Added	552	7	HB 1050
43-39A-21	Amended	552	8	HB 1050
43-39A-22	Amended	552	9	HB 1050
43-41-8	Amended	351	1	HB 579
43-41-9	Amended	417	42	SB 195
			43	SB 195
43-41-10	Amended	615	10	SB 388
43-47-6	Amended	615	10	SB 388
43-47-8	Amended	417	44	SB 195
43-50-21	Amended	615	11	SB 388
43-50-31	Amended	417	45	SB 195
43-50-40	Amended	417	46	SB 195
43-51-7	Amended	417	47	SB 195
44-2-191	Amended	621	3	SB 296
44-2-192	Amended	621	3	SB 296
44-2-193	Amended	621	3	SB 296
			4	SB 296
44-2-194	Amended	621	3	SB 296
			4	SB 296
44-2-195	Amended	621	3	SB 296
			4	SB 296
44-3-111	Amended	624	44	HB 1387
44-14-361.1	Amended	618	1	SB 362
44-14-363	Amended	553	1	HB 1147
44-14-518	Amended	553	2	HB 1147
45-1-6	Amended	680	26	SB 17
45-6-3	Amended	615	10	SB 388
45-7-7	Amended	680	27	SB 17
45-8-1	Amended	621	3	SB 296
			4	SB 296
45-8-13.1	Amended	621	4	SB 296
45-8-17	Amended	621	4	SB 296
45-9-4	Amended	418	20	SB 244
		621	2	SB 296
			3	SB 296
45-9-76	Amended	360	1-84	HB 1055
45-9-84.1	Amended	621	2	SB 296
			3	SB 296
45-10-26	Amended	680	28	SB 17
45-10-90	Amended	680	29	SB 17
45-10-91	Amended	680	29	SB 17
45-10-92	Amended	680	29	SB 17
45-10-93	Amended	615	10	SB 388
45-11-8	Amended	458	1	HB 980

	Effect	Act	Section	Bill/Resolution Number
Code Section—continued				
45-12-71	Amended	391	1	SB 206
45-12-72	Amended	621	3	SB 296
45-12-75	Amended	391	2	SB 206
45-12-78	Amended	621	3	SB 296
45-12-82	Amended	621	3	SB 296
45-12-83.1	Amended	621	2	SB 296
45-12-92	Amended	371	1	HB 1284
45-12-92.1	Added	360	1-84.1	HB 1055
45-12-93	Amended	387	1	SB 421
45-13-22	Amended	615	2	SB 388
45-13-24	Amended	615	3	SB 388
45-13-27	Amended	615	10	SB 388
45-13-41	Amended	615	10	SB 388
45-13-45	Amended	615	11	SB 388
45-14-20	Amended	621	2	SB 296
			3	SB 296
45-14-23	Amended	621	2	SB 296
45-15-35.1	Added	632	37	HB 540
45-16-25	Amended	503	1	HB 1095
45-16-27	Amended	414	3	HB 1322
45-16-32	Amended	503	2	HB 1095
45-18-1	Amended	624	45	HB 1387
45-18-2	Amended	624	45	HB 1387
45-18-5	Amended	624	45	HB 1387
45-18-5.1	Amended	624	45	HB 1387
45-18-5.2	Amended	624	45	HB 1387
45-18-6	Amended	624	45	HB 1387
45-18-7.1	Amended	624	45	HB 1387
45-18-7.2	Amended	624	45	HB 1387
45-18-7.3	Amended	624	45	HB 1387
45-18-7.5	Amended	624	45	HB 1387
45-18-7.6	Amended	624	45	HB 1387
45-18-7.7	Amended	624	45	HB 1387
45-18-7.8	Added	617	1	SB 363
45-18-9	Amended	624	45	HB 1387
45-18-10	Amended	624	45	HB 1387
45-18-12	Amended	624	45	HB 1387
45-18-13	Amended	621	2	SB 296
			3	SB 296
45-18-14	Amended	624	45	HB 1387
45-18-15	Amended	615	10	SB 388
		624	45	HB 1387
45-18-16	Amended	624	45	HB 1387
45-18-20	Amended	624	45	HB 1387
45-18-21	Amended	624	45	HB 1387
45-22-9	Amended	615	10	SB 388
46-2-33	Added	370	1	HB 1233
46-3-427	Amended	621	2	SB 296
46-3-436	Amended	621	2	SB 296
46-3-438	Amended	621	2	SB 296
46-4A-2	Amended	634	1	HB 244
46-4A-12	Amended	634	1	HB 244
46-4A-14	Amended	634	1	HB 244
46-5-70	Amended	360	1-85	HB 1055
46-5-73	Amended	360	1-86	HB 1055
46-5-100	Amended	360	1-87	HB 1055
46-5-134.1	Amended	624	46	HB 1387
46-5-166	Amended	671	3	HB 168
46-5-167	Amended	671	4	HB 168
46-5-222	Amended	671	5	HB 168
46-5-250	Added	671	6	HB 168

	Effect	Act	Section	Bill/Resolution Number
Code Section—continued				
46–5–251	Added	671	6	HB 168
46–5–252	Added	671	6	HB 168
46–7–3	Amended	447	2	SB 392
46–7–15	Amended	624	46	HB 1387
46–7–26	Amended	624	46	HB 1387
46–7–85.10	Amended	633	31	HB 396
46–7–92	Added	633	32	HB 396
46–8–123	Amended	621	2	SB 296
47–1–5	Amended	621	3	SB 296
			4	SB 296
47–1–7	Amended	681	65	SB 436
47–1–9	Amended	681	2	SB 436
47–1–13.1	Amended	681	64	SB 436
47–1–14	Amended	681	65	SB 436
47–1–62	Amended	457	1	HB 969
47–1–80.1	Amended	457	2	HB 969
47–1–81	Amended	681	64	SB 436
47–1–82	Amended	457	3	HB 969
		681	64	SB 436
47–2–1	Amended	681	3	SB 436
			64	SB 436
47–2–21	Amended	621	3	SB 296
47–2–25	Amended	681	65	SB 436
47–2–26	Amended	681	65	SB 436
47–2–28	Amended	681	4	SB 436
47–2–29	Amended	681	5	SB 436
47–2–58	Repealed and Reserved	681	6	SB 436
47–2–70	Amended	681	7	SB 436
47–2–71	Amended	681	8	SB 436
47–2–72	Amended	681	9	SB 436
47–2–90	Amended	681	10	SB 436
47–2–91	Amended	681	64	SB 436
47–2–95	Repealed	681	11	SB 436
47–2–96	Repealed and Reserved	681	12	SB 436
47–2–96.1	Repealed	681	13	SB 436
47–2–96.2	Repealed	681	14	SB 436
47–2–97	Repealed and Reserved	681	15	SB 436
47–2–110	Amended	455	1	HB 916
			2	HB 916
		681	16	SB 436
47–2–111	Amended	681	17	SB 436
47–2–120	Amended	681	18	SB 436
47–2–123	Amended	681	64	SB 436
47–2–125	Amended	450	1	HB 172
47–2–142	Repealed	681	19	SB 436
47–2–160	Repealed and Reserved	681	20	SB 436
47–2–161	Repealed and Reserved	681	21	SB 436
47–2–166	Repealed	681	22	SB 436
47–2–167	Repealed	681	23	SB 436
47–2–168	Repealed	681	24	SB 436
47–2–180	Repealed and Reserved	681	25	SB 436
47–2–200	Repealed and Reserved	681	26	SB 436
47–2–201	Amended	621	3	SB 296
	Repealed and Reserved	681	27	SB 436
47–2–222	Amended	681	64	SB 436
47–2–224	Repealed	681	28	SB 436
47–2–260	Amended	681	64	SB 436
47–2–261	Repealed and Reserved	681	29	SB 436
47–2–262	Amended	681	30	SB 436
47–2–266	Amended	681	31	SB 436
47–2–290	Amended	681	64	SB 436

Code Section	Effect	Act	Section	Bill/Resolution Number
Code Section—continued				
47-2-292	Amended	681	32	SB 436
47-2-298	Amended	681	33	SB 436
47-2-299	Repealed	681	34	SB 436
47-2-311	Repealed and Reserved	681	35	SB 436
47-2-318	Amended	393	1	HB 320
47-2-319	Repealed and Reserved	681	36	SB 436
47-2-325	Repealed and Reserved	681	37	SB 436
47-2-334	Amended	681	38	SB 436
47-2-352	Amended	681	64	SB 436
47-2-354	Amended	681	39	SB 436
47-3-1	Amended	457	4	HB 969
			5	HB 969
		681	40	SB 436
47-3-21	Amended	621	3	SB 296
47-3-23	Amended	681	65	SB 436
47-3-24	Amended	681	65	SB 436
47-3-27	Amended	681	64	SB 436
47-3-41.1	Amended	457	6	HB 969
47-3-60	Amended	681	41	SB 436
47-3-61	Repealed and Reserved	681	42	SB 436
47-3-65	Amended	681	43	SB 436
47-3-66	Amended	621	2	SB 296
		681	44	SB 436
47-3-67	Amended	621	2	SB 296
		681	45	SB 436
47-3-87	Repealed and Reserved	681	46	SB 436
47-3-93	Amended	457	7	HB 969
47-3-94	Repealed and Reserved	681	47	SB 436
47-3-101	Amended	457	8	HB 969
47-3-122	Amended	457	9	HB 969
			10	HB 969
47-4-2	Amended	681	48	SB 436
47-4-24	Amended	681	65	SB 436
47-4-26	Amended	681	65	SB 436
47-4-60	Amended	621	3	SB 296
47-4-80	Amended	681	49	SB 436
47-4-100	Amended	681	50	SB 436
47-4-106	Amended	457	11	HB 969
47-6-22	Amended	681	65	SB 436
47-6-40	Amended	681	51	SB 436
47-6-41	Repealed and Reserved	681	52	SB 436
47-6-42	Amended	681	53	SB 436
47-7-1	Amended	459	1	HB 1150
			2	HB 1150
47-7-22	Amended	681	65	SB 436
47-7-23	Amended	681	65	SB 436
47-7-61	Amended	459	3	HB 1150
			4	HB 1150
47-7-83	Amended	681	54	SB 436
47-7-100	Amended	459	5	HB 1150
47-7-103	Amended	459	6	HB 1150
47-7-104	Amended	459	7	HB 1150
47-7-124	Amended	459	8	HB 1150
47-7-127	Added	451	1	HB 249
47-7A-1	Repealed	459	9	HB 1150
		681	55	SB 436
47-7A-20	Repealed	459	9	HB 1150
		681	55	SB 436
47-7A-21	Repealed	459	9	HB 1150
		681	55	SB 436
47-7A-22	Repealed	459	9	HB 1150

	Effect	Act	Section	Bill/Resolution Number
Code Section—continued				
47–7A–22	Repealed	681	55	SB 436
47–7A–23	Repealed	459	9	HB 1150
		681	55	SB 436
47–7A–24	Repealed	459	9	HB 1150
		681	55	SB 436
47–7A–25	Repealed	459	9	HB 1150
		681	55	SB 436
47–7A–40	Repealed	459	9	HB 1150
		681	55	SB 436
47–7A–41	Repealed	459	9	HB 1150
		681	55	SB 436
47–7A–60	Repealed	459	9	HB 1150
		681	55	SB 436
47–7A–61	Repealed	459	9	HB 1150
		681	55	SB 436
47–7A–80	Repealed	459	9	HB 1150
		681	55	SB 436
47–7A–81	Repealed	459	9	HB 1150
		681	55	SB 436
47–7A–82	Repealed	459	9	HB 1150
		681	55	SB 436
47–7A–83	Repealed	459	9	HB 1150
		681	55	SB 436
47–7A–84	Repealed	459	9	HB 1150
		681	55	SB 436
47–7A–100	Repealed	459	9	HB 1150
		681	55	SB 436
47–7A–101	Repealed	459	9	HB 1150
		681	55	SB 436
47–7A–102	Repealed	459	9	HB 1150
		681	55	SB 436
47–7A–103	Repealed	459	9	HB 1150
		681	55	SB 436
47–7A–120	Repealed	459	9	HB 1150
		681	55	SB 436
47–7A–121	Repealed	459	9	HB 1150
		681	55	SB 436
47–7A–122	Repealed	459	9	HB 1150
		681	55	SB 436
47–7A–123	Repealed	459	9	HB 1150
		681	55	SB 436
47–7A–124	Repealed	459	9	HB 1150
		681	55	SB 436
47–7A–125	Repealed	459	9	HB 1150
		681	55	SB 436
47–7A–126	Repealed	459	9	HB 1150
		681	55	SB 436
47–7A–127	Repealed	459	9	HB 1150
		681	55	SB 436
47–8–2	Amended	621	3	SB 296
47–8–41	Amended	681	64	SB 436
47–8–67	Amended	681	64	SB 436
47–11–22	Amended	681	64	SB 436
			66	SB 436
47–11–23	Amended	681	65	SB 436
47–11–40	Amended	681	66	SB 436
47–11–50	Amended	681	64	SB 436
47–12–21	Amended	621	3	SB 296
47–14–23	Amended	681	65	SB 436
			66	SB 436
47–14–72	Amended	681	66	SB 436

	Effect	Act	Section	Bill/Resolution Number
Code Section—continued				
47-14-77	Amended	453	1	HB 486
47-14-79	Added	453	2	HB 486
47-16-21	Amended	621	3	SB 296
47-16-29	Amended	681	66	SB 436
47-16-41	Amended	681	64	SB 436
47-16-101	Amended	681	64	SB 436
			66	SB 436
47-16-102	Amended	681	64	SB 436
47-17-1	Amended	681	64	SB 436
47-17-23	Amended	681	65	SB 436
47-17-26	Amended	681	66	SB 436
47-17-41	Amended	631	1	HB 974
47-17-80	Amended	631	2	HB 974
47-18-2	Amended	682	1	HB 997
47-18-20	Amended	682	2	HB 997
47-18-21	Amended	682	2	HB 997
47-18-22	Amended	682	2	HB 997
47-18-40	Amended	681	64	SB 436
		682	3	HB 997
47-18-41	Amended	621	3	SB 296
		682	4	HB 997
47-18-43	Amended	682	5	HB 997
47-18-44	Amended	681	64	SB 436
47-18-60	Amended	682	6	HB 997
47-18-70	Amended	682	7	HB 997
47-19-1	Amended	621	3	SB 296
47-20-11	Repealed and Reserved	681	56	SB 436
47-20-12	Repealed and Reserved	681	57	SB 436
47-20-20	Amended	681	58	SB 436
47-20-21	Amended	621	3	SB 296
			4	SB 296
47-20-83.1	Amended	621	3	SB 296
47-21-22	Amended	681	65	SB 436
47-22-4	Amended	681	59	SB 436
47-22-6	Amended	681	65	SB 436
47-22-9	Amended	681	60	SB 436
47-23-25	Amended	681	64	SB 436
47-23-46	Amended	681	61	SB 436
47-23-47	Amended	681	64	SB 436
47-23-49	Repealed and Reserved	681	62	SB 436
47-23-50	Amended	681	63	SB 436
47-23-80	Amended	681	64	SB 436
47-23-81	Amended	621	2	SB 296
		681	64	SB 436
47-23-82	Amended	621	2	SB 296
47-23-124	Amended	681	64	SB 436
47-24-60	Amended	621	2	SB 296
			3	SB 296
47-25-81	Amended	681	66	SB 436
48-1-2	Amended	627	1	HB 1138
48-1-10	Added	396	2	SB 409
48-2-7	Amended	615	10	SB 388
48-2-12	Amended	615	10	SB 388
48-2-15	Amended	615	11	SB 388
48-2-17	Amended	621	2	SB 296
48-2-18	Amended	670	8-1	SB 346
48-2-82	Amended	621	2	SB 296
48-3-3	Amended	624	48	HB 1387
48-3-9	Amended	624	48	HB 1387
48-3-19	Amended	624	48	HB 1387
48-4-5	Amended	624	48	HB 1387

	Effect	Act	Section	Bill/Resolution Number
Code Section—continued				
48–4–63	Amended	624	48	HB 1387
48–4–78	Amended	624	48	HB 1387
48–5–2	Amended	670	5-1	SB 346
			5-2	SB 346
			5-3	SB 346
			5-4	SB 346
48–5–8	Amended	360	3-1	HB 1055
48–5–9.1	Added	670	9-2	SB 346
48–5–13	Amended	670	4-1	SB 346
48–5–15	Amended	499	1	HB 963
48–5–18	Amended	670	3-1	SB 346
48–5–23	Amended	670	9-1	SB 346
48–5–32.1	Amended	670	10-1	SB 346
48–5–41	Amended	644	1	HB 1186
48–5–41.2	Amended	624	48	HB 1387
48–5–48.3	Amended	624	48	HB 1387
48–5–52	Amended	499	2	HB 963
48–5–131	Amended	621	2	SB 296
48–5–291	Amended	670	4-2	SB 346
48–5–302	Amended	624	48	HB 1387
48–5–303	Amended	670	12-1	SB 346
48–5–304	Amended	621	2	SB 296
		670	11-1	SB 346
48–5–306	Amended	670	1-1	SB 346
48–5–311	Amended	670	2-1	SB 346
			4-3	SB 346
			6-1	SB 346
48–5–330	Amended	621	2	SB 296
48–5–346	Amended	615	10	SB 388
		621	2	SB 296
48–5–380	Amended	670	7-1	SB 346
48–5–421.1	Added	644	2	HB 1186
48–5–478.4	Amended	624	48	HB 1387
48–5–504	Amended	624	48	HB 1387
48–5–504.40	Amended	504	1	HB 1105
48–5B–1	Amended	670	6-2	SB 346
48–6–4	Amended	484	1	HB 1192
48–6–69	Amended	485	1	HB 1191
48–7–1	Amended	483	1	HB 1198
48–7–21	Amended	627	2	HB 1138
48–7–27	Amended	360	4-1	HB 1055
48–7–29.14	Amended	634	1	HB 244
		679	3	HB 1069
48–7–40.29	Added	679	1	HB 1069
48–7–40.30	Added	679	2	HB 1069
48–7–54	Amended	627	3	HB 1138
48–7–60	Amended	615	11	SB 388
48–7–112	Amended	615	10	SB 388
		621	2	SB 296
48–7–140	Repealed	382	1	HB 984
	Added	382	2	HB 984
48–7–141	Repealed	382	1	HB 984
48–7–142	Repealed	382	1	HB 984
48–7–143	Repealed	382	1	HB 984
48–7–144	Repealed	382	1	HB 984
48–7–145	Repealed	382	1	HB 984
48–7–146	Repealed	382	1	HB 984
48–7–147	Repealed	382	1	HB 984
48–7–148	Repealed	382	1	HB 984
48–7–149	Repealed	382	1	HB 984
48–7–167	Added	507	27	HB 1221

	Effect	Act	Section	Bill/Resolution Number
Code Section—continued				
48–7A–1	Repealed and Reserved	679	4	HB 1069
48–7A–3	Amended	679	5	HB 1069
48–8–2	Amended	507	1	HB 1221
48–8–3	Amended	507	2	HB 1221
48–8–6	Amended	507	3	HB 1221
		554	5	HB 277
		607	1	HB 1393
		624	48	HB 1387
48–8–14	Amended	507	4	HB 1221
48–8–17	Amended	507	5	HB 1221
48–8–17.1	Amended	507	6	HB 1221
48–8–30	Amended	507	7	HB 1221
48–8–31	Amended	507	8	HB 1221
48–8–32	Amended	507	9	HB 1221
48–8–38	Amended	507	10	HB 1221
48–8–39	Amended	507	11	HB 1221
48–8–45	Amended	507	12	HB 1221
48–8–49	Amended	507	13	HB 1221
48–8–50	Amended	507	14	HB 1221
48–8–52	Amended	507	15	HB 1221
48–8–58	Amended	507	16	HB 1221
48–8–59	Amended	507	17	HB 1221
48–8–68	Added	507	18	HB 1221
48–8–69	Added	507	18	HB 1221
48–8–70	Added	507	18	HB 1221
48–8–71	Added	507	18	HB 1221
48–8–72	Added	507	18	HB 1221
48–8–73	Added	507	18	HB 1221
48–8–74	Added	507	18	HB 1221
48–8–75	Added	507	18	HB 1221
48–8–76	Added	507	18	HB 1221
48–8–77	Added	507	18	HB 1221
48–8–82	Amended	507	19	HB 1221
48–8–87	Amended	507	20	HB 1221
48–8–89	Amended	639	1	HB 991
48–8–89.1	Amended	639	2	HB 991
			3	HB 991
48–8–92	Amended	639	4	HB 991
48–8–96	Amended	507	21	HB 1221
48–8–102	Amended	507	22	HB 1221
48–8–104	Amended	507	23	HB 1221
48–8–110.1	Amended	507	24	HB 1221
48–8–113	Amended	507	25	HB 1221
48–8–141	Amended	630	1	HB 1013
48–8–161	Amended	507	26	HB 1221
48–8–200	Amended	507	28	HB 1221
48–8–201	Amended	507	29	HB 1221
48–8–203	Amended	507	30	HB 1221
		679	6	HB 1069
48–8–204	Amended	507	31	HB 1221
48–8–240	Added	554	6	HB 277
48–8–241	Added	554	6	HB 277
48–8–242	Added	554	6	HB 277
		610	3	SB 520
48–8–243	Added	554	6	HB 277
48–8–244	Added	554	6	HB 277
48–8–244.1	Added	554	6	HB 277
48–8–245	Added	554	6	HB 277
48–8–246	Added	554	6	HB 277
48–8–247	Added	554	6	HB 277
48–8–248	Added	554	6	HB 277

	Effect	Act	Section	Bill/Resolution Number
Code Section—continued				
48-8-249	Added	554	6	HB 277
48-8-250	Added	554	6	HB 277
48-8-251	Added	554	6	HB 277
48-8-252	Added	554	6	HB 277
48-8-253	Added	554	6	HB 277
48-8-254	Added	554	6	HB 277
48-8-255	Added	554	6	HB 277
48-8-256	Added	554	6	HB 277
48-9-3	Amended	607	2	HB 1393
48-9-10	Amended	621	2	SB 296
48-9-36	Amended	621	2	SB 296
48-11-9	Amended	621	2	SB 296
48-11-15	Amended	621	2	SB 296
48-11-16	Amended	621	2	SB 296
48-13-20.1	Added	555	1	HB 1093
48-13-31	Amended	621	2	SB 296
48-13-51	Amended	606	1	HB 903
			2	HB 903
			3	HB 903
48-13-55	Amended	506	17	SB 131
48-14-3	Amended	621	2	SB 296
48-17-1	Amended	360	1-88	HB 1055
		468	1	SB 454
48-17-2	Amended	360	1-89	HB 1055
		468	2	SB 454
48-17-9	Amended	360	1-90	HB 1055
		468	3	SB 454
48-17-11	Amended	360	1-91	HB 1055
		468	4	SB 454
48-17-14	Amended	468	5	SB 454
48-17-15	Amended	468	6	SB 454
48-17-16	Added	468	7	SB 454
49-4-33	Amended	615	10	SB 388
49-4-53	Amended	615	10	SB 388
49-4-82	Amended	615	10	SB 388
49-4-156	Repealed	376	1	HB 1170
	Reserved	376	1	HB 1170
49-4-183	Amended	615	10	SB 388
49-4A-8	Amended	615	10	SB 388
		643	2-20	SB 308
49-5-12	Amended	615	10	SB 388
49-5-19	Amended	615	10	SB 388
49-5-41	Amended	424	1	HB 303
49-5-132	Amended	615	10	SB 388
		621	3	SB 296
49-5-220	Amended	615	11	SB 388
49-5-221	Amended	615	11	SB 388
49-5-273	Amended	615	10	SB 388
49-6-21	Amended	615	10	SB 388
50-1-9	Added	432	1	HB 1019
50-2-28	Amended	379	2	HB 1074
50-4-7	Amended	462	1	HB 1260
50-5-14	Amended	621	2	SB 296
			3	SB 296
50-5-16	Amended	621	2	SB 296
			3	SB 296
50-5-60.3	Amended	368	1-2	HB 981
50-5-60.4	Amended	615	10	SB 388
50-5-67	Amended	615	10	SB 388
50-5-69	Amended	418	21	SB 244
50-5-77	Amended	669	1	SB 194

	Effect	Act	Section	Bill/Resolution Number
Code Section—continued				
50-5-82	Amended	507	32	HB 1221
50-5-135	Amended	418	22	SB 244
50-5A-1	Amended	621	1	SB 296
50-5A-2	Amended	621	1	SB 296
50-5A-3	Amended	621	1	SB 296
50-5A-4	Amended	621	1	SB 296
50-5A-5	Amended	621	1	SB 296
50-5A-6	Amended	621	1	SB 296
50-5A-7	Amended	621	1	SB 296
50-5A-8	Amended	621	1	SB 296
50-5A-9	Amended	621	1	SB 296
50-5A-10	Amended	621	1	SB 296
50-5A-11	Amended	621	1	SB 296
50-5B-3	Amended	621	2	SB 296
50-6-32	Amended	630	2	HB 1013
		683	1	SB 389
50-7-8	Amended	615	10	SB 388
50-7-16	Amended	621	2	SB 296
50-7-18	Added	547	2	SB 449
50-7-41	Amended	621	2	SB 296
50-7-51	Amended	621	2	SB 296
50-7-70	Amended	360	1-92	HB 1055
50-8-7	Amended	615	10	SB 388
50-8-8	Amended	621	3	SB 296
		634	1	HB 244
50-8-13	Amended	634	1	HB 244
50-8-50	Added	467	1	HB 867
50-8-51	Added	467	1	HB 867
50-8-52	Added	467	1	HB 867
50-8-141	Amended	615	10	SB 388
50-8-170	Amended	634	1	HB 244
50-8-193	Amended	634	1	HB 244
50-9-9	Amended	379	3	HB 1074
50-9-13	Amended	425	1	HB 333
50-10-5	Amended	634	1	HB 244
50-12-64	Repealed and Reserved	547	3	SB 449
50-12-65	Repealed and Reserved	547	3	SB 449
50-12-66	Repealed and Reserved	547	3	SB 449
50-12-67	Repealed and Reserved	547	3	SB 449
50-12-68	Repealed and Reserved	547	3	SB 449
50-12-69	Repealed and Reserved	547	3	SB 449
50-12-69.1	Repealed and Reserved	547	3	SB 449
50-12-84	Amended	615	10	SB 388
50-13-2	Amended	468	8	SB 454
50-16-6	Amended	379	4	HB 1074
50-16-12	Amended	621	2	SB 296
			3	SB 296
50-16-14	Amended	379	5	HB 1074
50-16-18	Amended	505	1-1	HB 1128
50-16-32	Amended	621	3	SB 296
50-16-38	Amended	614	1	SB 455
50-17-2	Amended	621	2	SB 296
			3	SB 296
50-17-21	Amended	621	6	SB 296
50-17-22	Amended	375	1	HB 1258
		621	4	SB 296
50-17-23	Amended	621	3	SB 296
50-17-27	Amended	634	1	HB 244
50-17-50	Amended	621	3	SB 296
			4	SB 296
50-17-51	Amended	621	4	SB 296

	Effect	Act	Section	Bill/Resolution Number
Code Section—continued				
50–17–52	Amended	621	4	SB 296
50–17–53	Amended	621	4	SB 296
50–17–54	Amended	621	4	SB 296
50–17–56	Amended	621	4	SB 296
50–17–57	Amended	621	4	SB 296
50–17–59	Amended	621	4	SB 296
50–17–62	Amended	621	3	SB 296
			4	SB 296
50–17–63	Amended	621	2	SB 296
			4	SB 296
50–17–101	Amended	621	2	SB 296
50–18–2	Added	615	4	SB 388
50–18–20	Amended	615	5	SB 388
50–18–26	Amended	615	6	SB 388
50–18–27	Amended	615	7	SB 388
50–18–31	Amended	615	8	SB 388
50–18–37	Added	615	9	SB 388
50–18–72	Amended	409	1	HB 1086
			2	HB 1086
		418	23	SB 244
		451	2	HB 249
		643	2-21	SB 308
50–21–33	Amended	621	2	SB 296
			3	SB 296
50–22–2	Amended	545	5	HB 231
50–23–1	Amended	634	1	HB 244
50–23–2	Amended	634	1	HB 244
50–23–3	Amended	634	1	HB 244
50–23–4	Amended	634	1	HB 244
50–23–5	Amended	634	1	HB 244
			1A	HB 244
			2	HB 244
50–23–20	Amended	621	3	SB 296
50–23–25	Amended	634	1	HB 244
50–23–26	Amended	634	1	HB 244
50–23–28.1	Added	397	3	SB 380
50–23–30	Amended	634	1	HB 244
50–23–31	Amended	634	1	HB 244
50–23–32	Amended	634	1	HB 244
50–25–7.10	Amended	615	10	SB 388
50–27–13	Amended	621	3	SB 296
			4	SB 296
50–32–5	Added	554	7	HB 277
50–32–15	Amended	634	1	HB 244
50–32–39	Amended	634	1	HB 244
50–32–54	Amended	621	3	SB 296
50–37–1	Added	669	2	SB 194
50–37–2	Added	669	2	SB 194
50–37–3	Added	669	2	SB 194
50–37–4	Added	669	2	SB 194
50–37–5	Added	669	2	SB 194
50–37–6	Added	669	2	SB 194
50–37–7	Added	669	2	SB 194
50–37–8	Added	669	2	SB 194
51–12–5.1	Amended	621	2	SB 296
52–2–2	Amended	628	1	HB 1060
52–2–3	Amended	628	2	HB 1060
52–2–9	Amended	621	2	SB 296
		628	3	HB 1060
52–2–10	Amended	672	1	HB 958
52–2–11	Amended	628	4	HB 1060

	Effect	Act	Section	Bill/Resolution Number
Code Section—continued				
52-2-14	Amended	621	2	SB 296
52-2-19	Amended	628	5	HB 1060
52-2-23	Amended	628	6	HB 1060
52-2-31	Amended	628	7	HB 1060
52-2-33	Amended	628	8	HB 1060
52-2-36	Amended	628	9	HB 1060
52-7-13	Amended	373	2	SB 99
53-4-75	Added	493	1	SB 461
53-7-1	Amended	506	18	SB 131
53-12-1	Repealed and Reenacted	506	1	SB 131
53-12-2	Repealed and Reenacted	506	1	SB 131
53-12-3	Repealed and Reenacted	506	1	SB 131
53-12-4	Repealed and Reenacted	506	1	SB 131
53-12-5	Repealed and Reenacted	506	1	SB 131
53-12-6	Repealed and Reenacted	506	1	SB 131
53-12-7	Repealed and Reenacted	506	1	SB 131
53-12-20	Repealed and Reenacted	506	1	SB 131
53-12-21	Repealed and Reenacted	506	1	SB 131
53-12-22	Repealed and Reenacted	506	1	SB 131
53-12-22.1	Repealed and Reenacted	506	1	SB 131
53-12-23	Repealed and Reenacted	506	1	SB 131
53-12-24	Repealed and Reenacted	506	1	SB 131
53-12-25	Repealed and Reenacted	506	1	SB 131
53-12-26	Repealed and Reenacted	506	1	SB 131
53-12-27	Repealed and Reenacted	506	1	SB 131
53-12-28	Repealed and Reenacted	506	1	SB 131
53-12-40	Added	506	1	SB 131
53-12-41	Added	506	1	SB 131
53-12-42	Added	506	1	SB 131
53-12-43	Added	506	1	SB 131
53-12-44	Added	506	1	SB 131
53-12-45	Added	506	1	SB 131
53-12-50	Repealed	506	1	SB 131
53-12-51	Repealed	506	1	SB 131
53-12-52	Repealed	506	1	SB 131
53-12-53	Repealed	506	1	SB 131
53-12-54	Repealed	506	1	SB 131
53-12-55	Repealed	506	1	SB 131
53-12-56	Repealed	506	1	SB 131
53-12-57	Repealed	506	1	SB 131
53-12-58	Repealed	506	1	SB 131
53-12-59	Repealed	506	1	SB 131
53-12-60	Added	506	1	SB 131
53-12-61	Added	506	1	SB 131
53-12-62	Added	506	1	SB 131
53-12-63	Added	506	1	SB 131
53-12-64	Added	506	1	SB 131
53-12-65	Added	506	1	SB 131
53-12-70	Repealed	506	1	SB 131
53-12-71	Repealed	506	1	SB 131
53-12-72	Repealed	506	1	SB 131
53-12-73	Repealed	506	1	SB 131
53-12-74	Repealed	506	1	SB 131
53-12-80	Added	506	1	SB 131
53-12-81	Added	506	1	SB 131
53-12-82	Added	506	1	SB 131
53-12-83	Added	506	1	SB 131
53-12-90	Repealed	506	1	SB 131
53-12-91	Repealed	506	1	SB 131
53-12-92	Repealed	506	1	SB 131
53-12-93	Repealed	506	1	SB 131

	Effect	Act	Section	Bill/Resolution Number
Code Section—continued				
53-12-94	Repealed	506	1	SB 131
53-12-100	Added	506	1	SB 131
53-12-101	Added	506	1	SB 131
53-12-102	Added	506	1	SB 131
53-12-103	Added	506	1	SB 131
53-12-110	Repealed	506	1	SB 131
53-12-111	Repealed	506	1	SB 131
53-12-112	Repealed	506	1	SB 131
53-12-113	Repealed	506	1	SB 131
53-12-114	Repealed	506	1	SB 131
53-12-115	Repealed	506	1	SB 131
53-12-116	Repealed	506	1	SB 131
53-12-120	Added	506	1	SB 131
53-12-121	Repealed	506	1	SB 131
53-12-122	Repealed	506	1	SB 131
53-12-123	Repealed	506	1	SB 131
53-12-124	Repealed	506	1	SB 131
53-12-125	Repealed	506	1	SB 131
53-12-126	Repealed	506	1	SB 131
53-12-127	Repealed	506	1	SB 131
53-12-128	Repealed	506	1	SB 131
53-12-129	Repealed	506	1	SB 131
53-12-130	Repealed and Reenacted	506	1	SB 131
53-12-131	Repealed and Reenacted	506	1	SB 131
53-12-132	Repealed and Reenacted	506	1	SB 131
53-12-133	Repealed and Reenacted	506	1	SB 131
53-12-150	Repealed and Reenacted	506	1	SB 131
53-12-151	Repealed and Reenacted	506	1	SB 131
53-12-152	Repealed and Reenacted	506	1	SB 131
53-12-153	Repealed and Reenacted	506	1	SB 131
53-12-154	Added	506	1	SB 131
53-12-155	Added	506	1	SB 131
53-12-156	Added	506	1	SB 131
53-12-157	Added	506	1	SB 131
53-12-158	Added	506	1	SB 131
53-12-159	Added	506	1	SB 131
53-12-170	Repealed and Reenacted	506	1	SB 131
53-12-171	Repealed and Reenacted	506	1	SB 131
53-12-172	Repealed and Reenacted	506	1	SB 131
53-12-173	Repealed and Reenacted	506	1	SB 131
53-12-173.1	Repealed	506	1	SB 131
53-12-174	Repealed and Reenacted	506	1	SB 131
53-12-175	Repealed and Reenacted	506	1	SB 131
53-12-176	Repealed	506	1	SB 131
53-12-180	Added	506	1	SB 131
53-12-181	Added	506	1	SB 131
53-12-182	Added	506	1	SB 131
53-12-183	Added	506	1	SB 131
53-12-184	Added	506	1	SB 131
53-12-190	Repealed and Reenacted	506	1	SB 131
53-12-191	Repealed and Reenacted	506	1	SB 131
53-12-192	Repealed and Reenacted	506	1	SB 131
53-12-193	Repealed and Reenacted	506	1	SB 131
53-12-194	Repealed and Reenacted	506	1	SB 131
53-12-195	Repealed and Reenacted	506	1	SB 131
53-12-196	Repealed	506	1	SB 131
53-12-197	Repealed	506	1	SB 131
53-12-198	Repealed	506	1	SB 131
53-12-199	Repealed	506	1	SB 131
53-12-200	Added	506	1	SB 131
53-12-201	Added	506	1	SB 131

	Effect	Act	Section	Bill/Resolution Number
Code Section—continued				
53-12-202	Added	506	1	SB 131
53-12-203	Added	506	1	SB 131
53-12-204	Added	506	1	SB 131
53-12-210	Repealed and Reenacted	506	1	SB 131
53-12-211	Repealed and Reenacted	506	1	SB 131
53-12-212	Repealed and Reenacted	506	1	SB 131
53-12-213	Repealed and Reenacted	506	1	SB 131
53-12-214	Repealed and Reenacted	506	1	SB 131
53-12-215	Repealed and Reenacted	506	1	SB 131
53-12-216	Repealed and Reenacted	506	1	SB 131
53-12-217	Repealed and Reenacted	506	1	SB 131
53-12-218	Repealed and Reenacted	506	1	SB 131
53-12-219	Repealed and Reenacted	506	1	SB 131
53-12-220	Repealed and Reenacted	506	1	SB 131
53-12-221	Repealed and Reenacted	506	1	SB 131
53-12-222	Repealed and Reenacted	506	1	SB 131
53-12-230	Repealed and Reenacted	506	1	SB 131
53-12-231	Repealed and Reenacted	506	1	SB 131
53-12-232	Repealed and Reenacted	506	1	SB 131
53-12-233	Repealed	506	1	SB 131
53-12-234	Repealed	506	1	SB 131
53-12-240	Added	506	1	SB 131
53-12-241	Added	506	1	SB 131
53-12-242	Added	506	1	SB 131
53-12-243	Added	506	1	SB 131
53-12-244	Added	506	1	SB 131
53-12-245	Added	506	1	SB 131
53-12-246	Added	506	1	SB 131
53-12-247	Added	506	1	SB 131
53-12-250	Repealed	506	1	SB 131
53-12-251	Repealed	506	1	SB 131
53-12-252	Repealed	506	1	SB 131
53-12-253	Repealed	506	1	SB 131
53-12-254	Repealed	506	1	SB 131
53-12-255	Repealed	506	1	SB 131
53-12-256	Repealed	506	1	SB 131
53-12-257	Repealed	506	1	SB 131
53-12-258	Repealed	506	1	SB 131
53-12-259	Repealed	506	1	SB 131
53-12-260	Repealed and Reenacted	506	1	SB 131
53-12-261	Repealed and Reenacted	506	1	SB 131
53-12-262	Repealed and Reenacted	506	1	SB 131
53-12-263	Repealed and Reenacted	506	1	SB 131
53-12-264	Repealed and Reenacted	506	1	SB 131
53-12-265	Repealed	506	1	SB 131
53-12-270	Added	506	1	SB 131
53-12-280	Repealed and Reenacted	506	1	SB 131
53-12-281	Repealed	506	1	SB 131
53-12-282	Repealed	506	1	SB 131
53-12-283	Repealed	506	1	SB 131
53-12-284	Repealed	506	1	SB 131
53-12-285	Repealed	506	1	SB 131
53-12-286	Repealed	506	1	SB 131
53-12-287	Repealed	506	1	SB 131
53-12-288	Repealed	506	1	SB 131
53-12-289	Repealed	506	1	SB 131
53-12-290	Repealed and Reenacted	506	1	SB 131
53-12-291	Added	506	1	SB 131
53-12-292	Added	506	1	SB 131
53-12-300	Repealed and Reenacted	506	1	SB 131
53-12-301	Repealed and Reenacted	506	1	SB 131

	Effect	Act	Section	Bill/Resolution Number
Code Section—continued				
53–12–302	Repealed and Reenacted	506	1	SB 131
53–12–303	Added	506	1	SB 131
53–12–304	Added	506	1	SB 131
53–12–305	Added	506	1	SB 131
53–12–306	Added	506	1	SB 131
53–12–307	Added	506	1	SB 131
53–12–308	Added	506	1	SB 131
53–12–320	Added	506	1	SB 131
53–12–321	Added	506	1	SB 131
53–12–322	Added	506	1	SB 131
53–12–323	Added	506	1	SB 131
53–12–340	Added	506	1	SB 131
53–12–341	Added	506	1	SB 131
53–12–342	Added	506	1	SB 131
53–12–343	Added	506	1	SB 131
53–12–344	Added	506	1	SB 131
53–12–345	Added	506	1	SB 131
53–12–350	Repealed and Reenacted	506	1	SB 131
53–12–351	Repealed and Reenacted	506	1	SB 131
53–12–352	Repealed and Reenacted	506	1	SB 131
53–12–353	Repealed and Reenacted	506	1	SB 131
53–12–354	Repealed and Reenacted	506	1	SB 131
53–12–360	Added	506	1	SB 131
53–12–361	Added	506	1	SB 131
53–12–362	Added	506	1	SB 131
53–12–363	Added	506	1	SB 131
53–12–364	Added	506	1	SB 131
53–12–370	Repealed	506	1	SB 131
53–12–371	Repealed	506	1	SB 131
53–12–372	Repealed	506	1	SB 131
53–12–373	Repealed	506	1	SB 131
53–12–374	Repealed	506	1	SB 131
53–12–375	Repealed	506	1	SB 131
53–12–376	Repealed	506	1	SB 131
53–12–380	Added	506	1	SB 131
53–12–381	Added	506	1	SB 131
53–12–390	Repealed and Reenacted	506	1	SB 131
53–12–391	Repealed and Reenacted	506	1	SB 131
53–12–392	Repealed	506	1	SB 131
53–12–393	Repealed	506	1	SB 131
53–12–394	Repealed	506	1	SB 131
53–12–400	Added	506	1	SB 131
53–12–401	Added	506	1	SB 131
53–12–402	Added	506	1	SB 131
53–12–410	Added	506	1	SB 131
53–12–411	Added	506	1	SB 131
53–12–412	Added	506	1	SB 131
53–12–420	Added	506	1	SB 131
53–12–421	Added	506	1	SB 131
53–12–422	Added	506	1	SB 131
53–12–423	Added	506	1	SB 131
53–12–424	Added	506	1	SB 131
53–12–425	Added	506	1	SB 131
53–12–426	Added	506	1	SB 131
53–12–427	Added	506	1	SB 131
53–12–428	Added	506	1	SB 131
53–12–429	Added	506	1	SB 131
53–12–430	Added	506	1	SB 131
53–12–431	Added	506	1	SB 131
53–12–450	Added	506	1	SB 131
53–12–451	Added	506	1	SB 131

	Effect	Act	Section	Bill/Resolution Number
Code Section—continued				
53–12–452	Added	506	1	SB 131
53–12–453	Added	506	1	SB 131
53–12–454	Added	506	1	SB 131
53–12–455	Added	506	1	SB 131

TABLE OF CONTENTS

Part I

ARREST AND CRIMINAL INVESTIGATIVE PROCEDURES*

Chapter 1

Introduction

KeyCite®: Cases and other legal materials listed in KeyCite Scope can be researched through the KeyCite service on Westlaw®. Use KeyCite to check citations for form, parallel references, prior and later history, and comprehensive citator information, including citations to other decisions and secondary materials.

§ 1-1 General considerations

The importance of procedure in the area of substantive criminal law has, in recent years, received the attention it so rightly deserves by commentators and textbook writers alike. From a practical standpoint, the practitioner is well aware that cases can be won or lost on procedural grounds. Thus, this book is designed to aid Georgia practitioners in the handling of a criminal case. It is hoped that through the sequential examination of the various stages of the criminal process from arrest to final judgment, the reader will easily be able to find the point of law with which he is concerned.

While this book focuses on Georgia law, attention is given to federal constitutional law. It should be obvious to anyone who has even a passing knowledge of criminal law that in the past few years the Supreme Court's concern with the constitutional aspects of procedure has taken on great, if not a paramount, importance.

Criminal procedure has also been guided and influenced greatly by the federal courts and to a lesser extent by other sources, such as the American Bar Association Standards for Criminal Justice. In view of the importance of procedure in criminal cases, especially in light of the new sources of criminal procedure, many of which are not readily available to the average practitioner, it was felt that there was a need for this book.

§ 1-2 Scope and purpose

This book was conceived as a handbook of Georgia criminal procedure as practiced in our superior courts. Because of the interrelationship between pre-trial and trial practice, it soon became apparent that criminal procedure prior to trial would have to be included. Basically, however, this book remains a guide to those matters relating to trial practice in our courts of general criminal jurisdiction. Efforts have been made to refer to some of the rules and practices in state courts, city courts, or other special courts as those rules affect the trial of criminal cases.

This book is not intended to be, and is not, a book on substantive criminal law. The prosecution and defense of criminal cases are dealt with only in a general manner without any attempt to discuss the particularities of various kinds of prosecutions and their defenses.

Hopefully, this book will be helpful to those who will be involved in the trial of criminal cases.

This information is taken from* ***Daniel's Georgia Criminal Trial Practice, 2009-2010 Edition**, by Jack Goger (Thomson Reuters, 2009). Footnotes in the original volume were deleted to conserve space and reduce cost.*

This **Daniel's Georgia Criminal Trial Practice** data can also be accessed in its entirety on Westlaw at the sign-on **GACRMTRIAL**. The Westlaw sign-on **GA-HARRISON**, Georgia Harrison Analytical Library, contains documents from all available Georgia Harrison Analytical texts published by Thomson Reuters and The Harrison Company.

Chapter 2

Arrests

§ 2-1 Scope

This chapter involves the law relating to taking a person into custody in connection with a charge of violating a criminal law. The validity of an arrest has taken on new meaning with the federal constitutional application of the exclusionary rule. In addition to the material on arrests contained in this chapter, stop and frisk is discussed in Chapter 3, and search and seizure is discussed in Chapter 4, which contains sections on searches incident to a valid arrest and material on the question of probable cause. Custodial interrogation is discussed in Chapter 5, and Chapter 6 contains some material on arrest and identification procedures.

§ 2-2 Definitions of arrest

At the threshold, it must be understood that the word "arrest" has two distinct meanings. First, there is a common law, or in some states, a statutory meaning. Second, there is the federal constitutional meaning which has been recognized by the United States Supreme Court.

For the common law definition of the word "arrest," the Georgia Court of Appeals has stated:

"An arrest is the taking, seizing, or detaining of the person of another, either by touching or putting hands on him, or by any act indicating an intention to take such person into custody, and which subjects such person to the actual control and will of the person making the arrest. It is sufficient if the arrested person understands that he is in the power of the one arresting and submits in consequence thereof. The taking of another into custody for the purpose of investigating an alleged crime constitutes an arrest." See section 3-2, infra, on what constitutes a seizure.

The Georgia Supreme Court has more concisely said that "a person is under arrest whenever his liberty to come and go as he pleases is restrained, no matter how slight such restraint may be."

In Georgia, as provided by statute, it is not necessary that a person actually be touched in order to be considered arrested. If the person voluntarily submits or gives in on the condition that he will only be allowed his freedom of movement under the direction of the officer, the arrest is complete.

In addition, it has been held that the seizure of one's property from his immediate presence is the functional equivalent of the seizure of his person. This includes the seizure and retention of personal property or money when the authorities do not make it absolutely clear how they plan to reunite the suspect and his possessions at some time and place.

These statements represent the general common-law concept of arrest. However, this is not the present federal constitutional concept of the term "arrest" or the term "custodial arrest."

Under the federal constitutional concept of arrest, a greater degree of intrusion or restraint is required in order to have an arrest than that which was required at common law. For example, a "stop and frisk" in terms of federal constitutional law amounts to a seizure, not to an arrest; and it does not require probable cause. However, in common-law terms a "stop and frisk" at least generally appears to be an arrest. The person frisked is certainly at least slightly restrained. On the other hand, the United States Supreme Court in the *Terry* case made it clear that the Fourth Amendment applies to "seizures" as well as to arrests.

Thus, from a federal constitutional standpoint, the terms "seizure" and "arrest" or "custodial arrest" together seem to approximate the common-law concept of arrest. That is, the common-law term "arrest" applies, of course, to what the United States Supreme Court has called an "arrest" or "custodial arrest" from a federal constitutional standpoint, but the common-law term "arrest" also encompasses a "stop and frisk" or "seizure" as defined by the Supreme Court.

The nomenclature used by the United States Supreme Court is important because a "seizure" or "stop and frisk" is valid if based on reasonable suspicion, which is grounded upon specific and articulable facts, judged against an objective standard. However, when such a "search" is permissible the "search" accompanying such a seizure is much more restricted than in the case of a search incident to a lawful "arrest," as that term is used by the Supreme Court. There may not be a federal constitutional "arrest" in the absence of probable cause, but if there is probable cause (and the arrest is otherwise valid) the search conducted incident to such an arrest may be much broader than in the "stop and frisk" or "seizure" situation. However, where a person thought to be only an eyewitness to a shooting was asked to wait in the back of a police car until he could be questioned about the shooting, and the "witness" made an incriminating statement when a detective approached 17 minutes later, the court concluded that from a federal constitutional standpoint the seizure was reasonable and a less severe intrusion than a traditional arrest and thus declined to suppress the statement.

In *State v. Corbett,* the court held that whether or not a person has been constitutionally arrested depends upon "whether a reasonable person in the suspect's position would have thought the detention would not be temporary." In *State v. Davis,* Judge Johnson pointed out that "[a] person has been 'seized' within the meaning of the Fourth Amendment only if, in view of all of the circumstances surrounding the incident, a reasonable person would have believed that he was not free to leave. Examples of circumstances that might indicate a seizure, even where the person did not attempt to leave, would be the threatening presence of several officers, the display of a weapon by an officer, some physical touching of the person . . ., or the use of language or tone of voice indicating that compliance with the officer's request might be compelled."

It should be noted, however, that notwithstanding the foregoing, not every custodial restraint of an individual by a police officer will constitute an "arrest." A person taken into custody pursuant to an order of *civil* protective custody is not "arrested." In Lindsey v. State, for example, an individual who was detained, placed in handcuffs and into a police cruiser and secured while being served with a civil order authorizing the individual's detention for purposes of a mental evaluation was not deemed under "arrest" for purposes of a Fourth Amendment challenge to contraband found during the search.

In *Miranda v. State,* in an opinion by Judge, now Chief Justice, Benham, the Court of Appeals said there are at least three kinds of police-citizen encounters: (1) verbal encounters involving no coercion or detention, (2) brief "stops" or "seizures" which must be accompanied by reasonable suspicion, and (3) "arrests" which must be supported by probable cause.

In *Quinn v. State,* the court pointed out that "[n]ot all encounters between police officers and citizens involve seizures which implicate Fourth Amendment protections. . . . '[E]ven when officers have no basis for suspecting a particular individual, they may generally ask questions . . .; [and] ask to examine the individual's identification . . .;—as long as the police do not convey a message that compliance with their requests is required.' "

See section 3-2 et seq., infra, on facts justifying a stop and frisk and what constitutes a seizure.

§ 2-3 Immunity from arrest

Certain persons while performing or preparing to perform official duties may only be arrested for certain offenses. For example, such limited immunity from arrest applies to members of the General Assembly, and militiamen. The federal Constitution provides for this type of immunity from arrest for members of Congress and diplomats of a foreign nation; their families and staffs enjoy a broader immunity under a federal statute.

See section 2-20, infra, on arrest of peace officers.

§ 2-4 Delay in making an arrest

While it is often said that an officer is under a duty to arrest a defendant immediately without a warrant where a crime is committed in his presence, it is established in Georgia, and under the federal Constitution, that a defendant has no general right to an immediate arrest. The United States Supreme Court has held that the Sixth Amendment right to a speedy trial does not apply until the defendant has been indicted or arrested. However, in *United States v. Lovasco*, the Court has acknowledged that the due process clause "has a limited role to play in protecting against oppressive delay." If such a due process violation is asserted and there is "proof of actual prejudice" then it is said that the due process claim is ripe for adjudication, but this does not make the claim automatically valid. A delay for purposes of further investigation normally "does not deprive . . . [a defendant] of due process, even if his defense might have been somewhat prejudiced by the lapse of time." A defendant is entitled to a dismissal of his indictment where the delay is taken by the prosecution as "an intentional device to gain tactical advantage over the accused." The Court in *Lovasco* concluded that a good faith investigative delay of one and one half years did not amount to a due process violation. However, in determining whether or not a delay in obtaining an indictment after an arrest violates the Sixth Amendment right to a speedy trial, the Georgia Supreme Court has applied a less rigorous standard. The Georgia court has evaluated such a delay by the *Barker v. Wingo* standard which the United States Supreme Court has applied to a delay in trial after indictment. This standard is discussed in section 14-65, infra. Nevertheless, from a federal constitutional standpoint the general rule is that "[t]here is no constitutional right to be arrested."

While some states have considered a delay in arrest as a due process violation, it has been said that a dismissal of an indictment is required for pre-arrest or pre-indictment delay only if it is shown that (1) the delay caused substantial prejudice to the defendant's right to a fair trial and that (2) the delay was an intentional device to gain a tactical advantage over the defendant. Thus, it has been held that where a delay only results in a defendant's loss of ability to recall his whereabouts at the time of the alleged offense, the indictment will not be dismissed if there is no indication that the arrest was delayed in order to gain a tactical advantage over the defendant.

Additionally, even prior to *Chimel v. California,* it was held that an officer has no right to use such a delay as an excuse to wait until a defendant is at a particular place which the officer wishes to search incident to an arrest. However, if the officer waits to arrest for the purpose of giving the offender an opportunity to repeat the offense, such conduct alone is not objectionable.

§ 2-5 Place of arrest

Georgia provides by statute that, where necessary, an officer with a valid arrest warrant may break into a home to arrest a concealed offender. However, generally an officer has no right in the execution of a search warrant or a warrantless arrest to "break" the door in to arrest a defendant, without first stating his authority and purpose for demanding admission.

In *United States v. Watson,* the Supreme Court held that there may be a warrantless arrest of a suspect in a public place if the officer has probable cause to believe that the suspect has committed a felony. In *Payton v. New York,* the Court further held that an officer has no right to arrest a suspect in the suspect's home without an arrest warrant in the absence of exigent circumstances. However, *Payton* does not prevent a warrantless arrest in a common hallway of an apartment house, or where a defendant "is sitting on his porch," nor does it prevent an arrest in a defendant's home where the officer attempted to stop the defendant outside his home only to have the defendant retreat into his home. Likewise, in *Kendrick v. State,* the Georgia Court of Appeals held that a warrantless arrest effected after a valid consent to enter the home is not a Payton violation. Nevertheless, in *United States v. Winchenbach,* the court held that when officers have a search warrant for the defendant's residence and have probable cause to arrest him, they may arrest the defendant in his home without an arrest warrant.

In *Welsh v. Wisconsin,* the United States Supreme Court held that officers had no right to a warrantless entry of a defendant's home to arrest him for a non-jailable traffic offense in order to preserve evidence of his intoxication in the absence of other exigency. The Wisconsin Supreme Court had concluded that there were exigent circumstances based on the need to obtain a test of the blood alcohol level of the defendant and hot pursuit. The United States Supreme Court found that "there was no immediate or continuous pursuit of the . . . [defendant] from the scene of a crime," and thus no hot pursuit. The Court also held "that an important factor to be considered when determining whether any exigency exists is the gravity of the underlying offense for which the arrest is being made. Moreover, although no exigency is created simply because there is probable cause to believe that a serious crime has been committed, . . . application of the exigent-circumstances exception in the context of a home entry should rarely be sanctioned when there is probable cause to believe that only a minor offense . . . has been committed."

In *State v. Nichols,* an officer arrested the defendant in his father's home. The defendant backed into a car in the yard and when ordered to stop, he fled into the house. The court affirmed the validity of the arrest pointing out that "hot pursuit" need not involve a high speed chase.

In *McCauley v. State,* deputies responded to a domestic dispute where they found the wife of the defendant outside the residence crying and upset. She indicated that the defendant had been drinking and had struck and threatened her and their four-month-old infant. With the consent of the wife, the deputies entered the house and determined that the defendant was so impaired as to endanger the child. The appellate court affirmed the conviction, finding that the exigent circumstances justified the warrantless arrest of defendant in his home.

In *Steagald v. United States,* the United States Supreme Court held that an officer with an arrest warrant has no right to enter the home of a third party to search for the defendant unless the officer also has a search warrant to search the premises of the third party without his consent, or unless there are exigent circumstances.

In *King v. State,* a Georgia county deputy searched the residence of a third party in an attempt to execute an arrest warrant. The officer had been previously informed by the defendant that the person named in the arrest warrant no longer lived at that residence and was given permission by the defendant to search personal items of the former tenant that had been left at the residence. The court found that when the officer returned a second time, the fact that the defendant "started to back up in the doorway" and seemed "agitated" did not create exigent circumstances. Hence, it was error for the trial judge to deny a motion to suppress marijuana observed by the deputy in plain view after the officer entered the house.

The Eleventh Circuit in *United States v. Bulman,* while recognizing that there may be a lesser expectation of privacy in a motel room than a home, concluded that the Payton rule applied to the arrest of a defendant in his motel room. However, the Steagald rule is intended to protect the third party, whose home has been searched, and not the defendant who is arrested. Hence, it has been held where a defendant is arrested pursuant to an arrest warrant in a third party's home, without a search warrant, the defendant has no standing to move to suppress firearms and ammunition observed in plain view at the time of his arrest.

In *United States v. Reed,* the court said that the following factors may be considered in determining whether or not exigent circumstances exist to arrest a defendant in his home without an arrest warrant: (1) the gravity or violent nature of the offense; (2) whether the suspect is reasonably believed to be armed; (3) "a clear showing of probable cause . . . that the suspect committed the crime"; (4) a "strong reason to believe that the suspect is in the premises being entered"; (5) "a likelihood that the suspect will escape if not swiftly apprehended"; and (6) the peaceful circumstances of the entry by the officer.

In *United States v. Segura,* the Second Circuit found invalid the warrantless security check of the defendant's seventeenth floor apartment after his arrest in the lobby of the building.

§ 2-6 Procedure for arrest

In situations where a lawful arrest cannot be made without a warrant, the officer should have the warrant in his possession at the time of the arrest or so near at hand that it can be exhibited on demand. It has been said that an officer derives no authority or power from a warrant unless he has it with him and can display it. O.C.G.A. § 17-4-20 provides that an officer has a right to arrest with or without a warrant (1) if the offense was committed within his presence or within his immediate knowledge, or (2) if the offender is endeavoring to escape, or (3) if the officer has probable cause to believe an act of family violence has been committed, or (4) for other cause if there is likely to be a failure of justice from the want of a duly authorized officer to issue a warrant, or (5) if the officer has probable cause to believe that an offense involving physical abuse has been committed against a vulnerable adult who is defined as being a person 18 years old or older who is unable to protect himself or herself from physical or mental abuse.

In the absence of one of the five instances above, an officer generally has no right to arrest for a violation of a municipal ordinance or a misdemeanor unless the officer has a warrant in his possession at the time of the attempted arrest. This is said to be true because the officer is bound to have the warrant ready to be produced if asked for. For example, in *Croker v. State,* the court said that where the offense involved was a misdemeanor not committed in the presence of the officer and flight was not involved, the officer had no authority to arrest the defendant even though a warrant had been issued because the warrant was not accessible to the officer at the time. In the case of a felony, it is not necessary for the officer to have the warrant in his possession in order to make a valid arrest. Also, an officer may arrest without a warrant pursuant to O.C.G.A. § 17-4-20(a) or with probable cause. See section 2-13, infra. However, under Georgia law it has been held that if the officer wishes to arrest the defendant without a warrant, he should do so promptly. Without a warrant and in the absence of exigent circumstances, there is no right to make an arrest in a person's home. Moreover, even when an officer has an arrest warrant, the general rule requires that the officer knock and announce his presence before entering. See section 2-19, infra, on arrest warrants.

While it is provided by Georgia statute that where an officer has a warrant he may "break open the door of any house where the offender is concealed," and it is recognized that an officer may use such force as is reasonably necessary to arrest, nevertheless, he is not authorized to use any more force than is reasonably necessary. But see section 2-5, supra, on place of arrest. It has also been recognized that an officer may use more force to accomplish an arrest for a felony than for a misdemeanor.

In *Tennessee v. Garner,* the United States Supreme Court held a statute violative of the Fourth Amendment which permitted officers to use deadly force to prevent the escape of a suspected felon. The Court said that deadly force may not be used unless necessary to prevent escape and the officer has probable cause to believe that the suspect poses a significant threat of death or grave injury to the officer or others. In the case of a misdemeanor, an officer has no right to shoot merely to prevent his escape. This rule applies equally to an arrest for a violation of a municipal ordinance. However, even in the case of a misdemeanor, "in order to overcome declared, open and armed resistance to [the] execution of . . . [a warrant, an officer may] use such force as may be reasonably necessary to effect the arrest."

In 1986, Georgia added to O.C.G.A. § 17-4-20 a provision stating that an officer "may use deadly force to apprehend a suspected felon only when the officer reasonably believes that the suspect possesses a deadly weapon or any object, device, or instrument which, when used offensively against a person, is likely to or actually does result in serious bodily injury; when the officer reasonably believes that the suspect poses an immediate threat of physical violence to the officer or others; or when there is probable cause to believe that the suspect has committed a crime involving the infliction or threatened infliction of serious physical harm. Nothing in this Code section shall be construed so as to restrict such sheriffs or peace officers from the use of such reasonable nondeadly force as may be necessary to apprehend and arrest a suspected felon or misdemeanant."

Unless the person to be arrested knows that the person attempting to arrest him is an officer, the officer should notify him of his authority. Likewise, the person to be taken into custody should be notified of the offense with which he is being charged. If the officer has an arrest warrant, he should tell the suspect by what authority he is being arrested or should display the warrant to the accused. However, if a suspect knows he is being lawfully arrested by an officer, it is the duty of the suspect to submit quietly.

In the case of any offense involving a violation of any law or ordinance involving the operation, licensing, registration, maintenance or inspection of a motor vehicle, the officer may arrest by issuance of a citation if the offense was committed in the presence of the officer. If the offense results in an accident, an investigating officer may issue a citation regardless of whether the offense occurred in his presence. Also, a citation may be issued if the offense occurred before another officer. Any citation issued "shall enumerate the specific charges against the person and the date upon which the person is to appear and answer the charges." If the offense occurred before another officer, "the citation shall list the name of each officer and each must be present when the charges against the accused person are heard."

In *Atwater v. City of Lago Vista,* the United States Supreme Court held that an officer in Texas may, under the federal constitution, arrest the driver of an automobile for not wearing a seat belt even though the failure to utilize a seat belt is a non-jailable misdemeanor punishable only by a fine of not less than $25.00 or more than $50.00. Although the law permits officers to issue citations in lieu of arrest, the court pointed out that "the standard of probable cause 'applie[s] to all arrests, without the need to 'balance' the interests and circumstances involved in particular situations.' "

See *Criminal Arrest in Georgia,* Institute of Government, University of Georgia (1979), p. 34.

§ 2-7 Right to resist illegal arrest

Certain limitations exist on the power of an officer to arrest an individual. If the arrest is illegal and proceeds so far as to constitute an assault, the alleged offender may resist with such force as is reasonably necessary to prevent his arrest. However, an assault against an arresting officer is not justified unless the officer assaulted the person first. It is generally held that the killing of an individual who is illegally arresting another is manslaughter rather than murder. However, if the arresting officer intended to kill that individual prior to the attempted illegal arrest in order to effect the arrest, such a killing may amount to murder. The "law provides no right to resist a legal arrest." Where an arrest is unlawful, the person making the arrest may be subject to an action for damages and a possible action under the Civil Rights Act.

However, in *Green v. State,* a majority of the Court of Appeals held that where a person is charged with obstruction of a police officer, and his sole defense is that the arrest was illegal, it is not error for the trial judge to refuse to give a charge that "[e]very person has the right to resist an illegal arrest . . .," if the trial judge charges the essential elements of the obstruction offense requiring the state "to prove the lawfulness of the arrest in order to prove an essential element of the offense."

See section 2-11, infra, on probable cause to arrest.

§ 2-8 What persons have an officer's power to arrest?

Ordinarily the word "officer," for purposes of making an arrest, denotes a peace officer who is authorized by statute to make an arrest. An arrest by a security guard or a private citizen, or a citizen's arrest, is discussed in section 2-21, infra.

It should be noted that Georgia has provided by statute that no peace officer shall exercise the power to arrest if the officer has not complied with the Georgia Peace Officer Standards and Training Act. Also, in *Holstein v. State* the court held that an officer who has not completed the requirements of the Training Act may not obtain a search warrant. However, in *Davis v. State* the court held that an officer who has completed the training requirements of the statute may arrest even though he has not yet received his certification.

In *Williams v. State,* the court held that a federal DEA agent had no authority as an officer to make an arrest for a misdemeanor; however, the agent had the same right as any other citizen to arrest an offender who is committing a misdemeanor in his presence.

O.C.G.A. § 17-4-25 provides in part as follows:

"(a) Under a warrant issued by a judicial officer, an arresting officer may, in any county without regard to the residence of the arresting officer, arrest any person charged with a crime. It is the duty of the arresting officer to take the accused, with the warrant under which he was arrested, to the county in which the offense is alleged to have been committed, for examination before any judicial officer of that county."

This section does not apply to city police officers, but does apply to state officers and county police.

In *Watkins v. State,* the court held that under exigent circumstances a deputy sheriff has authority to make a warrantless arrest beyond the limits of his county.

See generally 6A C. J. S. Arrest § 17. See section 2-21, infra, on the authority of a private citizen to arrest, and section 2-20, infra, on arrest of peace officer. Generally, see section 2-13 et seq., infra, on arrest by an officer.

§ 2-9 Overview of prerequisites for warrantless arrests

In order to have a valid "stop and frisk" or "seizure" of a person in a federal constitutional sense, it is not necessary for an officer to have probable cause. An articulable suspicion is sufficient. See Chapter 3, infra. However, in order to have a valid arrest, the Fourth Amendment requires that there must be probable cause to believe that the suspect has violated the law, or is violating the law in the officer's presence. See section 2-2, supra, on the definition of an arrest.

By statute, Georgia has stated that an officer may arrest in five situations. However, the absolute prerequisite, which is sometimes lost sight of, is that from a federal constitutional standpoint an arrest is not valid unless there is probable cause, regardless of whether the situation falls within one of the five provisions of the Georgia statute authorizing an officer to make a warrantless arrest.

On the other hand, to have a valid arrest in the common law or Georgia tradition, one of the five statutory requirements must exist. Section 2-13 et seq., infra, discuss the question of whether or not one or more of the statutory requirements for an arrest can exist when there is no probable cause.

In summary, to have a valid arrest from both the federal constitutional and common law standpoint, there must first be probable cause. However, if one of the five situations of the Georgia statute exists there may be a valid "seizure" or "stop and frisk" in the federal constitutional sense, even in the absence of probable cause, if there is an articulable suspicion justifying the action.

§ 2-10 Probable cause—General

The Fourth Amendment provides as follows:

"The right of the people to be secure in their persons, houses, papers, and effects, against unreasonable searches and seizures, shall not be violated, and no Warrants shall issue, but upon probable cause, supported by Oath or affirmation, and particularly describing the place to be searched, and the persons or things to be seized."

In *Wong Sun v. United States,* the Supreme Court stated that regardless of whether an arrest is made with a warrant or without a warrant, such an arrest "must stand upon firmer ground than mere suspicion . . . though the arresting officer need not have in hand evidence which would suffice to convict. The quantum of information which constitutes probable cause—evidence which would 'warrant a man of reasonable caution in the belief' that a felony has been committed . . . must be measured by the facts of the particular case." In *Brown v. State,* the Georgia Court of Appeals said the "test of probable cause is whether it would justify a man of reasonable caution in believing that an offense has been or is being committed, and this requires merely a probability—less than a certainty but more than a mere suspicion or possibility." In arrests and searches the test, or requirement, of probable cause is objective; it is not a matter to be established by expert opinion nor a question of what the officer thought. However, "the judgment of seasoned officers should be treated with deference." Because of their expertise, these officers are 'able to perceive and articulate meaning in given conduct which would be wholly innocent to the untrained observer.' "

The same quantum of evidence is required to establish probable cause to arrest and probable cause to search. However, there are some different factual aspects of the two. In the case of an arrest without an arrest warrant, probable cause generally must exist before the arrest to believe that the particular person committed or is committing a particular offense, and there is little concern about whether or not the information is stale or current.

However, in the case of a search it is not necessary to name any person. A search and seizure is directed at a place. There is no constitutional requirement that a search warrant name the person who owns or has possession of the premises. In the case of a search there must be probable cause to believe that whatever is sought will be found at the place to be searched. Hence, the information may not be stale.

Lastly, it should be pointed out that even where there is probable cause to arrest a man, this does not mean that there is automatically probable cause to search his home, or place of business. Likewise, if there is probable cause to search a building, this does not mean that there is automatically probable cause to arrest the owner.

§ 2-11 Probable cause to arrest

As previously pointed out, in section 2-9, supra, there can be no valid arrest in the federal constitutional sense unless there is probable cause. And, shown in the last section, probable cause deals with probabilities, not certainties.

How is probable cause obtained? First of all:

"In order to have probable cause to make a warrantless arrest on the basis of personal observation, the presence of the peace officer at the place of observation, and the manner of observing, must be lawful, and this rule applies even where observations are made without entry into a private enclosure." In other words, the information used to establish probable cause must have been legally obtained.

Probable cause to arrest without a warrant has been said to be "a practical, non-technical conception affording the best compromise . . . for accommodating . . . often opposing interests. Requiring more would unduly hamper law enforcement. To allow less would be to leave law-abiding citizens at the mercy of the officers' whim or caprice."

In *Lewis v. State,* the Georgia Supreme Court said "[t]he test of probable cause is whether it would justify a person of reasonable caution in believing that an offense has been or is being committed, and this requires probability which is less than a certainty but more than mere suspicion or possibility."

Nevertheless, the factual basis supporting an officer's assessment of probable cause is at least as stringent as that which is applied when a magistrate weighs the facts in determining whether or not to issue an arrest warrant.

Probable cause must exist at the time of the arrest. In *Vaughn v. State,* the Georgia Supreme Court said:

"Whether that arrest was constitutionally valid depends in turn upon whether, at the moment the arrest was made, the officers had probable cause to make it—whether at that moment the facts and circumstances within their knowledge and of which they had reasonably trustworthy information were sufficient to warrant a prudent man in believing that the . . . [defendant] had committed or was committing an offense."

In determining whether or not probable cause to arrest exists, an officer may also consider what he knows, what he has seen, and what he has smelled. Thus, in *Berry v. State,* the court held that an officer, who had a degree in chemistry, who had received special training in drug identification, who knew the odor of hydrochloric acid, and who knew that hydrochloric acid is used to process cocaine and heroin, had probable cause to arrest a person fitting the drug courier profile when he detected the odor of hydrochloric acid. See section 3-4, infra, on drug courier profile.

In *State v. Batty,* a trial court's order finding that a police officer lacked probable cause to arrest the defendant for driving while intoxicated was affirmed where it appeared that the only objective evidence of impairment was the odor of alcohol. Although the stop of the defendant's motor vehicle was authorized because of a traffic violation, the trial court ruled that her arrest was not proper after she satisfactorily completed several field sobriety tests.

In *Banks v. State,* the court stated that "[f]light in connection with other circumstances may be sufficient probable cause to uphold" a warrantless arrest. In *State v. Willis*, the court held that where a defendant initially consented to a search and he then fled, these facts, "coupled with . . . [the defendant's] evasive answers regarding his presence in [a] high-crime area, would authorize a finding of probable cause to believe that the bulge in . . . [the defendant's] jacket pocket was contraband. . . ."

The standard for determining reliability of victims and informers in establishing probable cause for a warrantless arrest seem to be the same as in the case of evaluating an affidavit to determine probable cause for a search warrant. See section 4-7 et seq., infra, and see also 6A C. J. S. Arrest § 28 et seq.

In appraising the trustworthiness of information, and when an officer has to determine whether or not he has probable cause, the standard is an objective one, and subjective good faith alone is not sufficient. However, the known facts and reasonable inferences drawn therefrom may be evaluated from the standpoint of the expertise of the trained and experienced officer.

It must be remembered that it has been held that probable cause may rest upon the collective knowledge of the police when there is some degree of communication between them, rather than solely on the information possessed by the officer who actually makes the arrest. In *Paxton v. State,* the court pointed out that an NCIC printout is enough to establish probable cause to arrest. However, it must be remembered that under the rule of *Whiteley v. Warden,* if the officers initiating the NCIC report relating to the defendant did not themselves have probable cause, the arrest pursuant to the NCIC report would not be valid. But in *United States v. Hensley,* a stop-and-frisk situation, the United States Supreme Court held that the collective knowledge concept applies to police departments in two different states where the two departments are not engaging in a joint investigation. In *Hensley*, a "wanted flyer" was issued in Ohio and the stop was made in Kentucky. The Court did not discuss the lack of communication between the two different police departments involved but concluded that the "flyer" itself constituted articulable suspicion justifying a stop. See Chapter 3, infra, on stop and frisk. See section 2-26, infra, on the applicability of the exclusionary rule where there is a mistake in the indexing of a warrant.

The following section contains a discussion of some cases which have considered the problems of determining when probable cause exists.

See Chapter 3, infra, on an articulable suspicion justifying a stop or stop and frisk. See section 3-12, infra, for stop or arrest for the violation of a statute later determined to be unconstitutional. See section 2-19, infra, on arrest warrants.

§ 2-12 Probable cause to arrest—Illustrative cases

The case of *Brinegar v. United States* has been widely cited and relied on in discussing what facts are needed to constitute probable cause to arrest. In *Brinegar,* a government agent had parked beside a highway about five miles from a state line. The defendant drove by. The agent recognized the defendant and the car. The vehicle was proceeding in a direction away from a state in which liquor could be purchased and in the direction of an area where there was a demand for liquor even though the state was dry. The agent had arrested the defendant five months earlier for transporting liquor, had seen him loading liquor in a vehicle in the adjoining state at least twice in the last six months and knew he had a reputation for hauling liquor. The car seemed to be heavily loaded. The defendant tried unsuccessfully to outrun the agent. When the agent approached the car, he called the defendant by name and asked him how much liquor he had this time. The defendant told him not much. There was a case on the front seat which was visible or was covered with a lap robe. The Court concluded that there was probable cause to arrest the defendant.

In *Beck v. Ohio,* police officers who had received unspecified "information" and "heard" about the defendant and who "knew what he looked like" and knew that he had a gambling record, stopped the defendant as he was driving an automobile. Without an arrest or search warrant, the officers placed him under arrest and searched his car, finding nothing of interest. They took him to a police station, where they found some clearinghouse slips on his person, for the possession of which he was subsequently tried. The Court held that no probable cause for petitioner's arrest had been shown, and therefore the arrest, searches, and seizure of the slips were invalid.

In *Maryland v. Pringle,* the Supreme Court found that officers had probable cause to arrest the front-seat passenger of a vehicle where $763 was found in the car's glove compartment and cocaine was found in the backseat of the auto. The Court determined that the officer's discovery of the money and cocaine in their respective locations gave rise to the reasonable inference that the passenger "had knowledge of, and exercised reasonable control over, the cocaine." In addition, the Court distinguished *Ybarra v. Illinois* on the grounds that passengers in a private automobile will often be involved in a common enterprise, unlike a patron in a public tavern.

In *Draper v. United States,* a "special employee" of the Bureau of Narcotics, proven to be reliable in the past, informed a federal agent that the defendant, who was engaged in selling narcotics, was returning to Denver on a certain train and would be wearing certain articles of clothing. The Supreme Court upheld the conviction of Draper, stating that probable cause for arrest exists where an officer receives and corroborates very detailed information from a regular and reliable informer.

In *Smith v. State,* the court held that "where an informant supplies the information to one officer who then relays it to a fellow officer," the question of whether this information may be used to establish probable cause revolves around the reliability of the informant. Where the informant is found to be reliable, probable cause exists for the second officer. "However, where the officer *receiving the tip* could not establish the credibility of the informant, probable cause [is] not demonstrated." (Emphasis by the court.) See section 4-8 et seq., infra, on informers.

In *Wells v. State,* the court held that a tip from a reliable informant when corroborated by the personal observation of an investigating officer is sufficient to establish probable cause.

In *Taylor v. Alabama,* all of the members of the United States Supreme Court agreed there was no probable cause to arrest Taylor. The facts are summarized as follows: "In 1978, a grocery store in Montgomery, Ala., was robbed. There had been a number of robberies in this area, and the police had initiated an intensive manhunt in an effort to apprehend the robbers. An individual who was at that time incarcerated on unrelated charges told a police officer that 'he had heard that . . . Omar Taylor was involved in the robbery. . . .' This individual had never before given similar information to this officer, did not tell the officer where he had heard this information, and did not provide any details of the crime. This tip was insufficient to give the police probable cause to obtain a warrant or to arrest. . . ." Two officers arrested Taylor without a warrant. He was given *Miranda* warnings and fingerprinted. It was determined that his fingerprints matched prints found in the grocery. Based on this information, a warrant was obtained while Taylor was being interrogated. Taylor confessed.

The Court pointed out that the fingerprint information was obtained as a result of Taylor's illegal arrest and the arrest warrant was not valid. Since the confession was obtained through custodial interrogation after an illegal arrest, it was held to be inadmissible.

In *Hill v. California,* officers had sufficient evidence to constitute probable cause to arrest Hill. They went to his apartment without a warrant of any kind. When the officers knocked on a door, a man named Miller went to the door and was arrested. He fit the description of Hill but denied that he was Hill. He presented identification showing that he was Miller and said he was waiting for Hill. He said he knew nothing about any stolen property or guns, but there was a pistol in plain view on a coffee table. The officers were unimpressed with his explanation (which later proved to be true) and the search which they conducted produced evidence which the prosecution later sought to use in Hill's prosecution. The Court held that the officers reasonably mistook Miller for Hill, so Miller's arrest and the resulting search were valid. However, in *Commonwealth v. Collini,* the Pennsylvania Superior Court pointed out that while a reasonable mistaken belief may give probable cause to arrest, an *unreasonable* mistaken belief will not provide probable cause for an arrest.

In *Morris v. State,* the court held "that the defendant's failure to accurately repeat . . . [his] birthday and . . . social security number was sufficient evidence of a false identity as to provide probable cause" to arrest the defendant for giving a false name to a law enforcement officer. See section 3-12, infra, on when a "stop" becomes an "arrest."

In *Ledesma v. State,* the Georgia Supreme Court held probable cause to arrest was justified where Georgia officers received a teletype message from Missouri police that a named person was wanted for a felony in that state and the Georgia officers reasonably believed an arrest warrant had been issued in Missouri.

In *Alex v. State,* the court held that where a defendant refused to voluntarily submit to a search, when validly stopped, officers were authorized to detain him for a reasonable time in which to obtain a search warrant. Also, where under these circumstances the defendant pushed past the agents and shoved an officer with his forearm, the officers had probable cause to arrest him for battery and obstruction of an officer and to search him pursuant to the valid arrest. See section 4-26, infra.

In *Little v. State,* the defendant became a suspect in connection with the crimes of kidnapping and auto theft. There was no probable cause to arrest the defendant in connection with these crimes. The investigative officer found an old arrest warrant for the defendant on an unpaid traffic fine and arrested the defendant on that warrant so that he could be questioned about the kidnapping and the theft. He was given *Miranda* warnings, questioned and placed in a lineup where he was identified. The Georgia Court of Appeals held the arrest was valid and the evidence obtained as a result of the arrest was admissible.

In *Hamilton v. State,* the Georgia Court of Appeals, in considering probable cause to arrest, said "the officers were aware that a robbery had taken place less than an hour earlier. The manager-victim was able to identify a black sedan containing three passengers as transporting the probable robbers. A driver's license found at the scene established that Hamilton was probably one of the robbers or at least was present, and that Hamilton probably was driving a black 1967 or 1968 Plymouth Fury. At about 2:00 a.m., the officer saw a 1967 or 1968 black Plymouth Fury with three passengers less than an hour after the robbery about a mile from the scene of the robbery and the car gave indications of attempted evasion. Under such facts we have no hesitancy in concluding the officers had reasonable cause to stop the car and arrest its occupants."

However, in *United States v. Roper,* the Eleventh Circuit concluded that there was not probable cause to arrest the defendant for federal bail jumping at the time the defendant was stopped in an automobile. In this case, an Atlanta police officer saw a bail bondsman's flyer containing "a picture of Roper, his description, his driver's license number, a description of his automobile, and his auto tag number." The same day the officer saw a vehicle matching the description and the tag number described in the flyer. He confirmed through a radio check that the tag number was registered to Roper. However, the court concluded that the facts demonstrated an articulable suspicion justifying a stop. See section 3-7, infra, on articulable suspicion justifying a stop.

In *Chambers v. Maroney,* the United States Supreme Court summarized the facts of the case as follows:

"During the night . . . a . . . service station . . . was robbed by two men, each of whom carried and displayed a gun. The robbers took the currency from the cash register. . . . Two teenagers, who had earlier noticed a blue compact station wagon circling the block in the vicinity of the . . . station, then saw the station wagon speed away from a parking lot close to the . . . station. At the same time, they learned that the . . . station had been robbed. They reported to police, who arrived immediately, that four men were in the station wagon and one was wearing a green sweater. Kovacich told the police that one of the men who robbed him was wearing a green sweater. A trench coat and incriminating evidence was found in a search of the car. A description of the car and the two robbers was broadcast over the police radio. Within an hour, a light blue compact station wagon answering the description and carrying four men was stopped by the police about two miles from the . . . station. [The defendant] . . . was one of the men in the station wagon. He was wearing a green sweater and there was a trench coat in the car. The occupants were arrested [and incriminating evidence was found in a search of the car]." The Court concluded there was probable cause to arrest.

In *Davis v. State,* officers found an abandoned plane at a rural airport about 8:30 p.m. A wing of the plane had been damaged, and the door was open. The plane contained a number of bales of marijuana. About 7:00 a.m. the following morning, one of the officers discovered Davis walking on a highway about two-and-a-half miles from the airport. He wore nice clothes, but they seemed to be torn and ragged. The officer stopped Davis and found his clothes contained grass stains, were wet, and had a distinctive odor which smelled like the interior of the plane. The appellate court concluded there was probable cause to arrest Davis.

In *State v. Williams,* the court affirmed the trial court in finding there was no probable cause to arrest where the officer at the suppression hearing "testified that based on the following factors, he believed he had probable cause to transport Williams to the DEA office and procure a warrant to search him: (1) travel characteristics consistent with drug trafficking; (2) incorrect phone number given to Miami ticket agent; (3) manifestations of nervousness; (4) inconsistent answers regarding whom he was visiting in Miami; and (5) the roll of plastic wrap in his backpack." However, the appellate court concluded that "[w]hile these factors may give rise to a reasonable suspicion of illicit drug activity, they are insufficient even when combined to constitute probable cause to believe a suspect is transporting drugs."

Generally, an officer has no right to arrest a person merely because that person was present at the scene of the crime. However, in *United States v. Ashcroft,* the Fifth Circuit held that the agents had probable cause to arrest a man for conspiracy where he was present at two separate major cocaine transactions which were conducted in private.

In *Corbitt v. State,* the Georgia Court of Appeals found there was probable cause to arrest where an officer received information about drug transactions in a certain park, went to the park, and from a concealed position saw the defendant "lighting a half-used portion of [a] cigarette . . . holding it pinched between two fingers and drawing on it . . . in a different manner than you would a regular cigarette." The officer believed the defendant was smoking marijuana. He approached the defendant who moved his hand behind him and when he brought his hand in front of him, there was nothing in it. "A search of the area immediately behind the bench on which . . . [the defendant had been] sitting revealed a portion of what . . . [the officer] believed to be a marijuana cigarette." The defendant was then arrested.

In *Scott v. State,* at about 10:00 p.m. an officer received a telephone tip that three people were standing in front of a house known for drug sales on a designated street known as an area of drug activity. Officers immediately drove to the area in an unmarked patrol car. The three men separated on seeing the patrol car. The defendant started walking across the street. He was stopped by an officer who conducted a pat-down search. The court concluded that there was probable cause to believe the defendant had possession of contraband or was a party to possession. *Scott* could have been decided on the basis of articulable suspicion and stop and frisk since there was a frisk and a hard object justifying a search.

In *Copeland v. State,* the court pointed out that "[f]light in connection with other circumstances may be sufficient probable cause to uphold a warrantless arrest. . . . " Copeland was in an area known for "a high level of illegal drug use, had been walking in a suspicious manner with a suspected drug dealer, had walked away . . . when the officer attempted to question him, had admitted he was on parole, had voiced despair and run when asked if he had a weapon, and had pulled objects from his pockets and discarded them." The foregoing established probable cause to believe the defendant was committing a crime. In *Bigby v. State,* the court affirmed the trial court in finding that a "trained officer's detection of the odor of marijuana, together with . . . [the defendant's] flight . . . provided probable cause for his arrest."

In *Howie v. State,* there was evidence that the defendant "matched the physical description of the suspect which had been broadcasted on the police radio," but the description of the clothing did not exactly match those worn by the defendant. The defendant was "spotted across the street from the scene of the crime within minutes after it occurred, and he began to run when he saw the police officers." The appellate court affirmed the trial judge's ruling that there was probable cause to arrest the defendant.

In *Williams v. State,* the Georgia Court of Appeals concluded that there was probable cause to arrest. In this case, officers knew of a number of burglaries in which coins and jewelry were taken. In one burglary, Susan B. Anthony dollars and Kennedy half-dollars had been taken. All the burglaries were in Baldwin County between August and November inclusive. One morning in November, four brothers who frequently patronized a store apparently in Milledgeville purchased gasoline and beer with Kennedy half-dollars and Susan B. Anthony dollars. The clerk obtained the tag number of the vehicle and gave a description of the four occupants to the police.

Likewise, in *Horton v. State,* the Georgia Court of Appeals in a five-to-four decision held that there was probable cause to arrest the defendant. After one Dodson attempted to cash a stolen check in an A & P, he fled the store and walked directly to and conversed with the defendant before leaving in opposite directions. The store manager observed both men and unequivocally identified the defendant as the apparent aider and abettor, thereby providing probable cause to arrest.

In *Gober v. State,* the court held that when a gun of the same type as the murder weapon was found in the defendant's bedroom and the officers knew the defendant had used the victim's cellular telephone after the victim's death, there was probable cause to arrest the defendant.

In *Johnson v. State,* the defendant's arrest for driving on a suspended license was supported by probable cause despite the fact that the officer was advised that the defendant had not been served with notice of the suspension of his license. The court reasoned that once the officer observed the defendant driving, pulled him over for a headlight violation and then learned of the defendant's suspension, he then had sufficient probable cause to arrest the defendant. The court rejected Johnson's contention that the suspension was not effective since he did not receive written notice and concluded that actual or constructive notice would be sufficient. Furthermore, the court held that the officer should not be rendered powerless simply because he lacked information as to whether the defendant had actual or constructive knowledge and therefore, that he had probable cause to proceed with the arrest.

See Sheldon J. Shapiro, Annotation, "What Constitutes Probable Cause for Arrest—Supreme Court Cases," 28 L.Ed.2d 978 (1972). See section 2-14, infra, on other cases illustrating probable cause. See section 3-2 et seq., infra, on facts justifying a stop.

§ 2-13 Arrest by officer—General

In considering the question of warrantless arrests there are two possible considerations. Historically, the *first* concern was the provisions of a Georgia statute authorizing warrantless arrests under certain circumstances. The *second* concern addresses the question of whether or not the circumstances establish probable cause which authorized an arrest under the federal Constitution.

Except in the case of extradition matters, Georgia, by statute, authorizes warrantless arrests, as defined by the common law and Georgia authorities. Warrantless arrests may only be made in five situations which are set out in O.C.G.A. § 17-4-20(a). This section provides as follows:

"(a) An arrest for a crime may be made by a law enforcement officer either under a warrant or without a warrant if the offense is committed in such officer's presence or within such officer's immediate knowledge; if the offender is endeavoring to escape; if the officer has probable cause to believe that an act of family violence, as defined in O.C.G.A. § 19-13-1, has been committed; if the officer has probable cause to believe that an offense involving physical abuse has been committed against a vulnerable adult, who shall be for the purposes of this subsection a person eighteen years old or older who is unable to protect himself or herself from physical or mental abuse because of a physical or mental impairment; or for other cause if there is likely to be failure of justice for want of a judicial officer to issue a warrant."

This statute has been construed to be a codification of the common law with perhaps a slight enlargement of the power of arrest. It has been applied to all officers authorized to arrest and applied to violations of municipal ordinances, to misdemeanors, and to felonies.

Both the Georgia courts and the federal courts have expressed a preference for arrests pursuant to a warrant.

However, the United States Supreme Court has been reluctant to make such a preference a general constitutional mandate when the arrest is in public and is based on probable cause. But see section 2-5, supra, on the place of arrest.

In 1981, in *Vaughn v. State,* the Georgia Supreme Court pointed out that the federal constitutional standard for a warrantless arrest is less "stringent" than the requirements of O.C.G.A. § 17-4-20. However, in the 1982 landmark case of *Durden v. State*, the Georgia Supreme Court concluded that *"dual inquiries, one under federal law and one under state law, serve no useful purpose* and result in complicating the law. . . . [W]e find the state rule to be the same as the federal rule. *An arrest and search, legal under federal law, are legal under state law.*" (Emphasis added.) In short, the court held that if an officer has probable cause, he may arrest. In 1984, in *Bodiford v. State*, the Court of Appeals said that an arrest which is valid under the federal Constitution is valid in Georgia regardless of whether the statutory requirements have been met.

Georgia has a statute found in O.C.G.A. § 40-8-91 which requires the "marking" of motor vehicles used to make arrests for traffic violations. However, the statute has been held not to invalidate traffic arrests made in unmarked vehicles.

As discussed in section 2-11, supra, an officer has probable cause to arrest in the federal constitutional sense if at the time of the arrest the facts and circumstances, within the knowledge of the officer, and of which he had reasonably trustworthy information, were sufficient to warrant a prudent person in believing that the defendant had committed or was committing an offense, he has probable cause to arrest.

Lastly, it should be remembered that a violator of the law has no right to be promptly arrested. See section 2-4, supra.

See Kurtz, *Criminal Offenses and Defenses in Georgia* (4th ed.), p. 514. See section 2-5, supra, on place of arrest, and section 2-6, supra, on procedure for arrest.

§ 2-14 Arrest by officer—Offense committed in presence of officer

First, it should be kept in mind that an officer has no right to arrest, under both Georgia and federal law, unless there is probable cause. However, in federal constitutional terms, there may be a valid stop and frisk or "seizure" based on reasonable suspicion, grounded upon specific and articulable facts, judged against an objective standard. The federal "stop and frisk" is not an arrest.

Next we come to the question of what justifies a warrantless "arrest" in common law or traditional Georgia terms where the offense is committed in the presence of the officer. The Georgia statute authorizes a warrantless arrest if the offense is committed in the presence of the officer. However, the Georgia courts are no longer restricted by this statute. Generally, if there is probable cause for the arrest, an officer may arrest. If there is no probable cause, an officer may not arrest. See section 2-13, supra. However, in *Carranza v. State,* the Georgia Supreme Court held that where an offense is committed in a defendant's home in the presence of or in the immediate knowledge of an officer, there can be no arrest in that home unless there has been consent for the officer to enter or there are exigent circumstances. See section 2-5, supra, on place of arrest.

For example, in *Rockholt v. State,* probable cause to arrest was found where officers, while searching the premises of a drug supplier pursuant to a valid warrant, observed the defendant drive up and hurriedly attempt to leave when he saw the search in progress. The facts were sufficient to cause the officers to believe that the crime of possession of drugs was being committed in their presence. On the other hand, in *Stanley v. State,* the court concluded that there was not probable cause to arrest where police investigators had arranged to purchase four ounces of MDA and during the transaction undercover officers heard a horn sound continuously and saw the driver of the car motioning them over. Such actions were not sufficient for the officer to reasonably conclude that the defendant was in possession of MDA and thus committing a crime in the officer's presence.

See Kurtz, *Criminal Offenses and Defenses in Georgia* (4th ed.), p. 514. See section 2-11 et seq., supra, on probable cause to arrest.

§ 2-15 Arrest by officer—Offender is trying to escape

As noted in the previous section, an arrest may not be conducted in the absence of probable cause. However, a stop and frisk or "seizure," which does not rise to the level of an "arrest," may properly be conducted under the Constitution if it is based on reasonable suspicion, grounded upon specific and articulable facts, and judged against an objective standard.

With these important tenets in mind, we will explore what has justified a warrantless "arrest" in common law or traditional Georgia terms where the offender is attempting to escape.

The Georgia statute provides that an officer may arrest without a warrant if the offender is trying to escape or endeavoring to avoid arrest. It has been previously held that this exception does not apply where an offender simply fails to surrender to authorities. Based on this reasoning it was felt that the evidence must clearly show that the offender was attempting to escape immediately. Thus, it has been held that a policeman had no right to arrest a defendant simply because he walked away and refused to answer questions.

Probable cause has been recognized as playing an important part under the statute in *Watson* v. State. In this case, the court said that where the suspect was attempting to drive away in a car and officers had "sufficient facts and circumstances within their knowledge, based on reasonably trustworthy information, sufficient to warrant a prudent man in believing that the defendant had committed an offense [bank robbery]," an officer could validly stop the car.

Under the literal wording of *Vaughn v. State* and *Bodiford v. State,* the Georgia courts have brushed aside the statute on arrest and are now relying solely on the federal constitutional rule giving an officer the right to arrest whenever there is probable cause and not limiting this right by our statute. See section 2-13, supra.

See Kurtz, *Criminal Offenses and Defenses in Georgia* (4th ed.), p. 514.

§ 2-16 Arrest by officer—Act of family violence

In 1981, Georgia adopted a family violence act and in the process amended O.C.G.A. § 17-4-20. The amendment provides that an officer may arrest with or without a warrant if he has probable cause to believe that an act of family violence, as defined in O.C.G.A. § 19-13-1, has been committed. Presumably the words "probable cause" in the statute mean the same thing these words mean in the Fourth Amendment.

§ 2-17 Warrantless arrest by officer—Physical abuse against vulnerable adult

Effective January 1, 1998, O.C.G.A. § 17-4-20 authorizes an officer to arrest if the officer "has probable cause to believe that an offense involving physical abuse has been committed against a vulnerable adult," who is defined as a person 18 years of age or older and who is unable, either mentally or physically, to protect himself from physical or mental abuse.

§ 2-18 Warrantless arrest by officer—Failure of justice

It bears repeating that the right of arrest, in the federal constitutional sense, requires probable cause. However, the right to stop and frisk or "seize" requires something less: reasonable suspicion, grounded upon specific and articulable facts, judged against an objective standard.

Against this background, we will consider the question of what justifies a warrantless "arrest" in common law or traditional Georgia terms where, under the requirements of O.C.G.A. § 17-4-20, "for other cause there is likely to be failure of justice for want of a judicial officer to issue a warrant."

In 1966, in *Croker v. State,* the court referred to this "failure of justice" clause as being obscure. In the 1982 landmark case of *Durden v. State*, the court abandoned the Georgia arrest statute and held that any arrest valid under federal law is valid under Georgia law. In other words, if an officer has probable cause, he may arrest. If he does not have probable cause, he may not arrest. See section 2-13, supra. In *Fortson v. State*, the court pointed out "that if an officer acquires probable cause to arrest an accused outside his home, a failure of justice is likely to occur as a matter of law if the officer delays the arrest until a warrant is obtained."

See Kurtz, *Criminal Offenses and Defenses in Georgia* (4th ed.), p. 514.

§ 2-19 Arrest warrants

An arrest warrant has been said to consist of both an affidavit and a direction to an officer to arrest an offender and present him before a judicial officer. An affidavit and/or information must be presented to a magistrate before a valid warrant may be issued.

The verified facts presented to the magistrate need not all be set out in the affidavit, but such additional facts may be given in verified oral testimony or in another affidavit. However, the purpose of the verified facts submitted to a judicial officer is to present sufficient facts to enable the magistrate to make a judicial determination of whether or not there is probable cause to believe that a suspect is guilty of the offense charged.

O.C.G.A. § 17-4-41 requires that the affidavit contain the county in which the offense was committed, the time and date it was committed, the place of the offense, the party against whom the offense was committed, and a statement describing the offense. If the offense is theft, the affidavit must also describe the property alleged to have been stolen, the name of the owner, the value of such property, and the name of the person from whose possession the property was taken.

According to the statute, it "is the intent of these requirements that the accused person shall be informed of the specific charge against him and of all basic pertinent particulars pertaining thereto." While older cases have held that a general charge of "misdemeanor" is sufficient where a defendant is accused of committing a misdemeanor, it appears that such a "description" is no longer adequate under the statute.

The Fourth Amendment requires that a warrant "particularly describ[e] . . . the persons . . . to be seized." A warrant not naming the person to be arrested must describe him with some degree of certainty. A "John Doe" warrant without the name of the person to be arrested or such a description is not valid.

It has been held that an otherwise sufficient arrest warrant is not void because the affidavit fails to specify the time of day that the occurrence took place. However, a warrant which does not state the time other than the date, the place other than the county, or the party against whom the offense was committed, and does not describe the offense more specifically than as "passing a worthless check" is void. An affidavit which merely states the conclusion of a prosecutor, for example, that a defendant has exhibited a certain film which is obscene, is also insufficient. In *Devier v. State,* the Georgia Supreme Court held that the (verified) information supplied to the magistrate must be sufficient to establish probable cause, but the basis of the probable cause does not have to be established in the affidavit alone. It is sufficient if the affidavit and other verified information are sufficient to establish probable cause.

However, there is some relaxation of these requirements in extradition warrants. Thus, in 1975, the Georgia

Supreme Court held that an affidavit for an arrest warrant need not contain evidentiary facts. In *Smith v. Stynchcombe,* the Georgia Supreme Court stated that "the probable cause requirements of an affidavit on which a search warrant is issued" do not apply to arrest warrants. The court concluded that it should "require no more of a South Carolina arrest warrant affidavit *than we do in Georgia.*" (Emphasis added.) The court, in support of its position, cited an earlier extradition case which held that an affidavit for arrest in an extradition situation need only comply with the provisions of the Uniform Criminal Extradition Act, a statute which requires less detailed information than the present Georgia law for arrest warrants. Generally, see section 2-23, infra, and also 31A Am. Jur. 2d, Extradition § 59 and 35 C. J. S. Extradition § 16.

In addition to relaxed warrant requirements, it should be pointed out that in an extradition matter, no warrant is necessary in order to have a valid arrest. See section 2-23, infra.

In the federal area, the United States Supreme Court has held that the Fourth Amendment requirement of probable cause applies to both arrest warrants and search warrants. The Supreme Court, in *Whiteley v. Warden,* stated that before a warrant for either an *arrest* or search can issue, there must be sufficient information presented to the judicial officer to enable him to make "an independent judgment that probable cause exists for the warrant." The Court noted that when an arrest warrant is issued, it must meet the same probable cause requirements as a search warrant. Generally, see 5 Am. Jur. 2d Arrest § 12 et seq.

A mere conclusory statement that an accused is engaged in criminal activity is not valid. According to the United States Supreme Court, an affidavit is insufficient where it does not affirmatively state "that the affiant spoke with personal knowledge of the matters contained therein; it does not indicate any sources for . . . [affiant's] belief; and it does not set forth any other sufficient basis upon which a finding of probable cause could be made."

As previously pointed out in this section, an affidavit or verified information is presented before a magistrate so that he may determine whether or not probable cause exists. However, Georgia provides by statute that in making this decision the magistrate may also consider the facts which he knows. If there is probable cause, the magistrate may ordinarily issue an arrest warrant.

However, if the arrest warrant is for the arrest of a peace officer for any offense alleged to have been committed while in the performance of his duties, such a warrant "may be issued only by a judge of a superior court, a judge of a state court, or a judge of a probate court."

A form for an arrest warrant is set out in the Code

In *Watts v. Cannon,* the court held that an arresting officer, who was acting on reliable information that there was an outstanding felony warrant against the defendant, could arrest the defendant even though the officer did not have the warrant. The court cited and relied on a number of United States Supreme Court cases in justifying its conclusion. However, it should be kept in mind that the United States Supreme Court held, in *Whiteley v. Warden,* that where an arrest is made on a warrant which the officer learned about in a radio bulletin, the arrest is illegal unless the warrant was supported by probable cause. See section 2-26, infra, on arrest where warrant is quash or invalid.

In *State v. Stringer,* the court said "[t]he primary purpose of the bench warrant is to secure the presence of the defendant in court. Once the defendant appears in court, the bench warrant . . . has no force and effect."

O.C.G.A. § 17-4-47 was enacted in 1998. It provides that a judge may conduct applications for the issuance of arrest warrants by video conference. The video conference arrest warrant applications shall be conducted in such a manner that the judge conducting the hearing has visual and audible contact with all affiants and witnesses giving testimony.

For affidavit for arrest and an arrest warrant, see Goger, *Daniel's Georgia Criminal Trial Practice Forms* (6th ed.), § 4-58. See section 2-6, supra, on procedure for arrests and section 2-5, supra, on place of arrest.

§ 2-20 Magistrates who may issue arrest warrants

While there does not seem to be a Georgia case on the precise point, apparently a valid arrest warrant may only be issued by a neutral, detached magistrate. A unanimous United States Supreme Court held that where justices of the peace received five dollars for each search warrant issued, but nothing if they denied the application, the justices of the peace were neither neutral nor detached. This matter is discussed further in section 4-6, infra.

O.C.G.A. § 17-4-40 provides in part as follows: "Any judge of a superior, city, state, or magistrate court, or any municipal officer clothed by law with the powers of a magistrate may issue a warrant for the arrest of any offender against the penal laws, based on probable cause either on the judge's or officer's own knowledge or on the information of others given to the judge or officer under oath. Any retired judge or judge emeritus of a state court may likewise issue arrest warrants if authorized in writing to do so by an active judge of the state court of the county wherein the warrants are to be issued. . . . Any warrant for the arrest of a peace officer, law enforcement officer, teacher, or school administrator for any offense alleged to have been committed while in the performance of his or her duties may be issued only by a judge of a superior court, a judge of a state court, or a judge of a probate court." See section 4-2, infra, on search and seizure of documentary evidence in an attorney's possession.

§ 2-21 Arrests by a private citizen

O.C.G.A. § 17-4-60 provides as follows:

"A private person may arrest an offender if the offense is committed in his presence or within his immediate knowledge. If the offense is a felony and the offender is escaping or attempting to escape, a private person may arrest him upon reasonable and probable grounds of suspicion."

The foregoing Code section has been said to be a codification of the preexisting law. However, some distinctions have been pointed out between the statute and the common law.

The words of the statute, "in his presence" and "within his immediate knowledge" have been held to be synonymous. It has been held that where a suspect admits his guilt of shoplifting to the manager of the store, this places the commission of the crime within the immediate knowledge of the manager.

A citizen's arrest cannot be made for a mere violation of a city ordinance committed in the citizen's presence. If a misdemeanor is committed in the presence of a private citizen, he has a right of arrest if he arrests the offender at that time. However, if he does not immediately arrest, "his power to do so at all is gone." The statute apparently authorizes a citizen's arrest for a felony committed in the citizen's presence. Moreover, as Professor Kurtz points out, a private citizen may arrest upon probable cause if the offense involved was a felony and the offender is escaping or attempting to escape. However, he concludes by saying, "It would appear that no other citizens' arrest where the offense was committed outside the citizen's presence is authorized by Georgia law." The arrest powers of a private citizen are not increased because he has an arrest warrant. Despite the authority of a private citizen to arrest, there is no "legal duty on a private citizen to restrain or constrain someone who is drunk or otherwise impaired."

The authority of a citizen's arrest is extended by Georgia statutes to different types of security guards. Under the Georgia Private Detective and Security Agencies Act enacted in 1981, licensees or registrants under the Act have the same authority to arrest as private citizens, which is the authority to arrest for any violation of a misdemeanor or felony which occurs in their presence or within their immediate knowledge. Moreover, if the offense is a felony and the offender is escaping or attempting to escape a licensee or registrant may arrest upon probable cause.

A police officer generally has no greater authority to arrest outside of the city which employs him than a private citizen. However, if a city officer is in pursuit of an offender and unable to arrest him until he has left the city limits, the arrest is valid. However, in *Glazner v. State*, a majority of the Court of Appeals held that a municipal officer may arrest for traffic violations outside the city, even when not in hot pursuit for an offense committed in the city. Also a county police officer may arrest for a felony in another county if he has probable cause.

If a private person arrests a person, he must "without any unnecessary delay, take the person arrested before a judicial officer . . . or deliver the person and all effects removed from him to a peace officer of this state." If such a suspect is turned over to a law enforcement officer, the officer may take custody of the person arrested even if the officer has no such personal knowledge of the offense as would enable him to arrest the person without a warrant.

See Kurtz, *Criminal Offenses and Defenses in Georgia* (4th ed.), p. 514. Generally, see section 2-8, supra, on persons who may exercise an officer's power to arrest. Also, generally, see 5 Am. Jur. 2d Arrest §§ 34-36, 6A C. J. S. Arrest §§ 12-15, and *Criminal Arrest in Georgia,* Institute of Government, University of Georgia (1979), page 28 et seq.

§ 2-22 Custody and disposition after arrest

There are special statutory limitations relating to custody where an arrest is made by some officers with limited authority to arrest, and these statutory provisions do not follow a consistent pattern.

Where there is such a limitation, usually it is the duty of the arresting person to turn the suspect over to an officer having a general power of arrest. The preceding section discussed the disposition of a suspect who is arrested by a private citizen.

When a person is taken into custody, he is to be "booked" at the detention facility. It is the responsibility of the person having supervision over the facility to see that the name, age, and address of all persons arrested is recorded on appropriate records which are generally open to public inspection. However, generally, booking is not regarded as a part of the arrest process and a delay in booking or its absence will not affect a prior valid arrest. In *Franks v. State*, the Georgia Supreme Court limited the "booking exceptions" to *Miranda* and the Fifth Amendment "to requests for basic biographical data, such as the suspect's name, age, address, educational background, marital status, and other information required to complete an arrest form." See section 5-13, infra, on booking questions.

As a part of an officer's duty of keeping a suspect safe after arrest, officers may adopt reasonable measures to provide for the identification and recapture of a person in custody. Thus, officers generally are regarded as having the right to photograph the suspect as well as to take his measurements, weigh him and fingerprint him. In *Rivers v. State,* the court held that it is not necessary to obtain a defendant's consent before his photograph is taken. General questions asked incident to arrest and booking are not regarded as the functional equivalent of questioning, as that term is used in *Miranda.* However, in *Morris v. State,* the Georgia Court of Appeals stated that booking procedures are not per se exempt from the custodial interrogation requirements of *Miranda.* Thus, in *Franks v. State,* the court reversed the trial judge's admission of a statement made by defendant at booking in response to a question about how the defendant's arm was injured.

Also, there seems to be a general right to search a suspect at the detention facility, and, at least in serious cases, it seems that an officer has a right to have the prisoner remove his clothing. In the 1999 case of *Taylor v.*

State, the court held that it was reasonable that a female defendant could be ordered to remove her clothes by a female employee of a jail as part of the booking process if directed to do so by a police officer who had reason to believe the defendant had contraband hidden beneath her clothes. See section 5-13, infra, on interrogation.

In *Illinois v. Lafayette,* the United States Supreme Court held that officers may search the personal effects of a person under lawful arrest as part of the routine administrative procedure at a police stationhouse incident to booking and jailing the suspect. The court pointed out the "[p]olice conduct that would be impractical or unreasonable—or embarrassingly intrusive—on the street can more readily—and privately—be performed at the station . . . . [I]t is entirely proper for police to remove and list or inventory property found on the person or in the possession of an arrested person who is to be jailed . . . . A standardized procedure for making a list or inventory as soon as reasonable after reaching the stationhouse not only deters false claims but also inhibits theft or careless handling of articles taken from the arrested person. Arrested persons have also been known to injure themselves—or others—with belts, knives, drugs or other items on their person while being detained . . . . It is immaterial whether the police actually fear any particular package or container; the need to protect against such risk arises independently of a particular officer's subjective concerns." In this case, a shoulder bag was searched, and the Court concluded that, while the bag could have been sealed as a unit in a bag or box, the Constitution did not require such a less intrusive inventory. The same rule seems to apply to the search of a wallet at the police station. See section 4-26, infra, on the right to search a person incident to a lawful arrest.

In *Sears v. State,* the defendant was being booked into jail, and an officer conducting a routine inventory thumbed through a notebook, saw the word "killed," and seized the notebook. The defendant moved to suppress the notebook on the ground that private papers are not subject to seizure under O.C.G.A. § 17-5-21(a). The court affirmed the refusal of the trial judge to suppress. The court concluded that the term "private papers" is restricted to papers covered by privilege, such as attorney-client or doctor-patient.

In *Carter v. State,* the court held that where a defendant is arrested and in jail, the clothing worn by him at the time of arrest can be seized for evidence and searched without a warrant even if the clothing is no longer worn by the defendant and has been placed in the evidence room.

Georgia provides by statute that in all cases of arrest without a warrant, "the person arresting shall, without delay, convey the offender before the most convenient judicial officer authorized to receive an affidavit and issue a warrant . . . . No such imprisonment shall be legal beyond a reasonable time allowed for this purpose; and any person who is not brought before such judicial officer within 48 hours of arrest shall be released" "from imprisonment or custody until a warrant is obtained . . . ." However, the failure to have a commitment hearing within 48 hours does not render a conviction invalid nor does it automatically render a confession obtained during such unlawful detention inadmissible.

In the case of persons arrested pursuant to an arrest warrant, the officer "shall exercise reasonable diligence in bringing the person arrested before the judicial officer authorized to examine, commit, or receive bail and in any event to present the person arrested before a committing judicial officer within 72 hours after arrest. The accused shall be notified as to when and where the commitment hearing is to be held. An arrested person who is not notified before the hearing of the time and place of the commitment hearing shall be released." However, it should be noted that the statute does not actually require the holding of the commitment hearing within 72 hours but only requires that the suspect be brought before a magistrate during that time. Moreover, and perhaps in a more practical vein, the failure to have a timely commitment hearing is not generally a basis for dismissal of an indictment, and if an accused is indicted by a grand jury, without ever having had a preliminary hearing, this alone will not prevent a valid conviction at trial.

O.C.G.A. § 42-4-14 provides that Georgia jailers must make a reasonable effort to determine the nationality of the prisoners in their custody and the legality of their status. If the jailer finds that the prisoner is not in the country legally, he is to notify the United States Department of Homeland Security.

See sections 4-26 and 4-27, infra, on search of person and area incident to an arrest. See section 4-56, infra, on scope and intensity of searches. See section 2-25, infra, for cases holding that illegal arrest is no bar to prosecution.

§ 2-23 Extradition of fugitives—The Uniform Criminal Extradition Act

The basic provision for the interstate extradition of fugitives from justice is found in the Constitution of the United States, Article IV, Section 2, Paragraph 2: "A Person charged in any State with Treason, Felony, or other Crime, who shall flee from Justice, and be found in another State, shall on Demand of the executive Authority of the State from which he fled, be delivered up, to be removed to the State having Jurisdiction of the Crime." To implement this constitutional requirement, Georgia and most other states have enacted the Uniform Criminal Extradition Act, while the federal government has enacted a similar statute.

The Uniform Act places an affirmative constitutional duty on the governor of any state in which a fugitive is found to have him arrested and delivered up to the authorities of the state from which he fled. By law, a demand for extradition must be in writing and must allege (except in cases arising under O.C.G.A. § 17-13-25, discussed infra) that the accused was present in the demanding state at the time the alleged crime was committed, and that he subsequently fled the jurisdiction. The demand must be accompanied by a copy of an indictment against the accused, or by information supported by an affidavit in the state which has jurisdiction of the offense, or by a copy of an affidavit made before a magistrate of the demanding state, together with a copy of any warrant issued or by a copy of a judgment of conviction or of a sentence imposed in execution thereof, together with a statement by the governor of the demanding state that the accused has escaped from confinement or has broken the terms of his bail, probation, or parole. The indictment, affidavit or information must substantially charge the accused with having committed a crime under the law of the demanding state, and be authenticated by the governor of that state.

O.C.G.A. § 17-13-26 provides that when a demand for extradition is made upon the governor, he may call upon any state prosecuting officer, including the Attorney General, to investigate the demand and report whether or not the accused ought to be delivered to the demanding state.

O.C.G.A. § 17-13-24 provides that when a state wishes to have returned to that state a person charged with a crime in that state, but the accused is incarcerated in another state, the governor of the latter state may agree to extradite the prisoner, upon condition that, after he is tried in the demanding state, he be returned to the surrendering state to complete his sentence or to face pending criminal proceedings.

O.C.G.A. § 17-13-25 provides that this state may extradite, pursuant to the requirements of O.C.G.A. § 17-13-23, supra, any person who, although not present in the demanding state at the time the alleged crime was committed, nonetheless committed an act from outside the demanding state which intentionally resulted in a crime being committed within the demanding state.

In *Jenkins v. Garrison,* an Alabama application for extradition noted that Alabama did not contend that the petitioner was present within the state when the crimes were committed. However, the Georgia rendition warrant granting the extradition request stated that the petitioner committed the crimes in Alabama and was a "fugitive from justice." Although the warrant did not give the basis for its issuance, the warrant appeared to be issued pursuant to the mandatory terms of O.C.G.A. § 17-13-23 limiting extradition to a fugitive from justice found in another state, rather than pursuant to O.C.G.A. § 17-13-25 which does not hinge on whether the accused was present in the requesting state when the crimes were committed. Because of this discrepancy and because there was no evidence that gubernatorial discretion was exercised pursuant to O.C.G.A. § 17-13-25 when granting the rendition warrant, the court concluded that habeas corpus relief should have been granted.

When the governor of a state decides to extradite a fugitive to a demanding state, he must issue an arrest warrant, which must recite the facts necessary to the validity of its issuance. The warrant must authorize the peace officers to whom it is directed to arrest the fugitive and, subject to the provisions of O.C.G.A. §§ 17-13-20 et seq., discussed in this section, to deliver him up to the "duly authorized agent of the demanding state." The arresting officer is deemed to have the same authority to command assistance in arresting the fugitive as he has in any criminal process situation.

O.C.G.A. § 17-13-30 provides that before a fugitive is delivered up to the demanding state, he must first be brought before a judge of a court of record of the surrendering state. The judge must inform the accused of (1) "the demand made for his surrender," (2) the crime upon which the demand is based, and (3) his right to counsel.

Should the accused wish to contest the legality of the arrest, a reasonable time is allotted (by the judge of the surrendering state) to allow the accused to petition for habeas corpus relief. If a writ of habeas corpus is applied for, notice thereof shall be given to the prosecuting officer of the county where the arrest was made. The district attorney must answer and defend the habeas corpus unless the governor appoints the attorney general.

In *Michigan v. Doran,* the United States Supreme Court held that once the governor of a state has granted extradition, a court of that state, considering release on habeas corpus, can do no more than decide (1) whether the extradition documents on their face are in order, (2) whether the petitioner has been charged with a crime in the demanding state, (3) whether the petitioner is the person named in the demand for extradition, and (4) it may be necessary to determine whether the petitioner is a fugitive. In the 1998 case of *St. Lawrence v. Bartley,* the Georgia Supreme Court affirmed the granting of a petition for habeas corpus where the demand for extradition alleged that the petitioner was in the demanding state at the time of the alleged crime (see O.C.G.A. § 17-13-23). In this case, Bartley testified that she had not been in South Carolina since she was a toddler and was not a fugitive. Bartley also testified that her checks had been stolen from her and that the theft was reported to the police in Georgia. The court pointed out that although the warrant was prima facie evidence that Bartley had been in South Carolina, the state presented no other evidence that she was in South Carolina when the alleged crime was committed.

Once these requirements are met, any other defenses are to be decided in the demanding state. The guilt or innocence of the accused has no relevance in a habeas corpus proceeding to contest extradition, unless it involves identification of the petitioner as the one charged with the offense or one of the other three matters set out in *Doran.*

In *Oliver v. Barrett,* the Georgia Supreme Court held that "the mental competency of a fugitive is only relevant insofar as it concerns his ability to assist counsel in ascertaining and preparing for the limited issues to be decided in an extradition hearing."

Once the surrendering state makes an initial, prima facie showing that the extradition documents are in order, the burden of proof is on the defendant to show how his arrest and detention is unlawful. Thus, if the defendant contends he is not the person named in the governor's warrant, the burden is on him to show that he is not the person named. It has been said that the purpose of an extradition proceeding is merely to determine whether there is probable cause to transfer a criminal suspect from one jurisdiction to another to stand trial. However, it "is not appropriate for the habeas court to look behind the probable cause finding of the demanding state."

O.C.G.A. § 17-13-32 provides that the officers of both the surrendering state and the demanding state may use the jails of the surrendering state, when necessary, to confine the fugitive while en route, provided that the officers show proof to the keepers of the jails that the prisoner is in fact a fugitive subject to pending extradition proceedings.

O.C.G.A. § 17-13-33 provides that "any credible person" may initiate the extradition process by swearing out a warrant that a crime has been committed in another state and that the accused has been charged with that crime. The accused may then be arrested and brought before a magistrate to answer the complaint.

O.C.G.A. § 17-13-34 provides that a peace officer or a private citizen may arrest a person without a warrant upon reasonable information that the accused is charged in another state with a crime punishable by death or imprisonment for a term greater than one year. The accused must be brought before a magistrate with all practicable speed, where the arresting party must make a complaint under oath setting out the grounds of the arrest; and the accused must be given an opportunity to answer.

Where the magistrate finds that the person being held is the same person as the one who is charged with the alleged offense, and that he has fled from justice (except where O.C.G.A. § 17-13-25 is applicable), it is provided that the magistrate must, by warrant reciting the accusation, commit the accused to the county jail for up to 30 days, to permit an arrest of the accused under a warrant of the governor "on a requisition of the executive authority of the state" which has jurisdiction of the crime. The magistrate may also extend the incarceration for 60 additional days if the accused was not arrested under such a governor's warrant after the initial 30–day period expires, or the magistrate may discharge the accused.

O.C.G.A. § 17-13-36 provides that an accused fugitive may be admitted to bail unless the crime with which he is charged is punishable by death or life imprisonment in the demanding state.

O.C.G.A. § 17-13-39 provides that the governor, in his discretion, may surrender upon demand of the governor of another state any person found in this state, even though that person is incarcerated, on probation or parole, or is facing pending criminal charges in this state. The governor may condition the delivery of the prisoner upon such terms as he may stipulate, including the condition that the prisoner be returned to this state immediately after trial and before commencing the service of his sentence in the demanding state. No surrender of such a prisoner under this section is to be construed as a complete relinquishment of jurisdiction by the surrendering state over the prisoner. However, where the prisoner receives a sentence of death in the demanding state, that sentence may be carried out.

The governor may recall his warrant for the arrest of a fugitive or issue another warrant at any time.

A person brought into Georgia pursuant to the Uniform Criminal Extradition Act is immune from service of process in civil actions arising out of the same facts as the criminal proceedings for which he was extradited, until he has been convicted, or, if acquitted, until he has had a reasonable opportunity to return to the state from which he was extradited.

In *Palmer v. Dugger,* the Eleventh Circuit held that an indigent who remains in custody while awaiting extradition must get credit when he is sentenced for the time when he was in custody.

O.C.G.A. § 17-13-46 provides that a person arrested pursuant to the Uniform Criminal Extradition Act may waive procedural requirements of the extradition proceedings and may consent in writing to return to the demanding state. The accused must execute such a waiver in the presence of a judge of any court of record within the surrendering state. Before the execution of the waiver becomes valid, the judge must inform the accused of his right to be issued a warrant of extradition and to petition for habeas corpus relief as provided in O.C.G.A. § 17-13-30, discussed supra. Where a waiver has been duly executed, it is filed with the governor, and the accused is delivered to the agent of the demanding state. However, these provisions do not limit the rights of the accused to return to the demanding state voluntarily and without formality and therefore they are not exclusive.

O.C.G.A. § 17-13-47 provides that nothing in the Uniform Criminal Extradition Act is to be construed as limiting the powers of the surrendering state to try a fugitive (for crimes committed in the surrendering state) who has been demanded by another state. Thus, it seems that the surrendering state may retain the fugitive and delay extradition until the proceedings in the surrendering state have been terminated or regain custody of the accused in order to have a trial, sentencing or punishment for any offense committed in the surrendering state.

O.C.G.A. § 17-13-48 provides that after a fugitive has been extradited, he may be tried in the demanding state for other crimes which he allegedly committed in that state as well as those crimes specified in the warrant of extradition.

It has been held that there is no double jeopardy or collateral estoppel problem where a demand for extradition is rejected by the surrendering state, and a later demand based on the same criminal charge is accepted. It has also been held that the right to challenge the legality of extradition is deemed to have been waived by the fugitive by a failure to petition for habeas corpus relief; the matter cannot be raised after extradition at the trial in the demanding state upon the substantive crime charged.

Although an illegal arrest and extradition result in a civil rights violation actionable under 42 U. S. C. § 1983, it cannot be raised as a defense at the trial in the demanding state for the substantive crime charged.

Finally, it must be remembered that a person can only be extradited for a criminal offense and never for the purpose of enforcing the collection of a debt or any private purpose whatsoever, unless the failure to repay the debt also constitutes a crime in the demanding state. See section 14-66, infra, on Interstate Agreement on Detainers.

In *Oliver v. Barrett,* the court pointed out that while Georgia, by statute, "requires that extradition . . . be solely for the purpose of a criminal prosecution, it is not appropriate for the habeas court to look behind the probable cause finding of the demanding state."

Generally, see 35 C. J. S. Extradition § 2 et seq.; 31A Am. Jur. 2d Extradition § 22 et seq. See section 2-25, infra, on results of illegal arrests and kidnapping of a defendant and on the right of a court to try a defendant where he was illegally brought into the jurisdiction of the court. See Annotation, "Necessity That Demanding State Show Probable Cause to Arrest Fugitive in Extradition Proceedings," 90 A. L. R. 3rd 1085 (1979).

§ 2-24 The exclusionary rule—Background

The exclusionary rule, as that term is used in criminal procedure, refers in its broader aspects to the exclusion of some kind of evidence in a judicial proceeding. The term may be used in connection with the sustaining of a hearsay objection at trial, a ruling excluding evidence because of its irrelevancy, or any other valid reason for the non-admission of evidence.

In addition to the broader scope of the meaning of the "exclusionary rule," this term may be applied to a specific statute which provides that certain evidence is not to be admissible in one or more phases of a judicial proceeding. For example, certain confidential communications are excluded on the grounds of public policy. Also, a witness is not obligated to incriminate himself, and a defendant in a criminal case cannot be forced to give evidence for or against himself. By Georgia statute, a confession is not admissible unless it was "made voluntarily, without being induced by another by the slightest hope of benefit or remotest fear of injury." Also, by Georgia statute, any aggrieved defendant may move to suppress any evidence illegally seized in violation of O.C.G.A. §§ 17-5-1 et seq.

However, the term "exclusionary rule" is used most frequently in reference to the exclusion of evidence in some phase of a criminal proceeding as a result of a holding, independent of state law, of the United States Supreme Court. That decision held that evidence obtained by law enforcement officers in violation of the due process clause of the Fourteenth Amendment, or that clause and some provision of the Bill of Rights of the federal Constitution, is not admissible in state trials. In *Mowery v. State,* the Georgia Court of Appeals stated that "[t]he law does not favor exclusionary rules; they hinder the search for truth."

In the 1914 decision of *Weeks v. United States,* certain documents were taken from Weeks' room by a United States Marshal who had no authority to enter. The court held that private documents obtained as a result of an illegal search were not admissible as evidence against Weeks at his trial in federal court where he had demanded their return before trial. The court concluded that to admit into evidence such illegally seized evidence "would be to affirm by judicial decision a manifest neglect, if not an open defiance, of the prohibitions of the Constitution, intended for the protection of the people against such unauthorized action." In the 1920 decision of *Silverthorne Lumber Co. v. United States,* Justice Holmes stated that the Fourth Amendment would be reduced "to a form of words" without the use of the exclusionary rule to suppress evidence obtained by an unconstitutional search and seizure.

Nevertheless, the exclusionary rule in Fourth Amendment situations was not applied by the United States Supreme Court in state court proceedings until 1961. The landmark decision of *Mapp v. Ohio* was handed down during that year. *Mapp* involved the admission of evidence obtained in an illegal search and seizure. The majority held that the due process clause of the Fourteenth Amendment made the provisions of the Fourth Amendment applicable to the states; and, consequently, evidence obtained in violation of the Fourth Amendment could not be admitted in a state criminal proceeding. Thereafter, the exclusionary rule has been applied to the states.

In 1936, in *Brown v. Mississippi,* the United States Supreme Court, relying on the due process clause of the Fifth and Fourteenth Amendments, held that an involuntary confession was not admissible in a state criminal trial. In *Escobedo v. Illinois,* the confession which had been obtained was held inadmissible in a state criminal trial because the confession had been obtained in violation of the Sixth Amendment right to counsel, which was made applicable to the states by the Fourteenth Amendment. Two years later, in *Miranda v. Arizona,* the United States Supreme Court held that the Fifth Amendment was applicable to the states and that admissions and confessions not obtained in compliance with that opinion were not admissible in state or federal courts.

In the field of visual identification of a defendant, the United States Supreme Court in 1967 handed down a decision in *Gilbert v. California.* In that case, the Court held that a defendant in a state criminal trial had been denied his Sixth Amendment right to counsel, made applicable to the states through the Fourteenth Amendment, where he was identified at a lineup after indictment in the absence of his counsel. As a result, evidence of the pre-trial identification of the defendant was held to be inadmissible at his trial.

Lastly, it must be remembered that the federal constitutional exclusionary rule, as pronounced by the United States Supreme Court, represents the minimum constitutional protection due to a defendant in a criminal case. However, a state court may not interpret the federal Constitution to give a defendant any greater right or rights than that given by the interpretation of the federal Constitution by the United States Supreme Court. Nevertheless, a state court may interpret the constitution of the state to give a defendant broader protection than that provided by the federal Constitution as interpreted by the United States Supreme Court. This rule applies even when the wording of the state constitution is exactly like the wording of the federal Constitution on the particular matter. Also, Congress and the state legislatures may extend the exclusionary rule by legislation so as to give a defendant in a criminal case greater protection than he is entitled to under the federal Constitution.

See Wilkes, "A Most Deplorable Paradox: Admitting Illegally Obtained Evidence in Georgia—Past, Present and Future," 11 Ga. L. R. 105 (1976).

§ 2-25 The exclusionary rule—Present application at trial

The mere fact that an arrest or search is illegal does not prevent a criminal prosecution nor provide a defense to such a prosecution. In *Thompson v. State,* the court pointed out that "the illegality of an arrest neither bars prosecution or affects a conviction." In *Frisbie v. Collins,* the United States Supreme Court held that a court may try a defendant even where the defendant is forcibly abducted and brought within the jurisdiction of the court. In *Lujan v. Gengler,* the court held that where a defendant was kidnapped in a foreign country, not treated in a cruel or inhuman manner, and brought to this country, he was not entitled to be released because of the unconventional way in which he was brought to this county.

In *United States v. Alvarez-Machain,* the United States Supreme Court held that the kidnapping of a Mexican citizen in his home in that country and transporting him to Texas did not amount to a treaty violation nor prevent his trial.

However, primary evidence or evidence directly obtained from a defendant as a result of an arrest or a search and seizure invalid under the Fourth Amendment is not admissible against the defendant at his trial if he properly moves to suppress such evidence, except perhaps for purposes of impeachment. See section 3-12, infra, on fingerprinting when there is no probable cause to arrest.

It must be emphasized that the exclusionary rule which is applied to the United States Constitution applies only to *governmental action.* See section 4-59, infra.

The more difficult question is, what evidence derived from a violation of the Fourth Amendment must be suppressed where the evidence was not obtained directly or immediately from the defendant when the arrest or the search and seizure occurred?

In *Wong Sun v. United States,* the Court said:

"The exclusionary rule has traditionally barred from trial physical, tangible materials obtained either during or as a direct result of an unlawful invasion. It follows . . . that the Fourth Amendment may protect against the overhearing of verbal statements as well as against the more traditional seizure of 'papers and effects.' Similarly, testimony as to matters observed during an unlawful invasion has been excluded in order to enforce the basic constitutional policies . . . . Thus, verbal evidence which derives so immediately from an unlawful entry and an unauthorized arrest as the officers' action in the present case is no less the 'fruit' of official illegality than the more common tangible fruits of the unwarranted intrusion."

In *Silverthorne Lumber Co. v. United States,* Silverthorne had been held in contempt for refusal to obey a subpoena directing the production of certain documents. The government knew of the existence of the documents by reason of a prior illegal search and seizure. In reversing the conviction, the Court, in an opinion by Justice Holmes, said:

"The essence of a provision forbidding the acquisition of evidence in a certain way is that not merely evidence so acquired shall not be used before the court, but that it shall not be used at all. Of course this does not mean that the facts thus obtained become sacred and inaccessible. If knowledge of them is *gained from an independent source* they may be proved like any others, but the knowledge gained by the government's own wrong cannot be used by it . . . . (Emphasis added.)

Tainted evidence not obtained directly from the original invalid search and seizure or arrest has come to be known as derivative evidence or "fruit of the poisonous tree." This term was coined by Justice Frankfurter in *Nardone v. United States.* In that case, the Court noted a second exception to the rule that all derivative evidence must be excluded, by stating that such evidence could "become so attenuated as to dissipate the [original] taint."

The third exception to the rule that all evidence derived from unconstitutional action by officers was mentioned in a footnote of the case *Brewer v. Williams.*

The United States Supreme Court has never held that all derivative evidence is to be considered the "fruit of the poisonous tree" "simply because it would not have come to light *but* for the illegal actions of the police. Rather, the more apt question in such a case is 'whether granting establishment of the primary illegality, the evidence to which instant objection is made has been come at by exploitation of that illegality or instead by means sufficiently distinguishable to be purged of the primary taint.' " (Emphasis added.) However, there is no per se exclusion of in-court identification because of suggestive pre-trial identification procedures. See section 6-8, infra, on due process standard of identification.

As previously pointed out, the Supreme Court has at least given passing recognition to three exceptions to the broad language of *Silverthorne* indicating that evidence illegally obtained shall not be used to develop or find other evidence. These exceptions are stated in *United States v. Brookins* as follows: "[First] One form of insufficient connection between the fruit and the tree occurs if physical evidence, a witness' testimony, or the accused's statement has an attenuated link to the illegally secured evidence. . . . [Second] Another type of inadequate connection arises if the derivative evidence has an independent source from the illegally taken objects or statements. . . . A third category of insufficient connection obtains if the derivative evidence . . . would inevitably have been discovered during a police investigation without the aid of the illegally obtained evidence."

Initially the burden has been said to be on the defendant to show that the derivative evidence was obtained by the government as a result of the illegal search. Once this has been done, the government has the burden of establishing that the evidence is admissible under one of the three exceptions set out above.

The following three sections discuss when secondary or derivative evidence is admissible because of the good faith of the officer conducting a search pursuant to a warrant, an independent source, inevitable discovery, or attenuation.

See section 4-59, infra, on result of school searches.

§ 2-26 The exclusionary rule—Present application at trial—Good faith of officer conducting search pursuant to warrant

In the 1992 case of *Gary v. State,* the Georgia Supreme Court declined to follow the "good faith" exception found by the United States Supreme Court in *United States v. Leon.* The Georgia Court pointed out that a "[s]tate is free . . . to impose greater restrictions on police activity than those [the Supreme] Court holds to be necessary upon federal constitutional standards." The court then held that under the wording of O.C.G.A. § 17-5-30 the Georgia legislature said that "evidence seized by means of a warrant that is not supported by probable cause [must] be suppressed."

In *Leon,* the United States Supreme Court held that "the Fourth Amendment exclusionary rule . . . [does] not . . . bar the use in the prosecution's case-in-chief of evidence obtained by officers acting in reasonable reliance on a search warrant issued by a detached and neutral magistrate but ultimately found to be unsupported by probable cause."

In *Arizona v. Evans,* the United States Supreme Court extended the good faith exception to the exclusionary rule to cover errors by employees of the court. In this case, the defendant was arrested and contraband was recovered in a search incident to arrest. The arrest warrant for the defendant had been quashed, but, due to a clerical error by court employees, the computer did not indicate this. The court pointed out that the exclusionary rule was historically used to deter police misconduct and that because there was no police misconduct here, suppression was not necessary. In coming to this conclusion, the Court seemed impressed with the fact that this *type of mistake* occurred very infrequently and that the defendant made no showing that court employees are "inclined to ignore or subvert the Fourth Amendment." See section 4-20, infra, on execution of invalid warrant.

In *Herring v. United States,* the United States Supreme Court applied the reasoning of *Leon* and *Evans* to find that the exclusionary rule could not be used to suppress drugs and firearms found by officers in a search incident to arrest based on an arrest warrant later found to be defective. The Court held that the deterrent effect to police misconduct provided by the exclusionary rule was not served when the police mistakes were attenuated from the search and were no more than isolated negligence rather than "systemic error or reckless disregard of constitutional requirements."

In *Cunningham v. State,* the court affirmed a traffic stop where a patrolman checked with a dispatcher to determine whether a tag on a car belonged on another vehicle. The dispatcher gave erroneous information to the patrolman, who stopped the driver and then arrested him for driving under the influence. The court pointed out that there had been no bad faith and that it was just an "honest human mistake."

However, in *State v. White,* the Florida Supreme Court held that negligence of the sheriff's department in maintaining computer records "falls squarely within the class of governmental action that the exclusionary rule was designed to deter." During the stop of the defendant for a minor traffic violation, the deputy sheriff was informed of the existence of an outstanding warrant for the defendant. The defendant was arrested and contraband was discovered during a search of his car. Later it was discovered that the warrant was not outstanding but in fact had been served four days earlier by another deputy and the sheriff's office neglected to supply the computer with that information. The court also pointed out that the collective knowledge rule was also applicable here because other members of the sheriff's department knew that the warrant was no longer outstanding. See sections 2-11, supra, and 4-49, infra, on collective knowledge.

In *Harvey v. State,* the arresting officer ran the defendant's name through NCIC and it showed that there was a bench warrant for his arrest. Harvey was then placed under arrest and, in a search incident to that arrest, cocaine was discovered. At trial the defendant moved to suppress the cocaine because the bench warrant had been quashed a few days before the arrest. This information was not revealed in NCIC records when they were checked by the officer in the field. Nevertheless, the Georgia Supreme Court held that "in hindsight, [this Court] will not declare an arrest to be invalid when the arresting officer reasonably relied upon information which he had no reason to think was incorrect." Because the NCIC report was reliable enough to underlie the reasonable belief which is needed to establish probable cause, the court upheld the admission of the cocaine into evidence. Although the Leon "good faith" exception is not applicable in Georgia, the court in *Harvey* pointed out that it was not implicated here because "[t]he radio transmissions which confirmed the outstanding warrants established the necessary probable cause to arrest."

Also see section 4-22, infra, on good faith exclusionary exception as applied to a warrant not sufficiently particularizing items to be seized. See sections 3-2 and 4-45, infra, on invalidity of law authorizing a stop or search. See section 4-20, infra, on good faith mistaken belief of officer that area being searched was within scope of warrant.

§ 2-27 The exclusionary rule—Present application at trial—The independent source exception

"The essential aspect of the independent source rule is the existence of evidence which was not illegally seized and which in fact provided an independent basis for the discovery of the challenged evidence." Some courts have interpreted the independent source exception to require the government to show that the challenged evidence was acquired wholly apart from the original illegality. However, some other jurisdictions have interpreted this exception more broadly.

Two identification cases serve to illustrate the application of the independent source exception. In *Bynum v. United States,* the defendant had been illegally arrested and fingerprinted. However, the government sought to show that fingerprints which had previously been obtained by the FBI matched the fingerprints left at the scene of the crime. The court held that the older fingerprints were admissible in evidence along with the latent fingerprints taken from the scene.

In *United States v. Crews,* a victim was assaulted in a restroom on the grounds of the Washington Monument. She notified officers and gave a description of her assailant. Several days later, Crews was illegally arrested in the same area because he fit the description given. He was photographed and his picture identified by the victim in a photographic display. Crews was again taken into custody and identified at a lineup. The trial judge found that the victim's ability to identify Crews was based on her independent and untainted recollection of having seen him at the time of the crime and she was permitted to identify him at the trial. The Supreme Court concluded that the victim's presence in the courtroom at trial was not a result of police misconduct and Crews cannot claim immunity simply because his presence in court was precipitated by an unlawful arrest. Crews was not himself a suppressible fruit of an unlawful arrest. The "Fourth Amendment violation . . . yielded nothing of evidentiary value that the police did not already have in their grasp."

In *Murray v. United States,* the United States Supreme Court held that the exclusionary rule did not apply where officers illegally entered a warehouse and while there "observed in plain view numerous burlap-wrapped bales that were later found to contain marijuana . . ., [l]eft without disturbing the bales, kept the warehouse under surveillance, and did not reenter it until they had a search warrant" issued on the basis of information unrelated to the initial entry.

Generally, see 1 Ringel, *Searches and Seizures, Arrests and Confessions,* § 3.3(a) (Clark Boardman 1979).

§ 2-28 The exclusionary rule—Present application at trial—The inevitable discovery exception

The inevitable discovery exception permits the prosecution to justify the admission of evidence obtained as a result of an unlawful search by showing that the evidence would have been discovered later through legal means.

The Eleventh Circuit Court of Appeals refined the doctrine to also require that "the prosecution . . . demonstrate that the lawful means which made discovery inevitable were possessed by the police and were being actively pursued prior to the occurrence of the illegal conduct." In *Taylor v. State*, the Georgia Supreme Court concluded that as defined by the Eleventh Circuit, the inevitable discovery doctrine was consistent with prior application of the rule in Georgia and decided to expressly adopt it as the rule in this State.

A leading case on inevitable discovery is *Wayne v. United States,* in an opinion written by future Chief Justice Burger. In this case, the court, on the basis of *Wong Sun v. United States,* held a coroner's report concerning the cause of death to be admissible even though the body had been found as the result of an illegal search and seizure. The court pointed out that the body would have been found sooner or later and that the police would have been notified then. This case also demonstrates the close relationship which may exist between the inevitable discovery and independent source exceptions.

In *Nix v. Williams,* the United States Supreme Court considered Williams' second conviction. In the second *Williams* opinion, the Court approved the admissibility of evidence relating to the discovery and condition of the body of the victim since the prosecution had established by a preponderance of the evidence that the body would have been inevitably discovered in the same condition even if there had been no Sixth Amendment violation. The court noted that the prosecution is not required to prove the absence of bad faith on the part of the officers violating the defendant's constitutional rights.

In the 1987 Eleventh Circuit opinion in *United States v. Hernandez-Cano*, the court held that the inevitable discovery doctrine applied where an airline employee would have discovered cocaine even if an officer had not intervened and actually discovered the contraband.

Generally, see 1 Ringel, *Searches and Seizures, Arrests and Confessions,* § 3.3(b) (Clark Boardman 1979).

§ 2-29 The exclusionary rule—Present application at trial—Attenuation

The attenuation or purged taint exception to the rule that evidence derived from, or as a result of, an illegal arrest or search is inadmissible finds support in the fact that the United States Supreme Court has pointed out that it has never adopted a "but for" causation test. That is, the Court has not held that all evidence which would not have been discovered had it not been for the unconstitutional arrest or search and seizure must be excluded. The Supreme Court uses the term "attenuation" when referring to circumstances involving a tenuous connection between the violation of the defendant's constitutional rights and the discovery of the contested evidence. For example, in the case of a knock-and-announce violation that is the "but for" cause of the discovery of contested evidence, attenuation occurs when the causal connection is remote, or when "given a direct causal connection, the interest protected by the constitutional guarantee that has been violated would not be served by suppression of the evidence obtained."

In *Wong Sun v. United States,* federal narcotics agents entered without probable cause and chased Toy to his bedroom, where he was arrested. Toy made a statement implicating Yee. Narcotics were seized from Yee, who implicated Wong Sun. All defendants were arraigned and released. Within a few days, all three made statements to the Narcotics Bureau. The court agreed with Toy's contention that his statement and the drugs later seized from Yee were fruits of Toy's illegal arrest. However, the Court concluded that Wong Sun's statement which had been made to agents several days after arraignment was sufficiently attenuated to have dissipated the taint of his illegal arrest. The court pointed out that the taint of the illegal arrest was sufficiently purged by the independent act of the defendant in going to the office and making a statement after his arraignment. The fact that Wong Sun would not have gone to the office of the narcotics agents and made a statement had it not been for his illegal arrest did not prevent the admission of the statement.

In *Burnham v. State,* the Georgia Supreme Court held that "[t]he shorter the lapse in time between the illegal police activity and the defendant's statement, the more likely it is that the defendant's statement was the product of the illegal activity."

In *Brown v. Illinois,* the defendant was illegally arrested, given *Miranda* warnings, and within two hours of the time of his arrest he gave an inculpatory statement concerning a murder and later gave a second statement. The court concluded that the giving of *Miranda* warnings did not automatically break the causal chain so that the statement would be admissible, even if the statement had been made voluntarily under the Fifth Amendment. The court also reasoned that the second statement was the fruit of the first one and that it was not admissible. In the decision, the Court pointed out that each case must turn on its own facts. Of course, if a statement was not voluntarily made, it is not admissible for any purpose. In *Brown,* the Court enumerated some factors which may be considered in determining whether or not the illegal taint has been purged. Those factors are the following:

(1) *Miranda* warnings;

(2) Temporal proximity of the arrest and the confession;

(3) Presence of intervening circumstances;

(4) Purpose of the official misconduct; and

(5) Flagrancy of the official misconduct.

The burden of establishing the sufficiency of the attenuation from the illegality "rests squarely with the prosecution."

Wong Sun and *Brown* are based on Fourth Amendment violations. However, a different rule applies where there is a violation of the rules of *Miranda.* In *Oregon v. Elstad,* the United States Supreme Court considered a case in which the defendant was arrested, pursuant to a warrant, at his home in connection with a burglary. He was not given *Miranda* warnings, but he voluntarily made an incriminating statement in answer to some questions asked by the officer while sitting in the defendant's living room. One hour later, at police headquarters, he was administered *Miranda* warnings for the first time and he made a full confession, which was typed and signed. The defendant objected to the admissibility of the confession alleging that it was a result of the earlier incriminating statement. The defendant contended that a confession cannot be voluntary "once the cat is out of the bag." Writing for the majority, Justice O'Connor distinguished between "actual" coerced statements resulting from police misconduct and mere "technical" *Miranda* violations. Although the defendant was technically in custody while he was in his living room with the officer, there was no coercion. Because there was no coercion in the first interrogation, and the second confession came after the *Miranda* warnings were given, the second confession was admissible against the defendant. "The Fifth Amendment prohibits the prosecution in its case in chief only of *compelled* testimony. Failure to administer *Miranda* warnings creates a presumption of compulsion." However, "[a] subsequent administration of *Miranda* warnings to a suspect who has given a voluntary but unwarned statement ordinarily should suffice to remove the conditions that precluded admission of the earlier statement."

Elstad, however, does not afford police the opportunity to interrogate suspects without providing *Miranda* warnings with the intention of giving warnings after obtaining incriminating statements and then having the suspect repeat those statements. The United States Supreme Court rejected just such a practice in *Missouri v. Seibert,* where police attempted to circumvent *Miranda* by providing warnings mid-interrogation and post-confession. The opinion states that in determining whether "midstream *Miranda* warnings" could be effective, courts should consider: "the completeness and detail of the questions and answers to the first round of interrogation, overlapping contents of the two statements, the timing and setting of the first and second rounds, the continuity of police personnel, and the degree to which the interrogator's questions treated the second round as continuous with the first."

See section 2-31, note 7, infra, for an application of the Brown rule. Generally, see 1 Ringel, *Searches and Seizures, Arrests and Confessions,* § 3.3(c) (Clark Boardman 1979).

§ 2-30 The exclusionary rule—Present application at trial—Discovery of prosecution witness

In *United States v. Ceccolini,* the Court concluded that "the exclusionary rule should be invoked with much greater reluctance where the claim is based on a causal relationship between a constitutional violation and the discovery of a live witness than when a similar claim is advanced to support suppression of an inanimate object."

In arriving at this conclusion, the Court (1) rejected the contention of the government that the testimony of a live witness should never be excluded, and (2) reaffirmed the rule that verbal evidence may be the fruit of an unlawful arrest. However, the Court also said that the willingness of the witness to testify is material, since the witness might come forward and offer to testify on his own volition. The time, place and manner of the first questioning is of significance.

§ 2-31 The exclusionary rule—Present application at trial—Confessions obtained

See sections 5-13 and 5-26, infra, on admissibility under Georgia law of a confession made to a private person.

As previously pointed out in section 2-29, supra, an incriminating statement obtained from Toy in *Wong Sun v. United States* at the time of his illegal arrest was held to be a direct fruit of the unlawful arrest and therefore inadmissible. However, the statement of Wong Sun after his arraignment was admissible. Also as previously pointed out in section 2-29, supra, in *Brown v. Illinois,* the Court laid down some significant factors to be considered in determining the degree of attenuation which exists.

In *Dunaway v. New York,* the Court held that where a suspect is "picked up," taken to a police station, placed in an interrogation room, given *Miranda* warnings and makes incriminating statements, such statements are not admissible when the officers lacked probable cause to arrest. This is true even if *Miranda* warnings are given and the confession is "voluntary" for purposes of the Fifth Amendment. See section 11-1, infra, on a statement obtained after 48 hours following a warrantless arrest where there has been no probable cause hearing. The Supreme Court of Georgia cited and relied upon *Dunaway* in the 1986 case of *State v. Harris.*

In *Taylor v. Alabama,* the entire Court recognized that "a confession obtained through custodial interrogation after an illegal arrest should be excluded unless intervening events break the causal connection between the illegal arrest and the confession so that the confession is 'sufficiently an act of free will to purge the primary taint.' " In this case, the arrest had been without probable cause. In determining whether the primary taint has been purged, consideration should be given to the factors enumerated in *Brown v. Illinois,* which were discussed in section 2-29, supra. The *Taylor* majority concluded that the primary taint had not been purged. The dissenting justices disagreed. The following facts were discussed on the question of whether the taint had been purged:

(1) The conduct of the arresting officers had not been blatant.

(2) Taylor was told at the time of the arrest that he was being arrested for a robbery at a grocery.

(3) There was no police misconduct other than the arrest.

(4) Taylor was fingerprinted, placed in a lineup, and told that his fingerprints matched prints found in the store where the robbery had taken place.

(5) Taylor was given *Miranda* warnings on three occasions.

(6) Taylor was not represented by counsel.

(7) Taylor was in custody about six hours before he confessed.

(8) Taylor's girlfriend talked with him before he confessed. She was, however, emotionally upset at the time.

(9) Taylor was permitted to talk to a neighbor for a few minutes. Shortly after this conversation, he confessed.

However, in the 1980 case of *Rawlings v. Kentucky,* where Rawlings and some others were detained in a friend's home for about 45 minutes in a "congenial atmosphere" while a search warrant was obtained and *Miranda* warnings were given shortly before an incriminating statement was apparently volunteered, the statement was found to be admissible. The court emphasized the short duration of the detention and that there had been no flagrant misconduct by the officers.

Generally, if two confessions are made and the first is closely connected with the unlawful arrest, or search and seizure, the second confession is also regarded as not being admissible even if some time or intervening circumstances have occurred. In a sense, the second confession is regarded as being the fruit of the first. However, as in *Oregon v. Elstad,* this is not as likely to be true where the first confession was voluntary but is not admissible simply because of a technical *Miranda* violation.

Where a suspect is confronted with illegally seized items and he confesses to the crime involved, it seems that normally the confession would not be admissible.

In *Green v. State,* the arrest warrant contained no facts justifying that the defendant committed a murder. Since a statement was obtained from the defendant pursuant to the defective warrant, and was admitted at trial, the conviction was reversed. The dissenting opinion emphasized the good faith of the officers and cited *United States v. Williams.* The United States Supreme Court denied certiorari.

However, in *Thompson v. State,* in which Justice Smith dissented and Justice Weltner did not participate, the court held that a confession was admissible despite the fact that it was obtained as a result of an illegal arrest. Here the warrantless arrest was a violation of the Fourth Amendment since the defendant was in his home at the time of the arrest, there were no exigent circumstances; and the defendant did not consent to the arrest. The court emphasized the fact that the officers had probable cause to arrest, honestly thought they did not need an arrest warrant, and did not engage in any purposeful or flagrant misconduct.

Nevertheless, in *United States v. Johnson,* the United States Supreme Court held that the Payton rule, requiring an arrest warrant before a defendant may be arrested in his home in the absence of exigent circumstances, is to be applied retroactively to all cases in which the conviction was not final on the date of the *Payton* decision. *Payton* was decided in 1980. In *Johnson,* the Court held that it was error not to grant the motion to suppress the oral statement which Johnson made shortly after his warrantless arrest at home. The Ninth Circuit concluded in *Johnson* that the agents had probable cause to arrest. In fact, warrants had been obtained for the arrest of Johnson and another person known to have participated in the offense with him. At one point in *Johnson,* the Court stated, "The Government does not seriously suggest that the retroactivity of a given Fourth Amendment ruling should turn solely on the subjective state of a particular arresting officer's mind. Instead, it offers an 'objective' test: that law enforcement officers 'may properly be charged with knowledge' of all 'settled' Fourth Amendment law." This "objective test" was rejected, however, by the Court. It was reasoned that "if, as the Government argues, all rulings resolving unsettled Fourth Amendment questions should be nonretroactive, then, in close cases, law enforcement officials would have little incentive to err on the side of constitutional behavior."

In the 1990 case of *New York v. Harris,* the United States Supreme Court held that if a warrantless, nonconsensual, routine felony arrest in a suspect's home is supported by probable cause, it does not require the suppression of a statement made by the suspect after he was removed from his home. Similarly, in *Carranza v. State,* the Georgia Supreme Court, in a six to one decision, reached the same conclusion.

§ 2-32 The exclusionary rule—Present application at trial—Impeachment

In *Walder v. United States,* the defendant had been tried and convicted of purchasing and possessing heroin. On direct examination Walder testified that he never handled any narcotics. Over objection, on cross-examination the government asked Walder about the heroin unlawfully seized from his home earlier. He denied that narcotics had been taken from his home. The government then put on the stand one of the officers who participated in the unlawful search and seizure as well as the chemist who analyzed the seized heroin. The testimony was allowed and the conviction was affirmed because the defendant "opened the door" for cross-examination regarding his possession of the drugs.

In *Harris v. New York,* the defendant made statements to officers which were not admissible in the government's case in chief under *Miranda.* After Harris testified at trial, prior inconsistent statements he made were held to have been properly admitted for purposes of impeachment. Likewise, in *Michigan v. Harvey,* the Court held that "the prosecution may use a statement taken in violation of the [*Michigan v.*] *Jackson* prophylactic rule to impeach a defendant's false or inconsistent testimony." (*Jackson* is discussed in section 5-20, infra.)

However, the foregoing situation is to be distinguished from that which exists when a statement or confession was not voluntarily given. Thus, in *Mincey v. Arizona,* a statement obtained by officers from Mincey, while he was in the intensive care unit of a hospital in critical condition, as a result of questioning for four hours while he was in severe pain, was held not to have been voluntarily given. The court then concluded that a confession obtained in this manner could not be used for purposes of impeachment.

Also, the situations in *Walder* and *Harris* are to be distinguished from a case in which a prosecutor seeks to impeach the credibility of a defense *witness* by the use of illegally obtained evidence. *James v. Illinois* is such a case. In *James,* the Court concluded that to permit the impeachment of a defense witness with illegally obtained evidence would lead a defendant not to call the witness and "would not further . . . truthseeking . . . but would appreciably undermine the deterrent effect of the exclusionary rule. . . ." Hence, it is error to admit illegally obtained evidence for the purpose of impeaching a defense witness.

In *United States v. Havens,* the Court considered the admission into evidence of an illegally seized undershirt. On direct examination, Havens testified that he had had no activity with his co-defendant on his visit to Peru. On cross-examination, Havens testified that he had not participated in making a closed pocket on a tee-shirt which the customs officer found the co-defendant wearing. In rebuttal, an agent was permitted to testify to finding a tee-shirt in Havens' bag from which pieces had been cut which matched the pieces sewn to McLeroth's tee-shirt to form pockets which contained the cocaine. Also, the undershirt was admitted into evidence. The Court, in effect, affirmed the trial court and declined to restrict *Walder* to impeachment of direct testimony. The court concluded rather that the cross-examination grew reasonably out of Havens' direct testimony and was not a violation of his constitutional rights.

See Annotation, "Propriety of Using Otherwise Inadmissible Statement, Taken in Violation of *Miranda* Rule, to Impeach Criminal Defendant's Credibility—State Cases," 14 A. L. R. 4th 676 (1982).

§ 2-33 Real evidence discovered as a result of *Miranda* violation

Physical evidence discovered as a result of a *Miranda* violation need not be suppressed unless the interrogation involved actual coercion. The fruits from the unwarned statements of criminal suspects may thus be used as evidence against them in subsequent proceedings provided the statements made to the police were given voluntarily. Accordingly, in *Taylor v. State*, a murder weapon discovered through the *Miranda* tainted statement of the defendant was properly admitted at trial because the defendant's statement was voluntary albeit made without counsel, after a proper request for an attorney had been made by the defendant. However, in *Vergara v. State*, the court found that the fruits doctrine applied where there was a direct nexus between the interrogation and the discovery of the cocaine evidence after the defendant had requested counsel and ruled that the evidence should have been suppressed.

§ 2-34 The exclusionary rule—Present application—Non-trial proceedings

"When an attempt is made to apply the [exclusionary] rule in contexts other than the initial stages of a criminal prosecution, courts will balance the deterrent effect of the rule's use in the situation at hand against the cost to the government and society of losing the use of probative evidence."

It has been held in Georgia that evidence obtained from a search in violation of the Fourth Amendment may not be used to obtain a search warrant.

In the context of the Fifth Amendment, at least three decisions have concluded that evidence obtained in violation of *Miranda* may not be used to establish probable cause for a search and seizure. However, these cases are open to serious question after *Commonwealth v. White,* a 1977 United States Supreme Court decision where an equally divided court (Justice Powell did not participate) affirmed per curiam the Massachusetts Supreme Judicial Court's exclusion of evidence obtained in violation of *Miranda.*

In the area of grand jury investigations, the United States Supreme Court has held that a witness summoned to appear and testify before the grand jury may not refuse to answer questions on the ground that the questions were based on evidence obtained in an unlawful search and seizure. Also, it seems that it is not necessary to give *Miranda* warnings to a grand jury witness "who is called to testify about criminal activities in which he may have been personally involved."

In the case of parole or probation revocations, some courts have held that the exclusionary rule does not apply. However, in Georgia, at least in the case of probation proceedings, the exclusionary rule is applied.

Likewise, some courts have held that the exclusionary rule does not apply to sentencing proceedings, while other courts have applied the exclusionary rule.

See section 4-7, infra, on illegally obtained evidence being considered to establish probable cause, and section 2-25, supra. See section 5-26, infra, on admissibility of the fruits of an illegally obtained confession.

See sections 3-2 and 4-45, infra, on the application of the exclusionary rule where an officer relied on an invalid law. See section 30-7, infra, on admissibility of evidence obtained in violation of Fourth Amendment in a parole hearing.

§ 2-35 The exclusionary rule—Present application—Civil proceedings

In the case of a forfeiture or condemnation of an automobile, the United States Supreme Court referred to the proceedings as being quasi-criminal and held that the exclusionary rule applied.

However, in *United States v. Janis,* police officers, pursuant to an invalid warrant, conducted a search for evidence of bookmaking. Agents of the Internal Revenue Service were informed of Janis' arrest, resulting in an assessment against Janis for wagering taxes. The court held that the exclusionary rule should not be extended to forbid the use, in a civil proceeding by the federal government, of evidence illegally seized by a criminal law enforcement agent of a state because the likelihood of deterring law enforcement's conduct is not sufficient to outweigh societal costs imposed by the exclusion. Likewise, in *Immigration and Naturalization Service v. Lopez-Mendoza*, the Court held that the Fourth Amendment rule did not apply to a civil deportation proceeding.

In *Middleton v. Middleton,* the court held inadmissible a tape recorded conversation concerning a wife's extramarital affair made for use in a divorce case and made in violation of O.C.G.A. § 16-11-62, the anti-wiretapping statute.

Chapter 3

Stop–And–Frisk

§ 3-1 General considerations

The police have long felt the need to stop and question and search or frisk suspicious persons. Prior to *Mapp v. Ohio* and the exclusionary rule, the legality of such encounters was not considered to be of great importance and there were few reported cases which addressed the constitutionality of such stops and searches or frisks. However, after the *Mapp* decision in 1961 held that evidence obtained in violation of the Fourth Amendment was inadmissible in a state criminal prosecution, the validity of these searches or frisks began to receive much more attention. Also, the trend toward invalidating vagrancy, loitering, and disorderly conduct statutes further limited the right of officers to search or frisk suspicious persons.

In law enforcement parlance, a "stop" means "a temporary investigative detention of an individual short of an arrest." A "frisk" means the pat-down of an individual's outer clothing to determine whether he is carrying a weapon; a procedure not amounting to a full search. Thus, a stop and frisk represents two distinct occurrences. Even though the facts justify a stop, this does not mean that they justify a frisk. A frisk is more limited than a search incident to a valid arrest. Because both a stop and a frisk are less intrusive than a search incident to a valid arrest, they may be based on something less than probable cause.

The United States Supreme Court, in *Terry v. Ohio,* first considered the stop-and-frisk situation. The court concluded as follows: (1) In order to justify a stop and follow it with a frisk, the officer had to be able to point to specific and articulable facts which, taken together with reasonable inferences, judged against an objective standard, would justify a reasonable person in believing that the frisk was appropriate. This action may not be justified solely by a hunch, guess, or suspicion. (2) When an officer reasonably concludes that a suspicious person he is investigating at close range is armed and potentially dangerous to the officer or others, it would be unreasonable to prevent the officer from determining if he is armed and if so, to prevent him from disarming the person. (3) The sole justification for a frisk is to discover weapons so as to protect the officer and others. The court also pointed out that (4) a frisk is not justified by a need to seize evidence; (5) the frisk, like other searches, must be strictly tied to and justified by the circumstances which initially rendered it permissible; (6) the frisk must be limited to that which is necessary for the discovery of weapons which might be used to harm the officer or others nearby; (7) a stop-and-frisk is not outside the protection of the Fourth Amendment; (8) when a person is restrained so he cannot walk away, he has been seized; (9) a frisk is a serious intrusion on the person frisked; and (10) it is not necessary to have probable cause for an arrest in order to justify a stop-and-frisk.

The scope of the stop-and-frisk area was further delineated in *Sibron v. New York.* In this case, the officer did not have probable cause to arrest. The court concluded that he was looking for narcotics and had no reason to think Sibron was armed. However, the Court pointed out that even if there was probable cause for a limited search or pat-down of his outer clothing for weapons, there was no right to go into his pocket unless a weapon was found in the pat-down.

In *Terry,* the Court emphasized that the stop was solely to obtain weapons, but in *United States v. Hensley*, the United States Supreme Court pointed out that the stop could be based on an articulable suspicion that the person stopped was wanted for a completed felony. See section 3-7, infra.

In *Michigan v. Chesternut,* the United States Supreme Court held that an "investigatory pursuit" does not violate the Fourth Amendment unless a person has been "seized." Officers "can be said to have seized an individual 'only if, in view of all of the circumstances surrounding the incident, a reasonable person would have believed that he was not free to leave.' "

In *Pennsylvania v. Mimms,* two officers saw the defendant driving an automobile with an expired license plate. The defendant was stopped for the purpose of being issued a traffic summons. He was ordered to get out of the car. When he did, the officer noticed a large bulge under his jacket. The defendant was then frisked and a.38 revolver was found in his waistband. Later he was indicted for carrying a concealed weapon. The court first found that the order to get out of the car after the driver had been detained, was reasonable and therefore permissible under the Fourth Amendment. The court then ruled that the frisk was proper because the officer reasonably concluded that the person whom he legitimately stopped might be armed and presently dangerous. *Mimms* holds that when an officer observes a traffic violation and subsequently issues a citation, the officer may have the driver step out of the car. A number of cases have considered whether the right to have the driver exit the car automatically extends the right of an officer to have passengers in the stopped vehicle step out of the vehicle. This question was answered affirmatively in the 1997 opinion of *Maryland v. Wilson,* which held that "an officer making a traffic stop may order passengers to get out of the car pending completion of the stop." In addition, where the officer has reason to suspect in the context of a traffic stop that a passenger is armed and dangerous, the passenger may be frisked.

In 1979, the Court decided *Ybarra v. Illinois.* In this case, the defendant, Ybarra, was a bar patron at the time of the execution of a search warrant authorizing the search of the bar and one named employee for narcotics and related items. Ybarra was also searched and heroin was found. The court held that it was error to overrule the defendant's motion to suppress. The court found that the officer had no articulable suspicion justifying a weapon frisk, that the Fourth Amendment does not permit a pat down of a person for weapons unless the officer has a reasonable belief that the person is armed and dangerous, and that *Terry* does not permit a search for anything other than weapons. The court later pointed out that the search "was invalid because the police had no reason to believe . . . [Ybarra] had any special connection with the premises, and the police had no other basis for suspecting that he was armed or in possession of contraband." The 1998 Georgia Court of Appeals case of *Clark v. State* is very much like *Ybarra* in its facts and results.

However, in *Michigan v. Summers,* the Court considered an incident involving the execution of a warrant to search a house for narcotics. As the officers approached the house they met the defendant, who was leaving. They requested his assistance in gaining entrance to the house and detained him until they had searched the premises. After learning that the defendant owned the house and after discovering narcotics in the house, the defendant was arrested and searched. Heroin was discovered in his coat pocket. The court said that if there is probable cause to search a citizen's residence for contraband, "it is constitutionally reasonable to require that citizen to remain while officers of the law execute a valid warrant to search his home."

"An investigating officer need not have [an] 'articulable suspicion' before he can approach a stopped vehicle and talk with the driver." But see section 3-9, infra, on roadblocks.

In *Dunaway v. New York,* the defendant was implicated in a murder. The officers did not have "enough information to get a warrant" for the defendant's arrest, but he was "picked up" and brought in. Although the defendant was told he was not under arrest, he would have been physically restrained if he attempted to leave. He was placed in an interrogation room where he waived counsel, made statements and drew sketches that incriminated him. The court held that the defendant's statements and sketches should have been suppressed since the officers did not have probable cause to arrest the defendant and since the acts of taking the defendant into custody and transporting him to the police station could not be regarded as a mere stop approved in *Terry.*

In a plurality opinion, the Court in *United States v. Mendenhall* expanded the scope of frisks under *Terry.* In *Mendenhall,* Drug Enforcement Agency officers approached the defendant as she exited the plane. The officers identified themselves and asked to see her identification and plane ticket. They returned both the identification and ticket to the defendant and only then did they ask her to come with them to a nearby airport office. She consented to go to the office and once there, she further consented to a search of her person. The search revealed heroin. The court established that a person is "seized" only if, in view of all the circumstances, "a reasonable person would have believed that he was not free to leave." On these facts, the Court held that there was no objective reason for the defendant to believe that she was not free to walk away.

The Eleventh Circuit in *United States v. Rodriguez–Franco* held that a stop to obtain identification was not a seizure involving the Fourth Amendment.

In *Immigration and Naturalization Service v. Delgado,* the Court considered "factory surveys" conducted pursuant to a warrant in search of illegal aliens. Each "survey" lasted one to two hours. Agents were posted at factory exits while others asked employees one to three questions relating to citizenship. Four employees were questioned and their union filed an action challenging the constitutionality of the surveys and seeking injunctive relief. The court concluded that the "survey" did not result in the seizure of the entire work force, and the individuals were not seized when they were questioned while at work. In *Florida v. Bostick,* the United States Supreme Court considered a case which it found to be indistinguishable from *Delgado.* In *Bostick,* the question was whether officers without an articulable suspicion could board a bus at a scheduled stop and ask passengers for permission to search their baggage. The court held that the officers' practice of "working busses" is not per se unconstitutional. To determine if such an encounter constitutes a seizure, the Court modified *Mendenhall* in holding that "a court must consider all the circumstances . . . to determine whether the police conduct would have communicated to a reasonable person that the person *was not free to decline* the officers' requests or otherwise terminate the encounter. That rule applies to encounters that take place on a city street or in an airport lobby, and it applies equally to encounters on a bus."

The Supreme Court reversed the 11th Circuit Court of Appeals in *United States v. Drayton*, holding that the Fourth Amendment did not require police officers to advise bus passengers that they did not have to answer questions put to them as part of a routine drug interdiction effort. In the absence of any coercive police conduct, the court found that the cooperation of passengers was voluntary and consensual.

This reasoning was directly applied to traffic stops in Brendlin v. California. There, the United States Supreme Court addressed the question of whether a vehicle's passengers are seized for Fourth Amendment purposes and, thus, may challenge the stop's constitutionality. The Court held that, though a passenger, Brendlin was seized from the moment the car came to a halt because a reasonable person in his position would not feel "free to 'terminate the encounter' between the police and himself." However, the court expressly noted that "the relationship between driver and passenger is not the same in a common carrier as it is in a private vehicle, and the expectations of police officers and passengers differ accordingly." In *Solano-Rodriquez v. State,* the Georgia Court of Appeals applying the standard set out in *Florida v. Bostick* held that the proper test for determining when a seizure occurs on a bus is whether the passenger feels free to decline to answer an officer's questions rather than whether the passenger feels free to leave the bus since the passenger most likely has no desire to leave the bus.

See 6A C. J. S. Arrest § 38 et seq. See also Annotation, "Law Enforcement Officer's Authority Under Federal Constitution's Fourth Amendment, to Stop and Briefly Detain, and to Conduct Limited Protective Search Of or 'Frisk,' for Investigative Purposes, Person Suspected of Criminal Activity—Supreme Court Cases," 104 L.Ed.2d 1046 (1991).

§ 3-2 Facts justifying the stop—General

In *Terry v. Ohio,* the Court observed that "whenever a police officer accosts an individual and restrains his freedom to walk away he has 'seized' that person," but the Court did not discuss the exact point at which Terry was seized. The court said, however, in footnote number 16 on page 19 of the opinion, that all communications between an officer and a citizen do not involve a "seizure." "Only when the officer, by means of physical force or show of authority, has in some way restrained the liberty of a citizen may we conclude that a 'seizure' has occurred." Thus, in *Edwards v. State,* the Georgia Supreme Court held that there is "no seizure . . . when an individual voluntarily accompanies police in a spirit of cooperation."

It appears, therefore, that under some circumstances an officer may approach a person and ask him some questions even if the officer has no articulable suspicion. As Justice Harlan observed in his concurring opinion in *Terry,* a police officer has "the liberty (again, possessed by every citizen) to address questions to other persons, for ordinarily the person addressed has an equal right to ignore his interrogator and walk away." Justice White, also concurring in *Terry,* said there "is nothing in the Constitution which prevents a policeman from addressing questions to anyone on the streets." It has been held that an officer does not seize a passenger deplaning when the officer displays his credentials and asks permission of the passenger to talk with him.

In *Clark v. State,* the court pointed out that "merely refusing to identify oneself to a police officer is not a crime"; however, "one may commit obstruction when knowingly and willfully hindering an officer in investigating an offense committed by another." Thus, refusal to provide identification can be an obstruction.

In *State v. Dukes*, the court found that, although the defendant's sudden flight arguably gave officers articulable suspicion to detain him, such circumstances only gave the right to conduct a brief investigative stop, not to arrest for obstruction.

In Georgia it has been recognized that there are, "at least theoretically, three tiers of police-citizen encounters: (1) communication between police and citizens involving no coercion or detention and therefore without the compass of the Fourth Amendment, (2) brief 'seizures' that must be supported by reasonable suspicion, and (3) full-scale arrests that must be supported by probable cause." See section 2-2, supra, and section 4-26, infra, on arrests. See section 3-12, infra, on when a stop becomes an arrest.

In *Stokes v. State,* the court pointed out that it has "recognized a distinction between an officer's 'appropriately deferential' request for cooperation and a demand rising to the level of a stop. . . . [A]n officer's approach to a stopped vehicle and inquiry into the situation is not a 'stop' or 'seizure' but rather 'clearly falls within the realm of the first type of police-citizen encounter.' " Thus, police officers may "approach a citizen, ask for identification, ask him to roll down a window or step out of a car, and freely question him without any articulable suspicion, as long as the officers do not detain the citizen or create the impression that the citizen may not leave." Other examples of a first tier police-citizen encounter would include good faith intervention by police in what they believe to constitute emergency medical situations. In this context, police observation or inquiries which lead to the discovery of evidence of criminal activity may not be subject to suppression.

In *In the Interest of S. B.,* the court quoted with approval from the United States Supreme Court in *Florida v. Bostick* that "[m]erely approaching an individual and requesting that he give his consent for a search does *not* constitute a seizure and need *not* be supported by an articulable suspicion. [E]ven when officers have no basis for suspecting a particular individual, they may generally ask questions of that individual . . . and request consent to search . . . as long as the police do not convey a message that compliance with their requests is required." In *State v. Willis,* the court pointed out that "[e]ven when officers have no basis for suspecting a . . . [person], they may generally ask questions . . . to examine the individual's identification . . . and request consent to search. . . ." See section 3-9, infra, on consent during a roadblock and general considerations.

In the 1991 case of *California v. Hodari D.,* the United States Supreme Court considered a case in which officers drove up to a group of four or five persons in a high crime area and the group panicked and fled. One of the officers followed the defendant. When the officer had almost reached the defendant, "he tossed away what appeared to be a small rock. A moment later" the officer tackled the defendant. The rock turned out to be cocaine, and a motion to suppress was filed. The court said the only issue presented was whether the defendant had been "seized" within the meaning of the Fourth Amendment at the time the defendant dropped the drugs. Writing for the majority, Justice Scalia concluded that there was no seizure until the defendant was tackled; until he was physically stopped by the officer, the defendant had not yielded to the officer's show of authority. Therefore, the cocaine was not abandoned as a result of a seizure, and the motion to suppress was properly denied. See section 2-2, supra, on what constitutes an arrest.

A citizen who is walking away from an officer, however, may not be "detained" by the officer, and such a citizen is not obligated to answer questions, unless the officer has a specific reasonable articulable suspicion that the citizen is involved in criminal conduct. If the citizen answers the officer's questions, it generally does not seem to make any difference whether the officer had an articulable reasonable suspicion. But if the officer is to be justified in restraining the person who is approached, he must have such a reasonable articulable suspicion. The standard that is used must be an objective standard, but an officer may evaluate suspicious circumstances in the light of his own experience.

Not only may an officer approach a suspicious person and attempt to talk with him, but in the absence of coercion the officer may ask the person to accompany him to a nearby location to be searched. If the person agrees to do so and freely and voluntarily accompanies the officer, this generally amounts to a waiver or a consent and none of the person's Fourth Amendment rights have been violated. After reaching such place, and after being fully informed that he has a right to refuse to permit a search, if the suspected person intelligently and voluntarily consents to a search of his person and bag (if he has one) and contraband is discovered in the search, it is admissible against him if he is tried for a possessory offense. However, in *United States v. Place,* the United States Supreme Court said that an officer has authority "to make a *forcible stop* of a person when the officer has reasonable, articulable suspicion that the person has been, is, or is about to be engaged in criminal activity."

In *United States v. Cortez,* the United States Supreme Court expressly recognized the right to make an investigatory stop where there are sufficient objective manifestations "that the person stopped is, or is about to be, engaged in criminal activity." The court said:

"Based upon [the] whole picture the detaining officers must have a particularized and objective basis for suspecting the particular person stopped of criminal activity. . . . The idea that an assessment of the whole picture must yield a particularized suspicion contains two elements, each of which must be present before a stop is permissible. First, the assessment must be based upon all of the circumstances. The analysis proceeds with various objective observations, information from police reports, if such are available, and consideration of the modes or patterns of operation of certain kinds of lawbreakers. From these data, a trained officer draws inferences and makes deductions—inferences and deductions that might well elude an untrained person. . . .

"The second element contained in the idea that an assessment of the whole picture must yield a particularized suspicion is the concept that the process just described must raise a suspicion that the particular individual being stopped is engaged in wrongdoing."

In *Cortez,* the Court also said: "An investigatory stop must be justified by some objective manifestation that the person stopped is, or is about to be, engaged in criminal activity." The emphasis here is on the right of an officer to stop if he has an objective basis for suspecting the person stopped of criminal activity. In *Terry,* the emphasis seems to be that when an officer has an articulable suspicion "that criminal activity may be afoot and that the person with whom he is dealing may be armed and presently dangerous" there may be a valid "stop." *Cortez* indicates that the "armed and dangerous" element is not now essential.

While *Cortez* emphasizes the right of officers to stop where there is articulable suspicion that the suspect "is engaged in wrongdoing," in *United States v. Hensley* the Court pointed out that officers may stop if they have articulable suspicion that the suspect is wanted for a completed felony. See section 3-7, infra.

In *Herrington v. State,* the court pointed out that a specific, articulable suspicion justifying an investigatory stop of a vehicle "must be based on the totality of the circumstances, including objective observations, known information about the individual, patterns of certain kinds of lawbreakers, and inferences drawn and deductions made by trained law enforcement personnel."

In *Beck v. State,* the Georgia Court of Appeals pointed out that "[t]here is no requirement that the officer making the stop have all the information the original officer had about a suspect and the informant." In *State v. Pennyman* the court pointed out that "[t]he 'collective knowledge' rule provides that reasonable suspicion may exist based on the collective knowledge of the police when there is reliable communication between the officer supplying the information and the officer acting on that information instead of the arresting officer's knowledge alone. . . . [I]nformation provided by other officers as communicated in a 'be-on-the-lookout' dispatch provides the basis for reasonable and articulable suspicion to justify a stop." See section 3-7, infra. The method of establishing an articulable suspicion seems to be the same as that used in determining probable cause. See sections 4-7 and 4-49, infra. However, in *Kazeem v. State,* the Court of Appeals held that "[w]ithout the testimony of the officers who stopped and detained [the defendants], we do not know what information those officers had before making the stop and whether they had an objective and particularized basis for stopping the men. Therefore, the state has not met its burden of showing that the stop was justified," and the evidence should have been suppressed.

In order to justify further detention and questioning of a motorist once a routine traffic stop has ended, the officer must have a reasonable suspicion of criminal conduct. In the absence of reasonable suspicion, an officer's continued questioning and detention of the motorist becomes unlawful. As the Eleventh Circuit Court of Appeals observed in *United States v. Purcell*, "only unrelated questions which unreasonably prolong the detention are unlawful; detention, not questioning, is the evil at which *Terry's* prohibition is aimed. Questions which do not extend the duration of the initial seizure do not exceed the scope of an otherwise constitutional traffic stop."

In *Michigan v. Summers,* the United States Supreme Court said: "Although no special danger to the police is suggested by the evidence in this record, the execution of a warrant to search for narcotics is the kind of transaction that may give rise to sudden violence or frantic efforts to conceal or destroy evidence. The risk of harm to both the police and the occupants is minimized if the officers routinely exercise unquestioned command of the situation." Thus, in *Summers* the Court seems to be saying that there is a right to "stop" if the "transaction . . . may give rise to sudden violence or frantic efforts to conceal or destroy evidence." If this is true, an officer may "stop" to prevent destruction of evidence—this is an idea which is completely contrary to *Terry.*

In *Brown v. State,* the court said, "Investigative stops of vehicles are analogous to *Terry*-stops . . . and are invalid if based upon only unparticularized suspicion or hunch." Any stop of a moving vehicle has been treated as a detention, and, as pointed out in *Delaware v. Prouse*, an officer generally has no authority to make a stop of a vehicle unless he at least has a reasonable articulable suspicion that a traffic violation has occurred or that an occupant is otherwise subject to seizure, and such a stop constitutes a seizure of its occupants. See text discussing *Delaware v. Prouse* et seq., section 3-9, infra, on roadblocks. See section 3-7, infra, on stop based on a telephone tip. In the case of a parked automobile it has been held that officers have no authority to approach the car to order occupants to remain in the vehicle in the absence of a reasonable suspicion.

In *Montoya v. State,* the court held that "[e]ven the existence of an improper motivation on the part of an officer does not render a stop unreasonable. The validity of the stop depends not on the officer's actual state of mind but on an objective assessment of his actions in light of all the facts and circumstances confronting him at the time."

In *State v. Smith,* the defendant and a co-defendant were seated in a car on a public street during the afternoon in February. An officer stopped his patrol car, approached the defendant's car, and told the defendant to let the window down or open the door. The defendant opened the door. The officer then smelled marijuana, and observed a cigarette burning in the ashtray. The car was searched and marijuana found. The court said that the officer had no articulable suspicion at the time he approached the car and by "instructing the defendant to either roll down his window or open the door, the police officer 'seized' the defendant within the meaning of the Fourth Amendment." In *Tomlin v. State,* the appellate court affirmed the denial of a motion to suppress where an officer was driving behind a vehicle driven by the defendant. The officer "saw a passenger . . . smoking and then blowing smoke that smelled like marijuana out [of] the truck window." The officer notified another officer who stopped the vehicle and found marijuana. The court concluded that "smelling marijuana . . . was a specific articulable fact that gave rise to a reasonable suspicion that there was marijuana" in the defendant's vehicle.

In *Stanford v. State,* the Court of Appeals set out the standard of review for an order on a motion to suppress as follows:

> First, when a motion to suppress is heard by the trial judge, that judge sits as the trier of facts. The trial judge hears the evidence, and his findings based upon conflicting evidence are analogous to the verdict of a jury and should not be disturbed by a reviewing court if there is any evidence to support it. Second, the trial court's decision with regard to the questions of fact and credibility must be accepted unless clearly erroneous. Third, the reviewing court must construe the evidence most favorably to the upholding of the trial court's finding and judgment. (Cites omitted.)

Applying this standard in *State v. Jones*, the court affirmed the trial court's order granting a motion to suppress where the defendant was stopped by a police officer investigating the defendant's 30 day drive-out tag. After reviewing documents supplied by defendant, which demonstrated that the tag was in order, the officer detained the defendant with further questions while retaining the defendant's license. The officer requested permission to search the defendant's vehicle, which was given. Suppressing the cocaine found during the search, the trial court determined that the officer's continued detention and questioning of the defendant after having been provided adequate proof regarding the defendant's tag was unreasonable.

In *Brooks v. State,* the court said, "Brooks and a woman companion, driving along a U. S. highway in a pickup truck at about 2:30 a.m. were observed by a sheriff and his deputy to turn onto a side road leading into a woods. They followed the car for some distance, then flashed their top light and brought it to a stop. The sheriff and the defendant got out of their respective vehicles and in the illumination of the headlights the defendant was observed to have a plastic bag sticking out of his shirt pocket. . . ." The court held that there was no articulable suspicion justifying the stop and reversed the denial of the motion to suppress.

However, in *State v. Roberson,* a car was stopped at a roadblock. An officer recognized Roberson, a passenger, as being either a person who had escaped from jail or his brother. The officer asked what his name was. Roberson gave a false name. The court held that the officer had an articulable suspicion justifying the asking of the question. See section 3-9, infra, on roadblocks.

The stop must be a "brief stop." It has been said, if not sustained, that "indeed, it is the transitory nature of the stop that justifies the elimination of the probable cause requirement." In applying this standard, the Georgia Court of Appeals has said "it tortures the English language to say" a 40–minute stop is a brief stop or momentary detention. In *Schmidt v. State,* the court held that a 30–minute detention constituted an arrest. On the other hand, in *Sprauve v. State,* the same court held that a 30–minute stop until officers could get a drug dog was not excessive. In *United States v. Sharpe,* the United States Supreme Court said that in "assessing whether a detention is too long in duration to be justified as an investigative stop, we consider it appropriate to examine whether the police diligently pursued a means of investigation that was likely to confirm or dispel their suspicions quickly, during which time it was necessary to detain the defendant . . . . A court making this assessment should take care to consider whether the police are acting in a swiftly developing situation, and in such cases the court should not indulge in unrealistic second-guessing . . . . The question is not simply whether some other alternative was available, but whether the police acted unreasonably in failing to recognize or pursue it." In *United States v. Roper,* the Eleventh Circuit said, "The distinction between an arrest and an investigatory stop depends upon the nature and degree of the intrusion under all the facts of the particular encounter." See section 3-12, infra.

In *Terry,* the officer thought Terry and his companions were preparing for an armed robbery and the Court discussed a balancing of the interest of a suspected person and the public. However, in *Dunaway v. New York,* the Supreme Court rejected the concept of such a sliding scale where a person was held without probable cause for purposes of investigating an armed robbery and murder.

What situations justify an officer in stopping an individual? As it would be expected, this question may arise in an infinite variety of situations. Also, it must be kept in mind that the existence of one or two suspicious circumstances may not justify a stop, but the existence of several suspicious circumstances may justify a stop. Some of the more common circumstances that have been considered by the courts in determining the validity of a stop are discussed in the following sections of this chapter.

In *Brown v. State,* the court held, "[I]n determining when an investigative stop is unreasonably pretextual, the proper inquiry . . . is not whether the officer *could* validly have made the stop but whether under the same circumstances a reasonable officer *would* have made the stop in the absence of the invalid purpose. . . ." (Emphasis in original.) In *Guerrero v. State,* the court pointed out that even if there is articulable suspicion, an investigatory stop is pretextual unless a reasonable officer would have made the stop in the absence of the invalid purpose.

However, in *Brantley v. State,* the Georgia Court of Appeals followed the United States Supreme Court in *Whren v. United States,* in holding that from a federal constitutional standpoint, "when an officer sees a traffic offense occur, a resulting traffic stop does not violate the Fourth Amendment even if the officer has ulterior motives in initiating the stop, and even if a reasonable officer would not have made the stop under the same circumstances." In *Hines v. State*, the court pointed out that it is inconsequential whether or not a driver is ultimately cited for a traffic violation. See sections 3-3 and 4-26, infra.

In *Forsman v. State,* the court pointed out that the stop of a vehicle is authorized if the officer observes a traffic offense. The "failure to issue a citation or even an acquittal on an underlying traffic offense is of no consequence in determining the officer's [articulable suspicion necessary] to stop the vehicle. . . ."

In *Michigan v. DeFillippo,* the United States Supreme Court upheld a stop where an officer stopped a person, in good faith, pursuant to a city ordinance authorizing such a stop if the officer had reasonable cause to believe the suspect's behavior warrants further investigation. After the stop, but before a ruling on a motion to suppress, the ordinance had been held unconstitutional. See *Illinois v. Krull,* discussed in section 4-45, infra.

§ 3-3 Facts justifying the stop—Appearance

It has been held that an officer seeing a man with a bulge under his shirt near the scene of a homicide may stop him. The observance of a defendant, apparently with a weapon in his hand, standing behind a car in a parking lot (apparently at night) was found to justify a stop. In another case, however, where police obtained information about 1:30 a.m. that two persons in a restaurant were talking loud and might cause a disturbance and that one of them might be intoxicated, officers were held to have no right to stop two young, "hippy-looking" men who were simply walking down a sidewalk some five blocks from the restaurant.

In *State v. Williams,* the appellate court affirmed the granting of a motion to suppress where a patrolling officer observed four men during the morning standing on a curb near a housing project. No illegal or suspicious activity was seen. The officer testified his attention was drawn to them "as curb areas are popular locations for drug sales and the area around the housing project was known for drug activity." However, in *State v. Banks,* the court held that a stop was not justified by the "fact that a black man is standing [alone] next to an apartment building with his hand in his pocket at a reasonable hour. . . ."

In *State v. Kwiatkowski,* the appellate court affirmed the trial court in granting a motion to suppress evidence of marijuana found in a car. The case turned on the question of the validity of the "stop." Officers saw a car in a Department of Transportation parking lot in a "high drug area" with an out-of-state tag. The driver had a driver's license from still another state, one of the occupants seemed nervous, and they denied a request to search.

In *Brooks v. State,* however, the court held that an officer had no right to stop the driver of a pickup and his companion, where the pickup was being properly driven along a highway and the driver turned into a side road leading into the woods.

In *State v. Dubose,* officers were at a bus stop looking for a suspect in a murder which had occurred 24 hours earlier at the same bus stop. The men appeared to be gambling and drinking beer and wine. The court held that the officers had a right to approach the group, ask for identification and frisk the men for weapons. The men appeared to be engaged in criminal behavior and the officers conducted the pat-down search for their own protection.

An officer was held to be entitled to stop a van that was being driven slowly at 1:30 a.m. through the parking lot of a school when he knew that a nearby school had been burglarized numerous times. A lookout for a described car with a specified tag number justifies a stop of such car, even a number of miles away. See section 3-7, infra, on identification of auto used in the commission of a crime.

Although later overruled, the court in *Watson v. State,* the court held that an investigative stop was justified where the defendant was in a car having a "drive-out tag rather than a metal license tag" in view of the officer's "knowledge that many cars with drive-out tags turned out to have been stolen."

"[M]erely observing a can of beer in the hand of one who is otherwise driving a car or operating a boat in a safe manner does, in and of itself, constitute an articulable suspicion that a violation of . . . [the law] may be occurring so as to authorize a brief investigatory stop." Moreover, in *Darby v. State,* the trial court was affirmed in ruling that an officer's stop was not pretextual when he pulled the vehicle over to determine whether the crack in the "windshield . . . [had] a starburst or webbing effect" (made unlawful pursuant to O.C.G.A. § 40–8–73(e)).

In *State v. Burns,* the court affirmed the trial court in granting a motion to suppress. The officer had a "be on the lookout" alert for an older, yellow Monte Carlo occupied by two men, one believed to be a white man that had been involved in a purse snatching at a Lowe's store three days earlier. The officer testified that he saw an older yellow or tan Monte Carlo about two miles from the store. There appeared to be two occupants, although the windows were tinted. The court concluded the officer did not have a reasonable suspicion for the stop.

In *Whren v. United States,* the United States Supreme Court held that when an officer has probable cause to believe a driver has committed a traffic offense, the officer may stop the driver even if a reasonable officer would not have stopped the motorist absent some additional law enforcement objective. In *Maxwell v. State*, the court affirmed the denial of a motion to suppress where an officer followed a vehicle with the intention of finding "a violation and stop[ping] the vehicle." See section 4-26, infra, on pretextual arrests.

In *State v. Hammang,* an officer stopped a driver for driving without having her headlights on. The officer testified it was almost dark and all other cars he could see had their lights on. The driver was arrested for DUI and filed a motion to suppress based on the fact that the stop was at approximately 9:00 p.m., that sunset that day was at 8:34 p.m. and that she was not required to have her lights on until 9:04 pm. The grant of the motion to suppress was reversed by the appellate court. The court pointed out that "[i]f the officer acting in good faith believes an unlawful act has been committed, his actions are not rendered improper by a later legal determination that the defendant's actions were not a crime according to a technical legal definition or distinction determined to exist in the penal statute." See § 2-26, supra.

§ 3-4 Facts justifying the stop—Airport drug courier profile

The concept of the drug courier profile does not fit precisely into this general material on stop and frisk, but it seems to be more appropriate to discuss it here than elsewhere. General airport searches are discussed in section 4-34, infra. Searches of spectators to recreational events to find contraband are discussed in section 4-36, infra. Inasmuch as the airport drug courier profile stops are somewhat different from other stops discussed in this chapter, this section attempts to discuss not only when such a stop may be made or attempted, but it also discusses what action may be taken by officers after such a stop or attempted stop.

As background information, it should be pointed out that there are "three tiers of police-citizen encounters: [1] communication between police and citizen involving no coercion or detention and therefore without the compass of the Fourth Amendment, [2] brief 'seizures' that must be supported by reasonable suspicion, and [3] full-scale arrests that must be supported by probable cause."

Most cases have held that there is no right to stop a person at an airport simply because he fits the drug courier profile. In *United States v. Ballard,* the United States Court of Appeals for the Fifth Circuit defined the airport drug courier profile as "a compilation of factors considered . . . to be indicative of drug activity. Included among those characteristics listed are: (a) unusual nervousness; (b) no luggage or very limited luggage; (c) possession of an unusually large amount of cash, especially when in bills of small denominations; (d) unusual itinerary, taking circuitous routes from cities known to be source cities for narcotics, such as flying to New Orleans from Los Angeles by way of St. Louis; (e) arriving from a known narcotics source city; (f) paying for an airline ticket in currency of small denominations; (g) purchasing a one-way ticket; (h) use of an alias; (i) use of a false telephone number on an airline reservation; (j) placing a telephone call immediately upon arrival at the airport; and (k) travel by a known narcotics trafficker." The same case pointed out that the elements of the profile that were said to exist in that case did not "in any significant way operate to distinguish Ballard from the general public."

In *United States v. Mendenhall,* the United States Supreme Court was presented with the opportunity to clarify the legality of reliance on the drug courier profile. The question remains unsettled, however, due to lack of agreement on the basis of the decision among the justices forming the majority. While the officers' conduct in stopping and questioning the defendant was found to be lawful, two justices reached this conclusion on the basis that the stop did not constitute a seizure, and three concurring justices assumed that a seizure had occurred but found it justified by a reasonable and articulable suspicion, arising in part from factors included in the profile. The concurring justices noted that reliance on the profile would not necessarily establish a reasonable suspicion, noting that each case must be decided on its own facts. The four dissenting justices found that no reasonable and articulable suspicion of criminal activity had been shown and characterized the stop in question as one based on a mere hunch.

A later decision of the United States Supreme Court, in *Reid v. Georgia,* vacated a decision of the Georgia

Court of Appeals holding that there was a reasonable articulable suspicion justifying a stop since the suspect fell within the drug courier profile. The Supreme Court, in a brief per curiam decision with three dissents, did not discuss the "drug courier profile" generally, but the Court concluded that as a matter of law the stop was not justified where "(1) the petitioner had arrived from Fort Lauderdale, which the agent testified is a principal place of origin of cocaine sold elsewhere in the country, (2) the petitioner arrived in the early morning, when law enforcement activity is diminished, (3) he and his companion appeared to the agent to be trying to conceal the fact that they were traveling together, and (4) they apparently had no luggage other than their shoulder bags." The court pointed out that these circumstances "describe a very large category of presumably innocent travelers."

On remand, the Georgia Court of Appeals vacated its earlier decision and affirmed the trial judge's granting of the defendant's motion to suppress. The Georgia Supreme Court then granted certiorari and concluded that the United States Supreme Court found "that the evidence did not as a matter of law show a basis for an articulable or reasonable suspicion sufficient to justify any seizure of Reid, even a '*Terry* stop.' " The Georgia Supreme Court concluded that it must be first determined whether Reid was seized when he was first stopped. If he was seized at this point, the suppression of the trial judge must be sustained. However, the Georgia Supreme Court determined that there was no seizure in the initial encounter between the agent and Reid when it was suggested that Reid return to the terminal and he was requested to consent to a search. There was nothing to suggest that a reasonable person would have felt he was not free to go. Therefore, the initial approach was not a seizure. Hence, it was error for the trial judge to find that Reid was under arrest when the agent suggested that he go back to the terminal. The case was then remanded for further proceedings consistent with the opinion. Reid again applied to the United States Supreme Court for writ of certiorari, but the petition was denied.

In the Eleventh Circuit's en banc decision of *United States v. Berry,* the Court found no definitive guidance in the opinions of the United States Supreme Court to determine when an airport stop constitutes a seizure under the Fourth Amendment. The court stated that it would turn, therefore, to its own (Fifth Circuit's) opinions, which "though establishing a clearer line of precedent . . . form a confusing thicket. . . ." The *Berry* court concluded "that airport stops of individuals by police, if of extremely restricted scope and conducted in a completely non-coercive manner, do not invoke the Fourth Amendment." Of course, a seizure has occurred if " 'in view of all the circumstances surrounding the incident, a reasonable person would have believed that he was not free to leave.' "Whether or not a stop amounts to a seizure may turn on the tone of voice of the officer, the blocking of a person's path or "otherwise intercepting him to prevent his progress . . . , retaining an individual's ticket for more than a minimal amount of time or by taking a ticket over to a ticket counter," whether the officers made statements that an investigation had focused on the individual, informing an individual that an innocent person would cooperate with officers, and whether the passenger is informed that he is free not to consent to a search and is free to call a lawyer.

The *Berry* court pointed out that a match between the defendant and the drug courier profile characteristics does not, of itself, necessarily provide reasonable suspicion: "The profile is nothing more than an administrative tool of the police. The presence or absence of a particular characteristic on any particular profile is of *no* legal significance in the determination of reasonable suspicion." In *United States v. Robinson,* the court held that the Fourth Amendment aspects of *Berry* apply retroactively, at least to all convictions not final at the time the decision was rendered.

The Georgia Court of Appeals, in 1982, in *Berry v. State,* a case completely distinct from *United States v. Berry,* concluded that the "drug courier profile provides sufficient articulable and reasonable suspicion to authorize a '*Terry*-type' stop." Despite the fact that the Eleventh Circuit *Berry* case stated that "[t]he presence or absence of a particular characteristic on any particular profile is of *no* legal significance in the determination of reasonable suspicion," in the four to three decision of *Bothwell v. State,* the Georgia Supreme Court said that the profile characteristics are important in determining "whether there is a basis for a specific and articulable suspicion." In *Pullano v. State,* the Georgia Court of Appeals said that the drug courier profile plus information that the defendant "would be returning to Florida in a few hours, his apparent nervousness, the fact that he deplaned at least three or four minutes after the last passenger left" was sufficient to justify an investigatory stop. In *Murphy v. State,* the court pointed out that although the factors satisfying the drug courier profile are sufficient to justify a stop and frisk, they are still insufficient to establish probable cause for an arrest or search.

In *Rebeiro v. State,* the court said the drug courier profile plus the giving of a false name or obviously incorrect information may constitute probable cause for arrest. But in *Rebeiro* the court also said that where information given is not obviously false, probable cause does not exist.

In the 1989 case of *United States v. Sokolow,* the United States Supreme Court stated that in determining the validity of a stop, "[W]e must consider 'the totality of the circumstances—the whole picture.' "In approval of the denial of the motion to suppress, the Court pointed out that while no one of the factors testified to by officers was sufficient to justify the stop, "we think taken together they amount to reasonable suspicion. . . . A court sitting to determine the existence of reasonable suspicion must require the agent to articulate the factors leading to that conclusion, but the fact that these factors may be set forth in a *'profile'* does not somehow detract from their evidentiary significance as seen by a trained agent." (Emphasis added.) However, in *Gordon v. State,* the court pointed out that when a tipster provides "detailed information including [the defendant's] name, his physical description, a description of his clothing . . . , and information regarding his flight itinerary . . . [which were] independently verified . . . [it is sufficient] to justify an investigative stop."

The Fifth Circuit has held that where an individual consents to a pat-down of his outer garments and the officer pats him down in search of weapons or contraband and the officer feels a soft object in an inner pocket which he believes to be contraband, the officer may reach inside the jacket and remove the substance. The court concluded that this amounts only to a reasonable narcotics pat-down.

In *Florida v. Rodriguez,* the United States Supreme Court held that where plainclothes police officers approached citizens in an airport, identified themselves as police officers and asked if the citizens would step aside and talk, it was merely a "consensual encounter" and raised none of the citizens' Fourth Amendment rights. The court expressly did not decide whether continuing a discussion, which leads to a search, amounts to a "stop" requiring an articulable suspicion. However, the First Circuit has held that prolonged questioning may amount to a seizure.

In 1983, the United States Supreme Court decided *Florida v. Royer,* which is very much like the Georgia case of *Bothwell v. State. Bothwell* is discussed in section 3-13, infra. Royer purchased a one-way airline ticket to New York from Miami under an assumed name. He checked his two suitcases and went to the concourse leading to the boarding area. Two detectives approached Royer since they believed that he fit the drug courier profile. Upon request, Royer produced his ticket and driver's license which contained his correct name. When questioned, Royer explained that a friend had made the reservation for him under an assumed name. They informed Royer that they were narcotics officers and had reason to suspect him of transporting drugs. They retained Royer's ticket and driver's license and asked him to accompany them to a small room adjacent to the concourse. Without Royer's consent, one of the officers obtained his luggage and brought it to the room. Royer did not verbally respond to the detective's request that he consent to a search of his luggage, but he produced a key and unlocked one suitcase in which marijuana was found. Royer said that he did not know the combination to the lock on the other suitcase but that he did not object to its being opened. The officers pried the second suitcase open and found additional marijuana. Royer was then told he was under arrest. The trial court denied a motion to suppress. The Florida District Court of Appeal reversed, holding that Royer had been involuntarily confined within the small room without probable cause at the time of his consent to search, that the restraint exceeded that permitted by *Terry v. Ohio* and that his consent was tainted by the unlawful confinement. The Supreme Court affirmed. The plurality opinion of Justices White, Marshall, Powell and Stevens substantially agreed with the Florida District Court. Justice Brennan concurred in the result but complained that the plurality reached issues which did not have to be reached in order to affirm.

The syllabus of the Court states that "[w]hen the detectives identified themselves as narcotics agents, told . . . [the defendant] he was suspected of transporting narcotics, and asked him to accompany them to the police room, while retaining his airline ticket and driver's license and without indicating in any way that he was free to depart, [the defendant] was effectively seized for purposes of the Fourth Amendment. At the time [the defendant] produced the key to his suitcase, the detention to which he was then subjected was a more serious intrusion on his personal liberty than is allowable on mere suspicion of criminal activity. What had begun as a consensual inquiry in a public place escalated into an investigatory procedure in a police interrogation room, and [the defendant], as a practical matter, was under arrest at that time. Moreover, the detectives' conduct was more intrusive than necessary to effectuate an investigative detention otherwise authorized by the *Terry* line of cases." Also there was no probable cause to arrest the defendant at the time he consented to the search of his luggage.

In *United States v. Waksal,* the Eleventh Circuit held that where a suspect matching the "drug courier profile" is stopped at an airport, the stop amounts to a seizure where his ticket is obtained and retained, he is not told that he is free to leave and he is asked to accompany the officers to an office. On these facts, the defendant "could not reasonably have felt that he was free to leave."

See section 4-31, infra, on waiver and consent to a search. See section 3-13, infra, on retention of inanimate objects without probable cause. Also see section 4-34, infra, on airport searches connected with aircraft hijackings; section 4-35, infra, on searches on entering courthouses; and section 4-36, infra, on searches of persons entering places of entertainment and recreation. See Annotation, "Propriety of stop and search by law enforcement officers based solely on drug courier profile," 37 A. L. R. 5th 1 (1996) and Annotation, "Admissibility of drug courier profile testimony in criminal prosecution," 69 A. L. R. 5th 425 (1999).

§ 3-5 Facts justifying the stop—Ships and boats

In the 1983 United States Supreme Court case of *United States v. Villamonte–Marquez*, the Court reasoned that ships are not like automobiles in terms of the Fourth Amendment. The first Congress authorized the boarding of vessels even in the absence of suspicion. "[P]ermanent checkpoints [are not] practical on waters such as these where vessels can move in any direction at any time and need not follow established 'avenues' as automobiles must do. . . . [Also the] documentation requirements with respect to vessels are significantly different than the system of vehicle licensing. . . ." The government relied on 19 U. S. C. § 1581(a), which provided in part as follows: "Any officer of the customs may at any time go on board of any vessel . . . at any place in the United States . . . and examine the manifest and other documents and papers . . . and to this end may hail and stop such vessel . . . and use all necessary force to compel compliance." The court defined the issue as follows: "We are asked to decide whether the Fourth Amendment is offended when Customs officials, acting pursuant to this statute and without *any suspicion* of wrongdoing, board for inspection of documents a vessel that is located in waters providing ready access to the open sea." (Emphasis added.) The court concluded that there had not been any Fourth Amendment violation.

In *United States v. Gollwitzer,* the Eleventh Circuit held that a vessel capable of ocean travel could be stopped without reasonable suspicion where the ship was traveling in the Intracoastal Waterway. A few questions may be asked by customs officials and a visual inspection from the customs ship may be made. If what the officers see and the answers they receive provide a reasonable suspicion, the vessel may be boarded. The court suggested that this rule would not apply to smaller crafts which are incapable of ocean travel. In *United States v. Kubiak*, the Eleventh Circuit held that a Coast Guard has authority to stop a 31–foot Chris Craft vessel five or six miles from the coastline "in complete absence of suspicion of criminal activity." The court pointed out that the vessel was in "custom waters" and was subject to 14 U. S. C. § 89(a). In *United States v. Hidalgo-Gato*, the same circuit, while pointing out that the territorial waters of the United States extend out three miles from the coast, concluded that there is a contiguous 12–mile zone outside the territorial waters in which a vessel may be stopped, boarded, and searched by customs officials without probable cause or suspicion so long as the search is reasonable. This zone is regarded as the functional equivalent to the border.

In *United States v. One (1) 1982 28%2C International Vessel*, the Eleventh Circuit upheld the search of the lower deck of a ship stopped at a blockade for a routine check. Activity on the ship had been carried on to deceive observers into believing the ship was shrimping. Then the officer discovered that he had stopped the vessel under similar circumstances the previous month. The investigation had revealed "a deck sealed by screws . . . and a space beneath the deck that could not be accounted for."

However, in *Palmer v. State,* the Georgia Court of Appeals held that customs officials may make an investigative stop of a vessel on inland waters "if they are aware of articulable facts which justify a *reasonable suspicion* of illegal activity." Actually, the shrimp boat involved in *Palmer* was apparently in the ocean headed toward the open sea when it was stopped.

In *Jackson v. State,* the Georgia Court of Appeals held that O.C.G.A. § 52–7–25(b)(4) clearly authorized an enforcement officer of the Georgia Department of Natural Resources to stop a boat on Lake Lanier. The court declined to consider the stop under *Terry* standards and pointed out that the officer need not suspect wrongdoing. Such an officer is authorized "to make investigatory stops of watercraft for the sole purpose of *verifying* that the operator has the proper documentation and safety equipment. . . . [T]he boating public does not *necessarily* have the same expectation of privacy on regulated waterways as does the motoring public." In *Peruzzi v. State,* the Supreme Court turned back a constitutional challenge to the statute noting that Georgia now "joins a growing list of states that recognize the legitimacy of suspicionless boat safety inspections and their minimal impact on the privacy of boaters."

See section 3-7, infra, on report of a crime and section 3-8, infra, on a protective sweep.

§ 3-6 Facts justifying the stop—Conduct

An officer on routine patrol in a rural area where several burglaries had occurred was held entitled to stop a car from another county that was being driven slowly on a dirt road, where the passenger looked back and thereafter both the passenger and the driver started doing something in the back seat that caused the officer to think they were hiding something. An officer, however, does not have a reasonable and articulable suspicion to stop a man who went to his car, got in and drove off, after the officer saw him looking in the window of another car parked in a shopping center as though he were going to try to get in the car, when the officer knew that no damage had been done to the parked car. However, in *Darracott v. State,* the court upheld a stop where an officer saw several young people standing in a shopping center parking lot about midnight and there were beer cans and other litter scattered about and the defendant jumped in a vehicle and drove off as the officer approached. Also, the same result was reached in *Stanley v. State,* where the defendant saw a roadblock and backed up his vehicle in an "evasive action."

In *State v. Canidate,* an officer was responding to a call when he noticed a brown Nissan Maxima in the driveway of a house which he knew had previously been raided for drugs. When the officer was returning, he saw a brown Maxima coming toward him. Thinking the driver may have been buying drugs at the house, he pulled around behind the car. The officer said the car appeared to accelerate as he turned around behind it. The officer further testified that he was behind the car for 10 to 15 seconds when the car quickly pulled over into the parking lot of a real estate business. When asked why he was attempting to avoid the police, the driver explained he was trying to get to the real estate agent to see about buying a house. The trial judge found that the initial stop had been based on a hunch, not a particularized articulable suspicion. The appellate court affirmed the verdict and pointed out that the officer admitted that he did not have any basis for stopping the driver when he pulled in behind him. The court further noted that the act of pulling into the parking lot did not create an articulable suspicion.

In *Strawser v. State,* the appellate court reversed the trial court's denial of a defendant's motion to suppress where "a police officer . . . [had been] dispatched to pick up a . . . [wife] and daughter who were out walking in Warner Robins just before midnight." The wife of the defendant was crying and told the officer she had left the defendant's mother's home after arguing with the defendant. No physical altercation or violence was involved. The officer drove the defendant's wife to her mother-in-law's residence to get her belongings. While standing in front of the house, the defendant drove past the house to the end of the street, turned around and passed the house again. The officer thought it "odd" that the defendant did not stop at his mother's house, and followed the defendant "to get his side of the story." He asked the defendant why he did not stop and the defendant replied that he did not want to be arrested for driving under the influence. The appellate court concluded the conduct of the defendant was not sufficient to support a suspicion that the defendant was committing or was about to commit a crime.

In *Edgell v. State*, the Court of Appeals reversed the denial of a motion to suppress filed by the defendant passenger in a vehicle which was properly stopped by the arresting officer because of an expired tag. After ticketing the driver and impounding the vehicle, the officer instructed the defendant to exit the vehicle. Because the defendant acted nervously and pursuant to the officer's "routine" of patting down everyone whom he directs to exit a vehicle, he patted down the defendant over his protests. The officer arrested both the defendant and the driver when he felt a hard object in the defendant's pocket. Following the arrest, he placed his hand into the defendant's pockets and discovered a crack pipe and a small amount of marijuana. Concluding that the officer lacked any articulable suspicion that the defendant was engaged in any criminal activity, the court found that both the detention and the pat down were improper. The Court's observation is worth noting: "An individual's rights under the Fourth Amendment are not automatically waived . . . simply because he or she is asked to step out of a vehicle. The safety of officers is of extreme importance to this court. Nonetheless, our Constitution requires an officer to provide evidence to show that an act alleged to be performed for his safety was actually performed for that purpose in conformance with the requisite standards of *Terry*."

In *McDaniel v. State,* the Court of Appeals upheld an officer's investigative stop of a vehicle where the occupants had been seen peering into a parked car and upon seeing the police car, the driver "slammed on his brakes, turned off his headlights, and immediately put his vehicle in reverse. [The] [d]efendant raced away, unsuccessfully trying to enter a secure complex before abruptly speeding off again." In affirming, the court concluded that "[t]hese odd and evasive circumstances created a reasonable suspicion of criminal activity to permit a limited investigative stop. . . ."

In *State v. Billoups,* the court reversed the granting of a motion to suppress. Here two men broke and ran when they saw an officer about 2:30 a.m. in a high drug area. The court concluded there was probable cause to arrest but the incident seems to fit in better with stop and frisk cases. It is important to note that the court based its reversal on the totality of the circumstances surrounding the transaction. Flight in connection with other circumstances may be sufficient probable cause to uphold a warrantless arrest or search, the surrounding circumstances in this case being the time of night and the area and "certainly these circumstances [give] rise to an articulable suspicion . . . as to authorize a brief investigatory stop."

In *State v. Taylor,* the defendant approached an officer and said, "I believe you are looking for me." The confused officer said, "Is that right?" and seized the defendant. The appellate court affirmed the trial judge's conclusion that the comment did not provide the requisite articulable suspicion to justify the immediate seizure of defendant. "Nor did the fact that [defendant] was bicycling through a 'known drug area' give rise to articulable suspicion."

In *In the Interest of J. L. G.,* an anonymous call to police reported the presence of a person (whose clothing was described) with a hand gun. The officers arrived within minutes. The defendant was dressed as described and when he "saw the police car, he stuck his hand in his pocket, [and] turned away from the officers." When the officers started exiting their car, the defendant ran and refused to stop on command. The court affirmed the denial of a motion to suppress pointing out that there was an articulable suspicion justifying a stop and probable cause to arrest. In *Davis v. State,* the court pointed out that "[f]light may be evidence of a consciousness of guilt and may give rise to an articulable suspicion that a person is engaged in criminal activity . . . ."

In *Kingree v. State,* the court affirmed the denial of a motion to suppress where the officer stopped the defendant's car in an area known for drug arrests after witnessing two "lookouts" signaling to the driver, the passenger fleeing, and the driver backing the car away from the officer. These facts supported the officer's suspicion that he had interrupted a drug sale. However, in *Barnes v. State,* it was held that "mere presence in an area known to police for drug activity, without more, is insufficient to support a reasonable suspicion that one is engaged in or about to engage in criminal activity. 'An investigatory stop must be justified by some *objective* manifestation that the person stopped is, or is about to be, engaged in criminal activity.' " (Emphasis in original.) See section 3-8, infra, on environment issues relative to a stop.

In *Duke v. State,* the denial of the defendant's motion to suppress was reversed where "officers were watching an apartment for suspected drug sales" but "the only facts known by . . . officers were that . . . [the defendant] stopped his van in the apartment complex parking lot, he went down the stairs, he came back up the stairs and he left in van." This did not give the officers an objective basis for suspecting the defendant of criminal activities and justify the stop of his van.

"[A]s a general matter, the decision to stop an automobile is reasonable where the police have probable cause to believe that a traffic violation has occurred." An officer may stop a driver who is speeding or who has committed any other violation of the law. However, driving 49 miles per hour in a location where the speed limit is 70 miles per hour does not per se create a reasonable suspicion for stopping a car. See section 3-7, infra.

In *State v. Whitfield,* the court held that when an officer observes a motorist "weaving" this is sufficient to justify the officer in stopping the driver for a possible DUI violation, even if the weaving was in a single lane.

In *State v. Armstrong,* the court held that an officer is not required to know with certainty each element of a particular crime that could be established in order to make a valid stop. "If the officer acting in good faith believes that an unlawful act has been committed, his actions are not rendered improper by a later legal determination that the defendant's actions were not a crime according to a technical legal definition. . . ."

In *State v. Blair,* the court affirmed the trial court's granting of a motion to suppress. An officer stopped the car in which the defendant was riding in the back seat because the car was being driven with a dealer's drive-out tag. The officer said he was suspicious because no one produced any proof of ownership of the car. The occupants provided conflicting explanations of the purpose of their journey. All occupants appeared very nervous and the defendant was clutching a bag. The officer thought "something was going on," asked for permission to search and received a negative answer. As another officer drove up, the defendant fled with his bag, which was found to contain marijuana when he was arrested. Here, the officer stopped the car because of the tag. The stop was valid, but the evidence supports the trial judge's finding that the officer abandoned that investigation and held the occupants to conduct a search for drugs.

In *Berry v. State,* the Court of Appeals held that "the critical issue to the validity of a traffic stop is whether the officer had 'a particularized and objective basis for suspecting the particular person stopped of criminal activity.' " Applying this standard to a stop based upon the officer's suspicion that an auto *might* be stolen solely on the basis that it was being operated with a drive-out tag, the court concluded the stop was not authorized. Likewise, the court found in *Bius v. State,* that a stop was not warranted based upon an officer's suspicion that a vehicle *might* not be in compliance with motor vehicle registration laws solely because it was being driven with a drive-out tag.

In *Dorsey v. State,* an officer recognized Dorsey, who was driving a car. The officer had arrested him the year before on a bench warrant on a charge of being an habitual violator. The officer stopped Dorsey "because he knew that he might not have a driver's license." The court concluded that the officer had "specific and articulable facts" that warranted the stop for investigation.

Brisbane v. State is illustrative of a number of cases involving robberies at service stations in the very early morning hours. An armed robbery by three men occurred at one service station. Later, at about 3:45 a.m., while on routine patrol, an officer stopped at another station that had been the scene of a number of robberies. The officer noticed an automobile containing three occupants driving slowly by the station. Then the same vehicle approached the station again and slowed down again. The court held that the officer, who stopped the car, had a specific, articulable suspicion justifying the stop.

In *Bailey v. State,* an officer observed the defendant's car with a door open at a well-lit but closed service station about 2:00 a.m. The car was parked near a restroom and some vending machines. The station had been the scene of previous robberies and burglaries and the vending machine had been broken into on many occasions. As the officer approached the defendant, a co-defendant dropped or threw something from the car and the car left at a high rate of speed. The court concluded that the stop was authorized pursuant to *Terry.* However, in the Louisiana case of *State v. Blanton,* the court held that an investigatory stop was not justified merely because the defendant met some people at the airport who were under surveillance for drug violations, and drove them home.

In *Oboh v. State,* the court reversed the denial of a motion to suppress. The case turned on the validity of the defendant's stop. "The deputy simply saw a stranger drive a van (with bumper stickers with the insignia of a rental car agency) into a bank parking lot, observed bank tellers scrutinize the stranger as he was preparing to leave the bank's parking lot and was informed by one of the tellers that this stranger 'was acting very suspicious.' "

In *Edwards v. State,* the court held that an investigatory stop was authorized where the defendant sat in his truck during traffic signal cycle while pouring out what appeared to be beer. In *State v. Adams,* the court affirmed a stop of the driver of a vehicle where the officer saw the defendant changing lanes without giving a signal, even though the officer did not charge the defendant with improper lane change, but charged the defendant with driving under the influence based largely on information obtained at the time of the stop for illegal lane change. However, in *State v. Goodman,* the court held there were no articulable facts justifying a stop of the driver where the driver made a turn without signaling despite the presence of traffic behind him, since the statute contemplates instances in which a turn on a roadway can be made with reasonable safety without use of a turn signal, i.e., where a signal is not necessary to alert other drivers of a motorist's intention to turn.

In addition to the right to stop because of an articulable suspicion of a crime, the case of *Dickson v. State* holds that officers have a right to stop a person in an automobile who creates "a safety and traffic hazard."

In *Streicher v. State,* the court reversed the trial judge's denial of a motion to suppress where the officer saw the driver and passenger exchange places in an automobile, at about 8:30 a.m., when the car stopped at a stop sign. The officer did not suspect at the time that the occupants were engaged in criminal conduct, but in his experience every time something like this happened, he had found that there was intoxication or that someone did not have a driver's license. However, in *State v. Templeman,* the court affirmed the trial judge in finding that there was no articulable suspicion where the defendant stopped in the roadway 25 to 50 feet from an intersection for 45 to 60 seconds while facing a green traffic light in order to pick up a friend.

Two decisions worth comparing are *Crowley v. State* and *State v. Newton.* In *Crowley*, an officer stopped the defendant without "a particularized and objective basis for suspecting him of criminal activity," and then subsequently stopped him again after the individual fled. The Court of Appeals held that the defendant's flight provided sufficient reasonable suspicion to uphold the second detention. In contrast, the Court of Appeals in *Newton* concluded that an initial stop where officers exceeded the scope of *Terry* tainted the discovery of evidence found during a subsequent stop after the defendant fled. However, these two cases may be harmonized by the fact that the *Newton* Court did not directly address whether or not flight may provide an articulable suspicion to justify a consecutive stop of a suspect.

See section 4-21, infra, on frisk connected with execution of a search warrant.

§ 3-7 Facts justifying the stop—Report of a crime

In *Adams v. Williams,* the United States Supreme Court held that an officer was justified in approaching a man in a car in a high crime area during the early morning hours and in questioning him, where the officer had been told by a known informant that the suspect would be found there and that he was armed and carrying narcotics.

In *United States v. White,* an anonymous telephone tipster's information given to an officer plus the verification of some of the innocent details were said to add up to an articulable suspicion justifying a stop of the occupants of a car.

Conversely, "an *unverified* tip from an informant may not supply probable cause for a search or a warrant, [however,] if the information carries enough indicia of reliability, it will authorize a forcible stop of a suspect to maintain the status quo momentarily while obtaining more information."

In *Alabama v. White,* an officer received an anonymous phone call stating that "Vanessa White would be leaving 235–C Lynwood Terrace Apartments at a particular time in a brown Plymouth station wagon with the right taillight lens broken, that she would be going to Dobey's Motel, and that she would be in possession of about an ounce of cocaine inside a brown attache case." The officer drove to the Lynwood Terrace Apartments and saw a brown Plymouth station wagon with a broken right taillight in the parking lot in front of the 235 building. The officer saw the defendant leave the 235 building with nothing in her hands and enter the station wagon. The officer followed the Plymouth as it was driven in the most direct route to Dobey's Motel. The officer stopped the vehicle just before it reached Dobey's Motel. The officer informed the defendant she was stopped because she was suspected of carrying cocaine in the vehicle. He asked for and received permission to search the car. In the search he found an attache case which contained marijuana and in the defendant's pocket book he found cocaine. In upholding the stop, the court declined to say that an "anonymous caller could never provide the reasonable suspicion necessary for a *Terry* stop" but it concluded that "when the officers stopped . . . [the defendant], the anonymous tip had been sufficiently corroborated to furnish reasonable suspicion that . . . [the defendant] was engaged in criminal activity and that the investigative stop therefore did not violate the Fourth Amendment." In *State v. Williams,* the court quoted from *White* "that 'articulable suspicion' may not be grounded in an anonymous tip alone." See the excellent opinion of Judge Beasley in *State v. Ball,* which follows *White.*

In *Florida v. J. L.,* the United States Supreme Court pointed out that reasonable suspicion existed in *White,* but that case was "borderline." *Florida v. J. L.* then held that "[a]n anonymous tip that a person is carrying a gun is not, without more, sufficient to justify a police officer's stop and frisk. . . ." However, the court also pointed out that in *Florida v. J. L.,* "[a]ll the police had to go on . . . was the bare report of an unknown, unaccountable informant who neither explained how he knew about the gun nor supplied any basis for believing he had inside information about J. L." Furthermore, the court refused to grant an exception for cases involving firearms.

In *McKinley v. State,* the court reversed the trial judge's denial of a motion to suppress where police "received an anonymous telephone tip that four black males in a white Chevrolet Lumina van with Hillsborough County, Florida, license plates were attempting to sell cocaine on Butler Street in Camilla, Georgia." An officer in an unmarked car followed a white van occupied by two men to a parking lot in front of a convenience store and activated his blue light on his dash. As both the driver and the passenger were getting out of the van, the officer approached the driver and asked to see his driver's license and proof of insurance. The officer told the passenger to get back in the van and close the door. The driver produced his license and rental agreement for the van which did not list him as the renter or as an additional driver. Another officer arrived and told the passenger to get out of the van. Consent to search the van was given, but the appellate court held that the occupants of the van had been seized before the consent was given and that the consent was not freely given.

In *Johnson v. State,* the court held that a stop was not justified by "an anonymous telephone tip that two black men in a black truck were selling drugs on Lewis Street."

In *Tedford v. State,* the court affirmed the validity of a stop and frisk where officers received a call from the cook of a designated fast food restaurant who stated that "a customer approached him and said that he had been talking to a white male driving a blue vehicle with Georgia license tag number BX 307 outside the restaurant and that the man told the customer to leave the area because he was going to rob the restaurant. The officer who responded . . . testified that when he arrived he parked directly behind the vehicle matching the description . . . and that he immediately observed [the] defendant opening his door and exiting his vehicle."

In the Georgia case of *State v. Holton,* the court cited and relied on *Alabama v. White.* It emphasized that in that case and in the *Holton* case, the anonymous tipster predicted future behavior which was corroborated by observations of the police. The Georgia Court of Appeals said that such a prediction of future conduct and corroboration was necessary to authorize an investigative stop from an anonymous caller. However, in the Eleventh Circuit case of *United States v. Gibson,* the court held that an anonymous tip that a potentially armed person is in a public establishment justifies an investigative stop, without including information as to future conduct, in view of an overriding concern for the safety of the police and the public.

In *United States v. Kent,* the Eleventh Circuit acknowledged that a tip from an informant of unknown reliability will not ordinarily create a reasonable suspicion of criminality, but information from a known informant of unknown reliability has more indicia of reliability than an anonymous telephone tip. Also, corroboration of innocent details may change an otherwise insubstantial tip into a reasonable suspicion of criminal activity. Thus, where a known but unproved informant notified a Customs Patrol Officer that a white yacht-type, 50–foot vessel with three persons on board would be coming into the area of the Coral Gables Waterway within an hour carrying a load of marijuana, and a Customs vessel observed such a vessel about 45 minutes later and it was the only vessel observed in the area at that time, a stop and boarding was justified. See section 3-5, supra, on ships and boats.

In *Bentley v. State,* the court held that information provided by a known but untested confidential informant had more indicia of reliability than an anonymous tip.

In *Archer v. State,* the court held that the stop of the defendant was justified when "the details of that tip, including the predicted timing and route of a particular vehicle driven by a particular individual, were confirmed by the personal observations of the investigating officers."

Likewise, the Georgia Court of Appeals has upheld the action of an officer in stopping an individual where the officer had received a call from a known "civic" informer who stated that "an unknown black male, driving a 1978 gold Pontiac LeMans, was selling marijuana in 'nickel' bags at a specified location. The officer receiving the call . . . immediately departed for the location . . . and arrived within fifteen to twenty-five minutes." When the officer arrived he saw the defendant, who fit the description and was carrying a shopping bag, entering the only 1978 gold LeMans in the area. The court held that the officer had an articulable suspicion warranting the stop of the defendant as he tried to drive away.

In *Graves v. State,* an officer was executing a search warrant. Graves was present and the officer had been informed by a reliable informant that Graves always carried a weapon. The Georgia Court of Appeals held that a stop, and a later frisk, were justified.

In *Vansant v. State,* an officer stopped a white van. The officer had followed the vehicle for a half mile observing no traffic violation other than that the vehicle did not stop promptly when the flashing blue light was turned on. The only reason the van was stopped was because a white van had been involved in a hit and run accident about a mile away. The court concluded the facts did not justify an articulable suspicion. "[H]owever, . . . when an officer sees a traffic offense occur, a resulting traffic stop does not violate the Fourth Amendment even if the officer had ulterior motives in initiating the stop . . . " and even if the officer did not charge the defendant with the traffic offense observed. In *State v. Hall,* the court held there may be a *Terry* stop of an automobile if there is an initial minor traffic violation which an officer witnessed. However, the officer must have some other basis (i.e., the officer must have a reasonable suspicion of criminal conduct) for conducting additional questioning and searching a vehicle once a normal traffic stop has ended and the officer has told the motorist he is free to go. "Although this suspicion need not meet the standard of probable cause, it must be more than mere caprice or a hunch or an inclination." See section 4-26, infra.

In contrast to *Vansant*, the court in *State v. Harden* upheld a stop where police received a tip that an inebriated driver was about to leave a bank parking lot, and an officer shortly thereafter observed a vehicle leaving that location. The Court distinguished *Vansant* on the basis that in that case, the defendant's van was stopped a mile away from where the tipster observed the vehicle. Hence, it appears that police may stop a vehicle based on a tip that the driver is inebriated without corroboration of that tip as long as the officer can be reasonably certain that they are stopping the car described by the tipster.

In *Shorter v. State,* the court, citing *Vansant,* held that a general tip to be on the lookout for a white van may not create sufficient articulable suspicion. The court pointed out that "a more particularized description of a suspect vehicle" was needed to justify a *Terry* stop.

However, in *McSwain v. State,* the court held that "an officer's decision to broadcast a lookout" for a described car alone does not "create reasonable suspicion for another officer to stop the vehicle." Here there was no evidence of *collective* knowledge of officers which would give rise to reasonable suspicion that would justify a *Terry* stop.

In *Overand v. State,* the court concluded that "[a] dispatcher who reports a crime at a specified location gives police an articulable suspicion to investigate and detain individuals at the scene, particularly where police observations on arriving at the scene corroborate the dispatcher's report," and the officer is "not required to question dispatchers about the source of the information."

In *McGhee v. State,* the court stated "that when the police received a call to be on the lookout for a car . . . and the car in question roughly fit the description given for the lookout, this provided the basis for an articulable suspicion justifying the stop." See section 3-3, supra, on identification by tag number.

In *Smith v. State,* there had been an armed robbery about 2:30 a.m. The radio bulletin described "the perpetrators . . . [as] two black males armed with sawed-off shotguns and dressed in dark clothing, one of whom was wearing a gray colored toboggan hat." No vehicle description was given. About 3:05 a.m., a few miles away, an officer saw an automobile with a passenger wearing a gray toboggan hat; however, there were three men in the car. The court concluded that a stop of the vehicle was proper.

In *Dillard v. State,* an officer driving a police car saw the defendant drive into the driveway of a house which had been recently burglarized three times. When the defendant saw the officer, he stopped the car "and his passenger appeared to hide his head." The officer turned around to go back and the car had disappeared. The car was then located by officers in another subdivision. The court held that the stop which followed was justified.

In *Duffy v. State,* an officer learned at about 1:30 a.m. of an armed robbery and an assault which occurred around midnight. The officer was given the names of some possible suspects and a description of the car in which they left. The officer located a car with the description given and stopped the car. When the defendant got out, he had blood on his pants and the name of one of the suspects previously given. The court concluded that there was evidence supporting the stop and after the stop there was probable cause to arrest.

The Georgia Court of Appeals again found sufficient circumstances to justify a stop in *Butts v. State*, where, at about 3:00 a.m., an officer heard a broadcast stating that a black male had just committed an armed robbery in the immediate area in which he was patrolling. Ten or fifteen minutes after the robbery, he saw a black man running and stopped him. The court found that the officer had a reasonable articulable suspicion that justified the stop. The court did not discuss the very general description of the robber that had been given over the radio.

In *United States v. Hensley,* the United States Supreme Court held that officers in Kentucky were justified in stopping a person in an automobile pursuant to a police "flyer or bulletin [if it had] been issued on . . . articulable facts supporting a reasonable suspicion that the wanted person" had committed a felony in Ohio, and an objective reading of the flyer shows that the stopping officer had information which would warrant a man of reasonable caution to believe that the stop was proper.

In *Postell v. State,* the Georgia Supreme Court held that officers did not have an articulable suspicion justifying the stop of the defendant who was driving his car within 100 yards of the site of a purported drug delivery even though the defendant had been stopped several times before based on informant's tip that the defendant was a drug courier, but had never been found to be in possession of drugs. The officers had earlier received information from a known informant that a delivery was to be made to a certain address, and that one of several named persons might be serving as courier, but the defendant's name was not included.

In *State v. Mallory,* while an officer was arresting a person for a felony pursuant to a warrant, he saw the defendant approaching with his hands in his pockets. "When the officer took his badge out and started to approach the defendant, the defendant turned and walked away, whereupon the officer ordered the defendant to stop." The Georgia Court of Appeals held that the stop was justified in view of the circumstances and the fact that the officer had seen the arrestee with the defendant shortly before executing the warrant; the stop occurred at night in a poorly lighted area, and the officer wanted to be sure the defendant was not armed.

In *Williams v. State,* a druggist in an all-night drug store received a threat stating that a bomb was planted in the store and would be detonated remotely by the caller if the druggist did not deliver certain drugs to a designated point. There were a total of four calls between 2:00 and 4:00 a.m., and a police captain listened to the last call, which was at about 3:30 a.m. At about 4:00 a.m., while waiting for another call, "the druggist and captain were standing at the door of the pharmacy looking out upon a deserted shopping center parking lot." A car drove "from the area of an adjoining highway slowly across the parking lot. At the front door of the drug store, the car more or less stopped and the driver looked through the door and seemingly saw the druggist and presumably the police officer. The car then proceeded on out of the parking lot away from the area." The court concluded that the circumstances were sufficient to present an articulable suspicion justifying a stop of the car.

In *Clinkscale v. State,* there had been a theft of a truck from a business. The owner of the business gave the defendant's name as a suspect since he had formerly been an employee and had been in trouble before. While the officers were on the scene an employee told them that the suspect was riding toward the place of business on a bicycle. When the defendant apparently saw the officers he turned around and started back in the direction from which he had come. The court held that the officers had an articulable suspicion justifying a stop for questioning.

In *Evans v. State,* the officer was informed by the victim of a burglary that as he approached his home he saw "a truck leaving or coming up the highway from the area of his driveway" and the defendant was driving. Two or three hours later the officer saw the defendant driving a pickup. The driver did not stop immediately as directed, but he was pulled over by the officer. As the officer approached, he saw in the truck a number of items which had been taken in the burglary. The officer said he stopped the defendant to ask where he had been at the time of the burglary. The court concluded that the stop was justified and that after seeing the stolen items, he had probable cause to arrest the defendant and conduct a search incident to the arrest.

In *Starr v. State,* an armed robbery occurred about 3:35 p.m. The robber apparently left on foot. A radio lookout was posted for a "white male . . . , around 25 to 30 years of age, approximately six feet, medium build, mustache, possibly a beard, wearing some type of yellow cap, long white coat down below the knees, yellow gloves." An officer radioed that he had seen a man of medium build wearing "a yellow type hat and a long light-colored coat" running to the Colonial Motel. Another officer went to the motel and asked the clerk if he had rented a room to such a person who had not arrived in a car. Officers learned that a hitchhiker had just checked in. The clerk did not remember how he was dressed but remembered that he was fairly young and thought he had a mustache. The officers went to the room of the hitchhiker about 15 or 20 minutes after the robbery. The defendant answered the knock of the door. The court concluded that the "stop" was justified. When the door was opened, the officer saw a pair of yellow gloves and the defendant fit the description of the robber. The court said that at this point the officers had probable cause to arrest the defendant and they properly searched the room.

In *Tarwid v. State,* the court held illegal the stop of a vehicle on an interstate highway for traveling slightly under the maximum speed allowed. The court concluded that this conduct was not indicative that the driver was intoxicated and a radio transmission from a state trooper stating that he had given the driver a warning ticket in another county for speeding and that the vehicle "had shown signs of trafficking" in drugs did not justify the stop. However, in *Taylor v. State*, the appellate court affirmed the trial judge in finding that the officer was justified in stopping the defendant for driving 45 miles per hour in the center lane of I–20 because the driver was creating a traffic hazard. The court pointed out that driving "at such a slow speed as to impede the normal and reasonable movement of traffic" was a violation of O.C.G.A. § 40–6–184(a)(1).

See section 2-12, supra, on probable cause to arrest. See section 4-21, infra, on the right to stop and frisk incident to execution of a search warrant. See section 3-6, supra, on traffic violations.

§ 3-8 Facts justifying the stop—Environment

As previously indicated, the time and place of a stop often supply an important part in determining whether or not an officer has an articulable suspicion to justify a stop. A number of cases have emphasized the fact that the stop was made in a "high crime area." In *Bobo v. State*, the defendant was stopped because he was driving his truck at 2:00 a.m. in a residential area in which vandalism had been reported. However, the court concluded that the facts did not justify the stop. In *Attaway v. State*, the appellate court reversed the trial court's denial of a motion to suppress the evidence obtained from the investigative stop of a car. The officer, aware of past incidents of vandalism in the area, received information from the police dispatcher to be on the lookout for a small red vehicle that had reportedly circled around a named subdivision several times. The court held that the police might have been justified in closely observing the defendant's actions, but that the officer was not justified in making an investigative stop. In *Howden v. State*, the court reversed the trial court's denial of a motion to suppress where the officer "stopped defendant because it was late at night and defendant's warehouse is located in an area known for criminal activity." The defendant's van was backed up to the door of a closed warehouse. The defendant's van pulled out of the area a couple of minutes after the patrol car arrived. The appellate court held the stop which followed was not based on any particular fact that the defendant was engaged in or was about to engage in criminal activity. In *State v. Winnie*, the defendant, after entering a parking lot at 4:00 a.m., pulled away from an approaching officer. Although there was no indication that the officer's decision to stop the defendant was influenced by the defendant's decision to pull away, the court held that "there was no articulable suspicion for the stop."

In *Raulerson v. State,* the appellate court reversed the finding of the trial judge that there was an articulable suspicion justifying the stopping of an automobile where the defendant was driving at 1:20 a.m. between 25 and 30 m.p.h. in a 55 m.p.h. zone, turned onto a dirt road, and returned to the highway. However, in *Jones v. State,* the court affirmed the trial court's denial of a suppression motion where a car was stopped at 9:30 p.m. as it was leaving a new unoccupied subdivision in which some vandalism had occurred. The only unusual conduct referred to was that the vehicle did not have its lights turned on until the driver saw the officer's car. Likewise, in *Watson v. State,* the court affirmed a finding that the stop of an automobile was justified where an officer had seen the defendant and his two companions in a "high drug area" several times during the day and each time the occupants looked in the opposite direction.

In *Evans v. State,* the court affirmed the denial of a motion to suppress. The officer was patrolling in a high crime area at 12:45 a.m. when he noticed a motion detector had been set off at a convenience store. The officer had checked the store about 10 minutes earlier and found everything in order. Upon receipt of the alarm, the officer pulled out of a gasoline station and saw two persons in a 1969 Plymouth coming up the hill toward the officer about 1,000 yards from the convenience store. No other car or person was in sight. The officer went to the convenience store and noticed the glass in front had been knocked out and cartons of cigarettes were in the parking lot. The officer immediately left the store and followed the 1969 Plymouth. He stopped the car and observed a cigarette carton protruding from a garbage bag under the defendant's leg. The defendant was arrested. The yellow Plymouth was nearly identical to a "lookout" the officer had received earlier regarding other break-ins.

In *State v. Turntime,* the court reversed the granting of a motion to suppress where a defendant was stopped as he was walking in an apartment complex in which he did not live, looking in parked cars, at about 10:30 p.m. There had been a number of automobile break-ins in the area.

In *State v. Barnes,* the court found that a stop was legal where the defendant had stopped to pick up a known prostitute and drug user in the parking lot of a car wash at 12:56 a.m., the neighborhood residents had complained of drug use and prostitution at that particular car wash, and the defendant attempted to drive away rapidly when he realized he had been observed picking up his passenger. The court held that under the totality of the circumstances, the officer had the necessary "founded suspicion" that criminal activity was about to occur to justify a brief stop.

In *United States v. Magda,* the Fifth Circuit Court of Appeals found the officers had a sufficient, reasonable and articulable suspicion to stop a man they had seen exchange an object with another man. The exchange took place in an area in which there was a high incidence of narcotic transactions. In *Shaw v. State,* the court affirmed the conclusion of the trial judge holding that a stop was justified where the defendant was seen walking late at night in the vicinity of a burglarized apartment, carrying a dark object over his arm. In *Bozeman v. State,* the opinion affirmed the denial of a motion to suppress and held that a stop was justified where the defendant was in a high crime area and an officer saw him and a companion sitting for no apparent reason in a parked car in a remote part of a motel parking lot at 4:45 a.m. Furthermore, in *Illinois v. Wardlow,* the United States Supreme Court held that when, in an area known for drug trafficking, an officer sees a defendant look toward a police car and flee, those circumstances may give rise to a reasonable suspicion that the defendant is involved in criminal conduct. The court refused to hold that unprovoked flight from officers is always sufficient to justify a stop and reiterated that reasonable suspicion is to be determined by a totality of the circumstances. In *Brown v. Texas,* however, the Supreme Court found that there was no right to stop a suspicious-looking person seen in an alley during the day in a high crime area. Likewise, where officers staked out a ranch while awaiting a search warrant, it was held that they had no Fourth Amendment right to stop a car entering the ranch and frisk the occupants because they feared that the occupants might have had something to do with marijuana activities at that location.

In *Hughes v. State,* the Georgia Supreme Court concluded that "there is no objective manifestation that a person is, or is about to be, engaged in criminal activity merely because the person is a white man in a black neighborhood late at night, who picks up a black man at a location police consider a high-crime area, and who then drives slowly in a circular fashion through the neighborhood."

§ 3-9 Roadblocks

In *Delaware v. Prouse,* the defendant had been stopped at random by a patrolman. The patrolman had not observed any traffic violation or suspicious activity on the part of the defendant, and made the stop only to check the driver's license and the registration. The officer was not acting pursuant to any procedure pertaining to spot checks. During the stop, the patrolman saw marijuana in plain view on the floor of the car. In holding that the marijuana had been properly suppressed, the Court ruled that there must be at least an articulable and reasonable suspicion that a motorist is unlicensed, or that a car is not registered, or that an occupant is otherwise subject to seizure for violation of the law before a driver may be stopped.

In *Brower v. Inyo County,* the Court held that stopping a single motorist with a roadblock amounts to a "seizure" in Fourth Amendment terms. However, this rule does not apply to a roadblock where all vehicles are stopped for a license check.

Based upon its review of the United States Supreme Court's decision in *City of Indianapolis v. Edmond*, and the Georgia Supreme Court's decision in *LaFontaine v. State*, the Georgia Court of Appeals in *Baker v. State,* declared that the constitutional validity of a roadblock is dependent upon the presence of the following features: "(1) the record reflects that the decision to implement the checkpoint in question was made by supervisory officers and not officers in the field *and* that the supervision had a legitimate primary purpose. The phrase 'decision to implement' includes deciding to have this roadblock and where and when to have it . . . (2) all vehicles were stopped as opposed to random stops . . . (3) the delay to motorists was minimal . . . (4) the roadblock identification was well identified as a police checkpoint . . . (5) the screening officer's training and experience were sufficient to qualify him to make an initial determination as to which motorists would be given field tests for intoxication." The court expressly rejected the implication in prior decisions that these criteria were simply guidelines to be applied in weighing the "totality of the circumstances." Each of these factors is now a necessary prerequisite of constitutional proportion for a valid roadblock. As a result, in *Baker*, evidence obtained at the roadblock was ruled inadmissible because the state was unable to demonstrate at trial that the decision to implement the checkpoint had in fact been made by supervisory police personnel and not the field officers and there there was a legitimate primary purpose for the roadblock. Since *Baker*, the issue of whether a roadblock was duly authorized by supervising personnel often dictates the outcome of a contest to the admissibility of evidence seized at a roadblock. The state can expect to lose such contests if it fails to produce the responsible supervisory personnel at the hearing and has no other admissible evidence to establish the basis for the roadblock.

Roadblocks which have as a primary purpose the detection of general criminal wrongdoing will not survive scrutiny under the Fourth Amendment. In *Illinois v. Lidster,* the United States Supreme Court considered whether due process was offended by a police roadblock which was designed to question motorists about a crime which had been committed a week earlier at the roadblock location and at the approximate time the roadblock was being conducted. The court concluded that the roadblock was proper since its purpose was not a generalized criminal investigation of motorists and the passengers in their cars, but rather a request for help in connection with a criminal investigation. Approved legitimate purposes for roadblock checkpoints include: the interception of illegal aliens; sobriety; verification of driver licenses and vehicle registration; and emergency checkpoints to prevent an imminent terrorist attack or to catch a dangerous criminal thought to be in a particular area.

As noted by the Court in *Loney v. State*, features of a valid roadblock are not "absolute criteria which must be satisfied before a roadblock is legitimate. Rather, this Court looks to the totality of the circumstances surrounding the roadblock to determine whether the factors were satisfied."

In *O'Kelley v. State,* the Georgia Court of Appeals held that there is no "advanced publicity requirement in Georgia" for a roadblock. "Georgia law requires only that the roadblock be identified as a police checkpoint." In *Burns v. State,* the court held that the requirement that supervisory personnel designate the place for the roadblock was sufficiently met where the nightshift supervisor on that night authorized the roadblock even though another officer was the supervisor of the entire shift. In *Hardin v. State,* the court concluded that an auxiliary roadblock assigned to stop drivers attempting to avoid the central roadblock was within the requirements for a proper roadblock, even though its location was not explicitly authorized by supervisory personnel. The court's holding was premised on its finding that the general decision to implement the roadblock had been made by supervisory personnel.

In *Michigan Department of State Police v. Sitz,* the United States Supreme Court held that the Fourth Amendment was not violated where all motorists were stopped to check for signs of intoxication which were to be determined according to guidelines. In *LaFontaine v. State,* the court required that a "screening" officer at a roadblock checking for persons driving under the influence must have "training and experience . . . sufficient to qualify him to make an initial determination as to which motorists should be given field tests for intoxication."

In *United States v. Prichard,* the court held that a roadblock was constitutional on an interstate highway where officers started by stopping all cars but as soon as 10 cars were backed up, the officers would waive all stopped cars on through. The stops were held valid even though officers admitted that if they saw any evidence of crime while checking licenses and registrations, they planned to enforce the law.

In *Ledford v. State,* the trial judge was affirmed in finding a roadblock valid where "[e]very noncommercial vehicle was stopped at the roadblock, with the exception of noncommercial vehicles which had been checked at the roadblock in one direction and soon came through again in the other direction." But in *State v. Stearns,* the court found a roadblock arbitrary when the "trial court found that there were more than enough officers to stop vehicles traveling in both directions" but police had set up a roadblock north of a cluster of bars and only stopped vehicles being driven north.

In *Gamble v. State,* the court held valid a roadblock which officers set up primarily to check for licenses, insurance and registration; authorized by supervisory personnel; manned by qualified personnel; and identified as a police checkpoint. Motorists were delayed only briefly unless they were unable to produce requisite information. Officers only allowed cars to pass through unchecked when conditions on the road backed up traffic and created a potential safety hazard. However, in *State v. Manos* the appellate court affirmed the trial court in granting a motion to suppress material seized as a result of a roadblock. The court concluded that the problem with the roadblock was that all cars were stopped unless the officers got too backed up. In that event, officers let every car go until there were no more vehicles in sight before they started stopping cars again. The roadblock "was impermissibly based on an unfettered discretion granted to the field officer."

In *Gamble v. State,* the court held that when a car is validly stopped at a roadblock and the driver could not find proof of insurance, an officer was authorized to make a brief inquiry regarding the driver's and passenger's destination and to request consent to search the vehicle. Where an initial detention or seizure at a roadblock is valid, a secondary detention or seizure does not require additional proof of reasonable and articulable suspicion. In *McCray v. State,* the Court of Appeals upheld the detention of the defendant at a "secondary position" while an officer sought verification of the defendant's driver's license. At the initial roadblock stop the defendant produced a "tattered" license and was unable to furnish a vehicle registration. The court also upheld a subsequent search of the defendant's vehicle after a drug dog alerted officers to the presence of drugs in the defendant's car at that secondary stop. This court was satisfied that the roadblock was set up for a proper purpose, the defendant's detention was appropriate and allowing the dog to walk around the car did not unduly prolong the detention. Independent of the bona fides of a roadblock, evasive measures to avoid a roadblock may give rise to a reasonable suspicion of criminal activity on the part of police authorities. Thus, in *Taylor v. State*, the Court of Appeals affirmed the denial of the defendant's motion to suppress blood alcohol evidence obtained after the evasive and erratic effort of the defendant to avoid a roadblock.

See Annotation, "Validity of Police Roadblocks or Checkpoints for Purpose of Discovery of Alcoholic Intoxication—Post Sitz Cases," 74 A.L.R. 5th 319 (1999).

§ 3-10 The *Terry* frisk

In *Peters v. State,* the court pointed to United States Supreme Court holdings stating that there are

> at least theoretically, three tiers of police-citizen encounters: (1) communication between police and citizens involving no coercion or detention and therefore without the compass of the Fourth Amendment, (2) brief seizures that must be supported by reasonable suspicion, and (3) full-scale arrests that must be supported by probable cause. . . . In the first [tier] police officers may approach citizens, ask for identification, and freely question the citizen without any basis or belief that the citizen is involved in criminal activity, as long as the officers do not detain the citizen or create the impression that the citizen may not leave. The second tier occurs when the officer actually conducts a brief investigative *Terry* stop of the citizen. In this level, a police officer, even in the absence of probable cause, may stop persons and detain them briefly, when the officer has a particularized and objective basis for suspecting the persons are involved in criminal activity.

If there is a sufficient, articulable suspicion to stop a suspect, or if a suspect permits an officer to talk with him, the encounter must not go further than brief questioning of the suspect by the officer unless, after questioning, the officer has *probable cause* to believe the suspect has contraband or if the officer has a justified belief that the person stopped may be armed and dangerous. Likewise, an officer may check "for outstanding warrants or criminal histories on the occupants of a vehicle at a valid traffic stop," provided the officer has a justifiable safety concern during the stop.

If the officer at the end of the "stop phase" has probable cause to believe the suspect has contraband, he may arrest the suspect and then conduct a full-fledged search incident to the arrest. If the officer reasonably believes the suspect is armed and dangerous, he may frisk the suspect for weapons. The frisk, however, may not be justified by the desire to discover or prevent the destruction of evidence in the absence of probable cause and a valid stop alone does not justify a frisk.

Under the rule adopted in *Terry v. Ohio,* a "frisk" is a search within the meaning of the Fourth Amendment. The court in *Terry* also said, however, that unlike a search conducted incident to a lawful arrest, the scope of the frisk must be limited to an intrusion reasonably necessary to discover weapons on or about the person detained.

If a frisk is justified, an officer must ordinarily follow a two-step process. "The officer must pat down first, and then intrude beneath the surface only if he comes upon something which feels like a weapon." A number of courts have emphasized that an officer is not justified in concluding that a search may be conducted if the object felt is soft, but if the object is hard and of substantial size then the officer may remove the item. If an object is felt which the officer believes to be a weapon, the officer may only take such action as is necessary to examine the weapon, or, as McFadden did in *Terry,* remove the object. If the object obtained by the officer turns out to be an illegally concealed weapon or contraband, the officer may at that point arrest the suspect and then conduct a full-blown search.

In the 1993 case of *Minnesota v. Dickerson,* the United States Supreme Court held that "[i]f, while conducting a legitimate *Terry* search . . . the officer should . . . discover contraband other than weapons, he clearly cannot be required to ignore the contraband, and the Fourth Amendment does not require its suppression. . . ." If, however, the police lack a reasonable belief that an object felt is contraband or a weapon, the officer has no authority to squeeze, slide, or otherwise manipulate the contents of the defendant's pocket, after the officer knows the pocket does not contain a weapon, in order to determine if the object is contraband. In *Commonwealth v. Johnson,* the court concluded that there was probable cause to arrest where an officer during a *Terry* frisk felt a "crunchy, granular substance" in the defendant's crotch, since it was "immediately apparent" that the defendant possessed contraband. In *Seaman v. State*, Georgia recognized the "plain feel" doctrine and affirmed the denial of a motion to suppress where an experienced narcotics officer in the course of a *Terry* patdown felt what he believed to be a clear plastic baggie containing contraband. There was no evidence the officer "manipulated the object in [the defendant's] pocket in any way before identifying it." Further, in the Georgia case of *Buffington v. State*, the court also applied the "plain feel" test as to a crack pipe in the defendant's pocket because the police officer immediately recognized the pipe as a drug-related object. However, in *State v. Williams*, the court affirmed the suppression where the officer testified he searched the defendant's "pocket because he was concerned that the unidentified object which felt like a bag could be a weapon and because it could 'possibly' be contraband." In *Corley v. State*, after a stop, the officer frisked the defendant and felt and saw a bulge in the defendant's watch pocket. There was no evidence that led the officer to believe that the defendant had a weapon in his watch pocket. The defendant emptied his watch pocket when the officer told him to do so and an object which looked like marijuana was removed. The appellate court reversed the denial of the defendant's motion to suppress. See Annotation, "Application of 'Plain–Feel' Exception to Warrant Requirements—State Cases," 50 A.L.R. 5th 581 (1997).

Generally, in the absence of a pretextual stop, if the frisk does not produce a weapon or contraband, the encounter must be terminated at that point unless the officer has obtained probable cause for an arrest. See section 4-26, infra, on pretextual stops. However, in *McGugan v. State*, the officer felt a rather large hard object inside the defendant's inside jacket pocket. The officer asked the defendant to identify the object and the defendant did not respond. The deputy reached inside the defendant's pocket and removed a plastic bag containing a substance later identified as cocaine. The deputy testified he removed the object because the defendant failed to respond to the deputy's request to identify the object. The court concluded that the defendant's refusal to identify the object, coupled with his earlier reluctance to cooperate with the deputy, "created a reasonable suspicion that the defendant was armed" and justified the deputy in placing his hand in the defendant's pocket and removing the object. In *Redd v. State*, the court noted that "an individual's conduct in response to questioning or attempted questioning may rise to the level of probable cause to conduct an arrest or search." The court then held that when an officer has articulable suspicion authorizing a stop and frisk and the defendant "did not respond to the officer's questions, never allowed the officer to get close enough to question him or complete a limited patdown for weapons, ignored several requests to stop, and then fled into the woods," a nonconsensual investigation pursuant to *Terry* was authorized.

In cases where there is an illegal stop and search, which leads to the discovery of evidence of criminal conduct, the evidence may be admissible if the defendant was the subject of a valid outstanding warrant, despite the manner in which it was obtained if the defendant is arrested under the warrant. In *State v. Cooper*, the defendant was the passenger in a vehicle which was stopped and searched. The defendant sought to suppress the marijuana found in the car. At the time the vehicle was stopped the officer determined that the defendant was the subject of outstanding warrants and arrested him on the basis of these charges. The court concluded that once the warrants were discovered any taint to the evidence found during the search was "cleansed" and the search became justified as one incident to the arrest.

When the suspect is in a car and the articulable suspicion relates to any serious offense, the officer probably may have him get out of the car. Once the suspect is out of the car and on foot, it seems that he is like a pedestrian who has been stopped. In *Maryland v. Wilson,* the United States Supreme Court held that where the driver of a car is stopped for speeding, the "officer making a traffic stop may [also] order passengers to get out of the car pending completion of the stop." In *Rogers v. State,* the court held that "[a]n officer conducting a routine traffic stop may request and examine a driver's license and vehicle registration[,] and run a computer check on the documents." See section 4-26, infra, on search incident to a traffic arrest. In *State v. Blair,* the court pointed out that an investigatory traffic stop is "a brief stop, limited in time to that minimally necessary to investigate the allegation invoking suspicion, and limited in scope to identification and limited questioning reasonably related to the circumstances that justified the initiation of the momentary stop."

Evidence obtained from a pat down of a passenger in a motor vehicle conducted by an officer, who admitted that he was not concerned for his safety and administered the search as part of a routine followed in all cases where he directs someone to exit a vehicle, is subject to suppression.

§ 3-11 Extensions of the *Terry* frisk

The material in the foregoing section represents the traditional stereotyped approach to a *Terry* frisk. However, there seems to be an indication in United States Supreme Court opinions and decisions of a number of other courts indicating a departure from the traditional approach. For example, in *Michigan v. Summers,* the Court said that the right to "stop" is not limited to "momentary, on-the-street detention." In footnote 12 the Court said, "[T]he key principle of the Fourth Amendment is reasonableness—the balancing of competing interests. . . . If the purpose underlying a *Terry* stop—investigating possible criminal activity—is to be served, the police must under certain circumstances be able to detain the individual for longer than the brief time period involved in *Terry* and *Adams.*" In a like approach the Georgia Court of Appeals said that "[o]nce a '*Terry* stop' has been made, the legality of its scope 'is determined in each case by balancing the extent of the intrusion against the immediacy and importance of the interest in crime prevention or law enforcement which is sought to be advanced.' "

In *Hodges v. State,* the court affirmed the frisk where in addition to the standard *Terry* pat-down, the officer put his fingers under the defendant's "beltline [in the back], on the exterior of the shirt, to feel if there was a weapon secured under the clothing by the belt." This was deemed to be a reasonable search for weapons under the facts of the case which included the fact that the officer himself carried "his weapon in his back when he was off duty." The court also noted, among other things, that the event took place in the early morning hours while it was dark, that the officer went to that area following an emergency 911 call, and that the area was well known for the presence of guns and drugs.

In *Thomas v. State,* the court affirmed the conviction where a defendant exited an automobile and officers informed him that they had received information that he was carrying drugs. He kept placing his hand in his jacket pocket. After the defendant refused to obey an order to remove his hand from his pocket, the officer, fearing for his own safety, forcibly removed the defendant's hand from the pocket and reached in and found a bag containing the suspected heroin. At that point, the officer arrested the defendant and searched him and the automobile.

In *United States v. Sokolow,* the United States Supreme Court stated that officers are not obligated to use the "least intrusive means available to verify or dispel their suspicions."

As one commentator observed, "It is clear that there are several investigative techniques which may be utilized effectively in the course of a *Terry*-type stop. The most common is interrogation, which may include both a request for identification and inquiry concerning the suspicious conduct of the person detained. Sometimes the officer will communicate with others, either police or private citizens, in an effort to verify the explanation tendered or to confirm the identification or determine whether a person of that identity is otherwise wanted. Or, the suspect may be detained while it is determined if in fact an offense has occurred in the area, a process which might involve checking certain premises, locating and examining objects abandoned by the suspect, or talking with other people. If it is known that an offense has occurred in the area, the suspect may be viewed by witnesses to the crime. There is no reason to conclude that any investigative methods of the type just listed are inherently objectionable; they might cast doubt upon the reasonableness of the detention, however, if their use makes the period of detention unduly long or involves moving the suspect to another locale." 3 LaFave, *Search and Seizure,* § 9.2, pp. 36–37 (West 1978). See section 3-7, supra, on facts justifying a stop where there has been a crime reported.

However, in the 1995 opinion *Smith v. State,* the Georgia Court of Appeals does not speak in terms of exclusion of evidence discovered as a result of unjustified questioning during a stop. The court held that the "scope of the detention must be carefully tailored to its underlying justification." Thus, when a person is stopped for a possible DUI violation, the officer is justified to ask a driver "for his license to establish his identity, and to ask questions reasonably related to whether or not [the driver] was driving under the influence." Once an explanation has been given, the officer may "administer a statutorily authorized field sobriety test, or take any other reasonable steps to determine whether [the driver] was, as he originally suspected, driving under the influence." Questions pertaining to the possession of contraband are "beyond the permissible scope of the investigation." The court in *Migliore v. State* relied on *Smith* in holding that "[a]t the point the officer initiated the probe for drugs, he went beyond the permissible scope of the investigation and his further detention of the defendant went beyond that permitted by *Terry* and its progeny."

In *United States v. Purcell,* the 11th Circuit Court of Appeals held that a stop "may not last 'any longer than necessary to process the traffic violation' unless there is articulable suspicion of other illegal activity." In *United States v. Boyce,* the 11th Circuit gave the holding in *Purcell* some added definition by observing that there are only three situations in which a traffic stop may be prolonged: to investigate the driver's license and vehicle registration; to wait for the results of a criminal history check that is part of a routine traffic investigation; and, if there exists an "articulable suspicion of other illegal activity." Thus, when an officer's questioning and detention of the driver and the occupants of a motor vehicle exceeds the scope of reasonable permissible investigation, any evidence obtained as a result may be tainted and subject to suppression at trial.

In *Daniel v. State,* the Supreme Court of Georgia held that evidence obtained as a result of continued questioning and detention after the underlying basis for the initial traffic stop has concluded is not automatically subject to a constitutional challenge. "[W]e hold that a law enforcement officer's continued questioning of a vehicle's driver and passengers outside the scope of a valid traffic stop passes muster under the Fourth Amendment either when the officer has a reasonable articulable suspicion of other illegal activity or when the valid traffic stop has de-escalated into a consensual encounter." In *Daniel*, the police had no reason to suspect criminal activity which would warrant detaining the defendant beyond the scope of the initial stop. Nonetheless, the court concluded that under the totality of the circumstances surrounding the post traffic stop detention, the questioning was consensual in nature and hence the evidence obtained as a result thereof was the product of a lawful investigation and properly admitted at trial.

Following *Daniel*, however, the United States Supreme Court, in *Muehler v. Mena*, held that unless police questioning prolongs detention, the questioning does not amount to an additional seizure, "and, therefore, no additional Fourth Amendment justification" is required. Accordingly, in *Salmeron v. State*, the Supreme Court of Georgia abrogated the totality of the circumstances standard of *Daniel* and substituted the standard announced by the United States Supreme Court in *Muehler*.

As the Georgia Court of Appeals observed in *State v. Davis* following *Salmeron*, "even if police have no basis for suspecting that a person detained at a traffic stop is engaged in criminal activity unrelated to the stop, police may lawfully ask questions during the course of the stop about such unrelated activity, so long as the questioning does not prolong the stop beyond the time reasonably required to complete the purpose of the traffic stop." The court also noted in *Hayes v. State* that asking "the driver to step out of the vehicle does not unduly prolong the detention. Further, as a matter of Georgia law, it does not matter whether the request to search comes during the traffic stop or immediately thereafter."

The standard for whether or not an officer has reasonable suspicion to stop a vehicle centers on the totality of the circumstances surrounding a particular stop and whether the police questioning unduly prolongs an otherwise proper detention. The United States Supreme Court has expressly recognized that this standard includes analyzing both "innocent factors" and apparently "suspicious factors"

In *Simmons v. State,* the defendant was validly stopped for a traffic violation. The court pointed out that the appropriate legal standard for determining whether further questioning and a walk around the car with a narcotics dog were justified "is whether the officers had a *reasonable suspicion* [rather than probable cause] that [the defendant] was transporting illegal drugs." The appellate court held that the following did not establish such a reasonable suspicion: (1) the defendant and his passenger appeared nervous; (2) the defendant told officers that the vehicle rental agreement was in his wife's name, and his wife was not present; and (3) the defendant told officers he was nervous because the passenger was his girlfriend. After warning him for the traffic violation, the officer should not have detained the defendant further to ask him whether he was transporting narcotics and to walk a drug dog around his car. See section 3-12, infra, on when a stop becomes an arrest.

In *State v. Bibbins,* the Court of Appeals held that police questioning of a motorist during the course of a traffic stop, without more, does not rise to the level of a Fourth Amendment issue. The Court concluded that the 'scope' of a traffic detention has never been limited to the isolated traffic offense that led to the pullover but is broad enough to encompass identified, legitimate law enforcement goals relating to highway public safety, as long as the pursuit of those goals does not unreasonably prolong the duration of a valid, ongoing stop.

Adams v. Williams represents the exception to the general rule that an officer, at the time of the stop, is to talk with the suspect before determining whether or not to conduct a frisk. In this case, the officer approached Williams, reached to the spot where a gun was thought to be hidden and removed the gun. The court concluded that this conduct was reasonable. After obtaining the pistol, Williams was then arrested for the illegal possession of the weapon and searched as an incident to the arrest. In the Georgia case *Pace v. State,* officers in a high crime area saw the defendant standing in a parking lot. He stood there about eight minutes before the officers approached in a marked police car. The officers were suspicious that the defendant was there to sell drugs. When the defendant saw the police car, he turned and started walking away. The officers called him and he began acting very nervous and continued to walk away. When the officers approached him "he reached toward his right pocket and attempted several times to reach into it. They stopped him from going into the pocket because they were concerned for their safety . . . . They asked [the defendant] to put his hands on the police car, and the officer reached into the pocket and found [a] razor blade and drugs." There was no earlier pat-down. In affirming the admission of the evidence obtained from the pocket, the court pointed out that "[t]he law permits . . . officers to protect themselves from harm even when conducting a non-coercive lawful stop . . . . The usual police response will be to conduct a frisk, patting the individual's clothing in search of a weapon . . . . [However, a] pat down is not a prerequisite."

In *Davis v. State,* the court affirmed the trial judge in permitting an officer to testify that when he felt a hard object, he asked the defendant to remove it. The defendant pulled out a cigarette box. The trooper, concerned that the box might contain a razor blade or other small weapon, opened the box and found two marijuana cigarettes. The court said there was ample reason to believe the defendant was carrying a weapon.

In *Morris v. State,* the trial judge was affirmed in denying a defendant's motion to suppress contents found in a match box in the defendant's shirt pocket. The officer noticed a bulge in that area and asked the defendant what it was. The defendant told him it was matches. The officer then asked if the defendant would mind his examining the matches. The defendant said, "No, go ahead" and handed the box to the officer, who found "three plastic bags containing a white powdery substance."

In *United States v. Baker,* the Fourth Circuit held that "the reasonableness of a protective search depends on the factual circumstances of each case. . . . Thus, a pat down frisk is but one example of how a reasonable protective search may be conducted. . . . Balancing the officer's interest in self-protection against the resulting intrusion upon Baker's personal security, we hold that [the officer's] direction was reasonable under the circumstances." The officer instructed Baker to lift his shirt far enough to uncover a bulge near his waist so as to reveal the bulge. Baker had been stopped for a traffic violation. The bulge was caused by a gun.

In *State v. Williams,* the Nebraska Supreme Court found that the facts justified the forceful opening of a clenched fist as a part of a frisk where officers had received reports that people present were armed with knives and the defendant made a furtive gesture with her hand near the waistband of her pants. The officer was concerned about his safety and thought the defendant might be concealing a weapon.

Based on *Terry,* in 1983, the United States Supreme Court in *Michigan v. Long* approved a frisk or search of the passenger compartment of an automobile limited to areas in which a weapon might have been placed. The court said, "[t]he police searched the passenger compartment because they had reason to believe that the vehicle contained weapons. We hold that the protective search of the passenger compartment was reasonable under the principles articulated in *Terry* and other decisions of this Court." In another portion of the opinion the Court said "that the search of the passenger compartment of an automobile, limited to those areas in which a weapon may be placed or hidden, is permissible if the police officer possesses a reasonable belief based on 'specific and articulable facts which, taken together with the rational inferences from those facts, reasonably warrant' the officers in believing that the suspect is dangerous and the suspect may gain immediate control of weapons. . . . '[T]he issue is whether a reasonably prudent man in the circumstances would be warranted in the belief that his safety or that of others was in danger.' "

In *Holsey v. State,* the court held that "a law enforcement officer who detains a person for purposes of investigation should 'not be denied the opportunity to protect himself from attack by a hostile suspect' and may lawfully detain the person in a manner 'reasonably necessary to protect [his] personal safety and to maintain the status quo.' Other courts have held that, in sufficiently dangerous circumstances, law enforcement officers may effect and maintain investigatory detentions by drawing weapons and forcing defendants to lie face down with arms and legs spread. Such methods must be reserved for cases where plausible danger exists to the detaining officer's personal safety, but '[t]o require an officer to risk his life in order to make an investigatory stop would run contrary to the intent of *Terry v. Ohio* . . . .' [Footnotes omitted.]" In *United States v. Holt,* the court held that an officer making a traffic stop may ask the driver if there was a loaded gun in the car.

In *Jackson v. State,* the court held that, in the frisk stage, the officer was justified in handcuffing the defendant where he was regarded as being extremely violent.

In *United States v. Kent,* the Eleventh Circuit held that where Customs officials validly stop a vessel, they have a right to conduct a protective sweep after boarding the vessel.

In *Lansdown v. Commonwealth,* the court held that a frisk of a passenger of a vehicle was valid where the van had been stopped for being driven in a grossly reckless manner. The driver had tried to outrun the officers and the officers reasonably concluded that occupants might be armed.

In *Pitts v. State,* the court affirmed the action of an officer in conducting a "free air search" of the outside of a van by a German Shepherd dog after the officer obtained conflicting versions from the two occupants of the vehicle about their travel itinerary.

In the Delaware case of *Bromwell v. State,* the court upheld a "safety search" of a partially open cardboard box which did not appear to contain personal effects, as a part of the frisk of the man. However, in *State v. Noble,* the court stated that when a stop "has been made, the legality of its scope 'is determined in each case by balancing the extent of the intrusion against the immediacy and importance of the interest in crime prevention or law enforcement which is sought to be advanced.' "

In *State v. Key,* there were sufficient circumstances to "stop" an automobile. The two occupants said they were waiting for a girl to come home. It was about 2:40 a.m. The officer had the occupants get out and produce identification which they did. The officer saw an object "in the back seat . . . he suspected to be a person hiding under a blanket." He "again approached the car and 'reached in and checked' to see if his suspicion was correct. It was not." The object was a sleeping bag. The officer then apparently looked in "an ice chest sitting in the floor board." He found nothing but a can of beer inside. He also saw another beer can on the floor board on the driver's side. The officer then walked to the driver's side and "looked in through the window" with the aid of a flashlight; he "observed a clear plastic bag with a green, leafy substance . . . in the floorboard in front of the driver's seat." After seizing the suspected marijuana, he searched the passenger compartment, and, after finding a quantity of suspected marijuana, then searched the trunk and found additional suspected marijuana. The court concluded that the only difficulty with the search and seizure was the search of the cooler. The search of the cooler was not valid. However, the majority concluded that the intrusion into the cooler did not so taint the search procedure as to require the exclusion of the contraband later found in "plain view." In a dissenting opinion, Judge Sognier said the majority was in effect grafting "a healthy limb onto a 'poisonous tree.' "

In *Williams v. State,* the court affirmed the trial court's sanctioning of the opening of an automobile's unlocked trunk without probable cause when the officer thought someone was in the trunk who might pose a threat to his safety.

Some note should be taken of O.C.G.A. § 40-8-76.1(f) which prohibits an officer who stops a motorist because of a seat belt violation from bootstrapping that incident as probable cause for other criminal activity. However, as the court observed in Blitch v. State, O.C.G.A. § 40-8-76.1(f) does not preclude an officer from conducting a vehicle search with the drivers consent obtained during a lawful traffic stop for failure to wear a seatbelt.

§ 3-12 When does a "stop" become an "arrest"?

In *United States v. Roper,* the Eleventh Circuit acknowledged that "[t]he distinction between an arrest and an investigatory stop depends upon the nature and degree of the intrusion under all the facts of the particular encounter." However, the court concluded that the stop of an automobile was not converted into an arrest simply because the officer approached the stopped vehicle with a drawn gun. In *Hughes v. State,* a driver of an automobile was informed that he was not free to leave. The Georgia Supreme Court concluded that the evidence supported the conclusion of the trial judge that the defendant was under arrest. However, the "subjective intention of . . . [an] officer to detain the defendant had he attempted to leave is irrelevant except insofar as that intention may have been conveyed to the defendant."

In *Sultenfuss v. State,* the court found that (1) a stop "was not transformed into an arrest merely because one of the officers, who had physically struggled with appellant during a prior incident, drew his weapon on this occasion"; (2) requiring a defendant to step from an automobile did not transform a stop into an arrest; and (3) the detention of the defendant by blocking his car did not convert the confrontation into an arrest. In *Walton v. State,* the court concluded that a stop was not transformed into an "arrest merely because of the number of police cars used to effect the stop and the manner in which the police blocked his automobile." However, in *State v. Burks,* the court pointed out that after an "initial attempt to stop, '[f]light in connection with other circumstances may be sufficient probable cause to uphold a warrantless arrest or search.' "

In *People v. Vena,* the court concluded that a stop did not become an arrest even though officers transported suspects to the stationhouse in view of blizzard-type weather conditions. The court concluded that this was not more intrusive than detaining them in a field where they were captured or in a squad car.

However, in *Hayes v. Florida,* the United States Supreme Court held that where "there was no probable cause to arrest," officers have no right to take a suspect to the police station for the purpose of being fingerprinted. However, the Court pointed out that it was saying nothing which implied "that a brief detention in the field for the purpose of fingerprinting, where there is only reasonable suspicion . . . is necessarily impermissible under the Fourth Amendment." In *United States v. Guevara-Martinez*, the court held that when a defendant is illegally detained, his fingerprints, which were not taken as a part of the ordinary booking procedures, were not admissible.

In *People v. Hicks,* the New York Court of Appeals held that where there is a valid *Terry* stop the stop did not become an arrest and was valid even though the defendant was held about 10 minutes and transported to the crime scene for identification.

In the interesting Seventh Circuit case of *United States v. Chaidez,* the Court recognized that there were degrees of intrusion between what is required for a stop and what is required for an arrest. It said that a sliding scale should be applied. The probability requirement should be increased as the intuitiveness increases. There is no reason to "abandon the search for reasonableness when the intrusion falls between arrest and stop."

In *Kolender v. Lawson,* the United States Supreme Court considered the validity of a California statute which required "that an individual provide 'credible and reliable' identification when requested by a police officer who has reasonable suspicion of criminal activity to justify a *Terry* detention." The court held that the statute was unconstitutionally vague on its face and that it vests virtually complete discretion in the police to determine whether the suspect has satisfied the requirements of the statute. This California statute reminds one of the Georgia statute on loitering or prowling which is found in O.C.G.A. § 16–11–36, which is set out in part in the footnotes. This Georgia statute has been regarded as a separate and independent justification for a stop and interrogation. However, if a stop or an arrest is made pursuant to this Georgia statute, such a detention and an accompanying frisk or search which is otherwise valid would not seem to be invalid because of the unconstitutionality of the statute even if it is unconstitutional. Moreover, in *Bell v. State,* the Georgia Supreme Court held the Georgia loitering and prowling statute constitutional. In *Johnson v. State,* the appellate court reversed the trial court and found the defendant to have been seized where the defendant was asked for identification and what he was doing in the neighborhood. The defendant responded "Do I have to tell you?" and the officer responded affirmatively.

The Georgia Court of Appeals has observed: "[t]he United States Supreme Court has adopted a dual inquiry for evaluating the reasonableness of a lengthy investigative stop. First, we consider whether the officer's action was justified at its inception and second, whether it was reasonably related in scope to the circumstances which justified the interference in the first place. In assessing whether a detention is too long in duration to be justified as an investigative stop, we consider it appropriate to examine whether the police diligently pursued a means of investigation that was likely to confirm or dispel their suspicions quickly, during which time it was necessary to detain the defendant." (citations and punctuation omitted.) Reversing the suppression of evidence obtained following a consensual search initiated seventeen minutes after the initial traffic stop, the Eleventh Circuit stated in dicta: "Where at its inception a traffic stop is a valid one for a violation of the law, we doubt that a resultant seizure of no more than seventeen minutes can ever be unconstitutional on account of its duration: the detention is too short."

See section 2-12, supra, on probable cause which justifies an arrest. See section 2-2, supra, on seizures and arrests. See sections 4-26 and 4-27, infra, on searches incident to lawful arrest. See section 4-48 et seq., infra, on automobile searches. See section 3-11, supra, on duty of officer to release a suspect after completion of purpose of frisk.

§ 3-13 Brief retention of inanimate objects without probable cause

In *United States v. Van Leeuwen,* two 12–pound packages were deposited at a post office in Washington near the Canadian border. Both were mailed "air mail/registered." The mailer represented the packages as containing coins. One package was to be sent to California, the other to Tennessee. The postal clerk was suspicious and it was noticed that the return address given was that of a vacant housing area. The license plates on the mailer's car were from British Columbia. A policeman called on the California address and learned that the addressee was under investigation for dealing in illegal coins. The packages were held overnight until information could be obtained about the addressee in Tennessee. It was learned that the addressee there was under investigation for the same offense. A search warrant for the packages was issued and about 29 hours after the packages had been left with the post office, the warrant was executed. The packages were resealed and sent on their way. The mailer was convicted of illegally importing gold coins. The Supreme Court recognized that the Fourth Amendment applied to first class mail and that it could only be opened pursuant to a warrant. However, the Court concluded that the delaying of the packages until information could be obtained justifying the issuance of a warrant was not unreasonable under the Fourth Amendment. The court also drew an analogy between the facts of this case and those of *Terry.* See Annotation, "Warrantless Detention of Mail for Investigative Purposes as Violative of Fourth Amendment," 115 A. L. R. Fed. 439 (1993).

In *United States v. Klein,* the court found that the officers' observations and information received justified the detention of bags at an airport while the other investigation was being conducted. The court said that this was true even though there was no probable cause for an arrest of the owner. Additionally, although there was no probable cause for an arrest, the court found that there were grounds for a *Terry* stop. In *Yocham v. State,* the court said that while "one has a right under the Fourth Amendment to expect privacy of the contents of one's luggage, this right does not extend to the bags' exterior or to control of who actually handles them" once they have been checked. "Having the bags removed from the baggage cart pending further investigation was not an unreasonable seizure."

In *United States v. Place,* the United States Supreme Court said "when an officer's observations lead him reasonably to believe that a traveler is carrying luggage that contains narcotics, the principles of *Terry* and its progeny would permit the officer to detain the luggage briefly to investigate the circumstances that aroused his suspicion, provided that the investigative detention is properly limited in scope. . . . There is no doubt that the agents made a 'seizure' of Place's luggage for the purposes of the Fourth Amendment when, following his refusal to consent to a search, the agent told Place that he was going to take the luggage to a federal judge to secure issuance of a warrant. . . . At the outset, we must reject the Government's suggestion that the point at which probable cause for seizure of luggage from the person's presence becomes necessary is more distant than in the case of a *Terry* stop of the person himself. . . . The precise type of detention we confront here is seizure of personal luggage from the immediate possession of suspect for the purpose of arranging exposure to a narcotics detection dog. . . . [W]hen the police seize luggage from the suspect's custody, we think the limitations applicable to investigative detentions of the person should define the permissible scope of an investigative detention of the person's luggage on less than probable cause. Under this standard, it is clear that the police conduct here exceeded the permissible limits of a *Terry*-type investigative stop. The length of the detention of respondent's luggage alone precludes the conclusion that the seizure was reasonable in the absence of probable cause. . . . [T]he brevity of the invasion of the individual's Fourth Amendment interests is an important factor in determining whether the seizure is so minimally intrusive as to be justifiable on reasonable suspicion. . . . [I]n assessing the effect of the length of the detention, we take into account whether the police diligently purse their investigation. [] . . . [A]lthough we decline to adopt any outside time limitation for a permissible *Terry* stop, . . . we have never approved a seizure of the person for the prolonged 90–minute period involved here and cannot do so on the facts presented by this case. . . . [Also] the violation was exacerbated by the failure of the agents to accurately inform respondent of the place to which they were transporting his luggage, of the length of time he might be dispossessed, and of what arrangements would be made for return of the luggage if the investigation dispelled their suspicion."

In *Bothwell v. State,* the defendant "traveled alone, from an identified source city, flying under a false name, carried little or no luggage, purchased his expensive airline ticket in cash, acted very nervous, and had given false information to the airline." The stop was based solely on the drug courier profile. See section 3-4, supra. At the time of the stop, one of the officers took the defendant's ticket, retained it and took the defendant to a private office while retaining his boarding pass. He consented to a pat-down search of his person. At first he said he would consent to a search of his bag but after officers retrieved it, he withdrew his consent to the search of his bag. The agents retained the defendant's bag, but the defendant continued his flight to Phoenix. The agents obtained a drug dog. The dog indicated that there were narcotics in the bag. A search warrant was obtained, and a search produced cocaine. The defendant was arrested when he deplaned in Phoenix. In a four to three decision of the Georgia Supreme Court, the court affirmed the denial of the motion to suppress. See *Florida v. Royer,* discussed in section 3-4, supra.

In *State v. Foster,* the defendant fit the "drug courier profile." He was frisked but refused to consent to a search of a shaving bag he was carrying. The court held that the officers could briefly detain the bag under *Terry.* "[W]hen an officer's observations lead him reasonably to believe that a traveler is carrying luggage that contains narcotics, . . . the officer . . . [may] detain the luggage briefly to investigate the circumstances that aroused his suspicion, provided that the investigative detention is properly limited in scope." In this case, a dog sniffed the bag, detected narcotics in the bag, and the defendant was then arrested. The bag was then searched and cocaine was found in it.

In *Dawson v. State,* the Georgia Court of Appeals concluded that "[w]here a drug dog's alert is the *only* basis for suspecting the presence of contraband . . . , evidence that the dog has been extremely unreliable in the past may lead the trial court to conclude that the dog's alert, by itself, does not indicate a 'fair probability' of the presence of contraband. However, where there are additional indications of the presence of contraband . . . , the totality of the circumstances may support a finding of probable cause notwithstanding evidence of the dog's unreliability."

On the other hand, in *State v. Smith,* the defendant arrived at the Atlanta Airport from Fort Lauderdale, a source city. He looked around, staring at people. He appeared nervous. An agent followed the defendant to determine the name on his ticket. The agent learned from the ticket agent the defendant's name, destination, and the fact that the ticket had been paid for with a credit card. The agent called the call-back number in Fort Lauderdale and found it was a hotel there; he estimated that the defendant had remained there about 19 hours. When the defendant was approached, he produced "his ticket, driver's license, and his [real] name." The defendant said he had gone there to look at an airplane. As the defendant was questioned he seemed to become more nervous. He said he was not carrying contraband on his person or in his luggage. He consented to a search of his boots and had a considerable amount of money there. He was given *Miranda* warnings, was accused of carrying drugs in his luggage, and was warned that if he did not consent to a luggage search, he would, if possible, be met in Tulsa by officers and drug dogs. The defendant declined to consent. The agent then retrieved the defendant's checked suitcase, and the defendant was informed of his rights regarding the search of his suitcase. He was told that he was free to leave but that his suitcase would be retained. The defendant left for Tulsa while a search warrant was being obtained for the suitcase. When the suitcase was opened it was found to contain cocaine. The court affirmed the granting of the motion to suppress finding (1) that the stop was not justified by an articulable suspicion, and (2) that the scope of a *Terry* stop had been exceeded and the stop amounted to an illegal detention.

In *State v. Grant,* the court, while disapproving of the conclusion of the trial judge, concluded that a retention of luggage for about an hour was justified where officers acted diligently, the retention was not prolonged needlessly, the agents tried to make arrangements to return the luggage, and the intrusion was minimal and was justifiable.

See section 4-44, infra, on border searches and section 4-45, infra, on search of incoming international mail. See section 3-4, supra, on stops related to the airport drug courier profile. See section 4-34, infra, on searches at airports.

Chapter 4

Search And Seizure

§ 4-59 Results of illegal search

KeyCite®: Cases and other legal materials listed in KeyCite Scope can be researched through the KeyCite service on Westlaw®. Use KeyCite to check citations for form, parallel references, prior and later history, and comprehensive citator information, including citations to other decisions and secondary materials.

§ 4-1 Definitions of search and seizure

A search is a quest for information. The "term implies some exploratory investigation, or an invasion and quest, a looking for or seeking out . . . a prying into hidden places for that which is concealed." In *Maryland v. Macon,* the United States Supreme Court said, "A search occurs when 'an expectation of privacy that society is prepared to consider reasonable is infringed.' " In that case, the Court held that there was no search where an officer entered a bookstore and examined magazines "that were intentionally exposed to all" who entered the bookstore.

There is no search when an officer sees from a public road what is in plain view to the unaided eye or, apparently, when the officer sees something from business property generally used by and open to the public.

Based on the theory that "a search ordinarily implies a quest by an officer," the United States Supreme Court in *Wyman v. James* concluded that there was not a search by a social worker in making a home visit to a family receiving Aid to Families with Dependent Children money, even though the visit was to some extent investigative. In *United States v. DeBardeleben*, the court held that the insertion of the keys in the locks of a car was a minimum intrusion which did not amount to a search. See Annotation, "Attachment or Use of Transponder (Beeper) to Monitor Location of Airplane or Automobile as Constituting 'Search' Within Fourth Amendment," 57 A. L. R. Fed. 646 (1982). Also see section 4-2, infra, on protected areas and interests, and sections 14-74 to 14-78, infra, on expectation of privacy. See section 4-39, infra, on field tests of suspected drugs.

The act of taking and removing tangible personal property is a seizure. In *Maryland v. Macon*, the Supreme Court said, "A seizure occurs when 'there is some meaningful interference with an individual's possessory interests' in the property seized." No seizure was found in *Maryland* where an officer bought magazines he suspected were obscene that were on display in a store.

It has been held that where officers attempt to maintain a status quo until a warrant can be obtained, there is a seizure where the officers lock the premises or wait inside or outside for the arrival of a warrant. A seizure also occurs when intangible items are obtained, as in the case of overhearing or recording a telephone call improperly.

There is, however, no expectation of privacy in conversations which occur between a prisoner and a visitor in a prison or jail visiting area. Nor is there such an expectation in the case of a telephone call made from a police station reception area. Likewise, conversations between arrestees in the rear seat of a police patrol car which are secretly recorded have no reasonable expectation of privacy.

Finally, it must be noted that seizure of a person occurs not only in the case of an arrest, but also where a person is restrained so that he cannot walk away. See Chapter 2, supra, on arrest, and Chapter 3, supra, on stop-and-frisk.

§ 4-2 Protected areas and interests

Whatever areas and interests are protected by the Fourth Amendment are protected only against governmental action; individuals acting on their own initiative are not within the amendment's scope. See section 4-59, infra.

The Fourth Amendment states that people shall "be secure in their persons, houses, papers and effects, against unreasonable searches and seizures." An admirable opinion written by Judge Clark of the Georgia Court of Appeals contains the following: " 'A man's home is his castle. The storm and wind may enter, but the King cannot enter, and all the forces of the Crown cannot cross the threshold of his ruined tenement.' These words by Lord Eldon served as the basis for that portion of the Fourth Amendment in the Bill of Rights declaring that the people shall be secure in their houses against unreasonable searches and seizures. Our state Constitution contains almost identical language as used in the federal document." The Fourth Amendment protection has been extended beyond the home to people, automobiles, boats, the area within the curtilage of a house, apartments, hotel rooms, public telephone booths, offices, desks, a coin-operated locker in a bus station, a tent, and a refrigerator in a locked storage unit.

For example, a warrant authorizing the search of a house was held to give officers authority to search a U–Haul truck within the curtilage of the house. Marijuana found in a cooler about 100 yards from the defendant's house trailer at the end of a path from the trailer was also found to be in the curtilage of defendant's home. However, the curtilage concept does not prevent an officer without a warrant from approaching the front door of a house by the same route as would be used by any guest, delivery man, or postal employee. Likewise, the common areas of an apartment building, such as the lobby and the corridors, do not provide a tenant who resides there with a reasonable expectation of privacy where such areas are open and accessible to tenants, visitors, the landlord and its employees as well as the public. See section 4-42, infra. Generally, on curtilage, see section 4-19, infra.

The United States Supreme Court, in *Katz v. United States,* pointed out that the common law concept of trespass will no longer determine whether a violation of the Fourth Amendment has occurred, because the Fourth Amendment is intended to protect people, not simply places. However, a place is entitled to Fourth Amendment protection where an individual connected with the place has a reasonable expectation of privacy in that area. Generally, on expectation of privacy, see sections 14-74 to 14-78, infra. See section 4-27, infra, on seizure of premises while a search warrant is being obtained.

Generally, articles which can be seen with the naked eye from a place an officer is entitled to be are not protected, and this rule seems to apply to the other senses. Thus, in *Cox v. State*, the court stated that officers do not have to obtain prior judicial approval to listen to conversations from a hall outside an apartment or to place the naked ear next to the door to the apartment. In *Maryland v. Macon*, the United States Supreme Court held that there was no reasonable expectation of privacy in an obscene book on display in the public area of an adult bookstore, and the purchase of such a book was not a seizure.

In *United States v. King*, the Eleventh Circuit Court of Appeals held that a private contractor who accessed a military computer network on his personal computer while on a military base located in Saudi Arabia had no reasonable expectation of privacy as to the contents of files that were on a "shared" network, which enabled anyone on that network to access the files.

In *New York v. Burger,* the United States Supreme Court stated, "An expectation of privacy in commercial premises . . . is different from, and indeed less than, a similar expectation in an individual's home. . . . This expectation is particularly attenuated in commercial property employed in 'closely regulated' industries." The court then concluded that a state statute was constitutional which was enacted to combat auto theft which authorized a warrantless inspection of junkyards when certain criteria were followed.

In *United States v. Place,* the United States Supreme Court, in considering the sniffing by a dog of luggage of an airline passenger, said "the present course of investigation that the agents intended to pursue here—exposure of respondent's luggage, which was located in a public place, to a trained canine—did not constitute a 'search' within the meaning of the Fourth Amendment." However, in *Bond v. United States,* the Court held that an INS agent conducted an illegal search when he felt of the luggage in the overhead compartment of a bus. The agent detected a "brick-like object" in one of the bags and after receiving consent from the owner, searched and found methamphetamine. The court explained that while "a bus passenger . . . expects that his bag may be handled . . . [he] does not expect that other[s] . . . [will feel the bag] . . . in an exploratory manner."

In *Carter v. State,* the court held that the use of a dog to smell a package at a UPS station did not interfere with the defendant's possessory interest nor was it a search within the meaning of the Fourth Amendment.

As pointed out in section 4-27, infra, even though a container may be seized, this alone does not mean that the officer has the right to search the container. Abandoned premises and articles lose their protection; open fields and the public portions of business and commercial establishments are not protected.

Surveillance of a stall in public restrooms has sometimes been held to be protected and sometimes held not to be protected. In *Wylie v. State,* the Georgia Court of Appeals affirmed the denial of a motion to suppress where an officer entered a restroom, saw two pairs of feet facing each other under the partition around the commode stall. The officer then looked through the crack between the door and the adjacent wall "and saw two men ingesting a white powder which he took to be and which examination proved was in fact cocaine."

The exterior of a vehicle and articles which can be observed by the public from the outside are not protected. Similarly, in *New York v. Class,* the United States Supreme Court held that a motorist has no reasonable expectation of privacy in a motor vehicle identification number on the dashboard of the car, even if an object on the dash prevented an officer from reading the number from outside the vehicle which the officer had stopped for a traffic violation. The court also held that a gun, discovered by the officer when he leaned into the vehicle to uncover the identification number, was admissible against the defendant. See section 3-10, supra, on the "plain feel" doctrine.

In *United States v. Miller,* the United States Supreme Court held that a depositor had no Fourth Amendment interest in bank records consisting of microfilms of checks, deposit slips and other records relating to his bank account and that the subpoenaed records were the records of the bank and not the depositor's private papers. In *Braswell v. United States,* the United States Supreme Court held that there was no violation of the Fifth Amendment privilege of a sole stockholder of a corporation to require him, as custodian of the corporate records, to produce those records pursuant to a subpoena. However, in the Eleventh Circuit opinion of *In re Grand Jury Subpoena,* dated April 9, 1996, the court, relying on *Curcio v. United States*, held that the sole officer and director of a corporation could not be required to testify before a grand jury to the location of the corporate records after she asserted her Fifth Amendment privilege and stated that she did not possess the records. In *Smith v. Maryland*, the United States Supreme Court has held that there is no Fourth Amendment violation when a pen register is installed at the central telephone office to record the numbers dialed from a person's telephone. The Georgia Supreme Court, in *Kesler v. State*, cited and followed *Miller* in holding that neither the user of a telephone nor the subscriber to the telephone service has any expectation of privacy in telephone toll and billing records of the telephone company. However, in *Ellis v. State*, the Georgia Supreme Court, while recognizing that from a Fourth Amendment standpoint a pen register does not require a warrant, a warrant *is* required for a pen register under Georgia statutory law.

In *Skinner v. Railway Labor Executives' Association,* the United States Supreme Court held that a blood, urine, and breath test of employees involved in accidents for drugs is a "search" within the ambit of the Fourth Amendment. Even in the absence of a particularized suspicion of drug or alcohol use, the compelling governmental interest in railroad safety outweighs the limited intrusion upon the privacy interest of the employees, and such tests are admissible. The same Court handed down a decision in *National Treasury Employees Union v. Von Raab* on the same day as the *Skinner* case. In the *Von Raab* case, the Court held that the Customs Service may constitutionally require employees seeking promotions to positions requiring the carrying of firearms to undergo blood screening.

In *Chandler v. Miller,* the United States Supreme Court held invalid a Georgia statute requiring certain elective officials to certify that they have tested negative for drugs before qualifying for office. The court held that when public safety is not genuinely in jeopardy, the suspicionless search, no matter how unintrusive or conveniently arranged, is still a violation of the Fourth Amendment. The court pointed out that there was "no evidence of a drug problem among the State's elected officials . . . [that they] do not perform high risk, safety sensitive tasks, and the required certification immediately aids no interdiction effort."

In *Jackson v. State,* the Georgia Court of Appeals concluded that " 'there is no *constitutionally* protected right in a decedent's body. Rather, the courts have evolved the concept of quasi property in recognition of the interests of surviving relatives in the possession and control of decedents' bodies. We do not find this common law concept to be of constitutional dimension.' . . . [Hence, a defendant's] quasi-property interest in [a] stillborn fetus will not support a privacy claim sufficient to implicate the search and seizure provisions of the United States Constitution." (Emphasis in original.)

In *Ferguson v. Charleston, S.C.,* the United States Supreme Court, in a five to four decision, held a hospital's policy of conducting non-consensual drug tests on pregnant women and turning positive results over to police violates the Fourth Amendment. The court reasoned that the purpose behind the policy takes it outside prior rulings of the court upholding searches conducted under policies that dispense with usual Fourth Amendment requirements in order to serve "special needs" of law enforcement.

In *Stephenson v. State,* the court held that in response to harassing phone calls, there was no Fourth Amendment violation when a phone company employee traced a call, determined that it originated from the defendant's number, " 'trapped' the call by preventing the two phones from being disconnected from each other, and notified the police. Police went to defendant's residence, received permission to check his telephone and discovered that his line was dead. They also discovered that the phone line had been cut outside of the house. . . . The following day, . . . a telephone company employee and a police officer went to defendant's residence, and found no one at home. They went to where the line was cut outside of the house where the employee connected a test phone to the cut line. The police officer then spoke on the phone to another officer who was at the victim's phone . . . ."

There seems to be a division of authority on whether or not the use of "bugs" or electronic tracking devices violates the Fourth Amendment. However, in 1983, in *United States v. Knotts*, the United States Supreme Court held that there was no invasion of any legitimate expectation of privacy and no "search" or "seizure" within the contemplation of the Fourth Amendment in the use of a beeper to follow an object carried in an automobile on public roads and to a private residence. In *Knotts*, one Armstrong was purchasing chloroform to be used in the manufacture of drugs. Officers arranged to place a beeper inside a chloroform container which was sold to Armstrong. When Armstrong obtained the container, officers followed the car and maintained contact visually and with a monitor. Armstrong transferred the container to one Petschen. Petschen was then followed. Officers lost visual and "beeper" contact at one time but later located the container by the use of a helicopter. The container was then stationary at a cabin of Knotts. The officers then obtained a search warrant and discovered a drug laboratory at Knotts' cabin. The five gallon container was outside the cabin. The court pointed out that the surveillance amounted principally to following automobiles on public streets, that persons driving on public streets have no reasonable expectation of privacy, and that there was no indication that the beeper was used in any way to reveal the movement of the container in the cabin or in any way which would not have been visible to the naked eye outside the cabin.

In *United States v. Karo,* the United States Supreme Court held that, while the installation of a beeper in a drum of ether, with the consent of a dealer, was not a violation of the Fourth Amendment, there is such a violation where the beeper continued to be monitored after the drum had been placed in a private residence. Although the case was later overruled, the court in *Banks v. State,* the Georgia Court of Appeals summarized its holding as follows: "[O]fficers who find an apparently closed business unlocked during a normal security sweep may conduct a limited intrusion on the business premises for the sole purpose of securing the area and ensuring no intruders are present."

The Fourth Amendment does not protect against a misplaced confidence. Thus, where a person invites a guest into his home or room, the guest may later testify as to what he saw or heard while he was in the area into which he was invited, even though the guest is an undercover officer or is working with officers. Likewise, if such a guest is carrying a transmitter to which officers are listening, or if he is carrying a concealed recording device, there is no Fourth Amendment violation. See section 4-58, infra.

In *Zurcher v. Stanford Daily,* the United States Supreme Court held that a search warrant, rather than a subpoena duces tecum, may be used to search the premises of a third party who was not suspected of involvement in the underlying crime. See section 17-10, infra, on subpoenas for production of documents. However, by Georgia statute a search and seizure shall not be conducted without a warrant from a superior court judge, and no search warrant shall be issued for any evidence in the possession of an attorney who is not a criminal suspect unless the application specifies the place to be searched and shows that there is probable cause to believe that such evidence will be secreted or destroyed if a warrant is not issued.

In *Ledesma v. State,* the Georgia Supreme Court held that when officers recover property reported to be stolen, a good faith inventory of the property may be conducted.

In addition to the protection of the Fourth Amendment, as it is being applied by the United States Supreme Court, there is also a growing number of states which have extended greater protection to their citizens, through their own statutes and state constitutions, than that provided by the federal Constitution.

The United States Supreme Court in *United States v. Verdugo-Urquidez* held that the Fourth Amendment does not apply to the search and seizure by United States agents of property that is owned by a nonresident alien and located in a foreign country. See Annotation, "Expectation of Privacy in Internet Communications," 92 A. L. R. 5th 15 (2001).

Computers pose a unique challenge to the case law which has developed around such Fourth Amendment issues as expectation of privacy, probable cause, consent and the extent to which a computer's files may be searched. Although there is law developing in some recent cases, defense counsel, prosecutors and courts should proceed with caution where the subject of a police search resides within a suspect's computer.

It must be kept in mind that the failure to file a timely motion to suppress constitutes a waiver of any violation of the Fourth Amendment with respect to search and seizure.

Generally, see 1 LaFave, *Search and Seizure,* 220 et seq. (West 1978). See section 4-58, infra, on electronic surveillance. See section 5-22 et seq., infra, on non-testimonial evidence. See section 4-1, supra, on the definition of a "search" and a "seizure." See sections 14-74 to 14-78, infra, on expectation of privacy. See section 4-59, infra, on school searches. See Annotation, "Validity, Under Fourth Amendment, of 'Mail Cover,' " 57 A. L. R. Fed. 742 (1982). See section 4-42, infra, on material observed from a helicopter or plane.

§ 4-3 Property which may be seized

O.C.G.A. § 17–5–21 provides that a search warrant may issue for the seizure of the following:

(1) Any instruments, articles, or things, including the private papers of any person, which are designed, intended for use, or which have been used in the commission of the offense in connection with which the warrant is issued;

(2) Any person who has been kidnapped in violation of the laws of this state, who has been kidnapped in another jurisdiction and is now concealed within this state, or any human fetus or human corpse;

(3) Stolen or embezzled property;

(4) Any item, substance, object, thing, or matter, the possession of which is unlawful; or

(5) Any item, substance, object, thing, or matter, other than the private papers of any person, which is tangible evidence of the commission of the crime for which probable cause is shown.

When the peace officer is in the process of effecting a lawful search, nothing in this Code section shall be construed to preclude him from discovering or seizing any stolen or embezzled property, any item, substance, object, thing, or matter, the possession of which is unlawful, or any item, substance, object, thing, or matter, other than the private papers of any person, which is tangible evidence of the commission of a crime against the laws of this state.

In *Sears v. State,* the court held that the term "private papers" applies only "to papers covered by privilege (attorney-client, doctor-patient, etc.)."

While it is true that the above statute is couched in terms of a search pursuant to a warrant, it seems that the same persons or things might be seized pursuant to a lawful warrantless search if it is immediately apparent that the person or object falls within this Code section. See section 4-38 et seq., infra, on plain view.

In more general terms, in a lawful warrantless search, an officer may seize any contraband, stolen property, or mere evidence of a crime which he sees in plain view and which he immediately recognizes as such, provided that the scope of the search was strictly tied to and justified by the circumstances which rendered it permissible when initiated. Thus, in *United States v. Jones*, the court affirmed the trial court in approving a seizure of a handgun in plain view. The officer had been talking to the defendant through a closed screen door and there was another occupant of the room within arm's reach of the weapon.

Generally, see 68 Am. Jur. 2d Searches and Seizures § 85.

§ 4-4 Who may apply for a search warrant?

In Georgia, by statute any officer of this state or its political subdivisions, or a university, college or school charged with the duty of enforcing the criminal laws may file a written complaint for the issuance of a search warrant. An application for the issuance of a search warrant may be conducted by video conference and will be considered a written application if it satisfies statutory requirements. However, an officer is not entitled to obtain a search warrant unless he is certified pursuant to the provisions of O.C.G.A. §§ 35–8–1 et seq.. See section 2-8, supra.

In *State v. Harber,* the court held that where an officer was "not authorized to obtain and execute an extra-territorial search warrant, this lack of authority would constitute no more than a mere 'technical' defect" not affecting any substantial rights of the defendant.

§ 4-5 Judicial officers who may issue search warrants

Georgia statutes contain several references to the issuance of a search warrant by a "judicial officer." A judicial officer in the strict legal sense is one "who determines causes" between parties or who "renders decisions in a judicial capacity."

O.C.G.A. § 17–5–21 specifically provides that "any judicial officer authorized to hold a court of inquiry . . . may issue a search warrant." It has been expressly held that a magistrate may issue a search warrant for any area of the county in which his district lies. Judges of recorders' court or municipal court may issue search warrants apparently for any area within the municipality. In *Campbell v. State,* the court held that a judge of the Municipal Court of the City of College Park could sign a warrant in her home in Fulton County to be executed in Clayton County. The court reasoned that because the municipality of College Park crossed the Fulton County line into Clayton County, the judge's authority extended across the county line to the limits of the municipality. A judge pro hac vice of a municipal court may also issue a search warrant. In *State v. Kirkland,* the court held a judge of the Atlanta City Court lacked authority to authorize a search in Coweta County since no part of the City of Atlanta is in Coweta County. In *McLendon v. State,* the court upheld a warrant issued by a person sitting as a de facto magistrate. A juvenile court judge may issue a search warrant even in matters which are not concerned with juveniles. Of course, a superior court judge may issue a search warrant for execution in any county of his circuit and the warrant may be signed in any county of the circuit, regardless of the county in which the search is to be executed.

Prior to the enactment of the present Georgia statutes on search and seizure, it had been held that a deputy clerk could issue a search warrant if there existed express authorization by the legislature. However, such procedure has been recognized as not being valid in that "only a judicial officer can issue a [search] warrant."

Where a motion to suppress is filed and no issue is raised as to the authority of the magistrate to issue the search warrant, this amounts to a waiver of the right of the defendant to object.

In 2001, O.C.G.A. § 17–5–21.1 became effective and provides that a search warrant application may be heard by video conference under the conditions of the statute.

§ 4-6 Judicial officers who may issue search warrants—Neutral and detached magistrates

It is well recognized that the determination of whether probable cause exists to issue a search warrant must be made by a "neutral and detached magistrate." Thus, it has been held that a magistrate who serves as a weekend dispatcher for the police is disqualified from issuing a search warrant. Likewise, a magistrate who issues search warrants and then takes part in the searches is not regarded as neutral or detached. In *Connally v. Georgia,* it was held that a magistrate who is paid $5 for issuing a search warrant and receives no fee if he declines to do so is not a neutral and detached magistrate. However, this rule has not been applied retroactively. The Georgia Court of Appeals has concluded that each of these cases must be decided on its own facts and the "test . . . is whether . . . [the magistrate's] welfare is enhanced by positive action and not enhanced by negative action." The Georgia legislature in 1977 attempted to circumvent this problem by amending the statute providing compensation to a justice of the peace (now magistrate) by providing that he will be paid $5 regardless of whether he decides to issue a search warrant. However, the amended statute provides that the fee "shall not exceed $10.00, but this fee may be waived by the issuing magistrate." If the magistrate holds commitment hearings and obtains a fee for this service, the magistrate might be inclined to issue the search warrant so he could obtain fees incident to the preliminary hearing. In *Felker v. State*, the court held that a magistrate was not disqualified where he had a practice of not billing the county if he denied a search warrant but billing the county if he did. However, in *Rains v. State*, the court concluded that a magistrate issuing an arrest warrant is not disqualified by receiving warrant application forms from the county at no cost. Also it has been held that a magistrate is not to be regarded as disqualified to issue a search warrant where in the past in an unrelated incident he signed blank warrants to accommodate officers.

A magistrate is not disqualified merely because of personal association with police officers or regular visits to the sheriff's office and jail or because he was formerly a deputy sheriff. Likewise, an ex officio magistrate is not disqualified because he is also a coroner. In *Clark v. State*, the court held that a magistrate's neutrality was not impaired by the fact that the magistrate's son was a police officer for the same police department which obtained the search warrant where the son was not involved in the case in any way. In Judicial Qualification Opinion No. 101, the Commission concluded that any employee of a law enforcement body is disqualified by conflict of interest from serving as a magistrate.

Where a superior court judge personally impaneled a special investigative grand jury which indicted the defendant, and made suggestions to the district attorney concerning witnesses to be called, he was held not to be a neutral and detached magistrate. However, in *Beal v. State*, the court held that when a judge "notarized" an affidavit submitted in support of a warrant application, it did not keep him from being neutral and detached in examining or issuing the search warrant.

When a warrant is issued for the search and seizure of documentary evidence in the possession of an attorney, the court shall appoint a special master who is a member of the bar to accompany the person serving the warrant. The special master shall specify the items sought, and if the party fails to provide such items, he shall conduct a search. See section 4-2, supra, on warrants for the search and seizure of documentary evidence in an attorney's possession.

§ 4-7 Probable cause required for issuance of search warrant—General

A proceeding to obtain a search warrant can be initiated by "any officer of this state or its political subdivisions charged with the duty of enforcing the criminal laws." See section 2-8, supra, on officers who may obtain a search warrant. The Fourth Amendment provides that "no Warrants shall issue, but upon probable cause, supported by

§ 4-10 Probable cause required for issuance of search warrant—Observation of "informer" not appearing before magistrate

In general terms, anyone who gives an officer information is an informer. However, in the context of probable cause to search, the word often implies a person who is himself, to some extent, involved in unlawful activity. He may be a user of drugs, frequently he has been arrested, perhaps not infrequently he hopes for some special treatment because of his "helping" the police. On some occasions, the information is given because of jealousy, anger or "to get even" with the person "informed on." This is the kind of person whose credibility is discussed in this section.

A troublesome area in the law of search and seizure involves the credibility of information given to the affiant by an unnamed informer. For instance, although Georgia recognizes the validity of the "statement against interest" rule, it does not apply where the informant is unnamed. It is frequently said that the affidavit or sworn testimony before the magistrate must specifically state sufficient facts to show that the unnamed informer is reliable. In *Mitchell v. State*, the court pointed out that "when the information supplied by the informant is not corroborated, the magistrate must look to see whether the informant himself . . . [is] reliable." In *Pitts v. State*, the court pointed out that a magistrate, in determining reliability of an informer, may consider (1) the type of information previously supplied, (2) the use to which the information was put, and (3) the lapse of time since the information was furnished.

In *Aguilar v. Texas,* the United States Supreme Court held that where an affiant relies on information obtained from an informer, the affidavit must (1) state the underlying circumstances showing the informer's credibility, or the reliability of his information, *and* (2) state the underlying circumstances to support the conclusion that the informer had observed criminal activity. In other words, two essentials must be met: (1) There must be a showing of veracity of the informer and his information—the veracity prong of the two-prong test; and (2) there must be a showing of how or why the informer knew "the narcotics were where he claimed they were"—the basis of knowledge prong of the two-prong test.

The *first* prong of the Aguilar test, reliability of the informer, has often been established by including a statement in the affidavit that the informer has in the past given information which has led to arrests and convictions. Likewise, a statement that the informer has in the past given accurate information which led to the arrest of a person has been held to be sufficient. Where an informer, alleged to be reliable because of information given on two prior occasions which led to arrests, gave information received from an acquaintance, the Georgia Court of Appeals held the affidavit adequate despite the double hearsay objection.

The *second* prong of the Aguilar test has been said to require proof to support the informer's conclusion that criminal activity exists. Georgia courts have construed the second prong of the Aguilar test as requiring the affidavit to state how the information was obtained *or* to describe the criminal activity in such detail so that the magistrate can conclude that the informer's information is more than "a casual rumor circulating in the underworld," or a charge based on an individual's general reputation.

However, all of the foregoing material in this section must be examined in the light of the 1983 United States Supreme Court case of *Illinois v. Gates.* In *Gates* an anonymous letter received by police set out rather detailed information about the drug activities of Mr. and Mrs. Gates. Much of the information was corroborated, but there remained important gaps in the tip. The letter and an affidavit setting out what had been corroborated was used in obtaining a search warrant. A search pursuant to the warrant resulted in a discovery of a large amount of contraband. The Supreme Court said "an informant's 'veracity,' 'reliability' and 'basis of knowledge' are all highly relevant in determining the value of his report. . . . [H]owever . . . these elements should [not] be understood as entirely separate and independent requirements to be rigidly exacted in every case. . . . Rather . . . they should be understood simply as closely intertwined issues that may usefully illuminate the common sense, practical question whether there is 'probable cause' to believe that contraband or evidence is located in a particular place. . . . *[The] totality of the circumstances approach* is far more consistent with our prior treatment of probable cause . . . than is any rigid demand that specific 'tests' be satisfied by every informant's tip. Perhaps the central teaching of our decisions bearing on the probable cause standard is that it is a 'practical, non-technical conception.' . . . [P]robable cause is a fluid concept—turning on the assessment of probabilities in particular factual contexts—not readily, or even usefully, reduced to a neat set of legal rules . . . [T]he 'two-pronged test' directs analysis into two largely independent channels—the informant's 'veracity' or 'reliability' and his 'basis of knowledge.' There are persuasive arguments against according these two elements such independent status. Instead, they are better understood as relevant considerations in the totality of circumstances analysis that traditionally has guided probable cause determinations; a deficiency in one may be compensated for, in determining the overall reliability of a tip, by a strong showing as to the other, or by some other indicia of reliability. . . . [I]t is wiser to abandon the 'two-pronged test' established by our decisions in *Aguilar* and *Spinelli*. . . . In its place we reaffirm the totality of the circumstances analysis. . . ." It is important to recognize that the Court did not completely abandon the Aguilar–Spinelli test in *Gates;* the two prongs became part of a balancing test that includes the totality of the circumstances.

In *State v. Stephens,* the Georgia Supreme Court expressly adopted the rule of *Illinois v. Gates*, supra, stating (1) that "it is, at heart, a rule of subjectivity. One judge's 'probable cause' can be another judge's 'inarticulable suspicion' . . . [and (2)] that *Gates be considered as the* outer limit of probable cause. Accordingly we urge that arresting officers and magistrates make every effort to see that supporting affidavits reflect the maximum indication of reliability along the lines of *Aguilar-Spinelli*, whenever and wherever that shall be feasible."

In *Clark v. State,* the court held that *Gates* is to be applied retroactively.

In *Peacock v. State,* the court held that the " 'totality of the circumstances' is a less rigorous test than that of *Aguilar* and *Spinelli* . . . [and] an affidavit that would pass the former test must necessarily meet the 'totality of the circumstances' criterion." However, in *Langford v. State*, the court emphasized that veracity and basis of knowledge are still major concerns and that an affidavit for a search warrant must set forth sufficient facts from which the magistrate can independently determine the reliability of both the information and the informant.

In *Caswell v. State,* the affidavit, which was the sole basis of the warrant, established the reliability of the informant and adequately stated that "[d]uring the past five (5) days affiant has received information from a reliable confidential informant that Bert Caswell had a quantity of methamphetamines in his residence." However, concerning the informant's basis of knowledge, the appellate court pointed out that "[t]here was no indication in the affidavit as to whether this information came from the informant's personal knowledge so the informant's tip must be relegated to the status of a casual rumor." At the motion to suppress hearing there was additional information concerning the basis of the informant's knowledge other than that set out in the affidavit. However, the appellate court pointed out that this was irrelevant since it was not given to the magistrate at the time of the issuance of the warrant and reversed the trial court's denial of a motion to suppress.

In *State v. Goodrich,* the court affirmed the grant of a motion to suppress where the affidavit did not sufficiently set out facts from which the magistrate could independently determine the reliability of the information contained in the affidavit and the reliability of the informant.

In *VonLinsowe v. State,* the court pointed out that "[i]n order for the corroboration [by an officer] to be meaningful enough to show reliability, . . . the information corroborated must include 'a range of details relating not just to easily obtained facts and conditions existing at the time of the tip, but to future actions of third parties ordinarily not easily predicted.' . . . In short, the information corroborated will generally need to be a prediction of future behavior, as in [*Gates*] or something similar—that is, inside information not available to the general public." However, in *Wilson v. State*, the court held that this rule relating to a prediction of future behavior "applies to an anonymous telephone tip but not to a tip from a known reliable informant." For instance, in *Fiallo v. State,* the court held that "[m]erely confirming that the accused lives where the informant said he did is not sufficient corroboration of the information regarding illegal activity."

In *Kessler v. State,* the court held that it was not necessary for an affidavit to include the fact that the informant was a felon. See section 14-82, infra, on falsity of affidavits for search warrants. However, in *Perkins v. State,* the court pointed out that "officers seeking warrants should provide the magistrate with any information they have relevant to a CI's reliability or motivation, including criminal records and any payments made." In *Robertson v. State,* the court reversed the denial of a motion to suppress pointing out that the "officer's failure to inform the magistrate about the informant's criminal background, pending criminal charges and the possible revocation of his probation or parole, and his personal animosity toward . . . [the person whose home was searched] resulted in the magistrate being deprived of the opportunity to independently determine the reliability of the informant." If material information is knowingly or recklessly omitted, "the reviewing court should include it with other information provided the magistrate to determine whether probable cause to issue the warrant existed." "[H]owever, [if] the information directly known by the officers . . . was sufficient to establish probable cause," a reversal is not required.

In *Pettus v. State,* the court pointed out that "our courts have, on occasion, recognized the affiant's desire to protect the identity of a confidential informant by omitting certain details from the affidavit," such as the exact date drugs were seen on premises.

§ 4-11 Probable cause required for issuance of search warrant—Time

The time of the occurrence of the facts relied upon by the affiant is a prime element in establishing probable cause for the issuance of a search warrant. The magistrate must determine whether the facts presented create a reasonable belief that the same conditions described in the affidavit exist at the time of the presentation of the warrant. However, there has been some relaxation of the requirement of showing that the search warrant is not "stale." Thus, if from all the circumstances set out in the affidavit "there is a fair probability that contraband or evidence of a crime will be found in a particular place," a search warrant may be issued. In *Ayers v. State*, the court said that "the determination of staleness has been modified so that now that issue is included in the broad overview of 'totality of circumstances.' " As the Court of Appeals observed in *State v. Graddy,* "[t]he mere passage of time does not equate with staleness."

Where an affidavit contains no information relating to the time of the occurrence, a search warrant may not issue. However, in *Scott v. State,* the court held that "the absence of the precise time" the informant observed drug transactions is not necessarily fatal. When an affidavit uses the present tense in stating that a person is selling drugs at a specified location, this may sufficiently show that the information is current and not stale. An affidavit signed on a particular day stating that the informer had within five days prior thereto overheard a specified person state she was using cocaine and planned to use it over the upcoming weekend was held to be sufficient as to timeliness.

When an ongoing activity is described, the passage of time as to some of these events is less significant than in the case of a single, isolated transaction.

Generally, officers are permitted to obtain search warrants in advance when there is a probable cause to believe that the thing to be searched for *will be* at the location described when the search is executed even though the thing to be searched for is not at the location to be searched at the time of the issuance of a warrant.

In *United States v. Grubbs*, the Supreme Court held that such "anticipatory" warrants are not categorically unconstitutional and that a "triggering condition" is not required on the face of the warrant to satisfy the Fourth Amendment.

In *McLarty v. State,* a detective obtained a search warrant for drugs at the residence of the defendant but did not execute the warrant until an informant gave the detective confirming information that a person had just left the premises and that drugs were present. The appellate court affirmed the denial of defendant's motion to suppress.

While not directly related to the subject matter of this section, it should be kept in mind that a search warrant is void if not executed within 10 days from the date of issuance.

Generally, see 68 Am. Jur. 2d Searches and Seizures § 70. See also section 4-13, infra.

§ 4-12 Probable cause required for issuance of search warrant—Description of place and person to be searched

In order to allege probable cause, an affidavit must meet two essentials concerning the place and person to be searched: (1) an adequate description of the place or person and (2) facts to establish probable cause that the object sought is located at the described place.

The Fourth Amendment, the Georgia Constitution, and the Code all provide that the place to be searched be particularly described. In addition, according to the Georgia statute, if a warrant is to issue for the search of an individual, the person must be specifically described. The Constitution prohibits the issuance of a general warrant. A search warrant which does not particularly describe the place or person to be searched is considered a general warrant. However, the contents of the affidavit may be considered in determining the description of the place to be searched.

The description of the place to be searched must be sufficient to enable a prudent officer executing the warrant to locate the premises "definitely and with reasonable certainty." It has been pointed out that "[s]earch warrants are not directed at persons; they authorize the search of 'places' and the seizure of 'things,' and as a constitutional matter they need not even name the person from whom the things will be seized." The slight misspelling of the last name of the person occupying the premises will not necessarily render the affidavit and search warrant invalid, and if the property to be searched is clearly described, a search warrant using a completely incorrect first name does not void a search warrant for the premises.

In *Maryland v. Garrison,* the United States Supreme Court held that whether a mistake as to the place to be searched renders the warrant invalid depends upon the extent to which it was possible for an officer, acting reasonably, to discover a mistake either at the time the warrant was sought or at the time it was executed. Hence, the Georgia Court of Appeals held that a warrant to search a named theater located at "No. 13 West 11th Street" (in a named city) may be used to search a theater of the same name located at "No. 15 West 11th Street" where there is no such theater at the address set out. A search warrant to search lot 14K rather than 15K in a mobile home park was found sufficient where it was difficult to determine what the correct number was. A map was attached and the defendant's car was described and found at the site of the search. However, a warrant to search "283 Rock Springs" cannot be used to search "293 South Rock Springs."

An affidavit describing a room at one of two designated motels without giving a room number is insufficient. In the case of a warrant to search an apartment house, a dormitory, a motel, a duplex or a partitioned house, the warrant, on its face, must indicate more than a street address for the building. Where a two-story dwelling contained several front and back doors and separate mailboxes in front of each door, a warrant to search the entire first floor was held not to be sufficiently particular. However, where a single-family dwelling is rented by one person but occupied by several who pay rent to the lessee and there are no external signs of occupation by several families, a warrant to search the entire house is valid. In *Andrews v. State*, the court pointed out that where "several persons occupy the premises in common, sharing common living quarters but having separate bedrooms, the courts have held that a single warrant describing the entire premises is valid and justifies the search of the entire premises." Likewise, in *Newby v. State*, a warrant to search "for the person of defendant and the premises known as 2059 East Drive, Decatur, DeKalb County, Georgia" was held sufficiently definite where the warrant also provided that it was "requested for the above residence where [the defendant] rents a room."

In a town or small city, it may be sufficient to describe a building or home as the residence of a named person on a particular street in a specified county. However, it has been said that if "the name of the owner or occupant is not given, the description of the premises must be exact." Where a house was incorrectly described as being two-storied when it actually was one-storied but otherwise properly designated, the description was held to be sufficient since the officer could locate the building with "reasonable certainty." However, the description of the place to be searched as a named person's house trailer of a certain color located approximately one and one-half miles east of the intersection of two named roads "to a drive turning north to trailer park, said trailer being last on left in pines with a white station wagon sitting in yard" was found to be insufficient where no city or county was alleged. But in *Mosier v. State*, an affidavit and search warrant were headed "GEORGIA, GWINNETT COUNTY" and described the place to be searched as "6529 Norcross–Tucker Road." The defendant contended that the description was inadequate since the description did not name a county. The court took judicial notice that "Tucker, Georgia" is not an incorporated city, as contended by the defendant, but is merely a community encompassing portions of DeKalb and Gwinnett counties and concluded that the heading was sufficient to enable the officer "to ascertain with reasonable certainty" the place to be searched. See section 4-16 et seq., infra, on execution of search warrants.

A search warrant authorizing the seizure of records may or may not also authorize the seizure of a personal computer which may contain such records. In Grant v. State, the court held that if the warrant did not specify a computer or computer disks as items to be seized, those items could not be seized regardless of whether other permitted items could be found on the computer or computer disks. The court found no legal support for the trial court's decision that practical considerations and time constraints justified the overly extensive search. However, cases in other jurisdictions have held that computers may be seized where a warrant authorizes the seizure of records of certain types of crimes, such as drug-dealing, even though the police have no idea what is actually contained on the computers.

A search warrant for a car need not state the location of the vehicle if the description is sufficiently detailed. A warrant describing the person and place as "John Doe #Blue" and "on or about his person or auto (or truck) in the vicinity of Magnolia and Sunset, vehicle being either a green pickup truck or a blue and white Ford" was held sufficient since the affidavit contained a physical description of the individual.

The person or persons to be searched must also be described with particularity. This may be done by using the person's name or by describing him in some other manner. A warrant which states an alias as the name of a person is not invalid if in fact the individual is using the alias. However, a "John Doe" warrant which contains no description of the person to enable an officer to locate the person with reasonable certainty is void. A search warrant for a specified location and "all persons on the premises" is a general warrant as to a commercial customer in the place at the time of the search.

There is some older authority which holds that if a warrant provides for the search of "any other person on said premises who reasonably might be involved in the commission of the aforesaid violation of the laws of Georgia," this is regarded as sufficient particularity to justify the search of those persons present when the warrant is executed. But the addition of such words in a search warrant does not broaden the authority of an officer to search persons coming to the premises during the search or afterwards beyond the limited terms of O.C.G.A. § 17–5–28, which provides that an officer executing a warrant "may reasonably detain or search any person in the place at the time: (a) To protect himself from attack, or (b) To prevent the disposal or concealment of any instruments, articles or things particularly described in the warrant."

Generally, see 2 LaFave, *Search and Seizure* 72, § 4.5 (West 1978). See section 4-21, infra, on execution of a search warrant. See Annotation, "Search warrant: sufficiency of description of apartment or room to be searched in multiple-occupancy structure," 11 A. L. R. 3d 1330 (1967).

§ 4-13 Probable cause required for issuance of search warrant—reason for searching place and person

Not only must the place or person be particularly described, but the affidavit must contain sufficient facts to show the magistrate that there is probable cause for believing the object sought is located at the place described. However it has been held that "[a]n officer's inference that items sought will be at the place to be searched requires no more than 'a fair presumption' to be reasonable." It has been held that if a reliable informer has recently observed narcotics in the described premises, a finding of probable cause is justified without alleging facts to demonstrate that the informer knew the substance was a narcotic. However, in *State v. Law*, the court held that an affidavit for a search warrant "is not insufficient merely because it fails to show how the informant knew that the substance he saw was a narcotic." Nevertheless, it has been held that if stolen goods are seen on the premises, the informer must state sufficient facts to show how he knew the objects were stolen. An affidavit setting out general suspicious circumstances is insufficient. For example, observation of premises for several weeks, seeing known drug users and pushers there, seeing as many as 15 cars at the home at one time and general information that users and pushers hang around the house, do not add up to probable cause.

Frequently, officers may have probable cause to believe that a named person committed a burglary or possesses contraband. Without any additional facts, the cases are in conflict as to whether or not there is probable cause to believe that stolen goods or narcotics are in that individual's home.

Similar issues arise when the object of a search is a personal computer. Due to the ease with which files and data may be deleted over time, establishing probable cause to search these devices may be problematic. However, law enforcement officials now have various forensic tools which enable them to extrapolate data even long after deletion. In Buckley v. State, the court held that because the hard drive on the defendants computer was not perishable, previously obtained information that there were pornographic images on the computer was not stale. Thus, there was probable cause to search the computer.

In *McClain v. State,* the court pointed out that "[a]n officer's inference that items sought will be at the place to be searched requires no more than 'a fair presumption' to be reasonable."

It has been held that a well-defined path from the defendant's premises to a neighbor's property where marijuana was grown justifies issuing a search warrant for the defendant's home.

See section 4-11, supra, on timeliness of information.

§ 4-14 Probable cause required for issuance of search warrant—Person or thing to be seized

The warrant clause of the Fourth Amendment provides in pertinent part that "no Warrants shall issue, but upon probable cause, . . . particularly describing the place to be searched, and the persons or things to be seized." Further defining "persons or things," the Georgia Legislature established that a search warrant may be issued for the following: (1) any things or papers which are designed or intended for use, or have been used, in connection with a crime; (2) any person who has been kidnapped or any human fetus or corpse; (3) stolen or embezzled property; (4) anything which it is unlawful to possess; and (5) anything which is tangible evidence of the commission of a crime except private papers. However, "private papers" which are the instrumentalities of a crime may be seized even though not listed in a search warrant. Deposit slips and checks have been held not to be private papers.

In *Sanford v. Texas,* Justice Stewart expressed the unanimous view of the Supreme Court in holding that under the federal Constitution, the need to particularly describe the "things to be seized" is "accorded the most scrupulous exactitude when the 'things' are books and the basis for their seizure is the ideas they contain." However, in *Hunt v. State,* the Georgia Court of Appeals concluded that under the Georgia Constitution the requirements of *Sanford* for "scrupulous exactitude" applied to *all* search warrants.

The affidavit in support of a search warrant must describe with particularity the person or thing to be seized. In *United States v. Cook,* it was explained that "[a] general order to explore and rummage through a person's belongings is not permitted. The warrant must enable the searcher to reasonably ascertain and identify the things which are authorized to be seized. . . . Circumstances often make an exact description of the property impossible and in those cases the judicial officer issuing the warrant must weigh the practical necessities of law enforcement against the likelihood of a violation of the personal rights of the one whose premises and possessions are to be searched."

"The use of a generic term or a general description in a warrant, however, is acceptable to the judicial officer issuing the warrant only when a more specific description of the things to be seized is unavailable. Thus, in *United States v. Cortellesso,* the First Circuit upheld a warrant issued to search for and seize stolen clothing when the 'labels had been removed from the Pierre Cardin suits so that a more precise description would not have assisted the [searcher] and, that with respect to other stolen items, only a generic description was known.' Failure to employ the specificity available will invalidate a general description in a warrant." In *United States v. Bright*, the Fifth Circuit held that if the police had possessed a complete list of serial numbers of currency being sought, it would have been necessary to give them in the warrant description because "generic classifications in a warrant are acceptable only when a more precise description is not possible."

A description of "one statue of a Cobra Snake and other items that are fruits of the crime of burglary" is too general except as to the cobra statue. However, an affidavit which describes the things to be seized as "[f]ruits of the crime of the theft of a shipment of assorted shipment of clothing; traveral [sic] sport coats, suits, dresses, swimware [sic], handbags, taken 21 July, 1972, Tucker, Ga." has been held sufficient. In describing a pistol, it is not necessary to set out the exact caliber.

In *Lo-Ji Sales, Inc. v. New York*, the Court held that an open-ended search warrant which authorized the seizure of two films judicially determined to be obscene and the seizure of other items deemed to be obscene was a general warrant and invalid even when the magistrate went along to determine what articles were deemed to be obscene. See section 4-23, infra, on seizure of obscene material. Likewise, in *Dobbins v. State*, the Georgia Supreme Court concluded that the warrant which described the articles sought as "certain property and/or materials of a pornographic nature, to-wit, movies, pictures, and magazines which are contrary to the laws of Georgia" was a general warrant in violation of the Fourth Amendment. The *Dobbins* case concluded that the "warrant left the determination of what items were likely to be 'of a pornographic nature' entirely to the discretion of the officers executing the warrant."

However, in the child molestation case of *Cooper v. State,* the court concluded that a search warrant was valid which directed the seizure of "[a]ny video tape showing males/females involved in sexual intercourse or any sexual act" and "[a]ny magazine that shows nude males/females posing/involved in any sexual act . . ." used in the furtherance of the criminal act charged.

If a search warrant is general in nature, but also particularly describes certain articles to be seized, a motion to suppress based on the general nature of the warrant is valid only as to articles seized which were not particularly described. In other words, the valid portion of the search warrant should be severed from the invalid portion and the seizure pursuant to the valid portion should be sustained by the court at a suppression hearing.

See Annotation, "Sufficiency of Description of Business Records Under Fourth Amendment Requirement of Particularity in Federal Warrant Authorizing Search and Seizure," 53 A. L. R. Fed. 679 (1981). See also section 4-21, infra, on detention and search of person, and section 4-6, supra, on the necessity of having a neutral and detached magistrate.

§ 4-15 Issuance of search warrant

After the magistrate has considered affidavits, written complaints and/or sworn testimony, he must then make an independent determination of whether or not probable cause exists for the issuance of a search warrant. If the magistrate concludes probable cause exists then he should issue a search warrant. The magistrate has no right to issue a warrant to search a place not mentioned in the affidavit. When facts essential to a proper description of the place to be searched are omitted, this deficiency may not be supplied by the knowledge of the officers attempting to execute the warrant. The Georgia Code, surprisingly, does not contain a form for a search warrant, although certain requirements are set out.

The warrant should state the time and date of issuance. However, if the time of the issuance is not mentioned but it is shown that the warrant was issued prior to the search and seizure, the omission will be regarded only as an irregularity and will not void the warrant. The warrant should also command the search of the place described and the seizure of items enumerated.

A search warrant is not invalid where it is captioned "Superior Court of Hall County, Georgia," but is signed by a magistrate. "[T]he change in name of any court previously known as a police court, recorders court, mayors court, etc. 'shall not affect the validity of any action or prosecution.' "

The magistrate is charged with the duty of keeping a docket record of all warrants issued by him. The warrants shall be executed in duplicate and be directed to all peace officers in the state.

It now appears that a search warrant may be amended after it is issued. If, in such a situation, it were possible to amend the warrant, it would seem that it could only be done by the magistrate issuing it, and then only in conformity with the verified evidence on which the warrant was based. However, in *Green v. State,* the Georgia Supreme Court held that "an amendment to a search warrant may be authorized by a second judicial officer upon a proper showing of probable cause." In *State v. Sanders,* the court held that where an officer was about to execute a search warrant, but found the defendant to be registered in a different hotel room from the one mentioned in the search warrant, he could call the magistrate on the telephone and get the magistrate's consent to change the room number, make the change in the search warrant and search the room in which the defendant was registered. In *Oliver v. State,* a search warrant was issued to search "the residence . . . located at 506 Lamar St." The executing officer discovered that the house number was not correct. The next day he returned to the magistrate and orally requested that the number be changed from 506 to 206 on the warrant. Apparently, the number was changed before the search was conducted. The court concluded that the warrant was valid.

§ 4-16 Execution of search warrant—General

"Search warrants are not directed at persons; they authorize the search of 'places' and the seizure of 'things,' and as a constitutional matter they need not even name the person from whom the things will be seized." Thus, a warrant which allows the search of a person and his home does not permit the search of his person at his place of employment.

By statute, a search warrant must be executed within 10 days from the time of its issuance, and any warrant not executed within 10 days will be void. The warrant may be executed at any reasonable time within the 10–day period. When it is executed, the duplicate copy shall be left with the person from whom any articles are seized. It has been held that an officer may make a valid search after exhibiting to the defendant a photocopy of a search warrant rather than the original. Indeed, provided the officer executing the warrant properly informs the resident of the premises sought to be searched of the warrant's existence and if the search does not exceed the scope of the search authorized, the warrant need not be in the physical possession of the officer conducting the search provided it was issued based upon probable cause prior to the commencement of the search.

When necessary, reasonable force may be used to obtain entrance in order to execute a search warrant. The Georgia Code requires that a good-faith attempt be made to give verbal notice of the authority and purpose of the officers before force is used, and in the absence of such notice there is generally no right to enter a place to be searched. However, it has been held that the failure to give advance notice may be excused if such procedure would increase the officers' peril or lead to the destruction of evidence. See Annotation, "Sufficiency of showing of reasonable belief of danger to officers or others excusing compliance with 'knock and announce' requirement—state criminal cases," 17 A. L. R. 4th 301 (1982).

The same code section provides that after proper notice, or an attempt in good faith to give such notice, "necessary and reasonable force may be used to effect an entry."

§ 4-17 Who may search?

An officer has a right to apply for a search warrant. An officer having knowledge of exigent circumstances or a search warrant may conduct a search. Officers arriving after the original entry may take part in the search; however, "the later officials must confine their intrusion to the scope of the original invasion unless a warrant or one of the exceptions to the warrant requirement justifies a more thorough or wide ranging search."

§ 4-18 Execution of search warrant—Knock and announce

In the 1995 United States Supreme Court case of *Wilson v. Arkansas,* the Court unanimously held the "common-law 'knock-and-announce' principle forms a part of the reasonableness inquiry under the Fourth Amendment" in a search of a home. However, the Court stated that this was not a "rigid rule" and gave examples when the rule would be excused: (1) cases involving the safety of the officer, (2) cases where a felon has escaped and "retreats to his dwelling," and (3) cases where there is a risk of the destruction of evidence if advance notice is given. Then the Court pointed out that it "need not attempt a comprehensive catalog of the relevant countervailing factors here. For now, we leave to the lower courts the task of determining the circumstances under which an unannounced entry is reasonable under the Fourth Amendment."

In *Richards v. Wisconsin,* the United States Supreme Court rejected the blanket exception to the knock-and-announce requirement for felony drug investigations. The court recognized that even though threats of violence and the possibility of destruction of evidence are frequently present in felony drug investigations, these facts do not dispense with the need for a case-by-case evaluation of the manner in which the search is executed. A "no-knock" entry will be justified if the police have a reasonable suspicion that under the circumstances it would be dangerous, futile or it would inhibit a criminal investigation, such as allowing the destruction of evidence, to knock and announce their presence. "This standard . . . strikes the appropriate balance between the legitimate law enforcement concerns . . . and the individual privacy interests affected by no-knock entries."

In *United States v. Jones,* the court affirmed the trial judge in denying a motion to suppress where there had been a "wait" of 15 to 20 seconds between the "knock and announcement" and the time the officers entered an apartment of a suspected drug trafficker, over an objection of the defendant that he was not given time to respond. Similarly, in *United States v. Banks,* the United States Supreme Court held that it was reasonable for the officers to suspect imminent loss of evidence in a drug trafficking case after 15 to 20 seconds without a response based on the facts known to the officers at that time. In *United States v. Ramirez,* the Supreme Court held that the Fourth Amendment does not require "officers to [have] a higher standard . . . when a 'no-knock' entry results in the destruction of property" than when no property is damaged.

One Georgia case has specifically approved the issuance of a search warrant containing a "no-knock" provision where the facts set out in the affidavit demonstrated the potential of danger to the officer and destruction of evidence. Even without a "no-knock" provision in a search warrant, where officers knock, identify themselves, and receive no response, after a reasonable time they may use reasonable force to gain entrance. In *Swan v. State,* the Court of Appeals approved as reasonable a three to five second interval between the knock/announcement and the entry into the home. The Court found that the interval was sufficient in light of explicit judicial recognition that firearms are common to the drug trade. In Georgia it seems that even if there is no "no-knock" provision and even if the officers did not "knock and announce," the execution of a search warrant is still not illegal if exigent circumstances are found to exist, such as danger to the officers or destruction of evidence. In *Adams v. State,* the court held that even where a "no-knock" provision was erroneously included by the magistrate, this did not invalidate a search where the officers entered in a good faith belief that they were so authorized because of the peril created by the presence of a dangerous dog.

Violation of the knock-and-announce requirement does not necessitate application of the exclusionary rule. In *Hudson v. Michigan* the Supreme Court declined to suppress evidence obtained following a failure to knock-and-announce where the police had the ability to execute a previously obtained search warrant. The court went on to explain in dicta that, even if the failure to knock-and-announce is the "but-for" cause of discovery of the evidence sought to be excluded, such evidence may still be admitted where the causation is attenuated or where the deterrence benefits of suppression are outweighed by "substantial social costs." Attenuation occurs when the causal connection is remote, or when, "given a direct causal connection, the interest protected by the constitutional guarantee that has been violated would not be served by suppression of the evidence obtained." Because the knock-and-announce rule does not protect "one's interest in preventing the government from seeing or taking evidence described in a warrant," the *Hudson* court found that the presence of "but-for" causation would not have affected its ruling. See Annotation, "What constitutes compliance with knock-and-announce rule in search of private premises—state cases," 85 A. L. R. 5th 1 (2001) and 70 A. L. R. 3d 217 (1976).

§ 4-19 Execution of search warrant—Area to be searched—Curtilage

Officers may search the premises which are located at the place described in the search warrant. The right to search also includes the curtilage around a home. The right to search the curtilage of a dwelling includes the right to search "the yards and grounds of a particular address, its gardens, barns [and] buildings," as well as vehicles within the curtilage, but it does not include the right to search beyond the property lines of the dwelling specified in the warrant. In *Albert v. State,* the court referred to a service station as having a curtilage and approved of a search of a car at the station which was owned by a third person since the vehicle was deemed to be connected with the premises. But in *State v. Crank,* the court held that a search warrant for the defendant's home and vehicles located there did not authorize the following of the defendant's car for miles, then stopping and searching it. See section 4-2, supra, and section 4-42, infra.

In *Barton v. State,* the Georgia Court of Appeals stated that the word "premises" in a search warrant authorized the search of the home and a shed about 20 feet behind the house. The court stated that "premises" refers to the "entire living area used by its occupant. Living area may be otherwise expressed as the 'curtilage.' The word 'curtilage' includes yards and grounds of a particular address together with the gardens, barn and buildings thereon. . . . The principle of curtilage comes to us from the common law and traditionally has included outbuildings, which may be searched as part of the 'premises' though not specifically described so long as permission has been obtained to search the 'premises.' "

In *Payton v. State,* the court stated, "Whether the place searched is within the curtilage is to be determined from the facts, including its proximity or annexation to the dwelling, its inclusion within the general enclosure surrounding the dwelling, and its use and enjoyment as an adjunct to the domestic economy of the family."

In *Bunn v. State,* the court held that a resident of an apartment has a reasonable expectation of privacy in the curtilage around his apartment. However, in *Bayshore v. State,* the court concluded that the curtilage concept does not apply to a common area such as a parking area for use of occupants of apartments. See sections 4-2, supra, and 4-42, infra, on curtilage.

In *Espinoza v. State,* a search warrant was issued for "251–B Dickson Road." Officers searched both 251–B and 251–A, as well as the "stethoscope shaped" driveway, a part of which served both units. 251–A is on the left side of the duplex. Drugs were found in bushes several feet to the left of the 251–A driveway, outside the stethoscope. The resident of 251–A was indicted. The Georgia Court of Appeals found that the drugs were "not found within the curtilage shared by both apartments." Subsequently, the Georgia Supreme Court "granted the writ of certiorari to consider whether the Court of Appeals properly applied the concept of curtilage." The court explicitly stated, "We disapprove of the term 'common area curtilage,' on which the Court of Appeals relied." The court reversed on the ground that "police officers discovered the evidence within the curtilage of the defendant's apartment for which they did not have a search warrant." The court reasoned that "[t]he resident of 251–B would have no reasonable expectation of privacy in a portion of the yard that was not directly connected to that unit, its driveway, or its side of the duplex." The court affirmed the trial court's grant of a motion to suppress because the resident of 251–A "was the only resident who had a reasonable expectation of privacy in the yard outside the driveway leading to his unit." See Annotation, "Search and Seizure: Reasonable Expectation of Privacy in Driveways," 60 A. L. R. 5th 1 (1998).

Nevertheless, in *Maryland v. Garrison,* a description in a search warrant turned out to be ambiguous when the officers, acting in good faith, learned at the time of the execution of the warrant that there was a distinction between McWebb's apartment for which they had a search warrant, and the third floor of the building in that there were two apartments on that floor. Before the officers realized they were in the defendant's apartment rather than McWebb's apartment, they discovered contraband. The United States Supreme Court held that "a good-faith mistaken belief on the part of officers that the area being searched is within the scope of the warrant that is being executed does not mandate suppression." See section 4-12, supra, on description of place to be searched.

However, it must be remembered that while a search, justified by a search warrant, may not be extended beyond the dwelling described and its curtilage, no warrant is required to search an area beyond the curtilage of a house since no constitutional protection extends "to open fields, orchards, or other lands not an immediate part of the dwelling site." See section 4-42, infra.

§ 4-20 Execution of search warrant—Purpose of search

In 1999, the United States Supreme Court held in *Wilson v. Layne* that it is a Fourth Amendment violation to permit news media to enter a suspect's home to witness a search or arrest when their presence "was not in aid of the execution of the warrant."

In *Massachusetts v. Sheppard,* the United States Supreme Court considered a case in which a magistrate used an improper form when he intended to issue a search warrant. The warrant was issued by a magistrate at his home on Sunday. The officer had taken a form search warrant to the magistrate which was used in drug cases. The officer told the magistrate about this and the judge assured the officer he had made the necessary changes so that a search could be conducted for evidence related to a homicide. Actually, the warrant, as issued, provided only for a search for controlled substances. Without knowledge of the actual contents of the warrant, the officer searched and found evidence of the homicide. The court held that the exclusionary rule did not apply where the "officers reasonably believed that the search they conducted was authorized by a valid warrant." The court noted that the purpose of the exclusionary rule is to deter police misconduct. Because the defect of this warrant was caused by the judge's error, excluding the results of the search would not serve the goal of the exception. But see section 2-26, supra.

In general terms, an officer may search anywhere within the permissible area in which the object or objects of the search may be located, but not in an area in which the object of the search could not be located. Thus, an officer has no right to search desk drawers in search of a stolen television.

While officers may search in every place in which the object of the search warrant may be located, such officers must be careful to avoid unnecessary damage to the premises and personal property located therein.

In *Bradley v. State,* the court held that officers were entitled to search a camera bag of a resident of a house being searched even though the defendant was not named in the search warrant.

After a search of the designated area, an officer may apply for and obtain a second search warrant if probable cause is shown.

Generally, see section 4-14, supra, on person or thing to be seized and section 4-57, infra, on second search. See section 2-26, supra, on the application of the exclusionary rule where the officer acts in good faith pursuant to a warrant.

§ 4-21 Execution of search warrant—Detention and search of person present

O.C.G.A. § 17–5–28 provides that an officer in the execution of a search warrant may reasonably detain or search any person in the place at the time (a) to protect himself from attack or (b) to prevent the disposal or concealment of any instruments, articles, or things particularly described in the warrant. Officers may not broaden their power to search persons beyond the provisions of this Code section.

This Code section has been said to describe the maximum extent, consistent with the Constitution, to which officers may go in seizing persons not described in the search warrant. In *State v. Holmes,* the court pointed out that, in connection with the first statutory requirement, "the officer must be able to articulate specific facts that would support a reasonable belief or suspicion that the person to be searched was armed and dangerous."

In *Collins v. State,* the court held that the inclusion "in a search warrant of 'other persons' on the premises being searched" does not automatically convert an otherwise valid warrant into a general warrant. However, a warrant authorizing the search of places and persons for drugs in all automobiles located on a certain premises was found to be a general warrant and unconstitutional.

In *State v. Hawkins,* the court pointed out that in order to search a person under subsection (b) of the statute, "there must be a nexus between what the officers are authorized to search for[,] . . . the nature of the evidence sought, the environment in which the search is authorized, and the person searched." Where there was *probable cause* to believe those coming to a certain residence were carrying lottery tickets, the search of such individuals was held lawful despite the lack of express authorization by the warrant. In the absence of such probable cause, a third party entering premises which are being searched may not himself be searched where he has no opportunity to conceal any of the items described in the search warrant. In *State v. Anderson,* the court held that in the absence of "independent probable cause," a person present at the time of the search but not named in the warrant may be searched only (1) to protect the officer from attack or (2) to prevent disposal or concealment of contraband described in the warrant.

Searches of persons not named in a search warrant but found on the premises to be searched are illegal without an independent justification for a private search. If an officer has an articulable reasonable suspicion to think that a person on the premises is armed, he has a right to "pat-down" the person for weapons. In *McGugan v. State,* officers had obtained a search warrant to search a named individual and his residence for evidence relating to the sale of cocaine. A deputy remained outside to "secure the scene." The deputy saw the defendant drive by and then back into the driveway. The deputy approached the defendant's vehicle, identified himself, informed the defendant that a search was in progress and asked the defendant to step out of his vehicle. The defendant became nervous, looked around and did not get out. The deputy opened the door of the defendant's car and instructed the defendant for the third time to step outside. The defendant complied, but tried to pull away. The deputy frisked the defendant for weapons. The appellate court affirmed the trial court's finding that the frisk was justified by the officer's reasonable belief that the frisk was necessary to protect himself.

If an officer has probable cause to think that a person who is present is attempting to conceal the substance described in the warrant, he may arrest the person and have him empty his pockets. In *Travis v. State,* the court held that the defendant's presence at the time the search warrant for drugs was executed, coupled with his flight, provided probable cause to believe he had possession of contraband. Hence, his arrest was valid and a search conducted incident to the arrest was valid. On searches of persons present who are in some way described in the search warrant, see section 4-12, supra.

In *Ybarra v. Illinois,* the United States Supreme Court held that, where an officer is executing a warrant for the search of a bar and a certain named individual for narcotics and related items, a weapon frisk or a pat-down of Ybarra was not justified where the officer had no reasonable belief that he was armed and dangerous. The court also pointed out that a *Terry* frisk does not permit a search for anything other than weapons. In retrospect the Court said the search "was invalid because the police had no reason to believe . . . [Ybarra] had any special connection with the premises, and the police had no other basis for suspecting that he was armed or in possession of contraband."

In *State v. Varner,* the court affirmed the trial court in suppressing cocaine found in the defendant's pocket. When the search warrant was executed the defendant was present, but there was no evidence that he lived in the house. The officers handcuffed the people present. The officer asked the defendant if he had any drugs; he did not respond and simply looked at the ground. The officer asked the defendant for consent to search him; defendant again looked down and said nothing. "When the officer patted [the] defendant down, he felt what he stated was not a weapon but what he believed to be contraband in [the] defendant's front pocket." The agent reached into the defendant's pocket and retrieved a baggie containing what appeared to be crack cocaine. The officer could not articulate particular facts from which it would be reasonable to infer that the defendant was armed and dangerous.

However, in *Michigan v. Summers,* the United States Supreme Court considered an incident involving the execution of a warrant to search a house for narcotics. As the officers approached the house they met the defendant, who was leaving. They requested his assistance in gaining entrance to the house and then detained him until they had searched the premises. After learning that the defendant owned the house and after having discovered narcotics in the house, the defendant was arrested and searched. In his coat pocket heroin was found. The court said that if there is probable cause to search a citizen's residence for contraband "it is constitutionally reasonable to require that citizen to remain while officers of the law execute a valid warrant to search his home." In the 2001 case of *Illinois v. McArthur,* the United States Supreme Court held that where officers had probable cause to believe that the defendant had hidden contraband in his home, they could prevent the defendant from entering his home unaccompanied by an officer for about two hours while officers obtained a search warrant. However, in *State v. Mallard,* the Georgia Court of Appeals affirmed the trial court in granting a motion to suppress where the defendant was found to have possession of marijuana when he was stopped by an officer shortly after leaving a residence on which a warrant to search the house for marijuana was about to be executed. The officer stopped the defendant in order to determine if the owner of the house was in the car, and, after quickly determining that the owner of the house was not present and checking the defendant's driver's license, the officer asked the defendant if he had any marijuana. The defendant produced a baggy of marijuana. The officer had no information implicating the defendant of wrongdoing.

In *State v. Crank,* however, the Georgia Court of Appeals intimated that *Summers* may not justify following a defendant in a car for miles and then stopping him and forcing him to return to his house.

A person's suitcase or purse which he carries has been held to be included in his personal immunity from search so long as it is evident that it belongs to the owner. In *Hayes v. State,* police officers obtained a warrant to search "the person of . . . and the premises known as: the residence of Mark, being [a particularly described apartment]" for marijuana. The officers entered the apartment and found the defendant sleeping on the couch.

The defendant's suitcase was next to the couch. His name, "Daniel Hayes," was on the outside of the suitcase and the officer testified that immediately upon opening it he found an airline ticket issued in the defendant's name. The officer continued to search the suitcase and found a quantity of illegal drugs. The Georgia Court of Appeals held that because the officer had notice that the defendant was not the person specified in the warrant, and there was no independent justification for his arrest and subsequent search of his suitcase, the trial judge should have granted the defendant's motion to suppress. The same rule applies to a purse of a visitor which is near the visitor and evidently is owned by her. However, if a woman is in a house which is searched pursuant to a search warrant, and her pocketbook is on a bed in another room, it has been held that her purse may be searched even when there is no right to search her person. However, an officer's "investigation based on other similar and related incidents which, when studied as parts of a scheme or design, would lead the reasonable mind to light upon the particular suspect, comprises good probable cause."

In *Wright v. State,* the court pointed out that when there is no notice of ownership of personal property, "the police are entitled to assume that all objects within the premises [are] lawfully subject to [a] search" as a part of the premises to be searched under a warrant. "Whether the police . . . [knew or should have known] that an object belonged to a visitor must be determined by the trial court on the facts of each case; and the trial court's determination will be upheld if there is any evidence to support it . . . ."

See Annotation, "Sufficiency of description in warrant of person to be searched," 43 A. L. R. 5th 1 (1996). See section 4-7 et seq., supra, on probable cause to issue a search warrant for a person or thing to be seized. See sections 4-26 and 4-27, infra, on searches incident to a lawful arrest. Also see sections 4-22 and 4-27, infra, on protective sweeps. In addition, see section 4-22, infra, on search of personal items in premises searched. See Annotation, "Propriety of Search of Nonoccupant Visitor's Belongings Pursuant to Warrant Issued for Another's Premises," 51 A. L. R. 5th 375 (1997).

§ 4-22 Execution of search warrant—Property which may be seized—General

Generally, the Fourth Amendment permits law enforcement officers executing a search warrant to seize only those persons or items *"particularly"* described in the warrant. The fact that the officers make the decision as to what objects are listed in the warrant, and therefore subject to seizure, does not alone invalidate the warrant. In *Reaves v. State,* the court observed that while "a warrant cannot leave the determination of what articles fall within its description and are to be seized entirely to the judgment and opinion of the officer executing the warrant, the degree of specificity in the description is flexible and will vary with the circumstances involved." Thus, where the warrant identifies specified items of potential evidence, "residual clauses" such as "other items related to the crime of murder" or "evidence of child molestation and sexual exploitation of children" have been deemed sufficient to pass muster under the Fourth Amendment. However, in *Groh v. Ramirez,* the Supreme Court held that a warrant was facially invalid for "provid[ing] no description of the type of evidence sought," even though the application for the warrant adequately described the things to be seized. The court declined to allow the description contained in the application to be incorporated by reference into the actual warrant because the officer failed to leave a copy of the application at the premises to be searched. The court concluded that the search was unreasonable because the person whose premises were the subject of the search would have no way of ascertaining the proper subject and scope of the warrant. In *Battle v. State*, the Georgia Court of Appeals adopted *Groh.* The court noted that the "apparently widespread custom of preparing warrants which describe the place to be searched only by reference to the probable cause affidavit is not the better practice and should not be encouraged by judges who approve search warrants." The court concluded that a warrant which refers to another documents, e.g., the application, for a description of the premises to be searched and the things to be seized is invalid unless the other document is delivered and left at the subject premises.

Although the Fourth Amendment prevents officers from entering people's homes to conduct exploratory searches for evidence, both the search incident to a lawful arrest and plain view doctrines are used to justify seizure of property not listed in the search warrant if the discovery "resulted from a bona fide search for the items named in the warrant." Thus, an officer conducting a lawful search is not prevented "from seizing tangible evidence of the commission of a crime" if he has probable cause to believe it is such, despite the fact that it was not listed on the warrant.

If in the course of the execution of a search warrant, an officer obtains probable cause to arrest an individual found in the premises searched, the officer as an incident to the lawful arrest may search the individual and the area within his reach, lunge, or grab, and articles found are admissible not pursuant to the search warrant but pursuant to a search incident to a lawful arrest. Once a valid search warrant gets an officer into premises which he has a right to search, he does not have to close his eyes to obvious contraband which he sees in plain view while validly executing a search warrant for other articles.

From a federal constitutional standpoint, subject to some limitations hereinafter set out, and regardless of what objects are named in the search warrant, the following articles are also subject to seizure: (1) contraband, (2) stolen property, and (3) evidence of the commission of a crime.

An officer executing a valid warrant has a right to search any area in which the object sought might be located. However, he has no right to look where the object could not be located. Nevertheless, once the officer knows he has found what the search warrant directs him to seize, the search must stop.

The "plain view" doctrine "may not be used to extend a general exploratory search from one object to another until something incriminating at last emerges." However, when an officer is executing a warrant he may also seize not only what is described in the warrant, but also contraband, stolen property, or evidence of a crime in "plain view." See section § 4-41, infra.

Even when officers have received a consent to search for narcotics, they have no right to rummage through the premises and read through the defendant's papers in search of anything indicating that the defendant was engaged in illegal activity.

However, it has been held that a warrant sufficiently identifies items of a specific crime where a more precise description was not possible under the circumstances. In *United States v. Ladd*, the court upheld a warrant to seize all property relating to "smuggling, packing, distribution, and use of controlled substances."

In a case where a search warrant is issued to search a specified automobile for "tools and instrumentalities of the crime of burglary," the officers were found to be authorized in seizing and searching a small black leather bag found strapped under the hood of the car. In *Furfano v. State*, a search warrant was issued authorizing the search of a car for a "handgun, projectiles, blood, fingerprints, [and] other evidence pertaining to the crime of aggravated assault." A 35–millimeter film canister was among the items seized. The officer said it could have contained bullets or film which could have contained fingerprints. The court affirmed the denial of the motion to suppress.

In *Felker v. State,* a search warrant was issued in a rape case for hair and fibers; however, the court approved the seizure of lewd drawings.

In *Hale v. State,* the warrant authorized the seizure of "property or things consisting of evidence which tends to show that a crime has been committed or that a particular person has committed a crime." A two-page, handwritten letter to the defendant's wife was seized and the defendant was charged with forgery. The appellate court upheld the seizure of the letter which was used by a handwriting expert for comparison purposes.

Generally, the illegal seizure of items not authorized by the warrant or the plain view doctrine does not require the suppression of all articles, but only the suppression of those illegally seized. Nevertheless, if the officers' unlawful seizure of other materials led to the discovery of other evidence, this derivative evidence is not admissible. See section § 2-25, supra, on "fruits of the poisonous tree."

In *Lockhart v. State,* the Georgia Court of Appeals considered a case in which the officer alleged that an informer reported that the defendant was selling untax-paid whiskey and marijuana. The warrant obtained provided only for a search for untax-paid whiskey. When the officers went to execute the warrant, they took a "narcotics dog." No whiskey was found but marijuana was located by the dog. The appellate court reversed the trial judge's denial of the motion to suppress for three reasons: (1) the warrant did not particularly describe the thing to be seized; (2) the execution of a search "warrant may not exceed in scope the particular article or things to be seized"; and (3) in order "for the 'plain view' exception to the warrant requirement to be invoked, the sighting of the contraband not specified in the warrant must have been 'inadvertent.' "See section 4-2, supra, on curtilage.

In *United States v. Fitzgerald,* the court held a seizure of a pistol valid under the plain view doctrine even though some portions of the warrant did not sufficiently describe some of the items to be seized. The court said that it recognized that "police might be tempted to frame warrants in general terms, adding a few specific clauses in the hope that under the protection of those clauses they could engage in a general rummaging . . . and then contend that any incriminating evidence they recovered was found in plain view. . . . We believe, however, that careful administration of the rule will afford full protection to individual rights. First, magistrates must exercise vigilance to detect pretext and bad faith on the part of law enforcement officials. Second, courts should rigorously apply the exclusionary rule to evidence seized pursuant to the invalid portions of the warrant. Third, items not described in the sufficiently particular portions of the warrant will not be admissible unless it appears that (a) the police found the item in a place where one would reasonably have expected them to look in the process of searching for the objects described in the sufficiently particular portions of the warrant, (b) the police found the item before they found all the objects described in the sufficiently particular portions of the warrant (that is, before their lawful authority to search expired), and (c) the other requirements of the plain view rule—inadvertent discovery and probable cause to associate the item with criminal activity—are met."

In *Teems v. State,* while officers were executing a search warrant for drugs, the phone rang. It was answered by an officer. The caller asked for Ronald. The defendant was named Ronald, but the defendant was not present at the time. The officer replied that he was "Ronald." The caller said he "needed 300 Rubies and a quarter-of-a-pound of pot." The court held that the conversation was admissible.

Both the Eleventh Circuit and California have concluded that under the good faith exception of searches conducted pursuant to warrants, the particularity requirement for items to be seized has been relaxed to some extent insofar as the exclusionary rule is concerned. See section 2-26, supra, for the general application of the exclusionary rule where an officer conducts a search in good faith pursuant to a warrant.

See section 4-27, infra, on protective sweeps. See section 4-21, supra, on what property may be seized and searched pursuant to a search warrant. See Annotation, "Seizure of Books, Documents or Other Papers Under Search Warrant Not Describing Such Items," 54 A. L. R. 4th 391 (1987). See Annotation, "Validity of Search or Seizure of Computer, Computer Disk or Computer Peripheral Equipment," 84 A. L. R. 5th 1 (2000).

§ 4-23 Execution of search warrant—Property which may be seized—Obscene material

Because of First Amendment protection, it has been held that an officer has no authority to indiscriminately seize what he considers to be obscene publications without a prior judicial determination as to whether the material is, in fact, obscene. However, where an officer knows that a magistrate has determined that a certain issue of a certain magazine is probably obscene, he may seize a copy of the same issue of the same magazine from a store. Also, in *Simpson v. State,* the court held that sexual paraphernalia prohibited by O.C.G.A. § 16–12–80(b), which without doubt are designed primarily for the stimulation of genital organs and which are in plain view, may be confiscated.

In *New York v. P. J. Video, Inc.,* the United States Supreme Court pointed out that there is a distinction between seizing films to destroy them and the seizing of a single copy of a film for the bona fide purpose of preserving it as evidence in a criminal case. The court then held that no greater probable cause showing is necessary in the case of seizure of materials presumptively protected by the First Amendment than in other contexts. In order to establish probable cause to seize a copy of a film it is not necessary for the magistrate to actually view the film. It is sufficient if an officer has seen the film and he adequately describes the obscene nature of the film.

In *N & N, Inc. v. Veline,* the Georgia Supreme Court considered the seizure, pursuant to a warrant, of 42 eight-millimeter projectors. The Georgia case cited *Heller v. New York* and summarized its holding as follows: "[T]he Constitution does not require an adversary hearing on the issue of probable obscenity prior to the issuance of a warrant for the seizure of a film to be used as evidence where the issuing judge has viewed the film and found it to be obscene . . . . 'If such a seizure (for use as evidence) is pursuant to a warrant, issued after a determination of probable cause by a neutral magistrate, and, following the seizure, a prompt judicial determination of the obscenity issue in an adversary proceeding is available at the request of an interested party, the seizure is constitutionally permissible.' "

The *Veline* decision then remanded the case for an adversary hearing since it was obvious that N & N, Inc., wanted such a hearing. "In such a hearing evidence should be presented to allow the trial court to determine: (1) If the seizure was pursuant to a warrant (2) issued after a determination of probable cause (3) by a neutral magistrate; (4) that the projectors were used to show obscene films; and (5) the seizure was for the bona fide purpose to preserve the projectors as evidence, and (6) not to block distribution or exhibition of the films."

See section § 4-38 et seq., infra, on plain view. See section 4-14, supra, on description of obscene materials to be seized. See section 10-2, infra, on forfeitures.

§ 4-24 Return by officer

After the search has been completed, it is the duty of the officer to file a verified list of the items seized with the magistrate named in the warrant, or before a court having jurisdiction. However, failure to swear to the inventory will not invalidate the search and items seized and not listed on an inventory are not rendered inadmissible for this reason. By Georgia statute, on demand, the individual whose person or premises were searched shall be entitled to a copy of the inventory. However, such request should be made to the magistrate issuing the warrant and not to the trial judge or the district attorney.

A search pursuant to a warrant issued by a state court judge of one county for a search in that county is not invalidated by reason of the return being filed in that state court when the defendant is being tried for a felony in another county.

§ 4-25 Warrantless searches—General

There is a constitutional preference for searches pursuant to a warrant rather than without one. Under the Fourth Amendment, "a governmental search and seizure should represent both the efforts of the officer to gather evidence of wrongful acts and the judgment of the magistrate that the collected evidence is sufficient to justify invasion of a citizen's private premises. . . ."

Searches conducted without prior approval by a judge or magistrate are per se unreasonable subject only to a few "specifically established and well-delineated exceptions." In other words, "a search conducted pursuant to a search warrant, regular and proper on its face, is presumed to be valid and the burden is on the person who moves to suppress the items found to show that the search warrant was invalid." Thus, in cases which are close or marginal on the question of probable cause, if there is a warrant, the court should largely find there was probable cause, but if there is no warrant in such a case the court should find that there is an absence of probable cause. The preference for a warrant is also demonstrated by the fact that the exclusionary rule does not apply where officers demonstrate an objective reasonable reliance on a warrant later found not to be supported by probable cause.

In general terms, it has been said that in order to justify a warrantless search two essentials must exist: (1) It must be established that the circumstances at the time of the search were sufficient to require immediate action which necessitated not complying with the restrictions of the warrant requirement of the Fourth Amendment. (2) Also, and of equal importance, the manner and scope of the search which was conducted must be reasonably related to the justification of the search. In *Mincey v. Arizona,* the United States Supreme Court said that "the mere fact that law enforcement may be made more efficient can never by itself justify disregard of the Fourth Amendment. . . . The investigation of crime would always be simplified if warrants were unnecessary. But the Fourth Amendment reflects the views of those who wrote the Bill of Rights that the privacy of a person's home and property may not be totally sacrificed in the name of maximum simplicity in enforcement of the criminal law. . . . For this reason, warrants are generally required to search a person's home or his person unless 'the exigencies of the situation' make the needs of law enforcement so compelling that the warrantless search is objectively reasonable under the Fourth Amendment." In the 1999 case of *Flippo v. West Virginia,* the United States Supreme Court again "rejected the contention that there is a 'murder scene exception' to the Warrant Clause of the Fourth Amendment." However, if officers "reasonably believe a person is in need of immediate aid," they may make a prompt warrantless search of the murder scene.

In *United States v. Ross,* the Supreme Court held that a warrantless search which is authorized by an exception to the warrant requirement "is no broader and no narrower than a magistrate could legitimately authorize by warrant."

Exceptions to the warrant requirement may arise in the situations which are hereinafter listed. Also, the list includes a reference to the material contained in this book which relates to each of these exceptions.

(1) Search incident to a lawful arrest (§§ 4-26 and 4-27, infra).

(2) Valid stop-and-frisk (§ 4-28, infra, Chapter 3, supra).

(3) Where exigent circumstances exist (§ 4-29, infra).

(4) Where an officer is in hot pursuit (§ 4-30, infra).

(5) Where there is valid consent (§§ 4-31 through 4-33, infra).

(6) Airport searches (§ 4-34, infra).

(7) Courthouses and public buildings (§ 4-35, infra).

(8) Places of recreation and entertainment (§ 4-36, infra).

(9) Searches of abandoned property (§ 4-37, infra).

(10) Property in plain view (§ 4-39, infra).

(11) Property in open fields (§ 4-42, infra).

(12) Searches of probationers and inmates (§ 4-43, infra).

(13) Border searches (§ 4-44, infra).

(14) Administrative searches (§ 4-45, infra).

(15) Vehicle searches (§§ 4-46 through 4-55, infra).

The Fourth Amendment does not actually apply to "border searches." Also, some of the other situations are not true exceptions since the interest involved is not actually protected by the Fourth Amendment. Moreover, it has been said that some of the other exceptions to the warrant requirement listed above are actually not "true exceptions" in that the Fourth Amendment only prevents "unreasonable" searches and seizures and the so-called "exceptions," when they apply, are regarded as being reasonable.

§ 4-26 Warrantless searches—Incident to lawful arrest—Person

More than 50 years ago, Justice Cardozo wrote, "The peace officer empowered to arrest must be empowered to disarm. If he may disarm, he may search, lest a weapon be concealed." In *Washington v. Chrisman,* the United States Supreme Court said, "The absence of an affirmative indication that an arrested person might have a weapon available or might attempt to escape does not diminish the arresting officer's authority to maintain custody over the arrested person. . . . Every arrest must be presumed to present a risk of danger to the arresting officer." After an arrest, the officer has a right to remain literally at the defendant's elbow; and if the officer sees contraband while he is with or near the defendant, he may seize it.

In *Preston v. United States,* a unanimous Court held, "Unquestionably, when a person is lawfully arrested, the police have the right, without a search warrant, to make a contemporaneous search of the person of the accused for weapons or for the fruits of or implements used to commit the crime." In *Wade v. State,* the Georgia Court of Appeals stated that the motivation of a search pursuant to an arrest is irrelevant.

A search incident to an arrest will not be valid unless the arrest itself is lawful. In *Brock v. State*, the court held that an officer is not prevented from making an arrest for a traffic violation even though the officer is authorized to simply issue a traffic citation. The arrest may not be made as a pretext for conducting a search, and it will not be validated by what is found in the search. When the validity of an arrest is challenged, the burden is on the state to prove its legality. The arrest must generally precede the search or be substantially contemporaneous with the search. Where a search is incident to an arrest, the search is limited to the defendant and the area within his immediate control. Contraband or other fruits or instrumentalities of a crime may be seized in connection with the search. In *Lopez v. State,* a defendant's cell phone was confiscated at the time of his arrest and later examined for stored phone numbers of co-defendants involved in a drug trafficking scheme. The Court of Appeals did not disturb the trial court's order denying the motion to suppress because it was narrowly tailored to the circumstances of the case.

In the interesting case of *Sprinkles v. State,* the court pointed out that "[f]light after a lawful command to halt constitutes obstruction of an officer" and justifies an arrest for obstruction and the defendant may be searched as an incident of the arrest. However, the command to stop must be lawful. See sections 2-2 and 3-1, supra, on lawful stops.

The United States Supreme Court has held that the right to search incident to a valid arrest is an exception to the warrant requirement of the Fourth Amendment. "This general exception has historically been formulated into two distinct propositions. The first is that a search may be made of the *person* of the arrestee. . . . The second is that a search may be made of the area within the control of the arrestee." The remainder of this section is devoted to what is considered a search of the person.

If there is a valid custodial arrest, the officer may make a full search of the person. The extent of a search incident to a lawful arrest is not limited to a frisk, which has been discussed in Chapter 3, supra. In *Gustafson v. Florida,* the United States Supreme Court held that an officer "was entitled to make a full search" of Gustafson's person, incident to a lawful arrest for driving without a license. The court pointed out that where a defendant is arrested for driving without a license, it is immaterial (1) that the defendant had had no previous encounter with the arresting officer; (2) that only a minor offense was involved; (3) that no police regulations required the officer to take the defendant into custody; (4) that there was no police department policy requiring a full-scale search; and (5) that the officer had no fear of the defendant.

In the Michigan case of *People v. Chapman,* the court held that the right of a misdemeanant to bail immediately upon arrest does not limit the scope of a search incident to the arrest. See section 4-56, infra, on scope of a search.

In the Georgia case of *Baker v. State,* the court held that even though an officer could have only required the driver to surrender her license in lieu of bond or arrest for a minor traffic offense, this does not prevent the officer from taking the driver into custody and conducting an inventory search of her purse. In *Taylor v. State,* the Georgia Court of Appeals held that the search incident to the defendant's arrest was valid even though the officer would not have arrested the defendant for the offense if the defendant had consented to a search. Likewise, in the Texas case of *Williams v. State,* the court held that a search was valid where the defendant was guilty of a parking violation even though the formal arrest did not take place until after the search of the car and the reason for searching the car had little, if anything, to do with the parking violation. In *Williams v. State,* where an officer would not have stopped a vehicle for speeding had the officer not had a suspicion that it was carrying illicit drugs, the stop was, nonetheless, found valid. In *Jones v. State,* the court held "[t]he stop of a vehicle is authorized, and not pretextual, if the officer observed a traffic offense." In *Sanchez v. State,* the court held that when there is actual reason to take a defendant into custody because the officer believed he was violating the Georgia Controlled Substances Act, the arrest is not invalidated even though the initial charge was no proof of insurance and there was probable cause to believe he was guilty of that offense even though as a matter of fact he was not guilty of that offense. In *Whren v. United States,* the United States Supreme Court held that where a driver violated a traffic law, an officer *could stop* the vehicle even if the officer would not have stopped it had it not been for some other reason. In *Brantley v. State,* the Georgia Court of Appeals followed *Whren.* See sections 3-2 and 3-3, supra. See section 3-10, supra, on investigations following traffic stops.

However, under Georgia's seat belt law, absent additional offenses, an officer has no right to search a person or an automobile solely because an occupant of the front seat failed to wear a seat belt.

The defendant may be searched at the place of the arrest, and he may be searched at the jail when officers inventory his property, if this is part of the routine booking procedures. In *United States v. Edwards,* the Court said, "It is also plain that searches and seizures that could be made on the spot at the time of the arrest may legally be conducted later when the accused arrives at the place of detention."

However, any search of clothing or other property of the defendant at the police station should be done promptly, and it has been held that once property has been inventoried and put in storage, there is no right to a further examination of it without a search warrant.

Fingernail scrapings may be taken from an arrestee. There is a right to conduct a careful examination of the defendant's clothing and even to subject his clothing to a laboratory analysis. Although not sustained on appeal, it has also been held that when a suspect is arrested, his hands may be swabbed with cotton for purposes of a neutron activation test to determine the presence of the gunpowder residue.

In *United States v. Ross,* the United States Supreme Court abandoned the constitutional distinction between warrantless searches of "worthy" and "unworthy" containers. The court held that "a traveler who carries a toothbrush and a few articles of clothing in a paper bag or knotted scarf claims an equal right to conceal his possessions from official inspection as the sophisticated executive with the locked attache case. . . ." However, "the protection afforded by the [Fourth] Amendment varies in different settings. . . . A container carried at the time of arrest often may be searched without a warrant and even without specific suspicion concerning its contents."

It seems that if a woman's pocketbook is on a bed in another room, it is not considered a part of her person and it may not be searched as an incident to her lawful arrest. However, if a woman has a pocketbook in her possession at the time of her arrest, it seems that it is subject to a full search. See section 4-48, infra, on search of a vehicle as incident to a valid arrest.

Although a court may order a peace officer to apprehend a person pursuant to O.C.G.A. § 37-7-41(b) and, under certain conditions, take him or her to a drug treatment facility, the officer may not search the person who is the subject of the order. An apprehension is not the equivalent of an arrest which would warrant a search.

See section 4-27, infra, on seizures and searches around a person arrested, and section 4-55, infra, on inventories of automobiles. See section 3–7, infra, on automobile searches following a stop for a traffic violation. See section 4–57, infra, on second search of articles taken from an arrested defendant in an automobile. See section 2–22, supra, on search incident to "booking." See section 4-48, infra, on vehicle searches incident to an arrest. See section 3-2, supra, on investigative stops.

§ 4-27 Warrantless searches—Incident to lawful arrest—Articles and area around person arrested

In *Chimel v. California,* the United States Supreme Court established the validity of and limitations to a search of the area around an arrestee. The court held that officers have the right to search the defendant as well as the area within his "immediate control," or "wingspan," to remove any weapons and prevent the concealment or destruction of evidence. However, *Chimel* does not give arresting officers the authority to walk the defendant through his home so that they can search everywhere within his reach; nor does the case permit police to search "through all the desk drawers or other closed or concealed areas in [the] room itself."

O.C.G.A. § 17–5–1 provides that an officer has a right, incident to a lawful arrest, to search in the "immediate presence" of the person arrested for weapons to prevent the person from escaping, or to discover fruits of the crime or instruments used in commission of the crime for which the arrest is made. No Georgia cases have explicitly compared the meaning of the words "immediate control" in *Chimel* with the "immediate presence" language used in the statute. Presumptively, they mean the same thing.

An arrest cannot be used as a pretext to search a home where the true purpose for entering is to search and not to arrest the defendant who lives there. However, after a lawful arrest, the officer has a right to remain literally at the defendant's elbow; and if the officer sees contraband while he is with or near the defendant, he may seize it.

While there is no right to search an entire house incident to a lawful arrest, officers are authorized to make a "limited protective sweep in conjunction with an in-home arrest when the searching officer possesses a reasonable belief based on specific and articulable facts that the area to be swept harbors an individual posing a danger to those on the arrest scene." Such a sweep "may extend only to a cursory inspection of those spaces where a person may be found." In *Maryland v. Buie,* police officers had arrest warrants for two men. When they entered one defendant's home, they conducted a "protective sweep" and seized a red running suit observed in plain view. The United States Supreme Court upheld the "sweep" as well as the seizure because the defendant was wanted for a robbery in which the assailant wore a red running suit. See sections 4-21 and 4–22, supra, on what property may be seized and searched pursuant to a search warrant. In *Inglett v. State,* the court held "[p]olice officers are authorized to make a protective sweep in conjunction with an in-home arrest when they possess 'articulable facts which, taken together with the rational inferences from those facts, would warrant a reasonably prudent officer in believing that the area to be swept harbors an individual posing a danger to those on the arrest scene.' "

In *Belton v. New York,* the United States Supreme Court dealt with the scope of automobile searches when the occupants are arrested. The court held "when a policeman has made a lawful custodial arrest of the occupant of an automobile, he may, as a contemporaneous incident of that arrest, search the passenger compartment of that automobile." In *Thornton v. United States,* the Supreme Court held that *Belton* still applies "when an officer does not make contact until the person arrested has left the vehicle." However, in *Arizona v. Gant,* the Supreme Court held that *Belton* should not be construed to warrant a search incident to arrest which extends beyond the space within the defendant's immediate control. Even then, a search would only be justified by the arresting officer's reasonable belief that the area might contain a weapon or evidence of the crime for which the defendant was arrested. State and federal cases suggesting otherwise should be reviewed carefully in light of *Gant.* See sections 4-48 and 4–49, infra, on searches of vehicles and containers found therein.

When police search the area within the arrestee's "immediate control" or "immediate presence," they are sometimes allowed to search articles they find therein.

In *Chester v. State,* the court considered the search of a suitcase located in a house apparently owned by the defendant. Officers had a search warrant for the premises, and the suitcase had the defendant's surname on it. The court upheld the search even though the defendant's name did not appear in the warrant. The court pointed out that there is a distinction between the search of a suitcase of a visitor to the premises and the search of a suitcase of the owner of the premises.

In *State v. Browning,* police responded to a complaint of noise in an apartment. When a man opened the door, the officers observed four other persons in the apartment, one of whom was female. The man assured the officers they would keep the noise down and closed the door. As the door closed, the officers smelled marijuana, knocked on the door again, and heard a back door shut. When the officers entered the apartment there were only two men present, drug paraphernalia was in plain sight, and a woman's purse was "open" on the floor. An officer examined the contents of the purse and found marijuana. At trial the officer admitted he was searching the personal effects of a visitor and the judge granted the motion to suppress that evidence. The appellate court affirmed and concluded that the woman had a substantial interest in the privacy of all her possessions and that there was sufficient evidence to find that the purse had not been abandoned.

In *Rawlings v. Kentucky,* the United States Supreme Court denied a motion to suppress evidence discovered pursuant to a search warrant because the defendant did not have a reasonable expectation of privacy in the contents of a woman's purse, even though it was his belongings (illegal drugs) that were seized therein. In *Rawlings,* the defendant and others were kept in a house for about 45 minutes while police obtained a search warrant. The defendant contended that his admission of ownership of the drugs was a result of an illegal detention and that the search of his person was illegal. The court assumed that the detention was unconstitutional, but found that it was sufficiently attenuated from the admission to make the statement of ownership admissible. The search of the defendant's person was valid because it was incident to his arrest.

In *Segura v. United States,* the Court held that an earlier illegal entry into an apartment did not require suppression of evidence seized later pursuant to a valid warrant which was issued on information obtained by police before the illegal entry into the apartment.

See section § 2-25 et seq., supra, on results of illegal arrest. Also see section 4-48, infra, on search of vehicle incident to an arrest and section 4–49, infra, on probable cause to search a motor vehicle. See section 4–57, infra, on a second search of articles taken from an arrested defendant. See section 4-26, supra, on search of a person incident to a lawful arrest. See section 4-55, infra, on conducting an inventory of contents of a vehicle. See section 2–22, supra, on search at police stations.

§ 4-28 Warrantless searches—Valid stop-and-frisk

Stop-and-frisk situations are discussed in Chapter 3, supra.

§ 4-29 Warrantless searches—Exigent circumstances

A warrantless search may be valid in some emergency situations where there is an immediate necessity to search and no opportunity to obtain a warrant. Although "hot pursuit" is a type of emergency or exigent circumstance, it will be discussed separately in the following section. In *People v. Mitchell,* the court held that in order to establish the existence of an emergency situation, the following basic elements must appear: "(1) The police must have reasonable grounds to believe that there is an emergency at hand and an immediate need for their assistance for the protection of life or property. (2) The search must not be primarily motivated by intent to arrest and seize evidence. (3) There must be some reasonable basis, approximating probable cause, to associate the emergency with the area or place to be searched." In 2006, however, *Mitchell* was abrogated by *Brigham City v. Stuart*, wherein the U.S. Supreme Court held that a warrantless entry under exigent circumstances does not run afoul of the Fourth Amendment "as long as the circumstances, viewed *objectively*, justify [the] action." (Emphasis in original).

"Circumstances which have seemed relevant to courts include (1) the degree of urgency involved and the amount of time necessary to obtain a warrant, (2) reasonable belief that the contraband is about to be removed, (3) the possibility of danger to police officers guarding the site of the contraband while a search warrant is sought, (4) information indicating the possessors of the contraband are aware that the police are on their trail, and (5) the ready destructibility of the contraband and the knowledge 'that efforts to dispose of narcotics and to escape are characteristic behavior of persons engaged in the narcotics traffic.' " *United States v. Manning*, 448 F.2d 992, 998–999 (2d Cir.1971); *United States v. Davis,* 461 F.2d at 1031–1032.

In *Welsh v. Wisconsin,* the United States Supreme Court, in considering a warrantless home arrest, pointed out that the seriousness of the crime may be considered in determining whether exigent circumstances exist. The court said, "Our hesitation in finding exigent circumstances . . . is especially appropriate when the underlying offense for which there is probable cause to arrest is relatively minor. Before agents of the government may invade the sanctity of the home, the burden is on the government to demonstrate exigent circumstances that overcome the presumption of unreasonableness that attaches to all warrantless home entries. . . . When the government's interest is only to arrest for a minor offense, that presumption of unreasonableness is difficult to rebut, and the government usually should be allowed to make such arrests only with a warrant issued upon probable cause by a neutral and detached magistrate."

A number of cases have held that if there is probable cause to believe that contraband will be discovered, but would be destroyed unless there is an immediate search, the search may be conducted without a warrant. In *United States v. Rubin,* the Third Circuit held that where government agents have probable cause to believe that contraband is present and, based on surrounding circumstances or the information at hand, the agents have reason to conclude that the evidence will be destroyed or removed before they can secure a search warrant, a warrantless search is justified. The court cautioned that a case by case scrutiny of the circumstances is always necessary. According to *Rubin:*

"The emergency circumstances will vary from case to case, and the inherent necessities of the situation at the time must be scrutinized. Circumstances which have seemed relevant to courts include (1) the degree of urgency involved and the amount of time necessary to obtain a warrant, (2) reasonable belief that the contraband is about to be removed, (3) the possibility of danger to police officers guarding the site of the contraband while a search warrant is sought, (4) information indicating the possessors of the contraband are aware that the police are on their trail, and (5) the ready destructibility of the contraband and the knowledge 'that efforts to dispose of narcotics and to escape are characteristic behavior of persons engaged in the narcotics traffic' " (citations omitted).

In *Herring v. State*, an officer operating on a tip that a certain homeowner had drugs in his possession engaged in a permissible knock-and-talk procedure in order to investigate a report of a crime. Once the door was opened, the offer observed in plain view evidence of drug use. The officer also observed the defendant get up from a sofa and start walking toward the back of the hours. The court found the officer's warrantless entry to be justified by the likelihood that the contraband was in danger of immediate destruction.

Although the Supreme Court, in *Agnello v. United States,* stated that even when probable cause exists that evidence will be found in a certain area, a search for an article in a dwelling is unlawful in the absence of a search warrant, the Court alluded to the legality of a warrantless search where there is an emergency situation necessitating prompt action. If there is probable cause and no exigent circumstances, it may be permissible for officers to seize premises to secure the area while a search warrant is obtained; but generally, "they may not enter a home without a warrant merely because they plan to obtain one subsequently." The United States Supreme Court reversed a conviction resulting from the search of a house for narcotics where the state failed to show any exigent circumstances.

In *State v. Brannan,* the Georgia Court of Appeals said that "[a]lthough we review police actions from the standpoint of a hypothetical 'reasonable' officer, we must measure those actions from the foresight of an officer acting in a quickly developing situation and not from the hindsight of which judges have benefit."

In *Coker v. State,* the Georgia Court of Appeals held that "probable cause to believe that . . . [the defendant] had or was committing an offense standing alone does not authorize a warrantless search of his dwelling." See section 4-27, supra, on impoundment or securing premises pending issuance of a warrant.

In *Wayne v. United States,* then Judge, later Chief Justice Burger, in an opinion on exigent circumstances, stated that: "Breaking into a home by force is not illegal if it is reasonable in the circumstances. . . . [A] warrant is not required to break down a door to enter a burning home to rescue occupants or extinguish a fire, to prevent a shooting or to bring emergency aid to an injured person. The need to protect or preserve life or avoid serious injury is justification for what would be otherwise illegal absent an exigency or emergency. Fires or dead bodies are reported to police by cranks where no fires or bodies are to be found. Acting in response to reports of 'dead bodies,' the police may find the 'bodies' to be common drunks, diabetics in shock, or distressed cardiac patients. But the business of policemen and firemen is *to act,* not to speculate or meditate on whether the report is correct. People could well die in emergencies if police tried to act with the calm deliberation associated with the judicial process. Even the apparently dead often are saved by swift police response. A myriad of circumstances could fall within the terms 'exigent circumstances' . . . e.g., smoke coming out a window or under a door, the sound of gunfire in a house, threats from the inside to shoot through the door at police, reasonable grounds to believe an injured or seriously ill person is being held within."

If an officer reasonably believes there are wounded people in a home, he may enter without a warrant. The police have the right to enter without a warrant if they receive a credible call that an individual is dead in a house. Where officers find a man lying unconscious on a public street, they may search him to learn his identity and to obtain information about his medical history. If narcotics are discovered in the search, they are admissible if the defendant is tried for possession.

In a case where an officer found a vehicle parked at 3 a.m. with its motor running and a man lying on the front seat, the court concluded that the policeman had the right to try to rouse the man, and contraband found in the process was admissible. Likewise, a limited search of the trunk of an auto without a warrant was valid where officers smelled a strong odor of ether coming from the trunk and officers knew of its highly explosive character.

It must be remembered that probable cause does not permit a warrantless intrusion into one's home in the absence of a showing that the exigencies of the situation make such a search imperative. Thus, it has been held that an officer investigating a complaint about a loudly playing stereo in the early morning has no authority to enter an apartment uninvited when the defendant comes to the door in response to his knock.

In *United States v. Place,* the United States Supreme Court said, "Where law enforcement authorities have probable cause to believe that a container holds contraband or evidence of a crime, but have not secured a warrant, the Court has interpreted the Amendment to permit seizure of the property, pending issuance of a warrant to examine its contents, if the *exigencies* of the circumstances demand it or some other recognized exception to the warrant requirement is present. . . . For example, 'objects such as weapons or contraband found in a public place may be seized by the police without a warrant,' . . . because, under these circumstances, the risk of the item's disappearance or use for its intended purpose before a warrant may be obtained outweighs the interest in possession." (Emphasis added.) However, the mere "presence of contraband without more does not give rise to exigent circumstances."

In *Strozier v. State,* an officer saw marijuana plants in pots being watered by the defendant. The defendant was in a fenced yard standing at the corner of his carport. The trial court's determination that there were exigent circumstances was affirmed in view of the mobility of the plants. Conversely, in *Gates v. State,* the court held that exigent circumstances did not exist justifying seizure when a police officer observed marijuana growing on the defendant's property. However, if an occupant "sees" the officer, then the facts may amount to exigent circumstances and will justify an immediate seizure.

On the other hand, because of the mobility of the automobile, exigent circumstances justifying a warrantless search were found where officers received reliable information that a person possessed marijuana in a described automobile at a certain location. In *Meadows v. State*, officers received information describing the automobile defendant was driving and that the defendant was transporting cocaine to Cusseta from Columbus. Forty-five minutes later on the designated highway, an officer stopped Meadows, ordered him out of the car and patted him down for weapons and drugs. The officer removed a bag which appeared to contain cocaine residue. The appellate court affirmed the trial court in denying the motion to suppress the bag obtained in the search.

Likewise, the Georgia Court of Appeals has held that where the defendant was at an airport en route to another state, a search of his luggage was justified due to the exigent circumstance of insufficient time to obtain a warrant.

Where an officer, while executing a valid search warrant, answered a telephone call from the defendant, who mistook him for the resident, and made arrangements to meet the defendant to purchase marijuana, the warrantless arrest of the defendant and warrantless search were justified because the officer did not know in advance where the actual transaction was going to take place.

In *People v. Gardner,* the Illinois Appellate Court held that where an officer during a nighttime routine patrol found the door of a business unlocked, he had a right to enter to check for criminal conduct. In *People v. Cain,* the California Court of Appeals found exigent circumstances to exist when, during the early morning hours, law enforcement officers noticed the lights and television on in an apartment adjacent to the apartment of the victim of a brutal attack. There was no response to the officers' knock and the officers believed another victim might be inside. In upholding the warrantless search, the court pointed out that in such an exigent situation, the question is whether or not there "was . . . [a] threat so imminent and serious [that] a reasonable policeman would believe that a warrantless, emergency entry was necessary to save lives and property."

In a case where a defendant was arrested at a hospital for suspicion of murder following the death of his wife, the search of his home to see if there was any injured person was held reasonable under the circumstances. However, in *Mincey v. Arizona,* the United States Supreme Court pointed out that (1) "the seriousness of the offense under investigation [does not] itself [create] exigent circumstances," and (2) a warrantless search must be "strictly circumscribed by the exigencies which justify its initiation."

Nevertheless, *Mincey* continued to recognize "that the Fourth Amendment does not bar police officers from making warrantless entries and searches when they reasonably believe that a person within is in need of immediate aid. Similarly, when the police come upon the scene of a homicide, they may make a prompt warrantless search of the area to see if there are other victims or if a killer is still on the premises. . . .'The need to protect or preserve life or avoid serious injury is justification for what would be otherwise illegal absent an exigency or emergency.' " One of the cases cited in *Mincey* with approval was *People v. Mitchell.* Note, however, that in the 2006 decision of *Brigham City v. Stuart*, the U.S. Supreme Court abrogated *Mitchell* to the extent that it allows for consideration of an officer's subjective intent in making a warrantless entry of a home potentially occupied by persons in need of emergency assistance. A warrantless entry under such circumstances does not run afoul of the Fourth Amendment "as long as the circumstances, viewed *objectively*, justify [the] action." (Emphasis in original).

In *State v. Peterson,* the court held that "temporary care of minor children left without adult supervision by police requires police to care for the children until responsibility for their care and custody is undertaken by a responsible adult. . . . The absence of responsible adult supervision of children is an exigent circumstance justifying a warrantless entry."

In Burk v. State, the Georgia Court of Appeals adopted the lead taken by several other jurisdictions and held that "a reasonable belief that minors are consuming alcohol in a residence constitutes an exigent circumstance . . . ." The court cited as the basis for its ruling, public safety concerns as well as the likelihood that any evidence tending to show the crime of serving alcohol to minors would likely be destroyed if officers were forced to seek a warrant.

In *Thompson v. Louisiana,* the United States Supreme Court, in a 1984 per curiam opinion, held that a search was unlawful which had been conducted by two members of a homicide unit 35 minutes after officers arrived and found a corpse and an unconscious person who had attempted suicide. The homicide investigators conducted an exploratory search for about two hours. The first officers had already searched the premises for other victims and suspects. There was time to secure a warrant before the search.

Likewise, in *Ortega v. State,* the Wyoming Supreme Court upheld a murder scene check to determine the condition of the victim. In the process they observed blood stains. Although later overruled, the court held that the evanescent character of the blood justified a warrantless seizure.

Nevertheless, in *Overman v. State,* the Georgia Supreme Court held that officers who were called to the defendant's apartment where his former girlfriend had been shot and where the defendant consented to their entering had a right to "seize and secure possible evidence in plain view while investigating the scene." This right was said to include the right to seize a telephone tape recorder from the defendant's bedroom.

In *People v. Greene,* the court held that exigent circumstances existed justifying a warrantless entry where there was a " 'hang-up' call to 911, and the failure of a real person to answer an instant return call placed by the 911 system." Likewise, the 11th Circuit has held that where exigent circumstances demand an immediate response because of the possibility of danger to human life, a limited warrantless intrusion into a home may be justified by officers responding to a 911 call.

Likewise, in *Hatten v. State,* the court approved a murder scene warrantless search of the defendant's home and yard three to six hours after the police first arrived.

See section 4-56, infra, on scope and intensity of a search. See Annotation, "Belief That Burglary is in Progress or Has Been Recently Committed As Exigent Circumstances Justifying Warrantless Search of Premises," 64 A. L. R. 5th 637 (1998).

§ 4-30 Warrantless searches—Officer in hot pursuit

In *Warden v. Hayden,* the United States Supreme Court recognized the hot-pursuit exception to the warrant requirement. This case, which is typical of the hot-pursuit exception, involved a fleeing robber who entered a certain house. The police were informed of the robbery, knocked at the house, were admitted, and searched the entire house. Hayden was found in an upstairs bedroom feigning sleep, and he was arrested. Meanwhile, an officer discovered a shotgun and pistol in the adjoining bathroom, while another policeman found a jacket and trousers of the kind worn by the robber in a washing machine in the basement.

The Supreme Court affirmed the warrantless search, stating that under the exigencies of the situation, the search was imperative. "The Fourth Amendment does not require police officers to delay in the course of an investigation if to do so would gravely endanger their lives or the lives of others." Where speed is essential, a thorough search for persons and weapons is permissible to insure that the police can gain control of all weapons which can be used against them or to effect an escape.

In *Welsh v. Wisconsin,* the United States Supreme Court concluded that there was no "hot pursuit" where "there was no immediate or continuous pursuit of the . . . [defendant] from the scene of a crime."

In Georgia, the hot-pursuit exception was held to be applicable when officers, after a robbery, obtained an automobile license number which was traced to the defendant's wife and immediately proceeded to the defendant's residence where the defendant and the automobile were searched. In *Darby v. State,* the Georgia Court of Appeals recognized that to establish the hot pursuit exception to the warrant requirement, "[t]he critical elements that need to be satisfied . . . are (1) continuity of pursuit, and (2) immediacy of pursuit."

However, in the thought provoking Georgia case of *Hamrick v. State,* the court held that the doctrine of hot pursuit did not justify an arrest of a defendant in his home for a traffic violation (misdemeanor) where the circumstances did not make an immediate arrest necessary. See *Welsh v. Wisconsin,* supra, section 4-29, note 5 and accompanying text.

In the Fifth Circuit case of *United States v. Kreimes,* the court found that the warrantless search of a zippered piece of luggage was justified for the purpose of learning the identity of a person who fled from a truck which was found to be loaded with marijuana.

§ 4-31 Warrantless searches—Valid consent—General

A valid consent to a search eliminates an officer's need to obtain a warrant and the need for probable cause. However, a consent to search is not a consent to seize. Thus, an officer may only seize items which he has probable cause to believe are stolen or embezzled property, contraband, or instrumentalities or fruits of a crime. Likewise, consents have been strictly construed against the state; thus, it has been held that a consent to let an officer determine whether or not a key will fit a car is not a consent to a search of the car. It has been said that a consent to look inside a pick-up truck is not a consent to open a drawstring bag on the front seat. In *United States v. Elliott,* an officer asked the defendant if he could "look through the trunk [of a car] and see what you got in there? I don't want to look through each item." The officer also testified that he told the defendant he just wanted to see how things were packed. The defendant responded by releasing the trunk latch. The court held that this consent did not authorize the officer to conduct a thorough search of the contents of a bag located in the trunk. However, as pointed out in *Caster v. State,* a consent to a thorough search of everything found in a car is not limited "to a 'look inside' or 'in' the car and its contents." Thus, in *Caster* the court affirmed a finding that, because of the consent, an officer noticing a loose back seat was authorized to lift it and observe contraband.

It has been pointed out that "[c]onsent may be as limited as the consenter wishes. . . . The suspect is not required to call a halt when the search has gone beyond the scope of consent given; the burden remains on the [s]tate to show that the scope of the officer's search did not exceed the permission given." However, where a general consent to search is given, its validity should be regarded as continuing until the consent is revoked or otherwise withdrawn. Nonetheless, mere "acquiescence to a claim of lawful authority" will not suffice as consent to extend a *Terry* pat-down into a more intrusive search.

Where two or more officers undertake a warrantless search and one officer discovers contraband without actually knowing that one of the other officers has obtained a valid consent to search, the consent legitimized the search. In *State v. Sutton,* the court held that a valid written consent executed after a prior warrantless entry ratified the prior search.

The burden of proof is on the prosecution to show that the consent was, in fact, freely and voluntarily given. "The proper standard for a trial court's determination of whether there is consent to search is preponderance of the evidence," and it is not necessary for the judge to find beyond a reasonable doubt that consent was given. The same standard applies in determining the voluntariness of a consent to a search as pertains to confessions. Thus, a court looks to the totality of the surrounding circumstances.

In determining the question of voluntariness, the United States Supreme Court has considered such factors as the youth of the accused, his lack of education, failure to be informed of his constitutional rights, length of detention, prolonged nature of questioning, deprivation of food or sleep, and the psychological impact of these things on the accused. In *Schneckloth v. Bustamonte*, the United States Supreme Court held no single factor is controlling. In *Rogers v. State*, the court held that even where a person has been seized, if his "subsequent search was pursuant to a voluntary consent which was not a product of the illegal detention, the taint of that illegal detention would not require suppression of the evidence." In *VonLinsowe v. State*, the court held that where a defendant is being unlawfully detained, if the search was pursuant to a voluntary consent which was not a product of the illegal detention, the illegal detention would not require suppression of the evidence seized. "However, in order to eliminate any taint from an involuntary seizure or arrest, there must be proof both that the consent was voluntary and that it was not the product of the illegal detention. Proof of a voluntary consent alone is not sufficient. The relevant factors include temporal proximity of an illegal seizure and consent, intervening circumstances, and the purpose and flagrancy of the official misconduct."

In *Bowers v. State,* the defendant was stopped for "changing lanes without using a turn signal." There were no other vehicles in the area. After the defendant had been questioned in the cold for about 20 minutes, the defendant "consented" to a search of the car and contraband was found. The trial court denied a motion to suppress which the appellate court reversed. The court pointed out that a turn signal need not be given when the movement can be made with reasonable safety. There was no objective manifestation that the person being stopped was or was "about to be engaged in criminal activity." There was no significant lapse of time or intervening circumstances between the unlawful detention and the consent. "Therefore, . . . the consent was the product of the illegal detention. . . ." Likewise, in *Bolton v. State*, the Court of Appeals determined that the consent to search in that case was tainted by the police. If there is a lack of valid consent or a lack of exigent circumstances, any entry onto the subject premises is unreasonable. Thus any consent to search after an unwarranted entry or any evidence recovered in such a search would be considered tainted and thus subject to suppression.

In order to show a valid consent, it is not always essential for an officer to inform a person of his Fourth Amendment protections or his right to refuse to consent. However, a judge may "consider the absence of any attempt by . . . [an officer] to advise defendant of his constitutional rights . . ." in determining whether the State failed to satisfy its burden. In *State v. Westmoreland*, an officer, without articulable suspicion, asked the defendant and others if they would consent to be searched. The defendant asked if the officer had a search warrant. The officer replied that he did not need a warrant. The court pointed out that the answer was not true. It was held that when the evidence shows that a defendant must consent, "such evidence weighs heavily against a finding that [a] consent was voluntary."

If a suspect is given *Miranda* warnings and is informed that the results of a search may be used against him, the search is not considered the result of illegal coercion simply because there is no showing that he knew he could withhold his consent.

Where consent is obtained through coercion, it will not be deemed voluntary. In *Bumper v. North Carolina*, the consent to a search of a house by the defendant's grandmother was held to be involuntary where an officer falsely claimed to have a search warrant. Deception on the part of an officer may prevent a consent from being valid.

In *State v. Smith,* another North Carolina case, the Supreme Court of that state reversed the trial court and found no Fourth Amendment violation where officers without probable cause "proceed[ed] to the residence, knock[ed] on the door, and ask[ed] to be permitted inside. . . . [Inside] the officers inform[ed] the person that they . . . [are] investigating information that drugs are in the house. The officers then ask[ed] for [and received] . . . consent."

In *Darby v. State,* the court held that "[w]hen an officer represents to an accused that a warrant to search will be obtained if consent [to search] is refused and [the officer] does not have probable cause to secure the warrant, then the accused's consent is invalid." However, it has been held that deception on the part of an officer does not automatically prevent a consent from being valid, unless the method used offends due process. Thus, a consent to search is not invalid for the reason that the consent was given to an officer working outside his jurisdiction.

In *State v. Sims,* the Court of Appeals explained in the context of a warrantless search of an automobile that it is the unreasonable search and seizure which is prohibited by the Fourth Amendment. "The 'touchstone . . . is reasonableness' . . . [which] . . ., in turn, is measured in objective terms by examining the totality of the circumstances." Thus, "if the officer *continues to detain* the subject after the conclusion of the traffic stop and interrogates him to seek consent to search without reasonable suspicion of criminal activity, the officer has exceeded the scope of a permissible investigation of the initial traffic stop." Accordingly, what may begin as a reasonable setting in which to conduct a search may progress to one which, because of its "intensity and scope", violates the Fourth Amendment. The Court applied *Sims* in *Padron v. State*, to exclude contraband discovered during the search of a motor vehicle belonging to a Spanish-speaking couple whose proficiency in English was suspect. Admitting that he was acting only on a "hunch" when he requested leave to search the vehicle, the officer discovered cocaine in a suitcase in the trunk after the apparent protest of the driver that the search terminate. The officer did not present the couple with departmental consent to search forms printed in Spanish and did not request an interpreter until after the arrest was effected. The Court concluded that the officer never had a reasonable basis for conducting the search and that any "consent" obtained by the officer was the result of the coercive nature of the couple's detention during the search. *Salmeron v. State,* has since displaced *Padron* and the notice that an officer cannot question an individual on matters outside the scope of the reason for the stop. Instead, the court in *Salmeron* said the inquiry should be whether the police questioning unduly *prolonged* the detention initiated by the reason for the stop.

It has been held that the refusal of the defendant to consent to a search is not admissible since a defendant is not to be penalized for exercising a constitutional right.

See section 26-19, note 44, infra, on the validity of consent to warrantless searches as a condition of probation. Generally, see 2 LaFave, *Search and Seizure,* § 8.1 et seq. (West 1978). See section 3-11, supra, on extension of the *Terry* frisk. See section 4-2, supra, on admission because of misplaced confidence or deception. See section 5-10, infra, on statement made in presence of an acquaintance on the mistaken belief that the statement would not be revealed. See section 4-52, infra, on the nature of search of automobile permitted. See Goger, *Daniel's Georgia Handbook on Criminal Evidence* (2009 ed.), § 7–26, on the use which may be made of blood drawn from a driver under the implied consent statute.

§ 4-32 Warrantless searches—Valid consent by defendant

If the state seeks to justify a warrantless search on the theory that the defendant consented to the search, it "has the burden of proving that the consent was, *in fact,* freely and voluntarily given." In *State v. Williams,* the Georgia Court of Appeals pointed out that "although silence in the face of a request for permission to search may, when accompanied by other conduct, sometimes be interpreted as acquiescence, such 'acquiescence cannot . . . substitute for free consent.' "It has been held that if a search is "consented to" because the officer says he has a search warrant, the consent is not valid. In *Murphy v. State,* the court held that "[w]hen an officer represents to an accused that a warrant to search will be obtained if consent is refused, and does not have probable cause to secure a warrant, then the accused's consent is invalid." Likewise, a defendant who provides his consent to search after the police represent that they have the authority to enter and search the premises against the will of the defendant, if necessary, can still claim that the consent was not voluntary.

Some cases have treated a consent much like a confession and have concluded that if the consent was given because of an induced hope of reward, it is invalid. Also, it must be kept in mind that a person in police custody is in no position to refuse to comply with the demands of the officer. But generally, the validity of a defendant's consent to a search is determined by a totality of the circumstances. For example: (1) The fact that the defendant was in custody at the time the consent was given does not alone show that it was coerced. (2) The absence of proof that the defendant knew he could withhold his consent does not alone prevent the consent from being valid. (3) A threat to obtain a warrant does not alone invalidate the consent. However, all of these factors may be considered under the totality of the circumstances. In *Setser v. State*, the court held that "[a]lthough [a defendant's] consent may have been the product of his erroneous assumption, based on previous arrests, that the officers would proceed with a search anyway, such an erroneous assumption does not constitute coercion . . . and . . . [t]he consent was valid."

In *Lane v. State*, the court held that "[a] warrantless search may be upheld if the law enforcement officer conducting the search *reasonably* (albeit erroneously) believes the consent given was valid." (emphasis in original.)

In *Ohio v. Robinette,* the United States Supreme Court held that where a driver is stopped for a traffic offense, the failure of the officer to tell the driver that he was "free to go" did not alone prevent the driver's consent to search from being voluntary. The court emphasized (1) that the subjective thoughts of the officer are immaterial when he asks a driver to get out of the car if the officer was objectively justified in doing so; and (2) that the voluntariness of a consent "is a question of fact to be determined from all the circumstances."

Often the voluntariness of the defendant's consent turns on the meaning intended by his words, and it must be kept in mind that what may be a consent as to others may not always be regarded as a consent to law enforcement officers.

In *Gonzales v. State*, the Court of Appeals observed that once the investigation associated with a routine traffic stop has terminated, additional questioning or further searching of the vehicle must close in the absence of reasonable suspicion or valid consent. In this case, after stopping the defendants because of a partially obscured license plate, the officers continued questioning one of the defendants about whether there was any contraband in his car and searching the vehicle even after being told that the defendants would not consent to the search. The officer contended that his "reasonable suspicion" for the search was justified by the "nervousness" of the defendants. The Court ruled that "nervousness" without more is not sufficient to establish reasonable suspicion for detention and investigation for illicit drug activity.

In *Aranda v. State,* the court held that when there has been a general consent to a search of the person, this consent continues until it is either revoked or withdrawn and is not limited by a later statement of an officer that "it would not be 'a very detailed search,' it would be 'just a patdown of his outer clothing.' "

Acquiescence to apparent authority where the defendant is under arrest is not necessarily regarded as consent, and this seems to be particularly true if the defendant is under illegal arrest, or if an illegal search of one area has already taken place. The Eleventh Circuit has said "that the standard remains the same whether the defendant is in custody under arrest or merely stopped at the time of consent." A threat to arrest a defendant and all occupants of a house if a consent is not given may render the consent invalid.

A condition of a defendant's probation in a previous case that he submit himself, his premises, or motor vehicle to search by any law enforcement officer, and that any evidence seized is admissible against the defendant, was held in *State v. Bethune* to amount to a consent. In *State v. Hall,* the court affirmed the granting of a motion to suppress where a defendant was told that if he did not consent to a search of a car, the car would be impounded and he "would be arrested until they get a search warrant from the judge." See section 26-19, infra.

In a case from another jurisdiction, the court held that where a defendant refused to permit a search of his car, it was error to admit testimony of this exercise of his Fourth Amendment rights.

In the Texas case of *Brown v. State,* the court held that when a defendant placed a 911 call from her home, to which police were summoned, and stated that a crime had been committed by a third person, the caller impliedly consented to a search of the premises reasonably related to the routine investigation of the offense.

In the interesting Florida case of *Preces v. State,* the court held that there was no Fourth Amendment violation where undercover officers posing as potential buyers of marijuana were invited into the defendant's home and given an opportunity to inspect contraband, which they did.

In *Pupo v. State,* the court pointed out that to the extent the driver of a car had no authority to consent to a search, he clearly lacked standing to complain that the search violated the Fourth Amendment.

In *Beasley v. State,* the defendant consented to a urine test after he was told that the purpose of the results of the test were to be used in connection with the defendant's request for a bond. After the defendant tested positive for cocaine, he was charged with possession of cocaine. The court concluded that the consent was not voluntary since he had not been informed that he might be supplying evidence against himself in an independent criminal prosecution. However, in *Gadson v. State,* the defendant was arrested for assaulting a victim. He was given his *Miranda* rights and was asked for a sample of blood. He consented and signed a form consenting to give his blood without a search warrant and stating that anything found could be used as evidence in any court. The appellate court affirmed the admission of DNA evidence based on the blood in view of the defendant's freely and voluntarily given consent with "no limits on the scope of his consent." See Goger, *Daniel's Georgia Handbook on Criminal Evidence* (2009 ed.), § 7–26, on DNA examination of blood taken from driver under implied consent.

In *Cole v. State,* the court concluded that the defendant's consent to search his automobile was voluntary following a valid traffic stop made because of an improper lane change. After stopping the vehicle, the officer detected the smell of marijuana and requested permission to search the vehicle. The officer did admit that he might have stated that if the defendant did not consent, he would get a drug dog. The court ruled that the State did not have to affirmatively show that the officer did not make the statement. Rather, it is "up to the trial court to consider the weight to be given the possibility that it was made."

In *Fincher v. State*, the Court of Appeals noted that under appropriate circumstances the State may prove that consent to search given by the defendant or by an authorized third party after a search will serve to validate an otherwise illegal search.

See section 26-19, infra, on validity of consent to search as a condition of probation. See Annotation, "When is

Consent Voluntarily Given so as to Justify Search Conducted on Basis of That Consent—Supreme Court Cases," 148 A. L. R. Fed. 271 (1998).

§ 4-33 Warrantless searches—Valid consent by third person

In *Illinois v. Rodriguez,* the United States Supreme Court held that concerning the validity of a consent to search by a third person, the "consent to enter must 'be judged against an objective standard: would the facts available to the officer at the moment . . . warrant a man of reasonable caution in the belief that the consenting party had authority over the premises?' . . . If not, then warrantless entry without further inquiry is unlawful unless authority actually exists." Thus, "a warrantless search based on unauthorized consent could nonetheless be upheld if the law enforcement officer conducting the search *reasonably* (albeit erroneously) believed the consent given was valid."

A person may consent to a search if he possesses "common authority over or other sufficient relationship to the premises or effects sought to be inspected."

Common authority means "mutual use of the property by persons generally having joint access or control for most purposes, so that it is reasonable to recognize that any of the co-inhabitants has the right to permit the inspection in his own right and that the others have assumed the risk that one of their number might permit the common area to be searched." Thus, in *Atkins v. State,* the court held that the defendant's 17–year-old brother had sufficient authority to give a valid consent.

In *Park v. State,* officers went to the defendant's apartment and asked her 24–year-old daughter if she would mind looking around to see if she could find certain documents. The daughter consented. She found some of the documents which were given to the officers. The court did not regard this as a search by the officers and held the documents admissible.

In *Davis v. State,* the Georgia Supreme Court considered a case in which the defendant's ten-year-old stepson called 911 to report drugs in his home. The child had a key to the house and called his mother as soon as he got in from school. His mother came in from work about 4:30 p.m. He was not permitted to invite anyone into the house or to go outside during this period of about 1–½ hours. On the afternoon in question, he found what he believed to be drugs in his parents' bedroom. In making the call, the child acted on advice he received in a drug abuse class at school. In his call, he stated he would like to get some help for his parents. When the deputy arrived, he followed the child into the house and into the defendant's bedroom where the child obtained a mirror with white powder and a razor blade on it and pulled a bag of marijuana and "rolling papers" from a nightstand. The deputy saw a " 'marijuana joint' in an ashtray." The defendant contended that his stepson lacked authority to consent. The trial judge denied the motion to suppress. The Georgia Supreme Court held that the motion to suppress should have been granted. The court identified the following factors which should be considered in determining the validity of such a search: (1) "whether the minor lived on the premises; [2] whether the minor had a right of access to the premises and the right to invite others thereto; [3] whether the minor was of an age at which he or she could be expected to exercise at least minimal discretion; and [4] whether officers acted reasonably in believing that the minor had sufficient control over the premises to give a valid consent to search."

The court then emphasized the importance of examining "a child's mental maturity and his ability to understand the circumstances . . . and the consequences of his actions. . . . The younger a child the less likely that he or she can be said to have the minimal discretion required. . . ." The court concluded that based on the foregoing criteria, the child involved did not have authority to validly consent, the circumstances did not justify a finding of present danger to the child, nor were there exigent circumstances. Lastly, the court pointed out the facts of this case did not warrant affirmance under the "independent source" or "inevitable discovery exception." See section 2-27, supra, on the independent source exception, and section 2-28, supra, on the inevitable discovery exception. In 1997, Georgia enacted O.C.G.A. § 16–7–21, which provides that a minor may not permit a lawful entry if the "parent or guardian has previously given notice that such entry is forbidden or notice to depart." See Annotation, "Admissibility of Evidence Discovered in Search of Adult Defendant's Property or Residence Authorized by Defendant's Minor Child—State Cases," 51 A. L. R. 5th 425 (1997). Also see Annotation, "Admissibility of Evidence Discovered in Search of Adult Defendant's Property or Residence Authorized by Defendant's Minor Relative," 152 A. L. R. Fed. 475 (1999) and Annotation, "Admissibility of Evidence Discovered in Search of a Defendant's Property or Residence Authorized by Defendant's Spouse (resident or non-resident)—State Cases," 65 A. L. R. 5th (1999). However, the 1999 case of *Rainwater v. State*, the court, relying on *Davis*, said a 15–year-old gave valid consent to search her home.

It has been held that a father may consent to the search of his son's car which is parked on the father's premises. In *Fears v. State,* the court said that when the defendant left a bag at his sister's house, he assumed the risk that she might consent to a search of the bag and her consent was valid.

There have been cases involving all kinds of factual situations relating to third party consents. Some of the more significant situations will be mentioned here; others are referred to in the footnotes. Generally, a spouse or roommate can consent to a search of common premises. In order for the consent of a third party to be valid, that party must possess "common authority over or other sufficient relationship to the premises or effects sought to be inspected." Hence, the mere fact that a third person was present in a house does not mean that the third person could validly consent to a search of the house. However, in *Dover v. State,* the court held that where a husband had given his mother-in-law a key to his house and said she was welcome at any time, she had authority to enter the house in the absence of the owner and to consent to a search of the house when the circumstances reasonably indicated it might be necessary in the interest of the householders or safeguarding the house. The owner of a car may turn over to officers luggage of an acquaintance which has been placed in the automobile. However, in *United States v. Welch,* the court held that the consent of a male to search a rental car did not authorize the search of a purse found in the trunk which belonged to his female companion. If the owner of a car is present and the driver consents to a search, the driver's consent has been considered sufficient. An employer may give a valid consent to a search of the employer's truck which is driven by an employee. In *United States v. Jenkins,* the Court concluded that a driver of a rig has apparent authority to consent to a search of the trailer. On the other hand, a hotel clerk cannot validly consent to the search of a guest's room until it is vacated; a landlord cannot validly consent to the search of his tenant's quarters; and a nurse cannot consent to a search of a patient's clothing. See Annotation, "Admissibility of Evidence Discovered in Warrantless Search of Rental Property Authorized by Lessor of Property—State Cases," 61 A. L. R. 5th 149 (1998).

In *Browning v. State,* the court said, "An officer's belief that a third party has authority to consent to the search of another person's property should not only be based on information previously obtained in his investigation, but should also be based on the facts and circumstances existent at the time of the search."

In determining whether a consent given by a third party is voluntary, the "totality of circumstances" test is applicable, but it is not always necessary for the prosecution to establish that the person who consented knew that he had a right to refuse to consent.

An interesting question posed to the Georgia Court of Appeals was the validity of a consent to search given by one occupant to a premises where another occupant, also present at the time, had already refused such access to the police. In *Randolph v. State,* the court concluded that in a case involving a married couple, one spouse could not waive the other's right to privacy by allowing a police search in their residence after the other spouse had refused to permit the search. The court's decision was upheld by the Supreme Court of Georgia and the U.S. Supreme Court granted certiorari in order to resolve a split of authority among the Federal Courts of Appeal. In *Georgia v. Randolph,* the U.S. Supreme Court affirmed the judgment of the Supreme Court of Georgia, making clear, however, that their decision is strictly limited to those situations involving a physically present co-occupant objector. *Randolph* should not affect the capacity of the police to protect victims of domestic violence. For example, if the consenting occupant inside the dwelling indicates that he or she is in need of police protection, then police entry is justified regardless of the other occupant's refusal to consent.

However, in *Preston v. State,* the Georgia Court of Appeals held that police could not arrest the defendant at his home and then initiate a search of the home consented to by a live-in girlfriend that was not incident to the arrest without first informing the defendant the basis of the search and giving him an opportunity to object.

In *State v. Kuhnhausen,* the appellate court affirmed the grant of the defendant's motion to suppress evidence seized in a warrantless search of a mobile home shared by the defendant and his brother. Though the defendant's brother had consented to the search, the mobile home had been permanently divided with the construction of a wall and there was no interior access between the units. The court held that "one individual cannot waive the Fourth Amendment rights of another individual on their independent, separate, private property."

See Annotation, "Admissibility of Evidence Discovered in Search of Defendant's Property or Residence Authorized by Defendant's Adult Relative Other Than Spouse—State Cases," 55 A. L. R. 5th 125 (1998) (this annotation is almost 300 pages long); Annotation, "Admissibility of Evidence Discovered in Search of Defendant's Property or Residence Authorized by Defendant's Adult Relative Other Than Spouse," 160 A. L. R. Fed. 165 (2000); and Annotation, "Admissibility of Evidence Discovered in Search of Defendant's Property or Residence Authorized by One, Other Than Relative, Who is Co–Tenant or Common Resident With Defendant—State Cases," 68 A. L. R. 5th 343 (1999).

§ 4-34 Warrantless searches—Airport searches

The frequency of aircraft hijackings in the past has led to the adoption of measures to deal with the critical time when passengers board an airplane.

Federal Aviation Administration regulations require the presence of armed officers throughout the screening of departing passengers. Also, searches may be conducted in critical preboarding areas even if the passenger does not meet the FAA "profile" of a potential hijacker or otherwise appear suspicious. "[S]earch in an airport gate area or security checkpoint . . . [does] not require probable cause or even reasonable suspicion, but instead 'mere suspicion of possible illegal activity.' "Once commenced, a consent search may continue until the officers, in their professional judgment, conclude that no harm will result from the passenger boarding the plane.

The use of metal-detecting devices called magnetometers has been held to constitute a search under the Fourth Amendment. Georgia courts have approved the use of such devices as reasonable and have upheld the validity of the search or frisk based upon the magnetometer reading.

In some cases there has been an attempt to justify airport searches on the theory that a person traveling by airplane consents to airport security procedures. However, most cases seem to have rejected the implied consent theory, since such a "consent" is not freely and voluntarily given. "To make one choose between flying to one's destination and exercising one's constitutional right . . . in many situations [is] a form of coercion." Nevertheless, in *State v. Rosof,* the Georgia Court of Appeals held that persons "presenting themselves at a security check-point thereby consent automatically to a search" if there is a sign informing persons entering the area that they will be subject to search. Likewise, it has been said that when a "passenger presents himself at an airport security check-point, he has consented to the screening of his luggage by the X-ray machine." Most of the more recent cases have justified such security measures on the theory that although initially there is not enough probable cause to justify a search, if the passenger activates a magnetometer and follow-up procedures do not satisfy the officer, there is at least probable cause for a frisk. The courts have not been impressed with the distinction that a typical frisk situation is designed to protect the officer, whereas in the airport context the purpose of the frisk is to protect the passengers once the plane has departed, and it has been pointed out that an airport search is "not to be condemned as violating the Fourth Amendment simply because it does not precisely fit into one of the previously recognized categories for dispensing with a search warrant."

In *State v. Crisanti,* the court held that once a person who is subject to an investigatory stop admits a weapon is present, officers are privileged to search the area to uncover that weapon, and pointed out that the reasonableness of the action of officers is to be measured by the "foresight of the policeman on the scene. . . ."

In the 1980 case of *Shapiro v. State,* the Florida Supreme Court concluded that a passenger had no reasonable expectation of privacy which prevented his being searched for weapons or other devices which could be used in hijackings. Therefore, the court concluded, the Fourth Amendment did not apply.

The right to search without a warrant at an airport applies only to searches of passengers and the luggage they carry on board. In Georgia, it has been held that where an airline employee on his own initiative searches checked luggage which accidentally sprang open, the search is a private search not covered by the protection of the Fourth Amendment.

The search by Drug Enforcement Administration officers for drugs on passengers arriving in airports from other points in the United States, or the search of passengers arriving from foreign countries and passing through customs, are situations beyond the scope of this section.

Generally, on scope of a search and seizure, see section 4-56, infra. Also see section 3-4, supra, on drug courier profile and section 4-29, supra, on exigent circumstances. Generally, on airport searches, see 68 Am. Jur. 2d Searches and Seizures § 59 (1973), and 3 LaFave, *Search and Seizure* 327, § 10.6 (West 1978).

§ 4-35 Warrantless searches—Courthouses and public buildings

In the South Carolina case of *State v. Shelton,* the trial judge received reliable information that a party in a pending action carried a gun and had threatened one of the attorneys in the case. The trial judge ordered the party searched. The appellate court said:

"A trial judge has the inherent power to preserve order in his court and to see that justice is not obstructed by any person or persons. He has the authority to take such measures as appear reasonably necessary to secure orderly proceedings and to preserve the security of those participating in the trial or lawfully attending the proceedings. The exercise of this authority by the trial judge is not inhibited by the guarantees of the Fourth Amendment. Therefore, the Fourth Amendment protection against unreasonable searches and seizures is inapplicable to a courtroom in the exercise of the trial judge's authority and duty to preserve security and order."

However, generally a court does not know the identity of a person who is armed. Hence, where there are threats or have been acts of violence, magnetometers, or metal detecting devices, may be used to screen persons entering a courthouse.

In *McMorris v. Alioto,* the court in effect approved the requirement that persons entering a courthouse must pass through a metal detector. If the detector indicated the presence of metal, the person could empty his pockets and pass through the detector again. If the detector was activated again, the person was frisked before being permitted to enter. Briefcases and articles capable of concealing weapons were also subject to inspection. The court pointed out that any person could leave the courthouse without a further search or questioning if he activated the metal detector, and concluded that there was sufficient freedom from compulsion to meet the requirements of the Fourth Amendment.

In some cases, even more severe or intensive means of searching have been used. These security measures are sometimes said to be justified on a consent theory or on a theory of the inherent power of the court to maintain order.

See 3 LaFave, *Search and Seizure,* § 10.7(a) (West 1978); 1 Ringel, *Searches and Seizures,* Arrests and Confessions, § 16.3 (Clark Boardman 1979); Annotation, "Validity, Under Federal Constitution, of Search Conducted as Condition of Entering Public Building," 53 A. L. R. Fed. 888 (1981).

§ 4-36 Warrantless searches—Places of recreation and entertainment

Several cases have arisen involving the search of persons entering a stadium or some other such facility. These cases have arisen where spectators were required to submit to a search for drugs, alcohol, or weapons as a prerequisite to the right to enter. Justification of these checks or searches has generally been sought by drawing an analogy between such checks and airport searches. However, thus far the analysis has been rejected because (1) there is no showing of public necessity; (2) the intensity required of such a search, if it is to be effective, is intolerable; and (3) the searches have been used on a selective basis.

For the foregoing reasons such searches have been held unconstitutional if they are a result of government action.

See 1 Ringel, *Searches and Seizures, Arrests and Confessions,* § 16.4 (Clark Boardman 1979); 1 LaFave, *Search and Seizure,* § 10.7(a) (West 1978); Annotation, "Validity, Under Federal Constitution, of Search Conducted as Condition of Entering Public Building," 53 A. L. R. Fed. 888 (1981).

§ 4-37 Warrantless searches—Abandoned property

The United States Supreme Court has held that the Fourth Amendment does not apply to abandoned property.

Thus, if property has been abandoned it may be seized by officers without a warrant. Momentarily divesting oneself of contraband inside an automobile does not constitute abandonment. "The question of abandonment for Fourth Amendment purposes does not turn on strict property concepts but on whether the accused has relinquished his interest in the property to the extent that he no longer has a reasonable expectation of privacy . . . at the time of the search." "Abandonment is primarily a question of intent, and intent may be inferred from words spoken, acts done, and other objective facts. All relevant circumstances existing at the time of the alleged abandonment should be considered. Police pursuit or the existence of a police investigation does not of itself render abandonment involuntary." If a defendant abandons an automobile after being chased by police, he may not object to the search. In *Williams v. State,* the defendant's car "was found over 100 yards from the nearest home on land not belonging to the defendant: it was down a deserted field road, the tag and battery had been removed, and the vehicle was covered with freshly cut bushes and debris." The court said that the issue of abandonment is one of fact and will not be disturbed by an appellate court if there is any evidence to support it. Here there was adequate evidence to support a finding of abandonment. "In order to determine whether property has been abandoned, we must ask: Did the complaining party retain a legitimate expectation of privacy in the article allegedly abandoned?"

In *Berger v. State,* the court held that when a briefcase was left unlocked in the lobby of a hotel, an officer could open it and look in it to determine who the owner is. In *Ramsey v. State,* the court held that where a defendant denied ownership or any interest in a briefcase, this amounted to an abandonment of the briefcase and its contents and justified a warrantless search.

When a person drops or throws contraband away while he is being followed or approached by an officer, the property is treated as having been abandoned. This abandonment situation, in some parts of the country, has led to what has been commonly referred to as the "dropsy" cases and the "perjury routine" in which officers have been accused of routinely testifying that a defendant dropped the drugs when he saw the officer approaching. However, if the officer is attempting to make an illegal arrest which causes the defendant to dispose of the contraband, the property is not treated as having been abandoned. Likewise, where officers illegally stop a person and as a result of the stop the person abandons contraband, this is not regarded as voluntary abandonment and the contraband has been held not admissible.

However, if "a defendant is in a state of flight when he discards or abandons property . . . his being pursued does not result in the 'seizure' of property he abandoned." Hence, when a defendant is in a state of flight when he discards contraband, and has not submitted to any show of authority by the police, the contraband is "not discovered as a result of an illegal search or seizure, regardless of whether the police had probable cause to stop . . . [the defendant's] vehicle."

The case of *Abel v. United States* exemplifies an abandonment situation. In *Abel,* the defendant was arrested in his hotel room. After he had been taken away, an officer with the consent of the hotel manager searched the wastepaper basket in the room and discovered incriminating evidence. The court held the items had been abandoned and were thus admissible. However, a tenant who is evicted retains a reasonable expectation of privacy and an officer has no right to sift through his possessions before moving them onto the street.

Several cases involving the search of garbage cans placed on the street have held that the items in question were abandoned. See section 14-78, infra, on expectation of privacy. Likewise, it has been held that substances obtained from the feces of a hospitalized drug suspect are admissible. However, where personal property such as a wallet is merely lost and not abandoned, the owner does maintain an expectation of privacy, albeit a somewhat diluted one. Addressing the issue for the first time, the Court of Appeals in *Wolf v. State*, held that a person's expectations of privacy in their personal effects, does not vanish simply because the item is lost or mislaid. It is, however, diminished to the extent that police may examine the contents thereof in order to find the rightful owner. See Annotation, "Searches and Seizures: Reasonable Expectation of Privacy in Contents of Garbage or Trash Receptacle," 62 A. L. R. 5th 1 (1998).

In addition to personal property, the doctrine of abandonment also applies to real estate. In *Bloodworth v. State,* the defendant physically moved out of a house, but he retained possession until the day after the warrantless search. The court said that strict property concepts did not apply and the question was whether or not he had relinquished his interest in the property to such an extent that he no longer had a reasonable expectation of privacy. Therefore, the court concluded that the evidence authorized a finding that the premises had been abandoned.

In *Smith v. State,* a search was upheld on the theory of abandonment where the defendant was temporarily living elsewhere, the rent had not been paid for several months, the owner had initiated proceedings to take possession of the premises, the water had been turned off and the telephone disconnected several months before the search, and the house was said to be uninhabitable. In *Hollingsworth v. State,* the court upheld the warrantless search of an apparently vacant house which had been condemned by the city.

In *United States v. Tolbert,* the court held that the definition of the word "abandonment" has a traditional concept in property law, but the same word may have a different meaning under the Fourth Amendment. The court then concluded that the defendant had no expectation of privacy in a checked suitcase left in an air terminal where the defendant vociferously denied owning the suitcase. See sections 14-74 to 14-78, infra, on standing and expectation of privacy. See Annotation, "Search and Seizure: What Constitutes Abandonment of Personal Property Within Rule That Search and Seizure of Abandoned Property Is Not Unreasonable—Modern Cases," 40 A. L. R. 4th 382 (1985).

§ 4-38 Warrantless searches—Plain view—General

In a sense the plain view doctrine or rule is not an exception to the warrant requirement for a search. This is true in that articles discovered as a result of "plain view" are not discovered as a result of a search. No warrant is required since no search is conducted. Thus, the plain view doctrine is a seizure doctrine, not a search doctrine. However, absent exigent circumstances, an officer has no right to seize contraband unless he has a legal right to go where the contraband is located.

In *Texas v. Brown,* four Justices of the United States Supreme Court said that " '[p]lain view' is perhaps better understood, . . . not as an independent 'exception' to the warrant clause but simply as an extension of whatever the prior justification for the officer's 'access to an object' may be. The principle is grounded on the recognition that when a police officer has observed an object in 'plain view' the owner's remaining interests in the object are merely those of possession and ownership. . . . Likewise, it reflects the fact that requiring police to obtain a warrant once they have obtained a first-hand perception of contraband, stolen property or incriminating evidence generally would be a 'needless inconvenience,' . . . which might involve danger to the police and public."

The "plain view" exception to the warrant requirement is based on the theory that the discovery of the particular incriminating evidence is not the result of a search. In *Coolidge v. New Hampshire*, the Court said that in order for the plain view exception to apply, three requirements must be met: (1) the object must be inadvertently discovered, (2) the officer discovering the object must have a legal right to be where he is at the time of the discovery, and (3) it must be immediately apparent that the seized item is stolen property, contraband, or other fruits or evidence of a crime. However, in the 1990 case of *Horton v. California*, the United States Supreme Court held that the "inadvertent discovery requirement" of the plain view rule is no longer required.

In reading the cases on "plain view," it becomes readily apparent that these words in the Fourth Amendment context do not mean what they would seem to mean in lay English. It has been suggested that " '[o]pen view' is a better term to describe the non-intrusional visual observation from a vantage point outside a constitutionally protected area. The 'plain view doctrine' of Coolidge 'refers exclusively to the legal justification—the reasonableness—for the seizure of evidence . . . in the course of a constitutional search already in progress or in the course of an otherwise justifiable intrusion into a Constitutionally protected area. . . .' Because an 'open view' encompasses that which is readily observable or clearly visible from an observation point which is not within a constitutionally protected confine, this sighting of evidence needs no further justification for a seizure."

See section 4-22, supra, on property which may be seized when a warrant is executed. See section 4-40, infra, on enhanced vision of officer by the use of a light or binoculars. See section 4-42, infra, on aerial view of premises. See section 3-10, supra, on identification of a substance by feel.

§ 4-39 Warrantless searches—Plain view—Inadvertent discovery

In the 1990 case of *Horton v. California,* the United States Supreme Court held that "the absence of inadvertence" does not prevent a seizure from being valid under the plain view doctrine. The court pointed out that (1) "evenhanded law enforcement is best achieved by the application of objective standards of conduct, rather than standards that depend upon the subjective state of mind of the officer." (2) The inadvertence requirement is not required to prevent a "specific warrant" from being converted into a general warrant.

In *Nichols v. State,* the Georgia Court of Appeals followed *Horton*. However, in the 2006 case of *Mauge v. State,* the Court of Appeals listed inadvertent discovery as one of three requirements under the plain view doctrine.

For Georgia law before *Horton,* see *State v. Scott* and *Whittington v. State.*

§ 4-40 Warrantless searches—Plain view—Right of officer to be where he was at time of discovery

The officer must have a right to be where he is at the time he sees the item. Thus, looking into a motel window from a parking lot was held not objectionable because there existed no reasonable expectation of privacy, but if an officer goes on private property without a warrant and peers in a window and thus obtains probable cause for an arrest, the arrest and search incident to it are illegal. However, in *Pickens v. State,* the court held that the Fourth Amendment is not violated where an officer goes on private property only to the extent of knocking on outer doors, even if the officer does not have an articulable suspicion. In *State v. O'Bryant,* pursuant to an anonymous tip of possible drug dealing, officers went to the defendant's residence without a warrant to speak with the defendant. There was no response to their knock at the front door and the officers walked to the side of the house, knocked at a basement door and received no response. They noticed a Toyota truck parked in the driveway in which one of the officers had seen marijuana roaches in the ashtray on a prior occasion. At this time they saw through a tinted window what appeared to be a plastic bag of marijuana. One of the officers obtained a search warrant for the vehicle and the house. The search of the house yielded 20 pounds of marijuana. The appellate court affirmed the granting of the motion to suppress, pointing out that the officers had no right to be where they were when they looked into the Toyota.

It has been held in some jurisdictions that the use of a telescope to watch a defendant in his apartment was illegal and information so obtained was inadmissible. In *Patterson v. State,* the Georgia Court of Appeals held that it was proper for officers to use binoculars to watch a defendant harvest marijuana growing in a field. Also, such surveillance is proper under the open fields exception, which is discussed in the next section, and it is not to be compared with looking in a home.

The plain view doctrine does not apply to objects found while searching furniture or wastebaskets, nor will it justify an exploratory search from one object to another until incriminating evidence is found.

Despite the lesser expectation of privacy in a motor vehicle, it has been held that an officer has no authority to stick his head inside a windowless cargo van parked in a public place. The officer had found the sliding door open from 15 to 18 inches.

The plain view doctrine does not mean that the human senses may never be assisted in any way. In *United States v. Lee,* the United States Supreme Court held that the plain view doctrine was not violated where a search light was directed on a boat, revealing a number of cans of alcohol. The court also drew an analogy between the use of the search light and the use of field glasses and said that their use was constitutionally proper. Generally, courts have held that the use of a flashlight to see an object did not violate the concept of the plain view doctrine, particularly when related to automobiles. Also, the use of a flashlight in looking in an unlighted garage through an open door has been upheld. In *Kyllo v. United States,* the United States Supreme Court held that the warrantless use of a thermal imaging device to scan the home of the defendant in connection with an investigation involving an indoor marijuana farm was improper.

In the unusual Eleventh Circuit case of *United States v. Sentovich,* the court concluded that probable cause to obtain a search warrant could be based, in part, on the assertion of a DEA agent that he could smell marijuana inside of a closed suitcase at an airport.

In *Lo-Ji Sales, Inc. v. New York*, the Court said that "there is no basis for the notion that [where] a retail store invites the public to enter, it consents to wholesale searches and seizures that do not conform to Fourth Amendment guarantees."

In *Kilpatrick v. State,* an officer received a tip that the defendants had marijuana growing at their residence. He stated that the tip was insufficient to obtain a search warrant. He said he drove to the farm of Ken Kilpatrick's father to talk with the father about the tip. He entered a private road, drove by the father's home without stopping, drove down the road about one-half mile to the trailer in which the defendants lived, and saw marijuana growing outside the trailer. He then went back to get another officer, drove back to the trailer, and arrested Ken Kilpatrick, who consented to a search of the trailer where additional marijuana was found. The court held that the seizure of growing marijuana was not justified under the plain view doctrine since the defendants had a reasonable expectation of privacy at the trailer. The court also concluded that the consent to the search of the trailer was tainted by the illegal seizure of the growing marijuana and the illegal arrest.

In *Merriman v. State,* pursuant to an anonymous call that marijuana was growing in the defendant's backyard, officers went to the defendant's house and found the yard enclosed partly by a high brick wall and partly by a wooden fence about eight feet tall. They moved through a heavily wooded area behind the wooden fence and, looking through cracks in the fence, they saw growing marijuana. The seizure was affirmed.

See sections 4-31 and 4-32, supra, on inviting an undercover officer into a house to sell him contraband. See section 4-42, infra, on warrantless searches of open fields and on aircraft surveillance. See section 4-57, infra, on "second search" and a controlled delivery. See section 14-74, infra, on expectations of privacy and standing. See Annotation, "Permissibility and Sufficiency of Warrantless Use of Thermal Imager or Forward Looking Infra–Red Radar (F.L.I.R.)," 78 A. L. R. 5th 309 (2000).

§ 4-41 Warrantless searches—Plain view—Illegality of seized items immediately apparent

In *State v. David,* the Georgia Supreme Court pointed out that "[a]n officer's observation of . . . contraband from outside the apartment and his recognition of it as contraband, standing alone . . . [does] not authorize the officer to make a warrantless entry into the apartment to arrest the occupants and seize the material." For the plain view doctrine to authorize seizure, the officer must enter the home by consent or there must be exigent circumstances.

It must be immediately apparent to the officer that the object seized is subject to seizure. However, in *State v. Field,* the court held that where an officer sees suspicious items and he moves nothing but merely takes a closer look, this meets the requirements of immediate apparency of the plain view rule. In *State v. Sharer,* the Georgia Court of Appeals upheld the seizure of a brown bottle, two to three inches in height, with a white cap and no label of any sort. The bottle was opened and found to contain yellow capsules and blue pills. The bottle was found in plain view on the floor of an automobile. A further check of the car pursuant to a warrant led to the discovery of more bottles containing pills and capsules. The court concluded that having "lawfully discovered the pill bottles, the officers had probable cause to conclude from their location and appearance and the circumstances of their discovery that they contained contraband."

However, in *Stone v. State,* officers approached a truck and saw a brown paper bag on the floorboard. The bag had "enough torn places in it for the officers to see 'some white tablets, some white looking powder and some brownish material,' in plastic bags inside." One officer, who had been a policeman for six years, "had a suspicion" there were drugs in the bag. The trained officer testified that "to his personal knowledge what he observed, 'was not any controlled substance or was not anything that appeared to be a controlled substance.' "The court affirmed the holding of the trial judge that "the incriminating nature of the evidence" was not immediately apparent and that the seizure and search was not valid.

In *Texas v. Brown,* the United States Supreme Court considered the "immediately apparent" requirement of the plain view rule. Here a police officer stopped Brown at a driver's license checkpoint. The officer asked for his license, shined his flashlight into the car and saw an opaque party balloon, knotted near the tip, fall from Brown's hand to the seat. The officer was aware that drugs were frequently placed in such balloons. The officer then noticed small plastic vials, loose white powder and an open bag of party balloons in the glove compartment. Brown said he did not have a license with him and got out of the car as requested. The officer picked up the balloon which had fallen. The balloon seemed to have a powdery substance in the tied off portion. Brown was informed that he was under arrest, and the car was inventoried on the scene. A motion to suppress was denied by the trial judge. The Texas Court of Criminal Appeals reversed because the officer did not "*know* that 'incriminating evidence was before him when he seized the balloon.' "In a plurality opinion, the Supreme Court reversed. Chief Justice Burger and Justices Rehnquist, White, and O'Connor disregarded *Coolidge v. New Hampshire* as binding precedent and the opinion seems to go out of its way to point this out. The opinion says that "if, while lawfully engaged in an activity in a particular place, police officers perceive a suspicious object they may seize it immediately. . . . This rule merely reflects an application of the Fourth Amendment's central requirement of reasonableness to the law governing seizures of property. . . . [I]t is plain that . . . [the officer] possessed probable cause to believe that the balloon . . . contained an illicit substance." Justices Powell and Blackmun concurred in the judgment, saying that if probable cause must be shown to justify a seizure, it existed in this case, but they disagreed with the criticism of *Coolidge*. Justices Stevens, Brennan, and Marshall concurred in the judgment but said that the court failed to deal adequately with the search of the balloon as opposed to its seizure.

However, in *Arizona v. Hicks,* the United States Supreme Court held that "immediately apparent" means the officer must have probable cause to believe that the object is subject to seizure. Thus, while there is nothing to prevent an officer from recording serial numbers which may be easily seen, an officer may not move an article or turn it over to see the serial number unless there is probable cause where such moving of equipment is outside the scope of the exigency that justified the warrantless entry. However, in *Downey v. State,* the trial court was affirmed in denying a motion to suppress where officers conducted a search with the consent of the owner which was granted in connection with the execution of an arrest warrant for her son. During the search, one officer saw the stock of a rifle in a styrofoam gun box in the attic. He noted the serial number and handed the rifle down to be "cleared." The officer then went to his patrol car to check his notes from a previous burglary. The weapon was determined to be stolen.

In *Brown v. State,* the court recognized that "if the police see a person in possession of a highly suspicious object . . . which because of other circumstances is reasonably suspected to be contraband, and then observe that person make an apparent attempt to conceal that object from police view, probable cause is then present."

In *Whittington v. State,* officers were executing a search warrant for marijuana. In the attic they found a pillow case sewn together at both ends. They opened it and found 79 pieces of silverware of differing patterns. One of the officers said he recognized some of it as being of the same pattern as some which had been stolen. However, the owner was unable to describe the patterns which he said had been stolen. The court concluded that all of these facts, including the location, added up to probable cause to believe the silverware was stolen; and the seizure was, therefore, valid. Also, the court pointed out that "[i]t is not necessary under the law that the officer know with certainty that the item is stolen [or contraband] at the time of the seizure, only that there be probable cause to believe that this is the case." In *Mozier v. State,* a search warrant was issued to search for items taken from the victim, and where the affidavit stated that she had been beaten, the court upheld the seizure of brass knuckles.

In *United States v. Jacobsen,* the Supreme Court held that the DEA's field test of a white powder, discovered by an employee of a private freight carrier, was not a search within the meaning of the Fourth Amendment because it was sui generis. Thus, the motion to suppress was not valid.

See section 4-51, notes 2 and 7, infra, on "plain smell." See section 3-10, supra, notes 7 through 16, on objects identified by feel during a frisk. See section 4-29, supra, on exigent circumstances justifying seizure of contraband seen at a home.

§ 4-42 Warrantless searches—Open fields

Writing for the Court, in 1924, Justice Holmes held, in *Hester v. United States,* that the Fourth Amendment protects individuals in their "persons, houses, papers and effects" and its protection does not extend to open fields. Thus, it has been held that no search warrant is necessary for a search of an open field or orchard, or a beach, or some other such area. In *Oliver v. United States*, the Supreme Court seems to say the open fields doctrine applies to all land outside the curtilage regardless of how remote the land is and regardless of the efforts of the property owner to keep others out. The court said "that the term 'open fields' may include any unoccupied or undeveloped area outside of the curtilage. An open field need be neither 'open' nor a 'field' as those terms are used in common speech. . . . [A] thickly wooded area . . . may be an open field as that term is used in construing the Fourth Amendment."

In *United States v. Dunn,* the Court said that "the extent of the curtilage is determined by factors that bear upon whether an individual reasonably may expect that the area in question should be treated as the home itself. . . . [T]he central component of this inquiry [is] . . . whether the area harbors the 'intimate activity associated with the 'sanctity of a man's home and the privacies of life' . . . [C]urtilage questions should be resolved with particular reference to four factors: [1] the proximity of the area claimed to be curtilage to the home, [2] whether the area is included within an enclosure surrounding the home, [3] the nature of the uses to which the area is put, and [4] the steps taken by the resident to protect the area from observation by people passing by." The court then concluded that a barn was not located within the curtilage where it was located about 50 yards from a fence which surrounded the house.

Even prior to *Oliver,* the term "open field" was not limited to unfenced land. It has been applied to land posted with no trespassing signs and has not been limited to what is in plain view.

However, the area within the curtilage of a farm dwelling, as well as any building in that location, is protected. It has been held that a shed on a farm, located 45 to 60 yards from the house, is protected as being within the curtilage. However, a field separated by fence and some other objects has been found not to be within the curtilage even though it was only 35 feet from the residence. Likewise, the backyard of the house in which the defendant lives in a city is not within the open field doctrine, but is regarded as being within the curtilage of the house. However, the curtilage concept does not prevent an officer from going to the front door of a house by the same route which would be used by "any guest, deliveryman, postal employee, or other caller." In *State v. Lyons,* the Georgia Court of Appeals held that when, pursuant to a complaint, an officer went to the front door of a house which he reasonably believed to be occupied and he could get no response, he could enter the backyard even though fenced to reach the back door. The court distinguished the case from one where the officer entered the backyard for the purpose of conducting a warrantless search. In *Olson v. State,* the court treated an unoccupied abandoned house and its "curtilage" pursuant to the open fields doctrine. See sections § 4-2 and 4-19, supra.

In *Dow Chemical Co. v. United States,* the United States Supreme Court held that the open areas of an industrial complex are not analogous to the curtilage of a dwelling. The court found that aerial photographing of the complex from a plane in public navigable airspace was not a violation of the Fourth Amendment. Thus, the Court does not extend the coverage of the Fourth Amendment curtilage of an industrial complex to the extent of the protection of the curtilage of the home, but it still enjoys a greater protection than the true open field. See sections § 4-2 and 4-19, supra, on curtilage.

In *California v. Ciraolo,* decided the same day as *Dow Chemical,* the Court held that aerial naked-eye observation, from an altitude of 1,000 feet, of the fenced curtilage of a home did not violate the Fourth Amendment because there is no reasonable expectation of privacy within the curtilage of what could be seen by the naked eye from the navigable air space. Hence, the information obtained from these observations could be used to obtain a search warrant for the search and seizure of marijuana growing in the fenced yard.

In *Florida v. Riley,* the United States Supreme Court concluded that "surveillance of the interior of a partially covered greenhouse in a residential backyard from the vantage point of a helicopter located 400 feet above the greenhouse [does not constitute] a 'search' for which a warrant is required under the Fourth Amendment. . . ."

In *Thomas v. State,* the Georgia Court of Appeals considered a greenhouse located in a heavily wooded area on a two acre tract about 35 yards from a mobile home in which the defendant lived. The trial court concluded that the greenhouse was not within the curtilage of the house. The pilot of a Georgia State Patrol helicopter had just left a patch of marijuana in the area and was still operating at an altitude of 100 to 150 feet. He saw heavy green plants in the greenhouse but could not identify them. When he passed over the area again, he could see several trays of suspected marijuana on the outside of the property. The pilot radioed the information to deputies on the ground nearby. The deputies knocked on the door of the mobile home. When they received no response, they went to the greenhouse. No one else was present at the greenhouse, but they saw what appeared to be marijuana growing in trays outside the greenhouse and hundreds of marijuana plants inside. Based on the above information, a search warrant was obtained and a search conducted. The appellate court relied on the open fields doctrine and affirmed the denial of the motion to suppress.

In *Katz v. United States,* the United States Supreme Court emphasized that the Fourth Amendment protected persons and not places, and held that in determining whether the Fourth Amendment had been violated, the question was whether or not the officer's conduct "violated the privacy upon which [the defendant] justifiably relied." Prior to *Oliver,* some courts applied *Katz* to open fields cases. However, Georgia and a number of other jurisdictions have always followed *Hester.*

Generally, warrantless aerial observations have not been regarded as violative of the Fourth Amendment because it is said that no reasonable expectation of privacy is violated.

See section § 4-38 et seq., supra, on plain view warrantless searches. See Annotation, "Admissibility in Evidence of Aerial Photographs," 85 A. L. R. 5th 671 (2001).

§ 4-43 Warrantless searches—Jails, prisons, probationers, and inmates

A person on probation, like all other persons, has a right to be free from unreasonable searches and seizures. His probationary status is not an automatic exception to the warrant requirement.

The defendant's status as a probationer, however, is a circumstance to be considered in determining whether a search by a probation officer is reasonable. The Georgia Court of Appeals concluded that a warrantless search of a probationer is reasonable if, under all the circumstances, the probation officer acts reasonably to effectuate the legitimate operation of the probation supervisory process. Cases from some other jurisdictions have perhaps more strictly limited the Fourth Amendment protection of inmates and probationers.

In *Griffin v. Wisconsin,* the United States Supreme Court considered a state statute which authorized a warrantless search of a probationer's home by a probation officer where there are "reasonable grounds." The court held the statute to be constitutional and pointed out that although the Fourth Amendment requires that all home searches be reasonable, probationers and parolees "do not enjoy the 'absolute liberty to which every citizen is entitled, but only . . . conditional liberty properly dependent on observance of special 'restrictions.' . . . These restrictions are meant to assure that probation serves as a period of genuine rehabilitation and that the community is not harmed by probationers being at large.' "As a result, in *Fox v. State,* the Georgia Supreme Court has held that "[a]t a minimum, when a probationer has not consented to a search, a warrantless search of a probationer's home must be based upon reasonable grounds to believe that the probationer has contraband in the home or is engaged in some criminal activity there." Nevertheless, a waiver of Fourth Amendment rights may be valid if it has been negotiated through the plea bargaining process. However, if a defendant did not agree to the condition of probation, a waiver of Fourth Amendments rights is not valid. But in *Johnson v. State*, the court concluded that the defendant "impliedly consented" to a waiver of his Fourth Amendment rights where the defendant was specifically informed of the waiver at sentencing in the presence of counsel and his counsel did not object. In *Woody v. State*, the court held that where a defendant agrees to consent as a condition of probation, it is valid. In Samson v. California, the United States Supreme Court upheld the validity of a state statute that required all parolees to consent to a search of their premises when requested by law enforcement officers "with or without a search warrant and with or without cause." However, the waiver of Fourth Amendment rights provided as a condition of probation or parole cannot be used after the fact to justify a warrantless search by officers who were not aware of the waiver.

In *Howard v. State,* the Georgia Court of Appeals held that corrections officials have authority to condition a visit to a correctional institution on the willingness of the visitor to submit to a search for contraband or other items prohibited by O.C.G.A. § 42–5–15. The same case also held that where a warning sign has been placed at an entrance way stating that vehicles passing through the "guard line" of the prison are subject to a search, prison officials also have authority to search a vehicle of an employee parked inside the "guard line."

In *Hudson v. Palmer,* the United States Supreme Court held that "society is not prepared to recognize as legitimate any subjective expectation of privacy that a prisoner might have in his prison cell and that, accordingly, the Fourth Amendment proscription against unreasonable searches does not apply within the confines of a prison cell. The recognition of privacy rights for prisoners in their individual cells simply cannot be reconciled with the concept of incarceration and the needs and objectives of penal institutions." However, prisoners must "be accorded those rights not fundamentally inconsistent with imprisonment itself or incompatible with the objectives of incarceration."

In *State v. Henderson,* the court rejected the state's contention that a valid search warrant was not required before searching the defendant's cell, finding that when a search of a cell of a pretrial detainee is "conducted by representatives of the prosecution solely for the purpose of uncovering incriminating evidence which could be used against the detainee at trial, rather than out of concern for any of the legitimate prison objectives . . . , the pre-trial detainee retains a limited but legitimate expectation of privacy that he would be protected in such circumstances from an unreasonable search. . . ."

In *Franklin v. State,* the court recognized the right of officials to censor letters written by a defendant during pre-trial confinement as an aid to maintenance of discipline in the confinement facility. The court also concluded that an incriminating letter written by a defendant while incarcerated was admissible. In *Thomas v. State,* the Georgia Supreme Court held that "[f]or security and maintenance purposes, jail officials must have access to the cells and personal effects of all prisoners. . . . Letters found as a result of these searches . . . [are] not within the scope of the Fourth Amendment and . . . [are] therefore admissible."

In *Block v. Rutherford,* the United States Supreme Court held that an inmate in a jail has no due process right to be present during irregular "shake down" searches of cells.

However, in discussing the search of inmates' body cavities, the Court of Appeals in *McCullough v. State* stated that, while inmates have a decreased expectation of privacy and that body cavity searches may normally be conducted without a warrant, such searches must still be conducted in a reasonable manner. In order to justify such searches, the government "must show that a legitimate penological need necessitated the search, that the need could not have been satisfied by a more narrow means, and that the search and any consequent seizure were conducted in a reasonable manner." See section 4-56, infra, on scope and intensity of search.

See section 4-57, infra, on second search. See section 5-22, infra, on non-testimonial evidence under the United States Constitution. See section 26-19, infra, on the validity of consent to warrantless searches as a condition of probation. See section 14-78, infra, on expectation of privacy, and section 4-56, infra, on scope and intensity of a search. See Annotations, "Validity, Under Fourth Amendment, of Warrantless Search of Parolee or His Property by Parole Officer," 32 A. L. R. Fed. 155 (1977); "Fourth Amendment as Protecting Prisoner Against Unreasonable Searches and Seizures," 32 A. L. R. Fed. 601 (1977); "Censorship and Evidentiary Use of Unconvicted Prisoners' Mail," 52 A. L. R. 3d 548 (1973); "Censorship of Convicted Prisoners' 'Nonlegal' Mail," 47 A. L. R. 3d 1192 (1973).

§ 4-44 Warrantless searches—Border searches

A search at a border incident to the entrance of a person into the United States is not protected by the Fourth Amendment; hence, there is no warrant requirement for such searches. "Travelers may be . . . stopped in crossing an international boundary, because of national self-protection reasonably requiring one entering the country to identify himself as entitled to come in, and his belongings as effects which may be lawfully brought in."

Rules applying to border searches are important in Georgia since an airport at which passengers arrive after a non-stop flight from outside the country is "the functional equivalent to a border" of the United States. A search by customs agents of passengers at such an airport is not limited by the Fourth Amendment. Thus, a person and his baggage arriving at a customs area may be searched without the slightest suspicion even after the passenger has cleared the customs area.

There is authority which indicates that the defendant must be kept under constant surveillance from the time he leaves the customs area until he is searched in order to protect the privacy of the person and to ensure that any unlawful items found on him were not obtained in this country. However, the validity of a search removed from the customs area depends upon the totality of the circumstances, including the amount of time which has elapsed, the distance, and the extent of surveillance. See Annotation, "Validity of Warrantless Search Under Extended Border Doctrine," 102 A. L. R. Fed. 269 (1991).

While border searches are not controlled by the Fourth Amendment, the nature and extent of the search by custom officials is limited. Mere suspicion alone will not justify certain types of searches. If a customs official wishes to have a person disrobe, a real suspicion justifying the search must exist. It has been held that if an examination of body cavities is made, there must be a clear indication that contraband will be found. In *United States v. Ek,* the court said, "As a search becomes more intrusive, it must be justified by a corresponding higher level of suspicion of wrongdoing."

On April 16, 1984, the Eleventh Circuit handed down at least seven opinions involving the scope and intensity permitted in border searches in this Circuit. In *United States v. Vega–Barvo,* a border crossing case, the court held that a strip search requires a particularized "reasonable suspicion." This standard is met when "a person behaves in an articulably suspicious manner." "To determine the level of intrusiveness of a search we must focus on the indignity of the search. . . . [P]ersonal indignity suffered by the individual searched controls the level of suspicion required to make the search reasonable. . . . [T]hree factors . . . contribute to personal indignity . . . : (1) physical contact between the searcher and the person searched; (2) exposure of intimate body parts; and (3) use of force." The court then concluded that requiring a person to submit to a warrantless but properly taken x-ray at a hospital is no more intrusive than a strip search. The facts of the case justify a finding of reasonable suspicion that the defendant was a "mule" to carry cocaine in her digestive tract. In *United States v. Mosquera–Ramirez,* the court upheld the warrantless detention of 12 hours until the defendant discharged the contents of his stomach where there was reasonable suspicion and the defendant refused to consent to an x-ray examination. Likewise, in *United States v. Montoya de Hernandez,* a similar case, the United States Supreme Court upheld an incommunicado detention of 16 hours to await the defendant's bowel movement. Thereafter, a rectal examination was conducted pursuant to court order. In *United States v. Pino,* the court said that in order to conduct a rectal search "the facts must be sufficient to raise the level of required suspicion in the minds of experts . . . and . . . the review should not be an *ad hoc* determination of whether those facts would arouse the suspicion of the court, or an inexperienced person. . . . What is necessary are facts . . . which would cause these inspectors to reasonably believe that contraband was being carried internally and would be revealed in a rectal search: an articulable, particularized suspicion as to the person, and a particularized suspicion as to the location of the drugs."

The statutory provision for border searches does not provide for warrantless searches of residences, but only of people and vehicles. Hence, the Fifth Circuit has found that a warrantless search of the motel room of a person who had just entered the country was invalid. However, in *United States v. Richards,* the Fifth Circuit held that the border search exception permits the warrantless search of a piece of international mail, even after its delivery to the addressee, if there has been continuous surveillance of the mail and reasonable suspicion exists to believe that it contains contraband.

The Eleventh Circuit in *United States v. Chemaly* declined to decide whether the Fourth Amendment applied to passengers leaving the country. However, the court held that a warrant is required to search a person leaving for alleged currency violations under 31 U. S. C. § 5317.

See section 3-13, supra, on retention of inanimate objects without probable cause and section 4-45, infra, on search of incoming international mail. See section 3-5, supra, on stops and searches of vessels.

§ 4-45 Warrantless searches—Administrative searches

Border searches, airport searches, searches of prisoners, and perhaps parolees and probationers, may all be considered as a kind of administrative search. They have been discussed before and will not be considered further in this section.

In *Camara v. Municipal Court,* the United States Supreme Court considered a "safety inspection" of a dwelling by an employee of the Department of Health. Camara refused to permit a warrantless search and was convicted of violating an ordinance requiring occupants to submit to such inspections. The court concluded that in the absence of consent, a search warrant was required before an occupant had to submit to such an inspection. However, the Court also pointed out that a different kind of probable cause or a lesser degree of probable cause was required in the case of such an administrative search than that which is required in the traditional criminal search warrant. The court said that the probable cause required for such an administrative "area warrant" "must exist if reasonable legislative or administrative standards for conducting an area inspection are satisfied with respect to a particular dwelling. Such standards, which will vary with the municipal program being enforced, may be based upon the passage of time, the nature of the building (e.g., a multi-family apartment house), or the condition of the entire area, but they will not necessarily depend upon specific knowledge of the condition of the particular dwelling."

However, in *Wyman v. James,* the United States Supreme Court held that a home visit by a social worker to a family receiving Aid to Families with Dependent Children money was not a search in the traditional criminal law context of the Fourth Amendment; even if the visit had some characteristics of a search, it was reasonable, and no search warrant was required.

In *Illinois v. Krull,* the United States Supreme Court held that the exclusionary rule did not apply where officers, in good faith, relied on a statute authorizing a warrantless administrative search which was later held to violate the Fourth Amendment. See *Michigan v. DeFillippo,* discussed in section 3-2, supra. However, in *Yingsum Au v. State,* the Georgia Supreme Court applied the exclusionary rule where an officer relied on an ordinance of the City of Marietta in conducting a search and the court found the ordinance in violation of the Fourth Amendment.

In connection with the search of business premises the United States Supreme Court held in *United States v. Biswell* that when a federal treasury agent requests entry into a locked storeroom of a federally licensed firearms dealer for the purpose of inspecting firearms and ammunition, he has a right to conduct an inspection without first obtaining a search warrant. The court emphasized the broad authority which has historically been recognized in relation to dealers in alcohol and firearms. "When a dealer chooses to engage in this pervasively regulated business and to accept a federal license, he does so with the knowledge that his business records, firearms, and ammunition will be subject to effective inspection." Similarly, in *Donovan v. Dewey*, the Court held that an inspector acting under the Federal Mine Safety and Health Act could inspect a mine to insure compliance with health and safety standards without first obtaining a search warrant. The court discussed problems of mine safety and pointed out that the Act notifies operators that inspections will be conducted on a regular basis.

However, in *Marshall v. Barlow's, Inc.,* the United States Supreme Court held that an inspector working pursuant to the Occupational Safety and Health Act (OSHA) had no authority to conduct a warrantless inspection of the private areas of an ordinary business against which no complaints had been filed; but the Court again pointed out that probable "cause in the criminal law sense is not required" to obtain an administrative search warrant. Probable cause justifying an administrative search warrant may be based not only on specific evidence of an existing violation but also on a showing that "reasonable legislative or administrative standards for conducting an . . . inspection are satisfied with respect to a particular [establishment]."

In the fire investigations field, in *Michigan v. Tyler,* the Court held "that an entry to fight a fire requires no warrant, and that once in the building, officials may remain there for a reasonable time to investigate the cause of the blaze." However, a fire may be so devastating that no reasonable expectation of privacy interest remains. If the building is "totally consumed by the fire," there is no violation of the Fourth Amendment by a later warrantless search.

Administrative decisions involving tax levies were involved in *G. M. Leasing Corp. v. United States*. After determining that the corporation was the alter ego of a delinquent taxpayer, agents, acting without a warrant, seized several automobiles of the corporation from public streets, parking lots, and other open areas. The agents also went to the corporation's office in a cottage-type building and made a forced entry. No seizure was made. However, two days later they again entered the office without a warrant and seized books, records and other property. The Supreme Court concluded that the seizure of the automobiles did not violate the Constitution. However, the warrantless search and seizure of the articles from the office violated the Fourth Amendment since no exigent circumstances existed.

The search of incoming international mail was involved in *United States v. Ramsey*. In this case, a customs inspector found eight letter-size airmail envelopes in the same mail bag from Thailand. All eight envelopes appeared to have been addressed on the same typewriter. All were bulky and weighed from 3 to 6 times as much as normal international mail. He opened the envelopes without a warrant and found them to contain heroin.

The court concluded that the inspector had "reasonable cause to suspect" that the envelopes contained merchandise or contraband. Thus, the Fourth Amendment did not prohibit the action taken by the inspector because (a) border searches without probable cause and a warrant are reasonable within the meaning of the Fourth Amendment; (b) the inclusion of international mail within the border search exception does not represent any "extension" of that doctrine; (c) the border search exception is not based on exigent circumstances but is a longstanding historically recognized exception to the Fourth Amendment's general requirement that a warrant must be obtained; and (d) the opening of international mail under the guidelines of the statute, when the customs official has reason to believe the mail contains something other than correspondence, does not impermissibly chill free speech under the First Amendment. See section 3-1, supra, on factory surveys to locate illegal aliens.

However, in *New York v. Burger,* the United States Supreme Court pointed out that the expectation of privacy is greater in a home than in commercial premises and that there is no expectation of privacy in "[c]ertain industries [which] have a history of governmental oversight." Therefore, a warrant was not necessary for officers to conduct an inspection of a junkyard. The Supreme Court has applied this rule in the case of liquor dealers, firearms in a pawnshop, and mines.

See 3 LaFave, *Search and Seizure,* § 10.1 et seq. (West 1978); 1 Ringel, *Searches and Seizures, Arrests and Confessions*, § 14.1 et seq. (Clark Boardman 1979); 68 Am. Jur. 2d Searches and Seizures § 15; Annotation, "Fourth Amendment's Prohibition of Unreasonable Search and Seizure as Applied to Administrative Inspections of Private Property," 69 L.Ed.2d 1078 (1982). See Annotation, "State and local administrative inspection of and administrative warrants to search pharmacies," 29 A. L. R. 4th 264 (1984). See O.C.G.A. § 2–2–11 on agricultural inspection warrants.

§ 4-46 Warrantless searches—Vehicles—Overview of some United States Supreme Court cases

In *Carroll v. United States,* the defendant was driving a car from Detroit, to Grand Rapids, Michigan. Agents recognized his car, personally knew Carroll dealt in illegal liquor, and had seen the car on that highway before. The agents also knew the car had been used in the illegal liquor business, and because Detroit is located on an international boundary it was one of the most active centers for introducing illegal liquors into the country. These factors combined gave the agents reasonable cause to believe the defendant was carrying illegal liquor.

Because of this, the warrantless stop, search, and seizure was valid, since it was not reasonably practical to get a search warrant for a moving vehicle. In *Maryland v. Dyson,* the court reaffirmed *Carroll* and pointed out that the automobile exception provides that an officer may search a car without a warrant if he has probable cause to believe it contains contraband even if there are no exigent circumstances preventing the officer from getting a search warrant.

In *Chambers v. Maroney,* a service station attendant was robbed. The robbers and the vehicle they drove were described in a police broadcast. Within an hour, and within two miles of the station, a car and occupants were sighted and stopped by an officer. The occupants were arrested and the car was driven to the police station where it was searched without a warrant and incriminating evidence discovered. The court, in holding the search valid, pointed out that the validity of the search was not dependent on the right to arrest but was dependent on the reasonable cause the seizing officer has for his belief that the contents of the auto offend the law. Since there was probable cause to search where the car was stopped, it could also be searched after it had been towed to the police station.

In *Coolidge v. New Hampshire,* the court concluded that where Coolidge was arrested in his house there was no right to search his automobile parked in his drive as an incident to the arrest. Also, there was no right to search the vehicle based on probable cause since there were no exigent circumstances. The defendant was in custody. All the members of his immediate family were elsewhere, and guards had been placed at his home. The offense he was thought to have committed had taken place over four weeks before. The court also said, "The word 'automobile' is not a talisman in whose presence the Fourth Amendment fades away and disappears." Likewise, the search may not be justified under the plain view doctrine since its discovery was not inadvertent and there were no exigent circumstances.

§ 4-47 Warrantless searches—Vehicles—General

While the Fourth Amendment limitations apply to vehicles, warrantless examinations of automobiles have been upheld in circumstances in which a search of a home or office would not have been validated. The courts have recognized Fourth Amendment distinctions between homes and automobiles. The following factors have been given as reasons for a somewhat different application of the Fourth Amendment to vehicle searches: (1) The mobility of motor vehicles, as a matter of necessity, prevents rigorous enforcement of the warrant requirement; (2) an individual's expectation of privacy is less in an automobile; (3) automobiles are frequently subject to governmental regulations, such as those relating to licensing and inspection; and (4) the contents of impounded vehicles are routinely inventoried to protect the property of the owner, protect the officers against claims for lost or stolen property, and protect the police from potential danger.

Despite the foregoing considerations, the requirement of a search warrant for a vehicle has been said to be the general rule, and where there is a search without a warrant, the burden is on the government to show the search falls within one of the exceptions to the Fourth Amendment requirement of a warrant. Generally, the following exceptions or limitations may apply to the rule requiring a warrant:

(1) Search incident to a valid arrest.

(2) Where there is probable cause to search.

(3) Where the car is impounded or placed in storage.

(4) Where there is consent to the search.

(5) Search of a car at or near a border of the United States.

(6) Search of abandoned vehicle.

These exceptions to the warrant requirement will be discussed as listed above. Consent searches have been discussed earlier and border searches have been referred to previously.

It should be pointed out that where a defendant is arrested in a stolen automobile, he is said to have no standing or expectation of privacy which will enable him to object to an illegal search of the vehicle.

Also, the United States Supreme Court in *Cardwell v. Lewis* found that the owner of a car had no expectation of privacy in the exterior of his car. Here the defendant was suspected of having used his automobile to push the victim's vehicle over an embankment. The court said, " 'What a person knowingly exposes to the public, even in his own home or office, is not a subject of Fourth Amendment protection' . . . With the 'search' limited to the examination of the tire on the wheel and the taking of paint scrapings from the exterior of the vehicle left in the public parking lot, we fail to comprehend what expectation of privacy was infringed."

In *Illinois v. Caballes,* the United States Supreme Court held that the warrantless use of a drug-sniffing dog during a lawful traffic stop does not violate the defendant's legitimate privacy interests where the use of the dog does not impermissibly extend the traffic stop. In so holding, the Court distinguished *Kyllo v. United States,* stating, "The legitimate expectation that information about perfectly lawful activity will remain private is categorically distinguishable from respondent's hopes or expectations concerning the nondetection of contraband in the trunk of his car." As such, "[a] dog sniff conducted during a concededly lawful traffic stop that reveals no information other than the location of a substance that no individual has any right to possess, does not violate the Fourth Amendment."

See Annotation, "Validity, Under Federal Constitution, of Warrantless Search of Motor Vehicle—Supreme Court Cases," 66 L.Ed.2d 882 (1982). See section 14-78, infra, on examples of expectation of privacy.

§ 4-48 Warrantless searches—Vehicles—Incident to valid arrest

In the vehicle field it is frequently difficult to determine whether a search which was found to be valid by appellate courts was permitted on the theory that the search was incident to a valid arrest or because there was probable cause to conduct the search. Of course, both theories may apply in a given case. The two concepts have been confused and at times improperly lumped together, or used interchangeably. Yet they are different and much of the confusion which exists in the area of automobile searches has resulted from the failure to clearly separate the two concepts.

In *Chambers v. Maroney,* the United States Supreme Court said "that the search of an auto on probable cause proceeds on a theory wholly different from that justifying the search incident to an arrest: 'The right to search and the validity of the seizure are not dependent on the right to arrest. They are dependent on the reasonable cause the seizing officer has for belief that the contents of the automobile offend against the law.' "

In 1925 it was held that a search incident to an arrest is limited to the immediate area where the defendant is at the time of the arrest, and is to be made, for the most part, contemporaneously with the arrest. The purpose of a search incident to an arrest is to locate weapons and evidence related to the offense for which the arrest is made. The officer has a right, for his own personal safety and the safety of others, to locate weapons which might be used by the defendant in order to escape or to wound or kill an officer or other person. Likewise, the officer has a right to locate and preserve any evidence of the crime for which the defendant is arrested so as to prevent the defendant from destroying such evidence.

In *New York v. Belton,* the Court emphasized the need for a "straight forward rule" from a federal constitutional standpoint so that "a court will apply a settled principle to a recurring factual situation [so] that a person [can] . . . know the scope of his constitutional protection, . . . [and so] a policeman [can] know the scope of his authority." This was later referred to as a "bright line rule." The court then held "that when a policeman has made a lawful custodial arrest of the occupant of an automobile, he may, as a contemporaneous incident of that arrest, search the passenger compartment of that automobile." This right to search also applies to containers located in the passenger compartment. In *Glasco v. Commonwealth,* the Supreme Court of Virginia held that when a defendant was a "recent occupant" of a stopped car, officers may, under *Belton,* search the passenger compartment incident to an arrest even if the defendant had walked away from the vehicle at the time of the arrest.

The right to search the passenger compartment incident to a valid arrest is not lost at the time the defendant is placed in a police car and when the contents are no longer in the control of the defendant. The vehicle rule has been held applicable to a small airplane, a ship, a motor boat, and a wagon. In *New York v. Belton,* in a footnote, the Court said, " 'Container' here denotes any object capable of holding another object. It thus includes closed or open glove compartments, consoles, or other receptacles located anywhere within the passenger compartment, as well as luggage, boxes, bags, clothing, and the like. Our holding encompasses only the interior of the passenger compartment of an automobile and does not encompass the trunk." In *Boyd v. State,* the Georgia Court of Appeals held that under the Belton rule officers could search an open overnight bag in the open bed of a pickup when the officers arrested the occupants of the truck.

However, in *Knowles v. Iowa,* the United States Supreme Court refused to extend the bright line rule allowing a search incident to an arrest in a case in which the driver was stopped for speeding. The court held a state statute unconstitutional which provided "that the issuance of a citation in lieu of arrest 'does not affect the officer's authority to conduct an otherwise lawful search.' "The state supreme court had "interpreted this provision as providing authority to officers to conduct a full-blown search of an automobile and driver in those cases where police elect not to make a custodial arrest and instead issue a citation. . . ." The United States Supreme Court pointed out that neither of "the two historical rationales for the 'search incident to arrest' exception: (1) the need to disarm the suspect in order to take him into custody, and (2) the need to preserve evidence for later use at trial" justified a search in this case.

In *State v. Escobar,* the Georgia Court of Appeals affirmed the granting of a motion to suppress where there had been a valid arrest, a search of the interior of a van, and then the removal of a misaligned piece of molding from the outside of the vehicle. After the removal of the molding, with the aid of a flashlight and through a crack about an inch wide, officers "observed yellow and brown wrapped material. The compartment was later accessed by drilling into the vehicle, and eighteen individually wrapped kilogram packages of cocaine were recovered." It was the removal of the van's body molding that was outside the parameters of a legal search and thus illegal.

It has been held that the right to search containers found in the passenger compartment as an incident to a lawful arrest does not apply when the search occurred some five hours after the arrest. However, the United States Supreme Court by per curiam order vacated that judgment.

In *State v. Massenburg,* the North Carolina court held that under *Belton* a *locked* glove compartment may be searched incident to an arrest. In the Seventh Circuit case of *United States v. Veras,* the court held that under *Belton* an officer has a right to search a hidden compartment located between the top of the back seat and the rear window.

In 1977, the United States Supreme Court held that when a driver is stopped for driving a vehicle with an expired license plate, the officer may order the driver to step out of the automobile before he asks the driver for his driver's license. Apparently this rule will be applied to all cases where a defendant is stopped for a traffic violation. However, as pointed out in the chapter on stop-and-frisk, supra, an officer generally has no authority to make a stop of a vehicle unless he at least has a reasonable articulable suspicion that a traffic violation has occurred or that an occupant is otherwise subject to seizure.

However, where an officer stops a motorist for speeding and it is "the standard procedure when he arrested someone for a traffic violation . . . to issue the driver a standard citation and offer him the choice of leaving his driver's license with the [officer] . . . in lieu of bond or proceeding to the sheriff's office to make [a] . . . bond," the officer may not take the driver into custody and impound the car so as to make an inventory search. But in *Dixon v. State,* the court held that when a driver is arrested for speeding and having no proof of insurance or a driver's license, the passenger compartment may be validly searched even if it is later determined that the defendant had a valid license.

Of course, if there is a valid custodial arrest, the officer has the right to search the defendant. If there is a valid custodial arrest of a defendant in an automobile, as an incident of the arrest, the officer may search the passenger compartment of the car as set out above even after the defendant is removed from the immediate area of the automobile or even driven away by the police. In *Gooden v. State,* the court pointed out that the Belton rule does not apply in Georgia "where there is some necessity for the police to take custody of the vehicle and conduct an inventory search for the protection of the police department and the defendant."

In order to justify a search of an automobile as incident to an arrest, the initial arrest must be valid. There is no right to search an automobile as an incident of a valid arrest after it has been moved to another location. Unlike a search incident to a valid arrest, if there is *probable* cause to search the car at the scene of the arrest, then the search may be delayed until the defendant and the automobile have been taken to another location. However, where a defendant is arrested in his home and his car is parked on his drive, there is no right as an incident to the arrest to take the car to the police station and search it without a warrant. Likewise, where a defendant is arrested and found in possession of parking-meter keys, a search of his legally parked automobile a half-block away is not incident to the arrest. In *State v. Bell*, the Court of Appeals affirmed the trial court's order granting a motion to suppress evidence seized from the defendant's auto after the defendant had been arrested and charged with the offense of consuming alcohol in the vicinity of a liquor store in violation of a municipal ordinance. The court ruled that the seizure could not properly be characterized as a search incident to arrest because: the defendant had left his vehicle on his own initiative; the arrest was in no way related to the operation of the motor vehicle; and, the arresting officer's safety was never in jeopardy. In *State v. Lejeune*, the Supreme Court in reversing a trial court's order denying a motion to suppress based upon the "automobile exception" to the general requirement of a warrant for a search observed: "the 'automobile exception' cases do not hold that a search warrant is *never* needed to search a car. There is an automobile exception to the search warrant requirement, not an exemption." (emphasis in original). However, in a case where a driver is stopped for a defective taillight and then arrested for driving under the influence, the court held that the officer had the right to search the trunk of the car, not as an incident to the arrest, but because of facts giving the officer probable cause for searching the car for marijuana such as the odor of marijuana, a passenger being seen trying to throw something out of the car, and other facts.

In addition to a search incident to an arrest, the Georgia courts have recognized the limited right of officers to momentarily detain a citizen for a routine license check though there is no probable cause for an arrest. During a license check, probable cause for an arrest may be discovered by the officer. However, such license checks are "not [to] be used as a subterfuge to detain citizens for the purpose of searching their automobiles when they are under no founded suspicion." Roadblocks to check licenses are regarded as preventive therapy to determine if drivers meet the legislative determination of fitness to drive. See section 3-9, supra, on roadblocks. Nevertheless, an officer has no right to a *Terry* frisk of the driver of a vehicle simply because the officer is suspicious or because the defendant acts in a suspicious manner. Moreover, it has been held that even when there is a right to conduct a *Terry* frisk, if the occupants get out of the car and the officers are between the occupants and vehicle, there is no justification for one of the officers sticking his head in the vehicle to check for weapons.

In *State v. Watts,* in discussing the search of an auto, the court said that to establish probable cause for the issuance of a warrant by a magistrate or to establish exigent circumstances justifying a search without a warrant three elements are essential: "[1] that there is reason to accept the informer's reliability; [2] that the facts are sufficient to show how the informer obtained his information or that the criminal activity is described in such detail as to negate its being a mere rumor; and [3] that the information is current, not stale."

See section 2-11, supra, on probable cause to arrest without a warrant for an offense committed in the presence of an officer; sections 4-26 and 4-27, supra, on general searches incident to an arrest; and section 4-15, supra. In connection with the search of suitcases in a vehicle driven by a defendant at the time of his arrest, see sections 4-26 and 4-27, supra. See section 4-49, infra, on search of an automobile based on probable cause and section 3-11, supra, on frisk of a vehicle. See Annotation, "Validity, Under Federal Constitution, of Warrantless Search of Motor Vehicle—Supreme Court Cases," 66 L.Ed.2d 882, 887 (1982).

§ 4-49 Warrantless searches—Vehicles—Probable cause—General

In *Carroll v. United States,* the United States Supreme Court held that officers may search a stopped automobile without a warrant if there is probable cause to believe that contraband or other evidence of crime is within the vehicle and it is not practicable to secure a warrant. Thus, in the case of a motor vehicle, if there is probable cause to believe that it contains evidence which is seizable and there are exigent circumstances, an officer may conduct a warrantless search. In the 1996 case of *Pennsylvania v. Labron,* the United States Supreme Court held that a search of an automobile based on probable cause does not require exigent or unforeseen circumstances. " '[R]eady mobility' [amounts to] an exigency sufficient to excuse failure to obtain a search warrant. . . . If a car is readily mobile and probable cause exists to believe it contains contraband, the Fourth Amendment thus permits police to search the vehicle without more." The United States Supreme Court, in *Maryland v. Dyson* in 1999, upheld the stopping of a vehicle and a warrantless search of a vehicle based on probable cause even though there was sufficient time after the informant's tip to obtain a warrant and it would not have been significantly difficult to get a warrant. This has been said to be true because of the mobility of automobiles. A vehicle can quickly be moved out of the jurisdiction in which a warrant is obtained. However, the same rule has been applied to an automobile which has been rendered immobile as a result of a collision. The Carroll rule has been held to be applicable to an airplane.

In *Chambers v. Maroney,* the United States Supreme Court held that if there is probable cause to search the vehicle where it is stopped or located, the search may be delayed until the automobile is moved to another location. In *California v. Carney,* the Court applied the Carroll rule to an operable motor home on a public parking lot, and in *United States v. Hamilton,* the Ninth Circuit applied the Carroll rule to a motor home parked in a private drive.

It would be unreasonable to authorize officers to stop every automobile on the chance of finding contraband. In order to stop and search a car on a public highway, there must be probable cause for believing that the vehicle contains contraband. The "probable cause determination must be based on objective facts that could justify the issuance of a warrant by a magistrate and not merely on subjective good faith of the police officers." In addition, where the initial action of the police is improper, e.g., stopping a motorist without some objective basis for suspicion of wrongdoing, an intervening legitimate ground for stopping the driver, e.g., resisting arrest, may serve to purge the taint of an otherwise illegal stop and justify the use of any evidence seized in connection therewith.

In *Colorado v. Bannister,* the United States Supreme Court held that where there was probable cause to believe that articles appearing in plain view in an automobile were stolen property, the officer may seize the items without a search warrant. Also, in *People v. Superior Court of Orange County*, the California Court of Appeals held that officers may search a vehicle if they have probable cause to believe that a vehicle contains evidence of a crime, because no exigent circumstances need be shown aside from the mobility of the car. In *Michigan v. Thomas*, the United States Supreme Court held that a second search could be conducted by officers, without a search warrant, even after the vehicle had been immobilized by being in police custody. In *Boggs v. State*, the Georgia Court of Appeals held that where an officer has "probable cause to believe that contraband was contained somewhere in appellant's automobile, he was authorized to conduct a search of its contents, including the locked strongbox." In *California v. Acevedo*, the United States Supreme Court pointed out that "[t]o the extent that the Chadwick–Sanders rule protects privacy, its protection is minimal. . . . Sanders was explicitly undermined in Ross. [See section 4-52, infra.] . . . [I]t is better to adopt one clear-cut rule to govern automobile searches and eliminate the warrant requirement for closed containers set forth in Sanders. . . 'Probable cause to believe that a container placed in the trunk of [an automobile] contains contraband or evidence does not justify a search of the entire [vehicle].' . . . In the case before us, the police had probable cause to believe that the paper bag in the automobile's trunk contained marijuana. That probable cause now allows a warrantless search of the paper bag. . . . The police may search an automobile and the containers within it where they have probable cause to believe contraband or evidence is contained."

There must be at least as much probable cause for a vehicular search without a warrant as would be required to obtain a search warrant from a magistrate. In *Love v. State,* the Georgia Court of Appeals said, "An automobile search may be conducted without a warrant provided it is based on facts that would justify the issuance of a warrant." The facts known to the officers involved must be such as would lead a prudent man in the same circumstances to believe that contraband is illegally possessed in a vehicle or that tools or fruits of a crime are there. In *McKinney v. State,* the court held that exigent circumstances were not necessary to justify the warrantless search of an automobile. However, exigent circumstances plus a general inarticulable suspicion are not sufficient. The presence or absence of probable cause is to be determined from the totality of circumstances. The fact that it is the usual practice among officers to search stopped cars will not render a search valid.

The doctrine of collective knowledge of officers conducting a common investigation applies to the search of an automobile just as it applies to an arrest. See section 2-11, supra. Thus, the Georgia Court of Appeals, in *Parker v. State,* stated that especially "when an officer is operating under the exigent circumstances required for a warrantless search of a car, we cannot require a police officer to radio to another officer all the information he has about a suspect, the source of his information, and the background of his informant in order that the receiving officer may make an independent determination as to whether he has probable cause to stop and search the automobile in question. . . . [The] searching officer need not personally be aware of all the facts which would support a probable cause determination so long as it can be established by evidence that the searching officer's actions were the end result of a chain of information-sharing; one link of which is an officer in possession of the 'information requisite to support an independent judicial assessment of probable cause.' " However, in *Duke v. State*, the Court of Appeals acknowledged in response to a motion to suppress that the state was entitled to rely on the collective knowledge of law enforcement to satisfy the probable cause element to a warrantless search of an auto and its driver. However, while the arresting officer was acting appropriately by performing a stop and search, after receiving orders from his dispatch to stop a specific vehicle believed to be involved in drug activity, the Court nonetheless suppressed the evidence because the State failed to show the source of the information provided over the police radio or any reason for the order to make the stop. See sections 2-11, 3-2, 3-7, and 4-9, supra, on collective knowledge establishing an articulable suspicion.

See section 2-11, supra, on probable cause to arrest and section 4-7, supra, on probable cause to obtain a search warrant. See section 4-52, infra, on nature of search permitted. Also see section 4-29, supra, on exigent circumstances. Generally, see Annotation, "Validity, Under Federal Constitution, of Warrantless Search of Motor Vehicle—Supreme Court Cases," 66 L.Ed.2d 882, 889 (1982).

§ 4-50 Warrantless searches—Vehicles—Circumstances not amounting to probable cause

The following situations illustrate cases in which the Georgia Court of Appeals determined that probable cause to search a vehicle did not exist where (1) the police were notified by campus police from the local college to be on the lookout for a car fitting the description of a defendant's vehicle because of a campus traffic violation; (2) an officer recognized a driver as one he believed to possess marijuana and observed a cigarette paper in the car; (3) marijuana could not be seized from a car where an officer's most favorable testimony to the state was that he saw, through the window of the automobile and through the open aperture of the unlit glove compartment, a bag containing a substance he believed was contraband; (4) officers observed a man in a car who matched the description of a person who had reportedly recently retrieved a plastic bag from under some leaves, they had no right to search the man's car, even though they smelled alcohol from within the automobile; (5) an officer observed the passing of a paper bag from one car to another late at night, the car to which the bag is passed pulls away with its lights off, and, on stopping the vehicle, there is a paper sack which the officer partially sees behind the passenger seat; the officer asked, "What's in the paper bag?" and the driver said, "What paper bag?"; (6) there is no probable cause to search a car, which was not seen violating any law, but which was seen in a commercial district in the early morning hours approximately 500 yards from a place officers later learned had been burglarized; (7) likewise, the observation of black suspects near a Cadillac in the driveway of a residence in a "white" neighborhood and their shortly driving away did not constitute probable cause for an arrest for burglary; (8) officers had probable cause to search the defendant's car and the defendant was arrested a number of miles away from the car, there were found to be no exigent circumstances justifying a warrantless search where officers could have obtained a search warrant; and, (9) the "mere entry and exit of a house where drugs had been found six months earlier does not rise to the level of reasonable, articulable suspicion of a drug purchase" and hence would not provide the probable cause to stop the motor vehicle which took the defendant to and from the house.

§ 4-51 Warrantless searches—Vehicles—Circumstances amounting to probable cause

The observation by police officers of an object passed out of a car in exchange for money has been held to establish probable cause where the officers had reliable information that the car was being used to transport drugs. Where a car sped off when officers approached and officers noted the odor of marijuana when the car was stopped, there was probable cause to search the automobile. In *State v. Folk,* the court held that "a trained police officer's perception of the odor of burning marijuana, provided his ability to identify that odor is placed into evidence, constitutes sufficient probable cause to support the warrantless search of a vehicle," and pointed out that the court has previously found "the 'alert' of a trained narcotics dog, standing alone, sufficient to provide probable cause for the search of a vehicle."

In *Pittman v. State,* the court concluded that there was probable cause and exigent circumstances justifying a search of a car, including its trunk. Exigent circumstances seem clear. However, the report of the case fails to indicate how the known reliable informant obtained the information he furnished to the officer. The informant stated that the defendant was going to meet a black female at the Gulf station on Riverside Drive in the next few minutes and that the defendant would have a quantity of cocaine and be alone in a late model Oldsmobile Toronado. The officer went to the location, and the defendant arrived within five minutes alone in a car as described. The defendant walked behind the station and returned with a black female. The defendant looked around "apparently to see if the area was clear." Both persons got in the defendant's car and drove off. The officer stopped the car and searched it. The court pointed to "the detailed nature of his tip, and the corroboration of his information" as establishing probable cause.

Where a rape occurred in a red and white car in a rural area and such a vehicle was found with blood both on the inside and outside, a search of the car was held valid. After a high-speed chase, the arrest of a murder suspect has been held to constitute probable cause to search the interior of the car. However, it has been held that there is no probable cause to search a vehicle simply because an officer smells the odor of marijuana smoke.

§ 4-52 Warrantless searches—Vehicles—Nature of search permitted

It has been held in Georgia that where a car is speeding, the driver appears to be intoxicated, the odor of marijuana smoke is detected, a passenger is found to have marijuana, and the driver passes an alcohol intoximeter test, there is probable cause to search "every part of the vehicle and its contents that may conceal . . . contraband."

In *United States v. Ross,* officers received information from a reliable informant that a described person was selling narcotics and kept the contraband in the trunk of a car at a certain location. After locating the automobile, the officers left the area and returned about five minutes later. They observed the vehicle being driven away and stopped it. The interior of the car was searched, and one of the officers looked into the trunk, where he found a closed brown paper bag. He opened the bag and found glassine bags containing a white powder. Ross was charged with possession of heroin with intent to distribute. The officer also found a leather zipped pouch in the trunk. The Supreme Court held that the warrantless search of the bag and the pouch was valid. The court stated:

"A lawful search of fixed premises generally extends to the entire area in which the object of the search may be found and is not limited by the possibility that separate acts of entry or opening may be required to complete the search. Thus, a warrant that authorizes an officer to search a home for illegal weapons also provides authority to open closets, chests, drawers, and containers in which the weapon might be found. A warrant to open a footlocker to search for marijuana would also authorize the opening of packages found inside. A warrant to search a vehicle would support a search of every part of the vehicle that might contain the object of the search. When a legitimate search is under way, and when its purpose and its limits have been precisely defined, nice distinctions between closets, drawers, and containers, in the case of a home, or between glove compartments, upholstered seats, trunks, and wrapped packages, in the case of a vehicle, must give way to the interest in the prompt and efficient completion of the task at hand.

"This rule applies equally to all containers. . . .

"The scope of a warrantless search based on probable cause is no narrower—and no broader—than the scope of a search authorized by a warrant supported by probable cause. Only the prior approval of the magistrate is waived; the search otherwise is as the magistrate could authorize.

"The scope of a warrantless search of an automobile thus is not defined by the nature of the container in which the contraband is secreted. Rather, it is defined by the object of the search and the places in which there is probable cause to believe that it may be found. Just as probable cause to believe that a stolen lawnmower may be found in a garage will not support a warrant to search an upstairs bedroom, probable cause to believe that undocumented aliens are being transported in a van will not justify a warrantless search of a suitcase. Probable cause to believe that a container placed in the trunk of a taxi contains contraband or evidence does not justify a search of the entire cab. . . .

"The Fourth Amendment proscribes all unreasonable searches and seizures, and it is a cardinal principle that 'searches conducted outside the judicial process, without prior approval by judge or magistrate, are *per se* unreasonable under the Fourth Amendment—subject only to a few specifically established and well-delineated exceptions.' . . .

"The exception recognized in *Carroll* is unquestionably one that is 'specifically established and well-delineated.' We hold that the scope of the warrantless search authorized by that exception is no broader and no narrower than a magistrate could legitimately authorize by warrant. If probable cause justifies the search of a lawfully stopped vehicle, it justifies the search of every part of the vehicle and its contents that may conceal the object of the search."

In *United States v. Johns,* the United States Supreme Court held that where there is probable cause to search a vehicle and probable cause to search a package taken from the vehicle, it is not necessary to obtain a search warrant in order to search the package removed from the vehicle three days after its seizure.

The United States Supreme Court in *California v. Acevedo* held that where there is probable cause to search a vehicle for contraband and there is probable cause to search a paper bag or container found in the vehicle, officers may search the bag. *Acevedo* is discussed in section 4-49, supra. In *Wyoming v. Houghton,* the United States Supreme Court held that where probable cause exists to believe a vehicle contains contraband, the officer has a right to search any container large enough to conceal the object in the vehicle regardless of whether the container belongs to the driver or a passenger.

In *Florida v. Jimeno,* the Court held that a consent to search a vehicle included a consent to search a folded brown bag found on the floorboard. In *United States v. Jaras,* the Fifth Circuit held that the consent of a motorist to a search of the car he was driving did not amount to a consent to search suitcases in the trunk which were identified as belonging to a passenger, and the passenger's silence did not amount to a consent.

See sections 4-26 and 4-27, supra, on searches of articles around arrestee. Also see section 4-48, supra, on searches incident to the arrest of a driver of a vehicle, and section 4-53, infra, on searches of occupants of vehicles. See section 3-11, supra, on frisk of a motor vehicle. See section 4-29, supra, on exigent circumstances justifying a warrantless search.

§ 4-53 Warrantless searches—Vehicles—Search of occupants

Generally, it has been held that a passenger in an automobile may not be searched simply because the driver is stopped for speeding or for possession of contraband. However, in *Pennsylvania v. Mimms,* the Supreme Court held that where a driver is stopped for driving with an expired license plate, the officer may order him to get out of the car before looking at his driver's license. The dissenting opinion concludes that this case means a passenger in any vehicle stopped for a traffic violation may be ordered to get out of the car, but the majority opinion does not mention this. By mere presence in an automobile, a person does not lose his Fourth Amendment protection from search of his person. However, it has been held that if an officer alone is making an arrest for driving without a license and recognizes the passengers in the automobile as suspects in a recent crime, he may frisk them where there is a substantial risk of possible danger to his safety. It is not necessary that the officer be frightened by the threat of danger if he is aware of sufficient specific facts to suggest that he is in danger. In *Arizona v. Johnson,* the United States Supreme Court clarified the issue of whether police needed an articulable suspicion that the passenger in a vehicle stopped by the police has committed a crime before being subjected to a search. The court concluded that once the police detain the passenger by asking him or her to step out of the car, the passenger may be subject to search provided only that the police have reason to believe the passenger is armed.

Where a driver is arrested and there is probable cause to believe that evidence pertaining to the crime is in the automobile, the police officer may require the passengers to get out so that he may safely and effectively search the vehicle, and to prevent them from destroying the evidence. However, where defendants are stopped driving a stolen car and there is probable cause to arrest them, they may be searched incident to their arrests, like any one else who is arrested.

Pursuant to *Belton,* discussed in section 4-48, supra, a California court has held that where an occupant of an automobile is arrested, officers may search containers in the passenger compartment which belong to occupants who have not been arrested.

See sections 4-48 and 4-49, supra, on automobile searches. Also see sections 4-26 and 4-27, supra, on searches incident to an arrest. See section 14-76, infra, on standing of a passenger to challenge use of evidence seized following the search of a motor vehicle.

§ 4-54 Warrantless searches—Vehicles—Abandonment

Abandoned vehicles may generally be searched without a warrant. Sometimes such a warrantless search is said to be valid because the owner has no standing or expectation of privacy.

Strictly speaking, the question of whether or not a vehicle can be searched should probably turn on whether the owner had a reasonable expectation of privacy in the vehicle under all the circumstances existing. It has also been found that an automobile may be temporarily abandoned. A vehicle may be abandoned if it is given to another person. Also, a vehicle may be abandoned by leaving it at a service station for an unreasonable period of time. More commonly, a vehicle is deemed to have been abandoned when it has been chased by police, and after a wreck the driver flees.

§ 4-55 Warrantless searches—Vehicles—Inventory search after impound, put in storage, or condemned

In *South Dakota v. Opperman,* the United States Supreme Court held that, from a federal constitutional standpoint, a locked automobile impounded for a parking violation may be inventoried even if it has to be unlocked, and evidence discovered in the glove compartment during the process is admissible in evidence against the owner if the police department has a standard procedure of inventorying the contents of such vehicles.

In *Colorado v. Bertine,* the United States Supreme Court held that the Fourth Amendment does not prevent the "inventory search" of a closed container in the passenger compartment of an automobile which had been impounded, even if some less intrusive method might achieve the purpose of the inventory provided the inventory was carried out in compliance with standard police procedures. The court emphasized the importance of a "single familiar standard . . . to guide police officers."

In *Florida v. Wells,* the United States Supreme Court considered a case in which the defendant was arrested for driving under the influence of alcohol. Pursuant to permission, during an inventory search the officers found two marijuana cigarettes in the vehicle and a locked suitcase in the trunk. The suitcase contained a large amount of marijuana. The highway patrol had no policy on opening closed containers. Based on this, the Florida court suppressed evidence of the contraband found in the locked suitcase. In affirming, the United States Supreme Court pointed out that "[a] police officer may be allowed sufficient latitude to determine whether a particular container should or should not be opened in light of the nature of the search and characteristics of the container itself. Thus, while policies of opening all containers or of opening no containers are unquestionably permissible, it would be equally permissible, for example, to allow the opening of closed containers whose contents officers determine they are unable to ascertain from examining the containers exteriors. The allowance of the exercise of judgment based on concerns related to the purposes of an inventory search does not violate the Fourth Amendment." In *Martin v. State,* the court held that "[w]hether there was a department inventory policy and whether the officer knew it, if there was one, is not determinative of the issue although the existence of a policy would be relevant. . . . Justification of such a search, however, is premised upon the validity of the impoundment."

In *State v. Evans,* the Georgia Court of Appeals held that pursuant to standard procedure, an officer may unlock the trunk of an automobile and inventory an unlocked container found within even in the absence of probable cause. In *Michigan v. Thomas,* the United States Supreme Court upheld the search of an air vent under the dash after an earlier inventory search had disclosed contraband in the glove compartment. The court emphasized that the right to make a probable cause search is not lost by the impoundment of the vehicle.

Where there is such a standard policy, there is the right to inventory an impounded vehicle for the purpose of (1) protecting the owner's property while he is in custody or elsewhere; (2) protecting the officer against claims of the owner for alleged missing property; (3) protecting the public and the police from illegal weapons which might be contained in the car; and (4) determining whether the vehicle has been stolen. In *Pierce v. State,* the Georgia Court of Appeals said, "[i]nventory searches have two purposes: [1] to protect the vehicle and the property in it, and [2] to safeguard the police or other officers from claims of lost possessions." In conducting such an inventory, an officer may presumably check all areas of the automobile which he has reasonable probable cause to believe might contain any of the items to be inventoried. These areas normally include an inspection of the glove compartment, the trunk, the top of the seats, under the front seat and the floor of the automobile. In *Whatley v. State,* the court upheld an inventory conducted under the hood of a vehicle and said the areas examined need only be related to the purposes set out in *Opperman.* Of course, if in conducting such an inventory the officer finds contraband or stolen property, he may seize it. However, an inventory of the contents may not be used as a pretext for an investigatory police search. In *State v. Lowe,* the court pointed out that an impoundment "is valid only if there is some necessity for the police to take charge of [the car]. . . . In each instance, the ultimate test for the validity of the police's conduct is whether, under the circumstances then confronting the police, their conduct was reasonable within the meaning of the Fourth Amendment. . . . The existence of a department policy is relevant but not determinative:" of the right to impound and inventory.

If the impoundment is not valid, the inventory or search is not valid. Thus, where the owner of an automobile is arrested a half block away from his legally parked automobile and there is nothing to indicate the police intended to impound the car, the police may not search the car for the purpose of discovering fruits of the crime for which the defendant was arrested. Likewise, it has been held that where a defendant is arrested for speeding and driving under the influence while driving a borrowed car and the defendant asks that a passenger be permitted to return the car to the owner at a designated address, it is improper for the officer to have the vehicle impounded without seeking instructions from the owner. Where an owner makes his own arrangements to have his car towed away, an arresting officer has no right to conduct an inventory search of the vehicle.

It has been held that where an officer arrests the driver of an automobile for being drunk in a private parking lot owned by the driver, the officer has no right to call a wrecker and inventory the contents of the car. Likewise, officers have no right to impound a vehicle parked in a shopping mall where the owner is arrested. It has been held that where a defendant meets an undercover agent in a parking lot of a night club and goes into the building and comes back with a large amount of marijuana which is placed in the agent's car and the defendant is arrested, there is no right to impound and inventory the defendant's car. But where a defendant is arrested and separated from his automobile which is parked on a yellow curb and is obstructing traffic, the car can be impounded and inventoried. Likewise, where a driver is arrested driving under the influence and his car is impounded and inventoried, marijuana found in the trunk is admissible.

However, in *Mooney v. State,* the Georgia Supreme Court, in 1979, in a murder case said that the validity of a seizure and an inventory search is not dependent "upon the absolute necessity for the police to take charge of property to preserve it." The court cited with approval the case of *United States v. Gravitt,* in which police arrested men and seized and inventoried their car, which was parked at a motel. Their rent had been paid for two days beyond the time of the seizure of the car. However, officers had reason to expect that the detention would last much longer than two days. The court concluded that the car might have been stolen from the parking lot or some of the contents might have been taken; thus, it was convenient and reasonable for the car to be taken immediately after the arrest.

Nevertheless, in *Strobhert v. State,* the Georgia Court of Appeals reversed the denial of a motion to suppress. Here the defendant was arrested for possession of beer in a park. The defendant was standing by his lawfully parked car when arrested. The vehicle belonged to a member of his family. The defendant had a friend with him when he was arrested. The court held that while an absolute necessity to impound is not required, "a seizure must still be reasonable under the circumstances. . . . [Here] the impoundment was not reasonably necessary. . . . [T]he officer . . . did not even inquire into whether the companion could be trusted with the vehicle. The officer also had not asked about nor given appellant the opportunity to make alternative arrangements for the removal of the vehicle. . . ." There is no right of impoundment "when a driver is arrested and a reliable friend is present who may be authorized and capable of removing the vehicle or where the arrestee expresses some preference for a private towing service." In *Reed v. State,* a passenger was allowed to drive the vehicle from the place of the defendant's arrest to the sheriff's office. A check gave officers no reason to think the van had been stolen. The court reversed the trial judge after making a finding that the impoundment had not been reasonably necessary. But where a passenger in an automobile tells the arresting officer that he does not have any identification, the officer may assume that the passenger does not have a driver's license and impound the vehicle without offering to let him take it.

In Florida, a court held that an automobile slightly damaged in an accident may not be inventoried by officers simply because the owner is arrested, if the defendant has a friend who is willing to take charge of the vehicle. However, if a vehicle does not have a valid inspection sticker or proper lights (if arrest is at night), it would be unlawful for it to be operated by anyone; hence, officers are not obligated to let a friend of the arrested driver take the car. Likewise, if a car does not have a "valid license plate and current revalidation sticker, if required," it is illegal to operate such a vehicle and it may be impounded. An officer has no right to make an inventory search of a badly wrecked automobile if the driver is not under arrest and has a wrecker of his choice come to tow the car away.

It has been held that if a vehicle is lawfully seized for forfeiture or condemnation, it may apparently be "searched" without a warrant and not simply subjected to an "inventory" of its contents. In *Florida v. White,* the United States Supreme Court held that if officers have probable cause to believe a vehicle is subject to civil forfeiture, the officers may seize the vehicle if it is located in a public place.

Also, if there is probable cause to arrest a driver, the passenger compartment of a vehicle may be searched before the vehicle is impounded. See section 4-48, supra, on search of a vehicle incident to a valid arrest.

If a defendant fails to raise the issue of impoundment in a motion to suppress, there is no burden on the state to prove that the impoundment was proper.

In *State v. Haddock,* the court held that the trial judge "erred as a matter of law in granting . . . [a] motion to suppress" because the state failed to produce the impound inventory sheet.

See section 4-49, supra, on probable cause and exigent circumstances justifying a search.

§ 4-56 Scope and intensity of search

The validity of the scope of a search depends, generally, upon the reasonableness of the search in light of its purpose. A search which is initially valid may violate the Fourth Amendment because of "its intolerable intensity and scope." The "scope of [a] search must be 'strictly tied to and justified by' the circumstances which rendered its initiation permissible." Some of the limits of a search as they apply under the various circumstances have been discussed in those sections which deal with the particular situations.

In *United States v. Irizarry,* the First Circuit pointed out that the officers had no authority to search the space adjacent to an open ceiling tile in a motel bathroom after the occupant of the room had been arrested outside the motel room and then taken back inside after a crowd began to gather. The government contended that *Chimel v. California* did not apply because of exigent circumstances and probable cause to believe that the defendant possessed a pistol and contraband in the room. However, the Court concluded that there were no exigent circumstances after the defendant had been arrested. Hence, there was sufficient time to get a search warrant.

Even when officers are executing a valid search warrant, this does not mean that they may conduct an intensive examination of all parts of the premises described in the warrant. They may only look where the items described in the warrant might be. Thus, if an officer is executing a search warrant for a stolen television set, he has no right to rummage through desk drawers of other places too small to contain a television set. "The same meticulous investigation which would be appropriate in a search for two small canceled checks could not be considered reasonable where agents are seeking a stolen automobile or an illegal still."

Officers are justified in staying on premises only as long as it is necessary to conduct a reasonable search. A search warrant does not confer on the officer executing it the authority to make an unreasonable search. The officer must not exceed his authority and should be considerate of the comfort, convenience and feelings of the occupants. Officers are obligated to avoid unnecessary damage to the premises and to terminate the search as soon as the object of the search has been discovered.

Where officers, following information received from a reliable source, used a drug detection dog to sniff out marijuana in the defendant's suitcases at an airline terminal in a public area, the search was held to be reasonable. In *State v. Montford,* the court held that where there is a reasonable suspicion that a vehicle contains illegal drugs, an officer is authorized to walk a drug dog around the vehicle to see if the dog alerts for drugs. If "the dog alerted for drugs, that factor, combined with the factors prompting the use of the drug dog . . . established probable cause . . . authorizing the . . . search of [the car's] interior." However, it has also been held that a police officer has no right to take a trained dog into the baggage room, an area not open to the public, to sniff all the baggage in a general exploratory search or "fishing expedition."

Where officers make a warrantless entry in a search of a person believed to require immediate aid and they find a body, they may make a prompt warrantless search of the area to determine if there are other victims present or if the killer is still present. Likewise, officers may make a protective "sweep" of a house in which a body is discovered. See section 4-27, supra, on protective sweeps.

The courts seem to apply a rule of reason in determining the quantity of material which may be validly seized even where the search is legal. Thus, the seizure of the entire contents of a cabin or all of the defendant's files has been held unreasonable.

An inventory of an impounded or forfeited automobile is limited to (1) inventorying the owner's personal articles in the vehicle, (2) searching for illegal weapons, and (3) looking for evidence of ownership of the vehicle. In the case of a search of an automobile based on reasonable probable cause to believe that contraband or stolen property is in a vehicle, an officer may search any part of the automobile where it is reasonable to believe such articles might be concealed.

Except in the case of a border search, strip searches have been limited by *Rochin v. California*. In *Rochin*, the United States Supreme Court condemned the use of a stomach pump to forcibly seize swallowed narcotics by saying that such conduct "shocks the conscience." Strip searches of traffic offenders and misdemeanants are usually regarded as invalid. Officers generally have more authority to conduct strip searches of suspects of more serious offenses, and offenses associated with weapons or contraband, but even in these more serious cases, there still seems to be no general constitutional right to conduct a search of body cavities. In *Merriweather v. State*, the court affirmed the use of "a Heimlich Maneuver" to expel contraband from defendant's mouth. The court said that "[a]lthough forceful extraction of contraband from a criminal suspect implicates the Fourth Amendment and should be avoided whenever possible, a criminal suspect does not have a right to destroy evidence and 'the police are authorized to use reasonable but not excessive force in preventing the destruction or concealment of evidence.' "

However, in *Bell v. Wolfish,* the United States Supreme Court found no Fourth Amendment violation in requiring that a prisoner, after conviction, be required to submit to strip searches and to expose body cavities for visual inspection after each contact visit with a person from outside the institution and persons in jails and prisons. See section 4-43, supra, on search of probationers and inmates.

See section 3-13, supra, on retention of inanimate objects and section § 4-38 et seq., supra, on plain view. See section 4-26, supra, on search incident to a lawful arrest. See sections 5-22 and 5-23, infra, on the use of surgery on the human body to obtain evidence. See section 4-44, supra, on border searches. See section 4-31, supra, on consent. See Annotation, "Propriety of Search Involving Removal of Natural Substance or Foreign Object From Body by Actual or Threatened Force," 66 A. L. R. Fed. 119 (1984). See Annotation, "Validity, Under Federal Constitution, of Regulations, Rules, or Statutes Allowing Drug Testing of Students," 87 A. L. R. Fed. 148 (1988). See Annotation, "Federal and State Constitutions as Protecting Against Unreasonable Searches and Seizures," 85 A. L. R. 5th 261 (2001).

§ 4-57 Second search

The validity of an initial search, pursuant to a warrant or under an exception to the warrant requirement, generally will not sustain a later search of the same area unless a new warrant is obtained, or unless there again exists a right to search without a warrant. Thus, it has been held that where a prisoner is booked in jail and thoroughly searched, officers may not conduct a warrantless search several days later of his civilian clothes which were placed in the property room at the time of his arrest. However, generally a search of a person and his effects at the time of arrest does not prevent a search at the time the defendant reaches the station house.

In *People v. Richards,* the court held that a defendant has no reasonable expectation of privacy in items which were inventoried by police at the time of his processing. The item involved was a necklace which the defendant had at the time of his arrest. The Illinois Supreme Court pointed out that the necklace was not in any kind of container and that there was only a "second inspection" of it in order to give the victim of a theft an opportunity to see if she could identify the necklace as the one taken from her. The court concluded that there was no violation of the Fourth Amendment in such a "second inspection." In *Williams v. State*, the Georgia Supreme Court arrived at the same conclusion without considering expectation of privacy.

Likewise, in *Florida v. Meyers,* the United States Supreme Court held that where a vehicle has been impounded by officers at the time the defendant was arrested, a second warrantless search some eight hours later is valid even though the car has been retained in a locked secured area.

In *Michigan v. Tyler,* the United States Supreme Court held that the warrantless entry and inspection of fire marshals of a burning building is proper under the emergency exception to the warrant requirement. Also, their return some four hours later (after daylight) was treated as a continuation of their earlier investigation. However, a still later return and investigation required a search warrant. See section 4-45, supra, on administrative searches.

One exception to the second search doctrine is that which applies in the case of a controlled delivery. In *Illinois v. Andreas,* the United States Supreme Court held that where contraband is lawfully found in a sealed container and it is resealed by officers and delivered to the addressee under police supervision and there is "no substantial likelihood . . . that the contents of the shipping container were changed during . . . [a] gap in surveillance," it is not necessary for officers to obtain a warrant before seizing and again opening and searching the container. This is said to be true because there is no expectation of privacy in the contents of the container after it is first opened and found to contain contraband. "The simple act of resealing the container to make a controlled delivery does not operate to revive or restore the lawfully invaded privacy rights."

In *State v. Fultz,* the Georgia Court of Appeals, in a warrant situation and without citing *Andreas,* arrived at the same conclusion in reversing the grant of a motion to suppress. The trial court had concluded that there had not been a "controlled buy," apparently because the "purchaser" had not been searched before the "buy." The appellate court's reversal was actually based on the failure of the trial court to give sufficient deference to the magistrate's determination of probable cause. See section 4-7, supra, on probable cause.

In *State v. Johnston,* the manager of a mini-warehouse discovered that the locking device on a unit leased to the defendant had been cut. The manager opened the door and discovered several bags of pills. He recognized the pills as Quaalude, took a number of pills, closed the door, and called officers. When the officers arrived, the manager gave the officer the pills and told him what he had found. The officer then searched the unit. The court sustained the warrantless search on the theory that the defendant had no expectation of privacy after the manager had seen the pills.

See section 4-43, supra, on searches of prisoners and probationers. See section 4-20, supra, on obtaining a second search warrant. See section 4-26, supra, on search and/or seizure of clothing worn at time of arrest.

§ 4-58 Electronic surveillance—General

In *Osborn v. United States, Berger v. New York,* and *Katz v. United States,* the United States Supreme Court has shown that when appropriate procedural safeguards are met, a narrowly written statute providing for a system of electronic surveillance does not constitute an unreasonable search and seizure under the Fourth Amendment. The appropriate procedural safeguards required include (1) that an order permitting the surveillance (or an order renewing a previous order) be obtained from a neutral and detached judicial officer; (2) that the applicant show, with the particularity required of a search warrant, that there is probable cause that a crime has been or is being committed and that the defendant is responsible; (3) that the surveillance which is authorized be limited in time and scope to the investigation at hand, so as not to become a series of intrusions, searches, and seizures pursuant to a single showing of probable cause; (4) that the statute overcome the lack of notice by requiring a showing of exigent circumstances as a precondition to the judicial authorization; and (5) that the order be executed and the warrant returned with a dispatch. Of course, no prior judicial authorization is necessary where one party to the communication consents to the monitoring.

O.C.G.A. § 16–11–64.3 was enacted in 2000, providing for application process of an investigation warrant in an emergency situation. Specifically, it must be shown to the Attorney General or a district attorney with jurisdiction that the situation involves "the immediate danger of death or serious physical injury . . . [requiring] the immediate interception . . ." and that "[t]here are grounds upon which [a] . . . warrant pursuant to O.C.G.A. § 16–11–64 could be issued." Additionally, the Code section prevents the subsequent use of evidence obtained if the application is denied or the procurement is terminated prior to a warrant being issued.

In *Whatley v. State,* the court pointed out that "[t]he standard of probable cause for a wiretap authorization is the same as the standard for a regular search warrant."

All forms of electronic surveillance must be conducted pursuant to the Omnibus Crime Control and Safe

Streets Act (Title III) of 1968, as well as to the provisions of O.C.G.A. §§ 16–11–60 through 16–11–69, where those provisions are applicable. See Annotation, "Who May Apply or Authorize Application For Order to Intercept Wire or Oral Communications Under Title III of Omnibus Crime Control and Safe Streets Act of 1968 (18 U.S.C.A. §§ 2510, et seq.)," 169 A. L. R. Fed 169 (2001).

In *Porter v. State,* tapes of wiretapped conversations were made from February 20 to March 7; however, these tapes were not delivered to the superior court for sealing until March 28. The appellate court held that the defendants' motion to suppress the contents of the tapes should have been granted since the tapes were not submitted to the court for sealing *immediately* after the recording occurred as is required by 18 U.S.C.A. § 2518(8)(a).

In *King v. State,* the Georgia Supreme Court held that the harmless error rule did not apply where a trial judge failed to place a judicial seal on tapes which had been made pursuant to a wiretap order. The court pointed out that 18 U.S.C.A. § 2518(8) requires such a seal or a satisfactory explanation for its absence and the absence thereof prevents admissibility of the tapes.

But in *Williams v. State,* the Georgia Supreme Court held that failure to comply with O.C.G.A. § 16–11–64(b)(5) and (b)(6) did not require suppression of evidence unless the violation would result in prejudice to the defendant. However, the court concluded that violations that affect the quality or quantity of the evidence or the gathering or safeguarding of the evidence may require suppression.

The electronic "devices" regulated by O.C.G.A. § 16–11–60 et seq. include any instrument or apparatus used for overhearing, recording, intercepting, or transmitting sounds, or for observing, photographing, videotaping, recording, and transmitting visual images. A "surveillance warrant" may be issued for an act which endangers the security of the United States or the security of Georgia, or for a person who is committing or has committed the crime of treason, insurrection, rebellion, espionage, sabotage, or any felony involving bodily harm, or any crime involving arson, kidnapping, narcotics, dangerous drugs, or importing, manufacturing, delivering, distributing, dispensing, administering, selling or possessing with intent to distribute marijuana or any controlled substance, or burglary, prostitution, theft, blackmail, extortion, bribery, gambling, racketeering, or any felony involving alcoholic beverage laws or auto theft. In *Porter v. State,* the court pointed out that a warrant allowing wire interception must contain a statutory minimization provision.

The applicant for an electronic surveillance warrant must be the Attorney General or District Attorney having prosecutorial jurisdiction of a crime. Likewise, the issuing magistrate must be a Superior Court judge having jurisdiction of the crime. In *Evans v. State,* the court affirmed a superior court judge in Fulton County authorizing wiretaps of telephones in other counties. Under the system used, an inductor coil was placed in each county where each such telephone was located. Here the actual "listening post" was in Fulton County and the court concluded that the inductor coil was not a "device used to overhear, record or intercept . . ." within the meaning of the statute.

However, generally under both state and federal law a party to a telephone conversation may permit a third person to listen to the conversation without the knowledge of the other person, and an informant may conceal a radio transmitter or recorder and carry on a conversation without the knowledge of the other person. See Goger, *Daniel's Georgia Handbook on Criminal Evidence* (2009 ed.), § 9–16. In *United States v. Yonn,* the Eleventh Circuit applied the same rule to the warrantless planting of an electronic monitoring device in the defendant's motel room by government agents. The informer reserved the room for the defendant at his request. The device was then used to monitor the conversation between the defendant and the informer. In *Smith v. State,* the Court of Appeals ruled that consent to the monitoring of an inmate's phone calls may be implied where the institution in which the inmate is confined has a published policy which states that inmates' phone calls are monitored. Proof of such a policy or practice may consist of: lectures which describe the policy to inmates; written notices near the phones used by the inmates; manuals regarding such procedures which are provided to inmates; or recorded messages played on the prison phones before communication can begin.

In the 1992 case of *Salmon v. State,* the Georgia Court of Appeals held that under Georgia law as it then existed there was no prohibition against the interception of a cellular telephone conversation and that cellular telephone users had no justifiable expectation of privacy. However, in 1993 the Legislature enacted O.C.G.A. § 16–11–66.1, which has the effect of reversing *Salmon.* Under this statute, it is unlawful to intentionally intercept a cellular telephone conversation.

In the Georgia case of *Uhler v. State,* the court held that it is not necessary to make a written application in order to have the telephone company assist the state by tracing the "call-forwarding" process since this did not involve the interception of electric signals from the telephone lines.

In *United States v. Torres,* the Seventh Circuit held that Title III was not violated by a video surveillance or by surveillance of other than oral communications.

To be "aggrieved" under Georgia law and suppress the result of a wiretap, "the violation must have occurred on the movants' premises or the unlawfully heard conversation must have been of the movants themselves."

In *State v. Anderson,* the court considered O.C.G.A. § 16–11–64(b)(8) and held that one condition of the statute is "that there shall be no publication of the information obtained 'other than that necessary and essential to the preparation of and actual prosecution for the crime specified in the warrant.' . . . Any violation of this non-publication rule renders the wiretap an invasion of privacy and causes the 'evidence and information to be inadmissible in any criminal prosecution.' "

In *Williams v. State,* the court held as follows: (1) A failure to return the pen register warrant within 30 days of issuance, as required by O.C.G.A. § 16–11–64(b)(6), was not a basis for suppressing intercepted communications from the defendant's telephone because the defendant had no standing to complain of non-compliance with the statutory procedural safeguards when the pen register warrant was actually placed on his *mother's* telephone. (2) An application for a wiretap on the defendant's telephone did not have to show that conventional investigation techniques had been tried and failed, or were unlikely to be successful, because the purpose of this statute (18 U. S. C. § 2518(1)(c)) "is not to foreclose electronic surveillance until every other imaginable method of investigation has been unsuccessfully attempted, but simply to inform the issuing judge of the difficulties involved in the use of conventional techniques." (3) Although 18 U. S. C. § 2518(5) "requires an investigation warrant to contain a provision that the wiretap shall be conducted in such a way as to minimize the interception of communications unrelated to the investigation . . . ," it is sufficient if the issuing judge instructed the "district attorney, law enforcement officers, and agents [that they were] forbidden to record any conversations or discussions which [were] personal and private in nature or not specified in [the] warrant."

"Minor factual inaccuracies [in an affidavit] which are only peripherally relevant to the showing" of probable cause will not void a warrant for a wiretap.

The exclusionary rule generally applies to any information obtained in violation of Georgia law. In *Jordan v. State,* the court pointed out the difference between the United States and Georgia statutes regarding use of evidence obtained as a result of an illegal wiretap. 18 U. S. C. § 2515 provides that "no part of the contents of such [illegal] communication and *no evidence derived therefrom* may be received in evidence in any trial. . . ." (Emphasis in original.) However, O.C.G.A. § 16–11–67 does not contain any language precluding derivative evidence.

It is not reversible error for the trial judge to refuse to exclude spectators at a motion to suppress and conduct a closed hearing unless "the party seeking to close the hearing . . . advance[s] an over-riding interest that [he] is likely to be prejudiced. . . . [T]he closure must be no broader than necessary to protect that interest." See section 17-2, infra.

The exclusionary rule also applies to a violation of 18 U. S. C. § 2518(10)(a). This provision of the statute provides in part as follows:

"(10)(a) Any aggrieved person . . . may move to suppress the contents of any wire or oral communication intercepted pursuant to this chapter, or evidence derived therefrom, on the grounds that—

"(i) the communication was unlawfully intercepted;

"(ii) the order of authorization or approval under which it was intercepted is insufficient on its face; or

"(iii) the interception was not made in conformity with the order of authorization or approval.

"Such motion shall be made before the trial, hearing, or proceeding unless there was no opportunity to make such motion or the person was not aware of the grounds of the motion. . . ."

In addition to the foregoing, Georgia has a statute (O.C.G.A. § 16–11–62) prohibiting anyone from secretly intercepting a telephone call. O.C.G.A. § 16–11–67 provides that "[n]o evidence obtained [in violation of O.C.G.A. § 16–11–62] shall be admissible . . . except to prove" a violation of said statute. In *Jordan v. State,* the court implies (1) that an improper wiretap by a private individual "without the preknowledge and acquiescence of law enforcement authorities" will not prevent the use by the state of derivative evidence, and (2) the fruit of the poisonous tree doctrine and the inevitable discovery rule do not apply where there was no illegal conduct by state agents.

In *Barlow v. Barlow,* the court held that Georgia's wiretapping statutes apply to cordless telephone conversations.

See section 4-2, supra, on protected areas and interests. Generally, see Kurtz, *Criminal Offenses and Defenses in Georgia* (4th ed.), pp. 934–937, and see Goger, *Daniel's Georgia Criminal Trial Practice Forms* (6th ed.), § 14–196 et seq., on motion to suppress based on electronic surveillance. See Goger, *Daniel's Georgia Handbook on Criminal Evidence* (2009 ed.), § 9–16, on sound recordings and § 9–14 on method and location of surveillance. See section 4-2, supra, on pen registers and section 4-7, supra, on probable cause affidavits based on illegal wiretaps.

§ 4-59 Results of illegal search

The material contained in this section is in summary form. The exclusionary rule is treated in far greater depth in section 2-24 et seq., supra.

Generally, if a search or seizure is illegal, the articles obtained are not admissible in evidence in the prosecution's case in chief against a person who has standing to object to the search or seizure. However, the aggrieved party must make a timely motion to suppress the evidence. The person who conducts an illegal search or seizure may be liable in damages to the aggrieved person. Pursuant to O.C.G.A. § 17–5–30(a) "[a] defendant aggrieved by an unlawful search and seizure may move the court for the return of property, the possession of which is not otherwise unlawful and to suppress as evidence anything so obtained &dashl;" Because the code section applies only to a criminal defendant, a party to an administrative investigative proceeding can not rely upon it as authority for the recovery of evidence improperly seized by a state agency or its suppression in any future proceeding.

Evidence obtained in an illegal search and seizure can be used for purposes of impeachment of the aggrieved party if he testifies to facts contrary to those existing in the search or seizure. Likewise, illegally obtained evidence may be used to impeach a defendant's false testimony obtained in response to proper cross-examination which was reasonably suggested by the defendant's direct examination. Also, the exclusionary rule does not generally apply to civil proceedings.

In Georgia, the exclusionary rule is based not only on federal constitutional requirements as interpreted in *Mapp v. Ohio,* but also on statutory law.

Generally, the exclusionary rule, from a federal constitutional standpoint, applies only to governmental employees and does not apply to searches by private citizens. However, a joint operation of a credit card company and law enforcement officers has been held to be limited by the Fourth Amendment, and officers may not evade the requirements of the Fourth Amendment by the use of a private person to do what the officer could not do.

In *United States v. McGreevy,* Petrie was a full-time police officer who worked the midnight shift. He also worked for Federal Express about six hours a week doing security work and acting as liaison between the company and law enforcement agencies. He was called by the Federal Express station manager in regard to a suspicious package. He opened the package and found contraband. The court concluded that he was not acting under color of state law when he opened the package.

In *Goodwin v. State,* an off-duty police officer, while working security on private property, was instructed by his employer to stop all cars entering the premises. In doing so, he smelled alcohol on the breath of a driver and notified the police, who subsequently arrested the defendant. The court held that the defendant's claim that the initial stop lacked articulable suspicion and was not justified was without merit since the officer was "acting in his capacity as a hotel security officer and not attempting to search for incriminating evidence."

In *United States v. Miller,* the Ninth Circuit held that there are two critical factors to be considered in determining whether a private person was acting as an agent of the government in conducting a search: "(1) whether the government knew of or acquiesced in the intrusive conduct, and (2) whether the party performing the search intended to assist law enforcement efforts or to further his own ends." The court then concluded that a theft victim was not acting as an agent or instrumentality of law enforcement even though officers had asked the victim to help them identify the property stolen, agreed to his plan to enter the suspect's property for that purpose, and to some extent provided protection for him.

In *State v. Lovig,* the court said that the test is whether the private person, "in light of all circumstances of the case must be regarded as having acted as an 'instrument' or agent" of the government when he produced the evidence. In this regard, two cases worth comparing are *Cook v. State* and *Pruitt v. State.* In *Cook*, a statement made by the defendant to his father, who was also an F.B.I. agent, did not require suppression since, at the time it was made, the defendant's father was not acting in his capacity as a law enforcement officer but rather as a parent offering comfort to a troubled son. In *Pruitt*, the court ruled that evidence seized by a police officer father from his son's motor vehicle should have been suppressed since, under the totality of the circumstances, it never appeared that the police officer subordinated his official status to that of his parental status.

In *State v. Young,* the court considered a motion to suppress marijuana found by the assistant principal of a school on the person of a student. In refusing to uphold the suppression motion, the court concluded that persons conducting searches are to be divided into three groups: (1) searches by private persons, (2) searches by agents of the state, and (3) searches by law enforcement agents. The court said that searches by the second class of persons are not subject to the exclusionary rule, and that a principal or assistant principal of a school fits into this category.

Statements obtained by school officials acting in concert with or at the direction of police authorities may also be subject to exclusion. Whether the school officials were acting in such a capacity must be determined on a case by case basis by viewing the totality of the circumstances.

However, in *New Jersey v. T. L. O.,* the United States Supreme Court considered the validity of a search of a pupil by a public school official. The court found that the Fourth Amendment does apply to school officials, and that such officials act as representatives of the state, but that this conclusion does not mean probable cause is required for a search. The court concluded that under the Fourth Amendment a lesser standard of reasonableness is appropriate for school children. Thus, "the legality of a search of a student should depend simply on the reasonableness, under all the circumstances, of the search." There must be "reasonable grounds for *suspecting* that the search will turn up evidence that the student has violated or is violating either the law or the rules of the school." (Emphasis added.) "[T]he measures adopted [must be] reasonably related to the objective of the search and not excessively intrusive in the light of the age and sex of the student and the nature of the infraction."

In the 1987 case of *O'Connor v. Ortega,* the United States Supreme Court cited and relied on *T. L. O.* Ortega was a physician and psychiatrist who was Chief of Professional Education at a state hospital. Five of the Justices concluded that the state did not have probable cause to obtain a warrant to conduct a search of his desk or filing cabinet, where the search was reasonably limited in scope and was initiated for work-related non-investigative reasons. "In contrast to law enforcement officials, . . . public employers are not enforcers of the criminal law; instead, public employers have a direct and overriding interest in ensuring that the work of the agency is conducted in a proper and efficient manner. . . . Balanced against the substantial government interests in the efficient and proper operation of the workplace are the privacy interests of government employees in their place of work which, while not insubstantial, are far less than those found at home or in some other contexts. . . . '[S]pecial needs, beyond the normal need for law enforcement make the . . . probable-cause requirement impracticable. . . .' "

See section 4-56, supra, on drug tests of students. See section 14-74 et seq., infra, on the expectation of privacy. See an exhaustive annotation of over 250 pages entitled "Search Conducted by School Official or Teacher as Violation of Fourth Amendment or Equivalent State Constitutional Provision," 31 A. L. R. 5th 229 (1995). See section 2-26, supra, on erroneous information as constituting probable cause to arrest.

Chapter 5

Confessions And Self–Incrimination

§ 5-1 Confessions—Definition

Historically in Georgia, a confession has been regarded as a voluntary admission of guilt of every essential element of the crime involved, without including any legal excuse or justification. In order to be admissible, the confession must be made "without being induced by another by the slightest hope of benefit or remotest fear of injury." A number of older cases have emphasized that a statement which constitutes a confession must be so comprehensive as to include every essential element of the crime.

However, in 1974, in *Robinson v. State,* the Georgia Supreme Court held that an inculpatory statement may amount to a confession even though the defendant does not admit all the essential elements of the crime. In distinguishing between admissions and confessions, the court said that "the true determinant is whether the statement is offered by the accused as exculpatory or inculpatory." In *Robinson,* the defendant was charged with rape. He gave a statement which made no mention of penetration and stated only that everything started getting "fuzzy." However, Robinson did not state that he abandoned his attempt to rape, and unlike the statement in *Bloodworth v. State,* the statement of Robinson was considered a confession. In *Robinson,* the attack in question upon the child was admitted subject to the memory lapse, without justification, and the statement is not one from which the jury could infer innocence. "The statement, taken as a whole, can only be thought to have been given by Robinson for the purpose of assuming responsibility for the crime charged" and constitutes a confession. Since the *Robinson* decision, the courts have reaffirmed the rule laid down in that case several times.

Even when reference is made to a statement of the defendant, it is not necessary for the trial judge to give a charge distinguishing between a confession and an admission when there is no mention of a confession.

Confessions may be oral, written or recorded. If oral, they need not be reduced to writing. A confession may be partly oral and partly in writing. It has been held that a written confession must be contained in a single document. However, in view of *Robinson v. State,* this rule may not still be applicable.

The admissibility of a confession is not destroyed solely because it includes other transactions. See Goger,

Daniel's Georgia Handbook on Criminal Evidence (2009 ed.), § 4-48, on similar transactions, and § 4–58 on res gestae.

Where a hearing impaired person is legally arrested, if a qualified interpreter is not available one hour after the hearing impaired person has been taken into custody and a request has been forwarded to the Department of Human Resources, the arresting officer may interrogate or take a statement from the person, provided that "such interrogation and answers thereto shall be in writing and shall be preserved and turned over to the court" in the event the person is tried for the alleged offense. Additionally, an interpreter shall be provided and present during consultation between the hearing impaired person and the court appointed counsel. See Goger, *Daniel's Georgia Handbook on Criminal Evidence* (2009 ed.), § 6–6, on interpreters.

The trial court in *Newman v. State* suppressed the results of an interrogation where the police officers failed to comply with the provisions concerning the interrogation of deaf persons.

See section 5-2, infra, on admissions.

§ 5-2 Admissions—Definition

As pointed out in the last section, under present Georgia law, an "admission of the main fact, from which the essential elements of the criminal act may be inferred, amounts to an admission of the crime itself. If the main fact is admitted with a qualifying exclusion of a necessary ingredient of the crime charged, the crime is not confessed." Therefore, "a mere [admission] is made where the accused, though admitting to damaging circumstances, nonetheless attempts to deny responsibility for the crime charged by putting forward exculpatory or legally justifying facts. Thus . . . '[a] statement which includes facts or circumstances which show excuse or justification is not a confession of guilt even if it admits the main fact.' " For example, if a person is charged with burglary and he acknowledges that he entered the house, this is not a confession but it is an admission.

While it is sometimes difficult to distinguish between an admission and a confession, it is important for the trial judge to properly distinguish between the two when he instructs the jury. If the statement amounts to an admission and not a confession, it is error for the court to charge on confessions. However, a mere passing use of the word "confession" does not require a reversal even if the statement was an admission. The Georgia Supreme Court has said that "[i]f the trial judges would avoid the use of the word 'confession' in questionable cases and instead use the word 'admission' in each instance where they might otherwise use the word 'confession' or 'statement,' the entire problem would vanish." However, it has been held that the "quantum of evidence necessary to corroborate a confession is entirely for the jury to decide."

In *Griggs v. State,* the court concluded that under the facts of the case it was error to charge on a confession and on an incriminating statement and to let the jury determine which category the statement fell into. However, if a defendant does not admit that a statement is a confession, and if there is no request to charge on the need for corroboration of a confession, it is not error for the court to fail to so charge. An incriminating statement not amounting to a confession is an admission.

Under *Miranda v. Arizona,* both confessions and admissions are treated alike in determining their admissibility under the federal Constitution.

Where the state relies on a defendant's admission alone to establish an essential element of the case and the accused's inculpatory statement is coupled with exculpatory matter, the jury must consider both statements. However, this rule is inapplicable if there is other evidence contradicting the defendant's exculpatory statement.

See section 5-1, supra, on confessions. See section 10-2, infra, on admissions in pleadings in condemnation cases. See Goger, *Daniel's Georgia Handbook on Criminal Evidence* (2009 ed.), §§ 4–5 and 4-28, on the admissibility of admissions of a defendant.

§ 5-3 Admissibility—General

O.C.G.A. § 24–3–50 provides as follows:

"To make a confession admissible, it must have been made voluntarily, without being induced by another by the slightest hope of benefit or remotest fear of injury." Thus, according to this statute, there are three conditions which must exist before a pre-trial confession or admission is admissible in evidence at a criminal trial: (1) It must be made voluntarily. It must not be produced by or result from (2) "the slightest hope of benefit" or (3) the "remotest fear of injury." These essentials will be discussed in the following sections.

From a federal constitutional standpoint, the essential element of voluntariness is not to be regarded as being limited by the words "without being induced by another by the slightest hope of benefit or remotest fear of injury." Voluntariness based on a totality of *all* the surrounding facts and circumstances is an essential element of due process. In *Wan v. United States*, the United States Supreme Court said, "A confession is voluntary in law if, and only if, it was, in fact, voluntarily made."

O.C.G.A. § 24–3–53 provides as follows:

"All admissions shall be scanned with care, and confessions of guilt shall be received with great caution. A confession alone, uncorroborated by any other evidence, shall not justify a conviction." Blackstone wrote in the Eighteenth Century that confessions are regarded as "the weakest and most suspicious of all testimony; ever liable to be obtained by artifice, false hopes, promises of favour or menaces."

Despite the language of the statute, there is a line of Georgia cases stating that a "confession of guilt freely and voluntarily made by the accused, is direct evidence of the highest character and sufficient to authorize a conviction when corroborated by proof of the corpus delicti."

In *McGowan v. State,* the court held that the defendant has no standing to raise a question as to the violation of the witness' right not to be forced to give certain information. Also, a defendant "may not invoke another's privilege, even if the other is his co-defendant."

For motions to suppress statements, see Goger, *Daniel's Georgia Criminal Trial Practice Forms* (6th ed.), § 5–1 et seq. See Goger, *Daniel's Georgia Handbook on Criminal Evidence* (2009 ed.), §§ 1–22, 6–16, 6–36, and 8–9.

§ 5-4 Admissibility—Voluntariness—General

Today, as a result of *Miranda v. Arizona,* most litigation about confessions centers on the applicability of the Fifth Amendment. But until 1966, when *Miranda* was decided, the Court relied on other mechanisms for determining the validity of confessions. In the 1936 case *Brown v. Mississippi,* the United States Supreme Court gave the "voluntariness" test constitutional stature under the Due Process Clause of the Fourteenth Amendment in reversing the defendants' convictions that rested solely upon confessions extracted after they were severely beaten by police.

When determining voluntariness, the "totality of circumstances" that preceded the confession must be examined. In *Payne v. Arkansas,* the Court held that the defendant's confession was not "voluntary" because it came after he was held incommunicado for three days, was denied food for long periods of time, and was threatened by the chief of police that a lynch mob would get him if he did not confess.

In 1964, with the cases *Massiah v. United States* and *Escobedo v. Illinois,* the Supreme Court's focus shifted from "voluntariness" of confessions under the Due Process Clause to a defendant's right to "assistance of counsel" as provided by the Sixth Amendment. But, two years later, the Court decided *Miranda,* which made Fifth Amendment analysis the driving force behind inquiries into the admissibility of confessions.

However, the due process standard of voluntariness still applies, even where there is a Miranda violation in connection with a confession. If there is a Miranda violation, the statement obtained from the defendant is not admissible in the prosecution's case in chief. But the shield of "*Miranda* cannot be perverted into a license to use perjury" and a statement obtained from a defendant in violation of *Miranda* may be used to impeach an earlier statement made by the defendant during the trial if its "trustworthiness . . . satisfies legal standards." Similarly, *Miranda* does not require suppression of the physical fruits of a suspect's voluntary, but unwarned statements. However, in "*any* criminal trial the use against a defendant of his involuntary statement is a denial of due process." Of course, unless a confession or statement was given voluntarily, it fails to pass the Georgia statutory test.

In *Colorado v. Connelly,* the United States Supreme Court held that a confession cannot be held to be involuntary under the due process clause unless it is linked to coercion by government agents. The court then concluded that a confession was voluntary and hence admissible where the statement was made by the defendant because he thought he was being directed by God to confess.

In *King v. State,* the Georgia Supreme Court said voluntary "is practically synonymous with spontaneously, of his own free will; and not when overmastered by the will of another." But in a civil case it was held that an admission was not inadmissible simply because it was made after a polygraph examination.

Prolonged grilling prevents a confession from being voluntary. However, it has been held that the fact that a defendant is a drug addict and is undergoing withdrawal symptoms at the time of his confession does not alone make it involuntary. In *Ryan v. State,* the court held that "[t]he mere fact that a defendant was emotionally upset did not render [his statement] inadmissible." The giving of cigarettes and soft drinks to a suspect does not alone prevent a confession from being voluntarily given. In a dubious case, it has been held that if a defendant, while in a drunken stupor or asleep, makes an admission, the jury may determine whether or not it should be considered. In *Shelby v. State,* the Georgia Supreme Court affirmed a finding that a statement was freely and voluntarily given despite the fact that the defendant's blood alcohol level was .24 percent. A statement is not regarded as having been made involuntarily simply because the defendant was using drugs at the time it was given. In one case, however, where a defendant made a confession while in the hospital and under the influence of morphine, the statement was held to be involuntary. In *Brown v. State*, the court pointed out that "[i]lliteracy . . . 'does not dictate a determination that there has been no voluntary knowledgeable waiver.' " In *Vance v. Bordenkircher*, the court concluded that a confession in a murder case was voluntary even though given by a 15–year-old who had an I.Q. of 62 and a mental age of nine. In a similar case, *Willis v. State*, the court pointed out that "[a] mere showing that an accused . . . has a high blood alcohol level or may be suffering from some mental disability is not a sufficient basis to automatically exclude a statement." In *Horton v. State*, the court held that the fact officers did not inform the defendant she would be charged with murder until after she made a statement did not render the statement involuntary. In *Oliver v. State*, the court pointed out that the "mere showing that a person who confessed to a crime may have suffered from some mental disability is not a sufficient basis on which to exclude the statement." In a foreign case, the court held that a defendant has no right to introduce expert testimony showing that he was more likely to be induced to confess or more susceptible to being coerced. See Annotation, "Admissibility of Expert Testimony Regarding Reliability of Accused's Confession Where Accused Allegedly Suffered From Mental Disorder or Defect at Time of Confession," 82 A. L. R. 5th 591 (2000). Generally, see section 5-19, infra, on Miranda waivers.

It is not necessary for the trial judge to charge a jury on the necessity of voluntariness of a confession unless a timely written request has been filed.

Generally, a confession will be deemed admissible if, considering the totality of the circumstances, it was made voluntarily, "without being induced by hope of benefit or coerced by threats." However, in *State v. Gardner,* the Georgia Supreme Court held that a "confession made by one who is insane is not the product of 'a rational intellect and a free will,' and is, thus, not voluntarily made." Nevertheless, a person who is "mentally ill" may make a voluntary confession.

The United States Supreme Court held on non-constitutional grounds that a confession obtained during a delay in bringing a suspect before a magistrate rendered a confession inadmissible in *McNabb v. United States* and in *Mallory v. United States.* While most states have rejected the per se rule, some have followed it and Congress in 1968 in effect reversed these cases.

In Georgia, it has been held that a defendant who is arrested without a warrant is required to be presented before a magistrate within 48 hours or he must be released. However, it has been held that where the defendant is not presented before a magistrate within 48 hours after a warrantless arrest and a statement is obtained after the 48 hours, there is no right to a per se exclusion of the statement because the arrest is not necessarily violative of the federal Constitution and a violation of the Georgia statute does not automatically authorize a defendant to have the statement excluded. But see *County of Riverside v. McLaughlin,* which is discussed in section 11-1, infra. While there is no per se exclusion of such a statement, it must be remembered that where there is a warrantless arrest, the Fourth Amendment requires a probable cause determination "promptly after arrest." If a confession is obtained after a warrantless arrest but before a prompt probable cause hearing, it may be that it is subject to suppression as a violation of the Fourth Amendment. See section 2-24 et seq., supra, on the exclusionary rule.

In *Arizona v. Fulminante,* the United States Supreme Court held that the erroneous admission of a coerced confession can be harmless error.

See section 5-7, infra, on confessions obtained by trickery. See Annotation, "Admissibility of Confession as Affected by Delay in Arraignment of Prisoner," 19 A. L. R. 2d 1331 (1951). See Annotation, "Mental Subnormality of Accused as Affecting Voluntariness or Admissibility of Confession," 8 A. L. R. 4th 16 (1981). See also section 5-5, infra, on confessions obtained by a hope of benefit.

§ 5-5 Admissibility—Voluntariness—Hope of benefit

A confession which is obtained by a promise to confer a benefit on the suspect is involuntary and inadmissible. Where a confession is obtained by offering the defendant immunity, it is induced by a hope of reward and is inadmissible. Likewise, a promise to reduce or dismiss charges or recommend a relatively light sentence for the charge renders a confession involuntary. So, too, is a statement induced by the promise that the defendant would not be among those charged. A confession given to obtain the release from custody of the defendant's girlfriend has been held to be involuntary because of the circumstances surrounding the confession. This rule applies not only to full blown confessions, but to any sort of inculpatory admission or statement induced through "the slightest hope of benefit or the remotest fear of injury." In *Starr v. State*, for example, the court found on appeal that an incriminating statement made by the defendant during a taped interview with police investigators which placed him alone with the victim in a child molestation case should have been excluded at trial since it was induced by the hope of special considerations in the disposition of the case and was for that reason not made voluntarily. However, in Georgia it has been held that a confession obtained as a result of a promise of a collateral benefit is not excludable for that reason. See section 5-6, infra. Thus, in *Burton v. State*, the court held that an "officer's statement to the accused that substance abuse counseling was available was an offer of a collateral benefit which does not invalidate the [defendant's] statement."

An officer's promise to recommend a lighter punishment or statements to the effect that "everybody asks how cooperative has a suspect been with you" or that it would be better for him to make a confession have been regarded as holding out a hope of benefit. In *Askea v. State*, the court held that an investigator's statement to the defendant that his cooperation "would probably help him in court" impermissibly held out some hope of benefit. However, in *Lyles v. State*, the court pointed out that where a detective told the defendant he would let the district attorney know about his cooperation and this might result in a reduced sentence, no promises were made. Moreover, this defendant signed a form acknowledging that his statement was made without promise or hope of reward. Therefore, the Georgia Court of Appeals upheld the admissibility of the defendant's confession.

But a comment by an officer that it is always better to tell the truth does not invalidate a confession. If a defendant makes a confession implicating himself and others as a result of a plea bargain, but subsequently refuses to plead guilty and is tried, the confession is not admissible because it was given with the hope of benefit induced by another. However, in 1997 the Georgia Supreme Court in *Carswell v. State* held that an officer's agreement to tell the judge of the defendant's cooperation is not the kind of "hope of benefit" contemplated by O.C.G.A. § 24–3–50. Likewise, "[o]ffering to make known a suspect's confession to the district attorney and the trial judge is not an offer of benefit." In the same vein, a detective's suggestion made during the interrogation of a murder suspect that the suspect probably did not intend to murder the victim was not the equivalent of a hope of benefit, but mere routine police questioning designed to elicit a response from the suspect.

In *Patrick v. State,* the court held that a promise to keep a defendant out of Reidsville if he made a statement was not a promise of lighter punishment, was collateral in nature, and did not render a confession inadmissible. This was treated as being similar to a promise to inform the court of the defendant's cooperation. In *Arline v. State,* the court held that "the slightest hope of benefit" means "the hope of a lighter sentence." Where an officer tells a suspect that telling the truth "would probably help in court," this holds out some hope of reward.

However, in *Tyler v. State,* the court held that no hope of benefit was held out to the defendant where she was told that if she had anything to do with the crime, the best thing to do "was to go ahead and get it off her chest; that sometimes people did things for various reasons; . . . and whatever she told me I'd be willing to present it to the court." Also, where an officer tells a suspect that he will feel better if he confesses, this does not prevent the admission of a confession. In the questionable case of *Johnson v. State,* the court held that an agreement to put the defendant in a private cell, to seek psychiatric examination for the defendant, and to tell the judge of his cooperation, was held not to be the kind of hope of benefit which would keep a confession from being voluntary. In *White v. State,* the court held there was no "hope of benefit" where a defendant was to be transferred from a non-smoking jail to one where he could smoke. In *Duke v. State,* the court affirmed the admission of a statement where officers told defendant that if a third person committed the crime, then the defendant should tell the officers or risk being charged himself.

In *Sizemore v. State,* the court concluded that a defendant's statement was admissible when made to an officer who had "promised to let the defendant see his children [(the victims)] if he would make a statement."

In *Dickey v. State,* the court pointed out that the hope which prevents a confession from being admitted must be induced by someone other than the defendant. The fact that a defendant has a hope or fear which originates in the suspect's mind "from the seed of his own planting" will not result in the exclusion of his confession.

In *Williams v. State,* the court held that a statement was not the product of a "hope of reward" where defense counsel told the defendant that if the defendant made a statement, the district attorney might negotiate a sentence agreement. In *State v. Todd,* a majority of the appellate court reversed the trial court, which had held that an officer had induced the defendant's statement where the officer told the defendant that "if after we talk with you, we believe that probable cause doesn't exist, we are certainly not going to keep you arrested." The appellate court held that "this sort of mere truism, mere explanations of Todd's arrest and of the law, does not constitute an improper offer of some hope of benefit." Likewise, in *Heard v. State*, the court held that a confession was valid even though the defendant thought he could obtain a reduction in his bond if he confessed.

In *Tyson v. State,* the court indicated that implied promises based on a course of conduct with law enforcement officers over a number of years will not prevent a confession from being admissible.

See 1 Ringel, *Searches and Seizures, Arrests and Confessions,* § 25.2(c) (Clark Boardman 1979).

§ 5-6 Admissibility—Voluntariness—Fear of injury

A confession induced by fear on the part of the accused, as a result of a threat, is involuntary and not admissible. Thus, a confession made because of fear induced by torture is not admissible, and even advice by an officer to a suspect in custody, to the effect that if he knew anything he had better tell it, prevents a confession from being admissible.

In *Anderson v. State,* the appellate court held that the defendant's confession was not a result of a threat of injury or promise of benefit where the officer told the defendant that he was considering charging the defendant's girlfriend as an accessory to the crime. The court concluded that the officer's statement was a mere "truism" or recounting of facts.

In Lynumn v. Illinois, the Supreme Court held that an oral confession, which was made after the defendant had been told that "state financial aid for her infant children would be cut off, and her children taken away from her, if she did not 'cooperate,'" was involuntary. The court stated that "the confession cannot be deemed 'the product of a rational intellect and a free will.'" See section 5-5, supra.

In Garrity v. New Jersey, "police officers were investigated for allegedly fixing traffic tickets. The officers were informed that they could exercise their Fifth Amendment privilege against self-incrimination if they wished, but doing so would cost them their jobs. . . . The [United States] Supreme Court held that the statements obtained under threat of removal from office cannot be used . . . ."

In State v. Aiken, the Georgia Supreme Court adopted the totality of circumstances test used in *Garrity* for determining whether a public employees statement was coerced through an implied or express threat of termination. The Court observed:

> Factors that a court may consider include those discussed in the foregoing cases, including whether the State actor made an overt threat to the defendant of the loss of his job if he did not speak with investigators or whether a statute, rule, or ordinance of which the defendant was aware provided that the defendant would lose his job for failing to answer questions. If no express threat is present, the court may examine whether the defendant subjectively believed that he could lose his job for failing to cooperate and whether, if so, that belief was reasonable given the State action involved. In determining whether the defendants belief was objectively reasonable, the court may examine whether the defendant was aware of any statutes, ordinances, manuals, or policies that required cooperation and provided generally, without specifying a penalty, that an employee could be subject to discipline for failing to cooperate. The court may also consider whether the investigator implicitly communicated any threat of dismissal either in written or oral form; whether, before the interrogation began, the defendant was told he was free to leave at any time; and whether the defendant was told he had the right to have a lawyer present. A trial court, of course, is free to consider any other factor that it determines is relevant to the determination of voluntariness. We conclude that the totality of the circumstances test is in keeping with the spirit of *Garrity* and with the discretion our courts have historically enjoyed in determining whether a defendants statement is voluntary.
>
> (citations and footnotes omitted).

However, in State v. Stinson, the Georgia Court of Appeals held that this rule does not apply where there is neither an overt threat to terminate employment nor a subjective belief by such public employee that he would be terminated if he failed to answer questions.

In *Roberts v. State,* the court held that advising a defendant of the evidence the state has against him does not constitute coercion.

§ 5-7 Admissibility—Voluntariness—Trickery

The general rule is that the confession of a suspect, if freely and voluntarily made, is not rendered inadmissible although it is induced by some trick, artifice or deception, unless the trickery amounts to a violation of due process. O.C.G.A. § 24–3–51 provides as follows:

"The fact that a confession has been made under a spiritual exhortation, a promise of secrecy, or a promise of collateral benefit shall not exclude it."

While Georgia also has a code section which provides that an admission obtained by fraud is not admissible, this section has not been held to apply in criminal cases.

In *DeYoung v. State,* the court held that "[c]onfessions are admissible though obtained by artifice, trick, or deception, so long as the means employed to procure them are not calculated to elicit an untrue statement. . . . That a confession is obtained by such means does not preclude a finding that the confession was freely and voluntarily given." However, in *State v. Ritter*, the Georgia Supreme Court pointed out "that use of trickery and deceit to obtain a confession does not render it inadmissible, so long as the means employed are not calculated to procure an untrue statement." This principle cannot be allowed to supersede the requirements of O.C.G.A. § 24–3–50, however. "Thus, while deceit may not on its own render a statement inadmissible (where not calculated to procure an untrue statement), we hold that in looking to the totality of the circumstances . . . the employment of deceit may result in the inadmissibility of a statement in those situations where the particular deception used, by constituting a 'slightest hope of benefit or remotest fear of injury' under O.C.G.A. § 24–3–50, has induced a party to confess, thereby rendering the confession involuntary." Therefore, the court concluded that a statement obtained from the defendant was not admissible where the defendant was told that the victim was awake when he was actually dead. Likewise, the Georgia Supreme Court held in *Carswell v. State* that the statement obtained from the defendant was not subject to suppression even though the investigator told the defendant they were speaking "off the record" when they were being recorded. However, in *State v. Ritter* the Georgia Supreme Court pointed out that "deceit may result in the inadmissibility of a statement . . . where the particular deception used, by constituting a 'slightest hope of benefit or remotest fear of injury' . . . has induced a party to confess, thereby rendering the confession involuntary."

In *State v. Parks,* the Court of Appeals rejected the notion that the defendant's statement was not voluntary where he agreed to follow police officers to the station for the purpose of being questioned and, while there, was interrogated in a room where the door could not, in fact, be locked. With respect to the officers' employment of trickery during the questioning of the defendant, the court observed that "the use of trickery or deception does not bear on the issue of whether [the defendant] was in custody or reasonably believed himself to be in custody. (Citations omitted). Rather, trickery may compromise the *voluntariness* of a statement if it constitutes 'the slightest hope of benefit or remotest fear of injury.' "

In *Miranda v. Arizona,* the Supreme Court said, "[A]ny evidence that the accused was threatened, tricked, or cajoled into a waiver will, of course, show that the defendant did not voluntarily waive his privilege." Technically this language refers to the waiver of Miranda rights and not to the voluntariness of the confession itself, but it may indicate the attitude of the Court toward trickery. However, the United States Supreme Court never seems to have indicated any particular kind of trickery which would alone render a confession inadmissible. It has been said that a confession is not rendered inadmissible because of trickery or deception "as long as the means employed are not calculated to produce an untrue statement." See section 5-10, infra, on right to counsel.

Generally, see 1 Ringel, *Searches and Seizures, Arrests and Confessions,* § 25.2(d) (Clark Boardman 1979).

§ 5-8 Admissibility—Confession of juvenile

A confession from a juvenile is "scanned with more care and received with greater caution" than that of an adult. The provisions of O.C.G.A. § 15–11–47 apply to a confession by a juvenile even when the juvenile is tried as an adult. This statute provides in part as follows:

"A person taking a child into custody, with all reasonable speed and without first taking the child elsewhere, shall: (1) Forthwith release without bond the child to the child's parents . . . ; (3) Bring the child immediately before the juvenile court or promptly contact a juvenile court intake officer. The intake officer shall determine if the child should be released or detained. Prior to an informal detention hearing, the child shall be placed in detention, if necessary, only in such places as are authorized by O.C.G.A. § 15–11–48; or (4) Bring the child who is suspected of committing a delinquent act before the superior court of the county where the delinquent act occurred if the act is an act over which the superior court has exclusive or concurrent jurisdiction. . . .

"The person taking a child into custody shall promptly give notice thereof, together with a statement of the reason for taking the child into custody, to a parent, guardian, or other custodian and to the court. Any temporary detention or questioning of the child necessary to comply with this Code section shall conform to the procedures and conditions prescribed by this article and rules of court."

O.C.G.A. § 15–11–7(b) provides in part that "[a]n extrajudicial statement obtained in the course of violation of this article or one which would be constitutionally inadmissible in a criminal proceeding shall not be used against such child." However, the statute "does not require that one or both parents, or other responsible adult, be present during the questioning of a minor."

These provisions apply to both juvenile court proceedings and criminal cases. However, a confession is not to be automatically excluded if the provisions of the Juvenile Code are not complied with. In *Lattimore v. State,* the Georgia Supreme Court pointed out that "the issue to be considered is whether there is a knowing and intelligent waiver by . . . [the defendant] of his constitutional rights in making the incriminating statements. . . . [If a defendant] knowingly and intelligently waived his constitutional rights . . . and voluntarily made the statement in question . . ." it is not error for the trial judge to deny a motion to suppress the statement. Thus, in *Paxton v. State,* the court pointed out that the requirements of O.C.G.A. § 15–11–47(a)(2) are to be construed as directory and not mandatory. The same case also holds that there is no requirement that "an accused juvenile . . . be advised that he has a right to have a parent, guardian or adult present during questioning."

In *Marshall v. State,* the court affirmed the trial judge's finding that a confession of a 14–year-old juvenile was admissible. The defendant, after being arrested for murder, was taken first to the police station for booking and to obtain hair samples, rather than being handled as provided in O.C.G.A. § 15–11–47. The court stated that this did not amount to a per se violation of the Juvenile Code. The juvenile was advised of his rights, and both he and his mother signed a waiver of rights form. After booking, he was taken to the Youth Development Center for detention. The court pointed out that there is no requirement that one or both parents be present during questioning. The admissibility of such a confession from a juvenile is dependent upon the totality of the circumstances.

There are nine criteria to be considered in determining whether the waiver was voluntarily and knowingly given: (1) age of the accused; (2) education of the accused; (3) knowledge of the accused as to both the substance of the charge and the nature of his rights to consult with an attorney and remain silent; (4) whether the accused is held incommunicado or allowed to consult with relatives, friends or an attorney; (5) whether the accused is interrogated before or after formal charges are filed; (6) methods used in interrogation; (7) length of interrogation; (8) whether vel non the accused refuses to voluntarily give statements on prior occasions; and (9) whether the accused repudiates an extrajudicial statement at a later date. Where it appears that a juvenile delegates to a parent or guardian the decision to proceed without counsel, any subsequent statement may be subject to suppression as not being knowing and voluntary.

Statements obtained by school officials acting in concert with or at the direction of police authorities may also be subject to exclusion. Whether the school officials were acting in such a capacity must be determined on a case by case basis by viewing the totality of the circumstances.

§ 5-9 Admissibility—Massiah and Escobedo—Pre-*Miranda* theories based on the Sixth Amendment

The inadmissibility of incriminating statements obtained simply because of the absence of counsel was perhaps first recognized in 1964 by the United States Supreme Court in *Massiah v. United States.* In *Massiah* the Court held that the Sixth Amendment guarantee of "the assistance of counsel" in all "criminal prosecutions" is violated where government agents "deliberately elicit" post-indictment statements from a suspect in the absence of counsel. The fact that Massiah was already indicted when his incriminating statements were made is important to the decision of that case, as well as future Sixth Amendment cases, because the Sixth Amendment right to counsel only attaches at the initiation of adversary criminal proceedings. Therefore, before this "critical period of the proceedings," a suspect in a criminal investigation has no Sixth Amendment right to counsel. However, while the state may not use such statements in its case in chief, it may use the statements to impeach a defendant who elects to testify at trial.

Five weeks after *Massiah,* the United States Supreme Court decided *Escobedo v. Illinois.* Escobedo was arrested for murder, questioned, and then released the same day. He had counsel at the time of the initial arrest, and was later re-arrested and questioned again. During the second questioning, which lasted four hours, Escobedo was not permitted to speak with his lawyer, despite repeated requests to do so by both Escobedo and his attorney who was present at the police station while Escobedo was being questioned. Although the interrogation here was conducted before Escobedo was indicted, the Court noted that "in the context of this case, that fact should make no difference." Writing for the Court, Justice Goldberg narrowly held that (1) where an investigation "has begun to focus on a particular suspect, [(2)] the suspect has been taken into policy custody, [(3)] the police carry out a process of interrogations that lends itself to eliciting incriminating statements, [(4)] the suspect has requested and been denied an opportunity to consult with his lawyer, and [(5)] the police have not effectively warned him of his absolute constitutional right to remain silent, the accused has been denied 'the Assistance of Counsel' in violation of the Sixth Amendment . . . ."

In *Miranda v. Arizona,* the Court effectively limited the *Escobedo* holding to its facts.

§ 5-10 Admissibility—Right to counsel—The confusing relationship between the Fifth and Sixth Amendments

The Fifth Amendment provides that "[n]o person . . . shall be compelled in any criminal case to be a witness against himself." In *Miranda v. Arizona,* the United States Supreme Court interpreted the above quoted clause as providing a defendant with a right to have counsel present during custodial interrogation. The Sixth Amendment provides that "[i]n all criminal prosecutions, the accused shall . . . have the Assistance of Counsel for his defense." The Fifth Amendment refers to compulsion; the Sixth Amendment does not. Thus, there is an independent basis for the applicability of these two amendments. A statement or confession admissible under *Miranda* may be inadmissible under the Sixth Amendment. Thus, a voluntary statement made after the initiation of judicial proceedings by a defendant, either in custody or not in custody, in the absence of counsel may be inadmissible under the Sixth Amendment right to counsel. It is most difficult to generalize from the United States Supreme Court cases in this area; hence, the facts of each such case take on added significance.

In *Brewer v. Williams,* the defendant turned himself in in Davenport, Iowa, pursuant to telephone advice from his lawyer in Des Moines. He was booked in Davenport for abducting a 10–year-old girl in Des Moines. He was advised of his *Miranda* rights, conferred with a Davenport attorney, and was arraigned before a magistrate. The following day, officers from Des Moines drove the 160 miles to Davenport to get Williams. There was an express agreement that Williams was not to be questioned. On the way back, one of the officers talked with Williams extensively. The officer told Williams that they would be going back near the area where he thought the body had been disposed of and pointed out that the parents should be entitled to a Christian burial. It was snowing at the time and the officer said that after the snowstorm was over, they might not be able to find the body. Some time later Williams directed them to the body. The United States Supreme Court concluded that Williams' Sixth Amendment right to counsel had been violated and that, constitutionally, the case was indistinguishable from *Massiah.* Because adversary proceedings had begun against the defendant, he had a right to counsel when the officers interrogated him.

Rhode Island v. Innis was decided on the basis of whether or not there had been any custodial interrogation of the defendant. Innis had been arrested for a shotgun robbery. The defendant had been given *Miranda* warnings, and he said he wanted to talk with a lawyer. As he was being driven to the police station by two officers, one of the officers said to the other that there was a school for handicapped children in the area and a lot of children were running around. "God forbid one of them might find a weapon with shells . . . they might hurt themselves." The defendant interrupted the officers, stating that they should turn the car around and he would show them where the gun was located. The court concluded that the defendant volunteered the information and that it did not result from interrogation.

In *United States v. Henry,* the Court held that incriminating statements made to a cellmate, after the defendant was indicted, were in violation of the Sixth Amendment right to counsel. An FBI agent instructed the cellmate in advance to be alert to any statement made by the defendant, but not to initiate any conversation with the defendant and not to question him. The informer understood that he was to be paid if he furnished information.

In *Henry,* the Court distinguished *Hoffa v. United States.* Hoffa was convicted of endeavoring to bribe members of a jury who had tried him for an alleged earlier violation of the Taft–Hartley Act. A substantial part of the evidence against Hoffa was contributed by a paid informer named Partin, who testified to several incriminating statements made by Hoffa in his presence. The court concluded that (1) none of Hoffa's Fourth Amendment rights were violated because Partin was present by invitation and the conversations were knowingly carried on in his presence. All of Hoffa's statements were voluntary. The Fourth Amendment does not protect against the misplaced belief that Partin would not reveal the conversations; (2) Hoffa's Fifth Amendment rights were not violated because his incriminating statements were voluntary and not the product of coercion; (3) Hoffa's Sixth Amendment rights were not violated because the informer Partin was not present when Hoffa talked with his lawyer, and he could not complain that he was not taken into custody while the earlier trial was in progress even though the government had sufficient grounds for doing so.

In *Henry,* the Court said that in *Hoffa* there was no violation of the right to counsel by " 'deliberately eliciting incriminating statements.' . . . An accused speaking to a known government agent is typically aware that his statements may be used against him. . . . When the accused is in the company of a fellow inmate who is acting by prearrangement as a Government agent, the same cannot be said." The fact that Henry was incarcerated is also a factor because of the psychological inducement to reach for aid when a person is confined.

The *Henry* Court felt that *Hoffa* was different because, in *Hoffa,* the government used "incriminating statements from persons not in custody but suspected of criminal activity prior to the time charges [were] filed." In *Kuhlmann v. Wilson,* the United States Supreme Court held that the intentional placing of an informant in a cell with a defendant did not violate the Sixth Amendment where the informant does not take "some action, beyond merely listening, that was designed deliberately to elicit incriminating remarks." In *Illinois v. Perkins,* the United States Supreme Court held that *Miranda* warnings did not have to be given to an incarcerated suspect before an officer, posing as a fellow inmate, questioned the suspect.

The 1981 case of *Estelle v. Smith* should be considered. Smith was charged with murder. Apparently, defense counsel had been appointed to represent him. The trial judge, without notice to defense counsel, directed a psychiatric examination of Smith by a Dr. Grigson to determine Smith's competence to stand trial. Dr. Grigson was later called as a witness by the state to testify at the penalty stage of the bifurcated trial after Smith had been found guilty of murder. The psychiatrist testified that Smith was a severe sociopath and would continue his previous behavior. Smith was sentenced to death. The United States Supreme Court held that Smith's Sixth Amendment right to counsel was violated when he was sent to Dr. Grigson for evaluation, because defense counsel were not notified in advance that the psychiatric examination would encompass the issue of their client's future dangerousness, and Smith was denied his attorneys' assistance in making the decision of whether to submit to the examination and to what end the psychiatrist's findings could be used.

In *Maine v. Moulton,* the United States Supreme Court said that "the right to counsel granted by the Sixth and Fourteenth Amendments means at least that a person is entitled to the help of a lawyer at or after the time that judicial proceedings have been initiated against him." The court held that a recording of a conversation, made in the absence of counsel after the defendant had been indicted, between the defendant and a co-defendant who was a government informer, violated the Sixth Amendment.

However, in 1986, in *Moran v. Burbine,* the United States Supreme Court held that where a suspect was given *Miranda* warnings, and waived his right to remain silent, the waiver was not voided by (1) the failure of officers to inform suspect that counsel had been employed for him by a third person, or (2) in failing to inform suspect that counsel was attempting to reach him, or (3) by giving counsel misleading information regarding the officer's intention to interrogate the defendant. The court emphasized that the Sixth Amendment right to counsel did not apply until the initiation of adversary judicial proceedings, stating that *Escobedo* is now viewed not as a Sixth Amendment case but as a Fifth Amendment self-incrimination case. The court said that *Miranda* does not forbid such police deception relating to an attorney, and such conduct was not so offensive as to deprive the suspect of fundamental fairness guaranteed in the due process clause of the Fourteenth Amendment.

In *Cahill v. Rushen,* the Ninth Circuit held that a confession of the defendant after his conviction was not admissible when he was re-tried after obtaining a reversal of his earlier conviction. The defendant had told officers that the confession could not adversely affect him at that point, and he then confessed. The court concluded that there had been a denial of the defendant's right to counsel.

In *Spence v. State,* the court said that Georgia has limited the Massiah rule to post-indictment statements made outside the presence of counsel. In *Baxter v. State,* the Georgia Court of Appeals found *Henry* not to apply where the defendant made incriminating statements to two fellow inmates, who had encouraged the statements in the hope of lenient treatment. Since lenient treatment had not been promised by the state, the inmates were not state agents. See Goger, *Daniel's Georgia Handbook on Criminal Evidence* (2009 ed.), § 6–3.

In *United States v. Karr,* the Ninth Circuit held that the *Miranda* warnings plus being told that formal judicial proceedings had begun against him is sufficient information to enable a defendant to waive his Sixth Amendment right to counsel. In *Patterson v. Illinois,* the United States Supreme Court considered a post indictment statement made to an officer in absence of counsel. The defendant knew what he was charged with, was given *Miranda* warnings and signed a *Miranda* waiver. The court rejected Patterson's argument that the Sixth Amendment right to counsel is superior to "the fifth amendment right." The court then pointed out "that whatever warnings suffice for *Miranda* purposes will also be sufficient in the context of post indictment questioning."

In *Potter v. State*, the defendant, after being properly given his *Miranda* warnings, gave a voluntary statement while in custody. While the defendant was being interrogated, the public defender's office was attempting to gain access to the defendant to determine whether he qualified for and wanted its representation. The court rejected the defendant's argument that his statement should not have been admitted at trial because of the public defender's actions. In addition to noting that defendant had signed written waivers of his rights and had not invoked his right to counsel, the court observed that "[n]o attorney, acting without consulting [the defendant], was empowered to invoke a right to counsel for him."

In *Starks v. State,* the Georgia Supreme Court considered the admissibility of a non-custodial statement made to a probation officer. The court concluded that if the statement was obtained after the defendant had asserted his Sixth Amendment right to counsel, and the conversation had been initiated by the officer, the statement was not admissible.

Generally, see 1 Ringel, *Searches and Seizures, Arrests and Confessions,* § 29.1 et seq. (Clark Boardman 1979). See section 5-13, infra, on interrogation.

§ 5-11 Confessions and admissions—*Miranda v. Arizona*—General

Much controversy has centered around *Miranda v. Arizona,* handed down in 1966. However, thus far the United States Supreme Court has declined to reverse *Miranda* although it has had ample opportunity to do so. In a persuasive opinion in 1999, *United States v. Dickerson*, the Fourth Circuit held that the rules set out in *Miranda* are not required by the United States Constitution and that the provisions of 18 U. S. C. § 3501 contain the test for admitting confessions in federal courts. However, *Dickerson* was reversed by the United States Supreme Court, which held that *Miranda* was an interpretation of the requirements of the Constitution.

In essence, *Miranda* holds the following:

(1) The warnings established by *Miranda* govern unless other equally effective methods are found.

(2) "Volunteered statements of any kind are not barred" by *Miranda.*

(3) The rules apply when an individual in custody is first subjected to police questioning.

(4) The prescribed warnings must be given regardless of the knowledge of the person in custody.

(5) An individual is free to exercise his right to remain silent if he indicates in any manner at any time prior to or during questioning that he wishes to remain silent. If he does, questioning must cease immediately.

(6) If a statement is obtained in the absence of counsel, the prosecution has the burden of demonstrating that the defendant knowingly and intelligently waived his privilege against self-incrimination. A waiver of the privilege cannot be inferred from silence after the *Miranda* warnings have been given nor from the fact that a confession was obtained.

(7) An accused may not be penalized for exercising his privilege against self-incrimination.

(8) Unless and until warnings and waivers are demonstrated by the prosecution, no evidence obtained as a result of a violation of *Miranda* is admissible in evidence. However, it seems that generally statements made by a defendant in the absence of *Miranda* warnings are admissible where the primary purpose of questioning was to save the life of a victim. Thus, in *New York v. Quarles,* the United States Supreme Court held that it was not necessary for an officer to give *Miranda* warnings to a suspect in custody before asking "where is the gun"

because there were "overriding considerations of public safety" as measured by an objective standard. See Annotation on "public safety" exception to *Miranda,* 81 L.Ed.2d 990 (1986). See section 5-14, infra.

(9) The rules set forth in *Miranda* apply to both confessions and admissions.

The *Miranda* decision is not retroactive.

In *United States v. Mesa,* the Third Circuit held that a suspect barricaded in a motel room was not in custody when officers tried to talk him into a peaceful surrender. The fact that the motel was surrounded does not mean that the suspect was in custody.

In summary, it must be remembered that *Miranda* does not apply at all unless there are both (1) *custody* and (2) *interrogation.* If there is interrogation of an in-custody suspect, *Miranda* does apply. If *Miranda* is applicable, no statement obtained from a suspect is admissible unless both of the following requirements have been met: (1) The suspect must have been given *adequate warnings,* and (2) the suspect must have validly *waived* his right of silence.

If *Miranda* is applicable and there is a violation, the only result is the suppression of the in-custody statement and not a dismissal of the charges against the defendant.

§ 5-12 Confessions and admissions—Miranda v. Arizona—Custody

The necessity of giving the *Miranda* warnings exists *only* when an individual is questioned while in custody. According to *Miranda,* "custodial interrogation" means "questioning initiated by law enforcement officers after a person has been taken into custody or otherwise deprived of his freedom of action in any significant way." As a general rule, a person "who is the subject of a general on-the-scene investigation is not in custody," and neither the fact that the officer "would not have allowed any of the bystanders to leave until he had received some answers to his questions nor his conclusion that all of them were in his legal custody may be considered controlling on the issue of whether there had in fact been an official exercise of control or authority over the defendant amounting to an arrest." A person is not regarded as being in custody simply because he and other potential witnesses went to the jail, pursuant to request, and where they are called into an investigator's office individually for questioning. However, deprivation of freedom of action is an element to be considered in determining whether an individual is in custody. Thus, in *Reinhardt v. State,* the Georgia Supreme Court held that the defendant was in custody for *Miranda* purposes when he was questioned by officers in a hospital room.

In *Stansbury v. California,* the United States Supreme Court pointed out that *Miranda* warnings need only be given "where there has been such a restriction on a person's freedom as to render him 'in custody.' . . . [A] court must examine all of the circumstances surrounding the interrogation but 'the ultimate inquiry is simply whether there [was] a "formal arrest or restraint on freedom of movement." ' . . . [T]he initial determination of custody depends on the *objective* circumstances of the interrogation, not on the *subjective* views harbored by either the interrogating officers or the person being questioned. . . . [T]he only relevant inquiry is how a reasonable man in the suspect's shoes would have understood his situation. . . . [A] police officer's subjective view that the individual under questioning is a suspect, if undisclosed, does not bear upon the question [of] whether the individual is in custody for purposes of *Miranda.* "However, '[a]n officer's knowledge or beliefs may bear upon the custody issue if they are conveyed, by word or deed, to the individual being questioned . . . , [but] [t]hose beliefs are relevant only to the extent they would affect how a reasonable person in the position of the individual being questioned would gauge the breadth of his or her "freedom of action." ' "

In the 1995 United States Supreme Court case of *Thompson v. Keohane,* the Court concluded that two discrete inquiries are essential to a determination of "in custody for *Miranda* purposes: '[F]irst, what were the circumstances surrounding the interrogation; and second, given those circumstances, would a reasonable person have felt he or she was not at liberty to terminate the interrogation and leave. . . . [T]he court must apply an objective test. . . . The first inquiry . . . is distinctly factual. . . . The second inquiry . . . presents a 'mixed question of law and fact. . . .' " In *State v. Brannan,* the Georgia Court of Appeals said that in determining if a person is in custody, "we apply an objective standard and determine whether a reasonable person in his situation would have believed he was physically deprived of his freedom of action in a significant way." In *Hadley v. State,* the court pointed out that the factors to consider in determining whether or not a defendant was in custody "include: probable cause to arrest, substantive intent of the police, subjective belief of the defendant, and the focus of the investigation." In *Johnson v. State,* the court pointed out that the term "reasonable person" . . . "does not mean a person with a guilty conscience who knows as soon as they see the blue light that they will be arrested for matters known to them, but [which] are not as yet known to the police."

In *Hodges v. State,* the court cited *Stansbury* and held that there is no automatic need to Mirandize a person being questioned simply because the officer has probable cause to arrest.

In *Berkemer v. McCarty,* the United States Supreme Court pointed out that "detention of a motorist pursuant to a traffic stop is presumptively temporary and brief . . . [and] circumstances associated with the typical traffic stop are not such that the motorist feels completely at the mercy of the police. . . . In short, the atmosphere surrounding an ordinary traffic stop is substantially less 'police dominated' than that surrounding the kinds of interrogation at issue in *Miranda.* . . . [T]he usual traffic stop is more analogous to a so called '*Terry* stop. . . .' "

In *Crum v. State,* the Georgia Court of Appeals held that roadside questioning during the investigation of a routine traffic incident generally does not constitute a custodial situation. In *State v. Pastorini,* the court held that where an officer obtained the defendant's driver's license and insurance card while investigating an accident, and then administered field sobriety tests after observing signs of drunkenness, the defendant was not in custody as contemplated by *Miranda* until he was formally arrested. In *Sutton v. State,* the court pointed out that "an officer conducting a routine traffic stop may request and examine a driver's license and vehicle registration and run a computer check on the documents."

However, in *State v. O'Donnell,* the defendant was involved in a two car accident. The defendant left the scene and was almost immediately involved in a second accident, where he was arrested. An officer questioned him and had him perform field sobriety tests. The appellate court held that since the defendant was under arrest, "a *Miranda* warning must be given regardless of whether the questioning occurs in the context of a routine investigation of a traffic offense."

A *Terry* stop-and-frisk is regarded in Georgia as an investigative detention which does not in any significant way deprive a person of his freedom. Thus, questioning incident to a stop-and-frisk has been held not to amount to a custodial interrogation as contemplated by *Miranda.* See Goger, *Daniel's Georgia Handbook on Criminal Evidence* (2009 ed.), § 7–16.

In *Quinn v. State,* an officer with an arrest warrant for the defendant went to the defendant's house. "Before he placed defendant under arrest, the officer told defendant about the shooting incident, adding that he was 'not quite clear on everything that happened,' but that he did know that a 'shiny nickel weapon' was used. . . . Then he asked defendant if he owned a similar weapon. [The] [d]efendant replied that he did; he 'went inside,' brought the gun out and 'voluntarily' gave it to the officer." Thereupon, he was placed under arrest and then advised of his rights. The court affirmed the finding that there was no *Miranda* violation because he was not in custody until after the gun was handed to the officer.

The questioning of a person serving time for another crime is regarded as a custodial interrogation. In the absence of *Miranda* warnings or a valid waiver, any statement thus obtained is inadmissible. However, in *Minnesota v. Murphy,* the United States Supreme Court held that a defendant was not in custody at the time he made a confession to his probation officer in another case.

If a defendant, after an automobile collision, is found by the side of the road and questioned by the police, he is not regarded as being in custody at that time.

The Texas Court of Criminal Appeals has held that interrogation becomes custodial when the suspect admits committing the offense he is being questioned about.

In addition to *Miranda* warnings being required before a person in custody is questioned by police or representatives of the district attorney, the United States Supreme Court held in *Estelle v. Smith* that *Miranda* warnings have to be given before a psychiatric interview ordered by a trial judge on his own initiative where the defendant was being held for murder.

§ 5-13 Confessions and admissions—*Miranda v. Arizona*—Interrogation

Generally, on-the-scene questioning of citizens as to the facts surrounding a crime is not curtailed by *Miranda.* Routine police questioning not related to the investigation of the case does not amount to a custodial interrogation within the meaning of *Miranda.* An officer's question, "What are you doing here?" asked of a suspect who was apprehended at gunpoint is not an interrogation. The statement, volunteered by a defendant, "Well, you all got me," blurted out in a police car is admissible, even though not preceded by *Miranda* warnings. "Furthermore, a police officer's question, prompted by defendant's volunteered remark falls under the same exception."

A public safety exception to *Miranda* warnings is "not [dependent] upon the motivation for the individuals involved." This is a reversal of the holding in *State v. Overby,* which limited the exception to situations in which the *sole* purpose of questioning was for determining danger to persons at the scene.

Confessions which are volunteered are not affected by *Miranda.* In *Beeks v. State,* the defendant reported to the sheriff that a certain individual stole his car. While the defendant was in a car with two officers en route to report the theft, he made incriminating statements which were held voluntary and admissible.

The four cases making up the *Miranda* decision all involved action of law enforcement officials in attempting to get statements or confessions, and *Miranda* applies only to interrogations by law enforcement officers. The Georgia Supreme Court has held that questions asked by family members fall outside *Miranda* protection. In *Cook v. State,* the Georgia Supreme Court held that case by case analysis should be used when determining if the *Miranda* protections apply to the statements made by a child to a parent who is employed in law enforcement. Furthermore, the Georgia Court of Appeals has held that *Miranda* does not apply to the in-custody statement made to a caseworker of the Department of Family and Children Services in a cruelty to children case because the caseworker was not a law enforcement officer. Additionally, *Miranda* was held to be inapplicable in a situation where a private citizen was protecting his property. However, it has been pointed out that most of the courts considering the question have held that the requirements of *Miranda* apply to a statement obtained by a parole officer from questioning related to the parole function.

Once *Miranda* warnings are given and the suspect indicates his desire to remain silent, the questioning must cease. However, there is no blanket prohibition against subsequent questioning with the voluntariness of any later incriminating statement depending upon the facts of the individual case. However, in *Edwards v. Arizona,* the United States Supreme Court distinguished the right to remain silent from the right to counsel under the Fifth Amendment and held that "when an accused has invoked his right to have counsel present during custodial interrogation, a valid waiver of that right cannot be established by showing only that he responded to further police-initiated custodial interrogation even if he has been advised of his rights." See section 5-20, infra.

In *Rhode Island v. Innis,* the United States Supreme Court said that interrogation, as conceptualized in *Mi-*

randa, "must reflect a measure of compulsion above and beyond that inherent in custody itself . . . *Miranda* safeguards come into play whenever a person in custody is subjected to either express questioning or its *functional equivalent*. . . . [*Miranda* applies] to any words or actions on the part of the police (other than those normally attendant to arrest and custody) that the police should know are reasonably likely to elicit an incriminating response from the suspect. . . . A practice that the police should know is reasonably likely to evoke an incriminating response from a suspect thus amounts to interrogation" even if no direct question is asked. See section 14-27, infra, on discovery of a defendant's statements while in custody. However, in the 1990 case of *Illinois v. Perkins,* the United States Supreme Court held that *Miranda* warnings do not have to be given by an undercover policeman, posing as an inmate, before he questions an inmate about a crime the officer is investigating.

In *Carr v. State,* two defendants were arrested and placed in a patrol car where a hidden recorder recorded the conversation between the defendants. The court found that this was not interrogation and that officers "do not interrogate a suspect simply by hoping that he will incriminate himself."

In *Washington v. State,* where the defendant indicated that he did not wish to talk and stated that the police did not have any evidence against him, the court held that there was no interrogation where an officer informed the defendant of the evidence against him and the defendant then decided to talk. However, in *State v. Darby,* the court ruled that telling a suspect that he could only tell "his side" of things if he first signed a *Miranda* waiver was improper. The court noted that the suspect should have been advised that "he could make a voluntary statement but that he could not be interrogated by the officers without first signing the waiver."

In *Williams v. State,* the Georgia Supreme Court concluded that there was nothing to suggest that a sheriff should have known that his conduct was "reasonably likely to elicit an incriminating response from Williams" in taking him "back to the location where the killing occurred while he was still intoxicated and disoriented."

In *Johnson v. State,* the defendant, who was in custody on unrelated charges, was brought to the interview room for questioning where he was shown a picture of the victim prior to being informed of his *Miranda* rights. He stated, "I guess I know why I'm here now. I didn't shoot that man. I never got out of the car." The appellate court affirmed the action of the trial judge in admitting this statement in evidence as voluntary.

In *Shoemaker v. State,* an officer asked the driver of a car some questions. Both passengers responded with explanations. The Georgia Court of Appeals concluded that the spontaneous declaration of a passenger was not a result of police questioning of the declarant and was admissible.

In *Lazenby v. State,* the court affirmed the denial of a motion to suppress statements the defendant made while the arresting officer was attempting to read him his *Miranda* rights.

In *Pennsylvania v. Muniz,* the defendant was arrested for driving under the influence. He was taken routinely to a booking center and told that his voice and actions would be taped. Without being given *Miranda* warnings, he was asked questions about his name, address, height, weight, eye color, date of birth and current age. He was also asked and was not able to give the date of his sixth birthday. The United States Supreme Court held that the defendant's response to the date of his sixth birthday was testimonial and not admissible. The other questions were not regarded as interrogation. The taping of the sobriety test and incriminating statements of the defendant during the test were held admissible. See section 2-22, supra, on booking.

In Georgia it has been held that routine questions to the defendant at the time of arrest, such as the defendant's name or date of birth, are not generally regarded as interrogation. In *Edwards v. State,* the court found that there was no interrogation when a booking officer obtains information such as name, address, telephone number, social security number, date and place of birth, employer, height, and weight.

See section 5-19, infra, on waiver and assertion of *Miranda* rights. See section 5-10, supra, on confessions made to a cellmate.

§ 5-14 Confessions and admissions—*Miranda v. Arizona*—Warnings

As pointed out in section 5-11, supra, if there is in-custody interrogation by law enforcement officers and the prosecution wishes to introduce into evidence a statement by a defendant, it must be shown (1) that the defendant was adequately warned and (2) that he knowingly and intelligently waived his right to remain silent and his right to presence of counsel at the time of the interrogation.

In *Miranda,* the Court summarized the warnings required as follows: Prior to any questioning, the person must be warned (1) that he has a right to remain silent, (2) that any statement he makes *may* be used as evidence against him, (3) that he has a right to the presence of an attorney, and (4) that if he cannot afford an attorney, one will be appointed for him prior to any questioning if he so desires. If the accused indicates in any manner at any stage of the process that he wishes to consult with an attorney, questioning must cease. Likewise, if the individual is alone and indicates in any manner that he does not wish to be interrogated, the police may not question him. The mere fact that he may have answered some questions or volunteered statements does not deprive him of the right to refrain from answering any further inquiries until he has consulted with an attorney and thereafter consents to further questioning.

However, in *Duckworth v. Eagan,* the United States Supreme Court held that the *Miranda* warnings were satisfactory even though they contained a statement that the officers had "no way of giving you a lawyer, but one will be appointed for you, if you wish, if and when you go to court."

Miranda warnings are commonly given by reading them from a card which has been prepared for this purpose. However, an officer may give the warnings from memory rather than reading them. Many officers in Georgia currently use a *Miranda* warning card which contains the following material:

"1. You have the right to remain silent.

"2. Anything you say *can and will* be used against you in a court of law.

"3. You have the right to talk to a lawyer and have him present with you while you are being questioned.

"4. If you cannot afford to hire a lawyer, one will be appointed to represent you before any questioning, if you wish."

On the card quoted from above, a fifth statement is included:

"5. You can decide at any time to exercise these rights and not answer any questions or make any statements."

The reverse side of the card contains the following:

"WAIVER

"After the warning and in order to secure a waiver, the following questions should be asked and an affirmative reply secured to each question.

"1. Do you understand each of these rights I have explained to you?

"2. Having these rights in mind, do you wish to talk to us now?"

All of the warnings as prescribed in *Miranda* must be given, not just a part of them. Number 5 as set out above is not required.

The pre-questioning warnings must be given in a clear manner and in language understandable to the suspect. However, a person under arrest may be given a document containing the warnings. If the accused reads the warnings and signs a statement saying he clearly understands them, the warnings are generally considered to have been satisfactorily given even if the defendant later testifies that he did not comprehend all of the words.

In the opinion in *In the Interest of D. T. C.,* the court pointed out that the "facts that D. T. C. has an I.Q. of 64, has an intellectual deficiency and may be mentally retarded do not automatically invalidate his waiver of *Miranda* rights." In *Coppock v. State,* the Georgia Supreme Court held that "the fact that an individual may be moderately retarded is not sufficient to exclude . . . [his] statement."

Despite the broad language of *Miranda,* a number of courts have held that the need to give the prescribed warnings does not apply for routine traffic violations. Some of these courts have found an absence of the required custody, while others have regarded questions asked a driver as a limited on-the-scene investigation rather than an interrogation. However, if an officer determines that a driver should be arrested, *Miranda* warnings must be given. In the 1984 case of *Berkemer v. McCarty,* the United States Supreme Court held that *Miranda* safeguards must be complied with whenever there is custodial interrogation, regardless of the severity of the offense. However, the Court also pointed out that a routine traffic stop does not ordinarily amount to custody under *Miranda.* See section 5-12, supra, on traffic violations.

In *Foster v. State,* the Georgia Supreme Court held that statements made by officers to the defendant that his confession "was not going to hurt 'a thing' and that it would be 'as much for your benefit as ours . . .' " is not consistent with warnings required by *Miranda.*

It seems that in emergency situations, at least when there is not time to give *Miranda* warnings, questions asked to protect the safety of a person or persons are not prohibited by *Miranda.* See section 5-11, supra.

Generally, it is not necessary to inform a suspect of the nature of the offense with which he is being charged.

Although *Miranda* warnings must be given before questioning begins, it has been held that it is not necessary to repeat the warnings prior to a later session of interrogation if the interrogations are continuing in nature and separated by only a short time span. Where one investigating officer replaces another, a suspect who has been provided his rights and signed a waiver need not be given additional warnings where the lapse between the questioning was brief. In *McSears v. State*, the defendant was given *Miranda* warnings in connection with one case. Later during the interview, without *Miranda* warnings being given again, the defendant made a statement about another case. He was tried for the second case. The appellate court affirmed the admissibility of the admissions made during the interview relating to the second case. It has also been pointed out that if full warnings are given a defendant, at subsequent questionings it is not necessary that they be preceded by the complete warning if the defendant is reminded that he was previously advised of his rights. Where a defendant's attorney informs an officer that his client wishes to make a statement, there is no need to give the *Miranda* warnings. On the other hand, the United States Supreme Court has held inadmissible incriminating statements obtained by officers where there had been an agreement between the officers and the suspect's attorney that the suspect would not be questioned while being transported from one city to another.

§ 5-15 Confessions and admissions—*Miranda v. Arizona*—Warnings—Right to remain silent

Prior to any questioning, a person in custody must be warned of the right to remain silent. In fact, it appears that the remainder of the warnings are intended in large measure to implement this first warning. As noted in *Miranda,* an accused needs a warning concerning the right to remain silent because of the inherently compelling nature of in-custody interrogations.

The exercise of the right to remain silent must be unequivocal. Statements made by an accused after ambiguous assertions of the right, such as " . . . I can stop the interrogation. Right? Yes or no?" will not qualify and police may continue questioning. In addition, police are under no obligation to ask clarifying questions of the accused as to whether he or she fully comprehends the extent of the right to remain silent. Although acknowledging that such clarifying questions might be good police practice, the United States Supreme Court, in *Davis v. United States*, refused to apply such a rule where the right to counsel was concerned. Several federal courts and the Georgia Supreme Court in *Perez* have ruled that in the absence of an unequivocal assertion of the right to remain silent, police questioning of an accused in custody may proceed without any obligation on the part of the police to seek clarification of an accused's ambiguous statement about the right to remain silent.

If a defendant chooses to remain silent after receiving *Miranda* warnings, it is a violation of the Due Process Clause of the Fourteenth Amendment for the prosecution to use the accused's silence to impeach him. However, in *Jackson v. State,* the Georgia Supreme Court held that when a defendant on direct examination testifies that he made no statement, he may be cross-examined about his post-arrest silence. In *Osborne v. State,* the Georgia Court of Appeals held that "[t]he silence of an arrestee prior to his receipt of the *Miranda* warnings may be used by the State for purposes of impeachment." In *Fallen v. State,* "defense counsel elicited from his client the statement that he was never asked . . . to make a written statement." The court found no error in the district attorney bringing out on cross-examination that he was not asked to make a statement, because on being given his *Miranda* warnings, he elected to remain silent.

The Georgia Supreme Court has held this prohibition to be inapplicable to earlier cases where the issue was not raised in the trial court and to appeals which were completed before June 17, 1976, the date of the decision in *Doyle v. Ohio.* The rule against using a defendant's silence to impeach him does not apply retroactively in habeas corpus or other post-appeal attacks unless the point was properly raised in the trial court.

It is error for the trial judge to allow an officer "to testify that after being read his rights and after answering one question, the defendant refused to answer a second question and then said his lawyer would be available the next day. The defendant has the right to remain silent and to be represented by counsel and the exercise of these rights is not to be used as evidence against him."

However, if a defendant does not elect to remain silent and he makes a statement and if at trial he makes a different statement, the earlier statement is admissible for purposes of impeachment if the statement is freely and voluntarily made.

See section 5-20, infra, on duty to speak and tacit admissions. Also see section 7-7, subparagraph (5), infra. Also see section 5-19, infra, on questioning a defendant after he says he wants counsel.

§ 5-16 Confessions and admissions—*Miranda v. Arizona*—Warnings—Use in court of any statements

In summarizing the warning requirements, the United States Supreme Court in *Miranda* noted that any statement an accused makes "*may* be used against him." However, another part of the opinion goes on to state that the warnings should include a statement that "anything said *can and will* be used against the individual in court." It appears that a warning advising a suspect that any statement he makes "can and will" be used against him is not necessary.

§ 5-17 Confessions and admissions—*Miranda v. Arizona*—Warnings—Right to have counsel present

The right to have counsel present at an in-custody interrogation is "indispensable to the protection of the Fifth Amendment privilege." However, *Miranda* does not require an officer to inform a defendant how he can obtain counsel. Also, the Georgia Supreme Court has held that the *Miranda* warnings do not have to contain a statement that if during the course of questioning the suspect wishes an attorney, he may cease answering questions and will not be required to answer further questions until his attorney is present.

While questioning must cease when a suspect in custody says that he wants counsel, unless the right to counsel is later waived, a request to talk with some other person, such as a probation officer or a relative, does not require that questioning stop.

Signing a waiver to counsel after being told that counsel was not immediately available is still a valid waiver, even though the suspect was never provided with counsel during the interrogation. Likewise, a custodial statement was deemed properly admitted in Moore v. State, where the defendant agreed to an interrogation after signing a waiver and communicating, "I guess I'll get a lawyer too."

While a suspect has a right to invoke his right to counsel, this right is personal and cannot be invoked by another. Thus, where an attorney calls officers who have a defendant in custody and requests that questioning of the defendant cease until counsel arrives, this does not amount to an exercise of the defendant's right to counsel at the time of questioning. Likewise, in *Blanks v. State,* the Georgia Supreme Court held that where a suspect had been given the *Miranda* warnings a number of times, had waived his right to be silent, and was making a loud statement, officers were not obligated to inform him that an attorney had been hired for him and that the attorney wanted to confer with him. Moreover, in *Davis v. United States,* the United States Supreme Court held that for a defendant to invoke his right to counsel under the Fifth Amendment, the request must be unambiguous. The Georgia Supreme Court has since adapted the reasoning in *Davis* and in the absence of an unambiguous request for counsel, police may question an accused who has been properly advised of his rights to counsel.

§ 5-18 Confessions and admissions—*Miranda v. Arizona*—Warnings—Right to have counsel appointed

The *Miranda* warnings must effectively advise the accused of his right to a court-appointed counsel. However, it is not necessary to furnish counsel to a suspect where he can afford to employ an attorney on his own. Thus, it has been held that a warning is not defective if the provision for the appointment of counsel is omitted unless it appears that the defendant was indigent.

§ 5-19 Confessions and admissions—*Miranda v. Arizona*—Waiver—Right to remain silent

As previously pointed out in section 5-11, supra, if there is in-custody interrogation by the state or its representatives, a statement of the defendant obtained by officers is not admissible unless (1) the defendant was adequately warned (section 5-14, supra) and (2) the defendant validly waived his right of silence and, if counsel was not present, his right to the presence of counsel at the time of the interrogation.

An in-custody suspect must clearly and affirmatively waive his right to silence and counsel. A waiver cannot be implied from the silence of the suspect nor from the fact that a confession was obtained. There is no presumption that the defendant knowingly and intelligently waived his *Miranda* rights. In fact, the "courts must presume that a defendant did not waive his rights; the prosecution's burden is great." However, the failure of a suspect to expressly waive (in writing or orally) his right to remain silent does not automatically prevent the admission of a statement which he thereafter makes.

In *Michigan v. Mosley,* the defendant, who had been arrested in connection with certain robberies, exercised his right to remain silent after he was advised of his *Miranda* rights. More than two hours later, a different officer took the defendant to another part of the building, Mirandized the defendant again, and asked him questions about an unrelated holdup murder. At that time defendant made incriminating statements. The United States Supreme Court used a totality of circumstances analysis and held that the defendant's statements were obtained lawfully under the Fifth Amendment and were therefore properly admitted against him at trial. The court considered that (1) the defendant had been advised of his *Miranda* rights at both interrogations, (2) when the defendant exercised his right to remain silent at the first interrogation, the officer immediately ceased the questioning, and (3) the second interrogation occurred after a significant time lapse, was directed solely at the murder holdup, to which the defendant had not invoked his *Miranda* rights, and was conducted at another location in the building by another officer.

In the 2006 case of *Griffin v. State,* the Georgia Supreme Court considered the case of a defendant who sought to suppress incriminating statements where an officer honored the defendant's right to remain silent in the first interview, but then returned four days later to question the defendant about the same crime. The court affirmed the denial of the defendant's motion to suppress, holding that "a second interrogation regarding the same crime may also be constitutional under *Mosley* . . . where the initial invocation of the right to remain silent was scrupulously honored."

It has generally been held that it is not necessary to show that a suspect was informed of the charge against him. In *Vaughan v. State,* the court held that the failure of an officer "to advise a suspect as to the crimes about which he is to be questioned prior to the suspect's waiver of his *Miranda* rights is not relevant to the question of whether the suspect's waiver was knowing and voluntary."

In *Colorado v. Spring,* the United States Supreme Court held that the failure of an officer to inform a suspect that he would be questioned about a murder did not invalidate the interrogation. " '[O]ne who is told he is free to refuse to answer questions . . . [cannot] later complain that his answers were compelled.' . . . Here, the additional information could affect only the wisdom of a *Miranda* waiver, not its essentially voluntary and knowing nature. Accordingly, the failure of the law enforcement officials to inform Spring of the subject matter of the interrogation could not affect Spring's decision to waive his Fifth Amendment privilege in a constitutionally significant manner."

The fact that a person declined to sign a written waiver does not mean that a later statement which is obtained is automatically inadmissible. In *Moore v. State,* the Georgia Court of Appeals held that the defendant's refusal to sign a transcription of his confession, based on his belief that the unsigned statement could not be used against him, did not prevent the admissibility of the confession.

While the burden rests on the government to demonstrate that the defendant voluntarily, knowingly, and intelligently waived his privilege against self-incrimination and his right to retained or appointed counsel, where there is questioning of an in-custody suspect without the presence of an attorney, a defendant is not entitled to counsel to help him determine whether to waive his *Miranda* rights. In some jurisdictions, the state's burden of demonstrating an intelligent and knowing waiver is not met when only one officer testifies, when in fact two policemen were present at the time of the waiver, if there is a conflict in the evidence between the defendant and the testifying officer. However, Georgia has declined to follow these states.

In *Colorado v. Connelly,* the United States Supreme Court held that the burden placed on the state is to prove waiver by a preponderance of the evidence, and pointed out *Miranda* is concerned with governmental coercion and is not concerned "with moral and psychological pressures to confess emanating from sources other than official coercion."

In *United States v. Hernandez,* the Fifth Circuit pointed out that the "more times police inform a suspect of his rights in the face of his repeated invocation of one of those rights—the right to remain silent—the clearer it becomes that the police must not mean what they say. This is exactly the type of subtle coercive pressure which the *Miranda* opinion condemned."

Intoxication does not automatically prevent a valid waiver. A waiver by the defendant whose blood alcohol percentage was.27 has been upheld. Where a defendant had been shot and he contended that he was under the influence of alcohol and drugs and was suffering a great deal of pain, he was found to have understood and waived his *Miranda* rights when making a statement at a hospital. In *Felts v. State,* the Court of Appeals pointed out that "where a suspect is coherent and his demeanor indicates that he understands his rights and has waived those rights, intoxication will not be a defense."

Furthermore, a suspect need not have a great deal of intelligence to waive his *Miranda* rights. A waiver by a suspect with a mental age of 6 and I. Q. of 60 has been upheld. Likewise, the fact that a defendant is illiterate and was in a special education class when he was in school does not mean he is "incapable of understanding his *Miranda* rights when they are read to him." Also a waiver may be valid even though the "defendant may have been suffering from some mental condition" or is moderately retarded. In *Kerr v. State,* there was evidence that the defendant ranked in the lower 3% of the population in range of intelligence. The defendant contended that "he could not have made an *intelligent* waiver of *Miranda* rights, because he is not 'intelligent.' "In affirming the trial judge's finding that the defendant knowingly and voluntarily waived his *Miranda* rights, the court pointed out that there is no requirement that a suspect have a high or average degree of intelligence "but *requires* a knowing waiver."

Neither does an imperfect translation of a defendant's *Miranda* rights necessarily nullify an otherwise valid rights waiver. In *Nguyen v. State,* the court upheld the trial court's admission of the defendant's confession where the record showed that the defendant's *Miranda* rights were duly explained and that the defendant understood such rights. Under such circumstances, an imperfect translation of the defendant's rights will not foreclose a valid rights waiver.

It has been held that there is a distinction between the weight of the evidence required to show that a statement was made voluntarily and the evidence required to show a *Miranda* waiver. Thus, where an individual is "distraught, upset, weeping and obviously out of control" even if his statements were voluntary for the purpose of the Fifth Amendment, his condition may be such as to prevent a showing of "the higher standard . . . [required] with respect to waiver of the right to counsel that applies when the Sixth Amendment has attached." See section 5-4, supra.

In *United States v. Reyna,* the defendant underwent custodial interrogation without receiving the *Miranda* warnings and confessed. Immediately thereafter he was given the warnings, and he repeated the confession. The Fifth Circuit held that the "first" confession was tainted and that neither the "first" nor "second" confession was admissible. The confessions were said to be "so closely related in time and circumstance that they were one and the same." The idea is that the defendant "let the cat out of the bag" when he made the first statement.

However, in *Oregon v. Elstad,* the United States Supreme Court said that a "suspect who has once responded to unwarned . . . [and] uncoercive questioning is not thereby disabled from waiving his rights and confessing after he has been given the requisite *Miranda* warnings," even though he had made an admission of being present at the scene of the crime in response to his earlier questioning. In *Thornton v. State,* while in jail the defendant wrote a note to an investigator asking how he could "turn state's evidence." The investigator conducted a video interview with the defendant in which he proclaimed his innocence. No *Miranda* warnings had been given. The Georgia Supreme Court held that "[u]nwarned statements that are otherwise voluntary within the meaning of the Fifth Amendment must nevertheless be excluded from evidence under *Miranda.*"

In *Sliger v. State,* the Georgia Supreme Court held that the Unified Appeal Procedure giving the defendant an opportunity to state any objections he may have to defense counsel is not compelling the defendant to be a witness against himself.

It has been held that the best evidence of waiver by an in-custody suspect is a signed written waiver form. Such a waiver is set out in *Moody v. State.* However, there is no obligation on the state to give the defendant a copy of the signed waiver form, and there is no requirement that a copy of the waiver be furnished to defense counsel pursuant to a request for a copy of statements made by the defendant while in custody. See section 14-27, infra, for a request for a copy of such statements. Even when there is a valid waiver of counsel and a suspect begins to answer questions, he may at any time change his mind and exercise his right to remain silent. If he exercises this right, questioning must cease immediately.

§ 5-20 Confessions and admissions—*Miranda v. Arizona*—Waiver—Right to counsel

In *Edwards v. Arizona,* the United States Supreme Court established a per se rule, holding that once the *Miranda* right to counsel has been invoked, any further conversation between police and suspect (1) must be *initiated* by the suspect, and (2) "waivers of counsel must not only be voluntary, but constitute a knowing and intelligent relinquishment or abandonment of a known right or privilege." In *Edwards,* the defendant was arrested and Mirandized, after which he told police he wanted to "make a deal." Edwards then told officers he wanted "an attorney before making a deal" and the questioning ceased. The following morning, before the defendant had access to counsel, two different officers Mirandized the defendant again, he waived his rights, and confessed to the same crime about which he was questioned earlier. The court held that Edwards' incriminating statements should not have been admitted against him at trial.

The Georgia Supreme Court in *Gissendaner v. State* considered a case in which the lawyer, not the suspect, told officers he wanted to be present at any interviews between the suspect and officers. The court, in reversing the conviction, treated the statement of counsel as being the invocation by the suspect of her right to have counsel present before officers talked with the defendant.

In *Oregon v. Bradshaw,* the United States Supreme Court clarified what it means for a suspect to "initiate" a conversation under *Edwards.* In the plurality opinion, then Justice Rehnquist defined "initiation" of a conversation as when the suspect "evince[s] a willingness and desire for a generalized discussion about the investigation." In *Sanders v. State,* the Georgia Court of Appeals cited *Bradshaw* and said that where an in-custody defendant requests a lawyer, an analysis of whether the in-custody defendant who has invoked his right to counsel under *Miranda* "has later waived that right proceeds in two steps. First, a determination as to whether the *defendant* initiated further talks with the police, and second, if so, whether his waiver was shown to be voluntary under the totality of the circumstances."

Applying *Bradshaw,* the Supreme Court in *Connecticut v. Barrett* held that a suspect did not invoke his right to counsel within the meaning of *Edwards* where he received *Miranda* warnings and then stated that "he would not give police any written statements [without having counsel present] but [that] he had no problem in talking about the incident." The court regarded this statement as ambiguous; therefore, the oral statement which followed was admissible.

The Edwards rule applies where the right to counsel is invoked "during custodial interrogation." However, this situation is to be distinguished from that in *Michigan v. Mosley,* where the defendant was arrested and exercised his right to remain silent after receiving *Miranda* warnings. In *Moseley,* some hours after arrest and exercising his right to remain silent, another officer Mirandized the defendant and questioned him about an unrelated crime. The defendant made a statement which was admitted into evidence at trial. The Supreme Court affirmed the admission of the statement. In *Fields v. State,* the court cited *Moseley* and said *Fields* is similar to *Moseley* except in *Fields* officers sought the same information at each encounter. However, in *Fields* there was a 10–month period between the two instances and the defendant wished to make a statement at the later time. The court affirmed the admission of the statement.

In the 2006 case of *Griffin v. State,* the Georgia Supreme Court considered the case of a defendant who sought to suppress incriminating statements where an officer honored the defendant's right to remain silent in the first interview, but then returned four days later to question the defendant about the same crime. The court affirmed the denial of the defendant's motion to suppress, holding that "a second interrogation regarding the same crime may also be constitutional under *Mosley* . . . where the initial invocation of the right to remain silent was scrupulously honored."

In the 1986 case of *Michigan v. Jackson,* the United States Supreme Court held that where a defendant at arraignment requests counsel, the police may not thereafter initiate interrogation with the defendant. The court found the reasoning of *Edwards,* which was based on the Fifth Amendment, to apply with even greater force in this situation where the right was based on the Sixth Amendment right to counsel. *Jackson,* however, was overruled in *Montejo v. Louisiana.* The court found that *Jackson* was simply not tenable, at least with respect to a defendant's right to counsel where, after the appointment of counsel, the defendant voluntarily executes a proper waiver of counsel and speaks with police. The court said that *Jackson* was designed to prohibit police "badgering" and that *Miranda* warnings were sufficient to assure only voluntary waivers of counsel. Accordingly, police may not approach a represented defendant and request an interview without counsel being present provided only that the defendant is first advised of his right to counsel and then voluntarily waives that right.

In *McNeil v. Wisconsin,* the United States Supreme Court considered a case in which McNeil was represented by counsel at a bond hearing and was not released on bond, and then while still in jail and on the same day as the bond hearing, he was approached by officers, was given *Miranda* warnings, and was questioned about an unrelated murder, and he gave a statement. The court found that there had been no *Miranda* violation. The assertion of the Sixth Amendment right of counsel in one case does not bar the statement obtained in the unrelated case. Also, in *State v. Jenkins,* the same court held that "[t]he fact that . . . [the defendant] was questioned by a detective other than the one to whom he had made the request for counsel does not excuse the continued questioning after the request."

In *Texas v. Cobb,* the United States Supreme Court considered a case in which the defendant was charged with burglary and counsel was appointed for him in that case. Law enforcement officers approached the defendant and interrogated him about a murder which was factually related to the burglary. The court held that officers may interrogate the defendant about the other offense or offenses as long as the other offense or offenses have not been formally charged and the officers comply with the requirements of *Miranda.*

In *Vaughn v. State,* the Georgia Supreme Court cited and followed the rule of *Edwards.* However, the Georgia Supreme Court has held that "fruits" of a voluntary statement obtained in violation of *Edwards* are admissible even though the statement itself is not admissible at trial.

In *Roper v. State,* the Georgia Supreme Court held that "once an accused in custody invokes the right to counsel, he should not be subject to further interrogation by the authorities until counsel is *present,* unless the accused himself initiates further communication. . . ." (Emphasis added.) It is the duty of law enforcement authorities "to maintain a procedure to enable an officer who proposes to initiate an interrogation to determine whether a suspect has previously invoked the right to counsel. . . . The fact that the interrogating officers had no actual knowledge that . . . [the defendant] had made a request for counsel is constitutionally insignificant. . . . [The defendant's] negative answer to the question of whether he had a lawyer did not answer the question of whether he had invoked the right to counsel, nor could it constitute a waiver."

In *State v. Hatcher,* after the defendant was arrested "he was provided with and completed at the jail an 'eligibility affidavit form' for appointed counsel." The form stated that he could not afford a lawyer and wanted the court to appoint one for him. Two days later an investigator, who was generally aware of the booking procedures including the request for a lawyer, interviewed the defendant and gave him *Miranda* warnings. The defendant signed a waiver and made a confession. The Georgia Supreme Court held that the confession was admissible since "the form at issue was offered by the police and completed by appellant as a housekeeping measure; not for the questioning which was to take place a few days later, but as a prospective request for counsel 'when the government's role [would shift] from investigation to accusation.' . . . [T]he form was promulgated to satisfy an accused's Sixth Amendment right to counsel and cannot reasonably be read to constitute an invocation of right to counsel for purposes of the Fifth Amendment."

In *Cansler v. State,* the court held that "whether or not the detective knew of the request for an attorney is not dispositive. . . . [Also] the . . . [defendant's] later denial of the statement [does not] refute the contention that the detective initiated the interrogation."

In *Minnick v. Mississippi,* the defendant invoked his right to counsel. Counsel was then appointed and spoke with the defendant. Thereafter the police returned and, without an attorney, the defendant made statements later used against him at trial. The United States Supreme Court held that the fact that the defendant consulted with counsel did not suspend his Fifth Amendment rights in a way that would allow police to interrogate the defendant in the absence of his attorney, unless the defendant initiates the conversation and waives his rights.

In *Petty v. State,* the Georgia Supreme Court rejected the notion that *Edwards* had any application to a noncustodial interrogation and overruled *Nobles v. State,* to the extent it suggested that police must cease questioning an accused who is not in custody after he or she requests an attorney. In *Peebles v. State,* the court held that the assertion of the right to counsel does not render inadmissible any statement made by the defendant before he asserted the right of counsel. See Annotation, "What Constitutes Assertion of Right to Counsel Following *Miranda* Warnings—State Cases," 83 A. L. R. 4th 443.

However, in *State v. Bymes,* the Georgia Supreme Court held that because of "a 21–month break in custody between the initial interrogation and the final interrogation," *Edwards* did not apply; and in the 1994 case of *Wilson v. State,* the court held that *Edwards* did not apply where there was a seven-month break in custody.

It has been pointed out "that a waiver is possible if the request for counsel is equivocal." Thus, in Georgia it has been held that where a defendant was given *Miranda* warnings and an officer asked if he wanted to talk and the defendant said, "Well, it's no use," and the officer said it was up to him and asked again if he wanted to talk, and the defendant said yes and made a statement, there was no Edwards violation. However, in *Wilson v. State,* the United States Supreme Court held that once a defendant expresses a desire for counsel, questioning must cease and response to further interrogation cannot be used to cast doubt on the initial request. In *Lucas v. State,* the Georgia Supreme Court reversed the trial court, concluding that the defendant's statement during questioning that his lawyer told him not to say anything was an invocation of the Fifth Amendment. The concurring opinion by two justices stated that the officers should have sought clarification of his "equivocal request" before asking any other questions other than those related to whether or not the defendant wanted to stop talking.

In *Vasser v. State,* when the investigator mentioned the right to an attorney during the reading of the defendant's *Miranda* warnings, the defendant, in custody at the time, stated, "That's what I want. I want a lawyer." However, when the investigator again asked the defendant if he wanted an attorney at the conclusion of the *Miranda* warnings, the defendant responded, "It doesn't matter. I don't have nothing to hide." The investigator then proceeded to conduct an interrogation of the defendant, during the course of which the defendant asked, "After I beat this case, can I be a policeman, an investigator or something?" Finding that the defendant's question did not constitute an attempt to "initiate" conversation about the charges, the Court of Appeals held that the defendant clearly invoked his right to counsel and suppressed the in-custody statements.

In *Davis v. United States,* the defendant waived his right to remain silent and to have counsel, both orally and in writing. After being questioned for one and one-half hours the defendant said, "Maybe I should talk to a lawyer." The defendant was asked to clarify his comment to which he stated he was not asking for a lawyer. The defendant was then reminded of his rights and the questioning was continued. About one hour later the defendant said, "I think I want a lawyer before I say anything else." Questioning was stopped at this point. The United States Supreme Court held that "the suspect must unambiguously request counsel . . . [H]e must articulate his desire to have counsel present sufficiently clearly that a reasonable police officer in the circumstances would understand the statement to be a request for an attorney. If the statement fails to meet the requisite level of clarity, *Edwards* does not require that the officers stop questioning the suspect." The Georgia Supreme Court has expressly adopted *Davis* and has repudiated prior authority which required police to clarify ambiguous requests for counsel by a criminal suspect before interrogation could continue.

In *Berry v. State,* the Georgia Supreme Court held that if a request for counsel "was unambiguously limited to the taking of a polygraph examination and did not encompass the custodial interrogation," this did not prevent further questioning. In *Baird v. State,* the defendant said that he "might ought to talk to a lawyer" in response to a request to search his vehicle. The *Baird* court held (1) that this was not an assertion of his Fifth Amendment right to counsel, and (2) that where a limited request for counsel is made, officers are "required to honor [it] to no greater extent than the express limits of his reservation." Also, the court declined "to adopt a rule requiring officers to ask clarifying questions."

In *Hall v. State,* the Georgia Supreme Court pointed out that "where the accused asks a question that contains an ambiguous or equivocal reference to the availability of counsel, an interrogating officer must be given considerable latitude in formulating a reasonable and responsive answer."

In the interesting case of *Underwood v. State,* the defendant, after having been given his *Miranda* rights, handed the agents his lawyer's business card. On the back of "the card" there was a preprinted statement as follows: "I refuse to consent to any search of my premises, the location of my arrest, my car or my effects. I wish to exercise my rights under the fifth and sixth amendments to remain silent and to have my attorney present for any questioning or line up. If you ignore my wish to exercise these rights and attempt to procure a waiver I wish to confer with my attorney prior to any conversation with law enforcement agents on subject of waiver." When presented with the card, the officers "immediately terminated the interview." The court did not pass on the issue of "whether such an ambiguous act place[d] a burden on law enforcement officers to inquire whether any of the rights addressed on the preprinted business card are, in fact, being asserted." However, while the defendant was going back to the jail area, he stated "there were some things we could talk about." He was read the *Miranda* warnings and he signed the *Miranda* form. The appellate court affirmed the trial judge in admitting the defendant's statements which were given.

In *Ottis v. State,* the Georgia Supreme Court affirmed the conviction where the defendant said "she wished to talk to the detectives if her attorney was contacted." The detective was "unable to contact her attorney" and so informed the defendant. Then the defendant "initiated the discussion with the police which led to her spontaneous . . . statement placing her at the scene of the crimes, thereby knowingly and intelligently waiving the right she had invoked."

In *Gissendaner v. State,* a police investigator called the defendant, who was the focus of the investigation in the disappearance of her husband. He requested a meeting with the defendant. Later that day an attorney called and told the officer that counsel had met with defendant, that she wanted him to represent her, and that he wanted to be present at any interview between defendant and police. It was tentatively agreed that the three would meet on February 21. The officer did not hear from the attorney until February 21. On that day the officer went to the defendant's house and informed her that the body of her husband had been found. The defendant was arrested at her home about 1:30 a.m. on February 25. The defendant asked if she could call her attorney and was told she could not. The defendant was placed in a police car, and *Miranda* warnings were administered, and she agreed to talk with police. The Georgia Supreme Court reversed the conviction, finding that there had been a violation of *Edwards v. Arizona.*

In the 2000 case of *Lucas v. State,* the defendant told the interrogating officer that his "lawyer told me . . . to say nothing." Later during the interview the defendant said "[my lawyer] told me . . . to answer nothing." The interrogation continued without pause in both instances. The Georgia Supreme Court concluded "that under the circumstances . . . a reasonable police officer would have understood . . . [the defendant's] statements to be a request for counsel to be present during questioning." The court reversed the trial court's admission of the defendant's statement saying that it was "clearly erroneous."

Also, the Edwards rule does not apply unless the defendant is in custody. The Edwards rule also does not apply to a request of officers for routine booking information. However, in *Allen v. State,* the defendant was given *Miranda* warnings and stated "I'll talk to you after I've talked to my lawyer." The Georgia Supreme Court held that the defendant's initial invocation of his right to counsel could not have been clearer.

In *Mobley v. State,* the evidence showed that in less than 12 hours the defendant was questioned on three separate occasions. At the first questioning, he was given *Miranda* rights and refused to submit to questioning. Later the same day he was again approached by officers, advised of his *Miranda* rights, and questioned. He made an incriminating statement and said he wanted to talk with the sheriff. That evening he was approached by the sheriff and advised of his *Miranda* rights; he made an incriminating statement. The trial judge held that the statement made to the sheriff was freely and voluntarily made and therefore admissible. The Georgia Court of Appeals reversed based on *Edwards.* The court reasoned that the second interrogation was initiated by officers after the defendant asked for counsel and refused to talk. The court then said that in view of the totality of the circumstances, the third interrogation resulted from the unlawful second interrogation.

However, in *White v. State,* the Georgia Court of Appeals found no Edwards violation where, without making any statement, the defendant said he wanted counsel. Later, not knowing that the defendant had elected to remain silent, officers on an elevator with the defendant asked him if he did not want to make a statement. The defendant said he did, was given his *Miranda* rights and then confessed to the robbery.

In *Woodard v. State,* the Court of Appeals reversed the trial court order denying a motion to suppress statements made by the defendant in response to questions of police investigators after being advised of his *Miranda* rights and executing a written waiver of them. At the time he made the statements, he was represented by appointed counsel and because he had not initiated the conversations which led to the incriminating statements there was no waiver of his right to counsel.

In *Beck v. State*, the court pointed out that "the mere completion of an application to obtain appointed counsel, without more, is not sufficient to invoke the Fifth Amendment. . . ."

In *Arizona v. Roberson,* the defendant was arrested for burglary and given his warnings, at which point he stated that he wanted a lawyer "before answering any questions." Three days later, and as yet without counsel, a different officer Mirandized the defendant, he waived his rights, and implicated himself in another burglary. The United States Supreme Court held that Roberson's statements were inadmissible because the *Miranda* right to counsel is *not* offense specific.

In *Arizona v. Mauro,* the United States Supreme Court held that the defendant had waived his *Miranda* rights where the defendant stated that he did not want to answer questions without the presence of an attorney, but his wife insisted on talking with the defendant and was permitted to talk with him in the presence of an officer who openly recorded the conversation. The court concluded that the incriminating statements were not the result of interrogation by the officer.

In *Krier v. State,* where the defendant was arrested in New Orleans, the Georgia Supreme Court concluded that a request for counsel "in the asylum state [does not operate] to prevent any further inquiry by authorities in

[Georgia] as to whether the accused would like to speak to them, where [Georgia] authorities reasonably understood that no request for counsel had been made."

In the unusual case of *Roberson v. State,* the defendants were advised of their *Miranda* rights after arrest and invoked the right to counsel. The defendants' mother suggested to a television and radio reporter that the reporter interview one of the defendants in jail. Then the other defendant requested an interview. Consequently, the sheriff's office, on request, arranged the interviews. The police escorted the defendants to the interview but did not initiate or participate in the interview. The defendants signed waiver forms stating that they voluntarily agreed to the interviews, realizing they had the right to refuse and reserving the right to terminate the interviews at any time. The court affirmed the convictions finding that there was no violation of their rights to counsel.

The *Miranda* warnings currently in use by some Georgia officers are set out in section 5-14, supra. The opposite side of the card from which officers read the warnings states certain questions to be asked pertaining to waivers. These "waiver" questions have also been set out in section 5-14, supra. See section 5-13, supra, on the meaning of "interrogation." See section 5-15, supra, on the right to remain silent.

§ 5-21 Confessions and admissions—*Miranda v. Arizona*—Duty to speak

The application of the tacit admission rule in Georgia, at least in criminal cases, has been questioned for over half a century, although O.C.G.A. § 24–3–36, provides that acquiescence or silence when the circumstances require an answer, denial, or other conduct may amount to an admission. However, in *Mallory v. State,* the Georgia Supreme Court in a unanimous opinion held that in criminal cases a comment upon a defendant's silence or failure to come forward is "far more prejudicial than probative. Accordingly from the date of publication of the opinion, December 26, 1991, . . . such comment will not be allowed even where the defendant has not received *Miranda* warnings and where he takes the stand in his own defense." However, "not every reference to a defendant's invocation of the right to remain silent entitles a defendant to a reversal. Instead, the error may be found to be harmless beyond a reasonable doubt. The determination of harmless error must be made on a case by case basis, taking into consideration the facts, the trial context of the error, and the prejudice created thereby as juxtaposed against the strength of the evidence of defendant's guilt."

In *Doyle v. Ohio,* the United States Supreme Court held that an accused's silence after the giving of the *Miranda* warnings could not be used as evidence of his guilt. However, in *Fletcher v. Weir,* the United States Supreme Court stated that where a defendant had not been informed that he had a right to remain silent, there is no due process violation in permitting the defendant to be "cross examined as to his post-arrest silence when the defendant chooses to take the stand."

It must be kept in mind, however, that *Miranda* applies only where a defendant is in custody. Hence, in *Jenkins v. Anderson,* the Court held that the silence of a suspect who was not taken into custody for two weeks after a homicide could be constitutionally used for impeachment purposes on cross-examination when the suspect testifies to self-defense at his trial. The court pointed out that its decision does not force a state to allow impeachment by pre-arrest silence, but it shows that impeachment in such a situation does not violate the federal Constitution. But in Georgia non-Mirandized post arrest silence *is not admissible.*

In *Norris v. State,* the defendant contended he was coerced into escaping. The appellate court said that it could consider the failure of the defendant to tell an investigator about the coercion in determining whether the evidence was sufficient to justify his conviction.

In *DeBerry v. State,* the Georgia Supreme Court said that a defendant's Fifth Amendment rights were violated where an officer testified that the defendant made no statements to the police when arrested, but the failure of defense counsel to object waived the right of the defendant to later complain. The same right of silence was recognized where a defendant was given *Miranda* warnings, answered some questions, and then remained silent when he was asked a particularly incriminating question.

In *Gibbs v. State,* the prosecuting attorney asked an officer if the defendant provided the officer with any statement after he was in custody. The officer replied, "I advised him of his rights and he refused to give a statement." The court held that "the record shows an error of constitutional dimension." It is "fundamentally unfair to simultaneously afford a suspect a constitutional right to silence at arrest and yet allow the implication of that silence to be used against him. . . ."

In the unusual case of *Williams v. State,* the defendant pled temporary insanity at the time of the crime. In an effort to show that the defendant was not insane at that time, the state was permitted to show that at the time of defendant's arrest, he was given *Miranda* warnings and he elected to remain silent. However, in *Wainwright v. Greenfield,* the United States Supreme Court held that there was a violation of the Due Process Clause of the Fourteenth Amendment where the prosecutor used the defendant's silence, after he had been given *Miranda* warnings, as evidence of the defendant's sanity.

In *Jones v. Dugger,* the Eleventh Circuit held that there was no error in permitting an officer to testify to his observations of the mental condition of Jones at the time of questioning even if there had not been a valid *Miranda* waiver. The officer was not permitted to testify as to what Jones said, but he could testify that Jones seemed to be rational and well-oriented and his answers seemed to be responsive to the questions asked.

Even when there is an improper reference to the defendant's silence and the point has been preserved by proper objection, this does not automatically require reversal. The error may be considered to be harmless beyond a reasonable doubt. The test is whether the evidence of the election to remain silent pointed "directly at the substance of the defendant's defense or otherwise substantially prejudiced the defendant in the eyes of the jury."

See section 5-15, supra, on the right to remain silent and section 5-13, supra, on interrogation. Also, generally, see section 5-11, supra, on *Miranda*.

§ 5-22 Nontestimonial evidence—Under United States Constitution

In *Schmerber v. California,* the United States Supreme Court held that the compulsory taking of non-testimonial blood-sample evidence from a defendant does not violate the federal Constitution, although noting that the Fifth Amendment prevents the use of testimonial evidence in the situation where an accused is compelled to speak against himself. Likewise, in *South Dakota v. Neville,* the same Court held that the admission in evidence of a refusal of a defendant to submit to a blood-alcohol test is not a violation of the Fifth Amendment.

Thus, the federal Constitution does not entitle a defendant to refuse to submit to fingerprinting, photographing, or measurements. He must repeat words for identification, appear in court, assume certain positions, walk, make particular gestures, and furnish handwriting exemplars. If a defendant refuses to give handwriting exemplars, it is proper for the court in its charge, and for the prosecution in summation, to refer to the accused's failure to provide this non-testimonial evidence. However, it has been held that an unarrested suspect cannot be ordered by a court to furnish handwriting exemplars. Generally, a person may be required under the federal Constitution to give voice exemplars and handwriting exemplars to a grand jury. Likewise, it has been held that hair samples may be taken involuntarily from a defendant pursuant to a search warrant.

A defendant can be compelled to allow the removal of a bullet from his body by a physician pursuant to a search warrant if there is no risk involved in the procedure. However, a defendant cannot be compelled to undergo a risky operation to remove a bullet from the spinal cavity. In *Winston v. Lee,* the United States Supreme Court said, "The reasonableness of surgical intrusions beneath the skin depends on a case-by-case approach, in which the individual's interest in privacy and security are weighed against society's interest in conducting the procedure. . . . Schmerber . . . provides the appropriate framework of analysis for such cases." The court then concluded that the state had failed to demonstrate that surgical removal of the bullet would be reasonable in view of the evidence which the state had and the disputed evidence about the risks of such an operation.

In *Andresen v. Maryland,* the United States Supreme Court held that a defendant's incriminating business records are non-testimonial and thus admissible. In *Doe v. United States,* the United States Supreme Court held that there was no Fifth Amendment violation in requiring a depositor to sign a "consent directive" which directs foreign banks to disclose records of the depositor.

On incrimination by lineups, see section 6-4, infra. Also see section 4-26, supra, on searches incident to an arrest and section 4-32, supra, on consent to search. See section 21-3, infra, on voice exemplars as testimony. See section 5-13, supra, on video taping of sobriety tests.

§ 5-23 Nontestimonial evidence—Under Georgia Constitution and Georgia law

Georgia has long asserted that it grants more protection to its citizens than that afforded by the United States Constitution. The Georgia Constitution provides that "[n]o person shall be compelled to give testimony tending in any manner to criminate himself." The word "testimony" has been construed to limit the state from forcing the individual to present evidence, oral or real.

Georgia law regarding non-testimonial evidence has been summarized as follows:

"[N]o man is bound to accuse himself of any crime or to furnish any evidence to convict himself of any crime. . . . The constitutional guaranty protects one from being compelled to furnish evidence against himself, either in the form of oral confessions or incriminating admissions of an involuntary character, or of doing an act against his will which is incriminating in its nature."

The Georgia statute on self-incrimination provides as follows:

"No person, who shall be charged in any criminal proceeding with the commission of any indictable offense or any offense punishable on summary conviction shall be compellable to *give evidence* for or against himself." (Emphasis added.)

Thus, a defendant cannot be forced to do an affirmative act which would be incriminating such as placing his foot in a footprint near a burglary or placing his hand in his pocket and surrendering a pistol, based on these provisions. Likewise, it is improper for a district attorney during a trial to ask a defendant to stand and raise his shirt so as to reveal identifying scars on his chest, and a district attorney may not compel a defendant to produce handwriting exemplars or voice exemplars. However, it has been held that a high school student's state constitutional rights were not violated where the assistant principal asked the student to empty his pockets in the presence of the assistant principal, and that a law enforcement officer can obtain non-testimonial evidence from a prisoner.

In *Robinson v. State,* relying on *Creamer,* the Georgia Court of Appeals held that a defendant's state constitutional rights were not violated where, pursuant to a warrant, samples of blood and urine were taken to determine if he had cocaine in his system.

Also, in *Price v. State,* the court relied on *Creamer* in holding valid a search warrant which required a leg hair to be removed from a defendant who was not under arrest at the time. The court again emphasized that there is "a distinction between forcing an accused to *do* an act, and compelling him to *submit* to an act." (Emphasis in original.) The court explained that forcing a defendant to give evidence violates the right of the defendant not to incriminate himself, but forcing an accused to submit to the removal of a hair was not a violation of his rights.

In *Pinson v. State,* the Georgia Court of Appeals pointed out "that requiring a blood test for the purpose of proving or disproving paternity" would not compel a defendant to be a witness against himself within the meaning of the Fifth Amendment nor would the procedure compel him to give testimony tending to incriminate himself within the meaning of the Georgia Constitution.

In *Strong v. State,* testimony regarding the alcoholic content of a blood sample removed from the defendant for the intoxication test while he was unconscious in the hospital was held admissible in the defendant's trial for murder, a crime apparently committed by means of a motor vehicle, after the court concluded that the implied consent laws were inapplicable to a murder case. However in a routine driving under the influence case, the police must inform the driver that he has a choice of a blood, breath or urine test and the right to have an independent test made by someone of his own choosing.

As pointed out in the foregoing section, nothing in the United States Constitution prevents a defendant from being forced to give voice exemplars and in Georgia it has been held that a defendant may also be required to give such exemplars. However, there is older Georgia authority holding that a defendant may not be forced by court order to produce incriminating evidence. Thus, in *State v. Armstead,* the court held that a defendant cannot be forced to produce a handwriting exemplar to be used against him. However, the Georgia Court of Appeals has held that a defendant can be required to give voice exemplars and to repeat certain words in a lineup. Likewise, in *State v. Thornton,* the Georgia Supreme Court said, "We decline to extend our Constitution so far as would prohibit reasonable police practices, such as the taking of fingerprints [and] . . . taking . . . dental impressions. . . ."

In the interesting case of *Weems v. State,* the Georgia Supreme Court held that the Fourth Amendment right of a victim to be secure against an unreasonable search prevented a defendant from compelling a victim to undergo surgery for the removal of a bullet to be used in his defense. Likewise, in *Park v. State,* the court held that the defendant was not entitled to force the victim to be examined by an expert selected by the defendant.

Unlike the situation under the federal Constitution, in Georgia private papers which are merely tangible evidence of the commission of a crime may not be seized. However, it has been held that if the papers are the instrumentalities of a crime, they may be seized.

See section 6-12, infra, on voice identification. See section 5-22, supra, on compelling non-testimonial evidence under the federal Constitution and section 5-25, infra, on officers requiring an incriminating act. See Note, "The Georgia Right Against Self–Incrimination: Historical Anomaly or Vanguard of Justice?" 15 Georgia Law Review 1104 (1981). See Goger, *Daniel's Georgia Handbook on Criminal Evidence* (2009 ed.), § 7–29, on use of DNA results like fingerprints.

§ 5-24 Statutes requiring incriminating acts

If a statute requires a defendant to incriminate himself, he cannot be convicted for failing to comply with the terms of the statute. Therefore, a federal law requiring gamblers to pay a wagering tax and to register their names violates the privilege against self-incrimination under the Fifth Amendment. In one case, the United States Supreme Court held that a state statute infringes on the Fifth Amendment privilege against self-incrimination where it provides that if an officer of a political party, subpoenaed by a grand jury to testify concerning the conduct of his office, refuses to testify or to waive immunity against prosecution, he shall lose his office. However, in *California v. Byers,* a defendant charged with violating the "hit-and-run" law requiring a driver involved in a collision to stop at the scene and give his name and address was held not to suffer substantial risk of self-incrimination if he complied with the law, but rather to face the possibility of civil damages. However, in *Chandler v. Miller* the United States Supreme Court held unconstitutional a Georgia statute which required candidates running for certain offices to pass a urinalysis drug test before running for office. The court concluded that there was no "special need" for such tests.

In *Bd. Of Ed. Of Indep. Sch. Dist. No. 92 of Pottawatomie County v. Earls*, the United States Supreme Court approved a school district's policy which required all middle and high school students to consent to drug testing as a condition to participate in extracurricular activities. The Court based its decision on a finding that the policy was a reasonable device for detecting and preventing drug use among students.

Georgia has shown considerable reluctance in finding compelled acts to be so incriminating as to justify a defendant's refusal to act. Thus, in *Dennis v. State,* the Georgia Supreme Court held a statute valid which required a driver to drive his truck on a weighing scale, even though the law imposed a penalty on the driver for failure to follow such instructions.

In *Raines v. White,* the appellant Raines was a defendant in an action brought under O.C.G.A. §§ 19–7–40 et seq. to determine paternity. The defendant contended that O.C.G.A. § 19–7–45 was violative of the federal and state Constitutions. The court concluded that the defendant could be required to submit to a blood test as provided for in that section.

In *Keenan v. State,* the Georgia Supreme Court upheld the validity of O.C.G.A. § 40–6–392(d), holding that it was not error for the trial judge to admit the refusal of a defendant to take a state-administered breath test. In *Fantasia v. State,* the same court held that the defendant was not compelled by the state to submit to a breath test. "[T]he suspect has a choice which does not infringe upon his right against self-incrimination."

In *Garner v. United States,* the United States Supreme Court held that a federal income tax return in which the defendant stated he was a professional gambler was admissible against the defendant when he was charged with conspiracy to violate gambling laws. The defendant was said to have made the disclosure instead of claiming the privilege on his tax returns; his disclosures were not regarded as compelled incriminations.

See section 5-22, supra, on compelling non-testimonial evidence under the federal Constitution; section 5-23, supra, on non-testimonial evidence under the Georgia Constitution and law; and section 5-25, infra, on officers requiring incriminating acts.

§ 5-25 Officers requiring incriminating acts

In *Chafin v. State,* the defendant was required to sign a property receipt card which was kept in the normal course of business by the police department. The card was introduced at trial to allow a comparison of the signature with a signature on a motel registration form. The Georgia Supreme Court concluded that this was not a *Miranda* violation.

In *State v. Armstead,* the state filed a motion to compel the accused to produce handwriting exemplars. The Court of Appeals affirmed the trial court's decision to deny the motion, citing *Creamer v. State.* "[A]lthough evidence may be compulsorily adduced from an accused, it is constitutionally impermissible to compel an accused to perform an act which results in the production of incriminating evidence. . . . The distinction is between forcing an accused to *do* an act against his will and requiring an accused to *submit* to an act. While the latter 'takes evidence from the defendant' . . . and is constitutionally acceptable, the former compels the defendant, in essence, to *give* evidence which violates an individual's right not to incriminate himself." (Emphasis in original.)

The Court of Appeals recognized that the United States Supreme Court, in *Gilbert v. California*, held "that handwriting exemplars can be compelled," but asserted that the state can grant more (but not less) protection to its citizens than the federal Constitution. The *Armstead* court cited *Creamer*: " 'While the language in the United States Constitution has long been construed to be limited to "testimony," the Georgia Constitution has been construed to limit the State from forcing the individual to present *evidence*, oral or real.' "(Emphasis in original.) However, in a case involving a lineup, the Georgia Supreme Court cited *United States v. Wade*, and stated "one's voluntary consent to a lineup does not violate his Fifth Amendment right against self-incrimination, since the lineup process involves no compulsion of the accused to give evidence of a testimonial nature against himself." Similarly, the Georgia Supreme Court has held that a suspect can be forced to take part in a lineup. In *Graham v. State* the Georgia Court of Appeals held that the state has a right to demand the presence of the defendant so that he can be identified.

In *Tate v. State,* the Georgia Court of Appeals asserted that "[o]ur appellate courts have held, or recognized, that requiring a suspect in a criminal case to verbalize specified words for identification purposes, whether or not the words used are the same as those allegedly used during the commission of the offense, does not violate an accused's privilege against self-incrimination accorded the accused by the United States' Constitution and the state's statutes and Constitution." No Georgia cases were cited.

The idea that a suspect may be forced to speak certain words seems to be contrary to historic Georgia law which prevents a suspect from being forced to perform any affirmative act which might incriminate him. See section 5-23, supra.

Elder v. State involved testimony of witnesses in a murder trial where evidence was given that the defendant's foot fitted tracks leading from a field near the victim's house. The defendant, while under arrest and handcuffed, was brought by the sheriff and several others to the place where the tracks were being examined. The sheriff commanded the defendant to put his foot in the track. The Georgia Supreme Court held that this evidence should have been excluded, and because it was not, the case was remanded for a new trial. The court found that the defendant did not voluntarily put his foot in the track and stated: "the evidence as to the foot of the accused fitting the track should have been excluded upon objection being made thereto under the provision of the constitution of this State, which declares that 'No person shall be compelled to give testimony tending in any matter to criminate himself' . . . [W]e think in the present case, under the circumstances, there was such a show of force as amounted to the actual use of force and to coercion."

In *Rick v. State,* the defendant was convicted of possession of a certain drug and attempting to obtain the drug by forgery. A pharmacist who received the alleged forgery had written down the number of the defendant's driver's license. While testifying, the defendant was ordered to produce the license by the district attorney. The defendant's lawyer objected on Fourth Amendment grounds that the defendant's right against self-incrimination was violated. However, the Court of Appeals decided that it was not error for the trial judge to require him to produce his license and to admit the license into evidence. The court also pointed out that admission of the license was not harmful to the defendant because evidence had already been admitted regarding the defendant's license number.

In *Mobley v. State,* the court pointed out that compelling a defendant to undergo a psychiatric examination to determine his competency to stand trial and his insanity defense does not violate the defendant's privilege against self-incrimination.

See section 5-23, supra, on non-testimonial evidence under the Georgia Constitution and law. See section 5-4, supra, on coercing an employee to give a statement. See Goger, *Daniel's Georgia Handbook on Criminal Evidence* (2009 ed.), § 7–16 on performing a sobriety test without being warned against self-incrimination.

§ 5-26 Results of illegally obtained evidence

The material in this section is in summary form. The exclusionary rule is treated in far greater depth in section 2-24 et seq., supra.

From the standpoint of the federal exclusionary rule, any admission or confession of the defendant which is obtained in violation of the *Miranda* requirements is not admissible against the defendant if he makes a proper objection to the introduction of such evidence. Also if a confession or an admission is not freely and voluntarily made, it is not admissible. However, *Harris v. New York,* holds that if an accused makes a voluntary statement, even in the absence of proper *Miranda* warnings, it may be used to impeach him where the defendant testifies at trial. However, if the statement was not voluntarily made it may not be used even for purposes of impeachment. In addition, the admission of such a statement may constitute reversible error unless "the jury is expressly instructed that the evidence is admitted for the purpose of impeachment only, whether or not a request to so charge be made, and whether or not any exceptions are made to the charge as given."

Under Georgia law a confession is not admissible unless it was "made voluntarily, without being induced by another by the slightest hope of benefit or remotest fear of injury."

In *Griffin v. State,* the Georgia Court of Appeals held that under Georgia law, there must be a determination of voluntariness, regardless of whether the confession is obtained by an officer or a private person, before a statement is submitted to the jury for its consideration. Additionally, it is better practice for a hearing to be held outside the presence of the jury with both the state and the defendant given the opportunity to present evidence. Where the confession is obtained by a private actor who is not a state public law enforcement officer, there is no requirement that the suspect be provided with *Miranda* warnings.

In *Wilson v. Zant,* the Georgia Supreme Court concluded that the exclusionary rule did not apply to the fruits of a voluntary statement obtained in violation of *Edwards v. Arizona* even though the statement itself is inadmissible at trial. In the case of *United States v. Patane,* the District Court granted, and the Appellate court affirmed, the defendant's motion to suppress a firearm where the weapon was discovered as a result of the defendant's voluntary statements made without *Miranda* warnings. However, the United States Supreme Court reversed on the grounds that "[t]he Self-incrimination Clause . . . is not implicated by the admission into evidence of the physical fruit of a voluntary statement." Hence, neither *Miranda* nor the "fruits-of-the-poisonous-tree" doctrine requires suppression of physical evidence seized as a result of voluntary statements made in the absence of *Miranda* warnings.

The issue, however, may be different where the defendant's right to counsel has attached. In *Vergara v. State,* the defendant had requested counsel and sometime thereafter requested to speak with police investigators. The defendant's statements led to the discovery of contraband. The court concluded that based upon the totality of the circumstances, the state failed to show that the defendant had waived his previously invoked right to counsel and the fruits doctrine required the exclusion of the evidence.

Even if there is error on the part of the court in admitting such evidence, a reviewing court may still consider it harmless error and thus refuse to reverse the conviction. Also, a defendant lacks standing to attack a violation of the constitutional rights of a co-defendant who has confessed to a crime and thereby implicated the defendant.

See section 2-27, supra, on the effect of an illegal arrest on identification and section 6-9, infra, on the right to place a suspect in a lineup.

Chapter 6

Pre-Trial Identification

§ 6-1 Scope

In this chapter consideration is given to some methods of identifying a person, normally a defendant. A defendant may be identified in a number of ways, including eyewitness identification, photographic identification, voice identification, handwriting identification, fingerprint and palm print identification, footprint identification, and some other perhaps less commonly used methods of identification. This chapter is concerned only with eyewitness identification, photographic identification, and voice identification. Other methods of identification are treated elsewhere in this book.

§ 6-2 Eyewitness identification—Background

There have been cases in which a defendant was convicted of a crime because of the testimony of an eyewitness who incorrectly identified him as the person committing the crime. In some of these incidents, the evidence has been extremely weak. It has been stated that "erroneous identification of the accused constitutes the major cause of known wrongful convictions." Also, it has been said that the hazard of a mistaken eyewitness identification is particularly pronounced in a situation where the witness is a member of one race and the suspect is a member of another race.

It has been held that the fact that a victim cannot accurately describe the assailant to the police because of darkness and because he was attacked from the rear does not prevent an in-court identification. The Georgia Supreme Court has said that where an eyewitness positively identifies an assailant, this is not opinion evidence and consequently it is not error for the trial court to fail to charge on non-expert opinion evidence. However, Dr. Agnor, in his *Georgia Evidence,* refers to identification testimony as opinion testimony.

Until the case of *United States v. Wade,* decided in 1967 and discussed in the next section, it was generally thought that a jury question existed as to the identity of the defendant in all cases in which there was a dispute as to the identity of the perpetrator of a crime. It always has been true that the identity of a defendant as the guilty party may be shown by circumstantial evidence as well as direct evidence, but if the evidence is entirely circumstantial, it may be insufficient to support a conviction.

In *Wade,* the United States Supreme Court stated that eyewitness identification by the victim or witnesses is peculiarly riddled with dangers which may prevent a fair trial, and a major cause of miscarriages of justice result from mistaken identification. Despite the dangers which exist in eyewitness identifications, such identification is regarded as essential to most criminal cases. Yet, every experienced lawyer who tries criminal cases knows how devastating such eyewitness identification testimony frequently is, even when the witness has had very little opportunity to view the person who committed the crime. Nevertheless, the rule remains that generally, eyewitness testimony is admissible and the jury determines how much weight it should be given. However, there are situations so extreme that some such evidence is not admissible.

Identification testimony in court may conceivably come from three sources: (1) a witness pointing out the defendant in court; (2) asking the eyewitness if he has identified the defendant earlier; and (3) having a third person testify that the witness identified the defendant on an earlier occasion. However, Georgia has placed limitations on the third possibility which are discussed later in this section.

In the first situation there is no per se exclusionary rule. There is no authority for the proposition that an in-court identification is subject to the same safeguards required for a pre-trial identification at a line up or by way of a photographic array. However, if the pre-trial procedures have been such as to undermine the reliability of the eyewitness identification, there may be a due process violation. Thus, if the suggestiveness of the identification amounts to "a very substantial likelihood of irreparable misidentification" based on a totality of the circumstances, then such testimony of pre-trial identification is not admissible.

In the second situation and possibly in the third, where a defendant was identified by a witness or the victim at a pre-trial lineup or showup, there is a per se exclusionary rule which applies to the admission of such pre-trial identification testimony if the defendant had no opportunity to be represented by counsel at the lineup or showup and if the adversary criminal judicial proceeding had already been instituted against the defendant.

Also, in the second and third situations, there may be a less precise due process violation which may apply to such pre-trial identification testimony if (1) the identification procedure was so unduly suggestive (2) that it was conducive to irreparable mistaken identification.

Aside from the constitutional limitation which may require the exclusion of extrajudicial pre-trial identifications which are involved in situations two and three, there are other questions. In the second situation, Georgia and most jurisdictions seem to permit a witness to testify in court about his pre-trial identification of the defendant. In *United States v. Owens,* the United States Supreme Court held that there was no violation of the Confrontation Clause where there was testimony of an out-of-court identification statement of a witness who was present for trial as a witness and who had since lost his memory of the event so that he was not able to testify as to the basis for the identification. See Goger, *Daniel's Georgia Handbook on Criminal Evidence* (2009 ed.), § 1–27, on cross-examination. However, a few states will not permit such testimony on hearsay grounds or because it is regarded as unduly bolstering the in-court identification.

In the 2001 case of *White v. State,* the Georgia Supreme Court held that "[i]n the absence of some other viable hearsay exception, such as 'necessity' or 'res gestae,' a law enforcement officer may not testify to a pre-trial identification of the accused unless the person who actually made the identification testifies at trial and is subject to cross-examination." In *Abrams v. State*, the court affirmed the trial court in permitting an investigator to testify that the victim and an eyewitness identified the defendant, and over objection, the investigator testified that the victim told him the defendant "was the right size and the clothing was right." The court also pointed out that the victim and the eyewitness both testified and were available for cross-examination. See an excellent annotation, "Admissibility of Evidence as to Extrajudicial or Pretrial Identification of Accused," 71 A. L. R. 2d 449 (1960).

It is within a trial court's discretion whether or not to admit expert testimony regarding eyewitness identification. However, "[w]here eyewitness identification of the defendant is a key element of the State's case and there is no substantial corroboration of that identification by other evidence, trial courts may not exclude expert testimony without carefully weighing whether the evidence would assist the jury in assessing the reliability of eyewitness testimony and whether eyewitness testimony is the only effective way to reveal any weakness in an eyewitness identification." In *Brodes v. State,* the trial judge excluded expert testimony on the accuracy of eyewitness identification. The Appellate Court reversed, finding that the expert's testimony was "highly relevant" to the case, which involved "cross-racial identifications by victims who were at gunpoint . . . ." Following trial and conviction, *Brodes* eventually found its way to the Supreme Court of Georgia and there the Court reversed the trial court, which, relying on the pattern charge, instructed the jury that one of the factors it was to consider in reviewing the testimony of the eyewitnesses was the level of certainty in their identification. The Court was persuaded by the empirical research presented that there exists a distinct "lack of correlation between a witness's certainty in his or her identification of someone as the perpetrator of a crime and the accuracy of that identification . . . " The Court went on to "advise" trial courts to refrain from using the level of certainty factor as part of their eyewitness identification charge. However, *Brodes* in no way is an impediment to a witness testifying about his or her level of certainty of identification. Such testimony would, of course, be subject to challenge by way of "cross examination, expert testimony or the presentation of testimony from other eye witnesses."

The next section discusses in chronological order some United States Supreme Court decisions which have considered problems of eyewitness identification. Then the general aspects of lineups are treated followed by material on showups and photographic identification. Next, consideration is given to the right to counsel at the time of identification and then due process consideration is discussed. After material on motions for lineups there is a discussion on hearings on motions to suppress identification.

See Annotation, "Propriety of Requiring Suspect or Accused to Alter, or Refrain From Altering, Physical or Bodily Appearance," 24 A. L. R. 4th 592 (1983).

§ 6-3 Overview of some United States Supreme Court cases on eyewitness identification

On June 12, 1967, the United States Supreme Court handed down decisions in three landmark cases on eyewitness identification. The first case, in terms of where it is reported, is the case of *United States v. Wade.*

In *Wade,* the defendant was indicted for bank robbery some six months after the robbery. He was arrested about a week later. Fifteen days after counsel had been appointed for him, FBI agents, without notice to Wade's attorney, arranged to have two bank employees observe a lineup of Wade and five or six other prisoners. Before the lineup the bank employees observed, through an open door, Wade, who was standing in the hall with an FBI agent. The other five or six prisoners appeared and a lineup was conducted in the courtroom. Each person in the lineup was directed to say something like "put the money in the bag." Both employees identified Wade at the lineup. At trial both employees on direct examination identified Wade. Prior lineup identification was elicited from both employees on cross-examination. At the close of the testimony, defense counsel moved for a judgment of acquittal or alternatively to strike the courtroom identification on the ground that the lineup without notice to, and in the absence of, defense counsel violated the Sixth Amendment right to assistance of counsel and violated the Fifth Amendment. The Court of Appeals for the Fifth Circuit reversed and ordered a new trial at which the in-court identification evidence was to be excluded because of the Sixth Amendment violation and the court concluded that there had been no Fifth Amendment violation. The Supreme Court pointed out that a defendant is entitled to the presence of counsel "at any stage of the prosecution, formal or informal, in court or out, where counsel's absence might derogate from the accused's right to a fair trial." Identification may take the form of a lineup or showup "as in the present case, or presentation of the suspect alone to the witness . . . risks of suggestion attend either form of confrontation. . . ." "The presence of counsel at such critical confrontations . . . operates to assure that the accused's interests will be protected. . . ." The "presence of counsel itself can often avert prejudice and assure a meaningful confrontation at trial, there can be little doubt that for Wade the . . . lineup was a critical stage of the prosecution. . . ." Both Wade and his counsel should have been notified of the lineup and his counsel's presence should have been required unless this right was waived. Counsel's presence is necessary as an observer "to preserve the defendant's basic right to a fair trial as affected by his right meaningfully to cross-examine the witnesses against him and to have effective assistance of counsel at the trial itself." The court expressly left open the question of whether substitute counsel would suffice if the presence of his counsel would have resulted in prejudicial delay. The "accused's inability effectively to reconstruct at trial any unfairness that occurred at the lineup may deprive him of his only opportunity meaningfully to attack the credibility of the witnesses' courtroom identification."

In summary, the United States Supreme Court said that the court of appeals did not apply the proper test. The court directed the conviction vacated "pending a hearing to determine whether the in-court identifications had an independent source, or whether, in any event, the introduction of the evidence was harmless error . . . and . . . [directed] the District Court to reinstate the conviction or order a new trial, as may be proper." However, the Court pointed out that the Government must be given "the opportunity to establish by *clear and convincing* evidence that the in-court identifications were based upon observations of the suspect other than [at] the lineup identification." (Emphasis added.) The question to be determined in the trial court was whether the in-court identification was based on the lineup which was without counsel or whether it had an independent source. "Application of this test in the present context requires consideration of various factors; for example, [1] the prior opportunity to observe the alleged criminal act, [2] the existence of any discrepancy between any pre-lineup description and the defendant's actual description, [3] any identification prior to lineup of another person, [4] the identification by picture of the defendant prior to the lineup, [5] failure to identify the defendant on a prior occasion, and [6] the lapse of time between the alleged act and the lineup identification. [7] It is also relevant to consider those facts which despite the absence of counsel, are disclosed concerning the conduct of the lineup."

The second of the three cases to be reported was *Gilbert v. California.* After counsel had been appointed, a lineup was held in an auditorium after indictment for armed robbery of a savings and loan association. At trial Gilbert moved to strike the testimony of a cashier of the association on the ground that she identified him at the lineup which was conducted in the absence of his counsel. The trial judge denied a hearing at which the defendant sought to show that the witness' trial testimony was based at least in part on the lineup. On cross-examination the witness testified to her identification of the defendant at the lineup. Apparently other prosecution witnesses testified at the sentencing phase of the trial as to other robberies committed by the defendant and their lineup identification of the defendant. The conviction was vacated and the case remanded. The testimony of the witnesses at the sentencing phase of the case was subject to a per se exclusion because the defendant was not represented by counsel at the lineup identification. It was error for the trial judge to permit the in-court identification testimony of the witnesses at the savings and loan association without first determining that their testimony would not be tainted by the lineup. Unless "the California Supreme Court is 'able to declare a belief that it was harmless beyond a reasonable doubt' . . . Gilbert will be entitled on remand to a new trial or, if no prejudicial error is found on the guilt stage but only in the penalty stage, to whatever relief California law affords where the penalty stage must be set aside."

The last of the three cases is *Stovall v. Denno.* Stovall was arrested in 1961 the day after a doctor was stabbed to death in his kitchen and the doctor's wife also had been stabbed a number of times. The wife was placed in a hospital in critical condition and major surgery was performed on her. Stovall was brought to the wife's hospital room on the day after surgery for purposes of identification without being given an opportunity to obtain counsel. He was handcuffed and was the only black person in the room. After Stovall repeated a few words as directed, he was identified as the assailant. The victim testified at trial to her identification of Stovall in her room and also made an in-court identification of him. The state's conviction was attacked by federal habeas corpus. The Supreme Court concluded that the right to counsel at a lineup as recognized in *Wade* and *Gilbert* was to be applied only to identifications after June 12, 1967, the date of the decisions in those cases. However, even though the right to counsel at the time of an identification was not applied, Stovall still had a right to relief in the "event the confrontation . . . was so unnecessarily suggestive and conducive to irreparable mistaken identification that he was denied due process of law. . . . The practice of showing suspects singly to persons for the purpose of identification, and not as part of a lineup, has been widely condemned." However, whether or not due process has been violated depends on a totality of the circumstances surrounding it. Here the showing of Stovall to the victim was imperative. She was the only one who could have exonerated him. She might have died. The hospital was not far from the jail. She could not go to the jail and a lineup was out of the question. Hence, there was found to be no due process violation in the identification.

In *Simmons v. United States,* a savings and loan association in Chicago was robbed by two men in 1964. Officers located a car matching the one described by an employee of the association. A man named Andrews was a suspect. FBI agents obtained pictures of Andrews and Simmons from Andrews' sister who told agents that Andrews and Simmons were together on the day of the robbery. The agents showed the employees at least six snapshots which consisted mostly of group pictures of Andrews and Simmons. The pictures were exhibited to each employee separately. All of the employees identified Simmons, but none of them identified Andrews. They later reaffirmed their identification from pictures. Simmons claimed that the identification procedure fatally tainted his conviction. The United States Supreme Court pointed out that improper use of pictures may cause witnesses to err in identification and that the danger is increased where several pictures are displayed and the picture of one person recurs. However, despite the hazards, identification by photograph is widely used by officers. The court stated, "[W]e hold that each case must be considered on its own facts, and that convictions based on eyewitness identification at trial following a pretrial identification by photograph will be set aside on that ground only if the photographic identification procedure was so impermissibly suggestive as to give rise to a very substantial likelihood of irreparable misidentification." The court then pointed out that in this case photographic identification had to be resorted to. The perpetrators were still at large. The agents needed to determine if they were on the right tract. There was little likelihood of misidentification of Simmons. All employee witnesses identified Simmons. The bank had been well-lighted. The robbers did not wear masks. Andrews was not identified. Witnesses had no doubt. Hence, the identification procedures did not violate due process.

In *Foster v. California,* Davis, the night manager of a Western Union office, had been robbed by three men. Clay surrendered and implicated Foster and Grice. Only Davis and the robbers were witnesses to the crime. Davis was called to the police station to view a lineup of three men. Foster was about 6' tall, the other two in the lineup were about 5' 6". Foster wore a leather jacket similar to one worn by one of the robbers. Davis could not identify Foster positively but thought he was the man. Davis asked to talk with Foster and did so alone in a room with him. Davis was still uncertain. Ten days later police arranged another lineup. Foster was the only man in the second lineup who had been in the first. This time Davis was convinced that Foster was the man. At trial Davis testified to his identification of Foster in the lineups as set out above. The only other evidence against Foster was the testimony of Clay, an acknowledged accomplice in the robbery. The identification was made before the decision in *Wade.* However, the Court pointed out that judged by a totality of the circumstances, the conduct of an identification may be so unnecessarily suggestive and conducive to irreparable mistaken identity as to amount to a denial of due process. The court concluded that the facts of this case amounted to such a due process violation and reversed the conviction. The court concluded that *all* the identification testimony should have been excluded.

In *Kirby v. Illinois,* the defendant and a companion were arrested on a Chicago street. When officers reached the police station they learned that the day before a man named Shard had reported that he had been robbed by two men who had taken traveler's checks and his social security card. Kirby had the social security card and three checks. A police car was sent for Shard. When Shard entered the room at the police station he positively identified Kirby and his companion. Six weeks later Kirby and his companion were indicted. Their pre-trial motion to suppress Shard's testimony was denied. At trial Shard described his identification at the police station and made an in-court identification. In a plurality opinion the Supreme Court pointed out that the case did not involve any compulsory self-incrimination and hence the Fifth Amendment did not apply. As to the question of the right to counsel at identifications guaranteed by the Sixth Amendment and the per se exclusionary rule, the Court said that this right applies only after the initiation of judicial criminal proceedings. The right to counsel at identifications applies at any critical stage of a *prosecution* not merely when a suspect is arrested. In affirming the conviction, the Court pointed out that the due process clause adequately protects a person, who has not been formerly charged, from suggestive identifications and pointed out the interest of society in the prompt investigation of unsolved crimes. The decision does not discuss the suggestiveness of Kirby's identification from a due process standpoint.

In *Moore v. Illinois,* the defendant was arrested for rape. The victim appeared the next day at a preliminary hearing which was conducted to determine whether or not the defendant was to be bound over to the grand jury. The defendant's name was called and he was lead before the bench. The victim was in the courtroom and also was called by the judge. The prosecuting attorney outlined evidence connecting the defendant with the crime and moved for a continuance of the hearing until fingerprint evidence could be presented. The victim identified the defendant and a continuance was granted. Moore was not represented by counsel at the time. Counsel was appointed for Moore after he had been indicted. Defense counsel moved to suppress the identification of Moore by the victim because he was not represented by counsel. The motion was denied and at trial on direct examination the victim testified that she had identified Moore at the preliminary hearing and that she also had made an in-court identification. The defendant's conviction was affirmed by the Illinois courts and Moore sought a writ of habeas corpus in federal court. The Supreme Court pointed out (1) that the *Wade* per se exclusionary rule of pre-trial identification testimony applied to an uncounseled identification at a preliminary hearing. The right attaches "at or after the initiation of adversary judicial criminal proceedings—whether by way of formal charge, preliminary hearing, indictment, information, or arraignment." The court also pointed out that (2) counsel's presence can serve both his client's interests and those of the prosecution "by objecting to suggestive features of a procedure before they influence a witness' identification"; (3) the testimony of pre-trial identification elicited by the prosecution in its case-in-chief enhances the witnesses' in-court identification; (4) where testimony is the direct result of an illegal lineup, the prosecution is not entitled to an opportunity to show that the testimony had an independent source; (5) the right to have counsel present at an identification at or after the initiation of adversary criminal proceedings exists whether the identification is at a lineup, a one-on-one identification or a judicial proceeding. The denial of habeas corpus was reversed and the case was remanded for a determination of whether the failure to exclude that evidence was harmless constitutional error.

In *Neil v. Biggers,* the victim had been raped in 1965. She saw her assailant in the lighted house and then saw him in the moonlight for some 10 or 15 minutes. She gave a description of her assailant to officers. During the next seven months she was shown suspects in lineups and showups and some 30 or 40 photos. She did not identify any of them. The defendant, Biggers, was being held in jail on an unrelated charge and the victim was called to the police station to look at him. Officers said they were unable to get persons looking like Biggers so as to arrange a lineup, so a showup was conducted. At that showup, at the victim's request, Biggers said "shut up or I'll kill you." He was positively identified at that time and later convicted. The Tennessee Supreme Court affirmed and he filed a petition for habeas corpus in federal court asserting a due process violation. The United States Supreme Court concluded that the identification was unnecessarily suggestive but pointed out it "is the likelihood of misidentification which violates a defendant's right to due process . . . [s]uggestive confrontations are disapproved because they increase the likelihood of misidentification . . . the admission of evidence of a showup without more does not violate due process." The "central question [is] whether under the 'totality of the circumstances' the identification was reliable even though the confrontation procedure was suggestive. . . ." The "factors to be considered in evaluating the likelihood of misidentification include [1] the opportunity of the witness to view the criminal at the time of the crime, [2] the witness' degree of attention, [3] the accuracy of the witnesses' prior description of the criminal, [4] the level of certainty demonstrated by the witness at the confrontation, and [5] the length of time between the crime and the confrontation." After reviewing the facts of the case in light of the factors suggested, the Court concluded that there was no substantial likelihood of misidentification and held that the habeas corpus should not be granted.

In *United States v. Crews,* a woman was robbed by a male while she was in the women's restroom on the grounds of the Washington Monument. She gave officers a full description of her assailant. Several days later Crews was seen in the vicinity of the crime. He matched the earlier description. After an attempt to photograph him failed, he was taken into custody ostensibly as a suspected truant from school and apparently without probable cause. He was detained at police headquarters, briefly questioned, photographed and released. Thereafter the victim identified the photograph of Crews and later identified him at a lineup. He was indicted for the robbery. Defense counsel moved to suppress all identification testimony. The trial judge found that the victim's in-court identification was based upon her independent recollection untainted by the intervening identifications. It was conceded that testimony about the intervening photographic and lineup identifications were suppressible as a result of the Fourth Amendment violation, i.e., the unlawful arrest. The conviction was affirmed by the Supreme Court and the in-court identification was held admissible because there was support for the trial judge's finding that the victim's identification rested on her independent recollection of her initial encounter with the defendant, uninfluenced by the pre-trial identification.

In *United States v. Ash,* Ash and another were wanted in connection with a bank robbery. Acting on information, an FBI agent showed five black and white mug shots of black males of generally the same age, height and weight to four witnesses. All four made an uncertain identification of Ash. Ash was not in custody at the time and had not been charged. Trial finally was set almost three years after the crime. Shortly before trial, the prosecutor and an FBI agent showed five color photographs to the same witnesses. Three of the witnesses selected the picture of Ash. Ash was identified in court at trial and evidence of the pre-trial photographic identification was admitted. Ash was convicted and sought review. The appeal apparently was presented with the view that the defendant was entitled to a per se exclusion of the testimony relating to the pre-trial photographic identification. The Supreme Court pointed out that a photographic identification is not a trial-like stage and while there are some risks which exist there are also safeguards; and even if these safeguards fail, review is available under the due process standard. Therefore, the Sixth Amendment does not grant a right to counsel at photographic displays for the purpose of identification.

§ 6-4 Lineups

A lineup is distinguished from a showup by the fact that a lineup requires the witness to identify the alleged perpetrator of a crime from among a number of persons while a showup is a one-on-one identification whereby the witness is shown only one person and in effect asked if this is the person who committed the crime.

Lineups must be considered from two standpoints: First, in some situations there is a per se exclusion of the pre-trial identification testimony. Second, the due process standard must be considered. Due process considerations are discussed in section 6-8, infra.

Under the authority of *United States v. Wade* and *Moore v. Illinois,* there is a general per se exclusionary rule which applies to a pre-trial identification at or after the initiation of adversary judicial criminal proceedings unless the defendant is represented by counsel who is present at the time of the identification. In *Moore,* " 'adversary judicial criminal proceedings' were [said to be] initiated when a preliminary hearing was held," but this rule has been held not to apply where the pre-trial identification was at the place scheduled for a preliminary hearing but no evidence was introduced and the case was simply referred to juvenile court. In *Victorine v. State,* the Georgia Supreme Court continued to rely on a Georgia case decided before *Moore* and concluded that "there is no right to counsel at a pre-indictment photo lineup." In *Phillips v. State,* the Georgia Court of Appeals pointed out that the Sixth Amendment right to counsel at a lineup is *"offense-specific."* Thus, "[t]he right does not apply with respect to one offense where adversary proceedings have been commenced with respect to a different offense, but not that offense." In *Phillips*, the defendant had been indicted for burglary at the time of the lineup, but he had not yet been indicted for the unrelated charge of rape.

Nevertheless, a defendant may waive his right to the presence of counsel at a lineup. In *Jenkins v. State*, the Georgia Court of Appeals held that where defense counsel is notified of a lineup and he simply elects not to attend, this amounts to a waiver of the right to have counsel present. However, an identification in the absence of counsel at such time does not prevent an in-court identification at the time of trial if the in-court identification has an independent origin. Also, it must be remembered that there is no due process right to a pre-trial lineup.

A number of sets of rules or guidelines for lineup identifications have been suggested by and for various groups of law enforcement officers. These suggestions may be helpful to counsel attending a lineup and in connection with the cross-examination of witnesses who have given eyewitness identification testimony.

Some of the most important guidelines or rules which have been suggested are as follows:

(1) All persons in the lineup should be of the same general age and race and have similar characteristics.

(2) Clothing worn by each person should be similar.

(3) Any movements or statements should be made by each person in the lineup, one at a time. It now seems clear that under Georgia law a person in a lineup may be compelled to speak certain words.

(4) A color photograph of the lineup should be taken and developed as soon as possible.

(5) A witness should be prevented from seeing the defendant in custody prior to lineup.

(6) Witnesses should not be shown a photograph of the defendant before the lineup.

(7) If more than one person is to view a lineup, the witnesses should do so one at a time and out of the presence of the other.

(8) No actions should be taken or statements made to a witness to suggest that a suspect is standing in any particular place.

(9) As few persons as possible should be allowed in the room when the lineup is conducted.

(10) The witness, before entering the room where the lineup is to be conducted, should be given a form on which his identification can be marked and signed.

(11) There should be at least six persons in the lineup.

(12) Statements by persons in a lineup should not be requested unless a witness suggests it. If statements are made, all participants should repeat the same words.

(13) If counsel is present, he should be allowed to make suggestions.

(14) Prior to the lineup, the witness should give a detailed description of the perpetrator. This description should be reduced to writing before the lineup.

(15) If possible, law enforcement officers should not be used in lineups.

(16) Some authorities feel that "blank lineups"—lineups which are held in the absence of the suspect—should be utilized. Blank lineups could prevent a witness from picking out the person in the lineup looking most like the accused even if the person is not the perpetrator of the crime.

(17) The names and addresses of all persons participating in the lineup should be preserved.

In Georgia, it has been held that a suspect has no right to refuse to take part in a lineup. Generally, if a person is lawfully incarcerated on an unrelated charge, he may be forced to be a "stand in" in a lineup.

In *Foster v. State,* the Georgia Court of Appeals treated a pre-trial identification in the courtroom as a lineup. The court said that two witnesses to a robbery (who had never identified the defendant during a four-month period between the crime and the trial) were asked by a representative of the district attorney to identify the assailant from a group of defendants seated in the jury box of the courtroom, before the trial started. At the trial defense counsel objected to the identification testimony of one of these witnesses. The court concluded that if defense counsel was not present when the witness (who testified over objection as to the identity of the defendant) identified the defendant in the jury box, the admission of such pre-trial identification, and all of the witnesses' identification testimony, was error unless the trial judge determined that the witness' in-court identification had an origin independent "from her lineup identification, based on the standards set forth in . . . *Wade.*" The court distinguished *Foster* from *Prater v. State* where witnesses on their own initiative attended a court proceeding where they expected to see the defendant. The court indicated that *Wade* condemned state action in providing for identification in the absence of defense counsel. In *Robinson v. State,* the court found that there was no lineup where a witness on her own initiative attended an arraignment calendar call. The district attorney talked to the witness when she was noticed and asked if she could identify any of the robbers. The witness then pointed out the defendant. The court reasoned that the identification was not orchestrated by the police or the district attorney.

In *Ely v. State,* the court pointed out that evidence of such a courtroom identification arranged by the district attorney and without the knowledge of the defendant was not admissible under *Wade.* However, this alone does not prevent the witness, during the trial, from identifying the defendant if the trial identification has an independent origin.

In *Wiley v. State,* the court upheld the admissibility at trial of an identification at a "lineup" at which only the hands of participants were visible. The victim had previously given a detailed description of her assailant's hands. However, she had been unable to identify him at an earlier conventional lineup, presumably because her assailant was wearing a mask at the time of the crime. Because counsel was present at the lineup, the court properly applied the general two-step due process standard discussed in section 6-8, infra.

The statement of an officer to a witness before a lineup that a suspect had been arrested has been said to be no more suggestive than the lineup itself. However, such statements should be avoided.

In *Rivers v. State,* the court pointed out that a "lineup was not impermissibly suggestive because . . . [the defendant] was the only person to appear both in the photo array and the physical lineup."

See 29 Am. Jur. 2d, Evidence § 628 (1994) on suggestive lineups. Generally, see "Lineups and Showups: Admissibility and Effect of Pretrial Identification," 19 Am. Jur. Proof of Facts 2d 435; "Unreliability of Eyewitness Identification," 18 Am. Jur. Proof of Facts 2d 361. See also 29 Am. Jur. 2d Evidence § 371.4. See Annotation, "Admissibility of In–Court Identification as Affected by Pretrial Encounter That Was Not Result of Action by Police, Prosecutors and the Like," 86 A. L. R. 5th 463 (2001).

§ 6-5 Showups

As previously mentioned, a showup occurs when a witness views a single individual for purposes of identification. This means of identification is inherently suggestive and has been widely condemned when used by law enforcement officers.

Nonetheless, as the court observed in *Horne v. State,* "the identification need not be excluded as long as the identification was reliable notwithstanding any suggestive procedure under all the circumstances. The factors to be considered in evaluating the likelihood of misidentification include the opportunity of the witness to view the criminal at the time of the crime, the witness' degree of attention, the accuracy of the witness' prior description of the criminal, the level of certainty demonstrated by the witness at the confrontation, and the length of time between the crime and the confrontation." (Citations omitted.)

However, courts have generally upheld admission of in-court identification when the prior one-on-one showups were reasonably and fairly conducted at or near the time of the offense. Such early identification is needed (1) to guide officers in determining whether or not to look further for the perpetrator; (2) because the accuracy and reliability of identification is likely to be greater at that time; and (3) to permit the speedy release of an innocent person who is in custody. For these reasons, delays in identification of as much as two or three hours have not been condemned. However, an identification after a delay of as much as four or five hours has been held to be too suggestive.

In *M. A. K. v. State,* a juvenile was arrested and carried to the victim of a burglary to see if he were the burglar. The victim identified the juvenile. The Georgia statute, the material parts of which are set out in section 5-8, supra, provides that a "person taking a child into custody, with all reasonable speed and without first taking the child elsewhere, shall . . . [take] the child immediately before the juvenile court or promptly contact a juvenile court intake officer." The juvenile contended that this statute had been violated by taking him to the victim of the burglary for identification. The court held that the statute was directory and did not limit the authority of the officer to take the juvenile for identification.

After the exigencies connected with an identification shortly after an arrest have dissipated, there is a right to the presence of counsel at such identification at or after the initiation of the adversary criminal judicial proceeding. See section 6-4, supra. If this right to counsel is violated at such an identification there is a per se rule which prevents the admission of such pre-trial identification at the trial. However, this alone does not prevent an in-court identification at the time of trial.

If the showup or lineup takes place before the initiation of the adversary criminal judicial proceeding, but after the dissipation of the exigencies connected with the arrest, it seems that in-court testimony of the pre-trial identification will be excluded only if the pre-trial identification amounts to a due process violation, i.e., if it was so suggestive as to result in misidentification. However, here again, the tainted pre-trial identification does not automatically prevent a later in-court identification of the defendant at the time of trial.

An "accidental" identification of a defendant by a witness even after the initiation of the adversary criminal judicial proceeding will not automatically prevent in-court testimony of the pre-trial identification. Thus, in *Herron v. State,* the victim and her brother had been at the police station to view some pictures. The victim could not positively identify her assailant from the pictures but two of the pictures reminded her of her assailant. The defendant was then released and he left at the same time as the victim. The evidence was that the victim by chance saw the defendant. The victim then stated that the defendant was her assailant. The trial judge was affirmed in refusing to strike the one-on-one showup identification testimony because there was no showing that the confrontation was staged. The court concluded that the confrontation had not been arranged and thus there was no due process violation. There was said not to be a "very substantial likelihood of irreparable misidentification" and the pre-trial identification was not impermissibly suggestive. Hence, testimony of the pre-trial identification was admissible.

See section 6-8, infra, on due process and identification. See Annotation, "Admissibility of Evidence of Showup Identification as Affected by Allegedly Suggestive Showup Procedures," 39 A. L. R. 3d 791 (1971).

See 29 Am. Jur. 2d, Evidence § 629 (1994). Generally, see "Lineups and Showups: Admissibility and Effect of Pretrial Identification," 19 Am. Jur. Proof of Facts 2d 435; "Unreliability of Eyewitness Identification," 18 Am. Jur. Proof of Facts 2d 361.

§ 6-6 Picture identification

Much of what has been said about lineup and showup identification applies to an identification based on pictures, in that reliability is the linchpin of any identification procedure. However, there is one very important difference. Whereas there is generally a per se right to the exclusion of a pre-trial identification at a lineup or showup, at or after the initiation of the adversary judicial criminal proceeding if counsel is not present, no such automatic exclusion applies to testimony regarding a photographic identification.

In *United States v. Ash,* the United States Supreme Court concluded that the dangers of mistaken identification are not sufficient to require a per se exclusionary rule of testimony of a photographic identification. However, the admissibility of such testimony is still limited by the due process clause. In *Branch v. Estelle,* the Fifth Circuit pointed out that the distinction between a review of a corporal lineup and a photographic lineup is the fact that a photographic lineup can be reconstructed for purposes of trial and appellate court review. However, the court said that in a situation where officers fail to preserve the photographic array, there is a presumption that the array is impermissibly suggestive. Nevertheless, in *Daniel v. State,* the Georgia Court of Appeals held that the failure to preserve the photos used in a pre-trial lineup "merely goes to the weight to be afforded the pictorial lineup and not to its admissibility."

In *Brewer v. State,* the court affirmed the admission of a photograph of the defendant even though the photograph on the back contained the signature of the victim which had been placed there at the time she identified the photograph.

In *Huggins v. State,* the court held that testimony of a picture identification was admissible even though the pictures used had been lost ("the absence of the pictures at the time of trial . . . goes to the weight").

In the 2001 case of *White v. State,* the Georgia Supreme Court held that "[i]n the absence of some other viable hearsay exception, such as 'necessity' or 'res gestae,' a law enforcement officer may not testify to a pre-trial identification of the accused unless the person who actually made the identification testifies at trial and is subject to cross-examination."

The display of a single picture is regarded as being too suggestive. Hence, where there is such an impermissibly suggestive identification, it must be determined whether under a totality of the circumstances the display of a single photograph was conducive to irreparable mistaken identification. Even though the display of a single photograph is impermissibly suggestive, still this does not prevent an in-court identification if the in-court identification has an independent source.

If there are a number of pictures and the picture of one person appears more than once, or if an officer tells a witness that he has other evidence that one of the persons pictured committed the crime, the chance of misidentification increases. It has been held that the fact that the picture of the defendant was eight years old does not make the array impermissible.

Ideally the pictures presented should be of the same kind, size and appearance. In *Wright v. State,* the court held the photographic identification was not impermissibly suggestive where six photographs of black males who appeared to be about the same age as the defendant with similar medium complexion, hair, and no facial hair were presented to the victim. However, in *Cheeves v. State,* there was some indication that the backgrounds of some of the photographs were different, two of the photographs were slightly smaller than the others, and some of the persons pictured had on hats while others did not. The Georgia Court of Appeals affirmed the trial judge's action in overruling the defendant's request to exclude the eyewitness identification. Although the case was recently overruled, in *Heard v. State,* the court affirmed the trial judge's finding that the photo array was not impermissibly suggestive where the defendant's picture had a different colored background and his face may have been larger than the faces in the other photos. Likewise, in *Brewer v. State,* the court held that "[t]he contention that the shading and tone of defendant's photograph made . . . [the] identification procedure unduly suggestive is without merit." In *Padilla v. State,* the Georgia Supreme Court affirmed the trial court in the pre-trial identification of the defendant "even though he was the only mixed-race male in the photographs." In *Hendry v. State,* the court concluded that the fact that "the individuals in the photographs had on the same clothing as the individuals the witness saw in the show-up is not in and of itself impermissively [sic] suggestive." In *Jackson v. State,* the court held that a photographic lineup was not rendered impermissibly suggestive merely because the defendant's co-indictee was pictured in one of the six pictures displayed.

Nevertheless, in *Passman v. Blackburn,* a photographic identification was found to be impermissibly suggestive where officers used a single, colored photograph of a front view of the defendant and the remaining 11 pictures were black-and-white mug shots with front and side views. Also, the court pointed out that four of the black-and-white pictures were significantly smaller. Nevertheless, in *Graham v. State,* the court held, "The variance in size and texture in the pictures used does not render the procedure impermissibly suggestive." In *Colston v. State*, the court held that a photographic lineup was not impermissibly suggestive "because of the different backgrounds of the pictures, different sizes of the photographs and the fact that defendant's photograph was the second largest."

In the Tenth Circuit case of *United States v. Sanchez,* the court pointed out that "[t]he larger the number of pictures used in an array, the less likely it is that a minor difference, such as background color or texture, will have a prejudicial effect on selection. . . . Conversely, when a relatively low number of photographs are used . . . , minor differences such as background color can make a picture stand out, and can act to repeatedly draw a witness's eyes to that picture."

In asking a witness to view a photographic array, an officer should not tell the witness that the suspect has been arrested. However, a pre-trial photographic identification is not rendered impermissibly suggestive by an officer's telling the victim that there is a suspect in the seven pictures displayed.

It has been said pictures should be displayed to only one eyewitness at a time, and if there are other eyewitnesses they should not be present when the identification is being attempted. However, in a case where two photo spreads are used and only the defendant's picture appeared in both, the court concluded that the identification was not impermissibly defective.

Suggestions made by officers may cause a due process violation at the time of a photographic identification. The witness should not be informed that the defendant's picture is in the array, and no picture should be pointed out to a witness. In *Cridiso v. State,* the court said that "it may not be good practice for a police officer to indicate to a witness that he has chosen the 'right guy.' "However, the test for admissibility at trial following a tainted pre-trial identification (either photographic or physical) is "whether the in-court identification had an independent origin."

Georgia has recognized that a composite drawing of a suspect made up of data supplied by witnesses may be shown to a witness for purposes of identification. However, the inability of a victim to verbally convey the picture of the assailant to an artist has been held not to prevent a photo or physical identification. In *Williams v. State,* the court held that a composite drawing was not objectionable as hearsay where the police artist did not testify at trial. See Annotation, "Admissibility in Evidence of Composite Picture or Sketch Produced by Police to Identify Offender," 42 A. L. R. 3d 1217 (1972). Also, in Georgia it has been held that a defendant may be identified by permitting a witness to look through "mug" books.

Some psychologists believe that in an array of photographs, if one picture is not in line with the others, that is if it is "crooked" in the array, it is more likely to be picked out. Likewise, some have concluded that a picture of a person with a different expression from the persons in the other pictures or different clothing from the others is more likely to be selected.

In *Lynch v. State,* the defendant contended that the victim's in-court identification was tainted by a photographic lineup of eight photographs and that the array was misleading because the pictures (from chest up) showed the heights of the suspects. However, there was no testimony that the identification was based on any height information. The court concluded that in view of the totality of the circumstances, it was not error to admit the in-court identification testimony.

In the unusual case of *Gravitt v. State,* a picture was shown to the victim about two weeks before the victim was robbed and he was told that the defendant might rob him. Three days after the robbery the victim identified the defendant in a lineup. At trial the victim testified that his lineup identification had not been influenced by the picture. The court concluded that there was no substantial likelihood of misidentification and no due process violation in admitting the in-court identification.

In *Baier v. State,* an officer displayed three black and white photographs to the witness. Two of the pictures depicted the accused, including one with a mustache added. The witness tentatively identified the accused, pointing out that the mustache was incorrectly drawn. Later the witness saw him in a showup at jail and "recognized him." In reversing the conviction, the court concluded that there had been "an impermissibly suggestive photographic confrontation, followed by a suggestive in person confrontation at a critical stage of the proceedings conducted without counsel . . . making it impossible to determine that the courtroom identification is untainted. . . ." However, in *Futch v. State* the court stated that "[c]onvictions based on eyewitness identification at trial following a pretrial identification by photograph will be set aside only if the photographic identification procedure was so impermissibly suggestive as to give rise to a very substantial likelihood of irreparable misidentification. . . . Moreover, '(e)ven if a pretrial identification is tainted, an in-court identification is not constitutionally inadmissible if it does not depend upon the prior identification but has an independent origin.' "

It has been pointed out that a photographic array is a less reliable means of identification than a corporal lineup and that the use of such a less reliable identification is a factor which may be used in determining whether an identification was reliable. However, even though "a corporal lineup is the most reliable identification procedure and for that reason the most preferable, . . . a defendant has no constitutional right to a lineup."

In *Boscaino v. State,* the victim positively identified the defendant at a photographic lineup conducted three days after the incident. However, he could not positively identify the defendant in court. The court held that the failure to positively identify the defendant in court did not invalidate his earlier positive identification.

On the other hand, it was held in *Banks v. State* that "[t]he victims' failure to identify . . . [the defendant] from the photographic lineup does not require the conclusion that their in-court identification was based solely on the" viewing of the defendant in the courtroom at the time of trial.

Generally, see Annotations, "Admissibility of Evidence of Photographic Identification as Affected by Allegedly Suggestive Identification Procedures," 39 A. L. R. 3d 1000 (1971); "Lineups and Showups: Admissibility and Effect of Pretrial Identification," 19 Am. Jur. Proof of Facts 2d 435, 446; "Unreliability of Eyewitness Identification," 18 Am. Jur. Proof of Facts 2d 361. See also 29 Am. Jur. 2d Evidence (1994) § 630. See section 6-9, infra, on an arrest to take a suspect's picture. See Annotation, "Admissibility in Evidence of Composite Picture or Sketch Produced by Police to Identify Offender," 23 A. L. R. 5th 672 (1994), and Goger, *Daniel's Georgia Handbook on Criminal Evidence* (2009 ed.), § 7–8.

§ 6-7 Presence of counsel

As previously mentioned, defense counsel has a right to be present when his client is present at any kind of identification at or after the initiation of the adversary criminal proceeding. Conversely, there is no right to counsel at an identification before the initiation of the adversary criminal proceeding. Also, like most other rights, the presence of counsel may be waived. Nevertheless, the giving of the *Miranda* warning alone has been held not to constitute a waiver of the right to have counsel present at a lineup. Also, it may be possible to utilize substitute counsel if the defendant's counsel cannot be present or there would be a prejudicial delay in waiting for the defendant's counsel.

After the time at which the defendant constitutionally is entitled to counsel, when he is present for identification, the failure to have counsel present results in a per se exclusion of testimony of the pre-trial identification at least in the absence of an accidental or unanticipated identification or perhaps when the identification can be justified by exigent circumstances. If the defendant's right to counsel is violated, testimony of the pre-trial identification is inadmissible regardless of whether there was an independent source of the witness' identification at the confrontation.

However, the fact that there has been a pre-trial identification of a defendant in violation of his right to counsel does not necessarily mean that the in-court identification testimony of the witness is to be excluded. If the witness' in-court identification was independent of any tainted pre-trial identification, the in-court identification testimony is admissible.

As previously pointed out, however, the defendant is not entitled to be represented by counsel at a photographic identification regardless of when it takes place.

What is counsel's role at an identification? Clearly it is envisioned that counsel is present as a witness and so that he may better cross-examine the identifying witness or witnesses at trial. The idea of having defense counsel act as a witness at a critical stage of the proceeding may place the attorney in an unusual position. If there is a disagreement about what took place or the arrangement of the lineup, he may have to withdraw from the case in order to testify. However, in *Moore v. Illinois,* a more active role was suggested by the United States Supreme Court. The court said that defense counsel may object to suggestive features before they influence a witness' identification.

There is some older authority indicating that defense counsel can do nothing but observe and that he cannot prevent an unfair lineup nor make suggestions which must be followed. In addition, officers have authority to eject argumentative defense counsel from the lineup room if his efforts impede the efforts of officers to conduct the proceeding effectively. With the possible exception of the situation involving disruption of the proceeding, the validity of these views is at least open to question since *Moore.* However, if counsel does have a right to object or make suggestions, his failure to do so may amount to a waiver.

Generally, see "Lineups and Showups: Admissibility and Effect of Pretrial Identification," 19 Am. Jur. Proof of Facts 2d 435 and 22A C. J. S. § 616.

§ 6-8 Due process standard

The due process requirement applies to all testimony involving pre-trial identifications, at least in the absence of a waiver. These requirements apply to all lineups, showups, and photographic displays regardless of whether there was a constitutional right to the presence of counsel at the time. Thus, even if the right to counsel was waived by the defendant at the time of a pre-trial identification, it may still be possible for defense counsel to exclude testimony of the identification if the confrontation violated due process. The due process standard is the only standard which applies to a photographic pre-trial identification and it is the standard which applies to accidental confrontations and confrontations produced by exigent circumstances. Of course, it was the only standard which applied to pre-trial identifications before June 12, 1967.

The due process standard applies to two different kinds of identification testimony. First, it applies to the admissibility at trial of a pre-trial identification. Second, the due process standard applies to the question of whether or not the witness will be permitted to identify the defendant in court at the time of trial.

"It is error to allow testimony concerning a pre-trial identification of the defendant if the identification procedure was impermissibly suggestive and, under the totality of the circumstances, the suggestiveness gave rise to a substantial likelihood of misidentification." "A court need not consider whether there was a substantial likelihood of misidentification if it determines that the identification procedure was not impermissibly suggestive." "An identification procedure is impermissibly suggestive when it leads the witness to an 'all but inevitable identification' of the defendant as the perpetrator . . . or as was held in *Heyward v. State,*[] is the equivalent of the authorities telling the witness, 'This is our suspect.' "

In cases where there is a question of a due process violation in a pre-trial identification, testimony of the pre-trial identification is to be excluded if the violation was so suggestive as to result in misidentification. If the pre-trial identification "was so unnecessarily suggestive and conducive to mistaken identification" as judged by a totality of the circumstances surrounding it, the defendant is said to have been denied due process of law and testimony of the pre-trial identification should be excluded.

However, in the 2000 Georgia Supreme Court case of *Jones v. State,* the court held that "[w]hen a trial court concludes that an identification procedure is impermissibly suggestive, the issue becomes whether there was a substantial likelihood of irreparable misidentification. If not, then both the pre-trial and in-court identifications are admissible."

Insofar as admission of in-court identification where there is a question of whether or not due process has been violated, a two-step analysis now is used. First, the threshold inquiry is whether the identification procedure used was impermissibly suggestive, and only if it was, is the second question reached. Second, was there a substantial likelihood of irreparable misidentification? These questions are to be answered in the light of a totality of the circumstances surrounding the identification. Insofar as the question of likelihood of irreparable misidentification is concerned, it comes down "to the central question whether under the 'totality of the circumstances' the identification was reliable even though the confrontation was suggestive." In *Neil v. Biggers,* the United States Supreme Court said that the "factors to be considered in evaluating the likelihood of misidentification include [1] the opportunity of the witness to view the criminal at the time of the crime, [2] the witness' degree of attention, [3] the accuracy of the witness' prior description of the criminal, [4] the level of certainty demonstrated by the witness at the confrontation, and [5] the length of time between the crime and the confrontation." In *Semple v. State,* the court held that *Biggers* "deals with the suggestiveness of an identification procedure used by police, and applies only to state action."

However, in *Davis v. State,* the Georgia Court of Appeals recognized that even in a situation as "inherently suggestive" as a one-on-one showup, "any psychological effect a one-on-one showup may have on a potential witness is greatly diminished when that witness is a law enforcement officer who, through experience, training or both, has learned certain witness identification techniques and procedures."

A discrepancy between a pre-lineup description and the actual description, the identification of another person before a lineup, the failure to identify the defendant on an earlier occasion, the identification of the defendant by picture, and the lapse of time between the crime and the lineup are all significant factors to consider. However, in *Price v. State,* the court held that an identification is not "inherently unreliable" because of inconsistencies in the description given by the witness where the witness is available for cross-examination.

Where an identification is made, it is improper for an officer to tell the witness that he has chosen the right person.

In *Swicegood v. Alabama,* the court, on the basis of a due process violation in the identification of the defendant, pointed out that (1) the defendant, who was 35 years of age at the time, was 9 to 15 years older than the other participants in the lineup; (2) the two witnesses had an unsupervised opportunity to discuss the lineup between the first viewing when neither identified the defendant and the second viewing when they both positively identified the defendant; (3) one witness was allowed to view those in the lineup without masks although he had never seen the robber without a mask; (4) one witness had given only a very general description, and neither witness was asked to give a more precise description prior to the lineup; (5) neither witness had a good opportunity during the offense to see or hear the robber (one was locked in a closet the entire time and the other wore a blindfold covering her eyes for all except about two seconds, and her ears were covered for at least part of the time); (6) the lineup was held nearly three weeks after the robbery; (7) the in-court certainty may have been tainted by the remark of a police officer to the effect that the witnesses had identified the "right man"; and (8) even though the defendant generally fit the description of the witnesses, so did the others in the lineup. The court concluded that the lineup raised due process considerations sufficient enough to require an examination of the reliability of the identification. The court then examined each of the five factors set out in *Biggers* in light of the evidence in the present case and concluded by saying, "We cannot say that the likelihood of misidentification was slight or that the suggestiveness of the lineup was an uncorrupting influence. . . . [U]nder all the circumstances of this case, the suggestiveness of the lineup and the unreliability of the identifications coalesce to produce a due process violation."

In *Clark v. State,* the court held that a lineup was not impermissible because the defendant was the only person to appear in both an earlier pictorial identification and the lineup.

In *Hodnett v. State,* the Georgia Supreme Court pointed out that a lineup would not be flawed simply by an officer's telling a defendant to take a certain position in the lineup.

Lastly, the failure to hold any kind of pre-trial identification is not a due process violation of a defendant.

See section 6-5, supra, on showups.

Generally, see "Lineups and Showups: Admissibility and Effect of Pretrial Identification," 19 Am. Jur. Proof of Facts 2d 435 and "Unreliability of Eyewitness Identification," 18 Am. Jur. Proof of Facts 2d 361.

§ 6-9 Motions for lineups

In Georgia it has been said that a defendant has no right to refuse to participate in a lineup, at least if it is properly arranged and conducted. Even if he is on bond, it seems he may be required to appear for a lineup. Georgia courts do not seem to have considered expressly a situation in which law enforcement officers desire to have a suspect placed in a lineup even though they do not have sufficient probable cause to justify an arrest of the suspect. Most courts seem to hold that a suspect may not be forced to appear in a lineup unless there is probable cause to arrest the suspect. However, a person lawfully held in custody for one offense has been held not to have a right to complain when he is used as a "filler" in a lineup in connection with an unrelated offense. It has been held that when there is probable cause, pursuant to a warrant, there may be an arrest of a suspect for purposes of fingerprinting and photography. However, it seems that a grand jury at least may do so. Also, it should be remembered that if officers think they have probable cause for a valid arrest and they do not, this does not mean that in-court identification is automatically suppressible even if a picture made as a result of the illegal arrest was used as a means of a pre-trial identification.

Likewise, Georgia does not seem to have expressly passed on the question of whether or not a defendant on his own motion is entitled to a pre-trial lineup. Courts in other jurisdictions have differed on this question, some holding that a defendant under some circumstances is entitled to a pre-trial lineup and some holding that a defendant is not entitled to such a lineup.

§ 6-10 Admissibility of in-court identification testimony at trial

In sections 6-4 through 6-9, supra, the emphasis was on whether testimony of a pre-trial identification is admissible at trial. The thrust of this section is to determine when the pre-trial taint is so severe or the witness' view of the defendant so fleeting that a witness should be prevented from testifying at trial that "the defendant is the man I saw commit the crime." Some of the cases previously discussed in this chapter have considered this problem.

If a pre-trial identification arranged by officers violates the right to counsel or if there is a due process violation, such as was discussed above, then on motion it is the duty of the trial judge to determine whether the witness has an independent recollection of the appearance of the defendant which is based on having seen him at the time of the crime and which is independent of the tainted pre-trial identification. If the witness can testify independently of the pre-trial identification, the witness' in-court identification testimony is admissible. If the witness cannot testify in-court as to the defendant's identity independently of the tainted pre-trial identification, his in-court identification testimony should be excluded. In *Paxton v. State,* the Georgia Court of Appeals pointed out that an independent origin of an in-court identification may be shown by the fact that "the victim was able to give a precise and accurate description of his assailant before he viewed the photographic lineup."

If there is a tainted pre-trial identification and the state wishes to show that the witness should be permitted to identify the defendant in-court, the burden is on the state "to establish by clear and convincing evidence that the in-court identification . . . [would be] based upon the observations of the suspect" at some time other than at the tainted identification.

In *Tiller v. State,* the court pointed out that "even where a pretrial identification has been found to be tainted, a subsequent in-court identification is admissible if it does not depend on the prior, tainted identification but has some other independent basis."

In *Smith v. State,* the Georgia Court of Appeals considered whether a pre-trial photographic lineup was so impermissibly suggestive as to give rise to a substantial likelihood of irreparable misidentification. In determining whether the in-court identification was tainted, the court considered each of the five criteria set out in *Neil v. Biggers,* viz., (1) the opportunity of the witness to view the perpetrator at the time of the crime; (2) the witness' degree of attention; (3) the accuracy of the witness' prior description of the criminal; (4) the level of certainty demonstrated by the witness; and (5) the length of the time between the crime and the confrontation. The court then concluded that there was no substantial likelihood of misidentification at either the pre-trial or in-court identification.

It has been pointed out that reliability is to be determined from a totality of the circumstances. Thus, it has been held that an "in-court identification based upon the scene of the crime was not impermissibly tainted solely because the appellant sat at the defendant's table and was the only black male in the courtroom." Likewise, an in-court identification is not inadmissible solely because the victim was unable to identify the defendant at a lineup shortly after the crime or failed to identify the defendant at a photo lineup. In *Buckner v. State,* the court held that "uncertainty expressed by the victim regarding his in-court identification of [the defendant] was merely a factor to be considered by the jury in determining the weight of this testimony."

In *Brodes v. State,* the Georgia Supreme Court reversed the trial court, which, relying on the pattern charge, instructed the jury that one of the factors it was to consider in reviewing the testimony of the eyewitnesses was the level of certainty in their identification. The Court was persuaded by the empirical research presented that there exists a distinct "lack of correlation between a witness's certainty in his or her identification of someone as the perpetrator of a crime and the accuracy of that identification . . ." The Court went on to "advise" trial courts to refrain from using the level of certainty factor as part of their eyewitness identification charge. However, *Brodes* in no way is an impediment to a witness testifying about his or her level of certainty of identification. Such testimony would, of course, be subject to challenge by way of "cross examination, expert testimony or the presentation of testimony from other eye witnesses."

In *Clay v. State,* the court held that when the jury has been adequately charged on the presumption of innocence, reasonable doubt, burden of proof, credibility of witnesses and impeachment, there is no error should the court fail, *sua sponte,* to charge the jury on identification even if it constitutes the sole defense.

It should be pointed out that the United States Supreme Court held in *United States v. Crews* that where a defendant was illegally arrested and photographed and identified by the victim of the robbery by the picture and later in a pre-trial lineup, the victim was not prevented from identifying the defendant in court at the time of the trial where the trial judge found that her in-court identification was based on her original encounter with the defendant. However, it was conceded that her testimony as to the photographic identification and the lineup was suppressible as a result of the Fourth Amendment violation.

It must be emphasized that the failure of defense counsel to object to an in-court identification generally prevents a later attack based on an allegedly tainted prior identification. On the other hand, a pre-trial lineup or display of a photograph or photographs to a witness is not a prerequisite to an in-court identification.

It is within a trial court's discretion whether or not to admit expert testimony regarding eyewitness identification. However, "[w]here eyewitness identification of the defendant is a key element of the State's case and there is no substantial corroboration of that identification by other evidence, trial courts may not exclude expert testimony without carefully weighing whether the evidence would assist the jury in assessing the reliability of eyewitness testimony and whether eyewitness testimony is the only effective way to reveal any weakness in an eyewitness identification."

See 21A Am. Jur. 2d Criminal Law § 803. See Goger, *Daniel's Georgia Handbook on Criminal Evidence* (2009 ed.), § 7–8, on expert testimony relating to accuracy of eyewitness identification.

§ 6-11 Hearing on motion to suppress identification testimony

An objection to the admissibility of in-court identification may be raised at trial. Also, where there is a tainted pre-trial identification, most jurisdictions recognize the right of a defendant to file a pre-trial motion to suppress the in-court identification and to have an evidentiary hearing on the question raised.

In *Kemp v. State,* the Georgia Court of Appeals strongly indicated that the point should be raised before the trial starts and that a defendant may waive his right to an evidentiary hearing by not making a timely motion for such a hearing.

Regardless of how the point is raised, any such hearing should be conducted outside the presence of the jury. In *Watkins v. Sowders,* the United States Supreme Court concluded that while the Due Process Clause of the Fourteenth Amendment does not always require a hearing outside the presence of the jury, the "prudence of such a hearing has been emphasized by many decisions. . . . A judicial determination outside the presence of the jury of the admissibility of identification evidence may often be advisable. In some circumstances . . . such a determination may be constitutionally necessary. But it does not follow that the constitution requires a per se rule compelling such a procedure in every case."

In a motion to suppress identification testimony, the judge is the trier of fact and he is to determine credibility, weight, and conflicts in the evidence. It has been said that if there is evidence to support the ruling of the trial judge, the ruling will not be disturbed.

In *Moore v. State,* the court held that a trial judge may deny, without a hearing, a pre-trial motion to suppress identification testimony. The Georgia Court of Appeals held in *Davis v. State* that in reviewing the denial of a motion to suppress identification testimony, the appellate court may consider "the evidence adduced both at the suppression hearing and at trial."

See section 14-73, infra, on motions to suppress and motions in limine. For motions to suppress identification, see Goger, *Daniel's Georgia Criminal Trial Practice Forms* (6th ed.), §§ 6-1, 6-2, 6-3, 20-6, 20-7, 20-8, 20-9, 2-10 and 20-11.

§ 6-12 Voice identification

Much of what has been said about eyewitness identification applies to voice identification. For example, the California Court of Appeals has ruled that a defendant has a right to have his counsel present at a "voice lineup." Under the United States Constitution and under Georgia law, a defendant may be required to give voice exemplars and to repeat any words, including those which the witness said the perpetrator used at the time of the offense, and he may be forced to stand in a lineup. If a law enforcement officer requests individuals to speak over the telephone for purposes of identification and none of them refuse, the identification is admissible even though no *Miranda* warnings are given. See section 5-23, supra, on compelling a suspect to give non-testimonial evidence in Georgia.

Another difference between the two types of identification concerns their accuracy, particularly where spectrographic identification is used. Whereas eyewitness identification is frequently open to much dispute, voiceprints or spectrographic voice identifications are said to be quite accurate and are gaining acceptance in the scientific community. In fact, a voiceprint has been said to have the same accuracy as fingerprint identification. Some courts, however, have rejected voiceprints as unreliable.

One other distinction should be pointed out. While the general rule regards voice identification as direct testimony, the Georgia rule is that such testimony is opinion evidence and, consequently, is not admissible unless the witness testifies to the basis for his opinion.

In *Reese v. State,* the Georgia Court of Appeals declined to hold that where voice identification is involved, it is necessary to have persons in the lineup with a similar distinctive voice as that of the assailant.

In *Jefferson v. State,* the victim was approached from the rear, blindfolded, and raped. The assailant spoke to the victim a number of times, and she described his voice. While the defendant was being questioned at the police department on the day of the arrest, the police had the victim listen to the defendant's voice just outside the room where he was being questioned. The victim positively identified the voice of the defendant. The court concluded that the voice identification was admissible under the test of *Neil v. Biggers.* See section 6-3, supra. The Georgia court held that the factors to be considered in evaluating the likelihood of misidentification include (1) the opportunity to hear the voice at the time of the crime; (2) the degree of attention of the witness; (3) the witness' prior description of the voice; (4) the level of certainty of the witness at the time of confrontation; and (5) the length of time between the crime and the confrontation. The court then concluded that there was no substantial likelihood of irreparable misidentification.

Generally, see Goger, *Daniel's Georgia Handbook on Criminal Evidence* (2009 ed.), § 6–30, on the defendant as a witness, and § 9–6, on voice identification, and sections 5-22 and 5-23, supra, on non-testimonial evidence. See 1 Wharton's Criminal Evidence, § 189. See also 22A C. J. S. Criminal Law § 616(b)(4).

See 29 Am. Jur. 2d Evidence § 368, on identification by voice. See Annotations, "Admissibility of Evidence of Voice Identification of Defendant as Affected by Alleged Suggestive Voice Lineup Procedures," 55 A. L. R. 5th 423 (1998), and "Cautionary Instructions to Jury as to Reliability of, or Factors to Be Considered in Evaluating, Voice Identification Testimony," 17 A. L. R. 5th 851 (1994).

Part II

CRIMINAL OFFENSES—ELEMENTS OF A CRIME AND LAW ENFORCEMENT LIABILITY*

ARSON

I. Generally

At common law arson was defined as the malicious burning of the dwelling house of another. A crime against property, arson focused on the burning of the dwelling house because of the inherent danger to human life and safety. An intent to burn the dwelling house of another was required, as were fire and an actual burning, however slight. The "dwelling house" included the residence and buildings within the curtilage.

Arson is codified in Article 3 of Chapter 7 of Title 16 entitled "Arson and Explosives," where it is broken into three degrees. First and second degree arson, as defined by §§ 16-7-60 and 16-7-61, protect "structures," while third degree arson, as defined by § 16-7-62, protects personal property.

In 2004, the General Assembly expanded the scope of these statutes to prohibit and punish arsons committed during the commission of felonies.

II. Elements of Offense

Arson has three basic elements: (1) damage by fire or explosion; (2) the intentional act or direction of the defendant knowing that it will damage the protected structure of another; and (3) the lack of that other person's consent.

When an arson is committed during the commission of felony, the prosecution must prove the commission of the underlying felony in addition to the elements of the arson offense.

In 2008, the General Assembly in an effort to consolidate and harmonize the provisions relating to the arson of lands revised and redesignated § 16-7-28 as § 16-7-63.

A. Damage by Fire or Explosive

Unlike the common law, the Georgia statutes include damage by explosives as a basis for arson liability. In the context of criminal damage to property "fire or explosive" has been construed to require some sort of inflammable instrumentality controlled by human hands. That same construction would apparently apply to the arson statutes. Georgia has traditionally followed the common law view that any charring or burning, no matter how slight, constitutes damage within the meaning of the arson statute. The Court of Appeals, however, has broadened the term "damages" in the arson statute to include mere smoke damage, whether or not accompanied by charring or burning.

B. Criminal Intent

Arson is a crime of intention. The defendant must act with the intent to damage a protected structure. There is very little case law on the intent question as a distinct element, however, probably because the act of burning is very powerful evidence of the mens rea.

In an 1874 case, the Georgia Supreme Court held that if a prisoner burns a hole in the door of a guardhouse merely for the purpose of effecting his escape and not with intent to injure or destroy the building, he would not be guilty of arson. Given the present statute's definition of the mens rea as knowingly damaging the property of another, however, this case would probably be reversed if the question were litigated today. The intent to escape would be irrelevant, it could be argued, so long as the defendant knew that his act would damage the property.

The 1979 amendments to the arson statute added arson liability for knowingly directing another to do the acts which cause the prohibited damage.

In Altman v. State the court concluded that only one incendiary act and thus only one crime of arson was committed where the defendants, who carried a grudge against the victim, burned his cabin; the fire destroyed the first cabin and then spread to a second one, adjacent to the first. The court wrote that the act was "directed

---

This information is taken from* ***Kurtz, Criminal Offenses and Defenses in Georgia, 2010 Edition**, by Robert E. Cleary, Jr. (Thomson Reuters 2010). Footnotes in the original volume were deleted to conserve space and reduce cost.*

This **Kurtz, Criminal Offenses and Defenses in Georgia, 2010 Edition** data can also be accessed in its entirety on Westlaw at the sign-on **GACRIMOFDF**. The Westlaw sign-on **GAHARRISON**, Georgia Harrison Analytical Library, contains documents from all available Georgia Harrison Analytical texts published by Thomson Reuters and The Harrison Company.

not against individuals, since none happened to be present, but against the public interest in the protection of life and property in general. Therefore, only one crime was committed." While the *Altman* result could be defended as a lack of mens rea, it is not clear that the court's reasoning and broad language is appropriate. If the purpose of the arson statute is the protection of the security of a home, it would seem that the intentional burning of 10 homes is deserving of more punishment than the intentional burning of one home. The response, of course, to this approach is to argue that the disparate harms should and can be reflected in the punishment assessed, not in the number of convictions assessed.

In Alexander v. State, the defendant argued that the trial judge erred in denying his motion for directed verdict on the arson charge, since the state did not offer any evidence of the defendant's intent to burn the victim's apartment. The defendant did not dispute that it was he who struck the match that started the fire, but he claimed that it was an accident. The court held that the evidence presented by the state supported a finding that the defendant's striking of the match was not accidental. The evidence showed that the defendant had threatened the victim's life more than once before the fire and had physically abused the victim. The state's arson expert testified that the fire began in a puddle of gasoline on the floor which was ignited close to the floor, and that the extent of the defendant's injuries and the fact that the defendant's clothes were not burned made the version of the fire set forth in the defendant's written statement impossible.

In *Vega v. State*, the defendant argued that the evidence failed to show that he deliberately or intentionally set the fire to the abandoned building or that he had ignitable materials with him. Rather, the evidence only showed that he had tossed several tires onto the fire while it continued to grow larger. The court held, however, that § 16-7-60(a) does not require that the defendant personally set the fire or possess ignitable materials. The evidence would be sufficient where it shows that the defendant knowingly damaged or knowingly aided or abetted another to damage property by adding fuel to a fire.

C. Statutorily Protected Structures

The Georgia arson statute expands considerably the types of structures protected from damage. While at common law only dwellings were protected, § 16-7-60(a) describes the following as protected structures without regard to whether they are occupied, unoccupied or vacant: (1) dwelling houses, (2) buildings, vehicles, railroad cars, watercraft or other structures designed for use as dwellings, (3) any structure insured against loss or damage by fire or explosive, (4) any structure which is damaged with the intent to defeat, prejudice or defraud the rights of a spouse or co-owner. Additionally, first degree arson protects any structure which is damaged under such circumstances in which danger to human life is reasonably foreseeable. Section 16-7-61 defines second degree arson as the damaging of a structure not covered by § 16-7-60. This would appear to be limited to uninsured structures not designed as dwellings in which the damage was not done with the intent to defeat, prejudice or defraud the rights of a spouse or co-owner. Third degree arson is limited to the damaging of personal property.

D. Property of Another

The statutes continue the troublesome requirement that the property be that "of another." That phrase has embroiled many courts, including Georgia's, in arguments over whether property merely in another's possession is "of another." In Tukes v. State, the accused set fire to the house the occupants had already sold to him. The court found that the circumstance did not bar prosecution, stating that lawful occupancy constitutes the ownership contemplated by the statute, not legal title. This result is correct because the offense of arson is not so much an offense against property interests as it is against the security of the house. Since lawful occupancy by one in charge, rather than legal title, constitutes the ownership contemplated by the statute, alleging the "ownership" of the property by a person or entity is an unnecessarily minute description of an unnecessary fact in an indictment and need not be proved. The state need only present some evidence of lawful occupancy by another to satisfy this requirement of the statute.

Both § 16-7-60 and § 16-7-61 also now explicitly prohibit the burning of a structure used as a dwelling house in which anybody else has a security interest, such as a mortgage or lien. Thus, the mortgagor can be convicted of arson for burning his house. Two exceptions to the general requirement that the property damaged must belong to another are found in § 16-7-60(a)(3) and (4). The former subsection of first degree arson prohibits the burning of any insured structure and the latter bars the damaging of any structure, without regard to ownership, with the intent to defeat, prejudice, or defraud the rights of a spouse or co-owner. Thus, an individual who burns his own unmortgaged house would be guilty of first degree arson if it was done to defeat a spouse's rights upon divorce.

E. Reasonable Foreseeability of Danger to Human Life

To prove first degree arson under § 16-7-60(a)(5), it must be established that it was reasonably foreseeable that human life might be endangered by the accused's acts. The fact that the arson of one structure threatened a neighboring dwelling should be sufficient. For example, in Griffin v. State, evidence that the explosion of one house knocked out the windows of a neighboring dwelling located only 35 feet away supported a first degree arson conviction. Likewise, in Lawrence v. State, evidence that the defendant set the fire in her apartment and that the fire damaged ten units in the apartment complex was sufficient to support a first degree arson conviction.

In Vineyard v. State, a "reasonable foreseeability of danger to human life" was established where the evidence showed that the fire was set in a carpet plant, that the plant was occupied by several employees, and that although a wall separated the employees from the actual fire, they were in close proximity thereto and toxic smoke filled the area. In Helton v. State, the court held that the time of the fire, past midnight, plus the fact that the house was occupied by sleeping residents thereof was sufficient evidence of the potential for danger to human life.

In *Vega v. State*, the defendant claimed that, even if he had knowingly damaged the building by means of fire, he would not have had any way of knowing that he was endangering human life, because the building was abandoned, and the victim, who was in a small bedroom area, was so intoxicated that he was likely unconscious. The court found, however, that the evidence showed that the defendant had actual knowledge that he was endangering human life. The defendant's statements immediately after adding fuel to the fire and upon being restrained outside the building indicated that he knew that someone else was still in the building and probably died in the fire.

F. Lack of Consent

The final element of arson requires proof that the damage was done without the consent of all owners, any holder of a security interest or lien, or, under § 16-7-60(a)(3), the insurer. While lack of consent must be proven, a perfunctory statement by the defendant that he did not have the consent of the mortgagee will suffice, as will a similar statement about lack of consent made by the victim. The lack of consent can be established by circumstantial evidence.

G. Value of Property

The value of the property damaged need not be alleged or proven in prosecutions for first or second degree arson. For third degree arson, however, the state must prove the damaged personalty had a value of at least $25.

H. Address of Property

A variance between the specific address of the burned property alleged in the indictment and proof of the actual address at trial is not fatal where it is undisputed that the victims owned only one home and that home was burned. Thus, the defendant would not be entitled to a directed verdict of acquittal on this basis. Furthermore, if the address clearly is in dispute and hotly contested by the parties at trial, the disputed issue of fact must be decided by the jury and a directed verdict of acquittal would be inappropriate.

H.1. In Commission of Felonies

In 2004, the General Assembly seemingly expanded the scope of the arson statutes to prohibit and punish arsons committed during the commission of felonies. It can be inferred from the language of Section 4 of the 2004 Act that the General Assembly intended to enhance the punishment for arsons committed during the commission of felonies. This section provides that the Act "shall not apply to any offense committed prior to July 1, 2004. Any such offense shall be **punishable** as provided by the statue [sic] in effect at the time the offense was committed." (Emphasis supplied.) However, the Act did not add any enhanced punishment provisions for arsons committed during the commission of felonies nor did it substantively amend the existing punishment provisions. Because of this legislative oversight, arson offenses whether involving other felonies or not are subject to the same punishment provisions regardless of when they were committed, contrary to the mandate expressed in Section 4 of the Act. Moreover, this oversight renders the subsections added by the 2004 Act, §§ 16-7-60(b), 16-7-61(b), and 16-7-62(b), ineffective until the General Assembly can add provisions to the arson statutes that specifically punish arsons committed during the commission of felonies.

I. Jury Instructions

Where an indictment charges the defendant with committing first degree arson by a specific method, a charge to the jury that arson may be committed by a method not specified in the indictment can constitute error, if a modicum of evidence has been presented from which it could be inferred that the jury convicted the defendant of arson in a manner not charged in the indictment.

III. Presumption of Accidental Damage

There is one key presumption in Georgia arson law: it is presumed that any burning is the result of accidental or providential cause, rather than of criminal design. Thus, if nothing appears but the burning, the state must overcome this presumption. The effect of this presumption is illustrated by Riddings v. State.

In Riddings, the state proved that the defendants' mother had moved out of a house in response to the failure of her landlord and owner of the house to repair the water system, and that the defendants were in the vicinity of the house at the time of the occurrence of the fire. The defendants conceded their proximity, but denied setting the fire or any knowledge of how it started. The court held this evidence insufficient to overcome the presumption that the fire was accidental.

On the other hand, in Whitten v. State, testimony by firemen that there were four separate fires inside the burning building and that they smelled gasoline in two of the rooms was sufficient to overcome the presumption and establish the fire as incendiary in nature. The presumption of accidental burning is a reflection of and consistent with the generally announced burden on the state to prove the corpus delicti in any crime.

In the absence of a written request, the failure of the trial court to charge the jury that the law presumes every fire to be accidental until the state proves otherwise is not reversible error.

IV. Admissibility of Evidence

Because arson is usually accomplished by stealth, circumstantial evidence generally must be used to show both the guilt of the accused and the corpus delicti. The court in Grimes v. State provided a short list of the types of circumstantial evidence that is generally admissible: the isolation of the premises, the absence of any natural cause for the fire, the precautions taken to avoid a fire and the presence of oil or other inflammable material can all be introduced to show the corpus delicti. The motive and opportunity of the accused, his prior threats, subsequent admissions of fact and suspicious conduct on his part are also often used to establish the guilt of the accused.

Evidence of threats made by the defendant to the owner of the premises prior to its burning is admissible to show intent, as is evidence of an earlier attempt by the defendant to burn the building in question. Evidence of the defendant's commission of a similar arson for which he had not been convicted is admissible to show bent of mind and course of conduct. Evidence of motive is likewise admissible in the form of bad feelings between the defendant and the victim, the defendant's inability to pay his rent, the defendant's involvement in an unusually high number of prior fires, or the defendant's stated perception of his dire financial condition. Evidence of prior difficulties between the defendant and the victim is admissible for the purpose of establishing the nature of the victim's relationship with the defendant during the period immediately preceding the fire. This evidence is not inadmissible merely because it may incidentally place the defendant's character into evidence.

While evidence of another crime committed by the defendant would generally be inadmissible, evidence that cocaine was received by the defendant in partial payment for committing the arson would be admissible as part of the res gestae of the crime.

Suspicious circumstances, especially those involving conduct of the accused, are customarily admitted. In Lester v. State testimony of two neighbors stating that they had observed a man enter and leave a house in a surreptitious manner shortly before its burning was admitted. Typical are the cases in which the defendant is seen removing furniture or other items of personalty from a house shortly before its burning.

Officials are justified in entering a burning residence without a warrant to combat the fire and may remain for a reasonable time after it has been extinguished to investigate the cause of the fire. Photographs taken by an investigator of open drawers, of the insides of closets, and of rooms not damaged by the fire would be pertinent evidence in determining whether the fire was caused accidentally or intentionally. The absence of items from drawers, closets, and rooms could be construed as a suspicious circumstance indicating that the fire was not accidental. Because the investigator is properly in the residence collecting evidence concerning the cause of the fire, his photographs are not subject to suppression.

Direct evidence such as statements made by the defendant to his alleged co-conspirator, and descriptions of inflammable instrumentalities, such as clothing soaked with gasoline, and plastic bottles filled with gasoline is admissible and is often utilized by the state.

Expert testimony is often essential in an arson case. Because the fire in question often destroys everything in the building, prosecutors must rely heavily on experts' conclusions drawn from examining the building and any remains. An arson expert can testify to his conclusion that the building was destroyed by "two separate and very hot, fast-moving fires," leaving it to the jury to draw the inference of arson. Expert testimony can also be used to show motive. For example, in Griffin v. State there was expert testimony that most of the personalty listed on an insurance claim as lost in the fire had not, in fact, been in the burned house. This sufficiently established a motive for the fire.

When the trial court implicitly accepts a witness's expert qualifications, the state is not required to make a formal tender of the witness as an expert. When a witness is qualified as an expert in fire investigation, he is qualified to testify regarding the whole field. Most importantly, an expert is permitted to testify that in his opinion a fire was incendiary in nature as opposed to accidental. The fact that the expert's opinion may be based in part on facts not in evidence goes to the weight, not the admissibility, of his opinion.

Unless the defendant has placed his character in issue or has raised some defense which the profile is relevant to rebut, the state may not introduce expert testimony of a serial arsonist profile, nor may the state introduce character evidence showing the defendant's personality traits and personal history as its foundation for demonstrating that the defendant has the characteristics of a typical serial arsonist.

Firefighters can testify to their own personal sensory perceptions, and, after Parker v. State, firefighters can even offer their opinions as to the nature of the fire. In Parker, a volunteer firefighter who had 17 or 18 years experience and had helped fight the fire in question characterized the circumstances surrounding the event as "peculiar." The court held that he was qualified by his experience to offer such an opinion and that it would help the jury in evaluating his observations. In Carr v. State, two firefighters testified about such matters as backdrafts, vapor explosions, fire origins, and the use of accelerants. The court found no abuse of the trial court's discretion in permitting them to testify as experts. Both witnesses had considerable experience as firefighters, 20 years for one and 13 for the other. In Morrow v. State, the court held that the fire chief was competent to testify as an expert witness in explosive devices. He had attended arson schools and had also received specific training on explosive devices. Having fought fires for over 20 years in various capacities, he had experiences with gasoline fires and explosives, including four bombs. Even though the fire chief did not consider his experiences extensive and did not consider himself an explosives expert, such expressions of doubt did not render him unqualified.

In Carr v. State, the state presented testimony that a dog, trained to indicate the presence of chemical accelerants, had alerted at the site of a fire where investigators had already come to believe an accelerant was used. The Georgia Supreme Court held that the dog alert testimony was expert testimony subject to the requirements of scientific verifiability. The average layperson would not have been able to determine from merely watching the dog that chemicals which could have accelerated a fire were present. It was only by the dog handler's analysis of the dog's behavior that the conclusion could have been reached that an accelerant was used. However, since dog alerts to accelerants have not been shown to have the scientific reliability necessary to permit their use as substantive evidence of the presence of accelerants, the dog alert testimony was inadmissible. Because there was no other direct evidence of the presence of an accelerant, and thus no direct evidence of arson, the trial court's ruling that the testimony was admissible was reversible error.

Prior to 1995, the state's failure to provide the defendant upon written request with a copy of a fire scene investigator's written report resulted in the report being excluded from evidence in the state's case-in-chief or in rebuttal. The proper remedy for the state's failure to provide the written report was the exclusion of the written report rather than the granting of a mistrial. Any report that was based on the fire scene investigator's general knowledge gleaned from experience and training rather than on any tests performed on material taken from the scene did not constitute a "scientific report" and did not have to be produced by the state upon written request by the defendant. Effective January 1, 1995, the state's disclosure of a fire scene investigator's written report is regulated by Georgia's 1994 criminal discovery provisions. If the state fails to comply with these discovery provisions, the trial court may order compliance, grant a continuance, or, upon a showing of prejudice and bad faith, prohibit the state from introducing a fire scene investigator's written report not disclosed to the defendant.

V. *Sufficiency of Evidence*

There is no clear line that can be drawn to show what evidence is sufficient and what evidence is not sufficient to convict. Because arson cases usually rest in large part on circumstantial evidence, the factual patterns are so varied that it is difficult to find any common denominators. Nevertheless, certain types of factual circumstances are more persuasive than others.

A. *Presence at Scene of Crime*

Testimony that the defendant was present at the site of the alleged burning immediately prior to its inception has proven highly convincing as to guilt. Such evidence, although insufficient in itself to seal the fate of the accused, is particularly persuasive in conjunction with other evidence of guilt, or when the proof of the corpus delicti is particularly forceful. For example, in Maddox v. State the defendant's alleged co-conspirator connected the defendant with the alleged arson, the defendant admitted being with the co-conspirator shortly before the fire, and a witness testified to seeing a yellow automobile like the one owned by the defendant in and around the site of the fire before and after its occurrence. Such evidence was sufficient to convict the defendant of arson. In Collins v. State, the dweller testified that when she heard her boyfriend knocking on her window on the night in question, she yelled at him to leave as she was not going to let him in. Shortly thereafter, she heard noises at the kitchen door and called the police, who arrived to find the pickup truck and garage on fire. The court found this evidence of the boyfriend's presence at the scene of the fire along with other evidence sufficient to convict him of first degree arson. In Griffin v. State, although the evidence was circumstantial, it was held to be sufficient to convict the defendant of arson. In addition to his presence at the scene of the crime, the evidence showed that the defendant might have been motivated to start the fire because of animosity toward his estranged spouse for taking furniture from the marital home. Furthermore, the defendant's unexplained presence at the house approximately 30 minutes before the fire, his unusual and frightening demeanor which caused the estranged spouse to leave the house immediately before the fire, and his instantaneous exit after the fire was started were all circumstances which the jury could have relied on in finding the defendant guilty beyond a reasonable doubt. In Patterson v. State, witnesses testified that they saw the defendants standing beside a parked car. About 25 minutes later when the witnesses drove past the scene again, they saw the car totally engulfed in flames. Although neither of the defendants was present at that time, they admitted driving the car to the scene. Law enforcement authorities investigated and determined that the car had been doused with a flammable liquid and set afire. This evidence along with other evidence was held sufficient to convict the defendants of second degree arson.

In Murden v. State, a neighboring apartment dweller saw the defendant break into the apartment and then leave ten minutes later. She noticed that smoke was billowing out of the apartment door. The burned apartment belonged to the defendant's ex-girlfriend and she testified that after the fire the defendant called her and said that he "wasn't through" with her yet and that he wished that she and her baby "was in flames." After noting the establishment of the corpus delicti, the court held that under these circumstances "mere presence" was enough to indicate that the defendant was criminally responsible for the fire. When the proof of the corpus delicti is weak, however, the court will reverse convictions even though presence is admitted by the defendant.

The relationship between the proof of the corpus delicti and the guilt of the accused is probably greater than the courts admit. It is rare for the court to hold the evidence sufficient to establish the corpus delicti, but not sufficient to establish the accused as the criminal agency responsible. Often when the court is uneasy about the guilt of the accused, the court will almost invariably express its dissatisfaction with the proof of the corpus delicti.

B. *Suspicious Conduct*

While suspicious conduct of the accused is often used to help establish guilt, the courts have required a high degree of proof. In Powell v. State, for example, the corpus delicti was clearly proven. The accused, the owner of the arsoned dwelling, attempted to recover from his insurer for his "lost" furniture. The evidence presented at trial, however, revealed that the accused had moved the furniture out of his house the day before the burning and was presently storing the furniture several miles away under the name of a friend. Such conduct was held to establish defendant's guilt clearly.

In Jones v. State, however, the defendant's conduct did not rise to a sufficient level of "suspiciousness." There the only evidence adduced was that a house burned and the defendants, shortly thereafter, were found in possession of cottonseed stolen from the house without any showing as to how recent the theft was. In Campbell v. State the court concluded that there was evidence only of the defendant's presence at the crime scene. The court noted a "conspicuous absence of any evidence to show intent, motive, participation, conspiracy, counseling or encouragement of another party." In Solomon v. State, the evidence raised a suspicion against the defendant but not enough to connect him to the arson. Thus, the evidence was insufficient to convict the defendant where it revealed that the defendant and his wife were in the process of a divorce, that both had motive, that the defendant's personal possessions had been destroyed by the fire while the wife's personal possessions had been removed before the fire, and that both the defendant and his wife had access to the home. In Collins v. State, the court held that while the defendants obviously had the opportunity to start the fire, the perceived absence of clothing and family photographs in the mobile home, combined with the presence of photographs and "important" papers in their car and in one of the defendants' purse, was insufficient to establish a motive for starting the fire. Without more, the fact that they had exclusive access to the property, as many if not most property owners do, raised no inference of incendiarism on their part.

C. Threats

A threat made by the defendant is extremely persuasive evidence. So long as the threat is of reasonable specificity and there is at least some other thread of probative evidence this may be sufficient. A showing of ill-will between accused and prosecutor, plus a specific threat to burn the prosecutor's dwelling has been held sufficient to convict. The establishment of bad feeling and a general threat of harm, however, has been held insufficient.

D. Financial Distress

For the arson of one's own property great stress has been placed on the financial circumstances of the owners. In Kennedy v. State the court pointed out that the appellant was having a slow time in his building business and had recently renewed an insurance policy on the log cabin which was the subject of the arson. In Powell v. State the appellate court emphasized the appellants' "difficult financial condition . . . prior to the fire." In affirming the conviction, the court characterized the evidence as consistent with the state theory that the appellants sought to destroy their home, replace it elsewhere and escape their creditors. In Stephens v. State, despite the father's claim that the fire began accidentally, the court held that the evidence was sufficient to authorize his conviction for arson. The evidence showed that he "had fallen on severe financial hard times" with his sole remaining asset being the insurance policy on his home. There was also sufficient evidence to authorize the conviction of his son as an aider and abettor. Evidence of his son's "own financial distress" established his son's motive for complicity in the scheme to commit arson. In Steidl v. State, although the defendant denied conspiring with the ex-boyfriend of his daughter to burn his own house down, the court held that the evidence was sufficient to authorize his conviction for arson. Moreover, evidence that the defendant was behind on his mortgage payment and behind on payments to numerous other creditors and that, prior to the fire, the defendant had commented that he could get out of debt with insurance money if the house were burned down established the defendant's motive for the arson. In these cases, it should be noted, there was strong evidence of criminal agency in the fires.

VI. Relationship to Other Offenses

Important Notice about Repudiation of Actual or Same Evidence Test: The Georgia Supreme Court repudiated the actual evidence test in *Drinkard v. Walker*, 281 Ga. 211, 636 S.E.2d 530 (2006), because it found this test to be inconsistent with the statutory framework governing the prohibition against multiple convictions for included offenses in Georgia. This inconsistency resulted in years of confusion and unpredictable results. In its place, the court adopted the required evidence test and overruled any prior case law that is inconsistent with it. Thus, any prior case law applying the actual evidence test is no longer controlling and should not be relied upon to determine whether one offense is included in another under § 16-1-6(1). The discussion of such case law is included below only insofar as it may still be applicable to pending prosecutions that arose before the Drinkard decision. See MULTIPLE CONVICTIONS, II. Tests to Determine Presence of Multiple Convictions, for a complete discussion of the Drinkard decision.

Criminal damage to property in the second degree may, on the particular allegations and proof, be a lesser included offense of arson in the first degree, thus authorizing a conviction of the former on an indictment for the latter. When the evidence establishes without conflict that arson in the first degree occurred, and the defendant simply denies being the one who committed it, the crime of criminal damage to property merges with the crime of arson, and no charge on the lesser crime is required. Second degree criminal damage to property is necessarily a lesser included offense of second degree arson, since it differs from second degree arson only in the respect that a less serious injury or risk of injury or a lesser degree of culpability suffices to establish its commission.

Arson in the second degree is not a lesser included offense of arson in the first degree, where it is unrefuted that the property alleged and proven to be burned was that property included or described in the first degree arson statute. Also, arson in the third degree which refers specifically to personal property is not necessarily a lesser included offense of arson in the first degree, even though there is evidence that personal property was burned along with the dwelling.

Where the evidence shows a series of incendiary acts involving the property interests of different entities, multiple counts of arson should not be merged into a single conviction. However, where the evidence shows a succession of incendiary acts involving a single residence, such conduct constitutes one act of arson, that of burning of the residence. Since there is only one crime of arson, multiple counts of arson should be merged into a single conviction.

If the offense of burglary is completed before the offense of arson is committed, the two offenses do not merge as a matter of fact or law. Since the same facts are not necessary to prove the commission of both offenses, the defendant may be properly convicted and sentenced for each offense.

Where the evidence shows that the defendant intended to set fire to a house and that he set fire to clothing, i.e., to personal property, as a "substantial step toward the commission of that crime," a charge on attempted first degree arson would be authorized.

VII. Punishment

In Georgia, all three degrees of arson are felonies. Under § 16-7-60, first degree arson is punishable by imprisonment for one to twenty years or up to a $50,000 fine, or both. Second degree arson, under § 16-7-61, is punishable by one to ten years' imprisonment or a fine of up to $25,000 or both. Third degree arson, under § 16-7-62, is punishable by a fine of not more than $10,000 or imprisonment of one to five years, or both.

VIII. Arson of Lands

A. Prohibited Conduct

Section 16-7-63 prohibits (1) starting, causing, or procuring another to start or cause a fire with intent to damage in any woodlands, brush, field, or other lands that are not one's own and without the permission of the owner or the lessee having control of such property; (2) burning any brush, field, forest land, campfire, or debris, whether on one's own land or the lands of another, without taking the necessary precautions before, during, and after the fire to prevent the escape of the fire onto the lands of another; (3) causing a fire by discarding any lighted cigarette, cigar, debris, or any other flaming or smoldering material that may cause a forest fire; or (4) destroying or damaging any material or device used in the detection or suppression of wildfires.

B. Punishment

The offenses described in items (2), (3), and (4) above are punishable as misdemeanors.

The arson of lands in the third degree as described item (1) above is punishable by a fine not to exceed $10,000 or by imprisonment for not less than one nor more than five years, or both.

If the arson of lands as described in item (1) above results in a fire that burns more than five acres that are not one's own, the offense is classified as arson of lands in the second degree punishable by a fine of not more than $25,000 or by imprisonment for not less than one nor more than ten years, or both.

If the arson of lands as described in item (1) above is committed under such circumstances that it was reasonably foreseeable that human life might be endangered, the offense is classified as arson of lands in the first degree punishable by a fine of not more than $50,000 or by imprisonment for not less than one nor more than 20 years, or both.

C. Exceptions

Section 16-7-63 does not apply to any fire resulting from the operation of transportation machinery or equipment used in its normal or accustomed manner.

ASSAULT

See ATTEMPT AND SOLICITATION; SEXUAL ASSAULT AGAINST PERSONS IN CUSTODY OR UNDER SUPERVISION OR CARE OF ANOTHER. See also RECKLESS CONDUCT AND RELATED OFFENSES.

I. Generally

The common law of assault has been codified in the separate statutory crimes of simple assault and aggravated assault. Simple assault can be committed either by attempting to inflict a violent injury upon another or by placing another in reasonable apprehension of immediately receiving a violent injury. Aggravated assault consists of conduct constituting an assault in conjunction with either (1) the intent to murder, rape, or rob, (2) the use of a deadly weapon, or (3) the discharge of a firearm from within a motor vehicle toward another person without legal justification. Assault with the intent to murder, rape, or rob can also be punished as an attempt, but was included in the assault statute "from a deference to tradition."

II. Simple Assault

A. Generally

There are two types of simple assault: (1) the attempted battery type and (2) the apprehension of harm type.

While it is likely that any attempt to commit a battery constitutes an assault, the statute requires an attempt to inflict a "violent injury," rather than an attempt to commit a battery. Section 16-5-23, defining simple battery, distinguishes between a battery committed by causing physical harm and one committed by an insulting or provoking physical contact, and the court of appeals has insisted that the two types are separate. It might be argued, therefore, that an attempt to commit a battery of the insulting or provoking type is not an attempt to inflict a violent injury, and thus not an assault.

B. Attempted Battery Type

Because the attempted battery type of assault is defined in terms of attempt, it carries with it the considerable theoretical baggage which accompanies the attempt statute. Like other attempts, attempted battery assault is a specific intent crime, and the state must establish that the defendant intended to commit a violent injury. In addition, the prosecution must show that the defendant's actions constituted a "substantial step" toward the commission of a battery; mere preparation will not suffice. Thus, if the actor curses another and picks up rocks as if to throw them, but makes no attempt actually to throw the rocks, it has been held that he has not gone beyond preparation and is not guilty of an attempted battery assault.

As with any other attempt, however, if the defendant has gone beyond preparation, it is irrelevant that he is prevented from completing the battery or that the completion of the battery was physically impossible. Thus, if the defendant approaches his victim menacingly, with a brick in his hand which he is prevented from throwing only by the victim's pretense that he is armed, he is guilty of an attempted battery type of simple assault. The fact question of whether there has been a substantial step before prevention will often be close.

C. Reasonable Apprehension of Harm Type

The other type of simple assault is committed when one person places another in reasonable apprehension of immediately receiving a violent injury. The absence of an intent requirement in the statute would indicate that only an intent to commit an act which in fact places another in reasonable apprehension of injury is required, and not a specific intent to cause such apprehension.

The principal focus of the cases is on the actus reus question of whether the defendant's actions could have placed his victim in reasonable apprehension of immediate injury. A mere threat to commit a violent injury upon the person of another does not necessarily constitute an assault. Before there is an assault, there must be a threat to the victim (whether verbalized by the defendant or implied by his conduct) coupled with the apparent present ability of the defendant to carry out that threat. Lack of actual ability to carry out the threat is irrelevant, so long as the defendant had the apparent ability to do so from the victim's perspective. For example, aiming a toy pistol at another might very well constitute an assault, if the state can demonstrate that the victim reasonably apprehended an immediate violent injury.

Since § 16-5-20(a)(2) requires that the actor place his victim in reasonable apprehension of receiving an immediate violent injury, there would seem to be no liability for a "conditional assault," or a threat to injure another upon some as yet unrealized condition. For example, the threat, "If you don't stay away from my daughter, I'll kill you," (spoken to an undesirable, but nonthreatening suitor), is conditional and should not alone impose liability for assault. The actor's conduct at the time the conditional threat is delivered, however, may place his victim in reasonable apprehension of immediate injury, even though his words evidence only a conditional intent. Thus, where the defendant was drunk and holding a pistol to the chin of his victim at the time he issued a conditional threat, his assault conviction was affirmed because the jury could find that, under the circumstances, his victim reasonably apprehended an immediate injury.

D. Similar Offenses

Prior violent conduct that is sufficiently similar to the charged offense of simple assault is admissible for the limited purpose of establishing the defendant's bent of mind and course of conduct.

IIA. Assault of Unborn Child

A person commits the offense of assault of an unborn child when he, without legal justification, attempts to inflict violent injury to an unborn child. For the purposes of this offense, an unborn child is a member of the species homo sapiens at any stage of development who is carried in the womb. It should be noted that this definition has not adopted the common law limitation that affords protection only to those unborn children who are so far developed as to be ordinarily called "quick," i.e., so far developed as to be able to move or stir in the mother's womb. Rather, it affords protection to all unborn children at any stage of development.

III. Aggravated Assault

A. Generally

Analytically, there are two components to the proof of any aggravated assault under § 16-5-21. First, the defendant must commit an assault. Second, the assault must be committed either (1) with an intent to murder, to rape, or to rob, (2) with a deadly weapon, or (3) by discharging a firearm from within a motor vehicle toward another person without legal justification.

B. Mens Rea

1. Intent to Murder, Rape, or Rob

An assault with intent to murder, rape, or rob is a specific intent offense; the mens rea requirement is the specific intent to commit the particular crime. Thus, the courts have warned that a conviction for assault with intent to murder is improper if the facts indicate that the homicide would have been voluntary manslaughter rather than murder had the victim died. If a defendant shoots at his victim "as the result of a sudden, violent, and irresistible passion resulting from serious provocation," and misses, there will be no conviction for assault with intent to murder, although there would probably be a conviction for assault with a deadly weapon.

Intent to rape, when it is an essential element of the aggravated assault, may be shown by circumstantial evidence. Where it is an essential element of the aggravated assault, the failure to define the offense of rape in a jury instruction constitutes reversible error.

A defendant's denial of any intention to rape the victim, followed by his spontaneous assertion that he was unable to do so, would be directly relevant to an aggravated assault charge against him. The fact that a portion of his statement may incidentally be unfavorable to him does not render it inadmissible.

A defendant's belief that the victim was a female and his actions taken toward the victim in an effort to commit a rape would be sufficient to establish his intent to rape (i.e., have carnal knowledge with a female). That the victim turned out to be male, rendering an actual rape impossible, would not affect his culpability. The defendant's belief that the victim was a female would support a conviction of aggravated assault with intent to rape.

2. *Specific vs. General Intent*

Assault with intent to murder and assault with a deadly weapon do not have identical mens rea requirements. Where the defendant is charged with assault with intent to murder, the assault, coupled with the specific intent to commit murder, is the crime. Proof that the method of assault used by the defendant constituted a deadly or offensive weapon would not be required.

An assault committed by means of a deadly or offensive weapon, unlike an assault committed with the intent to murder, does not require a specific criminal intent; rather it requires only a general criminal intent, which in the case of simple assault, an essential element of aggravated assault, is a general intent to injure. Thus, where the defendant is charged with the attempted battery type of deadly weapon aggravated assault, the defendant's general intent to injure is an element of the offense. Proof of the defendant's use of a deadly or offensive weapon with the intended consequence being the attempted or the completed injury to the victim would be sufficient for conviction. Where the defendant is charged with the reasonable apprehension type of deadly weapon aggravated assault, however, a general intent to injure is not an element of the offense. Proof of the defendant's use of a deadly or offensive weapon which placed the victim in reasonable apprehension of immediately receiving a violent injury would be sufficient for conviction. In this type of deadly weapon aggravated assault, the state must show the intention to commit the act of using the deadly weapon, not the intention to make the victims apprehensive.

It is not necessary to charge the jury that an intent to injure is an essential element of aggravated assault. A general charge on intent would be sufficient to enable the jury to apply it to an assault count.

3. *Transferred Intent*

Where one intends to assault a victim with a deadly weapon and in the course of that assault another victim is injured, the original intent is transferred in law to the other victim as well. This principle of transferred intent does not apply, however, if a person, as the result of an unprovoked assault, shoots at his assailant, but misses him and instead hits a bystander. No guilt would attach to that person because the assault upon him would justify his shooting at the assailant.

4. *Intentionally Firing Gun into Group of People or at Another*

When a defendant intentionally shoots several times into a group of people intending to harm only one of them, a jury would be authorized to find him guilty of aggravated assault against each person in the group.

Firing shots with the intention of frightening a group of people establishes as a matter of law the offense of aggravated assault. Likewise, intentionally firing a gun at another, absent justification, is sufficient in and of itself to support a conviction of aggravated assault.

5. *Criminal Intent vs. Criminal Negligence*

Because the attempted battery type of deadly weapon aggravated assault cannot be committed by criminal negligence, a charge that criminal negligence can substitute for criminal intent would be error. Criminal intent and criminal negligence are not interchangeable in those instances where the mental culpability of the actor is the essential element that distinguishes two separate crimes, with separate penalties, for committing the same behavior. Such an instance exists with the attempted battery type of deadly weapon aggravated assault and reckless conduct: where the proscribed conduct is the result of the actor's criminal intent, the General Assembly has determined that the offense constitutes the felony of aggravated assault whereas that same conduct which is the result of the actor's criminal negligence supports a conviction only of reckless conduct.

A charge that criminal negligence can substitute for criminal intent would also be error for the reasonable apprehension type of deadly weapon aggravated assault. Because it is the state of mind of the victim that determines whether an aggravated assault of this type has been committed, there is no reason for a charge on criminal negligence at all.

6. Knowledge of Victim's Status as Peace Officer

An essential element of aggravated assault on a peace officer is that the defendant knew the victim was a peace officer. Thus, the jury must be charged that knowledge is an essential element of the crime.

However, where an indictment charges a defendant with felony murder predicated on an aggravated assault against a sheriff's deputy, the identification of the victim as a law enforcement officer would describe neither the murder charge nor the manner in which it was committed. Therefore, this identification would not be a material averment in the indictment and would not need to be proven, and it would be proper for the trial court to deny a defendant's motion for a jury instruction that the state bears the burden of proving beyond a reasonable doubt that the defendant knew that the victim was a law enforcement officer engaged in the performance of his duties at the time of the shooting.

7. Evidence Illustrating Motive, Intent, Plan, Scheme, Bent of Mind, or Course of Conduct

The following evidence has been held admissible to illustrate the defendant's motive, intent, plan, scheme, bent of mind, or course of conduct in committing an aggravated assault: (1) a conviction for a prior aggravated assault of a similar nature; (2) a conviction for a prior sexual offense similar in nature to a charge of aggravated assault with intent to rape; (3) a guilty plea to a prior voluntary manslaughter charge involving a stabbing incident of a similar nature; (4) evidence of prior difficulties, threats, or confrontations against the particular victim; (5) where the victim is the defendant's wife, evidence regarding the defendant's marital separations and relationship with another woman; (6) evidence of the defendant's previous beating of his spouse or mate; (7) evidence of a domestic situation in which the defendant demanded a sexual favor then assaulted the victim when she refused; (8) where the victim is a woman with whom the defendant is sexually and emotionally involved, a conviction for the prior murder of his wife; (9) evidence concerning the defendant's alleged participation in satanic worship; (10) evidence explaining gang culture; and (11) evidence concerning the defendant's expression of racial bias some time before the shooting.

If the defendant's previous conviction involved a different offense, a different victim, and was committed at a different time and in a different manner, his previous conviction is not admissible to show his state of mind in committing an aggravated assault.

C. Actus Reus

1. Assault with Intent to Murder, Rape, or Rob

The actus reus of the "assault with intent" type of aggravated assault was clarified in Bissell v. State. In this case where the defendant was charged with aggravated assault with intent to rape, the court reasoned that there is a "substantial step" requirement within this type of aggravated assault, but it relates to the simple assault element only. Thus, it is necessary for a conviction for aggravated assault to show a substantial step toward the commission of a battery, i.e., a simple assault. However, once that substantial step toward a battery is proven, it becomes aggravated assault so long as it was accompanied by an intent to commit rape. It need not be accompanied by a substantial step toward a rape. In fact, if there was a substantial step, the court said, "the crime would then become attempted rape." The court's conclusion, therefore, was that the actus reus of the "assault with intent" version of aggravated assault is the same as that for simple assault, with the only difference between the two crimes being the mens rea.

Where the charge is the "assault with intent" type of aggravated assault, the state is required to prove the commission of an assault with the intent to accomplish the more serious crime. The state is not required to prove the victim's reasonable apprehension of harm nor the likelihood that the weapon used would result in serious bodily injury.

2. Assault with a Deadly or Offensive Weapon

a. Types of Weapon

The great majority of aggravated assault cases involve the use of a weapon. There are two types of weapon under the statute: (1) a weapon that is deadly as a matter of law and (2) an object that, when used offensively, is likely to or actually does result in serious bodily injury. If the defendant is charged with committing the aggravated assault with a weapon that is deadly as a matter of law, it is inappropriate for the trial court to instruct the jury that deadly weapon aggravated assault is committed when the deadly weapon is "used offensively." The offensive use of a weapon applies only to an aggravated assault committed with an offensive weapon and does not apply to an aggravated assault committed with a weapon that is deadly as a matter of law.

Since an aggravated assault committed with an offensive weapon may be committed in more than one way, it is sufficient for the state to show that it was committed in any one of the separate ways listed in the indictment, even if the indictment uses the conjunctive rather than disjunctive form. Thus, where the evidence is sufficient to show that the defendant violated the statute in at least one of the ways alleged in the indictment, there is no fatal variance.

While the courts have been reluctant to hold that anything other than a firearm used as such is per se a deadly weapon, they have held that hands, fists, feet, dogs, lamps, shoes, blackjacks, motor vehicles, knives or pocketknives, waterbugs, metal pipes, small logs, cigarette lighters, lit cigarettes in conjunction with gasoline, and ceramic statues may be deadly or offensive weapons, depending upon the circumstances. Where a question exists as to whether an object could serve as a deadly or offensive weapon, it is proper for the trial court to define for the jury what constitutes a deadly or offensive weapon. The determination of whether a weapon is deadly or offensive is to be made by the jury, considering the manner in which the weapon was used.

It is not necessary for the state to admit into evidence the deadly weapon used by the defendant in order for the defendant to be found guilty of aggravated assault. Evidence of the victim's injuries, if any, may be used to show the weapon's deadliness. In the absence of any direct evidence that a deadly weapon was used in the assault against the victim, a jury can reasonably infer from evidence of the victim's injuries that the victim was indeed assaulted with a deadly weapon. However, there is no requirement that the victim actually be injured by the deadly weapon before a conviction for aggravated assault is authorized. Where the victim never actually received a violent injury, the jury's determination of whether the weapon was deadly would obviously have to be based upon factors other than the nature and extent of the victim's injuries.

b. Perception of Weapon's Deadliness

The determination of a weapon's deadliness depends upon whether the defendant is charged with deadly weapon aggravated assault or intent to murder aggravated assault. In the law of murder, the use of a deadly weapon is often used as evidence of an intent to kill, and the same is true where the charge is aggravated assault with the intent to murder. The Court of Appeals has indicated that in such cases the deadliness of the weapon is to be determined from the defendant's viewpoint, depending upon his perception of the weapon and its capabilities.

Where the charge is deadly weapon aggravated assault, however, it is the victim's reasonable apprehension of harm by an assault with a deadly weapon that establishes the crime of aggravated assault. The focus is on the victim's reasonable perception of the weapon, so that, for example, a shotgun which the defendant knows is missing its trigger and is incapable of firing would be a deadly weapon for purposes of deadly weapon aggravated assault if the victim reasonably perceived it as a normally functioning lethal weapon, even though it would not be a deadly weapon for purposes of establishing an intent to kill. This analysis, however, should apply only to a deadly weapon aggravated assault of the reasonable apprehension type. The victim's perception would hardly be relevant in the attempted battery type of deadly weapon aggravated assault.

c. Types of Assault

There are two types of deadly weapon aggravated assault under the statute: (1) the reasonable apprehension type and (2) the attempted battery type. In order to sustain a conviction of the first type, the state must demonstrate that the victim reasonably apprehended an immediate violent injury. In most instances, the victim's testimony that he saw a weapon and evidence of his reaction to it will articulate this type of deadly weapon aggravated assault. In order to sustain a conviction of the second type, the state must demonstrate that the defendant attempted to injure the victim. The victim's perception of the weapon and his reaction to it are irrelevant in this type of deadly weapon aggravated assault. Instead, the evidence must show that the defendant intended to commit a violent injury to the person of the victim and that the defendant's actions constituted an attempt toward the commission of that violent injury. Where an indictment sufficiently alleges deadly weapon aggravated assault of either type, the trial court may instruct the jury on both types of deadly weapon aggravated assault.

When in issue, the state of mind of the victim, including whether the victim had been placed under reasonable apprehension of injury or fear from an event, may be proved by indirect or circumstantial evidence. The victim's reasonable apprehension of a violent injury may be inferred from the conduct of the victim. Although the victim may not testify as to his apprehension and although the threat accompanying the use of the deadly weapon may have been indicative only of a conditional threat to inflict bodily harm, the jury can still determine from the circumstances that the victim, with a deadly weapon pointed at him, was in reasonable apprehension of immediately receiving a violent injury. The fact that a victim not available to testify at trial was severely wounded as a result of a shooting would certainly support an inference that he was placed in reasonable apprehension of his immediate safety. A victim who felt the flash and pressure of the weapon when it was fired could be found to be in reasonable apprehension of harm even though the weapon was not pointed at him. Also, a victim who heard a shot and fell to the ground to avoid being shot at again could be found to be in reasonable apprehension of immediately receiving a violent injury. Likewise, a victim, having fled for fear of being shot, could be found to be in reasonable apprehension of receiving a violent injury, even though he was not in the presence of the weapon when it was fired. A victim who continuously fought her armed attacker while screaming "Help me, God, help me Jesus, help me God, help me" could be found to be in reasonable apprehension of physical harm. Although the victim's awareness is not an essential element of the crime of aggravated assault, it has been held that a victim that was unquestionably asleep or passed out during the time of an aggravated assault could not have been placed in apprehension of receiving an injury. The corroboration of the victim's testimony is not required to prove deadly weapon aggravated assault.

A reasonable apprehension of harm cannot support an aggravated assault conviction without some evidence that the apprehension was aggravated by the defendant's use of a weapon. Absent any evidence that the defendant actually used a weapon against the victim, he cannot be found to have committed deadly weapon aggravated assault.

Since deadly weapon aggravated assault of the reasonable apprehension type is based upon the victim's perception of the assailant's weapon and her reaction to it and not upon the victim's fear of the assailant, a statement by the victim that she was not afraid of her assailant does not demand a verdict of acquittal for the assailant.

The aggravated assault statute does not differentiate between offensive and defensive threats of immediate bodily harm.

d. Possession of Weapon

In order to establish the crime of aggravated assault by the use of a firearm, there must be sufficient evidence that the defendant possessed the firearm. However, the state is not required to prove the victim was aware of the defendant's possession, nor is it required to produce physical evidence of gunfire, such as bullets, bullet holes, or expended shells, in order to establish this crime.

e. Firing Weapon into Group of People

Regardless of the number of shots fired, the act of firing a weapon into a group of people makes each individual in the group a separate victim. Where the defendant has been found guilty of multiple counts of aggravated assault under these circumstances, his convictions would not merge because the assaults were committed upon different victims.

f. Criminal Agency

Whether the victim's gunshot wound was self-inflicted or the result of the defendant's assault with a deadly weapon is a question for the jury to determine.

D. Party to Crime

A person who engages another in a fistfight while the other is simultaneously being beaten with an object by the person's confederate necessarily "aids and abets" the confederate in his assault upon the other, and is therefore a party to the crime committed by the confederate.

It is not necessary to place a weapon in the defendant's hands to find him guilty of being a party to the crime of aggravated assault.

Whether the defendant participated in an aggravated assault with intent to rob or abandoned the enterprise or was merely present is for the jury to determine.

E. Indictments

An indictment for aggravated assault which does not recite language from the Code must allege every essential element of the crime charged. An indictment which merely alleges that the accused used his hands in the commission of an assault fails to set forth the essential elements of aggravated assault. It fails to state that the accused attempted to use his hands as a deadly weapon or that he attempted to rape, rob, or murder the victim. Moreover, it fails to state that the accused intended to inflict a violent injury on the victim or that he placed the victim in reasonable apprehension of being injured violently. Without allegations setting forth the essential elements, the indictment is fatally defective and void, and incapable of supporting a conviction.

An indictment alleging an assault by use of an instrument which is not a deadly weapon per se is not required to be more specific regarding its use than indictments charging assault with an instrument which is a deadly weapon per se, as even the latter type of weapon, including guns, can be used in more than one way to commit an assault. So long as the indictment contains the necessary elements of the assault charged and clearly apprises the defendant of the allegation he must be prepared to defend against, the absence of language about the instrument's use can not be deemed to have rendered the indictment so vague as to be deficient.

Because the aggravated assault statute requires proof of only one act, inclusion in the indictment of more than one such act is mere surplusage, which is unnecessary to constitute the offense, need not be proved, and may be disregarded. Moreover, when an indictment alleges that an aggravated assault was committed by two means, the state need prove only one of the two acts constituting the crime to sustain a conviction.

An indictment charging a defendant in the statutory language of aggravated assault does not need to additionally charge in the language of simple assault in order to withstand demurrer.

Where the indictment charges the defendant with aggravated assault under § 16-5-21(a)(2), which requires only a showing of a general intent to injure, it would not be void for failing to expressly allege the criminal intent.

Where an indictment charges a defendant with committing an aggravated assault by one specific method, the defendant cannot be convicted of that offense based on a totally different, unspecified method. To do so would violate the defendant's rights under the Due Process Clause.

F. Jury Instructions

It is not necessary that a charge on simple assault be given in order to complete the definition of aggravated assault. The latter does not need the former to make it complete. It has been held, however, that where the defendant has been charged with assaulting the victim "with a firearm, a deadly weapon, by pointing said weapon at said person," a jury charge on deadly weapon aggravated assault that fails to include the requisite elements of assault is clearly inadequate. The offense could easily be confused with the misdemeanor offense of pointing a pistol at another. Under such a charge, there is a high probability that the jury would not be informed of the elements of aggravated assault sufficiently to determine whether the state has met its burden of proof.

Where an indictment charges the defendant with committing an aggravated assault by a specific method, a charge to the jury that aggravated assault may be committed by alternative methods, emphasizing a method of committing the crime not specified in the indictment, is reversible error. Yet the charge as a whole would not be erroneous if the trial court has also given a curative instruction limiting the jury's consideration to the method specified in the indictment or if the trial court has read the indictment verbatim to the jury. However, it should be noted that reading the charge as set forth in the indictment may not, under some circumstances, prevent the jury from being misled.

When the language of an indictment charges the defendant with causing the death of the victim "by shooting," it raises the possibility of aggravated assault both with a deadly weapon and intent to murder. As the language of such an indictment would be sufficient to put a defendant on notice of both grounds for aggravation, jury instructions that aggravated assault, as the underlying felony for a felony murder count, could be established with either "intent to murder" or use of a "deadly weapon" would be proper.

A charge stating that the term "serious bodily injury" as used in the aggravated assault statute means such injury as is likely to cause "death or great bodily harm" as used in the self-defense statute would not be a complete and correct statement of the law on aggravated assault and thus should not be given to a jury.

An instruction to the jury on the commission of aggravated assault by use of a deadly weapon that states that "[a] firearm when used as such is a deadly weapon as a matter of law" is a correct statement of the law and does not improperly direct a finding on the question of intent.

IV. Relationship to Other Offenses

Important Notice about Repudiation of Actual or Same Evidence Test: The Georgia Supreme Court repudiated the actual evidence test in *Drinkard v. Walker*, 281 Ga. 211, 636 S.E.2d 530 (2006), because it found this test to be inconsistent with the statutory framework governing the prohibition against multiple convictions for included offenses in Georgia. This inconsistency resulted in years of confusion and unpredictable results. In its place, the court adopted the required evidence test and overruled any prior case law that is inconsistent with it. Thus, any prior case law applying the actual evidence test is no longer controlling and should not be relied upon to determine whether one offense is included in another under § 16-1-6(1). The discussion of such case law is included below only insofar as it may still be applicable to pending prosecutions that arose before the Drinkard decision. See MULTIPLE CONVICTIONS, II. Tests to Determine Presence of Multiple Convictions, for a complete discussion of the Drinkard decision.

Prior to 1968, former GCA § 27-2508 provided that a person could not be convicted of assault with intent to commit an offense or of an attempt to commit an offense if it appeared that the crime intended or attempted was actually consummated. This rule was reversed by § 16-5-22, relating to assaults with the intent to commit an offense, and § 16-4-2, pertaining to attempts, which together were held to have repealed former GCA § 27-2508 by implication. The only limitation imposed by § 16-5-22 is that the defendant may not be convicted of both the assault and the completed crime.

There is no law authorizing the conviction for an attempt to commit a deadly weapon aggravated assault which itself is a particular type of attempt to commit a crime.

Stalking is not "in essence a common law assault." Since the act and intent elements of stalking differ from those of assault, it is clear that Georgia's stalking law proscribes intentional actions not covered by the assault statutes. Because of the differences between the two crimes, the rationale which makes attempted assault a legal impossibility and an absurdity does not apply to attempted stalking. Thus, attempted stalking is punishable as a criminal offense.

There is a great deal of case law concerning assault as a lesser included offense of other crimes. It is often advantageous for the defendant to have assault declared to be a lesser included offense of the indicted crime because it gives the jury an opportunity to render a "compromise" verdict, convicting the defendant for a lesser crime than that originally charged.

Georgia courts have held that simple assault is not necessarily a lesser included offense of deadly weapon aggravated assault. This is because the use of a deadly weapon elevates any simple assault into an aggravated assault.

A defendant is not entitled to a jury instruction on simple assault as a lesser included offense where the jury can find only an aggravated assault or no assault at all. Such would be the case where a deadly weapon was concededly or clearly involved in the assault or where the defendant's defense is essentially that no aggravated assault occurred. There are situations, however, when the record will support an instruction on simple assault. For example, if the deadly nature of the weapon used in an assault case is a contested issue, the defendant is entitled to an instruction on simple assault as a lesser included offense.

It has been held, for purposes of authorizing instruction and conviction of a lesser offense, that an offense is a lesser included offense of another offense if it is either necessarily included in the greater offense (that is, if all the essential elements of the lesser offense must necessarily be established as part of proving the commission of the greater offense) or if all the necessary elements of the lesser offense are alleged in the particular indictment charging the greater offense. The courts have held that the offenses of carrying a pistol without a license, carrying a concealed weapon, reckless conduct, and simple battery are not necessarily included in the offense of aggravated assault, and that the crime of terroristic threats and acts is not necessarily included in assault with intent to murder. Also, it has been held that simple assault is not a lesser included offense of terroristic threats, and that affray, as statutorily defined, is not a lesser included offense of aggravated assault.

Where there is no evidence that the defendant was merely firing at an occupied vehicle, a trial court's refusal to give a requested charge on terroristic acts as a lesser included offense of aggravated assault is not error.

Although it may be possible for simple assault to be a lesser included offense of child molestation, where the undisputed evidence shows that the defendant committed the crime of child molestation by fondling the victim with the requisite intent, a trial court's refusal to give a requested charge on simple assault as a lesser included offense is not error.

While aggravated assault with intent to commit rape may be a lesser included offense of rape in some cases, it is not so in every case because in many instances the offense of rape may undoubtedly be completed without the commission of an independent aggravated assault. The crime of aggravated assault with intent to rape is complete when there is a "substantial step" toward a battery of the victim, i.e., an assault, coupled with intent to rape. If there is a substantial step toward the rape itself, the crime would then become attempted rape. The acquittal of aggravated assault with intent to rape does not "necessarily include" a finding against rape. The offense for aggravated assault with intent to rape does not merge with the offense of burglary. The offense of aggravated assault with a deadly weapon does not merge with the offense of aggravated assault with intent to rape as a matter of fact where the aggravated assault with a deadly weapon was complete when the defendant grabbed the victim in the living room and wielded the knife, and where the subsequent aggravated assault with intent to rape occurred in the bedroom when the defendant bound the victim and made threatening statements concerning rape while the knife was on the dresser near his hand. The offense of child molestation does not merge with the offense of aggravated assault with intent to rape where the evidence shows that after the defendant pulled the victim's panties down and exposed his penis, he attempted to penetrate the victim's vagina with his penis. Aggravated assault and rape are separate offenses and do not merge, where the evidence used to prove the aggravated assault is not used to prove the force element of the rape. Where the evidence shows either the commission of the completed offense of aggravated assault with intent to rape or the commission of no offense, there is no error in the trial court's failure to charge the jury on the lesser offenses of battery and simple battery.

Where the offense constituting cruelty to children is based upon and committed in a way different from the offenses of child molestation and assault with intent to rape and is not satisfied by the introduction of the same evidence, there is no merger and the trial court may enter a separate conviction on cruelty to children.

Since the "assault" element of aggravated assault with intent to rob is contained within the "use of an offensive weapon" element of armed robbery and both crimes share the "intent to rob" element, there is no element of aggravated assault with intent to rob that is not contained in armed robbery. Therefore, an aggravated assault with intent to rob conviction would merge into an armed robbery conviction.

Aggravated assault with intent to rob would be necessarily included in armed robbery, but neither deadly weapon aggravated assault nor aggravated assault with intent to murder is necessarily included in armed robbery. Aggravated assault is not a lesser included offense of armed robbery as a matter of law, although it may be included as a matter of fact. Also, aggravated assault is not included in attempted armed robbery as a matter of law, although these two offenses may merge as a matter of fact. However, where the underlying facts show that one crime was completed prior to the second crime, so that the crimes are separate as a matter of law, there is no merger. Robbery by intimidation does not merge with aggravated assault with intent to rob as a matter of fact where the acts described by the victim constituted separate offenses. It also has been held that two simple assaults were separate offenses and were not as a matter of fact merely lesser included offenses of the offense of armed robbery. The crime of conspiracy to commit armed robbery does not merge with the crime of aggravated assault where the facts necessary to prove the conspiracy to commit armed robbery are not the same facts necessary to prove the aggravated assault. Because the offenses of robbery by force and aggravated assault on a person over the age of 65 years have different elements and prohibit different conduct, neither is included in the other as a matter of law. Nor are they included as a matter of fact where the state proves each offense by different facts.

Section 16-11-102 is not in conflict with, and does not take precedence over, §§ 16-5-20(a)(2) and 16-5-21(a)(2). The aggravated assault definition includes an element not contained in the pointing of a firearm definition, specifically: a resulting reasonable apprehension of immediate violent injury. Thus, if the victim is not placed in reasonable apprehension of immediate violent injury by the pointing of the firearm, only the misdemeanor of pointing a firearm (and not the felony of aggravated assault) has been committed. This would be the case where the victim was completely unaware that a firearm was pointed at him. On the other hand, if the pointing of the firearm placed the victim in reasonable apprehension of immediate violent injury, the felony of aggravated assault has occurred.

Where the evidence establishes either that the defendant committed the offenses of aggravated assault and murder by intentionally shooting and killing the victim or that he committed no offense at all because the pistol discharged accidentally, the trial court is not required to charge the jury regarding the offense of pointing a pistol at another as a lesser included offense of aggravated assault.

A charge of aggravated assault on a peace officer merges into a mutiny in a penal institution conviction because the aggravated assault charge is established by proof of less than all the facts required to establish the commission of mutiny.

In Jackson v. State, where the defendant struck a peace officer with a metal chair, the court held that the acquittal of the defendant of aggravated assault upon a peace officer does not compel the conclusion that the defendant did not act with the intent to cause serious bodily injury to the peace officer, since in aggravated assault upon a peace officer the court looks to the means by which one attempts to inflict injury; in the crime of mutiny in a penal institution, the court looks to the intended result.

Where an indictment alleging aggravated assault on a peace officer sufficiently puts the defendant on notice that he might be convicted of the lesser offense of felony obstruction of an officer and the evidence presented at trial would support such a charge, the trial court, upon written request, must charge the jury on the lesser included offense of felony obstruction. However, where there is overwhelming evidence that the defendant committed the aggravated assault, the failure to give the requested charge is harmless error.

Where the same conduct that proves aggravated assault on a police officer proves obstruction of the same officer, the two offenses merge for sentencing purposes and the defendant can be sentenced for only one.

Because the offense of leaving the scene of an accident has different elements than the offense of aggravated assault on a police officer, the two offenses do not merge as a matter of law.

Simple kidnapping and aggravated assault are not included in one another as a matter of law. Since simple kidnapping is consummated when the victim is seized, a prior or subsequent aggravated assault against the victim would constitute a crime separate from the kidnapping as a matter of fact. However, where an aggravated assault provides the "bodily injury" for a kidnapping with bodily injury charge, the two offenses legally merge.

Under the required evidence test, aggravated assault, aggravated battery, and kidnapping each require proof of at least one different element. Where the state presents independent evidence to prove each of these individual crimes as set forth in the indictment, the aggravated assault and aggravated battery can not be considered part of the single completed act of kidnapping with bodily injury and therefore do not merge with the kidnapping charge.

As a matter of law, aggravated assault with intent to rob is not a lesser included offense of kidnapping with bodily injury. The two offenses share no essential elements.

Where hijacking and kidnapping convictions are supported by different and additional facts from those supporting a conviction for aggravated assault, there is no merger of the offenses as a matter of fact.

If the evidence establishing false imprisonment is not used up in proving an aggravated assault charge, the two crimes, although occurring sequentially, constitute separate offenses since each is established by proof of different facts, i.e., each offense is a completed crime when the next is perpetrated on the victim.

Whether assault or aggravated assault is a lesser included offense in another offense (or whether another offense is included in aggravated assault) may also depend upon the allegations of the indictment in any particular case. If the indictment, in the course of setting forth the crime charged, alleges all the necessary elements of an assault, for example, then assault is a lesser included offense in that case, although it might not be in another case involving different factual allegations.

Although the element of physical or bodily harm is a requisite for battery, where the physical or bodily harm is committed with a deadly weapon, battery is not a lesser included offense. Where the indictment alleges assault with a deadly weapon and the evidence shows that an assault was committed with a deadly weapon, aggravated assault is proved beyond a reasonable doubt, and the evidence does not support a finding that the defendant committed a battery. Therefore, a trial court is not required to charge the jury on battery as a lesser included offense.

Where the facts adduced to support an aggravated assault charge in an indictment are the same facts used to support an aggravated battery charge in an indictment, the aggravated assault is a lesser included offense of the aggravated battery and the defendant may be convicted only for the aggravated battery. Where the aggravated assault and the aggravated battery are established by proof of different facts, the offenses do not merge in fact and the defendant may be convicted and sentenced for both offenses.

The rule of lenity applies when two statutes governing the same conduct are conflicting with respect to their prescribed punishments, i.e., where one statute punishes the same conduct to a lesser degree than the other statute. In such a situation, a defendant would be entitled to have the lesser of two penalties administered. Since aggravated assault and aggravated battery are both felonies, differing grades of punishment are not involved. Thus, the rule of lenity would not apply to a defendant's sentences for aggravated assault and aggravated battery.

If the aggravated assault of the victim is independent of the act causing the victim's death, the aggravated assault does not merge into the malice murder as a matter of fact. Moreover, if, in order to establish that the defendant committed aggravated assault as pled in the indictment, the state is required to show not only that he shot the victim but that he did so with the intent to rob him, the aggravated assault would not be established by proof of the same or less than all the facts required to establish proof of malice murder. Thus, the two crimes would not merge as a matter of fact. However, if the aggravated assault and murder of the victim arise out of the same act, a defendant's conviction on the aggravated assault charge would merge into the murder conviction.

Although attempt to commit murder and deadly weapon aggravated assault are two different crimes as a matter of law, because the one crime requires proof that the defendant intended to commit murder whereas the other crime does not require proof of such specific intent, deadly weapon aggravated assault merges into attempt to commit murder as a matter of fact where both crimes are based on allegations in the indictment that the defendant assaulted the victim with a deadly weapon and where each crime is established by proof of the same facts.

Where the evidence shows completion only of the greater offense of felony murder, that is, there is no evidence from which the jury can conclude that death resulted from a cause other than the aggravated assault inflicted by the defendant, the trial court is not required to offer aggravated assault to the jury as a lesser option.

Where the defendant is convicted of the voluntary manslaughter of one victim and the aggravated assault of another victim, the convictions do not merge as a matter of fact, even though only one shot was fired, striking both victims. One crime is not included within another if each crime affects a different victim. Thus, verdicts of guilty of voluntary manslaughter as to one victim and aggravated assault as to the other victim will be upheld.

Where there was one act committed upon one victim at the same time, either intentionally or accidentally, convictions of aggravated assault and involuntary manslaughter would be mutually exclusive verdicts. It would therefore be proper for the trial court to instruct the jury to continue deliberating on these two charges.

If evidence presented at trial supports allegations in an indictment that the defendant pointed a gun at the victim and threatened to shoot the victim, the jury would be authorized to find either that the defendant used a gun to place the victim in reasonable apprehension of immediately receiving a violent injury or that the defendant threatened to commit a crime of violence with the purpose of terrorizing the victim. In such a case, the offense of terroristic threats is included in the offense of aggravated assault with a deadly weapon as a matter of fact.

If the evidence does not show that two aggravated assaults upon the same victim were committed in a continuous and uninterrupted act but shows that one aggravated assault was completed before the other occurred, the two aggravated assaults are separate offenses and do not merge.

The aggravated assault and criminal trespass statutes differ in the classification of the interests that each statute seeks to protect: the person placed in reasonable apprehension of receiving serious bodily injury in the case of aggravated assault and the property of another in the case of criminal trespass. Thus, criminal trespass is not a lesser included offense of aggravated assault as a matter of law. Furthermore, inasmuch as an indictment alleges deadly weapon aggravated assault and therefore does not require the state to prove that the defendant interfered with the victim's property, criminal trespass is not a lesser included offense as a matter of fact.

Criminal damage to property in the first degree, which involves the deliberate and unauthorized interference with property, is not a lesser included offense of aggravated assault as a matter of law.

Because the elements of interference with government property are not included in the elements required for aggravated assault, the two offenses do not merge as a matter of law.

The offenses of aggravated stalking and aggravated assault do not merge as a matter of fact where the stalking is completed before the assault occurs.

Aggravated assault with a motor vehicle and hit-and-run with that same vehicle are not mutually exclusive verdicts. Duality is not an impossibility.

Reckless driving is a crime founded upon an act of criminal negligence rather than an intentional act. Aggravated assault with a motor vehicle, which is based on attempting to commit a violent injury to the person of another under § 16-5-20(a)(1), requires a finding of an intentional infliction of injury, which precludes the element of criminal negligence in reckless driving. Accordingly, a verdict of guilt as to aggravated assault with a motor vehicle based on § 16-5-20(a)(1) would be mutually exclusive with a verdict of guilt as to serious injury by vehicle predicated on reckless driving.

Because discharging a firearm near a public street is not a lesser included offense of aggravated assault, a trial court commits no error by refusing to merge the offenses during sentencing.

Although the weapon used to assault the victim is stolen, the offense of theft by receiving stolen property does not merge into the offense of aggravated assault as a matter fact because the theft offense requires proof that the defendant knew or should have known that the weapon was stolen. No such proof is required for an aggravated assault conviction.

The offense of possession of a firearm by a convicted felon does not merge into the offense of aggravated assault as a matter of fact because the possession offense requires proof that the defendant was a convicted felon, while the assault offense does not.

Instructing a jury that if they find the defendant guilty of deadly weapon aggravated assault, they necessarily have to find the defendant guilty of possession of a weapon during the commission of a crime is harmful error. Such an instruction prevents the jury from independently considering whether or not the defendant is guilty of the possession charge. A trial court cannot direct the jury to return a verdict of guilty in a criminal case no matter what the law or the evidence would require.

V. *Defenses and Exemptions*

A. *Simple Assault and Aggravated Assault*

Perhaps the most important of the defenses available in an assault or aggravated assault prosecution are the justification defenses set forth in Article 2 of Chapter 3 of Title 16, such as self-defense, defense of another, defense of property, and lawful arrest. Because of their importance and general applicability, these defenses are considered in separate topics of this work.

Since 1833 the law of Georgia has provided that: A person charged with simple assault or simple battery may introduce in evidence any opprobrious or abusive language used by the person against whom force was threatened or used and the trier of facts may, in its discretion, find that the words used were justification for simple assault or simple battery.

Section 16-5-25 is based upon a legislative determination that a person should not be held criminally liable when his passions are aroused by the abusive language of another, so long as the force employed is not disproportionate to the provocation which brought it about. The defense is available only to one charged with simple assault or simple battery, and it is not error to refuse an instruction on § 16-5-25 where the defendant is charged with murder or aggravated assault.

In determining whether the words used justified an assault or battery, the jury may consider circumstances such as the relative size and strength of the defendant and the victim, the degree of force used, and the initial use of abusive language by the defendant. The opprobrious language justifying an assault or battery must have been used in the defendant's presence and immediately prior to the assault, and, thus, words published in a newspaper will not justify an assault, even if they are "republished" by a statement such as "I put the publication in the paper as a man, and am responsible for it."

The defense has been fairly strictly construed. Grimaces or facial expressions of contempt are not "opprobrious or abusive language" which may justify an assault or battery, and the section is not a defense to a citation for criminal contempt for assaulting a witness in the courtroom. The defense is also unavailable to a police officer who assaults his prisoner, and insulting language used by a small child will not justify an assault by an adult upon the child.

Lack of knowledge of the victim's status as a police officer may be relevant in Georgia, as it is even in the federal system, to establish a defense of either self-defense or defense of others. Thus, if a defendant assaults an undercover officer while resisting arrest because he mistakenly believes the officer to be a private citizen, the facts should be examined to determine whether the use of force would have been justified against a private citizen. If so, then the defendant should not be punished for assault at all.

In a domestic dispute, a sibling who commits a simple assault or an aggravated assault against another sibling living or formerly living in the same household would be exempt from the enhanced punishment prescribed by the Crimes Against Family Members Act of 1999. Furthermore, a parent, guardian, or person acting in loco parentis who administers corporal punishment to a child would be exempt from the Act's enhanced punishment for simple assault. However, if the corporal punishment constitutes an aggravated assault, the parent would not be exempt under the Act.

Where an offense has been committed in the presence or within the immediate knowledge of a private citizen, he would be authorized by law to arrest the offender, and the offender would not be legally permitted to resist the arrest. Under these circumstances, jury instructions regarding an unlawful arrest by a private citizen and the offender's right to use force to resist such an unlawful arrest would not be authorized.

B. Assault of Unborn Child

There is nothing in the Code section outlining the offense of assault of an unborn child that permits the prosecution of (1) any person for conduct relating to an abortion for which the consent of the pregnant woman, or person authorized by law to act on her behalf, has been obtained or for which such consent is implied by law; (2) any person for any medical treatment of the pregnant woman or her unborn child; or (3) any woman with respect to her unborn child.

VI. Punishment

A. Simple Assault

Simple assault is a misdemeanor punishable under the general misdemeanor statute. However, simple assault is punishable as a misdemeanor of a high and aggravated nature when it is committed in a public transit vehicle or station, between family members, against an elder person, against a public school employee engaged in official duties or on school property, or against a pregnant female.

B. Assault of Unborn Child

Assault of an unborn child is a misdemeanor punishable under the general misdemeanor statute.

C. Aggravated Assault

Aggravated assault is a felony punishable by confinement from one to twenty years. However, aggravated assault is punishable by confinement from three to twenty years when it is committed against an elder person, in a public transit vehicle or station, or between family members. Aggravated assault is punishable by confinement from five to twenty years when it is committed against a correctional officer, by discharging a firearm from within a motor vehicle toward another person without legal justification, or by using a firearm against a student or teacher or other school personnel within a school safety zone. Aggravated assault is punishable by imprisonment from five to twenty years, by a fine from $50,000 to $200,000, or by both fine and imprisonment when it is committed during the theft of a commercial vehicle, its trailer, or its cargo. Finally, aggravated assault with intent to rape against a child under 14 years of age is punishable by imprisonment for not less than 25 nor more than 50 years. In addition, any person convicted of this offense is subject to the sentencing and punishment provisions of § 17-10-6.2, which requires the offender to receive a mandatory split sentence including a minimum sentence of imprisonment.

If the victim of an aggravated assault is a peace officer engaged in the performance of his official duties, the possible punishment is increased to not less than five nor more than twenty years. The case of Bundren v. State made it clear that a defendant must know his victim is a police officer for a conviction of the greater offense of assaulting a police officer. The court found that § 16-5-21(c) does not establish a separate crime of aggravated assault upon a police officer, but rather simply enhances the punishment when the victim happens to be a police officer. "Since it is necessary to prove intent, it therefore follows that knowledge is an essential element to the offense of the aggravated assault of a police officer." While this reasoning is less than clear, the result seems clearly correct in light of the statutory language which punishes those who "knowingly" make an assault on a police officer. The court concluded that "the jury must be charged that knowledge is an essential element to the crime."

The defendant's knowledge that the person he assaulted was a police officer can be established by direct and/or circumstantial evidence. The state is not required to prove the victim's certification in order to make a prima facie showing that he was acting as a police officer within the contemplation of the statute.

The Georgia Court of Appeals has held that it was not the intent of the legislature to create the offense of aggravated assault upon a police officer as a separate offense from aggravated assault. Its intent was to provide for a greater punishment for the offense of aggravated assault when the victim is a police officer. Thus, an indictment charging the defendant with aggravated assault is not required to identify the victim as a police officer in order for the greater punishment to be imposed.

A defendant who has inflicted a serious, disfiguring injury on the victim as a result of an aggravated assault can be ordered by the trial court upon conviction to pay restitution to the victim's insurance company. The amount of restitution ordered can not exceed the victim's damages. The defendant is not absolved from paying restitution caused by his assault merely because some of the victim's medical expenses had been discharged in bankruptcy. A defendant who has been acquitted of the aggravated assault of a victim cannot be held responsible for damages arising out of the aggravated assault. Thus, the defendant cannot be ordered by the trial court to pay restitution for the victim's injuries that were inflicted by a co-defendant.

BATTERY

See also ASSAULT; ATTEMPT AND SOLICITATION; SEXUAL BATTERY.

I. Generally

The Georgia criminal code has codified the common law of battery into the crimes of simple battery, battery, and aggravated battery, replacing such statutes as wife whipping and punishment of convicts without authority. Simple battery involves the offensive touching or intentional physical harming of another individual. Battery is committed when a person intentionally causes substantial physical harm or visible bodily harm to another. Aggravated battery, which replaces the old mayhem statute, is committed when a person renders a member of the victim's body useless or severely disfigures the victim.

II. Simple Battery

A. Generally.

There are three elements to simple battery: intent, causation, and a touching which is insulting, provoking, or harmful. Although prior law defined only one type of battery, § 16-5-23, while not altering the total content of the crime, provides for two separate offenses: one involving insulting or provoking contact and the other physical harm. The Court of Appeals has indicated that the offenses are distinct.

Although consent or lack thereof would be relevant in a case involving insulting or provoking contact, it would not be relevant in a case involving physical harm. It is the act and intent and results of the defendant's act which constitute the crime of simple battery involving physical harm. The attitude of the victim is not called into issue by these elements.

B. Intent

The defendant must intend to touch the victim in an insulting, provoking or harmful manner. Circumstantial evidence, of course, can be used to prove the element of intent. Evidence of the victim's wounds or the perpetrator's actions, for example, may show that the defendant was angry and possessed the requisite intent while touching the victim. Anger, however, need not be present, as intent may be shown without this emotion. Indeed, the courts have gone so far as to permit criminal negligence to satisfy the mens rea requirement. In J.A.T. v. State the court stated that even if the defendant were "sicking" his dog on the victim in sport, not intending to injure him, a battery could be found if such action amounted to criminal negligence.

Prior violent conduct that is sufficiently similar to the charged offense of simple battery is admissible for the limited purpose of establishing the defendant's bent of mind and course of conduct. Also, a prior difficulty between the defendant and the victim is admissible to show their relationship and to show the defendant's motive, intent, and bent of mind. The probative value of such evidence is not outweighed by any unfair prejudice.

C. Causation

In addition to intending to cause a prohibited touching, the defendant must also **actually** cause such contact. In the case of **harmful** contact, direct physical contact between the perpetrator and the victim is not necessary to prove this element, however. Because the statute provides that the defendant need only cause harm to the victim, the harm can be inflicted through an instrumentality which is set into motion by the defendant. Courts have found, for example, that this element was satisfied when a defendant set his dog on a victim, when the defendant drove an automobile which struck the victim, when a defendant drove his motorcycle into a victim, when the defendant threw bags at the victim, and when a victim was struck with a rock thrown by the defendant.

In the case of **insulting or provoking** contact, the statute requires that the defendant make "physical contact" with the victim. In light of the expansive reading historically given the language of the simple battery statute, the Georgia Court of Appeals has held that there is nothing in the statutory language which requires that the physical contact with the victim be made by the body of the defendant. Because direct physical contact is not required by the statute, an insulting or provoking contact can be caused by the defendant through the use of an instrumentality he has set in motion. For example, the Court of Appeals found that the state proved the occurrence of a physical contact with the victim when the evidence showed that the defendant brushed up against the victim with his camcorder while attempting to film under her dress in a store parking lot.

D. Prohibited Contact

Cases decided under the law prior to 1968, reading quite broadly the prior statutory definition of battery as "the unlawful beating of another," established that any intentional, nonconsensual physical contact may constitute a battery, and this appears to be the rule under the 1968 criminal code as well. Prior law, however, defined only one type of battery, "beating," which was broadly construed, while § 16-5-23 distinguishes between battery committed by causing physical harm to another and battery committed by making an insulting or provoking physical contact.

The Court of Appeals has indicated that conviction under an indictment charging a battery of the physical harm type is improper if only an offensive, but not painful, contact is shown.

Physical contact of an insulting nature is a form of simple battery separate from causing physical harm, and it must be charged specifically. Thus, a charge that simple battery may be committed either by intentionally making physical contact of an insulting or provoking nature or by causing physical harm, while a true statement of the elements of battery, is not a true statement of facts or law under which one can be convicted in the face of an accusation alleging only one form of simple battery. Such a charge is reversible error, unless the trial court in his charge to the jury also makes it clear that the defendant cannot be convicted of a form of simple battery other than what is set out in the accusation.

It is not necessary that the victim suffer great physical harm; the infliction of pain is sufficient harm under the statute.

IIA. Battery of Unborn Child

A person commits the offense of battery of an unborn child when he, without legal justification, intentionally inflicts physical harm upon an unborn child. For the purposes of this offense, an unborn child is a member of the species homo sapiens at any stage of development who is carried in the womb. It should be noted that this definition has not adopted the common law limitation that affords protection only to those unborn children who are so far developed as to be ordinarily called "quick," i.e., so far developed as to be able to move or stir in the mother's womb. Rather, it affords protection to all unborn children at any stage of development.

III. Battery and Family Violence Battery

A person commits battery when he intentionally causes: (1) substantial physical harm to another or (2) visible bodily harm to another. "Visible bodily harm" means bodily harm capable of being perceived by a person other than the victim and may include, but is not limited to, substantially blackened eyes, substantially swollen lips or other facial or body parts, or substantial bruises to body parts. Since the state is not limited by this statutory definition, it does not have to allege the specific visible bodily harm in order to make the indictment sufficiently technical and correct.

If the battery is committed against a past or present family member, then the battery constitutes the offense of family violence battery. It should be noted that a second conviction for family violence battery against the same or another family member carries a more severe punishment than a second conviction for battery. In no event is this proscription against family violence battery applicable to reasonable corporal punishment administered by a parent to a child.

When the General Assembly enacted the provision defining the offense of family violence battery in 1996, it did not create a new offense but rather a separate category of an existing offense. This provision simply enhances the penalty for the already prohibited act of battery when such involves family members. This definition also redefines any past battery conviction involving a family member to be a family violence battery conviction which can serve as basis for enhancing a defendant's penalty.

It is the act and intent and results of the defendant's act which constitute the crime of battery. The attitude of the victim, i.e., his consent or lack thereof, is not called into issue by these elements.

Whether or not a victim of intentional injury by another heals from his injuries is not the test of whether the victim suffered substantial physical harm. Whether substantial physical harm occurred is instead a question of fact for the jury to decide. Another question of fact the jury must decide is whether the defendant caused the victim's bodily injuries under circumstances constituting the offense of battery.

Evidence of prior difficulties between the defendant and the victim is admissible to illustrate the defendant's motive, intent, or bent of mind in committing a battery on the victim. Prior violent conduct that is sufficiently similar to the charged offense of battery is admissible for the limited purpose of establishing the defendant's bent of mind and course of conduct. Testimony as to the victim's statements regarding previous incidents of abuse made shortly after the infliction of her injuries is admissible as part of the res gestae even if such evidence incidentally places the defendant's character in evidence.

IV. Aggravated Battery

A person commits aggravated battery when he maliciously does any one of three things: (1) deprives a victim of a member of his body; (2) renders a member of a victim's body useless; or (3) seriously disfigures a victim.

The intent to maim, which was an element of the former offense of mayhem, is not an element of the offense of aggravated battery, which replaced the offense of mayhem in 1968. The mens rea language of the current statute requires that the defendant "maliciously" cause bodily harm to another. Evidence of a malicious intention to do one of the prohibited actus reus acts satisfies this requirement. Because the term "maliciously" has such obvious significance and common understanding, there is no need to define it in a jury charge.

Where the evidence shows that the defendant acted intentionally and without justification or serious provocation in firing a shot which struck an innocent bystander, the jury would be authorized to conclude that he acted maliciously. Although the defendant may not have intended to shoot the bystander, when the bystander has lost the use of his eye as a result of being struck by a bullet intended for another, the law transfers the original intent from the one against whom it was directed to the bystander who actually suffered from the shooting.

A prior offense that is sufficiently similar to the aggravated battery charged is admissible for the limited purpose of showing the defendant's bent of mind. However, if the purpose for which the prior offense is offered involves an issue which was resolved in the defendant's favor by a verdict of acquittal in the prior trial, evidence of the prior offense would be irrelevant and inadmissible.

For actus reus purposes, the focus of the statute is upon whether the defendant has maliciously caused the victim to suffer an enumerated physical injury, and the means employed so as maliciously to cause such an injury is not a mitigating factor that would serve to render the defendant guilty of any lesser crime. Also, the fact that the defendant's initial contact with the victim was not an immediate cause of the victim's bodily harm is not a mitigating factor. If the defendant by his initial contact sets in force a motion that ultimately results in the victim's bodily harm, he has committed an aggravated battery.

Also, for actus reus purposes, the courts have defined bodily members as any bodily part or organ, making an eye, a finger, a tooth, a genital organ, the brain, the rectum, or the nose a bodily member for purposes of the statute. There is no requirement that the bodily member be permanently rendered useless in order to constitute the crime of aggravated battery. Thus, the victim's substantial, albeit temporary, loss of use of a bodily member would be sufficient to support a conviction.

Medical testimony is not required to demonstrate the loss of use of a bodily member. The victim's testimony would be sufficient to establish her injuries.

There are no well-defined guidelines for the serious disfigurement element. The statute simply provides that any serious disfigurement of another person's body or member thereof constitutes aggravated battery. There is no requirement that, in addition to being serious, the disfigurement of the victim be permanent or immediately visible. Because the circumstances of each aggravated battery vary, what constitutes serious disfigurement will almost always be a question for the jury to resolve. This does not mean, however, that no threshold exists for determining whether disfiguring injuries meet the requisite level of seriousness for an aggravated battery charge. The serious disfigurement element requires an injury more severe than the visible wounds used to illustrate the visible bodily harm required to support a battery conviction. In other words, the injury must be more than a superficial wound, such as a scrape, bruise, discoloration, or swelling. Thus, where the state has adduced no evidence from which the jury can infer that the victim's injuries are more significant, grave, or severe than the superficial, visible wounds that would typically support a battery conviction, it has failed to carry its burden of proving the serious disfigurement element.

Where an indictment charges the defendant with committing an aggravated battery by a specific method, a charge to the jury that aggravated battery may be committed by alternative methods, emphasizing a method of committing the crime not specified in the indictment, is reversible error. Yet the charge as a whole would not be erroneous if the trial court has also given a curative instruction limiting the jury's consideration to the method specified in the indictment.

A victim who dies instantaneously from the first blow cannot be subjected to an aggravated battery.

If the victim of the aggravated battery is a peace officer as opposed to a civilian, then the crime carries a more severe punishment. If the victim is a state peace officer acting in concert with federal officials, then the defendant may also incur federal criminal liability.

An essential element of aggravated battery on a peace officer is that the defendant knew the victim was a peace officer. Thus, the jury must be charged that knowledge is an essential element of the crime.

IVA. Female Genital Mutilation

Any person who knowingly circumcises, excises, or infibulates, in whole or in part, the labia majora, labia minora, or clitoris of a female under 18 years of age is guilty of female genital mutilation. If the parent, guardian, or custodian of the minor female knowingly consents to or permits the mutilation, that person would likewise be guilty of this offense. Moreover, anyone who knowingly removes or causes or permits the removal of the minor female from this state for the purpose of mutilating her genitals would be guilty of the offense.

The statutory privileges provided by Chapter 9 of Title 24 do not apply to proceedings in which one of the parties to the privilege is charged with a crime against a female under 18 years of age. However, such person is compellable to give evidence only on the specific act for which the defendant is charged.

V. Relationship to Other Offenses

Important Notice about Repudiation of Actual or Same Evidence Test: The Georgia Supreme Court repudiated the actual evidence test in *Drinkard v. Walker*, 281 Ga. 211, 636 S.E.2d 530 (2006), because it found this test to be inconsistent with the statutory framework governing the prohibition against multiple convictions for included offenses in Georgia. This inconsistency resulted in years of confusion and unpredictable results. In its place, the court adopted the required evidence test and overruled any prior case law that is inconsistent with it. Thus, any prior case law applying the actual evidence test is no longer controlling and should not be relied upon to determine whether one offense is included in another under § 16-1-6(1). The discussion of such case law is included below only insofar as it may still be applicable to pending prosecutions that arose before the Drinkard decision. See MULTIPLE CONVICTIONS, II. Tests to Determine Presence of Multiple Convictions, for a complete discussion of the Drinkard decision.

The elements of battery are closely related to many other crimes which include elements of unpermitted physical contact. In cases where a battery is charged in conjunction with one of these other crimes, the verdicts must be consistent. If, for example, a defendant is charged with simple battery and obstructing a peace officer (by biting and kicking him), the defendant cannot be acquitted of the battery and convicted of the obstruction. Consistency was required because the conduct which constituted the battery was also the basis of the obstruction charge.

Battery is a lesser included offense of several crimes. The determination of whether an offense is a lesser included offense of another is especially important because that determination governs the possible liability of the defendant to double punishment as well as the jury charges to which he is entitled. A requested charge on simple battery need not be given, however, unless the evidence reasonably raises the issue or unless simple battery is, as a matter of law, an offense included in the specific crime for which the defendant was indicted. A defendant is not entitled to a jury charge on simple battery as a lesser included offense where his defense is essentially that no offense occurred or where his defense constitutes an absolute defense to any criminal liability whatsoever.

The question of merger will arise when a death occurs subsequent to a battery. The issue of whether there may be only one conviction of murder or two convictions, one for murder and the other for battery, ought to hinge on whether the death is the result of a single violation of the battery statute. If so, the battery ought to merge into the murder under the rule against multiple convictions. Whether a battery has been committed as part of the same transaction as the murder will often be a difficult factual question.

The crime most closely related to simple battery is simple assault; assault is often described as an attempted battery. Although former GCA § 27-2508 provided that a defendant may not be convicted of an assault where the evidence shows a completed battery, that section was implicitly repealed by § 16-5-22, which provides that a defendant may be convicted of an aggravated assault with intent to commit a major crime, even though the substantive crime itself was completed. Furthermore, former GCA § 27-2508 was repealed when it was not included in the O.C.G.A., effective November 1, 1982. Now, a defendant may be convicted for aggravated assault with intent to rape, for example, even if the rape was completed. This analysis and § 16-4-2, which states the same rule with respect to attempts generally, were applied to permit a conviction of simple assault, even though the battery was completed. Under § 16-5-22, a defendant cannot be convicted of both aggravated assault and the completed crime, and § 16-4-2 would similarly preclude a conviction for both simple assault and the resulting battery.

Simple battery may be as a matter of fact a lesser included offense of child molestation. It may also be as a matter of fact a lesser included offense of aggravated assault. Affray, as statutorily defined, is not a lesser included offense of simple battery.

The offense of simple battery merges into the offense of rape where the same impermissible touching—the hitting and slapping which constitutes simple battery—also supplies the element of force necessary for conviction of rape. If a jury finds a defendant guilty of the lesser included offense of simple battery at his rape trial, this finding amounts to an implicit acquittal of the defendant on the rape charge. Where the evidence shows that there was either a rape or that there was consensual sexual intercourse which was interrupted when the couple changed their minds, such evidence would not authorize charges on battery and simple battery as lesser included offenses. Where the evidence shows either the commission of a rape or no crime at all, such evidence would not authorize charges on battery and simple battery as lesser included offenses.

Where the evidence shows either the commission of the completed offenses of aggravated assault with intent to rape and child molestation or the commission of no offense, there is no error in the trial court's failure to charge the jury on the lesser offenses of battery and simple battery.

Simple battery could be a lesser included offense of battery, when the defendant is charged with intentionally causing visible bodily harm and the state does not prove that the harm was visible. If it is undisputed that the harm was visible, a charge on simple battery would be inapplicable.

The offense of simple battery merges into the offense of battery where each offense is established by proof of the same facts, except that the offense of battery requires proof that the defendant caused visible bodily harm. However, simple battery does not merge into battery as a matter of fact where the evidence independently establishes physical contact of an insulting and provoking nature separate from the infliction of visible bodily harm.

Simple battery is not a lesser included offense of felony obstruction of an officer. It is a separate and independent offense wherein the intent is to make physical contact or cause physical harm. Simply because the separate offense of simple battery could be prosecuted under the same set of facts that might support an obstruction conviction does not make simple battery a lesser included offense of obstruction under the law.

Since false imprisonment does not necessarily require an offensive touching as is required with simple battery, simple battery is not, by definition, a lesser included offense of false imprisonment.

The offense of battery is not a lesser included offense of false imprisonment, and the offenses do not merge as a matter of law. Nor do the offenses merge as a matter of fact where proof of each offense is distinct from proof of the other. That a distinct, separate offense, like battery, occurs during the ongoing course of another completed offense, like false imprisonment, does not in itself preclude conviction and sentence for each.

Since the offense of kidnapping with bodily injury is completed when the kidnapping and some bodily injury occurs, a prior or subsequent aggravated battery against the victim would constitute an offense separate from the kidnapping with bodily injury as a matter of fact. Similarly, where the offense of simple kidnapping is completed before the simple battery of the victim occurs, the simple battery constitutes an offense separate from the simple kidnapping as a matter of fact and law. However, where evidence of the battery is used to establish that the defendant injured the victim during the commission of the kidnapping, the battery is included in the offense of kidnapping with bodily injury as a matter of fact.

Under the required evidence test, aggravated assault, aggravated battery, and kidnapping each require proof of at least one different element. Where the state presents independent evidence to prove each of these individual crimes as set forth in the indictment, the aggravated assault and aggravated battery can not be considered part of the single completed act of kidnapping with bodily injury and therefore do not merge with the kidnapping charge.

Although the element of physical or bodily harm is a requisite for battery, where the physical or bodily harm is committed with a deadly weapon, battery is not a lesser included offense. Where the indictment alleges assault with a deadly weapon and the evidence shows that an assault was committed with a deadly weapon, aggravated assault is proved beyond a reasonable doubt, and the evidence does not support a finding that the defendant committed a battery. Therefore, a trial court is not required to charge the jury on battery as a lesser included offense.

Where there is no evidence whatsoever that the defendant's beating of the victim was a separate act but rather was part and parcel of the collective fatal attack on the victim, neither battery nor simple battery are lesser included offenses of malice murder as a matter of fact. Even if battery and simple battery are considered to be lesser included offenses, when the evidence shows completion only of the greater offense of malice murder, it is unnecessary for the trial court to charge on the lesser offenses.

If the evidence used to prove the defendant committed an aggravated battery is the same as that used to prove he committed a malice murder, the aggravated battery merges into the malice murder as a matter of fact, and a separate judgment of conviction and sentence for the aggravated battery should be vacated. If the aggravated battery of the victim is independent of the malicious act causing the victim's death, however, the aggravated battery does not merge with the malice murder as a matter of fact.

Where the facts adduced to support an aggravated assault charge in an indictment are the same facts used to support an aggravated battery charge in an indictment, the aggravated assault is a lesser included offense of the aggravated battery and the defendant may be convicted only for the aggravated battery. Where the aggravated assault and the aggravated battery are established by proof of different facts, the offenses do not merge in fact and the defendant may be convicted and sentenced for both offenses.

The rule of lenity applies when two statutes governing the same conduct are conflicting with respect to their prescribed punishments, i.e., where one statute punishes the same conduct to a lesser degree than the other statute. In such a situation, a defendant would be entitled to have the lesser of two penalties administered. Since aggravated assault and aggravated battery are both felonies, differing grades of punishment are not involved. Thus, the rule of lenity would not apply to a defendant's sentences for aggravated assault and aggravated battery.

Where the same evidence is used to support both obstruction and aggravated battery charges, one crime is included in the other, and the defendant cannot be sentenced for both.

A defendant is not entitled to a charge on the lesser offense of battery where the evidence establishes without dispute the commission of the greater offense of aggravated battery.

It has been held that aggravated battery may as a matter of fact merge with the greater offense of armed robbery or robbery by force. However, where the evidence shows that the robbery was complete before the aggravated battery occurred and where the evidence of neither offense was necessary to prove the other, there is no merger.

If the facts alleged in the indictment and the evidence presented at trial to establish the charged offense of cruelty to children are sufficient to establish the lesser included offense of battery as well, it is not error for the trial court to charge the jury on the offense of battery.

Cruelty to children, but not aggravated battery, requires proof that the victim was a child under the age of 18 who was caused cruel or excessive physical or mental pain. Aggravated battery, but not cruelty to children, requires proof that the victim was deprived of a member of his body or that such member was rendered useless or seriously disfigured. Therefore, each crime requires proof of at least one additional element which the other does not. Furthermore, the two crimes are not so closely related that multiple convictions are prohibited under other provisions of §§ 16-1-6 and 16-1-7. Accordingly, even if the same conduct establishes the commission of both aggravated battery and cruelty to children, the two crimes do not merge. Moreover, when the evidence establishes that the victim was subjected to multiple injuries in addition to the injury supporting an aggravated battery conviction, these additional injuries would support a cruelty to children conviction and the trial court's failure to merge the two offenses would not be erroneous.

The crime of reckless conduct is an instance of criminal negligence, rather than a culpable act of either general or specific criminal intent. Thus, where the evidence shows that the defendant committed a culpable act with criminal intent which resulted in the aggravated battery of the victim, a charge on reckless conduct is not authorized by the evidence.

VI. Defenses and Exemptions

A. Simple Battery.

There are three defenses to simple battery which, under most circumstances, are also applicable to simple assault. First, it is a defense to the crimes of assault and battery that the defendant was exercising his lawful authority as a police officer to make an arrest. The officer is justified in using only enough force to effect the arrest, however. Thus, the officer may use enough force to compel submission of the arrestee and, if need be, to defend himself.

Second, it is a common law defense to simple battery that the victim consented to the physical contact. A doctor who operates on a patient who consented to surgery, for example, has a defense to what would otherwise constitute a battery. Similarly, willing participants in contact sports cannot be convicted of battery when the contact is not likely to injure seriously or kill and is within the rules of the game. Although there is a dearth of Georgia cases on the subject, this defense is given substantial recognition by commentators.

Finally, under § 16-5-25, it is a defense to both simple assault and simple battery that the victim used opprobrious or abusive language. There has been very little recent indication as to just what kind of words constitute "opprobrious" or "abusive" language, but there are some limitations to the defense. If the defendant was the first person to use opprobrious words, then he is not entitled to invoke the defense. The defense is available only when the opprobrious words were uttered by the victim in the presence of the defendant. The defense of opprobrious language has been held unavailable to a police officer who commits a battery on his prisoner. It has also been held that this defense, being limited to the offenses of simple assault and simple battery, does not apply to the offenses of battery and aggravated battery.

Whether the assault or battery was justified by the victim's use of opprobrious words is a matter for the trier of fact to determine. The identity of the person who spoke the opprobrious words and the surrounding circumstances can be considered in order to make this determination. The Georgia Supreme Court held, for example, that opprobrious words uttered by a nine-year-old child did not justify an assault or battery upon that child by an adult. Presumably, opprobrious language by an insane or physically disabled person likewise would not justify an assault or battery.

Without any claim whatsoever by the defendant that he committed the offense because of abusive language, he is not entitled to a jury charge on abusive language as a justification for his committing the offense

The three defenses discussed above are not the only defenses available to a person on trial for the offense of simple battery. A defendant is entitled to assert the defense of self-defense/justification where there is some evidence presented which would authorize the consideration of this defense.

A charge of simple battery on an officer is subject to the affirmative defense that the person was resisting an unlawful arrest. However, a defendant's testimony that he did not resist the arrest would justify the trial court's refusal to give a jury charge on this affirmative defense.

In Pruitt v. State, the court held that the trial court erroneously admitted evidence of the battered woman syndrome in a case where the victim was a woman. The court did point out, however, that the Georgia Supreme Court has admitted such evidence where the defendant was a female asserting self-defense as a defense.

A.1. Battery of Unborn Child

There is nothing in the Code section outlining the offense of battery of an unborn child that permits the prosecution of (1) any person for conduct relating to an abortion for which the consent of the pregnant woman, or person authorized by law to act on her behalf, has been obtained or for which such consent is implied by law; (2) any person for any medical treatment of the pregnant woman or her unborn child; or (3) any woman with respect to her unborn child.

B. Family Violence Crimes.

In a domestic dispute, a sibling who commits a simple battery or an aggravated battery against another sibling living or formerly living in the same household would be exempt from the enhanced punishment prescribed by the Crimes Against Family Members Act of 1999. Furthermore, a parent, guardian, or person acting in loco parentis who administers corporal punishment to a child would be exempt from the Act's enhanced punishment for simple battery. However, if the corporal punishment constitutes an aggravated battery, the parent would not be exempt under the Act.

C. Female Genital Mutilation.

The proscription against female genital mutilation found in § 16-5-27 does not apply to procedures performed by or under the direction of a physician, a registered professional nurse, a certified nurse midwife, or a licensed practical nurse when necessary to preserve the physical health of the female. Also, this proscription does not apply to any autopsy or limited dissection as defined by § 45-16-21.

Consent of the minor female or of her parent, guardian, or custodian is not a defense to the offense of female genital mutilation. Moreover, religion, ritual, custom, or standard practice is not a defense to this offense.

VII. Punishment

A. Simple Battery

Simple battery is a misdemeanor punishable under the general misdemeanor statute. However, simple battery is punishable as a misdemeanor of a high and aggravated nature when it is committed (1) against an elder person or a pregnant female; (2) in a public transit vehicle or station; (3) against a police officer, law enforcement dog, correction officer, or detention officer engaged in carrying out official duties; (4) between family members; (5) against a person who is admitted to or receiving services from a health care facility for disabled adults or elder persons; (6) against a sports official while he is officiating an amateur contest or while he is on or exiting the property where he will officiate or has completed officiating an amateur contest; or (7) against a public school employee engaged in official duties or on school property.

A.1. Battery of Unborn Child

Battery of an unborn child is a misdemeanor punishable under the general misdemeanor statute.

B. Battery

Battery is a misdemeanor punishable under the general misdemeanor statute. Upon the second conviction for battery against the same victim, the defendant is punishable by imprisonment for not less than ten days nor more than 12 months, by a fine not to exceed $1,000, or both. Upon a third or subsequent conviction for battery against the same victim, the defendant is guilty of a felony punishable by imprisonment for not less than one nor more than five years. A person convicted of a second or subsequent offense of battery shall have his notice of conviction and photograph published in the legal organ of the county where he resides or where he was convicted.

A battery committed in a public transit vehicle or station, against a pregnant female, against an elder person, or against a sports official is punishable as a misdemeanor of a high and aggravated nature. A battery committed against a teacher or other school personnel, engaged in the performance of official duties or while on school property, is felony punishable by imprisonment for not less than one nor more than five years or by a fine of not more than $10,000, or both. Finally, a battery committed against a person who is admitted to or receiving services from a health care facility for disabled adults or elder persons is a felony punishable by imprisonment for not less than one nor more than five years or by a fine of not more than $2,000, or both.

C. Family Violence Battery

Upon a first conviction of family violence battery, the defendant will be guilty of and punished for a misdemeanor. Upon a second or subsequent conviction of family violence battery against the same or another victim, the defendant will be guilty of a felony and will be punished by imprisonment for not less than one nor more than five years. Moreover, a person convicted of a second or subsequent offense of family violence battery shall have his notice of conviction and photograph published in the legal organ of the county where he resides or where he was convicted.

With respect to conviction under recidivist statutes, the law recognizes that a nolo plea can constitute proof of a prior conviction. Thus, a trial court's consideration of a defendant's previous nolo contendere plea to the offense of battery for the purpose of adjudicating him guilty of felony family violence battery would not be error.

D. Aggravated Battery

Aggravated battery is normally a felony punishable by imprisonment for not less than one nor more than 20 years. However, an aggravated battery committed between family members is punishable by imprisonment for not less than three nor more than 20 years. An aggravated battery committed against an elder person, in a public transit vehicle or station, or upon a student or teacher or other school personnel within a school safety zone is punishable by imprisonment for not less than five nor more than 20 years. Finally, an aggravated battery committed upon a peace officer or a correctional officer, who is a victim in or on account of the performance of his official duties, is punishable by imprisonment for not less than ten nor more than 20 years.

E. Female Genital Mutilation.

Female genital mutilation is a felony punishable by imprisonment for not less than five nor more than 20 years.

VIII. Double Jeopardy

Although the General Assembly has enacted legislation vesting municipal courts with jurisdiction over various state misdemeanor offenses, it has not done so with respect to simple battery and battery, both state offenses. Because a municipal court lacks jurisdiction over these offenses, any prosecution of the offenses before such court is void and without effect as to a subsequent state court prosecution. The subsequent state court prosecution would not be barred on grounds of double jeopardy.

CRUELTY TO CHILDREN AND RELATED OFFENSES

See also DELINQUENCY, UNRULINESS, OR DEPRIVATION OF MINOR, CONTRIBUTING TO; PARENTAL DISCIPLINE DEFENSE; PARENTS AND CHILDREN, CRIMES RELATING TO.

I. Cruelty to Children

Prior to the 1968 revision of the criminal code, the cruelty to children statute applied to anyone who engaged in certain prohibited acts or omissions directed at a child. The 1968 statute, however, was limited in its application to a "parent, guardian, or other person supervising the welfare of or having immediate charge or custody" of a child under 18. The rationale for limiting the reach of the 1968 statute to individuals having control of the child was that the behavior proscribed by the statute prior to 1968 would be punishable under the general penal provisions relating to causing bodily harm. A special provision was desired, however, to punish a parent or one standing in loco parentis "who might seek to defend against outrageous acts toward a child by taking refuge in the concept of necessary corrective discipline."

In an apparent abandonment of the rationale on which the 1968 statute was based, the cruelty to children statute was amended by the General Assembly in 1978. Subsection (a) of § 16-5-70, which punishes willfully depriving a minor of necessary sustenance so as to jeopardize his health or well-being, still applies **only** to parents, guardians, or others "supervising the welfare of or having immediate charge or custody" of a minor. Subsection (b), however, now punishes **any person** who maliciously causes a minor "cruel or excessive physical or mental pain."

The cruelty to children statute was amended again by the General Assembly in 1996 so as to provide for first and second degrees of the offense. The General Assembly added language to subsections (a) and (b) of the statute which classified the offenses defined in those subsections as cruelty to children in the first degree and added a sentence to subsection (b) defining the offense of cruelty to children in the second degree. This sentence was added to protect children from witnessing violent crimes.

In 1999, the General Assembly changed the definition of cruelty to children in the second degree and set out this definition in subsection (c). When the General Assembly amended the statute again in 2004, it redesignated this definition as subsection (d) and reclassified this offense as cruelty to children in the third degree.

In an effort to further protect the well-being of this state's children, the General Assembly in 2004 enacted a child endangerment law. As part of this law, it enacted a new child neglect provision as subsection (c) of the statute and classified this new offense as cruelty to children in the second degree.

For statutes related to the offense of cruelty to children, see §§ 19-15-1 et seq., Child Abuse.

A. Elements

1. Cruelty to Children in the First Degree

As defined in subsections (a) and (b) of § 16-5-70, there are two types of cruelty to children in the first degree: (1) willfully depriving a child of necessary sustenance and (2) maliciously causing a child cruel or excessive physical or mental pain.

a. Willfully Depriving Child of Necessary Sustenance

In order to sustain a conviction of the first type of cruelty, the state must establish that (1) the defendant is a parent, guardian, or other person in charge of the child, (2) the child is under the age of 18, (3) the defendant willfully deprived the child of necessary sustenance, and (4) this deprivation jeopardized the child's health or well-being.

The Georgia Supreme Court in Caby v. State defined "necessary sustenance" as that which supports life. The defendant must be shown to have deprived the victim of "that necessary food and drink which is sufficient to support life and maintain health." Given that construction, the words used in the statute were held by the court not to be unconstitutionally vague. In addition, the Caby decision emphasizes that subsection (a) requires physical harm to the child, not mere neglect.

Whether the deprivation of necessary sustenance was done willfully is an issue for jury resolution.

The denial of necessary and appropriate medical care for a child under 18 years of age can constitute cruelty to a child when it causes the child "cruel or excessive physical or mental pain," but it does not constitute a denial of "sustenance." Being afraid because one might get in trouble is neither justification nor excuse for refusing to obtain medical care for one's injured child.

Where the defendant was indicted only for violation of § 16-5-70(a), the deprivation of necessary sustenance, charging the remainder of the Code section with respect to other offenses for which the defendant was not indicted might constitute reversible error. In such a case, the failure to charge the entire Code section on cruelty to children would not be erroneous.

b. Maliciously Causing Child Cruel or Excessive Physical or Mental Pain

In order to sustain a conviction of the second type of cruelty, the state must establish that (1) the child is under the age of 18, (2) the child suffered physical or mental pain, (3) the pain was cruel or excessive, (4) the defendant caused the pain, and (5) the defendant acted maliciously in doing so. A jury charge that recites the entire statutory definition of this type of cruelty does not constitute reversible error if the jury has also been given an instruction which confines the elements of the crime charged to those material allegations in the indictment.

The determination of what is cruel or excessive physical or mental pain is to be made by the jury. This determination need not depend solely on the victim's testimony.

Since the details of any cruel treatment inflicted on the victim are merely descriptive of the offensive act, it is not necessary that the state prove that the victim was injured in every way set forth in the indictment.

One method of proving the statutory element that the defendant caused cruel or excessive physical or mental pain would be the presentation of evidence that the child exhibited signs of suffering pain. However, evidence of the child's suffering may be unavailable in some cases. For instance, in one case there was expert testimony that the blows inflicted on a child were of such severity that the child was immediately rendered unconscious and was thereby incapable of exhibiting signs of suffering pain. The Georgia Supreme Court, however, held that the presentation of expert testimony that a particular action on the part of the defendant caused a child cruel or excessive physical pain was unnecessary since it was within the ken of the average juror presented with evidence that the child died after being subjected to multiple severe blows to the head by an adult to decide whether that adult caused the child cruel or excessive physical pain. Evidence of the child's age, the extent of her injuries, the nature of the assault to which the child was subjected, and the force with which the child was struck would be sufficient evidence from which a jury, applying generally accepted societal norms, could conclude whether the defendant caused the child cruel or excessive physical pain.

A jury charge on the offense of cruelty to children that includes as elements of the offense the infliction of both physical and mental pain does not constitute error where a jury, applying generally accepted societal norms, could deduce from the evidence that the child who endured a beating from the defendant suffered cruel and excessive mental pain in addition to the physical pain caused by the beating.

An indictment charging a defendant with first degree cruelty to children for unlawfully and maliciously causing cruel and excessive physical pain to the victim by touching his penis would sufficiently contain the elements of the offense intended to be charged and would apprise the defendant of what he must be prepared to meet. While it is true that touching does not necessarily entail pain, it would be clear from such a charge as a whole that the defendant is accused of touching the victim's penis in such a manner as to inflict pain. Such an indictment would not be subject to a special demurrer.

The malice element of the offense imports the absence of justification or excuse and the presence of actual intent to cause the harm produced or the wanton and willful doing of an act with the awareness that it is likely to produce the particular harm. The jury usually determines whether there was malice and such malice can be inferred from circumstantial evidence. There is no requirement that the jury find "actual hatred and ill will" in the heart of the defendant. Malice, for purposes of the statute, can be found on much less than deliberate intent to inflict the cruel act and by less than an abandoned and malignant heart. Where the defendant is charged with maliciously failing to seek medical care for the victim, there is no requirement that the jury find that the defendant had actual knowledge of the victim's specific injuries requiring care. Malice under § 16-5-70(b) does not require actual knowledge of the victim's injuries. The term "malice" is of such obvious significance and common understanding that there is no need to define it in a charge to the jury.

The offense of cruelty to children may be committed by raising a child in such unsanitary conditions that the child suffers cruel or excessive physical or mental pain. However, the basic elements of the offense must be shown by the evidence. Evidence of unsanitary conditions, alone, cannot serve to prove the element of malice in a prosecution for cruelty to children. There must be other evidence which would establish either that the defendant intended to cause harm to the child or that the defendant acted with awareness that such conduct was likely to cause harm.

c. *Children Protected by Statute*

By their terms, both subsections (a) and (b) of § 16-5-70 are designed to protect "child[ren] under the age of 18." While the statute's language could be construed to protect any person under the age of 18, by use of the word "child" rather than "person," it is arguable that the General Assembly may have been indicating less than total inclusion of all persons under the age of 18. In Collins v. State, a case decided before the statute had an age limit, the Georgia Supreme Court indicated that the cruelty to children statute was designed to protect those who are unable to protect themselves from the cruelty of older people because of their physical immaturity. Arguably, therefore, emancipated or married persons under the age of 18 may not be protected by the current statute. This point has not, however, been addressed by the appellate courts.

d. *Corporal Punishment*

Section 16-5-70 does not prohibit normal punishment of a child, and has traditionally been construed to provide a substantial amount of discretion in a parent's decision with respect to punishment. Some punishment, however, is simply impermissible as a matter of law. In Davis v. State, for instance, the defendant whipped a two-year-old child with a belt and then placed the child in scalding water as "punishment" for the child's having "violated the terms of toilet training." The court indicated that such treatment of the child could not be justified as punishment.

e. *Mother's Voluntary Relinquishment of Newborn Child*

The General Assembly enacted the Safe Place for Newborns Act of 2002 in order to prevent injuries to and deaths of newborn children caused by mothers who abandon them. Under this Act, a mother who leaves her newborn child in the physical custody of an employee, agent, or staff member of a medical facility is not subject to prosecution for the crime of cruelty to children. This exemption from prosecution is available only if the newborn child is no more than one week old at the time of relinquishment and only if the mother shows proof of her identity, if available, to the person with whom the newborn is left and provides her name and address.

1.1. Cruelty to Children in the Second Degree

In an effort to further protect the well-being of this state's children, the General Assembly in 2004 enacted a child endangerment law. As part of this law, it enacted a new child neglect provision as subsection (c) of the statute and classified this new offense as cruelty to children in the second degree. At the time of this enactment, Georgia was the only state without a child neglect statute. Without a statute proscribing criminally negligent conduct toward children, prosecutors had a difficult time prosecuting defendants for child neglect. Instead, they had to invoke other provisions of the Code in order to maintain such a prosecution. With the enactment of this new subsection (c), however, prosecutors now clearly have the statutory authority to prosecute defendants for neglecting children.

This new provision provides that a person commits the offense of cruelty to children in the second degree when he with criminal negligence causes a child under the age of 18 cruel or excessive physical or mental pain.

The General Assembly defined criminal negligence as "an act or failure to act which demonstrates a willful, wanton, or reckless disregard for the safety of others who might reasonably be expected to be injured thereby." While this provision certainly could not be used to prosecute a person for merely allowing a child to reside in a dirty house, it could be used to prosecute a person for allowing a child to reside in such unsanitary conditions that the child's health or safety would be endangered. Similarly, someone could not be prosecuted under this provision for failing to have a trigger lock on his gun but could be prosecuted for allowing a child to have access to a loaded gun that the child subsequently used to shoot himself. In both situations, a trier of fact could find criminal liability for willful, wanton, or reckless disregard for the child's safety.

The negligence necessary to constitute a crime is something more than that degree of negligence necessary to authorize recovery in a suit for damages. In construing the involuntary manslaughter statute prior to the 1968 Criminal Code, the Georgia Supreme Court held that "the negligence necessary . . . to constitute a crime is the equivalent of and, in fact, is recklessness . . . . Criminal negligence must be such as shows an indifference to the injurious results of the negligent acts. It must be inconsiderate of others. In order for one to be held to have been indifferent to the safety of others or inconsiderate of their welfare, it must appear that he knew, or that an ordinarily prudent person under similar circumstances would have known, that his act might probably endanger others." This construction would likewise be applicable to the "criminal negligence" requirement in subsection (c) of the cruelty to children statute.

2. Cruelty to Children in the Third Degree

In 1991, a majority of the Georgia Supreme Court held in Hall v. State that where the evidence showed that the defendant's two surviving children were present and witnessed their only brother being murdered by the defendant, the jury was entitled to conclude beyond a reasonable doubt that the defendant's two surviving children suffered "cruel and excessive mental pain" and that the defendant maliciously caused this pain by wantonly and willfully shooting his son "with an awareness of a plain and strong likelihood that such harm may result." Thus, the evidence was sufficient to support the defendant's conviction on two counts of cruelty to children.

In dissent, Justice Benham argued that the majority's interpretation of § 16-5-70(b) was overbroad. It was apparent from the language of this provision, Justice Benham argued, that the General Assembly intended to protect children from cruel conduct directed at them. This provision was not enacted to protect children from witnessing a violent crime. Thus, under Justice Benham's interpretation, the defendant's conduct did not constitute cruelty to children.

In 1996, the General Assembly added a sentence to § 16-5-70(b) to provide that "[a] person commits the offense of cruelty to children in the second degree when he intentionally allows a minor to witness the commission of a forcible felony." It appears that this sentence was added in response to Justice Benham's dissent. With this addition, the General Assembly manifested its intent not only to protect children from cruel conduct directed at them but to protect them from witnessing violent crimes as well.

In its enactment of the Crimes Against Family Members Act of 1999, the General Assembly eliminated the definition of cruelty to children in the second degree from subsection (b) and added a new definition of the offense in subsection (c) of the statute. When the General Assembly amended the statute again in 2004, it redesignated this definition as subsection (d) and reclassified this offense as cruelty to children in the third degree. Under the current definition, cruelty to children in the third degree is committed when the primary aggressor in a domestic dispute (1) intentionally allows a minor to witness the commission of a forcible felony, battery, or family violence battery or (2) commits any of these offenses knowing that a minor is present and sees or hears the act. This definition places the culpability for the offense solely on the primary aggressor in a domestic dispute. Thus, any victim of domestic violence who acts violently in self-defense during the dispute would not be punishable for this offense.

Children who see a battery are not mere witnesses to the crime, rather they are victims under the child cruelty statute. If a defendant knows that more than one child is present and that each child sees the same battery, there is more than one victim, and the defendant may be charged with more than one count of third degree cruelty to children. Moreover, notwithstanding the fact that each of the crimes is predicated on the children seeing the same battery, the crimes do not merge as a matter of fact or law for sentencing purposes.

A claim of self-defense by a victim of domestic violence would negate the essential element of intent if believed by the jury. Thus, where self-defense is the victim's sole defense to a cruelty charge, the trial court's failure to charge on self-defense would be harmful as a matter of law, even absent a request.

B. Reporting Statute; Temporary Protective Custody of Child

Section 19-7-5 is designed to protect children whose health and welfare are adversely affected and threatened by the conduct of those responsible for their care and to aid in the enforcement of § 16-5-70. The statute requires certain individuals who have reasonable cause to believe that a child has been abused to report or cause reports of that abuse to be made. Any other person may make such a report, but is not required to do so. Any person who makes such a report in good faith is immune from civil or criminal liability. Furthermore, a person who is required to report a suspected case of child abuse and who wilfully and knowingly fails to do so is guilty of a misdemeanor.

Although it is the intent of the reporting statute to cause the protective services of the state to be brought to bear on the situation in an effort to prevent further abuses, the state has no constitutional duty to protect a child against further violence. Its failure to do so does not constitute a violation of the Due Process Clause. Also, the reporting statute does not purport to create a private cause of action in tort in favor of a victim of child abuse whose death allegedly resulted from a physician's failure to discover and report the abuse.

A physician who is treating a child may take or retain temporary protective custody of the child without a court order and without parental consent if he has reasonable cause to believe that the child's life or health is in imminent danger as a result of suspected abuse or neglect. Any physician who is acting in good faith and in accordance with acceptable medical practice in the treatment of the child is immune from any civil or criminal liability that might otherwise be incurred or imposed as a result of taking or failing to take any action.

C. Evidentiary Matters

1. Direct Evidence of Mistreatment

a. Sufficiency of Evidence

The eyewitness testimony of a child's mother is sufficient, in and of itself, to support inferences that the accused acted with malice and that his acts caused the child cruel and excessive physical pain.

In Stone v. State the evidence showed the defendant had whipped his 14-year-old daughter for several hours with an ox whip while shouting abusive language, such as "damn you, I intend to kill you." The court noted that while "cruel," "unreasonable," and "malicious" are relative terms, the jury was authorized to find they included this conduct. The court upheld the conviction for cruelty to children even though the child bore no physical marks from the beating, and even though the child herself had testified that her father did not beat her cruelly.

In Messer v. State, the defendant beat a 13-year-old child with boards and poked her with needles so that she could not even remember going to bed. As a result of this treatment, the child required extensive medical care. The Court of Appeals held the evidence was sufficient to sustain a conviction for assault with intent to murder. It seems clear, that such evidence would, therefore, be sufficient to affirm a conviction for the lesser offense of cruelty to children.

In Remine v. State, the evidence established that the defendant beat his seven-year-old son with a metal studded belt for a period of 15 to 20 minutes as punishment for perceived misbehavior, inflicting severe bruises on his lower back, buttocks and legs. Photographs of the bruises were presented to the jury, and a police officer and a protective services worker testified as to the severity of the bruises. The court held that from this evidence the jury could have concluded that the defendant was guilty of cruelty to children.

In Weeks v. State, the victim testified that the defendant burned him with cigarettes. Photographs of the small circular sores corroborated this assertion. Even though a physician tentatively diagnosed the lesions as impetigo, that physician discredited the innocent explanation of poison ivy as the cause. The court held that this evidence was sufficient to authorize the jury's verdict that the defendant was guilty of cruelty to children.

In Glenn v. State, the evidence showed that the defendant caused her seven-year-old son to experience the physical and mental pain associated with forced anal sodomy so that she could obtain drugs from a dealer. The court held that the evidence was sufficient to support a conviction for cruelty to children.

In Mitchell v. State, the evidence showed that the defendant disciplined his eight-year-old son for bed wetting by forcing him to sit naked in a bathtub filled with very hot water and bleach (or some other caustic chemical) to wash his soiled bed linens. The child suffered severe burns to his feet, buttocks, and knuckles, which went untreated for five days. The court held that the evidence was sufficient to sustain the defendant's conviction.

In Boyce v. State, the evidence showed that the mother, who was later convicted of shooting her not quite two-year-old son, accused her daughter of the shooting from the outset. The court held that the mother's blaming of the little girl for such a violent act against a loved one which resulted in the girl manifesting observable psychological pathology could have authorized the jury to conclude that the mother inflicted on her daughter mental pain which was unreasonably cruel or excessive.

b. Admissibility of Evidence

In cruelty to children prosecutions, the direct evidence of mistreatment is often highly prejudicial. To the extent the evidence is offered for the sole purpose of arousing the passion or prejudice of the jury, it should be excluded. The scope of such a rule is, however, necessarily limited, because the prosecution must be given an opportunity to prove its case. To the extent the abuse was gruesome, the evidence will necessarily be equally gruesome. In Lister v. State, for example, the state offered photographs of the child's corpse. It was asserted that the admission of such pictures was inflammatory and irrelevant. The court held, however, that the state could properly introduce the photographs for the purpose of showing rope marks, bruises, and the denial of necessary sustenance. In Harmon v. State, the state exhibited the victim to the jury. The defendant asserted on appeal that the victim's physical presence had no probative value. The court disagreed. The victim had been shaken violently and choked by the defendant and as a result of her injuries, the victim was severely retarded, had cerebral palsy, and was permanently blind. The court held that the jury's observation of the victim could have either confirmed or contradicted the testimony regarding her condition.

In a § 16-5-70 prosecution tried in federal court under the Assimilative Crimes Act, which provides that crimes committed on federal reservations are tried in federal court under the relevant state criminal provisions, the district court had to decide whether evidence concerning the battered child syndrome was admissible. The battered child syndrome refers to a pattern of injuries which indicates that they were caused by intentional parental action rather than by accident. Relying on cases in other jurisdictions, the trial court admitted this evidence and was affirmed on appeal.

Where witnesses are qualified as experts in the field of child abuse and their testimony concerns the physical extent of the beatings, such evidence is relevant to the issue of excessive physical pain, an essential element of the crime of cruelty to children. However, where it is not beyond the ken of the average juror to determine from the evidence whether the defendant has caused the child excessive physical or mental pain, it is not permissible to present expert opinion testimony to the effect that the child has in fact suffered excessive physical pain and emotional abuse.

Expert testimony describing possible future trauma of children who have witnessed the murder of a sibling by a parent is admissible to counter an anticipated defense contention that, because the children exhibit no overt manifestations of trauma, they have not experienced cruel and excessive mental pain.

Expert testimony on the battered child syndrome is admissible to demonstrate that a child's fatal injuries were the result of an intentional act by someone, and not an accident. However, expert testimony that the childhood maltreatment syndrome or abused child syndrome was the "manner" in which the fatal injuries occurred, and that the fatal injuries occurred "in the process" of the childhood maltreatment syndrome is not admissible, since such testimony constitutes an opinion that the fatal injuries in fact resulted from child abuse, a conclusion that jurors would have the ability to reach for themselves.

Expert testimony, based on the expert's experience, that the type of injury sustained by the victim resembled those that she had seen before which were not accidental has been held admissible. Such testimony does not infringe upon the jury's role in deciding the ultimate issue.

An expert's testimony that the results of her professional observations and testing of the victim were "consistent with a child who has been . . . abused" has been held to be within the bounds of permissible expert testimony.

An expert may testify that a two-year-old child would not be physically capable of lifting a four-month-old baby out of a crib and throwing him on the floor because such a conclusion requires a specialized knowledge of the development and motor skills of infants and children that would be beyond the knowledge of the average juror.

Even though a treating physician may not be able to identify the specific cause of the child's injury, he may be versed enough to eliminate the defendant's theory as contraindicated. In Mitchell v. State, the court held that the trial court did not err in allowing the treating physician to rule out diaper rash as the cause of the child's buttocks burns, even though he could not identify which particular agent caused the burns.

A demonstration conducted by an expert witness in conjunction with his testimony as a means of illustrating the type of shaking involved in shaken infant syndrome is admissible. A showing of similarity in head and neck strength, control, and movement between the doll used in the demonstration and the real infant is not required as part of the foundation. While there should be substantial and reasonable similarity between the facts proved in the case and the facts upon which the demonstration is based, the facts need not be identical. If the doll and infant are sufficiently similar to assist the jury in considering the issue of how injuries of the type suffered in the case can result from violent shaking, the foundation is sufficient. Any dissimilarity between the conditions of the demonstration and the actual occurrence affects the weight rather than the admissibility of the evidence.

Where a witness has extensive experience and training with respect to fatal child abuse and specifically shaken baby syndrome, that background would be sufficient to allow the witness to give expert testimony regarding her professional evaluation of the victim's symptoms. The fact that she does not hold a medical degree would go only to the weight the jury may give her testimony.

2. Circumstantial Evidence of Mistreatment

The issue in Polk v. State, was whether there was sufficient circumstantial evidence to find that the injuries inflicted on a child occurred in Georgia. At the time of arrest in Brooks County, the child had fresh blood on its mouth and nose, indicating that some injury had been inflicted. Additionally, the defendant, the child's mother, displayed a complete lack of concern for the child and failed to get any aid. The court held that constituted sufficient circumstantial evidence that the cruel treatment occurred. While the precise issue before the Polk court was whether a crime had been committed in Georgia, as opposed to whether a crime had been committed at all, the case gives an indication of the type of circumstantial evidence the court will look to in a cruelty to children case. A cruelty to children conviction clearly can be sustained solely on the basis of circumstantial evidence.

In Morris v. State, the victim, the two-and-one-half-year-old son of the woman with whom the defendant was living, was brought to a hospital with bruises on his face, back, extremities, and buttocks. The court found the circumstantial evidence sufficient to have authorized the jury to believe the testimony of the doctors rather than that of the defendant regarding the nature of the injuries, and that the testimony would support an inference of malice. Moreover, given that the defendant admitted he was the only one present when the injuries occurred, the jury would have been authorized to infer as well that the defendant caused the injuries.

In King v. State, the victim, the defendant's 15-month-old son, died as a result of a blunt head trauma resulting in a skull fracture. The defendant testified that the child was well when he awoke on the morning in question and that the only persons present in the apartment that day were herself, her three-year-old son and the victim. There was evidence that the defendant told a neighbor that the child "fell and bumped his head." The results of the post mortem examination revealed a four-inch fracture in the thickest area of the skull, and a substantial area of bruising on the left side of the scalp. The medical examiner testified that such injuries could not result from a fall of one or two feet, but would require the force of an unbraced fall onto a concrete surface from a height of at least ten feet. The autopsy also showed a previous fracture of the left thigh bone and that the child suffered from failure to thrive. The court held that the evidence, although circumstantial, was sufficient to support the defendant's felony murder conviction, based on the underlying felony of cruelty to children. In Powell v. State, the evidence showed that the defendant cared for the two-month-old baby while her mother worked in the evenings. The baby had suffered nine fractured ribs, a fractured shin bone, retinal hemorrhages, swelling of the brain, and bleeding inside her head from two separate incidents of abuse. The pathologist testified that the cause of death was head injuries due to the shaken baby syndrome. His opinion was that the most recent incident would have been immediately apparent to any observer and occurred within two hours of her receiving medical attention. The court concluded that a rational trier of fact could have found the defendant guilty of felony murder and cruelty to children.

In Hooker v. State, the defendant was convicted of cruelty to children based on an incident which occurred while the defendant was changing the victim's diaper. At the next diaper changing, the victim was found to have a one-half centimeter bruise on the head of his penis. The examining physician opined that the injury was caused by a discrete blunt force, a pinching action, and that it was unlikely a child of the victim's age could have mustered sufficient force to create the bruise. The court concluded that the jury rationally could have found that the evidence excluded every reasonable hypothesis except that of the defendant's guilt.

In Harris v. State, the court found that there was ample evidence from which any rational trier of fact could have found beyond a reasonable doubt that the child's injuries were not accidental and that the defendant was guilty of cruelty to children. The burn marks on the child were inconsistent with the theory that the grease had been spilt or dripped on the child from above. Also, the child had more than 20 whip marks on his inner thighs, buttocks, and near his perineum. The defendant admitted that she got mad about her son constantly "messing in his diaper" and that she usually just "pop[s] him with her hand."

In Johnson v. State, the court concluded that the evidence was insufficient to support the defendant's conviction for felony murder, with cruelty to children being the underlying felony, in connection with the bludgeoning death of his infant nephew who was upstairs in the apartment with his mother and her boyfriend. No direct evidence was introduced at trial to establish that the defendant acted with malicious intent toward the baby or caused the baby to suffer physical pain. Nor was there any circumstantial evidence from which the jury could infer that the defendant mistreated the baby. It was shown only that the defendant was present in the apartment on the night of the murder, denied having committed the murder, called 911, and failed to assist in the police investigation.

3. Testimony or Statements of Child

Prior to 1989, the victim's testimony might have been inadmissible because the child was unable to understand the nature of an oath. Now, the competency statute permits child victims who do not understand the nature of an oath to testify and have their credibility judged by the jury. Under this statute, although a child is subject to a competency challenge on the ground that he does not have the use of reason, a child is not incompetent as a matter of law because of his infancy. This statute, however, does not expand the circumstances under which hearsay statements of a child may be admitted in evidence.

Because of the close relationship which often exists between the defendant and the victim in a cruelty to children prosecution, the direct testimony of the victim is often suspect. In Stone v. State, for example, the court upheld a cruelty to children conviction despite the testimony of the 14-year-old victim that her father had not cruelly beaten her. The court discounted such testimony indicating it was probably influenced by the child's fear of her father.

A child's declarations at the time of the incident are often admissible through testimony of another witness as exceptions to the hearsay rule, if they are part of the "res gestae." The res gestae includes excited utterances, declarations of physical feelings, and declarations concerning state of mind and motive.

Under the patient history exception to the hearsay rule, a victim's statements to a licensed professional counselor about being abused by the defendant are admissible. However, because these statements are hearsay, the defendant would be unable to attack the victim's credibility on cross-examination. Therefore, the defendant must be given the opportunity to introduce, without invoking the Child Hearsay Statute, the victim's prior inconsistent statements solely to impeach those statements admitted under the patient history exception.

Prior to 1995, the Child Hearsay Statute provided an exception to the hearsay rule only for statements concerning acts of physical abuse performed on the child making the statement. Thus, the Georgia Supreme Court held that the out-of-court statements of a child who observed the physical abuse of another child, but who was not himself a victim of such abuse, was not admissible as an exception to the hearsay rule under the statute. In 1995, the General Assembly amended the Child Hearsay Statute apparently in response to this holding to provide that statements made by a child concerning the physical abuse of another child which was performed in his presence are admissible as an exception to the hearsay rule. In 1998, however, the Georgia Supreme Court struck down this amendment because it found that it created disparate classes of identically-situated criminal defendants in violation of the Equal Protection Clauses of the state and federal constitutions. The 1995 amendment created a disparity in the substantive evidence admissible against criminal defendants charged with identical acts of physical abuse, based on nothing more than the age of the hearsay declarant. If the declarant were under the age of 14, more evidence would have been admissible against the defendant than if the declarant were over that age. The court found no rational basis for the disparity created by the amended statute. Since the court has struck down this amendment as unconstitutional, it cannot be used as a basis for admitting a child's statements as a witness to physical abuse committed in his presence. However, if the statements are merely cumulative of other evidence of the physical abuse, their admission does not constitute reversible error. Because the statute allows statements only from a victim of physical abuse, it would be inapplicable as a ground for admitting statements from a victim of mental cruelty. However, the statements of such a victim may be admitted as part of the res gestae.

Testimony concerning the techniques used in a videotaped interview of the victim involves an area of expertise beyond the ken of the average layman and, therefore, the defendant in a cruelty to children case is entitled to introduce expert testimony for the limited purpose of providing the jury with information about proper techniques for interviewing children and whether the interviewing techniques actually utilized were proper. The fact that this testimony indirectly involves the child's credibility does not render it inadmissible.

For a discussion of the Child Hearsay Statute and other related statutes, see SEXUAL OFFENSES AGAINST CHILDREN, IV. CHILD HEARSAY STATUTE.

4. *Similar Offenses or Prior Difficulties*

Where evidence is proffered showing similar offenses committed by the defendant against the same victim, the evidence is admissible to show motive, intent, plan, identity, bent of mind, or course of conduct.

Evidence of prior instances of neglect or abuse of the victim may be admitted as rebuttal evidence for impeachment purposes. The failure to comply with the notice requirements of Uniform Superior Court Rule 31.3 does not render such evidence inadmissible.

The defendant's prior cruel acts toward the victim are admissible as evidence demonstrating motive, intent, or bent of mind toward the victim, thereby establishing a logical, probative connection between the crime charged and the prior difficulty. Since Uniform Superior Court Rule 31.3 is not applicable to occurrences categorized as prior difficulties between the defendant and the victim, the failure to comply with the notice requirements of this rule does not render this evidence inadmissible. However, the admission of this evidence must be accompanied by an instruction from the trial court explaining the limited use to which the jury may put this evidence.

5. *Defendant's Impaired Perception*

Where the defendant's sole defense is that she suffered from a psychological condition that impaired her knowledge and perception of the abuse her spouse was inflicting on her child, expert testimony would be admissible to show that the defendant was not aware of the signs and symptoms of the abuse, even though a normally perceptive person would have been aware of it. This evidence would be admissible, just as evidence of a vision impairment or other sensory difficulty would be admissible, not as evidence of diminished capacity but as evidence of impaired perception. Learned sources from the expert's profession and the expert's psychological testing and interview of the defendant can serve as the factual basis for this testimony. It need not be based on evidence of any childhood abuse administered to the defendant. Furthermore, this testimony would be admissible even though it would go to the ultimate issue of whether the defendant had knowledge of her spouse's abuse, because the jury would have no way of reaching a conclusion on this issue without it.

D. *Relationship to Other Offenses*

Important Notice about Repudiation of Actual or Same Evidence Test: The Georgia Supreme Court repudiated the actual evidence test in *Drinkard v. Walker*, 281 Ga. 211, 636 S.E.2d 530 (2006), because it found this test to be inconsistent with the statutory framework governing the prohibition against multiple convictions for included offenses in Georgia. This inconsistency resulted in years of confusion and unpredictable results. In its place, the court adopted the required evidence test and overruled any prior case law that is inconsistent with it. Thus, any prior case law applying the actual evidence test is no longer controlling and should not be relied upon to determine whether one offense is included in another under § 16-1-6(1). The discussion of such case law is included below only insofar as it may still be applicable to pending prosecutions that arose before the Drinkard decision. See MULTIPLE CONVICTIONS, II. Tests to Determine Presence of Multiple Convictions, for a complete discussion of the Drinkard decision.

Aggravated assault is committed when one assaults another with intent to murder, rape, or rob, or assaults with a deadly weapon; cruelty to children is committed when one maliciously causes a child cruel or excessive pain. Depending on the allegations and proof in a particular case, therefore, cruelty to children is sometimes a lesser included offense of aggravated assault. In Williams v. State, the defendant, a babysitter, allegedly whipped a child fiercely after tying her hands and feet to a bed. The court upheld the conviction, holding that under the facts of the case cruelty to children was a lesser included offense of aggravated assault, the crime for which the defendant had been indicted.

It is clear that simple battery can be a lesser included offense of cruelty to children. But it must be clear that the evidence in the case can support a finding of simple battery. Thus, in Newton v. State, the court held that it was not error to fail to charge on simple battery. The defendant denied the allegations in the indictment and testified that the injuries to the child resulted from accident. On this evidence, therefore, the jury would have been authorized either to find the defendant guilty of the offense of cruelty to children or find him not guilty on the basis of accident. Under no view of the evidence would a conviction for simple battery have been authorized. It should be noted that if the defense is, for example, a claim that excessive pain or deprivation had not been shown, an instruction on simple battery would be authorized.

If the facts alleged in the indictment and the evidence presented at trial to establish the charged offense of cruelty to children are sufficient to establish the lesser included offense of battery as well, it is not error for the trial court to charge the jury on the offense of battery.

Where there is evidence that the defendant intended his actions and intended to cause pain, he would not be entitled to a charge on reckless conduct as a lesser included offense of cruelty to children in the first degree. Moreover, where the evidence shows either the commission of cruelty to children as charged, or the commission of no offense, the trial court is not required to charge the jury on the lesser included offense of reckless conduct.

Cruelty to children, but not aggravated battery, requires proof that the victim was a child under the age of 18 who was caused cruel or excessive physical or mental pain. Aggravated battery, but not cruelty to children, requires proof that the victim was deprived of a member of his body or that such member was rendered useless or seriously disfigured. Therefore, each crime requires proof of at least one additional element which the other does not. Furthermore, the two crimes are not so closely related that multiple convictions are prohibited under other provisions of §§ 16-1-6 and 16-1-7. Accordingly, even if the same conduct establishes the commission of both aggravated battery and cruelty to children, the two crimes do not merge. Moreover, when the evidence establishes that the victim was subjected to multiple injuries in addition to the injury supporting an aggravated battery conviction, these additional injuries would support a cruelty to children conviction and the trial court's failure to merge the two offenses would not be erroneous.

Where the offense constituting cruelty to children is based upon and committed in a way different from the offenses of child molestation and assault with intent to rape and is not satisfied by the introduction of the same evidence, there is no merger and the trial court may enter a separate conviction on cruelty to children.

Where the evidence demonstrates that cruelty to children and sexual battery counts are supported by separate facts, the two offenses do not merge as a matter of fact.

The offense of cruelty to children is separate and distinct from the offense of rape as a matter of fact, where the evidence used to established cruelty to children is not used to establish the rape.

Since the offense of cruelty to children requires the proof of at least one fact, the age of the victim, in addition to the facts used to establish the offense of malice murder, the offense of cruelty to children is not included as a matter of fact in the offense of malice murder.

Because malice murder does not include all of the essential elements of the offense of cruelty to children, the latter is not an included offense of malice murder, and a conviction for cruelty to children would not be authorized under a malice murder count of an indictment. It follows that the refusal to give a requested charge on cruelty to children as an included offense of malice murder would not be error.

While a conviction for cruelty to children may be authorized as an included offense of felony murder, if the defendant is convicted of malice murder, the erroneous failure to charge cruelty to children as an included offense of felony murder would be harmless.

Even if a jury finds a defendant guilty of the involuntary manslaughter of a child, a trial court would not be required to direct a verdict of acquittal on a cruelty to children charge. The two verdicts could indeed be consistent because the jury could have found from the evidence that the defendant maliciously caused the child excessive pain and that his actions caused the child's death, but that he may not have intended to kill the child.

Where two sequential but entirely different acts of cruelty have been committed against the same victim, a conviction and sentence for each would be authorized.

Even if the offenses of cruelty to children and contributing to the deprivation of a minor are based on similar facts, they have differing elements, and each requires proof of a fact not required to prove the other. Thus, the two offenses do not merge, and the jury would be authorized to find the defendant guilty of both.

E. Statute of Limitations

In 1987, the General Assembly amended § 17-3-1(c) by extending the limitations period for felonies against victims under 14 years of age from four to seven years. The age limitation of 14 years, however, was inconsistent with the age of majority specified in § 16-5-70(a) and (b). This inconsistency created disparate classes of identically-situated criminal defendants in violation of the Equal Protection Clauses of the state and federal constitutions. It created a disparity in the limitation periods applicable to identical felonies based on nothing more than the age of the victim. For instance, if a victim of first degree cruelty to children were under the age of 14, the limitations period for the prosecution against the defendant would have been seven years, rather than four years had the victim been over that age. Although identically-situated, a defendant committing the offense against a victim under the age of 14 would have had the disadvantage of a longer limitations period for his crime than a defendant committing the same offense against an older victim. There was no apparent rational basis for this disparate treatment of identically-situated defendants.

In order to cure § 17-3-1(c)'s constitutional infirmity and to eliminate this disparate treatment, the 2002 General Assembly increased the age limitation for the seven-year limitation period from 14 to 18 years of age. The increased age limitation in this provision is now consistent with the age of majority specified in § 16-5-70(a) and (b). Thus, all offenses of cruelty to children in the first degree are subject to the same seven-year limitation period for acts occurring on or after July 1, 2002. The four-year limitation period is no longer applicable to such acts occurring on or after that date.

At trial, the date of the offense need not be proved with preciseness, but only that it occurred during the period of limitations. It may be established by circumstantial evidence.

The state is not restricted to proving that the offense occurred on the date alleged in the indictment when the indictment does not specifically allege that the date of the offense is material.

F. Punishment

Cruelty to children in the first degree, according to § 16-5-70(e)(1), is a felony punishable by imprisonment for not less than five nor more than 20 years.

Cruelty to children in the second degree, according to § 16-5-70(e)(2), is a felony punishable by imprisonment for not less than one nor more than ten years.

Cruelty to children in the third degree, according to § 16-5-70(e)(3), is punishable as a misdemeanor upon the first or second conviction. A third or subsequent offense is a felony punishable by a fine not less than $1,000 nor more than $5,000 or imprisonment for not less than one year nor more than three years or punishable by both fine and imprisonment.

A defendant's continuing neglect, that is, his causing excessive physical or mental pain by failing to procure medical treatment for a child during a four-day period, cannot be punished as separate units of prosecution under § 16-5-70(b). Without evidence of a legislative intent to allow multiple punishments for the same course of conduct, acts that constitute a continuing criminal course of conduct are not punishable separately. Thus, the defendant's criminal conduct would constitute a single course of conduct spanning four days, not a separate offense for each day. In such a case, the four counts of cruelty to children should be merged for sentencing purposes.

II. Tattooing Body of Person Under Age of 18

It is unlawful for any unauthorized person to tattoo the body of any person under the age of 18. This offense is punishable as a misdemeanor.

III. Piercing Body of Person Under Age of 18

It is unlawful for any person to pierce the body, with the exception of the ear lobes, of any person under the age of 18 for the purpose of allowing the insertion of earrings, jewelry, or similar objects into the body, unless the prior written consent of a custodial parent or guardian is obtained. This prohibition does not apply if (1) the piercer has been furnished with proper identification showing that the individual is 18 years of age or older and (2) the piercer reasonably believes the individual to be 18 years of age or older. This offense is punishable as a misdemeanor.

IV. Reckless Abandonment of Child Under Age of One Year

A parent, guardian, or other person supervising the welfare of or having immediate charge or custody of a child under the age of one year commits the offense of reckless abandonment of a child when the person willfully and voluntarily physically abandons the child with the intention of severing all parental or custodial duties and responsibilities to the child and leaving the child in a condition which results in the death of the child. Reckless abandonment of a child is a felony punishable by imprisonment for not less than ten nor more than 25 years.

Where one leaves a child in a condition which results in the child's death, such act is to be accounted as the efficient, proximate cause of the death whenever it is made to appear that the act materially contributed to or accelerated the cause of death. In In Interest of B. L. M., a 15-year-old juvenile gave birth to a baby girl at her home. She placed the baby in a trash bag and placed the bag with the garbage on the porch. After the baby was discovered by the juvenile's mother, it was taken to the hospital where it died four days later. The pathologist who participated in the autopsy on the baby testified that the baby had numerous health problems. However, he consistently testified that the cause of death was a combination of the baby's prematurity and its exposure to the elements, and that he could not separate those two factors. The Court of Appeals held that although the baby's exposure was not the sole proximate cause of death, the trial court was authorized to find that it materially contributed to or accelerated the cause of death. Accordingly, the trial court was authorized to find that the juvenile's actions legally resulted in the baby's death.

V. Child Endangerment: Manufacturing Methamphetamine or Possessing Chemical Substance with Intent to Manufacture Methamphetamine in Presence of Child

In an effort to further protect the well-being of this state's children, the General Assembly in 2004 enacted a child endangerment law. As part of this law, it enacted § 16-5-73 to prohibit the manufacture of methamphetamine in the presence of children.

Any person who intentionally causes or permits a child under the age of 18 years to be present where he is manufacturing methamphetamine or possessing a chemical substance with the intent to manufacture methamphetamine is guilty of a felony punishable by imprisonment for not less than two nor more than 15 years.

If the child receives serious injury as a result of this offense, the person is guilty of a felony punishable by imprisonment for not less than five nor more than 20 years.

DEFENSE OF PROPERTY AND HABITATION

I. Generally

The use or threatened use of force to protect nonhabitation property is justified when and to the extent that the actor reasonably believes that it is necessary to prevent a trespass on or other tortious or criminal interference with real or personal property lawfully in the possession of the actor or a member of his immediate family or belonging to one whose property he is under a legal duty to protect. The use of deadly force to protect nonhabitation property, however, is not justified unless the actor reasonably believes it is necessary in order to prevent a forcible felony. In the context of the defense of property, the law of Georgia appears to conform generally to the principles followed in the majority of American jurisdictions.

This defense is not available to a spouse attempting to recover personal property taken by his estranged spouse. Under our current theft statutes, one spouse can never be guilty of the theft of property of the other spouse. Accordingly, where an estranged spouse takes personal property from the lawful possession of the other spouse, such conduct is neither tortious nor criminal interference within the meaning of the statute defining the defense, and therefore, the other spouse would not be justified in using force to regain possession of his personal property.

Where the defendant has failed to establish the defense of nonhabitation property as his sole defense, the trial court's failure to charge the jury sua sponte on this defense would not be erroneous.

The use or threatened use of force to protect a habitation is justified when and to the extent that the actor reasonably believes that it is necessary to prevent or terminate an unlawful entry into or attack upon a habitation. The use of deadly force to protect a habitation, however, is not justified unless (1) the actor reasonably believes that an entry that is made in a violent and tumultuous manner is attempted or made for the purpose of assaulting or offering personal violence to any person dwelling or being therein and that such force is necessary to prevent the assault or offer of personal violence; or (2) the actor, knowing or having reason to believe that an unlawful and forcible entry of his residence has occurred, uses that force against an intruder who is neither a family nor household member; or (3) the actor reasonably believes that the entry is made or attempted for the purpose of committing a felony therein and that such force is necessary to prevent the commission of the felony. The lack of limiting language in items (1) and (3) above similar to the language in item (2) that expressly excludes application of the habitation defense between family and household members shows that the General Assembly intended the habitation defense as outlined in items (1) and (3) to apply between co-inhabitants.

If the jury is to determine correctly whether a defendant's justification defense is authorized because he was defending himself against the use of unlawful force by a homeowner, it needs to know the law which authorizes a homeowner to use force to defend his home. Under these circumstances, a charge on the defense of habitation can be given even though that defense is not asserted by the defendant.

Defense of habitation is not available where there is no evidence that the victim was attempting to enter or attack a habitation when he was injured.

II. Lawful Possession

The first limitation on the use of force in the defense of property is the requirement of lawful possession of the property by the actor or a member of his family, or the existence of a legal duty on the actor's part to protect the property. This limitation, set forth in § 16-3-24, may permit the use of force in more situations than the rule in many jurisdictions, in that it allows the use of force to defend the property of another, not a member of the actor's family, to whom the actor owes a legal duty to protect his property.

The Georgia courts do not appear to have considered the existence of possession or legal duty either before or since the enactment of the 1968 criminal code, but § 16-3-24 is sufficiently clear on this point that it should raise few questions. The § 16-3-24 requirement of possession of the defended property can be contrasted with § 16-3-23 which deals with defense of habitation. The latter section contains no requirement that the habitation defended be that of the actor or of someone in a special relationship to him. Presumably, then, one is justified in using force to protect the habitation of a stranger to the same extent as in the case of one's own home. The courts have not addressed this aspect of § 16-3-23.

III. Deadly Force

A. Defense of Property

The major limitation on the use of force in the defense of property is the rule against using deadly force (that which is intended or likely to cause death or great bodily harm) to protect nonhabitation property where there is no apparent need to use such force to prevent a forcible felony. It is this limitation, formerly a part of the justifiable homicide statutes, which has received the most attention from the courts. An early case held that a killing to prevent the taking of a small amount of meat would be justified if the taking amounted to robbery, a felony "by violence or surprise" but the court seemed more concerned with the doctrine of voluntary manslaughter occasioned by provocation arousing an uncontrollable passion.

This rather broad justification for the use of deadly force in the defense of property was put in doubt by a later holding that one is never justified in killing to effect the recapture of stolen property, even if the original theft had been a felony, and by cases stating that to justify the use of deadly force, the injury threatened by the victim must be grave or severe, whether the threatened harm is to person or to property. This ambiguity in the description of the rule in this situation reflects the fact that permitting the use of deadly force in the defense of property raises significant policy questions concerning the conflict between property rights and personal rights: it can be argued persuasively that, although his act is unlawful, a thief ought not by his act be seen to forfeit his right to live.

The present requirement of a threatened forcible felony to justify the use of deadly force seems to balance properly these interests, restricting the use of deadly force to those situations in which personal safety is endangered. It should be noted that § 16-3-24 does not require a belief that the forcible felony is to be committed against the actor. Thus, the actor could justify his use of force to protect a spouse's property because of the threat of a forcible felony against the spouse.

B. Defense of Habitation

The use of deadly force in the defense of a habitation is less restricted than it is in the defense of other property. Prior to 2001, a resident's use of deadly force against an intruder was justified under two conditions: (1) if the resident reasonably believed that a violent and tumultuous entry was made for the purpose of assaulting or offering violence to a person within the residence or (2) if the resident reasonably believed that the entry was made for the purpose of committing a felony therein. The resident had to be acting under a reasonable belief that the deadly force was necessary to thwart the attack or felony in order for his actions to be justified. However, because home invasions generally are unexpected and often occur too quickly for a resident to make a reasonable decision about using deadly force, the General Assembly added a third condition to § 16-3-23 in 2001 in order to permit a resident's use of deadly force against an intruder without having to satisfy either of the two reasonableness requirements. Now, the justification for a resident's use of deadly force against an intruder can be based on the resident's mere knowledge or belief that the entry was unlawful and forcible. This amendment, of course, makes it "easier" for a resident to use deadly force because it contains no reasonableness requirement. "Essentially, homeowners can shoot first and ask questions later." This defense, however, is not available when the deadly force is used against a family or household member. Nor is the defense available when the deadly force is used against a unarmed neighbor who, after leaving the resident's home as instructed, tumultuously reenters it.

The lack of limiting language in § 16-3-23(1) and (3) similar to the language in subsection (2) that expressly excludes application of the habitation defense between family and household members shows that the General Assembly intended the habitation defense as outlined in subsections (1) and (3) to apply between co-inhabitants.

Section 16-3-23 seems to dispel some of the confusion that prevailed in this area prior to 1968. A number of cases decided under the prior law, which was a part of the law of justifiable homicide, were concerned with the question of whether the intended harm protected against had to be a felony in order to justify the use of deadly force. A complicated and somewhat confusing structure of rules was thus developed. For instance, if two or more persons sought entry into a habitation "in a riotous and tumultuous manner," manifestly intending to inflict serious injury upon the person of someone therein, the use of deadly force to repel the entry was justified, although the intended injury might not have amounted to a felony. If only one person sought unlawful entry, however, or if entry was sought in a manner not "riotous and tumultuous," a manifest intent to commit a felony had to be shown, unless the defender first unsuccessfully attempted to prevent entry by persuasion or other gentle means.

Because a resident awakened in the middle of the night by a stranger forcing entry into his home is unlikely to bear all of these factors in mind in deciding whether to respond with deadly force, the present law introduces a welcome simplicity to the defense of habitation, which should accord better with the expectations of the public. In the ordinary situation of a resident being awakened by stirrings in the night, there can be no doubt of a reasonable belief that a felony is in progress.

For purposes of § 16-3-23, a person's habitation can be a particular space in a jointly-occupied dwelling provided that the person has obtained the right to occupy that space and exclude any co-inhabitants therefrom. While this right can be obtained by clear agreement, the fact that a person sometimes locked herself in the master bedroom in the weeks preceding her shooting of the victim would be insufficient to establish a clear agreement between herself and the victim that the victim could not enter the bedroom. Under these circumstances, the bedroom would not constitute a habitation and breaking down the bedroom door would not constitute an unlawful entry into or attack upon a habitation. Accordingly, a jury charge on the defense of habitation would not be authorized.

C. Retreat Rule, No Duty to

In Johnson v. State, the Georgia Supreme Court observed that although the Code was silent as to the duty to retreat in self-defense cases, under the common law, a defendant claiming self-defense had no duty to retreat if he was not the aggressor. The General Assembly finally codified this common law principle when it enacted § 16-3-23.1 in 2006. This Code section provides that any person who uses threats or force in accordance with the law relating to self-defense, defense of habitation, or defense of property other than a habitation has no duty to retreat and has the right to stand his ground and use force, including deadly force.

IV. Unlawful Entry

For the defense of habitation to be applicable, it is essential that the entry defended against be unlawful. Thus, where a police officer investigating a wife-beating complaint was threatened with a shotgun if he entered the house, the denial of defendant's motion for a directed verdict of not guilty of aggravated assault was proper, as there was evidence from which a jury could find that the officer was making a lawful entry. Furthermore, the "mere fact that an arrest by an officer may be unlawful, without more, does not authorize the killing of the arresting officer." Also, where the defendant and his victim are married to each other (either by ceremonial or common law marriage), the defense is unavailable, presumably on the ground that the victim's entry is lawful. Similarly, the right to defend one's home from unlawful entry does not authorize the defendant to defend against an invited visitor who becomes unruly. If the entry was unlawful, however, the right to defend the habitation does not disappear once entry is gained, and if the necessity of force remains apparent, its use is justified.

The Georgia cases are silent on the question of whether one may use deadly force to resist dispossession of his home, as apparently are the cases from other jurisdictions. In the realm of non-deadly force, however, a landlord in Georgia enjoys no special status permitting him forcible entry. Thus, where a landlady went to her tenant's trailer to demand more rent and tried to force her way in, and the tenant slammed the trailer door on her fingers and threw water on her, the tenant's conviction by a judge without a jury of simple battery was reversed.

The general rule in most jurisdictions is that, just as one is not privileged to use deadly force in defense of property where there is no danger to persons involved, so one may not use a deadly trap or spring gun to defend his property from theft. In Bishop v. State, the defendant was found guilty of malice murder where an acquaintance of the defendant died as a result of wounds received from the defendant's spring gun or trap gun set up in the defendant's trailer. The court held that the use of deadly force to protect a habitation is justified only when the inhabitant "reasonably believes" the entry is made for the purpose of committing a felony. However, it was impossible for the defendant to form a reasonable belief in light of his absence from the trailer. Also, the courts have imposed civil liability for such conduct where a trespasser is injured, even if the trespasser is a thief. In the more recent of these cases, the court of appeals indicated that the defendant might be guilty of murder or manslaughter, but the issue was not squarely presented by a civil action for wrongful death.

V. Hot Pursuit

It is generally recognized that one may use force to regain possession of property wrongfully taken if done immediately after the taking or while in hot pursuit. No recent cases have addressed this issue, but early Georgia cases support this proposition, with the caveat that deadly force may never be used to effect recapture. While there is nothing in the current statutes that specifically authorizes such hot pursuit recapture, § 16-3-24 does specifically cover personal property and such hot pursuit recapture would certainly be aimed at the termination of the continuing trespass. As for a possible argument that once the taking had taken place the actor was no longer in possession, the court could very well find that possession had not moved to the wrongdoer, but only custody, with legal possession remaining in the wronged actor.

VI. Use of Force Against Property

The use of force in defense of property was applied in a relatively unusual setting. In State v. Moore, the defendant had been accustomed to using a driveway across the property of another for a number of years. When he was told by the other party that he could no longer use the driveway, he consulted an attorney and concluded that he had obtained a private way by prescription. The owner of the land across which the driveway ran also consulted an attorney, then constructed a chain link fence around his property, secured by a padlocked gate.

When the defendant ran his truck into the gate to open it, he was charged with criminal damage to property and convicted of criminal trespass. On appeal, the defendant claimed that the refusal of the trial judge to instruct the jury on § 16-3-24 was error. The trial court's refusal to instruct was apparently based on the section's language which authorizes the use of force "against another." The trial judge interpreted this to mean against the person of another. The court of appeals reversed, indicating that the defendant would be entitled to an acquittal if the jury was convinced that the defendant was acting under a reasonable belief that this was needed to protect his property in the prescriptive easement.

The Georgia Supreme Court, however, reversed the court of appeals and affirmed the conviction, relying on the criminal code definition of "another" as "person or persons other than the accused." While the supreme court did not mention it, additional support for its decision could be drawn from the requirement of § 16-3-24 that the property be in the defendant's possession. The notion of a prescriptive right being in a defendant's possession is hard to conceptualize. It might be argued that Moore reflects a strange ordering of values in that it protects the "victim's" property more than it protects his person. It seems, however, that the determination of such disputes as that in Moore ought to be left to civil litigation, rather than self-help. None of the immediacy which underlies the § 16-3-24 defense is present in Moore.

A different situation, however, might be presented if the use of force was directed at property in the aggressor's immediate possession. For example, if an intruder were entering the defendant's property and the defendant used force against the aggressor's dog which was accompanying him, for the purpose of repelling the trespass, it can be argued that § 16-3-24 would be a permissible defense. If confronted with that kind of situation, the court might be forced to rethink its Moore reliance on the definition of "another" and expand it to property owned by the aggressor. In either the Moore situation or the proposed hypothetical, it can be argued that the general justification defense of § 16-3-20(6) ought to be analyzed for possible applicability.

VII. Burden of Proof

As affirmative defenses, the burden of proof with regard to defense of habitation and defense of property rests upon the state. Thus, once the defendant has introduced enough evidence to raise the possibility of the applicability of § 16-3-23 or § 16-3-24, the state will have the burden of proving the non-existence of these defenses beyond a reasonable doubt.

VIII. Immunity from Civil Liability

A person who is justified in threatening or using force against another under the provisions of § 16-3-23, relating to the use of force in defense of a habitation, or § 16-3-24, relating to the use of force in defense of property other than a habitation, has no duty to retreat from the use of such force and is not liable to the person against whom the use of force was justified or to any person acting as an accomplice or assistant to such person in any civil action brought as a result of the threat or use of such force.

IX. Immunity from Criminal Prosecution

A person who uses threats or force in defense of a habitation or property other than a habitation or in accordance with the no duty to retreat rule is immune from criminal prosecution unless in the use of deadly force that person utilizes a weapon the carrying or possession of which is unlawful.

This statute must be construed to bar criminal proceedings against persons who use force under the circumstances set forth in § 16-3-23 or § 16-3-24. Further, as the statute provides that such person "shall be immune from criminal prosecution," the decision as to whether a person is immune under § 16-3-24.2 must be determined by the trial court before the trial of that person commences.

A convicted felon in possession of a weapon may not as a matter of law benefit from the pretrial immunity outlined in § 16-3-24.2.

As a potential bar to criminal proceedings which must be determined prior to a trial, immunity represents a far greater right than any encompassed by an affirmative defense, which may be asserted during trial but cannot stop a trial altogether. To avoid trial, a defendant bears the burden of showing that he is entitled to immunity under § 16-3-24.2 by a preponderance of the evidence. If a defendant cannot meet his burden of proving immunity prior to trial, he may nonetheless pursue an affirmative defense at trial, even though the affirmative defense may be based on the same statutory provision underlying a prior immunity motion. In this instance, the well-established burden of proof for affirmative defenses would be applicable during trial.

DISORDERLY CONDUCT CRIMES

See also CRIMINAL DEFAMATION; HARASSING PHONE CALLS; LOITERING OR PROWLING; TERRORISTIC THREATS AND ACTS; WEARING MASKS.

I. Generally

Disorderly conduct has been described as a petty offense chiefly against public order and decency. Whether conduct will violate a disorderly conduct statute will depend not only on the nature of the act and the accompanying mens rea, but also on the surrounding circumstances.

The offenses discussed below are grouped into categories generally along the lines of the evil which the statutes seek to avoid.

II. Disorderly Conduct Which Involves or Threatens Mob or Group Violence

A. Riot

A riot is defined by § 16-11-30 as a combination of two or more persons performing "an unlawful act of violence or any other act in a violent or tumultuous manner." Because the offense of rioting has undergone very little change since its initial codification in 1861, pre-1968 case law is helpful in understanding the meaning and coverage of the current statute.

The crime of riot has three elements: (1) a shared intent among two or more people (2) to do an unlawful act of violence or some other act in a violent and tumultuous manner and (3) a concert of action in furtherance of such an intent. Because these elements must coalesce, if only one of the rioters has the requisite intent, or if only one of the rioters acts in furtherance of the intent, there is no riot.

When proving the existence of a shared intent, it should be noted that it is not necessary to prove independently the existence of a previous plot or conspiracy on the part of the rioters. Rather, both a shared intent and a concert of action may be inferred from the manner in which the unlawful act of violence is committed. Because cooperation and joint action are required, however, two people fighting against each other does not constitute a riot.

The requirement of an intent to engage in an **act** of violence precludes a conviction for rioting upon proof that the defendant merely engaged in noisy or tumultuous behavior. The courts have, however, held that "violent behavior" short of a violent act is a sufficient act for riot. Therefore, people gathered together who commit no overt acts of violence but do commit some other act which is calculated to bring about a breach of the peace or to terrify people were held guilty of the offense of riot. This act was held to be violent and tumultuous conduct within the meaning of the statute.

A criminal riot does not require chaos or bedlam, notwithstanding the common connotation of the term "riot." For example, there was found to be sufficient evidence to support riot convictions when the defendants threatened their father, when the defendants chased their fishing partner and hurled objects at him, and when the defendants beat another person, giving him a bloody nose.

Because riot is a crime which involves multiple offenders, certain procedural guidelines must be noted. Section 17-8-4 adopts the traditional approach with regard to the severability of trials for joint offenders by providing for discretionary severance. If severance is granted and separate trials held, the acquittal or conviction of one party to the offense does not operate as an acquittal or conviction of others not tried even though joint action and the concurrence of two or more persons are required. On the other hand, if several persons were indicted and tried together for a riot and the proof showed the guilt of only one, all must be acquitted because the required multiplicity of action is missing. One may be convicted, however, even if his co-indictee has been exonerated if the indictment names persons unknown as co-rioters.

Rioting is a misdemeanor punishable under the general misdemeanor statute.

B. Inciting to Riot

Encouraging others to riot is also a crime. Section 16-11-31 punishes one who, with the intent to riot, advises or urges others to riot under circumstances which create a clear and present danger of a riot. This section covers intentional inciteful acts or conduct aimed at one's opponents as well as one's supporters.

The "clear and present danger" requirement in the statute was an obvious attempt to codify the First Amendment constitutional requirements for punishment of inciteful speech as they stood at the time of codification in 1968. However, the "clear and present danger" language has been interpreted in conformity with the most recent United States Supreme Court reformulation of the constitutional standard. In 1993, the Georgia Supreme Court applied this standard in Land v. State and held that since the defendant's conduct constituted inciting to riot and the evidence showed that a riot was imminent, the defendant's speech was not afforded any constitutional protection.

Inciting to riot is a misdemeanor punishable under the general misdemeanor statute.

C. Affray

Under § 16-11-32, the misdemeanor of affray has three elements. They are: (1) two or more people intentionally fighting (2) in a public place and (3) to the disturbance of the public tranquility.

The requirement that the people intentionally fight shields one from an affray conviction if his automatic reflexes would cause him to push back that which is about to destroy him. That is, for an assailant to be guilty of affray, he must be a "willing participant" in the conflict, as opposed to being the victim of an assault exercising the right of self-defense. Thus, the Court of Appeals vacated a conviction when the evidence showed that the "victim" was actually the aggressor and had approached the defendant in a menacing manner with a pool cue.

In order to find a violation of § 16-11-32, it must be shown that two willing participants engaged in a fight. Because both participants must have entered into the fight willingly and intentionally, the defense of one will inure to the benefit of the other. Thus, if the evidence shows that one of the two participants in a fight acted entirely in self-defense, while the other participant was the aggressor, neither is guilty of an affray. The Georgia Supreme Court has further held that the fight must include physical harm, so that an affray may not be committed by words alone.

The second element of affray is that the fight occur in a public place. "Public place" is defined by the criminal code as a "place where the conduct involved may reasonably be expected to be viewed by people other than members of the actor's family or household." The full meaning and import of the term "public place" for purposes of the statute has yet to be addressed by the Georgia Supreme Court.

The third element of affray is that the acts must tend to breach the peace and public tranquility. It is hard to envision what independent relevance this element has. It will invariably be satisfied if the other elements are met.

Where both participants are charged with affray, the successful defense of one of the participants operates as an acquittal of the other.

The fact that an aggravated assault took place in the context of an affray does not require the trial court to charge the jury on affray, where the indictment charged the defendant with aggravated assault. Affray, as statutorily defined, is not a lesser included offense of aggravated assault or even simple battery.

Ultimate Fighting matches encompass boxing, kick boxing, or contact karate. Under certain circumstances, the participants in an Ultimate Fighting match held in a public place and not regulated by the state boxing commission may be charged with the offense of affray.

D. Unlawful Assembly

Section 16-11-33 proscribes two separate types of unlawful assembly. Both are misdemeanors punishable under the general misdemeanor statute, § 17-10-3. The first type occurs when two or more persons assemble for the purpose of committing an unlawful act and fail to withdraw from the assembly upon a lawful command by a peace officer and **before** any member of the assembly has inflicted injury to the person or property of another. This type of unlawful assembly is in the nature of attempted riot. The second type occurs when two or more persons assemble, without authority of law, for the purpose of doing violence to the person or property of one supposed by the accused to be guilty of a violation of the law, or for the purpose of exercising correctional or regulative powers over any person by violence. This type of unlawful assembly can best be described as a lynch mob offense.

It should be noted that there is an affirmative defense of withdrawal. The defendant is not guilty if he withdraws either at any time before injury is inflicted or in response to a lawful order by a peace officer. The latter provision would indicate that an order to withdraw which was obeyed would be a defense even if the order came after injuries had been inflicted, as the defenses are written in the disjunctive, rather than the conjunctive.

Inasmuch as the proscriptions of § 16-11-33 are limited to assemblies which have an unlawful or violent purpose, § 16-11-33 would most likely withstand a First Amendment challenge.

On the facts of a particular case, unlawful assembly may be a lesser included offense of obstruction of a public passage.

No conviction for unlawful assembly may be had where the accused (or, indeed, any member of the assembled group) is also convicted of a completed crime against the person or property of another, where that completed crime was the purpose of the assembly. Thus, in Kerr v. State, the court held that because the defendants were properly convicted of criminal trespass, their convictions for unlawful assembly for the purpose of committing criminal trespass merged into the criminal trespass convictions.

E. Refusal to Disperse

Section 16-10-30 makes it a misdemeanor for a person in a gathering to refuse to obey the reasonable official request or order of a peace officer or firefighter to move, for the purpose of promoting the public safety by dispersing those gathered in dangerous proximity to a fire or other emergency.

F. Obstruction of Highways, Streets, Sidewalks, or Public Passages

It is a misdemeanor to obstruct purposely or recklessly any public passageway so that the passage is rendered impassable without unreasonable inconvenience or hazard. Liability does not attach, however, until the person so obstructing the passageway fails or refuses to cease the obstruction after receiving a reasonable official request or an order of a peace officer to do so.

In 1990 and 1991, two cases concerning the violation of this statute by abortion protesters were decided. In McMonagle v. State, the court held that a public passage that is temporarily barricaded by the police, that is not completely closed off to public access, and that is still usable and is used by the public does not cease to be a public passage so that in effect it cannot be protected from criminal obstruction. The court also held that the refusal of protestors to remove themselves after warning and their going "limp" and playing "dead" constitutes obstruction under the statute. Thus, anyone who exhorts protestors to go "limp" would be guilty of obstruction as a party to the crime. In Hoover v. State, the court held that an abortion conducted in compliance with the law would not constitute "imminent use of unlawful force" so as to justify the defendants' obstruction of a public passage during an abortion protest.

On the facts of a particular case, unlawful assembly may be a lesser included offense of obstruction of a public passage.

G. Criminal Interference with Government Property

Section 16-7-24(b) makes it a misdemeanor to forcibly interfere with or to obstruct the passage into or from government property. This statute is designed to replace pre-1968 GCA § 26-5502, which made it a misdemeanor to picket or demonstrate in a riotous manner on, around, or adjacent to state property.

III. Disorderly Conduct Which Involves Public Disturbance

A. Public Disturbance

"A person who recklessly or knowingly commits any act which may reasonably be expected to prevent or disrupt a lawful meeting, gathering, or procession is guilty of a misdemeanor." The crux of this offense is the creation of a public disturbance.

In State v. Fielden, the Georgia Supreme Court held that the language of § 16-11-34(a) is not unconstitutionally vague. Rather, it is clear and unambiguous. Reading the provision according to the natural and obvious import of its language, the court concluded that it provides a sufficiently definite warning to a person of ordinary intelligence of the prohibited conduct and further that it is not susceptible to arbitrary and discriminatory enforcement.

The court held, however, that § 16-11-34(a) is unconstitutionally overbroad because it stifles expression or conduct that is otherwise protected by the federal constitution. Under the literal language of the provision, any recklessly or knowingly committed act that could reasonably be expected to prevent or disrupt a lawful meeting, gathering or procession is a misdemeanor, regardless where it is committed, how trivial the act, its impact, or the intent of the actor other than the intent to commit the act itself. This provision thus applies to the reckless or knowing commission of such acts as heckling a referee at a sports venue, leaving on the audible ringer of a cellphone during a business symposium, changing lanes into a funeral procession on a rainy day, even playing the stereo loudly in an apartment while a neighbor hosts a dinner party. These examples demonstrate that the literal language of § 16-11-34(a) reaches conduct that is at once innocent and protected by the guarantees of free speech, thereby affecting and chilling constitutionally protected activity. Based on this analysis of the statutory language in § 16-11-34(a), the court concluded that it significantly impacts constitutionally permitted conduct without the requisite narrow specificity and fails to balance in a reasonable way the First Amendment rights of those desiring to express opposing points of view. Accordingly, the court found its overbreadth to be both real and substantial. Finding that curing the overbreadth in § 16-11-34(a) would be less a matter of reasonable judicial construction than a matter of substantial legislative revision, the court found that it lacked the authority to rewrite the provision to avoid its constitutional infirmities.

A paradigmatic case under § 16-11-34(a) is *Washington v. State*, where the defendants were protesting students whose conduct was held to be a public disturbance because the noise they created disrupted normal classroom activities. The conduct in question was singing and shouting which was considered to be a disturbance because it could not easily be ignored. The court indicated that if the conduct prosecuted had been merely the organizing activity, it would not in itself constitute a disturbance cognizable under the statute. The court implicitly found that students attending classes in the school to be a gathering or meeting, for clearly it was not a procession.

The *Washington* convictions were upheld based on circumstantial evidence connecting the disturbance to the defendants. While noting that the evidence was sharply conflicting, the court relied heavily on the testimony of the school principal that the singing and shouting appeared to emanate from the center of the group, where the defendants were situated. The court distinguished Tinker v. Des Moines Community School District, where the Supreme Court of the United States found a school protest to be constitutionally immune from disciplinary action on the basis of the non-disruptive nature of the silent protest at issue in *Tinker*.

A violation of § 16-11-34 was found to exist in Porter v. State where the defendants' conduct disrupted an ongoing church service. The defendants' conduct consisted of yelling, laughing, mocking and mimicking the service. Additionally, two co-participants who did not appeal their convictions brought copperhead snakes into the church. (Snake handling was not a part of the church service.) Under the foregoing circumstances, the Court of Appeals held that the evidence demonstrated that the behavior had a "disconcerting and disturbing effect" on the congregants and was sufficient to support the convictions.

Section 16-11-34 does not affect the powers which have been delegated to counties or to municipal corporations to pass ordinances to punish disorderly conduct within their jurisdiction. Where a municipality charges the defendant by using merely the words "disorderly conduct," it cannot be ascertained whether he is charged with the state offense or with a local ordinance; consequently, the charge against the defendant is too vague and indefinite to apprise him of the offense he allegedly committed.

B. Disruption of Senate or House of Representatives

Section 16-11-34.1 makes it unlawful for a person to recklessly and knowingly prevent or disrupt a session or meeting of the Senate or House of Representatives or any of its committees. It is unlawful to enter, occupy, or remain in the state capitol building or related buildings while one is in possession of a deadly weapon. It is unlawful to purposely and recklessly obstruct any passageway in Capitol Square. It is unlawful to willfully and knowingly without authorization enter or remain upon the floor or in any adjacent area of the Senate or House. It is unlawful to parade, demonstrate, or picket in the state capitol or its related buildings with intent to disrupt.

The first violation of § 16-11-34.1 is a misdemeanor. A second violation is a misdemeanor of a high and aggravated nature. A third or any subsequent violation is a felony punishable by imprisonment for not less than one nor more than three years.

B1. Disruption of Funeral or Memorial Services

1. Legislative Intent

In 2006, the General Assembly declared that the interest of persons in planning, participating in, and attending a funeral or memorial service for a deceased relative or loved one without unwanted impediment, disruption, disturbance, or interference was a substantial interest. The General Assembly further recognized the need to impose content neutral time, place, and manner restrictions on unwanted acts carried out with the intent to impede, disrupt, disturb, or interfere with such funeral or memorial service. In order to implement these restrictions, the General Assembly enacted § 16-11-34.2.

2. Prohibited Conduct

Under § 16-11-34.2, it is unlawful to engage in any disorderly or disruptive conduct with the intent to impede, disrupt, disturb, or interfere with the orderly conduct of any funeral or memorial service or with the normal activities and functions carried on in the facilities or buildings where the funeral or memorial service is taking place. Any or all of the following constitutes such disorderly or disruptive conduct:

(1) Displaying any visual images that convey fighting words or actual or imminent threats of harm directed to any person or property associated with the funeral or memorial service within 500 feet of the ceremonial site or location being used for the service at any time one hour prior to, during, or one hour after the posted time for the service;

(2) Uttering loud, threatening, or abusive language or singing, chanting, whistling, or yelling with or without noise amplification including, but not limited to, bullhorns, automobile horns, and microphones, such as would tend to impede, disrupt, disturb, or interfere with a funeral or memorial service within 500 feet of the ceremonial site or location being used for the service;

(3) Attempting to block or blocking pedestrian or vehicular access to the ceremonial site or location being used for a funeral or memorial service at any time one hour prior to, during, or one hour after the posted time for the service; or

(4) Conducting a public assembly, parade, demonstration, or other like event, either fixed or processional, within 500 feet of the ceremonial site or location being used for a funeral or memorial service at any time one hour prior to, during, or one hour after the posted time for the service.

3. *Punishment*

The disruption of a funeral or memorial is punishable a misdemeanor under the general misdemeanor statute.

C. *Disruption of Activities of School Campus or Facility*

Apparently in the wake of campus disorders, the General Assembly enacted § 16-11-35 in 1972. This Code section makes it a misdemeanor of a high and aggravated nature for a person, who is not a student or school employee, to enter a school campus or facility and fail to leave as directed by an administrative officer when it reasonably appears to the officer that the person is committing an act likely to interfere with the peaceful conduct of school activities or that the person has entered the campus or facility for the purpose of committing a disruptive act. The person must receive an order to leave from the school's chief administrative officer or his designee and must fail to leave before he is guilty of violating § 16-11-35.

The elements of this offense are almost identical to those for criminal trespass. Despite this similarity, the statutes defining the two offenses are not conflicting but coexist in harmony. The criminal trespass statute protects school campuses from unauthorized **use**, and § 16-11-35 protects school activities from unauthorized **disruption**. With the enactment of § 16-11-35, the General Assembly did not intend to exempt school campuses from the ambit of the criminal trespass statute. In other words, it did not intend that the act of remaining on school campuses for other than authorized educational purposes be criminalized only in the event that such presence also coincides with the commission or intent to commit "any act likely to interfere with the peaceful conduct of the activities of the campus." Thus, a defendant may be found to have violated the public property interest protected by the criminal trespass statute, regardless of the fact that his unauthorized activities may have posed no threat to the otherwise peaceful conduct of educational activities protected by § 16-11-35.

D. *Public Drunkenness*

The offense of public drunkenness is committed when an individual appears in an intoxicated condition in any public place and makes his intoxicated condition known by boisterousness, by indecent condition or act, or by vulgar, profane, loud, or unbecoming language. The requisites of § 16-11-41 are classically illustrated by the case of Moore v. State. In Moore, the defendant was discovered, uninvited, in the driveway of a private residence. The defendant's intoxicated condition was manifested by her blowing the horn of her automobile and by playing the radio at a high volume. Additionally, the defendant resisted police assistance, and was belligerent, using abusive and obscene language. The conviction was affirmed.

Merely appearing in public in a drunken condition does not violate § 16-11-41, because the public drunkenness statute is designed as a protection against the drunkard's conduct and not his mere presence. Consequently, drunkenness manifested by extreme stupor or a deep sleep is not a violation of state law. Thus, an individual who had "passed out" on the bench of an eating establishment with a partially empty fifth of liquor beside him, who was unsteady on his feet, and whose speech was slurred when he spoke was not guilty of public drunkenness. Likewise, a conviction would not be authorized where the evidence demonstrated only that the defendant had pulled off the road in his car and slept therein.

A conviction for public drunkenness is unauthorized where it appears that the defendant, although drunk, was not voluntarily in a public place. Involuntary presence would mean that the defendant had not committed the requisite actus reus. Thus, one cannot be removed by police officers or by anybody else from a place which is not a public place within the purview of the statute, be involuntarily placed in a public place, and then be convicted of public drunkenness.

Section 16-11-41 does not affect the powers delegated to counties or to municipal corporations to pass ordinances to punish drunkenness or disorderly conduct within their respective limits. The Court of Appeals has held that a city ordinance which is more restrictive than § 16-11-41 can withstand a challenge based on preemption by the state law so long as the municipal offense has some essential ingredient not an element of the state offense or the municipal offense lacks some element essential to the state offense. The Court of Appeals has also held that the prosecution must prove the existence of the public drunkenness ordinance in order to establish what acts constituted a violation of the ordinance.

Public drunkenness is not, as a matter of fact or law, a lesser included offense of driving under the influence of alcohol to the extent it is less safe to drive.

IV. Disorderly House Kept for Encouragement of Misbehavior or Common Disturbance of Neighborhood

A. Elements

Under § 16-11-44, one who keeps and maintains a disorderly house is guilty of a misdemeanor, punishable under the general misdemeanor statute, § 17-10-3. There are two elements to the crime: (1) the defendant must keep and maintain the house; and (2) the house must be a common, ill-governed, and disorderly establishment kept for the encouragement of gaming, drinking, or other misbehavior or kept in such a manner as to cause the common disturbance of the neighborhood or orderly citizens.

B. Keeps and Maintains

The defendant must be shown to be responsible for the keeping and maintaining of the dwelling in question; consequently, being a mere visitor to a disorderly house is not sufficient. A problem arises, however, when the dwelling is occupied by more than one person. If a family unit is involved, the courts have held that the violator is the head of the household unless he can produce evidence to the contrary. Traditionally, a husband's mere presence in the household was sufficient to establish him as its head even if his wife paid the rent. In light of the United States Supreme Court's decision in Orr v. Orr and the later repeal of Georgia's "head of the household" law, there is no longer a presumption that the male is the head of the household.

When the occupants of a dwelling are not members of the same immediate family, the state must show that the defendant is connected with the illicit activity; merely being an occupant of the quarters in which illicit activities transpire is insufficient. It would appear that the prosecution must show either knowledge of or active participation in the proscribed activity.

So far as § 16-11-44 proscribes the maintenance of a house to the encouragement of gambling or drinking on a general, customary or habitual basis, one of ordinary intelligence is given fair notice of what conduct is prohibited; and this section does not encourage arbitrary and erratic arrests and convictions.

C. Disorderly House

A disorderly house has been defined as "a house in which people abide or to which they resort to the disturbance of the neighborhood or for purposes which are injurious to the public morals, health, convenience, or safety."

In Fanning v. State the court reversed the defendant's conviction because there was no evidence the house was disorderly, even though a substantial amount of liquor was discovered on the premises. Quoting from Palfus v. State the court indicated that to be disorderly, a house must as a normal matter, as opposed to merely occasionally, be noisy, and the disturbance thus caused must be of a general nature, as opposed to merely disturbing one or two people. The court also indicated that merely being a tippling house is insufficient to sustain a conviction for disorderly house based on the phrase "injurious to the public morals, health, convenience or safety." This conception of what a "disorderly house" is was reaffirmed in the case of Clare v. State. In Clare, the court indicated that the defendant's apartment could not qualify as a disorderly house based on the noise emanating from it when the evidence failed to show a regular course of noisiness, or even that the defendant was particularly noisy on this occasion.

The type of proof necessary to prove a house is disorderly based on the phrase "to the common disturbance of the neighborhood" should be contrasted to the type required when the disorderly character is attributable because conduct within the house is alleged to be injurious to the public morality. The latter situation was at issue in Martin v. State. The primary issue on appeal was whether the character of a house may be proved by introducing evidence as to the reputation of the house. Approving this method of proof, the court indicated that under the public morality portion of the disorderly house proscription a house may be found to be disorderly, even if it is operated in a quiet manner, if it operates for purposes which are injurious to the public morality. In Martin, the defendant was apparently operating a bordello.

This interpretation of conduct punishable as contributing to a disorderly house was reiterated in Birdwell v. State. In Birdwell the court indicated "the charge of keeping and maintaining . . . a disorderly house to encourage idleness, gaming, drinking 'or other misbehavior,' may be shown by proof of repeated immoral acts of fornication and adultery committed therein with the knowledge and approval of defendant."

A building open to the public may constitute a disorderly house if the nature of the activity engaged therein tends to produce turmoil. For example, an ice-cream parlor which was the site of much drinking, dancing, fighting and loud cursing was considered to be a disorderly house, as was a restaurant which sold beer and wine, had a nickelodeon and was the scene of frequent arrests of drunken men.

V. Disorderly Conduct Statute

A. Generally

Prior to 1995, § 16-11-39 prohibited (1) the unprovoked use of "fighting words," (2) the unprovoked use of obscene and vulgar or profane language before a person under the age of 14, (3) engaging in indecent or disorderly conduct in a public place, and (4) the making of harassing phone calls.

When the General Assembly rewrote this statute in 1995, it retained the two provisions prohibiting the use of "fighting words" and the use of obscene and vulgar or profane language. It eliminated the provision prohibiting indecent or disorderly conduct, which was held to be unconstitutionally vague by the Georgia Supreme Court in 1990, and added two provisions which now clearly define the conduct that is prohibited under the statute, i.e., acts committed in a violent or tumultuous manner toward another person. The General Assembly also eliminated from the statute the provision prohibiting the making of harassing phone calls but enacted a new statute which now prohibits this offense.

B. Violent or Tumultuous Acts

Prior to 1995, former paragraph (3) of § 16-11-39 punished anyone who engaged in "indecent or disorderly conduct in the presence of another in any public place." The statute was totally silent as to the definition of "indecent or disorderly conduct." In 1990, the Georgia Supreme Court held that because the statute failed to define in any manner what was meant by indecent or disorderly conduct, it did not provide fair warning to persons of ordinary intelligence as to what it prohibited so that they might act accordingly, and it was thus too vague to justify the imposition of criminal punishment for its violation.

In 1995, when the General Assembly rewrote § 16-11-39, it eliminated the vague language of former paragraph (3) and added two provisions which now clearly define what acts constitute disorderly conduct and should provide fair warning as to what acts are prohibited under the statute. Section 16-11-39(a)(1) and (2) provide that one commits the offense of disorderly conduct when he (1) acts in a violent or tumultuous manner toward another person whereby that person is placed in reasonable fear of the safety of his life, limb, or health; or (2) acts in a violent or tumultuous manner toward another person whereby the property of that person is placed in danger of being damaged or destroyed.

C. Fighting Words

Section 16-11-39(a)(3) provides that one commits the offense of disorderly conduct when he uses "fighting words" without provocation in another's presence. These words can be either aimed at or descriptive of the listener in order to be proscribed by the statute. Obscene and vulgar or profane words do not constitute "fighting words" unless those words are also "opprobrious or abusive." It is important to note that actual response by the "victim" is not an element of the offense. Thus, if "fighting words" were used, they are punishable as soon as uttered, even though there is no response.

Specific threats to cause violence can constitute "fighting words" where they tend to provoke violent resentment. Moreover, the circumstances surrounding the incident are relevant to determine whether the defendant's statements were sufficient to incite the victim to take offensive action. Although the circumstances surrounding the utterance of the words can be crucial, circumstances cannot change harmless words into "fighting words."

Section 16-11-39(a)(3) was amended in 1974 in response to the United States Supreme Court's decision in the case of Gooding v. Wilson. The statute at issue in Gooding was similar to the pre-1974 version of § 16-11-39(a)(3), prohibiting the use of opprobrious words or abusive language tending to cause a breach of the peace. In Gooding, the United States Supreme Court, relying on Chaplinsky v. New Hampshire, held that the statute violated the First Amendment. In Chaplinsky, the Supreme Court had held that the First Amendment prohibits the states from punishing an individual for using certain words under a statute which is neither carefully drawn nor authoritatively construed to punish only unprotected speech, i.e., "fighting words." The Court defined "fighting words" as words which men of common intelligence would understand to be words likely to cause an average addressee to fight. Section 16-11-39(a)(3) was amended in 1974 to reflect that decision and is therefore limited by its terms to "fighting words."

The Georgia Court of Appeals in Brooks v. State applied the "fighting words" test in order to find that there was probable cause to arrest the defendant for violation of the opprobrious language statute where he called a policeman a dog in front of a crowd of 100 to 200 people. The Model Penal Code takes the position that "fighting words" directed at a police officer which might cause a personal disturbance on the part of the officer, but not a general disturbance, should not be punished. This, however, reflects a policy decision rather than a rule of constitutional law.

In 1914, the Georgia Court of Appeals in Elmore v. State rejected an argument similar to that adopted by the Model Penal Code. In Elmore the Court of Appeals was responding to the contention that a conviction should not lie for using "opprobrious words or abusive language 'tending to cause a breach of the peace' "if the language is directed at a police officer because a police officer cannot legally respond to vile language by assaulting one in his custody; therefore, the words cannot have a "tendency to cause a breach of peace." The court responded to this argument by indicating that it is perhaps because a police officer cannot respond with force that he should be legally protected from such verbal assault.

In another case, Bolden v. State, the Georgia Court of Appeals specifically rejected the position that a different standard should be used when opprobrious and abusive language is directed toward a police officer. The court observed that § 16-11-39(a)(3) makes no distinction based on the target of the utterance. The actus reus is committed when language is used which would be "fighting words" if evaluated against a reasonable person standard, regardless of the response or lack of response by the target of the utterance.

While this is true, the court **has** distinguished between opprobrious language used while under lawful arrest, and similar language used as "remonstrance against an illegal arrest." In Scott v. State, the Georgia Court of Appeals reversed the defendant's conviction for violating § 16-11-39 holding that "[o]pprobrious words heard only by the arresting officer and used in remonstrance to an illegal arrest do not constitute a violation of Code Ann. § 26-2610 [O.C.G.A. § 16-11-39]." Presumably, if others heard the language, that would alter the result.

Section 16-11-39(a)(3) requires the language used to be "without provocation." Because this is an element of the offense, the burden is upon the state to show lack of provocation. Whether the provocation proved is sufficient to justify the use of opprobrious words or abusive language is normally a jury question. Truth is not, however, a legal provocation for the use of opprobrious words.

In Shuler v. State, the defendant was indicted for simple battery and cruelty to children but was convicted only for the offense of using "fighting words." The defendant contended that the use of opprobrious language tending to incite a breach of peace was not a lesser included offense of cruelty to children. The court held, however, that the proof tracked the indictment which set forth words the defendant said to a student which would fall within the perimeter of that forbidden by the "fighting words" statute. While not specifically charged with using "fighting words," the defendant was indicted for using language which would tend to incite an immediate breach of the peace. Although the offense may not have been strictly a "lesser included" one within the scope of cruelty to children, the language of the indictment together with the evidence authorized the jury charge on "fighting words."

In Carroll v. State, the court held that "fighting words" was not a lesser included offense of terroristic threats as a matter of law because the crimes have different elements and prohibit generally different types of conduct. Furthermore, under the narrowly drawn indictment charging the defendant with terroristic threats, the trial court did not have the power to interpret the evidence so as to support a jury charge on the separate, unindicted, alternative offense of "fighting words."

D. Obscene and Vulgar or Profane Language

Section 16-11-39(a)(4) provides that one commits the offense of disorderly conduct when he uses, without provocation, "obscene and vulgar or profane language in the presence of or by telephone to a person under the age of 14 years which threatens an immediate breach of the peace."

The use of obscene and vulgar language may properly be subjected to state regulation. Under the current test established by the United States Supreme Court, material is obscene if the average person, applying contemporary community standards, would find that the material, taken as a whole, appeals to the prurient interest. Because "obscenity" is not subject to a very precise definition, what is obscene will vary over both time and space, rendering the precedential value of prior cases suspect. In the past, violations of § 16-11-39(a)(4) or statutes similar to it have been found when the defendant asked an eleven-year-old girl whether she had ever been laid; when the defendant addressed a female by saying, "Come here baby and kiss me, I am going to get into your pants;" when the defendant asked the female, "Will five dollars be enough. Do you want me to show you?;" and when the defendant inquired of one who was not his wife whether she would go to bed with him.

The last case to deal at length with the definition of the phrase "obscene and vulgar or profane language" pre-dated the Supreme Court's decision in Miller v. California. In Breaux v. State, over a strong dissent, the Georgia Supreme Court stated that "[l]anguage is obscene, vulgar or profane when, under the circumstances and manner in which such utterance was made, it would clearly offend a reasonable person's sense of decency." Although it is clear that a state may regulate obscene and profane speech, it is also clear that any such regulation must be pursuant either to a narrowly drawn statute or to a statute which has been authoritatively construed to reach only unprotected speech. The question then becomes whether § 16-11-39(a)(4) is such a statute.

In Chaplinsky v. New Hampshire the Supreme Court indicated that lewd, obscene and profane language is outside of the protection of the First Amendment. That decision, however, was arguably modified by the Supreme Court in Cohen v. California. In *Cohen* the Court appeared to indicate the language at issue was not subject to punishment because it did not fall into a category of speech which is regulable, i.e., obscenity, "fighting words," or libel. Apparently, conceding the defendant's statement could properly be classified as "offensive," the *Cohen* Court held that offensiveness was an insufficient ground to punish the defendant. Despite the Court's indication in *Cohen* that mere offensiveness is insufficient, an offensiveness standard appears to be the rule in Georgia as established in *Breaux*. As so construed, § 16-11-39(a)(4) is probably susceptible to a successful First Amendment challenge.

The relationship between paragraphs (3) and (4) of § 16-11-39(a) should be noted. Paragraphs (3) and (4) specify separate offenses, and a person may in one transaction so conduct himself as to be guilty of both of these offenses. The fact that the same language supports an element in each offense does not warrant merging of the convictions where other mutually exclusive elements of the offenses remain.

As currently construed under Breaux, paragraph (4) has a considerably broader sweep than paragraph (3). For example, in Rozier v. State the defendant was charged with violating § 16-11-39(a)(3) apparently for saying in the presence of a 16-year-old female and a five-year-old male, "How about some pussy?" The Georgia Court of Appeals reversed the conviction, indicating that "[t]his remark, when considered under the circumstances and in the context in which it was made, did not constitute 'fighting words.' " While the court did not discuss whether the defendant could have been convicted under § 16-11-39(a)(4), presumably, under Breaux, he could have been.

The mere use of obscene and vulgar or profane language does not constitute "fighting words" unless such language is also "opprobrious or abusive." In Crolley v. State, the defendant employed obscene, vulgar, and profane language in the course of venting his anger at one of his employees. However, the language employed by the defendant did not subject the employee to personal epithets or personal abuse. Giving § 16-11-39(a)(3) the required narrow and limited application, the court held that the evidence did not indicate that the defendant's conduct was sufficiently belligerent to incite an immediate breach of the peace. His language could not be fairly characterized as "fighting words" under the circumstances of the case. Accordingly, his conviction was reversed. The court stated, however, that had the employee been under the age of 14 and had the defendant been indicted for a violation of § 16-11-39(a)(4), the evidence might have possibly authorized a conviction.

As is the case with paragraph (3) of § 16-11-39(a), in order to violate paragraph (4) the language used must have been without provocation. Because the apparent intent of paragraph (4) is to protect children from scurrilous epithets, it might seem the provocation exception would apply only when the speaker is provoked by a member of the protected class. The court rejected such an argument in Ray v. State, however, permitting the provocation to come from a third party.

E. Presence Requirement

Paragraphs (3) and (4) of § 16-11-39(a) require the actus reus to occur in the presence of another. "Presence" has been construed to be conterminous with one's ability to hear. The presence requirement is not a strict liability element of the offense, however. Rather the prosecution must show the defendant knew, or that a reasonable person would have known, of the presence of others. This may be proved by circumstantial evidence, including the language the defendant used. Although the courts have never held that the victim must hear the offensive language, in Breaux v. State, the court said that the jury could have found that the victim understood the meaning of the defendant's language. If the victim's understanding of the language is an element of the offense, it would appear that hearing is likewise an element.

F. Venue

In those instances under § 16-11-39 where communications such as mailing, telegraphing or telephoning are necessary elements of the offense, venue is proper in the county where the "victim" is.

G. Jurisdiction

A state court does have jurisdiction to preside over the trial of the misdemeanor offense of disorderly conduct.

H. Punishment

The offense of disorderly conduct is a misdemeanor and is punishable under the general misdemeanor statute.

I. Disorderly Conduct Ordinances of Counties or Municipalities

Section 16-11-39 does not affect or limit the powers of counties or municipal corporations to adopt ordinances or resolutions prohibiting disorderly conduct within their respective limits.

Neither the trial courts nor the appellate courts may take judicial notice of the provisions of a disorderly conduct ordinance. Where such ordinance is relied upon, it must be pleaded and proved in the trial court. A prosecutor's failure to introduce the ordinance under which the defendant is charged results in a failure of proof, and the evidence would be insufficient as a matter of law to warrant the defendant's conviction for the ordinance violation.

DRUG-RELATED CRIMES

See MOTOR VEHICLE CRIMES; PENAL INSTITUTION CRIMES.

I. Generally

The Georgia Controlled Substances Act was enacted in 1974 at which time the Uniform Narcotic Drug Act was repealed. The Georgia Controlled Substances Act was contained in former GCA Title 79A. With the enactment of the Official Code of Georgia Annotated (O.C.G.A.), the Georgia Controlled Substances Act was incorporated in the criminal code of Georgia, effective November 1, 1982. This Act is now contained in chapter 13 of Title 16 of the O.C.G.A. The Dangerous Drug Act, provisions dealing with the sale or possession of model glue, and other general provisions dealing with drugs were also incorporated in this chapter of the Georgia criminal code.

The statutory framework of the Act will be dealt with first, followed by a brief discussion of related criminal provisions dealing with the licensing of pharmacists and pharmacies, dangerous drugs, model glue, and the Georgia Drug and Cosmetic Act. Because of the prevalence of prosecutions under the Act, this topic contains a detailed look at the case law interpreting the provisions of the Act. This topic concludes with a discussion of the punishment provisions of the Act and of the civil sanctions that may be imposed for a violation of the Act.

II. Controlled Substances Act

The Act contains five schedules of controlled substances each of which collects substances which are similar in their potential for abuse, medical importance and level of safety. Schedule I includes the most dangerous drugs and Schedule V the least dangerous. Section 16-13-30(a) enacts a broad prohibition of the purchase, possession, or control of any controlled substance. Section 16-13-30(b) prohibits the manufacture, delivery, distribution, dispensing, administration, possession with intent to distribute and sale of any controlled substance.

Schedule I drugs have a high potential for abuse, have no currently accepted medical use in treatment in the United States, and there is a lack of accepted safety for use under medical supervision. Schedule I includes certain opiates, opium derivatives, and hallucinogens (including LSD, mescaline, peyote phencyclidine, and tetrahydrocannabinol).

Schedule II drugs have a high potential for abuse, have currently accepted medical uses in treatment in the United States, and, if abused, may lead to severe psychological or physical dependence. Included in Schedule II are opium and opiates (including raw and powdered opium, codeine and morphine), cocaine, coca leaves, certain opiates (including methadone), stimulants (including amphetamine) and depressants (including amobarbital, secobarbital and pentobarbital).

Schedule III drugs have a potential for abuse less than those in Schedules I and II, have currently accepted medical uses in the United States, and, if abused, may lead to moderate or low physical dependence or high psychological dependence. Included in Schedule III are certain stimulants, certain depressants, substances containing limited narcotic concentrations, and anabolic steroids.

Schedule IV contains drugs with a low potential for abuse relative to the drugs in Schedule III, with currently accepted medical uses in the United States, and, if abused, may, relative to Schedule III drugs, lead to limited physical or psychological dependence.

Schedule V includes drugs with a low potential for abuse relative to Schedule IV drugs, with currently accepted medical uses in the United States, and, relative to Schedule IV drugs, if abused, may lead to limited physical or psychological dependence. Substances with very limited narcotic concentrations are included in Schedule V.

The specific drugs included in each schedule are listed in §§ 16-13-25 through 16-13-29. While the General Assembly enacted the original listings and has since modified them, the Act also provides for new inclusions or rescheduling through administrative action of the Board of Pharmacy. While the Supreme Court of Georgia, in Sundberg v. State, held a similar delegation of authority in a prior drug statute to be unconstitutional under the State Constitution, the delegation under the current Act has not yet been successfully challenged. In Harmon v. State, the court avoided ruling on the question because the defendant was convicted of the sale of a substance which had not been affected by any action of the Board of Pharmacy. It should be noted that, unlike the statute struck down in Sundberg, § 16-13-22 of the current Act contains a detailed list of factors which are to be considered by the Board of Pharmacy in rescheduling or adding substances. The 4-3 Sundberg decision stressed the fact that there were no guidelines in the delegation provision of that statute.

The most important criminal provisions of the Controlled Substances Act appear in §§ 16-13-30, 16-13-31, and 16-13-33. Section 16-13-30(a) prohibits the purchase, possession, or control of a controlled substance and subsection (b), the more serious crime, prohibits the manufacture, delivery, distribution, dispensing, administration, sale or possession with intent to distribute all controlled substances. Subsections (c) through (h) outline the punishment provisions for subsection (a) and (b) offenses with regard to each of the five schedules. Generally, subsection (b) offenses are more heavily punished than subsection (a) offenses and crimes involving the Schedule I and II substances are treated more severely than those involving Schedules III, IV and V. All are felonies and several provide enhanced punishment for recidivists.

Subsection (i) of § 16-13-30 outlines a felony for the possession, manufacture, delivery, distribution, dispensing, administration, purchase, sale or possession with intent to distribute of a counterfeit controlled substance. Subsection (j) broadly prohibits the possession, manufacture, delivery, distribution, dispensing, administration, purchase, sale or possession with intent to distribute of marijuana, an unscheduled drug. This offense is a felony, punishable by one to ten years imprisonment, with enhanced punishment for those whose violation involves more than 10 pounds of marijuana. Subsection (k) makes it unlawful for any person to hire, solicit, engage, or use an individual under the age of 17 years, in any manner, for the purpose of manufacturing, distributing, or dispensing, on behalf of the solicitor, any controlled substance, counterfeit substance, or marijuana unless the manufacturing, distribution, or dispensing is otherwise allowed by law. This offense is a felony punishable by imprisonment for not less than five years nor more than 20 years or by a fine not to exceed $20,000, or both. Subsection (l) outlines the punishment provisions for subsection (a) and (b) offenses with regard to flunitrazepam, a Schedule IV controlled substance. These offenses are punishable as felonies, and enhanced punishment is provided for recidivists.

Section 16-13-31 prohibits and punishes trafficking in (1) cocaine, (2) illegal drugs such as morphine or heroin, (3) marijuana, (4) methaqualone, and (5) methamphetamine or amphetamine. This Code section creates a schedule of punishments scaled to the amount of contraband involved, and there is a mandatory punishment for each gradation of the crime.

Section 16-13-31.1 prohibits and punishes trafficking in the amphetamine or methamphetamine commonly known as MDMA or ecstasy. This Code section creates a schedule of punishments scaled to the amount of MDMA or ecstasy involved, and there is a mandatory punishment for each gradation of the crime.

Section 16-13-33 makes it a crime to conspire or attempt to commit any offense under the Act. Unlike the general attempt and conspiracy crimes, however, the § 16-13-33 offenses are punishable to the same extent as the object offenses toward which they are directed. Under the Act, the conspiracy offense and the object offense are separate crimes and do not merge.

There are several other sections in the Act which define criminal offenses. Sections 16-13-32 through 16-13-32.2, the "Head Shop Act," make it a misdemeanor for any person or corporation, knowing the drug related nature of the object, to distribute to any person any drug related object.

Section 16-13-30.1 punishes the counterfeiting of controlled substances. The punishment provision imposes imprisonment of one to ten years and/or fine of up to $25,000. Section 16-13-30.2 provides that anyone who knowingly manufactures, distributes, or possesses with intent to distribute an imitation controlled substance is guilty of a misdemeanor of a high and aggravated nature. Where under the evidence § 16-13-30.2 cannot be considered a lesser included offense of § 16-13-30.1, one who has been charged with violating § 16-13-30.1 would not be entitled, upon request, to a charge on § 16-13-30.2 as a lesser included offense.

Both § 16-13-30.1 and § 16-13-30.2 prohibit the sale of fake illegal drugs. Using the same evidence, a reasonable trier of fact could find beyond a reasonable doubt that a defendant's conduct violates both § 16-13-30.1, a felony, and § 16-13-30.2, a misdemeanor. Because the same conduct constitutes both a felony and a misdemeanor, therefore, the rule of lenity requires that the defendant be subjected to the penalties for the misdemeanor, rather than the felony.

Section 16-13-30.3(b) prohibits any person, other than a pharmacist, medical practitioner, or retail distributor, from knowingly possessing any product that contains an excessive amount of ephedrine, pseudoephedrine, or phenylpropanolamine. In addition, this provision prohibits any person from possessing any amount of these substances with the intent to manufacture amphetamine or methamphetamine. A violation of § 16-13-30.3(b) is a felony punishable by imprisonment for not less than one nor more than ten years.

Section 16-13-30.3(b.1) limits the sale and manner of sale of products containing pseudoephedrine so as to limit their use in the unlawful manufacture of methamphetamine. This Code provision makes it a misdemeanor to offer such products for retail sale without blister packaging and by self-service. In addition, it is a misdemeanor under this provision to deliver in a single over the counter sale more than three packages of any product containing pseudoephedrine or any number of packages that contain a combined total of more than nine grams of pseudoephedrine. A knowing violation of either of these prohibitions is punishable by a fine of not more than $500. A second or subsequent violation is punishable by not more than six months' imprisonment or a fine of not more than $1,000, or both. In a prosecution for a violation of either of these prohibitions, a retailer who is in compliance with Georgia Meth Watch would be entitled to a defense if it can establish that the violation occurred unknowingly.

Section 16-13-30.3(b.1) also makes it a misdemeanor for a retail distributor to purchase any product containing pseudoephedrine from any person or entity other than a licensed manufacturer or a licensed wholesale distributor. A second or subsequent violation is punishable as a misdemeanor of a high and aggravated nature.

Section 16-13-30.3(d) prohibits any person from possessing, controlling, manufacturing, delivering, distributing, dispensing, administering, purchasing, selling, or possessing with intent to distribute any substance containing any amount of ephedrine, pseudoephedrine, phenylpropanolamine, or any of their salts, optical isomers, or salts of optical isomers which have been altered from their original condition so as to be powdered, liquefied, or crushed. This prohibition does not apply to any substance which is possessed or altered for a legitimate medical purpose. A violation of § 16-13-30.3(d) is a felony punishable by imprisonment for not less than one nor more than ten years.

The prohibitions in § 16-13-30.3 do not apply to certain pediatric products and products exempted by the Georgia State Board of Pharmacy.

Section 16-13-30.4(g)(1) prohibits any person who sells, transfers, receives, or possesses a product containing pseudoephedrine from (1) knowingly failing to comply with the statute's reporting requirements, (2) knowingly making a false statement in a required report or record, or (3) knowingly or deliberately failing to obtain a required license or permit. A violation of § 16-13-30.4(g)(1) is punishable as a misdemeanor on the first offense and as a misdemeanor of a high and aggravated nature on the second and subsequent offenses.

Section 16-13-30.4(g)(2) prohibits any person from possessing, selling, transferring, or otherwise furnishing a product containing pseudoephedrine with the knowledge or intent that the product will be used in the unlawful manufacture of a controlled substance. A violation of § 16-13-30.4(g)(2) is punishable as a felony by imprisonment for not less than one nor more than 15 years or by a fine not to exceed $100,000, or both.

Section 16-13-30.5(a) prohibits any person from possessing, whether acquired through theft or other means, any substance with the intent to (1) use such substance in the manufacture of a Schedule I or Schedule II controlled substance, or (2) knowingly convey such substance to another for use in the manufacture of a Schedule I or Schedule II controlled substance. A violation § 16-13-30.5(a) is punishable as a felony by imprisonment for not less than one nor more than 15 years or by a fine not to exceed $100,000, or both. Section 16-13-30.5 does not apply where possession was by a person authorized by law to dispense, prescribe, manufacture, or possess the substance in question.

The purpose of § 16-13-30.6 is to prohibit the purchase and sale of marijuana flavored products to minors in this state. Section 16-13-30.6 makes it a misdemeanor for any person knowingly to sell, deliver, distribute, or provide to a minor or knowingly to possess with intent to sell, deliver, distribute, or provide to a minor any marijuana flavored product. This offense is punishable by a fine of $500 for each offense. Each sale in violation of § 16-13-30.6 constitutes a separate offense. Section 16-13-30.6 also prohibits any minor from falsely representing to any person that such minor is 18 years of age or older with the intent to purchase or otherwise obtain any marijuana flavored product.

Sections 16-13-42 and 16-13-43 establish felonies for the violation of registration requirements for controlled substance manufacturers and dispensers, for the failure to keep required records, for the refusal to permit an entry for inspection, for the failure to comply with prescription requirements, and for other similar acts. Included in § 16-13-42 is a provision which makes it a felony knowingly to keep or maintain a structure which is used for violation of the Act. There apparently is very little criminal litigation under §§ 16-13-42 and 16-13-43 and their primary thrust apparently is administrative.

Section 16-13-32.3 makes it unlawful for any person knowingly or intentionally to use any communication facility in committing or in causing or facilitating the commission of any act or acts constituting a felony under the Controlled Substances Act. In the absence of circumstantial evidence that would exclude every other reasonable hypothesis save that of the defendant's guilt, the state must present direct evidence that the defendant used the communication facility to arrange the commission of the prohibited acts. While the state is required to present evidence that a communication facility was actually used, it is not required to present a transcript of monitored conversations in order to sustain a conviction. The identity of the callers and the content of the conversations may be inferred from the circumstances. Also, there must be evidence from which it can be inferred that the prohibited acts were carried out. However, the defendant does not have to directly participate in the subsequent prohibited acts that he had initially facilitated in order to be guilty of this offense. Each separate use of a communication facility is a separate offense. Each offense is punishable by a fine of not more than $30,000 or by imprisonment for not less than one nor more than four years, or both.

Section 16-13-32.4 makes it unlawful for any person to manufacture, distribute, dispense, or possess with intent to distribute a controlled substance or marijuana in, on, or within 1,000 feet of any real property owned by or leased to any public or private elementary school, secondary school, or school board used for elementary or secondary education. The first offense is punishable by imprisonment for not more than 20 years or a fine of not more than $20,000, or both. A second or subsequent offense is punishable by imprisonment for not less than five years nor more than 40 years or a fine of not more than $40,000, or both. It is mandatory for the court to impose a minimum sentence of five years which may not be suspended unless otherwise provided by law. A conviction for this offense will not merge with a conviction arising under any other provision of the Georgia Controlled Substances Act. Also, a sentence imposed for this offense will be served consecutively to any other sentence imposed.

It is no defense to a prosecution for this offense that (1) school was or was not in session at the time of the offense; (2) the real property was being used for other purposes besides school purposes at the time of the offense; or (3) the offense took place on a school vehicle. However, it is an affirmative defense that the prohibited conduct took place entirely within a private residence, that no person 17 years of age or younger was present in such private residence at any time during the commission of the offense, and that the prohibited conduct was not carried on for purposes of financial gain. This affirmative defense is not a defense with respect to any other offense involving a controlled substance or marijuana.

Section 16-13-32.5 makes it unlawful for any person to manufacture, distribute, dispense, or possess with intent to distribute a controlled substance or marijuana or a counterfeit substance in, on, or within 1,000 feet of any public park, playground, recreation center, or housing project, unless the manufacture, distribution, or dispensing is otherwise allowed by law. Because § 16-13-32.5(b) does not designate simple possession of contraband within 1,000 feet of a housing project as a prohibited act, a conviction for simple possession is not authorized under this provision. The first offense is punishable by imprisonment for not more than 20 years or a fine of not more than $20,000, or both. A second or subsequent offense is punishable by imprisonment for not less than five years nor more than 40 years or a fine of not more than $40,000, or both. It shall be mandatory for the court to impose a minimum sentence of five years which may not be suspended unless otherwise provided by law. A conviction for this offense will not merge with a conviction arising under any other provision of the Controlled Substances Act. Also, a sentence imposed for this offense will be served consecutively to any other sentence imposed. Where a defendant's prior convictions are only for violations of § 16-13-32.5, he is subject, as a habitual offender of this statute, to the specific recidivist provisions of § 16-13-32.5(c)(2), but where his prior convictions are for a mixed variety of felonies, he is subject, as a habitual felon, to the general recidivist provisions of § 17-10-7.

It is an affirmative defense to a prosecution for this offense that the prohibited conduct took place entirely within a private residence, that no person 17 years of age or younger was present in such private residence at any time during the commission of the offense, and that the prohibited conduct was not carried on for purposes of financial gain. This affirmative defense is not a defense with respect to any other offense involving a controlled substance, marijuana, or counterfeit substance.

Section 16-13-32.6 makes it unlawful for any person to illegally manufacture, distribute, dispense, or possess with intent to distribute a controlled substance or marijuana in, on, or within any real property designated as a drug-free commercial zone. The first offense is punishable by imprisonment for not more than 20 years or a fine of not more than $20,000, or both. A second or subsequent offense is punishable by imprisonment for not less than five years nor more than 40 years or a fine of not more than $40,000, or both. A sentence imposed for this offense will be served consecutively to any other sentence imposed. Also, a conviction for this offense will not merge with a conviction arising under any other provision of the Controlled Substances Act.

The Controlled Substances Act also includes detailed provisions outlining procedures for administrative inspections of "controlled premises" and procedures for the forfeiture of property involved in drug-related offenses. Among other things, all controlled substances and marijuana which have been manufactured, distributed, dispensed, held or acquired in violation of the Act are subject to forfeiture.

State and local agencies are subject to the requirements of the Controlled Substances Act, §§ 16-13-20 et seq., but are not subject to the requirements of the Dangerous Drug Act, §§ 16-13-70 et seq.

III. Related Criminal Provisions

In addition to the criminal provisions of the Controlled Substances Act, there are a number of criminal provisions outside of the Act which make it unlawful to engage in certain activities relating to drugs. Section 16-13-3 makes it a misdemeanor for any person to abandon, in a public place, any dangerous drug, poison, or controlled substance. Section 16-13-4 provides that a failure to obtain FDA approval for the sale of a controlled substance or a dangerous drug is a felony punishable by imprisonment of not less than one nor more than five years. Additionally, subsection (a) of § 16-13-2 provides for the conditional discharge of first offenders for the possession of a controlled substance. Moreover, subsection (c) provides for the conditional discharge of first offenders for controlled substance possession offenses as well as for nonviolent property offenses that are related to an accused's addiction to a controlled substance or alcohol. Although Georgia's appellate courts have consistently rejected addiction as a defense to a criminal act, the General Assembly with the enactment of § 16-13-2(c) in 2004 is obviously authorizing sentencing courts to consider addiction in mitigation of an addict's punishment as a first offender for controlled substance possession and nonviolent property offenses.

Under the law regulating pharmacists and pharmacies, it is a felony to engage in the practice of pharmacy without a license; to violate the law regulating drug researcher permits; and to violate the law regulating drug wholesalers, distributors, and suppliers. Otherwise, any violation of the law regulating pharmacists and pharmacies constitutes a misdemeanor. Specifically, it is a misdemeanor to sell or dispense prescription drugs through a vending machine; to distribute or deliver drugs or devices to or to receive drugs or devices from an unlicensed person or firm; to violate the law regulating the registration of third-party prescription program administrators; and to violate the law regulating the sale of poisons.

Under the Dangerous Drug Act, it is a misdemeanor to fail to place a required label on a "dangerous drug;" to write a prescription for a dangerous drug in violation of the statutory requirements; to obtain or attempt to obtain a dangerous drug by fraud, forgery, concealment of a material fact or use of a false name or address; for anyone to prescribe or order the dispensing of a dangerous drug except those who are licensed to do so, are doing so in the usual course of professional practice, and are doing so for a legitimate medical purpose; and to possess, have under one's control, manufacture, deliver, distribute, administer, sell, or possess with intent to distribute a counterfeit dangerous drug.

Under the Dangerous Drug Act, it is a felony to distribute or possess with the intent to distribute nitrous oxide, an anesthetic commonly known as "laughing gas," for any use other than for a medical treatment prescribed by the order of a licensed medical practitioner. This offense is punishable by imprisonment for not less than one year nor more than three years or by a fine not to exceed $5,000 or both. It is also a felony to distribute or possess with the intent to distribute to any person under 18 years of age nitrous oxide for any use other than for a medical treatment prescribed by the order of a licensed medical practitioner. This offense is punishable by imprisonment for not less than two years nor more than six years or by a fine not to exceed $10,000 or both. The Dangerous Drug Act, however, does not apply to any person who possesses, distributes, sells, or uses nitrous oxide for food preparation in a restaurant, for food service, or in household products.

Prior to 1991, the distribution of or possession with intent to distribute an anabolic steroid was punishable under the Dangerous Drug Act. In 1991, the General Assembly changed the classification of "anabolic steroid" from a dangerous drug to a Schedule III controlled substance. The distribution of or possession with intent to distribute an anabolic steroid is now punishable under the Controlled Substances Act. However, § 16-13-27.1 provides that certain anabolic steroid containing compounds, mixtures, or preparations have been exempted as Schedule III controlled substances by the United States Drug Enforcement Administration, as listed in 21 C. F. R. 1308.34, and are therefore exempted from § 16-13-27(6), the list of anabolic steroids included in Georgia's Schedule III controlled substances.

It is a misdemeanor to violate any provision of the Drug and Cosmetic Act. That Act is the state counterpart to the Federal Food, Drug and Cosmetic Act. Essentially, it makes unlawful the mislabeling of drugs, the adulteration of drugs, the sale or delivery of such drugs, the dissemination of false advertising and the giving of a false guaranty concerning a drug.

Section 16-13-96 makes it a misdemeanor for anyone to intentionally smell or inhale the fumes from any model glue or to intentionally possess, buy, sell, transfer possession, or receive possession of any model glue for the purpose of smelling or inhaling it.

Section 16-11-111 makes it a felony for any person to (1) purchase, possess, transfer, or distribute any amount of anhydrous ammonia knowing that it will be used unlawfully to manufacture a controlled substance; (2) possess, maintain, or transport any quantity of anhydrous ammonia in a container or receptacle other than a tank truck, tank trailer, rail tank car, bulk storage tank, field (nurse) tank, field applicator, or any other approved container; or (3) tamper with equipment manufactured to hold, apply, or transport anhydrous ammonia without the express consent of the owner of the equipment. A violation of § 16-11-111 is punishable by imprisonment for not less than one nor more than ten years and by a fine not to exceed $100,000. Furthermore, any person who violates the prohibition outlined in item (2) above is subject to civil penalties in accordance with § 40-16-6.

IV. Case Law

A. Possession

1. Possession and Possession with Intent to Distribute Distinguished

Although § 16-13-30 punishes many activities with regard to controlled substances, including manufacturing, delivering, distributing, dispensing, administering, selling, and purchasing, the most common charges are possession and possession with intent to distribute.

Possession (§ 16-13-30(a)) and possession with intent to distribute (§ 16-13-30(b)) should be distinguished. While it is clear that there is the common element of possession in both crimes, the state is required to prove the additional element of specific intent to distribute in order to establish a charge of possession with intent to distribute. A trial court's failure to instruct the jury correctly on this essential element is reversible error.

The prosecution may establish the defendant's intent to distribute without presenting any evidence of a drug transaction. The intent to distribute may be established by circumstantial evidence. This intent may be inferred from the quantity of the drug possessed and the manner in which it was packaged. In close cases, expert opinion testimony may be necessary to establish that the quantity and packaging of the drug would generally be for distribution, as opposed to personal use. Other evidence useful in establishing an intent to distribute is the presence of drug paraphernalia, the presence of a large amount of cash, the defendant's presence in an area where arrests for drug dealing are frequently made, and the defendant's criminal activity prior to his arrest. The defendant's criminal intent may also be established by evidence of his commission of a similar offense. However, the state must make a sufficient showing of similarity before the other offense can be introduced for the purpose of showing intent, and the trial court, upon request, must give a limiting instruction to the jury about the specific purpose for which the other offense can be considered. Where none of this additional evidence of intent is offered, a conviction for possession with intent to distribute cannot be sustained.

2. *Equal Access Rule*

a. *Presumption or Inference of Possession.*

"In the absence of any circumstances to the contrary, a presumption arises from proof of ownership and control of premises, an automobile, or other property that the owner is in control and possession of contraband found therein."

In the case of an automobile found containing contraband, no presumption arises that the driver or owner is in possession of the contraband, where there is any competent evidence that persons other than the accused have had access to or control of the vehicle for a period of time prior to the discovery of the contraband. When the accused presents competent evidence of equal access, a charge to the jury on presumption of possession is reversible error.

The presumption that the driver or owner of an automobile is in possession of all that is in the automobile is a rebuttable presumption of guilt against an driver or owner and may not be used as a presumption of innocence by an occupant of the automobile. The presumption applies only when the driver is in exclusive possession of the automobile and does not apply in a case involving evidence of joint possession with others. However, where the defendant's sole defense is that he was a mere passenger in the car, and that he was in neither actual nor constructive possession of the contraband, a full and complete charge on the law concerning possession is necessary, which requires, at a minimum, that the jury be informed of the elements of actual and constructive possession and the rebuttable presumption that all items found inside a vehicle belong to the owner and/or driver. The failure to give a requested charge on this rebuttable presumption is reversible error.

Where the evidence shows other persons had equal access to the contraband, and there is no evidence the defendant had complete possession and control of the car at any time, no presumption of possession arises. Without the presumption of possession and control, what is left is mere presence at the scene of a crime or, more to the point, mere presence near hidden contraband. As a matter of law, this is not enough to support a finding of criminal possession of the contraband beyond a reasonable doubt and to the exclusion of every other reasonable hypothesis. It should be noted that where the state does establish more than the defendant's mere presence in a vehicle in which contraband was found, neither the presumption of possession nor the equal access rule is applicable.

b. *Application of Rule*

A presumption of possession may be overcome by the application of the equal access rule. The equal access rule is simply a defense available to a defendant to whom a presumption of possession flows. Thus, the equal access rule is triggered only where the sole evidence of possession of the contraband found in a vehicle is the defendant's ownership or possession of the vehicle. The equal access rule is not available as a defense where there is no evidence of the defendant's ownership or exclusive control of the vehicle in which the contraband was found.

The equal access rule is inapplicable where the state's evidence is that the defendant actually and physically possessed the contraband. Nor does the rule apply, and no charge regarding the rule need be given, when the "contraband is not in an open, notorious and equally accessible area." Also, the equal access rule has no application where all persons allegedly having equal access to the contraband are alleged to have been in joint constructive possession of that contraband. The fact that some of the persons have pled guilty to an indictment does not necessarily defeat the inference that another person was in joint possession of the contraband with them, absent some indication that they or anyone else had claimed exclusive possession of it.

The equal access rule is inapplicable where the defendant must have had knowledge of the presence of the drug. Thus, in Quarles v. State, the court rejected an equal access defense based upon proof that marijuana plants were growing between corn plants, that the defendant had rented the field, that the marijuana plants had been carefully planted and cultivated, that the plants were clearly visible, and that the defendant was cultivating the crop at the time of his arrest. The equal access rule generally does not apply to cases involving marijuana plants growing on the land outside the owner's or lessee's residence, on the basis that such contraband is stationary. If the plants are not portable, the equal access rule is not applicable. Also, the equal access rule is not applicable to marijuana plants growing outside, because they, like other vegetation, require a period of months to grow, mature, and be harvested.

Evidence of the defendant's mere proximity to contraband in a vehicle to which someone else had earlier access along with his refusal to consent to a search of the vehicle is not sufficient, by itself, to overcome the equal access rule. Furthermore, the defendant's refusal to consent to the search of his vehicle cannot be used as evidence of guilty knowledge to support a conviction for possession.

c. *Evidence of Access*

In order to support a defense of equal access, the evidence must show that others actually had access to the premises and had the opportunity to commit the crime. Gee v. State presents the prototypical fact situation. In Gee, the defendant's conviction for possessing drugs was wholly dependent upon the proposition that the contraband was found at a place under the defendant's possession and control. In light of evidence that persons other than the defendant had liberal access to the place, the defendant's conviction was reversed. The court held that merely finding contraband on premises occupied by a defendant is not sufficient to support a conviction if it affirmatively appears from the evidence that persons other than the defendant had equal opportunity to commit the crime.

The evidence did not support a defense of equal access in Warren v. State. In this case, there was no evidence of anyone other than the defendant with equal access to the house. The defendant testified that he had locked the door to the house where the drugs were found. Also, there were no signs of an intruder when the door was unlocked on the day of the search. In light of this evidence, the court held that it did not affirmatively appear that someone other than the defendant had equal opportunity to commit the crime. Therefore, a failure to charge on equal access was not error.

Others merely being somewhere within the premises for a relatively short but unspecified time before drugs subsequently are found therein does not reasonably raise the defense of equal access. In Jones v. State, the court held that although there was a scant amount of evidence that some persons might have entered the premises to purchase drugs during the time when police surveillance was being conducted, there was no evidence these persons had equal access to that area where the closed paper bag containing the drugs was seized. Because the defense was not reasonably raised by the evidence, an instruction on the equal access defense was held not to be necessary.

Evidence of access to the premises by an unknown individual who accomplished a break-in is not that "equal access" which would shield a defendant from the presumption of possession of contraband found on the premises.

The equal access rule requires affirmative evidence of access to the defendant's residence by persons other than the defendant and members of his immediate household. In the absence of such evidence, an instruction on equal access is not authorized. Furthermore, even if the defendant demonstrates that nonresidents had equal access to his residence, other evidence demonstrating the defendant's possession of the contraband may be enough to make the instruction unnecessary.

When the evidence does not reasonably raise the issue of equal access, the trial court's refusal to instruct the jury on this issue is not error. Likewise, when the trial court elects not to instruct the jury on presumption of possession, an equal access instruction is not required.

The equal access rule requires affirmative evidence of access to a vehicle by persons other than the driver or owner of the vehicle. The fact that a vehicle may have been unlocked for a short time does not, standing alone, establish the "equal access" which would preclude the application of the presumption of possession of contraband found in the vehicle. Also, the fact that a vehicle was parked in another individual's driveway does not show that the other individual or anyone else had "equal access" to the vehicle and does not raise a reasonable doubt by rebutting the presumption of possession of contraband found in the vehicle.

Evidence of equal access is not an absolute defense to a charge of possession. The defendant is not entitled to a verdict of acquittal on grounds of equal access where there is other evidence of possession besides the defendant's ownership or possession of the vehicle. In other words, evidence of equal access does not necessarily exculpate the defendant. The totality of the evidence may be sufficient to connect the defendant to the possession of the drugs even though the evidence would have authorized a finding that others had equal access to them. Whether the evidence of equal access is sufficient to rebut the presumption of possession arising from the discovery of drugs in the premises or vehicle is a question properly left to the jury, under the totality of the evidence in the case. If the presumption of possession and control is unrebutted, the jury can then rationally find by inference that the driver and owner of the vehicle had direct physical control over the drugs, so as to be in actual possession of them; or that he had the power and intention to exercise dominion or control so as to be in constructive possession. Furthermore, if there is no credible evidence to support the defendant's claim that others in fact had access to the vehicle, the jury may disbelieve the claim and conclude that the only reasonable hypothesis is that the defendant had possession of the drugs.

Evidence of the defendant's commission of a similar drug offense can be used by the state to negate the defendant's claim of equal access.

3. *"Head of Household" Doctrine*

The "head of the household" doctrine is an old rule which provides a presumption that contraband found in a house belongs to the head of the household. The traditional head of household presumption in drug cases when combined with the statutory presumption that the husband is the head of the household (this statutory presumption was repealed by Acts 1983, p. 1309), came before the Georgia Supreme Court in Knighton v. State. The trial court had instructed the jury that contraband found in the house occupied by the defendant and his wife was presumed to be his. On appeal, the defendant asserted that the head of the household statute was gender-based discrimination in violation of the Constitution and, at any rate, the presumption, if valid at all, is only valid as a rebuttable presumption and the trial court erred in not informing the jury of that fact.

It must be emphasized that the Knighton court's holding affects only a particular type of head of household presumption, that is, one which is based on the gender of the participants. The general head of household presumption, that the head of the household is the possessor of contraband, still survives and can be charged to the jury so long as the identity of the head of the household is not based on the gender of the parties. For example, in Knighton itself, the court approved a gender neutral head of household instruction which states that "if you find that a person owns or is the lessee of a house or premises, you will be permitted, but not required, to presume that such person is in possession of the entire premises and all the property thereon or therein. However, this is a rebuttable presumption and may be overcome by evidence in the case that others had access to the premises." Thus, the head of the household still will be charged with a rebuttable presumption that he or she is the owner and possessor of the contraband found therein, subject to the equal access rule. In other words, notwithstanding the unconstitutionality of a rebuttable presumption of possession as against a husband, there is a viable rebuttable presumption of possession, without regard to gender or marital status, as against the owner or lessee of the premises where the contraband is found.

This gender-neutral head of household presumption has been upheld by the Court of Appeals. In Burdett v. State, the court held that the presumption was constitutional in that it is more likely than not that the head of household possesses items found in the house. The court held that so long as the jury is informed that the presumption may be rebutted it is not an unconstitutional burden-shifting instruction.

Where there is overwhelming evidence that a defendant had a possessory interest of some sort in the subject property, the state's failure to prove his specific interest and the giving of a head of household instruction constitutes, at most, harmless error.

4. *Circumstantial Evidence of Possession*

The gravamen of a possession charge is proof that the defendant actually or constructively possessed the substance. There is, however, no invariable requirement that the substance itself be produced.

a. *Actual Possession*

Actual possession, if present, is relatively easy to prove. Its proof generally consists of evidence that the substance was found on the defendant's person or circumstantial evidence pointing to actual possession.

As an example of the latter, in Phillips v. State, the court held actual possession had been proven. The evidence showed the following: the defendant had been observed drinking beer, he fled when the police approached, he had a brown paper bag in his hand, the police observed him holding the bag, ducking behind a trailer and emerging without the bag. The bag was subsequently discovered hidden under the steps to the trailer and containing drugs. Though circumstantial, the court held this sufficient to sustain a finding of actual possession by the defendant.

b. *Constructive Possession*

It is clear that circumstantial evidence can be sufficient to sustain a finding of constructive possession. In Gainer v. State, the evidence showed that the defendant was standing behind a counter and hesitated to move his foot. When he did a red triangle was observed sticking up between the floor boards. The police pulled up the loose boards and found marijuana. The conviction was affirmed. Likewise, the conviction in Clark v. State was affirmed, where evidence showed that the defendant was arrested in a room with two other men sitting around a low table on which there were drugs worth approximately $20,000 and devices for measuring, weighing, cutting and packing the drugs. In Reese v. State, the evidence showed that detectives found a brown paper bag that contained cocaine wrapped in aluminum foil near a church. A fingerprint examiner for the State Crime Lab testified that several fingerprints that matched the defendant's prints were found on pieces of the aluminum foil containing cocaine found in the bag, and that a white powdery substance, cocaine, was visible on three of the prints developed on the foil. The conviction was affirmed. In Brewster v. State, the evidence showed that a piece of cocaine was found in the yellow packet immediately after the defendant dropped the packet, after the defendant was seen to handle the contents of that same yellow packet by dumping them in his hand while participating in two apparent exchanges from that same packet. No one else was seen to handle the yellow packet. The court held that this evidence was at least circumstantial evidence of possession of the cocaine found in the balled-up candy wrapper, beyond a reasonable doubt and to the exclusion of every other reasonable hypothesis. In Williams v. State, the two officers testified that as they approached the group in front of the pool hall, they saw the defendant bend over the area in the fence where they later found the cocaine hidden. The officers observed the defendant's behavior and heard his response when his co-defendant told him that the cocaine was not in the cavity in the fence. The court held that there was sufficient evidence from which a rational trier of fact could have found that the defendant was guilty beyond a reasonable doubt of possessing the cocaine.

A case which may demonstrate the limits of the constructive possession doctrine is State v. Lewis. Here, the defendant was arrested as he opened or was about to open the door of a plane which contained marijuana. The lower court had reversed the conviction on the grounds that the defendant had not obtained possession of the contraband at the point of arrest. The Supreme Court disagreed, concluding that the evidence showed either that the defendant was in constructive possession of the marijuana at that point or that he was aiding and abetting another party in his constructive possession of the contraband.

In Gamble v. State, even though the defendant did not have actual physical control over the car at the time it was stopped, the court held that a rational jury could have concluded beyond a reasonable doubt that the defendant at least was in constructive possession of the contraband found in the car based on the circumstances surrounding the defendant's acquisition of the car; his nervousness upon seeing that the car had been stopped; the fact that he occupied the car immediately before turning it over to his co-defendant; and the evidence demonstrating that he exercised dominion and control over the car during the trip to and from Miami.

In Brooks v. State, the court held that the state failed to prove that the defendant was in joint constructive possession of the cocaine which another person hid in or near a cactus bush. The state's evidence, while showing the defendant's predisposition towards selling cocaine and even that he was dressed in a fashion common to street vendors of illicit substances, nonetheless failed to establish anything more than speculation as to a possible conspiracy with the other person.

In Merritt v. State, on the other hand, the court held that evidence of "drug sales" was part of the events witnessed by police, tying the defendant directly to the possession of cocaine found in the apartment. The sale of a plastic bag, believed in common experience to contain drugs, in exchange for money was an aspect of the charged criminal act and was admissible as res gestae although the defendant was, to his good fortune, not prosecuted for the sale of drugs. This evidence of "drug sales" and of cocaine and weighing scales in the apartment was sufficient to convict the defendant of possession of cocaine.

In Nolton v. State, the court held that although there was evidence in the case that other employees besides the defendant had access to the premises, the jury could reasonably have concluded that, as the employee in charge of the premises, the defendant enjoyed a right of access which was superior to that of anyone else other than the owner of the business, who denied any knowledge of the presence of the contraband.

In *Daughtery v. State*, the court held that evidence of the defendant's possession of approximately 58 grams of crack cocaine found in a briefcase hidden in the same room where the undercover officer made his purchase was sufficient to sustain the defendant's conviction on the cocaine trafficking charge. It was clear to the police officers conducting the search that the defendant was the individual in control of the scene inside the house. While the presence of others in the house might have been viewed as inculpating those individuals, their presence need not have been viewed as exculpating the defendant. It was for the jury to decide how to weigh and view that evidence.

In O'Neill v. State, the Georgia Supreme Court held that the Court of Appeals erroneously upheld the defendant's conviction for possession of methamphetamine based on his unconscious condition on a bed where the arresting officers found an ashtray containing two glass pipes used for smoking methamphetamine and a ring-sized jewelry box containing 2.8 grams of the drug. No evidence was introduced that the defendant's unconscious state was the result of smoking methamphetamine. Nor was any evidence introduced that excluded the possibility that the defendant was passed out on the bed for a reason unrelated to methamphetamine, such as from an excessive consumption of alcohol. Under these circumstances, the fact that the defendant was passed out could not have established that he had smoked methamphetamine as this fact did not exclude the reasonable possibility that the defendant's condition resulted from alcohol intoxication, exhaustion, or the ingestion of some legal substance other than methamphetamine.

c. *Mere Presence at Crime Scene vs. Constructive Possession*

Although circumstantial evidence may be enough to sustain a conviction, it is not enough if the court finds only "mere presence" has been shown. In Mitchell v. State, the court held the evidence proved presence alone. There the defendants were arrested in a house where cocaine and marijuana were found. The court reversed because there was no proof the defendants occupied or had control of the premises. In Myers v. State, the only evidence presented at trial in regard to the defendant was that he, a seventeen-year-old minor, lived in his mother's apartment where the contraband was found and circumstantial evidence that he fled the apartment when armed officers broke down the front door. The court held that the evidence was insufficient to form the basis of a conviction. No evidence was presented that the defendant participated in any activity associated with trafficking in cocaine. The court also held that the defendant's flight was a reasonable response and was not necessarily indicative of guilt. In Reid v. State, the court held that nothing more than mere presence at the scene of the crime was shown by the evidence. The informant did not testify, and the investigator's testimony regarding the substance of the information he received from the informant was inadmissible hearsay without probative value. Further, the evidence showed only that a certain amount of crack cocaine was found on the floorboard between the seat and the door on the passenger side of the car near where the defendant had been sitting and that the defendant denied he had seen the driver with any drugs that day. In Paden v. State, the court held that the circumstantial evidence and the reasonable inferences derived therefrom were insufficient to connect the defendant to the crack cocaine found at the residence of an admitted crack cocaine user, premises that the defendant did not regularly occupy. Moreover, others resided in the same house as the user and other residents used drugs in the user's bedroom. The fact that the defendant possessed over $200 when arrested and that he deposited money in the user's jail account did not connect him to the cocaine. The defendant offered a reasonable hypothesis for the events, and the state failed to prove he was in constructive possession of cocaine sufficient to sustain a conviction for possession with intent to distribute. In In Interest of A. D. C., the court found that there existed only a mere suspicion of the juvenile's participation as a party in the alleged offense of possessing with intent to distribute marijuana in, on, or within 1,000 feet of a public high school. The juvenile was in the same dressing room with another boy and departed the area just before marijuana was discovered on the other boy. Although the juvenile was found to have $269 in his possession, he was not found to be in possession of any controlled substances. Since a reasonable, unrebutted explanation was offered for the juvenile's lawful possession of this amount of money, his mere possession of it did not establish beyond a reasonable doubt that he was a party to the drug offense. In Brookshire v. State, the court concluded that the evidence presented failed to show that the defendant constructively possessed the marijuana. The evidence did not authorize, as a matter of law, a reasonable inference that the defendant knowingly exercised power and dominion over any portion of the marijuana in her son's car at the time of the arrest. Her son's statements showed only that he intended to meet the defendant that day and, at some point in the future, give her two ounces of marijuana in exchange for later payment. These statements were direct evidence of her son's intent to sell marijuana and did not show possession of marijuana by the defendant. Furthermore, since the statements were uncorroborated by other evidence, they could not support the defendant's conviction.

There are times, however, when the distinction between mere presence and constructive possession is very close. In Granger v. State, the convictions of two defendants were reversed on a "mere presence" theory. The evidence showed five individuals in a motel room. One tried to flush an armload of substances down the toilet; another had been observed earlier trying to rake something which appeared from the outside to be marijuana into a drawer where marijuana residue was subsequently discovered. The Granger court held that as to the two defendants, neither of whom had tried to flush the substances or rake them, only mere presence had been proven. In In the Interest of A. H., on the other hand, the convictions of two defendants were affirmed. The evidence showed six individuals in an apartment. Two of the individuals were caught in the rear of the apartment, apparently attempting to dispose of cocaine in the bathroom. However, because the defendants were found in the same small room in which cocaine was being prepared for retail sale and because there was evidence that they arrived only after the delivery of the cocaine was arranged, but well before the actual delivery took place, the court held that a rational trier of fact would be justified in concluding from this evidence that the defendants were more than merely present but were parties to the conversion of the cocaine from cake form into "rocks" suitably packaged in glassine bags for retail sale.

In Sanders v. State, the court held that there was sufficient evidence for the jury to find that the defendant constructively possessed the drugs, since it was established that he visited the apartment frequently, that he regularly used the bedroom there and that the drugs were in his immediate presence. The court held that this conclusion was not changed by the fact that the evidence would have authorized a finding that others had equal access to the same drugs.

In Widener v. State, the court held that the evidence showed the marijuana was not only within arm's reach of the defendant but in plain view and being smoked in the defendant's immediate presence at the time the police entered the home. Even though the officer did not testify that he saw the defendant or any other person at the coffee table in the act of smoking a marijuana cigarette, the trial court was authorized to find that the defendant was, at the least, in joint and constructive possession of the marijuana.

In McKenny v. State, the officers found rock cocaine in plain view on the kitchen counter and a scale of the type used for dealing drugs and a bag of marijuana in the kitchen cabinet. The court held that the fact that the defendant was in the house alone and possessed the key to the house, in which no evidence was found that any other person occupied it, was certainly sufficient evidence to show the defendant was in possession of the contents of the house.

In Shropshire v. State, the court held that sufficient circumstantial evidence was presented at trial to establish that the defendant had at least joint constructive possession of the contraband in the vehicle. There was evidence from which a jury could have concluded that the crack cocaine was visible, and that the defendant had access to it and the power to exercise control over it.

In Martin v. State, the court held that there was more than mere presence in the vicinity of contraband. There was no evidence that anyone else had equal access to the car, and the items were found in places in close proximity to and within the control of the driver.

In Christopher v. State, far more than "mere presence" at the scene of the crime was shown by the evidence presented at trial, whereby the jury could have concluded that the defendant either had actual physical possession of the contraband or else that the defendant aided and abetted in the crimes charged.

In Ward v. State, the court held that the evidence showed that the defendant's participation and knowledge amounted to something more than a "mere presence" at the scene of the crime and supported the state's theory that the defendant and his wife were both willing participants in the crime of manufacturing marijuana.

In Allen v. State, evidence in addition to the defendant's mere presence at the premises was presented, including the fact that the defendant's identification card was found in the same bag as that containing notes relating to a drug operation and the defendant's incriminating spontaneous statement. The court held that this evidence was sufficient to sustain the defendant's conviction for possession of methamphetamine.

In Okongwu v. State, there was not only proof that the defendant was present when the police raided his trailer, there was proof that he was standing next to the co-defendant just before she fled into the bathroom and stashed 17.8 grams of cocaine in the shower's soap dish. There was also proof that the defendant was monitoring local police activity just before the raid. Further, the state proved that the defendant fled when police officers appeared outside his trailer on another occasion, and that a dose of crack cocaine was found abandoned at the very spot where the defendant was sitting just before the officers appeared. The court held that this evidence was sufficient to sustain the defendant's conviction for possession of cocaine with intent to distribute.

In Blair v. State, the question for the factfinder was whether the defendant was merely present in the car in which marijuana was being smoked or whether he was participating in the smoking of the marijuana and thus in possession of it. Although the defendant maintained that only the driver was smoking the marijuana, the testimony of the two arresting officers, trained in drug detection and identification, established that the defendant's face was flushed, and his eyes were very glassy and bloodshot. Also, the defendant had the odor of marijuana about him, as though he had been smoking it, and he had the appearance of being intoxicated or under the influence of drugs. The green leafy material in the bags seized from the car tested positive for marijuana. The court held that the evidence was clearly sufficient to find the defendant guilty of marijuana possession.

In Hester v. State, the defendant, by his own evidence, showed that he was not merely one of the crowd. He was the one from the group of four males standing together who responded to the call from the car which stopped, ascertained that the occupant wanted to purchase "a good $20," and said he knew where it could be obtained. The trial court correctly ruled that this constituted more than mere presence, so as not to warrant a charge on mere presence.

d. Mere Spatial Proximity to Contraband vs. Constructive Possession

A finding of constructive possession must be based upon something more than the defendant's equal access to contraband or his mere "spatial proximity" to it. When the proximity of the contraband is coupled with such other facts and circumstances which sufficiently prove the defendant's connection to it, the totality of the evidence of the circumstances would be sufficient to establish his possession of the contraband. For instance, evidence of the presence of contraband in a close proximity to the defendant prior to his arrest, which is used to corroborate his confession, would be sufficient to justify his conviction for possession.

e. Controlled Delivery

In Myers v. State, a postal inspector delivered a package addressed to the defendant. The postal inspector told the defendant that he needed to get the parcel delivered to resolve whether it contained narcotics. In response, the defendant said that she would accept the package, although she would not sign for it. She stated that she would give the postal inspector permission to open the parcel so that the matter could be resolved. The postal inspector opened the package and found two baggies containing a green leafy substance later identified as marijuana and an unknown white powder. Drug-related items were later found in the defendant's vehicle and residence. Although the defendant contended that there was no evidence to connect her to the contraband and that she never took physical control of the package, the court held that there was sufficient circumstantial evidence to authorize her conviction for possession of marijuana with intent to distribute.

In Luke v. State, a GBI agent formulated a plan to make a controlled delivery of two packages containing marijuana to the residence of the defendant's father. After the defendant signed for the packages addressed to his father, he was arrested for receiving the marijuana. The court held that there simply was no evidence that the defendant had any knowledge that, when he signed for the delivery, those sealed, opaque packages contained contraband. A statement by another GBI agent that the defendant subsequently provided marijuana to a female was nonprobative hearsay and so could not constitute circumstantial evidence to establish the defendant's state of mind or knowledge at a prior time. In Perkins v. State, however, the court found that because the facts in the case were far different from those in Luke, Luke was not controlling. The court held that when the evidence was considered in its totality, i.e., when the circumstantial evidence connecting the defendant with the packages received during the controlled delivery was considered together with his false account about his relationship with the addressee, it was sufficient to authorize the trial court to conclude that the defendant was in fact the intended recipient of the packages and was aware of their contents. Accordingly, the evidence was sufficient to support the defendant's conviction for possession of marijuana with intent to distribute.

f. Presence of Metabolites in Bodily Fluid

The Court of Appeals has consistently held that the presence of cocaine metabolites in body fluid constitutes direct, positive evidence that the person who produced the body fluid possessed cocaine. The Georgia Supreme Court disapproved of this holding in Green v. State. In Green, the court held that the presence of cocaine metabolites in body fluid is direct evidence only of the fact that cocaine was introduced into the body producing the fluid, and is not direct evidence that the person possessed the cocaine. Rather, the presence of cocaine metabolites in body fluid is only circumstantial or indirect evidence that the person possessed cocaine.

g. Beaten Path Doctrine

In Blitch v. State, the court held that the "beaten path" doctrine allows connection of contraband found in close vicinity to a house so as to authorize rational jurors to conclude beyond reasonable doubt that the primary resident of that house owned or had control over the contraband. In Childers v. State, the court held that it is not essential that there be evidence linking the primary resident to the contraband in addition to the "beaten path" evidence, particularly when there is no evidence that others outside his immediate household had equal opportunity to commit the crime.

5. *Similar Offenses*

Evidence of a previous conviction for possession is admissible to show intent, motive, similarity of circumstances, and knowledge. In its presentation to the jury, the state must not merely submit into evidence a certified copy of the defendant's previous conviction. While the certified copy may be enough to establish that the defendant committed the independent offense, it does not establish the similarity or connection between that independent offense and the crime charged. The state must also present evidence to the jury to establish that similarity or connection. Although it is error to admit a certified copy of the defendant's previous indictment without any additional showing of similarity, this error is harmless if the evidence of the defendant's guilt is overwhelming.

Because the narratives contained in police reports generated in connection with police investigations do not have the reliability inherent in other documents that the courts have traditionally considered to be business records, the evidence contained in these narratives are not facts that should properly be admitted under the business records exception to the hearsay rule. Thus, it would be erroneous for a trial court to allow a police officer to read into evidence the narrative portion of a police report of which he had no personal knowledge and did not prepare for the purpose of demonstrating a similar transaction.

In order to provide defense counsel an opportunity to investigate the validity, relevance, or admissibility of similar transaction evidence, the state must notify the defense of its intent to introduce this evidence. The notice must specify the transaction to be introduced. In the absence of such notice, the admission of evidence about the transaction would be error. The state is not required to set out in its notice the lawful purposes for which it intends to use the evidence.

A defendant who preemptively introduces evidence of a prior conviction on direct examination may not on appeal claim that the admission of such evidence was error.

Upon request, the trial court must give a limiting instruction to the jury about the specific purpose for which the similar offense evidence can be considered. When a jury is informed that it can consider the similar offense evidence for the purpose of showing "the crimes charged in the case" and in considering an "element of the offense charged in this indictment," a fair risk exists that the jury will be confused and misled as to the proper limited use of this evidence to the prejudice of the defendant. The jury might improperly conclude that this evidence can be directly used to prove the crime charged or one or more of its elements. Since this language substantially expands the limited purposes for which the similar offense evidence can be used, it is overly broad and erroneous on its face.

The defendant's prior conviction for selling cocaine would be admissible in his trial for the possession of cocaine, where the prior conviction is presented not as evidence of bad character but as evidence to rebut a claim by the defendant that he does not fool with drugs.

A defendant who testifies may not be impeached by a prior felony conviction involving moral turpitude unless he first has placed his character into evidence. Thus, without the defendant placing his character into evidence, it would be improper for the state to use similar transaction evidence to attack his credibility.

6. *Prescriptions*

Prior to 1996, the Dangerous Drug Act provided that the possession of dangerous drugs prescribed for another person was legal only if the dangerous drugs were in the original prescription container. The possession of dangerous drugs prescribed for another person outside the original container was a misdemeanor. This provision of the Dangerous Drug Act applied exclusively to dangerous drugs, and there was no comparable provision which applied to controlled substances. In Black v. State, the Georgia Court of Appeals rejected the defendant's argument that because there was no comparable provision applicable to controlled substances, his possession of controlled substances, which were prescribed for his travelling companion but were possessed by the defendant outside the original prescription container, was not unlawful. The court found no indication that the General Assembly intended to authorize the possession of controlled substances (a felony) in these circumstances, while prohibiting the possession of dangerous drugs (a misdemeanor) under the same circumstances. Thus, the court upheld the defendant's conviction for the unlawful possession of controlled substances.

In 1996, the General Assembly, apparently in response to the defendant's argument in Black, amended the provision of the Dangerous Drug Act to make it applicable to controlled substances as well as dangerous drugs. Now, the possession of controlled substances or dangerous drugs prescribed for another person is legal only if such drugs are in the original prescription container and are labeled in accordance with the Georgia Drug and Cosmetic Act. Any person who possesses a controlled substance or dangerous drug prescribed for another person outside the original container or who possesses a drug which is not labeled in accordance with the law is guilty of a misdemeanor under the Dangerous Drug Act. It is interesting to note that with this 1996 amendment the possession of controlled substances under circumstances similar to those in Black would now be treated as a misdemeanor rather than as a felony offense.

In Hulsey v. State, the defendant was found guilty of unlawfully acquiring and obtaining possession of a controlled substance by altering a prescription. The Court of Appeals held that the trial court did not err in denying the defendant's motion for directed verdict of acquittal, because there was evidence linking the drug listed in the indictment (Darvocet) with the actual listed Schedule IV drug (Dextropropoxyphene). For purposes of the Georgia Controlled Substances Act, dextropropoxyphene and propoxyphene are chemically identical analgesics. The evidence showed that Darvocet N-100 is propoxyphene with acetaminophen and dextropropoxyphene is "Propoxyphene Napsylate." This circumstantial evidence was sufficient to authorize the jury's determination that the 90 Darvocet N-100 tablets the defendant fraudulently obtained were in fact the controlled substance dextropropoxyphene as alleged in the indictment.

Section 16-13-41(h) provides that it is unlawful for any practitioner to issue any prescription document signed in blank. In Raber v. State, the defendant argued that, because this provision does not define what a physician must do to "issue" a prescription document, he did not have fair notice that providing a pre-signed blank prescription pad to a member of his medical staff in the course of her employment would subject him to prosecution for a felony offense. Contrary to the defendant's argument, the Georgia Supreme Court held that properly construed, § 16-13-41(h) provides definite warning to persons of ordinary intelligence that the conduct alleged in the case was proscribed and therefore was not unconstitutionally vague. Section 16-13-41(h) proscribes the issuance of a prescription "document" rather than issuance of the prescription itself. It covers the circumstance where the prescription document, which identifies the practitioner by some preprinted information, is not filled in with any other required information except for the practitioner's signature and where this document is then given to another. This provision neither mentions nor implies that the practitioner must give the document to the ultimate user.

Also, in Raber the court rejected the defendant's argument that the language of § 16-13-41(h) allowed for arbitrary and discriminatory enforcement based upon unintended consequences of his conduct. The evidence showed that the nurse practitioner kept prescription pads pre-signed by the defendant in her residence, that her daughter admitted that she had stolen some of the prescription forms, and that another woman died from an apparent overdose of a drug which had been obtained by a prescription listing the defendant as the prescribing physician. The court found that it was not necessary to assess the surrounding circumstances in order to determine whether § 16-13-41(h) was violated. Evidence of the tragic death was relevant only because it eventually led to the discovery of the defendant's unlawful provision of the pre-signed prescription forms to his nurse practitioner. Thus, the death did not indicate that the prosecution's enforcement of the statute was arbitrary and discriminatory.

7. *Proof of Amount Possessed*

Unlike § 16-13-31, in which the requisite quantity and purity of cocaine which authorizes a conviction of trafficking in cocaine is specified in the statute, § 16-13-30 sets forth no quantities to distinguish mere possession and distribution. Knowledge of the amount of crack cocaine one would generally possess for personal use or the amount which might evidence distribution is not necessarily within the scope of the ordinary layman's knowledge and experience. Therefore, the testimony of an officer, qualified as an expert on drug use, that the amount of cocaine discovered would generally be for distribution, as opposed to personal use, is properly admissible.

Generally, the amount of a controlled substance which is possessed is not relevant to a conviction for possession. It has been held, therefore, that even if the amount possessed is so minute that it is not useable, a conviction will stand. There are situations, however, where the amount of substance possessed will be relevant to sentencing considerations. For example, under § 16-13-2, possession of an ounce or less of marijuana is a misdemeanor, while, under the general provisions of § 16-13-30(j), possession of more than an ounce is a felony. Thus, in a marijuana possession case, the amount of marijuana possessed will be an element of proof. In the absence of evidence to establish its weight, there is no basis for treating the offense as a felony.

The state's failure to give notice of the impending destruction of contraband and an opportunity to verify weight by independent weighing or by presence at the state's weighing, can lead to an insufficiency of admissible evidence of weight, an element of the crime.

It should also be noted that the placement of some substances in a particular schedule of controlled substances will depend on the amount of the substance involved in the crime. For example, codeine is listed in Schedule II (§ 16-13-26(1)(A)(vii)), but if the amount is not more than 1.8 grams per 100 milliliters, it is a Schedule III (§ 16-13-27(4)(B)) substance and if the amount is not more than 200 milligrams per 100 milliliters, it is a Schedule V (§ 16-13-29(1)(A)) substance. In one case, where it was uncertain whether the codeine possessed was a Schedule III or Schedule V amount, the court remanded for sentencing as a Schedule V amount. The court recognized that possession of both Schedule III and V drugs are governed by the same punishment section (§ 16-13-30(g)) but insisted that it had no way of knowing how the labelling of the substance would affect the length of sentence imposed. A resentencing was ordered.

8. *Indictments*

Where the defendant is indicted for misdemeanor possession of marijuana, evidence of the presence of tetrahydrocannabinol (THC) in the defendant's urine sample cannot sustain his conviction. A prosecution under the Controlled Substances Act for misdemeanor possession of marijuana cannot be instituted on the basis of a blood or urine test which shows "positive" for marijuana, because such positive showings will be based upon the presence of THC without the morphological features of the marijuana plant and are thus excluded from the definition of "marijuana" under the Act. Accordingly, it would appear that such prosecutions for possession of marijuana based upon positive blood or urine samples must be brought as felony prosecutions for possession of a Schedule I drug, i.e., THC. However, this rule may not control under the facts of a particular case. For instance, where evidence of the defendant's positive urine sample is used to corroborate the defendant's admission of possession, there would be no fatal variance between an allegation of misdemeanor possession of marijuana and the proof.

9. *Jury Instructions*

A trial court may charge the jury on constructive possession where there is sufficient evidence to support the charge. In Billingsley v. State, an officer testified that he observed the defendant retrieve cocaine from a pile of leaves on the side of the street and drop cocaine as he walked toward the officers. In each instance the evidence was sufficient to support a charge that the defendant knowingly had both the power and intention to exercise authority or control over the cocaine. Accordingly, the trial court did not err in giving the charge on constructive possession.

If circumstantial evidence exists raising a jury issue whether the defendant and another shared in the possession of the contraband, a charge on joint possession is authorized.

Where an indictment charges a defendant with committing the offense of possession with the intent to distribute, the trial court's reading of § 16-13-30(b) in its entirety does not constitute reversible error where the trial court has properly limited the jury's consideration of the evidence to the offense charged in the indictment.

10. Verdicts

When an indictment charges an offense and the jury returns a verdict of guilty on a lesser included offense, the verdict operates as an acquittal of the greater offense. Thus, if a jury returns a verdict on a lesser included offense, further deliberations are precluded. In Cantrell v. State, the jury returned a verdict of guilty of possession of cocaine. In so doing, the jury acquitted the defendant of the greater offense, possession of cocaine with intent to distribute. By refusing to accept the jury's verdict of guilty on the possession offense, the trial court forced the jury to reach unanimous agreement on the intent to distribute offense before considering the possession offense. However, where a jury deliberates a greater offense and an included offense, unanimity is not required for the greater offense before the jury can vote on the included offense. Thus, the Georgia Supreme Court concluded that the jury did not have to reach unanimous agreement on the intent to distribute offense before considering the possession offense.

B. Trafficking

1. Generally

The General Assembly has created trafficking offenses for (1) cocaine, (2) illegal drugs such as morphine or heroin, (3) marijuana, (4) methaqualone, and (5) methamphetamine or amphetamine, which are consolidated in § 16-13-31.

The General Assembly created another trafficking offense in 2004 for the amphetamine or methamphetamine commonly known as MDMA or ecstasy. This offense is defined in § 16-13-31.1.

2. Constitutionality

Section 16-13-31 survived an immediate constitutional attack in Paras v. State. The Georgia Supreme Court rejected the argument that the mandatory minimum sentencing deprived the sentencing judge of his discretion. The court also refused to find the statute in conflict with the parole authority given the State Board of Pardons and Paroles and rejected a claim that the sentencing provisions constituted cruel and unusual punishment under the Eighth Amendment. A vagueness attack on the wording of the statute was also denied by the court.

In Brugman v. State, the court held that, in clear language, § 16-13-31(e)(2) [now (g)(2)] contemplates only that the convicted trafficker will provide information about others involved in the crime for which he has been convicted. Section 16-13-31(e)(2) [now (g)(2)] does not, on its face, compel the defendant to exchange his own Fifth Amendment rights for a chance at a reduced sentence. The court also held that where any person is convicted under § 16-13-31 and provides "substantial assistance" to the authorities as contemplated by the statute, this information may be brought to the attention of the sentencing court by motion of either the district attorney or the defendant, or the sentencing court may make its own inquiry into the matter. The judge hearing the motion may then impose a reduced or suspended sentence if he finds that the defendant has rendered such substantial assistance. Such a construction of the statute assures that the power to impose sentence remains in the judiciary.

In Hardin v. State, the defendant contended that § 16-13-31(e), which makes it a felony to knowingly possess a mixture containing methamphetamine that exceeds twenty-eight grams, violated equal protection of the laws because it contained no purity requirement. The lack of this requirement, the defendant claimed, resulted in a disparate treatment of drug traffickers based on nothing more than the type of drug involved. The defendant's argument failed, according to the court, because the General Assembly is under no duty to treat all drugs and drug offenders the same and because the statute treats all traffickers in methamphetamine equally. The Generally Assembly can rationally employ different means to respond to the problems created by different drugs.

3. Actus Reus

a. Generally

The actus reus element for each of the trafficking offenses is similar: the selling, manufacturing, delivering, bringing into this state, or having possession of the requisite amount of contraband. It should be noted that the trafficking offenses, except for manufacturing methamphetamine or amphetamine, require proof of a threshold amount of the contraband. Thus, there must be at least 28 grams of cocaine; at least four grams of illegal drugs such as morphine, opium, or heroin; more than 10 pounds of marijuana; at least 200 grams of methaqualone; at least 28 grams of methamphetamine or amphetamine; or at least 28 grams of MDMA or ecstasy for the offense to be considered a trafficking offense.

There is no requirement in § 16-13-31 that the state allege and prove that a certain individual distributed the contraband. Proof of possession alone is sufficient to establish a violation of the statute.

Since trafficking may be committed in more than one way, it is sufficient for the state to show that it was committed in any one of the separate ways listed in the indictment, even if the indictment uses the conjunctive rather than disjunctive form. Thus, where the evidence is sufficient to show that the defendant violated § 16-13-31 in at least one of the ways alleged in the indictment, there is no fatal variance.

Where an indictment uses the conjunctive form but the trial court instructs the jury in the disjunctive pursuant to the language of § 16-13-31, there is no fatal variance between the instruction and the language of the indictment when the trial court also instructs the jury to review the indictment for the exact statement of the charge. Moreover, if it is proven that the defendant violated § 16-13-31 in either of the ways alleged in the indictment, he may be convicted.

Where an indictment charges a defendant with committing the offense of trafficking in only one way, a jury charge on the alternative ways by which trafficking may be committed does not constitute reversible error where the trial court has properly limited the jury's consideration of the evidence to the offense charged in the indictment.

A defendant can commit the crime of trafficking in one manner, by being involved with more than 28 grams of contraband. The quantity of contraband above 28 grams affects sentencing, however, not the manner in which the crime was committed. Thus, even where an indictment charges a defendant with trafficking in 200 grams or more of contraband, a jury instruction on trafficking in 28 grams or more would not constitute an erroneous instruction on a crime not alleged in the indictment.

Section 16-13-31(e)(2) treats pure amphetamine and a mixture containing amphetamine equally. It does not establish two different methods of trafficking based on the purity of the drug. Thus, where the state has charged the defendant with "trafficking in amphetamine," a jury instruction that trafficking in amphetamine may be accomplished by possessing "amphetamine or any mixture of amphetamine" would not create the possibility that the defendant could be convicted of an offense not charged.

By enacting § 16-13-31(b), the General Assembly clearly authorized a trafficking conviction based upon knowing possession of four or more grams of opium. Although a defendant may disagree that such possession establishes trafficking, the clear statutory language would govern his case.

b. The "Mixture" Containing the Controlled Substance

Despite compelling arguments that it was an unconstitutional classification scheme to impose greater punishment based on the total amount of "mixture" possessed, rather than on the total amount of cocaine possessed, and that it was irrational to punish less severely the possessor of 27 grams of pure cocaine than the possessor of 10 grams of cocaine in 20 grams of noncontraband, the Georgia Supreme Court in Lavelle v. State found the scheme in § 16-13-31 to be rationally related to the objectives of the legislature.

The Georgia appellate courts announced that part of the forbidden conduct under the trafficking in cocaine statute was the possession of any amount of cocaine in a "mixture" in which the total weight of the "mixture" was 28 grams or more.

In 1985, the legislature, despite the Georgia Supreme Court's construction of § 16-13-31(a) in Lavelle, struck the existing subsection and substituted in lieu thereof a new subsection (a). The legislature, apparently persuaded by the defendant's arguments in Lavelle, chose to omit the "mixture" language from both the description of the offense of trafficking in cocaine and from the penalty for trafficking in cocaine.

In Robinson v. State, Georgia Supreme Court held that when a statute making described conduct a crime is repealed prior to final judgment on a conviction, the repeal ends the prosecution if the legislature has not provided otherwise in a saving clause. In Robinson, the defendant was charged with the offense of trafficking in a mixture containing cocaine on February 5, 1985. On March 27, 1985, the legislature repealed the "mixture" language without including a saving clause. Thus, the defendant's conduct was no longer defined by the legislature as trafficking in cocaine; therefore, the prosecution in the case was at an end before the trial.

However, since the reversal of a conviction upon the authority of Robinson is the result of "trial error," i.e., a faulty or flawed indictment, rather than of evidentiary insufficiency, a second indictment omitting the "mixture" language would not constitute double jeopardy, and the retrial of the defendant would not be barred. In Bassett v. State, after the defendant's conviction was vacated upon the authority of Robinson, the defendant was re-indicted and again convicted of trafficking in cocaine based on an indictment that omitted the "mixture" language that rendered the previous indictment faulty. On appeal, the defendant again contended that he was being convicted of an offense which did not exist at the time the conduct in question occurred. However, with the omission of the "mixture" language from the second indictment, the court held that the act of knowingly bringing into the state or knowingly being in possession of more than 200 grams of cocaine constituted the offense of trafficking in cocaine both before and after the 1985 amendment to § 16-13-31.

It should be noted that the word "mixture" need not be recited in the indictment for the indictment to be considered faulty under the Robinson rule. If the word "substance" is used in an indictment as a synonym for "mixture," that indictment is as faulty under Robinson as an indictment using the word "mixture."

Although the Court of Appeals in Barrett v. State upheld the rule stated in Robinson v. State, it perceived the rule in a slightly different manner. In Barrett, the offense involved 428 grams of a mixture containing cocaine, of which 80 percent, or 342.4 grams, was proved to be pure cocaine. The court held that while clearly after July 1, 1985, the legislature no longer regarded as trafficking in cocaine the possession of an undetermined and perhaps infinitesimal amount of cocaine in a mixture, it was equally clear the legislature continued to regard, as trafficking in cocaine, the selling, manufacturing, delivering or bringing into this state and possession of 342.4 grams of pure cocaine, as was proved in this case. Thus, for a mixture containing an undetermined amount of cocaine, the prosecution would abate. For a mixture containing a determined amount of cocaine which violated the statute, even though the offense was redefined and harsher criminal sanctions reenacted, the prosecution would not abate. This perception of the Robinson rule was overruled by the Georgia Supreme Court in Gonzalez v. Abbott, because it conflicted with the court's decision in Bassett v. Lemacks. In Bassett, although there was proof at trial of a sufficient amount of pure cocaine in the "mixture" to violate § 16-13-31, the court held that the defendant's conviction for trafficking had to be set aside because the conduct with which he was charged and convicted, i.e., possessing "a mixture containing cocaine," was no longer defined as a crime in the statute at the time of his conviction. Thus, the prosecution in the case had abated.

As in Robinson, the defendant in Nichols v. State was indicted under former § 16-13-31(a) and was convicted after the statutory change. However, the defendant was charged with and found guilty of unlawfully and actually possessing "more than 28 grams of cocaine," not 28 grams of a **mixture containing cocaine**. Thus the defendant's conviction was authorized under the redefinition of the crime of trafficking in cocaine, as well as under former § 16-13-31(a), and was not violative of the mandate of Robinson.

In Gonzalez v. Abbott, the Eleventh Circuit Court of Appeals certified two questions of law to the Georgia Supreme Court to determine first, whether a conspiracy to traffick conviction may come under the Robinson rule, and second, whether such a conviction may come under the rule even though the indictment specifically alleged a quantity pertinent to the overt act element of conspiracy. The Georgia Supreme Court answered yes to both questions. Guided by the answers of the Georgia Supreme Court, the Eleventh Circuit Court of Appeals, based on the invalidity of the indictment, reversed the denial of the petitioner's habeas relief with regard to his conviction for conspiracy to traffick in cocaine.

In order to supersede and abolish the rule of common law stated by the Supreme Court of Georgia in the case of Robinson v. State, the 1987 legislature enacted § 16-1-11. This Code section provides that the repeal or amendment of any criminal statute will not affect or abate the status as a crime of any criminal act occurring prior to the effective date of the repeal or amendment. Nor will the prosecution for any criminal act be abated as the result of the repeal or amendment unless the legislature expressly declares otherwise.

It should also be noted that the 1986 legislature amended § 16-13-31(a) to provide punishments for trafficking in certain quantities of cocaine or of any "mixture" with a purity of 10 percent or more of cocaine. Where the "mixture" is of a purity of less than 10 percent, a person commits the felony offense of trafficking in cocaine, and shall be punished accordingly, if the total weight of the mixture multiplied by the percentage of cocaine contained in the mixture exceeds any of the quantities of cocaine specified in § 16-13-31(a)(1).

Thus, § 16-13-31 currently defines two methods of committing the crime of trafficking. One method deals with pure cocaine and the other with mixtures containing the statutorily required percentage of cocaine. In Barnett v. State, the grand jury returned a trafficking count within the indictment which specifically averred that trafficking had occurred due to the defendant's possession of 28 grams or more of (pure) cocaine; the count did not include an averment that trafficking occurred due to the defendant's possession of a mixture containing at least the statutorily required percentage of cocaine. The uncontroverted testimony of the crime lab chemist established that the substance analyzed had a total mixture weight of 33.9 grams and was 82.5 percent cocaine. Accordingly, the total weight of pure cocaine found in the mixture was only 27.9675 grams; less than the 28 grams averred in the trafficking count of the indictment. The court held that as only one means of offense commission was averred in the trafficking count of the grand jury's indictment and as the evidence at trial was insufficient to prove that trafficking had been committed in that manner, a fatal variance occurred.

In Byers v. State, the defendants were indicted and convicted for knowingly possessing "more than 28 grams of cocaine." Two bags of white powder, one with a gross weight of 31.7 grams and the other with a gross weight of 54.6 grams, were tested at the state crime laboratory. Although the forensic chemist who tested the substances testified that the test used did not indicate the presence of anything other than cocaine, he admitted that the test did not determine if certain commonly used adulterants were present in the substances, and that what percentage of the substances was pure cocaine "would be shear [sic] speculation." On these facts, the court held there was not sufficient evidence for a rational trier of fact to conclude that the defendants possessed at least 28 grams of pure cocaine.

In Bellamy v. State, the defendant asserted that because the forensic chemist who tested the drugs was unable to say whether the methamphetamine was pure or a mixture, there was a fatal variance between the indictment, which alleged that the substance was a mixture, and the proof at trial. The court found this assertion to be absurd and held that since § 16-13-31 treats pure methamphetamine and a mixture containing methamphetamine equally, any variance in the proof at trial regarding whether the methamphetamine was pure or a mixture was not fatal.

In *Clark v. State*, the court held that the absence of the word "purity" from the trafficking indictment did not render the indictment void. The court found that there is no substantive difference between an allegation that one knowingly possessed "any mixture with a purity of 10 percent or more of cocaine" and an allegation that one knowingly possessed "a mixture containing 10 percent or more of cocaine." They mean the same thing.

In Hill v. State, the state mixed the evidence from individual containers before testing. The trial court charged that the jury had to find that the defendant possessed 28 grams of methamphetamine, not a mixture thereof, in order to convict him for trafficking. This instruction set a higher standard of proof than required by the indictment. Because it was impossible to determine how much of the materials was methamphetamine and how much may have been simply ephedrine or something else, there was insufficient evidence to support a conviction based upon the jury charge. Nor was there sufficient evidence to support a trafficking conviction as alleged in the indictment. The defendant did not possess the mixture sent to the lab for testing. He merely possessed the component parts of that mixture. When the officer combined the components, it became impossible to determine if the defendant had possessed 28 grams of methamphetamine or even a 28-gram mixture containing methamphetamine.

c. Actual or Constructive Possession

Prior to 1988, § 16-13-31 prohibited knowing, "actual" possession of cocaine, illegal drugs, or marijuana. There were a number of cases ruling on what constituted "actual" possession. In Evans v. State, the court held that the legislature did not intend the phrase "actual possession" as found in the statute to mean that a person would be holding the controlled substance in his hand or have it physically on his person. Also, the legislature did not intend for a person to have the large amounts of a controlled substance that are proscribed by statute "on his person" in order to constitute actual possession. In most instances it would be physically impossible to have such large amounts on one's person. In Barrett v. State, the court held that "actual possession" referred not merely to physical custody but referred to actual active participation in the possession of such substances so as to be a party to the crime of trafficking.

From these cases it appeared that the courts ceased to distinguish "actual" from "constructive" possession. As a result of this lack of distinction between the two types of possession, the trial courts were instructing juries that they could find defendants guilty of trafficking based on their "actual" or "constructive" possession of a controlled substance, even though § 16-13-31 required "actual" possession. In Lockwood v. State, the Court of Appeals found no error in the trial court's charge to the jury that they were authorized to convict the defendant of trafficking in cocaine if the jury found beyond a reasonable doubt that he had actual or constructive possession of the cocaine. In Hamilton v. State, the court held that possession of a controlled substance may be either actual or constructive for purposes of a criminal prosecution under § 16-13-31. In Blaise v. State, the defendant was found guilty of trafficking for his "joint constructive possession of . . . cocaine." However, in Lockwood v. State, the Supreme Court in reviewing the Court of Appeals decision held that § 16-13-31 clearly required a finding of "actual" possession and not "constructive" possession. The Supreme Court's decision applied retroactively.

In 1988, the issue was ultimately resolved by the legislature when it eliminated the requirement that a person be in "actual" possession of a controlled substance in order to be found guilty of violating § 16-13-31. In view of this 1988 amendment, it is clear that the Supreme Court's decision in Lockwood is no longer controlling authority. Now, possession may be either actual or constructive, and it is not error for a trial court to give jury instructions on both types of possession. Indeed, where the central issue for the jury is whether the defendants had actual or constructive possession of the contraband, the trial court must charge the jury on the law of possession. However, when an indictment alleges only actual possession, it is reversible error for a trial court to charge the jury on "actual **or constructive possession**." Notwithstanding an indictment upon actual possession alone, when the evidence indisputably shows that the defendant knowingly had direct physical control over the contraband and not merely the power and intention to exercise dominion or control over it, a trial court's charge to the jury that it is authorized to convict the defendant of trafficking based on a finding of either actual or constructive possession does not constitute harmful error. Furthermore, when one is charged with conspiring with others to traffick in cocaine, it obviously is not error for the trial court to charge on constructive as well as actual possession.

The presumption that contraband is in the possession of the owner or driver of an automobile in no way bars the passenger from also being found guilty of possession because if two or more persons share actual or constructive possession of a thing, possession is joint.

Although each quantity of cocaine seized from a defendant may have been less than the statutory amount required to constitute trafficking and although each may have been in a different location, if it is shown that the defendant had actual possession of one quantity and constructive possession of the other quantity and if the two quantities combined meet the statutory amount required to constitute trafficking, this evidence would be sufficient to support a trafficking charge.

A person can not be in constructive possession of an entire kilogram of cocaine when he conducts an inspection, because he indisputably lacks the intention to exercise dominion or control over it until he has tested the sample. Upon tendering the purchase price to the seller, a person clearly possesses the intent to exercise control over all of the cocaine, but unless he acquires the power of control over it, he does not constructively possess it. Without proof of this power of control, the evidence would be insufficient to support a conviction for trafficking in cocaine.

In Hortman v. State, the defendant contended that the state failed to prove venue in Bibb County for the prosecution of his trafficking offense. He argued that since the element of dominion or control was cut off by law enforcement officials in Texas, no actual or constructive possession ever occurred in Bibb County. Law enforcement officers in Texas confiscated the boxes containing the marijuana and assumed control over them. Thereafter, notwithstanding the defendant's intent to exercise dominion and control over the marijuana, he no longer had the power to do so. Nor did any of his co-indictees have that power so as to make the defendant a party to the crime of trafficking. The evidence indisputably showed that it was Texas authorities who resealed the boxes of marijuana and sent them to the drug task force in Georgia via a different air freight carrier. Thus, the defendant and his co-conspirators lost control over the marijuana while it was still in Texas. Because the act of "knowingly bringing" a trafficking quantity of marijuana into Georgia was an essential element of the trafficking count in the indictment, and there was no proof of that element, the court held that the defendant's conviction for this offense could not stand.

d. *Proof of Amount Possessed*

Except for the trafficking offense of manufacturing methamphetamine or amphetamine, the state must show that the contraband weighed the threshold amount.

Where the state's electronic balance scales on which the contraband is weighed has a margin of error of less than one percent and the scales show that the contraband weighed the threshold amount, it is for the jury to decide whether the contraband weighed slightly more or slightly less than the threshold amount.

4. *Mens Rea*

Section 16-13-31 explicitly requires as the mens rea that the defendant must know he possesses the substance and he must know its identity. The statute is not, however, reasonably subject to the construction that the defendant must know or should know that the substance possessed weighs at least 28 grams.

An indictment charging a defendant with trafficking does not need to explicitly charge that he "knowingly" possessed the contraband, where it charges that the defendant had the contraband "under his control," which would be sufficient to infer the necessary criminal intent and to put the defendant on notice of the crime for which he is charged.

The knowledge element of a violation of § 16-13-31 can be proved by demonstrating either actual knowledge or deliberate ignorance. Deliberate ignorance is based on the alternative to the actual knowledge requirement at common law that if a party has his suspicions aroused but then deliberately omits to make further enquiries, because he wishes to remain in ignorance, he is deemed to have knowledge. A deliberate ignorance instruction is appropriate in a trafficking case when the facts support the inference that the defendant was aware of a high probability of the existence of the fact in question and purposely contrived to avoid learning all of the facts in order to have a defense in the event of a subsequent prosecution. Such an instruction does not obviate the state's burden of proving that the defendant had actual knowledge of the criminal activity.

In the prosecution of trafficking offenses wherein knowing possession constitutes an element of the crime, knowledge, of course, may be shown by circumstances which should excite suspicion in the mind of an ordinarily prudent man.

The defendant's testimony that he did not know the substance was in his possession does not mandate a finding of insufficient evidence that he knowingly possessed it. Rather, whether or not to believe such testimony is a question for the jury.

While mere presence at the scene of a crime is insufficient to convict one of being a party to the crime, presence, companionship, and conduct before and after the offense are circumstances from which one's participation in the criminal intent may be inferred. In Bowe v. State, the court held that although the defendant offered an explanation for his presence in the motel room when arrested, the jury was authorized to disbelieve that testimony and to infer from his presence and companionship with his co-defendants that he was guilty beyond a reasonable doubt of trafficking in cocaine.

Evidence of a separate earlier offense of possession of cocaine with intent to distribute is admissible to show bent of mind or course of conduct in the trial of a trafficking charge. However, the state must not merely submit into evidence a certified copy of the defendant's prior indictment and guilty plea to a charge of possession of cocaine. The state must also state the purpose for which the conviction is offered and must set forth the facts demonstrating the similarity between the offenses.

A jury's verdict finding the defendant guilty only of having the intention to traffick in cocaine amounts to an acquittal. There can be no finding of guilt without an inculpatory act in the case.

5. *Similar Offenses*

Where evidence is proffered showing prior or subsequent similar offenses of trafficking committed by the defendant, this evidence is admissible to show identity, plan, scheme, bent of mind, and course of conduct. However, before this evidence can be admitted, the trial court must conduct a hearing at which specified affirmative showings are made, and it must determine in the record that these showings have been made satisfactorily. Also, the trial court, upon request, must give a limiting instruction to the jury about the specific purpose for which this evidence can be considered. The trial court is not required to make an express finding that the probative value of the similar offense outweighs its prejudicial impact.

Where the date alleged in the indictment is not an essential averment, evidence of similar acts occurring within the statute of limitation is evidence of the crime charged and does not fall within the ambit of the rule relating to notice of the state's intention to present evidence of similar transactions.

6. *Conspiracy*

In Meyers v. State, the court held that since the ultimate purpose of the conspiracy was to sell, not to possess, marijuana, and since the possession and sale of a controlled substance are separate **and distinct crimes**, the offense of conspiracy to commit the offense of trafficking in marijuana by conspiring to sell more than 100 pounds but less than 2,000 pounds of marijuana was not committed when the conspirators first possessed the marijuana.

In Brown v. State, the court held that proof of a criminal agreement to import has no direct or necessary connection to proof of knowing and actual possession of the substance eventually imported. The prosecution of the federal crime of importation thus required proof of a fact not required in the prosecution for the possession offense and vice versa, and was therefore not a bar to the subsequent state prosecution. The federal conspiracy crime was not a lesser included offense of the state crime. The two crimes, whether the criminal agreement or the object of the agreement, were wholly different crimes.

It is reasonable to infer that one who conspires to import a large quantity of heroin into this country does so as part of a greater plan or scheme to traffic in heroin. This inference establishes a sufficient logical connection between the two crimes so that proof of the federal conspiracy crime tends to prove the trafficking crime. Thus, evidence of a defendant's prior federal conviction for conspiring to import a large quantity of heroin into this country is admissible as similar transaction evidence in his trial for trafficking in heroin.

When one is charged with conspiring with others to traffick in cocaine, it is not error for the trial court to charge on constructive as well as actual possession.

Evidence introduced on an invalid conspiracy to traffick in cocaine count is admissible on a valid conspiracy to traffick in marijuana count where it is relevant as evidence of the defendant's intent under the marijuana count.

Evidence corroborating a co-conspirator's testimony that the defendant actively participated in the conspiracy does not need to prove every element of the crime. It need only connect the defendant with the crime. Evidence of the defendant's conduct before, during and after the crime may be used to corroborate the co-conspirator's testimony.

7. *Party to Crime*

In Crenshaw v. State, the court held that a person could be a party to the crime of trafficking in the cocaine which was in another person's actual possession only if the person intentionally aided or abetted the other person so as to be in constructive possession of the contraband. The mere fact that a person may have known that another person was carrying cocaine would not authorize a finding that he aided and abetted him in the offense of trafficking. Likewise, a person's prior presence on a flight with the other person was not sufficient to show that he was a party to the crime.

"Actual possession," proof of which authorizes a conviction for trafficking, refers not merely to physical custody but refers to actual active participation in the possession of such substances so as to be a party to the crime of trafficking. Proof of actual possession may be by circumstantial evidence.

C. *Sale*

1. *Agent vs. Principal*

It is not necessary that the state prove the defendant was the principal in a drug transaction. In several cases the defendant argued that an agent does not actually control or sell the substance, and thus cannot be punished under a statute which seeks to punish the seller or the possessor. The court rejected the argument under the provision of the criminal code defining parties to a crime. One may be convicted of selling marijuana or a controlled substance even if he only acts as a procuring agent for another. Also, one may be convicted of selling a controlled substance even if he only acts as a lookout for the seller or as "human collateral" until the seller returns with the controlled substance.

The defendant's intent in agreeing to sell the controlled substance, whether real or feigned, is for the jury; and the jury's finding that the defendant was a willing participant in the illegal drug transaction will not be set aside unless clearly erroneous.

While the evidence surrounding a sale may show that the defendant never handled the money or contraband or made incriminating remarks, the jury can consider the defendant's involvement in a subsequent drug transaction to determine his intent to be an active participant in the sale and not merely a bystander.

2. *Completion of Sale*

The interesting question of first impression of when the sale of a drug is complete for purposes of the criminal law came before the Court of Appeals in Robinson v. State. In this case, the defendant was arrested after delivering the drug to a GBI agent but before any money changed hands. He appealed his conviction, asserting that while the indictment alleged a sale, the only act demonstrated by the evidence was a delivery. The court, however, concluded that dictum in a prior case was persuasive in demonstrating that a sale is completed when a seller delivers the goods. The court pointed out that this is the general rule in the drug context, citing an old federal case as authority.

In Willis v. State, the court held that it was not error for the trial court to fail to give the defendant's requested charge on the affirmative defense of abandonment of effort to commit a crime. The evidence showed that the defendant completed the crime of sale of cocaine by handing it to his wife and telling her to complete the sale. Because the defendant aided or abetted in the sale or procured another to make the sale, he was a party to the crime of selling cocaine and could be convicted thereof.

3. *Circumstantial Evidence of Sale*

In Hammond v. State, the court held that circumstantial evidence that the informant obtained the cocaine from the defendant considered with the officer's description of the monitored conversation between the informant and the defendant as well as his testimony concerning the defendant's possession and denial of possession of the money provided to the informant was sufficient to support the defendant's conviction for selling cocaine.

4. *Possession*

Neither actual nor constructive possession is an element of the offense of selling contraband.

5. *Similar Offenses*

Evidence of a previous cocaine sale is relevant to a defendant's intent and modus operandi and is admissible. However, the state's establishment of a prima facie case of similarity between the defendant's prior conviction for sale of cocaine and his subsequent sale of cocaine for which he is being tried does not satisfy its obligation to present proof on that issue at trial. There must be some evidence to establish between the prior crime and the crime on trial such similarity to and logical connection with each other so that proof of the prior crime tends to establish, by evidence of identity, bent of mind, or intent, the commission of the crime for which the defendant is on trial. The introduction of a certified copy of the defendant's prior conviction for the sale of cocaine is insufficient by itself. It should be noted that an independent sale of cocaine does not have to occur prior to the sale of cocaine of which the defendant is being tried to be admissible as other crimes or similar transactions evidence. The fact the independent sale occurred subsequently at most goes to the weight of the evidence and not its admissibility.

Proof of subsequent possession of some unused quantity of contraband is a sufficiently similar offense to be admissible in a trial for the sale of contraband. However, evidence that the defendant was in possession only of that cocaine which he ingested is not sufficiently similar to the sale of cocaine to be admissible in the defendant's trial for the sale of cocaine. Evidence of mere use of a drug (as opposed to its possession in some unused quantity) is not probative of motive, intent, plan or scheme to sell the drug; it is not sufficiently similar to the offense of the sale of that drug. Likewise, evidence of the defendant's prior drug sales is not sufficiently similar to the defendant's use of drugs to be admissible in his trial for possession of drugs in his bodily fluid. There are no significant similarities between the sale and the use of drugs, and the fact that the same type of drug was involved in both offenses does not render them similar.

The state must show a factual similarity between the defendant's "other" act of possessing drugs and the alleged act of selling drugs in order for evidence of the "other" act to be admissible to prove the defendant's identity as the seller of the drugs. It is the factual similarity of the defendant's possession of drugs on different occasions which renders it admissible to show his identity, and the differing intent with which he may have possessed the drugs on those separate occasions is not a bar to its admissibility for that limited purpose.

It should be noted that the trial court, upon request, must give a limiting instruction to the jury about the specific purpose for which the similar offense evidence can be considered.

A trial court has no authority to force the state to accept a defendant's offered stipulation of a prior conviction.

Evidence about an undercover officer's discussions with the defendant for possible future sales of cocaine that occurred during the crime on trial is not similar transaction evidence but is instead evidence of the circumstances of the transactions on trial, and is therefore admissible without the state giving notice of its intent to introduce such evidence. If the defendant's statement that he had sold cocaine on other occasions explains his involvement in the crime charged and is an integral part of his statements to police, his statement is admissible regardless of whether or not the separate crimes to which he confessed would otherwise be admissible as exceptions to the other transactions rule.

D. *Delivery or Distribution*

Section 16-13-30(b), which prohibits the unlawful delivery or distribution of cocaine, was not intended by the legislature to encompass the transmission of cocaine metabolites to a fetus that occurs when a pregnant woman ingests cocaine. This Code provision does not apply in these circumstances because at the time any transfer of cocaine metabolites takes place from the mother, the fetus is not considered a "person" within the meaning of the Controlled Substances Act. Also, the ordinary, logical, and common meanings of the terms "deliver" and "distribute" encompass only transfers that take place between one person and another person, outside the bodies of the persons involved.

Included within the definition of "delivery" set forth in § 16-13-21(7) is the "attempted transfer from one person to another." Although an attempt to commit a violation of the Georgia Controlled Substances Act is prohibited under § 16-13-33, the statutory definition of distribution under § 16-13-30 also includes the "attempt to transfer."

E. *Merger of Offenses*

Important Notice about Repudiation of Actual or Same Evidence Test: The Georgia Supreme Court repudiated the actual evidence test in *Drinkard v. Walker*, 281 Ga. 211, 636 S.E.2d 530 (2006), because it found this test to be inconsistent with the statutory framework governing the prohibition against multiple convictions for included offenses in Georgia. This inconsistency resulted in years of confusion and unpredictable results. In its place, the court adopted the required evidence test and overruled any prior case law that is inconsistent with it. Thus, any prior case law applying the actual evidence test is no longer controlling and should not be relied upon to determine whether one offense is included in another under § 16-1-6(1). The discussion of such case law is included below only insofar as it may still be applicable to pending prosecutions that arose before the Drinkard decision. See MULTIPLE CONVICTIONS, II. Tests to Determine Presence of Multiple Convictions, for a complete discussion of the Drinkard decision.

The Georgia Supreme Court dealt with a unit of prosecution issue in Tabb v. State. The defendant asserted that simultaneous possession of different Schedule II drugs constituted but one possession crime. The court rejected the argument, concluding that the General Assembly intended multiple punishment here. The court cited authority from prior Georgia decisions and elsewhere.

Where the averments of each count of an indictment refer to a different date on which the offense was alleged to have been committed, the date is made an essential averment of the transaction, and each count of the indictment is distinguishable. Thus, where the defendant is charged in three counts with having committed separate acts of selling cocaine on different dates, consecutive sentences may be imposed on each count.

A defendant cannot be convicted of both trafficking and possession with intent to distribute where the only evidence used to prove both offenses is the same quantity of drugs. In Iglesias v. State, the court held that the charge of possession with intent to distribute was a lesser included offense of trafficking as a matter of fact because the evidence required to convict the defendant of trafficking was the only evidence showing possession with intent to distribute. Thus, the defendant could not be convicted of both cocaine trafficking and also possession of cocaine with intent to distribute. However, where a portion of the drugs is used to prove the trafficking offense and the distinct remainder is used to prove the possession offense, there is no merger and the defendant may be convicted of both offenses. In Cassie v. State, the court held that there was no merger between the offense of trafficking and the offense of possession with intent to distribute, because the jury was authorized to find that the defendant was in actual possession of more than 28 grams of cocaine, parted with 27.6 grams to be sold, and retained possession of 19.2 grams. Likewise, in Timberlake v. State, the court held that there was no merger where, from the evidence that one quantity was larger than the other and that the two quantities were packaged separately and had slightly different purities, a jury could have concluded that the two quantities were intended to be utilized in different transactions.

A defendant cannot be convicted of both trafficking and possession with intent to distribute where both offenses arise from the same conduct. The intent to distribute which is necessary to the crime of possession of a substance under § 16-13-30(b) is satisfied by the reasonable inference that a person who possesses more than the 28 grams of cocaine under § 16-13-31 intends to distribute it. Therefore, the distribution offense contains no unique elements not satisfied by a trafficking offense, and the distribution offense would be included in the trafficking offense. Accordingly, consistent with the required evidence test adopted in the *Drinkard* decision, the two offenses merge.

A defendant cannot be convicted of both the sale and the possession of drugs where the only evidence used to prove both offenses is the same quantity of drugs. However, where the portion of the drugs actually sold is used to prove the sale and the distinct remainder is used to prove possession with intent to sell, there is no merger and the defendant may be convicted of both offenses. Likewise, when the defendant intends to sell only part and not all of the drugs in his possession, selling some and retaining the rest, the elements of both sale and simple possession have been satisfied as separate offenses, and the defendant may be convicted of both offenses.

Where cocaine with different trafficking weights is found in two separate locations in the defendant's home, the defendant should be charged with only one incident of trafficking in cocaine. The defendant's possession of all the cocaine in his home at the time of the incident is part of one continuous criminal act. Where the defendant has been erroneously charged and convicted of two trafficking offenses under these circumstances, his convictions will merge, and he will be susceptible to only one punishment.

In another case, however, the Court of Appeals held that double jeopardy did not attach to the defendant's prosecution for possession with intent to distribute in the county of his residence as a result of his guilty plea to possession with intent to distribute in another county. The defendant's act of possessing the marijuana with intent to distribute was not one continuous transaction. The defendant engaged in two separate courses of conduct at different times and locations with distinct quantities of contraband, even though he may have at some earlier time possessed all the marijuana in his home. The defendant himself removed a portion of the marijuana to a different location for a different purpose and was not in possession and control of all the marijuana at the time of either incident. The trial court therefore did not err in denying the defendant's motion for discharge and acquittal on the ground of double jeopardy.

Where the defendant is charged with possession with intent to distribute, it is not error for the trial court to charge the jury that should it find the defendant not guilty of this offense it would be authorized to consider whether the defendant committed the lesser offense of possession. Conviction of the greater offense of possession with intent to distribute renders harmless any error in a charge given for the lesser included offense of possession.

Where it is clear from the indictment and the evidence presented at trial that both the possession and the possession with intent to distribute convictions are based upon the same evidence, the trial court must merge the convictions and enter a sentence for only one of them.

In a trafficking case, where a jury issue exists regarding the type of possession, actual or constructive, exercised by the defendant, the lesser offense of possession is reasonably raised by the evidence and it is prejudicial error for the trial court to fail to instruct the jury on the lesser offense pursuant to the defendant's written request. Where an indictment for trafficking alleges that the defendant possessed more than 28 grams of cocaine, simple possession of cocaine is a lesser offense included as a matter of fact in the greater indicted offense of trafficking. Consequently, a written request to charge on simple possession would be adjusted to the evidence, and the trial court's refusal to give it would be error.

A defendant is not entitled to a charge on the lesser included offense of possession, where the evidence shows the completion of the greater offense, such as the possession of drugs with intent to distribute, the sale of drugs, the growing of marijuana, or trafficking, and there is no evidence raising the lesser offense of possession.

Possession of marijuana is not a necessary element of the crime of knowingly manufacturing marijuana by cultivating or planting, and so misdemeanor possession is not a lesser offense included in the crime of manufacturing as a matter of law, within the meaning of § 16-1-6. Similarly, possession of more than one ounce of marijuana is not, as a matter of law, a lesser included offense of manufacturing marijuana. Also, where the evidence required to establish the manufacturing charge is not required to prove possession, the two crimes do not merge as a matter of fact.

Merely because a conviction for possession with intent to distribute may result in life imprisonment is not controlling in determining whether such an offense is a greater or lesser included offense of trafficking.

The offense of abandonment is not a lesser included offense of possession but rather a separate offense. While it is possible that under the evidence the defendant committed the separate act of abandonment, that would not have any mitigating effect on his potential criminal culpability of the previous act of possession. It follows that a trial court may refuse a request to charge in connection with the entirely separate crime of abandonment.

In Davis v. State, the Court of Appeals held that attempted marijuana possession is a lesser included offense of marijuana possession, rejecting the defendant's assertion that attempt was not a **lesser included offense** within possession because the two offenses were defined in separate code sections and because they carried the same punishment. The court concluded that the attempt provision of the Georgia Controlled Substances Act (§ 16-13-33), rather than defining a separate and distinct crime, is exclusively a punishment provision designed to replace the punishment provision of the general attempt statute and concluded that the punishment aspect of an offense is irrelevant in the determination of whether that offense is included in another.

In contrast to the general conspiracy statute, which provides that the crime of conspiracy merges with the object crime when it is committed, conspiracy to possess marijuana with intent to distribute is not a lesser included offense of possession as a matter of fact or as a matter of law. They are separate crimes. Thus, an acquittal of the conspiracy offense is not an acquittal of the possession offense. In treating drug conspiracy on a par with drug possession, the legislature apparently made the policy decision that it was just as serious an offense.

Apparently, if one is indicted for conspiracy to violate the Georgia Controlled Substances Act under the general conspiracy statute and is also indicted for the object crime, the likely result will be the merger of the conspiracy into the object crime.

Where the evidence shows that the defendant's involvement in a drug transaction exceeded the use of mere language to solicit someone to commit the crime, criminal solicitation is not a lesser included offense of trafficking as a matter of law or fact. Thus, the defendant would not be entitled to a charge on criminal solicitation as a lesser included offense.

The offenses of driving while having marijuana or its metabolites present in the urine and possession of marijuana by ingestion merge as a matter of fact where there is no evidence independent of the blood analysis which shows any possession of marijuana by the defendant. Since all the evidence is used up in proving one crime, it is error for the trial court to sentence the defendant for both charges.

Convictions for possession of a drug-related object and possession of cocaine merge as a matter of fact where the only evidence used to establish the defendant's possession of the drug-related object is the circumstantial evidence used by the state to prove that he knowingly possessed cocaine residue on the object. Consequently, the trial court's failure to merge the two convictions and sentence the defendant only for possession of cocaine would constitute error.

F. *Exemptions or Exceptions Under Controlled Substances Act*

1. *Burden of Producing Evidence of Exception*

The Controlled Substances Act provides that the burden of coming forward with evidence of an exemption or an exception under the Act lies with the defendant. Thus, it is not part of the state's prima facie case that the defendant lies outside the statutory exceptions; rather, the defendant must present evidence that he is within one of the exceptions. A statutory exception amounts to an affirmative defense, with the initial burden of producing evidence to support the affirmative defense resting upon the defendant. Once a defendant raises the issue at trial, it is then incumbent upon the state to disprove the defense beyond a reasonable doubt.

2. *Specific Exceptions Within Code*

As for the specific exceptions, they are generally found within the Controlled Substances Act itself. However, exceptions may be found elsewhere in the Code. For example, there is an exception within the Dangerous Drug Act and an exception within the law regulating pharmacists and pharmacies which may be applicable in a prosecution under the Controlled Substances Act.

The specific exceptions which can be found in the Controlled Substances Act are to be found in § 16-13-35(b), which authorizes possession, manufacturing, dispensing, distribution and research by registered manufacturers, distributors, dispensers, and researchers, and in § 16-13-35(c), which authorizes possession for four groups of individuals: (1) employees of registered manufacturers and dispensers, (2) common carrier employees who possess in the usual course of business, (3) those who possess pursuant to a prescription written by an authorized person, and (4) those state officials who possess during the course of their employment. It should also be noted that § 16-13-52(d) grants the State Board of Pharmacy the power to authorize the possession of controlled substances for research purposes. Also, § 16-13-29.2 gives the State Board of Pharmacy the authority to exempt and control the sale of Schedule V controlled substances by rule. The Board's rules may allow the sale of these substances without the need for issuance of a prescription from a medical practitioner as long as they are sold only in a pharmacy.

3. *Reverse Sting Operations*

If legally maintained by law enforcement officers, controlled substances may be used by the officers in reverse sting operations. Since law enforcement officers are authorized by § 16-13-35(c)(4) to possess controlled substances while acting in the course of their official duties, there is no prohibition in the Controlled Substances Act against the retention and legal use of seized controlled substances not listed in Schedule I, so long as the owner of the drug is known and forfeiture proceedings have not been commenced. If the owner is unknown, however, the drug is summarily forfeited and must be destroyed in accordance with § 16-13-49(u)(1). This limitation effectively prevents a law enforcement agency, which possesses only summarily-forfeited controlled substances, from engaging in legal reverse sting operations. An agency would be able to engage in such operations only if it has properly identified, to the extent possible, the source of the drugs in its possession. However, because the failure to destroy a summarily-forfeited substance used in a reverse sting does not violate any of the defendant's constitutional rights, any evidence gathered by the police as a result of their use of the substance would not be subject to suppression. Moreover, the use of a drug in a reverse sting operation that the police should have destroyed earlier does not constitute police misconduct so outrageous that due process would require the reversal of the defendant's conviction.

4. *Controlled Substances Therapeutic Research Program*

Cancer and glaucoma patients participating in the Controlled Substances Therapeutic Research Program are immune from state prosecution for possession of marijuana as authorized by law. Physician, pharmacy, and pharmacist participants in this program are also immune from state prosecution for possession, distribution, and any other use of marijuana, which use is authorized by law.

5. *Medical Necessity*

The possession of marijuana which is purportedly being used for medicinal purposes but has not been prescribed by an authorized physician for one of the permitted therapeutic uses does not fall within any of the exceptions or immunities established by the General Assembly. Without evidence of a recognized exception or immunity for the defendant's possession of marijuana, a trial court may properly refuse to give a requested instruction on the defense of justification. Such an instruction could mislead the jury into believing that it could acquit the defendant if it finds that his conduct was justified because he thought that he derived some benefit from using the marijuana, notwithstanding the apparent illegality of possessing it.

The U. S. Supreme Court has held that there is no medical necessity exception for marijuana to the prohibitions in the federal Controlled Substances Act, even when a patient is seriously ill and lacks alternative avenues of relief. Although the Act does not explicitly abrogate the necessity defense, the court recognized that a medical necessity exception for marijuana is at odds with the terms of the Act and thus unavailable as a defense. The Act reflects a determination by Congress that marijuana has no medical benefits worthy of an exception outside the confines of a federal government-approved research project. Thus, medical necessity is not a defense to manufacturing and distributing marijuana.

6. *Claim of Right*

It has been held that in the absence of a defendant's claim of right to sell a substance, it is harmless error for a trial court to charge that any sale of a controlled substance is a violation of the Act (when the Act in fact provides for exceptions).

7. *Religious Exemptions under Federal Law*

In Gonzales v. O Centro Espirita Beneficente Uniao Do Vegetal, the federal government sought to prohibit a small religious sect from engaging in the practice of drinking a sacramental tea that contained a hallucinogen regulated under the federal Controlled Substances Act on the ground that the Act barred all use of the hallucinogen. The federal government contended that it had a compelling interest in the **uniform** application of the Controlled Substances Act, such that no exception to the ban on use of the hallucinogen could be made to accommodate the sect's sincere religious practice. Furthermore, it contended the regulatory regime established by the Act could not function with its necessary rigor and comprehensiveness if subjected to judicial exemptions.

Rejecting these contentions, the United States Supreme Court concluded that Congress's determination that the hallucinogen should be listed in Schedule I of the Controlled Substances Act did not provide a categorical answer that relieved the federal government of its obligation under the Religious Freedom Restoration Act (RFRA) to demonstrate that the compelling interest test was satisfied through application of the Controlled Substances Act to the particular claimant whose sincere exercise of religion was being substantially burdened. Moreover, the existence of statutory and regulatory exemptions for another Schedule I substance confirmed that the federal Controlled Substances Act did not preclude exceptions altogether and that the Act was amenable to judicially crafted exceptions. The court, therefore, found that the government did not demonstrate a compelling interest in the uniform application of the Controlled Substances Act by resting its argument on slippery-slope concerns that could be invoked in response to any RFRA claim for an exception to a generally applicable law, i.e., if the government makes an exception for one, it would have to make one for everyone; therefore, there are no exceptions. More specifically, the government failed to demonstrate that health concerns or the risk of diversion to recreational users provided a compelling interest in banning the sect's sacramental use of the hallucinogen.

G. *Evidentiary Considerations*

1. *Chain of Custody*

Because the substance at issue is generally analyzed by the State Crime Lab, the state must prove the substance tested was the same as the substance taken from the defendant. The current rule on proving chain of custody is derived from Pittman v. State and White v. State.

In *Pittman*, the court reversed a conviction for driving under the influence when the state had no proof of the chain of custody of the blood sample. The police officer who testified did not know by whom or by what means the sample was transmitted to the lab, or who received it there. "When a substance analyzed has passed through several hands its custody at all times should be accounted for. The evidence must not leave it to conjecture what has happened to it between the taking and the analysis."

The Supreme Court of Georgia in *White* clarified *Pittman* somewhat. In *White*, Gary Garner, a police officer, testified as to how he acquired the substance and the circumstances surrounding his subsequent delivery to the crime lab. The toxicologist who ran the tests and issued a report testified she had been given the substances by Garner. "In the absence of something to refute the conclusory statements of these witnesses, the testimony was sufficient to authorize the jury to find that Garner kept the items purchased from the accused . . . in his possession at all times until he delivered them to the [toxicologist.]" That was sufficient, according to the court, to prove chain of custody.

The appellate courts rarely reverse because the chain of custody was not adequately proven. If the evidence proves to a "reasonable certainty" the contraband given to the lab for analysis is the same as that taken from the defendant, and in the absence of any actual evidence (as opposed to speculation) of tampering, the chain of custody will be considered proven for purposes of appellate review. Meeks v. State is one of the rare cases where a conviction was reversed because the chain of custody was not adequately proven. In Meeks, the police officer testified the marijuana was placed in a briefcase and then turned over to the crime lab. He could not, however, remember what sort of container it was in, nor did he mark the container to show it contained evidence seized from the defendant.

Absent affirmative evidence of tampering, a crime lab and all its branch offices and employees are considered as a single link in the chain of custody. Since a chain of custody within the crime lab itself is not required, proof that the evidence was in the custody of the crime lab would establish the chain of custody.

Where there is no affirmative evidence of tampering or substitution, a missing link in the chain of custody does not alone require exclusion of the evidence. Thus, in *Franklin v. State*, where the testimony showed that the police placed the substance in a tamper-proof identifiable container and that the crime lab technician who tested the substance received it in the same container with no proof of tampering or substitution, the court held that the state met its burden of showing with reasonable certainty that the substance tested was the same as that seized, notwithstanding the fact that the individual who took the evidence from the police department to the crime lab was not identified.

2. *Right to Independent Analysis of Substance*

The Georgia Supreme Court in Patterson v. State held: "Where the defendant's conviction or acquittal is dependent upon the identification of the substance as contraband, due process of law requires that analysis of the substance not be left completely within the province of the state." The court further stated, however, that the defendant does not have an absolute, unqualified right to examine the evidence. Subsequent cases have defined the parameters of the right.

One of the first post-Patterson cases was Gilliland v. State. In a decision which reflected some of the factors the court considered important in ruling on a request for independent analysis, the court reversed the conviction. The court indicated the defendant's request came three months after he was indicted, one month after his motion to suppress was denied, and one month prior to trial. The request contained the name of the person the defendant wanted to administer the test and a statement that the defendant believed the state's test contained a substantial possibility of error.

The request for an independent analysis must be timely made. Furthermore, the defendant may waive his right to an independent analysis by not timely utilizing the court-ordered opportunity to conduct the analysis.

Unless a criminal defendant can show bad faith on the part of the police, the police's failure to preserve potentially useful evidence does not constitute a denial of due process of law. In Illinois v. Fisher, the United

States Supreme Court held that where police testing indicated that the chemical makeup of the substance inculpated, not exculpated, the defendant and it was undisputed that police acted in good faith and in accord with their normal practice when it destroyed the substance seized from the defendant, who had been a fugitive for over 10 years, the defendant failed to establish a due process violation. The existence of a pending discovery request filed by the defendant over 10 years earlier did not eliminate the necessity of showing bad faith on the part of police. Furthermore, the applicability of the bad-faith requirement depended not on the centrality of the contested evidence to the prosecution's case or the defendant's defense but on the distinction between material exculpatory evidence and potentially useful evidence. Since the substance destroyed in this case was, at best, potentially useful evidence, the bad-faith requirement applied.

When the state destroys a defendant's urine sample despite its known exculpatory value and despite a court order granting him access to it, and the defendant is unable to obtain comparable evidence by other reasonably available means, the defendant's right to due process has been violated and the trial court may dismiss the drug charges against him. Since the sample is not merely potentially useful but rather is clearly exculpatory, the defendant does not have to show that the state acted in bad faith in order to prove a due process violation.

The right to analyze independently the substance is clearly not absolute. A conviction will not be reversed, therefore, even if the defendant was not permitted to conduct an independent analysis if there is no real dispute about the identity of the substance. In Birge v. State, the defendant's conviction was affirmed because there was no bona fide dispute about what the substance was. During the search the police asked the defendant to get the marijuana. He handed them a substance which tested positive for marijuana. There never was a claim that it was not marijuana, and there was no denial of due process not to permit an independent analysis.

In Staples v. State, because the defendant did not challenge the chemical properties of the substance identified by an expert nor claim that the seized substance, by its nature, misidentified him as the perpetrator, the court held that it was not an abuse of the trial court's discretion to refuse to appoint an independent expert chemist for the defendant.

3. *Expert Evidence Regarding Identity of Substance*

Unquestionably, the best way to prove that a substance is contraband is through the use of a crime lab report. If, for some reason, that is not an available option (perhaps the chain of custody cannot be proven), the state may prove the substance is contraband through the testimony of the officer who seized it, after the officer has been qualified as an expert on contraband identification. It lies in the trial court's sound discretion to decide whether a witness has the learning or experience to be qualified as an expert in the field of drug identification. The exercise of this discretion will not be disturbed unless manifestly abused.

The Court of Appeals has stated, however, that the identity of a substance need not be established by expert testimony. The officer who seized the contraband can establish the identity of the substance by relating facts known or observed by him. A crime scene technician, who is trained and qualified to test for contraband, can establish the identity of the substance by testifying that the results of the tests performed on the substance were positive for contraband. The identity of the substance can also be established by the defendant stipulating or testifying that the substance is contraband and by making no claim that the substance is something other than contraband. However, it has been held that without expert testimony identifying the substance as contraband, a defendant's admission that he possessed contraband is insufficient to authorize a finding, beyond a reasonable doubt, that the substance is contraband.

Positive field test results are alone sufficient to sustain a conviction for selling or possessing cocaine. Positive test results from the state crime lab are not required. Thus, regardless of whether the substance found in the exhibit and tested by the crime lab was connected to the defendant, sufficient evidence arising from the field test would sustain a finding that the substance the defendant sold the officer was cocaine.

Where the defendant at trial admits to the identity of the substance, any alleged defect in the state's evidence on the identification of the substance becomes irrelevant. Such an admission, even if made after the state has concluded its case-in-chief, precludes any error in denying the defendant's motion for directed verdict based on evidentiary grounds.

Where the substance was part of the circumstances surrounding the defendant's arrest, witnesses for the state may refer to the "suspected" contraband, regardless of whether it has been positively identified.

Prior to 1995, the state was not permitted to bring into evidence a written crime lab report identifying a substance as contraband, if the state failed to furnish a copy of the report to the defendant upon his written request at least ten days prior to trial. The Court of Appeals held that this exclusionary rule did not apply to the "oral report" of a forensic scientist at trial regarding the identification of a suspect substance, nor did it apply to the testimony of a crime lab expert regarding individual test results that did not include any expression of the expert's conclusions or opinion. Effective January 1, 1995, the state's disclosure of a written crime lab report identifying a substance as contraband is regulated by Georgia's 1994 criminal discovery provisions. These provisions do not require actual service of the crime lab report upon defense counsel, but only make the report available for inspection and copying. If the state fails to comply with these discovery provisions, the trial court may order compliance, grant a continuance, or, upon a showing of prejudice and bad faith, prohibit the state from introducing a crime lab report not disclosed to the defendant.

Where a crime lab report has been admitted into evidence without objection and the forensic chemist has not read the results into evidence, the report is original evidence that may go out with the jury. It is not subject to the continuing witness objection.

Section 35-3-16, which was enacted by the General Assembly in 1994, authorized in any prosecution for a drug offense the admission in evidence of a sworn certificate of drug analysis by a state crime lab analyst. A properly executed certificate was "admissible evidence of the composition, quality, and quantity of the substance submitted to the laboratory for analysis." This certificate, rather than the lab analyst's testimony, was used to authenticate the results of the drug analysis.

In Miller v. State, the Georgia Supreme Court held that this certificate, as hearsay evidence, did not fit within any statutorily-recognized hearsay exception in Georgia. Since the certificate did not fall within a firmly rooted exception to the hearsay rule, the Confrontation Clause of the federal constitution barred receipt of the certificate in evidence without a preliminary showing of reliability or without determining that the lab analyst was not available to testify. The court found that the increased work demands of the state crime lab did not make a lab analyst "unavailable" to testify. The court also held that subsection (c) of § 35-3-16 did not guarantee a defendant the opportunity to cross-examine the lab analyst. A defendant's filing of an objection to the admission of the certificate only authorized the trial court to make a determination concerning the admissibility of the certificate and would not result in the lab analyst's appearance in court. When measured against the state constitution, the court found § 35-3-16 to be exceedingly troublesome. Because this Code section authorized the introduction of an ex parte affidavit into evidence against a criminal defendant, in contravention of the defendant's constitutional guaranty that he be confronted with the witnesses against him and be permitted to cross-examine them, it was unconstitutional. Also, requiring a defendant to request the presence of the witnesses against him and to explain why he requires their presence in order to be afforded his constitutional right of confrontation placed too heavy a burden on the assertion of a constitutional protection. Furthermore, the Code section impermissibly shifted the burden of proof from the state to the defendant against whom the state wished to introduce a certificate.

Apparently because of these constitutional infirmities, the General Assembly repealed § 35-3-16 in 1997.

In Melendez-Diaz v. Massachusetts, the United States Supreme Court held that the admission into evidence of testimonial affidavits of state laboratory analysts to prove that the material seized by police was cocaine would violate a defendant's Sixth Amendment right to confront the witnesses against him where the analysts did not testify in person.

Even if the printout from the machine testing the substance constitutes a writing, the best evidence rule does not bar introduction of the chemist's oral testimony regarding the test results. The issue is the existence of a fact, i.e., whether the substance tested has been identified, and not the contents or terms of the writing. Thus, the identity of a substance may be proved by both oral and written evidence. Furthermore, regardless of whether the chemist tested the substance or supervised the testing of the substance, his testimony regarding the results is admissible.

In Bostic v. State, the Court of Appeals affirmed a conviction for the sale of cocaine despite the defendant's claim that the trial court erred in permitting a forensic chemist to testify that the substance involved was cocaine. The defendant claimed that the trial court failed to determine whether the tests employed by the chemist reached a scientific state of verifiable certainty. The appellate court, while noting that it is the responsibility of the trial judge to satisfy himself of the competence of scientific evidence, concluded on the basis of its own research into the specific techniques involved, that any failure to expressly determine the validity of the test results was harmless. The dissenting judge accused the court of improperly taking judicial notice of the worth of such tests. He urged that the case be remanded for a specific finding of reliability by the trial court. However, it has been held that once a testing procedure has been recognized in a substantial number of courts, the trial court is authorized to take judicial notice, without receiving evidence, that the procedure used by the expert witness to identify the substance as cocaine has been established with verifiable certainty, or that it rests upon the laws of nature.

A forensic expert is allowed to testify that a urine specimen that he has analyzed is positive for a particular substance without quantifying the amount.

The "ontrack system" is a test performed on urine samples to detect the presence of marijuana or controlled substances. Until 2001, this test had not been recognized in a substantial number of courts as a reliable method of drug detection. Thus, in the absence of expert testimony that the test had been established with verifiable certainty or rested on the laws of nature, the results of such a test were not admissible. In 2001, however, one panel of the Court of Appeals upheld a trial court's finding that there was sufficient expert testimony presented in the case to establish that the techniques and procedures of the OnTrack TesTstik drug test have reached a scientific stage of verifiable certainty and that the test can be administered in a manner that ensures a reliable result. Nevertheless, another panel of the Court of Appeals concluded that it would be an abuse of discretion to admit drug testing evidence based solely on this one decision when it is unclear whether the same test was given in the case and when it is questionable whether the decision is directly relevant to the facts.

The state is not required to introduce evidence showing the validity and reliability of the scientific principles and techniques involved in the microscopic, thin layer chromatography and Duquenois-Levine tests. These tests have been recognized in a substantial number of courts as reliable methods for the identification of marijuana. Since these tests have been recognized by the courts, a trial judge may judicially notice, without taking evidence, that the tests have been established with verifiable certainty.

An expert does not have to perform "an exact test" to determine the purity of the mixture "down to a percentage." He can form an opinion as to the purity of the mixture in question based upon all his experience in analyzing thousands of other samples and upon the results of the particular tests performed on the samples taken from the mixture. The failure to conduct an "exact test" to determine the purity of the mixture down to a specific percentage would affect only the weight and not the admissibility of the expert's opinion regarding the purity thereof. The fact that the expert formed his conclusion as to purity based on raw data obtained by a technician does not render his conclusion hearsay. Furthermore, where the expert is available for full and searching cross-examination, the failure of the expert to test the sample independently, after observing the analytical test results obtained by others, goes only to the weight of the evidence and not to its admissibility.

In Paul v. State, a forensic chemist testified that the combined weight of the cocaine was 35.9 grams and that in his opinion each of the three bags contained cocaine of 100 percent purity. He based his opinion on his chemical analysis and his visual examination of the material, including the color tests. The court held that this testimony, in combination with the defendant's trial testimony, was sufficient to support a conviction of trafficking in 28 grams or more of cocaine with "a purity of 10 percent or more." Likewise, in Beauchene v. State, the court found that the state established the elements of the charged crime of trafficking in cocaine. The state's forensic chemist testified that the state's exhibit consisted of three bags which contained a total of 82.8 grams of cocaine of between 55 and 58 percent purity. Although the witness stated that she did not perform the full range of tests on one of the bags, she did determine that the purity of its contents was the same as that of the other two bags, and that the total weight of the contents of the bags on which she performed all the tests was 55 grams.

In Adams v. State, an expert concluded that a substance was cocaine by chemically testing two bags and determining, by expert tactile observation, that two other accompanying bags were identical or contained the same substance. The court concluded that there was a significant point in proof by chemical analysis as well as by expert analysis of appearance, or touch and feel.

In Means v. State, the court held that it was not necessary for the state to prove that each item seized contained cocaine. It was enough for the state to introduce evidence that random samples were taken and were found to contain 95 percent cocaine. From this evidence the jury could reasonably infer that all the items contained cocaine. The court also held that the total weight may be extrapolated from the average weight of the random samples where the evidence is undisputed as to the identity of the contraband.

In Cooper v. State, the court found that regardless of whether the substances found in the kitchen were confirmed as cocaine, the crime lab did confirm that the substance found in the coat pocket in the codefendant's bedroom closet as weighing 149 grams and as containing 73 percent cocaine. The bags of cocaine found in the bathroom also tested positive and cumulatively weighed one gram. The court held that the defendant's aiding and abetting the codefendant's trafficking operation at the house linked him to the cache of 149 grams of cocaine found in the bedroom, and the defendant's pill bottle linked him to the 19 small bags of cocaine found in the bathroom. This evidence supported the cocaine trafficking conviction of the defendant.

In Carroll v. State, the court held that the state did identify scientifically the found substances as marijuana when it admitted photographs of growing and harvested marijuana plants and actual specimens of what was seized and when the state's forensic chemist testified that specified tests performed on the leafy material confirmed the presence of marijuana.

In Burch v. State, the officer who seized the contraband testified that, based on his training and experience, the plants appeared to be marijuana. The analyst with the crime lab testified that tests performed by her indicated that the plant sample she tested was marijuana, but she could not positively identify it as marijuana. The jury was authorized to find that the reason the three tests were not positive was because the plants were young, had deteriorated, and the test sample was small. Circumstantial evidence in the form of materials used to grow marijuana was found in the vicinity of the plants. The court held that, cumulatively, this evidence was sufficient to authorize a rational trier of fact to find beyond a reasonable doubt that the plants were marijuana plants.

In Adkinson v. State, the court held that the evidence was insufficient to support the defendant's conviction of possession of marijuana with intent to distribute. A state chemist testified that, although he thought the green leafy material was marijuana, he did not test it, so he could not testify beyond a reasonable doubt that it was marijuana. Additional opinion testimony was properly allowed regarding the detectives' beliefs that the substance was marijuana, but no scientifically conclusive evidence was presented.

In Eason v. State, the court held that the defendant has the right to subpoena certain materials from the state crime lab chemist for the purpose of cross-examination. Those items which may be subpoenaed are limited to those memos, notes, graphs, computer print-outs, and other data the state crime lab chemist relied upon to support her testimony and opinion during her direct examination concerning the identity of the substance tested. To the extent that this information may be discoverable in a felony criminal case, its production is now governed by the Criminal Procedure Discovery Act and a defendant is entitled to this information only if he invokes the Act.

4. *Introduction of Substance into Evidence*

If the defendant does not object to the state crime lab technician's testimony concerning the identity of the substance, nor make a motion to suppress or otherwise object to testimony regarding the substance based on any taint in the chain of custody, the state will not be required to introduce the substance into evidence to establish its case.

5. *Expert Evidence Regarding Value of Substance*

"Formal" education is not a requisite to the admission of expert testimony. As a matter of common sense, the "street value" of drugs is more peculiarly in the ken of an officer working on the street or buying drugs incognito, and such an officer is more likely to be knowledgeable on that subject than a laboratory chemist who has no actual experience in the purchase of drugs on the street. Thus, such an officer's testimony as to the value of seized drugs, based on his knowledge of how drugs are packaged and what they sell for on the street, is admissible as evidence of the "street value" of those drugs.

6. Expert Evidence Regarding Therapeutic and Medicinal Effects of Marijuana

A defense witness's mere assertion of his own expertise as a "marijuana specialist" is not enough to qualify him as an expert concerning the therapeutic and medicinal effects of marijuana. The qualification of the witness must be based on evidence of his education, training, or experience in this field of study. Furthermore, even if properly qualified as an expert in the field, the witness would be precluded from testifying about the beneficial use of marijuana for certain physical ailments unless he has some firsthand knowledge about the defendant's alleged medical condition or any possible treatment for it.

7. Drug Paraphernalia

The state may present evidence that a crack cocaine pipe was found on the defendant's person at the time of his arrest for the sale of cocaine. Evidence regarding the crack pipe would be relevant to show that the defendant was involved in drug activity at the time of his arrest and would be particularly material in light of his denial that he had anything to do with the drug transaction at issue.

H. Head Shop Act

Section 16-13-32, the Head Shop Act, essentially prohibits the **knowing** sale of drug-related objects. Subsection (a) of the statute broadly defines drug-related objects and renders them contraband. It also prohibits advertising drug-related goods without a disclaimer that the goods are unavailable for distribution in Georgia. One convicted of a first offense is guilty of a misdemeanor, a second offense is made an aggravated misdemeanor and a third offense a felony.

A 1982 Eleventh Circuit Court of Appeals decision upheld the constitutionality of § 16-13-32. In High Ol' Times v. Busbee, the owners of certain head shops brought a declaratory judgment action, claiming that the statute was void for vagueness. The appellate court, in reversing a finding of unconstitutionality, found that a facial vagueness challenge is proper only in situations where the statute would be vague in all of its applications. It found that the statutes in question were not so broadly vague. In applying the vagueness inquiry to the facts of the case before it, the court found that the statutory language provided fair notice to vendors of the prohibited items. The court also found that the mere risk of future discriminatory enforcement would not render the statute void for vagueness in pre-enforcement litigation.

It should be noted that in related litigation former GCA § 26-9912 was held unconstitutional. Also § 16-13-1, which restricts the sale or distribution of drug paraphernalia to minors, was held to be unconstitutionally vague because the definition of drug-related object as any object "which an average person would reasonably conclude is intended to be used" with drugs did not even lend itself to a construction focused on the seller's intent. While the Eleventh Circuit Court of Appeals reversed the finding of the federal district court that Georgia's other head shop laws were unconstitutional, the state did not appeal the finding of unconstitutionality with regard to § 16-13-1. Thus, the finding that this Code section is unconstitutional in its entirety is final.

In § 16-13-32.1, the distribution, sale or possession with intent to distribute of **any** material which is intended by the defendant to be used for a wide range of activities related to the use of controlled substances or marijuana is prohibited. This is to be contrasted with § 16-13-32, which covers only objects which are built or designed for such purposes. Section 16-13-32.1(c) explains how intent is to be proven under the statute. Section 16-13-32.2 covers the same broad spectrum of materials and purposes as § 16-13-32.1 and punishes possession of such materials. Section 16-13-32.2 defines a misdemeanor, while section 16-13-32.1 is punished identically to section 16-13-32.

Two defendants argued that the enactment of § 16-13-32.1 was an implicit repeal of the earlier Head Shop Act, § 16-13-32. In State v. Gill, the defendants demurred to accusations of violation of the earlier statute on the ground that it had been repealed by the enactment of the later statute. The state appealed from the trial court's dismissal of the prosecutions. The Court of Appeals reversed, finding no repeal. The court concluded that there was no intent to repeal the earlier statute expressed in the legislation. It further held that the two statutes are not so repugnant that they cannot both exist simultaneously. The court accepted the state's contention that the two statutes reflect "simply a legislative effort to attack the problem—the marketing of drug related objects—from two different angles . . .. If X approached Y to sell him an item to help him smoke marijuana cigarettes and Y sold X an ordinary paper clip, Y would be guilty of violating OCGA § 16-13-32.1 since he specifically intended the paper clip for a drug related purpose. However, he would not be guilty of violating OCGA § 16-13-32 since the primary use of the paper clip, holding papers together, would not be drug related. On the other hand, if X approached Y and asked Y to sell him an exotic doorstop and Y sold X a water pipe . . . designed primarily for smoking marijuana, Y would be guilty of violating OCGA § 16-13-32, since the primary purpose of the object was drug related. However, Y would not be guilty of violating OCGA § 16-13-32.1 since the use that he specifically intended (doorstop) was not drug related."

The court went on to assert that the two statutes were actually complementary—"a legislative attempt to outlaw **all** transactions in drug related objects, both those specifically intended and those which would put a reasonable and prudent person on notice."

V. *Punishment*

A. *Possession and Possession with Intent to Distribute*

The Controlled Substances Act establishes a sliding scale of punishment depending on what schedule drug was possessed, and whether the defendant is convicted of possession or possession with intent to distribute. Schedule I and II drugs are the most dangerous and possession is punishable by imprisonment for two to 15 years. A second or subsequent conviction is punishable by imprisonment for five to 30 years.

Possession with intent to distribute Schedule I or Schedule II drugs is punishable by imprisonment for five to 30 years. Prior to July 1, 1996, a second or subsequent conviction was punishable by a mandatory life sentence. The constitutionality of the mandatory life sentence provision had been upheld against various challenges. In a number of cases, the Georgia Supreme Court rejected the claim that this provision was being enforced discriminatorily against African-Americans. The statistical evidence of selective enforcement was insufficient to meet the intentional discrimination test. However, in Stephens v. State, while a majority of the Georgia Supreme Court upheld the defendant's conviction against such a claim, a majority of the justices did not agree with the opinion upholding the conviction. The court was sharply divided on the issue of whether an inference of discriminatory intent could be drawn from the statistical evidence presented by the defendant. In particular Justice Thompson, after reviewing the statewide statistical evidence in his special concurring opinion, found it amiss that mandatory life sentences were being imposed only in those cases in which a district attorney, in the exercise of his discretion, informed a defendant that the state was seeking enhanced punishment. The statistics presented by the defendant were indicative of a statewide pattern of discrimination in the use of the mandatory life sentence provision, but he failed to prove a pattern of systematic discrimination by the district attorney in his jurisdiction. Thus, it was Justice Thompson's view that the judgment in the case had to be affirmed.

Nevertheless, it was Justice Thompson's opinion that the statistical evidence presented in the case served as notice to the General Assembly that the mandatory life sentence provision had been repealed de facto. A course of action that he recommended was that the General Assembly could choose to change the mandatory life sentence penalty to one of several sentencing options which the trial court could impose. The trial court could then exercise its discretion in the imposition of any enhanced punishment for a second or subsequent offense, and any abuse of this discretion would be subject to review and correction, if necessary.

Following Justice Thompson's recommendation, the General Assembly eliminated the mandatory life sentence provision in 1996. Section 16-13-30(d) now provides that upon conviction of a second or subsequent offense, the defendant "shall be imprisoned for not less than ten years nor more than 40 years or life imprisonment." Consequently, the sentencing judge retains the discretion either to impose any sentence within the statutory mandatory minimum and maximum sentence range or else to impose a life sentence.

The General Assembly further amended subsection (d) to make it applicable to all Schedule II controlled substances, including nonnarcotic as well as narcotic drugs. Finally, the General Assembly made subsection (a) of the general recidivist statute, which subjects a second-time felony offender to the maximum sentence prescribed for an offense, inapplicable to a sentence imposed for a second violation of § 16-13-30(b). However, the remaining provisions of the general recidivist statute are applicable for any subsequent violation. It has been held that the 1996 amendment cannot be applied retroactively.

Under the sentencing scheme prior to July 1, 1996, enhanced punishment for a second or subsequent offense was authorized only if (1) the state notified the defendant before trial of its intent to rely on the defendant's previous drug conviction, (2) the defendant's previous conviction was final at the time of this pretrial notification, and (3) the defendant's instant conviction was for a second violation, which occurred "second" in time to the previous violation. Apparently, these prerequisites for the imposition of enhanced punishment would still be applicable under the current sentencing scheme.

Possession of Schedule III, IV, or V drugs is punishable by imprisonment for one to five years. A second or subsequent conviction is punishable by imprisonment for one to ten years. Possession with intent to distribute these drugs is punishable by imprisonment for one to ten years.

Possession or possession with intent to distribute a counterfeit substance is punishable by imprisonment for one to ten years.

Possession of an ounce or less of marijuana is a misdemeanor punishable by imprisonment for up to twelve months or by a fine of up to $1,000, or both, or by public works not to exceed 12 months. Possession of over an ounce of marijuana is punishable generally by one to ten years imprisonment.

Possession of flunitrazepam, a Schedule IV controlled substance, is punishable by imprisonment for two to 15 years. A second or subsequent conviction is punishable by imprisonment for five to 30 years. Possession with intent to distribute this drug is punishable by imprisonment for five to 30 years. A second or subsequent conviction is punishable by imprisonment for ten to 40 years or life imprisonment. Subsection (a) of the general recidivist statute, which subjects a second-time felony offender to the maximum sentence prescribed for an offense, is inapplicable to a sentence imposed for a second offense, but that subsection and the remaining provisions of the general recidivist statute are applicable for any subsequent offense.

The punishments provided in § 16-13-30 do not preclude probation as a punishment. Where a portion of a defendant's sentence is reduced from imprisonment to probation, a fine of up to $100,000 is authorized as a condition of probation. Although § 16-13-30 makes no provision for the imposition of fines, § 17-10-8 generally permits imposition of a fine as a condition to probation when a sentence is probated in lieu of confinement.

B. Purchasing

There is no unconstitutional disparity between the prescribed punishments for possession and purchase of the same amount of marijuana. Since the purchasers of less than one ounce of marijuana commit a different crime than do the possessors of the same amount of contraband, a challenge to the constitutionality of the felony punishment prescribed for purchasing cannot be based upon the General Assembly's determination to provide a misdemeanor punishment for those who only possess the same amount of contraband. For equal protection purposes, the purchasers of less than one ounce of marijuana are not similarly situated to possessors of the same amount of contraband; only those accused of purchasing marijuana are similarly situated. Since the imposition of a felony punishment applies equally to all those accused of purchasing any amount of marijuana, there is no unconstitutional disparate treatment of similarly situated persons.

C. Trafficking

Section 16-13-31 provides punishments for the offenses of trafficking in (1) cocaine; (2) illegal drugs such as morphine, opium, or heroin; (3) marijuana; (4) methaqualone; and (5) methamphetamine or amphetamine. With regard to each of these offenses, § 16-13-31 creates a schedule of punishments scaled to the amount of contraband involved.

Likewise, § 16-13-31.1 punishes trafficking in the amphetamine or methamphetamine commonly known as MDMA or ecstasy. This Code section creates a schedule of punishments scaled to the amount of MDMA or ecstasy involved.

It should be noted that for each trafficking offense there is a mandatory punishment for each graduation of the offense. Thus, for example, those who are convicted of trafficking in cocaine or a cocaine mixture of 28 grams or more, but less than 200 grams, are subject to a mandatory minimum prison term of 10 years and a fine of $200,000; those convicted of trafficking in 200 grams or more, but less than 400 grams, are subject to a mandatory minimum prison term of 15 years and a fine of $300,000; and those convicted of trafficking in 400 grams or more are subject to a mandatory minimum prison term of 25 years and a fine of $1 million.

In Partridge v. State, the court held that trafficking in cocaine requires only that the threshold amount be shown, after which the quantity possessed bears only on punishment. The court further held that where the amount shown by the evidence would still show a violation of law, even if it did not meet the increment charged in the indictment, there would not be a material variance.

However, in Mallarino v. State, the court held that it is the quantity of drugs averred in the indictment of which the offender has been convicted, rather than the amount of drugs which the evidence establishes that the offender possessed in excess of the amount averred in the indictment, that controls in determining which mandatory minimum sentence is operative under § 16-13-31(a).

The holdings in these two cases appear to be contradictory but a closer examination reveals that they can be distinguished on the facts. In *Partridge*, even though the amount of cocaine shown by the evidence (319 grams of cocaine in a mixture of 450 grams) was less than the amount of cocaine charged in the indictment (400 grams of cocaine or cocaine mixture), the amount shown by the evidence met the standards for a finding of trafficking in a quantity of cocaine or cocaine mixture involving 400 grams or more and fell within the punishment provisions of § 16-13-31(a)(1)(C). While in *Mallarino*, the amount of cocaine charged in the indictment and the amount of cocaine for which the defendant was convicted was "greater than 28 grams." The appellate court could not determine from the verdict the maximum amount of cocaine which the jury found the defendant guilty of possessing. Thus, the court held that the minimum permissible sentence for trafficking in a quantity of cocaine or cocaine mixture involving 28 grams or more was controlled by § 16-13-31(a)(1)(A) instead of § 16-13-31(a)(1)(C), which punishes trafficking in a quantity of cocaine or cocaine mixture involving 400 grams or more.

Thus, it would appear that where there is no specific proof of the maximum amount possessed, it is the quantity of drugs averred in the indictment of which the offender has been convicted which authorizes the particular sentence. However, where there is specific proof of the maximum amount possessed, it is the amount possessed as shown by the evidence which authorizes the particular sentence, and not the language of the indictment. In Moon v. State, the indictment correctly charged the defendants with possession of more than "28 grams [of cocaine] with a purity in excess of 10%." However, since the conviction was authorized by proof of possession of 17,108 grams, the trial court was authorized by § 16-13-31(f) [now (h)] to sentence up to 30 years. The court held that the 25-year sentence was well within the mandatory minimum set at § 16-13-31(a)(1)(C) and the 30-year maximum set at § 16-13-31(f) [now (h)].

Similar punishment schedules are provided for each of the other trafficking offenses as well. The reader is left to consult the statute for specifics.

The General Assembly has expressed its intent that cocaine traffickers serve a ten-year minimum sentence, without the benefit of first offender treatment or probation for that ten-year term. It has determined that an adjudication of guilt cannot be withheld for a defendant who is found guilty of or pleads guilty to cocaine trafficking. Furthermore, the defendant's mandatory minimum prison sentence cannot be probated, and the defendant does not qualify for the drug-oriented first offender treatment in § 16-13-2(a). Under these circumstances, a convicted cocaine trafficker would not be eligible for general first offender treatment pursuant to § 42-8-60 or a probated prison sentence. Accordingly, a trial court does not have discretion to probate any portion of a sentence for trafficking in cocaine under the First Offender Act.

While there is mandatory sentencing for each of the trafficking offenses and while there is no deferring, probating, suspension or withholding of sentences, a statutory provision applicable to all the offenses permits the district attorney to request and the trial court to grant a reduced or suspended sentence upon a showing that the defendant has provided substantial assistance in the identification, arrest or conviction of any of his partners in the crime. This provision, however, does not by its terms **require** the trial court to impose a reduced or suspended sentence in the event a defendant has rendered such assistance but instead merely **authorizes** him to do so. Where the defendant's actions did not constitute substantial assistance sufficient to justify a reduced sentence below the mandatory minimum, it would be within the trial court's discretion to reject the defendant's request for a reduced sentence.

Any person who is guilty of trafficking in cocaine, illegal drugs, marijuana, or methamphetamine is punishable by imprisonment for not less than five years nor more than 30 years and by a fine not to exceed $1 million. This provision provides for a maximum punishment not provided for in the mandatory minimum punishments set out in § 16-13-31(a), (b), (c) and (e).

The rule of lenity applies when two statutes governing the same conduct are conflicting with respect to their prescribed punishments, i.e., where one statute punishes the same conduct to a lesser degree than the other statute. In such a situation, a defendant would be entitled to have the lesser of two penalties administered. In *Richards v. State*, the Georgia Court of Appeals held that this rule was inapplicable because the offense of manufacturing methamphetamine as described in § 16-13-30(b) was a lesser included offense of manufacturing/trafficking methamphetamine as outlined in § 16-13-31(f)(1). Furthermore, the most reasonable interpretation of the legislative intent in enacting § 16-13-31(f)(1) was to supplant the general punishment provision of § 16-13-30(b) with a specific and potentially more harsh punishment provision for manufacturing methamphetamine. Where a crime is penalized by a special law, the general provisions of the penal code are not applicable. Thus, since there was no uncertainty as to which of the two statutes applied in the case, the trial court was authorized to sentence the defendant for the greater felony offense after merging the lesser felony offense into it.

Any fact that enhances the penalty for a drug offense should be alleged in the indictment, submitted to the jury, and proved beyond a reasonable doubt. An indictment's failure to allege drug quantity, which fact when proven would subject a defendant to an enhanced sentence, is not a defect that would deprive a trial court of its power to adjudicate the case. This power can never be forfeited or waived. Rather, such a defect requires correction regardless of whether the defendant objected to it during trial. An appellate court cannot correct such a forfeited defect unless it finds the defect to be plain error that seriously affects the fairness, integrity, or public reputation of the trial. There would be no support for such a finding where there was overwhelming and essentially uncontroverted evidence that the offense involved a considerable quantity of drugs.

C.1. Possession of Drug-Related Objects

The same evidence can be used to prove both the offense of possession of a tool for the commission of crime, a felony, and the offense of possession of a drug-related object, a misdemeanor. Because the same conduct constitutes both a felony and a misdemeanor, the rule of lenity requires that a defendant be subjected to the penalties for the misdemeanor, rather than the felony.

D. Attempt and Conspiracy

Section 16-13-33 provides for the punishment of the crimes of attempt and conspiracy involving controlled substances. There is a great difference between § 16-4-8, the general conspiracy statute, and § 16-13-33, the attempt and conspiracy statute for controlled substances. Section 16-4-8 provides for only one-half the punishment which could be meted if the person committed the crime conspired to have been committed. The totally separate crime described in § 16-13-33 is given equal punishment status with the crime which is the conspiracy objective.

The General Assembly intended with the enactment of § 16-13-33 to supplant the general punishment provision with a specific (and potentially more harsh) punishment provision for attempt or conspiracy to possess controlled substances. Rather than one-half of the maximum sentence applicable to the substantive crime under § 16-4-6 or § 16-4-8, § 16-13-33 provides for potentially harsher punishment in the form of imprisonment not exceeding the maximum punishment prescribed for the Georgia Controlled Substances Act offense, the commission of which was the object of the attempt or conspiracy. The general and specific sentencing statutes are mutually exclusive, and there is no uncertainty as to which applies. Section 16-13-33 renders § 16-4-6 or § 16-4-8 inapplicable in prosecutions under the Georgia Controlled Substances Act.

Since the offense of attempted trafficking in cocaine under § 16-13-33 is punishable by imprisonment but contains no provision for a fine, the maximum fine which may be imposed as a condition of probation is $100,000 pursuant to § 17-10-8. Also, a conviction for conspiracy under § 16-13-33 does not authorize the imposition of a fine, but a fine not greater than $100,000 may be imposed as a condition of probation.

Although § 16-13-33 clearly provides for a potentially "harsher," i.e., maximum, sentence of imprisonment, that Code section does not require that the trial court impose a mandatory minimum term of imprisonment, or deny to the trial court the discretion it would otherwise have in determining whether the sentence it imposes is to be served entirely in prison.

VI. Civil Sanctions upon Conviction of Certain Controlled Substances Offenses

Upon being notified of a conviction of a licensed individual for any criminal offense involving the manufacture, distribution, trafficking, sale, or possession of a controlled substance or marijuana, the appropriate licensing authority shall suspend or revoke the license, permit, registration, certification, or other authorization to conduct a licensed occupation of such individual as provided by law. The failure of a licensed individual to notify the appropriate licensing authority of his conviction is considered grounds for revocation. A licensed individual who has been sanctioned may be entitled to reinstatement upon successful completion of a drug abuse treatment and education program approved by the licensing authority.

In addition to this sanction, the General Assembly in 1990 enacted a number of Code sections providing for the imposition of other civil sanctions on anyone convicted of an offense arising out of the unlawful manufacture, distribution, sale, possession, or use of marijuana, a controlled substance or other dangerous drug.

A person charged with a violation of the Georgia Controlled Substances Act who has tendered a plea of nolo contendere to the charges, when such plea has been accepted by the trial court, has been convicted of that offense for the purposes of consideration of an application for a firearms permit, and is thus statutorily ineligible for the issuance of such a permit.

A misdemeanor conviction for possession of less than an ounce of marijuana is not a crime of moral turpitude. Thus, such a conviction is not admissible for impeachment purposes.

Generally, a drug related offense classified as a felony is a felony involving moral turpitude which will remove a person's right to vote, but the right to vote may not be withheld until a conviction becomes final.

VII. Tax Liability

The 1990 General Assembly amended the Code title relating to revenue and taxation by adding a new chapter which provides in part that the use, possession, consumption, storage, or transfer of marijuana or any controlled substance is subject to a state excise tax. Each person who uses, possesses, consumes, stores, or transfers any such substance is liable for the tax, unless the person is lawfully in possession of such substance.

VIII. Drug Dealer Liability Act

The Drug Dealer Liability Act, enacted by the General Assembly in 1997, provides a civil remedy for damages to persons in a community injured as a result of illegal drug use. With this Act, the General Assembly intends to shift the cost of the damage caused by the existence of the illegal drug market in a community to those who illegally profit from that market and to establish the prospect of substantial monetary loss as a deterrent to those who have not yet entered into the illegal drug distribution market.

A person injured by an individual drug abuser may bring an action under the Act for damages against a person who participated in illegal marketing of the controlled substance used by the individual abuser. He may recover economic, noneconomic, and exemplary damages and reasonable attorneys' fees and costs, including, but not limited to, reasonable expenses for expert testimony.

IX. Enjoining or Abatement of Real Property Involved in Substantial Drug Related Activity

Any owner of real property who has actual knowledge that substantial drug related activity is being conducted on his property is guilty of maintaining a nuisance, and such real property shall be deemed a nuisance and may be enjoined or otherwise abated as provided by law.

HOMICIDE

See also ASSAULT; AVIATION CRIMES; COERCION DEFENSE; DEFENSE OF PROPERTY AND HABITATION; LAW ENFORCEMENT DEFENSE; MOTOR VEHICLE CRIMES; SELF-DEFENSE; WATER-RELATED CRIMES.

I. Generally

A. Specific Offenses

Fourteen offenses in the code involve the killing of a human being, the killing of a fetus or unborn child, or acts done with the intent to terminate a fetus as an element of the offense. Three of these offenses are the result of the 1968 codification consolidating all homicide offenses and abolishing such specific offenses of the pre-1968 criminal code as arson causing death and destroying or injuring a house with explosives resulting in death.

There are three major homicidal offenses: murder (§ 16-5-1), voluntary manslaughter (§ 16-5-2) and involuntary manslaughter (§ 16-5-3). Murder is the killing of another human being with malice aforethought or during the commission of a felony. Voluntary manslaughter is the killing of another human being resulting from a sudden and violent passion arising from a serious provocation. There are two types of involuntary manslaughter: (1) a killing caused by the commission of a non-felonious unlawful act and (2) a killing caused by the commission of a lawful act in an unlawful manner likely to cause death.

The eleven other homicidal offenses are assisting suicide (§ 16-5-5), criminal abortion (§ 16-12-140), partial-birth abortion (§ 16-12-144), feticide (§ 16-5-80), homicide by vehicle (§ 40-6-393), feticide by vehicle (§ 40-6-393.1), homicide by interference with an official traffic-control device or railroad sign or signal (§ 40-6-396), homicide by vessel (§ 52-7-12.2), feticide by vessel (§ 52-7-12.3), homicide by aircraft (§ 6-2-5.2), and perjury resulting in death (§ 16-10-70). The following is a brief description of each of these offenses. (1) Any person who publicly advertises or offers to intentionally and actively assist another person in the commission of suicide and commits any overt act to further that purpose is guilty of a felony. (2) Criminal abortion involves acts motivated by an intention to terminate the existence of a fetus. (3) Partial-birth abortion involves knowingly performing a partial vaginal delivery of a living human fetus before ending its life and completing the delivery. (4) Feticide is the willful killing of an unborn child so far developed as to be ordinarily called "quick" by any injury to the mother, which would be murder if it resulted in the death of the mother. (5) There are two degrees of homicide by vehicle. First degree vehicular homicide is the nonmalicious killing of another person through the violation of certain provisions of the Uniform Rules of the Road, while second degree vehicular homicide is the unintentional killing of another person through the violation of any other provision of the Uniform Rules. (6) There are two degrees of feticide by vehicle. First degree vehicular feticide is the killing of an unborn child so far developed as to be ordinarily called "quick" by any injury to the mother of such child through the violation of certain provisions of the Uniform Rules of the Road, which would be homicide by vehicle in the first degree if it resulted in the death of the mother. Second degree vehicular feticide involves the violation of any other provision of the Uniform Rules. (7) Homicide by interference with a traffic-control device or railroad sign is the nonmalicious killing of another person through the unlawful removal or defacement of a traffic-control device or railroad sign. (8) There are two degrees of homicide by vessel. Homicide by vessel in the first degree is the nonmalicious killing of another person through the violation of certain provisions of the Georgia Boat Safety Act, while homicide by vessel in the second degree is the unintentional killing of another person through the violation of any other provision of the Act. (9) There are two degrees of feticide by vessel. Feticide by vessel in the first degree is the killing of an unborn child so far developed as to be ordinarily called "quick" by any injury to the mother of such child through the violation of certain provisions of the Georgia Boat Safety Act, which would be homicide by vessel in the first degree if it resulted in the death of the mother. Homicide by vessel in the second degree involves the violation of any other provision of the Act. (10) Homicide by aircraft is the nonmalicious killing of another person through the operation of an aircraft while under the influence of alcohol or drugs. (11) The final homicidal offense is perjury resulting in death, which essentially is lying under oath which causes death.

Before a detailed examination of the specific homicidal offenses can be undertaken, an outline of the three basic elements of the corpus delicti of the nonabortion homicidal offenses will be presented. This is important because if there is a sufficiently proven corpus delicti it can corroborate a confession and, thus, authorize a conviction for the appropriate offense.

B. Corpus Delicti: Fact of Death

The single element common to all of the nonabortion homicidal offenses is the death of a human being. In these crimes, the corpus delicti, or body of the crime, very literally includes a body. The first question which must be asked, therefore, is whether a death of a human being has occurred. While this is an apparently simple question which normally is easily answered, recent medical developments have rendered it a more difficult decision in a legal context.

The question of whether there has been a death can occur on either end of the life cycle. On the one hand is the situation where there undoubtedly was a living human being at one point and the question is whether there has been a death. On the other extreme is the situation where the court must decide whether a human being ever existed.

The possible ambiguity about the death of a once-alive individual has developed because of the increasing sophistication of medical technology and its ability to keep people "alive" through life support systems. This phenomenon was vividly brought to the public's attention in In re Quinlan, where a father sought appointment as his daughter's guardian and permission to terminate life support systems to which she was attached. In that case, the victim was conceded by all parties to be alive, but the medical diagnosis was that her chances of revival to a "normal" form of life were virtually nil. The court eventually approved the appointment of the father as guardian and paved the way for the removal of life-support equipment.

While Quinlan did not squarely present the issue of whether there had been a death, such a situation in the criminal context easily can be imagined. For example, a defendant who shot a victim might claim that the doctor who terminated life support (or the family or guardian who ordered such termination) was responsible for the victim's death. A zealous prosecutor might decide to prosecute the doctor or consenting guardian for homicide.

The traditional legal definition of death has been the "stoppage of the circulation of the blood, and a cessation of . . . animal and vital functions . . .." Because of the increased ability of medical technology to maintain the breathing and circulation functions, however, many have urged the courts and legislatures to adopt a "brain death" definition of death. Under this approach, a person is dead when the brain (or an essential part thereof) ceases to function.

In 1975, Georgia joined the increasing number of jurisdictions adopting such a standard. Thus, under § 31-10-16, a person may be declared dead when there is "irreversible cessation of all functions of the entire brain . . .." While this statute is not without ambiguities, such as the silence as to specific tests to be administered to determine whether there has been such a cessation, it would seem that this definition, if used by a physician to declare the death of a victim, would make precise the time and agency of death. Once such a death had been declared, the doctor who later pulled the plug on life-support machinery would be absolved from criminal responsibility. The statute also cryptically adds that the concept of brain death shall not prohibit the use of "other medically recognized criteria for determining death." This would appear to permit a changing medical definition of death in the future to vary the content of the legal definition.

On the other end of the spectrum is the question of whether there has ever been a live human being. In Georgia, determining the death of a newly born or being-born infant has been governed by the born alive rule.

Thus, if a mother gives birth to her baby and subsequently kills it, there has been a nonabortion homicide only if the baby established an independent and separate existence from her. The fact that the baby breathed air has been held insufficient to establish the required independence because it is possible to breathe before complete separation from the mother. In such a situation, an abortion prosecution might be possible, although the abortion statute's language does not clearly indicate that self-aborting activities are proscribed. On the other hand, in a case where the medical examiner could not testify to an independent existence, the Georgia Supreme Court affirmed a murder conviction where the only evidence of independent existence was the testimony of two children that they heard the baby cry.

For a finding of criminal abortion, there is no analogue to the presence of the death of a human being. This is so because criminal abortion is defined not in terms of a termination of a fetus, but, rather, in terms of acts designed to produce a miscarriage or abortion. The elements of the crime and the exceptions mandated by the statute and the Constitution are discussed more fully below.

For a finding of feticide, feticide by vehicle, or feticide by vessel determining the death of an unborn child or fetus is governed by whether the fetus is so far developed as to be ordinarily called "quick," i.e., so far developed as to be able to move or stir in the mother's womb. The elements of the crime of feticide are discussed more fully below.

There is also the question, when the victim's body cannot be located, whether the evidence is sufficient to prove that the alleged victim is dead. In White v. State, the court held that there was overwhelming circumstantial evidence that the victim was dead. Blood stains were found in the victim's condominium. Witnesses testified that the defendant stated that he had slit the victim's throat in response to a homosexual advance and stated that the victim was dead. The defendant testified that he assumed, but did not know for certain, that the victim was dead as a result of injuries he inflicted on him. Further, as he put the victim in the victim's vehicle, the defendant noticed that the victim had grown "a little more stiffer," and as he left the victim in the woods alongside the highway, the victim still displayed no sign of life.

C. Corpus Delicti: Criminal Agency

The second element of the corpus delicti of the nonabortion homicidal crimes is the existence of a criminal agency as the cause of death. This element is normally easily proven by circumstantial evidence of the body's condition at the time of discovery. The court must be convinced that the circumstances exclude an inference of noncriminal homicide by natural causes, suicide, or accident. For example, in Peacock v. State, where there was testimony that a victim was shot twice in the head near a river and four days later a corpse was recovered in that river with one hole behind each ear and bullet fragments found in the corpse's brain, there was sufficient evidence to conclude violence or criminal agency. The court held that accident or suicide were sufficiently excluded. Likewise, in Reddick v. State, where the body of the deceased was found with the back of the skull crushed, throat cut, and stab wounds in the back, criminal agency was held to be shown. In Sorrells v. State, investigators discovered two badly decomposed bodies lying together in a bedroom. One was a man's body and the other was a woman's. It initially was assumed that the deaths had resulted from asphyxiation due to gas emanating from a heater in the bedroom. After the man's body was interred and the woman's body was cremated, investigators suspected that the deaths might be homicides. The man's body was exhumed, and the autopsy determined that the man died as the result of a shotgun blast. Despite the defendant's contention that the state failed to prove that the woman's death was a homicide as well, the evidence showed that the woman was engaged to and lived with the man and that, after two gunshots were overheard by neighbors, neither was seen alive ever again. In the defendant's own trial testimony, he acknowledged discovering and identifying the bodies. The court held that this evidence was sufficient to authorize a rational trier of fact to find proof beyond a reasonable doubt that the woman also had been murdered by a shotgun blast.

Whether suicide is a reasonable hypothesis is a question for the jury to determine. In Evans v. State, the defendant contended that the evidence was as consistent with a suicide as it was with a murder. Although the pathologist who performed the autopsy on the victim's body could not conclusively state whether the fatal wound was caused by the victim himself or another person, he testified that he was 90 percent certain that the wound was caused by someone other than the victim. Furthermore, no weapon was found near the body. The court held that where circumstantial evidence is sufficient to exclude every reasonable hypothesis save that of the homicide at the hands of the defendant, a guilty verdict will not be disturbed unless it is unsupportable as a matter of law.

An example of a case where the court found criminal agency not to have been proven beyond a reasonable doubt is Clay v. State. Here the evidence, outside of the defendant's confession, showed only that a human torso was found in the burned ruins of a gas station. Beginning with a presumption of noncriminal agency, the court held that the corpus delicti was not proven because there was no evidence of criminal agency, rejecting any reliance on the confession to corroborate the criminal agency element of the corpus delicti. The court held that while the corpus delicti can corroborate the defendant's confession, the reverse cannot also be permitted because to do this would be to "let a portion of the confession corroborate itself." Thus, the court made clear that a confession and a corpse are not necessarily sufficient in and of themselves to support a homicide conviction. Another case where the court found criminal agency had not been proven is Strozier v. State. In this case, the decedent was found face down in a street. After being admitted to a hospital, he died from his injuries. The defendant never acknowledged that the decedent was the person with whom he had an altercation or that the two were the same person. The court held that the investigating officer's hearsay testimony that he heard from an unknown source that someone named "Patrick" was linked to the attack against the decedent merely allowed the defendant to be tried based on rumor, gossip, and speculation. There was no other evidence introduced which connected the defendant to the death of the decedent. Furthermore, there was no conclusive proof that the decedent's death was the result of a criminal act rather than an accidental fall or traffic accident. The fact that the decedent was injured did not necessarily lead to the conclusion that he was the victim of a crime. Thus, there was no evidence upon which a rational trier of fact could have found the defendant guilty.

Criminal agency often becomes a crucial issue in cases where the victim is a young child and there are claims that death might have been caused by crib death or accidental means.

D. Corpus Delicti: Causation

The other element of the corpus delicti common to all the nonabortion homicidal crimes is that of causation. Because these crimes are all defined at least partially in terms of a particular result (the death), the linkage between the defendant's behavior and the result of death of the victim is crucially important. Whereas in other crimes the actus reus normally consists of the defendant's acts, in homicide the actus reus requires a showing of acts which lead to the prohibited result of death. The Georgia rule is that where the defendant's acts precede the victim's death, the defendant is the causative factor if the injuries inflicted by the defendant either (1) were the sole proximate cause of death, (2) directly and materially contributed to the occurrence of a subsequently accruing immediate cause of death, or (3) materially accelerated death. In fact, there is some limited authority that there is legal causation merely if the death would not have occurred "but for" the defendant's acts.

The Georgia courts have been very liberal in authorizing the submission of the causation issue to homicide juries. For example, in Martin v. State, the attending physician testified that the patient who died nine days after the automobile collision caused by the defendant was in "very satisfactory" condition immediately before death and seemed to be recovering. No autopsy was performed, the doctor conceded that a heart seizure could have caused death and, when asked if the collision injuries caused death, the physician said, "I can't say." The appellate court held that given the decedent's prior good health, there was enough evidence to go to a jury for a determination of whether the injuries at least materially contributed to the direct cause of death.

In Phipps v. State, the defendant contended that the trial court erred in refusing to grant a directed verdict of acquittal based on the fact that the medical experts could not positively state that the child's fatal head injuries were caused by intentional conduct rather than an accidental fall while the child was under the defendant's care and custody. Also, there was evidence that on prior occasions the child had been physically abused by others. The appellate court held that comparing the child's good physical condition at the time the defendant took him from his mother and shortly thereafter, with his injured condition at the time he and the defendant appeared at a fire station, and considering the acts of abuse admitted by the defendant, the evidence was sufficient to have authorized a finding that the defendant caused the child's death.

In Littles v. State, the victim's death was caused by a blood clot four months after defendant shot her. The attending physician testified that the shot left her weak and partially paralyzed, that a later psychosis "was consistent with her brain injury," and that inactivity caused by the paralysis and psychosis could have caused the clot. He also said he did not know whether the wound caused the death. The court held the evidence, although "not overwhelming," was sufficient to support a verdict.

In Adams v. State, after being shot by the defendant, the victim was hospitalized and underwent surgery for his injuries. While recuperating from his injuries, he suffered a stroke and died five days later. While there was conflicting evidence on the question whether there was sufficient evidence to connect the victim's stroke and resulting death to his gunshot injury, the court held that the testimony of two doctors that the gunshot and resulting surgery were contributing causes of the stroke which ultimately caused the victim's death was ample evidence to support the defendant's conviction for voluntary manslaughter.

In Lynch v. State, the defendant kicked his 76-year-old grandmother in the side. Her examination at a hospital revealed bruises but no internal injuries. Five days later, she was found to have a perforated bowel. Although she survived surgery, she died less than a month later of septicemia, triggered by the ruptured bowel. A physician testified that although there were circumstances other than beating and kicking which could have caused a perforation of the bowel, none of those circumstances applied to the victim. The court held that there was sufficient evidence to establish that the defendant caused the victim's death.

In Irby v. State, the state's expert opined that the cause of the victim's death was asphyxia, but he noted no signs of either internal or external trauma to any part of the body. While the doctor admitted the physical evidence did not absolutely rule out other natural causes of death, he testified the victim's recent medical history as reflected in her army medical records and the other circumstances of her death convinced him that she had been killed by her air being cut off by something such as a pillow or bag held over her face. The court held that it is not the doctor's expert opinion (or any other individual bit of evidence) alone, but the totality of the evidence that must be sufficient to convince the trier of fact "beyond a reasonable doubt." The court concluded that the evidence was sufficient in this case.

In Goodwin v. State, the defendant and the victim were roughhousing at work when the victim collapsed and died. The state's medical expert testified that there were virtually no signs of forcible injury on the victim's neck; the cause of death was not strangulation or asphyxiation but was heart dysrhythmia brought on by the pressure from the defendant's hands to the carotid sinus in the victim's neck; and the amount of pressure to the carotid sinus which could cause heart dysrhythmia might be as slight as that of a shirt collar around a neck. The court concluded that the evidence was sufficient to support the defendant's conviction for voluntary manslaughter.

In Miller v. State, the defendant while armed with a gun entered a home through a bedroom window and pointed the gun at the victims. One of the victims escaped and ran to the home of a neighbor who called police.

Before the police arrived, the victim suffered a fatal heart attack and the defendant left the home. The medical examiner testified that the victim's heart had been in bad condition and that the heart attack had been caused by the stress placed upon it by the emotional reaction to an armed intruder and the physical exertion of running over 100 feet to the neighbor's home. The court held that it was not error to deny the defendant's motion for directed verdict because the evidence was sufficient to authorize a conviction for felony murder with the underlying felony being burglary.

In Powell v. State, there was a dispute concerning who in a fracas delivered the blow that killed the victim. The associate medical examiner testified that the victim's skull was fractured by a blow near his eye from the blunt end of the axe blade swung by the defendant. He compared each possible weapon at the scene with the injury and concluded that only the axe blade could have delivered the fatal blow. He also observed that the victim's shirt was dry, undermining the defense's theory that the victim was struck in the eye with a pressure washer wielded by another person in the fracas. Testimony of the state's experiments with the pressure washer also countered that theory. The court held that this evidence was sufficient to exclude every other reasonable theory so as to justify a finding of guilt beyond a reasonable doubt.

In Roberts v. State, the defendant admitted that he stabbed the two victims, and eyewitnesses testified to those events. A detective testified without objection that he observed the deceased victim bleeding and receiving medical treatment; and that the victim had died as a result of the stab wounds. The court held that this evidence was sufficient to prove the essential element of causation.

In Skaggs v. State, the defendant argued that the evidence was not sufficient to authorize his conviction, because the victim died from injuries sustained in a fall onto the concrete rather than from the blows to his head. The court, however, found that while the immediate cause of the victim's death was the injuries he suffered in the fall, the fall itself was the direct and immediate result of the blows administered by defendant. The only intervening force was gravity. It was reasonably foreseeable, and certainly not abnormal, that one who was struck in the nose and then kicked in the face with a steel-toed boot might fall to the ground and suffer a serious bodily injury. It did not matter that the defendant never intended for the victim to fall and sustain a fatal injury as the result. To authorize the felony murder conviction, the state was required only to prove the defendant's intent to commit aggravated assault. The court concluded that the evidence showed the commission of aggravated assault with a deadly weapon and that the injuries the victim received in the aggravated assault ultimately caused his death.

A fairly common situation which arises with regard to the causation issue is the defendant who administers a mortal wound but claims that the negligence or mistreatment of a doctor or nurse has intervened to cut off his original criminal liability. The Georgia rule, consistent with that of other states, is that improper medical treatment is not normally a supervening cause. Reiterated by the appellate courts, the rule is that the only situation in which such negligence will cut off the defendant's liability is where treatment of a nonmortal wound is so negligently performed that it can fairly be said that the treatment, not the original wound, caused the death. Although such a statement rightfully can be criticized as being somewhat circular, it seems clear that only gross mistreatment, such as the application of "unwholesome salves or medicines," will be held to intervene and serve to cut off the defendant's criminal liability. In other words, a certain amount of medical negligence can be seen to be foreseeable and, therefore, is not a supervening legal cause.

In Green v. State, the victim died of a stress ulcer in the hospital a week after the defendant stabbed her. Although the experts at trial disputed the primary cause of death, they agreed that stress caused the ulcer. The evidence at trial was sufficient for the jury to find that the defendant stabbed his wife, thus setting in motion a series of events that resulted in her death, and that the hospital's treatment of her wound with the pain killer Toradol was a secondary, rather than intervening, cause of death. The court concluded that the trial court did not err in its charges on causation.

In Johnson v. State, the defendant contended that his acquittal was mandated because the state failed to exclude beyond a reasonable doubt the possibility that death may have resulted from the improper removal of life-support systems from the victim rather than from injuries caused by him. The court found that the question of whether removing the support systems met procedural requirements was not an issue in the case. The treating doctor's testimony established that the victim was legally dead before the systems were removed and that her death was caused by the subdural hematomas that were the result of the defendant's blows to the victim's face. Moreover, the defendant offered no objection to the treating doctor's testimony that a second doctor had, in fact, conducted an independent examination and declared the victim brain-dead before the systems were disconnected.

In Woods v. State, the medical experts testified at trial that the victim never regained consciousness after being hit by one of the defendants, spent the last two years in a deep coma in a hospital or nursing home, and died as a result of the head injuries that had rendered him unconscious. The court held that any problems with the victim's medical treatment would have been a secondary cause of death, rather than the intervening cause. As a result, the decision of trial counsel to rely on the theory of self-defense was a tactical decision that was within the range of reasonable professional assistance. Thus, counsel were not ineffective for failing to investigate and present the victim's medical treatment as the cause of his death.

In Shields v. State, the pathologist testified that if the victim had not been shot, she would not have been paralyzed, would not have developed the deep vein thrombosis, would not have needed the anticoagulant drug Coumadin, and thus would not have suffered the intracerebral hemorrhage that killed her approximately six months after the shooting. The defendant contended that this evidence was circumstantial and did not exclude the reasonable hypothesis that the death was the result of an unexplained hemorrhage that was unrelated to the gunshot wounds. The court rejected this contention and found that the only cause of the victim's death supported by the evidence was that it was the result of an intracerebral hemorrhage caused by the anticoagulant drug Coumadin. While it was possible that the hemorrhage was caused by something other than the Coumadin, there was no medical evidence to support such a possibility. Thus, even if the evidence of causation was circumstantial, the jury was authorized to reject as unreasonable other possible causes of the brain hemorrhage that were only theoretical and to resolve the issue of causation of the victim's death adversely to the defendant.

Prior to July 1, 2007, any person who falsified or forged the living will of another with the intent to cause a withholding or withdrawal of life-sustaining procedures contrary to the wishes of the patient and, thereby, because of any such act, directly caused life-sustaining procedures to be withheld or withdrawn and death thereby to be hastened was subject to prosecution for criminal homicide. There was a similar provision concerning a person who falsified or forged a health care power of attorney. The law required that the living will or health care power of attorney be in "written" form. If there was no evidence of these documents in "written" form, a person could not be subject to criminal liability on the ground that he falsified or forged a living will or health care power of attorney.

Effective July 1, 2007, the General Assembly revised this law in its entirety so as to provide for an advance directive of health care which combines the concepts of the living will and the health care power of attorney into a single legal document. Notwithstanding this revision, the General Assembly enacted a savings clause for any living will or health care power of attorney executed prior to this effective date. The revised law does not apply to, affect, or invalidate documents executed under the prior law nor does it affect any claim, right, or remedy that accrued prior to its effective date. It should be noted that the revised law, similar to the prior law, provides that any person who falsifies or forges an advance directive for health care of another or who willfully conceals or withholds personal knowledge of an amendment or revocation of an advance directive for health care with the intent to cause a withholding or withdrawal of life-sustaining procedures or the withholding or withdrawal of the provision of nourishment or hydration contrary to the intent of the declarant and thereby, because of such act, directly causes life-sustaining procedures or the provision of nourishment or hydration to be withheld or withdrawn and death thereby to be hastened would be subject to prosecution for criminal homicide.

An inventive claim has been made by several defendants who have claimed that the acts of the **victim** cut off the defendant's criminal liability. In Patterson v. State, the victim was a 15-year-old girl who died after she jumped out of a car where the defendant was making romantic advances to her. The court held that the victim's voluntary act of jumping out could be attributed to the defendant if the jumping was the natural and probable consequence of the defendant's original acts. The Patterson court indicated that the grading of the resulting homicide as murder or voluntary manslaughter would depend upon whether the victim's acts were reasonable under the circumstances and whether the victim's acts naturally tended toward death or not. In Thornton v. State, the defendant was held guilty of murder where the evidence indicated that the immediate cause of death was the victim's jumping into a ditch to avoid the defendant's attacks. In Wyrick v. State, the Court of Appeals affirmed an involuntary manslaughter verdict where the death was caused by the defendant's pursuing the victim in an unprovoked assault and the victim was struck by a car in avoiding the assault. In Mansfield v. State, the victim escaped a beating which was being administered by the defendant and two others. The victim was pursued by the attackers and, in the process, went off a nearby dock into a river and drowned. The homicide conviction was upheld. In Dyers v. State, the court held that notwithstanding the victim's refusal of immediate medical treatment after the defendant's attack, the evidence was sufficient to authorize the jury to find that the victim's death was caused by injuries inflicted upon him by the defendant.

In at least one situation, however, the court has held that the victim's acts did serve to cut off the defendant's liability for the ensuing death. In Thacker v. State, the defendant was indicted for involuntary manslaughter arising out of a drag racing incident in which the decedent was competing against the defendant. The indictment charged unlawful act involuntary manslaughter in that the defendant was violating several provisions of the motor vehicle code and, thus, caused the decedent's death. The immediate cause of death was the decedent's loss of control of his car. The defendant's demurrer to the indictment was overruled by the trial court. The Georgia Court of Appeals reversed the trial court's action, holding that the facts indicated that the defendant was not the "proximate cause" of the death of the victim. The decedent's loss of control was the cause of the death and this act, in the court's analysis, was not chargeable to the defendant. While this fact situation can be distinguished from the earlier ones in that here, unlike the prior cases, no compulsion on the victim was being exerted by the defendant, this case may also be explained on some rudimentary assumption of the risk notion. The decedent may be seen as an equally culpable wrongdoer whose death will not be attributed to the defendant. In this analysis, Thacker may stand for the broader proposition that the deaths of co-conspirators or accomplices ordinarily will not be seen to have been caused by a defendant's violation of the law.

The expiration of a year and a day between the defendant's acts and the victim's death can no longer serve to cut off the defendant's criminal liability. At common law, to constitute the offense of criminal homicide death must have occurred within a year and a day from the infliction of the wound. This common-law rule, not having been expressly changed by statute, prevailed in Georgia. The year-and-a-day rule provided a limit to prosecutions for murder and eliminated speculation as to causation at a time when medical science was much less sophisticated and cause was difficult to prove. In 1968, the General Assembly adopted a new criminal code that was intended to supersede the common law. Because the year-and-a-day rule was not included as part of what was intended to be a comprehensive criminal code, the adoption of the criminal code in 1968 ended the viability of the year-and-a-day rule in this state. In 1991, the General Assembly with the enactment of § 16-5-4 made statutory the Georgia Supreme Court's ruling in State v. Cross, that the year-and-a-day rule is not the law of

Georgia.

A defense that someone or something else other than the defendant caused the victim's death necessarily challenges only the identity of the person or event which inflicted the fatal injury on the victim. It does not call into question uncontroverted evidence that the injury, however or by whomever inflicted, was the sole cause of the victim's death. Unless the defendant adduces evidence that the other injuries sustained by the victim were related to the medical reasons for the victim's death or that this evidence otherwise casts a light on the identity of the person or event which inflicted the fatal injury on the victim, there is no abuse of the trial court's discretion in excluding evidence of any injuries other than the injury that caused the victim's death.

In State v. Williams, the court held that failure to allege a precise time of death in an indictment for murder rendered the indictment subject to demurrer. It was unclear, said the court, whether the indictment alleged death at the point of cessation of heartbeat, at the point of brain death, or at somatic death. The failure to either allege the time of death or to allege the method of death relied upon by the state rendered the indictment too uncertain. The court did not indicate which definition of death is appropriate or whether alternatives are available to the prosecution.

In Phillips v. State, the court held that an indictment failing to specify the cause of death is sufficient when the circumstances of the case will not admit of greater certainty in stating the means of death.

An indictment charging the defendant with causing the victim's death by two methods would put the defendant on notice that he needs to defend against proof that he caused the victim's death by both of these methods. Thus, an instruction to the jury that it can find the defendant guilty if it finds that he caused the victim's death by either or both methods would not require the defendant to defend against a cause of death that was not alleged in the indictment and would not operate to subject the defendant to a later prosecution for the same offense.

E. Admissibility of Evidence

The admissibility of certain kinds of evidence in homicide trials has been dealt with in numerous cases.

1. Battered Syndromes

In Smith v. State, the Georgia Supreme Court reversed a conviction for the erroneous exclusion of testimony by a clinical psychologist concerning the "battered woman syndrome." The psychologist would have testified to the phenomenon of battered women and that the defendant (a woman who killed her live-in boyfriend) fell within the battered woman profile. The court held that this evidence should have been admitted as part of the defendant's claim of self-defense. The court concluded that "the expert's testimony explaining why a person suffering from battered woman's syndrome would not leave her mate, would not inform police or friends, and would fear increased aggression against herself, would be such conclusions that jurors could not ordinarily draw for themselves." Thus, the expert testimony was admissible. However, whether the defendant shot her mate in self-defense is not a question outside the ken of the average juror, and is not a proper subject for expert testimony.

In another case, however, the court refused to reverse a murder conviction where similar evidence was offered. The terse analysis in Mullis v. State does not reveal much of the court's reasoning. It may be that the defendant did not offer evidence of self-defense in her testimony. The opinion seems to indicate that the only defense was accident.

In Chapman v. State, the Georgia Supreme Court held that although evidence of the "battered woman syndrome" is admissible, it is not a separate defense. Rather, evidence of the syndrome is admissible in an attempt to show that the defendant had a mental state necessary for the defense of justification although the actual threat of harm does not immediately precede the homicide.

In Pugh v. State, the court held that as evidence of the "battered woman syndrome" is admissible for the purposes of establishing (1) reasonable fear of the wife in connection with a claim of self-defense and (2) general character for violence of the husband, such evidence may not be excluded because the defendant failed to satisfy the basis for admissibility of the same evidence as relevant to insanity, mental illness, or mental incompetency. The court emphasized that the fact that such evidence is admissible in connection with an issue of self-defense, does not mean that it can be used to raise the issues of insanity, mental illness, or mental incompetency without prior compliance with the notice provisions of Uniform Superior Court Rule 31.4 [now Rule 31.5].

The rationale for the admission of expert testimony on the battered woman syndrome should not be applied to a case merely because the defendant's expert would testify that the defendant's actions were "activated and driven by the same psychological dynamics" as those in the battered woman syndrome. This rationale was pronounced by the Georgia Supreme Court in Smith v. State as the result of a need to treat a complex area of human response and behavior. If the facts of a case do not create a comparable need, expert testimony providing a psychological explanation for the defendant's actions is not relevant to the jury's consideration of his justification defense.

A number of factors must be considered in determining whether a self-defense claim based on the battered person syndrome has been established. These factors include evidence of a close personal relationship between the defendant and the victim; a pattern of physical, sexual, or psychological abuse; and a reasonable apprehension of harm. If there is only limited or no evidence of these factors in a case, then the evidence does not rise to the level of battering necessary to rely on the battered person syndrome as a basis for a self-defense claim. Therefore, expert testimony that the defendant suffers from the syndrome would be inadmissible. Verbal or emotional abuse can warrant the introduction of expert testimony on the battered person syndrome. However, the psychological abuse inflicted on the defendant must have been of such an extreme nature that it engendered in the defendant a reasonable belief in the imminence of the victim's use of unlawful force. Psychological abuse which humiliates, embarrasses, or abases an individual, when unaccompanied by other acts or verbal statements giving rise to a reasonable fear of imminent physical harm, cannot alone justify the admission of expert testimony on the battered person syndrome.

Consistent with the concept of the battered person syndrome as an evidentiary component of the defense of justification, the General Assembly amended the law relating to self-defense in 1993 to provide that in a prosecution for murder or manslaughter, if a defendant raises a justification defense, the defendant, in order to establish the defendant's reasonable belief that the use of force or deadly force was immediately necessary, may be permitted to offer (1) relevant evidence that the defendant had been the victim of acts of family violence or child abuse committed by the deceased and (2) relevant expert testimony regarding the condition of the mind of the defendant at the time of the offense, including those relevant facts and circumstances relating to the family violence or child abuse that are the bases of the expert's opinion. Thus, a defendant who was a prior victim of abuse may offer battered person syndrome evidence to illustrate his or her reasonable belief in the imminence of the victim's use of unlawful force. Evidence that the defendant suffered from battered person syndrome is only another circumstance which, if believed by the jury, would authorize a finding that a reasonable person, who had experienced prior physical abuse such as was endured by the defendant, would reasonably believe that the use of force against the victim was necessary, even though that belief may have been, in fact, erroneous. The General Assembly's provision for the admissibility of relevant expert testimony regarding the condition of the defendant's mind in a situation of abuse has not otherwise changed the rule in homicides where justification is raised as a defense, namely, that justification is based upon the fears of a reasonable person, not upon the reasonable fears of the defendant.

Where the defendant's expert avers on direct examination that the defendant did suffer from the battered person syndrome and did believe death or great bodily injury was imminent, the trial court may permit the state's expert to testify in rebuttal.

Any error in precluding a defense expert from testifying about post-traumatic stress disorder would be harmless where there was extensive testimony concerning the victim's acts of violence and extensive testimony concerning the battered woman syndrome that was cumulative of testimony the expert would have given on the disorder.

Where a defense expert testifies that he relied upon the defendant's medical records in reaching the conclusion that his client was not malingering of faking the battered-person claim, it is permissible for the prosecutor to cross-examine the expert about those records.

It should be noted that a jury is not required to believe the testimony of defense witnesses supporting a battered-person claim but is authorized to find, instead, that the defendant intentionally shot the victim under circumstances which did not constitute self-defense.

Specific instructions on the battered person syndrome are appropriate when warranted by the evidence and requested by the defendant. In Smith v. State, the Georgia Supreme Court announced the rule that when a battered person syndrome self-defense claim has been properly established, the trial court should give specific jury instructions on justification by self-defense which are tailored to explain how the defendant's experiences as a battered person affected that defendant's state of mind at the time of the killing. Thus, in addition to the general instruction on justification, an instruction must be given to explain to the jury the relevancy of the battered person syndrome evidence as it relates to the reasonableness of the defendant's belief that the use of deadly force was immediately necessary to defend herself against the victim's imminent use of unlawful force.

Evidence that the defendant suffered abuse at the hands of others may not be used in determining whether she acted with the fear of a reasonable person under the circumstances. An instruction to the jury on this principle would be a correct statement of the law.

Although evidence of actual danger immediately preceding the homicide would not authorize instructions on the battered person syndrome, the mere fact that the defendant offers this evidence in furtherance of a justification defense does not mean that battered person syndrome instructions would be unauthorized as a matter of law. A defendant who pursues alternative defense theories is entitled to requested instructions on both theories, if there is some evidence to support each theory. Thus, if the defendant offers, in addition to evidence of actual danger immediately preceding the homicide, evidence of the battered person syndrome to show his reasonable, but erroneous, belief that danger was imminent, then the trial court should give requested instructions on the battered person syndrome.

To make a prima facie showing of self-defense based upon the battered person syndrome, a defendant should present the opinion testimony of an expert as well as independent testimony regarding the historical facts upon which the expert relies. If the defendant presents testimony regarding the historical facts but presents no expert testimony whatsoever, he fails to make a prima facie showing of the battered person syndrome, and the trial court would not be obligated to give requested instructions on that syndrome.

There is no general mandate requiring a trial court, when responding to a jury's request for a recharge on the justification defense, to also recharge on all principles asserted in connection with that defense. Rather, the trial court in its discretion may recharge the jury in full or only upon the point or points requested. By confining the scope of recharge so as only to answer the jury's specific questions, the trial court does not mislead or confuse the jurors, nor does it effectively curtail the jury's consideration of the principles connected with the defense.

The defendant is not entitled to the effective assistance of her expert. Thus, even if the expert mistakenly testifies that the defendant was suffering from the battered person syndrome, while, in fact, she was suffering from the rape trauma syndrome, the defendant would not be deprived of her due process right to a fair trial.

A colloquy between the trial court and defense expert that has the beneficial effect of educating the jury as well as informing the trial court on the evolution of the battered person syndrome, upon which the defendant predicates his defense, does not constitute an erroneous expression of opinion on the issues to be decided in the case in violation of § 17-8-57. The "plain error" principle would have no application under these circumstances.

In Sanders v. State, the Georgia Supreme Court ruled that evidence of the "battering parent syndrome" was not admissible as part of the state's case-in-chief in a prosecution of a mother for the murder of her child. The court held that while the state witness did not explicitly testify that the defendant fit the profile of the battering parent, the implication of the testimony was clear. The reasonable juror could be expected to match the profile to the characteristics of the defendant and conclude from this that the defendant had murdered her baby.

The Sanders court held that the state may not introduce such evidence unless the defendant has placed his or her character in issue or has asserted a defense which the battering parent syndrome could serve to rebut. The court found that the admission of the testimony in this case was erroneous, but affirmed the conviction on a finding of harmless error. The court did not identify which defenses in this kind of case would be rebuttable by introduction of the battering parent syndrome.

In another admissibility case, Payne v. State, the court held that evidence of the battered child syndrome was admissible against the defendant who was convicted of the murder of a 22-month-old child. The court held that this testimony was admissible to rebut the defense theory of accident or mistake.

Where the defendant is not claiming to have committed the homicide in self-defense but rather attempting to mitigate the element of intent in pursuit of a verdict of voluntary manslaughter, testimony regarding the victim's abuse of the defendant showing that the defendant was undergoing emotional and physical turmoil at the time of the homicide would not be relevant. Such testimony would not be relevant because the question in a voluntary manslaughter case is not whether the provocation proffered by the defendant was sufficient to excite a deadly passion in the particular defendant. Rather, it is whether such provocation was sufficient to excite such passion in a reasonable person.

2. *Victim's Reputation for Violence*

A great deal of litigation has revolved around attempts by homicide defendants to introduce evidence concerning the victim's general reputation for violence or specific acts of violence toward the defendant or toward others. Normally, the purpose of this evidence is to establish a self-defense defense or to support the defendant's theory that any homicide was voluntary manslaughter and not murder. The Georgia Supreme Court in Bennett v. State set out a synthesis of the law in this area. The following appears with citations omitted:

> Generally, the reputation or character of a murder victim for violence is irrelevant and inadmissible in criminal proceedings . . .. However, when relying on the defense of justification in a homicide case the accused may offer evidence of the violent character of the deceased victim if he makes a prima facie showing that the victim was the aggressor and was assailing the defendant, and that the defendant was honestly seeking to defend himself. Once the defendant makes a prima facie case for justification, he may offer evidence of the victim's general reputation for violence, including the victim's general reputation for a specific type of violence, such as for shooting people. Such evidence is admissible to corroborate the defendant's testimony that the victim was violent on the occasion in question and to show the defendant's state of mind (reasonable fear) at the time of the incident in question. Moreover, although the defendant may not prove the victim's general reputation for violence by specific acts of violence, if the defendant makes out a prima facie case for justification, he may offer evidence of 'prior specific assaults by the deceased upon the defendant to illustrate his contention that he reasonably believed he had to use deadly force to defend himself.'

It should be noted that even in situations where the defendant might have been permitted by the above rules to introduce evidence concerning the victim's general reputation for violence, he was not permitted to introduce evidence concerning specific acts of violence on other individuals. These rules have been cited and applied in a number of cases.

In Lolley v. State, Justice Weltner stated in his special concurring opinion that the rule reflected in Bennett v. State ought to be changed to permit evidence of specific acts of violence against third persons in cases where a defendant claims justification. In Chandler v. State, the court found the reasoning of Justice Weltner's special concurring opinion persuasive and held that the rule concerning prior specific acts of violence by the victim should be changed for future cases to comport with the special concurrence of Justice Weltner in Lolley v. State. Thus, as of September 12, 1991, evidence of specific acts of violence by a victim against third persons is admissible where the defendant claims justification. In *Chandler*, the court also imposed certain procedures to govern the introduction of such evidence. For example, the defendant must give advance notice to the state of his intention to introduce such evidence for that evidence to be admissible. Also, the defendant's notice must specify the dates, places, and names of the third persons involved. An inability to pinpoint the dates of the incidents would go to the weight of the evidence, not its admissibility. It should be noted, however, that the notice by itself does not make the evidence admissible; the defendant must also present a legitimate claim of justification. The procedures governing the introduction of such evidence were incorporated into the Uniform Superior Court Rules in 1993. The defendant must comply with these procedures only when he is seeking to introduce evidence of the victim's specific acts of violence against third persons. His compliance with these procedures is not required when he is seeking to introduce evidence of his prior difficulties with the victim to support a claim of justification. Finally, the defendant must establish by competent evidence that the victim's prior act involved violence.

The rule adopted in *Chandler* has been held to be applicable to prior acts of molestation and sexual assault by the victim against third persons. Where a defendant is seeking to establish the victim's propensity for seeking out and sexually assaulting young men and boys in a manner consistent with his claim of justification, evidence of the victim's prior acts of molestation and sexual assault is highly relevant to that defense and should be admitted. Since acts of forcible molestation and sexual assault, by their very nature, involve violence, a showing that the victim's actions were accompanied by independent acts of violence is not required for the purpose of establishing the defendant's claim of justification.

Since revenge for the molestation of one's child is not a material exculpatory factor in a criminal case, evidence of the victim's alleged commission of prior acts of molestation, standing alone, would not be admissible in defense of a homicidal act. Only if the defendant acted in accordance with the legally recognized exculpatory motive of justification, rather than revenge, would evidence of the victim's bad character and specific acts of molestation be admissible on the defendant's behalf. Otherwise, such evidence would constitute an irrelevant attack on the character of the deceased victim who could not answer the charges of molestation being asserted against him.

In response to the defendant's claim of justification and to evidence that the victim was the first aggressor, the state may present evidence of the victim's reputation for peacefulness.

If evidence offered by the defendant renders the desired inferences of lack of motive and self-defense more probable than they would be without the evidence, it is relevant and should be admitted. In Smith v. State, the court held that evidence that the victim carried a sawed-off shotgun and solicited a person to help commit a robbery and murder rendered the defendant's desired inferences of lack of motive and self-defense more probable because it supported his claim that he and the victim had gone into the woods to test-fire their guns in anticipation of a robbery and because it showed that the victim possessed one of the shotguns and therefore could have fired at the defendant first. Thus, evidence of the victim's alleged possession and solicitation offenses prior to the shooting was relevant and should have been admitted. Further, because the state could not point to a specific victim of the alleged offenses, they did not constitute specific acts of violence by the victim against a third party. Thus, the pretrial notice provisions governing the introduction of evidence of such acts was inapplicable to the alleged offenses.

3. *Victim's State of Mind*

The general rule is that evidence of threats previously made by the victim but uncommunicated to the defendant is not admissible on the question of whether the defendant was justified in killing the victim. However, such evidence may be admitted as an exception to the hearsay rule when offered not for the truth of the matter asserted but to show the victim's state of mind. This evidence is only admissible when there is a conflict in the evidence as to who started the fight, to corroborate evidence of threats which in fact were communicated, and to establish the attitude of the victim. Where the evidence adduced belies the defendant's contention that the uncommunicated threat showed the victim's state of mind, the hearsay exception does not apply.

Where the victim's statement, "I can't stand the SOB," on the night of the murder is the only evidence of animus between the victim and the defendant, it is admissible to show the victim's state of mind and attitude at the time of the crime.

Evidence which tends to show the victim's state of mind in regard to the defendant may be relevant in instances in which the defendant claims self-defense.

4. *Victim's Statements Prior to Death*

Testimony as to the victim's statements in regard to what had transpired prior to the infliction of his fatal injuries is admissible under the "dying declaration" exception to the hearsay rule. The fact that the victim did not see the assailant does not automatically render his identification of the accused inadmissible. Also, testimony as to the victim's statements made shortly after the infliction of his fatal injuries is admissible under the res gestae exception to the hearsay rule.

Testimony as to a victim's statement that the defendant was out to get him or do anything to kill him is admissible under the necessity exception to the hearsay rule where necessity and particularized guarantees of trustworthiness have been established. Formerly, the victim's death, in and of itself, was sufficient to satisfy the necessity component of the exception. However, the Georgia Supreme Court has held that death or unavailability of the victim cannot alone satisfy the necessity component without allowing the exception to swallow the rule. Additionally, the proponent of the evidence must show that the statement is relevant to a material fact and that the statement is more probative on that material fact than other evidence that may be procured and offered. The trustworthiness component is satisfied if the trial court, after examining the totality of the circumstances surrounding the making of the statements sought to be introduced, determines that there are sufficient indicia of reliability. Where the hearsay statements of the victim are not "testimonial" in nature, indicia of reliability other than the opportunity for cross-examination are constitutionally permissible considerations in applying the necessity exception to Georgia's hearsay rule. The admission of "testimonial" hearsay statements without the opportunity for cross-examination, however, constitutes error but would be harmless where there is no reasonable probability that the statements contributed to the verdict.

A victim's statements alleging an attack by the defendant on the victim that are made in response to a police officer's questions during a time when there is no longer an ongoing emergency are testimonial in nature, and it is a violation of the Confrontation Clause of the Sixth Amendment to admit the hearsay account of the attack over a defendant's objection where the defendant has had no previous opportunity for cross-examination.

Since there is nothing inherent in the attorney-client relationship that suggests a spouse will naturally utter a truthful statement in consulting an attorney about a divorce, there is no bright-line rule that any statement of a deceased spouse to a divorce attorney about the other spouse's violence during the marriage is admissible under the necessity exception to the hearsay rule. Rather, the totality of the circumstances surrounding the making of the out-of-court statement determines whether there is sufficient indicia of trustworthiness.

Testimony as to the victim's statement, which was precipitated by the defendant's death threat against him and which was the result of a spontaneous reaction, is admissible under the excited utterance exception to the hearsay rule. Testimony as to the victim's statements made during an argument with the defendant, when offered to prove the fact of the argument itself and not the truth or falsity of its contents, is admissible as original evidence to show the increasing tension between the defendant and the victim.

For a victim's conversation with a witness about prior difficulties with the defendant to be admissible under § 24-3-2, the conversation must be known to the defendant. Then if and only if the defendant's conduct or motives are relevant to the issues being tried, the conversation upon which the defendant acted would be admissible. It is admissible because it represents original evidence to prove the very fact that such a conversation occurred, not its truth or falsity.

5. *Victim's Medical Records*

Hospital records pertaining to the admission and treatment of the victim that contain recordations of acts, transactions, occurrences, and events that are normally recorded during the course of a hospital's business are excepted from the rule prohibiting the admission of hearsay and thus are admissible.

American Red Cross records showing the victim's blood group are admissible under the business records exception to the hearsay rule when the state lays the proper foundation by offering the testimony of an American Red Cross employee demonstrating that blood grouping is determined by machine testing and thus the matter constitutes objective factual data maintained in the regular course of business. Also, the records must contain neither opinion nor diagnosis. These records are not the type of investigation-generated written scientific report subject to discovery by the defendant.

6. *Victim's Alcohol Use*

Where the defendant fails to show what, if any, effect alcohol had on the victim at the time of the fatal incident, the trial court is authorized to exclude evidence of the victim's alcohol use.

An expert may not testify about the effects of alcohol on the victim unless evidence of the victim's blood alcohol level has been properly admitted at trial. A report showing the blood alcohol level of the victim is admissible when the defendant lays a proper foundation for either the admission of the report or the expert's testimony regarding the test results contained in the report by showing that the witness is familiar with the method of record keeping or that he can testify that the entry of the test results was made in the regular course of business at the time the test was conducted or within a reasonable time thereafter.

7. *Victim's Drug Use*

Where the defense cannot demonstrate how the use of drugs contributed to the behavior of the victim at the time of the shooting that would be relevant to the defendant's justification defense, evidence of the victim's drug use is properly excluded as being too speculative. Moreover, where evidence of the victim's prior drug use would not tend to prove his reputation for violence nor the reasonableness of the defendant's claim that the use of deadly force was necessary, it is properly excluded.

Where the connection between the victim's cocaine abuse and the infection that contributed to his death amounts to nothing more than sheer speculation, the trial court's exclusion of any mention of the victim's cocaine use from the evidence would not be erroneous.

8. *Victim's Character*

Where the defendant does not assert a defense of justification, evidence of the murder victim's character, such as his conflict with a third party, is irrelevant and inadmissible.

Incidental characterizations of the victim that are relevant to the facts of the murder are admissible.

Testimony regarding the victim's reckless behavior on the night in question is allowed so the jury can consider whether the victim's recklessness on the subject evening contributed to his death. However, evidence regarding prior instances of such behavior is irrelevant.

Evidence regarding the victim's homosexuality would be admissible to the extent it is relevant to the defendant's claim of self-defense against the victim's unwelcome homosexual advances. However, evidence of the victim's homosexual relationships presented merely to attack the victim's character would not be admissible.

9. *Victim's Identity*

The actual bones and body parts of the victim are admissible where the gruesome appearance of such evidence has not been caused by any act of the state and where such evidence is relevant to prove the identity of the victim and to show the location of the victim's fatal wound.

A photograph of a deceased victim is admissible to prove the victim's identity. While it is preferable for the trial court to admit the photograph of the victim alone, without extraneous material that is unnecessary to aid in fendant and the co-defendant showing the existence of a relationship between the two; (16) evidence that the defendant was a drug dealer, that he used drugs with and sold drugs to the victim, and that there was a dispute between him and the victim regarding drugs; (17) evidence that the intended murder victim had stolen narcotics from the defendant; (18) evidence that the defendant was arrested on a drug charge a few days before the victim's murder; (19) evidence of the defendant's membership in a satanic group; (20) evidence of the defendant's membership in a gang; (21) evidence of the defendant's racist beliefs and Klan affiliation; (22) a notebook possessed by the defendant containing hieroglyphic religious drawings and references to the occult; (23) evidence of a movie possessed by the defendant which depicts the conduct with which the defendant is charged; (24) a weapon possessed by the defendant; and (25) evidence that the defendant was a fugitive from another jurisdiction.

Evidence of the defendant's motive is relevant, even though it may incidentally place his character in evidence. Evidence of motive is not subject to the notice and hearing requirements of Uniform Superior Court Rules 31.1 and 31.3.

The introduction of improper evidence that goes to a motive to kill is harmless error where there is a conviction for felony murder which requires no such motive.

15.1. Defendant's Tattoos

A photograph of a tattoo on the body of the defendant is admissible when it is evidence of a possible motive for the crime or when it is used for purposes of identification. A photograph of the defendant's tattoo is irrelevant, however, when it is used to establish that the defendant acted in conformity with the tattoo. The existence of a tattoo, in and of itself, does not establish a defendant's propensity to act in conformance with that depicted in the tattoo. Thus, where the prosecution presents evidence of a defendant's tattoo which depicts a weapon similar to that involved in the crime, its admission would constitute error when its only purpose is to establish the defendant's propensity to use such a weapon. Nevertheless, where the erroneous admission of such evidence does not contribute to the verdict, it does not constitute reversible error.

Where the elicitation of the defendant's unguarded response to a perceived confidante regarding the circumstances of the crimes in which they had both participated was clearly designed to procure an unfiltered, genuine statement from the defendant and where there is no evidence that the police investigative techniques were designed to induce the slightest hope of benefit or fear of injury in the confidante, the defendant's resulting inculpatory statements during the secretly-taped telephone conversation between the defendant and the confidante would not be considered involuntary and therefore inadmissible under § 24-3-50.

16. Videotapes and Photographs

Videotapes, like still photographs, are admissible when relevant to an issue, even if inflammatory. A videotape showing the position of the victim's body at the crime scene is admissible.

Pre-autopsy photographs taken of the victim are relevant to the nature of the victim's wounds and cause of death and are therefore admissible. A post-autopsy photograph of the victim that does not depict any alteration of the body which may have occurred during the autopsy is also relevant to show the wound that caused the decedent's death. Since such a photograph does not show a material fact which became apparent only because of the autopsy, the state is not required to lay a foundation for its admission. A post-autopsy photograph depicting an alteration of the victim's body is admissible when it is necessary to show some material fact which became apparent only because of the autopsy. The defendant's admission that he killed the victim does not render photographs of the victim's body inadmissible.

17. Medical Examiner's and Other Experts' Testimony

The medical examiner who performed the autopsy should be permitted to express his opinion as to causation where his conclusion is one which jurors would not ordinarily be able to draw for themselves, i.e., the conclusion is beyond the ken of the average layman. However, where the factors which led the medical examiner to his conclusion that the victim's death was a homicide are factors well within the knowledge and understanding of the jury, where his investigation did not lead to that conclusion, and where his expertise was not needed or used in reaching that conclusion, the medical examiner should not be permitted to testify that, in his opinion, the manner of death, as opposed to the cause of death, was due to homicide. Likewise, a medical examiner should not be permitted to testify that the childhood maltreatment syndrome or abused child syndrome was the "manner" in which the fatal injuries occurred, and that the fatal injuries occurred "in the process" of the childhood maltreatment syndrome, since such testimony constitutes an opinion that the fatal injuries in fact resulted from child abuse, a conclusion that jurors would have the ability to reach for themselves. While the better practice is for medical examiners to be instructed not to state a conclusion that the death resulted from homicide, such a conclusion does not improperly invade the province of the jury if the conclusion merely reiterates and underscores the medical examiner's previous testimony as to causation and if the jury can reach no conclusion, based on this testimony, other than that the death was a homicide.

If the autopsy report of a prior medical examiner has been admitted under the business records exception to the hearsay rule, it is permissible for the current medical examiner to read aloud the report as redacted. Furthermore, even though the current medical examiner's opinion is based on facts contained in the report, his opinion does not constitute the restatement of the diagnostic opinion of another expert.

Where the victim's body has not been found, the medical examiner who has observed the crime scene should be allowed to give expert opinion testimony as to whether a death had occurred.

A medical examiner, who has been qualified as an expert in ballistics, may testify as to the significance of gunpowder residue found on the victim's shirt. Likewise, a forensic pathologist, who has been qualified to testify based on special knowledge derived from experience or study, may state an opinion as to the distance between the gun and the victim and the angle of trajectory of the bullet which entered his body. A treating physician of the victim, who has been qualified as an expert in the field of emergency medicine with experience in treating stab wounds, may testify regarding the force required to cause the victim's fatal injury.

A medical expert for the defense, who is a trained physician licensed to practice in this state, is qualified to testify on pathological matters. However, his testimony will be limited to matters within his own personal knowledge and facts admitted at trial and presented to him in the form of hypothetical questions.

The opinion of a crime lab expert that a hair found at the crime scene and the defendant's hair sample have a common origin is admissible under § 24-9-67. The fact that the expert does not discount the victim as the possible source of the hair goes to the weight to be given the evidence, not its admissibility.

A crime scene reconstructionist, who has been qualified as an expert in the field of behavioral science, may testify that a perpetrator might move or cover a victim's body to depersonalize the victim because a close relationship existed between the perpetrator and the victim.

The admission of testimony of the state's toxicologist that he had reviewed the work of the doctor who had originally prepared the toxicology report relating to the deceased victim and reached the same conclusion that the victim's blood sample tested negative for cocaine would not violate the defendant's constitutional right to confront the witnesses against him. The state toxicologist, having reviewed the data and testing procedures to determine the accuracy of the report, may base his opinion on data gathered by the doctor. His opinion then is more than a mere conduit for the doctor's findings.

18. Death Certificates

Conclusions on a death certificate of the events leading up to the death or regarding whether the cause of death was intentional or accidental are inadmissible. However, because the word "Homicide" is nothing more than an indication of the immediate agency of death, its exclusion from the death certificate upon its admission into evidence is not required. Where the cause of death on the death certificate is consistent with the testimony of the coroner who issued it, the certificate contains no improper hearsay which would preclude its admission.

A death certificate properly completed by a medical examiner is considered prima facie evidence of both the death itself and the cause of the death. A death certificate is accorded initial prima facie evidentiary value regardless of the examiner's credibility. For this reason, death certificates that are properly redacted to show only prima facie evidence of the fact that a death occurred and the causes of the death are not subject to the "continuing witness" rule and may go out with the jury.

19. Murder Weapon

A weapon may be admissible if the identification is sufficient to allow the jury to decide, under the evidence relative to identification, whether it is the identical weapon used by the defendant. Because the pretrial procedures used to determine the constitutional admissibility of identification testimony do not apply when the identity of a weapon is concerned, the exclusionary remedy is also inapplicable. Any suggestiveness in the identification of the weapon is relevant to the weight, not the admissibility, of the evidence. Thus, the proper manner for contesting identification testimony is by cross-examination at trial, not by a pretrial motion to suppress. The jury, not the trial court, decides whether the identification of the weapon is dependable and accurate.

A warrant issued and executed at the request of the lead detective investigating a victim's murder makes it more probable that the gun recovered pursuant to that warrant is the murder weapon involved in the case. This fact is consequential to the determination of the prosecution against the defendant. Accordingly, a trial court would not abuse its discretion in overruling a defendant's objections, based solely on relevancy, to admission of the search warrant used to recover the murder weapon.

A weapon that was not actually used in the commission of a murder, but which is similar to that which was so used, is generally admissible into evidence. A murder weapon that has been dismantled and perhaps reassembled in a different manner while undergoing tests for fingerprints is still admissible in evidence. Where the murder weapon has not been recovered, the state may offer evidence, such as a piece of the victim's skull, to prove the size and character of the weapon used.

The atomic absorption test, which is used to detect trace elements of metals found in gunshot residue, has been held to be scientifically reliable and, therefore, admissible at trial.

The existence of technological advances that purportedly have made the metals found in gun residue more common in the environment, the failure to test the gun itself, and the lack of "blind testing," go to the weight to be accorded the atomic absorption test rather than to its admissibility.

Both the gun and the cartridge involved in a murder are distinct and recognizable physical objects which can be identified upon observation, obviating the necessity of a chain of custody showing.

20. Chain of Custody

When the state seeks to introduce into evidence an item that is subject to the chain of custody rule, it must establish with reasonable assurance that the item seized is the same as the item being offered into evidence. The chain of custody requirements apply only after the state has taken possession of an item. Absent affirmative evidence of tampering, challenges to evidence that focus on the period before the state took possession are governed by general rules of relevance and authentication. If there is a sufficient evidentiary connection between the defendant and the item received by the police, the item is admissible. Any doubt regarding this connection goes to the weight of the evidence not its admissibility, and the jury is charged with deciding how much weight to give evidence.

F. Venue

In homicide cases, charges taken verbatim from § 17-2-2(c) and (h) do not improperly impose a burden on defendants to disprove that venue was properly laid. Rather than creating burden-shifting presumptions regarding venue, § 17-2-2 provides the means by which a jury can ensure that the constitutional mandate of establishing venue beyond a reasonable doubt has been satisfied in cases where the state has brought forth evidence to establish venue and the defendant has introduced evidence intended to counter that showing. The statute does not require any compulsory or permissive presumptions to be drawn regarding whether venue in a particular forum is proper.

Nonetheless, in order to more clearly effectuate the intention of § 17-2-2 and to alleviate defendants' concerns about the creation of burden-shifting presumptions, the Georgia Supreme Court instructed that in future cases the better practice would be for trial courts, when charging juries, to refrain from quoting § 17-2-2(c) and (h) verbatim. Instead, trial courts should give to juries the charges quoted in the court's opinion in Napier v. State.

II. Murder and Manslaughter

A. Defined

Sections 16-5-1, 16-5-2, and 16-5-3 define the three major homicidal crimes: murder, voluntary manslaughter and involuntary manslaughter. That which generally distinguishes murder from manslaughter is the presence of malice aforethought, although a limited group of homicides are murder even though performed without malice. That which distinguishes voluntary from involuntary manslaughter is the intention to kill. An intentional, non-malicious killing is voluntary manslaughter, while an unintended non-malicious killing is usually involuntary manslaughter.

A homicide which is neither justifiable nor malicious could be either accident or felony murder, but not manslaughter.

B. Murder

1. Malice Murder

a. Mens Rea

The mens rea for malice murder is malice, which can be described simply as an intention to kill another human being. Section 16-5-1 identifies two kinds of malice: express and implied. The presence of two types of malice in the statute can be attributed to prior statutory drafting. The Georgia Supreme Court has never spent a great deal of time in distinguishing between the two kinds of malice, but it appears that express malice is that which is proven by the defendant's own actions outside the killing itself. For example, in Sheppard v. State the court said that evidence that the defendant deliberately aimed the car at the victims, that he was previously hostile toward the victims, that there were previous ill feelings between one of the victims and the defendant, and that defendant threatened the only surviving victim was sufficient to support what the court held was a finding of express malice. In Patterson v. State, the defendant urged that there was no proof of his intention to kill. The court held, however, that from the facts and circumstances of the case the jury was authorized to find that the defendant's killing of the victim was intentional and malicious. The defendant became angry because the victim had not repaid a small loan. After stating that he would shoot the victim, the defendant obtained a gun and, accompanied by several friends, confronted the victim. Although the defendant contended that he shot the victim to protect one of his friends, there was significant evidence to the contrary. After first shooting the victim in the leg, the defendant deliberately took aim and fired two shots into the victim's head. In Hansley v. State, the defendant contended that the state failed to prove malice. However, the evidence showed that the defendant, who had fought with the victim before, left the fight to get a gun from a friend's car, yelled that the victim would not get away this time, and fired several shots at the victim, who was attempting to enter his car. The court held that this evidence was more than sufficient to prove malice. In Somchith v. State, the defendant contended that the evidence did not show malice murder but only voluntary manslaughter provoked by the victim's sexual involvement with another man and their argument about it. However, the court held that ample evidence was presented to allow the jury to infer malice. The evidence showed that the defendant secured a pistol earlier on the day of the shooting and that he shot the victim not once, but four times, including a contact wound to the head. In Brown v. State, the defendant contended that evidence of the victim's alleged molestation of the defendant's daughter should have been admitted to show that he acted without malice. The court disagreed. Evidence only of past molestation of the child did not show that the defendant acted lawfully with present justification when he shot the victim, but showed that the defendant was motivated solely by revenge for the past molestation and authorized a finding that he was guilty of malice murder. In Sapp v. State, the court held that the jury was authorized to discredit the defendant's testimony that he lacked the malice necessary for murder and find based on the defendant's behavior before the shooting, the obscene comment he made about the victim, and his actions afterwards, that the defendant possessed the requisite malice when he shot and killed the victim. In Frezghi v. State, the defendant contended that the evidence showed only that he committed voluntary manslaughter, because the state did not contradict his testimony that the victim first stabbed him during an argument and that he became angry, took the knife from her, and could not control himself. The court, however, concluded that the evidence, including the numerous stab wounds and the cruel and deliberate nature of the final wound, was sufficient to authorize the jury to find the defendant guilty of malice murder. In Thomas v. State, the defendant contended that the state failed to present evidence that he acted with malice. The court, however, held that evidence that an electrical cord was wrapped twice around the victim's neck and then was tightened by repeatedly twisting the cord around a broom handle and that the defendant did not initially report the victim's purported threatening behavior supported the trial court's finding the defendant guilty of malice murder. The defendant's testimony that the victim provoked him did not establish, as a matter of law, that he did not act with malice since the existence of provocation does not preclude the existence of malice. In Hill v. State, the defendant contended he should not have been convicted of malice murder as there was no evidence of malice. The court, however, held that the circumstances of the defendant's attack on the victim were sufficient for the jury to find that he acted with the required malice. Although the defendant testified that his only intent was to rob the victim, he also testified that he observed that the victim was elderly and infirm to the point that he had to rest after a short walk and used an inhalant medication, and that he hit the victim hard enough to knock him to the ground.

This mens rea of express malice is not to be confused with premeditation which some jurisdictions define as the mental state required for first degree murder. Premeditation is not an element of murder in Georgia, and the malice which is required for murder can be formed in an instant so long as it is present at the time of the act of killing and, therefore, it is no defense that there was an insufficient amount of time for malice to be formed.

Motive is not an essential element of the crime of malice murder. Although motive may be relevant to the issues of intent and malice, it is not a separate element of the crime which must be proven by the state. While motive is not an essential element in the proof of the crime of murder, the state is entitled to present evidence to establish that there was a motive. The defendant, however, is not entitled to present evidence of a motive for his act which would not otherwise constitute a viable defense to his criminal liability.

Of course, the intention to kill, like any other intention, is rarely capable of proof out of the mouth of the defendant or through specific prior acts connected to him or her. It is the relatively rare defendant who will admit such an intention, unless he or she is claiming some justification defense. Therefore, the murder statute and the cases under it provide that there can be a finding by the trier of fact of implied malice. Although most murders in which this implied malice provides the mens rea can be described as intentional killings, there are situations in which the killing is unintentional but is committed with such an extreme indifference to human life ("abandoned and malignant heart" in the language of § 16-5-1) that the law finds such a killing to be as culpable as an intentional killing and, thus, murder.

Since "malice aforethought" is an essential element of murder, it should be defined by the trial court when it charges the jury on the statutory definition of murder. However, if the defendant does not request such a charge and the evidence is overwhelming that the killing took place intentionally and without justification or serious provocation, the failure to define malice does not require reversal.

A trial court's failure to charge on implied malice is not harmful when the jury is instructed that it must find actual malice before finding the defendant guilty of malice murder.

b. Deadly Weapon Doctrine

While the statute identifies two situations in which "implied" malice shall be found ("where no considerable provocation appears" and "abandoned and malignant heart"), the most fruitful kind of evidence which has been relied upon for a finding of implied malice has been the use of a deadly weapon, like a gun or knife. The courts had traditionally held that when a defendant used a deadly weapon to kill there was enough evidence to find the presence of malice. The method by which this was usually expressed was a two-step analysis which stated that (1) upon a showing of the use of a deadly weapon the law presumed intent and (2) the law presumed every intentional homicide to be malicious.

i. Jury Instructions: Former Practice

The traditional methods of informing the jury of the effect of the use of a deadly weapon, however, were subjected to repeated constitutional attacks. In Patterson v. State, for example, the defendant claimed that presenting the jury with the instructions that "the law **presumes** the intent to kill" from the use of a deadly weapon and "the law **presumes** every intentional homicide to be malicious until the contrary is **established**"(emphasis added) constituted an unconstitutional shift of the burden of proof as well as an unconstitutional set of presumptions because there was no rational connection between the fact proved and the fact presumed.

While the Georgia Supreme Court recognized that malice was the mens rea element of murder and that United States Supreme Court authority forbade the placing of the burden of proof on the defendant with regard to an element of the offense, the Georgia court held that the two above-quoted charges did not unconstitutionally place the burden of proof on the defendant. In the court's language, these two instructions did "not shift any burden of proof or persuasion to defendant." The court characterized the effect of these instructions as placing only a burden of production on the defendant, which was permitted by the relevant United States Supreme Court authority.

While the Patterson analysis itself seemed questionable in light of the language of the malice presumption that it would exist until the contrary was **established**, it was apparent that United States Supreme Court authority on this issue implicitly overruled Patterson on its facts. In Sandstrom v. Montana, the court held that a trial court instruction almost identical to that in Patterson, to the effect that "the law presumes that a person intends the ordinary consequences of his voluntary acts," was unconstitutional in that it violated the Fourteenth Amendment's requirement that the state prove every element of a criminal offense beyond a reasonable doubt. Sandstrom held that regardless of what the Montana Supreme Court held was the actual legal effect of such a presumption, a reasonable juror, when told that "the law presumes," could have interpreted the instruction as creating either a conclusive presumption or at least a burden-shifting one, and either such interpretation was unconstitutional in a criminal case. Under Sandstrom, therefore, it was apparent that at least Patterson's malice instruction (which spoke in terms of the contrary being "established") and, possibly, also the intent presumption were subject to the same constitutional infirmities as the Sandstrom instructions. Sandstrom mandated that great caution should be used in the instruction of juries with regard to the deadly weapon doctrine.

Our appellate courts were often faced with the question of whether particular jury instructions violated the Sandstrom mandate which forbade both conclusive presumptions and jury instructions which shifted the burden of persuasion concerning intent or malice to the defendant. In Johnson v. State, the court reversed a murder conviction for violation of the principles of Sandstrom. The court concluded that the deadly weapon instruction given in the case could have been interpreted by the jury to be a conclusive one. This was erroneous under Sandstrom because it relieved the state of its burden to prove every element of murder beyond a reasonable doubt.

As for the second presumption, that an intentional killing is murder, the Johnson court found that despite the fact that the jury was told that the presumption was rebuttable, it could have interpreted the instruction as requiring the defendant to disprove murder by some quantum of proof. This would have shifted the burden of persuasion to the defendant. The court did not identify, however, which portion of the instruction could have led the reasonable juror to conclude that the defendant had to satisfy a burden of persuasion with regard to the presumption of murder.

This latter holding of Johnson constituted a movement by the court toward more protection of the defendant. In Hosch v. State, the court had held that the murder presumption had to include language indicating that it was rebuttable. In Johnson, however, the court conceded that this language was present and yet reversed anyway. It is noteworthy that the Johnson court, in striking down the murder presumption instruction, cited no other Georgia cases and relied solely on Sandstrom and Mullaney v. Wilbur. This indicated movement by the Georgia court beyond its established precedent.

The Georgia Supreme Court advised lower courts that Sandstrom errors could be avoided by more careful instructions on the finding of intent and malice. In Rivers v. State, the court stated that since Sandstrom, it had disapproved and would continue to disapprove the practice of casting criminal jury instructions in terms of presumptions. The better practice would be for the instructions to be cast in terms of permissible inferences which might be drawn from the purposeful activity of the defendant. Such instructions, when combined with the ordinary direction that the jury had to find all elements of the crime to be present beyond a reasonable doubt, were undoubtedly consistent with the mandate of the United States Supreme Court.

However, our courts later determined that a trial court's substitution of the term "infers" in lieu of the term "presumes" did not necessarily render benign an otherwise unconstitutionally burden-shifting charge. When a trial court directed the jury to infer an essential element of the crime and that the inference was rebuttable, it unconstitutionally relieved the State of its burden of proof. The use of either term was not conclusive of whether an instruction was permissive or mandatory. The difference between a permissive inference and mandatory presumption was found in the presence or absence of "language of command" such as "shall be." Where such "language of command" was absent from instructions on criminal intent, phrases such as "intent may be inferred . . . ," or "it is reasonable to infer . . . ," or "you may draw the inference that . . . ," were clearly permissive in nature and were not in violation of Sandstrom. Furthermore, it had been held that an instruction containing such a phrase did not improperly comment on the evidence.

In Franklin v. State, the Georgia Supreme Court found that reasonable jurors would not have interpreted the instruction on the rebuttable presumption of intent and on accident as being conclusive or as shifting the burden of persuasion to the defendant. It also rejected the argument that an instruction defining implied malice was unconstitutional as a burden shifting instruction under Sandstrom. The court concluded that a definition differed from a presumption as was at issue in Sandstrom.

In a federal habeas corpus case based on the Georgia trial, however, the Eleventh Circuit Court of Appeals found that the instruction on intent violated Sandstrom. In Franklin v. Francis, the court found that the additional charge to the jury that criminal intent was not presumed and that the state had to prove every element of the crime beyond a reasonable doubt did **not** cure the unconstitutionality of the instruction. The U.S. Supreme Court affirmed the Court of Appeals' decision. The Franklin decision in the Supreme Court cast grave doubt on the continuing validity of a number of Georgia Supreme Court decisions approving instructions on the ground that the general instructions on proof beyond a reasonable doubt and the presumption of innocence cured any burden-shifting infirmity.

The finding of a violation of Sandstrom was not per se a finding of reversible error. In several cases, both the state and federal courts found Sandstrom violations to be harmless constitutional error.

In 1983, the Supreme Court of the United States, however, cast doubt on the scope of the applicability of harmless error in the context of Sandstrom violations. In Connecticut v. Johnson, the jury was instructed that there was a conclusive presumption that every person intends the natural and probable consequences of his or her act, a clear Sandstrom error. The state court reversed the conviction without addressing the state's contention that the error was harmless. On appeal to the United States Supreme Court, the state asserted that the state supreme court had committed error in failing to consider the possibility of harmless error. In a fragmented decision without a majority opinion, the Supreme Court affirmed the state supreme court's action. It would seem that Johnson established that a certain number of Sandstrom errors were automatically reversible constitutional error. The court itself was not certain of the precise boundary line between automatically reversible error and possible harmless error. The only possible exception to the rule of automatic reversible error mentioned by the plurality contemplated instructions where the conviction was for a crime other than the one where the erroneous instruction was given or instructions in cases where the defendant conceded the presence of intent.

In 1986, the Supreme Court of the United States clearly held that the harmless-error analysis was applicable in cases of Sandstrom error. In Rose v. Clark, the court held that the taint of an unconstitutional burden-shifting jury instruction may be harmless, where it appeared beyond a reasonable doubt that the error complained of did not contribute to the verdict obtained. To say that an error did not contribute to the verdict was to find that error unimportant in relation to everything else the jury considered on the issue in question, as revealed in the record.

ii. Jury Instructions: Current Practice

In 1995, the Georgia Supreme Court indicated its movement beyond the precedent established by its prior decisions by strongly discouraging the practice of instructing a jury that it might infer the intent to kill from the defendant's use of a deadly weapon, especially where the jury was not also instructed that it could use its discretion to determine whether to make the authorized inference. The court suggested that the better practice would be, in the absence of some special request from the jury, not to emphasize particular circumstances such as the use of a deadly weapon and to indicate what inferences might arise therefrom. Rather, general charges on intent and circumstantial evidence would ordinarily be sufficient. Apparently, because many trial courts failed to follow what the court recognized as the better practice, it made a clear departure from its established precedent by disapproving of the practice of giving a "use of a deadly weapon" instruction in a murder trial. The court held that this practice constitutes error regardless of whether the jury is also instructed that it has the discretion to make the authorized inference. The court mandated that our trial courts should now merely give the jury a simple instruction on intent. The court made its holding applicable to all cases in the "pipeline," i.e., cases pending on direct review or not yet final as of March 2, 2001, but did not make it applicable to convictions challenged on habeas corpus.

Instructing a jury that it can infer the defendant's intent to kill based upon his use of a deadly weapon would constitute harmless error, however, where the jury has convicted the defendant of felony murder rather than malice murder. Unlike malice murder, felony murder does not require intent to kill; rather, the defendant only must have intended to commit the underlying felony. Furthermore, such error does not require reversal where the state has presented overwhelming evidence of the defendant's intent to kill. Also, where the defendant neither objected to the charge at trial nor reserved objections to the overall charge, the error would be waived on appeal.

Where the issue at trial is not whether the killing was intentional but whether it was justified based on a battered-person claim, the giving of a deadly weapon charge on the uncontested issue of intent to kill would constitute harmless error.

c. Abandoned and Malignant Heart

Another method of proving implied malice is through the extreme nature of the act itself. In many of these situations, the defendant may be able to state honestly that there was no intention to kill the victim, but the law will permit the defendant's act to be labelled murder because of its wantonness or reckless disregard for human life. The Georgia Supreme Court has written that malice "may arise from a reckless disregard for human life." Evidence that the defendant acted in reckless disregard for human life is, for purposes of demonstrating his guilt of the crime of malice murder, as equally probative as evidence that he acted with a specific intent to kill. Thus, an instruction to the jury that a reckless disregard for human life may be equivalent to a specific intent to kill would be a correct statement of the law. Such an instruction would not authorize a malice murder conviction based upon proof that the defendant caused the death of another through any and all acts of criminal negligence.

An instruction that states that malice may be inferred from an abandoned or malicious heart would not create an unconstitutional presumption which would shift the burden of proof to the defendant. The instruction would clearly inform the jury that intent to kill is an element of malice. Furthermore, such an instruction would not create an unconstitutional mandatory presumption of intent. It would merely inform the jury that they are permitted to infer malice from the circumstances surrounding the commission of the offense, but they would not be required to so infer. Finally, the instruction would not relieve the jury of the duty of finding that a killing occurred and that the defendant participated in the killing.

Specific fact situations in which the courts have affirmed a finding of such extreme disregard for human life as to be the equivalent of malice are (1) shooting a rifle at the victim while aiming one and a half feet over his head at a distance of 40-60 yards; (2) stabbing a victim many times with an ice pick; (3) repeatedly whipping a child with a rope; (4) smothering a victim by covering her mouth to prevent her continued screaming during a sexual assault; (5) shooting a victim by means of a spring gun or trap gun; (6) shooting in the immediate vicinity of occupied houses and fleeing the scene without seeking care for the victim; (7) repeatedly shooting into a house believed to be occupied by a person who supposedly robbed the shooter; (8) conducting a robbery while the victim after being shot lay alive but bleeding; (9) shooting into a crowd; and (10) keeping one's finger on the trigger of a loaded, cocked weapon while driving intoxicated at a high rate of speed and turning around in the driver's seat so that the barrel of the weapon made contact with victim's neck before he was shot.

The primary use of the abandoned and malignant heart theory of implied malice had been in cases of murder by vehicle. The Georgia Court of Appeals, however, held that with the enactment in 1974 of § 40-6-393 (the vehicular homicide statute) a murder charge could not be predicated upon a homicide resulting from "reckless disregard for the safety of persons" as that phrase was used in the reckless driving statute (§ 40-6-390), since that offense was expressly made "homicide by vehicle in the first degree" by § 40-6-393. The Georgia Supreme Court agreed with this holding and thought "that implicit within it lies the conclusion that 'reckless disregard for the safety of persons' cannot serve as implied malice aforethought, i.e., an abandoned and malignant heart, so as to authorize a murder conviction." The court later found this language to be in conflict with its subsequent unambiguous holdings wherein implied malice is defined as conduct which exhibits a reckless disregard for human life. To the extent that this language ever had any viability as authority for a contrary definition of implied malice, it clearly was no longer support for that proposition. The court found the definition of implied malice adopted in its subsequent holdings to be controlling.

Although the vehicular homicide statute has displaced the involuntary manslaughter statute as to vehicular homicides, it has not displaced the general malice murder statute. The vehicular homicide statute applies only to vehicular homicides caused "without malice aforethought" and "without an intention to do so." Thus, malice murder by vehicle, just as malice murder by other means, still falls under the general malice murder statute. In Anderson v. State, the defendant's conviction for malice murder by vehicle was predicated on evidence of the defendant's implied malice. The evidence showed that the defendant drove, at a speed of 68 miles per hour, across the center line striking head-on another vehicle, without attempting to brake his vehicle or otherwise avoid the collision, and killed the driver of the other vehicle. The court held the defendant's statement to law enforcement officers that he regretted the victim's death, "but it had to be somebody," was evidence of an intent to kill someone else in order to take his own life. In Chester v. State, the court upheld the defendant's conviction for malice murder by vehicle, where the jury's finding of implied malice was based on evidence that at the time of the accident the defendant was angry at women, and was speeding and drunk. Although he was drunk, he knew that he struck two girls, and that one of the girls was in the bed of his truck. Moreover, he knowingly dumped this girl's body at an isolated abandoned railroad track, thus making it highly unlikely that anyone would render aid to her to save her life.

d. Absence of Provocation

While the statute (§ 16-5-1) provides that malice is implied "where no considerable provocation appears," this does not provide an independent means of proving or disproving malice. In other words, the absence of provocation does not prove the existence of malice. Nor does the existence of provocation prove its absence. The proof of implied malice will depend either on an inference of intent or on the presence of an abandoned or malignant heart, probably the former. The presence of the provocation language is a relic of the statutory language prior to 1968 and is essentially a means of distinguishing murder from voluntary manslaughter.

Evidence of anger is not, as a matter of law, a showing of the provocation necessary to set aside a finding of malice. Thus, even where there is evidence that the victim angered the defendant, the jury may still determine from all the facts and circumstances that the killing, rather than being the result of considerable provocation, was intentional and malicious.

e. Party to Crime

The state is not required to prove that the defendant was the "triggerman" in order to prove him guilty of malice murder. Even assuming the defendant did not shoot the victim, if there is evidence that he intentionally aided or abetted the commission of the murder or that he intentionally advised, encouraged, or procured another to commit the murder, there would be sufficient evidence to support a finding of guilt.

The defendant need not have inflicted the fatal wound on the victim. If there is evidence that he was a willing participant in the harassing, chasing, and beating of the victim which led to the fatal outcome, the jury would be authorized to infer from the defendant's conduct that he aided and abetted the murder.

f. Verdicts

Malice murder is defined as the killing of another "with malice aforethought, either express or implied." Vehicular homicide is defined as killing another while operating a car, "without malice aforethought" and "without an intention to do so." Hence, when a jury returns verdicts finding the defendant guilty of the malice murder and vehicular homicide of another, the jury has convicted the defendant of killing both with **and** without malice aforethought. Obviously, the two verdicts are mutually exclusive, and it is proper for the trial court to refuse to accept these verdicts and send the jury back to continue its deliberations.

However, guilty verdicts for malice murder and felony murder are not mutually exclusive as a matter of law. A guilty verdict for felony murder does not constitute a finding that the murder was committed without malice aforethought, but that the murder was committed while in the commission of another felony offense "irrespective of malice." In other words, the presence or absence of malice is irrelevant to the commission of felony murder. Nor are the two verdicts mutually exclusive as a matter of fact where the evidence authorizes the jury to conclude that the defendant committed the murder while in the commission of a felony but also acted with malice aforethought.

The doctrine of mutually exclusive verdicts applies only where the jury returns multiple convictions as to crimes which are mutually exclusive of each other. This doctrine does not apply where there is a verdict of guilty and another of not guilty.

Since a jury's inability to agree on a verdict is not itself a verdict, a verdict which shows "no agreement" on a malice murder count and guilty on a felony murder count does not constitute a mutually exclusive verdict.

Where the jury has convicted the defendant of malice murder, it is not required to return a verdict on voluntary manslaughter.

g. Sentencing

Where a defendant is charged with the malice murder of separate victims in different counts and is found guilty on each count, he may be sentenced separately on each count to run consecutively for the reason that the killing of different persons constitutes separate crimes.

2. Felony Murder

One type of felonious homicide is murder even though the traditionally required malice is not present. Section 16-5-1(c) provides that when a person "causes the death of another human being" while "in the commission of a felony," he is guilty of murder. Dating from the early English common law, the felony-murder rule provides an exception to the general doctrine of mens rea that the mental element for one offense cannot render a defendant criminally liable for another offense. Here the mens rea of the underlying felony is permitted to substitute for the malice normally required for murder. Because of the proliferation of felonies and a feeling that not all of them merit inclusion in the felony-murder side which bypasses the malice requirement, the felony-murder rule has been limited by many jurisdictions to encompass only "inherently dangerous" felonies or certain specifically listed felonies. The rule itself has come under great attack by commentators, some of whom have described it as an "anachronism" and some who have called for its abolition. It has been suggested that felony murder is not necessary in light of the availability of "abandoned and malignant heart" implied malice as a prosecutorial device to convict extreme behavior which results in unintended killing.

a. Felonies Which Trigger the Rule

i. Limitations on Application of Rule

Georgia's statutory felony-murder provision reflects the very traditional broad phraseology. No limitation of the kind of felonies which trigger the rule is mentioned, and the only language change from the rule's standard statement of "in the commission **or in the attempted commission of**" a felony is the elimination of the emphasized phrase. This is not a substantive change at all, because under the present code the criminal attempt to commit a felony is itself a felony and, thus, would trigger the felony-murder rule.

Given the broad language of the Georgia statute, any limitation of the rule had to come judicially. Prior to 1992, the Georgia courts displayed very little willingness to limit the application of the rule to only inherently dangerous felonies. For example, the courts indicated or held that the felonies of escape, cruelty to children, and conspiracy could be used to support felony-murder convictions. In 1992, the Georgia Supreme Court decided to limit the application of the rule to any felony that is either dangerous per se or that, by the attendant circumstances, creates a foreseeable risk of death. The court also noted that under these circumstances there must be a sufficient connection between the felony and the homicide in order to trigger the rule. The court, applying this limitation in Ford v. State, held that the status felony of possession of a firearm by a convicted felon was not sufficient to support a conviction for felony murder, because the felony was neither inherently dangerous nor life-threatening under the circumstances of the homicide. In Hulme v. State, on the other hand, the court held that in this state a defendant may be convicted of felony murder based on the underlying felony of distributing a controlled substance if that felony is inherently dangerous to human life and if the defendant directly causes the death of the victim while in the commission of the felony. However, the court expressly stated that this holding does not mean that every delivery or distribution of a controlled substance that results in death can support a felony murder conviction.

In Ross v. State, the court held that pointing a loaded gun at another person may be an unlawful act amounting to an aggravated assault. Moreover, the act can support a finding of felony murder, even if the assault is upon the homicide victim.

ii. Modified Merger Doctrine

In Baker v. State, the Georgia Supreme Court in a detailed exposition addressed the issue of whether an underlying aggravated assault should support a felony-murder conviction or should properly be "merged" into the homicide and the entire transaction analyzed for the presence or absence of malice. In Baker, the defendant fired two shots at the decedent with the first missing and the second killing. The prosecution proceeded on a felony-murder theory, asserting aggravated assault as the underlying felony. In this kind of situation, many jurisdictions would reject the use of the aggravated assault as the underlying felony, limiting the permissible underlying felonies to those which are "independent" of the killing conduct. It has been suggested that convicting someone of felony murder in this situation is "bootstrapping," and since the vast majority of killings include an aggravated assault, "bootstrapping" would result in relieving prosecutors of the burden of proving malice or an intent to kill as element of all such killings.

The Georgia Supreme Court, however, rejected the proposed limitation to "independent" felonies. A major reason, according to the majority opinion, was Georgia's criminal homicide scheme which would provide no other criminal punishment for an accidental (nonintentional) killing committed during a felony. According to the court, such a death could not be "unlawful act" involuntary manslaughter under § 16-5-3(a) because that is limited to nonfelonious unlawful acts. It could not be "criminal negligence" involuntary manslaughter under § 16-5-3(b) because that is limited to behavior which is lawful, yet conducted in an unlawful way. Finally, according to the court, it could only be voluntary manslaughter under § 16-5-2 if it were done in the heat of passion. Thus, the court reasoned, if nonintentional killings during felonies were not felony murder, they would escape punishment.

The Baker reasoning is curious at best. Taken on its own terms, the court's analysis overlooks the fact that malice can be implied if the killing exhibits an abandoned and malignant heart. It is submitted that extremely negligent behavior during a forcible felony would qualify under this rubric for a malice murder conviction. In fact, a persuasive argument could be made that virtually any crime when committed through the use of a weapon capable of killing illustrated an "abandoned and malignant heart." There is, therefore, a "pigeonhole" within murder for many accidental deaths caused by the commission of a felony.

While it might be surmised that Baker's approval of aggravated assault as a permissible underlying felony will turn all intentional killings into felony murder and, thus, unfairly provide prosecutors a short cut around the malice requirement to murder convictions, this assumption is more apparent than real. Even under Baker, the state will have to prove the commission of an aggravated assault. Under § 16-5-21, an aggravated assault conviction requires proof of either (1) the use of a deadly weapon or (2) an intent to murder, rape, or rob. Thus, the prosecutor's task will not be significantly different or easier in felony murder than it is in malice murder. If he can prove the use of a deadly weapon for aggravated assault, he probably can also use the deadly weapon to prove malice. If he can demonstrate an intent to murder for purposes of aggravated assault, he can prove malice for malice murder. If he can show only an intent to rob or rape for the aggravated assault, he is proving the kind of independent felony which even an anti-Baker ruling would permit to serve as the underlying felony in felony murder.

Post-Baker litigation indicates that the court may not be taking quite as rigid a stance toward the felony-murder rule as Baker indicated. In Malone v. State, the defendant, indicted for felony murder, urged reconsideration of Baker because he claimed that it would preclude a charge on voluntary manslaughter in his trial, because even in a voluntary manslaughter there usually is an aggravated assault which would make the killing felony murder under Baker. The defendant, therefore, argued that Baker would effectively eliminate voluntary manslaughter as an authorized verdict in homicide cases. Voluntary manslaughter is, by definition, an intentional killing which results in death. Thus, there will always be an aggravated assault included in a voluntary manslaughter and, the defendant argued, every voluntary manslaughter will become a felony murder.

The Malone court, however, refused to overrule Baker, asserting that the defendant's argument proceeded from an incorrect premise. The court held that where the killing was based upon a serious provocation and heat of passion, a voluntary manslaughter instruction was permissible under a felony-murder indictment and that voluntary manslaughter would be an authorized verdict. The reasoning was rather sparse and consisted only in the court's flat statement that the crime of voluntary manslaughter involves a less culpable mental state than the "real or imputed" malice which the felony-murder doctrine is designed to supply in a murder prosecution.

The fact is, however, that an aggravated assault still occurs in every voluntary manslaughter. The court never directly addressed that fact and, it can be concluded, must have held that there are two grades of aggravated assault: one which is not in the heat of passion which can support a felony-murder conviction and another which is in the heat of passion which cannot support a felony-murder conviction. Under this approach not all felonies can support a felony-murder conviction, despite the apparently conflicting rule of Baker. Another exception to the apparently broad rule of Baker was also suggested by Malone when it said that voluntary manslaughter itself was not a felony which could support a felony-murder conviction. Of course, if the contrary were true there could never be a voluntary manslaughter conviction because all such crimes would be felony murder.

The concerns expressed in Baker and Malone discussed above were alleviated by the Georgia Supreme Court in Edge v. State. In Edge, the court recognized the unfairness of this state's "strict liability" felony-murder rule, which allows the "bootstrapping" of an assault charge to support a felony-murder conviction, in those instances where the killings could have been reduced, on the ground of mitigation, to manslaughter. Instead of adopting the "merger doctrine" in toto to rectify this unfairness, which would preclude felony murder based on any aggravated assault by the defendant on the victim, the court adopted a modified version of the doctrine, which would preclude a felony murder conviction only where it would prevent an otherwise warranted verdict of voluntary manslaughter. Stated another way, if there is but one assault and that assault could form the basis of either felony murder or voluntary manslaughter, a verdict of felony murder may not be returned if the jury finds that the assault is mitigated by provocation and passion. This modified "merger doctrine" applies only where the aggravated assault is perpetrated against the homicide victim and is an integral part of the killing and where there is evidence that the aggravated assault was provoked by the homicide victim. The modified "merger doctrine" does not apply where the evidence shows that the aggravated assault resulting in the victim's death was directed against someone other than the homicide victim. Nor does the doctrine apply where the evidence shows that the underlying felony, such as armed robbery, was independent of the killing itself.

iii. Jury Instructions

The court in Edge v. State also stated that its holding would require some precision in the charge to the jury where the evidence would authorize a conviction for felony murder or voluntary manslaughter. A sequential charge requiring the jury to consider voluntary manslaughter only if it has considered and found the defendant not guilty of malice murder and felony murder would not be appropriate. Instead, the trial court should instruct the jury so as to ensure adequate consideration of charges for both forms of homicide. Sequential charges on underlying felonies that are independent of the killing itself and on lesser included offenses are not prohibited under the rationale in *Edge*.

If a trial court has given a sequential charge to the jury in violation of *Edge*, a defendant who has reserved his right to raise objections to the jury charge on appeal is entitled to a new trial. However, if the sequential charge given was requested by the defendant, he cannot assert on appeal that the charge was erroneous. Even if the defendant's trial preceded *Edge*, he cannot subsequently contend that it was error to give a sequential charge if he previously failed to comply with the applicable procedures for securing review of that issue. Even though the trial court has given an improper sequential charge to the jury, if it is evident from the record that the verdict of felony murder was the product of adequate consideration of charges for both forms of homicide rather than of any prejudicial emphasis communicated by the improper sequential charge, the defendant's conviction for felony murder will be upheld.

With the jury's consideration of malice, it must also consider the element of provocation. If the jury finds that the defendant committed the homicide with malice, it necessarily finds that the element of provocation does not exist or is insufficient to overcome the jury's finding of malice whether express or implied. With this finding of malice, voluntary manslaughter is eliminated from the jury's consideration, rendering any sequential charge given by a trial court in connection with felony murder and voluntary manslaughter harmless error. Likewise, if the evidence does not authorize consideration of voluntary manslaughter as a possible verdict, a sequential charge does not amount to reversible error.

Even absent an objection to a sequential charge or to a jury's verdict finding a defendant guilty of felony murder, appellate review of the trial court's failure to apply the modified merger rule cannot be waived, because a conviction which should have been merged into another as a matter of fact or law is void.

A felony which is an included offense of another felony which is charged in an indictment may constitute the underlying felony upon which conviction of felony murder may be grounded, given adequate proof and correct jury instructions. Correct jury instructions must identify the included offense as a felony and must specify its essential elements, as well as the elements of felony murder. Unless an adequate instruction on the included offense is given to the jury, that offense cannot serve as a basis for a felony murder conviction.

When the language of an indictment charges the defendant with causing the death of the victim "by shooting," it raises the possibility of aggravated assault both with a deadly weapon and intent to murder. As the language of such an indictment would be sufficient to put a defendant on notice of both grounds for aggravation, jury instructions that aggravated assault, as the underlying felony for a felony murder count, could be established with either "intent to murder" or use of a "deadly weapon" would be proper.

Since there is only one offense of murder which can be committed **either** with malice aforethought **or** while in the commission of a felony, a trial court's use of the term "murder" in connection with its instructions on a felony murder charge would not be error.

There is no requirement to define the word "homicide" in instructing the jury on felony murder.

iv. Indictments

In order to satisfy due process when an indictment charges a compound felony such as felony murder, the count charging the compound offense must contain the essential elements of the predicate offense, or the indictment must contain a separate count charging the predicate offense completely, or the indictment must elsewhere allege facts showing how the compound offense was committed.

The defendant need not be charged with the independent crime of aggravated assault against the murder victim in order to be convicted of felony murder while in the commission of an aggravated assault.

An indictment that omits an essential element of the predicate felony in a felony murder count can nonetheless satisfy the requirements of due process as long as the indictment charges the predicate felony completely in a separate count.

v. Multiple Underlying Felonies

While a defendant may not be sentenced for two murders where there is only one victim, where there are multiple underlying felonies, the state is not required to elect between them when charging the defendant with felony murder. The appropriate manner for charging felony murder in instances where more than one underlying felony is alleged is to indict for one count of felony murder, and enumerate the multiple underlying felonies.

Where a defendant has been charged in a single count with felony murder based on multiple underlying felonies and the jury has returned a general verdict of guilty on the felony murder count without delineating which of the underlying felonies served as the predicate for the felony murder conviction, the defendant's conviction must be set aside. However, if the trial court has entered a judgment of conviction and sentence only on the verdict finding the defendant guilty of malice murder, any issue concerning the felony murder count is moot.

The fact that the jury has acquitted the defendant for the underlying felony committed against the victim does not affect the validity of its guilty verdict for felony murder, where the defendant has been found guilty of multiple underlying felonies committed against others during the same incident.

vi. Sentencing

If a jury returns guilty verdicts of felony murder, voluntary manslaughter, and aggravated assault, in the absence of an objection to the form of the verdicts, a trial court is not under a duty to sentence the defendant for the crime of felony murder. The trial court may find as a matter of law that the jury's finding of voluntary manslaughter precludes a conviction on the felony murder charge and may sentence the defendant on the voluntary manslaughter charge.

A trial court may not sentence a defendant for felony murder and voluntary manslaughter based on the same underlying aggravated assault. By definition, a defendant found guilty of voluntary manslaughter lacks the mens rea required to commit felony murder in that any malice which would have been imputed from the underlying felony has been mitigated by the provocation which induced the crime of voluntary manslaughter.

Where there is only one murder victim, it is incorrect to sentence the defendant twice for felony murder. The judgment of conviction and sentence on one of the felony murder counts must be vacated. Once this count is vacated, the underlying felony is no longer merged as a matter of law, and the trial court should sentence the defendant for the underlying felony.

When a jury finds a defendant guilty of two counts of felony murder involving the same victim, it is within the trial court's discretion to choose to merge one underlying felony rather than the other into the felony murder count for which the defendant is sentenced, thus leaving the other underlying felony for independent sentencing.

The trial court's imposition of illegal, multiple sentences for the felony murder of only one victim is not an ambiguity in a jury verdict that must be resolved by the Georgia Supreme Court's imposition of a rule of law. Rather, it is an error of law which is best resolved by the exercise of the trial court's sentencing discretion. Thus, such a case must be remanded to the trial court so that it may exercise its discretion in determining which felony murder conviction sentence is to be imposed.

b. Causation

It is clear that there are other judicial limitations on the Georgia felony-murder rule. In 1992, the Georgia Supreme Court decided to limit the application of the rule to any felony that is either dangerous per se or that, by the attendant circumstances, creates a foreseeable risk of death. The court also noted that under these circumstances there must be a sufficient connection between the felony and the homicide in order to trigger the rule. This indicates the court's willingness to impose a causation requirement into the felony-murder rule. The statute itself does not explicitly do so.

In Durden v. State, the court dealt with a causation issue in the context of a felony-murder conviction. The defendant was committing a burglary when the store owner came upon the scene. There was an exchange of gunfire, but the owner was not injured. However, he died soon afterward of cardiac arrest. The defendant argued that his felony-murder conviction was unauthorized because he administered no physical injury to the victim or, alternatively, that there was no causation demonstrated.

The court affirmed the conviction, rejecting the early common law requirement of physical harm as a prerequisite for criminal responsibility for homicide and finding causation. The court pointed out that the medical examiner had testified that the cardiac arrest had been caused by the victim's small coronary arteries and the stress of events. The court applied the traditional test of causation and found that the jury was authorized to find beyond a reasonable doubt that the felony had caused the death of the victim.

In Minor v. State, the defendant was convicted of felony murder with the underlying felony being rape. About three hours after having been raped, and while being questioned in her home by the police, the victim collapsed and died from a heart attack. The victim had a severely diseased heart and was significantly overweight at the time of the rape. The state's experts testified both that the victim had in fact been raped, as opposed to having had consensual sex, and that the rape had caused the heart attack. The court concluded that a rational trier of fact could have been persuaded beyond a reasonable doubt that the defendant's sexual intercourse with the victim was not consensual and that the victim's heart attack was caused by the stress of the rape.

In State v. Crane, the defendants were indicted for felony murder where the victim was a co-felon in the attempted burglary who was actually killed by the homeowner whose home was the target of the burglary. While other jurisdictions are split on the issue, this was a case of first impression in Georgia and the Georgia Supreme Court held that the felony-murder rule is not applicable in this situation. The focus was on the statutory requirement in the felony-murder provision of § 16-5-1(c) that the defendant "cause" the death of the victim. The court said that this provision could require either direct causation by the defendant or indirect causation. To cover the instant situation, the court said, it would have to adopt a reading which permitted indirect causation to be sufficient. The court held that while it would favor such a construction, it was bound by the general principle favoring the strict construction of penal statutes against the state and in favor of the accused. The court thus affirmed the dismissal of the indictments by the lower court and left the question of the scope of the rule to the General Assembly.

The construction that the court adopted in Crane was applied in a situation involving the death of an innocent bystander. In Hill v. State, the defendant shot and killed a police officer in a gunfight. The officer, responding to the defendant's shot, returned fire and killed a bystander. Since it was clear that the defendant did not directly cause the bystander's death, the court held that his felony murder conviction had to be set aside.

Crane and Hill were distinguished by the Georgia Supreme Court in Scott v. State. In this case, while the defendant and the victim were in the process of detonating an explosive device for the purpose of destroying public property, the device exploded and killed the victim. The court held that the defendant's conduct came squarely within the language of the felony-murder statute, because the victim's death resulted from conduct of the defendant and the victim who were acting in concert with a felonious purpose. Similarly, in Vasser v. State, the court held that the defendant could be convicted of felony murder, although he had no knowledge of the victim's involvement in the arson, because the victim was acting in concert with a codefendant in committing the crime when his death occurred.

In Hyman v. State, the defendant falsely told police that his fugitive friend was not in his house. When a police officer looked into a closet in the house, the defendant's friend fatally shot the officer. Applying the principles enunciated in State v. Crane and Hill v. State the Georgia Supreme Court held that the murder in this case was only indirectly attributable to the defendant's false statement. Rather, the defendant's friend directly caused the officer's death, and there was no evidence whatsoever that the defendant was acting in concert with his friend or was otherwise a party to the actual shooting. Because the defendant did not directly cause the officer's death, the court reversed his conviction for felony murder.

In State v. Cross, the defendant was indicted for felony murder with the underlying felony being cruelty to children. The indictment alleged that the defendant's shaking of the child victim resulted in injuries that caused the child's death over a year later. The court found no merit in the defendant's contention that the victim must die during the commission of the underlying felony. Instead, the court held that the felony-murder statute requires that the death need only be **caused** by an injury which occurred during the res gestae of the felony.

In McCoy v. State, the defendant was indicted for felony murder and arson in the first degree. The court held that the evidence was sufficient to show that a fireman's death was directly attributable to the defendant's felonious conduct in deliberately setting a fire. The fireman came to the scene as a direct result of the fire, the protective cover over the well into which the fireman fell was burned away by the fire, and the fireman died as a result of breathing the concentrated smoke from the fire.

Where two persons are engaged in mutual combat and as a result of their assault upon each other a bystander dies, both are guilty of felony murder. In such a case, transferred intent has no applicability to felony murder, which does not require proof of intent, transferred or otherwise, as an element of the homicide.

The Supreme Court of the United States has ruled on the permissibility of the death sentence for the nontriggerman in a felony-murder case. In Enmund v. Florida, the Court was dealing with a rather familiar type of case in which two felony accomplices are charged with felony murder in a case based on the killing by one of them during the commission of a felony. The defendant, the nonkilling accomplice, argued that the death penalty to which he was sentenced was unconstitutional in violation of the Eighth Amendment. In a 5-4 decision, the Court vacated the death sentence because there was an "absence of proof that [the defendant] killed or attempted to kill" and the sentence was handed down "regardless of whether [the defendant] intended or contemplated that life would be taken [in the felony] . . . ." The narrowness of the holding ought to be emphasized. It seems clear that the Court was not ruling out the possibility that a death sentence would be constitutional where the nontriggerman intended the death of the victim or anticipated that lethal force would be involved in the underlying felony.

Thus, the Supreme Court of the United States held in Tison v. Arizona that the reckless disregard for human life implicit in knowingly engaging in criminal activities known to carry a grave risk of death represents a highly culpable mental state, a mental state that may be taken into account in making a capital sentencing judgment when that conduct causes its natural, though also not inevitable, lethal result. Major participation in the felony committed, combined with reckless indifference to human life, is sufficient to satisfy the criminal culpability requirement found in Enmund v. Florida.

c. "In Commission of"

The phrase "in the commission of" also may prove to be a limitation on the felony murder rule. In Jones v. State, the court held that a killing which took place after the "technical" completion of the underlying felony could be indictable as felony murder if it took place within the felony's res gestae. Also, in State v. Cross, the court held that the victim need not die during the commission of the underlying felony. The death need only be caused by an injury which occurred during the felony's res gestae. While ambiguous, the phrase "in the commission of" certainly indicates that at some point the felony's commission will end for purposes of invoking the felony-murder rule. It has been suggested that an analysis of whether the res gestae is completed should concentrate on the "time, place and continuity of action" of the underlying felony.

In Collier v. State, the court was faced with the question of when a felony terminates for the purposes of the felony-murder rule. In its first detailed analysis of this question, the court canvassed authority from other jurisdictions and concluded that an arrest would terminate the felony, but only if it was one where the custody was "complete" and the surrender was "complete and continuous." The fact that post-crime pursuit is delayed does not terminate the felony. Generally, the court said, an underlying felony continues during the escape phase of the felony if there is continuous pursuit immediately organized. The felony terminates when the defendant has arrived at a place of seeming security or when pursuit ceases. On the facts, the court found that the jury could have believed that the felony had not yet ceased. The case involved a homicide of a police officer who arrested the defendant after his commission of an armed robbery. The court also reiterated the familiar rule that conviction of both the underlying felony as well as felony murder is improper.

d. Party to Crime

A defendant who helps his accomplice shoot the victim and who then obtains the gun from the accomplice and shoots the victim again may be convicted of felony murder. Since the defendant becomes culpable for the crime once he intentionally aids or abets his accomplice, the mere fact that the victim may have already been dead when the defendant shot him would be of no consequence.

A person who commits a felony may be convicted of felony murder for a homicide that results during the commission of that felony, without regard to whether the person intended to kill the victim or directly acted to commit the murder.

3. Relationship Between Malice Murder and Felony Murder

In Georgia, a defendant may be convicted of an offense embraced by the allegations of the indictment if the evidence supports such a charge. Therefore, to the extent that a malice murder indictment alleges the commission of a felony in addition to the killing and there is evidence to support that allegation, the jury can be instructed on and is authorized to return a verdict of felony murder. Thus, in Cromer v. State, the Georgia Supreme Court wrote that "[t]here was no error in charging on felony murder under an indictment for malice murder." The court cited the *Baker* case discussed above to reject the contention that felony murder is an inappropriate charge where the only felony suggested by the evidence is the aggravated assault which directly led to the death.

A defendant's claim of error in the underlying felony portion of a felony murder charge would be moot if he has been convicted of malice murder.

A malice murder can be committed in the commission of an armed robbery where the unlawful intent required for malice murder exists. A party concerned in the commission of that armed robbery may be charged with and convicted of malice murder. In order to convict a party to an armed robbery under a malice murder indictment, the intent that must be attributed to the party so as to render him guilty of malice murder is the accomplice's malicious intent to commit the murder, not the accomplice's intent to commit the armed robbery. Thus, a trial court must charge the jury that to find a party to an armed robbery guilty of malice murder it must find that the accomplice who shot and killed the robbery victim did so while acting with the unlawful intention to kill, i.e., with malice. To instruct the jury that it must find the party guilty of malice murder upon a finding that the accomplice murdered the victim while acting with the intent to commit armed robbery, i.e., with the intent necessary for felony murder improperly instructs the jury to return a verdict of guilty of a type of murder not charged in the indictment or included as an offense in the jury instructions.

An indictment for a single homicide which may have been committed in more than one way can take one of two recognized forms. One such form is indictment by means of a single count which contains alternative allegations as to the various ways in which the homicide may have been committed. In addition to this single count form of indictment, there is the alternative counts form in which each count alleges that the defendant committed the same homicide in one of a number of separate ways. The Georgia Supreme Court has held that an indictment on alternative counts does not constitute an inherently prejudicial form of pleading.

When both malice and felony murder are alleged as alternative and separate counts, a felony murder count that alleges that the causing of bodily harm was malicious, not that the commission of the complete crime of aggravated battery was malicious, is not merely another allegation of malice murder couched in felony murder language. A defendant might have had malice in the form of the intent to cause bodily harm with no malice in the form of the intent to kill, and yet death might still occur; in such a case the defendant would be guilty of felony murder but not malice murder. Accordingly, such an indictment alleging both malice murder and felony murder predicated on an aggravated battery does not allege malice murder twice but, instead, properly charges malice murder and felony murder as distinct, alternative counts.

An indictment for both malice murder and felony murder does not place an unfair burden on the defendant to have to defend against two separate crimes, where the trial court's jury instructions make clear that while the state may seek a murder conviction under alternate theories, the defendant can be convicted of only one count of murder. There is no rule forcing the state to elect between malice and felony murder before presenting the case to the jury.

It is clear, however, that the rule against multiple convictions embodied in § 16-1-7(a) forbids a conviction on the same set of facts of both felony murder and malice murder. Thus, in Pressley v. State, the court held that where there is only one victim and the jury returns verdicts of guilty of malice murder and felony murder the latter conviction must be vacated. In Smith v. State, the court held that when the elements of malice and an underlying felony both exist in a murder case, the law does not preclude verdicts of guilty of both malice and felony murder. Yet where there is a single victim, the defendant may be sentenced on either but not both. In Matthews v. State, the court held that since there was only one murder victim and the defendant was found guilty of both counts, i.e., malice and felony murder, the trial court correctly ruled that the two counts merged, and sentenced the defendant to only one life sentence. Even if the jury erroneously imposes sentences for both malice and felony murder, a new sentencing trial is not required because the void felony murder sentence does not affect the validity of malice murder sentence. In Barker v. State, the court held that because there were only two homicides and the evidence supported the convictions for malice murder, the felony murder convictions merged into the malice murder convictions by operation of law. Thus, the judgments of conviction and sentences on the felony murder counts had to be vacated.

When valid guilty verdicts are returned on both alternative counts of malice and felony murder, the alternative felony murder count is vacated by operation of § 16-1-7. Since the felony murder conviction has been statutorily vacated, there is no felony murder count into which the underlying felony can merge. Thus, it is proper for the trial court to treat the felony murder count as merely surplusage and then to proceed to determine whether a separate sentence on the underlying felony may be authorized for lack of merger, as a matter of fact, into the extant malice murder conviction.

Verdicts are mutually exclusive where a guilty verdict on one count logically excludes a finding of guilt on the other. Thus, the rule against mutually exclusive verdicts applies to multiple guilty verdicts which cannot be logically reconciled. The rule is not implicated where verdicts of guilty of felony murder and not guilty of malice murder are returned.

Guilty verdicts for malice murder and felony murder are not mutually exclusive as a matter of law. A guilty verdict for felony murder does not constitute a finding that the murder was committed without malice aforethought, but that the murder was committed while in the commission of another felony offense "irrespective of malice." In other words, the presence or absence of malice is irrelevant to the commission of felony murder. Nor are the two verdicts mutually exclusive as a matter of fact where the evidence authorizes the jury to conclude that the defendant committed the murder while in the commission of a felony but also acted with malice aforethought.

Since a jury's inability to agree on a verdict is not itself a verdict, a verdict which shows "no agreement" on a malice murder count and guilty on a felony murder count does not constitute a mutually exclusive verdict.

An acquittal of malice murder does not preclude a conviction of felony murder.

In *Milam v. State*, the Georgia Supreme Court abolished the rule that inconsistent verdicts in irreconcilable conflict in criminal cases warranted reversal, because it is not generally within the court's power to make inquiries into the jury's deliberations or to speculate about the reasons for any inconsistency between guilty and not guilty verdicts. The court has, however, recognized an exception to the abolition of this rule, i.e., when instead of being left to speculate about the unknown motivations of the jury, the appellate record makes clear the jury's reasoning why it found the defendant not guilty of one of the charges. In such a case, the court need not speculate whether the jury verdict was the product of lenity or of legal error, and the rules regarding inconsistent verdicts are not applicable. The court may then decide whether the jury's finding of not guilty of one charge requires vacation of the judgment entered on the guilty verdicts returned on the other charges in the case. In *Turner v. State*, the court found that as both § 16-3-20 and the trial court's repeated instruction to the jury made clear, the jury's finding of justification as to the malice murder count applied to the felony murder and aggravated assault charges based on the same conduct. In light of the jury's express finding of justification, the court held that it was error for the trial court to enter judgment on the jury verdicts finding the defendant guilty of felony murder and aggravated assault.

4. Relationship Between Murder and Other Crimes.

Important Notice about Repudiation of Actual or Same Evidence Test: The Georgia Supreme Court repudiated the actual evidence test in *Drinkard v. Walker*, 281 Ga. 211, 636 S.E.2d 530 (2006), because it found this test to be inconsistent with the statutory framework governing the prohibition against multiple convictions for included offenses in Georgia. This inconsistency resulted in years of confusion and unpredictable results. In its place, the court adopted the required evidence test and overruled any prior case law that is inconsistent with it. Thus, any prior case law applying the actual evidence test is no longer controlling and should not be relied upon to determine whether one offense is included in another under § 16-1-6(1). The discussion of such case law is included below only insofar as it may still be applicable to pending prosecutions that arose before the Drinkard decision. See MULTIPLE CONVICTIONS, II. Tests to Determine Presence of Multiple Convictions, for a complete discussion of the Drinkard decision.

On the trial of a murder case, if there be any evidence, however slight, as to whether the offense is murder or voluntary manslaughter, an instruction as to the law of both offenses should be given to the jury. If the evidence in a trial on a murder indictment indicates the presence of such facts as would make the killing voluntary or involuntary manslaughter, a conviction for the appropriate manslaughter crime is authorized under § 16-1-6.

It is also clear that in a felony-murder indictment the underlying felony is a lesser included offense, and there can be a conviction of only the felony if the evidence supports such a finding. It is equally clear, however, that because the felony in a felony-murder case is a lesser included offense of the murder, the rule against multiple convictions (§ 16-1-7) forbids conviction of both felony murder and the underlying felony. However, when the underlying felony is committed upon one victim and the felony murder charged in another count in the same indictment is committed upon another victim, the underlying felony does not merge with the felony murder conviction and it is proper for the trial court to enter convictions and sentences for both the felony murder and the underlying felony.

Where the evidence shows completion only of the greater offense of felony murder, that is, there is no evidence from which the jury can conclude that death resulted from a cause other than the aggravated assault inflicted by the defendant, the trial court is not required to offer aggravated assault to the jury as a lesser option.

In felony murder cases, trial courts are not constitutionally required to instruct juries on lesser related homicide offenses that are not lesser included offenses of the felony murder charge.

Where two or more felonies are involved in a felony-murder case, only one felony is required to support a felony-murder conviction, and only one felony need be merged with that conviction. Prior to 1993, in order to determine which of two or more felonies should have merged with the felony-murder conviction when the jury failed to specify the underlying felony, the Georgia Supreme Court applied the "chain of circumstances" analysis to hold that the initial felony which began the "chain of circumstances" leading to the victim's death merged with the murder conviction. In Thompson v. State, the court rejected this analysis as being purely speculative in determining what in fact the jury intended as the underlying felony. Now, where it is unclear which of two or more felonies is the underlying felony for a felony murder conviction, the trial court must merge the most severe (in terms of potential punishment).

A defendant may be convicted of an offense included in the underlying felony charged in a felony-murder indictment. Thus, if the evidence would authorize a finding that the accused committed an offense "included" in the underlying felony charged in a felony murder indictment and if that included offense is a misdemeanor, then a guilty verdict as to felony-grade involuntary manslaughter would be authorized.

The verdicts of guilty of felony murder and involuntary manslaughter are not mutually exclusive as a matter of law. Nor are they as a matter of fact where the jury can conclude from the defendant's actions that he committed a felony against one person which would support the felony murder and that he acted recklessly toward another person, and therefore, is guilty of involuntary manslaughter as well.

A mutually exclusive verdict may be rendered in a particular case, however, where the offenses or acts alleged in the indictment as underlying the felony murder and involuntary manslaughter counts reflect that the jury, in order to find the defendant guilty on both counts, necessarily reached two positive findings of fact that cannot logically mutually exist. For instance, in Jackson v. State the Georgia Supreme Court concluded that the jury's verdict finding the defendant guilty of felony murder predicated upon a § 16-5-20(a)(1) aggravated assault on the victim was mutually exclusive of a verdict finding him guilty of involuntary manslaughter predicated upon reckless conduct in regard to the same act involving the same victim at the same instance of time. The jury convicted the defendant of killing the victim with criminal intent **and** with criminal negligence, that is, of killing both with and without an intention to do so. The two verdicts were obviously mutually exclusive. Because it was both legally and logically impossible to convict the defendant of both felony murder and involuntary manslaughter, the court reversed both mutually exclusive convictions and ordered a new trial.

The rule against mutually exclusive verdicts applies to multiple guilty verdicts which cannot be logically reconciled. The rule is not implicated where verdicts of not guilty by reason of insanity of malice murder and guilty but mentally ill of the remaining offenses are returned. Moreover, the fact that the verdicts might be factually inconsistent is of no avail to the defendant. It is well settled that factual inconsistencies in verdicts rendered in the same case do not afford a ground for setting aside a conviction.

Under § 16-1-7(a)(1), it is proper to convict and sentence a defendant for that crime which includes all others. Since a misdemeanor can be an included crime in a felony, misdemeanor-involuntary manslaughter can be an included crime in felony murder. Where the evidence shows that a homicide occurred in the commission of both a felony and an included misdemeanor, there is no inconsistency or ambiguity in verdicts of guilt as to misdemeanor-involuntary manslaughter and felony murder. Accordingly, it is not error to merge the included misdemeanor into the felony and then to merge the underlying felony into the felony murder count. When the misdemeanor merges into the felony, the predicate for the defendant's conviction for involuntary manslaughter is eliminated, but the felony remains as the basis for the defendant's conviction for murder. Thus, the trial court may properly enter the judgment of conviction and sentence on the jury's verdict finding the defendant guilty of the offense of felony murder.

Where the acts alleged in the indictment fit the requirements for both felony murder and vehicular homicide, the defendant may be prosecuted for each crime. Although the defendant may not be properly sentenced for each crime, that does not prevent his trial on both charges.

When valid guilty verdicts are returned on both alternative counts of felony murder and vehicular homicide, the alternative vehicular homicide count is vacated by operation of § 16-1-7. Since the vehicular homicide conviction has been statutorily vacated, there is no vehicular homicide count into which the underlying traffic offense can merge. Thus, it is proper for the trial court to treat the vehicular homicide count as merely surplusage and then to proceed to determine whether a separate sentence on the underlying traffic offense may be authorized for lack of merger, as a matter of fact, into the extant felony murder conviction. This analysis applies as well when valid guilty verdicts are returned on both alternative counts of felony murder and involuntary manslaughter.

Where felony murder and vehicular homicide in the first degree are based on separate and distinct underlying actions, it is neither legally nor logically impossible to convict the defendant of both offenses.

There is one situation in which the rule against multiple convictions prevents conviction of both malice murder and an underlying felony. This is illustrated in Burke v. State and involves the use of the conspiracy/complicity doctrine. In Burke, the defendant was convicted of the malice murder of the victim of an armed robbery. He, however, was not the actual killer and his liability for the armed robbery was premised on the fact that he was a co-conspirator with the actual perpetrator. Under these circumstances, the court held that the malice of the killer was properly imputed to the defendant because the defendant was the killer's co-conspirator in the armed robbery and the malice murder "was a probable consequence of that armed robbery."

On these facts, however, because the defendant's malice murder conviction depended upon the participation in the armed robbery, the court ordered the defendant's armed robbery conviction vacated, finding that in this kind of case the latter was included in the former. Thus, the nontriggerman conspirator could have been convicted of only malice murder, while the actual triggerman could have been convicted of **both** the armed robbery **and** malice murder. This latter double conviction did not violate § 16-1-7(a) because the triggerman's malice murder conviction did not depend upon (and therefore did not include) participation in the armed robbery.

Robbery by force and malice murder are separate crimes which do not merge as a matter of law. Moreover, they do not merge as a matter of fact where each crime is proved by distinct elements absent from the proof of the other.

Because the intent relevant to a conviction for felony murder is the underlying intent for the felony and because intent to kill, as well as mitigating factors such as provocation and passion, are irrelevant to that intent, a jury's verdict of guilty of felony murder does not constitute a finding that the defendant did not act with provocation and passion in assaulting the victim and does not conflict with the jury's verdict of guilty of voluntary manslaughter. Under these circumstances, the verdicts are not mutually exclusive. A trial court may not sentence a defendant for felony murder and voluntary manslaughter based on the same underlying aggravated assault. By definition, a defendant found guilty of voluntary manslaughter lacks the mens rea required to commit felony murder in that any malice which would have been imputed from the underlying felony has been mitigated by the provocation which induced the crime of voluntary manslaughter. Moreover, a trial court may not sentence a defendant for both offenses because there is only one victim. To convict and sentence the defendant for both offenses would improperly subject him to multiple convictions and punishments for one crime.

In Ward v. State, the court held that the final clause of the feticide statute does not preclude a defendant's conviction for both murder of the mother and feticide.

Malice murder and kidnapping with bodily injury do not merge as a matter of law, and they do not merge as a matter of fact since there is no requirement that the state prove the existence of malice aforethought to establish the charge of kidnapping with bodily injury, though malice aforethought must be proven for the murder charge, and there is no requirement that the state prove the victim is unlawfully abducted to establish the murder charge, though such unlawful abduction must be proven to establish kidnapping with bodily injury.

Where there is no evidence whatsoever that the defendant's beating of the victim was a separate act but rather was part and parcel of the collective fatal attack on the victim, neither battery nor simple battery are lesser included offenses of malice murder as a matter of fact. Even if battery and simple battery are considered to be lesser included offenses, when the evidence shows completion only of the greater offense of malice murder, it is unnecessary for the trial court to charge on the lesser offenses.

If the evidence used to prove the defendant committed an aggravated battery is the same as that used to prove he committed a malice murder, the aggravated battery merges into the malice murder as a matter of fact, and a separate judgment of conviction and sentence for the aggravated battery should be vacated.

If the aggravated battery of the victim is independent of the malicious act causing the victim's death, the aggravated battery does not merge with the malice murder as a matter of fact. Likewise, if the aggravated assault of the victim is independent of the act causing the victim's death, the aggravated assault does not merge into the malice murder as a matter of fact. Moreover, if, in order to establish that the defendant committed aggravated assault as pled in the indictment, the state is required to show not only that he shot the victim but that he did so with the intent to rob him, the aggravated assault would not be established by proof of the same or less than all the facts required to establish proof of malice murder. Thus, the two crimes would not merge as a matter of fact. However, if the aggravated assault and murder of the victim arise out of the same incident, a defendant's conviction on the aggravated assault charge would merge into the murder conviction.

Verdicts of not guilty on a murder count and guilty on an aggravated assault count are neither inconsistent nor mutually exclusive.

Because malice murder does not include all of the essential elements of the offense of cruelty to children, the latter is not an included offense of malice murder, and a conviction for cruelty to children would not be authorized under a malice murder count of an indictment. It follows that the refusal to give a requested charge on cruelty to children as an included offense of malice murder would not be error.

While a conviction for cruelty to children may be authorized as an included offense of felony murder, if the defendant is convicted of malice murder, the erroneous failure to charge cruelty to children as an included offense of felony murder would be harmless.

Because a defendant cannot be both a party to a crime and an accessory after the crime, a felony murder conviction is void as a matter of law when a jury convicts a defendant of hindering the apprehension of a criminal as a lesser included offense of murder.

5. Double Jeopardy

The grant of mistrial as to a count of murder does not prevent the state from trying the defendant again for murder and the lesser included offense of voluntary manslaughter, if the termination of trial was proper. If the jury is unable to reach a verdict on a murder count, the termination of the trial is not improper. In such a case, a second trial on both the charge of murder and the lesser included offense of voluntary manslaughter will not violate the defendant's right to be tried once for the same offense.

Where the jury has stated that they found the defendant not guilty of malice murder but were deadlocked as to the other offenses before them, the trial court's declaration of a mistrial does not terminate the original jeopardy to which the defendant was subjected for the other offenses. Rather, jeopardy for these offenses is continuing.

Thus, an acquittal on the indicted offense of malice murder would not bar retrial on the lesser included unindicted offense of voluntary manslaughter to which continuing jeopardy had attached in the first trial.

Where the jury was unable to reach a verdict on a felony murder count, with deadly weapon aggravated assault as the underlying felony, but was able to reach a verdict of acquittal on an aggravated assault with intent to rob count, if the verdict reflects that the jury intended to and did acquit the defendant solely on the charge of aggravated assault with intent to rob, the state's prosecution of the defendant for felony murder based on the separate underlying felony of deadly weapon aggravated assault is not barred as a successive prosecution in violation of the defendant's double jeopardy rights. Furthermore, unless it can be established that the jury necessarily found that the defendant did not assault the victim with a deadly weapon, the mere possibility that the jury may have done so does not bar the state's prosecution of the defendant for felony murder based on the deadly weapon aggravated assault.

When a trial court rules on a defendant's motion for new trial that the evidence was insufficient to warrant the imposition of a life sentence for a felony murder guilty verdict, the trial court is essentially stating that the evidence was insufficient to authorize the underlying felony murder guilty verdict itself. Since the trial court has found the evidence legally insufficient, the Double Jeopardy Clause precludes the further prosecution of the defendant for felony murder.

If a defendant is found guilty of both felony murder and the underlying felony, the conviction for the underlying felony merges with the felony murder conviction. However, it does not necessarily follow that double jeopardy bars retrial when a trial ends in an acquittal of felony murder and a mistrial on the underlying felony. The acquittal on the felony murder does not necessarily imply acquittal on the underlying felony. Thus, retrial on the underlying felony would be permissible under the doctrine of continuing jeopardy.

Although the statutory aggravating circumstances enumerated in § 17-10-30(b) may function as elements of the greater offense of capital murder for the limited purpose of implicating the constitutional right of trial by jury, they are not offenses, but rather they are procedural standards designed to control a jury's discretion in capital cases in order to ensure against capricious and arbitrary enforcement of the death penalty. Accordingly, aggravating circumstances are not offenses for purposes of the constitutional guarantee against double jeopardy. Therefore, the fact that a jury finds that the offenses of armed robbery and burglary are aggravating factors in sentencing a defendant for murder would not preclude separate convictions for committing those offenses.

Double-jeopardy protections are not triggered when the jury deadlocks at the defendant's first sentencing proceeding for murder and the trial court prescribes a sentence of life imprisonment pursuant to state law. The Double Jeopardy Clause is not implicated because neither the jury nor the judge has "acquitted" the defendant in this initial sentencing proceeding by entering findings sufficient to establish legal entitlement to the life sentence, i.e., findings that the state failed to prove one or more aggravating circumstances beyond a reasonable doubt. In such a case, where the defendant appeals the conviction and succeeds in having it set aside, jeopardy has not terminated, so that the life sentence imposed in connection with the initial conviction raises no double-jeopardy bar to a death sentence on retrial.

5.1. Statute of Limitations

Section § 17-3-1(a), in permitting the commencement of a prosecution for "murder" at any time, applies on its face to both malice murder and felony murder. The running of the statute of limitations on the underlying felony is irrelevant to a prosecution for felony murder. Furthermore, a felony murder conviction is not dependent upon the successful prosecution of the underlying felony. Thus, the expiration of the limitations period for the underlying felony does not preclude a prosecution for felony murder.

An indictment is not rendered defective because a felony murder count incorporates by reference an underlying felony count which must be stricken. Even if the underlying felony count is stricken due to the expiration of the statute of limitations, it remains a part of the indictment to the extent that it is incorporated into the felony murder count.

An underlying felony that is separately charged in an indictment for felony murder cannot remain as a separate count, where, ordinarily, it would be barred by the statute of limitations. Thus, where the limitations period for the felony has expired, the trial court's application of the statute of limitations to bar the underlying felony count would be correct. Nevertheless, a conviction for the underlying felony may ultimately be appropriate, as it is a lesser included offense of the felony murder count. Furthermore, although the underlying felony is no longer the subject of a separate count, it remains in the indictment as part of the felony murder count into which it is incorporated.

The statute of limitations applicable in a criminal case is that which relates to the offense charged in the indictment, and not to any minor offense included therein of which the accused might be found guilty. Thus, the statute of limitations applicable to the lesser included offense of voluntary manslaughter would not bar a conviction of that offense under an indictment for murder, since there is no statutory limitation as to indictments for murder.

6. Punishment

The punishment for murder is either life imprisonment, imprisonment for life without parole, or death.

Prior to 2009, a sentence of life without parole was an alternative sentence to a sentence of death, dependent upon the state also seeking the death penalty. The death penalty provisions had to be utilized in order to implement the life without parole sentencing option. Thus, the state was barred from seeking life without parole unless it had filed a notice of intent to seek the death penalty. In 2009, the General Assembly amended § 16-5-1(d) to allow a sentence of life without parole to be imposed for the offense of murder independent of a death penalty prosecution and repealed Code sections inconsistent with such sentencing.

In a jury trial, the determination of which penalty is administered is left to the jury in a separate proceeding conducted after the guilt/innocence phase of the trial. The sentencing procedure is discussed at length elsewhere and is beyond the scope of this book.

C. Manslaughter

Except for felony murder and homicide by vehicle, all nonmalicious criminal homicide is manslaughter. Georgia has two types of manslaughter: voluntary and involuntary. The former is the intentional "heat of passion" killing that is viewed as less criminal than murder, yet not quite justified enough to render it noncriminal. The latter includes unintentional killings of two varieties: (1) "criminal negligence" which is not to the level of "abandoned and malignant heart" murder and (2) killings arising out of "unlawful acts" which are not felonies so as to invoke the felony-murder rule.

1. Voluntary Manslaughter

Section 16-5-2 punishes those who cause a human being's death under "circumstances which would otherwise be murder" if the defendant's acts were the sole result of a "sudden, violent, and irresistible passion" which is caused by "serious provocation." The statute is careful to add, perhaps redundantly, that such a passion cannot be found if there was a "sufficient" cooling off time between the provocation and the killing.

Inherent in the statutory definition is the requirement that the killing be intentional. Thus, the only intentional criminal killings which are not malicious (and, therefore, murder) are those where the killer's intention is attributable to the finding of provocation envisioned by § 16-5-2 and the killing passion it creates. The killer's intention can be proved by circumstantial evidence. Whether the killing was intentional is a matter for the jury to determine. A claim by the killer that the killing was unintentional would establish the absence of an essential element of the offense. Without evidence of an intention to kill, an instruction on voluntary manslaughter would not be authorized.

Voluntary manslaughter can be seen as a crime which is a creature of compromise. The law, while refusing to find the defendant's act noncriminal or justified because it was in self-defense, defense of others, defense of property, etc., nevertheless makes some allowances for the frailties of human nature and punishes for less than murder. It is important, however, to recognize that while this is a "compromise" crime, it cannot always be offered to a murder jury as a compromise verdict. Evidence must exist to support a finding of provocation, passion, and lack of cooling off time. Theoretically, if there is not sufficient evidence to support such a finding, a voluntary manslaughter verdict will be overturned. Thus, if the only evidence before the jury is that which would support a murder conviction and that which would support an alibi or justification defense and there is no evidence to support a provocation claim, a voluntary manslaughter instruction is neither required or authorized. It has been held, however, that where there is no evidence supporting voluntary manslaughter but, rather, a murder conviction is "demanded" by the evidence, a voluntary manslaughter conviction will be permitted to stand. To this extent, therefore, the courts can be seen to be authorizing the use of a voluntary manslaughter verdict as a "compromise" verdict. In essence, the defendant on appeal is denied relief because things could have been worse for him.

a. Provocation

The statute requires proof of "serious" provocation sufficient to excite a deadly passion in a reasonable person. Whether the provocation was sufficient to excite a deadly passion in a particular defendant is of no moment. It is a question of law for the trial court to determine whether there is slight evidence that the defendant acted as the result of sudden, violent, and irresistible passion resulting from serious provocation in order to support a charge on voluntary manslaughter. The question of whether the provocation was serious enough is normally left to the trier of fact. However, certain patterns can be discerned from the cases with regard to provocation.

i. Mutual Combat

The provocation in most voluntary manslaughter cases is "mutual combat." Dating from an 1860 Georgia case, the mutual combat doctrine holds that if the parties were in a fight pursuant to a mutual intent to fight and were both armed, a killing resulting from the altercation will be no more than voluntary manslaughter. It is clear that both parties must have been at fault and "mutually willing to fight because of a sudden quarrel." Thus, if a defendant was acting merely to repel an unprovoked attack, this act is not mutual combat but self-defense which would, if the jury made such a finding, justify the killing. Thus, where there is no evidence that the victim was armed and the evidence showed that whatever force he used was in self-defense to ward off an unprovoked attack by the defendant, a voluntary manslaughter instruction is not required.

Where one shoots at another intending to kill him under such circumstances that the killing, if accomplished, would be voluntary manslaughter, but the shot misses the intended victim and accidentally kills an innocent third person, the homicide will be voluntary manslaughter. In Coker v. State, the Georgia Court of Appeals applied this principle to the facts of the case. The evidence showed that while the defendant was standing his ground to engage in mutual combat, shots were exchanged between his group and another group, and a shot fired by someone other than the defendant strayed and killed a bystander. This evidence was held sufficient to support the defendant's conviction for voluntary manslaughter as a party to the crime. However, in Willis v. State, the Georgia Supreme Court held that where two people were engaged in mutual combat and as a result of their assault upon each other a bystander died, both were guilty of felony murder.

It has been held that mutual combat is something more than a fist fight or scuffle. Thus, evidence that showed only that there had been an argument between the defendant and the deceased did not authorize a mutual combat voluntary manslaughter charge, although one court did approve a conviction where the evidence, in the court's analysis, showed only a "heated family disturbance." "Boxing" or fighting prior to a homicide does not constitute the kind of provocation which would warrant a charge on voluntary manslaughter.

Mutual combat is not a complete defense to a murder charge; rather, it is a defense which, if accepted by the jury, may result in reduction of the crime to voluntary manslaughter. However, if the defendant has withdrawn from the mutual combat and has effectively communicated his intent to do so but later kills in self-defense, then the killing may be justified and the defendant may be found not guilty. Jury instructions on these principles, rather than being conflicting, would adequately convey to the jury the duty to withdraw or retreat from mutual combat.

Because the mutual combat charge authorizes a jury to find the defendant guilty of voluntary manslaughter in lieu of murder, it is a charge that benefits a defendant and, as such, a convicted defendant's complaint that it was improper to give the charge would be without merit.

ii. Words Combined with Other Circumstances

It has long been the law in Georgia, as in most other states, that mere words cannot provide the kind of provocation which is the basis of a voluntary manslaughter conviction. A 1978 Georgia Supreme Court case held that this rule had formerly been "embedded in the . . . statutory law of Georgia" and that this rule was still a part of § 16-5-2. As one court wrote, the "indignation may be great, and the passion may be strong; but if aroused by words alone, they are insufficient to . . . reduce a homicide from murder to manslaughter." It has been held, however, that words can be combined with other circumstances to justify a killing. It would seem, therefore, that words could be combined with other circumstances so as to be sufficient provocation for voluntary manslaughter.

In 1988, the Georgia Supreme Court held that although the statutory law of Georgia no longer contained the proposition found in the Code of 1933 that "[i]n all cases of voluntary manslaughter, there must be some actual assault upon the person killing, or an attempt by the person killed to commit a serious personal injury on the person killing," the proposition nonetheless remained a part of Georgia's law of voluntary manslaughter.

iii. Physical Contact by Victim

Physical contact by the victim has been deemed sufficient to raise the issue of voluntary manslaughter, as in Butts v. State, where the victim slapped the defendant. In Addison v. State, a severe slap on the head was held to raise the question of voluntary manslaughter and, where there was a previous history of threats exchanged between the defendant and the victim and the victim had dated the defendant's wife, a bumping of the defendant's car by the victim along with a rush toward the car by the victim was held to authorize a voluntary manslaughter conviction.

In most cases where the victim has committed a battery on the defendant, it will be urged by the defendant that the killing was justified in self-defense. The crucial distinction here, at the intersection between justifiable and criminal homicide, is the motive with which the defendant acts. If he is acting out of passion or anger it will be voluntary manslaughter, while if he is acting out of a motive to prevent injury it will be self-defense. Whether the defendant acted in the heat of passion or in self-defense is a matter for the jury to determine. It should also be noted that the fear engendered by danger can be sufficient provocation to excite the passion necessary for voluntary manslaughter.

It is readily seen that the defendant's motive will often be a close question, and a jury verdict for voluntary manslaughter will usually be left undisturbed on appeal. In White v. State, the court held that a voluntary manslaughter verdict will be supported where the jury can conclude that the defendant acted out of a fear of an offense "less than a felony." This is because the self-defense defense of § 16-3-21 authorizes only a force reasonable under the circumstances and a killing can never be reasonable if the victim's offense is only that of a crime less than a felony. Of course, simple battery is such an offense. Thus, if the only reasonable fear that a defendant had was that of a simple battery, self-defense is not present and voluntary manslaughter is authorized.

iv. Adulterous Conduct

Adultery as a provocation has been held not only to reduce a killing from murder to manslaughter but to justify a killing, according to the "unwritten law." Thus, in Henderson v. State, the Court of Appeals held that killing a paramour in order to prevent adultery would be justifiable homicide, although killing the spouse would not be so since it would terminate the marriage. The Supreme Court of Georgia in Burger v. State, however, described this traditional rule as "uncivilized" and held that an instruction on justifiable homicide in the killing of a spouse or paramour should not be given. The *Burger* court, however, left open the possibility that, on the facts of a particular case, adultery might be sufficient provocation as to support a voluntary manslaughter verdict. In Brooks v. State, the court noted that although the victim used words to make the defendant aware of her adultery, it was the victim's adulterous conduct, rather than her words describing that conduct, which served as sufficient provocation authorizing a charge on voluntary manslaughter.

It is submitted that the *Burger* holding with regard to adultery ought to govern trial court instructions and appellate court analysis in all voluntary manslaughter cases. Rather than establish categorical rules that certain fact situations do or do not show sufficient provocation, the court should grant juries a fairly free rein in these cases and should take the issue of provocation from the jury only in extremely rare circumstances. This appears to reflect the treatment of the issue in the Georgia courts.

The rationale underlying the court's decision finding adulterous conduct as sufficient provocation would also be applicable to sexual conduct involving a defendant's illicit lover and another man. Nevertheless, a request to charge on provocation caused by the illicit lover's "adulterous conduct" would be inapt in such a case. Adultery can be committed only by married persons, not illicit lovers. Thus, a trial court's refusal to give such a charge would be proper.

A lover's engaging in an act of consensual sex with her ex-husband can serve as sufficient provocation to reduce a homicide from murder to voluntary manslaughter. However, evidence of such conduct does not demand a finding of voluntary manslaughter. Even where one claims sexual jealousy as the provocation for a killing, it is generally a question for a jury to determine whether the slayer acted from passion or revenge. If the evidence authorizes a finding that the slayer shot to avenge himself against the ex-husband's past acts, rather than as the result of any present provocation resulting from the reconciliation of the ex-spouses, the jury would be authorized to find proof of malice murder rather than voluntary manslaughter.

In a special concurring opinion in Ricketts v. State, Chief Justice Fletcher, rather than joining in the majority's approval of the Suggested Pattern Jury Instruction on adultery in murder cases, found that it failed to fully apprise a jury of the law of this state that adulterous conduct can serve as sufficient provocation to reduce homicide from murder to voluntary manslaughter. In order to provide juries with a clearer statement of the law in future prosecutions involving a defense of voluntary manslaughter because of adulterous conduct, Chief Justice Fletcher urged trial courts to first define voluntary manslaughter and then charge as follows:

> A spouse's adulterous conduct may serve as serious provocation sufficient to cause a person to act as the result of a sudden, violent, and irresistible passion. What circumstances will present a situation so as to excite such passion and exclude all idea of deliberation or malice is a matter for the jury to determine. If the evidence shows, beyond a reasonable doubt, that the killing was done by the defendant without malice, and without a spirit of revenge, but under a violent, sudden impulse of passion, then you would be authorized to find the defendant guilty of voluntary manslaughter.

Recognizing the validity of Chief Justice Fletcher's opinion, the drafters of the Suggested Pattern Jury Instructions changed the pattern charge on adultery in 2003 by adding language specifically stating that "[y]ou may consider whether adultery amounts to provocation, which would mitigate the killing." This change in the pattern charge reflects a consensus view among trial judges in this state that an adultery charge is incomplete and potentially misleading when it fails to make explicit the notion that adultery may constitute provocation sufficient to mitigate a killing.

Notwithstanding this change in the pattern charge, the trial court in Shields v. State gave to the jury an adultery charge that was modeled after the former pattern charge and that omitted the language adopted in 2003 which reiterates that adultery can amount to provocation. Despite this omission, the majority in Shields held that the charge as given left the door open for the jury to consider whether such killing was committed in circumstances which would constitute voluntary manslaughter. Moreover, in the context of the trial court's charge as a whole, the majority held that the instruction in no way misled the jury or hindered the defendant's ability to attempt a defense of voluntary manslaughter.

Where the defendant's contention that he acted with irresistible passion as a result of the victim's adulterous conduct is not his sole defense and is not supported by the evidence, the trial court's failure to charge the jury on voluntary manslaughter would not be error.

v. Insufficient Provocation

Evidence of anger is not, as a matter of law, a showing of the provocation necessary to set aside a finding of malice. Thus, even where there is evidence that the victim angered the defendant, the jury may still determine from all the facts and circumstances that the killing, rather than being the result of considerable provocation, was intentional and malicious.

The desire to prevent a drug user from using drugs again is not sufficient provocation to reduce murder to voluntary manslaughter. Also, where the only evidence relating to provocation is the defendant's assertion that the victims refused to sell drugs to him, a charge on voluntary manslaughter is not warranted.

Finally, a charge on voluntary manslaughter is not warranted when the only alleged evidence of provocation is the victim resisting a forcible felony.

b. Passion

The intentional killing in a voluntary manslaughter case has to result from a provocation to passion. According to the statute, this passion has to be "sudden, violent, and irresistible." A Georgia Supreme Court case has described it as that which "excludes all idea of deliberation or malice." Although normally the passion will be anger, there is authority that fear will suffice.

However, sexual passion is not within the "passion" which is part of the voluntary manslaughter definition. The question of the existence of and sufficiency of the passion is one for the jury. The jury ought to be required to find not only that the reasonable person acting under these circumstances would have reacted passionately but also that this defendant actually did. Otherwise the provocative circumstances would be merely granting a license to kill.

c. *Cooling Off*

Section 16-5-2 provides that if there was a time period between the provocation and the killing long enough for "the voice of reason and humanity to be heard," there is not voluntary manslaughter but murder. The statute allocates the determination of this question to the jury. Ordinarily, it will be left to the jury to decide whether there was a cooling off period during which a reasonable person would have cooled off and whether this defendant actually had cooled off.

Although the jury is the judge of whether there was a sufficient cooling off period, it is a question of law for the trial court to determine whether there is slight evidence that the defendant acted as the result of sudden, violent and irresistible passion resulting from serious provocation. The trial court can conclude as a matter of law that the incident did not constitute even slight evidence of provocation because of a cooling off period between the incident and the killing and, therefore, can refuse to charge the jury as to voluntary manslaughter.

d. *Improper Sequential Jury Instructions*

Where the evidence would authorize a conviction for felony murder or voluntary manslaughter, a sequential charge requiring the jury to consider voluntary manslaughter only if it has considered and found the defendant not guilty of malice murder and felony murder is not appropriate. Instead, the trial court should instruct the jury so as to ensure adequate consideration of charges for both forms of homicide.

If a trial court has given a sequential charge to the jury in violation of Edge v. State, a defendant who has reserved his right to raise objections to the jury charge on appeal is entitled to a new trial. However, if the sequential charge given was requested by the defendant, he cannot assert on appeal that the charge was erroneous. Even if the defendant's trial preceded Edge, he cannot subsequently contend that it was error to give a sequential charge if he previously failed to comply with the applicable procedures for securing review of that issue. Even though the trial court has given an improper sequential charge to the jury, if it is evident from the record that the verdict of felony murder was the product of adequate consideration of charges for both forms of homicide rather than of any prejudicial emphasis communicated by the improper sequential charge, the defendant's conviction for felony murder will be upheld.

With the jury's consideration of malice, it must also consider the element of provocation. If the jury finds that the defendant committed the homicide with malice, it necessarily finds that the element of provocation does not exist or is insufficient to overcome the jury's finding of malice, whether express or implied. With this finding of malice, voluntary manslaughter is eliminated from the jury's consideration, rendering any sequential charge given by a trial court in connection with felony murder and voluntary manslaughter harmless error. Likewise, if the evidence does not authorize consideration of voluntary manslaughter as a possible verdict, a sequential charge does not amount to reversible error.

Even absent an objection to a sequential charge or to a jury's verdict finding a defendant guilty of felony murder, appellate review of the trial court's failure to apply the modified merger rule cannot be waived, because a conviction which should have been merged into another as a matter of fact or law is void.

e. *Imperfect Self-Defense*

In a minority of other states, "imperfect self-defense" is a form of voluntary manslaughter where the killing is committed with an honest but unreasonable belief in the necessity of using deadly force. Because "imperfect self-defense" as a form of voluntary manslaughter is not recognized in this state, it is not error for a trial court to refuse to give a requested charge on "imperfect self-defense."

f. *Verdicts*

If a jury returns guilty verdicts of felony murder, voluntary manslaughter, and aggravated assault, in the absence of an objection to the form of the verdicts, a trial court is not under a duty to sentence the defendant for the crime of felony murder. The trial court may find as a matter of law that the jury's finding of voluntary manslaughter precludes a conviction on the felony murder charge and may sentence the defendant on the voluntary manslaughter charge.

A trial court may not sentence a defendant for felony murder and voluntary manslaughter based on the same underlying aggravated assault. By definition, a defendant found guilty of voluntary manslaughter lacks the mens rea required to commit felony murder in that any malice which would have been imputed from the underlying felony has been mitigated by the provocation which induced the crime of voluntary manslaughter. Moreover, a trial court may not sentence a defendant for both offenses because there is only one victim. To convict and sentence the defendant for both offenses would improperly subject him to multiple convictions and punishments for one crime.

Because the intent relevant to a conviction for felony murder is the underlying intent for the felony and because intent to kill, as well as mitigating factors such as provocation and passion, are irrelevant to that intent, a jury's verdict of guilty of felony murder does not constitute a finding that the defendant did not act with provocation and passion in assaulting the victim and does not conflict with the jury's verdict of guilty of voluntary manslaughter. Under these circumstances, the verdicts are not mutually exclusive.

In a case presenting an unusual situation involving possible verdicts of felony murder or voluntary manslaughter and excluding any possible verdict of malice murder, the court held that a charge on voluntary manslaughter that merely referred to malice to distinguish voluntary manslaughter from an intentional killing was not reversible error.

Where the defendant is convicted of the voluntary manslaughter of one victim and the aggravated assault of another victim, the convictions do not merge as a matter of fact, even though only one shot was fired, striking both victims. One crime is not included within another if each crime affects a different victim. Thus, verdicts of guilty of voluntary manslaughter as to one victim and aggravated assault as to the other victim will be upheld.

Where the jury has convicted the defendant of malice murder, it is not required to return a verdict on voluntary manslaughter.

f.1. Relationship Between Voluntary Manslaughter and Other Crimes

Important Notice about Repudiation of Actual or Same Evidence Test: The Georgia Supreme Court repudiated the actual evidence test in *Drinkard v. Walker*, 281 Ga. 211, 636 S.E.2d 530 (2006), because it found this test to be inconsistent with the statutory framework governing the prohibition against multiple convictions for included offenses in Georgia. This inconsistency resulted in years of confusion and unpredictable results. In its place, the court adopted the required evidence test and overruled any prior case law that is inconsistent with it. Thus, any prior case law applying the actual evidence test is no longer controlling and should not be relied upon to determine whether one offense is included in another under § 16-1-6(1). The discussion of such case law is included below only insofar as it may still be applicable to pending prosecutions that arose before the Drinkard decision. See MULTIPLE CONVICTIONS, II. Tests to Determine Presence of Multiple Convictions, for a complete discussion of the Drinkard decision.

If the aggravated assault of the victim is independent of the killing itself, the aggravated assault does not merge into the voluntary manslaughter as a matter of fact.

Where the jury was authorized to conclude from the evidence either that the defendant intentionally shot the victim, in which case he was guilty of voluntary manslaughter, or that the gun discharged accidentally, in which case he was guilty of no crime, the trial court's refusal to charge the jury on the lesser included offense of involuntary manslaughter would not be error.

g. Punishment

Voluntary manslaughter is a felony punishable, under § 16-5-2, by imprisonment for one to 20 years.

2. Involuntary Manslaughter

Section 16-5-3 provides for two different types of involuntary manslaughter. Subsection (a) defines felony involuntary manslaughter as an unintentional killing which results from the commission of an unlawful yet nonfelonious act. Subsection (b) defines misdemeanor involuntary manslaughter as an unintentional killing which results from the commission of a lawful act in an unlawful manner. Note, however, that a trial court's charge to the jury should not designate one form of involuntary manslaughter as "felony" and the other as "misdemeanor." The former can be described as "unlawful act" involuntary manslaughter while the latter is the "criminal negligence" type of involuntary manslaughter.

The common ground shared by both types of involuntary manslaughter is that of unintentional killing. A verdict for involuntary manslaughter is not authorized and instructions are not required where the evidence makes it plain that the act was done intentionally. Thus, where the victim's body showed nine gunshot wounds in the back, the court held, as a matter of law, that involuntary manslaughter was not at issue. Likewise, the court refused to order involuntary manslaughter instructions where the victim died as the result of 15 blows with a blunt instrument or where the victim died as the result of repeated stabbing with a knife. An involuntary manslaughter instruction is not warranted even if it is the sole defense if the evidence does not support the charge. It is important to note that while evidence which could support the proof of an unintentional killing is necessary for an involuntary manslaughter instruction, it is not necessarily sufficient. Thus, where the evidence shows a lack of intent to kill but the presence of a felony by the defendant, no theory of involuntary manslaughter is available. However, if the evidence does not demand a finding that the victim's death was the result of a felony and there is some evidence that the victim's death occurred unintentionally, an involuntary manslaughter instruction is warranted and should be given to the jury upon a proper request.

Even if the evidence is consistent with a finding that the victim was intentionally killed, the jury can still properly find that the defendant unintentionally killed the victim during the commission of a misdemeanor.

Unlike voluntary manslaughter, involuntary manslaughter does not contain an element that mitigates a greater offense. Thus, the prohibition against giving a sequential charge to the jury to consider possible verdicts in a particular sequence, which would eliminate the jury's full consideration of any mitigating factor, is inapplicable in a case involving involuntary rather than voluntary manslaughter.

a. "Unlawful Act" Involuntary Manslaughter

It has been held that an "unlawful act other than a felony" sufficient to trigger § 16-5-3(a) is "an act condemned by some statute or valid municipal ordinance of this state." Thus, most § 16-5-3(a) prosecutions will be based on a violation of a misdemeanor statute or a local ordinance. It would appear that the word "unlawful" does not authorize the court to make ad hoc determinations that behavior not prohibited by the criminal code is, nevertheless, unlawful. This view is fortified in § 16-2-1 by its abolition of common law crimes and by its requirement of a statutory violation before a crime can be punished.

Where the evidence in a case affords no basis whatsoever for a finding that the killing was unintentional or that the defendant was guilty of a misdemeanor rather than felony, it is proper for the trial court to refuse to charge the jury on involuntary manslaughter involving an unintentional killing during an unlawful act other than a felony.

The majority of "unlawful act" involuntary manslaughter convictions formerly were based on violations of the motor vehicle code. At the present time, however, deaths arising out of a violation of the motor vehicle code must be prosecuted under § 40-6-393. The courts have indicated that unintentional killings arising out of simple battery, simple assault, and reckless conduct would constitute § 16-5-3(a) violations. In fact, a violation of § 16-11-102, pointing a pistol, has been held sufficient to support an instruction under § 16-5-3(a). It should be emphasized that if the only evidence in the case indicates an aggravated assault under § 16-5-21 through the use of a loaded pistol, this offense will be felony murder even if the killing is unintentional, because § 16-5-3(a) requires a **nonfelonious** unlawful act and § 16-5-21 describes a felony.

In a § 16-5-3(a) prosecution, while the state will not have the burden of proving an intention to kill, it will be required to show the requisite mens rea for a violation of the underlying unlawful act. Thus, in Solomon v. State, the court held that the state must show an intent to commit the unlawful act itself or reckless conduct which violates the statute defining the unlawful act. It is submitted that this latter route to an involuntary manslaughter conviction ought to be available only when recklessness would be sufficient culpability for conviction of the underlying offense itself. In other words, new mens rea requirements for the underlying unlawful act ought not be created in manslaughter prosecutions.

Another requirement in a § 16-5-3(a) prosecution is that of causation. It must appear from the evidence that the death was caused by the violation of the statute defining the underlying unlawful act. For example, in Burns v. State, the Georgia Supreme Court held that it was not error for the trial court to fail to charge on involuntary manslaughter. The court found no merit in the defendant's argument that the victim's death was caused by his carrying a pistol without a license in violation of § 16-11-128. According to the court, there was no showing of a causal relationship between the defendant's not having complied with the state's licensing laws and the victim's death. Likewise, in Carlton v. State, the Court of Appeals found no merit in the defendant's argument that felony involuntary manslaughter should have been charged based upon his carrying a concealed weapon in violation of § 16-11-126. The concealment, while unlawful, did not cause the death. The firing of the gun did so. In Hill v. State, the Court of Appeals held that a rational trier of fact, relying on the evidence at trial, could have found the defendant guilty of involuntary manslaughter with simple battery as the underlying unlawful act. It was uncontroverted that the defendant was bouncing and shaking the child on his knee immediately before the child lost consciousness and went limp. The causal relationship between the defendant's physical contact with the child and the child's death was supported by the testimony of the pediatrician and the medical examiner that the child's death resulted from "Shaken Baby Syndrome."

Although a charge of involuntary manslaughter in the commission of an unlawful act involving use of a firearm can be based on an allegation that the unintentional killing was caused by the defendant's commission of misdemeanor offenses such as pointing the firearm at the victim or reckless conduct with the firearm, such a charge cannot be based on an allegation that the unintentional death was caused solely by the defendant's unlawful possession of the firearm. Since there would be no allegation that the defendant committed an unlawful act under circumstances that could be the proximate cause of the unintentional death, the involuntary manslaughter indictment would be fatally defective.

b. *"Criminal Negligence" Involuntary Manslaughter*

It is a misdemeanor to kill another human being while performing a "lawful act in an unlawful manner likely to cause death or great bodily harm." The courts have grappled with the precise definition of what conduct this statute punishes. In the Georgia Supreme Court's most detailed description of the conduct prohibited by § 16-5-3(b), the court described it as "criminal negligence [that] shows an indifference to the injurious results of the negligent acts." The court made clear that criminal negligence is more than civil or tort negligence and held it "must appear that [the defendant] knew, or that an ordinarily prudent person under similar circumstances would have known, that his act might probably endanger others."

If there is sufficient evidence to raise an issue as to whether the victim's death was the result of the defendant's criminally negligent conduct, the appellate courts have held that it is error for a trial court to refuse to charge the jury on this grade of involuntary manslaughter. In Prince v. State, the defendant made his brother leave his home by threatening him with a gun. While the defendant handled the gun, the gun "went off" and killed the brother. Although the defendant was in lawful possession of the home and was authorized to order his brother to leave, his handling of the gun was criminally negligent conduct. This evidence was sufficient to raise the issue of involuntary manslaughter for the jury's consideration, and the jury should have been instructed accordingly. Likewise, in Teasley v. State, the defendant shot open a locked box, and the bullet apparently ricocheted off the box and killed the victim who was lying on the floor nearby. Although it was lawful for the defendant to shoot open the locked box, it was criminally negligent to do so in close proximity to the victim. The Georgia Supreme Court held that the evidence was ample to raise an issue for the jury's consideration as to the defense of involuntary manslaughter. Thus, the trial court's refusal to charge the jury on involuntary manslaughter was error.

c. *Involuntary Manslaughter v. Accident*

By definition, involuntary manslaughter involves an unintended killing. Likewise, the § 16-2-2 defense of accident is an assertion that the death, while factually caused by the defendant, was unintentionally caused. In fact, because the courts limit involuntary manslaughter to **criminal** negligence, the defendant who asserts that his actions were, at worst, tortiously negligent is asserting an accident defense. Because the determination of whether particular behavior is merely tortiously or, instead, criminally negligent is merely one of degree, it seems clear that most, if not all, cases presenting an asserted accident defense will likewise present an involuntary manslaughter case as well. For example, in Sirmans v. State, the defendant testified that as he grabbed the gun the "bullet went off." While he was arguing for total exoneration under § 16-2-2, it certainly ought to have been within reason that a jury could have found that the defendant's actions were criminally negligent.

Some cases appear to say that where the defense is accident, involuntary manslaughter is not presented. These cases, however, all arose in the context of a defense assertion on appeal that the trial judge should have, sua sponte, charged involuntary manslaughter and can be explained as reflecting an unwillingness to permit the defendant to take his chances on an accident acquittal and then seek a new trial on involuntary manslaughter. This defense technique is no longer permissible under State v. Stonaker, which requires defendants to request charges in writing on lesser offenses. If defendants, therefore, in "accident" cases also seek involuntary manslaughter instructions in the future, it is suggested that in most situations such instructions will be warranted. The difference between accident and involuntary manslaughter is often one of degree and the defendant who seeks to place the latter possibility before the jury ought to be permitted to do so. However, such instructions will not be warranted where there is no evidence that the defendant unintentionally shot the victim by the commission of an unlawful act other than a felony, or where there is no evidence that the defendant accidentally shot the victim by the commission of a lawful act in an unlawful manner.

d. Involuntary Manslaughter v. Self-Defense

Just as some homicide defendants have asserted that their accident defense testimony raised the possibility of involuntary manslaughter, others who have testified to self-defense have claimed a right to § 16-5-3(b) involuntary manslaughter instructions. The essence of the claim is that where a defendant denies an intention to kill yet does so while acting in self-defense a jury ought to be able to conclude that, even if self-defense was not shown under § 16-3-21 because the force used was excessive, the defendant's acts were lawful (self-defense) yet done in an unlawful manner (with excessive force). Thus, the elements of § 16-5-3(b)—lack of intention, lawful act, unlawful manner—would be present. In 1975, the Georgia Supreme Court recognized that this analysis was defensible, but refused to reverse a conviction for failure to instruct on involuntary manslaughter because the defendant had not sought the instructions at trial.

There has been a great deal of litigation concerning the necessity and appropriateness of involuntary manslaughter instructions in situations where the defendant claims self-defense as a primary defense. In the paradigmatic case, the defendant argues as an alternative to his complete defense of self-defense that the homicide could be viewed as involuntary manslaughter under § 16-5-3(b) in that he was performing a lawful act (self-defense) in an unlawful manner (excessive force). In the ordinary case, the defendant's testimony will be that he was simply using the homicide-producing instrumentality to scare the deceased. This question has continued to be confronted by the appellate courts and the Georgia Supreme Court has attempted to make the law in the area more precise.

In Crawford v. State, the defendant shot the decedent, assertedly in defense of self and habitation. On trial for murder, he interposed those two defenses and additionally requested a jury instruction on involuntary manslaughter under § 16-5-3(b), which the trial court refused to give. The Georgia Supreme Court affirmed the conviction and took the opportunity to attempt to set out the law in this area. After reviewing the case law dating back to 1908, the court held that "it is not necessary to give a request to charge . . . as to involuntary manslaughter, Code § 26-1103(b) [O.C.G.A. § 16-5-3], where the defendant asserts that he or she fired a gun in self-defense." The court distinguished earlier cases in which a homicide defendant was held entitled to such an instruction as involving **other** instrumentalities, such as brake sticks and knives. The distinguishing factor, according to the court, is that "the deadly force of a gun is known to all." Therefore, by using a gun the defendant has committed the separate crime of reckless conduct (§ 16-5-60) and, therefore, cannot be said to have committed a lawful act for purposes of involuntary manslaughter.

Crawford is an admirable attempt to clarify the law in the area. The court decided that the intentional use of a gun is simply inconsistent with the lack of intent to kill which is a prerequisite in involuntary manslaughter. Because most of the cases appear to deal with situations where the defendant used a gun, this would appear to cover most cases. After the decision in Crawford, which dealt with the use of a gun in self-defense, the question of how to handle nongun cases remained open. That is, what if the defendant used something other than a gun in self-defense? Would that defendant be entitled to a charge on involuntary manslaughter?

In Saylors v. State, the Georgia Supreme Court dealt with a nongun case. In Saylors, the defendant used a three-inch pocket knife in self-defense and asserted error in the failure to charge the jury on involuntary manslaughter. The Supreme Court affirmed, relying on Crawford. While recognizing the difference in the weapons used, the court concluded that the "soundness of [the Crawford] reasoning is undeniable, and leads inevitably to this conclusion: a defendant who seeks to justify homicide under the 'self-defense' statute . . . is not entitled to an additional instruction on involuntary manslaughter in the course of a lawful act . . . whatever the implement of death." While not citing it, Saylors implicitly approved Fitzhugh v. State, a Court of Appeals decision reaching the same conclusion. The question left open in Crawford has been answered.

Post-Crawford litigation in both the Supreme Court and the Court of Appeals is consistent with, although not always explicit in, its reliance on Crawford.

In Williams v. State, the Georgia Supreme Court specifically rejected the defendant's claim that intentionally shooting in the direction of a victim to scare him would authorize an instruction on § 16-5-3(b). The defendant testified that he was attempting to shoot over the victim's head to scare him but that his aim was bad. He contended that the theory of involuntary manslaughter was applicable because a jury could have found that he was acting in self-defense (the lawful act) but used excessive force (the unlawful manner).

The court responded to the defendant's claim by pointing out that if his testimony was to be believed, his act was either justified and no crime at all or it constituted the felony of aggravated assault. In neither case could the evidence be interpreted as demonstrating a lawful act in an unlawful manner. The intention to pull the trigger sufficed to make the Crawford rule applicable and render the misdemeanor involuntary manslaughter instruction unnecessary. Failure to instruct as to that crime was not error.

An involuntary manslaughter instruction is not authorized where the defendant created an emergency requiring a killing and then claimed self-defense. In Rhode v. State, the court held that even if it were admitted that the defendant shot the unarmed victim when he resisted the burglary of his home and the murder of his two children, such admission would not have shown that the defendant committed the lawful act of self-defense. Therefore, a charge on involuntary manslaughter involving a lawful act committed in an unlawful manner was not warranted.

d.1. Involuntary Manslaughter v. "Parental Reasonable Discipline" Justification Defense

A homicide defendant who relies on the "parental reasonable discipline" justification defense is not entitled to an additional instruction on involuntary manslaughter in the course of a lawful act because if the defendant was justified in administering reasonable parental discipline, he is guilty of no crime. Furthermore, if the defendant was not so justified, the homicide does not fall within the "lawful act" predicate of § 16-5-3(b) since, in the rejecting the defense, the jury has determined thereby that the act was not lawful.

e. Relationship Between "Unlawful Act" Involuntary Manslaughter and "Criminal Negligence" Involuntary Manslaughter

The question of whether a defendant indicted under § 16-5-3(a) can instead be convicted of a violation of § 16-5-3(b) has arisen several times. The courts which considered the question have held that if the indictment allegations are broad enough and the proof is sufficient, such a conviction would be authorized. Thus, where the defendant was charged with having ignored a stop sign and killing the driver of a pickup truck, the court held that a § 16-5-3(b) conviction was authorized where the defendant insisted he had complied with the stop sign. In fact, it can be argued that every § 16-5-3(a) indictment includes a charge of § 16-5-3(b) because, in the language of § 16-1-6, the latter crime consists of only "a less culpable mental state" than the former. Subsection (a) must include proof of an intent to commit the "unlawful act," while criminal negligence, a less culpable mental state than intent, suffices to convict under subsection (b).

f. Relationship Between Involuntary Manslaughter and Other Crimes

When valid guilty verdicts are returned on both alternative counts of felony murder and involuntary manslaughter, the alternative involuntary manslaughter count is vacated by operation of § 16-1-7. Since the involuntary manslaughter conviction has been statutorily vacated, there is no involuntary manslaughter count into which the underlying misdemeanor offense can merge. Thus, it is proper for the trial court to treat the involuntary manslaughter count as merely surplusage and then to proceed to determine whether a separate sentence on the underlying misdemeanor offense may be authorized for lack of merger, as a matter of fact, into the extant felony murder conviction.

Where the jury is authorized to conclude from the evidence either that the defendant intentionally shot the victim, in which case he would be guilty of voluntary manslaughter, or that the gun discharged accidentally, in which case he would be guilty of no crime, the trial court's refusal to charge the jury on the lesser included offense of involuntary manslaughter would not be error.

Where the evidence shows either the commission of the completed offense of felony murder or the commission of no offense, the trial court is not required to charge the jury on involuntary manslaughter as a lesser included offense.

g. Verdicts

A jury verdict that has found the defendant guilty of involuntary manslaughter, in spite of the trial court's instructions to the jury only on the law of murder and voluntary manslaughter, is not a proper verdict. After the jury has returned such a verdict and the trial court has determined prior to the verdict's publication in open court that the verdict is not a proper one, the trial court should return the jury for further deliberation with direction to return a verdict within range of instructions on murder and voluntary manslaughter originally given to it. The jury must return a verdict that is responsive to the issues framed by the indictment and the evidence and given to the jury in the trial court's instructions.

If the trial court's instructions on "unlawful act" involuntary manslaughter are correct statements of the law and if the jurors have correctly applied these instructions to the facts as found by them, the jury's verdict of guilty is a proper one. Evidence that, because of a misunderstanding of the trial court's instructions, the jurors believed that they were finding the defendant guilty of a misdemeanor, rather than a felony, and that they would not have voted to find the defendant guilty had they known that "unlawful act" involuntary manslaughter was punishable as a felony does not impeach the verdict. The legal status of the offense of involuntary manslaughter as a felony or misdemeanor and the resulting punishment if a guilty verdict is returned, is of absolutely no concern to the jury.

The verdicts of guilty of felony murder and involuntary manslaughter are not mutually exclusive as a matter of law. Nor are they as a matter of fact where the jury can conclude from the defendant's actions that he committed a felony against one person which would support the felony murder and that he acted recklessly toward another person, and therefore, is guilty of involuntary manslaughter as well.

A mutually exclusive verdict may be rendered in a particular case, however, where the offenses or acts alleged in the indictment as underlying the felony murder and involuntary manslaughter counts reflect that the jury, in order to find the defendant guilty on both counts, necessarily reached two positive findings of fact that cannot logically mutually exist. For instance, in Jackson v. State the Georgia Supreme Court concluded that the jury's verdict finding the defendant guilty of felony murder predicated upon a § 16-5-20(a)(1) aggravated assault on the victim was mutually exclusive of a verdict finding him guilty of involuntary manslaughter predicated upon reckless conduct in regard to the same act involving the same victim at the same instance of time. The jury convicted the defendant of killing the victim with criminal intent **and** with criminal negligence, that is, of killing both with and without an intention to do so. The two verdicts were obviously mutually exclusive. Because it was both legally and logically impossible to convict the defendant of both felony murder and involuntary manslaughter, the court reversed both mutually exclusive convictions and ordered a new trial.

The rule against mutually exclusive verdicts applies only where the convictions result from the same act involving the same victim at the same instant. Where the victim sustains several injuries, convictions for both intentional and negligent crimes are not mutually exclusive. In *Waits v. State*, for example, the Georgia Supreme Court held that the criminal intent required for aggravated assault, aggravated battery, and cruelty to children did not logically exclude the criminal negligence element of reckless conduct because the victim sustained numerous injuries. A rational trier of fact could have found that the victim initially suffered non-fatal injuries which resulted from the defendant's frequently negligent care. Thus, because the evidence showed that the crime of reckless conduct occurred prior to the other offenses and that the conviction for that crime was not based upon the same conduct as the other crimes, the reckless conduct verdict did not logically exclude any other verdict.

Where there was one act committed upon one victim at the same time, either intentionally or accidentally, convictions of aggravated assault and involuntary manslaughter would be mutually exclusive verdicts. It would therefore be proper for the trial court to instruct the jury to continue deliberating on these two charges.

Under § 16-1-7(a)(1), it is proper to convict and sentence a defendant for that crime which includes all others. Since a misdemeanor can be an included crime in a felony, misdemeanor-involuntary manslaughter can be an included crime in felony murder. Where the evidence shows that a homicide occurred in the commission of both a felony and an included misdemeanor, there is no inconsistency or ambiguity in verdicts of guilt as to misdemeanor-involuntary manslaughter and felony murder. Accordingly, it is not error to merge the included misdemeanor into the felony and then to merge the underlying felony into the felony murder count. When the misdemeanor merges into the felony, the predicate for the defendant's conviction for involuntary manslaughter is eliminated, but the felony remains as the basis for the defendant's conviction for murder. Thus, the trial court may properly enter the judgment of conviction and sentence on the jury's verdict finding the defendant guilty of the offense of felony murder.

Even if a jury finds a defendant guilty of the involuntary manslaughter of a child, a trial court would not be required to direct a verdict of acquittal on a cruelty to children charge. The two verdicts could indeed be consistent because the jury could have found from the evidence that the defendant maliciously caused the child excessive pain and that his actions caused the child's death, but that he may not have intended to kill the child.

h. Punishment

Under § 16-5-3, "unlawful act" involuntary manslaughter is a felony punishable by imprisonment for one to ten years. "Criminal negligence" involuntary manslaughter is punishable as a misdemeanor under § 17-10-3.

D. Assisting Suicide

Any person who publicly advertises, offers, or holds himself out as offering that he will intentionally and actively assist another person in the commission of suicide and commits any overt act to further that purpose is guilty of a felony. This offense is punishable by imprisonment for not less than one nor more than five years.

Any person who knowingly and willfully commits any act which destroys the volition of another, such as fraudulent practices upon such person's fears, affections, or sympathies; duress; or any undue influence whereby the will of one person is substituted for the wishes of another, and thereby intentionally causes or induces such other person to commit or attempt to commit suicide is guilty of a felony. This offense is punishable by imprisonment for not less than one nor more than ten years.

The Code provisions that make it unlawful to assist another person in the commission of suicide do not affect any of the laws, in whole or in part, that may be applicable to the withholding or withdrawal of medical or health care treatment, including but not limited to, laws related to a living will, a durable power of attorney for health care, an advance directive for health care, or a written order not to resuscitate.

The United States Supreme Court has held that a state's prohibition on assisting suicide does not violate the Due Process Clause of the Fourteenth Amendment. The "right" to assistance in committing suicide is not a fundamental liberty interest protected by the Due Process Clause. Also, such a prohibition satisfies the constitutional requirement that it be rationally related to legitimate government interests. The court has also held that a prohibition on assisting suicide does not violate the Equal Protection Clause of the Fourteenth Amendment. The distinction between refusing lifesaving medical treatment and assisted suicide is neither arbitrary nor irrational. Logic and contemporary practice support the judgment that the two acts are different, and a state may therefore, consistent with the federal constitution, treat them differently. The reasons for recognizing and acting on this distinction are valid and important public interests which easily satisfy the constitutional requirement that a legislative classification bear a rational relation to some legitimate end.

Even if there is evidence that a defendant committed murder for the purpose of obtaining a death sentence, the defendant's execution by the state would not constitute an assisted suicide. The defendant is being sentenced to death not because of his own desire to die but because of the nature of his crimes. Furthermore, the jury, not the defendant, makes the final determination that death is the appropriate punishment for his crimes. The fact that the defendant agrees with the jury's determination that his crimes deserve death is immaterial.

III. Homicidal Offenses Not Found in Article 1 of Chapter 5 of Title 16

A. Generally

A number of offenses outside of Article 1 of Chapter 5 of Title 16 can be described as homicidal offenses in that they include as an element either a killing of a person, a killing of a fetus or unborn child, or an attempted termination of a fetus. These offenses are: criminal abortion (§ 16-12-140), partial-birth abortion (§ 16-12-144), feticide (§ 16-5-80), concealing death (§ 16-10-31), homicide by vehicle (§ 40-6-393), feticide by vehicle (§ 40-6-393.1), homicide by interference with an official traffic-control device or railroad sign or signal (§ 40-6-396), homicide by vessel (§ 52-7-12.2), feticide by vessel (§ 52-7-12.3), homicide by aircraft (§ 6-2-5.2), and perjury resulting in death (§ 16-10-70).

B. Abortion

1. Criminal Abortion

In 1973, the United States Supreme Court in Roe v. Wade and Doe v. Bolton imposed severe limitations on how the abortion of fetuses can be criminally punished by the states. Viewing the problem as one which involves the conflicting interests of the mother and society, the Court held that during the first trimester of pregnancy a mother has an absolute right to an abortion. After the first trimester, however, a societal interest in maternal health becomes compelling and can support regulations aimed at protecting such health. Finally, the societal interest in the possibility of life in the fetus permits state criminal punishment of all nontherapeutic abortions performed after the fetus has become viable, i. e., capable of an independent existence apart from the mother.

In 1992, a 5-4 majority of the United States Supreme Court in Planned Parenthood of Southeastern Pennsylvania v. Casey held that Roe v. Wade was still the law of the land, but that the states are nevertheless free to restrict abortion as long as they do not place an "undue burden" on the woman, which was Justice O'Connor's test in her concurring opinion in the *Webster* case. Utilizing this "undue burden" test, the majority held that Pennsylvania could not force a woman to notify her husband about an abortion. The state could, however, impose a 24-hour waiting period; require doctors to tell women about other options to abortions so as to provide "informed consent"; demand parental notification for minors; and make doctors provide statistical information about patients.

The current Georgia abortion statute, codified at §§ 16-12-140 to 16-12-143, was enacted in 1973 in response to the United States Supreme Court decision invalidating the prior law as violative of the pregnant woman's rights under the Due Process Clause of the federal constitution. The current statutory scheme is rather curious. Under § 16-12-140, it is a crime for a person to administer any substance or use any means with the intent to produce a miscarriage or abortion. This section refers to "exceptions" in § 16-12-141. While one would assume, therefore, that § 16-12-141 would contain a list of situations in which the acts prohibited by § 16-12-140 could be performed, this is clearly not the case. Although subsection (a) of § 16-12-141 provides that an abortion deemed "necessary" by a physician "based upon his best clinical judgment" is always permitted, it also provides that a partial-birth abortion by a duly licensed physician or layperson is prohibited. Subsection (b) prohibits post-first trimester abortions performed without licensed physicians and outside of licensed hospitals, licensed ambulatory surgical centers, or licensed abortion facilities, and subsection (c) prohibits post-second trimester abortions which are not deemed to be necessary to the preservation of the mother's "life or health."

Subsections (b) and (c), while written in the form of prohibitions, apparently are designed to permit all other abortions. In other words, all first trimester abortions can be performed anywhere (not just in licensed hospitals, licensed ambulatory surgical centers, or licensed abortion facilities), and second trimester abortions can be performed without a showing of medical necessity to protect the mother's life or health, so long as they are performed in a licensed hospital, a licensed ambulatory surgical center, or a licensed abortion facility. This is the obvious intent of the statute because otherwise it would clearly violate the Roe v. Wade and Doe v. Bolton guidelines.

Subsection (d) of § 16-12-141 provides record keeping requirements for those who perform abortions.

Section 16-12-142(a), which was formerly subsection (e), provides that hospitals need not admit patients seeking abortions and that individuals who have objections to the performance of all abortions cannot be held liable for a refusal to perform one. Also, § 16-12-141(b), which was enacted in 2006, provides that a pharmacist who states in writing an objection to any abortion is not required to fill a prescription for a drug if the purpose of the drug is to terminate a pregnancy and that such refusal cannot be the basis for any claim for damages or for any disciplinary or recriminatory action. However, the objecting pharmacist must make all reasonable efforts to locate another pharmacist who is willing to fill such prescription or immediately return the prescription to the prescription holder. Moreover, this provision cannot be construed to authorize a pharmacist to refuse to fill a prescription for birth control medication, including any process, device, or method to prevent pregnancy and including any drug or device approved by the federal Food and Drug Administration for such purpose.

As for the constitutionality of the statutory scheme, it seems to be in essential compliance with relevant United States Supreme Court authority, with one exception. Certainly the requirement of § 16-12-141(b) of a licensed hospital, a licensed ambulatory surgical center, or a licensed abortion facility for post-first trimester abortions is a legitimate regulation which effectuates the state interest in maternal health. Also, the record-keeping requirement of § 16-12-141(d) is reasonably related to a legitimate state interest in health and the United States Supreme Court has upheld a similar provision. Section 16-12-141(c), however, which forbids abortions after the second trimester of pregnancy without certification of necessity to protect the mother's life or health may suffer from a constitutional defect.

Roe and later cases permit the state to bar abortions after **viability**. In one of its abortion decisions, the Court emphasized that viability is a medical concept and its determination must be left to physicians. While it normally occurs at the end of the second trimester (between 24-28weeks), it varies from pregnancy to pregnancy. The Court, therefore, stressed that "neither the legislature nor the courts may proclaim one of the elements entering into the ascertainment of viability—be it **weeks of gestation** or fetal weight or any other single factor—as the determinant of when the state has a compelling interest in the life or health of the fetus. Viability is the critical point. And we have recognized no attempt to stretch the point of viability one way or the other." (Emphasis added). It would appear that § 16-12-141(c) in proscribing post-second trimester elective abortions has done exactly that which the Court condemned—isolated the number of weeks of gestation as the dividing line between legal and illegal elective abortions instead of using the entire concept of viability. To the extent that the statute punishes post-second trimester, pre-viability abortions, it would appear to violate the constitutional right to an elective (nontherapeutic) abortion as announced in Roe and explained in Colautti.

Additionally, it ought to be noted that there is an apparent inconsistency within § 16-12-141 itself. Subsection (a) appears to validate an abortion at any point in pregnancy when the physician determines that it is "necessary." The decision as to necessity is left to the physician's "best clinical judgment." The subsection points out that nothing in the article "shall be construed to prohibit" such an abortion, commonly known as a therapeutic abortion. However, subsection (c) appears to do exactly that, by stating that "[n]o abortion . . . shall be performed after the second trimester unless the physician and two consulting physicians certify that the abortion is necessary in their best clinical judgment to preserve the life or health of the woman." Although this regulation would be constitutional to the extent that it applies after viability, it certainly appears to restrict the right to an abortion set up by subsection (a). The courts have not yet been called upon to resolve this apparent conflict.

In 1985, the General Assembly enacted a statute dealing with disposal of aborted fetuses. Under the statute, all those hospitals and clinics where abortions are performed or occur spontaneously and laboratories to which aborted fetuses are delivered must provide for the disposal of the aborted fetuses by "cremation, interment, or other manner approved of by the commissioner of community health." Annual reports to the commissioner are also required concerning the disposal. Violation of the statute is punishable by a fine of between $1,000 and $5,000. In 2005, the General Assembly added a provision to this statute that requires physicians or their agents to submit to the Department of Community Health annual parental notification report forms with the requested data entered accurately and completely. The amended statute also provides for penalties and remedies for the failure to provide such reports.

In a case involving abortion protestors, the Georgia Court of Appeals held that an abortion conducted in compliance with the law would not constitute "imminent use of unlawful force" so as to justify the defendants' obstruction of a public passage during an abortion protest.

In Hillman v. State, the defendant was indicted under § 16-12-140 for allegedly using a handgun to shoot herself in the abdomen "with intent to produce a miscarriage and an abortion of her unborn child." The Court of Appeals held that a pregnant woman cannot be prosecuted under the statute for allegedly performing a criminal abortion on herself. By its plain meaning, the statute does not criminalize a pregnant woman's actions in securing an abortion, regardless of the means utilized. The court rejected the state's construction and overbroad application of the statute which would have encompassed the defendant's conduct. Under such a construction, a woman would have been at risk of a criminal indictment for virtually any perceived self-destructive behavior during her pregnancy which could have caused a late term miscarriage. Finally, the court held that regardless of whether the pregnant woman acts alone or with assistance, she cannot be charged under the statute, as the statute is specifically directed to prevent the conduct of persons other than the pregnant woman.

2. *Partial-Birth Abortion*

In 1997, the General Assembly enacted a statute prohibiting partial-birth abortions. A partial-birth abortion is an abortion in which the person performing the abortion partially vaginally delivers a living human fetus before ending the life of the fetus and completing the delivery. Any person who knowingly performs a partial-birth abortion and thereby ends the life of a human fetus is punishable by a fine not to exceed $5,000, imprisonment for not more than five years, or both.

This prohibition does not apply to a partial-birth abortion that is necessary to save the life of the mother because her life is endangered by a physical disorder, physical illness, or physical injury, including a life-endangering condition caused by or arising from the pregnancy itself, provided that no other medical procedure will suffice to save the mother's life.

A woman upon whom a partial-birth abortion has been performed is not subject to prosecution for violating this law.

The father of the fetus and the parents of the mother, if she was under the age of 18 at the time of the abortion, may obtain appropriate relief in a civil action, unless the pregnancy resulted from the plaintiff's criminal conduct or the plaintiff consented to the abortion. Such relief includes money damages for all injuries, psychological and physical, and statutory damages equal to three times the cost of the partial-birth abortion.

It should be noted that United States District Court Judge J. Owen Forrester has refused to issue an injunction against the enforcement of this law. The judge stated that "the state has a legitimate and compelling interest in regulating the manner in which abortions are performed after the fetus is viable." The judge had ruled earlier in an interim order that the law applies only to viable fetuses. The state settled the case challenging the constitutionality of this law by stipulating that the law applies only to the medical procedure known as intact dilation and extraction and applies only to viable fetuses, that is, fetuses that could live outside the womb. "The effect of the settlement was to define precisely, and to limit, what kind of abortions are prohibited." This limitation of the statute's prohibition to the intact dilation and extraction of a viable fetus avoids the constitutional defect found in a partial-birth abortion statute of another state. Since the language of that state's statute could be construed to cover a much broader category of abortion procedures, it was found by the U.S. Supreme Court to place an undue burden upon a woman's right to terminate her pregnancy before viability. However, like the other state's statute, our statute is constitutionally defective for another reason. Although it provides an exception for those instances when partial-birth abortion is necessary to preserve the life of the mother, it lacks any exception for the preservation of the mother's health. The law requires a health exception in order to validate even a postviability abortion regulation.

3. *Parental Notification Act*

In 1987, the General Assembly enacted the Parental Notification Act. The Act provided that no physician or other person should perform an abortion upon an unemancipated minor under the age of 18 years unless the child's parent or guardian was properly notified.

A preliminary injunction enjoining the implementation of the Parental Notification Act sought by Planned Parenthood was granted by United States District Court Judge Robert Hall. The court found (1) the verification procedures of the Act were unconstitutionally burdensome and failed to provide adequate alternative means of verification, and (2) the promulgated Juvenile Court Rules requiring the inclusion on certain court documents of the minor's name and Social Security number failed to guarantee that minor constitutionally adequate anonymity in seeking judicial waiver by not requiring that the juvenile court record be sealed.

In 1988, the Parental Notification Act was amended to correct these constitutional infirmities but was again held unconstitutional. The United States District Court held that the failure of the statute to recognize more expeditious forms of written notice under § 15-11-112(a)(1)(C) was the only constitutional defect in the statutory scheme not remediable by an amendment to the Uniform Juvenile Court Rules. The court went on to find a number of defects in these rules.

In 1990, the United States Supreme Court struck down a Minnesota parental notification law which required minor women to notify both biological parents and had no judicial bypass procedure. However, the court upheld an Ohio one-parent abortion notification law which provided a judicial bypass alternative for minor women who could not notify their parents. (Note that Georgia's Parental Notification Act is a one-parent notification law with a judicial bypass procedure.)

In 1991, the Eleventh Circuit Court of Appeals, guided by these two United States Supreme Court decisions, held that the federal district court improperly enjoined the implementation of Georgia's Parental Notification Act. The court held that the Act's notification requirements taken together do not unduly burden the minor's abortion decision and that the Act's judicial bypass procedure does survive constitutional scrutiny.

Any person who violates the provisions of the Act shall be guilty of a misdemeanor, and any person who intentionally encourages another to provide false information pursuant to the Act shall be guilty of a misdemeanor.

4. *Woman's Right to Know Act*

In 2005, the General Assembly enacted the Woman's Right to Know Act. Under this Act, no abortion can be performed in this state except with the voluntary and informed consent of the female upon whom the abortion is to be performed. Except in the case of a medical emergency, consent to an abortion is voluntary and informed if and only if the female is informed at least 24 hours before the abortion of (1) the particular medical risks to her associated with the particular abortion procedure to be employed, when medically accurate; (2) the probable gestational age of the unborn child at the time the abortion would be performed; and (3) the medical risks associated with carrying the unborn child to term. In addition, the female must be informed (1) that medical assistance benefits may be available for prenatal care, childbirth, and neonatal care; (2) that the father will be liable pursuant to § 19-7-49(a) to assist in the support of her child; (3) how to obtain a list of health care providers, facilities, and clinics that offer to perform ultrasounds free of charge; and (4) that she has the right to review printed materials provided by the state that describe the unborn child, list agencies that offer alternatives to abortion, and contain information on fetal pain.

The female must certify in writing, prior to the abortion, that the information described above has been furnished to her and that she has been informed of her opportunity to review the printed materials provided by the state. For all cases in which an ultrasound has been performed prior to conducting an abortion or a pre-abortion screen, the female must certify in writing that (1) she was provided the opportunity to view the fetal image and hear the fetal heartbeat; (2) whether or not she elected to view the sonogram; and (3) whether or not she elected to listen to the fetal heartbeat, if present. Prior to the performance of the abortion, the physician who is to perform the abortion or the physician's qualified agent must receive a copy of these written certifications and retain them on file with the female's medical record for at least three years following the date of receipt.

When a medical emergency compels the performance of an abortion, the physician must inform the female prior to the abortion, if medically reasonable and prudent, of the medical indications supporting the physician's judgment that an abortion is medically necessary to avert her death or that a 24-hour delay would create serious risk of substantial or irreversible impairment of a major bodily function. Any physician who so informs the female can not be held civilly liable for failure to obtain informed consent to an abortion.

C. Feticide

1. Legislative Background

The General Assembly enacted the original feticide statute in 1876. When the General Assembly revised the criminal code in 1968, it found the feticide statute along with a plethora of other pre-1968 statutes relating to specific types of homicide to be archaic and unnecessary. Since the General Assembly deliberately designed the homicide statutes of the 1968 criminal code to have general applicability, it decided not to include those pre-1968 statutes relating to specific types of homicide. However, apparently recognizing that there was a need for the feticide statute in the criminal code, the General Assembly resurrected the statute and incorporated it into the code in 1982. The General Assembly then amended the statute in 2006 so as to revise the definition of feticide, to prohibit the voluntary manslaughter of an unborn child, and to provide for exceptions.

2. Definition of Offense

In 2006, the General Assembly revised the definition of feticide in three ways. First, it eliminated the common law limitation that afforded protection only to those unborn children who were "so far developed as to be ordinarily called 'quick,' "i.e., so far developed as to be able to move or stir in the mother's womb. Now, the statute affords protection to all unborn children at any stage of development. Second, the General Assembly added the phrase that the cause of the unborn child's death must be "without legal justification." It would appear that this phrase permits a defense to criminal liability where the defendant can show that a justification defense applies to his case. Finally, the General Assembly added the provision that a person can commit feticide if he causes the death of the unborn child "when in the commission of a felony." With the addition of this language to the statute, the General Assembly has incorporated a rule very similar to the felony-murder rule found in the homicide statute. This rule permits the substitution of the mens rea of the underlying felony for the malice normally required for murder.

With these revisions the statute now provides that "[a] person commits the offense of feticide if he or she willfully and without legal justification causes the death of an unborn child by any injury to the mother of such child, which would be murder if it resulted in the death of such mother, or if he or she, when in the commission of a felony, causes the death of an unborn child." This offense is punishable by life imprisonment.

Although feticide is, of course, related to criminal abortion, the feticide statute is designed to prohibit a very different kind of conduct. While the criminal abortion statute prohibits conduct performed in compliance with the mother's will, the feticide statute prohibits conduct performed against her will. Indeed, the statute apparently requires that the offender act with the requisite mens rea for murder or felony murder.

3. Voluntary Manslaughter of Unborn Child

A person commits the offense of voluntary manslaughter of an unborn child when that person causes the death of the child under circumstances which would otherwise be feticide and if such person acts solely as the result of a sudden, violent, and irresistible passion resulting from serious provocation sufficient to excite such passion in a reasonable person. However, if there should have been an interval between the provocation and the killing sufficient for the voice of reason and humanity to be heard, of which the jury in all cases is the judge, the killing will be attributed to deliberate revenge and be punished as feticide. The offense of voluntary manslaughter of an unborn child is punishable as a felony by imprisonment for not less than one nor more than 20 years.

4. Exceptions

Nothing in the feticide statute can be construed to permit the prosecution of (1) any person for conduct relating to an abortion for which the consent of the pregnant woman, or person authorized by law to act on her behalf, has been obtained or for which such consent is implied by law; (2) any person for any medical treatment of the pregnant woman or her unborn child; or (3) any woman with respect to her unborn child.

5. Constitutional Issues and Construction of Statute

Since the 2006 General Assembly eliminated from the definition of feticide the common law limitation that afforded protection only to those unborn children who were "so far developed as to be ordinarily called 'quick,' "any case law construing this term would no longer be controlling authority for offenses committed on or after July 1, 2006, the effective date of the enactment. The case law discussion construing this term is included below to the extent that it may still be applicable to offenses committed before that date.

The 1982 feticide statute came under constitutional attack in *Brinkley v. State*, where the defendant claimed that the use of the word "quick" rendered it unconstitutionally vague. The Georgia Supreme Court, in rejecting this claim, cited a number of cases interpreting the 1876 feticide statute which used the same word. The court held that the word "quick" meant the point at which the "fetus is able to move in its mother's womb" and found that the trial court had correctly instructed the jury on that definition.

Because of the lengthy history of judicial definition of the word, there was no constitutional infirmity. The court concluded that the 1982 statute informed all of what actions the state prohibited with sufficient definiteness that ordinary people could understand. The court also pointed out that there was nothing in the United States Supreme Court abortion jurisprudence which cast any doubt on the validity of the statute. In those cases, "the court dealt with a balance between a woman's right of privacy affording her the choice to decide the question of abortion . . . as against the state's interest in safeguarding health, maintaining medical standards, and in protecting potential life. . . . But here we deal with the interest of the state in protecting both the mother and the fetus from the intentional wrongdoing of a third party who can claim no right for his actions."

In *Smith v. Newsome*, the Eleventh Circuit Court of Appeals held that the 1982 feticide statute was not unconstitutionally vague. The court held that the case law of Georgia had long adopted the common law understanding of "quick" as when the fetus is so far developed as to be capable of movement within the mother's womb. Furthermore, rather than adding vagueness, the final clause of the 1982 feticide statute contributed specificity to the offense. Finally, the distinction between sentences required by the 1982 feticide statute and the criminal abortion statute was rationally related to legitimate governmental purposes.

In *Ward v. State*, the Georgia Supreme Court held that the clause, "by any injury to the mother of such child, which would be murder if it resulted in the death of such mother," would not preclude a defendant's conviction for both murder of the mother and feticide. The court found that this language contributes specificity to the offense. A jury must make a factual finding that the defendant's actions, had they resulted in death to the mother, would have constituted murder. Moreover, as long as neither offense is included in the other as a matter of law or of fact, it would not be error to convict a defendant of both offenses.

D. Concealing Death

Another homicide-related statute punishes anyone who, by concealing the death of any other person, hinders a discovery of whether or not that person was unlawfully killed. This offense is a felony punishable by imprisonment for not less than one nor more than ten years, a fine of not less than $1,000 nor more than $5,000, or both. This statute would apparently punish the concealment of all deaths because all deaths would raise the possibility of an unlawful killing.

E. Homicide by Vehicle

Prior to 1974, unintended, vehicular deaths provided a fruitful source for prosecutions under the involuntary manslaughter statute (§ 16-5-3). This source was diverted to another statute (§ 40-6-393) when the General Assembly created the offense of homicide by vehicle in 1974. With the creation of this offense, the General Assembly excepted unintended, vehicular deaths from other forms of involuntary manslaughter. Now, such deaths must be prosecuted and punished under the homicide by vehicle statute rather than the involuntary manslaughter statute.

Under the homicide by vehicle statute, if an unintended death occurs through the violation of the statutes punishing the failure to stop for a stopped school bus, the failure to stop at the scene of an accident, reckless driving, driving under the influence, or fleeing a police officer, it is first degree homicide by vehicle and punishable by three to 15 years' imprisonment. All other violations of the motor vehicle code which result in unintended deaths are second degree homicide by vehicle and are punishable as misdemeanors.

For further analysis of § 40-6-393, see MOTOR VEHICLE CRIMES.

F. Feticide by Vehicle

The offenses of feticide by vehicle in the first degree and in the second degree are punishable under § 40-6-393.1. See MOTOR VEHICLE CRIMES.

G. Homicide by Interference with Official Traffic-Control Device or Railroad Sign or Signal

The offense of homicide by interference with an official traffic-control device or railroad sign or signal is punishable under § 40-6-396. See MOTOR VEHICLE CRIMES.

H. Homicide by Vessel

The offenses of homicide by vessel in the first degree and in the second degree are punishable under § 52-7-12.2. See WATER-RELATED CRIMES.

I. Feticide by Vessel

The offenses of feticide by vessel in the first degree and in the second degree are punishable under § 52-7-

12.3. See WATER-RELATED CRIMES.

J. Homicide by Aircraft

The offense of homicide by aircraft is punishable under § 6-2-5.2. See AVIATION CRIMES.

K. Homicide by Perjury

Section 16-10-70 provides that those who cause death by their perjury are subject to enhanced punishment under the perjury statute. For further analysis of the perjury statutes, see PERJURY AND RELATED CRIMES.

IMPEDING ARREST OR PROSECUTION

See also LAW ENFORCEMENT DEFENSE.

I. Generally

There are ten code sections punishing behavior that interferes with the arrest or prosecution of violators of the criminal law. Four of the crimes (hindering apprehension, obstructing a law enforcement officer, giving a false name, address, or birthdate, and removing the firearm, chemical spray, or baton of a law enforcement officer) concentrate on behavior before or at the arrest stage, while five other crimes (compounding a crime, tampering with evidence, attempting to murder or threatening a witness in an official proceeding, intimidating a witness in an official proceeding, and intimidating a juror or court officer) are more likely to occur later in the prosecution process. The last crime, false report of a crime, punishes behavior which interferes with the law enforcement process by triggering it unnecessarily.

II. Interference with Arrest

A. Hindering Apprehension or Punishment of a Criminal

Section 16-10-50 replaces and broadens the coverage of code sections in the criminal code prior to 1968. The mens rea of this felony is an intent to hinder the apprehension or punishment of a person who the actor knows or has reason to believe is either (1) a felon, (2) an escaped inmate, or (3) an escaped prisoner. There are two alternative actus reus elements, either of which will suffice for conviction. The actor must either (1) harbor or conceal the felon, inmate, or prisoner or (2) conceal or destroy evidence of the crime committed by such a person. The latter actus reus is similar to the actus reus of § 16-10-94, which makes it a misdemeanor to tamper with evidence. The latter statute punishes those who destroy, alter, conceal, or disguise evidence or make, devise, prepare, or plant false evidence.

Once a person has concealed the evidence of a crime with the intent of protecting himself and another from punishment, the crime of hindering the apprehension of a criminal is complete. The fact that the person later reveals to the police the place where the evidence is concealed does not result in the abandonment of the crime. Thus, the defense of abandonment is not available to this person.

Section 16-10-50 has not been utilized to any great extent since its enactment in 1968 as part of the revised criminal code. One decision involved a prosecution for armed robbery in which one of the defendants complained that the testimony of a state witness who had harbored him after flight from the scene would require corroboration, it being the testimony of an accomplice. The court rejected the defense argument, pointing out that § 16-10-50 is designed to punish those formerly known as accessories after the fact and that such individuals are not parties to the crime under § 16-2-20 of the current code. Under this statutory scheme, one may not be convicted as a party to the crime and also be convicted as an accessory after the fact. Thus, where one has been convicted as a party to the crime, his conviction for hindering the apprehension of a criminal must be set aside.

A predecessor statute to § 16-10-50 was upheld in one case against a charge of unconstitutional vagueness and was held in another case to cover the situation where the defendant had actual knowledge of facts which would give him good reason to believe that the person harbored was guilty of a crime. Although the latter holding was perhaps questionable in light of the language of the prior statute which required the defendant to "know" the harbored person to be guilty, the present statute would clearly authorize the same result. It punishes those who hinder the apprehension of those they "know" or have "reasonable grounds to believe" are guilty of a felony or are escaped inmates or prisoners. This mens rea permits conviction not only for intentional activity but also for negligent activity.

Section 16-10-50, which is punishable by one to five years' imprisonment, can be seen as punishing a subset of the behavior covered by the crime of obstruction of law enforcement officers (§ 16-10-24(a)). It seems clear that an individual could not be convicted of violating both § 16-10-50 and § 16-10-24(a) on the basis of the same acts and that § 16-10-24(a) would be a lesser included offense of § 16-10-50 in that any violation of the latter statute would necessarily be a violation of the former. It should be noted that a violation of § 16-10-24(a) is punishable as a misdemeanor.

B. Giving False Name, Address, or Birthdate to Law Enforcement Officers

1. Generally

The drafters of the 1968 criminal code added § 16-10-25 to the criminal law of Georgia, promising that it would "greatly aid law enforcement." This statute makes it a misdemeanor to give a false name, address, or birthdate to a law enforcement officer who is in the lawful discharge of his official duties with the intent to mislead the officer. This statute is not written in terms of misleading only law enforcement officers of this state. It applies to any law enforcement officer. There is no requirement in the statute that the false name be given to any particular officer. Thus, there would be no fatal variance in a case where the indictment names one officer, but the evidence shows that another officer was given the false name.

It is uncertain what the purpose of this statute is since it covers behavior all of which could be punishable under § 16-10-24(a), obstruction of law enforcement officers, and since it punishes that behavior as a misdemeanor, as does § 16-10-24(a). A 1975 case, for example, held that giving an arresting officer a false name was a violation of § 16-10-24.

2. *Proof of Defendant's Real Name*

There must be some evidence that the name given in the subject incident was false. Generally this is established by some proof of the defendant's real name. In Agony v. State, the court held that the evidence did not establish that the name given in this incident was false as opposed to the names in the prior incidents being false. The evidence simply established that on three different occasions the defendant had given different names to a law enforcement officer. It did not support even an inference that the defendant gave a false name to a law enforcement officer on this occasion rather than on prior occasions. No other evidence of identification, such as a driver's license, and no testimony of anyone familiar with the defendant's real name was presented. As the state failed to present sufficient evidence to find the defendant guilty beyond a reasonable doubt of giving a false name, the defendant's conviction had to be reversed.

3. *Lawful Discharge of Official Duties*

In order to establish a violation of § 16-10-25, the evidence must show that the law enforcement officer was acting lawfully in the discharge of his official duties. In Scott v. State, the court addressed the content of the lawful duties of a law enforcement officer. In this case, the defendants were charged with giving a false name to a police officer who had arrested them for a misdemeanor. The court held that since the policeman had not witnessed the misdemeanor, the arrest would have been unlawful and, thus, the false name would have been given to the police officer while he was acting unlawfully. The court was quick to point out, however, that the policeman would have had the right to question the defendants before the misdemeanor arrest and giving a false name during such questioning would have occurred during the policeman's lawful carrying out of his duties and, therefore, would have violated § 16-10-25. In Rajappa v. State, the court held that the police officers acted reasonably in assuming that the defendant's 15-year-old daughter had sufficient control over the premises and that the daughter's consent was sufficient to authorize their entry into the premises to conduct a warrantless search. Thus, the police officers were acting lawfully in the discharge of their duties when the defendant gave them a false name.

Where circumstances do not provide an officer with articulable suspicion that the law has been or is about to be violated, the officer's act of detaining and questioning an individual is nothing more than a police-citizen encounter outside the scope of his official police duties. In Holt v. State, the defendant's only transgression was his presence in a car with a cracked windshield which was traversing the wrong parking lot, at the wrong time. The court held that because the officer could not articulate a particularized reason for questioning the defendant, other than his sense that the defendant was "making kind of furtive movements like [he was] nervous about something," and because the officer admitted that he had no basis for believing that the defendant had engaged in, was engaging in, or was about to engage in criminal activity, the officer was not lawfully discharging his official duties when he questioned the defendant. The defendant therefore did not violate § 16-10-25 when he gave the officer a false name and date of birth, and his conviction had to be reversed. In Wynn v. State, however, the court found that the officers did not lack articulable suspicion that a violation of the law had occurred. Indeed, the facts available to the officers upon their initial approach of the defendant and discovery of the open container of beer resting in plain view provided information, satisfying a probable cause standard, that the defendant was in violation of the state's open container law. Thus, the court held that there was sufficient evidence that the officers' act of questioning the defendant was more than a consensual inquiry and was within the scope of the officers' official duties so that a jury could have determined that the defendant's use of a false name was a violation of § 16-10-25.

A law enforcement officer who has identified himself as such is not required to inform anyone to whom he speaks of the nature of his inquiry in order to be in the lawful discharge of his official duties. Thus, a defendant who gives an officer a false name but corrects his misstatement before he becomes aware of the nature of the officer's inquiry would still be guilty of the offense of giving a false name to a law enforcement officer.

4. *Intent to Mislead*

Whether the requisite intent to mislead is manifested by the circumstances is a question for the trier of fact. The issue to be decided is not whether the officer was actually misled but whether the defendant intended to mislead him.

The quantum of proof necessary to find an intent to mislead a law enforcement officer was at issue in Johnson v. State. In Johnson, the defendant when arrested for a traffic violation gave the officer one name and then gave another the following day. The defendant claimed that he used both names on occasion, but admitted that the name first given did not appear on his birth certificate, social security card, or previous driver's license. The court upheld the conviction. This was the only evidence which was before the court and the court's affirmance here indicates that the mere commission of the prohibited act probably will be enough for a finding of the prohibited mens rea. A similar situation arose in Rajappa v. State. In Rajappa, the question was whether the defendant could be guilty of giving a false name when by custom of her native country she had two last names and when the name she gave to the police was one of those names. The court held that there was ample evidence from which the trial court could have concluded that the defendant intended to deceive the police by giving that name. Evidence of the defendant's educational background indicated that she was familiar with the customs of the United States. Also, the police officers testified that the defendant identified herself as "Mini Venkateswara" but later showed them a driver's license bearing the name "Padmini Rajappa" and admitted that was her name.

In Grisson v. State, the court held that the officer's testimony was sufficient to establish the fact that the defendant, when stopped at a license/insurance card checkpoint, did not produce a valid driver's license but instead gave a false name and date of birth. The criminal intent to mislead the officer as to the defendant's identity could have been inferred from the documentary evidence indicating that the defendant personally received notice that his driver's license and driving privileges had been revoked in Georgia for a minimum of five years.

5. *Admissibility of Evidence*

The giving of a false name to a law enforcement officer during the investigation of a crime is evidence which indicates a consciousness of guilt on the part of the defendant and is admissible against him. Also, the giving of a false name to a law enforcement officer at the time of arrest is admissible as evidence regarding the circumstances of the defendant's arrest.

Asking for a person's name and birthdate during the process of an arrest is not reasonably likely to elicit a response which incriminates one in the commission of a crime and, therefore, is not interrogation. No Miranda warnings are necessary in this situation. Thus, the failure to provide Miranda warnings would not render an officer's testimony about the defendant's giving a false name and birthdate inadmissible.

6. *Probable Cause for Arrest*

A suspect's failure to accurately repeat his birthday and social security number is sufficient evidence of a false identity as to provide probable cause for his arrest.

7. *Relationship to Other Offenses*

Important Notice about Repudiation of Actual or Same Evidence Test: The Georgia Supreme Court repudiated the actual evidence test in *Drinkard v. Walker*, 281 Ga. 211, 636 S.E.2d 530 (2006), because it found this test to be inconsistent with the statutory framework governing the prohibition against multiple convictions for included offenses in Georgia. This inconsistency resulted in years of confusion and unpredictable results. In its place, the court adopted the required evidence test and overruled any prior case law that is inconsistent with it. Thus, any prior case law applying the actual evidence test is no longer controlling and should not be relied upon to determine whether one offense is included in another under § 16-1-6(1). The discussion of such case law is included below only insofar as it may still be applicable to pending prosecutions that arose before the Drinkard decision. See MULTIPLE CONVICTIONS, II. Tests to Determine Presence of Multiple Convictions, for a complete discussion of the Drinkard decision.

While the offense of giving a false name requires that the fraud be perpetrated against a law enforcement officer, the offense of forgery in the first degree does not. Also, a forgery has to involve a writing, while giving a false name does not. As such, the two offenses do not merge as a matter of law. Furthermore, where the forgery is completed long before the defendant ever gives his false name to a law enforcement officer, the two offenses do not merge as a matter of fact.

C. *Obstruction of Law Enforcement Officers*

1. *Generally*

The criminal statutes prior to 1968 dealt with obstruction of an officer serving legal process and executing a sentence. These statutes were replaced in 1968 by a criminal statute that prohibited the knowing and willful obstruction or hindrance of a law enforcement officer in the lawful discharge of his official duties. This offense was punishable as misdemeanor.

In 1986, this statute was stricken and replaced by the current criminal statute. The current statute establishes two different grades of the offense of obstruction: misdemeanor obstruction and felony obstruction. If the obstruction or hindrance of an officer neither offers nor does violence to his person, it is punishable as a misdemeanor. If the resistance, obstruction, or opposition offers or does violence to his person, it is punishable as a felony by imprisonment for not less than one nor more than five years.

A jury charge that the definition of misdemeanor obstruction is identical to felony obstruction except that "misdemeanor obstruction is not offering to do violence, but simply resisting arrest" communicates all the elements of misdemeanor obstruction in a manner not likely to mislead a jury. However, the better practice would be to charge fully on both misdemeanor and felony obstruction.

2. *Mens Rea*

The mens rea for both misdemeanor and felony obstruction is knowing and willful action. Because the statutory mens rea requires knowing and willful activity, it is apparent that the individual who obstructs a policeman without knowledge of his status is not guilty of a violation of § 16-10-24. Very few cases presenting this fact situation under § 16-10-24 have been identified, however. This may be because other criminal sanctions exist with penalties just as severe. For example, simple assault or simple battery would normally be present in many of these situations. In a case which does not include such an actus reus, however, it would seem that the defendant who was hindering or obstructing the law enforcement officer without knowledge of his status would not be guilty of obstruction.

The willfulness of the defendant's actions can be established by presenting evidence of similar instances of crimes against police officers. Such evidence has been held to be admissible to show the defendant's motive, intent, and bent of mind, and to show that this is a typical way in which the defendant deals with the police.

3. *Actus Reus*

a. *Means of Obstruction*

The effectiveness of the pre-1968 obstruction statute, which defined its actus reus in terms of "obstruct, resist, or oppose," was diminished by the fact that it failed to specify the means of obstruction. The courts confined the statute's application to assaults, thus rendering the statute largely superfluous. As early as 1886, the Georgia courts interpreted that statute as requiring the use or threatened use of force. In McBride v. State, the court held that the statute required the use or threatened use of force together with the ability and the apparent intent to carry such threat into effect.

The 1968 obstruction statute, which defined its actus reus in terms of "obstructs or hinders," likewise failed to specify the means of obstruction. However, the drafters of the statute did state that the statute covered "the obstruction of law enforcement in general by the use of violence, threat of violence, or other unlawful means." In Samples v. State, the court held that the 1968 statute required proof of "forcible" resistance or opposition to the officer in the performance of his duties.

In 1986, the 1968 obstruction statute was stricken and replaced by the current statute, which establishes two different grades of the offense: misdemeanor obstruction and felony obstruction. The actus reus of misdemeanor obstruction is essentially the same as the 1968 statute. However, the misdemeanor obstruction provision does not require proof of "force" or "violence" in order to secure a conviction. This requirement is contained only in the felony obstruction provision. A conviction for felony obstruction requires proof that the defendant offered or did "violence" to the person of an officer. Thus, under the current statute, the actus reus for misdemeanor obstruction is the obstruction or hindrance of a law enforcement officer in the lawful discharge of his official duties other than by offering or doing violence to his person. Argument, flight, stubborn obstinance, and lying are all examples of conduct that may satisfy the obstruction element. The actus reus for felony obstruction is the resistance, obstruction, or opposition of any statutorily protected officer in the lawful discharge of his official duties by offering or doing violence to his person. Injury of the officer is not an element of felony obstruction.

Since the offense of misdemeanor obstruction does not contain the element of "violence" (as does the offense of felony obstruction), any allegations regarding the means by which a defendant committed violence on a police officer are unnecessary with regard to a conviction for misdemeanor obstruction and need not be proved.

Where an indictment alleges that the offense of felony obstruction was committed by "using loud and profane language and by fighting [the] officer," the state is not required to prove that the defendant physically fought with the officer. Since the word "fighting" denotes not only a physical struggle but also a verbal disagreement, it is enough for the state to show that the defendant verbally threatened the officer and acted in opposition to his authority.

Where an accusation charges the defendant with obstruction by interfering with the execution of a warrant but the defendant is convicted of obstruction by interfering with the officers' reverse sting operation, there would be no fatal variance between the accusation and the proof at trial where there is evidence that the execution of the search warrant and the sting operation occurred simultaneously.

The determination of the content of the actus reus requirement of the obstruction statute has been a fruitful source of case law. The case law indicates that the statute clearly covers verbal exchanges. Threats and abusive language which hinder or obstruct the officer in the lawful discharge of his official duties would constitute misdemeanor obstruction, while threats of violence would constitute felony obstruction. Where the offense is grounded on a verbal exchange, it is for the jury to determine whether the speech must reasonably be interpreted as a threat of violence constituting the offense of felony obstruction.

A threat of future violence, by itself, could constitute felony obstruction. However, an obstruction conviction cannot stand where there is no evidence that such threats obstructed the officer's completion of his law enforcement duties.

Other obstruction convictions have been affirmed (1) where there were repeated attempts to come onto the premises where policemen were attempting to execute a search warrant; (2) where the defendant, after being instructed by an officer not to do so, informed a third party of the presence of police and warned him not to go into a home where officers were conducting a search and a reverse sting operation; (3) where the defendant returned to the scene of a fatal shooting after being told by officers on several occasions to leave the scene; (4) where the defendant gave false information to the police officer trying to serve a warrant on another person; (5) where the defendant gave false information to a booking officer; (6) where the defendant refused to be fingerprinted; (7) where the defendant willfully refused to obey an officer; (8) where the defendant refused to remain at an alleged crime scene pending a brief official police investigation; (9) where the defendant did not respond at all to the officer's orders and forced the officer to get a warrant in an effort to effectuate his arrest; (10) where the defendant refused to provide the officer with identification; (11) where the defendant ignored repeated requests by the officer to produce her driver's license; (12) where by his statements and actions the defendant deliberately misled the officer into mistaking him for his brother; (13) where the defendant spit on the officer while refusing to identify himself; (14) where an inmate refused to enter his cell and hit a correctional officer; (15) where the defendant purposefully kicked and attempted to bite officers as they were assisting in an investigation; (16) where the defendant, when an officer began to frisk him, struck the officer in the chest and violently resisted the officer's attempt to subdue him; (17) where the defendant attacked an officer, who was attempting to escort the defendant's companion away from a bar, by tackling him from behind and driving him into a door resulting in an injury to his hand; (18) where the defendant pushed an officer attempting to take him into custody and ran away from the officer; (19) where the defendant violently resisted arrest for violating a city ordinance against disorderly conduct; (20) where the defendant shouted and cursed so that an officer could not hear what a spouse was saying concerning a domestic disturbance; (21) where the defendant hid or destroyed evidence; (22) where the defendant backed her vehicle into the officer's patrol car; and (23) where the defendant fled on foot from an officer. The holding in this last case is limited by the fact that an obstruction conviction for flight cannot be upheld if there is evidence that the defendant halted when ordered to do so or if there is no evidence that the pursuing officer, in a show of lawful authority, ordered the defendant to halt. A mere verbal exchange, boldly obnoxious and contemptuous conduct, a failure to provide identification of a person sought by the police, a mere refusal to give one's name to an officer, and a failure to respond immediately to an officer do not constitute violations of the statute.

Some of the above holdings must be reviewed in light of the United States Supreme Court decision in City of Houston v. Hill. There the United States Supreme Court found a municipal ordinance, which provided that it was "unlawful for any person to . . . in any manner oppose, molest, abuse or interrupt any policeman in the execution of his duty," to be substantially overbroad in that it prohibited willful and intentional verbal interruptions of police officers. The court stated that the freedom of individuals verbally to oppose or challenge police action without thereby risking arrest is one of the principal characteristics which distinguishes a free nation from a police state. The court's holding reflects the constitutional requirement that, in the face of verbal challenges to police action, officers and municipalities must respond with restraint. However, the decision does not leave municipalities powerless to punish physical obstruction of police action.

It is unnecessary for the state to prove that the defendant is guilty of the underlying crime that caused the officer to act in order to prove him guilty of obstruction of the officer.

An instruction on a specific means of obstruction, even though abstractly correct, should not be given to the jury unless authorized by the evidence. An unauthorized instruction could allow the jury to find the defendant guilty of the crime of obstruction under a theory unsupported by the evidence. When such an instruction is given, if it should be confusing or misleading to the jury, a new trial will be required.

Even if the trial court instructs the jury on both means of committing felony obstruction under the statute, any error in doing so would be harmless if the trial court gives a curative instruction which clearly limits the jury's consideration to the means alleged in the indictment.

b. Law Enforcement Officer

Proof that the law enforcement officer is certified is not an essential element of the offense. In Dennis v. State, one of the arresting officers had just completed his basic training course at the police academy and was a sworn reserve officer with arrest powers. The court held that this evidence was sufficient to show that the officer was a "law enforcement officer" within the meaning of the statute.

c. Lawful Discharge of Official Duties

While many of § 16-10-24 cases are those in which the defendant is charged with resisting an officer's attempt to arrest him, interference with the lawful discharge of any of the law enforcement official's duties will constitute a violation of the statute. Thus, in Allen v. State, the court upheld a conviction of a bouncer who interfered with the entrance of a sheriff into a private club when the sheriff was trying to deliver a permit to the club's owner. Likewise, in Mason v. State, a third party's interference with attempts to serve a warrant was held to be within the statute's proscription. In Banks v. State, the court held that the retrieval and preservation of evidence was within the lawful discharge of an officer's duties and that an attack on an officer performing such a duty constituted a violation of the statute. In Vaughn v. State, the court held that an officer trying to investigate a complaint of domestic violence and to ensure that everything was all right at a house was within the lawful discharge of his duties and that the defendant's actions in resisting arrest constituted obstruction of an officer. In Walker v. State, the court held that an officer who responded to a domestic dispute call was acting in the lawful discharge of his duties when he, because of his concern for the safety of himself and the victim, attempted to search the defendant for weapons. A law enforcement officer is authorized to conduct a pat-down search of an individual when he reasonably believes him to be armed or otherwise dangerous to the officer or others. Evidence of the defendant's failure to comply with the officer's attempt to search him was sufficient to authorize his conviction for obstruction. In Animashaun v. State, the court held that an officer, who was present at an apartment for the purpose of avoiding a confrontation between a husband and wife when the wife returned to the apartment to retrieve her possessions, was in the lawful discharge of his official duty when the husband interfered with the officer's attempt to maintain the peace.

In Duncan v. State, the court held that a police officer moonlighting as a bouncer was performing his lawful duties when acting as a bouncer. The court pointed out that law enforcement officials have a 24-hour duty to maintain the public peace. The court found its decision supported by strong public policy reasoning. "The presence of uniformed officers in places susceptible to breaches of the peace deters unlawful acts and conduct by patrons . . .. The public knows the uniform and the badge stand for the authority of the government."

Unless contradicted by other evidence, proof that one acted as a law enforcement officer is prima facie evidence that he was such an officer and was lawfully discharging his official duties. In Miller v. State, the officer testified that he was on duty and was lawfully discharging his duty when he attempted to reach into the arrestee's pocket to obtain his car keys so that a wrecker could pull his car from a ditch. During this attempt, the arrestee, who was sitting in the patrol car, grabbed and pulled the officer toward the car causing him to strike his head on the roof of the car. The defense did not present any evidence to contradict the officer's testimony. Thus, there was sufficient evidence to support the arrestee's conviction for felony obstruction.

Upon an individual being found guilty of a misdemeanor that contemplates imprisonment, law enforcement officials possess the duty and power to contain that individual for the purposes of carrying out the sentence. In Scott v. State, the court held that once the defendant refused to pay a fine for a traffic violation, the officers were authorized to carry out the alternative sentence of a jail term. The officers' attempts to restrain the defendant were simply a function of their continuing duty to control a person arrested, tried, and sentenced under the law. The evidence therefore supported the conclusion that the officers were acting pursuant to an official duty.

A question may arise as to the validity of resistance or obstruction of an attempt to serve process, such as a writ of possession, which is invalid. It has been stated as a matter of general law that resisting process valid on its face is illegal obstruction of law enforcement, even where there might be some underlying illegality not apparent from the face of the document. Conversely, it has been held that resisting or obstructing process which is patently void is not a crime. The purpose of these two rules is to adjust the tension between two public policies: one which favors the protection of law enforcement officials in the performance of their jobs and one which favors the protection of private citizens from illegal intrusions on their privacy and/or liberty.

The only Georgia authority in this area seems to prefer the latter policy to the former. In Searcy v. State, the court reversed an obstruction conviction because the affidavit upon which the fieri facias was based was insufficient. There is no indication that this irregularity appeared on the face of the process being served. In Gibson v. State, although the court held valid an indictment for obstruction of justice, it pointed out that evidence of a procedural failure in issuing the writ which had been resisted would be admissible at trial, implying that if the issuing magistrate had failed to require the plaintiff to post bond, resistance to the writ would not be criminal. In both of these cases, now over ninety years old, the court indicated that nonapparent irregularities in the process would justify resistance or obstruction. These cases, however, predate the current statute which seems to limit the private citizen's right to interfere with the work of law enforcement officials. A court, when confronted by Searcy and Gibson, might find them inconsistent with the current statute's broadening of the crime of obstruction.

One of the most important of a law enforcement official's duties is that of arresting violators of the law. The question of when a policeman is acting within his duty and the consequences of his acting outside it is thus a very important question under § 16-10-24. A defendant who is arrested by a law enforcement official and charged with obstruction of that arrest under § 16-10-24 may very well claim that the official's behavior placed him beyond the scope of his official duties and that the resistance was, therefore, justified. The standard for determining whether an officer was lawfully discharging his duties such that an individual's conduct would constitute obstruction is whether a reasonable suspicion existed to stop the individual charged with obstruction.

In Brown v. State, the court upheld a conviction for impeding arrest where the arresting officer was in hot pursuit of an arrestee who fled from the street into the defendant's house. Citing United States Supreme Court authority, the court held that a suspect cannot defeat a lawful arrest in public by fleeing into a private home. Thus, the pursuing officer was lawfully performing his duty to arrest, and the trial judge's refusal to instruct the jury concerning the presence of "exigent circumstances" was not erroneous.

In Animashaun v. State, the court upheld the defendant's conviction for felony obstruction, even though the officers' entry into the defendant's apartment was without a warrant. The defendant's wife willingly gave the officers her key to the apartment. At that point in time, she still possessed common authority over the premises, and the officers' entry based upon her consent was authorized.

In Brown v. State, the court concluded that the arresting officers were engaged in the lawful discharge of their official duties even though they did not have a search warrant, there were no exigent circumstances, and there was no evidence of the homeowner's proper consent allowing them to enter his home to arrest a probation violator who did not reside there. The court found that the officers had probable cause and a warrant for the violator's arrest. This gave the officers the authority to enter the third person's home to execute the arrest warrant.

In Strickland v. State, the officer not only had probable cause to arrest the defendant for obstructing the Emergency Medical Technicians (EMTs), the defendant's continued interference with the EMTs' attempt to fulfill their duty and examine the still-unattended poison victim was an exigent circumstance that would have justified the officer's entry onto private property without a warrant. The evidence showed the officer was in the lawful pursuit of his duty when the defendant offered to do violence to his person.

In Sanders v. State, the court held that probable cause existed to stop the driver of a vehicle and make a warrantless arrest of him for driving too fast for conditions. The jury was authorized to infer that the defendant as passenger knew that a police officer was attempting to perform his official duty of arresting the driver, and to find that the defendant by fleeing deliberately took action to delay, hamper or impede the officer in the performance of this duty.

In In Interest of C. W., the officer had been told by a subdivision resident that the juvenile was driving his go-cart in a dangerous manner and on private yards, which his own observations in part confirmed. When the officer attempted to stop the juvenile by signaling him with his siren so he could investigate and give a warning, the juvenile unlawfully fled. The court held that from that point, the officer was justified in apprehending the juvenile and was lawfully discharging his duties when the juvenile threatened him.

In Norman v. State, the court held that the defendant's failure to stop running after the detective identified himself as a police officer and yelled stop several times and the defendant's continued struggling with the detective after he was detained provided the probable cause for his arrest for obstruction.

In Singleton v. State, the court held that the officers were in the lawful discharge of their duties when they responded to a disorderly person call and when a radio transmission, which confirmed the outstanding warrants, established the necessary probable cause to arrest the defendant.

In Dennis v. State, the evidence showed that before the officers confronted the defendant, they had probable cause to believe he had committed battery on his wife. The court held that because the officers were acting in the lawful discharge of their duties during the incident, the defendant's resistance constituted obstruction.

In Hall v. State, the court held that the officer was acting in the lawful discharge of his official duties when he stopped the defendant's vehicle for the offense of driving an improperly equipped vehicle.

In Reagin v. State, the court held that the officer had probable cause to believe that the defendant had been driving while under the influence. The officer saw the defendant sitting in a parked car drinking from a can. The defendant attempted to conceal the can as the officer approached his car. The officer had direct knowledge of the defendant's apparent intoxication and had been told by the defendant that he drove to the rest stop only 15 minutes before the officer's arrival. It was immaterial to the legality of the arrest that the defendant was acquitted of the charge of driving under the influence. Evidence of the defendant's physical resistance to his arrest was sufficient to authorize his conviction for obstruction.

In Williams v. State, the court held that there was ample evidence from which a rational trier of fact could have concluded that the officer had probable cause to arrest the defendant for being drunk in public and to find beyond a reasonable doubt that he was guilty of misdemeanor obstruction. The fact that the trial court granted a directed verdict of acquittal as to the charge of public drunk was immaterial to the officer's probable cause to arrest the defendant.

A dispatcher who reports a crime at a specified location gives police an articulable suspicion to investigate and detain individuals at the scene, particularly where police observations on arriving at the scene corroborate the dispatcher's report. Thus, in Overand v. State, the court held that the evidence sustained a finding of an articulable suspicion. Police observations of a white female arguing vigorously with a white male in the driveway of the reported crime scene corroborated the information received from the dispatcher. While demanding that the female stay, police also discovered a pistol, further corroborating the dispatcher's report. Thus, since the police had an articulable suspicion to detain and question the female suspect, they were in the lawful discharge of their official duties when she refused to remain at the crime scene.

In Wynn v. State, the court found that the officers did not lack articulable suspicion that a violation of the law had occurred. Indeed, the facts available to the officers upon their initial approach of the defendant and discovery of the open container of beer resting in plain view provided information, satisfying a probable cause standard, that the defendant was in violation of the state's open container law. Thus, the court held that there was sufficient evidence that the officers' act of questioning the defendant was more than a consensual inquiry and was within the scope of the officers' official duties so that a jury was authorized to conclude that the lawful discharge of official duties element of felony obstruction had been proven beyond a reasonable doubt.

In Youhoing v. State, the court held that through the use of his senses and based on his conversation with the defendant, examination of her license, and the location of her car in a fire lane in front of a fast-food restaurant, the officer easily gained the personal knowledge and probable cause necessary to initiate an arrest. Due to the general exigencies involving the transient motoring public, no warrant was required for the arrest to be lawful. The officer's decision to implement a full custodial arrest, rather than a non-custodial arrest by issuing a citation, was lawful and authorized. Thus, evidence that the defendant intentionally hindered the officer by her actions when he attempted to place her under custodial arrest was sufficient to support her conviction for misdemeanor obstruction.

Where circumstances do not provide an officer with articulable suspicion that the law has been or is about to be violated, the officer's act of stopping an individual is nothing more than a police-citizen encounter outside the scope of his official police duties. In In Interest of J.T., the court initially held that because the state failed to prove the existence of the local ordinance against loitering in a known drug area, it was unable to show that the officer was in the lawful discharge of his official duties the first time he tried to stop the juvenile. The court also found that during the officer's three encounters with the juvenile, he never had any particular and objective reason to suspect the juvenile of criminal activity. Because the officer had no lawful basis for stopping the juvenile, even briefly, the court held that the juvenile did not obstruct the officer by refusing to stop.

4. Right to Resist Illegal Arrest or Excessive Force Arrest

a. Common Law Right to Resist

The right to resist forcibly an arrest which is unlawful because there is no arrest warrant when a warrant is needed or there is no probable cause was established in the English common law by 1710 and carried over to the United States. Some jurisdictions have modified this right, and the Model Penal Code advocates its total abolition on the grounds that such resistance by an arrestee is usually futile and often dangerous and that the issue of an arrest's legality is better left to resolution in later court proceedings.

An arrest is not unlawful within the common law right to resist, if the arrest is authorized by statute, even though the statute may later be declared unconstitutional. In Johnson v. State, the court held that the fact that the state was barred from securing the defendant's conviction for disorderly conduct, because the disorderly conduct statute was subsequently declared unconstitutional, was immaterial to the defendant's guilt for obstruction of the law enforcement officer. It was the legality of the defendant's arrest for disorderly conduct, not his actual conviction for disorderly conduct, that was material to his guilt for obstruction of the law enforcement officer. Thus, the defendant did not have the legal right to resist his arrest, and his motion for a directed verdict of acquittal on the obstruction charge was properly denied.

b. Lack of Probable Cause to Arrest

Because an officer making an arrest without probable cause is not lawfully discharging his official duties, physical resistance to such an arrest is not a violation of § 16-10-24. In Wagner v. State, there was no evidence that the defendant was unruly or threatened to breach the peace or even that the officer thought he was drunk. The defendant's sole offense was to refuse to give his name. The court held that this mere refusal was not probable cause for arrest. Thus, the arrest was unlawful and the defendant's physical resistance to the arrest did not violate the statute. In Brooks v. State, the evidence showed that at the moment the officers decided to seize the defendant, the facts and circumstances within the knowledge of the officers and of which they had reasonable trustworthy information were not sufficient to warrant a prudent man to believe that the defendant had committed an offense. As the officers lacked probable cause or articulable suspicion such as would have authorized the seizure, the defendant was entitled to resist the unlawful arrest by attempting to "push through" an officer to effect his escape. Since the evidence showed that the officer was not in the lawful discharge of his official duties, the defendant's conviction for obstruction was not authorized. In Woodward v. State, there was no evidence that the defendant presented a security threat, that it was unlawful for her to be in the building housing the sheriff's department, or that anyone had instructed her not to enter the second floor. A belligerent telephone call earlier in the day, without more, was not disorderly conduct and did not constitute probable cause for an arrest. As there was no evidence that the deputy was in the lawful discharge of his duties when he arrested the defendant, she had the right to resist with all force necessary for that purpose, and her conviction for felony obstruction was not authorized. In Land v. State, considering that all evidence of the contraband found in the defendant's house should have been suppressed and that the detectives gained entry to the house using an invalid search warrant, the court concluded that there was no proof that the officers were authorized to arrest the defendant. Without such evidence, the state could not establish that the detectives were lawfully discharging their official duties. Accordingly, the defendant's conviction for the offense of obstruction of a law enforcement officer was not authorized by the evidence.

In *State v. Ealum*, the state could not show that the defendants committed a new crime in the presence of law enforcement officers sufficient to purge the taint of the officers' prior unlawful entry into the trailer. Since the officers in the case were not lawfully discharging their duties at the time of the defendants' alleged obstructing behavior, obstruction charges would not properly lie against the defendants. Thus, the court upheld that trial court's granting of the defendants motion to suppress all tangible physical evidence, statements, and testimony resulting from the unlawful entry into their trailer.

c. Limitations on Amount Force Used to Resist Arrest

A related, although separate, question which might arise in a § 16-10-24 prosecution would be resistance to a lawful arrest which is being effectuated through the use of excessive force. In this situation, the general rule is that reasonable force may be used by the arrestee to thwart such force by the arresting officer.

The right of an arrestee to resist forcibly an illegal arrest was announced in Georgia in 1892. In Thomas v. State, the court indicated that shooting at a police officer making an illegal arrest would not be murder, but only manslaughter, presumably because this response by the arrestee was a lawful act (resistance) performed in an unlawful manner (killing). Thomas, thus, established two principles: (1) forcible resistance of an illegal arrest is permitted, and (2) there are limits to the amount of force permissible. The precise scope of the amount of force permissible was described by the Georgia Supreme Court in Perdue v. State, as "force sufficient to prevent the consummation of the arrest." Perdue suggested that even deadly force could be used in such a situation, but that it must await the use of "greater force" by the arresting officer. Taken together, Thomas and Perdue seem to indicate that an ordinary arrest could be resisted by ordinary force and an arrest being carried out with deadly force could be resisted with deadly force.

As for a lawful arrest made with an excessive use of force, the Georgia cases support the rule that such excessive force can be resisted by proportionate force and will not be seen as an obstruction of officers. In Mullis v. State, the court held that an arrestee would be justified in killing an arresting officer who used excessive force in effectuating a lawful (or unlawful) arrest. In describing such excessive force, the court mentioned unprovoked assaults with deadly weapons which were, or could reasonably be seen by the arrestee to be, intended to kill the arrestee. It should be stressed that in such a situation the killing would not be merely reduced from murder to manslaughter, but totally justified. This result is totally consistent with, and can be viewed as part of, the law of self-defense. To the extent that the policeman's force is excessive it is illegal and can be defended against.

It is axiomatic that neither the right to resist an unlawful arrest nor the right to resist an excessive force arrest is a license to act without restraint. The defendant must actually have been acting to resist the arrest and cannot later use the fact of the illegal or excessive force arrest as an excuse for striking the officer. As the court wrote in Napper v. State, "the rule applies only in those cases where the attack upon the officer is, as a matter of fact and not merely as a theory, made in defense of one's liberty . . . ."

d. *Jury Instructions*

The right to resist forcibly an illegal arrest was reiterated by the Court of Appeals in Brooks v. State. The Brooks court, however, seemed to be placing new restrictions on the right. In Brooks, the defendant was being arrested and grabbed for the officer's gun. He claimed, as a defense to simple assault, that he was resisting an illegal arrest. The court rejected the defendant's claim of an entitlement to an instruction on the right to resist an illegal arrest on the grounds that an arrestee can never assault an officer unless the officer has first assaulted him within the meaning of § 16-5-20, the simple assault statute.

The Brooks court held that since the officer had not placed the defendant in "reasonable apprehension of immediately receiving a violent injury," in the language of § 16-5-20(a)(2), the failure to instruct on the right to resist an illegal arrest was not error. This case appears to be in direct contradiction to an earlier case which described an illegal arrest itself as an assault justifying the use of force to prevent the completion of the arrest. In many situations, the Brooks rule will be satisfied in that the defendant will be able to demonstrate fear of violent injury at the hands of the police officer, but to the extent that a Brooks-type assault by the police officer is not present, the holding serves to limit the traditional right to resist forcibly an illegal arrest. To this extent, the Georgia courts may have been influenced by those urging limitation of the traditional right.

In Williams v. State, the court held that where the defendant testified that he struck the officer in defense of his wife, not in resistance to an unlawful arrest, it was not error for the trial court to charge the jury that it was not to consider the legality or illegality of the defendant's arrest. Nor did the trial court err in preventing defense counsel from arguing the "illegality" of the arrest.

An arrest is not unlawful within the common law right to resist if the officer has probable cause to make the arrest. In Cordis v. State, the court held that the evidence provided the requisite probable cause to arrest. The officer had seen the defendant drive around the restaurant and, upon questioning him, observed the odor of alcoholic beverages, an open container, slurred speech, bloodshot eyes, and balance problems. The defendant's subsequent acquittal on the DUI and open container charges was irrelevant to the probable cause issue. Thus, an instruction on the right to resist an unlawful arrest was not authorized by the evidence.

If the defendant has made no showing that an unlawful or illegal arrest had taken place, he would not be entitled to a charge on the right to resist an unlawful or illegal arrest by the use of force. Furthermore, if there is no evidence to support a charge on the right to resist unlawful force used in making a legal arrest, the defendant would not be entitled to such a charge.

Where an offense has been committed in the presence or within the immediate knowledge of a private person, he would be authorized by law to arrest the offender, and the offender would not be legally permitted to resist the arrest. Under these circumstances, jury instructions regarding an unlawful arrest by a private person and the offender's right to use force to resist such an unlawful arrest would not be authorized.

5. *Right to Resist Allegedly Improper Sentence*

When an individual has been tried, convicted, and in the process of satisfying the court's judgment, he cannot plead an allegedly improper sentence as justification for obstruction of an officer attempting to carry out the sentence imposed by the court. At that stage of the judicial process, the proper course of action is the employment of the appeals process to correct the error rather than resorting to physical resistance.

6. *Defenses*

Even if the defendant made an effort to get away, and not to stand and fight, this is no defense to a felony obstruction charge.

The alleged unlawfulness of the defendant's arrest is not an affirmative defense to an obstruction charge. An affirmative defense requires that the defendant admit the crime in order to raise the defense. By alleging that the arrest was unlawful, the defendant is not admitting the crime of obstruction but is asserting that the state has failed to prove an essential element of that crime. If the jury were to determine that the arrest was unlawful, it would be required to acquit the defendant because of the state's failure to prove an essential element, not because the defendant's resistance was justified. Thus, where the trial court has properly instructed the jury on the essential elements of the crime of obstruction and on the state's burden of proving each element beyond a reasonable doubt, it is not required to give the additional, requested instruction on a person's right to resist an unlawful arrest.

7. *Admissibility of Evidence*

Documents involving internal affairs investigations of the arresting officer, his personnel evaluations, internal department memorandums, training evaluations, and other similar matters are not admissible unless the defense is attempting to impeach the officer and has made a showing that the documents contain contradictory statements previously made by the officer as to matters relevant to his testimony and to the case.

A videotape which has captured part of the physical altercation between the defendant and the officer has substantial probative value toward establishing the facts and nature of that altercation. There is no substantial danger that the defendant would be unfairly prejudiced if the videotape is shown to a jury. To the extent that the videotape does not capture the entire course of events between the defendant and the officer and does not capture the audio portion of the encounter, other forms of evidence such as oral testimony may be presented. Moreover, the jury is authorized to consider any incompleteness of the videotape in determining the amount of weight and credibility to accord it.

A prior conviction for misdemeanor obstruction, which involves neither violence nor moral turpitude, is not admissible for impeachment purposes.

When the subject matter of an inquiry relates to numerous facts perceived by the senses that cannot be adequately described and presented to the jury, a witness may state his impressions drawn from, and opinions based upon, the facts and circumstances observed by him or the effect which they produced upon his mind. This rule applies to witnesses who personally observed the events to which they are testifying and, essentially, authorizes such eyewitnesses to present a shorthand impression of those events in situations where language fails to adequately convey their observations to the jury with the same force and clearness as they appeared to the witness. This rule would not apply, however, to a witness who did not personally observe any part of the events. In *Bly v. State*, for instance, the Georgia Supreme Court held that the investigating officer's testimony that he thought that the arresting officer acted appropriately as a police officer in the line of duty during the traffic stop was not a shorthand rendition of fact, because it was not based on facts and circumstances observed by him. Rather, the investigating officer's testimony constituted an opinion that was based upon his second-hand assessment of the same evidence presented by the state to the jury and was therefore inadmissible.

Even assuming that expert testimony is needed to enable an average juror to understand the standard of conduct for a police officer during a traffic stop, where no evidence is introduced at trial regarding the elements and constituent factors that guide an expert to his conclusions, his testimony would not be admissible. Moreover, whether or not a police officer, according to his version of events, acted appropriately in the line of duty is a matter regarding which the jurors can make an equally intelligent judgment of their own, independently of the opinion of an expert. Accordingly, such testimony would not be admissible as expert opinion on an issue beyond the ken of the average layperson.

Finally, the investigating officer's testimony that the arresting officer acted appropriately during the traffic stop would improperly bolster the credibility of the arresting officer, the victim of the offenses for which the defendant is being tried. Considering the critical nature of the investigating officer's testimony and its potential to influence the jury, the trial court's admission of such testimony would constitute harmful error, entitling the defendant to a new trial.

8. Relationship to Other Offenses

Important Notice about Repudiation of Actual or Same Evidence Test: The Georgia Supreme Court repudiated the actual evidence test in *Drinkard v. Walker*, 281 Ga. 211, 636 S.E.2d 530 (2006), because it found this test to be inconsistent with the statutory framework governing the prohibition against multiple convictions for included offenses in Georgia. This inconsistency resulted in years of confusion and unpredictable results. In its place, the court adopted the required evidence test and overruled any prior case law that is inconsistent with it. Thus, any prior case law applying the actual evidence test is no longer controlling and should not be relied upon to determine whether one offense is included in another under § 16-1-6(1). The discussion of such case law is included below only insofar as it may still be applicable to pending prosecutions that arose before the Drinkard decision. See MULTIPLE CONVICTIONS, II. Tests to Determine Presence of Multiple Convictions, for a complete discussion of the Drinkard decision.

Neither obstruction of an officer nor terroristic threats is included in the other as a matter of law or fact. Obstruction of an officer requires proof of different elements not included in terroristic threats. The crimes are mutually independent and each is aimed at prohibiting specific conduct.

Simple battery is not a lesser included offense of felony obstruction of an officer. It is a separate and independent offense wherein the intent is to make physical contact or cause physical harm. Simply because the separate offense of simple battery could be prosecuted under the same set of facts that might support an obstruction conviction does not make simple battery a lesser included offense of obstruction under the law.

Where the same evidence is used to support both obstruction and aggravated battery charges, one crime is included in the other, and the defendant cannot be sentenced for both.

Where misdemeanor obstruction of an officer is a lesser included offense of the indicted offense of felony obstruction, the trial court may charge the jury as to a possible verdict of misdemeanor obstruction as a lesser included offense. Where the evidence shows completion of the greater offense of felony obstruction, it is not necessary for the trial court to charge on such lesser included offenses as misdemeanor obstruction or simple assault.

Where an indictment alleging aggravated assault on a police officer sufficiently puts the defendant on notice that he might be convicted of the lesser offense of felony obstruction of an officer and the evidence presented at trial would support such a charge, the trial court, upon written request, must charge the jury on the lesser included offense of felony obstruction. However, where there is overwhelming evidence that the defendant committed the aggravated assault, the failure to give the requested charge is harmless error.

Where the same conduct that proves aggravated assault on a police officer proves obstruction of the same officer, the two offenses merge for sentencing purposes and the defendant can be sentenced for only one.

Because the offense of leaving the scene of an accident has different elements than the offense of felony obstruction, the two offenses do not merge as a matter of law.

Where the defendant's actions were directed against individual law enforcement officers during a single confrontation, his actions constitute separate crimes which do not merge in fact or law. Because there are separate victims, it is proper for the trial court to treat the individual obstruction counts as discrete offenses for sentencing.

Under the facts presented in Gibson v. State, the Court of Appeals found that the crime of obstructing an officer was included in the crime of fleeing or attempting to elude an officer. The indictment's allegations for fleeing or attempting to elude an officer were sufficient also to satisfy the elements of the offense of obstruction. Under the facts, there was no material distinction between "willfully" disobeying the officer's order as prohibited by § 40-6-395(a) and disobeying it "knowingly and willfully" as prohibited by § 16-10-24(a). Because the defendant's testimony provided evidence satisfying the required elements of the offense of obstruction, the court held that the trial court erred in refusing to give the requested charge on obstruction as a lesser included offense. Since the evidence supporting the greater charge was in conflict, the error was not harmless. The defendant was therefore entitled to a new trial.

9. *Civil Cause of Action*

Section 16-10-24 sets forth a criminal penalty for knowingly obstructing or hindering police in the discharge of their official duties and does not expressly provide for a civil cause of action as a remedy for a violation. Moreover, there is nothing in the language of the statute or in the criminal statutory scheme that provides a basis to infer that the legislature intended to create an implicit civil cause of action for damages caused by violation of the statute.

D. *Removal or Attempt to Remove Firearm, Chemical Spray, or Baton from Law Enforcement Officer*

It is a felony for any person knowingly to remove or attempt to remove a firearm, chemical spray, or baton from the possession of a law enforcement officer who is lawfully acting within the course and scope of his employment. The prosecution must prove that the person knew or had reason to know that the law enforcement officer was employed as such. This offense is punishable by imprisonment for not less than one nor more than five years or a fine of not more than $10,000, or both.

This offense constitutes a separate offense, and a sentence may be imposed separately from and consecutive to or concurrent with a sentence for any other offense related to the act or acts establishing the removal offense.

III. *Interference with Prosecution*

A. *Compounding a Crime*

Two offenses, compounding a crime (§ 16-10-90) and tampering with evidence (§ 16-10-94), concentrate on behavior likely to occur after the institution of proceedings against a criminal defendant. Compounding a crime is derived from the common law which originally made it a felony to bargain with a thief not to prosecute or to prosecute "faintly" in order to assure his acquittal. This crime was known as theft-bote and eventually became a misdemeanor more generally encompassing the acceptance of any valuable consideration in return for an agreement not to prosecute for any offense.

Under the current Georgia statute, the crime of compounding a crime is committed when an individual accepts, after institution of criminal proceedings and without permission of the court or prosecuting attorney, any benefit in consideration of a promise not to prosecute or aid in prosecution of a criminal offense. If the offense being prosecuted is a felony, then compounding is likewise a felony, punishable by a fine of up to $1,000 and/or one to five years' imprisonment. Compounding a misdemeanor is a misdemeanor.

Case law under the predecessor statutes does exist and ought to be examined. In Stancel v. State, the defendant accepted $500 from a person alleged to have assaulted him with intent to kill. The agreement was ostensibly to settle a civil suit for damages and the only evidence of violation of the compounding statute was the fact that the defendant absented himself from the assault prosecution. The court reversed the conviction on the grounds that there must be evidence of an agreement not to prosecute and the simple failure to appear to testify was not sufficient.

The language of § 16-10-90, which punishes a promise "express or implied," may be broader than the Stancel statute and a court might find that failure to appear in court would be sufficient evidence of an implied promise. It is also important to note that there was evidence in Stancel that the defendant had been informed, during the negotiations for the $500, of the existence of the crime of compounding and insisted that this was not the purpose of the agreement.

There is also early authority that for prosecution of compounding a felony there had to be proof that the antecedent crime which was alleged to have been compounded had actually been committed. In Hays v. State, the court wrote that "[t]here could be no compounding of a crime unless there was a crime to compound." It should be noted that prosecutions for compounding a misdemeanor statute punished those who were "informing or prosecuting under pretense of any penal law." The court, in Sheppard v. State, held that such language evinced a legislative intent to punish those who were using the criminal prosecution to benefit themselves and, thus, did not require a showing that the antecedent crime had actually been committed. Section 16-10-90, which does not simply define the actus reus of the offense as "compounding the crime," as the Hays statute did, but rather defines it in terms of an agreement "not to prosecute or aid in the prosecution of a criminal offense," would appear not to require proof of the commission of the antecedent offense.

Under the current statute, it has been held that the offense of compounding a crime is separate and apart from the underlying offense and is not, per se, based upon the successful prosecution of the offense attempted to be compounded. The crucial date is the date of the consummated agreement to conceal the crime, or abstain from prosecution, or to withhold evidence. If, on that date, the underlying criminal proceedings have been instituted, and are then pending, and the unlawful agreement is reached, the offense is complete.

B. Tampering with Evidence

Destruction of evidence was a common law offense, now codified in § 16-10-94 (tampering with evidence). This was not formerly a separate offense in Georgia, but was held to be punishable under a pre-1968 statute punishing "any . . . offense against public justice." A 1970 decision held that statute to include destruction of evidence.

The mens rea of § 16-10-94 can be satisfied with any one of three alternative intents: an intent to prevent the apprehension of any person, an intent to cause the wrongful apprehension of any person, or the intent to obstruct the prosecution or defense of any person. The crime is committed when the defendant, with any one of these intents, "knowingly destroys, alters, conceals, or disguises physical evidence or makes, devises, prepares, or plants false evidence."

The defendant's destruction or alteration of evidence of a crime committed by him can be considered by a jury in order to determine the intent of the defendant to commit the crime.

It should be noted that concealment or destruction of evidence is an alternative actus reus in the crime of hindering apprehension or punishment of a criminal under § 16-10-50. The relationship between the two statutes naturally, therefore, arises. It would appear that § 16-10-94 encompasses a broader universe of behavior. While concealment or destruction is covered by § 16-10-94, many additional types of behavior are covered. Destruction of evidence of any crime is covered by § 16-10-94, while § 16-10-50 only covers destruction of evidence of a felony. It also appears that the latter statute requires a knowledge or reason to believe on the part of the defendant that a particular person has committed a crime, while § 16-10-94 would be applicable where the defendant destroyed that which he knew was evidence of a crime even when he did not know the identity of the perpetrator.

While it has not been decided in this state whether a prosecution must be initiated before § 16-10-94 can be violated, other state courts have held that it is not necessary for the prosecution already to have begun and that the offense may be committed by one having knowledge of an official investigation even before a grand jury proceeding has begun.

Any person who tampers with evidence involving the prosecution or defense of a felony and involving another person commits a felony punishable by imprisonment for not less than one nor more than three years. However, any person who tampers with evidence involving the prosecution or defense of a serious violent felony and involving another person commits a felony punishable by imprisonment for not less than one nor more than ten years. Finally, any person who tampers with evidence involving the prosecution or defense of a misdemeanor is punishable under the general misdemeanor statute.

By its own terms, § 16-10-94(a) contemplates that a person may commit the offense by tampering with evidence in his own case or in that of another person. The term "involving another person" found in § 16-10-94(c), however, refers to a third-party perpetrator of the underlying crime and thus imposes felony punishment only when a person commits the tampering offense involving the prosecution or defense of the third-party perpetrator. Thus, where the state has not presented any allegations or evidence indicating that the defendant committed the tampering offense to prevent the apprehension or prosecution of anyone other than himself, there would be no evidence to support the imposition of a felony sentence under the sentencing provisions of § 16-10-94(c). Rather, the trial court in such a case would be required to impose misdemeanor punishment for the defendant's tampering offense.

A related statute provides that any person who, with intent to conceal any material fact relating to a potential claim or cause of action, knowingly and willfully destroys, alters, or falsifies any health record shall be guilty of a misdemeanor.

C. Murder Attempts or Threats Designed to Prevent Testimony, Production of Evidence, or Communication of Information to Authorities Relating to Criminal Activities

In 1998, the General Assembly found that witness intimidation would likely always be a factor in the prosecution of cases involving criminal gang activity. Thus, it enacted a statute to prohibit such conduct. An official proceeding need not be pending or about to be instituted before a violation of the statute can be found. Under the statute, any person who attempts to kill another person, with intent to prevent (1) a person's attendance or testimony in an official proceeding; (2) the production of a record, document, or other object in an official proceeding; or (3) a person's communication of information to authorities relating to criminal activities, is guilty of a felony punishable by imprisonment for not less than ten nor more than 20 years.

Furthermore, any person who threatens, causes, or attempts to cause physical or economic harm to or threatens to damage or damages the property of another person or a member of his family or household, with the intent to hinder, delay, prevent, or dissuade any person from (1) attending or testifying in an official proceeding; (2) reporting in good faith to the authorities information relating to criminal activities; (3) arresting or seeking the arrest of another person in connection with criminal activities; or (4) causing a criminal prosecution or a probation revocation proceeding to be sought or instituted, is guilty of a felony punishable by imprisonment for not less than two years nor more than ten years or by a fine of not less than $10,000 nor more than $25,000, or both.

Any violation of this law is considered a separate offense and does not merge with any other offense.

D. Intimidation of Witnesses

In 1998, the General Assembly found that witness intimidation would likely always be a factor in the prosecution of cases involving criminal gang activity. Thus, it amended § 16-10-93 by adding a provision to prohibit such conduct. An official proceeding need not be pending or about to be instituted before a violation of the provision can be found. Under the statute, it is unlawful for any person to use intimidation, physical force, threats, corrupt persuasion, or misleading conduct for the purpose of (1) influencing, delaying, or preventing the testimony of any person in an official proceeding; (2) causing or inducing any person to withhold or destroy evidence, to evade legal process, or to be absent from the proceeding; or (3) hindering, delaying, or preventing a person's communication of information to authorities relating to criminal activities. Any person convicted of violating this law is guilty of a felony punishable by imprisonment for not less than two nor more than ten years or by a fine of not less than $10,000 nor more than $20,000, or both.

Any violation of this law is considered a separate offense and does not merge with any other offense.

E. Intimidation of, Impeding, or Injury of Jurors or Court Officers

Section 16-10-97 provides that a person, who by threat or force or by any threatening letter or communication, intimidates, impedes, or injures any grand juror, petit juror, or any court officer while in or on account of the discharge of such juror's or officer's duties, is punishable by a fine of not more than $5,000 or by imprisonment for not more than five years, or both.

The phrase "while in the discharge of such . . . officer's duties" should not be read so as to restrict the application of § 16-10-97(1) only to those threats or other attempts to intimidate or impede which occur while the case is actually pending before the court officer. Rather, the General Assembly intended by this language simply to limit the application of this paragraph to those situations which arise out of or are related to the performance of the court officer's official duties, whether the proscribed activities occur while the court officer is actively engaged on the matter giving rise to the offense or whether the proscribed activities occur at some other juncture.

A private probation officer is an officer of the court within the meaning of § 16-10-97. Protecting probation officers from intimidation and injury comports with the obvious legislative intent behind the statute, i.e., to protect the integrity of the judicial system by protecting those who occupy positions of trust, command, and authority within it.

F. False Report of Crime

The final provision which punishes interference with arrest or prosecution of a criminal offense is § 16-10-26 which makes it a misdemeanor to give a false report or cause a false report of crime to be given to a law enforcement officer or agency of the state. The behavior it punishes seems likely to be identical to that under the crime of false statements, § 16-10-20, which is a felony. A defendant who gave a false report of a crime and was prosecuted under the latter statute would, however, undoubtedly argue that where two statutes punish the same behavior, that which more specifically covers the behavior at issue is the only one which can be prosecuted. This is similar to an argument accepted by the Georgia courts that where involuntary manslaughter is committed by the use of a car, it must be prosecuted under the more specific vehicular homicide statute which punishes the same behavior.

Section 16-10-26 sets forth a criminal penalty for knowingly giving a false report of a crime to police and does not expressly provide for a civil cause of action as a remedy for a violation. Moreover, there is nothing in the language of the statute or in the criminal statutory scheme that provides a basis to infer that the legislature intended to create an implicit civil cause of action for damages caused by violation of the statute.

It should be noted that under the Motor Vehicle Certificate of Title Act, a related statute provides that any person who knowingly makes a false report to a peace officer or the state revenue commissioner of the theft or conversion of a vehicle is guilty of a misdemeanor of a high and aggravated nature.

LAW ENFORCEMENT DEFENSE

See also IMPEDING ARREST OR PROSECUTION.

I. Generally

Under § 16-3-20(4), **reasonable** conduct performed in the course of making a **lawful** arrest is justified and is a defense to criminal prosecution. This principle contains two distinct requirements: the arrest made or attempted must be **lawful** and the conduct of the arresting party must be **reasonable**. The arrest's legality depends upon the status of the arresting party, the offense for which the arrest was made, and the circumstances under which the arresting party obtained knowledge of the offense and under which the arrest is attempted. On the other hand, the reasonableness of the arresting party's conduct depends primarily upon the nature of the offense for which the arrest is made and the conduct of the arrestee in response to the attempt to arrest him.

The law governing the legality of arrests and of the use of force to effect an arrest has developed in a variety of contexts. Many of the cases concern prosecution of an arrestee for his conduct in resisting arrest; others are appeals from convictions of an arresting party for making an unlawful arrest or for the excessive use of force in effecting an otherwise lawful arrest. Still others are cases concerned with the admissibility of evidence obtained in a search incident to an allegedly unlawful arrest, and a few cases involve civil actions against arresting parties for unlawful arrests or excessive force. To the extent that the issues in these cases overlap, the courts have been consistent in their decisions on the legality of arrests and the reasonableness of force employed. Although there is no assurance that the courts will not develop somewhat different rules in different contexts in the future, the law of arrest should be the same in each of these types of cases.

II. Lawfulness

A. Generally

The basic limitation on the lawfulness of an arrest is the requirement that the arresting party have probable cause to believe the arrestee has committed an offense. A warrantless arrest made without probable cause or an arrest for conduct which does not constitute a violation of the penal laws is false imprisonment and punishable as such. Similarly, the malicious issuance or execution of a manifestly illegal warrant is punishable as false imprisonment under color of legal process. The motive of the arresting party, however, is irrelevant, and ill will toward the arrestee will not invalidate an otherwise lawful arrest.

It should be noted that members of the General Assembly and members of the state militia enjoy a qualified immunity from arrest while in pursuit of their official duties. Presumably, therefore, an arrest under such circumstances would be unlawful, although there are no cases discussing this issue.

B. Arrests by Police Officers

The lawfulness of an arrest by a police officer is governed by § 17-4-20(a), which provides that a police officer may make an arrest "either under a warrant or without a warrant if the offense is committed in such officer's presence or within such officer's immediate knowledge; if the offender is endeavoring to escape; if the officer has probable cause to believe that an act of family violence . . . has been committed; if the officer has probable cause to believe that an offense involving physical abuse has been committed against a vulnerable adult . . . ; or for other cause if there is likely to be failure of justice for want of a judicial officer to issue a warrant." This has been construed as "a codification of the common law on the subject of arrest, with perhaps a slight enlargement of the power of arrest," and the decisions are generally in accord with the rules followed in the majority of American jurisdictions. Although it was previously held that § 17-4-20 stated the only circumstances in which an officer may make a warrantless arrest, the enactment of the Uniform Criminal Extradition Act in 1951 added a provision permitting a warrantless arrest "upon reasonable information that the accused stands charged in the courts of a state with a crime punishable by death or imprisonment for a term exceeding one year," and this has been held an expansion of the authority stated in § 17-4-20. It should be noted that a police officer who does not comply with the provisions of the Georgia Peace Officer Standards and Training Act is limited to the arrest powers of a private citizen. While, as a private citizen, a non-complying officer may effect an arrest under certain circumstances, § 17-5-20 expressly forbids the issuance of a search warrant on the application of a private citizen.

Although a police officer may arrest for any offense with a warrant, if the arrest is such that a warrant is required the warrant must be in the possession of the arresting officer or of one nearby who is working with him, unless an immediate arrest is necessary to prevent a "failure of justice." Whether an arrest is necessary in order to prevent a failure of justice is ordinarily a jury question.

A police officer may make an immediate arrest without a warrant for any offense committed in his presence, whether the offense be a felony, a misdemeanor, or a violation of a municipal ordinance. If the arrest is not made at the time the offense is committed or immediately thereafter, however, a warrant is required, at least in the case of an arrest for a misdemeanor or ordinance violation, unless the delay is caused by the arrestee's flight and subsequent pursuit. The requirement that the offense be committed "in his presence" has been construed to have the same meaning as the phrase "within his immediate knowledge" in § 17-4-60, defining the arrest powers of a private citizen; that is, if the officer obtains knowledge of the offense by means of any of his senses, the offense is committed "in his presence." On the other hand, if the officer cannot learn of the offense without searching the arrestee, the offense is not committed "in his presence."

Where an individual commits an offense in his or her home and that offense is committed "in [the] presence or within [the] immediate knowledge" of a police officer, the officer is authorized to arrest the individual in the home without a warrant only where the officer's entry into the home is by consent or where there are exigent circumstances. Absent exigent circumstances or consent, a neutral judicial officer must be allowed to assess whether the police have probable cause to make an arrest in the home.

Although § 17-4-20(a) states that a police officer may make an arrest without a warrant if "the offender is endeavoring to escape," this principle is limited by holdings that an officer generally may not arrest for a misdemeanor or an ordinance violation not committed in his presence, even if the arrestee is attempting to escape. A police officer may, however, arrest an escaped misdemeanor convict without a warrant.

Referring to the provision in § 17-4-20(a) that an officer may make a warrantless arrest when "there is likely to be failure of justice for want of a judicial officer to issue a warrant," the Court of Appeals has said that "[w]hat the . . . phrase includes is obscure . . .." Only two cases appear to apply this provision. The first involved a police officer who was given a warrant to execute, but returned the warrant when he could not find the arrestee. Shortly thereafter, the officer was involved in a near-collision in his squad car. Stopping the other driver, the officer recognized the person named in the warrant, arrested him, and searched his car. The fruits of the search were not suppressed because the arrest was necessary to prevent a "failure of justice." In the second, a county sheriff was informed by a warehouse owner that he had witnessed an on duty police officer break into his warehouse and steal $130 in marked bills. Seeking to arrest the defendant before he went off duty and had an opportunity to dispose of the evidence, the sheriff obtained a warrant from a justice of the peace, but was unable to execute it because it was improperly issued. Unable to obtain a proper warrant before the defendant was to go off duty, the sheriff arrested him without a warrant. The arrest was lawful because delay in making the arrest would have caused a "failure of justice" by giving the defendant time to rid himself of the marked money.

Section 17-4-20(d) provides: "No law enforcement agency . . . shall adopt or promulgate any rule, regulation, or policy which prohibits a peace officer from using that degree of force to apprehend a suspected felon which is allowed by the statutory and case law of this state." Under this provision, therefore, no local government or state agency could be more restrictive on law enforcement officials than the courts or legislature. If a certain amount of force is permitted by statute or case law (as indicated, the law on excessive force is case law, not statutory), no governmental restriction of that level of force can be promulgated. It is not clear whether this change in the language of § 17-4-20(d) reflects a change in the actual substantive content of the law. At the least, it certainly makes the law clearer. Under prior law, the other governmental agencies were barred from enacting policies "in conflict" with the state law.

C. Arrests by Private Citizens

The authority of a private citizen to make an arrest depends upon whether he is doing so on his own or is assisting a police officer. A private citizen summoned to assist a police officer has the same authority as the officer, and one who reasonably and in good faith volunteers his assistance is likewise protected from criminal liability to the same extent as the officer.

If he acts on his own, however, his authority is more narrow. The mere possession of a warrant by a private person does not make an arrest lawful, although the arrest is legal if he is assisting a police officer who has a warrant. Under § 17-4-60, a private citizen may arrest for an offense committed in his presence or, if the offender is escaping, upon reasonable and probable grounds to suspect that the arrestee has committed a felony. The section has been construed as a codification of the common law on the authority of a private citizen to make an arrest, and it, thus, does not authorize an arrest for an ordinance violation or a misdemeanor which is not a breach of the peace even when it is committed in his presence.

Many jurisdictions provide that citizens' arrests made where the offense was not committed in the presence of the citizen are legal only where the offense actually was committed. In these jurisdictions, the citizen must act not only reasonably, but accurately. There is no Georgia law on this point, probably because a probable cause arrest is authorized by § 17-4-60 in the only situation in which a citizen might make an arrest where the offense did not take place in his presence: where there was a felony committed and the offender is escaping. It would appear that no other citizens' arrest where the offense was committed outside the citizen's presence is authorized by Georgia law. As in the case of a police officer, a citizen's arrest for an offense committed in his presence must be made at the time of the offense; a later arrest is invalid. A private person may also make a warrantless arrest upon reasonable information under the Uniform Criminal Extradition Act. It should be noted that arrest powers of private citizens are given to private detectives and security guards in certain situations.

D. Arrests by Nuclear Power Facility Security Officers

A security officer, including a contract security officer, employed by a federally licensed nuclear power facility or licensee thereof has the authority in order to secure that facility to search any person on the premises of the facility or the properties adjacent to it if the facility is under imminent threat or danger, pursuant to a written agreement entered into with the local enforcement agency having jurisdiction over the facility, for the purpose of determining if the person possesses unauthorized weapons, explosives, or other similarly prohibited material. If the person objects to the search, he must be detained or required to immediately vacate the premises. Any person refusing to submit to a search and refusing to vacate the premises of the facility upon the request of a security officer is guilty of a misdemeanor.

In accordance with a nuclear security plan approved by the United States Nuclear Regulatory Commission or other federal agency authorized to regulate nuclear facility security, a security officer, including a contract security officer, employed by a federally licensed nuclear power facility or licensee thereof has the authority in order to secure that facility to detain any person located on the premises of the facility or on the properties adjacent thereto if the facility is under imminent threat or danger, pursuant to a written agreement entered into with the local law enforcement agency having jurisdiction over the facility, where there is reasonable suspicion to believe that the person poses a threat to the security of the facility, regardless of whether the prohibited act occurred in the officer's presence. In the event of that person's detention, the law enforcement agency having jurisdiction over the facility must be immediately contacted. The detention can not exceed the amount of time reasonably necessary to allow for law enforcement officers to arrive at the facility.

III. Reasonableness of Force Employed

For the arresting party's conduct to be justified, not only must the arrest have been lawful, but the arresting party's conduct must have been reasonable. This issue generally arises in cases wherein it is alleged that excessive force was employed to effect or attempt an arrest. Although all of these cases have involved arrests by police officers, it is likely that the same principles apply to arrests by private citizens; however, the private citizen has much less license to use force than the law enforcement official.

In Bennett v. State the Court of Appeals dealt with the use of the defense by a hybrid type of defendant, a bail bondsman. While the court correctly concluded that the bail bondsman ought not to have a greater license to use force than a law enforcement official, it left unanswered the more difficult question of whether less license is authorized. In other words, shall the bondsman be treated as a law enforcement official or a private citizen or sui generis with regard to the amount of force which can be used in facilitating an arrest?

The cardinal rule on the use of force to effect an arrest is that the arresting officer may use enough force to effect the arrest and no more; even simply pointing a pistol at the arrestee is unlawful if not reasonably necessary to effect the arrest. If the arrestee resists, the officer may use only that amount of force necessary to obtain submission. A further limitation is imposed in the case of arrests for a misdemeanor or an ordinance violation: the use of deadly force is never justified to effect an arrest for such an offense unless the arresting officer is met with armed resistance.

Although it was said in McAllister v. State that a police officer has no right to shoot or kill an arrestee if the latter is not seeking to resist arrest by force, but only to escape it by flight, it is possible that this rule is restricted to misdemeanor and ordinance violation arrests. The United States Supreme Court, in Tennessee v. Garner, has held that the use of deadly force in the effectuation of an arrest is limited by the Constitution to situations involving violent felons. The Court held that the Fourth Amendment, in restricting the police to "reasonable" arrest practices, prohibits the use of deadly force where the fleeing felon is unarmed and nondangerous. The Court did state, however, that "if the suspect threatens the officer with a weapon or there is probable cause to believe that he has committed a crime involving the infliction or threatened infliction of serious physical harm, deadly force may be used if necessary to prevent escape . . .." This ruling should not work a change in Georgia law which already seemed to have limited the use of deadly force in this way.

Often the arrestee, in resisting arrest, presents a threat to the safety of the arresting party. In that event, the arresting party may employ a greater degree of force in self-defense if necessary, than he would be justified in using to effect the arrest without resistance and this is true without regard to the lawfulness of the arrest. If an unlawful arrest is attempted for the purpose of bringing about this result, however, the killing of the arrestee is murder.

The killing of a fleeing misdemeanant is murder, voluntary manslaughter, or involuntary manslaughter in the commission of an unlawful act, depending upon the circumstances. A police officer attempting an illegal arrest who is met with resistance not disproportionate to the degree of force he is employing and who kills the arrestee is guilty of murder. An unintentional killing in the course of an unlawful arrest is at least involuntary manslaughter in the commission of an unlawful act.

Sheriffs and peace officers may use deadly force to apprehend a suspected felon only when (1) the officer reasonably believes that the suspect possesses a deadly weapon, or (2) the officer reasonably believes that the suspect poses an immediate threat of physical violence to the officer or others, or (3) there is probable cause to believe that the suspect has committed a crime involving the infliction or threatened infliction of serious physical harm. Police officers being tried for a homicide that occurred while they were acting in the line of duty in response to a report that the suspect possessed a deadly weapon are entitled upon request to a jury instruction tracking this statutory language on the use of deadly force by police officers. A justification charge applicable to ordinary citizens would be wholly inadequate to inform the jury of the law applicable to police officers acting in the line of duty.

Employees of state and county correctional institutions, jails, and other places of lawful confinement or peace officers of any agency in the state may use deadly force when reasonably necessary to prevent escapes or apprehend escapees from such institutions.

Security officers, including contract security officers, employed by federally licensed nuclear power facilities or licensees thereof have the authority in order to secure those facilities to threaten or use force against another in defense of those facilities and the persons therein as provided for under §§ 16-3-21 and 16-3-23.

MOTOR VEHICLE CRIMES

See also DECEPTIVE PRACTICES; HOMICIDE; NATURAL RESOURCES, CRIMES RELATING TO; PROPERTY DAMAGE CRIMES; THEFT CRIMES.

I. Generally

Title 40 is designed primarily to regulate behavior concerning motor vehicles and traffic. Criminal provisions concerning the Uniform Rules of the Road, the registration and licensing of vehicles, the certificates of titles of vehicles, the identification of vehicles or vehicle parts, driver's licenses, and the safety of vehicles are to be found in this title. In addition to this title, there are provisions in several other titles which have some effect on the operation of motor vehicles.

II. Serious Traffic Offenses Under the Uniform Rules of the Road

A. Generally

Enacted in 1974, the Uniform Rules of the Road regulate behavior on the state's roads. Various sections prescribe the rules concerning, for example, traffic signs; right of way; rights and duties of pedestrians; turning, starting, and signaling; speed restrictions; and stopping, standing and parking. Except for sections which provide some other specific punishment, a violation defined in any provision of the Uniform Rules of the Road is a misdemeanor.

Section 40-1-1 is an extensive definitional section, applicable to the entire title on motor vehicles and traffic. The territorial coverage of the Uniform Rules of the Road is generally limited to publicly maintained roads with six exceptions: (1) where a different place is referred to in a particular code section, (2) where a vehicle is operated at a shopping center or parking lot that is used as a through or connector street, (3) anywhere the offense involved is reckless driving, driving under the influence, or homicide by vehicle, (4) any parking area where the offense involved is hit and run, striking an unattended vehicle, or striking a fixture, (5) where a vehicle is operated on any private property that fronts on coastal marshlands or estuarine area, and (6) where a vehicle is operated within a privately owned residential area located in a county or municipality. The rules apply, where appropriate, to riding animals or animal drawn vehicles. The rules are inapplicable to those working on the highways while they are doing so. Those who are operating authorized emergency vehicles or law enforcement vehicles are exempted from general coverage of the rules and are subject only to some general constraints.

The most serious traffic offenses of the Uniform Rules of the Road are set out in Article 15 of Chapter 6 of Title 40. They are reckless driving (§ 40-6-390), driving under the influence (§ 40-6-391), homicide by vehicle (§ 40-6-393), feticide by vehicle (§ 40-6-393.1), serious injury by vehicle (§ 40-6-394), fleeing or attempting to elude a police officer (§ 40-6-395), homicide or serious injury by interference with an official traffic-control device or railroad sign or signal (§ 40-6-396), and aggressive driving (§ 40-6-397).

B. Reckless Driving

1. Generally

Section 40-6-390 punishes those who drive "in reckless disregard for the safety of persons or property." A similarly worded predecessor statute withstood a challenge that it was unconstitutionally vague. In Lancaster v. State, the Court of Appeals held that the statute was precise enough. In defining the content of reckless conduct, the court stressed that it is more than mere negligence and approvingly quoted a law dictionary definition which described it as a "contemptuous willingness to injure and disregard of the consequences to others."

Considering the general standard and the variety of types of behavior possibly included in the definition, a listing of situations covered by the statute would be fruitless. It should be noted, however, that the court has held that intoxication evidence is relevant to the issue of recklessness. It should also be noted that while § 40-6-390 is a misdemeanor itself with enhanced punishment for repeat offenders, it is rarely used in prosecutions by itself. Almost invariably, the section is utilized only as the underlying crime in a prosecution under § 40-6-393 for homicide by vehicle.

Speeding, unaccompanied by other traffic violations, can form the basis for a reckless driving conviction if the state presents evidence that a defendant was driving at an excessive rate of speed given the posted speed limit and the driving conditions existing at the time.

2. Indictments or Accusations

The exact location is not a material element of reckless driving, and an indictment is sufficiently certain if it charges that the offense was committed in a particular county. Thus, a variance between the exact location of the reckless driving alleged in the indictment and that proved at trial is not fatal.

One panel of the Court of Appeals has held that if an accusation charging someone with reckless driving is worded so plainly that the nature of the offense is easily understood, the failure to allege the essential element of "disregard for the safety of persons or property" does not render the accusation invalid. However, another panel has held that if the accusation fails to include this crucial language, it is substantively defective. Until the Court of Appeals reconciles this conflict in its decisions, the better practice would be for the state to include this language in its accusations for reckless driving.

Where an indictment charging the defendant with reckless driving alleges that the offense was committed conjunctively in separate ways and the state offers proof to show commission of the offense in any one of these ways, a jury charge in the disjunctive is not error.

A count charging a defendant with reckless driving based on marijuana consumption is not subject to dismissal as a violation of equal protection. Although the Georgia Supreme Court has determined that § 40-6-391(a)(6) is unconstitutional as a denial of equal protection because of its disparate treatment of legal and illegal marijuana users, in a prosecution of reckless driving based on marijuana consumption, it does not matter whether the defendant consumed the marijuana legally or illegally. The charge merely includes the fact that marijuana was found in the defendant's blood because it is relevant to the jury's determination that the defendant drove in reckless disregard for the safety of persons or property, which is what the state must prove beyond a reasonable doubt. The state does not have to prove the defendant guilty of driving under the influence of marijuana.

No victim need be named in an indictment for reckless driving because, unlike the offense of aggressive driving, reckless driving is not directed toward a specific person. Instead, it is the act of driving in such a manner as to demonstrate a reckless disregard for all people or property generally, whether or not any specific person or property is in fact endangered at the time of the indicted act. Thus, precisely the same reckless acts of driving cannot be punished multiple times by simply naming a different person or property that the acts allegedly endangered. Consequently, the counts of an indictment charging the accused with the same acts of reckless driving directed toward each of the passengers of a vehicle would be subject to demurrer as a matter of law.

2.1. Admissibility of Evidence

Where an accused is charged with reckless driving, test results showing his use of drugs are admissible because the reckless driving violation could have been precipitated by the drug usage.

Evidence of the hazardous design and consequent malfunctioning of an intersection during the time of a collision and evidence of the corrective measures taken by the Department of Transportation since the collision, demonstrating its knowledge of the intersection's hazardous design, would be relevant to negate the elements of criminal negligence and proximate cause in regard to a reckless driving charge and to support a defendant's affirmative defense of accident. Furthermore, evidence of subsequent modifications to the intersection would be relevant not only to attempt to show that there were known flaws in the intersection, and hence known dangers, at the time of the collision but also that the Department of Transportation was the responsible party. Such evidence would be relevant and admissible as tending to exonerate the defendant.

3. Relationship to Other Offenses

Important Notice about Repudiation of Actual or Same Evidence Test: The Georgia Supreme Court repudiated the actual evidence test in *Drinkard v. Walker*, 281 Ga. 211, 636 S.E.2d 530 (2006), because it found this test to be inconsistent with the statutory framework governing the prohibition against multiple convictions for included offenses in Georgia. This inconsistency resulted in years of confusion and unpredictable results. In its place, the court adopted the required evidence test and overruled any prior case law that is inconsistent with it. Thus, any prior case law applying the actual evidence test is no longer controlling and should not be relied upon to determine whether one offense is included in another under § 16-1-6(1). The discussion of such case law is included below only insofar as it may still be applicable to pending prosecutions that arose before the Drinkard decision. See MULTIPLE CONVICTIONS, II. Tests to Determine Presence of Multiple Convictions, for a complete discussion of the Drinkard decision.

If the jury reveals which of the lesser included offenses serves as the foundation for finding a person to have been a "less safe" driver under the DUI statute or for finding a person guilty under the vehicular homicide statute, a sentence on the remaining lesser offense of reckless driving may be appropriate. Since reckless driving requires a reckless disregard for the safety of another person, an element not required by the DUI statute to be alleged and proven, it is not a lesser included offense as a matter of law. It also is not a lesser included offense as a matter of fact, unless the accusation includes an allegation of reckless disregard for the safety of another person and there is proof of such at trial.

Where the evidence shows that different facts establish the offenses of speeding and reckless driving, a conviction for speeding does not factually merge into a conviction for reckless driving. However, where the state uses up the evidence that the defendant was speeding to prove the reckless driving offense, the speeding conviction factually merges into the reckless driving conviction. Although it would be proper to prosecute the defendant for both speeding and reckless driving, he can be convicted and sentenced only for reckless driving.

C. Aggressive Driving

In an effort to reduce the number of traffic accidents and deaths caused by what is commonly known as road rage, the General Assembly enacted § 40-6-397 in 2001 to prohibit and punish this behavior.

Under § 40-6-397, a person commits the offense of aggressive driving when he operates any motor vehicle with the intent to annoy, harass, molest, intimidate, injure, or obstruct another person, including without limitation violating § 40-6-42 (overtaking and passing of vehicles), 40-6-48 (driving on roadways laned for traffic), 40-6-49 (following too closely), 40-6-123 (turning movements and required signals), 40-6-184 (driving at such a slow speed as to impede the movement of traffic), 40-6-312 (operating motorcycles on roadways laned for traffic), or 40-6-390 (reckless driving) with such intent. Any person convicted of aggressive driving is guilty of a misdemeanor of a high and aggravated nature.

Aggressive driving, unlike most other traffic offenses, is not a strict liability offense. Thus, aggressive driving will be more difficult to prove because the state must establish more than the mere intent to do the act which results in the traffic violation. Rather, it must establish that the traffic violation was committed with the specific intent to "annoy, harass, molest, intimidate, injure, or obstruct another person." The issue of intent is a question for the finder of fact.

Section 40-6-397 does not limit the applicability of the offense as going toward another **driver**. Rather, the state may indict a suspect for aggressive driving against any or all of the occupants of the vehicle and may attempt to show that the suspect operated his vehicle with the specific intent to "annoy, harass, molest, intimidate, injure, or obstruct" each person therein.

D. Homicide by Vehicle

1. Generally

As a result of the enactment of Georgia's vehicular homicide statute in 1974, a vehicular homicide which formerly was prosecuted as involuntary manslaughter must now be prosecuted under the vehicular homicide statute. Section 40-6-393 establishes two different grades of the offense of vehicular homicide: homicide by vehicle in the first degree and homicide by vehicle in the second degree. If the death results from a violation of § 40-6-163(a) (duty to stop before reaching a school bus stopped on the highway with visual signals in operation), § 40-6-390 (reckless driving), § 40-6-391 (driving under the influence), or § 40-6-395(a) (fleeing a police officer), the offense is homicide by vehicle in the first degree, which is a felony punishable by imprisonment for not less than three nor more than 15 years. Also, if the death results from an accident involving the driver and the driver leaves the scene of the accident in violation of 40-6-270(b) (duty to stop at the scene of the accident to give information and to render reasonable assistance), the offense is likewise homicide by vehicle in the first degree, which is a felony punishable by imprisonment for not less than three nor more than 15 years. Finally, if the death results from a habitual violator's operation of a motor vehicle while his license is in revocation, the offense is homicide by vehicle in the first degree but is punishable by imprisonment for not less than five nor more than 20 years.

If the death results from a violation of any other provision of the title on motor vehicles and traffic, the offense is homicide by vehicle in the second degree, which is punishable as a misdemeanor. Any provision of the title which does not set forth a specific violation cannot form the basis for this offense.

A violation of § 40-6-391(k)(1) is a valid statutory predicate for first degree vehicular homicide.

The plain language of § 40-6-393(a) makes clear that a person is guilty of homicide by vehicle if he causes the death of another, without malice aforethought, by illegally overtaking a school bus, driving recklessly, driving under the influence, or fleeing or attempting to elude an officer. There is nothing in the statute that would prevent a person of ordinary intelligence from understanding that actions taken to elude police that result in the death of another person could lead to a prosecution and conviction for first degree homicide by vehicle.

2. Causation

It is clear that some relationship between the traffic violation and the death must be demonstrated. In Johnson v. State, the court upheld an instruction which stated that in order to find the defendant guilty of first degree homicide by vehicle, the jury must find a violation of the Uniform Rules of the Road and must then find that such violation was the direct and proximate cause of the victim's death. The trial court properly defined proximate cause as "the act or omission [which] played a substantial part in bringing about or actually causing the injury or damage and . . . the injury or damage was either a direct result or a reasonably probable consequence of the act or omission."

The state's showing of proximate cause may be based upon direct or circumstantial evidence. Thus, the state is not required to produce direct evidence showing that the defendant's impaired driving ability proximately caused the collision.

If the defendant could have reasonably anticipated or foreseen intervening acts that might have caused the fatal accident, the causal connection is not broken and the defendant would be responsible for all of the consequences resulting from the intervening acts.

Where the defendant's theory of intervening criminal causation is not supported by the facts or the evidence, the trial court is not obligated to give an instruction on this theory.

An instruction on sudden emergency is not appropriate in a vehicular homicide case.

Inasmuch as the defendant's conduct is a substantial factor in causing the victim's death, it is a proximate cause of the victim's death, and the victim's failure to wear a seat belt can play no role in determining whether the defendant is guilty of vehicular homicide.

Although §§ 40-6-391(a)(1) and 40-6-393(a) require the state to prove only that the intoxicated driver caused the victim's death as a result of driving under the influence to the extent it was less safe for him to drive, the negligent operation of the vehicle by the defendant and the behavior of the victim remain relevant to the issue of causation in a vehicular homicide case. Where the evidence supports a finding that the victim's death resulted from an unavoidable accident but also supports a fault-based finding, it is for the jury to determine whether, in the absence of the defendant's negligent operation of his vehicle, the decedent's death could have been avoided.

In a vehicular homicide case, evidence of the other driver's drug use is inadmissible when it is intended only to impugn his character and has no relevance to any disputed issues in the case. However, evidence that the other driver may have been impaired by drug use, and thereby less able to avoid a fatal accident, would clearly be relevant in such a case. The conduct of all drivers involved in the accident is relevant to the extent it may impact the jury's determination of which driver's actions caused the fatality or whether the fatality resulted from an unavoidable accident.

The other driver's possible impairment would not be rendered irrelevant by expert testimony that the defendant's actions left the other driver with no way to avoid the accident. Whether or not the other driver was impaired, and whether or not his impairment contributed to the accident, would be for the jury to determine after considering all the relevant evidence.

The language of § 40-6-393(d) clearly requires that the state prove not only that the accused was operating a motor vehicle after having been declared a habitual violator, but that such act caused the death of another person.

Prior to 2008, a conviction for first degree vehicular homicide predicated on a hit-and-run required proof of all the elements of felony hit-and-run plus the additional element that the defendant's violation of § 40-6-270(b) was a contributing cause of the victim's death. The Court of Appeals's previous interpretation of § 40-6-393(a) in *Klaub v. State*, as not including a requirement that the defendant cause the victim's death through his failure to stop and render assistance after the accident, eliminated a key element that distinguished first degree vehicular homicide through a hit-and-run from the offense of felony hit-and-run and therefore overruled this interpretation. Thus, where the evidence in *Henry v. State* showed only that the driver caused the victim's death and then failed to stop and render assistance, the court concluded there was no evidence of causation that could sustain the defendant's conviction of first degree vehicular homicide through a violation of § 40-6-270(b) and remanded the case to the trial court for sentencing on the lesser included offense of felony hit-and-run.

In 2008, apparently dissatisfied with the result in *Henry v. State*, the General Assembly eliminated from § 40-6-393(a) the requirement that the defendant cause the victim's death through his failure to stop and render assistance after the accident. The General Assembly replaced this requirement with a new definition of first degree vehicular homicide predicated on a hit-and-run. This offense is committed when the defendant causes the victim's death by causing the accident that kills him and when the defendant then leaves the scene of the accident in violation of § 40-6-270(b). Under this definition, the contributing cause of the victim's death is not the defendant's violation of § 40-6-270(b) but his causing of the fatal accident. Thus, where the evidence shows that the defendant caused the victim's death by accident and then failed to stop and render assistance, there would be evidence of causation that could sustain the defendant's conviction of first degree vehicular homicide. With the enactment of this definition, the General Assembly has apparently overruled the decision in *Henry*. Since this decision is no longer controlling authority, it should not be followed.

3. Intention or Criminal Negligence

Except for aggressive driving, violations of the Uniform Rules of the Road are strict liability offenses. Thus, in most cases the criminal intent that the state must prove is simply the intent to do the act which results in the violation of the law, and not the specific intent to commit the crime itself. In Hoffer v. State, where the defendant was convicted of running a red light and of homicide by vehicle in the second degree, the court held that the state was not required to prove that the defendant intentionally drove through a red light, or even that the defendant knew that the light was red. The state was simply required to prove that the defendant intended to drive his car through the intersection at a point in time when the red light facing the defendant's lane of travel was red.

Criminal negligence is applicable to first degree homicide by vehicle. In Johnson v. State, the Court of Appeals approved the trial court's instruction on criminal negligence. Despite the fact that the vehicular homicide statute does not explicitly include any requirement of culpability other than that which attaches to the predicate traffic violation, the court pointed out that a traffic violation constitutes criminal negligence when the violation is " 'intentional, wilful, or wanton, or [when] the violation, though unintentional, is accompanied by recklessness or is under circumstances from which probable death or injury to others might be reasonably anticipated.' "

An instruction as to criminal negligence has also been held applicable to second degree homicide by vehicle. However, where the theory of criminal negligence is not supported by the facts or the evidence, the trial court is not obligated to give such an instruction.

It is for the jury to determine whether the defendant operated his vehicle in a criminally negligent manner in violation of a traffic safety statute or whether he operated it in response to an emergency situation created by the victim's vehicle when it obstructed the roadway.

3.1. Party to Crime

Where there is evidence to support a finding that the defendant was a party to the underlying crime of driving under the influence of alcohol and that his actions played a substantial part in causing the victims' deaths, such evidence would be sufficient to convict him of homicide by vehicle even though he was neither driving nor riding in the car involved in the fatal accident.

4. Indictments

An indictment charging a violation of § 40-6-393 must make clear which grade of the offense is being charged: homicide by vehicle in the first degree or homicide by vehicle in the second degree. An indictment which directly tracks the language of § 40-6-393(a) is sufficient to charge a defendant with homicide by vehicle in the first degree. This offense may be charged in various ways in different counts of an indictment to meet the evidence. An indictment which contains such alternative counts is not subject to a special demurrer. Finally, the indictment must allege the traffic violation that was the proximate cause of the victim's death.

An indictment that omits an essential element of the predicate traffic offense in a homicide by vehicle count can nonetheless satisfy the requirements of due process as long as the indictment charges the predicate traffic offense completely in a separate count.

As to an indictment for the commission of vehicular homicide in the first degree, a verdict of guilty of vehicular homicide in the second degree may be returned thereon, such a verdict not constituting an unauthorized amendment of the indictment. This would be especially true where the very indictment itself alleges the defendant's commission of a less culpable traffic offense as a separate count. The entirely separate less culpable traffic offense does not merge into the more culpable traffic offense. Thus, it is possible to return a verdict of guilt as to DUI and a verdict of guilt as to second degree vehicular homicide.

Homicide by vehicle punishes behavior which would otherwise be "unlawful act" involuntary manslaughter.

The courts have held that an indictment for "involuntary manslaughter" alleging facts which bring the case under § 40-6-393 is valid, but can support only a § 40-6-393 conviction because an indictment is to be judged by its allegations, not the label it places on them. A very significant practical difference occurs, however, when the homicide by vehicle is of the misdemeanor variety (i.e., the traffic violation was not a violation of § 40-6-163(a), 40-6-270(b), § 40-6-390, § 40-6-391 or § 40-6-395(a)). In this situation, what otherwise would be a felonious involuntary manslaughter is only misdemeanor homicide by vehicle under § 40-6-393(c) and the punishment is less.

The distinction between "unlawful act" involuntary manslaughter and misdemeanor homicide by vehicle was challenged by the state as unconstitutional in State v. Edwards. In that case, the state argued that classifying homicides by vehicle resulting from traffic violations differently from other homicides in the commission of unlawful acts was an unconstitutional classification denying equal protection of the law. The Georgia Supreme Court rejected this argument, holding that the legislation defining homicide by vehicle and prescribing misdemeanor punishment in certain cases did not treat persons similarly situated differently. The General Assembly was authorized to find that "unlawful act" involuntary manslaughter differs from homicide by vehicle.

Where the acts alleged in the indictment fit the requirements for both felony murder and vehicular homicide, the defendant may be prosecuted for each crime. Although the defendant may not be properly sentenced for each crime, that does not prevent his trial on both charges.

5. *Similar Transactions*

Before introducing evidence regarding the defendant's prior accidents, the state must provide written notice of its intent to use such evidence to the defendant's counsel and file it with the trial court at least ten days before trial, unless the time period is altered by the judge. The judge must then hold an evidentiary hearing to determine if the evidence should be admitted. The defendant's failure to object to the lack of notice and the required hearing does not constitute a waiver of the procedure. The lack of notice and the required hearing can constitute harmful error entitling the defendant to a new trial if the admitted evidence does not demonstrate substantial relevancy for a proper purpose or if such relevancy is substantially outweighed by the danger of unfair prejudice.

6. *Relationship to Other Offenses*

Important Notice about Repudiation of Actual or Same Evidence Test: The Georgia Supreme Court repudiated the actual evidence test in *Drinkard v. Walker*, 281 Ga. 211, 636 S.E.2d 530 (2006), because it found this test to be inconsistent with the statutory framework governing the prohibition against multiple convictions for included offenses in Georgia. This inconsistency resulted in years of confusion and unpredictable results. In its place, the court adopted the required evidence test and overruled any prior case law that is inconsistent with it. Thus, any prior case law applying the actual evidence test is no longer controlling and should not be relied upon to determine whether one offense is included in another under § 16-1-6(1). The discussion of such case law is included below only insofar as it may still be applicable to pending prosecutions that arose before the Drinkard decision. See MULTIPLE CONVICTIONS, II. Tests to Determine Presence of Multiple Convictions, for a complete discussion of the Drinkard decision.

Concerning double jeopardy protection, homicide by vehicle is analogous to felony murder. Just as a defendant cannot be convicted and sentenced for both murder and the underlying felony in felony murder, in a § 40-6-393 prosecution based, for example, on driving under the influence, there cannot be sentencing both for driving under the influence and homicide by vehicle. A traffic violation underlying the offense of vehicular homicide constitutes a lesser included offense, and conviction of both offenses is proscribed. Accordingly, a conviction for such an underlying offense would merge into the offense of vehicular homicide.

When valid guilty verdicts are returned on both alternative counts of felony murder and vehicular homicide, the alternative vehicular homicide count is vacated by operation of § 16-1-7. Since the vehicular homicide conviction has been statutorily vacated, there is no vehicular homicide count into which the underlying traffic offense can merge. Thus, it is proper for the trial court to treat the vehicular homicide count as merely surplusage and then to proceed to determine whether a separate sentence on the underlying traffic offense may be authorized for lack of merger, as a matter of fact, into the extant felony murder conviction.

Where felony murder and vehicular homicide in the first degree are based on separate and distinct underlying actions, it is neither legally nor logically impossible to convict the defendant of both offenses.

In Brock v. State, the defendant had already pleaded to driving under the influence when the state later tried to prosecute under § 40-6-393. The court held that the rule against successive prosecutions prevented the second prosecution because both the DUI and the homicide were within the jurisdiction of the same court and had been known by the prosecutor. While the court did not purport to reach the claim that the second prosecution also violated the rule against multiple convictions, it did describe the DUI conviction here as a lesser included offense of § 40-6-393. Thus, since conviction of both the greater and the lesser offense is precluded by statute, it would seem clear that even if both prosecutions had been brought at the same time only one conviction could stand.

Where a person is charged with felony vehicular homicide, a probate court does not have jurisdiction to try the person for that charge, and § 40-6-376(d)'s restrictions on jurisdiction over underlying offenses apply. This provision narrowly divests a court of jurisdiction over certain underlying traffic offenses charged against the particular person whose vehicular homicide charge cannot also be considered by that court. The purpose of § 40-6-376(d) is to prevent, whether by inadvertence or chicanery, the separation of the underlying traffic offense from the vehicular homicide and its disposition in another court, thereby preventing prosecution of the vehicular homicide because of double jeopardy. Thus, because a judgment entered by a probate court on an underlying traffic offense of a felony vehicular homicide would be "null and void" under § 40-6-376(d), a defendant cannot plead prior jeopardy if subsequently indicted for the vehicular homicide in a court having jurisdiction thereof.

In State v. LeMay, the court held that where the state sought to prosecute a defendant on the greater offense of vehicular homicide and the lesser included offense of driving under the influence in a single prosecution, and the defendant received a mistrial on the greater offense, the remaining conviction of the lesser offense did not bar retrial of the greater offense. Of course, the court held should the defendant be convicted of vehicular homicide on retrial, the trial court must set aside the conviction of driving under the influence since it was an offense included in vehicular homicide.

Where a jury has reached an unspecified agreement on the lesser included offense of DUI but still is in disagreement as to the additional elements of the greater offense of vehicular homicide, which has DUI and reckless driving as the underlying offenses, the trial court does not have to stop all deliberations and require the jury to return a verdict on the lesser included offense, thereby precluding all further deliberations on the greater offense. A jury may agree on some elements of an offense but require more deliberative time on other elements. Under these circumstances, requiring further deliberations which eventually result in a guilty verdict on both DUI and vehicular homicide would not be erroneous.

In a first degree vehicular homicide case, where the undisputed evidence shows that the defendant was operating the motor vehicle while his license was revoked due to habitual violator status, it is not error to refuse to give a charge on second degree vehicular homicide. Although the evidence shows the defendant unintentionally caused the death of the victim while speeding or failing to maintain a lane, the lesser offense of second degree vehicular homicide is not available to him because of his habitual violator status.

Where one is charged with the vehicular homicide of different people in different counts and is found guilty on each count, he may be sentenced separately on each count to run consecutively for the reason that the killing of different people constitutes separate crimes even though done at the same time with one stroke of the same death-dealing instrument. Thus, even though the vehicular homicide counts arise from a single incident, they do not merge for sentencing purposes.

7. *Murder by Vehicle*

With the enactment in 1974 of the vehicular homicide statute (§ 40-6-393), a murder charge cannot be predicated upon a vehicular homicide resulting from "reckless disregard for the safety of persons" as that phrase is used in the reckless driving statute (§ 40-6-390). Such an offense is expressly made "homicide by vehicle in the first degree" by § 40-6-393. Thus, an allegation in an indictment of "reckless disregard for human life and safety of persons using [the] highway" will not support an indictment for murder.

Although the vehicular homicide statute has displaced the involuntary manslaughter statute as to vehicular homicides, it has not displaced the general malice murder statute. The vehicular homicide statute applies only to vehicular homicides caused "without malice aforethought" and "without an intention to do so." Thus, malice murder by vehicle, just as malice murder by other means, still falls under the general malice murder statute. In Anderson v. State, the defendant's conviction for malice murder by vehicle was predicated on evidence of the defendant's implied malice. The evidence showed that the defendant drove, at a speed of 68 miles per hour, across the center line striking head-on another vehicle, without attempting to brake his vehicle or otherwise avoid the collision, and killed the driver of the other vehicle. The court held the defendant's statement to law enforcement officers that he regretted the victim's death, "but it had to be somebody," was evidence of an intent to kill someone else in order to take his own life. In Chester v. State, the court upheld the defendant's conviction for malice murder by vehicle, where the jury's finding of implied malice was based on evidence that at the time of the accident the defendant was angry at women, and was speeding and drunk. Although he was drunk, he knew that he struck two girls, and that one of the girls was in the bed of his truck. Moreover, he knowingly dumped this girl's body at an isolated abandoned railroad track, thus making it highly unlikely that anyone would render aid to her to save her life.

Under an indictment for murder by vehicle, homicide by vehicle rather than involuntary manslaughter is the lesser included offense applicable to the case. If sufficiently supported by the evidence, a conviction for homicide by vehicle can be obtained but not for involuntary manslaughter.

7.1. *Defenses*

An instruction on accident or misfortune would be authorized in vehicular homicide/DUI cases, if there is evidence that the defendant could not have avoided the collision due to circumstances beyond his control.

When the DUI predicate offense is set out only as an element of the offense of vehicular homicide and not as a separate crime for which the defendant risks separate criminal liability, the state has not commenced a prosecution against the defendant for DUI to which the misdemeanor statute of limitation applies. Rather, the state has commenced a prosecution for vehicular homicide only, and the four-year limitation period applies.

8. *Verdicts*

Malice murder is defined as the killing of another "with malice aforethought, either express or implied." Vehicular homicide is defined as killing another while operating a car, "without malice aforethought" and "without an intention to do so." Hence, when a jury returns verdicts finding the defendant guilty of the malice murder and vehicular homicide of another, the jury has convicted the defendant of killing both with and without malice aforethought. Obviously, the two verdicts are mutually exclusive, and it is proper for the trial court to refuse to accept these verdicts and send the jury back to continue its deliberations.

Given the statutory definitions of first and second degree vehicular homicide, it cannot be said that verdicts finding a defendant guilty of first degree vehicular homicide by reckless driving in the deaths of two victims are mutually exclusive of verdicts finding him guilty of second degree vehicular homicide in the deaths of two other victims. A finding of second degree vehicular homicide does not mandate a conclusion that the defendant did not drive in a reckless manner. The jury could have believed that although the defendant was reckless, that reckless driving did not cause the two other deaths. Instead, the jury might have concluded that some other traffic offense caused these deaths.

9. Unborn Child Not Person Within Meaning of Statute

In Billingsley v. State the court stated that the legislature did not intend for the term "person" as used in the vehicular homicide statute to encompass unborn children. The court supported this interpretation by the fact that the legislature re-enacted a feticide statute in 1982, a course of action which would have been unnecessary had unborn children been considered persons within the meaning of the existing homicide statutes. Because an unborn child cannot be considered a "person" within the meaning of § 40-6-393, the court concluded that the appellant's conviction of vehicular homicide arising from the death of an unborn child must be reversed.

However, in *State v. Hammett*, the court found that an unborn child who was delivered through an emergency Caesarean section and who lived approximately eleven hours before dying from the injuries he had received in a vehicular accident was a "person" under § 40-6-393(b) [now (c)] at the time of his death. The court held that it was not the victim's status at the time the injuries were inflicted that determined the nature of the crime, such as vehicular homicide, but that it was the victim's status at the time of death which was the determinative factor.

Apparently, these two decisions served as the impetus for the General Assembly's enactment in 1991 of the feticide by vehicle statute, which is discussed below.

E. Feticide by Vehicle

A person commits the offense of feticide by vehicle in the first degree if he causes the death of an unborn child by any injury to the mother of such child which would be homicide by vehicle in the first degree as provided in § 40-6-393(a), (b), or (d) if it resulted in the death of the mother. The offense of feticide by vehicle in the first degree is punishable by imprisonment for not less than three years nor more than 15 years.

A person commits the offense of feticide by vehicle in the second degree if he causes the death of an unborn child by any injury to the mother of such child by violating any provision of the title on motor vehicles and traffic other than § 40-6-390 (reckless driving) or § 40-6-391 (driving under the influence), which would be homicide by vehicle in the second degree as provided in § 40-6-393(c) if it resulted in the death of such mother. The offense of feticide by vehicle in the second degree is punishable as a misdemeanor.

Apparently, the feticide by vehicle statute was enacted because the conviction of a defendant in a vehicular homicide case involving the death of an unborn child could not be upheld, as an unborn child is not considered a "person" under the vehicular homicide statute. A defendant's conviction for vehicular homicide in such a case could be upheld only if the unborn child had been injured in a vehicular accident and had died from the injuries after his birth, i.e., after he had become a "person" under the vehicular homicide statute.

For a discussion of the feticide statute, see HOMICIDE.

F. Serious Injury by Vehicle

In 1979, the General Assembly enacted § 40-6-394, which makes it a felony to seriously injure a person through the violation of § 40-6-390 (reckless driving) or § 40-6-391 (driving under the influence). The punishment for this offense is imprisonment for not less than one nor more than 15 years.

Serious injury is described in the statute as bodily harm which deprives a person of a member of his body, renders a member of his body useless, seriously disfigures his body or a member thereof, or causes organic brain damage rendering his body or any member thereof useless. There is no requirement that, in addition to being "serious," the member of the victim be permanently rendered useless. Whether the bodily harm to the victim constitutes serious disfigurement is a jury question. Although there are no well-defined guidelines for the serious disfigurement element, the Georgia Supreme Court has held that the language of § 40-6-394 is not so vague and ambiguous as to fail to place a defendant on notice as to what type of injuries would constitute serious disfigurement.

Where the victim's serious injuries were not the result of some unforeseeable intervening act but were substantially caused by the defendant's criminal acts, some other factor contributing to the victim's injuries would not break the causal connection between the defendant's wrongful conduct and those injuries. The finder of fact would be authorized to find the defendant guilty of serious injury by vehicle.

Whether the evidence is sufficient to show that the victim died immediately upon impact or that he survived but died shortly thereafter as a result of serious bodily harm caused by the impact is an issue for the jury to resolve.

Where it is alleged in one count of an indictment that the defendant's act of driving under the influence seriously injured the victim by rendering a member of his body useless and it is alleged in another count that the same act seriously injured the victim by rendering another member of his body useless, the defendant can be prosecuted on both of these counts but cannot be convicted and sentenced on both. The single instance of the defendant's act of driving under the influence is "used up" in proving one of the counts and cannot be used again as the predicate for a conviction and sentence on the other.

Photographs taken of the victim while hospitalized are relevant to show the seriousness of the victim's injuries. Also, a videotape depicting the rehabilitation of the seriously injured victim is relevant and has probative value in that it illustrates for the jury the extent of the victim's injuries.

A separate conviction for driving under the influence or a separate conviction for reckless driving can merge into a conviction for causing serious injury by vehicle.

Reckless driving is a crime founded upon an act of criminal negligence rather than an intentional act. Aggravated assault with a motor vehicle, which is based on attempting to commit a violent injury to the person of another under § 16-5-20(a)(1), requires a finding of an intentional infliction of injury, which precludes the element of criminal negligence in reckless driving. Accordingly, a verdict of guilt as to aggravated assault with a motor vehicle based on § 16-5-20(a)(1) would be mutually exclusive with a verdict of guilt as to serious injury by vehicle predicated on reckless driving.

G. *Homicide or Serious Injury by Interference with Official Traffic-Control Device or Railroad Sign or Signal*

In 1996, the General Assembly enacted § 40-6-396, adding two more offenses to its classification of serious traffic offenses.

Any person who, without malice aforethought, causes the death of another person by violating § 40-6-26(a) commits the offense of homicide by interference with an official traffic-control device or railroad sign or signal. The punishment for this offense is imprisonment for not less than two not more than 15 years.

Any person who, without malice aforethought, causes bodily harm to another person by violating § 40-6-26(a) commits the offense of serious injury by interference with an official traffic-control device or railroad sign or signal. Serious injury is described in the statute as bodily harm which deprives a person of a member of his body, renders a member of his body useless, seriously disfigures his body or a member thereof, or causes organic brain damage rendering his body or any member thereof useless. The punishment for this offense is imprisonment for not less than one nor more than five years.

H. *Driving Under the Influence*

1. *Generally*

By far the most heavily litigated motor vehicle crime is § 40-6-391 which punishes drivers or operators of vehicles whose ability is impaired by alcohol or drugs. It punishes those who drive or who are in actual physical control of moving vehicles if they are in one of six conditions: (1) under the influence of alcohol to the extent that it is less safe for the person to drive; (2) under the influence of any drug to the extent that it is less safe for the person to drive; (3) under the intentional influence of any glue, aerosol, or other toxic vapor to the extent that it is less safe for the person to drive; (4) under the combined influence of any two or more of these substances to the extent that it is less safe for the person to drive; (5) the person's alcohol concentration is 0.08 grams or more at any time within three hours after such driving or being in actual physical control from alcohol consumed before such driving or being in actual physical control ended; or (6) there is any amount of marijuana or a controlled substance present in the person's blood or urine, or both, including the metabolites and derivatives of each or both without regard to whether or not any alcohol is present in the person's breath or blood. The statute also punishes those who drive or who are in actual physical control of moving commercial motor vehicles while there is 0.04 percent or more by weight of alcohol in their blood, breath, or urine and punishes those persons under the age of 21 who drive or who are in actual physical control of any moving vehicle while their alcohol concentration is 0.02 grams or more at any time within three hours after such driving or being in physical control from alcohol consumed before such driving or being in actual physical control ended.

The statute also provides that the offense of endangering a child by driving under the influence of alcohol or drugs is committed when a person under the influence transports in a motor vehicle a child under the age of 14 years. This offense does not merge with the offense of driving under the influence for the purpose of prosecution.

2. *Constitutional Issues and Statutory Construction*

In Cargile v. State the Georgia Supreme Court held that there was sufficient definiteness in the DUI statute. The court pointed out that it had previously rejected vagueness attacks on the predecessor statute and found that the phrase "driving under the influence of alcohol" is universally recognized and understood "and is not indefinite or unintelligible."

In Head v. State the Georgia Supreme Court rejected an attack on § 40-6-391 which claimed a violation of due process in the failure to require distributors of alcoholic beverages to inform consumers as to what quantity of the beverage is required to make them intoxicated under the law. The court said that the statutory language was sufficient to inform potential defendants of their legal responsibilities.

In Bohannon v. State, the Georgia Supreme Court upheld the constitutionality of the three-hour rule found in § 40-6-391(a)(5). The court held that this provision was reasonably related to a legitimate state interest and was neither vague nor overbroad.

In Love v. State, the Georgia Supreme Court concluded that § 40-6-391(a)(6), which prohibits driving while marijuana residue is circulating in the bodily fluids, bore a rational relationship to the legitimate state purpose of public safety. For this reason, the provision was not an unconstitutional denial of equal protection. However, it violated equal protection for another reason. The statute allowed a driver with metabolites of legally-used marijuana in his bodily fluids to be convicted only if it was established that he was "rendered incapable of driving safely," while a driver with metabolites of illegally-used marijuana could be convicted without evidence of impairment. This disparate treatment was predicated on whether the marijuana use was legally sanctioned. In light of the rational relationship between the statute and the legitimate state purpose of public safety and the fact that the effects of legally-used marijuana were indistinguishable from the effects of illegally-used marijuana, the court concluded that the legislative distinction between users of legal and illegal marijuana was not directly related to the public safety purpose of the legislation. The Court of Appeals, however, has held that there is nothing in this decision which states that the statute is unconstitutional when applied to those convicted of driving with a detectable level of cocaine in their system. Furthermore, there would never be an instance of a legal cocaine user so as to make the statute unconstitutional as a denial of equal protection.

In Barnett v. State, the Georgia Supreme Court held that § 40-6-391(k), which sets forth the blood alcohol concentration standard for underage drivers, bore a reasonable relationship to the legitimate state purposes of protecting the public safety and safeguarding the physical well-being of children. Since the General Assembly had a rational basis for enacting this provision, the provision did not violate the defendant's equal protection rights by setting forth a standard that was different from the standard for persons above age 21.

In Proo v. State, the Court of Appeals held that it is apparent that the intent of the legislature in its 1988 amendment to § 40-6-391 was to make uniform the standards for different types of intoxication, i.e., to apply the "less safe" standard to both alcohol and drug intoxication, and that its intent was clearly not the repeal of criminal sanctions for driving under the influence of alcohol.

In State v. Kachwalla, the Georgia Supreme Court held that because "less safe to drive" found in § 40-6-391(a) and "rendered incapable of driving safely" found in § 40-6-391(b) set the same standard of impairment necessary to establish that a driver is driving under the influence of alcohol or other intoxicating substance, one accused of violating § 40-6-391(a)(2) does not suffer unconstitutional disparate treatment under the statute.

In Lockett v. State, the Court of Appeals concluded that the General Assembly used the terms "alcohol concentration" expressed in grams and "percent . . . by weight of alcohol" interchangeably. Alcohol concentration expressed in grams and percentage of alcohol by weight are simply two phrases which indicate blood alcohol level is measured using the weight of pure alcohol in a certain volume of blood. When the terms are considered in their statutory context, it is clear the General Assembly was concerned with providing accurate evidence as to the amount of alcohol or drug in a person's blood at the alleged time, regardless of whether the chemical test is performed on the driver's blood, breath, or urine. Thus, the trial court did not err by denying the defendant's motion to suppress because the Intoxilyzer 5000 rendered his results in "alcohol concentration" rather than "by weight of alcohol" as required by § 40-6-391(i).

In Noble v. State, the Georgia Supreme Court rejected the defendant's claim that § 40-6-391(a)(5) was unconstitutionally vague because the term "breath" was not defined therein. When measured by a common understanding of the term, the court found that § 40-6-391(a)(5) provided more than adequate notice to a person of ordinary intelligence that driving with an alcohol concentration in excess of 0.08 grams, as measured by grams of alcohol per liters of breath, was criminal conduct.

3. Jury Instructions

A charge to the jury that includes all of the provisions of § 40-6-391(a), although some of them are not applicable, may confuse or mislead the jury and may be reversible error.

A charge defining "alcohol concentration" as "grams of alcohol per 100 milliliters of blood or grams of alcohol per 210 liters of breath" should not be give to a jury where it is not relevant to the case and would only confuse and mislead the jury.

An instruction on driving under the influence that does not inform the jury that it may convict the defendant of DUI based on the odor of alcohol alone, or unduly emphasize evidence of such an odor, but specifically informs the jury that such an odor alone is insufficient evidence upon which to base a conviction would not be erroneous.

4. Indictments or Accusations

The phrase "driving under the influence," with respect to both alcohol and drugs, and the phrase "to the extent it is less safe for the person to drive" are not two separate elements but are equivalent concepts describing the same physical condition. Thus, an indictment that alleges that the defendant was "driving under the influence . . . contrary to the laws of [this] State" is sufficient to charge the defendant with a crime under § 40-6-391. The failure to also allege "to the extent that it was less safe for the person to drive" would not require the quashing of the indictment.

An indictment charging a defendant with driving under the influence of alcohol or drugs, which does not specify "to the extent it was less safe for the person to drive," is an indictment that charges the defendant with violating § 40-6-391(a) in one of the three ways specified by subsections (a)(1), (2), or (3) [now (4)]. Such an indictment, however, would not put a defendant on notice that he or she could be convicted under § 40-6-391(a)(4) or

(5) [now (a)(5) or (6)], which do not contain the phrase "under the influence" and do not require the state to prove impaired driving ability. Thus, an indictment, which alleges that the defendant caused the death of the victim by driving his vehicle "in reckless disregard for the safety of persons and property by driving under the influence of drugs," only puts the defendant on notice that he can be convicted if the drugs made him a less safe driver under § 40-6-391(a)(2). The indictment does not put the defendant on notice that he can be convicted solely on the physical act of driving with any amount of drugs in his blood or urine under § 40-6-391(a)(5) [now (a)(6)]. Because this indictment only alleges that the defendant was "driving under the influence of drugs" and thus only puts him on notice that he can be convicted of vehicular homicide based on a violation of § 40-6-391(a)(2), the defendant cannot be found guilty based on a violation of § 40-6-391(a)(5) [now (a)(6)].

While it is impermissible to join distinct offenses in a single count of an indictment or accusation, the Georgia Supreme Court has held in Lester v. State that § 40-6-391 establishes one crime and that subsections (a)(1) and (a)(4) [now (a)(5)] merely set out two different methods of proving the same crime. An indictment or accusation is not subject to the objection of duplicity or multifariousness where these alternative methods of violating § 40-6-391(a) are alleged in a single count. Further, it has been held that an accusation charging a violation of § 40-6-391, which does not specify whether subsection (a)(1) or (a)(4) [now (a)(5)] will be the method of proof used, is not harmful error. Where the state does charge the defendant with two alternative counts of DUI arising from the same conduct, a defect in one count does not affect the validity of the other, alternative count. The state is not required to elect to prosecute under one subsection or the other. Where there is evidence to support a verdict of guilty under either subsection, the jury is not required to disclose the subsection on which it based its verdict. It is clear, however, that the substantive double jeopardy rule forbids convictions being entered under both subsections predicated on the same conduct. If the offenses charged under both subsections are based on the same conduct, they merge under the rule.

Where a defendant is tried on an accusation which charges him with violating only § 40-6-391(a)(4) [now (a)(5)], the state cannot prove the defendant violated § 40-6-391(a) other than by driving while having 0.12 percent [now 0.08 percent] or more by weight of alcohol in his blood. Accordingly, circumstantial evidence of the defendant's intoxication at the time of his arrest would not be admissible in the case as proof that he had violated § 40-6-391(a)(1). Such evidence is, however, admissible as evidence of the circumstances surrounding the defendant's arrest for having violated § 40-6-391(a)(4) [now (a)(5)].

In Purser v. State, the Court of Appeals construed § 40-6-391(a)(4) [now (a)(5)] to prohibit **both** driving with a blood-alcohol concentration of 0.12 grams [now 0.08 grams] or more and driving with a blood-alcohol concentration that measures 0.12 grams [now 0.08 grams] or more at any time within three hours of ceasing to drive. Under this construction, the state does not have the burden of proving that a person registering such a blood-alcohol concentration shortly after driving also possessed such a blood-alcohol concentration at the time he was in control of the vehicle.

Where the defendant is charged with violating § 40-6-391(a)(3) [now (a)(4)], that the evidence showed use only of alcohol and not of drugs does not create a fatal variance between the accusation and the proof.

Where the defendant is charged with violating § 40-6-391(a)(6) by having marijuana and its metabolites present in his urine while driving, the fact that the evidence deals with metabolites in the blood rather than in the urine does not create a fatal variance between the accusation and the proof. The presence of marijuana metabolites in the blood is circumstantial evidence from which a jury can conclude that they were also present in the urine, as specifically charged.

The definition of "marijuana" contained in the Controlled Substances Act is inapplicable to offenses indicted under the Motor Vehicles Act. The definition of "marijuana" contained in the Motor Vehicles Act includes tetrahydrocannabinol (THC) in the definition for purposes of determining whether one is driving under the influence thereof. Indeed, since THC in the blood or urine is the method by which the presence of marijuana is detected, THC must be considered "marijuana" in order for § 40-6-391(a)(6) to even be actionable. Thus, no fatal variance exists between an allegation of driving under the influence of marijuana and proof of the presence of THC in the defendant's urine.

The terms "alcohol concentration" and "grams" as used in an accusation are not necessary facts which the state is required to prove, and the state's failure to offer proof in those specific terms does not amount to a fatal variance between the allegata and probata. The word "concentration" as used in an accusation does not mean something other than "the amount of alcohol in a person's blood." Moreover, although the test results are expressed in numbers which represent the percentage of alcohol in the blood by weight, or grams, those results frequently have been referred to without qualifying them with either the term "percent" or the term "grams." Thus, evidence adduced that shows test results of 0.12 and 0.11 would be sufficient to show an unlawful blood alcohol level.

The inclusion on the Uniform Traffic Citation (UTC) of a test result does not preclude the state from proving its case by other admissible evidence. The test result, which is noted on the UTC in a separate section pertaining to tests administered, is simply not a part of the formal charge made. Although such notations and remarks on a UTC may apprise the defendant of the nature of the charges against him, that does not necessarily mean they constitute formal allegations which must be proven at trial.

Where no prosecution has actually commenced on a Uniform Traffic Citation (UTC), the fact that the charges in a subsequent accusation are different from those in the UTC issued to the defendant does not affect the accusation's validity.

A Uniform Traffic Citation (UTC) charging a violation of § 40-6-391(a)(1) to (5) alleges a single statutory offense. The various subsections under § 40-6-391(a) are not different offenses in and of themselves, but different methods of proving a violation of § 40-6-391(a), which may be charged in one count. Thus, the UTC would not be subject to a motion to quash on the basis that it charges more than one offense.

Where a Uniform Traffic Citation (UTC) uses the term "DUI" and indicates a violation of "Code Section 40-6-391," it would put a defendant on notice that he could be prosecuted for less safe DUI, per se DUI, or both.

If the accusation refers to the DUI statute, § 40-6-391, the absence of the statutory language "drive or be in actual physical control of a moving vehicle" does not render the accusation defective, technically or otherwise.

The description of the DUI offense charged prevails over any provision of the DUI statute cited. Thus, where the count charges the accused with "unlawfully driv[ing] a moving vehicle while there was any amount of marijuana in the accused's urine," which clearly tracks the language of § 40-6-391(a)(6), it is not rendered misleading by the fact that it incorrectly cites subsection (a)(5) rather than (a)(6). Since this count would properly place the accused on notice that he is being charged under § 40-6-391(a)(6), which clearly prohibits the presence of "metabolites" in the driver's urine, it is of no consequence that the count does not specifically set forth that the accused unlawfully drove a moving vehicle with a "metabolite" of marijuana.

The trial court may submit the issue of driving under the influence to the jury even though the accusation does not state the date on which the offense occurred. When the date is not an essential element of the case, the state is only required to prove that the incident occurred within the two year statute of limitation period prior to the filing of the accusation.

5. Actus Reus

The crime of driving under the influence to the extent that it is less safe to drive consists of three actus reus elements: (1) the driving or actual physical control of a moving vehicle, (2) the circumstance of being under the influence, and (3) impaired driving ability. Although the third element requires proof of impaired driving ability, it does not require proof of an actual unsafe act. No mens rea is specified by the statute, so nothing more than voluntary action need be shown.

As for the actus reus of driving or being in actual physical control of a moving vehicle, under a predecessor statute, which defined the actus reus as "operating" a vehicle, it was held that steering the car after a push by others was covered by the statute. It would seem that being in actual physical control of a moving vehicle, under the current statutory language, would also cover such a situation. On the other hand, the holding in Flournoy v. State, which construed the term "operating" to include sitting in a stationary car with the motor running, would apparently no longer be valid because of the requirement of a moving vehicle by § 40-6-391. However, in Phillips v. State, the facts were similar to those in the Flournoy case, but the court held that although no one saw the defendant driving the vehicle, the circumstantial evidence demonstrated that he had been in physical control of a moving vehicle shortly before the police arrived. It should be noted, however, that it is not a crime merely to occupy a parked automobile while under the influence of alcohol.

As for the actus reus of being under the influence, the question has arisen as to what being "under the influence" means. It is clear that it need not be proven that the defendant was in a total stupor. In Harper v. State, the court held that the state must show that the defendant's intoxication was such that it was less safe to operate the vehicle than it would have been if he were not affected by the intoxicating liquor. Although this standard can be described as a minimal one, the Harper court rejected a jury instruction which authorized a conviction where the defendant was under the influence of an intoxicant "to any extent whatsoever." In Wallace v. State, on the other hand, the court held that a charge is harmfully incomplete where it does not inform the jury that being under the influence of alcohol means that consumption of alcohol has rendered the defendant a less safe driver. In Gilmore v. State, the court held that the investigating officer's detection of a strong odor of alcohol on the defendant and the defendant's involvement in an accident constitutes evidence of impaired driving ability caused by alcohol.

It should be noted, however, that the statute does not require the state to show that the person actually committed an unsafe act, nor does it require the jury to find that the driver was actually unsafe. The statute simply requires a finding that the person was a less safe driver than he would have been if he were not under the influence of alcohol. Thus, under the statute, a jury can consistently find that a person's driving, although not unsafe, was less safe than if the person were not under the influence of alcohol.

Where the defendant has been charged with violating § 40-6-391(a)(3), the state is required to prove only that the defendant was under the influence of a glue, aerosol, or other toxic vapor to the extent that it was less safe for him to drive. Because the presence of a specific chemical is not an essential element of the crime, the state is not required to prove the chemical composition of the inhalant. Rather, the identity of the inhalant may be established circumstantially.

As for the actus reus of being under the influence "per se," the state does not have to prove that the defendant was a less safe driver by virtue of his intoxication. A showing that the defendant's blood-alcohol concentration was 0.08 grams or more is all that is necessary to prove that he is under the influence. Moreover, the state does not have to prove that the defendant was under the influence at the time of driving. The state need only prove that the defendant's blood-alcohol concentration was 0.08 grams or more at the time of the test or at any time within three hours of driving or being in control of a vehicle.

As for the actus reus of having any amount of a controlled substance present in the defendant's blood or urine, or both, a showing that the defendant's blood or urine contained an amount greater than zero is all that is required. The state is not required to prove that the defendant's driving ability was impaired or that he was a less safe driver. If there is conflicting evidence concerning the presence of the controlled substance in the defendant's blood, a finding by the trier of fact that the evidence showing its presence was more reliable than that showing its absence will not be disturbed on appeal if there is any evidence to sustain the finding.

It has been held that merely observing a can of beer in the hand of one who is otherwise driving a car in a safe manner does, in and of itself, constitute an articulable suspicion that a violation of § 40-6-391 may be occurring so as to authorize a brief investigatory stop. Even though such an observation may not demonstrate probable cause to believe that such a violation is actually occurring, it does demonstrate an articulable suspicion warranting further investigation into whether the imbibing operator of the car nevertheless has a blood-alcohol level of .12 percent [now 0.08 percent] or greater.

The exact location is not a material element of driving under the influence, and an accusation is sufficiently certain if it charges that the offense was committed in a particular county.

6. Admissibility of Evidence

a. Opinions and Observations as to Intoxication

The admissibility of certain kinds of evidence has been litigated often in connection with the current and predecessor statutes. It has been held that lay witnesses can express their opinions as to intoxication; police officers can express their opinions as to intoxication and as to the extent of intoxication that would render the defendant a less safe driver; and testimony regarding the speed and manner of driving is admissible to show intoxication. Evidence of post-driving drinking can be used to show drinking while driving, but testimony that the witness has seen the defendant drinking at other times is not admissible. However, if a defense witness testifies that the defendant did not appear intoxicated on the day of his arrest, the state is entitled to cross-examine that witness to determine the facts upon which the witness's observation was based, including the witness's observations of the defendant's drinking on previous occasions.

A mug shot that has been identified as fairly and accurately representing the defendant's appearance shortly after his arrest is admissible where the incident of driving under the influence is being re-created for the jury and the defendant's appearance is "some evidence" of his intoxication.

The failure to give Miranda warnings does not require the suppression of a police officer's testimony about his mere observations of the suspect at the scene of the traffic stop.

b. Field Sobriety Test Results

If there exists a reasonable and articulable suspicion that a driver may be intoxicated, he may be detained by the police and field sobriety tests may be administered in order to determine whether he had been driving under the influence. In order for the field sobriety test results to be admissible at trial, the state must offer evidence that the arresting officer had a reasonable and articulable suspicion to justify the administration of the tests. The trial court must closely scrutinize the facts of the case to ensure that reasonable suspicion actually was present at the initiation of the DUI investigation and was not invented after the arrest to cover a scheme of screening routine traffic stops without observing constitutional safeguards. Routine traffic stops cannot be used as a screening device for DUI offenders absent specific facts authorizing such inquiry in a case.

A screening officer at a roadblock need only be sufficiently trained to enable him to make a determination as to which motorists should be asked to take the field sobriety tests. Evidence of the officer's considerable experience in handling DUI arrests would be sufficient to establish his ability to make a reasoned judgment as to which motorists should be asked to take the tests.

Although there is no statutory scheme covering field sobriety tests and other initial screening tests, lack of such a scheme does not prevent the admission of field sobriety test results into evidence at trial. A law enforcement officer who has been properly qualified may testify about the effects of alcohol consumption on the body and how field sobriety tests are designed to detect someone who has been drinking. The officer may testify regarding these tests without first requiring expert testimony as a foundation for admission.

The results of field sobriety tests constitute admissible evidence of probable cause to support an arrest for driving under the influence. The fact that the arresting officer did not fully comply with every National Highway Traffic Safety Administration guideline for administration of the tests does not destroy the probative value of the tests and render them inadmissible, but affects only the weight and credibility of the behavioral observations made by the officer.

Because a defendant generally is not in custody or under arrest at the time field sobriety tests are administered, Miranda warnings generally are not necessary prior to administering the tests. The fact that the defendant may have no apparent way of leaving or that he owes a legal duty to remain at the scene for other reasons does not mean that he is in custody for Miranda purposes. Furthermore, the results of field sobriety tests given without the benefit of Miranda warnings need not be excluded under the Fifth Amendment of the United States Constitution because the results of these tests are not evidence of a testimonial or communicative nature. Likewise, any slurring of speech and other evidence of lack of muscular coordination revealed by a defendant's responses to an officer's direct questions constitute nontestimonial components of those responses and thus are not inadmissible. Even if the defendant's performance on the tests is influenced by his relatively minor injuries, this would be a factor affecting the weight of this evidence, not its admissibility. If the trial court finds, however, that the defendant was under arrest at the time he took the field sobriety tests and that the officer failed to give the required Miranda warnings, it is proper for the trial court to suppress the field sobriety test results. In order to make this finding the trial court must determine whether the officer made any statement or overt act that would cause a reasonable person to believe that he was under arrest and not temporarily detained during the investigation. The officer's "belief" that probable cause existed to make the arrest does not determine when the arrest was effectuated.

If the defendant is not under arrest at the time of his refusal to perform additional field sobriety tests, his refusal would not be protected by the privilege against self-incrimination. Accordingly, evidence of his refusal would be admissible at trial.

Section 40-6-392 deals only with chemical tests for alcohol or drugs in blood. It is inapplicable to field sobriety tests. Accordingly, the General Assembly's failure to state in § 40-6-392 that the refusal to submit to field sobriety tests is admissible in evidence against a defendant is neither significant nor an indication of legislative intent to make such refusals inadmissible in evidence.

The horizontal gaze nystagmus (HGN) test can provide competent evidence that the defendant was impaired by some substance. Although this evidence might not be sufficient to sustain a conviction for driving under the influence of marijuana, this sign of impairment together with red, glassy eyes and the smell of marijuana can be used to determine whether probable cause exists to arrest a person for driving under the influence.

The horizontal gaze nystagmus (HGN) test is an accepted, common procedure that has reached a state of verifiable certainty in the scientific community and is admissible as a basis upon which an officer can determine that a driver was impaired by alcohol. Evidence of the HGN test is admissible without first requiring expert testimony as a foundation for its admission. The HGN test is admissible as valid to show a symptom indicative of, though not determinative of, the presence of alcohol. An arresting officer's testimony that the HGN test results showed a certain level of impairment caused by alcohol is also admissible. An officer's testimony about his observations while administering the HGN test are admissible even though he is not qualified to testify about the results of the test. Evidence of the improper administration of the HGN test goes to the weight of the test and not to its admissibility. It has yet to be decided whether the results of the "hippus" test would be admissible as evidence of being under the influence.

If the National Highway Traffic Safety Administration's rules and procedures for administering sobriety tests are not part of a police officer's training in Georgia, the cross-examination of an officer regarding these rules and procedures would be irrelevant. Furthermore, if the state chooses to have the officer testify as a lay witness and describe the actions of the defendant in performing the sobriety tests without referring to NHTSA procedures, cross-examination on these procedures is irrelevant, regardless of whether the officer is trained in them or not.

A conviction under § 40-6-391(a)(5) does not require the state to prove impaired driving ability. Thus, even if the results of the field sobriety tests should have been excluded, it is highly probable that such error would not contribute to the judgment. The breath test results alone would provide sufficient proof of the per se violation. Any error in denying a defendant's motion to suppress the results of the field sobriety tests would therefore be harmless.

In Howell v. State, the court held that the trial court did not err in instructing the jury that "[f]ield sobriety evaluations, as with any other form of evaluation, may be subject to human error in their administration or interpretation, and the burden of showing such errors rests with the party who is challenging the weight of said evidence." The jury instruction did not relate to any element of the crime. It was merely an application of the principle, as contained in § 24-4-1, that the burden of proving a fact generally lies upon the party who is asserting it. The charge was not burden shifting under Sandstrom.

c. *Silent Witness Law*

Under the silent witness theory, a videotape of the commission of an alleged DUI offense constitutes independent probative evidence of what it shows. Authentication of the subject videotape is always required. The foundational requirements for the admissibility of videotapes under the silent witness theory are (1) expert testimony establishing that the videotape had not been altered or manipulated; (2) testimony establishing the date and place the videotape was taken; and (3) testimony establishing the identity of the relevant participants depicted. The admission of a videotape under the silent witness theory does not violate the rights provided to the defendant by the Confrontation Clause.

In 1996, the General Assembly enacted the silent witness law which establishes significantly different foundational requirements for the admissibility of a videotape in the absence of an authenticating witness. By this enactment, the General Assembly has implicitly rejected the theory adopted by the Court of Appeals. Section 24-4-48 provides for the admissibility of a videotape when the authenticating witness is unavailable and when the videotape tends to show reliably the fact or facts for which it is offered. This Code section also provides for the admissibility of a videotape made by a self-operating camera, such as a patrol car camera, when the videotape tends to show reliably the fact or facts for which it is offered. However, the date and time must be contained on the videotape and must be shown to have been made contemporaneously with the events depicted. The chain of custody requirement does not apply to such a videotape because it is a distinct and recognizable physical object that can be identified upon observation.

d. *Defendant's Statements or Responses to Arresting Officer*

When a police officer is conducting a preliminary on-the-scene investigation to determine the nature of the situation, no Miranda warning is necessary, and the driver's statements or responses to the officer's questions are admissible. The fact that the officer retains the driver's license for a short period during the course of the investigation does not necessarily mean that the driver is in custody, even if at that point, by leaving, the driver could be arrested for violating state law. Furthermore, because ordinary traffic stops do not involve custody for purposes of Miranda, evidence is not inadmissible for lack of Miranda warnings. However, if the trial court finds that the driver was under arrest at the scene of the initial stop and the officer failed to give the required warnings, it is proper for the trial court to suppress reference to conversations between the driver and the police. But if the driver while in custody made his statements voluntarily and not in response to any form of custodial questioning and interrogation by the police, his statements would not be inadmissible for lack of Miranda warnings. However, a remark made by an officer after the driver's arrest, which the officer should have known was reasonably likely to elicit an incriminating response from the driver, would amount to interrogation. In the absence of Miranda warnings, the driver's post-arrest response to such a remark would be involuntary and therefore inadmissible.

Under our criminal discovery provisions, the defendant is entitled to have a copy of any statement made by him while in police custody. However, since a preliminary on-the-scene investigation does not constitute a custodial situation, the state is not required to furnish to the defendant statements he made to an officer at the scene. Thus, the state's failure to produce those statements for the defense pursuant to a demand under the discovery provisions does not render those statements inadmissible.

e. *Defendant's Identification as Driver of Vehicle*

In a DUI trial, when the factual issue of the identity of the driver is brought into dispute by the testimony of a defense witness that he, and not the defendant, had been driving the vehicle at the time of the accident, the state may introduce a hospital intake report made after the accident, showing that the defense witness had stated that he had been the passenger. Once a proper foundation has been laid, the report is admissible as a business record to impeach the defense witness by proof of a prior inconsistent statement which happened to be recorded in the ordinary course of the hospital's intake procedures.

Testimony by an officer, who did not observe the defendant operating the vehicle, that he was informed by another at the scene of the arrest and in the presence of the defendant that the defendant had been operating the vehicle is admissible under the res gestae exception to the hearsay rule.

A deputy coroner, who is a licensed paramedic and whose testimony is carefully limited by the trial court to the manner and cause of the defendant's and the victim's injuries, may testify that the defendant's injuries were consistent with a finding that he was the driver of the vehicle at issue.

f. *Defendant's Alcohol Consumption*

Because a defendant's reputation for sobriety does not tend to prove or disprove whether the defendant's alcohol consumption on the night in question rendered him a less safe driver, such evidence is irrelevant and therefore not admissible.

Where there is evidence that the defendant participated in drinking at a neighbor's apartment, it would not be an abuse of discretion for the trial court to admit evidence that other individuals in the neighbor's apartment were also drinking alcohol.

g. *Defendant's Prior DUI Offenses*

Where there are sufficient similarities between prior offenses and the offense charged in a DUI case, the admission of the prior offenses is warranted to show course of conduct and bent of mind. The fact that the defendant did not "contest" the prior offenses is of no relevance in determining whether they were of sufficient factual similarity to warrant their admission for those purposes. Because the admission of evidence of prior offenses is the exception rather than the rule, the state has the burden of ensuring that the necessary requirements are met before such evidence may be admitted. This includes ensuring that the defendant is given sufficient notice of the state's intent to present evidence of the prior offenses, that the hearing on the prior offenses is taken down or recorded, and that the trial court's determination that the state has made the three affirmative showings is on the record. Otherwise, the admission of such evidence is improper. It should also be noted that a limiting instruction about the specific purpose for which the prior offenses can be considered must be given to the jury by the trial court upon request by the defense. Unless the defense has explicitly requested that the limiting instruction be given immediately upon the admission of evidence of prior offenses or otherwise has asserted any such right, the trial court's giving of the limiting instruction in its closing charge to the jury would not constitute reversible error.

h. *Officer's Entry into Defendant's Home*

Upon a showing of probable cause to arrest for the offenses of DUI or reckless driving, either of these offenses would be sufficiently serious criminal activity to justify an officer's warrantless, nonconsensual entry into a suspect's home to arrest him, if exigent circumstances exist to justify the entry. Where the officer has no probable cause to arrest the suspect for DUI before entry is made into his home, the suspicion that the suspect drove his car under the influence of alcohol would provide no basis for the officer's entry into the home to investigate that suspicion without a warrant or consent. Even if there is probable cause to arrest the suspect for reckless driving before entry is made into the home, since the reckless operation of the car and the consequent threat to public safety would be at an end, exigent circumstances would no longer exist justifying a nonconsensual, warrantless entry to arrest for this offense. Under these circumstances, any questioning of the suspect inside his home would violate his Fourth Amendment right to be secure in his home from unreasonable searches or seizures. Thus, all evidence obtained during the questioning would be inadmissible at trial. However, other evidence obtained after the suspect has complied with the officer's request to step outside his home would still be admissible.

i. Officer's Search of Vehicle

When an officer arrests a driver for DUI, the officer may conduct a warrantless search of the passenger compartment of the driver's vehicle for the purpose of obtaining evidence of intoxication.

j. Officer's Response to Defendant

An intake officer's response, as testified to by the defendant to prove the truth of her testimony that she had requested an independent test, would be an out-of-court statement inadmissible under the hearsay rule.

k. Expert Testimony

An expert witness may testify as to what effect a 0.16 Blood Alcohol Content (BAC) has on a person's ability to drive a motor vehicle. The qualitative relationship between a quantitative BAC and driving ability is beyond the ken of the average juror.

An arresting officer with over four years of law enforcement experience, training in DUI detection and field sobriety testing, and involvement in over a hundred DUI arrests would be qualified to testify about the effects of alcohol consumption on the body.

A defense expert, who is unfamiliar with the workings of the Intoxilyzer 5000, would not be qualified to testify as an expert on infrared breath-testing machines.

Expert testimony that the defendant's blood-alcohol content was.11 grams percent was held to be admissible, even though the defendant's blood was tested approximately two hours after the collision. Although the expert did not pinpoint the amount of alcohol in the defendant's blood at the time of the collision, he testified that it takes approximately 30 minutes for the level of blood alcohol to peak and that it diminishes over time. The clear implication of the expert's testimony was that the defendant's blood alcohol level exceeded.11 grams percent at the time of the collision.

Evidence of an independent blood test taken by the defendant several hours after his arrest is not admissible without expert testimony showing the relevancy of the test results to the defendant's blood alcohol level at the time of his arrest.

Where evidence of the defendant's exposure to paint fumes has been presented, expert testimony about the effect of substances within the paint on the defendant's breath test results is limited to the substance proven to have been present in the paint to which the defendant was exposed. The expert may not testify about the effect of other substances unless evidence providing a basis for his opinion has been admitted into evidence.

Where there is evidence of the defendant's physical activities prior to his taking the state-administered test, a defense expert should be allowed to testify about how alcohol is absorbed and eliminated by the human body, how a reading on the Intoxilyzer 5000 might be elevated because of these activities, and how another machine might possibly yield a different alcohol concentration.

A forensic expert is allowed to testify that a urine specimen that he has analyzed is positive for particular substances without quantifying the amounts. Once the arresting officer has testified to the degree of impairment as manifested by the defendant's behavior, the forensic expert is allowed to testify that such behavior would be consistent with the behavior of someone who was under the influence of those substances, and that the influence of those substances would impair the person's ability to operate an automobile safely. An expert is also allowed to testify, based on his knowledge and experience, on the characteristics of a drug that the disclosed scientific test results had shown to be present in the defendant's system.

Absent the chemical analysis referenced in former § 40-6-392(b), a defense expert's testimony about the defendant's blood alcohol content based upon the Widmark formula is irrelevant, and the only issue is whether the defendant's driving ability was impaired by alcohol to the point he was less safe to drive.

l. Certificate of Blood or Urine Analysis

Section 35-3-16, which was enacted by the General Assembly in 1994, authorized in any prosecution for the offense of driving under the influence of alcohol or drugs the admission in evidence of a sworn certificate of blood or urine analysis by a state crime lab analyst. A properly executed certificate was "admissible evidence of the composition, quality, and quantity of the substance submitted to the laboratory for analysis." This certificate, rather than the lab analyst's testimony, was to be used to authenticate the results of the blood or urine analysis.

In Miller v. State, the Georgia Supreme Court held that this certificate, as hearsay evidence, did not fit within any statutorily-recognized hearsay exception in Georgia. Since the certificate did not fall within a firmly rooted exception to the hearsay rule, the Confrontation Clause of the federal constitution barred receipt of the certificate in evidence without a preliminary showing of reliability or without determining that the lab analyst was not available to testify. The court found that the increased work demands of the state crime lab did not make a lab analyst "unavailable" to testify. The court also held that subsection (c) of § 35-3-16 did not guarantee a defendant the opportunity to cross-examine the lab analyst. A defendant's filing of an objection to the admission of the certificate only authorized the trial court to make a determination concerning the admissibility of the certificate and would not result in the lab analyst's appearance in court. When measured against the state constitution, the court found § 35-3-16 to be exceedingly troublesome. Because this Code section authorized the introduction of an ex parte affidavit into evidence against a criminal defendant, in contravention of the defendant's constitutional guaranty that he be confronted with the witnesses against him and be permitted to cross-examine them, it was unconstitutional. Also, requiring a defendant to request the presence of the witnesses against him and to explain why he requires their presence in order to be afforded his constitutional right of confrontation placed too heavy a burden on the assertion of a constitutional protection. Furthermore, the Code section impermissibly shifted the burden of proof from the state to the defendant against whom the state wished to introduce a certificate.

Apparently because of these constitutional infirmities, the General Assembly repealed § 35-3-16 in 1997.

m. Blood Alcohol Level Test Results

The test results of persons other than the defendant would shed no light on the issue of whether the defendant was under the influence of alcohol to the extent that it was less safe for him to drive. Any mere disparity between the defendant's test results and those of others charged with DUI would not be reflective of the differing effect that a given blood alcohol level might have on the ability of different individuals to drive safely. Thus, questioning a witness whether the defendant's test was low compared to those normally given to people who are charged with DUI is not allowable.

Upon a proper foundation being laid, a hospital record is admissible under the business record exception to the hearsay rule to show the test results of a hospital-administered test of the defendant's blood alcohol level. Since the hospital record is admissible under this exception, it bears an "indicia of reliability" sufficient to satisfy the Confrontation Clause.

Valid breath test results, which are otherwise determined to be inadmissible on procedural grounds, may be properly admitted for impeachment purposes.

The length of time one is detained in a police car before being transported to jail affects the weight, not the admissibility, of breath test results.

A photocopy of the results of the state-administered test showing the defendant's blood-alcohol level may be admitted into evidence without accounting for the original.

The results of a random drug test administered by a probation office shortly after a probationer's DUI arrest would be relevant to his defense. The statutorily created privilege protecting the confidentiality of probation records must, under these circumstances, yield to an accused's constitutional right to information which is material to his defense. Because the administrative process to obtain information contained in probation records fails to include any requirement for timeliness of production or the automatic right to material essential to a defense in a criminal proceeding, there is no merit to the position that the procedures set forth in the statute provide the accused with an adequate means to obtain the confidential records. Therefore, under these circumstances, the statute unconstitutionally limits the accused's constitutional right to compulsory process.

An acquittal on a per se DUI charge in one trial does not necessarily include a finding that the breath test results are unreliable for any purpose. The fact that some level of alcohol was detected in the defendant's system after his arrest would be relevant to a less safe driver charge in a second trial of the defendant. Thus, the state is not precluded by the doctrine of collateral estoppel from introducing evidence of the breath test results in the second trial.

7. Sufficiency of Evidence

As for the quantum of evidence sufficient to support a § 40-6-391 conviction, the leading case is Stephens v. State. In Stephens there was no direct evidence of the defendant having driven the car in question, the only witnesses having first seen him staggering up an embankment away from a car. The blood test establishing intoxication was not administered until one hour after the accident. Faced with a line of cases seeming to require direct testimony from a witness who had seen the defendant driving, the court affirmed the conviction based on the positive blood test and the defendant's admission that he had been alone in the car. The mere failure of direct testimony of anyone who saw the defendant driving did not, in the court's view, preclude a finding of guilt. Also, it has been held that the absence of testimony concerning the defendant's unsafe driving would be immaterial to establishing a violation of the statute.

"If circumstantial evidence may be used in establishing" more serious crimes, the court in Stephens v. State opined, "[T]here is simply no logic . . . for holding that it cannot be used in establishing the guilt of one charged with [DUI]." The prior contrary cases were overruled. The Stephens rule has since been applied to affirm a conviction in a case where the defendant made no admission at all. It should be noted that the confession of a defendant alone is not sufficient for a conviction. As in other crimes, there must be corroborating evidence from another source to establish the corpus delicti.

When driving under the influence of alcohol is alleged, the presence of alcohol must be proven by the state. Even though there is evidence of unsafe driving, unless there is some evidence of alcohol indicia, the evidence will be insufficient to convict the defendant of driving under the influence of alcohol.

In Campbell v. State, the officer, prior to stopping the defendant for another matter, did not see anything about the defendant's driving that indicated he was driving under the influence of alcohol. However, the court held that evidence of the alcohol content of the defendant's blood combined with evidence of the defendant's bloodshot eyes and unsteadiness on his feet was sufficient to convict the defendant of driving under the influence of alcohol.

In Hurd v. State, after the defendant was stopped at a roadblock, the officer noticed a strong odor of alcohol and that the defendant's eyes were red. Also, the defendant's intoximeter test registered.10 approximately 30 minutes after the stop. The court held that this evidence was sufficient to convict the defendant and that the evidence introduced by the defendant did not rebut as a matter of law the presumption of intoxication created by the intoximeter test results. It should be noted that the statutory basis for this presumption of intoxication was eliminated by the General Assembly in 2001.

In Banks v. State, the officer testified that the results of the state-administered tests were.121 and.116 and that the machine tested specifically for alcohol. The jury was charged concerning the statutory definitions of alcohol concentration and the requirements for conviction. The court held that even though no evidence was presented explaining the meaning of ".121 and.116," the evidence was sufficient to support the defendant's conviction of driving with an unlawful alcohol concentration.

In Potts v. State, the court held that where the defendant had refused to take the state-requested test, an officer's opinion based upon his experience and observations that the defendant was intoxicated to the extent that he was a less safe driver was sufficient to support a conviction. However, in Clay v. State, the court concluded that the officer's opinion that the defendant was under the influence of alcohol to the extent that it was less safe for him to drive was without evidentiary foundation. The jury rejected the results of the defendant's intoximeter test as being unreliable, based on the testimony of his expert. The sole evidentiary basis offered by the officer for his opinion consisted of his observations that the defendant's "eyes were red and glassy, and he had an odor of alcoholic beverage about his breath." However, it was established without dispute that the defendant's eyes normally appeared red and bloodshot, and the mere fact that he had an odor of alcohol on his breath clearly was not sufficient, in and of itself, to give rise to an inference that he was intoxicated. Like Clay, the jury in Gilbert v. State rejected the results of the defendant's intoximeter test. However, unlike Clay, the officer's testimony showing that the defendant was in an intoxicated state was not the sole evidence adduced to support the defendant's conviction. The officer also testified that he discovered the defendant at the scene of an accident beside a damaged vehicle that the defendant admitted driving. The court held that the officer's testimony was sufficient to support the defendant's conviction.

In Davis v. State, even less evidence was presented in support of the verdict than was adduced in Clay. In Davis, two witnesses testified that they observed the defendant drinking out of a beer can earlier in the evening before the accident, and the investigating officers testified that they smelled alcohol at the accident scene but could not trace the source. The court held that evidence that defendant consumed alcohol did not prove that he was under the influence of alcohol to the extent he was a less safe driver, and that evidence that the officers smelled alcohol at the scene was also insufficient, especially given other evidence that passengers with the defendant had been drinking as well. Additionally, although there was evidence that the defendant was a less safe driver, no evidence was adduced to show that he was a less safe driver **as a result of** being under the influence of alcohol. Moreover, the defendant rebutted the charge of DUI by introducing the results of a blood test performed three hours after the accident, which was negative for alcohol and drugs.

In Sieveking v. State, the intoximeter test was administered but its results were suppressed because of an inadequate implied consent notice. Nevertheless, the evidence was sufficient to support the conviction for driving under the influence. In addition to the officer's testimony that the defendant showed all six possible indications of impairment on the HGN test, the officer testified that he showed four of eight possible clues of impairment when performing the heel-to-toe test. The alcosensor test was positive, there was an odor of alcoholic beverage from inside the car, the defendant's eyes were glassy, and he was unsteady on his feet. The court held that the jury was authorized to consider these as reliable indicators that the defendant was impaired by alcohol to the extent it was less safe for him to drive.

The manner of the defendant's driving can support a reasonable inference that, as a result of alcohol consumption, the defendant was a less safe driver. In Heath v. State, the trial court refused to admit the blood test results into evidence because the state failed to lay a proper foundation for admission. Nevertheless, there was evidence that while at the emergency room following the accident, the officer saw the defendant exhibiting signs of intoxication in that he had a strong odor of alcohol and was acting in a belligerent manner. In addition to signs of intoxication, evidence of the accident showed that despite good driving conditions, the defendant slammed with great force into the rear of a clearly visible car stopped in his lane of traffic without applying his brakes. The Court of Appeals held that there was evidence authorizing a reasonable inference that only a short time passed between the time of the accident and the time of the officer's observations of the defendant's signs of intoxication. The manner in which the accident occurred, i.e., the defendant's failure to apply brakes prior to the collision, also supported a reasonable inference that, as a result of alcohol consumption, the defendant was not as alert or physically capable and was a less safe driver. In Gentry v. State, the court held that evidence that the defendant was driving under the influence of alcohol and cocaine, along with evidence that the fatal collision occurred when he lost control of the vehicle while traveling at a high rate of speed in excess of the posted speed limit, was sufficient to allow the jury to conclude that the defendant was a less safe driver as a result of the influence of the alcohol and cocaine. In Lanier v. State, the court held there was sufficient evidence to show that the defendant operated his vehicle in a less safe manner. The officer testified that the defendant failed to heed his audible and visible signals to stop at the intersection where road flares and flashing blue lights had been posted. After the defendant traveled an additional 100 yards before stopping, the officer detected a strong odor of alcohol about the defendant and that his eyes were red, his speech was slurred, and he was unsteady on his feet.

In Johnson v. State, the court found that the defendant's refusal to take the state-administered chemical test was circumstantial evidence of his intoxication. Furthermore, although the videotape of the stop refuted the officer's testimony that the defendant's speech was slurred, the officer also testified that the defendant's eyes were bloodshot, his pupils dilated, and his face was flushed. Additionally, the officer testified about the manner in which the defendant was driving, specifically that he came up fast behind other cars and abruptly passed them. Finally, although there were deviations from protocol in the manner in which the field sobriety tests were conducted, the videotape clearly showed that the defendant failed on several occasions to follow the officer's instructions on how to perform the tests, which was an indicator that he was under the influence of intoxicants. The court held that the evidence was sufficient to authorize the trier of fact to find that the defendant was under the influence to the extent that it was less safe for him to drive.

The failure of an officer to testify to any less safe behavior on the defendant's part does not render the evidence insufficient to support the conviction. An officer's opinion is not critical to establish the fact of the defendant's less safe driving, as the trier of fact can form its own opinion based on the indicia pointing to that fact. For instance, the circumstantial evidence of the defendant's physical appearance and demeanor would be sufficient for the trier of fact to determine that the defendant was less safe to drive in his condition.

Evidence that the defendant had ingested cocaine is by itself insufficient to support a conviction of driving under the influence in violation of § 40-6-391(a)(2). There must be additional evidence from which the jury can infer that the defendant was under the influence of cocaine to the extent that he was a less safe driver, such as evidence of his physical condition or conduct at the time of arrest. Evidence presented by expert witnesses indicating the adverse physical and psychological effects of cocaine in the system is sufficient evidence from which a jury can infer that such adverse effects on the defendant's body and psyche could have rendered him a "less safe" driver.

Notwithstanding the Intoxilyzer 5000's margin of error, properly admitted Intoxilyzer results would provide ample evidence of a defendant's guilt of a per se charge.

Expert testimony to the effect that the defendant's blood-alcohol content at the time of the accident was between.105 and .13 percent was held sufficient when combined with other evidence, even though the analysis of the defendant's blood sample obtained following the accident revealed a blood-alcohol content of .08 percent.

Evidence establishing that the defendant's test results indicated a blood alcohol concentration of.21 grams percent along with expert testimony from a trauma team nurse and physician that the defendant was under the influence of alcohol upon his arrival at the hospital to the extent that his motor abilities and reaction time were impaired by alcohol was held sufficient to allow the jury to conclude that the defendant was under the influence of alcohol to the extent that he was a less safe driver.

Where there is no evidence as to the alcohol content of the blood, in order to find one guilty of driving under the influence there must be some definite evidence as to the quantity of alcohol consumed and as to the time span over which the alcohol was consumed. However, the failure to show the quantity of alcohol consumed and the time span in which it was consumed will not prevent a trier of fact from determining whether the defendant was a less safe driver where there is evidence about the defendant's conduct and his manner of unsafe driving.

8. *Chemical Tests*

a. *Generally*

Although a § 40-6-391 conviction can be obtained without the introduction of chemical tests of a bodily substance, most prosecutions do include such evidence. The introduction of evidence of chemical tests is governed by § 40-6-392. This section's detailed set of rules determines admissibility in both civil and criminal trials.

b. *Licensed Individual and Certified Testing Instrument Required for State-Administered Test*

In order for a test result to be considered valid, the state must prove that the test was performed according to the requirements of § 40-6-392(a)(1)(A). Substantial compliance with these statutory requirements can be established by circumstantial evidence arising from the testimony of the chemist who operated the machine and performed the test.

It should be noted that charging a jury that the chemical analysis of a person's breath "shall be considered valid" if it has been performed according to these statutory requirements creates a mandatory presumption in violation of the person's due process rights under the federal and state constitutions. Such a charge constitutes harmful error where the person's defense is that the breath-testing instrument overstated his true blood alcohol concentration and that the amount of alcohol he admitted drinking did not render him a less safe driver.

The statute requires that the test be performed according to methods approved by the Division of Forensic Sciences of the Georgia Bureau of Investigation. Approval of these methods through the Administrative Procedure Act is not required for the test results to be admissible at trial. The lack of testimony regarding the Division of Forensic Sciences' unpublished guidelines and compliance or noncompliance with them does not affect the admissibility of these results.

It is sufficient for an operator to testify to the facts upon which a trial court can base a conclusion that the chemical test complied with § 40-6-392(a)(1)(A). It is not necessary that the operator additionally testify to his opinion that the test was performed according to methods approved by the Division of Forensic Sciences.

The statute also requires that the test be performed by a competent, licensed individual; and blood used for a blood test must be drawn by a qualified person. As to this last requirement, the results of a blood test are inadmissible unless the state presents competent evidence showing that the blood was withdrawn by a person qualified under the statute. Introducing privately held records related to the blood drawer's employee training would not be an acceptable method of proving his qualifications. Given the potential impact on the defendant's right of confrontation, acceptable methods of proving the blood drawer's qualifications would be by his testimony at trial or by introducing the statutorily authorized certification. Because this certification falls within the firmly rooted hearsay exception for public records, it may be admitted to establish the qualifications of the blood drawer without violating a defendant's right of confrontation under the federal and state constitutions. Another acceptable method, added by the General Assembly in 2001, would be by the testimony, under oath, of the blood drawer's supervisor or medical records custodian that the blood drawer was properly trained and authorized to draw blood as an employee of the medical facility or employer.

A licensed individual does not have to have an expert's knowledge of the underlying scientific principles governing the functioning of the testing device. Nor does he have to know how to calibrate the device.

An Intoxilyzer's insufficient sample reading on its face fails to produce a Blood Alcohol Content evaluation. An officer/operator is not required either by statute or by GBI guidelines to go behind the insufficient sample reading and perform an evaluation of the numeric air flow volume, which may vary from subject to subject.

The statute also requires that the test be performed on a machine that is operated with all its electronic and operating components prescribed by its manufacturer properly attached and in good working order. The operation and maintenance of the machine must be approved and certified by the Division of Forensic Sciences. A 1995 Act made these requirements retroactively applicable to all cases pending on April 25, 1995.

The Division, in cooperation with the Georgia Peace Officer Standards and Training Council, must provide for the training and certification of operators of breath test equipment. A copy of the operator's certificate is prima-facie evidence in any civil, criminal, or administrative proceeding that the operator was qualified to operate the equipment.

c. State-Administered Tests

i. Initial Alcohol Screening Test

If there exists a reasonable and articulable suspicion that a person is intoxicated, he may be detained by the police and an initial alcohol screening test may be administered in order to determine if it is safe for him to drive.

Since a person is not under arrest when an initial alcohol screening breath test is administered and since § 40-6-392 is inapplicable to the initial alcohol screening breath test, there is no requirement that administration of the screening test be preceded by advising the person of his right to an independent test. Since the person is not in police custody, there is no requirement that the request to undergo the screening test be preceded by Miranda warnings. Nor is there a requirement that the request be preceded by a reading of the implied consent notice.

The results of this testing device are admissible as evidence if its design is approved by the Division of Forensic Sciences. These results are admissible to show the presence of alcohol rather than the amount of alcohol percentage. Although the state rules and regulations provide that an initial alcohol screening breath test may be performed, an arresting officer is not required to give such a test.

Because a person is not in police custody at the time the initial alcohol screening breath test is requested, the constitutional and state statutory protections against self-incrimination are not applicable. Accordingly, evidence of a person's prearrest refusal to undergo the screening test is not rendered inadmissible by the lack of Miranda warnings prior to the test.

The state is not required to establish a foundation of the alco-sensor's acceptability before evidence of a defendant's refusal to submit to testing can be admissible. Nor is the state required to establish the same foundation for admitting an alco-sensor refusal as evidence as it must to admit an alco-sensor test result as evidence when the device has not actually been used in the former situation.

Informing a suspect that he is not entitled to an attorney prior to taking an alco-sensor test but is entitled to one once arrested and taken to jail is not a misleading statement that would render evidence of the suspect's failure to take the test inadmissible.

ii. Breath-Testing Instruments

Breath tests other than the initial screening test may be conducted on an approved breath-testing instrument. An instrument which determines the amount of alcohol in one's breath (by whatever means) and calculates therefrom the blood alcohol content performs a "chemical analysis" or "chemical test" pursuant to § 40-6-392(a)(1). An approved breath-testing instrument is considered accurate if properly operated.

The results of such a test are admissible as evidence if the state establishes that the instrument has been approved for use in this state. At one time, a properly authenticated record or testimony from the director of the state crime lab was required to authenticate the director's approval of the instrument used in a case. Now, if the state establishes that the instrument has been approved for use in this state as specified by administrative rule or as authorized by the Director of the Division of Forensic Sciences, the test results of the instrument are admissible. It has been held that where the Director of the Division of Forensic Sciences has issued a permit for the operation of an instrument, it may be inferred that its design has been approved by him and thus the results of the test are admissible. It has also been held that even when an instrument has had one of its components disengaged by the manufacturer, if the instrument as modified has been approved in accordance with the statutory requirements, the test results of the instrument are admissible. This holding, however, has been legislatively overruled by the 1994 amendment to § 40-6-392. For the test results of an instrument to be considered valid and thus admissible under this amendment, the instrument must have all of its electronic and operating components prescribed by its manufacturer properly attached and in good working order. A 1995 Act made this requirement retroactively applicable to all cases pending on April 21, 1995.

The state must establish that the instrument has been maintained in good operating condition in order for test results of the instrument to be admissible. The Director of the Division of Forensic Sciences is required to cause each instrument to be checked periodically for calibration and operation and a record of the results of all such checks to be maintained. There is a presumption that the Director has caused the instrument used to administer a breath test to be checked periodically for calibration, and the defendant must adduce sufficient competent evidence to overcome this presumption.

Beginning in 1995, each time an inspector from the Division of Forensic Sciences inspects an approved breath-testing instrument, he must certify that the instrument has all of its electronic and operating components prescribed by its manufacturer properly attached and in good working order. When properly prepared and executed, the inspector's certificate is self-authenticating, is admissible in any court of law, and satisfies the requirement that the Division certify that the instrument is being properly operated and maintained. A 1995 Act made these certification requirements retroactively applicable to all cases pending on April 25, 1995.

An inspection certificate prepared under § 40-6-392(f) is a record made and promulgated in the regular course of business. It is not made in an investigatory or adversarial setting; nor is it generated in anticipation of the prosecution of a particular defendant. Thus, an inspection certificate is not testimonial hearsay that would be inadmissible under Crawford v. Washington.

Because this self-authenticating certificate comes within the firmly rooted hearsay exception for business records, the certificate, upon a proper foundation being established, may be admitted at trial without violating a defendant's right of confrontation under the federal and state constitutions. Likewise, printouts attached to the certificate purporting to be the test results from the inspection, upon an adequate foundation being laid, may be admitted as business records without violating the defendant's right of confrontation. There is no requirement that, in order to lay a proper foundation, the person who conducted the inspection, or someone who actually witnessed it, appear in court to testify about the inspection or the completion of the certificate. It should be noted, however, that the foundation for the admission of the certificate under the business records exception is rendered unnecessary if the statutory foundation requirements have been satisfied. These requirements are: (1) the certificate must be signed under oath by the inspector; and (2) the certificate must contain the requisite language of § 40-6-392(f). Once completed as specified under the statute, the certificate is admissible in any court of law without further proof. There is no requirement that the state attach the test cards to the certificate. Furthermore, there is no requirement that certification and inspection of a machine occur on the same day as the testing or that the machine be inspected directly before and after each test. Nor is there a requirement that the certificate be prepared on the day of inspection. Any discrepancy between the date of inspection and the date of the certificate goes to the weight of the evidence and not its admissibility. This certificate is not the type of investigation-generated written scientific report subject to the state's criminal discovery provisions. Thus, the certificate may be introduced even though it has not been provided to the defendant before trial. A photocopy of the certificate may be admitted into evidence where the state has accounted for the absence of the original. The photocopy does not need to be certified to be admissible.

If the state fails to produce the certificate, it must establish by other admissible evidence that the statutory foundation requirements have been met. For instance, the fact the machine had all its requisite parts and was in good working order can be established circumstantially through the testimony of the technician who operated the machine and performed the test or through the testimony of an area supervisor who bases her opinion on certain documents printed by the machine during its most recent inspection by another officer. A malfunction of the printer or internal clock does not affect the admissibility of the test results but goes to the weight of those results. The statute does not require that a machine, which is working properly according to Division of Forensic Sciences approved diagnostic tests, be taken apart and each component tested individually in order to lay the required foundation for the admission of the test results.

A pretrial motion in limine is the proper vehicle by which to interpose an objection to the admissibility of test results on the basis of noncompliance with the statutory foundation requirements. The trial court's determination of admissibility, pursuant to these requirements, controls this matter of law, and the state is not required to reprove the legal issue of admissibility to the jury. Since this determination of admissibility is never a jury question, a jury instruction as to the foundational requirements would not be authorized. There is no requirement, however, that the foundation be laid outside the presence of the jury; the contemporaneous objection rule applies when presenting such preliminary, foundational evidence.

Due process under the federal constitution and the Georgia Constitution does not require that law enforcement agencies preserve breath samples in order to introduce breath-analysis tests at trial. Nor does due process require that an independent expert be allowed to examine the instrument that was used to test the defendant's breath.

Prior to January 1, 1995, breath tests to determine blood alcohol concentration were usually conducted on the Intoximeter 3000 machine. Having been decommissioned on December 31, 1994, this machine is no longer used in this state and its test results are no longer admissible in court. Effective January 1, 1995, breath tests are to be conducted on the Intoxilyzer 5000 machine. However, the Director of the Division of Forensic Sciences is authorized to approve the design of any other type of breath alcohol analyzer used in this state. There is a procedural difference between the use of the Intoxilyzer 5000 and the Intoximeter 3000. The Intoximeter 3000 only required one breath sample. The Intoxilyzer 5000 requires two breath samples that must be within 0.020 grams of each other. If the two samples are not within this narrow window, the test will not be considered valid. If the samples fall within the window but differ, the operator is instructed to use the lower reading. Apparently, because of this procedural difference, the General Assembly amended § 40-6-392 to provide that in all cases where the arrest is made on or after January 1, 1995, and the state selects breath testing, two sequential breath samples are to be requested for the testing of alcohol concentration. For either or both of these sequential samples to be admissible in the state's or plaintiff's case-in-chief, the readings cannot differ from each other by an alcohol concentration of greater than 0.020 grams and the lower of the two results is determinative for accusation and indictment purposes and administrative license suspension purposes. No more than two sequential series of a total of two adequate breath samples each are to be requested by the state. Both of the sequential test results may be admitted into evidence and may go out with the jury. Any margin for error relates to the weight rather than the admissibility of the results. The results are admissible without testimony as to what significance should be attributed to them. The credibility of a defense expert's attack upon the reliability of the results is an issue for the jury to resolve.

Because § 40-6-392(a)(1)(B) clearly contemplates the admission of both sequential test results, it does not limit the state to using only the lower of two samples to prosecute a DUI charge and in excluding evidence of the result of the second breath sample solely on that basis.

Cross-examination regarding the Intoxilyzer 5000 would be irrelevant in a case where only the Intoximeter 3000 was utilized.

A trial court may not instruct the jury that the Intoxilyzer 5000 machine's margin for error does not diminish the evidentiary value of the test results. Such a conclusion is rightly within the jury's domain. While it is within the province of the trial court to determine the admissibility of the test results, it is within the province of the jury to determine what weight should be given to those results.

While the defendant may always introduce evidence of the possibility of error or circumstances that might have caused the Intoxilyzer 5000 to malfunction, he is not entitled to an instruction that such evidence may be considered by the jury in evaluating evidence of the defendant's blood alcohol level. The absence of such an instruction would not deprive him of the defense that the test results were incorrect.

An Intoxilyzer 5000's margin of error relates to the weight given to the test results rather than to their admissibility. In addition, these results are direct evidence of guilt. The evidence supporting a per se charge would not be rendered insufficient simply because the Intoxilyzer's margin of error brings a test result below Georgia's legal limit for blood-alcohol content. Thus, even if the evidence establishes a margin of error, the defendant would not be entitled to a directed verdict on this basis.

After instructing the jury that the relationship between alcohol in the blood and in the breath is a ratio of 1 to 2,100, the trial court may, but is not required to, instruct the jury that it can give the test results the weight that it deems fit, including no weight at all.

While the defendant may attack the Intoxilyzer 5000 test by attempting to show the machine was not in good working order and thus not operating properly when he was tested, he is not entitled to admission of evidence as a matter of law that is of remote relevance, if any, to the operating condition of the machine on the date of his test. In one case, the trial court ruled a "service work order" for the machine inadmissible as not relevant. The defendant proffered that the work order and the arresting officer's testimony would have shown that various parts of the machine were replaced and that the machine was malfunctioning months after the defendant's test. The Court of Appeals held that in the absence of any other evidence which would have linked the proffered evidence with the condition of the machine on the date of the defendant's test, the proffered evidence would not have logically raised a reasonable inference that the machine was not in good working order on that date. Thus, the trial court did not abuse its discretion.

iii. Authority to Request Test and Analyze Sample

Once an arrest for driving under the influence is made, an officer is authorized by the implied consent law to request a chemical test. However, the implementation of the implied consent law is not restricted solely to arrests for driving under the influence. If a person is under arrest for "any offense" arising out of acts concerning which the arresting officer has at least "reasonable grounds" to believe that a violation of § 40-6-391 has occurred, the officer may request a chemical test, even if then short of probable cause to arrest for driving under the influence.

The coincidence of probable cause to arrest a suspect for a violation of the DUI statute and the suspect's actual arrest, albeit for a non-DUI offense, means that the suspect is, as a matter of law, arrested for an offense arising out of acts alleged to have been committed in violation of the DUI statute. Thus, the defendant's arrest for such an offense would not subject the results of his state-administered breath test to suppression.

Formerly, if a person was "involved in any traffic accident resulting in serious injuries or fatalities," the officer was authorized by § 40-5-55(a) to request a chemical test without first placing that person under arrest. In 2003, however, the Georgia Supreme Court held that this provision authorizes unreasonable searches and seizures in violation of the state and federal constitutions to the extent that it requires chemical testing of the operator of a motor vehicle involved in a traffic accident resulting in serious injuries or fatalities regardless of any determination of probable cause. In the absence of probable cause that the operator has violated the DUI statute, an officer would not be legally authorized to inform the operator of his implied consent rights. Consequently, informing the operator of these rights would be misleading, and any consent based upon this misrepresentation would be invalid. Thus, the results of a blood test procured pursuant to § 40-5-55(a) would have to be excluded at trial.

The Supreme Court's decision makes it clear that § 40-5-55(a) is unconstitutional to the extent that it can be interpreted to require an individual to submit to chemical testing **solely** because that individual was involved in a traffic accident resulting in serious injuries or fatalities. On the other hand, where an individual has been involved in a traffic accident resulting in serious injuries or fatalities **and** the investigating officer has probable cause to believe that the individual was driving under the influence of alcohol or other drugs, the constitutional infirmities are no longer present, and the ensuing search is both warranted and constitutional. In such a case, § 40-5-55 does not require that the individual be arrested in order to trigger his implied consent to testing. This is so because the individual may be so incapacitated as a result of the traffic accident that a formal arrest would be unwarranted under the circumstances. Furthermore, an individual involved in such an accident, rather than someone who is merely stopped while driving, is on notice that some inquiry will be made regarding the cause of and responsibility for the accident, and this knowledge would give context to the subsequent reading of implied consent rights.

In circumstances where there has been no traffic accident resulting in serious injuries or fatalities, but the investigating officer has probable cause to believe that the suspect was driving under the influence of alcohol or other drugs, the statutory mandates of § 40-5-55 require an arrest prior to any reading of implied consent rights. The arrest necessary before the reading of implied consent, however, does not have to be a formal arrest in which the officer explicitly states to the suspect that he has been arrested. Implied consent is triggered at the point that the suspect is not free to leave and a reasonable person in his position would not believe that the detention is temporary, regardless of whether a formal arrest has occurred.

In *Cornwell v. State*, the Georgia Supreme Court held that the implied consent statute (§ 40-5-55) as applied to the defendant was not unconstitutional because it allowed for the warrantless compelled testing of a driver's bodily fluids without proof of the existence of exigent circumstances. Since a driver is deemed to have consented to tests of his bodily substances when probable cause exists to arrest him for an alleged violation of § 40-6-391, the court found that the existence of exigent circumstances is wholly irrelevant. Indeed, where the driver has been arrested based on probable cause and the state has complied with the statutory implied consent requirements, the driver cannot complain that testing done by the state for the presence of alcohol and drugs violated his rights under the state and federal constitutions to be free from unreasonable searches and seizures.

Prior to 1998, the plain language of § 40-5-67.1(a) authorized the arresting officer to select a breath test and a urine test or a blood test and a urine test. In State v. Warmack, the Court of Appeals held that nothing in the statutory scheme authorized the officer to require, as opposed to request, additional testing after the officer selected a breath test. Once the officer designated the test, the statute provided no authority for making another selection when the officer became dissatisfied with the results of the state-administered test. Under these circumstances, the defendant had a right to refuse any additional testing. Apparently dissatisfied with this result, the General Assembly amended the language of § 40-5-67.1(a) in 1998 to provide that an officer has the authority to designate which test or tests are to be administered "initially and may subsequently require a test or tests of any substances not initially tested." The General Assembly found, contrary to the decision in Warmack, that the officer "should be allowed to initially require a combination of tests and should subsequently be allowed to require additional tests of any substance not initially tested." Now that this amendment authorizes an officer to require subsequent tests, a request to undergo additional testing need not be preceded by Miranda warnings. The statutory scheme also provides that where a person is involved in a traffic accident resulting in serious injuries or fatalities, the investigating officer is authorized to designate which test or tests must be administered, provided that a blood test with drug screen may also be administered. This testing must be administered "as soon as practicable under the circumstances." This testing is permitted only if the investigating officer has probable cause to believe that the individual involved in the accident was driving under the influence of alcohol or other drugs.

The authority of an officer to require additional samples for retesting will be limited by the reasonableness of the delay and reasonableness of the inconvenience to the person. An officer may take a portion of the blood legitimately drawn during the person's independent test and may send the sample to the crime lab for subsequent testing, either for control purposes or for potential rebuttal evidence, or both.

Nothing in the statutory scheme prohibits an officer from requesting multiple tests at one time. However, in all cases where the arrest is made on or after January 1, 1995, if the officer selects breath testing, he can request no more than two sequential series of a total of two adequate breath samples each. If both the first and second samples produce printed alcohol concentration analyses, the officer is without authority to conduct another breath test on the defendant.

The import of the language in § 40-5-55 is that the arresting officer must have reasonable grounds to believe that the suspect has been driving under the influence before requesting that a chemical test be performed. There is nothing in that language that would exclude testing for drugs as well as alcohol as long as the suspect is properly advised pursuant to the implied consent notice that the tests were being administered for the purpose of determining whether he was under the influence of alcohol or drugs. Although § 40-5-55 goes on to provide that, subject to § 40-6-392, the officer must designate whether a breath, urine, or blood test will be performed, that language means that the officer must advise the suspect of which test or tests he is requesting the suspect undergo. This language does not require the officer to request that the crime lab test for drugs as well as alcohol. Thus, the officer's failure to make such a request would not render the test results inadmissible.

Nothing in the statutory scheme relating to chemical testing or implied consent states that an officer who obtains consent for more than one chemical test is required to administer all of the tests for which consent was obtained. As long as a defendant's right to an independent chemical test is clear, an officer may obtain consent for more than one chemical test and then elect which consented-to test or tests will be administered.

If the state has a blood sample analyzed by the state crime lab, the blood test itself is state-administered. The fact that the drawing of the blood may have been done at an independent medical facility does not affect admissibility.

The scope of the consent granted by a defendant to a test to determine alcohol or drug content of blood, as well as the legislative intent embodied in the implied consent statutes, may be derived from the wording of the implied consent notice read to a defendant. The notice requests a defendant to submit to a test "for the purpose of determining if you are under the influence of alcohol or drugs." The representations in the notice concerning the nature of the test to be performed or the use to which the test results will be applied are binding upon the state. Consequently, the test results can be used against a defendant only for the purpose of determining whether he was driving "under the influence of alcohol or drugs" or has committed some other driving-related offense. Thus, while the test results can be used for the purpose of determining whether the defendant was driving with the presence of drugs in his blood, they cannot be used as the sole basis for a drug possession charge, nor can a blood sample be subjected to additional DNA testing so that it may be used as the basis for a sexual offense charge. These uses would exceed the scope of the consent granted by the defendant.

Whatever a hospital consent form may say or lead a defendant to believe, it has no bearing on the state's right to test the defendant's blood and urine for alcohol or drugs pursuant to the consent given by the defendant after receiving the required implied consent notice. Nothing on such a form, including a statement signed by the arresting officer, can be construed as action taken by the state in violation of the statutory requirements of implied consent.

Our implied consent law does not permit a suspect under arrest for driving under the influence to withdraw his consent to a state-administered blood test before the sample is analyzed.

In 2005, the Georgia Supreme Court held in *State v. Collier* that an officer did not have the authority to seek a search warrant to compel a person to submit blood and urine samples for drug testing when that person had invoked his right under the implied consent law to refuse such testing. Section 40-5-67.1(d) plainly required that if an individual did not consent to the designated chemical test, then no test was to be administered. This precluded any discretion on the part of the officer to attempt to obtain such testing. Furthermore, the legislatively-created sanctions for refusing such testing did not include being compelled to submit to testing through the use of a search warrant.

In 2006, apparently disapproving of this construction of the statute, the General Assembly enacted a provision that legislatively overrules the Supreme Court's decision in *Collier*. This provision states that nothing in § 40-5-67.1 should be deemed to preclude the acquisition or admission of evidence of a violation of § 40-6-391 if obtained by voluntary consent or a search warrant as authorized by the constitution or laws of this state or the United States. Because this amendment, which took effect in July 2006, is not merely a procedural or evidentiary change but one eliminating a defendant's substantive right to refuse to submit to testing, it should not be applied retroactively.

iv. Authority to Administer Test to Unconscious Person

The test can be administered without the actual consent of the tested party if he is unconscious, dead or otherwise incapable of refusal. In this situation, the statute provides that the original implied consent to such tests expressed by driving on state roads is operative to authorize the test administration. Yet there is no statutory requirement compelling the state to conduct a test.

The provision authorizing a test in this situation has withstood a constitutional attack based on the privilege against self-incrimination. In Strong v. State, the Georgia Supreme Court relied heavily on Schmerber v. California, a United States Supreme Court decision which rejected a Fifth Amendment self-incrimination attack on a similar California procedure.

An Equal Protection attack on the statutory scheme was raised in Williams v. State. The defendant, who had been unconscious at the time of the test, sought to have the evidence of the test excluded on the grounds that had he been conscious he could have refused to have the test administered and he ought to be treated equally with conscious individuals. The court rejected the claim summarily, over a vigorous dissent which argued that § 40-6-392 requires actual consent to the test and that the implied consent provision of § 40-5-55(b) requires total compliance with § 40-6-392.

There is nothing in the statutes or case law which requires the state to take and retain blood samples for use by an unconscious defendant in the event he desires an independent test by someone of his own choosing after regaining consciousness.

Where an individual has been involved in a traffic accident resulting in serious injuries or fatalities and the investigating law enforcement officer has probable cause to believe that the individual was driving under the influence of alcohol or other drugs, the drawing of the individual's blood while he is unconscious is both warranted and constitutional. However, the mere odor of alcohol emanating from the unconscious individual would not be sufficient to establish probable cause. There must be other evidence of impairment such as the individual's unsafe driving act on which to base probable cause to draw his blood while he is unconscious.

v. Legality of Test

There has been considerable litigation concerning the appropriate procedural device by which to raise the issue of the legality of the state-administered tests. In State v. Johnston the court held that allegations of noncompliance with the statute or departmental regulations are not properly cognizable in a pretrial motion to suppress, but pointed out that a trial judge **can choose** to treat such a motion as a motion in limine and decide the issues it presents before trial. The court also held that a motion to suppress hearing contemplates the suppression of tangible evidence only, but refused to decide the question of how to litigate the admissibility of testimonial or nontangible evidence before trial. A grant of a motion in limine is directly appealable by the state under § 5-7-1.

The courts have been hesitant to suppress evidence based on the state's noncompliance with administrative rules. Such rules and regulations are not construed to have the force and effect of law, but are deemed to be policy statements. Thus, in State v. Richardson, the court held that the breath test was not subject to suppression because the officer failed to comply with the "20-minute rule" of the department, which requires officers to wait 20 minutes to observe the defendant prior to the giving of a breath test. In several other cases the appellate courts held that minor violations of administrative rules were not enough to cause exclusion of the test results.

Although a police vehicle used to make a traffic arrest is required to be distinctly marked with the name of the police agency, a traffic arrest made in an unmarked vehicle is not invalid. Thus, an officer in an unmarked vehicle, who has observed erratic driving, is authorized to arrest the driver, and the driver's arrest, being legal, cannot be the basis for suppressing his breath test results.

Formerly, a person involved in a traffic accident resulting in a serious injury was deemed by operation of law to have given consent to a chemical test of his bodily substances for the presence of alcohol or any other drug. The results of a chemical test given under these circumstances was not subject to suppression. In 2003, however, the Georgia Supreme Court held that this provision of the law authorized an unreasonable search and seizure in violation of the state and federal constitutions to the extent that it required chemical testing of the operator of a motor vehicle involved in a traffic accident resulting in serious injuries or fatalities regardless of any determination of probable cause. Thus, the results of a chemical test procured pursuant to this provision would be subject to suppression at trial.

The Supreme Court's decision makes it clear that § 40-5-55(a) is unconstitutional to the extent that it can be interpreted to require an individual to submit to chemical testing **solely** because that individual was involved in a traffic accident resulting in serious injuries or fatalities. On the other hand, where an individual has been involved in a traffic accident resulting in serious injuries or fatalities **and** the investigating officer has probable cause to believe that the individual was driving under the influence of alcohol or other drugs, the constitutional infirmities are no longer present, and the ensuing search is both warranted and constitutional. In such a case, § 40-5-55 does not require that the individual be arrested in order to trigger his implied consent to testing. This is so because the individual may be so incapacitated as a result of the traffic accident that a formal arrest would be unwarranted under the circumstances. Furthermore, an individual involved in such an accident, rather than someone who is merely stopped while driving, is on notice that some inquiry will be made regarding the cause of and responsibility for the accident, and this knowledge would give context to the subsequent reading of implied consent rights.

An officer's failure to read the defendant his Miranda rights prior to requesting and obtaining a urine sample or prior to administering the state-administered breath test does not render the test results inadmissible. Moreover, because the test results are not evidence of a testimonial or communicative nature, their admission would not violate the defendant's Fifth and Fourteenth Amendment rights. Also, their admission would not violate the defendant's statutory right against self-incrimination because, although he is in custody when he takes the test, that right is not applicable until he has been charged in a criminal proceeding.

d. Implied Consent Notices

Prior to January 1, 1993, the arresting officer in his implied consent notice was required to inform the DUI suspect (1) that §§ 40-5-55 and 40-6-392 required him to submit to state-administered chemical tests for the purpose of determining alcoholic or drug content, (2) that he had the right to an additional test by personnel of his own choosing, and (3) that his refusal to submit to the state-administered chemical tests would result in the suspension of his driver's license for 6 to 12 months. The General Assembly revised the requirements relative to a DUI suspect's implied consent rights in 1992, 1994, 1995, 1997, 1998, and 2001. Now, there are separate implied consent notices for (1) suspects under age 21, (2) suspects age 21 or over, and (3) suspects who are commercial motor vehicle drivers. The arresting officer is required to select and read to the suspect the appropriate implied consent notice. Each notice informs the suspect (1) that Georgia law requires him to submit to state-administered chemical testing for the purpose of determining if he is under the influence of alcohol or drugs, (2) what will be the consequences if he refuses state-administered testing, (3) what will be the consequences if he submits to state-administered testing and the results indicate that he is under the influence "per se," and (4) that after submitting to state-administered testing he is entitled to additional testing at his own expense and from qualified personnel of his own choosing. Once a suspect has been informed of his implied consent rights, he is deemed to have been properly advised of those rights and the results of any chemical testing or his refusal to submit to such testing is admissible into evidence against him. Failure to provide any notice as set out above does not invalidate the suspension of any driver's license.

Prior to 2006, in all cases in which police officers requested a chemical test of a person's blood, urine, or other bodily substances in connection with the operation of a motor vehicle for the purpose of determining whether the driver was under the influence of alcohol or drugs, they had to give the notice or warning required by the implied consent statute. Police officers were not permitted to circumvent the implied consent statute by merely requesting consent without giving any implied consent notice or warning. In 2006, the General Assembly added subsection (d.1) to § 40-5-67.1 which provides that nothing in § 40-5-67.1 should be deemed to preclude the acquisition or admission of evidence of a violation of § 40-6-391 if obtained by voluntary consent or a search warrant as authorized by the constitution or laws of this state or the United States. This amendment eliminates the need to give an implied consent warning where an individual "voluntarily" agrees to testing. This amendment not only changes the substance of the implied consent warning, it does away with the requirement that the warning be given at all where an officer manages to otherwise lawfully obtain consent to testing. This is not merely a procedural or evidentiary change, but one eliminating a defendant's substantive right to refuse to submit to testing. Therefore, this amendment, which took effect in July 2006, should not be applied retroactively.

Prior to 1995, although the implied consent notice given to a DUI suspect had to be complete, informing the suspect of all the types of tests available to him and of his right to choose his own qualified person to administer the test, the notice did not have to track the exact language of the implied consent statute. The General Assembly in its 1995 Regular Session amended § 40-5-67.1(b) to provide that a law enforcement officer is **required** to give to the suspect the appropriate implied consent notice in the language specified in the statute. This amendment was effective April 21, 1995.

In Martin v. State, the Court of Appeals found that Section 5 of the amending Act provided that § 40-5-67.1(b) applied to all cases pending on April 21, 1995, the date that the Governor approved the amended statute. Since the defendant's case was pending on April 21, 1995, the implied consent notice prescribed by the amended statute was required to be given to the defendant. Obviously, since the defendant was arrested and given his implied consent notice on September 10, 1994, the arresting officer could not have given the specific implied consent notice prescribed by the amended statute. Nevertheless, inasmuch as the General Assembly made the amended statute applicable to pending cases, the Court of Appeals, after comparing the notice given to the notice required, found the notice to be insufficient.

The General Assembly in its 1995 Extraordinary Session added subsection (b.1) to § 40-5-67.1 in response to the Court of Appeals decision in Martin v. State. This amendment was effective August 18, 1995. Under subsection (b.1), § 40-5-67.1(b) applied to any case wherein the request for chemical testing was made regarding an offense committed on or after April 21, 1995. Section 40-5-67.1(b) did not apply to any case wherein the request for chemical testing was made regarding an offense committed prior to April 21, 1995, in which case the former provisions governing the content of implied consent notices applied.

In State v. Martin, the Georgia Supreme Court concluded that the Court of Appeals's opinion had to be reversed pursuant to the August 1995 amendment. Although the Court of Appeals correctly applied the April 1995 amendment at the time its opinion was rendered, the August amendment rendered the April amendment applicable only to those stops made after April 21, 1995. The Supreme Court concluded that the August amendment was valid under the state and federal constitutions and by its plain language it applied to the defendant's case. Thus, the implied consent notice given the defendant satisfied the applicable statutory requirement under former law, and the trial court did not err by denying the defendant's motion in limine to suppress his breath test results.

For offenses committed on or after April 21, 1995, the Court of Appeals held that the arresting officer was required to read the **exact** language mandated by § 40-5-67.1(b). Substantial compliance with the statute was not sufficient. Strict compliance, which meant reading the notices exactly as written in the statute, was required. Apparently disapproving of this construction of the statute, the General Assembly found and declared in 1998 that while DUI suspects "should be informed of their rights regarding the administration of chemical testing, no such suspect is entitled to a notice which tracks the exact language of the implied consent statute . . . " The notice must "be read in its entirety but need not be read exactly so long as the substance of the notice remains unchanged." Thus, contrary to holdings of the Court of Appeals, "substantial" rather than "strict" compliance is the applicable standard. This 1998 amendment is retroactive in its application.

The purpose of the requirement that the notice be read in its "entirety" is to ensure that the officer read through the entire notice rather than only a portion of it. Thus, a notice that has been read all the way through but has had a word omitted would still satisfy this requirement, and a trial court would be able to consider whether the substance of the notice has been changed by the omission. As long as the notice's meaning has not been affected, the omission of a word would not alter its substance.

In Klink v. State, the Georgia Supreme Court upheld the constitutionality of § 40-5-67.1 against a challenge that it violated due process. The court concluded that the choices provided by the implied consent notices in the statute are not so incomplete, misleading, or coercive that no real choices exist. Furthermore, the implied consent notices do not violate due process because they fail to include a notice that the test results may be used against the suspect at trial. The court also upheld the implied consent statute against an equal protection challenge in Lutz v. State. The court held that the statute does not provide different administrative penalties for people who drive under the influence of alcohol than it provides for people who drive under the influence of other, illegal drugs. Both groups of impaired drivers are subject to having their licenses suspended administratively without having been prosecuted for DUI.

Merely because the notices set forth in the implied consent statute inform suspects that their refusal to submit to a bodily alcohol concentration test may result in a driver's license suspension and may also be introduced against them at trial, it does not follow that the notices are defective for failing to inform suspects that the state is permitted to use alcohol concentration test results in a DUI prosecution. The failure to so inform the suspect does not render his consent to take the test unknowing and involuntary. Chemical tests may be administered to the suspect without first notifying him that the test results may be used in a DUI prosecution. Accordingly, the use of the test results at the suspect's DUI prosecution would not violate his rights under the Fourth Amendment.

The implied consent notice to be given to commercial motor vehicle driver suspects is to be read to drivers of commercial vehicles, not to drivers of private vehicles who happen to hold commercial driver's licenses.

In circumstances where there has been no traffic accident resulting in serious injuries or fatalities, the investigating officer should inform the suspect of his implied consent rights at the time of arrest or as close to that time as circumstances warrant. The suspect must be **arrested** before he can be deemed to have given consent to have a chemical test performed to determine the presence of alcohol or other drugs. The existence of mere probable cause to arrest is not sufficient. Thus, even where there is probable cause to arrest for a violation of § 40-6-391, an implied consent notice given to a suspect several days prior to his arrest for DUI can in no way be considered contemporaneous to that arrest and would therefore be inappropriate. Under these circumstances, the suspect's refusal to submit to a chemical test would be warranted, and evidence of this refusal would be inadmissible at trial.

On the other hand, where an individual has been involved in a traffic accident resulting in serious injuries or fatalities **and** the investigating officer has probable cause to believe that the individual was driving under the influence of alcohol or other drugs, chemical testing is both warranted and constitutional. In such a case, § 40-5-55 does not require that the individual be arrested in order to trigger his implied consent to testing. This is so because the individual may be so incapacitated as a result of the traffic accident that a formal arrest would be unwarranted under the circumstances. Furthermore, an individual involved in such an accident, rather than someone who is merely stopped while driving, is on notice that some inquiry will be made regarding the cause of and responsibility for the accident, and this knowledge would give context to the subsequent reading of implied consent rights.

It should be noted, however, if the injury suffered in the accident is not one of the serious injuries specified in § 40-5-55(c), the rules associated with the reading of an implied consent notice to a suspect following a traffic accident with serious injuries or fatalities would not apply. Rather, the defendant's implied consent rights must be analyzed under that portion of § 40-5-55(a) regarding an individual who has been **arrested** for any offense arising out of acts alleged to have been committed in violation of § 40-6-391.

Based on the plain wording of § 40-5-55(a), which requires only that the person be involved in a traffic accident resulting in serious injuries or fatalities, there is no requirement that the serious injury or fatality occur prior to reading the implied consent warnings, only that an individual be deemed to have given consent "when" or "if" this circumstance exists. It is not unreasonable to expect that in some cases it will not be evident or known to police that the accident resulted in a serious injury or fatality until long after the accident itself has occurred. In *Snyder v. State*, the trooper had probable cause to believe that the defendant was driving under the influence of alcohol based upon his observations at the scene and the result of the AlcoSensor test. Because the traffic accident also subsequently resulted in a fatality, the defendant was therefore deemed to have consented to a test of his blood. Accordingly, his arrest was not required prior to the reading of the implied consent warnings.

The officer has no duty to repeat the notices and rights to a suspect and is not required to give the notices to a suspect who is unconscious. The implied consent law is not violated if an officer other than the arresting officer informs the suspect of his rights.

Miranda warnings are not required prior to the giving of an implied consent notice to a DUI suspect in police custody. Furthermore, the notice itself need not inform the suspect of the privilege against self-incrimination. Because the suspect's consent to take the state-administered test is neither testimonial nor communicative in nature, it is not protected by the privilege against self-incrimination. Thus, the absence of Miranda warnings would not require the suppression of the suspect's consent under federal law. Also, the suspect's consent is not protected by the statutory right against self-incrimination because, although he is in custody when he consents to take the test, that right is not applicable until he has been charged in a criminal proceeding.

A suspect is not entitled to advice of counsel when confronted with a decision as to whether to submit to a test under the implied consent law or with a decision as to whether to request an independent examination. Thus, evidence as to the test should be suppressed where the suspect is misled by an officer's statement to believe that he is entitled to advice of counsel prior to submitting to the test.

In the event of a multi-car collision involving more than one drunk driver, simultaneously informing the drunk drivers of their implied consent rights will not result in the suppression of a state-administered breath test result, if the drivers are also independently informed of their rights before they are subjected to a state-administered test.

Sections 40-5-67.1 and 40-6-392(a)(3) do not require that implied consent notices be read only in English. Nor do they require that the notices be read to suspects in their native language. They only require that the notices be read to the suspects. The statutes thus, on their face, do not create a classification of English-speaking and non-English-speaking suspects. Absent a showing that these statutes were enacted or applied with a discriminatory purpose, they do not violate equal protection. Furthermore, implied consent notices are a matter of legislative grace, and due process does not require that the notices be given in languages that suspects understand.

Where the arresting officer cannot communicate to the suspect his implied consent rights because the suspect cannot speak English, any failure to obtain an additional test is justifiable and the results of the state-administered test are admissible.

Where a defendant, who speaks only broken English, testifies through an interpreter that he did not understand his implied consent notices, the state may seek to impeach the defendant by questioning him concerning any prior DUI arrests during which chemical tests had been performed on his bodily substances. The fact that the defendant had submitted to chemical tests after having been given the notices on prior occasions increases the likelihood that he understood the notices on this occasion. The probative value of the elicited testimony would outweigh its prejudicial effect. Since the state is seeking to impeach the defendant with evidence concerning the circumstances of his arrest, not his criminal conviction, it is not required to prove the prior convictions by introducing certified copies or otherwise.

If the arresting officer cannot communicate to the suspect his implied consent rights because the suspect is hearing impaired, the officer or his department is required by the hearing impaired law to request a qualified interpreter from the Department of Human Resources once the suspect is taken into custody. If no such request is made and no qualified interpreter is present, the suspect cannot be properly informed of his implied consent rights, and the results of the state-administered test are not admissible in any criminal proceeding against the suspect. When the request has been made for an interpreter and the required one-hour waiting period lapses, the officer may proceed with his investigation under the implied consent law. If, however, the suspect intelligently waives the one-hour requirement, then the officer may proceed with written interrogatories and the suspect should answer in writing.

The state must show that the arresting officer properly advised the suspect of his implied consent rights. If the state fails to make this showing, the state-administered test results are inadmissible. Formerly, the arresting officer's testimony that he read the suspect his implied consent rights from a card that he carried for that purpose constituted a prima facie showing that the officer informed the suspect of his implied consent rights. Since this card now contains notices for three different types of DUI suspects, one of which the arresting officer must select and read to the suspect, the officer's mere conclusory statement that he read the suspect his implied consent rights as set forth on a card issued to him by his department would fail to meet the state's burden of proving compliance with the implied consent notice requirements. The state must now present further evidence specifying the substance of the notice allegedly given. For instance, testimony from the arresting officer that he read the Georgia implied consent law from 1997 for suspects over 21 and the officer's recitation of a portion of the notice given at trial would be sufficient to prove compliance with these requirements.

Where the arresting officer, at a hearing on a motion in limine, erroneously testifies that he read the suspect the incorrect implied consent notice, the state, realizing that the officer had done so after he had been excused, may be allowed to reopen the evidence and use a videotape of the traffic stop to demonstrate that the officer gave incorrect testimony at the hearing and that he actually gave the suspect the correct implied consent notice. Since the videotape contradicts the officer's testimony, the rule against impeaching one's own witness would be inapplicable.

Sufficient compliance with the implied consent statute is also established by evidence showing that the suspect was given timely notice of his implied consent rights and thereafter made no request for an independent chemical test. It has been held that the state has only to show that the suspect, after being advised of his rights, did not refuse to submit to the state-administered test. The state need not show compliance with the implied consent statute's mandatory language where the defense has expressly stipulated, at trial, that the implied consent notice was given. Inherent in such a stipulation is that the implied consent notice was valid.

An inaccurate notice will render the state-administered blood alcohol test inadmissible. The erroneous admission of this test probably will not affect a conviction for driving while under the influence of alcohol to the extent that it was less safe for the defendant to drive, where other evidence, including the arresting officer's observation of the defendant's driving, is amply sufficient to support the defendant's conviction.

Breath test results, which were suppressed because an inaccurate notice was given to the defendant, may be subsequently admitted by the trial court to allow the state to rebut a defendant's expert opinion concerning the amount of alcohol in the defendant's body at the time of his arrest.

An arresting officer's failure to file a DPS 1205 form immediately after the defendant's arrest in order to initiate administrative license suspension proceedings does not render the implied consent notice given to the defendant defective or misleading.

The implied consent notice should not be read before the administration of the alcosensor test because that may mislead the suspect into believing that he is required to submit to that test. However, unless the suspect can show that the timing of the reading of the notice was so confusing that he was unable to make an intelligent decision about whether to submit to the state-administered test, it will not render the results of the state-administered test inadmissible.

The "under 21" implied consent notice is not misleading as to the purpose of the breath test. It specifically informs the suspect that the purpose of the test is to determine whether he was driving under the influence of alcohol and that a 0.02 blood alcohol concentration (BAC) will result in such violation. The presence of the prohibited 0.02 BAC renders the suspect under the influence of alcohol for purposes of the notice. Thus, the suspect's consent to testing for the purpose of determining whether he was driving under the influence does not limit the state to prosecution solely under the less safe driver provisions of our DUI laws but includes prosecution for the presence of alcohol under the per se BAC provisions as well.

License suspension is a true and legitimate consequence of refusing to submit to or submitting and failing the test. There is no unlawful coercion where the officer merely informs the arrestee of the permissible range of sanctions that the state may ultimately be authorized to impose. The fact that his license is not ultimately suspended does not mean he was not informed of the true and legitimate consequences of a refusal or a failed test.

In 2004, the Court of Appeals held that by threatening to obtain a search warrant in order to obtain the necessary samples by force, the police would be misleading the suspect about the consequences of refusing to consent to the requested tests. Where police mislead a suspect about his implied consent rights, any consent based upon the misrepresentation would be invalid. All results of such coerced tests should therefore be excluded. Apparently dissatisfied with this result, the General Assembly amended § 40-5-67.1 in 2006 to provide that nothing in this Code section should be deemed to preclude the acquisition or admission of evidence of a violation of § 40-6-391 if obtained by voluntary consent or a search warrant as authorized by the constitution or laws of this state or the United States. Because this amendment, which took effect in July 2006, is not merely a procedural or evidentiary change but one eliminating a defendant's substantive right to refuse to submit to testing, it should not be applied retroactively.

The DUI suspect not only has a right to an independent test of his own choosing, but also, under § 40-6-392(a)(4), has the right to be informed about this right. It has been held that the failure to inform the suspect of this right to an independent test will render the state's test evidence inadmissible in both criminal and civil cases.

In State v. Dull, the court held that Steed v. City of Atlanta, as only a two-judge decision, possessed no precedential value. The court declined to endorse the novel requirement announced in Steed. Neither the Court of Appeals nor the Supreme Court, prior to Steed, ever construed § 40-6-391 as requiring an affirmative showing of waiver or an actual request of an additional chemical test. In summary, the failure to inform a defendant of the right to an additional chemical test, and not the failure to obtain and show a waiver affirmatively, renders inadmissible the results of a chemical test administered at the request of the arresting officer. Where there is a conflict over whether a defendant was advised of his right to an additional test, resolution of the question of credibility is for the trial court.

The Court of Appeals has made it clear that the admissibility of chemical tests is a question of law for the judge to decide and, therefore, the jury need not be informed of the provisions of § 40-6-392(a) dealing with the requirement of notification to the defendant of alternative means of testing.

It should be noted that a defendant can complain only about a failure to warn him of his own rights. In Johnson v. State, a defendant was held to be without standing to object to the admission of a chemical test administered to a third party.

e. Independent or Additional Test Requested by Suspect

After the suspect has been informed of his right to an independent test, he must effectively communicate to the officer a desire for an independent test. This right is invoked by some statement of the suspect that reasonably can be construed in light of the circumstances to be an expression of a desire for an independent test. The officer is not required to ask the suspect where and by whom he wishes the independent test performed. It is the responsibility of the suspect, not of the officer, to designate the specifics of the independent testing and the officer must be apprised by the suspect of those specifics before the officer has a duty to facilitate the suspect's election. Accordingly, any interpretation of the applicable statutory provisions as would preclude the arresting officer from engaging in any further inquiry with regard to the specifics of the suspect's election of an independent test must be rejected. If the suspect does not apprise the officer of those specifics, the officer's action in taking the suspect to the nearest hospital in accordance with departmental policy would be reasonable.

The officer must make a reasonable effort to accommodate the suspect who seeks an independent test and must permit the suspect or afford him the opportunity to make the necessary arrangements. Obtaining bond is not a prerequisite to the officer's reasonable accommodation of the suspect.

The suspect's request must be made within a reasonable time after his arrest. A request made after the suspect has been informed of his implied consent rights but before the state-administered test has been given is not premature but timely. Also, the suspect may request more than one test, for example, a breath test and a blood test.

After the suspect has made the necessary arrangements for his independent test, he has the right to be transported to the place of testing. However, there is no duty on the part of an officer to transport a suspect to a hospital that has refused to perform the test without a doctor's order. If the suspect has elected to be taken to a facility that only would draw but not test the blood sample, it is the responsibility of the suspect to request thereafter to be transported to a place where the sample can be tested.

The cost of the independent test, to be administered by a qualified person of the suspect's own choosing, must be borne by the suspect, at least where he is able to pay. Who pays for the blood test, however, does not affect admissibility.

Since the statutes entitle a suspect to have an "additional" test, not necessarily an independent test, he may affirmatively choose at his own expense to have the state's qualified testing officer perform an additional breath test. Upon his affirmative request, the suspect should be permitted to obtain a second, state-administered breath test.

Where there is a conflict over whether the suspect requested and was denied an independent test, resolution of the question of credibility is for the trial court. If there is evidence to support the trial court's finding of fact that the suspect did not request an independent test, it would not be clearly erroneous for the trial court to deny the suspect's motion to suppress.

The failure to allow a suspect to obtain an independent test requires the suppression of the results of the breath test, unless the state presents evidence at the suppression hearing from which the trial court can find that the failure to respond to the suspect's timely request was justified. Although depriving the suspect of the means of obtaining an independent test would render the state's test inadmissible, it would not warrant the dismissal of the entire case where there is sufficient competent evidence to find him guilty of driving under the influence.

Separate and apart from the statutory right, created by § 40-6-392(a), to an independent test when the state administers an alcohol concentration test, a defendant in a DUI case has a due process right to establish potentially exculpatory evidence if he requests an independent chemical test. The only meaningful time for obtaining such evidence is at the time of arrest. While it may be true that a defendant is denied his statutory right to "a chemical test or tests" if he is not permitted to order the test of his choice, his due process rights are not denied if he is not permitted to order the test of his choice, so long as he is provided the opportunity to establish potentially exculpatory evidence by a competent and approved method.

While the statutory scheme adequately safeguards the defendant's equal protection and due process rights to gather exculpatory evidence through an independent test, the procedure mandates that the defendant voluntarily submit, first, to a state-administered test. If the defendant refuses to cooperate with the state-administered test, he intentionally refuses and rejects the very protection provided by the statutory scheme, thereby waiving not only his statutory right to an independent test but also his due process right to obtain exculpatory evidence for use in his defense.

The suspect's refusal to provide the second breath sample as provided in § 40-6-392(a)(1)(B) does not constitute a refusal to comply with the state's request to provide a breath sample. Accordingly, as long as the suspect provides the state with one admissible breath sample, he retains his right to an independent analysis of his blood.

Because an independent test is not performed at either the request or direction of a law enforcement officer, it is not subject to the dictates of § 40-6-392, and the party seeking to admit the test results must satisfy the trial court that the results are admissible pursuant to the rules of evidence. Documentary evidence of an independent test designed to measure a person's alcohol concentration level may be admitted into evidence under the business records exception to the hearsay rule, when the party seeking to admit the test results lays a proper foundation by offering the testimony of the custodian of records of the laboratory where the independent test was conducted. Also, the document may be admitted under this exception where it contains only the numerical result of the alcohol concentration level test performed on the defendant's blood and contains no opinions in addition to the test result. The exclusion of independent test results can be harmful error if these results would tend to create doubt concerning the accuracy of the results of the first test.

The state may not introduce the results of an additional, but not independent, blood alcohol test requested by the suspect as the result of a deficient notice. The failure to properly advise a suspect of his right to an independent, additional blood alcohol test prevents the state from introducing the results of the additional test. These results must be excluded from the state's case-in-chief just as the results of the state's test are excluded. The failure to give a proper notice invalidates the results of any test.

f. Refusal to Submit to State-Administered Test

A suspect has a right to refuse to submit to the state-administered chemical tests under the implied consent law. To be a correct and complete statement of the law, a jury instruction on the suspect's right to refuse must also instruct the jury that evidence of the suspect's refusal may be used against him at trial.

It has been held that a failure to inform the suspect of his right to an additional independent test not only bars the admission of the results of the state test, but also justifies a refusal to submit to the state test. In Garrett v. Department of Public Safety, the Georgia Supreme Court held that a refusal to be tested is justified and can, therefore, not be the basis of a driver's license suspension where the suspect was not warned of his right to an independent test.

The Garrett case points out a very important fact. In most situations, an actual consent by the suspect must be obtained before the state-administered chemical test will be performed. If the suspect refuses to submit to the state test, no test will be performed. Although § 40-6-392 gives the suspect the right to an additional test, it does not satisfy his obligation to submit to the state-administered test. Thus, if the suspect refuses to take the state-administered test, he has no right to an additional test.

A suspect may rescind his initial refusal to submit to a chemical test if such rescission is made in accordance with the following guidelines. A subsequent consent after a refusal to take a chemical test must be made (1) within a very short and reasonable time after the prior first refusal; (2) when a test administered upon the subsequent consent would still be accurate; (3) when testing equipment is still readily available; (4) when honoring the request would result in no substantial inconvenience or expense to the police; and (5) when the suspect requesting the test has been in the custody of the arresting officer and under observation for the whole time since arrest. Once the trial court has ruled in a hearing on a motion in limine to exclude evidence concerning the suspect's attempted rescission of his initial refusal to take the chemical test, the defense may not present this evidence during trial in order to impeach the state's witnesses on this issue.

In *Howell v. State*, upon being read implied consent warnings by one of the arresting officers, the defendant unequivocally revoked his implied consent. Without engaging the defendant in further discourse, the officer arrested him and transported him to a police station where he directed another officer to administer the breath test. The second officer instructed the defendant to blow into the breath testing device. There was no evidence the defendant was asked a second time whether he would consent to a state-administered test and no evidence that he rescinded his refusal and thereafter consented. He was thus administered a breath test simply because he did not refuse to cooperate. The court could not deem such a procedure to be fair or such actions by an officer to be reasonable. Consequently, the trial court erred in denying the defendant's motion to suppress.

A police officer may attempt to persuade a suspect to rescind his initial refusal to submit to chemical testing, so long as any procedure utilized by an officer in attempting to persuade a defendant to rescind his refusal is fair and reasonable. In *Stapleton v. State*, the Court of Appeals held that police conduct met this fair and reasonable requirement. Although the defendant clearly refused to take a breath test when asked at the scene, she rescinded that refusal by agreeing to take the test at the police station. No evidence was presented showing that the officer coerced or threatened the defendant to take the test or that she was intimidated in any way by the officer's request. Under these circumstances, the court determined that the officer did not act unreasonably when he again asked the defendant to take a breath test following her initial refusal at the scene. Therefore, the court affirmed the trial court's denial of the defendant's motion to suppress the test results.

Prior to 1993, there was neither a statutory nor a constitutional requirement that the arresting officer inform the suspect of the consequences of the refusal to submit to the state-administered test. Where the arresting officer did inform the suspect of the consequences of the refusal, it was held that the giving of such information to a suspect did not, as a matter of law, unlawfully coerce his submission to the state-administered test. Effective January 1, 1993, the arresting officer is required by statute to inform the suspect of the consequences of his refusal at the time the state-administered test is requested. The arresting officer's repeatedly informing the suspect, after she has initially refused to submit to the state-administered test, that if she does not submit to the test, the officer will have to suspend her driver's license for one year has been found not to be harmful. Such a statement is not false or misleading and directly and personally brings home to the suspect the consequences of her refusal.

Prior to 1995, the arresting officer had to inform a nonresident suspect in a separate notice that the consequences of his refusal to submit to the state-administered test would be the loss of his driving privileges, "at least on the highways of this state," for the statutorily specified period of time. Since this language is now a part of the implied consent notices prescribed by § 40-5-67.1(b), which the arresting officer is required to select and read to each suspect, a separate notice for nonresident suspects is no longer required.

In 1989, the General Assembly enacted the Uniform Commercial Driver's License Act in order to implement the mandatory provisions of the federal Commercial Motor Vehicle Safety Act of 1986. Under the federal Act, Georgia's disqualification of a driver from operating a commercial motor vehicle, based on his refusal to submit to alcohol testing, in fact **does disqualify** the driver from driving anywhere in the United States for at least one year. Therefore, the Court of Appeals has held that this state's informed consent statute is an accurate statement of the consequences of refusing testing. Far from being coercive, the notice gives sufficient information for drivers of commercial vehicles to make truly informed decisions about whether to submit to testing and the impact of that decision on their careers.

An officer's failure to warn a commercial driver that the refusal to submit to the state-administered test will also lead to the suspension of his personal driving privileges does not necessarily require the suppression of the test results. Where a commercial driver has been misinformed about his implied consent rights, suppression is not required if the misinformation did not affect his decision whether to consent to testing.

The suspect's refusal to submit to the state test results in the administrative suspension of his Georgia driver's license or his privilege to drive in this state or results in his disqualification as a driver of a commercial motor vehicle. The period of suspension or disqualification begins to run upon receipt by the department of the arresting officer's sworn report. The suspension or disqualification is subject to review. Because the state does not have a full opportunity at a license suspension hearing to litigate the question of whether a suspect refused testing, it is not collaterally estopped from presenting evidence on that issue at the suspect's DUI trial.

The refusal to take the state-administered test is admissible "in any criminal trial" and in any civil trial. This refusal itself may be considered as positive evidence creating an inference that the test would show the presence of the prohibited substance. However, this evidence, alone, is insufficient to sustain a conviction of driving under the influence.

The Georgia courts have held that the admission of the suspect's refusal to take the test does not violate the state constitution or the state statutory protection against self-incrimination. Accordingly, evidence of the suspect's consent or refusal to take the test is not rendered inadmissible by the lack of Miranda warnings at the time of arrest. Because the choice afforded a suspect under the "implied consent" statute does not rise to the level of constitutional self-incrimination, it is improper for a trial court to apply the "totality of circumstances" test to determine whether the suspect's consent to the test was freely and voluntarily given.

Even if the suspect is in custody at the time of a request to undergo additional state testing, evidence of his refusal to undergo the testing would not be rendered inadmissible by the lack of Miranda warnings.

Unless encumbered by a physical or medical limitation, a person submitting to a breathalyzer test may be considered to have refused to comply if an adequate breath sample has not been provided. As such, instructions given by a trial court regarding the evidentiary ramifications of such a refusal are both proper and warranted.

Where the undisputed evidence shows that a Spanish-speaking suspect spoke some English, did communicate with the arresting officer, and effectively withdrew his consent, an instruction that an uncommunicative suspect is incapable of withdrawing his consent by refusing to submit to a state-administered test would not be adjusted to the evidence. Furthermore, an instruction that the suspect's refusal can be considered as evidence creating an inference that the test would show the presence of alcohol or drugs is proper where the jury is also instructed that the inference is rebuttable and where the suspect is allowed to attempt to rebut it with evidence that he did not understand the implied consent notices.

It should be noted that the arresting officer's failure without cause to read the implied consent notice to the suspect at the time of his arrest renders evidence of the suspect's refusal to take the state-administered test inadmissible. Furthermore, an arresting officer's failure to comply with the statutory requirements for conveying the implied consent notice to a hearing-impaired suspect would entitle the suspect to refuse to take the state-administered test, and the admission of the suspect's justified refusal would constitute reversible error. Also, if the implied consent notice given to a suspect in its totality contains inaccurate, misleading, and/or inapplicable information, such that the suspect is thereby deprived of making an informed choice under the implied consent statute, the suspect's refusal to take to the state-administered test is rendered inadmissible.

Even if the implied consent notice given to the suspect correctly informs him of his rights, a subsequent misleading explanation of those rights would still make it impossible for the suspect to make an informed decision under the implied consent statute. Furthermore, even if the officer did not intend to mislead, if the suspect is misled or misinformed as to his rights, his ability to make an informed decision would be impaired, thereby rendering evidence of his refusal to take the state-administered test inadmissible.

Under the Georgia Supreme Court's current construction of § 40-5-55(a), consent is implied only if a person has been **arrested** for a violation of § 40-6-391 or if a person has been involved in a traffic accident resulting in serious injuries or fatalities **and** the investigating officer has probable cause to believe that the person was violating § 40-6-391. Consequently, where there has been no traffic accident resulting in serious injuries or fatalities, the suspect must be **arrested** before he can be deemed to have given consent to have a chemical test performed to determine the presence of alcohol or other drugs. The existence of mere probable cause to arrest is not sufficient. Thus, even where there was probable cause to arrest for a violation of § 40-6-391, an implied consent notice given to a suspect several days prior to his arrest for DUI could in no way be considered contemporaneous to that arrest and would therefore be inappropriate. Under these circumstances, the suspect's refusal to submit to a chemical test would be warranted, and evidence of this refusal would be inadmissible at trial.

The law does not require an officer to ensure that a suspect be provided an environment free from a non-state actor's "bad advice" when deciding whether to cooperate with a properly administered implied consent notice, especially when that advice does not inure to the state's benefit and especially when the suspect is equally free to ignore such advice. Thus, an officer's act of placing a contentious suspect in the backseat of his patrol car with another suspect would not provide a sufficient basis for suppression of the other suspect's subsequent refusal to submit to chemical testing, absent any allegation and evidence of defect in the implied consent notice and absent any allegation and evidence that the other suspect did not understand his rights under the notice.

Absent a showing of bad faith or a constitutional violation, an officer's misrepresentation to a suspect that the arrest is being videotaped does render evidence of the suspect's refusal to submit to a blood test inadmissible.

In 2005, the Georgia Supreme Court held in *State v. Collier* that an officer did not have the authority to seek a search warrant to compel a person to submit blood and urine samples for drug testing when that person had invoked his right under the implied consent law to refuse such testing. Section 40-5-67.1(d) plainly required that if an individual did not consent to the designated chemical test, then no test was to be administered. This precluded any discretion on the part of the officer to attempt to obtain such testing. Furthermore, the legislatively-created sanctions for refusing such testing did not include being compelled to submit to testing through the use of a search warrant.

In 2006, apparently disapproving of this construction of the statute, the General Assembly enacted a provision that legislatively overrules the Supreme Court's decision in *Collier*. This provision states that nothing in § 40-5-67.1 should be deemed to preclude the acquisition or admission of evidence of a violation of § 40-6-391 if obtained by voluntary consent or a search warrant as authorized by the constitution or laws of this state or the United States. Because this amendment, which took effect in July 2006, is not merely a procedural or evidentiary change but one eliminating a defendant's substantive right to refuse to submit to testing, it should not be applied retroactively.

Where the prosecution has been prevented from presenting evidence concerning the defendant's refusal to take a blood test, it is proper for the trial court to exclude comment by defense counsel on the inability of the prosecution to present evidence of an alcohol test. It would be manifestly unfair to prevent the prosecution from presenting this evidence and at the same time comment on the prosecution's failure to do so.

Where evidence of the defendant's refusal to submit to the state-administered test has been admitted at trial, the prosecution may argue in closing that the defendant's refusal shows that he was conscious of his impairment and guilt. It would be a reasonable inference for the prosecution to make that the defendant's refusal stemmed from a fear that the results would be unfavorable.

In all cases where the arrest is made on or after January 1, 1995, and the state selects breath testing, two sequential breath samples must be requested for the testing of alcohol concentration. No more than two sequential series of a total of two adequate breath samples each shall be requested by the state. However, after an initial test in which the instrument indicates an adequate breath sample was given for analysis, any subsequent refusal to give additional breath samples cannot be construed as a refusal for purposes of suspension of a driver's license. A refusal to give an adequate sample or samples on any subsequent breath, blood, urine, or other bodily substance test does not affect the admissibility of the results of any prior samples. Where the suspect does provide an adequate breath sample as defined in the statute, his failure or refusal to provide a second adequate breath sample does not constitute a complete refusal to submit to the state-administered test. Thus, any evidence regarding the failure or refusal to provide the second breath sample is inadmissible.

g. *Discovery of Test Results*

The discovery rule regarding chemical tests in DUI cases grants the defendant access to "full information concerning the test." Under this rule, the results generated by the use of a gas chromatograph to test the blood alcohol content of the defendant's blood are discoverable. Thus, the defendant has the right to subpoena the printed results generated by the gas chromatograph for the purpose of cross-examination, and if the subpoena is not unreasonable and oppressive, it may not be quashed by the trial court.

A request for blood test results from the state must be timely made. The state must provide the defendant the actual test results, and the omission of these results from the forensic laboratory reports supplied to the defense by the state constitutes reversible error. When a written scientific report is furnished late, the appropriate remedy is not for the trial court to exclude the results of the test but to grant a continuance or recess upon timely request by the defendant.

Where the arresting officer has provided the defendant with a copy of his breath test results at the time the tests were administered, any failure by the state to provide the same pursuant to the defendant's discovery request for any written scientific reports is harmless.

Horizontal gaze nystagmus (HGN) test results constitute a scientific report discoverable under § 17-16-23. The officer's findings are not merely data recordation or notes but are based on a scientific analysis of the defendant's performance of a recognized test. Oral communication of the results to the defendant and even an "open file" policy of the prosecutor do not relieve the state of its burden to furnish a written report to the defendant. The failure to furnish this report requires exclusion of not only the report but also the officer's oral testimony as to the results of the test. However, unless the defendant can show how this evidence has harmed him, its admission constitutes harmless error.

A certificate of inspection of the Intoxilyzer is not discoverable as a scientific report under § 17-16-23.

The prosecution is not required to comply with a defendant's notice to produce documents relating to the Intoxilyzer, such as log sheets showing the results of tests performed on other subjects, service and operation manuals, inspection reports, and service and repair records. Where the prosecutor states at trial without contradiction that the requested documents are not in his possession, he has no duty to produce them.

Because a Brady motion calls for the production of exculpatory evidence known to the prosecution but unknown to the defense, it does not reach evidence of the defendant's performance on field sobriety tests, as that evidence is known to the defense. In preparing his defense, the defendant would have recited his performance to defense counsel or to an expert for evaluation. Moreover, even if the defendant is unaware of his performance on the tests, no Brady violation occurs where evidence of his performance becomes available to him at trial.

Since a DUI suspect's medical records clearly are protected by the right to privacy guaranteed by the state constitution, they cannot be disclosed without the suspect's consent unless their production is required by state law. In the absence of waiver and without notice to the suspect or an opportunity to object, it is not appropriate under § 24-9-40(a) for the state in a criminal case to subpoena a suspect's own personal medical records which are then in the possession of a physician, hospital, or health care facility.

When there is no attempt by the defense to push for discovery of a gas chromatograph printout, no refusal by the state to produce that document, and no request by the defense for a continuance for additional time to examine it, there would be no abuse of the trial court's discretion in admitting the testimony of the state's expert witness concerning this printout, despite the prosecutor's failure to produce it before trial.

h. *Chain of Custody*

The courts have insisted that the chain of custody of bodily substance samples between extraction and testing must be established for the admissibility of the test results. In Pittman v. State, the Court of Appeals held that there had to be an accounting of who took the sample, how it was labelled, how it was sent to the state crime laboratory and who received it at the lab. The Georgia Supreme Court, in 1968, however, insisted that the custody chain need not be absolutely air-tight. "The circumstances need only establish reasonable assurance of the identity of the sample." Even contamination would not render a blood sample inadmissible.

When a urine sample is routinely handled and nothing in the record raises a suspicion that the urine tested was other than that taken from the defendant, the evidence of tests on such urine is admissible.

i. *Right to Independent Analysis of Blood Sample*

In order to prevail upon a claim that the defendant's due process rights under the Fourth Amendment to the federal constitution were violated by the state's destruction of his blood sample before he had an opportunity to independently test it, the defendant must show bad faith. Bad faith is a question of fact for the trial court to determine, and the trial court's finding will not be disturbed on appeal if there is any evidence to support it. If there is evidence to support a finding that the defendant failed to show bad faith, the trial's court decision to allow the blood test results into evidence will be upheld.

j. Exceptions

Locomotive engineers are not required, under Georgia's Implied Consent Act, to submit to chemical tests to determine the presence of alcohol or drugs after a train/automobile collision at a grade crossing.

9. Inferences of Intoxication or Nonintoxication

Section 40-6-392(b) constructs a scheme whereby (1) a test result showing an alcohol concentration of 0.05 grams or less may give rise to an inference of nonintoxication and (2) a test result of an alcohol concentration in excess of 0.05 grams but less than 0.08 grams will not give rise to an inference of intoxication or nonintoxication but may be considered by the trier of fact with other evidence to determine intoxication. A test result showing an alcohol concentration of 0.08 grams or more in the person's blood, breath, or urine is sufficient to determine intoxication per se without resort to any inference. The General Assembly's lowering of the alcohol concentration necessary to establish intoxication per se to 0.08 grams or more in 2001 rendered obsolete the provision for 0.08 grams or more as an alcohol concentration giving rise to an inference of intoxication. Therefore, the General Assembly deleted this inference from the scheme outlined in § 40-6-392(b). Nevertheless, it is clear that under this scheme a conviction can be returned where a test result between 0.05 and 0.08 grams is combined with other evidence to establish intoxication.

This statutory scheme does not apply to a person driving a commercial motor vehicle. In such a case, if there was at the time alleged or within three hours after driving or being in actual physical control of a moving vehicle from alcohol consumed before such driving or being in actual physical control ended an alcohol concentration of 0.04 grams or more in the person's blood, breath, or urine, the person shall be in violation of § 40-6-391(i). Nor does this statutory scheme apply to a person under the age of 21. In such a case, if there was at the time alleged or within three hours after driving or being in actual physical control of a moving vehicle from alcohol consumed before such driving or being in actual physical control ended an alcohol concentration of 0.02 grams or more in the person's blood, breath, or urine, the person shall be in violation of § 40-6-391(k).

Former § 40-6-392(b)(3) provided that a certain level of alcohol concentration would give rise to a presumption of intoxication. There were a number of decisions ruling on whether a jury charge given in the language of § 40-6-392(b)(3) created an unconstitutional, burden-shifting presumption that a person with a certain level of alcohol concentration was intoxicated. With the deletion of § 40-6-392(b)(3) in 2001, there is no longer a statutory basis for giving such a charge. Thus, the prior decisions are no longer controlling authority and should not be followed.

It is not necessary that a blood alcohol level test administered by a hospital in providing medical treatment be performed in compliance with the procedures of § 40-6-392(a) in order to be considered a valid test for the purpose of applying the inferences permitted under § 40-6-392(b).

In Stevenson v. State, the court rejected the defendant's contention that § 40-6-391(a)(5) [now (a)(6)] created an impermissible irrebuttable presumption that a person with a trace, no matter how minuscule, of marijuana in his system is an unsafe driver. The court held that this subsection criminalizes a specific act: driving or being in control of a moving vehicle while there is any amount of marijuana or controlled substance in a person's blood or urine. The state must prove the elements of this offense beyond a reasonable doubt, but those elements do not include impaired driving ability.

A jury instruction that the defendant's refusal to submit to a chemical test is admissible against him does not mandate the jury to infer guilt from the refusal. It merely informs the jury that it may consider the fact.

10. Defenses

The basic defense in a DUI case will probably be an attack on the presence of one of the actus reus elements, either the driving or actual physical control of the moving vehicle or the circumstance of being under the influence. No mens rea is specified by the statute, so nothing more than voluntary action need be shown.

In Cook v. State, the court rejected a claim of chronic alcoholism as a DUI defense. The Cook court held that this was voluntary intoxication. If the court were convinced, however, under § 16-3-4, that there was involuntary intoxication, it would seem that there would be a defense.

It is not a defense to a violation of § 40-6-391 that prior to the time of the defendant's arrest, he had been taking a prescription drug, the major component of which was alcohol. The fact that a person is legally entitled to use a drug is not a defense. However, unless that person is rendered incapable of driving safely as a result of using a drug which he is legally entitled to use, he is not in violation of the DUI statute. The state is not required to negate the possibility that one's high blood alcohol level was caused by something other than his consumption of alcoholic beverages. Once the state establishes a prima facie case, it is up to the defense to overcome such evidence; the state need not disprove beyond a reasonable doubt every fact constituting any and all affirmative defenses related to the culpability of the accused.

A person may not defend against a charge that he was driving under the influence of alcohol to the extent that it was less safe to drive by showing that his impaired driving ability resulted from legal drug use as well as alcohol consumption.

Where a jury finds that a defendant was not driving under the influence of involuntary intoxication but was driving under the influence of voluntary intoxication, there can be no logical conclusion that his voluntary intoxication was the result of accident or misfortune. In such a case, the failure to charge the jury on the defense of accident or misfortune would not be reversible error.

A charge on accident or misfortune would be authorized in vehicular homicide/DUI cases, however, if there is evidence that the defendant could not have avoided the collision due to circumstances beyond his control.

Without a factual or legal basis to justify a DUI violation, a charge on justification would be unwarranted.

There is no immunity from prosecution for DUI because the act was committed on private property rather than a public road.

11. Relationship to Other Offenses

Important Notice about Repudiation of Actual or Same Evidence Test: The Georgia Supreme Court repudiated the actual evidence test in *Drinkard v. Walker*, 281 Ga. 211, 636 S.E.2d 530 (2006), because it found this test to be inconsistent with the statutory framework governing the prohibition against multiple convictions for included offenses in Georgia. This inconsistency resulted in years of confusion and unpredictable results. In its place, the court adopted the required evidence test and overruled any prior case law that is inconsistent with it. Thus, any prior case law applying the actual evidence test is no longer controlling and should not be relied upon to determine whether one offense is included in another under § 16-1-6(1). The discussion of such case law is included below only insofar as it may still be applicable to pending prosecutions that arose before the Drinkard decision. See MULTIPLE CONVICTIONS, II. Tests to Determine Presence of Multiple Convictions, for a complete discussion of the Drinkard decision.

If the jury reveals which of the lesser included offenses serves as the foundation for finding a person to have been a "less safe" driver under the DUI statute, sentences of the remaining lesser offenses may be appropriate. Since reckless conduct requires harm or danger to "another person," an element not required by the DUI statute to be alleged and proven, it is not a lesser included offense as a matter of law. It also is not a lesser included offense as a matter of fact, unless the accusation includes an allegation of harm or danger to another person and there is proof of such at trial.

Where the facts alleged in the accusation with regard to the DUI charge are not sufficient to establish the lesser traffic offenses as well, the lesser traffic offenses cannot merge with the DUI charge as a matter of fact, regardless of the evidence adduced at trial. Furthermore, where there is ample evidence supporting the DUI charge absent evidence of the other traffic offenses, there is no merger because the evidence required to prove the other traffic offenses has not been "used up" proving the DUI charge.

Public drunkenness is not, as a matter of fact or law, a lesser included offense of driving under the influence of alcohol to the extent it is less safe to drive.

A defendant who has been convicted of only one of two offenses involving driving under the influence of drugs, as contained in two counts of an indictment, has not been subjected to double jeopardy.

Where under the facts in a case the offense of driving under the influence is a lesser included offense in the violation of a probationary license offense under the habitual violator statute, the offenses merge, and the defendant may not be convicted of the lesser included offense of driving under the influence.

The offenses of driving while having marijuana or its metabolites present in the urine and possession of marijuana by ingestion merge as a matter of fact where there is no evidence independent of the blood analysis which shows any possession of marijuana by the defendant. Since all the evidence is used up in proving one crime, it is error for the trial court to sentence the defendant for both charges.

A single act of driving under the influence of multiple substances is a single offense. As the defendant has committed only one offense of driving under the influence, he may not be subjected to multiple punishment for being under the influence of multiple substances.

Where charges for driving under the influence of alcohol to the extent it was less safe and driving under the influence of drugs are not predicated upon precisely the same conduct, the defendant may be convicted and sentenced on both charges.

Where two DUI charges are based on the same conduct, the evidence will not support convictions of two separate offenses. Even though the trial court enters only a single sentence, if that sentence applies to both DUI counts of the accusation, by definition the trial court has convicted the defendant of two counts of DUI. Unless the trial court merges one count into the other or indicates that the sentence applies only to one count, the sentence applies to both counts and is improper.

12. Punishment

The punishment for DUI is set out in § 40-6-391(c). A repeat offender is treated more harshly than a first or second offender. Section 40-5-63(a) expressly requires that the driver's license of any person convicted of violating § 40-6-391 shall by operation of law be suspended, unless the driver's license has been previously suspended pursuant to §§ 40-5-67.1 and 40-5-67.2. The driver's license of any person convicted of a drug related offense pursuant to § 40-6-391 shall be suspended according to the requirements of § 40-5-75. Furthermore, each charge for which a conviction was obtained must be treated as a separate transaction for the purpose of imposing a license suspension, even if the convictions arise from a single incident.

The punishment for driving or being in actual physical control of any moving commercial motor vehicle while there is 0.04 percent or more by weight of alcohol in the person's blood, breath, or urine is set out in § 40-6-391(i).

The punishment for a person under the age of 21 driving or being in actual physical control of any moving vehicle while the person's alcohol concentration is 0.02 grams or more is set out in § 40-6-391(k). Any term of imprisonment served is subject to the provisions of § 17-10-3.1. The driver's license of any person convicted of violating § 40-6-391(k) shall be suspended as provided by § 40-5-57.1.

The punishment for a licensed school bus driver driving a school bus in violation of § 40-6-391 is set out in § 40-6-391.3.

A person convicted of violating § 40-6-391 a second or subsequent time within a five-year period shall have his notice of conviction along with his photograph published in the legal organ of the appropriate county. Any motor vehicle operated by a person who has been declared a habitual violator for three DUI violations and whose license has been revoked and who is arrested and charged with another DUI violation, is declared to be contraband and subject to forfeiture to the state, provided that the forfeiture shall not be absolute unless the defendant is finally convicted of such offense.

Without a showing that there is no rational relationship between the state's compelling interest in protecting the public's safety and the distinction drawn between first offenders contained in § 40-6-391(f), the Georgia Supreme Court held that the exclusion of DUI offenses from the coverage of the First Offender Act does not violate a defendant's right to the equal protection of the laws guaranteed by the federal and state constitutions.

In 1998, Heidi Marie Flye along with her children were killed in a motor vehicle collision which involved a drunk driver who had been convicted of driving under the influence in this state less than a year before the collision. In 1999, the General Assembly found that these deaths could have been prevented had the driver been required to have an ignition interlock device installed on his vehicle. If the drunk driver's vehicle had been equipped with such a breath testing device, it would have prevented him from starting his vehicle and driving it. In an effort to strengthen the laws requiring the installation and use of ignition interlock devices the General Assembly enacted what is now commonly known and cited as Heidi's Law. However, Heidi's Law could not be effectively implemented due to several inconsistencies within the law itself and with other Code provisions. Thus, it was extensively revised by the General Assembly in 2000. The law was revised again in 2001. Section 42-8-111 now provides that in addition to any other provision of probation, upon a resident's second or subsequent conviction of driving under the influence within a five-year period, for which he is granted probation, the sentencing court is required to order as a condition of probation that the person must have installed and must maintain in each motor vehicle registered in his name for a six-month period a functioning, certified ignition interlock device, unless the court exempts the person from these requirements based upon the court's determination that they would subject the person to undue financial hardship. Furthermore, that person must have installed and must maintain in any other motor vehicle to be driven by him during the six-month period a functioning, certified ignition interlock device. He is not allowed during that period to drive any motor vehicle whatsoever that is not so equipped.

In the event the court finds that the person has violated the terms of his probation, his driving privilege will be revoked by the Department of Driver Services for one year from the date of probation revocation. Upon a second violation during the same period, his driving privilege will be revoked by the department for five years from the date of the second probation revocation.

A probationer must notify any person who rents, leases, or loans a motor vehicle to him of his driving restriction. Anyone who knowingly rents, leases, or loans a motor vehicle to the probationer without a functioning, certified ignition interlock device is guilty of a misdemeanor. A probationer who requests or solicits another person to blow into the ignition interlock device or to start the motor vehicle for the purpose of providing him with an operable vehicle is guilty of a misdemeanor. Likewise, any person who blows into the device or starts the motor vehicle for the purpose of providing the probationer with an operable vehicle is guilty of a misdemeanor. Finally, anyone who tampers with or circumvents the operation of the device is guilty of a misdemeanor.

The punishment for the offense of endangering a child by driving under the influence of alcohol or drugs is in accordance with § 16-12-1(d), relating to the offense of contributing to the delinquency, unruliness, or deprivation of a child. This offense does not merge with the offense of driving under the influence for the purpose of sentencing.

For additional penalty assessments for violations relating to driving under the influence of alcohol or drugs to be used for compensating innocent victims of crime, see § 15-21-112.

13. Tort Liability of Police Officers

A police officer, who has observed a noticeably intoxicated driver, has no duty to protect a member of the general public from the negligence of the intoxicated driver by arresting or otherwise restraining the intoxicated driver from continuing to drive. Before a special duty can be imposed on the police officer to protect an individual from the negligence of the intoxicated driver, there must be a special relationship either between the police officer and the individual which sets the individual apart from the general public or between the police officer and the intoxicated driver which imposes a duty on the officer to control the driver's conduct. If, when the police officer encounters the intoxicated driver, the individual is not an identifiable victim in immediate danger of harm, there is no special relationship and no special duty to protect the individual from the intoxicated driver's negligence. If the police officer's encounter with the intoxicated driver is a passing one, there is no special relationship and no special duty imposed, because the police officer exercises no control over the intoxicated driver. Although a police officer has authority to arrest a driver without a warrant where an offense is committed in his presence or within his immediate knowledge, this authority alone does not create a duty to arrest for purposes of a tort action.

14. Double Jeopardy

The actions taken by a school to attempt to correct a defendant's drunken on-campus behavior in order to protect others would not be punitive but remedial and would not bar a subsequent criminal prosecution of the defendant on a DUI charge.

I. Fleeing or Attempting to Elude Pursuing Police Officer

Under § 40-6-395(a), any driver who willfully fails or refuses to obey a police officer's signal to stop his vehicle is guilty of a misdemeanor of a high and aggravated nature. This provision helps to fill in part of the gap left by § 16-10-52, which covers only escapes from custody or confinement. In order to show a violation of this provision, the state must show that the officer allegedly eluded was in the required uniform and that his vehicle was appropriately marked. It should be noted, however, that this provision applies whether the pursuing police officer is in his vehicle or on foot. The state must also show that the signal to bring the vehicle to a stop was given in the manner alleged. The driver's willfulness may be established circumstantially.

In *Harbuck v. State*, the Georgia Supreme Court rejected the defendant's contention that § 40-6-395(a) was an unconstitutional delegation of legislative authority because its lack of standards for measuring driver compliance with a police directive to stop resulted in a violation of the statute being defined by the judgment of the arresting officer giving that directive. The court held that the General Assembly's failure to include within the statute the amount of time that must elapse or the distance that must be traveled before the driver's failure to stop becomes criminal conduct is not an improper delegation of legislative authority to the arresting officer. The officer, by acting on his determination that he has probable cause to believe a crime is being committed, is exercising the executive branch function of enforcing the law, not the legislative function of defining what constitutes a crime.

The *Harbuck* court also held that § 40-6-395(a) was not unconstitutional for failing to have within it a justification defense. There is no constitutional requirement that a statute criminalizing certain conduct must contain a statement that a justification defense may be asserted. Moreover, such a requirement is unwarranted given the existing statutory defense that "[t]he fact that a person's conduct is justified is a defense to prosecution for any crime based on that conduct."

Because the offense can be committed by a defendant's failure to respond to a visual signal of the officer either by hand or by emergency light, the failure to allege which type of visual signal the defendant was given would subject an accusation to a special demurrer.

The focus in the statute is on the officer or vehicle being identified clearly as a police officer or police vehicle, and not on any particular officer. Thus, there would be no fatal variance in a case where the indictment alleges that the defendant fled from one officer, but the evidence shows that he fled from another.

Inasmuch as § 40-6-395(a) does not require a lawful stop, a defendant cannot argue that an officer's lack of an articulable suspicion to stop him rendered the evidence insufficient to support his conviction.

Under § 40-6-395(b)(5), anyone who, while fleeing or attempting to elude a pursuing police vehicle or police officer in an attempt to escape arrest for **any** offense other than a violation of the Uniform Rules of the Road, operates his vehicle in excess of 30 miles an hour above the posted speed limit, strikes or collides with another vehicle or a pedestrian, flees in traffic conditions which place the general public at risk of receiving serious injuries, or leaves the state is guilty of a felony punishable by a fine of $5,000, by imprisonment for not less than one year nor more than five years, or by both fine and imprisonment. The sentence for this offense cannot be suspended, probated, deferred, or withheld, and the charge cannot be reduced to a lesser offense, merged with any other offense, or served concurrently with any other offense.

Where all of the evidence is used to prove the crime of felony fleeing or attempting to elude, a misdemeanor conviction for fleeing or attempting to elude would merge into the greater offense.

Since the offense of felony fleeing or attempting to elude requires proof of additional material elements, it cannot merge with the offense of felony habitual violator. Moreover, by law a sentence for felony fleeing or attempting to elude cannot be merged with that of another offense.

Under the facts presented in Gibson v. State, the Court of Appeals found that the crime of obstructing an officer was included in the crime of fleeing or attempting to elude an officer. The indictment's allegations for fleeing or attempting to elude an officer were sufficient also to satisfy the elements of the offense of obstruction. Under the facts, there was no material distinction between "willfully" disobeying the officer's order as prohibited by § 40-6-395(a) and disobeying it "knowingly and willfully" as prohibited by § 16-10-24(a). Because the defendant's testimony provided evidence satisfying the required elements of the offense of obstruction, the court held that the trial court erred in refusing to give the requested charge on obstruction as a lesser included offense. Since the evidence supporting the greater charge was in conflict, the error was not harmless. The defendant was therefore entitled to a new trial.

Where the felony of fleeing or attempting to elude a police officer results in the death of another person, it can serve as the predicate felony supporting a felony murder conviction.

Unless there is evidence that a passenger in the vehicle acted in concert with the driver in an effort to flee from police, the passenger would be entitled to a directed verdict in his favor on a charge of fleeing from police.

Section 40-6-395(c) punishes those who impersonate a law enforcement official by means of a falsely labelled vehicle or motorcycle. The subsection also punishes those who impersonate law enforcement officials in order to control traffic. Because this subsection has no specific penalty, this offense is punishable as a misdemeanor under § 40-6-1.

III. Other Traffic Offenses Under the Uniform Rules of the Road

A. Driving Too Fast for Conditions

Some appellate court litigation has developed concerning the other traffic offenses under the Uniform Rules of the Road. Section 40-6-180 prohibits driving a vehicle at a speed "greater than is reasonable and prudent under the conditions and having regard for the actual and potential hazards then existing." A predecessor statute which was similarly worded was upheld against a claim that the statute was unconstitutionally vague in Teague v. Keith. The Teague case, however, was a **civil** case as are many cases involving the Uniform Rules of the Road because of the tort doctrine of negligence per se. The Teague court emphasized that this was not a criminal case, relying strongly on a prior Georgia Supreme Court case which made the civil/criminal distinction in dicta and which suggested that a similarly worded statute was unconstitutional in a criminal context. An identical kind of analysis was adopted by the court in Eidson v. Felder in connection with the predecessor statute to § 40-6-123, concerning the proper procedure for turning. In light of these decisions it would appear that a statute may be precise enough in the civil context, yet unconstitutionally vague in the criminal context. The Teague case would appear to doom § 40-6-180 as a criminal statute.

However, it should be noted that §§ 40-6-181 and 40-6-182 are much more specific in expressing speed restrictions in miles per hour and in authorizing administrative establishment of speed limits. Section 40-6-180 meets constitutional certainty requirements when read together with § 40-6-181. In Bilbrey v. State, the Georgia Supreme Court held that while § 40-6-180 standing alone does not meet these requirements, the statute furnishes sufficient criteria when read in conjunction with § 40-6-181. When read together, the code sections make it reasonably clear that when a vehicle encounters one of the listed road conditions or other hazards caused by weather or highway conditions, the law requires a reduction in speed below the maximum posted limit. Although the statutory scheme is not as specific as some, when read as a whole it gives sufficient warning of what conduct is unlawful. This is the result due process requires.

B. Racing

Another statute that has come before the appellate courts for an important interpretation is § 40-6-186(b), which deals with speed races and drag racing. In Perkins v. State, the court held that the section sets out two crimes: (1) racing or speed contests and (2) drag races, the latter of which requires prearranged courses, finish lines, etc. If the defendant is charged with one of the offenses, the court said, it is error to inform the jury with regard to the other one. In Dodd v. State, the court, finding sufficient evidence of racing, held that it was not legally significant that the automobiles involved in the race were capable of going faster than they were or that the distance between the automobiles basically stayed the same.

B.1. Driving with Suspended, Canceled, or Revoked Vehicle Registration

No motor vehicle registration may be issued or renewed unless the tag agent receives satisfactory proof of minimum insurance coverage of the vehicle and, in the case of a private passenger vehicle, proof that such coverage was initially issued for a minimum term of six months.

Any person who knowingly drives a motor vehicle on any public road or highway of this state at a time when the vehicle registration is suspended, canceled, or revoked is guilty of a misdemeanor.

For a first conviction or a plea of nolo contendere, the defendant is subject to imprisonment for not more than 12 months. In addition, there may be imposed a fine of not less than $500 nor more than $1,000, at the discretion of the court.

For a second or subsequent conviction within five years as measured from the dates of previous arrests for which convictions were obtained or pleas of nolo contendere were accepted to the date of the current arrest for which a conviction is obtained or a plea of nolo contendere accepted, the defendant, being guilty of a high and aggravated misdemeanor, is subject to imprisonment for not less than ten days nor more than 12 months. In addition, there may be imposed a fine of not less than $1,000 nor more than $2,500.

When the Department of Driver Services receives a record of the defendant's conviction, it will extend the period of suspension or revocation of the vehicle's registration for six months and suspend the defendant's driver's license.

C. Other Minor Traffic Offenses

Other relatively minor traffic offenses upon which cases have been litigated include (1) section 40-6-181, exceeding the maximum motor vehicle speed limit; (2) section 40-6-2, willfully failing to obey a lawful order of a police officer who is directing, controlling, or regulating traffic; (3) section 40-6-71, failing to yield the right of way when turning left; (4) section 40-6-72, failure to yield right of way; (5) section 40-6-74, failing to yield to an emergency vehicle; (6) section 40-6-140, failing to yield to a train; (7) section 40-6-163, failing to stop for a school bus which has actuated its flashers and stop-arm; (8) section 40-6-48(1), improperly changing lanes; (9) section 40-6-72(b), disregarding a stop sign; (10) section 40-6-97(b), standing "on a highway for the purpose of soliciting employment, business, or contributions from the occupant of any vehicle;" (11) section 40-6-10, failing to produce proof of insurance; and (12) section 40-6-253(b), consuming an alcoholic beverage or possessing an open alcoholic beverage container while in the passenger area of a motor vehicle.

Another particularly noteworthy offense is the misdemeanor set out in § 40-6-298. Section 40-6-290 et seq., dealing with bicycle riding, sets up certain rules, and § 40-6-298(b) forbids parents and guardians from authorizing or knowingly permitting their children or wards to violate any of these provisions. Thus, a parent who is aware of his child's persistent violation of these provisions and does not halt this behavior is guilty of a misdemeanor.

Other noteworthy statutes include §§ 40-6-270, 40-6-271, 40-6-272, 40-6-273, and 40-6-275, which set up a series of duties for drivers who are involved in accidents with the precise content of duties dependent on the nature of the accident. The failure to stop at and return to the scene of an accident involving death, personal injury, or damage to a vehicle (§ 40-6-270) and the failure to notify the driver of an unattended vehicle of the name and address of the driver striking the unattended vehicle (§ 40-6-271) provide criminal punishment, while the other duties are criminally enforced by § 40-6-1.

D. Defenses

Since most violations of the Uniform Rules of the Road are strict liability offenses, the absence of a criminal scheme or undertaking or of criminal negligence is not available as a defense to one charged with such a violation. Thus, an instruction on the defense of accident would not be authorized.

Where the defendant is charged with a strict liability crime, such as a traffic violation, he is entitled to a justification charge upon a proper evidentiary showing, if he meets the statutory requirements of § 16-3-20, and the entire charge does not otherwise fairly present the defendant's theory to the jury. In such a case, the defendant admits the conduct but is not precluded from showing that his actions were justified under § 16-3-20. Thus, where the defendant's testimony could support a justification charge and it is the sole defense, such a charge should be given by the trial court whether or not requested by the defendant.

IV. Offenses Involving Title Certificates, Identification of Motor Vehicles or Motor Vehicle Parts, and License Plates

A. Generally

Section 40-3-90 makes it a felony to, with fraudulent intent, (1) alter, forge or counterfeit a title certificate, (2) alter or forge an assignment of a title certificate or security interest, (3) knowingly possess or use an altered, forged or counterfeit title certificate, (4) give false information in connection with the obtaining of a title certificate, (5) alter or forge a notice of additional lienholder or security interest holder, or (6) wilfully violate any provision of the Motor Vehicle Certificate of Title Act after having been convicted for a prior violation of the Act.

Section 40-2-72 makes it a felony, punishable by two to five years in prison, to violate the provisions for disabled veterans' license tags to be found in §§ 40-2-69 to 40-2-71.

Section 40-4-22(a) makes it a felony to knowingly buy, sell, receive, dispose of, conceal, use, or possess any motor vehicle, or any part thereof, from which the manufacturer's serial numbers or other distinguishing numbers or identifying marks have been removed, defaced, covered, altered, or destroyed for the purpose of concealing or misrepresenting the vehicle's identity. The guilty knowledge of the alteration has been held to be the gist of the offense and a conviction has been upheld where the defendant sold a car with altered tags and claimed he would produce a bill of sale which he never did.

Section 40-2-7 makes it a misdemeanor to remove a license plate from a vehicle or to affix to a vehicle a license plate not authorized by law for use on it with intent to conceal or misrepresent the identity of the vehicle or its owner. Section 40-2-5 makes it a misdemeanor of a high and aggravated nature (1) to remove or transfer a license plate from the motor vehicle for which such license plate was issued; (2) to sell or otherwise transfer or dispose of a license plate upon or for use on any motor vehicle other than the vehicle for which such license plate was issued; (3) to buy, receive, use, or possess for use on a motor vehicle any license plate not issued for use on such motor vehicle; or (4) to operate a motor vehicle bearing a license plate which was improperly removed or transferred from another vehicle.

Under prior law, the courts recognized an overlap of these two statutes. Although the court in Dismuke v. State purported to distinguish between affixing (§ 40-2-7) and using (§ 40-2-5) an improper license plate, it was clear that the affixing of the plate could be prosecuted as a use. In Studdard v. State, the court held that where the car was a stolen car and the license plate was stolen from another vehicle, there had to be some proof of knowledge of the stolen nature of either one in order to show an intent to conceal the car's true identity.

Under § 40-2-136(a), upon a person's second or subsequent conviction of violating § 40-6-391 within five years, as measured from the dates of previous arrests for which convictions were obtained to the date of the current arrest for which a conviction is obtained, the trial court must issue an order requiring that the license plates of all motor vehicles registered in that person's name be surrendered to the court. The commissioner must revoke each such license plate upon receiving notice from the trial court. It is a misdemeanor for that person to obtain a new license plate or plates before he has been issued a limited driving permit or probationary driver's license or before his driver's license has been reissued or reinstated, whichever first occurs.

B. Mens Rea

Three cases in the early 1920's interpreting predecessor statutes to current provisions deal with the issue of the required mental element in traffic offenses. Traffic offenses have often been described as "strict liability" offenses in that no culpability is required for conviction. This statement is generally true in Georgia with the important caveat that there is a mental awareness element involved, even if the offense is otherwise a "strict liability" one. In Davis v. State, the defendant was prosecuted under the predecessor to § 40-2-41, which punishes the failure to display a license plate. The defendant asserted that he was aware that he did not have a license plate but that it had been stolen the night before his arrest. He had, in fact, been told by the sheriff that he could drive without a plate until he got a replacement. His conviction was affirmed. In Harden v. State, on the other hand, a conviction under the same statute was reversed where the defendant had a license plate on his car at the beginning of his trip but it apparently was stolen or fell off during the trip without his knowledge.

Davis and Harden are not in conflict and, when taken together, indicate that, while no intent to violate the law need be shown, an intent to do the prohibited act is necessary. Thus, for example, it is not necessary to prove an awareness that running a red light is illegal, but an intent to run the red light is proven by the act of doing so. Therefore, the Harden defendant won a reversal because he did not intend to drive the car without a license plate, while Davis definitely did intend to do so even though it was for a very good reason.

As the court wrote in Nelson v. State, interpreting a predecessor statute to former GCA § 68-1702, "criminal intent is simply the intent to do the act which results in the violation of the law and not the intent to commit the crime itself." It should be noted that while most of the traffic regulations in the title on motor vehicles and traffic have no explicit mens rea requirements, some include words like "knowingly" or "wilfully." These words import a mens rea element beyond the mere intent to do the prohibited act.

V. Offenses Involving Drivers' Licenses

A. Generally

Chapter 5 of Title 40 contains a number of criminal provisions relating to drivers' licenses. For example, § 40-5-120 punishes three specific acts as misdemeanors and additionally makes it a misdemeanor to violate any of the chapter's regulatory provisions. Section 40-5-2(g) makes it a misdemeanor of a high and aggravated nature for anyone knowingly and willfully to (1) disclose, distribute, or sell a driver's record or personal information to an unauthorized recipient or for an unauthorized purpose, or (2) make a misrepresentation or false statement in order to obtain access to or information from the department's records.

B. Driving without Being Licensed or with Suspended, Disqualified, or Revoked License

Except when a license has been revoked as a habitual violator, any person who drives a motor vehicle on any public highway of this state without being licensed or at a time when his privilege to drive is suspended, disqualified, or revoked is guilty of a misdemeanor.

Generally, the state must show that the defendant had actual or legal notice of the suspension of his license in order for his conviction to be sustained. The state may satisfy this evidentiary requirement by showing that the defendant had notice of the suspension by operation of law automatically upon his conviction for DUI. A Georgia Crime Information Center (GCIC) driver's license history is admissible to show the fact of suspension, but only if the state tenders a certified copy of a department record or proves that the driving record was obtained from a computer terminal lawfully connected to the GCIC computer. Where the state does not satisfy this foundational requirement or does not even offer the defendant's driving history into evidence, it fails to prove that the defendant's license was suspended. Furthermore, a police officer's statement at trial that his computer check of the defendant revealed a suspended license would also fail to establish the fact of suspension. This unsworn representation as to the contents of the defendant's driving record does not qualify as evidence. Finally, a Uniform Traffic Citation, on which the officer has written that the defendant's license was suspended, cannot be used as evidence of his guilt.

Since driving with a suspended license after proper notification from the department is a strict criminal liability offense, the state is not required to show mens rea or guilty intent on the part of the violator.

Whether the convictions or charges serving as the basis for the suspension are either expunged from the defendant's record or subject to collateral attack on constitutional grounds is not an issue. The offense of driving a motor vehicle when one's privilege to do so has been suspended is an offense separate and distinct from the offenses which led to the suspension. Until the license is reinstated, it is illegal to drive.

Prior to 2006, where a defendant's license had been suspended under § 40-5-56 for failing to appear at a hearing for a traffic offense, unless the arresting officer verified and placed the service date on the uniform citation issued to the defendant, under the clear mandate of former § 40-5-121(b)(1), no charge of driving with a suspended license could be made against the defendant. With the General Assembly's elimination of this unnecessary and cumbersome requirement in 2006, this holding is no longer controlling authority.

Where there are sufficient similarities between prior incidents of driving with a suspended license and the offense charged, the admission of the prior incidents would be authorized to show course of conduct.

Upon a first conviction or plea of nolo contendere within a five-year period, as measured from the dates of previous arrests for which convictions were obtained to the date of the current arrest for which a conviction is obtained or a plea of nolo contendere is accepted, the defendant must be fingerprinted and punished by imprisonment for not less than two days nor more than 12 months, and there may be imposed in addition thereto a fine of not less than $500 nor more than $1,000. Such fingerprints, taken upon conviction, are forwarded to the Georgia Crime Information Center where an identification number is assigned to the defendant for the purpose of tracking any future violations by the same defendant.

Upon a second and third conviction within a five-year period, the defendant would be guilty of a high and aggravated misdemeanor punishable by imprisonment for not less than ten days nor more than 12 months, and there may be imposed in addition thereto a fine of not less than $1,000 nor more than $2,500.

Upon a fourth or subsequent conviction within a five-year period, the defendant would be guilty of a felony punishable by imprisonment for not less than one year nor more than five years, and there may be imposed in addition thereto a fine of not less than $2,500 nor more than $5,000.

C. Driving After Being Declared Habitual Violator

1. Elements

a. Generally

In prosecutions under § 40-5-58(c), the state is required to prove that the defendant was declared a habitual violator; that his license was revoked; that he received notice that his license was revoked because of his status as a habitual violator; and that he operated a motor vehicle in this state without having obtained a valid driver's license. Evidence of all these material allegations may be submitted by means of a properly certified document or by means of relevant portions of the defendant's driving record. However, the defendant's entire driving record, especially that portion listing numerous prior traffic offenses, is immaterial to the offense of operating a motor vehicle after being declared an habitual violator and should not be submitted.

The elements of the habitual violator offense do not include any specific location in which the habitual violator operates a motor vehicle. Therefore, the location alleged in the indictment, with the exception of the county, is immaterial and pure surplusage.

b. Habitual Violator Declaration

A "habitual violator" is any person who has been arrested and convicted three or more times within a five-year period of various offenses, such as DUI and vehicular homicide. Section 40-5-58(b) sets out the procedure by which the department declares a person to be a habitual violator.

In 1995, the Court of Appeals concluded in Wilson v. Miles that three separate and unrelated transactions were required to supply the three "arrests and convictions" needed for a habitual violator declaration. The court found that by adding the phrase "singularly or in combination" as paragraph (3) of § 40-5-58(a) in 1987, the General Assembly evidenced its intent that "arrested and convicted" within the five-year period meant that the charges "singularly or in combination" had to result from three separate incidents, regardless of the number of enumerated offenses charged during any singular incident. However, the General Assembly, apparently disapproving of this construction of the statute, expressly defined "singularly or in combination" in 1996 to mean that the department "is to treat each charge for which a conviction was obtained as a separate transaction when determining whether or not a person has the requisite convictions" needed for a habitual violator declaration.

A "conviction" for purposes of habitual violator status includes a plea of nolo contendere, a forfeiture of bail or collateral, the payment of a fine, a plea of guilty, or a finding of guilt on a traffic violation charge, regardless of whether the sentence is suspended, probated, or rebated. The Court of Appeals has held that this includes nolo pleas entered before January 1, 1976, the effective date of the statute. Convictions from other states cannot be attacked collaterally in habitual violator prosecutions in this state so long as they are regular on their face.

The Georgia Supreme Court has held that § 40-5-58 is **not** a recidivist statute so that the prior convictions which caused the license revocation need not be alleged in the indictment. The validity of the prior convictions is not an issue, and a person cannot make it one by defending on the ground that one or more of the convictions have been set aside following the prohibited driving, or on the ground that one or more of the offenses of which the person was convicted and which were used to support his habitual violator status have been eliminated by a change in the law.

c. Notification of Habitual Violator Status

The essence of the habitual violator offense is not the existence of the prior convictions but rather driving a vehicle after receiving notice that one's license has been revoked as an habitual violator. Because notification of one's habitual violator status is an essential element of the offense, the state is required to present proof of compliance with the notification provisions of § 40-5-58(b) in order to establish that the revocation was valid. The date upon which the requisite notice was given to the habitual violator is relevant to whether his subsequent act of driving is punishable as a felony or a misdemeanor. A nonlicensed habitual violator who drives within five years of notification of his status as such is punishable for a felony, whereas a nonlicensed habitual violator who drives more than five years after the notification of his status as such is punishable for a misdemeanor.

A variance between the notice date alleged in the indictment and the date proved at trial is not fatal if the indictment does not allege that the date is material to the charge. Absent a showing that the date is material, the state can prove the elements of the offense by proof that the defendant drove a vehicle within five years of the time he was notified of his habitual violator status.

Under § 40-5-66(a), a person aggrieved by a final decision declaring him a habitual violator has a statutory right of appeal to superior court. Moreover, the Department of Driver Services has also granted such a person a right to pursue an internal administrative review within the department before appealing to superior court. On the other hand, there is no statute or administrative rule granting administrative law judges operating under the Office of State Administrative Hearings the authority to review a ruling by the department that someone is a habitual violator. Because administrative law judges lack jurisdiction to review the department's habitual violator declaration, an administrative law judge's ruling on the issue would be void and of no effect.

d. Operating Motor Vehicle Without Valid Driver's License

Once a license has been revoked, driving a motor vehicle subjects the defendant to the provisions of § 40-5-58(c). The statute prohibits a person who has been declared a habitual violator and whose license has been revoked from operating a vehicle anywhere in the state, including on a private thoroughfare. The defendant's operation of the vehicle may be proven by circumstantial evidence. The term "operate" as used in § 40-5-58(c) does not necessarily mean driving a vehicle, although it can include driving. Thus, a person who has been declared a habitual violator and who has been discovered by police officers asleep in the driver's seat of a motor vehicle which is stopped in the roadway with its engine running, its transmission in gear, and its lights on would be operating a motor vehicle in violation of the statute.

It is not necessary that a traffic offender have a driver's license to be classified a "habitual violator." When a habitual violator is notified of his classification, what is suspended is his right "to operate a motor vehicle in this state." Once this right has been suspended, driving a motor vehicle subjects the defendant to the statute's felony provisions.

An individual may not avoid prosecution for operating a motor vehicle in this state after having been declared an habitual violator by obtaining a valid license from another state.

The premature and erroneous issuance of a Georgia driver's license to an habitual violator is not adequate to show as a matter of law that the defendant's driving privileges have been properly reinstated. Administrative lapses notwithstanding, the fact that the defendant has obtained a driver's license does not give him permission to drive. Ignorance of the laws to this effect is no excuse.

e. Operating Motor Vehicle While Having Probationary License

A violation of a probationary license under the habitual violator statute does not require that the state prove a nonbusiness purpose at the time of the offense. Proof of driving under the influence would be sufficient.

2. Admissibility of Prior Habitual Violator Convictions

Evidence of prior "habitual violator convictions" is admissible to show the defendant's bent of mind and course of conduct with regard to a habitual violator count in an indictment. However, the state must not merely submit into evidence certified copies of the defendant's prior "habitual violator convictions." The state must also present evidence showing the similarity of the prior convictions and the crimes charged.

3. Defenses

An habitual violator's driving a motor vehicle without a driver's license may be justified under circumstances "which stand upon the same footing of reason and justice" as those defenses enumerated in the criminal code.

The mere fact that a person may be ignorant of the continued existence of his habitual violator status and the resultant consequences does not, in and of itself, afford him any defense to a felony charge for violating the statute.

4. Double Jeopardy

In State v. Gilder, the court held that a defendant could not be convicted of the misdemeanor offense of driving with a revoked driver's license (§ 40-5-121) and then later prosecuted for the felony offense of habitual violator (§ 40-5-58(c)) for the same act of driving.

5. Lesser Included Offenses

Important Notice about Repudiation of Actual or Same Evidence Test: The Georgia Supreme Court repudiated the actual evidence test in Drinkard v. Walker, because it found this test to be inconsistent with the statutory framework governing the prohibition against multiple convictions for included offenses in Georgia. This inconsistency resulted in years of confusion and unpredictable results. In its place, the court adopted the required evidence test and overruled any prior case law that is inconsistent with it. Thus, any prior case law applying the actual evidence test is no longer controlling and should not be relied upon to determine whether one offense is included in another under § 16-1-6(1). The discussion of such case law is included below only insofar as it may still be applicable to pending prosecutions that arose before the Drinkard decision. See MULTIPLE CONVICTIONS, II. Tests to Determine Presence of Multiple Convictions, for a complete discussion of the Drinkard decision.

Where an indictment charges a defendant with the offense of felony habitual violator and the proof at trial shows that the defendant only committed the offense of misdemeanor habitual violator, there is no fatal variance between the offense charged in the indictment and the offense actually proved at trial. In addition to defining the offense of felony habitual violator, § 40-5-58(c)(1) by its terms defines a misdemeanor lesser included offense of operating a motor vehicle after revocation of a driver's license and before issuance of a new license. This misdemeanor offense differs from the offense of felony habitual violator only in that it does not require the element of operating the motor vehicle within five years of notice of revocation. Since the misdemeanor offense does not contain this element, any allegation in an indictment regarding the time at which the defendant committed the offense of operating a motor vehicle after revocation of his license and before issuance of a new license is an unnecessary description of an unnecessary fact that need not be proved at trial.

Where under the facts in a case the offense of driving under the influence is a lesser included offense in the violation of a probationary license offense under the habitual violator statute, the offenses merge, and the defendant may not be convicted of the lesser included offense of driving under the influence.

Since the offense of felony fleeing or attempting to elude requires proof of additional material elements, it cannot merge with the offense of felony habitual violator. Moreover, by law a sentence for felony fleeing or attempting to elude cannot be merged with that of another offense.

6. Punishment

Under § 40-5-58(c)(1), a habitual violator whose driver's license has been revoked and who is later convicted of driving a vehicle before being issued a driver's license or before the expiration of five years from such revocation, whichever occurs first, may be fined for not less than $750 or may be sentenced to a term of not less than one nor more than five years' imprisonment, or both. If a habitual violator is convicted of driving a vehicle after the expiration of five years from such revocation but before being issued a driver's license, he is guilty of a misdemeanor.

Under § 40-5-58(c)(2), a person who has been declared a habitual violator as a result of three or more DUI convictions within a five-year period of time, as measured from the dates of previous arrests for which convictions were obtained to the date of the most recent arrest for which a conviction was obtained, and who is thereafter convicted of operating a motor vehicle during such period of revocation, prior to the issuance of a probationary license or before the expiration of five years, is guilty of the felony of habitual impaired driving and is punishable by a fine of not less than $1,000 or by imprisonment for not less than one nor more than five years, or both.

Section 17-10-7(b) only authorizes recidivist sentencing for a repeat "serious violent felony" offender. The habitual violator offense does not fall within the definition of "serious violent felony." Thus, an habitual violator cannot be sentenced as a recidivist under § 17-10-7(b). Likewise, an habitual violator cannot be sentenced as a recidivist under § 17-10-7(c), which disallows parole, unless he has been convicted for a fourth offense. An habitual violator who has been convicted for a third offense can be sentenced as a recidivist only under § 17-10-7(a), which requires the trial judge to impose the longest sentence prescribed for a subsequent offense but allows the trial judge, in his discretion, to probate or suspend that sentence.

D. Suspension or Revocation of Driver's License for DUI Arrest or Conviction

Section 40-5-67.1(c) requires that the driver's license, permit, or nonresident operating privilege of any driver, who is under arrest for DUI or who was involved in a traffic accident resulting in serious injuries or fatalities, be administratively suspended if the state-administered chemical test results indicate that he is under the influence "per se" in violation of § 40-6-391. Section 40-5-67.2 sets forth the terms and conditions of the suspension upon the first, second, third, and subsequent suspensions. An administrative license suspension pursuant to § 40-5-67.1 is counted toward fulfillment of any period of suspension subsequently imposed as a result of a conviction for DUI which arises out of the same violation for which the administrative license suspension was imposed. An administrative license suspension pursuant to § 40-5-67.1 runs concurrently with any revocation of such driver's license pursuant to a subsequent determination that such person is a habitual violator. Section 40-5-67.1(c) also provides that the driver of a commercial motor vehicle is disqualified from operating a motor vehicle for a minimum period of one year if the state-administered chemical test results indicate an alcohol concentration of 0.04 grams or more.

Credit for an administrative license suspension will be given **only** against a subsequent suspension under the DUI statute, where both are imposed as a result of the same arrest. Since an habitual violator revocation does not result from the same arrest as does an administrative license suspension, but rather, results from the accumulation of three separate DUI convictions within a period of five years, an administrative license suspension cannot be credited against a subsequent habitual violator revocation. Moreover, credit cannot be given because § 40-5-67.2(b) provides that the suspension runs concurrently with any revocation of the driver's license. The term "concurrently" simply means that the suspension and the revocation time periods each begin on the date of its imposition and that each will end on its prescribed date, unaffected by the existence or termination of the other.

Section 40-5-67.1(d) requires that the driver's license, permit, or nonresident operating privilege of any driver, who is under arrest for DUI or who was involved in a traffic accident resulting in serious injuries or fatalities, be suspended for a period of one year if that driver refuses, upon the request of a law enforcement officer, to submit to a state-administered chemical test. If the driver of a commercial motor vehicle refuses to take the state-administered chemical test, this Code section requires that he be disqualified from operating a commercial motor vehicle and that his driver's license, permit, or nonresident operating privilege be suspended, subject to review as provided by law.

If the driver has refused to submit to the state-administered test, the law enforcement officer who requested the test must submit a sworn report to the Department of Public Safety that the officer had reasonable grounds to believe the arrested person had been driving under the influence of alcohol and that the person had refused to submit to the test upon his request. This sworn statement is customarily completed on a form known as DPS Form 1205. After the department receives this form, it is required to suspend the driver's license for one year. In an administrative hearing requested by the driver to challenge the suspension, where the arresting officer testifies in person as to the events of the driver's arrest, this form clearly is not necessary to the resolution of any of the issues at the hearing. Furthermore, since the department is not required to make an initial showing that the license was suspended, it need not tender this form into evidence. In reviewing the suspension of a driver's license for failure to submit to a state-administered alcohol test, the administrative law judge (ALJ) must determine "[w]hether at the time of the request for the test or tests the officer informed the person of the person's implied consent rights and the consequence of submitting or refusing to submit to such test." If there is evidence to support a finding that the driver was properly advised of his implied consent rights, the suspension will be upheld.

Under the double jeopardy clauses of the state and federal constitutions, an administrative license suspension does not constitute punishment foreclosing further punishment arising out of a prosecution for driving under the influence. An administrative license suspension for driving under the influence is reasonably related and not disproportional to the state's longstanding remedial purpose in removing dangerous and habitually negligent drivers from its roadways. The driver's license is suspended by a designated public officer in an administrative setting, rather than as punishment in consequence of a criminal prosecution. Despite carrying the sting of punishment, the primary purpose of the suspension is not to deter the driver or seek retribution.

Because the fee for the restoration of one's driving privilege is not a fine and is not required to be paid, but is rather a voluntary payment, it cannot be considered punitive or a sanction for purposes of double jeopardy.

An accidental license suspension for DUI does not constitute punishment for purposes of double jeopardy. Even though the defendant himself may choose to treat his license suspension as lawful in order to obtain relief from the suspension more expeditiously, his actions of attending DUI classes and paying a $210 reinstatement fee do not convert the license suspension into a punishment flowing from an erroneous DUI conviction. Although the defendant suffers harm, he does not suffer from the prosecutorial power of the state.

An administrative hearing is a determination as to the suspension of one's driving privilege within this state, outside the merits of the pending criminal DUI charge. The "winning" of such hearing does not result in the acquittal of the defendant on the pending DUI charge or the return of the defendant's plastic license, which by statute remains in the trial court's possession until disposition of the DUI charge. Accordingly, due process is not violated by the failure to return a defendant's plastic license simply because an administrative hearing was resolved in the defendant's favor, when the rationale for the confiscation of the license in the first place, a pending DUI charge, has not been so resolved.

Section 40-5-63(a) expressly requires that the driver's license of any person convicted of violating § 40-6-391 shall by operation of law be suspended, unless the driver's license has been previously suspended pursuant to §§ 40-5-67.1 and 40-5-67.2. The driver's license of any person convicted of a drug related offense pursuant to § 40-6-391 shall be suspended according to the requirements of § 40-5-75. Furthermore, each charge for which a conviction was obtained must be treated as a separate transaction for the purpose of imposing a license suspension, even if the convictions arise from a single incident. Section 40-5-63(a) sets forth the lengths and terms of suspensions upon the first, second and third convictions of DUI, and subsection (b) states that the period of suspension begins on the date of the DUI conviction. It thus appears that the General Assembly intended § 40-5-63 to effectuate suspension or revocation upon a conviction for DUI, the notice being the trial for violation of § 40-6-391, i.e., notice "by operation of law." Consequently, due process does not require that one be afforded a hearing before the decision suspending his license is made.

A premature and erroneous license reinstatement is not adequate to show as a matter of law that the defendant's driving privileges have been properly reinstated. Administrative lapses notwithstanding, the fact that a driver has his driver's license reinstated does not give him permission to drive in contravention of § 40-5-63(a)(1). Ignorance of the laws to this effect is no excuse.

Section 40-5-57.1(a) requires the suspension of the driver's license of any person under 21 years of age convicted of violating § 40-6-391.

VI. Offenses Involving Motor Vehicle Safety

The Motor Vehicle Safety Responsibility Act has a general misdemeanor provision which, barring another special penalty, makes the violation of any provision of the Act a misdemeanor. The Act also has two specific statutes punishing certain violations more precisely. They are § 40-9-7 (willfully failing to return a suspended driver's license to the Department of Driver Services) and § 40-9-8 (operating a motor vehicle during a driver's license suspension).

Section 40-8-7 makes it a misdemeanor for any person to drive or move, or for the owner to cause or knowingly permit to be driven or moved, on any street or highway any vehicle or combination of vehicles (1) which is in such unsafe condition as to endanger any person; (2) which does not contain those parts or is not at all times equipped with such lights and other equipment in proper condition and adjustment as required by law; or (3) which is not equipped in the manner provided by law.

Section 40-8-7 is a strict criminal liability statute. Although the state is required to prove that the accused intended to do the act or make the omissions prohibited, it is not required to prove a mental fault. The fact that there is no criminal scheme or undertaking or criminal negligence is not a defense to a violation of this statute.

PROPERTY DAMAGE CRIMES

See also ARSON; BOMBS, EXPLOSIVES, AND CHEMICAL AND BIOLOGICAL WEAPONS; DISORDERLY CONDUCT CRIMES.

I. Criminal Damage to Property

A. Generally

Criminal damage to property essentially codifies the common law of malicious mischief. Prior to 1968, the law of malicious mischief included many highly particularized offenses. Now, most acts of malicious mischief, at least those related to property, are consolidated into §§ 16-7-22 and 16-7-23.

At common law, malicious mischief was the malicious destruction of, or damage to, the property of another. Section 16-7-22 defines first degree criminal damage to property as (1) the knowing interference with any property so as to endanger human life or (2) the knowing interference by force or violence with any public utility service or any public transportation or communication system. Section 16-7-23 proscribes two types of activity as second degree criminal damage to property: (1) intentional damage of another's property without his consent in excess of $500; or (2) reckless or intentional damage of another's property by means of fire or explosive.

B. Elements

1. Actus Reus

The core of the actus reus for the violation of §§ 16-7-22 and 16-7-23 is an act which damages property. The possible acts which satisfy this description are obviously infinitely varied. Specific examples, however, include running over a mailbox with a car, throwing rocks at a building, smashing into a gate, destroying a gutter carrying water from a well, and destruction of a tombstone in a private burial ground. Under the present statutory formulation these acts would constitute second degree criminal damage to property because they do not constitute threats to human life or interference with a public utility service or public transportation or communication systems.

The actus reus of first degree criminal damage to property omits the traditional requirement of damage and punishes those who "interfere" with property in a certain extremely reckless manner or who "interfere" with certain public facilities. It is not clear which activities will be held to "interfere" which would not also damage, but it does seem clear that the present statutory language is broader than the law prior to 1968. Acts which would appear to satisfy the requirement are wrecking a street car through the use of dynamite, obstruction of a railroad track, digging ditches and stretching wire across a road and placing debris and nails on a road, and shooting a shotgun loaded with bird shot into a dwelling.

The phrase "in a manner so as to endanger human life" has been construed by the Georgia Supreme Court to mean reckless endangerment rather than actual endangerment. Under this construction, it need only be shown that the defendant's reckless behavior created a risk of danger to others. A showing of actual harm is not required. Thus, a person who fires gunshots into an inhabited dwelling where people are likely to be present endangers human life within the meaning of the statute. The fact that the occupants of the dwelling were not physically present does not lessen the risk of danger to others nor the recklessness of the defendant's behavior.

2. Mens Rea

The mens rea of malicious mischief was troublesome at common law and remains so under the Georgia statutory formulation. The majority rule has been that malice must be directed toward the owner or possessor of the damaged or destroyed property rather than merely against the property. Georgia has never followed this rule. Under the law prior to 1968, it was necessary to prove only that the act of mischief was done "wantonly and recklessly." This is apparently still the law since the statutes simply employ mens rea terms such as "knowingly," "intentionally," and "recklessly."

It has been held, however, that lack of ill-will in general or the presence of a good motive may negate the required mens rea. For example, in Carstorphen v. State, the complainant had placed a lock on an elevator which he and the defendant both had a legal right to use. The defendant broke the lock only to gain access to the elevator. The court held the defendant not guilty of malicious mischief because he did not act with a malicious intent or motive. It is uncertain whether this is still good law under the present statutory formulation, which no longer requires malice, but punishes merely intentional behavior.

3. Protected Property

Both real and personal property, as well as public property, are protected by §§ 16-7-22 and 16-7-23. While animals are protected by the cruelty to animals provision (§ 16-12-4), owners of livestock and other animals of quantifiable value are arguably also protected from damage to their animals by the criminal damage provisions.

Under the law prior to 1968, the property damaged did not need to have value. This apparently is still the general rule, although § 16-7-23(a)(1) requires the damaged property be worth over $500 for criminal liability to attach under that provision. While more than $500 worth of damage is an essential element of § 16-7-23(a)(1), rigid and exact methods of proof are not required. It should be noted that the expense to the owner of the damaged property for labor in dealing with the damage is not the element which must exceed $500 and cannot be used as a substitute for the value of the damage to the property.

4. Requirement of Damage

Generally, there is no question about whether there has been damage. Occasionally, however, that will be an issue. In Adams v. State, for example, the defendant was charged with willfully damaging a monument in a private burial ground. The monument was located on property owned by the defendant. It was knocked over by a bulldozer being operated under the defendant's instructions and was taken to a gully and buried. The monument remained intact, even while buried. Nevertheless, the court found the monument to have been damaged; its dismantling and removal separated it from the grave, of which it had become an integral part.

Mere inconvenience to the owner, however, does not satisfy the damage requirement. In Pollett v. State the defendant wilfully removed wood from a woodrack of another, but did not injure the wood. On appeal the court held the defendant was not guilty of malicious mischief, notwithstanding the inconvenience to the owner of the wood who was put to the expense and trouble of replacing the wood on the rack. This is consistent with Adams because there is not the same permanent relationship between wood and a rack as that which exists between a tombstone and a grave. Similarly, Howard v. State held that malicious mischief is not committed when one removes a post which has been placed in the ground preparatory to erecting a fence, so long as the post itself is not injured. A different result should obtain if the fence has been completed, even if the post is removed unscathed, because the posts and wire would then form an integral whole capable of being criminally damaged by the removal of a part.

5. Ownership of Property

The law prior to 1968 was unclear both as to the necessity of proving ownership and as to the quantum of proof sufficient to satisfy the requirement. It should be noted that while § 16-7-23 speaks in terms of property of another, § 16-7-22 protects all property.

Under the law prior to 1968, the victim must have had more than a use interest or easement in the property in question. In Grant v. State the indictment alleged the defendant destroyed a bridge which was the property of four named individuals. The proof showed the four individuals had, at most, an easement in the bridge. The court reversed the conviction, holding the evidence did not prove the allegations of the indictment. Perhaps had the indictment stated more generally that the bridge belonged to the community of persons who used it to get to church and to the mill, the defendant would have been properly convicted.

Also, under the law prior to 1968, an oral assertion of ownership of real property was inadmissible to prove ownership if properly objected to. If there was no objection, an oral assertion of ownership was sufficient if the indictment alleged ownership by that person. Where there was no evidence indicating ownership by a particular entity, it was error to charge the jury that if the entity was in possession of the property and used the property that ownership might be inferred.

Under the present law, lawful occupancy by one in charge constitutes ownership, and the question of legal title is not involved. In Rash v. State, the court held that since a divorce decree awarded the former wife title to and "use" of the house, even though the former husband had not yet complied with the court order to give his former wife a quitclaim deed, the wife's legal occupancy was shown and the contested element of ownership in the offense of criminal damage to property in the second degree was proved.

If both the state and the defendant introduce evidence of ownership, it becomes a question of fact for the jury.

Criminal damage to property in the first degree is not a crime against ownership. It is a crime against the state involving the unauthorized interference with property in a manner that endangers human life. Section 16-7-22(a) does not expressly or impliedly qualify or limit in any way the scope of the term "human life" as used therein. Thus, this offense is committed where the human life endangered is that of tenants, rather than the owners, of the property.

C. Admissibility of Evidence

The most frequently litigated admissibility problem in criminal damage to property cases involves the question of value under § 16-7-23(a)(1) which requires that damage exceed $500 (formerly $100). This element is generally proven by asking the owner to state the property's value. Unless the owner is an expert appraiser, however, this method of proof raises problems with the opinion rule. In Van Voltenburg v. State the official in charge of the vehicle maintenance compound testified that the gate into which the defendant had smashed had sustained $150 to $175 worth of damage. On cross-examination, the witness admitted that he had estimated the amount of damage himself; he had bought the gates new and knew their value. The court found the testimony admissible as a statement of fact rather than opinion because he was testifying from his own personal knowledge based on the purchase of the gates.

The Court of Appeals has expressed its willingness to allow into evidence similar statements or opinions without resorting to classifying them as statements of fact. In Hiatt v. State, the witness was the property manager for an apartment complex, a position he had held for about six months. He testified he had purchased approximately $2,000 worth of furniture during the month before trial. Although he had not replaced any of the furniture damaged in this particular incident, he had noted the replacement cost at wholesale plus 10% for items identical to those damaged. He testified on the extent of damage to each item and its replacement cost. The court held that testimony as to value is permissible if the witness adequately shows that he has had an opportunity to form a correct opinion.

Evidence of prior difficulties between the defendant and the owner of the property is admissible to show intent in criminal damage to property cases. In Mullen v. State, the court held that evidence of the defendant's prior attacks on a homeowner was admissible to show his state of mind and motive for firing two shots into the owner's home.

Properly identified photographs depicting the damaged property have been held admissible.

D. Sufficiency of Evidence

Sufficiency of the evidence in criminal damage to property cases is generally raised in the context of questioning whether an act admittedly committed constitutes criminal damage to property. Cases dealing with the sufficiency of the evidence introduced to show that the accused committed the alleged acts are rare.

The quantum of proof sufficient to satisfy the requirement of more than $100 (now $500) worth of damage under § 16-7-23(a)(1) was considered in Hayes v. State. At trial, the witness was never asked to state the value of a C.B. radio before and after the incident. He did state its purchase price, length of ownership, condition before, and that it was "broken to pieces" afterward. The court held that the evidence was sufficient for the jury to conclude that the damage exceeded $100 (now $500) since the jury is allowed to draw from its own experience in forming estimates of the market value of everyday objects. In Holbrook v. State, an equipment operator for a construction company testified that he was familiar with the approximate value of trucks used in the construction business and that the damaged truck was worth "around $17,000" before the damage, and less than $1,000 after the damage. The court held that given this testimony regarding the extent of the damage, as well as the photographs of the truck properly admitted into evidence, the jury had sufficient evidence to determine that the value of damage was in excess of $500. In Spann v. State, evidence of damage in excess of $500 was established by the opinion testimony of the investigating police officer testifying as a lay witness and the photographs he took at the scene. The photographs, depicting in graphic detail extensive damage to the victim's car, fully corroborated the officer's estimate of the value of the damage done to the victim's vehicle. The court held that this evidence was sufficient for the jury to find the defendant guilty of criminal damage to property in the second degree.

In Hildebrand v. State, however, the state offered no proof of any amounts paid for repair of the property damaged and presented no photographs depicting the property damaged, so there was no competent evidence from which the jury could determine that the value of the damage for which defendant was responsible was in excess of $500, an essential element of the indicted crime. Thus, the court held that the trial court erred in denying the defendant's motion for directed verdict of acquittal on this charge. In *In the Interest of A. F.*, the only evidence of damage in excess of $500 was the victim's testimony that she obtained an estimate to repair her van in the amount of $605 from "the dealer." She acknowledged that the damage to her van was not repaired for this price. The victim's testimony about the repair estimate she obtained was inadmissible hearsay. Since this hearsay was the only evidence establishing the amount of damage to the victim's van, the juvenile's adjudication of delinquency for criminal damage to property in the second degree had to be vacated.

To sustain a § 16-7-22(a)(1) conviction, the evidence must be sufficient to show that the defendant's actions endangered human life. For example, in Simmons v. State the evidence showed the defendant fired a shotgun loaded with bird shot into a dwelling. The evidence further showed that the owner's mother was lying in a room directly in line with the point of entry of the gunshot although none of the shot entered her room. The court upheld the defendant's conviction under § 16-7-22(a)(1), holding the evidence was sufficient on the issue of endangering human life. In Robinson v. State, the evidence showed that the defendant fired a .357 magnum and hit the rear tire on the driver's side of the victim's car as the victim sat in the driver's seat. The court held the evidence established the commission of criminal damage to property in the first degree beyond a reasonable doubt.

E. Defenses Peculiar to Criminal Damage to Property

Because the crime is defined in terms of property "of another," the principal defense in a second degree criminal damage to property prosecution is the "claim of right" defense, a specific application of the mistake of fact defense. "Claim of right" requires the accused to establish that he had a good faith belief that he had an ownership interest in the property in question. A mere assertion of ownership, although made at the time the property was injured or destroyed and subsequently repeated, does not require a finding that the accused acted under an honest claim of right, especially in the absence of any evidence to support such a claim. It should be emphasized that since the property protected by § 16-7-22 is **all** property, not just that of another, the "claim of right" defense should not be recognized in a § 16-7-22 case. In other words, if interference with the defendant's own property endangers human life it violates § 16-7-22.

Abandonment is an available defense to a second degree criminal damage to property prosecution although it may be difficult to establish. In Adams v. State, the defense was not available despite the fact that the burial ground in question had fallen into a state of ruin and that there had been no burials for years. The court held that it would not be legally abandoned so long as there were markers on the graves sufficient to put one on notice that it was a burial ground. It may be, however, that a different result would be reached if the subject matter of the offense was something less hallowed than a cemetery plot.

The standard jury charges on provocation do not pertain to property offenses. The concept of provocation is inapplicable because it presupposes that the victim provoked the offense.

F. Relationship to Other Offenses

Important Notice about Repudiation of Actual or Same Evidence Test: The Georgia Supreme Court repudiated the actual evidence test in *Drinkard v. Walker*, 281 Ga. 211, 636 S.E.2d 530 (2006), because it found this test to be inconsistent with the statutory framework governing the prohibition against multiple convictions for included offenses in Georgia. This inconsistency resulted in years of confusion and unpredictable results. In its place, the court adopted the required evidence test and overruled any prior case law that is inconsistent with it. Thus, any prior case law applying the actual evidence test is no longer controlling and should not be relied upon to determine whether one offense is included in another under § 16-1-6(1). The discussion of such case law is included below only insofar as it may still be applicable to pending prosecutions that arose before the Drinkard decision. See MULTIPLE CONVICTIONS, II. Tests to Determine Presence of Multiple Convictions, for a complete discussion of the Drinkard decision.

As defined in § 16-7-22(a)(1), criminal damage to property in the first degree is a felonious act which is inherently dangerous or life-threatening and that felony can, therefore, support a felony murder conviction.

The provision of § 16-7-23(a)(2) which punishes reckless or intentional damage of another's property by means of fire or explosives raises the obvious question of the relationship between this crime and the three arson crimes of §§ 16-7-60, 16-7-61, and 16-7-62. This will be an important question in two situations: the determination of whether § 16-1-7(a) will permit multiple punishments for both arson and criminal damage to property on the basis of the same act (the question of multiple convictions) and whether a criminal damage to property conviction is authorized as a lesser included offense in a trial on an arson indictment.

For purposes of the rule against multiple punishments, it has been held that § 16-7-23(a)(2) is included within first degree arson, which punishes damage by fire of a protected structure under circumstances which endanger human life, because the former's proscriptions punish the same conduct as § 16-7-60, requiring only a less culpable mental state. Thus, despite the fact that there were multiple victims, only one conviction could be had for the same act. In D.C.A. v. State, the court held § 16-7-23(a)(2) to be included necessarily within § 16-7-61 (second degree arson) so as to authorize a conviction of the former under an indictment charging the latter. (Actually, the proceeding was in juvenile court.)

It does seem clear that anybody who violates § 16-7-61 will necessarily have violated § 16-7-23(a)(2). This will also be true of those who violate §§ 16-7-60 and 16-7-62. In fact, given the breadth of the three arson statutes, it is hard to identify any behavior which is a violation of § 16-7-23(a)(2) which is not also a violation of one of the arson crimes.

Two Court of Appeals cases dealt with convictions of interference with government property as lesser included offenses where the indictment alleged criminal damage to property. In Hack v. State, the indictment charged the defendant with violating the criminal damage to property statute by intentionally damaging "a certain 1982 Ford automobile, the property of the Clayton County Board of Commissioners in excess of $100." The trial evidence demonstrated only $2 worth of damage, and therefore, the trial judge did not submit the criminal damage to property allegation to the jury, but instead instructed on interference with government property (see III., E. Criminal Interference with Government Property, infra). Under § 16-7-24(a), that crime punishes one who "destroys, damages, or defaces government property." The jury convicted the defendant of the offense of interference with government property. The appellate court, relying on Porter v. State, reversed the conviction, holding that interference with government property is not a lesser included offense of criminal damage to property.

It is contended that both of these cases are incorrect. The courts in both cases have overlooked the familiar rule in Georgia that an offense may be a lesser included offense of another, either as a matter of law or as a matter of the pleading in the indictment. That is, on an indictment charging crime X, a conviction of crime Y can be returned if either (1) Y is necessarily charged any time X is charged or (2) the elements of Y were charged in the indictment in the particular case. It is clear that the elements of interference with government property were alleged in the Hack indictment. That crime requires that the property be that of the government and that the defendant have damaged, destroyed, or defaced it. These allegations were made and evidence on these allegations was introduced at trial.

While the *Porter* court correctly identified the general rules about conviction of a lesser included offense as stated above, it made a crucial error in applying these rules to the issue before it. It overturned the interference with government property conviction because, in its words, "[c]onspicuously missing from the greater . . . offense of criminal damage to property is any necessity of proving the governmental nature of ownership . . .." What the court was confusing here was the type of allegation which is **required** to be made in an indictment and those which are **actually** made. While the state might not be **forced** to allege that the damaged property was that of the government in a criminal damage to property indictment, if it **does** so describe the property as governmental, it would appear that an interference with government property conviction would be appropriate. It is not clear whether the Porter case is correctly decided on its facts because the opinion does not indicate what was alleged in the indictment. It is clear, however, that the Hack court ignored the language of the indictment before it.

It has been held that criminal trespass is a lesser included offense of criminal damage to property in the second degree. Criminal trespass cannot be considered, as a matter of fact, a lesser included offense of criminal damage to property in the first degree where the only evidence of "interference" in the case is an intentional, life-endangering act and where there is no evidence of a mere knowing and malicious interference with the property of another without his consent. Also, criminal trespass as a lesser offense of burglary and criminal damage to property in the second degree do not constitute the same offense as a matter of fact or law, and it is not error for a trial court to impose consecutive sentences for these separate offenses.

Criminal damage to property in the first degree, which involves the deliberate and unauthorized interference with property, is not a lesser included offense of aggravated assault as a matter of law.

Where the evidence used to support a stalking charge is the same evidence used to support a criminal damage to property charge, the two offenses merge as a matter of law.

G. Punishment

Both first and second degree criminal damage to property are felonies. The former is punishable by imprisonment of one to ten years, while the latter is punishable by imprisonment for one to five years.

Where the defendant has pled guilty to criminal trespass as a lesser included offense of criminal damage to property in the second degree, in the absence of any agreement on the damage to the property, the $500 limit set forth in § 16-7-21(a) is the maximum amount that a trial court can order the defendant to pay as restitution for damage to the property.

II. Criminal Trespass

A. Generally

Section 16-7-21 replaces pre-1968 statutes which were extremely limited in scope, distinguishing, for example, enclosed from unenclosed land, and cultivated from uncultivated land. The present statute eliminates these out-dated distinctions and is drafted in more general terms. Under § 16-7-21, criminal trespass can now be committed in five different ways: (1) intentionally damaging property of another in an amount less than or equal to $500 or interfering with the use or possession of another's property; (2) entering the land, premises, or vehicle of another for an "unlawful purpose"; (3) entering the land or premises of another after receiving notice that such entry is forbidden; (4) remaining on the land or premises or within the vehicle of another after being told to leave; and (5) intentionally defacing, mutilating, or defiling any military grave marker, monument, memorial, or plaque that is privately owned or located on privately owned land.

B. Elements of Offense

1. Actus Reus

The actus reus of § 16-7-21(a) is the "interference" with the use or possession of property belonging to another without his consent. This is an addition to prior law. It has been held that under this provision where the defendant is interfering with access to the property of another, it is immaterial whether he is actually on the property. Section 16-7-21(a) also includes those acts which constitute criminal damage to property, but which cause $500 or less of damage. The state is not required to prove the actual ownership of the damaged property, only that it belonged to someone other than the defendant. Where the damaged property is an "everyday object," the jury may draw from its own experience in forming an estimate of its value. Where there is no evidence as to whether the amount of damage done is more or less than $500, no conviction can stand.

In a most unrevealing decision, the court in Benton v. State stated that evidence that the defendant was found crawling out of a fan duct from a laundry where clothes were found strewn about "did not appear to warrant an instruction on subsection (a) of our criminal trespass statute." The court volunteered no explanation of why the acts of the defendant did not constitute criminal trespass as defined by § 16-7-21(a), and a strong argument can be made that they did.

The actus reus of § 16-7-21(b) is generally satisfied if the defendant either enters or remains after receiving notice to leave a clearly defined area within the ownership of another.

The actus reus of § 16-7-21(e) is satisfied if the defendant defaces, mutilates, or defiles a privately owned military grave marker, monument, memorial, or plaque.

2. Mens Rea

Intent is expressly required by § 16-7-21. Case law prior to 1968 defined the mens rea in terms of commission of an act malevolently, with an evil purpose, without any ground for believing the act to be lawful, and without regard for the property rights of the owner of the property. Section 16-7-21(a) may very well require a similar state of mind since it requires one "knowingly and maliciously" to interfere with the property of another. The intent with which this act is done is peculiarly a question of fact for the jury to determine. The rest of the statute calls for either a knowing or an intentional mens rea. Thus, as was the case under the law prior to 1968, if the act alleged to be a trespass is committed in good faith under a claim of ownership, there can be no conviction. Furthermore, one charged with trespass cannot be convicted unless he is aware of his conduct and aware of the attendant circumstances.

In Black v. State, for example, Lockett, who had the right to cut wood anywhere on the lands of Clare, gave the defendant, a young boy, permission to cut wood. Clare apparently had misled Lockett as to the property boundaries and, as a result, the boy cut wood from the land of the complainant while in the presence of Lockett and the complainant's agent. Neither informed the defendant that he was trespassing. The court held that the element of wilfulness had not been proved, and, in fact, had been clearly disproved.

Although a defendant is not obligated to produce any evidence, in order to assert a good faith defense, there must be evidence to support it. In Haygood v. State, the defendant urged that no criminal intent was shown because she was acting on a good faith belief that she was trimming a neighbor's hedge on her property. However, there was no evidence of any survey showing that the boundary lay along the line where the defendant cut the hedge, and there was no evidence that the defendant ever contended or believed the property line lay where she cut the hedge. The only evidence of where the property line might have been was the prior marked survey, and the jury could have found that the defendant knowingly ignored it when she cut a foot-wide encroachment on her neighbor's property with her hedge clippers.

Criminal trespass is usually a "specific intent" crime, i.e., the defendant must intend to do something more than the mere act committed. Under § 16-7-21(b)(2) and (b)(3), the accused must enter or remain on the premises of another, knowing that he has been given notice forbidding his presence. Under § 16-7-21(b)(1) entry must be made with the intent to commit an unlawful act.

3. Protected Property

Compared to the law prior to 1968, § 16-7-21 substantially broadens the types of property upon or in which trespass can be committed. In a direct break with prior law, § 16-7-21(b) expressly includes within its coverage land, premises, and certain types of locomotive structures (vehicles, railroad cars, aircraft, and watercraft). The term "premises" has been interpreted to mean the land and the buildings located on it and to include property owned or used for public purposes. "Property" as used in § 16-7-21(a) should be defined to reach substantially the same types of property covered by § 16-7-23(a)(1). Section 16-7-21(e) expressly includes within in its coverage all privately owned military grave markers, monuments, memorials, or plaques.

4. Notice Element

Notice is the essential element of § 16-7-21(b)(2) and (b)(3) prosecutions. As under the law prior to 1968, the state must prove that the notice given was intended to apply to the particular property in question and was conveyed in understandable terms. In Murphey v. State the owner of a store told the defendant while he was inside the store to " . . . leave my premises and never set foot upon my place again." The defendant immediately left the store, walked down a road, climbed over a fence, and walked across a path over a pasture owned by the store owner. The owner had allowed neighbors to travel that path for seven years, and it was the most direct way for the defendant to go home. The defendant testified that he had never been forbidden to walk that way. The court overturned the trespass conviction on the ground that the notice was insufficient to inform the defendant of the owner's position regarding the pasture. According to the court, an order to leave the "premises" was not an explicit notice not to use a path.

However, an "explicit" reference to the property the defendant is forbidden to enter is not required, where there have been repeated and unequivocal notices to the defendant that he should stay away from **any premises** occupied by the complainant. In Stockwell v. State, the court held that although the complainant's admonition that the defendant was to stay away from her "everywhere" would not necessarily authorize his conviction for criminal trespass on land or premises other than those in which the complainant had a possessory interest, this fact did not otherwise demonstrate that the complainant's admonition would not authorize the defendant's conviction for criminal trespass upon those lands or premises in which the complainant did have a possessory interest.

The notice to leave certain premises usually applies to the entire premises, and not to just one location on the premises. In Kerr v. State, the court found no merit in the defendant's argument that he was not warned by an abortion clinic administrator to leave after he changed locations on the premises, because in her warning the administrator demanded that he leave **the premises**, not just the one location. In McCrosky v. State, the court rejected the defendant's argument that the evidence of notice was insufficient because the written notice did not specifically mention the medical research facility owned by the university. The defendant received one written and two verbal warnings to leave the university campus on the day of the demonstration. The written notice issued by the officer to the defendant on the parking deck clearly extended to all university property and not just the parking deck. The court found the notice was reasonable under the circumstances and sufficiently explicit to apprise the defendant of the property she was forbidden to enter.

A notice can bar entry completely or bar entry for a specific purpose, so long as the notice requirements are met.

In Scott v. State the court was faced with the differing notice requirements of § 16-7-21(b)(2) and (b)(3), which lie in the time of the giving of the notice. According to the court, while subsection (b)(3) is violated if the defendant enters lawfully, but remains after being told to leave, subsection (b)(2) is violated when the defendant enters after being told not to.

In Scott, the complainant had refused the defendant's request to come to her home and sit with her. At 3:00 a.m., the defendant quietly walked into the apartment and awakened the complainant. She immediately screamed, "Get out" and the defendant hurriedly left. In upholding a § 16-7-21(b)(2) conviction, the court found no error in the trial judge's refusal to instruct the jury that a trespasser is entitled to sufficient time to depart after being so ordered. Noting the aforementioned difference between subsections (b)(2) and (b)(3), the court concluded that the defendant's statement that he left immediately would create an issue if he were being prosecuted under § 16-7-21(b)(3), but that it was not an issue under § 16-7-21(b)(2) where the essence of the offense is entry **after** notice denying entry.

It is necessary that the person giving notice under § 16-7-21 have a legally sufficient relationship with the property. The statute itself states that the owner or a rightful occupant is qualified to give notice. Additionally, an agent of the owner is also qualified. In Perry v. State, the person giving notice to the accused that his entry into a motel was forbidden testified that he was a detective on the local police force. There was no evidence that he was the owner, occupant, or agent of the owner of the premises. This lack of evidence was held to be fatal to a § 16-7-21(b)(2) prosecution. Similarly, in Jackson v. State, the court held that the evidence failed to establish an essential element of the offense because there was no evidence that, when the officer gave the notice to the defendant, he was acting as the authorized representative of the owner or rightful occupant of the apartment.

If a police officer's conduct in arresting a criminal trespasser is in the discharge of his official functions, it is immaterial whether the police officer is an agent of the owner. In Rembert v. Arthur Schneider Sales, the court held that once a customer refused to leave a store after being asked to leave by the owner in the police officer's presence, the customer became a criminal trespasser. The police officer was authorized by law, not by his employment with the owner, to arrest the customer.

In Hope v. State, the defendant contended that there was no showing that the City of Atlanta, owner of the airport, had specifically authorized a police officer to prohibit him from going onto the airport property. The court held that a police officer, whether possessing power of arrest or not, is a representative of the city of which he is a sworn officer while protecting the property of that city, wherever located. Also, an officer holds, at a minimum, the same status with regard to criminal trespass as does a maintenance man or security guard for a private owner.

While hearsay evidence concerning notice may be presented to explain an officer's conduct and can be considered by the trier of fact when determining if the officer had probable cause to arrest a trespasser, such evidence cannot be used as original evidence to prove that the defendant had notice not to be present on the subject property. In Patterson v. State, the only evidence presented by the state that the defendant was given notice to depart from the address and refused to do so was the arresting officer's hearsay testimony that the occupant of that address told the defendant to leave his porch on another occasion. The court held that while this evidence could be considered to explain the arresting officer's conduct, it could not be used to prove that the defendant had notice not to be present on the porch. Thus, because the state failed to prove the essential element of notice beyond a reasonable doubt, the defendant's conviction for criminal trespass had to be reversed.

Prior to 1997, § 16-7-21 was totally silent concerning the authority to rescind a previous notice barring entry to property. However, there was some case law authority for the proposition that entry, although previously forbidden, may be granted by the permission of a person legally entitled to withhold the right. Based on this proposition, the Court of Appeals held in Hutson v. State that a minor of appropriate maturity was a "rightful occupant" of her parents' home for purposes of the criminal trespass statute and thus entitled to grant the right of entry. Because her invitation conveyed authority to the defendant, her boyfriend, to disregard the earlier notice of her parents that he was barred from the home, the court reversed his conviction for criminal trespass. In 1997, the General Assembly amended § 16-7-21, obviously in response to the Court of Appeals' decision in Hutson, to provide that "permission to enter or invitation to enter given by a minor who is or is not present on or in the property of the minor's parent or guardian is not sufficient to allow lawful entry of another person upon the [property] . . . if such parent or guardian has previously given notice that such entry is forbidden . . . " In light of this 1997 amendment, it thus appears that Hutson v. State is no longer controlling authority.

To be guilty of criminal trespass, a person who has been advised to leave must be given a reasonable amount of time to do so. What constitutes a reasonable amount of time under the circumstances is a question for the jury.

5. *"Unlawful Purpose."*

The "unlawful purpose" requirement of § 16-7-21(b)(1) has been a troublesome one. This element requires that the accused have the intent to commit an act in addition to the act of entering the premises. In many cases that unlawful purpose will be theft. Where the intent to steal is proved, the criminal trespass merges with or is included within burglary, § 16-7-1, so that double conviction would be barred. If there is no evidence to support a finding of a nonfelonious unlawful purpose, a trespass conviction is **not** authorized. On the other hand, if, in a burglary prosecution, the jury might have believed that the defendant entered for an unlawful purpose other than the commission of a felony or theft, the defendant is entitled, upon request, to a charge on trespass.

A defendant who has requested a charge on criminal trespass may not rely on a jury verdict acquitting him of greater offenses, such as burglary and kidnapping, as a determination that the state failed to prove that he entered a residence "for an unlawful purpose." A verdict of guilty as to criminal trespass would not be without evidentiary support where the evidence would have authorized a conviction for burglary or kidnapping.

C. *Admissibility of Evidence*

The Georgia courts have been liberal in the evidence they have permitted to be introduced to prove notice as required in subsection (b). Cases have admitted evidence which is highly prejudicial to the defendant and of questionable probative value on the issue of notice. For example, in Gasaway v. State when asked why the defendant had been forbidden to enter a skating rink, the owner of the rink testified that there had been "a lot of trouble out there," that the defendant "was always coming out there fighting," and that the defendant was drunk when he came to the rink. The court upheld the admissibility of the evidence as probative of the complainant's conduct in forbidding the defendant access to the premises despite claims of prejudice and irrelevance.

D. *Sufficiency of Evidence*

Few reported criminal trespass cases consider the question of the sufficiency of the evidence and those that do tend to lack extensive analysis. This is probably due to the simplicity of the offense—all that need be proven is an entry after notice of forbiddance or a remaining after a request to leave.

Section 16-7-21(b)(2) (entry after prior notice) cases generally involve an establishment's attempts to prevent the entry of "undesirables," and convictions in these cases are generally affirmed. In Walker v. State, the evidence showed that a prostitute was warned by hotel security guards that she would be arrested for criminal trespass if she came back to the hotel and that she returned. That was held to be sufficient. In McCrosky v. State, the court upheld the sufficiency of the evidence where the evidence showed that a university police officer announced over a megaphone that anyone crossing the barricade would be arrested. After the protestor crossed over the line of barricades, she was immediately arrested by other officers. The evidence also showed that another officer previously had given the protestor a criminal trespass warning informing her that she would be subject to arrest if she ever returned to university property at any time in the future. In Gasaway v. State, evidence that the defendant had entered the complainant's skating rink several times in a drunken condition, that he had created disturbances at the place, that the complainant previously had forbidden the defendant to come on the premises, and that the nature of the complainant's business was such that his customers were mostly children, was upheld as sufficient. In Ivey v. State, the court upheld the sufficiency of the evidence where it showed that the defendant was served with prior notice of banishment from the housing authority property. However, he was later discovered on the property engaging in a verbal dispute with his fiancee. In Hammond v. State, the defendant had been issued a notice barring his entry on university property for the purpose of sleeping. He was later found sleeping on university property late at night. The court held that the evidence was sufficient to authorize the defendant's conviction for criminal trespass.

Section 16-7-21(b)(3) (remaining after request to leave) cases often involve similar circumstances. In Rowles v. State, evidence that a season passholder at an amusement park was drunk, staggering and abusive, was repeatedly asked to leave, and finally arrested after assaulting a guard was sufficient to convict under § 16-7-21(b)(3). In Strozier v. State, it was held that though an apartment has common entrance ways and halls, evidence that an apartment dweller made repeated requests for one to leave her property was sufficient to find one guilty of criminal trespass. In Reid v. State, a hospital security guard testified that he told the defendant to leave the room in which he was on the telephone but he refused. The court held that this alone was sufficient evidence of criminal trespass. Whether the defendant, after being advised to leave, left within a reasonable time under the circumstances was a question for the factfinder to decide. Many § 16-7-21(b)(3) cases involve students making demands of or protesting to school officials. So long as the evidence establishes a refusal to leave after a clear and fair request to leave by the official in charge, the courts have upheld the convictions.

For § 16-7-21(b)(1) (entry with an unlawful purpose) cases, the evidence is very similar in nature to that required for a burglary conviction. The evidence must show that the defendant in fact entered the premises of the victim and must show that the alleged unlawful act occurred on the victim's property. The evidence must, however, indicate a purpose in entering other than to commit a theft or felony. This will sometimes be presented by the defendant's own testimony. In Wells v. State, the state's evidence in a burglary prosecution showed that the defendant entered through the window of a house in the early hours of the morning, struggled with the victim, and then fled through the window by which he entered. Because the fact finder could have believed the entry was for an unlawful purpose other than a theft or felony, this evidence was sufficient to sustain a verdict for the lesser offense of criminal trespass.

Finally, it should be noted that because criminal trespass is a misdemeanor, the rule requiring corroboration of an accomplice's testimony does not apply. Thus, a conviction can be upheld on the sole basis of an accomplice's testimony.

E. Defenses

The most prevalent defense to a criminal trespass charge is that the alleged trespass was committed under a claim of right. Older cases hold that no conviction can be had where the defendant entered the land or premises in question with a good faith claim of ownership or possessory rights in the property. If proven, such a defense negates the requisite mens rea. This defense should still exist under the current statute. The Supreme Court of Georgia has held that an agent who believes in good faith that his principal is the owner of and entitled to possession of the premises can not be found guilty of criminal trespass if he goes upon the premises in obedience to the directions of his principal. Because both joint tenants have a valid ownership interest, one joint tenant can not be criminally prosecuted by the other joint tenant for trespass to the property in which they share ownership.

The claim of right defense most often involves the rights of tenants and their guests. A tenant who in good faith claims possession of land, under one who has a bona fide claim of title, can not be convicted of trespass. Further, because a tenant is entitled to the undisturbed enjoyment of his possession, the landlord has no right to exercise any control over who may enter the premises or over the conduct of the tenant's guests, so long as they are there for a lawful purpose and do not infringe upon any right of the landlord.

A 1977 case considered the extent to which a contractual right to be on the premises constitutes a defense to a § 16-7-21 charge. In Rowles v. State, the accused asserted that the contractual right to be on the premises embodied in his season pass to an amusement park provided him with a defense to the charge of criminal trespass. The court concluded that the season pass was not unqualified permission from the owner for the passholder to be present in any condition.

In State v. Moore, the issue before the court was whether the defendant had a defense to a trespass charge where he removed a fence which interfered with his access to his property. In an unusual ordering of values, the court held that while § 16-3-24(a) permits the use of force against a **person** to terminate the tortious interference with the defendant's property, it does not permit force to be used against the **property** of another. Furthermore, the court held that it was no defense that the complainant had wrongfully obstructed the driveway and thus interfered with the defendant's ability to get to his property.

In Watson v. State, the defendant contended that title to the store products had passed to him when he identified them and placed them in his cart and consequently he was not refusing to leave the premises after being told to do so by the store manager, but was merely refusing to abandon property which was rightfully his. The court disagreed and held that even assuming that title to the store products had passed to the defendant, the fact that the defendant had "title" to the store products could not serve as a basis for allowing him to ignore the store manager's demand that he leave, thereby violating a criminal statute.

F. Constitutional Issues

Our criminal trespass statutes have been subjected to repeated constitutional attack. The statutes have been attacked as being unconstitutionally vague, as being violative of the First Amendment rights of freedom of assembly and speech, and as being applied in violation of the Equal Protection Clause. In a series of cases during the early 1960s, mostly involving black civil rights groups, the Georgia Supreme Court upheld the legitimacy of the then existing criminal trespass statute until decisions by the United States Supreme Court forced it to reverse its position.

Few cases have considered the constitutionality of the various provisions of the current statute. In Mixon v. State the words "unlawful purpose" contained in § 16-7-21(b)(1) were alleged to be unconstitutionally vague. The Georgia Supreme Court disagreed on the ground that the phrase "unlawful purpose" had to be construed in context as part of former GCA Chapter 26-15, "Criminal Damage to Property," and that the words required a purpose to violate a criminal law.

A 1973 case challenged the constitutionality of § 16-7-21(b)(3) (remaining on premises after notice to leave given). In Daniel v. State the court held that the defendant's conviction for remaining on public school premises after being directed to depart constituted no denial of freedom of speech and assembly because conduct employed in exercising those freedoms must not constitute a trespass upon property owned or occupied by others.

In the 1989 case of United States v. Gilbert, the federal district court determined that the defendant's use of a federal building as a residence constituted a trespass under Georgia law. The federal government sought to enjoin this activity. However, as a defense, the defendant argued that his activity was expressive and therefore protected by the First Amendment. The court, assuming that the activity was expressive and thus protected, held that an injunction aimed at enjoining the defendant's use of the federal building as a residence, was a reasonable time, place, and manner restriction under the First Amendment. First, such an injunction would be content-neutral. Second, such an injunction could be narrowly tailored to further the significant governmental interest in preserving the aesthetics of the building. Finally, such an injunction would leave open many alternate channels of communication to the defendant.

Where a person is on state property solely for expressive purposes and where there is no valid restriction forbidding such conduct, as a matter of law that person is on state property under the "authority" of the free speech guarantees of the First Amendment. In such a case, that person cannot be convicted of criminal trespass because the state would not be able to prove that he was present "without authority," an essential element of criminal trespass. In Langton v. State, the defendant was convicted of criminal trespass for remaining in the parking lot of a Georgia Department of Labor facility after being directed to leave by a security guard and by the supervisor of the facility. The defendant's defense was that her presence was authorized because she was engaged in expressive activity protected by the First Amendment. Specifically, she was distributing leaflets encouraging older workers to unite in order to gain political power to oppose age discrimination. The court found that a purported state restriction, which was the basis for the defendant being asked to leave, forbidding the distribution of all written communication on all state property without regard to the intended use of any particular sites would be unreasonable under the "public forum analysis." For that reason, the court held that the restriction was unconstitutional and did not validly restrict the defendant's right to be present for the purpose of expressive activity.

In a 1979 case, State v. Raybon, the Georgia Supreme Court upheld § 16-7-21(b)(3), this time against a Due Process and Equal Protection attack. The case was correctly decided, but its factual setting raises a rather interesting problem. The property owner in Raybon was the Greyhound bus station manager. He dealt with "derelicts" by reading them a printed notice which they were to sign, which tells them to leave the bus station and never return. In Raybon, the defendant returned five hours after being given notice to depart, and returned without a legitimate reason to do so. Under those facts, a criminal trespass conviction seems appropriate. The manager testified, however, that he intended his notice to include all returns, both for legitimate and illegitimate reasons. It is questionable whether the criminal law can or ought to be used to punish a person who enters a business establishment to conduct legitimate business, merely because of his prior misconduct. Of course, on the Raybon facts this issue was not presented.

G. Relationship to Other Offenses

Important Notice about Repudiation of Actual or Same Evidence Test: The Georgia Supreme Court repudiated the actual evidence test in *Drinkard v. Walker*, 281 Ga. 211, 636 S.E.2d 530 (2006), because it found this test to be inconsistent with the statutory framework governing the prohibition against multiple convictions for included offenses in Georgia. This inconsistency resulted in years of confusion and unpredictable results. In its place, the court adopted the required evidence test and overruled any prior case law that is inconsistent with it. Thus, any prior case law applying the actual evidence test is no longer controlling and should not be relied upon to determine whether one offense is included in another under § 16-1-6(1). The discussion of such case law is included below only insofar as it may still be applicable to pending prosecutions that arose before the Drinkard decision. See MULTIPLE CONVICTIONS, II. Tests to Determine Presence of Multiple Convictions, for a complete discussion of the Drinkard decision.

The relationship between § 16-7-21(b)(1) (entry for an unlawful purpose) and § 16-7-1 (burglary) has been troublesome to the Georgia courts, resulting in conflicting opinions and confusing language. The confusion arises from the fact that the burglary statute requires an entry with an intent to commit a felony or a theft. Because an intent to commit a felony is necessarily an unlawful purpose, the Georgia courts have been left with the question of whether a criminal trespass conviction is authorized when the evidence shows an intent to commit a theft or felony.

The Court of Appeals, in a number of cases, has stated that if the intent to steal is proven, § 16-7-21(b)(1) merges with § 16-7-1. Thus, in Reese v. State, the court held that where the evidence discloses only an intent to commit a theft, a charge on criminal trespass is not proper. Where the evidence discloses that the accused might have entered for an unlawful purpose other than the commission of a felony or theft, a charge on criminal trespass is authorized.

These cases place a severe limitation on the "unlawful purpose" language of § 16-7-21(b)(1). The cases necessarily limit it to situations where the intent was to commit only a misdemeanor.

In Coney v. State, the court upheld a burglary conviction, holding the evidence sufficient to show an intent to commit a felony. The court found no error in the trial judge's charging on criminal trespass because the inclusion of the charge on criminal trespass favored the defendant. Coney may be seen as inconsistent with Reese because the appellate court affirmed a conviction where improper instructions were given, but the two cases together simply suggest that if the evidence shows an intent to commit a theft or felony, the judge will not be reversed for charging or not charging on criminal trespass. A defendant convicted of the lesser offense under such a charge hardly will be in any position to assert the error in instruction, since it ordinarily will have been at his request and in his favor.

In Brewer v. State, the court held that the trial court did not err in failing to give the defendant's written request to charge on criminal trespass as a lesser included offense of burglary. The defendant's evidence of alibi did not reasonably raise the inference that he unlawfully entered the home with a less culpable mental state than the felonious intent of a burglar as charged in the indictment.

In Munoz v. State, the court held it was not error for the trial court to refuse to give the defendant's requested charge on criminal trespass as a lesser included offense of burglary, where the uncontradicted evidence showed completion of the greater offense so that the charge on the lesser offense was not required.

In Bradshaw v. State, the court held that where the defendant denied entering the premises, there was no error in refusing to charge on criminal trespass as a lesser included offense of burglary.

In Dix v. State, the court held that it was not error for the trial court to refuse to give the defendant's requested charge on criminal trespass as a lesser included offense of entering an automobile with an intent to commit a theft, where there was sufficient evidence to support the jury's verdict that the defendant was guilty of the greater offense.

It should be noted that even where the defendant is entitled to a charge on § 16-7-21(b)(1) as a lesser included offense, he must comply with the rules laid down by the Georgia Supreme Court in State v. Stonaker. In Burton v. State the Court of Appeals applied Stonaker, finding no error in a failure to charge on criminal trespass where the accused neglected to make a written request for the charge.

In Waugh v. State, the Supreme Court held that the trial court's refusal to give the defendant's requested charge on criminal trespass as a lesser included offense of criminal damage to property in the first degree was not error. Criminal trespass could not be considered, as a matter of fact, a lesser included offense because the only evidence of "interference" in the case was the life-endangering act of intentionally dropping a rock into the path of on-coming traffic, which was used to establish the offense of criminal damage to property in the first degree. There was no evidence of a mere knowing and malicious "interference" with the property of another without his consent, which is required to establish the offense of criminal trespass.

In Merrell v. State, the Court of Appeals held that criminal trespass is a lesser included offense of criminal damage to property in the second degree and, thus, the trial court can instruct the jury with regard to the former offense in a trial based on an indictment for the latter.

In Williams v. State, the trial court charged § 16-7-21(b) of the criminal trespass statute as the lesser included offense of burglary. The jury thereafter found the defendant guilty of criminal trespass, but not of burglary. The Georgia Court of Appeals found that the crimes for which the defendant was convicted, i.e., criminal trespass as a lesser offense of burglary and criminal damage to property in the second degree, did not constitute the same offense as a matter of fact or law, and the trial court did not err in imposing consecutive sentences for these separate offenses.

In Kerr v. State, the court held that a violation of subsection (a) and a violation of subsection (b)(3) of § 16-7-21 did not merge as a matter of law because each required proof of different elements. The court also held that the two violations did not merge as a matter of fact where evidence showed that the defendants interfered with the use of the property by making ingress to and egress from the property difficult, thereby violating subsection (a), but other evidence also showed that defendants were on the property and that they refused to leave after being told to do so by the properly identified authorized representative of the owner of the property, thereby violating subsection (b)(3).

No conviction for unlawful assembly may be had where the accused (or, indeed, any member of the assembled group) is also convicted of a completed crime against the person or property of another, where that completed crime was the purpose of the assembly. Thus, in Kerr v. State, the court held that unlawful assembly for the purpose of committing criminal trespass was included in the crime of criminal trespass, because the defendants were properly convicted of criminal trespass.

The aggravated assault and criminal trespass statutes differ in the classification of the interests that each statute seeks to protect: the person placed in reasonable apprehension of receiving serious bodily injury in the case of aggravated assault and the property of another in the case of criminal trespass. Thus, criminal trespass is not a lesser included offense of aggravated assault as a matter of law. Furthermore, inasmuch as an indictment alleges deadly weapon aggravated assault and therefore does not require the state to prove that the defendant interfered with the victim's property, criminal trespass is not a lesser included offense as a matter of fact.

H. Punishment

Criminal trespass is a misdemeanor punishable under the general misdemeanor statute.

The misdemeanor offense of criminal trespass does not involve moral turpitude. A conviction for this offense is not admissible to impeach a witness's testimony at trial.

Where the defendant has pled guilty to criminal trespass as a lesser included offense of criminal damage to property in the second degree, in the absence of any agreement on the damage to the property, the $500 limit set forth in § 16-7-21(a) is the maximum amount that a trial court can order the defendant to pay as restitution for damage to the property.

III. Related Offenses

A. Damaging, Destroying, or Secreting Property to Defraud Another

Section 16-9-53, which replaces three pre-1968 statutes, makes it a criminal offense for one to damage, destroy, or secret property to defraud another person. The act must be done knowingly and with the intent to defraud. It applies to any property of whatever class or character and the property in question may be owned by the defendant or another person. Section 16-9-53 is a felony, carrying a penalty of imprisonment from one to five years.

There have been few cases decided under this or predecessor statutes. In Jarrett v. State, the defendant was convicted under § 16-9-53 for secreting property in order to defraud another. The claim on appeal was that the property had not been hidden, and therefore there had been no secreting. The evidence showed that the property was visible from several vantage points and was in plain view to those who entered the defendant's property. The court, on appeal, rejected the assertion that to secret property it must be hidden in the literal sense. According to the court, the prosecution need only show that the property had been "placed where it is unlikely to be discovered." On the facts of the case, the court found that a jury could have found that the property had been so placed and the conviction was affirmed.

One old case sheds some light on the types of evidence that can be admitted. In McElhannon v. State, the defendant was charged with mutilating and destroying a corporation's books with the intent to defraud and injure the corporation. The court held that because one of the alleged motives for the perpetration of the offense was concealment of a misappropriation, it was proper for the state to show that shortly before the incident the accused had been seen gambling. Furthermore, evidence which tended to show that there had been no misappropriation of the funds of the corporation, but that its losses had been sustained in the due course of its business, was admissible, as was evidence that a third party was mismanaging the corporation.

Few cases have considered the sufficiency of evidence in a prosecution for defrauding another by damaging property. In Powell v. State, the court upheld a conviction based on the following facts. The furnishings of the house arsoned by the defendant owner were insured; they had been removed at night by the defendant two days before the fire and stored in a distant city in a location rented in the name of a friend. When the house was saved, the absence of furnishings was explained by the defendant to his insurance carrier by stating unknown parties had taken everything of value. At no time did the defendant inform the authorities or his insurance carrier that the items were in fact removed by him and were safely in storage. The court found this evidence sufficient for the jury to conclude that the insured furnishings were removed and secreted knowingly and with intent to defraud another.

One question that may arise is whether burning to defraud an insurer under § 16-9-53 constitutes a lesser included offense of arson, so as to preclude double conviction. This question should be answered in the negative because the offenses involve completely different intents and are designed to punish different types of deleterious behavior. Under the law prior to 1968, one case held that burning to defraud an insurer is not a lesser offense of third-degree arson, thus permitting a burning to defraud prosecution to proceed after an acquittal for arson. One case under the current law, in fact, upheld convictions for both arson and secreting property to defraud another on the basis of the same acts.

Endangering a security interest is not a lesser included offense of secreting property to defraud another as a matter of law. Nor is it a lesser included offense as a matter of fact where the indictment has narrowly charged the defendant with secreting a property interest to defraud another and the facts alleged in the indictment are insufficient to establish endangering a security interest. Based on the facts alleged in the indictment and the evidence presented at trial, the trial court may appropriately deny a defendant's request to charge the jury on endangering a security interest as a lesser included offense.

B. Criminal Use of an Article with an Altered Identification Mark

Section 16-9-70 prohibits the criminal use of an article with an altered identification mark. Although the statute's title speaks in terms of an altered identification mark, its language punishes only the use of an article with a **removed** identification mark. It is unclear whether a change of one or two numbers would be within the statute's proscription. The proscription applies only to a **manufacturer's** number or identification mark. It does not apply to a number or identification affixed by a user or owner. The statute broadly defines "use," as buying, selling, receiving, disposing of, concealing, or having in one's possession such an altered article. "Article" is defined with laborious specificity as a mechanical or electrical device, appliance, contrivance, material, vessel as defined in § 52-7-3, or other piece of apparatus or equipment, other than a motor vehicle. The statute explicitly requires that the accused know that the identification mark has been removed for the purpose of concealing or destroying the identity of the article. Subsection (c) excludes from the operation of the statute alterations made in the ordinary course of business. Criminal use of an article with an altered identification mark is a felony punishable by imprisonment for one to five years.

In Brooks v. State, the Georgia Supreme Court upheld the constitutionality of § 16-9-70 against a claim that it was too vague to be enforceable.

Perhaps the key element in a § 16-9-70 prosecution is the proof of knowledge on the part of the defendant that the identification number has been removed. In Rogers v. State, the defendant asserted that such knowledge had not been proven. The court, on appeal, held that knowledge can be proven by circumstantial evidence. While this is certainly true, the court went further and described such proof as "constructive knowledge," a potentially confusing term. While there can be no doubt that the mens rea of this offense can be proven by circumstantial evidence, there also ought to be no doubt what the mens rea is—knowledge.

If by "constructive knowledge" the court means knowledge of this defendant proven by circumstantial evidence, it is correct. If, on the other hand, it defines "constructive knowledge" to mean knowledge of facts from which the defendant **ought** to have known of the situation, it is revising the legislative definition of the mens rea of the statute. A jury must be told that it must find knowledge by the defendant, but that knowledge can be proven by something other than direct testimony by the defendant that he knew. To punish defendants for what they ought to have known under the circumstances is to punish them for negligence which is not the mens rea outlined by the statute.

No clear line can yet be discerned as to what evidence is sufficient to convict under this statute. A number of reported cases have considered the question. In Rogers v. State, the evidence showed that the police found a pistol with gouge marks on the butt which obliterated the serial number. The defendant testified, with corroboration by his wife and friend, that his friend gave him the pistol as collateral for a loan and that he (the defendant) did not own the pistol. The defendant admitted noticing the scratch marks but testified that he did not know that the serial number was not on the pistol. The court held that the evidence was sufficient for the jury to conclude that the serial number had been obliterated, that it had been done for the purpose of concealing the pistol's identity, and that the defendant knew this.

On the other hand, in Blair v. State, a stereo stolen from a pawnshop was subsequently located on display in defendant's store. The testimony established that a wooden strip bearing an identification number would normally have been glued to the unit at the time it was manufactured and that this strip was no longer affixed when the stereo was recovered. There was no direct evidence that a number was affixed to the stereo at the time it was stolen from the pawnshop, except that the owner's daughter testified that she thought a number was so affixed. Although the daughter also testified that the identification numbers of all items in the shop were routinely recorded, she did not produce a number for the stereo. The court concluded that in the absence of any clear indication that the identification number was affixed to the stereo prior to its theft, there was no basis for an inference that it had been removed purposefully and reversed the conviction.

In Power v. State, the defendant testified at trial that he had purchased a rifle with an altered identification mark eight years earlier when he was approximately 15 years old, and that he knew at the time that the serial mark had been obliterated. The defendant's uncle testified that he was present at the sale of the gun and that either he or the defendant inquired of the seller why there was no identification mark on the gun. The seller told them not to worry about it. The court concluded that the evidence showed only that the defendant was aware the serial number had been removed, and that there was no evidence, direct or circumstantial, to show that he knew the serial number had been removed for the purpose of concealing the identity of the rifle. Thus, the defendant's motion for directed verdict should have been granted.

In Fulton v. State, the court held that the jury's verdict of guilty as to possession of a firearm by a convicted felon was not mutually exclusive of its verdict of not guilty regarding criminal use of an article with an altered identification mark. Prior to taking the pistol from his girl friend, the defendant had never had the pistol in his possession. The jury was authorized to find that the defendant had no knowledge that the serial number under the hand grips on the gun had been altered. Thus, the jury was authorized to acquit, because the state had failed to prove the essential elements of knowledge and intent as to the criminal use of the pistol with an altered serial number, even though possession of the pistol, itself, was proven.

Evidence showing that the defendant was arrested in possession of a weapon with the serial number removed, immediately after confronting the victim, would be sufficient to authorize a charge concerning the criminal use of an article with an altered identification mark.

C. Removal of Collars or Identifying Items or Marks from Animals

Section 16-9-71 makes it unlawful for any person without the express permission of the owner or lessee of an animal to remove a collar, tag, tattoo, or any identification mark artificially attached to or imprinted on an animal for the purposes of identification which causes or is likely to cause the loss of the animal to the owner. This offense is punishable as a misdemeanor.

D. *Vandalism to a Place of Worship*

Section 16-7-26 makes it a criminal offense maliciously to deface or desecrate a church, synagogue, or other place of public religious worship. This felony carries a penalty of imprisonment from one to five years.

E. *Criminal Interference with Government Property*

Under § 16-7-24, it is a felony, punishable by one to five years in prison, to destroy, damage, or deface government property. Additionally, it is a misdemeanor to forcibly interfere with or to obstruct the passage into or from government property. "Government property" includes all property, whether real or personal, of the federal government, the state, any political subdivision thereof, or any government agency. Government ownership of the property is an essential element of the offense that may be established by direct or circumstantial evidence.

It is likely that anyone committing the acts prohibited by § 16-7-24 would also be guilty of committing other crimes, such as theft, criminal damage to property, or criminal trespass. Nevertheless, the drafters of the code thought it desirable to have a specific statute directed to the protection of government property which would supply a needed aid to law enforcement officers.

Because the elements of interference with government property are not included in the elements required for aggravated assault, the two offenses do not merge as a matter of law.

Damaging government property may be justified under circumstances "which stand upon the same footing of reason and justice" as those defenses enumerated in the criminal code.

F. *Mutilating, Defacing, Defiling, or Abusing Contemptuously Any Publicly or Privately Owned Military Monument, Plaque, Marker, or Memorial*

Section 50-3-1(b)(1) makes it a misdemeanor for any person to mutilate, deface, defile, or abuse contemptuously any publicly owned military monument, plaque, marker, or memorial dedicated to the military personnel of this state, the United States of America or the several states thereof, or the Confederate States of America or the several states thereof. Furthermore, under this provision, it is a misdemeanor for any officer, body, or representative of state or local government or any department, agency, authority, or instrumentality thereof to remove or conceal from display any such monument, plaque, marker, or memorial for the purpose of preventing the visible display of it.

Section 50-3-1(b)(4) makes it unlawful for any person acting without authority to mutilate, deface, defile, abuse contemptuously, relocate, remove, conceal, or obscure any privately owned monument, plaque, marker, or memorial which is dedicated to, honors, or recounts the military service of any past or present military personnel of this state, the United States of America or the several states thereof, or the Confederate States of America or the several states thereof. Any person or entity who suffers injury or damages as a result of a violation of this law may bring an action individually or in a representative capacity against the person committing the violation to seek injunctive relief and to recover general and exemplary damages sustained as a result of his unlawful actions.

G. *Damaging, Injuring, or Interfering with Property of Public Utility Companies, Municipalities or Political Subdivisions*

Section 16-7-25 prohibits any person from intentionally and without authority injuring or destroying any apparatus (including, but not limited to, meters, pipes, conduits, wires, lines, posts, or lamps) belonging to a company or political subdivision engaged in the manufacture or sale of electricity, water, gas, telephone, or other public services. The statute also prohibits anyone from intentionally preventing a meter from properly registering the quantity of service supplied; interfering with the proper action of such company or political subdivision; intentionally diverting any services of such company or political subdivision; or intentionally using or causing to be used any service manufactured, sold or distributed by such company or political subdivision without its consent.

The statute creates a presumption which will force defendants to produce evidence. Subsection (b) creates a rebuttable presumption of liability against the person who, with knowledge of the tampering or diversion, receives the benefit of the service without proper charge. This portion of the statute may be in conflict with § 16-2-6 which provides that a person will not be presumed to act with criminal intention and juries ought to be informed of permissible inferences which can be drawn instead of in terms of a presumption.

The Court of Appeals in Dougherty v. State cited both § 16-7-25 and § 16-2-6 but did not discuss the apparent conflict. Instead, the court merely announced that the evidence was sufficient to establish the requisite intent for a conviction under § 16-7-25. The evidence showed that the defendant's power service was disconnected and the meter sealed. Approximately five weeks later, police found the meter unsealed with a load on it and the lights and television turned on in defendant's house. The defendant denied playing the television set but admitted using electrical power on that date.

Violation of § 16-7-25 is a misdemeanor and, as such, is subject to the provisions of the general misdemeanor punishment section.

H. Injuring, Tearing Down or Destruction of Mailboxes; Injuring, Defacing or Destruction of Mail

Section 16-7-27 prohibits the willful destruction or injury of mail receptacles or mail. Since its enactment, no reported cases have considered it. On its face, however, it would appear to be a lesser included offense of criminal trespass as proscribed by § 16-7-21(a). Furthermore, it may be preempted by federal law governing the postal service.

Violation of § 16-7-27 is a misdemeanor, punishable under the general misdemeanor statute.

I. Litter Prevention and Abatement

1. Littering

Section 16-7-43(b) makes it a misdemeanor to litter on public or private property. In addition to imposing punishment under the general misdemeanor statute, the court may direct the violator to pick up and remove his and other litter from the public street, highway, or right of way upon which he has deposited litter or may direct him to pick up and remove any and all litter from any public beach, public park, or private right of way.

O.C.G.A. § 16-7-43(g) also makes it a misdemeanor to willfully obstruct, resist, impede, or interfere with any person appointed to enforce this state's litter prevention law or local littering ordinances or to retaliate or discriminate in any manner against this person as a reprisal for any act or omission.

Section 16-7-47(d) makes it a misdemeanor for any person to dump any refuse or other material into a container other than household garbage, if a local government has clearly marked that container for "household garbage only." It is also a misdemeanor for any person to set fire to the contents of, indiscriminately scatter or disperse the contents of, or otherwise vandalize any containers provided by a local government for the dumping of trash or garbage.

2. Egregious Littering

Section 16-7-52 makes it unlawful for any person to intentionally dump egregious litter, unless authorized to do so by law or by a duly issued permit, (1) in or on any public highway, road, street, alley, or thoroughfare, including any portion of the right of way thereof, or on any other public lands except in containers or areas lawfully provided for such dumping; (2) in or on any fresh-water lake, river, canal, or stream or tidal or coastal water of the state; or (3) in or on any private property, unless prior consent of the owner has been given and unless such dumping will not adversely affect the public health and is not in violation of any other state law, rule, or regulation.

Under § 16-7-53, egregious littering is punishable either as a misdemeanor of a high and aggravated nature or as a felony depending upon type of litter involved. Each day a continuing violation occurs constitutes a separate violation.

3. Placement of Posters, Signs, or Advertisements

Section 16-7-58 makes it a misdemeanor to place posters, signs, or advertisements (1) on any public property or building or on any private property unless the owner or the occupier as authorized by the owner has given permission to place the posters, signs, or advertisements on the property or (2) on any property zoned for commercial or industrial uses if the placement of such posters, signs, or advertisements conflicts with any zoning laws or ordinances.

Any poster, sign, or advertisement placed in violation of § 16-7-58 constitutes a public nuisance, and the officials having jurisdiction of the public property or building, including without limitation law enforcement officers, may remove or direct the removal of the same.

Each poster, sign, or advertisement placed in violation of § 16-7-58 constitutes a separate offense.

J. Criminal Trespass by Motor Vehicles

Acts 1990, p. 2048, eff. Jan. 1, 1991, repealed § 16-7-29 which prohibited criminal trespass by motor vehicles. However, this same Act enacted a similar Code section at § 40-6-252.

K. Tampering with Operation of Electronic Monitoring Devices

In 2004, the General Assembly found that because of prison and jail overcrowding and the high cost of incarceration electronic monitoring devices, under appropriate conditions and limitations, would provide cost effective alternatives to, or bridges to and from, incarceration. Moreover, it found that these devices would offer effective means to track offenders and might reduce criminal recidivism.

Section 16-7-29 is designed to encourage the use of electronic monitoring devices while at the same time discourage interference with these devices. This Code section provides that it is a felony punishable by not less than one nor more than five years for any person to knowingly and without authority remove, destroy, or circumvent the operation of an electronic monitoring device which is being used for the purpose of monitoring a person who is complying with a home arrest program as set forth in § 42-1-8 or who is wearing the device as a condition of bond or pretrial release, probation, or parole. It is likewise a felony for any person to knowingly and without authority request or solicit any other person to remove, destroy, or circumvent the operation of an electronic monitoring device which is being used for these purposes.

RAPE

See also ASSAULT; MISTAKE DEFENSE; SEXUAL OFFENSES AGAINST CHILDREN.

I. Generally

Defined as the carnal knowledge of a woman, forcibly and against her will, rape is one of the few sex-specific offenses in the criminal code. For that reason it is unusual, but it is peculiar for other reasons as well. It is one of very few crimes in which nonconsent is an element of the offense. Moreover, until legislation in 1976 overturned prior law, the complainant's reputation for chastity was admissible on the issue of whether she consented to the intercourse on the occasion in question, and prior specific acts of sexual intercourse with men other than the defendant were held admissible for that purpose as well. The latter rule was based on a belief that a woman's consent to the sexual advances of one man implies her consent to those of another. The fear that a vindictive woman's lies would result in the conviction of an innocent man also accounted for the now repealed statutory proviso which required corroborating evidence to support a rape conviction.

Another result of the definition of rape as a crime which can be committed only by men against women is that the statute is subject to constitutional attack as gender-based discrimination violative of the Equal Protection Clause of the Fourteenth Amendment. Several such attacks, one of which was successful, have been brought against sex-specific rape and statutory rape statutes in past years. The Georgia Supreme Court, however, has upheld § 16-6-1 against an Equal Protection attack, finding that the statute serves important public interests in protecting women from "physical injury, psychological trauma and possible pregnancy." Even though the rape statute is designed to punish male offenders, it is clear that a woman can be convicted of rape if she aids or abets in the commission of the crime.

II. Elements

The prosecution must show three elements to prove a case of rape: (1) carnal knowledge, (2) force, and (3) lack of consent.

A. Carnal Knowledge or Penetration

Section 16-6-1 defines carnal knowledge as "any penetration of the female sex organ by the male sex organ." The cases make clear that the statute is to be read literally here; any penetration, however slight, is sufficient to constitute this element of the offense and may be proved by indirect or circumstantial evidence, as well as direct evidence. However, the evidence must show that the victim's vagina was penetrated by a male sex organ. Thus, evidence that shows that the victim had been sexually molested by the insertion of a wedge-shaped object into her vagina does not show such penetration. Although in most cases the state will introduce medical evidence of penetration, there is authority that the victim's testimony that the defendant "raped" her is sufficient to show that penetration did, in fact, occur. Other than the penetration of the female sex organ by the male sex organ, the infliction of physical injury is not an element of the offense of rape. Also, ejaculation is not an element of rape, and it is not necessary that the examining physician find semen in the victim's body.

A person who aids and abets in the commission of a rape is a party to the rape and may be charged and convicted of rape even though he did not actually have sexual intercourse with the victim.

B. Force

Although force and lack of consent are clearly two separate elements of the crime of rape and the older cases emphasized the distinction between the two, analysis of each is intertwined with the other. The older cases required the state to prove the use of such physical force as was necessary to overcome the victim's resistance to the defendant's attack. It is clear today, however, that the element of force will be proven if the defendant's words or acts were sufficient to instill in the victim a reasonable apprehension of bodily harm, violence, or other dangerous consequences to herself or others.

In 1977, the Georgia Supreme Court differentiated between the elements of force and lack of consent in forcible rape cases involving underage victims by holding that lack of consent, but not force, was established by proof of the victim's age. Thus, force was a necessary element of common-law or forcible rape against an underage victim. The state was required to prove this element by acts of force or mental coercion rather than by presuming force as a matter of law based on the victim's age. In 1998, the Georgia Supreme Court reaffirmed its holding but found that there was a troubling inconsistency in the way our law dealt with forcible rape and other sexual offenses when the victim was a young child. At common law, rape included consensual relations with a female under ten years of age. As the legal age of consent increased, however, it became necessary in rape cases to distinguish between different categories of underage females. Since a presumption of force supplied by the victim's age would apply to all categories of underage females, even sexually active teenagers, it was abandoned. Such a presumption would not only have ignored the wide variety of factual situations in rape cases but would have been contrary to the trend in criminal law to create meaningful grading distinctions among the different forms of the offense. Yet the abandonment of this presumption left young victims of rape without the same protection the presumption still afforded young victims of other sexual offenses. In order to resolve this inconsistency, the Georgia Supreme Court urged the General Assembly to enact an additional definition of forcible rape which would provide that a man is guilty of rape if "the female is less than 10 years old." In 1999, the General Assembly did as the court urged and changed the definition of rape to provide that a person commits the offense of rape when he has carnal knowledge of "[a] female who is less than ten years of age." The General Assembly intended this phrase to refer only to chronological age, not to overall cognitive age or overall age equivalence. Enacting this definition reestablishes the common-law rule and the common-sense principle that sexual intercourse with a female under ten years of age is a forcible act constituting rape as a matter of law. This enactment overrules the Georgia Supreme Court's holding to the extent that it applies to females who are less than ten years of age. Where the victim is ten years of age or older but under the age of consent, the state still cannot presume the element of force as a matter of law but must prove it as a factual matter. Actual force against the victim may be proved by circumstantial evidence.

In a rape case involving a victim rendered insensible by sleep or intoxication, only constructive force, i.e., the force that is necessary to effect the penetration, need be shown to satisfy the force requirement. Where there is evidence of the victim's excessive alcohol consumption at the time of the rape, a jury instruction on constructive force would be authorized.

C. Lack of Consent

The former requirement of proof that the victim's nonconsent be evidenced by physical resistance with all her strength until completion of the act by the defendant has given way to the more realistic requirement that the victim must not have freely consented to the intercourse. In fact, the victim need not have physically resisted at all, if fear or intimidation was the reason for failure to do so.

The victim's testimony that the sexual acts were committed against her will would be sufficient to support the defendant's conviction of rape, the issue of her credibility being for the jury to decide. In order to determine whether the alleged victim freely consented to the intercourse, the question is not whether the victim's testimony as to her lack of consent is reasonable; nor is it whether the victim's apprehension was reasonable. The question is whether the state has proved, beyond a reasonable doubt, that the acts of the accused were not freely consented to by the alleged victim. This is a question of fact for the jury to decide. The jury is entitled to reject the defendant's claim of a consensual sexual encounter and accept the victim's testimony depicting nonconsensual, forcible intercourse.

In a rape case involving an underage victim, the victim's lack of consent is established by proof that she was under the age of consent.

If the victim is rendered insensible at the time of the attack by sleep, intoxication, or mental incompetence, she is incapable of consent and its absence need not be shown. Indeed, there is nothing in § 16-6-1 which precludes a finding of rape if the victim is not alive at the moment of penetration.

When the victim is a mentally incapacitated adult incapable of giving valid consent to a sexual act, the principle mandating that force be proved is simply not applicable. The issue for the jury to decide in such a case is whether the victim was capable of knowingly and intelligently consenting to sexual intercourse. Thus, notwithstanding the lack of evidence of force, evidence of the victim's inability to give proper consent to sexual intercourse would be sufficient to authorize the jury to convict the defendant of rape.

Evidence of the victim's physical or mental condition before or at the time of the commission of the offense is admissible insofar as it bears on the question of consent.

III. Evidence

A. Corroboration

The traditional rules of evidence in rape cases reflect a lack of confidence in the victim's credibility and great concern that innocent defendants will be convicted. The corroboration requirement repealed in 1978 was one of the devices used to guard against the possibility that a jury would be unfairly swayed by the complaint of a vengeful woman. Until July 1, 1978, § 16-6-1 provided that "no conviction shall be had on the unsupported testimony of the female." Prior to the requirement's deletion from the statute, the Georgia Supreme Court had consistently held, however, that a complaint of rape was sufficiently corroborated if some evidence, other than the victim's testimony, tended to prove that the crime had been committed. It was not necessary that the supportive evidence either connect the defendant to the crime or show beyond a reasonable doubt that the crime was committed.

The deletion of the corroboration requirement was attacked as an unconstitutional shift of the burden of proof in Tucker v. State. In Tucker, the defendant argued that the amended statute permits a mere allegation by the victim to place the burden of proof on the defendant in violation of the Due Process Clause. The court rejected the argument, pointing out that the state still had the burden of proving beyond a reasonable doubt all the elements of the crime. The statute merely defines what would be sufficient; it does not require a conviction or place any ultimate burden on the defendant. It should be noted that the corroboration requirement remains in the statutory rape statute. There is not and has never been any requirement that the testimony of the victim of an attempted forcible rape be corroborated.

Apparently, the corroboration of a rape victim's testimony still may be necessary where the victim testifies that the acts were committed forcibly and against her will and the defendant testifies that the acts were all with the victim's consent.

Evidence of a purported rape victim's state of mind following the attack may corroborate her claim that she was raped.

B. Victim's Prior Sexual Behavior

1. Exclusionary Rule Prior to Rape Shield Statute

A second evidentiary device traditionally used to protect against the conviction of innocent defendants was the admission of evidence of the victim's prior sexual misconduct both to prove the victim's consent as well as to impeach her testimony generally. This was formerly permitted as an exception to the Code provision that the general character of the parties and their conduct in other transactions are irrelevant. The use of the victim's prior sexual misconduct to impeach her testimony was premised on the belief that an unchaste woman lacks the general traits of truth and veracity. Its use to show consent was based on the belief that consent to one man's advances implies consent to another's. In 1974, the Georgia Supreme Court rejected both of these traditional rationales in Lynn v. State, holding that evidence of specific acts of prior sexual intercourse with men other than the defendant was inadmissible either for impeachment or for the purpose of showing consent.

2. Rape Shield Statute

In 1976, the Georgia General Assembly enacted what is commonly described as the Rape Shield Statute (§ 24-2-3), thereby modifying the scope of Lynn's exclusionary rule. Defining the complaining witness's "past sexual behavior" as including, but not being limited to, evidence of her (1) marital history, (2) mode of dress, and (3) general reputation for promiscuity, nonchastity, or sexual mores contrary to the community standards, the General Assembly generally forbade the introduction of such evidence in rape prosecutions.

The 1976 Rape Shield Statute contained two exceptions to its exclusionary rule. The past sexual behavior of the complaining witness was not admissible unless the trial court (1) found that the past sexual behavior directly involved the participation of the accused or (2) found that the evidence expected to be introduced supported an inference that the defendant could have reasonably believed that the complaining witness consented to the conduct complained of in the prosecution.

In 1989, the General Assembly amended subsection (b) of the statute by substituting the word "and" for the word "or." This amendment, which reduced the two exceptions to one, strengthened the Rape Shield Statute's exclusionary rule by narrowing the range of admissible evidence of a complaining witness's alleged past sexual behavior. The current exception in subsection (b) has been construed to relate only to past sexual behavior involving the complaining witness and the accused. Now, in order for evidence of a complaining witness's past sexual behavior to be introduced under subsection (b), it must directly involve the accused **and** support an inference that the accused reasonably believed the complaining witness consented.

In addition to the amendment to subsection (b), the General Assembly in 1989 created another very limited exception in paragraph (2) of subsection (c). Under this exception, evidence is admissible if it "is so highly material that it will substantially support a conclusion that the accused reasonably believed that the complaining witness consented to the conduct complained of and that justice mandates the admission of such evidence." Evidence introduced under this exception need not relate to prior behavior between the complaining witness and the accused. However, before evidence of the complaining witness's prior behavior may be introduced, the accused must show some connection between the prior behavior and himself. This connection may be shown by evidence of any behavior or verbal exchange that concerned the accused, by evidence of behavior that related to the incident at issue, or by evidence of behavior that could legitimately be claimed to have prompted a belief in consent on the occasion at issue.

The exceptions within the statute may seem to threaten to swallow up the general rule of inadmissibility. Prior to Lynn and the statute, the defendant was traditionally seeking to introduce the sexual history of the complaining witness for the purpose of showing consent, and the exceptions appear to permit the introduction of this same evidence for the same purpose. Thus, it might seem that the exceptions return the law to its pre-Lynn status. This is not true, however, for two reasons.

First, while the evidence is admissible to show consent (or at least to show a mistake of fact which is a defense under § 16-3-5), the statute, in requiring the defense to notify the judge of its intent to introduce such evidence and in requiring an in camera hearing before the jury hears the evidence, eliminates the possibility that a jury will hear prejudicial evidence concerning the complaining witness's past sexual history and then later be told to ignore it because an insufficient amount of evidence has been introduced. Second, and more importantly, the evidence of past sexual misconduct must be such as to support a belief **on the part of the defendant** that the complaining witness was consenting. Thus, no longer will the jury be able simply to rely on an inference that those who have consented before have consented again. For example, if the complaining witness has a reputation for unchastity in the community, it would seem that the defendant would at least have to demonstrate that he knew of such a reputation before such evidence possibly could be admitted under either exception. Indeed, cases under the statute indicate such evidence may not be admitted even with such a demonstration. Without such a linkage to the defendant, it is hard to conceive of how this evidence could show a belief on the defendant's part that the complaining witness was consenting.

Because of the danger of a jury inferring from any evidence of past sexual misconduct by the complaining witness that she consented to the sexual intercourse at issue, the statute does not permit the introduction of the evidence directly to the jury. Before such introduction is permitted, the defense must notify the judge of its intent to introduce such evidence, and the judge in an in camera proceeding must be convinced that the evidence is sufficient to show the complaining witness's past sexual involvement with the defendant and to support an inference of the complaining witness's consent. Only after the judge finds that any of the evidence introduced at the hearing is admissible under the statute, or is so highly material that it will substantially support a conclusion that the accused reasonably believed that the complaining witness consented to the conduct complained of and that justice mandates the admission of such evidence, will the jury hear the evidence. This statute provides the exclusive means for admitting evidence relating to the past sexual behavior of the complaining witness in prosecutions for rape.

The introduction of evidence prohibited by the Rape Shield Statute gives the trial court grounds to find manifest necessity for a mistrial. Thus, a single unanswered question by defense counsel about the victim's sexual history may alone give rise to the manifest necessity for a mistrial.

3. Case Law Under Rape Shield Statute

While the 1989 amendment to the Rape Shield Statute changes the standard for admitting evidence of the victim's past sexual behavior, the procedure to be followed and the types of cases covered by the statute remain unchanged. For this reason, most of the prior case law still applies. However, the discussion of the case law that follows should be read in light of the 1989 amendment.

In its initial application of the 1976 Rape Shield Statute, the Court of Appeals indicated that it would be construed very strictly against a defendant who sought to use one of the statutory exceptions. In Johnson v. State, the defendant sought to introduce testimony from two men that they had previously had sexual intercourse with the victim. Defense counsel claimed that this was proper impeachment testimony to counter the victim's statement, in response to questioning on direct and cross-examination, that she was a virgin at the time of the incident and had told the defendant so. Upholding the trial court's refusal even to hold a hearing on the admissibility of such evidence, the court held that this evidence could not fit within the consent exception. While the court's ruling could be explained by the fact that there was no evidence linking the past sexual behavior with the defendant's knowledge so that it could support an inference of consent in his mind, the court's language was much more broad. Its reasoning was that the evidence was inadmissible because the purpose of the Rape Shield Statute was to eliminate the reasoning that "if she did it once, she did it again." The court did not admit the possibility that if the defendant was aware of such prior behavior he reasonably might have inferred consent on the victim's part.

In its second treatment of the 1976 Rape Shield Statute, the Court of Appeals again upheld the refusal of a trial court to admit evidence of past sexual behavior by the victim. In Parks v. State, the defendant offered testimony by the defendant's and the victim's co-worker that the co-worker had had sexual relations with the victim on the one date he had had with her after knowing her for eight months. The court held that this was not admissible under the consent exception because "[n]othing remotely suggests that the defendant could, except as the result of an attack of megalomania, have inferred from these facts that the victim would consent to his sexual demands." Again, no specific mention was made as to whether the evidence might show that the defendant was aware of the prior sexual behavior.

Evidence of the defendant's knowledge or awareness of the victim's prior sexual behavior, which could have supported a reasonable belief that the victim consented to the conduct complained of, was admissible under the consent exception of the 1976 Rape Shield Statute. Lack of such knowledge rendered evidence of the victim's prior sexual behavior inadmissible. For example, in Lamar v. State, the defendant sought to introduce evidence of the victim's sexual experience. The court affirmed the trial court's refusal to admit the evidence. The trial testimony showed that the two had met only an hour before the rape. The court said that the prior behavior could not have involved the defendant, thereby excluding the first statutory exception. As for the consent exception, the court said that "in that short time, it is unlikely that the appellant would discover any past sexual activity on the part of his youthful victim that could justify his claim that she consented to intercourse." Likewise, in Burley v. State, the defendant testified that the complainant told him that she was having some unspecified "marital problems." The court affirmed the trial court's refusal to admit evidence of the complainant's prior marital problems and held that the defendant's "lack of knowledge that the victim's marital problem related to infidelity could have had no reasonable bearing on whether the victim would consent to the conduct complained of." Also, in Jones v. State, the court affirmed the trial court's refusal to introduce evidence offered by the defendant to show that the victim had engaged in sexual intercourse with three young men, because the defendant had no knowledge of the alleged conduct between the victim and three young men.

This type of evidence now comes within the exception carved out in paragraph (2) of subsection (c) of the present Rape Shield Statute. However, the evidence is more circumscribed than it was formerly, as it now must be "so highly material that it will substantially support" a finding that the defendant reasonably believed that the victim consented to the conduct complained of and it must be such that "justice mandates the admission of such evidence."

There must be sufficient evidence of the victim's past sexual behavior and of the defendant's awareness of the details of that behavior in order to qualify for the exceptions set out in the present Rape Shield Statute. In Postell v. State, the court affirmed the trial court's conclusion that the evidence was insufficient to qualify for those exceptions. The only evidence proffered by the defendant at the hearing was that, prior to the incident at issue, the victim told the defendant she had been previously raped, and that she may have contracted an infection as a result. There was no evidence that the defendant was made aware of the details of the previous rape.

The exception in subsection (b) of the present Rape Shield Statute relates only to past sexual behavior involving the defendant and the victim. In Smith v. State, the court held that the trial court did not err in refusing to allow evidence regarding the victim's alleged past sexual behavior. The witness' testimony that the victim had offered him sexual favors in exchange for drugs or money could not support any inference that the defendant reasonably believed that the victim consented to sexual intercourse because it did not refer to any past sexual behavior involving the victim and the defendant, and because the defendant did not even know about the alleged incident until after he had been charged with the rape. Also, the defendant testified during the in camera hearing that he was unaware of the victim's reputation for offering sex in exchange for drugs. In Hicks v. State, the court held that the trial court did not err by excluding portions of a conversation between the defendant and the victim immediately prior to and during the course of the alleged criminal acts. The conversation involved the victim's past sexual abuse by others and her emotional problems as a result of the abuse. The past sexual abuse did not involve the defendant, and he admitted that he had not met the victim prior to the date of the assault.

The exception in subsection (b) is applicable only if both of its requirements are satisfied. The victim's past sexual behavior must not only directly involve the defendant; it must also support an inference that the defendant reasonably believed the victim consented. In Larocque v. State, the court held that the trial court properly excluded evidence of the victim's past sexual relationship with the defendant, including their mutual participation in "rough sex." Although the victim's past sexual behavior did directly involve the defendant, the trial court concluded that the defendant's offer of proof did not support an inference that the defendant could have reasonably believed that the victim consented to the conduct complained of in the case. Thus, the exception in subsection (b) was not applicable. In Davis v. State, the trial court concluded that the defendant had no reason to believe the victim had consented to sex, even if she had done so previously as the defendant alleged, inasmuch as she was beaten and had to run naked through the woods for help. In light of this evidence, the defendant's claim of prior consensual sex with the victim did not support an inference that he could have reasonably believed she consented on the night of the offense. Accordingly, the trial court did not abuse its discretion by excluding evidence of prior sexual activity between the defendant and the victim.

While the defense is allowed under the Rape Shield Statute to present evidence of the past sexual relationship between the parties, it is not allowed to present evidence about the relationship which injects an improper element of emotionalism into the case. In Cook v. State, the defense was allowed to present evidence of the past sexual relationship between the defendant and the victim and evidence of the argument which preceded the rape but was not allowed to present evidence of the substance of that argument, i.e., the victim's decision to have an abortion. The court held that the defendant was not denied an opportunity to present evidence of his sole defense. The trial court did not prohibit him from explaining his presence in the victim's home or his subsequent act to console her. However, since evidence of the abortion only injected an improper element of emotionalism into the case, the trial court properly ruled that this evidence was irrelevant to the issue of consent.

In Singleton v. State, the court held that the Rape Shield Statute applies by its terms to "any prosecution for rape" and, therefore, excludes such evidence from all parts of the trial. The defendants had asserted that the victim's prior sexual behavior was admissible as relevant in mitigation of punishment. The court responded that "the philosophy behind the appellants' argument is precisely that which the statute seeks to eliminate, i.e., that women of promiscuous sexual reputation are entitled to less protection under the rape laws than women of chaste reputation."

A defendant desiring to introduce evidence of the victim's past sexual behavior must comply with the procedure outlined in the Rape Shield Statute for that evidence to be admissible. In Tenant v. State, the defendant complained that certain evidence concerning the victim's past sexual behavior was admissible and that the trial judge wrongfully excluded it. The court rejected the claim because the defendant had not followed the statutory procedure for the introduction of such evidence. The Rape Shield Statute requires the defendant to give prior notice to the trial judge of his intention to use the evidence, whereupon the trial judge shall conduct an in camera hearing to focus on the defendant's offer of proof. The defendant had not given such notice to the trial judge and did not request an in camera hearing to determine if such evidence was admissible. In Tremble v. State, the defendant asked the victim on cross-examination to explain the fact that dark brown caucasian pubic hairs were found on her which were inconsistent with her own. The defendant in the case was black and the victim caucasian. The court found that the trial court properly excluded this evidence because the defendant sought to introduce testimony concerning the past sexual behavior of the victim and the statutory procedure for such introduction had not been complied with. In Banks v. State, while the defendant did give the trial court prior notice of his intent to introduce evidence of prior sexual relations with the victim, he failed to include certain evidence in his proffer. At no time did he proffer that the treating nurse would testify that the victim admitted to a prior act of voluntary intercourse. The defendant completely bypassed the procedural safeguards by failing to give any notice of an intent to ask the nurse about the sexual history contained in the admissions report. The court held that this failure rendered any reference to the statement inadmissible.

The state is not allowed under the Rape Shield Statute to argue or introduce evidence that the victim was a virgin at the time of the attack. In Herndon v. State, the court held that evidence that the victim was a virgin, that is, that she had not had prior sexual relations, was inadmissible. Thus, it was erroneous for the trial court to allow statements about the victim's virginity during the prosecutor's opening statement and during the examining physician's testimony. Although any evidence of physical injuries the victim received during the commission of the rape, including the condition of the hymen, would be admissible, for the prosecutor and the examining physician to call the victim a "virgin" would be to comment on her prior sexual history needlessly. Nonetheless, the court found the trial court's error to be harmless because the evidence against the defendant was overwhelming. In Veal v. State, the court held it was harmless error for the trial court to deny the defendant's motion in limine to preclude the rape victim from testifying that during the attack she told the defendant she was a virgin. Since the Rape Shield Statute provides the exclusive means for admitting this type of evidence in rape cases, the court held that it was error for the trial court to admit this testimony as part of the res gestae. However, the defendant was not harmed by this error, since the Rape Shield Statute protects the rape victim, not the accused, from admission of this type of evidence. Moreover, the defendant's defense was based upon a claim of mistaken identity, not alleged consent by the victim.

Evidence of the victim's motherhood is inadmissible under the Rape Shield Statute. The only possible desired inference arising from the victim's motherhood is that, because she had had prior sexual experience with someone other than the defendant, she consented to his indecent liberties on this occasion. Such inference is clearly prohibited under the statute and does not come within any exception under subsection (b).

In an important case, the Georgia Supreme Court held that certain testimony was not covered by the Rape Shield Statute, and thus, its exclusion by the trial court was reversible error. In Villafranco v. State, the defendants sought to introduce evidence that shortly before they met the complaining witness on the night of the alleged crime, she had told her friend that she wanted to go to a party to see if she could "get some nookey." They claimed that this evidence was relevant to her state of mind at the time of the admitted sexual intercourse with the defendants, which they claimed was consensual. The state argued to the trial court that this was evidence of prior sexual behavior which was not admissible under either exception of subsection (b) of the 1976 Rape Shield Statute.

The Georgia Supreme Court held that the exclusion of the evidence was erroneous. The court pointed out that the statement was made very close to the time of the sexual intercourse. Equally important, according to the court, was the fact that the victim was constant in her desire to go to a party. The court held that it was relevant to the question of the victim's state of mind and was not evidence of prior sexual behavior.

Like the holding in Villafranco v. State, the Court of Appeals in Raines v. State, held that certain evidence was relevant to the question of the victim's state of mind and was not evidence of prior sexual behavior. In Raines, the court held that the victim's testimony regarding her prior rape was relevant to explain her contemporaneous state of mind and conduct in failing to physically resist the defendant. The court also held that the victim's testimony was not barred under the Rape Shield Statute, because that provision precludes the introduction of evidence of the victim's past sexual behavior, and a prior rape committed against the victim has nothing whatsoever to do with her past sexual behavior. Although evidence regarding a victim's prior rape is admissible for the purpose approved in Raines, such evidence is not admissible to support a defendant's argument that the prior rape was not rape, but consensual sexual behavior, and that therefore it would be reasonable to infer that the victim consented to the present conduct.

In *Taylor v. State*, the defendant sought to introduce evidence of the victim's subsequent rape in order to show that the lack of injury to the victim's hymen following the alleged incidents with the defendant would have made it less likely that those incidents occurred. The court held that the trial court properly excluded the evidence based on its finding that no evidence showed that the later rape of the victim by her father was similar in force or penetration to the acts perpetrated by the defendant and, therefore, that the injury to the hymen from the later rape was not probative of showing whether the defendant had earlier engaged in sexual intercourse with the victim. Moreover, since no exception to the Rape Shield Statute applied, the court held that inquiry into the victim's sexual history was properly foreclosed.

Evidence of the victim's religious beliefs pertaining to sexual intercourse outside of marriage may be relevant to the question of the victim's state of mind. In Postell v. State, the Court of Appeals indicated that evidence that the victim told the defendant she could not have sexual intercourse with him because her church taught that it was wrong would be admissible to show the victim's state of mind on the issue of consent. However, additional evidence that had no purpose other than to create the inference that the victim had conducted herself in a chaste manner in accordance with those religious beliefs would not be admissible under the Rape Shield Statute.

The Georgia Supreme Court, in Villafranco v. State, held that the trial court erroneously excluded evidence of statements made by the victim to a co-worker before the incident that she never wore underpants. The victim had testified at trial that she was wearing underpants on the night of the incident. The testimony of the victim's co-worker was offered to impeach the victim's testimony and corroborate the testimony of one of the defendants that the victim was not wearing underpants on the night in question. The court held that the "rape shield law is not applicable to evidence offered to impeach the prosecution's principal witness as to her mode of dress at the time in question."

In reaching its conclusion that the evidence was admissible, the Georgia Supreme Court referred favorably to a concurring opinion in an earlier Court of Appeals case, Parks v. State, which argued that the right of impeachment "is inviolable and should never be abridged." The court noted only that it was applying the principle espoused by the earlier concurrence "under the facts of this case." It is submitted that a broad application of such an exception to the Rape Shield Statute would threaten the statute's very existence and efficacy.

Cross-examination about a victim's motive for lying, after the defendant has made a proffer which directly contradicts the victim's prior testimony, has been held to be reasonable cross-examination, but the defendant must first satisfy the requirements of the Rape Shield Statute. In Gibbs v. State, the only proffer made by the defendant concerning the victim's possible pregnancy as a motive for lying was his defense counsel's mere statement, and this statement was found to be unavailing for purposes of meeting the requirements of the Rape Shield Statute. In Green v. State, the evidence the defendant sought to introduce was precisely the type of irrelevant, prejudicial evidence the Rape Shield Statute was intended to exclude. Evidence that the 13-year-old victim had engaged in sexual activity with other males might have inflamed or impassioned the jury and would have done little, if anything, to support the defendant's theory that the victim falsely accused him of rape in order to explain a pregnancy. Moreover, the evidence showed that the victim could not have been pregnant at the time she reported the rape. In Griffin v. State, the defendant sought to cross-examine the victim regarding her relationship with the chief assistant district attorney because that relationship might have affected her motives, biases, and interests in testifying. The court held that evidence of such behavior was inadmissible under the Rape Shield Statute. Evidence concerning a romantic relationship between the victim and the recused prosecuting attorney would not have contributed materially to the guilt or innocence of the defendant as to the incident at issue but rather would have injected irrelevant and prejudicial matter. In McIntosh v. State, the defendant sought during cross-examination to impeach the victim on her statement that she was taking medication during the time of the rape because someone close to her had died. The court disagreed with the defendant's assertion that the Rape Shield Statute did not protect the victim in this instance because her explanation was "specious" and, therefore, subject to challenge. The court found that the trial court did not abuse its discretion by determining that an inquiry into the facts regarding this issue was not relevant to the case. Indeed, it was apparent that the true purpose of eliciting such testimony was to show the jury that the victim had been involved with three men within a seven-month period, which was clearly prohibited under the Rape Shield Statute.

Insofar as the permissible scope of cross-examination in a rape prosecution is concerned, § 24-2-3(a) only bars evidence regarding the **sexual** aspects of a prior relationship. Evidence merely that the victim has or had a romantic relationship with another man would not reflect on her character for sexual behavior. Therefore, so long as the defense confines its questioning to the non-sexual nature of the victim's former relationships, the Rape Shield Statute would not be a basis for curtailing its cross-examination of the victim. Applying this construction of the statute in Richardson v. State, the Georgia Supreme Court held that because the defense's proposed inquiry was confined to the existence of a relationship with an ex-boyfriend and whether the desire to reestablish that relationship was a motive to make a false claim of rape, the trial court erred in relying upon the statute to preclude the defense from cross-examining the victim in this regard.

Several Court of Appeals cases make clear that the Rape Shield Statute will exclude not only direct questioning concerning the victim's prior sexual behavior, but also indirect questioning. In Myers v. State, the defendant sought to introduce testimony by a defense witness that the victim had a reputation for "partying." The trial court excluded this evidence and the Court of Appeals affirmed, concluding that the "only possible relevance of such evidence would rest upon the innuendo that 'partying' equates to prior sexual behavior." Likewise, in Grant v. State, the defendant asked the victim on cross-examination whether she had gonorrhea at the time of the alleged rape. The trial court sustained an objection to the question on the basis of the Rape Shield Statute and was affirmed on appeal. The court rejected the defendant's theory of defense which asserted that this question was designed to impeach the victim's claim that the rapist gave her gonorrhea. Despite that theory, the court pointed out that there were only two exceptions to the 1976 Rape Shield Statute (prior sex with the defendant and evidence of consent) and neither was met in this case. However, in White v. State, the Court of Appeals agreed with the defendant's argument that the excluded medical testimony regarding an infectious discharge discovered in the victim's body within hours after the alleged rape was not evidence of the victim's past sexual behavior in violation of the Rape Shield Statute but was relevant to the defendant's claim that he did not penetrate the victim because of the victim's gross physical condition. The testimony was also admissible to impeach the victim's claim that she was not diagnosed with vaginal infections after the alleged rape and to challenge the victim's claim that the defendant was the cause of her vaginal infections. Similarly, in Reece v. State, the defendant objected to the evidence introduced by the state in that it implied and suggested that the defendant had given the victim a venereal or vaginal disease and that he therefore committed the crimes charged. The court held that the defendant should have been allowed, in a proper fashion, to show by his wife's medical records, or otherwise, that his wife was then undergoing medical treatment and tests for pregnancy and showed no sign of this disease, and therefore, by logical extension, that the defendant did not have the disease. The court held that allowing this vital defense to be put forward did not offend the Rape Shield Statute, even if it might suggest by deduction that if the defendant did not have the disease, and did not transmit it to the victim, then someone else might have done so.

In Gibbs v. State, the defendant sought to impeach the victim through her cross-examination, plus that of the doctor to the effect that she said the defendant raped her on additional occasions. His sole intention was to "attack the credibility of the victim," to cause a reasonable doubt that the incidents in the indictment even happened. The Court of Appeals held that the trial court properly disallowed this evidence since the defendant did not seek to invoke either one of the statutory exceptions of the 1976 Rape Shield Statute and since evidence of rape, not being consensual sexual behavior, was not admissible under the statute.

In Martin v. State, the defendant sought to introduce evidence concerning photographs and intimate letters written by the victim to her husband while he was incarcerated at a correctional institution, as a way "to attack the victim's credibility." This evidence would have illustrated the purported similarities between the vivid sexual descriptions the victim had depicted in her letters and the victim's details of the lewd words and sexual activities of the defendant, and it would have allowed the defendant to show that the victim was not a "sweet, innocent thing." The court held that because the defendant failed to show a valid purpose for this evidence, it was properly excluded under the present Rape Shield Statute.

In Sweeney v. State, the defendant sought to introduce evidence that the victim had recorded a phone-sex-tape. The court held that evidence of a prior sex tape made by the victim did not support an inference that the defendant could have reasonably believed the victim consented to the attempted sexual intercourse. In fact, the defendant's defense was not that of consent but that the attempted rape never happened and the victim fabricated the entire incident in response to his alleged threat to reveal her sexual activities, including the phone-sex-tape, to other people. Because there was no claim of the victim's consent, the trial court correctly ruled that the Rape Shield Statute barred evidence of the sex tape.

In Johnson v. State, the defendant sought to introduce that portion of his statement to police which referred to the victim as a "well known whore." The court held that even assuming the statement to be true, it was no defense to rape. Thus, there was no error in the trial court's granting of the state's motion in limine, premised on the Rape Shield Statute, to exclude this portion of the defendant's statement.

Finally, in George v. State, the court held that where the questions posed by defense counsel did not directly reflect on the complainant's past sexual behavior, the possibility that they might have been construed as implicating past sexual conduct could have been eliminated with a corrective instruction to the jury.

Prior to 2005, the courts applied the proscriptions set forth in the Rape Shield Statute in nonrape prosecutions. In Roberts v. State, for instance, the defendant was charged with kidnapping with bodily injury. The alleged bodily injury involved rape and aggravated sodomy. The court held that because the alleged rape and aggravated sodomy constituted evidence of bodily injury, the reasons why evidence of prior sexual experience were inadmissible under the Rape Shield Statute were equally applicable in this case. Thus, the trial court properly precluded the defendant's right to cross examine the victim about her prior sexual conduct with other men. In other decisions, the Court of Appeals found the Rape Shield Statute applicable in prosecutions for aggravated assault with intent to rape, statutory rape, child molestation, and incest.In *Abdulkadir v. State*, however, the Georgia Supreme Court disapproved of these decisions because it found that the statute, by its plain terms, applied only to prosecutions for rape. While there might be compelling policy reasons to apply the Rape Shield Statute in prosecutions for crimes other than rape, the General Assembly's express limitation of the statute's applicability to prosecutions for rape excluded its application in prosecutions for all other crimes. Since the courts are not authorized to expand a statute's application beyond its plain terms, the Supreme Court stated that any expansion of the Rape Shield Statute's applicability had to come from the General Assembly, as it alone is entrusted with the authority to amend existing laws.

In response to this decision, the General Assembly, apparently recognizing that there were compelling policy reasons for the expansion of the Rape Shield Statute's applicability, amended the statute in 2005 so that it is now expressly applicable not only in prosecutions for rape but also in prosecutions for aggravated sodomy, aggravated child molestation, and aggravated sexual battery. This amendment applies to all trials that commence on or after July 1, 2005.

Although the applicability of the Rape Shield Statute was not at issue in Hardy v. State, the court there pointed out that even this reform statute has not moved juries entirely out of the area of speculating about past sexual experiences and their correlation with the likelihood of a present consent to sexual intercourse. In this case, the defendant successfully sought, through the statutory procedure, to introduce evidence of the victim's prior sexual activity. This tactic was, in fact, successful in that although the indictment was for rape, the conviction was for simple battery. The court pointed out, however, that "[p]roof of present consent in a rape trial, then, is different from proof of consent to any other crime. In other crimes the proffered evidence and the inference it supports must logically relate within a particular factual context . . . . In rape cases, however, proof of prior consent without regard to identity of persons or similarity of circumstances may be admitted to allow the jury to weigh . . . the probability of consent with respect to an entire class of 'unchaste' women . . . "

The court here, of course, was referring to the exception which, as was previously suggested, might threaten to swallow up the general exclusionary rule in the Rape Shield Statute: evidence of prior sexual behavior which might lead to a present belief by the defendant that the victim was consenting. The court noted that once the judge admits such evidence after the statutory in camera hearing, there is no effective review of the decision and the court does not consider any prejudice to the victim which the admission might present. The court concluded that even under this statute "a jury may still acquit or convict a [rape] defendant . . . upon spurious assessments of the complainant's character which are simply not relevant to present day consent." The court seems to be suggesting that evidence of prior sexual behavior is not relevant to present day consent.

The Court of Appeals has held that in appropriate cases the fact that the victim of a rape was pregnant would be relevant and admissible. In Thomas v. State, the victim was 9 months pregnant at the time of the incident and testified to that fact. The defendant claimed that the evidence was inadmissible, relying on an early Georgia case which held that evidence of the victim's pregnancy was inadmissible as irrelevant. The court, however, distinguished the earlier case on its facts, pointing out that in the earlier case there was no evidence concerning the stage of pregnancy at the time of the rape. The court said that "[w]hile the mere fact of pregnancy of an alleged rape victim may not be relevant to the issue of consent of a victim, when the alleged victim is in her fortieth week of pregnancy, it can be argued by both sides that her physical condition has relevance to the issue of consent." The court also pointed out that the advanced pregnancy could help to explain the victim's delay in reporting the crime to police. She had testified that she delayed her report of the crime to the police because she was worried about her unborn child and wanted to get to the hospital.

In Smith v. State, the Georgia Supreme Court held that the Rape Shield Statute does not bar admission of testimony regarding the victim's alleged past false accusations against persons other than the defendant. Such evidence does not involve the victim's past sexual conduct but rather the victim's propensity to make false statements regarding sexual misconduct. Before such evidence can be admitted, however, the trial court must make a threshold determination outside the presence of the jury that a reasonable probability of falsity exists. This rule, authorizing evidence of prior false accusations of rape in a rape trial, does not apply where there is no evidence that the victim accused any individual in connection with her prior claim that she was raped.

C. *Victim's Drug Use*

Whether the victim used drugs in the past or was generally knowledgeable about illegal drugs is irrelevant to the issue of whether a defendant committed the offense of rape. Rape is no more lawful when committed against a woman who uses drugs than it is against one who does not use drugs.

While the victim may not be discredited because of a discrepancy as to a wholly immaterial matter, the victim's consumption of drugs shortly before the incident is not immaterial, inasmuch as it may have affected her recollection of events. Under these circumstances, the exclusion of evidence of the victim's drug use would be erroneous.

Evidence of the victim's decision to submit to the AZT drug regimen, despite its negative side effects and unproven effectiveness, would be admissible insofar as it tends to show that the victim would not have voluntarily consented to unprotected sex with the defendant knowing that he was HIV positive.

D. *Victim's Filing of Civil Suit Against Defendant*

The cross-examination of the victim about filing a civil suit against the defendant without any factual basis for such cross-examination is impermissible.

D.1. *Victim's Involuntary Psychiatric Examination*

Since there is no statutory authority nor case law in this state that mandates the involuntary psychiatric examination of a rape victim, there would be no abuse of discretion for the trial court to deny a defendant's motion for such an examination of the victim.

E. *Defendant's Prior Activity*

While the Rape Shield Statute allows the victim's prior sexual activity to be admitted in certain situations as an exception to the general rule of nonadmissibility of character and prior acts, another exception to this general rule permits certain evidence concerning the rape defendant to be introduced. Where evidence is proffered showing similar offenses committed by the defendant in the same locality, at about the same time, the evidence is admissible for the purpose of demonstrating motive, plan, scheme, bent of mind, or course of conduct. For example, in McNeal v. State, evidence was introduced that on two other occasions the defendant approached the witness while she was standing at a bus stop early in the morning in the same general vicinity as the occurrence complained of, grabbed her by the throat, forced her into the woods, and raped her. The court held that this evidence was admissible to show the defendant's motive, scheme, and course of conduct.

Evidence that the defendant had on other occasions pursued a similar course of conduct showing a similar state of mind has also been held relevant to the plausibility of the victim's testimony, including her identification of the defendant as the rapist. In Payne v. State, the court admitted the testimony of two other women that at about the same hour within three weeks' time and in the same geographical area as the scene of the incident, each was followed home from work by the same car and attacked by the defendant, who carried a jacket over his shoulder, as she left her car to enter her home. The court held that the testimony was admissible to corroborate the victim's testimony, including her identification of the defendant as the rapist.

This exception to the rule against admission of evidence of other crimes is applied liberally in prosecutions for rape and for sex crimes generally, so that such evidence has been held relevant not only to the question of the identity of the assailant, but also to whether the victim in the instant case consented.

To obtain admission of evidence of the defendant's prior rape as a similar transaction, the state must show that (1) the evidence is admitted for a proper purpose; (2) there is sufficient evidence that the defendant committed the prior rape; and (3) there is a logical connection or similarity between the prior rape and the charged rape so that proof of the former tends to prove the latter. The state must satisfy these three requirements by a preponderance of the evidence. The trial court's finding that the state's evidence met the standard of proof necessary for the admission of similar transaction evidence will not be disturbed on appeal unless clearly erroneous.

If the issue of intent to rape involved in a case was in dispute in a previous trial and that issue was resolved in the defendant's favor by his acquittal, the state is precluded under the collateral estoppel doctrine from relitigating that issue. However, where the issue of intent to rape in a previous trial had not been resolved in the defendant's favor, the state would not be estopped from presenting in its case evidence of the prior incident. Likewise, though the issue of consent in a previous rape trial had been resolved in the defendant's favor by his acquittal, evidence of this prior incident would be admissible in a subsequent rape trial, where the issue involved in the subsequent trial is the identity of the defendant rather than the consent of the victim. Also, the fact that a grand jury had no-billed a rape charge against the defendant resulting from a prior incident does not preclude the admission of the evidence, since the no-bill left unresolved the issue of whether the defendant was in fact the perpetrator of the prior offense.

Evidence of a prior conviction of simple battery is admissible as a similar transaction to a rape charge, where the simple battery conviction involved a previous rape charge dismissed because of a venue problem.

By pleading guilty to a prior sexual assault, the defendant waives his right to challenge the victim's statements regarding the incident. Therefore, when the victim is unavailable to testify in a subsequent rape trial, the admission of her statements as evidence of a similar transaction committed by the defendant does not violate the defendant's right under the Confrontation Clause.

If there was a lengthy interval between a prior sexual assault involving the defendant and the victim's interview at the police station, the victim's narrative statement given to a police officer at the station would not qualify as res gestae. Thus, allowing the state to prove the similar transaction by introducing the victim's statement as part of the res gestae would be clearly erroneous.

Since force is an essential element of rape, the victim's testimony as to the defendant's violence and the victim's fear of him is relevant and admissible. Lack of resistance, induced by fear, is force, and may be shown by the prosecutrix' state of mind from her prior experience with the defendant and subjective apprehension of danger from him. That this evidence may incidentally place the defendant's character in issue does not make it inadmissible.

Evidence of the defendant's prior violent encounter with the victim is admissible in a rape trial. However, the state must show that (1) the evidence is introduced to show the ongoing physical violence problem between the defendant and the victim; (2) there is sufficient evidence about the prior violent encounter; and (3) there is a marked similarity between the prior violent encounter and the rape charged at trial.

Evidence that the defendant threatened the victim prior to raping her is admissible as part of the res gestae even if such evidence incidentally places his character in evidence.

Evidence of prior difficulties between the defendant and the victim is admissible to show the state of feeling between the two and the defendant's bent of mind and course of conduct toward the victim. For this evidence to be admissible, the state must establish a logical, probative connection between the difficulties and the crimes charged.

A counselor's pamphlets, which concerned "date rape" and various misconceptions concerning rape, were held not to be inadmissible hearsay. The pamphlets were not entered to prove their truth but were used to explain the defendant's statement about the pamphlets and to explain his prior conduct.

In a prosecution for a sexual offense, evidence of sexual paraphernalia found in the defendant's possession is inadmissible unless it shows the defendant's lustful disposition toward the sexual activity with which he is charged or his bent of mind to engage in that activity. Under this rule, sexually explicit material cannot be introduced merely to show a defendant's interest in sexual activity. It can only be admitted if it can be linked to the crime charged.

Evidence regarding the defendant's drug use is admissible if it serves to explain his motive for raping the victim.

F. Hearsay

It has been consistently held that testimony that the victim made a complaint to those to whom complaint would naturally be made, shortly after the commission of the offense, is admissible in evidence as exception to the hearsay rule. The rule has been extended to allow the witness to relate the details of the victim's complaint as well. On the other hand, the victim's delay in reporting the rape can be considered by the jury in determining her credibility. However, the jury may determine from the evidence that the victim's delay in reporting the rape was the result of her fear of the defendant and did not indicate subsequent fabrication.

Evidence of the victim's outcry statements regarding the defendant's sexual acts against her would be sufficient to establish the essential elements of rape. The fact that at trial the victim has disavowed her prior statements would go to the weight and credibility that the jury wishes to assign to the state's otherwise sufficient evidence.

Under the "patient history" exception to the hearsay rule, a victim's statements to an emergency room physician that she had been assaulted and raped by the defendant are admissible.

A prior consistent statement of the victim is not admissible unless (1) the veracity of the victim's testimony has been placed in issue at trial, (2) the victim is present at trial, and (3) the victim is available for cross-examination. The victim's veracity is placed in issue so as to permit the introduction of a prior consistent statement only if affirmative charges of recent fabrication, improper influence, or improper motive are raised during cross-examination. Otherwise, the victim's prior consistent statement is pure hearsay evidence which cannot be admitted merely to corroborate the victim or to bolster the victim's credibility in the eyes of the jury. If there is no charge of recent fabrication or of improper influence or motive, the trial court's failure to sustain an objection to admission of the victim's prior consistent statement as improper bolstering would constitute harmful error unless, before the statement is admitted, the victim has testified without objection that she had given a pretrial statement to the police and that it was consistent with her trial testimony. Under the circumstances, the reading of the statement would not have contributed to the verdict.

Where the victim's veracity is at issue, a sexual assault nurse examiner may testify as to what the victim told her regarding the incident. The victim's statement, if consistent with her trial testimony, would be admissible as substantive evidence of the matter asserted.

As a general rule, allowing the written statement of the alleged victim to go out with the jury violates the continuing witness rule. However, this error is harmless if the evidence contained in the statement has also been brought out during the trial and the evidence of guilt is overwhelming.

G. DNA Identification of Defendant

It has been held that DNA identification techniques can produce reliable results. An evidentiary hearing to determine the admissibility of the state's DNA test results must he held by the trial court prior to its decision to allow the results into evidence. There must be sufficient evidence elicited at this hearing to support the trial court's determination that DNA testing procedures used by the state's serologist were performed in an acceptable manner and were capable of producing reliable results. The state's serologist may testify as to the DNA testing and results in the case where there is sufficient evidence to support his qualifications as an expert. These results must establish the defendant's guilt only beyond a reasonable doubt. Mathematical certainty is not required. The fact that DNA testing has a margin of error goes only to the weight and credibility that the jury wishes to assign to this evidence.

Expert testimony explaining that the term "with a reasonable scientific certainty" is used in a DNA report only when the frequency shows a rare occurrence, which the expert defines as an occurrence of once in above ten billion, has been held to be necessary to explain the results of the defendant's testing and is neither improper nor bolstering.

If the state wishes to use a scientific report containing the DNA test results of the defendant at trial, it must provide a copy of the report to the defense "no later than ten days prior to trial, or as otherwise ordered by the court." While there are a number of remedies for the state's failure to comply with this requirement, because of the complexity of DNA analysis and testing, merely permitting defense counsel a few days prior to trial to inspect the report would not afford him adequate time for trial preparation. Under these circumstances, the appropriate remedy would be to grant a continuance.

Although a defendant has the right to receive a copy of the results of any State Crime Lab DNA test, if such a test has been conducted at the State's request, he has no right to seek, and the trial court has no authority to order, that the State Crime Lab conduct tests for the defendant's benefit. Thus, a defendant in a criminal case is not entitled to a continuance pending receipt of the results of State Crime Lab DNA test which has not been requested by the State.

In order to obtain funds to hire an expert witness to test the state's DNA evidence independently, an indigent defendant is required to show (1) why the evidence is critical; (2) what type of scientific testimony is needed; (3) what the expert proposes to do regarding the evidence; and (4) the anticipated costs for the services.

If there is other evidence positively identifying the defendant as the person who raped the victim, DNA identification evidence is not "critical" evidence concerning the defendant's guilt or innocence. In such a case, the defendant is not entitled at his expense on motion timely made to have an expert of his choosing examine the DNA identification evidence.

The testimony of a defense expert, who has only reviewed the lab notes and results of the state-directed DNA tests, is properly excluded where he has no personal knowledge of the testing procedures or results and where no DNA evidence has been introduced which would have allowed him to be examined by the use of a hypothetical question.

DNA test results are like fingerprints which are maintained on file by law enforcement officials for use in further investigations. Thus, the sharing of DNA evidence between law enforcement officials in different counties does not require an independent warrant.

Where a search warrant affidavit contains sufficient facts to establish probable cause that the defendant committed the rape and specifies the material evidence to be collected, DNA identification evidence would not be subject to a motion to suppress. Furthermore, since the presence of defense counsel is not required for the execution of the warrant, the absence of counsel when the blood is drawn would not subject the evidence to suppression.

Where there is evidence that a detective informed a suspect that his DNA sample would be used for comparison with other such samples and that no limits were placed on the scope of the suspect's consent, a trial court in a hearing on a motion to suppress would be authorized to conclude that the detective did not deceive the suspect in violation of his Fourth Amendment rights.

H. Medical Examination of Victim

When evidence relating to an allegation of rape is collected in the course of a medical examination of the victim, the law enforcement agency investigating the alleged rape is responsible for the cost of the medical examination to the extent that expense is incurred for the limited purpose of collecting evidence.

The state's failure to preserve a rape kit purportedly containing evidence from the physical examination of the victim does not deprive the defendant of due process where the rape kit evidence is immaterial to the case and the state did not act in bad faith in failing to preserve the evidence.

Where the state seeks to introduce evidence of a rape kit and blood vials, it need only show with reasonable certainty that the evidence is the same as that obtained from the victim and that there has been no tampering or substitution. The fact the state crime lab personnel who received the evidence are not identified and, therefore, do not testify at trial is not fatal to the chain of custody.

A medical diagram depicting the location of injuries to the victim's genitalia can be used as a tool to explain an expert's testimony and is not subject to a continuing witness objection.

I. Expert Testimony

A doctor's expert opinion testimony on issues to be decided by the jury, even the ultimate issue, i.e., consent, is admissible where the conclusion of the expert is one which jurors would not ordinarily be able to draw for themselves, i.e., the conclusion is beyond the ken of the average layman. Thus, medical opinion testimony by the doctor who examined the victim after the rape that he observed lacerations or tears in the victim's perineum which were consistent with an act of nonconsensual sexual intercourse but not consistent with an act of consensual sexual intercourse would be admissible, since the significance of tears in the perineum would be beyond the ken of the average layman.

Where defense counsel elicits expert testimony unfavorable to his client, even when that testimony constitutes an opinion of ultimate fact which invades the province of the jury, defense counsel will not be heard to object to it, no matter how prejudicial it may be, if it is a direct and pertinent response to the question propounded.

A psychologist for the state is permitted to give her expert opinion that a mentally retarded victim is incapable of consenting to sexual intercourse. Expert opinion testimony dealing with the victim's level of mental retardation and its effect on her capacity to consent, which involves no improper legal conclusion, may be admitted to assist the jury in reaching its verdict.

A registered nurse, who has acted as a rape counselor, may testify as to the existence of certain typical patterns of behavior exhibited by victims of rape, and she may testify as to behavior she has observed in the victim in a rape case. The nurse's testimony does not amount to an expert opinion as to whether the victim had been raped.

A registered nurse, who has received specialized professional training in the examination of victims of sexual assaults and in the collection of evidence from such crimes and who has worked as a sexual assault nurse examiner at a rape crisis center, would be qualified to testify as an expert in the field of examination of sexual assault victims.

Even though a trial court has discretion to qualify a witness as an expert, the witness's testimony must relate to the scientific or technical knowledge within his area of expertise. In Prickett v. State, the court held that there was insufficient evidence that the witness had special knowledge about post traumatic stress disorder and rape trauma syndrome. While the witness's testimony may have shown him to be an expert in counseling, the state failed to present any evidence that this special knowledge of counseling included an expertise in the psychological theories of post traumatic stress disorder and rape trauma syndrome. The trial court abused its discretion in allowing the counselor's testimony to go far beyond the proved area of his expertise. In Thomas v. State, on the other hand, the court found no abuse of discretion in the trial court's qualification of the witness as an expert on victims of sexual abuse, including rape. Further, the witness's testimony regarding the number of women who delay in reporting a rape or who fail to report it all was clearly related to knowledge within the witness's area of expertise. Thus, there was no error in the admission of her testimony.

Where the defendant is seeking to undermine the victim's credibility through illustrating her failure to initiate an outcry for help, expert opinion testimony regarding the "learned helplessness" of women in abusive relationships is relevant to explain the victim's behavior. The possibility that this testimony may touch on the victim's credibility does not render it inadmissible. Since testimony regarding the typical characteristics of an abuser would improperly place the defendant's character in issue, however, the trial court must limit the testimony to what is necessary to rebut any defense or issue raised by the defendant.

In *Harris v. State*, the Court of Appeals found that expert testimony that it was a common misconception that people make up rape allegations for the purpose of revenge implicitly went to the ultimate issue to be decided by the jury, namely, whether the victim had fabricated the rape allegation against the defendant. It was not beyond the ken of the average juror to determine whether and under what circumstances a rape allegation had been fabricated. Accordingly, the court held that the expert's testimony should not have been allowed. The admission of the improper testimony did not mandate a new trial, however, because based on the strength of the evidence against the defendant it was highly improbable that the expert's testimony contributed to the judgment.

An expert witness may testify as to the existence of certain typical patterns of behavior exhibited by victims of rape, as long as the jury is permitted to draw for itself the final conclusion as to whether the victim in the case at hand was raped.

IV. Marital Rape

At English common law, a man could not be convicted of raping his wife. The genesis of this rule was apparently an analysis by a seventeenth century treatise writer who stated that "the husband cannot be guilty of a rape committed . . . upon his lawful wife, for by their mutual matrimonial consent and contract the wife hath given up herself in this kind unto her husband, which she cannot retract." While this defense of the marital rape exemption may seem out of place in our current era of sexual equality, the exemption has had significant staying power in American jurisdictions. As recent as 1983, 34 American jurisdictions had codified the rule. The Model Penal Code, in fact, suggests that the marital rape exemption be adopted at least in situations where there has not been a judicial decree of separation. The Commentaries to the Code argue that "the law of rape, if applied to spouses, would thrust the prospect of criminal sanctions into the ongoing process of adjustment in the marital relationship." The Commentaries further argue that the "gravity of the crime of forcible rape derives not merely from its violent character but also from its achievement of a particularly degrading kind of unwanted intimacy. Where the attacker stands in an ongoing relation of sexual intimacy, that evil, as distinct from the force used to compel submission, may well be thought qualitatively different."

The marital rape exemption, however, has been under heavy fire and several state courts have construed their rape statutes to punish husbands who rape their wives. In Warren v. State, the Georgia Supreme Court joined the trend toward rejecting the exemption. The defendant was indicted for raping his wife at a time when the couple was living together. He appealed the denial of his pretrial motion to dismiss the indictment. Phrasing the issue as "When a woman says I do, does she give up her right to say I won't?," Justice Smith for a unanimous court affirmed the lower court's action. Pointing out that Hale's statement was made at a time when marriages were indissoluble and when "[w]ives were subservient to their husbands, her identity was merged into his, her property became his property, and she took his name for her own," Justice Smith concluded that none of the justifications offered for the rule were satisfactory. He found Hale's implied consent theory to be "without logical meaning" and that it "obviously conflicts with our Constitutional and statutory laws and our regard for all citizens of this State." (Emphasis in original.) The court, responding to the modern justification for the rule stating that wives would fabricate rape charges in the midst of marital strife, held that "[t]here is no other crime we can think of in which all of the victims are denied protection simply because someone might fabricate a charge . . . ." (Emphasis in original.) The court also pointed out that in states which have rejected the exemption there has not been a flood of rape complaints by wives.

The court concluded its analysis by pointing out that there has never been any explicit statutory marital rape exemption in the Georgia statute and the words of the current statute are broader than the traditional common law definition of rape which was the language of the former rape statute. The court also pointed out that the 1968 redraft of the Georgia criminal code was patterned largely after the Model Penal Code which, as pointed out above, includes an explicit marital rape exemption. The court, therefore, concluded that the choice of language made by the 1968 drafters was considered. The Warren court went on to hold that the aggravated sodomy statute also does not contain an exemption for husbands charged with committing the crime on their wives. The court also rejected a claim that the application of the rape statute to the defendant in this case constituted a violation of the Due Process Clause's notice requirements. The court held that its ruling was "a first application of these statutes to this particular set of facts, this is not an unforeseeable judicial enlargement of criminal statutes that are narrowly drawn."

In 1996, the General Assembly amended the rape statute to expressly provide that "[t]he fact that the person allegedly raped is the wife of the defendant shall not be a defense to a charge of rape."

In marital rape cases, evidence of recent prior marital difficulties between husband and wife is admissible. The state of feelings between the then husband and wife is clearly relevant because the issue is whether the subject sex acts were forced or consensual.

V. *Attempted Rape*

The prosecution must show three elements to prove a case of attempted rape. It must prove that the defendant (1) intended to have forcible and nonconsensual carnal knowledge of the victim; and (2) took a substantial step toward committing rape; but (3) failed to consummate the rape.

On the trial of a rape case, where there is some evidence, however slight, of attempted rape, it is not error for the trial court to charge the law in relation to that issue.

In pleading guilty to criminal attempt to commit rape, a defendant admits he intended to commit the specific crime of rape and took a substantial step toward that end. Because the crime attempted is related to a sexually violent offense (i.e., rape), the defendant is required to comply with the sexual offender registration requirements of § 42-1-12.

VI. *Statute of Limitations*

Prior to 1996, the statute of limitations for a prosecution for rape was seven years. In 1996, the General Assembly extended the limitations period for forcible rape to 15 years. The limitations period for attempted rape is four years.

The 1996 amendment, which extends the period of limitation for forcible rape to 15 years, applies to offenses not barred at the time of the effective date of the amendment, so that a prosecution may be commenced at any time within the newly established period. This amendment, however, cannot operate to revive a rape offense that was barred at the time of the effective date, since that would make the amendment ex post facto.

In 1992, the General Assembly with the enactment of § 24-4-60 authorized the creation of a state deoxyribonucleic acid (DNA) data bank of samples obtained from convicted sex offenders in order to determine and retain the identification characteristics specific to these offenders. In 2000, the General Assembly broadened the scope of this statute by requiring the obtaining of DNA samples from all convicted felons and the storing of these samples in the data bank. An examination of these samples revealed that many matched the DNA evidence of old, unsolved rape cases. Despite this evidence, the state could not prosecute the convicted felons because the limitation periods for their crimes had expired. Remedial legislation was necessary to enable the state to use identification evidence derived from the state's DNA data bank to prosecute convicted felons for certain crimes even though the limitation periods previously established by law had expired.

Accordingly, the General Assembly eliminated the statute of limitations for any rape occurring on or after July 1, 2002, when DNA evidence is used to establish the identity of the accused. A sufficient portion of the physical evidence tested for DNA, however, must be preserved and available for testing by the accused. Furthermore, if the DNA evidence does not establish the identity of the accused, the limitation on the prosecution reverts to the 15-year period specified in § 17-3-1(b).

VII. *Selective Prosecution*

To support a claim of selective prosecution for rape, the defendant must show that others generally are not prosecuted for the same misconduct and that a discriminatory motive for the prosecution exists. Without such a showing, the defendant's claim will fail.

VIII. Punishment

The rape statute provides that one convicted of rape must be punished by death, by life imprisonment without parole, by life imprisonment, or by a split sentence that is a term of imprisonment for not less than 25 years and not exceeding life imprisonment, followed by probation for life. Any person convicted of rape is also subject to the sentencing and punishment provisions of §§ 17-10-6.1 and 17-10-7, which provide for mandatory minimum sentences and sentences for life without possibility of parole in certain cases and provide restrictions on the authority of the State Board of Pardons and Paroles to grant paroles.

A plurality of the United States Supreme Court held in Coker v. Georgia that the imposition of the death penalty for the rape of an adult woman who has not been killed is cruel and unusual punishment under the Eighth Amendment. By referring only to an adult woman throughout its opinion, however, the plurality limited its findings to the rape of an adult, leaving open the question whether death would be a disproportionate penalty for the rape of a child. The Supreme Court of Louisiana, construing that state's rape statute, has held that given the appalling nature of the crime, the severity of the harm inflicted upon the victim, and the harm imposed on society, death would not be a disproportionate penalty for the rape of a child. The court also found that the class of defendants eligible for the death penalty would be sufficiently narrow so as not to lead to arbitrary and capricious application. Since our rape statute, as amended in 1999, now expressly affords protection to females who are "less than ten years of age" and still includes a death penalty provision, it would appear that the death penalty may be applied in cases involving the rape of a child. However, whether death is a disproportionate penalty for such a crime is question that must be answered by the Georgia Supreme Court.

In Collins v. State, the Georgia Supreme Court, construing the definition of "capital felony" together with the decision in Coker v. Georgia, concluded that convictions of rape are no longer convictions of capital felonies for appellate jurisdictional purposes. However, rape is still considered a capital felony for purposes of determining statutory aggravating circumstances under the death penalty statute.

The death penalty for rape is not unconstitutional where the victim is killed.

Rape, whose seriousness has not changed, was a capital offense at the time the speedy trial statutes were enacted. Since the removal of the sentencing option of imposing the death penalty does not reflect on the General Assembly's original determination that the state should be allowed more time to prepare a rape case, rape is still considered a capital offense for purposes of the speedy trial statutes.

IX. Relationship to Other Offenses

Important Notice about Repudiation of Actual or Same Evidence Test: The Georgia Supreme Court repudiated the actual evidence test in *Drinkard v. Walker*, 281 Ga. 211, 636 S.E.2d 530 (2006), because it found this test to be inconsistent with the statutory framework governing the prohibition against multiple convictions for included offenses in Georgia. This inconsistency resulted in years of confusion and unpredictable results. In its place, the court adopted the required evidence test and overruled any prior case law that is inconsistent with it. Thus, any prior case law applying the actual evidence test is no longer controlling and should not be relied upon to determine whether one offense is included in another under § 16-1-6(1). The discussion of such case law is included below only insofar as it may still be applicable to pending prosecutions that arose before the Drinkard decision. See MULTIPLE CONVICTIONS, II. Tests to Determine Presence of Multiple Convictions, for a complete discussion of the Drinkard decision.

The law of Georgia is clear that a defendant under indictment for a particular crime can be convicted of other offenses. To warrant conviction of a lesser offense on an indictment charging a greater offense, it is essential (1) that the allegations describing the greater offense contain all essential averments relating to the lesser offense or (2) that the greater offense necessarily include all the essential ingredients of the lesser. In either situation, however, before a verdict of the lesser offense can be authorized there must be evidence in the record supporting a finding of that crime.

While aggravated assault with intent to commit rape may be a lesser included offense of rape in some cases, it is not so in every case because in many instances the offense of rape may undoubtedly be completed without the commission of an independent aggravated assault. The crime of aggravated assault with intent to rape is complete when there is a "substantial step" toward a battery of the victim, i.e., an assault, coupled with intent to rape. If there is a substantial step toward the rape itself, the crime would then become attempted rape. The acquittal of aggravated assault with intent to rape does not "necessarily include" a finding against rape. Aggravated assault and rape are separate offenses and do not merge, where the evidence used to prove the aggravated assault is not used to prove the force element of the rape.

In order for a crime to be included in another crime it must be established by proof of the same or less than all the facts. Because the additional fact of marriage must be shown in order to prove adultery, adultery is not included in the offense of rape.

As a matter of law, fornication cannot be forcible and against the woman's will. Thus, fornication is not a lesser included offense of rape.

Depending on what the indictment alleges, statutory rape could be an authorized verdict on a rape indictment. Because the crimes of rape and statutory rape are separate offenses which require proof of different elements, they are not included within each other as a matter of law. Furthermore, even where the evidence at trial shows that there was only one act of sexual intercourse, the crime of statutory rape is not included, as a matter of fact, in the crime of rape. The fact that the act of sexual intercourse supports an element in each crime does not warrant merging of the sentences where other mutually exclusive elements of the crimes remain.

The offense of child molestation may be included as a matter of fact in an indictment charging the offense of rape, where the victim is under the age of consent. In such a case it is reversible error to refuse to give a requested charge on child molestation as a lesser included offense of the rape charge. However, a defendant is not entitled to a jury instruction on child molestation as a lesser included offense of rape where the jury is only authorized by the evidence to find the defendant either guilty or not guilty of rape.

Although child molestation becomes included within rape as a matter of fact if the victim is under the age of consent, child molestation is not included within rape as a matter of law because, unlike rape, child molestation requires proof that the victim was under the age of consent. If a rape indictment does not allege that the victim was under the age of consent, the defendant has not been placed on notice that he should be prepared to defend himself against the charges of both rape and child molestation. Without such notice, the trial court is not authorized, sua sponte, to instruct the jury on child molestation as a lesser included offense of rape. If the trial court so instructs jury and the jury convicts the defendant of the lesser included offense of child molestation, due process will not allow the conviction to stand.

The offense of child molestation does not merge into the offense of rape where the evidence shows that the defendant fondled the victim and, in an entirely separate incident later that evening, raped her.

Where the child molestation count of an indictment alleges actions that are factually contained in the attempted rape count, the child molestation offense merges into the attempted rape offense as a matter of fact. While the defendant can be prosecuted for both offenses, if he is convicted of both, the trial court must merge the child molestation conviction into the attempted rape conviction for sentencing purposes.

The offense of aggravated child molestation merges as a matter of fact into the offense of rape, where the evidence shows that the injuries the victim sustained as a result of the rape are the same injuries that serve as the basis for the offense of aggravated child molestation. However, an aggravated child molestation conviction would not merge as a matter of fact into a rape conviction for sentencing purposes, where the evidence shows that the defendant sexually assaulted the victim twice.

Incest and rape have at least one element each not necessary to prove the other. Neither incest nor rape can be proved by only the same facts proving the other. Thus, neither incest nor rape is included in the other as a matter of law. Also, incest and rape do not merge as a matter of fact where more than one instance of sexual intercourse occurred, permitting conviction for each offense based on separate occasions. Furthermore, the crime of incest is not included within the crime of rape as a matter of fact even where only one instance of sexual intercourse occurred. The fact that the act of sexual intercourse supports an element in each crime does not warrant merging of the sentences where other mutually exclusive elements of the crimes remain.

The offense of cruelty to children is separate and distinct from the offense of rape as a matter of fact, where the evidence used to establish cruelty to children is not used to establish the rape.

The offense of simple battery merges into the offense of rape where the same impermissible touching—the hitting and slapping which constitutes simple battery—also supplies the element of force necessary for conviction of rape. If a jury finds a defendant guilty of the lesser included offense of simple battery at his rape trial, this finding amounts to an implicit acquittal of the defendant on the rape charge. Where the evidence shows that there was either a rape or that there was consensual sexual intercourse which was interrupted when the couple changed their minds, such evidence would not authorize charges on battery and simple battery as lesser included offenses. Where the evidence shows either the commission of a rape or no crime at all, such evidence would not authorize charges on battery, simple battery, and sexual battery as lesser included offenses.

Where the evidence in a case establishes that the offenses of sexual battery and rape were two separate and distinct offenses, sexual battery would not be a lesser included offense of rape and a verdict of guilty on the sexual battery charge would not operate as an exoneration and acquittal on the rape charge.

Since each of the offenses of aggravated anal sodomy, aggravated oral sodomy, and rape contains at least one element not contained in the others, the aggravated sodomy offenses cannot merge as a matter of law into the rape offense.

The offense of burglary does not merge with the offenses of rape and aggravated sodomy. To establish the offense of burglary, the state needs to prove only that the defendant entered the victim's home without authority and with the intent to commit the rape and aggravated sodomy. It does not have to prove that the defendant actually committed these offenses to establish the burglary offense.

Acquittal on an aggravated sodomy charge does not preclude the findings of fact necessary for a conviction for rape. The elements of the crimes are different, and the jury can choose to convict on the rape charge and acquit on the aggravated sodomy charge without any inconsistency.

In Cardoza v. State, the defendant committed four rapes against the same victim within a certain time period. Although occurring sequentially, one after the other, each of the rapes constituted a separate offense since each was established by proof of different facts, i.e., each offense was a completed crime when the next was perpetrated upon the victim. Under such circumstances, the same conduct is not being punished twice nor is one act included in the other so as to proscribe the separate conviction and punishment for each act.

One act of rape is not legally included in another, separate act of rape so as to require reversal under a conflict theory.

Where a terroristic threat conviction is supported by separate and distinct facts from those necessary for an attempted rape conviction, the convictions do not merge.

For a discussion about rape as a lesser included offense of kidnapping with bodily injury, see KIDNAPPING.

X. Civil Liability

The rapist is subject not only to the sanctions of the criminal law, but can be held liable civilly as well. Furthermore, there is authority for the proposition that if the rape is committed by the defendant while he is acting within the scope of his employment, his employer may also be held liable. In an action for damages, the rape need be established only by the preponderance of the evidence, the civil standard of proof. No special damages need be shown. On proof of the assault the law will presume that the plaintiff was damaged. Further, the victim may also be granted punitive or exemplary damages, the measure of which is left to the "enlightened conscience of impartial jurors."

XI. Rape Victim Confidentiality Statute

One other provision of the criminal code is pertinent to rape. Section 16-6-23 provides that publication of the name or identity of any woman who may have been either raped or assaulted with an intent to rape is a misdemeanor. Although the case was later overruled, in Cox Broadcasting Corp. v. Cohn, the Georgia Supreme Court, after rejecting an argument that the criminal statute created a civil right of action for damages, granted a right of privacy action under Georgia tort law. On appeal, the United States Supreme Court reversed, holding that civil liability could not be based on the publication of a rape victim's name, but failed to address the validity of the criminal statute. The broad language used by the Court in its decision, however, indicates that the statute is unconstitutional in imposing a criminal sanction on the exercise of freedom of the press.

In The Florida Star v. B. J. F., the United States Supreme Court held that imposing damages on a newspaper for publishing a rape victim's name obtained from a police report violated the First Amendment. Adopting a test enunciated in this United States Supreme Court decision as the basis for evaluating an action for common law invasion of privacy, the Georgia Supreme Court in Macon Telegraph Publishing Co. v. Tatum held that a victim cannot recover damages from a newspaper for an invasion of privacy based on its publication of the victim's name in connection with a sexual assault. Once a person becomes the victim of a crime, she loses her right to keep her name private and becomes the object of a legitimate public interest. A newspaper has the right under the federal and state constitutions to accurately report the facts regarding the incident, including the victim's name. In Dye v. Wallace, the Georgia Supreme Court, finding the rationale in the Florida Star case to be fully applicable to § 16-6-23, held that the statute contravenes the First and Fourteenth Amendments of the federal constitution. Under the circumstances of the case, the court found that the imposition of civil liability was too precipitous a means of advancing the state's interest in guarding against the dissemination of the victim's identity.

In Doe v. Board of Regents of the University System of Georgia, the Georgia Court of Appeals held that a police incident report that involves a false claim of rape is a public record obtainable under the Open Records Act. The report of a crime, whether the report is true or false, is a matter of public interest and is a subject of legitimate public inquiry. However, the rape victim confidentiality statute creates a specific and discrete exemption from the Open Records Act. Under this statute, the identity of a victim as revealed in a police incident report is protected from disclosure. The statute does not require that the matter be established as true in order for the identity of the victim to be protected. The statute covers the identity of one who "may have been" a victim. Thus, under the Open Records Act, a newspaper is entitled to such a police incident report, but under the rape victim confidentiality statute, the victim's name and identifying information must be redacted.

ROBBERY

See also ASSAULT; THEFT CRIMES.

I. Generally

Common law robbery was, in effect, compound larceny, because it was a combination of larceny and assault. More particularly, it was defined as the felonious and forcible taking of the property of another from his person, or in his presence, against his will, by putting him in fear. As compared to the common law definition, Georgia law prior to 1968 defined robbery as the wrongful, fraudulent, and violent taking of money, goods, or chattels from the person of another with intent to steal.

The 1968 revision of the criminal code recodified the offense of robbery, but left the law substantially unaltered. In the current code, § 16-8-40 provides that a person commits robbery when, with intent to commit theft, he takes property of another from the person or the immediate presence of another by use of force, intimidation, or sudden snatching. Armed robbery is defined in § 16-8-41, as the taking of another's property with intent to commit theft from the person or immediate presence of another by use of an offensive weapon.

II. Elements

A. Generally

Analytically, the offenses of robbery and armed robbery have four separate elements. In both offenses there must be an intent to commit a theft, a taking of property of another, and the taking must be from the person or from the immediate presence of another. The fourth element requires that the taking be accompanied by "force." In the case of robbery, that "force" may be either actual force, intimidation, or a sudden snatching, while in the case of armed robbery the "force" must be the use of an offensive weapon. Included within the notion of force is the requirement that the taking be against the victim's will.

Since the particular location of an armed robbery is not an element of the offense, it is not necessary that the indictment specify the exact location in which the offense occurred, so long as it is alleged that the offense occurred within the county.

B. Intent to Commit Theft

The intent to commit a theft is essential to the completed offenses of robbery and armed robbery and failure to so inform the jury is, if harmful, reversible error.

In an armed robbery case, the state is not required to prove that the defendant had the intent to commit **armed** robbery, but merely that he had the intent to commit theft and did so with an offensive weapon or any device having the appearance of a weapon.

One case expressly found that a jury could find the requisite intent to commit theft where the defendant entered a liquor store, reached into his pocket for a pistol, and said " . . . I came after the . . . money." It will be rare that such direct evidence will be available and circumstantial evidence will normally be utilized.

Evidence of an armed robbery previously committed by a defendant is admissible as relevant to his motive, plan, scheme, bent of mind, and course of conduct as to a later committed armed robbery. However, before this evidence can be admitted, the trial court must conduct a hearing at which specified affirmative showings are made. The State must show: (1) that the evidence is not being introduced for some improper purpose but rather for an appropriate purpose which is an exception to the general rule of inadmissibility; (2) sufficient evidence to show the accused committed the other offense; and (3) sufficient connection or similarity between the other offense and the crime charged such that proof of the former tends to prove the latter. The trial court must determine in the record that these showings have been made satisfactorily. Also, the trial court, upon request, must give a limiting instruction to the jury about the specific purposes for which this evidence can be considered. Furthermore, the trial court, upon request, must fully instruct the jury that the defendant is not on trial for the prior robbery and that before the jury can consider the prior robbery, it must first determine whether the defendant actually committed that crime, and if so, whether it is similar enough to the robbery with which the defendant is presently charged, that proof of the prior robbery, in light of the limited purposes for which it is introduced, tends to prove the latter robbery.

Other evidence held to be admissible to establish the defendant's motive, intent, bent of mind, or course of conduct include: (1) the defendants' joint and separate bad financial condition for a year prior to the robbery, including evidence of bad checks and overdrawn accounts up to two months before the robbery; (2) dispossessory warrants filed against the defendant less than a month prior to the robbery; (3) the defendant's having money to pay his parole fees the day after the robbery, after being months in arrears on those fees; (4) the defendant's observation of the place he is charged with robbing; and (5) the defendant's statements made before or after the robbery.

Evidence of the defendant's motive in perpetrating the robbery is clearly admissible and is not rendered inadmissible by the fact that it incidentally puts his character in issue. Furthermore, the state is not required to give notice of its intent to present such evidence.

Regardless of whether a defendant intended to take another's property and withhold it permanently, his intent to take it for his own temporary use without the owner's authorization evinces an intent to commit a theft.

With respect to the crime of armed robbery, there must be intent to commit theft, but it is not necessary that such intent exist for any particular period of time before the armed robbery, rather, the intent simply must exist concurrent in time with the act. Furthermore, it does not matter that the defendant did not have the intent to commit a theft at the time he used force against the victim. Once he takes property belonging to the victim, he has committed the offense of robbery regardless of when his intent to take the property arose.

The violent taking of money or property from the person of another by force or intimidation, without the consent of the owner, with the intent of converting the same to the use of the taker for the payment of a demand claimed to be due him by one from whom the money or property is so taken, constitutes the offense of robbery. The taker cannot under such circumstances justify the taking and be excused of the offense of robbery on the ground that the person from whom the money or property was so taken was indebted to him, and that the taking was to pay the debt.

C. Takes Another's Property

The Georgia Supreme Court has held that the slightest movement of property is a taking. Consequently, the taking element would be satisfied by evidence that the defendant temporarily took control of the property just before being apprehended for the robbery. Return of the property, of course, does not negate the taking element. It should also be noted that the taking element can be proven by circumstantial evidence.

The taking in an armed robbery is complete once control over the property is transferred from the victim to the armed robber. When the armed robber uses his weapon to force the victim to drop the property, he exercises complete control over that property. That his exercise of control is brief and ultimately unsuccessful is immaterial.

Thus, the armed robber need not physically touch the property to complete the taking.

The property aspect of this element is satisfied where another's "property" is taken regardless of the exact value of that property. It is not necessary, therefore, to prove the exact value of the items taken, but only to show that the items had some value.

An over-inclusive list of items alleged to have been taken in an indictment for armed robbery is not fatal to the validity of a conviction.

Although evidence of recent unexplained (or unsatisfactorily explained) possession of stolen property may be sufficient to give rise to an inference that the defendant took the property, the sufficiency of the evidence to support a robbery conviction must still be adjudged by the totality of the evidence under the reasonable doubt standard.

Finally, "another" is defined by statute as a person or persons other than the accused. Therefore, it is clear that a robbery indictment is not fatally flawed by the fact that it alleges ownership of the property in the victim, who turns out to have been only a custodian of the property for the real owner. Similarly, an armed robbery indictment that alleges ownership of the property in a bailee having possession of the property when it was stolen is sufficient as a matter of law, and the defense should not be allowed to highlight for the jury any variance between the allegations of the indictment and the proof at trial concerning the title of the stolen property.

The identity of the person alleged to have been robbed is not an essential element of the crime so as to create a fatal variance. Moreover, it is not incumbent upon the state to prove the identity of the victim in order to convict the defendant of armed robbery.

It is not clear whether the fact that the defendant had an interest in the subject property would be important. For example, he might be taking partnership property from a partner.

D. From the Person or Immediate Presence of Another

Robbery is a crime against possession and is not affected by concepts of ownership. Thus, one may be charged with robbery even when the object of the intended theft is contraband, in which the victim could have no legitimate property rights. Furthermore, one may rob only a person and not a corporate entity or an object such as a cash drawer.

A defendant, who is temporarily given some property by the possessor who retains possession, is guilty of a trespass to possession and larceny if he then absconds with the goods.

When, in a single transaction, an individual robs one individual of more than one item or of property belonging to two individuals, only one crime of robbery is committed. However, when, in a single transaction, an individual robs two individuals of property in their possession, that individual may be convicted of two counts of armed robbery even though the property may have been jointly owned by the two individuals.

The requirement that the taking be from "the person" of the victim is self-evident. Thus, where the victim testified that the defendant took his billfold which contained $2.00, the conviction for robbery was upheld. The Georgia Supreme Court has commented, however, that there "is a surprising absence of cases" defining the scope of the concept of "immediate presence." In Welch v. State, however, the court approvingly cited dicta in an earlier case which extended the definition of "immediate presence" so far that it is hardly recognizable. In Welch, the court affirmed a conviction for robbery when the evidence showed the victim was approximately three-tenths of a mile away from the actual taking of the money. In Morgan v. State, the Court of Appeals held that since the victim fled the scene after he was threatened with a knife and the property was stolen before he could even drive away, that was sufficient to constitute a theft from his immediate presence. In Wilson v. State, the Court of Appeals held that evidence that the victim was in charge of the cash drawer from which money was taken while she stepped away briefly to alert her manager was sufficient to show a taking from her immediate presence. In Gido v. State, after the defendant used force to push the victim down an embankment and throw her between two bushes, he picked up money dropped by the victim. The Court of Appeals held that although the defendant did not take the money directly from the victim, it was in her immediate possession at the time of the robbery. In Culver v. State, the Court of Appeals held that there was sufficient evidence from which the jury could have inferred that the defendant stole the $600 from the victim's purse after the aggravated assault and rape. The defendant told the victim to stay on the bed or he would kill her, and he remained in her home a few minutes before leaving. Although the victim could not see what the defendant was doing because she had something over her face, the jury could have found that the victim was aware that her life and personal property were at risk while the defendant terrorized her and remained in her home. In Booker v. State, the Court of Appeals held that the evidence authorized the jury to find that the money retrieved by the defendant from the victim's personal possessions in the apartment from which the victim had leaped was within his immediate presence. In Meyers v. State, the Court of Appeals held that, considering that the victim was held at gunpoint in his living room while property was taken from his bedroom, the theft was not too far afield to be outside the victim's immediate presence.

Although the victim's "person" and his "immediate presence" are separated by the word "or" in the statutory definition of robbery, the word "or" is employed in such a way that it specifically incorporates into the definition the principle that the victim's "person" includes the entire area within his "immediate presence." Because they are mutually inclusive, rather than exclusive, concepts, there is no fatal variance between an indictment which charges that property was taken from the victim's person and proof which shows that the taking was from the victim's immediate presence.

The mere fact that the property was taken directly from someone other than the person alleged in the indictment does not create a fatal variance, if the evidence shows that the person alleged in the indictment was sufficiently close to the taking so that it occurred within his immediate presence or within the sphere of his protective influence.

The requirement that the property be taken "from the person or the immediate presence" of the victim is satisfied by the slightest change of location whereby the dominion of the property is (even temporarily) transferred from the victim to the perpetrator. Thus, in Dillard v. State, the Court of Appeals held that even though the victim remained in or near the vehicle at all times following her abduction, the victim's vehicle was clearly taken from her person or immediate presence when she was abducted and forced into the back seat of her vehicle.

In an indictment for armed robbery, the allegation of a use of an offensive weapon to accomplish the taking necessarily gives rise to the inference that the property was taken "from the person or the immediate presence of another." Where an indictment gives rise to such an inference, it need not explicitly state this essential element in order to sufficiently inform the defendant of the charges against him.

Where an indictment for armed robbery properly charges conjunctively that the defendant took property "from the person and immediate presence" of the victim and the state offers proof to show commission of the offense by either method, a jury charge in the disjunctive pursuant to the language of the statute is not error.

E. "Force" Requirement

1. By "Force"

This theory of the modus operandi of robbery focuses on the force or violence displayed by the robber, rather than on any resistance or violence on the victim's part. Under this conception of the force requirement, the Georgia Court of Appeals has upheld robbery convictions when it was shown that (1) the robber removed a wrist watch with sufficient "force" to stop the victim from walking and to spin the victim around; (2) the robber took money out of a cash register while grabbing the victim's arm; (3) the robber grabbed the victim around the neck and then grabbed his wallet and left; (4) the robber picked up money dropped by the victim after he used force to push her down an embankment and throw her between two bushes; (5) the robber took the victim's purse after he slapped her and threw her down three times; and (6) the robber drove off in the victim's car as the victim was running away after he was grabbed and hit by another. Because of this focus on the robber and not the victim, it is not necessary that the victim be conscious or even alive at the time of the taking.

"Force" implies actual personal violence, a struggle, and a personal outrage committed upon the person of the victim which precedes the defendant's nonconsensual taking of the property.

The force essential to a robbery can either precede the taking or occur contemporaneously with it. Thus, where there is proof that the defendant's use of force preceded the theft of an automobile, the fact that his victim was dead at the time of the actual taking would not prevent a conviction for robbery by force.

Although the assailant has custody of an item pursuant to the victim's consent, possession of the item does not change to the assailant until the victim, by means of violence, has been dissuaded from seeking its return. That being so, it is the force which effects the taking.

2. By Intimidation

Robbery by intimidation is not a lesser included offense of robbery by force, but rather a different method of committing robbery. Robbery by intimidation is the same as putting in fear at common law, and focuses on constructive force, as is present when a person is induced through fear to part with his property. The intimidation must take the form of a threat, coercion, or placing the victim in fear of immediate bodily injury to himself or to another. One court found this element to be satisfied when a gas station attendant placed gasoline in a car and was later informed while looking into the end of a shotgun barrel that he should forego any thought of collecting the money due. In another case, this element was found to be satisfied when the defendant had his hand in his jacket pocket and pointed at the victim as though he had a weapon concealed in the pocket, and told the victim to give him all the money in the register drawer.

There is no requirement that a reasonable man standard be applied in order to authorize a conviction for robbery by intimidation. A conviction is authorized by the actual apprehension of danger on the part of the victim. The relevance of a reasonable man standard occurs only where the law presumes actual apprehension of danger from evidence that there was just ground for it. Thus, a jury charge omitting a reference to a reasonable man standard for determining apprehension of danger would be more advantageous to the defendant than required and would not be erroneous.

3. By Sudden Snatching

This theory of "force" is satisfied where the victim is relieved of some possession so quickly that he does not have time to react, even though he is aware of the taking.

If the victim is aware of the taking of property from his immediate presence before the taking is complete, the offense committed is robbery by sudden snatching. If the victim is not aware of the taking until it is complete, the offense committed is not robbery by sudden snatching but rather theft by taking.

It is not necessary to show that the defendant employed violence and that the victim resisted in order to prove robbery by sudden snatching. However, if such evidence is adduced at trial, it would not amount to a fatal variance between the allegations and proof that would preclude the defendant's conviction for robbery by sudden snatching.

4. Armed Robbery Modus Operandi

Armed robbery is distinguished from robbery by the requirement that the force element be satisfied by use of an offensive weapon. The offensive weapon must be used prior to or contemporaneously with the taking. Thus, where the taking is completed after the victim has been shot and killed, a conviction for armed robbery is authorized. Where the taking is completed while the victim is asleep before she is awakened and sexually assaulted at gunpoint, no armed robbery has occurred. In this situation, § 16-8-41 "clearly contemplates that the offensive weapon be used as a concomitant to a taking which involves the use of actual force or intimidation (constructive force) against another person." If there is ample evidence of the use of actual force, evidence of constructive force or intimidation is unnecessary.

Although the victim may not have actually seen the taking of his property during the armed robbery, if the victim was clearly aware that his life and property were at risk, there would be sufficient evidence of force to support an armed robbery conviction.

The jury is entitled to reject the defendant's claim that he did not produce the offensive weapon until after the taking and accept the victim's testimony depicting an armed robbery.

Armed robbery does not occur unless the robber's use of an offensive weapon directly or indirectly induces the possessor of property to relinquish possession to the robber. If the possessor acts in concert with the robber and relinquishes control over the property pursuant to their pre-arranged agreement, an essential element of robbery, i. e., force or intimidation, is missing. In such a case, since the possessor can admit the charge that she aided and abetted the robber by relinquishing possession of the property voluntarily and still be innocent of armed robbery, an indictment charging the possessor with felony murder, with the armed robbery as the underlying felony, is fatally defective.

All participants in a plan to commit armed robbery are responsible for the criminal acts that are a probable consequence of the plan and are committed while executing it. Moreover, a participant may be convicted despite not being the actual perpetrator of the armed robbery. Where the evidence is sufficient to find the defendant guilty of armed robbery as a party to the offense, it need not be shown that the defendant personally wielded a gun during the commission of the robbery. Furthermore, a defendant can be convicted of armed robbery even though he might not have had knowledge that his accomplice was going to use a weapon to perpetrate it, so long as it can be found that the defendant was a party to the offense and that the use of the weapon by the accomplice was naturally or necessarily done in furtherance of the conspiracy to commit the robbery even though not part of the original agreement.

In several gasoline theft cases the Court of Appeals has held that the required taking occurs when the attendant asks for payment and is refused, rather than when the gasoline is pumped into the vehicle. Accordingly, the inquiry into the validity of an armed robbery conviction focuses on whether the refusal of payment was accomplished by use of an offensive weapon.

Although the statute does not specifically define "offensive weapon," this element has been held to be satisfied even though the defendant asserted that the gun was only a cap pistol. The court did not, however, articulate the reason for finding an offensive weapon in this case. A possible inference from the case, however, is that the character of the weapon will be determined by the victim's reasonable apprehension rather than the actual offensive nature of the weapon. Thus, if the article or device appears to the victim to be an offensive weapon, it is no defense that the defendant did not actually have a gun or other offensive weapon in his possession when he committed the robbery.

An armed robber need not use an offensive weapon in a menacing or threatening manner to accomplish the robbery. Rather, the victim need only be aware of the defendant's use of a weapon which has the desired forceful effect of assisting to accomplish the robbery.

Since the purpose of using "any replica, article, or device having the appearance of [an offensive] weapon" is to create a reasonable apprehension on the part of the victim that an offensive weapon is being used, it is immaterial whether such apprehension is created by use of the sense of vision or by any other sense, provided that the apprehension is reasonable under the circumstances. Thus, the weapon does not have to be visible as far as being in the hand of or shown to the victim by the accused in order to convict him of armed robbery. The legislature intended § 16-8-41 to encompass armed robbers who have concealed offensive weapons in their pockets or under wraps or other devices. However, while the presence of a weapon during the commission of a robbery may be established without proof that the weapon was actually seen, some physical manifestation of a weapon is required or some evidence from which the presence of a weapon may be inferred. If an indictment alleges that an armed robbery was committed with the "use of a knife," the proof must show it. Evidence that the victim saw "something shiny" in the defendant's hand would be insufficient. However, evidence that the defendant used a weapon of a similar nature capable of inflicting the same character of injury upon the victim as the knife alleged in the indictment would not constitute a fatal variance.

Where an indictment specifically charges the defendant with committing an armed robbery by use of an offensive weapon, a trial court's jury instruction, which recites the entire armed robbery statute, is unlikely to mislead the jury into convicting the defendant of armed robbery by any other means than as charged in the indictment if the evidence shows that an offensive weapon was used in the commission of the robbery and if the trial court reads directly from the indictment in the course of instructing the jury.

An armed robbery indictment, which alleges that the defendant intended to commit theft by taking the victims' money "by use of an offensive weapon, to wit: a firearm," would not be void merely because it fails to specify the type or caliber of the weapon. The law does not require such specificity in describing the weapon used to perpetrate an armed robbery.

In a case dealing with the federal bank robbery statute, the U.S. Supreme Court concluded that an unloaded gun is a "dangerous weapon." First, a gun is an article that is typically and characteristically dangerous; the use for which it is manufactured and sold is a dangerous one, and the law reasonably may presume that such an article is always dangerous even though it may not be armed at a particular time or place. In addition, the display of a gun instills fear in the average citizen; as a consequence, it creates an immediate danger that a violent response will ensue. Finally, a gun can cause harm when used as a bludgeon.

Although the state must prove the defendant was in possession of an offensive weapon during the armed robbery, it is not required to prove the victim's awareness of the defendant's possession. Nor is the state required to prove the use of a gun containing ammunition. In fact, it does not have to prove that the gun was loaded.

The victim's testimony about the defendant's use of a weapon is sufficient to establish the element of use of an offensive weapon. However, the victim's testimony is not required if there is testimony from other witnesses which establishes this element of the offense. Also, it has been held that a doctor's testimony concerning the nature and extent of a victim's injuries and photographs depicting a victim's injuries are clearly relevant to show that a robbery was committed by use of an offensive weapon.

III. Miscellaneous

A. Punishment

Robbery is punishable by one to twenty years' imprisonment. Robbery of a person who is 65 years of age or older is punishable by five to twenty years' imprisonment.

Armed robbery is punishable by death, life imprisonment, or imprisonment from ten to twenty years. This offense is also punishable according to the sentencing and punishment provisions of §§ 17-10-6.1 and 17-10-7, which provide for mandatory minimum sentences and sentences for life without possibility of parole in certain cases and provide restrictions on the authority of the State Board of Pardons and Paroles to grant paroles. Armed robbery is not a reducible felony under § 17-10-5.

Taking what is perceived as a mandate from the United States Supreme Court, the Georgia Supreme Court has held that the death sentence cannot constitutionally be imposed in an armed robbery case where the victim does not die. However, armed robbery, as an alleged contemporaneous capital felony, would support a death sentence for murder.

Prior to 1995, a defendant who had been convicted of a second or subsequent armed robbery had to be sentenced by the trial court to imprisonment for not less than ten years. Under current law, a defendant who has been convicted once of an armed robbery or another "serious violent felony" and who after such first conviction subsequently commits and is convicted of an armed robbery for which he is not sentenced to death must be sentenced by the trial court to imprisonment for life without parole.

The armed robbery statute allows for the imposition of a life sentence or a determinate sentence, whether or not the offender was sentenced as a recidivist. If a defendant charged with armed robbery is indicted as a recidivist, the trial court is authorized to sentence the defendant under the general recidivist statute to the longest period of time prescribed for the punishment of armed robbery, i.e., life imprisonment. Where a defendant charged with armed robbery is not indicted as a recidivist, the trial court is likewise authorized to sentence the defendant to life imprisonment based on an exercise of its judicial discretion as applied to the facts of the case and the aggravating factor of the defendant's prior felony conviction for armed robbery. If a defendant charged with armed robbery is indicted as a "serious violent felony" recidivist, the trial court is authorized to sentence the defendant to imprisonment for life without parole.

There is a special punishment provision for those who intentionally inflict bodily injury in the course of an armed robbery in which a controlled substance is taken from a pharmacy or wholesale druggist. A minimum of fifteen years' imprisonment is mandated for those who commit such a crime.

Because the current statutory language prohibits modification of a sentence for armed robbery, the act of a judge in probating a sentence for armed robbery is void.

The crimes of armed robbery and theft by receiving are mutually exclusive of each other, and a defendant cannot be convicted of both crimes where the crimes involved the same property.

B. Forfeiture of Property Used in Armed Robbery

All motor vehicles, tools, and weapons which are used or intended for use in any manner in the commission of or to facilitate the commission of an armed robbery are subject to forfeiture.

C. Relationship of Robbery and Armed Robbery to Other Offenses

Important Notice about Repudiation of Actual or Same Evidence Test: The Georgia Supreme Court repudiated the actual evidence test in *Drinkard v. Walker*, 281 Ga. 211, 636 S.E.2d 530 (2006), because it found this test to be inconsistent with the statutory framework governing the prohibition against multiple convictions for included offenses in Georgia. This inconsistency resulted in years of confusion and unpredictable results. In its place, the court adopted the required evidence test and overruled any prior case law that is inconsistent with it. Thus, any prior case law applying the actual evidence test is no longer controlling and should not be relied upon to determine whether one offense is included in another under § 16-1-6(1). The discussion of such case law is included below only insofar as it may still be applicable to pending prosecutions that arose before the Drinkard decision. See MULTIPLE CONVICTIONS, II. Tests to Determine Presence of Multiple Convictions, for a complete discussion of the Drinkard decision.

A number of cases in the area of robbery and armed robbery have considered the problem of determining what are lesser included offenses because of the language found in § 16-8-41(a) that: "The offense of robbery by intimidation shall be a lesser included offense in the offense of armed robbery." Most decisions in this area involve a defendant who was convicted of armed robbery and is seeking a new trial with instructions on robbery by intimidation. If the evidence clearly supports only an armed robbery conviction, then no new trial is required.

Soon after the 1968 revision of the criminal code it was held that if the evidence authorized a conviction for armed robbery it **could not authorize** a conviction for the lesser offense of robbery by intimidation. In these cases, therefore, the failure of the judge to charge the jury on robbery by intimidation was held not to be error. Then, in Holcomb v. State, the Georgia Supreme Court was confronted by this certified question from the Court of Appeals: "Where the evidence establishes that an accused committed a robbery by the use of an offensive weapon may he or his co-conspirator be convicted of the 'lesser included offense' of robbery by intimidation?" The Holcomb court answered that the "could not authorize" terminology in prior cases was incorrect and stated that "we should have held that the failure to charge on robbery by intimidation was not error because the evidence did not **demand** a charge on that offense." In other words, if on the record, the jury has evidence from which it can conclude that only robbery by intimidation was committed, it should be so instructed. Since this decision, failure to charge robbery by intimidation is still not reversible error if **all** the credible "evidence showed completion of the greater offense of armed robbery, so that the charge on the lesser offense was not required."

Likewise, it is not necessary to charge on the lesser included offenses of robbery and theft by taking, where the evidence demonstrates completion of the greater offense of armed robbery and there is no evidence raising the lesser offenses. Nor is it necessary to charge on the lesser included offense of theft by taking, where the evidence demonstrates that the offense, if any, is robbery by sudden snatching and there is no evidence of the lesser offense or where the evidence demonstrates that the defendant committed the robbery either by use of a replica of a handgun or by intimidation. Nor is it necessary to charge on the lesser included offense of robbery by force or criminal attempt where the evidence demonstrates either the completion of the greater offense of armed robbery or no offense at all. A new trial, however, has been ordered where the trial judge failed to instruct on the lesser offenses and the evidence was such that the jury could have found the defendant guilty of only robbery by intimidation or theft by taking.

It is not error for a trial court to instruct a jury that before it can consider the lesser offense of theft by taking, it has to reject the other charges of armed robbery and robbery by intimidation. The jury's prior consideration of armed robbery or robbery by intimidation would not eliminate evidence from the jury's consideration which might authorize instead a verdict for theft by taking.

Where there is evidence to warrant the charge, the trial court may charge the jury that it can consider theft by deception as a lesser included offense of robbery.

For purposes of the § 16-1-7(a) rule against multiple convictions, armed robbery has been held to be a lesser included offense of felony murder, but not malice murder. Thus, an individual normally may stand convicted both of armed robbery and malice murder on the same set of facts.

Robbery by force and malice murder are separate crimes which do not merge as a matter of law. Moreover, they do not merge as a matter of fact where each crime is proved by distinct elements absent from the proof of the other.

Since the "assault" element of aggravated assault with intent to rob is contained within the "use of an offensive weapon" element of armed robbery and both crimes share the "intent to rob" element, there is no element of aggravated assault with intent to rob that is not contained in armed robbery. Therefore, an aggravated assault with intent to rob conviction would merge into an armed robbery conviction.

Aggravated assault is not a lesser included offense of armed robbery as a matter of law, although it may be included as a matter of fact. Deadly weapon aggravated assault may be as a matter of fact a lesser offense included in armed robbery. Aggravated assault is not included in attempted armed robbery as a matter of law, although these two offenses may merge as a matter of fact. However, where the underlying facts show that one crime was completed prior to the second crime, so that the crimes are separate as a matter of law, there is no merger. The crime of conspiracy to commit armed robbery does not merge with the crime of aggravated assault where the facts necessary to prove the conspiracy to commit armed robbery are not the same facts necessary to prove the aggravated assault. Robbery by intimidation does not merge with aggravated assault with intent to rob as a matter of fact where the acts described by the victim constituted separate offenses. Because the offenses of robbery by force and aggravated assault on a person over the age of 65 years have different elements and prohibit different conduct, neither is included in the other as a matter of law. Nor are they included as a matter of fact where the state proves each offense by different facts.

The offense of possession of a firearm during the commission of a felony does not merge into the offense of armed robbery upon convictions for both.

Since the rule against inconsistent verdicts has been abolished, a defendant's acquittal on a possession of a firearm charge does not require an acquittal on an armed robbery charge. The acquittal on the one charge and a conviction on the other may reflect a compromise or lenity by the jury rather than inconsistent factual conclusions.

Robbery and armed robbery do not merge as a matter of law where separate incidents involved different actions, different specific objectives or intents, and different victims. Robbery is not a lesser included offense of armed robbery where the evidence clearly establishes that the robbery was committed through the use of a weapon, and there is no evidence from which a jury can find that the robbery was committed without the use of such a weapon.

Robbery by force and armed robbery do not merge where the evidence shows that the acts constituting the offenses, although committed sequentially, were committed in different ways and where proof of the elements of the offenses were not satisfied by the introduction of the same evidence.

Simple battery is not as a matter of law an offense included in robbery by force. Aggravated battery may as a matter of fact merge with the greater offense of armed robbery or robbery by force. However, where the evidence shows that the robbery was complete before the aggravated battery occurred and where the evidence of neither offense was necessary to prove the other, there is no merger.

Neither theft by receiving nor theft by deception is a lesser included offense of armed robbery. Motor vehicle theft is not a lesser included offense of armed robbery as a matter of fact, where the evidence used to establish the motor vehicle theft is not the same evidence used to establish the armed robbery.

It has been held that the offenses of armed robbery and kidnapping can merge under certain factual situations. There is, however, not an automatic merger simply because two offenses may arise from the same series of events. It has been held that the offenses of armed robbery and kidnapping with bodily injury do not merge as a matter of fact or law, where the evidence of either offense is not necessary to prove the other. Thus, there was no merger, where the evidence showed that simple kidnapping was complete before the defendant armed with a pistol took money from the victim. It was not until after the victim handed the defendant the money that the defendant shot him in the leg. This additional, gratuitous violence followed, and was not an element of, the already completed act of armed robbery. The shooting was the bodily injury which aggravated the already completed simple kidnapping. Also, there was no merger where the evidence showed that the kidnapping was complete upon the defendant's pointing the gun at the victim's head and forcing him to drive the truck away; armed robbery occurred upon the defendant's tying the victim up and assuming control of the truck, using the gun to acquire and maintain superiority. The offenses of kidnapping with bodily injury and robbery by force do not merge as a matter of fact where the evidence shows that the kidnapping was complete before the robbery was effectuated.

Under Georgia's statutory double jeopardy provisions, there is no prohibition against a defendant's being convicted of both burglary and a completed criminal offense, such as armed robbery, after gaining entry into the dwelling, as each offense has distinct elements.

Using what could be described as a time sequence analysis in order to determine whether there was inclusion on the facts, the Court of Appeals in Barnett v. State held that the charge of terroristic threats did not merge with the charge of armed robbery. The evidence was sufficient to show the robbery was complete, in that the money from the cash register was in the defendant's possession before he made the alleged threat to the victim that he would kill her if she moved. Thus, the threat was not part of the armed robbery, but the evidence was sufficient to show that it was made with the purpose of terrorizing the victim to effect his escape from the scene of the robbery.

In State v. Smith, the Court of Appeals held that the trial court improperly merged eight of twelve armed robbery counts into four counts under an "incident location" theory. The record showed that each of the counts merged by the court for sentencing purposes involved separate individuals. Thus, the defendant's action against each individual was a separate crime and could not merge in fact or law.

While in some cases robbery by intimidation may be a lesser included offense of armed robbery, where the two offenses involve two separate incidents with two separate victims, the defendant would be properly convicted of both offenses because under these circumstances the offenses do not merge as a matter of law.

D. Venue

Venue for the offenses of robbery and armed robbery is the county where the taking occurred. Venue has been held to be proven where the victim testifies that the robbery occurred at her home and testifies later that her home is in a certain county.

E. Defenses

A claim of right is a defense to the crime of theft, not robbery by sudden snatching or armed robbery. To allow a claim of right defense to these offenses, within which the use of force is implicit, would sanction the use of force to claim the property.

Whether the defendant participated in an attempted robbery or abandoned the enterprise is for the jury to determine.

F. Statute of Limitations

In 1992, the General Assembly with the enactment of § 24-4-60 authorized the creation of a state deoxyribonucleic acid (DNA) data bank of samples obtained from convicted sex offenders in order to determine and retain the identification characteristics specific to these offenders. In 2000, the General Assembly broadened the scope of this statute by requiring the obtaining of DNA samples from all convicted felons and the storing of these samples in the data bank. An examination of these samples revealed that many matched the DNA evidence of old, unsolved rape cases. Despite this evidence, the state could not prosecute the convicted felons because the limitation periods for their crimes had expired. Remedial legislation was necessary to enable the state to use identification evidence derived from the state's DNA data bank to prosecute convicted felons for certain crimes even though the limitation periods previously established by law had expired.

Accordingly, the General Assembly eliminated the statute of limitations for any armed robbery occurring on or after July 1, 2002, when DNA evidence is used to establish the identity of the accused. A sufficient portion of the physical evidence tested for DNA, however, must be preserved and available for testing by the accused. Furthermore, if the DNA evidence does not establish the identity of the accused, the limitation on the prosecution reverts to the seven-year period specified in § 17-3-1(b).

SEXUAL OFFENSES AGAINST CHILDREN

See also CONSENSUAL SEXUAL INTERCOURSE OR MARRIAGE; CRIME PREVENTION DEFENSE; OBSCENITY; RAPE; UNNATURAL SEXUAL ACTS.

I. Statutory Rape

A. Elements

Statutory rape, § 16-6-3, is one of four sexual offenses in the criminal code primarily designed to protect children from deviant sexual conduct. Defined as sexual intercourse with a person under the age of 16 years, statutory rape is the only one of the four sexual offenses against children which requires nothing more than a general mens rea. The reason for this may be that statutory rape often causes extensive physical harm to its victim, while sexual offenses, such as child molestation and enticing a child for indecent purposes, are less likely to cause such harm.

In any event, it is clear that a conviction for statutory rape will be had upon proof of two elements: that the defendant engaged in sexual intercourse with the victim and that the victim was less than 16 years of age. Neither force nor lack of consent need be shown. The statute can be used, therefore, to punish a person who engages in consensual sexual intercourse, as the statute creates a conclusive presumption that a person under the age of 16 years is legally incapable of consenting to sexual relations. Furthermore, apparently one may be convicted of statutory rape even though he or she had an actual and reasonable belief that the victim was above the age of 16 years because knowledge of the victim's age is not part of the statute's mens rea.

In 1999, the General Assembly changed the definition of forcible rape to provide that a person commits the offense when he has carnal knowledge of "[a] female who is less than ten years of age." The enactment of this definition reestablished the common-law rule that rape includes consensual relations with a female under ten years of age and the common-sense principle that sexual intercourse with a female under ten years of age is a forcible act constituting rape as a matter of law. By extending the application of the forcible rape statute to sexual intercourse with females under ten years of age, the General Assembly has implicitly limited the application of the statutory rape statute. Before the enactment of this definition, all sexual intercourse with females under the age of consent was subject to the application of the statutory rape statute. Under the current statutory scheme, sexual intercourse with a female under ten years of age is no longer subject to the application of the statutory rape statute but is instead subject to the application of the forcible rape statute. Sexual intercourse with a female under ten years of age, which had to be prosecuted in many cases in the past as statutory rape because of the extreme difficulty of proving force, must now be prosecuted and punished under the forcible rape statute. This statutory scheme, however, may be subject to constitutional attack as a violation of equal protection guarantees by reason of its underinclusion of male victims and female perpetrators.

B. Attempt

An indictment charging a defendant with attempted statutory rape is not subject to a general demurrer merely because it fails to allege an essential element of the completed crime. An element that is essential in proving the completed crime does not mean that it is indispensable in proving criminal attempt. The relevant question is whether the acts alleged in the indictment constitute a substantial step toward the commission of the crime. What constitutes a substantial step is a question of degree, and depends upon the circumstances of each case. Where it cannot be said as a matter of law that the alleged acts do not constitute a substantial step, the indictment is not fatally defective for failure to allege the commission of a crime.

C. Evidence

1. Corroboration Requirement

Although the requirement that a victim's testimony be corroborated has been deleted from the forcible rape statute, corroboration is still required in statutory rape. The standard for corroborating the victim's testimony in statutory rape cases is the same as that which was applied to forcible rape cases. Traditionally, both the commission of the crime and the identity of the defendant had to be verified by independent testimony. Today, however, only the fact of the commission of the crime need be corroborated by other evidence; independent identification evidence no longer need be introduced. The requirement is satisfied so long as there is **some** independent evidence which tends to prove that the incident occurred as alleged.

In any case, the sufficiency of the evidence is a question for the jury's determination, which will not be disturbed by the appellate courts if any corroborating evidence was introduced. For example, the victim's testimony has been held sufficiently corroborated by her outcry or report of the incident to the police or some other person, by her description of the clothing that the defendant was wearing at the time of the attack, by her actions and demeanor following the attack, and even by her letter to a relative describing the attack. It has also been held that the victim's testimony may be corroborated by the defendant's inculpatory statements, by the victim's prior consistent statements as recounted by others, by a psychotherapist's testimony that the victim showed signs of child sexual abuse syndrome, and by medical evidence. The Georgia Supreme Court has held, furthermore, that a lie detector test can be used to corroborate the testimony of the victim of statutory rape, at least where there had been a pretest stipulation between the state and the defendant.

2. Victim's Behavior

In statutory rape cases, since the illegal sexual or carnal intercourse is with a victim under the age of consent, the issues of consent and chastity are not material, and it would serve no useful purpose to allow a thorough and sifting examination as to the victim's credibility in regard to such issues. The defendant, therefore, is precluded from cross-examining the victim on these issues.

Notwithstanding this exclusionary rule, the Court of Appeals found in a number of its decisions that the Rape Shield Statute applied in statutory rape cases even though the statute's exceptions relating to consent and the accused's prior participation were inapplicable. Thus, without exception, inquiring into the victim's past sexual behavior was not permitted. The Georgia Supreme Court, however, implicitly disapproved of these decisions in Abdulkadir v. State because it found that the Rape Shield Statute, by its plain terms, applied only in prosecutions for rape. While there might be compelling policy reasons to apply the Rape Shield Statute in prosecutions for sexual crimes other than rape, the General Assembly's express limitation of the statute's applicability to prosecutions for rape excluded its application in prosecutions for all other sexual crimes. Since the courts are not authorized to expand a statute's application beyond its plain terms, the Supreme Court stated that any expansion of the Rape Shield Statute's applicability had to come from the General Assembly, as it alone is entrusted with the authority to amend existing laws.

In response to this decision, the General Assembly, apparently recognizing that there were compelling policy reasons for the expansion of the Rape Shield Statute's applicability, amended the statute in 2005 so that it is now expressly applicable not only in prosecutions for rape but also in prosecutions for aggravated sodomy, aggravated child molestation, and aggravated sexual battery. This amendment applies to all trials that commence on or after July 1, 2005. It should be noted, however, that this 2005 amendment does not abrogate the exclusionary rule previously applied in statutory rape cases. Any consideration as to the Rape Shield Statute's present inapplicability in statutory rape cases is pretermitted because evidence of the victim's past sexual behavior would be inadmissible and properly excluded based on the established precedent of the Georgia Supreme Court.

Testimony regarding the victim's alleged past false accusations against persons other than the defendant is admissible in statutory rape cases. Before ruling on the admissibility of such evidence, the trial court must make a threshold determination outside the presence of the jury that a reasonable probability of falsity existed.

3. Similar Offenses

As is true in prosecutions for many of the sexual offenses in the criminal code, the courts are fairly lenient in permitting the introduction of evidence of similar offenses in which the defendant was involved for the purpose of establishing the defendant's identity, motive, intent, plan or scheme, or bent of mind. Thus, testimony that the defendant had been involved in a prior, forcible rape is admissible as similar transaction evidence in a statutory rape case. However, there must exist a sufficient similarity or connection between the prior independent crime and the statutory rape charged in the case in order for the evidence to be admissible at trial. It should be noted that such evidence is not necessarily limited to the defendant's previous illegal conduct.

4. Other Acts of Intercourse with the Defendant

Statements by the victim of previous acts of sexual intercourse with the defendant is admissible as evidence of prior difficulties between the defendant and the victim. The prosecution's failure to provide notice of this evidence to the defense prior to trial does not render the evidence inadmissible.

Evidence of an unindicted act of intercourse occurring a few days after the indicted act of intercourse was committed may be properly admitted as res gestae.

D. Constitutional Issues

A constitutionally based attack was made on Georgia's statutory rape statute based on a claim that the statute violated the Equal Protection Clause in that it protected females exclusively and penalized males exclusively. This claim of unconstitutionality was rejected by the Georgia Supreme Court in Barnes v. State. In Barnes, the court held that the gender-based classification in the statutory rape statute was substantially related to the legislative objectives of protecting young girls from the unique physical and psychological damage resulting from sexual intercourse with males. Additionally, and more importantly, the child molestation statute provided penalties identical to those for statutory rape. Thus, a woman engaging in sexual intercourse with a male child less than 14 years of age, while violating a different statute, was subject to the same penalties as a man who committed statutory rape. These statutes, according to the court, provided a general statutory scheme giving protection to both male and female children under the age of 14, regardless of the offender's gender.

Another constitutionally based attack was made on Georgia's statutory rape statute based on a claim that it was a violation of equal protection under the law to adjudge a male juvenile to be delinquent for the statutory rape of an underage female without holding the female to any sort of responsibility. This claim of unconstitutionality was also rejected by the Georgia Supreme Court in In the Interest of B. L. S. The Georgia Supreme Court, basing its decision on its holding in Barnes, held that because the child molestation statute provided penalties identical to those for statutory rape, a female "child" under the age of 17 who engaged in sexual intercourse with a male who was under the age of 14 was subject to the same delinquency adjudication as a male "child" who was adjudged to be delinquent by reason of his commission of statutory rape. Thus, the statutory rape statute was not invalid as depriving the male juvenile of equal protection of the law.

In dissent, Justice Sears argued that while young boys were in as much need of protection from premature sexual intercourse with adults as were young girls, they did not get the same protection under the child molestation statute as young girls did under the statutory rape statute. Justice Sears argued that the lenient sentencing options provided in the child molestation statute, which were not available in the statutory rape statute, lessened the penalties that could be imposed on female perpetrators and lessened the protection available to young boys. Also, application of the two statutes could easily result in a harsher penalty being assessed against a male criminal defendant than the penalty imposed against a similarly situated female defendant. Thus, Georgia's statutory rape law, as written, violated constitutional equal protection guarantees by reason of the underinclusion of male victims and female perpetrators.

It appears that the General Assembly, recognizing the validity of Justice Sears' argument, decided to gender neutralize the statutory rape statute in 1995 in order to extend that statute's coverage to those formerly excluded, i.e., to male victims and female perpetrators. In light of this 1995 amendment, it thus appears that the holdings of the Georgia Supreme Court in Barnes v. State and *In the Interest of B. L. S.* are no longer controlling.

In Phagan v. State, the defendant contended that the 1995 amendment to the statutory rape statute, which expanded the coverage of the statute to minors under the age of 16, was unconstitutional when applied to him since he had lawfully engaged in consensual sexual activity with the minor before the effective date of the amendment, and was thereby entitled, under the auspices of the constitutional right of privacy, to continue the activity. The Georgia Supreme Court disagreed with this contention. Whatever privacy interest the defendant invoked to protect his consensual sexual activity with a 15-year-old female not his spouse did not offer a safehaven from the 1995 amendment's criminalization of the conduct. In raising the age at which a minor may consent to sexual intercourse, the General Assembly acted to further the state's compelling interests in safeguarding young people. In light of these compelling interests, the trial court properly upheld the age amendment against the defendant's constitutional challenge.

E. Relationship to Other Offenses

Important Notice about Repudiation of Actual or Same Evidence Test: The Georgia Supreme Court repudiated the actual evidence test in *Drinkard v. Walker*, 281 Ga. 211, 636 S.E.2d 530 (2006), because it found this test to be inconsistent with the statutory framework governing the prohibition against multiple convictions for included offenses in Georgia. This inconsistency resulted in years of confusion and unpredictable results. In its place, the court adopted the required evidence test and overruled any prior case law that is inconsistent with it. Thus, any prior case law applying the actual evidence test is no longer controlling and should not be relied upon to determine whether one offense is included in another under § 16-1-6(1). The discussion of such case law is included below only insofar as it may still be applicable to pending prosecutions that arose before the Drinkard decision. See MULTIPLE CONVICTIONS, II. Tests to Determine Presence of Multiple Convictions, for a complete discussion of the Drinkard decision.

Although no other sexual offense has been held to be a necessarily included offense of statutory rape, on the facts of particular cases incest, child molestation, and fornication could be lesser included offenses of statutory rape.

The statutory rape and child molestation statutes are part of a legislative framework aimed at protecting children from sexual exploitation and abuse. As part of a coordinated scheme relating to the same subject matter, the Georgia Supreme Court found in Dixon v. State that these statutes had to be construed together to determine how the General Assembly intended to treat conduct involving a victim who was 14 or 15 years of age and a defendant who was no more than three years older than the victim. Construing these statutes together as they appeared in the Code in 2004 showed a clear legislative intent to prosecute such conduct as misdemeanor statutory rape rather than felony child molestation. First, in 1996 the General Assembly amended the statutory rape statute specifically to eliminate any discretion over whether to punish conduct meeting the misdemeanor statutory rape criteria as either felony or misdemeanor statutory rape. When the General Assembly eliminated this discretion, it intended the misdemeanor provision to have exclusive application to conduct falling within its parameters. Allowing the state to retain the discretion to prosecute the same conduct as either misdemeanor statutory rape or felony child molestation would have defeated this legislative intent. Second, since the misdemeanor statutory rape provision was far more specific concerning such conduct than the child molestation statute, this more specific provision should have prevailed over the general statute and any prosecution should have proceeded under this provision. Third, the misdemeanor statutory rape provision reflected the most recent legislative judgment regarding the appropriate punishment for such conduct. Since the General Assembly most recently declared that sex between teenagers less than three years apart should have been punished as misdemeanor statutory rape, and not felony child molestation, that judgment would have to prevail. Finally, given the conflict between the two statutes concerning their prescribed punishments, the rule of lenity would require that a defendant receive only the lesser of the two possible punishments.

Notwithstanding this construction in Dixon, the Georgia Supreme Court encouraged the General Assembly to examine this case and make a more recognizable distinction between statutory rape, child molestation, and the other sexual crimes, and to clarify the sort of conduct that would qualify for the minimum sentence accompanying a conviction for aggravated child molestation. The court stated that the conflicting nature of the statutory scheme relating to sexual conduct, especially with respect to teenagers, might lead to inconsistent results. Under the statutes as they appeared in 2004, it was entirely possible that teenagers could have been convicted of aggravated child molestation and received the concomitant ten-year minimum sentence, if they willingly engaged in sexual activity, but stopped short of the actual act of sexual intercourse, so long as one experienced slight pain or received even minor injuries incidental to the act.

In 2006, the General Assembly responded to the court's concern about the conflict and lack of clarity in this statutory scheme. It prescribed, in accord with the statutory rape statute, misdemeanor punishment for teenagers within a certain age range who willingly engage in sexual activity that constitutes child molestation or aggravated child molestation. Moreover, the General Assembly explicitly provided that an act of sodomy is the sort of conduct that would qualify for misdemeanor punishment accompanying a teenager's conviction for aggravated child molestation. By limiting the sexual activity that can serve as the basis of a charge of misdemeanor aggravated child molestation to an act of sodomy, the General Assembly is expressing a clear legislative intent that an act of sexual intercourse between teenagers within a certain age range does not qualify as aggravated child molestation. Rather, the misdemeanor statutory rape provision would apply exclusively to such sexual activity.

It is error to convict a person of child molestation and statutory rape for the same conduct. He may be prosecuted for both offenses, but he may not be convicted of both. However, the offense of child molestation does not merge into the offense of statutory rape where the evidence shows that the defendant fondled the victim and, in an entirely separate incident later that evening, raped her. Likewise, the offenses do not merge where the evidence shows that the offense of child molestation was complete when the defendant without regard to his subsequent acts removed the clothing of the victim with the requisite intent, and where the evidence shows that the offense of statutory rape was not initiated until the defendant without regard to his previous acts began to engage in sexual intercourse with the underage victim.

Because the crimes of rape and statutory rape are separate offenses which require proof of different elements, they are not included within each other as a matter of law. Furthermore, even where the evidence at trial shows that there was only one act of sexual intercourse, the crime of statutory rape is not included, as a matter of fact, in the crime of rape. The fact that the act of sexual intercourse supports an element in each crime does not warrant merging of the sentences where other mutually exclusive elements of the crimes remain.

The fact that an underage child is incapable of consenting to an act of sexual intercourse under the statutory rape statute would not preclude a finding that an unmarried child who voluntarily has sexual intercourse with another person commits the delinquent act of fornication and therefore is in need of treatment and rehabilitation.

F. Punishment

Except as provided in § 16-6-3(c), statutory rape is a felony punishable by imprisonment for not less than one nor more than 20 years. However, if the person convicted of statutory rape was 21 years of age or older, the offense would be punishable by imprisonment for not less than ten nor more than 20 years. In addition to these punishments, an offender would be subject to the sentencing and punishment provisions of § 17-10-6.2, which requires the offender to receive a mandatory split sentence including a minimum sentence of imprisonment.

Section 16-6-3(c) provides a lesser punishment for a statutory rape involving teenagers. If the victim was at least 14 but less than 16 years of age and the person convicted of statutory rape was 18 years of age or younger and was no more than four years older than the victim, the statutory rape would be punishable only as a misdemeanor.

In *Phagan v. State*, the Georgia Supreme Court held that this sentencing scheme, which provides harsher punishment for older persons found guilty of statutory rape, does not violate the Equal Protection Clause. The General Assembly could have reasonably decided that persons beyond a certain age should have sufficient maturity and judgment to be held responsible for conduct which might be excusable in a younger person. Thus, the General Assembly had a rational basis for enacting the amendment calling for disparate sentences based on the age of the perpetrator.

The rule of lenity applies when two statutory provisions governing the same conduct are conflicting with respect to their prescribed punishments, i.e., where one provision punishes the same conduct to a lesser degree than the other provision. In such a situation, a defendant would be entitled to have the lesser of two penalties administered. In *Orr v. State*, the Court of Appeals found that because the indictment made no mention of the defendant's age, its allegations only set forth a charge of felony statutory rape. The jury was only charged as to this species of rape and, thus, its verdict had to be reasonably construed as finding the defendant guilty of statutory rape as charged. Accordingly, the trial court was not compelled under the rule of lenity to impose misdemeanor punishment, and its imposition of felony punishment did not constitute error.

Where two or more charges of statutory rape differ from one another only with respect to the averment of date and where the date is not made an essential element in any of the charges, if all the dates alleged fall within the period of the statute of limitation, only one sentence can be imposed. This rule applies in prosecutions for multiple sexual assaults against child victims where the state finds it impractical to treat the dates specified in the charges as material averments.

II. Child Molestation and Aggravated Child Molestation

A. Elements

1. Mens Rea

While statutory rape is a general intent offense, the other three sexual offenses against children found in the criminal code, child molestation, aggravated child molestation, and enticing a child for indecent purposes, are specific intent offenses.

Whether the defendant had the requisite intent when he committed the act of molestation is a matter for jury resolution. Case law provides some assistance as to what showing of intent is necessary to satisfy the statute. A showing of a "general plan" of the defendant to use the child to gratify the defendant's lust or passions or sexual desires is not required by the statute. Furthermore, the defendant need not have intended to actually use the child's body in some physical capacity in order to commit an act of molestation. It is sufficient if the defendant utilizes or capitalizes on the child's mere presence as a witness to his intentional immoral or indecent act, provided the act is accomplished "with the intent to arouse or satisfy the sexual desires" of either the child or the defendant. The courts have held that the jury can infer the requisite intent of "arousing or satisfying sexual desires" from the commission of the proscribed act. However, proof of the defendant's actual arousal is not required. In a juvenile proceeding, a showing that the juvenile had the intent or knowledge of an adult is not required; all that needs to be shown is that the juvenile committed the proscribed act with the intent to satisfy his own sexual desires.

Implicit in an indictment charging a defendant with child molestation is that the act of molestation was committed with an intent to arouse or satisfy the defendant's or the child's sexual desires. Thus, the indictment need not expressly allege the defendant's specific intent with regard to that act.

2. Actus Reus

a. Child Molestation: Immoral or Indecent Acts Involving Child

The child molestation statute prohibits the commission of "any immoral or indecent act to or in the presence of or with any child under the age of 16 years," when such act is accompanied by an intent "to arouse or satisfy the sexual desires" of either the child or the actor.

The statute does not define "immoral or indecent act." However, the lack of a precise definition most likely does not render the statute vulnerable to a Fourteenth Amendment attack on vagueness grounds. As the commentary to the 1968 revision of the criminal code points out, the child molestation statute "substantially restates the law embodied" in the statute's predecessor, which was upheld by the Georgia Supreme Court in the face of such an attack. Whether the defendant committed an indecent or immoral act in the presence of the victim is a question for the jury to decide.

Society as reflected in the jury's verdict determines whether the indicted sexual act is immoral or indecent. The child's view of the sexual act is irrelevant. Thus, evidence that a 14-year-old victim consented to the act of sexual intercourse with the defendant and that he later bragged about it to others would not be relevant to show that the act of sexual intercourse was not immoral or indecent to the child.

Case law provides some assistance in defining the prohibited act. Clearly, no penetration is required for child molestation to occur. Merely fondling the child's body, accompanied by the requisite intent, will constitute the offense. Whether the child was clothed or unclothed is not a factor in determining whether the act is "immoral or indecent." While the statutory language makes clear that an indecent act short of touching will suffice, there must be sufficient contact between the defendant and the victim to constitute the crime of child molestation. In other words, they must be together in order for the crime to be committed. For instance, showing a sexually explicit videotape to a child in one's home or soliciting a child to engage in sexual activities while in the child's bedroom would satisfy the "presence" requirement of the statute because there would be sufficient contact with the child, but engaging in a sexually explicit telephone conversation with a child would not, because the only contact with the victim would be through the telephone. Although the statute requires that the defendant perform the indecent act in the child's presence, it does not require the child to observe the entire act. As long as the child can see the person and the person is aware of the presence of the child, there is no specific limit to how far away that person can be before he can no longer be considered to be in the presence of the child.

Obviously, commission of any of the acts constituting the crime of public indecency would be sufficient to constitute the actus reus of child molestation, as the two statutes are in pari materia and should, therefore, be construed together. For instance, consenting sexual intercourse between husband and wife would be transformed from acceptable and protected marital conduct into an immoral and indecent act, where the act is committed openly and intentionally in the presence of children. By such conduct, the husband and wife have converted their residence from a constitutionally protected zone of privacy into a public place, thereby subjecting their conduct to criminal prosecution.

Because injury is not a necessary element of the crime of child molestation, the state has no duty to establish that the victim was hurt.

The offense of child molestation is a crime against the person, and every child involved in an incident is a victim of this crime. Thus, where the defendant allegedly exposed his penis during two separate incidents to a number of children as they were getting off their school bus, the defendant was properly indicted on eight counts of child molestation, one count for each victim, rather than on two counts, one count for each instance of exposure.

An indictment need not allege the details of the offense but may charge the defendant with child molestation in the general language of the statute. Where a count in an indictment charges a defendant with committing child molestation in more than one way, it is sufficient for the state to show that it was committed in at least one of the ways alleged in that count, even if the count used the conjunctive rather than disjunctive form. Accordingly, the trial court may instruct the jury that it can convict the defendant of child molestation if it finds that the defendant committed the offense in either of the ways specified in the indictment.

A jury charge reciting the entire statutory definition of child molestation is not in violation of a defendant's due process rights where it does not suggest that the jury can convict the defendant of child molestation in any way other than by the method specified in the indictment and where it instructs the jury that the state bears the burden of proving every material allegation in the indictment. Moreover, such a charge does not constitute error where the evidence does not raise a reasonable probability that the jury convicted the defendant of committing the offense by a method not specified in the indictment or where the trial court has properly limited the elements of the offense to those acts charged in the indictment. It should be noted, however, that in the absence of any request for a limiting instruction, there is no error in failing to give one.

b. Child Molestation: Electronically Transmitting Images of Immoral or Indecent Acts to Child

The child molestation statute also prohibits the electronic transmission of images of a person engaging in, inducing, or otherwise participating in any immoral or indecent act to a child under the age of 16 years with the intent to arouse or satisfy the sexual desires of either the child or the person.

A person is subject to prosecution in this state pursuant to § 17-2-1 for engaging in this prohibited conduct while (1) either within or outside of this state if such conduct involves a child who resides in this state, or (2) within this state if such conduct involves a child who resides within or outside this state.

c. Aggravated Child Molestation: Physical Injury or Sodomy Involving Child

The aggravated child molestation statute defines the offense as the commission of an act of child molestation which physically injures the child or involves an act of sodomy. If there is evidence of physical injury in the case, it is not necessary for the state to prove sodomy.

Where an indictment charges the defendant with committing the offense in only one of these ways, a jury charge reciting the entire statutory definition of aggravated child molestation is reversible error, when it raises a reasonable possibility that the jury, relying upon the evidence presented at trial, may convict the defendant of committing the offense in a way not alleged in the indictment. However, the jury charge as a whole does not constitute error if the trial court has sufficiently limited the jury's consideration to the elements of the offense as charged in the indictment and if the indictment is before the jury to aid them in their deliberations.

Since child molestation is an element of aggravated child molestation, it is proper for the trial court to define child molestation for the jury. Although it would be better practice for the trial court in an aggravated child molestation case involving sodomy to define "sodomy" in its charge to the jury, in the absence of a request, the failure to do so is not reversible error.

3. Victim's Age

In order to convict a defendant of the offense of child molestation, the state must prove that the victim was under the age of 16 at the time of the acts alleged in the indictment. The Georgia Supreme Court has upheld the 1995 amendment, which expanded the coverage of the child molestation statute to include minors under the age of 16, against a constitutional challenge.

4. Victim's Consent and Knowledge of Victim's Age

The language of the statute does not indicate whether consent of the child or lack of knowledge of the child's age constitutes a valid defense to a prosecution for child molestation. However, the statutory history implies that they do not. Pre-1968 GCA § 26-1301a and two other provisions were codified together, constituting Chapter 26-13A of the criminal code prior to 1968. Pre-1968 GCA § 26-1301a prohibited child molestation, while pre-1968 GCA § 26-1302a prohibited enticement of a child with immoral intent. The third provision, pre-1968 GCA § 26-1303a, provided that neither the child's consent to the immoral conduct nor lack of knowledge of the child's age would constitute a defense to prosecution for the two substantive offenses. The statutes no longer contain this language. However, in its introductory note and accompanying table illustrating the relationship between pre-1968 and 1968 criminal code provisions, the drafters indicated that the substance of pre-1968 GCA § 26-1303a was transferred to the enticing a child for indecent purposes statute, § 16-6-5, in the 1968 revision. Therefore, although its survival is not at all clear, the drafters apparently intended to retain the pre-1968 rule that neither consent nor lack of knowledge of age constitutes a defense to a prosecution for **either** child molestation or enticing a child for indecent purposes.

Moreover, in Coker v. State, the Court of Appeals held that considerations of "consent" and "force" and "against the will" of the child are irrelevant in child molestation cases. Also, it has been held that sexual acts directed to children are, in law, forcible and against the will. Furthermore, in Veasey v. State, the Court of Appeals held that since knowledge of the child's age is not an element of the offense, a mistaken belief as to the child's age would not justify the act. Finally, in *Schultz v. State*, the Court of Appeals held that an instruction to the jury that knowledge is not an element of the offenses of child molestation or aggravated child molestation would be a correct statement of law.

5. *Knowledge of Victim's Identity*

A conflict between the defendant's and the victim's testimony concerning whether the defendant fondled the victim under the mistaken belief that she was his wife is a matter of credibility for the jury to resolve.

Because the practice of identifying a minor victim by initials in an indictment does not put a defendant on notice of the particular person against whom he allegedly committed the crime, the victim's initials are insufficient in an indictment challenged pretrial.

6. *Gender of Defendant and Victim*

Most of the child molestation cases involve the commission of the offense by a male upon a female. The statute makes clear, however, that the offender and the victim can be persons of either sex. Therefore, as the drafting committee noted, a woman can be convicted of child molestation if she engages in sexual intercourse with a male child of the requisite age.

7. *Relationship of Defendant and Victim*

The General Assembly, by enacting § 16-6-4, intended to protect children in this state under the age of 16 from sexual predators and offenders. From this perspective, it is obvious that the most reasonable interpretation of the statute, and the only one that does not result in unreasonable or absurd consequences, is that this statute criminalizes the act of child molestation when perpetrated on **any** child under the age of 16, not just the legitimate descendants of the offender. To construe otherwise would lead to the absurd result of de-criminalizing the molestation of a step-child, an illegitimate child, or any other child who is not the legitimate descendant of a defendant. Such a construction was not the intention of the General Assembly. Accordingly, an indictment would not be void for failing to assert the child's relationship with the defendant as an essential element of child molestation.

B. *Attempt*

A person who performs any act which constitutes a substantial step toward the commission of the crime of child molestation would be guilty of criminal attempt. For example, although driving a van, rolling down a window, and holding up money before children is each a lawful act, when these individual, seemingly innocuous, acts are taken together and combined with the uttered words "Let me stick my hand down your pants," there is evidence of an act inexplicable as a lawful act. Thus, evidence of these combined acts would be sufficient for a conviction of criminal attempt to commit child molestation. A conviction for criminal attempt would likewise be supported by evidence that the defendant entered the victim's house with the intent to engage in sexual activity and thereupon sat nude on the victim's bed while she was in it or by evidence that the defendant left the victim only when she pushed him away, having taken a substantial step toward the molestation of the victim by kissing her, by attempting to place his tongue in her mouth (although not actually doing so), and by fondling her buttocks.

An indictment charging a defendant with criminal attempt is not subject to a general demurrer merely because it fails to allege that the attempt was committed in the physical presence of the intended victim. The mere fact that physical presence is an essential element of the completed crime of child molestation does not mean that it is indispensable in proving criminal attempt. The relevant question is whether the acts alleged in the indictment constitute a substantial step toward the commission of the crime. What constitutes a substantial step is a question of degree, and depends upon the circumstances of each case. Where it cannot be said as a matter of law that the alleged acts do not constitute a substantial step, the indictment is not fatally defective for failure to allege the commission of a crime.

C. *Party to Crime*

One can be convicted as a party to the crime of aggravated child molestation if the evidence shows that he intentionally aided and abetted another in anally sodomizing the victim.

D. *Admissibility of Evidence*

1. *Victim's Testimony*

It should be remembered that although the courts allow the jury to infer intent in child molestation cases even where no specific evidence is presented on that issue, the jury will, indeed, be required to find beyond a reasonable doubt an intent on the defendant's part. On the same set of facts, child molestation may be easier to prove than statutory rape, as one can be convicted of child molestation on the uncorroborated testimony of the victim. Even if the victim has made no immediate outcry and has recanted her story, these circumstances do not render her testimony against the defendant insufficient. It is for the jury to resolve such conflicts in the evidence and to assess the victim's credibility.

Prior consistent and inconsistent statements of the victim constitute substantive evidence which the jury can credit or not as it sees fit. However, unless the victim's veracity has affirmatively been placed in issue, the victim's prior consistent statement is pure hearsay evidence which cannot be admitted merely to bolster the victim's credibility in the eyes of the jury. The victim's veracity is placed in issue so as to permit the introduction of a prior consistent statement only if affirmative charges of recent fabrication, improper influence, or improper motive are raised during cross-examination. Even then, the prior consistent statement may not be admitted unless it has been determined that it was made before the improper motive or influence came into existence or before the time of the alleged recent fabrication.

If the victim's testimony shows that he had a motive to falsify his testimony, it demands a charge on the credibility of witnesses. However, since the mere possibility of a motive to testify falsely does not evidence a manifest purpose to do so, nor establish that the victim's testimony was willfully or knowingly false, the trial court is not required to instruct the jury that the victim's testimony, if it is willfully and knowingly false, must be disregarded entirely unless corroborated by circumstances or other unimpeached evidence.

Whether the defendant should be allowed to interview the child victim before she testifies at trial is a question properly addressed to the child's custodian. The Department of Family & Children Services (DFACS), when acting as the child's legal custodian, may make this decision. However, it cannot be compelled to submit the child to a pretrial interview. A defendant who has sought to compel DFACS to make this decision cannot later complain that the decision should have been made by the child's guardian ad litem.

Prior to 1989, before a child was allowed to testify in a child molestation case, he had to demonstrate at a competency hearing that he understood the nature of an oath, and the issue of a child's competency to testify was left to the discretion of the trial judge. In 1989, the General Assembly amended the competency statute to remedy the evil of having all children subject to a competency challenge on the ground that they did not understand the nature of an oath. Now, the statute provides that in criminal cases involving child molestation a child is deemed legally competent to testify. A child is allowed to testify regardless of his understanding of the nature of an oath and is allowed to have his credibility judged by the jury. The trial judge is not required to make an express determination that the child is competent based on the child's understanding of the nature of an oath before allowing him to testify. To the degree that a child understands that he is to tell the truth, the child is in effect under oath. Since the General Assembly has carved out this exception, the prerequisite administration of the oath otherwise called for by § 24-9-60 has been obviated when the child does not comprehend its nature. The child simply becomes an unsworn witness, made so because incapable of taking an oath. It should be noted that although a child is no longer subject to a competency challenge on the ground that he does not understand the nature of an oath, a child, like an adult, is still subject to a competency challenge on the ground that he does not have the use of reason because of mental retardation. In the absence of a specific challenge as to a victim's ability to reason, the trial judge is not required to conduct a competency hearing.

The credibility of a child victim is exclusively within the province of the jury and may not be impermissibly bolstered by the judgment of another witness that the child victim is credible. However, a statement that clearly is not an opinion as to the child's credibility but is simply an observation by the witness that he found the child to be articulate is not bolstering.

Testimony about a child victim's truthfulness may not be presented to the jury to prove the child's reliability under the child hearsay statute. The state cannot use the child hearsay statute to eviscerate the rule against improper bolstering.

The victim may testify about acts of molestation that the defendant has not been charged with committing if those acts are a part of the res gestae of the defendant's continued sexual exploitation of the victim.

Permitting drawings made by the victim to go out with the jury, after a social worker has identified the drawings as made during the victim's outcry testimony to her, does not violate the continuing witness rule where the drawings served only as tools used during the social worker's interview with the victim and they do not substantively impact on the issue of the defendant's guilt.

Under the plain terms of the Reciprocal Discovery Act, a defendant is not entitled to the victim's oral, unrecorded statement. There can be no "possession, custody, or control" of a witness' statement which has neither been recorded nor committed to writing. Accordingly, if, but only if, the victim's statement had been recorded or committed to writing other than in "notes or summaries made by counsel," would it be discoverable.

2. *Expert Testimony*

In child molestation cases, expert testimony of a child sexual abuse syndrome is competent evidence that the jury may accept or reject for consideration in its determination of whether the child in fact was abused and, if so, whether the defendant did it. However, an expert may not testify as to his opinion as to whether the child had been abused sexually unless the inference to be drawn from facts in evidence is beyond the ken of the jurors, that is, unless the jurors, for want of specialized knowledge, skill, or experience, are incapable of drawing from facts in evidence such an inference for themselves.

A physician, based on his physical examination of the victim as well as on the history related to him by the victim, may no longer opine directly that an act of abuse actually occurred. Rather, the physician may testify only that his findings are consistent with the occurrence of abuse. Where an expert does testify that an act of sexual abuse actually occurred, the trial court's cautionary instructions to the jury to disregard that portion of the expert's testimony would prevent any error from occurring.

Although the distinction may seem fine, there is a legal difference between an expert opinion that the victim's examination and behavior was consistent with sexual abuse and an opinion that the victim was sexually abused. In the first situation, the testimony is a permissible expression of the expert's opinion based on factors beyond the ken of the average juror. The jury is permitted to draw for itself the final conclusion as to whether the victim had, in fact, been sexually abused. In the second situation, however, the weight of the expert is put behind a factual conclusion which invades the province of the jury by providing a direct answer to the ultimate issue: was the victim sexually abused?

In most cases of sexual abuse, there will be no physical evidence of the abuse. Rather, the evidence of abuse will be comprised of the medical history provided by the victim. This medical history is made up of a list of discrete medical and/or psychological symptoms. The average juror, lacking training as a physician, psychiatrist, or psychologist, would not be able to draw an inference on his own whether these symptoms are indicative of abuse. Therefore, it is permissible for an expert to testify that the symptoms and history described by the victim are consistent with the occurrence of abuse. While this evidence might indirectly reflect on the victim's credibility, it would nonetheless be admissible as evidence linking the defendant to the crime.

While an expert may testify generally about the ability of children of a certain age group to distinguish between the truth and a lie, an expert may not testify that he believes the victim is capable of distinguishing truth from fantasy. Such testimony essentially amounts to improper bolstering of the victim's credibility, which is a matter solely within the province of the jury. Where the trial court takes corrective measures immediately upon the introduction of expert testimony going to the victim's credibility and during its main charge to the jury at a later time in the trial, the trial court's refusal to grant a mistrial would not be an abuse of discretion.

Furthermore, an expert may not give an opinion on the victim's credibility or express an opinion on the ultimate issue of the defendant's guilt for the purpose of rehabilitating the credibility of the victim whose veracity has been attacked.

While expert opinion testimony that directly addresses the credibility of the victim is prohibited, testimony that bolsters the credibility of the indicted allegations of sexual abuse is not. The state can establish the credibility of the indicted acts of sexual abuse through expert testimony. The fact that the testimony may also indirectly, though necessarily, involve the child's credibility does not render it inadmissible. For instance, although an expert's foundation testimony that the victim was initially referred to him for the treatment of alleged sexual abuse may indicate his belief in the victim's credibility, this testimony does not constitute an improper bolstering. Such testimony has an impact only on the credibility of the allegations of abuse. It does not directly address the credibility of the victim or express a direct opinion that the victim was sexually abused.

The testimony of experts that certain medical or scientific tests resulted in findings consistent with molestation would not constitute improper bolstering of the victim's credibility. Such testimony would be admissible and proper.

A detective, who has been properly qualified as an expert witness, may testify about the capacity of child victims to specifically recall the dates when offenses against them took place.

Without a basis upon an investigating detective's professional knowledge, skill, or observations, his opinion that the defendant was the perpetrator of the offense would be improper, and its admission would be erroneous. Furthermore, questions by the state eliciting such an opinion would likewise be improper and therefore erroneous.

An expert, who has been properly qualified in the area of forensic evaluation of child sexual abuse victims, may testify that it is not unusual for a child to endure sexual abuse, yet keep it a secret, even where the child may have a safe outlet to report the abuse.

A pediatric nurse practitioner, who has been properly qualified in the examination of abused children, may provide an assessment of a child's psychological state as it relates to her physical examination of the child. Based on her experience and training, the nurse would be in a position to draw inferences that could not be drawn by the average layperson.

Since expert opinion testimony is not required to assist a jury in determining whether or not the victims were truthful in their reports of abuse, particularly when the opinion is based upon inadmissible hearsay regarding alleged prior abuse of the victims by unidentified third parties, a defense expert's conclusion that the victims had fabricated their reports as result of projection or pay back is properly excluded.

Expert testimony concerning the creation of false memories in children may be permissible, provided that the party seeking to present the testimony shows that the expert's opinion is based on facts within his personal knowledge or other facts admitted into evidence.

Expert testimony regarding a victim's gender identity disorder and its correlation with sexual abuse is both relevant and admissible.

The recurrence of compulsive behaviors and the likelihood of a person with compulsive behavior rehabilitating himself without treatment are subject matters not within the scope of the ordinary laymen's knowledge and experience, and thus expert evidence regarding these matters is properly admissible in a case where the defendant denies having molested the victim and testifies that his self-rehabilitation ended his compulsive incestuous behavior prior to the alleged child molestation. Expert testimony that the defendant does not fit the psychological profile of a child or adolescent sex abuser is not admissible, where the jury, without the help of expert opinion, can determine the credibility and truthfulness of all the various witnesses at trial and can form independent opinions as to the defendant's capability of performing the acts he was accused of. Likewise, "profile testimony" that, in the opinion of an expert, a defendant who is on trial for sex crimes against a child is or is not a pedophile does not constitute admissible expert testimony. Expert opinion testimony concerning what the defendant's intent was at the time of a prior conviction for child molestation is speculative in nature and should be excluded.

A jury is free to reject expert opinion testimony about the defendant's lack of intent to arouse or satisfy sexual desires and substitute their own knowledge and experience.

The fact that the witness does not hold a license to practice psychology in this state is not determinative of his qualifications as an expert. The trial court may qualify the witness based on testimony regarding his education and experience. Moreover, questions concerning the witness's qualifications, experience, and close working relationship with the state go to the credibility of his testimony, not its admissibility.

The specifics of the expert's work on other child molestation cases for the particular district attorney's office prosecuting the defendant's case are irrelevant to the expert's qualifications and are inadmissible.

A conflicting expert opinion on results of a test used by the psychologist who interviewed the victims goes to the weight rather than the admissibility of the testimony.

3. *Scientific Evidence*

Given the rejection by other states of penile plethysmograph evidence as reliable evidence of a defendant's sexual deviancy, and particularly the uncertainty within the scientific community of its reliability, it is inadmissible in Georgia.

4. *Hearsay*

Under the "patient history" exception to the hearsay rule, a child's statements about what sexual acts were committed are admissible, but her statements about who committed the acts are not admissible. Under the res gestae exception to the hearsay rule, a doctor is allowed to testify about statements made by the victim concerning acts of molestation by the defendant even though the acts are not charged in the indictment.

5. *Defendant's Behavior*

As in rape and statutory rape cases, evidence of other offenses of a similar nature, the occurrence of which is not too remote in time, is admissible in child molestation cases to show the defendant's intent, bent of mind, or general plan to use children to gratify his sexual desires, especially where those offenses show a proclivity for a particular kind of abnormal sexual activity. Furthermore, proof of the defendant's predilection for pederasty is relevant and admissible to show his state of mind toward young victims and to establish his pattern of sexual predation. In fact, one case indicates that an act which in itself is not unlawful, committed by the defendant some time after he molested the child, is admissible to show the defendant's state of mind at the time of the offense. Prior inappropriate or questionable noncriminal behavior of the defendant is also admissible and relevant as tending to show his lustful disposition. However, before evidence of a similar offense can be admitted, the trial court must conduct a hearing at which specified affirmative showings are made. The state must show: (1) that the evidence is not being introduced for some improper purpose but rather for an appropriate purpose which is an exception to the general rule of inadmissibility; (2) sufficient evidence that the accused committed the other offense; and (3) a sufficient connection or similarity between the other offense and the crime charged such that proof of the former tends to prove the latter. Also, the trial court must give a limiting instruction to the jury, but only upon request, about the specific purposes for which this evidence can be considered. It should also be noted that it is impermissible for the state to introduce evidence of a large number of these similar offenses before it offers any evidence concerning the charges contained in the indictment on trial.

Since there is no apparent material difference between prior and subsequent difficulties evidence, evidence of subsequent difficulties, like evidence of prior difficulties, would not be subject to the similar transaction evidence requirements of Uniform Superior Court Rule 31.3. The mere fact that a sexual incident involving the defendant and the victim allegedly occurred a few months after, as opposed to some time before, the indicted offense would not alter the more important fact that the incident arose from the relationship between the two. Moreover, just like evidence of a prior difficulty, evidence of a defendant's subsequent act toward the same victim is admissible as evidence of the relationship between the victim and the defendant, as it may show the defendant's motive, intent, and bent of mind in committing the act against the victim which resulted in the charge for which the defendant is being prosecuted.

As with evidence of prior difficulties, when evidence of subsequent difficulties is admitted, the trial court is not required to give a limiting charge in the absence of a request for such a charge.

In a prosecution for a sexual offense, evidence of sexual paraphernalia found in the defendant's possession is inadmissible unless it shows the defendant's lustful disposition toward the sexual activity with which he is charged or his bent of mind to engage in that activity. Under this rule, sexually explicit material cannot be introduced merely to show a defendant's interest in sexual activity. It can only be admitted if it can be linked to the crime charged and if the state can lay a proper foundation showing a connection between the defendant and the material. This new rule of evidence may be applied retroactively. Since evidence of the defendant's lustful disposition in general can have a prejudicial effect on the jury's determination as to his credibility and guilt, its admission can constitute harmful error, requiring a new trial for the defendant. Its admission can constitute harmless error, however, where there is overwhelming evidence of the defendant's guilt or where the evidence is not patently salacious and its sexual nature is ambiguous.

It matters not that the sexually explicit material may not show the exact act or a similar act between persons of age, sex, or relationship equivalent to that of the victim and the defendant. Any inconsistency in the identification of the material goes to the weight rather than the admissibility of the evidence.

If the pornographic images possessed by the defendant do not depict him engaging in sexual activity with a minor but merely portray illegal acts similar to those for which he is being tried, the admission of the images is not subject to Uniform Superior Court Rule 31.3, governing the admission of similar transaction evidence.

In a child molestation case, the unindicted acts of vaginal and anal intercourse against the victim would be admissible, not as similar transaction evidence involving independent offenses, but as evidence of the defendant's prior acts toward the victim. The prior acts are evidence of the relationship between the victim and the defendant and may show the defendant's motive, intent, and bent of mind in committing the child molestation.

Even though a defendant is not charged with certain conduct committed during the child molestation, evidence of such conduct may be presented at trial as long as it is relevant to the crime charged. In *Ortiz v. State*, the court held that the defendant failed to show that the trial court abused its discretion in admitting evidence that tended to prove that the defendant placed his penis on the child's vagina simply because that evidence also indicated that some penetration may have occurred at that time or that the defendant also may have touched the child's vagina with his hand, even though the state did not charge the defendant with such conduct. The determination of the weight to be accorded such evidence was for the jury.

In an aggravated child molestation case, evidence of the defendant's prior activities that can be construed as indicative of his homosexual tendencies is of some relevancy to the issue of the defendant's sexual orientation. Evidence of homosexuality (and indications of such sexual preferences) are admissible to show a defendant's bent of mind toward the sexual activity with which he is charged. Also, evidence of the defendant's bisexual nature is admissible to prove intent, motive, plan, scheme, and bent of mind.

Evidence that the defendant was abused as a child is irrelevant to the question of whether he committed the crime of child molestation and is inadmissible.

Evidence of a suicide attempt by a defendant accused of child molestation is relevant as possibly indicating a consciousness of guilt and is admissible for whatever weight the jury chooses to assign. Also, evidence of the defendant's suicide attempts after being accused of another, similar act of child molestation is relevant to show identity in the similar transaction.

Where evidence of the defendant's acts of family violence is relevant to show the child victim's reasons for not reporting the acts of molestation sooner, it is not rendered inadmissible because it incidentally puts the defendant's character in issue.

Character witnesses for the defense cannot testify about specific instances of the defendant's caring for young girls. Such evidence is not admissible because it amounts to self-serving declarations of nonculpability to prove a character trait. Furthermore, character witnesses cannot testify about the defendant's reputation in the community for treating children appropriately. Since the import of such testimony would be that the defendant did not have a reputation for molesting children, it is inadmissible.

The defendant's admission which is otherwise competent and admissible is not to be excluded simply because the admission was made before or after the taking of a lie detector test.

6. Victim's Behavior

The Court of Appeals has held that an exclusionary rule applicable in rape cases is also applicable in child molestation cases, i.e., the victim's past sexual behavior is irrelevant in the determination of whether he was molested by the defendant. The defendant, therefore, is precluded from cross-examining the victim on this point. Under this rule, the state is likewise precluded from asking the victim questions concerning his past sexual behavior. Nor may evidence be admitted to discredit the victim by showing his preoccupation with sex.

Notwithstanding this exclusionary rule, the Court of Appeals found in a number of its decisions that the Rape Shield Statute was applicable in child molestation cases and could serve as the basis for excluding evidence of the victim's past sexual behavior. The Georgia Supreme Court, however, disapproved of these decisions in Abdulkadir v. State because it found that the Rape Shield Statute, by its plain terms, applied only in prosecutions for rape. While there might be compelling policy reasons to apply the Rape Shield Statute in prosecutions for sexual crimes other than rape, the General Assembly's express limitation of the statute's applicability to prosecutions for rape excluded its application in prosecutions for all other sexual crimes. Since the courts are not authorized to expand a statute's application beyond its plain terms, the Supreme Court stated that any expansion of the Rape Shield Statute's applicability had to come from the General Assembly, as it alone is entrusted with the authority to amend existing laws.

In response to this decision, the General Assembly, apparently recognizing that there were compelling policy reasons for the expansion of the Rape Shield Statute's applicability, amended the statute in 2005 so that it is now expressly applicable not only in prosecutions for rape but also in prosecutions for aggravated sodomy, aggravated child molestation, and aggravated sexual battery. This amendment applies to all trials that commence on or after July 1, 2005. It should be noted, however, that this 2005 amendment does not abrogate the exclusionary rule previously applied in child molestation cases. Any consideration as to the limitation of the Rape Shield Statute's applicability in child molestation cases is pretermitted because evidence of the victim's past sexual behavior would be inadmissible and properly excluded based on the established precedent of the appellate courts of this state.

While evidence of a victim's past sexual history is not usually admissible, such evidence may be admissible if shown to be relevant. The fact that evidence may be inadmissible for one purpose does not warrant its exclusion when it is relevant for another purpose. Thus, if evidence of the victims' naivete and lack of sexual experience or education would explain why the defendant was able to abuse them the way he did, the trial court's admission of this evidence for the limited purpose of showing the defendant's superiority of knowledge and the victims' naivete and lack of familiarity with sexual things would not constitute an abuse of discretion.

Where the state has elicited medical testimony suggesting that the victim may have contracted a sexually transmitted disease from the defendant, the defendant may introduce additional medical evidence showing that while the victim had tested positive for the disease, he had not. As long as this evidence is introduced for the purpose of corroborating a defense that the defendant did not molest the victim, and not for the purpose of exploring the victim's past or other sexual behavior, it does not offend any exclusionary rule.

Generally, evidence of a prior unrelated molestation of the victim is not admissible to explain the victim's knowledge of sexual acts. However, evidence of a prior molestation of the victim would be admissible to show that someone other than the defendant caused the injuries to the victim. Also, when evidence of the child abuse accommodation syndrome is introduced at trial, evidence that the victim had been molested by someone other than the defendant may be admissible to establish other possible causes for the behavioral symptoms exhibited by the victim.

A third party conviction for child molestation is not direct evidence of an alternative explanation for the victim's claims of child molestation. Such evidence does not lessen the defendant's culpability with regard to the victim's assertions against him. It does not follow that if, tragically, a child has been abused by multiple offenders, the child's claim of abuse against a specific offender is abrogated by the fact of prior abuse, alone.

Questioning a child other than the victim about sexual abuse by a nondefendant in order to demonstrate that the victim may have learned about sex by witnessing the other child's abuse is violative of the other child's privacy interests, unduly speculative, and irrelevant to the issue of whether the defendant molested the victim. This is particularly true when the molestation of the other child occurred when the victim was a mere infant.

Testimony regarding the victim's alleged past false accusations against persons other than the defendant is admissible in child molestation cases. Before ruling on the admissibility of such evidence, the trial court must make a threshold determination outside the presence of the jury that a reasonable probability of falsity exists. The fact that an accusation is not prosecuted is insufficient to establish its falsity. If the trial court, after considering the context and circumstances of the past false accusation, determines that it was the result of coercion and duress from victim's alleged abuser, it would not be an abuse of the trial court's discretion to exclude testimony about the accusation. If the victim, when confronted with evidence of a prior false accusation, testifies that she does not remember the prior incident, the victim's testimony concerning her molestation should not be disregarded entirely if it is plausible that the victim's failure of memory is due to the lapse of time since the occurrence of the prior incident and if the victim's testimony concerning her molestation is corroborated by the testimony of others and by other evidence. A caseworker is not allowed to give his opinion that the victim has made prior false accusations of molestation, because such evidence addresses the credibility of the witness.

The defendant is entitled to cross-examine an outcry witness about his prior false allegations of molestation in order to attack his credibility.

Evidence about the victim's sexual dreams are not admissible unless the defendant is able to show a connection between the victim's dreams and the alleged acts committed by the defendant.

Where there is a complete absence of any evidence from the defense that it would be necessary to violate the victim's psychologist-patient privilege, the trial court may limit the defense's cross-examination of the victim's therapist and thereby prevent the defense from engaging in a fishing expedition to dredge up evidence of domestic problems totally unrelated to the act of molestation.

Without proof that the victim knew that her mother had been sexually abused or other proof that the mother improperly influenced the victim's testimony, the prior sexual abuse of the victim's mother is irrelevant and should be excluded. Furthermore, if there is no proof that the victim may have been confusing the defendant with another person when he accused the defendant of molestation, evidence concerning improper acts committed by that person toward the victim's mother is not sufficiently probative to warrant its admission.

7. Videotapes Depicting Defendant and Victim Engaging in Sexual Conduct

The admission of videotapes depicting the defendant and the victim engaging in sexual conduct is error if the proper foundation has not been laid. In those circumstances not covered by the "silent witness" law, a videotape is admissible where the operator of the machine which produced it or one who personally witnessed the recorded events testifies that the videotape accurately portrayed what the witness saw take place at the time the events occurred. Applying this standard to the facts in Phagan v. State, the Georgia Supreme Court was constrained to conclude that the videotapes played for the jury were not authenticated. The jury watched two videotapes which appeared to depict the defendant and the minor without anyone testifying that what the jury was seeing was an accurate portrayal of what actually occurred. In light of this evidentiary deficiency, the court had to reverse the defendant's conviction for aggravated child molestation because the erroneously admitted videotape contained the only evidence supporting the charge.

8. Civil Actions Arising out of Incidents Underlying Criminal Prosecution

Evidence of the victim's threatened civil action against the state as a result of the incident that underlies the criminal case against the defendant is a proper subject for cross-examination. The victim's financial interest in the threatened civil action is relevant because it goes to the victim's bias or interest in the criminal case. The victim's financial interest is not diminished by the fact that the defendant in the civil action is someone other than the criminal defendant. Where the criminal case against the defendant hinges on the victim's credibility, the defendant should be permitted to argue that the threatened civil action provides a motive for the victim to fabricate the incident underlying the criminal case. Under these circumstances, the exclusion of the evidence would constitute harmful error.

E. Statute of Limitations

Evidence of child molestation is not restricted to the day mentioned in the indictment, but may extend to any appropriate date previous to the finding in the indictment and within the statute of limitation for the prosecution of the offense charged. However, if the indictment charges the defendant with child molestation committed in a specific manner, evidence of any unindicted prior acts committed in an entirely different manner is inadmissible as direct evidence of the offense charged. An indictment that charges the defendant with committing the offense on and between certain dates, the exact date being to the grand jurors unknown, sufficiently specifies a date. Circumstantial evidence is sufficient to authorize a finding that the offense charged occurred within the period of limitations.

Where the date alleged in the indictment is not an essential averment, evidence of similar acts occurring within the statute of limitation is evidence of the crime charged and does not fall within the ambit of the rule relating to notice of the state's intention to present evidence of similar transactions. However, it has been held that the "continuous transaction" or res gestae exception that is provided in the rule is not so broad as to cover acts committed months prior or subsequent to the offense charged, nor to acts committed almost a year after the offense charged.

In 1987, the Georgia Court of Appeals decided in Sears v. State that the statute of limitation for the offense of child molestation was not tolled because the offense was unknown due to the victim's infancy, his lack of awareness of the criminality of the defendant's alleged conduct, and/or his purported fear of the defendant. The applicable statute of limitation, § 17-3-1(c), contained no exception or condition that would toll its operation. Since there was no statutory basis for the exceptions espoused by the state, the court was compelled to give effect to the clear expression of legislative will that the prosecution had to be commenced within the period specified by the statute regardless of the victim's infancy.

Apparently recognizing the need for an exception that would toll the limitation period for certain offenses against minors, the General Assembly enacted in 1992 § 17-3-2.1, which provides that if a victim of the offense of cruelty to children or of certain sexual offenses is under 16 years of age on the date of the violation, the statute of limitation is tolled until the victim has reached the age of 16 or the violation is reported to a law enforcement agency, prosecuting attorney, or other governmental agency, whichever occurs earlier. This code section only applies to offenses occurring on or after July 1, 1992.

This enactment evinces the General Assembly's intent that the statute of limitation for certain offenses against minors should be tolled by the infancy of the victim until such time as the victim is 16 years of age. However, this legislative intent cannot be construed to establish an exception to the limitation period specified in § 17-3-1(c) for those felonies committed against minors under the age of fourteen, which predate July 1, 1992. In these cases, the victims' infancy does not toll the statute's operation, and the prosecutions must be brought within seven years. Had the General Assembly intended a different result, it could have amended § 17-3-1 to provide for tolling or omitted the date limitation from § 17-3-2.1(b).

In 1987, the General Assembly amended § 17-3-1(c) by extending the limitations period for felonies against victims under 14 years of age from four to seven years. This amendment only applied to offenses committed after July 1, 1987. Thus, for victims under 14 years of age, there could have been two applicable limitation periods: a seven-year limitation period for offenses committed after July 1, 1987, and a four-year limitation period for such offenses committed before that date.

The 1987 General Assembly drafted § 17-3-1(c) so that the age limitation specified in this provision was the same as the statutory age of consent at that time, which was 14 years of age. Thus, all molestations were subject to the same seven-year limitations period. When the age of consent specified in § 16-6-4 was increased to 16 years of age in 1995, however, the General Assembly neglected to increase the age limitation in § 17-3-1(c). Thus, the age limitation specified in § 17-3-1(c) was inconsistent with the age of consent specified in § 16-6-4. This inconsistency created disparate classes of identically-situated criminal defendants in violation of the Equal Protection Clauses of the state and federal constitutions. It created a disparity in the limitation periods applicable to identical felonies based on nothing more than the age of the victim. For instance, if a molestation victim were under the age of 14, the limitations period for the prosecution against the defendant would have been seven years, rather than four years had the victim been over that age. Although identically-situated, a defendant committing the offense against a victim under the age of 14 would have had the disadvantage of a longer limitations period for his crime than a defendant committing the same offense against an older victim. There was no apparent rational basis for this disparate treatment of identically-situated defendants.

In order to cure § 17-3-1(c)'s constitutional infirmity and to eliminate this disparate treatment, the 2002 General Assembly increased the age limitation for the seven-year limitation period from 14 to 18 years of age. The increased age limitation in this provision is now consistent with the age of consent specified in § 16-6-4. Now, all molestations are again subject to the same seven-year limitations period for acts occurring on or after July 1, 2002. The four-year limitation period is no longer applicable to such acts occurring on or after that date.

In 1992, the General Assembly with the enactment of § 24-4-60 authorized the creation of a state deoxyribonucleic acid (DNA) data bank of samples obtained from convicted sex offenders in order to determine and retain the identification characteristics specific to these offenders. In 2000, the General Assembly broadened the scope of this statute by requiring the obtaining of DNA samples from all convicted felons and the storing of these samples in the data bank. An examination of these samples revealed that many matched the DNA evidence of old, unsolved rape cases. Despite this evidence, the state could not prosecute the convicted felons because the limitation periods for their crimes had expired. Remedial legislation was necessary to enable the state to use identification evidence derived from the state's DNA data bank to prosecute convicted felons for certain crimes even though the limitation periods previously established by law had expired.

Accordingly, the General Assembly eliminated the statute of limitations for any aggravated child molestation occurring on or after July 1, 2002, when DNA evidence is used to establish the identity of the accused. A sufficient portion of the physical evidence tested for DNA, however, must be preserved and available for testing by the accused. Furthermore, if the DNA evidence does not establish the identity of the accused, the limitation on the prosecution reverts to the seven-year period specified in § 17-3-1(c).

E.1. Selective Prosecution

To support a claim of selective prosecution for aggravated child molestation, the defendant must show that others generally are not prosecuted for the same misconduct and that a discriminatory motive for the prosecution exists. Without such a showing, the defendant's claim will fail.

F. Punishment

1. Child Molestation

Except as provided in § 16-6-4(b)(2), a first offense of child molestation is a felony punishable by imprisonment for not less than five nor more than 20 years. In addition, the first offender is subject to the sentencing and punishment provisions of § 17-10-6.2, which requires the first offender to receive a mandatory split sentence including a minimum sentence of imprisonment, and § 17-10-7. Upon the first offender's incarceration, the Department of Corrections must provide counseling to him.

Except as provided in § 16-6-4(b)(2), a second or subsequent offense of child molestation is a felony punishable by imprisonment for not less than ten nor more than 30 years or by life imprisonment. In addition, the repeat offender is subject to the sentencing and punishment provisions of §§ 17-10-6.2 and 17-10-7. If the state intends to seek a punishment of life imprisonment, it must provide written notice to the repeat offender prior to trial.

Section 16-6-4(b)(2) provides a lesser punishment for a child molestation involving teenagers. If the victim was at least 14 but less than 16 years of age and the person convicted of child molestation was 18 years of age or younger and was no more than four years older than the victim, the child molestation would be punishable only as a misdemeanor and would not be subject to the sentencing and punishment provisions of § 17-10-6.2.

A conviction for child molestation is not inconsistent with a defendant's acquittals on charges of statutory rape and enticing a child for indecent purposes. In addition, the acquittals do not preclude the findings of fact necessary to support a conviction for child molestation as a trier of fact can believe a part of a witness' testimony and discredit other parts.

2. Aggravated Child Molestation

Except as provided in § 16-6-4(d)(2), the offense of aggravated child molestation is a felony punishable by life imprisonment or by a split sentence that is a term of imprisonment for not less than 25 years and not exceeding life imprisonment, followed by probation for life. In addition, the offender is subject to the sentencing and punishment provisions of §§ 17-10-6.1 and 17-10-7, which provide for mandatory minimum sentences and sentences for life without possibility of parole in certain cases and provide restrictions on the authority of the State Board of Pardons and Paroles to grant paroles.

Section 16-6-4(d)(2) provides a lesser punishment for an aggravated child molestation involving teenagers. In such a case, the offense of aggravated child molestation would be punishable as a misdemeanor and would not be subject to the sentencing and punishment provisions of § 17-10-6.1 only when (1) the victim was at least 13 but less than 16 years of age, (2) the offender was 18 years of age or younger and was no more than four years older than the victim, and (3) the basis of the aggravated child molestation charge involved an act of sodomy.

Where two charges of aggravated child molestation are indistinguishable in that all of the averments are identical, this lack of particularization permits the imposition of only one sentence. However, where the averments of each count of an indictment refer to a different date, the date is made an essential averment of the transaction, and each count of the indictment is distinguishable. Thus, where the defendant is charged in two counts with having committed separate acts of child molestation upon the same victim on different dates in different years, sentence may be imposed on both counts. Moreover, sequential but separate acts of child molestation against the same victim will support separate convictions.

3. Constitutional Issues

In Odett v. State, the Georgia Supreme Court held that there was a rational basis for treating child molestation based on an act of sodomy differently from child molestation based on an act of intercourse. Contrary to the defendant's contention, the court found no legal or factual support for the argument that oral sodomy was less intrusive to the victim than intercourse and, therefore, deserving of similar treatment in child molestation cases. The General Assembly could have reasonably concluded that the psychological well-being of a minor was more damaged by an act of sodomy than by an act of intercourse and that child molestation based on an act of sodomy warranted a greater punishment. Thus, the different treatment did not violate the defendant's equal protection and due process rights under the federal and state constitutions.

In Widner v. State, the Georgia Supreme Court held that the defendant's mandatory minimum sentence for aggravated child molestation did not violate his constitutional right of privacy. The defendant's act of sodomy with the minor was not protected by any privacy right.

The Due Process Clause is not violated where a trial court declines to permit the jury to be made aware during the guilt phase of the trial that, if found guilty of aggravated child molestation, the defendant would be required by law to be imprisoned for a minimum number of years without any possibility of early release.

Since the societal consensus in Georgia or the United States does not oppose sentencing youthful offenders convicted of violent offenses to long terms of incarceration, the Georgia Supreme Court has concluded that application of the mandatory minimum sentencing scheme to a youthful sexual offender, even in the face of an excellent prognosis for rehabilitation, does not violate the constitutional prohibition against the imposition of cruel and unusual punishment.

In *Humphrey v. Wilson*, the Georgia Supreme Court concluded that the habeas court properly ruled that the teenage offender's sentence of ten years in prison for having consensual oral sex with a fifteen-year-old girl when he was only seventeen years old constituted cruel and unusual punishment. The court found that recent legislative amendments, substituting misdemeanor punishment for the teenage offender's conduct in place of felony punishment and relieving such teenage offenders from registering as sex offenders, represented a seismic shift in the General Assembly's view of the gravity of oral sex between two willing teenage participants. Acknowledging that no one had a better sense of the evolving standards of decency in this state than our elected representatives, the court concluded that the amendments to §§ 16-6-4 and 42-1-12 reflected a decision by the people of this state that the severe felony punishment and sex offender registration imposed on the teenage offender made no measurable contribution to acceptable goals of punishment. Notwithstanding society's significant interest in protecting children from premature sexual activity, the court further acknowledged that the teenage offender's crime did not rise to the level of culpability of adults who prey on children and that, for the law to punish the teenage offender as it would an adult, with the extraordinarily harsh punishment of ten years in prison without the possibility of probation or parole, appeared to be grossly disproportionate to his crime. Accordingly, the Georgia Supreme Court, considering the nature of the teenager offender's offense, concluded that his ten-year sentence did not further a legitimate penological goal and thus, since the sentence was grossly disproportionate to his crime, constituted cruel and unusual punishment under both the state and federal constitutions. Because the minimum punishment for the crime for which the teenage offender was convicted constituted cruel and unusual punishment, the court remanded the case to the habeas court for it to enter an order reversing his conviction and sentence and discharging him from custody.

4. Similar Transaction Evidence

The trial court may consider the similar transaction evidence presented at trial in determining the defendant's sentence.

The designation of a person as a sexual offender is neither a sentence nor a punishment but simply a regulatory mechanism and status resulting from the conviction of certain crimes. As such, there is no requirement that the offender be given notice that he will have to register as a sexual offender.

The sexual offender registration requirement is not a punishment. Consequently, a lifetime registration requirement does not extend the maximum sentence allowed under § 16-6-4. Additionally, the registration requirements must be met regardless of whether they are included as a term of probation. Thus, the trial judge is not required to confine the sexual offender registration requirements to the sentencing parameters of the offense for which the defendant is convicted nor is the trial judge authorized to do so as the registration requirements are statutory, not subject to the trial judge's discretion.

G. Relationship to Other Offenses

Important Notice about Repudiation of Actual or Same Evidence Test: The Georgia Supreme Court repudiated the actual evidence test in *Drinkard v. Walker*, 281 Ga. 211, 636 S.E.2d 530 (2006), because it found this test to be inconsistent with the statutory framework governing the prohibition against multiple convictions for included offenses in Georgia. This inconsistency resulted in years of confusion and unpredictable results. In its place, the court adopted the required evidence test and overruled any prior case law that is inconsistent with it. Thus, any prior case law applying the actual evidence test is no longer controlling and should not be relied upon to determine whether one offense is included in another under § 16-1-6(1). The discussion of such case law is included below only insofar as it may still be applicable to pending prosecutions that arose before the Drinkard decision. See MULTIPLE CONVICTIONS, II. Tests to Determine Presence of Multiple Convictions, for a complete discussion of the Drinkard decision.

On the facts of a particular case, child molestation may be an lesser included offense of sodomy. Similarly, public indecency and simple battery may be lesser included offenses of child molestation, depending upon allegations of the indictment and the facts established by the prosecution.

Although the evidence shows that several acts of child molestation were committed at the same time and place, the offenses do not merge where none of the evidence supporting each count of child molestation is used up in proving a different count.

The statutory rape and child molestation statutes are part of a legislative framework aimed at protecting children from sexual exploitation and abuse. As part of a coordinated scheme relating to the same subject matter, the Georgia Supreme Court found in Dixon v. State that these statutes had to be construed together to determine how the General Assembly intended to treat conduct involving a victim who was 14 or 15 years of age and a defendant who was no more than three years older than the victim. Construing these statutes together as they appeared in the Code in 2004 showed a clear legislative intent to prosecute such conduct as misdemeanor statutory rape rather than felony child molestation. First, in 1996 the General Assembly amended the statutory rape statute specifically to eliminate any discretion over whether to punish conduct meeting the misdemeanor statutory rape criteria as either felony or misdemeanor statutory rape. When the General Assembly eliminated this discretion, it intended the misdemeanor provision to have exclusive application to conduct falling within its parameters. Allowing the state to retain the discretion to prosecute the same conduct as either misdemeanor statutory rape or felony child molestation would have defeated this legislative intent. Second, since the misdemeanor statutory rape provision was far more specific concerning such conduct than the child molestation statute, this more specific provision should have prevailed over the general statute and any prosecution should have proceeded under this provision. Third, the misdemeanor statutory rape provision reflected the most recent legislative judgment regarding the appropriate punishment for such conduct. Since the General Assembly most recently declared that sex between teenagers less than three years apart should have been punished as misdemeanor statutory rape, and not felony child molestation, that judgment would have to prevail. Finally, given the conflict between the two statutes concerning their prescribed punishments, the rule of lenity would require that a defendant receive only the lesser of the two possible punishments.

Notwithstanding this construction in Dixon, the Georgia Supreme Court encouraged the General Assembly to examine this case and make a more recognizable distinction between statutory rape, child molestation, and the other sexual crimes, and to clarify the sort of conduct that would qualify for the minimum sentence accompanying a conviction for aggravated child molestation. The court stated that the conflicting nature of the statutory scheme relating to sexual conduct, especially with respect to teenagers, might lead to inconsistent results. Under the statutes as they appeared in 2004, it was entirely possible that teenagers could have been convicted of aggravated child molestation and received the concomitant ten-year minimum sentence, if they willingly engaged in sexual activity, but stopped short of the actual act of sexual intercourse, so long as one experienced slight pain or received even minor injuries incidental to the act.

In 2006, the General Assembly responded to the court's concern about the conflict and lack of clarity in this statutory scheme. It prescribed, in accord with the statutory rape statute, misdemeanor punishment for teenagers within a certain age range who willingly engage in sexual activity that constitutes child molestation or aggravated child molestation. Moreover, the General Assembly explicitly provided that an act of sodomy is the sort of conduct that would qualify for misdemeanor punishment accompanying a teenager's conviction for aggravated child molestation. By limiting the sexual activity that can serve as the basis of a charge of misdemeanor aggravated child molestation to an act of sodomy, the General Assembly is expressing a clear legislative intent that an act of sexual intercourse between teenagers within a certain age range does not qualify as aggravated child molestation. Rather, the misdemeanor statutory rape provision would apply exclusively to such sexual activity.

Child molestation may be a lesser included offense of statutory rape. However, the offense of child molestation does not merge into the offense of statutory rape where the evidence shows that the defendant fondled the victim and, in an entirely separate incident later that evening, raped her. Likewise, the offenses do not merge where the evidence shows that the child molestation was complete when the defendant without regard to his subsequent acts removed the clothing of the victim with the requisite intent, and where the evidence shows that the statutory rape was not initiated until the defendant without regard to his previous acts began to engage in sexual intercourse with the underage victim.

The offense of child molestation may be included as a matter of fact in an indictment charging the offense of rape, where the victim is under the age of consent. In such a case it is reversible error to refuse to give a requested charge on child molestation as a lesser included offense of the rape charge. However, a defendant is not entitled to a jury instruction on child molestation as a lesser included offense of rape where the jury is only authorized by the evidence to find the defendant either guilty or not guilty of rape.

Although child molestation becomes included within rape as a matter of fact if the victim is under the age of consent, child molestation is not included within rape as a matter of law because, unlike rape, child molestation requires proof that the victim was under the age of consent. If a rape indictment does not allege that the victim was under the age of consent, the defendant has not been placed on notice that he should be prepared to defend himself against the charges of both rape and child molestation. Without such notice, the trial court is not authorized, sua sponte, to instruct the jury on child molestation as a lesser included offense of rape. If the trial court so instructs jury and the jury convicts the defendant of the lesser included offense of child molestation, due process will not allow the conviction to stand.

The offense of child molestation does not merge with the offense of aggravated assault with intent to rape where the evidence shows that after the defendant pulled the victim's panties down and exposed his penis, he attempted to penetrate the victim's vagina with his penis.

Where the child molestation count of an indictment alleges actions that are factually contained in the attempted rape count, the child molestation offense merges into the attempted rape offense as a matter of fact. While the defendant can be prosecuted for both offenses, if he is convicted of both, the trial court must merge the child molestation conviction into the attempted rape conviction for sentencing purposes.

Statutory rape may be a lesser included offense of aggravated child molestation where both offenses are in fact based upon the same, single act of sexual intercourse.

The offense of aggravated child molestation merges as a matter of fact into the offense of rape, where the evidence shows that the injuries the victim sustained as a result of the rape are the same injuries that serve as the basis for the offense of aggravated child molestation. However, an aggravated child molestation conviction would not merge as a matter of fact into a rape conviction for sentencing purposes, where the evidence shows that the defendant sexually assaulted the victim twice.

Child molestation and incest do not merge as a matter of fact where the evidence shows that the defendant committed the indecent and immoral acts of lifting his minor daughter's nightgown and lying on top of her immediately before committing the incestuous act of intercourse.

The offense of child molestation does not merge into the offense of aggravated sodomy where the offenses are based on separate acts. Where the evidence establishes only one act of sodomy, the proof of which is necessary to prove the child molestation count as alleged in an indictment, the offense of sodomy is included as a matter of fact in the offense of child molestation. Where a victim testifies to several consecutive acts of sodomy and to yet another entirely separate act of sodomy, all of which occurred one morning, this evidence would authorize a jury to find that more than one instance of sodomy occurred, permitting conviction for both aggravated child molestation and aggravated sodomy based on separate occasions. Where the evidence establishes two incidents, each involving only one act of sodomy, and where the same act of sodomy is the basis of an aggravated child molestation charge and an aggravated sodomy charge in each of two indictments, it is proper to prosecute the defendant in both indictments for both aggravated child molestation and aggravated sodomy, but he should be convicted and sentenced under each indictment for only one of the two rather than for both.

Where the defendant's conduct satisfies the elements of aggravated child molestation, the state is not required to prosecute only the lesser crime of simple sodomy. It may prosecute the defendant under any or all statutes that fit his conduct.

Child molestation and aggravated child molestation do not merge as a matter of fact or law where each transaction constitutes a separate offense since each is established by proof of different facts, i.e., each offense is a completed crime when the next is perpetrated upon the victim. Likewise, two counts of child molestation that are supported by different facts constitute separate offenses, so that the two counts do not merge as a matter of fact or law.

A trial court is authorized to charge the jury on child molestation as a lesser included offense of aggravated child molestation so long as the charge is supported by the evidence and the indictment sufficiently places the defendant on notice of the conduct which he must defend at trial.

Since a jury verdict finding the defendant guilty of the lesser included offense of attempted aggravated child molestation would not constitute an implicit acquittal on the greater offense of aggravated child molestation, subsequent prosecution on the greater offense would not be barred by double jeopardy. A jury verdict returned on a greater offense instruction sufficiently erroneous so as to demand retrial could not be deemed an unambiguous verdict that would bar retrial. Furthermore, the failure to file a written plea in bar before the second trial would operate as a waiver of a subsequent challenge on procedural double jeopardy grounds.

In Taylor v. State, the court held that the offense of kidnapping with bodily harm was proved by showing asportation of the victim and the blow to his head, and was completed prior to the sodomy. Thus, there was no merger as a matter of fact because the facts used to prove the crime of aggravated child molestation were different from those used to show the essential elements of kidnapping.

Where the offense of false imprisonment can be proved by facts different from the offense of child molestation, the two offenses do not merge.

The offense of cruelty to children is separate and distinct from the offense of aggravated child molestation as matter of fact, where the evidence used to establish cruelty to children is not used to establish the aggravated child molestation.

Where the offense constituting cruelty to children is based upon and committed in a way different from the offenses of child molestation and assault with intent to rape and is not satisfied by the introduction of the same evidence, there is no merger and the trial court may enter a separate conviction on cruelty to children.

Where the evidence shows either the commission of the completed offense of child molestation or the commission of no offense, there is no error in the trial court's failure to charge the jury on the lesser offenses of battery and simple battery.

The offenses of child molestation and sexual battery have different elements and protect different classifications of victims. Accordingly, the offense of sexual battery is not included in the offense of child molestation as a matter of law. Where the indictment in a case is narrowly tailored to the offense of child molestation and where the evidence presented at trial supports that offense, sexual battery is not included in child molestation as a matter of fact. However, in a case where the facts alleged in the indictment for child molestation also include all of the elements of sexual battery, sexual battery can be a lesser included offense of child molestation as a matter of fact. A charge on sexual battery as a lesser included offense of child molestation is required when the indictment puts the defendant on notice that he could be convicted of the lesser included offense **and** the evidence presented at trial is sufficient to establish the lesser included offense consistent with these averments.

Where the evidence is sufficient to convict the defendant of either child molestation or sexual battery, the trial court would be authorized to merge the lesser offense of sexual battery into the greater offense of child molestation.

The rule of lenity applies when two statutes governing the same conduct are conflicting with respect to their prescribed punishments, i.e., where one statute punishes the conduct as a misdemeanor while the other statute punishes the same conduct as a felony. In such a situation, a defendant would be entitled to have the lesser of two penalties administered. This rule would be inapplicable, however, in a case where the defendant was found guilty of both child molestation and sexual battery arising out of the same conduct involving the victim. Since both crimes are felonies, different grades of punishment would not be involved. Furthermore, there would be no uncertainty concerning the applicable penal statute to be used in sentencing the defendant. Thus, the trial court's merging of a sexual battery conviction into a child molestation conviction for sentencing purposes would not be error.

The offense of sexual battery is committed when the defendant intentionally makes nonconsensual, physical contact with the intimate body parts of another, not when another makes physical contact with the defendant's intimate body parts. Thus, letting a child touch one's penis would not constitute sexual battery, and evidence of such conduct would not warrant a charge on sexual battery as a lesser included offense of child molestation. Furthermore, where the evidence shows sexual activity rather than mere touching, a charge on sexual battery would not be warranted.

The offenses of child molestation and aggravated sexual battery do not merge where the two offenses are alleged in separate counts of an indictment and each count alleges actions that are not factually or legally contained in the other count and where the evidence presented at trial supports each of the separate actions. Where there is no evidence of such separate actions, however, the offenses merge as a matter of fact.

Enticing a child for indecent purposes has an asportation element not found in either criminal attempt or child molestation. Child molestation and enticement are separate offenses, and the combination of attempt with child molestation does not bring it within the purview of enticement. However, if the enticement count of an indictment specifically alleges that the defendant enticed the child for the purpose of child molestation, in order to prove the enticement count, the prosecution must prove all the facts used to prove the child molestation count. Therefore, the offenses merge as a matter of fact and the defendant cannot be convicted and sentenced for both. If both counts do not contain the same factual allegations, there is no merger. Thus, where the defendant obtains a directed verdict on the enticement count, neither collateral estoppel nor res judicata nor double jeopardy will preclude his conviction on the child molestation count.

If requested by the defendant, a charge on public indecency as a lesser included offense of child molestation is required where the indictment put the defendant on notice that he could be convicted of the lesser included offense and the evidence presented at trial was sufficient to establish the lesser included offense consistent with averments in the indictment. The failure to give such a charge, however, would constitute harmless error where there is overwhelming evidence of the defendant's guilt of child molestation.

Contributing to the delinquency of a minor is not included in the offense of child molestation as a matter of law or fact since the two offenses share no essential elements and are directed to different acts. Consequently, proof of one offense would not serve to prevent conviction on the other. Accordingly, there would be no error in refusing to charge the jury on the separate offense of contributing to the delinquency of a minor.

III. Enticing Child for Indecent Purposes

A. Elements

Section 16-6-5, enticing a child for indecent purposes, punishes certain activity directed toward committing the crime of child molestation. One commits the offense when he or she "solicits, entices, or takes" a child under the age of 16 years to any place for the purpose of molesting the child or committing indecent acts. As the language of the statute suggests, the gist of the offense is the taking, enticing, alluring, or persuading of the child; the act of molesting the child is **not** an element of § 16-6-5.

The crime of enticing a child for indecent purposes requires the showing of a **joint operation** of the act of enticing a child and the intention to commit acts of indecency or child molestation. Although the jury can infer the prohibited intent from the subsequent molestation of the child, acts occurring after the enticement do not establish the crime. There must be evidence that the defendant did, in fact, entice or take the child if the defendant is to be convicted of enticing a child for indecent purposes.

Any unlawful asportation, however slight, is sufficient to show the "taking" element of the offense of enticing a child for indecent purposes. This element is satisfied whether the "taking" involves physical force, enticement, or persuasion. The concept of asportation relates to movement. Thus, there must be evidence that the defendant caused the child to move towards a place for indecent purposes. Where there is evidence of luring and/or enticing there need be no evidence of actual molestation.

The statute does not define the term "indecent act." However, because the statute refers to both indecent acts **and** child molestation, it would be reasonable to assume that "indecent acts" are different from those acts punished by the child molestation statute. Even though the meaning of "indecent acts" is not clear, the predecessor to the statute, which stated the prohibited purpose as that of taking "immoral, improper, or indecent liberties" with the child, was upheld against a claim that the statute was unconstitutionally vague.

The drafting committee apparently intended to retain the rule that neither consent nor lack of knowledge of the child's age constitutes a defense to prosecution under the statute.

The General Assembly, by enacting § 16-6-5, intended to protect children in this state under the age of 16 from sexual predators and offenders. From this perspective, it is obvious that the most reasonable interpretation of the statute, and the only one that does not result in unreasonable or absurd consequences, is that this statute criminalizes the act of enticement of a child for indecent purposes when perpetrated on **any** child under the age of 16, not just the legitimate descendants of the offender. To construe otherwise would lead to the absurd result of de-criminalizing the enticement of a step-child, an illegitimate child, or any other child who is not the legitimate descendant of a defendant. Such a construction was not the intention of the General Assembly. Accordingly, an indictment would not be void for failing to assert the child's relationship with the defendant as an essential element of enticement of a child for indecent purposes.

B. Attempt

An indictment charging a defendant with attempting to entice a child for indecent purposes is not subject to a general demurrer merely because it fails to allege that the attempt involved the asportation of the victim. The mere fact that asportation is an essential element of the completed crime of enticing a child for indecent purposes does not mean that it is indispensable in proving criminal attempt. The relevant question is whether the acts alleged in the indictment constitute a substantial step toward the commission of the crime. What constitutes a substantial step is a question of degree, and depends upon the circumstances of each case. Where it cannot be said as a matter of law that the alleged acts do not constitute a substantial step, the indictment is not fatally defective for failure to allege the commission of a crime.

C. Venue

The crime of enticing a child for indecent purposes is complete when the child is enticed with the requisite intent, regardless of the ultimate site whereat the enticer contemplates that the act of indecency or child molestation is to be perpetrated. Thus, in order to prove venue, the prosecution must show that the child was "enticed" with the requisite intent in the county wherein the defendant is being prosecuted. It is immaterial that the evidence also shows that the defendant actually took the child into a county other than that wherein he is being prosecuted.

C.1. Admissibility of Evidence

Even if a child has had sexual conversations with others, such evidence would not support an inference that the defendant therefore could have reasonably believed that she consented to his crime of enticing her for indecent purposes. Thus, refusing to allow the defendant to question the victim about such purported conversations would not be error.

D. Punishment

Except as provided in § 16-6-5(c), the offense of enticing a child for indecent purposes is a felony punishable by imprisonment for not less than ten nor more than 30 years. In addition, the offender is subject to the sentencing and punishment provisions of § 17-10-6.2, which requires the offender to receive a mandatory split sentence including a minimum sentence of imprisonment.

Section 16-6-5(c) provides a lesser punishment where the enticement for indecent purposes involves teenagers. If the victim was at least 14 but less than 16 years of age and the person convicted of enticing a child for indecent purposes was 18 years of age or younger and was no more than four years older than the victim, the enticement of a child for indecent purposes would be punishable only as a misdemeanor and would not be subject to the sentencing and punishment provisions of § 17-10-6.2.

E. Relationship to Other Offenses

Important Notice about Repudiation of Actual or Same Evidence Test: The Georgia Supreme Court repudiated the actual evidence test in *Drinkard v. Walker*, 281 Ga. 211, 636 S.E.2d 530 (2006), because it found this test to be inconsistent with the statutory framework governing the prohibition against multiple convictions for included offenses in Georgia. This inconsistency resulted in years of confusion and unpredictable results. In its place, the court adopted the required evidence test and overruled any prior case law that is inconsistent with it. Thus, any prior case law applying the actual evidence test is no longer controlling and should not be relied upon to determine whether one offense is included in another under § 16-1-6(1). The discussion of such case law is included below only insofar as it may still be applicable to pending prosecutions that arose before the Drinkard decision. See MULTIPLE CONVICTIONS, II. Tests to Determine Presence of Multiple Convictions, for a complete discussion of the Drinkard decision.

On the facts of a particular case, enticing a child for indecent purposes may be a lesser included offense of kidnapping.

Enticing a child for indecent purposes has an asportation element not found in either criminal attempt or child molestation. Child molestation and enticement are separate offenses, and the combination of attempt with child molestation does not bring it within the purview of enticement. However, if the enticement count of an indictment specifically alleges that the defendant enticed the child for the purpose of child molestation, in order to prove the enticement count, the prosecution must prove all the facts used to prove the child molestation count.

Therefore, the offenses merge as a matter of fact and the defendant cannot be convicted and sentenced for both. If both counts do not contain the same factual allegations, there is no merger. Thus, where the defendant obtains a directed verdict on the enticement count, neither collateral estoppel nor res judicata nor double jeopardy will preclude his conviction on the child molestation count.

IV. Child Hearsay Statute

The Child Hearsay Statute provides that a statement made by a child under the age of 14 years describing any act of sexual contact or physical abuse performed with or on the child by another or performed with or on another in the presence of the child is admissible in evidence by the testimony of the person or persons to whom made if the child is available to testify in the proceedings and the trial court finds that the circumstances of the statement provide sufficient indicia of reliability. Thus, the statute's only limitations on the admissibility of the evidence are the child's availability to testify and the sufficiency of the indicia of reliability surrounding the statement. The child's veracity need not be at issue nor does the child need to be unresponsive for the evidence to be admitted at trial.

The fact that the child was not under the age of 14 at the time her statement was made does not affect the admissibility of the witness's testimony as a prior consistent statement, if the child's veracity has been placed in issue, and the child is present at trial and thoroughly cross-examined about the truthfulness of her statement.

There is no requirement in the Child Hearsay Statute that the state provide the defense with pretrial notice of its intention to introduce child hearsay statements in evidence.

The trial court is not required to make a finding of necessity before admitting a child hearsay statement into evidence. Although the trial court can conduct a hearing outside the presence of the jury to determine whether the circumstances of the statement provide sufficient indicia of reliability before receiving testimony concerning that statement, the trial court is not required to make that determination prior to receiving the testimony. However, when the state seeks to support its argument for reliability with inadmissible testimony, the trial court is required to conduct a separate hearing outside the presence of the jury to avoid the presentation of this inadmissible testimony.

The statutory requirement of "sufficient indicia of reliability" can otherwise be met if, after both parties have rested at trial, the record contains competent evidence which would support a finding of reliability. The factors which the trial court may consider in determining reliability, when applicable, include but are not limited to the following: (1) the atmosphere and circumstances under which the statement **was made** (including the time, the place, and the people present thereat); (2) the spontaneity of the child's statement to the persons present; (3) the child's age; (4) the child's general demeanor; (5) the child's condition (physical or emotional); (6) the presence or absence of threats or promise of benefits; (7) the presence or absence of drugs or alcohol; (8) the child's general credibility; (9) the presence or absence of any coaching by parents or other third parties before or at the time of the child's statement, and the type of coaching and circumstances surrounding the same; and, the nature of the child's statement and type of language used therein; and (10) the consistency between repeated out-of-court statements by the child. Any alleged inconsistencies in the victim's statements, however, would be a matter for the jury's consideration in weighing the evidence, not a matter of admissibility.

Where the defendant has a sufficient opportunity to contest the indicia of reliability as to the out-of-court statements of the child through extensive cross-examination of the witness, there is no requirement for expert testimony to establish the reliability of the child's out-of-court statements. Further, the question of a particular child's credibility is not properly the subject of expert testimony as it is reserved for the jury.

A trial court's expression of opinion in an unrequested, gratuitous recitation of the Child Hearsay Statute that the child's statement had sufficient indicia of reliability could influence the jurors conclusions about the truth of the victim's statements. This expression of opinion, at least impliedly, as to the veracity of the victim would be improper under § 17-8-57 and would require reversal.

The trial court is not required to determine the competency of a child witness during an investigative interview before the substance of that interview can be admitted into evidence.

By its terms, the Child Hearsay Statute allows the prosecution to satisfy its burden of proof under certain circumstances by introducing the alleged victim's hearsay declarations without putting the victim on the stand. If the prosecution invokes the Child Hearsay Statute to introduce out-of-court declarations by the alleged victim, before the state rests, the trial court must, at the request of either party, cause the alleged victim to take the stand. The trial court must then inform the jury that it is the court who has called the child as a witness, and that both parties have the opportunity to examine the child. The trial court must then allow both parties to examine and cross-examine the child as though the Child Hearsay Statute has not been invoked. If the child testifies before the jury and is subject to cross-examination, there is no violation of the defendant's Sixth Amendment right to confront witnesses. That the defendant chooses not to cross-examine the victim does not alter the result; it is the opportunity, not the follow-through, that is the determinative factor. Even if the child is unresponsive to a number of questions as put by the defendant, there is still no violation of the defendant's constitutional confrontation right so as to require that the child's out-of-court statements be stricken. If the child actually testifies in the case, the witness's testimony concerning the child's out-of-court statements is otherwise admissible. There is no requirement that the child's testimony corroborate the witness's testimony concerning the out-of-court statements. If after this examination and cross-examination of the child the trial court finds the victim "qualified" to testify, the court is not required to conduct a competency hearing itself.

With this procedure, the defendant would not be placed in the position of calling the alleged victim to the stand in order to exercise his rights under the Sixth Amendment, and thereby possibly causing the jurors to resent the defendant for forcing the child to take the stand and undergo cross-examination.

Conflicts between the statement and the testimony of the child at trial would not necessarily render the former inadmissible, but would rather present a question of credibility of the witness to be resolved by the trier of fact.

The Child Hearsay Statute also applies to the out-of-court statements made by a child under the age of 14 concerning the sexual abuse that he or she may have suffered, regardless of whether or not the child is the actual victim in the case. However, if the child is not available to testify, his statements do not fall within the hearsay exception and are not admissible.

In 1993, the Georgia Court of Appeals held that statements made by the victim to the witness about sexual contact between the defendant and another child was not admissible evidence under the Child Hearsay Statute. That statute provided an exception to the hearsay rule only for statements concerning acts of sexual conduct or physical abuse performed on the child making the statement. In 1995, the General Assembly amended the Child Hearsay Statute apparently in response to this holding to provide that statements made by a child concerning sexual contact between the defendant and another child, which was performed in the child's presence, are admissible as an exception to the hearsay rule. In 1998, however, the Georgia Supreme Court struck down this amendment because it found that it created disparate classes of identically-situated criminal defendants in violation of the Equal Protection Clauses of the state and federal constitutions. The 1995 amendment created a disparity in the substantive evidence admissible against criminal defendants charged with identical acts of molestation, based on nothing more than the age of the hearsay declarant. If the declarant were under the age of 14, more evidence would have been admissible against the defendant than if the declarant were over that age. The court found no rational basis for the disparity created by the amended statute. Since the court has struck down this amendment as unconstitutional, it cannot be used as a basis for admitting a child's statements as a witness to sexual conduct committed in his presence.

Statements made by a victim **to a witness** about sexual contact between the defendant **and another child** are not admissible under the Child Hearsay Statute, where the victim did not witness the sexual contact. The admission of the statements, however, would constitute harmless error where they are cumulative of other properly admitted testimony concerning the sexual contact.

Furthermore, portions of a handwritten note and a videotaped interview in which the declarant stated that the victim told the declarant that the defendant had sexual contact with the victim constitutes double hearsay inadmissible under the Child Hearsay Statute, since the declarant did not witness the sexual contact involving the victim. However, in light of other properly admitted cumulative evidence of the sexual contact, the erroneous admission of the handwritten note and videotaped interview would not necessitate reversal.

A prior act of molestation committed against the child of a witness, who has been permitted to relate statements made by the child about sexual acts committed against the victims, is relevant to show any possible bias against the accused child molester that the witness may entertain, unconsciously or deliberately.

Child hearsay statements obtained through an interpreter, rather than directly from the victim, are admissible. Answers communicated through an interpreter are made to the person asking the question, despite the existence of an interpreter.

If a defendant's directions to a victim about what he wanted the victim to do were an integral part of his offenses, they are admissible as part of the res gestae. In such a case, a witness's testimony regarding what the victim said the defendant told her to do is admissible.

Under the Child Hearsay Statute, a tape recording of an interview between the victim and a social worker is not susceptible to a hearsay objection. A videotape of an interview between the victim and a police officer is admissible where the videotape provides sufficient indicia of reliability. Any inconsistency in the child's statements during the interview does not invalidate the interview but is simply one of the many factors the trial court is required to consider in determining threshold reliability. Also, any conflict between the statements and trial testimony does not render the statements inadmissible but rather presents a question of credibility to be resolved by the jury.

Testimony concerning the techniques used in a videotaped interview of the victim involves an area of expertise beyond the ken of the average layman and, therefore, the defendant in a child molestation case is entitled to introduce expert testimony for the limited purpose of providing the jury with information about proper techniques for interviewing children and whether the interviewing techniques actually utilized were proper. The fact that this testimony indirectly involves the child's credibility does not render it inadmissible.

There is no requirement that a child be placed under oath prior to the videotaping of an out-of-court interview in order for this documentary evidence, which contains a contemporaneous record of the child's statements, to be admissible. The playing of the videotape at trial does not constitute an impermissible bolstering of the victim's testimony. Audio and videotape interviews with the victim are not depositions, and therefore, the state is not required to notify the defendant before the interviews are conducted.

Allowing the jury to replay the victim's videotaped interview in the jury room during its deliberations, over the objection of defense counsel, violates the continuing witness rule. This error is harmful if the trial court has failed to caution the jurors against placing undue emphasis on the videotape or to place any limits on the number of times or manner in which they should view it and if the other evidence against the defendant is not overwhelming.

There is nothing in the language of the Child Hearsay Statute to suggest that the General Assembly's intent was that only adults could present testimony under the statute; instead, any competent person may present such testimony. Nothing in the statute restricts the statement to use solely in connection with the specific allegation for which the defendant is on trial. The statement may be admitted as similar transaction evidence. Nothing in the statute limits the number of statements that may be introduced. Thus, the state may introduce any number of the victim's prior consistent statements.

The Child Hearsay Statute applies not only in cases where the defendant is indicted for offenses requiring proof of sexual contact or physical abuse. It is also applies in cases where the sexual contact between the victim and the perpetrator is merely verbal. Accordingly, the descriptions by child victims of their sexual enticement or solicitation by the defendant would involve sexual contact for purposes of the hearsay statute. The admission of videotaped interviews of such victims would, therefore, be appropriate under the statute.

In White v. Illinois, the defendant was convicted by a jury of aggravated criminal sexual assault of a four-year-old child. The child never testified at the defendant's trial. Others were permitted to testify regarding the child's out-of-court statements describing the assault. The defendant objected to admission of their testimony on hearsay grounds. The United States Supreme Court held that permitting the challenged testimony did not violate the defendant's Sixth Amendment Confrontation Clause right. The Confrontation Clause does not require that, before a trial court admits such testimony under the "spontaneous declaration" and "medical examination" exceptions to the hearsay rule, the prosecution must either produce the declarant at trial or the trial court must find that the declarant is unavailable. Where proffered hearsay has sufficient guarantees of reliability to come within a firmly rooted exception to the hearsay rule, the Confrontation Clause is satisfied.

V. Testimony of Youthful Witnesses

Legislation has been enacted to protect youthful witnesses in trials of sex offenses. In any criminal trial where a person under 16 is testifying concerning any sex offense, the trial court must clear the courtroom of all persons except parties to the action and their immediate families, attorneys and their secretaries, court officers, jurors, court reporters, and the media. A familiar person may be allowed to sit or stand near a youthful witness during his testimony.

Additionally, in trials where a child who is 10 years of age or younger is alleged to have been the victim of cruelty to children, rape, statutory rape, child molestation, aggravated child molestation, or sexual assault while in the custody of another, a statute provides that the trial court may order that the child's testimony be taken outside the courtroom and shown in the courtroom by means of a two-way closed circuit television. An order may be granted only if (1) the testimony is taken during the criminal trial proceeding, and (2) the judge determines that testimony by the child victim in the courtroom will result in the child's suffering serious emotional distress such that the child cannot reasonably communicate. The statute also provides who may question the child and who may be in the room with the child during his testimony. During the child's testimony, the defendant will be in the courtroom and will be allowed to communicate with the persons in the room where the child is testifying by any appropriate electronic method.

In Kentucky v. Stincer, the United States Supreme Court held that because the defendant had the opportunity for full and effective cross-examination of the two child witnesses during trial, and because of the nature of the competency hearing, the defendant's rights under the Confrontation Clause and under the Due Process Clause were not violated by his exclusion from the competency hearing of the two children.

In Coy v. Iowa, the United States Supreme Court held that a one-way screen which is specifically designed to enable the complaining witnesses to avoid viewing the defendant as they give their testimony violated the defendant's right to a face to face encounter. However, in Ortiz v. State, the Georgia Supreme Court held that the mere fact that the trial court used its discretion in allowing the victims to sit at an angle where they would not have to directly face the defendant in no way violated the defendant's constitutional right to confrontation. The defendant had the full opportunity to confront each victim with a thorough and sifting cross-examination and to expose each victim to the court and jury.

In Pennsylvania v. Ritchie, the case involved a parent's sexual abuse of his minor child. The United States Supreme Court held that the compulsory process clause of the United States Constitution does not give a defendant the right to discover the names of potential witnesses or favorable evidence. The rights under the compulsory process provision are better analyzed under the due process clause of the Constitution. In this case the court held that the state's confidential child abuse information may be kept from the defendant subject only to an in-camera inspection by the trial judge.

In the unusual circumstance in which a spouse is also the minor victim, the victim/spouse's testimony can be compelled concerning the crime of statutory rape for which the defendant/spouse is charged.

VI. Civil Liability

Any civil action for recovery of damages suffered as a result of childhood sexual abuse must be commenced within five years of the date the plaintiff attains the age of majority.

A charge to the jury on the inability of a child under 14 years of age to consent to sexual intercourse may be relevant in criminal cases involving a child's ability to consent to criminal acts, but it is not relevant in civil negligence cases involving a 13-year-old child's ability to appreciate dangers of his environment and to avoid consequences associated with exposure to such dangers. Under such circumstances, the matter of a child's ability to appreciate dangers of the environment is ordinarily left as a question of fact for the jury rather than as a matter of law for the trial court.

A failure by a county agency handling the cases of sexually abused and exploited children to follow its sexual abuse and exploitation protocol does not constitute an affirmative or other defense to prosecution of a sexual abuse or exploitation offense, nor does a failure by the agency to follow the protocol give rise to a civil cause of action.

VII. Registration of Convicted Child Sexual Offenders

In 1996, the United States Congress enacted a provision which provides for the release of information to the public about convicted sexual offenders. This enactment is commonly referred to as Megan's Law, named after Megan Kanka, a seven-year-old child who was sexually assaulted and murdered by a convicted sexual offender who lived in her neighborhood. Georgia's Megan's Law provides that the Georgia Bureau of Investigation or any sheriff maintaining records required by the state sexual offender registry statute must, in addition to the requirement to inform the public of the presence of sexual offenders in each community, release such other relevant information collected pursuant to this statute that is necessary to protect the public from these sexual offenders. Each sheriff has the authority to determine what that information will be and in what manner it will be released. The United States Supreme Court has found such a notification system to be a civil, nonpunitive regulatory measure. Therefore, its retroactive application would not violate the Ex Post Facto Clause of the federal constitution.

When a person, who has been convicted of a crime for which he is required to register as a sexual offender under § 42-1-12, makes his first report to a sheriff after his release from confinement, placement on probation, or upon establishing residency in the county, the sheriff must cause a notice of that person's conviction and release from confinement to be published. The notice must contain the convicted person's photograph taken at the time of his arrest; his name and address; the date, time, and place of arrest, if available; and the disposition of the case. The notice must be published at or near the time the person registers with the sheriff at least once, and, at the sheriff's option, may be published more than once, in the legal organ of the appropriate county. The notice must also include the address of the Georgia Bureau of Investigation website for additional information regarding the state sexual offender registry.

The state sexual offender registry statute would apply to a defendant convicted of criminal attempt to commit child molestation and criminal attempt to entice a child for indecent purposes, even though no actual minor was involved in the attempt. Interpreting the statute to require an actual minor in a criminal attempt is not supported by either the plain language of § 42-1-12(a)(4)(B) [now (a)(9)(B)] or the underlying legislative intent. Furthermore, an actual minor is not a required element in an attempt to commit these offenses. The defendant's intent and his substantial steps toward the commission of these offenses establish the criminal attempt even if it is impossible to complete the intended offenses because the targeted victim is an adult male police officer posing in an Internet sting operation as a 14-year-old girl looking for pen pals, rather than an actual minor.

VIII. Residency, Employment, and Loitering Restrictions of Registered Sexual Offenders

No registered sexual offender may reside within 1,000 feet of any child care facility, church, school, or area where minors congregate. In addition, no registered sexual offender may be employed by or volunteer at any child care facility, school, or church or by or at any business or entity that is located within 1,000 feet of a child care facility, a school, or a church. Finally, no sexually dangerous predator may be employed by or volunteer at any business or entity that is located within 1,000 feet of an area where minors congregate.

Notwithstanding any county or municipal ordinance or resolution adopted pursuant to state law, no registered sexual offender may loiter, as prohibited by § 16-11-36, at any child care facility, school, or area where minors congregate.

Any registered sexual offender who knowingly violates these prohibitions is guilty of a felony punishable by imprisonment for not less than ten nor more than 30 years.

IX. Disqualification of First Offender Probationers for Employment with Schools, Child Welfare Agencies, and Child Day-Care Centers

The discharge of a first offender probationer without adjudication of guilt may be used to disqualify him for employment with a public or private school, child welfare agency, or child day-care center if he was discharged after prosecution for the offense of child molestation, sexual battery, enticing a child for indecent purposes, sexual exploitation of a child, pimping, pandering, or incest.

THEFT CRIMES

See also ATTEMPT AND SOLICITATION; BURGLARY; COMPUTER SYSTEMS PROTECTION, CRIMES RELATING TO; CREDIT CARD AND FINANCIAL TRANSACTION CARD CRIMES; DECEPTIVE PRACTICES; DEFENSE OF PROPERTY AND HABITATION; FORGERY AND RELATED OFFENSES; GAME AND FISH CRIMES; MISTAKE DEFENSE; MOTOR VEHICLE HIJACKING; PROPERTY DAMAGE CRIMES; PUBLIC REVENUE AND TAXATION, CRIMES RELATING TO; RESIDENTIAL MORTGAGE FRAUD; ROBBERY; TAINTED PUBLIC TRANSACTIONS; TELEMARKETING ACTIVITIES, CRIMES RELATING TO; TELEPHONE AND TELEGRAPH SERVICES, CRIMES RELATING TO; TRANSPORTATION PASSENGER SAFETY, CRIMES RELATING TO.

I. Generally

The 1968 criminal code revision had a great impact on Georgia's theft provisions. Faced with a morass of statutes which included forty-two code sections on larceny alone, the drafters eliminated such offenses as larceny of dog, larceny of oysters or shells, and theft of baled cotton and, instead, established several broad crimes. The common law of England recognized three separate theft crimes: larceny, embezzlement, and false pretenses. These common law crimes were arrested in their expansion by the courts; thus, legislative gap-filling was required to cover all of the anti-social behavior which merited punishment. This resulted in a number of statutes in Georgia, for example, designed to overcome the common law's restrictive definition of property subject to larceny and another group of statutes expanding the types of offenders who were covered by the embezzlement or fraudulent conversion provisions.

The approach taken by the revisers was twofold: first, a general theft by taking statute, § 16-8-2, was enacted to punish all those who "unlawfully take" or "being in lawful possession thereof, unlawfully appropriates any property of another with the intention of depriving him of the property, regardless of the manner in which the property is taken or appropriated." This consolidation statute had an evident purpose of abolishing the major distinction drawn by the common law between offenders who trespassed on possession (larceny) and offenders who lawfully obtained property and **then** converted it (embezzlement). In response to the rigid common law limitation on the property which is subject to the theft crimes, the drafters defined property in § 16-1-3(13) of the criminal code to include anything of value.

The consolidation statute itself is not without ambiguity. The drafters, while defining the crime as encompassing both unlawful taking and unlawful appropriation, do not define either phrase. The drafters apparently recognized this by stating that "[i]n **some** instances, conduct which will amount to an unlawful taking is obvious." Presumably, these instances include all trespasses against possession, the common law definition of larceny.

"In other instances," the drafters added, "a devious course of conduct will be so designed as to take on the appearance of legality, resulting in what should be theft." Here, the drafters were obviously referring to those who obtain title to property by deceitful means. This, under the statute, is an unlawful taking even though the victim's consent means there is no trespass to possession. This type of acquisition was formerly covered by the crime of false pretenses. The language of § 16-8-2 punishing, on the other hand, unlawful appropriation refers to the situation formerly covered by embezzlement or fraudulent conversion statutes where the offender lawfully gained possession, but not title, to property and then converted. Thus, the means of acquisition traditionally covered by larceny and false pretenses is unlawful taking, and embezzlement is unlawful appropriation. All are punished by § 16-8-2.

The second part of the drafter's scheme seems the product of caution. In its short series of specific theft crimes, the code assures that these specific means of unlawful taking or appropriation are punished by the criminal law. The drafters themselves recognized that there would be a "certain amount" of overlap between § 16-8-2 and the following sections punishing theft by deception (§ 16-8-3), theft by extortion (§ 16-8-16), theft of lost or mislaid property (§ 16-8-6), theft by receiving stolen property (§ 16-8-7), theft of services (§ 16-8-5), theft by conversion (§ 16-8-4), and theft of a trade secret (§ 16-8-13). The drafters laid this to the fact that unlawful taking was not defined in § 16-8-2. In this sense, these specific theft crimes could just as easily have been included as illustrative subsections of § 16-8-2.

Given the overlap between § 16-8-2 and the other statutes, the question naturally arises as to which statute ought to be used in a specific indictment. In Stull v. State, the defendant had obtained property by writing to the victims on false letterheads representing himself to be a business concern. The state prosecuted the defendant under § 16-8-2. The defendant appealed, claiming that any such prosecution ought to be brought under § 16-8-3, the theft by deception statute, claiming that this provision more particularly prohibited such behavior. The Georgia Supreme Court rejected this argument, stating that "[w]hile the indictment in this case . . . might more appropriately have been brought under § 26-1803 [O.C.G.A. § 16-8-3], the language of § 26-1802 [O.C.G.A. § 16-8-2] is broad enough to encompass the facts proved in this case, [and since the punishment is identical and double jeopardy would protect the defendant from multiple prosecutions or convictions] no harm was done to the accused by reason of the fact that he was not charged under § 26-1803 [O.C.G.A. § 16-8-3]."

Stull makes clear that § 16-8-3 prohibits one of the types of theft proscribed in § 16-8-2. In addition, embezzlement, punished in § 16-8-4, has also been held to be included within the broad language of § 16-8-2. It should be apparent, however, that not all of the other specific theft crimes are covered in the general statute. For example, no case has been found where receipt of stolen property has been prosecuted under § 16-8-2. The language of the latter section does not seem to embrace that kind of behavior.

It has been held that the phrase "regardless of the manner in which the property is taken or appropriated," found in the theft by taking statute, renders the statute sufficiently broad to encompass thefts or larcenies perpetrated by deception and theft by conversion. Thus, the state may indict an individual for theft by taking, yet prove the elements of theft by deception.

Although § 16-8-2 consolidates the offenses of larceny, embezzlement, and false pretenses, the elements of at least one of these traditional theft offenses must be proven for conviction under § 16-8-2. The court has also held that a defendant has the right to an indictment which informs him of the charges against him and he cannot be convicted of acts not charged. In Walker v. State, the indictment charged the defendant with unlawfully taking certain tools from the victim's car. The proof showed that the defendant was actually in lawful possession of the tools under a security agreement. Thus, when the defendant violated the security agreement by refusing to return the tools he was unlawfully appropriating them, but not unlawfully taking them. Because the proof was fatally variant from the charge, the court reversed the theft by taking conviction over a four-judge dissent. The court advised prosecutors that whenever exigencies of proof exist as to whether an offense was committed in one of two methods proscribed by a statute, the prosecution may charge the accused in separate counts of a single indictment and let the jury select which method the evidence supports.

It has been held error for a trial court to give the entire § 16-8-2 in a charge, emphasizing and explaining words in a method of commission of the offense which was not charged, and in failing to give a limiting instruction concerning which method could be considered by the jury.

II. Individual Theft Crimes

A. Theft by Taking

In addition to its role as a consolidation statute, § 16-8-2 also has its own independent significance. Most of the cases which have been prosecuted under § 16-8-2 have been what formerly would have been larceny cases. Unlike embezzlement and false pretenses cases which can be brought under either § 16-8-2 or one of the other statutes, there is no alternative section under which a larceny may be charged, except for larceny of a particular kind of property. The only other cases which appear to be brought under § 16-8-2 are those in which the state is not certain which of the other two traditional crimes, embezzlement or false pretenses, has been committed. In that case, the wisest course is to bring a prosecution under § 16-8-2 and charge the entire statutory language in the indictment.

If a defendant has (1) unlawfully taken or misappropriated and (2) carried away (3) property of another (4) with the requisite intent, he has violated § 16-8-2. Each element of the offense must be proven, just as though the defendant had been charged with common law larceny.

Unless it is alleged in an indictment charging a defendant with theft by taking that the exact date or dates of the offense are unknown to the grand jurors, the indictment must specifically identify the date of the alleged offense (if it arises out of a single occurrence) or the dates (if it arises out of a series of thefts).

The definitions contained in the Uniform Commercial Code, including the definitions of "holder in due course" and "negotiable instrument," are inapplicable to a prosecution for criminal attempt to commit theft by taking. A defendant cannot require the state to prove as additional elements of a crime requirements engrafted from another, unrelated body of law.

1. Unlawful Taking or Misappropriation

For a taking to be unlawful, it must be without the permission of the owner or other person in lawful possession. Because theft by taking is a crime against possession, a property owner may be guilty if he takes the property out of the lawful possession of another who has a lien or security interest in the property. In Henry v. State, the owner of a bicycle and suit of clothes was guilty of larceny when he stole the items from a pledgee who held them as security for the room and board she had supplied the owner. Similarly, in Ayers v. State, an owner was guilty of stealing his property from the possession of the sheriff who had lawfully seized the property under levy.

The manner in which the theft occurred is not necessarily determinative of whether the theft was an unlawful taking or an unlawful appropriation. Instead, the question is whether the defendant had the requisite intent to deprive the owner of the property at the time he received the items. In Spray v. State, the court found no variance between the allegations contained in the indictment and the proof adduced at trial. Simply because the defendant went through appropriate channels and obtained the property under color of his position as chief of police, did not mean that he could not be indicted for and found guilty of an unlawful taking. It was clear from the evidence that the defendant intended to deprive the state of its property at the time of his receipt of the items and was, thus, guilty of an unlawful taking as alleged in the indictment.

An appropriation is unlawful when a person in lawful possession of another's property appropriates that property to his own use without the permission of the owner. When a theft by taking involves the misappropriation of property, the state must prove that the property initially came into the defendant's hands lawfully. In Wilson v. State, a local government employee was indicted for the misappropriation of cash bonds and fines that he had collected for a local government. The employee argued that his motion for a directed verdict should have been granted because the state presented no evidence that he had the legal authority to collect the cash bonds and fines. Therefore, the state failed to prove that the employee came into "lawful possession" of the cash bonds and fines. The court held that the cash bonds and fines collected by the local government employee did come into his possession lawfully. Because local government officials are presumed to do their duty, the state was entitled to the unrebutted presumption that the officials had authorized the employee to collect bonds and fines in accordance with the requirements of the local government's charter.

In Stevens v. State, a GBI agent gave the defendant $600 with which he was to purchase one-half ounce of cocaine. Instead of purchasing the cocaine, the defendant fled with the money. The defendant contended that he legally possessed the money as a result of an illegal contract for the sale of drugs. However, the court stated that it was incorrect to characterize the case as an action to enforce a contract. The court held that the defendant was not entitled to a directed verdict because there was undisputed evidence that the defendant, being in lawful possession of $600, did unlawfully appropriate the money with the intention of depriving the agent of it.

In Thomas v. State, although the owner of the vehicle gave the defendant permission to drive her car during the day, she did not give him permission to keep it for several days. The owner's son testified that the last time he saw the car before it was stolen, the defendant was driving it. The court held that this evidence was sufficient to authorize the jury's finding the defendant guilty of theft by taking.

In Parker v. State, the defendant, a truck driver, was provided with a company credit card to be used only for the purchase of gasoline. A cashier befriended by the defendant testified that, with his agreement, she used the credit card to obtain cash and cigarettes from the store, while falsely indicating on the credit receipts that gas had been purchased. Both shared the misappropriated money and merchandise. In corroboration of this testimony, another driver testified that the defendant showed him how to misappropriate money with the cashier's help. The court held that the evidence amply supported the defendant's conviction for theft by taking.

2. Asportation

A second element is "asportation" or "carrying away." This element is usually easily met as it has been held that a "[l]arceny is completed when there is an asportation, however slight, and although the goods are not removed from the land of the owner." Also, the concealing of property is sufficient asportation to satisfy this requirement. In cases where a thief does not literally take and asport the subject property but causes some innocent third person to do so, the third person is deemed to act as the agent of the thief and asportation is imputed to the thief.

3. Property of Another

A third element requires that the property taken be that of another. Although an owner is guilty of theft of his own property if it is lawfully in another's possession, at common law property which was owned jointly or by partnership could not be stolen by one joint owner or partner. Similarly, spouses could not be convicted of stealing property from one another. Under present Georgia law, it is clear from § 16-8-1(3) that spousal property remains exempt from theft by taking by either spouse; however, as to jointly held or partnership property, § 16-8-1(3) provides that "property of another" includes all property in which anyone other than the accused has an interest. Thus a partner could be convicted of theft of partnership property.

Lawful possession of property is sufficient, for the purposes of the theft by taking statute, to make the property in question the property of the victim. Thus, ownership of stolen property can be alleged in the person having actual lawful possession, even though that person is only a bailee or a consignee, or even though that person has transferred title to the stolen property to another.

In another case addressing the definition of "property of another," the Court of Appeals held that where a defendant took property from a merchant upon the promise to pay the purchase price later, the failure to return the property or to pay the price was not theft by taking. The fact that the merchant had the right to future payment was not the kind of interest contemplated by § 16-8-1(3). The transaction vested title in the defendant and the property was no longer that "of another."

If, with fraudulent intent, the defendant gets leave to take possession of the property only and then appropriates it to himself, he is guilty of theft by taking. While the defendant's intent is thus to appropriate the property, the consent which he fraudulently obtains from the victim covers no more than possession. Title to the property, rather than passing to the defendant, remains with the victim. Likewise, where the victim does not convey to the defendant his entire interest in the property, but delivers no more than possession until certain other specific conditions are met, the victim retains a security interest in the property.

In a case dealing with theft by taking by a bank teller, the court held that during the depositing and collecting stage of a check, there is a dual proprietary interest in the item—one by the depositor, and another by the depositary bank. Each would be entitled to assert his interest in the property to the exclusion of all others except the true owner. However, when there may be confusion as to title, one charged with theft by taking will not be heard to raise nice and delicate questions as to the title of the article stolen.

Where an employee kept and installed in his house the doors and windows of his employer in order to settle a salary dispute, a jury could find this type of possession unlawful, amounting and adding up to theft by taking.

In a case involving the theft of property seized while the defendant was performing his duties as a county law enforcement officer, the defendant argued that the stolen money was not the property of the county or any other state or political subdivision at the time of misappropriation because it had not then been forfeited under state law. The Georgia Court of Appeals, however, found that the evidence showed that the misappropriated money was seized by county deputies pursuant to lawful police investigations and was therefore subject to forfeiture under state law. Consequently, the county had a vested interest in the stolen money the moment the money was used during the commission of any underlying criminal acts. This evidence along with testimony that the deputies were required to turn in all money found or seized to the county was held sufficient to authorize the jury's finding that the defendant stole money belonging to the county and that he conspired with another law enforcement officer to defraud a state or political subdivision by taking government property.

In a case involving the misappropriation of cash bonds and fines collected by a local government employee, the employee argued that his motion for a directed verdict should have been granted because the state failed to prove that the cash that he misappropriated was the property of the local government. The evidence showed that the local government had the authority to accept cash bonds. Thus, the local government had a property right in the cash that it accepted. The court held that the evidence was legally sufficient to show that the cash was the property of the local government.

At common law, only personalty could be a subject of larceny. This requirement led to some undesirable results. For example, if a thief severed property from realty and took the removed property, a larceny was not committed; but if the owner severed the property and then the thief stole it, a larceny was committed. The criminal code prior to 1968 changed this by providing that property detached from realty automatically became personalty. Also, the criminal code prior to 1968 ended the common law rule that intangibles, documents, and instruments could not be subjects of larceny. Although the current criminal code does not specifically reject the common law definition of property subject to theft, § 16-1-3(13) of the criminal code defines the concept very broadly to include "anything of value," which includes "real estate, tangible and intangible personal property, contract rights," etc. It seems clear that the common law definitions of property subject to theft are no longer applicable.

When the property taken is currency, it is not necessary for the indictment charging the defendant with theft by taking to specifically identify the form of the currency taken. The identification of the property taken as lawful U. S. currency is sufficient.

It should be noted that it is not essential to the proof of the corpus delicti of the crime of theft by taking that the stolen property be recovered and displayed at trial.

4. Mens Rea

The mens rea of common law larceny was an "intent to steal" or "animus furandi." The requisite intent was an intent to deprive the victim of the possession and enjoyment of property permanently. Thus, if one intended at the time of taking to return the property, he had not committed common law larceny. Although it is not free from ambiguity, it appears that the mens rea requirement of § 16-8-2 is different from the traditional larceny mens rea. The language of the statute punishes the defendant who "unlawfully takes or, being in lawful possession thereof, unlawfully appropriates any property of another with the intention of depriving him of the property . . .."

Arguably, because of the construction of the sentence the "intention of depriving" mens rea refers only to unlawful appropriation and not unlawful taking. Under this interpretation, the mens rea for the unlawful taker would be the traditional larceny mens rea, with all of the case law surrounding that concept. This, however, certainly is not compelled by the statutory language or warranted by the general purpose in consolidating and assimilating the former common law crimes. It seems unlikely that in a consolidation statute which punishes wrongful behavior "regardless of the manner" in which the wrong was committed, that the General Assembly intended to retain two distinctive mens rea for the two different branches of § 16-8-2. Thus, it seems that the statutory mens rea applies to both the unlawful taker and the unlawful appropriator.

The question remains as to what is an "intention to deprive." The current criminal code answers that question in § 16-8-1(1) by stating that to deprive is to withhold either "permanently or **temporarily**" or to dispose of property "so as to make it unlikely that the owner will recover it." Thus, while at common law an intent to return the property would negate the requisite mens rea of an intent permanently to deprive the victim, this no longer is the law in Georgia. An intent to withhold even temporarily will satisfy the mens rea of § 16-8-2. As the Court of Appeals wrote in Martin v. State, "[o]nce criminal intent . . . was proved, it became irrelevant whether the deprivation . . . was permanent or temporary." Thus, an intent to merely use the property of another without the owner's authorization would evince an intent to commit a theft.

One's impression that he has a right to hold property hostage for the payment of a debt does not excuse what would otherwise be a theft by taking. Thus, evidence of such an impression would not establish a mens rea defense.

As an element of the offense, the presence of the requisite mens rea must be proven by the prosecution beyond a reasonable doubt. As with all crimes, in theft prosecutions intent will normally be proven through the use of circumstantial evidence and will be a question for the jury to decide. To the extent that the defendant can raise a reasonable doubt about this element of the crime being present, he will have a mens rea "defense."

When the alleged taking occurs when a defendant fails to perform under a contract with the victim, the real issue is whether the defendant accepted or retained the victim's money with no intention to satisfy his obligations under the contract. Whether the defendant intended to fulfill his contractual obligations when he took the victim's money is a question for the jury.

The Court of Appeals has questioned whether good faith constitutes a proper legal defense to a charge of theft by taking. Nevertheless, by asserting that he has acted in good faith, a defendant essentially asserts that he lacked criminal intent. Thus, if the jury is properly instructed on criminal intent, the trial court does not err in failing to charge the jury on good faith.

It has been held that evidence of prior similar crimes is admissible to show the defendant's state of mind or scheme in committing a theft offense. However, there must be sufficient similarity or connection between the prior independent crimes and the offense charged, that proof of the former tends to prove the latter.

In Hawkins v. State, the defendant was charged with theft by taking of a piece of heavy machinery. He entered the machinery, started it and moved it 2,000 feet before it became mired in the mud. While affirming the conviction, the court stated that if the jury had believed the defense testimony that he had intended merely to damage the machinery there would have to be an acquittal for lack of intent. The court found, however, that there was evidence to support the jury's rejection of the defendant's testimony.

In Cook v. State, the defendant's theft of money was not included in his theft of a motor vehicle. Although the money was in the motor vehicle at the time the motor vehicle was stolen, the defendant was not aware of its presence and thus lacked the requisite intent to steal the money. However, the defendant's act of physically taking the money from its hiding place, coupled with the then present intent to steal it, was thus a second criminal act against the property of the victim, which was separate and distinct from the earlier theft of the motor vehicle.

5. *Claim of Right*

Another mens rea defense to theft by taking, as well as to most of the other theft offenses, is the traditional "claim of right" defense in which the defendant takes property under a belief that it is his or that he has an entitlement to it. This defense (as well as some related defenses) is codified at § 16-8-10. Paragraph (2) is the traditional claim of right defense which is an assertion by the defendant that he "[a]cted under an honest claim of right to the property or service involved or under a right to acquire or dispose of it as he did." The two other § 16-8-10 defenses are a claim that the defendant "[w]as unaware that the property or service was that of another" and a claim that the defendant took property which was offered for sale with the intent to pay for it promptly or believing that the owner would have consented to the taking.

The relationship between § 16-8-10 and a defense of lack of intent is uncertain. On the one hand, the statute can be seen to be merely an assurance that lack of intent can be shown by the defendant charged under § 16-8-2 or any of the theft crimes to which it is applicable. In fact, the drafters of the criminal code themselves enigmatically describe the statute as setting out "defenses [which] are intended to make sure that a defendant on trial for theft shall have the opportunity to show the absence of the necessary mental element for the crime of theft." On the other hand, the statute itself is labelled an affirmative defense, which normally connotes a defense which becomes relevant only after the elements of the crime are proven. Also, if the § 16-8-10 defenses are solely negation of the mens rea, one wonders as to the purpose in adding the statute to the criminal code at all. Surely any criminal defendant has the right to disprove the presence of one of the elements of the crime or, more precisely, to raise the requisite reasonable doubt which is all that is necessary to prevent a finding of one of the elements of a crime.

Regardless of what the intention of the drafters was with regard to the relationship between § 16-8-10 and the negation of the mens rea, the Georgia Court of Appeals has held that the § 16-8-10 defenses are not the same as that of lack of intent.

In Breland v. State, the defendant was implicated in a scheme whereby two other individuals stole gasoline trucks and filled them with gasoline stolen from a wholesaler which was then delivered to gas station owners. The defendant's claim was that he did not know the gasoline was stolen and that he thought he was assisting the rightful owner in disposing of it. The trial court's refusal to charge on the claim of right defense of § 16-8-10 was upheld by the Court of Appeals.

The court said that the defense being raised by the testimony was a lack of intent, not a claim of right, and the failure to give the claim of right jury instruction was not error. It is submitted that while there is a distinction between a claim of right and a lack of intent defense, the distinction was wrongly applied in Breland. The intent to violate § 16-8-2 was present, even under the defendant's testimony. The intent was to take away the gasoline from the victim. The mitigation claimed by the defendant was that the wholesaler had given permission. This is part of the affirmative defense outlined by § 16-8-10(2). He was acting under a belief that he had a right to dispose of the gasoline as he did.

Two other cases illustrate true lack of intent defenses. In Mathis v. State, the defendant was charged under § 16-8-2 after being found in possession of cameras, speakers, and tapes. He testified that he had been looking for the rightful owner. This truly is not a claim of right defense. He knew it was somebody's property, and he was not claiming that he had permission to have it. Thus, § 16-8-10(1) and (2) were not implicated. The claim clearly was that he had no intention to withhold the goods from the actual owner. This is a claim that he lacked the intention to deprive and is a claim which seeks to negate the mens rea of § 16-8-2.

Likewise, in Bremer v. State, a theft by receiving defendant claimed that he did not know that stereo equipment he bought at a very low price was stolen. He unsuccessfully sought a charge on § 16-8-10, but the appellate court affirmed the denial of his request. His claim was not a claim of right but a negation of the mens rea of theft by receiving, which is knowledge or reason to believe that the goods are stolen. Bremer's correct conclusion should be contrasted with Breland's incorrect conclusion. Here, the lack of knowledge of the stolen character of the goods did negate an element of § 16-8-7, whereas the Breland defendant's claim was not one which negated the mens rea of depriving the possessor of the goods which is the mental element of § 16-8-2.

However, in one case the defendant's acting on what he thought was an honest claim of right was found to negate his criminal intent to deprive the victims of the property. In Edens v. State, the court reversed the defendant's conviction based on the trial court's findings that the defendant did not possess the criminal intent necessary for theft by taking, in that his intent was to repossess an item under an honest claim of right after the purchasers defaulted on their payments.

In Grant v. State, the court held that had the defendant been on trial either for stealing the vehicle from a third party or for receiving stolen property, then a charge to the effect that he could not be found guilty if he had acted under an honest claim of right would certainly have been appropriate and necessary. However, inasmuch as he was indicted and tried for stealing the vehicle directly from the dealer, such a charge was not required.

Where claim of right is a defendant's only real defense, a trial court's failure to charge on claim of right is reversible error. However, raising the hue and cry of "sole defense" does not mandate that a charge on claim of right be given without some evidence to support it.

Another important case involving § 16-8-10 concerns an interpretation of § 16-8-10(3) which provides a defense for those who take property offered for sale with an intent to pay promptly or reasonably believing that the owner of the property would consent to the taking. In Cox v. State, the defendant was a clerk in a convenience store who gave his friends a great deal of merchandise which was being offered for sale. His trial testimony was that he intended to repay the owner at the time of his next payday which was the following week.

The trial court failed to give a § 16-8-10(3) instruction, presumably because the contemplated repayment was not prompt. The Court of Appeals reversed, finding that the facts raised a question of fact and that the jury should have been instructed as to § 16-8-10(3). It is apparent that the court was interpreting the paying "promptly" language of § 16-8-10(3) and, it might be added, was permitting the jury to give a rather broad interpretation to "promptly."

6. Actus Reus

It should be noted that a theft of several items from the same owner or possessor at the same time is all one crime. In Breland v. State, the defendant was convicted of stealing two trucks from Gulf Oil and then taking the trucks to a gasoline storage facility where gasoline was stolen from a bailee of Gulf Oil. The court held that the theft of the trucks constituted one theft. The court cited an old Georgia case, for the proposition that the taking of several items from one owner in one transaction was a single theft. The court also upheld, however, the conviction for a separate count of theft for the taking of the gasoline because it happened at a different time and place. It should be apparent that the line at which a continuing historical happening becomes a series of separate "transactions" is ephemeral, at best.

Likewise ephemeral is the dividing line between sufficient and insufficient evidence of the taking to support a conviction. Therefore, no attempt is made here to catalogue all cases raising this issue. Several cases provide an insight into the sufficiency question. In Wadley v. State, the defendant sold four maple chairs worth $57 each at retail for $5 each to a pawnshop. Shortly thereafter, police recovered two shipping cartons outside the shop. Each apparently had contained two chairs identical to the ones sold by the defendant. The warehouse of the furniture company which made the chairs was nearby and four chairs like those sold by the defendant had been reported missing. The court affirmed the conviction despite the defendant's assertion that the failure to identify these precise chairs as the stolen ones rendered the state's case insufficient.

In McClean v. State, the defendant was found in possession of goods identified as being stolen from the victim's mobile camper a month before. Despite the defendant's assertion that he had owned the goods at all times and testimony indicating a fleeing third party on the night of the theft, the court upheld the conviction. The court's action authorized theft by taking convictions on the sole basis of possession of recently stolen goods. This was a rather startling holding, particularly when contrasted with the well established rule that such evidence standing alone is insufficient to support a conviction for theft by receiving stolen goods.

In Bankston v. State the court held that recent possession of stolen goods will not automatically support a guilty verdict for theft. Instead, recent possession is to be viewed as probative evidence of the crime, and reviewed along with the other evidence in the case to determine whether any rational juror could find the defendant guilty beyond a reasonable doubt. In the trial of a theft by taking case, the jury should be instructed on the principle of recent unexplained possession in terms of a permissible inference.

Evidence of recent unexplained possession of stolen property will authorize but not require the trier of fact to infer guilt and an appellate court may find it sufficient in itself to support a conviction for the crime of theft by taking. Such evidence is sufficient in itself to support a conviction only if the jury has found "that the presumed fact (the defendant committed the crime) follows from the proved facts (proof of a theft and recent, unexplained possession of stolen goods by the defendant) beyond a reasonable doubt." The jury is not compelled to accept a defendant's explanation for his possession of stolen goods.

In Reed v. State, after buying a large quantity of yarn from a creditor, the defendant was unable to pay for this yarn under the terms of a purchase agreement. The creditor suggested an arrangement whereby she could gradually pay off the indebtedness by buying and selling yarn on the creditor's behalf. The defendant subsequently violated the agreement by selling a large quantity of yarn and retaining the proceeds herself rather than remitting them to the creditor. The court held that there was sufficient competent evidence to support a conviction for theft by taking.

Whether the defendant was in a fiduciary relationship with the victim is a jury question. In Hanson v. State, the evidence showed that on eleven separate dates the defendant cleared to zero the running daily totals on the computerized cash register, pocketed the money received from the sales up to that point, and reported only those sales that were made from the time the register was cleared until the close of business. The court found that evidence of the defendant's position as an assistant manager, with responsibility for closing out the cash register and accounting for the money made, was sufficient for a jury to find that a fiduciary relationship existed. In Eads v. State, the evidence showed that an elderly victim executed a power of attorney to the defendant, authorizing him to "sign, endorse, receive, deposit or issue checks" on her behalf and that the defendant placed the victim's endorsement on the back of her checks, cashed them, and appropriated the funds. The court held that in appropriating the funds, the defendant was clearly guilty of theft of the victim's property "in breach of his fiduciary obligation" to her. In Manous v. State, the court held that the evidence was sufficient to convict the defendant of theft by taking $1,123,900 in money belonging to an elderly victim. The defendant gained the victim's complete devotion and dependence and acquired complete control of her affairs. The victim's mental state had deteriorated seriously. The victim had signed checks made out to the defendant in various amounts, and the defendant had signed checks on the victim's account. Eventually the victim had only $3.90 in her bank account. Although the victim had expressed her desire to give the defendant what he needed, she testified that she did not intend to give the defendant all of her money.

A theft by taking conviction may be obtained on a confession although corroborated only by proof of the corpus delicti. In McCant v. State, the testimony of an analyst for a restaurant chain that one of its stores lost over $3,000 due to fraudulent refunds established the corpus delicti. Witness testimony and documentary evidence that the defendant was shift manager during each of the times the store experienced excessive refunds and negative sales and that the shift manager had to approve all refunds provided sufficient corroboration of the defendant's admission to the chain's employees that he took approximately $5,000 from the store by processing fraudulent refunds and that he used the money to pay his bills.

In Jordan v. State, the court held that proof that an office manager cashed or deposited into her own account more than $500 worth of unauthorized business checks was sufficient to support the jury's verdict that she committed theft by taking.

In motor vehicle theft cases, there is no requirement that the engine of the vehicle be running or that the thief successfully navigate the vehicle onto a street before the crime is complete. In Travis v. State, a witness noticed a vehicle rolling backwards across a parking lot. The vehicle, with its plastic back window cut, had no lights on, the engine was not running, and the doors were closed. After the vehicle hit the back of the witness's vehicle, the defendant got out and tried to leave the scene. Given these facts, the court concluded that a rational trier of fact could have found proof of the defendant's guilt of theft by taking.

In Dukes v. State, the evidence showed that at the request of the lienholder the defendant and his former employee picked up a repossessed motor vehicle from the lienholder's parking lot. The defendant later sold the motor, transmission, and door of the vehicle to a salvage business. The defendant then informed a representative of the lienholder that he forgot to pick up the vehicle. The vehicle was subsequently reported stolen. The court held that there was ample evidence to authorize the defendant's conviction for theft by taking of the motor vehicle.

In Matthews v. State, the evidence showed that while misrepresenting his employment with a corporation, the defendant negotiated the rental of a van for that corporation from a rental car agency. Further misrepresenting his employment with that corporation, the defendant signed the lease for the van. The defendant was never an employee of the corporation. The van originally leased was replaced with a second van under a second lease. The leases for both vans had been extended a number of times. After the final extension of the second lease had expired, the second van was not returned, no rental fee was ever paid, and the defendant did not contact the agency. The agency reported the van as possibly stolen, and the police in a neighboring state found the van burned at a housing project with the defendant present at the scene. The defendant presented the police with the expired lease for the van. The court held that there was sufficient evidence to support the defendant's conviction for theft by taking. The jury was authorized to determine that the defendant did not intend to pay any rental fee and that in retaining possession of the vans beyond the terms of the leases the defendant intended to appropriate the vans with the intention of at least temporarily depriving the rental car agency of the vans.

In Grant v. State, there was no direct evidence that the defendant was an accessory before the fact to the driver's theft by taking the truck. The circumstantial evidence could have supported the defendant's version of events that he did not participate in the theft of the truck and did not learn that the truck was stolen until after he began riding around with the driver, at which time, he tried to help the driver sell the truck. The court held that because the evidence did not exclude the reasonable hypothesis that the driver had stolen the truck without the defendant's knowledge or participation, the defendant's conviction for theft by taking the truck was insupportable as a matter of law.

In Locklear v. State, the undisputed evidence showed that other people had access to the body shop's bank deposit bag at the time it disappeared and there was no evidence of the defendants' possession of it. In order to convict the defendants of theft, the state had to present more that the coincidence of two thefts occurring around the time the defendants visited two different establishments. The court found that the state failed to demonstrate the defendants' participation in the thefts and to exclude other reasonable hypotheses for the disappearance of the money. The state showed nothing more that the defendants' presence in the wrong place at the wrong time.Thus, the circumstantial evidence was insufficient as a matter of law to support their convictions for felony theft by taking.

In Bradford v. State, the court held that there was sufficient evidence from which the jury was authorized to find beyond a reasonable doubt that the defendants committed the charged thefts by intentionally deceiving the victim lenders. The defendants ostensibly arranged for investors to buy residential rental property. Unbeknownst to the investors, the defendants created false and fraudulent loan application documents in order to qualify the investors for the mortgages. Based on the false loan documents, lenders agreed to loan money to the investors. The defendants then bought each house in question at fair market value and, on the same day, "flipped" the house by selling it to their investor at a greatly inflated price. The defendants used the proceeds from the "flip" sale to the investor to pay off their own earlier purchase of the house, and they kept the difference between the low price they had paid for the house and the higher price paid by the investor who eventually defaulted on the loan.

Overcharging for services or goods furnished in and of itself does not constitute a violation of the theft by taking statute, but charging for services or goods not performed or delivered could constitute such a violation.

In certain cases in order to prove theft by taking beyond a reasonable doubt, the state must present evidence which would eliminate the possibility that some other person had access to the stolen property during the critical period before the property was discovered missing.

It is within the province of the jury to accept the state's evidence that the defendant stole the property and reject the defendant's evidence that he had the permission and consent of the owner to take the property on the occasion upon which the theft charge was predicated.

7. *Relationship to Other Offenses*

Important Notice about Repudiation of Actual or Same Evidence Test: The Georgia Supreme Court repudiated the actual evidence test in *Drinkard v. Walker*, 281 Ga. 211, 636 S.E.2d 530 (2006), because it found this test to be inconsistent with the statutory framework governing the prohibition against multiple convictions for included offenses in Georgia. This inconsistency resulted in years of confusion and unpredictable results. In its place, the court adopted the required evidence test and overruled any prior case law that is inconsistent with it. Thus, any prior case law applying the actual evidence test is no longer controlling and should not be relied upon to determine whether one offense is included in another under § 16-1-6(1). The discussion of such case law is included below only insofar as it may still be applicable to pending prosecutions that arose before the Drinkard decision. See MULTIPLE CONVICTIONS, II. Tests to Determine Presence of Multiple Convictions, for a complete discussion of the Drinkard decision.

Theft by taking may be, but is not always, a lesser included offense of burglary. Where theft by taking and burglary counts are based on the theft of different property, the theft by taking offense is not a lesser included offense of burglary.

The offense of conspiracy to defraud a state or political subdivision does not merge with the underlying offense of theft by taking.

Motor vehicle theft is not a lesser included offense of armed robbery as a matter of fact, where the evidence used to establish the motor vehicle theft is not the same evidence used to establish the armed robbery.

Where there is no evidence that the motor vehicle was taken from the victim by means other than hijacking with a firearm, a charge on the lesser included offense of motor vehicle theft is not authorized.

If the victim is aware of the taking of property from his immediate presence before the taking is complete, the offense committed is robbery by sudden snatching. If the victim is not aware of the taking until it is complete, the offense committed is not robbery by sudden snatching but rather theft by taking.

Theft by receiving is not a crime included in the crime of theft by taking. The crimes of theft by taking and theft by receiving are mutually exclusive. Accordingly, a conviction of theft by receiving would bar a subsequent prosecution for theft by taking.

Because different elements must be demonstrated to find a defendant guilty of both theft by taking and entering an automobile, as a matter of both law and fact, these offenses do not merge.

Where the evidence shows either that the defendant intended to take a car and was caught while taking it or that he was trying to stop a runaway car and committed no crime at all, there would be no evidence that he entered the car with the intent to commit a theft or felony therein. Thus, a charge on entering an automobile would not be warranted.

B. *Theft by Shoplifting*

Theft by shoplifting is treated specially in the criminal code in § 16-8-14. Formerly subsection (b) of § 16-8-2, the General Assembly severed this portion of the statute in 1978 when it added penalty provisions peculiar to shoplifting. Shoplifting could certainly have been prosecuted under the former larceny or false pretenses statutes and also under current § 16-8-2. Yet there have always been special statutes aimed at this type of theft because of recurrent problems in proving intent and asportation. For example, because one is usually impliedly authorized to pick up and examine goods in a retail establishment, it is difficult at times to determine when an unauthorized asportation occurs. Also, it is difficult to prove lack of intent to pay for goods at any time before leaving a store. The statute remedies these problems by identifying particular types of behavior as the actus reus of shoplifting in contrast with the general language defining the actus reus of § 16-8-2.

1. *Actus Reus*

When done with the requisite mens rea, the following acts violate the shoplifting statute: (1) concealment or taking possession of goods or merchandise, (2) altering the price tag or mark of goods or merchandise, (3) transferring goods or merchandise from one container to another, (4) switching labels or price tags on merchandise, and (5) wrongfully causing the amount paid to be less than the merchant's stated price. It should be noted that goods or merchandise are covered by the first three provisions, but only merchandise is explicitly covered by the fourth. It also should be noted that the first three provisions specifically apply only to stores or retail establishments while the fourth is not, by its terms, so limited. Another inconsistency occurs between the description of the mens rea and the actus reus language. Apparently inadvertently, the mens rea is framed in terms of merchandise only, while the first three types of actus reus specifically mention "goods or merchandise."

Reasonable certainty of ownership is all that is required to establish this element of the offense. In Lanier v. State, the court held that it could have been inferred from the loss prevention employee's testimony that the stolen coats were owned by the department store. This evidence of ownership was sufficient.

Any variance between the allegation in the indictment and the proof at trial concerning the precise identity of the victim of the theft would not be fatal, so long as the defendant has been fully informed of the charges against him and there is no danger of a second prosecution for the same shoplifting offense.

Where the defendant is charged with "taking possession" under § 16-8-14(a)(1) and the evidence shows that he did in fact take possession of the goods, the fact that the state might also have charged him with interchanging price tags under § 16-8-14(a)(4) would not create a fatal variance in the proof.

2. *Mens Rea*

As for the mens rea, this statute, unlike § 16-8-2, provides three alternative mens reas. Instead of merely punishing the individual who intends to deprive the owner of property, as in § 16-8-2, the shoplifting statute punishes those who commit one of the actus reus provisions with the intent **either** (1) to appropriate the property to his own use without paying for it, (2) to deprive the owner of the possession of it, or (3) to deprive the owner of the value of it. It would appear that these mens rea provisions are broader than that of § 16-8-2.

For example, it would seem that under mens rea (1) the individual who removes a toy from the shelf of the store and plays with it without intending to purchase it has committed shoplifting. Likewise, the individual who browses through a magazine or newspaper will have violated the statute. In both of these situations, the defendant will have committed actus reus (1) (taking possession of the property) along with mens rea (1) (intending to use the property without an intention of paying for it).

Mens rea (2) has given rise to some discussion of when there is actually an intent to deprive the owner of the possession of the goods. The appellate courts have been faced with the problem of determining whether the owner who permits people to take goods off the shelves is or is not being deprived of possession. In K-Mart Corp. v. Coker, the Georgia Supreme Court has resolved this problem by holding that the intent to deprive the owner of the possession and value of the goods can be inferred from the defendant's conduct, and that the defendant's failure to remove the goods from the store does not negate the criminal intent that the statute requires.

Mens rea (3) (intending to deprive the owner of the value of the goods) would appear to be satisfied where the evidence shows that the defendant took possession of the goods and then solicited a refund for those goods without those goods having been previously purchased.

Where an accusation charges the defendant with committing theft by shoplifting with only one of the three intents specified in the statute, instructing the jury on all three intents would not constitute reversible error where the evidence does not create a reasonable possibility that the jury could have convicted the defendant of committing the offense with either one of the other intents only. For example, where the evidence shows that the offense was committed with all three intents, the jury would not be able to find the defendant guilty of having either or both of the other intents without also finding him guilty of having the intent charged in the accusation. Thus, instructing the jury on all three intents would be harmless.

Secrist v. State dealt with the mens rea provisions of § 16-8-14. In this case, the defendant was charged with shoplifting and the state introduced an out-of-court statement by the defendant that stated "I did take a pair of leather earrings and a wallet from the shop. I was going to let Irvin take their cost from my earnings." The defendant was apparently an employee of the shop that was victimized. The trial judge instructed the jury with regard to this statement as a confession.

The defendant appealed, claiming that this was not a confession because it contained a negation of the mens rea by announcing an intention to have the employer deduct the value of the goods from future earnings. The majority rejected the defendant's argument, concluding that while this statement may have negated an intent to deprive the owner of the value of the goods, it certainly did not negate an intention to deprive the owner of possession or to appropriate the merchandise to his own use. Thus, this was a complete admission of the crime alleged in the accusation and an instruction on confessions was held proper. The dissenting judge urged that the statement asserted a claim of right defense under § 16-8-10 and, thus, was not a complete confession.

The dissenting judge's point seems to be well taken. The claim of right defense does serve as an affirmative defense which concedes the presence of the requisite mens rea. It should be noted, however, that the General Assembly, when it removed the shoplifting offense from § 16-8-2 in 1978 to a separate section, did not change the coverage of the claim of right defense of § 16-8-10. Thus, at the time of Secrist § 16-8-10, which by its terms applies to prosecutions under § 16-8-2, applied to shoplifting which was a § 16-8-2 offense at that time. Now, however, it is a § 16-8-14 offense and the coverage of § 16-8-10 does not explicitly extend to that kind of prosecution, which may be a legislative oversight.

Evidence of prior similar shoplifting incidents are admissible to show the defendant's motive, plan, scheme, and bent of mind in committing a subsequent shoplifting offense. That the other incidents involved other stores and other kinds of merchandise does not render them dissimilar to the subsequent offense.

3. Relationship to Other Offenses

Important Notice about Repudiation of Actual or Same Evidence Test: The Georgia Supreme Court repudiated the actual evidence test in *Drinkard v. Walker*, 281 Ga. 211, 636 S.E.2d 530 (2006), because it found this test to be inconsistent with the statutory framework governing the prohibition against multiple convictions for included offenses in Georgia. This inconsistency resulted in years of confusion and unpredictable results. In its place, the court adopted the required evidence test and overruled any prior case law that is inconsistent with it. Thus, any prior case law applying the actual evidence test is no longer controlling and should not be relied upon to determine whether one offense is included in another under § 16-1-6(1). The discussion of such case law is included below only insofar as it may still be applicable to pending prosecutions that arose before the Drinkard decision. See MULTIPLE CONVICTIONS, II. Tests to Determine Presence of Multiple Convictions, for a complete discussion of the Drinkard decision.

Although theft by deception may be a lesser included offense of shoplifting as a matter of fact, where the undisputed evidence shows the completion of the offense of shoplifting or no offense at all, the trial court is not required to charge the jury on the lesser included offense of theft by deception.

A trial court's denial of a defense request for a charge on misdemeanor theft by shoplifting does not constitute error where the evidence shows either the commission of felony shoplifting or no offense at all.

In the absence of a request, the trial court is not required to instruct sua sponte on misdemeanor theft by taking as a lesser included offense of felony theft by shoplifting.

4. Punishment

There are two grades of shoplifting: misdemeanor and felony. Shoplifting goods worth $300 or less in value is punishable as a misdemeanor. However, there is enhanced punishment for subsequent offenses. Prior felony or misdemeanor convictions for shoplifting serve as the basis for imposing this enhanced punishment. A conviction of a second offense requires, in addition to or in lieu of any imprisonment which might be imposed, a fine of at least $250 which may not be suspended or probated. A conviction of a third offense requires, in addition to or in lieu of any fine which might be imposed, imprisonment for not less than 30 days or confinement in a community correctional facility for a period of 120 days or a monitored house arrest for a period of 120 days. In addition to this confinement, the defendant may be required to undergo psychological evaluation and treatment at his expense. The imprisonment or confinement may not be suspended, probated, deferred, or withheld. A conviction of a fourth or subsequent offense is punishable as a felony by imprisonment for not less than one nor more than ten years. The first year of the sentence may not be suspended, probated, deferred, or withheld. Shoplifting goods worth more than $300 is a felony punishable by imprisonment for not less than one nor more than ten years. Also, shoplifting from three separate stores or retail establishments within one county, within a seven-day period, and with the goods from each theft worth more than $100 is a felony punishable by imprisonment for not less than one nor more than ten years. This provision was enacted in 2000 to provide enhanced punishment for shoplifters belonging to organized crime groups who steal large quantities of a particular item from the same retail chain within a county during a short period of time.

The statute defines "value" as the actual retail price of the goods at the time and place of the offense and provides that the unaltered price tag shall be prima facie evidence of value and ownership. Value is not an essential element of the crime of theft by shoplifting. It is only if there is a factual issue as to whether the value is greater than $300 that the jury must determine value in order to assist the trial court in determining the appropriate sentence. If the evidence does not raise a factual issue relating to value, a charge to the jury on valuation is not necessary.

The General Assembly amended O.C.G.A. § 16-8-14(b)(1)(C) in 1997 so that the fourth or subsequent conviction for shoplifting shall be a felony. This amendment was enacted to remedy a deficiency in the prior statute whereby the courts could consider only prior misdemeanor shoplifting convictions. Thus, the General Assembly intended that as to convictions of shoplifting occurring after the effective date of the 1997 amendment, **any** prior shoplifting conviction shall be considered in determining if the defendant has committed felony shoplifting. Under this construction of the statute, a foreign shoplifting conviction—whether misdemeanor or felony—may be considered when determining whether a current Georgia shoplifting charge is a fourth offense felony.

Section 16-8-14(b)(1)(C) provides a specific sentencing scheme for defendants convicted four or more times for shoplifting and gives the trial court discretion to sentence the defendants to a term of not less than one nor more than ten years. By contrast, the applicable general recidivist sentencing scheme set forth in § 17-10-7(a) provides that any defendant with a prior felony conviction who thereafter is convicted of another felony must be given the maximum sentence, which in a shoplifting case would require imposition of the maximum ten-year sentence set out in § 16-8-14(b)(1)(C). Because nothing in the specific sentencing scheme in § 16-8-14(b)(1)(C) permits application of conflicting provisions in the general recidivist sentencing scheme in § 17-10-7(a), the specific scheme controls. Thus, despite a shoplifting defendant's prior felony convictions, the trial court has discretion under § 16-8-14(b)(1)(C) to sentence him to a term of not less than one nor more than ten years.

Section 16-8-14, which provides for sentence enhancement based on the number of prior shoplifting convictions, does not apply where none of the defendant's prior felony convictions involved shoplifting. In such a case, the trial court must sentence the defendant under the general recidivist statute, § 17-10-7(c), rather than under the specific shoplifting statute, § 16-8-14.

A person may be convicted of felony shoplifting where the subject of the felony is less than $300 in value, if the person has been previously convicted three or more times for such an offense. The prior convictions must be alleged in the indictment. However, it has been held that so long as the defendant is indicted as a fourth offender, there is no requirement for the indictment to list a previous conviction provided the state's intent to present such evidence at the sentencing phase is made known to the defendant prior to his trial.

Although the state may list the defendant's prior convictions supporting recidivist treatment in the indictment, it is not required to present evidence of the defendant's recidivism to the jury during the guilt/innocence phase of the trial where there is no other legal basis for the consideration thereof. Therefore, it would be error for the trial court to read the indictment to the jury without redacting the references to the defendant's recidivism and prior convictions.

C. Theft by Fraudulent Use of Retail Sales Receipts and Universal Product Code Labels

Recent technological developments have enabled shoplifters to use more sophisticated methods to commit their crimes. For instance, new technology has been used to produce large quantities of fraudulent Universal Product Code (UPC) labels, which are then sold to shoplifters to ply their trade. After purchasing an item, the shoplifter will substitute the item's "valid UPC label with a fraudulent one programmed for a much higher value." The shoplifter will then use a fraudulent sales receipt and the fraudulent UPC label to obtain a refund at the higher value. Section 16-8-17 was enacted in 2000 specifically to proscribe this method of shoplifting and the manufacture of fraudulent retail sales receipts and UPC labels.

A person who, with intent to cheat or defraud a retailer, possesses, uses, utters, transfers, makes, alters, counterfeits, or reproduces a retail sales receipt or a Universal Product Code label which results in a theft of property worth more than $300 in value commits a felony punishable by imprisonment for not less than one nor more than three years or by a fine or both. However, if the property is taken from three separate stores or retail establishments within one county, within a seven-day period, and with the property from each theft worth more than $100 in value, the person commits a felony punishable by imprisonment for not less than one nor more than ten years.

A person who, with intent to cheat or defraud a retailer, possesses 15 or more fraudulent retail sales receipts or Universal Product Code labels or possesses a device the purpose of which is to manufacture fraudulent receipts or labels commits a felony punishable by imprisonment for not less than one nor more ten years.

D. Theft by Deception

Section 16-8-3 codifies the crime of theft by deception, punishing those who obtain "property by any deceitful means or artful practice with the intention of depriving the owner of the property." The drafters were apparently influenced greatly by the formulation of theft by deception in Model Penal Code § 223.3. The theft by deception statute appears to combine the common law crimes of false pretenses (obtaining title from the victim by deceit) and larceny by trick (obtaining mere possession by deceit and later converting). The broad language of this statute has been held to encompass fraudulent bid-rigging schemes.

1. Mens Rea

The statute's mens rea is twofold. First, there must be an intent to deprive. An intent to deprive is the intent to withhold the property of another either permanently or temporarily or to dispose of the property so as to make it unlikely that the owner will recover it. Second, there must be an intent to act deceptively. Thus, the actor who mistakenly believes something himself cannot be guilty if he persuades the "victim" to act on that mistaken belief. Whether an intent to deceive has been established is a jury question. The jury's inference of intent can be supported by circumstantial evidence.

2. Actus Reus

a. Generally

The more difficult issue in this area has been in defining the actus reus. Theft by deception and its predecessors (false pretenses and larceny by trick) are not crimes of stealth, but rather crimes that are committed face to face, often in a business context. Therefore, courts and legislatures traditionally have not defined the actus reus of this crime too broadly for fear that this would allow the use of the criminal sanction to punish mere failures to live up to contracts. Thus, the majority view rejects false pretenses convictions where the defendant has made a false promise, that is, he has promised to do something in the future without any intention actually to perform the promise. While perhaps conceding that such an act is a fraudulent one worthy of punishment, most courts refuse to punish such behavior because of a feared difficulty in distinguishing a false promise from a broken one, in which the defendant intends to perform at the time of the making of the promise but then fails to do so. These courts fear that juries will leap from evidence that the promise was not performed to the conclusion that the defendant never **intended** to perform it. This would render it a crime to fail to pay a debt. Thus, even though a false promise can be seen to be a misrepresentation of a present fact (the fact being the state of mind of the defendant), most courts reject false pretense prosecutions based on this set of facts.

In defining theft by deception's actus reus, § 16-8-3 reflects a wariness of defining deception too broadly. Five specific methods of deception are identified and only one authorizes a conviction for a false promise and, even then, not all false promises are punished. A person deceives if he intentionally (1) "creates or confirms" a victim's false impression about an "existing fact or past event" which the defendant knew or believed was false; (2) "fails to correct" a previously created false impression; (3) prevents "another" from obtaining relevant information about the transfer of property; (4) fails to disclose any legal impediment to the enjoyment of property, such as a lien or adverse claim, regardless of whether the impediments are matters of public record; or (5) makes a false promise of performance of services. In this last method of deception, the statute explicitly forbids conviction solely on the evidence of a failure to perform a promised service. The statute does not indicate that these methods of deception are the exclusive means of violating the statute. Even if the catalogue of deceptive acts is meant to be exhaustive, however, the statute additionally punishes artful practices, which are not defined at all.

It is clear that the actus reus is **not** specifically limited to spoken words but includes nonverbal behavior which creates or confirms the false impression. In fact, in at least two situations ("failure to correct" and "failure to disclose"), the statute creates an affirmative obligation to act, thus breaching the traditional distinction in the criminal law between misfeasance and nonfeasance.

b. Creating False Impression of Existing Fact or Past Event

The careful description in paragraphs (b)(1) and (2) of the act of the defendant in creating a "false impression" of a fact or event should also be noted. This makes it clear that statements of literal truth (half-truths) can subject the actor to liability if they are intentionally made in order to create a false impression. The actor must know or believe that the created impression (which itself must have been intentionally created or confirmed) is false. Without knowledge, or at least belief, that an impression is false, there can be no intent to deceive. Finally, it should be noted that the statute skirts the question of whether an intentional misstatement of the law can be the basis of a conviction. Although many courts refuse to convict in this situation on the ground that everyone, including the victim, is presumed to know the law, the Georgia law prior to 1968 was to the contrary. Although the current statute does not explicitly cover misstatements of law, such statements can certainly be described as creating a false impression of an existing fact,i.e., the state of the law. Particularly in light of pre-1968 case law, it is assumed that misstatements of law are covered by the statute.

Most of the case law decided under § 16-8-3 deals with paragraph (b)(1) and whether the defendant had created a "false impression" about an existing fact or past event. One troublesome area has been the use of worthless checks as a means of obtaining property. In Dunphy v. State, a theft by deception conviction was upheld where the defendant obtained a real estate option by writing a worthless check and "covering" it with another worthless check. In one sentence, the court concluded that the evidence supported the verdict, without specifically addressing the question of whether the presentation of a worthless check is a misrepresentation of the current status of the drawer's bank account. Dunphy is further complicated by the fact that the seller of the real estate option who received the check actually was paid by the drawee bank so that it is not clear whether the seller or the bank was the victim.

The Court of Appeals, in the same year, reversed a theft by deception conviction based on a somewhat similar set of facts. In Croy v. State, the defendant uttered two worthless checks to a used car dealer for a total of twenty cars. The parties had been dealing for several years with each other and the "victim" testified that in this case the defendant had "asked for one week" on the draft. The understanding between the parties, therefore, was that the check would not be presented to the drawee for a week. The check was worthless when given to the "victim" and the defendant never deposited covering funds. The court held this was not sufficient for a § 16-8-3 conviction.

Under these circumstances, the court found that the only representation made by the defendant was that in a week there would be sufficient funds. This was a representation about future events and not covered by paragraph (b)(1). The court analogized this situation to that of delivery of a postdated check and said that, under these circumstances, the victim's "loss results from his absolute confidence in the party making the promise" not from any deceit or artful practice.

It is apparent that what distinguishes Croy from Dunphy is the extrinsic agreement not to present the check immediately. The court did not explicitly face the question of a check delivered without any extraneous understandings or agreements. It should be noted that the writing of a bad check itself is a crime under other code provisions.

In another case, the defendant told the victim that he would send a check for the purchase of the new car in a few days while "creating the impression" that he had money in the bank to cover any such check. Because of the creating of the false impression, this would be sufficient to warrant a § 16-8-3 conviction, but the court reversed the conviction for other reasons. Likewise, in Harris v. State, where the defendant obtained titles to two cars after creating the false impression that he owned valuable stock and would be selling it and sending the proceeds to the seller, the court found that this would be sufficient to support a conviction. Again, however, the failure of the trial court to instruct the jury that a false promise of future performance cannot form the basis of theft by deception resulted in a reversal of the conviction and a new trial. Harris is also notable because the defendant's behavior was largely nonverbal in that he stood by while the seller checked out the value of the stock which he owned in a particular company, but failed to inform the seller that his stock was actually that of another company of the same name and was worthless.

In Arnold v. State, the defendant was convicted of theft by deception in obtaining $250,000 by intentionally and falsely representing to investors that he owned certain real property to secure an investment and that he had conveyed the property to the investors, when in fact he never owned the property and thus could not convey it. The court rejected the defendant's assertion that the investors relied on only a promise to do something in the future. The court held that the state proved beyond a reasonable doubt that the representation forming the basis of the theft by deception referred to a presently existing fact. Both prior to and at the closing, the defendant, orally and by documents, falsely represented to the investors that he presently owned the offered collateral. Moreover, the check was not handed over to the defendant's agent until the fraudulently signed security deed was delivered.

In Adams v. State, the court held that proof of the victim's reliance upon a false impression as to an existing fact authorized the defendant's conviction for theft by deception even though there was evidence of other contributing inducements, such as his representations as to future events. The fact that the defendant also made representations as to future events, which are not prohibited by paragraph (b)(1), did not affect the evidence supporting his conviction.

It has been held that evidence of the defendant's express promise or representation is required in order to establish his creation of a false impression in another. In Wilburn v. State, the defendant was charged with obtaining wages from two employers through the creation of a false impression of fact by working for both of them during the same period of time under employment agreements requiring him to work for each of them exclusively. The court held that the evidence was insufficient to support his convictions. The evidence did not establish that the defendant's employment with either of the two companies in question had been conditioned on any express promise or representation by him to the effect that he would work exclusively for those companies. Also, both employers denied that the defendant had received any compensation to which he was not entitled.

A 1978 case illustrates the requirement of paragraph (b)(1) that there actually be a deception of the victim. In Perdue v. State, the defendant was an administrator of a CETA program who was obtaining payoffs from employees and their families. The court reversed the conviction with regard to one victim who testified that she was paying the defendant $15 weekly to keep her daughter on the CETA payroll. The victim testified that she knew she was being "ripped off" and the court apparently held that in such a case there is no creation of a false impression about a fact. The victim knew that there should be no payment made.

On the other hand, when the defendant told other victims that they had to pay anywhere from $1 to $1.50 weekly for things such as "supplies" and "work permits" the court upheld the convictions on the grounds that the defendant had created the false impression in the minds of the victims that such payments were legitimate and that she was authorized to collect them. Perdue indicates that the "victim's" gullibility and actual knowledge will have an effect on the defendant's liability for theft by deception. It should be noted that in many situations in which the victim is aware of what is going on, a theft by extortion prosecution under § 16-8-16 will be warranted.

As a matter of law, a valid contractual merger clause executed by two or more parties in an arm's length business transaction precludes any subsequent claim of theft by deception based upon pre-contractual, oral representations. Any impressions based upon these representations would be superseded by a merger clause that expressly puts the parties on notice that the agreement's terms supersede any and all prior representations not contained therein. Under the express terms of such an agreement, a party cannot reasonably rely upon and thus cannot be deceived by these representations. Therefore, any pre-contractual misrepresentations cannot form the basis of a post-contractual claim of theft by deception.

c. Preventing Victim from Acquiring Pertinent Information about Property

Section 16-8-3(b)(3) provides that theft by deception can be committed if the defendant prevents the victim from acquiring information pertinent to the disposition of his property. In Adams v. State, the court found that evidence that the defendant threatened the victim when she asked about her money was sufficient to support his conviction under this paragraph of the statute.

d. Obtaining Property

It has been held that a defendant in a § 16-8-3 prosecution must actually have obtained the property. Thus, in Stewart v. State, the court held that a defendant who obtained money for the corporation of which he was president and part owner could not be guilty of theft by deception because there was no proof that defendant received any benefit, with all of the funds paid by the victims going directly into the corporate account. Although this holding may be viewed as being compelled by the statutory language describing a defendant who "obtains" property, it seems an overly restrictive interpretation. Even assuming that no money was directly received by the Stewart defendant, it seems obvious that, at the least, the value of his partial ownership in the corporation was increased by his behavior. He thus "obtained" property, in the form of increased value for his assets. Even without any increase in value in defendant's holdings, it seems that an actor who "altruistically" deceives X to benefit Y ought to be guilty of theft by deception. In Interagency, Inc. v. Danco Financial Corp., the court held that the plaintiff proffered sufficient evidence to show that the defendants did personally obtain the funds. Even though the $8,500 check was initially to be placed in a corporate trust account, there was substantial evidence that because of the defendants' close identity of interests, they each, jointly and severally, directly profited from the funds.

Although it must be shown in a theft by deception prosecution that the defendant actually obtained the property, there is no requirement of proof of pecuniary loss by the victim. Thus, in Harrell v. State, evidence that showed that the defendant obtained a vehicle of the dealership, albeit for less than one day, was sufficient under the statute.

In Markowitz v. Wieland, the plaintiffs argued that they were given a warranty agreement which provided that structural defects in their home would be covered for ten years and that the contractor failed to repair the defects as warranted, causing a decrease in the market value of their home. The court held, however, that to sustain an action for theft by deception the plaintiffs had to show that the contractor obtained their property. An unrealized diminution in the value of the property did not equate to the contractor obtaining the property as the plaintiffs were still the owners. Therefore, the theft by deception claim failed.

e. Exceptions

Section 16-8-3(c) excludes from characterization as "deceitful means" or "artful practices" false matters which have no "pecuniary significance" and exaggerated statements unlikely to deceive ordinary people. Thus, the statute continues the traditional requirement of materiality by requiring that the defendant obtain the property "by" the prohibited acts and by specifically excluding from the actus reus those matters having "no pecuniary significance." The statute also continues the traditional refusal to punish puffery or opinions.

The Court of Appeals has construed "pecuniary significance" to mean that the misrepresentation or false impression upon which a prosecution is based must somehow relate to the theft of the property at issue. In other words, a charge of theft by deception cannot be sustained where the only falsity proven is completely unconnected to the theft of the property. In Adams v. State, the court found that the jury could have interpreted the defendant's misrepresentation regarding his position at the company to have "pecuniary significance" because it was used to induce the victim to part with her money. The jury could have found that by inflating his employment status, the defendant hoped to persuade the victim that he was better qualified to invest her retirement funds. The evidence sustained a finding, therefore, that the defendant created a false impression of his qualifications to handle the victim's money. Furthermore, although the better practice would have been to present specific testimony that the victim relied upon this impression, the court found that the evidence was sufficient for the jury to infer reliance based upon the victim's decision to hand over her funds to the defendant for investment in a music business. Thus, there was sufficient evidence for the jury to find the defendant guilty of theft by deception.

3. Defenses

Any lack of diligence by a victim to prevent a theft by deception affords no defense to the accused.

4. Relationship to Other Offenses

Important Notice about Repudiation of Actual or Same Evidence Test: The Georgia Supreme Court repudiated the actual evidence test in *Drinkard v. Walker*, 281 Ga. 211, 636 S.E.2d 530 (2006), because it found this test to be inconsistent with the statutory framework governing the prohibition against multiple convictions for included offenses in Georgia. This inconsistency resulted in years of confusion and unpredictable results. In its place, the court adopted the required evidence test and overruled any prior case law that is inconsistent with it. Thus, any prior case law applying the actual evidence test is no longer controlling and should not be relied upon to determine whether one offense is included in another under § 16-1-6(1). The discussion of such case law is included below only insofar as it may still be applicable to pending prosecutions that arose before the Drinkard decision. See MULTIPLE CONVICTIONS, II. Tests to Determine Presence of Multiple Convictions, for a complete discussion of the Drinkard decision.

Although theft by deception may be a lesser included offense of shoplifting as a matter of fact, where the undisputed evidence shows the completion of the offense of shoplifting or no offense at all, the trial court is not required to charge the jury on the lesser included offense of theft by deception.

Where there is evidence to warrant the charge, the trial court may charge the jury that it can consider theft by deception as a lesser included offense of robbery.

Where the same evidence is used to prove the defendant's guilt on three counts each alleging in identical terms theft by deception of one of the three pieces of equipment, the three charged offenses merge as a matter of fact into one theft by deception offense for purposes of conviction and sentencing.

E. Theft by Extortion

Section 16-8-16 expands the common-law misdemeanor of extortion which punished public officials who demanded fees to which they were not entitled to protect against a broader range of coerced transfers of property. Anyone who obtains property by threatening to do one of six things is guilty of the felony of theft by extortion. Modeled closely after Model Penal Code § 223.4, the statute punishes those who threaten to (1) inflict bodily injury on either the victim or anyone else; (2) accuse anyone of a criminal offense; (3) disseminate material subjecting someone to hatred, contempt, or ridicule or impairing someone's credit or business reputation; (4) take or withhold action as a public official or cause a public official to take or withhold action; (5) bring about or continue a collective unofficial action "if the property is not demanded or received for the benefit of the group;" and (6) cooperate or not cooperate with respect to another's legal claim or defense.

While most states punish the threat itself, Georgia is in the minority of states which require there be an actual **obtaining** of the property for conviction of extortion. The drafters explained this by pointing out that the theft statutes were designed to protect property, not individuals. Of course, under the appropriate circumstances, the threatener who does not succeed in obtaining the property will be guilty of attempted theft by extortion and prosecuted under the general criminal attempt statute, § 16-4-1.

Although the statute does not specifically articulate a mens rea requirement, it seems clear that the use of the verb "threaten" as part of the actus reus connotes purposeful activity. Thus, a defendant's behavior presumably must have as its purpose the threatening of one of the prohibited acts. It is unclear what the drafters intended by the use of "unlawfully" in defining the prohibited act of obtaining property. The use of the word by the drafters is apparently intentional, however, because the Model Penal Code section upon which the Georgia statute is based does not include the term.

As for the actus reus, it is clear that, unlike some statutes which require that the threats be in writing, the Georgia statute imposes no such requirement. Some of the prohibited kinds of threats raise questions about the relationship between extortion and other crimes. For example, threatening bodily injury unless property is transferred (as specified in paragraph (a)(1)) appears similar to robbery. The armed robbery defendant in Sanders v. State, asserted that extortion ought to have been charged as a lesser included offense. The court, in rejecting this argument, pointed out that the robbery statute (§ 16-8-40) punishes only those who threaten to inflict immediate serious bodily harm to the victim, while § 16-8-16 punishes threats to inflict any bodily injury. Thus, extortion may be committed by threatening future and/or nonserious bodily injury.

Paragraph (a)(4) dealing with public officials refusing to take or taking official action in return for property raises questions about the intersection between bribery (§ 16-10-2) and extortion. It would seem that the distinction is based on the initiator of the transfer of property. If the initiator is the private individual, the offense is bribery, while if the public official initiates the transfer and coerces the private individual, the offense is extortion. The distinction may be very important in that bribery carries a much heavier possible punishment than extortion. It should also be noted that the bribery statute punishes the acceptor as well as the offeror of bribes. This may make it crucial to separate the coercing public official from the merely accepting public official. It may seem anomalous, but given the punishment schemes for the two statutes, it will be in the public official's interest to have been an extortionist rather than merely the acceptor of a bribe. It should be noted, however, that there are two wrongdoers in bribery and only one in extortion.

It is interesting to note that, in contrast to Georgia law, under federal law an affirmative act of inducement by a public official, such as a demand, is not an element of the offense of extortion "under color of official right" prohibited by the Hobbs Act. Even though the public official has not initiated the transaction, his acceptance of a bribe constitutes an implicit promise to use his official position to serve the interests of the bribe-giver. The federal government need only show that a public official has obtained a payment to which he was not entitled, knowing that the payment was made in return for official acts.

It is also interesting to note that under federal law an explicit promise or undertaking to perform or not to perform an action as a public official would constitute the crime of extortion. In McCormick v. United States, the United States Supreme Court held that the receipt of political contributions by an elected official under color of official right constitutes the crime of extortion under the federal Hobbs Act, but only if the payments are made in return for an explicit promise or undertaking by the official to perform or not to perform an official act. In such situations the official asserts that his official conduct will be controlled by the terms of the promise or undertaking.

A pre-1968 Georgia case explored the relationship between theft by extortion and false pretenses (theft by deception). In Jackson v. State, the defendant falsely represented himself to be a law enforcement officer and threatened his victim with a false criminal accusation unless money was paid. The Georgia Supreme Court reversed a false pretenses conviction, holding that although there was a deception, the victim's payment of the money was actuated by the coercion. Thus, this was, therefore, extortion and **not** false pretenses. Thus, the difference between extortion and false pretenses is the difference between coercion and deception.

It should be stressed that paragraph (a)(2) forbids gaining property by threatening a criminal accusation. It appears, therefore, that it is generally no defense that the extortion victim actually committed the crime which the extortionist threatened to expose. The defendant may, indeed, have a privilege or duty to expose such activity, but paragraph (a)(2) makes clear that he should not use this as a means of obtaining property. When a private individual takes money to keep a crime quiet, he is violating the same type of duty that a public official has to perform his statutory responsibilities.

Likewise, it should be noted that paragraph (a)(3) is not limited to explicit threats to disseminate derogatory information. In Williams v. State, the Court of Appeals held that the threat need not be explicit. The co-defendant called the victim and offered to sell him incriminating photographs taken of the victim and a woman not his wife. The court held that given the circumstances a failure to prove an explicit threat was not fatal to the state's case.

Although the six paragraphs of § 16-8-16(a) cover most of the threats which might be made by an extortionist, the drafters rejected an omnibus Model Penal Code provision, § 223.4(g), which would have punished threats to "inflict any other harm which would not benefit the actor." This broad provision would punish, for example, the employer who demanded a kickback from his employees or the school teacher who demanded money from students in return for good grades. These actions do not appear to be illegal under § 16-8-16.

A statutory affirmative defense is provided by § 16-8-16(c). A defendant is privileged to threaten criminal accusation, dissemination of derogatory information, official action, or the giving or withholding of testimony, to the extent that the defendant was honestly claiming restitution or indemnification for "harm done in the circumstance to which such accusation, exposure, legal action, or other official action relates." Thus, the person who believes himself to be the victim of an embezzlement can threaten to make criminal charges unless the alleged embezzler makes restitution of the amount the defendant believes to have been embezzled.

Likewise, the defendant can threaten to expose derogatory information about the "victim" to the extent and only to the extent that he believes these derogatory facts have caused the defendant injury. Of course, even if without criminal liability, both of the above individuals run the risk of civil liability for defamation if their charges prove to be false. This statutory affirmative defense can be seen as the analogue to the § 16-8-10 claim of right defense which does not apply to theft by extortion.

A special venue provision, § 16-8-16(b), provides venue in the county where the threat was either made or received or the county in which the property was obtained.

The punishment provision for extortion is not § 16-8-12, which punishes most of the theft crimes and is based on a monetary dividing line between misdemeanor and felony theft. All extortion, regardless of the amount extorted, is a felony under § 16-8-16(d), punishable by one to ten years' imprisonment.

F. Theft of Lost or Mislaid Property

Section § 16-8-6 is a special provision dealing with thefts of lost or mislaid property. It punishes the individual who "comes into control of property that he knows or learns to have been lost or mislaid and appropriates the property to his own use without first taking reasonable measures to restore the property to the owner." The statute's actus reus is comprised of two elements: the action of appropriating the property to the defendant's own use and the omission of reasonable efforts to return the property to the rightful owner.

It should be noted that the mens rea requirement is that the party act with knowledge that the property is lost or mislaid. It is irrelevant when this knowledge is obtained because the statute punishes those who come into control of property, knowing or later learning of its lost or mislaid nature. Although direct evidence of such knowledge will be rare, the circumstances surrounding acquisition ought to be probative on this question. Thus, the nature of the property, the location of its "finding," and the presence or absence of identifying marks ought to be relevant in the determination of the defendant's knowledge.

There have been a number of decisions concerning § 16-8-6. In Royal v. State, the court reversed the defendant's conviction because the state failed to prove that the property was lost or mislaid. Instead, the state proved by its own witness that the property was neither lost or mislaid but was actually stolen.

In two decisions, it was held that the evidence was sufficient to support the defendant's conviction for theft of lost or mislaid property. In English v. State, the defendant split $4,000 with another county deputy knowing that the money was found on the roadside near a vehicle that had been stopped pursuant to a police investigation. However, the defendant made no attempt to restore the money to its rightful owner and he made no attempt to determine whether the money was used for illegal activities. He simply took the money and did not report it to the county sheriff. There was also testimony that the deputies were required to turn in all money found or seized to the county sheriff. In Davenport v. State, the defendant deposited $95 in his checking account, but the bank erroneously credited his account with a deposit of $9,500. After confirming the erroneous amount in his account, the defendant promptly withdrew the money and closed his account. After the bank discovered the error, the defendant admitted that the money was not his. He offered but failed to repay the bank.

The claim of right affirmative defense of § 16-8-10 is applicable to § 16-8-6 prosecutions but it appears that proof of unawareness that the property was that of another, which is an affirmative defense under § 16-8-10(1), is actually an element of the offense, on which the state will bear the burden of proof. If the defendant is unaware that it belongs to someone else, he cannot know of its lost or mislaid character.

G. Theft of Services

Section 16-8-5 punishes those who "knowingly" and "with the intent to avoid payment" obtain commercially available "services, accommodations, entertainment, or the use of personal property" by deception. This broad provision displaces prior law which protected only some services, like hotel accommodations, from theft.

The same broad coverage can be and, in fact, is obtained by the expansive definition of the property protected by the general theft by taking statute. Section 16-1-3(13), both in its explicit inclusion of services as part of "property" and in its general definition of property as "anything of value," appears to be the type of statute which would protect commercially offered services, accommodations, etc. under the general theft by taking statute, § 16-8-2. Thus, it seems clear that §§ 16-8-2 and 16-8-5 overlap.

The mens rea of theft of services clearly requires a showing of "knowingly" obtaining commercial services. Thus, it would seem that the defendant who could generate a reasonable doubt that he knew there was a price for the services would be entitled to an acquittal. The mens rea also explicitly requires an intent to avoid payment, which has been described by the Court of Appeals as the "essential ingredient of the offense." The intent to avoid payment can be proven by circumstantial evidence. The statutory language requiring action by deception also imports an additional mens rea requirement. Because deception by its nature requires intentional activity, not only must the defendant know he is obtaining commercial services and intends not to pay for them, but he must intend to fool the vendor into giving him the services. The defendant who announces an intention not to pay the vendor has not violated § 16-8-5. This last mens rea element is hidden because of the extreme unlikelihood that a defendant would act this way or that the victim would part with the services upon hearing such an announcement.

A number of § 16-8-5 cases that reached the appellate courts resulted in reversals for failure to prove the mens rea. In Adams v. State, the defendant rented a pump for a day. Because it did not work properly he exchanged it the next day. Nothing was said about extra charges. On the third day, when he returned the second pump and paid for only one day's rental he was charged under § 16-8-5. The court reversed, holding that the state had failed to prove an intent to avoid payment and deception. There was no evidence that the defendant was aware that the vendor expected a charge for the second day, so he could hardly be shown to have intended to avoid the payment. In Roberson v. State, the defendant stopped payment on a check when dissatisfied with the quality of work. The court held that the evidence of stopping payment and refusing to discuss the matter with the prosecuting witness would "tend to show an intent to avoid payment." But the defendant's evidence of a reason why he stopped payment left the circumstantial evidence in equipoise and caused a reversal.

However, in Nichols v. State, the appellate court affirmed the defendant's conviction and held that the state did prove the mens rea elements of deception and an intent to avoid payment. There was direct evidence that the defendant obtained services, that is, the lodging, by deception. In obtaining the apartment, he used the name of another and stolen identification. There was also circumstantial evidence of an intent to avoid payment. The defendant changed locks on the apartment at least twice and became delinquent in his rent. The landlord obtained a writ of possession against the defendant who filed an answer in another's name.

The actus reus of obtaining the services by deception is straightforward. It should be noted that the deception is not enough for a § 16-8-5 conviction. There must be an actual obtaining. It has been held that the surreptitious and unauthorized entrance and use of a vacant apartment is one of the forms of obtaining "accommodations" clearly encompassed within the meaning of the statute. Also, the surreptitious and unauthorized use of electricity or electrical energy within the apartment is one of the forms of obtaining "services" within the meaning of the statute.

The claim of right defense of § 16-8-10 is applicable to a § 16-8-5 prosecution.

H. Theft by Conversion

Two separate statutes deal with theft by conversion which supplants the pre-1968 law of embezzlement. Under § 16-8-4, theft by conversion is committed when an individual has lawfully obtained another's property, including but not limited to leased or rented personal property, under an obligation (either contractual or otherwise) to apply or dispose of the property in a particular fashion, but that individual violates the obligation and knowingly converts the property to his own use. The statute is applicable regardless of whether the original obligation required use of the actual property or the use of an equivalent amount of the defendant's property. The other conversion statute, § 16-8-15, deals with the conversion of payments for property improvements.

1. *"Lawfully Obtained."*

At common law, the essential distinction between embezzlement and larceny was in the means of acquisition. In larceny, the obtaining of the goods by the defendant was unlawful in that it was a trespass against the possession of the owner. On the other hand, the embezzler's means of acquisition were lawful. Section 16-8-4 continues this distinction by punishing only those who convert after lawfully obtaining the property but rejects the sometimes arcane distinction in theft law between custody and possession. Many courts hold that while the custodian who converts is guilty of larceny, the possessor who converts is guilty of embezzlement. The Georgia statute speaks only of obtaining the property, thus covering both custodians and possessors.

Having been presented with a statute which abolishes the custody/possession distinction, the Court of Appeals, in Partain v. State, may have inadvertently reinserted the possession requirement. A municipal building inspector was charged under § 16-8-4 with receiving money under an arrangement with a contractor whereby the contractor paid one-half the normal inspection fee to the defendant and did not have to pay the rest. Apparently, the defendant kept the funds for himself. The defendant's § 16-8-4 conviction was reversed because, in the court's words, "the defendant was never in lawful possession of [the] funds." While the conviction was properly reversed, the court ought to have spoken in terms of unlawfully obtaining rather than unlawful possession.

2. *Property of Another*

The property protected by § 16-8-4 includes anything of value and, while it must be property of another, partnership property is protected by this statute under § 16-8-1(3) which defines "property of another" as any property in which another person has an interest. This rule merely continues the preexisting Georgia law on the subject. It should be noted that spousal property, under § 16-8-1(3), is not the property of another and, thus, not protected by § 16-8-4. In 1988, the General Assembly amended § 16-8-4 to include "leased or rented personal property" as the property protected by the statute.

One cannot be convicted of theft by conversion for selling his equitable interest in property, since an essential element of the offense, possession of the property of another, would be missing. In King v. State, the court stated that a grantor of a deed to secure debt retains an equitable interest in property. Thus, the grantor had an interest in the property which he was free to sell to a business creditor, subject to the deed to secure debt. The business creditor purchased the grantor's equitable interest in the property. The security deed remained as a lien on the property, and the grantor remained liable to holder of the deed. However, it was clear that the money the grantor received was not the holder's, but his own, for the sale of his equitable interest in the property. Thus, an essential element of theft by conversion, possession by the accused of the funds of another person, was missing.

3. *Obligation to Apply or Dispose of Property in Certain Way*

Not only must the § 16-8-4 defendant have obtained property of another in a lawful way, there must be either a legal or contractual obligation to apply or dispose of the funds or property in a particular fashion. It is the violation of this agreement by conversion that is the essence of the crime. It would appear that the disposition or application contemplated by the drafters would be one for the property owner's benefit. Thus, the employee who absconds with money he was supposed to use to pay his employer's debts clearly satisfies this element of the crime. Likewise, the bank teller who makes off with funds he was supposed to deposit in the bank's cash box has satisfied this element. (Under the Georgia definition, this would be theft by conversion with either depositor or bank as victim.)

The more difficult question would be the defendant who borrows property and then converts. Does this behavior violate an obligation? Yes, clearly there is an obligation to return the goods. But whether this is the kind of obligation contemplated by the statute is uncertain. In at least most of the situations contemplated by the statute the application or disposition is to be made to a third person. Here, of course, the disposition would be back to the owner. It should be noted that the pre-1968 law of larceny after trust, which was the equivalent of embezzlement, did not cover conversion by borrowers.

The Court of Appeals has indicated that it will examine the terms of any alleged agreement very carefully before finding a violation of it. This approach is consistent with the traditional strict construction of penal statutes. In Baker v. State, the defendant agreed to construct a steeple for $325. He was prosecuted when it was discovered that the materials cost only $100. The court reversed because there was nothing in the agreement limiting the amount he was to retain for his labor and services in constructing the steeple.

In Hill v. State, the victim freely gave $2,500 to the defendant in return for the defendant's promise personally to provide certain future services. After the defendant attempted but failed to provide the services, the victim requested the return of his $2,500 and the defendant presented him with a check in that amount. However, the check was not honored because of insufficient funds. The court reversed the defendant's conviction. The evidence showed that the victim gave no specific directions as to **how** the $2,500 was to be applied by the defendant. The victim's only interest after freely parting with the cash was in receiving the future services that the defendant had agreed to perform on his behalf or in receiving a refund if those future services did not produce the desired result. The court concluded that this evidence would not authorize a finding that the defendant obtained the $2,500 from the victim "under an agreement or other known legal obligation to make a specified application" thereof.

In Lovell v. State, the victim agreed to engage the defendant to do cabinetry work. The court held that neither the defendant's written agreement with the victim nor the victim's testimony showed that the defendant was obligated to apply any portion of the contract price to specific cabinet materials of identifiable quality. There simply was no evidence of the defendant's failure to apply funds in a manner specified in any agreement. Consequently, the evidence was insufficient to authorize the jury's verdict that the defendant committed theft by conversion, as it merely showed that the defendant failed to perform his contract to deliver cabinets.

4. Conversion

To be convicted under § 16-8-4, the defendant must not only violate the agreement or obligation but must also convert the property to his own use. The clearest example of satisfaction of this element would be a defendant who took some personal property which he was supposed to transfer to X for the owner's benefit but instead sold it, leased it, or otherwise disposed of it to Y. Nowhere does the code define "convert," but in the civil context it has been held to consist of "any distinct act of dominion wrongfully asserted over one's property in denial of his right or inconsistent with it." The problems in proving a conversion under § 16-8-4, however, are that the evidence is usually circumstantial; the converted property can be, and usually is, money; and the statute applies where the agreement contemplates the defendant's using his own property of equivalent value to satisfy the terms of the agreement, rather than the actual property of another which the defendant has obtained.

A defendant can satisfy the terms of an agreement, but still violate the statute by converting the victim's funds from their intended and agreed-upon application to the defendant's own use. In Cochran v. State, the victims acknowledged that they did, indeed, receive their share of the property for the funds that they tendered, and the evidence showed that all of the funds were used to purchase the property. However, the court held that the jury was authorized to find that the defendants converted the victims' money by using those funds to purchase most of the defendants' share in the property because the evidence showed that the victims' money, which provided approximately 83 percent of the purchase price, paid not only for the victims' 50 percent share of the property but also for 33 percent of the defendants' 37.5 percent share of the property.

Section 16-8-4(a) does not require the converted funds to be titled in the accused's name; it merely sets forth that the funds or property be knowingly converted to the accused's "own use." Thus, in Cochran v. State, the court held that although the evidence reflected that the property purchased with the converted funds was titled in the name of the defendant's wife, given the fact that the defendant routinely purchased property under his wife's name, the jury was authorized to conclude that the conversion which the defendant was instrumental in performing was for his use.

Proof of conversion vel non lies in the explanation or failure to explain proved discrepancies between amounts received and disbursements going toward the fulfillment of the contract. In Cox v. State, it appeared without contradiction from the state's evidence that the defendant did not use the money to pay the victim's automobile insurance premium. The evidence showed that, instead, the defendant abandoned his insurance office without notifying the victim. Although the defendant purportedly established an office in another town, he failed to return the victim's telephone calls, and the victim was unable to find him in that town. This evidence was sufficient to authorize the jury to infer that the defendant fraudulently converted the money to his own use.

The courts have emphasized that conversion is a separate requirement for violation of the agreement. If the only proof is that the contract was breached, then no conviction shall lie. In Baker v. State, the defendant contractor was paid money to build a house and, despite payments being made by the prospective homeowners, unpaid bills still existed. Stressing that the "gravamen of the offense . . . is fraudulent conversion, not failure to comply with a contractual obligation," the court said that the mere unpaid bills did not necessarily prove a conversion to the contractor's own use.

First, the materials may have simply cost more than the contractor expected. Second, the agreement may have permitted payment of labor costs before payment of material costs and the materials might be covered by the last, unpaid installment of the contract price. At any rate, mere existence of unpaid bills did not prove that the contractor had converted the money to his own use. The court hinted that the continued existence of unpaid bills after payment delivered to defendant for the explicit purpose of paying the bills might suffice for proof of conversion. The court, in a later opinion in the same case, reversed the conviction for lack of evidence of conversion. While Baker indicates that breach of the contract is not sufficient proof of conversion it would seem to be necessary. One can hardly be held to be a convertor if one is complying with the agreement.

Baker was distinguished in Jackson v. State where the Court of Appeals held the evidence sufficient in another § 16-8-4 prosecution involving a construction contract. Here, unlike in Baker, the defendant himself testified that he had received the money from his clients, had an obligation to pay for materials, and had, instead, spent the money for other purposes.

Since Baker and Jackson, the General Assembly has enacted § 16-8-15 which punishes all those who, having received payment for improvements to property, use the proceeds "for any other purpose than to pay for labor or service performed on or materials furnished by his order for this specific improvement while any amount for which he may be or become liable for such labor, services, or materials remains unpaid commits a felony." This would seem to make precise the obligation of a contractor and impose these obligations as a matter of law, regardless of the actual contractual arrangements. Thus, payments made for improving real property are frozen, by law, in the hands of the improver until **all** debts to suppliers are satisfied.

To convict a defendant under § 16-8-15, it is necessary to prove the creation of a trust described in the indictment and a fraudulent breach of it in the manner alleged. In Teston v. State, although the indictment charged the defendant with misappropriation of "proceeds of payments made to him on account of improving certain real property, to wit: a house being built for Debbie Harrell in Coffee County," the court found that the evidence did not establish that the defendant was entrusted with funds for the specific purpose (the Harrell house construction) set forth in the indictment. Harrell made no payments to the defendant for construction of a house, nor had she entered into a contract to purchase the house from the defendant. The funds drawn by the defendant pursuant to his construction loan with the bank were shown by the loan documents to be for "business—construction," and not only for "a house being built for Debbie Harrell." Further, the loan was secured by the defendant's assets, not by Harrell.

The constructive trust fund doctrine imposes a constructive trust in favor of subcontractors and material suppliers on funds paid by the owner to a contractor. A subcontractor or material supplier, in order to invoke the constructive trust fund doctrine, must file a valid lien pursuant to the Georgia lien statutes. In Doyle Dickerson Co. v. Durden, the Court of Appeals noted that there is nothing in § 16-8-15 which makes explicit provision for the creation of a constructive trust in favor of subcontractors and material suppliers. Also, the violation of this statute does not automatically give rise to a civil cause of action on the part of one who claims to have been injured thereby since reference must be made to the applicable provisions of tort law.

A general problem with identifying a conversion under § 16-8-4 is that, by its terms, the statute applies when the defendant was permitted, under the agreement, to use his own property of equivalent value to satisfy the agreement, rather than the actual property of the victim. Because the victim's property may be money, how does one know when there has been a conversion? For example, before § 16-8-15 was enacted, if the construction contract did not require the actual check delivered to the homebuilder to be delivered to suppliers, and the check was simply deposited in the contractor's checking account, at what point could it be said that there had been a conversion? When the next check was written on the account? When the account balance went below the level of outstanding debts? When it was exhausted? This is a difficulty which is hard to overcome without direct evidence or an admission of conversion.

5. *Mens Rea*

The statutory language requires that the conversion be done "knowingly." In Baker v. State, the court interpreted this to mean fraudulent conversion or an intent not to return. The court in Jackson v. State held that fraudulent intent was what distinguished a criminal conversion from a breach of contract. This fraudulent intent can be established by circumstantial evidence. An intent to return equivalent property has been held not to negate this intent in a pre-1968 embezzlement case. Also, it has been held that later acquiescence by the owner of the property does not negate the intent at the time of the conversion.

A statutory presumption of intent to convert is constructed in § 16-8-4(b), where a government employee or financial institution employee fails to pay an account upon a lawful demand. The value of this presumed intention is questionable if there also must be a proof of an act of conversion. Surely, the failure to pay will not suffice for a showing of a conversion.

It should be noted that the claim of right affirmative defense of § 16-8-10 applies to § 16-8-4 prosecutions. Thus, there is no theft by conversion if there is an honest belief of the defendant that he was authorized to dispose of the property the way he did.

Notwithstanding the statutory presumption that "[a] failure to pay for material or labor furnished for [real] property improvements [is] prima-facie evidence of intent to defraud," § 16-8-15 requires the state to prove not only a general criminal intent but also a specific intent to defraud beyond a reasonable doubt.

6. *Separate Offenses*

Where the defendant has committed three prohibited acts of theft by conversion against the same victim, based on three separate failures to apply three separate payments to the purpose specified for each such payment, three sequential but entirely separate crimes have been committed against the victim, and a conviction and separate sentence for each crime is authorized.

7. *Constitutionality*

In Smith v. State, the defendant urged the Georgia Supreme Court to strike down § 16-8-4 as unconstitutional because it provided for imprisonment for debt and involuntary servitude and it was violative of due process. The court rejected the defendant's argument on the grounds that the punishment was not for the contractual debt, rather for the conversion of the victim's property by the defendant. The court found inapposite a prior state case in which the court struck down a statute which punished an employer's willful failure to pay his employees' wages. In that case, the court said, there was a presumption of fraud implied from the fact of legal indebtedness. No similar presumption is operative under § 16-8-4. Instead, this statute creates a form of larceny after trust and not criminal punishment for indebtedness. In dissent, Justice Gunter complained that because the statute, by its terms, is applicable where the original agreement between the parties permits the defendant to treat the owner's property as his own and permits the defendant to use his own property of equivalent value to carry out his obligations under the agreement, that the statute permits imprisonment for debt. In other words, the dissent urged that in that kind of agreement not only is it hard to identify the conversion, there is no conversion and the only "act" being punished is the status of indebtedness.

The focus of Justice Gunter's dissent was the "agreement" provision which punishes the defendant who converts in violation of the agreement. The statute also punishes those who convert in violation of "other known legal obligation." The constitutionality of the latter provision was at issue in Jackson v. State. The Court of Appeals in Jackson rejected, by a bare majority, the claim of the four dissenters that this provision rendered the statute unconstitutional. The Jackson dissenters made this claim because the "other known legal obligation" language would make "every employee, who receives a salary, a criminal if he did not use that salary for paying his 'known legal obligation[s].' " The dissent apparently overlooked the statutory requirement that the converted property be that of another. When an employee receives earned wages, the money is **not** the property "of another;" it is his property.

In Connally v. State, the Georgia Supreme Court rejected the defendant's constitutional challenge to the theft by conversion statute and affirmed his conviction because the state constitution does not forbid imprisonment for criminal conduct, even though the criminal conduct also results in a civil debt. The state constitution prohibits prosecutions based **solely** on the failure to repay a lawful debt. The theft by conversion statute, however, requires more than proof of a failure to comply with any contractual obligation. It requires proof of criminal intent: the knowing appropriation of funds or property belonging to another. Because the statute requires proof of a criminal intent, it does not violate the constitutional prohibition against imprisonment for debt.

The court also rejected the defendant's contention that the theft by conversion statute is unconstitutionally vague. The defendant, who was a trustee of several trusts, took money from those trusts for his personal use. The court found that the statute provides more than adequate notice to a person of ordinary intelligence that a trustee's intentional appropriation of trust funds for his personal use and for speculative business ventures is criminal conduct.

8. Conversion of Leased Personal Property

In 1988, the General Assembly repealed § 16-8-19, which prohibited the conversion of leased personal property. However, in the same act the General Assembly amended the theft by conversion statute, § 16-8-4, to include "leased or rented personal property" as the property protected by that statute.

In 1994, the General Assembly further amended the theft by conversion statute to include leased or rented personal property having a replacement cost value greater than $100 and personal property such as heavy equipment, tractors, and farm equipment as the property protected by that statute. A person is presumed to have knowingly converted such personal property in his possession or under his control by virtue of a lease or rental agreement if that person fails to return the personal property within five days, Saturdays, Sundays, and holidays excluded, after the owner of the personal property or the owner's agent has mailed to that person a letter demanding return of the personal property.

In Sherrod v. State, the Georgia Supreme Court found the statutory presumption in § 16-8-4(c)(2) to be mandatory. This provision mandates the finding of all the elements of the crime of theft by conversion of leased property when the state merely proves that the demand letter was sent in accordance with the statute. Accordingly, the court declared this mandatory presumption to be unconstitutional. Since this presumption applied to elements of the crime that were at issue in the case and since evidence of the defendant's guilt was not overwhelming, the court considered the state's reliance upon the presumption to be harmful error.

I. Other Theft Crimes

Two theft offenses are defined solely on the basis of the type of property taken. Section 16-8-13 punishes theft of a trade secret and § 16-8-20 punishes livestock thefts. From the wording of the two statutes, it is clear that, as for the mens rea and actus reus provisions, they are virtually identical to the general prohibition of theft by taking (§ 16-8-2).

Section 16-8-13 has a $100 dividing line between felony and misdemeanor, unlike the $500 dividing line of § 16-8-12. Also, the § 16-8-13 felony offense (which is not reducible) carries a one to five year prison sentence and a fine of not more than $50,000 in contrast to the one to ten years' imprisonment under § 16-8-12.

Livestock theft, for purposes of § 16-8-20, is a felony punishable by one to ten years' imprisonment and a $1,000 fine. If the fair market value of the livestock is less than $100 the theft is a misdemeanor.

A final specific theft crime defined in terms of the type of property taken is found at § 16-8-21. This statute makes it a misdemeanor to take a shopping cart from a store or to abandon it anywhere except the parking lot on the store premises. Section 16-8-21(d) requires that the store owner post at least three copies of the statute in the store before the removal of a shopping cart becomes a crime.

J. Stolen Property Offenses

Included in the criminal code are four separate offenses dealing with offenders who have some connection to stolen property other than having stolen it. These offenses are theft by receiving stolen property, theft by receiving property stolen in another state, theft by bringing stolen property into this state, and retail property fencing.

1. Theft by Receiving Stolen Property

The most important of the stolen property offenses is theft by receiving stolen property (§ 16-8-7). There are two parts to the actus reus and two parts to the mens rea of this crime.

a. *Actus Reus*

The first part of the actus reus is written in the alternative. The defendant who "receives, disposes of, or retains" the forbidden property has committed the actus reus. Thus, there need be no proof of the transfer of the goods to the defendant, and the retention of property after guilty knowledge is obtained is criminal. This changes Georgia law prior to 1968 which required a concurrence of guilty knowledge and the acquisition of the property. In addition to the alternative means of satisfying the first part of the actus reus, the statute itself defines "receiving," one of the alternatives, very broadly to include "acquiring possession or control or lending on the security of the property." This provision indicates that for purposes of this statute obtaining a security interest in a piece of property is analogous to controlling or possessing it.

The Court of Appeals has decided a number cases concerning what evidence will sustain a finding of possession or control of stolen property. In Williamson v. State, the court held that merely because the gun in question was found under the defendant's seat in an automobile was not enough to sustain a finding of possession. Similarly, in London v. State, considering the lack of direct evidence as to the defendant's possession of or control over the stolen guns and the number of people who had equal access to the places in the apartment where the guns ultimately were found, the court concluded that there was insufficient evidence to sustain a finding of possession or control. In Thomas v. State, however, evidence showing that the defendant had five cartridges in his pocket at the time of his arrest, which were similar to those in the gun at the time of its theft, and that he hid the gun shortly before his arrest was enough to sustain a finding of possession. In Dukes v. State, the court held that the investigating officer's hearsay testimony that the owner of the vehicle informed him that she wanted to have a warrant issued for the defendant's arrest for the theft of her vehicle was not probative evidence that the defendant received or was in possession of the stolen vehicle. In Greenwood v. State, the court held that the defendant's statement, that the stolen truck was his, could be considered as evidence of possession or receipt of the stolen property. In Watkins v. State, the court held that when the victim was placed in the trunk of his automobile or his liberty otherwise restricted by being subjected involuntarily to the will of the defendant's co-conspirators, the co-conspirators were in control and possession of the automobile sufficient to support the conviction of the defendant, who joined the conspiracy later, for theft by receiving stolen property. The evidence was overwhelming that the victim at no time regained possession and control over his vehicle during the course of the conspiracy, notwithstanding his physical presence in the vehicle.

One cannot be convicted of the crime of receiving stolen property absent exercise of control over the stolen goods, or if one is a passenger, intentionally aiding and abetting the commission of the crime. In In Interest of C. W., no evidence was presented by the state that the juvenile ever retained, disposed of, acquired possession of, or controlled the stolen van, nor was any evidence presented of any affirmative act by the juvenile that rose to the level of aiding and abetting the crime. All evidence indicated that the juvenile was simply along for the ride. Thus, the juvenile's adjudication of delinquency for the offense of theft by receiving stolen property had to be reversed.

In Clark v. State, the Court of Appeals held that the essence of this portion of the actus reus was the act of the defendant in obtaining the property from another person. While this is undoubtedly true about the receiving alternative, the words "dispose" and "retain" hardly connote the same requirement of a third person. On its facts, Clark is undoubtedly correct in holding that collateral estoppel forbids the same person from being convicted for both "receiving" and stealing the property because those two situations are contradictory, but it is not equally clear that a defendant's double jeopardy rights would be violated by convictions for both theft and retention or both theft and disposing.

Where a defendant is indicted for "retaining" stolen property, it is not necessary for the state to show how and when the defendant came to have possession, so long as there is sufficient evidence that he retained the stolen property with guilty knowledge. In Floyd v. State, police officers observed a rental truck being driven to the rear of a department store. One of the officers found the truck parked behind the store. A burglary suspect later identified as the defendant was pursued and apprehended, and the key to the truck was found in his pocket. A police officer later determined that the truck had been stolen. The court held that this evidence was sufficient to show retention of stolen property.

The second part of the actus reus is that the goods must be stolen goods. There is no doubt that stolen property includes all property taken in what traditionally would be larceny. As for property obtained by embezzlement or false pretenses, although there is authority from other jurisdictions that such property is not stolen, it would seem that the legislative purpose in consolidating the pre-1968 theft crimes would require adoption of the view that property originally obtained by embezzlement and false pretenses is stolen property.

In Poole v. State, the assistant manager of the victimized store testified that the property was stolen and that the merchandise bore the store label, which would have been removed if sold. The Court of Appeals held that this evidence was sufficient proof of the stolen nature of the goods. The court has also stated that identification of the victim is not a part of the required proof in a theft by receiving case.

In *Lopez v. State*, the arresting officer found in the car in which the defendant was a passenger a pistol, stamped "Restricted to Law Enforcement Government Only" and fully loaded with Winchester "black talon" hollow-point bullets, ammunition police officers use. The officer reported the serial number on the weapon to dispatch, who told the officer that the pistol had been reported stolen. The officer testified that such a weapon was not available for public sale and could only have been obtained by theft or on the black market. The Court of

Appeals found, however, that the officer's testimony that radio dispatch identified the pistol as stolen was nonprobative hearsay. Furthermore, the fact that the weapon was labeled for law enforcement use only and loaded with police-issue ammunition did not exclude the possibility that the weapon may have been given away or sold on the black market in violation of the warning. Consequently, the court held that the circumstantial evidence of a larcenous taking was insufficient to sustain the defendant's conviction for theft by receiving.

The state, of course, bears the burden of proving that the goods in the defendant's possession were the ones proven to have been stolen. In Causey v. State, where the indictment and proof showed that "cotton pajamas" had been stolen and the search of the defendant's premises yielded "739 assorted ladies smocks," the court reversed the conviction for failure to prove the stolen nature of the goods in the defendant's possession. Likewise, in Johnson v. State, the court reversed a § 16-8-7 conviction where the only evidence that the goods were the subject of a theft was the testimony of a company official that it would be "unlikely" that the goods had been sold legitimately by the manufacturer. In Dunbar v. State, however, the court upheld the defendant's conviction because it found that the state had proved the ownership and identity of the stolen vehicle. The year, make, model, and tag number of the vehicle driven by the defendant at the time of his arrest were identified by the victim and the arresting officer at trial and matched the description of the vehicle set out in the indictment as the vehicle stolen from the victim. In Johnson v. State, the defendants' convictions were upheld even though the owner of the getaway car did not testify. Two of the defendants admitted to a law enforcement officer that the getaway car had been stolen, and there was evidence that the car's steering column was busted in such a way as to indicate to an investigating officer that the vehicle had been stolen.

The technical quality of an owner's interest need not be pursued in a prosecution for theft by receiving, because ownership is important only in the sense of whether the goods were owned by someone other than the accused. In Greeson v. State, the court held that the variance between the indictment and the evidence concerning the ownership of the stolen vehicle was not fatal. The state showed that someone other than the defendant owned the vehicle, and the indictment gave sufficient notice of the property which was the subject of the prosecution.

Under the law prior to 1968, an essential element of receiving stolen goods was that the goods were stolen by some person other than the defendant. Under the present law, the state is not required to prove that the defendant did not steal the goods.

Where direct and uncontested evidence identifies the defendant as the original thief, the defendant cannot be convicted of theft by receiving.

b. Mens Rea

The most heavily litigated portion of § 16-8-7 is the mens rea requirement that the defendant "know or should know" that the goods were stolen. As long ago as 1886, in Cobb v. State, the Georgia Supreme Court acknowledged that " . . . it is rare that knowledge can be brought home to the receiver of . . . goods stolen by somebody who knows what the receiver knew touching the fact that they were stolen. The circumstances, the time, the secrecy, all the transactions before, at the time and afterwards, may be brought to bear upon what was the knowledge of the receiver . . .." The wording of the current statute eases the state's burden somewhat in that knowledge need not be coincident with the acquiring of the goods because the statute punishes the retention of stolen goods with guilty knowledge. The state is also aided in that the statute does not require subjective awareness. The defendant who should have, but did not, know of the goods' stolen character is guilty. Permitting the jury to convict on negligence, however, does not change the prosecutor's burden much in actuality because in a circumstantial evidence case the most important factor in determining what the defendant actually knew is the surrounding circumstances which indicate what he should have known. Whether the defendant possessed the requisite guilty knowledge that the property was stolen is for the jury to decide.

The rule with regard to the sufficiency of evidence of guilty knowledge is easily stated but not quite as easily applied. "Unexplained possession of recently stolen goods can be used **in conjunction with other evidence** to infer guilty knowledge, but **standing alone** it will not . . . authorize a conviction."

The question of how much and what type of "other evidence" is required is often before the courts. While every prosecutor would like to be able to introduce testimony from the thief that he told the defendant the goods were stolen, this is understandably rare. In affirming convictions, the courts have relied upon a number of factors in the transactions as indicating guilty knowledge, such as (1) the removal of identification marks; (2) attempting to disguise the stolen property; (3) the marked discrepancy between purchase and market price; (4) nighttime transactions; (5) trafficking in weapons "on the street"; (6) the urgency of the seller to deal with the defendant; (7) common knowledge that this type of goods is often stolen; (8) the lack of paperwork showing ownership; (9) contradictory statements concerning one's ownership and possession of property; (10) evidence showing that stolen merchandise is often traded for illegal drugs along with evidence that the defendant was guilty of trafficking in cocaine; (11) the defendant's knowledge of his companion's propensity for theft together with evidence that the car belonged to someone else; (12) the defendant's knowledge of the perpetrators' crimes and his assistance in disposing of some of the stolen property; (13) an acknowledgment of the amount of stolen money remaining and an awareness that the defendants were living thousands of dollars beyond their means; and (14) the use of cash instead of checks. Also, the defendant's reaction to law enforcement officials in denying the possession of the goods, fleeing upon the approach of law enforcement officials, throwing the goods from a car as police approach, and hiding the goods shortly before his arrest have been relied upon by the courts.

In a few cases, the Court of Appeals has affirmed § 16-8-7 convictions on extremely weak evidence. For example, in G. W. v. State, the court pointed to the defendant's failure to explain his possession (which ought to be irrelevant under Higginbotham) and the fact that the defendant was found in possession of a car key to another car on the same lot as the stolen car. The court did not explain how this demonstrated knowledge of the stolen nature of the car. In Poole v. State, the only evidence in addition to the possession was the fact that the defendant threw the goods in question out of his car when approached. The court decided this was evidence of guilty retention of stolen goods knowing they were stolen. In Hurston v. State, although there was sufficient evidence to show that the passenger of a vehicle was aware that it was stolen, thereby satisfying the mens rea requirement of the statute, the only evidence the court found to satisfy the actus reus requirement of possession, control, or retention of the stolen vehicle was that the driver left the passenger alone in the vehicle with the motor running when he went into a convenience store. The evidence in these cases does not seem much stronger, if at all, than the evidence in which the court has reversed convictions because the only evidence was that the defendant was found in the same car as the stolen goods, the defendant tried twice to pawn the goods, the defendant tried to keep police out of the motel room where a stolen gun was hidden in a drawer, or the defendant called a later recipient to get rid of the goods because "they was in hot water."

The definition of theft by receiving stolen property involves another mental element in that the intent to restore the property to the owner is made a defense to a § 16-8-7 prosecution. This might indicate that an intent to deprive is an element which is part of the prosecution's burden, but no cases have held this. The provision might as easily be read as simply providing an affirmative defense on which the defendant bears the initial burden of presenting evidence while the state bears the ultimate burden of proof once the defense has been introduced into the case. The statutory claim of right affirmative defense found in § 16-8-10 is applicable to this as well as most of the other theft offenses.

It is the opinion of the Attorney General that stolen property acquired by a pawn shop remains the property of the original owner. If a pawnbroker does not know at the time of acquiring an item that it is stolen property, but later discovers that the item has been stolen and retains it, the pawnbroker has committed the offense of theft by receiving stolen property.

Evidence of a prior similar theft by receiving incident is admissible to show the defendant's state of mind, that is, whether he intended to retain property he knew or should have known was stolen.

c. Double Jeopardy

In seeking dismissal of a pending charge for theft by receiving on the basis of double jeopardy, the defendant has the burden of proving the facts necessary to establish that the pending charge was committed by the same act and thus constitutes the same offense as the charge under which he was put in jeopardy. In the absence of facts establishing that there was only one offense, the defendant has failed to carry his burden and the denial of his substantive double jeopardy claim would be proper.

d. Relationship to Other Offenses

Important Notice about Repudiation of Actual or Same Evidence Test: The Georgia Supreme Court repudiated the actual evidence test in *Drinkard v. Walker*, 281 Ga. 211, 636 S.E.2d 530 (2006), because it found this test to be inconsistent with the statutory framework governing the prohibition against multiple convictions for included offenses in Georgia. This inconsistency resulted in years of confusion and unpredictable results. In its place, the court adopted the required evidence test and overruled any prior case law that is inconsistent with it. Thus, any prior case law applying the actual evidence test is no longer controlling and should not be relied upon to determine whether one offense is included in another under § 16-1-6(1). The discussion of such case law is included below only insofar as it may still be applicable to pending prosecutions that arose before the Drinkard decision. See MULTIPLE CONVICTIONS, II. Tests to Determine Presence of Multiple Convictions, for a complete discussion of the Drinkard decision.

Theft by receiving a motor vehicle is not a lesser included offense of motor vehicle hijacking. The offense of theft by receiving is intended to catch the person who buys or receives the stolen vehicle, as distinct from the principal thief.

Theft by receiving stolen property is not a lesser included offense of armed robbery but is a separate offense proved by an entirely different set of facts.

Although the weapon used to assault the victim is stolen, the offense of theft by receiving stolen property does not merge into the offense of aggravated assault as a matter fact because the theft offense requires proof that the defendant knew or should have known that the weapon was stolen. No such proof is required for an aggravated assault conviction.

A defendant can not be guilty both of theft by taking and theft by receiving the same property. As a matter of law, the crimes are mutually exclusive, and the defendant can not be sentenced on both. Although the crimes are mutually exclusive, the state may charge the defendant with both to provide alternative charges for the jury to choose if the state fails to carry the burden on identity.

Because the offenses of entering an automobile and theft by receiving involve different proscribed conduct and have distinctive elements, they do not merge as a matter of law. However, these offenses may merge as a matter of fact based on the evidence presented at trial.

Erroneously instructing a jury on the unindicted offense of theft by receiving stolen property, unless prejudicial or harmful as revealed by the entire record, does not require or demand reversal.

A conviction for kidnapping would not be void as mutually exclusive of a prior conviction of theft by receiving stolen property. The crime of kidnapping contains no element that the accused either stole property or received stolen property. Because the two crimes have completely different elements, convictions based on them would not be mutually exclusive on the ground that a finding of guilt on the essential elements of one crime by definition excludes a finding of guilt based on an essential element of the other.

2. *Theft by Receiving Property Stolen in Another State and Theft by Bringing Stolen Property into this State*

Section 16-8-8 creates the crime of theft by receiving property stolen in another state. This section is identical in language to § 16-8-7, but it deals only with property stolen outside of Georgia. In Golden v. State, the court had held that receiving goods stolen in another state was not illegal because it was not larceny to bring stolen goods into the state. The court suggested corrective legislation and the predecessor of § 16-8-8 was enacted. Another statutory provision, the predecessor of present § 16-8-9, was enacted making it illegal to bring stolen property into the state with knowledge that it was stolen.

Subsequent to the original enactments of these statutes in 1918, it was held that in a prosecution for knowingly receiving stolen property, it was not necessary for the state to show that the subject property was stolen in Georgia, thereby minimizing, if not destroying altogether, the need for this corrective legislation. The drafters of the 1968 criminal code did not find it necessary to include these statutes in the code. However, with the enactment of § 16-8-8 and § 16-8-9 in 1972, these statutes are again a part of the criminal code.

The guilty knowledge of § 16-8-9 can be established by direct or circumstantial evidence and can be inferred from circumstances which would, in the opinion of the jury, lead a reasonable person to believe that the property was stolen.

Evidence regarding the defendant's gang activity may be admitted to establish his motive for bringing stolen property into this state.

3. *Retail Property Fencing*

a. *Definition of Offense*

Section 16-8-5.2 defines two types of retail property fencing. A person commits one type when he receives, disposes of, or retains retail property which was unlawfully taken or shoplifted over a period not to exceed 180 days with the intent to (1) transfer, sell, or distribute such retail property to a retail property fence or (2) attempt or cause such retail property to be offered for sale, transfer, or distribution for money or other things of value.

Whoever knowingly receives, possesses, conceals, stores, barters, sells, or disposes of retail property with the intent to distribute any retail property which is known or should be known to have been taken or stolen in violation of this law with the intent to distribute the proceeds, or to otherwise promote, manage, carry on, or facilitate this offense commits the other type of retail property fencing.

b. *Inference of Intent to Profit from Scheme*

It is not necessary in any prosecution under § 16-8-5.2 for the state to prove that any intended profit was actually realized. The trier of fact may infer that a particular scheme or course of conduct was undertaken for profit from all of the attending circumstances.

c. *Defenses*

It is not a defense that the property was obtained by means other than through the commission of a theft offense if the property was explicitly represented to the accused as being obtained through the commission of a theft.

d. *Forfeiture of Property*

Any property constituting proceeds derived from or realized through a violation of § 16-8-5.2 is subject to forfeiture to the State of Georgia except that no property of any owner shall be forfeited, to the extent of the interest of such owner, by reason of an act or omission established by such owner to have been committed or omitted without knowledge or consent of such owner. The procedure for forfeiture and disposition of forfeited property is provided for under § 16-13-49.

e. *Separate Offense*

Each violation of § 16-8-5.2 constitutes a separate offense.

J.1. *Inference of Intent to Avoid Payment Due for Rental or Lease of Personal Property in Prosecutions of Certain Theft Crimes*

The trier of fact may infer that the accused intended to avoid payment due for the rental or lease of any personal property in a prosecution for theft by taking, theft by deception, theft by conversion, or theft of services, if a person knowingly (1) used false identification; (2) provided false information on a written contract; (3) made, drew, uttered, executed, or delivered an instrument for the payment of money on any bank or other depository in exchange for present consideration, knowing that it would not be honored by the drawee; (4) abandoned any property at a location that is not the location agreed upon for return and that would not be reasonably known to the owner; (5) returned any property to a location that would not reasonably be known to the owner without notifying the owner; or (6) returned any property at a time beyond posted business hours of the owner.

No person can be convicted of these theft crimes, however, where there was an agreement to delay payment for such property or services or the accused made payment in full within two business days after returning the property or obtaining the services.

K. Venue

Although the general venue provision for criminal actions requires that a crime be prosecuted in the county "where the crime was committed," certain theft offenses have their own special venue provision which is much broader. According to § 16-8-11, the prosecution of these certain theft offenses is properly brought "in any county in which the accused exercised control over the property which was the subject of the theft." The provisions of § 16-8-11 simply continue preexisting theft venue provisions.

In 1994, § 16-8-11 was amended to provide that in any prosecution for theft by conversion in which there is a written rental agreement for personal property, the crime is considered to have been committed in the county in which the accused signed the rental agreement.

The state cannot establish venue by means of acts that are not an element of a theft offense by merely alleging that the acts constituted an "ongoing effort" to conceal the already completed theft offense. While efforts to conceal a theft offense may amount to the separate offense of concealing evidence of a crime, such actions do not form part of the theft offense.

Four theft offenses are not specifically covered by the venue provisions of § 16-8-11. These theft offenses include theft by extortion (§ 16-8-16), entering an automobile or other motor vehicle with intent to commit a theft or felony (§ 16-8-18), livestock theft (§ 16-8-20), and the removal or abandonment of shopping carts (§ 16-8-21). These offenses are covered by the general venue provision for criminal actions (§ 17-2-2).

Circumstantial as well as direct evidence may be used to prove venue in theft cases.

L. Punishment for Certain Theft Crimes

Section 16-8-12 establishes a general punishment scheme which covers most theft crimes. The scheme punishes on the basis of the value of the property stolen, the type of property stolen, the nature of the offender, or the age of the victim.

If the property which was the subject of the theft was $500 or less in value, a person convicted of any of the theft offenses covered by § 16-8-12 shall be punished as for a misdemeanor. If the property which was the subject of the theft exceeded $500 in value, a person convicted of the theft shall be punished by imprisonment for not less than one nor more than ten years or, in the discretion of the trial judge, as for a misdemeanor. There can only be one sentence and conviction if several items are stolen as part of a continuous criminal act.

As originally enacted, § 16-8-12, which provides for the punishment of theft by taking and other theft crimes, overlapped and conflicted with former § 16-8-17, which provided for the punishment of theft of a motor vehicle or a motor vehicle part. Both sections provided for the punishment of the theft of a motor vehicle. Section 16-8-12 provided for punishment of one to ten years imprisonment, while former § 16-8-17 provided for punishment of three to seven years imprisonment.

In Chandler v. State, the Court of Appeals in its holding on venue acknowledged that a motor vehicle theft was a theft by taking and stated that former § 16-8-17 merely provided the punishment for motor vehicle theft. However, in Simmons v. State the court acknowledged that a 1978 amendment, which raised the felony property value level of § 16-8-12, had "impliedly repealed" former § 16-8-17. The court based its conclusion upon language in the amendment's preamble describing the act's purpose as being "to change the penalty provisions relating to the crimes of theft; to repeal conflicting laws . . . ." Simmons held, therefore, that sentencing under § 16-8-12 was proper for theft of a motor vehicle. Apparently, the court viewed the 1978 legislative action as a purposeful reenactment of one of two conflicting provisions which thereby repealed the other statute.

Section § 16-8-17 was repealed by the General Assembly in 1981. The theft of a motor vehicle or a motor vehicle part is considered a theft by taking under § 16-8-2 and is now punished as provided in § 16-8-12(a)(5). Under § 16-8-12(a)(5), if the property which was the subject of the theft was a motor vehicle or was a motor vehicle part or component which exceeded $100 in value, the offense is punishable by imprisonment for not less than one nor more than ten years. In the trial judge's discretion, the felony may be reduced to a misdemeanor. Any person who is convicted of a second or subsequent offense is punishable by imprisonment for not less than one year nor more than 20 years. Subsequent offenses are punishable under § 17-10-7.

Section 16-8-12(a)(5)(A) permits felony punishment for the theft of a motor vehicle, regardless of value, and requires evidence of value exceeding $100 only where a motor vehicle part or component was the subject of the theft. This reading of the statute comports with § 16-8-18, which defines as a felony the entry of a person into a motor vehicle with intent to commit a theft. If the entry into the motor vehicle with the intent to steal is a felony, the actual theft of the car (as defined in the theft statutes and as punished in § 16-8-12) should be no less.

If a theft or a fraudulent act was committed by a person engaged in telemarketing, in any activity on the Internet, or in home repair or improvement work, the offense is punishable by imprisonment for not less than one nor more than ten years. In the trial judge's discretion, the felony may be reduced to a misdemeanor. Any person who is convicted of a second or subsequent offense is punishable by imprisonment for not less than one nor more than 20 years. Subsequent offenses are punishable under § 17-10-7.

If any amount of anhydrous ammonia, as defined in § 16-11-111, is the subject of the theft, the offense is punishable by imprisonment for not less than one nor more than ten years, a fine not to exceed the amount provided by § 17-10-8, or both.

If the property is taken by a fiduciary in breach of his fiduciary obligation or by a government or financial institution officer or employee, the punishment is imprisonment for not less than one nor more than 15 years, a fine not to exceed the amount provided by § 17-10-8, or both. As the drafters of the 1968 criminal code explained, a theft committed by persons in these categories is punished more severely "[b]ecause it is necessary to maintain the integrity of fiduciaries and employees of governments and financial institutions."

The theft of a memorial to the dead or any ornamentation, flower, tree, or shrub placed on, adjacent to, or within any enclosure of a memorial to the dead, is punishable by imprisonment for not less than one nor more than three years.

If a privately owned military grave marker, monument, memorial, or plaque is the subject of the theft and its value is $300 or less, the offense is punishable by imprisonment for not less than one nor more than three years. If its value is more than $300, the offense is punishable by imprisonment for not less than three nor more than five years.

If a destructive device, explosive, or firearm is the subject of the theft offense, the offense is punishable by imprisonment for not less than one nor more than ten years.

If a vehicle engaged in the commercial transportation of cargo or its trailer, semitrailer, container, or cargo is the subject of the theft offense, the offense is punishable by imprisonment for not less than three nor more than ten years, by a fine not less than $5,000 nor more than $50,000, and, if applicable, the revocation of the defendant's commercial driver's license in accordance with § 40-5-151, or any combination of such penalties.

If the property of the theft was ferrous metals or regulated metal property, as such terms are defined in § 10-1-350, and the sum of the aggregate amount of such property, in its original and undamaged condition, plus any reasonable costs which are or would be incurred in the repair or the attempt to recover any property damaged in the theft or removal of such regulated metal property, exceeds $500, the offense is punishable by imprisonment for not less than one nor more than five years, a fine of not more than $5,000, or both.

Any person who commits the offense of theft by deception when the property which was the subject of the theft exceeded $500 in value and the offense was committed against a person who is 65 years of age or older is punishable by imprisonment for not less than five nor more than ten years.

The theft of a growing or otherwise unharvested commercial agricultural product which is being grown or produced as a crop is punishable by a fine of not less than $500 and not more than the maximum fine otherwise authorized by law. This minimum fine is not subject to suspension, stay, or probation. The minimum fine is not required in any case in which a sentence of confinement is imposed and the sentence of confinement is not suspended, stayed, or probated. However, in such a case the imposition of any otherwise authorized fine is not prohibited.

The Georgia Supreme Court has held that, despite the dividing line between felony and misdemeanor theft, theft by taking is only one crime, and the punishment for that crime is controlled by the value of the property taken. Therefore, in Mack v. Ricketts, a felony sentence was upheld when the evidence showed felony-level theft, despite the ambiguity in the indictment with respect to the value of the stolen property.

It should be noted that while value is not an element of either theft by taking or theft by receiving, it is relevant for distinguishing between a misdemeanor and a felony for sentencing. Thus, an indictment must allege whether the value of the property taken is over $500 in order to apprise a defendant of whether the offense charged is a misdemeanor or felony. The indictment need not allege the specific amount taken. Value, however, is not relevant to the punishment to be imposed for theft by taking of an automobile. Proof that the item stolen was an automobile is sufficient to support a felony sentence. Thus, any allegation in an indictment concerning the value of the automobile is mere surplusage and need not be proven.

The state carries the burden of proving the value of stolen property, and a showing of any value will support a conviction carrying misdemeanor punishment. In proving value the state may not rely solely on the price, unless the theft was from a retail establishment and then the retail value may be conclusive. The employees of a retail establishment who are familiar with the stolen item are competent to testify as to its retail value. An owner does not have to be an expert to testify as to the value of his property, or that property under his control, provided he has experience or familiarity with such values.

Opinion evidence as to the value of an item has probative value and may be admitted if a foundation is laid showing that the witness has some knowledge, experience, or familiarity with the value of the property or similar property and if the witness gives reasons for the value assessed and has had an opportunity for forming a correct opinion. The fact that his opinion as to value is based in part on hearsay goes to the weight of his testimony and is not a basis for excluding it. A jury is not bound by opinion evidence, however, and it may draw from its own experience in reaching a valuation as to "everyday objects." The jury's awareness of the market value of such "everyday objects," coupled with evidence concerning the cost, time of purchase, and condition of the stolen property would be sufficient to authorize a conviction.

When the only evidence as to value indicates that the theft by taking should carry felony punishment, the trial court is not required to charge the jury that they might recommend the defendant be punished for the misdemeanor grade of the offense.

The cost of the property to the owner, although relevant on the question of value, is not the ultimate determinant. Nor is the replacement cost. The value of stolen property which is the subject of the theft is the fair cash market value either at the time and place of the theft or at any time during the receipt or concealment of the property. The defendant is chargeable with a felony if the stolen property exceeds $500 in value under this criteria; there is no requirement that the value of the property be known to the defendant either when he received the property or thereafter. Thus, evidence that the defendant was in receipt of a stolen lottery ticket at a time when it still had a redemption value of $5,000 would be sufficient to support his conviction for felony theft by receiving stolen property.

In a guilty plea hearing, a negotiated agreement to tender a guilty plea to a "felony" theft offense necessarily incorporates the defendant's voluntary admission of the existence of the factual element that the stolen property had a value greater than $500. This would be a sufficient substitute for evidence of the actual value of the stolen property, so as to authorize the imposition of a felony sentence for the theft offense to which the defendant has pled guilty.

III. Motor Vehicle Chop Shop and Stolen and Altered Property Act

Any person who knowingly and with intent (1) owns, operates, or conducts a chop shop; (2) transports any motor vehicle or motor vehicle part to or from a location knowing it to be a chop shop; or (3) sells, transfers, purchases, or receives any motor vehicle or motor vehicle part either to or from a location knowing it to be a chop shop is guilty of a felony punishable by imprisonment for not less than three years nor more than ten years, by a fine of not more than $100,000, or by both such fine and imprisonment.

Any person who knowingly alters, counterfeits, defaces, destroys, disguises, falsifies, forges, obliterates, or removes a vehicle identification number with the intent to misrepresent the identity or prevent the identification of a motor vehicle or motor vehicle part is guilty of a felony punishable by imprisonment for not less than one year nor more than ten years, by a fine of not more than $50,000, or by both such fine and imprisonment.

Any person who buys, disposes, sells, transfers, or possesses a motor vehicle or motor vehicle part with knowledge that the vehicle identification number of the motor vehicle or motor vehicle part has been altered, counterfeited, defaced, destroyed, disguised, falsified, forged, obliterated, or removed is guilty of a felony punishable by imprisonment for not less than one year nor more than ten years, by a fine of not more than $50,000, or by both such fine and imprisonment. This provision does not apply to legitimate motor vehicle scrap processors, nor does it apply to any owner or authorized possessor of a motor vehicle after it has been recovered by law enforcement authorities after having been reported stolen.

Under the Act, the offenses of attempt, conspiracy, solicitation, aiding and abetting, and being an accessory after the fact are all felonies punishable by imprisonment for not less than one year nor more than five years, by a fine of not more than $25,000, or by both such fine and imprisonment.

No prosecution shall be brought and no person shall be convicted of any violation under the Act where the acts of such person otherwise constituting a violation were done in good faith in order to comply with the laws or regulations of any state or territory of the United States or of the United States government.

In addition to the above punishments, the Act also provides for restitution, for the seizure of personal property used or possessed in connection with any violation of the Act, for the forfeiture of the seized personal property, and for civil relief from conduct constituting a violation of the Act.

UNLAWFUL EAVESDROPPING AND SURVEILLANCE AND RELATED CRIMES

See also PEEPING TOM.

I. Generally

Part 1 of Article 3 of Chapter 11 of Title 16 contains four related substantive offenses. The offense of "Peeping Tom" is treated separately. The two remaining offenses are unlawful eavesdropping and surveillance (§ 16-11-62) and possession, sale, and distribution of eavesdropping devices (§ 16-11-63).

The provisions of Part 1 of Article 3 of Chapter 11 of Title 16 of the criminal code were designed to address the problems associated with the great possibility in modern society of invasion of an individual's right to privacy resulting from the proliferation of electronic eavesdropping devices and surveillance devices. These problems are also covered by federal legislation. The Georgia invasion of privacy statutes are supplemental to and not inconsistent with the federal law. It should be stressed that both the federal and state statutes are applicable in Georgia state courts and both must be complied with in order to render wiretap evidence admissible in Georgia state proceedings. However, where the state statutes delineate greater restrictions on interceptions and, therefore, provide greater protection to individual privacy rights than federal law, the state statutes are not preempted by the federal law and should be applied in a state proceeding.

II. Unlawful Eavesdropping and Surveillance

Section 16-11-62 sets forth the general prohibition of eavesdropping and surveillance. Section 16-11-62(1) declares that it is unlawful for "[a]ny person in a clandestine manner intentionally to overhear, transmit, or record or attempt to overhear, transmit, or record the private conversation of another which shall originate in any private place." Paragraph (4) makes it unlawful for "[a]ny person intentionally and secretly to intercept by the use of any device, instrument, or apparatus the contents of a message sent by telephone, telegraph, letter, or by any other means of private communication." This provision has been broadly construed to prohibit the interception of all types of telephone conversations, including those made on cordless telephones. Except as otherwise provided by law, these prohibitions include interceptions by family members. Moreover, these prohibitions apply only to the intentional interception of conversations. Thus, a conversation that is inadvertently recorded would not be inadmissible under the statute.

The remaining paragraphs of § 16-11-62 proscribe related invasions of privacy, not necessarily limited to those involving a "device." For example, paragraph (3) makes it unlawful for any person "to go on or about the premises of another or any private place, except as otherwise provided by law, for the purpose of invading the privacy of others by eavesdropping upon their conversations or secretly observing their activities." Paragraph (6) makes it unlawful for any person "to sell, give, or distribute, without legal authority, to any person or entity any photograph, videotape, or record, or copies thereof, of the activities of another which occur in any private place and out of public view without the consent of all persons observed." Additionally, the final omnibus paragraph (7) prohibits "any other acts of a nature similar to those set out in paragraphs (1) through (6) . . . which invade the privacy of another."

There are three major exceptions to the general prohibition in § 16-11-62. These exceptions are concerned with consent, law enforcement officers, and Public Service Commission licenses. The Georgia courts have run into difficulty in determining the contours of the consent exception, but these problems apparently have now been resolved.

In addition to these major exceptions, there is an express exception for observing, photographing, or recording the activities of incarcerated individuals. Since a police car is much like a jail cell, no reasonable expectation of privacy exists for an arrestee seated in the police car. Thus, the recording of a post-arrest conversation in the back seat of the police car does not offend the state's wiretapping statutes. Likewise, since a prisoner has no reasonable expectation of privacy in the calls he places to nonattorneys from jail, the admission of the prisoner's recorded calls at trial would not violate his right to privacy.

There is also an express exception for observing, photographing, or recording the activities of others for the purpose of security, crime prevention, or crime detection. This exception applies to the activities of persons (1) who are on an owner's or occupier's real property or an approach thereto in areas where there is no reasonable expectation of privacy or (2) who are within the curtilage of one's residence. In the latter situation, a photograph, videotape, or record made by the resident, or a copy thereof, may be disclosed to the district attorney or a law enforcement officer and is admissible in a judicial proceeding without the consent of the person observed, photographed, or recorded.

There is no exception in the statute for illegal or immoral conversations even if these conversations can be so characterized. Waiver of privacy can not be based on the content of the conversation, otherwise all criminal conversations would be admissible.

A. Consent Exception

1. Consent by Party to Conservation

The primary problem for the courts in this area had been the delineation of the exceptions to § 16-11-62. This problem had been compounded by the language of the consent exception. Section 16-11-66 provided:

> "Nothing in Code Section 16-11-62 shall prohibit the interception, recording, and divulging of a message sent by telephone, telegraph, letter, or any other means of communication when the **sender and receiver** thereof expressly or impliedly consent thereto or in those instances wherein the message is initiated or instigated by a person and the message constitutes the commission of a crime or is directly in the furtherance of a crime, provided at least one party thereto consents." (Emphasis added.)

The language of § 16-11-66 suggested that both parties to a conversation had to consent to the interception or recording of a message, except where such message constituted the commission of a crime or was in direct furtherance of a crime. If the message fell within the latter category, only one person had to consent to authorize an interception. It appeared that all other recording of the conversation was outside the § 16-11-66 exception and, thus, illegal under § 16-11-62.

The above interpretation was a literal interpretation of the exception. However, in interpreting § 16-11-62, the Georgia courts had not always taken a "literal" approach to § 16-11-66. The question of the scope of the consent exception had been litigated in a situation where one of the parties to a conversation recorded the conversation without the knowledge of the other party. If the conversation was not the actual commission of a crime or in direct furtherance, § 16-11-66 appeared to be unavailable to authorize the tape recording.

In Cross v. State, the Georgia Court of Appeals, in analyzing such a situation, held that § 16-11-62 prohibited only nonparties to a conversation from recording or divulging information. Accordingly, it was not unlawful for a party to a conversation to record or transmit a conversation without the knowledge or consent of the other party. Thus, there was no need even to utilize the consent exception. The court justified this interpretation of § 16-11-62 by pointing out that the section's focus was on the overhearing of a conversation, which necessarily involved a nonparty to the conversation. In effect, the court construed § 16-11-62 to incorporate the "misplaced trust" doctrine set out in Hoffa v. United States, under which individuals always are seen to run the risk that those to whom they speak in confidence will betray their trust. The court did recognize that in the situation it was addressing, § 16-11-66 was made "redundant" by its interpretation of § 16-11-62.

Cross sparked a judicial debate that lasted for several years. Several decisions were rendered in which the court adopted a position contrary to the holding in Cross. However, it apparently was settled that Cross correctly stated Georgia law, and the consent exception was largely unnecessary. As the Georgia Supreme Court stated in

Mitchell v. State:

> . . . the General Assembly intended:
>
> (1) Code § 26-3001(a) [O.C.G.A. § 16-11-62(1)] to prohibit third parties from intercepting in a clandestine manner a private conversation between two or more parties; except under the conditions of
>
> (2) Code § 26-3006 [O.C.G.A. § 16-11-66], which allows a third party to intercept, record and divulge the conversation, (a) where the parties to the conversation consent, or (b) where the message is a crime or is directly in furtherance of a crime and one party to the conversation consents;
>
> * * *
>
> (4) none of these Code sections prohibits the actual parties to the conversation from recording or divulging it.

Between 1973 when Cross was decided and 1977 when the Georgia Supreme Court adopted the Cross analysis in Mitchell, several cases relied on the consent exception to find no violation of § 16-11-62. In retrospect, these interpretations of § 16-11-66 were unnecessary because under Cross and Mitchell there were no violations of the terms of § 16-11-62 itself.

In 1993, the General Assembly amended the language of the consent exception, apparently in conformance with the Cross/Mitchell rationale. Now, § 16-11-66(a) provides:

> (a) Nothing in Code Section 16-11-62 shall prohibit a person from intercepting a wire, oral, or electronic communication where such person is a party to the communication or one of the parties to the communication has given prior consent to such interception.

A confidential informant's consent to having his conversation monitored by a police officer during a controlled drug buy is implied by the fact that he has permitted the officer to place a body bug on him.

2. Child Consent Procedures; Parental Exception

Prior to 1993, the state could record a child's telephone conversation on its own without having first obtained an investigation warrant as long as it had the valid consent of the child. In Dobbins v. State, police officers, with the consent of the child's father, had arranged for the recording of incriminating phone calls between the child and her molester. The Georgia Supreme Court held that since the evidence showed that the state had obtained neither an investigation warrant nor the valid consent of the child, the recorded telephone conversation containing several incriminating statements made by the defendant to the child was not admissible. The court held further that the father could not consent, on behalf of his child, to the state's recording of the conversation.

The Dobbins decision spurred the General Assembly to amend § 16-11-66 in 1993. This Code section was amended to provide that the telephone conversations of a child under 18 years of age may be recorded and divulged if, upon written application by a private citizen, law enforcement agency, or prosecutor's office, a judge of a superior court and the child consent to such taping. This application does not have to comply with the procedures required for the issuance of an investigation warrant. Consent to the taping could be given only by order of the judge after making certain findings and determinations. Although the Act amending this Code section was originally introduced with a provision allowing for a parent's vicarious consent to the recording of a child's telephone conversation with a suspect, the final version of the Act placed "the decision to grant permission to record [such conversations] in the hands of judges **alone** as long as certain guidelines [were] followed." Thus, as was held by the Court of Appeals in Bishop v. State, the language of the amendment clearly precluded a parent's vicarious consent to the recording of his child's telephone conversation with a suspect.

The Court of Appeals, however, recognized that this amendment created numerous evidentiary problems in cases when the child is under significant criminal influence by another and the child does not recognize the genuine risk that this influence poses for him. For instance, even if the state or the parents in such a case were to petition a superior court judge for permission to record the telephone conversations between the child and the suspect, the judge would be precluded from issuing his order as long as the child, while under the influence of the suspect, refuses to consent and participate in the recording. Nevertheless, since the language of the amendment was so clear and unambiguous, the court was not authorized to construe it otherwise so that it would have permitted the admission of the tape recordings. Rather, the court found that it was solely the task of the General Assembly to amend the Code section to allow the admission into evidence of tape recordings "made by parents with a good faith, objectively reasonable basis for concern regarding the safety of their children as victims of criminal conduct of another."

At the Court of Appeals' urging, the General Assembly undertook the task of amending the child consent procedures in its 2000 Session. It created a parental exception to these procedures with the enactment of subsection (d) of § 16-11-66. Adopting some of the language used by the court in its decision, this subsection provides that "[t]he provisions of this article shall not be construed to prohibit a parent or guardian of a child under 18 years of age, with or without the consent of such minor child, from monitoring or intercepting telephonic conversations of such minor child with another person by use of an extension phone located within the family home, or electronic or other communications of such minor child from within the family home, for the purpose of ensuring the welfare of such minor child. If the parent or guardian has a reasonable or good faith belief that such conversation or communication is evidence of criminal conduct involving such child as a victim or an attempt, conspiracy, or solicitation to involve such child in criminal activity affecting the welfare or best interest of such child, the parent or guardian may disclose the content of such telephonic conversation or electronic communication to the district attorney or a law enforcement officer. A recording or other record of any such conversation or communication made by a parent or guardian in accordance with this subsection that contains evidence of criminal conduct involving such child as a victim or an attempt, conspiracy, or solicitation to involve such child in criminal activity shall be admissible in a judicial proceeding except as otherwise provided in subsection

(b) of this Code section." A superior court may give retroactive effect to this enactment.

With the enactment of the parental exception in 2000, Bishop v. State is overruled to the extent that it holds that a parent cannot vicariously consent to the recording of his child's telephone conversation with a suspect. The enactment makes it clear that consent may be given either by order of a judge of a superior court upon written application or by the parent or guardian of the child as provided by the parental exception. Furthermore, the enactment broadens the scope of the child consent procedures to include, in addition to telephone conversations, conversations conducted by "electronic communication," such as e-mail.

Although the child's consent is required before a superior court judge can issue an order authorizing the recording of the child's conservation by a third party, the child alone lacks the capacity to consent to the recording, even if age ten or older. Thus, as a matter of law, the child alone is incapable of giving consent to the recording of his phone calls by a third party either by implication or by subsequent ratification.

However, the child consent procedures apply only to a third party's interception of a child's telephone conversation and does not prohibit a child who is an actual party to the conversation from recording and divulging it.

B. Law Enforcement Exception

Another exception to the prohibitions of § 16-11-62 is found in § 16-11-64 which provides that a law enforcement officer acting in his official capacity can be exempted by following certain procedures.

The Georgia Supreme Court was faced with a constitutional challenge to § 16-11-64 in Granese v. State. The statute was challenged on the basis of the First, Fourth, Sixth, and Fourteenth Amendments. The court found all of these challenges to be meritless. No First Amendment violation exists because § 16-11-64 does not make private speech the equivalent of public property. There is no Fourth or Fourteenth Amendment violation because § 16-11-64 does not authorize a general search. Finally, the court held that § 16-11-64 does not deprive an individual of his Sixth Amendment right to counsel because no custodial interrogation is involved.

1. Warrant Procedures

As part of Georgia's Support of the War on Terrorism Act of 2002, the General Assembly eliminated the state procedures for the issuance of surveillance warrants and replaced these procedures with a new provision subjecting the issuance of such warrants solely to the terms, conditions, and procedures provided for by federal law. Since the state procedures arguably provided greater protection to individual privacy rights than the federal procedures, the Act's elimination of these procedures effectively enhances state law enforcement's capability to surveil an individual but to the detriment of individual privacy rights. The General Assembly obviously determined that less protection was necessary in order to assist the federal government in its war on terrorism.

a. Current Procedures

As enacted in 2002, § 16-11-64(c) provides that upon written application, under oath, of the prosecuting attorney having jurisdiction over prosecution of the crime under investigation, or the Attorney General, made before a judge of superior court, the court may issue an investigation warrant permitting the use of a surveillance device, as defined in § 16-11-60, for the surveillance of a person or place to the extent the warrant is consistent with and subject to the terms, conditions, and procedures provided for by Chapter 119 of Title 18 of the United States Code Annotated, as amended.

b. Former Procedures

Since warrant procedures are now required to be "consistent with and subject to the terms, conditions, and procedures provided for by Chapter 119 of Title 18 of the United States Code Annotated, as amended," the former state procedures are no longer controlling and should not be followed. These procedures, however, are similar to those applicable under federal law. Hence, the case law discussion construing the former procedures is included below to the extent that it may have some applicability under the current procedures and insofar as it is still applicable to prosecutions arising before the effective date of Georgia's Support of the War on Terrorism Act of 2002.

Former paragraphs (1) through (7) of § 16-11-64(b) prescribed the warrant procedures that law enforcement officers had to follow in order to engage in electronic surveillance activities. These as well as the federal procedures had to be satisfied in order to render the surveillance evidence admissible in Georgia courts. Unless they were satisfied, any evidence obtained would have been in violation of § 16-11-62 and therefore inadmissible. For example, in State v. Toomey, an investigator from the sheriff's office was called on to investigate the unauthorized use of a business phone. After being told that the phone was being used for trafficking in illegal drugs, the investigator himself listened in on these conversations and then obtained a search warrant. The trial court's sustaining of a motion to suppress evidence pursuant to this warrant was upheld on appeal because the procedures required by § 16-11-64 had not been complied with. Thus, the investigator was in violation of § 16-11-62, and the evidence was inadmissible.

The warrant procedures of § 16-11-64 had to be complied with only when law enforcement officers were attempting to use an eavesdropping "device," as that term was defined in § 16-11-60. Other types of eavesdropping could have been engaged in by law enforcement officers. Thus, in Satterfield v. State, the court held that the provisions did not apply where the police overheard a conversation by listening through a thin wall. In Rautenstrauch v. State, the court held that § 16-11-64 did not prevent a law enforcement officer from surreptitiously going upon the premises of another and overhearing a conversation through a window. Of course, whether a law enforcement action passed muster under the Fourth Amendment of the United States Constitution was an entirely different question.

A warrant under § 16-11-64 could have been issued only when there was probable cause to believe that one of the crimes specified in former paragraph (1) of § 16-11-64(b) had been or was being committed. The former paragraph (1) crimes were generally very serious crimes. In Orkin v. State, the defendant, who was charged with conspiracy to commit murder, argued that (1) conspiracy was not one of these crimes because it was not specifically listed in former paragraph (1) and (2) conspiracy was not a "felony involving bodily harm" which was specifically listed in former paragraph (1). The court rejected these arguments, holding that conspiracy to commit murder was a felony involving bodily harm within the meaning of former paragraph (1). The court thus indicated that it would look at the specific facts of a felony to ascertain whether it involved bodily harm rather than looking at felonies in a categorical fashion to determine whether conspiracy, for example, always involved bodily harm.

A warrant to use a videotape camera to depict evidence of a hunter's illegal activities, which instrument or apparatus clearly was a "device" within the meaning of § 16-11-60, would not have been obtainable under the former procedures because a warrant could have been issued only for specified serious felonies, not for misdemeanors. Moreover, a warrant for use of such a device would not have been needed by a law enforcement officer who, in performing his duties, did not invade a private place.

Assuming that the alleged crime being investigated was one of those enumerated in former paragraph (1) of § 16-11-64(b), the question often arose whether the warrant itself was valid. In several cases, an attack on the investigation warrant or the warrant procedure was based on federal law which provided for nonadmissibility of evidence obtained in violation of its provisions. In Orkin v. State, for example, the court held that the warrant issued was sufficiently specific to comply with both state and federal law. The warrant stated which phones were to be tapped and which conversations were to be overheard (those between a named third party and other "unknown persons"). One of the "unknown persons" turned out to be the defendant.

Prior to 2000, the authority to apply for and issue a surveillance warrant in this state was restricted to the circuit wherein the device was to be physically placed. In Granese v. State, the court held that approval of a warrant by the superior court judge of the circuit wherein the wiretap device was to be placed comported with both state and federal requirements. The court further held that the judge's orders were sufficiently complied with by the use of a manual recording device even though the order called for the use of an automatic device. In King v. State, the court held that the application for a wiretap warrant was sufficient to demonstrate the state's compliance with the statutory requirements. The application reflected that it was made in writing under oath to the appropriate superior court judge, by the district attorney of the circuit where the wiretap was placed.

In 2000, the General Assembly eliminated this territorial restriction and expanded the scope of the authority to apply for and issue a surveillance warrant to include any crime over which the prosecuting attorney and the superior court judge have jurisdiction. Notwithstanding the significant changes to the surveillance warrant procedures wrought by Georgia's Support of the War on Terrorism Act of 2002, this expanded jurisdictional authority is still provided for in § 16-11-64(c). Thus, as long as they have jurisdiction over a crime, the prosecuting attorney can apply for and the superior court judge can issue a warrant for the placement of a surveillance device in any judicial circuit where the crime is being committed.

2. Disclosure of Wiretap Information

Prior to the enactment of Georgia's Support of the War on Terrorism Act of 2002, an additional protection against privacy invasion was contained in § 16-11-64. Former paragraph (8) of § 16-11-64(b) provided that there could be no disclosure of wiretap information unless it was "necessary and essential" to the prosecution of the crime specified in the warrant. Thus, even if all warrant procedures had been complied with, any unnecessary or nonessential publication of evidence obtained under the warrant rendered such evidence inadmissible. With the elimination of this provision in 2002, the disclosure of wiretap information must now be "consistent with and subject to the terms, conditions, and procedures provided for by Chapter 119 of Title 18 of the United States Code Annotated, as amended." In other words, any disclosure of wiretap information must be made in compliance with the federal counterpart to former paragraph (b)(8), i.e., 18 U. S. C. § 2517. Under the federal statute, the disclosure must be "appropriate to the proper performance of the official duties of the officer making or receiving the disclosure." With the General Assembly's adoption of this federal standard in place of the state standard, the state standard is no longer controlling and should not be applied to determine whether the disclosure of wiretap information is authorized. Since the state standard arguably provided greater protection to individual privacy rights than the federal standard, its elimination effectively enhances state law enforcement's capability to share information in a criminal investigation but to the detriment of individual privacy rights. The case law discussion construing both the former "necessary and essential" standard and the former state warrant procedures is included below only insofar as it may still be applicable to prosecutions arising before the effective date of Georgia's Support of the War on Terrorism Act of 2002.

In Orkin v. State, two publications of tape recordings were alleged to be unnecessary. The tapes were played to the intended murder victim in order to verify Orkin's voice. In addition, the tapes were played in court for the purpose of conducting sound-level tests. Only district attorney office staff members were present. The court held that the terms necessary and essential "do not mean 'indispensable.' " The court stated:

> The construction to be given the statute is rather what is reasonably necessary and essential to the preparation of and

actual prosecution for a crime. What is reasonable will depend upon the facts of a given case and must necessarily rest in the controlled discretion of the district attorney, subject to review by the trial court. Where there is evidence to support the decision of a trial judge . . . that decision will not be disturbed on appeal.

Using this standard, the court found that the "necessary and essential" test had been satisfied. The evidence showed that only limited portions of the tape had been played and that measures had been taken to prevent unnecessary playing of the tapes.

In an extraordinary motion for new trial, based on newly discovered evidence, the Orkin defendant later alleged that the intended murder victim's attorney was present during the playing of the tapes. A majority of the Court of Appeals held this was permissible. On certiorari, the Georgia Supreme Court upheld this decision, although it acknowledged "an admittedly close set of facts." A dissenter urged that the Court of Appeals had erroneously constructed an "attorney exception" to the "necessary and essential" test and that the case ought to stand on the application of the "necessary and essential" test alone.

In a number of decisions, the Court of Appeals failed to correctly apply the statutory standard for determining whether disclosure of wiretap information was authorized. In determining whether the disclosure was "necessary and essential," the Court of Appeals failed to balance the state's interest in disclosing the information with the protection of the citizen's privacy. For instance, in Van Nice v. State, the court held that the statute authorized the disclosure of wiretap information to other law enforcement agencies and officials even though it broadened the scope of the pending investigation and gave probable cause to seek additional wiretaps and to intercept the conversations of additional parties. In Uhler v. State, the court stated that even if the wiretap information was shared with other law enforcement agencies, such disclosure did not cause the information to be inadmissible at trial. In King v. State, the court held that the state properly released the wiretap information to the federal Drug Enforcement Agency to pursue evidence of interstate drug traffic in connection with the state investigation. In Ayers v. State, the court held that the trial court did not abuse its discretion in refusing to suppress the wiretap information because of the district attorney's action in disseminating the information to an IRS agent in furtherance of the investigation. Likewise, in State v. Anderson, the court held that even though the agent may have acted solely as an IRS agent in preparing a tax assessment, at the time the wiretap evidence was disclosed to him he was acting as an agent of the state. Accordingly, the trial court erred by holding that the IRS agent's listening to the wiretaps was an unauthorized disclosure of the information. In Anderson v. State, the Georgia Supreme Court reversed the Court of Appeals' decision and implicitly overruled that court's other decisions suggesting a contrary holding. Although the court recognized the need and importance for such disclosure where the prosecution of the crime specified in the warrant reasonably required it, the mere fact that disclosure was made to another law enforcement agency for assistance or for the prosecution of any crime within its jurisdiction did not abrogate the statutory requirement that the disclosure had to be reasonably necessary and essential to the preparation of and actual prosecution of the crime or crimes alleged in the warrant. Wiretap information disclosed to another law enforcement agency was not admissible unless the state could show that the crimes charged reasonably required the assistance and expertise of the other agency in order to effect their prosecution.

It has been held that disclosure of information to a magistrate to obtain a search warrant of a residence directly related to the crime specified in the wiretap warrant was proper.

Former paragraph (8) of § 16-11-64(b) was held not to automatically override the principle of openness of criminal proceedings or the First Amendment and turn criminal proceedings into closed events. A defendant seeking closure under the statute had to establish such overriding interest that would have required a closure as a matter of law.

In a request for public access to documents containing information gained through wiretaps, the Georgia Supreme Court held that former paragraph (8) of § 16-11-64(b) prohibited the public disclosure of such information and that the trial court should have deleted from the documents information obtained under a warrant authorizing a wiretap.

The U. S. Supreme Court has held that the First Amendment does provide protection to a publisher's repeated intentional disclosure of a lawfully obtained but illegally intercepted cellular telephone conversation about a matter of public concern.

While former paragraph (8) of § 16-11-64(b), relating to disclosure of information gathered under a wiretap, contained a provision requiring exclusion of such evidence where it was improperly disclosed, former paragraph (5) of § 16-11-64(b) did not contain a similar exclusionary rule with respect to handling of the application for a wiretap warrant and related documents. Accordingly, despite the state's failure to strictly comply with the statutory requirements of former paragraph (5) of § 16-11-64(b), in the absence of evidence that the documents were improperly disclosed or tampered with, the wiretap evidence would have been admissible.

In United States v. Hayes, the federal district court was faced with the question of whether Georgia law would have kept evidence obtained by means of wiretapping from a federal grand jury. In this case, a Georgia district attorney was subpoenaed to appear as a witness before a federal grand jury. He was instructed to bring certain records relating to the interception of communications made by a certain individual. In a motion to quash, the district attorney stated that supplying the grand jury with the information requested would have constituted a violation of Georgia law. The federal court held that complying with the order of the federal grand jury would not have constituted a violation of the Georgia law, noting that the Code provisions were concerned with the admissibility of evidence in Georgia as opposed to federal courts and that, in any event, Georgia law would have been ineffectual under the Supremacy Clause of the federal constitution.

In Connally v. State, the court held that the defendant's right to confront the witnesses against him was not denied by the refusal of the state to reveal the identity of an informer who permitted a detective to overhear a conversation between the informant and the defendant. The defendant asserted that only the informer could have countered the detective's claim that consent was given. The court held that the mere possibility that the police might have been impeached was not enough to require disclosure of the informer's identity.

Under the provisions of former paragraph (7) of § 16-11-64(b), the prosecution had to disclose to the defendant any transcripts of wiretap evidence obtained pursuant to a warrant. The Court of Appeals, however, found this provision inapplicable where the transcripts were obtained pursuant to the consent of one of the parties to the conversation under § 16-11-66.

3. *Providing Facilities or Technical Assistance*

Under former subsection (d) of § 16-11-64, communication carriers, their officers, employees and agents were authorized to provide facilities or technical assistance to persons authorized by warrant to intercept a wire communication. The General Assembly eliminated this provision in its Support of the War on Terrorism Act of 2002. With the elimination this provision, similar federal statutes are now controlling. Since former subsection (d) is similar to these statutes, the case law discussion construing this subsection is included below to the extent that it may have some applicability under the federal statutes and insofar as it is still applicable to prosecutions arising before the effective date of Georgia's Support of the War on Terrorism Act of 2002.

In Uhler v. State, the court held that since the process employed by a telephone company in tracing the "call-forwarding" process did not involve "interception of a wire or oral communication," written application requesting the issuance of an order directing the telephone company to assist the State was not required. In Gonzalez v. State, the court held that although a telephone company started installing a line for electronic surveillance at the request of a police officer three days before a warrant authorizing such surveillance was obtained, the installation was not complete until the date the warrant issued. Further, no device capable of intercepting wire communications was placed on the line by the telephone company. Any error in the telephone company's actions was harmless, as no eavesdropping or recording of wire communications was conducted without a warrant as a result of its action.

C. *Law Enforcement Emergency Exceptions*

1. *Pen Register or Trap and Trace Devices*

An investigative or law enforcement officer specifically designated by a prosecuting official may have installed and use a pen register or trap and trace device if he reasonably determines that (1) an emergency situation exists which requires the installation and use of the device before a court order can, with due diligence, be obtained and (2) there are grounds upon which the order could be entered authorizing the device's installation and use. The emergency situation must involve either an immediate danger of death or serious bodily injury to a person or conspiratorial activities characteristic of organized crime. Furthermore, a court order approving the installation or use of the device must be issued in accordance with § 16-11-64.1 within 48 hours of the time the device is installed.

Because pen registers are not among the devices governed by § 16-11-64, the 20-day limit for investigative warrants issued under that Code section do not apply to a pen register order. Rather, such a pen register order would be governed by § 16-11-64.1, which contains no time limitation.

2. *Electronic Surveillance Devices*

In the event of an emergency situation, an investigative or law enforcement officer specifically designated by a prosecuting official may utilize an electronic surveillance device to intercept the wire, oral, or electronic communications or to observe, monitor, or record the activities of the person or persons involved in the emergency situation. Before the device can be utilize by the officer, the prosecuting official must determine that (1) an emergency situation exists involving the immediate danger of death or serious physical injury to a person; (2) the situation requires the immediate interception of the communications or surveillance of the activities of any person involved in the situation before a court order can, with due diligence, be obtained; and (3) there are grounds upon which an investigation warrant could be issued. Furthermore, an application for an investigation warrant must be made pursuant to § 16-11-64 with 48 hours after the interception or surveillance commences.

If an application for an investigation warrant is granted, the interception or surveillance must be conducted in accordance with § 16-11-64, except that the interception or surveillance continues only so long as the emergency situation exists.

Where an application for an investigation warrant is denied or the interception or surveillance is terminated without an investigation warrant having been issued, the contents of any intercepted communications or other surveillance are not admissible in any court of this state except to prove violations of the wiretap law. The contents of any intercepted communications or other surveillance effected without an investigation warrant having been issued are confidential and must not be disclosed except to prove violations of the wiretap law.

D. *Public Service Commission Exception*

The final exception to the provisions of § 16-11-62 is found in § 16-11-65, which permits the Public Service Commission to license the use of interception equipment for the purpose of business service improvement. The commission is not authorized to issue a license "until the applicant has demonstrated to the commission a clear, apparent, and logically reasonable need for the use of the equipment in connection with a legitimate business activity of the user or subscriber and demonstrated to the satisfaction of the commission that it will be operated by persons of good moral character and that the equipment will be used in a lawful manner and in conformity with the tariffs filed for the equipment."

The commission is authorized to revoke a license "when it is established to the satisfaction of the commission that the equipment is being used in an unlawful manner contrary to the tariff applicable to the equipment or in a manner contrary to the purposes and uses for which the license had been issued." The commission may also revoke a license if it is discovered that a material misrepresentation was made in applying for the license.

The commission can promulgate rules and regulations relating to the issuance and revocation of licenses and is further permitted to "adopt any and all appropriate rules and regulations of any sort to ensure the privacy of telephonic and telegraphic communications." A violation of such rules constitutes a violation of Part 1 of Article 3 of Chapter 11 of Title 16.

The Georgia Attorney General has issued an opinion stating that a license to use telephone service observing equipment may be revoked upon proof that the licensee is recording conversations on the grounds that said activity is contrary to the purposes and uses for which the license was issued. The recording of conversations is not authorized by the commission's grant of authority to intercept, as the use of the term "recording" is not included within the term "interception" by the enabling legislation.

As part of the public service commission exception, § 16-11-65(d) provides that duly authorized employees of any telephone company regulated by the Public Service Commission are exempted from the provisions of Part 1 of Article 3 of Chapter 11 of Title 16 with respect to "the reasonable and limited intercepting of telephone communications under circumstances reasonably calculated to assure the privacy of telephone communications when such interception is accomplished solely for the purpose of maintaining the quality of service furnished to the public or for the purpose of preventing the unlawful use of telephone service."

III. Possession, Sale, or Distribution of Eavesdropping Devices

The provisions of § 16-11-62, which are designed to prohibit electronic eavesdropping, are bolstered by § 16-11-63, which forbids anyone other than law enforcement officers from possessing, selling, or distributing eavesdropping devices.

An eavesdropping device is any instrument or apparatus which by virtue of its size, design, and method of operation has no normal or customary function or purpose other than to permit the user thereof secretly to intercept, transmit, listen to, or record private conversations of others.

IV. Punishment

Both unlawful eavesdropping and surveillance and the possession, sale, or distribution of eavesdropping devices are felonies, punishable by imprisonment for one to five years and/or a fine of up to $10,000. Law enforcement officers acting in good faith reliance on the statute or a court order have a defense to criminal prosecution.

V. Interception of Cellular Radio Telephone Communications

In 1992, the Georgia Court of Appeals, in a two-judge decision that possessed no precedential value, held that § 16-11-62(4) did not prohibit the interception of a cellular telephone conversation. Unlike landline telephone communications, cellular telephone communications were not considered private, because cellular telephones transmitted "FM" radio waves for anyone to hear. Thus, cellular telephone users had no justifiable expectation of privacy.

In 1993, the General Assembly enacted former § 16-11-66.1, apparently in response to the Court of Appeals decision, to specifically prohibit the interception of cellular radio telephone communications.

The General Assembly, however, eliminated this prohibition in its Support of the War on Terrorism Act of 2002 apparently because in 2000 the Georgia Supreme Court broadly construed the terms "telephone" and "private communication" as used in § 16-11-62(4) to include all types of telephones and telephone communications. Because individuals engaged in conversations on the telephone, whether landline, cordless, or cellular, expect their conversations to be private, the court held that § 16-11-62(4) protects these conversations from interception. This construction rendered the protection afforded by former § 16-11-66.1 redundant and therefore ripe for elimination by the General Assembly in 2002.

V.A. Required Disclosure of Stored Wire or Electronic Communications and Transactional Records

As part of Georgia's Support of the War on Terrorism Act of 2002, the General Assembly enacted a new § 16-11-66.1 in order to provide state law enforcement officers access to stored wire and electronic communications and transactional records.

A law enforcement officer, a prosecuting attorney, or the Attorney General may require the disclosure of stored wire or electronic communications, as well as transactional records pertaining thereto, to the extent and under the procedures and conditions provided for by the laws of the United States.

A provider of electronic communication service or remote computing service must provide the contents of, and transactional records pertaining to, wire and electronic communications in its possession or reasonably accessible thereto when a requesting law enforcement officer, a prosecuting attorney, or the Attorney General complies with the provisions for access thereto set forth by the laws of the United States.

Search warrants for production of stored wire or electronic communications and transactional records pertaining thereto have state-wide application or application as provided by the laws of the United States when issued by a judge with jurisdiction over the criminal offense under investigation and to which the records relate.

A subpoena for the production of stored wire or electronic communications and transactional records pertaining thereto may be issued at any time upon a showing by a law enforcement official, a prosecuting attorney, or the Attorney General that the subpoenaed material relates to a pending criminal investigation.

The failure to comply with a request for disclosure is punishable as contempt.

V.B. *Civil Liability of Broker for Unlawful Purchase, Acquisition, Sale, or Release of Telephone Records*

A. Legislative Findings

The General Assembly has found that telephone records can be of great use to criminals because the customer information contained in call logs listed in such records include a wealth of personal data. These records are sometimes accessed without authorization of the customer by an employee of the telephone service provider selling the data or by a data broker or other person who pretends to be the owner of the telephone and who convinces the telephone company's employees to release the data to such person. The General Assembly enacted the Telephone Records Privacy Protection Act in 2006 in order to prohibit the unlawful obtaining or release of a customer's telephone records.

B. Prohibited Conduct

It is unlawful for any telephone records broker to purchase, acquire, sell, or release the telephone records of any person who is a Georgia resident or to attempt to purchase, acquire, sell, or release the telephone record of any third party who is a Georgia resident. This prohibition applies whether the customer's telephone record is obtained by the telephone records broker directly from a telecommunications company or from any other third-party source. A person is considered a Georgia resident if the individual has a Georgia billing address.

C. Civil Penalty

This prohibited conduct is punishable by a civil fine in an amount not to exceed $10,000 for each violation. The prosecuting attorney or the Attorney General is authorized to prosecute the civil case. Each telephone record purchased, acquired, sold, or released and each attempt to purchase, acquire, sell, or release a telephone record constitutes a separate violation.

D. Tort Liability

Any violation constitutes a tort and creates a right of action in the person or entity whose telephone records have been purchased, acquired, sold, or released for which damages may be recovered. Special damages may be inferred by the violation. Reasonable attorney's fees should be awarded to the plaintiff where the plaintiff has prevailed in the underlying action.

E. Law Enforcement Exception

This prohibition does not prevent any action by a law enforcement agency or any officer, employee, or agent of a law enforcement agency to obtain the telephone records or personal identifying information of any third party who is a Georgia resident in connection with the performance of the official duties of the agency, officer, employee, or agent.

VI. *Evidentiary Impact of Violations of Part 1 of Article 3 of Chapter 11 of Title 16*

The basic evidentiary rule relating to criminal invasions of privacy is contained in § 16-11-67 which states: "No evidence obtained in a manner which violates any of the provisions of this part shall be admissible in any court of this state except to prove violations of this part."

The importance of this statute cannot be overestimated. Indeed, because law enforcement officers, the most likely violators of this part, have a good faith defense to § 16-11-62 criminal prosecutions under § 16-11-64(e), the primary function of this statute has not been as a criminal statute, but as an exclusionary rule to bar wiretap evidence in trials of other substantive offenses.

This exclusionary rule applies to administrative procedural violations associated with electronic surveillance warrants. However, procedural violations do not require the exclusion of evidence derived from electronic surveillance, where the defendant makes no showing of prejudice or harm to his privacy interest resulting from the state's noncompliance with these procedures.

Assuming that the exclusionary rule of § 16-11-67 applies, an additional question remains as to its scope. Typically, the evidence sought to be introduced will be the evidence of the intercepted communication itself. In such case, admissibility depends upon compliance with the provisions of this part. However, in Cauley v. State, the court was faced with a different problem. In that case, the prosecution sought to introduce certain physical evidence alleged to have been the product of an unlawfully overheard conversation. The court held that the motion to suppress was properly overruled. Citing the United States Supreme Court case of Wong Sun v. United States, which established the "fruit of the poisonous tree" doctrine, the court found that the evidence in question "was not derived from an exploitation of the [illegally intercepted call] but instead by means sufficiently distinguishable to be purged of any taint attaching to that call." The court implied, however, that evidence obtained through the exploitation of illegal eavesdropping would be inadmissible under the "fruit of the poisonous tree" doctrine. Although the Wong Sun doctrine is based on the Fourth Amendment, Cauley's extension of the statutory exclusionary rule would seem to be warranted under a rationale of discouraging statutory violations.

In Duncan v. State, the court held that evidence seized as a result of an illegal wiretap should have been suppressed. Since the affidavit and application for the wiretap relied upon tainted information from an illegal pen register, then any evidence gathered as a result of the wiretap was also tainted under the "fruit of the poisonous tree" doctrine.

In Dobbins v. State, the court held that the defendant's incriminating statements should not have been admitted into evidence as they were the fruit of an illegal recording of his telephone conversation with the victim and were therefore tainted by its illegality.

In Jordan v. State, the court upheld the trial court's denial of the defendant's motion to suppress evidence derivative of an illegal wiretap by a private individual. The tape illegally made by the private individual was not allowed to be used for any purpose at trial. However, there having been no illegal conduct by state agents involved in the individual's initial taping, the court held that the "fruit of the poisonous tree" doctrine was not applicable to exclude the remaining tapes by an informant and an undercover agent which were legally made subsequent to the initial taping.

In Quintrell v. State, the court held that since a conservation ranger is given by statute the power "[t]o go upon property outside of buildings, posted or otherwise, in the performance of [his] duties," a hunter can not reasonably expect his illegal activities on private property to be safe from surveillance by the ranger. Furthermore, because the special protection accorded by the Fourth Amendment is not extended to the open fields, entry on posted private property by a ranger does not constitute trespass onto a zone of privacy. Thus, the ranger's videotaping of the hunter's illegal activities would not constitute an unlawful surveillance which would subject the videotape to suppression.

Sections 16-11-62 and 16-11-67, while applicable to the content of telephone conversations, do not extend to include telephone company records. Also, the disclosure of information concerning what numbers were dialed from a particular phone is not prohibited.

VII. Civil Liability

An eavesdropping victim can bring a civil action under Georgia's eavesdropping act. If the conduct in intercepting and disclosing the victim's conversations rises to the requisite level of outrageousness, it will support an emotional distress claim.

Part III
CRIMINAL CODE OF GEORGIA, CRIMINAL PROCEDURE AND MISCELLANEOUS CRIMINAL PROVISIONS

TITLE 3

ALCOHOLIC BEVERAGES

CHAPTER 2

STATE ADMINISTRATION AND ENFORCEMENT

Article 2

Article 2

Enforcement

§ 3–2–30. Powers and duties of special agents and enforcement officers of department

(a) Persons appointed by the commissioner as special agents or enforcement officers of the department, in the enforcement of this title and other laws of this state with respect to the manufacture, transportation, distribution, sale, storage, or possession of alcoholic beverages, shall have the authority throughout the state to:

(1) Obtain and execute warrants for arrest of persons charged with violations of such laws;

(2) Obtain and execute search warrants in the enforcement of such laws;

(3) Arrest without warrant any person violating such laws in the officer's presence or within his immediate knowledge when there is likely to be a failure of enforcement of such laws for want of a judicial officer to issue a warrant;

(4) Make investigations in the enforcement of such laws and, in connection with the investigations, to go upon any property outside of buildings, posted or otherwise, in the performance of official duties;

(5) Seize and take possession of all property which is declared contraband under such laws; and

(6) Carry firearms while performing their duties.

(b) Each special agent or enforcement officer shall file with the commissioner a public official's bond in the amount of $1,000.00, the cost of which shall be paid by the department.

(c) Nothing in this title shall be construed so as to relieve any special agent or enforcement officer, after making an arrest, from the duties imposed generally to obtain a warrant promptly and, without undue delay, to return arrested persons before a person authorized to examine, commit, or receive bail, as required by general law.

(d) After an agent or enforcement officer has accumulated 25 years of service with the department, upon leaving the department under honorable conditions, such agent or enforcement officer shall be entitled as part of such officer's compensation to retain his or her weapon and badge pursuant to regulations promulgated by the commissioner.

(e) As used in this subsection, the term "disability" means a disability that prevents an individual from working as a law enforcement officer. When a special agent or an enforcement officer leaves the department as a result of a disability arising in the line of duty, such special agent or an enforcement officer shall be entitled as part of such officer's compensation to retain his or her weapon and badge in accordance with regulations promulgated by the commissioner.

Laws 1963, p. 135, §§ 1, 2; Laws 1980, p. 1573, § 1; Laws 1981, p. 1269, § 12; Laws 1996, p. 1074, § 1; Laws 2004, Act 784, § 1, eff. July 1, 2004; Laws 2005, Act 19, § 3, eff. April 7, 2005.

Formerly Code 1933, § 5A–350.

Historical and Statutory Notes

The 2004 amendment by Act 784 added subsec. (e).

The 2005 amendment by Act 19 was a provision contained in a correction bill.

§ 3–2–31. Assistance by enforcement officers to local authorities in criminal cases

(a) Upon a request by the governing authority of any municipality or county, the sheriff or chief of a county police force, the judge of the superior court of any county, or the Governor, the commissioner, in unusual circumstances, may and, in the case of an order from the Governor, shall direct special agents and enforcement officers of the department to render assistance in:

(1) Any criminal case;

(2) The prevention of violations of law; or

(3) Detecting and apprehending those violating any criminal laws of this state, any other state, or the United States.

(b) This Code section shall not apply solely to agents who enforce this title but shall apply to all agents of the department with law enforcement powers.

Laws 1978, p. 1490, § 1; Laws 1980, p. 1573, § 1.

Formerly Code 1933, § 5A–351.

§ 3–2–32. Agents authorized to enter premises to enforce provisions of title

The commissioner and his agents may enter upon the licensed premises of any person engaged in the manufacture, transportation, distribution, sale, storage, or possession of alcoholic beverages at any time for the purpose of inspecting the premises and enforcing this title and shall have access during the inspection to all books, records, and supplies relating to the manufacture, transportation, distribution, sale, storage, or possession of alcoholic beverages.

Laws 1937–38, Ex. Sess., p. 103, § 8; Laws 1977, p. 1316, § 1; Laws 1980, p. 1573, § 1.

Formerly Code 1933, § 58–817; Code 1933, § 5A–352.

§ 3–2–33. Untaxed alcoholic beverages declared contraband; seizure; disposition

(a) Except as otherwise specifically provided for by law, it is unlawful for any person to sell, possess, conceal, store, or convey any alcoholic beverage on which any tax or license fee imposed by this title has not been paid.

(b) Any peace officer or authorized agent of the commissioner shall declare as contraband any alcoholic beverage:

(1) Not reported for collection of taxes under a reporting system established by the commissioner;

(2) Found in any county, municipality, or unincorporated area of any county where the sale of alcoholic beverages is not lawful when the alcoholic beverage is intended for use or sale contrary to law; or

(3) Sold, conveyed, or possessed, concealed, stored, or held for sale by any person who has not first obtained all licenses required by this title.

(c) Except as otherwise provided in this title, all contraband alcoholic beverages seized shall be immediately delivered to the commissioner or to persons designated by him to receive the contraband alcoholic beverages.

Laws 1980, p. 1573, § 1; Laws 1981, p. 1269, § 14; Laws 1985, p. 1118, § 1; Laws 2006, Act 510, § 5, eff. July 1, 2006.

Formerly Code 1933, § 5A–354.

Historical and Statutory Notes

The 2006 amendment by Act 510, in par. (b)(1), deleted "bearing the required tax stamps or markings as provided by this title or not" following "Not".

§ 3–2–34. Disposition of contraband alcoholic beverages

(a) All alcoholic beverages upon which no taxes have been paid to this state or any other state and which are not specifically exempt from the taxes imposed by law shall be destroyed by the peace officer or agent of the commissioner seizing the beverages, except that a small quantity of the illicit alcoholic beverage may be retained for purposes of evidence in the proper court; and then the illicit alcoholic beverage shall be destroyed immediately.

(b) All contraband alcoholic beverages upon which the taxes have been paid either to this state or to any other state shall be either destroyed or sold at public sale as provided by law.

Laws 1980, p. 1573, § 1; Laws 1981, p. 1269, § 15.

Formerly Code 1933, § 5A–355.

§ 3–2–35. Seizure and disposition of contraband, generally

(a) The commissioner and his agents shall seize and take possession of any contraband found in the possession of any person in violation of this title.

(b) Upon seizure, the commissioner or his agent shall give a receipt to the person from whom the contraband property was seized, if known, identifying the property seized and indicating from whom seized and the place of seizure.

(c) A copy of the receipt shall be:

(1) Filed in the office of the commissioner and shall be a public record open to public inspection; and

(2) Posted at the courthouse of the county in which the contraband was seized.

(d) Any person desiring to make claim to the contraband property shall file a claim with the commissioner at his office in Atlanta within ten days from the day of seizure. The commissioner, within 30 days of receipt of any such claim, shall afford the claimant a hearing in which to show his entitlement to the seized items. The burden of proof at such hearing shall be upon the claimant to establish his claim to the items seized and to show compliance with or justification for noncompliance with this Code section. The commissioner shall enter a written order granting or denying the claim within 30 days from the date of the hearing.

(e) An appeal from the commissioner's order may be taken to the Superior Court of Fulton County by filing with the commissioner, within 15 days from the date of the decision, a notice of appeal to the Superior Court of Fulton County. The appeal shall be based upon the record made before the commissioner; and the commissioner, upon the filing of a notice of appeal, shall transmit the record and appropriate documents to the superior court within 30 days from the date of the filing of notice of appeal. The superior court shall review the record for errors of law, violation of constitutional or statutory provisions, violation of the statutory authority of the agency, lawfulness of the procedure, lack of any evidence to support the decision, and arbitrariness and abuse of discretion. However, the court shall not substitute its judgment for that of the hearing officer as to the weight of evidence on questions of fact.

(f) All alcoholic beverages upon which the taxes have been paid to either this state or any other state shall be disposed of as follows:

(1) In the case of malt beverage, the seized goods shall be destroyed by the commissioner or his authorized agent;

(2) In the case of wine, the seized goods shall be sold by the commissioner at public sale, except that, where seized wine is determined by the commissioner to be unfit for human consumption, it shall be destroyed;

(3) In the case of distilled spirits, the seized goods shall be sold by the commissioner at public sale, except that, where seized distilled spirits are determined by the commissioner to be unfit for human consumption, the distilled spirits shall be destroyed.

(g) This Code section shall not apply to unlawfully manufactured alcoholic beverages.

Laws 1980, p. 1573, § 1; Laws 1981, p. 1269, § 16; Laws 1982, p. 3, § 3.

Formerly Code 1933, § 5A–356.

§ 3–2–36. Prosecution of violators of liquor laws

The commissioner or his agents shall secure warrants or other criminal process against any person who violates any provision of this title in counties and municipalities where the sale of alcoholic beverages is not authorized and in counties and municipalities where the sale of alcoholic beverages is authorized but where the alcoholic beverages are being sold contrary to law. The commissioner or his agents shall prosecute such offenders.

Laws 1937–38, Ex. Sess., p. 103, § 17; Laws 1972, p. 207, § 8; Laws 1980, p. 1573, § 1; Laws 1981, p. 1269, § 13.

Formerly Code 1933, § 5A–353.

CHAPTER 3

REGULATION OF ALCOHOLIC BEVERAGES GENERALLY

Article 2

Article 3

Article 2

Prohibited Acts

§ 3–3–20. Sale of alcoholic beverages on Sundays and election days prohibited; exceptions

(a) Except as provided in subsection (d) of this Code section or except as specifically authorized by law, no person knowingly and intentionally shall sell or offer to sell alcoholic beverages on Sunday.

(b)(1) As used in this subsection, the term "day" means that period of time beginning with the opening of the polls and ending with the closing of the polls.

(2)(A) Except as provided in subparagraph (B) of this paragraph and paragraph (3) of this subsection, in any county or municipality in which the sale of alcoholic beverages is authorized, the sale of alcoholic beverages in compliance with such authorization shall be authorized and legal on any election day.

(B) The local governing authority of any county in which the sale of alcoholic beverages is authorized and the local governing authority of any municipality in which the sale of alcoholic beverages is authorized may, by ordinance, prohibit the sale of alcoholic beverages on any election days. In any case where the governing authority of a county or municipality has passed an ordinance prohibiting the sale of alcoholic beverages on any election days as authorized by this subparagraph, such prohibition shall apply only within the territorial boundaries for which the election is held but such territorial boundaries shall not include any property owned or operated by a county, municipality, or other political subdivision of this state for airport purposes if no person resides on such publicly owned or operated property.

(3)(A) Notwithstanding any other provisions of this subsection, it shall be unlawful for any person to sell alcoholic beverages within 250 feet of any polling place or of the outer edge of any building within which such polling place is established on primary or election days.

(B) Any person violating the provisions of this paragraph shall be guilty of a misdemeanor.

(c) The governing authority of any county or municipality may, by ordinance or resolution, prohibit the sale of alcoholic beverages on Christmas Day.

(d)(1) In all municipalities within any county having a population of 400,000 or more according to the United States decennial census of 1990 or any future such census in which the sale of alcoholic beverages is lawful, alcoholic beverages may be sold on Sundays between the hours of 12:30 P.M. and 12:00 Midnight at festivals. As used in this paragraph, the term "festival" means a specific outdoor public celebration or gathering for which a license or permit has been issued by the appropriate governing authority which involves the use either of public parks or public streets and which includes entertainment, dancing, music, dramatic productions, art exhibition, parades, or the sale of merchandise, food or alcohol, or any combination of the foregoing; and which of necessity requires for its successful execution the provision and coordination of municipal services to a degree significantly over and above that which the city routinely provides under ordinary everyday circumstances. The definition of "festival," as used in this paragraph, does not include events which are solely parades, foot races, or political demonstrations unless such parade, foot race, or political demonstration is proposed as an integral part of a larger "festival," as defined in this paragraph.

(2) Notwithstanding the provisions of this subsection, all persons and entities selling alcoholic beverages pursuant to this subsection shall fully comply with all other applicable state and local license and permit requirements.

Laws 1937, p. 148, §§ 6, 7; Laws 1937–38, Ex. Sess., p. 103, § 14; Laws 1971, p. 864, § 1; Laws 1972, p. 721, § 1; Laws 1977, p. 1236, § 1; Laws 1977, p. 1316, § 1; Laws 1980, p. 1573, § 1; Laws 1981, p. 460, § 1; Laws 1981, p. 1269, § 19; Laws 1982, p. 890, § 1; Laws 1984, p. 1688, § 1; Laws 1985, p. 1508, § 1; Laws 1986, p. 10, § 3; Laws 1992, p. 1694, § 1; Laws 2000, p. 1405, § 1.

Formerly Code 1933, § 58–813; Code 1933, § 5A–507.

§ 3–3–21. Sales of alcoholic beverages near church, school, or housing authority property; prohibitions

(a)(1) No person knowingly and intentionally may sell or offer to sell:

(A) Any distilled spirits in or within 100 yards of any church building or within 200 yards of any school building, educational building, school grounds, or college campus;

(B) Any wine or malt beverages within 100 yards of any school building, school grounds, or college campus. This subparagraph shall not apply at any location for which a license has been issued prior to July 1, 1981, nor to the renewal of such license. Nor shall this subparagraph apply at any location for which a new license is applied for if the sale of wine and beer was lawful at such location at any time during the 12 months immediately preceding such application;

(C) Any distilled spirits, wine, or malt beverages within 100 yards of an alcoholic treatment center owned and operated by this state or any county or municipal government therein. This paragraph shall not apply to any business having a license in effect on July 1, 1981.

(2) As used in this subsection, the term "school building" or "educational building" shall apply only to state, county, city, or church school buildings and to such buildings at such other schools in which are taught subjects commonly taught in the common schools and colleges of this state and which are public schools or private schools as defined in subsection (b) of Code Section 20–2–690.

(b) Nothing contained in this Code section shall prohibit the licensing of the sale or distribution of alcoholic beverages by:

(1) Hotels of 50 rooms or more which have been in continuous operation for a period of at least five years preceding July 1, 1981;

(2) Bona fide private clubs, owning their own homes, subject to licensing under Chapter 7 of this title; and

(3) Licensees for the retail sale of alcoholic beverages for consumption on the premises only who shall be subject to regulation as to distances from churches, schools, and colleges by counties and municipalities.

(c) For purposes of this Code section, distances shall be measured by the most direct route of travel on the ground.

(d)(1) In counties having a population of not less than 175,000 nor more than 195,000, according to the United States decennial census of 1970 or any future such census, the distances provided in subparagraph (a)(1)(A) of this Code section for separation of businesses licensed under this title from churches and schools shall be measured as follows:

(A) From the property line of the tract on which is located the business regulated under this title;

(B) To the property line of the tract on which is located the church, school ground, or college campus; and

(C) Along a straight line which describes the shortest distance between the two property lines.

(2) No license in effect on April 13, 1979, shall be revoked before its date of expiration by reason of the method of measurement set out in this subsection if the license was granted in reliance on another method of measurement. No application for a license or for a renewal shall be denied by reason of the method of measurement set out in this subsection if the application is for premises for which a license was granted prior to April 13, 1979, in reliance on another method of measurement.

(e)(1) As used in this subsection, the term "housing authority property" means any property containing 300 housing units or fewer owned or operated by a housing authority created by Article 1 of Chapter 3 of Title 8, the "Housing Authorities Law."

(2) No person knowingly and intentionally may sell any alcoholic beverages for consumption on the premises within 100 yards of any housing authority property. This subsection shall not apply at any location for which a license has been issued prior to July 1, 2000, nor to the renewal of such license. Nor shall this subsection apply at any location for which a new license is applied for if the sale of alcoholic beverages for consumption on the premises was lawful at such location at any time during the 12 months immediately preceding such application.

Laws 1808, Cobb's 1851 Digest, p. 851; Laws 1890–91, p. 132, § 1; Laws 1935, p. 73, § 15B; Laws 1937, p. 148, § 2; Laws 1937–38, Ex. Sess., p. 103, § 9; Laws 1945, p. 447, §§ 1, 2; Laws 1973, p. 610, § 1; Laws 1980, p. 1573, § 1; Laws 1981, p. 1265, § 1; Laws 1981, p. 1269, § 20; Laws 1998, p. 1300, § 2; Laws 1999, p. 81, § 3; Laws 2000, p. 1653, § 1.

Formerly Code 1863, § 4448; Code 1868, § 4490; Code 1873, § 4575; Code 1882, § 4575; Penal Code 1895, § 434; Penal Code 1910, § 435; Code 1933, § 58–601; Code 1933, § 5A–508.

§ 3–3–21.1. Possession of alcoholic beverages on public school grounds

(a) Except as provided in subsection (b) of this Code section, no person shall possess any alcoholic beverages upon the grounds or within any structure of a public elementary school; public high school; or public trade, vocational, or industrial school.

(b) Subsection (a) of this Code section shall not apply to any situation where alcoholic beverages are used by a teacher for educational purposes nor to any situation where alcoholic beverages are used in a religious ceremony or observance.

Laws 1981, p. 625, § 1.

Formerly Code 1933, § 5A–508.1.

§ 3–3–22. Furnishing alcoholic beverages to intoxicated persons

No alcoholic beverage shall be sold, bartered, exchanged, given, provided, or furnished to any person who is in a state of noticeable intoxication.

Laws 1937–38, Ex. Sess., p. 103, § 15; Laws 1953, Nov.-Dec. Sess., p. 283, § 1; Laws 1980, p. 1206, §§ 2, 5; Laws 1980, p. 1573, § 1; Laws 1981, p. 1269, § 21.

Formerly Code 1933, § 5A–509.

§ 3–3–23. Furnishing alcoholic beverages to, and purchase of alcoholic beverages by, persons under 21 years of age prohibited; possession of alcoholic beverages by persons under 21 years of age prohibited; exceptions; proper identification; procedure where false identification tendered

(a) Except as otherwise authorized by law:

(1) No person knowingly, directly or through another person, shall furnish, cause to be furnished, or permit any person in such person's employ to furnish any alcoholic beverage to any person under 21 years of age;

(2) No person under 21 years of age shall purchase, attempt to purchase, or knowingly possess any alcoholic beverage;

(3) No person under 21 years of age shall misrepresent such person's age in any manner whatever for the purpose of obtaining illegally any alcoholic beverage;

(4) No person knowingly or intentionally shall act as an agent to purchase or acquire any alcoholic beverage for or on behalf of a person under 21 years of age; or

(5) No person under 21 years of age shall misrepresent his or her identity or use any false identification for the purpose of purchasing or obtaining any alcoholic beverage.

(b) The prohibitions contained in paragraphs (1), (2), and (4) of subsection (a) of this Code section shall not apply with respect to the sale, purchase, or possession of alcoholic beverages for consumption:

(1) For medical purposes pursuant to a prescription of a physician duly authorized to practice medicine in this state; or

(2) At a religious ceremony.

(c) The prohibitions contained in paragraphs (1), (2), and (4) of subsection (a) of this Code section shall not apply with respect to the possession of alcoholic beverages for consumption by a person under 21 years of age when the parent or guardian of the person under 21 years of age gives the alcoholic beverage to the person and when possession is in the home of the parent or guardian and such parent or guardian is present.

(d) The prohibition contained in paragraph (1) of subsection (a) of this Code section shall not apply with respect to sale of alcoholic beverages by a person when such person has been furnished with proper identification showing that the person to whom the alcoholic beverage is sold is 21 years of age or older. For purposes of this subsection, the term "proper identification" means any document issued by a governmental agency containing a description of the person, such person's photograph, or both, and giving such person's date of birth and includes, without being limited to, a passport, military identification card, driver's license, or an identification card authorized under Code Sections 40–5–100 through 40–5–104. "Proper identification" shall not include a birth certificate and shall not include any traffic citation and complaint form.

(e) If such conduct is not otherwise prohibited pursuant to Code Section 3–3–24, nothing contained in this Code section shall be construed to prohibit any person under 21 years of age from:

(1) Dispensing, serving, selling, or handling alcoholic beverages as a part of employment in any licensed establishment;

(2) Being employed in any establishment in which alcoholic beverages are distilled or manufactured; or

(3) Taking orders for and having possession of alcoholic beverages as a part of employment in a licensed establishment.

(f) Testimony by any person under 21 years of age, when given in an administrative or judicial proceeding against another person for violation of any provision of this Code section, shall not be used in any administrative or judicial proceedings brought against such testifying person under 21 years of age.

(g) Nothing in this Code section shall be construed to modify, amend, or supersede Chapter 11 of Title 15.

(h) In any case where a reasonable or prudent person could reasonably be in doubt as to whether or not the person to whom an alcoholic beverage is to be sold or otherwise furnished is actually 21 years of age or older, it shall be the duty of the person selling or otherwise furnishing such alcoholic beverage to request to see and to be furnished with proper identification as provided for in subsection (d) of this Code section in order to verify the age of such person; and the failure to make such request and verification in any case where the person to whom the alcoholic beverage is sold or otherwise furnished is less than 21 years of age may be considered by the trier of fact in determining whether the person selling or otherwise furnishing such alcoholic beverage did so knowingly.

(i) Any retailer or retail consumption dealer, or any person acting on behalf of such retailer or retail consumption dealer, who upon requesting proper identification from a person attempting to purchase alcoholic beverages from such retailer or retail consumption dealer pursuant to subsection (h) of this Code section is tendered a driver's license which indicates that such driver's license is falsified, is not the driver's license of the person presenting it, or that such person is under the age of 21 years, the person to whom said license is tendered shall be authorized to either write down the name, address, and license number or to seize and retain such driver's license and in either event shall immediately thereafter summon a law enforcement officer who shall be authorized to seize the license either at the scene or at such time as the license can be located. The procedures and rules connected with the retention of such license by the officer shall be the same as those provided for the acceptance of a driver's license as bail on arrest for traffic offenses pursuant to Code Section 17–6–11.

Laws 1981, p. 1269, § 22; Laws 1985, p. 753, §§ 1, 3; Laws 1985, p. 782, §§ 1, 2; Laws 1986, p. 789, §§ 1, 2; Laws 1988, p. 1372, § 1; Laws 1989, p. 1227, § 1; Laws 1997, p. 1085, § 1.

Formerly Code 1933, § 5A–510.

§ 3–3–23.1. Unlawful sale of alcoholic beverages to, and unlawful purchase and possession of alcoholic beverages by, any person under 21 years of age

(a) It is unlawful for any person knowingly to violate any prohibition contained in Code Section 3–3–23, relating to furnishing alcoholic beverages to, and purchasing, attempting to purchase, and possession of alcoholic beverages by, a person under 21 years of age.

(b)(1) Any person convicted of violating any prohibition contained in subsection (a) of Code Section 3–3–23 shall, upon the first conviction, be guilty of a misdemeanor, except that any person convicted of violating paragraph (2) of subsection (a) of Code Section 3–3–23 shall, upon the first conviction, be guilty of a misdemeanor and shall be punished by not more than six months' imprisonment or a fine of not more than $300.00, or both and except that any person convicted of violating paragraph (4) of subsection (a) of Code Section 3–3–23 shall, upon the first conviction, be guilty of a misdemeanor of a high and aggravated nature.

(2) Any person convicted of violating any prohibition contained in subsection (a) of Code Section 3–3–23 shall, upon the second or subsequent conviction, be guilty of a misdemeanor of a high and aggravated nature, except that any person convicted of violating paragraph (2) of subsection (a) of Code Section 3–3–23 shall, upon the second or subsequent conviction, be guilty of a misdemeanor.

(3) In addition to any other penalty provided for in paragraphs (1) and (2) of this subsection, the driver's license of any person convicted of attempting to purchase an alcoholic beverage in violation of paragraph (2) of subsection (a) of Code Section 3–3–23 upon the first conviction shall be suspended for six months and upon the second or subsequent conviction shall be suspended for one year.

(c) Whenever any person who has not been previously convicted of any offense under this Code section or under any other law of the United States or this or any other state relating to alcoholic beverages pleads guilty to or is found guilty of a violation of paragraph (2) or (3) of subsection (a) of Code Section 3–3–23, the court, without entering a judgment of guilt and with the consent of such person, may defer further proceedings and place such person on probation upon such reasonable terms and conditions as the court may require. The terms of probation shall preferably be such as require the person to undergo a comprehensive rehabilitation program (including, if necessary, medical treatment), not to exceed three years, designed to acquaint such person with the ill effects of alcohol abuse and with knowledge of the gains and benefits which can be achieved by being a good member of society. Upon violation of a term or condition of probation, the court may enter an adjudication of guilt and proceed accordingly. Upon fulfillment of the terms and conditions of probation, the court shall discharge such person and dismiss the proceedings against him or her. Discharge and dismissal under this subsection shall be without court adjudication of guilt and shall not be deemed a conviction for purposes of this subsection or for purposes of disqualifications or disabilities imposed by law upon conviction of a crime. Discharge and dismissal under this subsection may occur only once with respect to any person.

(d) Unless the officer has reasonable cause to believe such person is intoxicated, a law enforcement officer may arrest by issuance of a citation, summons, or accusation a person accused of violating any provision of Code Section 3–3–23. The citation, summons, or accusation shall enumerate the specific charges against the person and either the date upon which the person is to appear and answer the charges or a notation that the person will be later notified of the date upon which the person is to appear and answer the charges. If the person charged shall fail to appear as required, the judge having jurisdiction of the offense may issue a warrant or other order directing the apprehension of such person and commanding that such person be brought before the court to answer the charges contained within the citation, summons, or accusation and the charge of his or her failure to appear as required. Nothing in this subsection shall be construed to invalidate an otherwise valid arrest by citation, summons, or accusation of a person who is intoxicated.

(e) A law enforcement officer arresting a person by the issuance of a citation, summons, or accusation under subsection (d) of this Code section may require any such person having a driver's license or instruction permit to deposit such license or permit with the arresting officer in order to ensure the appearance of such person to answer the charges against him or her. The procedures and rules connected with the acceptance of such license or permit and subsequent disposition of the case shall be the same as provided for the acceptance of a driver's license as bail on arrest for traffic offenses pursuant to Code Section 17–6–11.

(f) In addition to any other punishment or sentence, the court may order all persons convicted under subsection (b) of this Code section or sentenced under subsection (c) of this Code section to complete a DUI Alcohol or Drug Use Risk Reduction Program prescribed by the Department of Driver Services within 120 days of such conviction or sentence. Failure to complete such program within 120 days shall be contempt of court and shall be punished by a fine of not more than $300.00 or 20 days imprisonment, or both. If the conviction or sentence results from a charge of unlawful possession of alcoholic beverages while operating a motor vehicle, the court shall report such conviction or sentence to the Department of Driver Services within ten days after conviction or sentencing.

Laws 1981, p. 862, § 3; Laws 1981, p. 1269, § 64; Laws 1982, p. 3, § 3; Laws 1985, p. 753, §§ 2, 4; Laws 1985, p. 782, § 3; Laws 1992, p. 2746, § 1; Laws 1997, p. 1085, § 2; Laws 1998, p. 1106, § 1; Laws 2002, p. 415, § 3; Laws 2005, Act 68, § 2–1, eff. July 1, 2005; Laws 2006, Act 510, § 7, eff. July 1, 2006.

Formerly Code 1933, § 5A–9901.1.

Historical and Statutory Notes

The 2005 amendment by Act 68, in subsec. (f), substituted "Department of Driver Services" for "Department of Human Resources" in the first sentence and "Department of Driver Services" for "Department of Motor Vehicle Safety" in the second sentence.

The 2006 amendments by Act 510, in subsec. (d), substituted "any provision" for "only paragraph (2) of subsection (a)"; and in subsecs. (d) and (e), inserted ", summons, or accusation" following "citation" throughout.

§ 3–3–24. Persons under 18 years of age not to be allowed or required to serve, sell, or take orders for alcoholic beverages; exceptions

(a) No person shall allow or require a person in his employment under 18 years of age to dispense, serve, sell, or take orders for any alcoholic beverages.

(b) This Code section shall not prohibit persons under 18 years of age who are employed in supermarkets, convenience stores, breweries, or drugstores from selling or handling alcoholic beverages which are sold for consumption off the premises.

Laws 1958, p. 640, §§ 1, 2; Laws 1974, p. 460, § 1; Laws 1976, p. 409, § 1; Laws 1980, p. 1573, § 1; Laws 1981, p. 1269, § 22.

Formerly Code 1933, § 5A–510; Code 1933, § 5A–511.

§ 3–3–24.1. Definition; penalty

(a) For purposes of this Code section, the term "business establishment primarily engaged in the retail sale of alcoholic beverages in unbroken packages" means an individual, partnership, corporation, association, or other business entity which derives from its retail sale of alcoholic beverages in unbroken packages at least 75 percent of its total annual gross income.

(b) Reserved.

(c) Any person violating this Code section shall be guilty of a misdemeanor, except that the violation of this Code section by a person under 17 years of age shall constitute a delinquent act under Chapter 11 of Title 15 and not a misdemeanor.

Laws 1981, p. 1269, § 25; Laws 1982, p. 3, § 3; Laws 1994, p. 237, § 2.

Formerly Code 1933, § 5A–519.

§ 3–3–24.2. Posting of laws concerning sales to underage persons; contents of notice; punitive action against violators

(a) Each retail business establishment in this state which is licensed to sell alcoholic beverages of any kind shall post in a conspicuous place or places a notice which shall contain the provisions of the laws of this state which deal with the unlawful sale of such items to underage persons and the penalties for violating such laws.

(b) The department shall prepare, print, and distribute the notices required by subsection (a) of this Code section. The notices shall contain those provisions of the law of this state which the department determines will best inform the citizens of this state of the relevant provisions of the law regarding sale of alcoholic beverages to underage persons.

(c) The commissioner may take punitive action against violators, up to and including revocation of the state retail dealer's license of any retail business establishment which fails to comply with this Code section. The undertaking of any punitive action allowed under this Code section shall not prohibit criminal prosecution for sale to underage persons.

Laws 1981, p. 1269, § 26.

Formerly Code 1933, § 5A–520.

§ 3–3–25. Furnishing alcoholic beverages to prisoners or inmates of places of confinement and possession on grounds or within 200 yards of certain buildings prohibited; exceptions

(a) No person knowingly and intentionally shall:

(1) Offer for sale, sell, barter, exchange, give, provide, or furnish alcoholic beverages to:

(A) Any person confined in any jail, penal institution, correctional facility, or other lawful place of confinement; or

(B) Any person who is a patient or lawful inmate of the Central State Hospital;

(2) Offer for sale any alcoholic beverages within 200 yards of any building of the Central State Hospital which was in existence on July 1, 1977; or

(3) Introduce or possess any alcoholic beverages upon the grounds of the Central State Hospital or in the buildings of the Georgia War Veterans Home.

(b) Nothing contained in this Code section shall prevent or prohibit:

(1) The administration of alcohol by the staff of the above-mentioned institutions to any prisoner, patient, or lawful inmate in strict compliance with the prescription of a licensed physician; or

(2) The staff members of the Central State Hospital and the Georgia War Veterans Home who maintain their domicile on the grounds of these institutions from possessing alcoholic beverages for their own consumption or for that of their families or persons invited to their homes, except patients or lawful inmates of these institutions.

(c) No person shall knowingly allow any other person to violate this Code section.

Laws 1874, p. 92, § 1; Laws 1875, p. 328, § 1; Laws 1977, p. 183, § 1; Laws 1977, p. 1247, § 1; Laws 1980, p. 1573, § 1.

Formerly Code 1882, § 1374a; Penal Code 1895, § 437; Penal Code 1910, § 437; Code 1933, § 58–607; Code 1933, § 5A–512.

§ 3–3–26. Breaking of package on the premises

No retail dealer shall knowingly and intentionally allow or permit the breaking of any package or packages containing alcoholic beverages on the premises where sold or allow or permit the drinking of the contents of such package or packages on the premises where sold. This Code section shall not apply with respect to sales pursuant to a license for consumption on the premises.

Laws 1937–38, Ex. Sess., p. 103, § 9; Laws 1980, p. 1573, § 1.

Formerly Code 1933, § 5A–513.

§ 3–3–27. Prohibitions on distillation, manufacture, making, transporting, shipping, receiving, or possessing of alcoholic beverages; failure to file proper reports or bond, pay tax or license fees, prohibited; stills to be destroyed; penalties

(a) No person knowingly and intentionally shall:

(1) Distill, manufacture, or make any distilled spirits, except as permitted by this title;

(2) Manufacture, make, brew, or ferment any malt beverages or wine, except as permitted by this title;

(3) Transport, ship, receive, possess, sell, offer to sell, distribute, or in any manner use any alcoholic beverages or alcohol, except as permitted by this title;

(4) Fail to file any report required by this title;

(5) File any report required by this title that is either intentionally false or fraudulent, or both;

(6) Fail to pay any tax or license fee imposed or authorized by this title unless specifically exempted from such payment;

(7) Fail to have a sufficient bond filed with the commissioner as required by this title; or

(8) Evade or violate, or conspire to evade or violate, any provision of this title.

(b) Any apparatus, article, or other tangible personal property used in the unlawful distillation, manufacture, or making of any alcoholic beverages is declared contraband and shall be destroyed by the officers or agents seizing the property or otherwise disposed of as the commissioner directs.

(c) Any person who violates the provisions of:

(1) Paragraph (1) of subsection (a) of this Code section shall be guilty of a felony and, upon conviction thereof, shall be punished by imprisonment for not less than one year nor more than five years;

(2) Paragraphs (2) through (8) of subsection (a) of this Code section shall be guilty of a misdemeanor.

Laws 1980, p. 1573, § 1; Laws 1981, p. 1269, § 65.

Formerly Code 1933, §§ 5A–514, 5A–9902.

§ 3–3–27.1. Transportation of alcoholic beverages into State; report to commissioner

Except with respect to alcoholic beverages lawfully possessed pursuant to Code Section 3–3–8, no person, common carrier, or contract carrier shall transport any alcoholic beverage into this state unless such transportation is immediately reported to the commissioner. Each such report shall show the consignor and consignee, the quantity delivered, and such other information as required by the commissioner.

Laws 1981, p. 1269, § 23.

Formerly Code 1933, § 5A–514.1.

§ 3–3–28. Repealed by Laws 2005, Act 96, § 1, eff. July 1, 2005

Historical and Statutory Notes

Repealed § 3–3–28, prohibiting the reuse, counterfeiting, or forging of tax stamps, was derived from Laws 1937-38, Ex. Sess., p. 103, § 11; Laws 1980, p. 1573, § 1; Code 1933, § 5A–515. The repealing law also reserved the section designation.

§ 3–3–29. Possession, sale, or purchase of unstamped distilled spirits

Except as otherwise expressly provided for by law, no person knowingly and intentionally shall possess, sell, or purchase any distilled spirits upon which the taxes imposed by this title have not been paid.

Laws 1937–38, Ex. Sess., p. 103, § 11; Laws 1980, p. 1573, § 1; Laws 1993, p. 464, § 1.

Formerly Code 1933, § 5A–516.

§ 3–3–30. Foreign trade zones

(a) Any provision of this title to the contrary notwithstanding, any public or private corporation which has been granted the privilege of establishing, operating, and maintaining a foreign trade zone by the Foreign Trade Zones Board in accordance with an act of Congress, approved June 18, 1934, entitled "An Act to provide for the establishment, operation and maintenance of foreign trade zones in ports of entry of the United States, to expedite and encourage foreign commerce and for other purposes,"[1] may store alcoholic beverages, until the termination of such privilege, within the boundaries of such foreign trade zone. Any public or private corporation which has been granted the privilege of establishing, operating, or maintaining a foreign trade zone may also distribute alcoholic beverages to destinations outside this state.

(b) Nothing contained in this Code section shall authorize the sale at retail of any alcoholic beverages within the boundaries of a foreign trade zone if the sale would otherwise be prohibited by the laws of this state.

Laws 1981, p. 1269, § 24.

Formerly Code 1933, § 5A–518.

[1] Foreign Trade Zones Act, 19 U.S.C.A. § 81a.

§ 3–3–31. Prohibition on shipment of alcoholic beverages by persons in another state or country to unauthorized persons in this state; legislative intent

The General Assembly finds, determines, and declares that the direct shipment of alcoholic beverages by persons in the business of selling alcoholic beverages in other states or countries to residents of this state in violation of this title poses a serious threat to the public health, safety, revenue, and the economy of Georgia. The General Assembly further finds, determines, and declares that the present penalties for illegal direct shipments of alcoholic beverages to residents of this state are inadequate to ensure compliance with the provisions of this title and that the measures provided for in Code Section 3–3–32 are fully consistent with the powers conferred upon the State of Georgia by the Twenty-first Amendment to the Constitution of the United States.

Laws 1997, p. 399, § 1; Laws 1998, p. 128, § 3.

§ 3–3–32. Penalty; exceptions

(a) Any person in the business of selling alcoholic beverages in another state or country who knowingly and intentionally ships or causes to be shipped any alcoholic beverages directly to any resident of this state who does not hold a valid manufacturer's, importer's, broker's, or wholesaler's license issued by the State of Georgia is in violation of this chapter.

(b) Any person found by the commissioner to be in violation of subsection (a) of this Code section shall be issued a cease and desist order by certified mail or statutory overnight delivery. Any person who, after receiving a cease and desist order, is found by the commissioner to be in violation of subsection (a) of this Code section for a second or subsequent occurrence, within a two-year period of the first violation, shall be guilty of a felony and, upon conviction thereof, shall be punished by a fine not to exceed $10,000.00. This subsection shall not apply to any person who has registered brands for sale with the commissioner pursuant to Code Section 3–4–152, 3–5–31 or 3–6–22 and who shall have current licenses and posted adequate surety bonds as required by this title; provided, however, violations of the provisions of subsection (a) of this Code section shall constitute grounds for the commissioner to take appropriate administrative action against such person, including suspension or cancellation of license and forfeiture of bonds.

(c) This Code section shall not apply to the direct shipment of sacramental alcoholic beverages to bona fide religious organizations as authorized by the commissioner.

Laws 1997, p. 399, § 1; Laws 1998, p. 128, § 3; Laws 2000, p. 1589, § 3.

§ 3–3–33. Vaporized forms of alcoholic beverages; alcohol vaporizing devices; misdemeanor violations

(a) As used in this Code section, the term:

(1) "Alcohol vaporizing device" means any device, machine, or process that mixes any alcoholic beverages with pure oxygen or other gas to produce a vaporized product for the purpose of consumption by inhalation.

(2) "Licensed premises" means any premises in which alcoholic beverages are sold or dispensed for consumption on the premises and shall include any premises which are required by law to be licensed to sell or dispense alcoholic beverages for consumption on the premises.

(3) "Operator" means an owner, license holder, operator, manager, or person in charge of any licensed premises.

(b)(1) No person shall purchase, offer for sale or use, sell, or use any vaporized form of an alcoholic beverage produced by an alcohol vaporizing device. This paragraph shall not apply to a product that contains alcohol as otherwise lawfully prescribed by a health care practitioner who is licensed under Title 43.

(2) No person shall own or possess any alcohol vaporizing device, including but not limited to any machine known as an Alcohol Without Liquid (AWOL) machine. This paragraph shall not apply to any nebulizer or atomizer used to supply a product that contains alcohol as otherwise lawfully prescribed by a health care practitioner who is licensed under Title 43.

(c) No operator shall keep or allow to be kept on the licensed premises thereof any vaporized form of an alcoholic beverage produced by an alcohol vaporizing device.

(d) Any person convicted of a violation of this Code section shall be guilty of a misdemeanor. Any person convicted of a violation of this Code section involving the offer for sale or use to a person under the age of 21 shall be guilty of a misdemeanor, except that upon the second or subsequent conviction such person so convicted shall be guilty of a misdemeanor of a high and aggravated nature.

Laws 2008, Act 499, § 1, eff. July 1, 2008.

Article 3

Prohibited Conduct on Licensed Premises

§ 3–3–40. Definitions

As used in this article, the term:

(1) "Licensed premises" means any premises in which alcoholic beverages are sold or dispensed for consumption on the premises and shall include any premises which are required by law to be licensed to sell or dispense alcoholic beverages for consumption on the premises.

(2) "Operator" means and includes the owner, license holder, operator, manager, and person in charge of any licensed premises.

Laws 1988, p. 212, § 1.

§ 3–3–41. Certain nude and sexual conduct, use of devices or objects to perform or simulate such conduct, and showing and displaying of pictures, etc., prohibited

(a) No person shall perform on licensed premises acts of or acts which constitute or simulate:

(1) Sexual intercourse, masturbation, sodomy, bestiality, oral copulation, flagellation, or any sexual acts which are prohibited by law;

(2) The touching, caressing, or fondling of the breast, buttocks, anus, or genitals; or

(3) The displaying of any portion of the female breast below the top of the areola or the displaying of any portion of any person's pubic hair, anus, cleft of the buttocks, vulva, or genitals.

(b) No person shall use on licensed premises artificial devices or inanimate objects to perform, simulate, or depict any of the prohibited conduct or activities described in subsection (a) of this Code section.

(c) It shall be unlawful for any person to show, display, or exhibit, on licensed premises, any film, still picture, electronic reproduction, or any other visual reproduction or image of any act or conduct described in subsection (a) or (b) of this Code section.

Laws 1988, p. 212, § 1.

§ 3–3–42. Solicitation of drinks by certain persons prohibited

It shall be unlawful for any person employed or working in any capacity in any licensed premises to solicit or encourage patrons to purchase drinks to be consumed by or otherwise disposed of by any such person so employed or working.

Laws 1988, p. 212, § 1.

§ 3–3–43. Permitting persons to view acts performed on other premises from the licensed premises prohibited

No operator shall knowingly permit any person in the licensed premises to view from the licensed premises, by glass partition or other artifice, an act or conduct described in Code Section 3–3–41 and performed on premises other than the licensed premises.

Laws 1988, p. 212, § 1.

§ 3–3–44. Permitting persons to remove alcoholic beverages to other premises for certain purposes prohibited

No operator shall knowingly permit any person to remove any alcoholic beverage sold or dispensed on the licensed premises to adjacent or other premises for the purpose of viewing any conduct or activity prohibited on the licensed premises by this article; provided, however, that this Code section shall not be applicable to a person who removes an alcoholic beverage to his home or place of abode.

Laws 1988, p. 212, § 1.

§ 3–3–45. Employing, encouraging, permitting, or assisting persons to engage in certain conduct prohibited

It shall be unlawful for any operator to employ, encourage, permit, or assist any person to engage in any conduct or activity in violation of this article.

Laws 1988, p. 212, § 1.

§ 3–3–46. Penalties

(a) The violation of any provision of this article by the operator of any licensed premises shall constitute grounds for the suspension and revocation of any and all alcoholic beverage licenses issued to such operator.

(b) Any person who violates any provision of this article shall be guilty of a misdemeanor of a high and aggravated nature.

Laws 1988, p. 212, § 1.

CHAPTER 5

MALT BEVERAGES

Article 1

General Provisions

§ 3–5–5. Conditions under which kegs of malt beverages may be sold at retail

(a) As used in this Code section, the term:

(1) "Keg" means any brewery-sealed container or barrel containing, by liquid volume, more than two gallons of malt beverage.

(2) "Retail dealer," "retail licensee," or "licensee" means a person holding either a retail dealer license, a permit issued by the commissioner authorizing the sale of alcoholic beverages for consumption only on the premises for a period not to exceed one day, or a beverage alcohol caterer license.

(b) No person licensed under this chapter shall sell malt beverages at retail by the keg except as provided in subsections (c), (d), and (e) of this Code section. The commissioner may take punitive action against violators, up to and including revocation of the state retail dealer's license of any licensed retail dealer who fails to comply with this Code section. The undertaking of any punitive action allowed under this Code section shall not prohibit criminal prosecution for sale to underage persons.

(c) Each retail licensee selling kegs containing malt beverages for consumption off licensed premises shall require each keg purchaser to present a Georgia driver's license or other proper identification at the time of purchase. The licensee shall record for each keg sale: the date of sale; the size of keg; the keg identification number; the amount of container deposit; the name; address; date of birth of the purchaser; and the form of identification presented by such purchaser. The purchaser shall sign a statement at the time of purchase attesting to the accuracy of the purchaser's name and address, the location where the contents of the keg will be consumed, and acknowledging that a violation of Code Section 3–3–23, as it relates to furnishing alcoholic beverages to persons under the age of 21 years, may result in civil liability, criminal prosecution, or both. The licensee shall retain the identification form and purchaser's signed statement attesting to the accuracy of the purchaser's name and address and acknowledging that a violation of Code Section 3–3–23, as it relates to furnishing alcoholic beverages to persons under the age of 21 years, may result in civil liability, criminal prosecution, or both, for a minimum of six months following the sale of the keg.

(d) Each keg sold at retail for consumption off licensed premises shall be labeled with the name and address of the retail licensee, the keg identification number, and the state alcohol license number of the business. The Department of Revenue will prescribe the form of registration label or tag to be used for this purpose. The registration label or tag shall be supplied by the Department of Revenue without fee and securely affixed to the keg by the licensee making the sale. In addition to the label or tag, the Department of Revenue shall provide guidelines to the licensee on the information to be recorded on the identification form required under subsection (c) of this Code section.

(e) The licensee shall record the date of return of the keg on the identification form required under subsection (c) of this Code section. If there is no label or tag affixed to the keg or if the identification number is not legible, the licensee shall indicate this fact on the identification form required under subsection (c) of this Code section. The licensee shall not refund a deposit for a keg that is returned without the required label or tag and identification number intact and legible.

(f) The removal of the required label shall be unlawful until such time that it is lawfully returned to the retailer by the purchaser. Possession of a keg without the required label and identification number shall be unlawful and subject to penalty pursuant to Code Section 3–3–9.

Laws 2001, p. 1100, § 1; Laws 2002, p. 415, § 3.

CHAPTER 10

SALE OR POSSESSION OF DISTILLED SPIRITS IN DRY COUNTIES AND MUNICIPALITIES

Section

§ 3–10–5. Allowing use of premises

It is unlawful for any person to permit the use of any premises which he owns or controls for the unlawful sale, manufacture, or other unlawful disposition of distilled spirits.

Laws 1915, Ex. Sess., p. 77, § 5; Laws 1980, p. 1573, § 1.

Formerly Code 1933, § 58–105; Code 1933, § 5A–7103.

§ 3–10–6. Forfeiture of rights of lessee or tenant

The unlawful manufacture, sale, or keeping for sale or disposition of any distilled spirits shall work, at the option of the landlord, a forfeiture of the rights of any lessee or tenant under any lease or contract for rent of the premises where the unlawful act is performed by the lessee or tenant or by any agent, servant, clerk, or employee of the lessee or tenant with the latter's knowledge or permission.

Laws 1915, Ex. Sess., p. 77, § 6; Laws 1980, p. 1573, § 1.

Formerly Code 1933, § 58–106; Code 1933, § 5A–7108.

TITLE 4

ANIMALS

CHAPTER 3

LIVESTOCK RUNNING AT LARGE OR STRAYING

§ 4–3–3. Livestock running at large prohibited

No owner shall permit livestock to run at large on or to stray upon the public roads of this state or any property not belonging to the owner of the livestock, except by permission of the owner of such property.

Laws 1953, Jan.-Feb. Sess., p. 380, § 3; Laws 1953, Nov.-Dec. Sess., p. 395, § 4.

§ 4–3–4. Duty of officers to impound; impounding by others

(a) It shall be the duty of the sheriff, his deputies, or any other county law enforcement officer to impound livestock found to be running at large or straying. Owners or operators of farms may also impound such livestock, provided that the livestock is kept in a suitable place and cared for properly; such owners or operators shall receive the feed and care fee allowed in Code Section 4–3–10.

(b) If an owner or operator of a farm impounds livestock, it shall be his duty to notify the owner of such livestock immediately. If the owner of the livestock is unknown and is not determined within three days, the person who impounds the livestock shall notify the sheriff of such impoundment; and the sheriff shall transport the livestock as soon as possible to a county pound as provided for in Code Section 4–3–11. The sheriff shall then follow the procedure set out in this chapter as if he had originally impounded such livestock.

Laws 1953, Jan.-Feb. Sess., p. 380, § 4; Laws 1953, Nov.-Dec. Sess., p. 395, § 5.

§ 4–3–12. Permitting livestock to run at large; releasing impounded livestock

Any owner of livestock who intentionally or knowingly permits the same to run at large or stray upon the public roads of this state or any property not belonging to the owner of the livestock unless by permission of the owner of such property, or any person who shall release livestock, after being impounded, without authority of the impounder, shall be guilty of a misdemeanor and, upon conviction thereof, shall be punished by imprisonment in the county jail not exceeding six months, or by fine not exceeding $500.00, or by both fine and imprisonment.

Laws 1953, Jan.-Feb. Sess., p. 380, § 12; Laws 1953, Nov.-Dec. Sess., p. 395, § 6.

CHAPTER 8

DOGS

Article 1

Article 1

General Provisions

§ 4–8–1. Dumping dead dog on property of another

No person shall intentionally abandon a dead dog on any private property belonging to another unless the person so doing shall have first obtained permission from the owner of the property on which the dog is being left and the provisions of Code Section 4–5–3 are complied with in full.

Laws 1969, p. 831, § 1.

§ 4–8–2. Dumping dead dog on public property or public right-of-way

No person shall abandon a dead dog on any public property or public right of way unless the place in which the dog is being left is a public dump or other facility designed for receiving such and has been designated by the local governmental authorities as a public facility for receiving trash or refuse and the provisions of Code Section 4–5–3 are complied with in full.

Laws 1969, p. 831, § 2.

§ 4–8–3. Abandoning dogs

No person shall release a dog on any property, public or private, with the intention of abandoning the dog.

Laws 1969, p. 831, § 3.

§ 4–8–4. Liability for damage done by dogs

(a) The owner or, if no owner can be found, the custodian exercising care and control over any dog which goes upon the land of another and causes injury, death, or damage directly or indirectly to any livestock or poultry shall be civilly liable to the owner of the livestock or poultry for damages, death, or injury caused by the dog. The liability of the owner or custodian of the dog shall include consequential damages.

(b) This Code section is to be considered cumulative of other remedies provided by law. There is no intent to do away with or limit other causes of action which might inure to the owner of any livestock or poultry.

Laws 1969, p. 831, § 4.

§ 4–8–5. Performing cruel acts on, or harming, maiming or killing dogs

(a) No person shall perform a cruel act on any dog; nor shall any person harm, maim, or kill any dog, or attempt to do so, except that a person may:

(1) Defend his person or property, or the person or property of another, from injury or damage being caused by a dog; or

(2) Kill any dog causing injury or damage to any livestock or poultry.

(b) The method used for killing the dog shall be designed to be as humane as is possible under the circumstances. A person who humanely kills a dog under the circumstances indicated in subsection (a) of this Code section shall incur no liability for such death.

(c) This Code section shall not be construed to limit in any way the authority or duty of any law enforcement officer, dog or rabies control officer, humane society, or veterinarian.

Laws 1969, p. 831, § 5.

§ 4–8–6. Permitting female dog in heat to roam free

No owner or custodian of any dog in heat shall permit the dog to roam or run free beyond the limits of his property.

Laws 1969, p. 831, § 6.

§ 4–8–6.1. Removal of dog collar; permission

(a) For the purposes of this Code section, the term "collar" means any electronic or radio transmitting collar that has the purpose of tracking the location of a dog.

(b) No person shall remove a collar from a dog without permission from the dog's owner with the intention of preventing or hindering the owner from locating such dog, and if such dog is lost or killed as a result of the violator's removal of such collar, the violator shall be required to pay the dog's owner restitution in the amount of the actual value of the dog and any associated veterinary expenses.

(c) This Code section shall not apply to an owner or lessee of real property who removes a collar from a dog caught on his or her owned or leased property while such dog remains on such property if such owner or lessee gives notice of such action within 24 hours to the county or municipal law enforcement agency having territorial jurisdiction.

Laws 2008, Act 540, § 1, eff. July 1, 2008.

§ 4–8–7. Violations relating to dogs

Except as provided in Code Sections 16–12–4 and 16–12–37, any person who violates any provision of this article shall be guilty of a misdemeanor.

Laws 1969, p. 831, § 7; Laws 1988, p. 824, § 1; Laws 2000, p. 754, § 3.

TITLE 10

COMMERCE AND TRADE

CHAPTER 1

SELLING AND OTHER TRADE PRACTICES

Article 6

Article 12

Article 6

Interstate Purchase of Rifles and Shotguns

§ 10–1–100. Purchase by Georgia residents in other states

Residents of the State of Georgia may purchase rifles and shotguns in any state of the United States, provided such residents conform to applicable provisions of statutes and regulations of the United States, of the State of Georgia, and of the state in which the purchase is made.

Laws 1969, p. 804, § 1; Laws 2002, p. 977, § 1.

§ 10–1–101. Purchase in state by residents of other states

Residents of any state of the United States may purchase rifles and shotguns in the State of Georgia, provided such residents conform to applicable provisions of statutes and regulations of the United States, of the State of Georgia, and of the state in which such persons reside.

Laws 1969, p. 804, § 2; Laws 2002, p. 977, § 1.

Article 12

Ticket Scalping

§§ 10–1–310, 10–1–311. Repealed by Laws 2001, p. 752, § 1, eff. July 1, 2001

TITLE 15

COURTS

CHAPTER 8

CITY COURTS

§ 15–8–1. City courts as courts of record

City courts created by special Act of the General Assembly shall be courts of record.

Laws 1924, p. 83, § 1.

Formerly Code 1933, § 24–2204.

§ 15–8–2. Judge disqualified for other municipal office

It shall be illegal for the judge of any city court to also hold any municipal office or appointment in the city where the court is held.

Laws 1878–79, p. 137, § 1.

Formerly Code 1933, § 24–2203.

§ 15–8–3. Judges may preside in other city courts; power and authority

(a) The judges of the various city courts may preside in any of the city courts established by the General Assembly in the same manner as the superior court judges preside in the courts of one another; and any city court judge may exercise all the powers, duties, and functions devolved upon the judge of the city court over which he is called to preside by the request of the judge of such city court where the judge is disqualified or is providentially prevented from trying a case.

(b) Any judge of any city court in this state may preside and act in any other city court in this state upon the request of the regular judge thereof, and when so presiding and acting the judge shall have full power and authority over all matters pending in the court.

Laws 1899, p. 48, § 1; Laws 1929, p. 443, § 1.

Formerly Civil Code 1910, § 4828; Code 1933, § 24–2201.

§ 15–8–4. Transfer of criminal cases to superior courts when judge is disqualified

The several judges of the city courts, on the call of any criminal case in the courts in which the presiding judge is disqualified, may pass an order transferring the case for trial to the superior court of the county in which the city court is located. When the case is so transferred, it shall be tried in the superior court as though it had originated therein.

Laws 1920, p. 277, § 1.

Formerly Code 1933, § 24–2202.

§ 15–8–5. Deputy clerk; appointment, bond, oath of office, and powers

The clerks of the city courts shall each have the power to appoint a deputy clerk and may require from him a bond with good security. The deputy clerks shall take the same oath as the clerks do before entering upon the discharge of their duties; and their powers and duties shall be the same as those of the clerk, for as long as the principal continues in office and not longer. For the faithful performance of their duties the deputy clerks and their securities shall be bound. The appointment of deputy clerks shall be in writing and shall be entered upon the minutes of the court.

Laws 1902, p. 106, §§ 1, 2.

Formerly Civil Code 1910, § 4829; Code 1933, § 24–2301.

§ 15–8–6. Power to preside in municipal court in certain counties

Any judge of any city court or like court may, when authorized to do so by the governing authorities of any city having a population of more than 350,000 according to the United States decennial census of 1950 or any future such census, preside in the municipal court, by whatever name called, of such city. When so presiding, such judge shall have full power and authority in all matters pending in the court, including the trial of all offenses against the ordinances of the city.

Laws 1955, p. 192, § 1; Laws 1982, p. 2107, § 8.

Formerly Code 1933, § 24–2204.

CHAPTER 10

MAGISTRATE COURTS

Article 1

Article 1

General Provisions

§ 15–10–1. One magistrate court in each county

There shall be one magistrate court in each county of the state which shall be known as the Magistrate Court of ____ County.

Laws 1983, p. 884, § 2–1.

§ 15–10–2. Jurisdiction and powers

Each magistrate court and each magistrate thereof shall have jurisdiction and power over the following matters:

(1) The hearing of applications for and the issuance of arrest and search warrants;

(2) Issuance of warrants and related proceedings as provided in Article 4 of Chapter 6 of Title 17, relating to bonds for good behavior and bonds to keep the peace;

(3) The holding of courts of inquiry;

(4) The trial of charges of violations of county ordinances and penal ordinances of state authorities;

(5) The trial of civil claims including garnishment and attachment in which exclusive jurisdiction is not vested in the superior court and the amount demanded or the value of the

property claimed does not exceed $15,000.00, provided that no prejudgment attachment may be granted;

(6) The issuance of summons, trial of issues, and issuance of writs and judgments in dispossessory proceedings and distress warrant proceedings as provided in Articles 3 and 4 of Chapter 7 of Title 44;

(7) The punishment of contempts by fine not exceeding $200.00 or by imprisonment not exceeding ten days or both;

(8) The administration of any oath which is not required by law to be administered by some other officer;

(9) The granting of bail in all cases where the granting of bail is not exclusively committed to some other court or officer;

(10) The issuing of subpoenas to compel attendance of witnesses in the magistrate court and subpoenas for the production of documentary evidence before the magistrate court;

(11) Such other matters as are committed to their jurisdiction by other general laws;

(12) The trial and sentencing of misdemeanor violations of Code Section 16–9–20, relating to criminal issuance of bad checks, as provided by Article 10 of this chapter;

(13) The execution or subscribing and the acceptance of written waivers of extradition in the same manner provided for in Code Section 17–13–46; and

(14) The trial and sentencing of misdemeanor violations of other Code sections as provided by Article 13 of this chapter.

Laws 1983, p. 884, § 2–1; Laws 1985, p. 1003, § 1; Laws 1986, p. 701, § 1; Laws 1987, p. 399, § 1; Laws 1987, p. 448, § 1; Laws 1987, p. 1032, § 1; Laws 1989, p. 320, § 1; Laws 1989, p. 338, § 1; Laws 1999, p. 834, § 1; Laws 2000, p. 1155, § 1; Laws 2008, Act 471, § 15, eff. May 12, 2008.

§ 15–10–2.1. Misdemeanor violations relating to littering and related environmental offenses

(a) Subject to the provisions of subsection (b) of this Code section, in addition to any other jurisdiction vested in the magistrate courts, such courts shall have the right and power to conduct trials, receive pleas of guilty, and impose sentence upon defendants for violating any provision of Part 2, Part 3, or Part 3A of Article 2 of Chapter 7 of Title 16 or Code Section 32–6–51 or 40–6–248.1 that is punishable for its violation as a misdemeanor. Such jurisdiction shall be concurrent with other courts having jurisdiction over such violations.

(b) A magistrate court shall not have the power to dispose of misdemeanor cases as provided in subsection (a) of this Code section unless the defendant shall first waive in writing a trial by jury. If the defendant does not waive a trial by jury, the defendant shall notify the court and, if reasonable cause exists, the defendant shall be immediately bound over to a court in the county having jurisdiction to try the offense wherein a jury may be impaneled.

Laws 2006, Act 538, § 3–6, eff. July 1, 2006.

Historical and Statutory Notes

Laws 2006, Act 538, § 5–1, provides:

"This Act shall become effective upon its approval by the Governor [April 21, 2006] or upon its becoming law without such approval for purposes of adopting local ordinances to become effective on or after July 1, 2006; and for all other purposes, this Act shall become effective on July 1, 2006."

Former § 15–10–2.1 was repealed by Laws 1985, p. 352, § 1, effective March 20, 1985.

§ 15–10–3. Oath; certificate; commission

(a) All magistrates, constables, and clerks of magistrate court shall before entering on the duties of their offices subscribe before the judge of the probate court the oaths prescribed by Code Sections 45–3–1 and 45–3–13 and the following oath:

"I swear or affirm that I will duly and faithfully perform all the duties required of me as (magistrate, constable, or clerk of magistrate court) of ____ County."

(b)(1) The clerk of superior court shall make an entry of the oath of each officer on the minutes of the superior court.

(2) In the case of constables and clerks, the chief judge of the superior court shall issue to the officer taking the oath a certificate which shall serve as the officer's commission.

(3) All magistrates shall be issued a commission under the seal of the office of the Governor as provided in Code Section 45–3–31. In the case of magistrates or an appointed chief magistrate, the appointing authority shall issue to the magistrate or chief magistrate taking the oath a certificate of appointment. A copy of such certificate shall be forwarded to the office of the Secretary of State.

(c) In the case of a probate judge serving as a magistrate, a clerk of superior court serving as clerk of magistrate court, or a sheriff or sheriff's deputy serving as constable, no oath, certificate, or commission shall be required except the oath and commission of the probate judge as probate judge, clerk of superior court as clerk of superior court, or sheriff or deputy as such.

Laws 1983, p. 884, § 2–1; Laws 1984, p. 1096, § 1; Laws 1987, p. 398, § 1.

§ 15–10–4. Sessions of court

The magistrate court shall not have fixed terms. The chief magistrate shall provide for sessions of court to be held at such times and in such places, within or without the county seat, as are necessary or convenient.

Laws 1983, p. 884, § 2–1.

§ 15–10–5. Offices, courtrooms, supplies, and equipment

The county governing authority shall provide suitable offices and courtrooms for the use of the magistrate court and shall supply all fixtures, supplies, and equipment necessary for the proper functioning of the magistrate court.

Laws 1983, p. 884, § 2–1.

§ 15–10–6. Local rules

The chief magistrate may with the approval of the chief judge of superior court adopt local rules for the court not inconsistent with law and the rules adopted by the Supreme Court.

Laws 1983, p. 884, § 2–1.

§ 15–10–7. Council of Magistrate Court Judges; creation; membership; officers; purpose; expenses

(a) There is created a council of magistrate court judges to be known as the "Council of Magistrate Court Judges." The council shall be composed of the chief magistrates, magistrates, and senior magistrates of the magistrate courts of this state. The council is authorized to organize itself and to develop a constitution and bylaws. The officers of said council shall consist of a president, a first vice president, a second vice president, a secretary, a treasurer, and such other officers as the council shall deem necessary. The council shall have an executive committee composed of two representatives from each judicial administrative district. No senior magistrate shall serve as an officer of the council or as a regular representative of a judicial administrative district to the executive committee of the council.

(b) It shall be the purpose of the council to effectuate the constitutional and statutory responsibilities conferred upon it by law, to further the improvement of the magistrate courts and the administration of justice, to assist the chief magistrates, magistrates, and senior magistrates throughout the state in the execution of their duties, and to promote and assist in the training of chief magistrates, magistrates, and senior magistrates.

(c) Expenses of the administration of the council shall be paid from state funds appropriated for that purpose, from federal funds available to the council for that purpose, or from other appropriate sources.

Laws 1988, p. 461, § 2; Laws 1993, p. 910, § 3.

§ 15–10–8. Retired magistrates authorized to perform marriage ceremonies

A retired magistrate of a magistrate court of any county of this state shall be vested with the same authority as an active judge of this state for the purpose of performing marriage ceremonies. For purposes of this Code section, a retired magistrate of a magistrate court shall be one who has served not less than eight years.

Laws 1990, p. 297, § 1.

Article 2

Magistrates

§ 15–10–20. Chief magistrate; number of magistrates in each county; term of office; bond; superior court judges removed from office as result of federal court order to become special judges of magistrate court

(a) Each magistrate court shall have a chief magistrate and may have one or more other magistrates. Such magistrates shall be the judges of the magistrate court and shall be known as magistrates of the county. Unless otherwise provided by local law, the number of magistrates in each county shall be fixed from time to time by majority vote of the judges of the superior court of the county, but no magistrate shall be removed from office during a term of office except for cause as provided by Code Sections 15–10–24 and 15–10–25. The number of magistrates authorized for the county shall be one magistrate until increased by the judges of superior court or by local law; but this subsection shall not operate to remove a magistrate from office during his term of office.

(b) The term of office of any magistrate taking office prior to January 1, 1985, shall expire on December 31, 1984, except that this subsection shall not operate to shorten any term of office in violation of Article VI, Section X, Paragraph II of the Constitution. The term of office of any magistrate taking office on or after January 1, 1985, shall be for four years beginning on the first day of an odd-numbered year, except that in selecting magistrates to fill newly created positions or if otherwise necessary, a magistrate may be selected for a term of less than four years to expire on the last day of an even-numbered year.

(c)(1) Unless otherwise provided by local law, all magistrates, other than the officers becoming magistrates pursuant to Code Section 15–10–120, who are selected to take office prior to January 1, 1985, shall be selected as provided in this subsection. The judges of the superior court of the county shall by majority vote appoint as chief magistrate either an officer becoming a magistrate pursuant to Code Section 15–10–120 or some other person meeting the qualifications specified in subsection (a) of Code Section 15–10–22. Any other magistrates, other than the officers becoming magistrates pursuant to Code Section 15–10–120, shall be appointed by the chief magistrate with the consent of the judges of superior court.

(2)(A) If the chief magistrate so selected is an officer becoming a magistrate pursuant to Code Section 15–10–120, then his term as chief magistrate will be as provided by this paragraph.

(B) If the term which he was serving on June 30, 1983, will expire on the last day of 1984 or 1986, then his term as chief magistrate will likewise expire on the last day of 1984 or 1986.

(C) If the term which he was serving on June 30, 1983, will expire other than on the last day of 1984 or 1986, then his term as chief magistrate shall expire on December 31, 1984, even though he is granted a longer term as magistrate by Article VI, Section X, Paragraph II of the Constitution; but his term as magistrate shall not be shortened in violation of said Paragraph of the Constitution. In any case covered by this subparagraph, the person whose term as chief magistrate expires December 31, 1984, but who is granted by the Constitution a longer term as magistrate shall be eligible to succeed himself for a four-year term as chief magistrate beginning January 1, 1985, if he resigns his current term as magistrate prior to beginning such four-year term as chief magistrate.

(d) Unless otherwise provided by local law, all magistrates taking office on or after January 1, 1985, shall be selected as provided in this subsection. The chief magistrate shall be elected by the voters of the county at the general election next preceding the expiration of the term of the incumbent chief magistrate, in a partisan election in the same manner as county officers are elected, for a term beginning on the first day of January following his election. His successors shall likewise be elected quadrennially thereafter for terms beginning on the first day of January following their election. Magistrates other than the chief magistrate shall be appointed by the chief magistrate with the consent of the judges of superior court. The term of a magistrate so appointed shall run concurrently with the term of the chief magistrate by whom he was appointed.

(e) Unless otherwise provided by local law, a vacancy in the office of chief magistrate shall be filled by an appointment by majority vote of the judges of superior court for the remainder of the unexpired term; and a vacancy in the office of any other magistrate shall be filled by an appointment by the chief magistrate with the consent of the judges of superior court for the remainder of the unexpired term. If, however, a vacancy occurs which does not reduce the number of magistrates for the county below the number of magistrates authorized for the county, then such vacancy shall not be filled.

(f) The General Assembly may by local law provide for the number of magistrates of a county, provide for a different method of selecting magistrates than that specified in subsections (c) and (d) of this Code section, and provide for a different method of filling vacancies than that specified in subsection (e) of this Code section.

(g) The General Assembly may at any time provide by local law that the probate judge shall serve as chief magistrate or magistrate and provide for compensation of the probate judge in his or her capacity as chief magistrate or magistrate; and in such a case the chief magistrate or magistrate shall not be separately elected but shall be the probate judge.

(h) Each magistrate taking office after July 1, 1985, shall before entering on the performance of his duties execute bond in the amount of $25,000.00 for the faithful performance of his duties. Each magistrate in office on July 1, 1985, shall execute such a bond not later than September 1, 1985. The amount of bond required of the magistrate or magistrates of any county may be increased by local law. Such bonds shall be subject to all provisions of Chapter 4 of Title 45 in the same manner as bonds of other county officials. The premiums due on such bonds shall be paid by the fiscal authority of the county out of county funds.

(i)(1) Any person who is holding office on January 1, 1994, as a judge of the superior courts of this state, whether within the term for which elected or appointed or otherwise, and who subsequent to such date and prior to December 31, 1996, is effectively removed from such office by federal court order shall upon such removal become a special judge of the magistrate court as provided for in this subsection. As used in this subsection, the term "federal court order" shall mean only an order of a federal court which is entered in a civil action challenging under federal law or federal constitutional provisions (or both) the validity of the manner of selection of superior court judges in this state. A person shall be considered as effectively removed from office by such an order if the order by its terms prohibits such person's continued service as a judge of the superior courts without by the terms of the order allowing such person a meaningful opportunity to seek an appointment or election as a judge of the superior courts which would take effect within 30 days following such removal. Nothing in this subsection shall apply with respect to any removal from office resulting from criminal conduct or other malfeasance on the part of the person removed from office.

(2) Any person becoming a special judge of the magistrate court pursuant to this subsection shall become a special judge of the magistrate court of the county in which such person resides. Any such special judge of the magistrate court shall serve for a term of office expiring December 31, 1996. The Governor shall issue to each such special judge of the magistrate court a commission stating the date of commencement and expiration of such term of office.

(3) Any special judge of the magistrate court serving pursuant to this subsection shall have all the same powers and duties as any other judge of such magistrate court.

(4) Any special judge of the magistrate court serving pursuant to this subsection shall be compensated and reimbursed for expenses in such amount or amounts as are now or hereafter provided by law for a judge of the superior courts, such compensation to be payable from state funds in the same manner as now or hereafter provided by law for a judge of the superior courts.

(5) The provisions of this subsection shall control over any other conflicting provisions of this chapter.

Laws 1983, p. 884, § 2–1; Laws 1984, p. 22, § 15; Laws 1984, p. 442, § 1; Laws 1984, p. 1096, § 2; Laws 1985, p. 149, § 15; Laws 1985, p. 636, § 1; Laws 1994, p. 607, § 2; Laws 1996, p. 1231, § 3.

§ 15–10–20.1. Reelection of magistrates performing ordered military duty

(a) Any elected chief magistrate or elected magistrate who is performing ordered military duty, as defined in Code Section 38–2–279, shall be eligible for reelection in any primary or general election which may be held to elect a successor for the next term of office, and may qualify in absentia as a candidate for reelection to such office. The performance of ordered military duty shall not create a vacancy in such office during the term for which such judge was elected.

(b) Where the giving of written notice of candidacy is required, any elected chief magistrate or elected magistrate who is performing ordered military duty may deliver such notice by mail, agent, or messenger to the proper elections official. Any other act required by law of a candidate for the office of chief magistrate or magistrate judge may, during the time such official is on ordered military duty, be performed by an agent designated in writing by the absent chief magistrate or magistrate judge.

Laws 2009, Act 75, § 1, eff. April 30, 2009.

§ 15–10–21. Chief magistrate to assign cases and decide disputes

The chief magistrate shall assign cases among the several magistrates of the county and shall decide any disputes between the magistrates of the county.

Laws 1983, p. 884, § 2–1.

§ 15–10–22. Qualifications of magistrates

(a) Each magistrate shall have been a resident of the county for one year next preceding the beginning of his term of office and shall as of such date be at least 25 years of age and shall possess a high school diploma or its equivalent. However, an officer becoming a magistrate pursuant to Code Section 15–10–120 shall be eligible to the office of magistrate without the necessity of meeting these qualifications. Additional qualifications for the office of chief magistrate or magistrate or both may be imposed by local law.

(b) A magistrate who is an attorney may practice in other courts but may not practice in the magistrate's own court or appear in any matter as to which that magistrate has exercised any jurisdiction.

Laws 1983, p. 884, § 2–1; Laws 1984, p. 1096, § 3; Laws 1987, p. 430, § 1.

§ 15–10–23. Minimum salaries

(a)(1) As used in this Code section, the term "full-time capacity" means, in the case of a chief magistrate, a chief magistrate who regularly exercises the powers of a magistrate as set forth in Code Section 15–10–2 at least 40 hours per workweek. In the case of all other magistrates, such term means a magistrate who was appointed to a full-time magistrate position and who regularly exercises the powers of a magistrate as set forth in Code Section 15–10–2 at least 40 hours per workweek.

(2) Unless otherwise provided by local law, effective January 1, 2006, the chief magistrate of each county who serves in a full-time capacity other than those counties where the probate judge serves as chief magistrate shall receive a minimum annual salary of the amount fixed in the following schedule:

Population	Minimum Salary
0–5,999	$ 29,832.20
6,000–11,889	40,967.92
11,890–19,999	46,408.38
20,000–28,999	49,721.70
29,000–38,999	53,035.03
39,000–49,999	56,352.46
50,000–74,999	63,164.60
75,000–99,999	67,800.09
100,000–149,999	72,434.13
150,000–199,999	77,344.56
200,000–249,999	84,458.82
250,000–299,999	91,682.66
300,000–399,999	101,207.60
400,000–499,999	105,316.72
500,000 or more	109,425.84

The minimum salary for each affected chief magistrate shall be fixed from the table in this subsection according to the population of the county in which the chief magistrate serves as determined by the United States decennial census of 2000 or any future such census; provided, however, that such annual salary shall be recalculated in any year following a census year in which the Department of Community Affairs publishes a census estimate for the county prior to July 1 that is higher than the immediately preceding decennial census. Notwithstanding the provisions of this subsection, unless otherwise provided by local law, effective January 1, 1996, in any county in which more than 70 percent of the population according to the United States decennial census of 1990 or any future such census resides on property of the United States government which is exempt from taxation by this state, the population of the county for purposes of this subsection shall be deemed to be the total population of the county minus the population of the county which resides on property of the United States government.

(3) All other chief magistrates shall receive a minimum monthly salary equal to the hourly rate that a full-time chief magistrate of the county would receive according to paragraph (2) of this subsection multiplied by the number of actual hours

worked by the chief magistrate as certified by the chief magistrate to the county governing authority.

(4) Unless otherwise provided by local law, each magistrate who serves in a full-time capacity other than the chief magistrate shall receive a minimum monthly salary of $3,851.46 per month or 90 percent of the monthly salary that a full-time chief magistrate would receive according to paragraph (2) of this subsection, whichever is less.

(5) All magistrates other than chief magistrates who serve in less than a full-time capacity or on call shall receive a minimum monthly salary of the lesser of $22.22 per hour for each hour worked as certified by the chief magistrate to the county governing authority or 90 percent of the monthly salary that a full-time chief magistrate would receive according to paragraph (2) of this subsection; provided, however, that notwithstanding any other provisions of this subsection, no magistrate who serves in less than a full-time capacity shall receive a minimum monthly salary of less than $592.58 unless a magistrate waives such minimum monthly salary in writing.

(6) Magistrates shall be compensated solely on a salary basis and not in whole or in part from fees. The salaries and supplements of all magistrates shall be paid in equal monthly installments from county funds.

(b) The amounts provided in subsection (a) of this Code section, as increased by the supplement, if any, provided by subsection (d) of Code Section 15–10–105, shall be increased by multiplying said amounts by the percentage which equals 5 percent times the number of completed four-year terms of office served by any chief magistrate or magistrate where such terms have been completed after December 31, 1995, effective the first day of January following the completion of each such period of service.

(c) On and after July 1, 2006, whenever the employees in the classified service of the State Personnel Administration receive a cost-of-living increase or general performance based increase of a certain percentage or a certain amount, the amounts provided in subsection (a) of this Code section, as increased by the supplement, if any, provided by subsection (d) of Code Section 15–10–105 and as increased by the application of longevity increases pursuant to subsection (b) of this Code section, shall be increased by the same percentage or same amount applicable to such state employees. If the cost-of-living increase or general performance based increase received by state employees is in different percentages or different amounts as to certain categories of employees, the amounts provided in subsection (a) of this Code section, as increased by the supplement, if any, provided by subsection (d) of Code Section 15–10–105 and as increased by the application of longevity increases pursuant to subsection (b) of this Code section, shall be increased by a percentage or an amount not to exceed the average percentage or average amount of the general increase in salary granted to the state employees. The Office of Planning and Budget shall calculate the average percentage increase or average amount increase when necessary. The periodic changes in the amounts provided in subsection (a) of this Code section, as increased by the supplement, if any, provided by subsection (d) of Code Section 15–10–105 and as increased by the application of longevity increases pursuant to subsection (b) of this Code section, as authorized by this subsection, shall become effective on the first day of January following the date that the cost-of-living increases or general performance based increases received by state employees become effective; provided, however, that if the cost-of-living increases received by state employees become effective on January 1, such periodic changes in the amounts provided in subsection (a) of this Code section, as increased by the supplement, if any, provided by subsection (d) of Code Section 15–10–105 and as increased by the application of longevity increases pursuant to subsection (b) of this Code section, as authorized by this subsection, shall become effective on the same date that the cost-of-living increases or general performance based increases received by state employees become effective.

(d) The county governing authority may supplement the minimum annual salary of the chief or other magistrate in such amount as it may fix from time to time, but no such magistrate's compensation or supplement shall be decreased during any term of office. Nothing contained in this subsection shall prohibit the General Assembly by local law from supplementing the annual salary of any magistrates.

(e) The General Assembly may by local law fix the compensation of any or all of a county's magistrates. The chief magistrate or magistrate shall be entitled to the greater of the compensation established by local law, including any supplement by the county governing authority, or the minimum annual salary stated in subsection (a) of this Code section but in no event to both.

(f) This Code section shall apply to any chief magistrate who is also serving as a judge of a civil court which is provided for in Article VI, Section I, Paragraph I of the Constitution of the State of Georgia of 1983. In such case, the salary of such chief magistrate shall be as provided by the local governing authority of the county.

(g) The salaries and supplements of senior magistrates shall be paid from county funds at a per diem rate equal to the daily rate that a full-time chief magistrate of the county would receive under paragraph (2) of subsection (a) of this Code section; provided, however, that the minimum annual and monthly salaries provided for in this Code section shall not apply to senior magistrates.

Laws 1983, p. 884, § 2–1; Laws 1988, p. 424, § 1; Laws 1989, p. 426, § 1; Laws 1993, p. 910, § 4; Laws 1995, p. 562, § 1; Laws 1998, p. 1159, §§ 11, 12; Laws 2001, p. 902, § 8; Laws 2002, p. 1088, § 1; Laws 2006, Act 649, § 6, eff. July 1, 2006; Laws 2006, Act 851, § 1, eff. July 1, 2006; Laws 2009, Act 155, § 1, eff. July 1, 2009.

Historical and Statutory Notes

In 2001, the Code Commission, in the first sentence of par. (a)(1), substituted "means, in the case of a chief magistrate, a" for "means in the case of a chief magistrate means a". See § 28–9–5.

§ 15–10–23.1. Monthly expense allowance

In addition to any salary, fees, or expenses now or hereafter provided by law, unless a magistrate waives such expenses in writing, the governing authority of each county is authorized to provide as contingent expenses for the operation of the office of magistrate court, and payable from county funds, a monthly expense allowance to each magistrate of not less than the amount fixed in the following schedule:

Population	Minimum Monthly Expenses
0– 11,889	$ 100.00
11,890– 74,999	200.00
75,000–249,999	300.00
250,000–499,999	400.00
500,000 or more	500.00

Laws 2001, p. 902, § 9; Laws 2006, Act 851, § 2, eff. July 1, 2006.

§ 15–10–24. Discipline, removal, and involuntary retirement

Magistrates shall be subject to discipline, removal, and involuntary retirement by the Judicial Qualifications Commission in accordance with Article VI, Section VII, Paragraph VII of the Constitution.

Laws 1983, p. 884, § 2–1; Laws 1990, p. 336, § 1.

§ 15–10–25. Training requirements

(a) All magistrates shall periodically satisfactorily complete a training course as provided in Article 8 of this chapter. All senior magistrates shall periodically satisfactorily complete a training course as provided in Code Section 15-10-223.

(b) The Georgia Magistrate Courts Training Council shall keep records of training completed by magistrates and senior magistrates.

(c) Subject to the provision of Code Section 15-10-24, if any magistrate or senior magistrate does not satisfactorily complete the required training in any year, the Georgia Magistrate Courts Training Council shall promptly notify the Judicial Qualifications Commission which shall recommend removal of the magistrate from office unless the Judicial Qualifications Commission finds that the failure was caused by facts beyond the control of the magistrate or senior magistrate.

(d) The reasonable costs and expenses of such training shall be paid by the county governing authority from county funds.

Laws 1983, p. 884, § 2-1; Laws 1984, p. 1096, § 4; Laws 1990, p. 336, § 2; Laws 1993, p. 910, § 5.

§ 15-10-26. Local ordinances not to be inconsistent with local Acts

In any case in which action is authorized under this chapter to be taken by local Act or local ordinance, no local ordinance shall be enacted which is inconsistent with a local Act.

Laws 1983, p. 884, § 2-1.

§ 15-10-27. Judge of civil court to serve as chief magistrate in certain counties

(a) With respect to any county in which there exists a civil court of the county continued in existence by Article VI, Section X, Paragraph I, subparagraph (5) of the Constitution and in which there are as of June 30, 1983, no officers who will become magistrates pursuant to Code Section 15-10-120, the provisions of this Code section shall control over any other conflicting provisions of this chapter.

(b) In any county subject to this Code section the judge of such civil court shall serve as chief magistrate for a term of office concurrent with his term as judge of civil court. The chief judge of superior court of any such county shall fix the compensation to be received by the chief magistrate for his services as chief magistrate, and such compensation may be less than the minimum salary otherwise specified by this chapter.

(c) In any county subject to this Code section the clerk of civil court shall serve as clerk of magistrate court and the sheriff and deputies of civil court shall serve as constables of magistrate court.

(d) A civil court judge who appoints an attorney or another trial judge to act as judge pro tempore of the civil court may provide that the attorney or judge so appointed shall also serve as magistrate pro tempore for the magistrate court.

Laws 1983, p. 884, § 2-1; Laws 1987, p. 484, § 1.

Article 3

Civil Proceedings

§ 15-10-40. Article to govern civil proceedings

This article shall govern civil proceedings in the magistrate court.

Laws 1983, p. 884, § 2-1.

§ 15-10-41. No jury trials; appeals

(a) There shall be no jury trials in the magistrate court.

(b)(1) Except as otherwise provided in this subsection, appeals may be had from judgments returned in the magistrate court to the state court of the county or to the superior court of the county and the same provisions now provided for by general law for appeals contained in Article 2 of Chapter 3 of Title 5 shall be applicable to appeals from the magistrate court, the same to be a de novo appeal. The provisions of said Article 2 of Chapter 3 of Title 5 shall also apply to appeals to state court.

(2) No appeal shall lie from a default judgment or from a dismissal for want of prosecution after a nonappearance of a plaintiff for trial. Any voluntary dismissal by the plaintiff or by order of the court for want of prosecution shall be without prejudice except that the filing of a second such dismissal shall operate as an adjudication upon the merits. Review, including review of a denial of a postjudgment motion to vacate a judgment, shall be by certiorari to the state court of that county or to the superior court of that county.

Laws 1983, p. 884, § 2-1; Laws 1984, p. 1096, § 5; Laws 1986, p. 701, § 2; Laws 1987, p. 1009, § 1; Laws 1993, p. 974, § 1; Laws 2008, Act 720, § 1, eff. July 1, 2008.

§ 15-10-42. Proceedings not subject to "Georgia Civil Practice Act"

Proceedings in the magistrate court shall not be subject to Chapter 11 of Title 9, the "Georgia Civil Practice Act."

Laws 1983, p. 884, § 2-1.

§ 15-10-43. Commencement of action; service; answer

(a) Actions shall be commenced by the filing of a statement of claim, including the last known address of the defendant, in concise form and free from technicalities. The plaintiff or his or her agent shall sign and verify the statement of claim by oath or affirmation. At the request of any individual, the judge or clerk may prepare the statement of claim and other papers required to be filed in an action. The statement of claim shall include a brief statement of the claim giving the defendant reasonable notice of the basis for each claim contained in the statement of claim and the address at which the plaintiff desires to receive the notice of hearing.

(b) A copy of the verified statement of claim shall be served on the defendant personally, or by leaving a copy thereof at the defendant's dwelling or usual place of abode with some person of suitable age and discretion then residing therein, or by delivering a copy of the claim to an agent authorized by appointment or by law to receive service of process, and such service shall be sufficient. Service of said process shall be made within the county as provided in this Code section. Service outside the county shall be by second original as provided in Code Section 9-10-72. Said service shall be made by any official or person authorized by law to serve process in the superior court, by a constable, or by any person sui juris who is not a party to, or otherwise interested in, the action, who is specially appointed by the judge of said court for that purpose. When the claim and notice are served by a private individual, such individual shall make proof of service by affidavit, showing the time and place of such service on the defendant.

(c) An answer to the claim must be filed with the court or orally presented to the judge or clerk of the court within 30 days after service of the statement of claim on the defendant to avoid a default. The answer shall be in concise form and free from technical requirements, but must admit or deny the claim of the plaintiff. The answer shall contain the address at which the defendant desires to receive the notice of hearing. If the answer is presented to the judge or clerk orally, the judge or clerk shall reduce the answer to writing. A copy of the answer shall be forwarded to the plaintiff and defendant with the notice of hearing. If an answer is timely filed or presented, the court shall within ten days of filing or presentation of the answer notify the defendant and the plaintiff of the calling of a hearing on the claim. The notice shall include the date, hour, and location of the hearing, which date shall be not less than 15 nor more than 30 days after the date the notice is given. The notice shall be served on the plaintiff and the defendant by mail or personal service to the address given by the plaintiff at the time he or she files his or her claim and the address given by the defendant at the time he or she files or presents his or her answer. The date of mailing shall be the date the notice is given. The clerk shall enter a certificate of service.

(d) Upon failure of the defendant to answer the claim within 30 days after service of the statement of claim, the defendant shall be in default. The defaulting party may open the default upon filing an answer and upon payment of costs within 15 days of default. If the defendant is still in default after the expiration of 15 days after the answer is due, the plaintiff shall be entitled to a default judgment without further proof if the claim is for liquidated damages. When the claim is for unliquidated damages, the plaintiff must offer proof of the damage amount. Separate notice of the date and time of the unliquidated damages hearing shall be sent to the defendant at his or her service address. The defendant shall be allowed to submit evidence at that hearing on the issue of the amount of damage only.

(e)(1) When a hearing is scheduled pursuant to subsection (c) of this Code section, upon failure of the defendant to appear for the hearing, the plaintiff shall be entitled to have the defendant's answer stricken and a default judgment entered; provided, however, that no default judgment shall be granted if the defendant appears at trial through counsel. If the claim is for liquidated damages, the plaintiff shall be entitled to take a judgment in the amount set forth in the complaint without further proof. If the claim is for unliquidated damages, the plaintiff shall proceed to prove his or her damages and take judgment in an amount determined by the judge.

(2) When a hearing is scheduled pursuant to subsection (d) of this Code section, upon failure of the defendant to appear, the plaintiff shall be entitled to submit proof of the damages and take judgment in an amount determined by the judge.

(3) If the plaintiff fails to appear for a hearing scheduled pursuant to either subsection (c) or (d) of this Code section, the court on motion of the defendant, or on its own motion, may dismiss the plaintiff's complaint, with or without prejudice, in the discretion of the court.

(f) At any time before final judgment, the court, in its discretion, upon payment of costs, may allow the default to be opened for providential cause preventing the filing of required pleadings or for excusable neglect or where the judge, from all the facts, shall determine that a proper case has been made for the default to be opened, on terms to be fixed by the court. In order to allow the default to be thus opened, the showing shall be made under oath, shall set up a meritorious defense, shall offer to plead instanter, and shall announce ready to proceed with the trial.

(g) Notwithstanding the provisions of Code Section 15–10–42, the magistrate court may grant relief from a judgment under the same circumstances as the state court may grant such relief. Requests for relief from judgments pursuant to this Code section in the magistrate court shall be by filing a written motion which sets forth the issues with reasonable specificity. The procedure shall then be the same as in other cases except the court may assess costs as seem just.

(h) A complaint in equity to set aside a judgment of the magistrate court may be brought under the same circumstances as a complaint to set aside a judgment in a court of record.

(i) Nothing in this chapter shall be construed to prohibit an employee of any corporation or other legal entity from representing the corporation or legal entity before the magistrate court.

Laws 1983, p. 884, § 2–1; Laws 1984, p. 22, § 15; Laws 1985, p. 627, § 1; Laws 1986, p. 701, § 3; Laws 1993, p. 974, § 2; Laws 1997, p. 922, § 1; Laws 2008, Act 720, § 2, eff. July 1, 2008.

§ 15–10–44. Trial; dismissal; continuance

(a) The trial shall be conducted on the day set for the hearing, or at such later time as the judge may set. Immediately prior to the trial of any case, the judge shall counsel the parties to make an earnest effort to settle the controversy by conciliation. If the parties fail to settle their differences without a trial, the judge shall proceed with the hearing on its merits.

(b) The judge shall conduct the trial in such manner as to do substantial justice between the parties according to the rules of substantive law. All rules and regulations relating to pleading, practice, and procedure shall be liberally construed so as to administer justice.

(c) If the plaintiff fails to appear, the action may be dismissed for want of prosecution, the defendant may proceed to a trial on the merits, or the case may be continued as the judge may direct. If both parties fail to appear, the judge may continue the case, order the same dismissed for want of prosecution, or make any other just and proper disposition thereof, as justice may require.

Laws 1983, p. 884, § 2–1.

§ 15–10–45. Counterclaims

(a) If any defendant has a claim against the plaintiff arising out of the transaction or occurrence that is the subject matter of the plaintiff's claim, which claim does not require for its adjudication the presence of third parties over whom the court cannot obtain jurisdiction, such claim must be asserted by the defendant at or before the hearing on plaintiff's claim or thereafter be barred.

(b) If any defendant has a claim against the plaintiff other than a compulsory counterclaim described in subsection (a) of this Code section, such claim may be asserted by the defendant at or before the hearing on the plaintiff's claim.

(c) If any defendant asserts a claim against the plaintiff, the defendant shall file with the court a statement of the claim in concise form and free from technicalities. The defendant's claim shall give the plaintiff reasonable notice of the basis for each claim contained in the statement of claim. The defendant shall sign and verify the statement of claim by oath or affirmation. At the request of a defendant, the judge or clerk may prepare the statement.

(d) If the amount of a counterclaim exceeds the jurisdictional limits of the magistrate court, the case shall be transferred to any court of the county which has jurisdictional limits which exceed the amount of the counterclaim. If there is more than one court to which the action may be transferred, the parties may agree on the court to which the action shall be transferred, and, in the absence of any agreement, the judge of the magistrate court shall determine the court to which the action shall be transferred. If there is no other court to which the action may be transferred, it shall be transferred to the superior court of the county.

(e) A counterclaim may in the discretion of the magistrate be tried either separately or jointly with the plaintiff's claim.

Laws 1983, p. 884, § 2–1; Laws 1984, p. 22, § 15; Laws 1984, p. 1096, § 6; Laws 2008, Act 720, § 3, eff. July 1, 2008.

§ 15–10–46. Staying judgments and executions; partial payments

(a) When the judgment is to be rendered and the party against whom it is to be entered requests it, the judge shall inquire fully into the earnings and financial status of such party and shall have full discretionary power to stay the entry of judgment, to stay execution, and to order partial payments in such amounts, over such periods, and upon such terms as seem just under the circumstances and as will assure a definite and steady reduction of the judgment until it is fully and completely satisfied.

(b) The judge of the magistrate court shall not be obligated to collect such deferred partial payments on judgments so rendered but, if the plaintiff so requests, he may do so at the expense of the plaintiff for clerical and accounting costs incurred thereby, not to exceed 10 percent of each payment.

Laws 1983, p. 884, § 2–1.

§ 15–10–47. Money judgments

(a) Except where otherwise provided by law, the general laws and rules applicable to the effect, recordation, execution, and enforcement of money judgments in civil cases in the superior courts of this state shall be applicable to and govern the magistrate courts.

(b) Upon the issuance of any execution by the magistrate court, the clerk of the magistrate court shall immediately transmit a copy of the execution to the clerk of superior court of the county. The fee of the clerk of superior court for recording the execution on the general execution docket shall be charged and collected by the magistrate court contemporaneously with or prior to the issuance of the execution but not before the entry of judgment in the action; and such fee shall be transmitted by the clerk of magistrate court to the clerk of superior court together with the copy of the execution. The clerk of the superior court shall immediately enter the execution upon the general execution docket in the same manner as executions issued by the superior court, without the necessity of any action by the plaintiff in fi. fa.

Laws 1983, p. 884, § 2–1; Laws 1984, p. 1096, § 7; Laws 1986, p. 701, § 4; Laws 1987, p. 320, § 1.

§ 15–10–48. Form of statement of claim, verification, and notice

The statement of claim, verification, and notice shall be in substantially the following form:

Magistrate Court of ________ County

State of Georgia

____

Plaintiff

____

Address

v.

____

Defendant

Statement of Claim

(Here the plaintiff or, at his or her request, the court will insert a brief statement of the plaintiff's claim or claims giving the defendant reasonable notice of the basis for each claim and, if the action is on a contract, either express or implied, the original statement of the plaintiff's claim which is to be filed with the court may be verified by the plaintiff or his or her agent as follows:)

STATE OF GEORGIA

COUNTY OF ________

__________________, being first duly sworn on oath, says the foregoing is a just and true statement of the amount owing by defendant to plaintiff, exclusive of all setoffs and just grounds of defense.

____

Plaintiff or agent

Sworn and subscribed before me this _____ day of ____________, ____.

____

Notary public
or attesting
official

Notice

TO: ____________

Defendant

____

Home Address

or

____

Business Address

You are hereby notified that ____________________ has made a claim and is requesting judgment against you in the sum of _______ dollars ($_____), as shown by the foregoing statement. The court will hold a hearing upon this claim at (address of court) at a time to be set after your answer is filed.

YOU ARE REQUIRED TO FILE OR PRESENT AN ANSWER TO THIS CLAIM WITHIN 30 DAYS AFTER SERVICE OF THIS CLAIM UPON YOU. IF YOU DO NOT ANSWER, JUDGMENT BY DEFAULT WILL BE ENTERED AGAINST YOU. YOUR ANSWER MAY BE FILED IN WRITING OR MAY BE GIVEN ORALLY TO THE JUDGE.

If you have witnesses, books, receipts, or other writings bearing on this claim, you should bring them with you at the time of hearing.

If you wish to have witnesses summoned, see the court at once for assistance.

If you have any claim against the plaintiff, you should notify the court at once.

If you admit the claim, but desire additional time to pay, you must come to the hearing in person and state the circumstances to the court.

You may come with or without an attorney.

____

Magistrate of
_____ County

Laws 1983, p. 884, § 2–1; Laws 1999, p. 81, § 15; Laws 2008, Act 720, § 4, eff. July 1, 2008.

§ 15–10–49. Procedure in attachment cases, garnishment cases, and dispossessory proceedings

(a) Procedure in attachment cases shall be subject to Chapter 3 of Title 18, except that there shall be no prejudgment attachment granted in the magistrate court.

(b) Procedure in garnishment cases shall be subject to Chapter 4 of Title 18.

(c) Procedure in dispossessory proceedings and in distress warrant proceedings shall be subject to Articles 3 and 4 of Chapter 7 of Title 44.

Laws 1983, p. 884, § 2–1; Laws 1986, p. 701, § 5.

§ 15–10–50. Post-judgment interrogatories in aid of judgments

(a) In aid of any judgment or execution issued by any court in this state upon which the unpaid balance does not exceed the jurisdictional amount for civil claims in magistrate court as provided in paragraph (5) of Code Section 15–10–2, the judgment creditor or his successor in interest when that interest appears of record, may, in addition to any other process or remedy provided by law, examine the judgment debtor by propounding the interrogatories specified in this Code section in the manner provided in this Code section.

(b) If the judgment or execution concerning which interrogatories are being propounded was issued by the magistrate court, the judgment creditor may, after the entry of judgment, file the form interrogatories specified in this Code section with the clerk of the same magistrate court, along with costs of $10.00. Interrogatories filed under this subsection shall be served upon the judgment debtor by certified mail or statutory overnight delivery.

(c) Interrogatories propounded pursuant to a judgment entered in any other court shall be filed as a new civil action and shall be accompanied by the filing and service fees required for civil actions in that magistrate court. Interrogatories propounded under this subsection shall be served upon the judgment debtor in the manner provided for service of process in civil actions in magistrate court.

(d) The interrogatories, verification, and notice shall be in substantially the following form:

Magistrate Court of ________ County
State of Georgia

________________	
Plaintiff	Current Civil Action File No. ____________
________________	
Address	
________________	
v.	Original Civil Action File No. ____________
________________	
Defendant	Court where original judgment entered:
________________	________________
Address	
________________	

INTERROGATORIES

TO: _____, Defendant in the above-styled action:

The Plaintiff in the above-styled action requests that you answer the following interrogatories separately, fully, and under oath and serve such answers on said plaintiff at plaintiff's address shown above by mail or hand delivery within 30 days after the service of these interrogatories.

1. List your full name, home phone number, and address, including apartment number and ZIP Code.

2. List the name, address, and phone number of your employer(s).

3. Describe and state the location of each piece of real estate in which you own any interest.

4. Give the name, address, phone number, and a description of the nature of any business venture in which you own any interest.

5. List the names, addresses, and phone numbers of all persons who owe money to you and specify the amounts owed.

6. List the names and addresses of all banks or savings institutions where you have any sums of money deposited and identify the accounts by number.

7. List and give the present location of all items of personal property owned by you that have a value of more than $100.00.

VERIFICATION

STATE OF GEORGIA, COUNTY OF _____

_____, being first duly sworn on oath, says the foregoing are true and complete answers to the interrogatories propounded by plaintiff to defendant.

Sworn and subscribed
before me, this ________
day of ____________, _____.

________________	________________
Notary public or attesting official	Defendant

NOTICE

YOU ARE REQUIRED TO PROVIDE COMPLETE ANSWERS TO THE ABOVE–STATED QUESTIONS TO THE PLAINTIFF WITHIN 30 DAYS AFTER SERVICE OF THESE INTERROGATORIES UPON YOU. IF YOU DO NOT ANSWER, OR DO NOT ANSWER COMPLETELY, YOU MAY BECOME SUBJECT TO THE SANCTIONS PROVIDED BY LAW FOR CONTEMPT OF COURT. IF YOU NEED FURTHER INSTRUCTION OR IF YOU NEED ASSISTANCE IN ANSWERING THE QUESTIONS CONTACT THE COURT AT ONCE.

(e) The court in its discretion may limit the number of times interrogatories may be propounded upon a judgment debtor, may relieve a judgment debtor of the obligation to answer one or more propounded interrogatories, and may for good cause shown enlarge the time for answering any interrogatory. The court may if necessary compel the answering of interrogatories, but the sanction of contempt shall be applied only after notice and an opportunity for hearing and a showing of willful failure to answer or willful failure to answer fully and truthfully.

(f) An evasive or incomplete answer to an interrogatory shall be treated as a failure to answer.

(g) Notwithstanding the provisions of Code Section 15–10–42, the judgment creditor or a successor in interest when that interest appears of record may, in addition to any other process or remedy provided by law, utilize the discovery provisions set forth in Code Section 9–11–69.

Laws 1985, p. 1003, § 2; Laws 1988, p. 267, § 1; Laws 1990, p. 886, §§ 1, 2; Laws 1996, p. 365, § 1; Laws 1999, p. 81, § 15; Laws 2000, p. 1589, § 3; Laws 2008, Act 720, § 5, eff. July 1, 2008.

Historical and Statutory Notes

In 2008, the Code Commission, in subsec. (b), inserted a comma following "by the magistrate court". See § 28–9–5.

§ 15–10–51. Clerk or deputy clerk may be authorized to sign notice or summons in pending civil actions

The chief magistrate of each county may, by local rule of court, authorize the clerk of the magistrate court or one or more deputy clerks of the court to sign any notice or summons in any civil action pending in the court.

Laws 1985, p. 636, § 2.

Formerly Code 1981, § 15–10–50.

§ 15–10–52. Action by assignee of obligee to show action in name of original obligee by assignee

The style of any action, other than a proceeding brought pursuant to Chapter 7 of Title 44, relating to landlord and tenant, brought in the magistrate court by the assignee of the obligee of any obligation shall show the action in the name of the original obligee by the assignee.

Laws 2000, p. 880, § 1.

§ 15–10–53. Filing by electronic means; electronic signature and verification; service; challenge to authenticity; fees

(a) Any magistrate court may provide for the filing of civil, garnishment, distress warrant, dispossessory, foreclosure, abandoned motor vehicle, and all other noncriminal actions, claims, answers, counterclaims, pleadings, postjudgment interrogatories, and other documents by electronic means.

(b) Any pleading or document filed electronically shall be in a format prescribed by the court.

(c) Any pleading or document filed electronically shall include the electronic signature of the person filing the pleading or document as defined in Code Section 10–12–2.

(d) Any pleading or document filed electronically which is required to be verified, verified under oath, or be accompanied by an affidavit may include such verification, oath, or affidavit by one of the following methods:

(1) As provided in Code Section 10–12–11;

(2) By oath or affirmation of the party filing the pleading at the time of the trial of the case;

(3) By supplemental verified pleading; or

(4) By electronic verification, oath, or affidavit in substantially the following form:

"By affixing this electronic verification, oath, or affidavit to the pleading(s) submitted to the court and attaching my electronic signature hereon, I do hereby swear or affirm that the statements set forth in the above pleading(s) are true and correct.

Date:_________ Electronic Signature:_________"

(e) Service of any claim or complaint filed electronically shall be made as provided by law. Service of all subsequent pleadings and notices may be made electronically only on a party who has filed pleadings electronically; service on all other parties shall be made by such other means as are provided by law. Each pleading or document which is required to be served on other parties shall include a certificate of service indicating the method by which service on the other party has been made. An electronic certificate of service shall be made in substantially the following form:

"By affixing this electronic certificate of service to the pleading(s) or document(s) submitted to the court and attaching my electronic signature hereon, I do hereby swear or affirm that I have this date served the opposing party with a copy of this pleading by e-mail or placing a copy in regular mail with sufficient postage thereon to the following address: (set forth address of opposing party).

Date:_________ Electronic Signature:_________"

(f) Nothing in this Code section shall prevent a party from contesting an electronic pleading, document, or signature on the basis of forgery or fraud. Any pleading or document found by the court to have been fraudulently filed shall be stricken from the record.

(g) Where the authenticity or the integrity of an electronic pleading, document, or signature is challenged, the proponent of the electronic pleading, document, or signature shall have the burden of proving that the electronic pleading, document, or signature is authentic.

(h) Upon the receipt of any pleading or other document filed electronically, the clerk of magistrate court shall notify the filer of receipt of the pleading or document. Such notice shall include the date and time the court accepted the pleading or document as filed.

(i) Any pleading or document filed electronically shall be deemed filed as of the time the clerk of court gains electronic control of the document.

(j) When the filing of the pleading or document requires the payment of a fee, the clerk of magistrate court may establish procedures for the payment of such fees connected with such filing. The filing of any such pleading or document shall create an obligation by the party to pay such fee to the clerk of court instanter.

(k) The clerk of court may assess an additional transaction fee or fees for each electronic filing and electronic payment.

Laws 2000, p. 1580, § 1; Laws 2009, Act 141, § 3, eff. July 1, 2009.

Historical and Statutory Notes

In 2000, the Code Commission redesignated § 15–10–52, which was enacted by Laws 2000, p. 1580, § 1, as § 15–10–53. See § 28–9–5.

Article 4

Violation of Ordinances of Counties and State Authorities

§ 15–10–60. Violations of county ordinances and ordinances of state authorities; punishment; suspended sentences

(a) This article governs trials of violations of county ordinances and ordinances of state authorities, which violations may be punished by incarceration or monetary penalty. Nothing in this chapter shall grant to any county or state authority more authority to enact or enforce such ordinances than the county or state authority has independently of this chapter. The punishment imposed for any ordinance violation shall not exceed a fine of $1,000.00 or six months' imprisonment or both, provided the judge shall probate not less than 120 days of any sentence imposed, except as otherwise provided by general law, and shall not exceed the maximum punishment specified by the ordinance. In the event a sentence is revoked, a defendant shall not serve more than 60 days in a county jail.

(b) The trial court may suspend the service of the sentence imposed in the case upon such terms and conditions as it may prescribe for the payment of the fine, for performance of community service in lieu of a fine or incarceration, for the payment of restitution to a victim, or other condition relating to the underlying offense. Service of the sentence, when so suspended, shall not begin unless and until ordered by the court having jurisdiction thereof, after a hearing as in cases of revocation of probated sentences, because of the failure or refusal of the defendant to comply with the terms and conditions upon which service of a sentence was suspended. Service of all or any part of any sentence suspended upon such conditions may be ordered to commence by the trial court any time before the expiration of one year from the date of the sentence after a hearing and a finding by the court that the defendant has failed or refused to comply with the terms and conditions upon which service of the sentence was suspended.

Laws 1983, p. 884, § 2–1; Laws 1984, p. 22, § 15; Laws 1987, p. 448, § 2; Laws 1993, p. 910, § 1; Laws 2000, p. 1155, § 2; Laws 2003, Act 168, § 1, eff. July 1, 2003.

Historical and Statutory Notes

The 2003 amendment by Act 168 rewrote subsec. (a) which had read as follows:

"(a) This article governs trials of violations of county ordinances and ordinances of state authorities, which violations may be punished by incarceration or monetary penalty. Nothing in this chapter shall grant to any county or state authority more authority to enact or enforce such ordinances than the county or state authority has independently of this chapter. The punishment imposed for any ordinance violation shall not exceed a fine of $1,000.00 or 60 days' imprisonment or both, except as otherwise provided by general law, and shall not exceed the maximum punishment specified by the ordinance."

§ 15–10–61. Removal of case to state or superior court

There shall be no jury trials in the magistrate court. Any defendant who is charged with one or more ordinance violations may, at any time before trial, demand that the case be removed for a jury trial to the state court of the county or to the superior court of the county if there is no state court. Such a demand shall be written. Upon such a demand the court shall grant the demand. Failure to so demand removal of the case shall constitute a waiver of any right to trial by jury which the defendant may otherwise have.

Laws 1983, p. 884, § 2–1; Laws 1987, p. 448, § 2.

§ 15–10–62. Prosecutions to be upon citation or accusation; service; arrest of accused

(a) Prosecutions for violations of county ordinances shall be upon citation as provided in Code Section 15–10–63 or upon accusation by the county attorney or such other attorney as the county governing authority may designate. Prosecutions for violations of ordinances of state authorities shall be upon citation as provided in Code Section 15–10–63 or upon accusation by such attorney as the state authority may designate. Such attorney shall be the prosecuting attorney in cases tried upon accusation.

(b) Accusations of violations of ordinances and citations shall be personally served upon the person accused. Each accusation shall state the time and place at which the accused is to appear for trial. The accused shall not be arrested prior to the time of trial, except for the offenses of public drunkenness or disorderly conduct and except that ordinances of state authorities may provide for immediate arrest; provided, however, that the accused may be arrested prior to the time of trial for the violation of a county ordinance relating to loitering; and provided, further, that any defendant who fails to appear for trial shall thereafter be arrested on the warrant of the magistrate and required to post a bond for his or her future appearance.

Laws 1983, p. 884, § 2–1; Laws 1984, p. 1096, § 8; Laws 1985, p. 149, § 15; Laws 1987, p. 448, § 2; Laws 1994, p. 292, § 1.

§ 15–10–63. Prosecutions upon citation

(a) The governing authority of any county or any state authority may provide that ordinance violations may be tried upon citations with or without a prosecuting attorney as well as upon accusations.

(b) Each citation shall state the time and place at which the accused is to appear for trial, shall identify the offense with which the accused is charged, shall have an identifying number by which it shall be filed with the court, shall indicate the identity of the accused and the date of service, and shall be signed by the county or authority agent who completes and serves it.

(c) Prosecutions for violations of ordinances upon citations shall be commenced by the completion, signing, and service of a citation by any agent of the county who is authorized by the county governing authority to issue citations or by an agent of the state authority who is authorized by the authority to issue citations. A copy of the citation shall be personally served upon the accused; and the original shall promptly be filed with the court.

(d) No person shall be arrested prior to the time of trial, except for the offenses of public drunkenness or disorderly conduct or as authorized by ordinance of a state authority; provided, however, that the accused may be arrested prior to the time of trial for the violation of a county ordinance relating to loitering; and provided, further, that any defendant who fails to appear for trial shall be arrested thereafter on the warrant of the magistrate and required to post a bond for his or her future appearance.

Laws 1983, p. 884, § 2–1; Laws 1984, p. 1096, § 9; Laws 1985, p. 149, § 15; Laws 1987, p. 448, § 2; Laws 1994, p. 292, § 2; Laws 2000, p. 880, § 2.

§ 15–10–63.1. Cash bonds

(a) The chief magistrate of each county may by written order establish a schedule of cash bonds for the personal appearance in court of any person charged with a violation of an ordinance. The chief magistrate shall designate the officer or officers authorized to accept cash bonds pursuant to the schedule of bonds published by the court. In no event shall any officer or agent who is authorized to issue citations be authorized to accept a cash bond at the time of or in conjunction with the issuance of any citation. The officer accepting a cash bond shall issue a receipt for the bond to the person charged with the violation.

(b) Any person who is accused by citation but has not been arrested may, but shall not be required to, give a cash bond for his personal appearance in court for trial. If a person who has given a cash bond fails to appear for trial, the failure to appear shall be deemed to constitute a guilty plea and such cash bond shall be forfeited upon the call of the case for trial. It shall not be necessary for the county to take any further action to forfeit the cash bond. Forfeiture of a cash bond shall be deemed to constitute imposition and payment of a fine and shall be a bar to a subsequent prosecution of the accused for the violation. The court may, however, in any case enter an order pursuant to which bond forfeiture shall not be deemed to constitute imposition of a sentence and subsequent prosecution shall not be barred; and in any such case the amount of the bond forfeited shall be credited against any fine subsequently imposed.

(c) It shall be the duty of the clerk of magistrate court to furnish the officer or officers authorized under the order with a book of blank receipts consecutively numbered in triplicate and readily distinguishable and identifiable. The receipts shall be completed by the officers when accepting a cash bond so as to show the name of the person cited or arrested, the date of citation or arrest, nature of the offense, amount of cash bond given, and the name of the receiving officer. The receiving officer shall deliver a copy of the receipt to the person cited or arrested at the time the cash bond is given and shall file the original together with the cash bond with the clerk of the magistrate court not later than the next succeeding business day following the date of issuance of the receipt.

Laws 1985, p. 417, § 1; Laws 1987, p. 448, § 2.

§ 15–10–64. Executions; confinement

(a) Execution may issue immediately upon any fine imposed by the court and not immediately paid.

(b) The sheriff of the county shall receive and house all persons sentenced to confinement for contempt or arrested or sentenced to confinement for violation of ordinances.

Laws 1983, p. 884, § 2–1; Laws 1984, p. 1096, § 10; Laws 1987, p. 448, § 2.

§ 15–10–65. Review by certiorari

Review of convictions shall be by certiorari to the superior court.

Laws 1983, p. 884, § 2–1; Laws 1987, p. 448, § 2.

§ 15–10–66. Prosecuting attorney

The county attorney or another attorney designated by the county governing authority may act as prosecuting attorney for violations of county ordinances; and any attorney designated by the affected state authority may act as prosecuting attorney for violation of state authority ordinances.

Laws 1983, p. 884, § 2–1; Laws 1987, p. 448, § 2.

Article 8

Magistrate Training

§ 15–10–130. Short title

This article shall be known and may be cited as "The Georgia Magistrate Courts Training Council Act."

Laws 1983, p. 884, § 2–1.

§ 15–10–131. Definitions

As used in this article, the term:

(1) "Certified magistrate" means a magistrate judge who has the appropriate required certificate of training issued by the council and on file with the council or a magistrate judge who is exempt from such training by subsection (d) of Code Section 15–10–137.

(2) "Council" means the Georgia Magistrate Courts Training Council.

(3) "School" means any school, college, university, academy, or training program approved by the council and the Judicial Council of Georgia which offers basic, in-service, advanced, specialized, or continuing judicial training or a combination thereof and includes within its meaning a combination of course curriculum, instructors, and facilities which meet the standards required by the council.

Laws 1983, p. 884, § 2–1; Laws 1985, p. 1416, § 1; Laws 1990, p. 8, § 15.

§ 15–10–132. Georgia Magistrate Courts Training Council; creation; membership; terms

(a) There is established a council which shall be known and designated as the "Georgia Magistrate Courts Training Council" and which shall be composed of the director of the Administrative Office of the Courts or such director's designee, which member shall not be a voting member, and five magistrate judges, either elected or appointed, who shall be appointed by the president of the Council of Magistrate Court Judges, with approval of the council's executive committee, for terms of two years.

(b) Membership on the council does not constitute public office and no member shall be disqualified from holding office by reason of his membership.

(c) Members of the Georgia Justice Courts Training Council serving as of June 30, 1983, shall continue on and automatically become members of the Georgia Magistrate Courts Training Council with the same term and office as held on June 30, 1983.

Laws 1983, p. 884, § 2–1; Laws 1997, p. 922, § 2; Laws 1999, p. 81, § 15.

§ 15–10–133. Oath of office by council, certificate of appointment

Immediately and before entering upon the duties of office, the members of the Georgia Magistrate Courts Training Council shall take the oath of office and shall file the same in the office of the Judicial Council, which, upon receiving the oath of office, shall issue to each member a certificate of appointment.

Laws 1983, p. 884, § 2–1.

§ 15–10–134. Organization of council; officers; quorum; minutes; reports

(a) A chairman and vice chairman shall be elected at the first meeting of each calendar year.

(b) The director of the Administrative Office of the Courts or his designee shall serve as secretary to the council.

(c) A simple majority of the members of the council shall constitute a quorum for the transaction of business.

(d) The council shall maintain minutes of its meetings and such other records as it deems necessary.

(e) The council shall report at least annually to the Governor and to the General Assembly as to its activities.

Laws 1983, p. 884, § 2–1; Laws 1990, p. 8, § 15.

§ 15–10–135. Compensation

The members of the council shall receive no salary but shall be reimbursed for their reasonable and necessary expenses actually incurred in the performance of their functions; provided, however, that such expenses shall not exceed those allowed to members of the General Assembly.

Laws 1983, p. 884, § 2–1.

§ 15–10–136. Functions, powers and responsibilities

The council is vested with the following functions, powers, and responsibilities:

(1) To make all the necessary rules and regulations to carry out this article;

(2) To cooperate with and secure the cooperation of every department, agency, or instrumentality of the state government or its political subdivisions in furtherance of the purposes of this article;

(3) To approve schools and to prescribe minimum qualifications for instructors at approved schools;

(4) To issue a certification to any magistrate judge satisfactorily complying with an approved training program established;

(5) To do any and all things necessary or convenient to enable it wholly and adequately to perform its duties and to exercise the power granted to it; and

(6) To prescribe, by rules and regulations, the minimum requirements for curricula and standards composing the initial in-service, advanced, specialized, and continuing training courses for certification.

Laws 1983, p. 884, § 2–1.

§ 15–10–137. Training certification requirements

(a) Any person who takes office as a magistrate on July 1, 1983, and who was certified under the former Justice Courts Training Council shall satisfactorily complete 40 hours of training prior to December 31, 1984, in order to become certified under this article.

(b) Any person who becomes a magistrate between July 1, 1983, and June 30, 1998, shall satisfactorily complete 40 hours of training in the performance of his or her duties and shall attend the first scheduled training session held after the date of his or her election or appointment in order to become certified under this article. In order to become certified under this article, any person who becomes a magistrate on or after July 1, 1998, shall satisfactorily complete 80 hours of training specified by the council concerning the performance of his or her duties during the first two years after becoming a magistrate.

(b.1) Any person who becomes a magistrate on or after July 1, 1998, shall complete during the initial year of service as a magistrate a program of orientation activities established by the council and conducted under the guidance and supervision of an experienced adviser or mentor magistrate or judge.

(c)(1) In order to maintain the status of a certified magistrate judge, each person certified as such shall complete 20 hours of additional training per annum during each calendar year after the year of his or her initial certification in which he or she serves as a magistrate judge.

(2) For the calendar years 2009 and 2010 only, the council may suspend, in whole or in part, the training requirements of this subsection. If the council suspends such requirements, and if any magistrate judge has completed all or a portion of the required training prior to suspension of the training requirements, credit for the training so completed shall be carried over and applied to calendar year 2010 or 2011.

(d) Notwithstanding any other provision of this article, any magistrate who is also an active member of the State Bar of Georgia shall be certified as a certified magistrate by the council without being required to complete any training otherwise required by subsection (b) of this Code section but shall be required to complete the mentor program of subsection (b.1) of this Code section within 12 months of taking office as magistrate and the annual training required by subsection (c) of this Code section, commencing with the first full calendar year following the year in which such a magistrate takes office.

Laws 1983, p. 884, § 2–1; Laws 1984, p. 22, § 15; Laws 1984, p. 1096, § 12; Laws 1985, p. 1416, § 2; Laws 1990, p. 8, § 15; Laws 1998, p. 185, § 1; Laws 2002, p. 1073, § 1; Laws 2009, Act 110, § 2, eff. May 4, 2009.

Article 9

Magistrate Court Serving as Municipal Court

§ 15–10–150. Counties and municipalities authorized to contract concerning municipal court services

The governing authority of any county may contract with the governing authority of any municipality within the county for the county to furnish municipal court services to the municipality as authorized by this article; and the governing authorities of municipalities are likewise authorized to enter into such contracts with county governing authorities.

Laws 1986, p. 787, § 1.

§ 15–10–151. Provisions of contracts; approval of chief magistrate

Any contract entered into pursuant to this article shall provide that the county shall furnish municipal court services to the municipality through the officers, employees, and facilities of the magistrate court of the county. Any contract so entered into shall not become effective unless it is approved by the chief magistrate then in office; and no such contract shall extend beyond the term of the chief magistrate then in office.

Laws 1986, p. 787, § 1.

§ 15–10–152. Authority of judges and other officers and personnel of magistrate court

When a contract entered into pursuant to this article has become effective, the judges of the magistrate court shall have full authority to act as judges of the municipal court of the municipality; and the other officers and personnel of the magistrate court shall have full authority to act as officers and personnel of the municipal court.

Laws 1986, p. 787, § 1.

§ 15–10–153. Style of judges, pleadings, etc.; dockets and records to be kept separate

When acting as officers of the municipal court all judges and other officers of the magistrate court shall be styled as judges and officers of the municipal court; and all pleadings, process, and papers of the municipal court shall be styled as such and not as pleadings, process, and papers of the magistrate court. The dockets and other records of the municipal court shall be kept separately from those of the magistrate court.

Laws 1986, p. 787, § 1.

§ 15–10–154. Limitations upon punishment for violations of municipal ordinances

Any limitations upon the punishment which may be imposed for violations of municipal ordinances which are contained in the charter of the municipality shall continue to control in municipal courts operated under this article, and if no such limitation exists the maximum punishment imposed shall not exceed a fine of $1,000.00 or six months' imprisonment or both, unless some other general law authorizes greater punishment. Other charter provisions not in conflict with this article shall continue to apply in municipal courts operated under this article.

Laws 1986, p. 787, § 1.

§ 15–10–155. Exceptions

(a) Except as provided in subsection (b) of this Code section, the authority granted to municipalities by this article shall not apply to:

(1) A municipality whose charter does not authorize a municipal court;

(2) A municipality whose charter provides for the election, as judge or judges and not as members of the municipal governing authority, of the judge or judges of a court having jurisdiction over municipal ordinance violations; or

(3) A municipality whose charter expressly provides that the municipality shall not have the authority granted by this article.

(b) The authority granted to municipalities by this article shall, notwithstanding the provisions of subsection (a) of this Code section, apply to any municipality if as of June 30, 1983, jurisdiction over violation of its ordinances was by law vested in a magistrate court in existence on that date.

Laws 1986, p. 787, § 1; Laws 1987, p. 3, § 15.

Article 10

Deposit Account Fraud Prosecutions

§ 15–10–200. Trials of misdemeanor violations

This article governs trials of misdemeanor violations of Code Section 16–9–20, relating to deposit account fraud, which violations shall be punishable as provided in subsection (b) of Code Section 16–9–20.

Laws 1987, p. 1032, § 2; Laws 1994, p. 1787, § 2.

§ 15–10–201. Jury trial; waiver

There shall be no jury trials in the magistrate court. Any person charged with one or more misdemeanor violations of Code Section 16–9–20 may, at any time before trial, demand that the case be removed to the state court of the county or to the superior court of the county if there is no state court. Such demand shall be written. Upon such written demand the court shall grant the demand. Failure to so demand removal of the case shall constitute a waiver of any right to trial by jury which the defendant may otherwise have had and of any other right which could have been secured by such a demand.

Laws 1987, p. 1032, § 2; Laws 1988, p. 13, § 15.

§ 15–10–202. Practice and procedure

(a) Prosecution for a misdemeanor violation of Code Section 16–9–20 may proceed by arrest, as provided in Chapter 4 of Title 17, and an accusation, as provided in Code Section 17–7–71, or by citation.

(b) Each citation shall be based upon an affidavit as in the issuance of an arrest warrant and said citation shall state the time and place at which the accused is to appear for trial, shall identify the offense with which the accused is charged, shall have an identifying number by which it shall be filed with the court, shall indicate the identity of the accused and the date of service, and shall be signed by a judge or clerk of the magistrate court.

(c) Prosecutions upon citations shall be commenced by the completion and signing of the citation by a judge or clerk of the magistrate court and service of the citation by a law enforcement officer. A copy of the citation shall be personally served upon the accused and the original shall promptly be filed with the court.

(d) If the prosecution is proceeding upon citation, the accused shall not be arrested prior to the time of trial; but any defendant who fails to appear for trial shall be arrested thereafter on the warrant of a judge of the magistrate court and required to post a bond for his future appearance. If the accused demands removal of the case to the state or superior court, the magistrate court may require that the accused post a bond for his future appearance in the state or superior court.

(e) The prosecuting attorney of the court in which the case would have been tried if a demand for removal had been made shall be responsible for the prosecution of the case in the magistrate court.

Laws 1987, p. 1032, § 2; Laws 2000, p. 880, § 3.

§ 15–10–203. Optional procedure for forfeiture of no contest cash bonds on misdemeanor bad check violations as final disposition

(a) The chief magistrate of each county may by written order establish a schedule of no contest cash bonds which the accused may post when arrested or accused by warrant or citation pursuant to subsection (d) of Code Section 15–10–202. The schedule of no contest cash bond amounts shall be sufficient to cover court costs, minimum fines as set forth in Code Section 16–9–20, and restitution in the full amount of the dishonored check. At the time of posting a no contest cash bond, the receipt shall contain the following language: "IF YOU GIVE A NO CONTEST CASH BOND AND FAIL TO APPEAR FOR TRIAL, THIS BOND MAY BE FORFEITED AND, IF SO FORFEITED, SHALL CONSTITUTE A MISDEMEANOR GUILTY PLEA AND A WAIVER OF CERTAIN CONSTITUTIONAL RIGHTS," which shall be acknowledged by the person arrested.

(b) A person arrested or accused by warrant or citation pursuant to subsection (d) of Code Section 15–10–202 who does not wish to post a no contest cash bond may post a property bond or standard appearance bond to assure his or her future appearance in court.

(c) If a person who gives a no contest cash bond fails subsequently to appear for trial, such failure shall constitute a guilty plea and the no contest cash bond shall be forfeited, unless the court proceeds under the provisions of subsection (d) of this Code section. It shall not be necessary for the state to take any further action to forfeit the no contest cash bond. Forfeiture of a no contest cash bond shall be considered to constitute imposition and payment of a fine and restitution and, if so considered, shall be a bar to a subsequent prosecution of the accused for the violation in accordance with Code Section 16–9–20.

(d) If the judge determines at the time of the nonappearance at trial of the defendant in his or her sole discretion that substantial justice will not be accomplished by the forfeiture of the no contest cash bond amount and the disposition of the charges with prejudice, the posting of the no contest cash bond shall not be considered a plea of guilty nor constitute a bar to a subsequent prosecution of the defendant for the violation, and any moneys posted under the no contest cash bond shall be held in the court's registry pending subsequent prosecution, and the defendant shall be served with a citation for a reasonable future appearance date, and, in default of the defendant's appearance, the court shall issue a bench warrant for the defendant's arrest.

(e) Upon a conviction under a subsequent prosecution, the proceeds of any no contest cash bond shall be applied and distributed toward restitution, fine, and court costs imposed by the court.

(f) If a defendant posts a property bond or standard appearance bond and thereafter fails to appear at the designated time, a bench warrant shall be issued for such person and the bond shall be forfeited as provided by Code Section 17–6–17.

Laws 1994, p. 865, § 1.

Article 11

Senior Magistrates

§ 15–10–220. Appointment

There is created the office of senior magistrate. Subject to the approval of the governing authority, any chief magistrate of this state may appoint to the office of senior magistrate any retired chief magistrate, magistrate, or judge who prior to retirement served at least eight consecutive years as chief magistrate or magistrate, or a combination of such offices, or served eight consecutive years as a judge of a court of record or juvenile court, or a combination of such offices. A senior magistrate need not be a member of the State Bar of Georgia, unless required by local law. The term of an appointment made pursuant to this Code section shall not exceed the current term of the appointing officer.

Laws 1993, p. 910, § 2.

§ 15–10–221. Duties

Upon the request of any chief magistrate of this state, a senior magistrate may discharge all of the duties of a magistrate and may assume and exercise all of the jurisdiction, power, and authority of a magistrate.

Laws 1993, p. 910, § 2.

§ 15–10–222. Oath

Before entering on the duties of his or her office, a senior magistrate shall subscribe before the judge of the probate court in which he or she is first appointed the oath prescribed in Code Section 45–3–1 and the following oath:

"I swear or affirm that I will duly and faithfully perform all the duties required of me as senior magistrate and that I will support the Constitution of the United States and the Constitution of Georgia."

Laws 1993, p. 910, § 2.

§ 15–10–223. Training

In order to maintain the status of senior magistrate, a senior magistrate shall complete the 20 hours of training provided for in subsection (c) of Code Section 15–10–137 in each calendar year in which he or she serves as a senior magistrate.

Laws 1993, p. 910, § 2.

Article 13

Trials of Certain Misdemeanors

§ 15–10–260. Concurrent criminal jurisdiction over certain misdemeanor marijuana possession, shoplifting, alcohol violations relating to minors, and criminal trespass

(a) This article governs trials of misdemeanor violations of Code Sections 16–13–30 and 16–13–2, relating to possession of less than one ounce of marijuana; Code Section 16–8–14, relating to theft by shoplifting of $300.00 or less; Code Section 3–3–23, relating to furnishing alcoholic beverages to, and purchase and possession of alcoholic beverages by, a person under 21 years of age; and Code Section 16–7–21, relating to criminal trespass.

(b) Magistrate courts are authorized to conduct trials and impose sentences for violations of misdemeanors specified in subsection (a) of this Code section; provided, however, that the violation must have occurred in the unincorporated area of the county.

(c) A person convicted of violation of a misdemeanor specified in subsection (a) of this Code section shall be punished as provided in paragraphs (1) through (4) of this subsection as follows:

(1) For possession of less than one ounce of marijuana, as provided in subsection (b) of Code Section 16–13–2;

(2) For theft by shoplifting, as provided in paragraph (1) of subsection (b) of Code Section 16–8–14;

(3) For furnishing alcoholic beverages to, and purchase and possession of alcoholic beverages by, a person under 21 years of age, as provided in Code Section 3–3–23.1; and

(4) For criminal trespass, as provided in subsection (d) of Code Section 16–7–21.

(d) The jurisdiction of magistrate courts to try and dispose of the misdemeanor violations enumerated in subsection (a) of this Code section shall be concurrent with the jurisdiction of any other courts having jurisdiction to try and dispose of such cases.

Laws 2000, p. 1155, § 3.

§ 15–10–261. Jury trial; waiver

There shall be no jury trials in the magistrate court. A magistrate court shall not have the power to dispose of the misdemeanor offenses enumerated in subsection (a) of Code Section 15–10–260 unless the defendant shall first waive in writing a trial by jury. If the defendant does not waive a trial by jury, the defendant shall notify the court and, if probable cause exists, the defendant shall be immediately bound over to a court in the county having jurisdiction to try the offense wherein a jury may be impaneled.

Laws 2000, p. 1155, § 3.

§ 15–10–262. Procedures relating to citation arrest or accusation; prosecuting attorneys

(a) Prosecution for misdemeanor violations authorized in this article may proceed by citation, summons, arrest, citation and arrest, or by arrest warrant as provided in Chapter 4 of Title 17, or by an accusation as provided in Code Section 17–7–71.

(b) The solicitor general of counties having solicitors general, or the county attorney or another attorney designated by the county governing authority, may act as the prosecuting attorney of the magistrate court in proceedings under this article.

Laws 2000, p. 1155, § 3.

§ 15–10–263. No contest cash bonds and related procedures

(a) The chief magistrate of each county may by written order establish a schedule of no contest cash bonds which the accused may post when arrested or accused by warrant or citation pursuant to this article. The schedule of no contest cash bond amounts shall be sufficient to cover court costs and minimum fines as set forth in the Code section applicable to the alleged offense. At the time of posting a no contest cash bond, the receipt shall contain the following language: "IF YOU GIVE A NO CONTEST CASH BOND AND FAIL TO APPEAR FOR TRIAL, THIS BOND MAY BE FORFEITED AND, IF SO FORFEITED, SHALL CONSTITUTE A MISDEMEANOR GUILTY PLEA AND A WAIVER OF CERTAIN CONSTITUTIONAL RIGHTS," which shall be acknowledged by the person arrested.

(b) A person arrested or accused by warrant or citation pursuant to this article who does not wish to post a no contest cash bond may post a property bond or standard appearance bond to assure his or her future appearance in court.

(c) If a person who gives a no contest cash bond fails subsequently to appear for trial, such failure shall constitute a guilty plea and the no contest cash bond shall be forfeited, unless the court proceeds under the provisions of subsection (d) of this Code section. It shall not be necessary for the state to take any further action to forfeit the no contest cash bond. Forfeiture of a no contest cash bond shall be considered to constitute imposition and payment of a fine and, if so considered, shall be a bar to a subsequent prosecution of the accused for the violation.

(d) If the judge determines at the time of the nonappearance at trial of the defendant in his or her sole discretion that substantial justice will not be accomplished by the forfeiture of the no contest cash bond amount and the disposition of the charges with prejudice, the posting of the no contest cash bond shall not be considered a plea of guilty nor constitute a bar to a subsequent prosecution of the defendant for the violation, and any moneys posted under the no contest cash bond shall be held in the court's registry pending subsequent prosecution, and the defendant shall be served with a citation for a reasonable future appearance date, and, in default of the defendant's appearance, the court shall issue a bench warrant for the defendant's arrest.

(e) Upon a conviction under a subsequent prosecution, the proceeds of any no contest cash bond shall be applied and distributed toward the fine and court costs imposed by the court.

(f) If a defendant posts a property bond or standard appearance bond and thereafter fails to appear at the designated time, a bench warrant shall be issued for such person and the bond shall be forfeited as provided by Code Section 17–6–17.

Laws 2000, p. 1155, § 3.

CHAPTER 11

JUVENILE PROCEEDINGS

Article 1

Part 1

Part 2

Part 3

Part 4

Article 1

Juvenile Proceedings

Part 1

General Provisions

§ 15–11–1. Construction and purpose

This chapter shall be liberally construed to the end:

(1) That children whose well-being is threatened shall be assisted and protected and restored, if possible, as secure law-abiding members of society;

(2) That each child coming within the jurisdiction of the court shall receive, preferably in his or her own home, the care, guidance, and control that will be conducive to the child's welfare and the best interests of the state; and

(3) That when a child is removed from the control of his or her parents the court shall secure for the child care as nearly as possible equivalent to that which his or her parents should have given the child.

Laws 1971, p. 709, § 1; Laws 2000, p. 20, § 1.

Formerly Code 1933, § 24A–101.

Historical and Statutory Notes

The 2000 amendment inserted gender neutral referents.

Uniform Law

This section is based upon § 1 of the Uniform Law Commissioners' Model Juvenile Court Act. See 9A Uniform Laws Annotated, Master Edition, or ULA Database on Westlaw.

§ 15–11–2. Definitions

As used in this chapter, the term:

(1) "Adult" means any individual who is not a child under the definition in paragraph (2) of this Code section.

(1.1) "Biological father" means the male who impregnated the biological mother resulting in the birth of the child.

(2) "Child" means any individual who is:

(A) Under the age of 17 years;

(B) Under the age of 21 years, who committed an act of delinquency before reaching the age of 17 years, and who has been placed under the supervision of the court or on probation to the court; or

(C) Under the age of 18 years, if alleged to be a "deprived child" or a "status offender" as defined by this Code section.

(3) "Community rehabilitation center" means a rehabilitation and custodial center established within a county for the purpose of assisting in the rehabilitation of delinquent and unruly children in a neighborhood and family environment in cooperation with community educational, medical, and social agencies, which center meets the following requirements:

(A) Is located within any county having a juvenile court presided over by at least one full-time judge exercising jurisdiction exclusively over juvenile matters; and

(B) Is operated by a nonprofit corporation organized under Chapter 3 of Title 14, the "Georgia Nonprofit Corporation Code," and has a full-time chief executive officer. The charter, bylaws, and method of selecting the board of directors and chief executive officer of such nonprofit corporation shall be subject to the unanimous approval of the chief judge of the judicial circuit in which the county is located, the judge or judges of the juvenile court, the superintendent of the county school district, and the commissioner of corrections, which approval shall be in writing and shall be appended to the charter and bylaws of the nonprofit organization. Any amendment of the charter or bylaws of the nonprofit corporation shall be subject to the same written approval as the original charter and bylaws.

(4) "Court" or "juvenile court" means the court exercising jurisdiction over juvenile matters.

(4.1) "Criminal justice purposes" means the performance of any activity directly involving the investigation, detection, apprehension, detention, pretrial release, post-trial release, prosecution, adjudication, correctional supervision, or rehabilitation of children or adults who are accused of, convicted of, or charged with crimes or the collection, storage, and dissemination of criminal history record information.

(5) "Custodian" means:

(A) A person, other than a parent or legal guardian, who stands in loco parentis to the child or a person to whom legal custody of the child has been given by order of a court; or

(B) A public or private agency or other private organization licensed or otherwise authorized by law to receive and provide care for a child to which legal custody of the child has been given by order of a court.

(6) "Delinquent act" means:

(A) An act designated a crime by the laws of this state, or by the laws of another state if the act occurred in that state, under federal laws, or by local ordinance, and the crime does not fall under subparagraph (C) of paragraph (12) of this Code section and is not a juvenile traffic offense as defined in Code Section 15–11–73;

(B) The act of disobeying the terms of supervision contained in a court order which has been directed to a child who has been adjudged to have committed a delinquent act; or

(C) Failing to appear as required by a citation issued with regard to a violation of Code Section 3–3–23.

(7) "Delinquent child" means a child who has committed a delinquent act and is in need of treatment or rehabilitation.

(8) "Deprived child" means a child who:

(A) Is without proper parental care or control, subsistence, education as required by law, or other care or control necessary for the child's physical, mental, or emotional health or morals;

(B) Has been placed for care or adoption in violation of law;

(C) Has been abandoned by his or her parents or other legal custodian; or

(D) Is without a parent, guardian, or custodian.

No child who in good faith is being treated solely by spiritual means through prayer in accordance with the tenets and practices of a recognized church or religious denomination by a duly accredited practitioner thereof shall, for that reason alone, be considered to be a "deprived child."

(8.1) "Identification data" means the fingerprints, name, race, sex, date of birth, and any other unique identifiers of the child.

(9) "Judge" means judge or judges of the court exercising jurisdiction over juvenile matters. Such term shall not mean or include an associate juvenile court judge or associate juvenile court traffic judge unless specifically so stated.

(10) "Juvenile court intake officer" means the juvenile court judge, associate juvenile court judge, court service worker, or person employed as a juvenile probation or intake officer designated by the juvenile court judge or, where there is none, the superior court judge, which person is on duty for the purpose of determining whether any child taken into custody should be released or detained and, if detained, the appropriate place of detention. Each superior or juvenile court judge shall provide for one of the above persons to be on duty or on call as an intake officer during each 24 hour period.

(10.1) "Legal father" means a male who:

(A) Has legally adopted a child;

(B) Was married to the biological mother of that child at the time the child was conceived or was born, unless such paternity was disproved by a final order pursuant to Article 3 of Chapter 7 of Title 19;

(C) Married the legal mother of the child after the child was born and recognized the child as his own, unless such paternity was disproved by a final order pursuant to Article 3 of Chapter 7 of Title 19;

(D) Has legitimated the child by a final order pursuant to Code Section 19–7–22; or

(E) Has legitimated the child pursuant to Code Section 19–7–21.1

and who has not surrendered or had terminated his rights to the child.

(10.2) "Legal mother" means the female who is the biological or adoptive mother of the child and who has not surrendered or had terminated her rights to the child.

(10.3) "Parent" means either the legal father or the legal mother of the child.

(10.4) "Putative father registry" means the registry established and maintained pursuant to subsections (d) and (e) of Code Section 19–11–9.

(10.5) "Shelter care" means:

(A) A licensed foster home or home approved by the court which may be a public or private home or the home of the noncustodial parent or a relative; or

(B) A facility operated by a licensed child welfare agency.

(11) "Status offender" means a child who is charged with or adjudicated of an offense which would not be a crime if it were committed by an adult, in other words, an act which is only an offense because of the perpetrator's status as a child. Such offenses shall include, but are not limited to, truancy, running away from home, incorrigibility, and unruly behavior.

(12) "Unruly child" means a child who:

(A) While subject to compulsory school attendance is habitually and without justification truant from school;

(B) Is habitually disobedient of the reasonable and lawful commands of his or her parent, guardian, or other custodian and is ungovernable;

(C) Has committed an offense applicable only to a child;

(D) Without just cause and without the consent of his or her parent or legal custodian deserts his or her home or place of abode;

(E) Wanders or loiters about the streets of any city, or in or about any highway or any public place, between the hours of 12:00 Midnight and 5:00 A.M.;

(F) Disobeys the terms of supervision contained in a court order which has been directed to such child, who has been adjudicated unruly; or

(G) Patronizes any bar where alcoholic beverages are being sold, unaccompanied by such child's parents, guardian, or custodian, or possesses alcoholic beverages; and

(H) In any of the foregoing, is in need of supervision, treatment, or rehabilitation; or

(I) Has committed a delinquent act and is in need of supervision, but not of treatment or rehabilitation.

Laws 1950, p. 367, § 3; Laws 1951, p. 291, § 2; Laws 1968, p. 1013, § 1; Laws 1971, p. 709, § 1; Laws 1973, p. 579, § 1; Laws 1973, p. 882, § 2; Laws 1976, p. 1064, §§ 1, 2; Laws 1977, p. 700, § 1; Laws 1977, p. 1237, § 1; Laws 1981, p. 862, § 1; Laws 1982, p. 3, § 15; Laws 1985, p. 283, § 1; Laws 1985, p. 1313, § 1; Laws 1986, p. 1017, § 1; Laws 1990, p. 1691, § 1; Laws 1990, p. 1930, § 1; Laws 1992, p. 1983, § 1; Laws 1997, p. 1686, § 1; Laws 1998, p. 128, § 15; Laws 1998, p. 842, § 1; Laws 2000, p. 20, § 1; Laws 2003, Act 3, § 1, eff. July 1, 2003; Laws 2003, Act 268, § 1, eff. July 1, 2003; Laws 2008, Act 580, § 9, eff. July 1, 2008.

Formerly Code 1933, § 24A–401.

Historical and Statutory Notes

The 2000 amendment restructured this chapter into parts and modified statutory references to reflect this restructuring. In addition the amendment inserted gender neutral referents.

The 2003 amendment by Act 3 rewrote par. (5) which had read:

(5) " 'Custodian' means a person, other than a parent or legal guardian, who stands in loco parentis to the child or a person to whom legal custody of the child has been given by order of a court, and who has the rights and duties provided in Code Section 15–11–13."

The 2003 amendment by Act 268, in subpar. (C) of par. (2), inserted "or a 'status offender' " after "child".

The 2008 amendment by Act 580, in par. (10.1), rewrote subpars. (D) and (E), which formerly read:

"(D) Has been determined to be the father by a final paternity order pursuant to Article 3 of Chapter 7 of Title 19; or

"(E) Has legitimated the child by a final order pursuant to Code Section 19–7–22".

Uniform Law

This section is based upon § 2 of the Uniform Law Commissioners' Model Juvenile Court Act. See 9A Uniform Laws Annotated, Master Edition, or ULA Database on Westlaw.

§ 15–11–3. Appeals; supersedeas

In all cases of final judgments of a juvenile court judge, appeals shall be taken to the Court of Appeals or the Supreme Court in the same manner as appeals from the superior court. However, no such judgment or order shall be superseded except in the discretion of the judge; rather, the judgment or order of the court shall stand until reversed or modified by the reviewing court.

Laws 1915, p. 35, § 17; Laws 1916, p. 58, § 5; Laws 1935, p. 399, §§ 4, 7; Laws 1950, p. 367, § 27; Laws 1951, p. 291, § 30; Laws 1956, p. 69, § 6; Laws 1968, p. 1013, § 18; Laws 1971, p. 709, § 1; Laws 2000, p. 20, § 1.

Formerly Code 1933, § 24–2417; Code 1933, § 24A–3801; Code 1981, § 15–11–64.

Historical and Statutory Notes

The 2000 amendment which restructured this chapter redesignated this section from § 15–11–64.

Uniform Law

This section is based upon § 59 of the Uniform Law Commissioners' Model Juvenile Court Act. See 9A Uniform Laws Annotated, Master Edition, or ULA Database on Westlaw.

§ 15–11–3.1. Renumbered as § 15–11–18.1 by Laws 2000, p. 20, § 1

§ 15–11–4. Court of inquiry; court of record; issuance of warrants

(a) *Court of inquiry.* The juvenile court shall have jurisdiction to act as a court of inquiry with all the powers and rights allowed courts of inquiry in this state and to examine or investigate into the circumstances or causes of any conduct or acts of any person 17 years of age or over that may be in violation of the laws of this state whenever the person is brought before the court in the course of any proceeding instituted under this article. The court shall cause the person to be apprehended and brought before it upon either a writ of summons, a warrant duly issued, or by arrest. Where, after hearing evidence, the court has reasonably ascertained that there is probable cause to believe that the person has committed a misdemeanor or felony as prescribed under the laws of this state, the court shall commit, bind over to the court of proper jurisdiction in this state, or discharge the person. When justice shall require, the court shall cause the person to make the bond or bail as the court shall deem proper under the circumstances, to cause the person to appear before the court of proper jurisdiction in this state to be acted upon as provided by law.

(b) *Court of record.* The juvenile court is a court of record, having a seal. The judge and the judge's duly appointed representatives shall each have power to administer oaths and affirmations.

(c) *Issuance of warrants by juvenile court judge.* The juvenile court judge and associate juvenile court judge shall have authority to issue a warrant for the arrest of any child for an offense committed against the laws of this state, based either on personal knowledge or the information of others given under oath.

Laws 1950, p. 367, §§ 2, 30; Laws 1951, p. 291, § 33; Laws 1957, p. 307, § 1; Laws 1965, p. 433, § 1; Laws 1968, p. 1013, §§ 19, 21; Laws 1971, p. 709, § 1; Laws 1973, p. 882, § 9; Laws 1986, p. 1017, § 1; Laws 1991, p. 627, § 4; Laws 1995, p. 619, § 7; Laws 1997, p. 1681, § 4; Laws 1998, p. 653, § 7; Laws 1998, p. 842, § 5; Laws 2000, p. 20, § 1.

Formerly Code 1933, § 24A–3901; Code 1981, § 15–11–65.

Historical and Statutory Notes

The 2000 amendment, which restructured this chapter into parts and modified statutory references to reflect this restructuring, renumbered this section from § 15–11–65. In addition the amendment inserted gender neutral referents.

§ 15–11–4.1. Renumbered as § 15–11–20 by Laws 2000, p. 20, § 1

§ 15–11–5. Contempt powers; other sanctions

(a) In addition to all other inherent powers of the court to enforce its lawful orders, the court may punish a person for contempt of court for willfully disobeying an order of the court or for obstructing or interfering with the proceedings of the court or the enforcement of its orders, subject to the law relating to the procedures therefor and the limitations thereon.

(b) In addition or as an alternative to the punishment provided in subsection (a) of this Code section, after notice and opportunity for hearing, the court may impose any or all of the following sanctions when a parent, guardian, or other custodian willfully violates any order issued by the court directed to that parent, guardian, or other custodian:

(1) Require the parent, guardian, or other custodian of the child to make restitution in an amount not to exceed $2,500.00 for any damage or loss caused by the child's wrongful act;

(2) Impose a fine not to exceed $1,000.00;

(3) Reimburse the state for the costs of detention, treatment, or rehabilitation of the child;

(4) Require the parent, guardian, or other custodian of the child to perform court approved community service designed to contribute to the ability of the parent, guardian, or other custodian to provide proper parental care and supervision of the child; or

(5) Require the parent, guardian, or other custodian of the child to enter into a contract or plan as a part of the disposition of any charges against the child, so as to provide for the supervision and control of the child by the parent, guardian, or custodian and reunification of the child with the parent, guardian, or custodian.

Laws 1950, p. 367, § 26; Laws 1951, p. 291, § 29; Laws 1971, p. 709, § 1; Laws 1996, p. 868, § 5; Laws 2000, p. 20, § 1.

Formerly Code 1933, § 24A–3601; Code 1981, § 15–11–62.

Historical and Statutory Notes

The 2000 amendment which restructured this chapter redesignated this section from § 15–11–62.

Uniform Law

This section is based upon § 58 of the Uniform Law Commissioners' Model Juvenile Court Act. See 9A Uniform Laws Annotated, Master Edition, or ULA Database on Westlaw.

§ 15–11–5.1. Renumbered as § 15–11–62 by Laws 2000, p. 20, § 1

§ 15–11–6. Right to counsel

(a) *"Indigent person" defined.* An indigent person is one who at the time of requesting counsel is unable without undue financial hardship to provide for full payment of legal counsel and all other necessary expenses for representation.

(b) *Right to legal representation.* Except as otherwise provided under this article, a party is entitled to representation by legal counsel at all stages of any proceedings alleging delinquency, unruliness, incorrigibility, or deprivation and if, as an indigent person, a party is unable to employ counsel, he or she is entitled to have the court provide counsel for him or her. If a party appears without counsel, the court shall ascertain whether such party knows of his or her right to counsel and to be provided with counsel by the court if he or she is an indigent person. The court may continue the proceeding to enable a party to obtain counsel and shall provide counsel for an unrepresented indigent person upon the request of such a person. Counsel must be provided for a child not represented by the child's parent, guardian, or custodian. If the interests of two or more parties conflict, separate counsel shall be provided for each of them.

Laws 1968, p. 1013, § 11; Laws 1971, p. 709, § 1; Laws 1986, p. 1017, § 1; Laws 1990, p. 1930, § 2; Laws 2000, p. 20, § 1.

Formerly Code 1933, § 24A–2001; Code 1981, § 15–11–30.

Historical and Statutory Notes

The 2000 amendment, which restructured this chapter into parts and modified statutory references to reflect this restructuring, renumbered this section from § 15–11–30. In addition the amendment inserted gender neutral referents.

Uniform Law

This section is based upon § 26 of the Uniform Law Commissioners' Model Juvenile Court Act. See 9A Uniform Laws Annotated, Master Edition, or ULA Database on Westlaw.

§ 15–11–7. Other basic rights

(a) A party is entitled to the opportunity to introduce evidence and otherwise be heard in his or her own behalf and to cross-examine adverse witnesses.

(b) A child charged with a delinquent act need not be a witness against or otherwise incriminate himself or herself. An extrajudicial statement obtained in the course of violation of this article or one which would be constitutionally inadmissible in a criminal proceeding shall not be used against such child. Evidence illegally seized or obtained shall not be received over objection to establish the allegations made against a child. A confession validly made by the child out of court is insufficient to support an adjudication of delinquency unless it is corroborated in whole or in part by other evidence.

Laws 1968, p. 1013, § 11; Laws 1971, p. 709, § 1; Laws 1986, p. 1017, § 1; Laws 2000, p. 20, § 1.

Formerly Code 1933, § 24A–2002; Code 1981, § 15–11–31.

Historical and Statutory Notes

The 2000 amendment, which restructured this chapter into parts and modified statutory references to reflect this restructuring, renumbered this section from § 15–11–31. In addition the amendment inserted gender neutral referents.

Uniform Law

This section is based upon § 27 of the Uniform Law Commissioners' Model Juvenile Court Act. See 9A Uniform Laws Annotated, Master Edition, or ULA Database on Westlaw.

§ 15–11–8. Costs and expenses for care of child

(a) The following expenses shall be a charge upon the funds of the county upon certification thereof by the court:

(1) The cost of medical and other examinations and treatment of a child ordered by the court;

(2) The cost of care and support of a child committed by the court to the legal custody of an individual or a public or private agency other than the Department of Juvenile Justice, but the court may order supplemental payments, if such are necessary or desirable;

(3) Reasonable compensation for services and related expenses of counsel appointed by the court, where appointed by the court to represent the child and when appointed by the court to conduct the proceedings;

(4) Reasonable compensation for a guardian ad litem;

(5) The expense of service of summons, notices, and subpoenas, travel expenses of witnesses, transportation, subsistence, and detention of the child, and other like expenses incurred in the proceedings under this chapter; and

(6) The cost of counseling and counsel and advice required or provided under the provisions of Code Sections 15–11–57 and 15–11–68.

(b) If, after due notice to the parents or other persons legally obligated to care for and support the child and after affording them an opportunity to be heard, the court finds that they are financially able to pay all or part of the costs and expenses stated in subsection (a) of this Code section, the court may order them to pay the same and prescribe the manner of payment. In addition, the court may order payment from the parents or other legally obligated persons to reimburse all or part of the costs and expenses of the Department of Human Services for treatment, care, and support of the child. Unless otherwise ordered, payment shall be made to the clerk of the court for remittance to the person or agency, including the Department of Human Services, to whom compensation is due or, if the costs and expenses have been paid by the county, to the appropriate officer of the county.

Laws 1915, p. 35, §§ 31, 32; Laws 1950, p. 367, § 23; Laws 1951, p. 291, § 26; Laws 1968, p. 1013, § 16; Laws 1971, p. 709, § 1; Laws 1974, p. 1126, § 8; Laws 1985, p. 149, § 15; Laws 1986, p. 1017, § 1; Laws 1992, p. 1983, § 16; Laws 1992, p. 2137, § 1; Laws 1992, p. 2474, § 2; Laws 1997, p. 1453, § 1; Laws 2000, p. 20, § 1; Laws 2009, Act 102, § 2–2, eff. July 1, 2009.

Formerly Code 1933, §§ 24–2431, 24–2432; Code 1933, § 24A–3401; Code 1981, § 15–11–56.

Historical and Statutory Notes

The 2000 amendment, which restructured this chapter into parts and modified statutory references to reflect this restructuring, renumbered this section from § 15–11–56. In addition the amendment inserted gender neutral referents.

The 2009 amendment by Act 102 substituted "Department of Human Services" for "Department of Human Resources" throughout the section.

Uniform Law

This section is based upon § 52 of the Uniform Law Commissioners' Model Juvenile Court Act. See 9A Uniform Laws Annotated, Master Edition, or ULA Database on Westlaw.

§ 15–11–9. Guardian ad litem

(a) As used in this Code section, the term "court appointed special advocate" shall have the same meaning as set forth in Code Section 15–11–9.1.

(b) The court at any stage of a proceeding under this article, on application of a party or on its own motion, shall appoint a guardian ad litem for a child who is a party to the proceeding if the child has no parent, guardian, or custodian appearing on the child's behalf or if the interests of the parent, guardian, or custodian appearing on the child's behalf conflict with the child's interests or in any other case in which the interests of the child require a guardian. A party to the proceeding or the employee or representative of a party to the proceeding shall not be appointed. In deprivation cases, a person appointed as a child's guardian ad litem must have received before the appointment training appropriate to the role that is administered or approved by the Office of the Child Advocate and may be an attorney or court appointed special advocate, or both. For attorneys, the preappointment training required pursuant to this Code section shall be satisfied within attorneys' existing continuing legal education obligations and shall not require attorneys to complete additional training hours in addition to those currently required by the State Bar of Georgia. The Office of the Child Advocate shall exempt from the training required by this Code section attorneys who have practiced as guardians ad litem in juvenile court deprivation proceedings for three or more years and, when such determination is made by the court, have demonstrated a proficiency in child representation.

Laws 1951, p. 291, § 24; Laws 1968, p. 1013, § 15; Laws 1971, p. 709, § 1; Laws 1986, p. 1017, § 1; Laws 1998, p. 652, § 1; Laws 2000, p. 20, § 1; Laws 2005, Act 150, § 1, eff. May 4, 2005; Laws 2007, Act 231, § 1, eff. May 24, 2007.

Formerly Code 1933, § 24A–3301; Code 1981, § 15–11–55.

Historical and Statutory Notes

The 2000 amendment which restructured this chapter redesignated this section from § 15–11–55.

The 2005 amendment by Act 150 rewrote subsec. (b). Prior to amendment subsec. (b) had read:

"(b) The court at any stage of a proceeding under this article, on application of a party or on its own motion, shall appoint a guardian ad litem for a child who is a party to the proceeding if the child has no parent, guardian, or custodian appearing on the child's behalf or if the interests of the parent, guardian, or custodian appearing on the child's behalf conflict with the child's interests or in any other case in which the interests of the child require a guardian. A party to the proceeding or the employee or representative of a party to the proceeding shall not be appointed. In deprivation cases, an attorney or court appointed special advocate, or both, may be appointed as the child's guardian ad litem."

In 2005, the Code Commission, in the third sentence of subsec. (b), deleted a comma following "Office of the Child Advocate". See § 28–9–5.

The 2007 amendment by Act 231, in subsec. (a), substituted "shall have the same meaning as set forth in Code Section 15–11–9.1" for "means a volunteer who has been screened and trained regarding deprivation, child development, and juvenile court procedures and has been appointed as a guardian ad litem by the court in a deprivation case".

Uniform Law

This section is based upon § 51 of the Uniform Law Commissioners' Model Juvenile Court Act. See 9A Uniform Laws Annotated, Master Edition, or ULA Database on Westlaw.

§ 15–11–9.1. Court appointed special advocate (CASA)

(a) As used in this Code section, the term:

(1) "Court appointed special advocate" or "CASA" means a community volunteer who:

(A) Has been screened and trained regarding deprivation, child development, and juvenile court procedures;

(B) Has met all of the requirements of an affiliate court appointed special advocate program;

(C) Is being actively supervised by an affiliate court appointed special advocate program; and

(D) Has been appointed as a lay guardian ad litem by the court in a juvenile court deprivation proceeding.

(2) "Affiliate court appointed special advocate program" means a locally-operated program operating with the approval of the local juvenile court which screens, trains, and supervises volunteers to advocate for the best interest of abused and neglected children in deprivation proceedings.

(b)(1) Before executing duties as a CASA, and upon completion of all the requirements of an affiliate court appointed special advocate program, a CASA shall be sworn in by a judge of the juvenile court in the court or circuit in which he or she wishes to serve. A CASA shall not be assigned a case prior to being sworn in by a juvenile court judge as set forth in this paragraph.

(2) If a juvenile court judge determines that a child involved in a deprivation proceeding needs a CASA, the judge shall have the authority to appoint a CASA, and in such circumstance shall sign an order appointing a CASA at the earliest possible stage of the proceedings. Such order shall impose on a CASA all the duties, rights, and responsibilities set forth in this Code section.

(c) The role of a CASA in juvenile court deprivation proceedings shall be to advocate for the best interests of the child.

(d) In all cases to which a CASA is assigned, except as ordered by the judge, a CASA shall:

(1) Conduct an independent assessment to determine the facts and circumstances surrounding the case;

(2) Maintain regular and sufficient in-person contact with the child;

(3) Submit written reports to the court regarding the child's best interests;

(4) Advocate for timely court hearings to obtain permanency for the child;

(5) Request a judicial citizen review panel or judicial review of the case;

(6) Collaborate with the child's attorney, if any;

(7) Attend all court hearings and other proceedings to advocate for the child's best interests;

(8) Monitor compliance with the case plan and all court orders; and

(9) Review all court related documents.

(e) As a lay guardian ad litem, a CASA shall not be required to:

(1) Engage in activities which could reasonably be construed as the practice of law; or

(2) Obtain legal counsel or other professional services for a child.

(f)(1) Except as provided in Article 5 of this chapter, the "Georgia Child Advocate for the Protection of Children Act," a CASA shall be notified of all court hearings, judicial reviews, judicial citizen review panels, and other significant changes of circumstances of the child's case to which the CASA has been appointed to the same extent and in the same manner as the parties to the case are notified of such matters.

(2) A CASA shall be notified of the formulation of any case plan of the child's case to which the CASA has been appointed and may be given the opportunity to be heard by the court about such plans.

(g) Upon presentation of an order appointing a CASA as a guardian ad litem, such CASA shall have access to all records and information relevant to the child's case to which such CASA has been appointed when such records and information are not otherwise protected from disclosure pursuant to Code Section 19–7–5. Such records and information shall not include records and information provided under Article 5 of this chapter, the "Georgia Advocate for the Protection of Children Act," or provided under Chapter 4A of Title 49. The CASA's right to access such records shall be as otherwise authorized by law.

(h)(1) All records and information acquired, reviewed, or produced by a CASA during the course of his or her appointment shall be deemed confidential and shall not be disclosed except as ordered by the court.

(2) Except as provided in Code Section 49–5–41, any CASA who discloses confidential information obtained during the course of his or her appointment shall be guilty of a misdemeanor. CASA's shall maintain all information and records regarding mental health, developmental disability, and substance abuse according to the confidentiality requirements contained in Code Section 37–3–166, 37–4–125, or 37–7–166, as applicable.

(i) Any CASA authorized and acting in good faith, in the absence of fraud or malice, and in accordance with the duties required by this Code section shall have immunity from any liability, civil or criminal, that might otherwise be incurred or imposed as a result of taking or failing to take any action pursuant to this Code section. This Code section shall not be construed as imposing any additional duty on a CASA which is not already otherwise imposed by law.

(j)(1) The court may remove a CASA from a case upon finding that the CASA has acted in a manner contrary to the child's best interest, or if the court otherwise deems continued service as unwanted or unnecessary.

(2) The court may discharge a CASA for nonparticipation in a case or upon finding that the CASA has acted in a manner contrary to the mission and purpose of the affiliate court appointed special advocate program.

Laws 2007, Act 231, § 2, eff. May 24, 2007; Laws 2008, Act 471, § 15, eff. May 12, 2008.

Historical and Statutory Notes

The 2008 amendment by Act 471 was a provision contained in a correction bill.

Former § 15–11–9.1 was renumbered as § 15–11–24.3 by Laws 2000, p. 20, § 1.

§ 15–11–10. Community based risk reduction programs

(a) As used in this Code section, the term "program" means a community based risk reduction program established pursuant to this Code section.

(b) Any court may by order establish within the geographical jurisdiction of the court a court approved community based risk reduction program for the purpose of utilizing available community resources in assessment and intervention in cases of delinquency, deprivation, or unruliness. Subject to the procedures, requirements, and supervision established in the order creating such program, any individual and any public or private agency or entity may participate in the program.

(c) In any jurisdiction within which a program has been established, when a child comes before the court for disposition in any case involving delinquency, deprivation, or unruliness, the court may order that an assessment be made of the child and the circumstances resulting in the child being before the court. The assessment would be developed by assembling existing information and individualized plans of the agencies involved in providing services to the child and his or her family. The court may further order that, if the assessment demonstrates a need therefor, a case plan may be developed by a panel representing community agencies as authorized by the court, which plan may be amended or revised from time to time by the court or by the panel taking into consideration requests for revision made by a parent, the parents, or a guardian. Upon request, the child or the parents, or both, may be present during any review of the child's case by the panel. Such case plan shall contain the proposed actions and alternatives for the proper and efficient use of available community resources to assist the child. The case plan shall be served on the child and the child's parent, parents, or guardian. Included with the case plan shall be a cover letter which contains the following information: (1) sources to explain to the recipient of the case plan the process, procedures, and penalties for not responding to the court order in the prescribed time period; and (2) the deadline for responding to the court order and stating objections to the case plan or any portion thereof, which shall be ten days from the date of service. If no objection is made or if the child, parent, parents, or guardian consents to the case plan, the case plan shall be incorporated into and made a part of the disposition order entered in the case by entry of a supplemental order. The case plan may be modified by the court at any time the child is under the jurisdiction of the court. If a child or a parent or guardian objects to the case plan, the court shall conduct a hearing, at which the court may decline to adopt the case plan or may confirm or modify the case plan. In implementing a case plan, the court shall have available all of the protective powers set forth in Code Section 15–11–11, without the necessity of a show cause hearing, unless objection is made to the case plan. Code Section 15–11–11 should provide interventions reasonably necessary to effect the appropriate treatment plan for the protection and benefit of the child.

(d) Notwithstanding any provision contained in this article, in this Code, or in any rule or regulation adopted by any department, board, or agency of the state to the contrary, the court and any individual, public or private agency, or other entity participating in a program established pursuant to this Code section may exchange, as necessary, information, medical records, school records, records of adjudication, treatment records, and any other records or information which may aid in the assessment of and intervention with the children and families in the program. Such information shall be used by such individuals and agencies only for the purposes provided in this Code section and as authorized by the court for the purpose of implementing the case plan and for the purposes permitted under each agency's own rules and regulations. Such information shall not be released to any other individual or agency except as may be necessary to effect the appropriate treatment or intervention as provided in the case plan. Such information shall otherwise remain confidential and the court may punish any violations of confidentiality as contempt of court. Any person who authorizes or permits any person or agency not listed in Code Section 49–5–41, Code Section 19–7–5, or this Code section to have access to such records concerning reports of child abuse declared confidential by Code Section 49–5–40 shall be guilty of a misdemeanor. Any person who knowingly and under false pretenses obtains or attempts to obtain records or reports of child abuse declared confidential by Code Section 49–5–40 or information contained therein except as authorized by Code Section 49–5–41, Code Section 19–7–5, or this Code section shall be guilty of a misdemeanor. Records made confidential by Code Section 49–5–40 and information obtained from such records may not be made a part of any record which is open to the public except that a district attorney may use and make public that record or information in the course of any criminal prosecution for any offense which constitutes or results from child abuse. This Code section shall not abridge the provisions of Code Section 37–3–166, 37–4–125, or 37–7–166 relating to confidentiality of patient or client records and shall not serve to destroy or in any way abridge the confidential or privileged character thereof.

(e)(1) As part of a program, a court may implement or adopt an early intervention program designed to identify children and families who are at risk of becoming involved with the court through petitions alleging that a child is delinquent, deprived, or unruly. Such early intervention program shall be for the purpose of developing and implementing intervention actions or plans to divert the children and their families from becoming involved in future cases in the court. The involvement of the judge of the court shall be for the limited purpose of facilitating the development of the program and for the purpose of protecting the confidentiality of the children and families participating in the program.

(2) As part of such an early intervention program, the court may enter into protocol agreements with school systems within the court's jurisdiction, the county department of family and children services, the county department of health, any state or local department or agency, any mental health agency or institution, local physicians or health care providers, licensed counselors and social workers, and any other social service, charitable, or other entity or any individual functioning within the jurisdiction of the court and with any other agency or individual providing educational or treatment services to families and children within the jurisdiction of the court. Such protocol agreements shall authorize those persons and agencies entering into them to exchange confidential information in the same manner and subject to the same restrictions, conditions, and penalties as provided in subsection (d) of this Code section.

(3) When any agency or entity participating in a protocol agreement under this subsection identifies a child who is at risk of becoming delinquent, deprived, or unruly, the agency or entity shall refer the case to a multiagency staffing panel. The panel shall develop a multiagency intervention plan for the child. The child or the parents, or both, may be present during any review of the child's case by the panel. The parents or guardian of the child shall be notified of the plan by the agency making the referral or by a person or entity designated by the panel to administer the program. The staff of the court, but not

the judge, shall work with the other agencies involved to educate the parents and the child on the importance of following the plan and on the consequences if either the parents or the child is referred to the court. If an intervention plan is developed for a child and the parent or parents or guardian consents to the plan, the failure to comply with the plan or any portion thereof may constitute the basis for a referral to the department of family and children services as shall be provided in the protocol agreement.

Laws 1994, p. 417, § 1; Laws 2000, p. 20, § 1.

Formerly Code 1981, § 15-11-66.

Historical and Statutory Notes

The 2000 amendment, which restructured this chapter into parts and modified statutory references to reflect this restructuring, renumbered this section from § 15-11-66.

§ 15-11-11. Protective orders

(a) On application of a party or on the court's own motion, the court may make an order restraining or otherwise controlling the conduct of a person if an order of disposition of a child has been or is about to be made in a proceeding under this article and due notice of the application or motion and the grounds therefor and an opportunity to be heard thereon have been given to the person against whom the order is directed. Such an order may require any such person:

(1) To stay away from the home or the child;

(2) To permit a parent to visit the child at stated periods;

(3) To abstain from offensive conduct against the child, the child's parent, or any person to whom custody of the child is awarded;

(4) To give proper attention to the care of the home;

(5) To cooperate in good faith with an agency to which custody of a child is entrusted by the court or with an agency or association to which the child is referred by the court;

(6) To refrain from acts of commission or omission that tend to make the home not a proper place for the child;

(7) To ensure that the child attends school pursuant to any valid law relating to compulsory attendance;

(8) To participate with the child in any counseling or treatment deemed necessary after consideration of employment and other family needs; and

(9) To enter into and complete successfully a substance abuse program approved by the court.

(b) After notice and opportunity for hearing afforded to a person subject to a protective order, the order may be modified or extended for a further specified period, or both, or may be terminated if the court finds that the best interests of the child and the public will be served thereby.

(c) Protective orders may be enforced by citation to show cause for contempt of court by reason of any violation thereof and, where protection of the welfare of the child so requires, by the issuance of a warrant to take the alleged violator into custody and bring him or her before the court.

Laws 1971, p. 709, § 1; Laws 1980, p. 1013, § 2; Laws 1984, p. 562, § 1; Laws 1986, p. 1017, § 1; Laws 1996, p. 474, § 2; Laws 2000, p. 20, § 1.

Formerly Code 1933, § 24A-3401; Code 1933, § 24A-3401a; Code 1981, § 15-11-57.

Historical and Statutory Notes

The 2000 amendment, which restructured this chapter into parts and modified statutory references to reflect this restructuring, renumbered this section from § 15-11-57. In addition the amendment inserted gender neutral referents.

Uniform Law

This section is based upon § 53 of the Uniform Law Commissioners' Model Juvenile Court Act. See 9A Uniform Laws Annotated, Master Edition, or ULA Database on Westlaw.

§ 15-11-12. Investigation and report

(a) If the allegations of a petition alleging delinquency, unruliness, or deprivation are admitted by a party or if notice of a hearing under Code Section 15-11-30.2 has been given, the court prior to the hearing on need for treatment or rehabilitation and disposition may direct that a social study and report in writing to the court be made by the probation officer of the court or other person designated by the court, concerning the child, the child's family, the child's environment, and other matters relevant to disposition of the case. If the allegations of the petition are not admitted and notice of a hearing under Code Section 15-11-30.2 has not been given, the court shall not direct the making of the study and report until after the court has heard the petition upon notice of hearing given pursuant to this article and has found that the child committed a delinquent act or is an unruly or deprived child.

(b) During the pendency of any proceeding, the court may order the child to be examined at a suitable place by a physician or psychologist and may also order medical or surgical treatment of a child who is suffering from a serious physical condition or illness which, in the opinion of a licensed physician, requires prompt treatment, even if the parent, guardian, or other custodian has not been given notice of a hearing, is not available, or without good cause informs the court of his or her refusal to consent to the treatment.

Laws 1915, p. 35, § 32; Laws 1950, p. 367, §§ 12, 19; Laws 1951, p. 291, § 13; Laws 1971, p. 709, § 1; Laws 1986, p. 1017, § 1; Laws 2000, p. 20, § 1.

Formerly Code 1933, § 24-2432; Code 1933, § 24A-2101; Code 1981, § 15-11-32.

Historical and Statutory Notes

The 2000 amendment, which restructured this chapter into parts and modified statutory references to reflect this restructuring, renumbered this section from § 15-11-32. In addition the amendment inserted gender neutral referents.

Uniform Law

This section is based upon § 28 of the Uniform Law Commissioners' Model Juvenile Court Act. See 9A Uniform Laws Annotated, Master Edition, or ULA Database on Westlaw.

§ 15-11-13. Rights and duties of legal custodian

A custodian to whom legal custody has been given by the court under this article has the right to physical custody of the child, the right to determine the nature of the care and treatment of the child, including ordinary medical care, and the right and duty to provide for the care, protection, training, and education and the physical, mental, and moral welfare of the child, subject to the conditions and limitations of the order and to the remaining rights and duties of the child's parents or guardian.

Laws 1971, p. 709, § 1; Laws 1986, p. 1017, § 1; Laws 2000, p. 20, § 1.

Formerly Code 1933, § 24A-2901; Code 1981, § 15-11-43.

Historical and Statutory Notes

The 2000 amendment which restructured this chapter redesignated this section from § 15-11-43.

Uniform Law

This section is based upon § 38 of the Uniform Law Commissioners' Model Juvenile Court Act. See 9A Uniform Laws Annotated, Master Edition, or ULA Database on Westlaw.

§ 15–11–14. Emergency care and supervision of child without court order

(a) Notwithstanding Code Section 15–11–45 or any other provision of law, the Department of Human Services is authorized to provide emergency care and supervision to any child without seeking a court order for a period not to exceed seven days when:

(1) As a result of an emergency or illness, the person who has physical and legal custody of the child or children is unable to provide for the care and supervision of the child or children, and such person or a law enforcement officer, emergency personnel employed by a licensed ambulance provider, fire rescue personnel, or a hospital administrator or his or her designee requests that the department exercise such emergency custody; and

(2) The child or children are not at imminent risk of abuse or neglect, other than the risks arising from being without a caretaker.

During such period, the department shall endeavor to place the child or children with a relative of the parent or guardian, in shelter care, or in emergency foster care or shall make other appropriate placement arrangements. The department shall have the same rights and powers with regard to the child or children as does the custodial parent or other legal custodian.

(b) Immediately upon receiving custody of the child or children, the department shall begin a diligent search for a relative or other designee of the parent who can provide for the care and supervision of the child or children.

(c) At any time during such seven-day period, upon the parent or guardian's notification to the department that the parent or guardian, or a relative or designee thereof, is able to provide care to and exercise control over the child or children, the department shall release the child or children to the person having custody of the child or children at the time the child or children were taken into the custody of the department or to such person's relative or designee except as provided in subsection (d) of this Code section.

(d) Upon the expiration of such seven-day period, if the child or children have not been released pursuant to subsection (c) of this Code section or if the department determines that there is an issue of neglect, abandonment, or abuse, the department shall promptly contact a juvenile court intake officer or bring the child or children before the juvenile court pursuant to Code Section 15–11–47 or 15–11–49. If, upon making an investigation, the intake or other authorized officer of the court finds that shelter care is warranted for the child or children, then, for purposes of this chapter, the child or children shall be deemed to have been placed in shelter care at the time such finding was made. The department may take such other and further actions under this article and all other provisions of law, as are authorized and appropriate, with regard to the child or children.

(e) During the period when a child is in the care and supervision of the department pursuant to this Code section, the department shall have the same authority to consent to medical treatment for the child as does the child's custodial parent or other legal custodian.

(f) The department and its successors, agents, assigns, and employees shall be immune from any and all liability for providing care and supervision for a child pursuant to subsection (a) of this Code section, for consenting to medical treatment for the child pursuant to subsection (e) of this Code section, and for releasing the child pursuant to subsection (c) of this Code section.

Laws 1999, p. 1232, § 1; Laws 2000, p. 20, § 1; Laws 2000, p. 136, § 15; Laws 2009, Act 102, § 2–2, eff. July 1, 2009.

Formerly Code 1981, § 15–11–17.1.

Historical and Statutory Notes

The 2009 amendment by Act 102 substituted "Department of Human Services" for "Department of Human Resources" throughout the section.

§ 15–11–15. Temporary protective custody of child by physician without court order and without parental consent

(a) Notwithstanding Code Section 15–11–45 or any other provision of law, a physician, licensed to practice medicine in the State of Georgia in accordance with Article 2 of Chapter 34 of Title 43, who is treating a child may take or retain temporary protective custody of the child, without a court order and without the consent of a parent, guardian, or custodian, provided that:

(1) The physician has reasonable cause to believe that the child is in a circumstance or condition that presents an imminent danger to the child's life or health as a result of suspected abuse or neglect; and

(2) There is not sufficient time for a court order to be obtained under this article for temporary custody of the child before the child may be removed from the presence of the physician.

(b) A physician detaining a child in temporary custody shall:

(1) Make reasonable and diligent efforts to inform the parents, guardian, or custodian of the child of the whereabouts of the child;

(2) As soon as possible, make a report of the suspected abuse or neglect which caused him or her to take temporary custody of the child, as required by subsection (e) of Code Section 19–7–5, and inform the child welfare agency designated by the Department of Human Services to which such report is made that the child has been detained in temporary custody as provided in this Code section; and

(3) Not later than 24 hours after the child is detained in temporary custody:

(A) Contact a juvenile court intake officer as provided in paragraph (2) of subsection (a) of Code Section 15–11–47, and inform such intake officer that the child is in imminent danger to his or her life or health as a result of suspected abuse or neglect; or

(B) Contact a law enforcement officer who shall take the child into custody and promptly bring the child before a juvenile court intake officer as provided in Code Sections 15–11–47 and 15–11–48.

(c) A child who meets the requirements for inpatient admission shall be retained in the hospital or institution until such time as the child is medically ready for discharge. Upon notification by the hospital or institution to the department that a child who is not eligible for inpatient admission or who is medically ready for discharge has been taken into custody by a physician in accordance with subsection (b) of this Code section, provided that the child has been placed in the custody of the Department of Human Services, the department shall take physical custody of the child within six hours of being notified.

(d) If the intake officer determines that the child is to be detained, in accordance with Code Sections 15–11–46 and 15–11–48 and subsection (a) of Code Section 15–11–49 and the court orders that the child be detained in the legal custody of the Department of Human Services, acting by and through any of the county departments of family and children services, then:

(1) If the child remains in the physical care of the physician, the department shall take physical possession of the child within six hours of being notified by the physician, unless the child meets the criteria for admission to a hospital, or other medical institution or facility where he or she has been detained in the temporary custody by a physician; or

(2) If the child has been brought before the juvenile court by a law enforcement officer, the department shall promptly take physical possession of the child.

(e) If the child is not released, then the court shall notify the child's parents, guardian, or other custodian, the physician, and the Department of Human Services of the detention hearing which is to be held within 72 hours as provided in subsection (c) of Code Section 15-11-49.

(f) If the intake officer determines that the child should not be detained, the child shall be released pursuant to the provisions set forth in Code Section 15-11-49.

(g) If after the detention hearing the child is not released, the physician shall file the petition required by subsection (e) of Code Section 15-11-49 in accordance with this article, provided that such physician continues to believe that the child's life or health is in danger as a result of suspected abuse or neglect.

(h) Any hospital or physician authorized and acting in good faith and in accordance with acceptable medical practice in the treatment of a child under this Code section shall have immunity from any liability, civil or criminal, that might otherwise be incurred or imposed as a result of taking or failing to take any action, pursuant to this Code section. This Code section shall not be construed as imposing any additional duty not already otherwise imposed by law.

Laws 2000, p. 231, § 3; Laws 2009, Act 102, § 2-2, eff. July 1, 2009.

Historical and Statutory Notes

The 2000 amendment, which restructured this chapter into parts and modified statutory references to reflect this restructuring, renumbered this section from § 15-11-17.1. In addition the amendment inserted gender neutral referents.

The 2009 amendment by Act 102 substituted "Department of Human Services" for "Department of Human Resources" throughout the section.

§ 15-11-16. Renumbered as § 15-11-30 by Laws 2000, p. 20, § 1

§ 15-11-17. Renumbered as § 15-11-45 by Laws 2000, p. 20, § 1

§ 15-11-17.1. Renumbered as § 15-11-14 by Laws 2000, p. 20, § 1

Part 2

Juvenile Court Administration

§ 15-11-18. Creation of juvenile courts; term, compensation, and qualifications of judges; presiding judges; practice of law by judges; action by superior court judges

(a) *Creation.* There is created a juvenile court in every county in the state.

(b) *Appointment; authority; judgeships in existence on or before October 1, 2000.* The judge or a majority of the judges of the superior court in each circuit in the state may appoint one or more qualified persons as judge of the juvenile courts of the circuit. Such superior court judge or judges shall establish the total number of circuit-wide juvenile court judges and shall establish whether the judge or judges shall be full time or part time, or a combination of full time and part time. Each circuit-wide judge appointed will have the authority to act as judge of each juvenile court in each county of the circuit. If no person is appointed as a juvenile court judge for the circuit, then the superior court judge or judges of the circuit shall assume the duties of the juvenile court judge in all counties in the circuit in which a separate juvenile court judgeship had not been established as part of the duties of the superior court judge. All juvenile court judgeships, their methods of compensation, selection, and operation, established on or before October 1, 2000, shall continue until such time as one or more circuit-wide juvenile court judges are appointed. However, in any circuit where a superior court judge assumes the duties of the juvenile court judge, such circuit shall not be entitled to the state funds provided for in subsection (d) of this Code section.

(c) *Fulfilling preexisting terms; jurisdiction.* When one or more circuit-wide juvenile court judges are appointed, any juvenile court judge in office at that time shall be authorized to fulfill his or her term of office. The jurisdiction of each judge shall be circuit wide.

(d) *Terms and compensation of judges.*

(1) Each juvenile court judge appointed under this Code section shall serve for a term of four years. Except as otherwise provided by law, the compensation of the full-time or part-time juvenile court judges shall be set by the superior court as provided in subsection (h) of this Code section with the approval of the governing authority or governing authorities of the county or counties for which the juvenile court judge is appointed.

(2) The state, out of funds appropriated to the judicial branch of government, shall contribute toward the salary of the judges on a per circuit basis in the following amounts:

(A) Each circuit with one or more juvenile court judges who are not superior court judges assuming the duties of juvenile court judges shall receive a state grant of $85,000.00;

(B) In addition to the base amount set out in subparagraph (A) of this paragraph, each circuit which on or after October 1, 2000, has more than four superior court judges is eligible for additional state grants. For each superior court judge who exceeds the base of four judges, the circuit shall be eligible for an additional grant in an amount equal to one-fourth of the base amount of the state grant set out in subparagraph (A) of this paragraph;

(C) In those circuits where the judge or judges of the superior court elect to use the state grant provided in this paragraph for one or more part-time judges, the amount of the state grant shall be as follows:

(i) For each part-time judge who works one day weekly .... $ 17,000.00

(ii) For each part-time judge who works two days weekly 34,000.00

(iii) For each part-time judge who works three days weekly 51,000.00

(iv) For each part-time judge who works four days weekly 68,000.00;

provided, however, that a grant for one or more part-time judges shall not exceed the amount the circuit is eligible for in accordance with subparagraphs (A) and (B) of this paragraph;

(D) Reserved;

(E) Reserved; and

(F) All state grants provided by this paragraph shall be spent solely on salaries for juvenile court judges and shall not be used for any other purposes.

(3) After the initial appointments and prior to any subsequent appointment or reappointment of any part-time or full-time juvenile court judge under this Code section, the judge or judges responsible for making the appointment shall publish notice of the opening on the juvenile court once a month for three months prior to such appointment or reappointment in the official legal organs of each of the counties in the circuit where the juvenile court judge has venue. The expense of such publication shall be paid by the county governing authority in the county where such notice or notices are published.

(e) *Qualifications of judges.* No person shall be judge of the juvenile court unless, at the time of his or her appointment, he or she has attained the age of 30 years, has been a citizen of the state for three years, and has practiced law for five years. A juvenile court judge shall be eligible for reappointment.

(f) *Presiding judge.* In the event that more than one juvenile court judge is appointed, one shall be designated presiding judge.

(g) *Practice of law by judges.* It shall be unlawful for any full-time juvenile court judge to engage in any practice of law outside his or her role as a juvenile court judge. It shall be unlawful for a part-time judge of any juvenile court to engage directly or indirectly in the practice of law in his or her own name or in the name of another as a partner in any manner in any case, proceeding, or matter of any kind in his or her own court or in any other court in any case, proceeding, or any other matters of which his or her own court has pending jurisdiction or has had jurisdiction. It shall be unlawful for any juvenile court judge, full time or part time, to give advice or counsel to any person on any matter of any kind whatsoever which has arisen directly or indirectly in his or her own court, except such advice or counsel as he or she is called upon to give while performing the duties of a juvenile court judge.

(h) *Action by superior court judges.* In any case in which action under this Code section is to be taken by the superior court judge of the circuit, such action shall be taken as follows:

(1) Where there are one or two judges, such action shall be taken by the chief judge of the circuit; and

(2) Where there are more than two judges, such action shall be taken by a majority vote of the judges of the circuit.

(i) *Administration and expenses.* Each juvenile court created under this article shall be assigned and attached to the superior court of the county for administrative purposes. The governing authority of the county of residence of each juvenile court judge shall offer the juvenile court judge or judges insurance benefits and any other benefits except retirement or pension benefits equivalent to those offered to employees of the county, with a right to contribution from other counties in the circuit for a pro rata contribution toward the costs of such benefits, based on county population. Counties shall continue to provide membership in retirement plans available to county employees for any juvenile court judge in office before July 1, 1998, who did not become a member of the Georgia Judicial Retirement System provided by Chapter 23 of Title 47. Except as otherwise provided by subsection (d) of this Code section, all expenditures of the court are declared to be an expense of the court and payable out of the county treasury with the approval of the governing authority or governing authorities of the county or counties for which the juvenile court judge is appointed.

(j) *Applicability.*

(1) To the extent that the provisions of this Code section conflict with a local constitutional amendment authorizing the election of a juvenile court judge and with the provisions of a local Act authorized by such local constitutional amendment to provide for the term of office, vacancies in office, qualifications, compensation, and full-time or part-time status of a juvenile court judge or judges, the provisions of such local constitutional amendment and such local Act shall govern.

(2) The state grants provided by subsection (d) of this Code section shall be provided to any circuit encompassing a juvenile court governed by the provisions of a local constitutional amendment and a local Act in the same manner as other circuits, except that, in any circuit with one or more elected juvenile court judges, the elected juvenile court judge who is senior in duration of service as a juvenile court judge shall establish, subject to other applicable provisions of law, the total number of circuit-wide juvenile court judges, whether the judge or judges shall be full time or part time or a combination of full time and part time, and the compensation of any part-time juvenile court judge or judges.

(k) *Simultaneous service by judges.*

(1) No person who is serving as a full–time juvenile court judge after appointment as judge pursuant to this Code section shall at the same time hold the office of judge of any other class of court of this state.

(2) The provisions of paragraph (1) of this subsection shall also apply to any person serving as a juvenile court judge after being elected juvenile court judge pursuant to a local law authorized by a constitutional amendment providing for the election of one or more juvenile court judges.

(3) Nothing in this subsection shall prevent any duly appointed or elected juvenile court judge from sitting by designation as a superior court judge pursuant to Code Section 15–1–9.1 or as otherwise provided by law.

Laws 1908, p. 1107, § 2; Laws 1915, p. 35, §§ 1, 21; Laws 1916, p. 58, § 3; Laws 1935, p. 399, §§ 5, 6; Laws 1950, p. 367, §§ 2, 4, 5; Laws 1951, p. 291, §§ 2, 3, 4; Laws 1956, p. 69, §§ 1, 3; Laws 1956, p. 799, § 1; Laws 1962, p. 518, § 1; Laws 1963, p. 621, § 1; Laws 1968, p. 1013, §§ 1, 2, 2A; Laws 1971, p. 709, § 1; Laws 1974, p. 586, § 1; Laws 1974, p. 1126, § 1; Laws 1982, p. 3, § 15; Laws 1982, p. 2199, § 1; Laws 1984, p. 22, § 15; Laws 1985, p. 149, § 15; Laws 1986, p. 1017, § 1; Laws 1992, p. 908, § 1; Laws 1998, p. 513, § 6; Laws 2000, p. 20, § 1; Laws 2000, p. 1094, § 1; Laws 2001, p. 4, § 15; Laws 2002, p. 1162, § 1; Laws 2005, Act 19, § 15, eff. April 7, 2005; Laws 2005, Act 86, § 1, eff. July 1, 2005; Laws 2006, Act 453, § 15(1), eff. April 14, 2006; Laws 2006, Act 453, § 15, eff. Jan. 1, 2007.

Formerly Penal Code 1910, § 886; Code 1933, §§ 24–2401, 24–2421; Code 1933, § 24A–201; Code 1981, § 15–11–3.

Historical and Statutory Notes

The 2000 amendment by Act 467, which restructured this chapter into parts and modified statutory references to reflect this restructuring, renumbered this section from § 15–11–3. In addition the amendment inserted gender neutral referents.

The 2000 amendment by Act 742 substantially rewrote this section which, as so amended, was given effect as the section text.

The 2001 amendment was a correction bill.

The 2002 amendment added subsec. (k).

The 2005 amendment by Act 19, inserted "Simultaneous service by judges" between subsec. (k) and par. (1) of the subsec.

The 2005 amendment by Act 86 rewrote subsec. (d), par. (2), which had read:

"(2) The state, out of funds appropriated to the judicial branch of government, shall contribute toward the salary of the judges on a per circuit basis in the following amounts:

"(A) Each circuit with one or more juvenile court judges who are not superior court judges assuming the duties of juvenile court judges shall receive a state grant of $ 85,000.00. Such state funds shall be spent solely on salaries for juvenile court judges and shall not be used for any other purposes.

"(B) In addition to the base amount set out in subparagraph (A) of this paragraph, each circuit which on or after October 1, 2000, has more than four superior court judges is eligible for additional state grants. For each superior court judge who exceeds the base of four judges, the circuit shall be eligible for an additional grant in an amount equal to one-fourth of the base amount of the state grant set out in subparagraph (A) of this paragraph. Such additional state grants shall be spent solely on salaries for juvenile court judges and shall not be used for any other purposes.

"(C) In those circuits where the judge or judges of the superior court elect to use the state grant provided in this Code section for one or more part-time judges, the amount of the state grant shall be as follows:

(i) For each part-time judge who works one day weekly $17,000.00
(ii) For each part-time judge who works two days weekly 34,000.00
(iii) For each part-time judge who works three days weekly 51,000.00
(iv) For each part-time judge who works four days weekly 68,000.00;

"provided, however, that a grant for one or more part-time judges shall not exceed the amount the circuit is eligible for in accordance with subparagraphs (A) and (B) of this paragraph."

In 2005, the Code Commission, in subsec. (d), par. (2), reserved subpar. (D) subsequent to its repeal, effective January 1, 2007 and substituted "judges and" for "judges, and" in the first sentence of division (i), and reserved subpar. (E) until it became effective on January 1, 2007, and substituted "judges and" for "judges, and" in the first sentence of division (i). See § 28–9–5.

The 2006 amendments by Act 453 were provisions contained in a correction bill.

Laws 2006, Act 453, § 55, provides in part:

"(b)(1) Paragraph (2) of Section 15 of this Act shall become effective on January 1, 2007."

In 2008, the Code Commission, reserved the designation of subpar. (d)(2)(E), and added "; and" at the end of the subparagraph. See § 28–9–5.

§ 15–11–18.1. Commissioning of juvenile court judges; submission of orders of appointment of associate juvenile court judges to Council of Juvenile Court Judges

(a) Whenever a juvenile court judge is appointed pursuant to Code Section 15–11–18, it shall be the duty of the clerk of the superior court to forward to the Secretary of State and to the Council of Juvenile Court Judges a certified copy of the order of appointment. The order of appointment shall set out the name of the person appointed, the term of office, the effective date of the appointment, the name of the person being succeeded, if any, and whether the office was vacated by resignation, death, or otherwise. Upon receipt of said order, the Secretary of State shall issue a commission as for superior court judges.

(b) Whenever an associate juvenile court judge is appointed to serve in a juvenile court, the clerk of the court shall forward a certified copy of the order of appointment to the Council of Juvenile Court Judges.

Laws 1984, p. 565, § 1; Laws 1990, p. 1691, § 2; Laws 2000, p. 20, § 1.

Formerly Code 1981, § 15–11–3.1.

Historical and Statutory Notes

The 2000 amendment, which restructured this chapter into parts and modified statutory references to reflect this restructuring, renumbered this section from § 15–11–3.1.

§ 15–11–19. Council of Juvenile Court Judges

(a) All of the judges and associate judges of the courts exercising jurisdiction over children shall constitute a Council of Juvenile Court Judges. The council shall annually elect from among its members a judge to serve as presiding judge and chairperson of the council. The council shall meet at stated times to be fixed by it, on call of the chairperson. It may establish general policies for the conduct of courts exercising jurisdiction over children and may promulgate uniform rules and forms governing procedures and practices of the courts. It shall publish in print or electronically an annual report of the work of the courts exercising jurisdiction over children, which shall include statistical and other data on the courts' work and services, research studies it may make of the problems of children and families dealt with by the courts, and any recommendations for legislation. The council is authorized to inspect and copy records of the court, law enforcement agencies, and the Department of Human Services for the purpose of compiling statistical data on children.

(b) Subject to the approval of the council, the presiding judge shall appoint a chief administrative and executive officer for the council, who shall have the title of director of the council. Under the general supervision of the presiding judge and within the policies established by the council, the director shall:

(1) Provide consultation to the courts regarding the administration of court services and the recruitment and training of personnel;

(2) Make recommendations to the council for improvement in court services;

(3) With the approval of the presiding judge, appoint consultants and necessary clerical personnel to perform the duties assigned to the council and the director;

(4) Collect necessary statistics and prepare an annual report of the work of the courts;

(5) Promulgate in cooperation with the Department of Juvenile Justice or any successor department or agency standard procedures for coordinating state and local probation services throughout the state; and

(6) Perform such other duties as the presiding judge shall specify.

Laws 1950, p. 367, § 33; Laws 1971, p. 709, § 1; Laws 1978, p. 1512, § 1; Laws 1991, p. 627, § 1; Laws 1992, p. 1983, § 2; Laws 1997, p. 1453, § 1; Laws 2000, p. 20, § 1; Laws 2009, Act 102, § 2–2, eff. July 1, 2009; Laws 2010, Act 615, § 10, eff. June 3, 2010.

Formerly Code 1933, § 24A–501; Code 1981, § 15–11–4.

Historical and Statutory Notes

The 2000 amendment, which restructured this chapter into parts and modified statutory references to reflect this restructuring, renumbered this section from § 15–11–4. In addition the amendment inserted gender neutral referents.

The 2009 amendment by Act 102 substituted "Department of Human Services" for "Department of Human Resources" throughout the section.

The 2010 amendment by Act 615, in subsec. (a), inserted "in print or electronically" following "publish" throughout the subsection.

§ 15–11–20. Training seminars

(a) The Council of Juvenile Court Judges, in conjunction with the Institute of Continuing Judicial Education of Georgia, shall establish seminars for all judges and associate juvenile court judges exercising juvenile court jurisdiction and may make provisions relative to those seminars by court rules properly adopted; provided, however, that said judges shall receive credit for attending seminars outside of this state only in circumstances of hardship as determined by the Council of Juvenile Court Judges.

(b) These seminars shall offer instruction and training in juvenile law and procedure, child development and psychology, sociological theories relative to delinquency and breakdown of the family structure, and such other training and activities as the council may determine would promote the quality of justice in the juvenile court system.

(c) Expenses of administration of this seminar program and actual expenses incurred by the judges or associate juvenile court judges in attending these seminars shall be paid from state funds appropriated for the council for that purpose, from federal funds available to the council for that purpose, or from other appropriate sources. These expenses for judges and associate juvenile court judges shall not exceed the allowances allowed members of the General Assembly.

(d) Each judge and associate juvenile court judge exercising juvenile jurisdiction shall participate in at least one seminar established or approved by the Council of Juvenile Court Judges each year and meet such rules as established by the council pertaining to such training. Superior court judges may meet this requirement by attending seminars held in conjunction with the seminars for superior court judges provided by the Institute of Continuing Judicial Education of Georgia. Judges and associate juvenile court judges shall not exercise juvenile court jurisdiction after January 1, 1983, unless the Council of Juvenile Court Judges certifies that annual training has been accomplished or unless the judge is in the first year of his or her initial appointment;

provided, however, that the council may in hardship cases extend deadlines for compliance with this Code section.

Laws 1981, p. 1390, § 1; Laws 1990, p. 1691, § 3; Laws 1995, p. 783, §§ 1, 2; Laws 1998, p. 653, § 4; Laws 2000, p. 20, § 1.

Formerly Code 1933, § 24A–502; Code 1981, § 15–11–4.1.

Historical and Statutory Notes

The 2000 amendment, which restructured this chapter into parts and modified statutory references to reflect this restructuring, renumbered this section from § 15–11–4.1.

§ 15–11–21. Associate juvenile court judges

(a) The judge may appoint one or more persons to serve as an associate juvenile court judge in juvenile matters on a full-time or part-time basis. The associate juvenile court judge shall serve at the pleasure of the judge, and his or her salary shall be fixed by the judge with the approval of the governing authority or governing authorities of the county or counties for which the associate juvenile court judge is appointed. The salary of each associate juvenile court judge shall be paid from county funds.

(b) Each associate juvenile court judge shall have the same qualifications as required for a judge of the juvenile court as provided in subsection (e) of Code Section 15–11–18; provided, however, that any person serving as an associate juvenile court judge on July 1, 2007, shall be qualified for appointment thereafter to serve as an associate juvenile court judge.

(c) In any case or class of cases involving alleged delinquent, unruly, or deprived children, the judge shall determine whether such case shall be conducted by the judge or by the associate juvenile court judge in the manner provided by this article.

(d) Upon the conclusion of a hearing before an associate juvenile court judge, the associate juvenile court judge shall sign and file an order of the court which sets forth the decision made by the associate juvenile court judge. A copy of the order shall be given to the parties to the proceedings.

(e) A rehearing may be ordered by the judge at any time and, except for detention hearings or probable cause hearings, shall be ordered if a party files a written request therefor within five days after receiving a copy of the order of the associate juvenile court judge.

Laws 1915, p. 35, § 29; Laws 1950, p. 367, § 6; Laws 1951, p. 291, § 5; Laws 1971, p. 709, § 1; Laws 1982, p. 2199, § 2; Laws 1986, p. 1017, § 1; Laws 1990, p. 1691, § 4; Laws 1991, p. 627, § 2; Laws 1994, p. 562, § 1; Laws 1998, p. 653, § 5; Laws 2000, p. 20, § 1; Laws 2007, Act 236, § 1, eff. July 1, 2007; Laws 2007, Act 325, § 1, eff. July 1, 2007; Laws 2008, Act 471, § 15, eff. May 12, 2008.

Formerly Code 1933, § 24–2429; Code 1933, § 24A–701; Code 1981, § 15–11–10.

Historical and Statutory Notes

The 2000 amendment, which restructured this chapter into parts and modified statutory references to reflect this restructuring, renumbered this section from § 15–11–10.

The 2007 amendment by Act 236, in subsec. (a), deleted the last sentence which had read "Except as provided in subsection (b) of this Code section, an associate juvenile court judge shall be a member of the State Bar of Georgia or shall be a graduate of a law school; provided, however, that any person serving as a referee on July 1, 1983, shall be qualified for appointment thereafter to serve as an associate juvenile court judge."; and rewrote subsec. (b). Prior to amendment subsec. (b) had read:

"(b) In each county having a population of 75,000 or more according to the United States decennial census of 1990 or any such future census and which employs a full-time juvenile court judge, each associate juvenile court judge appointed after July 1, 1994, shall have the same qualifications as required for a judge of the juvenile court as provided in subsection (e) of Code Section 15–11–18; provided, however, that any person serving as a referee on July 1, 1983, shall be qualified for appointment thereafter to serve as an associate juvenile court judge."

The 2007 amendment by Act 325 rewrote subsec. (c) which had read:

"(c) The judge may direct that hearings in any case or class of cases involving alleged delinquent, unruly, or deprived children shall be conducted in the first instance by the associate juvenile court judge in the manner provided by this article. If a party so requests, the hearing shall be conducted by the judge except for detention hearings or probable cause hearings, which shall be conducted by the associate juvenile court judge if directed to do so by the judge."

The 2008 amendment by Act 471 was a provision contained in a correction bill.

§ 15–11–22. Associate juvenile court traffic judges

(a) The judge may appoint one or more persons to serve at the pleasure of the judge as associate juvenile court traffic judges on a full-time or part-time basis. An associate juvenile court traffic judge shall be a member of the State Bar of Georgia or shall be otherwise qualified by experience and training. The compensation of the associate juvenile court traffic judges shall be fixed by the judge with the approval of the governing authority of the county and shall be paid in equal monthly installments from county funds, unless otherwise provided by law.

(b) The court may direct that any case or class of cases arising under Code Section 15–11–73 shall be heard in the first instance by an associate juvenile court traffic judge who shall conduct the hearing in accordance with Code Section 15–11–73. Upon the conclusion of the hearing, the associate juvenile court traffic judge shall file an order of the court with a copy thereof to the child and other parties to the proceedings.

Laws 1971, p. 709, § 1; Laws 1990, p. 1691, § 6; Laws 1991, p. 627, § 3; Laws 2000, p. 20, § 1.

Formerly Code 1933, § 24A–3102; Code 1981, § 15–11–50.

Historical and Statutory Notes

The 2000 amendment, which restructured this chapter into parts and modified statutory references to reflect this restructuring, renumbered this section from § 15–11–50.

§ 15–11–23. Pro tempore juvenile court judges

In the event of the disqualification, illness, or absence of the judge of the juvenile court, the judge of the juvenile court may appoint any attorney at law resident in the judicial circuit in which the court lies, any judge or senior judge of the superior courts, or any duly appointed juvenile court judge to serve as judge pro tempore of the juvenile court. In the event the judge of the juvenile court is absent or unable to make such appointment, the judge of the superior court of that county may so appoint. The person so appointed shall have the authority to preside in the stead of the disqualified, ill, or absent judge and shall be paid from the county treasury such emolument as the appointing judge shall prescribe; provided, however, that the emolument shall not exceed the compensation received by the regular juvenile court judge for such services.

Laws 1916, p. 58, § 4; Laws 1950, p. 367, § 5; Laws 1960, p. 200, § 1; Laws 1962, p. 150, § 1; Laws 1971, p. 709, § 1; Laws 1974, p. 1126, § 9; Laws 1977, p. 812, § 1; Laws 2000, p. 20, § 1.

Formerly Code 1933, § 24–2442; Code 1933, § 24A–3701; Code 1981, § 15–11–63.

Historical and Statutory Notes

The 2000 amendment, which restructured this chapter into parts and modified statutory references to reflect this restructuring, renumbered this section from § 15–11–63.

§ 15–11–24. Clerks and other personnel

The judge of the juvenile court shall have the authority to appoint clerks and any other personnel necessary for the execution of the purposes of this chapter. The compensation of the employees shall be fixed by the judge, with the approval of the governing authority of the county. The salaries of the employees shall be paid out of county funds. All appointments shall be made from eligible lists secured from the local merit boards in those counties where such boards exist or from lists established by competitive examinations conducted by the court. The appointment, salary, tenure, and all other conditions of employment of the employees shall be in accordance with the laws and regulations governing the merit system in operation or such rules and regulations as are established by the court. Any employee of the court may be removed for cause by the judge of the court, the reasons therefor to be assigned in writing.

Laws 1950, p. 367, §§ 7, 8; Laws 1951, p. 291, § 6; Laws 1953, p. 352, § 1; Laws 1971, p. 709, § 1; Laws 1985, p. 149, § 15; Laws 1986, p. 1017, § 1; Laws 2000, p. 20, § 1.

Formerly Code 1933, § 24A–603; Code 1981, § 15–11–9.

Historical and Statutory Notes

The 2000 amendment, which restructured this chapter into parts and modified statutory references to reflect this restructuring, renumbered this section from § 15–11–9.

§ 15–11–24.1. Appointment and salaries of probation officers

The judge may appoint one or more probation officers who shall have the powers and duties stated in Code Section 15–11–24.2. The salaries of the probation officers shall be fixed by the judge with the approval of the governing authority of the county or counties for which they are appointed and shall be payable from county funds.

Laws 1915, p. 35, §§ 22, 30; Laws 1916, p. 58, § 3; Laws 1950, p. 367, § 7; Laws 1951, p. 291, § 6; Laws 1953, p. 352, § 1; Laws 1971, p. 709, § 1; Laws 2000, p. 20, § 1.

Formerly Code 1933, §§ 24–2422, 24–2430; Code 1933, § 24A–601; Code 1981, § 15–11–7.

Historical and Statutory Notes

The 2000 amendment, which restructured this chapter into parts and modified statutory references to reflect this restructuring, renumbered this section from § 15–11–7.

Uniform Law

This section is based upon § 5 of the Uniform Law Commissioners' Model Juvenile Court Act. See 9A Uniform Laws Annotated, Master Edition, or ULA Database on Westlaw.

§ 15–11–24.2. Duties of probation officers

A probation officer:

(1) Shall make investigations, reports, and recommendations to the court as directed by this article;

(2) Shall receive and examine complaints and charges of delinquency, unruly conduct, or deprivation of a child for the purpose of considering the commencement of proceedings under this article;

(3) Shall supervise and assist a child placed on probation or in the protective supervision or care of such probation officer by order of the court or other authority of law;

(4) Shall make appropriate referrals to other private or public agencies of the community if their assistance appears to be needed or desirable;

(5) May take into custody and detain a child who is under the supervision or care of such probation officer as a delinquent, unruly, or deprived child if the probation officer has reasonable cause to believe that the child's health or safety or that of another is in imminent danger, or that the child may abscond or be removed from the jurisdiction of the court, or when so ordered by the court pursuant to this article. A probation officer may not conduct accusatory proceedings against a child who is or may be under such probation officer's care or supervision;

(6) Shall perform all other functions designated by this chapter or by order of the court pursuant thereto. Any of the functions specified in this Code section may be performed in another state if authorized by the court located in this state and permitted by the laws of the other state; and

(7) Other laws to the contrary notwithstanding, no county juvenile intake or probation officer or staff of the Department of Juvenile Justice serving as juvenile intake or probation officer shall be liable for the acts of any child not detained or taken into custody as provided in paragraph (5) of this Code section when, in the judgment of such officer, such detention or custody is not warranted.

Laws 1915, p. 35, § 26; Laws 1950, p. 367, § 8; Laws 1951, p. 291, § 8; Laws 1971, p. 709, § 1; Laws 1974, p. 1126, § 3; Laws 1986, p. 1017, § 1; Laws 1993, p. 438, § 1; Laws 1997, p. 1453, § 1; Laws 2000, p. 20, § 1.

Formerly Code 1933, § 24–2426; Code 1933, § 24A–602; Code 1981, § 15–11–8.

Historical and Statutory Notes

The 2000 amendment, which restructured this chapter into parts and modified statutory references to reflect this restructuring, renumbered this section from § 15–11–8. In addition the amendment substituted reference to child for juvenile.

Uniform Law

This section is based upon § 6 of the Uniform Law Commissioners' Model Juvenile Court Act. See 9A Uniform Laws Annotated, Master Edition, or ULA Database on Westlaw.

§ 15–11–24.3. Transfer of probation and intake services and employees to Department of Juvenile Justice

(a) As used in this Code section, the term:

(1) "Department" means the Department of Juvenile Justice.

(2) "Probation and intake employees" means any probation officer specified in Code Section 15–11–24.1 and any personnel of a juvenile court to whom are delegated the duties of an intake officer under this article, other than a juvenile court judge, associate juvenile court judge, or court service worker.

(3) "Probation and intake services" means those services provided by probation and intake employees for the juvenile court of a county.

(b) After June 30, 1992, the intake and probation services of the juvenile court of each county may be transferred to and become a part of the state-wide juvenile and intake services and fully funded through the department. The intake and probation employees of juvenile courts of those counties whose intake and probation services are transferred pursuant to this Code section shall become employees of the department on the date of such transfer and on and after that date such employees shall be subject to the salary schedules and other personnel policies of the department, except that the salaries of such employees shall not be reduced as a result of becoming employees of the department.

(c) The intake and probation services of the juvenile court of a county may be transferred to the department pursuant to this Code section by local Act of the General Assembly which approves such transfer and becomes effective after June 30, 1992.

(d) Persons who were probation and intake employees of the juvenile court of a county on June 30, 1996, but who were transferred as probation and intake employees to and became a part of the state-wide juvenile and intake services system fully funded through the department before January 1, 1999, shall be covered employees in the classified service of the State Personnel Administration.

Laws 1991, p. 1823, § 1; Laws 1999, p. 81, § 15; Laws 2000, p. 20, § 1; Laws 2000, p. 1258, § 1; Laws 2009, Act 155, § 1, eff. July 1, 2009.

Formerly Code 1981, § 15–11–9.1.

Historical and Statutory Notes

The 2000 amendment by Act 467, which restructured this chapter into parts and modified statutory references to reflect this restructuring, renumbered this section from § 15–11–9.1.

The 2000 amendment by Act 793 added subsec. (d).

The 2009 amendment by Act 155 substituted "State Personnel Administration" for "state merit system" throughout the section.

§ 15–11–25. Training requirements for juvenile court clerks

(a) Any person who is appointed as or is performing the duties of a clerk of the juvenile court after July 1, 2000, shall satisfactorily complete 20 hours of training in the performance of the duties of a clerk of the juvenile court within the first 12 months following such appointment or the first performance of such duties.

(b) Any person who is appointed as or is performing the duties of a clerk of the juvenile court for any year after 2000, other than the year in which such person satisfactorily completes any initial training required under subsection (a) of this Code section, shall satisfactorily complete in that year 12 hours of additional training in the performance of such person's duties as clerk.

(c) The training required by this Code section shall be provided by the Institute of Continuing Judicial Education of Georgia. Upon satisfactory completion of such training, a certificate issued by such institute shall be placed into the minutes of the juvenile court record in the county in which such person serves as a clerk of the juvenile court. All reasonable expenses of such training including, but not limited to, any tuition fixed by such institution shall be paid from county funds by the governing authority of the county for which the person serves as a clerk of the juvenile court, unless funding is provided from other sources.

(d) A judge of the juvenile court shall appoint a clerk pro tempore for that court for the period of training in order for the regular clerk to attend training required by this Code section. Such clerk pro tempore shall not be required to meet the training otherwise required by this Code section for performing the clerk's duties.

(e) The provisions of this Code section shall not apply to clerks of juvenile courts who also act as clerks of superior courts and who already have mandatory training requirements in such capacity.

Laws 2000, p. 1102, § 2.

§ 15–11–26. Renumbered as § 15–11–39, § 15–11–49.1 by Laws 2000, p. 20, § 1

§ 15–11–27. Renumbered as § 15–11–39.1 by Laws 2000, p. 20, § 1

Part 3

Jurisdiction and Venue

§ 15–11–28. Jurisdiction over juveniles

(a) *Exclusive original jurisdiction.* Except as provided in subsection (b) of this Code section, the court shall have exclusive original jurisdiction over juvenile matters and shall be the sole court for initiating action:

(1) Concerning any child:

(A) Who is alleged to be delinquent;

(B) Who is alleged to be unruly;

(C) Who is alleged to be deprived;

(D) Who is alleged to be in need of treatment or commitment as a mentally ill or mentally retarded child;

(E) Who is alleged to have committed a juvenile traffic offense as defined in Code Section 15–11–73; or

(F) Who has been placed under the supervision of the court or on probation to the court; provided, however, that such jurisdiction shall be for the sole purpose of completing, effectuating, and enforcing such supervision or a probation begun prior to the child's seventeenth birthday; or

(2) Involving any proceedings:

(A) For obtaining judicial consent to the marriage, employment, or enlistment in the armed services of any child if such consent is required by law;

(B) Under the Interstate Compact on Juveniles, or any comparable law, if enacted or adopted in this state;

(C) For the termination of the legal parent-child relationship and the rights of the biological father who is not the legal father of the child, other than that in connection with adoption proceedings under Article 1 of Chapter 8 of Title 19, in which the superior courts shall have concurrent jurisdiction to terminate the legal parent-child relationship and the rights of the biological father who is not the legal father of the child;

(D) Under Article 3 of this chapter, relating to prior notice to a parent or guardian relative to an unemancipated minor's decision to seek an abortion; or

(E) Brought by a local board of education pursuant to Code Section 20–2–766.1.

(b) *Criminal jurisdiction.*

(1) Except as provided in paragraph (2) of this subsection, the court shall have concurrent jurisdiction with the superior court over a child who is alleged to have committed a delinquent act which would be considered a crime if tried in a superior court and for which the child may be punished by loss of life, imprisonment for life without possibility of parole, or confinement for life in a penal institution.

(2)(A) The superior court shall have exclusive jurisdiction over the trial of any child 13 to 17 years of age who is alleged to have committed any of the following offenses:

(i) Murder;

(ii) Voluntary manslaughter;

(iii) Rape;

(iv) Aggravated sodomy;

(v) Aggravated child molestation;

(vi) Aggravated sexual battery; or

(vii) Armed robbery if committed with a firearm.

(A.1) The granting of bail or pretrial release of a child charged with an offense enumerated in subparagraph (A) of this paragraph shall be governed by the provisions of Code Section 17–6–1.

(B) After indictment, the superior court may after investigation and for extraordinary cause transfer any case involving a child 13 to 17 years of age alleged to have committed any offense enumerated in subparagraph (A) of this paragraph which is not punishable by loss of life, imprisonment for life without possibility of parole, or confinement for life in a penal institution. Any such transfer shall be appealable by the State of Georgia pursuant to Code Section 5–7–1. Upon such a transfer by the superior court, jurisdiction shall vest in the juvenile court and jurisdiction of the superior court shall terminate. Any case transferred by the superior court to the juvenile court pursuant to this subparagraph shall be subject to the designated felony provisions of Code Section 15–11–63 and the transfer of the case from superior court to juvenile court shall constitute notice to the child that such case is subject to the designated felony provisions of Code Section 15–11–63.

(C) Before indictment, the district attorney may, after investigation and for extraordinary cause, decline prosecution in the superior court of a child 13 to 17 years of age alleged to have committed an offense specified in subparagraph (A) of this paragraph. Upon declining such prosecution in the superior court, the district attorney shall immediately cause a petition to be filed in the appropriate juvenile court for adjudication. Any case transferred by the district attorney to the juvenile court pursuant to this subparagraph shall be subject to the designated felony provisions of Code Section 15–11–63 and the transfer of the case from superior court to juvenile court shall constitute notice to the child that such case is subject to the designated felony provisions of Code Section 15–11–63.

(D) The superior court may transfer any case involving a child 13 to 17 years of age alleged to have committed any offense enumerated in subparagraph (A) of this paragraph and convicted of a lesser included offense not included in subparagraph (A) of this paragraph to the juvenile court of the county of the child's residence for disposition. Upon such a transfer by the superior court, jurisdiction shall vest in the juvenile court and jurisdiction of the superior court shall terminate.

(E) Within 30 days of any proceeding in which a child 13 to 17 years of age is convicted of certain offenses over which the superior court has exclusive jurisdiction as provided in subparagraph (A) of this paragraph or adjudicated delinquent on the basis of conduct which if committed by an adult would constitute such offenses, the superior court shall provide written notice to the school superintendent or his or her designee of the school in which such child is enrolled or, if the information is known, of the school in which such child plans to be enrolled at a future date. Such notice shall include the specific criminal offense that such child committed. A local school system to which the child is assigned may request further information from the court's file.

(c) *Custody and support jurisdiction.*

(1) Where custody is the subject of controversy, except in those cases where the law gives the superior courts exclusive jurisdiction, in the consideration of these cases the juvenile court shall have concurrent jurisdiction to hear and determine the issue of custody and support when the issue is transferred by proper order of the superior court.

(2)(A) In any case where a child is alleged to be a deprived child as defined in paragraph (8) of Code Section 15–11–2, the juvenile court upon a finding of deprivation shall have jurisdiction to order temporary child support for such child to be paid by that person or those persons determined to be legally obligated to support such child. In determining such temporary child support, the juvenile court shall apply the child support guidelines provided in Code Section 19–6–15. Where there is an existing order of a superior court or other court of competent jurisdiction setting child support for the child, the juvenile court may order the child support obligor in the existing order to make such payments instead to the caretaker of the child on a temporary basis but shall not otherwise modify the terms of the existing order. A copy of the juvenile court's order shall be filed in the clerk's office of the court that entered the existing order. The juvenile court shall have jurisdiction to order temporary child support for the child to be paid by any other person determined to be legally obligated to support such child.

(B) Temporary child support orders entered pursuant to subparagraph (A) of this paragraph shall be enforceable by the juvenile court through the contempt powers of the juvenile court as provided in Code Section 15–11–5 so long as the juvenile court is entitled to exercise jurisdiction over the deprivation case.

(d) *Age limit for new actions.* The juvenile court shall not have jurisdiction to initiate any new action against an individual for acts committed after he or she has reached the age of 17 years. This subsection does not affect the court's jurisdiction to enter extension orders pursuant to Code Section 15–11–58.

(e) *Concurrent jurisdiction as to legitimation petitions.*

(1) The juvenile court shall have concurrent jurisdiction to hear any legitimation petition transferred to the juvenile court by proper order of the superior court.

(2) The juvenile court shall have jurisdiction to hear any legitimation petition filed pursuant to Code Section 19–7–22 as to a child with respect to whom a deprivation proceeding is pending in the juvenile court at the time the legitimation petition is filed.

(3) Notwithstanding the provisions of paragraphs (1) and (2) of this subsection, after a petition for legitimation is granted, if a demand for a jury trial as to support has been properly filed by either parent, then the case shall be transferred to superior court for such jury trial.

Laws 1915, p. 35, § 2; Laws 1935, p. 399, § 1; Laws 1950, p. 367, § 9; Laws 1951, p. 291, § 9; Laws 1953, Nov.-Dec. Sess., p. 87, § 3; Laws 1955, p. 610, § 1; Laws 1956, p. 603, § 1; Laws 1968, p. 1013, § 3; Laws 1971, p. 709, § 1; Laws 1973, p. 882, § 1; Laws 1977, p. 181, § 1; Laws 1979, p. 1179, § 1; Laws 1979, p. 1404, § 1; Laws 1985, p. 149, § 15; Laws 1987, p. 1013, § 1; Laws 1990, p. 1572, § 1; Laws 1994, p. 1012, § 14; Laws 1997, p. 1064, § 2; Laws 1997, p. 1436, § 3; Laws 1997, p. 1681, § 1; Laws 2000, p. 20, § 1; Laws 2000, p. 618, § 2; Laws 2002, p. 1162, § 2; Laws 2003, Act 377, § 1, eff. July 1, 2003; Laws 2009, Act 171, § 3, eff. July 1, 2009.

Formerly Code 1933, § 24–2402; Code 1933, § 24A–301; Code 1981, § 15–11–5.

Historical and Statutory Notes

The 2000 amendment by Act 467, which restructured this chapter into parts and modified statutory references to reflect this restructuring, renumbered this section from § 15–11–5. In addition the amendment substituted reference to child for juvenile and provided gender neutral referents.

The 2000 amendment by Act 685 added subsec. (a)(2)(E).

The 2002 amendment substituted in the second sentence of subsec. (b)(2)(C) for "withdraw the case and lodge it" the words "cause a petition to be filed".

The 2003 amendment by Act 377 rewrote subsec. (c) which had read as follows:

"(c) *Concurrent custody and support jurisdiction.* Where custody is the subject of controversy, except in those cases where the law gives the superior courts exclusive jurisdiction, in the consideration of these cases the juvenile court shall have concurrent jurisdiction to hear and determine the issue of custody and support when the issue is transferred by proper order of the superior court."

The 2009 amendment by Act 171, in subsec. (a), par. (2), subpar. (C), inserted "Article 1 of".

§ 15–11–29. Venue

(a) A proceeding under this article may be commenced in the county in which the child resides. If delinquent or unruly conduct is alleged, the proceeding may be commenced in the county in which the acts constituting the alleged delinquent or unruly conduct occurred. If deprivation is alleged, the proceeding may be brought in the county in which the child is present when it is commenced; provided, however, that for the convenience of the parties and witnesses, the court may transfer the proceeding to the county in which the child resides. If the proceeding is transferred, certified copies of all legal and social documents and records pertaining to the proceeding on file with the clerk of court shall accompany the transfer. A juvenile court judge, an associate juvenile court judge, a judge pro tempore of the juvenile court, or any person sitting as a juvenile court judge may conduct hearings in connection with any proceeding under this article in any county within the judicial circuit.

(b) When a superior court judge sits as juvenile court judge, hearings in connection with any proceeding under this article may be heard before the judge in any county within the judicial circuit over which the judge presides.

Laws 1950, p. 367, § 28; Laws 1951, p. 291, § 9; Laws 1953, Nov.-Dec. Sess., p. 87, § 3; Laws 1968, p. 1013, § 3; Laws 1971, p. 709, § 1; Laws 1986, p. 1017, § 1; Laws 1995, p. 774, § 1; Laws 1998, p. 653, § 1; Laws 2000, p. 20, § 1.

Formerly Code 1933, § 24A–1101; Code 1981, § 15–11–15.

Historical and Statutory Notes

The 2000 amendment, which restructured this chapter into parts and modified statutory references to reflect this restructuring, renumbered this section from § 15–11–15.

Uniform Law

This section is based upon § 11 of the Uniform Law Commissioners' Model Juvenile Court Act. See 9A Uniform Laws Annotated, Master Edition, or ULA Database on Westlaw.

§ 15–11–30. Transfer to county of residence or retention of jurisdiction

(a) As used in this Code section, the term:

(1) "Adjudicating court" means the juvenile court which makes a finding that a child has committed an unruly or delinquent act.

(2) "Nonresident child" means a child who is a resident of a county of this state other than a county encompassed by the circuit of the adjudicating court.

(3) "Resident child" means a child who is a resident of a county encompassed by the circuit of the adjudicating court.

(b) Except as provided in subsection (c) of this Code section, if the adjudicating court finds that a nonresident child has committed an unruly or delinquent act, the adjudicating court may after adjudication of delinquency or unruliness retain jurisdiction over the disposition of the nonresident child or may transfer the proceeding to the county of the child's residence for disposition. Like transfer may be made if the residence of the child changes pending the proceeding. Prior to making any order for disposition of the nonresident child, the adjudicating court shall, if it retains jurisdiction, communicate to the court of the county of the child's residence the fact of the adjudication of delinquency or unruliness. This communication shall state the date upon which the adjudicating court plans to enter an order for disposition of the nonresident child and shall request any information or recommendations relevant to the disposition of the nonresident child. Any such recommendation shall be considered by but shall not be binding upon the adjudicating court in making its order for disposition.

(c) If the adjudicating court finds that a nonresident child has committed an unruly or delinquent act and that the court has jurisdiction over one or more resident children who also participated in the same delinquent or unruly act, then the adjudicating court may retain jurisdiction over the disposition of the nonresident child or may transfer the proceedings as provided in subsection (b) of this Code section. Prior to making any order for disposition of the nonresident child the adjudicating court shall, if it retains jurisdiction, communicate to the court of the county of the child's residence the fact of the adjudication of delinquency or unruliness. This communication shall state the date upon which the adjudicating court plans to enter an order for disposition of the nonresident child and shall request any information or recommendations relevant to the disposition of the nonresident child. Any such recommendations shall be considered by but shall not be binding upon the adjudicating court in making its order for disposition.

(d) When any case is transferred pursuant to subsection (b) of this Code section certified copies of all legal and social documents and records pertaining to the case on file with the clerk of the court shall accompany the transfer.

Laws 1971, p. 709, § 1; Laws 1983, p. 829, § 1; Laws 1984, p. 22, § 15; Laws 1995, p. 774, § 2; Laws 2000, p. 20, § 1.

Formerly Code 1933, § 24A–1201; Code 1981, § 15–11–16.

Historical and Statutory Notes

The 2000 amendment, which restructured this chapter into parts and modified statutory references to reflect this restructuring, renumbered this section from § 15–11–16.

Uniform Law

This section is based upon § 12 of the Uniform Law Commissioners' Model Juvenile Court Act. See 9A Uniform Laws Annotated, Master Edition, or ULA Database on Westlaw.

§ 15–11–30.1. Appointment of guardian; jurisdiction over custody and support cases

(a)(1) The court is vested with jurisdiction to appoint a guardian of the person or property of any child and with jurisdiction over proceedings involving any child whose custody is the subject of controversy. Any such appointment shall be made pursuant to the same requirements of notice and hearing as are provided for appointments of guardians of the persons and properties of minors by the judge of the probate court.

(2)(A) In addition to the jurisdiction to appoint guardians pursuant to paragraph (1) of this subsection, the juvenile court shall be vested with jurisdiction to appoint a permanent guardian for a child whose custody is a subject of controversy before the court as a result of an adjudication that the child is deprived in accordance with Part 6 of this article. Prior to the entry of such an order, the court shall:

(i) Find that reasonable efforts to reunify the child with his or her parent would be detrimental to the child in accordance with subsection (h) of Code Section 15–11–58 or find that the living parents or parent of the child have consented to the permanent guardianship;

(ii) Find that termination of parental rights and adoption and, if the proposed guardian is not a relative of the child, that placement with a fit and willing relative, is not in the best interest of the child;

(iii) Find that the proposed permanent guardian can provide a safe and permanent home for the child;

(iv) Find that the appointment of a permanent guardian for the child is in the best interest of the child and that the individual chosen as the child's permanent guardian is the individual most appropriate to be the child's permanent guardian taking into consideration the best interest of the child; and

(v) If the child is 14 years of age or older, find that the appointment of a permanent guardian for the child is in the best interest of the child and that the individual chosen by such child as the child's permanent guardian is the individual most appropriate to be the child's permanent guardian taking into consideration the best interest of the child.

(B) The court may enter an order of support on behalf of the child against the parents of the child in accordance with paragraph (2) of subsection (c) of Code Section 15–11–28.

(C) Orders under subparagraph (A) of this paragraph shall:

(i) Remain in effect until the child reaches the age of 18 or becomes emancipated;

(ii) Not be subject to review by the court except as provided in subparagraph (D) of this paragraph; and

(iii) Establish a reasonable visitation schedule which allows the child to maintain meaningful contact with his or her parents through personal visits, telephone calls, letters, or other forms of communication or specifically include any restriction on a parent's right to visitation.

(D) The court shall retain jurisdiction over a guardianship action under this paragraph for the sole purpose of entering an order following the filing of a petition to modify, vacate, or revoke the guardianship and to appoint a new guardian. The superior courts shall have concurrent jurisdiction for enforcement or modification of any child support or visitation order entered pursuant to this Code section. The guardianship shall be modified, vacated, or revoked based upon a finding, by clear and convincing evidence, that there has been a material change in the circumstances of the child or the guardian and that such modification, vacation, or revocation of the guardianship order and the appointment of a new guardian is in the best interest of the child. Appointment of a new guardian shall be subject to the provisions of this paragraph.

(E) Notice of a guardianship petition pursuant to this paragraph shall be given in accordance with subsection (c) of Code Section 29–2–17 except that, if the parents have consented to the guardianship, notice of the petition shall not be required to be given to the individuals listed in division (vii) of subparagraph (F) of this paragraph. The hearing shall be conducted in accordance with Code Section 29–2–18, to determine the best interest of the child, and in reaching its determination the court shall consider subparagraph (A) of this paragraph.

(F) The petition for the appointment of a permanent guardian pursuant to this paragraph shall set forth:

(i) A statement of the facts upon which the court's jurisdiction is based;

(ii) The name and date of birth of the child;

(iii) The name, address, and county of domicile of the petitioner and the petitioner's relationship to the child, if any, and, if different from the petitioner, the name, address, and county of domicile of the individual nominated by the petitioner to serve as guardian and that individual's relationship to the child, if any;

(iv) A statement that:

(I) Reasonable efforts to reunify the child with his or her parent would be detrimental to the child in accordance with subsection (h) of Code Section 15–11–58 or that the living parents or parent of the child have consented to the permanent guardianship;

(II) Termination of parental rights and adoption and, if the proposed guardian is not a relative of the child, that placement with a fit and willing relative is not in the best interest of the child;

(III) The proposed guardian can provide a safe and permanent home for the child;

(IV) The appointment of a permanent guardian for the child is in the best interest of the child and that the individual chosen as the child's guardian is the individual most appropriate to be the child's permanent guardian taking into consideration the best interest of the child; and

(V) If the child is 14 years of age or older, that the appointment of a permanent guardian for the child is in the best interest of the child and that the individual chosen by such child as the child's permanent guardian is the individual most appropriate to be the child's permanent guardian taking into consideration the best interest of the child;

(v) A statement of whether the child was born out of wedlock and, if so, the name and address of the biological father, if known;

(vi) Whether, to the petitioner's knowledge, there exists any notarized or witnessed document made by a parent of the child that deals with the guardianship of the child and the name and address of any designee named in the document;

(vii) In addition to the petitioner and the nominated guardian and, if the parents have not consented to the permanent guardianship, the names and addresses of the following relatives of the child whose whereabouts are known:

(I) The adult siblings of the child; provided, however, that not more than three adult siblings need to be listed;

(II) If there is no adult sibling of the child, the grandparents of the child; provided, however, that not more than three grandparents need to be listed; or

(III) If there is no grandparent of the child, any three of the nearest adult relatives of the child determined according to Code Section 53–2–1 of the "Revised Probate Code of 1998";

(viii) Whether a temporary guardian has been appointed for the child or a petition for the appointment of a temporary guardian has been filed or is being filed; and

(ix) The reason for any omission in the petition for appointment of a permanent guardian for the child in the event full particulars are lacking.

(G) A guardian of the person of a child appointed under this paragraph shall have the rights and duties of a permanent guardian as are provided in Code Sections 29–2–21, 29–2–22, and 29–2–23 and shall take the oath required of a guardian as provided in Code Section 29–2–24.

(b) Other courts, in handling divorce, alimony, habeas corpus, or other cases involving the custody of a child or children, may transfer the question of the determination of custody, support, or custody and support to the juvenile court for investigation and a report back to the superior court or for investigation and determination. If the referral is for investigation and determination, then the juvenile court shall proceed to handle the matter in the same manner as though the action originated under this article in compliance with the order of the superior court. At any time prior to the determination of any such question, the juvenile court may transfer the jurisdiction of the question back to the referring superior court.

Laws 1915, p. 35, § 35; Laws 1950, p. 367, §§ 10, 21; Laws 1951, p. 291, §§ 10, 24; Laws 1968, p. 1013, §§ 4, 15; Laws 1971, p. 709, § 1; Laws 1974, p. 1126, § 2; Laws 1986, p. 1017, § 1; Laws 2000, p. 20, § 1; Laws 2003, Act 377, § 2, eff. July 1, 2003; Laws 2008, Act 795, § 1, eff. July 1, 2008.

Formerly Code 1933, § 24–2435; Code 1933, § 24A–302; Code 1981, § 15–11–6.

Historical and Statutory Notes

The 2000 amendment, which restructured this chapter into parts and modified statutory references to reflect this restructuring, renumbered this section from § 15–11–6.

The 2003 amendment by Act 377 rewrote subsec. (b) which had read as follows:

"(b) Courts of record, in handling divorce, alimony, or habeas corpus cases involving the custody of a child or children, may transfer the question of the determination of custody and support to the juvenile court for investigation and a report back to the superior court or for investigation and determination. If the referral is for investigation and determination, then the juvenile court shall proceed to handle the matter in the same manner as though the action originated under this article in compliance with the order of the superior court. At any time prior to the determination of such question, the juvenile court may transfer the jurisdiction of the question back to the referring superior court."

The 2008 amendment by Act 795 rewrote this section, which formerly read:

"(a) The court is vested with jurisdiction to appoint a guardian of the person or property of any child and with jurisdiction over proceedings involving any child whose custody is the subject of controversy. Any such appointment shall be made pursuant to the same requirements of notice and hearing as are provided for appointments of guardians of the persons and properties of minors by the judge of the probate court.

"(b) Other courts, in handling divorce, alimony, habeas corpus, or other cases involving the custody of a child or children, may transfer the question of the determination of custody, support, or custody and support to the juvenile court for investigation and a report back to the superior court or for investigation and determination. If the referral is for investigation and determination, then the juvenile court shall proceed to handle the matter in the same manner as though the action originated under this article in compliance with the order of the superior court. At any time prior to the determination of any such question, the juvenile court may transfer the jurisdiction of the question back to the referring superior court."

§ 15–11–30.2. Transfer to other courts after filing of petition

(a) After a petition has been filed alleging delinquency based on conduct which is designated a crime or public offense under the laws, including local ordinances, the court before hearing the petition on its merits may transfer the offense for prosecution to the appropriate court having jurisdiction of the offense if:

(1) A hearing on whether the transfer should be made is held in conformity with Code Sections 15–11–6, 15–11–7, and 15–11–41;

(2) Notice in writing of the time, place, and purpose of the hearing is given to the child and his or her parents, guardian, or other custodian at least three days before the hearing;

(3) The court in its discretion determines there are reasonable grounds to believe that:

(A) The child committed the delinquent act alleged;

(B) The child is not committable to an institution for the mentally retarded or mentally ill; and

(C) The interests of the child and the community require that the child be placed under legal restraint and the transfer be made; and

(4) The child:

(A) Was at least 15 years of age at the time of the alleged delinquent conduct; or

(B) Was 13 or 14 years of age and either committed an act for which the punishment is loss of life or confinement for life in a penal institution or committed aggravated battery resulting in serious bodily injury to a victim.

(b) After a petition has been filed alleging delinquency based on conduct which is designated a crime or public offense under the laws, including local ordinances, the court before hearing the petition on its merits shall transfer the offense for prosecution to the appropriate court having jurisdiction of the offense if:

(1) A hearing on whether the transfer should be made is held in conformity with Code Sections 15–11–6, 15–11–7, and 15–11–41;

(2) Notice in writing of the time, place, and purpose of the hearing is given to the child and the child's parents, guardian, or other custodian at least three days before the hearing;

(3) The court in its discretion determines there are reasonable grounds to believe that the child while confined to a youth development center committed the offense of murder, voluntary manslaughter, aggravated assault, or aggravated battery as defined in Chapter 5 of Title 16; and

(4) The child was at least 14 years of age at the time of the alleged conduct described in paragraph (3) of this subsection.

(c) The transfer terminates the jurisdiction of the juvenile court over the child with respect to an adjudication of delinquency as to the delinquent acts alleged in the petition.

(d) No child, either before or after reaching 17 years of age, shall be prosecuted for an offense previously committed unless the case has been transferred as provided in this Code section.

(e) Statements made by the child at any hearing under this article are not admissible against the child over objection in the criminal proceedings following the transfer.

(f) This Code section shall not apply to any proceeding within the exclusive jurisdiction of the superior court pursuant to subparagraph (b)(2)(A) of Code Section 15–11–28.

Laws 1915, p. 35, § 16; Laws 1950, p. 367, § 11; Laws 1951, p. 291, § 11; Laws 1953, Nov.-Dec. Sess., p. 87, §§ 1, 2; Laws 1955, p. 581, § 1; Laws 1971, p. 709, § 1; Laws 1973, p. 882, § 6; Laws 1978, p. 1758, § 1; Laws 1986, p. 1017, § 1; Laws 1990, p. 1930, § 4; Laws 1994, p. 1012, § 25; Laws 2000, p. 20, § 1; Laws 2000, p. 1419, § 2.

Formerly Code 1933, § 24–2416; Code 1933, § 24A–2501; Code 1981, § 15–11–39.

Historical and Statutory Notes

The 2000 amendment by Act 467, which restructured this chapter into parts and modified statutory references to reflect this restructuring, renumbered this section from § 15–11–39. In addition the amendment substituted reference to child for juvenile and provided gender neutral referents.

The 2000 amendment by Act 862 substantially rewrote subsec. (a) which formerly provided:

"(a) Except as otherwise provided in subsection (b) of this Code section, after a petition has been filed alleging delinquency based on conduct which is designated a crime or public offense under the laws, including local ordinances, the court before hearing the petition on its merits may transfer the offense for prosecution to the appropriate court having jurisdiction of the offense if:

"(1) A hearing on whether the transfer should be made is held in conformity with Code Sections 15–11–28, 15–11–30, and 15–11–31:

"(2) Notice in writing of the time, place, and purpose of the hearing is given

to the child and his parents, guardian, or other custodian at least three days before the hearing;

"(3) The court in its discretion determines there are reasonable grounds to

believe that:

"(A) The child committed the delinquent act alleged;

"(B) The child is not committable to an institution for the mentally retarded or mentally ill; and

"(C) The interests of the child and the community require that the child be placed under legal restraint and the transfer be made; and

"(4) The child was at least 15 years of age at the time of the alleged delinquent conduct or the child was 13 or 14 years of age and committed an act for which the punishment is loss of life or confinement for life in a penal institution."

§ 15–11–30.3. Mandatory transfers when child 15 years of age or older has committed designated felony act

(a) After a petition has been filed alleging that a child 15 years of age or older has committed a designated felony act, the court shall follow the procedure specified in this Code section if the designated felony act alleged to have been committed would have constituted the crime of burglary if done by an adult and the child has been found at separate court appearances to have committed acts which would have constituted the crime of burglary if done by an adult on three or more previous occasions.

(b) If this Code section applies, the court shall hold a hearing in conformity with Code Sections 15–11–6, 15–11–7, and 15–11–41. Notice shall be given in writing of the time, place, and purpose of the hearing to the child and the child's parents, guardian, or other custodian at least three days before the hearing.

(c) If at the hearing the court determines that there are reasonable grounds to believe that the child committed the designated felony act alleged, the court shall transfer the offense to superior court for prosecution. The transfer terminates the jurisdiction of the juvenile court over the child with respect to the designated felony act alleged. The transfer order shall constitute a determination by a court of inquiry that there is probable cause to commit the child as a defendant to the criminal court competent to try the child. After such a transfer, until and unless a judgment of guilt is entered and sentence pronounced, the child shall be detained only as provided in subsection (a) of Code Section 15–11–48.

(d) Upon the transfer of any matter to superior court under this Code section, the district attorney shall after investigation report to the judge whether the matter should be retransferred to juvenile court; and the superior court may upon such a report or on its own motion order the matter retransferred to juvenile court. After such a retransfer, the provisions of subsection (d) of Code Section 15–11–63 shall apply as in other cases.

(e) The provisions of this Code section shall not apply to a smash and grab burglary.

Laws 1982, p. 1871, § 3; Laws 1982, p. 1871, § 6; Laws 2000, p. 20, § 1; Laws 2010, Act 674, § 1, eff. July 1, 2010.

Formerly Code 1933, § 24A–2502; Code 1981, § 15–11–39.1.

Historical and Statutory Notes

The 2000 amendment, which restructured this chapter into parts and modified statutory references to reflect this restructuring, renumbered this section from § 15–11–39.1. In addition the amendment substituted reference to child for juvenile and provided gender neutral referents.

The 2010 amendment by Act 674 added subsec. (e).

§ 15–11–30.4. Transfers to juvenile court

If it appears to any court in a criminal proceeding or a quasi-criminal proceeding that the defendant is a child, except in cases where the superior court has exclusive or concurrent jurisdiction as provided in subsection (b) of Code Section 15–11–28, the case shall forthwith be transferred to the juvenile court together with a copy of the accusatory pleading and all other papers, documents, and transcripts of testimony relating to the case. The transferring court shall order that the child be taken forthwith to the juvenile court or to a place of detention designated by the court or shall release him or her to the custody of his or her parent, guardian, custodian, or other person legally responsible for him or her, to be brought before the juvenile court at a time designated by that court. The accusatory pleading may serve in lieu of a petition in the juvenile court unless that court directs the filing of a petition.

Laws 1915, p. 35, §§ 14, 15; Laws 1935, p. 399, § 3; Laws 1950, p. 367, § 10; Laws 1951, p. 291, § 10; Laws 1968, p. 1013, § 4; Laws 1971, p. 709, § 1; Laws 1973, p. 882, § 3; Laws 1994, p. 1012, § 16; Laws 2000, p. 20, § 1.

Formerly Code 1933, §§ 24–2414, 24–2415; Code 1933, § 24A–901; Code 1981, § 15–11–13.

Historical and Statutory Notes

The 2000 amendment, which restructured this chapter into parts and modified statutory references to reflect this restructuring, renumbered this section from § 15–11–13. In addition the amendment substituted reference to child for juvenile.

§ 15–11–30.5. Transfers when disposition incorporates reunification plan

Whenever an order of disposition incorporates a reunification plan and the residence of the parent is not in the county of the court with jurisdiction or the residence of the parent changes to a county other than the county of the court with jurisdiction, the court may transfer jurisdiction to the juvenile court of the residence of the parent or parents to whom reunification is directed. Said transferring court shall provide the receiving court within 30 days of the filing of the transfer order with certified copies of the adjudication order, the order of disposition, the order of transfer, the case plan, and such other court documents deemed necessary by the sending court to enable the receiving court to assume jurisdiction over the matter. Compliance with this Code section shall terminate jurisdiction in the transferring court and initiate jurisdiction in the receiving court.

Laws 1998, p. 653, § 3; Laws 2000, p. 20, § 1.

Formerly Code 1981, § 15–11–41.1.

Historical and Statutory Notes

The 2000 amendment, which restructured this chapter into parts and modified statutory references to reflect this restructuring, renumbered this section from § 15–11–41.1.

§ 15–11–31. Renumbered as § 15–11–7 by Laws 2000, p. 20, § 1

§ 15–11–32. Renumbered as § 15–11–12 by Laws 2000, p. 20, § 1,

§ 15–11–33. Renumbered as § 15–11–56, § 15–11–65 by Laws 2000, p. 20, § 1

§ 15–11–34. Renumbered as § 15–11–55 by Laws 2000, p. 20, § 1

Part 4

Commencement and Conduct of Proceedings

§ 15–11–35. Commencement of proceedings

A proceeding under this article may be commenced:

(1) By transfer of a case from another court as provided in Code Section 15–11–30.4;

(2) As provided in Code Section 15–11–73 in a proceeding charging a juvenile traffic offense;

(3) By the court accepting jurisdiction as provided in Code Section 15–11–88 or accepting supervision of a child as provided in Code Section 15–11–90;

(4) In other cases of alleged delinquency, unruliness, or deprivation by the filing of a petition as provided in this article. The petition and all other documents in the proceeding shall be entitled "In the interest of ____, a child," except upon appeal, in which event the anonymity of the child shall be preserved by appropriate use of initials; or

(5) In other cases as provided by law.

Laws 1915, p. 35, § 3; Laws 1950, p. 367, § 12; Laws 1951, p. 291, § 12; Laws 1968, p. 1013, § 5; Laws 1971, p. 709, § 1; Laws 1986, p. 1017, § 1; Laws 2000, p. 20, § 1.

Formerly Code 1933, § 24–2403; Code 1933, § 24A–801; Code 1981, § 15–11–11.

Historical and Statutory Notes

The 2000 amendment, which restructured this chapter into parts and modified statutory references to reflect this restructuring, renumbered this section from § 15–11–11.

Uniform Law

This section is based upon § 8 of the Uniform Law Commissioners' Model Juvenile Court Act. See 9A Uniform Laws Annotated, Master Edition, or ULA Database on Westlaw.

§ 15–11–35.1. Renumbered as § 15–11–66.1 by Laws 2000, p. 20, § 1

§ 15–11–36. Subpoenas

Upon application of a party, the court, or any authorized officer of the court, the clerk of the court shall issue, or the court on its own motion may issue, subpoenas requiring attendance and testimony of witnesses and production of papers at any hearing under this article.

Laws 1971, p. 709, § 1; Laws 1986, p. 1017, § 1; Laws 2000, p. 20, § 1.

Formerly Code 1933, § 24A–1501; Code 1981, § 15–11–22.

Historical and Statutory Notes

The 2000 amendment, which restructured this chapter into parts and modified statutory references to reflect this restructuring, renumbered this section from § 15–11–22.

Uniform Law

This section is based upon § 18 of the Uniform Law Commissioners' Model Juvenile Court Act. See 9A Uniform Laws Annotated, Master Edition, or ULA Database on Westlaw.

§ 15–11–36.1. Renumbered as § 15–11–57 and § 15–11–68 by Laws 2000, p. 20, § 1

§ 15–11–37. Preliminary determination before filing of petition

A petition alleging delinquency, deprivation, or unruliness of a child shall not be filed unless the court or a person authorized by the court has determined and endorsed upon the petition that the filing of the petition is in the best interest of the public and the child.

Laws 1950, p. 367, § 12; Laws 1971, p. 709, § 1; Laws 2000, p. 20, § 1.

Formerly Code 1933, § 24A–1601; Code 1981, § 15–11–23.

Historical and Statutory Notes

The 2000 amendment, which restructured this chapter into parts and modified statutory references to reflect this restructuring, renumbered this section from § 15–11–23.

Uniform Law

This section is based upon § 19 of the Uniform Law Commissioners' Model Juvenile Court Act. See 9A Uniform Laws Annotated, Master Edition, or ULA Database on Westlaw.

§ 15–11–38. Who may make petition

Subject to Code Section 15–11–37, the petition alleging delinquency, deprivation, or unruliness of a child may be made by any person, including a law enforcement officer, who has knowledge of the facts alleged or is informed and believes that they are true.

Laws 1915, p. 35, § 3; Laws 1950, p. 367, § 12; Laws 1971, p. 709, § 1; Laws 2000, p. 20, § 1.

Formerly Code 1933, § 24–2403; Code 1933, § 24A–1602; Code 1981, § 15–11–24.

Historical and Statutory Notes

The 2000 amendment, which restructured this chapter into parts and modified statutory references to reflect this restructuring, renumbered this section from § 15–11–24.

Uniform Law

This section is based upon § 20 of the Uniform Law Commissioners' Model Juvenile Court Act. See 9A Uniform Laws Annotated, Master Edition, or ULA Database on Westlaw.

§ 15–11–38.1. Contents of petition

The petition shall be verified and may be on information and belief. It shall set forth plainly:

(1) The facts which bring the child within the jurisdiction of the court, with a statement that it is in the best interest of the child and the public that the proceeding be brought and, if delinquency or unruly conduct is alleged, that the child is in need of supervision, treatment, or rehabilitation, as the case may be;

(2) The name, age, and residence address, if any, of the child on whose behalf the petition is brought;

(3) The names and residence addresses, if known to petitioner, of the parents, guardian, or custodian of the child and of the child's spouse, if any; or, if neither the child's parents, nor the child's guardian, nor the child's custodian resides or can be found within the state or if their respective places of residence address are unknown, the name of any known adult relative residing within the county or, if there is none, the known adult relative residing nearest to the location of the court; and

(4) If the child is in custody and, if so, the place of his or her detention and the time the child was taken into custody.

Laws 1915, p. 35, § 3; Laws 1950, p. 367, § 12; Laws 1951, p. 291, § 12; Laws 1968, p. 1013, § 5; Laws 1971, p. 709, § 1; Laws 2000, p. 20, § 1.

Formerly Code 1933, § 24–2403; Code 1933, § 24A–1603; Code 1981, 15–11–25.

Historical and Statutory Notes

The 2000 amendment, which restructured this chapter into parts and modified statutory references to reflect this restructuring, renumbered this section from § 15–11–25. In addition the amendment substituted reference to child for juvenile and provided gender neutral referents.

Uniform Law

This section is based upon § 21 of the Uniform Law Commissioners' Model Juvenile Court Act. See 9A Uniform Laws Annotated, Master Edition, or ULA Database on Westlaw.

§ 15–11–39. Time for hearing; summons

(a) After the petition has been filed the court shall set a hearing thereon, which, if the child is in detention, shall not be later than ten days after the filing of the petition. In the event the child is not in detention, the court shall set a hearing thereon which shall be not later than 60 days from the date of the filing of the petition.

(b) The court shall direct the issuance of a summons to the parents, guardian, or other custodian, a guardian ad litem, and any other persons who appear to the court to be proper or necessary parties to the proceeding, requiring them to appear before the court at the time fixed to answer the allegations of the petition. The summons shall also be directed to the child if he or she is 14 or more years of age or is alleged to be a delinquent or unruly child. A copy of the petition shall accompany the summons unless the summons is served by publication, in which case the published summons shall indicate the general nature of the allegations and where a copy of the petition can be obtained.

(c) The court may endorse upon the summons an order directing the parents, guardian, or other custodian of the child to appear personally at the hearing and directing the person having the physical custody or control of the child to bring the child to the hearing. In the event a parent, guardian, or other custodian of the child willfully fails to appear personally at the hearing after being ordered to so appear, or the parent, guardian, or other custodian of the child willfully fails to bring the child to the hearing after being so directed, the court may enter any order authorized by and in accordance with the provisions of Code Section 15–11–5.

(d) The summons shall state that a party is entitled to counsel in the proceedings and that the court will appoint counsel if the party is unable without undue financial hardship to employ counsel.

(e) A party other than the child may waive service of summons by written stipulation or by voluntary appearance at the hearing. If the child is present at the hearing, the child's counsel, with the consent of the parent, guardian, other custodian, or guardian ad litem, may waive service of summons in the child's behalf.

Laws 1915, p. 35, §§ 4, 5; Laws 1950, p. 367, § 13; Laws 1951, p. 291, § 14; Laws 1968, p. 1013, § 6; Laws 1971, p. 709, § 1; Laws 1974, p. 1126, § 4; Laws 1996, p. 868, § 4; Laws 2000, p. 20, § 1; Laws 2002, p. 1162, § 3.

Formerly Code 1933, §§ 24–2404, 24–2405; Code 1933, § 24A–1701; Code 1981, § 15–11–26.

Historical and Statutory Notes

The 2000 amendment, which restructured this chapter into parts and modified statutory references to reflect this restructuring, renumbered this section from § 15–11–26. In addition the amendment substituted reference to child for juvenile and provided gender neutral referents.

The 2002 amendment twice in subsec. (a) substituted for "fix a time for" the words "set a" preceding "hearing".

Uniform Law

This section is based upon § 22 of the Uniform Law Commissioners' Model Juvenile Court Act. See 9A Uniform Laws Annotated, Master Edition, or ULA Database on Westlaw.

§ 15–11–39.1. Service of summons

(a) If a party to be served with a summons is within this state and can be found, the summons shall be served upon him or her personally at least 24 hours before the hearing. If a party to be served is within this state and cannot be found but his or her address is known or can with reasonable diligence be ascertained, the summons may be served upon such party by mailing him or her a copy thereof by registered or certified mail or statutory overnight delivery at least five days before the hearing. If a party to be served is outside this state but he or she can be found or his or her address is known or his or her whereabouts or address can with reasonable diligence be ascertained, service of the summons may be made either by delivering a copy thereof to such party personally or by mailing a copy to him or her by registered or certified mail or statutory overnight delivery at least five days before the hearing.

(b) If, after reasonable effort, a party to be served with a summons cannot be found and such party's post office address cannot be ascertained, whether he or she is within or outside this state, the court may order service of the summons upon him or her by publication in accordance with Code Sections 9–11–4 and 9–11–5. The hearing shall not be earlier than five days after the date of the last publication.

(c) Service of the summons may be made by any suitable person under the direction of the court.

(d) The court may authorize the payment from county funds of the costs of service and of necessary travel expenses incurred by persons summoned or otherwise required to appear at the hearing.

Laws 1915, p. 35, § 6; Laws 1950, p. 367, § 14; Laws 1951, p. 291, § 15; Laws 1968, p. 1013, § 7; Laws 1971, p. 709, § 1; Laws 2000, p. 20, § 1; Laws 2000, p. 1589, § 3.

Formerly Code 1933, § 24–2406; Code 1933, § 24A–1702; Code 1981, § 15–11–27.

Historical and Statutory Notes

The 2000 amendment by Act 467, which restructured this chapter into parts and modified statutory references to reflect this restructuring, renumbered this section from § 15–11–27. In addition the amendment provided gender neutral referents.

The 2000 amendment by Act 918 provided alternatively to the use of certified mail the use of statutory overnight delivery.

§ 15–11–39.2. Interlocutory order of disposition where summons served by publication

(a) If service of summons upon a party is made by publication, the court may conduct a provisional hearing upon the allegations of the petition and enter an interlocutory order of disposition if:

(1) The petition alleges delinquency, unruly conduct, or deprivation of the child;

(2) The summons served upon any party:

(A) States that prior to the final hearing on the petition designated in the summons a provisional hearing thereon will be held at a specified time and place;

(B) Requires the party who is served other than by publication to appear and answer the allegations of the petition at the provisional hearing;

(C) States further that findings of fact and orders of disposition made pursuant to the provisional hearing will become final at the final hearing unless the party served by publication appears at the final hearing; and

(D) Otherwise conforms to Code Section 15–11–39; and

(3) The child is personally before the court at the provisional hearing.

(b) All provisions of this article applicable to a hearing on a petition, to orders of disposition, and to other proceedings dependent thereon shall apply under this Code section, but findings of fact and orders of disposition shall have only interlocutory effect pending final hearing on the petition. The rights and duties of the party served by publication are not affected except as provided in subsection (c) of this Code section.

(c) If the party served by publication fails to appear at the final hearing on the petition, the findings of fact and interlocutory orders made shall become final without further evidence and shall be governed by this article as if made at the final hearing. If the party appears at the final hearing, the findings and orders shall be vacated and disregarded and the hearing shall proceed upon the allegations of the petition without regard to this Code section.

Laws 1971, p. 709, § 1; Laws 1986, p. 1017, § 1; Laws 2000, p. 20, § 1.

Formerly Code 1933, § 24A–1901; Code 1981, § 15–11–29.

Historical and Statutory Notes

The 2000 amendment, which restructured this chapter into parts and modified statutory references to reflect this restructuring, renumbered this section from § 15–11–29.

§ 15–11–40. Modification or vacation of orders; probation revocation

(a) An order of the court shall be set aside if:

(1) It appears that it was obtained by fraud or mistake sufficient therefor in a civil action;

(2) The court lacked jurisdiction over a necessary party or of the subject matter; or

(3) Newly discovered evidence so requires.

(b) An order of the court may also be changed, modified, or vacated on the ground that changed circumstances so require in the best interest of the child, except an order committing a delinquent child to the Department of Juvenile Justice, after the child has been transferred to the physical custody of the Department of Juvenile Justice, or an order of dismissal. An order granting probation to a child found to be delinquent or unruly may be revoked on the ground that the conditions of probation have not been observed.

(c) Any party to the proceeding, the probation officer, or any other person having supervision or legal custody of or an interest in the child may petition the court for the relief provided in this

Code section. The petition shall set forth in clear and concise language the grounds upon which the relief is requested.

(d) After the petition is filed, the court shall fix a time for hearing and shall cause notice to be served, as a summons is served under Code Section 15–11–39.1, on the parties to the proceeding or those affected by the relief sought. After the hearing, which may be informal, the court shall deny or grant relief as the evidence warrants.

Laws 1915, p. 35, § 27; Laws 1951, p. 291, § 22; Laws 1956, p. 527, § 1; Laws 1968, p. 1013, § 14; Laws 1971, p. 709, § 1; Laws 1992, p. 1983, § 15; Laws 1997, p. 1453, § 1; Laws 2000, p. 20, § 1.

Formerly Code 1933, § 24–2427; Code 1933, § 24A–2801; Code 1981, § 15–11–42.

Historical and Statutory Notes

The 2000 amendment, which restructured this chapter into parts and modified statutory references to reflect this restructuring, renumbered this section from § 15–11–42.

§ 15–11–40.1. Probation management program

(a) For purposes of this Code section, the term:

(1) "Department" means the Department of Juvenile Justice.

(2) "Graduated sanctions' means:

(A) Verbal and written warnings;

(B) Increased restrictions and reporting requirements;

(C) Community service;

(D) Referral to treatment and counseling programs in the community;

(E) Weekend programming;

(F) Electronic monitoring, as such term is defined in Code Section 42–8–151;

(G) Curfew;

(H) An intensive supervision program; or

(I) A home confinement program.

(3) "Hearing officer" means a department employee or county juvenile probation office employee, as applicable, who has been selected and appointed by the department or county juvenile probation office, as applicable, to hear cases alleging violations of probation for administrative sanctioning. A hearing officer shall not be a probation officer who has direct supervision over the child who is the subject of the hearing.

(4) "Probation management program" means a special condition of probation that includes graduated sanctions.

(5) "Secure probation sanctions program" means secure confinement of seven, 14, or 30 days.

(b) In addition to any other terms or conditions of probation provided for under this chapter, the court may require that children who receive a disposition of probation:

(1) Be ordered to a probation management program; or

(2) Be ordered to a secure probation sanctions program by a probation officer or hearing officer.

(c) Where a child has been ordered to a probation management program or secure probation sanctions program, the court shall retain jurisdiction throughout the period of the probated sentence and may modify or revoke any part of a probated sentence as provided in Code Section 15–11–40.

(d)(1) The department in jurisdictions where the department is authorized to provide probation supervision, or the county juvenile probation office in jurisdictions where probation supervision is provided directly by the county, as applicable, shall be authorized to establish rules and regulations for graduated sanctions as an alternative to judicial modifications or revocations for probationers who violate the terms and conditions of a probation management program.

(2) The department or county juvenile probation office, as applicable, shall not sanction probationers for violations of conditions of probation if the court has expressed an intention in a written order that such violations be heard by the court.

(e) The department or county juvenile probation office, as applicable, shall impose only those restrictions equal to or less restrictive than the maximum sanction established by the court.

(f) The secure probation sanctions program shall be established by the department. Exclusion of a child from a secure probation sanctions program otherwise authorized by this Code section to enter such program shall be mutually agreed upon by the Council of Juvenile Court Judges and the department. The secure probation sanctions program shall be available to the juvenile courts to the extent that each secure facility has capacity for such offenders within its facilities. Prior to reaching full capacity, the department shall inform the various juvenile courts of its capacity constraints.

(g)(1) When requesting the secure probation sanctions program, probation officers supervising a child under a probation management program shall provide an affidavit to the court specifying:

(A) The elements of the child's probation program;

(B) The child's failures to respond to graduated sanctions in the community; and

(C) The child's number of violations and the nature of each violation.

(2) If a probation officer fails to document the violations and specify how the child has failed to complete a probation management program, such child shall be ineligible to enter the secure probation sanctions program.

(3) A child may enter the secure probation sanctions program if ordered by the court and:

(A) The probation officer has complied with the provisions of paragraph (1) of this subsection and the criteria set by the department for entrance into such program and the child has had three or more violations of probation; or

(B) A child in a probation management program and his or her parent or guardian, or a child in such program and his or her attorney, admit to three or more violations of such program and sign a waiver accepting the sanction proposed by the probation officer.

(4) Each new violation of a condition of a probated sentence may result in a child being sentenced to the secure probation sanctions program; provided, however, that if a child is sentenced to the secure probation sanctions program and completes all program components in the seven, 14, and 30 day programs, such child shall be ineligible to attend the secure probation sanctions program for a future violation of a condition of the same probated sentence.

(h)(1) When a violation of a condition of probation occurs, a child may have an administrative hearing conducted by a hearing officer. If the hearing officer determines by a preponderance of the evidence that such child violated the conditions of probation, the probation officer shall be authorized to impose graduated sanctions or a secure probation sanctions program. A child's failure to comply with a sanction imposed under this paragraph shall constitute another violation of probation.

(2) The hearing officer's decision shall be final unless such child files, within five days of the service of such decision, a written demand with the hearing officer for review of such decision. Such demand shall not stay the sanction decision. The hearing officer shall issue a response to such demand within five days of receiving such demand.

(3) If the hearing officer insists on the sanction, such decision shall be final unless the child files an appeal in the court that originally adjudicated the child. Such appeal shall be filed within ten days of the date of the decision of the hearing officer.

(4) The appeal shall first be reviewed by the court upon the record. At the court's discretion, a de novo hearing may be held on the decision. The filing of the appeal shall not stay the sanction decision.

(5) Where the court does not act on the appeal within 15 days of the date of the filing of the appeal, the sanction decision shall be affirmed by operation of law.

Laws 2010, Act 674, § 2, eff. July 1, 2010.

Historical and Statutory Notes

Laws 2010, Act 674, § 10, provides:

"This Act shall become effective on July 1, 2010, and Sections 2 and 5 of this Act shall apply to any child sentenced to probation on and after July 1, 2010; the former provisions of Code Section 15–11–66 shall continue to apply to any child sentenced to probation prior to July 1, 2010."

§ 15–11–41. Conduct of hearings

(a) All hearings shall be conducted by the court without a jury. Any hearing may be adjourned from time to time within the discretion of the court as set forth in subsection (b) of Code Section 15–11–56.

(b) The proceedings shall be recorded by stenographic notes or by electronic, mechanical, or other appropriate means, unless such recording is waived by the child and the child's parent, guardian, or attorney.

(c) In any proceeding before the juvenile court, the judge, upon the court's own motion, may request the assistance of the district attorney or a member of the district attorney's staff to conduct the proceedings on behalf of the petitioner. If for any reason the district attorney is unable to assist, the judge may appoint legal counsel for such purpose.

Laws 1915, p. 35, § 11; Laws 1950, p. 367, § 18; Laws 1951, p. 291, § 21; Laws 1968, p. 1013, §§ 12, 20; Laws 1971, p. 709, § 1; Laws 1974, p. 1126, § 5; Laws 1980, p. 416, § 2; Laws 1989, p. 824, § 1; Laws 1992, p. 2419, § 1; Laws 1995, p. 619, § 1; Laws 1997, p. 1681, § 2; Laws 1998, p. 606, § 1; Laws 2000, p. 20, § 1; Laws 2002, p. 1162, § 4.

Formerly Code 1933, § 24–2411; Code 1933, § 24A–1801; Code 1981, § 15–11–28.

Historical and Statutory Notes

The 2000 amendment, which restructured this chapter into parts and modified statutory references to reflect this restructuring, renumbered this section from § 15–11–26. In addition the amendment substituted reference to child for juvenile and provided gender neutral referents and deleted former subsecs. (c) and (c.1) pertaining to exclusions from and admissions to juvenile court hearings, respectively.

The 2002 amendment substantially rewrote the section which prior thereto provided:

"(a) All hearings shall be conducted by the court without a jury. Any hearing may be adjourned from time to time within the discretion of the court as set forth in subsection (d) of Code Section 15–11–56.

"(b) Unless waived by the child and the child's parent, guardian, or attorney, the proceedings shall be recorded by stenographic notes or by electronic, mechanical, or other appropriate means.

"(c) In any proceeding before the juvenile court, the judge, upon the court's own motion, may request the assistance of the district attorney or a member of the district attorney's staff to conduct the proceedings on behalf of the petitioner. If for any reason the district attorney is unable to assist, the judge may appoint legal counsel for such purpose.

"(d) In any delinquency proceeding in which a petition has been filed, the district attorney or a member of the district attorney's staff shall conduct the proceedings on behalf of the state if requested to do so by the juvenile court if the state is not otherwise represented by a solicitor of the juvenile court. Notwithstanding any other provisions of law to the contrary, in any delinquency proceedings conducted by the district attorney or a member of the district attorney's staff, the district attorney or staff member shall be entitled to complete access to all court files, probation files, hearing transcripts, delinquency reports, and any other juvenile court records which may be of assistance to the district attorney or staff member in the conduct of such delinquency proceedings. It shall be the duty of the clerk and probation officers of the juvenile court to assist the district attorney or staff member in obtaining any such files, transcripts, reports, or records, or copies thereof, as may be requested by the district attorney or staff member. In any such case, the petition shall be dismissed by the court upon the motion of the district attorney setting forth that there is not sufficient evidence to warrant the further conduct of the proceeding.

"(e) (1) In any delinquency proceeding in which a petition has been filed, the juvenile court shall notify any victim of a delinquent child's alleged offense that the victim may submit a victim impact statement if:

"(A) The delinquent child, in committing a felony, caused physical, psychological, or economic injury to the victim; or

"(B) The delinquent child, in committing a misdemeanor, caused serious physical injury or death to the victim.

"(2) A victim impact statement submitted by a victim shall be attached to the case file and may be used by the district attorney or the judge during any stage of the proceedings against the child involving predisposition, disposition, or determination of restitution.

"(3) A victim impact statement shall:

"(A) Identify the victim of the offense and the perpetrator;

"(B) Itemize any economic loss suffered by the victim as a result of the offense;

"(C) Identify any physical injury suffered by the victim as a result of the offense along with its seriousness and permanence;

"(D) Describe any change in the victim's personal welfare or familial relationships as a result of the offense;

"(E) Identify any request for psychological services initiated by the victim or the victim's family as a result of the offense; and

"(F) Contain any other information related to the impact of the offense upon the victim that the court requires.

"(4) The victim may complete the victim impact statement form and submit such form to the juvenile court. If the victim is unable to do so because of such victim's mental, emotional, or physical incapacity, or because of such victim's age, the victim's attorney or a family member may complete the victim impact statement form on behalf of the victim.

"(5) The court shall, in the manner prescribed by rule of court, provide the child with a copy of the victim impact statement within a reasonable time prior to any hearing at which it is to be considered and allow the child to have the opportunity to rebut the victim's written statements.

"(6) No disposition of the child shall be invalidated because of failure to comply with the provisions of this Code section. This Code section shall not be construed to create any cause of action or any right of appeal on behalf of any person.

"(f) At any hearing on a petition alleging deprivation of a child, the court shall make and file its findings as to whether the child is a deprived child, as defined in paragraph (8) of Code Section 15–11–2, and whether such deprivation is found to have been the result of alcohol or other drug abuse."

§ 15–11–41.1. Renumbered as § 15–11–30.5 by Laws 2000, p. 20, § 1

§ 15–11–42. Renumbered as § 15–11–40 by Laws 2000, p. 20, § 1

§ 15–11–43. Renumbered as § 15–11–13 by Laws 2000, p. 20, § 1

§ 15–11–44. Renumbered as § 15–11–87 by Laws 2000, p. 20, § 1

Part 5

Arrest and Detention

§ 15–11–45. Taking into custody

(a) A child may be taken into custody:

(1) Pursuant to an order of the court under this article, including an order to an employee of the Department of Juvenile Justice designated in accordance with paragraph (2) of subsection (i) of Code Section 49–4A–8 or to an employee of

the Department of Corrections, to apprehend a child who has escaped from an institution or facility operated either by the Department of Juvenile Justice or the Department of Corrections or a child who has been placed under supervision and who has broken the conditions thereof;

(2) Pursuant to the laws of arrest;

(3) By a law enforcement officer or duly authorized officer of the court if there are reasonable grounds to believe that the child has committed a delinquent act or if there are reasonable grounds to believe that he or she is an unruly child;

(4) By a law enforcement officer or duly authorized officer of the court if there are reasonable grounds to believe that the child is suffering from illness or injury or is in immediate danger from his or her surroundings and that his or her removal is necessary;

(5) By a law enforcement officer or duly authorized officer of the court if there are reasonable grounds to believe that the child has run away from his or her parents, guardian, or other custodian;

(6) By a law enforcement officer or duly authorized officer of the court if a parent or guardian of a child has contacted a law enforcement agency and reported that the child is absent from parental custody without consent and a facility created pursuant to paragraph (2) of subsection (e) of Code Section 15–11–47 is available; or

(7) By a law enforcement officer or duly authorized officer of the court if a child is violating a curfew and a facility created pursuant to paragraph (2) of subsection (e) of Code Section 15–11–47 is available.

(b) The taking of a child into custody is not an arrest, except for the purpose of determining its validity under the Constitution of this state or of the United States.

(c) When a child who is taken into custody pursuant to this article has committed an act which would constitute a felony under the laws of this state if committed by an adult, the juvenile court, within 48 hours after it learns of the taking into custody, shall notify the district attorney or duly authorized assistant district attorney of the judicial circuit in which the juvenile proceedings are to be instituted.

Laws 1908, p. 1107, § 6; Laws 1950, p. 367, § 16; Laws 1951, p. 291, § 17; Laws 1955, p. 581, § 2; Laws 1968, p. 1013, § 9; Laws 1971, p. 709, § 1; Laws 1976, p. 1066, § 3; Laws 1980, p. 416, § 1; Laws 1986, p. 1017, § 1; Laws 1992, p. 1983, § 3; Laws 1994, p. 1012, § 17; Laws 1995, p. 863, § 2; Laws 1997, p. 1453, § 1; Laws 2000, p. 20, § 1.

Formerly Penal Code 1910, § 892; Code 1933, § 24A–1301; Code 1981, § 15–11–17.

Historical and Statutory Notes

The 2000 amendment, which restructured this chapter into parts and modified statutory references to reflect this restructuring, renumbered this section from § 15–11–17.

Uniform Law

This section is based upon § 13 of the Uniform Law Commissioners' Model Juvenile Court Act. See 9A Uniform Laws Annotated, Master Edition, or ULA Database on Westlaw.

§ 15–11–46. Detention

A child taken into custody shall not be detained or placed in shelter care prior to the hearing on the petition unless:

(1) The child's detention or care is required to protect the person or property of others or of the child;

(2) The child may abscond or be removed from the jurisdiction of the court;

(3) The child has no parent, guardian, or custodian or other person able to provide supervision and care for him or her and return him or her to the court when required; or

(4) An order for the child's detention or shelter care has been made by the court pursuant to this article.

Laws 1971, p. 709, § 1; Laws 1986, p. 1017, § 1; Laws 2000, p. 20, § 1.

Formerly Code 1933, § 24A–1401; Code 1981, § 15–11–18.

Historical and Statutory Notes

The 2000 amendment, which restructured this chapter into parts and modified statutory references to reflect this restructuring, renumbered this section from § 15–11–18. In addition the amendment substituted reference to child for juvenile and provided gender neutral referents.

Uniform Law

This section is based upon § 14 of the Uniform Law Commissioners' Model Juvenile Court Act. See 9A Uniform Laws Annotated, Master Edition, or ULA Database on Westlaw.

§ 15–11–46.1. Interim control or detention of accused children

(a) As a matter of public policy, restraints on the freedom of accused children prior to adjudication shall be imposed only when there is probable cause to believe that the accused child did the act of which he or she is accused and there is clear and convincing evidence that the child's freedom should be restrained.

(b) The imposition of interim control or detention on an accused child may be considered for the purposes of:

(1) Protecting the jurisdiction and process of the court;

(2) Reducing the likelihood that the child may inflict serious bodily harm on others during the interim period; or

(3) Protecting the accused child from imminent bodily harm upon his or her request.

(c) Interim control or detention shall not be imposed on an accused child:

(1) To punish, treat, or rehabilitate the child;

(2) To allow parents to avoid their legal responsibilities;

(3) To satisfy demands by a victim, the police, or the community;

(4) To permit more convenient administrative access to the child; or

(5) To facilitate further interrogation or investigation.

(d) Whenever an accused child cannot be unconditionally released, conditional or supervised release that results in the least necessary interference with the liberty of the child shall be favored over more intrusive alternatives.

(e) Whenever the interim curtailment of an accused child's freedom is permitted under this Code section, the exercise of authority shall reflect the following values:

(1) Respect for the privacy, dignity, and individuality of the accused child and his or her family;

(2) Protection of the psychological and physical health of the child;

(3) Tolerance of the diverse values and preferences among different groups and individuals;

(4) Assurance of equality of treatment by race, class, ethnicity, and sex;

(5) Avoidance of regimentation and depersonalization of the child;

(6) Avoidance of stigmatization of the child; and

(7) Assurance that the child has been informed of his or her right to consult with an attorney and that if the child cannot afford an attorney, one will be provided.

Laws 1989, p. 838, § 1; Laws 1991, p. 346, § 1; Laws 2000, p. 20, § 1.

Formerly Code 1981, § 15–11–18.1.

Historical and Statutory Notes

The 2000 amendment, which restructured this chapter into parts and modified statutory references to reflect this restructuring, renumbered this section from § 15–11–18.1. In addition the amendment substituted reference to child for juvenile and provided gender neutral referents.

§ 15–11–47. Procedure after taking child into custody

(a) *Release to parents; delivery to medical facility, intake officer, or court.* A person taking a child into custody, with all reasonable speed and without first taking the child elsewhere, shall:

(1) Forthwith release without bond the child to the child's parents, guardian, or other custodian upon their promise to bring the child before the court when requested by the court;

(2) Forthwith deliver the child to a medical facility if the child is believed to suffer from a serious physical condition or illness which requires prompt treatment and, upon delivery, shall promptly contact a juvenile court intake officer. Immediately upon being notified by the person taking a child into custody, the intake officer shall determine if such child should be released, detained, or brought before the court. Prior to an informal detention hearing or committal hearing authorized under Code Sections 17–6–15 and 17–6–16 and Articles 1, 2, and 8 of Chapter 7 of Title 17, the child shall be placed in detention, if necessary, only in such places as are authorized by Code Section 15–11–48;

(3) Bring the child immediately before the juvenile court or promptly contact a juvenile court intake officer. The intake officer shall determine if the child should be released or detained. Prior to an informal detention hearing, the child shall be placed in detention, if necessary, only in such places as are authorized by Code Section 15–11–48; or

(4) Bring the child who is suspected of committing a delinquent act before the superior court of the county where the delinquent act occurred if the act is an act over which the superior court has exclusive or concurrent jurisdiction as provided in subsection (b) of Code Section 15–11–28; however, pending a commitment hearing authorized under Code Sections 17–6–15 and 17–6–16 and Articles 1, 2, and 8 of Chapter 7 of Title 17 or an indictment, the child shall be returned and placed in detention, if necessary, only in such places as are authorized by Code Section 15–11–48.

(b) *Failure of parent to bring child before court.* If a parent, guardian, or other custodian, when requested, willfully fails to bring the child before the court as provided in subsection (a) of this Code section, the court may issue its order directing that the child be taken into custody and brought before the court and, in addition, may enter any order authorized by and in accordance with the provisions of Code Section 15–11–5. If it is necessary to place the child in detention prior to his or her appearance in court, the child shall be placed in a facility as authorized by Code Section 15–11–48.

(c) *Notice; temporary detention or questioning.* The person taking a child into custody shall promptly give notice thereof, together with a statement of the reason for taking the child into custody, to a parent, guardian, or other custodian and to the court. Any temporary detention or questioning of the child necessary to comply with this Code section shall conform to the procedures and conditions prescribed by this article and rules of court.

(d) *Bail.* All children subject to the jurisdiction of the juvenile court and alleged to be delinquent or unruly shall have the same right to bail as adults; and the judge shall admit to bail all children under the court's jurisdiction in the same manner and under the same circumstances and procedures as are applicable to adults accused of the commission of crimes. Any person having legal custody or an adult blood relative or stepparent shall be entitled to post bail but shall be required immediately to return the child to the individual or entity having legal custody of the child.

(e) *Treatment of unruly child.*

(1) With respect to a child suspected of being unruly as defined in paragraph (12) of Code Section 15–11–2 or a child who is in violation of a curfew, a person taking such a child into custody shall not exercise custody over the child except for a period of 12 hours. A child taken into custody may be detained in a holding facility for unruly children as provided for in paragraph (2) of this subsection. If a parent or guardian has not assumed custody of the child at the end of such period or if the child has not been brought before the juvenile court or if an intake officer has not made a detention decision, the child shall be released from custody. In no case shall such a child in custody be detained in a jail.

(2) Counties and municipalities are authorized to establish facilities where a child who is suspected of being unruly or who is in violation of a curfew may be informally detained until the parent or guardian assumes custody of the child. Immediately after a child is brought into such a facility, every effort shall be made to contact the parent or guardian of the child. A child shall not be restrained in a cell or other such place apart from other children unless such child engages in disruptive or unruly behavior while at the holding facility.

Laws 1915, p. 35, § 13; Laws 1950, p. 367, § 16; Laws 1951, p. 291, § 17; Laws 1955, p. 581, § 2; Laws 1968, p. 1013, § 9; Laws 1969, p. 760, § 1; Laws 1971, p. 709, § 1; Laws 1973, p. 882, § 4; Laws 1977, p. 1237, § 2; Laws 1986, p. 1017, § 1; Laws 1987, p. 3, § 15; Laws 1994, p. 1012, § 18; Laws 1995, p. 863, § 3; Laws 1996, p. 868, § 3; Laws 2000, p. 20, § 1; Laws 2006, Act 476, § 1, eff. July 1, 2006.

Formerly Code 1933, § 24–2413; Code 1933, § 24A–1402; Code 1981, § 15–11–19.

Historical and Statutory Notes

The 2000 amendment, which restructured this chapter into parts and modified statutory references to reflect this restructuring, renumbered this section from § 15–11–19. In addition the amendment substituted reference to child for juvenile and provided gender neutral referents.

The 2006 amendment by Act 476, in subsec. (d), deleted ", on application of the parent or guardian," following "delinquent and unruly", and added "Any person having legal custody or an adult blood relative or stepparent shall be entitled to post bail but shall be required immediately to return the child to the individual or entity having legal custody of the child." at the end of the subsection.

Uniform Law

This section is based upon § 15 of the Uniform Law Commissioners' Model Juvenile Court Act. See 9A Uniform Laws Annotated, Master Edition, or ULA Database on Westlaw.

§ 15–11–48. Place of detention; data on child detained

(a) *Allegation of delinquency.* A child alleged to be delinquent may be detained only in:

(1) A licensed foster home or a home approved by the court which may be a public or private home or the home of the noncustodial parent or of a relative;

(2) A facility operated by a licensed child welfare agency; or

(3) A detention home or center for delinquent children which is under the direction or supervision of the court or other public authority or of a private agency approved by the court.

(b) *Allegation of capital or violent offense.* A child alleged to have committed an offense over which the superior court has exclusive or concurrent jurisdiction under subsection (b) of Code Section 15–11–28 shall be detained pending a commitment hearing under Code Sections 17–6–15 and 17–6–16 and Articles 1, 2, and 8 of Chapter 7 of Title 17 or an indictment only in a facility described in paragraphs (1) through (3) of subsection (a) of this Code section unless it appears to the satisfaction of the court in which the case is pending that public safety and protection reasonably require detention in the jail and the court so orders, but only where the detention is in a room separate and removed from those for adults and constructed in such a way that there can be no physical contact between a child and an adult offender.

(c) *Transfer following indictment.* Following an indictment for an offense over which the superior court has exclusive or concurrent jurisdiction under subsection (b) of Code Section 15–11–28 or following the transfer of a case to any court for criminal prosecution under Code Section 15–11–30.2, the child shall be held only in a facility described in paragraphs (1) through (3) of subsection (a) of this Code section unless it appears to the satisfaction of the superior court that public safety and protection reasonably require detention in the jail and the court so orders, but only where the detention is in a room separate and removed from those for adults and constructed in such a way that there can be no physical contact between a child and an adult offender.

(d) *Notification of court by official of jail.* The official in charge of a jail or other facility for the detention of adult offenders or persons charged with crime shall immediately inform the juvenile court or a duly authorized officer of the juvenile court if a person who is or appears to be under the age of 17 years is received at the facility and shall bring him or her before the court upon request or deliver him or her to a detention or shelter care facility designated by the court; provided, however, the official in charge of a jail or other facility for the detention of adult offenders or persons charged with a crime shall immediately inform the court in which the case is pending or a duly authorized officer of such court if a person who is or appears to be 13 to 17 years of age and who is alleged to have committed any offense enumerated in subparagraph (b)(2)(A) of Code Section 15–11–28 is received at the facility and shall bring him or her before the court upon request or deliver him or her to a detention facility designated by the court. Such child shall not be held in the jail but may be held in a temporary holding area outside of the jail constructed as such for not longer than six hours pending transfer to the detention facility. For purposes of this Code section, the term "jail" shall include not only the cells, but any other secured area of the jail adjacent to the cells in which adult offenders are held or through which they are transported.

(e) *Allegation of unruliness.* A child unruly or alleged to be unruly who has not been released from custody as provided in subsection (e) of Code Section 15–11–47 may be detained or placed in shelter care only in the facilities stated in paragraphs (1) and (2) of subsection (a) of this Code section or in a secure juvenile detention facility for a period not to exceed 72 hours; provided, however, upon written order of the judge having jurisdiction of the case and upon good cause shown, a child alleged to be unruly may be detained for one additional period not to exceed 48 hours; provided, further, that no child alleged to be or found to be unruly who has not previously been adjudicated unruly may be detained in a secure juvenile detention facility unless such child is alleged to be under the court's jurisdiction as provided in subparagraph (D) of paragraph (12) of Code Section 15–11–2 and then shall be detained in that facility only so long as is required to effect the child's return home or to ensure the child's presence at a scheduled court appearance when the child has previously failed to appear for a scheduled court appearance. In the event a child alleged to be unruly comes within the purview of the Interstate Compact on Juveniles and the proper authorities of a demanding state have made an official return request to the proper authorities of this state, the Interstate Compact on Juveniles shall apply to the child.

(f) *Allegation of deprivation.* A child alleged to be deprived may be placed in shelter care only in the facilities stated in paragraphs (1) and (2) of subsection (a) of this Code section or in a shelter care facility operated by the court. The actual physical placement of a child pursuant to this subsection shall require the approval of the judge of the juvenile court or his or her designee.

(g) *Data to be maintained.* All facilities that detain children for pretrial detention shall maintain the following data on each child detained:

(1) Name;

(2) Date of birth;

(3) Sex;

(4) Race;

(5) Offense or offenses for which being detained;

(6) Date of and authority for confinement;

(7) Date of and authority for release or transfer; and

(8) Where transferred or to whom released.

Such data shall be recorded and retained by the facility for three years and shall be made available for inspection during normal business hours by any court exercising juvenile court jurisdiction, by the Department of Juvenile Justice, by the Department of Corrections, and by the Georgia Council of Juvenile Court Judges.

Laws 1908, p. 1107, § 6; Laws 1915, p. 35, § 18; Laws 1950, p. 367, §§ 16, 17; Laws 1951, p. 291, § 17; Laws 1955, p. 581, § 2; Laws 1968, p. 1013, § 9; Laws 1971, p. 709, § 1; Laws 1973, p. 882, § 5; Laws 1977, p. 1237, §§ 3–5; Laws 1979, p. 774, § 1; Laws 1985, p. 1313, §§ 2, 3; Laws 1987, p. 479, § 1; Laws 1989, p. 1716, § 1; Laws 1990, p. 1351, § 1; Laws 1992, p. 1983, § 4; Laws 1994, p. 1012, § 19; Laws 1995, p. 863, § 4; Laws 1997, p. 1453, § 1; Laws 1999, p. 81, § 15; Laws 2000, p. 20, § 1.

Formerly Penal Code 1910, § 893; Code 1933, § 24–2418; Code 1933, § 24A–1403; Code 1981, § 15–11–20.

Historical and Statutory Notes

The 2000 amendment, which restructured this chapter into parts and modified statutory references to reflect this restructuring, renumbered this section from § 15–11–20. In addition the amendment substituted reference to child for juvenile and provided gender neutral referents.

Uniform Law

This section is based upon § 16 of the Uniform Law Commissioners' Model Juvenile Court Act. See 9A Uniform Laws Annotated, Master Edition, or ULA Database on Westlaw.

§ 15–11–49. Release from detention or shelter care; hearing

(a) If a child is brought before the court or delivered to a detention or shelter care facility designated by the court, the intake or other authorized officer of the court shall immediately make an investigation and release the child unless it appears that the child's detention or shelter care is warranted or required under Code Section 15–11–46.

(b) If a child is so released and the case is to be prosecuted further other than by informal adjustment, a petition under Code Section 15–11–38.1 shall be made and presented to the court within 30 days.

(c)(1) If a child alleged to be delinquent is not so released, an informal detention hearing shall be held promptly and not later than 72 hours after the child is placed in detention or shelter care to determine whether detention or shelter care of the child is required under Code Section 15–11–46, provided that, if the 72 hour time period expires on a Saturday, Sunday, or legal holiday, the hearing shall be held on the next day which is not a Saturday, Sunday, or legal holiday.

(2) If a child alleged to be unruly is not so released, the informal detention hearing shall be held promptly and not later than 72 hours after the child is placed in detention or shelter care as provided in subsection (e) of Code Section 15–11–48.

(3) If a child alleged to be deprived is not so released, the informal detention hearing shall be held promptly and not later than 72 hours after the child is placed in shelter care as provided in subsection (f) of Code Section 15–11–48, provided

that, if the 72 hour time period expires on a Saturday, Sunday, or legal holiday, the hearing shall be held on the next day which is not a Saturday, Sunday, or legal holiday.

(4) Reasonable notice of the hearing specified in this subsection, either oral or written, stating the time, place, and purpose of the detention hearing, shall be given to the child and, if they can be found, to the child's parents, guardian, or other custodian. In the event the child's parents, guardian, or other custodian cannot be found, the court shall forthwith appoint a guardian ad litem. Prior to the commencement of the hearing, the court shall inform the parties of their right to counsel and to appointed counsel if they are indigent persons and of the child's right to remain silent with respect to any allegations of delinquency or unruly conduct.

(d) If the child is not so released and a parent, guardian, custodian, or guardian ad litem has not been notified of the hearing and did not appear or waive appearance at the hearing and files the affidavit of such person showing these facts, the court shall rehear the matter without unnecessary delay and shall order the child's release unless it appears from the hearing that the child's detention or shelter care is required under Code Section 15–11–46.

(e) If the child is not so released, a petition under Code Section 15–11–38.1 shall be made and presented to the court within 72 hours of the detention hearing; provided, however, that, if the child not so released is alleged to be a deprived child, a petition under Code Section 15–11–38.1 shall be made and presented to the court within five days of the detention hearing.

Laws 1971, p. 709, § 1; Laws 1977, p. 1237, § 6; Laws 1985, p. 1313, § 4; Laws 1986, p. 1097, § 1; Laws 2000, p. 20, § 1.

Formerly Code 1933, § 24A–1404; Code 1981, § 15–11–21.

Historical and Statutory Notes

The 2000 amendment, which restructured this chapter into parts and modified statutory references to reflect this restructuring, renumbered this section from § 15–11–21. In addition the amendment substituted reference to child for juvenile and provided gender neutral referents.

Uniform Law

This section is based upon § 17 of the Uniform Law Commissioners' Model Juvenile Court Act. See 9A Uniform Laws Annotated, Master Edition, or ULA Database on Westlaw.

§ 15–11–49.1. Order to take child into immediate custody

If it appears from a filed affidavit or from sworn testimony before the court that the conduct, condition, or surroundings of the child are endangering the child's health or welfare or those of others or that the child may abscond or be removed from the jurisdiction of the court or will not be brought before the court, notwithstanding the service of the summons, the court may endorse upon the summons an order that a law enforcement officer shall serve the summons and take the child into immediate custody and bring the child forthwith before the court.

Laws 1915, p. 35, §§ 4, 5; Laws 1950, p. 367, § 13; Laws 1951, p. 291, § 14; Laws 1968, p. 1013, § 6; Laws 1971, p. 709, § 1; Laws 1974, p. 1126, § 4; Laws 1996, p. 868, § 4; Laws 2000, p. 20, § 1.

Formerly Code 1933, §§ 24–2404, 24–2405; Code 1933, § 24A–1701; Code 1981, § 15–11–26.

Historical and Statutory Notes

The 2000 amendment, which restructured this chapter into parts and modified statutory references to reflect this restructuring, renumbered this section from § 15–11–26(d). In addition the amendment substituted reference to child for juvenile and provided gender neutral referents.

§ 15–11–50. Commitment to penal institution prohibited

A child shall not be committed to a penal institution or other facility used primarily for the execution of sentences of persons convicted of a crime; provided, however, that this Code section shall not be construed as prohibiting the direct commitment of a child to the custody of the Department of Corrections for detention in a designated youth confinement unit as provided in this article.

Laws 1915, p. 35, §§ 12, 19; Laws 1950, p. 367, § 19; Laws 1951, p. 291, § 19; Laws 1968, p. 1013, § 10; Laws 1971, p. 709, § 1; Laws 1986, p. 1017, § 1; Laws 1990, p. 1930, § 3; Laws 1992, p. 1983, § 12; Laws 1994, p. 1012, § 23; Laws 1996, p. 823, § 1; Laws 1997, p. 1064, § 5; Laws 1997, p. 1453, § 1; Laws 1998, p. 128, § 15; Laws 2000, p. 20, § 1.

Formerly Code 1933, §§ 24–2412, 24–2419; Code 1933, § 24A–2401; Code 1981, § 15–11–38.

Historical and Statutory Notes

The 2000 amendment, which restructured this chapter into parts and modified statutory references to reflect this restructuring, renumbered this section from § 15–11–38(c).

§ 15–11–51. Release of child from detention; notification to victim

(a) As used in this Code section, the term:

(1) "Notice" shall have the same meaning as set forth in Code Section 17–17–3.

(2) "Victim" shall have the same meaning as set forth in Code Section 17–17–3.

(3) "Violent delinquent act" means the commission, attempt to commit, conspiracy to commit, or solicitation of another to commit a delinquent act which if committed by an adult would constitute:

(A) A serious violent felony as defined by Code Section 17–10–6.1;

(B) A designated felony as defined by Code Section 15–11–63;

(C) Stalking or aggravated stalking as provided by Article 7 of Chapter 5 of Title 16; or

(D) Any attempt to commit, conspiracy to commit, or solicitation of another to commit an offense enumerated in subparagraphs (A) through (C) of this paragraph.

(b) If a child accused of a violent delinquent act is detained pending adjudication as provided by Code Sections 15–11–46.1 and 15–11–47, the juvenile court intake officer shall provide notice to the victim, whenever practicable, that such child is to be released from detention not less than 24 hours prior to such child's release from detention.

(c) Not less than 48 hours prior to the release from detention of a child who has been adjudicated to have committed a violent delinquent act, the juvenile court intake officer shall, whenever practicable, provide notice to the victim of such pending release.

(d) Notification need not be given unless the victim has expressed a desire for such notification and has provided the juvenile court intake officer with a current address and telephone number. It shall be the duty of the juvenile court intake officer to advise the victim of his or her right to notification and of the requirement of the victim's providing a primary and personal telephone number to which such notification shall be directed.

Laws 2009, Act 112, § 1, eff. May 4, 2009.

Historical and Statutory Notes

Former § 15–11–51 was repealed by Laws 1986, p. 1017, § 3, eff. July 1, 1986.

§§ 15-11-52 to 15-11-53. Repealed by Laws 1986, p. 1017, § 3, eff. July 1, 1986

Part 6

Deprivation

§ 15-11-54. Findings; findings with regard to result of alcohol or drug abuse; disposition

(a) *Findings.* After hearing the evidence on any petition alleging deprivation, the court shall make and file its findings as to whether the child is a deprived child. If the court finds that the child is not a deprived child, it shall dismiss the petition and order the child discharged from any detention or other restriction theretofore ordered in the proceeding.

(b) *Findings with regard to result of alcohol abuse or drug abuse.* If the court finds that a child is deprived, the court shall also make and file a finding as to whether such deprivation is the result of alcohol abuse or drug abuse by a parent or guardian.

(c) *Disposition.* The court shall proceed immediately or at a postponed hearing to make a proper disposition of the case in accordance with Code Section 15-11-55 if the court finds from clear and convincing evidence that the child is deprived.

Laws 2002, p. 1162, § 5.

§ 15-11-55. Disposition of deprived child

(a) If the child is found to be a deprived child, the court may make any of the following orders of disposition best suited to the protection and physical, mental, and moral welfare of the child:

(1) Permit the child to remain with his or her parents, guardian, or other custodian, including a putative father, subject to conditions and limitations as the court prescribes, including supervision as directed by the court for the protection of the child;

(2)(A) Subject to conditions and limitations as the court prescribes, transfer temporary legal custody to any of the persons or entities described in this paragraph. Without limiting the generality of the foregoing, such conditions and limitations shall include a provision that the court shall approve or direct the retransfer of the physical custody of the child back to the parents, guardian, or other custodian either upon the occurrence of specified circumstances or in the discretion of the court. Any such retransfer of physical custody may be made subject to such further conditions and limitations as the court prescribes, including supervision for the protection of the child. The persons or entities to whom or which temporary legal custody may be transferred shall include the following:

(i) Any individual including a putative father who, after study by the probation officer or other person or agency designated by the court, is found by the court to be qualified to receive and care for the child;

(ii) An agency or other private organization licensed or otherwise authorized by law to receive and provide care for the child;

(iii) Any public agency authorized by law to receive and provide care for the child; provided, however, that for the purpose of this Code section, the term "public agency" shall not include the Department of Juvenile Justice; or

(iv) An individual in another state with or without supervision by an appropriate officer under Code Section 15-11-89.

(B) Except for dispositions pursuant to paragraph (1) of subsection (a) of Code Section 15-11-66 and Code Section 15-11-67, within 30 days after the removal of a child from the custody of the parent or parents of the child, the Department of Human Services shall exercise due diligence to identify a parent or relative of the child or other persons who have demonstrated an ongoing commitment to the child. All identified adult relatives of the child, subject to exceptions due to family or domestic violence, shall be provided with notice:

(i) Specifying that the child has been or is being removed from parental custody;

(ii) Explaining the options the relative has to participate in the care and placement of the child and any options that may be lost by failing to respond to the notice;

(iii) Describing the process for becoming an approved foster family home and the additional services and supports available for children placed in approved foster homes; and

(iv) Describing any financial assistance for which the relative may be eligible.

(C) The results of such search and notification shall be documented in writing and filed with the court by the time of the first review. During such 30 day period, the court may order that the child be placed in the temporary legal custody of the Department of Human Services or any other appropriate entity or person.

(D) The court shall order in its preliminary disposition that the parent or other legal guardian of the child shall provide within ten days the names and addresses of all relatives and other persons who might be considered as possible placements for the child. The parties shall have an ongoing duty to supplement this information during the course of the case at each judicial review or citizen panel review. The court shall include in all published summons a notice that this information must be provided.

(E) The Council of Juvenile Court Judges shall be authorized to create uniform rules and forms to implement the provisions of this paragraph; or

(3) Without making any of the orders specified in paragraphs (1) and (2) of this subsection, transfer custody of the child to the court of another state exercising jurisdiction over children if authorized by and in accordance with Code Section 15-11-87 if the child is or is about to become a resident of that state.

(b) Unless a child found to be deprived is found also to be delinquent, such child shall not be committed to or confined in an institution or other facility designed or operated for the benefit of delinquent children.

(c) Notwithstanding any other provision of law, the court after transferring temporary legal custody of a child to the Division of Family and Children Services within the Department of Human Services may at any time conduct sua sponte a judicial review of the current placement plan being provided to said child. After its review the court may order the division to comply with the current placement plan, order the division to devise a new placement plan within available division resources, or make any other order relative to placement or custody outside the Department of Human Services as the court finds to be in the best interest of the child. Placement or a change of legal custody by the court outside the Department of Human Services shall relieve the department of further responsibility for the child so placed.

(d) The policy of this state is that children in the custody of the Division of Family and Children Services should have stable placements. Not less than five days in advance of any placement change, the division shall notify the court, a child who is 14 years of age or older, the child's parents, guardian, or other custodian, and any attorney of record of such change in the location of the child's placement while the child is in the division's custody; provided, however, that if the child's health or welfare may be endangered by any delay in changing the child's placement, only the court and any attorney of record shall be notified of such placement change within 24 hours of such change. A child who is 14 years of age or older, the child's parents, guardian, or other custodian, and any attorney of record may request a hearing with regard to the child's case plan or the permanency plan in order for the court to consider the change in the location of the child's placement and any changes to the case plan or permanency plan resulting from the child's change in placement location. Such hearing shall be held within five days of receiving notice of a change in the location of the child's placement and prior to any such placement change, unless the child's health or welfare may be endangered by any delay in changing the child's placement. At the hearing to consider the child's case plan and permanency plan, the court shall consider the case plan and permanency plan recommendations made by the division, including a recommendation as to the location of the placement of the child, and shall make findings of fact upon which the court relied in determining to reject or accept the case plan or permanency plan and the recommendations made by the division, including the location of the child's placement. If the court rejects the recommendations of the division, the court shall demonstrate that the division's recommendations were considered and explain why it did not follow the recommendations. If the court rejects the division's case plan and permanency plan recommendations, including the change in the location of the placement of the child, the court may order the division to devise a new case plan and permanency plan recommendation, including a new recommendation as to the location of the child within the resources of the department, or make any other order relative to placement or custody outside the Department of Human Services as the court finds to be in the best interest of the child and consistent with this subsection. Placement or a change of legal custody by the court outside the Department of Human Services shall relieve the department of further responsibility for the child so placed.

(e) A juvenile court shall not be required to make an order of disposition pursuant to this Code section regarding a child who is discharged from a facility in which the child was hospitalized or habilitated pursuant to Chapter 3, 4, or 7 of Title 37 unless the child is to be discharged into the physical custody of any person who had such custody when the court made its most recent finding that such child was deprived.

(f) If a child is found to be a deprived child and the deprivation is found to have been the result of alcohol or other drug abuse by a parent or guardian, as specified in subsection (b) of Code Section 15-11-54, and the court orders transfer of temporary legal custody of the child, as provided in paragraph (2) of subsection (a) of this Code section, the court is authorized to further order that legal custody of the child may not be transferred back to the child's custodian or guardian whose abuse of alcohol or another drug resulted in the child's deprivation unless such person undergoes substance abuse treatment and random substance abuse screenings and those screenings remain negative for a period of no less than six consecutive months.

Laws 1915, p. 35, § 9; Laws 1916, p. 58, § 2; Laws 1950, p. 1107, § 19; Laws 1951, p. 291, § 21; Laws 1968, p. 1013, § 13; Laws 1971, p. 709, § 1; Laws 1993, p. 1716, § 1; Laws 1998, p. 606, § 2; Laws 2000, p. 20, § 1; Laws 2002, p. 1162, § 6; Laws 2003, Act 3, § 2, eff. July 1, 2003; Laws 2007, Act 325, § 2, eff. July 1, 2007; Laws 2009, Act 37, § 1, eff. July 1, 2009; Laws 2009, Act 102, § 2-2, eff. July 1, 2009; Laws 2010, Act 418, § 10, eff. July 1, 2010.

Formerly Code 1933, § 24-2409; Code 1933, § 24A-2301; Code 1981, § 15-11-34.

Historical and Statutory Notes

The 2000 amendment, which restructured this chapter into parts and modified statutory references to reflect this restructuring, renumbered this section from § 15-11-34. In addition the amendment substituted reference to child for juvenile and provided gender neutral referents.

The 2002 amendment rewrote subsec. (e) which formerly provided:

"(e) If a child is found to be a deprived child and the deprivation is found to have been the result of alcohol or other drug abuse, as specified in subsection (f) of Code Section 15-11-41, and the court orders transfer of temporary legal custody of the child, as provided in paragraph (2) of subsection (a) of this Code section, the court is authorized to further order that legal custody of the child may not be transferred back to the person having custody of the child when the deprivation occurred unless such person undergoes substance abuse treatment and random substance abuse screenings and those screenings remain negative for a period of no less than six consecutive months."

The 2003 amendment by Act 3 in subsec. (a), par. (2), substituted "." for "; or" at the end of subpar. (D), and added the paragraph beginning "Except for dispositions..." following subpar. (D).

The 2007 amendment by Act 325, in subsec. (a), inserted "provided, however, that for the purpose of this Code section, the term 'public agency' shall not include the Department of Juvenile Justice;" in subpar. (2)(C); in subsec. (c), inserted "legal" following "Placement or a change of"; inserted a new subsec. (d); and redesignated former subsecs. (d) and (e) as (e) and (f).

The 2009 amendment by Act 37 rewrote the par. (a)(2) which had read:

"(2) Subject to conditions and limitations as the court prescribes, transfer temporary legal custody to any of the persons or entities described in this paragraph. Without limiting the generality of the foregoing, such conditions and limitations shall include a provision that the court shall approve or direct the retransfer of the physical custody of the child back to the parents, guardian, or other custodian either upon the occurrence of specified circumstances or in the discretion of the court. Any such retransfer of physical custody may be made subject to such further conditions and limitations as the court prescribes, including supervision for the protection of the child. The persons or entities to whom or which temporary legal custody may be transferred shall include the following:

"(A) Any individual including a putative father who, after study by the probation officer or other person or agency designated by the court, is found by the court to be qualified to receive and care for the child;

"(B) An agency or other private organization licensed or otherwise authorized by law to receive and provide care for the child;

"(C) Any public agency authorized by law to receive and provide care for the child; provided, however, that for the purpose of this Code section, the term 'public agency' shall not include the Department of Juvenile Justice; or

"(D) An individual in another state with or without supervision by an appropriate officer under Code Section 15-11-89.

"Except for dispositions pursuant to paragraph (1) of subsection (a) of Code Section 15-11-66 and Code Section 15-11-67, before transferring temporary legal custody in an order of disposition under this paragraph a reasonably diligent search for a parent or relative of the child or other persons who have demonstrated an ongoing commitment to the child shall be conducted by the court and the Department of Human Resources. Such search shall be completed within 90 days from the date on which the child was removed from the home, the results of such search documented in writing and filed with the court at the time of the first review. During such 90 day period, the child may be placed in the temporary legal custody of the Department of Human Resources or any other appropriate entity or person; or"

The 2009 amendment by Act 102 substituted "Department of Human Services" for "Department of Human Resources" throughout the section.

In 2009, the Code Commission, due to irreconcilable conflicts, treated the amendment of subpars. (a)(2)(B) and (a)(2)(C) by Laws 2009, Act 37, § 1, as superseded by Laws 2009, Act 102, § 2-2. See Butts County v. Strahan, 107 S.E. 163, 151 Ga. 417 (1921).

The 2010 amendment by Act 418, in subsec. (a), par. (2), subpar. (B), substituted "within 30 days after the removal of a child from the custody of the parent or parents of the child, the Department of Human Services shall exercise due diligence to identify" for "before transferring temporary legal custody in an order of disposition under this paragraph a reasonably diligent search for", deleted "shall be conducted by the court and the Department of Human Services. Such search shall be completed within 90 days from the date on which the child was removed from the home" after "commitment to the child", added "All identified adult relatives of the child, subject to exceptions due to family or domestic violence, shall be provided with notice" and divs. (i) to (iv); in subpar. (C), inserted "and notification" after "such search", substituted "by the time" for "at the time", substituted "30 day" for "90 day" and inserted "the court may order that" preceding "the child".

Uniform Law

This section is based upon § 30 of the Uniform Law Commissioners' Model Juvenile Court Act. See 9A Uniform Laws Annotated, Master Edition, or ULA Database on Westlaw.

§ 15–11–55.1. Notice of hearings or other proceedings to foster parents and preadoptive parents or relatives providing care for child

In advance of any hearing or other proceeding to be held with respect to a child pursuant to Code Section 15–11–55 or a deprivation hearing to be held with respect to a child pursuant to paragraph (3) of subsection (c) of Code Section 15–11–49 and Code Sections 15–11–39 and 15–11–39.2, the court shall provide notice or shall direct that a party shall provide notice of such hearing or other proceeding, including their right to be heard at such hearing or other proceeding, to the foster parents of the child, and to any preadoptive parents or relatives providing care for the child, consistent with the form and timing of notice to parties; provided, however, that this provision shall not be construed to require a foster parent, preadoptive parent, or relative caring for the child to be made a party to the hearing solely on the basis of such notice and right to be heard.

Laws 2007, Act 248, § 2, eff. May 24, 2007.

§ 15–11–56. Hearing; findings; disposition

(a) *Evidence.* In dispositional hearings under subsection (c) of Code Section 15–11–54 and in all proceedings involving custody of a child, all information helpful in determining the questions presented, including oral and written reports, may be received by the court and relied upon to the extent of its probative value even though not otherwise competent in the hearing on the petition. The parties or their counsel shall be afforded an opportunity upon request to examine and controvert written reports so received and to cross-examine individuals making the reports, except that portions of such reports not relied on by the court in reaching its decision which, if revealed, would be prejudicial to the interests of the child or any party to the proceeding may be withheld in the court's discretion. Confidential sources of information need not be disclosed.

(b) *Continuances; scheduling.* On its own motion or that of a party, the court may continue the hearings under subsection (c) of Code Section 15–11–54 for a reasonable period to receive reports and other evidence bearing on the disposition of a child. In this event, the court shall make an appropriate order for protection of the child during the period of the continuance. In scheduling investigations and hearings, the court shall give priority to proceedings in which a child has been removed from his or her home before an order of disposition has been made.

Laws 1951, p. 291, § 21; Laws 1968, p. 1013, § 12; Laws 1971, p. 709, § 1; Laws 1992, p. 1983, § 5; Laws 2000, p. 20, § 1; Laws 2002, p. 1162, § 7.

Formerly Code 1933, § 24A–2201; Code 1981, § 15–11–33.

Historical and Statutory Notes

The 2000 amendment, which restructured this chapter into parts and modified statutory references to reflect this restructuring, renumbered this section from § 15–11–33(a), (b), (d), and (e). In addition the amendment substituted reference to child for juvenile and provided gender neutral referents.

The 2002 amendment substantially rewrote this section which, prior thereto, provided:

"(a) Findings. After hearing the evidence on any petition alleging delinquency, unruliness, or deprivation, the court shall make and file its findings as to whether the child is a deprived child or, if the petition alleges that the child is delinquent or unruly, after hearing the evidence the court shall make and file its findings as to whether the acts ascribed to the child were committed by the child. If the court finds that the child is not a deprived child or that the allegations of delinquency or unruly conduct have not been established, it shall dismiss the petition and order the child discharged from any detention or other restriction theretofore ordered in the proceeding.

"(b) Disposition. The court shall proceed immediately or at a postponed hearing to make a proper disposition of the case if the court finds from clear and convincing evidence that the child:

"(1) Is deprived;

"(2) Is in need of treatment or rehabilitation as a delinquent child; or

"(3) Is in need of treatment or rehabilitation or supervision as an unruly child.

"(c) Evidence. In dispositional hearings under subsection (b) of this Code section and in all proceedings involving custody of a child, all information helpful in determining the questions presented, including oral and written reports, may be received by the court and relied upon to the extent of its probative value even though not otherwise competent in the hearing on the petition. The parties or their counsel shall be afforded an opportunity upon request to examine and controvert written reports so received and to cross-examine individuals making the reports, except that portions of such reports not relied on by the court in reaching its decision which, if revealed, would be prejudicial to the interests of the child or any party to the proceeding may be withheld in the court's discretion. Confidential sources of information need not be disclosed.

"(d) Continuances; scheduling. On its own motion or that of a party, the court may continue the hearings under this Code section for a reasonable period to receive reports and other evidence bearing on the disposition or the child's need for treatment or rehabilitation. In this event, the court shall make an appropriate order for detention of the child or for the child's release from detention subject to supervision of the court during the period of the continuance. In scheduling investigations and hearings, the court shall give priority to proceedings in which a child is in detention or has otherwise been removed from his or her home before an order of disposition has been made."

§ 15–11–56.1. Renumbered as § 15–11–71 by Laws 2000, p. 20, § 1

§ 15–11–57. Counseling or counsel and advice for deprived child

When any child is before a juvenile court and such child is found by the court to be a deprived child, the court shall be authorized, in addition to any other disposition authorized by this article, to order such child and such child's parents or guardian to participate in counseling or in counsel and advice as determined by the court. Such counseling and counsel and advice may be provided by the court, court personnel, probation officers, professional counselors or social workers, psychologists, physicians, qualified volunteers, or appropriate public, private, or volunteer agencies as directed by the court and shall be designed to assist in deterring future conditions of deprivation, or other conduct or conditions which would be harmful to the child or society.

Laws 1992, p. 2474, § 1; Laws 1998, p. 128, § 15; Laws 1998, p. 653, § 2; Laws 1998, p. 854, § 1; Laws 2000, p. 20, § 1.

Formerly Code 1981, § 15–11–36.1.

Historical and Statutory Notes

The 2000 amendment, which restructured this chapter into parts and modified statutory references to reflect this restructuring, renumbered this section from § 15–11–36.1. In addition the amendment rephrased the section which prior thereto provided:

"When any child is before a juvenile court and such child is found by the court to have committed a delinquent act, to be a deprived child, to be an unruly child, or to have committed a juvenile traffic offence as defined in Code Section 15–11–49, the court shall be authorized, in addition to any other disposition authorized by this article, to order such child and such child's parents or guardian to participate in counseling or in counsel and advice as determined by the court. Such counseling and counsel and advice may be provided by the court, court personnel, probation officers, professional counselors or social workers, psychologists, physicians, qualified volunteers, or appropriate public, private, or volunteer agencies as directed by the court and shall be designed to assist in deterring future delinquent or unruly acts, conditions of deprivation, or other conduct or conditions which would be harmful to the child or society."

§ 15–11–58. Reunification services

(a) A court's order removing a child from the child's home shall be based upon a finding by that court that continuation in the home would be contrary to the welfare of the child. If the court places custody of the child in the Division of Family and Children Services of the Department of Human Services, the court shall also determine as a finding of fact whether reasonable efforts were made by the Division of Family and Children Services of the Department of Human Services and any other appropriate agencies to preserve and reunify families prior to the placement of a child in the custody of the Department of Human Services, to prevent or eliminate the need for removal of the child from that child's home, and to make it possible for the child to return safely to the child's home. Such findings shall also be made at every subsequent review of the court's order under this chapter.

(1) In determining reasonable efforts to be made with respect to a child, as described in this subsection, and in making such reasonable efforts, the child's health and safety shall be the paramount concern;

(2) Except as provided in paragraph (4) of this subsection, reasonable efforts shall be made to preserve and reunify families:

(A) Prior to the placement of a child in the custody of the Department of Human Services, to prevent or eliminate the need for removing the child from the child's home; and

(B) To make it possible for a child to return safely to the child's home;

(3) If continuation of reasonable efforts of the type described in paragraph (2) of this subsection is determined to be inconsistent with the permanency plan for the child, reasonable efforts shall be made to place the child in a timely manner in accordance with the permanency plan and to complete whatever steps are necessary to finalize the permanent placement of the child;

(4) Reasonable efforts of the type described in paragraph (2) of this subsection shall not be required to be made with respect to a parent of a child if a court of competent jurisdiction has determined that:

(A) The parent has subjected the child to aggravated circumstances which may include but need not be limited to abandonment, torture, chronic abuse, and sexual abuse;

(B) The parent has:

(i) Committed murder of another child of the parent;

(ii) Been convicted of the murder of the other parent of the child;

(iii) Committed voluntary manslaughter of another child of the parent;

(iv) Aided or abetted, attempted, conspired, or solicited to commit murder or voluntary manslaughter of another child of the parent; or

(v) Committed a felony assault that results in serious bodily injury to the child or another child of the parent; or

(C) The parental rights of the parent to a sibling have been terminated involuntarily;

(5) If reasonable efforts of the type described in paragraph (2) of this subsection are not made with respect to a child as a result of a determination made by a court of competent jurisdiction in accordance with paragraph (4) of this subsection:

(A) A permanency hearing in accordance with subsection (*o*) of this Code section shall be held for the child within 30 days after such determination; and

(B) Reasonable efforts shall be made to place the child in a timely manner in accordance with the permanency plan and to complete whatever steps are necessary to finalize the permanent placement of the child; and

(6) Reasonable efforts to place a child for adoption or with a legal guardian may be made concurrently with reasonable efforts of the type described in paragraph (2) of this subsection.

(b) Within 30 days of the date a child who is placed in the custody of the Department of Human Services is removed from the home and at each subsequent review of the disposition order, the Division of Family and Children Services of the Department of Human Services must submit a written report to the court which shall either include a case plan for a reunification of the family or include a statement of the factual basis or bases for determining that a plan for reunification is not appropriate. Such report shall become a discrete part of the case record in a format determined by the Division of Family and Children Services of the Department of Human Services and shall be made available to the parents or guardian of the foster child. The contents of the report shall be determined at a meeting to be held by the Division of Family and Children Services of the Department of Human Services in consultation with the judicial citizen review panel, if one is designated by the court for such purpose, and the parents and children, when available. The parents shall be given written notice of the meeting at least five days in advance and shall be advised that the report will be submitted to the court for consideration to become an order of the court. The report submitted to the court shall also contain any dissenting recommendations of the judicial citizen review panel, if applicable, and any recommendations of the parents, if such are available.

(c) If the report contains a plan for reunification services, such plan if adopted by the court shall be in effect until modification by the court. The plan shall address each reason requiring removal and shall contain at least the following:

(1) The purpose for which the child was placed in foster care, including a statement of the reasons why the child cannot be adequately protected at home and the harm which may occur if the child remains in the home, and shall also include a description of the services offered and the services provided to prevent removal of the child from the home;

(2) A discussion of how the plan is designed to achieve a placement in a safe setting that is the least restrictive, most family-like, and most appropriate setting available and in close proximity to the home of the parents, consistent with the best interests and special needs of the child;

(3) A clear description of the specific actions to be taken by the parents and the specific services to be provided by the Division of Family and Children Services of the Department of Human Services or other appropriate agencies in order to bring about the identified changes that must be made in order for the child to be safely returned home; provided, however, that all services and actions required of the parents which are not directly related to the circumstances necessitating separation cannot be made conditions of the return of the child without further court review;

(4) Specific time frames in which the goals of the plan are to be accomplished to fulfill the purpose of the reunification plan;

(5) The person within the Division of Family and Children Services of the Department of Human Services or other agency who is directly responsible for ensuring that the plan is implemented;

(6) Consideration of the advisability of a reasonable visitation schedule which allows the parents to maintain meaningful contact with their children through personal visits, telephone calls, and letters;

(7) A statement that reasonable efforts have been made and a requirement that reasonable efforts shall be made for so long as the child remains in the custody of the department:

(A) To place siblings removed from their home in the same foster care, kinship, guardianship, or adoptive placement, unless the Division of Family and Children Services documents that such a joint placement would be contrary to the safety or well-being of any of the siblings; and

(B) In the case of siblings removed from their home who are not so jointly placed, for frequent visitation or other ongoing interaction between the siblings, unless the Division of Family and Children Services documents that such frequent visitation or other ongoing interaction would be contrary to the safety or well-being of any of the siblings;

(8) Provisions ensuring the educational stability of the child while in foster care, including:

(A) An assurance that the placement of the child in foster care takes into account the appropriateness of the current educational setting and the proximity to the school in which the child is enrolled at the time of placement;

(B) An assurance that the state agency has coordinated with appropriate local educational agencies to ensure that the child remains in the school in which the child is enrolled at the time of placement; or

(C) If remaining in such school is not in the best interests of the child, an assurance by the Division of Family and Children Services that such division and the local educational agencies have cooperated to assure the immediate and appropriate enrollment in a new school, with all of the educational records of the child provided to such new school; and

(9) A requirement that the Division of Family and Children Services of the Department of Human Services case manager and staff, and, as appropriate, other representatives of the child, provide the child with assistance and support in developing a transition plan that is personalized at the direction of the child; includes specific options on housing, health insurance, education, local opportunities for mentors and continuing support services, and work force supports and employment services; and is as detailed as the child may elect in the 90 day period immediately prior to the date on which the child will attain 18 years of age.

(d) If the submitted report contains a proposed plan for reunification services, and no hearing is requested as provided in this Code section, the court shall enter a dispositional order or supplemental order incorporating all elements of the plan for reunification services which the court finds essential to reunification of the child with his or her family, specifying what must be accomplished by all parties before reunification of the family can be achieved. If the report contains a plan for reunification services, a copy of the report must be transmitted to the parents at the same time the report is transmitted to the court, along with written notice that the report will be considered by the court without a hearing unless, within five days from the date the copy of the report was received, the parents request a hearing before the court to review the report. The Division of Family and Children Services of the Department of Human Services shall provide the custodian of the child, the foster parents of the child, and any preadoptive parents or relatives providing care for the child with a copy of those portions of the court approved plan that involve the permanency goal and the services to be provided to the child. The provisions of subsection (p) of this Code section concerning notice, opportunity to be heard, authority of the court, and content of the court's order are applicable to proceedings under this subsection.

(e) If the report submitted to the court does not contain a plan for reunification services, upon proper notice being provided to the parents, the court shall, no later than 30 days following the filing of the report, hold a hearing to review the report and the determination that a plan for reunification services is not appropriate.

(f) When a recommendation is made that reunification services are not appropriate and should not be allowed, the report shall address each reason requiring removal and shall contain at least the following:

(1) The purpose for which the child was placed in foster care, including a statement of the reasons why the child cannot be adequately and safely protected at home and the harm which may occur if the child remains in the home, and a description of the services offered and the services provided to prevent removal of the child from the home;

(2) A clear statement describing all of the reasons supporting a finding that reasonable efforts to reunify a child with the child's family will be detrimental to the child, and that reunification services therefore need not be provided, including specific findings as to whether any of the grounds for terminating parental rights exist, as set forth in subsection (b) of Code Section 15–11–94 or paragraph (4) of subsection (a) of this Code section; and

(3) The statements, provisions, and requirements found in paragraphs (7) and (8) of subsection (c) of this Code section.

(g) At the hearing held for the purpose of reviewing the determination by the Division of Family and Children Services of the Department of Human Services that a reunification plan is not appropriate, the representative of the Division of Family and Children Services shall notify the court whether and when it intends to proceed with termination of parental rights at that time. If the Division of Family and Children Services indicates that it does not intend to petition for the termination of parental rights, the court may appoint a guardian ad litem and charge such guardian with the duty of determining whether termination proceedings should be commenced.

(h) When reviewing the determination by the Division of Family and Children Services of the Department of Human Services that a reunification plan is not appropriate, the court shall determine by clear and convincing evidence whether reasonable efforts to reunify a child with his or her family will be detrimental to the child and that reunification services, therefore, should not be provided or should be terminated. There shall be a presumption that reunification services should not be provided if the court finds by clear and convincing evidence that:

(1) The parent has unjustifiably failed to comply with a previously ordered plan designed to reunite the family;

(2) A child has been removed from the home on at least two previous occasions and reunification services were made available on those occasions;

(3) Any of the grounds for terminating parental rights exist, as set forth in subsection (b) of Code Section 15–11–94; or

(4) Any of the circumstances set out in paragraph (4) of subsection (a) of this Code section exist, making it unnecessary to provide reasonable efforts to reunify.

(i)(1) If the court has entered an order finding that reasonable efforts to reunify a child with his or her family would be detrimental to the child in accordance with subsection (h) of this Code section and if the court finds that referral for termination of parental rights and adoption is not in the best interest of the child, the court may, upon proper petition, enter a custody order which shall remain in effect until the child's eighteenth birthday:

(A) Placing the child in the custody of a relative of the child if such a person is willing and, after study by the probation officer or other person or agency designated by the court, is found by the court to be qualified to receive and care for the child;

(B) Placing the child in the custody of any nonrelative individual who, after study by the probation officer or other person or agency designated by the court, is found by the court to be qualified to receive and care for the child;

(C) Placing the child in the custody of a suitable individual custodian in another state pursuant to the provisions of Code Section 15–11–89; or

(D) In the case where the court has found a compelling reason that a placement pursuant to subparagraph (A), (B), or (C) of this paragraph is not in the child's best interest, placing the child in the custody of an agency or organization licensed or otherwise authorized by law to receive and provide care for the child which is operated in a manner that provides such care, guidance, and control as would be provided in a family home as defined in the court's order.

Such order may be modified following a petition for modification by a party or upon motion of the court pursuant to Code Section 15–11–40.

(2) A probation officer, judicial citizen review panel established by the court, or other person or agency designated by the court shall, after study or review, submit a report to the

court addressing whether the custodian to whom custody of a child has been given pursuant to this Code section continues to be qualified to receive and care for the child within:

(A) Thirty–six months of an order placing a child in the custody of a relative pursuant to subparagraph (A) of paragraph (1) of this subsection and every 36 months thereafter; or

(B) Twelve months of an order placing a child in the custody of a nonrelative, an out-of-state custodian, or an agency or organization licensed or otherwise authorized by law to receive and provide care for the child pursuant to subparagraph (B), (C), or (D) of paragraph (1) of this subsection and every 12 months thereafter.

(3) Whenever a child is placed in the custody of an agency or organization licensed or otherwise authorized by law to receive and provide care for the child pursuant to subparagraph (D) of paragraph (1) of this subsection, such agency or organization shall be charged with the responsibility of notifying the court within ten days in the event its license is placed on probation, suspended, revoked, or surrendered and, in such event, the court shall conduct a judicial review within ten days of such notification to determine whether another placement should be made for the child.

(j) At the hearing required by subsection (e) of this Code section, the court shall hold a permanency hearing in accordance with subsection (*o*) of this Code section and shall consider and incorporate a permanency plan for the child in its order which shall comply with subsection (*o*) of this Code section.

(k) Except as otherwise provided by law, an order of disposition placing a deprived child in foster care under the supervision of the Division of Family and Children Services of the Department of Human Services shall continue in force for 12 months after the date the child is considered to have entered foster care or until sooner terminated by the court. For the purposes of this Code section, the date the child is considered to have entered foster care shall be the date of the first judicial finding that the child has been subjected to child abuse or neglect, or the date that is 60 days after the date on which the child is removed from the home, whichever is earlier. All cases of children in foster care in the custody of the Division of Family and Children Services of the Department of Human Services shall be initially reviewed within 90 days of the entering of the dispositional order but no later than six months following the child's placement and shall be conducted by the juvenile court judge, by an associate juvenile court judge or judge pro tempore, or by judicial citizen review panels established by the court, as the court directs, meeting such standards and using such procedures as shall be established by court rule by the Supreme Court of Georgia, with the advice and consent of the Council of Juvenile Court Judges. At the time of each review of every case of a child in foster care in the custody of the Division of Family and Children Services of the Department of Human Services, a representative of the Division of Family and Children Services shall notify the court whether such division intends to proceed with the termination of parental rights at that time. If such division indicates that it does not intend to petition for the termination of parental rights at that time, the court may appoint a guardian ad litem and charge such guardian with the duty of determining whether termination proceedings should be commenced. In the event the review is conducted by judicial citizen review panels, the panel shall transmit its report, including its findings and recommendations and those of such division, along with such division's proposed revised plan for reunification or other permanency plan, if necessary, to the court and the parents within five days after the review. Any party may request a hearing on the proposed revised plan in writing within five days after receiving a copy of such plan. The Division of Family and Children Services of the Department of Human Services shall provide the custodian of the child, the foster parents of the child, and any preadoptive parents or relatives providing care for the child with a copy of those portions of the report of the judicial citizen review panel that involve the recommended permanency goal and the recommended services to be provided to the child. Following such initial review, additional periodic reviews shall be held at six-month intervals. The provisions of subsection (p) of this Code section concerning notice, opportunity to be heard, authority of the court, and content of the court's order are applicable to proceedings under this subsection.

(*l*) If no hearing is requested or scheduled by the court on its own motion, the court shall review the proposed revised plan and enter a supplemental order incorporating a revised plan as part of its disposition in the case. In the event that a hearing is held, the court shall, after hearing evidence, enter a supplemental order incorporating all elements that the court finds essential in the proposed revised plan. The provisions of subsection (p) of this Code section concerning notice, opportunity to be heard, authority of the court, and content of the court's order are applicable to proceedings under this subsection. The judge's supplemental order shall be entered within a reasonable time from the conclusion of the hearing or expiration of the time for the hearing to be requested and shall also provide one of the following:

(1) That the child return to the home of his or her parents, legal guardian, or custodian with or without court imposed conditions;

(2) That the child continue in the current custodial placement and that the current placement is appropriate for the child's needs; or

(3) That the child continue in the current custodial placement but that the current placement plan is no longer appropriate for the child's needs and direct the department to devise another plan within available resources. The new plan must be submitted within ten days for court approval. Copies of any court approved revised plan shall be furnished to all parties. The Division of Family and Children Services of the Department of Human Services shall provide the custodian of the child, the foster parents of the child, and any preadoptive parents or relatives providing care for the child with a copy of those portions of the court approved revised plan that involve the permanency goal and the services to be provided to the child.

In the event that the judicial citizen review panel determines that the parents have unjustifiably failed to comply with the ordered plan designed to reunite the family and that such failure is significant enough to warrant consideration of termination of parental rights, the panel may make a recommendation to the guardian ad litem of the child, the Division of Family and Children Services of the Department of Human Services, and the intake officer of the court that a petition for termination of parental rights should be prepared. Any such party or officer of the court shall file a petition if, upon examination, they find sufficient evidence. In the event that no guardian ad litem has been appointed when the judicial citizen review panel recommends that a petition to terminate parental rights be filed, the court shall have the authority to appoint a guardian ad litem who shall have the duty to determine whether termination proceedings should be commenced.

(m) In the event that a child has been in foster care under the responsibility of the Division of Family and Children Services of the Department of Human Services for 15 of the most recent 22 months, or, if the court has determined a child to be an abandoned infant, as set forth in subsection (b) of Code Section 15–11–94, or has made a determination that the parent has committed murder of another child of the parent; been convicted of the murder of the other parent of the child; committed voluntary manslaughter of another child of the parent; aided or abetted, attempted, conspired, or solicited to commit murder or voluntary manslaughter of another child of the parent, or committed felony assault that has resulted in serious bodily injury to the child or to another child of the parent, the department shall file a petition to terminate the parental rights of the child's parents or, if such a petition has been filed by another party, seek to be joined as a party to the petition, and, concurrently, to identify, recruit, process, and approve a qualified family for an adoption, unless, at the option of the Division of Family and Children Services of the

Department of Human Services, the child is being cared for by a relative; the case plan documents a compelling reason for determining that filing such a petition would not be in the best interests of the child; or the Division of Family and Children Services of the Department of Human Services has not provided to the family of the child, consistent with the specific time frames for the accomplishment of the case plan goals, such services deemed necessary for the safe return of the child to the child's home.

(n) The court which made the order may extend its duration for not more than 12 months if:

(1) A hearing is held upon motion of the Division of Family and Children Services of the Department of Human Services prior to the expiration of the order;

(2) Reasonable notice of the factual basis of the motion and of the hearing and opportunity to be heard are given to the parties affected; and

(3) The court finds that the extension is necessary to accomplish the purposes of the order extended.

(*o*)(1) With respect to each child in the custody of the Department of Human Services, a permanency hearing shall be held no later than 30 days after the Division of Family and Children Services of the Department of Human Services has submitted a written report to the court which does not contain a plan for reunification services as provided in subsection (j) of this Code section, or no later than 12 months after the child is considered to have entered foster care, whichever comes first. Thereafter, a permanency hearing shall be held not less frequently than every 12 months during the time the child continues in the custody of the Department of Human Services. A permanency hearing may be held by the court at the time of the hearing on a motion to extend custody permitted by subsection (n) of this Code section. The provisions of subsection (p) of this Code section concerning notice, opportunity to be heard, authority of the court, and content of the court's order are applicable to proceedings under this paragraph.

(2) At the time of the permanency hearing, the Division of Family and Children Services of the Department of Human Services shall submit for the court's consideration a report recommending a permanency plan for the child which shall include whether and, if applicable, when the child shall be returned to the parent or parents; referred for termination of parental rights and adoption; referred for legal guardianship; placed permanently with a fit and willing relative; or, in the case where the division has provided a compelling reason that none of the foregoing options would be in the best interest of the child, placed in another planned permanent living arrangement. The report shall include documentation of the steps to be taken by the Division of Family and Children Services of the Department of Human Services to finalize the permanent placement of the child. When the permanency plan recommended is referral for termination of parental rights and adoption, such report shall include child specific recruitment efforts such as the use of state, regional, and national adoption exchanges, including electronic exchange systems. The provisions of subsection (p) of this Code section concerning notice, opportunity to be heard, authority of the court, and content of the court's order are applicable to proceedings under this paragraph.

(3) The permanency hearing may be conducted as the court directs by the juvenile court judge or by an associate juvenile court judge or judge pro tempore. The court may also direct that the permanency hearing be conducted by a judicial citizen review panel established by the court in the manner provided in subsection (k) of this Code section, unless the permanency hearing is one required under subsection (j) of this Code section as a result of a recommendation that reunification services are not appropriate. The judicial citizen review panel may conduct its hearing in the same manner as it conducts a case review under subsection (k) of this Code section. The provisions of subsection (p) of this Code section concerning notice, opportunity to be heard, authority of the court, and content of the court's order are applicable to proceedings under this paragraph.

(A) The panel shall transmit its report, including its findings and recommendations and those of the Division of Family and Children Services, to the court and the parties within five days after such hearing. The report of the judicial citizen review panel shall include all the elements required in paragraphs (5) and (6) of this subsection. Any party may request a hearing on the proposed permanency plan by submitting a request in writing within five days of receiving a copy of such plan. If a hearing is not requested, the court shall review the proposed permanency plan and enter a supplemental order incorporating all elements required by paragraphs (5) and (6) of this subsection that the court finds essential in the proposed permanency plan. In the event a hearing before the court is requested on the report transmitted by the judicial citizen review panel, the court shall, after hearing evidence, enter a supplemental order incorporating all the elements required in paragraphs (5) and (6) of this subsection.

(B) If a permanency hearing is held before the court, the court shall, after hearing evidence, enter a supplemental order incorporating all elements of the proposed permanency plan required by paragraphs (5) and (6) of this subsection that the court finds essential in the proposed permanency plan.

(4) The parents, the custodian of the child, the foster parents of the child, any preadoptive parent or relative providing care for the child, and other parties shall be given written notice of a permanency hearing at least five days in advance and shall be advised that the permanency plan recommended by the Division of Family and Children Services of the Department of Human Services will be submitted to the court for consideration to become an order of the court. Procedural safeguards shall be applied with respect to parental rights pertaining to the removal of the child from the home of his or her parents, to a change in the child's placement, and to any determination affecting visitation privileges of parents. Procedural safeguards shall also be applied to assure that the court or the judicial citizen review panel conducting a permanency hearing, including any hearing regarding transition of the child from foster care to independent living, shall consult, in an age-appropriate manner, with the child regarding the proposed permanency or transition plan for such child. The provisions of subsection (p) of this Code section concerning notice, opportunity to be heard, authority of the court, and content of the court's order are applicable to proceedings under this paragraph.

(5) The permanency plan incorporated in the court's order shall include whether and, if applicable, when the child shall be returned to the parent or parents, referred for termination of parental rights and adoption, referred for legal guardianship, or placed permanently with a fit and willing relative. If the court finds that there is a compelling reason that it would not be in the child's best interests to be returned to the parent or parents, referred for termination of parental rights and adoption, referred for legal guardianship, or placed permanently with a fit and willing relative, then the court's order shall document the compelling reason and provide that the child should be placed in another planned permanent living arrangement as defined in the court's order. The provisions of subsection (p) of this Code section concerning notice, opportunity to be heard, authority of the court, and content of the court's order are applicable to proceedings under this paragraph.

(6) The court or judicial citizen review panel which conducts the permanency hearing shall determine, as a finding of fact, whether the Division of Family and Children Services of the Department of Human Services has made reasonable efforts to finalize the permanency plan which is in effect at the time of the hearing. Further, the court or the judicial citizen review

panel, if applicable, shall determine as a finding of fact whether, in the case of a child placed out of the state, the out-of-state placement continues to be appropriate and in the best interest of the child and, in the case of a child who has attained the age of 14, shall determine the services needed to assist the child to make a transition from foster care to independent living. Also, in the case of a child whose permanency plan provides that the child will not be returned to the parent, the court or judicial citizen review panel, if applicable, shall consider in-state and out-of-state placement options for such child. Such findings of fact shall be made a part of the report of the judicial citizen review panel to the court and any supplemental order entered by the court.

(7) A supplemental order of the court adopting the permanency plan shall be entered within 30 days after the court has determined that reunification efforts will not be made by the Division of Family and Children Services of the Department of Human Services, if applicable, or within 12 months after the child is considered to have entered foster care, whichever is first, and at least every 12 months thereafter while the child is in foster care, unless the court finds good cause why such order cannot be entered by that time. The supplemental order shall include a requirement that the Division of Family and Children Services of the Department of Human Services case manager and staff, and, as appropriate, other representatives of the child, provide the child with assistance and support in developing a transition plan that is personalized at the direction of the child; includes specific options on housing, health insurance, education, local opportunities for mentors and continuing support services, and work force supports and employment services; and is as detailed as the child may elect in the 90 day period immediately prior to the date on which the child will attain 18 years of age.

(p) In advance of each review, hearing, or other proceeding to be held with respect to a child pursuant to this Code section, the court shall provide written notice or shall direct that a party shall provide written notice of such review, hearing, or other proceeding, including their right to be heard at such review, hearing, or other proceeding to the custodian of the child, to the foster parents of the child, and to any preadoptive parents or relatives providing care for the child, consistent with the form and timing of notice to parties; provided, however, that this provision shall not be construed to require a custodian, foster parent, preadoptive parent, or relative caring for the child to be made a party to the review, hearing, or other proceeding solely on the basis of such notice and opportunity to be heard. At each such review, hearing, or proceeding, the court in its discretion, based upon the evidence, may enter an order accepting or rejecting any report of the Division of Family and Children Services of the Department of Human Services, ordering an additional evaluation, appointing a guardian ad litem, or undertaking such other review as it deems necessary and appropriate to determine the disposition that is in the child's best interest. The court's order may incorporate all or part of the report of the Division of Family and Children Services of the Department of Human Services. In its order the court shall include findings of fact which reflect the court's consideration of the oral and written testimony offered by the parents, the custodian of the child, the foster parents of the child, any preadoptive parents or relatives providing care for the child who are required to be provided with notice and a right to be heard in any review, hearing, or proceeding to be held with respect to the child, and the Division of Family and Children Services of the Department of Human Services. A disposition may be made under the terms of this Code section only if the court finds that such disposition is in the best interest of the child.

Laws 1971, p. 709, § 1; Laws 1974, p. 1126, § 6; Laws 1984, p. 794, § 1; Laws 1986, p. 1017, § 2; Laws 1990, p. 8, § 15; Laws 1990, p. 1765, § 1; Laws 1992, p. 1983, § 14; Laws 1992, p. 2184, § 1; Laws 1996, p. 474, § 1; Laws 1997, p. 933, § 1; Laws 1997, p. 1453, § 1; Laws 1998, p. 854, § 2; Laws 1998, p. 908, § 1; Laws 2000, p. 20, § 1; Laws 2002, p. 1162, §§ 8, 9; Laws 2002, p. 1173, § 1; Laws 2003, Act 3, §§ 3, 4, eff. July 1, 2003; Laws 2004, Act 596, § 1, eff. July 1, 2004; Laws 2007, Act 248, §§ 3 to 5, eff. May 24, 2007; Laws 2009, Act 102, § 2–2, eff. July 1, 2009; Laws 2010, Act 469, §§ 1 to 3, eff. May 27, 2010.

Formerly Code 1933, § 24A–2701; Code 1981, § 15–11–41.

Historical and Statutory Notes

The 2000 amendment, which restructured this chapter into parts and modified statutory references to reflect this restructuring, renumbered this section from § 15–11–41 (b) to (r). In addition the amendment substituted reference to child for juvenile and provided gender neutral referents and inserted "judicial" preceding "citizens review panel".

The 2002 amendments substantially rewrote this section which prior thereto provided:

"(a) A court's order removing a child from the child's home shall be based upon a finding by that court that continuation in the home would be contrary to the welfare of the child. The court shall also determine as a finding of fact whether reasonable efforts were made by the Division of Family and Children Services of the Department of Human Resources and any other appropriate agencies to preserve and reunify families prior to the placement of a child in foster care, to prevent or eliminate the need for removal of the child from that child's home, and to make it possible for the child to return safely to the child's home. Such findings shall also be made at every subsequent review of the court's order under this chapter.

"(1) In determining reasonable efforts to be made with respect to a child, as described in this subsection, and in making such reasonable efforts, the child's health and safety shall be the paramount concern;

"(2) Except as provided in paragraph (4) of this subsection, reasonable efforts shall be made to preserve and reunify families:

"(A) Prior to the placement of a child in foster care, to prevent or eliminate the need for removing the child from the child's home; and

"(B) To make it possible for a child to return safely to the child's home;

"(3) If continuation of reasonable efforts of the type described in paragraph (2) of this subsection is determined to be inconsistent with the permanency plan for the child, reasonable efforts shall be made to place the child in a timely manner in accordance with the permanency plan and to complete whatever steps are necessary to finalize the permanent placement of the child;

"(4) Reasonable efforts of the type described in paragraph (2) of this subsection shall not be required to be made with respect to a parent of a child if a court of competent jurisdiction has determined that:

"(A) The parent has subjected the child to aggravated circumstances which may include but need not be limited to abandonment, torture, chronic abuse, and sexual abuse;

"(B) The parent has:

"(i) Committed murder of another child of the parent;

"(ii) Committed voluntary manslaughter of another child of the parent;

"(iii) Aided or abetted, attempted, conspired, or solicited to commit murder or voluntary manslaughter of another child of the parent; or

"(iv) Committed a felony assault that results in serious bodily injury to the child or another child of the parent; or

"(C) The parental rights of the parent to a sibling have been terminated involuntarily;

"(5) If reasonable efforts of the type described in paragraph (2) of this subsection are not made with respect to a child as a result of a determination made by a court of competent jurisdiction in accordance with paragraph (4) of this subsection:

"(A) A permanency hearing shall be held for the child within 30 days after such determination; and

"(B) Reasonable efforts shall be made to place the child in a timely manner in accordance with the permanency plan and to complete whatever steps are necessary to finalize the permanent placement of the child; and

"(6) Reasonable efforts to place a child for adoption or with a legal guardian may be made concurrently with reasonable efforts of the type described in paragraph (2) of this subsection.

"(b) Within 30 days of the date of removal of the child from the home and at each subsequent review of the disposition order, the Division of Family and Children Services of the Department of Human Resources must submit a written report to the court which shall either include a case plan for a reunification of the family or include a statement of the factual basis or bases for determining that a plan for reunification is not appropriate. Such report shall become a discrete part of the case record in a format determined by the Division of Family and Children Services of the Department of Human Resources and shall be made available to the parents or guardian of the foster child. The contents of the report shall be determined at a meeting to be held by the Division of Family and Children Services of the Department of Human Resources in consultation with the judicial citizen review panel, if one is designated by the court for such purpose, and the parents and children, when available. The parents shall be given written notice of the meeting at least five days in advance and shall be advised that the report will be submitted to become an order of the court. The report submitted to the court shall also contain any dissenting recommendations of the judicial citizen review panel, if applicable, and any recommendations of the parents, if such are available.

"(c) If the report contains a plan for reunification services, such plan if adopted by the court shall be in effect until modification by the court. The plan shall address each reason requiring removal and shall contain at least the following:

"(1) The purpose for which the child was placed in foster care, including a statement of the reasons why the child cannot be adequately protected at home and the harm which may occur if the child remains in the home and shall also include a description of the services offered and the services provided to prevent removal of the child from the home;

"(2) A discussion of how the plan is designed to achieve a placement in a safe setting that is the least restrictive, most family-like, and most appropriate setting available and in close proximity to the home of the parents, consistent with the best interests and special needs of the child;

"(3) A clear description of the specific actions to be taken by the parents and the specific services to be provided by the Division of Family and Children Services of the Department of Human Resources or other appropriate agencies in order to bring about the identified changes that must be made in order for the child to be safely returned home; provided, however, that all services and actions required of the parents which are not directly related to the circumstances necessitating separation cannot be made conditions of the return of the child without further court review;

"(4) Specific time frames in which the goals of the plan are to be accomplished to fulfill the purpose of the reunification plan;

"(5) The person within the Division of Family and Children Services of the Department of Human Resources or other agency who is directly responsible for ensuring that the plan is implemented; and

"(6) Consideration of the advisability of a reasonable visitation schedule which allows the parents to maintain meaningful contact with their children through personal visits, telephone calls, and letters.

"(d) If the submitted report contains a proposed plan for reunification services, and no hearing is requested as provided in this Code section, the court shall enter a dispositional order or supplemental order incorporating all elements of the plan for reunification services which the court finds essential to reunification of the child with his or her family, specifying what must be accomplished by all parties before reunification of the family can be achieved. If the report contains a plan for reunification services, a copy of the report must be transmitted to the parents at the same time the report is transmitted to the court, along with written notice that the report will be made the order of the court unless, within five days from the date the copy of the report was received, the parents request a hearing before the court to review the report.

"(e) If the report submitted to the court does not contain a plan for reunification services, upon proper notice being provided to the parents, the court shall, no later than 30 days following the filing of the report, hold a permanency hearing to review the report and the determination that a plan for reunification services is not appropriate.

"(f) When a recommendation is made that reunification services are not appropriate and should not be allowed, the report shall address each reason requiring removal and shall contain at least the following:

"(1) The purpose for which the child was placed in foster care, including a statement of the reasons why the child cannot be adequately and safely protected at home and the harm which may occur if the child remains in the home and a description of the services offered and the services provided to prevent removal of the child from the home; and

"(2) A clear statement describing all of the reasons supporting a finding that reasonable efforts to reunify a child with the child's family will be detrimental to the child, and that reunification services therefore need not be provided, including specific findings as to whether any of the grounds for terminating parental rights exist, as set forth in subsection (b) of Code Section 15–11–94 or paragraph (4) of subsection (a) of this Code section.

"(g) At the permanency hearing held for the purpose of reviewing the determination by the Division of Family and Children Services of the Department of Human Resources that a reunification plan is not appropriate, the representative of the Division of Family and Children Services shall notify the court whether and when it intends to proceed with termination of parental rights at that time. If the Division of Family and Children Services indicates that it does not intend to petition for the termination of parental rights, the court may appoint a guardian ad litem and charge such guardian with the duty of determining whether termination proceedings should be commenced.

"(h) When reviewing the determination by the Division of Family and Children Services of the Department of Human Resources that a reunification plan is not appropriate, the court shall determine by clear and convincing evidence whether reasonable efforts to reunify a child with his or her family will be detrimental to the child and that reunification services, therefore, should not be provided or should be terminated. There shall be a presumption that reunification services should not be provided if the court finds by clear and convincing evidence that:

"(1) The parent has unjustifiably failed to comply with a previously ordered plan designed to reunite the family;

"(2) A child has been removed from the home on at least two previous occasions and reunification services were made available on those occasions;

"(3) Any of the grounds for terminating parental rights exist, as set forth in subsection (b) of Code Section 15–11–94; or

"(4) Any of the circumstances set out in paragraph (4) of subsection (a) of this Code section exist, making it unnecessary to provide reasonable efforts to reunify.

"(i) If, after a judicial hearing in which the court finds that reunification is not in the best interests of the child and custody is granted to a relative, the custody order shall remain in effect until the child's eighteenth birthday unless modified following a petition for modification by a party pursuant to Code Section 15–11–40. Within 36 months of the custody order and every 36 months thereafter, a probation officer, judicial citizen review panel established by the court, or other person or agency designated by the court shall, after study or review, submit a report to the court addressing whether the relative with custody continues to be qualified to receive and care for the child. A copy of the report shall be mailed to the parents at their last known address.

"(j) Whenever the permanency plan is adoption or placement in another permanent home, the report submitted to the court shall document the steps to be taken by the Division of Family and Children Services of the Department of Human Resources to find an adoptive family or other permanent living arrangement for the child; to place the child with an adoptive family, a fit and willing relative, a legal guardian, or in another planned permanent living arrangement; and to finalize the adoption or legal guardianship. At a minimum, such documentation shall include child specific recruitment efforts such as the use of state, regional, and national adoption exchanges including electronic exchange systems.

"(k) Except as otherwise provided by law, an order of disposition placing a deprived child in foster care under the supervision of the Division of Family and Children Services of the Department of Human Resources shall continue in force for 12 months after the date the child is considered to have entered foster care or until sooner terminated by the court. For the purposes of this subsection, the date the child is considered to have entered foster care shall be the date of the first judicial finding that the child has been subjected to child abuse or neglect, or the date that is 60 days after the date on which the child is removed from the home, whichever is earlier. All cases of children in foster care in the custody of the Division of Family and Children Services of the Department of Human Resources shall be initially reviewed within 90 days of the entering of the dispositional order but no later than six months following the child's placement and shall be conducted by the juvenile court judge, by an associate juvenile court judge or judge pro tempore, or by judicial citizen review panels established by the court, as the court directs, meeting such standards and using such procedures as shall be established by court rule by the Supreme Court of Georgia, with the advice and consent of the Council of Juvenile Court Judges. At the time of each review of every case of a child in foster care in the custody of the Division of Family and Children Services of the Department of Human Resources, a representative of the Division of Family and Children Services shall notify the court whether such division intends to proceed with the termination of parental rights at that time. If such division indicates that it does not intend to petition for the termination of parental rights at that time, the court may appoint a guardian ad litem and charge such guardian with the duty of determining whether termination proceedings should be commenced. In the event the review is conducted by judicial citizen review panels, the panel shall transmit its report, including its findings and recommendations and those of such division, along with such division's proposed revised plan for reunification or other permanency plan, if necessary, to the court and the parents within five days after the review. Any party may request a hearing on the proposed revised plan in writing within five days after receiving a copy of such plan. Following such initial review, additional periodic reviews shall be held at six-month intervals. The foster parents, if any, of a child and any preadoptive parent or relative providing care for the child shall be provided with notice of and an opportunity to be heard in any review or hearing to be held with respect to the child, except that this provision shall not be construed to require that any foster parent, preadoptive parent, or relative providing care for the child be made a party to such a review or hearing solely on the basis of such notice and opportunity to be heard.

"(*l*) If no hearing is requested or scheduled by the court on its own motion, the court shall review the proposed revised plan and enter a supplemental order incorporating a revised plan as part of its disposition in the case. In the event that a hearing is held, the court shall, after hearing evidence, enter a supplemental order incorporating all elements that the court finds essential in the proposed revised plan. The judge's supplemental order shall be entered within a reasonable time from the conclusion of the hearing or expiration of the time for the hearing to be requested and shall also provide one of the following:

"(1) That the child return to the home of his or her parents, legal guardian, or custodian with or without court imposed conditions;

"(2) That the child continue in the current custodial placement and that the current placement is appropriate for the child's needs; or

"(3) That the child continue in the current custodial placement but that the current placement plan is no longer appropriate for the child's needs and direct the department to devise another plan within available resources. The new plan must be submitted within ten days for court approval. Copies of any court approved revised plan shall be furnished to all parties.

"In the event that the judicial citizen review panel determines that the parents have unjustifiably failed to comply with the ordered plan designed to reunite the family and that such failure is significant enough to warrant consideration of termination of parental rights, the panel may make a recommendation to the guardian ad litem of the child, the Division of Family and Children Services of the Department of Human Resources, and the intake officer of the court that a petition for termination of parental rights should be prepared. Any such party or officer of the court shall file a petition if, upon examination, they find sufficient evidence. In the event that no guardian ad litem has been appointed when the judicial citizen review panel recommends that a petition to terminate parental rights be filed, the court shall have the authority to appoint a guardian ad litem who shall have the duty to determine whether termination proceedings should be commenced.

"(m) In the event that a child has been in foster care under the responsibility of the Division of Family and Children Services of the Department of Human Resources for 15 of the most recent 22 months, or, if the court has determined a child to be an abandoned infant, as set forth in subsection (b) of Code Section 15-11-94, or has made a determination that the parent has committed murder of another child of the parent; committed voluntary manslaughter of another child of the parent; aided or abetted, attempted, conspired, or solicited to commit murder or voluntary manslaughter of another child of the parent, or committed felony assault that has resulted in serious bodily injury to the child or to another child of the parent, the department shall file a petition to terminate the parental rights of the child's parents or, if such a petition has been filed by another party, seek to be joined as a party to the petition, and, concurrently, to identify, recruit, process, and approve a qualified family for an adoption, unless, at the option of the Division of Family and Children Services of the Department of Human Resources, the child is being cared for by a relative; the case plan documents a compelling reason for determining that filing such a petition would not be in the best interests of the child; or the Division of Family and Children Services of the Department of Human Resources has not provided to the family of the child, consistent with the specific time frames for the accomplishment of the case plan goals, such services deemed necessary for the safe return of the child to the child's home.

"(n) The court which made the order may extend its duration for not more than 12 months if:

"(1) A hearing is held upon motion of the Division of Family and Children Services of the Department of Human Resources prior to the expiration of the order, which hearing shall, after the making of appropriate findings of fact, determine the permanency plan for the child. Such a permanency plan shall state whether and, if applicable, when the child shall be returned to the parent or referred for termination of parental rights and placed for adoption or referred for legal guardianship. In cases where the Division of Family and Children Services of the Department of Human Resources has documented to the court a compelling reason for determining that it would not be in the best interest of the child to return home, be referred for termination of parental rights, be placed for adoption, or be placed with a fit and willing relative or with a legal guardian, the permanency plan shall state that the child shall be placed in another planned permanent living arrangement. The permanency plan shall also state whether reunification services, if in effect, should be continued. With respect to a child placed out of state, procedural safeguards shall be applied as to whether the out-of-state placement continues to be appropriate and in the best interest of the child, and, in the case of a child who has attained age 16, the services needed to assist the child to make a transition from foster care to independent living. Procedural safeguards shall also be applied with respect to parental rights pertaining to the removal of the child from the home of his or her parents, to a change in the child's placement, and to any determination affecting visitation privileges of parents;

"(2) Reasonable notice of the factual basis of the motion and of the hearing and opportunity to be heard are given to the parties affected, including foster parents, if any, of a child and any preadoptive parent or relative providing care for the child except that this provision shall not be construed to require that any foster parent, preadoptive parent, or relative providing care for the child be made a party to such a review or hearing solely on the basis of such notice and opportunity to be heard; and

"(3) The court finds that the extension is necessary to accomplish the purposes of the order extended.

"(*o*) Except as otherwise provided by law, any other order of disposition in a proceeding involving delinquency, unruliness, or deprivation, except in an order involving the appointment of a guardian of the person or property of a child, continues in force for not more than two years. The court may sooner terminate its order or extend its duration for further periods. An order of extension may be made if:

"(1) A hearing is held prior to the expiration of the order upon motion of a party or on the court's own motion;

"(2) Reasonable notice of the factual basis of the motion and of the hearing and opportunity to be heard are given to the parties affected;

"(3) The court finds that the extension is necessary to accomplish the purposes of the order extended; and

"(4) The extension does not exceed two years from the expiration of the prior order.

"(p) Except as provided in Code Section 15-11-70, the court may terminate an order of disposition or extension prior to its expiration, on or without an application of a party, if it appears to the court that the purposes of the order have been accomplished.

"(q) Unless otherwise provided by law, when the child reaches 21 years of age all orders affecting him or her then in force terminate and he or she is discharged from further obligation or control."

The 2003 amendment by Act 3 rewrote the section which had read:

"(a) A court's order removing a child from the child's home shall be based upon a finding by that court that continuation in the home would be contrary to the welfare of the child. If the court places custody of the child in the Division of Family and Children Services of the Department of Human Resources, the court shall also determine as a finding of fact whether reasonable efforts were made by the Division of Family and Children Services of the Department of Human Resources and any other appropriate agencies to preserve and reunify families prior to the placement of a child in the custody of the Department of Human Resources, to prevent or eliminate the need for removal of the child from that child's home, and to make it possible for the child to return safely to the child's home. Such findings shall also be made at every subsequent review of the court's order under this chapter.

"(1) In determining reasonable efforts to be made with respect to a child, as described in this subsection, and in making such reasonable efforts, the child's health and safety shall be the paramount concern;

"(2) Except as provided in paragraph (4) of this subsection, reasonable efforts shall be made to preserve and reunify families:

"(A) Prior to the placement of a child in the custody of the Department of Human Resources, to prevent or eliminate the need for removing the child from the child's home; and

"(B) To make it possible for a child to return safely to the child's home;

"(3) If continuation of reasonable efforts of the type described in paragraph (2) of this subsection is determined to be inconsistent with the permanency plan for the child, reasonable efforts shall be made to place the child in a timely manner in accordance with the permanency plan and to complete whatever steps are necessary to finalize the permanent placement of the child;

"(4) Reasonable efforts of the type described in paragraph (2) of this subsection shall not be required to be made with respect to a parent of a child if a court of competent jurisdiction has determined that:

"(A) The parent has subjected the child to aggravated circumstances which may include but need not be limited to abandonment, torture, chronic abuse, and sexual abuse;

"(B) The parent has:

"(i) Committed murder of another child of the parent;

"(ii) Committed voluntary manslaughter of another child of the parent;

"(iii) Aided or abetted, attempted, conspired, or solicited to commit murder or voluntary manslaughter of another child of the parent; or

"(iv) Committed a felony assault that results in serious bodily injury to the child or another child of the parent; or

"(C) The parental rights of the parent to a sibling have been terminated involuntarily;

"(5) If reasonable efforts of the type described in paragraph (2) of this subsection are not made with respect to a child as a result of a determination made by a court of competent jurisdiction in accordance with paragraph (4) of this subsection:

"(A) A permanency hearing in accordance with subsection (*o*) of this Code section shall be held for the child within 30 days after such determination; and

"(B) Reasonable efforts shall be made to place the child in a timely manner in accordance with the permanency plan and to complete whatever steps are necessary to finalize the permanent placement of the child; and

"(6) Reasonable efforts to place a child for adoption or with a legal guardian may be made concurrently with reasonable efforts of the type described in paragraph (2) of this subsection.

"(b) Within 30 days of the date a child who is placed in the custody of the Department of Human Resources is removed from the home and at each subsequent review of the disposition order, the Division of Family and Children Services of the Department of Human Resources must submit a written report to the court which shall either include a case plan for a reunification of the family or include a statement of the factual basis or bases for determining that a plan for reunification is not appropriate. Such report shall become a discrete part of the case record in a format determined by the Division of Family and Children Services of the Department of Human Resources and shall be made available to the parents or guardian of the foster child. The contents of the report shall be determined at a meeting to be held by the Division of Family and Children Services of the Department of Human Resources in consultation with the judicial citizen review panel, if one is designated by the court for such purpose, and the parents and children, when available. The parents shall be given written notice of the meeting at least five days in advance and shall be advised that the report will be submitted to become an order of the court. The report submitted to the court shall also contain any dissenting recommendations of the judicial citizen review panel, if applicable, and any recommendations of the parents, if such are available.

"(c) If the report contains a plan for reunification services, such plan if adopted by the court shall be in effect until modification by the court. The plan shall address each reason requiring removal and shall contain at least the following:

"(1) The purpose for which the child was placed in foster care, including a statement of the reasons why the child cannot be adequately protected at home and the harm which may occur if the child remains in the home and shall also include a description of the services offered and the services provided to prevent removal of the child from the home;

"(2) A discussion of how the plan is designed to achieve a placement in a safe setting that is the least restrictive, most family-like, and most appropriate setting available and in close proximity to the home of the parents, consistent with the best interests and special needs of the child;

"(3) A clear description of the specific actions to be taken by the parents and the specific services to be provided by the Division of Family and Children Services of the Department of Human Resources or other appropriate agencies in order to bring about the identified changes that must be made in order for the child to be safely returned home; provided, however, that all services and actions required of the parents which are not directly related to the circumstances necessitating separation cannot be made conditions of the return of the child without further court review;

"(4) Specific time frames in which the goals of the plan are to be accomplished to fulfill the purpose of the reunification plan;

"(5) The person within the Division of Family and Children Services of the Department of Human Resources or other agency who is directly responsible for ensuring that the plan is implemented; and

"(6) Consideration of the advisability of a reasonable visitation schedule which allows the parents to maintain meaningful contact with their children through personal visits, telephone calls, and letters.

"(d) If the submitted report contains a proposed plan for reunification services, and no hearing is requested as provided in this Code section, the court shall enter a dispositional order or supplemental order incorporating all elements of the plan for reunification services which the court finds essential to reunification of the child with his or her family, specifying what must be accomplished by all parties before reunification of the family can be achieved. If the report contains a plan for reunification services, a copy of the report must be transmitted to the parents at the same time the report is transmitted to the court, along with written notice that the report will be made the order of the court unless, within five days from the date the copy of the report was received, the parents request a hearing before the court to review the report.

"(e) If the report submitted to the court does not contain a plan for reunification services, upon proper notice being provided to the parents, the court shall, no later than 30 days following the filing of the report, hold a hearing to review the report and the determination that a plan for reunification services is not appropriate.

"(f) When a recommendation is made that reunification services are not appropriate and should not be allowed, the report shall address each reason requiring removal and shall contain at least the following:

"(1) The purpose for which the child was placed in foster care, including a statement of the reasons why the child cannot be adequately and safely protected at home and the harm which may occur if the child remains in the home and a description of the services offered and the services provided to prevent removal of the child from the home; and

"(2) A clear statement describing all of the reasons supporting a finding that reasonable efforts to reunify a child with the child's family will be detrimental to the child, and that reunification services therefore need not be provided, including specific findings as to whether any of the grounds for terminating parental rights exist, as set forth in subsection (b) of Code Section 15–11–94 or paragraph (4) of subsection (a) of this Code section.

"(g) At the hearing held for the purpose of reviewing the determination by the Division of Family and Children Services of the Department of Human Resources that a reunification plan is not appropriate, the representative of the Division of Family and Children Services shall notify the court whether and when it intends to proceed with termination of parental rights at that time. If the Division of Family and Children Services indicates that it does not intend to petition for the termination of parental rights, the court may appoint a guardian ad litem and charge such guardian with the duty of determining whether termination proceedings should be commenced.

"(h) When reviewing the determination by the Division of Family and Children Services of the Department of Human Resources that a reunification plan is not appropriate, the court shall determine by clear and convincing evidence whether reasonable efforts to reunify a child with his or her family will be detrimental to the child and that reunification services, therefore, should not be provided or should be terminated. There shall be a presumption that reunification services should not be provided if the court finds by clear and convincing evidence that:

"(1) The parent has unjustifiably failed to comply with a previously ordered plan designed to reunite the family;

"(2) A child has been removed from the home on at least two previous occasions and reunification services were made available on those occasions;

"(3) Any of the grounds for terminating parental rights exist, as set forth in subsection (b) of Code Section 15–11–94; or

"(4) Any of the circumstances set out in paragraph (4) of subsection (a) of this Code section exist, making it unnecessary to provide reasonable efforts to reunify.

"(i) If, after a judicial hearing in which the court finds that reunification is not in the best interests of the child and custody is granted to a relative, the custody order shall remain in effect until the child's eighteenth birthday unless modified following a petition for modification by a party pursuant to Code Section 15–11–40. Within 36 months of the custody order and every 36 months thereafter, a probation officer, judicial citizen review panel established by the court, or other person or agency designated by the court shall, after study or review, submit a report to the court addressing whether the relative with custody continues to be qualified to receive and care for the child. A copy of the report shall be mailed to the parents at their last known address.

"(j) At the hearing required by subsection (e) of this Code section, the court shall hold a permanency hearing in accordance with subsection (*o*) of this Code section and shall consider and incorporate a permanency plan for the child in its order which shall comply with subsection (*o*) of this Code section.

"(k) Except as otherwise provided by law, an order of disposition placing a deprived child in foster care under the supervision of the Division of Family and Children Services of the Department of Human Resources shall continue in force for 12 months after the date the child is considered to have entered foster care or until sooner terminated by the court. For the purposes of this Code section, the date the child is considered to have entered foster care shall be the date of the first judicial finding that the child has been subjected to child abuse or neglect, or the date that is 60 days after the date on which the child is removed from the home, whichever is earlier. All cases of children in foster care in the custody of the Division of Family and Children Services of the Department of Human Resources shall be initially reviewed within 90 days of the entering of the dispositional order but no later than six months following the child's placement and shall be conducted by the juvenile court judge, by an associate juvenile court judge or judge pro tempore, or by judicial citizen review panels established by the court, as the court directs, meeting such standards and using such procedures as shall be established by court rule by the Supreme Court of Georgia, with the advice and consent of the Council of Juvenile Court Judges. At the time of each review of every case of a child in foster care in the custody of the Division of Family and Children Services of the Department of Human Resources, a representative of the Division of Family and Children Services shall notify the court whether such division intends to proceed with the termination of parental rights at that time. If such division indicates that it does not intend to petition for the termination of parental rights at that time, the court may appoint a guardian ad litem and charge such guardian with the duty of determining whether termination proceedings should be commenced. In the event the review is conducted by judicial citizen review panels, the panel shall transmit its report, including its findings and recommendations and those of such division, along with such division's proposed revised plan for reunification or other permanency plan, if necessary, to the court and the parents within five days after the review. Any party may request a hearing on the proposed revised plan in writing within five days after receiving a copy of such plan. Following such initial review, additional periodic reviews shall be held at six-month intervals. The foster parents, if any, of a child and any preadoptive parent or relative providing care for the child shall be provided with notice of and an opportunity to be heard in any review or hearing to be held with respect to the child, except that this provision shall not be construed to require that any foster parent, preadoptive parent, or relative providing care for the child be made a party to such a review or hearing solely on the basis of such notice and opportunity to be heard.

"(*l*) If no hearing is requested or scheduled by the court on its own motion, the court shall review the proposed revised plan and enter a supplemental order incorporating a revised plan as part of its disposition in the case. In the event that a hearing is held, the court shall, after hearing evidence, enter a supplemental order incorporating all elements that the court finds essential in the proposed revised plan. The judge's supplemental order shall be entered within a reasonable time from the conclusion of the hearing or expiration of the time for the hearing to be requested and shall also provide one of the following:

"(1) That the child return to the home of his or her parents, legal guardian, or custodian with or without court imposed conditions;

"(2) That the child continue in the current custodial placement and that the current placement is appropriate for the child's needs; or

"(3) That the child continue in the current custodial placement but that the current placement plan is no longer appropriate for the child's needs and direct the department to devise another plan within available resources. The new plan must be submitted within ten days for court approval. Copies of any court approved revised plan shall be furnished to all parties.

"In the event that the judicial citizen review panel determines that the parents have unjustifiably failed to comply with the ordered plan designed to reunite the family and that such failure is significant enough to warrant consideration of termination of parental rights, the panel may make a recommendation to the guardian ad litem of the child, the Division of Family and Children Services of the Department of Human Resources, and the intake officer of the court that a petition for termination of parental rights should be prepared. Any such party or officer of the court shall file a petition if, upon examination, they find sufficient evidence. In the event that no guardian ad litem has been appointed when the judicial citizen review panel recommends that a petition to terminate parental rights be filed, the court shall have the authority to appoint a guardian ad litem who shall have the duty to determine whether termination proceedings should be commenced.

"(m) In the event that a child has been in foster care under the responsibility of the Division of Family and Children Services of the Department of Human Resources for 15 of the most recent 22 months, or, if the court has determined a child to be an abandoned infant, as set forth in subsection (b) of Code Section 15–11–94, or has made a determination that the parent has committed murder of another child of the parent; committed voluntary manslaughter of another child of the parent; aided or abetted, attempted, conspired, or solicited to commit murder or voluntary manslaughter of another child of the parent, or committed felony assault that has resulted in serious bodily injury to the child or to another child of the parent, the department shall file a petition to terminate the parental rights of the child's parents or, if such a petition has been filed by another party, seek to be joined as a party to the petition, and, concurrently, to identify, recruit, process, and approve a qualified family for an adoption, unless, at the option of the Division of Family and Children Services of the Department of Human Resources, the child is being cared for by a relative; the case plan documents a compelling reason for determining that filing such a petition would not be in the best interests of the child; or the Division of Family and Children Services of the Department of Human Resources has not provided to the family of the child, consistent with the specific time frames for the accomplishment of the case plan goals, such services deemed necessary for the safe return of the child to the child's home.

"(n) The court which made the order may extend its duration for not more than 12 months if:

"(1) A hearing is held upon motion of the Division of Family and Children Services of the Department of Human Resources prior to the expiration of the order;

"(2) Reasonable notice of the factual basis of the motion and of the hearing and opportunity to be heard are given to the parties affected; and

"(3) The court finds that the extension is necessary to accomplish the purposes of the order extended.

"(*o*) With respect to each child in the custody of the Department of Human Resources, a permanency hearing shall be held no later than 30 days after the Division of Family and Children Services of the Department of Human Resources has submitted a written report to the court which does not contain a plan for reunification services as provided in subsection (j) of this Code section, or no later than 12 months after the child is considered to have entered foster care, whichever comes first. Thereafter, a permanency hearing shall be held not less frequently than every 12 months during the time the child continues in the custody of the Department of Human Resources. A permanency hearing may be held by the court at the time of the hearing on a motion to extend custody permitted by subsection (n) of this Code section.

"(1) At the time of the permanency hearing, the Division of Family and Children Services of the Department of Human Resources shall submit for the court's consideration a report recommending a permanency plan for the child which shall include whether and, if applicable, when the child shall be returned to the parent or parents; referred for termination of parental rights and adoption; referred for legal guardianship; placed permanently with a fit and willing relative; or, in the case where the division has provided a compelling reason that one of the foregoing options would not be in the best interest of the child, placed in another planned permanent living arrangement. The report shall include documentation of the steps to be taken by the Division of Family and Children Services of the Department of Human Resources to finalize the permanent placement of the child. When the permanency plan recommended is referral for termination of parental rights and adoption, such report shall include child specific recruitment efforts such as the use of state, regional, and national adoption exchanges, including electronic exchange systems.

"(2) The permanency hearing may be conducted as the court directs by the juvenile court judge or by an associate juvenile court judge or judge pro tempore. The court may also direct that the permanency hearing be conducted by a judicial citizen review panel established by the court in the manner provided in subsection (k) of this Code section, unless the permanency hearing is one required under subsection (j) of this Code section as a result of a recommendation that reunification services are not appropriate. The judicial citizen review panel may conduct its hearing in the same manner as it conducts a case review under subsection (k) of this Code section.

"(A) In the event that the permanency hearing is conducted by a judicial citizen review panel, the panel shall transmit its report, including its findings and recommendations and those of the Division of Family and Children Services, to the court and the parties within five days after such hearing. The report of the judicial citizen review panel shall include all the elements required in paragraphs (4) and (5) of this subsection. Any party may request a hearing on the proposed permanency plan by submitting a request in writing within five days of receiving a copy of such plan. If a hearing is not requested, the court shall review the proposed permanency plan and enter a supplemental order incorporating all elements required by paragraphs (4) and (5) of this subsection. In the event a hearing before the court is requested on the report transmitted by the judicial citizen review panel, the court shall, after hearing evidence, enter a supplemental order incorporating all the elements required in paragraphs (4) and (5) of this subsection.

"(B) If a permanency hearing is held before the court, the court shall, after hearing evidence, enter a supplemental order incorporating all elements of the proposed permanency plan required by paragraphs (4) and (5) of this subsection.

"(3) The parents and other parties shall be given written notice of a permanency hearing at least five days in advance and shall be advised that the permanency plan recommended by the Division of Family and Children Services of the Department of Human Resources will be submitted to become an order of the court. Procedural safeguards shall be applied with respect to parental rights pertaining to the removal of the child from the home of his or her parents, to a change in the child's placement, and to any determination affecting visitation privileges of parents. In addition, the foster parents, if any, of a child and any preadoptive parent or relative providing care for the child shall receive written notice of the permanency hearing at least five days in advance and shall be given an opportunity to be heard; provided, however, that this provision shall not be construed to require a foster parent, preadoptive parent, or relative caring for the child to be made a party to the hearing solely on the basis of such notice and opportunity to be heard.

"(4) The permanency plan incorporated in the court's order shall include whether and, if applicable, when the child shall be returned to the parent or parents, referred for termination of parental rights and adoption, referred for legal guardianship, or placed permanently with a fit and willing relative. If the court finds that there is a compelling reason that it would not be in the child's best interests to be returned to the parent or parents, referred for termination of parental rights and adoption, referred for legal guardianship, or placed permanently with a fit and willing relative, then the court's order shall document the compelling reason and provide that the child should be placed in another planned permanent living arrangement.

"(5) The court or judicial citizen review panel which conducts the permanency hearing shall determine, as a finding of fact, whether the Division of Family and Children Services of the Department of Human Resources has made reasonable efforts to finalize the permanency plan which is in effect at the time of the hearing. Further, the court or the judicial citizen review panel, if applicable, shall determine as a finding of fact whether, in the case of a child placed out of the state, the out-of-state placement continues to be appropriate and in the best interest of the child and, in the case of a child who has attained the age of 14, shall determine the services needed to assist the child to make a transition from foster care to independent living. Such findings of fact shall be made a part of the report of the judicial citizen review panel to the court and any supplemental order entered by the court.

"(6) A supplemental order of the court adopting the permanency plan must be entered within 30 days after the court has determined that reunification efforts will not be made by the Division of Family and Children Services of the Department of Human Resources, if applicable, or within 12 months after the child is considered to have entered foster care, whichever is first, and at least every 12 months thereafter while the child is in foster care, unless the court finds good cause why such order cannot be entered by that time."

The 2004 amendment by Act 596, in subpar. (a)(4)(B), inserted new div. (ii) and redesignated former divs. (ii), (iii), and (iv) as new divs. (iii), (iv), and (v) respectively; and in subsec. (m), inserted "been convicted of the murder of the other parent of the child;" following "murder of another child of the parent;".

The 2007 amendment by Act 248, in par. (4) of subsec. (*o*), inserted "Procedural safeguards shall also be applied to assure that the court or the judicial citizen review panel conducting a permanency hearing, including any hearing regarding transition of the child from foster care to independent living, shall consult, in an age–appropriate manner, with the child regarding the proposed permanency or transition plan for such child."; in par. (6) of subsec. (*o*), inserted "Also, in the case of a child whose permanency plan provides that the child will not be returned to the parent, the court or judicial citizen review panel, if applicable, shall consider in–state and out–of–state placement options for such child." and deleted "The provisions of subsection (p) of this Code section concerning notice, opportunity to be heard, authority of the court, and content of the court's order are applicable to proceedings under this paragraph." following "entered by the court." at the end of the paragraph; and, in subsec. (p), substituted "review, hearing, or other proceeding" for "review or hearing" three times in the first clause of the first sentence and once in the fourth sentence, and substituted "review, hearing, or other proceeding" for "hearing" in the proviso clause of the first sentence and in the second sentence.

The 2009 amendment by Act 102 substituted "Department of Human Services" for "Department of Human Resources" throughout the section.

The 2010 amendment by Act 469, in subsec. (c), added pars. (7) through (9); in subsec. (f), added par. (3); and in subsec. (*o*), in the first sentence of par. (7) replaced "must" with "shall", and added new second sentence.

§ 15–11–58.1. Proceedings involving deprivation of children

(a) Except as otherwise provided by law, an order of disposition in a proceeding involving deprivation, except an order involving the appointment of a guardian of the person or property of a child, continues in force for not more than two years. The court may sooner terminate its order or extend its duration for further periods. An order of extension may be made if:

(1) A hearing is held prior to the expiration of the order upon motion of a party or on the court's own motion;

(2) Reasonable notice of the factual basis of the motion and of the hearing and opportunity to be heard are given to the parties affected;

(3) The court finds that the extension is necessary to accomplish the purposes of the order extended; and

(4) The extension does not exceed two years from the expiration of the prior order.

(b) The court may terminate an order of disposition of a child adjudicated as deprived or an extension of such a disposition order prior to its expiration, on or without an application of a party, if it appears to the court that the purposes of the order have been accomplished.

(c) Unless otherwise provided by law, when a child adjudicated as deprived reaches 18 years of age all orders affecting him or her then in force terminate and he or she is discharged from further obligation or control.

Laws 2003, Act 377, § 3, eff. July 1, 2003.

Historical and Statutory Notes

Former § 15–11–58.1 was renumbered as § 15–11–80 by Laws 2000, p. 20, § 1.

§ 15–11–59. Renumbered as § 15–11–82 by Laws 2000, p. 20, § 1

§ 15–11–60. Renumbered as § 15–11–83 by Laws 2000, p. 20, § 1

§ 15–11–61. Renumbered as § 15–11–79.2 by Laws 2000, p. 20, § 1

Part 7

Delinquent and Unruly Children

§ 15–11–62. Child 13 to 17 years of age convicted of certain violent crimes; confinement in youth confinement unit

(a) A child 13 to 17 years of age convicted of any offense enumerated in subparagraph (b)(2)(A) of Code Section 15–11–28 shall be committed to the custody of the Department of Corrections; provided, however, that any child in the custody of the Department of Corrections shall be housed in a designated youth confinement unit until reaching the age of 17 notwithstanding that such child was tried and convicted as an adult in superior court. Any designated youth confinement unit in which a child is housed shall be designed to ensure that children are at all times housed separately from any adult offender incarcerated in the facility in which such youth confinement unit is located and shall be designed to facilitate rehabilitation of such children, which shall mean that a youth confinement unit shall be of a nondormitory design whenever possible and whenever such facilities become available and staffed by personnel who have received specialized training in the field of juvenile justice. All designated youth confinement units shall provide to children 13 to 17 years of age who have been sentenced to such units as a result of a conviction in superior court as an adult of an offense enumerated in subparagraph (b)(2)(A) of Code Section 15–11–28 life skills training, academic or vocational training, and substance abuse and violence prevention counseling to the extent that appropriations are available for such activities.

(b) When given legal custody over a child for confinement in a youth confinement unit as provided under this Code section, the Department of Corrections shall have:

(1) The right of physical possession of the child;

(2) The right and duty to protect, train, and discipline the child;

(3) The responsibility to provide the child with food, clothing, shelter, and education;

(4) The right to determine the facility in which the child shall be confined; and

(5) The right and duty to provide or obtain for a child medical, hospital, psychiatric, surgical, or dental care or services as may be considered appropriate and necessary by competent medical authority without securing prior consent of parents or legal guardians.

Laws 1994, p. 1012, § 15; Laws 1995, p. 783, § 3; Laws 2000, p. 20, § 1.

Formerly Code 1981, § 15-11-5.1.

Historical and Statutory Notes

The 2000 amendment, which restructured this chapter into parts and modified statutory references to reflect this restructuring, renumbered this section from § 15-11-5.1. In addition the amendment substituted reference to child for juvenile or youth and provided gender neutral referents.

§ 15-11-63. Designated felony acts; restrictive custody

(a) As used in this Code section, the term:

(1) "A carefully arranged and monitored home visit" means a home visit during which a child is monitored by appropriate personnel of the Department of Juvenile Justice designated pursuant to regulations of the commissioner of juvenile justice.

(2) "Designated felony act" means an act which:

(A) Constitutes a second or subsequent offense under subsection (b) of Code Section 16-11-132 if committed by a child 13 to 17 years of age;

(B) If done by an adult, would be one or more of the following crimes:

(i) Kidnapping or arson in the first degree, if done by a child 13 or more years of age;

(ii) Aggravated assault, arson in the second degree, aggravated battery, robbery, armed robbery not involving a firearm, or battery in violation of Code Section 16-5-23.1 if the victim is a teacher or other school personnel, if done by a child 13 or more years of age;

(iii) Attempted murder or attempted kidnapping, if done by a child 13 or more years of age;

(iv) Reserved;

(v) Hijacking a motor vehicle, if done by a child 13 or more years of age;

(vi) Any violation of Code Section 16-7-82, 16-7-84, or 16-7-86 if done by a child 13 or more years of age;

(vii) Any other act which, if done by an adult, would be a felony, if the child committing the act has three times previously been adjudicated delinquent for acts which, if done by an adult, would have been felonies;

(viii) Any violation of Code Section 16-13-31, relating to trafficking in cocaine, illegal drugs, marijuana, or methamphetamine;

(ix) Any criminal violation of Code Section 16-14-4, relating to racketeering;

(x) Any violation of Code Section 16-10-52, relating to escape, if the child involved in the commission of such act has been previously adjudicated to have committed a designated felony; or

(xi) Any violation of Code Section 16-7-2;

(C) Constitutes a second or subsequent adjudication of delinquency based upon a violation of Code Section 16-7-85 or 16-7-87;

(C.1) Constitutes any violation of Code Section 16-15-4, relating to criminal street gangs;

(C.2) Constitutes a second or subsequent adjudication of delinquency based on a violation of Code Section 16-11-127.1 or is a first violation of Code Section 16-11-127.1 involving:

(i) Any weapon, as such term is defined in Code Section 16-11-127.1, together with an assault;

(ii) A firearm as defined in paragraph (2) of subsection (a) of Code Section 16-11-131; or

(iii) A dangerous weapon or machine gun as defined in Code Section 16-11-121;

(D) Constitutes an offense within the exclusive jurisdiction of the superior court pursuant to subparagraph (b)(2)(A) of Code Section 15-11-28 which is transferred by the superior court to the juvenile court for adjudication pursuant to subparagraph (b)(2)(B) of Code Section 15-11-28 or which is transferred by the district attorney to the juvenile court for adjudication pursuant to subparagraph (b)(2)(C) of Code Section 15-11-28; or

(E) Constitutes a second or subsequent violation of Code Sections 16-8-2 through 16-8-9, relating to theft, if the property which was the subject of the theft was a motor vehicle.

(3) "Intensive supervision" means the monitoring of a child's activities on a more frequent basis than regular aftercare supervision, pursuant to regulations of the commissioner of juvenile justice.

(b) Where a child is found to have committed a designated felony act, the order of disposition shall be made within 20 days of the conclusion of the dispositional hearing and shall include a finding based on a preponderance of the evidence as to whether, for the purposes of this Code section, the child does or does not require restrictive custody under this Code section, in connection with which the court shall make specific written findings of fact as to each of the elements set forth in paragraphs (1) through (5) of subsection (c) of this Code section as related to the particular child. If the court finds that restrictive custody under this Code section is not required, the order of disposition shall be as otherwise provided in this article. If the court finds that restrictive custody is required, it shall continue the proceeding and enter an order of disposition for restrictive custody. Every order under this Code section shall be a dispositional order, shall be made after a dispositional hearing, and shall state the grounds for the order.

(c) In determining whether restrictive custody is required, the court shall consider:

(1) The needs and best interests of the child;

(2) The record and background of the child;

(3) The nature and circumstances of the offense, including whether any injury involved was inflicted by the child or another participant;

(4) The need for protection of the community; and

(5) The age and physical condition of the victim.

(d) Notwithstanding subsection (c) of this Code section, the court shall order restrictive custody in any case where the child is found to have committed a designated felony act in which the child inflicted serious physical injury upon another person who is 62 years of age or more.

(e) When the order is for restrictive custody in the case of a child found to have committed a designated felony act:

(1) The order shall provide that:

(A) The child shall be placed in the custody of the Department of Juvenile Justice for an initial period of five years;

(B) The child shall initially be confined in a youth development center for a period set by the order, to be not less than 12 nor more than 60 months; provided, however, that time spent in secure detention prior to placement in a youth development center shall be counted toward the period set by the order; and provided, further, that where the order of the court is made in compliance with subsection (f) of this Code section, the child shall initially be confined in a youth development center for 18 months;

(C) After the period set under subparagraph (B) of this paragraph, the child shall be placed under intensive supervision for a period of 12 months; and

(D) The child may not be released from a youth development center or transferred to a nonsecure facility during the period provided in subparagraph (B) of this paragraph nor may the child be released from intensive supervision during the period provided in subparagraph (C) of this paragraph, unless by court order. No home visits shall be permitted during the first six-month period of confinement in a youth development center unless authorized by the court except for emergency visits for medical treatment or severe illness or death in the family. All home visits must be carefully arranged and monitored while a child is confined in a youth development center, whether such confinement is pursuant to a court order or otherwise;

(2) During the placement or any extension thereof:

(A) After the expiration of the period provided in subparagraph (C) of paragraph (1) of this subsection, the child shall not be released from intensive supervision without the written approval of the commissioner of juvenile justice or such commissioner's designated deputy;

(B) While in a youth development center, the child may be permitted to participate in all youth development center services and programs and shall be eligible to receive special medical and treatment services, regardless of the time of confinement in the youth development center. After the first six months of confinement in a youth development center, a child may be eligible to participate in youth development center sponsored programs including community work programs and sheltered workshops under the general supervision of a youth development center staff outside of the youth development center; and, in cooperation and coordination with the Department of Human Services, the child may be allowed to participate in state sponsored programs for evaluation and services under the Division of Rehabilitation Services of the Department of Labor and the Department of Behavioral Health and Developmental Disabilities;

(C) The child shall not be discharged from the custody of the Department of Juvenile Justice unless a motion therefor is granted by the court, which motion shall not be made prior to the expiration of one year of custody; and

(D) Unless otherwise specified in the order, the Department of Juvenile Justice shall report in writing to the court not less than once every six months during the placement on the status, adjustment, and progress of the child; and

(3) Upon the expiration of the initial period of placement in a youth development center, or any extension thereof, the placement may be extended on motion by the Department of Juvenile Justice, after a dispositional hearing, for an additional period of 12 months, provided that no initial placement or extension of custody under this Code section may continue beyond the individual's twenty-first birthday.

(f) When the order is for restrictive custody in the case of a child found to have committed any designated felony act and such child has been found by a court to have committed a designated felony act on a prior occasion, regardless of the age of the child at the time of commission of such prior act, the order of the court shall be made pursuant to subparagraph (e)(1)(B) of this Code section.

(g) The Department of Juvenile Justice shall retain the power to continue the confinement of the child in a youth development center or other program beyond the periods specified by the court within the term of the order.

(h) Any court making a finding or adjudication that a child has committed a designated felony act shall identify the school last attended by such child and the school which such child intends to attend and shall transmit a copy of such adjudication or finding to the principals of the school which the child last attended and the school which the child intends to attend within 15 days of the adjudication or finding. Such information shall be subject to notification, distribution, and requirements as provided in Code Section 20–2–671.

Laws 1980, p. 1013, § 1; Laws 1982, p. 1871, §§ 1, 2, 4, 5; Laws 1984, p. 22, § 15; Laws 1986, p. 192, § 1; Laws 1986, p. 277, § 1; Laws 1986, p. 1017, § 1; Laws 1987, p. 3, § 15; Laws 1987, p. 1012, § 1; Laws 1989, p. 46, § 1; Laws 1992, p. 1983, §§ 9–11; Laws 1994, p. 1012, §§ 21, 22; Laws 1994, p. 1625, § 2; Laws 1996, p. 416, § 1; Laws 1997, p. 1061, § 2; Laws 1997, p. 1064, § 4; Laws 1997, p. 1453, §§ 1, 2; Laws 1998, p. 270, § 2; Laws 1999, p. 81, § 15; Laws 2000, p. 20, § 1; Laws 2000, p. 1137, § 2; Laws 2002, p. 1324, § 1–1; Laws 2009, Act 102, § 2–7, eff. July 1, 2009; Laws 2010, Act 465, § 1, eff. May 25, 2010; Laws 2010, Act 674, §§ 3, 4, eff. July 1, 2010.

Formerly Code 1933, §§ 24A–2301A, 24A–2302A; Code 1981, § 15–11–37.

Historical and Statutory Notes

The 2000 amendment by Act 467, which restructured this chapter into parts and modified statutory references to reflect this restructuring, renumbered this section from § 15–11–37. In addition the amendment substituted reference to child for juvenile or youth and provided gender neutral referents.

The 2000 amendment by Act 751 modified language to reflect the transfer of division of rehabilitation services from department of human resources to department of labor.

The 2002 amendment in subsec. (e)(2)(B) substituted for "Division of Mental Health, Mental Retardation, and Substance Abuse" the words Division of Mental Health, Developmental Disabilities, and Addictive Diseases of the Department of Human Resources.

The 2009 amendment by Act 102 in par. (e)(2), substituted "cooperation and coordination with the Department of Human Services" for "cooperation and coordination with the Department of Human Resources" and "Department of Behavioral Health and Developmental Disabilities" for "Division of Mental Health, Developmental Disabilities, and Addictive Diseases of the Department of Human Resources" in subpar. (B).

The 2010 amendment by Act 465, in subsec. (a), par. (2), deleted and reserved subpar. (B), subdiv. (iv) which prior thereto had read "The carrying or possession of a weapon in violation of subsection (b) of Code Section 16–11–127.1", and added subpar. (C.2).

The 2010 amendment by Act 674, in subsec. (a), par. (2), subpar. (B), added div. (xi); in subsec. (e), par. (1), subpar. (B), deleted "subsequent to the date of the order and" after "secure detention".

§ 15–11–64. Termination of proceedings relating to a runaway child

Any proceeding or other processes or actions relating to a child in which the sole allegation is that the child deserted without cause the child's home or place of abode for the first time shall be terminated or dismissed upon the request of the parent or legal custodian of the child.

Laws 1977, p. 1237, § 7; Laws 2000, p. 20, § 1.

Formerly Code 1933, § 24A–802; Code 1981, § 15–11–12.

Historical and Statutory Notes

The 2000 amendment, which restructured this chapter into parts and modified statutory references to reflect this restructuring, renumbered this section from § 15–11–12. In addition the amendment provided gender neutral referents.

§ 15–11–64.1. Conduct of delinquency proceeding by district attorney or staff

In any delinquency proceeding in which a petition has been filed, the district attorney or a member of the district attorney's staff shall conduct the proceedings on behalf of the state if requested to do so by the juvenile court if the state is not otherwise represented by a solicitor of the juvenile court. Notwithstanding any other provisions of law to the contrary, in any delinquency proceedings conducted by the district attorney or a member of the district attorney's staff, the district attorney or staff member shall be entitled to complete access to all court files, probation files, hearing transcripts, delinquency reports, and any other juvenile court records which may be of assistance to the district attorney or staff member in the conduct of such delinquency proceedings. It shall be the duty of the clerk and probation officers of the juvenile court to assist the district attorney or staff member in obtaining any such files, transcripts, reports, or records, or copies thereof, as may be requested by the district attorney or staff member. In any such case, the petition shall be dismissed by the court upon the motion of the district attorney setting forth that there is not sufficient evidence to warrant the further conduct of the proceeding.

Laws 2002, p. 1162, § 10.

§ 15–11–64.2. Victim impact form in delinquency proceeding

(a) In any delinquency proceeding in which a petition has been filed, the juvenile court shall notify any victim of a delinquent child's alleged delinquent act that the victim may submit a victim impact form as provided in Code Section 17–10–1.1 if:

(1) The allegedly delinquent child, in conduct which would constitute a felony if committed by an adult, caused physical, psychological, or economic injury to the victim; or

(2) The allegedly delinquent child, in conduct which would constitute a misdemeanor if committed by an adult, caused serious physical injury or death to the victim.

(b) The provisions of subsection (e) of Code Section 17–10–1.1 shall apply to the use and disclosure of the victim impact form.

(c) The victim may complete the victim impact form and submit such form to the juvenile court. If the victim is unable to do so because of such victim's mental, emotional, or physical incapacity, or because of such victim's age, the victim's attorney or a family member may complete the victim impact form on behalf of the victim.

(d) Prior to the imposition of a dispositional order for an allegedly delinquent child, the juvenile court shall permit the victim to address the juvenile court and present any information or opinions that concern the victim or the victim's family, including the impact of the delinquent act on the victim, the harm caused by the allegedly delinquent child and the delinquent act, the need for restitution, or the terms of the disposition order. Such statement shall be given in the presence of the allegedly delinquent child and shall be subject to cross-examination. The prosecuting attorney and the allegedly delinquent child shall be afforded the opportunity to explain, support, or deny the victim's statement. It shall be the duty of the juvenile court to advise the victim of the right to address the court prior to the entry of a dispositional order for a delinquent child. The victim shall have the discretion to exercise the right to be present and be heard at the dispositional hearing. If the victim is voluntarily absent from the dispositional hearing, such absence shall constitute a waiver of the rights provided by this subsection.

(e) Except as provided in subsection (d) of this Code section, no disposition of the child shall be invalidated because of failure to comply with the provisions of this Code section. This Code section shall not be construed to create any cause of action or any right of appeal on behalf of the victim, the state, or the accused; provided, however, that if the court intentionally fails to comply with this Code section, the victim may file a complaint with the Judicial Qualifications Commission.

Laws 2002, p. 1162, § 10; Laws 2010, Act 403, § 1, eff. July 1, 2010.

Historical and Statutory Notes

The 2010 amendment by Act 403 rewrote the section which had read as follows:

"(a) In any delinquency proceeding in which a petition has been filed, the juvenile court shall notify any victim of a delinquent child's alleged offense that the victim may submit a victim impact statement if:

"(1) The allegedly delinquent child, in conduct which would constitute a felony if committed by an adult, caused physical, psychological, or economic injury to the victim; or

"(2) The allegedly delinquent child, in conduct which would constitute a misdemeanor if committed by an adult, caused serious physical injury or death to the victim.

"(b) A victim impact statement submitted by a victim shall be attached to the case file and may be used by the district attorney or the judge during any stage of the proceedings against the child involving predisposition, disposition, or determination of restitution.

"(c) A victim impact statement shall:

"(1) Identify the victim of the offense and the perpetrator;

"(2) Itemize any economic loss suffered by the victim as a result of the offense;

"(3) Identify any physical injury suffered by the victim as a result of the offense along with its seriousness and permanence;

"(4) Describe any change in the victim's personal welfare or familial relationships as a result of the offense;

"(5) Identify any request for psychological services initiated by the victim or the victim's family as a result of the offense; and

"(6) Contain any other information related to the impact of the offense upon the victim that the court requires.

"(d) The victim may complete the victim impact statement form and submit such form to the juvenile court. If the victim is unable to do so because of such victim's mental, emotional, or physical incapacity, or because of such victim's age, the victim's attorney or a family member may complete the victim impact statement form on behalf of the victim.

"(e) The court shall, in the manner prescribed by rule of court, provide the child with a copy of the victim impact statement within a reasonable time prior to any hearing at which it is to be considered and allow the child to have the opportunity to rebut the victim's written statements.

"(f) No disposition of the child shall be invalidated because of failure to comply with the provisions of this subsection. This subsection shall not be construed to create any cause of action or any right of appeal on behalf of any person."

§ 15–11–65. Dispositional hearing for delinquent or unruly child; evidence; continuances; scheduling

(a) *Dispositional hearing for delinquent or unruly child.* If the court finds on proof beyond a reasonable doubt that the child committed the acts by reason of which he or she is alleged to be delinquent or unruly, it shall proceed immediately or at a later time to conduct a dispositional hearing for the purpose of hearing evidence as to whether the child is in need of treatment, rehabilitation, or supervision and shall make and file its findings thereon. If the court finds that the allegations of delinquency or unruly conduct have not been established, it shall dismiss the petition and order the child discharged from any detention or other restriction theretofore ordered in relation to the allegations. If the child is to be held in custody at a detention facility between the adjudicatory hearing and the dispositional hearing, the court shall conduct the dispositional hearing within 30 days of the adjudicatory hearing unless the court makes and files written findings of fact explaining the need for the delay. In the absence of evidence to the contrary, evidence sufficient to warrant a finding that acts have been committed which constitute a felony is also sufficient to sustain a finding that the child is in need of treatment or rehabilitation. If the court finds that the child is not in need of treatment, rehabilitation, or supervision, it shall dismiss the proceeding and discharge the child from any detention or other restriction theretofore ordered.

(b) *Evidence.* In dispositional hearings under subsection (a) of this Code section and in all proceedings involving custody of a child, all information helpful in determining the questions presented, including oral and written reports, may be received by the court and relied upon to the extent of its probative value even though not otherwise competent in the hearing on the petition. The parties or their counsel shall be afforded an opportunity upon request to examine and controvert written reports so received and to cross-examine individuals making the reports, except that portions of such reports not relied on by the court in reaching its decision which, if revealed, would be prejudicial to the interests of the child or any party to the proceeding may be withheld in the court's discretion. Confidential sources of information need not be disclosed.

(c) *Continuances; scheduling.* On its own motion or that of a party, the court may continue the hearings under this Code section for a reasonable period to receive reports and other evidence bearing on the disposition or the child's need for treatment or rehabilitation. In this event, the court shall make an appropriate order for detention of the child or for the child's release from detention subject to supervision of the court during the period of the continuance. In scheduling investigations and hearings, the court shall give priority to proceedings in which a child is in detention or has otherwise been removed from his or her home before an order of disposition has been made.

Laws 1951, p. 291, § 21; Laws 1968, p. 1013, § 12; Laws 1971, p. 709, § 1; Laws 1992, p. 1983, § 5; Laws 2000, p. 20, § 1; Laws 2002, p. 1162, § 11.

Formerly Code 1933, § 24A–2201; Code 1981, § 15–11–33.

Historical and Statutory Notes

The 2000 amendment, which restructured this chapter into parts and modified statutory references to reflect this restructuring, renumbered this section from § 15–11–33(c) and (d). In addition the amendment provided gender neutral referents.

The 2002 amendment rewrote subsec. (a) and added subsec. (c). Prior to amendment subsec. (a) provided:

"(a) Dispositional hearing for delinquent or unruly child. If the court finds on proof beyond a reasonable doubt that the child committed the acts by reason of which he or she is alleged to be delinquent or unruly, it shall proceed immediately or at a later time to conduct a dispositional hearing for the purpose of hearing evidence as to whether the child is in need of treatment, rehabilitation, or supervision and shall make and file its findings thereon. If the child is to be held in custody at a detention facility between the adjudicatory hearing and the dispositional hearing, the court shall conduct the dispositional hearing within 30 days of the adjudicatory hearing. If the dispositional hearing is conducted more than 30 days after the adjudicatory hearing, the court shall make and file written findings of fact explaining the need for the delay. In the absence of evidence to the contrary, evidence sufficient to warrant a finding that acts have been committed which constitute a felony is also sufficient to sustain a finding that the child is in need of treatment or rehabilitation. If the court finds that the child is not in need of treatment, rehabilitation, or supervision, it shall dismiss the proceeding and discharge the child from any detention or other restriction theretofore ordered."

§ 15–11–66. Disposition of delinquent child

(a) At the conclusion of the dispositional hearing provided in subsection (a) of Code Section 15–11–65, if the child is found to have committed a delinquent act and is subsequently determined to be in need of treatment or rehabilitation, the court may make any of the following orders of disposition best suited to the child's treatment, rehabilitation, and welfare:

(1) Any order authorized by Code Section 15–11–55 for the disposition of a deprived child;

(2) An order placing the child on probation under conditions and limitations the court prescribes, under the supervision of:

(A) The probation officer of the court or the court of another state as provided in Code Section 15–11–89;

(B) Any public agency authorized by law to receive and provide care for the child; or

(C) The chief executive officer of any community rehabilitation center acknowledging in writing such officer's willingness to accept the responsibility for the supervision of the child;

(3) An order placing the child in an institution, camp, or other facility for delinquent children operated under the direction of the court or other local public authority;

(4) An order committing the child to the Department of Juvenile Justice;

(5) An order requiring that the child make such restitution as defined in paragraph (7) of Code Section 17–14–2. Such order may remain in force and effect simultaneously with any other order of the court, including, but not limited to, an order of commitment to the Department of Juvenile Justice. While an order requiring restitution is in effect, the enforcement thereof may be transferred to the Department of Juvenile Justice. In the event that the child changes his or her place of residence while the order is still in effect, the court may transfer enforcement of its order to the juvenile court of the county of the child's residence and its probation staff; however, no order of restitution shall be enforced while such child is in placement at a youth development center unless the commissioner of juvenile justice certifies that a restitution program is available at such facility. Payment of funds under this paragraph shall be made by the child or the child's family or employer directly to the clerk of the juvenile court entering the order or another employee of that court designated by the judge, and that court shall disburse such funds in the manner authorized in the order;

(6) An order requiring that the child perform community service in a manner prescribed by the court and under the supervision of an individual designated by the court; or

(7) An order requiring the child to remit to the general fund of the county a sum not to exceed the maximum applicable to an adult for commission of any of the following offenses: homicide by vehicle, manslaughter resulting from the operation of a motor vehicle, any felony in the commission of which a motor vehicle is used, hit and run or leaving the scene of an accident, racing on highways or streets, using a motor vehicle in fleeing or attempting to elude an officer, fraudulent or fictitious use of a license, driving under the influence of alcohol or drugs, possession of controlled substances or marijuana, driving without proof of minimum required motor vehicle insurance, or any violation of the Code sections contained in Title 40 which is properly adjudicated as a delinquent act.

(b)(1) At the conclusion of the dispositional hearing provided in subsection (a) of Code Section 15–11–65, if the child is found to have committed a delinquent act, the court may, in addition to any other treatment or rehabilitation, suspend the driver's license of such child for any period not to exceed the date on which the child becomes 18 years of age or, in the case of a child who does not have a driver's license, prohibit the issuance of a driver's license to such child for any period not to exceed the date on which the child becomes 18 years of age. The court shall retain the driver's license for a period of suspension and return it to the offender at the end of such period. The court shall notify the Department of Driver Services of any such actions taken pursuant to this subsection.

(2)(A) If the child is adjudicated for the commission of a delinquent act, the court may in its discretion in those cases involving:

(i) An offense that would be a felony if committed by an adult; or

(ii) An offense that would be a misdemeanor of a high and aggravated nature if committed by an adult and involving bodily injury or harm or substantial likelihood of bodily injury or harm, in addition to any other treatment or rehabilitation,

order the child to serve up to a maximum of 30 days in a youth development center, or after assessment and with the court's approval, in a treatment program provided by the Department of Juvenile Justice or the juvenile court.

(B) A child ordered to a youth development center under this paragraph and detained in a secured facility pending placement in the youth development center shall be given credit for time served in the secured facility awaiting placement. On and after July 1, 2013, the maximum number of days that the court may order a child to serve in a youth development center under this paragraph shall be increased to 60 days.

(b.1) Notwithstanding the provisions of subsections (a) and (b) of this Code section, at the conclusion of the dispositional hearing provided in subsection (a) of Code Section 15–11–65, if the child is found to have committed a delinquent offense which would be a violation of subsection (k) of Code Section 40–6–391 if committed by an adult, the court shall make an order of disposition which, for purposes of the child's rehabilitation, imposes the same penalty, period of confinement, and period of community service provided in Code Section 40–6–391 which are applicable to an adult convicted of violating subsection (k) of Code Section 40–6–391, with any such period of confinement to be served in an institution, camp, or other facility for delinquent children operated under the direction of the court or other local public authority or, if no such facility is available, in a regional youth detention center, provided that such child shall be kept segregated from all children other than those confined for violating subsection (k) of Code Section 40–6–391. A previous finding that the child committed such a delinquent offense shall be deemed a previous conviction for purposes of this subsection. The judge shall have the same authority and discretion regarding allowing service of confinement on weekends or during nonworking hours as is provided under subsection (a) of Code Section 17–10–3.1.

(c) In any case in which a child who has not achieved a high school diploma or the equivalent is placed on probation, the court may require as a condition of probation that the child pursue a course of study designed to lead to achieving a high school diploma or the equivalent; and, in any case in which such a condition of probation may be imposed, the court shall give express consideration to whether such a condition should be imposed.

Laws 1908, p. 1107, § 9; Laws 1915, p. 35, § 9; Laws 1916, p. 58, § 2; Laws 1950, p. 1107, § 19; Laws 1951, p. 291, § 21; Laws 1968, p. 1013, § 13; Laws 1973, p. 579, § 2; Laws 1982, p. 3, § 15; Laws 1982, p. 2199, § 3; Laws 1983, p. 539, § 1; Laws 1984, p. 894, § 1; Laws 1990, p. 1691, § 5; Laws 1991, p. 1030, § 1; Laws 1992, p. 1983, § 6; Laws 1994, p. 1012, § 19.5; Laws 1997, p. 760, § 1A; Laws 1997, p. 1453, §§ 1, 2; Laws 2000, p. 20, § 1; Laws 2001, p. 739, § 1; Laws 2002, p. 415, § 15; Laws 2002, p. 1162, § 12; Laws 2005, Act 57, § 1, eff. July 1, 2005; Laws 2005, Act 68, § 5–1, eff. July 1, 2005; Laws 2006, Act 453, § 15, eff. April 14, 2006; Laws 2009, Act 36, § 1, eff. April 21, 2009; Laws 2010, Act 674, § 5, eff. July 1, 2010.

Formerly Penal Code 1910, § 895; Code 1933, § 24–2409; Code 1933, § 24A–2302; Code 1981, § 15–11–35.

Historical and Statutory Notes

The 2000 amendment, which restructured this chapter into parts and modified statutory references to reflect this restructuring, renumbered this section from § 15–11–35. In addition the amendment provided gender neutral referents.

The 2001 amendment added at the end of the fourth sentence of subsec. (b) "or, after assessment and with the court's approval, in a treatment program provided by the Department of Juvenile Justice or the juvenile court."

The 2002 amendment by Act 462 was a correction.

The 2002 amendment by Act 934 substituted for references to "adjudicatory hearing" references to "dispositional hearing provided in subsection (a) of Code Section 15–11–65".

The 2005 amendment by Act 57 rewrote subsec. (b) which had read:

"(b) At the conclusion of the dispositional hearing provided in subsection (a) of Code Section 15–11–65, if the child is found to have committed a delinquent act, the court may, in addition to any other treatment or rehabilitation, suspend the driver's license of such child for any period not to exceed the date on which the child becomes 18 years of age or, in the case of a child who does not have a driver's license, prohibit the issuance of a driver's license to such child for any period not to exceed the date on which the child becomes 18 years of age. The court shall retain the driver's license for a period of suspension and return it to the offender at the end of such period. The court shall notify the Department of Motor Vehicle Safety of any such actions taken pursuant to this subsection. If the child is adjudicated for the commission of a delinquent act, the court may in its discretion, in addition to any other treatment or rehabilitation, order the child to serve up to a maximum of 90 days in a youth development center, or after assessment and with the court's approval, in a treatment program provided by the Department of Juvenile Justice or the juvenile court."

The 2005 amendment by Act 68, in subsec. (b), substituted "Department of Driver Services" for "Department of Motor Vehicle Safety".

The 2006 amendment by Act 453 was a provision contained in a correction bill.

The 2009 amendment by Act 36, in par. (1) of subsec. (b), substituted "30 days" for "60 days", and inserted "On and after July 1, 2011, the maximum number of days that the court may order a child to serve in a youth development center under this paragraph shall be increased to 60 days."

The 2010 amendment by Act 674, rewrote subsec. (b) which had read:

"(b)(1) At the conclusion of the dispositional hearing provided in subsection (a) of Code Section 15–11–65, if the child is found to have committed a delinquent act, the court may, in addition to any other treatment or rehabilitation, suspend the driver's license of such child for any period not to exceed the date on which the child becomes 18 years of age or, in the case of a child who does not have a driver's license, prohibit the issuance of a driver's license to such child for any period not to exceed the date on which the child becomes 18 years of age. The court shall retain the driver's license for a period of suspension and return it to the offender at the end of such period. The court shall notify the Department of Driver Services of any such actions taken pursuant to this subsection. If the child is adjudicated for the commission of a delinquent act, the court may in its discretion in those cases involving: (A) a violation of probation involving another adjudicated delinquent act and upon the court making a finding of fact that the child has failed to respond to the graduated alternative sanctions set forth in paragraph (2) of this subsection; (B) an offense that would be a felony if committed by an adult; or (C) an offense that would be a misdemeanor of a high and aggravated nature if committed by an adult and involving bodily injury or harm or substantial likelihood of bodily injury or harm, in addition to any other treatment or rehabilitation, order the child to serve up to a maximum of 30 days in a youth development center, or after assessment and with the court's approval, in a treatment program provided by the Department of Juvenile Justice or the juvenile court. A child ordered to a youth development center under this paragraph and detained in a secured facility pending placement in the youth development center shall be given credit for time served in the secured facility awaiting placement. On and after July 1, 2011, the maximum number of days that the court may order a child to serve in a youth development center under this paragraph shall be increased to 60 days.

"(2) The Department of Juvenile Justice, in conjunction with the Council of Juvenile Court Judges of Georgia, shall establish and monitor a graduated alternative sanctions program for children on probation. The graduated alternative sanctions program shall be implemented in each judicial circuit in consultation with the judge of the juvenile court. The graduated alternative sanctions program may include, but shall not be limited to, community service, electronic monitoring, increased reporting or intensive supervision, home confinement, day or evening reporting centers, or treatment intervention."

Laws 2010, Act 674, § 10, provides:

"This Act shall become effective on July 1, 2010, and Sections 2 and 5 of this Act shall apply to any child sentenced to probation on and after July 1, 2010; the former provisions of Code Section 15–11–66 shall continue to apply to any child sentenced to probation prior to July 1, 2010."

Uniform Law

This section is based upon § 31 of the Uniform Law Commissioners' Model Juvenile Court Act. See 9A Uniform Laws Annotated, Master Edition, or ULA Database on Westlaw.

§ 15–11–66.1. Disposition of child adjudged to have committed delinquent act constituting AIDS transmitting crime; HIV testing

(a) Any term used in this Code section and defined in Code Section 31–22–9.1 shall have the meaning provided for such term in Code Section 31–22–9.1.

(b) As part of any order of disposition regarding a child adjudged to have committed a delinquent act constituting an AIDS transmitting crime, the court may in its discretion and after conferring with the director of the health district, as such officer is provided for in Code Section 31–3–15, order that child to submit to an HIV test within 45 days following the adjudication of delinquency and shall mail the Department of Juvenile Justice a copy of such order within three days following the issuance thereof.

(c) The Department of Juvenile Justice, within 30 days following receipt of the copy of order under subsection (b) of this Code section, shall arrange for the HIV test for the child ordered to submit thereto.

(d) Any child sentenced to the custody and control of the Department of Corrections or the Department of Juvenile Justice shall be HIV tested in accordance with the policies and procedures of the respective department.

(e) If a child is required by this Code section to submit to an HIV test and is thereby determined to be infected with HIV, that determination and the name of the child shall be deemed to be AIDS confidential information and shall be reported to:

(1) The Department of Juvenile Justice or the Department of Corrections, as the case may be, and the Department of Community Health, the latter of which may disclose the name of the child if necessary to provide and shall provide counseling to each victim of that child's AIDS transmitting crime or to any parent or guardian of any victim who is a minor or incompetent person, if the Department of Juvenile Justice or the Department of Corrections believes the crime posed a reasonable risk of transmitting HIV to the victim;

(2) The court which ordered the HIV test; and

(3) Those persons in charge of any facility to which the child has been confined by order of the court. In addition to any other restrictions regarding the confinement of children, a child determined to be an HIV infected person may be confined in that facility separately from any other children in that facility other than those who have been determined to be infected with HIV if:

(A) That child is reasonably believed to be sexually active while confined;

(B) That child is reasonably believed to be sexually predatory either during or prior to detention; or

(C) The commissioner of juvenile justice or the commissioner of corrections, as the case may be, reasonably determines that other circumstances or conditions exist which indicate that separate confinement would be warranted.

Laws 1988, p. 1799, § 2; Laws 1992, p. 1983, § 7; Laws 1994, p. 1012, § 20; Laws 1997, p. 1453, §§ 1, 2; Laws 2000, p. 20, § 1; Laws 2009, Act 102, § 1–13, eff. July 1, 2009.

Formerly Code 1981, § 15–11–35.1.

Historical and Statutory Notes

The 2000 amendment, which restructured this chapter into parts and modified statutory references to reflect this restructuring, renumbered this section from § 15–11–35.1. In addition the amendment substituted reference to "child" for "juvenile".

The 2009 amendment by Act 102, in subsec. (e), substituted "Department of Community Health" for "Department of Human Resources" in par. (1).

§ 15–11–67. Disposition of unruly child

If the child is found to be unruly, the court may make any disposition authorized for a delinquent child except that, if commitment to the Department of Juvenile Justice is ordered, the court shall first find that the child is not amenable to treatment or rehabilitation pursuant to paragraph (1), (2), or (3) of subsection (a) of Code Section 15–11–66.

Laws 1908, p. 1107, § 9; Laws 1915, p. 35, § 9; Laws 1916, p. 58, § 2; Laws 1950, p. 1107, § 19; Laws 1951, p. 291, § 21; Laws 1968, p. 1013, § 13; Laws 1971, p. 709, § 1; Laws 1992, p. 1983, § 8; Laws 1997, p. 1453, § 1; Laws 2000, p. 20, § 1.

Formerly Penal Code 1910, § 895; Code 1933, § 24–2409; Code 1933, § 24A–2303; Code 1981, § 15–11–36.

Historical and Statutory Notes

The 2000 amendment, which restructured this chapter into parts and modified statutory references to reflect this restructuring, renumbered this section from § 15–11–36.

Uniform Law

This section is based upon § 32 of the Uniform Law Commissioners' Model Juvenile Court Act. See 9A Uniform Laws Annotated, Master Edition, or ULA Database on Westlaw.

§ 15–11–68. Counseling or counsel and advice for child found to have committed delinquent act, to be unruly child, or to have committed juvenile traffic offense

When any child is before a juvenile court and such child is found by the court to have committed a delinquent act, to be an unruly child, or to have committed a juvenile traffic offense as defined in Code Section 15–11–73, the court shall be authorized, in addition to any other disposition authorized by this article, to order such child and such child's parents or guardian to participate in counseling or in counsel and advice as determined by the court. Such counseling and counsel and advice may be provided by the court, court personnel, probation officers, professional counselors or social workers, psychologists, physicians, qualified volunteers, or appropriate public, private, or volunteer agencies as directed by the court and shall be designed to assist in deterring future delinquent or unruly acts or other conduct or conditions which would be harmful to the child or society.

Laws 1992, p. 2474, § 1; Laws 1998, p. 128, § 15; Laws 1998, p. 653, § 2; Laws 1998, p. 854, § 1; Laws 2000, p. 20, § 1; Laws 2001, p. 4, § 15.

Formerly Code 1981, § 15–11–36.1.

Historical and Statutory Notes

The 2000 amendment, which restructured this chapter into parts and modified statutory references to reflect this restructuring, renumbered this section from § 15–11–36.1. In addition the amendment deleted "conditions of deprivation" preceding "or other conduct" in the first sentence.

§ 15–11–69. Counsel and advice with view to informal adjustment

(a) Before a petition is filed, the probation officer or other officer of the court designated by the court, subject to the court's direction, may give counsel and advice to the parties with a view to an informal adjustment if it appears that:

(1) The admitted facts bring the case within the jurisdiction of the court;

(2) Counsel and advice without an adjudication would be in the best interest of the public and the child; and

(3) The child and the child's parents, guardian, or other custodian consent thereto with knowledge that consent is not obligatory.

(b) The giving of counsel and advice cannot extend beyond three months from the day commenced unless extended by the court for an additional period not to exceed three months and does not authorize the detention of the child if not otherwise permitted by this article.

(c) An incriminating statement made by a participant to the person giving counsel or advice and in the discussion or conferences incident thereto shall not be used against the declarant over objection in any hearing except in a hearing on disposition in a juvenile court proceeding or in a criminal proceeding against such declarant after conviction for the purpose of a presentence investigation.

(d) If a child is alleged to have committed a designated felony act as defined in Code Section 15-11-63, the case shall not be subject to informal adjustment, counsel, or advice without the prior written notification of the district attorney or his or her authorized representative.

Laws 1971, p. 709, § 1; Laws 1986, p. 1017, § 1; Laws 1997, p. 1064, § 3; Laws 2000, p. 20, § 1.

Formerly Code 1933, § 24A-1001; Code 1981, § 15-11-14.

Historical and Statutory Notes

The 2000 amendment, which restructured this chapter into parts and modified statutory references to reflect this restructuring, renumbered this section from § 15-11-14. In addition the amendment provided gender neutral referents.

Uniform Law

This section is based upon § 10 of the Uniform Law Commissioners' Model Juvenile Court Act. See 9A Uniform Laws Annotated, Master Edition, or ULA Database on Westlaw.

§ 15-11-70. Duration of orders of disposition; extensions of duration

(a) Except as provided in subsection (b) of this Code section, an order of disposition committing a delinquent or unruly child to the Department of Juvenile Justice continues in force for two years or until the child is sooner discharged by the Department of Juvenile Justice. The court which made the order may extend its duration for an additional two years subject to like discharge, if:

(1) A hearing is held upon motion of the Department of Juvenile Justice prior to the expiration of the order;

(2) Reasonable notice of the factual basis of the motion and of the hearing and an opportunity to be heard are given to the child and the parent, guardian, or other custodian; and

(3) The court finds that the extension is necessary for the treatment or rehabilitation of the child.

(b) If the court commits a delinquent child to the Department of Juvenile Justice for a delinquent act which if done by an adult would be the crime of murder, then the court's commitment may continue until the child's twenty-first birthday. The court shall determine whether any or all of the child's commitment should include an order for restrictive custody by making specific written findings of fact using the elements set forth in paragraphs (1) through (5) of subsection (c) of Code Section 15-11-63. Any child committed to the Department of Juvenile Justice under the provisions of this subsection shall not be released from confinement or discharged from the custody of the Department of Juvenile Justice unless a motion for early release is granted by the court. The court which made the order of commitment may shorten the duration of its order if:

(1) A hearing is held prior to the expiration of the order upon motion of a party or on the court's own motion;

(2) Reasonable notice of the factual basis of the motion and of the hearing and an opportunity to be heard are given to the parties affected; and

(3) The court finds that the discharge is necessary to accomplish the purposes of the original order and for the treatment or rehabilitation of the child.

(c) Except as provided in subsection (b) of this Code section, any other order of disposition in a proceeding involving delinquency or unruliness, except an order involving the appointment of a guardian of the person or property of a child, continues in force for not more than two years. The court may sooner terminate its order or extend its duration for further periods. An order of extension may be made if:

(1) A hearing is held prior to the expiration of the order upon motion of a party or on the court's own motion;

(2) Reasonable notice of the factual basis of the motion and of the hearing and opportunity to be heard are given to the parties affected;

(3) The court finds that the extension is necessary to accomplish the purposes of the order extended; and

(4) The extension does not exceed two years from the expiration of the prior order.

(d) The court may terminate an order of disposition of a child adjudicated as delinquent or unruly or an extension of such a disposition order prior to its expiration, on or without an application of a party, if it appears to the court that the purposes of the order have been accomplished.

(e) Unless otherwise provided by law, when a child who has been adjudicated as delinquent or unruly reaches 21 years of age all orders affecting him or her then in force terminate and he or she is discharged from further obligation or control.

Laws 1971, p. 709, § 1; Laws 1974, p. 1126, § 6; Laws 1984, p. 794, § 1; Laws 1986, p. 1017, § 2; Laws 1990, p. 8, § 15; Laws 1990, p. 1765, § 1; Laws 1992, p. 1983, § 14; Laws 1992, p. 2184, § 1; Laws 1996, p. 474, § 1; Laws 1997, p. 933, § 1; Laws 1997, p. 1453, § 1; Laws 1998, p. 854, § 2; Laws 1998, p. 908, § 1; Laws 2000, p. 20, § 1; Laws 2002, p. 1162, § 13; Laws 2006, Act 541, § 3, eff. July 1, 2006.

Formerly Code 1933, § 24A-2701; Code 1981, § 15-11-41.

Historical and Statutory Notes

The 2000 amendment, which restructured this chapter into parts and modified statutory references to reflect this restructuring, renumbered this section from § 15-11-41(a).

The 2002 amendment designated the existing provisions as subsec. (a) and added subsecs. (b) to (d).

The 2006 amendment by Act 541, in subsec. (a), substituted "Except as provided in subsection (b) of this Code Section" for "Except as otherwise provided by law"; redesignated subsecs. (b) through (d) as (c) through (e) respectively and added new subsec. (b); and in newly designated subsec. (c), substituted "Except as provided in subsection (b) of this Code Section" for "Except as otherwise provided by law".

Laws 2006, Act 541, § 2, provides:

"This part shall be known and may be cited as the 'Amy's [so in original] Law.' "

§ 15-11-71. Supervision fees

(a) The purpose of this Code section is to allow the juvenile courts of Georgia to collect supervision fees from those who are placed under the courts' formal or informal supervision in order that the court may use those fees to expand the provision of the following types of ancillary services:

(1) Housing in nonsecure facilities that meet the requirements of Code Section 15-11-48;

(2) Educational services, tutorial services, or both;

(3) Counseling and diagnostic testing;

(4) Mediation;

(5) Transportation to and from court ordered services;

(6) Truancy intervention services;

(7) Restitution programs; and

(8) Job development or work experience programs.

(b) The juvenile court may order each delinquent or unruly child who receives supervision under paragraph (2), (5), or (6) of subsection (a) of Code Section 15–11–66 or Code Section 15–11–67 or counsel and advice pursuant to Code Section 15–11–69 to pay:

(1) An initial court supervision user's fee of not less than $10.00 nor more than $200.00; and

(2) A court supervision user's fee of not less than $2.00 nor more than $30.00 for each month that the child receives supervision

to the clerk of the court. The child and each parent, guardian, or legal custodian of the child may be jointly and severally liable for the payment of the fee and shall be subject to the enforcement procedure stated in subsection (b) of Code Section 15–11–8. The judge shall attempt to provide that any such fees shall be imposed on such terms and conditions as shall assure that the funds for the payment are from moneys earned by the child. All moneys collected by the clerk under this subsection shall be transferred to the county treasurer, or such other county official or employee who performs duties previously performed by said treasurer, who shall deposit the moneys into a county supplemental juvenile services fund. The governing authority of the county shall appropriate moneys from the county supplemental juvenile services fund to the juvenile court for the court's discretionary use in providing supplemental community based services described in subsection (a) of this Code section to offenders who are children. These funds shall be administered by the county and the court may draw upon them by submitting invoices to the county. The county supplemental juvenile services fund may be used only for these services. Any moneys remaining in the fund at the end of the county fiscal year shall not revert to any other fund but shall continue in the county supplemental juvenile services fund. The county supplemental juvenile services fund may not be used to replace other funding of services.

(c) For the purpose of this Code section, the term "guardian" or "legal custodian" shall not be interpreted or construed to include the Department of Human Services or the Department of Juvenile Justice.

Laws 1990, p. 1871, § 1; Laws 1993, p. 931, § 1; Laws 1997, p. 1064, § 6; Laws 2000, p. 20, § 1; Laws 2005, Act 161, § 1, eff. July 1, 2005; Laws 2009, Act 102, § 2–2, eff. July 1, 2009.

Formerly Code 1981, § 15–11–56.1.

Historical and Statutory Notes

The 2000 amendment, which restructured this chapter into parts and modified statutory references to reflect this restructuring, renumbered this section from § 15–11–56.1. In addition the amendment substituted references to "child" for "juvenile" and provided gender neutral referents.

The 2005 amendment by Act 161, in subsec. (a), inserted a new par. (6) and redesignated former pars. (6) and (7) as pars. (7) and (8); in subsec. (b), substituted "paragraph (2), (5), or (6) of subsection (a)" for "paragraph (5) of subsection (a)" and substituted "Code Section 15–11–66 or Code Section 15–11–67 or counsel and advice pursuant to" for "Code Section 15–11–66, Code Section 15–11–67, or paragraph (2) of subsection (a) of"; and inserted "or the Department of Juvenile Justice" in subsec. (c).

The 2009 amendment by Act 102 substituted "Department of Human Services" for "Department of Human Resources" throughout the section.

§ 15–11–72. Order of disposition not conviction of crime

An order of disposition or other adjudication in a proceeding under this article is not a conviction of a crime and does not impose any civil disability ordinarily resulting from a conviction nor operate to disqualify the child in any civil service application or appointment.

Laws 1915, p. 35, §§ 12, 19; Laws 1950, p. 367, § 19; Laws 1951, p. 291, § 19; Laws 1968, p. 1013, § 10; Laws 1971, p. 709, § 1; Laws 1986, p. 1017, § 1; Laws 1990, p. 1930, § 3; Laws 1992, p. 1983, § 12; Laws 1994, p. 1012, § 23; Laws 1996, p. 823, § 1; Laws 1997, p. 1064, § 5; Laws 1997, p. 1453, § 1; Laws 1998, p. 128, § 15; Laws 2000, p. 20, § 1.

Formerly Code 1933, §§ 24–2412, 24–2419; Code 1933, § 24A–2401; Code 1981, § 15–11–38.

Historical and Statutory Notes

The 2000 amendment, which restructured this chapter into parts and modified statutory references to reflect this restructuring, renumbered this section from § 15–11–38(a).

Uniform Law

This section is based upon § 33 of the Uniform Law Commissioners' Model Juvenile Court Act. See 9A Uniform Laws Annotated, Master Edition, or ULA Database on Westlaw.

§ 15–11–73. Juvenile traffic offenses

(a) *Definition.* Except as provided in subsection (c) of this Code section, a juvenile traffic offense consists of a violation by a child under the age of 17 of:

(1) A law or local ordinance governing the operation of a moving motor vehicle upon the streets or highways of this state or upon the waterways within or adjoining this state; or

(2) Any other motor vehicle traffic law or local ordinance if the child is taken into custody and detained for its violation or is transferred to the juvenile court by the court hearing the charge.

(b) *Jurisdiction.* Notwithstanding the provisions of Title 40 which grant jurisdiction over traffic court offenses to certain courts, the juvenile court shall have exclusive original jurisdiction over juvenile traffic offenses.

(c) *Exceptions.* The following offenses shall be delinquent offenses and shall not be handled as juvenile traffic offenses: homicide by vehicle, manslaughter resulting from the operation of a vehicle, any felony in the commission of which a motor vehicle is used, racing on highways and streets, using a motor vehicle in fleeing or attempting to elude an officer, fraudulent or fictitious use of a license, hit and run or leaving the scene of an accident, driving under the influence of alcohol or drugs, possession of a controlled substance or marijuana, and any other offense for which driving privileges may be suspended or revoked for an adult.

(d) *Nature of offense.* A juvenile traffic offense is not an act of delinquency unless the case is transferred to the delinquency calendar as provided in subsection (i) of this Code section.

(e) *Procedure.* The summons, notice to appear, or other designation of a citation accusing a child of committing a juvenile traffic offense constitutes the commencement of the proceedings in the court of the county in which the alleged violation occurred and serves in place of a summons and petition under this article. These cases shall be filed and heard separately from other proceedings of the court. If the child is taken into custody on the charge, Code Sections 15–11–46 and 15–11–49 shall apply. If the child is, or after commencement of the proceedings becomes, a resident of another county of this state, the court in the county where the alleged traffic offense occurred may retain jurisdiction over the entire case.

(f) *Hearing.* The court shall fix a time for a hearing and shall give reasonable notice thereof to the child and, if their address is known, to the parents, guardian, or custodian. If the accusation made in the summons, notice to appear, or other designation of a citation is denied, an informal hearing shall be held at which the parties shall have the right to subpoena witnesses, present evidence, cross-examine witnesses, and appear by counsel. The hearing shall be open to the public.

(g) *Disposition.* If the court finds on the admission of the child or upon the evidence that the child committed the offense charged, it may make one or more of the following orders:

(1) Reprimand, counsel, or warn the child and the child's parents; provided, however, that this dispositional order is not available for any offense listed in subsection (c) of this Code section;

(2) As a matter of probation or if the child is committed to the custody of the state, order the Department of Driver Services to suspend the child's privilege to drive under stated conditions and limitations for a period not to exceed 12 months;

(3) Require the child to attend a traffic school approved by the Department of Driver Services or a substance abuse clinic or program approved by either the Department of Behavioral Health and Developmental Disabilities or the Council of Juvenile Court Judges for a reasonable period of time;

(4) Order the child to remit to the general fund of the county a sum not exceeding the maximum applicable to an adult for a like offense;

(5) Require the child to participate in a program of community service as specified by the court;

(6) Impose any sanction authorized by Code Section 15–11–66, 15–11–67, or 15–11–68; or

(7) Place the child on probation subject to the conditions and limitations imposed by Title 40 on probation granted to adults for like offenses, but such probation shall be supervised by the court as provided in Code Section 15–11–66.

(h) *Fines.* If a fine is assessed under paragraph (4) of subsection (g) of this Code section, such fine shall be subject to all additions and penalties as specified under this title and Title 47.

(i) *Transfer to delinquency calendar.* In lieu of the preceding orders, if the evidence indicates the advisability thereof, the court may transfer the case to the delinquency calendar of the court and direct the filing and service of a summons and petition in accordance with this article. The judge so ordering is disqualified, upon objection, from acting further in the case prior to an adjudication that the child committed a delinquent act.

(j) *Reporting procedure.* Upon finding that the child has committed a juvenile traffic offense or a delinquent offense which would be a violation of Title 40 if committed by an adult, the court shall forward, within ten days, a report of the final adjudication and disposition of the charge to the Department of Driver Services; provided, however, that this procedure shall not be applicable to those cases which have been dismissed or in which the child and the child's parents have been reprimanded, counseled, or warned by the court pursuant to paragraph (1) of subsection (g) of this Code section. The Department of Driver Services shall record the adjudication and disposition of the offense on the child's permanent record and such adjudication and disposition shall be deemed a conviction for the purpose of suspending or revoking the individual's driver's license. Such record shall also be available to law enforcement agencies and courts as are the permanent traffic records of adults.

Laws 1971, p. 709, § 1; Laws 1983, p. 1000, § 17; Laws 1986, p. 1017, § 1; Laws 1991, p. 94, § 15; Laws 1991, p. 1030, § 2; Laws 1992, p. 6, § 15; Laws 2000, p. 20, § 1; Laws 2002, p. 415, § 15; Laws 2005, Act 68, § 5–2, eff. July 1, 2005; Laws 2009, Act 102, § 3–2, eff. July 1, 2009.

Formerly Code 1933, § 24A–3101; Code 1981, § 15–11–49.

Historical and Statutory Notes

The 2000 amendment, which restructured this chapter into parts and modified statutory references to reflect this restructuring, renumbered this section from § 15–11–49. In addition the amendment substituted references to "child" for "juvenile" and provided gender neutral referents.

The 2002 amendment was a correction bill.

The 2005 amendment by Act 68 in subsec. (g)(2) and (3) substituted "Department of Driver Services" for "Department of Motor Vehicle Safety" and also in par. (3) substituted "approved" for "conducted" following "attend a traffic school"; and, in subsec. (j) substituted "Department of Driver Services" for "Department of Motor Vehicle Safety" twice.

The 2009 amendment by Act 102 substituted "Department of Behavioral Health and Developmental Disabilities" for "Department of Human Resources" throughout the section.

Uniform Law

This section is based upon § 44 of the Uniform Law Commissioners' Model Juvenile Court Act. See 9A Uniform Laws Annotated, Master Edition, or ULA Database on Westlaw.

Part 7A

Discovery Proceedings

§ 15–11–75. Discovery procedures; limitations; orders

(a) *Request for discovery.* In all cases in which a child is charged with having committed a delinquent act as defined in Code Section 15–11–2, the child shall, upon written request to the person or entity prosecuting the case having actual custody, control, or possession of the material to be produced, have full access to the following for inspection, copying, or photographing:

(1) A copy of the complaint;

(2) A copy of the petition;

(3) The names and last known addresses and telephone numbers of each witness to the occurrence which forms the basis of the charge;

(4) A copy of any written statement made by the child or any witness that relates to the subject matter concerning the testimony of the witness that the prosecuting attorney or entity prosecuting the case intends to call as a witness;

(5) Transcriptions, recordings, and summaries of any oral statement of the child or of any witness, except the product of counsel;

(6) Any scientific or other report which is intended to be introduced at the hearing or that pertains to physical evidence which is intended to be introduced;

(7) Photographs and any physical evidence which are intended to be introduced at the hearing; and

(8) Copies of the police incident report and supplemental report, if any, regarding the occurrence which forms the basis of the charge.

(b) *Reciprocal discovery.* If the child requests disclosure of information pursuant to subsection (a) of this Code section, it shall be the duty of the child to promptly make the following available for inspection, copying, or photographing to the prosecuting attorney or the entity prosecuting the case:

(1) The names and last known addresses and telephone numbers of each witness to the occurrence which forms the basis of the defense;

(2) Any scientific or other report which is intended to be introduced at the hearing or that pertains to physical evidence which is intended to be introduced;

(3) Photographs and any physical evidence which are intended to be introduced at the hearing; and

(4) A copy of any written statement made by any witness that relates to the subject matter concerning the testimony of the witness that the child intends to call as a witness.

(c) *Timing of response to discovery.* A request for discovery or reciprocal discovery shall be complied with promptly and not later than 48 hours prior to the adjudicatory hearing except when later compliance is made necessary by the timing of the request. If the request for discovery is made fewer than 48 hours prior to the adjudicatory hearing, the discovery response shall be produced in a timely manner. If, subsequent to providing a discovery response in compliance with this Code section, the existence of additional evidence is found, it shall be promptly provided to the person or child making the discovery request.

(d) *Alibi.*

(1) Upon written request by the prosecuting attorney or entity prosecuting the case stating the time, date, and place at which the alleged delinquent act was committed, the child shall serve upon the prosecuting attorney or entity prosecuting the case a written notice of the child's intention to offer a defense of alibi. Such notice by the child shall state the specific place or places at which the child claims to have been at the time of the alleged delinquent act and the names, addresses, dates of birth, and telephone numbers of the witnesses, if known to the child, upon whom the child intends to rely to establish such alibi unless previously supplied. A request for alibi evidence shall be complied with promptly and not later than 48 hours prior to the adjudicatory hearing except when later compliance is made necessary by the timing of the request. If the request for alibi evidence is made fewer than 48 hours prior to the adjudicatory hearing, the alibi evidence shall be produced in a timely manner. If the defendant withdraws the notice of intention to rely upon an alibi defense, the notice and intention to rely upon an alibi defense are not admissible. However the prosecuting attorney or entity prosecuting the case may offer any other evidence regarding alibi.

(2) The prosecuting attorney or entity prosecuting the case shall serve upon the child a written notice stating the names, addresses, dates of birth, and telephone numbers of the witnesses, if known to the state, upon whom the state intends to rely to rebut the child's evidence of alibi unless previously supplied.

(e) *Order granting discovery; limitations; sanctions.* If a request for discovery is refused, application may be made to the court for a written order granting discovery. Motions for discovery shall certify that a request for discovery was made and was refused. An order granting discovery shall require reciprocal discovery. Notwithstanding the provisions of subsection (a) of this Code section, the court may deny, in whole or in part, or otherwise limit or set conditions concerning the discovery response upon a sufficient showing by a person or entity to whom a request for discovery is made that disclosure of the information would:

(1) Jeopardize the safety of a party, witness, or confidential informant;

(2) Create a substantial threat of physical or economic harm to a witness or other person;

(3) Endanger the existence of physical evidence;

(4) Disclose privileged information; or

(5) Impede the criminal prosecution of a minor who is being prosecuted as an adult or the prosecution of an adult charged with an offense arising from the same transaction or occurrence.

(f) *Failure to comply.* If at any time during the course of the proceedings it is brought to the attention of the court that a person or entity has failed to comply with an order issued pursuant to this Code section, the court may grant a continuance, prohibit the party from introducing in evidence the information not disclosed, or enter such other order as the court deems just under the circumstances.

(g) *Court discretion.* Nothing contained in this Code section shall prohibit the court from ordering the disclosure of any information that the court deems necessary and appropriate for proper adjudication.

(h) *Confidentiality of discovery responses.* Any material or information furnished to the child pursuant to this part shall remain in the exclusive custody of the child and shall only be used during the pendency of the case and shall be subject to such other terms and conditions as the court may provide.

(i) *Danger of proceeding pro se.* If a child proceeds pro se, the court shall instruct the child concerning the danger of proceeding pro se and his or her rights under this Code section.

Laws 2003, Act 61, § 1, eff. July 1, 2003.

Historical and Statutory Notes

Laws 2003, Act 61, § 2, provides:

"This Act shall become effective on July 1, 2003, and shall apply to all cases in which a petition is filed on or after that date."

Part 8

Access to Records and Hearings

§ 15–11–78. Exclusion from and admission to hearings of general public

(a) As used in this Code section, the term "deprivation proceeding" means a court proceeding stemming from a petition alleging that a child is a deprived child.

(b) The general public shall be admitted to:

(1) An adjudicatory hearing involving an allegation of a designated felony pursuant to Code Section 15–11–63;

(2) An adjudicatory hearing involving an allegation of delinquency brought in the interest of any child who has previously been adjudicated delinquent; provided, however, the court shall close any delinquency hearing on an allegation of sexual assault or any delinquency hearing at which any party expects to introduce substantial evidence related to matters of deprivation;

(3) Any child support hearing;

(4) Any hearing in a legitimation action filed pursuant to Code Section 19–7–22;

(5) At the court's discretion, any dispositional hearing involving any proceeding under this article; or

(6) Any hearing in a deprivation proceeding, except as otherwise provided in subsection (c) of this Code section.

(c) The court may close the hearing in a deprivation proceeding only upon making a finding upon the record and issuing a signed order as to the reason or reasons for closing all or part of a hearing in such proceeding and stating that:

(A) The proceeding involves an allegation of an act which, if done by an adult, would constitute a sexual offense under Chapter 6 of Title 16; or

(B) It is in the best interest of the child. In making such a determination, the court shall consider such factors as:

(i) The age of the child;

(ii) The nature of the allegations;

(iii) The effect that an open court proceeding will have on the court's ability to reunite and rehabilitate the family unit; and

(iv) Whether the closure is necessary to protect the privacy of a child, of a foster parent or other caretaker of a child, or of a victim of domestic violence.

(d) The court may close a hearing or exclude a person from a hearing in any proceeding on its own motion, by motion of a party to the proceeding, or by motion of a child who is the subject of the proceeding or the child's attorney or guardian ad litem.

(e) Only the parties, their counsel, witnesses, persons accompanying a party for his or her assistance, the victim, and any other persons as the court finds have a proper interest in the proceeding or in the work of the court may be admitted by the court to hearings from which the public is excluded; provided, however, that when the conduct alleged in the deprivation proceeding could give rise to a criminal or delinquent prosecution, attorneys for the prosecution and the defense shall be admitted.

(f) The court may refuse to admit a person to a hearing in any proceeding upon making a finding upon the record and issuing a signed order that the person's presence at the hearing would:

(1) Be detrimental to the best interest of a child who is a party to the proceeding;

(2) Impair the fact-finding process; or

(3) Be otherwise contrary to the interest of justice.

(g) The court may temporarily exclude any child from a termination of parental rights hearing except while allegations of his or her delinquency or unruly conduct are being heard.

(h) Any request for installation and use of electronic recording, transmission, videotaping, or motion picture or still photography of any judicial proceeding shall be made to the court at least two days in advance of the hearing. The request shall be evaluated by the court pursuant to the standards set forth in Code Section 15–1–10.1.

(i) The judge may order the media not to release identifying information concerning any child or family members or foster parent or other caretaker of a child involved in hearings open to the public.

(j) The general public shall be excluded from proceedings in juvenile court unless such hearing has been specified as one in which the general public shall be admitted to pursuant to this Code section.

Laws 1915, p. 35, § 11; Laws 1950, p. 367, § 18; Laws 1951, p. 291, § 21; Laws 1968, p. 1013, §§ 12, 20; Laws 1971, p. 709, § 1; Laws 1974, p. 1126, § 5; Laws 1980, p. 416, § 2; Laws 1989, p. 824, § 1; Laws 1992, p. 2419, § 1; Laws 1995, p. 619, § 1; Laws 1997, p. 1681, § 2; Laws 1998, p. 606, § 1; Laws 2000, p. 20, § 1; Laws 2009, Act 67, § 1, eff. Jan. 1, 2010; Laws 2010, Act 403, § 2, eff. July 1, 2010.

Formerly Code 1933, § 24–2411; Code 1933, § 24A–1801; Code 1981, § 15–11–28.

Historical and Statutory Notes

The 2000 amendment, which restructured this chapter into parts and modified statutory references to reflect this restructuring, renumbered this section from § 15–11–28(c) and (c.1).

The 2009 amendment by Act 67 rewrote the section which had read:

"(a) Except as otherwise provided by subsection (b) of this Code section, the general public shall be excluded from hearings involving delinquency, deprivation, or unruliness. Only the parties, their counsel, witnesses, persons accompanying a party for his or her assistance, and any other persons as the court finds have a proper interest in the proceeding or in the work of the court may be admitted by the court. The court may temporarily exclude the child from the hearing except while allegations of his or her delinquency or unruly conduct are being heard.

"(b) The general public shall be admitted to:

"(1) An adjudicatory hearing involving an allegation of a designated felony pursuant to Code Section 15–11–63;

"(2) An adjudicatory hearing involving an allegation of delinquency brought in the interest of any child who has previously been adjudicated delinquent; provided, however, the court shall close any delinquency hearing on an allegation of sexual assault or any delinquency hearing at which any party expects to introduce substantial evidence related to matters of deprivation;

"(3) Any child support hearing;

"(4) Any hearing in a legitimation action filed pursuant to Code Section 19–7–22; or

"(5) At the court's discretion, any dispositional hearing involving any proceeding under this article."

Laws 2009, Act 67, § 6, provides:

"This Act shall become effective on January 1, 2010, and shall not apply to any juvenile court proceeding filed before that date. Any such proceeding filed before January 1, 2010, shall be governed by the statute in effect at the time the juvenile court proceeding was filed."

The 2010 amendment by Act 403, in subsec. (e), added "the victim" to the list of persons who may be admitted to hearings.

§ 15–11–79. Inspection of court files and records

(a) Except as provided in subsection (b) of this Code section, all files and records of the court in a proceeding under this article are open to inspection only upon order of the court.

(b) Subject to the requirements of subsection (a) of Code Section 15–11–56, subsection (b) of Code Section 15–11–65, and Code Section 15–11–79. 2, the general public shall be allowed to inspect court files and records for cases arising under Code Section 15–11–73 or any complaint, petition, or order from any case that was open to the public pursuant to paragraphs (1) through (5) of subsection (b) of Code Section 15–11–78. The general public shall be allowed to inspect court files and records for proceedings involving a legitimation petition under the jurisdiction of the juvenile court pursuant to paragraph (1) or (2) of subsection (e) of Code Section 15–11–28.

(c)(1) The judge may permit authorized representatives of recognized organizations compiling statistics for proper purposes to inspect and make abstracts from official records under whatever conditions upon their use and distribution the judge may deem proper and may punish by contempt any violation of those conditions.

(2) The judge may permit any school principal or any school guidance counselor, school social worker, or school psychologist who is certified under Chapter 2 of Title 20 and who is counseling a child as a part of such counseling person's school employment duties to review official records of the court in any proceeding under this chapter concerning that child, including but not limited to records of that child's controlled substance or marijuana abuse, which records are protected by Code Section 49–5–41.1, under whatever conditions that the judge may deem proper and may punish by contempt any violation of those conditions.

(d) The judge shall permit authorized representatives of the Department of Juvenile Justice, the Department of Corrections, the Governor's Office for Children and Families, and the Council of Juvenile Court Judges to inspect and extract data from any court files and records for the purpose of obtaining statistics on children and to make copies pursuant to the order of the court.

(e) Notwithstanding any other provision of law, the complaint, petition, order of adjudication, and order of disposition in any delinquency case in which the child has been adjudicated to be delinquent for a violation of the criminal laws of this state shall be disclosed upon request of counsel for the state or the accused for use preliminarily to or in conjunction with a subsequent juvenile or criminal proceeding in a court of record.

Laws 1915, p. 35, § 11; Laws 1950, p. 367, § 30; Laws 1951, p. 291, § 33; Laws 1957, p. 307, § 1; Laws 1968, p. 1013, § 19; Laws 1971, p. 709, § 1; Laws 1978, p. 1512, § 2; Laws 1986, p. 1017, § 1; Laws 1990, p. 1930, § 5; Laws 1992, p. 1983, § 17; Laws 1993, p. 979, § 1; Laws 1994, p. 97, § 15; Laws 1995, p. 619, § 2; Laws 1997, p. 1064, § 7; Laws 1997, p. 1453, § 1; Laws 1997, p. 1681, § 3; Laws 2000, p. 20, § 1; Laws 2002, p. 1162, § 14; Laws 2008, Act 562, § 10, eff. July 1, 2008; Laws 2009, Act 67, § 2, eff. Jan. 1, 2010.

Formerly Code 1933, § 24–2411; Code 1933, § 24A–3501; Code 1981, § 15–11–58.

Historical and Statutory Notes

The 2000 amendment, which restructured this chapter into parts and modified statutory references to reflect this restructuring, renumbered this section from § 15–11–58. In addition the amendment substituted references to "child" for "student" and "children" for "juveniles".

The 2002 amendment modified a subsection reference in the first sentence of subsec. (b).

The 2008 amendment by Act 562 substituted "Governor's Office for Children and Families" for "Children and Youth Coordinating Council" throughout the section.

The 2009 amendment by Act 67, in subsec. (b), inserted "paragraphs (1) through (5) of" preceding "subsection (b) of Code Section 15-11-78".

Laws 2009, Act 67, § 6, provides:

"This Act shall become effective on January 1, 2010, and shall not apply to any juvenile court proceeding filed before that date. Any such proceeding filed before January 1, 2010, shall be governed by the statute in effect at the time the juvenile court proceeding was filed."

Uniform Law

This section is based upon § 54 of the Uniform Law Commissioners' Model Juvenile Court Act. See 9A Uniform Laws Annotated, Master Edition, or ULA Database on Westlaw.

§ 15-11-79.1. Use of disposition and evidence

The disposition of a child and evidence adduced in a hearing in the juvenile court may not be used against such child in any proceeding in any court other than for a proceeding for delinquency or unruliness, whether before or after reaching majority, except in the establishment of conditions of bail, plea negotiations, and sentencing in felony offenses; and, in such excepted cases, such records of dispositions and evidence shall be available to district attorneys and superior court judges and the accused and may be used in the same manner as adult records.

Laws 1915, p. 35, §§ 12, 19; Laws 1950, p. 367, § 19; Laws 1951, p. 291, § 19; Laws 1968, p. 1013, § 10; Laws 1971, p. 709, § 1; Laws 1986, p. 1017, § 1; Laws 1990, p. 1930, § 3; Laws 1992, p. 1983, § 12; Laws 1994, p. 1012, § 23; Laws 1996, p. 823, § 1; Laws 1997, p. 1064, § 5; Laws 1997, p. 1453, § 1; Laws 1998, p. 128, § 15; Laws 2000, p. 20, § 1.

Formerly Code 1933, §§ 24-2412, 24-2419; Code 1933, § 24A-2401; Code 1981, § 15-11-38.

Historical and Statutory Notes

The 2000 amendment, which restructured this chapter into parts and modified statutory references to reflect this restructuring, renumbered this section from § 15-11-38(b).

§ 15-11-79.2. Sealing of files and records

(a) Upon dismissal of a petition or complaint alleging delinquency or unruliness, or, in a case handled through informal adjustment, following completion of the informal adjustment, the court shall order the sealing of the files and records in the case, including those specified in Code Sections 15-11-82 and 15-11-83.

(b) On application of a person who has been adjudicated delinquent or unruly or on the court's own motion, and after a hearing, the court shall order the sealing of the files and records in the proceeding, including those specified in Code Sections 15-11-82 and 15-11-83, if the court finds that:

(1) Two years have elapsed since the final discharge of the person;

(2) Since the final discharge of the person he or she has not been convicted of a felony or of a misdemeanor involving moral turpitude or adjudicated a delinquent or unruly child and no proceeding is pending against the person seeking conviction or adjudication; and

(3) The person has been rehabilitated.

(c) Reasonable notice of the hearing required by subsection (b) of this Code section shall be given to:

(1) The district attorney;

(2) The authority granting the discharge if the final discharge was from an institution or from parole; and

(3) The law enforcement officers or department having custody of the files and records if the files and records specified in Code Sections 15-11-82 and 15-11-83 are included in the application or motion.

(d) Upon the entry of the order the proceeding shall be treated as if it had never occurred. All index references shall be deleted and the person, the court, the law enforcement officers, and the departments shall properly reply that no record exists with respect to the person upon inquiry in any matter. Copies of the order shall be sent to each agency or official therein named and shall also be sent to the deputy director of the Georgia Crime Information Center. Inspection of the sealed files and records thereafter may be permitted by an order of the court upon petition by the person who is the subject of the records and only by those persons named in the order or to criminal justice officials upon petition to the court for official judicial enforcement or criminal justice purposes.

(e) The court may seal any record containing information identifying a victim of an act which, if done by an adult, would constitute a sexual offense under Chapter 6 of Title 16.

Laws 1971, p. 709, § 1; Laws 1995, p. 619, § 6; Laws 1998, p. 842, § 4; Laws 2000, p. 20, § 1; Laws 2002, p. 1162, § 15; Laws 2009, Act 67, § 3, eff. Jan. 1, 2010.

Formerly Code 1933, § 24A-3504; Code 1981, § 15-11-61.

Historical and Statutory Notes

The 2000 amendment, which restructured this chapter into parts and modified statutory references to reflect this restructuring, renumbered this section from § 15-11-61. In addition the amendment provided gender neutral referents.

The 2002 amendment deleted subsection (b), redesignated subsections (a), (c), and (d) as subsections (b), (d), and (e), respectively, and inserted new subsections (a) and (c). Prior to deletion, former subsec. (b) provided:

"(b) Reasonable notice of the hearing shall be given to:

"(1) The district attorney;

"(2) The authority granting the discharge if the final discharge was from an institution or from parole; and

"(3) The law enforcement officers or department having custody of the files and records if the files and records specified in Code Sections 15-11-82 and 15-11-83 are included in the application or motion."

The 2009 amendment by Act 67 rewrote subsec. (e) which had read:

"(e) Except as otherwise provided by the court, no order sealing files and records under this Code section may be issued regarding any proceeding in which the general public may not be excluded from the hearing under subsection (a) or (b) of Code Section 15-11-78."

Laws 2009, Act 67, § 6, provides:

"This Act shall become effective on January 1, 2010, and shall not apply to any juvenile court proceeding filed before that date. Any such proceeding filed before January 1, 2010, shall be governed by the statute in effect at the time the juvenile court proceeding was filed."

Uniform Law

This section is based upon § 57 of the Uniform Law Commissioners' Model Juvenile Court Act. See 9A Uniform Laws Annotated, Master Edition, or ULA Database on Westlaw.

§ 15-11-80. Notice to school superintendent

Within 30 days of any proceeding in which a child is adjudicated delinquent for a second or subsequent time or any adjudicatory proceeding involving a designated felony, the court shall provide written notice to the school superintendent or his or her designee of the school in which such child is enrolled or, if the information is known, of the school in which such child plans to be enrolled at a future date. Such notice shall include the specific delinquent act or designated felony act that such child committed.

Laws 1995, p. 619, § 3; Laws 2000, p. 20, § 1.

Formerly Code 1981, § 15-11-58.1.

Historical and Statutory Notes

The 2000 amendment, which restructured this chapter into parts and modified statutory references to reflect this restructuring, renumbered this section from § 15-11-58.1.

§ 15–11–81. Preservation and destruction of records; computer retrieval

(a) *Records.* Subject to the earlier sealing of certain records pursuant to Code Section 15–11–79.2, the juvenile court shall make and keep records of all cases brought before it and shall preserve the records pertaining to a child in accordance with the common records retention schedules for courts approved by the State Records Committee pursuant to Code Section 50–18–92. Thereafter, the court may destroy such records, except that records of cases where orders were entered permanently depriving a parent of the custody of a child and records of cases involving a petition for legitimation of a child filed pursuant to Code Section 19–7–22 shall be preserved permanently. The court shall notify the deputy director of the Georgia Crime Information Center upon the destruction of any such felony records. The juvenile court shall make official minutes consisting of all petitions and orders filed in a case and any other pleadings, certificates, proofs of publication, summonses, warrants, and other writs which may be filed therein and shall make social records consisting of records of investigation and treatment and other confidential information. The provisions of this subsection notwithstanding, identification data shall be maintained and shall be disseminated to criminal justice officials for official judicial enforcement or criminal justice purposes as provided in Code Section 35–3–33.

(b) *Records, dockets, indexes, files.* Nothing in this chapter shall restrict or otherwise prohibit a juvenile court clerk from electing to store for computer retrieval any or all records, dockets, indexes, or files; nor shall a juvenile court clerk be prohibited from combining or consolidating any books, dockets, files, or indexes in connection with the filing for record of papers of the kind specified in this chapter or any other law, provided that any automated or computerized record-keeping method or system shall provide for the systematic and safe preservation and retrieval of all books, dockets, records, or indexes. When the clerk of a juvenile court elects to store for computer retrieval any or all records, the same data elements used in a manual system shall be used, and the same integrity and security maintained.

Laws 1950, p. 367, §§ 2, 30; Laws 1951, p. 291, § 33; Laws 1957, p. 307, § 1; Laws 1965, p. 433, § 1; Laws 1968, p. 1013, §§ 19, 21; Laws 1971, p. 709, § 1; Laws 1973, p. 882, § 9; Laws 1986, p. 1017, § 1; Laws 1991, p. 627, § 4; Laws 1995, p. 619, § 7; Laws 1997, p. 1681, § 4; Laws 1998, p. 653, § 7; Laws 1998, p. 842, § 5; Laws 2000, p. 20, § 1.

Formerly Code 1933, § 24A–3901; Code 1981, § 15–11–65.

Historical and Statutory Notes

The 2000 amendment, which restructured this chapter into parts and modified statutory references to reflect this restructuring, renumbered this section from § 15–11–65.

§ 15–11–82. Law enforcement records

(a) Except as provided in Code Sections 15–11–79 and 15–11–83, law enforcement records and files concerning a child shall be kept separate from the records and files of arrests of adults.

(b) Unless a charge of delinquency is transferred for criminal prosecution under Code Section 15–11–30.2, or the interest of national security requires, or the case is one in which the general public may not be excluded from the hearings under Code Section 15–11–78, or the court otherwise orders in the interest of the child, the records and files shall not be open to public inspection nor shall their contents be disclosed to the public.

(c) Inspection of the records and files is permitted by:

(1) A juvenile court having the child before it in any proceeding;

(2) Counsel for a party to the proceedings, with the consent of the court;

(3) The officers of public institutions or agencies to whom the child is committed;

(4) Law enforcement officers of this state, the United States, or any other jurisdiction when necessary for the discharge of their official duties;

(5) A court in which the child is convicted of a criminal offense, for the purpose of a presentence report or other dispositional proceeding;

(6) Officials of penal institutions and other penal facilities to which the child is committed;

(7) A parole board in considering the child's parole or discharge or in exercising supervision over the child; or

(8) Any school superintendent, principal, assistant principal, school guidance counselor, school social worker, school psychologist certified under Chapter 2 of Title 20, or school law enforcement officer appointed pursuant to Chapter 2, 3, or 8 of Title 20 when necessary for the discharge of his or her official duties.

(d) The court shall allow authorized representatives of the Department of Juvenile Justice, the Department of Corrections, and the Council of Juvenile Court Judges to inspect and copy law enforcement records for the purpose of obtaining statistics on children.

(e) Any law enforcement records and files involving an offense over which the superior court shall have exclusive jurisdiction as provided in paragraph (2) of subsection (b) of Code Section 15–11–28 shall be kept and reported in the same manner as the records and files of adults.

(f) Access to fingerprint records submitted to the Georgia Bureau of Investigation pursuant to Code Section 15–11–83 shall be limited to the administration of criminal justice purposes as defined in Code Section 15–11–2.

Laws 1950, p. 367, § 16; Laws 1951, p. 291, § 19; Laws 1968, p. 1013, § 10; Laws 1971, p. 709, § 1; Laws 1978, p. 1512, § 3; Laws 1990, p. 1930, § 6; Laws 1992, p. 1983, § 18; Laws 1995, p. 619, § 4; Laws 1997, p. 828, § 1; Laws 1997, p. 1064, § 8; Laws 1997, p. 1453, § 1; Laws 1998, p. 128, § 15; Laws 1998, p. 842, § 2; Laws 2000, p. 20, § 1; Laws 2009, Act 67, § 4, eff. Jan. 1, 2010.

Formerly Code 1933, § 24A–3502; Code 1981, § 15–11–59.

Historical and Statutory Notes

The 2000 amendment, which restructured this chapter into parts and modified statutory references to reflect this restructuring, renumbered this section from § 15–11–59. In addition the amendment substituted reference to "children" for "juveniles".

The 2009 amendment by Act 67, in subsec. (b), deleted "subsection (a) or (b) of" preceding "Code Section 15–11–78".

Laws 2009, Act 67, § 6, provides:

"This Act shall become effective on January 1, 2010, and shall not apply to any juvenile court proceeding filed before that date. Any such proceeding filed before January 1, 2010, shall be governed by the statute in effect at the time the juvenile court proceeding was filed."

Uniform Law

This section is based upon § 55 of the Uniform Law Commissioners' Model Juvenile Court Act. See 9A Uniform Laws Annotated, Master Edition, or ULA Database on Westlaw.

§ 15–11–83. Children's fingerprints, photographs, and names

(a)(1) Every child charged with an act which would be a felony if committed by an adult, other than those status offender crimes as defined in Code Section 15–11–2, shall be fingerprinted and photographed upon being taken into custody. Fingerprints and photographs of children shall be taken and filed separately from those of adults by law enforcement officials to be used in investigating the commission of crimes and to be made available as provided in this article and as may be directed by the court.

(2) Law enforcement agencies may photograph a child who for any reason has been placed in the custody and control of the Department of Juvenile Justice and who has absconded and subsequently returned to such custody. Photographs shall be maintained in accordance with paragraph (1) of this subsection.

(b) All children sentenced to the custody of the Department of Corrections shall be fingerprinted. The fingerprinting of child inmates will be processed in accordance with the Department of Corrections' policies for adult inmates.

(c) Fingerprint files and photographs of children may be inspected by law enforcement officers when necessary for criminal justice purposes and for the discharge of their official duties. The names and addresses of children who have been fingerprinted or photographed and the offense or offenses charged shall be made available in the discretion of the court to the appropriate department of family and children services and school superintendent. This information may be disseminated by the appropriate school superintendent to the child's teachers and counselors in the superintendent's discretion. Other inspections may be authorized by the court in individual cases upon a showing that it is necessary in the public interest.

(d) If a child has been charged with an offense that if committed by an adult would be a felony, or if the case is transferred to another court for prosecution, the child's fingerprints, personal identification data, and other pertinent information shall be forwarded to the Georgia Crime Information Center of the Georgia Bureau of Investigation. The Georgia Crime Information Center shall create a juvenile fingerprint file and enter the data into the computerized criminal history files. The Georgia Bureau of Investigation shall act as the official state repository for juvenile history data and is authorized to disseminate such data for the purposes specified in Code Section 15–11–82.

(e) Upon application of the child, fingerprints and photographs of a child shall be removed from the file and destroyed if a petition alleging delinquency is not filed or the proceedings are dismissed after either a petition is filed or the case is transferred to the juvenile court as provided in Code Section 15–11–30.4 or the child is adjudicated not to be a delinquent child. The court shall notify the deputy director of the Georgia Crime Information Center when fingerprints and photographs are destroyed pursuant to this subsection, and the Georgia Bureau of Investigation shall treat such records in the same manner as expunged records pursuant to subsection (c) of Code Section 35–3–37.

(f) Except as provided in this Code section, without the consent of the judge, a child shall not be photographed after he or she is taken into custody unless the case is transferred to another court for prosecution.

(g)(1) The name or picture of any child under the jurisdiction of the juvenile court for the first time shall not be made public by any news media, upon penalty of contempt under Code Section 15–11–5, except as otherwise provided in paragraph (2) of this subsection or as authorized by an order of the court.

(2) It shall be mandatory upon the judge of the juvenile court or his or her designee to release the name of any child with regard to whom a petition has been filed alleging the child committed a designated felony act or alleging the child committed a delinquent act if the child has previously been adjudicated delinquent or if the child has previously been before the court on a delinquency charge and adjudication was withheld. No person, firm, or corporation shall be guilty of any offense by making public the name or picture of any such child.

Laws 1950, p. 367, §§ 16, 30; Laws 1951, p. 291, §§ 19, 33; Laws 1957, p. 307, § 1; Laws 1968, p. 1013, §§ 10, 19; Laws 1971, p. 709, § 1; Laws 1973, p. 882, § 8; Laws 1982, p. 928, §§ 1, 2; Laws 1984, p. 22, § 15; Laws 1994, p. 1012, § 26; Laws 1995, p. 619, § 5; Laws 1998, p. 653, § 6; Laws 1998, p. 842, § 3; Laws 2000, p. 20, § 1; Laws 2002, p. 836, § 1.

Formerly Code 1933, § 24A–3503; Code 1981, § 15–11–60.

Historical and Statutory Notes

The 2000 amendment, which restructured this chapter into parts and modified statutory references to reflect this restructuring, renumbered this section from § 15–11–60.

The 2002 amendment designated subsec. (a)(1) and added subsec. (a)(2).

Uniform Law

This section is based upon § 56 of the Uniform Law Commissioners' Model Juvenile Court Act. See 9A Uniform Laws Annotated, Master Edition, or ULA Database on Westlaw.

§ 15–11–84. Government departments, boards, and agencies sharing nonconfidential information in order to serve the best interest of a child

(a) As used in this Code section, the term "governmental entity" shall mean the court, superior court, the Department of Juvenile Justice, the Department of Behavioral Health and Developmental Disabilities, the Division of Family and Children Services of the Department of Human Services, county departments of family and children services, or public school, as such term is defined in Code Section 16–11–35.

(b) Governmental entities and state, county, municipal, or consolidated government departments, boards, or agencies shall exchange with each other all information not held as confidential pursuant to federal law and relating to a child which may aid a governmental entity in the assessment, treatment, intervention, or rehabilitation of a child, notwithstanding Code Section 15–1–15 or 15–11–9.1, subsection (d) of Code Section 15–11–10, or Code Section 15–11–66.1, 15–11–75, 15–11–81, 15–11–82, 15–11–174, 20–2–751.2, 20–14–40, 24–9–40.1, 24–9–41, 24–9–42, 26–4–5, 26–4–80, 26–5–17, 31–5–5, 31–33–6, 37–1–53, 37–2–9.1, 42–5–36, 42–8–40, 42–8–106, 49–5–40, 49–5–41, 49–5–41.1, 49–5–44, 49–5–45, 49–5–183, 49–5–184, 49–5–185, or 49–5–186, in order to serve the best interest of the child. Information which is shared pursuant to this subsection shall not be utilized to assist in the prosecution of the child in juvenile court or superior court or utilized to the detriment of the child.

(c) Information released pursuant to this Code section shall not change or rescind the confidential nature of such information and such information shall not be subject to public disclosure or inspection unless otherwise provided by law.

Laws 2009, Act 67, § 5, eff. Jan. 1, 2010; Laws 2010, Act 624, § 15, eff. June 3, 2010.

Historical and Statutory Notes

Laws 2009, Act 67, § 6, provides:

"This Act shall become effective on January 1, 2010, and shall not apply to any juvenile court proceeding filed before that date. Any such proceeding filed before January 1, 2010, shall be governed by the statute in effect at the time the juvenile court proceeding was filed."

In 2009, the Code Commission, in subsec. (a), substituted "Department of Behavioral Health and Developmental Disabilities" for "Division of Mental Health, Developmental Disabilities, and Addictive Diseases within the Department of Human Resources", substituted "of" for "within", and substituted "Human Services" for "Human Resources". See § 28–9–5.

The 2010 amendment by Act 624 was a provision contained in a correction bill.

§ 15–11–85. Renumbered as § 15–11–98 by Laws 2000, p. 20, § 1

§ 15–11–86. Renumbered as § 15–11–99 by Laws 2000, p. 20, § 1

Part 9

Interstate Proceedings

§ 15–11–87. Disposition of nonresident child

(a) If the court finds that a child who has been adjudged to have committed a delinquent act or to be unruly or deprived is or is about to become a resident of another state which has adopted the Uniform Juvenile Court Act or a substantially similar act which includes provisions corresponding to this Code section and Code Section 15–11–88, the court may defer the hearing on the need for treatment or rehabilitation and disposition and may request by any appropriate means the juvenile court of the child's residence or prospective residence to accept jurisdiction of the child.

(b) If the child becomes a resident of another state while on probation or under protective supervision under order of a court of this state, the court may request the juvenile court of the county of the state in which the child has become a resident to accept jurisdiction of the child and to continue his or her probation or protective supervision.

(c) Upon receipt and filing of an acceptance, the court of this state shall transfer custody of the child to the accepting court and cause the child to be delivered to the person designated by that court to receive custody of the child. It also shall provide that court with certified copies of the order adjudging the child to be a delinquent, unruly, or deprived child, of the order of transfer, and, if the child is on probation or under protective supervision under order of the court, of the order of disposition. It also shall provide that court with a statement of the facts found by the court of this state and any recommendations and other information it considers of assistance to the accepting court in making a disposition of the case or in supervising the child on probation or otherwise.

(d) Upon compliance with subsection (c) of this Code section the jurisdiction of the court of this state over the child is terminated.

Laws 1971, p. 709, § 1; Laws 2000, p. 20, § 1.

Formerly Code 1933, § 24A–3001; Code 1981, § 15–11–44.

Historical and Statutory Notes

The 2000 amendment, which restructured this chapter into parts and modified statutory references to reflect this restructuring, renumbered this section from § 15–11–44. In addition the amendment inserted gender neutral referents.

Uniform Law

This section is based upon § 39 of the Uniform Law Commissioners' Model Juvenile Court Act. See 9A Uniform Laws Annotated, Master Edition, or ULA Database on Westlaw.

§ 15–11–88. Disposition of resident child received from another state

(a) If a juvenile court of another state which has adopted the Uniform Juvenile Court Act or a substantially similar act which includes provisions corresponding to this Code section and Code Section 15–11–87 requests a court of this state to accept jurisdiction of a child found by the requesting court to have committed a delinquent act or to be an unruly or deprived child and the court of this state finds, after investigation, that the child is or is about to become a resident of the county in which the court presides, it shall promptly and not later than 14 days after receiving the request issue its acceptance in writing to the requesting court and shall direct its probation officer or other person designated by it to take physical custody of the child from the requesting court and bring the child before the court of this state or make other appropriate provisions for the child's appearance before the court.

(b) Upon the filing of certified copies of the orders of the requesting court determining that the child committed a delinquent act or is an unruly or deprived child and committing the child to the jurisdiction of a court of this state, the court of this state shall immediately fix a time for a hearing on the need for treatment or rehabilitation and disposition of the child or on the continuance of any probation or protective supervision.

(c) The hearing and notice thereof and all subsequent proceedings shall be governed by this article. The court may make any order of disposition permitted by the facts and this article. The orders of the requesting court are conclusive that the child committed the delinquent act or is an unruly or deprived child and of the facts found by the court in making the orders, subject only to Code Section 15–11–40. If the requesting court has made an order placing the child on probation or under protective supervision, a like order shall be entered by the court of this state. The court may modify or vacate the order in accordance with Code Section 15–11–40.

Laws 1971, p. 709, § 1; Laws 1986, p. 1017, § 1; Laws 2000, p. 20, § 1.

Formerly Code 1933, § 24A–3002; Code 1981, § 15–11–45.

Historical and Statutory Notes

The 2000 amendment, which restructured this chapter into parts and modified statutory references to reflect this restructuring, renumbered this section from § 15–11–45.

Uniform Law

This section is based upon § 40 of the Uniform Law Commissioners' Model Juvenile Court Act. See 9A Uniform Laws Annotated, Master Edition, or ULA Database on Westlaw.

§ 15–11–89. Ordering out-of-state supervision

(a) Subject to the provisions of this article governing dispositions and to the extent that funds of the county are available, the court may place a child in the custody of a suitable person in another state. On obtaining the written consent of a juvenile court of another state which has adopted the Uniform Juvenile Court Act or a substantially similar act which includes provisions corresponding to this Code section and Code Section 15–11–90, the court of this state may order that the child be placed under the supervision of a probation officer or other appropriate official designated by the accepting court. One certified copy of the order shall be sent to the accepting court and another shall be filed with the clerk of the governing authority of the county of the requesting court of this state.

(b) The reasonable cost of the supervision, including the expenses of necessary travel, shall be borne by the county of the requesting court of this state. Upon receiving a certified statement signed by the judge of the accepting court of the cost incurred by the supervision, the court of this state shall certify if it appears that the sum so stated was reasonably incurred and shall file it with the appropriate officials of the county for payment. The appropriate officials shall thereupon issue a warrant for the sum stated payable to the appropriate officials of the county of the accepting court.

Laws 1971, p. 709, § 1; Laws 1986, p. 1017, § 1; Laws 2000, p. 20, § 1.

Formerly Code 1933, § 24A–3003; Code 1981, § 15–11–46.

Historical and Statutory Notes

The 2000 amendment, which restructured this chapter into parts and modified statutory references to reflect this restructuring, renumbered this section from § 15–11–46.

Uniform Law

This section is based upon § 41 of the Uniform Law Commissioners' Model Juvenile Court Act. See 9A Uniform Laws Annotated, Master Edition, or ULA Database on Westlaw.

§ 15–11–89.1. Powers of out-of-state probation officers

If a child has been placed on probation or protective supervision by a juvenile court of another state which has adopted the Uniform Juvenile Court Act or a substantially similar act which includes provisions corresponding to this Code section and the child is in this state with or without the permission of that court, the probation officer of that court or other person designated by that court to supervise or take custody of the child has all the powers and privileges in this state with respect to the child as are given by this article to like officers or persons of this state, including the rights of visitation, counseling, control, direction, taking into custody, and returning to that state.

Laws 1971, p. 709, § 1; Laws 1986, p. 1017, § 1; Laws 2000, p. 20, § 1.

Formerly Code 1933, § 24A–3005; Code 1981, § 15–11–48.

Historical and Statutory Notes

The 2000 amendment, which restructured this chapter into parts and modified statutory references to reflect this restructuring, renumbered this section from § 15–11–48.

Uniform Law

This section is based upon § 43 of the Uniform Law Commissioners' Model Juvenile Court Act. See 9A Uniform Laws Annotated, Master Edition, or ULA Database on Westlaw.

§ 15–11–90. Supervision under out-of-state order

(a) Upon receiving a request from a court exercising jurisdiction over children of another state which has adopted the Uniform Juvenile Court Act or a substantially similar act which includes provisions corresponding to this Code section and Code Section 15–11–89 to provide supervision of a child under the jurisdiction of that court, a court of this state may issue its written acceptance to the requesting court and may designate its probation or other appropriate officer who is to provide supervision, stating the probable cost per day therefor.

(b) Upon the receipt and filing of a certified copy of the order of the requesting court placing the child under the supervision of the officer so designated, the officer shall arrange for the reception of the child from the requesting court, shall provide supervision pursuant to the order and this article, and shall report thereon from time to time to the requesting court, including in the report any recommendations which he or she may have.

(c) The court in this state from time to time shall certify to the requesting court the cost of supervision that has been incurred and shall request payment therefor from the appropriate officials of the county of the requesting court to the appropriate officials of the county of the accepting court.

(d) The court of this state at any time may terminate supervision by notifying the requesting court. In that case, or if the supervision is terminated by the requesting court, the probation officer supervising the child shall return the child to a representative of the requesting court authorized to receive the child.

Laws 1971, p. 709, § 1; Laws 1986, p. 1017, § 1; Laws 2000, p. 20, § 1.

Formerly Code 1933, § 24A–3004; Code 1981, § 15–11–47.

Historical and Statutory Notes

The 2000 amendment, which restructured this chapter into parts and modified statutory references to reflect this restructuring, renumbered this section from § 15–11–47. In addition the amendment substituted reference to "children" for "juveniles" and added gender neutral referents.

Uniform Law

This section is based upon § 42 of the Uniform Law Commissioners' Model Juvenile Court Act. See 9A Uniform Laws Annotated, Master Edition, or ULA Database on Westlaw.

§ 15–11–91. Renumbered as § 15–11–104 by Laws 2000, p. 20, § 1

§ 15–11–92. Renumbered as § 15–11–105 by Laws 2000, p. 20, § 1

Article 2

Termination of Parental Rights

§ 15–11–93. Scope and duration of order

An order terminating the parental rights of a parent under this article is without limit as to duration and terminates all the parent's rights and obligations with respect to the child and all rights and obligations of the child to the parent arising from the parental relationship, including rights of inheritance. The parent is not thereafter entitled to notice of proceedings for the adoption of the child by another, nor has the parent any right to object to the adoption or otherwise to participate in the proceedings.

Laws 1986, p. 1017, § 4; Laws 2000, p. 20, § 1.

Formerly Code 1981, § 15–11–80.

Historical and Statutory Notes

The 2000 amendment, which restructured this chapter into parts and modified statutory references to reflect this restructuring, renumbered this section from § 15–11–80.

Uniform Law

This section is based upon § 49 of the Uniform Law Commissioners' Model Juvenile Court Act. See 9A Uniform Laws Annotated, Master Edition, or ULA Database on Westlaw.

§ 15–11–94. Conditions and procedures under which parental rights may be terminated

(a) In considering the termination of parental rights, the court shall first determine whether there is present clear and convincing evidence of parental misconduct or inability as provided in subsection (b) of this Code section. If there is clear and convincing evidence of such parental misconduct or inability, the court shall then consider whether termination of parental rights is in the best interest of the child, after considering the physical, mental, emotional, and moral condition and needs of the child who is the subject of the proceeding, including the need for a secure and stable home. If the court finds clear and convincing evidence of the circumstance provided in paragraph (5) of subsection (b) of this Code section, the court shall presume that termination of parental rights is in the best interest of the child.

(b) Except as provided in subsections (e) through (h) of Code Section 15–11–96, the court by order may terminate the parental rights of a parent with respect to the parent's child if:

(1) The written consent of the parent, acknowledged before the court, has been given; provided, however, that acknowledgment before the court is not necessary where the parent or parents voluntarily surrender the child for adoption as provided by subsection (e) of Code Section 19–8–4, 19–8–5, 19–8–6, or 19–8–7;

(2) A decree has been entered by a court of competent jurisdiction of this or any other state ordering the parent, guardian, or other custodian to support the child, and the parent, guardian, or other custodian has wantonly and willfully failed to comply with the order for a period of 12 months or longer;

(3) The parent has abandoned the child or the child was left under circumstances that the identity of the parent is unknown and cannot be ascertained despite diligent searching, and the parent has not come forward to claim the child within three months following the finding of the child;

(4)(A) The court determines parental misconduct or inability by finding that:

(i) The child is a deprived child, as such term is defined in Code Section 15–11–2;

(ii) The lack of proper parental care or control by the parent in question is the cause of the child's status as deprived;

(iii) Such cause of deprivation is likely to continue or will not likely be remedied; and

(iv) The continued deprivation will cause or is likely to cause serious physical, mental, emotional, or moral harm to the child.

(B) In determining whether the child is without proper parental care and control, the court shall consider, without being limited to, the following:

(i) A medically verifiable deficiency of the parent's physical, mental, or emotional health of such duration or nature as to render the parent unable to provide adequately for the physical, mental, emotional, or moral condition and needs of the child;

(ii) Excessive use of or history of chronic unrehabilitated abuse of intoxicating liquors or narcotic or dangerous drugs or controlled substances with the effect of rendering the parent incapable of providing adequately for the physical, mental, emotional, or moral condition and needs of the child;

(iii) Conviction of the parent of a felony and imprisonment therefor which has a demonstrable negative effect on the quality of the parent-child relationship;

(iv) Egregious conduct or evidence of past egregious conduct of the parent toward the child or toward another child of a physically, emotionally, or sexually cruel or abusive nature;

(v) Physical, mental, or emotional neglect of the child or evidence of past physical, mental, or emotional neglect of the child or of another child by the parent; and

(vi) Injury or death of a sibling under circumstances which constitute substantial evidence that such injury or death resulted from parental neglect or abuse.

(C) In addition to the considerations in subparagraph (B) of this paragraph, where the child is not in the custody of the parent who is the subject of the proceedings, in determining whether the child is without proper parental care and control, the court shall consider, without being limited to, whether the parent without justifiable cause has failed significantly for a period of one year or longer prior to the filing of the petition for termination of parental rights:

(i) To develop and maintain a parental bond with the child in a meaningful, supportive manner;

(ii) To provide for the care and support of the child as required by law or judicial decree; and

(iii) To comply with a court ordered plan designed to reunite the child with the parent or parents; or

(5) The parent has been convicted of the murder of the child's other parent.

(c) If the court does not make an order of termination of parental rights, it may grant an order under Code Section 15–11–55 if the court finds from clear and convincing evidence that the child is a deprived child.

Laws 1986, p. 1017, § 4; Laws 1990, p. 1425, § 1; Laws 1990, p. 1572, § 2; Laws 1991, p. 94, § 15; Laws 1996, p. 474, § 3; Laws 1997, p. 143, § 15; Laws 1999, p. 252, § 1; Laws 2000, p. 20, § 1; Laws 2004, Act 596, § 2, eff. July 1, 2004.

Formerly Code 1981, § 15–11–81.

Historical and Statutory Notes

The 2000 amendment, which restructured this chapter into parts and modified statutory references to reflect this restructuring, renumbered this section from § 15–11–81.

The 2004 amendment by Act 596, in subsec. (a), inserted "If there is clear and convincing evidence of such parental If the court finds clear and convincing evidence of the circumstance provided in paragraph (5) of subsection (b) of this Code section, the court shall presume that termination of parental rights is in the best interest of the child." at the end; and in subsec. (b), added par. (5).

Uniform Law

This section is based upon § 47 of the Uniform Law Commissioners' Model Juvenile Court Act. See 9A Uniform Laws Annotated, Master Edition, or ULA Database on Westlaw.

§ 15–11–95. Petition

(a) The petition to terminate parental rights and all subsequent court documents in the proceeding shall be entitled "In the matter of ____, a child.", except upon appeal, in which event the anonymity of the child shall be preserved by appropriate use of initials. The petition shall be in writing.

(b) The petition shall be made, verified, and endorsed by the court as provided in Article 1 of this chapter for a petition alleging deprivation.

(c) The petition shall state clearly that an order for termination of parental rights is requested and that the effect thereof will be as stated in Code Section 15–11–93, and shall set forth in ordinary and concise language the facts required by Code Section 15–11–38.1.

(d) When a petition seeks termination of the rights of a biological father who is not the legal father and who has not surrendered his rights to the child, the petition shall be amended to include a certificate from the putative father registry disclosing the name, address, and social security number of any registrant acknowledging paternity of the child pursuant to subparagraph (d)(2)(A) of Code Section 19–11–9 or indicating the possibility of paternity of a child of the child's mother pursuant to subparagraph (d)(2)(B) of Code Section 19–11–9 for a period beginning no later than two years immediately prior to the child's date of birth. Such certificate shall document a search of the registry on or after the date of the filing of the petition and shall include a statement that the registry is current as to filings of registrants as of the date of the petition or as of a date later than the date of the petition.

Laws 1986, p. 1017, § 4; Laws 1997, p. 1686, § 2; Laws 2000, p. 20, § 1.

Formerly Code 1981, § 15–11–82.

Historical and Statutory Notes

The 2000 amendment, which restructured this chapter into parts and modified statutory references to reflect this restructuring, renumbered this section from § 15–11–82.

Uniform Law

This section is based upon § 48 of the Uniform Law Commissioners' Model Juvenile Court Act. See 9A Uniform Laws Annotated, Master Edition, or ULA Database on Westlaw.

§ 15–11–96. Summons; rights of biological fathers

(a) Upon filing of the petition, summons shall be issued forthwith on the child's parents, guardian, lawful custodian, and on the person presently having physical custody of the child.

(b) A copy of the petition shall be attached to the summons in all cases other than service by publication. When served by publication, the notice shall indicate the general nature of the allegations and where a copy of the petition may be obtained by the child's parents, guardian, lawful custodian, and the person presently having physical custody of the child. Such copy shall be available from the court during business hours. A free copy shall be available to the parent or, upon request, shall be mailed to the parent. All summons shall contain a statement to the effect that the hearing is for the purpose of terminating parental rights.

(c) The summons shall require the person who has physical custody of the child to appear personally and to bring the child before the court at the time and place stated in the summons. Where, at the court's discretion, it is deemed in the interest of the child that the child need not be brought before the court, the court may so indicate. The summons shall be served at least 30 days before the time set for the hearing, and a copy of the petition shall be served together with the summons and shall be made in the manner provided in Code Section 9–11–4, relating to service in civil practice.

(d) If the paternity of a child born out of wedlock has been established in a judicial proceeding to which the father was a party prior to the filing of the petition, the father shall be served with summons as provided by this article. Such father has the right to be heard unless he has relinquished all paternal rights with reference to the child.

(e) If there is a biological father who is not the legal father of a child and he has not executed a surrender as specified in paragraph (2) of subsection (e) of Code Section 19–8–4, 19–8–5, 19–8–6, or 19–8–7 he shall be notified of the proceedings pursuant to this Code section in the following circumstances:

(1) If his identity is known to the petitioner or the petitioner's attorney;

(2) If he is a registrant on the putative father registry who has acknowledged paternity of the child in accordance with subparagraph (d)(2)(A) of Code Section 19–11–9;

(3) If he is a registrant on the putative father registry who has indicated possible paternity of a child of the child's mother in accordance with subparagraph (d)(2)(B) of Code Section 19–11–9 during a period beginning two years immediately prior to the child's date of birth; or

(4) If the court finds from the evidence, including but not limited to the affidavit of the mother executed in compliance with the court's requirement pursuant to subsection (g) of this Code section in the form provided in subsection (h) of Code Section 19–8–26, that such biological father who is not the legal father has performed any of the following acts:

(A) Lived with the child;

(B) Contributed to the child's support;

(C) Made any attempt to legitimate the child; or

(D) Provided support or medical care for the mother either during her pregnancy or during her hospitalization for the birth of the child.

(f) Notification provided for in subsection (e) of this Code section shall be given to a biological father who is not a legal father by the following methods:

(1) Registered or certified mail or statutory overnight delivery, return receipt requested, at his last known address, which notice shall be deemed received upon the date of delivery shown on the return receipt;

(2) Personal service, which notice shall be deemed received when personal service is perfected; or

(3) Publication once a week for three weeks in the official organ of the county where the petition has been filed and of the county of his last known address, which notice shall be deemed received upon the date of the last publication.

If feasible, the methods specified in paragraph (1) or (2) of this subsection shall be used before publication.

(g) If there is a biological father who is not the legal father of the child and the identity of such biological father is not known to the petitioner or the petitioner's attorney, then the court shall be authorized to require the mother to execute an affidavit regarding such father in the form provided in subsection (h) of Code Section 19–8–26 or show cause before the court if she refuses. If the court finds from the evidence including but not limited to the affidavit of the mother that such biological father who is not the legal father has not performed any of the following acts:

(1) Lived with the child;

(2) Contributed to the child's support;

(3) Made any attempt to legitimate the child; or

(4) Provided support or medical care for the mother either during her pregnancy or during her hospitalization for the birth of the child,

and the petitioner provides a certificate from the putative father registry stating that there is no entry on the putative father registry either acknowledging paternity of the child or indicating possible paternity of a child of the child's mother for a period beginning no later than two years immediately prior to the child's date of birth, then it shall be rebuttably presumed that the biological father who is not the legal father is not entitled to notice of the proceedings. Absent evidence rebutting the presumption, then no further inquiry or notice shall be required by the court and the court shall enter an order terminating the rights of such biological father to the child.

(h) When notice is given pursuant to subsection (e) of this Code section, it shall advise such biological father who is not the legal father that he loses all rights to the child and will not be entitled to object to the termination of his rights to the child unless, within 30 days of receipt of such notice, he files:

(1) A petition to legitimate the child pursuant to Code Section 19–7–22 or an acknowledgment of legitimation pursuant to Code Section 19–7–21.1; and

(2) Notice of the filing of the petition to legitimate or acknowledgment of legitimation with the court in which the action under this Code section is pending.

(i) A biological father who is not the legal father loses all rights to the child and the court shall enter an order terminating all such father's rights to the child and such father may not thereafter object to the termination of his rights to the child if within 30 days from his receipt of the notice provided for in subsection (e) of this Code section he:

(1) Does not file a legitimation petition and give notice as required in subsection (h) of this Code section;

(2) Files a legitimation petition which is subsequently dismissed for failure to prosecute; or

(3) Files a legitimation petition and the action is subsequently concluded without a court order declaring a finding that he is the legal father of the child.

Laws 1986, p. 1017, § 4; Laws 1990, p. 1572, § 3; Laws 1991, p. 94, § 15; Laws 1997, p. 1686, § 3; Laws 2000, p. 20, § 1; Laws 2000, p. 1589, § 3; Laws 2008, Act 580, § 10, eff. July 1, 2008.

Formerly Code 1981, § 15–11–83; Code 1981, § 96.

Historical and Statutory Notes

The 2000 amendment by Act 467, which restructured this chapter into parts and modified statutory references to reflect this restructuring, renumbered this section from § 15–11–83.

The 2000 amendment by Act 918 provided for delivery by statutory overnight delivery alternatively with certified mail.

The 2008 amendment by Act 580, in subsec. (h), par. (1), inserted "or an acknowledgment of legitimation pursuant to Code Section 19–7–21.1" following the citation to Code Section 19–7–22; and in par. (2) inserted "or acknowledgment of legitimation" following "Notice of the filing of the petition to legitimate".

§ 15–11–97. Sanctions for failure to be served or failure to obey summons

(a) If any person named in and properly served with summons shall without reasonable cause fail to appear or, when directed in the summons, to bring the child before the court, then the court may issue a rule nisi against such person, directing the person to appear before the court to show cause why such person should not be held in contempt of court.

(b) If the summons cannot be served or if the person to whom the summons is directed fails to obey it, the court may issue an order to take the child into protective custody.

Laws 1986, p. 1017, § 4; Laws 2000, p. 20, § 1.

Formerly Code 1981, § 15–11–84.

Historical and Statutory Notes

The 2000 amendment, which restructured this chapter into parts and modified statutory references to reflect this restructuring, renumbered this section from § 15–11–84.

§ 15–11–98. Appointment of counsel and guardians ad litem

(a) In any proceeding for terminating parental rights or any rehearing or appeal thereon, the court shall appoint an attorney to represent the child as the child's counsel and may appoint a separate guardian ad litem or a guardian ad litem who may be the same person as the child's counsel.

(b) If the parent or parents of the child desire to be represented by counsel but are indigent, the court shall appoint an attorney for such parent or parents, which shall be a charge upon the funds of the county upon certification thereof by the court in the same manner as authorized for other expenses under Code Section 15–11–8.

Laws 1986, p. 1017, § 4; Laws 2000, p. 20, § 1.

Formerly Code 1981, § 15–11–85.

Historical and Statutory Notes

The 2000 amendment, which restructured this chapter into parts and modified statutory references to reflect this restructuring, renumbered this section from § 15–11–85. In addition the amendment substituted reference to "children" for "juveniles" and added gender neutral referents.

§ 15–11–99. Standard of proof

In all proceedings under this article, the standard of proof to be adduced to terminate parental rights shall be by clear and convincing evidence.

Laws 1986, p. 1017, § 4; Laws 2000, p. 20, § 1.

Formerly Code 1981, § 15–11–86.

Historical and Statutory Notes

The 2000 amendment, which restructured this chapter into parts and modified statutory references to reflect this restructuring, renumbered this section from § 15–11–86.

§ 15–11–100. Physical or mental examinations

The court may require a physical or mental evaluation of any parent, stepparent, guardian, or child involved in a proceeding under this article.

Laws 1986, p. 1017, § 4; Laws 2000, p. 20, § 1.

Formerly Code 1981, § 15–11–87.

Historical and Statutory Notes

The 2000 amendment, which restructured this chapter into parts and modified statutory references to reflect this restructuring, renumbered this section from § 15–11–87.

§ 15–11–101. Confidentiality of testimony of parties

The record of the testimony of the parties adduced in any proceeding under this article shall not be admissible in any civil, criminal, or any other cause or proceedings in any court against a person named as respondent for any purpose whatsoever, except in subsequent deprivation or termination proceedings involving the same child or deprivation or termination proceedings involving the same respondent under this article.

Laws 1986, p. 1017, § 4; Laws 2000, p. 20, § 1.

Formerly Code 1981, § 15–11–88.

Historical and Statutory Notes

The 2000 amendment, which restructured this chapter into parts and modified statutory references to reflect this restructuring, renumbered this section from § 15–11–88.

§ 15–11–102. Hearings

The court shall conduct hearings, where appropriate, in accordance with Code Section 15–11–39.2.

Laws 1986, p. 1017, § 4; Laws 2000, p. 20, § 1.

Formerly Code 1981, § 15–11–89.

Historical and Statutory Notes

The 2000 amendment, which restructured this chapter into parts and modified statutory references to reflect this restructuring, renumbered this section from § 15–11–89.

§ 15–11–103. Custody of child following termination proceedings; adoption

(a) Upon the entering of an order terminating the parental rights of a parent, a placement may be made only if the court finds that such placement is in the best interest of the child and in accordance with the child's court approved permanency plan created pursuant to Code Section 15–11–58. In determining which placement is in the child's best interest, the court shall enter findings of fact reflecting its consideration of the following:

(1) The child's need for a placement that offers the greatest degree of legal permanence and security;

(2) The least disruptive placement alternative for the child;

(3) The child's sense of attachment and need for continuity of relationships; and

(4) Any other factors the court deems relevant to its determination.

(b) A placement effected under the provisions of this Code section shall be conditional upon the person who is given permanent custody or who is granted an adoption of the child agreeing to abide by the terms and conditions of the order of the court.

(c) The court shall transmit a copy of every final order terminating the parental rights of a parent to the Office of Adoptions of the Department of Human Services within 15 days of the filing of such order.

(d) The custodian has authority to consent to the adoption of the child, the child's marriage, the child's enlistment in the armed forces of the United States, and surgical and other medical treatment for the child.

(e) In those cases in which the court has placed the child pursuant to a permanency plan of adoption, if a petition seeking the adoption of the child is not filed within six months after the date of the disposition order, the court shall then, and at least every six months thereafter as long as the child remains unadopted, review the circumstances of the child to determine what efforts have been made to assure that the child will be adopted. The court may then enter such orders as it deems necessary to further the adoption, including but not limited to another placement. In those cases where parental rights to the child were terminated without the designation of a permanent guardian or adoptive family, the court shall, at least every six months thereafter as long as the child remains subject to the jurisdiction of the court, review the circumstances of the child to determine that placement in the family home-like setting continues to be in the child's best interest.

Laws 1986, p. 1017, § 4; Laws 1991, p. 602, § 1; Laws 1996, p. 474, § 4; Laws 1999, p. 252, § 2; Laws 2000, p. 20, § 1; Laws 2003, Act 3, § 5, eff. July 1, 2003; Laws 2003, Act 207, § 1, eff. July 1, 2003; Laws 2004, Act 489, § 1, eff. July 1, 2004; Laws 2009, Act 37, § 2, eff. July 1, 2009; Laws 2009, Act 102, § 2-2, eff. July 1, 2009; Laws 2010, Act 418, § 11, eff. July 1, 2010.

Formerly Code 1981, § 15-11-90.

Historical and Statutory Notes

The 2000 amendment, which restructured this chapter into parts and modified statutory references to reflect this restructuring, renumbered this section from § 15-11-90. In addition the amendment added gender neutral referents.

The 2003 amendment by Act 3 rewrote the section which had read:

"(a)(1) If, upon the entering of an order terminating the parental rights of a parent, there is no parent having parental rights, the court shall first attempt to place the child with a person related to the child by blood or marriage or with a member of the child's extended family. A thorough search for a suitable family member shall be made by the court and the Department of Human Resources in attempting to effect this placement. A placement effected under this paragraph shall be conditioned upon the family member who is given permanent custody or who is granted an adoption of the child agreeing to abide by the terms and conditions of the order of the court. A placement shall be made under the terms of this paragraph only if such a placement is in the best interest of the child.

"(2) If no placement of the child is effected under paragraph (1) of this subsection, the court may make any of the following dispositions: commit the child to the custody of the Department of Human Resources or to a licensed child-placing agency willing to accept custody for the purpose of placing the child for adoption or, in the absence of an adoption, in a foster home, or take other suitable measures for the care and welfare of the child.

"(b) The court shall transmit a copy of every final order terminating the parental rights of a parent to the Division of Family and Children Services Adoption Unit of the Department of Human Resources within 15 days of the filing of such order.

"(c) The custodian has authority to consent to the adoption of the child, the child's marriage, the child's enlistment in the armed forces of the United States, and surgical and other medical treatment for the child.

"(d) If a petition seeking the adoption of the child is not filed within one year after the date of the disposition order, the court shall then, and at least yearly thereafter as long as the child remains unadopted, review the circumstances of the child to determine what efforts have been made to assure that the child will be adopted. The court may then enter such orders as it deems necessary to further the adoption, including but not limited to another placement."

The 2003 amendment by Act 207, in subsec. (b) (redesignated as subsec. (c) by Act 3), substituted "Office of Adoptions" for "Division of Family and Children Services Adoption Unit".

The 2004 amendment by Act 489, in subsec. (e), substituted "within six months" for "within one year", and substituted "every six months" for "yearly" twice.

The 2009 amendment by Act 37 rewrote the section which had read:

"(a)(1) If, upon the entering of an order terminating the parental rights of a parent, there is no parent having parental rights, the court shall first attempt to place the child with a person related to the child by blood or marriage or with a member of the child's extended family if such a person is willing and, after study by the probation officer or other person or agency designated by the court, is found by the court to be qualified to receive and care for the child, if the court determines such placement is the most appropriate for and in the best interest of the child. A placement effected under this paragraph shall be conditioned upon the family member who is given permanent custody or who is granted an adoption of the child agreeing to abide by the terms and conditions of the order of the court.

"(2) If no placement of the child is effected under paragraph (1) of this subsection, the court may commit the child to the custody of the Department of Human Resources or to a licensed child-placing agency willing to accept custody for the purpose of placing the child for adoption, if the court determines such placement is the most appropriate for and in the best interest of the child.

"(3) If no placement of the child is effected under paragraph (1) or (2) of this subsection, the court may commit the child to a suitable individual on the condition that the person becomes the guardian of the person of the child pursuant to the court's authority under Code Section 15-11-30.1, if the court determines such placement is the most appropriate for and in the best interest of the child.

"(4) If no placement of the child is effected under paragraph (1), (2), or (3) of this subsection, the court may commit the child to the custody of the Department of Human Resources or to a licensed child-placing agency willing to accept custody for the purpose of placing the child in a foster home, if the court determines such placement is the most appropriate for and in the best interest of the child.

"(5) If no placement of the child is effected under paragraph (1), (2), (3), or (4) of this subsection, the court may commit the child to the custody of an agency or organization authorized by law to receive and provide care for children which is operated in a manner that provides such care, guidance, and control as would be provided in a family home as defined in the court's order, if the court determines that such placement is the most appropriate for and in the best interest of the child.

"(6) If no placement of the child is effected under paragraph (1), (2), (3), (4), or (5) of this subsection, the court may take other suitable measures for the care and welfare of the child.

"(b) A placement may be made under the terms of this Code section only if the court finds that such placement is in the best interest of the child.

"(c) The court shall transmit a copy of every final order terminating the parental rights of a parent to the Office of Adoptions of the Department of Human Resources within 15 days of the filing of such order.

"(d) The custodian has authority to consent to the adoption of the child, the child's marriage, the child's enlistment in the armed forces of the United States, and surgical and other medical treatment for the child.

"(e) Except in those cases where the child was placed pursuant to paragraph (3) or (5) of subsection (a) of this Code section, if a petition seeking the adoption of the child is not filed within six months after the date of the disposition order, the court shall then, and at least every six months thereafter as long as the child remains unadopted, review the circumstances of the child to determine what efforts have been made to assure that the child will be adopted. The court may then enter such orders as it deems necessary to further the adoption, including but not limited to another placement. In those cases where the child was placed with a guardian of the child's person pursuant to paragraph (3) of subsection (a) of this Code section, the guardian shall report to the court in the same manner and at the same frequency as is required for guardians of the person of minors appointed by the judge of the probate court. In those cases where the child was placed pursuant to paragraph (5) of subsection (a) of this Code section, the court shall, at least every six months thereafter as long as the child remains subject to the jurisdiction of the court, review the circumstances of the child to determine that placement in the family home-like setting continues to be in the child's best interests."

The 2009 amendment by Act 102 substituted "Department of Human Services" for "Department of Human Resources" throughout the section.

In 2009, the Code Commission, due to irreconcilable conflicts, treated the amendment of this section by Laws 2009, Act 37, § 2, as superseded by Laws 2009, Act 102, § 2-2. See Butts County v. Strahan, 107 S.E. 163, 151 Ga. 417 (1921).

The 2010 amendment by Act 418 rewrote subsec. (a) which had read as follows:

"(a)(1) If, upon the entering of an order terminating the parental rights of a parent, there is no parent having parental rights, the court shall first attempt to place the child with a person related to the child by blood or marriage or with a member of the child's extended family if such a person is willing and, after study by the probation officer or other person or agency designated by the court, is found by the court to be qualified to receive and care for the child, if the court determines such placement is the most appropriate for and in the best interest of the child. A placement effected under this paragraph shall be conditioned upon the family member who is given permanent custody or who is granted an adoption of the child agreeing to abide by the terms and conditions of the order of the court.

"(2) If no placement of the child is effected under paragraph (1) of this subsection, the court may commit the child to the custody of the Department of Human Services or to a licensed child-placing agency willing to accept custody for the purpose of placing the child for adoption, if the court determines such placement is the most appropriate for and in the best interest of the child.

"(3) If no placement of the child is effected under paragraph (1) or (2) of this subsection, the court may commit the child to a suitable individual on the condition that the person becomes the guardian of the person of the child pursuant to the court's authority under Code Section 15–11–30.1, if the court determines such placement is the most appropriate for and in the best interest of the child.

"(4) If no placement of the child is effected under paragraph (1), (2), or (3) of this subsection, the court may commit the child to the custody of the Department of Human Services or to a licensed child-placing agency willing to accept custody for the purpose of placing the child in a foster home, if the court determines such placement is the most appropriate for and in the best interest of the child.

"(5) If no placement of the child is effected under paragraph (1), (2), (3), or (4) of this subsection, the court may commit the child to the custody of an agency or organization authorized by law to receive and provide care for children which is operated in a manner that provides such care, guidance, and control as would be provided in a family home as defined in the court's order, if the court determines that such placement is the most appropriate for and in the best interest of the child.

"(6) If no placement of the child is effected under paragraph (1), (2), (3), (4), or (5) of this subsection, the court may take other suitable measures for the care and welfare of the child."

§ 15–11–104. Conflicting provisions; notice of hearing or other proceeding to foster parents and preadoptive parents or relatives providing care for child

In a proceeding under this article, the provisions of Article 1 of this chapter shall apply unless in conflict with this article. In advance of any hearing or other proceeding to be held with respect to a child pursuant to this article, the court shall provide written notice or shall direct that a party shall provide written notice of such hearing or other proceeding, including their right to be heard at such hearing or other proceeding, to the foster parents of the child and to any preadoptive parents or relatives providing care for the child, consistent with the form and timing of notice to parties; provided, however, that this provision shall not be construed to require a foster parent, preadoptive parent, or relative caring for the child to be made a party to the hearing solely on the basis of such notice and right to be heard.

Laws 1986, p. 1017, § 4; Laws 2000, p. 20, § 1; Laws 2007, Act 248, § 6, eff. May 24, 2007.

Formerly Code 1981, § 15–11–91.

Historical and Statutory Notes

The 2000 amendment, which restructured this chapter into parts and modified statutory references to reflect this restructuring, renumbered this section from § 15–11–91.

The 2007 amendment by Act 248 added the second sentence.

§ 15–11–105. Construction

Nothing in this article shall be construed as affecting the rights of a parent other than the parent who is the subject of the proceedings.

Laws 1986, p. 1017, § 4; Laws 2000, p. 20, § 1.

Formerly Code 1981, § 15–11–92.

Historical and Statutory Notes

The 2000 amendment, which restructured this chapter into parts and modified statutory references to reflect this restructuring, renumbered this section from § 15–11–92.

§ 15–11–106. Time of hearings; order of disposition

Provided that no just cause has been shown for delay, all hearings contemplated by this article shall be conducted within 90 days of the date a petition to terminate parental rights is filed pursuant to Code Section 15–11–95. Provided that no just cause has been shown by written finding of fact by the court for delay, an order of disposition shall be issued by the juvenile court no later than 30 days after the conclusion of the hearing on the petition to terminate parental rights. This Code section shall not affect the right to request a rehearing or the right to appeal the juvenile court's order.

Laws 1995, p. 1359, § 1; Laws 2000, p. 20, § 1; Laws 2005, Act 75, § 2, eff. May 2, 2005.

Formerly Code 1981, § 15–11–93.

Historical and Statutory Notes

The 2000 amendment, which restructured this chapter into parts and modified statutory references to reflect this restructuring, renumbered this section from § 15–11–93.

The 2005 amendment by Act 75 rewrote the section which had read:

"All hearings contemplated by this article shall be conducted in an expedient manner. An order of disposition shall be issued by the juvenile court no later than one year after the filing of the petition required by Code Section 15–11–95, provided that no just cause has been shown for delay. This Code section shall not affect the right to request a rehearing or the right to appeal the juvenile court's order."

Article 3

Parental Notification

§ 15–11–110. Short title

This article shall be known and may be cited as the "Parental Notification Act."

Laws 1987, p. 1013, § 2; Laws 1988, p. 13, § 15; Laws 1988, p. 661, § 1.

§ 15–11–111. Definitions

As used in this article, the term:

(1) "Abortion" means the use or prescription of any instrument, medicine, drug, or any other substance or device with the intent to terminate the pregnancy of a female known to be pregnant. The term "abortion" shall not include the use or prescription of any instrument, medicine, drug, or any other substance or device employed solely to increase the probability of a live birth, to preserve the life or health of the child after live birth, or to remove a dead unborn child who died as a result of a spontaneous abortion. The term "abortion" also shall not include the prescription or use of contraceptives.

(2) "Proper identification" means any document issued by a governmental agency containing a description of the person, the person's photograph, or both, including, but not limited to, a driver's license, an identification card authorized under Code Sections 40–5–100 through 40–5–104 or similar identification card issued by another state, a military identification card, a passport, or an appropriate work authorization issued by the United States Immigration and Customs Enforcement Division of the Department of Homeland Security.

(3) "Unemancipated minor" means any person under the age of 18 who is not or has not been married or who is under the care, custody, and control of such person's parent or parents, guardian, or the juvenile court of competent jurisdiction.

Laws 1987, p. 1013, § 2; Laws 1988, p. 661, § 1; Laws 2005, Act 400, § 1, eff. May 10, 2005; Laws 2008, Act 471, § 15, eff. May 12, 2008.

Historical and Statutory Notes

The 2005 amendment by Act 400 rewrote the section, which had read:

"As used in this article, the term:

"(1) 'Abortion' means the intentional termination of human pregnancy with an intention other than to produce a live birth or to remove a dead fetus.

"(2) 'Unemancipated minor' means any person under the age of 18 who is not or has not been married or who is under the care, custody, and control of such person's parent or parents, guardian, person standing in loco parentis, or the juvenile court of competent jurisdiction."

The 2008 amendment by Act 471 was a provision contained in a correction bill.

§ 15–11–112. Notification requirements; waiver; court order

(a) No physician or other person shall perform an abortion upon an unemancipated minor under the age of 18 years unless:

(1)(A) The minor seeking an abortion shall be accompanied by a parent or guardian who shall show proper identification and state that the parent or guardian is the lawful parent or guardian of the minor and that the parent or guardian has been notified that an abortion is to be performed on the minor;

(B) The physician or the physician's qualified agent gives at least 24 hours' actual notice, in person or by telephone, to a parent or guardian of the pending abortion and the name and address of the place where the abortion is to be performed; provided, however, that, if the person so notified indicates that he or she has been previously informed that the minor was seeking an abortion or if the person so notified has not been previously informed and he or she clearly expresses that he or she does not wish to consult with the minor, then in either event the abortion may proceed in accordance with Chapter 9A of Title 31; or

(C) The physician or a physician's qualified agent gives written notice of the pending abortion and the address of the place where the abortion is to be performed, sent by certified mail, return receipt requested with delivery confirmation, addressed to a parent or guardian at the usual place of abode of the parent or guardian. Unless proof of delivery is otherwise sooner established, such notice shall be deemed delivered 48 hours after mailing. The time of mailing shall be recorded by the physician or agent in the minor's file. The abortion may be performed 24 hours after the delivery of the notice; provided, however, that, if the person so notified certifies in writing that he or she has been previously informed that the minor was seeking an abortion or if the person so notified has not been previously informed and he or she certifies in writing that he or she does not wish to consult with the minor, then in either event the abortion may proceed in accordance with Chapter 9A of Title 31; and

(2) The minor signs a consent form stating that she consents, freely and without coercion, to the abortion.

(b) If the unemancipated minor or the physician or a physician's qualified agent, as the case may be, elects not to comply with any one of the requirements of subparagraph (a)(1)(A), (a)(1)(B), or (a)(1)(C) of this Code section, or if the parent or legal guardian of the minor cannot be located, the minor may petition, on the minor's own behalf or by next friend, any juvenile court in the state for a waiver of such requirement pursuant to the procedures provided for in Code Section 15–11–114. The juvenile court shall assist the minor or next friend in preparing the petition and notices required pursuant to this Code section. Venue shall be lawful in any county, notwithstanding Code Section 15–11–29.

(c) No abortion shall be performed unless the requirements of subparagraph (a)(1)(A), (a)(1)(B), or (a)(1)(C) of this Code section have been met or the minor has obtained a court order waiving such requirements.

Laws 1987, p. 1013, § 2; Laws 1988, p. 661, § 1; Laws 2001, p. 4, § 15; Laws 2005, Act 400, § 2, eff. May 10, 2005.

Historical and Statutory Notes

The 2001 amendment was a correction bill.

The 2005 amendment by Act 400 rewrote the section, which had read:

"(a) No physician or other person shall perform an abortion upon an unemancipated minor under the age of 18 years unless:

"(1)(A) The minor seeking an abortion shall furnish a statement, signed by a parent, guardian, or person standing in loco parentis and such minor, stating that such parent, guardian, or person standing in loco parentis is the lawful parent or guardian of such minor, or is the person standing in loco parentis of such minor, and that such parent, guardian, or person standing in loco parentis has been notified that an abortion is to be performed on such minor; or

"(B) The physician or an agent gives at least 24 hours' actual notice, in person or by telephone, to a parent, guardian, or person standing in loco parentis of the minor, of the pending abortion and the name and address of the place where the abortion is to be performed; provided, however, that, if the person so notified indicates that he or she has been previously informed that the minor was seeking an abortion or if the person so notified has not been previously informed and he or she clearly expresses that he or she does not wish to consult with the minor, then in either event the abortion may proceed immediately; or

"(C) The physician or an agent gives written notice of the pending abortion and the address of the place where the abortion is to be performed, sent by regular mail, addressed to a parent, guardian, or person standing in loco parentis of the minor at the usual place of abode of the parent, guardian, or person standing in loco parentis. Unless proof of delivery is otherwise sooner established, such notice shall be deemed delivered 48 hours after mailing. The time of mailing shall be recorded by the physician or agent in the minor's file. The abortion may be performed 24 hours after the delivery of the notice; provided, however, that, if the person so notified indicates that he or she has been previously informed that the minor was seeking an abortion or if the person so notified has not been previously informed and he or she clearly expresses that he or she does not wish to consult with the minor, then in either event the abortion may proceed immediately; and

"(2) The minor signs a consent form stating that she consents, freely and without coercion, to the abortion.

"(b) If the unemancipated minor or the physician or an agent, as the case may be, elects not to comply with any one of the notification requirements of subparagraph (a)(1)(A), (a)(1)(B), or (a)(1)(C) of this Code section, or if the parent, legal guardian, or person standing in loco parentis of such minor cannot be located, such minor may petition, on such minor's own behalf or by next friend, any juvenile court in the state for a waiver of such requirement pursuant to the procedures provided for in Code Section 15–11–114. Such juvenile court shall assist the minor or next friend in preparing the petition and notices required pursuant to this Code section. Venue shall be lawful in any county, notwithstanding Code Section 15–11–29."

§ 15–11–113. Hearing; notification of date, time and place

Notwithstanding Code Sections 15–11–38, 15–11–38.1, and 15–11–39, the unemancipated minor or next friend shall be notified of the date, time, and place of the hearing in such proceedings at the time of filing the petition. The hearing shall be held within three days of the date of filing, excluding Saturdays, Sundays, and holidays. The parents or guardian or person standing in loco parentis of the unemancipated minor shall not be served with the petition or with a summons or otherwise notified of the proceeding. If a hearing is not held within the time prescribed in this Code section, the petition shall be deemed granted.

Laws 1987, p. 1013, § 2; Laws 1988, p. 661, § 1; Laws 2001, p. 4, § 15.

Historical and Statutory Notes

The 2001 amendment was a correction bill.

§ 15–11–114. Court proceedings; appellate review

(a) An unemancipated minor may participate in proceedings in the court on such minor's own behalf and the court shall advise such minor of the right to court appointed counsel and shall provide such minor with such counsel upon request or if such minor is not already adequately represented.

(b) All court proceedings under this Code section shall be conducted in a manner to preserve the complete anonymity of the parties and shall be given such precedence over other pending matters as is necessary to ensure that a decision is reached by the court as expeditiously as is possible under the circumstances of the case. In no event shall the name, address, birth date, or social security number of such minor be disclosed.

(c) The requirement of subparagraph (a)(1)(A), (a)(1)(B), or (a)(1)(C) of Code Section 15–11–112 shall be waived if the court finds either:

(1) That the unemancipated minor is mature enough and well enough informed to make the abortion decision in consultation with her physician, independently of the wishes of such minor's parent or guardian; or

(2) That the notice to a parent or, if the minor is subject to guardianship, the legal guardian pursuant to Code Section 15–11–112 would not be in the best interests of the minor.

(d) A court that conducts proceedings under this Code section shall issue written and specific factual findings and legal conclusions supporting its decision and shall order that a record of the evidence be maintained. The juvenile court shall render its decision within 24 hours of the conclusion of the hearing and a certified copy of same shall be furnished immediately to the minor. If the juvenile court fails to render its decision within 24 hours after the conclusion of the hearing, then the petition shall be deemed granted. All juvenile court records shall be sealed in a manner which will preserve anonymity.

(e) An expedited appeal completely preserving the anonymity of the parties shall be available to any unemancipated minor to whom the court denies a waiver of notice. The appellate courts are authorized and requested to issue promptly such rules as are necessary to preserve anonymity and to ensure the expeditious disposition of procedures provided by this Code section. In no event shall the name, address, birth date, or social security number of such minor be disclosed during the expedited appeal or thereafter.

(f) No filing fees shall be required of any unemancipated minor who uses the procedures provided by this Code section.

Laws 1987, p. 1013, § 2; Laws 1988, p. 13, § 15; Laws 1988, p. 661, § 1; Laws 2005, Act 400, § 3, eff. May 10, 2005.

Historical and Statutory Notes

The 2005 amendment by Act 400, in subsec. (c), deleted "notification" preceding "requirement" in the introductory language, substituted "parent or guardian" for "parent, guardian, or person standing in loco parentis" in par. (1), and deleted "or person standing in loco parentis" following "legal guardian" in par. (2).

§ 15–11–115. Applicability of law

The requirements and procedures of this article shall apply to all unemancipated minors within this state whether or not such persons are residents of this state.

Laws 1987, p. 1013, § 2; Laws 1988, p. 661, § 1.

§ 15–11–116. Exceptions based upon medical emergency

This article shall not apply when, in the best clinical judgment of the attending physician on the facts of the case before him, a medical emergency exists that so complicates the condition of the minor as to require an immediate abortion. A person who performs an abortion as a medical emergency under the provisions of this Code section shall certify in writing the medical indications on which this judgment was based when filing such reports as are required by law.

Laws 1987, p. 1013, § 2; Laws 1988, p. 661, § 1.

§ 15–11–117. Civil and criminal immunities

Any physician or any person employed or connected with a physician, hospital, or health care facility performing abortions who acts in good faith shall be justified in relying on the representations of the unemancipated minor or of any other person providing the information required under this article. No physician or other person who furnishes professional services related to an act authorized or required by this article and who relies upon the information furnished pursuant to this article shall be held to have violated any criminal law or to be civilly liable for such reliance, provided that the physician or other person acted in good faith.

Laws 1987, p. 1013, § 2; Laws 1988, p. 661, § 1.

§ 15–11–118. Violations

Any person who violates the provisions of this article shall be guilty of a misdemeanor and any person who intentionally encourages another to provide false information pursuant to this article shall be guilty of a misdemeanor.

Laws 1987, p. 1013, § 2; Laws 1988, p. 661, § 1.

Article 4

Mental Health

§ 15–11–149. Disposition of mentally ill or mentally retarded child

(a) *Study and report.* If, at any time, the evidence indicates that a child may be suffering from mental retardation or mental illness, the court may commit the child to an appropriate institution, agency, or individual for study and report on the child's mental condition.

(b) *Determination of disability.* The juvenile court judge shall determine whether a child has been determined to be handicapped as defined in 20 U.S.C. Sections 1401(a)(1) and 1401(a)(15). If there is an Individualized Education Program (IEP) as defined in 20 U.S.C. Section 1401(a)(20), it shall be made a part of the dispositional hearing record.

(c) *Commitment.* If it appears from the study and report undertaken pursuant to subsection (a) of this Code section that the child is committable under the laws of this state as a mentally retarded or mentally ill child, the court shall order the child detained and shall proceed within ten days to commit the child to the Department of Behavioral Health and Developmental Disabilities.

(d) *Other disposition or transfer.* If the child is found not to be committable, the court shall proceed to the disposition or transfer of the child as otherwise provided by Article 1 of this chapter.

(e) *Applicability of Code Section 15–11–62.* The provisions of Code Section 15–11–62 shall not apply to any child 13 to 15 years of age who is found to be suffering from mental illness or mental retardation. Any such child shall not be committed to the Department of Corrections but shall be committed to the Department of Behavioral Health and Developmental Disabilities as provided in this Code section.

Laws 1971, p. 709, § 1; Laws 1973, p. 882, § 7; Laws 1986, p. 1017, § 1; Laws 1987, p. 3, § 15; Laws 1992, p. 1983, § 13; Laws 1994, p. 1012, § 24; Laws 2000, p. 20, § 2; Laws 2002, p. 1324, § 1–2; Laws 2006, Act 541, § 1, eff. July 1, 2006; Laws 2007, Act 18, § 15, eff. May 11, 2007; Laws 2009, Act 102, § 3–4, eff. July 1, 2009.

Formerly Code 1933, § 24A–2601; Code 1981, § 15–11–40.

Historical and Statutory Notes

The 2000 amendment, which restructured this chapter into parts and modified statutory references to reflect this restructuring, renumbered this section from § 15–11–40.

The 2002 amendment in two instances substituted "Division of Mental Health, Developmental Disabilities, and Addictive Diseases of the Department of Human Resources" for "Division of Mental Health, Mental Retardation, and Substance Abuse of the Department of Human Resources."

The 2006 revision of Article 4 of Chapter 11 by Act 541 reenacted the section without amendment.

The 2007 amendment by Act 18 was a provision contained in a correction bill.

The 2009 amendment by Act 102 substituted "Department of Behavioral Health and Developmental Disabilities" for "Division of Mental Health, Developmental Disabilities, and Addictive Diseases of the Department of Human Resources" throughout the section.

§ 15–11–150. Legislative purpose

(a) The purpose of this article is to:

(1) Set forth procedures for a determination of mental incompetency and a declaration of dependency for any child while the child is determined to be not mentally competent; and

(2) Provide a mechanism for the development and implementation of a mental competency plan for treatment, habilitation, support, or supervision, within current resources, for any child who is determined to be not mentally competent to participate in an adjudication or disposition hearing and is adjudicated dependent upon the court.

(b) The provisions of this article shall not apply to any case in which the superior court has jurisdiction pursuant to Code Section 15–11–62.

Laws 1999, p. 507, § 1; Laws 2000, p. 20, § 2; Laws 2006, Act 541, § 1, eff. July 1, 2006.

Historical and Statutory Notes

The 2000 amendment restructured this chapter into parts and modified statutory references to reflect this restructuring.

The 2006 revision of Article 4 of Chapter 11 by Act 541 reenacted the section without amendment.

§ 15–11–151. Definitions

As used in this article, the term:

(1) "Dependent" means a child who is alleged to have committed a delinquent or unruly act, is found not mentally competent to stand trial by the court, and has charges pending which have not been dismissed by the court.

(2) "Judge" means any judge, associate judge, or judge pro tempore of the court exercising jurisdiction over juvenile matters.

(3) "Mental competency plan" means an interagency treatment, habilitation, support, or supervision plan developed at an interagency meeting of state or local agency representatives, parties, and other interested persons, which is achievable within the limits of current resources, following a court's finding that a child is not mentally competent and dependent upon the court and submitted to the court for approval as part of the disposition of the dependency case. The goal of a mental competency plan is supervision, to bring or restore the child to mental competency such that he or she is able to participate in adjudication, a disposition hearing for delinquency or unruliness, or a proceeding regarding transfer to superior court.

(4) "Mental competency proceedings" means hearings conducted to determine whether a child is mentally competent to participate in adjudication, a disposition hearing, or a transfer proceeding held pursuant to this chapter.

(5) "Mentally competent" means having sufficient present ability to understand the nature and objectives of the proceedings, against himself or herself, to comprehend his or her own situation in relation to the proceedings, and to render assistance to the defense attorney in the preparation and presentation of his or her case in all adjudication, disposition, or transfer hearings held pursuant to this chapter. The child's age or immaturity may be used as the basis for determining the child's competency.

(6) "Mentally ill" means having a disorder of thought or mood which significantly impairs judgment, behavior, capacity to recognize reality, or ability to cope with the ordinary demands of life.

(7) "Mental retardation" means a state of significant subaverage general intellectual functioning existing concurrently with deficits in adaptive behavior and originating in the developmental period.

(8) "Plan manager" means a person who is under the supervision of the court and is appointed by the court to convene a meeting of all relevant parties for the purpose of developing a mental competency plan. Said person is responsible for collecting all previous histories of the child including evaluations, assessments, and school records.

(9) "Qualified examiner" means a licensed psychologist or psychiatrist who has expertise in child development and has received training in forensic evaluation procedures through formal instruction, professional supervision, or both.

Laws 1999, p. 507, § 1; Laws 2000, p. 20, § 2; Laws 2006, Act 541, § 1, eff. July 1, 2006.

Historical and Statutory Notes

The 2000 amendment, which restructured this chapter into parts and modified statutory references to reflect this restructuring, reenacted this section without change.

The 2006 amendment by Act 541, in par. (1), added "to stand trial" following "not mentally competent"; in par. (5), added "The child's age of immaturity may be used as the basis for determining the child's competency." at the end of the paragraph; redesignated pars. (6) and (7) as pars. (8) and (9) respectively, and added new pars. (6) and (7).

§ 15–11–152. Stay of proceedings regarding child who may not be mentally competent; evaluation of child's mental condition

(a) If at any time after the filing of a petition alleging delinquency or unruliness the court has reason to believe that the child named in the petition may not be mentally competent, the court on its own motion or on the motion of the attorney representing the child, any guardian ad litem for the child, the child's parent or legal guardian, or the attorney representing the state may stay all delinquency or unruly conduct proceedings relating to that petition and order an evaluation of the child's mental condition. Prior to the administration of any such evaluation, the court shall appoint an attorney to represent the child if the child is not yet represented by counsel. All time limits under Article 1 of this chapter for adjudication and disposition of that petition are tolled during the evaluation, adjudication, and disposition phases of the mental competency proceeding.

(b) An evaluation ordered under subsection (a) of this Code section shall be conducted by a qualified examiner who shall consider whether the child is mentally competent. If the qualified examiner determines that the child is not competent, the qualified examiner shall complete a full mental health evaluation, study, and report pursuant to Code Section 15–11–149. If the basis for questioning the child's mental competency concerns a problem with intellectual functioning, mental retardation, mental illness, maturity, or a learning disability, the qualified examiner must be a psychiatrist or licensed psychologist. The juvenile court shall provide the qualified examiner with any law enforcement or court records necessary for understanding the petition alleging delinquency or unruliness. The attorney for the child may provide the qualified examiner with any records from any other available sources that are deemed necessary for the mental competency evaluation.

(c) A qualified examiner who conducts an evaluation under subsection (b) of this Code section shall submit a written report to the court, within 30 days from receipt of the court order requiring the evaluation, which report shall contain the following:

(1) The reason for the evaluation;

(2) The evaluation procedures used, including any psychometric instruments administered, any records reviewed, and the identity of any persons interviewed;

(3) Any available pertinent background information;

(4) The results of a mental status exam, including the diagnosis and description of any psychiatric symptoms, cognitive deficiency, or both;

(5) A description of abilities and deficits in the following mental competency functions:

(A) The ability to understand and appreciate the nature and object of the proceedings;

(B) The ability to comprehend his or her situation in relation to the proceedings; and

(C) The ability to render assistance to the defense attorney in the preparation of his or her case;

(6) An opinion regarding the potential significance of the child's mental competency, strengths, and deficits;

(7) An opinion regarding whether or not the child should be considered mentally competent; and

(8) A specific statement for the basis for a determination of incompetence.

(d) If, in the opinion of the qualified examiner, the child should not be considered mentally competent, the qualified examiner shall complete a full mental health evaluation and report pursuant to Code Section 15–11–149, and such report shall also include the following:

(1) A diagnosis made as to whether there is a substantial probability that the child will attain mental competency to participate in adjudication, a disposition hearing, and a transfer hearing in the foreseeable future;

(2) A recommendation as to the appropriate treatment setting and whether residential or nonresidential treatment is required or appropriate;

(3) Where appropriate, recommendations for the general level and type of remediation necessary for significant deficits; and

(4) Where appropriate, recommendations for modifications of court procedure which may help compensate for mental competency weaknesses.

(e) The court in its discretion may grant the qualified examiner an extension in filing the evaluation report.

(f) Copies of the written evaluation report shall be provided by the court to the attorney representing the child, the attorney representing the state, the prosecuting attorney or a member of his or her staff, and any guardian ad litem for the child no later than five working days after receipt of the report by the court.

(g) Upon a showing of good cause by any party or upon the court's own motion, the court may order additional examinations by other qualified examiners. In no event shall more than one examination be conducted by a qualified examiner employed by the Department of Behavioral Health and Developmental Disabilities.

(h) No statement made by a child or information obtained in the course of an evaluation, hearing, or other proceeding provided for in this Code section, whether the evaluation is with or without the consent of the child, shall be admitted into evidence against the child in any future proceeding in the state's case-in-chief.

Laws 1999, p. 507, § 1; Laws 2000, p. 20, § 2; Laws 2006, Act 541, § 1, eff. July 1, 2006; Laws 2009, Act 102, § 3–2, eff. July 1, 2009.

Historical and Statutory Notes

The 2000 amendment, which restructured this chapter into parts and modified statutory references to reflect this restructuring, reenacted this section without change.

The 2006 amendment by Act 541, in subsec. (a), added "the child's parent or legal guardian," after "guardian ad litem for the child," and added "Prior to the administration of any such evaluation, the court shall appoint an attorney to represent the child if the child is not yet represented by counsel." following "child's mental condition."; in subsec. (b), added "If the qualified examiner determines that the child is not competent, the qualified examiner shall complete a full mental health evaluation, study, and report pursuant to Code Section 15–11–149." following "child is mentally competent.", added "mental illness, maturity," following "mental retardation,", and deleted "probation officers of" preceding "juvenile court shall provide"; in subsec. (c), added new par. (8); rewrote subsec. (d); and in subsec. (f), substituted "prosecuting attorney" for "district attorney". Prior to amendment, subsec. (d) had read:

"(d) If, in the opinion of the qualified examiner, the child should not be considered mentally competent, the evaluation report shall also include the following:

"(1) A diagnosis made as to whether there is a substantial probability that the child will attain mental competency to participate in adjudication, a disposition hearing, and a transfer hearing in the foreseeable future;

"(2) Recommendations for the general level and type of remediation necessary for significant deficits; and

"(3) Recommendations for modifications of court procedure which may help compensate for mental competency weaknesses."

The 2009 amendment by Act 102 substituted "Department of Behavioral Health and Developmental Disabilities" for "Department of Human Resources" throughout the section.

§ 15–11–153. Mental competency hearings; findings by court

(a) A hearing to determine mental competency shall be conducted within 60 days after the initial court order for evaluation. At least ten days' prior written notice of the hearing shall be transmitted to the child, any parent, guardian, or other legal custodian of the child, any guardian ad litem for the child, the attorney representing the child, and the attorney representing the state. Ten days' prior written notice of the hearing shall be served on the prosecuting attorney for all mental competency proceedings in which the prosecuting attorney, or a member of the prosecuting attorney's staff, may participate. The hearing may be continued by the court for good cause shown.

(b) The burden of proving that the child is not mentally competent shall be on the child. The standard of proof necessary for proving mental incompetency shall be a preponderance of the evidence.

(c) At the hearing to determine mental competency, the attorney representing the child and the attorney representing the state shall have the right to:

(1) Present evidence;

(2) Call and examine witnesses;

(3) Cross-examine witnesses; and

(4) Present arguments.

The qualified examiner appointed by the court shall be considered the court's witness and shall be subject to cross-examination by both the attorney representing the child and the attorney representing the state.

(d) The court's findings of fact shall be based on any evaluations of the child's mental condition conducted by qualified examiners appointed by the court and any evaluations of the child's mental condition conducted by independent evaluators hired by the parties and any additional evidence presented.

(e) If the court finds that the child is mentally competent, the proceedings which have been suspended shall be resumed and the time limits under Article 1 of this chapter for adjudication and disposition of the petition shall begin to run from the date of the order finding the child mentally competent.

(f) If the court finds that the child is not mentally competent, the child shall be adjudicated dependent by the court. At the time the child is adjudicated dependent upon the court, the court shall appoint a guardian ad litem to represent the best interests of the child if a guardian ad litem has not been appointed previously.

(g) All court orders determining incompetency shall include specific written findings by the court as to the nature of the incompetency and whether the child requires a secure or nonsecure treatment.

(h) Copies of the court's findings shall be transmitted to the same parties to whom notice of the hearing was provided within ten days following the issuance of those findings.

Laws 1999, p. 507, § 1; Laws 2000, p. 20, § 2; Laws 2006, Act 541, § 1, eff. July 1, 2006.

Historical and Statutory Notes

The 2000 amendment, which restructured this chapter into parts and modified statutory references to reflect this restructuring, reenacted this section without change.

The 2006 amendment by Act 541 rewrote the section which had read:

"(a) A hearing of mental competency shall be conducted within 60 days after the initial court order for evaluation. At least ten days' prior written notice of the hearing shall be transmitted to the child, any parent, guardian, or other legal custodian of the child, any guardian ad litem for the child, the attorney representing the child, and the attorney representing the state. Ten days' prior written notice of the hearing shall be served on the district attorney, for all mental competency proceedings in which the district attorney, or a member of the district attorney's staff, may participate. The hearing may be continued by the court for good cause shown.

"(b) At the hearing of mental competency, the attorney representing the child and the attorney representing the state shall have the right to:

"(1) Present evidence;

"(2) Call and examine witnesses;

"(3) Cross-examine witnesses; and

"(4) Present arguments.

"The qualified examiner appointed by the court shall be considered the court's witness and shall be subject to cross-examination by both the attorney representing the child and the attorney representing the state.

"(c) The court's findings of fact shall be based on any evaluations of the child's mental condition conducted by qualified examiners appointed by the court and any evaluations of the child's mental condition conducted by independent evaluators hired by the parties. The burden of proving that the child is not mentally competent shall be on the child. The standard of proof necessary for proving mental incompetency shall be a preponderance of the evidence. Copies of the court's findings shall be transmitted to the same parties to whom notice of the hearing was provided within ten days following the issuance of those findings.

"(d) If the court finds that the child is mentally competent, the proceedings which have been suspended shall be resumed and the time limits under Article 1 of this chapter for adjudication and disposition of the petition shall begin to run from the date of the order finding the child mentally competent.

"(e) If the court finds that the child is not mentally competent, the child may be adjudicated dependent by the court. If the court determines that a child alleged to have committed an act which is a misdemeanor if committed by an adult or an unruly act is not mentally competent, and the child is adjudicated dependent, the court may dismiss the petition without prejudice. A child who is thus found not to be mentally competent shall not be subject to discretionary transfer to superior court, adjudication, disposition, or modification of disposition as long as such mental incompetency exists. At the time the child is adjudicated dependent upon the court, the court shall appoint a guardian ad litem to represent the best interests of the child if a guardian ad litem has not been appointed previously."

§ 15–11–153.1. Finding of mental incompetency; dismissal of petition; transfer to state court

(a) If the court determines that a child is mentally incompetent, is dependent, or is alleged to have committed an unruly act or an act which would be a misdemeanor if committed by an adult, the court may dismiss the petition without prejudice.

(b) A child who is found to be mentally incompetent shall not be subject to discretionary transfer to superior court, adjudication, disposition, or modification of disposition provided that the mental incompetency exists.

Laws 2006, Act 541, § 1, eff. July 1, 2006.

Historical and Statutory Notes

In 2006, the Code Commission, in subsec. (a), inserted "or" following ", is dependent,". See § 28–9–5.

§ 15–11–153.2. Transfer of proceedings; jurisdiction

(a) If at any time following an adjudication of dependency, the court determines that the child is a resident of a county of this state other than the county in which the court sits, the court may transfer the proceeding to the county of the child's residence unless the act alleged would be a felony if committed by an adult.

(b) When any case is transferred pursuant to this Code section, certified copies of all legal, social history, health, or mental health records pertaining to the case on file with the clerk of the court shall accompany the transfer. Compliance with this Code section shall terminate jurisdiction in the sending court and initiate jurisdiction in the receiving court.

(c) If the child's mental competency is restored, jurisdiction of the case may be returned to the sending court.

Laws 2006, Act 541, § 1, eff. July 1, 2006.

§ 15–11–154. Plan manager; mental competency plan

(a) Upon an adjudication of dependency, the court having jurisdiction of the case shall appoint a plan manager who may be any guardian ad litem for the child or may be any other person who is under the supervision of the court. The person so appointed shall submit a mental competency plan to the court within 30 days of the court's adjudication of dependency. That plan shall include the following:

(1) The specific deficits the plan is attempting to address, including supervision, mental competency, or mental competency restoration;

(2) An outline of the specific provisions for supervision of the child for protection of the community and the child;

(3) An outline of a plan designed to provide for treatment, habilitation, support, or supervision services in the least restrictive environment achievable within the limits of current resources;

(4) If the plan recommends treatment in a secure environment, certification by the plan manager that all other appropriate community based treatment options have been exhausted; and

(5) Identification of all parties, including the child, agency representatives, and other persons responsible for each element of the plan.

The court in its discretion may grant the plan manager an extension in filing the mental competency plan.

(b)(1) The mental competency plan shall be developed at a meeting of all relevant parties convened by the plan manager. The plan manager shall request that the following persons attend the meeting:

(A) Any parent, guardian, or other legal custodian of the child;

(B) The attorney representing the child;

(C) The attorney representing the state;

(D) Any guardian ad litem of the child;

(E) Mental health or mental retardation representatives;

(F) Any probation officer or caseworker who works with the child;

(G) A representative from the child's school; and

(H) Any family member of the child who has shown an interest and involvement in the child's well-being.

(2) The plan manager may request that other relevant persons attend the mental competency plan meeting including but not limited to the following:

(A) A representative from the Division of Public Health of the Department of Community Health;

(B) A child protective services worker; and

(C) Representatives of the public and private resources to be utilized in the plan.

(3) The plan manager shall be responsible for collecting all previous histories of the child, including but not limited to previous evaluations, assessments, and school records, and for making such histories available for consideration by the persons at the meeting.

(4) Before the disposition hearing and review hearings, the plan manager shall be responsible for convening a meeting of all parties and representatives of all agencies.

(5) The plan manager and persons enumerated in paragraph (1) of subsection (b) of this Code section shall identify to the court any person who should provide testimony at such hearing.

(6) The plan manager shall be responsible for monitoring the competency plan, presenting to the court amendments to such plan as needed, and presenting evidence to the court for the reapproval of such plan at subsequent review hearings.

Laws 1999, p. 507, § 1; Laws 2000, p. 20, § 2; Laws 2006, Act 541, § 1, eff. July 1, 2006; Laws 2010, Act 624, § 15, eff. June 3, 2010.

Historical and Statutory Notes

The 2000 amendment, which restructured this chapter into parts and modified statutory references to reflect this restructuring, reenacted this section without change.

The 2006 amendment by Act 541 rewrote the section which had read:

"(a) If at any time following an adjudication of dependency, the court determines that the child is a resident of a county of this state other than the county in which the court sits, the court may transfer the proceeding to the county of the child's residence unless the act alleged would be a felony if committed by an adult. When any case is transferred pursuant to this Code section, certified copies of all legal, social history, health, or mental health records pertaining to the case on file with the clerk of the court shall accompany the transfer. Compliance with this Code section shall terminate jurisdiction in the sending court and initiate jurisdiction in the receiving court. If the child's mental competency is restored, jurisdiction of the case may be returned to the sending court.

"(b) Upon an adjudication of dependency, the court having jurisdiction of the case shall appoint a plan manager who may be any guardian ad litem for the child or may be any other person who is under the supervision of the court. The person so appointed shall submit a mental competency plan to the court within 30 days of the court's adjudication of dependency. That plan shall include the following:

"(1) The specific deficits the plan is attempting to address, including supervision, mental competency, or mental competency restoration;

"(2) An outline of the specific provisions for supervision of the child for protection of the community and the child;

"(3) An outline of a plan designed to provide for treatment, habilitation, support, or supervision services achievable within the limits of current resources; and

"(4) Identification of all parties, including the child, agency representatives, and other persons responsible for each element of the plan.

"The court in its discretion may grant the plan manager an extension in filing the mental competency plan.

"(c)(1) The mental competency plan shall be developed at a meeting of all relevant parties convened by the plan manager. The plan manager shall request that the following persons attend the meeting:

"(A) Any parent, guardian, or other legal custodian of the child;

"(B) The attorney representing the child;

"(C) The attorney representing the state;

"(D) Any guardian ad litem of the child;

"(E) Mental health or mental retardation representatives;

"(F) Any probation officer or caseworker who works with the child; and

"(G) A representative from the child's school.

"(2) The plan manager may request that other relevant persons attend the mental competency plan meeting including but not limited to the following:

"(A) A representative from the division of public health;

"(B) A child protective services worker;

"(C) Representatives of the public and private resources to be utilized in the plan; and

"(D) Any family member of the child who has shown an interest and involvement in the child's well-being.

"(3) The plan manager shall be responsible for collecting all previous histories of the child, including but not limited to previous evaluations, assessments, and school records, and for making such histories available for consideration by the persons at the meeting."

The 2010 amendment by Act 624 was a provision contained in a correction bill.

§ 15–11–155. Disposition hearing on mental competency plan; commitment of child to certain agencies; continuing jurisdiction

(a) The court shall hold a disposition hearing for the purpose of approving the mental competency plan within 30 days after the mental competency plan has been submitted to the court. Thereafter, the court shall hold a hearing for the purpose of reviewing the child's condition and approving the mental competency plan every six months during the child's dependency.

(b) The persons required to be notified of the mental competency disposition hearing and witnesses identified by the plan manager shall be given at least ten days' prior notice of the disposition hearing and any subsequent hearing to review the child's condition and shall be afforded an opportunity to be heard at any such hearing. The victim, if any, of the child's delinquent or unruly act shall also be provided with the same ten days' prior notice regarding any such hearing and shall be afforded an opportunity to be heard and to present a victim impact form to the court at any such hearing. The judge shall make a determination regarding sequestration of witnesses in order to protect the privileges and confidentiality rights of the child.

(c) At the disposition hearing, the court shall enter an order incorporating a mental competency plan as part of the disposition. At the time of disposition, a child who has been adjudicated a dependent of the court shall be placed in an appropriate treatment setting. If a dependent child is housed in a detention or youth development facility at the time of disposition, such child shall be moved to an appropriate treatment setting within five business days.

(d) If the court determines at any time that the child will not become competent to proceed, the court may dismiss the delinquency petition. If, at the end of the two-year period following the date of the order of incompetence, the child has not attained competence and there is no substantial evidence that the child will attain competence within a year, the court shall dismiss the delinquency petition. If appropriate, the court may order that civil commitment proceedings be initiated. Such proceedings shall be instituted not less than 60 days prior to the dismissal of the delinquency petition.

(e) The prosecuting attorney or a member of the prosecuting attorney's staff may seek civil commitment pursuant to Chapters 3 and 4 of Title 37. If, during the disposition hearing or any subsequent review hearing, the court determines that the child meets criteria for commitment and that services are available under the relevant laws for commitment to any agency or agencies for treatment, habilitation, support, or supervision, the court may commit the child to an appropriate agency or agencies for services under applicable law.

(f) At any time, in the event of a change in circumstances regarding the child, the court on its own motion or on the motion of the attorney representing the child, any guardian ad litem for the child, the attorney for the state, or the plan manager may set a hearing for review of the mental competency plan and any proposed amendments to that plan. The court may issue an appropriate order incorporating an amended mental competency plan.

(g) At the disposition hearing and at every review hearing, the court shall consider whether the petition alleging delinquency or unruliness should be withdrawn, maintained, or dismissed, without prejudice, upon grounds other than the child's not being mentally competent. If the court dismisses the petition, the state may seek to refile petitions alleging felonies if the child is later determined to be mentally competent. The state may also seek transfer to superior court if the child is later determined to be mentally competent.

(h)(1) If the court determines that a child alleged to have committed an act which is a felony if committed by an adult is not mentally competent and the child is adjudicated as a dependent, the court shall retain jurisdiction of the child for up to two years after the date of the order of adjudication. The order may be extended for additional two-year periods as provided in subsection (a) of Code Section 15–11–58.1.

(2) If the court determines that a child alleged to have committed an act which is a misdemeanor if committed by an adult or an unruly act is not mentally competent and the child is adjudicated as a dependent, the court shall retain jurisdiction of the child for up to 120 days following the disposition order incorporating the mental competency plan. The order may not be extended by the court.

(i) If the court finds that a child is not mentally competent to stand trial, any party may file at any time a motion for a rehearing on the issue of the child's mental incompetency. The court shall grant such motion upon a showing by the moving party that there are reasonable grounds to believe that the child is now mentally competent. If this motion is granted, the court shall proceed as provided in Code Sections 15–11–152, 15–11–153, 15–11–153.1, 15–11–153.2, 15–11–154, and this Code section and shall enter findings of fact as to the child's mental competency.

(j) If a child is under a mental competency plan when the child reaches the age of 18, the plan manager shall make a referral to appropriate adult services.

Laws 1999, p. 507, § 1; Laws 2000, p. 20, § 2; Laws 2005, Act 19, § 15, eff. April 7, 2005; Laws 2006, Act 541, § 1, eff. July 1, 2006; Laws 2010, Act 403, § 3, eff. July 1, 2010.

Historical and Statutory Notes

The 2000 amendment restructured this chapter into parts and modified statutory references to reflect this restructuring.

The 2005 amendment by Act 19 was a provision contained in a correction bill.

The 2006 amendment by Act 541 rewrote the section which had read:

"(a) The court shall hold a disposition hearing for the purpose of approving the mental competency plan within 30 days after the mental competency plan has been submitted to the court. Thereafter, the court shall hold a hearing for the purpose of reviewing the child's condition and approving the mental competency plan every six months during the child's dependency. Before the disposition hearing and any review hearings, the plan manager shall be responsible for convening a meeting of all parties, representatives of all agencies, and other persons responsible for the plan and for identifying to the court any persons who should provide testimony at such hearing.

"(b) The persons required to be notified of the mental competency hearing and witnesses identified by the plan manager shall be given at least ten days' prior notice of the disposition hearing and any subsequent hearing to review the child's condition and shall be afforded an opportunity to be heard at any such hearing. The victim, if any, of the child's delinquent or unruly act shall also be provided with the same ten days' prior notice regarding any such hearing and shall be afforded an opportunity to be heard and to present a victim impact statement to the court at any such hearing. The judge shall make a determination regarding sequestration of witnesses in order to protect the privileges and confidentiality rights of the child.

"(c) At the disposition hearing, the court shall enter an order incorporating a mental competency plan as part of the disposition. If, upon subsequent review, the court determines that the child may be mentally competent, the court shall proceed as provided in Code Sections 15–11–152, 15–11–153, and 15–11–154 and enter findings of fact as to the child's mental competency.

"(d) At any time, in the event of a change in circumstances regarding the child, the court on its own motion or on the motion of the attorney representing the child, any guardian ad litem for the child, the attorney for the state, or the plan manager may set a hearing for review of the mental competency plan and any proposed amendments to that plan. The court may issue an appropriate order incorporating an amended mental competency plan.

"(e) At the disposition hearing and at every review hearing, the court shall consider whether the petition alleging delinquency or unruliness should be withdrawn, maintained, or dismissed, without prejudice, upon grounds other than the child's not being mentally competent. If the court dismisses the petition, the state may seek to refile petitions alleging felonies if the child is later determined to be mentally competent. The state may also seek transfer to superior court if the child is later determined to be mentally competent.

"(f) The district attorney or a member of his or her staff may seek civil commitment pursuant to Chapters 3 and 4 of Title 37. If, during the disposition hearing or any subsequent review hearing, the court determines that the child meets criteria for commitment and that services are available under the relevant Code provisions for commitment to any agency or agencies for treatment, habilitation, support, or supervision, the court may commit the child to an appropriate agency or agencies for services under applicable law.

"(g)(1) If the court determines that a child alleged to have committed an act which is a felony if committed by an adult is not mentally competent and the child is adjudicated as a dependent, the court shall retain jurisdiction of the child for up to two years after the date of the order of adjudication. The order may be extended for additional two-year periods as provided in subsection (a) of Code Section 15–11–58.1.

"(2) If the court determines that a child alleged to have committed an act which is a misdemeanor if committed by an adult or an unruly act is not mentally competent and the child is adjudicated as a dependent, the court shall retain jurisdiction of the child for up to 120 days following the disposition order incorporating the mental competency plan. The order may not be extended by the court.

"(h) If the court finds that a child is not mentally competent to stand trial, any party may file at any time a motion for a rehearing on the issue of the child's mental incompetency. The court shall grant such motion upon a showing by the moving party that there are reasonable grounds to believe that the child is now mentally competent. If this motion is granted, the court shall proceed as provided in Code Sections 15–11–152, 15–11–153, 15–11–154, and this Code section and shall enter findings of fact as to the child's mental competency.

"(i) If a child is under a mental competency plan when the child reaches the age of 18, the plan manager shall make a referral to appropriate adult services."

The 2010 amendment by Act 403, in subsec. (b), substituted "victim impact form" for "victim impact statement".

Article 5

Child Advocate for the Protection of Children

§ 15-11-170. Short title; legislative intent

(a) This article shall be known and may be cited as the "Georgia Child Advocate for the Protection of Children Act."

(b) In keeping with this article's purpose of assisting, protecting, and restoring the security of children whose well-being is threatened, it is the intent of the General Assembly that the mission of protection of the children of this state should have the greatest legislative and executive priority. Recognizing that the needs of children must be attended to in a timely manner and that more aggressive action should be taken to protect children from abuse and neglect, the General Assembly creates the Office of the Child Advocate for the Protection of Children to provide independent oversight of persons, organizations, and agencies responsible for providing services to or caring for children who are victims of child abuse and neglect, or whose domestic situation requires intervention by the state. The Office of the Child Advocate for the Protection of Children will provide children with an avenue through which to seek relief when their rights are violated by state officials and agents entrusted with their protection and care.

Laws 2000, p. 243, § 1.

§ 15-11-171. Definitions

As used in this article, the term:

(1) "Advocate" or "child advocate" means the Child Advocate for the Protection of Children established under Code Section 15-11-172.

(2) "Agency" shall have the same meaning and application as provided for in paragraph (1) of subsection (a) of Code Section 50-14-1.

(3) "Child" or "children" means an individual receiving protective services from the division, for whom the division has an open case file, or who has been, or whose siblings, parents, or other caretakers have been the subject of a report to the division within the previous five years.

(4) "Department" means the Department of Human Services.

(5) "Division" means the Division of Family and Children Services of the Department of Human Services.

Laws 2000, p. 243, § 1; Laws 2009, Act 102, § 2-2, eff. July 1, 2009.

Historical and Statutory Notes

The 2009 amendment by Act 102 substituted "Department of Human Services" for "Department of Human Resources" throughout the section.

§ 15-11-172. Creation of Office of Child Advocate for the Protection of Children; administrative assignment; staff and personnel; contracts

(a) There is created the Office of the Child Advocate for the Protection of Children. The Governor, by executive order, shall create a nominating committee which shall consider nominees for the position of the advocate and shall make a recommendation to the Governor. Such person shall have knowledge of the child welfare system, the juvenile justice system, and the legal system and shall be qualified by training and experience to perform the duties of the office as set forth in this article.

(b) The advocate shall be appointed by the Governor from a list of at least three names submitted by the nominating committee for a term of three years and until his or her successor is appointed and qualified and may be reappointed. The salary of the advocate shall not be less than $60,000.00 per year, shall be fixed by the Governor, and shall come from funds appropriated for the purposes of the advocate.

(c) The Office of the Child Advocate for the Protection of Children shall be assigned to the Office of Planning and Budget for administrative purposes only, as described in Code Section 50-4-3.

(d) The advocate may appoint such staff as may be deemed necessary to effectively fulfill the purposes of this article, within the limitations of the funds available for the purposes of the advocate. The duties of the staff may include the duties and powers of the advocate if performed under the direction of the advocate. The advocate and his or her staff shall receive such reimbursement for travel and other expenses as is normally allowed to state employees, from funds appropriated for the purposes of the advocate.

(e) The advocate shall have the authority to contract with experts in fields including but not limited to medicine, psychology, education, child development, juvenile justice, mental health, and child welfare, as needed to support the work of the advocate, utilizing funds appropriated for the purposes of the advocate.

(f) Notwithstanding any other provision of state law, the advocate shall act independently of any state official, department, or agency in the performance of his or her duties.

(g) The advocate or his or her designee shall be an ex officio member of the State-wide Child Abuse Prevention Panel.

Laws 2000, p. 243, § 1.

§ 15-11-173. Duties of advocate

The advocate shall perform the following duties:

(1) Identify, receive, investigate, and seek the resolution or referral of complaints made by or on behalf of children concerning any act, omission to act, practice, policy, or procedure of an agency or any contractor or agent thereof that may adversely affect the health, safety, or welfare of the children;

(2) Refer complaints involving abused children to appropriate regulatory and law enforcement agencies;

(3) Coordinate and supervise the work of the Georgia Child Fatality Review Panel created by Code Section 19-15-4 and provide such staffing and administrative support to the panel as may be necessary to enable the panel to carry out its statutory duties;

(4) Report the death of any child to the chairperson of the child fatality review subcommittee of the county in which such child resided at the time of death, unless the advocate has knowledge that such death has been reported by the county medical examiner or coroner, pursuant to Code Section 19-15-3, and to provide such subcommittee access to any records of the advocate relating to such child;

(5) Provide periodic reports on the work of the Office of the Child Advocate for the Protection of Children, including but not limited to an annual written report for the Governor and the General Assembly and other persons, agencies, and organizations deemed appropriate. Such reports shall include recommendations for changes in policies and procedures to improve the health, safety, and welfare of children and shall be made expeditiously in order to timely influence public policy;

(6) Establish policies and procedures necessary for the Office of the Child Advocate for the Protection of Children to accomplish the purposes of this article including without limitation providing the division with a form of notice of availability

of the Office of the Child Advocate for the Protection of Children. Such notice shall be posted prominently, by the division, in division offices and in facilities receiving public moneys for the care and placement of children and shall include information describing the Office of the Child Advocate for the Protection of Children and procedures for contacting that office; and

(7) Convene quarterly meetings with organizations, agencies, and individuals who work in the area of child protection to seek opportunities to collaborate and improve the status of children in Georgia.

Laws 2000, p. 243, § 1; Laws 2008, Act 562, § 3, eff. July 1, 2008.

Historical and Statutory Notes

The 2008 amendment by Act 562 redesignated pars. (3) through (6) as pars. (4) through (7), and added new par. (3).

§ 15–11–174. Rights and powers of advocate; motions to quash subpoenas; judicial actions

(a) The advocate shall have the following rights and powers:

(1) To communicate privately, by mail or orally, with any child and with each child's parent or guardian;

(2) To have access to all records and files of the division concerning or relating to a child, and to have access, including the right to inspect, copy, and subpoena records held by clerks of the various courts, law enforcement agencies, service providers, including medical and mental health, and institutions, public or private, with whom a particular child has been either voluntarily or otherwise placed for care or from whom the child has received treatment within the state. To the extent any such information provides the names and addresses of individuals who are the subject of any confidential proceeding or statutory confidentiality provisions, such names and addresses or related information which has the effect of identifying such individuals shall not be released to the public without the consent of such individuals. The Office of the Child Advocate for the Protection of Children is bound by all confidentiality safeguards provided in Code Sections 49–5–40 and 49–5–44. Anyone wishing to obtain records held by the Office of the Child Advocate shall petition the original agency of record where such records exist;

(3) To enter and inspect any and all institutions, facilities, and residences, public and private, where a child has been placed by a court or the division and is currently residing. Upon entering such a place, the advocate shall notify the administrator or, in the absence of the administrator, the person in charge of the facility, before speaking to any children. After notifying the administrator or the person in charge of the facility, the advocate may communicate privately and confidentially with children in the facility, individually or in groups, or the advocate may inspect the physical plant. To the extent possible, entry and investigation provided by this Code section shall be conducted in a manner which will not significantly disrupt the provision of services to children;

(4) To apply to the Governor to bring legal action in the nature of a writ of mandamus or application for injunction pursuant to Code Section 45–15–18 to require an agency to take or refrain from taking any action required or prohibited by law involving the protection of children;

(5) To apply for and accept grants, gifts, and bequests of funds from other states, federal and interstate agencies, independent authorities, private firms, individuals, and foundations for the purpose of carrying out the lawful responsibilities of the Office of the Child Advocate for the Protection of Children;

(6) When less formal means of resolution do not achieve appropriate results, to pursue remedies provided by this article on behalf of children for the purpose of effectively carrying out the provisions of this article; and

(7) To engage in programs of public education and legislative advocacy concerning the needs of children requiring the intervention, protection, and supervision of courts and state and county agencies.

(b)(1) Upon issuance by the advocate of a subpoena in accordance with this article for law enforcement investigative records concerning an ongoing investigation, the subpoenaed party may move a court with appropriate jurisdiction to quash said subpoena.

(2) The court shall order a hearing on the motion to quash within five days of the filing of the motion to quash, which hearing may be continued for good cause shown by any party or by the court on its own motion. Subject to any right to an open hearing in contempt proceedings, such hearing shall be closed to the extent necessary to prevent disclosure of the identity of a confidential source; disclosure of confidential investigative or prosecution material which would endanger the life or physical safety of any person or persons; or disclosure of the existence of confidential surveillance, investigation, or grand jury materials or testimony in an ongoing criminal investigation or prosecution. Records, motions, and orders relating to a motion to quash shall be kept sealed by the court to the extent and for the time necessary to prevent public disclosure of such matters, materials, evidence, or testimony.

(c) The court shall, at or before the time specified in the subpoena for compliance therewith, enter an order:

(1) Enforcing the subpoena as issued;

(2) Quashing or modifying the subpoena if it is unreasonable and oppressive; or

(3) Conditioning enforcement of the subpoena on the advocate maintaining confidential any evidence, testimony, or other information obtained from law enforcement or prosecution sources pursuant to the subpoena until the time the criminal investigation and prosecution are concluded. Unless otherwise ordered by the court, an investigation or prosecution shall be deemed to be concluded when the information becomes subject to public inspection pursuant to Code Section 50–18–72. The court shall include in its order written findings of fact and conclusions of law.

Laws 2000, p. 243, § 1; Laws 2001, p. 859, § 1; Laws 2002, p. 415, § 15; Laws 2007, Act 248, § 1, eff. May 24, 2007.

Historical and Statutory Notes

The 2001 amendment designated the existing section as subsec. (a) and added subsecs. (b) and (c).

The 2002 amendment was a correction bill.

The 2007 amendment by Act 248, in par. (2) of subsec. (a), substituted a period for the semicolon following "such individuals" and added "The Office of the Child Advocate for the Protection of Children is bound by all confidentiality safeguards provided in Code Sections 49–5–40 and 49–5–44. Anyone wishing to obtain records held by the Office of the Child Advocate shall petition the original agency of record where such records exist;".

§ 15–11–175. Discrimination or retaliation prohibited against persons making complaints or providing information

(a) No person shall discriminate or retaliate in any manner against any child, parent or guardian of a child, employee of a facility, agency, institution or other type of provider, or any other person because of the making of a complaint or providing of information in good faith to the advocate, or willfully interfere with the advocate in the performance of his or her official duties.

(b) Any person violating subsection (a) of this Code section shall be guilty of a misdemeanor.

Laws 2000, p. 243, § 1.

§ 15–11–176. Investigation of complaints

The advocate shall be authorized to request an investigation by the Georgia Bureau of Investigation of any complaint of criminal misconduct involving a child.

Laws 2000, p. 243, § 1.

§ 15–11–177. Child Advocate Advisory Committee

(a) There is established a Child Advocate Advisory Committee. The advisory committee shall consist of:

(1) One representative of a not for profit children's agency appointed by the Governor;

(2) One representative of a for profit children's agency appointed by the President of the Senate;

(3) One pediatrician appointed by the Speaker of the House of Representatives;

(4) One social worker with experience and knowledge of child protective services who is not employed by the state appointed by the Governor;

(5) One psychologist appointed by the President of the Senate;

(6) One attorney appointed by the Speaker of the House of Representatives from the Children and the Courts Committee of the State Bar of Georgia; and

(7) One juvenile court judge appointed by the Chief Justice of the Supreme Court of Georgia.

Each member of the advisory committee shall serve a two-year term and until the appointment and qualification of such member's successor. Appointments to fill vacancies in such offices shall be filled in the same manner as the original appointment.

(b) The advisory committee shall meet a minimum of three times a year with the advocate and his or her staff to review and assess the following:

(1) Patterns of treatment and service for children;

(2) Policy implications; and

(3) Necessary systemic improvements.

The advisory committee shall also provide for an annual evaluation of the effectiveness of the Office of the Child Advocate for the Protection of Children.

Laws 2000, p. 243, § 1.

Article 6

Emancipation of Minors

§ 15–11–200. Definitions

As used in this article, the term:

(1) "Emancipation" means termination of the rights of the parents to the custody, control, services, and earnings of a minor.

(2) "Minor" means a person who is at least 16 but less than 18 years of age.

(3) "Parents" has the same meaning as set forth in Code Section 15–11–2.

Laws 2006, Act 466, § 1, eff. July 1, 2006.

§ 15–11–201. Conditions under which emancipation may occur

(a) Emancipation may occur by operation of law or pursuant to a petition filed by a minor with the juvenile court as provided in this article.

(b) An emancipation occurs by operation of law:

(1) When a minor is validly married;

(2) When a person reaches the age of 18 years; or

(3) During the period when the minor is on active duty with the armed forces of the United States.

(c) An emancipation occurs by court order pursuant to a petition filed by a minor with the juvenile court as provided in Code Sections 15–11–202 through 15–11–207.

Laws 2006, Act 466, § 1, eff. July 1, 2006.

§ 15–11–202. Petition

A minor seeking emancipation shall file a petition for emancipation in the juvenile court in the county where the minor resides. The petition shall be signed and verified by the minor, and shall include:

(1) The minor's full name and birth date, and the county and state where the minor was born;

(2) A certified copy of the minor's birth certificate;

(3) The name and last known address of the minor's parents or guardian, and if no parent or guardian can be found, the name and address of the minor's nearest living relative residing within this state;

(4) The minor's present address and length of residency at that address;

(5) A declaration by the minor indicating that he or she has demonstrated the ability to manage his or her financial affairs; the minor may include any information he or she considers necessary to support the declaration;

(6) A declaration by the minor indicating that he or she has the ability to manage his or her personal and social affairs; the minor may include any information he or she considers necessary to support the declaration; and

(7) The names of adults who have personal knowledge of the minor's circumstances and believe that under those circumstances emancipation is in the best interest of the minor. Such individuals may include any of the following:

(A) Physician or osteopath licensed pursuant to Chapter 34 of Title 43;

(B) Registered professional nurse or licensed practical nurse licensed pursuant to Chapter 26 of Title 43;

(C) Psychologist licensed pursuant to Chapter 39 of Title 43;

(D) Professional counselor, social worker, or marriage and family therapist licensed pursuant to Chapter 10A of Title 43;

(E) School guidance counselor, school social worker, or school psychologist;

(F) School administrator, school principal, or school teacher;

(G) Member of the clergy;

(H) Law enforcement officer; or

(I) Attorney.

Laws 2006, Act 466, § 1, eff. July 1, 2006.

§ 15–11–203. Summons and time for answer

(a) Upon filing the petition, a copy of the petition for emancipation and a summons to appear at the hearing shall be served on the minor's parents or guardian, if applicable, upon any individual who provided an affidavit as set forth in paragraph (7) of Code Section 15–11–202, and any other individual named in the petition.

(b) Any individual served with the petition for emancipation may file an answer to such petition in the juvenile court within 30 days of being served.

Laws 2006, Act 466, § 1, eff. July 1, 2006.

§ 15–11–204. Appointment of counsel and guardian ad litem; affidavits of adults supporting emancipation

(a) After a petition for emancipation is filed, the court may:

(1) Assign an employee of the court or appoint a guardian ad litem to investigate the allegations of the petition and to file a report containing the results of the investigation with the court, including a recommendation as to whether it is in the best interest of the minor that the petition for emancipation be granted;

(2) Appoint an attorney for the minor; and

(3) Appoint an attorney for the minor's parents or guardian if they are indigent and if they oppose the petition.

(b) After a petition for emancipation is filed, the court shall seek an affidavit from each individual identified in the petition pursuant to paragraph (7) of Code Section 15–11–202 which describes why the individual believes the minor should be emancipated.

Laws 2006, Act 466, § 1, eff. July 1, 2006.

§ 15–11–205. Hearing; burden of proof; required findings

(a) The hearing on the petition for emancipation shall be before a judge; and the court shall issue an emancipation order if it determines that emancipation is in the best interest of the minor and the minor establishes:

(1) That the minor's parent or guardian does not object to the petition; or if a parent or guardian objects to the petition, that the best interest of the child is served by allowing the emancipation to occur by court order;

(2) That the minor is a resident of this state;

(3) That the minor has demonstrated the ability to manage his or her financial affairs, including proof of employment or other means of support; the term "other means of support" does not include general assistance or aid received from means-tested public assistance programs such as Temporary Assistance for Needy Families or similar programs under Title IV–A of the federal Social Security Act;

(4) That the minor has the ability to manage his or her personal and social affairs, including, but not limited to, proof of housing; and

(5) That the minor understands his or her rights and responsibilities under this article as an emancipated minor.

(b) A minor who petitions the court for emancipation shall have the burden of showing by a preponderance of evidence that emancipation should be ordered.

(c) If the court issues an emancipation order, the court shall retain a copy of the order until the emancipated minor becomes 25 years of age.

(d) An emancipation obtained by fraud is voidable. Voiding an emancipation order does not affect an obligation, responsibility, right, or interest that arose during the period of time the order was in effect.

(e) The minor or a parent or guardian of the minor may appeal the court's grant or denial of an emancipation petition. The appeal shall be filed in the Court of Appeals.

Laws 2006, Act 466, § 1, eff. July 1, 2006; Laws 2008, Act 471, § 15, eff. May 12, 2008.

Historical and Statutory Notes

The 2008 amendment by Act 471 was a provision contained in a correction bill.

§ 15–11–206. Rescission of emancipation order; effects

(a) A minor emancipated by court order may petition the juvenile court that issued the emancipation order to rescind such order.

(b) A copy of the petition for rescission and a summons shall be served on the minor's parents or guardian.

(c) The court shall grant the petition and rescind the order of emancipation if it finds:

(1) That the minor is indigent and has no means of support;

(2) That the minor and the minor's parents or guardian agree that the order should be rescinded; or

(3) That there is a resumption of family relations inconsistent with the existing emancipation order.

(d) If a petition for rescission is granted, the court shall issue an order rescinding the emancipation order and retain a copy of the order until the minor becomes 25 years of age.

(e) Rescission of an emancipation order does not alter any contractual obligations or rights or any property rights or interests that arose during the period of time that the emancipation order was in effect.

(f) The minor or a parent or guardian of the minor may appeal the court's grant or denial of a petition for rescission of an emancipation order. The appeal shall be filed in the Court of Appeals.

Laws 2006, Act 466, § 1, eff. July 1, 2006; Laws 2007, Act 18, § 15, eff. May 11, 2007.

Historical and Statutory Notes

The 2007 amendment by Act 18 was a provision contained in a correction bill.

§ 15–11–207. Rights of emancipated minor; limitations; parents or guardians not liable for debts

(a) A minor emancipated by operation of law or by court order shall be considered to have the rights and responsibilities of an adult, except for those specific constitutional and statutory age requirements regarding voting, use of alcoholic beverages, and other health and safety regulations relevant to the minor because of his or her age. The rights of a minor to receive any transfer of property or money pursuant to "The Georgia Transfers to Minors Act" under Article 5 of Chapter 5 of Title 44; under the Uniform Transfers to Minors Act, the Uniform Gift to Minors Act, or other substantially similar act of another state; or pursuant to a trust agreement shall not be affected by a declaration of an emancipation under this article.

(b) A minor shall be considered emancipated for the purposes of, but not limited to:

(1) The right to enter into enforceable contracts, including apartment leases;

(2) The right to sue or be sued in his or her own name;

(3) The right to retain his or her own earnings;

(4) The right to establish a separate domicile;

(5) The right to act autonomously, and with the rights and responsibilities of an adult, in all business relationships, including, but not limited to, property transactions and obtaining accounts for utilities, except for those estate or property matters that the court determines may require a conservator or guardian ad litem;

(6) The right to earn a living, subject only to the health and safety regulations designed to protect those under the age of 18 regardless of their legal status;

(7) The right to authorize his or her own preventive health care, medical care, dental care, and mental health care, without parental knowledge or liability;

(8) The right to apply for a driver's license or other state licenses for which he or she might be eligible;

(9) The right to register for school;

(10) The right to apply for medical assistance programs and for other welfare assistance, if needed;

(11) The right, if a parent, to make decisions and give authority in caring for his or her own minor child; and

(12) The right to make a will.

(c) The parents or guardian of a minor emancipated by court order are not liable for any debts incurred by the minor during the period of emancipation.

Laws 2006, Act 466, § 1, eff. July 1, 2006.

§ 15–11–208. Emancipated minor not a deprived child; duty to support; ability to marry

(a) The duty to provide support for a minor child shall continue until an emancipation order is granted.

(b) A minor emancipated under this article shall not be considered a "deprived child" for purposes of Part 6 of Article 1 of this chapter.

(c) The provisions set forth in Code Section 19–3–2 regarding age limitations to contract for marriage shall apply to a minor who has become emancipated under this article.

Laws 2006, Act 466, § 1, eff. July 1, 2006; Laws 2008, Act 471, § 15, eff. May 12, 2008.

Historical and Statutory Notes

The 2008 amendment by Act 471 was a provision contained in a correction bill.

CHAPTER 13

OFFICERS OF COURT GENERALLY

Article 1

Article 1

Liability for Official Acts

§ 15–13–1. Officers of court liable to suits, etc.

All sheriffs, deputy sheriffs, coroners, jailers, constables, and other officers of court shall be liable to all actions and disabilities which they incur in respect of any matter or thing relating to or concerning their respective offices.

Laws 1792, Cobb's 1851 Digest, p. 576.

Formerly Code 1863, § 3852; Code 1868, § 3872; Code 1873, § 3948; Code 1882, § 3948; Civil Code 1895, § 4769; Civil Code 1910, § 5341; Code 1933, § 24–201.

§ 15–13–2. Liability of sheriffs to parties

Any sheriff shall be liable to an action for damages or an attachment for contempt of court, at the option of the party, whenever it appears that the sheriff has injured the party by:

(1) Making a false return;

(2) Neglecting to arrest a defendant;

(3) Neglecting to levy on the property of the defendant;

(4) Neglecting to pay over to the plaintiff or his attorney any moneys collected by the sheriff by virtue of any fi. fa. or other legal process; or

(5) Neglecting to make a proper return of any writ, execution, or other process put into the hands of the sheriff.

Laws 1799, Cobb's 1851 Digest, p. 576.

Formerly Code 1863, § 3853; Code 1868, § 3873; Code 1873, § 3949; Code 1882, § 3949; Civil Code 1895, § 4770; Civil Code 1910, § 5342; Code 1933, § 24–202.

§ 15–13–3. Money collected by officers may be demanded, etc.; evidence of date and service of demand

(a) If any sheriff, coroner, magistrate, constable, clerk of the superior court, or attorney at law fails, upon application, to pay to the proper person or his attorney any money he may have in his hands which he may have collected by virtue of his office, the party entitled thereto or his attorney may serve such officer with a written demand for the same. If not then paid, for such neglect or refusal the officer shall be compelled to pay interest at the rate of 20 percent per annum upon the sum he has in his hands from the date of the demand, unless good cause is shown to the contrary.

(b) A copy of the demand produced in court, verified by affidavit stating when and where the original was served upon the officer, shall be prima-facie evidence of the date and service thereof.

Laws 1822, Cobb's 1851 Digest, p. 578; Laws 1841, Cobb's 1851 Digest, p. 579; Laws 1983, p. 884, § 4–1.

Formerly Code 1863, §§ 3854, 3855; Code 1868, §§ 3874, 3875; Code 1873, §§ 3950, 3951; Code 1882, §§ 3950, 3951; Civil

Code 1895, §§ 4771, 4772; Civil Code 1910, §§ 5343, 5344; Code 1933, §§ 24–206, 24–207.

§ 15–13–4. Rules nisi against officers

The judges of the superior courts, judges of the probate courts, and magistrates, respectively, upon application, may grant rules nisi against all officers subject thereto, which rules nisi shall contain a full statement of the case in which the officer is called upon to show cause and also of the time and place of hearing. The officer called on by the rule nisi shall be served with a copy thereof within a reasonable time before the hearing.

Laws 1841, Cobb's 1851 Digest, p. 580; Laws 1983, p. 884, § 4–1.

Formerly Code 1863, § 3857; Code 1868, § 3877; Code 1873, § 3953; Code 1882, § 3953; Civil Code 1895, § 4774; Civil Code 1910, § 5346; Code 1933, § 24–209.

§ 15–13–5. Answer to rule nisi; subsequent proceedings

The officer called on by rule nisi, as provided in Code Section 15–13–4, shall fully respond in writing to the rule, which answer shall be under oath taken at the time the answer is filed. If the answer is not denied, the rule shall be discharged or shall be made absolute, depending on whether the court deems the answer sufficient. The movant of the rule may traverse the truth of the answer, in which case an issue shall be made and tried by a jury at the same term unless good cause for continuance is shown, which may be done only once by each party. Upon the trial of such issue the court shall discharge the rule or shall make the rule absolute, depending on whether the verdict of the jury is for or against the officer.

Laws 1840, Cobb's 1851 Digest, p. 579.

Formerly Code 1863, § 3858; Code 1868, § 3878; Code 1873, § 3954; Code 1882, § 3954; Civil Code 1895, § 4775; Civil Code 1910, § 5347; Code 1933, § 24–210.

§ 15–13–6. When officer may be ruled without notice

If a sheriff or other officer designedly absents himself from his court, the presiding judge or justice, when required by plaintiffs in execution or their attorneys, shall grant a rule absolute against the sheriff or other officer without the notice provided for in Code Section 15–13–4 unless it is proved at such term of the court that the sheriff or other officer, from sickness, is not able to attend the court.

Laws 1841, Cobb's 1851 Digest, p. 579.

Formerly Code 1863, § 3859; Code 1868, § 3879; Code 1873, § 3955; Code 1882, § 3955; Civil Code 1895, § 4777; Civil Code 1910, § 5349; Code 1933, § 24–212.

§ 15–13–7. Magistrates and constables, when ruled

Magistrates and constables shall be considered officers of the superior court so far as to be subject to be ruled under similar conditions as are provided in relation to any other officer of the court and shall be subject to all the penalties as are provided in case of a rule absolute against sheriffs and other officers of the court when they, or either of them, refuse or neglect to collect or to pay over any money which they may have received or collected in their official capacities.

Laws 1820, Cobb's 1851 Digest, p. 649; Laws 1839, Cobb's 1851 Digest, p. 651; Laws 1876, p. 37, § 1; Laws 1983, p. 884, § 4–1; Laws 1984, p. 22, § 15.

Formerly Code 1863, § 3865; Code 1968, § 3885; Code 1873, § 3961; Code 1882, § 3961; Civil Code 1895, §§ 4060, 4782; Civil Code 1910, §§ 4657, 5354; Code 1933, § 24–205.

§ 15–13–8. Officers may be ruled after going out of office

Sheriffs, deputy sheriffs, coroners, clerks of the superior courts, magistrates, and constables shall be subject to the rule and order of the courts at any and all times after they have retired from their respective offices, in such cases and in like manner as they would have been had they remained in office.

Laws 1813, Cobb's 1851 Digest, p. 202; Laws 1983, p. 884, § 4–1.

Formerly Code 1863, § 3856; Code 1868, § 3876; Code 1873, § 3952; Code 1882, § 3952; Civil Code 1895, § 4773; Civil Code 1910, § 5345; Code 1933, § 24–208.

§ 15–13–9. Deputy sheriffs subject to rule, etc.

All deputy sheriffs shall be liable to be ruled and attached in the same way and manner as sheriffs. However, the liability of the sheriff shall not be affected by any such proceeding against his deputy when the same is not effective.

Laws 1841, Cobb's 1851 Digest, p. 580.

Formerly Code 1863, § 3863; Code 1868, § 3883; Code 1873, § 3959; Code 1882, § 3959; Civil Code 1895, § 4780; Civil Code 1910, § 5352; Code 1933, § 24–203.

§ 15–13–10. Service of rule against sheriff and deputy

Whenever the sheriff or his deputy is a party to any rule or is interested therein and there is no coroner or other lawful officer of the county to execute the same, it shall be the duty of the judge or justice of the court to appoint pro tempore a special officer to carry out and effectuate the order of the court, for which the appointed officer shall be allowed the usual fees of sheriffs for like service.

Laws 1840, Cobb's 1851 Digest, p. 580.

Formerly Code 1863, § 3864; Code 1868, § 3884; Code 1873, § 3960; Code 1882, § 3960; Civil Code 1895, § 4781; Civil Code 1910, § 5353; Code 1933, § 24–204.

§ 15–13–11. Lien of rule absolute

When a rule absolute has been obtained against any officer for the payment of money, as provided in Code Sections 15–13–4 and 15–13–5, the rule shall constitute the same lien upon the property, both real and personal, of the officer as an ordinary judgment at law; and, if not punctually paid, the demand shall thereafter draw interest at the rate of 20 percent per annum. The plaintiff may have either an attachment or an execution issued upon the rule absolute and may have either of the processes returned and the other issued, at pleasure.

Laws 1858, p. 90, § 1.

Formerly Code 1863, § 3860; Code 1868, § 3880; Code 1873, § 3956; Code 1882, § 3956; Civil Code 1895, § 4778; Civil Code 1910, § 5350; Code 1933, § 24–214.

§ 15–13–12. Date of lien

Unless otherwise provided by law, a rule absolute granted against a sheriff, constable, or other officer who has defaulted in his duty shall constitute a lien on his property from the date of rendition but shall be of equal date with other judgments rendered against the officer within the same term of court.

Formerly Code 1863, § 1994; Code 1868, § 1984; Code 1873, § 2001; Code 1882, § 2001; Civil Code 1895, § 2826; Civil Code 1910, § 3376; Code 1933, § 24–215.

§ 15–13–13. Practice on money rules

(a) Where money is in the hands of an officer, he may pay it over to the plaintiff by whose process it was raised, unless other claimants deposit their liens with him. Notice to retain is insufficient unless accompanied by a lien.

(b) Money raised by legal process not being subject to levy and sale, the court in making distribution shall proceed upon equitable principles.

(c) All parties intervening shall, by appropriate pleading, set forth the ground of their claim to the fund.

(d) All persons interested who are notified in writing by the sheriff or movant of the pendency of the rule shall be bound by the judgment of distribution.

Formerly Civil Code 1895, § 4776; Civil Code 1910, § 5348; Code 1933, § 24–211.

§ 15–13–14. Default of officers, how punished

If any sheriff or other officer fails to make a proper return of all writs, executions, and other processes put into his hands or fails to pay over all moneys received on such executions on his being required to do so by the court, he shall be liable for contempt and may be fined, imprisoned, or removed from office in the manner prescribed by the Constitution and laws of this state.

Laws 1799, Cobb's 1851 Digest, p. 577.

Formerly Code 1863, § 3861; Code 1868, § 3881; Code 1873, § 3957; Code 1882, § 3957; Civil Code 1895, § 4779; Civil Code 1910, § 5351; Code 1933, § 24–213.

CHAPTER 16

SHERIFFS

Article 1

Article 1

General Provisions

§ 15–16–1. Qualification, term of office, training, etc.

(a) *Intent.* The General Assembly declares it to be in the best interests of the citizens of this state that qualifications and standards for the office of sheriff be determined and set so as to improve both the capabilities and training of those persons who hold the office of sheriff. With the increase of crime continuing as a major social problem in this state and with the understanding that the sheriff is the basic law enforcement officer of the several counties of this state, it is declared to be the intent of the General Assembly that proper qualifications and standards be required of the person holding the office of sheriff so as to increase the effectiveness and capabilities of the several sheriffs of this state as law enforcement officers to combat crime.

(b) *General requirements.* Except as otherwise provided in this Code section, sheriffs are elected, qualified, commissioned, hold their offices for the same term, and are subject to the same disabilities as the clerks of the superior courts.

(c) *Qualifications.*

(1) No person shall be eligible to hold the office of sheriff unless such person:

(A) At the time of qualifying as a candidate for the office of sheriff is a citizen of the United States;

(B) Has been a resident of the county in which he or she seeks the office of sheriff for at least two years immediately preceding the date of qualifying for election to the office;

(C) At the time of qualifying as a candidate for the office of sheriff is a registered voter;

(D) At the time of qualifying as a candidate for the office of sheriff has attained the age of at least 25 years;

(E) At the time of qualifying as a candidate for the office of sheriff has obtained a high school diploma or its recognized equivalent in educational training as established by the Georgia Peace Officer Standards and Training Council;

(F) Has not been convicted of a felony offense or any offense involving moral turpitude contrary to the laws of this state, any other state, or the United States; provided, however, that a plea of nolo contendere to a felony offense or any offense involving moral turpitude contrary to the laws of this state shall have the same effect as a plea of guilty, thereby disqualifying such a person from holding the office of sheriff;

(G) Is fingerprinted and a search made of local, state, and national fingerprint files to disclose any criminal record, which fingerprints are to be taken under the direction of the judge of the probate court and must be taken on or before, but no later than, the close of qualification for election to the office of sheriff;

(H) At the time of qualifying as a candidate for the office of sheriff gives a complete written history of his or her places of residence for a period of six years immediately preceding his or her qualification date, giving the house number or RFD number, street, city, county, and state;

(I) At the time of qualifying as a candidate for the office of sheriff gives a complete written history of his or her places of employment for a period of six years immediately preceding his or her qualification date, giving the period of time employed and the name and address of his or her employer; and

(J) Is a registered peace officer as provided in Code Section 35–8–10 or is a certified peace officer as defined in Chapter 8 of Title 35. Any person who is not a registered or certified peace officer at the time such person assumes the office of sheriff shall be required to complete satisfactorily the requirements for certification as a peace officer as provided in Chapter 8 of Title 35 within six months after such person takes office; provided, however, that an extension of the time to complete such requirements may be granted by the Georgia Peace Officer Standards and Training Council upon the presentation of evidence by a sheriff that he or she was unable to complete the basic training course and certification requirements due to illness, injury, military service, or other reasons deemed sufficient by such council. The Georgia Peace Officer Standards and Training Council shall make every effort to ensure that space is available for newly elected sheriffs who are not certified or registered peace officers to attend the course as soon as possible after such persons take office. Such council shall notify the appropriate judge of the probate court whenever a newly elected sheriff who is not certified fails to become certified as a peace officer pursuant to the requirements of this subparagraph.

(2) Each person offering his or her candidacy for the office of sheriff shall, within 60 days prior to or at the time such person qualifies:

(A) File with the officer before whom such person has qualified to seek the office of sheriff a certified copy of his or her birth certificate and a certified copy of his or her high school diploma or certified proof of its recognized equivalent in education training as established by the Georgia Peace Officer Standards and Training Council; and

(B) Swear or affirm before the officer before whom such person has qualified to seek the office of sheriff that he or she meets all of the qualifications required by this subsection, except as otherwise provided in subparagraph (J) of paragraph (1) of this subsection, and that he or she has complied with the requirements of subparagraph (G) of paragraph (1) of this subsection no later than the close of qualification for election to the office of sheriff.

(3) Each person offering to run for the office of sheriff and who is otherwise qualified shall be allowed, six months prior to qualifying and at his or her own expense, to attend the basic mandate course for peace officers. The Georgia Peace Officer Standards and Training Council shall work to ensure that space is available for such individuals to attend the course.

(d) *Exemption.* The requirements of subparagraphs (c)(1)(D), (c)(1)(E), (c)(1)(F), (c)(1)(H), (c)(1)(I), and (c)(1)(J) of this Code section shall be deemed to have been met by any person who is currently serving as a duly qualified and elected sheriff of one of the several counties of this state.

Laws 1799, Cobb's 1851 Digest, p. 198; Laws 1977, p. 1171, § 1; Laws 1978, p. 244, § 1; Laws 1981, p. 1334, §§ 1, 2; Laws 1982, p. 3, § 15; Laws 1984, p. 579, § 1; Laws 1984, p. 1369, § 1; Laws 1986, p. 606, § 1; Laws 1989, p. 1091, § 3; Laws 1990, p. 8, § 15; Laws 1992, p. 2112, § 1; Laws 1993, p. 724, §§ 1, 2; Laws 1994, p. 521, § 1; Laws 1997, p. 952, § 1; Laws 1998, p. 224, § 1.

Formerly Code 1863, § 320; Code 1868, § 381; Code 1873, § 345; Code 1882, § 345; Civil Code 1895, § 4368; Civil Code 1910, § 4902; Code 1933, § 24–2801.

§ 15–16–3. Training course for newly elected sheriffs; intent of law; compensation for attendance; cost of course of training

(a) *Intent.* The General Assembly declares it to be the purpose of this Code section to promote the orderly transfer of the law enforcement power of the several counties of this state in connection with the expiration of the term of office of the sheriff and the taking of office of the newly elected sheriff. The interest of the State of Georgia requires that such transitions in the office of the sheriff be accomplished so as to assure continuity in the conduct of the peace-keeping functions of the several counties of this state. Any disruption occasioned by the transfer of the law enforcement power to a person not properly versed and trained in law enforcement and the operations of the office of sheriff is declared to be detrimental to the safety and well-being of the citizens of the several counties of this state and of the entire state. Accordingly, it is the intent of the General Assembly that appropriate training be required of sheriffs who are newly elected so as to avoid or minimize any disruption in the performance of the duties and responsibilities or the authority of the sheriffs of the several counties of this state. This training shall be generally devoted to contemporary law enforcement, investigation, judicial process, and correction practices and specifically shall be germane to the duties and operational functions of the office of sheriff in the several counties of this state. Further, the purpose of this Code section is to promote professionalism within the office of sheriff by ensuring the highest possible quality of law enforcement training is offered to each sheriff on an annual basis. Accordingly, it is the intent of the General Assembly that appropriate ongoing training be required of all sheriffs. This training shall be generally devoted to contemporary law enforcement, investigation, judicial process, and corrections practices and specifically shall be germane to the duties and operational functions of the office of sheriff in the several counties of this state.

(b) *Sheriffs-elect specialized training.* Any person elected to the office of sheriff in a county of this state who was not serving as a duly elected or appointed sheriff on or before July 1, 1976, shall enroll in, attend, and successfully complete a course of sheriffs-elect specialized training and instruction established and provided by the Georgia Sheriffs' Association with the assistance of the Georgia Public Safety Training Center. Such course of instruction shall be held every four years at a time to be designated by the Georgia Sheriffs' Association. Any newly elected sheriff who is unable to attend such training course when it is offered because of medical disability or providential cause shall, within one year from the date such disability or cause terminates, complete a course of instruction as determined by the Georgia Sheriffs' Association and approved by the Georgia Peace Officer Standards and Training Council. Any newly elected sheriff who does not fulfill the obligations of this subsection shall lose his or her power of arrest.

(c) *Compensation.* A newly elected sheriff who enrolls in and attends a course of training and instruction as described in subsection (b) of this Code section shall be paid compensation for his or her attendance on a weekly basis at the successful completion of each week's training. The compensation shall be paid by the Georgia Sheriffs' Association using funds appropriated by the state for such purpose or from federal funds available for such purpose. The compensation shall be in an amount equal to a proportionate part of the annual salary to be received by the new sheriff of the least populated county in this state for each week spent in attendance at the course of training and instruction. For the purposes of this Code section, five days of training and instruction shall be considered one week.

(d) *Costs.* The cost of training, housing, travel, and meals appropriate to the course of training and instruction shall be paid by the Georgia Sheriffs' Association from state funds appropriated for such purpose or from federal funds available for such purpose.

(e) *Annual training.*

(1) From and after July 1, 1997, no person shall be eligible to hold the office of sheriff unless he or she attends a minimum of 20 hours' training annually as may be selected by the Georgia Sheriffs' Association.

(2) The basis for the minimum annual requirement of in-service training shall be the calendar year. Sheriffs who satisfactorily complete the sheriffs-elect specialized training in accordance with the provisions of this Code section after April 1 in any calendar year shall be excused from the minimum annual training requirement for the calendar year during which the sheriffs-elect specialized training course is completed.

(3) A waiver of the requirement of minimum annual in-service training may be granted by the Georgia Peace Officer Standards and Training Council, in its discretion, upon the presentation of evidence by a sheriff that he or she was unable to complete such training due to medical disability, providential cause, or other reason deemed sufficient by the council.

(4) Any person who fails to complete the minimum annual in-service training required under this Code section and who has not received a waiver of such requirement pursuant to paragraph (3) of this subsection shall not perform any of the duties of sheriff involving the power of arrest until such training shall have been successfully completed. In addition, the Governor may suspend from office without pay for a period of 90 days any sheriff who fails to complete the minimum annual in-service training required under this Code section. The probate judge of the county of the sheriff's residence shall appoint a person who meets the qualifications for sheriff pursuant to this Code section to assume the duties and responsibilities of the office of sheriff during any such period of suspension.

Laws 1976, p. 423, §§ 1, 2; Laws 1982, p. 3, § 15; Laws 1984, p. 22, § 15; Laws 1997, p. 952, § 2.

§ 15–16–10. Duties; defaulting sheriffs or deputies; contempt of court; removal

(a) It is the duty of the sheriff:

(1) To execute and return the processes and orders of the courts and of officers of competent authority, if not void, with due diligence, when delivered to him for that purpose, according to this Code;

(2) To attend, by himself or his deputy, upon all sessions of the superior court of the county and also upon sessions of the probate court whenever required by the judge thereof and, while the courts are in session, never to leave same without the presence of himself or his deputy, or both, if required;

(3) To attend, in the same manner specified in paragraph (2) of this subsection, at the place or places of holding an election at the county site, on the day of an election, from the opening to the closing of the polls, and to take under his charge all subordinate officers present, as police to preserve order;

(4) To publish sales, citations, and other proceedings as required by law and to keep a file of all newspapers in which his official advertisements appear, in the manner required of clerks of the superior courts;

(5) To keep an execution docket wherein he must enter a full description of all executions delivered to him and the dates of their delivery, together with all his actions thereon, and to have the same ready for use in any court of his county;

(6) To keep a book in which shall be entered a record of all sales made by process of court or by agreement of the parties under the sanction of the court, describing accurately the property and the process under which sold, the date of the levy and sale, the purchaser, and the price;

(7) To receive from the preceding sheriff all unexecuted writs and processes and proceed to execute the same; to carry into effect any levy or arrest made by a predecessor; to put purchasers into possession, and to make titles to purchasers at his or her predecessor's sales, when not done by his or her predecessor;

(8) To perform such other duties as are or may be imposed by law or which necessarily appertain to his or her office;

(9) To exercise the same duties, powers, and arrest authority within municipalities which such officer exercises in the unincorporated areas of counties; and

(10) To develop and implement a comprehensive plan for the security of the county courthouse and any courthouse annex. Prior to the implementation of any security plan, the plan shall be submitted to the chief judge of the superior court of the circuit wherein the courthouse or courthouse annex is located for review. The chief judge shall have 30 days to review the original or any subsequent security plan. The chief judge may make modifications to the original or any subsequent security plan. The sheriff shall provide to the county governing authority the estimated cost of any security plan and a schedule for implementation 30 days prior to adoption of any security plan. A comprehensive plan for courthouse security shall be considered a confidential matter of public security. Review of a proposed security plan by the governing authority shall be excluded from the requirements of Code Section 50–14–1 and any such review shall take place as provided in Code Section 50–14–3. Such security plan shall also be excluded from public disclosure pursuant to paragraph (15) of subsection (a) of Code Section 50–18–72. The sheriff shall be the official custodian of the comprehensive courthouse security plan and shall determine who has access to such plan and any such access and review shall occur in the sheriff's office or at a meeting of the county governing authority held as provided in paragraph (9) of Code Section 50–14–3; provided, however, that the sheriff shall make the original security plan available upon request for temporary, exclusive review by any judge whose courtroom or chambers is located within the courthouse or courthouse annex or by any commissioner of the county in which the courthouse or courthouse annex is located. The sheriff shall be responsible to conduct a formal review of the security plan not less than every four years.

(b) If any sheriff or deputy fails to comply with any provision of subsection (a) of this Code section, he shall be fined for a contempt as the clerk of the superior court is fined in similar cases. Code Section 15–6–82, as to removal, shall also apply to sheriffs.

(c) In all counties of this state having a population of not less than 625,000 nor more than 725,000 according to the United States decennial census of 2000 or any future such census, it shall be the duty of the sheriffs of such counties to receive, confine, feed, and care for all persons charged with the violation of any ordinances of such counties in the same manner as persons charged with an indictable offense, whether such person charged with the violation of an ordinance is being held pending a hearing before the recorder's courts of such counties or has been sentenced by the recorder's courts to imprisonment in the county jail.

(d) Nothing in this Code section shall restrict or otherwise prohibit a sheriff or a deputy sheriff or clerk acting under the authority of a sheriff from electing to store for computer retrieval any or all records, dockets, books, indices, or files; nor shall a sheriff or a deputy sheriff or clerk acting under the authority of a sheriff be prohibited from combining or consolidating any records, dockets, books, indices, or files in connection with the maintenance of any records of the kind specified or required in this Code section or any other law, provided that any automated or computerized record-keeping method or system shall provide for the systematic and safe preservation and retrieval of all such records, dockets, books, indices, or files. When the sheriff or a deputy sheriff or clerk acting under the authority of the sheriff elects to store for computer retrieval any or all records, the same data elements used in a manual system shall be used, and the same integrity and security maintained.

Laws 1799, Cobb's 1851 Digest, p. 574; Laws 1810, Cobb's 1851 Digest, p. 577; Laws 1818, Cobb's 1851 Digest, p. 858; Laws 1820, Cobb's 1851 Digest, p. 480; Laws 1823, Cobb's 1851 Digest, p. 52; Laws 1853–54, p. 28, § 4; Laws 1905, p. 106, § 1; Laws 1964, p. 2885, § 1; Laws 1981, p. 3, § 2; Laws 1981, p. 4238, § 1; Laws 1982, p. 3, § 15; Laws 1982, p. 2107, § 14; Laws 1992, p. 6, § 15; Laws 1992, p. 1230; Laws 1993, p. 1688, § 1; Laws 2000, p. 844, § 1; Laws 2002, p. 1473, § 1; Laws 2006, Act 647, § 1, eff. July 1, 2006.

Formerly Code 1863, §§ 336, 340; Code 1868, §§ 397, 401; Code 1873, §§ 361, 366; Code 1882, §§ 361, 366; Civil Code 1895, §§ 4380, 4386; Civil Code 1910, §§ 4914, 4920; Code 1933, §§ 24–2813, 24–2814.

§ 15–16–13. Contract for law enforcement services to municipality

(a) The sheriffs of the various counties of this state are authorized to contract with the governing body of any municipal corporation located within their respective counties, with the written consent of the governing authority of the county, for the purpose of providing law enforcement services to the municipal corporation. Such contracts may include undertakings by the sheriff to perform any police function, to exercise any police power, or to render any police service on behalf of the contracting municipal corporation. Upon the execution of any such contract and within the limitations contained in the contract, the sheriff and his deputies may exercise the same powers as possessed by the contracting municipal corporation with respect to police services and all powers necessary or incidental thereto.

(b) Any contract authorized by this Code section shall not affect, impair, or limit the authority or powers of the municipal corporation or of the sheriff except as otherwise specified in the contract. Sheriffs shall have the same duties, powers, and arrest authority within municipalities which such officers have in unincorporated areas of counties. The duties, powers, and arrest authority of sheriffs shall not be limited, impaired, or affected in any way upon a sheriff and a municipality entering into a contract for the sheriff to provide additional duties or services to a municipality. Nothing in this Code section shall be construed so as to limit, affect, diminish, or impair the rights, powers, or duties of any county or municipal police department as set forth in Code Section 36–8–5 or any law creating or authorizing the creation of a municipal police department.

(c) Such contracts shall provide for the reimbursement of the county for the costs incurred by the sheriff in providing contract services, including, but not limited to, the compensation of deputy sheriffs and other personnel, the costs of funding retirement benefits, insurance, workers' compensation and other fringe benefits for deputies and personnel, the costs of training deputies and other personnel, and the costs of equipment, materials, supplies, and utilities to the extent that such equipment, materials, supplies, and utilities are not furnished by the contracting municipal corporation. Each contract shall provide for the ascertainment of the cost of providing contract services and shall be of such duration as may be agreed upon, unless in conflict with any other general law or the Constitution of this state.

(d) All payments made by a municipal corporation under the terms of any contract authorized by this Code section shall be made to the general fund of the county. Any funds paid into the general fund of the county pursuant to such a contract shall be used for the purposes provided for in this Code section and in the contract and shall be paid by the governing authority of the county.

(e) Any other law to the contrary notwithstanding, the sheriff is authorized to employ such additional deputies and personnel as may be provided for in any contract authorized by this Code section and to purchase such automobiles, equipment, materials, supplies, and utilities as may be provided for in any such contract, the compensation, benefits, expenses, and costs of which shall be paid or funded by the governing authority of the county in an amount or amounts not exceeding the contract payments made by the municipal corporation into the general fund of the county.

(f) This Code section shall not apply to any county of 800,000 population or more according to the United States decennial census of 2000 or any future such census.

Laws 1974, p. 542, §§ 1–4, 4A; Laws 1993, p. 1688, § 2; Laws 2002, p. 1473, § 1.

§ 15–16–14. Administration of oaths

Sheriffs and their legal deputies may administer oaths in all cases where, in discharge of the duties of the office of sheriff, it is legal for them to take bond and security or any affidavit which by law suspends the further execution of process in their hands. Such oaths, when so taken, shall be as legal and binding and subject to the same penalty as to perjury as are oaths when administered by any other officer.

Laws 1873, p. 51, § 1.

Formerly Code 1873, § 362; Code 1882, § 362; Civil Code 1895, § 4382; Civil Code 1910, § 4916; Code 1933, § 24–2819.

§ 15–16–24. Liability for misconduct of jailer

Sheriffs are liable for the misconduct of their jailers as they are liable for their deputies; and persons injured by a jailer have the same option in bringing an action on the jailer's bond that they have in bringing an action on the deputy's bond, provided that the sheriff shall not be liable for such misconduct and no claim or cause of action against the sheriff for such misconduct shall exist unless one of the following conditions exists:

(1) The sheriff personally benefited financially from the act complained of;

(2) The sheriff was personally aware of and had actual knowledge of the act complained of and had actual knowledge that the act was illegal, was contrary to law, or was the breach of a duty imposed by law and either acted to cause or failed to prevent the act complained of; or

(3) The sheriff failed to exercise ordinary care and diligence to prevent the condition or act which proximately caused the injury complained of.

Laws 1980, p. 493, § 1; Laws 1982, p. 3, § 15.

Formerly Code 1863, § 335; Code 1868, § 396; Code 1873, § 360; Code 1882, § 360; Civil Code 1895, § 4379; Civil Code 1910, § 4913; Code 1933, § 24–2812.

CHAPTER 24

SEXUAL ASSAULT PROTOCOL

Section

§ 15–24–1. Definitions

As used in this chapter, the term:

(1) "Protocol committee" or "committee" means a multidisciplinary, multiagency sexual assault committee established for a county pursuant to Code Section 15–24–2. The protocol committee is charged with developing local protocols to investigate and prosecute alleged cases of sexual assault.

(2) "Sexual assault" means rape, sodomy, aggravated sodomy, incest, sexual battery, and aggravated sexual battery as those terms are defined in Chapter 6 of Title 16.

Laws 2004, Act 519, § 3, eff. July 1, 2004.

§ 15–24–2. Sexual assault protocol; committee

(a) Each judicial circuit shall be required to establish a sexual assault protocol as provided in this Code section.

(b) The chief superior court judge of each judicial circuit shall establish a sexual assault protocol committee as provided in subsection (c) of this Code section and shall appoint an interim chairperson who shall preside over the first meeting. The chief superior court judge shall appoint persons to fill any vacancies on the committee. Thus established, the committee shall thereafter elect a chairperson from its membership.

(c)(1) Each of the following agencies of the judicial circuit shall designate a representative to serve on the committee:

(A) The office of the sheriff of each sheriff's office in the judicial circuit;

(B) The office of the district attorney;

(C) The magistrate court;

(D) The office of the chief of police of a county of each county within the judicial circuit in counties which have a county police department;

(E) The office of the chief of police of the largest municipality in the county of each county within the judicial circuit; and

(F) The county board of health of each county within the judicial circuit.

(2) In addition to the representatives serving on the committee as provided for in paragraph (1) of this subsection, the chief superior court judge shall designate:

(A) A local citizen of the judicial circuit;

(B) A representative of a sexual assault or rape crisis center serving the judicial circuit or, if no such center exists, then a local citizen; and

(C) A health care professional who performs sexual assault examinations within the judicial circuit or, if no such person exists, then a local citizen.

(3) If any designated agency fails to carry out its duties relating to participation on the committee, the chief superior court judge of the circuit may issue an order requiring the participation of such agency. Failure to comply with such order shall be cause for punishment as for contempt of court.

(d) The protocol committee shall adopt a written sexual assault protocol, a copy of which shall be furnished to each agency in the judicial circuit that handles cases of sexual assault. The protocol shall be a written document outlining in detail the procedures to be used in investigating, collecting evidence, paying for expenses related to evidence collection, and prosecuting cases arising from alleged sexual assault and shall take into consideration the provisions of Article 4 of Chapter 5 of Title 17. The protocol may provide for different procedures to be used within particular municipalities or counties within the judicial circuit. The protocol committee shall adopt a written sexual assault protocol no later than December 31, 2004. The protocol committee may incorporate sexual assault protocols used in the judicial circuit as they existed on or before July 1, 2004.

(e) The purpose of the protocol shall be to ensure coordination and cooperation between all agencies involved in sexual assault cases so as to increase the efficiency of all agencies handling such cases and to minimize the stress created for the alleged sexual assault victim by the legal and investigatory process; provided, however, that a failure by an agency to follow the protocol shall not constitute an affirmative or other defense to prosecution of a sexual assault, preclude the admissibility of evidence, nor shall a failure by an agency to follow the protocol give rise to a civil cause of action.

(f) Upon completion of the writing of the sexual assault protocol, the protocol committee shall continue in existence and shall meet at least annually for the purpose of evaluating the effectiveness of the protocol and appropriately modifying and updating same.

Laws 2004, Act 519, § 3, eff. July 1, 2004; Laws 2008, Act 539, § 1, eff. May 12, 2008.

Historical and Statutory Notes

The 2008 amendment by Act 539, in subsec. (d), added "and shall take into consideration the provisions of Article 4 of Chapter 5 of Title 17" in the second sentence; and in subsec. (e), added "preclude the admissibility of evidence," in the last sentence.

TITLE 16

CRIMES AND OFFENSES

CHAPTER 1

GENERAL PROVISIONS

§ 16–1–1. Title

This title shall be known and may be cited as the "Criminal Code of Georgia."

Laws 1968, p. 1249, § 1.

Formerly Code 1933, § 26–101.

§ 16–1–2. General purposes

The general purposes of this title are:

(1) To forbid and prevent conduct which unjustifiably and inexcusably causes or threatens substantial harm to individual or public interests;

(2) To give fair warning of the nature of the conduct forbidden and the sentence authorized upon conviction;

(3) To define that which constitutes each crime; and

(4) To prescribe penalties which are proportionate to the seriousness of crimes and which permit recognition of differences in rehabilitation possibilities among individual criminals.

Laws 1968, p. 1249, § 1.

Formerly Code 1933, § 26–102.

§ 16–1–3. Definitions

As used in this title, the term:

(1) "Affirmative defense" means, with respect to any affirmative defense authorized in this title, unless the state's evidence raises the issue invoking the alleged defense, the defendant must present evidence thereon to raise the issue. The enumeration in this title of some affirmative defenses shall not be construed as excluding the existence of others.

(2) "Agency" means:

(A) When used with respect to the state government, any department, commission, committee, authority, board, or bureau thereof; and

(B) When used with respect to any political subdivision of the state government, any department, commission, committee, authority, board, or bureau thereof.

(3) "Another" means a person or persons other than the accused.

(4) "Conviction" includes a final judgment of conviction entered upon a verdict or finding of guilty of a crime or upon a plea of guilty.

(5) "Felony" means a crime punishable by death, by imprisonment for life, or by imprisonment for more than 12 months.

(6) "Forcible felony" means any felony which involves the use or threat of physical force or violence against any person.

(7) "Forcible misdemeanor" means any misdemeanor which involves the use or threat of physical force or violence against any person.

(8) "Government" means the United States, the state, any political subdivision thereof, or any agency of the foregoing.

(9) "Misdemeanor" and "misdemeanor of a high and aggravated nature" mean any crime other than a felony.

(10) "Owner" means a person who has a right to possession of property which is superior to that of a person who takes, uses, obtains, or withholds it from him and which the person taking, using, obtaining, or withholding is not privileged to infringe.

(11) "Peace officer" means any person who by virtue of his office or public employment is vested by law with a duty to maintain public order or to make arrests for offenses, whether that duty extends to all crimes or is limited to specific offenses.

(12) "Person" means an individual, a public or private corporation, an incorporated association, government, government agency, partnership, or unincorporated association.

(13) "Property" means anything of value, including but not limited to real estate, tangible and intangible personal property, contract rights, services, choses in action, and other interests in or claims to wealth, admission or transportation tickets, captured or domestic animals, food and drink, and electric or other power.

(14) "Prosecution" means all legal proceedings by which a person's liability for a crime is determined, commencing with the return of the indictment or the filing of the accusation, and including the final disposition of the case upon appeal.

(15) "Public place" means any place where the conduct involved may reasonably be expected to be viewed by people other than members of the actor's family or household.

(16) "Reasonable belief" means that the person concerned, acting as a reasonable man, believes that the described facts exist.

(17) "State" means the State of Georgia, all land and water in respect to which this state has either exclusive or concurrent jurisdiction, and the airspace above such land and water.

(18) "Without authority" means without legal right or privilege or without permission of a person legally entitled to withhold the right.

(19) "Without his consent" means that a person whose concurrence is required has not, with knowledge of the essen-

tial facts, voluntarily yielded to the proposal of the accused or of another.

Laws 1833, Cobb's 1851 Digest, p. 780; Laws 1968, p. 1249, § 1; Laws 1970, p. 236, § 1; Laws 1973, p. 292, § 3; Laws 1982, p. 3, § 16.

Formerly Code 1863, § 6; Code 1868, § 5; Code 1873, § 5; Code 1882, § 5; Penal Code 1895, § 2; Penal Code 1910, § 2; Code 1933, § 26–101; Code 1933, § 26–401.

§ 16–1–4. Code governs crimes

No conduct constitutes a crime unless it is described as a crime in this title or in another statute of this state. However, this Code section does not affect the power of a court to punish for contempt or to employ any sanction authorized by law for the enforcement of an order, civil judgment, or decree.

Laws 1968, p. 1249, § 1.

Formerly Code 1933, § 26–201.

§ 16–1–5. Presumption of innocence and proof beyond reasonable doubt

Every person is presumed innocent until proved guilty. No person shall be convicted of a crime unless each element of such crime is proved beyond a reasonable doubt.

Laws 1968, p. 1249, § 1.

Formerly Code 1933, § 26–501.

§ 16–1–6. Included crime

An accused may be convicted of a crime included in a crime charged in the indictment or accusation. A crime is so included when:

(1) It is established by proof of the same or less than all the facts or a less culpable mental state than is required to establish the commission of the crime charged; or

(2) It differs from the crime charged only in the respect that a less serious injury or risk of injury to the same person, property, or public interest or a lesser kind of culpability suffices to establish its commission.

Laws 1968, p. 1249, § 1.

Formerly Code 1933, § 26–505.

§ 16–1–7. Multiple prosecutions for same conduct

(a) When the same conduct of an accused may establish the commission of more than one crime, the accused may be prosecuted for each crime. He may not, however, be convicted of more than one crime if:

(1) One crime is included in the other; or

(2) The crimes differ only in that one is defined to prohibit a designated kind of conduct generally and the other to prohibit a specific instance of such conduct.

(b) If the several crimes arising from the same conduct are known to the proper prosecuting officer at the time of commencing the prosecution and are within the jurisdiction of a single court, they must be prosecuted in a single prosecution except as provided in subsection (c) of this Code section.

(c) When two or more crimes are charged as required by subsection (b) of this Code section, the court in the interest of justice may order that one or more of such charges be tried separately.

Laws 1968, p. 1249, § 1; Laws 1982, p. 3, § 16.

Formerly Code 1933, § 26–506.

§ 16–1–8. Effect of former prosecution

(a) A prosecution is barred if the accused was formerly prosecuted for the same crime based upon the same material facts, if such former prosecution:

(1) Resulted in either a conviction or an acquittal; or

(2) Was terminated improperly after the jury was impaneled and sworn or, in a trial before a court without a jury, after the first witness was sworn but before findings were rendered by the trier of facts or after a plea of guilty was accepted by the court.

(b) A prosecution is barred if the accused was formerly prosecuted for a different crime or for the same crime based upon different facts, if such former prosecution:

(1) Resulted in either a conviction or an acquittal and the subsequent prosecution is for a crime of which the accused could have been convicted on the former prosecution, is for a crime with which the accused should have been charged on the former prosecution (unless the court ordered a separate trial of such charge), or is for a crime which involves the same conduct, unless each prosecution requires proof of a fact not required on the other prosecution or unless the crime was not consummated when the former trial began; or

(2) Was terminated improperly and the subsequent prosecution is for a crime of which the accused could have been convicted if the former prosecution had not been terminated improperly.

(c) A prosecution is barred if the accused was formerly prosecuted in a district court of the United States for a crime which is within the concurrent jurisdiction of this state if such former prosecution resulted in either a conviction or an acquittal and the subsequent prosecution is for the same conduct, unless each prosecution requires proof of a fact not required in the other prosecution or unless the crime was not consummated when the former trial began.

(d) A prosecution is not barred within the meaning of this Code section if:

(1) The former prosecution was before a court which lacked jurisdiction over the accused or the crime; or

(2) Subsequent proceedings resulted in the invalidation, setting aside, reversal, or vacating of the conviction, unless the accused was thereby adjudged not guilty or unless there was a finding that the evidence did not authorize the verdict.

(e) Termination under any of the following circumstances is not improper:

(1) The accused consents to the termination or waives by motion to dismiss or other affirmative action his right to object to the termination; or

(2) The trial court finds that the termination is necessary because:

(A) It is physically impossible to proceed with the trial;

(B) Prejudicial conduct in or out of the courtroom makes it impossible to proceed with the trial without injustice to the defendant;

(C) The jury is unable to agree upon a verdict; or

(D) False statements of a juror on voir dire prevent a fair trial.

Laws 1968, p. 1249, § 1; Laws 1982, p. 3, § 16.

Formerly Code 1933, § 26–507.

§ 16–1–9. Application of title to crimes committed before and after enactment

This title shall govern the construction and punishment of any crime defined in this title committed on and after July 1, 1969, as well as the construction and application of any defense. This title does not apply to or govern the construction or punishment of any crime committed prior to July 1, 1969, or the construction or application of any defense. Such a crime must be construed and punished according to the law existing at the time of the commission thereof in the same manner as if this title had not been enacted.

Laws 1833, Cobb's 1851 Digest, p. 838; Laws 1968, p. 1249, § 1.

Formerly Code 1863, § 4550; Code 1868, § 4570; Code 1873, § 4664; Code 1882, § 4664; Penal Code 1895, § 18; Penal Code 1910, § 18; Code 1933, § 26–103; Code 1933, § 26–103.

§ 16–1–10. Punishment for other crimes

Any conduct that is made criminal by this title or by another statute of this state and for which punishment is not otherwise provided, shall be punished as for a misdemeanor.

Laws 1865–66, p. 233, § 2; Laws 1968, p. 1249, § 1.

Formerly Code 1863, § 4395; Code 1868, § 4436; Code 1873, § 4509; Code 1882, § 4509; Penal Code 1895, § 334; Penal Code 1910, § 339; Code 1933, § 26–5001; Code 1933, § 26–104.

§ 16–1–11. Repeal of criminal statute not to abate status as crime of criminal acts which occurred prior to such repeal

The repeal, repeal and reenactment, or amendment of any law of this state which prohibits any act or omission to act and which provides for any criminal penalty therefor, whether misdemeanor, misdemeanor of a high and aggravated nature, or felony, shall not affect or abate the status as a crime of any such act or omission which occurred prior to the effective date of the Act repealing, repealing and reenacting, or amending such law, nor shall the prosecution of such crime be abated as a result of such repeal, repeal and reenactment, or amendment unless the General Assembly expressly declares otherwise in the Act repealing, repealing and reenacting, or amending such law.

Laws 1987, p. 260, § 1.

CHAPTER 2

CRIMINAL LIABILITY

Article 1

Article 2

Article 1

Culpability

§ 16–2–1. Definition of crime

(a) A "crime" is a violation of a statute of this state in which there is a joint operation of an act or omission to act and intention or criminal negligence.

(b) Criminal negligence is an act or failure to act which demonstrates a willful, wanton, or reckless disregard for the safety of others who might reasonably be expected to be injured thereby.

Laws 1833, Cobb's 1851 Digest, p. 779; Laws 1968, p. 1249, § 1; Laws 2004, Act 439, § 2, eff. July 1, 2004.

Formerly Code 1863, § 4188; Code 1868, § 4227; Code 1873, § 4292; Code 1882, § 4292; Penal Code 1895, § 31; Penal Code 1910, § 31; Code 1933, § 26–201; Code 1933, § 26–601.

Historical and Statutory Notes

The 2004 amendment by Act 439 designated the existing text as subsec. (a) and added subsec. (b).

Laws 2004, Act 439, § 6, provides:

"This Act shall become effective on July 1, 2004, and shall apply to all crimes which occur on or after that date."

§ 16–2–2. Misfortune or accident not a crime

A person shall not be found guilty of any crime committed by misfortune or accident where it satisfactorily appears there was no criminal scheme or undertaking, intention, or criminal negligence.

Laws 1833, Cobb's 1851 Digest, p. 779; Laws 1968, p. 1249, § 1.

Formerly Code 1863, § 4198; Code 1868, § 4237; Code 1873, § 4302; Code 1882, § 4302; Penal Code 1895, § 40; Penal Code 1910, § 40; Code 1933, § 26–404; Code 1933, § 26–602.

§ 16–2–3. Presumption of sound mind and discretion

Every person is presumed to be of sound mind and discretion but the presumption may be rebutted.

Laws 1968, p. 1249, § 1.

Formerly Code 1933, § 26–606.

§ 16–2–4. Acts presumed to be wilful

The acts of a person of sound mind and discretion are presumed to be the product of the person's will but the presumption may be rebutted.

Laws 1968, p. 1249, § 1.

Formerly Code 1933, § 26–603.

§ 16–2–5. Consequences presumed intended

A person of sound mind and discretion is presumed to intend the natural and probable consequences of his acts but the presumption may be rebutted.

Laws 1968, p. 1249, § 1.

Formerly Code 1933, § 26–604.

§ 16–2–6. Intention a question of fact

A person will not be presumed to act with criminal intention but the trier of facts may find such intention upon consideration of the words, conduct, demeanor, motive, and all other circumstances connected with the act for which the accused is prosecuted.

Laws 1833, Cobb's 1851 Digest, p. 779; Laws 1968, p. 1249, § 1.

Formerly Code 1863, § 4189; Code 1868, § 4228; Code 1873, § 4298; Code 1882, § 4293; Penal Code 1895, § 32; Penal Code 1910, § 32; Code 1933, § 26–202; Code 1933, § 26–605.

Article 2

Parties to Crimes

§ 16–2–20. Parties to crime; punishment

(a) Every person concerned in the commission of a crime is a party thereto and may be charged with and convicted of commission of the crime.

(b) A person is concerned in the commission of a crime only if he:

(1) Directly commits the crime;

(2) Intentionally causes some other person to commit the crime under such circumstances that the other person is not guilty of any crime either in fact or because of legal incapacity;

(3) Intentionally aids or abets in the commission of the crime; or

(4) Intentionally advises, encourages, hires, counsels, or procures another to commit the crime.

Laws 1968, p. 1249, § 1.

Formerly Code 1933, § 26–801.

§ 16–2–21. Trial and conviction of parties who did not directly commit the crime

Any party to a crime who did not directly commit the crime may be indicted, tried, convicted, and punished for commission of the crime upon proof that the crime was committed and that he was a party thereto, although the person claimed to have directly committed the crime has not been prosecuted or convicted, has been convicted of a different crime or degree of crime, or is not amenable to justice or has been acquitted.

Laws 1968, p. 1249, § 1.

Formerly Code 1933, § 26–802.

§ 16–2–22. Criminal responsibility of corporations

(a) A corporation may be prosecuted for the act or omission constituting a crime only if:

(1) The crime is defined by a statute which clearly indicates a legislative purpose to impose liability on a corporation, and an agent of the corporation performs the conduct which is an element of the crime while acting within the scope of his office or employment and in behalf of the corporation; or

(2) The commission of the crime is authorized, requested, commanded, performed, or recklessly tolerated by the board of directors or by a managerial official who is acting within the scope of his employment in behalf of the corporation.

(b) For the purposes of this Code section, the term:

(1) "Agent" means any director, officer, servant, employee, or other person who is authorized to act in behalf of the corporation.

(2) "Managerial official" means an officer of the corporation or any other agent who has a position of comparable authority for the formulation of corporate policy or the supervision of subordinate employees.

Laws 1968, p. 1249, § 1.

Formerly Code 1933, § 26–803.

CHAPTER 3

DEFENSES TO CRIMINAL PROSECUTIONS

Article 1

Responsibility

§ 16–3–1. Minimum age

A person shall not be considered or found guilty of a crime unless he has attained the age of 13 years at the time of the act, omission, or negligence constituting the crime.

Laws 1968, p. 1249, § 1.

Formerly Code 1933, § 26–701.

§ 16–3–2. Mental capacity; insanity

A person shall not be found guilty of a crime if, at the time of the act, omission, or negligence constituting the crime, the person did not have mental capacity to distinguish between right and wrong in relation to such act, omission, or negligence.

Laws 1968, p. 1249, § 1.

Formerly Code 1933, § 26–702.

§ 16–3–3. Delusional compulsion

A person shall not be found guilty of a crime when, at the time of the act, omission, or negligence constituting the crime, the person, because of mental disease, injury, or congenital deficiency, acted as he did because of a delusional compulsion as to such act which overmastered his will to resist committing the crime.

Laws 1968, p. 1249, § 1.

Formerly Code 1933, § 26–703.

§ 16–3–4. Intoxication

(a) A person shall not be found guilty of a crime when, at the time of the act, omission, or negligence constituting the crime, the person, because of involuntary intoxication, did not have sufficient mental capacity to distinguish between right and wrong in relation to such act.

(b) Involuntary intoxication means intoxication caused by:

(1) Consumption of a substance through excusable ignorance; or

(2) The coercion, fraud, artifice, or contrivance of another person.

(c) Voluntary intoxication shall not be an excuse for any criminal act or omission.

Laws 1833, Cobb's 1851 Digest, p. 779; Laws 1968, p. 1249, § 1.

Formerly Code 1863, § 4197; Code 1868, § 4236; Code 1873, § 4301; Code 1882, § 4301; Penal Code 1895, § 39; Penal Code 1910, § 39; Code 1933, § 26–403; Code 1933, § 26–704.

§ 16–3–5. Mistake of fact

A person shall not be found guilty of a crime if the act or omission to act constituting the crime was induced by a misapprehension of fact which, if true, would have justified the act or omission.

Laws 1968, p. 1249, § 1; Laws 1969, p. 857, § 3.

Formerly Code 1933, § 26–705.

Article 2

Justification and Excuse

§ 16–3–20. Justification as a defense

The fact that a person's conduct is justified is a defense to prosecution for any crime based on that conduct. The defense of justification can be claimed:

(1) When the person's conduct is justified under Code Section 16–3–21, 16–3–23, 16–3–24, 16–3–25, or 16–3–26;

(2) When the person's conduct is in reasonable fulfillment of his duties as a government officer or employee;

(3) When the person's conduct is the reasonable discipline of a minor by his parent or a person in loco parentis;

(4) When the person's conduct is reasonable and is performed in the course of making a lawful arrest;

(5) When the person's conduct is justified for any other reason under the laws of this state; or

(6) In all other instances which stand upon the same footing of reason and justice as those enumerated in this article.

Laws 1968, p. 1249, § 1; Laws 1999, p. 81, § 16.

Formerly Code 1933, § 26–901.

§ 16–3–21. Use of force in defense of self or others, including justifiable homicide; conflicting rules

(a) A person is justified in threatening or using force against another when and to the extent that he or she reasonably believes that such threat or force is necessary to defend himself or herself or a third person against such other's imminent use of unlawful force; however, except as provided in Code Section 16–3–23, a person is justified in using force which is intended or likely to cause death or great bodily harm only if he or she reasonably believes that such force is necessary to prevent death or great bodily injury to himself or herself or a third person or to prevent the commission of a forcible felony.

(b) A person is not justified in using force under the circumstances specified in subsection (a) of this Code section if he:

(1) Initially provokes the use of force against himself with the intent to use such force as an excuse to inflict bodily harm upon the assailant;

(2) Is attempting to commit, committing, or fleeing after the commission or attempted commission of a felony; or

(3) Was the aggressor or was engaged in a combat by agreement unless he withdraws from the encounter and effectively communicates to such other person his intent to do so and the other, notwithstanding, continues or threatens to continue the use of unlawful force.

(c) Any rule, regulation, or policy of any agency of the state or any ordinance, resolution, rule, regulation, or policy of any county, municipality, or other political subdivision of the state which is in conflict with this Code section shall be null, void, and of no force and effect.

(d) In a prosecution for murder or manslaughter, if a defendant raises as a defense a justification provided by subsection (a) of this Code section, the defendant, in order to establish the defendant's reasonable belief that the use of force or deadly force was immediately necessary, may be permitted to offer:

(1) Relevant evidence that the defendant had been the victim of acts of family violence or child abuse committed by the deceased, as such acts are described in Code Sections 19–13–1 and 19–15–1, respectively; and

(2) Relevant expert testimony regarding the condition of the mind of the defendant at the time of the offense, including those relevant facts and circumstances relating to the family violence or child abuse that are the bases of the expert's opinion.

Laws 1833, Cobb's 1851 Digest, p. 785; Laws 1968, p. 1249, § 1; Laws 1975, p. 1209, § 1; Laws 1993, p. 1716, § 2; Laws 2001, p. 1247, § 1.

Formerly Code 1863, § 4230; Code 1868, § 4267; Code 1873, § 4333; Code 1882, § 4333; Penal Code 1895, § 73; Penal Code 1910, § 73; Code 1933, § 26–1014; Code 1933, § 26–902.

Historical and Statutory Notes

The 2001 amendment to subsec. (a) inserted gender neutral language and the words "except as provided in Code Section 16–3–23,".

§ 16–3–22. Persons rendering assistance to law enforcement officers

(a) Any person who renders assistance reasonably and in good faith to any law enforcement officer who is being hindered in the performance of his official duties or whose life is being endangered by the conduct of any other person or persons while performing his official duties shall be immune to the same extent as the law enforcement officer from any criminal liability that might otherwise be incurred or imposed as a result of rendering assistance to the law enforcement officer.

(b) The official report of the law enforcement agency shall create a rebuttable presumption of good faith and reasonableness on the part of the person who assists the law enforcement officer.

(c) The purpose of this Code section is to provide for those persons who act in good faith to assist law enforcement officers whose health and safety is being adversely affected and threatened by the conduct of any other person or persons. This Code section shall be liberally construed so as to carry out the purposes thereof.

Laws 1967, p. 745, §§ 1, 2.

Formerly Code 1933, § 27–219.

§ 16–3–23. Use of force in defense of habitation

A person is justified in threatening or using force against another when and to the extent that he or she reasonably believes that such threat or force is necessary to prevent or terminate such other's unlawful entry into or attack upon a habitation; however, such person is justified in the use of force which is intended or likely to cause death or great bodily harm only if:

(1) The entry is made or attempted in a violent and tumultuous manner and he or she reasonably believes that the entry is attempted or made for the purpose of assaulting or offering personal violence to any person dwelling or being therein and that such force is necessary to prevent the assault or offer of personal violence;

(2) That force is used against another person who is not a member of the family or household and who unlawfully and forcibly enters or has unlawfully and forcibly entered the residence and the person using such force knew or had reason to believe that an unlawful and forcible entry occurred; or

(3) The person using such force reasonably believes that the entry is made or attempted for the purpose of committing a felony therein and that such force is necessary to prevent the commission of the felony.

Laws 1833, Cobb's 1851 Digest, p. 785; Laws 1968, p. 1249, § 1; Laws 2001, p. 1247, § 2.

Formerly Code 1863, § 4229; Code 1868, § 4266; Code 1873, § 4332; Code 1882, § 4332; Penal Code 1895, § 72; Penal Code 1910, § 72; Code 1933, § 26–1013; Code 1933, § 26–903.

Historical and Statutory Notes

The 2001 amendment inserted gender neutral language and the provisions comprising par. (2), and redesignated former par. (2) as par. (3).

§ 16–3–23.1. Use of force in defense of habitation, property, self, or others; no duty to retreat

A person who uses threats or force in accordance with Code Section 16–3–21, relating to the use of force in defense of self or others, Code Section 16–3–23, relating to the use of force in defense of a habitation, or Code Section 16–3–24, relating to the use of force in defense of property other than a habitation, has no duty to retreat and has the right to stand his or her ground and use force as provided in said Code sections, including deadly force.

Laws 2006, Act 599, § 1, eff. July 1, 2006.

§ 16–3–24. Use of force in defense of property

(a) A person is justified in threatening or using force against another when and to the extent that he reasonably believes that such threat or force is necessary to prevent or terminate such other's trespass on or other tortious or criminal interference with real property other than a habitation or personal property:

(1) Lawfully in his possession;

(2) Lawfully in the possession of a member of his immediate family; or

(3) Belonging to a person whose property he has a legal duty to protect.

(b) The use of force which is intended or likely to cause death or great bodily harm to prevent trespass on or other tortious or criminal interference with real property other than a habitation or personal property is not justified unless the person using such force reasonably believes that it is necessary to prevent the commission of a forcible felony.

Laws 1968, p. 1249, § 1.

Formerly Code 1933, § 26–904.

§ 16–3–24.1. "Habitation" and "personal property" defined

As used in Code Sections 16–3–23 and 16–3–24, the term "habitation" means any dwelling, motor vehicle, or place of business, and "personal property" means personal property other than a motor vehicle.

Laws 1998, p. 1153, § 1.1.

§ 16–3–24.2. Immunity from criminal prosecution where use of threats or force is justified

A person who uses threats or force in accordance with Code Section 16–3–21, 16–3–23, 16–3–23.1, or 16–3–24 shall be immune from criminal prosecution therefor unless in the use of deadly force, such person utilizes a weapon the carrying or possession of which is unlawful by such person under Part 2 or 3 of Article 4 of Chapter 11 of this title.

Laws 1998, p. 1153, § 1.2; Laws 1999, p. 81, § 16; Laws 2006, Act 599, § 2, eff. July 1, 2006.

Historical and Statutory Notes

The 2006 amendment by Act 599 substituted "Code Section 16-3-21, 16-3-23, 16-3-23.1," for "Code Section 16-3-23" and substituted "in the use of deadly force," for "any deadly force used by".

§ 16–3–25. Entrapment as a defense

A person is not guilty of a crime if, by entrapment, his conduct is induced or solicited by a government officer or employee, or agent of either, for the purpose of obtaining evidence to be used in prosecuting the person for commission of the crime. Entrapment exists where the idea and intention of the commission of the crime originated with a government officer or employee, or with an agent of either, and he, by undue persuasion, incitement, or deceitful means, induced the accused to commit the act which the accused would not have committed except for the conduct of such officer.

Laws 1968, p. 1249, § 1.

Formerly Code 1933, § 26–905.

§ 16–3–26. Coercion as a defense

A person is not guilty of a crime, except murder, if the act upon which the supposed criminal liability is based is performed under such coercion that the person reasonably believes that performing the act is the only way to prevent his imminent death or great bodily injury.

Laws 1833, Cobb's 1851 Digest, p. 780; Laws 1968, p. 1249, § 1.

Formerly Code 1863, § 4202; Code 1868, § 4238; Code 1873, § 4303; Code 1882, § 4303; Penal Code 1895, § 41; Penal Code 1910, § 41; Code 1933, § 26–402; Code 1933, § 26–906.

§ 16–3–27. Benefit of clergy

Since it is no longer needed or appropriate, the ancient device of benefit of clergy shall not exist.

Laws 1833, Cobb's 1851 Digest, p. 837; Laws 1968, p. 1249, § 1.

Formerly Code 1863, § 4547; Code 1868, § 4567; Code 1873, § 4661; Code 1882, § 4661; Penal Code 1895, § 17; Penal Code 1910, § 17; Code 1933, § 26–102; Code 1933, § 26–202.

§ 16–3–28. Affirmative defenses

A defense based upon any of the provisions of this article is an affirmative defense.

Laws 1968, p. 1249, § 1.

Formerly Code 1933, § 26–907.

Article 3

Alibi

§ 16–3–40. Alibi as a defense

The defense of alibi involves the impossibility of the accused's presence at the scene of the offense at the time of its commission. The range of the evidence in respect to time and place must be such as reasonably to exclude the possibility of presence.

Formerly Penal Code 1895, § 992; Penal Code 1910, § 1018; Code 1933, § 38–122.

CHAPTER 4

CRIMINAL ATTEMPT, CONSPIRACY, AND SOLICITATION

§ 16–4–1. Criminal attempt

A person commits the offense of criminal attempt when, with intent to commit a specific crime, he performs any act which constitutes a substantial step toward the commission of that crime.

Laws 1968, p. 1249, § 1.

Formerly Code 1933, § 26–1001.

§ 16–4–2. Criminal attempt conviction lawful though crime was committed

A person may be convicted of the offense of criminal attempt if the crime attempted was actually committed in pursuance of the attempt but may not be convicted of both the criminal attempt and the completed crime.

Laws 1968, p. 1249, § 1.

Formerly Code 1933, § 26–1004.

§ 16–4–3. Charge of crime includes criminal attempt

A person charged with commission of a crime may be convicted of the offense of criminal attempt as to that crime without being specifically charged with the criminal attempt in the accusation, indictment, or presentment.

Laws 1968, p. 1249, § 1.

Formerly Code 1933, § 26–1005.

§ 16–4–4. Impossibility no defense

It is no defense to a charge of criminal attempt that the crime the accused is charged with attempting was, under the attendant circumstances, factually or legally impossible of commission if such crime could have been committed had the attendant circumstances been as the accused believed them to be.

Laws 1968, p. 1249, § 1.

Formerly Code 1933, § 26–1002.

§ 16–4–5. Abandonment of effort as defense

(a) When a person's conduct would otherwise constitute an attempt to commit a crime under Code Section 16–4–1, it is an affirmative defense that he abandoned his effort to commit the crime or in any other manner prevented its commission under circumstances manifesting a voluntary and complete renunciation of his criminal purpose.

(b) A renunciation of criminal purpose is not voluntary and complete if it results from:

(1) A belief that circumstances exist which increase the probability of detection or apprehension of the person or which render more difficult the accomplishment of the criminal purpose; or

(2) A decision to postpone the criminal conduct until another time.

Laws 1968, p. 1249, § 1.

Formerly Code 1933, § 26–1003.

§ 16–4–6. Punishment

(a) A person convicted of the offense of criminal attempt to commit a crime punishable by death or by life imprisonment shall be punished by imprisonment for not less than one year nor more than 30 years.

(b) A person convicted of the offense of criminal attempt to commit a felony, other than a felony punishable by death or life imprisonment, shall be punished by imprisonment for not less than one year nor more than one-half the maximum period of time for which he or she could have been sentenced if he or she had been convicted of the crime attempted, by one-half the maximum fine to which he or she could have been subjected if he or she had been convicted of the crime attempted, or both.

(c) A person convicted of the offense of criminal attempt to commit a misdemeanor shall be punished as for a misdemeanor.

Laws 1968, p. 1249, § 1; Laws 2007, Act 255, § 1, eff. July 1, 2007.

Formerly Code 1933, § 26–1006.

Historical and Statutory Notes

The 2007 amendment by Act 255, in subsec. (a), substituted "30" for "ten"; and in subsec. (b), added ", other than a felony punishable by death or life imprisonment," and made the subsection gender neutral.

Laws 2007, Act 255, § 2, provides:

"This Act shall become effective on July 1, 2007, and shall apply to all crimes committed on and after that date."

§ 16–4–7. Criminal solicitation

(a) A person commits the offense of criminal solicitation when, with intent that another person engage in conduct constituting a felony, he solicits, requests, commands, importunes, or otherwise attempts to cause the other person to engage in such conduct.

(b) A person convicted of the offense of criminal solicitation to commit a felony shall be punished by imprisonment for not less than one nor more than three years. A person convicted of the offense of criminal solicitation to commit a crime punishable by death or by life imprisonment shall be punished by imprisonment for not less than one nor more than five years.

(c) It is no defense to a prosecution for criminal solicitation that the person solicited could not be guilty of the crime solicited.

(d) The provisions of subsections (a) through (c) of this Code section are cumulative and shall not supersede any other penal law of this state.

Laws 1978, p. 903, § 1.

Formerly Code 1933, §§ 26–1007, 26–1008, 26–1009.

§ 16–4–8. Conspiracy to commit a crime

A person commits the offense of conspiracy to commit a crime when he together with one or more persons conspires to commit any crime and any one or more of such persons does any overt act to effect the object of the conspiracy. A person convicted of the offense of criminal conspiracy to commit a felony shall be punished by imprisonment for not less than one year nor more than one-half the maximum period of time for which he could have been sentenced if he had been convicted of the crime conspired to have been committed, by one-half the maximum fine to which he could have been subjected if he had been convicted of such crime, or both. A person convicted of the offense of criminal conspiracy to commit a misdemeanor shall be punished as for a misdemeanor. A person convicted of the offense of criminal conspiracy to commit a crime punishable by death or by life imprisonment shall be punished by imprisonment for not less than one year nor more than ten years.

Laws 1833, Cobb's 1851 Digest, p. 808; Laws 1968, p. 1249, § 1; Laws 1969, p. 857, § 14; Laws 1977, p. 601, § 2.

Formerly Code 1863, § 4387; Code 1868, § 4425; Code 1873, § 4497; Code 1882, § 4497; Penal Code 1895, § 118; Penal Code 1910, § 120; Code 1933, § 26–1901; Code 1933, § 26–3201.

§ 16–4–8.1. Conviction of conspiracy to commit a crime where crime actually committed

A person may be convicted of the offense of conspiracy to commit a crime, as defined in Code Section 16–4–8, even if the crime which was the objective of the conspiracy was actually committed or completed in pursuance of the conspiracy, but such person may not be convicted of both conspiracy to commit a crime and the completed crime.

Laws 1996, p. 679, § 1.

§ 16–4–9. Withdrawal of co-conspirator

A coconspirator may be relieved from the effects of Code Section 16–4–8 if he can show that before the overt act occurred he withdrew his agreement to commit a crime.

Laws 1968, p. 1249, § 1; Laws 1969, p. 857, § 14.

Formerly Code 1933, § 26–3202.

§ 16–4–10. Domestic terrorism

(a) As used in this Code section, "domestic terrorism" means any violation of, or attempt to violate, the laws of this state or of the United States which:

(1) Is intended or reasonably likely to injure or kill not less than ten individuals as part of a single unlawful act or a series of unlawful acts which are interrelated by distinguishing characteristics; and

(2)(A) Is intended to intimidate the civilian population of this state, any of its political subdivisions, or of the United States;

(B) Is intended to alter, change, or coerce the policy of the government of this state or any of its political subdivisions by intimidation or coercion; or

(C) Is intended to affect the conduct of the government of this state or any of its political subdivisions by use of destructive devices, assassination, or kidnapping.

(b) Notwithstanding any other provision of law, any person who commits, attempts to commit, conspires to commit, or solicits, coerces, or intimidates another to commit a violation of the laws of this state or of the United States for the purpose of domestic terrorism shall, except in cases for which the death penalty may be imposed and the state has served notice of its intention to seek the death penalty, be sentenced to the maximum term of imprisonment and a fine not to exceed the amount prescribed by Code Section 17–10–8, which penalty shall not be suspended, stayed, probated, or withheld.

(c) In addition to any other provision of law, evidence that a person committed an offense for which the death penalty may be imposed under the laws of this state for the purpose of domestic terrorism shall be admissible during the sentencing phase as a statutory aggravating circumstance. It shall be the duty of the judge to consider, or to instruct the jury to consider, in addition to the statutory aggravating circumstances provided in Code Section 17–10–30, that the offense was committed for the purpose of domestic terrorism.

Laws 2002, p. 1284, § 2.

CHAPTER 5

CRIMES AGAINST THE PERSON

Article 1

Homicide

§ 16–5–1. Murder

(a) A person commits the offense of murder when he unlawfully and with malice aforethought, either express or implied, causes the death of another human being.

(b) Express malice is that deliberate intention unlawfully to take the life of another human being which is manifested by external circumstances capable of proof. Malice shall be implied where no considerable provocation appears and where all the circumstances of the killing show an abandoned and malignant heart.

(c) A person also commits the offense of murder when, in the commission of a felony, he causes the death of another human being irrespective of malice.

(d) A person convicted of the offense of murder shall be punished by death, by imprisonment for life without parole, or by imprisonment for life.

Laws 1833, Cobb's 1851 Digest, p. 783; Laws 1968, p. 1249, § 1; Laws 2009, Act 62, § 1, eff. April 29, 2009.

Formerly Code 1863, § 4217; Code 1868, § 4254; Code 1873, § 4320; Code 1882, § 4320; Penal Code 1895, § 60; Penal Code 1910, § 60; Code 1933, § 26–1002; Code 1933, § 26–1101.

Historical and Statutory Notes

The 2009 amendment by Act 62, in subsec. (d), inserted ", by imprisonment for life without parole,".

Laws 2009, Act 62, §§ 8 to 11, provide:

"SECTION 8. Except as provided in this section, the provisions of this Act shall apply only to those offenses committed after the effective date of this Act. With express written consent of the state, an accused whose offense was committed prior to the effective date of this Act may elect in writing to be sentenced under the provisions of this Act, provided that: (1)

jeopardy for the offense charged has not attached or (2) the accused has been sentenced to death but the conviction or sentence has been reversed on appeal and the state is not barred from seeking prosecution after the remand.

"SECTION 9. Except as provided in Section 8 of this Act, the amendment or repeal of a Code section by this Act shall not affect any sentence imposed by any court of this state prior to the effective date of this Act.

"SECTION 10. A person may be sentenced to life without parole without the prosecutor seeking the death penalty under the laws of this state.

"SECTION 11.(a) This Act shall become effective upon its approval by the Governor or upon its becoming law without such approval and shall apply to all crimes committed on and after such date, and except as provided in Section 8 of this Act, the law as set forth in Section 2 and in Sections 3 through 7 of this Act as it existed prior to the effective date of this Act shall apply to all offenses committed on and before such date.

"(b) The provisions of this Act shall not affect or abate the status as a crime of any such act or omission which occurred prior to the effective date of the Act repealing, repealing and reenacting, or amending such law, nor shall the prosecution of such crime be abated as a result of such repeal, repeal and reenactment, or amendment."

§ 16–5–2. Voluntary manslaughter

(a) A person commits the offense of voluntary manslaughter when he causes the death of another human being under circumstances which would otherwise be murder and if he acts solely as the result of a sudden, violent, and irresistible passion resulting from serious provocation sufficient to excite such passion in a reasonable person; however, if there should have been an interval between the provocation and the killing sufficient for the voice of reason and humanity to be heard, of which the jury in all cases shall be the judge, the killing shall be attributed to deliberate revenge and be punished as murder.

(b) A person who commits the offense of voluntary manslaughter, upon conviction thereof, shall be punished by imprisonment for not less than one nor more than 20 years.

Laws 1833, Cobb's 1851 Digest, pp. 783, 784; Laws 1858, p. 99, § 1; Laws 1968, p. 1249, § 1.

Formerly Code 1863, §§ 4222, 4223; Code 1868, §§ 4259, 4260; Code 1873, §§ 4325, 4326; Code 1882, §§ 4325, 4326; Penal Code 1895, §§ 65, 66; Penal Code 1910, §§ 65, 66; Code 1933, §§ 26–1007, 26–1008; Code 1933, § 26–1102.

§ 16–5–3. Involuntary manslaughter

(a) A person commits the offense of involuntary manslaughter in the commission of an unlawful act when he causes the death of another human being without any intention to do so by the commission of an unlawful act other than a felony. A person who commits the offense of involuntary manslaughter in the commission of an unlawful act, upon conviction thereof, shall be punished by imprisonment for not less than one year nor more than ten years.

(b) A person commits the offense of involuntary manslaughter in the commission of a lawful act in an unlawful manner when he causes the death of another human being without any intention to do so, by the commission of a lawful act in an unlawful manner likely to cause death or great bodily harm. A person who commits the offense of involuntary manslaughter in the commission of a lawful act in an unlawful manner, upon conviction thereof, shall be punished as for a misdemeanor.

Laws 1833, Cobb's 1851 Digest, p. 784; Laws 1951, p. 737, § 1; Laws 1968, p. 1249, § 1; Laws 1984, p. 397, § 1.

Formerly Code 1863, §§ 4224, 4225, 4226; Code 1868, §§ 4261, 4262, 4263; Code 1873, §§ 4327, 4328, 4329; Code 1882, §§ 4327, 4328, 4329; Penal Code 1895, §§ 67, 68, 69; Penal Code 1910, §§ 67, 68, 69; Code 1933, §§ 26–1009, 26–1010; Code 1933, § 26–1103.

§ 16–5–4. Death not have to occur within certain time to be homicide

In order to be a homicide punishable under this article, death need not have occurred within a year and a day from the date of the injury alleged to have caused such death.

Laws 1991, p. 719, § 1.

§ 16–5–5. Assisting suicide

(a) As used in this Code section, the term:

(1) "Intentionally and actively assisting suicide" means direct and physical involvement, intervention, or participation in the act of suicide which is carried out free of any threat, force, duress, or deception and with understanding of the consequences of such conduct.

(2) "Suicide" means the intentional and willful termination of one's own life.

(b) Any person who publicly advertises, offers, or holds himself or herself out as offering that he or she will intentionally and actively assist another person in the commission of suicide and commits any overt act to further that purpose is guilty of a felony and, upon conviction thereof, shall be punished by imprisonment for not less than one nor more than five years.

(c) Any person who knowingly and willfully commits any act which destroys the volition of another, such as fraudulent practices upon such person's fears, affections, or sympathies; duress; or any undue influence whereby the will of one person is substituted for the wishes of another, and thereby intentionally causes or induces such other person to commit or attempt to commit suicide shall be guilty of a felony and, upon conviction thereof, shall be punished by imprisonment for not less than one nor more than ten years.

(d) The provisions of this Code section shall not be deemed to affect any of the laws, in whole or in part, that may be applicable to the withholding or withdrawal of medical or health care treatment, including, but not limited to, laws related to a living will, a durable power of attorney for health care, an advance directive for health care, or a written order not to resuscitate.

Laws 1994, p. 1370, § 1; Laws 2007, Act 48, § 5, eff. July 1, 2007.

Historical and Statutory Notes

The 2007 amendment by Act 48, in subsec. (d), inserted "an advance directive for health care," near the end of the subsection.

Article 2

Assault and Battery

§ 16–5–20. Simple assault

(a) A person commits the offense of simple assault when he or she either:

(1) Attempts to commit a violent injury to the person of another; or

(2) Commits an act which places another in reasonable apprehension of immediately receiving a violent injury.

(b) Except as provided in subsections (c) through (h) of this Code section, a person who commits the offense of simple assault shall be guilty of a misdemeanor.

(c) Any person who commits the offense of simple assault in a public transit vehicle or station shall, upon conviction thereof, be punished for a misdemeanor of a high and aggravated nature. For purposes of this Code section, "public transit vehicle" means a bus, van, or rail car used for the transportation of passengers within a system which receives a subsidy from tax revenues or is operated under a franchise contract with a county or municipality of this state.

(d) If the offense of simple assault is committed between past or present spouses, persons who are parents of the same child, parents and children, stepparents and stepchildren, foster parents and foster children, or other persons excluding siblings living or formerly living in the same household, the defendant shall be punished for a misdemeanor of a high and aggravated nature. In no event shall this subsection be applicable to corporal punishment administered by a parent or guardian to a child or administered by a person acting in loco parentis.

(e) Any person who commits the offense of simple assault against a person who is 65 years of age or older shall, upon conviction thereof, be punished for a misdemeanor of a high and aggravated nature.

(f) Any person who commits the offense of simple assault against an employee of a public school system of this state while such employee is engaged in official duties or on school property shall, upon conviction of such offense, be punished for a misdemeanor of a high and aggravated nature. For purposes of this Code section, "school property" shall include public school buses and stops for public school buses as designated by local school boards of education.

(g) Any person who commits the offense of simple assault against a female who is pregnant at the time of the offense shall, upon conviction thereof, be punished for a misdemeanor of a high and aggravated nature.

(h) Nothing in this Code section shall be construed to permit the prosecution of:

(1) Any person for conduct relating to an abortion for which the consent of the pregnant woman, or person authorized by law to act on her behalf, has been obtained or for which such consent is implied by law;

(2) Any person for any medical treatment of the pregnant woman or her unborn child; or

(3) Any woman with respect to her unborn child.

For the purposes of this subsection, the term "unborn child" means a member of the species homo sapiens at any stage of development who is carried in the womb.

Laws 1833, Cobb's 1851 Digest, p. 787; Laws 1968, p. 1249, § 1; Laws 1991, p. 971, §§ 1, 2; Laws 1999, p. 381, § 2; Laws 1999, p. 562, § 2; Laws 2004, Act 560, § 1, eff. July 1, 2004; Laws 2005, Act 19, § 16, eff. April 7, 2005; Laws 2006, Act 654, § 1, eff. July 1, 2006.

Formerly Code 1863, §§ 4256, 4257; Code 1868, §§ 4291, 4292; Code 1873, §§ 4357, 4358; Code 1882, §§ 4357, 4358; Penal Code 1895, §§ 95, 96; Penal Code 1910, §§ 95, 96; Code 1933, §§ 26–1401, 26–1402; Code 1933, § 26–1301.

Historical and Statutory Notes

The 2004 amendment by Act 560 added subsec. (f).

Laws 2004, Act 560, § 9(b), provides:

"Part I of this Act shall become effective on July 1, 2004, and shall apply to offenses committed on or after such date."

The 2005 amendment by Act 19 was a provision contained in a correction bill.

The 2006 amendment by Act 654, in subsec. (b), substituted "through (h)" for "through (f)"; and added new subsecs. (g) and (h).

Laws 2006, Act 654, § 5, provides:

"This Act shall become effective on July 1, 2006, and shall apply to all offenses committed on or after such date."

§ 16–5–21. Aggravated assault

(a) A person commits the offense of aggravated assault when he or she assaults:

(1) With intent to murder, to rape, or to rob;

(2) With a deadly weapon or with any object, device, or instrument which, when used offensively against a person, is likely to or actually does result in serious bodily injury; or

(3) A person or persons without legal justification by discharging a firearm from within a motor vehicle toward a person or persons.

(b) Except as provided in subsections (c) through (k) of this Code section, a person convicted of the offense of aggravated assault shall be punished by imprisonment for not less than one nor more than 20 years.

(c) A person who knowingly commits the offense of aggravated assault upon a peace officer while the peace officer is engaged in, or on account of the performance of, his or her official duties shall, upon conviction thereof, be punished by imprisonment for not less than five nor more than 20 years.

(d) Any person who commits the offense of aggravated assault against a person who is 65 years of age or older shall, upon conviction thereof, be punished by imprisonment for not less than three nor more than 20 years.

(e)(1) As used in this subsection, the term "correctional officer" shall include superintendents, wardens, deputy wardens, guards, and correctional officers of state, county, and municipal penal institutions who are certified by the Georgia Peace Officer Standards and Training Council pursuant to Chapter 8 of Title 35 and employees of the Department of Juvenile Justice who are known to be employees of the department or who have given reasonable identification of their employment. The term "correctional officer" shall also include county jail officers who are certified or registered by the Georgia Peace Officer Standards and Training Council pursuant to Chapter 8 of Title 35.

(2) A person who knowingly commits the offense of aggravated assault upon a correctional officer while the correctional officer is engaged in, or on account of the performance of, his or her official duties shall, upon conviction thereof, be punished by imprisonment for not less than five nor more than 20 years.

(f) Any person who commits the offense of aggravated assault in a public transit vehicle or station shall, upon conviction thereof, be punished by imprisonment for not less than three nor more than 20 years. For purposes of this Code section, "public transit vehicle" has the same meaning as in subsection (c) of Code Section 16–5–20.

(g) Any person who commits the offense of aggravated assault upon a person in the course of violating Code Section 16–8–2 where the property that was the subject of the theft was a vehicle engaged in commercial transportation of cargo or any appurtenance thereto, including without limitation any such trailer, semitrailer, container, or other associated equipment, or the cargo being transported therein or thereon, shall upon conviction be punished by imprisonment for not less than five years nor more than 20 years, a fine not less than $50,000.00 nor more than $200,000.00, or both such fine and imprisonment. For purposes of this subsection, the term "vehicle" includes without limitation any railcar.

(h) A person convicted of an offense described in paragraph (3) of subsection (a) of this Code section shall be punished by imprisonment for not less than five nor more than 20 years.

(i) Any person who commits the offense of aggravated assault involving the use of a firearm upon a student or teacher or other school personnel within a school safety zone as defined in paragraph (1) of subsection (a) of Code Section 16–11–127.1 shall, upon conviction thereof, be punished by imprisonment for not less than five nor more than 20 years.

(j) If the offense of aggravated assault is committed between past or present spouses, persons who are parents of the same child, parents and children, stepparents and stepchildren, foster parents and foster children, or other persons excluding siblings living or formerly living in the same household, the defendant shall be punished by imprisonment for not less than three nor more than 20 years.

(k) Any person who commits the offense of aggravated assault with intent to rape against a child under the age of 14 years shall be punished by imprisonment for not less than 25 nor more than 50 years. Any person convicted under this subsection shall, in addition, be subject to the sentencing and punishment provisions of Code Section 17–10–6.2.

(*l*) A person who knowingly commits the offense of aggravated assault upon an officer of the court while such officer is engaged in, or on account of the performance of, his or her official duties shall, upon conviction thereof, be punished by imprisonment for not less than five nor more than 20 years. As used in this subsection, the term "officer of the court" means a judge, attorney, clerk of court, deputy clerk of court, court reporter, court interpreter or probation officer.

Laws 1833, Cobb's 1851 Digest, pp. 787–789; Laws 1840, Cobb's 1851 Digest, p. 788; Laws 1866, p. 151, § 1; Laws 1968, p. 1249, § 1; Laws 1976, p. 543, § 1; Laws 1982, p. 1242, § 2; Laws 1984, p. 900, § 1; Laws 1985, p. 628, § 1; Laws 1991, p. 971, §§ 3, 4; Laws 1994, p. 1012, § 8; Laws 1994, p. 1920, §§ 1, 2; Laws 1996, p. 988, § 1; Laws 1997, p. 1453, § 1; Laws 1999, p. 381, § 3; Laws 2000, p. 1626, § 1; Laws 2003, Act 9, § 16, eff. May 14, 2003; Laws 2004, Act 793, § 1, eff. July 1, 2004; Laws 2006, Act 571, § 4, eff. July 1, 2006; Laws 2010, Act 646, § 1, eff. July 1, 2010.

Formerly Code 1863, §§ 4250, 4258, 4259, 4260; Code 1868, §§ 4285, 4293, 4294, 4295; Code 1873, §§ 4351, 4359, 4360, 4361; Code 1882, §§ 4351, 4359, 4360, 4361; Penal Code 1895, §§ 97, 98, 99, 100; Penal Code 1910, §§ 97, 98, 99, 100; Code 1933, §§ 26–1403, 26–1404, 26–1405, 26–1406; Code 1933, § 26–1302.

Historical and Statutory Notes

The 2000 amendment added the second sentence to subsec. (e)(1).

The 2003 amendment by Act 9, in subsec. (b), substituted "(c) through (i)" for "(c), (d), (e), (f), (g), (h), and (i)".

The 2004 amendment by Act 793 inserted subsec. (f.1).

The 2006 amendment by Act 571, in subsec. (b), substituted "through (k)" for "through (i)"; redesignated subsecs. (f.1) through (i) as subsecs. (g) through (j); and added new par. (k).

Laws 2006, Act 571, §§ 1 and 30, provide:

"SECTION 1. The General Assembly finds and declares that recidivist sexual offenders, sexual offenders who use physical violence, and sexual offenders who prey on children are sexual predators who present an extreme threat to the public safety. Many sexual offenders are extremely likely to use physical violence and to repeat their offenses; and some sexual offenders commit many offenses, have many more victims than are ever reported, and are prosecuted for only a fraction of their crimes. The General Assembly finds that this makes the cost of sexual offender victimization to society at large, while incalculable, clearly exorbitant. The General Assembly further finds that the high level of threat that a sexual predator presents to the public safety, and the long-term effects suffered by victims of sex offenses, provide the state with sufficient justification to implement a strategy that includes:

"(1) Incarcerating sexual offenders and maintaining adequate facilities to ensure that decisions to release sexual predators into the community are not made on the basis of inadequate space;

"(2) Requiring the registration of sexual offenders, with a requirement that complete and accurate information be maintained and accessible for use by law enforcement authorities, communities, and the public;

"(3) Providing for community and public notification concerning the presence of sexual offenders;

"(4) Collecting data relative to sexual offenses and sexual offenders;

"(5) Requiring sexual predators who are released into the community to wear an electronic monitoring system for the rest of their natural life and to pay for such system; and

"(6) Prohibiting sexual predators from working with children, either for compensation or as a volunteer.

"The General Assembly further finds that the state has a compelling interest in protecting the public from sexual offenders and in protecting children from predatory sexual activity, and there is sufficient justification for requiring sexual offenders to register and for requiring community and public notification of the presence of sexual offenders. The General Assembly declares that in order to protect the public, it is necessary that the sexual offenders be registered and that members of the community and the public be notified of a sexual offender's presence. The designation of a person as a sexual offender is neither a sentence nor a punishment but simply a regulatory mechanism and status resulting from the conviction of certain crimes. Likewise, the designation of a person as a sexual predator is neither a sentence nor a punishment but simply a regulatory mechanism and status resulting from findings by the Sexual Offender Registration Review Board and a court if requested by a sexual offender."

"SECTION 30. (a) This Act shall become effective July 1, 2006.

"(b) Any person required to register pursuant to the provisions of Code Section 42–1–12, relating to the state sexual offender registry, and any person required not to reside within areas where minors congregate, as prohibited by Code Section 42–1–13 [see § 42–1–15], shall not be relieved of the obligation to comply with the provisions of said Code sections by the repeal and reenactment of said Code sections.

"(c) The provisions of this Act shall not affect or abate the status as a crime of any such act or omission which occurred prior to the effective date of the Act repealing, repealing and reenacting, or amending such law, nor shall the prosecution of such crime be abated as a result of such repeal, repeal and reenactment, or amendment."

The 2010 amendment by Act 646 added subsec. (*l*).

§ 16–5–22. Assault conviction lawful though intended crime was committed

A person may be convicted of the offense of assault with intent to commit a crime if the crime intended was actually committed as a result of the assault but may not be convicted of both the assault and completed crime.

Laws 1968, p. 1249, § 1.

Formerly Code 1933, § 26–1303.

§ 16–5–23. Simple battery

(a) A person commits the offense of simple battery when he or she either:

(1) Intentionally makes physical contact of an insulting or provoking nature with the person of another; or

(2) Intentionally causes physical harm to another.

(b) Except as otherwise provided in subsections (c) through (i) of this Code section, a person convicted of the offense of simple battery shall be punished as for a misdemeanor.

(c) Any person who commits the offense of simple battery against a person who is 65 years of age or older or against a female who is pregnant at the time of the offense shall, upon conviction thereof, be punished for a misdemeanor of a high and aggravated nature.

(d) Any person who commits the offense of simple battery in a public transit vehicle or station shall, upon conviction thereof, be punished for a misdemeanor of a high and aggravated nature. For purposes of this Code section, "public transit vehicle" has the same meaning as in subsection (c) of Code Section 16–5–20.

(e) Any person who commits the offense of simple battery against a police officer, law enforcement dog, correction officer, or detention officer engaged in carrying out official duties shall, upon conviction thereof, be punished for a misdemeanor of a high and aggravated nature.

(f) If the offense of simple battery is committed between past or present spouses, persons who are parents of the same child, parents and children, stepparents and stepchildren, foster parents and foster children, or other persons excluding siblings living or formerly living in the same household, the defendant shall be punished for a misdemeanor of a high and aggravated nature. In no event shall this subsection be applicable to corporal punishment administered by a parent or guardian to a child or administered by a person acting in loco parentis.

(g) A person who is an employee, agent, or volunteer at any facility licensed or required to be licensed under Code Section 31–7–3, relating to long-term care facilities, or Code Section 31–7–12, relating to personal care homes, or who is required to be licensed pursuant to Code Section 31–7–151 or 31–7–173, relating to home health care and hospices, who commits the offense of simple battery against a person who is admitted to or receiving services from such facility, person, or entity shall be punished for a misdemeanor of a high and aggravated nature.

(h) Any person who commits the offense of simple battery against a sports official while such sports official is officiating an amateur contest or while such sports official is on or exiting the property where he or she will officiate or has completed officiating an amateur contest shall, upon conviction thereof, be punished for a misdemeanor of a high and aggravated nature. For the purposes of this Code section, the term "sports official" means any person who officiates, umpires, or referees an amateur contest at the collegiate, elementary or secondary school, or recreational level.

(i) Any person who commits the offense of simple battery against an employee of a public school system of this state while such employee is engaged in official duties or on school property shall, upon conviction of such offense, be punished for a misdemeanor of a high and aggravated nature. For purposes of this Code section, "school property" shall include public school buses and stops for public school buses as designated by local school boards of education.

Laws 1833, Cobb's 1851 Digest, p. 788; Laws 1968, p. 1249, § 1; Laws 1987, p. 557, § 1; Laws 1991, p. 971, §§ 5, 6; Laws 1992, p. 2055, § 1; Laws 1993, p. 91, § 16; Laws 1997, p. 907, § 1; Laws 1999, p. 381, § 4; Laws 1999, p. 562, § 3; Laws 2000, p. 16, § 1; Laws 2004, Act 560, § 2, eff. July 1, 2004; Laws 2005, Act 19, § 16, eff. April 7, 2005.

Formerly Code 1863, § 4262; Code 1868, § 4297; Code 1873, § 4363; Code 1882, § 4363; Penal Code 1895, § 102; Penal Code 1910, § 102; Code 1933, § 26–1408; Code 1933, § 26–1304.

Historical and Statutory Notes

The 2000 amendment substituted reference to subsec. (h) for (g) near the beginning of subsec. (b), and added subsec. (h).

The 2004 amendment by Act 560 added subsec. (i).

Laws 2004, Act 560, § 9(b), provides:

"Part I of this Act shall become effective on July 1, 2004, and shall apply to offenses committed on or after such date."

The 2005 amendment by Act 19 was a provision contained in a correction bill.

§ 16–5–23.1. Battery

(a) A person commits the offense of battery when he or she intentionally causes substantial physical harm or visible bodily harm to another.

(b) As used in this Code section, the term "visible bodily harm" means bodily harm capable of being perceived by a person other than the victim and may include, but is not limited to, substantially blackened eyes, substantially swollen lips or other facial or body parts, or substantial bruises to body parts.

(c) Except as provided in subsections (d) through (*l*) of this Code section, a person who commits the offense of battery is guilty of a misdemeanor.

(d) Upon the second conviction for battery against the same victim, the defendant shall be punished by imprisonment for not less than ten days nor more than 12 months, by a fine not to exceed $ 1,000.00, or both. The minimum sentence of ten days for a second offense shall not be suspended, probated, deferred, stayed, or withheld; provided, however, that it is within the authority and discretion of the sentencing judge to:

(1) Allow the sentence to be served on weekends by weekend confinement or during the nonworking hours of the defendant. A weekend shall commence and shall end in the discretion of the sentencing judge, and the nonworking hours of the defendant shall be determined in the discretion of the sentencing judge; or

(2) Suspend, probate, defer, stay, or withhold the minimum sentence where there exists clear and convincing evidence that imposition of the minimum sentence would either create an undue hardship upon the defendant or result in a failure of justice.

(e) Upon a third or subsequent conviction for battery against the same victim, the defendant shall be guilty of a felony and shall be punished by imprisonment for not less than one nor more than five years. The minimum sentence provisions contained in subsection (d) of this Code section shall apply to sentences imposed pursuant to this subsection.

(f) If the offense of battery is committed between past or present spouses, persons who are parents of the same child, parents and children, stepparents and stepchildren, foster parents and foster children, or other persons living or formerly living in the same household, then such offense shall constitute the offense of family violence battery and shall be punished as follows:

(1) Upon a first conviction of family violence battery, the defendant shall be guilty of and punished for a misdemeanor; and

(2) Upon a second or subsequent conviction of family violence battery against the same or another victim, the defendant shall be guilty of a felony and shall be punished by imprisonment for not less than one nor more than five years. In no event shall this subsection be applicable to reasonable corporal punishment administered by parent to child.

(g) Any person who commits the offense of battery in a public transit vehicle or station shall, upon conviction thereof, be punished for a misdemeanor of a high and aggravated nature. For purposes of this Code section, "public transit vehicle" has the same meaning as in subsection (c) of Code Section 16–5–20.

(h) Any person who commits the offense of battery against a female who is pregnant at the time of the offense shall, upon conviction thereof, be punished for a misdemeanor of a high and aggravated nature.

(i) Any person who commits the offense of battery against a teacher or other school personnel engaged in the performance of official duties or while on school property shall, upon conviction thereof, be punished by imprisonment for not less than one nor more than five years or a fine of not more than $10,000.00, or both. For purposes of this Code section, "school property" shall include public school buses and public school bus stops as designated by local school boards of education.

(j) Except as otherwise provided in subsection (e) and paragraph (2) of subsection (f) of this Code section, any person who commits the offense of battery against a person who is 65 years of age or older shall, upon conviction thereof, be punished for a misdemeanor of a high and aggravated nature.

(k) A person who is an employee, agent, or volunteer at any facility licensed or required to be licensed under Code Section 31–7–3, relating to long-term care facilities, or Code Section 31–7–12, relating to personal care homes, or who is required to be licensed pursuant to Code Section 31–7–151 or 31–7–173, relating to home health care and hospices, who commits the offense of battery against a person who is admitted to or receiving services from such facility, person, or entity shall, upon conviction thereof, be punished by imprisonment for not less than one nor more than five years, or a fine of not more than $ 2,000.00, or both.

(*l*) Any person who commits the offense of battery against a sports official while such sports official is officiating an amateur contest or while such sports official is on or exiting the property where he or she will officiate or has completed officiating an amateur contest shall, upon conviction thereof, be punished for a misdemeanor of a high and aggravated nature. For purposes of this Code section, the term "sports official" means any person who officiates, umpires, or referees an amateur contest at the collegiate, elementary or secondary school, or recreational level.

Laws 1987, p. 1010, § 1; Laws 1991, p. 971, §§ 7, 8; Laws 1996, p. 449, § 1; Laws 1997, p. 907, § 2; Laws 1997, p. 1064, § 9; Laws 1998, p. 128, § 16; Laws 1999, p. 562, § 4; Laws 2000, p. 16, § 1; Laws 2004, Act 560, § 3, eff. July 1, 2004.

Historical and Statutory Notes

The 2000 amendment substituted reference to subsec. (*l*) for (k) near the beginning of subsec. (c), and added subsec. (*l*).

The 2004 amendment by Act 560, in subsec. (i), deleted the comma following "school personnel" and added the second sentence beginning with "For purposes of this Code section".

Laws 2004, Act 560, § 9(b), provides:

"Part I of this Act shall become effective on July 1, 2004, and shall apply to offenses committed on or after such date."

§ 16–5–24. Aggravated battery

(a) A person commits the offense of aggravated battery when he or she maliciously causes bodily harm to another by depriving him or her of a member of his or her body, by rendering a member of his or her body useless, or by seriously disfiguring his or her body or a member thereof.

(b) Except as provided in subsections (c) through (h) of this Code section, a person convicted of the offense of aggravated battery shall be punished by imprisonment for not less than one nor more than 20 years.

(c) A person who knowingly commits the offense of aggravated battery upon a peace officer while the officer is engaged in, or on account of the performance of, his or her official duties shall, upon conviction thereof, be punished by imprisonment for not less than ten nor more than 20 years.

(d) Any person who commits the offense of aggravated battery against a person who is 65 years of age or older shall, upon conviction thereof, be punished by imprisonment for not less than five nor more than 20 years.

(e)(1) As used in this subsection, the term "correctional officer" shall include superintendents, wardens, deputy wardens, guards, and correctional officers of state, county, and municipal penal institutions who are certified by the Georgia Peace Officer Standards and Training Council pursuant to Chapter 8 of Title 35 and employees of the Department of Juvenile Justice who are known to be employees of the department or who have given reasonable identification of their employment. The term "correctional officer" shall also include county jail officers who are certified or registered by the Georgia Peace Officer Standards and Training Council pursuant to Chapter 8 of Title 35.

(2) A person who knowingly commits the offense of aggravated battery upon a correctional officer while the correctional officer is engaged in, or on account of the performance of, his or her official duties shall, upon conviction thereof, be punished by imprisonment for not less than ten nor more than 20 years.

(f) Any person who commits the offense of aggravated battery in a public transit vehicle or station shall, upon conviction thereof, be punished by imprisonment for not less than five nor more than 20 years. For purposes of this Code section, "public transit vehicle" has the same meaning as in subsection (c) of Code Section 16–5–20.

(g) Any person who commits the offense of aggravated battery upon a student or teacher or other school personnel within a school safety zone as defined in paragraph (1) of subsection (a) of Code Section 16–11–127.1 shall, upon conviction thereof, be punished by imprisonment for not less than five nor more than 20 years.

(h) If the offense of aggravated battery is committed between past or present spouses, persons who are parents of the same child, parents and children, stepparents and stepchildren, foster parents and foster children, or other persons excluding siblings living or formerly living in the same household, the defendant shall be punished by imprisonment for not less than three nor more than 20 years.

Laws 1833, Cobb's 1851 Digest, pp. 786, 787; Laws 1968, p. 1249, § 1; Laws 1976, p. 543, § 2; Laws 1982, p. 3, § 16; Laws 1984, p. 900, § 2; Laws 1985, p. 628, § 2; Laws 1991, p. 971, §§ 9, 10; Laws 1994, p. 1012, § 9; Laws 1996, p. 988, § 2; Laws 1997, p. 1453, § 1; Laws 1999, p. 381, § 5; Laws 2000, p. 1626, § 2; Laws 2003, Act 9, § 16, eff. May 14, 2003.

Formerly Code 1863, § 4238; Code 1868, § 4273; Code 1873, § 4339; Code 1882, § 4339; Penal Code 1895, § 83; Penal Code 1910, § 83; Code 1933, § 26–1201; Code 1933, § 26–1305.

Historical and Statutory Notes

The 2000 amendment added the second sentence to subsec. (e)(1).

The 2003 amendment by Act 9, in subsec. (b), substituted "(c) through (h)" for "(c), (d), (e), (f), (g), and (h)".

§ 16–5–25. Opprobrious or abusive language may be justification

A person charged with the offense of simple assault or simple battery may introduce in evidence any opprobrious or abusive language used by the person against whom force was threatened or used; and the trier of facts may, in its discretion, find that the words used were justification for simple assault or simple battery.

Laws 1833, Cobb's 1851 Digest, p. 786; Laws 1968, p. 1249, § 1.

Formerly Code 1863, § 4576; Code 1868, § 4597; Code 1873, § 4694; Code 1882, § 4694; Penal Code 1895, § 103; Penal Code 1910, § 103; Code 1933, § 26–1409; Code 1933, § 26–1306.

§ 16–5–26. Notice of conviction; publication

(a) The clerk of the court in which a person is convicted of a second or subsequent violation of Code Section 16–5–20 and is sentenced pursuant to subsection (d) of such Code section, Code Section 16–5–23 and is sentenced pursuant to subsection (f) of such Code section, or Code Section 16–5–23.1 shall cause to be published a notice of conviction for such person. Such notice of conviction shall be published in the manner of legal notices in the legal organ of the county in which such person resides or, in the case of nonresidents, in the legal organ of the county in which the person was convicted. Such notice of conviction shall be one column wide by two inches long and shall contain the photograph taken by the arresting law enforcement agency at the time of arrest; the name and address of the convicted person; the date, time, and place of arrest; and the disposition of the case and shall be published once in the legal organ of the appropriate county in the second week following such conviction or as soon thereafter as publication may be made.

(b) The convicted person for which a notice of conviction is published pursuant to this Code section shall be assessed $25.00 for the cost of publication of such notice and such assessment shall be imposed at the time of conviction in addition to any other fine imposed.

(c) The clerk of the court, the publisher of any legal organ which publishes a notice of conviction, and any other person involved in the publication of an erroneous notice of conviction shall be immune from civil or criminal liability for such erroneous publication, provided that such publication was made in good faith.

Laws 2004, Act 560, § 3A, eff. July 1, 2004; Laws 2005, Act 19, § 16, eff. April 7, 2005.

Historical and Statutory Notes

Laws 2004, Act 560, § 9(b), provides:

"Part I of this Act shall become effective on July 1, 2004, and shall apply to offenses committed on or after such date."

The 2005 amendment by Act 19 was a provision contained in a correction bill.

§ 16–5–27. Female genital mutilation

(a) Any person:

(1) Who knowingly circumcises, excises, or infibulates, in whole or in part, the labia majora, labia minora, or clitoris of a female under 18 years of age;

(2) Who is a parent, guardian, or has immediate custody or control of a female under 18 years of age and knowingly consents to or permits the circumcision, excision, or infibulation, in whole or in part, of the labia majora, labia minora, or clitoris of such female; or

(3) Who knowingly removes or causes or permits the removal of a female under 18 years of age from this state for the purpose of circumcising, excising, or infibulating, in whole or in part, the labia majora, labia minora, or clitoris of such female

shall be guilty of female genital mutilation.

(b) A person convicted of female genital mutilation shall be punished by imprisonment for not less than five nor more than 20 years.

(c) This Code section shall not apply to procedures performed by or under the direction of a physician, a registered professional nurse, a certified nurse midwife, or a licensed practical nurse licensed pursuant to Chapter 34 or 26, respectively, of Title 43 when necessary to preserve the physical health of the female. This Code section shall also not apply to any autopsy or limited dissection as defined by Code Section 45–16–21 which is conducted in accordance with Article 2 of Chapter 16 of Title 45.

(d) Consent of the female under 18 years of age or the parent, guardian, or custodian of the female under 18 years of age shall not be a defense to the offense of female genital mutilation. Religion, ritual, custom, or standard practice shall not be a defense to the offense of female genital mutilation.

(e) The statutory privileges provided by Chapter 9 of Title 24 shall not apply to proceedings in which one of the parties to the privilege is charged with a crime against a female under 18 years of age, but such person shall be compellable to give evidence only on the specific act for which the defendant is charged.

Laws 2005, Act 157, § 1, eff. July 1, 2005.

§ 16–5–28. Assault of unborn child

(a) For the purposes of this Code section, the term "unborn child" means a member of the species homo sapiens at any stage of development who is carried in the womb.

(b) A person commits the offense of assault of an unborn child when such person, without legal justification, attempts to inflict violent injury to an unborn child.

(c) Any person convicted of the offense of assault of an unborn child shall be guilty of a misdemeanor.

(d) Nothing in this Code section shall be construed to permit the prosecution of:

(1) Any person for conduct relating to an abortion for which the consent of the pregnant woman, or person authorized by law to act on her behalf, has been obtained or for which such consent is implied by law;

(2) Any person for any medical treatment of the pregnant woman or her unborn child; or

(3) Any woman with respect to her unborn child.

Laws 2006, Act 654, § 1, eff. July 1, 2006.

Historical and Statutory Notes

Laws 2006, Act 654, § 5, provides:

"This Act shall become effective on July 1, 2006, and shall apply to all offenses committed on or after such date."

§ 16–5–29. Battery of an unborn child

(a) For the purposes of this Code section, the term "unborn child" means a member of the species homo sapiens at any stage of development who is carried in the womb.

(b) A person commits the offense of battery of an unborn child when such person, without legal justification, intentionally inflicts physical harm upon an unborn child.

(c) A person convicted of the offense of battery of an unborn child shall be guilty of a misdemeanor.

(d) Nothing in this Code section shall be construed to permit the prosecution of:

(1) Any person for conduct relating to an abortion for which the consent of the pregnant woman, or person authorized by law to act on her behalf, has been obtained or for which such consent is implied by law;

(2) Any person for any medical treatment of the pregnant woman or her unborn child; or

(3) Any woman with respect to her unborn child.

Laws 2006, Act 654, § 1, eff. July 1, 2006.

Historical and Statutory Notes

Laws 2006, Act 654, § 5, provides:

"This Act shall become effective on July 1, 2006, and shall apply to all offenses committed on or after such date."

Article 3

Kidnapping, False Imprisonment, and Related Offenses

§ 16–5–40. Kidnapping

(a) A person commits the offense of kidnapping when such person abducts or steals away another person without lawful authority or warrant and holds such other person against his or her will.

(b)(1) For the offense of kidnapping to occur, slight movement shall be sufficient; provided, however, that any such slight movement of another person which occurs while in the commission of any other offense shall not constitute the offense of kidnapping if such movement is merely incidental to such other offense.

(2) Movement shall not be considered merely incidental to another offense if it:

(A) Conceals or isolates the victim;

(B) Makes the commission of the other offense substantially easier;

(C) Lessens the risk of detection; or

(D) Is for the purpose of avoiding apprehension.

(c) The offense of kidnapping shall be considered a separate offense and shall not merge with any other offense.

(d) A person convicted of the offense of kidnapping shall be punished by:

(1) Imprisonment for not less than ten nor more than 20 years if the kidnapping involved a victim who was 14 years of age or older;

(2) Imprisonment for life or by a split sentence that is a term of imprisonment for not less than 25 years and not exceeding life imprisonment, followed by probation for life, if the kidnapping involved a victim who is less than 14 years of age;

(3) Life imprisonment or death if the kidnapping was for ransom; or

(4) Life imprisonment or death if the person kidnapped received bodily injury.

(e) Any person convicted under this Code section shall, in addition, be subject to the sentencing and punishment provisions of Code Sections 17–10–6.1 and 17–10–7.

(f) The offense of kidnapping is declared to be a continuous offense, and venue may be in any county where the accused exercises dominion or control over the person of another.

Laws 1833, Cobb's 1851 Digest, p. 788; Laws 1876, p. 39, § 1; Laws 1880–81, p. 74, § 1; Laws 1937, p. 489, § 1; Laws 1953, Nov.-Dec. Sess., p. 99, § 1; Laws 1968, p. 1249, § 1; Laws 1982, p. 970, § 1; Laws 1994, p. 1959, § 4; Laws 2006, Act 571, § 5, eff. July 1, 2006; Laws 2009, Act 88, § 1, eff. July 1, 2009.

Formerly Code 1863, §§ 4266, 4267; Code 1868, §§ 4301, 4302; Code 1873, §§ 4367, 4368; Code 1882, §§ 4367, 4368; Penal Code 1895, §§ 109, 110; Penal Code 1910, §§ 109, 110; Code 1933, §§ 26–1601, 26–1602, 26–1603; Code 1933, § 26–1311.

Historical and Statutory Notes

The 2006 amendment by Act 571 rewrote the section which had read:

"(a) A person commits the offense of kidnapping when he abducts or steals away any person without lawful authority or warrant and holds such person against his will.

"(b) A person convicted of the offense of kidnapping shall be punished by imprisonment for not less than ten nor more than 20 years, provided that a person convicted of the offense of kidnapping for ransom shall be punished by life imprisonment or by death and provided, further, that, if the person kidnapped shall have received bodily injury, the person convicted shall be punished by life imprisonment or by death. Any person convicted under this Code section shall, in addition, be subject to the sentencing and punishment provisions of Code Sections 17–10–6.1 and 17–10–7."

Laws 2006, Act 571, §§ 1 and 30, provide:

"SECTION 1. The General Assembly finds and declares that recidivist sexual offenders, sexual offenders who use physical violence, and sexual offenders who prey on children are sexual predators who present an extreme threat to the public safety. Many sexual offenders are extremely likely to use physical violence and to repeat their offenses; and some sexual offenders commit many offenses, have many more victims than are ever reported, and are prosecuted for only a fraction of their crimes. The General Assembly finds that this makes the cost of sexual offender victimization to society at large, while incalculable, clearly exorbitant. The General Assembly further finds that the high level of threat that a sexual predator presents to the public safety, and the long-term effects suffered by victims of sex offenses, provide the state with sufficient justification to implement a strategy that includes:

"(1) Incarcerating sexual offenders and maintaining adequate facilities to ensure that decisions to release sexual predators into the community are not made on the basis of inadequate space;

"(2) Requiring the registration of sexual offenders, with a requirement that complete and accurate information be maintained and accessible for use by law enforcement authorities, communities, and the public;

"(3) Providing for community and public notification concerning the presence of sexual offenders;

"(4) Collecting data relative to sexual offenses and sexual offenders;

"(5) Requiring sexual predators who are released into the community to wear an electronic monitoring system for the rest of their natural life and to pay for such system; and

"(6) Prohibiting sexual predators from working with children, either for compensation or as a volunteer.

"The General Assembly further finds that the state has a compelling interest in protecting the public from sexual offenders and in protecting children from predatory sexual activity, and there is sufficient justification for requiring sexual offenders to register and for requiring community and public notification of the presence of sexual offenders. The General Assembly declares that in order to protect the public, it is necessary that the sexual offenders be registered and that members of the community and the public be notified of a sexual offender's presence. The designation of a person as a sexual offender is neither a sentence nor a punishment but simply a regulatory mechanism and status resulting from the conviction of certain crimes. Likewise, the designation of a person as a sexual predator is neither a sentence nor a punishment but simply a regulatory mechanism and status resulting from findings by the Sexual Offender Registration Review Board and a court if requested by a sexual offender."

"SECTION 30. (a) This Act shall become effective July 1, 2006.

"(b) Any person required to register pursuant to the provisions of Code Section 42–1–12, relating to the state sexual offender registry, and any person required not to reside within areas where minors congregate, as prohibited by Code Section 42–1–13 [see § 42–1–15], shall not be relieved of the obligation to comply with the provisions of said Code sections by the repeal and reenactment of said Code sections.

"(c) The provisions of this Act shall not affect or abate the status as a crime of any such act or omission which occurred prior to the effective date of the Act repealing, repealing and reenacting, or amending such law, nor shall the prosecution of such crime be abated as a result of such repeal, repeal and reenactment, or amendment."

The 2009 amendment by Act 60, in subsec. (a), substituted "such person abducts or steals away another" for "he abducts or steals away any" and inserted "other" and "or her"; redesignated subsec. (b) and (c) as subsecs. (d) and (e) and added new subsecs. (b), (c), and (f).

The 2009 amendment by Act 88 duplicated the amendment by Act 60.

§ 16–5–41. False imprisonment

(a) A person commits the offense of false imprisonment when, in violation of the personal liberty of another, he arrests, confines, or detains such person without legal authority.

(b) A person convicted of the offense of false imprisonment shall be punished by imprisonment for not less than one nor more than ten years.

(c) Any person convicted under this Code section wherein the victim is not the child of the defendant and the victim is less than 14 years of age shall, in addition, be subject to the sentencing and punishment provisions of Code Section 17–10–6.2.

Laws 1833, Cobb's 1851 Digest, p. 788; Laws 1968, p. 1249, § 1; Laws 2006, Act 571, § 6, eff. July 1, 2006.

Formerly Code 1863, §§ 4263, 4264; Code 1868, §§ 4298, 4299; Code 1873, §§ 4364, 4365; Code 1882, §§ 4364, 4365; Penal Code 1895, §§ 106, 107; Penal Code 1910, §§ 106, 107; Code 1933, §§ 26–1501, 26–1502; Code 1933, § 26–1308.

Historical and Statutory Notes

The 2006 amendment by Act 571 added subsec. (c).

Laws 2006, Act 571, §§ 1 and 30, provide:

"SECTION 1. The General Assembly finds and declares that recidivist sexual offenders, sexual offenders who use physical violence, and sexual offenders who prey on children are sexual predators who present an extreme threat to the public safety. Many sexual offenders are extremely likely to use physical violence and to repeat their offenses; and some sexual offenders commit many offenses, have many more victims than are ever reported, and are prosecuted for only a fraction of their crimes. The General Assembly finds that this makes the cost of sexual offender victimization to society at large, while incalculable, clearly exorbitant. The General Assembly further finds that the high level of threat that a sexual predator presents to the public safety, and the long-term effects suffered by victims of sex offenses, provide the state with sufficient justification to implement a strategy that includes:

"(1) Incarcerating sexual offenders and maintaining adequate facilities to ensure that decisions to release sexual predators into the community are not made on the basis of inadequate space;

"(2) Requiring the registration of sexual offenders, with a requirement that complete and accurate information be maintained and accessible for use by law enforcement authorities, communities, and the public;

"(3) Providing for community and public notification concerning the presence of sexual offenders;

"(4) Collecting data relative to sexual offenses and sexual offenders;

"(5) Requiring sexual predators who are released into the community to wear an electronic monitoring system for the rest of their natural life and to pay for such system; and

"(6) Prohibiting sexual predators from working with children, either for compensation or as a volunteer.

"The General Assembly further finds that the state has a compelling interest in protecting the public from sexual offenders and in protecting children from predatory sexual activity, and there is sufficient justification for requiring sexual offenders to register and for requiring community and public notification of the presence of sexual offenders. The General Assembly declares that in order to protect the public, it is necessary that the sexual offenders be registered and that members of the community and the public be notified of a sexual offender's presence. The designation of a person as a sexual offender is neither a sentence nor a punishment but simply a regulatory mechanism and status resulting from the conviction of certain crimes. Likewise, the designation of a person as a sexual predator is neither a sentence nor a punishment but simply a regulatory mechanism and status resulting from findings by the Sexual Offender Registration Review Board and a court if requested by a sexual offender."

"SECTION 30. (a) This Act shall become effective July 1, 2006.

"(b) Any person required to register pursuant to the provisions of Code Section 42–1–12, relating to the state sexual offender registry, and any person required not to reside within areas where minors congregate, as prohibited by Code Section 42–1–13 [see § 42–1–15], shall not be relieved of the obligation to comply with the provisions of said Code sections by the repeal and reenactment of said Code sections.

"(c) The provisions of this Act shall not affect or abate the status as a crime of any such act or omission which occurred prior to the effective date of the Act repealing, repealing and reenacting, or amending such law, nor shall the prosecution of such crime be abated as a result of such repeal, repeal and reenactment, or amendment."

§ 16–5–42. False imprisonment under color of legal process

When the arrest, confinement, or detention of a person by warrant, mandate, or process is manifestly illegal and shows malice and oppression, an officer issuing or knowingly and maliciously executing the same shall, upon conviction thereof, be removed from office and punished by imprisonment for not less than one nor more than ten years.

Laws 1833, Cobb's 1851 Digest, p. 788; Laws 1895, p. 63, §§ 1, 2; Laws 1968, p. 1249, § 1.

Formerly Code 1863, § 4265; Code 1868, § 4300; Code 1873, § 4366; Code 1882, § 4366; Penal Code 1895, § 108; Penal Code 1910, § 108; Code 1933, § 26–1503; Code 1933, § 26–1309.

§ 16–5–43. Malicious confinement of sane person

A person who maliciously causes the confinement of a sane person, knowing such person to be sane, in any asylum, public or private, shall, upon conviction thereof, be punished by imprisonment for not less than one nor more than ten years.

Laws 1890–91, p. 237, § 4; Laws 1968, p. 1249, § 1.

Formerly Penal Code 1895, § 560; Penal Code 1910, § 575; Code 1933, § 26–1504; Code 1933, § 26–1310.

§ 16–5–44. Aircraft hijacking

(a) A person commits the offense of hijacking an aircraft when he (1) by use of force or (2) by intimidation by the use of threats or coercion places the pilot of an aircraft in fear of immediate serious bodily injury to himself or to another and causes the diverting of an aircraft from its intended destination to a destination dictated by such person.

(b) The offense of hijacking is declared to be a continuing offense from the point of beginning, and jurisdiction to try a person accused of the offense of hijacking shall be in any county of this state over which the aircraft is operated.

(c) A person convicted of the offense of hijacking an aircraft shall be punished by death or life imprisonment.

Laws 1969, p. 741, § 1.

Formerly Code 1933, § 26–3301.

§ 16–5–44.1. Motor vehicle hijacking

(a) As used in this Code section:

(1) "Firearm" means any handgun, rifle, shotgun, or similar device or weapon which will or can be converted to expel a projectile by the action of an explosive or electrical charge and includes stun guns and tasers as defined by subsection (a) of Code Section 16–11–106, as amended, and any replica, article, or device having the appearance of a firearm.

(2) "Motor vehicle" means any vehicle which is self-propelled.

(3) "Weapon" means an object, device, or instrument which when used against a person is likely to or actually does result in serious bodily injury or death or any replica, article, or device having the appearance of such a weapon including, but not limited to, any object defined as a weapon by Code Section 16–11–127.1 or as a dangerous weapon by Code Section 16–11–121.

(b) A person commits the offense of hijacking a motor vehicle when such person while in possession of a firearm or weapon obtains a motor vehicle from the person or presence of another by force and violence or intimidation or attempts or conspires to do so.

(c) A person convicted of the offense of hijacking a motor vehicle shall be punished by imprisonment for not less than ten nor more than 20 years and a fine of not less than $10,000.00 nor more than $100,000.00, provided that any person who has previously committed an offense under the laws of the United States or of Georgia or of any of the several states or of any foreign nation recognized by the United States which if committed in Georgia would have constituted the offense of hijacking a motor vehicle shall be punished by imprisonment for life and a fine of not less than $100,000.00 nor more than $500,000.00. For purposes of this subsection, "state" shall include the District of Columbia and any territory, possession, or dominion of the United States.

(d) The offense of hijacking a motor vehicle shall be considered a separate offense and shall not merge with any other offense; and the punishment prescribed by subsection (c) of this Code section shall not be deferred, suspended, or probated.

(e) Any property which is used, intended for use, derived, or realized, directly or indirectly, from a violation of this Code section is forfeited to the state and no property interest shall exist therein. Any action declaring such forfeiture shall be governed by the provisions of Code Section 16–13–49.

Laws 1994, p. 1625, § 3.

§ 16–5–45. Interference with custody

(a) As used in this Code section, the term:

(1) "Child" means any individual who is under the age of 17 years or any individual who is under the age of 18 years who is alleged to be a deprived child as such is defined in Code Section 15–11–2, relating to juvenile proceedings.

(2) "Committed person" means any child or other person whose custody is entrusted to another individual by authority of law.

(3) "Lawful custody" means that custody inherent in the natural parents, that custody awarded by proper authority as provided in Code Section 15–11–45, or that custody awarded to a parent, guardian, or other person by a court of competent jurisdiction.

(b)(1) A person commits the offense of interference with custody when without lawful authority to do so the person:

(A) Knowingly or recklessly takes or entices any child or committed person away from the individual who has lawful custody of such child or committed person;

(B) Knowingly harbors any child or committed person who has absconded; or

(C) Intentionally and willfully retains possession within this state of the child or committed person upon the expiration of a lawful period of visitation with the child or committed person.

(2) A person convicted of the offense of interference with custody shall be punished as follows:

(A) Upon conviction of the first offense, the defendant shall be guilty of a misdemeanor and shall be fined not less than $ 200.00 nor more than $ 500.00 or shall be imprisoned for not less than one month nor more than five months, or both fined and imprisoned;

(B) Upon conviction of the second offense, the defendant shall be guilty of a misdemeanor and shall be fined not less than $ 400.00 nor more than $ 1,000.00 or shall be imprisoned for not less than three months nor more than 12 months, or both fined and imprisoned; and

(C) Upon the conviction of the third or subsequent offense, the defendant shall be guilty of a felony and shall be punished by imprisonment for not less than one nor more than five years.

(c)(1) A person commits the offense of interstate interference with custody when without lawful authority to do so the person knowingly or recklessly takes or entices any minor or committed person away from the individual who has lawful custody of such minor or committed person and in so doing brings such minor or committed person into this state or removes such minor or committed person from this state.

(2) A person also commits the offense of interstate interference with custody when the person removes a minor or committed person from this state in the lawful exercise of a visitation right and, upon the expiration of the period of lawful visitation, intentionally retains possession of the minor or committed person in another state for the purpose of keeping the minor or committed person away from the individual having lawful custody of the minor or committed person. The offense is deemed to be committed in the county to which the minor or committed person was to have been returned upon expiration of the period of lawful visitation.

(3) A person convicted of the offense of interstate interference with custody shall be guilty of a felony and shall be imprisoned for not less than one year nor more than five years.

Laws 1968, p. 1249, § 1; Laws 1978, p. 1420, § 1; Laws 1982, p. 970, § 2; Laws 1986, p. 1325, § 1; Laws 1987, p. 561, § 1; Laws 1999, p. 81, § 16; Laws 2000, p. 20, § 5.

Formerly Code 1933, § 26–1312.

Historical and Statutory Notes

The 2000 amendment in subsec. (a)(3) substituted reference to section 15–11–45 for 15–11–17.

§ 16–5–46. Trafficking a person for labor or sexual servitude

(a) As used in this Code section, the term:

(1) "Coercion" means:

(A) Causing or threatening to cause bodily harm to any person, physically restraining or confining any person, or threatening to physically restrain or confine any person;

(B) Exposing or threatening to expose any fact or information that if revealed would tend to subject a person to criminal or immigration proceedings, hatred, contempt, or ridicule;

(C) Destroying, concealing, removing, confiscating, or possessing any actual or purported passport or other immigration document, or any other actual or purported government identification document, of any person; or

(D) Providing a controlled substance, as such term is defined by Code Section 16–13–21, to such person.

(2) "Deception" means:

(A) Creating or confirming another's impression of an existing fact or past event which is false and which the accused knows or believes to be false;

(B) Maintaining the status or condition of a person arising from a pledge by that person of his or her personal services as security for a debt, if the value of those services as reasonably assessed is not applied toward the liquidation of the debt or the length and nature of those services are not respectively limited and defined, or preventing a person from acquiring information pertinent to the disposition of such debt; or

(C) Promising benefits or the performance of services which the accused does not intend to deliver or perform or knows will not be delivered or performed. Evidence of failure to deliver benefits or perform services standing alone shall not be sufficient to authorize a conviction under this Code section.

(3) "Labor servitude" means work or service of economic or financial value which is performed or provided by another person and is induced or obtained by coercion or deception.

(4) "Sexual servitude" means:

(A) Any sexually explicit conduct as defined in paragraph (4) of subsection (a) of Code Section 16–12–100 for which anything of value is directly or indirectly given, promised to, or received by any person, which conduct is induced or obtained by coercion or deception or which conduct is induced or obtained from a person under the age of 18 years; or

(B) Any sexually explicit conduct as defined in paragraph (4) of subsection (a) of Code Section 16–12–100 which is performed or provided by any person, which conduct is induced or obtained by coercion or deception or which conduct is induced or obtained from a person under the age of 18 years.

(b) A person commits the offense of trafficking a person for labor servitude when that person knowingly subjects or maintains another in labor servitude or knowingly recruits, entices, harbors, transports, provides, or obtains by any means another person for the purpose of labor servitude.

(c) A person commits the offense of trafficking a person for sexual servitude when that person knowingly subjects or maintains another in sexual servitude or knowingly recruits, entices, harbors, transports, provides, or obtains by any means another person for the purpose of sexual servitude.

(d) Any person who commits the offense of trafficking a person for labor or sexual servitude shall be guilty of a felony, and upon conviction thereof, shall be punished by imprisonment for not less than one nor more than 20 years. Any person who commits the offense of trafficking a person for labor or sexual servitude against a person who is under the age of 18 years shall be guilty of a felony, and upon conviction thereof, shall be punished by imprisonment for not less than ten nor more than 20 years.

(e) Prosecuting attorneys and the Attorney General shall have concurrent authority to prosecute any criminal cases arising under the provisions of this Code section and to perform any duty that necessarily appertains thereto.

(f) Each violation of this Code section shall constitute a separate offense and shall not merge with any other offense.

(g) A corporation may be prosecuted under this Code section for an act or omission constituting a crime under this Code section only if an agent of the corporation performs the conduct which is an element of the crime while acting within the scope of his or her office or employment and on behalf of the corporation and the commission of the crime was either authorized, requested, commanded, performed, or within the scope of his or her employment on behalf of the corporation or constituted a pattern of illegal activity that an agent of the company knew or should have known was occurring.

Laws 2006, Act 457, § 3, eff. July 1, 2007.

Historical and Statutory Notes

Laws 2006, Act 457, § 10(b), provides: "Section 3 of this Act shall become effective on July 1, 2007, and shall not apply to any offense committed prior to July 1, 2007."

Article 4

Reckless Conduct

§ 16–5–60. Reckless conduct; HIV infected persons

(a) Any term used in this Code section and defined in Code Section 31–22–9.1 shall have the meaning provided for such term in Code Section 31–22–9.1.

(b) A person who causes bodily harm to or endangers the bodily safety of another person by consciously disregarding a substantial and unjustifiable risk that his act or omission will cause harm or endanger the safety of the other person and the disregard constitutes a gross deviation from the standard of care which a reasonable person would exercise in the situation is guilty of a misdemeanor.

(c) A person who is an HIV infected person who, after obtaining knowledge of being infected with HIV:

(1) Knowingly engages in sexual intercourse or performs or submits to any sexual act involving the sex organs of one person and the mouth or anus of another person and the HIV infected person does not disclose to the other person the fact of that infected person's being an HIV infected person prior to that intercourse or sexual act;

(2) Knowingly allows another person to use a hypodermic needle, syringe, or both for the introduction of drugs or any other substance into or for the withdrawal of body fluids from the other person's body and the needle or syringe so used had been previously used by the HIV infected person for the introduction of drugs or any other substance into or for the withdrawal of body fluids from the HIV infected person's body and where that infected person does not disclose to the other person the fact of that infected person's being an HIV infected person prior to such use;

(3) Offers or consents to perform with another person an act of sexual intercourse for money without disclosing to that other person the fact of that infected person's being an HIV infected person prior to offering or consenting to perform that act of sexual intercourse;

(4) Solicits another person to perform or submit to an act of sodomy for money without disclosing to that other person the fact of that infected person's being an HIV infected person prior to soliciting that act of sodomy; or

(5) Donates blood, blood products, other body fluids, or any body organ or body part without previously disclosing the fact of that infected person's being an HIV infected person to the person drawing the blood or blood products or the person or entity collecting or storing the other body fluids, body organ, or body part,

is guilty of a felony and, upon conviction thereof, shall be punished by imprisonment for not more than ten years.

(d) A person who is an HIV infected person or hepatitis infected person and who, after obtaining knowledge of being infected with HIV or hepatitis, commits an assault with the intent to transmit HIV or hepatitis, using his or her body fluids (blood, semen, or vaginal secretions), saliva, urine, or feces upon:

(1) A peace officer while the peace officer is engaged in the performance of his or her official duties or on account of the peace officer's performance of his or her official duties; or

(2) A correctional officer while the correctional officer is engaged in the performance of his or her official duties or on account of the correctional officer's performance of his or her official duties is guilty of a felony and, upon conviction thereof, shall be punished by imprisonment for not less than five nor more than 20 years.

Laws 1968, p. 1249, § 1; Laws 1988, p. 1799, § 3; Laws 2003, Act 54, § 1, eff. July 1, 2003.

Formerly Code 1933, § 26–2910.

Historical and Statutory Notes

The 2003 amendment by Act 54 added new subsec. (d).

§ 16–5–61. Hazing students in connection with membership, etc., in school organization

(a) As used in this Code section, the term:

(1) "Haze" means to subject a student to an activity which endangers or is likely to endanger the physical health of a student, regardless of a student's willingness to participate in such activity.

(2) "School" means any school, college, or university in this state.

(3) "School organization" means any club, society, fraternity, sorority, or a group living together which has students as its principal members.

(4) "Student" means any person enrolled in a school in this state.

(b) It shall be unlawful for any person to haze any student in connection with or as a condition or precondition of gaining acceptance, membership, office, or other status in a school organization.

(c) Any person who violates this Code section shall be guilty of a misdemeanor of a high and aggravated nature.

Laws 1988, p. 694, § 1; Laws 1990, p. 1690, § 1.

Article 5

Cruelty to Children

§ 16–5–70. Cruelty to children

(a) A parent, guardian, or other person supervising the welfare of or having immediate charge or custody of a child under the age of 18 commits the offense of cruelty to children in the first degree when such person willfully deprives the child of necessary sustenance to the extent that the child's health or well-being is jeopardized.

(b) Any person commits the offense of cruelty to children in the first degree when such person maliciously causes a child under the age of 18 cruel or excessive physical or mental pain.

(c) Any person commits the offense of cruelty to children in the second degree when such person with criminal negligence causes a child under the age of 18 cruel or excessive physical or mental pain.

(d) Any person commits the offense of cruelty to children in the third degree when:

(1) Such person, who is the primary aggressor, intentionally allows a child under the age of 18 to witness the commission of a forcible felony, battery, or family violence battery; or

(2) Such person, who is the primary aggressor, having knowledge that a child under the age of 18 is present and sees or hears the act, commits a forcible felony, battery, or family violence battery.

(e)(1) A person convicted of the offense of cruelty to children in the first degree as provided in this Code section shall be punished by imprisonment for not less than five nor more than 20 years.

(2) A person convicted of the offense of cruelty to children in the second degree shall be punished by imprisonment for not less than one nor more than ten years.

(3) A person convicted of the offense of cruelty to children in the third degree shall be punished as for a misdemeanor upon the first or second conviction. Upon conviction of a third or subsequent offense of cruelty to children in the third degree, the defendant shall be guilty of a felony and shall be sentenced to a fine not less than $1,000.00 nor more than $5,000.00 or imprisonment for not less than one year nor more than three years or shall be sentenced to both fine and imprisonment.

Laws 1878–79, p. 162, § 3; Laws 1968, p. 1249, § 1; Laws 1978, p. 228, § 1; Laws 1981, p. 683, § 1; Laws 1995, p. 957, § 2; Laws 1996, p. 1071, § 1; Laws 1999, p. 381, § 6; Laws 2004, Act 439, § 3, eff. July 1, 2004.

Formerly Code 1882, § 4612h; Penal Code 1895, § 708; Penal Code 1910, § 758; Code 1933, § 26–8001; Code 1933, § 26–2801.

Historical and Statutory Notes

The 2004 amendment by Act 439 rewrote subsecs. (c), (d), and (e) which had read:

"(c) Any person commits the offense of cruelty to children in the second degree when:

"(1) Such person, who is the primary aggressor, intentionally allows a child under the age of 18 to witness the commission of a forcible felony, battery, or family violence battery; or

"(2) Such person, who is the primary aggressor, having knowledge that a child under the age of 18 is present and sees or hears the act, commits a forcible felony, battery, or family violence battery.

"(d) A person convicted of the offense of cruelty to children in the first degree as provided in this Code section shall be punished by imprisonment for not less than five nor more than 20 years.

"(e) A person convicted of the offense of cruelty to children in the second degree shall be punished as for a misdemeanor upon the first or second conviction. Upon conviction of a third or subsequent offense of cruelty to children in the second degree, the defendant shall be guilty of a felony and shall be sentenced to a fine not less than $1,000.00 nor more than $5,000.00 or imprisonment for not less than one year nor more than three years or shall be sentenced to both fine and imprisonment."

Laws 2004, Act 439, § 6, provides:

"This Act shall become effective on July 1, 2004, and shall apply to all crimes which occur on or after that date."

§ 16–5–71. Tattooing the body of any person under the age of 18

(a) It shall be unlawful for any person to tattoo the body of any person under the age of 18, except that a physician or osteopath licensed under Chapter 34 of Title 43, or a technician acting under the direct supervision of such licensed physician or osteopath, and in compliance with Chapter 9 of Title 31 shall be authorized to mark or color the skin of any person under the age of 18 by pricking in coloring matter or by producing scars for medical or cosmetic purposes.

(b) Any person violating the provisions of subsection (a) of this Code section shall be guilty of a misdemeanor.

Laws 1987, p. 443, § 1; Laws 1994, p. 446, § 1.

§ 16–5–71.1. Piercing the body of any person under the age of 18

(a) It shall be unlawful for any person to pierce the body, with the exception of the ear lobes, of any person under the age of 18 for the purpose of allowing the insertion of earrings, jewelry, or similar objects into the body, unless the prior written consent of a custodial parent or guardian of such minor is obtained; provided, however, that the prohibition contained in this subsection shall not apply if:

(1) Such person has been furnished with proper identification showing that the individual is 18 years of age or older; and

(2) The person reasonably believes such minor to be 18 years of age or older.

(b) Any person violating the provisions of subsection (a) of this Code section shall be guilty of a misdemeanor.

Laws 1996, p. 645, § 1.

§ 16–5–72. Reckless abandonment of a child

(a) A parent, guardian, or other person supervising the welfare of or having immediate charge or custody of a child under the age of one year commits the offense of reckless abandonment of a child when the person willfully and voluntarily physically abandons such child with the intention of severing all parental or custodial duties and responsibilities to such child and leaving such child in a condition which results in the death of said child.

(b) Any person who violates subsection (a) of this Code section shall be guilty of a felony and shall, upon conviction thereof, be punished by imprisonment for not less than ten nor more than 25 years.

Laws 1989, p. 1605, § 1.

§ 16–5–73. Definitions

(a) As used in this Code section, the term:

(1) "Chemical substance" means anhydrous ammonia, as defined in Code Section 16–11–111; ephedrine, pseudoephedrine, or phenylpropanolamine, as those terms are defined in Code Section 16–13–30.3; or any other chemical used in the manufacture of methamphetamine.

(2) "Child" means any individual who is under the age of 18 years.

(3) "Intent to manufacture" means but is not limited to the intent to manufacture methamphetamine, which may be demonstrated by a chemical substance's usage, quantity, or manner or method of storage, including but not limited to storing it in proximity to another chemical substance or equipment used to manufacture methamphetamine.

(4) "Methamphetamine" means methamphetamine, amphetamine, or any mixture containing either methamphetamine or amphetamine, as described in Code Section 16-13-26.

(5) "Serious injury" means an injury involving a broken bone, the loss of a member of the body, the loss of use of a member of the body, the substantial disfigurement of the body or of a member of the body, or an injury which is life threatening.

(b)(1) Any person who intentionally causes or permits a child to be present where any person is manufacturing methamphetamine or possessing a chemical substance with the intent to manufacture methamphetamine shall be guilty of a felony and, upon conviction thereof, shall be punished by imprisonment for not less than two nor more than 15 years.

(2) Any person who violates paragraph (1) of this subsection wherein a child receives serious injury as a result of such violation shall be guilty of a felony and, upon conviction thereof, shall be punished by imprisonment for not less than five nor more than 20 years.

Laws 2004, Act 439, § 4, eff. July 1, 2004; Laws 2005, Act 19, § 16, eff. April 7, 2005.

Historical and Statutory Notes

Laws 2004, Act 439, § 6, provides:

"This Act shall become effective on July 1, 2004, and shall apply to all crimes which occur on or after that date."

The 2005 amendment by Act 19 was a provision contained in a correction bill.

Article 6

Feticide

§ 16-5-80. Feticide

(a) For the purposes of this Code section, the term "unborn child" means a member of the species homo sapiens at any stage of development who is carried in the womb.

(b) A person commits the offense of feticide if he or she willfully and without legal justification causes the death of an unborn child by any injury to the mother of such child, which would be murder if it resulted in the death of such mother, or if he or she, when in the commission of a felony, causes the death of an unborn child.

(c) A person convicted of the offense of feticide shall be punished by imprisonment for life.

(d) A person commits the offense of voluntary manslaughter of an unborn child when such person causes the death of an unborn child under circumstances which would otherwise be feticide and if such person acts solely as the result of a sudden, violent, and irresistible passion resulting from serious provocation sufficient to excite such passion in a reasonable person; provided, however, that, if there should have been an interval between the provocation and the killing sufficient for the voice of reason and humanity to be heard, of which the jury in all cases shall be the judge, the killing shall be attributed to deliberate revenge and be punished as feticide.

(e) A person convicted of the offense of voluntary manslaughter of an unborn child shall be guilty of a felony and shall be punished by imprisonment for not less than one nor more than 20 years.

(f) Nothing in this Code section shall be construed to permit the prosecution of:

(1) Any person for conduct relating to an abortion for which the consent of the pregnant woman, or person authorized by law to act on her behalf, has been obtained or for which such consent is implied by law;

(2) Any person for any medical treatment of the pregnant woman or her unborn child; or

(3) Any woman with respect to her unborn child.

Laws 1982, p. 2499, § 1; Laws 2006, Act 654, § 2, eff. July 1, 2006.

Historical and Statutory Notes

The 2006 amendment by Act 654 rewrote the section which had read:

"(a) A person commits the offense of feticide if he willfully kills an unborn child so far developed as to be ordinarily called 'quick' by any injury to the mother of such child, which would be murder if it resulted in the death of such mother.

"(b) A person convicted of the offense of feticide shall be punished by imprisonment for life."

Laws 2006, Act 654, § 5, provides:

"This Act shall become effective on July 1, 2006, and shall apply to all offenses committed on or after such date."

Article 7

Stalking

§ 16-5-90. Stalking

(a)(1) A person commits the offense of stalking when he or she follows, places under surveillance, or contacts another person at or about a place or places without the consent of the other person for the purpose of harassing and intimidating the other person. For the purpose of this article, the terms "computer" and "computer network" shall have the same meanings as set out in Code Section 16-9-92; the term "contact" shall mean any communication including without being limited to communication in person, by telephone, by mail, by broadcast, by computer, by computer network, or by any other electronic device; and the place or places that contact by telephone, mail, broadcast, computer, computer network, or any other electronic device is deemed to occur shall be the place or places where such communication is received. For the purpose of this article, the term "place or places" shall include any public or private property occupied by the victim other than the residence of the defendant. For the purposes of this article, the term "harassing and intimidating" means a knowing and willful course of conduct directed at a specific person which causes emotional distress by placing such person in reasonable fear for such person's safety or the safety of a member of his or her immediate family, by establishing a pattern of harassing and intimidating behavior, and which serves no legitimate purpose. This Code section shall not be construed to require that an overt threat of death or bodily injury has been made.

(2) A person commits the offense of stalking when such person, in violation of a bond to keep the peace posted pursuant to Code Section 17-6-110, standing order issued under Code Section 19-1-1, temporary restraining order, temporary protective order, permanent restraining order, permanent protective order, preliminary injunction, or permanent injunction or condition of pretrial release, condition of probation, or condition of parole in effect prohibiting the harassment or intimidation of another person, broadcasts or publishes, including electronic publication, the picture, name, address, or phone number of a person for whose benefit the bond, order, or condition was made and without such person's consent in such a manner that causes other persons to harass or intimidate such person and the person making the broadcast or publication knew or had reason to believe that such broadcast or publication would cause such person to be harassed or intimidated by others.

(b) Except as provided in subsection (c) of this Code section, a person who commits the offense of stalking is guilty of a misdemeanor.

(c) Upon the second conviction, and all subsequent convictions, for stalking, the defendant shall be guilty of a felony and shall be punished by imprisonment for not less than one year nor more than ten years.

(d) Before sentencing a defendant for any conviction of stalking under this Code section or aggravated stalking under Code Section 16–5–91, the sentencing judge may require psychological evaluation of the offender and shall consider the entire criminal record of the offender. At the time of sentencing, the judge is authorized to issue a permanent restraining order against the offender to protect the person stalked and the members of such person's immediate family, and the judge is authorized to require psychological treatment of the offender as a part of the sentence, or as a condition for suspension or stay of sentence, or for probation.

Laws 1993, p. 1534, § 1; Laws 1998, p. 885, § 1; Laws 2000, p. 1283, § 1.

Historical and Statutory Notes

The 2000 amendment to subsec. (a) designated par. (1), inserted therein "terms 'computer' and 'computer network' shall have the same meanings as set out in Code Section 16–9–92; the term 'contact' shall mean any communication including without being limited to communication in person, by telephone, by mail, by broadcast, by computer, by computer network, or by any other electronic device; and the place or places that contact by telephone, mail, broadcast, computer, computer network, or any other electronic device is deemed to occur shall be the place or places where such communication is received. For the purpose of this article, the", and added par. (2).

§ 16–5–91. Aggravated stalking

(a) A person commits the offense of aggravated stalking when such person, in violation of a bond to keep the peace posted pursuant to Code Section 17–6–110, temporary restraining order, temporary protective order, permanent restraining order, permanent protective order, preliminary injunction, good behavior bond, or permanent injunction or condition of pretrial release, condition of probation, or condition of parole in effect prohibiting the behavior described in this subsection, follows, places under surveillance, or contacts another person at or about a place or places without the consent of the other person for the purpose of harassing and intimidating the other person.

(b) Any person convicted of a violation of subsection (a) of this Code section shall be guilty of a felony and, upon conviction thereof, shall be punished by imprisonment for not less than one nor more than ten years and by a fine of not more than $ 10,000.00. The provisions of subsection (d) of Code Section 16–5–90 apply to sentencing for conviction of aggravated stalking.

Laws 1993, p. 1534, § 1; Laws 1995, p. 911, § 1; Laws 1998, p. 885, § 2; Laws 2002, p. 862, § 1.

Historical and Statutory Notes

The 2002 amendment inserted in subsec. (a) "good behavior bond,".

§ 16–5–92. Exceptions

The provisions of Code Sections 16–5–90 and 16–5–91 shall not apply to persons engaged in activities protected by the Constitution of the United States or of this state or to persons or employees of such persons lawfully engaged in bona fide business activity or lawfully engaged in the practice of a profession.

Laws 1993, p. 1534, § 1.

§ 16–5–93. Victims entitled to notice of release from custody of person arrested for and charged with stalking or aggravated stalking

(a) The victim of stalking or aggravated stalking shall be entitled to notice of the release from custody of the person arrested for and charged with the offense of stalking or aggravated stalking and to notice of any hearing on the issue of bail for such person. No such notice shall be required unless the victim provides a landline telephone number other than a pocket pager or electronic communication device number to which such notice can be directed.

(b) The law enforcement agency, prosecutor, or court directly involved with the victim at the outset of a criminal prosecution for the offense of stalking or aggravated stalking shall advise the victim of his or her right to notice and of the requirement of the victim's providing a landline telephone number other than a pocket pager or electronic communication device number to which the notice of custodial release or bail hearing can be directed. Such victim shall transmit the telephone number described in this subsection to the court and custodian of the person charged with stalking or aggravated stalking.

(c) Upon receipt of the telephone number, the custodian of the person charged with stalking or aggravated stalking shall take reasonable and necessary steps under the circumstances to notify the victim of the person's release from custody. Such notice shall, at a minimum, include:

(1) Prior to the person's release, placing a telephone call to the number provided by the victim and giving notice to the victim or any person answering the telephone who appears to be sui juris or by leaving an appropriate message on a telephone answering machine; and

(2) Following the person's release, if the custodian is unable to notify the victim by the method provided in paragraph (1) of this subsection, telephoning the number provided by the victim no less than two times in no less than 15 minute intervals within one hour of custodial release and giving notice to the victim or to any person answering the telephone who appears to be sui juris or by leaving an appropriate message on a telephone answering machine.

(d) Upon receipt of the telephone number, the court conducting a hearing on the issue of bail shall take reasonable and necessary steps under the circumstances to notify the victim of any scheduled hearing on the issue of bail. Such notice shall, at a minimum, include placing a telephone call to the number provided by the victim prior to any scheduled hearing on the issue of bail.

(e) Notwithstanding any other provision of this Code section, a scheduled bail hearing or the release of the person charged with stalking or aggravated stalking shall not be delayed solely for the purpose of effectuating notice pursuant to this Code section for a period of more than 30 minutes.

(f) Upon the person's release or escape from custody after conviction and service of all or a portion of a sentence, notification to the victim shall be provided by the State Board of Pardons and Paroles as set forth in Code Sections 42–9–46 and 42–9–47.

(g) This Code section shall not apply to a custodian who is transferring a person charged with stalking or aggravated stalking to another custodian in this state.

(h) As used in this Code section, the term "custodian" means a warden, sheriff, jailer, deputy sheriff, police officer, officer or employee of the Department of Juvenile Justice, or any other law enforcement officer having actual custody of an inmate.

(i) A custodian or his or her employing agency shall not be liable in damages for a failure to provide the notice required by this Code section, but the custodian shall be subject to appropriate disciplinary action including termination for such failure.

Laws 1993, p. 1534, § 1; Laws 1997, p. 1453, § 1.

§ 16–5–94. Restraining orders, protective orders, and approval of consent orders to prevent recurrence of stalking

(a) A person who is not a minor who alleges stalking by another person may seek a restraining order by filing a petition alleging conduct constituting stalking as defined in Code Section 16–5–90. A person who is not a minor may also seek relief on behalf of a minor by filing such a petition.

(b) Jurisdiction for such a petition shall be the same as for family violence petitions as set out in Code Section 19–13–2.

(c) Upon the filing of a verified petition in which the petitioner alleges with specific facts that probable cause exists to establish that stalking by the respondent has occurred in the past and may occur in the future, the court may order such temporary relief ex parte as it deems necessary to protect the petitioner or a minor of the household from stalking. If the court issues an ex parte order, a copy of the order shall be immediately furnished to the petitioner.

(d) The court may grant a protective order or approve a consent agreement to bring about a cessation of conduct constituting stalking. Orders or agreements may:

(1) Direct a party to refrain from such conduct;

(2) Order a party to refrain from harassing or interfering with the other;

(3) Award costs and attorney's fees to either party; and

(4) Order either or all parties to receive appropriate psychiatric or psychological services as a further measure to prevent the recurrence of stalking.

(e) The provisions of subsections (c) and (d) of Code Section 19–13–3, subsections (b), (c), and (d) of Code Section 19–13–4, and Code Section 19–13–5, relating to family violence petitions, shall apply to petitions filed pursuant to this Code section, except that the clerk of court may provide forms for petitions and pleadings to persons alleging conduct constituting stalking and to any other person designated by the superior court pursuant to this Code section as authorized to advise persons alleging conduct constituting stalking on filling out and filing such petitions and pleadings.

Laws 1998, p. 885, § 3; Laws 1999, p. 81, § 16.

§ 16–5–95. Violation of family violence order

(a) A person commits the offense of violating a family violence order when the person knowingly and in a nonviolent manner violates the terms of a family violence temporary restraining order, temporary protective order, permanent restraining order, or permanent protective order issued against that person pursuant to Article 1 of Chapter 13 of Title 19, which:

(1) Excludes, evicts, or excludes and evicts the person from a residence or household;

(2) Directs the person to stay away from a residence, workplace, or school;

(3) Restrains the person from approaching within a specified distance of another person; or

(4) Restricts the person from having any contact, direct or indirect, by telephone, pager, facsimile, e-mail, or any other means of communication with another person, except as specified in the order.

(b) Any person convicted of a violation of subsection (a) of this Code section shall be guilty of a misdemeanor.

(c) Nothing contained in this Code section shall prohibit a prosecution for the offense of stalking or aggravated stalking that arose out of the same course of conduct; provided, however, that, for purposes of sentencing, a violation of this Code section shall be merged with a violation of any provision of Code Section 16–5–90 or 16–5–91 that arose out of the same course of conduct.

Laws 2003, Act 298, § 1, eff. July 1, 2003.

§ 16–5–96. Notice of conviction; publication

(a) The clerk of the court in which a person is convicted of a second or subsequent violation of Code Section 16–5–90 or 16–5–91 shall cause to be published a notice of conviction for such person. Such notice of conviction shall be published in the manner of legal notices in the legal organ of the county in which such person resides or, in the case of nonresidents, in the legal organ of the county in which the person was convicted. Such notice of conviction shall be one column wide by two inches long and shall contain the photograph taken by the arresting law enforcement agency at the time of arrest; the name and address of the convicted person; the date, time, and place of arrest; and the disposition of the case and shall be published once in the legal organ of the appropriate county in the second week following such conviction or as soon thereafter as publication may be made.

(b) The convicted person for which a notice of conviction is published pursuant to this Code section shall be assessed $25.00 for the cost of publication of such notice and such assessment shall be imposed at the time of conviction in addition to any other fine imposed.

(c) The clerk of the court, the publisher of any legal organ which publishes a notice of conviction, and any other person involved in the publication of an erroneous notice of conviction shall be immune from civil or criminal liability for such erroneous publication, provided that such publication was made in good faith.

Laws 2004, Act 560, § 3B, eff. July 1, 2004; Laws 2005, Act 19, § 16, eff. April 7, 2005.

Historical and Statutory Notes

Laws 2004, Act 560, § 9(b), provides:

"Part I of this Act shall become effective on July 1, 2004, and shall apply to offenses committed on or after such date."

The 2005 amendment by Act 19 was a provision contained in a correction bill.

Article 8

Protection of Elder Persons

§ 16–5–100. Cruelty to a person who is 65 years of age or older

(a) A guardian or other person supervising the welfare of or having immediate charge or custody of a person who is 65 years of age or older commits the offense of cruelty to a person who is 65 years of age or older when the person willfully deprives a person who is 65 years of age or older of health care, shelter, or necessary sustenance to the extent that the health or well-being of a person who is 65 years of age or older is jeopardized.

(b) The provisions of this Code section shall not apply to a physician nor any person acting under a physician's direction nor to a hospital, skilled nursing facility, hospice, nor any agent or employee thereof who is in good faith following a course of treatment developed in accordance with accepted medical standards or who is acting in good faith in accordance with a living will, a durable power of attorney for health care, an advance directive for health care, an order not to resuscitate, or the instructions of the patient or the patient's lawful surrogate decision maker, nor shall the provisions of this Code section require any physician, any institution licensed in accordance with Chapter 7 of Title 31 or any employee or agent thereof to provide health care services or shelter to any person in the absence of another legal obligation to do so.

(b.1) The provisions of this Code section shall not apply to a guardian or other person supervising the welfare of or having immediate charge or control of a person who is 65 years of age or older who in good faith provides treatment by spiritual means alone through prayer for the person's physical or mental condition, in lieu of medical treatment, in accordance with the practices of and written notarized consent of the person.

(c) A person convicted of the offense of cruelty to a person who is 65 years of age or older as provided in this Code section shall be punished by imprisonment for not less than one nor more than 20 years.

Laws 2000, p. 1085, § 2; Laws 2002, p. 648, § 1; Laws 2007, Act 48, § 6, eff. July 1, 2007.

Historical and Statutory Notes

The 2002 amendment inserted in subsec. (a) reference to health care and shelter, inserted a new subsec. (c), and rewrote subsec. (b) which as enacted in 2000 provided:

"The provisions of this Code section shall not apply to a physician nor any person acting under his or her direction nor to a hospital, skilled nursing facility, nor any agent or employee thereof who is acting in good faith in accordance with a living will as provided in Chapter 32 of Title 31, a durable power of attorney for health care as provided in Chapter 36 of Title 31, or the instructions of the patient or the patient's lawful surrogate decision maker."

In 2002, the Code Commission redesignated subsec. (c), which was added by Laws 2002, p. 648, § 1, as subsec. (b.1). See § 28–9–5.

The 2007 amendment by Act 48, in subsec. (b), substituted "a physician's" for "his or her" preceding "direction nor to a hospital", deleted "as provided in Chapter 32 of Title 31" following "living will", "power of attorney for health care", and "not to resuscitate"; and inserted "an advance directive for health care," preceding "an order not to resuscitate".

Article 9

Publishing of Notice of Conviction and Release

§ 16–5–110. Notice of conviction and release published in legal organ

(a) When a person who has been convicted of a crime for which that person is required to register under Code Section 42–1–12 makes his or her first report to a sheriff after such person's release from confinement, placement on probation, or upon establishing residency in the county, the sheriff shall cause to be published a notice of conviction and release from confinement of such person. Such notice shall be one column wide by two inches long and shall contain the photograph taken by the arresting law enforcement agency at the time of arrest; the name and address of the convicted person; if available, the date, time, and place of arrest; and the disposition of the case. The notice shall be published at or near the time the person registers with the sheriff at least once, and, at the sheriff's option, may be published more than once, in the legal organ of the appropriate county. The notice shall include the address of the Georgia Bureau of Investigation website for additional information regarding the sexual offender registry.

(b) The convicted person for which a notice of conviction and release from confinement is published pursuant to subsection (a) of this Code section shall be assessed $25.00 for the cost of publication of such notice, and such assessment shall be imposed at the time of reporting to the sheriff's office.

(c) The sheriff, the publisher of any legal organ which publishes a notice of conviction and release from confinement, and any other person involved in the publication of an erroneous notice of conviction and release from confinement shall be immune from civil or criminal liability for such erroneous publication, provided that such publication was made in good faith.

Laws 2005, Act 74, § 1, eff. July 1, 2005; Laws 2006, Act 453, § 16, eff. April 14, 2006; Laws 2006, Act 571, § 7, eff. July 1, 2006; Laws 2007, Act 18, § 16, eff. May 11, 2007.

Historical and Statutory Notes

The 2006 amendment by Act 453 was a provision contained in a correction bill.

The 2006 amendment by Act 571 rewrote subsec. (a) which had read:

"(a) When a person who has been convicted of a crime for which that person is required to register under Code Section 42–1–12 makes his or her first report to a sheriff after such person's release from confinement, the sheriff shall cause to be published a notice of conviction and release from confinement of such person. Such notice shall be published in the manner of legal notices in the legal organ of the county in which person resides. Such notice shall be one column wide by two inches long and shall contain the photograph taken by the arresting law enforcement agency at the time of arrest or a subsequent photograph, the name and address of the convicted person, and the date, time, place of arrest, and disposition of the case and shall be published once in the legal organ of the appropriate county in the second week following such person's release from confinement or as soon thereafter as publication may be made. The notice shall include the address of the Georgia Bureau of Investigation website for additional information regarding the sexual offender registry."

Laws 2006, Act 571, §§ 1 and 30, provide:

"SECTION 1. The General Assembly finds and declares that recidivist sexual offenders, sexual offenders who use physical violence, and sexual offenders who prey on children are sexual predators who present an extreme threat to the public safety. Many sexual offenders are extremely likely to use physical violence and to repeat their offenses; and some sexual offenders commit many offenses, have many more victims than are ever reported, and are prosecuted for only a fraction of their crimes. The General Assembly finds that this makes the cost of sexual offender victimization to society at large, while incalculable, clearly exorbitant. The General Assembly further finds that the high level of threat that a sexual predator presents to the public safety, and the long-term effects suffered by victims of sex offenses, provide the state with sufficient justification to implement a strategy that includes:

"(1) Incarcerating sexual offenders and maintaining adequate facilities to ensure that decisions to release sexual predators into the community are not made on the basis of inadequate space;

"(2) Requiring the registration of sexual offenders, with a requirement that complete and accurate information be maintained and accessible for use by law enforcement authorities, communities, and the public;

"(3) Providing for community and public notification concerning the presence of sexual offenders;

"(4) Collecting data relative to sexual offenses and sexual offenders;

"(5) Requiring sexual predators who are released into the community to wear an electronic monitoring system for the rest of their natural life and to pay for such system; and

"(6) Prohibiting sexual predators from working with children, either for compensation or as a volunteer.

"The General Assembly further finds that the state has a compelling interest in protecting the public from sexual offenders and in protecting children from predatory sexual activity, and there is sufficient justification for requiring sexual offenders to register and for requiring community and public notification of the presence of sexual offenders. The General Assembly declares that in order to protect the public, it is necessary that the sexual offenders be registered and that members of the community and the public be notified of a sexual offender's presence. The designation of a person as a sexual offender is neither a sentence nor a punishment but simply a regulatory mechanism and status resulting from the conviction of certain crimes. Likewise, the designation of a person as a sexual predator is neither a sentence nor a punishment but simply a regulatory mechanism and status resulting from findings by the Sexual Offender Registration Review Board and a court if requested by a sexual offender."

"SECTION 30. (a) This Act shall become effective July 1, 2006.

"(b) Any person required to register pursuant to the provisions of Code Section 42–1–12, relating to the state sexual offender registry, and any person required not to reside within areas where minors congregate, as prohibited by Code Section 42–1–13 [see § 42–1–15], shall not be relieved of the obligation to comply with the provisions of said Code sections by the repeal and reenactment of said Code sections.

"(c) The provisions of this Act shall not affect or abate the status as a crime of any such act or omission which occurred prior to the effective date of the Act repealing, repealing and reenacting, or amending such law, nor shall the prosecution of such crime be abated as a result of such repeal, repeal and reenactment, or amendment."

In 2006, the Code Commission, due to irreconcilable conflicts, treated the amendment of this section by Laws 2006, Act 453, § 16, as superseded by Laws 2006, Act 571, § 7. See Butts County v. Strahan, 107 S.E. 163, 151 Ga. 417 (1921).

The 2007 amendment by Act 18 was a provision contained in a correction bill.

CHAPTER 6

SEXUAL OFFENSES

§ 16–6–1. Rape

(a) A person commits the offense of rape when he has carnal knowledge of:

(1) A female forcibly and against her will; or

(2) A female who is less than ten years of age.

Carnal knowledge in rape occurs when there is any penetration of the female sex organ by the male sex organ. The fact that the person allegedly raped is the wife of the defendant shall not be a defense to a charge of rape.

(b) A person convicted of the offense of rape shall be punished by death, by imprisonment for life without parole, by imprisonment for life, or by a split sentence that is a term of imprisonment for not less than 25 years and not exceeding life imprisonment, followed by probation for life. Any person convicted under this Code section shall, in addition, be subject to the sentencing and punishment provisions of Code Sections 17–10–6.1 and 17–10–7.

(c) When evidence relating to an allegation of rape is collected in the course of a medical examination of the person who is the victim of the alleged crime, the law enforcement agency investigating the alleged crime shall be responsible for the cost of the medical examination to the extent that expense is incurred for the limited purpose of collecting evidence.

Laws 1833, Cobb's 1851 Digest, p. 787; Laws 1866, p. 151, § 1; Laws 1960, p. 266, § 1; Laws 1968, p. 1249, § 1; Laws 1978, p. 3, § 1; Laws 1994, p. 1959, § 5; Laws 1996, p. 1115, § 1; Laws 1997, p. 6, § 2; Laws 1999, p. 666, § 1; Laws 2006, Act 571, § 8, eff. July 1, 2006.

Formerly Code 1863, §§ 4248, 4249; Code 1868, §§ 4283, 4284; Code 1873, §§ 4349, 4350; Code 1882, §§ 4349, 4350; Penal Code 1895, §§ 93, 94; Penal Code 1910, §§ 93, 94; Code 1933, §§ 26–1301, 26–1302; Code 1933, § 26–2001.

Historical and Statutory Notes

The 2006 amendment by Act 571, in subsec. (b), substituted "a split sentence that is a term of imprisonment for not less than 25 years and not exceeding life imprisonment, followed by probation for life" for "imprisonment for not less than ten nor more than 20 years".

Laws 2006, Act 571, §§ 1 and 30, provide:

"SECTION 1. The General Assembly finds and declares that recidivist sexual offenders, sexual offenders who use physical violence, and sexual offenders who prey on children are sexual predators who present an extreme threat to the public safety. Many sexual offenders are extremely likely to use physical violence and to repeat their offenses; and some sexual offenders commit many offenses, have many more victims than are ever reported, and are prosecuted for only a fraction of their crimes. The General Assembly finds that this makes the cost of sexual offender victimization to society at large, while incalculable, clearly exorbitant. The General Assembly further finds that the high level of threat that a sexual predator presents to the public safety, and the long-term effects suffered by victims of sex offenses, provide the state with sufficient justification to implement a strategy that includes:

"(1) Incarcerating sexual offenders and maintaining adequate facilities to ensure that decisions to release sexual predators into the community are not made on the basis of inadequate space;

"(2) Requiring the registration of sexual offenders, with a requirement that complete and accurate information be maintained and accessible for use by law enforcement authorities, communities, and the public;

"(3) Providing for community and public notification concerning the presence of sexual offenders;

"(4) Collecting data relative to sexual offenses and sexual offenders;

"(5) Requiring sexual predators who are released into the community to wear an electronic monitoring system for the rest of their natural life and to pay for such system; and

"(6) Prohibiting sexual predators from working with children, either for compensation or as a volunteer.

"The General Assembly further finds that the state has a compelling interest in protecting the public from sexual offenders and in protecting children from predatory sexual activity, and there is sufficient justification for requiring sexual offenders to register and for requiring community and public notification of the presence of sexual offenders. The General Assembly declares that in order to protect the public, it is necessary that the sexual offenders be registered and that members of the community and the public be notified of a sexual offender's presence. The designation of a person as a sexual offender is neither a sentence nor a punishment but simply a regulatory mechanism and status resulting from the conviction of certain crimes. Likewise, the designation of a person as a sexual predator is neither a sentence nor a punishment but simply a regulatory mechanism and status resulting from findings by the Sexual Offender Registration Review Board and a court if requested by a sexual offender."

"SECTION 30. (a) This Act shall become effective July 1, 2006.

"(b) Any person required to register pursuant to the provisions of Code Section 42–1–12, relating to the state sexual offender registry, and any person required not to reside within areas where minors congregate, as prohibited by Code Section 42–1–13 [see § 42–1–15], shall not be relieved of the obligation to comply with the provisions of said Code sections by the repeal and reenactment of said Code sections.

"(c) The provisions of this Act shall not affect or abate the status as a crime of any such act or omission which occurred prior to the effective date of the Act repealing, repealing and reenacting, or amending such law, nor shall the prosecution of such crime be abated as a result of such repeal, repeal and reenactment, or amendment."

§ 16–6–2. Sodomy; aggravated sodomy

(a)(1) A person commits the offense of sodomy when he or she performs or submits to any sexual act involving the sex organs of one person and the mouth or anus of another.

(2) A person commits the offense of aggravated sodomy when he or she commits sodomy with force and against the will of the other person or when he or she commits sodomy with a person who is less than ten years of age. The fact that the person allegedly sodomized is the spouse of a defendant shall not be a defense to a charge of aggravated sodomy.

(b)(1) Except as provided in subsection (d) of this Code section, a person convicted of the offense of sodomy shall be punished by imprisonment for not less than one nor more than 20 years and shall be subject to the sentencing and punishment provisions of Code Section 17–10–6.2.

(2) A person convicted of the offense of aggravated sodomy shall be punished by imprisonment for life or by a split sentence that is a term of imprisonment for not less than 25 years and not exceeding life imprisonment, followed by probation for life. Any person convicted under this Code section of the offense of aggravated sodomy shall, in addition, be subject to the sentencing and punishment provisions of Code Sections 17–10–6.1 and 17–10–7.

(c) When evidence relating to an allegation of aggravated sodomy is collected in the course of a medical examination of the person who is the victim of the alleged crime, the law enforcement agency investigating the alleged crime shall be financially responsible for the cost of the medical examination to the extent that expense is incurred for the limited purpose of collecting evidence.

(d) If the victim is at least 13 but less than 16 years of age and the person convicted of sodomy is 18 years of age or younger and is no more than four years older than the victim, such person shall be guilty of a misdemeanor and shall not be subject to the sentencing and punishment provisions of Code Section 17–10–6.2.

Laws 1833, Cobb's 1851 Digest, p. 787; Laws 1949, p. 275, § 1; Laws 1968, p. 1249, § 1; Laws 1994, p. 1959, § 7; Laws 1996, p. 1115, § 2; Laws 1997, p. 6, § 3; Laws 2000, p. 1346, § 1; Laws 2006, Act 571, § 9, eff. July 1, 2006.

Formerly Code 1863, §§ 4251, 4252; Code 1868, §§ 4286, 4287; Code 1873, §§ 4352, 4353; Code 1882, §§ 4352, 4353; Penal Code 1895, §§ 382, 383; Penal Code 1910, §§ 373, 374; Code 1933, §§ 26–5901, 26–5902; Code 1933, § 26–2002.

Validity

This section has been held unconstitutional in the case of Powell v. State, 1998, 270 Ga. 327, 510 S.E.2d 18.

Historical and Statutory Notes

The 2000 amendment inserted in the second sentence of subsec. (a) "or when he or she commits sodomy with a person who is less than ten years of age", and substituted "30" for "20" years at the end of the second sentence to subsec. (b).

The 2006 amendment by Act 571 in subsec. (a), added paragraph designations; rewrote subsec. (b); and added subsec. (d). Prior to amendment subsec. (b) had read:

"(b) A person convicted of the offense of sodomy shall be punished by imprisonment for not less than one nor more than 20 years. A person convicted of the offense of aggravated sodomy shall be punished by imprisonment for life or by imprisonment for not less than ten nor more than 30 years. Any person convicted under this Code section of the offense of aggravated sodomy shall, in addition, be subject to the sentencing and punishment provisions of Code Sections 17–10–6.1 and 17–10–7."

Laws 2006, Act 571, §§ 1 and 30, provide:

"SECTION 1. The General Assembly finds and declares that recidivist sexual offenders, sexual offenders who use physical violence, and sexual offenders who prey on children are sexual predators who present an extreme threat to the public safety. Many sexual offenders are extremely likely to use physical violence and to repeat their offenses; and some sexual offenders commit many offenses, have many more victims than are ever reported, and are prosecuted for only a fraction of their crimes. The General Assembly finds that this makes the cost of sexual offender victimization to society at large, while incalculable, clearly exorbitant. The General Assembly further finds that the high level of threat that a sexual predator presents to the public safety, and the long-term effects suffered by victims of sex offenses, provide the state with sufficient justification to implement a strategy that includes:

"(1) Incarcerating sexual offenders and maintaining adequate facilities to ensure that decisions to release sexual predators into the community are not made on the basis of inadequate space;

"(2) Requiring the registration of sexual offenders, with a requirement that complete and accurate information be maintained and accessible for use by law enforcement authorities, communities, and the public;

"(3) Providing for community and public notification concerning the presence of sexual offenders;

"(4) Collecting data relative to sexual offenses and sexual offenders;

"(5) Requiring sexual predators who are released into the community to wear an electronic monitoring system for the rest of their natural life and to pay for such system; and

"(6) Prohibiting sexual predators from working with children, either for compensation or as a volunteer.

"The General Assembly further finds that the state has a compelling interest in protecting the public from sexual offenders and in protecting children from predatory sexual activity, and there is sufficient justification for requiring sexual offenders to register and for requiring community and public notification of the presence of sexual offenders. The General Assembly declares that in order to protect the public, it is necessary that the sexual offenders be registered and that members of the community and the public be notified of a sexual offender's presence. The designation of a person as a sexual offender is neither a sentence nor a punishment but simply a regulatory mechanism and status resulting from the conviction of certain crimes. Likewise, the designation of a person as a sexual predator is neither a sentence nor a punishment but simply a regulatory mechanism and status resulting from findings by the Sexual Offender Registration Review Board and a court if requested by a sexual offender."

"SECTION 30. (a) This Act shall become effective July 1, 2006.

"(b) Any person required to register pursuant to the provisions of Code Section 42–1–12, relating to the state sexual offender registry, and any person required not to reside within areas where minors congregate, as prohibited by Code Section 42–1–13 [see § 42–1–15], shall not be relieved of the obligation to comply with the provisions of said Code sections by the repeal and reenactment of said Code sections.

"(c) The provisions of this Act shall not affect or abate the status as a crime of any such act or omission which occurred prior to the effective date of the Act repealing, repealing and reenacting, or amending such law, nor shall the prosecution of such crime be abated as a result of such repeal, repeal and reenactment, or amendment."

§ 16–6–3. Statutory rape

(a) A person commits the offense of statutory rape when he or she engages in sexual intercourse with any person under the age of 16 years and not his or her spouse, provided that no conviction shall be had for this offense on the unsupported testimony of the victim.

(b) Except as provided in subsection (c) of this Code section, a person convicted of the offense of statutory rape shall be punished by imprisonment for not less than one nor more than 20 years; provided, however, that if the person so convicted is 21 years of age or older, such person shall be punished by imprisonment for not less than ten nor more than 20 years. Any person convicted under this subsection of the offense of statutory rape shall, in addition, be subject to the sentencing and punishment provisions of Code Section 17–10–6.2.

(c) If the victim is at least 14 but less than 16 years of age and the person convicted of statutory rape is 18 years of age or younger and is no more than four years older than the victim, such person shall be guilty of a misdemeanor.

Laws 1918, p. 259, §§ 1, 2; Laws 1968, p. 715, § 1; Laws 1995, p. 957, § 3; Laws 1996, p. 871, § 1; Laws 1996, p. 1115, § 3; Laws 2006, Act 571, § 10, eff. July 1, 2006.

Formerly Code 1933, §§ 26–1303, 26–1304; Code 1933, § 26–2018.

Historical and Statutory Notes

The 2006 amendment by Act 571 rewrote the section which had read:

"(a) A person commits the offense of statutory rape when he or she engages in sexual intercourse with any person under the age of 16 years and not his or her spouse, provided that no conviction shall be had for this offense on the unsupported testimony of the victim.

"(b) A person convicted of the offense of statutory rape shall be punished by imprisonment for not less than one nor more than 20 years; provided, however, that if the person so convicted is 21 years of age or older, such person shall be punished by imprisonment for not less than ten nor more than 20 years; provided, further, that if the victim is 14 or 15 years of age and the person so convicted is no more than three years older than the victim, such person shall be guilty of a misdemeanor."

Laws 2006, Act 571, §§ 1 and 30, provide:

"SECTION 1. The General Assembly finds and declares that recidivist sexual offenders, sexual offenders who use physical violence, and sexual offenders who prey on children are sexual predators who present an extreme threat to the public safety. Many sexual offenders are extremely likely to use physical violence and to repeat their offenses; and some sexual offenders commit many offenses, have many more victims than are ever reported, and are prosecuted for only a fraction of their crimes. The General Assembly finds that this makes the cost of sexual offender victimization to society at large, while incalculable, clearly exorbitant. The General Assembly further finds that the high level of threat that a sexual predator presents to the public safety, and the long-term effects suffered by victims of sex offenses, provide the state with sufficient justification to implement a strategy that includes:

"(1) Incarcerating sexual offenders and maintaining adequate facilities to ensure that decisions to release sexual predators into the community are not made on the basis of inadequate space;

"(2) Requiring the registration of sexual offenders, with a requirement that complete and accurate information be maintained and accessible for use by law enforcement authorities, communities, and the public;

"(3) Providing for community and public notification concerning the presence of sexual offenders;

"(4) Collecting data relative to sexual offenses and sexual offenders;

"(5) Requiring sexual predators who are released into the community to wear an electronic monitoring system for the rest of their natural life and to pay for such system; and

"(6) Prohibiting sexual predators from working with children, either for compensation or as a volunteer.

"The General Assembly further finds that the state has a compelling interest in protecting the public from sexual offenders and in protecting children from predatory sexual activity, and there is sufficient justification for requiring sexual offenders to register and for requiring community and public notification of the presence of sexual offenders. The General Assembly declares that in order to protect the public, it is necessary that the sexual offenders be registered and that members of the community and the public be notified of a sexual offender's presence. The designation of a person as a sexual offender is neither a sentence nor a punishment but simply a regulatory mechanism and status resulting from the conviction of certain crimes. Likewise, the designation of a person as a sexual predator is neither a sentence nor a punishment but simply a regulatory mechanism and status resulting from findings by the Sexual Offender Registration Review Board and a court if requested by a sexual offender."

"SECTION 30. (a) This Act shall become effective July 1, 2006.

"(b) Any person required to register pursuant to the provisions of Code Section 42–1–12, relating to the state sexual offender registry, and any person required not to reside within areas where minors congregate, as prohibited by Code Section 42–1–13 [see § 42–1–15], shall not be relieved of the obligation to comply with the provisions of said Code sections by the repeal and reenactment of said Code sections.

"(c) The provisions of this Act shall not affect or abate the status as a crime of any such act or omission which occurred prior to the effective date of the Act repealing, repealing and reenacting, or amending such law, nor shall the prosecution of such crime be abated as a result of such repeal, repeal and reenactment, or amendment."

§ 16–6–4. Child molestation; aggravated child molestation

(a) A person commits the offense of child molestation when such person:

(1) Does any immoral or indecent act to or in the presence of or with any child under the age of 16 years with the intent to arouse or satisfy the sexual desires of either the child or the person; or

(2) By means of an electronic device, transmits images of a person engaging in, inducing, or otherwise participating in any immoral or indecent act to a child under the age of 16 years with the intent to arouse or satisfy the sexual desires of either the child or the person.

(b)(1) Except as provided in paragraph (2) of this subsection, a person convicted of a first offense of child molestation shall be punished by imprisonment for not less than five nor more than 20 years and shall be subject to the sentencing and punishment provisions of Code Sections 17–10–6. 2 and 17–10–7. Upon a defendant being incarcerated on a conviction for a first offense, the Department of Corrections shall provide counseling to such defendant. Except as provided in paragraph (2) of this subsection, upon a second or subsequent conviction of an offense of child molestation, the defendant shall be punished by imprisonment for not less than ten years nor more than 30 years or by imprisonment for life and shall be subject to the sentencing and punishment provisions of Code Sections 17–10–6.2 and 17–10–7; provided, however, that prior to trial, a defendant shall be given notice, in writing, that the state intends to seek a punishment of life imprisonment.

(2) If the victim is at least 14 but less than 16 years of age and the person convicted of child molestation is 18 years of age or younger and is no more than four years older than the victim, such person shall be guilty of a misdemeanor and shall not be subject to the sentencing and punishment provisions of Code Section 17–10–6.2.

(c) A person commits the offense of aggravated child molestation when such person commits an offense of child molestation which act physically injures the child or involves an act of sodomy.

(d)(1) Except as provided in paragraph (2) of this subsection, a person convicted of the offense of aggravated child molestation shall be punished by imprisonment for life or by a split sentence that is a term of imprisonment for not less than 25 years and not exceeding life imprisonment, followed by probation for life, and shall be subject to the sentencing and punishment provisions of Code Sections 17–10–6.1 and 17–10–7.

(2) A person convicted of the offense of aggravated child molestation when:

(A) The victim is at least 13 but less than 16 years of age;

(B) The person convicted of aggravated child molestation is 18 years of age or younger and is no more than four years older than the victim; and

(C) The basis of the charge of aggravated child molestation involves an act of sodomy shall be guilty of a misdemeanor and shall not be subject to the sentencing and punishment provisions of Code Section 17–10–6.1.

(e) A person shall be subject to prosecution in this state pursuant to Code Section 17–2–1 for any conduct made unlawful by paragraph (2) of subsection (a) of this Code section which the person engages in while:

(1) Either within or outside of this state if, by such conduct, the person commits a violation of paragraph (2) of subsection

(a) of this Code section which involves a child who resides in this state; or

(2) Within this state if, by such conduct, the person commits a violation of paragraph (2) of subsection (a) of this Code section which involves a child who resides within or outside this state.

Laws 1950, p. 387, § 1; Laws 1953, Nov.-Dec. Sess., p. 408, § 1; Laws 1968, p. 1249, § 1; Laws 1984, p. 685, § 1; Laws 1984, p. 1495, § 1; Laws 1985, p. 283, § 1; Laws 1987, p. 617, § 1; Laws 1992, p. 6, § 16; Laws 1993, p. 715, § 1; Laws 1994, p. 1959, § 6; Laws 1995, p. 957, § 4; Laws 1997, p. 1578, § 1; Laws 2006, Act 571, § 11, eff. July 1, 2006; Laws 2009, Act 149, § 1, eff. May 5, 2009.

Formerly Code 1933, § 26–2019.

Historical and Statutory Notes

The 2006 amendment by Act 571 rewrote the section which had read:

"(a) A person commits the offense of child molestation when he or she does any immoral or indecent act to or in the presence of or with any child under the age of 16 years with the intent to arouse or satisfy the sexual desires of either the child or the person.

"(b) A person convicted of a first offense of child molestation shall be punished by imprisonment for not less than five nor more than 20 years. Upon such first conviction of the offense of child molestation, the judge may probate the sentence; and such probation may be upon the special condition that the defendant undergo a mandatory period of counseling administered by a licensed psychiatrist or a licensed psychologist. However, if the judge finds that such probation should not be imposed, he or she shall sentence the defendant to imprisonment; provided, further, that upon a defendant's being incarcerated on a conviction for such first offense, the Department of Corrections shall provide counseling to such defendant. Upon a second or subsequent conviction of an offense of child molestation, the defendant shall be punished by imprisonment for not less than ten years nor more than 30 years or by imprisonment for life; provided, however, that prior to trial, a defendant shall be given notice, in writing, that the state intends to seek a punishment of life imprisonment. Adjudication of guilt or imposition of sentence for a conviction of a second or subsequent offense of child molestation, including a plea of nolo contendere, shall not be suspended, probated, deferred, or withheld.

"(c) A person commits the offense of aggravated child molestation when such person commits an offense of child molestation which act physically injures the child or involves an act of sodomy.

"(d)(1) A person convicted of the offense of aggravated child molestation shall be punished by imprisonment for not less than ten nor more than 30 years. Any person convicted under this Code section of the offense of aggravated child molestation shall, in addition, be subject to the sentencing and punishment provisions of Code Sections 17–10–6.1 and 17–10–7.

"(2) The court sentencing a person who has been convicted of a first offense of aggravated child molestation when the victim is 16 years of age or younger at the time of the offense is authorized to require, before sentencing, that the defendant undergo a psychiatric evaluation to ascertain whether or not medroxyprogesterone acetate chemical treatment or its equivalent would be effective in changing the defendant's behavior. If it is determined by a qualified mental health professional that such treatment would be effective, the court may require, as a condition of probation and upon provisions arranged between the court and the defendant, the defendant to undergo medroxyprogesterone acetate treatment or its chemical equivalent which must be coupled with treatment by a qualified mental health professional. In case of a person sentenced to probation who is required to undergo such treatment or its chemical equivalent and is in the custody of a law enforcement agency or confined in a jail at the time of sentencing, when he or she becomes eligible for probation, such person shall begin medroxyprogesterone acetate treatment and counseling prior to his or her release from custody or confinement. A person sentenced to probation who is required to undergo such treatment and who is not in the custody of a law enforcement agency or confined in a jail at the time of sentencing shall be taken into custody or confined until treatment can begin. Additional treatment may continue after such defendant's release from custody or confinement until the defendant demonstrates to the court that such treatment is no longer necessary. No such treatment shall be administered until such person has been fully informed of the side effects of hormonal chemical treatment and has consented to the treatment in writing. The administration of the treatment shall conform to the procedures and conditions set out in subsection (c) of Code Section 42–9–44.2.

"(3) Any physician or qualified mental health professional who acts in good faith in compliance with the provisions of this Code section and subsection (c) of Code Section 42–9–44.2 in the administration of treatment or provision of counseling provided for in this Code section shall be immune from civil or criminal liability for his or her actions in connection with such treatment or counseling."

Laws 2006, Act 571, §§ 1 and 30, provide:

"SECTION 1. The General Assembly finds and declares that recidivist sexual offenders, sexual offenders who use physical violence, and sexual offenders who prey on children are sexual predators who present an extreme threat to the public safety. Many sexual offenders are extremely likely to use physical violence and to repeat their offenses; and some sexual offenders commit many offenses, have many more victims than are ever reported, and are prosecuted for only a fraction of their crimes. The General Assembly finds that this makes the cost of sexual offender victimization to society at large, while incalculable, clearly exorbitant. The General Assembly further finds that the high level of threat that a sexual predator presents to the public safety, and the long-term effects suffered by victims of sex offenses, provide the state with sufficient justification to implement a strategy that includes:

"(1) Incarcerating sexual offenders and maintaining adequate facilities to ensure that decisions to release sexual predators into the community are not made on the basis of inadequate space;

"(2) Requiring the registration of sexual offenders, with a requirement that complete and accurate information be maintained and accessible for use by law enforcement authorities, communities, and the public;

"(3) Providing for community and public notification concerning the presence of sexual offenders;

"(4) Collecting data relative to sexual offenses and sexual offenders;

"(5) Requiring sexual predators who are released into the community to wear an electronic monitoring system for the rest of their natural life and to pay for such system; and

"(6) Prohibiting sexual predators from working with children, either for compensation or as a volunteer.

"The General Assembly further finds that the state has a compelling interest in protecting the public from sexual offenders and in protecting children from predatory sexual activity, and there is sufficient justification for requiring sexual offenders to register and for requiring community and public notification of the presence of sexual offenders. The General Assembly declares that in order to protect the public, it is necessary that the sexual offenders be registered and that members of the community and the public be notified of a sexual offender's presence. The designation of a person as a sexual offender is neither a sentence nor a punishment but simply a regulatory mechanism and status resulting from the conviction of certain crimes. Likewise, the designation of a person as a sexual predator is neither a sentence nor a punishment but simply a regulatory mechanism and status resulting from findings by the Sexual Offender Registration Review Board and a court if requested by a sexual offender."

"SECTION 30. (a) This Act shall become effective July 1, 2006.

"(b) Any person required to register pursuant to the provisions of Code Section 42–1–12, relating to the state sexual offender registry, and any person required not to reside within areas where minors congregate, as prohibited by Code Section 42–1–13 [see § 42–1–15], shall not be relieved of the obligation to comply with the provisions of said Code sections by the repeal and reenactment of said Code sections.

"(c) The provisions of this Act shall not affect or abate the status as a crime of any such act or omission which occurred prior to the effective date of the Act repealing, repealing and reenacting, or amending such law, nor shall the prosecution of such crime be abated as a result of such repeal, repeal and reenactment, or amendment."

The 2009 amendment by Act 149, in subsec. (a), substituted "such person" for "he or she does", designated par. (1), in new par. (1), inserted "Does" and "; or", inserted par. (2); and added subsec. (e).

§ 16–6–5. Enticing a child for indecent purposes

(a) A person commits the offense of enticing a child for indecent purposes when he or she solicits, entices, or takes any child under the age of 16 years to any place whatsoever for the purpose of child molestation or indecent acts.

(b) Except as provided in subsection (c) of this Code section, a person convicted of the offense of enticing a child for indecent purposes shall be punished by imprisonment for not less than ten nor more than 30 years. Any person convicted under this Code section of the offense of enticing a child for indecent purposes shall, in addition, be subject to the sentencing and punishment provisions of Code Section 17–10–6.2.

(c) If the victim is at least 14 but less than 16 years of age and the person convicted of enticing a child for indecent purposes is 18 years of age or younger and is no more than four years older than the victim, such person shall be guilty of a misdemeanor and shall not be subject to the sentencing and punishment provisions of Code Section 17–10–6.2.

Laws 1950, p. 387, § 2; Laws 1953, Nov.-Dec. Sess., p. 408, § 2; Laws 1968, p. 1249, § 1; Laws 1984, p. 1495, § 2; Laws 1992, p. 6, § 16; Laws 1992, p. 2131, § 1; Laws 1995, p. 957, § 5; Laws 2006, Act 571, § 12, eff. July 1, 2006.

Formerly Code 1933, § 26–2020.

Historical and Statutory Notes

The 2006 amendment by Act 571, rewrote subsec. (b) and added subsec. (c). Prior to amendment, subsec. (b) had read:

"(b) A person convicted of the offense of enticing a child for indecent purposes shall be punished by imprisonment for not less than one nor more than 20 years. Upon a first conviction of the offense of enticing a child for indecent purposes, the judge may probate the sentence; and such probation may be upon the special condition that the defendant undergo a mandatory period of counseling administered by a licensed psychiatrist or a licensed psychologist. However, if the judge finds that such probation should not be imposed, he shall sentence the defendant to imprisonment. Upon a second or third conviction of such offense, the defendant shall be punished by imprisonment for not less than five years. For a fourth or subsequent conviction of the offense of enticing a child for indecent purposes, the defendant shall be punished by imprisonment for 20 years. Adjudication of guilt or imposition of sentence for a conviction of a third, fourth, or subsequent offense of enticing a child for indecent purposes, including a plea of nolo contendere, shall not be suspended, probated, deferred, or withheld."

Laws 2006, Act 571, §§ 1 and 30, provide:

"SECTION 1. The General Assembly finds and declares that recidivist sexual offenders, sexual offenders who use physical violence, and sexual offenders who prey on children are sexual predators who present an extreme threat to the public safety. Many sexual offenders are extremely likely to use physical violence and to repeat their offenses; and some sexual offenders commit many offenses, have many more victims than are ever reported, and are prosecuted for only a fraction of their crimes. The General Assembly finds that this makes the cost of sexual offender victimization to society at large, while incalculable, clearly exorbitant. The General Assembly further finds that the high level of threat that a sexual predator presents to the public safety, and the long-term effects suffered by victims of sex offenses, provide the state with sufficient justification to implement a strategy that includes:

"(1) Incarcerating sexual offenders and maintaining adequate facilities to ensure that decisions to release sexual predators into the community are not made on the basis of inadequate space;

"(2) Requiring the registration of sexual offenders, with a requirement that complete and accurate information be maintained and accessible for use by law enforcement authorities, communities, and the public;

"(3) Providing for community and public notification concerning the presence of sexual offenders;

"(4) Collecting data relative to sexual offenses and sexual offenders;

"(5) Requiring sexual predators who are released into the community to wear an electronic monitoring system for the rest of their natural life and to pay for such system; and

"(6) Prohibiting sexual predators from working with children, either for compensation or as a volunteer.

"The General Assembly further finds that the state has a compelling interest in protecting the public from sexual offenders and in protecting children from predatory sexual activity, and there is sufficient justification for requiring sexual offenders to register and for requiring community and public notification of the presence of sexual offenders. The General Assembly declares that in order to protect the public, it is necessary that the sexual offenders be registered and that members of the community and the public be notified of a sexual offender's presence. The designation of a person as a sexual offender is neither a sentence nor a punishment but simply a regulatory mechanism and status resulting from the conviction of certain crimes. Likewise, the designation of a person as a sexual predator is neither a sentence nor a punishment but simply a regulatory mechanism and status resulting from findings by the Sexual Offender Registration Review Board and a court if requested by a sexual offender."

"SECTION 30. (a) This Act shall become effective July 1, 2006.

"(b) Any person required to register pursuant to the provisions of Code Section 42–1–12, relating to the state sexual offender registry, and any person required not to reside within areas where minors congregate, as prohibited by Code Section 42–1–13 [see § 42–1–15], shall not be relieved of the obligation to comply with the provisions of said Code sections by the repeal and reenactment of said Code sections.

"(c) The provisions of this Act shall not affect or abate the status as a crime of any such act or omission which occurred prior to the effective date of the Act repealing, repealing and reenacting, or amending such law, nor shall the prosecution of such crime be abated as a result of such repeal, repeal and reenactment, or amendment."

§ 16–6–5.1. Sexual assault

(a) As used in this Code section, the term:

(1) "Actor" means a person accused of sexual assault.

(2) "Intimate parts" means the genital area, groin, inner thighs, buttocks, or breasts of a person.

(3) "Psychotherapy" means the professional treatment or counseling of a mental or emotional illness, symptom, or condition.

(4) "Sexual contact" means any contact between the actor and a person not married to the actor involving the intimate parts of either person for the purpose of sexual gratification of the actor.

(5) "School" means any educational program or institution instructing children at any level, pre-kindergarten through twelfth grade, or the equivalent thereof if grade divisions are not used.

(b) A person who has supervisory or disciplinary authority over another individual commits sexual assault when that person:

(1) Is a teacher, principal, assistant principal, or other administrator of any school and engages in sexual contact with such other individual who the actor knew or should have known is enrolled at the same school; provided, however, that such contact shall not be prohibited when the actor is married to such other individual;

(2) Is an employee or agent of any probation or parole office and engages in sexual contact with such other individual who the actor knew or should have known is a probationer or parolee under the supervision of the same probation or parole office;

(3) Is an employee or agent of a law enforcement agency and engages in sexual contact with such other individual who the actor knew or should have known is being detained by or is in the custody of any law enforcement agency;

(4) Is an employee or agent of a hospital and engages in sexual contact with such other individual who the actor knew or should have known is a patient or is being detained in the same hospital; or

(5) Is an employee or agent of a correctional facility, juvenile detention facility, facility providing services to a person with a disability, as such term is defined in Code Section 37–1–1, or a facility providing child welfare and youth services, as such term is defined in Code Section 49–5–3, who engages in sexual contact with such other individual who the actor knew or should have known is in the custody of such facility.

(c) A person who is an actual or purported practitioner of psychotherapy commits sexual assault when he or she engages in sexual contact with another individual who the actor knew or should have known is the subject of the actor's actual or purported treatment or counseling or the actor uses the treatment or counseling relationship to facilitate sexual contact between the actor and such individual.

(d) A person who is an employee, agent, or volunteer at any facility licensed or required to be licensed under Code Section 31–7–3 or 31–7–12 or who is required to be licensed pursuant to

Code Section 31–7–151 or 31–7–173 commits sexual assault when he or she engages in sexual contact with another individual who the actor knew or should have known had been admitted to or is receiving services from such facility or the actor.

(e) Consent of the victim shall not be a defense to a prosecution under this Code section.

(f) A person convicted of sexual assault shall be punished by imprisonment for not less than one nor more than 25 years or by a fine not to exceed $100,000.00, or both; provided, however, that:

(1) Except as provided in paragraph (2) of this subsection, any person convicted of the offense of sexual assault of a child under the age of 16 years shall be punished by imprisonment for not less than 25 nor more than 50 years and shall, in addition, be subject to the sentencing and punishment provisions of Code Section 17–10–6.2; and

(2) If at the time of the offense the victim of the offense is at least 14 years of age but less than 16 years of age and the actor is 18 years of age or younger and is no more than four years older than the victim, such person shall be guilty of a misdemeanor and shall not be subject to the sentencing and punishment provisions of Code Section 17–10–6.2.

Laws 1983, p. 721, § 1; Laws 1990, p. 1003, § 1; Laws 1991, p. 1108, § 1; Laws 1992, p. 6, § 16; Laws 1992, p. 1940, § 1; Laws 1999, p. 562, § 5; Laws 2006, Act 571, § 13, eff. July 1, 2006; Laws 2010, Act 389, § 2, eff. May 20, 2010.

Historical and Statutory Notes

The 2006 amendment by Act 571, in subsec. (a), par. (4), substituted "between the actor and a person not married to the actor involving the intimate parts of either person for the purpose of sexual gratification of the actor" for "for the purpose of sexual gratification of the actor with the intimate parts of a person not married to the actor"; in subsec. (b), added "or she" preceding "engages in sexual contact" in the first sentence, substituted "ten nor more that 30 years" for "one nor more than three years" in the second sentence, and added "; provided, however, that any person convicted of the offense of sexual assault under this subsection of a child under the age of 14 years shall be punished by imprisonment for not less than 25 years nor more than 50 years. Any person convicted under this subsection of the offense of sexual assault shall, in addition, be subject to the sentencing and punishment provisions of Code Section 17–10–6.2."; in subsec. (c), par. (4), substituted "ten nor more than 30 years" for "one nor more than three years", and added "; provided, however, that any person convicted of the offense of sexual assault under this subsection of a child under the age of 14 years shall be punished by imprisonment for not less than 25 nor more than 50 years. Any person convicted under this subsection of the offense of sexual assault shall, in addition, be subject to the sentencing and punishment provisions of Code Section 17–10–6.2."; and in subsec. (d), substituted "ten nor more than 30 years" for "one nor more than five years" and added "Any person convicted under this subsection of the offense of sexual assault shall, in addition, be subject to the sentencing and punishment provisions of Code Section 17–10–6.2."

Laws 2006, Act 571, §§ 1 and 30, provide:

"SECTION 1. The General Assembly finds and declares that recidivist sexual offenders, sexual offenders who use physical violence, and sexual offenders who prey on children are sexual predators who present an extreme threat to the public safety. Many sexual offenders are extremely likely to use physical violence and to repeat their offenses; and some sexual offenders commit many offenses, have many more victims than are ever reported, and are prosecuted for only a fraction of their crimes. The General Assembly finds that this makes the cost of sexual offender victimization to society at large, while incalculable, clearly exorbitant. The General Assembly further finds that the high level of threat that a sexual predator presents to the public safety, and the long-term effects suffered by victims of sex offenses, provide the state with sufficient justification to implement a strategy that includes:

"(1) Incarcerating sexual offenders and maintaining adequate facilities to ensure that decisions to release sexual predators into the community are not made on the basis of inadequate space;

"(2) Requiring the registration of sexual offenders, with a requirement that complete and accurate information be maintained and accessible for use by law enforcement authorities, communities, and the public;

"(3) Providing for community and public notification concerning the presence of sexual offenders;

"(4) Collecting data relative to sexual offenses and sexual offenders;

"(5) Requiring sexual predators who are released into the community to wear an electronic monitoring system for the rest of their natural life and to pay for such system; and

"(6) Prohibiting sexual predators from working with children, either for compensation or as a volunteer.

"The General Assembly further finds that the state has a compelling interest in protecting the public from sexual offenders and in protecting children from predatory sexual activity, and there is sufficient justification for requiring sexual offenders to register and for requiring community and public notification of the presence of sexual offenders. The General Assembly declares that in order to protect the public, it is necessary that the sexual offenders be registered and that members of the community and the public be notified of a sexual offender's presence. The designation of a person as a sexual offender is neither a sentence nor a punishment but simply a regulatory mechanism and status resulting from the conviction of certain crimes. Likewise, the designation of a person as a sexual predator is neither a sentence nor a punishment but simply a regulatory mechanism and status resulting from findings by the Sexual Offender Registration Review Board and a court if requested by a sexual offender."

"SECTION 30. (a) This Act shall become effective July 1, 2006.

"(b) Any person required to register pursuant to the provisions of Code Section 42–1–12, relating to the state sexual offender registry, and any person required not to reside within areas where minors congregate, as prohibited by Code Section 42–1–13 [see § 42–1–15], shall not be relieved of the obligation to comply with the provisions of said Code sections by the repeal and reenactment of said Code sections.

"(c) The provisions of this Act shall not affect or abate the status as a crime of any such act or omission which occurred prior to the effective date of the Act repealing, repealing and reenacting, or amending such law, nor shall the prosecution of such crime be abated as a result of such repeal, repeal and reenactment, or amendment."

The 2010 amendment by Act 389 rewrote the section which had read:

"(a) As used in this Code section, the term:

"(1) 'Actor' means a person accused of sexual assault.

"(2) 'Intimate parts' means the genital area, groin, inner thighs, buttocks, or breasts of a person.

"(3) 'Psychotherapy' means the professional treatment or counseling of a mental or emotional illness, symptom, or condition.

"(4) 'Sexual contact' means any contact between the actor and a person not married to the actor involving the intimate parts of either person for the purpose of sexual gratification of the actor.

"(b) A probation or parole officer or other custodian or supervisor of another person referred to in this Code section commits sexual assault when he or she engages in sexual contact with another person who is a probationer or parolee under the supervision of said probation or parole officer or who is in the custody of law or who is enrolled in a school or who is detained in or is a patient in a hospital or other institution and such actor has supervisory or disciplinary authority over such other person. A person convicted of sexual assault shall be punished by imprisonment for not less than ten nor more than 30 years; provided, however, that any person convicted of the offense of sexual assault under this subsection of a child under the age of 14 years shall be punished by imprisonment for not less than 25 nor more than 50 years. Any person convicted under this subsection of the offense of sexual assault shall, in addition, be subject to the sentencing and punishment provisions of Code Section 17–10–6.2.

"(c)(1) A person commits sexual assault when such person has supervisory or disciplinary authority over another person and such person engages in sexual contact with that other person who is:

"(A) In the custody of law; or

"(B) Detained in or is a patient in a hospital or other institution.

"(2) A person commits sexual assault when, as an actual or purported practitioner of psychotherapy, he or she engages in sexual contact with another person who the actor knew or should have known is the subject of the actor's actual or purported treatment or counseling, or, if the treatment or counseling relationship was used to facilitate sexual contact between the actor and said person.

"(3) Consent of the victim shall not be a defense to a prosecution under this subsection.

"(4) A person convicted of sexual assault under this subsection shall be punished by imprisonment for not less than ten nor more than 30 years; provided, however, that any person convicted of the offense of sexual assault under this subsection of a child under the age of 14 years shall be punished by imprisonment for not less than 25 nor more than 50 years. Any person convicted under this subsection of the offense of sexual assault shall, in addition, be subject to the sentencing and punishment provisions of Code Section 17–10–6.2.

"(d) A person who is an employee, agent, or volunteer at any facility licensed or required to be licensed under Code Section 31–7–3, relating to long-term care facilities, or Code Section 31–7–12, relating to personal care homes, or who is required to be licensed pursuant to Code Section 31–7–151 or 31–7–173, relating to home health care and hospices, commits sexual assault when such person engages in sexual contact with another person who has been admitted to or is receiving services from such facility, person, or entity. A person convicted of sexual assault pursuant to this subsection shall be punished by imprisonment for not less than ten nor more than 30 years, or a fine of not more than $5,000.00, or both. Any violation of this subsection shall constitute a separate offense. Any person convicted under this subsection of the offense of sexual assault shall, in addition, be subject to the sentencing and punishment provisions of Code Section 17–10–6.2."

§ 16–6–6. Bestiality

(a) A person commits the offense of bestiality when he performs or submits to any sexual act with an animal involving the sex organs of the one and the mouth, anus, penis, or vagina of the other.

(b) A person convicted of the offense of bestiality shall be punished by imprisonment for not less than one nor more than five years.

Laws 1833, Cobb's 1851 Digest, p. 787; Laws 1880–81, p. 74, § 1; Laws 1968, p. 1249, § 1.

Formerly Code 1863, §§ 4253, 4254; Code 1868, §§ 4288, 4289; Code 1873, §§ 4354, 4355; Code 1882, §§ 4354, 4355; Penal Code 1895, §§ 384, 385; Penal Code 1910, §§ 375, 376; Code 1933, §§ 26–5903, 26–5904; Code 1933, § 26–2004.

§ 16–6–7. Necrophilia

(a) A person commits the offense of necrophilia when he performs any sexual act with a dead human body involving the sex organs of the one and the mouth, anus, penis, or vagina of the other.

(b) A person convicted of the offense of necrophilia shall be punished by imprisonment for not less than one nor more than ten years.

Laws 1977, p. 315, § 1.

Formerly Code 1933, § 26–2022.

§ 16–6–8. Public indecency

(a) A person commits the offense of public indecency when he or she performs any of the following acts in a public place:

(1) An act of sexual intercourse;

(2) A lewd exposure of the sexual organs;

(3) A lewd appearance in a state of partial or complete nudity; or

(4) A lewd caress or indecent fondling of the body of another person.

(b) A person convicted of the offense of public indecency as provided in subsection (a) of this Code section shall be punished as for a misdemeanor except as provided in subsection (c) of this Code section.

(c) Upon a third or subsequent conviction for public indecency for the violation of paragraph (2), (3), or (4) of subsection (a) of this Code section, a person shall be guilty of a felony and shall be punished by imprisonment for not less than one nor more than five years.

(d) For the purposes of this Code section only, "public place" shall include jails and penal and correctional institutions of the state and its political subdivisions.

(e) This Code section shall be cumulative to and shall not prohibit the enactment of any other general and local laws, rules, and regulations of state and local authorities or agencies and local ordinances prohibiting such activities which are more restrictive than this Code section.

Laws 1833, Cobb's 1851 Digest, p. 815; Laws 1865–66, p. 233, § 2; Laws 1968, p. 1249, § 1; Laws 1991, p. 966, § 1; Laws 1992, p. 6, § 16; Laws 1996, p. 312, § 1; Laws 1996, p. 354, § 1.

Formerly Code 1863, § 4420; Code 1868, § 4461; Code 1873, § 4535; Code 1882, § 4535; Penal Code 1895, § 390; Penal Code 1910, § 381; Code 1933, § 26–6101; Code 1933, § 26–2011.

§ 16–6–9. Prostitution

A person commits the offense of prostitution when he or she performs or offers or consents to perform a sexual act, including but not limited to sexual intercourse or sodomy, for money or other items of value.

Laws 1968, p. 1249, § 1; Laws 2001, p. 92, § 3.

Formerly Code 1933, § 26–2012.

Historical and Statutory Notes

The 2001 amendment rewrote this section which formerly provided:

"A person commits the offense of prostitution when he performs or offers or consents to perform an act of sexual intercourse for money."

§ 16–6–10. Keeping a place of prostitution

A person having or exercising control over the use of any place or conveyance which would offer seclusion or shelter for the practice of prostitution commits the offense of keeping a place of prostitution when he knowingly grants or permits the use of such place for the purpose of prostitution.

Laws 1943, p. 568, § 1; Laws 1968, p. 1249, § 1; Laws 1970, p. 236, § 3.

Formerly Code 1933, § 26–2014.

§ 16–6–11. Pimping

A person commits the offense of pimping when he or she performs any of the following acts:

(1) Offers or agrees to procure a prostitute for another;

(2) Offers or agrees to arrange a meeting of persons for the purpose of prostitution;

(3) Directs or transports another person to a place when he or she knows or should know that the direction or transportation is for the purpose of prostitution;

(4) Receives money or other thing of value from a prostitute, without lawful consideration, knowing it was earned in whole or in part from prostitution; or

(5) Aids or abets, counsels, or commands another in the commission of prostitution or aids or assists in prostitution where the proceeds or profits derived therefrom are to be divided on a pro rata basis.

Laws 1918, p. 267, § 1; Laws 1968, p. 1249, § 1; Laws 1970, p. 236, § 2; Laws 2003, Act 216, § 1, eff. June 2, 2003.

Formerly Code 1933, § 26–6201; Code 1933, § 26–2013.

Historical and Statutory Notes

The 2003 amendment by Act 216, inserted "or she" in the first sentence; and in par. (3), substituted "Directs or transports another person to a place when he or she knows or should know that the direction or transportation is for the purpose of prostitution" for "Directs another to a place knowing such direction is for the purpose of prostitution"

§ 16–6–12. Pandering

A person commits the offense of pandering when he or she solicits a person to perform an act of prostitution in his or her own behalf or in behalf of a third person or when he or she knowingly assembles persons at a fixed place for the purpose of being solicited by others to perform an act of prostitution.

Laws 1968, p. 1249, § 1; Laws 1970, p. 236, § 5; Laws 1988, p. 1797, § 1; Laws 1998, p. 1301, § 1.

Formerly Code 1933, § 26–2016.

§ 16–6–13. Punishment for keeping a place of prostitution, pimping or pandering

(a) Except as otherwise provided in subsection (b) of this Code section, a person convicted of any of the offenses enumerated in Code Sections 16–6–10 through 16–6–12 shall be punished as for a misdemeanor of a high and aggravated nature. A person convicted of the offense enumerated in Code Section 16–6–9 shall be punished as for a misdemeanor.

(b) A person convicted of keeping a place of prostitution, pimping, or pandering when such offense involves keeping a place of prostitution for, the pimping for, or the solicitation of a person under the age of 18 years to perform an act of prostitution or the assembly of two or more persons under the age of 18 years at a fixed place for the purpose of being solicited by others to perform an act of prostitution shall be guilty of a felony and shall be punished by imprisonment for a period of not less than five nor more than 20 years and such convicted person shall be fined not less than $2,500.00 nor more than $10,000.00. Adjudication of guilt or imposition of a sentence for a conviction of a second or subsequent offense when such offense involves keeping a place of prostitution for, the pimping for, or pandering of a person under the age of 18 years pursuant to this subsection, including a plea of nolo contendere, shall not be suspended, probated, deferred, or withheld.

(c)(1) The clerk of the court in which a person is convicted of pandering shall cause to be published a notice of conviction for each such person convicted. Such notices of conviction shall be published in the manner of legal notices in the legal organ of the county in which such person resides or, in the case of nonresidents, in the legal organ of the county in which the person was convicted. Such notice of conviction shall be one column wide by two inches long and shall contain the photograph taken by the arresting law enforcement agency at the time of arrest, name, and address of the convicted person and the date, time, place of arrest, and disposition of the case and shall be published once in the legal organ of the appropriate county in the second week following such conviction or as soon thereafter as publication may be made.

(2) The convicted person for which a notice of conviction is published pursuant to this subsection shall be assessed the cost of publication of such notice and such assessment shall be imposed at the time of conviction in addition to any other fine imposed pursuant to this Code section.

(3) The clerk of the court, the publisher of any legal organ which publishes a notice of conviction, and any other person involved in the publication of an erroneous notice of conviction shall be immune from civil or criminal liability for such erroneous publication, provided such publication was made in good faith.

(d) In addition to any other penalty authorized under subsections (a) and (b) of this Code section, a person convicted of an offense enumerated in Code Sections 16–6–9 through 16–6–12 shall be fined $ 2,500.00 if such offense was committed within 1,000 feet of any school building, school grounds, public place of worship, or playground or recreation center which is used primarily by persons under the age of 17 years.

Laws 1968, p. 1249, § 1; Laws 1970, p. 236, § 4; Laws 1988, p. 1797, § 2; Laws 1992, p. 6, § 16; Laws 1998, p. 1301, § 2; Laws 2001, p. 92, § 4; Laws 2003, Act 382, § 1.1, eff. June 4, 2003.

Formerly Code 1933, § 26–2015.

Historical and Statutory Notes

The 2001 amendment rewrote subsec. (b) which formerly provided:

"(b) A person convicted of pandering when such offense involves the solicitation of a person under the age of 17 years to perform an act of prostitution or the assembly of two or more persons under the age of 17 years at a fixed place for the purpose of being solicited by others to perform an act of prostitution shall be guilty of a felony and shall be fined not less than $2,500.00 nor more than $10,000.00 or shall be imprisoned for not less than one year nor more than five years, or both fined and imprisoned. Adjudication of guilt or imposition of sentence for a conviction of a second or subsequent offense of pandering involving a person under the age of 17years pursuant to this subsection, including a plea of nolo contendere, shall not be suspended, probated, deferred, or withheld."

The 2003 amendment by Act 382, in subsec. (b), substituted "convicted of keeping a place of prostitution, pimping, or pandering when such offense involves keeping a place of prostitution for, the pimping for, or the solicitation" for "convicted of pimping or pandering when such offense involves the pimping for or the solicitation", deleted "of pimping or pandering involving" following "second or subsequent offense", and inserted "when such offense involves keeping a place of prostitution for, the pimping for, or pandering of".

§ 16–6–13.1. Testing for sexually transmitted diseases of persons convicted of pandering

(a) Any term used in this Code section and defined in Code Section 31–22–9.1 shall have the meaning provided for such term in Code Section 31–22–9.1.

(b) Upon a verdict or plea of guilty or a plea of nolo contendere to the offense of pandering, the court in which that verdict is returned or plea entered shall as a condition of probation or a suspended sentence require the defendant in such case to submit to testing for sexually transmitted diseases within 45 days following the date of the verdict or plea and to consent to release of the test results to the defendant's spouse if the defendant is married; provided, however, that a defendant who is not a resident of this state shall, upon a verdict or plea of guilty or a plea of nolo contendere, be ordered by the court to undergo immediate testing for sexually transmitted diseases and shall remain in the custody of the court until such testing is completed. The clerk of the court, in the case of a defendant who is a resident of this state, shall mail, within three days following the date of that verdict or plea, a copy of that verdict or plea to the Department of Community Health. The tests for sexually transmitted diseases required under this subsection shall be limited to the eight most common sexually transmitted diseases as determined by the Department of Community Health.

(c) The Department of Community Health, within 30 days following the notification under subsection (b) of this Code section, shall arrange for the tests for the person required to submit thereto. Such person shall bear the costs of such tests.

(d) Any person required under this Code section to submit to testing for sexually transmitted diseases who fails or refuses to submit to the tests arranged pursuant to subsection (c) of this Code section shall be subject to such measures deemed necessary by the court in which the verdict was returned or plea entered to require voluntary submission to the tests.

Laws 1998, p. 1301, § 3; Laws 2009, Act 102, § 1–4, eff. July 1, 2009.

Historical and Statutory Notes

The 2009 amendment by Act 102 substituted "Department of Community Health" for "Department of Human Resources" throughout the section.

§ 16–6–13.2. Forfeiture of motor vehicles operated by persons convicted of pimping or pandering; exceptions

(a) As used in this Code section, the term:

(1) "Costs" means, but is not limited to:

(A) All expenses associated with the seizure, towing, storage, maintenance, custody, preservation, operation, or sale of the motor vehicle; and

(B) Satisfaction of any security interest or lien not subject to forfeiture under this Code section.

(2) "Court costs" means, but is not limited to:

(A) All court costs, including the costs of advertisement, transcripts, and court reporter fees; and

(B) Payment of receivers, conservators, appraisers, accountants, or trustees appointed by the court pursuant to this Code section.

(3) "Governmental agency" means any department, office, council, commission, committee, authority, board, bureau, or division of the executive, judicial, or legislative branch of a state, the United States, or any political subdivision thereof.

(4) "Interest holder" means a secured party within the meaning of Code Section 11–9–102 or the beneficiary of a perfected encumbrance pertaining to an interest in a motor vehicle.

(5) "Motor vehicle" or "vehicle" means any motor vehicle as defined in Code Section 40–1–1.

(6) "Owner" means a person, other than an interest holder, who has an interest in a motor vehicle and is in compliance with any statute requiring its recordation or reflection in public records in order to perfect the interest against a bona fide purchaser for value.

(7) "Proceeds" means property derived directly or indirectly from, maintained by, or realized through an act or omission and includes any benefit, interest, or property of any kind without reduction for expenses incurred for acquisition, maintenance, or any other purpose.

(b)(1) An action filed pursuant to this Code section shall be filed in the name of the State of Georgia and may be brought by the prosecuting attorney having jurisdiction over any offense which arose out of the same conduct which made the motor vehicle subject to forfeiture. Such prosecuting attorney may bring an action pursuant to this Code section in the superior court in the county where the motor vehicle was seized or in the county where conduct occurred which made the motor vehicle subject to forfeiture.

(2) Any action brought pursuant to this Code section may be compromised or settled in the same manner as other civil actions.

(c)(1) Any motor vehicle operated by a person to facilitate a violation of Code Section 16–6–11 where the offense involved the pimping of a person under the age of 18 years to perform an act of prostitution and involved a motor vehicle or operated by a person who has been convicted of or pleaded nolo contendere for two previous violations of Code Section 16–6–11 or 16–6–12 involving a motor vehicle within a five-year period and who is convicted or pleads nolo contendere to a third violation of Code Section 16–6–11 or 16–6–12 involving a motor vehicle within the same five-year period is declared to be contraband and subject to forfeiture to the state, as provided in this Code section.

(2) For the purpose of this subsection, a violation of Code Section 16–6–11 or 16–6–12 involving a motor vehicle shall mean a violation of Code Section 16–6–11 or 16–6–12 in which a motor vehicle is used to violate said Code section or in which the violation occurred.

(d) A property interest shall not be subject to forfeiture under this Code section if the owner of such interest or interest holder establishes that such owner or interest holder:

(1) Is not legally accountable for the conduct giving rise to its forfeiture, did not consent to it, and did not know of the conduct;

(2) Holds the motor vehicle jointly or in common with a person whose conduct gave rise to its forfeiture and such owner did not consent to such conduct and did not know of the conduct;

(3) Does not hold the motor vehicle for the benefit of or as nominee for any person whose conduct gave rise to its forfeiture, and, if the owner or interest holder acquired the interest through any such person, the owner or interest holder acquired it as a bona fide purchaser for value without knowingly taking part in an illegal transaction; or

(4) Acquired the interest:

(A) Before the conduct giving rise to its forfeiture, and the person whose conduct gave rise to its forfeiture did not have the authority to convey the interest to a bona fide purchaser for value at the time of the conduct; or

(B) After the completion of the conduct giving rise to its forfeiture:

(i) As a bona fide purchaser for value without knowingly taking part in an illegal transaction; and

(ii) At the time the interest was acquired, was reasonably without cause to believe that the motor vehicle was subject to forfeiture or likely to become subject to forfeiture under this Code section.

(e)(1) Upon learning of the address or phone number of the company which owns any rented or leased vehicle which is present at the scene of an arrest or other action taken pursuant to this Code section, the seizing law enforcement agency shall immediately contact the company to inform it that the vehicle is available for the company to take possession.

(2) In any case where a vehicle which is the only family vehicle is determined to be subject to forfeiture, the court may, if it determines that the financial hardship to the family as a result of the forfeiture and sale outweighs the benefit to the state from such forfeiture, order the title to the vehicle transferred to such other family member who is a duly licensed operator and who requires the use of such vehicle for employment or family transportation purposes. Such transfer shall be subject to any valid liens and shall be granted only once.

(f)(1) A motor vehicle which is subject to forfeiture under this Code section may be seized by any law enforcement officer of this state or of any political subdivision thereof who has power to make arrests or execute process or a search warrant issued by any court having jurisdiction over the motor vehicle. A search warrant authorizing seizure of a motor vehicle which is subject to forfeiture pursuant to this Code section may be issued on an affidavit demonstrating that probable cause exists for its forfeiture or that the motor vehicle has been the subject of a previous final judgment of forfeiture in the courts of this state. The court may order that the motor vehicle be seized on such terms and conditions as are reasonable.

(2) A motor vehicle which is subject to forfeiture under this Code section may be seized without process if there is probable cause to believe that the motor vehicle is subject to forfeiture under this Code section or the seizure is incident to an arrest or search pursuant to a search warrant or to an inspection under an inspection warrant.

(g)(1) When a motor vehicle is seized pursuant to this Code section, the sheriff or law enforcement officer seizing the same shall report the fact of seizure, in writing, within 20 days thereof to the prosecuting attorney of the county where the seizure was made.

(2) Within 30 days from the date of seizure, a complaint for forfeiture shall be initiated as provided for in subsection (l) or (m) of this Code section.

(3) If the state fails to initiate forfeiture proceedings against a motor vehicle seized for forfeiture by notice of pending forfeiture within the time limits specified in paragraphs (1) and (2) of this subsection, the motor vehicle must be released on the request of an owner or interest holder, pending further proceedings pursuant to this Code section, unless the motor vehicle is being held as evidence.

(h)(1) Seizure of a motor vehicle by a law enforcement officer constitutes notice of such seizure to any person who was present at the time of seizure who may assert an interest in the motor vehicle.

(2) When a motor vehicle is seized pursuant to this Code section, the prosecuting attorney, sheriff, or law enforcement officer seizing the same shall give notice of the seizure to any owner or interest holder who is not present at the time of seizure by personal service, publication, or the mailing of written notice:

(A) If the owner's or interest holder's name and current address are known, by either personal service or mailing a copy of the notice by certified mail or statutory overnight delivery to that address;

(B) If the owner's or interest holder's name and address are required by law to be on record with a government agency to perfect an interest in the motor vehicle but the owner's or interest holder's current address is not known, by mailing a copy of the notice by certified mail or statutory overnight delivery, return receipt requested, to any address on the record; or

(C) If the owner's or interest holder's address is not known and is not on record as provided in subparagraph (B) of this paragraph or the owner's or interest holder's interest is not known, by publication in two consecutive issues of a newspaper of general circulation in the county in which the seizure occurs.

(3) Notice of seizure must include a description of the motor vehicle, the date and place of seizure, the conduct giving rise to forfeiture, and the violation of law alleged.

(i) A motor vehicle taken or detained under this Code section is not subject to replevin, conveyance, sequestration, or attachment. The seizing law enforcement agency or the prosecuting attorney may authorize the release of the motor vehicle if the forfeiture or retention is unnecessary or may transfer the action to another agency or prosecuting attorney by discontinuing forfeiture proceedings in favor of forfeiture proceedings initiated by the other law enforcement agency or prosecuting attorney. An action under this Code section may be consolidated with any other action or proceeding under this title relating to the same motor vehicle on motion by an interest holder and must be so consolidated on motion by the prosecuting attorney in either proceeding or action. The motor vehicle is deemed to be in the custody of the State of Georgia subject only to the orders and decrees of the superior court having jurisdiction over the forfeiture proceedings.

(j) If a motor vehicle is seized under this Code section, the prosecuting attorney may:

(1) Remove the motor vehicle to a place designated by the superior court having jurisdiction over the forfeiture proceeding;

(2) Remove the motor vehicle to a storage area, within the jurisdiction of the court, for safekeeping;

(3) Provide for another governmental agency, a receiver appointed by the court pursuant to Chapter 8 of Title 9, an owner, or an interest holder to take custody of the motor vehicle and remove it to an appropriate location within the county where the motor vehicle was seized; or

(4) Require the sheriff or chief of police of the political subdivision where the motor vehicle was seized to take custody of the motor vehicle and remove it to an appropriate location for disposition in accordance with law.

(k) As soon as possible, but not more than 30 days after the seizure of a motor vehicle, the seizing law enforcement agency shall estimate the value of the motor vehicle seized.

(*l*) If the estimated value of the motor vehicle seized is $ 25,000.00 or less, the prosecuting attorney may elect to proceed under the provisions of this subsection in the following manner:

(1) Notice of the seizure of such motor vehicle shall be posted in a prominent location in the courthouse of the county in which the motor vehicle was seized. Such notice shall include a description of the motor vehicle, the date and place of seizure, the conduct giving rise to forfeiture, a statement that the owner of such motor vehicle has 30 days within which a claim must be filed, and the violation of law alleged;

(2) A copy of the notice, which shall include a statement that the owner of such motor vehicle has 30 days within which a claim must be filed, shall be served upon an owner, interest holder, or person in possession of the motor vehicle at the time of seizure as provided in subsection (h) of this Code section and shall be published for at least three successive weeks in a newspaper of general circulation in the county where the seizure was made;

(3) The owner or interest holder may file a claim within 30 days after the second publication of the notice of forfeiture by sending the claim to the seizing law enforcement agency and to the prosecuting attorney by certified mail or statutory overnight delivery, return receipt requested;

(4) The claim must be signed by the owner or interest holder under penalty of perjury and must set forth:

(A) The caption of the proceedings as set forth on the notice of pending forfeiture and the name of the claimant;

(B) The address at which the claimant will accept mail;

(C) The nature and extent of the claimant's interest in the motor vehicle;

(D) The date, identity of the transferor, and circumstances of the claimant's acquisition of the interest in the motor vehicle;

(E) The specific provision of this Code section relied on in asserting that the motor vehicle is not subject to forfeiture;

(F) All essential facts supporting each assertion; and

(G) The precise relief sought;

(5) If a claim is filed, the prosecuting attorney shall file a complaint for forfeiture as provided in subsection (m) of this Code section within 30 days of the actual receipt of the claim. A person who files a claim shall be joined as a party; and

(6) If no claim is filed within 30 days after the second publication of the notice of forfeiture, all right, title, and interest in the motor vehicle is forfeited to the state and the prosecuting attorney shall dispose of the motor vehicle as provided in subsection (s) of this Code section.

(m)(1) When a complaint is filed pursuant to this Code section, the motor vehicle which is the subject of the action shall be named as the defendant and the action shall be in rem. The complaint shall be verified on oath or affirmation by a duly authorized agent of the state in a manner required by the laws of this state. Such complaint shall describe the motor vehicle with reasonable particularity; state that it is located within the county or will be located within the county during the pendency of the action; state its present custodian; state the name of the owner or interest holder, if known; allege the essential elements of the violation which is claimed to exist; state the place of seizure, if the motor vehicle was seized; and conclude with a prayer of due process to enforce the forfeiture.

(2) A copy of the complaint and summons shall be served on any person known to be an owner or interest holder and any person who was in possession of the motor vehicle at the time of seizure:

(A) Service of the complaint and summons shall be as provided in subsections (a), (b), (c), and (d) of Code Section 9-11-4;

(B) If the owner, interest holder, or person who was in possession of the motor vehicle at the time of seizure is unknown or resides out of the state or departs the state or cannot after due diligence be found within the state or conceals himself or herself so as to avoid service, notice of the proceeding shall be published once a week for two successive weeks in the newspaper in which the sheriff's advertisements are published. Such publication shall be deemed notice to any and all persons having an interest in or right affected by such proceeding and from any sale of the motor vehicle resulting therefrom, but shall not constitute notice to an interest holder unless that person is unknown or resides out of the state or departs the state or cannot after due diligence be found within the state or conceals himself or herself to avoid service; and

(C) If a motor vehicle which has not been seized is the subject of the action, the court may order the sheriff or another law enforcement officer to take possession of the motor vehicle.

(3) An owner of or interest holder in the motor vehicle may file an answer asserting a claim against the motor vehicle in the action in rem. Any such answer shall be filed within 30 days after the service of the summons and complaint. Where service is made by publication and personal service has not been made, an owner or interest holder shall file an answer within 30 days of the date of final publication. An answer must be verified by the owner or interest holder under penalty of perjury. In addition to complying with the general rules applicable to an answer in civil actions, the answer must set forth:

(A) The caption of the proceedings as set forth in the complaint and the name of the claimant;

(B) The address at which the claimant will accept mail;

(C) The nature and extent of the claimant's interest in the motor vehicle;

(D) The date, identity of transferor, and circumstances of the claimant's acquisition of the interest in the motor vehicle;

(E) The specific provision of this Code section relied on in asserting that the motor vehicle is not subject to forfeiture;

(F) All essential facts supporting each assertion; and

(G) The precise relief sought.

(4) If at the expiration of the period set forth in paragraph (3) of this subsection no answer has been filed, the court shall order the disposition of the seized motor vehicle as provided for in this Code section.

(5) If an answer is filed, a hearing must be scheduled by the court to be held within 60 days after service of the complaint unless continued for good cause and must be held by the court without a jury.

(n) No person claiming an interest in a motor vehicle subject to forfeiture under this Code section may intervene in a trial or appeal of a criminal action.

(*o*) In conjunction with any civil or criminal action brought pursuant to this Code section:

(1) The court, on application of the prosecuting attorney, may enter any restraining order or injunction; require the execution of satisfactory performance bonds; appoint receivers, conservators, appraisers, accountants, or trustees; or take any action to seize, secure, maintain, or preserve the availability of a motor vehicle subject to forfeiture under this Code section, including issuing a warrant for its seizure and writ of attachment, whether before or after the filing of a complaint for forfeiture;

(2) A temporary restraining order under this Code section may be entered on application of the prosecuting attorney, without notice or an opportunity for a hearing, if the prosecuting attorney demonstrates that:

(A) There is probable cause to believe that the motor vehicle with respect to which the order is sought, in the event of final judgment or conviction, would be subject to forfeiture under this Code section; and

(B) Provision of notice would jeopardize the availability of the motor vehicle for forfeiture;

(3) Notice of the entry of a restraining order and an opportunity for a hearing must be afforded to persons known to have an interest in the motor vehicle. The hearing must be held at the earliest possible date consistent with the date set in subsection (b) of Code Section 9-11-65 and is limited to the issues of whether:

(A) There is a probability that the state will prevail on the issue of forfeiture and that failure to enter the order will result in the motor vehicle's being destroyed, conveyed, encumbered, removed from the jurisdiction of the court, concealed, or otherwise made unavailable for forfeiture; and

(B) The need to preserve the availability of the motor vehicle through the entry of the requested order outweighs the hardship on any owner or interest holder against whom the order is to be entered;

(4) If a motor vehicle is seized for forfeiture without a previous judicial determination of probable cause or order of forfeiture or a hearing under paragraph (2) of this subsection, the court, on an application filed by an owner of or interest holder in the motor vehicle within 30 days after notice of its seizure or actual knowledge of such seizure, whichever is earlier, and complying with the requirements for an answer to an in rem complaint, and after five days' notice to the prosecuting attorney where the motor vehicle was seized, may issue an order to show cause to the seizing law enforcement agency for a hearing on the sole issue of whether probable cause for forfeiture of the motor vehicle then exists. The hearing must be held within 30 days unless continued for good cause on motion of either party. If the court finds that there is no probable cause for forfeiture of the motor vehicle, the motor vehicle must be released pending the outcome of a judicial proceeding which may be filed pursuant to this Code section; and

(5) The court may order a motor vehicle that has been seized for forfeiture to be sold to satisfy a specified interest of any interest holder, on motion of any party, and after notice and a hearing, on the conditions that:

(A) The interest holder has filed a proper claim and:

(i) Is authorized to do business in this state and is under the jurisdiction of a governmental agency of this state or of the United States which regulates financial institutions, securities, insurance, or real estate; or

(ii) Has an interest that the prosecuting attorney has stipulated is exempt from forfeiture;

(B) The interest holder must dispose of the motor vehicle by commercially reasonable public sale and apply the proceeds first to its interest and then to its reasonable expenses incurred in connection with the sale or disposal; and

(C) The balance of the proceeds, if any, must be returned to the actual or constructive custody of the court, in an interest-bearing account, subject to further proceedings under this Code section.

(p) A defendant convicted in any criminal proceeding is precluded from later denying the essential allegations of the criminal offense of which the defendant was convicted in any proceeding pursuant to this Code section, regardless of the pendency of an appeal from that conviction; however, evidence of the pendency of an appeal is admissible. For the purposes of this Code section, a conviction results from a verdict or plea of guilty, including a plea of nolo contendere.

(q) In hearings and determinations pursuant to this Code section:

(1) The court may receive and consider, in making any determination of probable cause or reasonable cause, all evidence admissible in determining probable cause at a preliminary hearing together with inferences therefrom;

(2) There is a rebuttable presumption that any motor vehicle of a person is subject to forfeiture under this Code section if the state establishes probable cause to believe that the person has engaged in conduct giving rise to forfeiture while using or operating said motor vehicle;

(3) In any contested proceeding to determine if a motor vehicle should be forfeited as provided in this Code section, the prosecuting attorney on behalf of the state must prove that the vehicle is subject to forfeiture pursuant to subsection (c) of this Code section by a preponderance of the evidence; and

(4) In any contested proceeding to determine if a motor vehicle should be forfeited as provided in this Code section, an owner of a property interest or interest holder must prove that the property is exempted from forfeiture pursuant to subsection (d) of this Code section by a preponderance of the evidence.

(r)(1) Any motor vehicle declared to be forfeited under this Code section vests in this state at the time of commission of the conduct giving rise to forfeiture together with the proceeds of the motor vehicle after that time. Any motor vehicle or proceeds transferred later to any person remain subject to forfeiture and thereafter must be ordered to be forfeited unless the transferee claims and establishes in a hearing under this Code section that the transferee is a bona fide purchaser for value and the transferee's interest is exempt under subsection (d) of this Code section.

(2) On entry of judgment for a person claiming an interest in the motor vehicle that is subject to proceedings to forfeit a motor vehicle under this Code section, the court shall order that the motor vehicle or interest in the motor vehicle be released or delivered promptly to that person.

(s)(1) When a motor vehicle is forfeited under this Code section, the court may:

(A) Order the motor vehicle to be sold, and the proceeds of such sale shall be used for payment of all expenses of the forfeiture and sale including, but not limited to, the expenses of seizure, towing, maintenance of custody, advertising, and court costs. The remainder of the proceeds of a sale of a forfeited motor vehicle, after payment of the expenses, shall be expended by the local governing authority for drug treatment, rehabilitation, prevention, or education or any other program which responds to problems created by drug or substance abuse; or

(B) Upon application of the seizing law enforcement agency or any other law enforcement agency of state, county, or municipal government permit the agency to retain the motor vehicle for official use in law enforcement work.

(2) Where a motor vehicle is to be sold pursuant to this subsection, the court may direct that such motor vehicle be sold by:

(A) Judicial sale as provided in Article 7 of Chapter 13 of Title 9; provided, however, that the court may establish a minimum acceptable price for such motor vehicle; or

(B) Any commercially feasible means.

(t) An acquittal or dismissal in a criminal proceeding shall preclude civil proceedings under this Code section.

(u) For good cause shown, the court may stay civil forfeiture proceedings during the pendency of a related criminal action resulting from a violation of this chapter.

(v) This Code section must be liberally construed to effectuate its remedial purposes.

Laws 1999, p. 472, § 1; Laws 2000, p. 1589, § 3; Laws 2001, p. 94, § 3; Laws 2001, p. 362, § 29.

Historical and Statutory Notes

The 2000 amendment substituted "certified mail or statutory overnight delivery" for "certified mail" in three instances.

The 2001 amendment by Act 20 rewrote subsec. (c) which formerly provided:

"(c)(1) Any motor vehicle operated by a person who has been convicted of or pleaded nolo contendere for two previous violations of code Section 16–6–12 involving a motor vehicle within a five-year period and who is convicted or pleads nolo contendere to a third violation of Code Section 16–6–12 involving a motor vehicle within the same five-year period is declared to be contraband and subject to forfeiture to the state, as provided in this Code section, provided that said forfeiture shall not be absolute unless the defendant is convicted of said offense.

"(2) For the purpose of this subsection a violation of Code Section 16–6–12 involving a motor vehicle shall mean a violation of Code Section 16–6–12 in which a motor vehicle is used to violate said Code section or in which the violation occurred."

The 2001 amendment by Act 191 in subsec. (a)(4) substituted reference to section "11–9–102" for "11–9–105".

§ 16–6–13.3. Forfeiture of proceeds or money used for or derived from pimping involving minors

(a) Any proceeds or money which is used, intended for use, used in any manner to facilitate, or derived from a violation of Code Section 16–6–11, wherein any of the persons involved in performing an act of prostitution is under the age of 18, is contraband and forfeited to the state and no person shall have a property interest in it. Such proceeds or money may be seized or detained in the same manner as provided in Code Section 16–13–49 and shall not be subject to replevin, conveyance, sequestration, or attachment.

(b) Within 60 days of the date of the seizure of proceeds or money pursuant to this Code section, the district attorney shall initiate forfeiture or other proceedings as provided in Code Section 16–13–49. An owner or interest holder, as defined by subsection (a) of Code Section 16–13–49, may establish as a defense to the forfeiture of proceeds or money which is subject to forfeiture under this Code section the applicable provisions of subsection (e) or (f) of Code Section 16–13–49. Proceeds or money which is forfeited pursuant to this Code section shall be disposed of and distributed as provided in Code Section 16–13–49, provided that no less than 50 percent of the money and proceeds forfeited under this Code section shall be distributed to the local governing authority to be distributed to local or statewide programs serving the child victims of the crime which are funded or operated by state or local governmental agencies.

(c) If the proceeds or money subject to forfeiture cannot be located; has been transferred or conveyed to, sold to, or deposited with a third party; is beyond the jurisdiction of the court; has been substantially diminished in value while not in the actual physical custody of a receiver or governmental agency directed to maintain custody of the proceeds or money; or has been commingled with other property that cannot be divided without difficulty, the court shall order the forfeiture of any proceeds or money of a claimant or defendant up to the value of proceeds or money found by the court to be subject to forfeiture under this Code section in accordance with the procedures set forth in subsection (x) of Code Section 16–13–49.

(d) The provisions of paragraphs (3), (4), and (5) of subsection (x) and subsection (z) of Code Section 16–13–49 shall be applicable to any proceedings brought pursuant to this Code section.

Laws 2001, p. 94, § 4; Laws 2003, Act 9, § 16, eff. May 14, 2003.

Historical and Statutory Notes

The 2003 amendment by Act 9, in subsec. (a), substituted "or derived" for "or is derived".

§ 16–6–14. Pandering by compulsion

A person commits the offense of pandering by compulsion when he or she by duress or coercion causes a person to perform an act of prostitution and, upon conviction thereof, shall be punished by imprisonment for not less than one nor more than ten years.

Laws 1968, p. 1249, § 1; Laws 2001, p. 92, § 5.

Formerly Code 1933, § 26–2017.

Historical and Statutory Notes

The 2001 amendment inserted gender neutral language.

§ 16–6–15. Solicitation of sodomy

(a) A person commits the offense of solicitation of sodomy when he solicits another to perform or submit to an act of sodomy. Except as provided in subsection (b) of this Code section, a person convicted of solicitation of sodomy shall be punished as for a misdemeanor.

(b) A person convicted of solicitation of sodomy when such offense involves the solicitation of a person or persons under the age of 18 years to perform or submit to an act of sodomy for money shall be guilty of a felony and shall be punished by imprisonment for a period of not less than five nor more than 20 years and shall be fined not less than $ 2,500.00 nor more than $ 10,000.00.

Laws 1968, p. 1249, § 1; Laws 1988, p. 1797, § 3; Laws 2001, p. 92, § 6.

Formerly Code 1933, § 26–2003.

Historical and Statutory Notes

The 2001 amendment rewrote subsec. (b) which formerly provided:

"(b) A person convicted of solicitation of sodomy when such offense involves the solicitation of a person under the age of 17 years to perform or submit to an act of sodomy for money shall be guilty of a felony and shall be fined not less than $1,000.00 nor more than $5,000.00 or shall be imprisoned for not less than one year nor more than five years, or both fined and imprisoned."

§ 16–6–16. Masturbation for hire

(a) A person, including a masseur or masseuse, commits the offense of masturbation for hire when he erotically stimulates the genital organs of another, whether resulting in orgasm or not, by manual or other bodily contact exclusive of sexual intercourse or by instrumental manipulation for money or the substantial equivalent thereof.

(b) A person committing the offense of masturbation for hire shall be guilty of a misdemeanor.

Laws 1975, p. 402, § 1.

Formerly Code 1933, § 26–2021.

§ 16–6–17. Unlawful for masseur or masseuse to massage any person in certain buildings, structures or places; definitions

(a) It shall be unlawful for any masseur or masseuse to massage any person in any building, structure, or place used for the purpose of lewdness, assignation, prostitution, or masturbation for hire.

(b) As used in this Code section, the term:

(1) "Masseur" means a male who practices massage or physiotherapy, or both.

(2) "Masseuse" means a female who practices massage or physiotherapy, or both.

(c) Any person who violates this Code section shall be guilty of a misdemeanor.

Laws 1975, p. 402, § 3.

§ 16–6–18. Fornication

An unmarried person commits the offense of fornication when he voluntarily has sexual intercourse with another person and, upon conviction thereof, shall be punished as for a misdemeanor.

Laws 1833, Cobb's 1851 Digest, pp. 814, 815; Laws 1865–66, p. 233, § 2; Laws 1968, p. 1249, § 1.

Formerly Code 1863, § 4419; Code 1868, § 4460; Code 1873, § 4534; Code 1882, § 4534; Penal Code 1895, § 381; Penal Code 1910, § 372; Code 1933, § 26–5801; Code 1933, § 26–2010.

§ 16–6–19. Adultery

A married person commits the offense of adultery when he voluntarily has sexual intercourse with a person other than his spouse and, upon conviction thereof, shall be punished as for a misdemeanor.

Laws 1833, Cobb's 1851 Digest, pp. 814, 815; Laws 1865–66, p. 233, § 2; Laws 1968, p. 1249, § 1.

Formerly Code 1863, § 4419; Code 1868, § 4460; Code 1873, § 4534; Code 1882, § 4534; Penal Code 1895, § 381; Penal Code 1910, § 372; Code 1933, § 26–5801; Code 1933, § 26–2009.

§ 16–6–20. Bigamy

(a) A person commits the offense of bigamy when he, being married and knowing that his lawful spouse is living, marries another person or carries on a bigamous cohabitation with another person.

(b) It shall be an affirmative defense that the prior spouse has been continually absent for a period of seven years, during which time the accused did not know the prior spouse to be alive, or that the accused reasonably believed he was eligible to remarry.

(c) A person convicted of the offense of bigamy shall be punished by imprisonment for not less than one nor more than ten years.

Laws 1833, Cobb's 1851 Digest, p. 814; Laws 1910, p. 61, § 1; Laws 1968, p. 1249, § 1.

Formerly Code 1863, §§ 4415, 4416; Code 1868, §§ 4456, 4457; Code 1873, §§ 4530, 4531; Code 1882, §§ 4530, 4531; Penal Code 1895, §§ 376, 377, 378; Penal Code 1910, §§ 367, 368, 369; Code 1933, §§ 26–5601, 26–5602, 26–5603; Code 1933, § 26–2007.

§ 16–6–21. Marrying a bigamist

(a) An unmarried man or woman commits the offense of marrying a bigamist when he marries a person whom he knows to be the wife or husband of another.

(b) It shall be an affirmative defense that the prior spouse of the bigamist has been continually absent for a period of seven years, during which time the accused did not know the prior spouse of the bigamist to be alive, or that the accused reasonably believed the bigamist was eligible to remarry.

(c) A person convicted of the offense of marrying a bigamist shall be punished by imprisonment for not less than one nor more than ten years.

Laws 1833, Cobb's 1851 Digest, p. 814; Laws 1968, p. 1249, § 1.

Formerly Code 1863, § 4417; Code 1868, § 4458; Code 1873, § 4532; Code 1882, § 4532; Penal Code 1895, § 379; Penal Code 1910, § 370; Code 1933, § 26–5604; Code 1933, § 26–2008.

§ 16–6–22. Incest

(a) A person commits the offense of incest when such person engages in sexual intercourse or sodomy, as such term is defined in Code Section 16–6–2, with a person whom he or she knows he or she is related to either by blood or by marriage as follows:

(1) Father and child or stepchild;

(2) Mother and child or stepchild;

(3) Siblings of the whole blood or of the half blood;

(4) Grandparent and grandchild;

(5) Aunt and niece or nephew; or

(6) Uncle and niece or nephew.

(b) A person convicted of the offense of incest shall be punished by imprisonment for not less than ten nor more than 30 years; provided, however, that any person convicted of the offense of incest under this subsection with a child under the age of 14 years shall be punished by imprisonment for not less than 25 nor more than 50 years. Any person convicted under this Code section of the offense of incest shall, in addition, be subject to the sentencing and punishment provisions of Code Section 17–10–6.2.

Laws 1833, Cobb's 1851 Digest, p. 814; Laws 1886, p. 30, § 1; Laws 1916, p. 51, § 1; Laws 1968, p. 1249, § 1; Laws 2006, Act 571, § 14, eff. July 1, 2006; Laws 2010, Act 389, § 3, eff. May 20, 2010.

Formerly Code 1863, § 4418; Code 1868, § 4459; Code 1873, § 4533; Code 1882, § 4533; Penal Code 1895, § 380; Penal Code 1910, § 371; Code 1933, § 26–5701; Code 1933, § 26–2006.

Historical and Statutory Notes

The 2006 amendment by Act 571, made the section gender neutral; in subsec. (b), substituted "ten nor more than 30 years" for "one nor more than 20 years" and added "; provided, however, that any person convicted of the offense of incest under this subsection with a child under the age of 14 years shall be punished by imprisonment for not less than 25 nor more than 50 years. Any person convicted under this Code section of the offense of incest shall, in addition, be subject to the sentencing and punishment provisions of Code Section 17–10–6.2."

Laws 2006, Act 571, §§ 1 and 30, provide:

"SECTION 1. The General Assembly finds and declares that recidivist sexual offenders, sexual offenders who use physical violence, and sexual offenders who prey on children are sexual predators who present an extreme threat to the public safety. Many sexual offenders are extremely likely to use physical violence and to repeat their offenses; and some sexual offenders commit many offenses, have many more victims than are ever reported, and are prosecuted for only a fraction of their crimes. The General Assembly finds that this makes the cost of sexual offender victimization to society at large, while incalculable, clearly exorbitant. The General Assembly further finds that the high level of threat that a sexual predator presents to the public safety, and the long-term effects suffered by victims of sex offenses, provide the state with sufficient justification to implement a strategy that includes:

"(1) Incarcerating sexual offenders and maintaining adequate facilities to ensure that decisions to release sexual predators into the community are not made on the basis of inadequate space;

"(2) Requiring the registration of sexual offenders, with a requirement that complete and accurate information be maintained and accessible for use by law enforcement authorities, communities, and the public;

"(3) Providing for community and public notification concerning the presence of sexual offenders;

"(4) Collecting data relative to sexual offenses and sexual offenders;

"(5) Requiring sexual predators who are released into the community to wear an electronic monitoring system for the rest of their natural life and to pay for such system; and

"(6) Prohibiting sexual predators from working with children, either for compensation or as a volunteer.

"The General Assembly further finds that the state has a compelling interest in protecting the public from sexual offenders and in protecting children from predatory sexual activity, and there is sufficient justification for requiring sexual offenders to register and for requiring community and public notification of the presence of sexual offenders. The General Assembly declares that in order to protect the public, it is necessary that the sexual offenders be registered and that members of the community and the public be notified of a sexual offender's presence. The designation of a person as a sexual offender is neither a sentence nor a punishment but simply a regulatory mechanism and status resulting from the conviction of certain crimes. Likewise, the designation of a person as a sexual predator is neither a sentence nor a punishment but simply a regulatory mechanism and status resulting from findings by the Sexual Offender Registration Review Board and a court if requested by a sexual offender."

"SECTION 30. (a) This Act shall become effective July 1, 2006.

"(b) Any person required to register pursuant to the provisions of Code Section 42–1–12, relating to the state sexual offender registry, and any person required not to reside within areas where minors congregate, as prohibited by Code Section 42–1–13 [see § 42–1–15], shall not be relieved of the obligation to comply with the provisions of said Code sections by the repeal and reenactment of said Code sections.

"(c) The provisions of this Act shall not affect or abate the status as a crime of any such act or omission which occurred prior to the effective date of the Act repealing, repealing and reenacting, or amending such law, nor shall the prosecution of such crime be abated as a result of such repeal, repeal and reenactment, or amendment."

The 2010 amendment by Act 389, in subsec. (a), added "or sodomy, as such term is defined in Code Section 16–6–2," following "sexual intercourse" and substituted "such person" for "the person" in the introductory paragraph, made subsection gender neutral, and made other nominal changes.

§ 16–6–22.1. Sexual battery

(a) For the purposes of this Code section, the term "intimate parts" means the primary genital area, anus, groin, inner thighs, or buttocks of a male or female and the breasts of a female.

(b) A person commits the offense of sexual battery when he or she intentionally makes physical contact with the intimate parts of the body of another person without the consent of that person.

(c) Except as otherwise provided in this Code section, a person convicted of the offense of sexual battery shall be punished as for a misdemeanor of a high and aggravated nature.

(d) A person convicted of the offense of sexual battery against any child under the age of 16 years shall be guilty of a felony and, upon conviction thereof, shall be punished by imprisonment for not less than one nor more than five years.

(e) Upon a second or subsequent conviction under subsection (b) of this Code section, a person shall be guilty of a felony and, upon conviction thereof, shall be imprisoned for not less than one nor more than five years and, in addition, shall be subject to the sentencing and punishment provisions of Code Section 17–10–6.2.

Laws 1990, p. 1003, § 2; Laws 2003, Act 216, § 1.1, eff. June 2, 2003; Laws 2006, Act 571, § 15, eff. July 1, 2006.

Historical and Statutory Notes

The 2003 amendment by Act 216, in subsec. (c), substituted "Except as otherwise provided in this Code section, a person convicted" for "A person convicted"; and inserted new subsec. (d).

The 2006 amendment by Act 571 made the section gender neutral and rewrote subsec. (c) which had read:

"(c) Except as otherwise provided in this Code section, a person convicted of the offense of sexual battery shall be punished as for a misdemeanor of a high and aggravated nature."

Laws 2006, Act 571, §§ 1 and 30, provide:

"SECTION 1. The General Assembly finds and declares that recidivist sexual offenders, sexual offenders who use physical violence, and sexual offenders who prey on children are sexual predators who present an extreme threat to the public safety. Many sexual offenders are extremely likely to use physical violence and to repeat their offenses; and some sexual offenders commit many offenses, have many more victims than are ever reported, and are prosecuted for only a fraction of their crimes. The General Assembly finds that this makes the cost of sexual offender victimization to society at large, while incalculable, clearly exorbitant. The General Assembly further finds that the high level of threat that a sexual predator presents to the public safety, and the long-term effects suffered by victims of sex offenses, provide the state with sufficient justification to implement a strategy that includes:

"(1) Incarcerating sexual offenders and maintaining adequate facilities to ensure that decisions to release sexual predators into the community are not made on the basis of inadequate space;

"(2) Requiring the registration of sexual offenders, with a requirement that complete and accurate information be maintained and accessible for use by law enforcement authorities, communities, and the public;

"(3) Providing for community and public notification concerning the presence of sexual offenders;

"(4) Collecting data relative to sexual offenses and sexual offenders;

"(5) Requiring sexual predators who are released into the community to wear an electronic monitoring system for the rest of their natural life and to pay for such system; and

"(6) Prohibiting sexual predators from working with children, either for compensation or as a volunteer.

"The General Assembly further finds that the state has a compelling interest in protecting the public from sexual offenders and in protecting children from predatory sexual activity, and there is sufficient justification for requiring sexual offenders to register and for requiring community and public notification of the presence of sexual offenders. The General Assembly declares that in order to protect the public, it is necessary that the sexual offenders be registered and that members of the community and the public be notified of a sexual offender's presence. The designation of a person as a sexual offender is neither a sentence nor a punishment but simply a regulatory mechanism and status resulting from the conviction of certain crimes. Likewise, the designation of a person as a sexual predator is neither a sentence nor a punishment but simply a regulatory mechanism and status resulting from findings by the Sexual Offender Registration Review Board and a court if requested by a sexual offender."

"SECTION 30. (a) This Act shall become effective July 1, 2006.

"(b) Any person required to register pursuant to the provisions of Code Section 42–1–12, relating to the state sexual offender registry, and any person required not to reside within areas where minors congregate, as prohibited by Code Section 42–1–13 [see § 42–1–15], shall not be relieved of the obligation to comply with the provisions of said Code sections by the repeal and reenactment of said Code sections.

"(c) The provisions of this Act shall not affect or abate the status as a crime of any such act or omission which occurred prior to the effective date of the Act repealing, repealing and reenacting, or amending such law, nor shall the prosecution of such crime be abated as a result of such repeal, repeal and reenactment, or amendment."

§ 16–6–22.2. Aggravated sexual battery

(a) For the purposes of this Code section, the term "foreign object" means any article or instrument other than the sexual organ of a person.

(b) A person commits the offense of aggravated sexual battery when he or she intentionally penetrates with a foreign object the sexual organ or anus of another person without the consent of that person.

(c) A person convicted of the offense of aggravated sexual battery shall be punished by imprisonment for life or by a split sentence that is a term of imprisonment for not less than 25 years and not exceeding life imprisonment, followed by probation for life, and shall be subject to the sentencing and punishment provisions of Code Sections 17–10–6.1 and 17–10–7.

Laws 1990, p. 1003, § 2; Laws 1994, p. 1959, § 8; Laws 2006, Act 571, § 16, eff. July 1, 2006.

Historical and Statutory Notes

The 2006 amendment by Act 571 made the section gender neutral and rewrote subsec. (c) which had read:

"(c) A person convicted of the offense of aggravated sexual battery shall be punished by imprisonment for not less than ten nor more than 20 years. Any person convicted under this Code section shall, in addition, be subject to the sentencing and punishment provisions of Code Sections 17–10–6.1 and 17–10–7."

Laws 2006, Act 571, §§ 1 and 30, provide:

"SECTION 1. The General Assembly finds and declares that recidivist sexual offenders, sexual offenders who use physical violence, and sexual offenders who prey on children are sexual predators who present an extreme threat to the public safety. Many sexual offenders are extremely likely to use physical violence and to repeat their offenses; and some sexual offenders commit many offenses, have many more victims than are ever reported, and are prosecuted for only a fraction of their crimes. The General Assembly finds that this makes the cost of sexual offender victimization to society at large, while incalculable, clearly exorbitant. The General Assembly further finds that the high level of threat that a sexual predator presents to the public safety, and the long-term effects suffered by victims of sex offenses, provide the state with sufficient justification to implement a strategy that includes:

"(1) Incarcerating sexual offenders and maintaining adequate facilities to ensure that decisions to release sexual predators into the community are not made on the basis of inadequate space;

"(2) Requiring the registration of sexual offenders, with a requirement that complete and accurate information be maintained and accessible for use by law enforcement authorities, communities, and the public;

"(3) Providing for community and public notification concerning the presence of sexual offenders;

"(4) Collecting data relative to sexual offenses and sexual offenders;

"(5) Requiring sexual predators who are released into the community to wear an electronic monitoring system for the rest of their natural life and to pay for such system; and

"(6) Prohibiting sexual predators from working with children, either for compensation or as a volunteer.

"The General Assembly further finds that the state has a compelling interest in protecting the public from sexual offenders and in protecting children from predatory sexual activity, and there is sufficient justification for requiring sexual offenders to register and for requiring community and public notification of the presence of sexual offenders. The General Assembly declares that in order to protect the public, it is necessary that the sexual offenders be registered and that members of the community and the public be notified of a sexual offender's presence. The designation of a person as a sexual offender is neither a sentence nor a punishment but simply a regulatory mechanism and status resulting from the conviction of certain crimes. Likewise, the designation of a person as a sexual predator is neither a sentence nor a punishment but simply a regulatory mechanism and status resulting from findings by the Sexual Offender Registration Review Board and a court if requested by a sexual offender."

"SECTION 30. (a) This Act shall become effective July 1, 2006.

"(b) Any person required to register pursuant to the provisions of Code Section 42–1–12, relating to the state sexual offender registry, and any person required not to reside within areas where minors congregate, as prohibited by Code Section 42–1–13 [see § 42–1–15], shall not be relieved of the obligation to comply with the provisions of said Code sections by the repeal and reenactment of said Code sections.

"(c) The provisions of this Act shall not affect or abate the status as a crime of any such act or omission which occurred prior to the effective date of the Act repealing, repealing and reenacting, or amending such law, nor shall the prosecution of such crime be abated as a result of such repeal, repeal and reenactment, or amendment."

§ 16–6–23. Publication of name or identity of female raped or assaulted; punishment

(a) It shall be unlawful for any news media or any other person to print and publish, broadcast, televise, or disseminate through any other medium of public dissemination or cause to be printed and published, broadcast, televised, or disseminated in any newspaper, magazine, periodical, or other publication published in this state or through any radio or television broadcast originating in the state the name or identity of any female who may have been raped or upon whom an assault with intent to commit the offense of rape may have been made.

(b) This Code section does not apply to truthful information disclosed in public court documents open to public inspection.

(c) Any person or corporation violating this Code section shall be guilty of a misdemeanor.

Laws 1911, p. 179, §§ 1, 2; Laws 1968, p. 1249, § 1.

Formerly Code 1933, § 26–2105; Code 1933, § 26–9901.

Validity

This section has been held unconstitutional in the case of Dye v. Wallace, 2001, 274 Ga. 257, 553 S.E.2d 561.

§ 16–6–24. Ordinances proscribing loitering for purpose of procuring others to engage in sexual acts for hire

Nothing contained in this chapter shall prevent any county or municipality from adopting ordinances which proscribe loitering or related activities in public for the purpose of procuring others to engage in any sexual acts for hire.

Laws 1979, p. 131, § 1.

Formerly Code 1933, § 26–2023.

§ 16–6–25. Assisting sexual offender in eluding law

(a) As used in this Code section, the term "law enforcement unit" means any agency, organ, or department of this state, or a subdivision or municipality thereof, whose primary functions include the enforcement of criminal or traffic laws; the preservation of public order; the protection of life and property; or the prevention, detection, or investigation of crime. Such term shall also include the Department of Corrections and the State Board of Pardons and Paroles.

(b) Any person who knows or reasonably believes that a sexual offender, as defined in Code Section 42–1–12, is not complying, or has not complied, with the requirements of Code Section 42–1–12 and who, with the intent to assist such sexual offender in eluding a law enforcement unit that is seeking such sexual offender to question him or her about, or to arrest him or her for, his or her noncompliance with the requirements of Code Section 42–1–12:

(1) Harbors, attempts to harbor, or assists another person in harboring or attempting to harbor such sexual offender;

(2) Conceals, attempts to conceal, or assists another person in concealing or attempting to conceal such sexual offender; or

(3) Provides information to the law enforcement unit regarding such sexual offender which the person knows to be false information commits a felony and shall be punished by imprisonment for not less than five nor more than 20 years.

Laws 2006, Act 571, § 17, eff. July 1, 2006; Laws 2007, Act 18, § 16, eff. May 11, 2007.

Historical and Statutory Notes

Laws 2006, Act 571, §§ 1 and 30, provide:

"SECTION 1. The General Assembly finds and declares that recidivist sexual offenders, sexual offenders who use physical violence, and sexual offenders who prey on children are sexual predators who present an extreme threat to the public safety. Many sexual offenders are extremely likely to use physical violence and to repeat their offenses; and some sexual offenders commit many offenses, have many more victims than are ever reported, and are prosecuted for only a fraction of their crimes. The General Assembly finds that this makes the cost of sexual offender victimization to society at large, while incalculable, clearly exorbitant. The General Assembly further finds that the high level of threat that a sexual predator presents to the public safety, and the long-term effects suffered by victims of sex offenses, provide the state with sufficient justification to implement a strategy that includes:

"(1) Incarcerating sexual offenders and maintaining adequate facilities to ensure that decisions to release sexual predators into the community are not made on the basis of inadequate space;

"(2) Requiring the registration of sexual offenders, with a requirement that complete and accurate information be maintained and accessible for use by law enforcement authorities, communities, and the public;

"(3) Providing for community and public notification concerning the presence of sexual offenders;

"(4) Collecting data relative to sexual offenses and sexual offenders;

"(5) Requiring sexual predators who are released into the community to wear an electronic monitoring system for the rest of their natural life and to pay for such system; and

"(6) Prohibiting sexual predators from working with children, either for compensation or as a volunteer.

"The General Assembly further finds that the state has a compelling interest in protecting the public from sexual offenders and in protecting children from predatory sexual activity, and there is sufficient justification for requiring sexual offenders to register and for requiring community and public notification of the presence of sexual offenders. The General Assembly declares that in order to protect the public, it is necessary that the sexual offenders be registered and that members of the community and the public be notified of a sexual offender's presence. The designation of a person as a sexual offender is neither a sentence nor a punishment but simply a regulatory mechanism and status resulting from the conviction of certain crimes. Likewise, the designation of a person as a sexual predator is neither a sentence nor a punishment but simply a regulatory mechanism and status resulting from findings by the Sexual Offender Registration Review Board and a court if requested by a sexual offender."

"SECTION 30. (a) This Act shall become effective July 1, 2006.

"(b) Any person required to register pursuant to the provisions of Code Section 42–1–12, relating to the state sexual offender registry, and any person required not to reside within areas where minors congregate, as prohibited by Code Section 42–1–13 [see 42–1–15], shall not be relieved of the obligation to comply with the provisions of said Code sections by the repeal and reenactment of said Code sections.

"(c) The provisions of this Act shall not affect or abate the status as a crime of any such act or omission which occurred prior to the effective date of the Act repealing, repealing and reenacting, or amending such law, nor shall the prosecution of such crime be abated as a result of such repeal, repeal and reenactment, or amendment."

The 2007 amendment by Act 18 was a provision contained in a correction bill.

CHAPTER 7

DAMAGE TO AND INTRUSION UPON PROPERTY

Article 1

Burglary

§ 16–7–1. Burglary

(a) A person commits the offense of burglary when, without authority and with the intent to commit a felony or theft therein, he enters or remains within the dwelling house of another or any building, vehicle, railroad car, watercraft, or other such structure designed for use as the dwelling of another or enters or remains within any other building, railroad car, aircraft, or any room or any part thereof. A person convicted of the offense of burglary, for the first such offense, shall be punished by imprisonment for not less than one nor more than 20 years. For the purposes of this Code section, the term "railroad car" shall also include trailers on flatcars, containers on flatcars, trailers on railroad property, or containers on railroad property.

(b) Upon a second conviction for a crime of burglary occurring after the first conviction, a person shall be punished by imprisonment for not less than two nor more than 20 years. Upon a third conviction for the crime of burglary occurring after the first conviction, a person shall be punished by imprisonment for not less than five nor more than 20 years. Adjudication of guilt or imposition of sentence shall not be suspended, probated, deferred, or withheld for any offense punishable under this subsection.

Laws 1833, Cobb's 1851 Digest, p. 790; Laws 1858, p. 98, § 1; Laws 1865–66, p. 232, § 2; Laws 1866, p. 151, § 1; Laws 1868, p. 16, § 1; Laws 1878–79, p. 65, §§ 1, 2; Laws 1968, p. 1249, § 1; Laws 1977, p. 895, § 1; Laws 1978, p. 236, § 1; Laws 1980, p. 770, § 1.

Formerly Code 1863, §§ 4283, 4285; Code 1868, §§ 4320, 4322; Code 1873, §§ 4386, 4388; Code 1882, §§ 4386, 4388; Penal Code 1895, §§ 149, 150; Penal Code 1910, §§ 146, 147; Code 1933, §§ 26–2401, 26–2402; Code 1933, § 26–1601.

§ 16–7–2. Smash and grab burglary

(a) As used in this Code section, the term "retail establishment" means an establishment that sells goods or merchandise from a fixed location for direct consumption by a purchaser and includes establishments that prepare and sell meals or other edible products either for carry out or service within the establishment.

(b) A person commits the offense of smash and grab burglary when he or she intentionally and without authority enters a retail establishment with the intent to commit a theft and causes damage in excess of $500.00 to such establishment without the owner's consent.

(c) A person convicted of smash and grab burglary shall be guilty of a felony and, upon conviction, shall be punished by imprisonment for not less than two nor more than 20 years, by a fine of not more than $100,000.00, or both; provided, however, that upon a second or subsequent conviction, he or she shall be punished by imprisonment for not less than five nor more than 20 years, by a fine of not more than $100,000.00, or both.

Laws 2010, Act 674, § 6, eff. July 1, 2010.

Article 2

Criminal Trespass and Damage to Property

Part 1

General Provisions

§ 16–7–20. Possession of tools for the commission of crime

(a) A person commits the offense of possession of tools for the commission of crime when he has in his possession any tool, explosive, or other device commonly used in the commission of burglary, theft, or other crime with the intent to make use thereof in the commission of a crime.

(b) A person convicted of the offense of possession of tools for the commission of crime shall be punished by imprisonment for not less than one nor more than five years.

Laws 1910, p. 135, §§ 1, 2; Laws 1968, p. 1249, § 1.

Formerly Code 1933, § 26–2701; Code 1933, § 26–1602.

§ 16–7–21. Criminal trespass

(a) A person commits the offense of criminal trespass when he or she intentionally damages any property of another without consent of that other person and the damage thereto is $ 500.00 or less or knowingly and maliciously interferes with the possession or use of the property of another person without consent of that person.

(b) A person commits the offense of criminal trespass when he or she knowingly and without authority:

(1) Enters upon the land or premises of another person or into any part of any vehicle, railroad car, aircraft, or watercraft of another person for an unlawful purpose;

(2) Enters upon the land or premises of another person or into any part of any vehicle, railroad car, aircraft, or watercraft of another person after receiving, prior to such entry, notice from the owner, rightful occupant, or, upon proper identification, an authorized representative of the owner or rightful occupant that such entry is forbidden; or

(3) Remains upon the land or premises of another person or within the vehicle, railroad car, aircraft, or watercraft of another person after receiving notice from the owner, rightful occupant, or, upon proper identification, an authorized representative of the owner or rightful occupant to depart.

(c) For the purposes of subsection (b) of this Code section, permission to enter or invitation to enter given by a minor who is or is not present on or in the property of the minor's parent or guardian is not sufficient to allow lawful entry of another person upon the land, premises, vehicle, railroad car, aircraft, or watercraft owned or rightfully occupied by such minor's parent or guardian if such parent or guardian has previously given notice that such entry is forbidden or notice to depart.

(d) A person who commits the offense of criminal trespass shall be guilty of a misdemeanor.

(e) A person commits the offense of criminal trespass when he or she intentionally defaces, mutilates, or defiles any grave marker, monument, or memorial to one or more deceased persons who served in the military service of this state, the United States of America or any of the states thereof, or the Confederate States of America or any of the states thereof, or a monument, plaque, marker, or memorial which is dedicated to, honors, or recounts the military service of any past or present military personnel of this state, the United States of America or any of the states thereof, or the Confederate States of America or any of the states thereof if such grave marker, monument, memorial, plaque, or marker is privately owned or located on land which is privately owned.

Laws 1882–83, p. 121, § 1; Laws 1959, p. 173, § 1; Laws 1960, p. 142, § 1; Laws 1968, p. 1249, § 1; Laws 1969, p. 857, § 5; Laws 1979, p. 764, § 1; Laws 1985, p. 484, § 1; Laws 1985, p. 1491, § 1; Laws 1997, p. 526, § 1; Laws 2001, p. 1153, § 1.

Formerly Penal Code 1895, § 220; Penal Code 1910, § 217; Code 1933, § 26–3002; Code 1933, § 26–1503.

Historical and Statutory Notes

The 2001 amendment added subsec. (e).

§ 16–7–22. Criminal damage to property in the first degree

(a) A person commits the offense of criminal damage to property in the first degree when he:

(1) Knowingly and without authority interferes with any property in a manner so as to endanger human life; or

(2) Knowingly and without authority and by force or violence interferes with the operation of any system of public communication, public transportation, sewerage, drainage, water supply, gas, power, or other public utility service or with any constituent property thereof.

(b) A person convicted of the offense of criminal damage to property in the first degree shall be punished by imprisonment for not less than one nor more than ten years.

Laws 1968, p. 1249, § 1.

Formerly Code 1933, § 26–1501.

§ 16–7–23. Criminal damage to property in the second degree

(a) A person commits the offense of criminal damage to property in the second degree when he:

(1) Intentionally damages any property of another person without his consent and the damage thereto exceeds $500.00; or

(2) Recklessly or intentionally, by means of fire or explosive, damages property of another person.

(b) A person convicted of the offense of criminal damage to property in the second degree shall be punished by imprisonment for not less than one nor more than five years.

Laws 1968, p. 1249, § 1; Laws 1985, p. 484, § 2; Laws 1985, p. 1491, § 2; Laws 2008, Act 530, § 2, eff. July 1, 2008.

Formerly Code 1933, § 26–1502.

Historical and Statutory Notes

The 2008 amendment by Act 530 deleted par. (3) of subsec. (a), which had read as follows:

"(3) With intent to damage, starts a fire on the land of another without his consent."

§ 16–7–24. Criminal interference with government property

(a) A person commits the offense of interference with government property when he destroys, damages, or defaces government property and, upon conviction thereof, shall be punished by imprisonment for not less than one nor more than five years.

(b) A person commits the offense of interference with government property when he forcibly interferes with or obstructs the passage into or from government property and, upon conviction thereof, shall be punished as for a misdemeanor.

Laws 1968, p. 1249, § 1.

Formerly Code 1933, § 26–2613.

§ 16–7–25. Damaging, injuring or interfering with property of public utility companies, municipalities or political subdivisions

(a) It shall be unlawful for any person intentionally and without authority to injure or destroy any meter, pipe, conduit, wire, line, post, lamp, or other apparatus belonging to a company, municipality, or political subdivision engaged in the manufacture or sale of electricity, gas, water, telephone, or other public services; intentionally and without authority to prevent a meter from properly registering the quantity of such service supplied; in any way to interfere with the proper action of such company, municipality, or political subdivision; intentionally to divert any services of such company, municipality, or political subdivision; or otherwise intentionally and without authority to use or cause to be used, without the consent of the company, municipality, or political subdivision, any service manufactured, sold, or distributed by the company, municipality, or political subdivision.

(b) Where there is no evidence to the contrary, the person performing any of the illegal acts set forth in subsection (a) of this Code section and the person who with knowledge of such violation receives the benefit of such service without proper charge as a result of the improper action shall be presumed to be responsible for the act of tampering or diversion.

(c) This Code section shall be cumulative to and shall not prohibit the enactment of any other general and local laws, rules, and regulations of state or local authorities or agencies and local ordinances prohibiting such activities which are more restrictive than this Code section.

(d) Any person who violates this Code section shall be guilty of a misdemeanor.

Laws 1897, p. 69, § 1; Laws 1916, p. 153, § 1; Laws 1957, p. 490, §§ 1–5; Laws 1976, p. 773, § 1; Laws 1978, p. 1658, § 1.

Formerly Penal Code 1910, § 783; Code 1933, §§ 26–3801, 26–3802; Code 1933, § 26–1507.

§ 16–7–26. Vandalism to a place of worship

(a) A person commits the offense of vandalism to a place of worship when he maliciously defaces or desecrates a church, synagogue, or other place of public religious worship.

(b) A person convicted of the offense of vandalism to a place of worship shall be punished by imprisonment for not less than one nor more than five years.

Laws 1967, p. 457, § 1; Laws 1968, p. 1249, § 1.

Formerly Code 1933, § 26–1505.

§ 16–7–27. Injuring, tearing down or destruction of mailboxes; injuring, defacing or destruction of mail

(a) It shall be unlawful for any person willfully or maliciously to injure, tear down, or destroy any mailbox or receptacle intended or used for the receipt or delivery of mail or willfully or maliciously to injure, deface, or destroy any mail deposited therein.

(b) Any person who violates this Code section shall be guilty of a misdemeanor.

Laws 1979, p. 619, § 1.

Formerly Code 1933, § 26–1508.

§ 16–7–28. Renumbered § 16–7–63 by Laws 2008, Act 530, § 3, eff. July 1, 2008

§ 16–7–29. Removal, destruction, or circumvention of electronic monitoring devices; penalties

(a) For purposes of this Code section, the term "electronic monitoring device" shall include any device that is utilized to track the location of a person.

(b) It shall be unlawful for any person to knowingly and without authority remove, destroy, or circumvent the operation of an electronic monitoring device which is being used for the purpose of monitoring a person who is:

(1) Complying with a home arrest program as set forth in Code Section 42–1–8;

(2) Wearing an electronic monitoring device as a condition of bond or pretrial release;

(3) Wearing an electronic monitoring device as a condition of probation;

(4) Wearing an electronic monitoring device as a condition of parole; or

(5) Wearing an electronic monitoring device as required in Code Section 42–1–14.

(c) It shall be unlawful for any person to knowingly and without authority request or solicit any other person to remove, destroy, or circumvent the operation of an electronic monitoring device which is being used for the purposes described in subsection (b) of this Code section.

(d) Any person who violates this Code section shall be guilty of the offense of tampering with the operation of an electronic monitoring device and shall be punished by imprisonment for not less than one nor more than five years.

Laws 2004, Act 587, § 2, eff. Jan. 1, 2005; Laws 2005, Act 19, § 16, eff. April 7, 2005; Laws 2006, Act 453, § 16, eff. April 14, 2006; Laws 2010, Act 389, § 4, eff. May 20, 2010.

Historical and Statutory Notes

Laws 2004, Act 587, § 1, provides:

"The General Assembly finds that the safety of the public is a paramount concern and that prison and jail overcrowding and the high cost of incarceration demand a cost effective and innovative approach to protecting communities from dangerous offenders while at the same time providing alternatives to, or bridges to and from incarceration. Under appropriate conditions and limitations, electronic monitoring devices provide the criminal justice system with a tool that should be considered under proper circumstances. Electronic monitoring devices offer effective means to track individuals and may reduce criminal recidivism as well as provide the state with monetary savings since the cost of an electronic monitoring device is far less than the cost of incarcerating an individual and an individual may be able to pay for the device. The criminal penalties provided by this Act are designed to encourage the use of electronic monitoring devices while at the same time discourage interference with these devices."

Laws 2004, Act 587, § 4, provides:

"This Act shall become effective on January 1, 2005."

The 2005 amendment by Act 19, designated subsecs. (a), (b), and (c) as (b), (c), and (a) respectively; in newly designated subsec. (b), substituted "electronic monitoring device" for "electronic monitor"; and in subsec. (d), substituted "five" for "5".

The 2006 amendment by Act 453 was a provision contained in a correction bill.

Former § 16–7–29 was repealed by Laws 1990, p. 2048, § 5a, eff. January 1, 1991.

The 2010 amendment by Act 389, in subsec. (b), added par. (5).

Part 2

Littering Public and Private Property

Historical and Statutory Notes

Laws 2006, Act 538, §§ 1–1 and 5–1, provide:

"SECTION 1–1. This Act shall be known and may be cited as the 'Comprehensive Litter Prevention and Abatement Act of 2006.'"

"SECTION 5–1. This Act shall become effective upon its approval by the Governor [April 21, 2006] or upon its becoming law without such approval for purposes of adopting local ordinances to become effective on or after July 1, 2006; and for all other purposes, this Act shall become effective on July 1, 2006."

§ 16–7–40. Repealed by Laws 2006, Act 538, § 2–1, eff. July 1, 2006

Historical and Statutory Notes

The repealed section, relating to the short title of the part, was derived from Laws 1970, p. 494, § 1; Laws 1990, p. 8, § 16. The repealing law also reserved the section designation.

§ 16–7–41. Repealed by Laws 1981, p. 1758, § 1, eff. April 17, 1981

Historical and Statutory Notes

The repealed section designation was reserved by Laws 2006, Act 538, § 2–1.

§ 16–7–42. Definitions

As used in this part, the term:

(1) "Litter" means any discarded or abandoned:

(A) Refuse, rubbish, junk, or other waste material; or

(B) Dead animals that are not subject to the provisions of Code Section 4–5–4.

(2) "Public or private property" means the right of way of any road or highway; any body of water or watercourse or the shores or beaches thereof; any park, playground, building, refuge, or conservation or recreation area; residential or farm properties, timberlands, or forests; or any commercial or industrial property.

Laws 1970, p. 494, § 3; Laws 1990, p. 8, § 16; Laws 1993, p. 496, § 1; Laws 2006, Act 538, § 2–1, eff. July 1, 2006.

Historical and Statutory Notes

The 2006 amendment by Act 538 rewrote the section which had read:

"As used in this part, the term:

"(1) 'Litter' means all discarded sand, gravel, slag, brickbats, rubbish, waste material, tin cans, refuse, garbage, trash, debris, dead animals, or other discarded materials of every kind and description which are not waste as such term is defined in paragraph (6) of Code Section 16–7–51.

"(2) 'Public or private property' means the right of way of any road or highway; any body of water or watercourse or the shores or beaches thereof; any park, playground, building, refuge, or conservation or recreation area; and residential or farm properties, timberlands, or forests."

Laws 2006, Act 538, § 5–1, provides:

"This Act shall become effective upon its approval by the Governor [April 21, 2006] or upon its becoming law without such approval for purposes of adopting local ordinances to become effective on or after July 1, 2006; and for all other purposes, this Act shall become effective on July 1, 2006."

§ 16–7–43. Unlawful activities

(a) It shall be unlawful for any person or persons to dump, deposit, throw, or leave or to cause or permit the dumping, depositing, placing, throwing, or leaving of litter on any public or private property in this state or any waters in this state, unless:

(1) The area is designated by the state or by any of its agencies or political subdivisions for the disposal of litter and the person is authorized by the proper public authority to so use such area;

(2) The litter is placed into a nondisposable litter receptacle or container designed for the temporary storage of litter and located in an area designated by the owner or tenant in lawful possession of the property; or

(3) The person is the owner or tenant in lawful possession of such property or has first obtained consent of the owner or tenant in lawful possession or unless the act is done under the personal direction of the owner or tenant, all in a manner consistent with the public welfare.

(b)(1) Any person who violates subsection (a) of this Code section shall be guilty of a misdemeanor.

(2) In addition to the punishment provided under paragraph (1) of this subsection:

(A) In the sound discretion of the court, the person may be directed to pick up and remove from any public street or highway or public right of way for a distance not to exceed one mile any litter the person has deposited and any and all litter deposited thereon by anyone else prior to the date of execution of sentence; or

(B) In the sound discretion of the judge of the court, the person may be directed to pick up and remove from any public beach, public park, private right of way, or, with the prior permission of the legal owner or tenant in lawful possession of such property, any private property upon which it can be established by competent evidence that the person has deposited litter, any and all litter deposited thereon by anyone prior to the date of execution of sentence.

(c) The court may publish the names of persons convicted of violating subsection (a) of this Code section.

(d) Any county, municipality, consolidated government, or law enforcement agency thereof of this state which is empowered by Code Section 16–7–45 or other law to enforce the provisions of this Code section or local littering ordinances may, in its discretion, appoint any person who is a citizen of the United States, is of good moral character, and has not previously been convicted of a felony to enforce the provisions of this Code section or local littering ordinances within the county, municipality, or consolidated government in which the appointing agency exercises jurisdiction. Each person appointed pursuant to this Code section shall take and subscribe an oath of office as prescribed by the appointing authority. Any person appointed and sworn pursuant to this subsection shall be authorized to enforce the provisions of this Code section or local littering ordinances in the same manner as any employee or law enforcement officer of this state or any county, municipality, or consolidated government of this state subject to the limitations provided in subsections (e) and (f) of this Code section.

(e) No person appointed pursuant to subsection (d) of this Code section shall be deemed a peace officer under the laws of this state or:

(1) Be deemed to be an employee of or receive any compensation from the state, county, municipality, consolidated government, or appointing law enforcement agency;

(2) Be required to complete any training or be certified pursuant to the requirements of Chapter 8 of Title 35;

(3) Have the power or duty to enforce any traffic or other criminal laws of the state, county, municipality, or consolidated government;

(4) Have the power to possess and carry firearms and other weapons for the purpose of enforcing the littering laws; or

(5) Be entitled to any indemnification from the state, county, municipality, or consolidated government for any injury or property damage sustained by such person as a result of attempting to enforce the littering laws of this state or any local government.

(f) Notwithstanding any law to the contrary, neither the state nor any county, municipality, or consolidated government of this state or any department, agency, board, or officer of this state or any county, municipality, or consolidated government of this state shall be liable or accountable for or on account of any act or omission of any person appointed pursuant to this Code section in connection with such person's enforcement of the provisions of this Code section or local littering ordinances.

(g) It shall be unlawful for any person willfully to obstruct, resist, impede, or interfere with any person appointed pursuant to this Code section in connection with such person's enforcement of this Code section or local littering ordinances or to retaliate or discriminate in any manner against such person as a reprisal for any act or omission of such person. Any violation of this subsection shall be punishable as a misdemeanor.

Laws 1970, p. 494, §§ 4, 5; Laws 1971, p. 886, § 1; Laws 1974, p. 454, § 1; Laws 1982, p. 3, § 16; Laws 1987, p. 813, § 1; Laws 1995, p. 315, § 1; Laws 2002, p. 637, § 2; Laws 2006, Act 538, § 2–1, eff. July 1, 2006.

Historical and Statutory Notes

The 2002 amendment increased fines in subsec. (b), modified the subdivision designations therein and substituted "court" for "court in which the conviction is obtained" in subsec. (b)(2)(B), and added subsecs. (d) to (g).

The 2006 amendment by Act 538, in subsec. (a), substituted "area" for "property" twice in par. (1), inserted "so" following "public authority to", and substituted "a nondisposable litter receptacle or container designed for the temporary storage of litter and located in an area designated by the owner or tenant in lawful possession of the property" for "a litter receptacle or container installed on such property" in par. (2); in subsec. (b), designated the introductory paragraph as par (1), in newly designated par. (1) deleted "and, upon conviction thereof, shall be punished as follows:" and inserted a period in its place, deleted former par. (1) which had read "By a fine of not less than $200.00 nor more than $1,200.00; and", and inserted the introductory phrase of par. (2) beginning "In addition to the punishment"; in subsec. (d), inserted the reference to consolidated government three times, and inserted "by Code Section 16–7–45 or other law"; in subsec. (e), inserted the reference to consolidated government three times, and substituted "traffic or other criminal laws" for "other traffic or criminal laws"; in subsec. (f), substituted the reference to consolidated government for the reference to political subdivision twice; and made nonsubstantive changes.

Laws 2006, Act 538, § 5–1, provides:

"This Act shall become effective upon its approval by the Governor [April 21, 2006] or upon its becoming law without such approval for purposes of adopting local ordinances to become effective on or after July 1, 2006; and for all other purposes, this Act shall become effective on July 1, 2006."

§ 16–7–44. Litter dumped from vehicle or other conveyance; trier of fact; discretion

(a) Whenever litter is thrown, deposited, dropped, or dumped from any motor vehicle, boat, airplane, or other conveyance in violation of Code Section 16–7–43, the trier of fact may in its discretion and in consideration of the totality of the circumstances infer that the operator of the conveyance has violated this part.

(b) Except as provided in subsection (a) of this Code section, whenever any litter which is dumped, deposited, thrown, or left on public or private property in violation of Code Section 16–7–43 is discovered to contain any article or articles, including but not limited to letters, bills, publications, or other writings which display the name of a person thereon in such a manner as to indicate that the article belongs or belonged to such person, the trier of fact may in its discretion and in consideration of the totality of the circumstances infer that such person has violated this part.

Laws 1970, p. 494, § 6; Laws 1984, p. 1489, § 1; Laws 1990, p. 8, § 16; Laws 2006, Act 538, § 2–1, eff. July 1, 2006.

Historical and Statutory Notes

The 2006 amendment by Act 538 substituted "the trier of fact may in its discretion and in consideration of the totality of the circumstances infer" for "it shall be prime–facie evidence" in subsec. (a); and substituted "the trier of fact may in its discretion and in consideration of the totality of the circumstances infer" for "it shall be a rebuttable presumption" in subsec. (b).

Laws 2006, Act 538, § 5–1, provides:

"This Act shall become effective upon its approval by the Governor [April 21, 2006] or upon its becoming law without such approval for purposes of adopting local ordinances to become effective on or after July 1, 2006; and for all other purposes, this Act shall become effective on July 1, 2006."

§ 16–7–45. Enforcement

All law enforcement agencies, officers, and officials of this state or any political subdivision thereof or any enforcement agency, officer, or any official of any commission or authority of this state or any political subdivision thereof is authorized, empowered, and directed to enforce compliance with this part.

Laws 1970, p. 494, § 7; Laws 1985, p. 149, § 16; Laws 1990, p. 8, § 16; Laws 2006, Act 538, § 2–1, eff. July 1, 2006.

Historical and Statutory Notes

The 2006 amendment by Act 538 inserted "or authority" following "any commission".

Laws 2006, Act 538, § 5–1, provides:

"This Act shall become effective upon its approval by the Governor [April 21, 2006] or upon its becoming law without such approval for purposes of adopting local ordinances to become effective on or after July 1, 2006; and for all other purposes, this Act shall become effective on July 1, 2006."

§ 16–7–46. Receptacles to be provided

All public authorities and agencies having supervision of properties of this state are authorized, empowered, and instructed to establish and maintain receptacles for the deposit of litter at appropriate locations where the property is frequented by the public, to post signs directing persons to the receptacles and serving notice of the provisions of this part, and to otherwise publicize the availability of litter receptacles and requirements of this part.

Laws 1970, p. 494, § 8; Laws 1990, p. 8, § 16; Laws 2006, Act 538, § 2–1, eff. July 1, 2006.

Historical and Statutory Notes

The 2006 amendment by Act 538 amended the section without change.

Laws 2006, Act 538, § 5–1, provides:

"This Act shall become effective upon its approval by the Governor [April 21, 2006] or upon its becoming law without such approval for purposes of adopting local ordinances to become effective on or after July 1, 2006; and for all other purposes, this Act shall become effective on July 1, 2006."

§ 16–7–47. Containers provided by local government; designation as suitable for dumping household garbage; vandalizing containers; violations

(a) As used in this Code section, the term "household garbage" means animal, vegetable, and fruit refuse matter and other refuse matter ordinarily generated as by-products of a household or restaurant, such as tin cans, bottles, paper, cardboard, plastics, and wrapping or packaging materials.

(b) The governing authority of each county, municipality, or consolidated government of this state which provides containers for the dumping of trash or garbage therein shall be authorized to designate any or all such containers as being suitable for the dumping therein of household garbage only. If a container is clearly marked "household garbage only," it shall be unlawful for any person to dump any refuse or other material into the container other than household garbage.

(c) It shall be unlawful for any person to set fire to the contents of, indiscriminately scatter or disperse the contents of, or otherwise vandalize any containers provided by any county, municipality, or consolidated government for the dumping of trash or garbage.

(d) Any person who violates subsection (b) or (c) of this Code section shall be guilty of a misdemeanor.

Laws 1979, p. 831, §§ 1–3; Laws 2006, Act 538, § 2–1, eff. July 1, 2006.

Historical and Statutory Notes

The 2006 amendment by Act 538 inserted ", municipality, or consolidated government" in subsecs. (b) and (c).

Laws 2006, Act 538, § 5–1, provides:

"This Act shall become effective upon its approval by the Governor [April 21, 2006] or upon its becoming law without such approval for purposes of adopting local ordinances to become effective on or after July 1, 2006; and for all other purposes, this Act shall become effective on July 1, 2006."

§ 16–7–48. Enforcement of local laws, rules, or regulations; adoption and violation of local ordinances

(a) Nothing in this part shall limit the authority of any state agency, county, municipality, or consolidated government to enforce any other laws, rules, or regulations relating to litter.

(b) Nothing within this part shall be construed to prohibit the adoption of local ordinances regulating and controlling litter within the jurisdiction of any county, municipality, or consolidated government. Violation of such ordinances shall be punished as provided in the municipal charter or local ordinances.

Laws 1981, p. 1758, § 1; Laws 2006, Act 538, § 2–1, eff. July 1, 2006.

Historical and Statutory Notes

The 2006 amendment by Act 538 rewrote the section which had read:

"Nothing within this part shall be construed to prohibit the adoption of local ordinances regulating and controlling litter within the corporate limits of a municipality. Violation of such ordinances shall be punished as provided in the municipal charter."

Laws 2006, Act 538, § 5–1, provides:

"This Act shall become effective upon its approval by the Governor [April 21, 2006] or upon its becoming law without such approval for purposes of adopting local ordinances to become effective on or after July 1, 2006; and for all other purposes, this Act shall become effective on July 1, 2006."

Part 3

Egregious Litter Control

Historical and Statutory Notes

Laws 2006, Act 538, §§ 1–1 and 5–1, provide:

"SECTION 1–1. This Act shall be known and may be cited as the 'Comprehensive Litter Prevention and Abatement Act of 2006.' "

"SECTION 5–1. This Act shall become effective upon its approval by the Governor [April 21, 2006] or upon its becoming law without such approval for purposes of adopting local ordinances to become effective on or after July 1, 2006; and for all other purposes, this Act shall become effective on July 1, 2006."

§ 16–7–50. Repealed by Laws 2006, Act 538, § 2–2, eff. July 1, 2006

Historical and Statutory Notes

The repealed section, relating to the short title of the part, was derived from Laws 1993, p. 496, § 2. The repealing law also reserved the section designation.

§ 16–7–51. Definitions

As used in this part, the term:

(1) "Biomedical waste" means that term as defined in paragraph (1.1) of Code Section 12–8–22.

(2) "Commercial purpose" means for the purpose of economic gain.

(3) "Dump" means to throw, discard, place, deposit, discharge, burn, or dispose of a substance.

(4) "Egregious litter" means all litter, as such term is defined in paragraph (1) of Code Section 16–7–42, exceeding ten pounds in weight or 15 cubic feet in volume; any discarded or abandoned substance in any weight or volume if biomedical waste, hazardous waste, or a hazardous substance; or any substance or material dumped for commercial purposes.

(5) "Hazardous substance" means that term as defined in paragraph (4) of Code Section 12–8–92.

(6) "Hazardous waste" means that term as defined in paragraph (10) of Code Section 12–8–62.

Laws 1993, p. 496, § 2; Laws 2006, Act 538, § 2–2, eff. July 1, 2006.

Historical and Statutory Notes

The 2006 amendment by Act 538 rewrote the section which had read:

"As used in this part, the term:

"(1) 'Biomedical waste' means that term as defined in paragraph (1.1) of Code Section 12–8–22 on January 1, 1993.

"(2) 'Commercial purpose' means for the purpose of economic gain.

"(3) 'Dump' means to throw, discard, place, deposit, discharge, burn, or dispose of a substance.

"(4) 'Hazardous substance' means that term as defined in paragraph (4) of Code Section 12–8–92 on January 1, 1993.

"(5) 'Hazardous waste' means that term as defined in paragraph (10) of Code Section 12–8–62 on January 1, 1993.

"(6) 'Waste' means all discarded substances and materials whatsoever exceeding ten pounds in weight or 15 cubic feet in volume, or any such substance in any weight or volume if biomedical waste, hazardous waste, a hazardous substance, or any such substance or material dumped for commercial purposes. Such term includes, without limitation, sand; gravel; slag; brickbats; rubbish; waste material; tin cans; refuse; garbage; trash; debris; dead animals; bottles; boxes; containers; papers; tobacco products; tires; appliances; mechanical equipment or parts; building or construction materials; tools; machinery; wood; motor vehicles and motor vehicle parts; vessels; aircraft equipment; waste oil; batteries; antifreeze; sludge from a waste-water treatment facility, water supply treatment plant, or air pollution control facility; air contaminants from any source or facility; and any other discarded material or substance of every kind and description resulting from domestic, industrial, commercial, mining, or governmental operations."

Laws 2006, Act 538, § 5–1, provides:

"This Act shall become effective upon its approval by the Governor [April 21, 2006] or upon its becoming law without such approval for purposes of adopting local ordinances to become effective on or after July 1, 2006; and for all other purposes, this Act shall become effective on July 1, 2006."

§ 16–7–52. Unlawful activities

It shall be unlawful for any person to intentionally dump egregious litter unless authorized to do so by law or by a duly issued permit:

(1) In or on any public highway, road, street, alley, or thoroughfare, including any portion of the right of way thereof, or on any other public lands except in containers or areas lawfully provided for such dumping;

(2) In or on any fresh-water lake, river, canal, or stream or tidal or coastal water of the state; or

(3) In or on any private property, unless prior consent of the owner has been given and unless such dumping will not adversely affect the public health and is not in violation of any other state law, rule, or regulation.

Laws 1993, p. 496, § 2; Laws 2006, Act 538, § 2–2, eff. July 1, 2006.

Historical and Statutory Notes

The 2006 amendment by Act 538 substituted "intentionally dump egregious litter" for "dump waste" in the introductory paragraph.

Laws 2006, Act 538, § 5–1, provides:

"This Act shall become effective upon its approval by the Governor [April 21, 2006] or upon its becoming law without such approval for purposes of adopting local ordinances to become effective on or after July 1, 2006; and for all other purposes, this Act shall become effective on July 1, 2006."

§ 16–7–53. Dumping egregious litter; violations

(a) Any person who intentionally dumps egregious litter in violation of Code Section 16–7–52 in an amount not exceeding 500 pounds in weight or 100 cubic feet in volume which is not biomedical waste, hazardous waste, or a hazardous substance and not for commercial purposes shall be guilty of a misdemeanor of a high and aggravated nature. For purposes of this subsection, each day a continuing violation occurs shall constitute a separate violation.

(b) Any person who intentionally dumps egregious litter in violation of Code Section 16–7–52 in an amount exceeding 500 pounds in weight or 100 cubic feet in volume which is not biomedical waste, hazardous waste, or a hazardous substance and not for commercial purposes shall upon the first offense be guilty of a misdemeanor of a high and aggravated nature. Upon the second and each subsequent offense such person shall be guilty of a felony and, upon conviction thereof, shall be fined not more than $25,000.00 for each violation or imprisoned for not more than five years, or both; provided, however, that the portion of any term of imprisonment exceeding two years shall be probated conditioned upon payment of a fine imposed under this subsection. For purposes of this subsection, each day a continuing violation occurs shall constitute a separate violation.

(c) Any person who intentionally dumps egregious litter in violation of Code Section 16–7–52 in any quantity if the substance is biomedical waste, hazardous waste, or a hazardous substance or if the dumping is for commercial purposes shall be guilty of a felony and, upon conviction thereof, shall be fined not more than $25,000.00 for each violation or imprisoned for not more than five years, or both; provided, however, that the portion of any term of imprisonment exceeding two years shall be probated conditioned upon payment of a fine imposed under this subsection. For purposes of this subsection, each day a continuing violation occurs shall constitute a separate violation.

(d) In addition to the penalties provided in subsections (a) and (b) of this Code section, the court may order the violator to remove or render harmless any egregious litter dumped in violation of Code Section 16–7–52, repair or restore property damaged by or pay damages resulting from such dumping, or perform public service related to the removal of illegally dumped egregious litter or to the restoration of an area polluted by such substance.

(e)(1) The court shall cause to be published a notice of conviction for each person convicted of violating any provision of this Code section. Such notices of conviction shall be published in the manner of legal notices in the legal organ of the county in which such person resides or, in the case of a nonresident, in the legal organ of the county in which the person was convicted. Such notice of conviction shall contain the name and address of the convicted person; date, time, and place of arrest; and disposition of the case and shall be published once in the legal organ of the appropriate county in the second week following such conviction or as soon thereafter as publication may be made.

(2) The convicted person for which a notice of conviction is published pursuant to this subsection shall be assessed the cost of publication of such notice, and such assessment shall be imposed at the time of conviction in addition to any other fine imposed pursuant to this Code section.

(3) The clerk of the court, the publisher of any legal organ which publishes a notice of conviction, and any other person involved in the publication of an erroneous notice of conviction shall be immune from civil or criminal liability for such erroneous publication, provided such publication was made in good faith.

Laws 1993, p. 496, § 2; Laws 2006, Act 538, § 2–2, eff. July 1, 2006.

Historical and Statutory Notes

The 2006 amendment by Act 538 rewrote the section which had read:

"(a) Any person who dumps waste in violation of Code Section 16–7–52 in an amount not exceeding 500 pounds in weight or 100 cubic feet in volume which is not biomedical waste, hazardous waste, or a hazardous substance and not for commercial purposes shall be guilty of a misdemeanor of a high and aggravated nature. For purposes of this subsection, each day a continuing violation occurs shall constitute a separate violation.

"(b) Any person who dumps waste in violation of Code Section 16–7–52 in an amount exceeding 500 pounds in weight or 100 cubic feet in volume shall upon the first offense be guilty of a misdemeanor of a high and aggravated nature and shall upon the second and each subsequent offense be guilty of a felony and, upon conviction thereof, shall be fined not more than $25,000.00 for each violation or imprisoned for not more than two years, or both. For purposes of this subsection, each day a continuing violation occurs shall constitute a separate violation.

"(c) Any person who dumps waste in violation of Code Section 16–7–52 in any quantity if the waste is biomedical waste, hazardous waste, or a hazardous substance or if the dumping is for commercial purposes shall be guilty of a felony and, upon conviction thereof, shall be fined not more than $25,000.00 for each violation or imprisoned for not more than two years, or both. For purposes of this subsection, each day a continuing violation occurs shall constitute a separate violation.

"(d) In addition to the penalties provided in subsections (a) and (b) of this Code section, the court may order the violator to remove or render harmless any waste dumped in violation of Code Section 16–7–52, repair or restore property damaged by or pay damages resulting from such dumping, or perform public service related to the removal of illegally dumped waste or to the restoration of an area polluted by such waste."

Laws 2006, Act 538, § 5–1, provides:

"This Act shall become effective upon its approval by the Governor [April 21, 2006] or upon its becoming law without such approval for purposes of adopting local ordinances to become effective on or after July 1, 2006; and for all other purposes, this Act shall become effective on July 1, 2006."

§ 16–7–53.1. Violations while driving, moving, or operating a vehicle; vehicle impound

(a) Whenever a person has been arrested for a violation of Code Section 16–7–52 committed while driving, moving, or operating a vehicle, the arresting law enforcement agency may impound the vehicle that the person was driving, moving, or operating at the time of arrest until such time as the arrestee claiming the vehicle meets the conditions for release in subsection (b) of this Code section or a person other than the arrestee meets the conditions for release in subsection (c) of this Code section.

(b) A vehicle impounded pursuant to this Code section shall not be released unless the person claiming the vehicle:

(1) Presents a valid driver's license, proof of ownership or lawful authority to operate the motor vehicle, and proof of valid motor vehicle insurance for that vehicle; and

(2) Is able to operate the vehicle in a safe manner and would not be in violation of Title 40.

(c) A vehicle impounded pursuant to this Code section may be released to a person other than the arrestee only if:

(1) The vehicle is not owned or leased by the person under arrest and the person who owns or leases the vehicle claims the vehicle and meets the conditions for release in subsection (b) of this Code section; or

(2) The vehicle is owned or leased by the arrestee, the arrestee gives written permission to another person to operate the vehicle, and the conditions for release in subsection (b) of this Code section are met.

(d) A law enforcement agency impounding a vehicle pursuant to this Code section may charge a reasonable fee for towing and storage of the vehicle. The law enforcement agency may retain custody of the vehicle until that fee is paid.

Laws 2006, Act 538, § 2–2, eff. July 1, 2006.

Historical and Statutory Notes

Laws 2006, Act 538, § 5–1, provides:

"This Act shall become effective upon its approval by the Governor [April 21, 2006] or upon its becoming law without such approval for purposes of adopting local ordinances to become effective on or after July 1, 2006; and for all other purposes, this Act shall become effective on July 1, 2006."

§ 16–7–54. Litter containing articles displaying person's name; trier of fact; discretion

Whenever any egregious litter which is dumped in violation of Code Section 16–7–52 is discovered to contain any article or articles, including but not limited to letters, bills, publications, or other writings which display the name of a person thereon, addressed to such person or in any other manner indicating that the article belongs or belonged to such person, the trier of fact may in its discretion and in consideration of the totality of the circumstances infer that such person has violated this part.

Laws 1993, p. 496, § 2; Laws 2006, Act 538, § 2–2, eff. July 1, 2006.

Historical and Statutory Notes

The 2006 amendment by Act 538 substituted "egregious litter" for "waste" and substituted "the trier of fact may in its discretion and in consideration of the totality of the circumstances infer" for "it shall be a rebuttable presumption".

Laws 2006, Act 538, § 5–1, provides:

"This Act shall become effective upon its approval by the Governor [April 21, 2006] or upon its becoming law without such approval for purposes of adopting local ordinances to become effective on or after July 1, 2006; and for all other purposes, this Act shall become effective on July 1, 2006."

§ 16–7–55. Enforcement of local laws, rules, or regulations; adoption and violation of local ordinances

(a) Nothing in this part shall limit the authority of any state agency, county, municipality, or consolidated government to enforce any other laws, rules, or regulations relating to egregious litter or the management of solid, biomedical, or hazardous waste.

(b) Nothing within this part shall be construed to prohibit the adoption of local ordinances regulating and controlling egregious litter within the jurisdiction of any county, municipality, or consolidated government. Violation of such ordinances shall be punished as provided in the municipal charter or local ordinances.

Laws 1993, p. 496, § 2; Laws 2006, Act 538, § 2–2, eff. July 1, 2006.

Historical and Statutory Notes

The 2006 amendment by Act 538 rewrote the section which had read:

"Nothing in this part shall limit the authority of any state agency to enforce any other laws, rules, or regulations relating to waste or the management of solid, biomedical, or hazardous waste."

Laws 2006, Act 538, § 5–1, provides:

"This Act shall become effective upon its approval by the Governor [April 21, 2006] or upon its becoming law without such approval for purposes of adopting local ordinances to become effective on or after July 1, 2006; and for all other purposes, this Act shall become effective on July 1, 2006."

§ 16–7–56. Construction

Nothing in this part shall be construed so as to repeal, supersede, amend, or modify any provision of Title 12.

Laws 1993, p. 496, § 2; Laws 2006, Act 538, § 2–2, eff. July 1, 2006.

Historical and Statutory Notes

The 2006 amendment by Act 538 amended this section without change.

Laws 2006, Act 538, § 5–1, provides:

"This Act shall become effective upon its approval by the Governor [April 21, 2006] or upon its becoming law without such approval for purposes of adopting local ordinances to become effective on or after July 1, 2006; and for all other purposes, this Act shall become effective on July 1, 2006."

Part 3A

Placement of Posters, Signs and Advertisements

Historical and Statutory Notes

Laws 2006, Act 538, §§ 1–1 and 5–1, provide:

"SECTION 1–1. This Act shall be known and may be cited as the 'Comprehensive Litter Prevention and Abatement Act of 2006.'"

"SECTION 5–1. This Act shall become effective upon its approval by the Governor [April 21, 2006] or upon its becoming law without such approval for purposes of adopting local ordinances to become effective on or after July 1, 2006; and for all other purposes, this Act shall become effective on July 1, 2006."

§ 16–7–58. Placement of posters, signs and advertisements on public or private property; permission and limitations; violations

(a) It shall be unlawful for any person to place posters, signs, or advertisements:

(1) On any public property or building, unless the owner thereof or the occupier as authorized by such owner has given permission to place such posters, signs, or advertisements on such property; provided, however, that signs within the rights of way of public roads shall be governed by Code Section 32–6–51;

(2) On any private property unless the owner thereof or the occupier as authorized by such owner has given permission to place such posters, signs, or advertisements on such property; and, provided, further that no municipal, county, or consolidated government may restrict by regulation or other means the length of time a political campaign sign may be displayed or the number of signs which may be displayed on private property for which permission has been granted; or

(3) On any property zoned for commercial or industrial uses if the placement of such posters, signs, or advertisements conflicts with any zoning laws or ordinances.

(b) Any poster, sign, or advertisement placed in violation of paragraph (1) of subsection (a) of this Code section is declared to be a public nuisance, and the officials having jurisdiction of the public property or building, including without limitation law enforcement officers, may remove or direct the removal of the same.

(c) Each poster, sign, or advertisement placed in violation of this Code section shall constitute a separate offense.

(d) Any person who violates this Code section shall be punished the same as for littering under Code Section 16–7–43.

Laws 1971, p. 624, §§ 1, 3; Laws 1983, p. 471, § 1; Laws 2001, Ex. Sess., p. 335, § 4; Laws 2006, Act 538, § 2–3, eff. July 1, 2006; Laws 2006, Act 727, § 1, eff. May 3, 2006.

Formerly Code 1981, §§ 21–1–1, 21–2–3.

Historical and Statutory Notes

Laws 2006, Act 538, § 2–3, renumbered former § 21–2–3 as § 16–7–58 and amended the section. The amendment, in subsec. (a), in the introductory paragraph, substituted "place posters, signs, or advertisements" for "place campaign posters, signs, and advertisements", deleted former par. (1), redesignated former pars. (2) and (3) as pars. (1) and (2), in new par. (1), inserted ", unless the owner thereof or the occupier as authorized by such owner has given permission to place such posters, signs, or advertisements on such property; provided, however, that signs within the rights of way of public roads shall be governed by Code Section 32–6–51", in new par. (2), inserted "or the occupier as authorized by such owner" following "owner thereof", and substituted "such posters, signs, or advertisements" for "such campaign posters, signs, and advertisements", deleted former par. (4) which had been reserved, redesignated former par. (5) as par. (3), and in new par. (3), substituted "such posters, signs, or advertisements" for "such campaign posters, signs, and advertisements"; inserted new subsecs. (b) and (c); redesignated former subsec. (b) as subsec. (d); and in new subsec. (d), substituted "shall be punished the same as for littering under Code Section 16–7–43" for "shall be guilty of a misdemeanor". Prior to deletion, former par. (a)(1) had read:

"(1) Within the right of way of any public streets, roads, or highways;".

Laws 2006, Act 538, § 5–1, provides:

"This Act shall become effective upon its approval by the Governor [April 21, 2006] or upon its becoming law without such approval for purposes of adopting local ordinances to become effective on or after July 1, 2006; and for all other purposes, this Act shall become effective on July 1, 2006."

Laws 2006, Act 727, § 1, effective May 3, 2006, amended § 21–2–3 (renumbered as this section by Act 538, effective July 1, 2006). The amendment, in subsec. (a), in the introductory paragraph, substituted "place posters, signs, or advertisements" for "place campaign posters, signs, and advertisements", deleted former par. (1), redesignated former pars. (2) and (3) as pars. (1) and (2), in new par. (1), inserted ", unless the owner thereof or the occupier as authorized by such owner has given permission to place such posters, signs, or advertisements on such property; provided, however, that signs within the rights of way of public roads shall be governed by Code Section 32–6–51", in new par. (2), inserted "or the occupier as authorized by such owner" following "owner thereof", substituted "such posters, signs, or advertisements" for "such campaign posters, signs, and advertisements", and inserted "; and, provided, further that no municipal, county, or consolidated government may restrict by regulation or other means the length of time a political campaign sign may be displayed or the number of signs which may be displayed on private property for which permission has been granted" following "on such property", deleted former par. (4) which had been reserved, redesignated former par. (5) as par. (3), and in new par. (3), substituted "such posters, signs, or advertisements" for "such campaign posters, signs, and advertisements". Prior to deletion, former par. (a)(1) had read:

"(1) Within the right of way of any public streets, roads, or highways;".

Laws 2006, Act 727, § 7, effective May 3, 2006, provides:

"In the event any section, subsection, sentence, clause, or phrase of this Act shall be declared or adjudged invalid or unconstitutional, such declaration or adjudication shall affect and invalidate the whole of the section in which such matter appears herein, but shall in no manner affect the other sections, subsections, sentences, clauses, or phrases of this Act, which shall remain of full force and effect as if the section, subsection, sentence, clause, or phrase so declared or adjudged invalid or unconstitutional were not originally a part hereof. The General Assembly declares that it would have passed the remaining parts of this Act if it had known that such part or parts hereof would be declared or adjudged invalid or unconstitutional, but would not have passed any section of this Act containing or constituting an invalid or unconstitutional provision."

Article 3

Arson and Explosives

§ 16–7–60. Arson in the first degree

(a) A person commits the offense of arson in the first degree when, by means of fire or explosive, he or she knowingly damages or knowingly causes, aids, abets, advises, encourages, hires, counsels, or procures another to damage:

(1) Any dwelling house of another without his or her consent or in which another has a security interest, including but not limited to a mortgage, a lien, or a conveyance to secure debt, without the consent of both, whether it is occupied, unoccupied, or vacant;

(2) Any building, vehicle, railroad car, watercraft, or other structure of another without his or her consent or in which another has a security interest, including but not limited to a mortgage, a lien, or a conveyance to secure debt, without the consent of both, if such structure is designed for use as a dwelling, whether it is occupied, unoccupied, or vacant;

(3) Any dwelling house, building, vehicle, railroad car, watercraft, aircraft, or other structure whether it is occupied, unoccupied, or vacant and when such is insured against loss or damage by fire or explosive and such loss or damage is accomplished without the consent of both the insurer and the insured;

(4) Any dwelling house, building, vehicle, railroad car, watercraft, aircraft, or other structure whether it is occupied, unoccupied, or vacant with the intent to defeat, prejudice, or defraud the rights of a spouse or co-owner; or

(5) Any building, vehicle, railroad car, watercraft, aircraft, or other structure under such circumstances that it is reasonably foreseeable that human life might be endangered.

(b) A person also commits the offense of arson in the first degree when, in the commission of a felony, by means of fire or explosive, he or she knowingly damages or knowingly causes, aids, abets, advises, encourages, hires, counsels, or procures another to damage anything included or described in subsection (a) of this Code section.

(c) A person convicted of the offense of arson in the first degree shall be punished by a fine of not more than $50,000.00 or by imprisonment for not less than one nor more than 20 years, or both.

Laws 1924, p. 192, § 1; Laws 1949, p. 1118, § 2; Laws 1968, p. 1249, § 1; Laws 1976, p. 1497, § 1; Laws 1979, p. 935, § 1; Laws 2004, Act 576, § 1, eff. July 1, 2004.

Formerly Code 1933, § 26–2208; Code 1933, § 26–1401.

Historical and Statutory Notes

The 2004 amendment by Act 576, made the section gender neutral; redesignated former subsec. (b) as subsec. (c); and inserted new subsec. (b).

Laws 2004, Act 576, § 4, provides:

"This Act shall become effective on July 1, 2004. This Act shall not apply to any offense committed prior to July 1, 2004. Any such offense shall be punishable as provided by the statue [so in original] in effect at the time the offense was committed."

§ 16–7–61. Arson in the second degree

(a) A person commits the offense of arson in the second degree as to any building, vehicle, railroad car, watercraft, aircraft, or other structure not included or described in Code Section 16–7–60 when, by means of fire or explosive, he or she knowingly damages or knowingly causes, aids, abets, advises, encourages, hires, counsels, or procures another to damage any building, vehicle, railroad car, watercraft, aircraft, or other structure of another without his or her consent or in which another has a security interest, including but not limited to a mortgage, a lien, or a conveyance to secure debt, without the consent of both.

(b) A person also commits the offense of arson in the second degree as to any building, vehicle, railroad car, watercraft, aircraft, or other structure not included or described in Code Section 16-7-60 when, in the commission of a felony, by means of fire or explosive, he or she knowingly damages or knowingly causes, aids, abets, advises, encourages, hires, counsels, or procures another to damage any building, vehicle, railroad car, watercraft, aircraft, or other structure of another without his or her consent or in which another has a security interest, including but not limited to a mortgage, a lien, or a conveyance to secure debt, without the consent of both.

(c) A person convicted of the offense of arson in the second degree shall be punished by a fine of not more than $25,000.00 or by imprisonment for not less than one nor more than ten years, or both.

Laws 1924, p. 192, § 2; Laws 1949, p. 1118, § 3; Laws 1968, p. 1249, § 1; Laws 1976, p. 1497, § 2; Laws 1979, p. 935, § 2; Laws 1985, p. 149, § 16; Laws 2004, Act 576, § 2, eff. July 1, 2004.

Formerly Code 1933, § 26-2209; Code 1933, § 26-1402.

Historical and Statutory Notes

The 2004 amendment by Act 576, made the section gender neutral; redesignated former subsec. (b) as subsec. (c); and inserted new subsec. (b).

Laws 2004, Act 576, § 4, provides:

"This Act shall become effective on July 1, 2004. This Act shall not apply to any offense committed prior to July 1, 2004. Any such offense shall be punishable as provided by the statue [so in original] in effect at the time the offense was committed."

§ 16-7-62. Arson in the third degree

(a) A person commits the offense of arson in the third degree when, by means of fire or explosive, he or she knowingly damages or knowingly causes, aids, abets, advises, encourages, hires, counsels, or procures another to damage:

(1) Any personal property of another without his or her consent or in which another has a security interest, including but not limited to a lien, without the consent of both and the value of the property is $25.00 or more;

(2) Any personal property when such is insured against loss or damage by fire or explosive and the loss or damage is accomplished without the consent of both the insurer and insured and the value of the property is $25.00 or more; or

(3) Any personal property with the intent to defeat, prejudice, or defraud the rights of a spouse or co-owner and the value of the property is $25.00 or more.

(b) A person also commits the offense of arson in the third degree when, in the commission of a felony, by means of fire or explosive, he or she knowingly damages or knowingly causes, aids, abets, advises, encourages, hires, counsels, or procures another to damage anything included or described in subsection (a) of this Code section.

(c) A person convicted of the offense of arson in the third degree shall be punished by a fine not to exceed $10,000.00 or by imprisonment for not less than one nor more than five years, or both.

Laws 1924, p. 192, §§ 3, 4; Laws 1949, p. 1118, § 4; Laws 1968, p. 1249, § 1; Laws 1976, p. 1497, § 3; Laws 1979, p. 935, § 3; Laws 2004, Act 576, § 3, eff. July 1, 2004.

Formerly Code 1933, § 26-2210; Code 1933, § 26-1403.

Historical and Statutory Notes

The 2004 amendment by Act 576, made the section gender neutral; redesignated former subsec. (b) as subsec. (c); and inserted new subsec. (b).

Laws 2004, Act 576, § 4, provides:

"This Act shall become effective on July 1, 2004. This Act shall not apply to any offense committed prior to July 1, 2004. Any such offense shall be punishable as provided by the statue [so in original] in effect at the time the offense was committed."

§ 16-7-63. Engaging in certain activities relating to use of fires and ignited objects

(a) It shall be unlawful:

(1) To, with intent to damage, start, cause, or procure another to start or cause a fire in any woodlands, brush, field, or other lands that are not one's own and without the permission of the owner or the lessee having control of such property;

(2) To burn any brush, field, forest land, campfire, or debris, whether on one's own land or the lands of another, without taking the necessary precautions before, during, and after the fire to prevent the escape of such fire onto the lands of another. The escape of such fire shall be prima-facie evidence that necessary precautions were not taken;

(3) For any person to cause a fire by discarding any lighted cigarette, cigar, debris, or any other flaming or smoldering material that may cause a forest fire; or

(4) To destroy or damage any material or device used in the detection or suppression of wildfires.

(b) This Code section shall not apply to fire resulting from the operation of transportation machinery or equipment used in its normal or accustomed manner.

(c)(1) Any person who violates paragraph (2), (3), or (4) of subsection (a) of this Code section shall be guilty of a misdemeanor.

(2) Any person who violates paragraph (1) of subsection (a) of this Code section shall be guilty of arson of lands in the third degree and shall be punished the same as provided by subsection (c) of Code Section 16-7-62 for arson in the third degree.

(3) Any person whose violation of paragraph (1) of subsection (a) of this Code section results in a fire that burns more than five acres that are not one's own shall be guilty of arson of lands in the second degree and shall be punished the same as provided by subsection (c) of Code Section 16-7-61 for arson in the second degree.

(4) Any person who violates paragraph (1) of subsection (a) of this Code section under such circumstances that it was reasonably foreseeable that human life might be endangered shall be guilty of arson of lands in the first degree and shall be punished the same as provided by subsection (c) of Code Section 16-7-60 for arson in the first degree.

Laws 1833, Cobb's 1851 Digest, p. 824; Laws 1865-66, p. 233, § 2; Laws 1898, p. 60, § 1; Laws 1949, p. 1118, § 8; Laws 1956, p. 737, § 8; Laws 1971, p. 577, §§ 1, 2; Laws 2008, Act 530, § 3, eff. July 1, 2008.

Formerly Code 1981 § 16-7-28

Historical and Statutory Notes

This section, added as § 16-7-28, was renumbered by Laws 2008, Act 530, § 3, effective July 1, 2008.

The 2008 amendment by Act 530 renumbered the section; and rewrote par. (1) of subsec. (a) and subsec. (c), which had read as follows:

"(1) To start, cause, or procure another to start a fire in any woodlands, brush, field, or any other lands not one's own or leased and without the permission of the owner;"

"(c) Any person who violates subsection (a) of this Code section shall be guilty of a misdemeanor."

§ 16–7–64. Repealed by Laws 1996, p. 416, § 2, eff. May 1, 1996

Article 4

Bombs, Explosives, and Chemical and Biological Weapons

§ 16–7–80. Definitions

As used in this article, the term:

(1) "Bacteriological weapon" or "biological weapon" means any device which is designed in such a manner as to permit the intentional release into the population or environment of microbial or other biological agents or toxins whatever their origin or method of production in a manner not otherwise authorized by law or any device the development, production, or stockpiling of which is prohibited pursuant to the "Convention on the Prohibition of the Development, Production, and Stockpiling of Bacteriological (Biological) and Toxin Weapons and Their Destruction," 26 U.S.T. 583, TIAS 8063.

(2) "Commissioner" means the Safety Fire Commissioner.

(3) "Conviction" means an adjudication of guilt of or a plea of guilty or nolo contendere to the commission of an offense against the laws of this state, any other state or territory, the United States, or a foreign nation recognized by the United States. Such term includes any such conviction or plea notwithstanding the fact that sentence was imposed pursuant to Article 3 of Chapter 8 of Title 42. Such term also includes the adjudication or plea of a juvenile to the commission of an act which if committed by an adult would constitute a crime under the laws of this state.

(4) "Destructive device" means:

(A) Any explosive, incendiary, or over-pressure device or poison gas which has been configured as a bomb; a grenade; a rocket with a propellant charge of more than four ounces; a missile having an explosive or incendiary charge of more than one-quarter ounce; a poison gas; a mine; a Molotov cocktail; or any other device which is substantially similar to such devices;

(B) Any type of weapon by whatever name known which will or may be readily converted to expel a projectile by the action of an explosive or other propellant, through a barrel which has a bore diameter of more than one-half inch in diameter; provided, however, that such term shall not include a pistol, rifle, or shotgun suitable for sporting or personal safety purposes or ammunition; a device which is neither designed or redesigned for use as a weapon; a device which, although originally designed for use as a weapon, is redesigned for use as a signaling, pyrotechnic, line throwing, safety, or similar device; or surplus military ordnance sold, loaned, or given by authority of the appropriate official of the United States Department of Defense;

(C) A weapon of mass destruction;

(D) A bacteriological weapon or biological weapon; or

(E) Any combination of parts either designed or intended for use in converting any device into a destructive device as otherwise defined in this paragraph.

(5) "Detonator" means a device containing a detonating charge that is used to initiate detonation in an explosive, including but not limited to electric blasting caps, blasting caps for use with safety fuses, and detonating cord delay connectors.

(6) "Director" means the director of the Georgia Bureau of Investigation.

(7) "Distribute" means the actual, constructive, or attempted transfer from one person to another.

(8) "Explosive" means any chemical compound or other substance or mechanical system intended for the purpose of producing an explosion capable of causing injury to persons or damage to property or containing oxidizing and combustible units or other ingredients in such proportions or quantities that ignition, fire, friction, concussion, percussion, or detonator may produce an explosion capable of causing injury to persons or damage to property, including but not limited to the substances designated in Code Section 16–7–81; provided, however, that the term explosive shall not include common fireworks as defined by Code Section 25–10–1, model rockets and model rocket engines designed, sold, and used for the purpose of propelling recoverable aero models, or toy pistol paper caps in which the explosive content does not average more than 0.25 grains of explosive mixture per paper cap for toy pistols, toy cannons, toy canes, toy guns, or other devices using such paper caps unless such devices are used as a component of a destructive device.

(9) "Explosive ordnance disposal technician" or "EOD technician" means:

(A) A law enforcement officer, fire official, emergency management official, or an employee of this state or its political subdivisions or an authority of the state or a political subdivision who is certified in accordance with Code Section 35–8–13 and members of the Georgia National Guard who are qualified as explosive ordnance disposal technicians under the appropriate laws and regulations when acting in the performance of their official duties; and

(B) An official or employee of the United States, including but not limited to a member of the armed forces of the United States, who is qualified as an explosive ordnance disposal technician under the appropriate laws and regulations when acting in the performance of his or her official duties.

(10) "Felony" means any offense punishable by imprisonment for a term of one year or more, and includes conviction by a court-martial under the Uniform Code of Military Justice for an offense which would constitute a felony under the laws of the United States. A conviction of an offense under the laws of a foreign nation shall be considered a felony for the purposes of this article if the conduct giving rise to such conviction would have constituted a felony under the laws of this state or of the United States if committed within the jurisdiction of this state or the United States at the time of such conduct.

(11) "Hoax device" or "replica" means a device or article which has the appearance of a destructive device.

(12) "Incendiary" means a flammable liquid or compound with a flash point of 150 degrees Fahrenheit or less as determined by Tagliabue or equivalent closed-cup device, including but not limited to, gasoline, kerosene, fuel oil, or a derivative of such substances.

(13) "Over-pressure device" means a frangible container filled with an explosive gas or expanding gas which is designed or constructed so as to cause the container to break or fracture in a manner which is capable of causing death, bodily harm, or property damage.

(14) "Poison gas" means any toxic chemical or its precursors that through its chemical action or properties on life processes causes death or permanent injury to human beings; provided, however, that such term shall not include:

(A) Riot control agents, smoke, and obscuration materials or medical products which are manufactured, possessed, transported, or used in accordance with the laws of the United States and of this state;

(B) Tear gas devices designed to be carried on or about the person which contain not more than one-half ounce of the chemical;

(C) Pesticides, as provided in paragraph (12) of Code Section 16–7–93.

(15) "Property" means any real or personal property of any kind including money, choses in action, and other similar interests in property.

(16) "Public building" means any structure which is generally open to members of the public with or without the payment of an admission fee or membership dues including, but not limited to structures owned, operated, or leased by the state, the United States, any of the several states, or any foreign nation or any political subdivision or authority thereof; any religious organization; any medical facility; any college, school, or university; or any corporation, partnership, or association.

(17) "Weapon of mass destruction" means any device which is designed in such a way as to release radiation or radioactivity at a level which will result in internal or external bodily injury or death to any person.

Laws 1996, p. 416, § 3.

§ 16–7–81. List of explosive materials

The following materials are explosives within the meaning of this article:

(1) Acetylides of heavy metals;

(2) Aluminum containing polymeric propellant;

(3) Aluminum ophorite explosive;

(4) Amatex;

(5) Amatol;

(6) Ammonal;

(7) Ammonium nitrate explosive mixtures, cap sensitive;

(8) Ammonium nitrate explosive mixtures, noncap sensitive;

(9) Aromatic nitro-compound explosive mixtures;

(10) Ammonium perchlorate explosive mixtures;

(11) Ammonium perchlorate composite propellant;

(12) Ammonium picrate (picrate of ammonia, Explosive D);

(13) Ammonium salt lattice with isomorphously substituted inorganic salts;

(14) Ammonium tri-iodide;

(15) ANFO (ammonium nitrate-fuel oil);

(16) Baratol;

(17) Baronol;

(18) BEAF (1,2–bis (2,2–difluoro–2–nitroacetoxyethane));

(19) Black powder;

(20) Black powder based explosive mixtures;

(21) Blasting agents, nitro-carbo-nitrates, including noncap sensitive slurry and water-gel explosives;

(22) Blasting caps;

(23) Blasting gelatin;

(24) Blasting powder;

(25) BTNEC (bis (trinitroethyl) carbonate);

(26) Bulk salutes;

(27) BTNEN (bis (trinitroethyl) nitramine);

(28) BTTN (1,2,4 butanetriol trinitrate);

(29) Butyl tetryl;

(30) Calcium nitrate explosive mixture;

(31) Cellulose hexanitrate explosive mixture;

(32) Chlorate explosive mixtures;

(33) Composition A and variations;

(34) Composition B and variations;

(35) Composition C and variations;

(36) Copper acetylide;

(37) Cyanuric triazide;

(38) Cyclotrimethylenetrinitramine (RDX);

(39) Cyclotetramethylenetetranitramine (HMX);

(40) Cyclonite (RDX);

(41) Cyclotol;

(42) DATB (diaminotrinitrobenzene);

(43) DDNP (diazodinitrophenol);

(44) DEGDN (diethyleneglycol dinitrate);

(45) Detonating cord;

(46) Detonators;

(47) Dimethylol dimethyl methane dinitrate composition;

(48) Dinitroethyleneurea;

(49) Dinitroglycerine (glycerol dinitrate);

(50) Dinitrophenol;

(51) Dinitrophenolates;

(52) Dinitrophenyl hydrazine;

(53) Dinitroresorcinol;

(54) Dinitrotoluene-sodium nitrate explosive mixtures;

(55) DIPAM;

(56) Dipicryl sulfone;

(57) Dipicrylamine;

(58) Display fireworks;

(59) DNDP (dinitropentano nitrile);

(60) DNPA (2,2–dinitropropyl acrylate);

(61) Dynamite;

(62) EDDN (ethylene diamine dinitrate);

(63) EDNA;

(64) Ednatol;

(65) EDNP (ethyl 4,4–dinitropentanoate);

(66) Erythritol tetranitrate explosives;

(67) Esters of nitro-substituted alcohols;

(68) EGDN (ethylene glycol dinitrate);

(69) Ethyl-tetryl;

(70) Explosive conitrates;

(71) Explosive gelatins;

(72) Explosive mixtures containing oxygen-releasing inorganic salts and hydrocarbons;

(73) Explosive mixtures containing oxygen-releasing inorganic salts and nitro bodies;

(74) Explosive mixtures containing oxygen-releasing inorganic salts and water insoluble fuels;

(75) Explosive mixtures containing oxygen-releasing inorganic salts and water soluble fuels;

(76) Explosive mixtures containing sensitized nitromethane;

(77) Explosive mixtures containing tetranitromethane (nitroform);

(78) Explosive nitro compounds of aromatic hydrocarbons;

(79) Explosive organic nitrate mixtures;

(80) Explosive liquids;

(81) Explosive powders;

(82) Flash powder;

(83) Fulminate of mercury;

(84) Fulminate of silver;

(85) Fulminating gold;

(86) Fulminating mercury;

(87) Fulminating platinum;

(88) Fulminating silver;

(89) Gelatinized nitrocellulose;

(90) Gem-dinitro aliphatic explosive mixtures;

(91) Guanyl nitrosamino guanyl tetrazene;

(92) Guanyl nitrosamino guanylidene hydrazine;

(92.1) Guncotton;

(92.2) Heavy metal azides;

(92.3) Hexamitrostrilbene;

(92.4) Hexanite;

(92.5) Hexanitrodiphenylamine;

(92.6) Hexogen;

(93) Hexogene or octogene and a nitrated N-methylaniline;

(94) Hexolites;

(95) HMX (cyclo–1,3,5,7–tetramethylene–2,4,6,8–tetranitramine; Octogen);

(96) Hydrazinium nitrate/hydrazine/aluminum explosive system;

(97) Hydrazoic acid;

(98) Igniter cord;

(99) Igniters;

(100) Initiating tube systems;

(101) KDNBF (potassium dinitrobenzo-furoxane);

(102) Lead azide;

(103) Lead mannite;

(104) Lead mononitroresorcinate;

(105) Lead picrate;

(106) Lead salts, explosive;

(107) Lead styphnate (styphnate of lead, lead trinitroresorcinate);

(108) Liquid nitrated polyol and trimethylolethane;

(109) Liquid oxygen explosives;

(110) Magnesium ophorite explosives;

(111) Mannitol hexanitrate;

(112) MDNP (methyl 4,4–dinitropentanoate);

(113) MEAN (monoethanolamine nitrate);

(114) Mercuric fulminate;

(115) Mercury oxalate;

(116) Mercury tartrate;

(117) Metriol trinitrate;

(118) Minol–2 (40% TNT, 40% ammonium nitrate, 20% aluminum);

(119) MMAN (monomethylamine nitrate); methylamine nitrate;

(120) Mononitrotoluene-nitroglycerin mixture;

(121) Monopropellants;

(122) NIBTN (nitroisobutametriol trinitrate);

(123) Nitrate sensitized with gelled nitroparaffin;

(124) Nitrated carbohydrate explosive;

(125) Nitrated glucoside explosive;

(126) Nitrated polyhydric alcohol explosives;

(127) Nitrates of soda explosive mixtures;

(128) Nitric acid and a nitro aromatic compound explosive;

(129) Nitric acid and carboxylic fuel explosive;

(130) Nitric acid explosive mixtures;

(131) Nitro aromatic explosive mixtures;

(132) Nitro compounds of furane explosive mixtures;

(133) Nitrocellulose explosive;

(134) Nitroderivative of urea explosive mixture;

(135) Nitrogelatin explosive;

(136) Nitrogen trichloride;

(137) Nitrogen tri-iodide;

(138) Nitroglycerine (NG, RNG, nitro, glyceryl trinitrate, trinitroglycerine);

(139) Nitroglycide;

(140) Nitroglycol (ethylene glycol dinitrate, EGDN);

(141) Nitroguanidine explosives;

(142) Nitroparaffins Explosive Grade and ammonium nitrate mixtures;

(143) Nitronium perchlorate propellant mixtures;

(144) Nitrostarch;

(145) Nitro-substituted carboxylic acids;

(146) Nitrourea;

(147) Octogen (HMX);

(148) Octol (75% HMX, 25% TNT);

(149) Organic amine nitrates;

(150) Organic nitramines;

(151) PBX (RDX and plasticizer);

(152) Pellet powder;

(153) Penthrinite composition;

(154) Pentolite;

(155) Perchlorate explosive mixtures;

(156) Peroxide based explosive mixtures;

(157) PETN (nitropentaerythrite, pentaerythrite tetranitrate, pentaerythritol tetranitrate);

(158) Picramic acid and its salts;

(159) Picramide;

(160) Picrate of potassium explosive mixtures;

(161) Picratol;

(162) Picric acid (manufactured as an explosive);

(163) Picryl chloride;

(164) Picryl fluoride;

(165) PLX (95% nitromethane, 5% ethylenediamine);

(166) Polynitro aliphatic compounds;

(167) Polyolpolynitrate-nitrocellulose explosive gels;

(168) Potassium chlorate and lead sulfocyanate explosive;

(169) Potassium nitrate explosive mixtures;

(170) Potassium nitroaminotetrazole;

(171) Pyrotechnic compositions;

(172) PYX (2,6–bis(picrylamino)–3,5–dinitropyridine);

(173) RDX (cyclonite, hexogen, T4,cyclo–1,3, 5,-trimethylene–2,4,6,-rinitramine; hexahydro–1,3,5–trinitro-S-triazine);

(174) Safety fuse;

(175) Salutes, (bulk);

(176) Salts of organic amino sulfonic acid explosive mixture;

(177) Silver acetylide;

(178) Silver azide;

(179) Silver fulminate;

(180) Silver oxalate explosive mixtures;

(181) Silver styphnate;

(182) Silver tartrate explosive mixtures;

(183) Silver tetrazene;

(184) Slurried explosive mixtures of water, inorganic oxidizing salt, gelling agent, fuel, and sensitizer, cap sensitive;

(185) Smokeless powder;

(186) Sodatol;

(187) Sodium amatol;

(188) Sodium azide explosive mixture;

(189) Sodium dinitro-ortho-cresolate;

(190) Sodium nitrate-potassium nitrate explosive mixture;

(191) Sodium picramate;

(192) Special fireworks;

(193) Squibs;

(194) Styphnic acid explosives;

(195) Tacot (tetranitro–2,3,5,6–dibenzo–1,3a,4,6a tetrazapentalene);

(196) TATB (triaminotrinitrobenzene);

(197) TATP (triacetone triperoxide);

(198) TEGDN (triethylene glycol dinitrate);

(199) Tetrazene (tetracene, tetrazine, l(5–tetrazolyl)–4–guanyl tetrazene hydrate);

(200) Tetranitrocarbazole;

(201) Tetryl (2,4,6 tetranitro-N-methylaniline);

(202) Tetrytol;

(203) Thickened inorganic oxidizer salt slurried explosive mixture;

(204) TMETN (trimethylolethane trinitrate);

(205) TNEF (trinitroethyl formal);

(206) TNEOC (trinitroethylorthocarbonate);

(207) TNEOF (trinitroethylorthoformate);

(208) TNT (trinitrotoluene, trotyl, trilite, triton);

(209) Torpex;

(210) Tridite;

(211) Trimethylol ethyl methane trinitrate composition;

(212) Trimethylolthane trinitrate-nitrocellulose;

(213) Trimonite;

(214) Trinitroanisole;

(215) Trinitrobenzene;

(216) Trinitrobenzoic acid;

(217) Trinitrocresol;

(218) Trinitro-meta-cresol;

(219) Trinitronaphthalene;

(220) Trinitrophenetol;

(221) Trinitrophloroglucinol;

(222) Trinitroresorcinol;

(223) Tritonal;

(224) Urea nitrate;

(225) Water bearing explosives having salts of oxidizing acids and nitrogen bases, sulfates, or sulfamates, cap sensitive;

(226) Water-in-oil emulsion explosive compositions;

(227) Xanthamonas hydrophilic colloid explosive mixture.

Laws 1996, p. 416, § 3; Laws 2000, p. 1562, § 1.

Historical and Statutory Notes

The 2000 amendment inserted pars. (92.1) through (92.6).

§ 16–7–82. Possession, manufacture, etc., of destructive devices except as provided in this law

(a) It shall be unlawful for any person to possess, manufacture, transport, distribute, possess with the intent to distribute, or offer to distribute a destructive device except as provided in this article.

(b) Any person convicted of a violation of this Code section shall be punished by imprisonment for not less than three nor more than 20 years or, by a fine of not more than $25,000.00 or both or, if the defendant is a corporation, by a fine of not less than $25,000.00 nor more than $100,000.00 or not fewer than 5,000 nor more than 10,000 hours of community service or both.

Laws 1996, p. 416, § 3.

§ 16–7–83. Possession, manufacture, etc., of destructive devices except as provided in this law

(a) It shall be unlawful for any person who is under indictment for or who has been convicted of a felony by a court of this state, any other state, the United States including its territories, possessions, and dominions, or a foreign nation to possess, manufacture, transport, distribute, possess with the intent to distribute, or offer to distribute a destructive device, detonator, explosive, poison gas, or hoax device.

(b) It shall be unlawful for any person knowingly to distribute a destructive device, detonator, explosive, poison gas, or hoax device to any person:

(1) Who he or she knows or should know is under indictment for or has been convicted of a felony by a court of this state, any other state, the United States including its territories, possessions, and dominions, or a foreign nation; or

(2) Who he or she knows or should know has been adjudicated to be mentally incompetent or mentally ill by a court of this state, any other state, or the United States including its territories, possessions, and dominions.

(c) Any person convicted of a violation of this Code section shall be punished, in the case of an individual, by imprisonment for not less than one nor more than 15 years or by a fine of not more than $25,000.00 or both or, if the defendant is a corporation, by a fine of not less than $10,000.00 nor more than $75,000.00 or not fewer than 1,000 nor more than 5,000 hours of community service or both.

(d) Notwithstanding any other provision of law, the Department of Behavioral Health and Developmental Disabilities shall make available to any law enforcement agency or district attorney of this state such information as may be necessary to establish that a person has been adjudicated by any court to be mentally incompetent or mentally ill.

(e) The provisions of this Code section shall not apply to:

(1) Any person who has been pardoned for a felony by the President of the United States, the State Board of Pardons and Paroles, or the person or agency empowered to grant pardons under the constitution or laws of any other state or of a foreign nation and, by the terms of the pardon, has expressly been authorized to receive, possess, distribute, or transport a destructive device, explosive, poison gas, or detonator; or

(2) A person who has been convicted of a felony, but who has been granted relief from the disabilities imposed by the laws of the United States with respect to the acquisition, receipt, transfer, shipment, or possession of explosives by the secretary of the United States Department of the Treasury pursuant to 18 U.S.C. 845, may apply to the Board of Public Safety for relief from the disabilities imposed by this Code section in the same manner as is provided in subsection (d) of Code Section 16–11–131. The board may grant such relief under the same standards and conditions as apply to firearms.

Laws 1996, p. 416, § 3; Laws 2009, Act 102, § 3–2, eff. July 1, 2009.

Historical and Statutory Notes

The 2009 amendment by Act 102 substituted "Department of Behavioral Health and Developmental Disabilities" for "Department of Human Resources" throughout the section.

§ 16–7–84. Distribution of destructive device, explosive, poison gas, or detonator to person under 21 years of age

(a) It shall be unlawful for any person to distribute or to offer to distribute a destructive device, explosive, poison gas, or detonator to any person who is under 21 years of age.

(b) Any person convicted of a violation of this Code section shall be punished, in the case of an individual, by imprisonment for not less than one nor more than three years or by a fine of not more than $10,000.00 or both or, if the defendant is a corporation, by a fine of not more than $20,000.00 or not fewer than 3,000 hours of community service or both.

Laws 1996, p. 416, § 3.

§ 16–7–85. Manufacture, possession, etc., of hoax device or replica of destructive device or detonator

(a) It shall be unlawful for any person to manufacture, possess, transport, distribute, or use a hoax device or replica of a destructive device or detonator with the intent to cause another to believe that such hoax device or replica is a destructive device or detonator.

(b) Any person convicted of a violation of this Code section shall be punished by imprisonment for not more than one year or by a fine of not more than $10,000.00 or both or, if the defendant is a corporation, a fine of not less than $1,000.00 or not fewer than 500 hours of community service or both for each such hoax device or replica; provided, however, that if such person communicates or transmits to another that such hoax device or replica is a destructive device or detonator with the intent to obtain the property of another person or to interfere with the ability of another person to conduct or carry on the ordinary course of business, trade, education, or government, such violation shall be punished by imprisonment for not less than one year nor more than five years or by a fine of not more than $25,000.00 or both or, if the defendant is a corporation, a fine of not less than $50,000.00 or not fewer than 1,000 nor more than 10,000 hours of community service or both for each such hoax device or replica.

Laws 1996, p. 416, § 3.

§ 16–7–86. Conspiracy

It shall be unlawful for any person to attempt or conspire to commit any offense prohibited by this article. Any person convicted of a violation of this Code section shall be punished by imprisonment or community service; by a fine; or by both such punishments not to exceed the maximum punishment prescribed for the offense the commission of which was the object of the attempt or conspiracy.

Laws 1996, p. 416, § 3.

§ 16–7–87. Obstruction of law enforcement officers

It shall be unlawful for any person knowingly to hinder or obstruct any explosive ordnance technician, law enforcement officer, fire official, emergency management official, animal trained to detect destructive devices, or any robot or mechanical device designed or utilized by a law enforcement officer, fire official, or emergency management official of this state or of the United States in the detection, disarming, or destruction of a destructive device. Any person convicted of a violation of this Code section shall be punished as provided in subsection (b) of Code Section 16–10–24.

Laws 1996, p. 416, § 3.

§ 16–7–88. Possession, transportation, receipt, or use of destructive device or explosive with intent to kill, injure or intimidate or to destroy any public building

(a) Any person who possesses, transports, or receives or attempts to possess, transport, or receive any destructive device or explosive with the knowledge or intent that it will be used to kill, injure, or intimidate any individual or to destroy any public building shall be punished by imprisonment for not less than ten nor more than 20 years or by a fine of not more than $125,000.00 or both or, if the defendant is a corporation, by a fine of not less than $125,000.00 nor more than $200,000.00 or sentenced to perform not fewer than 10,000 nor more than 20,000 hours of community service or both.

(b) In addition to any other penalty imposed under the laws of this state or of the United States, any person who shall use or attempt to use any destructive device or explosive to kill or injure any individual, including any public safety officer performing duties as a direct or proximate result of a violation of this subsection, or to destroy any public building shall be imprisoned for not less than 20 nor more than 40 years or fined the greater of the cost of replacing any property that is destroyed or $250,000.00 or both or, if the defendant is a corporation, fined the greater of the cost of replacing any property which is destroyed or $1 million or sentenced to perform not fewer than 20,000 nor more than 40,000 hours of community service or both.

(c) Any other provision of law to the contrary notwithstanding, no part of any sentence imposed pursuant to subsection (a) or (b) of this Code section shall be probated, deferred, suspended, or withheld and no person sentenced pursuant to subsection (a) or (b) of this Code section shall be eligible for early release, leave, work release, earned time, good time, or any other program administered by any agency of the executive or judicial branches of this state which would have the effect of reducing or mitigating such sentence until the defendant has completed the minimum sentence as provided by subsection (a) or (b) of this Code section.

Laws 1996, p. 416, § 3; Laws 1997, p. 512, § 1.

§ 16–7–89. Each violation a separate offense

Each violation of the provisions of this article shall be considered a separate offense.

Laws 1996, p. 416, § 3.

§ 16–7–90. Records and reports

It shall be the duty of any person authorized by paragraph (1) or (2) of Code Section 16–7–93 to manufacture, possess, transport, distribute, or use a destructive device, detonator, explosive, or hoax device within the state:

(1) To maintain such records as may be required pursuant to Title 25. Such records may be inspected by the Commissioner or the director or such officers' designees or any law enforcement officer or fire official during normal business hours; and

(2) To report promptly the loss or theft of any destructive device, detonator, explosive, or hoax device to the Georgia Bureau of Investigation.

Laws 1996, p. 416, § 3.

§ 16–7–91. Searches and inspections

The Commissioner or director or such officers' designees or any law enforcement officer or fire official may obtain an inspection warrant as provided in Code Section 25–2–22.1 to conduct a search or inspection of:

(1) Any person licensed pursuant to Title 25 to manufacture, possess, transport, sell, distribute, or use a destructive device or detonator within the state;

(2) Any person licensed pursuant to Chapter 7 of Title 2 to manufacture, possess, transport, sell, or distribute or use pesticides; or

(3) Any property where such pesticide, destructive device, or detonator is manufactured, possessed, transported, distributed, or used.

Laws 1996, p. 416, § 3.

§ 16–7–92. Power to compel attendance of witnesses and production of documents

In any case where there is reason to believe that a destructive device, detonator, explosive, or hoax device has been manufactured, possessed, transported, distributed, or used in violation of this article or Title 25 or that there has been an attempt or a conspiracy to commit such a violation, the Attorney General, any district attorney, the director, or such persons as may be designated in writing by such officials shall have the same power to compel the attendance of witnesses and the production of evidence before such official in the same manner as the state fire marshal as provided in Code Sections 25–2–27, 25–2–28, and 25–2–29.

Laws 1996, p. 416, § 3.

§ 16–7–93. Exceptions

The provisions of Code Sections 16–7–82, 16–7–84, 16–7–85, and 16–7–86 shall not apply to:

(1) Any person authorized to manufacture, possess, transport, distribute, or use a destructive device or detonator pursuant to the laws of the United States, as amended, or pursuant to Title 25 when such person is acting in accordance with such laws and any regulations issued pursuant thereto;

(2) Any person licensed as a blaster by the Commissioner pursuant to Chapter 8 of Title 25, when such blaster is acting in accordance with the laws of the state and any regulations promulgated thereunder and any ordinances and regulations of the political subdivision or authority of the state where blasting operations are being performed;

(3) Fireworks, as defined by Code Section 25–10–1 and any person authorized by the laws of this state and of the United States to manufacture, possess, distribute, transport, store, exhibit, display, or use fireworks;

(4) A law enforcement, fire service, or emergency management agency of this state, any agency or authority of a political subdivision of this state, or the United States and any employee or authorized agent thereof while in performance of official duties and any law enforcement officer, fire official, or emergency management official of the United States or any other state while attending training in this state;

(5) The armed forces of the United States or of this state;

(6) Research or educational programs conducted by or on behalf of a college, university, or secondary school which have been authorized by the chief executive officer of such educational institution or his or her designee and which is conducted in accordance with the laws of the United States and of this state;

(7) The use of explosive materials in medicines and medicinal agents in forms prescribed by the most recent published edition of the official United States Pharmacopoeia or the National Formulary;

(8) Small arms ammunition and reloading components thereof;

(9) Commercially manufactured black powder in quantities not to exceed 50 pounds, percussion caps, safety and pyrotechnic fuses, quills, quick and slow matches, and friction primers intended to be used solely for sporting, recreational, or cultural purposes in antique firearms or antique devices; or

(10) An explosive which is lawfully possessed in accordance with the rules adopted pursuant to Code Section 16–7–94.

Laws 1996, p. 416, § 3.

§ 16–7–94. Exception as to agricultural activities

After consultation with the Commissioner of Agriculture or his or her designee, the Board of Public Safety may except by rule any explosive or quantity of explosive for use in legitimate agricultural activities. A copy of any such rule shall be furnished to the Commissioner of Agriculture.

Laws 1996, p. 416, § 3.

§ 16–7–95. Seizure and forfeiture of property

(a) All property which is subject to forfeiture pursuant to Code Section 16–13–49 which is, directly or indirectly, used or intended for use in any manner to facilitate a violation of this article or any proceeds derived or realized therefrom shall be considered contraband. Except as provided in subsection (b) of this Code section, such property may be seized and shall be forfeited to the state as provided in Code Section 16–13–49. A property interest shall not be subject to forfeiture under this Code section if the owner of such interest or interest holder establishes any of the provisions of subsection (e) of Code Section 16–13–49.

(b) On application of the seizing law enforcement agency, the superior court may authorize the seizing law enforcement agency to destroy or transfer to any agency of this state or of the United States which can safely store or render harmless any destructive device, explosive, poison gas, or detonator which is subject to forfeiture pursuant to this Code section if the court finds that it is impractical or unsafe for the seizing law enforcement agency to store such destructive device, explosive, poison gas, or detonator. Such application may be made at any time after seizure. Any destruction authorized pursuant to this subsection shall be made in the presence of at least one credible witness or shall be recorded on film, videotape, or other electronic imaging method. Any such film, videotape, or other electronic imaging method shall be admissible as evidence in lieu of such destructive device, explosive, poison gas, or detonator. The court may also direct the seizing agency or an agency to which such destructive device, explosive, poison gas, or detonator is transferred to make a report of the destruction, take samples, or both.

(c) The provisions of subsection (b) of this Code section shall not prohibit an explosive ordnance technician, other law enforcement officer, or fire service personnel from taking action which will render safe an explosive, destructive device, poison gas, or detonator or any object which is suspected of being an explosive, destructive device, poison gas, or detonator without the prior approval of a court when such action is intended to protect lives or property.

Laws 1996, p. 416, § 3; Laws 1997, p. 143, § 16; Laws 1997, p. 512, § 2.

§ 16–7–96. Evidence; photographs, videotapes, or other identification

(a) Photographs, videotapes, or other identification or analysis of a destructive device, explosive, poison gas, or detonator duly identified by an explosive ordnance disposal technician or a person qualified as a forensic expert in the area of destructive devices shall be admissible in any civil or criminal trial in lieu of the destructive device or detonator.

(b) If a destructive device, explosive, poison gas, or detonator which has been rendered safe is introduced into evidence in any criminal or civil action, it shall be the duty of the clerk of court immediately to photograph the same and to transfer custody of the destructive device or detonator to the director or his or her designee or an explosive ordnance disposal technician.

Laws 1996, p. 416, § 3.

§ 16–7–97. Exception as to fertilizers, propellant actuated devices or tools, and pesticides

The provisions of this article shall not apply to:

(1) Fertilizers, propellant actuated devices, or propellant activated industrial tools manufactured, imported, distributed, or used for their intended purposes; or

(2) A pesticide which is manufactured, stored, transported, distributed, possessed, or used in accordance with Chapter 7 of Title 2, the federal Insecticide, Fungicide, and Rodenticide Act, 61 Stat. 163, as amended, and the federal Environmental Pesticide Control Act of 1972, Pub. L. 92–516, as amended.[1]

Laws 1996, p. 416, § 3.

[1] 7 U.S.C.A. § 136 et seq.

CHAPTER 8

OFFENSES INVOLVING THEFT

Article 1

Article 2

Article 3

Article 4

Article 5

Article 1

Theft

§ 16–8–1. Definitions

As used in this article, the term:

(1) "Deprive" means, without justification:

(A) To withhold property of another permanently or temporarily; or

(B) To dispose of the property so as to make it unlikely that the owner will recover it.

(2) "Financial institution" means a bank, insurance company, credit union, building and loan association, investment trust, or other organization held out to the public as a place of deposit of funds or medium of savings or collective investment.

(3) "Property of another" includes property in which any person other than the accused has an interest but does not include property belonging to the spouse of an accused or to them jointly.

Laws 1968, p. 1249, § 1.

Formerly Code 1933, § 26–1801.

§ 16–8–2. Theft by taking

A person commits the offense of theft by taking when he unlawfully takes or, being in lawful possession thereof, unlawfully appropriates any property of another with the intention of depriving him of the property, regardless of the manner in which the property is taken or appropriated.

Laws 1833, Cobb's 1851 Digest, p. 791; Laws 1968, p. 1249, § 1; Laws 1974, p. 468, § 1; Laws 1975, p. 876, § 1; Laws 1978, p. 2257, § 1.

Formerly Code 1863, § 4290; Code 1868, § 4327; Code 1873, § 4393; Code 1882, § 4393; Penal Code 1895, § 155; Penal Code 1910, § 152; Code 1933, § 26–2602; Code 1933, § 26–1802.

§ 16–8–3. Theft by deception

(a) A person commits the offense of theft by deception when he obtains property by any deceitful means or artful practice with the intention of depriving the owner of the property.

(b) A person deceives if he intentionally:

(1) Creates or confirms another's impression of an existing fact or past event which is false and which the accused knows or believes to be false;

(2) Fails to correct a false impression of an existing fact or past event which he has previously created or confirmed;

(3) Prevents another from acquiring information pertinent to the disposition of the property involved;

(4) Sells or otherwise transfers or encumbers property intentionally failing to disclose a substantial and valid known lien, adverse claim, or other legal impediment to the enjoyment of the property, whether such impediment is or is not a matter of official record; or

(5) Promises performance of services which he does not intend to perform or knows will not be performed. Evidence of failure to perform standing alone shall not be sufficient to authorize a conviction under this subsection.

(c) "Deceitful means" and "artful practice" do not, however, include falsity as to matters having no pecuniary significance, or exaggeration by statements unlikely to deceive ordinary persons in the group addressed.

Laws 1968, p. 1249, § 1.

Formerly Code 1933, § 26–1803.

§ 16–8–4. Theft by conversion

(a) A person commits the offense of theft by conversion when, having lawfully obtained funds or other property of another including, but not limited to, leased or rented personal property, under an agreement or other known legal obligation to make a specified application of such funds or a specified disposition of such property, he knowingly converts the funds or property to his own use in violation of the agreement or legal obligation. This Code section applies whether the application or disposition is to be made from the funds or property of another or from the accused's own funds or property in equivalent amount when the agreement contemplates that the accused may deal with the funds or property of another as his own.

(b) When, under subsection (a) of this Code section, an officer or employee of a government or of a financial institution fails to pay on an account, upon lawful demand, from the funds or property of another held by him, he is presumed to have intended to convert the funds or property to his own use.

(c)(1) As used in this subsection, the term "personal property" means personal property having a replacement cost value greater than $ 100.00, excluding any late fees and penalties, and includes heavy equipment as defined in paragraph (2) of Code Section 10–1–731 and tractors and farm equipment primarily designed for use in agriculture.

(2) Any person having any personal property in such person's possession or under such person's control by virtue of a lease or rental agreement who fails to return the personal property within five days, Saturdays, Sundays, and holidays excluded, after a letter demanding return of the personal property has been mailed to such person by certified or registered mail or statutory overnight delivery, return receipt requested, at such person's last known address by the owner of the personal property or by the owner's agent shall be presumed to have knowingly converted such personal property to such person's own use in violation of such lease or agreement.

(3) In the event that any personal property is not returned as provided for in the lease or rental agreement and the court orders the lessor or renter to pay replacement costs, replacement costs shall include but not be limited to:

(A) The market value of the personal property. The market value shall be established by the owner of the property by providing from a supplier of such or reasonably similar personal property a current quotation of the value of the personal property which is of like quality, make, and model of the personal property being replaced. The value to be awarded shall be the higher of:

(i) The value on the date when the conversion occurred; or

(ii) The value on the date of the trial;

(B) All rental charges from the date the rental agreement was executed until the date of the trial or the date that the property was recovered, if recovered; and

(C) Interest on the unpaid balance each month at the current legal rate from the date the court orders the lessor or renter to pay replacement costs until the date the judgment is satisfied in full.

(4) If as a part of the order of the court the lessor or renter is placed on probation, supervision of said probation shall not be terminated until all replacement costs, fees, charges, penalties, interest, and other charges are paid in full. All payments relative to this Code section shall be made to the appropriate court of jurisdiction and the court shall make distribution to the owner within 30 days of receipt thereof.

(5) In the event that the owner incurs any expenses in the process of locating a lessor or renter who did not return any personal property according to the lease or rental agreement, the court shall provide that the lessor or renter reimburse the owner for those expenses which may include, but not be limited to, credit reports, private detective fees, investigation fees, fees charged by a law enforcement agency for such services as police reports, background checks, fees involved with swearing out a warrant for incarceration, and any other bona fide expenses.

Laws 1968, p. 1249, § 1; Laws 1969, p. 857, § 16; Laws 1988, p. 763, § 1; Laws 1994, p. 650, § 1; Laws 1997, p. 414, §§ 1, 2; Laws 2000, p. 1589, § 4.

Formerly Code 1933, § 26–1808.

Validity

This section has been held unconstitutional, in part, in the case of Sherrod v. State, 2006, 280 Ga. 275, 627 S.E.2d 36.

Historical and Statutory Notes

The 2000 amendment amendment substituted in subsec. (c)(2) "certified mail or statutory overnight delivery" for "certified mail".

§ 16–8–5. Theft of services

A person commits the offense of theft of services when by deception and with the intent to avoid payment he knowingly obtains services, accommodations, entertainment, or the use of personal property which is available only for compensation.

Laws 1968, p. 1249, § 1.

Formerly Code 1933, § 26–1807.

§ 16–8–5.1. Avoiding payment due for rental or lease of personal property; intent; agreements to delay payment

The trier of fact may infer that the accused intended to avoid payment due for the rental or lease of any personal property in any prosecution pursuant to Code Section 16–8–2, relating to theft by taking; 16–8–3, relating to theft by deception; 16–8–4, relating to theft by conversion; or 16–8–5, relating to theft of services; if a person knowingly:

(1) Used false identification;

(2) Provided false information on a written contract;

(3) Made, drew, uttered, executed, or delivered an instrument for the payment of money on any bank or other depository in exchange for present consideration, knowing that it would not be honored by the drawee;

(4) Abandoned any property at a location that is not the location agreed upon for return and that would not be reasonably known to the owner;

(5) Returned any property to a location that would not reasonably be known to the owner without notifying the owner; or

(6) Returned any property at a time beyond posted business hours of the owner.

No person shall be convicted under Code Section 16–8–2, relating to theft by taking; 16–8–3, relating to theft by deception; 16–8–4, relating to theft by conversion; or 16–8–5, relating to theft of services; where there was an agreement to delay payment for such property or services or the accused makes payment in full within two business days after returning the property or obtaining the services.

Laws 2005, Act 318, § 1, eff. July 1, 2005; Laws 2006, Act 453, § 16, eff. April 14, 2006.

Historical and Statutory Notes

The 2006 amendment by Act 453 was a provision contained in a correction bill.

§ 16–8–5.2. Retail property fencing; forfeiture of property

(a) As used in this Code section, the term:

(1) "Retail property" means any new article, product, commodity, item, or component intended to be sold in retail commerce.

(2) "Retail property fence" means a person or entity that buys, sells, transfers, or possesses with the intent to sell or transfer retail property that such person knows or should have known was stolen.

(3) "Value" means the retail value of the item as stated or advertised by the affected retail establishment, to include applicable taxes.

(b) A person commits the offense of retail property fencing when such persons receives, disposes of, or retains retail property which was unlawfully taken or shoplifted over a period not to exceed 180 days with the intent to:

(1) Transfer, sell, or distribute such retail property to a retail property fence; or

(2) Attempt or cause such retail property to be offered for sale, transfer, or distribution for money or other things of value.

(c) Whoever knowingly receives, possesses, conceals, stores, barters, sells, or disposes of retail property with the intent to distribute any retail property which is known or should be known to have been taken or stolen in violation of this subsection with the intent to distribute the proceeds, or to otherwise promote, manage, carry on, or facilitate an offense described in this subsection, shall have committed the offense of retail property fencing.

(d)(1) It shall not be necessary in any prosecution under this Code section for the state to prove that any intended profit was actually realized. The trier of fact may infer that a particular scheme or course of conduct was undertaken for profit from all of the attending circumstances.

(2) It shall not be a defense to violating this Code section that the property was obtained by means other than through the commission of a theft offense if the property was explicitly represented to the accused as being obtained through the commission of a theft.

(e) Any property constituting proceeds derived from or realized through a violation of this Code section shall be subject to forfeiture to the State of Georgia except that no property of any owner shall be forfeited under this subsection, to the extent of the interest of such owner, by reason of an act or omission established by such owner to have been committed or omitted without knowledge or consent of such owner. The procedure for forfeiture and disposition of forfeited property under this subsection shall be as provided for under Code Section 16–13–49.

(f) Each violation of this Code section shall constitute a separate offense.

Laws 2008, Act 581, § 1, eff. July 1, 2008.

§ 16–8–6. Theft of lost or mislaid property

A person commits the offense of theft of lost or mislaid property when he comes into control of property that he knows or learns to have been lost or mislaid and appropriates the property to his own use without first taking reasonable measures to restore the property to the owner.

Laws 1968, p. 1249, § 1.

Formerly Code 1933, § 26–1805.

§ 16–8–7. Theft by receiving stolen property

(a) A person commits the offense of theft by receiving stolen property when he receives, disposes of, or retains stolen property which he knows or should know was stolen unless the property is received, disposed of, or retained with intent to restore it to the owner. "Receiving" means acquiring possession or control or lending on the security of the property.

(b) In any prosecution under this Code section it shall not be necessary to show a conviction of the principal thief.

Laws 1833, Cobb's 1851 Digest, pp. 807, 808; Laws 1961, p. 118, § 1; Laws 1968, p. 1249, § 1; Laws 1969, p. 857, § 4.

Formerly Code 1863, §§ 4382, 4383; Code 1868, §§ 4420, 4421; Code 1873, §§ 4488, 4489; Code 1882, §§ 4488, 4489; Penal Code 1895, §§ 171, 172; Penal Code 1910, §§ 168, 169; Code 1933, §§ 26–2620, 26–2621; Code 1933, § 26–1806.

§ 16–8–8. Theft by receiving property stolen in another State

A person commits the offense of theft by receiving property stolen in another state when he receives, disposes of, or retains stolen property which he knows or should know was stolen in another state, unless the property is received, disposed of, or retained with intent to restore it to the owner.

Laws 1918, p. 272, § 1; Laws 1972, p. 841, § 2.

Formerly Code 1933, § 26–2623; Code 1933, § 26–1816.

§ 16–8–9. Theft by bringing stolen property into this State

A person commits the offense of theft by bringing stolen property into this state when he brings into this state any property which he knows or should know has been stolen in another state.

Laws 1918, p. 272, § 2; Laws 1972, p. 841, § 1.

Formerly Code 1933, § 26–2622; Code 1933, § 26–1815.

§ 16–8–10. Claim of right

It is an affirmative defense to a prosecution for violation of Code Sections 16–8–2 through 16–8–7 that the person:

(1) Was unaware that the property or service was that of another;

(2) Acted under an honest claim of right to the property or service involved or under a right to acquire or dispose of it as he did; or

(3) Took property or service exposed for sale intending to purchase and pay for it promptly or reasonably believing that the owner, if present, would have consented.

Laws 1968, p. 1249, § 1.

Formerly Code 1933, § 26–1810.

§ 16–8–11. Venue

In a prosecution under Code Sections 16–8–2 through 16–8–9 and 16–8–13 through 16–8–15, the crime shall be considered as having been committed in any county in which the accused exercised control over the property which was the subject of the theft. In addition, in any prosecution under Code Section 16–8–4 in which there is a written rental agreement for personal property, the crime shall also be considered to have been committed in the county in which the accused signed the rental agreement.

Laws 1968, p. 1249, § 1; Laws 1972, p. 841, § 3; Laws 1994, p. 650, § 2.

Formerly Code 1933, § 26–1811.

§ 16–8–12. Punishment

(a) A person convicted of a violation of Code Sections 16–8–2 through 16–8–9 shall be punished as for a misdemeanor except:

(1) If the property which was the subject of the theft exceeded $500.00 in value, by imprisonment for not less than one nor more than ten years or, in the discretion of the trial judge, as for a misdemeanor;

(2) If the property was any amount of anhydrous ammonia, as defined in Code Section 16–11–111, by imprisonment for not less than one nor more than ten years, a fine not to exceed the amount provided by Code Section 17–10–8, or both;

(3) If the property was taken by a fiduciary in breach of a fiduciary obligation or by an officer or employee of a government or a financial institution in breach of his or her duties as such officer or employee, by imprisonment for not less than one nor more than 15 years, a fine not to exceed the amount provided by Code Section 17–10–8, or both;

(4) If the crime committed was a violation of Code Section 16–8–2 and if the property which was the subject of the theft was a memorial to the dead or any ornamentation, flower, tree, or shrub placed on, adjacent to, or within any enclosure of a memorial to the dead, by imprisonment for not less than one nor more than three years. Nothing in this paragraph shall be construed as to cause action taken by a cemetery, cemetery owner, lessee, trustee, church, religious or fraternal organization, corporation, civic organization, or club legitimately attempting to clean, maintain, care for, upgrade, or beautify a grave, gravesite, tomb, monument, gravestone, or other structure or thing placed or designed for a memorial of the dead to be a criminal act;

(5)(A) The provisions of paragraph (1) of this subsection notwithstanding, if the property which was the subject of the theft was a motor vehicle or was a motor vehicle part or component which exceeded $100.00 in value or if the theft or unlawful activity was committed in violation of subsection (b) of Code Section 10–1–393.5 or in violation of subsection (b) of Code Section 10–1–393.6 or while engaged in telemarketing conduct in violation of Chapter 5B of Title 10, by imprisonment for not less than one nor more than ten years or, in the discretion of the trial judge, as for a misdemeanor; provided, however, that any person who is convicted of a second or subsequent offense under this paragraph shall be punished by imprisonment for not less than one year nor more than 20 years.

(B) Subsequent offenses committed under this paragraph, including those which may have been committed after prior felony convictions unrelated to this paragraph, shall be punished as provided in Code Section 17–10–7;

(6)(A) As used in this paragraph, the term:

(i) "Destructive device" means a destructive device as such term is defined by Code Section 16–7–80.

(ii) "Explosive" means an explosive as such term is defined by Code Section 16–7–80.

(iii) "Firearm" means any rifle, shotgun, pistol, or similar device which propels a projectile or projectiles through the energy of an explosive.

(B) If the property which was the subject of the theft offense was a destructive device, explosive, or firearm, by imprisonment for not less than one nor more than ten years;

(7) If the property which was the subject of the theft is a grave marker, monument, or memorial to one or more deceased persons who served in the military service of this state, the United States of America or any of the states thereof, or the Confederate States of America or any of the states thereof, or a monument, plaque, marker, or memorial which is dedicated to, honors, or recounts the military service of any past or present military personnel of this state, the United States of America or any of the states thereof, or the Confederate States of America or any of the states thereof, and if such grave marker, monument, memorial, plaque, or marker is privately owned or located on privately owned land, by imprisonment for not less than one nor more than three years if the value of the property which was the subject of the theft is $300.00 or less, and by imprisonment for not less than three years and not more than five years if the value of the property which was the subject of the theft is more than $300.00;

(8) If the property that was the subject of the theft was a vehicle engaged in commercial transportation of cargo or any appurtenance thereto, including without limitation any such trailer, semitrailer, container, or other associated equipment, or the cargo being transported therein or thereon, by imprisonment for not less than three years nor more than ten years, a fine not less than $5,000.00 nor more than $50,000.00, and, if applicable, the revocation of the defendant's commercial driver's license in accordance with Code Section 40–5–151, or any combination of such penalties. For purposes of this paragraph, the term "vehicle" includes without limitation any railcar; or

(9) Notwithstanding the provisions of paragraph (1) of this subsection, if the property of the theft was ferrous metals or regulated metal property, as such terms are defined in Code Section 10–1–350, and the sum of the aggregate amount of such property, in its original and undamaged condition, plus any reasonable costs which are or would be incurred in the repair or the attempt to recover any property damaged in the theft or removal of such regulated metal property, exceeds $500.00, by imprisonment for not less than one nor more than five years, a fine of not more than $5,000.00, or both.

(b) Except as otherwise provided in paragraph (5) of subsection (a) of this Code section, any person who commits the offense of theft by deception when the property which was the subject of the theft exceeded $500.00 in value and the offense was committed against a person who is 65 years of age or older shall, upon conviction thereof, be punished by imprisonment for not less than five nor more than ten years.

(c) Where a violation of Code Sections 16–8–2 through 16–8–9 involves the theft of a growing or otherwise unharvested commercial agricultural product which is being grown or produced as a crop, such offense shall be punished by a fine of not less than $500.00 and not more than the maximum fine otherwise authorized by law. This minimum fine shall not in any such case be subject to suspension, stay, or probation. This minimum fine shall not be required in any case in which a sentence of confinement is imposed and such sentence of confinement is not suspended, stayed, or probated; but this subsection shall not prohibit imposition of any otherwise authorized fine in such a case.

Laws 1968, p. 1249, § 1; Laws 1972, p. 841, § 4; Laws 1978, p. 1457, § 1; Laws 1981, p. 1552, § 1; Laws 1981, p. 1576, § 1; Laws 1982, p. 1371, § 2; Laws 1984, p. 900, § 3; Laws 1986, p. 1228, § 1; Laws 1992, p. 6, § 16; Laws 1994, p. 359, § 1; Laws 1996, p. 231, § 4; Laws 1996, p. 416, § 4; Laws 1997, p. 1507, § 4; Laws 1998, p. 643, § 5; Laws 2000, p. 1085, § 3; Laws 2001, p. 1153, § 2; Laws 2003, Act 29, § 1, eff. May 15, 2003; Laws 2004, Act 793, § 2, eff. July 1, 2004; Laws 2006, Act 545, § 1, eff. July 1, 2006; Laws 2007, Act 345, § 4, eff. July 1, 2007; Laws 2009, Act 150, § 4, eff. July 1, 2009.

Formerly Code 1933, § 26–1812.

Historical and Statutory Notes

The 2000 amendment to subsec. (a)(2) made the provision gender neutral and inserted at the end ", a fine not to exceed the amount provided by Code Section 17–10–8, or both".

The 2001 amendment added subsec. (a)(6).

The 2003 amendment by Act 29, in subsec. (a), substituted "16–8–2 through 16–8–9" for "16–8–2 to 16–8–9" in the introductory paragraph, inserted a new par. (2), and redesignated former pars. (2) through (6) as pars. (3) through (7); in subsec. (b), substituted a reference to paragraph (5) for a reference to paragraph (4); and in subsec. (c) substituted "16–8–2 through 16–8–9" for "16–8–2 to 16–8–9".

The 2004 amendment by Act 793, in subsec. (a), added par. (8).

The 2006 amendment by Act 545, in subsec. (a), par. (8), substituted "and, if applicable, the revocation of the defendant's commercial driver's license in accordance with Code Section 40–5–151, or any combination of such penalties" for "or both such fine and imprisonment".

The 2007 amendment by Act 345, in subsec. (a), added par. (9).

The 2009 amendment by Act 150, in subsec. (a), par. (9), inserted "sum of the" preceding "aggregate amount" and inserted ", plus any reasonable costs which are or would be incurred in the repair or the attempt to recover any property damaged in the theft or removal of such regulated metal property" preceding "exceeds $500.00".

§ 16–8–13. Theft of a trade secret

(a) As used in this Code section, the term:

(1) "Article" means any object, material, device, substance, or copy thereof, including any writing, record, recording, drawing, sample, specimen, prototype, model, photograph, microorganism, blueprint, or map.

(2) "Copy" means any facsimile, replica, photograph, or other reproduction of an article and any note, drawing, or sketch made of or from an article.

(3) "Representing" means describing, depicting, containing, constituting, reflecting, or recording.

(4) "Trade secret" means information, without regard to form, including, but not limited to, technical or nontechnical data, a formula, a pattern, a compilation, a program, a device, a method, a technique, a drawing, a process, financial data, financial plans, product plans, or a list of actual or potential customers or suppliers which is not commonly known by or available to the public and which information:

(A) Derives economic value, actual or potential, from not being generally known to, and not being readily ascertainable by proper means by, other persons who can obtain economic value from its disclosure or use; and

(B) Is the subject of efforts that are reasonable under the circumstances to maintain its secrecy.

(b) Any person who, with the intent to deprive or withhold from the owner thereof the exclusive use of a trade secret, or with an intent to appropriate a trade secret to his or her own use or to the use of another, does any of the following:

(1) Takes, uses, or discloses such trade secret to an unauthorized person;

(2) Acquires knowledge of such trade secret by deceitful means or artful practice; or

(3) Without authority, makes or causes to be made a copy of an article representing such trade secret

commits the offense of theft of a trade secret and, upon conviction thereof, shall be punished by imprisonment for not less than one nor more than five years and by a fine of not more than $50,000.00, provided that, if the value of such trade secret, and any article representing such trade secret that is taken, is not more than $100.00 such person shall be punished as for a misdemeanor.

(c) In a prosecution for any violation of this Code section, a court shall preserve the secrecy of an alleged trade secret by reasonable means, which may include granting protective orders in connection with discovery proceedings, holding in camera hearings, sealing the records of the action, and ordering any person involved in the litigation not to disclose an alleged trade secret without prior court approval.

(d) For the purposes of this Code section, a continuing theft by any person constitutes a single claim against that person, but this Code section shall be applied separately to the claim against each person who receives a trade secret from another person who committed the theft.

(e) This Code section shall not affect:

(1) Contractual duties or remedies, whether or not based on theft of a trade secret; or

(2) The provisions of Code Sections 10–1–761 through 10–1–767, pertaining to civil offenses and remedies involving the misappropriation of a trade secret, or other civil or criminal laws that presently apply or in the future may apply to any transaction or course of conduct that violates this Code section.

Laws 1965, p. 647, §§ 1, 2; Laws 1966, p. 425, §§ 1, 2, 5; Laws 1968, p. 1249, § 1; Laws 1992, p. 6, § 16; Laws 1995, p. 1051, § 1.

Formerly Code 1933, § 26–1809.

§ 16–8–14. Theft by shoplifting

(a) A person commits the offense of theft by shoplifting when he alone or in concert with another person, with the intent of appropriating merchandise to his own use without paying for the same or to deprive the owner of possession thereof or of the value thereof, in whole or in part, does any of the following:

(1) Conceals or takes possession of the goods or merchandise of any store or retail establishment;

(2) Alters the price tag or other price marking on goods or merchandise of any store or retail establishment;

(3) Transfers the goods or merchandise of any store or retail establishment from one container to another;

(4) Interchanges the label or price tag from one item of merchandise with a label or price tag for another item of merchandise; or

(5) Wrongfully causes the amount paid to be less than the merchant's stated price for the merchandise.

(b)(1) A person convicted of the offense of theft by shoplifting, as provided in subsection (a) of this Code section, when the property which was the subject of the theft is $ 300.00 or less in value shall be punished as for a misdemeanor; provided, however, that:

(A) Upon conviction of a second offense for shoplifting, where the first offense is either a felony or a misdemeanor, as defined by this Code section, in addition to or in lieu of any imprisonment which might be imposed, the defendant shall be fined not less than $ 250.00 and the fine shall not be suspended or probated;

(B) Upon conviction of a third offense for shoplifting, where the first two offenses are either felonies or misdemeanors, or a combination of a felony and a misdemeanor, as defined by this Code section, in addition to or in lieu of any fine which might be imposed, the defendant shall be punished by imprisonment for not less than 30 days or confinement in a "special alternative incarceration-probation boot camp," probation detention center, diversion center, or other community correctional facility of the Department of Corrections for a period of 120 days or shall be sentenced to monitored house arrest for a period of 120 days and, in addition to either such types of confinement, may be required to undergo psychological evaluation and treatment to be paid for by the defendant; and such sentence of imprisonment or confinement shall not be suspended, probated, deferred, or withheld; and

(C) Upon conviction of a fourth or subsequent offense for shoplifting, where the prior convictions are either felonies or misdemeanors, or any combination of felonies and misdemeanors, as defined by this Code section, the defendant commits a felony and shall be punished by imprisonment for not less than one nor more than ten years; and the first year of such sentence shall not be suspended, probated, deferred, or withheld.

(2) A person convicted of the offense of theft by shoplifting, as provided in subsection (a) of this Code section, when the property which was the subject of the theft exceeds $ 300.00 in value commits a felony and shall be punished by imprisonment for not less than one nor more than ten years.

(3) A person convicted of the offense of theft by shoplifting, as provided in subsection (a) of this Code section, when the property which was the subject of the theft is taken from three separate stores or retail establishments within one county during a period of seven days or less and when the property which was the subject of each theft exceeds $ 100.00 in value, commits a felony and shall be punished by imprisonment for not less than one nor more than ten years.

(c) In all cases involving theft by shoplifting, the term "value" means the actual retail price of the property at the time and place of the offense. The unaltered price tag or other marking on property, or duly identified photographs thereof, shall be prima-facie evidence of value and ownership of the property.

(d) Subsection (b) of this Code section shall in no way affect the authority of a sentencing judge to provide for a sentence to be served on weekends or during the nonworking hours of the defendant as provided in Code Section 17–10–3, relative to punishment for misdemeanors.

Laws 1957, p. 115, §§ 1, 3; Laws 1978, p. 2257, § 2; Laws 1983, p. 457, § 1; Laws 1997, p. 1394, § 1; Laws 1998, p. 578, § 1; Laws 2000, p. 870, § 1.

Formerly Code 1933, § 26–1802.1.

Historical and Statutory Notes

The 2000 amendment added subsec. (b)(3).

§ 16–8–15. Theft by conversion of payments for property improvements

(a) Any architect, landscape architect, engineer, contractor, subcontractor, or other person who with intent to defraud shall use the proceeds of any payment made to him on account of improving certain real property for any other purpose than to pay for labor or service performed on or materials furnished by his order for this specific improvement while any amount for which he may be or become liable for such labor, services, or materials remains unpaid commits a felony and, upon conviction thereof, shall be punished by imprisonment for not less than one year nor more than five years or upon the recommendation of the jury or in the discretion of the trial judge, punished for a misdemeanor, provided that, in addition to the above sanctions, where a corporation's agent acts within the scope of his office or employment and on behalf of the corporation and with intent to defraud uses such proceeds for purposes other than for property improvements or where a corporation's board of directors or managerial official, the latter acting within the scope of his employment and on behalf of the corporation recklessly tolerates or, with intent to defraud, authorizes, requests, or commands the use of such proceeds for purposes other than for property improvements, the corporation commits a felony and, upon conviction thereof, shall be punished by a fine of not less than $1,000.00 nor more than $5,000.00.

(b) A failure to pay for material or labor furnished for such property improvements shall be prima-facie evidence of intent to defraud.

Laws 1941, p. 480, § 1; Laws 1976, p. 1456, § 1; Laws 1982, p. 3, § 16.

Formerly Code 1933, § 26–1808.1.

§ 16–8–16. Theft by extortion

(a) A person commits the offense of theft by extortion when he unlawfully obtains property of or from another person by threatening to:

(1) Inflict bodily injury on anyone or commit any other criminal offense;

(2) Accuse anyone of a criminal offense;

(3) Disseminate any information tending to subject any person to hatred, contempt, or ridicule or to impair his credit or business repute;

(4) Take or withhold action as a public official or cause an official to take or withhold action;

(5) Bring about or continue a strike, boycott, or other collective unofficial action if the property is not demanded or received for the benefit of the group in whose interest the actor purports to act; or

(6) Testify or provide information or withhold testimony or information with respect to another's legal claim or defense.

(b) In a prosecution under this Code section, the crime shall be considered as having been committed in the county in which the threat was made or received or in the county in which the property was unlawfully obtained.

(c) It is an affirmative defense to prosecution based on paragraph (2), (3), (4), or (6) of subsection (a) of this Code section that the property obtained by threat of accusation, exposure, legal action, or other invocation of official action was honestly claimed as restitution or indemnification for harm done in the circumstance to which such accusation, exposure, legal action, or other official action relates or as compensation for property or lawful services.

(d) A person convicted of the offense of theft by extortion shall be punished by imprisonment for not less than one nor more than ten years.

Laws 1968, p. 1249, § 1; Laws 1992, p. 6, § 16.

Formerly Code 1933, § 26–1804.

§ 16–8–17. Theft resulting from unlawful use of retail sales receipts or Universal Product Code labels

(a)(1) Except as provided in paragraph (2) of this subsection, a person who, with intent to cheat or defraud a retailer, possesses, uses, utters, transfers, makes, alters, counterfeits, or reproduces a retail sales receipt or a Universal Product Code label which results in a theft of property which exceeds $ 300.00 in value commits a felony and shall be punished by imprisonment for not less than one nor more than three years or by a fine or both.

(2) A person convicted of a violation of paragraph (1) of this subsection, when the property which was the subject of the theft resulting from the unlawful use of retail sales receipts or Universal Product Code labels is taken from three separate stores or retail establishments within one county during a period of seven days or less and when the property which was the subject of each theft exceeds $ 100.00 in value, commits a felony and shall be punished by imprisonment for not less than one nor more than ten years.

(b) A person who, with intent to cheat or defraud a retailer, possesses 15 or more fraudulent retail sales receipts or Universal Product Code labels or possesses a device the purpose of which is to manufacture fraudulent retail sales receipts or Universal Product Code labels will be guilty of a felony and punished by imprisonment for not less than one nor more than ten years.

Laws 2000, p. 870, § 2; Laws 2001, p. 4, § 16.

Historical and Statutory Notes

The 2001 amendment modified language correctively.

§ 16–8–18. Entering automobile

If any person shall enter any automobile or other motor vehicle with the intent to commit a theft or a felony, he shall be guilty of a felony and, upon conviction thereof, shall be punished by imprisonment for not less than one nor more than five years, or, in the discretion of the trial judge, as for a misdemeanor.

Laws 1933, p. 111, § 1; Laws 1976, p. 186, § 1.

Formerly Code 1933, § 26–2637; Code 1933, § 26–1813.1.

§ 16–8–19. Repealed by Laws 1988, p. 763, § 2, eff. July 1, 1988

§ 16–8–20. Livestock theft

(a) A person commits the offense of livestock theft when he unlawfully takes or, being in lawful possession thereof, unlawfully appropriates any livestock of another with the intention of depriving the owner of such livestock.

(b) For the purposes of this Code section, the term "livestock" means horses, cattle, swine, sheep, goats, rabbits, and any domestic animal produced as food for human consumption.

(c) Any person committing the offense of livestock theft commits a felony and, upon conviction thereof, shall be punished by imprisonment for not less than one nor more than ten years and by a fine of $1,000.00; provided, however, that, if the fair market value of the livestock taken or appropriated is $100.00 or less, the person shall be guilty of a misdemeanor.

(d) For the purposes of this Code section, if any livestock is killed or mutilated and a portion thereof taken, the value of the whole animal while alive or his entire carcass, whichever is greater, shall be considered for the purpose of distinguishing between a misdemeanor offense and a felony offense.

Laws 1974, p. 1006, § 1; Laws 1995, p. 244, § 10; Laws 2008, Act 534, § 7, eff. May 12, 2008.

Formerly Code 1933, § 26–1817.

Historical and Statutory Notes

Laws 2008, Act 534, § 7, in subsec. (b), removed ratites from the scope of the subsection.

§ 16–8–21. Removal, larceny, or abandonment of shopping carts; penalties

(a) As used in this Code section, "shopping cart" means those pushcarts of the type which are commonly provided by grocery stores, drugstores, or other merchant stores or markets for the use of the public in transporting commodities in stores and markets and incidentally from the store to a place outside the store.

(b) It shall be unlawful for any person to remove a shopping cart from the premises, posted as provided in subsection (d) of this Code section, of the owner of such shopping cart without the consent, given at the time of such removal, of the owner or of his agent, servant, or employee. For the purpose of this Code section, the premises shall include all the parking area set aside by the owner or on behalf of the owner for the parking of cars for the convenience of the patrons of the owner.

(c) It shall be unlawful for any person to abandon a shopping cart upon any public street, sidewalk, way, or parking lot other than a parking lot on the premises of the owner.

(d) The owner of the store in which the shopping cart is used shall post in at least three prominent places in his store and at each exit therefrom a printed copy of this Code section, which copy shall be printed in type no smaller than 12 points.

(e) Any person who violates subsection (b) or (c) of this Code section shall be guilty of a misdemeanor.

Laws 1975, p. 848, § 1.

Article 2

Robbery

§ 16–8–40. Robbery

(a) A person commits the offense of robbery when, with intent to commit theft, he takes property of another from the person or the immediate presence of another:

(1) By use of force;

(2) By intimidation, by the use of threat or coercion, or by placing such person in fear of immediate serious bodily injury to himself or to another; or

(3) By sudden snatching.

(b) A person convicted of the offense of robbery shall be punished by imprisonment for not less than one nor more than 20 years.

(c) Notwithstanding any other provision of this Code section, any person who commits the offense of robbery against a person who is 65 years of age or older shall, upon conviction thereof, be punished by imprisonment for not less than five nor more than 20 years.

Laws 1833, Cobb's 1851 Digest, p. 791; Laws 1903, p. 43, § 1; Laws 1957, p. 261, § 1; Laws 1968, p. 1249, § 1; Laws 1984, p. 900, § 4.

Formerly Code 1863, § 4286; Code 1868, § 4323; Code 1873, § 4389; Code 1882, § 4389; Penal Code 1895, § 151; Penal Code 1910, § 148; Code 1933, § 26–2501; Code 1933, § 26–1901.

§ 16–8–41. Armed robbery; robbery by intimidation

(a) A person commits the offense of armed robbery when, with intent to commit theft, he or she takes property of another from the person or the immediate presence of another by use of an offensive weapon, or any replica, article, or device having the appearance of such weapon. The offense of robbery by intimidation shall be a lesser included offense in the offense of armed robbery.

(b) A person convicted of the offense of armed robbery shall be punished by death or imprisonment for life or by imprisonment for not less than ten nor more than 20 years.

(c)(1) The preceding provisions of this Code section notwithstanding, in any case in which the defendant commits armed robbery and in the course of the commission of the offense such person unlawfully takes a controlled substance from a pharmacy or a wholesale druggist and intentionally inflicts bodily injury upon any person, such facts shall be charged in the indictment or accusation and, if found to be true by the court or if admitted by the defendant, the defendant shall be punished by imprisonment for not less than 15 years.

(2) As used in this subsection, the term:

(A) "Controlled substance" means a drug, substance, or immediate precursor in Schedules I through V of Code Sections 16–13–25 through 16–13–29.

(B) "Pharmacy" means any place licensed in accordance with Chapter 4 of Title 26 wherein the possessing, displaying, compounding, dispensing, or retailing of drugs may be conducted, including any and all portions of any building or structure leased, used, or controlled by the licensee in the conduct of the business licensed by the State Board of Pharmacy at the address for which the license was issued. The term pharmacy shall also include any building, warehouse, physician's office, or hospital used in whole or in part for the sale, storage, or dispensing of any controlled substance.

(C) "Wholesale druggist" means an individual, partnership, corporation, or association registered with the State Board of Pharmacy under Chapter 4 of Title 26.

(d) Any person convicted under this Code section shall, in addition, be subject to the sentencing and punishment provisions of Code Sections 17–10–6.1 and 17–10–7.

Laws 1833, Cobb's 1851 Digest, p. 791; Laws 1858, p. 98, § 1; Laws 1890–91, p. 83, § 1; Laws 1937, p. 490, § 1; Laws 1957, p. 261, §§ 2, 3; Laws 1968, p. 1249, § 1; Laws 1969, p. 810, § 1; Laws 1976, p. 1359, § 1; Laws 1981, p. 1266, § 1; Laws 1985, p. 1036, § 1; Laws 1994, p. 1959, § 3; Laws 1999, p. 81, § 16.

Formerly Code 1863, §§ 4287, 4288; Code 1868, §§ 4324, 4325; Code 1873, §§ 4390, 4391; Code 1882, §§ 4390, 4391; Penal Code 1895, §§ 152, 153; Penal Code 1910, §§ 149, 150; Code 1933, §§ 26–2502, 26–2503; Code 1933, § 26–1902.

Article 3

Criminal Reproduction and Sale of Recorded Material

§ 16–8–60. Recorded material; unauthorized reproductions, manufacture, distribution and sale

(a) It is unlawful for any person, firm, partnership, corporation, or association knowingly to:

(1) Transfer or cause to be transferred any sounds or visual images recorded on a phonograph record, disc, wire, tape, videotape, film, or other article on which sounds or visual images are recorded onto any other phonograph record, disc, wire, tape, videotape, film, or article without the consent of the person who owns the master phonograph record, master disc, master tape, master videotape, master film, or other device or article from which the sounds or visual images are derived; or

(2) Sell; distribute; circulate; offer for sale, distribution, or circulation; possess for the purpose of sale, distribution, or circulation; cause to be sold, distributed, or circulated; cause to be offered for sale, distribution, or circulation; or cause to be possessed for sale, distribution, or circulation any article or device on which sounds or visual images have been transferred, knowing it to have been made without the consent of the person who owns the master phonograph record, master disc, master tape, master videotape, master film, or other device or article from which the sounds or visual images are derived.

(b) It is unlawful for any person, firm, partnership, corporation, or association to sell; distribute; circulate; offer for sale, distribution, or circulation; or possess for the purposes of sale, distribution, or circulation any phonograph record, disc, wire, tape, videotape, film, or other article on which sounds or visual images have been transferred unless such phonograph record, disc, wire, tape, videotape, film, or other article bears the actual name and address of the transferor of the sounds or visual images in a prominent place on its outside face or package.

(c) This Code section shall not apply to any person who transfers or causes to be transferred any such sounds or visual images:

(1) Intended for or in connection with radio or television broadcast transmission or related uses;

(2) For archival purposes; or

(3) Solely for the personal use of the person transferring or causing the transfer and without any profit being derived by the person from the transfer.

(d) Every person convicted of violating this Code section shall be guilty of a felony and shall be punished as follows:

(1) Upon the first conviction of violating this Code section, by a fine of not less than $500.00 nor more than $25,000.00, by imprisonment for not less than one year nor more than two years, or both such fine and imprisonment;

(2) Upon the second conviction of violating this Code section, by a fine of not less than $1,000.00 nor more than $100,000.00, by imprisonment for not less than one year nor more than three years and the judge may suspend, stay, or probate all but 48 hours of any term of imprisonment, or both such fine and imprisonment; or

(3) Upon the third or subsequent conviction of violating this Code section, by a fine of not less than $2,000.00 nor more than $250,000.00, by imprisonment for not less than two nor more than five years and the judge may suspend, stay, or probate all but six days of any term of imprisonment, or both such fine and imprisonment.

(e) This Code section shall neither enlarge nor diminish the right of parties to enter into a private contract.

(f)(1) Any phonograph record, disc, wire, tape, videotape, film, or other article onto which sounds or visual images have been transferred shall be subject to forfeiture to the State of Georgia except that no property of any owner shall be forfeited under this paragraph, to the extent of the interest of such owner, by reason of an act or omission established by such owner to have been committed or omitted without knowledge or consent of such owner.

(2) The procedure for forfeiture and disposition of forfeited property under this subsection shall be as provided for under Code Section 16–13–49.

(g) For purposes of imposing restitution pursuant to Chapter 14 of Title 17 when a person is convicted pursuant to this Code section, the court shall consider damages to any owner or lawful producer of a master phonograph record, master disc, master tape, master videotape, master film, or other device or article from which sounds or visual images are derived. Restitution shall be based upon the aggregate wholesale value of lawfully manufactured and authorized recorded devices corresponding to the nonconforming recorded devices involved in the violation of this Code section and shall also include reasonable investigative costs related to the detection of the violation of this Code section.

Laws 1975, p. 44, § 1; Laws 1978, p. 1938, § 1; Laws 1986, p. 652, § 1; Laws 1988, p. 13, § 16; Laws 2008, Act 448, § 1, eff. July 1, 2008.

Historical and Statutory Notes

The 2008 amendment by Act 448, in subsec. (c), substituted "shall not" for "does not"; rewrote subsec. (d); and added subsecs. (f) and (g). Prior to revision subsec. (d) read:

"(d) Violation of this Code section is a felony and is punishable upon conviction by a fine of not more than $25,000.00 or by imprisonment for not less than one year nor more than two years, or both fine and imprisonment; second or subsequent violations of this Code section shall be punishable upon conviction by a fine of not more than $100,000.00 or by imprisonment for not less than one year nor more than three years, or both fine and imprisonment."

§ 16-8-61. Sale, rental, loan, etc. of video movies unlawful unless official rating prominently displayed on covering

(a) As used in this Code section, the term:

(1) "Official rating" means the official rating of a motion picture by the Classification and Rating Administration of the Motion Picture Association of America.

(2) "Video movie" means a videotape, video cassette, video disc, any prerecorded video display or visual depiction, any prerecorded device that can be converted to a visual depiction, or other reproduction or reconstruction of a motion picture.

(b) No person may sell, rent, loan, or otherwise disseminate or distribute for monetary consideration a video movie unless the official rating of the motion picture from which the video movie is copied is clearly and prominently displayed in boldface type on the outside of the cassette, case, jacket, or other covering containing the video movie. Such video movie shall be clearly and prominently marked as "not rated" if:

(1) The motion picture from which the video movie is copied has no official rating;

(2) The official rating of the motion picture from which the video movie is copied is not readily available to such person; or

(3) The video movie has been altered so that its content materially differs from the motion picture.

(c) Any person who violates subsection (b) of this Code section shall, upon conviction thereof, be punished by a fine of not more than $100.00.

Laws 1987, p. 1384, § 1.

§ 16-8-62. Film piracy; violations and penalties

(a) As used in this Code section, the term:

(1) "Audiovisual recording device" means any device capable of recording or transmitting a motion picture, or any part thereof, using any technology now known or later developed.

(2) "Facility" shall not include a personal residence.

(b) Any person who knowingly operates the recording function of an audiovisual recording device while a motion picture is being exhibited, without the consent of the owner, operator, or lessee of the exhibition facility and of the licensor of the motion picture being exhibited, shall be guilty of film piracy.

(c) The provisions of this Code section shall not be construed to prevent any lawfully authorized investigative, law enforcement, or intelligence personnel of the state or federal government from operating any audiovisual recording device in a facility where a motion picture is being exhibited as part of their official duties or activities.

(d) This Code section is not applicable to a person who operates an audiovisual recording device in a retail establishment solely to demonstrate the use of the device for sales purposes.

(e) A prosecution under this Code section shall not preclude obtaining any other civil or criminal remedy under any other provision of law.

(f) Violation of this Code section is a misdemeanor of a high and aggravated nature and punishable upon conviction as provided in Code Section 17-10-4. A second or subsequent conviction for violation of this Code section shall be punishable as a felony.

Laws 2004, Act 663, § 1, eff. July 1, 2004.

Article 4

Motor Vehicle Chop Shops and Stolen and Altered Property

§ 16-8-80. Short title

This article shall be known and may be cited as the "Motor Vehicle Chop Shop and Stolen and Altered Property Act."

Laws 1991, p. 1805, § 1.

§ 16-8-81. Legislative intent

(a) The General Assembly finds and declares the following:

(1) The annual number of reported motor vehicle thefts has exceeded 1 million. Approximately 50 percent of all larcenies reported to law enforcement authorities in the United States are directed against motor vehicles. The recovery rate of stolen motor vehicles has decreased significantly during the most recent decade;

(2) Thefts of motor vehicles and the disposition of stolen motor vehicles and motor vehicle parts are becoming more professional in nature. Such theft and disposition activities have attracted criminal elements which have used intimidation and violence as a means of obtaining increased control of such activities;

(3) The theft of motor vehicles has brought increased and unnecessary burdens to motor vehicle users and taxpayers, as the national financial cost of motor vehicle related theft offenses currently approaches $5 billion annually;

(4) Prosecutors should give increased emphasis to the prosecution of persons committing motor vehicle thefts, with particular emphasis given to professional motor vehicle theft operations and to persons engaged in the dismantling of stolen motor vehicles for the purpose of trafficking in stolen motor vehicle parts; and

(5) Traditional law enforcement strategies and techniques that concentrate on bringing criminal penalties to bear on motor vehicle thieves, but do not focus on chop shops that are heavily involved in the dismantling of stolen motor vehicles or the distribution of motor vehicle parts and that do not enlist the assistance of private enforcement and use civil sanctions, are inadequate to control motor vehicle theft, as well as related offenses. Comprehensive strategies must be formulated; more effective law enforcement techniques must be developed; evidentiary, procedural, and substantive laws must be strengthened; and criminal penalties and civil sanctions must be enhanced.

(b) The General Assembly, therefore, concludes that for the protection of the general public interest, the "Motor Vehicle

Chop Shop and Stolen and Altered Property Act" shall be enacted.

Laws 1991, p. 1805, § 1.

§ 16-8-82. Definitions

As used in this article, the term:

(1) "Chop shop" means any building, lot, or other premise where one or more persons knowingly engage in altering, destroying, disassembling, dismantling, reassembling, or storing any motor vehicle or motor vehicle part known to be illegally obtained by theft, fraud, or conspiracy to defraud in order to either:

(A) Alter, counterfeit, deface, destroy, disguise, falsify, forge, obliterate, or remove the identification, including the vehicle identification number of such motor vehicle or motor vehicle part, in order to misrepresent the identity of such motor vehicle or motor vehicle part or to prevent the identification of such motor vehicle or motor vehicle part; or

(B) Sell or dispose of such motor vehicle or motor vehicle part.

(2) "Motor vehicle" includes every device in, upon, or by which any person or property is or may be transported or drawn upon a highway which is self-propelled or which may be connected to and towed by a self-propelled device and also includes any and all other land based devices which are self-propelled but which are not designed for use upon a highway, including, but not limited to, farm machinery and construction equipment.

(3) "Person" includes a natural person, company, corporation, unincorporated association, partnership, professional corporation, and any other legal entity.

(4) "Unidentifiable" means that the uniqueness of a motor vehicle or motor vehicle part cannot be established by either expert law enforcement investigative personnel specially trained and experienced in motor vehicle theft investigative procedures and motor vehicle identification examination techniques or by expert employees of not for profit motor vehicle theft prevention agencies specially trained and experienced in motor vehicle theft investigation procedures and motor vehicle identification examination techniques.

(5) "Vehicle identification number" includes, but is not limited to, a number or numbers, a letter or letters, a character or characters, a datum or data, a derivative or derivatives, or a combination or combinations thereof, used by the manufacturer or the Department of Revenue for the purpose of uniquely identifying a motor vehicle or motor vehicle part.

Laws 1991, p. 1805, § 1; Laws 2002, p. 415, § 16; Laws 2003, Act 9, § 16, eff. May 14, 2003; Laws 2005, Act 68, § 6-1, eff. July 1, 2005.

Historical and Statutory Notes

The 2002 amendment to par. (5) substituted for "Revenue" the words "Motor Vehicle Safety".

The 2003 amendment by Act 9, in par. (4), substituted "not for profit" for "not-for-profit".

The 2005 amendment by Act 68, in par. (5), substituted "Department of Revenue" for "Department of Motor Vehicle Safety".

§ 16-8-83. Offenses and penalties

(a) Any person who knowingly and with intent:

(1) Owns, operates, or conducts a chop shop;

(2) Transports any motor vehicle or motor vehicle part to or from a location knowing it to be a chop shop; or

(3) Sells, transfers, purchases, or receives any motor vehicle or motor vehicle part either to or from a location knowing it to be a chop shop

shall be guilty of a felony and, upon conviction thereof, shall be punished by imprisonment for not less than three years nor more than ten years, by a fine of not more than $100,000.00, or by both such fine and imprisonment.

(b) Any person who knowingly alters, counterfeits, defaces, destroys, disguises, falsifies, forges, obliterates, or removes a vehicle identification number with the intent to misrepresent the identity or prevent the identification of a motor vehicle or motor vehicle part shall be guilty of a felony and, upon conviction thereof, shall be punished by imprisonment for not less than one year nor more than ten years, by a fine of not more than $50,000.00, or by both such fine and imprisonment.

(c)(1) Any person who buys, disposes, sells, transfers, or possesses a motor vehicle or motor vehicle part with knowledge that the vehicle identification number of the motor vehicle or motor vehicle part has been altered, counterfeited, defaced, destroyed, disguised, falsified, forged, obliterated, or removed shall be guilty of a felony and, upon conviction thereof, shall be punished by imprisonment for not less than one year nor more than ten years, by a fine of not more than $50,000.00, or by both such fine and imprisonment.

(2) The provisions of paragraph (1) of this subsection shall not apply to a motor vehicle scrap processor who, in the normal legal course of business and in good faith, processes a motor vehicle or motor vehicle part by crushing, compacting, or other similar methods, provided that any vehicle identification number is not removed from the motor vehicle or motor vehicle part prior to or during any such processing.

(3) The provisions of paragraph (1) of this subsection shall not apply to any owner or authorized possessor of a motor vehicle recovered by law enforcement authorities after having been stolen or where the condition of the vehicle identification number of the motor vehicle or motor vehicle part is known to or has been reported to law enforcement authorities. It shall be presumed that law enforcement authorities have knowledge of all vehicle identification numbers on a motor vehicle or motor vehicle part which are altered, counterfeited, defaced, disguised, falsified, forged, obliterated, or removed when law enforcement authorities deliver or return the motor vehicle or motor vehicle part to its owner or authorized possessor after it has been recovered by law enforcement authorities after having been reported stolen.

(d) A person commits the offense of attempted operation of a chop shop when, with the intent to commit a violation proscribed by subsection (a), (b), or (c) of this Code section, the person does any act which constitutes a substantial step toward the commission of a violation proscribed by subsection (a), (b), or (c) of this Code section; and such person shall be guilty of a felony and, upon conviction thereof, shall be punished by imprisonment for not less than one year nor more than five years, by a fine of not more than $25,000.00, or by both such fine and imprisonment.

(e) A person commits the offense of conspiracy when, with the intent that a violation proscribed by subsection (a), (b), or (c) of this Code section be committed, the person agrees with another to the commission of a violation proscribed by subsection (a), (b), or (c) of this Code section; and such person shall be guilty of a felony and, upon conviction thereof, shall be punished by imprisonment for not less than one year nor more than five years, by a fine of not more than $25,000.00, or by both such fine and imprisonment. No person may be convicted of conspiracy under this subsection unless an act in furtherance of such agreement is alleged and proved to have been committed by that person or a coconspirator.

(f) A person commits the offense of solicitation when, with the intent that a violation proscribed by subsection (a), (b), or (c) of this Code section be committed, the person commands, encourages, or requests another to commit a violation proscribed by subsection (a), (b), or (c) of this Code section; and such person shall be guilty of a felony and, upon conviction thereof, shall be punished by imprisonment for not less than one year nor more than five years, by a fine of not more than $25,000.00, or by both such fine and imprisonment.

(g) A person commits the offense of aiding and abetting when, either before or during the commission of a violation proscribed by subsection (a), (b), or (c) of this Code section and with the intent to promote or facilitate such commission, the person aids, abets, agrees, or attempts to aid another in the planning or commission of a violation proscribed by subsection (a), (b), or (c) of this Code section; and such person shall be guilty of a felony and, upon conviction thereof, shall be punished by imprisonment for not less than one year nor more than five years, by a fine of not more than $25,000.00, or by both such fine and imprisonment.

(h) A person is an accessory after the fact who maintains, assists, or gives any other aid to an offender while knowing or having reasonable grounds to believe the offender has committed a violation under subsection (a), (b), or (c) of this Code section; and such person shall be guilty of a felony and, upon conviction thereof, shall be punished by imprisonment for not less than one year nor more than five years, by a fine of not more than $25,000.00, or by both such fine and imprisonment.

(i) No prosecution shall be brought and no person shall be convicted of any violation under this Code section where the acts of such person otherwise constituting a violation were done in good faith in order to comply with the laws or regulations of any state or territory of the United States or of the United States government.

(j) The sentence imposed upon a person convicted of any violation of this Code section shall not be reduced to less than one year of imprisonment for a second conviction or less than five years for a third or subsequent conviction, and no sentence imposed upon a person for a second or subsequent conviction of any violation of this Code section shall be suspended or reduced until such person shall have served the minimum period of imprisonment provided for in this Code section. A person convicted of a second or subsequent violation of this Code section shall not be eligible for probation, parole, furlough, or work release.

(k)(1) In addition to any other punishment, a person who violates this Code section shall be ordered to make restitution to the lawful owner or owners of the stolen motor vehicle or vehicles or the stolen motor vehicle part or parts, to the owner's insurer to the extent that the owner has been compensated by the insurer, and to any other person for any financial loss sustained as a result of a violation of this Code section.

(2) For purposes of this Code section, the term:

(A) "Financial loss" shall include, but not be limited to, loss of earnings, out-of-pocket and other expenses, repair and replacement costs, and claims payments.

(B) "Lawful owner" shall include an innocent bona fide purchaser for value of a stolen motor vehicle or motor vehicle part who does not know that the motor vehicle or part is stolen or an insurer to the extent that such insurer has compensated a bona fide purchaser for value.

(3) The court shall determine the extent and method of restitution required under this subsection. In an extraordinary case, the court may determine that the best interests of the victim and justice would not be served by ordering restitution. In any such case, the court shall make and enter specific written findings on the record concerning the extraordinary circumstances presented which mitigated against restitution.

Laws 1991, p. 1805, § 1; Laws 1992, p. 6, § 16.

§ 16–8–84. Seizure of motor vehicle, motor vehicle part, tool, implement, or instrumentality used or possessed in violation of law

(a) Any tool, implement, or instrumentality, including, but not limited to, a motor vehicle or motor vehicle part, used or possessed in connection with any violation of Code Section 16–8–83 may be seized by a member of a state or local law enforcement agency upon process issued by any court of competent jurisdiction.

(b) Seizure of property described in subsection (a) of this Code section may be made by a member of a state or local law enforcement agency without process if:

(1) The seizure is made in accordance with any applicable law or regulation;

(2) The seizure is incident to inspection under an administrative inspection warrant;

(3) The seizure is incident to a search made under a search warrant;

(4) The seizure is incident to a lawful arrest;

(5) The seizure is made pursuant to a valid consent to search;

(6) The property seized has been the subject of a prior judgment in favor of the state in a criminal proceeding or in an injunction or forfeiture proceeding under Code Section 16–8–86; or

(7) There are reasonable grounds to believe that the property is directly or indirectly dangerous to the health or safety of the public.

(c) When property is seized pursuant to this Code section, the seizing agency may:

(1) Place the property under seal; or

(2) Remove the property to a place selected and designated by the seizing agency.

Laws 1991, p. 1805, § 1.

§ 16–8–85. What is subject to forfeiture; forfeiture proceedings

(a) The following are subject to forfeiture unless obtained by theft, fraud, or conspiracy to defraud and the rightful owner is known or can be identified and located:

(1) Any tool;

(2) Any implement; or

(3) Any instrumentality, including, but not limited to, any motor vehicle or motor vehicle part, whether or not owned by the person from whose possession or control it was seized, which is used or possessed either in violation of Code Section 16–8–83 or to promote or facilitate a violation of Code Section 16–8–83.

(b) Any motor vehicle, other conveyance, or motor vehicle part used by any person as a common carrier is subject to forfeiture under this Code section where the owner or other person in charge of the motor vehicle, other conveyance, or motor vehicle part is a consenting party to a violation of Code Section 16–8–83.

(c)(1) Any motor vehicle, motor vehicle part, other conveyance, tool, implement, or instrumentality is not subject to forfeiture under this Code section by reason of any act or omission which the owner proves to have been committed or omitted without the owner's knowledge or consent.

(2) Seizing agencies shall utilize their best efforts to identify any seized motor vehicle or motor vehicle part to determine ownership or the identity of any other person having a right or interest in a seized motor vehicle or motor vehicle part. In its reasonable identification and owner location attempts, the seizing agency shall cause the stolen motor vehicle files of the Georgia Bureau of Investigation to be searched for stolen or wanted information on motor vehicles similar to the seized motor vehicle or consistent with the seized motor vehicle part.

(3) Where a motor vehicle part has an apparent value in excess of $ 1,000.00:

(A) The seizing agency shall consult with an expert of the type specified in paragraph (4) of Code Section 16–8–82; and

(B) The seizing agency shall also request searches of the on-line and off-line files of the National Crime Information Center and the National Automobile Theft Bureau when the Georgia Bureau of Investigation and Georgia Crime Information Center files have been searched with negative results.

(d) A forfeiture of a motor vehicle, motor vehicle part, or other conveyance encumbered by a bona fide security interest is subject to the interest of the secured party where the secured party neither had knowledge of nor consented to the act or omission forming the ground for the forfeiture.

(e) Property, as described in subsection (a) of this Code section, which is seized and held for forfeiture shall not be subject to replevin and is subject only to the order and judgments of a court of competent jurisdiction hearing the forfeiture proceedings.

(f)(1) A prosecutor in the county where the seizure occurs shall bring an action for forfeiture in a court of competent jurisdiction. The forfeiture action shall be brought within 60 days from the date of seizure except where the prosecutor in the sound exercise of discretion determines that no forfeiture action should be brought because of the rights of property owners, lienholders, or secured creditors or because of exculpatory, exonerating, or mitigating facts and circumstances.

(2) The prosecutor shall give notice of the forfeiture proceeding by mailing a copy of the complaint in the forfeiture proceeding to each person whose right, title, or interest is of record in the Department of Revenue, the Department of Transportation, the Federal Aviation Agency, or any other department or agency of this state, any other state or territory of the United States, or of the federal government if such property is required to be registered with any such department or agency.

(3) Notice of the forfeiture proceeding shall be given to any other such person as may appear, from the facts and circumstances, to have any right, title, or interest in or to the property.

(4) The owner of the property or any person having or claiming right, title, or interest in the property may within 60 days after the mailing of such notice file a verified answer to the complaint and may appear at the hearing on the action for forfeiture.

(5) The prosecutor shall show at a forfeiture hearing, by a preponderance of the evidence, that such property was used in the commission of a violation of Code Section 16–8–83 or was used or possessed to facilitate such violation.

(6) The owner of such property may show by a preponderance of the evidence that the owner did not know, and did not have reason to know, that the property was to be used or possessed in the commission of any violation or that any of the exceptions to forfeiture are applicable.

(7) Unless the prosecutor shall make the showing required of it, the court shall order the property released to the owner. Where the prosecutor has made such a showing, the court may order that:

(A) The property be destroyed by the agency which seized it or some other agency designated by the court;

(B) The property be delivered and retained for use by the agency which seized it or some other agency designated by the court; or

(C) The property be sold at public sale.

(g) A copy of a forfeiture order shall be filed with the sheriff of the county in which the forfeiture occurs and with each federal or state department or agency with which such property is required to be registered. Such order, when filed, constitutes authority for the issuance to the agency to whom the property is delivered and retained for use or to any purchaser of the property of a certificate of title, registration certificate, or other special certificate as may be required by law in consideration of the condition of the property.

(h) Proceeds from sale at public auction, after payment of all reasonable charges and expenses incurred by the agency designated by the court to conduct the sale in storing and selling the property, shall be paid into the general fund of the county of seizure.

(i) No motor vehicle, either seized under Code Section 16–8–84 or forfeited under this Code section, shall be released by the seizing agency or used or sold by an agency designated by the court unless any altered, counterfeited, defaced, destroyed, disguised, falsified, forged, obliterated, or removed vehicle identification number is corrected by the issuance and affixing of either an assigned or replacement vehicle identification number plate as may be appropriate under laws or regulations of this state.

(j) No motor vehicle part having any altered, counterfeited, defaced, destroyed, disguised, falsified, forged, obliterated, or removed vehicle identification number may be disposed of upon forfeiture except by destruction thereof, except that this subsection shall not apply to any such motor vehicle part which is assembled with and constitutes part of a motor vehicle.

(k) No motor vehicle or motor vehicle part shall be forfeited under this Code section solely on the basis that it is unidentifiable. Instead of forfeiture, any seized motor vehicle or motor vehicle part which is unidentifiable shall be the subject of a written report sent by the seizing agency to the Department of Revenue, which report shall include a description of the motor vehicle or motor vehicle part, including its color, if any; the date, time, and place of its seizure; the name of the person from whose possession or control it was seized; the grounds for its seizure; and the location where the same is held or stored.

(*l*) When a seized unidentifiable motor vehicle or motor vehicle part has been held for 60 days or more after the notice to the Department of Revenue specified in subsection (k) of this Code section has been given, the seizing agency, or its agent, shall cause the motor vehicle or motor vehicle part to be sold at a public sale to the highest bidder. Notice of the time and place of sale shall be posted in a conspicuous place for at least 30 days prior to the sale on the premises where the motor vehicle or motor vehicle part has been stored.

(m) When a seized unidentifiable motor vehicle or motor vehicle part has an apparent value of $ 1,000.00 or less, the seizing agency shall authorize the disposal of the motor vehicle or motor vehicle part, provided that no such disposition shall be made sooner than 60 days after the date of seizure.

(n) The proceeds of the public sale of an unidentifiable motor vehicle or motor vehicle part shall be deposited into the general fund of the state, county, or municipal corporation employing the seizing agency after deduction of any reasonable and necessary towing and storage charges.

(*o*) Seizing agencies shall utilize their best efforts to arrange for the towing and storing of motor vehicles and motor vehicle parts in the most economical manner possible. In no event shall the owner of a motor vehicle or a motor vehicle part be required to pay more than the minimum reasonable costs of towing and storage.

(p) A seized motor vehicle or motor vehicle part that is neither forfeited nor unidentifiable shall be held subject to the order of the court in which the criminal action is pending or, if a request for its release from such custody is made, until the prosecutor has notified the defendant or the defendant's attorney of such request and both the prosecution and defense have been afforded a reasonable opportunity for an examination of the property to determine its true value and to produce or reproduce, by photographs or other identifying techniques, legally sufficient evidence for introduction at trial or other criminal proceedings. Upon expiration of a reasonable time for the completion of the examination, which in no event shall exceed 14 days from the date of service upon the defense of the notice of request for return of property as provided in this subsection, the property shall be released to the person making such request after satisfactory proof of such person's entitlement to the possession thereof. Notwithstanding the foregoing, upon application by either party with notice to the other, the court may order retention of the property if it determines that retention is necessary in the furtherance of justice.

(q) When a seized vehicle is forfeited, restored to its owner, or disposed of as unidentifiable, the seizing agency shall retain a report of the transaction for a period of at least one year from the date of the transaction.

(r) When an applicant for a certificate of title or salvage certificate of title presents to the Department of Revenue proof that the applicant purchased or acquired a motor vehicle at public sale conducted pursuant to this Code section and such fact is attested to by the seizing agency, the Department of Revenue shall issue a certificate of title or a salvage certificate of title, as determined by the state revenue commissioner, for such motor vehicle upon receipt of the statutory fee, a properly executed application for a certificate of title or other certificate of ownership, and the affidavit of the seizing agency that a state assigned number was applied for and affixed to the motor vehicle prior to the time that the motor vehicle was released by the seizing agency to the purchaser.

Laws 1991, p. 1805, § 1; Laws 1992, p. 6, § 16; Laws 2000, p. 951, § 12–2; Laws 2005, Act 68, § 6–2, eff. July 1, 2005.

Historical and Statutory Notes

The 2000 amendment, effective July 1, 2001, throughout the section substituted for "Revenue" the words "Motor Vehicle Safety".

The 2005 amendment by Act 68, in subsecs. (f)(2), (k), and (*l*), substituted "Department of Revenue" for "Department of Motor Vehicle Safety"; and, in subsec. (r), substituted "Department of Revenue" for "Department of Motor Vehicle Safety" twice and substituted "state revenue commissioner" for "commissioner of motor vehicle safety".

§ 16–8–86. Civil actions

(a) The Attorney General, any prosecutor, or any aggrieved person may institute a civil action against any person in a court of competent jurisdiction seeking relief from conduct constituting a violation of any provision of this article. If the plaintiff in such action proves the alleged violation, or its threat, by a preponderance of the evidence, any court of competent jurisdiction after due provision for the rights of innocent persons shall grant relief by entering any appropriate order or judgment, including, but not limited to:

(1) Ordering any defendant to be divested of any interest in any property;

(2) Imposing reasonable restrictions upon the future activities or investments of any defendant, including prohibiting any defendant from engaging in the same type of endeavor as the defendant was engaged in previously;

(3) Ordering the suspension or revocation of a license, permit, or prior approval granted by any public agency or any other public authority; or

(4) Ordering the surrender of the charter of a corporation organized under the laws of this state or the revocation of a certificate authorizing a foreign corporation to conduct business within this state upon a finding that the board of directors or a managerial agent acting on behalf of the corporation, in conducting the affairs of the corporation, has authorized or engaged in conduct made unlawful by this article and that, for the prevention of future criminal conduct, the public interest requires the charter of the corporation be surrendered and the corporation dissolved or the certificate to conduct business in this state revoked.

(b) In a proceeding under this Code section, injunctive relief shall be granted in conformity with the principles that govern the granting of relief from injury or threatened injury in other cases, but no showing of special or irreparable injury shall have to be made. Pending final determination of a proceeding under this Code section, a temporary restraining order or a preliminary injunction may be issued upon a showing of immediate danger of significant injury, including the possibility that any judgment for money damages might be difficult to execute, and, in a proceeding initiated by an aggrieved person, upon the execution of proper bond against injury for an injunction improvidently granted.

(c) Any person injured, directly or indirectly, by conduct constituting a violation by any person of Code Section 16–8–83 shall, in addition to any other relief, have a cause of action for threefold the actual damages sustained by the person.

(d) A final judgment or decree rendered against the defendant in any civil or criminal proceeding shall estop the defendant in any subsequent civil action or proceeding brought by any person as to all matters to which the judgment or decree would be an estoppel as between the parties to the civil or criminal proceeding.

(e) Notwithstanding any other provision of law providing for a shorter period of limitations, a civil action under this Code section may be commenced at any time within five years after the conduct made unlawful under Code Section 16–8–83 terminates or the cause of action accrues or within any longer statutory period that may be applicable. If any action is brought by a prosecutor to punish, prevent, or restrain any activity made unlawful under Code Section 16–8–83, the running of the period of limitations shall be suspended during the pendency of such action and for two years following its termination.

(f) Personal service of any process in an action under this Code section may be made upon any person outside the state if the person has engaged in any conduct constituting a violation of Code Section 16–8–83 in this state. The person shall be deemed to have thereby submitted to the jurisdiction of the courts of this state for the purposes of this subsection.

(g) Obtaining any civil remedy under this Code section shall not preclude obtaining any other civil or criminal remedy under this article or any other provision of law. Civil remedies under this Code section are supplemental and not exclusive.

Laws 1991, p. 1805, § 1.

Article 5

Residential Mortgage Fraud

§ 16–8–100. Short title

This article shall be known and may be cited as the "Georgia Residential Mortgage Fraud Act."

Laws 2005, Act 162, § 2, eff. May 5, 2005.

Historical and Statutory Notes

Laws 2005, Act 162, § 1, provides:

"The General Assembly finds and declares that fraud involving residential mortgages is at an all-time high in the United States and in Georgia. Mortgage lending institutions and borrowers have suffered hundreds of millions of dollars in losses due to residential mortgage fraud. Homeowners in neighborhoods plagued by mortgage fraud have witnessed the deterioration of their neighborhoods. Fraudulently inflated property values in their neighborhoods have resulted in substantial increases in property taxes. The General Assembly therefore concludes that for the protection of the general public, and particularly for the protection of borrowers, homeowners, lending institutions, and the integrity of the mortgage lending process, the "Georgia Residential Mortgage Fraud Act" shall be enacted."

§ 16–8–101. Definitions

As used in this article, the term:

(1) "Mortgage lending process" means the process through which a person seeks or obtains a residential mortgage loan

including, but not limited to, solicitation, application, or origination, negotiation of terms, third-party provider services, underwriting, signing and closing, and funding of the loan. Documents involved in the mortgage lending process include, but are not limited to, uniform residential loan applications or other loan applications; appraisal reports; HUD–1 settlement statements; supporting personal documentation for loan applications such as W–2 forms, verifications of income and employment, bank statements, tax returns, and payroll stubs; and any required disclosures.

(2) "Pattern of residential mortgage fraud" means one or more misstatements, misrepresentations, or omissions made during the mortgage lending process that involve two or more residential properties, which have the same or similar intents, results, accomplices, victims, or methods of commission or otherwise are interrelated by distinguishing characteristics.

(3) "Person" means a natural person, corporation, company, limited liability company, partnership, trustee, association, or any other entity.

(4) "Residential mortgage loan" means a loan or agreement to extend credit made to a person, which loan is secured by a deed to secure debt, security deed, mortgage, security interest, deed of trust, or other document representing a security interest or lien upon any interest in one-to-four family residential property located in Georgia including the renewal or refinancing of any such loan.

Laws 2005, Act 162, § 2, eff. May 5, 2005; Laws 2006, Act 453, § 16, eff. April 14, 2006.

Historical and Statutory Notes

The 2006 amendment by Act 453 was a provision contained in a correction bill.

§ 16–8–102. Residential mortgage fraud; elements

A person commits the offense of residential mortgage fraud when, with the intent to defraud, such person:

(1) Knowingly makes any deliberate misstatement, misrepresentation, or omission during the mortgage lending process with the intention that it be relied on by a mortgage lender, borrower, or any other party to the mortgage lending process;

(2) Knowingly uses or facilitates the use of any deliberate misstatement, misrepresentation, or omission, knowing the same to contain a misstatement, misrepresentation, or omission, during the mortgage lending process with the intention that it be relied on by a mortgage lender, borrower, or any other party to the mortgage lending process;

(3) Receives any proceeds or any other funds in connection with a residential mortgage closing that such person knew resulted from a violation of paragraph (1) or (2) of this Code section;

(4) Conspires to violate any of the provisions of paragraph (1), (2), or (3) of this Code section; or

(5) Files or causes to be filed with the official registrar of deeds of any county of this state any document such person knows to contain a deliberate misstatement, misrepresentation, or omission.

An offense of residential mortgage fraud shall not be predicated solely upon information lawfully disclosed under federal disclosure laws, regulations, and interpretations related to the mortgage lending process.

Laws 2005, Act 162, § 2, eff. May 5, 2005.

§ 16–8–103. Venue

For the purpose of venue under this article, any violation of this article shall be considered to have been committed:

(1) In the county in which the residential property for which a mortgage loan is being sought is located;

(2) In any county in which any act was performed in furtherance of the violation;

(3) In any county in which any person alleged to have violated this article had control or possession of any proceeds of the violation;

(4) If a closing occurred, in any county in which the closing occurred; or

(5) In any county in which a document containing a deliberate misstatement, misrepresentation, or omission is filed with the official registrar of deeds.

Laws 2005, Act 162, § 2, eff. May 5, 2005.

§ 16–8–104. Authority of Attorney General and district attorneys

District attorneys and the Attorney General shall have the authority to conduct the criminal investigation and prosecution of all cases of residential mortgage fraud under this article or under any other provision of this title. Nothing in this Code section shall be construed to preclude otherwise authorized law enforcement agencies from conducting investigations of offenses related to residential mortgage fraud.

Laws 2005, Act 162, § 2, eff. May 5, 2005; Laws 2010, Act 678, § 1, eff. July 1, 2010.

Historical and Statutory Notes

The 2010 amendment by Act 678 added the second sentence.

§ 16–8–105. Violation is a felony; penalties

(a) Any person violating this article shall be guilty of a felony and, upon conviction, shall be punished by imprisonment for not less than one year nor more than ten years, by a fine not to exceed $5,000.00, or both.

(b) If a violation of this article involves engaging or participating in a pattern of residential mortgage fraud or a conspiracy or endeavor to engage or participate in a pattern of residential mortgage fraud, said violation shall be punishable by imprisonment for not less than three years nor more than 20 years, by a fine not to exceed $100,000.00, or both.

(c) Each residential property transaction subject to a violation of this article shall constitute a separate offense and shall not merge with any other crimes set forth in this title.

Laws 2005, Act 162, § 2, eff. May 5, 2005.

§ 16–8–106. Forfeiture of property

All real and personal property of every kind used or intended for use in the course of, derived from, or realized through a violation of this article shall be subject to forfeiture to the state. Forfeiture shall be had by the same procedure set forth in Code Section 16–14–7. District attorneys and the Attorney General may commence forfeiture proceedings under this article.

Laws 2005, Act 162, § 2, eff. May 5, 2005.

CHAPTER 9

FORGERY AND FRAUDULENT PRACTICES

Article 1

Article 2

Article 3

Article 4

Article 5

Section

Article 6

Part 1

Part 2

Part 3

Part 4

Article 7

Article 8

Article 9

Article 1

Forgery and Related Offenses

§ 16–9–1. Forgery in the first degree

(a) A person commits the offense of forgery in the first degree when with intent to defraud he knowingly makes, alters, or possesses any writing in a fictitious name or in such manner that the writing as made or altered purports to have been made by another person, at another time, with different provisions, or by authority of one who did not give such authority and utters or delivers such writing.

(b) A person convicted of the offense of forgery in the first degree shall be punished by imprisonment for not less than one nor more than ten years.

Laws 1968, p. 1249, § 1; Laws 1969, p. 857, § 6.

Formerly Code 1933, § 26–1701.

§ 16–9–2. Forgery in the second degree

(a) A person commits the offense of forgery in the second degree when with the intent to defraud he knowingly makes, alters, or possesses any writing in a fictitious name or in such manner that the writing as made or altered purports to have been made by another person, at another time, with different provisions, or by authority of one who did not give such authority.

(b) A person convicted of the offense of forgery in the second degree shall be punished by imprisonment for not less than one nor more than five years.

Laws 1968, p. 1249, § 1; Laws 1969, p. 857, § 6; Laws 1982, p. 3, § 16.

Formerly Code 1933, § 26–1702.

§ 16–9–3. Definition of writing

For purposes of Code Sections 16–9–1 and 16–9–2, the word "writing" includes, but is not limited to, printing or any other method of recording information, money, coins, tokens, stamps, seals, credit cards, badges, trademarks, and other symbols of value, right, privilege, or identification.

Laws 1968, p. 1249, § 1.

Formerly Code 1933, § 26–1703.

§ 16–9–4. Possession, display, use, manufacture, alteration, sale, or distribution of false, fictitious, fraudulent, or altered identification document

(a) As used in this Code section, the term:

(1) "Access device" means a unique electronic identification number, address, description, or routing code or a device containing a unique electronic identification number, address, description, or routing code issued to an individual which permits or facilitates entry into a facility or computer or provides access to the financial resources, including, but not limited, to the credit resources of the individual to whom the device or card is issued.

(2) "Description" means any identifying information about a person, including, but not limited to, date of birth, place of birth, address, social security number, height, weight, hair or eye color, or unique biometric data such as fingerprint, voice print, retina or iris image, DNA profile, or other unique physical representation.

(3) "Government agency" means any agency of the executive, legislative, or judicial branch of government or political subdivision or authority thereof of this state, any other state, the United States, or any foreign government or international governmental or quasi-governmental agency recognized by the United States or by any of the several states.

(4) "Identification document" means:

(A) Any document or card issued to an individual by a government agency or by the authority of a government agency containing the name of a person and a description of the person or such person's photograph, or both, and includes, without being limited to, a passport, visa, military identification card, driver's license, or an identification card;

(B) Any document issued to an individual for the purpose of identification by or with the authority of the holder of a trademark or trade name of another, as these terms are defined in Code Section 10–1–371, that contains the trademark or trade name and the name of the person to whom the document is issued and a description of the person or the person's photograph, or both; or

(C) Any access device.

(b)(1) It shall be unlawful for any person to knowingly possess, display, or use any false, fictitious, fraudulent, or altered identification document.

(2) It shall be unlawful for any person to knowingly manufacture, alter, sell, distribute, deliver, possess with intent to sell, deliver, or distribute, or offer for sale, delivery, or distribution a false, fraudulent, or fictitious identification document or any identification document which contains any false, fictitious, or fraudulent statement or entry.

(3) It shall be unlawful for any person to knowingly manufacture, alter, sell, distribute, deliver, possess with the intent to sell, deliver, or distribute, or offer for sale, delivery, or distribution any identification document containing the trademark or trade name of another without the written consent of the owner of the trademark or trade name.

(4) It shall be unlawful for any person to knowingly possess, display, or use any false, fictitious, fraudulent, or altered identification document containing the logo or legal or official seal of a government agency or any colorable imitation thereof in furtherance of a conspiracy or attempt to commit a violation of the criminal laws of this state or of the United States or any of the several states which is punishable by imprisonment for one year or more.

(5) It shall be unlawful for any person to knowingly manufacture, alter, sell, distribute, deliver, possess with the intent to sell, deliver, or distribute, or offer for sale or distribution any other identification document containing the logo or legal or official seal of a government agency or any colorable imitation thereof without the written consent of the government agency.

(6) It shall be unlawful for any person to knowingly possess, display, or use an identification document issued to or on behalf of another person without the permission or consent of the other person for a lawful purpose, unless the identification document is possessed, displayed, or used with the intent to restore it to the other person or government agency or other entity that issued the identification document to the person.

(c)(1) Except as provided in paragraph (2) or (3) of this subsection, any person who violates the provisions of paragraph

(1), (3), or (6) of subsection (b) of this Code section shall be guilty of a misdemeanor.

(2) Except as provided in paragraph (3) of this subsection, any person who violates the provisions of paragraph (1), (3), or (6) of subsection (b) of this Code section for the second or any subsequent offense shall be guilty of a felony and shall be punished by a fine of not more than $25,000.00 or by imprisonment for not more than three years, or both.

(3) Except as provided in paragraph (5) of this subsection, any person who manufactures, alters, sells, distributes, delivers, receives, possesses, or offers for sale or distribution three or more identification documents in violation of the provisions of subsection (b) of this Code section shall be punished by imprisonment for not less than three nor more than ten years, a fine not to exceed $100,000.00, or both.

(4) Except as provided in paragraph (3) or (5) of this subsection, any person who violates the provisions of paragraph (2), (4), or (5) of subsection (b) of this Code section shall be punished by imprisonment for not less than one nor more than five years, a fine not to exceed $100,000.00, or both.

(5) Any person who is under 21 years of age and violates the provisions of subsection (b) of this Code section for the purpose of the identification being used to obtain entry into an age restricted facility or being used to purchase a consumable good that is age restricted, shall, upon a first conviction thereof, be guilty of a misdemeanor and upon a second or subsequent conviction shall be punished as for a misdemeanor of a high and aggravated nature.

(6) Any person convicted of an attempt or conspiracy to violate the provisions of subsection (b) of this Code section shall be punished by imprisonment, by a fine, or by both such punishments not to exceed the maximum punishment prescribed for the offense the commission of which was the object of the attempt or conspiracy.

(d) Each violation of this Code section shall constitute a separate offense.

(e) Any violation of this Code section shall be considered to have been committed in any county of this state in which the evidence shows that the identification document was manufactured, altered, sold, displayed, distributed, delivered, received, offered for sale or distribution, or possessed.

(f) The provisions of this Code section shall not apply to any lawfully authorized investigative, protective, or intelligence activity of an agency of the United States, this state, or any of the several states or their political subdivisions or any activity authorized under Chapter 224 of Title 18 of the United States Code or any similar such law relating to witness protection.

(g) It shall not be a defense to a violation of this Code section that a false, fictitious, fraudulent, or altered identification document contained words indicating that it is not an identification document.

(h)(1) Any property which is used, intended for use, or used in any manner to facilitate a violation of this Code section is contraband and forfeited to the state and no person shall have a property interest in it. Such property may be seized or detained in the same manner as provided in Code Section 16–13–49 and shall not be subject to replevin, conveyance, sequestration, or attachment.

(2) Within 60 days of the date of the seizure of contraband pursuant to this Code section, the district attorney shall initiate forfeiture or other proceedings as provided in Code Section 16–13–49. An owner or interest holder, as defined by subsection (a) of Code Section 16–13–49, may establish as a defense to the forfeiture of property which is subject to forfeiture under this Code section the applicable provisions of subsection (e) or (f) of Code Section 16–13–49. Property which is forfeited pursuant to this Code section shall be disposed of and distributed as provided in Code Section 16–13–49.

(3) If property subject to forfeiture cannot be located; has been transferred or conveyed to, sold to, or deposited with a third party; is beyond the jurisdiction of the court; has been substantially diminished in value while not in the actual physical custody of a receiver or governmental agency directed to maintain custody of the property; or has been commingled with other property that cannot be divided without difficulty, the court shall order the forfeiture of any property of a claimant or defendant up to the value of property found by the court to be subject to forfeiture under this subsection in accordance with the procedures set forth in subsection (x) of Code Section 16–13–49.

(4) The provisions of paragraphs (3), (4), and (5) of subsection (x) and subsection (z) of Code Section 16–13–49 shall be applicable to any proceedings brought pursuant to this subsection.

(i) It shall be an affirmative defense to the manufacturing, selling, or distributing of identification documents that contain false, fictitious, or altered information that the person manufacturing, selling, or distributing the documents used due diligence to ascertain the truth of the information contained in the identification document.

Laws 1988, p. 760, § 1; Laws 2002, p. 551, § 1; Laws 2008, Act 714, § 1, eff. July 1, 2008; Laws 2009, Act 70, § 1, eff. Oct. 1, 2009.

Historical and Statutory Notes

The 2002 amendment rewrote this section which, prior thereto, provided:

"(a) As used in this Code section, the term "identification document" means any document issued by a government agency containing a description of the person or such person's photograph, or both, and giving such person's date of birth, and includes without being limited to a passport, military identification card, driver's license, or an identification card authorized under Code Sections 40–5–100 through 40–5–104.

"(b) (1) It shall be unlawful for any person to knowingly manufacture, sell, or distribute a false identification document.

"(2) Any person who violates paragraph (1) of this subsection on the first offense shall be guilty of a misdemeanor. Any person who violates paragraph (1) of this subsection for the second or any subsequent offense shall be guilty of a felony and shall be punished by a fine of not more than $5,000.00 or by imprisonment for not more than three years, or both."

The 2008 amendment by Act 714 rewrote subsec. (c), which formerly read:

"(c)(1) Except as provided in paragraph (2) or (3) of this subsection, any person who violates paragraph (1), (2), (3), or (6) of subsection (b) of this Code section shall be guilty of a misdemeanor.

"(2) Any person who violates paragraph (2), (3), or (6) of subsection (b) of this Code section for the second or any subsequent offense shall be guilty of a felony and shall be punished by a fine of not more than $25,000.00 or by imprisonment for not more than three years, or both.

"(3) Any person who manufactures, alters, sells, distributes, delivers, receives, possesses, or offers for sale or distribution three or more identification documents in violation of subsection (b) of this Code section shall be punished by imprisonment for not less than three nor more than ten years, a fine not to exceed the amount specified by Code Section 17–10–8, or both.

"(4) Any person who violates paragraph (4) or (5) of subsection (b) of this Code section shall be punished by imprisonment for not less than one nor more than five years, a fine not to exceed the amount specified by Code Section 17–10–8, or both.

"(5) Any person convicted of an attempt or conspiracy to violate subsection (b) of this Code section shall be punished by imprisonment, by a fine, or by both such punishments not to exceed the maximum punishment prescribed for the offense the commission of which was the object of the attempt or conspiracy."

Laws 2008, Act 714, § 2, provides:

"This Act shall become effective on July 1, 2008, and shall apply to all offenses committed on or after that date."

The 2009 amendment by Act 70 rewrote subsec. (g) which had read:

"(g) It shall not be a defense to a violation of this Code section that a document contained words indicating that it is not an identification document unless there appears on the front and back of such document the word "novelty" which is in a color which is not transparent on the design of the document, is in block letters not less than 40 point type in size, and is indelible ink."

Laws 2009, Act 70, § 2, provides:

"This Act shall become effective on October 1, 2009, and shall apply to offenses committed on or after such date."

§ 16–9–5. Manufacture, sale, distribution, or possession of counterfeit or false proof of insurance document

(a) As used in this Code section, the term "proof of insurance document" means any document issued by, on behalf of, or purportedly on behalf of an insurer to a motor vehicle policyholder or applicant for motor vehicle coverage, which document is designed to constitute proof or evidence of the minimum motor vehicle liability insurance required by law for the purposes of Code Section 40–6–10.

(b)(1) It shall be unlawful for any person knowingly to manufacture, sell, or distribute a counterfeit or false proof of insurance document.

(2) It shall be unlawful for any person to possess a counterfeit or false proof of insurance document.

(3) A proof of insurance document shall be deemed counterfeit or false if the proof of insurance document has been altered, modified, or originally issued in any manner which contains false information concerning the insurer, the owner, the motor vehicle, or the insurance thereon.

(c)(1) Any person who violates paragraph (1) of subsection (b) of this Code section on the first offense shall be guilty of a misdemeanor. Any person who violates paragraph (1) of subsection (b) of this Code section for the second or any subsequent offense shall be guilty of a felony and shall be punished by a fine of not more than $ 5,000.00 or by imprisonment for not more than three years, or both.

(2) Any person who violates paragraph (2) of subsection (b) of this Code section shall be guilty of a misdemeanor.

Laws 1990, p. 1440, § 1; Laws 1991, p. 94, § 16; Laws 2000, p. 429, § 2.

Historical and Statutory Notes

The 2000 amendment to subsec. (a) deleted "card, paper, or other" preceding "document issued".

§ 16–9–6. Breach of fiduciary obligation against person who is 65 years of age or older

Unless a greater penalty is specifically provided in this chapter, any violation of this chapter by a fiduciary in breach of a fiduciary obligation against a person who is 65 years of age or older shall be punished by imprisonment for not less than one nor more than 15 years, a fine not to exceed the amount provided by Code Section 17–10–8, or both.

Laws 2000, p. 1085, § 4.

Article 2

Deposit Account Fraud

§ 16–9–20. Deposit account fraud

(a) A person commits the offense of deposit account fraud when such person makes, draws, utters, executes, or delivers an instrument for the payment of money on any bank or other depository in exchange for a present consideration or wages, knowing that it will not be honored by the drawee. For the purposes of this Code section, it is prima-facie evidence that the accused knew that the instrument would not be honored if:

(1) The accused had no account with the drawee at the time the instrument was made, drawn, uttered, or delivered;

(2) Payment was refused by the drawee for lack of funds upon presentation within 30 days after delivery and the accused or someone for him or her shall not have tendered the holder thereof the amount due thereon, together with a service charge, within ten days after receiving written notice that payment was refused upon such instrument. For purposes of this paragraph:

(A) Notice mailed by certified or registered mail or statutory overnight delivery evidenced by return receipt to the person at the address printed on the instrument or given at the time of issuance shall be deemed sufficient and equivalent to notice having been received as of the date on the return receipt by the person making, drawing, uttering, executing, or delivering the instrument. A single notice as provided in subparagraph (B) of this paragraph shall be sufficient to cover all instruments on which payment was refused and which were delivered within a ten-day period by the accused to a single entity, provided that the form of notice lists and identifies each instrument; and

(B) The form of notice shall be substantially as follows:

"You are hereby notified that the following instrument(s)

Number	Date	Amount	Name of Bank
______	______	______	______
______	______	______	______
______	______	______	______
______	______	______	______
______	______	______	______

drawn upon ____ and payable to ____, (has) (have) been dishonored. Pursuant to Georgia law, you have ten days from receipt of this notice to tender payment of the total amount of the instrument(s) plus the applicable service charge(s) of $ ____ and any fee charged to the holder of the instrument(s) by a bank or financial institution as a result of the instrument(s) not being honored, the total amount due being ____ dollars and ____ cents. Unless this amount is paid in full within the specified time above, a presumption in law arises that you delivered the instrument(s) with the intent to defraud and the dishonored instrument(s) and all other available information relating to this incident may be submitted to the magistrate for the issuance of a criminal warrant or citation or to the district attorney or solicitor-general for criminal prosecution."; or

(3) Notice mailed by certified or registered mail or statutory overnight delivery is returned undelivered to the sender when such notice was mailed within 90 days of dishonor to the person at the address printed on the instrument or given by the accused at the time of issuance of the instrument.

(b)(1) Except as provided in paragraphs (2) and (3) of this subsection and subsection (c) of this Code section, a person convicted of the offense of deposit account fraud shall be guilty of a misdemeanor and, upon conviction thereof, shall be punished as follows:

(A) When the instrument is for less than $ 100.00, a fine of not more than $ 500.00 or imprisonment not to exceed 12 months, or both;

(B) When the instrument is for $ 100.00 or more but less than $ 300.00, a fine of not more than $ 1,000.00 or imprisonment not to exceed 12 months, or both; or

(C) When more than one instrument is involved and such instruments were drawn within 90 days of one another and each is in an amount less than $ 100.00, the amounts of such separate instruments may be added together to arrive at and be punishable under subparagraph (B) of this paragraph.

(2) Except as provided in paragraph (3) of this subsection and subsection (c) of this Code section, a person convicted of the offense of deposit account fraud, when the instrument is

for an amount of not less than $ 300.00 nor more than $ 499.99, shall be guilty of a misdemeanor of a high and aggravated nature. When more than one instrument is involved and such instruments were given to the same entity within a 15 day period and the cumulative total of such instruments is not less than $ 300.00 nor more than $ 499.99, the person drawing and giving such instruments shall upon conviction be guilty of a misdemeanor of a high and aggravated nature.

(3) Except as provided in subsection (c) of this Code section, a person convicted of the offense of deposit account fraud, when the instrument is for $ 500.00 or more, shall be guilty of a felony and, upon conviction thereof, shall be punished by a fine of not less than $ 500.00 nor more than $ 5,000.00 or by imprisonment for not more than three years, or both.

(4) Upon conviction of a first or any subsequent offense under this subsection or subsection (c) of this Code section, in addition to any other punishment provided by this Code section, the defendant shall be required to make restitution of the amount of the instrument, together with all costs of bringing a complaint under this Code section. The court may require the defendant to pay as interest a monthly payment equal to 1 percent of the amount of the instrument. Such amount shall be paid each month in addition to any payments on the principal until the entire balance, including the principal and any unpaid interest payments, is paid in full. Such amount shall be paid without regard to any reduction in the principal balance owed. Costs shall be determined by the court from competent evidence of costs provided by the party causing the criminal warrant or citation to issue; provided, however, that the minimum costs shall not be less than $ 25.00. Restitution may be made while the defendant is serving a probated or suspended sentence.

(c) A person who commits the offense of deposit account fraud by the making, drawing, uttering, executing, or delivering of an instrument on a bank of another state shall be guilty of a felony and, upon conviction thereof, shall be punished by imprisonment for not less than one nor more than five years or by a fine in an amount of up to $ 1,000.00, or both.

(d) The prosecuting authority of the court with jurisdiction over a violation of subsection (c) of this Code section may seek extradition for criminal prosecution of any person not within this state who flees the state to avoid prosecution under this Code section.

(e) In any prosecution or action under this Code section, an instrument for which the information required in this subsection is available at the time of issuance shall constitute prima-facie evidence of the identity of the party issuing or executing the instrument and that the person was a party authorized to draw upon the named account. To establish this prima-facie evidence, the following information regarding the identity of the party presenting the instrument shall be obtained by the party receiving such instrument: the full name, residence address, and home phone number.

(1) Such information may be provided by either of two methods:

(A) The information may be recorded upon the instrument itself; or

(B) The number of a check-cashing identification card issued by the receiving party may be recorded on the instrument. The check-cashing identification card shall be issued only after the information required in this subsection has been placed on file by the receiving party.

(2) In addition to the information required in this subsection, the party receiving an instrument shall witness the signature or endorsement of the party presenting such instrument and as evidence of such the receiving party shall initial the instrument.

(f) As used in this Code section, the term:

(1) "Bank" shall include a financial institution as defined in this Code section.

(2) "Conviction" shall include the entering of a guilty plea, the entering of a plea of nolo contendere, or the forfeiting of bail.

(3) "Financial institution" shall have the same meaning as defined in paragraph (21) of Code Section 7-1-4 and shall also include a national bank, a state or federal savings bank, a state or federal credit union, and a state or federal savings and loan association.

(4) "Holder in due course" shall have the same meaning as in Code Section 11-3-302.

(5) "Instrument" means a check, draft, debit card sales draft, or order for the payment of money.

(6) "Present consideration" shall include without limitation:

(A) An obligation or debt of rent which is past due or presently due;

(B) An obligation or debt of state taxes which is past due or presently due;

(C) An obligation or debt which is past due or presently due for child support when made for the support of such minor child and which is given pursuant to an order of court or written agreement signed by the person making the payment;

(D) A simultaneous agreement for the extension of additional credit where additional credit is being denied; and

(E) A written waiver of mechanic's or materialmen's lien rights.

(7) "State taxes" shall include payments made to the Georgia Department of Labor as required by Chapter 8 of Title 34.

(g) This Code section shall in no way affect the authority of a sentencing judge to provide for a sentence to be served on weekends or during the nonworking hours of the defendant as provided in Code Section 17-10-3.

(h)(1) Any party holding a worthless instrument and giving notice in substantially similar form to that provided in subparagraph (a)(2)(B) of this Code section shall be immune from civil liability for the giving of such notice and for proceeding as required under the forms of such notice; provided, however, that, if any person shall be arrested or prosecuted for violation of this Code section and payment of any instrument shall have been refused because the maker or drawer had no account with the bank or other depository on which such instrument was drawn, the one causing the arrest or prosecution shall be deemed to have acted with reasonable or probable cause even though he, she, or it has not mailed the written notice or waited for the ten-day period to elapse. In any civil action for damages which may be brought by the person who made, drew, uttered, executed, or delivered such instrument, no evidence of statements or representations as to the status of the instrument involved or of any collateral agreement with reference to the instrument shall be admissible unless such statements, representations, or collateral agreement shall be written simultaneously with or upon the instrument at the time it is delivered by the maker thereof.

(2) Except as otherwise provided by law, any party who holds a worthless instrument, who complies with the requirements of subsection (a) of this Code section, and who causes a criminal warrant or citation to be issued shall not forfeit his or her right to continue or pursue civil remedies authorized by law for the collection of the worthless instrument; provided, however, that if interest is awarded and collected on any amount ordered by the court as restitution in the criminal case, interest shall not be collectable in any civil action on the same amount. It shall be deemed conclusive evidence that any action is brought upon probable cause and without malice where such party holding a worthless instrument has complied with the provisions of subsection (a) of this Code section regardless of whether the criminal charges are dismissed by a court due to payment in full of the face value of the instrument and applicable service charges subsequent to the date that affidavit

for the warrant or citation is made. In any civil action for damages which may be brought by the person who made, drew, uttered, executed, or delivered such instrument, no evidence of statements or representations as to the status of the instrument involved or of any collateral agreement with reference to the instrument shall be admissible unless such statements, representations, or collateral agreement shall be written simultaneously with or upon the instrument at the time it is delivered by the maker thereof.

(i) Notwithstanding paragraph (2) of subsection (a) of this Code section or any other law on usury, charges, or fees on loans or credit extensions, any lender of money or extender of other credit who receives an instrument drawn on a bank or other depository institution given by any person in full or partial repayment of a loan, installment payment, or other extension of credit may, if such instrument is not paid or is dishonored by such institution, charge and collect from the borrower or person to whom the credit was extended a bad instrument charge. This charge shall not be deemed interest or a finance or other charge made as an incident to or as a condition to the granting of the loan or other extension of credit and shall not be included in determining the limit on charges which may be made in connection with the loan or extension of credit or any other law of this state.

(j) For purposes of this Code section, no service charge or bad instrument charge shall exceed $30.00 or 5 percent of the face amount of the instrument, whichever is greater, except that the holder of the instrument may also charge the maker an additional fee in an amount equal to that charged to the holder by the bank or financial institution as a result of the instrument not being honored.

(k) An action under this Code section may be prosecuted by the party initially receiving a worthless instrument or by any subsequent holder in due course of any such worthless instrument.

Laws 1959, p. 252, §§ 1–3; Laws 1968, p. 1249, § 1; Laws 1974, p. 705, § 1; Laws 1975, p. 482, § 1; Laws 1977, p. 1266, §§ 1, 2; Laws 1978, p. 2020, § 1; Laws 1980, p. 1034, § 1; Laws 1980, p. 1147, §§ 1–3; Laws 1981, p. 1550, § 1; Laws 1983, p. 484, § 1; Laws 1983, p. 485, § 1; Laws 1983, p. 1189, §§ 1, 2; Laws 1984, p. 22, § 16; Laws 1984, p. 1435, § 1; Laws 1985, p. 708, § 1; Laws 1986, p. 209, § 1; Laws 1987, p. 983, § 1; Laws 1988, p. 268, § 1; Laws 1988, p. 762, § 1; Laws 1989, p. 1570, § 1; Laws 1990, p. 8, § 16; Laws 1994, p. 1787, § 3; Laws 1995, p. 910, §§ 1, 2; Laws 1996, p. 748, § 10; Laws 1996, p. 1014, §§ 1, 2; Laws 1999, p. 720, § 1; Laws 2000, p. 1352, § 1; Laws 2000, p. 1589, § 4; Laws 2003, Act 9, § 16, eff. May 14, 2003; Laws 2003, Act 196, § 1, eff. July 1, 2003.

Formerly Code 1933, § 26–1704; Code 1933, § 41A–9909.

Historical and Statutory Notes

The 2000 amendment by Act 837 inserted following the form in subsec. (a)(2) "and any fee charged to the holder of the instrument(s) by a bank or financial institution as a result of the instrument(s) not being honored", deleted in subsec. (b)(4) following "under this Code section" the words "plus the amount of any fees charged to the holder of the instrument by a bank or financial institution as a result of the instrument not being honored.", redefined the statutory reference in "bank" in subsec. (f)(1), inserted in subsec. (f)(3) "and shall also include a national bank, a state or federal savings bank, a state or federal credit union, and a state or federal savings and loan association", added subsec. (f)(7), and inserted at the end of subsec. (j) ", except that the holder of the instrument may also charge the maker an additional fee in an amount equal to that charged to the holder by the bank or financial institution as a result of the instrument not being honored."

The 2000 amendment by Act 918 substituted in subsecs. (a)(2)(A) and (a)(3) "certified mail or statutory overnight delivery" for "certified mail".

The 2003 amendment by Act 9, in subsec. (f), redesignated par. (7) as par. (4), and redesignated pars. (4) through (6) as pars. (5) through (7), respectively.

The 2003 amendment by Act 196, in subsec. (j), substituted "$30.00" for "$25.00".

§ 16–9–21. Printing, executing, or negotiating checks knowing check information is in error, fictitious, or assigned to another account holder

(a) It shall be unlawful for any person to print or cause to be printed checks, drafts, orders, or debit card sales drafts, drawn upon any financial institution or to execute or negotiate any check, draft, order, or debit card sales draft knowing that the account number, routing number, or other information printed on such check, draft, order, or debit card sales draft is in error, fictitious, or assigned to another account holder or financial institution.

(b) Any person who violates subsection (a) of this Code section shall be punished by a fine of not more than $5,000.00 or by imprisonment for not less than one year nor more than five years, or both.

Laws 1989, p. 1570, § 2; Laws 1994, p. 1787, § 4.

Article 3

Illegal Use of Financial Transaction Cards

§ 16–9–30. Definitions

As used in this article, the term:

(1) "Acquirer" means a business organization, financial institution, or an agent of a business organization or financial institution that authorizes a merchant to accept payment by financial transaction card for money, goods, services, or anything else of value.

(2) "Automated banking device" means any machine which when properly activated by a financial transaction card and personal identification code may be used for any of the purposes for which a financial transaction card may be used.

(3) "Cardholder" means the person or organization named on the face of a financial transaction card to whom or for whose benefit the financial transaction card is issued by an issuer.

(4) "Expired financial transaction card" means a financial transaction card which is no longer valid because the term for which it was issued has elapsed.

(5) "Financial transaction card" or "FTC" means any instrument or device, whether known as a credit card, credit plate, bank services card, banking card, check guarantee card, debit card, or by any other name, issued with or without fee by an issuer for the use of the cardholder:

(A) In obtaining money, goods, services, or anything else of value;

(B) In certifying or guaranteeing to a person or business the availability to the cardholder of funds on deposit that are equal to or greater than the amount necessary to honor a draft or check payable to the order of such person or business; or

(C) In providing the cardholder access to a demand deposit account, savings account, or time deposit account for the purpose of:

(i) Making deposits of money or checks therein;

(ii) Withdrawing funds in the form of money, money orders, or traveler's checks therefrom;

(iii) Transferring funds from any demand deposit account, savings account, or time deposit account to any other demand deposit account, savings account, or time deposit account;

(iv) Transferring funds from any demand deposit account, savings account, or time deposit account to any credit card accounts, overdraft privilege accounts, loan accounts, or any other credit accounts in full or partial satisfaction of any outstanding balance owed existing therein;

(v) For the purchase of goods, services, or anything else of value; or

(vi) Obtaining information pertaining to any demand deposit account, savings account, or time deposit account.

(5.1) "Financial transaction card account number" means a number, numerical code, alphabetical code, or alphanumeric code assigned by the issuer to a particular financial transaction card and which identifies the cardholder's account with the issuer.

(6) "Issuer" means the business organization or financial institution or its duly authorized agent which issues a financial transaction card.

(7) "Personal identification code" means a numeric or alphabetical code, signature, photograph, fingerprint, or any other means of electronic or mechanical confirmation used by the cardholder of a financial transaction card to permit authorized electronic use of that financial transaction card.

(8) "Presenting" means those actions taken by a cardholder or any person to introduce a financial transaction card into an automated banking device with or without utilization of a personal identification code or merely displaying or showing, with intent to defraud, a financial transaction card to the issuer or to any person or organization providing money, goods, services, or anything else of value or to any other entity.

(9) "Receives" or "receiving" means acquiring possession of or control of or accepting a financial transaction card as security for a loan.

(10) "Revoked financial transaction card" means a financial transaction card which is no longer valid because permission to use it has been suspended or terminated by the issuer.

Laws 1960, p. 1113, § 1; Laws 1968, p. 1249, § 1; Laws 1969, p. 128, § 1; Laws 1970, p. 529, §§ 1, 2; Laws 1980, p. 1083, § 1; Laws 1990, p. 304, § 1; Laws 1996, p. 371, § 1.

Formerly Code 1933, § 26–1705.

§ 16–9–31. Financial transaction card theft

(a) A person commits the offense of financial transaction card theft when:

(1) He takes, obtains, or withholds a financial transaction card from the person, possession, custody, or control of another without the cardholder's consent; or who, with knowledge that it has been so taken, obtained, or withheld, receives the financial transaction card with intent to use it or to sell it or to transfer it to a person other than the issuer or the cardholder;

(2) He receives a financial transaction card that he knows to have been lost, mislaid, or delivered under a mistake as to the identity or address of the cardholder and he retains possession with intent to use it or sell it or to transfer it to a person other than the issuer or the cardholder;

(3) He, not being the issuer, sells a financial transaction card or buys a financial transaction card from a person other than the issuer; or

(4) He, not being the issuer, during any 12 month period receives two or more financial transaction cards in the names of persons which he has reason to know were taken or retained under circumstances which constitute a violation of paragraph (3) of subsection (a) of Code Section 16–9–33 and paragraph (3) of this subsection.

(b) Taking, obtaining, or withholding a financial transaction card without consent of the cardholder or issuer is included in conduct defined in Code Section 16–8–2 as the offense of theft by taking.

(c) Conviction of the offense of financial transaction card theft is punishable as provided in subsection (b) of Code Section 16–9–38.

(d) When a person has in his possession or under his control two or more financial transaction cards issued in the names of persons other than members of his immediate family or without the consent of the cardholder, such possession shall be prima-facie evidence that the financial transaction cards have been obtained in violation of subsection (a) of this Code section.

Laws 1969, p. 128, § 1; Laws 1980, p. 1083, § 1; Laws 1992, p. 6, § 16.

Formerly Code 1933, § 26–1705.2; Code 1933, § 26–1705.1.

Validity

This section has been held unconstitutional, in part, in the case of Mohamed v. State, 2003, 276 Ga. 706, 583 S.E.2d 9.

§ 16–9–32. Forgery of financial transaction card

(a) A person commits the offense of financial transaction card forgery when:

(1) With intent to defraud a purported issuer; a person or organization providing money, goods, services, or anything else of value; or any other person, he falsely makes or falsely embosses a purported financial transaction card;

(2) With intent to defraud a purported issuer; a person or organization providing money, goods, services, or anything else of value; or any other person, he falsely encodes, duplicates, or alters existing encoded information on a financial transaction card or utters such a financial transaction card; or

(3) He, not being the cardholder or a person authorized by him, with intent to defraud the issuer; a person or organization providing money, goods, services, or anything else of value; or any other person, signs a financial transaction card.

(b) A person falsely makes a financial transaction card when he makes or draws in whole or in part a device or instrument which purports to be the financial transaction card of a named issuer but which is not such a financial transaction card because the issuer did not authorize the making or drawing or when he alters a financial transaction card which was validly issued.

(c) A person falsely embosses a financial transaction card when without authorization of the named issuer he completes a financial transaction card by adding any of the matter other than the signature of the cardholder, which an issuer requires to appear on the financial transaction card before it can be used by a cardholder.

(d) A person falsely encodes a financial transaction card when without authorization of the purported issuer he records, erases, or otherwise alters magnetically, electronically, electromagnetically, or by any other means whatsoever information on a financial transaction card which will permit acceptance of that card by any automated banking device.

(e) Conviction of the offense of financial transaction card forgery shall be punishable as provided in subsection (b) of Code Section 16–9–38.

(f) When a person other than the purported issuer possesses two or more financial transaction cards which are falsely made, falsely encoded, or falsely embossed, such possession shall be prima-facie evidence that said cards were obtained in violation of paragraph (1) or (2) of subsection (a) of this Code section.

Laws 1969, p. 128, § 1; Laws 1980, p. 1083, § 1.

Formerly Code 1933, § 26–1705.3; Code 1933, § 26–1705.2.

§ 16–9–33. Financial transaction card fraud

(a) A person commits the offense of financial transaction card fraud when with intent to defraud the issuer; a person or organization providing money, goods, services, or anything else of value; or any other person, he:

(1) Uses for the purpose of obtaining money, goods, services, or anything else of value:

(A) A financial transaction card obtained or retained or which was received with knowledge that it was obtained or retained in violation of Code Section 16–9–31 or 16–9–32;

(B) A financial transaction card which he or she knows is forged, altered, expired, revoked, or was obtained as a result of a fraudulent application in violation of subsection (d) of this Code section; or

(C) The financial transaction card account number of a financial transaction card which he or she knows has not in fact been issued or is forged, altered, expired, revoked, or was obtained as a result of a fraudulent application in violation of subsection (d) of this Code section;

(2) Obtains money, goods, services, or anything else of value by:

(A) Representing without the consent of the cardholder that he or she is the holder of a specified card;

(B) Presenting the financial transaction card without the authorization or permission of the cardholder;

(C) Falsely representing that he or she is the holder of a card and such card has not in fact been issued; or

(D) Giving, orally or in writing, a financial transaction card account number to the provider of the money, goods, services, or other thing of value for billing purposes without the authorization or permission of the cardholder for such use;

(3) Obtains control over a financial transaction card as security for debt;

(4) Deposits into his account or any account by means of an automated banking device a false, fictitious, forged, altered, or counterfeit check, draft, money order, or any other such document not his lawful or legal property; or

(5) Receives money, goods, services, or anything else of value as a result of a false, fictitious, forged, altered, or counterfeit check, draft, money order, or any other such document having been deposited into an account via an automated banking device, knowing at the time of receipt of the money, goods, services, or item of value that the document so deposited was false, fictitious, forged, altered, or counterfeit or that the above-deposited item was not his lawful or legal property.

(b) A person who is authorized by an issuer to furnish money, goods, services, or anything else of value upon presentation of a financial transaction card by the cardholder or any agent or employee of such person commits the offense of financial transaction card fraud when, with intent to defraud the issuer or the cardholder, he:

(1) Furnishes money, goods, services, or anything else of value upon presentation of a financial transaction card obtained or retained in violation of Code Section 16–9–31 or a financial transaction card which he knows is forged, expired, or revoked;

(2) Alters a charge ticket or purchase ticket to reflect a larger amount than that approved by the cardholder; or

(3) Fails to furnish money, goods, services, or anything else of value which he represents in writing to the issuer that he has furnished.

(c) Conviction of the offense of financial transaction card fraud as provided in subsection (a) or (b) of this Code section is punishable as provided in subsection (a) of Code Section 16–9–38 if the value of all money, goods, services, and other things of value furnished in violation of this Code section or if the difference between the value actually furnished and the value represented to the issuer to have been furnished in violation of this Code section does not exceed $ 100.00 in any six-month period. Conviction of the offense of financial transaction card fraud as provided in subsection (a) or (b) of this Code section is punishable as provided in subsection (b) of Code Section 16–9–38 if such value exceeds $ 100.00 in any six-month period.

(d) A person commits the offense of financial transaction card fraud when, upon application for a financial transaction card to an issuer, he knowingly makes or causes to be made a false statement or report relative to his name, occupation, employer, financial condition, assets, or liabilities or willfully and substantially overvalues any assets or willfully omits or substantially undervalues any indebtedness for the purpose of influencing the issuer to issue a financial transaction card. Financial transaction card fraud as provided in this subsection is punishable as provided in subsection (b) of Code Section 16–9–38.

(e) A cardholder commits the offense of financial transaction card fraud when he willfully, knowingly, and with an intent to defraud the issuer; a person or organization providing money, goods, services, or anything else of value; or any other person submits verbally or in writing to the issuer or any other person any false notice or report of the theft, loss, disappearance, or nonreceipt of his financial transaction card and personal identification code. Conviction of the offense of financial transaction card fraud as provided in this subsection is punishable as provided in subsection (b) of Code Section 16–9–38.

(f) A person authorized by an acquirer to furnish money, goods, services, or anything else of value upon presentation of a financial transaction card or a financial transaction card account number by a cardholder or any agent or employee of such person, who, with intent to defraud the issuer, acquirer, or cardholder remits to an issuer or acquirer, for payment, a financial transaction card record of a sale, which sale was not made by such person, agent, or employee, commits the offense of financial transaction card fraud. Conviction of the offense of financial transaction card fraud as provided in this subsection shall be punishable as provided in subsection (b) of Code Section 16–9–38.

(g) In any prosecution for violation of this Code section, the state is not required to establish that all of the acts constituting the crime occurred in this state or within one city, county, or local jurisdiction, and it is no defense that some of the acts constituting the crime did not occur in this state or within one city, county, or local jurisdiction. Except as otherwise provided by Code Section 17–2–2, for purposes of venue the crime defined by this Code section shall be considered as having been committed in the county where the commission of the crime commenced.

(h) For purposes of this Code section, revocation shall be construed to include either notice given in person or notice given in writing to the person to whom the financial transaction card and personal identification code was issued. Notice of revocation shall be immediate when notice is given in person. The sending of a notice in writing by registered or certified mail or statutory overnight delivery in the United States mail, duly stamped and addressed to such person at his last address known to the issuer, shall be prima-facie evidence that such notice was duly received after seven days from the date of deposit in the mail. If the address is located outside the United States, Puerto Rico, the Virgin Islands, the Canal Zone, and Canada, notice shall be presumed to have been received ten days after mailing by registered or certified mail or statutory overnight delivery.

Laws 1969, p. 128, § 1; Laws 1980, p. 1083, § 1; Laws 1990, p. 304, § 2; Laws 1992, p. 6, § 16; Laws 1996, p. 371, §§ 2, 3; Laws 2000, p. 1589, § 3.

Formerly Code 1933, §§ 26–1705.1, 26–1705.4; Code 1933, § 26–1705.3.

Historical and Statutory Notes

The 2000 amendment substituted twice in subsec. (h) "certified mail or statutory overnight delivery" for "certified mail".

§ 16–9–34. Criminal possession of financial transaction card forgery devices

(a) A person commits the offense of criminal possession of financial transaction card forgery devices when:

(1) He is a person other than the cardholder and possesses two or more incomplete financial transaction cards with intent to complete them without the consent of the issuer; or

(2) With knowledge of its character, he possesses machinery, plates, or any other contrivance designed to reproduce instruments purporting to be financial transaction cards of an issuer who has not consented to the preparation of such financial transaction cards.

(b) A financial transaction card is incomplete if part of the matter, other than the signature of the cardholder, which an issuer requires to appear on the financial transaction card before it can be used by a cardholder has not yet been stamped, embossed, imprinted, encoded, or written upon.

(c) Conviction of the offense of criminal possession of financial transaction card forgery devices is punishable as provided in subsection (b) of Code Section 16–9–38.

Laws 1969, p. 128, § 1; Laws 1980, p. 1083, § 1; Laws 1982, p. 3, § 16.

Formerly Code 1933, § 26–1705.5; Code 1933, § 26–1705.4.

§ 16–9–35. Criminal receipt of goods and services fraudulently obtained

A person commits the offense of criminally receiving goods and services fraudulently obtained when he receives money, goods, services, or anything else of value obtained in violation of subsection (a) of Code Section 16–9–33 with the knowledge or belief that the same were obtained in violation of subsection (a) of Code Section 16–9–33. Conviction of the offense of criminal receipt of goods and services fraudulently obtained is punishable as provided in subsection (a) of Code Section 16–9–38 if the value of all money, goods, services, and anything else of value obtained in violation of this Code section does not exceed $100.00 in any six-month period. Conviction of the offense of criminal receipt of goods and services fraudulently obtained is punishable as provided in subsection (b) of Code Section 16–9–38 if such value exceeds $100.00 in any six-month period.

Laws 1969, p. 128, § 1; Laws 1980, p. 1083, § 1.

Formerly Code 1933, § 26–1705.6; Code 1933, § 26–1705.5.

§ 16–9–36. Rebuttable presumption of criminal receipt of goods and services fraudulently obtained

A person who obtains at a discount price a ticket issued by an airline, railroad, steamship, or other transportation company from other than an authorized agent of such company, which ticket was acquired in violation of subsection (a) of Code Section 16–9–33 without reasonable inquiry to ascertain that the person from whom it was obtained had a legal right to possess it shall be rebuttably presumed to know that such ticket was acquired under circumstances constituting a violation of subsection (a) of Code Section 16–9–33 if the ticket shows on its face that it was issued through the use of a financial transaction card or that it is otherwise nonrefundable.

Laws 1969, p. 128, § 1; Laws 1980, p. 1083, § 1.

Formerly Code 1933, § 26–1705.7; Code 1933, § 26–1705.6.

§ 16–9–36.1. Criminal factoring of financial transaction card records

Any person who, without the acquirer's express authorization, employs or solicits an authorized merchant or any agent or employee of such merchant to remit to an issuer or acquirer, for payment, a financial transaction card record of a sale, which sale was not made by such merchant, agent, or employee, commits the offense of criminal factoring of financial transaction card records. Conviction of criminal factoring of financial transaction card records shall be punishable as provided in subsection (b) of Code Section 16–9–38.

Laws 1990, p. 304, § 3.

§ 16–9–37. Unauthorized use of financial transaction card

Any person who has been issued or entrusted with a financial transaction card for specifically authorized purposes, provided such authorization is in writing stating a maximum amount charges that can be made with the financial transaction card, and who uses the financial transaction card in a manner and for purposes not authorized in order to obtain or purchase money, goods, services, or anything else of value shall be punished as provided in subsection (a) of Code Section 16–9–38.

Laws 1969, p. 128, § 1; Laws 1980, p. 1083, § 1.

Formerly Code 1933, § 26–1705.8; Code 1933, § 26–1705.7.

§ 16–9–38. Punishment and penalties

(a) A person who is subject to the punishment and penalties of this subsection shall be fined not more than $1,000.00 or imprisoned not less than one year nor more than two years, or both.

(b) A person subject to punishment under this subsection shall be guilty of a felony and shall be punished by a fine of not more than $5,000.00 or imprisonment for not less than one year nor more than three years, or both.

Laws 1969, p. 128, § 1; Laws 1972, p. 861, § 1; Laws 1980, p. 1083, § 1.

Formerly Code 1933, § 26–1705.9; Code 1933, § 26–1705.8.

§ 16–9–39. Publication of information regarding schemes, devices, means, or methods for financial transaction card fraud or theft of telecommunication services

(a) As used in this Code section, "publish" means the communication or dissemination of information to any one or more persons either orally, in person, by telephone, radio or television, or in a writing of any kind, including without limitation a letter, memorandum, circular, handbill, newspaper or magazine article, or book.

(b) A person who publishes the number or code of any existing, canceled, revoked, or nonexistent telephone number, credit number, or other credit device, or method of numbering or coding which is employed in the issuance of telephone numbers, credit numbers, or other credit devices with knowledge or reason to believe that it may be used to avoid the payment of any lawful telephone or telegraph toll charge under circumstances evidencing an intent to have such telephone number, credit number, credit device, or method of numbering or coding so used shall be punished as provided in subsection (a) of Code Section 16–9–38.

(c) An offense under this Code section may be deemed to have been committed at either the place at which the publication was initiated, at which publication was received, or at which the information so published was utilized to avoid or attempt to avoid payment of any lawful telephone or telegraph charge.

Laws 1972, p. 473, § 1; Laws 1980, p. 1083, § 1.

Formerly Code 1933, § 26–1705.10; Code 1933, § 26–1705.9.

Article 4

Fraud and Related Offenses

§ 16–9–50. Deceptive business practice

(a) A person commits the offense of using a deceptive business practice when in the regular course of business he knowingly:

(1) Uses or possesses for use a false weight or measure or any other device for falsely determining or recording any quality or quantity;

(2) Sells, offers, or exposes for sale or delivers less than the represented quality or quantity of any commodity; or

(3) Takes or attempts to take more than the represented quantity of any commodity when as buyer he furnishes the weight or measure.

(b) Any person who commits the offense of using a deceptive business practice shall be guilty of a misdemeanor.

Laws 1968, p. 1249, § 1.

Formerly Code 1933, § 26–1706.

§ 16–9–51. Endangering security interest

(a) Except as provided in subsection (b) of this Code section, a person who destroys, removes, conceals, encumbers, transfers, or otherwise deals with property subject to a security interest with intent to hinder enforcement of that interest shall be guilty of a misdemeanor.

(b) A person who destroys, removes, conceals, encumbers, transfers, or otherwise deals with property subject to a security interest with intent to hinder enforcement of that security interest and in so doing does damage to such property in an amount greater than $500.00 shall be guilty of a misdemeanor of a high and aggravated nature.

(c) In a prosecution under this Code section the crime shall be considered as having been committed in any county where any act in furtherance of the criminal scheme was done or caused to be done.

Laws 1968, p. 1249, § 1; Laws 1988, p. 299, § 1.

Formerly Code 1933, § 26–1707.

§ 16–9–52. Improper solicitation of money by use of invoice for goods, etc. not ordered

(a) A person commits the offense of improper solicitation of money when he solicits payment of money by another by means of a statement or invoice or any writing that could reasonably be interpreted as a statement or invoice for goods not yet ordered or for services not yet performed and not yet ordered, unless there appears on the face of the statement or invoice or writing in 30 point boldface type the following warning:

"This is a solicitation for the order of goods or services and you are under no obligation to make payment unless you accept the offer contained herein."

(b) Any person who violates subsection (a) of this Code section shall be guilty of a misdemeanor.

(c) In addition to other remedies, any person damaged by noncompliance with subsection (a) of this Code section is entitled to damages in the amount equal to three times the sum solicited.

Laws 1968, p. 322, §§ 1–3; Laws 1969, p. 857, § 7; Laws 1985, p. 149, § 16.

Formerly Code 1933, § 26–1708.

§ 16–9–53. Damaging, destroying, or secreting property to defraud another

(a) A person commits the offense of damaging, destroying, or secreting property to defraud another person when he knowingly and with intent to defraud another person damages, destroys, or secretes any property of whatever class or character, whether the property of himself or of another person.

(b) A person convicted of the offense of damaging, destroying, or secreting property to defraud another person shall be punished by imprisonment for not less than one nor more than five years.

Laws 1968, p. 1249, § 1.

Formerly Code 1933, § 26–1504.

§ 16–9–54. Fraudulent telephone solicitation

(a) In making a telephone solicitation for the purpose of the sale of goods or services or for the purpose of seeking charitable contributions, it shall be unlawful for any person to make false statements regarding the purpose of the solicitation, the person or persons represented by the solicitor, or the person or persons benefiting from the solicitation.

(b) Any person who violates subsection (a) of this Code section shall be guilty of a misdemeanor.

Laws 1977, p. 601, § 1.

Formerly Code 1933, § 26–1710.

§ 16–9–55. Fraudulently obtaining or attempting to obtain public housing

(a) Any person who obtains or attempts to obtain or who establishes or attempts to establish eligibility for, and any person who knowingly or intentionally aids or abets such person in obtaining or attempting to obtain or in establishing or attempting to establish eligibility for, any public housing or a reduction in public housing rental charges or any rent subsidy or payment from a tenant in connection with public housing to which such person would not otherwise be entitled, by means of a false statement, failure to disclose information, impersonation, or other fraudulent scheme or device shall be guilty of a misdemeanor.

(b) As used in this Code section, "public housing" means housing which is constructed, operated, maintained, financed, or subsidized by the state, a county, a municipal corporation, the Georgia Housing and Finance Authority, a housing authority, or by any other political subdivision or public corporation of the state or its subdivisions.

(c) Notice of subsection (a) of this Code section shall be printed on the application form for public housing and shall be displayed in the office where such application is made.

Laws 1977, p. 1332, §§ 1, 2; Laws 1980, p. 405, § 2; Laws 1989, p. 1242, § 1; Laws 1991, p. 1653, § 2–3.

Formerly Code 1933, § 26–1710; Code 1933, § 26–1710.1.

§ 16–9–56. Fraudulent attempts to obtain refunds

(a) It shall be unlawful for any person to give a false or fictitious name, address, or telephone number as that person's own or to give the name, address, or telephone number of any other person without that other person's knowledge and approval for the purpose of obtaining or attempting to obtain a refund for merchandise returned to a business establishment or a refund on a ticket or other document which is evidence of a service purchased from a business establishment, which service is yet to be performed.

(b) Any person who violates this Code section shall be guilty of a misdemeanor.

Laws 1974, p. 490, § 1; Laws 1978, p. 1985, § 1; Laws 1994, p. 850, § 1.

Formerly Code 1933, § 26–1709.

§ 16–9–57. Representing peace officer organization without authority

(a) It shall be unlawful for any person to solicit or accept a fee, consideration, or donation or to offer for sale or to sell advertising as a representative of a peace officer organization or fire service organization or under the guise of representing a peace officer organization or fire service organization unless such person is employed by, is acting pursuant to the authority of, or is a member of such organization.

(b) As used in this Code section, the term:

(1) "Fire service" shall include any person duly elected, appointed, or employed to engage in fire fighting.

(2) "Peace officer" shall include any person duly elected, appointed, or employed to engage in public law enforcement work.

(c) Any person, firm, association, or corporation violating subsection (a) of this Code section shall be guilty of a misdemeanor and, upon conviction thereof, shall be punished by a fine of not more than $500.00 or by imprisonment for not more than 30 days, or both.

(d) Any person, firm, association, or corporation violating subsection (a) of this Code section through the use of some form of communication across the boundaries of the state, whether such communication is by mail, by the use of any electronic device including but not limited to the use of a telephone or telegraph, or by any other means, shall be guilty of a felony and, upon conviction thereof, shall be punished by imprisonment for not less than one year nor more than three years or by a fine of not less than $1,000.00 nor more than $5,000.00, or both.

Laws 1974, p. 1221, §§ 1–3; Laws 1985, p. 411, § 1.

§ 16–9–58. Failure to pay for agricultural products or chattels; penalty

Any person, either on his or her own account or for others, who with fraudulent intent shall buy cotton, corn, rice, crude turpentine, spirits of turpentine, rosin, pitch, tar, timber, pulpwood, Christmas trees, pine needles, horticultural crops, poultry and poultry products, cattle, hogs, sheep, goats, ratites, horses, mules, pecans, peaches, apples, watermelons, cantaloupes, or other products or chattels and fail or refuse to pay therefor within 20 days following receipt of such products or chattels or by such other payment due date explicitly stated in a written contract agreed to by the buyer and seller, whichever is later, shall be guilty of a misdemeanor; except that if the value of the products or chattels exceeded $500.00 such person shall be guilty of a felony and, upon conviction thereof, shall be imprisoned for not less than one year nor more than five years.

Laws 1983, p. 485, § 2; Laws 1995, p. 244, § 11; Laws 2003, Act 93, § 1, eff. July 1, 2003.

Historical and Statutory Notes

The 2003 amendment by Act 93 rewrote the section which had read:

"Any person, either on his or her own account or for others, who shall buy cotton, corn, rice, crude turpentine, spirits of turpentine, rosin, pitch, tar, timber, pulpwood, poultry and poultry products, cattle, hogs, sheep, goats, ratites, horses, mules, pecans, peaches, apples, watermelons, cantaloupes, or other products or chattels and shall fail or refuse to pay therefor or shall make way with or dispose of the same before he or she shall have paid therefor unless credit shall be expressly extended therefor shall be guilty of a felony and, upon conviction thereof, shall be imprisoned for not less than one year nor more than five years."

§ 16–9–59. Operating credit repair services organization

(a) As used in this Code section, the term:

(1) "Buyer" means any individual who is solicited to purchase or who purchases the services of a credit repair services organization.

(2)(A) "Credit repair services organization" means any person who, with respect to the extension of credit to a buyer by others, sells, provides, or performs, or represents that he can or will sell, provide, or perform, in return for the payment of money or other valuable consideration any of the following services:

(i) Improving a buyer's credit record, history, or rating;

(ii) Obtaining an extension of credit for a buyer;

(iii) Providing advice or assistance to a buyer with regard to either division (i) or (ii) of this subparagraph.

(B) "Credit repair services organization" does not include:

(i) Any person authorized to make loans or extensions of credit under the laws of this state or the United States who is subject to regulation and supervision by this state or the United States;

(ii) Any bank or savings and loan institution whose deposits or accounts are eligible for insurance by the Federal Deposit Insurance Corporation or the Savings Association Insurance Fund of the Federal Deposit Insurance Corporation;

(iii) Any nonprofit organization exempt from taxation under Section 501(c)(3) of the Internal Revenue Code of 1986;

(iv) Any person licensed as a real estate broker by this state if the person is acting within the course and scope of that license;

(v) Any person licensed to practice law in this state if the person renders services within the course and scope of his or her practice as an attorney;

(vi) Any broker-dealer registered with the Securities and Exchange Commission or the Commodity Futures Trading Commission if the broker-dealer is acting within the course and scope of those regulatory agencies; or

(vii) Any consumer reporting agency as defined in the federal Fair Credit Reporting Act (15 U.S.C. 1681–1681t).

(3) "Extension of credit" means the right to defer payment of debt or to incur debt and defer its payment, offered or granted primarily for personal, family, or household purposes.

(b) A person commits the offense of operating a credit repair services organization when he or she owns, operates, or is affiliated with a credit repair services organization.

(c) Any person who commits the offense of operating a credit repair services organization shall be guilty of a misdemeanor.

Laws 1987, p. 1413, § 1; Laws 1988, p. 13, § 16.

§ 16–9–60. Foreclosure fraud

(a) For purposes of this Code section, the term "foreclosure fraud" shall include any of the following: knowingly or willfully representing that moneys provided to or on behalf of a debtor, as defined in Code Section 44–14–162.1 in connection with property used as a dwelling place by said debtor, are a loan if in fact they are used to purchase said property or such debtor's interest therein; or knowingly or willfully making fraudulent representation to a debtor about assisting the debtor in connection with said property.

(b) Any person who by foreclosure fraud purchases or attempts to purchase residential property by means of such fraudulent scheme shall be guilty of a felony.

(c) A person who violates subsection (b) of this Code section shall be punished by imprisonment for not less than one year nor more than three years or by a fine of not less than $1,000.00 nor more than $5,000.00, or both.

Laws 1988, p. 1469, § 1; Laws 1989, p. 12, § 1.

§ 16–9–61. Misrepresenting origin or ownership of timber or agricultural commodities

(a) A person commits the crime of misrepresenting the origin or ownership of timber or agricultural commodities when, in the course of a sale, attempted sale, delivery, or other completed or attempted transaction regarding timber or agricultural commodities, he or she knowingly, willfully, and with criminal intent to defraud makes a false statement or knowingly, willfully, and with criminal intent to defraud causes a false statement to be made with regard to any specific ownership of the timber or agricultural commodities or with regard to the location or ownership of the land where the timber was cut or the agricultural commodities were harvested.

(b) Misrepresenting the origin of timber or agricultural commodities shall be punished, upon conviction, as for a misdemeanor; except that if the property which was the subject of the misrepresentation exceeded $500.00 in value, it shall be a felony offense punishable upon conviction by a sentence of imprisonment of not less than one year and not exceeding five years.

Laws 1996, p. 943, § 1.

Article 5

Removal or Alteration of Identification from Property

§ 16–9–70. Criminal use of an article with an altered identification mark

(a) A person commits the offense of criminal use of an article with an altered identification mark when he or she buys, sells, receives, disposes of, conceals, or has in his or her possession a radio, piano, phonograph, sewing machine, washing machine, typewriter, adding machine, comptometer, bicycle, firearm, safe, vacuum cleaner, dictaphone, watch, watch movement, watch case, or any other mechanical or electrical device, appliance, contrivance, material, vessel as defined in Code Section 52–7–3, or other piece of apparatus or equipment, other than a motor vehicle as defined in Code Section 40–1–1, from which he or she knows the manufacturer's name plate, serial number, or any other distinguishing number or identification mark has been removed for the purpose of concealing or destroying the identity of such article.

(b) A person convicted of the offense of criminal use of an article with an altered identification mark shall be punished by imprisonment for not less than one nor more than five years.

(c) This Code section does not apply to those cases or instances where any of the changes or alterations enumerated in subsection (a) of this Code section have been customarily made or done as an established practice in the ordinary and regular conduct of business by the original manufacturer or by his duly appointed direct representative or under specific authorization from the original manufacturer.

Laws 1974, p. 434, § 1; Laws 2006, Act 456, § 2, eff. April 14, 2006.

Formerly Code 1933, § 26–1506.

Historical and Statutory Notes

The 2006 amendment by Act 456, in subsec. (a), substituted "vessel as defined in Code Section 52–7–3, or other" for "or"; and inserted gender neutral language.

§ 16–9–71. Removal of collars or identifying items or marks

(a) It shall be unlawful for any person without the express permission of the owner or lessee of an animal to remove a collar, tag, tattoo, or any identification mark artificially attached to or imprinted on an animal for the purposes of identification which causes or is likely to cause the loss of the animal to the owner thereof.

(b) Any person who violates subsection (a) of this Code section shall be guilty of a misdemeanor.

Laws 1980, p. 1062, § 1.

Formerly Code 1933, § 26–2802.1.

Article 6

Computer Systems Protection

Part 1

Computer Related Crimes Generally

§ 16–9–90. Short title

This article shall be known and may be cited as the "Georgia Computer Systems Protection Act."

Laws 1991, p. 1045, § 1; Laws 1996, p. 6, § 16.

§ 16–9–91. Legislative intent

The General Assembly finds that:

(1) Computer related crime is a growing problem in the government and in the private sector;

(2) Such crime occurs at great cost to the public, since losses for each incident of computer crime tend to be far greater than the losses associated with each incident of other white collar crime;

(3) The opportunities for computer related crimes in state programs, and in other entities which operate within the state, through the introduction of fraudulent records into a computer system, unauthorized use of computer facilities, alteration or destruction of computerized information files, and stealing of financial instruments, data, or other assets are great;

(4) Computer related crime operations have a direct effect on state commerce;

(5) Liability for computer crimes should be imposed on all persons, as that term is defined in this title; and

(6) The prosecution of persons engaged in computer related crime is difficult under previously existing Georgia criminal statutes.

Laws 1991, p. 1045, § 1.

§ 16–9–92. Definitions

As used in this article, the term:

(1) "Computer" means an electronic, magnetic, optical, hydraulic, electrochemical, or organic device or group of devices which, pursuant to a computer program, to human instruction, or to permanent instructions contained in the device or group of devices, can automatically perform computer operations with or on computer data and can communicate the results to another computer or to a person. The term includes any connected or directly related device, equipment, or facility which enables the computer to store, retrieve, or communicate computer programs, computer data, or the results of computer operations to or from a person, another computer, or another device. This term specifically includes, but is not limited to, mail servers and e–mail networks. This term does not include a device that is not used to communicate with or to manipulate any other computer.

(2) "Computer network" means a set of related, remotely connected computers and any communications facilities with the function and purpose of transmitting data among them through the communications facilities.

(3) "Computer operation" means computing, classifying, transmitting, receiving, retrieving, originating, switching, storing, displaying, manifesting, measuring, detecting, recording, reproducing, handling, or utilizing any form of data for business, scientific, control, or other purposes.

(4) "Computer program" means one or more statements or instructions composed and structured in a form acceptable to a computer that, when executed by a computer in actual or modified form, cause the computer to perform one or more computer operations. The term "computer program" shall include all associated procedures and documentation, whether or not such procedures and documentation are in human readable form.

(5) "Data" includes any representation of information, intelligence, or data in any fixed medium, including documentation, computer printouts, magnetic storage media, punched cards, storage in a computer, or transmission by a computer network.

(6) "Electronic communication" means any transfer of signs, signals, writing, images, sounds, data, or intelligence of any nature transmitted in whole or in part by a wire, radio, electromagnetic, photoelectronic, or photo–optical system that affects interstate or foreign commerce, but does not include:

(A) Any wire or oral communication;

(B) Any communication made through a tone–only paging device;

(C) Any communication from a tracking device; or

(D) Electronic funds transfer information stored by a financial institution in a communications system used for the electronic storage and transfer of funds.

(7) "Electronic communication service" means any service which provides to its users the ability to send or receive wire or electronic communications.

(8) "Electronic communications system" means any wire, radio, electromagnetic, photoelectronic, photo–optical, or facilities for the transmission of wire or electronic communications, and any computer facilities or related electronic equipment for the electronic storage of such communications.

(9) "Electronic means" is any device or apparatus which can be used to intercept a wire, oral, or electronic communication other than:

(A) Any telephone or telegraph instrument, equipment, or facility, or any component thereof,

(i) Furnished to the subscriber or user by a provider of electronic communication service in the ordinary course of its business and used by the subscriber or user in the ordinary course of its business or furnished by such subscriber or user for connection to the facilities of such service and used in the ordinary course of its business; or

(ii) Used by a provider of electronic communication service in the ordinary course of its business or by an investigative or law enforcement officer in the ordinary course of his or her duties; or

(B) A hearing aid or similar device being used to correct subnormal hearing to better than normal.

(10) "Electronic storage" means:

(A) Any temporary, intermediate storage of wire or electronic communication incidental to its electronic transmission; and

(B) Any storage of such communication by an electronic communication service for purposes of backup protection of such communication.

(11) "Financial instruments" includes any check, draft, money order, note, certificate of deposit, letter of credit, bill of exchange, credit or debit card, transaction–authorizing mechanism, or marketable security, or any computer representation thereof.

(12) "Law enforcement unit" means any law enforcement officer charged with the duty of enforcing the criminal laws and ordinances of the state or of the counties or municipalities of the state who is employed by and compensated by the state or any county or municipality of the state or who is elected and compensated on a fee basis. The term shall include, but not be limited to, members of the Department of Public Safety, municipal police, county police, sheriffs, deputy sheriffs, and agents and investigators of the Georgia Bureau of Investigation.

(13) "Property" includes computers, computer networks, computer programs, data, financial instruments, and services.

(14) "Remote computing service" means the provision to the public of computer storage or processing services by means of an electronic communications system.

(15) "Services" includes computer time or services or data processing services.

(16) "Use" includes causing or attempting to cause:

(A) A computer or computer network to perform or to stop performing computer operations;

(B) The obstruction, interruption, malfunction, or denial of the use of a computer, computer network, computer program, or data; or

(C) A person to put false information into a computer.

(17) "Victim expenditure" means any expenditure reasonably and necessarily incurred by the owner to verify that a computer, computer network, computer program, or data was or was not altered, deleted, damaged, or destroyed by unauthorized use.

(18) "Without authority" includes the use of a computer or computer network in a manner that exceeds any right or permission granted by the owner of the computer or computer network.

Laws 1991, p. 1045, § 1; Laws 1992, p. 6, § 16; Laws 2005, Act 46, § 3, eff. July 1, 2005.

Historical and Statutory Notes

The 2005 amendment by Act 46 rewrote par. (1); redesignated pars. (6), (7), (8), (9), (10), (11) as (11), (13), (15), (16), (17), (18) respectively; and added new pars. (6) through (10), (12), and (14). Prior to amendment, par. (1) had read:

"(1) 'Computer' means an electronic, magnetic, optical, electrochemical, or other high-speed data processing device or system performing computer operations with or on data and includes any data storage facility or communications facility directly related to or operating in conjunction with such device; but such term does not include an automated typewriter or typesetter, portable hand-held calculator, household appliance, or other similar device that is not used to communicate with or to manipulate any other computer."

§ 16–9–93. Criminal liability and penalties for crimes of computer theft, trespass, invasion of privacy, forgery, and password disclosure

(a) *Computer Theft.* Any person who uses a computer or computer network with knowledge that such use is without authority and with the intention of:

(1) Taking or appropriating any property of another, whether or not with the intention of depriving the owner of possession;

(2) Obtaining property by any deceitful means or artful practice; or

(3) Converting property to such person's use in violation of an agreement or other known legal obligation to make a specified application or disposition of such property

shall be guilty of the crime of computer theft.

(b) *Computer Trespass.* Any person who uses a computer or computer network with knowledge that such use is without authority and with the intention of:

(1) Deleting or in any way removing, either temporarily or permanently, any computer program or data from a computer or computer network;

(2) Obstructing, interrupting, or in any way interfering with the use of a computer program or data; or

(3) Altering, damaging, or in any way causing the malfunction of a computer, computer network, or computer program, regardless of how long the alteration, damage, or malfunction persists

shall be guilty of the crime of computer trespass.

(c) *Computer Invasion of Privacy.* Any person who uses a computer or computer network with the intention of examining any employment, medical, salary, credit, or any other financial or personal data relating to any other person with knowledge that such examination is without authority shall be guilty of the crime of computer invasion of privacy.

(d) *Computer Forgery.* Any person who creates, alters, or deletes any data contained in any computer or computer network, who, if such person had created, altered, or deleted a tangible document or instrument would have committed forgery under Article 1 of this chapter, shall be guilty of the crime of computer forgery. The absence of a tangible writing directly created or altered by the offender shall not be a defense to the crime of computer forgery if a creation, alteration, or deletion of data was involved in lieu of a tangible document or instrument.

(e) *Computer Password Disclosure.* Any person who discloses a number, code, password, or other means of access to a computer or computer network knowing that such disclosure is without authority and which results in damages (including the fair market value of any services used and victim expenditure) to the owner of the computer or computer network in excess of $500.00 shall be guilty of the crime of computer password disclosure.

(f) *Article not Exclusive.* The provisions of this article shall not be construed to preclude the applicability of any other law which presently applies or may in the future apply to any transaction or course of conduct which violates this article.

(g) *Civil Relief; Damages.*

(1) Any person whose property or person is injured by reason of a violation of any provision of this article may sue therefor and recover for any damages sustained and the costs of suit. Without limiting the generality of the term, "damages" shall include loss of profits and victim expenditure.

(2) At the request of any party to an action brought pursuant to this Code section, the court shall by reasonable means conduct all legal proceedings in such a way as to protect the secrecy and security of any computer, computer network, data, or computer program involved in order to prevent possible recurrence of the same or a similar act by another person and to protect any trade secrets of any party.

(3) The provisions of this article shall not be construed to limit any person's right to pursue any additional civil remedy otherwise allowed by law.

(4) A civil action under this Code section must be brought within four years after the violation is discovered or by exercise of reasonable diligence should have been discovered. For purposes of this article, a continuing violation of any one subsection of this Code section by any person constitutes a single violation by such person.

(h) *Criminal Penalties.*

(1) Any person convicted of the crime of computer theft, computer trespass, computer invasion of privacy, or computer forgery shall be fined not more than $50,000.00 or imprisoned not more than 15 years, or both.

(2) Any person convicted of computer password disclosure shall be fined not more than $5,000.00 or incarcerated for a period not to exceed one year, or both.

Laws 1991, p. 1045, § 1.

§ 16–9–93.1. Transmission of data through computer network, etc., using name, trade name, trademark, etc., to falsely identify person, organization, or representative transmitting such data

(a) It shall be unlawful for any person, any organization, or any representative of any organization knowingly to transmit any data through a computer network or over the transmission facilities or through the network facilities of a local telephone network for the purpose of setting up, maintaining, operating, or exchanging data with an electronic mailbox, home page, or any other electronic information storage bank or point of access to electronic information if such data uses any individual name, trade name, registered trademark, logo, legal or official seal, or copyrighted symbol to falsely identify the person, organization, or representative transmitting such data or which would falsely state or imply that such person, organization, or representative has permission or is legally authorized to use such trade name, registered trademark, logo, legal or official seal, or copyrighted symbol for such purpose when such permission or authorization has not been obtained; provided, however, that no telecommunications company or Internet access provider shall violate this Code section solely as a result of carrying or transmitting such data for its customers.

(b) Any person violating subsection (a) of this Code section shall be guilty of a misdemeanor.

(c) Nothing in this Code section shall be construed to limit an aggrieved party's right to pursue a civil action for equitable or monetary relief, or both, for actions which violate this Code section.

Laws 1996, p. 1505, § 1.

§ 16–9–94. Venue

For the purpose of venue under this article, any violation of this article shall be considered to have been committed:

(1) In the county of the principal place of business in this state of the owner of a computer, computer network, or any part thereof;

(2) In any county in which any person alleged to have violated any provision of this article had control or possession of any proceeds of the violation or of any books, records, documents, or property which were used in furtherance of the violation;

(3) In any county in which any act was performed in furtherance of any transaction which violated this article; and

(4) In any county from which, to which, or through which any use of a computer or computer network was made, whether by wires, electromagnetic waves, microwaves, or any other means of communication.

Laws 1991, p. 1045, § 1; Laws 1992, p. 6, § 16.

Part 2

Deceptive Commercial E-Mail

§ 16–9–100. Definitions

As used in this part, the term:

(1) "Advertiser" means a person or entity that advertises through the use of commercial e-mail.

(2) "Automatic technical process" means the actions performed by an e-mail service provider's or telecommunications carrier's computers or computer network while acting as an intermediary between the sender and the recipient of an e–mail.

(3) "Commercial e-mail" means any e-mail message initiated for the purpose of advertising or promoting the lease, sale, rental, gift, offer, or other disposition of any property, services, or extension of credit.

(4) "Direct consent" means that the recipient has expressly consented to receive e–mail advertisements from the advertiser or initiator, either in response to a clear and conspicuous request for direct consent or at the recipient's own initiative.

(5) "Domain" means any alphanumeric designation which is registered with or assigned by any domain name registrar, domain name registry, or other domain name registration authority as part of an electronic address on the Internet.

(6) "Domain owner" means, in relation to an e–mail address, the actual owner at the time an e–mail is received at that address of a domain that appears in or comprises a portion of the e–mail address. The registrant of a domain is presumed to be the actual owner of that domain.

(7) "E–mail" means an electronic message that is sent to an e–mail address and transmitted between two or more telecommunications devices, computers, or electronic devices capable of receiving electronic messages, whether or not the message is converted to hard copy format after receipt, viewed upon transmission, or stored for later retrieval. The term includes electronic messages that are transmitted through a local, regional, or global computer network.

(8) "E–mail address" means a destination, commonly expressed as a string of characters, to which e–mail can be sent or delivered. An e–mail address consists of a user name or mailbox, the "@" symbol, and reference to a domain.

(9) "E–mail service provider" means any person, including an Internet service provider, that is an intermediary in sending or receiving e–mail or that provides to end–users of the e–mail service the ability to send or receive e–mail.

(10) "False or misleading," when used in relation to a commercial e–mail, means that:

(A) The header information includes an originating or intermediate e–mail address, domain name, or Internet protocol address which was obtained by means of false or fraudulent pretenses or representations;

(B) The header information fails to accurately identify the computer used to initiate the e–mail;

(C) The subject line of the e–mail is intended to mislead a recipient about a material fact regarding the content or subject matter of the e–mail;

(D) The header information is altered or modified in a manner that impedes or precludes the recipient of the e–mail or an e–mail service provider from identifying, locating, or contacting the person who initiated the e–mail;

(E) The header information or content of the commercial e–mail, without authorization and with intent to mislead, references a personal name, entity name, trade name, mark, domain, address, phone number, or other personally identifying information belonging to a third party in such manner as would cause a recipient to believe that the third party authorized, endorsed, sponsored, sent, or was otherwise involved in the transmission of the commercial e–mail;

(F) The header information or content of the commercial e–mail contains false or fraudulent information regarding the identity, location, or means of contacting the initiator of the commercial e-mail; or

(G) The commercial e–mail falsely or erroneously states or represents that the transmission of the e–mail was authorized on the basis of:

(i) The recipient's prior direct consent to receive the commercial e–mail; or

(ii) A preexisting or current business relationship between the recipient and either the initiator or advertiser.

(11) "Header information" means those portions of an e–mail message which designate or otherwise identify:

(A) The sender;

(B) All recipients;

(C) An alternative return e–mail address, if any; and

(D) The names or Internet protocol addresses of the computers, systems, or other means used to send, transmit, route, or receive the e–mail message.

The term does not include either the subject line or the content of an e–mail message.

(12) "Incident" means the contemporaneous initiation in violation of this part of one or more commercial e–mails containing substantially similar content.

(13) "Initiate" or "initiator" means to transmit or cause to be transmitted a commercial e–mail, but does not include the routine transmission of the commercial e–mail through the network or system of a telecommunications utility or an e–mail service provider.

(14) "Internet protocol address" means the unique numerical address assigned to and used to identify a specific computer or computer network that is directly connected to the Internet.

(15) "Minor" means any person under the age of 18 years.

(16) "Person" means a person as defined by Code Section 16–1–3 and specifically includes any limited liability company, trust, joint venture, or other legally cognizable entity.

(17) "Preexisting or current business relationship," as used in connection with the sending of a commercial e–mail, means that the recipient has made an inquiry and has provided his or her e–mail address, or has made an application, purchase, or transaction, with or without consideration, regarding products or services offered by the advertiser.

(18) "Protected computer" means any computer that, at the time of an alleged violation of any provision of this part involving that computer, was located within the geographic boundaries of the State of Georgia.

(19) "Recipient" means any addressee of a commercial e–mail advertisement. If an addressee of a commercial e–mail has one or more e–mail addresses to which a commercial e–mail is sent, the addressee shall be deemed to be a separate recipient for each e–mail address to which the e–mail is sent.

(20) "Routine transmission" means the forwarding, routing, relaying, handling, or storing of an e–mail message through an automatic technical process. The term shall not include the sending, or the knowing participation in the sending, of commercial e–mail advertisements.

Laws 2005, Act 46, § 4, eff. July 1, 2005.

Historical and Statutory Notes

Laws 2005, Act 46, §§ 1 and 2, provide:

"Section 1. This Act shall be known and may be cited as the "Georgia Slam Spam E–mail Act.

"Section 2. The General Assembly finds and declares that electronic mail has become an important and popular means of communication, relied on by millions of Georgians on a daily basis for personal and commercial purposes. The low cost and global reach of electronic mail make it convenient and efficient. Electronic mail serves as a catalyst for economic development and frictionless commerce. The General Assembly further finds that the convenience and efficiency of electronic mail is threatened by an ever–increasing glut of deceptive commercial electronic mail. The senders of these electronic messages engage in a variety of fraudulent and deceptive practices to hide their identities, to disguise the true source of their electronic mail, and to evade the criminal and civil consequences of their actions. Deceptive commercial electronic mail imposes costs upon its ultimate recipients who are forced to receive, review, and delete unwanted messages and upon the electronic mail service providers forced to carry the messages. The General Assembly further finds that our state has a paramount interest in protecting its businesses and citizens from the deleterious effects of deceptive commercial electronic mail, including the impermissible shifting of cost and economic burden that results from the false and fraudulent nature of deceptive commercial electronic mail. Georgia's enforcement of this interest imposes no additional burden upon the senders of such electronic mails in relation to the laws of any other state, in that such enforcement requires nothing more than the senders' forbearance from active deception."

§ 16–9–101. Initiation of deceptive commercial e-mail

Any person who initiates a commercial e–mail that the person knew or should have known to be false or misleading that is sent from, passes through, or is received by a protected computer shall be guilty of the crime of initiation of deceptive commercial e–mail.

Laws 2005, Act 46, § 4, eff. July 1, 2005.

§ 16–9–102. Violations; penalties

(a) Any person convicted of a violation of Code Section 16–9–101 shall be guilty of a misdemeanor and punished by a fine of not more than $1,000.00 or by imprisonment of not more than 12 months, or both, except:

(1) Where the volume of commercial e–mail transmitted exceeded 10,000 attempted recipients in any 24 hour period;

(2) Where the volume of commercial e–mail transmitted exceeded 100,000 attempted recipients in any 30 day period;

(3) Where the volume of commercial e–mail transmitted exceeded one million attempted recipients in any one–year period;

(4) Where the revenue generated from a specific commercial e–mail exceeded $1,000.00;

(5) Where the total revenue generated from all commercial e–mail transmitted to any e–mail service provider or its subscribers exceeded $50,000.00; or

(6) Where any person knowingly hires, employs, uses, or permits any minor to assist in the transmission of commercial e–mail in violation of Code Section 16–9–101,

the person shall be guilty of a felony and punished by a fine of not more than $50,000.00 or by imprisonment of not more than five years, or both.

(b) For the second conviction of Code Section 16–9–101 within a five–year period, as measured from the dates of previous arrests for which convictions were obtained to the date of the current arrest for which a conviction is obtained, the person shall be guilty of a felony and punished by a fine of not more than $50,000.00 or by imprisonment of not more than five years, or both. For the purpose of this subsection, the term "conviction" shall include a plea of nolo contendere.

Laws 2005, Act 46, § 4, eff. July 1, 2005.

§ 16–9–103. Venue

For the purpose of venue under this part, any violation of this part shall be considered to have been committed:

(1) In the county of the principal place of business in this state of the owner of an involved protected computer, computer network, or any part thereof;

(2) In any county in which any person alleged to have violated any provision of this part had control or possession of any proceeds of the violation or of any books, records, documents, or property which were used in furtherance of the violation;

(3) In any county in which any act was performed in furtherance of any transaction which violated this part; and

(4) In any county from which, to which, or through which any use of an involved protected computer or computer network was made, whether by wires, electromagnetic waves, microwaves, or any other means of communication.

Laws 2005, Act 46, § 4, eff. July 1, 2005.

§ 16–9–104. Attorney General concurrent jurisdiction

The Attorney General shall have concurrent jurisdiction with the district attorneys and solicitors–general to conduct the criminal prosecution of violations of this part.

Laws 2005, Act 46, § 4, eff. July 1, 2005.

§ 16–9–105. Standing to assert civil action

(a) The following persons shall have standing to assert a civil action under this part:

(1) Any e–mail service provider whose protected computer was used to send, receive, or transmit an e–mail that was sent in violation of this part; and

(2) A domain owner of any e–mail address to which a deceptive commercial e–mail is sent in violation of this part, provided that the domain owner also owns a protected computer at which the e–mail was received.

(b) Any person who has standing and who suffers personal, property, or economic damage by reason of a violation of any provision of this part may initiate a civil action for and recover the greater of:

(1) Five thousand dollars plus expenses of litigation and reasonable attorney's fees;

(2) Liquidated damages of $1,000.00 for each offending commercial e–mail, up to a limit of $2 million per incident, plus expenses of litigation and reasonable attorney's fees; or

(3) Actual damages, plus expenses of litigation and reasonable attorney's fees.

Laws 2005, Act 46, § 4, eff. July 1, 2005.

§ 16–9–106. Separate offenses; application of other laws policy of provider

(a) Any crime committed in violation of this part shall be considered a separate offense.

(b) The provisions of this part shall not be construed as limiting or precluding the application of any other provision of law which applies to any transaction or course of conduct which violates this part.

(c) Nothing in this part shall be construed to limit or restrict the adoption, implementation, or enforcement by an e–mail service provider or Internet service provider of a policy of declining to transmit, receive, route, relay, handle, or store certain types of e-mail.

Laws 2005, Act 46, § 4, eff. July 1, 2005.

§ 16–9–107. Action against e-mail service provider

There shall be no cause of action under this part against an e-mail service provider on the basis of its routine transmission of any commercial e-mail over its computer network.

Laws 2005, Act 46, § 4, eff. July 1, 2005.

Part 3

Investigative Authority

§ 16–9–108. Authority of Attorney General and district attorneys; failure to obey subpoena

(a) In any investigation of a violation of this article or any investigation of a violation of Code Section 16–12–100, 16–12–100.1, 16–12–100.2, 16–5–90, or Article 8 of Chapter 9 of Title 16 involving the use of a computer in furtherance of the act, the Attorney General or any district attorney shall have the power to administer oaths; to call any party to testify under oath at such investigation; to require the attendance of witnesses and the production of books, records, and papers; and to take the depositions of witnesses. The Attorney General or any such district attorney is authorized to issue a subpoena for any witness or a subpoena to compel the production of any books, records, or papers.

(b) In case of refusal to obey a subpoena issued under this Code section to any person and upon application by the Attorney General or district attorney, the superior court in whose jurisdiction the witness is to appear or in which the books, records, or papers are to be produced may issue to that person an order requiring him or her to appear before the court to show cause why he or she should not be held in contempt for refusal to obey the subpoena. Failure to obey a subpoena may be punished by the court as contempt of court.

Laws 2005, Act 46, § 4, eff. July 1, 2005.

§ 16–9–109. Authority of law enforcement units, the Attorney General, and district attorneys

(a) Any law enforcement unit, the Attorney General, or any district attorney who is conducting an investigation of a violation of this article or an investigation of a violation of Code Section 16–12–100, 16–12–100.1, 16–12–100.2, or 16–5–90 or Article 8 of this chapter involving the use of a computer, cellular telephone, or any other electronic device used in furtherance of the act may require the disclosure by a provider of electronic communication service or remote computing service of the contents of a wire or electronic communication that is in electronic storage in an electronic communications system for 180 days or less pursuant to a search warrant issued under the provisions of Article 2 of Chapter 5 of Title 17 by a court with jurisdiction over the offense under investigation. Such court may require the disclosure by a provider of electronic communication service or remote computing service of the contents of a wire or electronic communication that has been in electronic storage in an electronic communications system for more than 180 days as set forth in subsection (b) of this Code section.

(b)(1) Any law enforcement unit, the Attorney General, or any district attorney may require a provider of electronic communication service or remote computing service to disclose a record or other information pertaining to a subscriber to or customer of such service, exclusive of the contents of communications, only when any law enforcement unit, the Attorney General, or any district attorney:

(A) Obtains a search warrant as provided in Article 2 of Chapter 5 of Title 17;

(B) Obtains a court order for such disclosure under subsection (c) of this Code section; or

(C) Has the consent of the subscriber or customer to such disclosure.

(2) A provider of electronic communication service or remote computing service shall disclose to any law enforcement unit, the Attorney General, or any district attorney the:

(A) Name;

(B) Address;

(C) Local and long distance telephone connection records, or records of session times and durations;

(D) Length of service, including the start date, and types of service utilized;

(E) Telephone or instrument number or other subscriber number or identity, including any temporarily assigned network address; and

(F) Means and source of payment for such service, including any credit card or bank account number of a subscriber to or customer of such service when any law enforcement unit, the Attorney General, or any district attorney uses a subpoena authorized by Code Section 16–9–108, 35–3–4.1, or 45–15–17 or a grand jury or trial subpoena when any law enforcement unit, the Attorney General, or any district attorney complies with paragraph (1) of this subsection.

(3) Any law enforcement unit, the Attorney General, or any district attorney receiving records or information under this subsection shall not be required to provide notice to a subscriber or customer. A provider of electronic communication service or remote computing service shall not disclose to a subscriber or customer the existence of any search warrant or subpoena issued pursuant to this article nor shall a provider of electronic communication service or remote computing service disclose to a subscriber or customer that any records have been requested by or disclosed to any law enforcement unit, the Attorney General, or any district attorney pursuant to this article.

(c) A court order for disclosure issued pursuant to subsection (b) of this Code section may be issued by any superior court with jurisdiction over the offense under investigation and shall only issue such court order for disclosure if any law enforcement unit, the Attorney General, or any district attorney offers specific and articulable facts showing that there are reasonable grounds to believe that the contents of an electronic communication, or the records or other information sought, are relevant and material to an ongoing criminal investigation. A court issuing an order pursuant to this Code section, on a motion made promptly by a provider of electronic communication service or remote computing service, may quash or modify such order, if compliance with such order would be unduly burdensome or oppressive on such provider.

(d)(1) Any records supplied pursuant to this part shall be accompanied by the affidavit of the custodian or other qualified witness, stating in substance each of the following:

(A) The affiant is the duly authorized custodian of the records or other qualified witness and has authority to certify the records;

(B) The copy is a true copy of all the records described in the subpoena, court order, or search warrant and the records were delivered to the attorney, the attorney's representative, or the director of the Georgia Bureau of Investigation or the director's designee;

(C) The records were prepared by the personnel of the business in the ordinary course of business at or near the time of the act, condition, or event;

(D) The sources of information and method and time of preparation were such as to indicate its trustworthiness;

(E) The identity of the records; and

(F) A description of the mode of preparation of the records.

(2) If the business has none or only part of the records described, the custodian or other qualified witness shall so state in the affidavit.

(3) If the original records would be admissible in evidence if the custodian or other qualified witness had been present and testified to the matters stated in the affidavit, the copy of the records shall be admissible in evidence. When more than one person has knowledge of the facts, more than one affidavit shall be attached to the records produced.

(4) No later than 30 days prior to trial, a party intending to offer such evidence produced in compliance with this subsection shall provide written notice of such intentions to the opposing party or parties. A motion opposing the admission of such evidence shall be filed within ten days of the filing of such notice, and the court shall hold a hearing and rule on such motion no later than ten days prior to trial. Failure of a party to file such motion opposing admission prior to trial shall constitute a waiver of objection to such records and affidavit. However, the court, for good cause shown, may grant relief from such waiver.

Laws 2005, Act 46, § 4, eff. July 1, 2005; Laws 2006, Act 453, § 16, eff. April 14, 2006; Laws 2007, Act 202, § 1, eff. May 23, 2007.

Historical and Statutory Notes

The 2006 amendment by Act 453 was a provision contained in a correction bill.

The 2007 amendment by Act 202, in subsec. (a), substituted "Code Section 16-12-100, 16-12-100.1, 16-12-100.2, or 16-5-90 or Article 8 of this chapter involving the use of a computer, cellular phone, or any other electronic device used" for "Code Section 16-12-100, 16-12-100.1, 16-12-100.2, 16-5-90 or Article 8 of Chapter 9 of Title 16 involving the use of a computer"; in subsec. (b), substituted "Code Section 16-9-108, 35–3–4.1, or 45-15-17" for "Code Section 16-9-108 or 45-15-17"; and in subpar. (d)(1)(B), substituted ", the attorney's representative, or the director of the Georgia Bureau of Investigation or the director's designee;" for "or the attorney's representative;".

Part 4

Identifying Information

§ 16–9–109.1. False representation in the use of internet or electronic mail to induce another to provide identifying information; penalties; immunity

(a) As used in this part, the term:

(1) "Electronic mail message" means a message sent to a unique destination, commonly expressed as a string of characters, consisting of a unique user name or mailbox, commonly referred to as the "local part," and a reference to an Internet domain, commonly referred to as the "domain part," whether or not displayed, to which an electronic message can be sent or delivered.

(2) "Employer" includes a business entity's officers, directors, parent corporation, subsidiaries, affiliates, and other corporate entities under common ownership or control within a business enterprise.

(3) "Identifying information" means, with respect to an individual, any of the following:

(A) Social security number;

(B) Driver's license number;

(C) Bank account number;

(D) Credit card or debit card number;

(E) Personal identification number or PIN;

(F) Automated or electronic signature;

(G) Unique biometric data;

(H) Account password; or

(I) Any other piece of information that can be used to access an individual's financial accounts or to obtain goods or services.

(4) "Internet" shall have the meaning set forth in paragraph (10) of Code Section 16–9–151.

(5) "Web page" means a location that has a single uniform resource locator or other single location with respect to the Internet.

(b)(1) It shall be unlawful for any person with intent to defraud, by means of a web page, electronic mail message, or otherwise through use of the Internet, to solicit, request, or take any action to induce another person to provide identifying information by representing himself, herself, or itself to be a business without the authority or approval of such business.

(2) It shall be unlawful for any person, with actual knowledge, conscious avoidance of actual knowledge, or willfully, to possess with intent to use in a fraudulent manner, sell, or distribute any identifying information obtained in violation of paragraph (1) of this subsection.

(c) Any person who intentionally violates subsection (b) of this Code section shall be guilty of a felony and shall be punished by imprisonment for not less than one nor more than 20 years, a fine of not less than $1,000. 00 nor more than $500,000.00, or both.

(d)(1) No employer shall be held criminally liable under this Code section as a result of any actions taken:

(A) With respect to computer equipment used by its employees, contractors, subcontractors, agents, leased employees, or other staff which the employer owns, leases, or otherwise makes available or allows to be connected to the employer's network or other computer facilities when such equipment is used for an illegal purpose without the employer's knowledge, consent, or approval; or

(B) By employees, contractors, subcontractors, agents, leased employees, or other staff who misuse an employer's computer equipment for an illegal purpose without the employer's knowledge, consent, or approval.

(2) No person shall be held criminally liable under this Code section when its protected computers, computer equipment, or software product has been used by unauthorized users to violate this Code section without such person's knowledge, consent, or approval.

(e) This Code section shall not apply to a telecommunications provider's or Internet service provider's good faith transmission or routing of, or intermediate temporary storing or caching of, identifying information.

(f) No provider of an interactive computer service may be held liable in a civil action under any law of this state, or any of its political subdivisions, for removing or disabling access to content on an Internet website or other online location controlled or operated by such provider, when such provider believes in good faith that such content has been used to engage in a violation of this part.

Laws 2008, Act 529, § 1, eff. July 1, 2008.

Article 7

Motor Vehicle Sales and Transfers

§ 16–9–110. Sale of motor vehicles not manufactured to comply with federal emission and safety standards

(a) It shall be unlawful for any person, firm, or corporation knowingly to sell, transfer, or otherwise convey any motor vehicle which was not manufactured to comply with federal emission and safety standards applicable to new motor vehicles as required by 42 U.S.C. Section 7401 through Section 7642, known as the federal Clean Air Act, as amended, and as required by 15 U.S.C. Section 1381 through Section 1431, known as the National Traffic and Motor Vehicle Safety Act of 1966, as amended, unless and until the United States Customs Service or the United States Department of Transportation and the United States Environmental Protection Agency have certified that the motor vehicle complies with such applicable federal standards.

(b) Any person convicted of violating subsection (a) of this Code section shall be guilty of a misdemeanor.

Laws 1985, p. 692, § 1; Laws 1992, p. 6, § 16; Laws 1996, p. 6, § 16.

§ 16–9–111. Installation practices involving air bags

Any person who knowingly installs or reinstalls any object in lieu of and other than an air bag which was designed in accordance with federal safety regulations for the make, model, and year of the vehicle as part of a vehicle inflatable restraint system shall be guilty of a misdemeanor of a high and aggravated nature.

Laws 2002, p. 629, § 1.

Article 8

Identity Fraud

§ 16–9–120. Definitions

As used in this article, the term:

(1) "Administrator" means the administrator appointed under Part 2 of Article 15 of Chapter 1 of Title 10, the "Fair Business Practices Act of 1975."

(2) "Business victim" means any individual or entity that provided money, credit, goods, services, or anything of value to someone other than the intended recipient where the intended recipient has not given permission for the actual recipient to receive it and the individual or entity that provided money, credit, goods, services, or anything of value has suffered financial loss as a direct result of the commission or attempted commission of a violation of this article.

(3) "Consumer victim" means any individual whose personal identifying information has been obtained, compromised, used, or recorded in any manner without the permission of that individual.

(4) "Identifying information" shall include, but not be limited to:

(A) Current or former names;

(B) Social security numbers;

(C) Driver's license numbers;

(D) Checking account numbers;

(E) Savings account numbers;

(F) Credit and other financial transaction card numbers;

(G) Debit card numbers;

(H) Personal identification numbers;

(I) Electronic identification numbers;

(J) Digital or electronic signatures;

(K) Medical identification numbers;

(L) Birth dates;

(M) Mother's maiden name;

(N) Selected personal identification numbers;

(O) Tax identification numbers;

(P) State identification card numbers issued by state departments; or

(Q) Any other numbers or information which can be used to access a person's or entity's resources.

(5) "Resources" includes, but is not limited to:

(A) A person's or entity's credit, credit history, credit profile, and credit rating;

(B) United States currency, securities, real property, and personal property of any kind;

(C) Credit, charge, and debit accounts;

(D) Loans and lines of credit;

(E) Documents of title and other forms of commercial paper recognized under Title 11;

(F) Any account, including a safety deposit box, with a financial institution as defined by Code Section 7–1–4, including a national bank, federal savings and loan association, or federal credit union or a securities dealer licensed by the Secretary of State or the federal Securities and Exchange Commission; and

(G) A person's personal history, including but not limited to records of such person's driving records; criminal, medical, or insurance history; education; or employment.

Laws 1998, p. 865, § 2; Laws 2002, p. 551, § 2.

Historical and Statutory Notes

The 2002 amendment rewrote this article. Prior to amendment 16–9–120 provided:

"There is created the criminal offense of financial identity fraud."

§ 16–9–121. Elements of offense

(a) A person commits the offense of identity fraud when he or she willfully and fraudulently:

(1) Without authorization or consent, uses or possesses with intent to fraudulently use identifying information concerning a person;

(2) Uses identifying information of an individual under 18 years old over whom he or she exercises custodial authority;

(3) Uses or possesses with intent to fraudulently use identifying information concerning a deceased individual;

(4) Creates, uses, or possesses with intent to fraudulently use any counterfeit or fictitious identifying information concerning a fictitious person with intent to use such counterfeit or fictitious identification information for the purpose of committing or facilitating the commission of a crime or fraud on another person; or

(5) Without authorization or consent, creates, uses, or possesses with intent to fraudulently use any counterfeit or fictitious identifying information concerning a real person with intent to use such counterfeit or fictitious identification information for the purpose of committing or facilitating the commission of a crime or fraud on another person.

(b) A person commits the offense of identity fraud by receipt of fraudulent identification information when he or she willingly accepts for identification purposes identifying information which he or she knows to be fraudulent, stolen, counterfeit, or fictitious. In any prosecution under this subsection it shall not be necessary to show a conviction of the principal thief, counterfeiter, or fraudulent user.

(c) The offenses created by this Code section shall not merge with any other offense.

(d) This Code section shall not apply to a person under the age of 21 who uses a fraudulent, counterfeit, or other false identification card for the purpose of obtaining entry into a business establishment or for purchasing items which he or she is not of legal age to purchase.

Laws 1998, p. 865, § 2; Laws 1999, p. 81, § 16; Laws 2002, p. 551, § 2; Laws 2007, Act 241, § 4, eff. May 24, 2007; Laws 2010, Act 501, § 1, eff. July 1, 2010.

Historical and Statutory Notes

The 2002 amendment rewrote this article. Prior to amendment 16–9–121 provided:

"A person commits the offense of financial identity fraud when without the authorization or permission of another person and with the intent unlawfully to appropriate financial resources of that other person to his or her own use or to the use of a third party he or she:

"(1) Obtains or records identifying information which would assist in accessing the financial resources of the other person; or

"(2) Accesses or attempts to access the financial resources of the other person through the use of identifying information. Such identifying information shall include but not be limited to:

"(A) Social security numbers;

"(B) Driver's license numbers;

"(C) Checking account numbers;

"(D) Savings account numbers;

"(E) Credit card numbers;

"(F) Debit card numbers;

"(G) Personal identification numbers;

"(H) Electronic identification numbers;

"(I) Digital signatures; or

"(J) Any other numbers or information which can be used to access a person's financial resources."

The 2007 amendment by Act 241 rewrote the section which had read:

"A person commits the offense of identity fraud when without the authorization or permission of a person with the intent unlawfully to appropriate resources of or cause physical harm to that person, or of any other person, to his or her own use or to the use of a third party he or she:

"(1) Obtains or records identifying information of a person which would assist in accessing the resources of that person or any other person; or

"(2) Accesses or attempts to access the resources of a person through the use of identifying information."

Laws 2007, Act 241, § 7, provides:

"This Act shall become effective upon its approval by the Governor or upon its becoming law without such approval and Section 4 shall apply to all offenses occurring on or after such date."

The 2010 amendment by Act 501, in subsec. (a), in pars. (1), (4) and (5) substituted "person" for "individual", and made other incidental changes.

§ 16–9–122. Unlawful acts; punishment

It shall be unlawful for any person to attempt or conspire to commit any offense prohibited by this article. Any person convicted of a violation of this Code section shall be punished by imprisonment or community service, by a fine, or by both such punishments not to exceed the maximum punishment prescribed for the offense the commission of which was the object of the attempt or conspiracy.

Laws 2002, p. 551, § 2.

Historical and Statutory Notes

The 2002 amendment rewrote this article. Prior to amendment 16–9–122 provided:

"The administrator appointed under Code Section 10–1–395 shall have the authority to investigate any complaints regarding financial identity fraud. In conducting such investigations the administrator shall have all investigative powers which are available to the administrator under Part 2 of Article 15 of Chapter 1 of Title 10, the |LSQUOŒFair Business Practices Act of 1975.' "

§ 16–9–123. Investigation of complaints

The administrator appointed under Code Section 10–1–395 shall have the authority to investigate any complaints of consumer victims regarding identity fraud. In conducting such investigations the administrator shall have all investigative powers which are available to the administrator under Part 2 of Article 15 of Chapter 1 of Title 10, the "Fair Business Practices Act of 1975." If, after such investigation, the administrator determines that a person has been a consumer victim of identity fraud in this state, the administrator shall, at the request of the consumer victim, provide the consumer victim with certification of the findings of such investigation. Copies of any and all complaints received by any law enforcement agency of this state regarding potential violations of this article shall be transmitted to the Georgia Bureau of Investigation. The Georgia Bureau of Investigation shall maintain a repository for all complaints in the State of Georgia regarding identity fraud. Information contained in such repository shall not be subject to public disclosure. The information in the repository may be transmitted to any other appropriate investigatory agency or entity. Consumer victims of identity fraud may file complaints directly with the Governor's Office of Consumer Affairs, the Georgia Bureau of Investigation, or with local law enforcement. Employees of the Governor's Office of Consumer Affairs may communicate with consumer victims. Any and all transmissions authorized under this Code section may be transmitted electronically, provided that such transmissions are made through a secure channel for the transmission of such electronic communications or information, the sufficiency of which is acceptable to the Governor's Office of Consumer Affairs. Nothing in this Code section shall be construed to preclude any otherwise authorized law enforcement or prosecutorial agencies from conducting investigations and prosecuting offenses of identity fraud.

Laws 1998, p. 865, § 2; Laws 2002, p. 551, § 2; Laws 2008, Act 570, § 1, eff. May 13, 2008.

Formerly Code 1981, § 16–9–122.

Historical and Statutory Notes

The 2002 amendment rewrote this article. Prior to amendment 16–9–123 provided:

"The Attorney General shall have the authority to conduct the criminal prosecution of all cases of financial identity fraud or to refer them to the district attorney in the county where the crime was committed."

The 2008 amendment by Act 570 substituted "Georgia Bureau of Investigation" for "Governor's Office of Consumer Affairs" in two places; and inserted ", Georgia Bureau of Investigation, or with local law enforcement".

§ 16–9–124. Conduct of criminal investigation

The Attorney General and prosecuting attorneys shall have the authority to conduct the criminal prosecution of all cases of identity fraud.

Laws 1998, p. 865, § 2; Laws 2002, p. 551, § 2.

Formerly Code 1981, § 16–9–123.

Historical and Statutory Notes

The 2002 amendment rewrote this article. Prior to amendment 16–9–124 provided:

"In any criminal proceeding brought pursuant to this article, the crime shall be considered to have been committed in any county in which any part of the financial identity fraud took place, regardless of whether the defendant was ever actually in such county."

§ 16–9–125. Venue

The General Assembly finds that identity fraud involves the use of identifying information which is uniquely personal to the consumer or business victim of that identity fraud and which information is considered to be in the lawful possession of the consumer or business victim wherever the consumer or business victim currently resides or is found. Accordingly, the fraudulent use of that information involves the fraudulent use of information that is, for the purposes of this article, found within the county where the consumer or business victim of the identity fraud resides or is found. Accordingly, in a proceeding under this article, the crime will be considered to have been committed in any county where the person whose means of identification or financial information was appropriated resides or is found, or in any county in which any other part of the offense took place, regardless of whether the defendant was ever actually in such county.

Laws 1998, p. 865, § 2; Laws 2002, p. 551, § 2.

Formerly Code 1981, § 16–9–124.

Historical and Statutory Notes

The 2002 amendment rewrote this article. Prior to amendment 16–9–125 provided:

"A violation of this article shall be punishable by imprisonment for not less than one nor more than ten years."

§ 16–9–125.1. Law enforcement agency jurisdiction

(a) A person who has learned or reasonably believes that he or she has been the victim of identity fraud may contact the local law enforcement agency with jurisdiction over his or her actual residence for the purpose of making an incident report. The law enforcement agency having jurisdiction over the complainant's residence shall make a report of the complaint and provide the complainant with a copy of the report. Where jurisdiction for the investigation and prosecution of the complaint lies with another agency, the law enforcement agency making the report shall forward a copy to the agency having such jurisdiction and shall advise the complainant that the report has been so forwarded.

(b) Nothing in this Code section shall be construed so as to interfere with the discretion of a law enforcement agency to allocate resources for the investigation of crimes. A report created pursuant to this Code section is not required to be counted as an open case file.

Laws 2007, Act 241, § 5, eff. May 24, 2007.

§ 16–9–126. Punishment

(a) A violation of this article, other than a violation of Code Section 16–9–122, shall be punishable by imprisonment for not less than one nor more than ten years or a fine not to exceed $100,000.00, or both. Any person who commits such a violation for the second or any subsequent offense shall be punished by imprisonment for not less than three nor more than 15 years, a fine not to exceed $250,000.00, or both.

(b) A violation of this article which does not involve the intent to commit theft or appropriation of any property, resource, or other thing of value that is committed by a person who is less than 21 years of age shall be punishable by imprisonment for not less than one nor more than three years or a fine not to exceed $ 5,000.00, or both.

(c) Any person found guilty of a violation of this article may be ordered by the court to make restitution to any consumer victim or any business victim of such fraud.

(d) Each violation of this article shall constitute a separate offense.

(e) Upon a conviction of a violation of this article, the court may issue any order necessary to correct a public record that contains false information resulting from the actions which resulted in the conviction.

Laws 1998, p. 865, § 2; Laws 2002, p. 551, § 2; Laws 2007, Act 241, § 6, eff. May 24, 2007.

Formerly Code 1981, § 16–9–125.

Historical and Statutory Notes

The 2002 amendment rewrote this article. Prior to amendment 16–9–126 provided:

"In addition to being imprisoned as provided in Code Section 16–9–125, a person found guilty of financial identity fraud may be ordered by the court to make restitution to any victims of such fraud."

The 2007 amendment by Act 241 redesignated subsecs. (b) through (d) as subsecs. (c) through (e), and added new subsec. (b).

In 2007, the Code Commission, in subsec. (b), inserted a comma following "resource" and deleted a comma following "21 years of age". See § 28–9–5.

§ 16–9–127. Authority of administrator

The administrator shall have authority to initiate any proceedings and to exercise any power or authority in the same manner as if he or she were acting under Part 2 of Article 15 of Chapter 1 of Title 10, as regards violations or potential violations of this article.

Laws 1998, p. 865, § 2; Laws 2002, p. 551, § 2.

Formerly Code 1981, § 16–9–126.

Historical and Statutory Notes

The 2002 amendment rewrote this article. Prior to amendment 16–9–127 provided:

"The prohibitions set forth in Code Section 16–9–121 shall not apply to:

"(1) The lawful obtaining of credit information in the course of a bona fide consumer or commercial transaction;

"(2) The lawful, good faith exercise of a security interest or a right to offset by a creditor or a financial institution; or

"(3) The lawful, good faith compliance by any party when required by any warrant, levy, garnishment, attachment, court order, or other judicial or administrative order, decree, or directive.

"These exemptions will not apply to a person intending to further a scheme to violate Code Section 16–9–121."

§ 16–9–128. Exemptions

(a) The prohibitions set forth in Code Sections 16–9–121 and 16–9–122 shall not apply to nor shall any cause of action arise under Code Sections 16–9–129 and 16–9–131 for:

(1) The lawful obtaining of credit information in the course of a bona fide consumer or commercial transaction;

(2) The lawful, good faith exercise of a security interest or a right to offset by a creditor or a financial institution;

(3) The lawful, good faith compliance by any party when required by any warrant, levy, garnishment, attachment, court order, or other judicial or administrative order, decree, or directive; or

(4) The good faith use of identifying information with the permission of the affected person.

(b) The exemptions provided in subsection (a) of this Code section will not apply to a person intending to further a scheme to violate Code Section 16–9–121 or 16–9–122.

(c) It is not necessary for the state to negate any exemption or exception in this article in any complaint, accusation, indictment, or other pleading or in any trial, hearing, or other proceeding under this article involving a business victim. In such cases the burden of proof of any exemption or exception is upon the business victim claiming it.

Laws 2002, p. 551, § 2; Laws 2010, Act 501, § 2, eff. July 1, 2010.

Historical and Statutory Notes

The 2010 amendment by Act 501, in subsec. (a), in par. (4), substituted "person" for "individual".

§ 16–9–129. Business victims; damages, attorney's fees, and costs

Any business victim who is injured by reason of any violation of this article shall have a cause of action for the actual damages sustained and, where appropriate, punitive damages. Such business victim may also recover attorney's fees in the trial and appellate courts and the costs of investigation and litigation reasonably incurred.

Laws 2002, p. 551, § 2.

§ 16–9–130. Consumer victims; damages, attorney's fees, and costs; procedure

(a) Any consumer victim who suffers injury or damages as a result of a violation of this article may bring an action individually or as a representative of a class against the person or persons engaged in such violations under the rules of civil procedure to seek equitable injunctive relief and to recover general and punitive damages sustained as a consequence thereof in any court having jurisdiction over the defendant; provided, however, punitive damages shall be awarded only in cases of intentional violation. A claim under this article may also be asserted as a defense, setoff, cross-claim, or counterclaim or third-party claim against such person.

(b) A court shall award three times actual damages for an intentional violation.

(c) If the court finds in any action that there has been a violation of this article, the consumer victim injured by such violation shall, in addition to other relief provided for in this Code section and irrespective of the amount in controversy, be awarded reasonable attorney's fees and expenses of litigation incurred in connection with said action.

(d) It shall not be a defense in any action under this article that others were, are, or will be engaged in like practices.

(e) In any action brought under this article the administrator shall be served by certified or registered mail or statutory overnight delivery with a copy of the initial complaint and any amended complaint within 20 days of the filing of such complaint. The administrator shall be entitled to be heard in any such action, and the court where such action is filed may enter an order requiring any of the parties to serve a copy of any other pleadings in an action upon the administrator.

Laws 2002, p. 551, § 2.

§ 16–9–131. Criminal prosecution

Whenever an investigation has been conducted by the Governor's Office of Consumer Affairs under this article and such investigation reveals conduct which constitutes a criminal offense, the administrator shall forward the results of such investigation to the Attorney General or other prosecuting attorney of this state who shall commence any criminal prosecution that he or she deems appropriate.

Laws 2002, p. 551, § 2.

§ 16–9–132. Cumulative nature of law

This article is cumulative with other laws and is not exclusive. The rights or remedies provided for in this article shall be in addition to any other procedures, rights, remedies, or duties provided for in any other law or in decisions of the courts of this state dealing with the same subject matter.

Laws 2002, p. 551, § 2.

Article 9

Computer Security

§ 16–9–150. Short title

This article shall be known and may be cited as the "Georgia Computer Security Act of 2005."

Laws 2005, Act 389, § 1, eff. May 10, 2005.

§ 16–9–151. Definitions

As used in this article, the term:

(1) "Advertisement" means a communication, the primary purpose of which is the commercial promotion of a commercial product or service, including content on an Internet website operated for a commercial purpose.

(2) "Authorized user," with respect to a computer, means a person who owns or is authorized by the owner or lessee to use the computer.

(3) "Cause to be copied" means to distribute or transfer computer software or any component thereof. Such term shall not include providing:

(A) Transmission, routing, provision of intermediate temporary storage, or caching of software;

(B) A storage medium, such as a compact disk, website, or computer server, through which the software was distributed by a third party; or

(C) An information location tool, such as a directory, index, reference, pointer, or hypertext link, through which the user of the computer located the software.

(4) "Computer software" means a sequence of instructions written in any programming language that is executed on a computer. Such term shall not include a text or data file, a web page, or a data component of a web page that is not executable independently of the web page.

(5) "Computer virus" means a computer program or other set of instructions that is designed to degrade the performance of or disable a computer or computer network and is designed to have the ability to replicate itself on other computers or computer networks without the authorization of the owners of those computers or computer networks.

(6) "Consumer" means an individual who resides in this state and who uses the computer in question primarily for personal, family, or household purposes.

(6.1) "Covered file-sharing program" means a computer program, application, or software that enables the computer on which such program, application, or software is installed to designate files as available for searching by and copying to one or more other computers, to transmit such designated files directly to one or more other computers, and to request the transmission of such designated files directly from one or more other computers. Covered file-sharing program does not mean a program, application, or software designed primarily to operate as a server that is accessible over the Internet using the Internet Domain Name System, to transmit or receive e-mail messages, instant messaging, real-time audio or video communications, or real-time voice communications, to provide network or computer security, network management, hosting and backup services, maintenance, diagnostics, or technical support or repair, or to detect or prevent fraudulent activities.

(7) "Damage" means any significant impairment to the integrity or availability of data, software, a system, or information.

(8) "Execute," when used with respect to computer software, means the performance of the functions or the carrying out of the instructions of the computer software.

(9) "Intentionally deceptive" means any of the following:

(A) By means of an intentionally and materially false or fraudulent statement;

(B) By means of a statement or description that intentionally omits or misrepresents material information in order to deceive the consumer; or

(C) By means of an intentional and material failure to provide any notice to an authorized user regarding the download or installation of software in order to deceive the consumer.

(10) "Internet" means the global information system that is logically linked together by a globally unique address space

based on the Internet Protocol or its subsequent extensions; that is able to support communications using the Transmission Control Protocol/Internet Protocol suite, its subsequent extensions, or other Internet Protocol compatible protocols; and that provides, uses, or makes accessible, either publicly or privately, high level services layered on the communications and related infrastructure described in this paragraph.

(11) "Person" means any individual, partnership, corporation, limited liability company, or other organization, or any combination thereof.

(12) "Personally identifiable information" means any of the following:

(A) A first name or first initial in combination with a last name;

(B) Credit or debit card numbers or other financial account numbers;

(C) A password or personal identification number required to access an identified financial account;

(D) A social security number; or

(E) Any of the following information in a form that personally identifies an authorized user:

(i) Account balances;

(ii) Overdraft history;

(iii) Payment history;

(iv) A history of websites visited;

(v) A home address;

(vi) A work address; or

(vii) A record of a purchase or purchases.

Laws 2005, Act 389, § 1, eff. May 10, 2005; Laws 2006, Act 453, § 16, eff. April 14, 2006; Laws 2010, Act 422, § 1, eff. July 1, 2010.

Historical and Statutory Notes

The 2006 amendment by Act 453 was a provision contained in a correction bill.

The 2010 amendment by Act 422, added par. (6.1).

§ 16–9–152. Prohibited copying of spyware software onto computer

(a) It shall be illegal for a person or entity that is not an authorized user, as defined in Code Section 16–9–151, of a computer in this state to knowingly, willfully, or with conscious indifference or disregard cause computer software to be copied onto such computer and use the software to do any of the following:

(1) Modify, through intentionally deceptive means, any of the following settings related to the computer's access to, or use of, the Internet:

(A) The page that appears when an authorized user launches an Internet browser or similar software program used to access and navigate the Internet;

(B) The default provider or web proxy the authorized user uses to access or search the Internet; or

(C) The authorized user's list of bookmarks used to access web pages;

(2) Collect, through intentionally deceptive means, personally identifiable information that meets any of the following criteria:

(A) It is collected through the use of a keystroke-logging function that records all keystrokes made by an authorized user who uses the computer and transfers that information from the computer to another person;

(B) It includes all or substantially all of the websites visited by an authorized user, other than websites of the provider of the software, if the computer software was installed in a manner designed to conceal from all authorized users of the computer the fact that the software is being installed; or

(C) It is a data element described in subparagraph (B), (C), or (D) of paragraph (12) of Code Section 16–9–151, or in division (12)(E)(i) or (12)(E)(ii) of Code Section 16–9–151, that is extracted from the consumer's or business entity's computer hard drive for a purpose wholly unrelated to any of the purposes of the software or service described to an authorized user;

(3) Prevent, without the authorization of an authorized user, through intentionally deceptive means, an authorized user's reasonable efforts to block the installation of, or to disable, software, by causing software that the authorized user has properly removed or disabled to automatically reinstall or reactivate on the computer without the authorization of an authorized user;

(4) Intentionally misrepresent that software will be uninstalled or disabled by an authorized user's action, with knowledge that the software will not be so uninstalled or disabled; or

(5) Through intentionally deceptive means, remove, disable, or render inoperative security, antispyware, or antivirus software installed on the computer.

(b) Nothing in this Code section shall apply to any monitoring of, or interaction with, a user's Internet or other network connection or service, or a protected computer, by a telecommunications carrier, cable operator, computer hardware or software provider, or provider of information service or interactive computer service for network or computer security purposes, diagnostics, technical support, repair, network management, network maintenance, authorized updates of software or system firmware, authorized remote system management, or detection or prevention of the unauthorized use of or fraudulent or other illegal activities in connection with a network, service, or computer software, including scanning for and removing software proscribed under this article.

Laws 2005, Act 389, § 1, eff. May 10, 2005; Laws 2007, Act 18, § 16, eff. May 11, 2007.

Historical and Statutory Notes

The 2007 amendment by Act 18 was a provision contained in a correction bill.

§ 16–9–153. Prohibited copying of adware software or computer viruses onto computer

(a) It shall be illegal for a person or entity that is not an authorized user, as defined in Code Section 16-9-151, of a computer in this state to knowingly, willfully, or with conscious indifference or disregard cause computer software to be copied onto such computer and use the software to do any of the following:

(1) Take control of the consumer's or business entity's computer by doing any of the following:

(A) Transmitting or relaying commercial electronic mail or a computer virus from the consumer's or business entity's computer, where the transmission or relaying is initiated by a person other than the authorized user and without the authorization of an authorized user;

(B) Accessing or using the consumer's or business entity's modem or Internet service for the purpose of causing damage to the consumer's or business entity's computer or of causing an authorized user or a third party affected by such conduct to incur financial charges for a service that is not authorized by an authorized user;

(C) Using the consumer's or business entity's computer as part of an activity performed by a group of computers for the purpose of causing damage to another computer, including, but not limited to, launching a denial of service attack; or

(D) Opening multiple, sequential, stand-alone advertisements in the consumer's or business entity's Internet browser without the authorization of an authorized user and with knowledge that a reasonable computer user cannot close the advertisements without turning off the computer or closing the consumer's or business entity's Internet browser;

(2) Modify any of the following settings related to the computer's access to, or use of, the Internet:

(A) An authorized user's security or other settings that protect information about the authorized user for the purpose of stealing personal information of an authorized user; or

(B) The security settings of the computer for the purpose of causing damage to one or more computers; or

(3) Prevent, without the authorization of an authorized user, an authorized user's reasonable efforts to block the installation of, or to disable, software, by doing any of the following:

(A) Presenting the authorized user with an option to decline installation of software with knowledge that, when the option is selected by the authorized user, the installation nevertheless proceeds; or

(B) Falsely representing that software has been disabled.

(b) Nothing in this Code section shall apply to any monitoring of, or interaction with, a user's Internet or other network connection or service, or a protected computer, by a telecommunications carrier, cable operator, computer hardware or software provider, or provider of information service or interactive computer service for network or computer security purposes, diagnostics, technical support, repair, network management, network maintenance, authorized updates of software or system firmware, authorized remote system management, or detection or prevention of the unauthorized use of or fraudulent or other illegal activities in connection with a network, service, or computer software, including scanning for and removing software proscribed under this article.

Laws 2005, Act 389, § 1, eff. May 10, 2005.

§ 16–9–154. Deceptive inducement of installation of software

(a) It shall be illegal for a person or entity that is not an authorized user, as defined in Code Section 16–9–151, of a computer in this state to do any of the following with regard to such computer:

(1) Induce an authorized user to install a software component onto the computer by intentionally misrepresenting that installing software is necessary for security or privacy reasons or in order to open, view, or play a particular type of content;

(2) Deceptively causing the copying and execution on the computer of a computer software component with the intent of causing an authorized user to use the component in a way that violates any other provision of this Code section;

(3) Prevent reasonable efforts to block the installation, execution, or disabling of a covered file-sharing program on the computer; or

(4) Install, offer to install, or make available for installation, reinstallation, or update a covered file-sharing program on the computer without first providing clear and conspicuous notice to the authorized user of the computer showing which files on that computer will be made available to the public, obtaining consent from the authorized user to install the covered file-sharing program, and requiring affirmative steps by the authorized user to activate any feature on the covered file-sharing program that will make files on that computer available to the public. Such notice shall be redisplayed each time a change occurs in the list of files that will be made available to the public.

(b) Nothing in this Code section shall apply to any monitoring of, or interaction with, a user's Internet or other network connection or service, or a protected computer, by a telecommunications carrier, cable operator, computer hardware or software provider, or provider of information service or interactive computer service for network or computer security purposes, diagnostics, technical support, repair, network management, network maintenance, authorized updates of software or system firmware, authorized remote system management, or detection or prevention of the unauthorized use of or fraudulent or other illegal activities in connection with a network, service, or computer software, including scanning for and removing software proscribed under this article.

Laws 2005, Act 389, § 1, eff. May 10, 2005; Laws 2010, Act 422, § 2, eff. July 1, 2010.

Historical and Statutory Notes

The 2010 amendment by Act 422, in subsec. (a), added pars. (3) and (4) and made other incidental changes.

§ 16–9–155. Violations; penalties

(a) Any person who violates the provisions of paragraph (2) of Code Section 16–9–152, subparagraph (a)(1)(A), (a)(1)(B), or (a)(1)(C) of Code Section 16-9-153, or paragraph (2) of subsection (a) of Code Section 16-9-153 shall be guilty of a felony and, upon conviction thereof, shall be sentenced to imprisonment for not less than one nor more than ten years or a fine of not more than $3 million, or both.

(b) The Attorney General may bring a civil action against any person violating this article to enforce the penalties for the violation and may recover any or all of the following:

(1) A civil penalty of up to $100.00 per violation of this article, or up to $100,000.00 for a pattern or practice of such violations;

(2) Costs and reasonable attorney's fees; and

(3) An order to enjoin the violation.

(c) In the case of a violation of subparagraph (a)(1)(B) of Code Section 16–9–153 that causes a telecommunications carrier to incur costs for the origination, transport, or termination of a call triggered using the modem of a customer of such telecommunications carrier as a result of such violation, the telecommunications carrier may bring a civil action against the violator to recover any or all of the following:

(1) The charges such carrier is obligated to pay to another carrier or to an information service provider as a result of the violation, including, but not limited to, charges for the origination, transport, or termination of the call;

(2) Costs of handling customer inquiries or complaints with respect to amounts billed for such calls;

(3) Costs and reasonable attorney's fees; and

(4) An order to enjoin the violation.

(d) An Internet service provider or software company that expends resources in good faith assisting consumers or business entities harmed by a violation of this chapter, or a trademark owner whose mark is used to deceive consumers or business entities in violation of this chapter, may enforce the violation and may recover any or all of the following:

(1) Statutory damages of not more than $100.00 per violation of this article, or up to $1 million for a pattern or practice of such violations;

(2) Costs and reasonable attorney's fees; and

(3) An order to enjoin the violation.

Laws 2005, Act 389, § 1, eff. May 10, 2005; Laws 2006, Act 453, § 16, eff. April 14, 2006.

Historical and Statutory Notes

The 2006 amendment by Act 453 was a provision contained in a correction bill.

§ 16–9–156. Criminal and civil liability

(a) For the purposes of this Code section, the term "employer" includes a business entity's officers, directors, parent corporation, subsidiaries, affiliates, and other corporate entities under common ownership or control within a business enterprise. No employer may be held criminally or civilly liable under this article as a result of any actions taken:

(1) With respect to computer equipment used by its employees, contractors, subcontractors, agents, leased employees, or other staff which the employer owns, leases, or otherwise makes available or allows to be connected to the employer's network or other computer facilities; or

(2) By employees, contractors, subcontractors, agents, leased employees, or other staff who misuse an employer's computer equipment for an illegal purpose without the employer's knowledge, consent, or approval.

(b) No person shall be held criminally or civilly liable under this article when its protected computers have been used by unauthorized users to violate this article or other laws without such person's knowledge, consent, or approval.

(c) A manufacturer or retailer of computer equipment shall not be liable under this Code section, criminally or civilly, to the extent that the manufacturer or retailer is providing third-party branded software that is installed on the computer equipment that the manufacturer or retailer is manufacturing or selling.

Laws 2005, Act 389, § 1, eff. May 10, 2005.

§ 16–9–157. Preemption of other laws

The General Assembly finds that this article is a matter of state-wide concern. This article supersedes and preempts all rules, regulations, codes, ordinances, and other laws adopted by any county, municipality, consolidated government, or other local governmental agency regarding spyware and notices to consumers from computer software providers regarding information collection.

Laws 2005, Act 389, § 1, eff. May 10, 2005.

CHAPTER 10

OFFENSES AGAINST PUBLIC ADMINISTRATION

Article 1

Article 2

Article 3

Article 4

Article 5

Article 1

Abuse of Governmental Office

§ 16–10–1. Violation of oath by public officer

Any public officer who willfully and intentionally violates the terms of his oath as prescribed by law shall, upon conviction thereof, be punished by imprisonment for not less than one nor more than five years.

Laws 1968, p. 1249, § 1.

Formerly Code 1933, § 26–2302.

§ 16–10–2. Bribery

(a) A person commits the offense of bribery when:

(1) He or she gives or offers to give to any person acting for or on behalf of the state or any political subdivision thereof, or of any agency of either, any benefit, reward, or consideration to which he or she is not entitled with the purpose of influencing him or her in the performance of any act related to the functions of his or her office or employment; or

(2) A public official, elected or appointed, or an employee of this state or any agency, authority, or entity of the state, or any county or municipality or any agency, authority, or entity thereof, directly or indirectly solicits, receives, accepts, or agrees to receive a thing of value by inducing the reasonable belief that the giving of the thing will influence his or her performance or failure to perform any official action. A thing of value shall not include:

(A) Food or beverage consumed at a single meal or event;

(B) Legitimate salary, benefits, fees, commissions, or expenses associated with a recipient's nonpublic business, employment, trade, or profession;

(C) An award, plaque, certificate, memento, or similar item given in recognition of the recipient's civic, charitable, political, professional, or public service;

(D) Food, beverages, and registration at group events to which all members of an agency, as defined in paragraph (1) of subsection (a) of Code Section 21–5–30.2, are invited. An agency shall include the Georgia House of Representatives, the Georgia Senate, committees and subcommittees of such bodies, and the governing body of each political subdivision of this state;

(E) Actual and reasonable expenses for food, beverages, travel, lodging, and registration for a meeting which are provided to permit participation or speaking at the meeting;

(F) A commercially reasonable loan made in the ordinary course of business;

(G) Any gift with a value less than $100.00;

(H) Promotional items generally distributed to the general public or to public officers;

(I) A gift from a member of the public officer's immediate family; or

(J) Food, beverage, or expenses afforded public officers, members of their immediate families, or others that are associated with normal and customary business or social functions or activities;

provided, however, that receiving, accepting, or agreeing to receive anything not enumerated in subparagraphs (A) through (J) of this paragraph shall not create the presumption that the offense of bribery has been committed.

(b) A person convicted of the offense of bribery shall be punished by a fine of not more than $5,000.00 or by imprisonment for not less than one nor more than 20 years, or both.

Cobb's 1851 Digest, p. 805; Laws 1865–66, p. 233, § 1; Laws 1949, p. 274, § 1; Laws 1959, p. 34, § 18; Laws 1968, p. 1249, § 1; Laws 1991, p. 1749, § 1; Laws 1992, p. 1075, § 17.

Formerly Code 1863, §§ 4364, 4365; Code 1868, §§ 4402, 4403; Code 1873, §§ 4469, 4470; Code 1882, §§ 4469, 4470; Penal Code 1895, §§ 267, 268; Penal Code 1910, §§ 270, 271; Code 1933, §§ 26–4101, 26–4102; Code 1933, § 26–2301.

§ 16–10–3. Receiving funds for enforcement of penal laws or regulations

(a) Except as otherwise provided in this Code section, any officer or employee of the state or any agency thereof who receives from any private person, firm, or corporation funds or other things of value to be used in the enforcement of the penal laws or regulations of the state is guilty of a misdemeanor.

(b) Except as otherwise provided in this Code section, any officer or employee of a political subdivision who receives from any private person, firm, or corporation funds or other things of value to be used in the enforcement of the penal laws or regulations of the political subdivision of which he is an officer or employee is guilty of a misdemeanor.

(c) Nothing contained within this Code section shall be deemed or construed so as to prohibit any law enforcement officer of the state or any political subdivision thereof:

(1) From being employed by private persons, firms, or corporations during his off-duty hours when such employment is approved in writing by the chief or head, or his duly designated agent, of the law enforcement agency by which such law enforcement officer is employed; or

(2) From soliciting for or accepting contributions of equipment or of funds to be used solely for the purchase of equipment to be used in the enforcement of the penal laws or regulations of this state or any political subdivision thereof when such acceptance is approved in writing by the chief or head, or his duly designated agent, of the law enforcement agency by which such law enforcement officer is employed.

Laws 1958, p. 333, § 1; Laws 1959, p. 34, § 3; Laws 1968, p. 1249, § 1; Laws 1972, p. 1147, § 1; Laws 1987, p. 906, § 1.

Formerly Code 1933, § 26–2303.

§ 16–10–4. Improperly influencing legislative action

Text of section effective until January 10, 2011. See also, section effective January 10, 2011.

(a) Any officer or employee of the state or any agency thereof who asks for or receives anything of value to which he is not entitled in return for an agreement to procure or attempt to procure the passage or defeat the passage of any legislation by the General Assembly, or procure or attempt to procure the approval or disapproval of the same by the Governor shall, upon conviction thereof, be punished by imprisonment for not less than one nor more than five years.

(b) Any officer or employee of a political subdivision who asks for or receives anything of value to which he is not entitled in return for an agreement to procure or attempt to procure the passage or defeat the passage of any legislation by the legislative body of the political subdivision of which he is an officer or employee shall, upon conviction thereof, be punished by imprisonment for not less than one nor more than five years.

Laws 1959, p. 34, § 1; Laws 1964, p. 261, § 1; Laws 1968, p. 1249, § 1.

Formerly Code 1933, § 26–2304.

§ 16–10–4. Improperly influencing legislative action

Text of section effective January 10, 2011. See also, section effective until January 10, 2011.

(a) Any officer or employee of the state or any agency thereof who asks for or receives anything of value to which he or she is not entitled in return for an agreement to procure or attempt to procure the passage or defeat the passage of any legislation by the General Assembly, or procure or attempt to procure the approval or disapproval of the same by the Governor, shall be guilty of a felony and, upon conviction thereof, shall be punished by a fine of not more than $100,000.00 or by imprisonment for not less than one nor more than five years, or both.

(b) Any officer or employee of a political subdivision who asks for or receives anything of value to which he or she is not entitled in return for an agreement to procure or attempt to procure the passage or defeat the passage of any legislation by the legislative body of the political subdivision of which he or she is an officer or employee shall be guilty of a felony and, upon conviction thereof, shall be punished by a fine of not more than $100,000.00 or by imprisonment for not less than one nor more than five years, or both.

Laws 1959, p. 34, § 1; Laws 1964, p. 261, § 1; Laws 1968, p. 1249, § 1; Laws 2010, Act 680, § 24, eff. Jan. 10, 2011.

Formerly Code 1933, § 26–2304.

Historical and Statutory Notes

The 2010 amendment by Act 680 rewrote the section which had read:

"(a) Any officer or employee of the state or any agency thereof who asks for or receives anything of value to which he is not entitled in return for an agreement to procure or attempt to procure the passage or defeat the passage of any legislation by the General Assembly, or procure or attempt to procure the approval or disapproval of the same by the Governor shall, upon conviction thereof, be punished by imprisonment for not less than one nor more than five years.

"(b) Any officer or employee of a political subdivision who asks for or receives anything of value to which he is not entitled in return for an agreement to procure or attempt to procure the passage or defeat the passage of any legislation by the legislative body of the political subdivision of which he is an officer or employee shall, upon conviction thereof, be punished by imprisonment for not less than one nor more than five years."

Laws 2010, Act 680, § 30, provides in part:

"This Act shall become effective on January 10, 2011, and shall apply to all reports filed on and after such date; provided, however, that if Code Section 45–12–92.1 as enacted by HB 1055 at the regular session of the 2010 General Assembly does not become law" .

Code Section 45–12–92.1 was enacted by Laws 2010, Act 360 (HB 1055), effective May 12, 2010.

§ 16–10–5. Officer or employee improperly influencing another officer or employee

Text of section effective until January 10, 2011. See also, section effective January 10, 2011.

(a) Any officer or employee of the state or any agency thereof who asks for or receives anything of value to which he is not entitled in return for an agreement to influence or attempt to influence official action by any other officer or employee of the state or any agency thereof shall, upon conviction thereof, be punished by imprisonment for not less than one nor more than five years.

(b) Any officer or employee of a political subdivision who asks for or receives anything of value to which he is not entitled in return for an agreement to influence or attempt to influence official action by any other officer or employee of that political subdivision shall, upon conviction thereof, be punished by imprisonment for not less than one nor more than five years.

Laws 1878–79, p. 175, § 1; Laws 1968, p. 1249, § 1.

Formerly Code 1882, § 4470a; Penal Code 1895, § 269; Penal Code 1910, § 272; Code 1933, § 26–4103; Code 1933, § 26–2305.

§ 16–10–5. Officer or employee improperly influencing another officer or employee

Text of section effective January 10, 2011. See also, section effective until January 10, 2011.

(a) Any officer or employee of the state or any agency thereof who asks for or receives anything of value to which he or she is not entitled in return for an agreement to influence or attempt to influence official action by any other officer or employee of the state or any agency thereof shall be guilty of a felony and, upon conviction thereof, shall be punished by a fine of not more than $100,000.00 or by imprisonment for not less than one nor more than five years, or both.

(b) Any officer or employee of a political subdivision who asks for or receives anything of value to which he or she is not entitled in return for an agreement to influence or attempt to influence official action by any other officer or employee of that political subdivision shall be guilty of a felony and, upon conviction thereof, shall be punished by a fine of not more than $100,000.00 or by imprisonment for not less than one nor more than five years, or both.

Laws 1878–79, p. 175, § 1; Laws 1968, p. 1249, § 1; Laws 2010, Act 680, § 25, eff. Jan. 10, 2011.

Formerly Code 1882, § 4470a; Penal Code 1895, § 269; Penal Code 1910, § 272; Code 1933, § 26–4103; Code 1933, § 26–2305.

Historical and Statutory Notes

The 2010 amendment by Act 680 rewrote the section which had read:

"(a) Any officer or employee of the state or any agency thereof who asks for or receives anything of value to which he is not entitled in return for an agreement to influence or attempt to influence official action by any other officer or employee of the state or any agency thereof shall, upon conviction thereof, be punished by imprisonment for not less than one nor more than five years.

"(b) Any officer or employee of a political subdivision who asks for or receives anything of value to which he is not entitled in return for an agreement to influence or attempt to influence official action by any other officer or employee of that political subdivision shall, upon conviction thereof, be punished by imprisonment for not less than one nor more than five years."

Laws 2010, Act 680, § 30, provides in part:

"This Act shall become effective on January 10, 2011, and shall apply to all reports filed on and after such date; provided, however, that if Code Section 45–12–92.1 as enacted by HB 1055 at the regular session of the 2010 General Assembly does not become law" .

Code Section 45–12–92.1 was enacted by Laws 2010, Act 360 (HB 1055), effective May 12, 2010.

§ 16–10–6. Officer or employee of political subdivision or local authority selling to employing political subdivision or local authority

(a) As used in this Code section, the term "employing local authority" means a local authority or board created by a local Act of the General Assembly or a local constitutional amendment or created by general law and requiring activation by an ordinance or resolution of a local governing authority.

(b) Any employee, appointed officer, or elected officer of a political subdivision, hereafter referred to as "employing political subdivision," or agency thereof or any employee or appointed officer of an employing local authority who for himself or herself or in behalf of any business entity sells any real or personal property to:

(1) The employing political subdivision or employing local authority;

(2) An agency of the employing political subdivision;

(3) A political subdivision for which local taxes for education are levied by the employing political subdivision; or

(4) A political subdivision which levies local taxes for education for the employing political subdivision

shall, upon conviction thereof, be punished by imprisonment for not less than one nor more than five years.

(c) Subsection (b) of this Code section shall not apply to:

(1) Sales of personal property of less than $800.00 per calendar quarter;

(2) Sales of personal property made pursuant to sealed competitive bids made by the employee, appointed officer, or elected officer, either for himself or herself or on behalf of any business entity; or

(3) Sales of real property in which a disclosure has been made:

(A) To the judge of the probate court of the county in which the purchasing political subdivision or local authority is wholly included or, if not wholly included in any one county, to the judge of the probate court of any county in which the purchasing political subdivision or local authority is partially included and which shall have been designated by the purchasing political subdivision or local authority to receive such disclosures, provided that if the sale is made by the judge of the probate court, a copy of such disclosure shall also be filed with any superior court judge of the superior court of the county;

(B) At least 15 days prior to the date the contract or agreement for such sale will become final and binding on the parties thereto;

(C) Which shows that an employee, appointed officer, or elected officer of an employing political subdivision or agency thereof or of an employing local authority has a personal interest in such sale, which interest includes, without being limited to, any commission, fee, profit, or similar benefit and which gives the name of such person, his or her position in the political subdivision or agency or local authority, the purchase price, and location of the property.

(d) Any contract or transaction for a sale made in accordance with subsection (c) of this Code section shall be valid and no employee, appointed officer, or elected officer shall be subject to civil liability for any such sale.

Laws 1968, p. 1249, § 1; Laws 1972, p. 542, § 1; Laws 1975, p. 854, § 1; Laws 1979, p. 536, § 1; Laws 1980, p. 733, § 1; Laws 1982, p. 2107, § 15; Laws 1983, p. 1326, § 2; Laws 1984, p. 22, § 16; Laws 1986, p. 10, § 16; Laws 1994, p. 607, § 9; Laws 1998, p. 593, § 1; Laws 2003, Act 9, § 16, eff. May 14, 2003; Laws 2010, Act 405, § 1, eff. July 1, 2010.

Formerly Code 1933, § 26–2306.

Historical and Statutory Notes

The 2003 amendment by Act 9 substituted "appointed" for "appointive" and substituted "elected" for "elective" in the introductory paragraph of subsec. (b), par. (2) of subsec. (c), and subpar. (3)(C) of subsec. (c).

The 2010 amendment by Act 405, in subsec. (c), par. (1), substituted "$800.00" for "$200.00" and added subsec. (d).

§ 16–10–7. False acknowledgment of appearance or oath

Any officer authorized to administer oaths or to take and certify acknowledgments who knowingly makes a false acknowledgment, certificate, or statement concerning the appearance before him or the taking of an oath or affirmation by any person is guilty of a misdemeanor.

Laws 1959, p. 34, § 14; Laws 1968, p. 1249, § 1.

Formerly Code 1933, § 26–2310.

§ 16–10–8. False official certificates or writings

An officer or employee of the state or any political subdivision thereof or other person authorized by law to make or give a certificate or other writing who knowingly makes and delivers such a certificate or writing containing any statement which he knows to be false shall, upon conviction thereof, be punished by imprisonment for not less than one nor more than five years.

Laws 1959, p. 34, § 16; Laws 1968, p. 1249, § 1.

Formerly Code 1933, § 26–2311.

§ 16–10–9. Enforcement of separation of powers provision of Constitution

(a) It shall be unlawful for:

(1) Members of the General Assembly to accept or hold office or employment in the executive branch of the state government or any agency thereof or in the judicial branch of the state government;

(2) Judges of courts of record or their clerks and assistants to accept or hold office or employment in the executive branch of the state government or any agency thereof or in the legislative branch of the state government; or

(3) Officers or employees of the executive branch of the state government to accept or hold office or employment in the legislative or judicial branches of the state government.

(b) A person who knowingly disburses or receives any compensation or money in violation of this Code section is guilty of a misdemeanor.

(c) Nothing in this Code section shall be construed to apply to any officer or employee of the executive branch who has taken a leave of absence without pay from his post for temporary service as an employee of the legislative branch while it is in session and during the authorized stay-over period.

Laws 1959, p. 34, § 7; Laws 1961, p. 42, § 1; Laws 1968, p. 1249, § 1.

Formerly Code 1933, § 26–2309.

Article 2

Obstruction of Public Administration and Related Offenses

§ 16–10–20. False statements and writings; concealment of facts

A person who knowingly and willfully falsifies, conceals, or covers up by any trick, scheme, or device a material fact; makes a false, fictitious, or fraudulent statement or representation; or makes or uses any false writing or document, knowing the same to contain any false, fictitious, or fraudulent statement or entry, in any matter within the jurisdiction of any department or agency of state government or of the government of any county, city, or other political subdivision of this state shall, upon conviction thereof, be punished by a fine of not more than $1,000.00 or by imprisonment for not less than one nor more than five years, or both.

Laws 1976, p. 483, § 1; Laws 1979, p. 1068, § 1; Laws 1982, p. 3, § 16.

Formerly Code 1933, § 26–2408.

§ 16–10–21. Conspiracy to defraud state or political subdivision

(a) A person commits the offense of conspiracy to defraud the state when he conspires or agrees with another to commit theft of any property which belongs to the state or to any agency thereof or which is under the control or possession of a state officer or employee in his official capacity. The crime shall be complete when the conspiracy or agreement is effected and an overt act in furtherance thereof has been committed, regardless of whether the theft is consummated. A person convicted of the offense of conspiracy to defraud the state shall be punished by imprisonment for not less than one nor more than five years.

(b) A person commits the offense of conspiracy to defraud a political subdivision when he conspires or agrees with another to commit theft of any property which belongs to a political subdivision or to any agency thereof or which is under the control or possession of an officer or employee of a political subdivision in his official capacity. The crime shall be complete when the conspiracy or agreement is effected and an overt act in furtherance thereof has been committed, regardless of whether the theft is consummated. A person convicted of the offense of conspiracy to defraud a political subdivision shall be punished by imprisonment for not less than one nor more than five years.

Laws 1872, p. 25, § 1; Laws 1968, p. 1249, § 1.

Formerly Code 1882, § 4493; Penal Code 1895, § 287; Penal Code 1910, § 291; Code 1933, § 26–4201; Code 1933, § 26–2307.

§ 16–10–22. Conspiracy in restraint of free and open competition

(a) A person who enters into a contract, combination, or conspiracy in restraint of trade or in restraint of free and open competition in any transaction with the state or any agency thereof, whether the transaction is for goods, materials, or services, shall, upon conviction thereof, be punished by imprisonment for not less than one nor more than five years. The crime of conspiracy in restraint of free and open competition in transactions with the state shall be complete when the contract, combination, or conspiracy is effected and an overt act in furtherance thereof has been committed.

(b) A person who enters into a contract, combination, or conspiracy in restraint of trade or in restraint of free and open competition in any transaction with a political subdivision or any agency thereof, whether the transaction is for goods, materials, or services, shall, upon conviction thereof, be punished by imprisonment for not less than one nor more than five years. The crime of conspiracy in restraint of free and open competition in transactions with political subdivisions shall be complete when the contract, combination, or conspiracy is effected and an overt act in furtherance thereof has been committed.

(c) A person who is convicted of or who pleads guilty to a violation of subsection (a) or (b) of this Code section as a result of any contract, combination, or conspiracy in restraint of trade or in restraint of free and open competition in any transaction which was entered into or carried out, in whole or in part, on or after July 1, 1985, shall be ineligible to submit a bid on, enter into, or participate in any contract with any department, agency, branch, board, or authority of the state or any county, municipality, board of education, or other political subdivision thereof for a period of five years following the date of the conviction or entry of the plea.

Laws 1959, p. 34, § 6; Laws 1964, p. 261, § 6; Laws 1968, p. 1249, § 1; Laws 1985, p. 1184, § 1.

Formerly Code 1933, § 26–2308.

§ 16–10–23. Impersonating an officer

A person who falsely holds himself out as a peace officer or other public officer or employee with intent to mislead another into believing that he is actually such officer commits the offense of impersonating an officer and, upon conviction thereof, shall be punished by a fine of not more than $1,000.00 or by imprisonment for not less than one nor more than five years, or both.

Laws 1968, p. 1249, § 1; Laws 1986, p. 1059, § 1.

Formerly Code 1933, § 26–2405.

§ 16–10–24. Obstruction of officers

(a) Except as otherwise provided in subsection (b) of this Code section, a person who knowingly and willfully obstructs or hinders any law enforcement officer in the lawful discharge of his official duties is guilty of a misdemeanor.

(b) Whoever knowingly and willfully resists, obstructs, or opposes any law enforcement officer, prison guard, correctional officer, probation supervisor, parole supervisor, or conservation ranger in the lawful discharge of his official duties by offering or doing violence to the person of such officer or legally authorized person is guilty of a felony and shall, upon conviction thereof, be punished by imprisonment for not less than one nor more than five years.

Laws 1833, Cobb's 1851 Digest, p. 806; Laws 1865–66, p. 233, § 2; Laws 1968, p. 1249, § 1; Laws 1986, p. 484, § 1.

Formerly Code 1863, § 4370; Code 1868, § 4408; Code 1873, § 4476; Code 1882, § 4476; Penal Code 1895, § 306; Penal Code 1910, § 311; Code 1933, § 26–4401; Code 1933, § 26–2505.

Historical and Statutory Notes

The 2002 amendment by Act 787 and by Act 952 each provided that the terms "fireman" and "firemen" wherever the same shall occur be substituted by the terms "firefighter" and "firefighters".

§ 16–10–24.1. Obstructing or hindering firefighter in discharge of his duties

(a) As used in this Code section, the term "firefighter" means:

(1) Any person who is employed as a professional firefighter on a full-time basis for at least 40 hours per week by any county, municipal, or state fire department when such person has responsibility for preventing and suppressing fires, protecting life and property, enforcing municipal, county, or state fire prevention codes, or enforcing any law or ordinance pertaining to the prevention or control of fires;

(2) Any volunteer firefighter as the term "volunteer firefighter" is defined by paragraph (7) of Code Section 47–7–1 as said paragraph (7) exists on January 1, 1988; or

(3) Any person employed as a professional firefighter on a full-time basis for at least 40 hours per week by a person or corporation which has a contract with a municipality or county to provide fire prevention and fire-fighting services for such municipality or county when such person has responsibility for preventing and suppressing fires, protecting life and property, enforcing municipal or county fire prevention codes, or enforcing any municipal or county ordinances pertaining to the prevention and control of fires.

(b) Except as otherwise provided in subsection (c) of this Code section, a person who knowingly and willfully obstructs or hinders any firefighter in the lawful discharge of the firefighter's official duties is guilty of a misdemeanor.

(c) Whoever knowingly and willfully resists, obstructs, or opposes any firefighter in the lawful discharge of the firefighter's official duties by offering or doing violence to the person of such firefighter is guilty of a felony and shall, upon conviction thereof, be punished by imprisonment for not less than one nor more than five years.

Laws 1988, p. 301, § 1; Laws 1991, p. 755, § 1; Laws 2002, p. 660, § 4; Laws 2002, p. 1259, § 11.

§ 16–10–24.2. Obstructing or hindering emergency medical technician, emergency medical professional, or properly identified person working under direction of emergency medical professional in discharge of his duties

(a) As used in this Code section, the term:

(1) "Emergency medical professional" means any person performing emergency medical services who is licensed or certified to provide health care in accordance with the provisions of Chapter 11, Chapter 26, or Chapter 34 of Title 43.

(2) "Emergency medical technician" means any person who has been certified as an emergency medical technician, cardiac technician, paramedic, or first responder pursuant to Chapter 11 of Title 31.

(b) Except as otherwise provided in subsection (c) of this Code section, a person who knowingly and willfully obstructs or hinders any emergency medical technician, any emergency medical professional, or any properly identified person working under the direction of an emergency medical professional in the lawful discharge of the official duties of such emergency medical technician, emergency medical professional, or properly identified person working under the direction of an emergency medical professional is guilty of a misdemeanor.

(c) Whoever knowingly and willfully resists or obstructs any emergency medical technician, any emergency medical professional, or any properly identified person working under the direction of an emergency medical professional in the lawful discharge of the official duties of the emergency medical technician, emergency medical professional, or properly identified person working under the direction of an emergency medical professional by threatening or doing violence to the person of such emergency medical technician, emergency medical professional, or properly identified person working under the direction of an emergency medical professional is guilty of a felony and shall, upon conviction thereof, be punished by imprisonment for not less than one nor more than five years.

Laws 1994, p. 331, § 1; Laws 1996, p. 835, § 1; Laws 1999, p. 81, § 16.

§ 16–10–24.3. Interfering with calls for emergency assistance

Any person who verbally or physically obstructs, prevents, or hinders another person with intent to cause or allow physical harm or injury to another person from making or completing a 9–1–1 telephone call or a call to any law enforcement agency to request police protection or to report the commission of a crime is guilty of a misdemeanor and shall, upon conviction thereof, be punished by a fine not to exceed $1,000.00 or imprisonment not to exceed 12 months, or both.

Laws 1998, p. 608, § 1; Laws 2005, Act 134, § 1, eff. July 1, 2005.

Historical and Statutory Notes

The 2005 amendment by Act 134 substituted "9–1–1" for "911".

§ 16–10–25. Giving false name to officers

A person who gives a false name, address, or date of birth to a law enforcement officer in the lawful discharge of his official duties with the intent of misleading the officer as to his identity or birthdate is guilty of a misdemeanor.

Laws 1968, p. 1249, § 1; Laws 1989, p. 224, § 1.

Formerly Code 1933, § 26–2506.

§ 16–10–26. False report of a crime

A person who willfully and knowingly gives or causes a false report of a crime to be given to any law enforcement officer or agency of this state is guilty of a misdemeanor.

Laws 1968, p. 983, §§ 1, 2; Laws 1969, p. 857, § 11.

Formerly Code 1933, § 26–2509.

§ 16–10–27. False fire alarm

A person who transmits in any manner to a fire department, public or private, or to any other group which is organized for the purpose of preventing or controlling fires a false report of a fire, knowing at the time that there is no reasonable ground for believing that such fire exists, is guilty of a misdemeanor.

Laws 1937, p. 373, §§ 1, 2; Laws 1968, p. 1249, § 1.

Formerly Code 1933, § 26–2608.

§ 16–10–28. False public alarm

(a) As used in this Code section, the term:

(1) "Destructive device" means a destructive device as such term is defined by Code Section 16–7–80.

(2) "Hazardous substance" means a hazardous substance as such term is defined by Code Section 12–8–92.

(b) A person who transmits in any manner a false alarm to the effect that a destructive device or hazardous substance of any nature is concealed in such place that its explosion, detonation, or release would endanger human life or cause injury or damage to property, knowing at the time that there is no reasonable ground for believing that such a destructive device or hazardous substance is concealed in such place, commits the offense of transmitting a false public alarm and, upon conviction thereof, shall be punished by imprisonment for not less than one nor more than five years or by a fine of not less than $ 1,000.00, or both.

(c) In addition to any other penalty imposed by law for a violation of this Code section, the court may require the defendant to make restitution to any affected public or private entity for the reasonable costs or damages associated with the offense including, without limitation, the actual value of any goods, services, or income lost as a result of such violation. Restitution made pursuant to this subsection shall not preclude any party from obtaining any other civil or criminal remedy available under any other provision of law. The restitution authorized by this subsection is supplemental and not exclusive.

Laws 1968, p. 1249, § 1; Laws 1996, p. 416, § 5; Laws 2002, p. 1094, § 3.

Formerly Code 1933, § 26–2609.

Historical and Statutory Notes

The 2002 amendment added at the end of subsec. (b) "or by a fine of not less than $1,000.00, or both" and added subsec. (c).

§ 16–10–29. Requesting ambulance service with knowledge that no reasonable need for such service exists

(a) It shall be unlawful for any person to transmit in any manner a request for ambulance service to any person, firm, or corporation furnishing ambulance service, public or private, knowing at the time of making the request for ambulance service that there exists no reasonable need for such ambulance service.

(b) Any person who violates subsection (a) of this Code section shall be guilty of a misdemeanor.

Laws 1977, p. 797, §§ 1, 2.

§ 16–10–30. Refusal to disperse at request of officer or firefighter

A person in a gathering who refuses to obey the reasonable official request or order of a peace officer or firefighter to move, for the purpose of promoting the public safety by dispersing those gathered in dangerous proximity to a fire or other emergency, is guilty of a misdemeanor.

Laws 1968, p. 1249, § 1; Laws 2002, p. 660, § 4; Laws 2002, p. 1259, § 11.

Formerly Code 1933, § 26–2606.

Historical and Statutory Notes

The 2002 amendment by Act 787 and by Act 952 each provided that the terms "fireman" and "firemen" wherever the same shall occur be substituted by the terms "firefighter" and "firefighters".

§ 16–10–31. Concealing death

A person who, by concealing the death of any other person, hinders a discovery of whether or not such person was unlawfully killed is guilty of a felony and upon conviction shall be punished by imprisonment for not less than one nor more than ten years, a fine of not less than $1,000.00 nor more than $5,000.00, or both.

Laws 1968, p. 1249, § 1; Laws 1997, p. 923, § 1.

Formerly Code 1933, § 26–1104.

§ 16–10–32. Attempted killing or threats to prevent information on criminal activity from being communicated to law enforcement or to the courts

(a) Any person who attempts to kill another person with intent to:

(1) Prevent the attendance or testimony of any person in an official proceeding;

(2) Prevent the production of a record, document, or other object, in an official proceeding; or

(3) Prevent the communication by any person to a law enforcement officer, prosecuting attorney, or judge of this state of information relating to the commission or possible commission of a criminal offense or a violation of conditions of probation, parole, or release pending judicial proceedings

shall be guilty of a felony and, upon conviction thereof, shall be punished by imprisonment for not less than ten nor more than 20 years.

(b) Any person who threatens or causes physical or economic harm to another person or a member of such person's family or household, threatens to damage or damages the property of another person or a member of such person's family or household, or attempts to cause physical or economic harm to another person or a member of such person's family or household with the intent to hinder, delay, prevent, or dissuade any person from:

(1) Attending or testifying in an official proceeding;

(2) Reporting in good faith to a law enforcement officer, prosecuting attorney, or judge of a court of this state, or its political subdivisions or authorities, the commission or possible commission of an offense under the laws of this state or a violation of conditions of probation, parole, or release pending judicial proceedings;

(3) Arresting or seeking the arrest of another person in connection with a criminal offense; or

(4) Causing a criminal prosecution, or a parole or probation revocation proceeding, to be sought or instituted, or assisting in such prosecution or proceeding

shall be guilty of a felony and, upon conviction thereof, shall be punished by imprisonment for not less than two years nor more than ten years or by a fine of not less than $10,000.00 nor more than $25,000.00, or both.

(c)(1) For the purposes of this Code section, the term "official proceeding" means any hearing or trial conducted by a court of this state or its political subdivisions, a grand jury, or an agency of the executive, legislative, or judicial branches of government of this state or its political subdivisions or authorities.

(2) An official proceeding need not be pending or about to be instituted at the time of any offense defined in this Code section.

(3) The testimony, record, document, or other object which is prevented or impeded or attempted to be prevented or impeded in an official proceeding in violation of this Code section need not be admissible in evidence or free of a claim of privilege.

(4) In a prosecution for an offense under this Code section, no state of mind need be proved with respect to the circumstance:

(A) That the official proceeding before a judge, court, magistrate, grand jury, or government agency is before a judge or court of this state, a magistrate, a grand jury, or an agency of state or local government; or

(B) That the judge is a judge of this state or its political subdivisions or that the law enforcement officer is an officer or employee of the State of Georgia or a political subdivision or authority of the state or a person authorized to act for or on behalf of the State of Georgia or a political subdivision or authority of the state.

(5) A prosecution under this Code section may be brought in the county in which the official proceeding, whether or not pending or about to be instituted, was intended to be affected or in the county in which the conduct constituting the alleged offense occurred.

(d) Any crime committed in violation of subsection (a) or (b) of this Code section shall be considered a separate offense.

Laws 1998, p. 270, § 4.

§ 16–10–33. Remove or attempt to remove firearm, chemical spray, or baton from person acting within course of employment

(a) It shall be unlawful for any person knowingly to remove or attempt to remove a firearm, chemical spray, or baton from the possession of another person if:

(1) The other person is lawfully acting within the course and scope of employment; and

(2) The person has knowledge or reason to know that the other person is employed as:

(A) A peace officer as defined in paragraph (8) of Code Section 35–8–2;

(B) A probation officer, or other employee with the power of arrest, by the Department of Corrections;

(C) A parole supervisor, or other employee with the power of arrest, by the State Board of Pardons and Paroles;

(D) A jail officer or guard by a county or municipality and has the responsibility of supervising inmates who are confined in a county or municipal jail or other detention facility; or

(E) A juvenile correctional officer by the Department of Juvenile Justice and has the primary responsibility for the supervision and control of youth confined in such department's programs and facilities.

(b) Any person who violates subsection (a) of this Code section shall, upon conviction thereof, be punished by imprisonment for not less than one nor more than five years or a fine of not more than $ 10,000.00, or both.

(c) A violation of this Code section shall constitute a separate offense. A sentence imposed under this Code section may be imposed separately from and consecutive to or concurrent with a sentence for any other offense related to the act or acts establishing the offense under this Code section.

Laws 2000, p. 1267, § 1; Laws 2001, p. 4, § 16.

Historical and Statutory Notes

The 2001 amendment was a correction bill.

Article 3

Escape and Other Offenses Related to Confinement

§ 16–10–50. Hindering apprehension or punishment of a criminal

(a) A person commits the offense of hindering the apprehension or punishment of a criminal when, with intention to hinder the apprehension or punishment of a person whom he knows or has reasonable grounds to believe has committed a felony or to be an escaped inmate or prisoner, he:

(1) Harbors or conceals such person; or

(2) Conceals or destroys evidence of the crime.

(b) A person convicted of the offense of hindering apprehension or punishment of a criminal shall be punished by imprisonment for not less than one nor more than five years.

Laws 1833, Cobb's 1851 Digest, p. 808; Laws 1876, p. 114, § 1; Laws 1968, p. 1249, § 1.

Formerly Code 1863, § 4384; Code 1868, § 4422; Code 1873, § 4490; Code 1882, §§ 4490, 4490a; Penal Code 1895, §§ 321, 322; Penal Code 1910, §§ 326, 327; Code 1933, §§ 26–4601, 26–4602; Code 1933, § 26–2503.

§ 16–10–51. Bail jumping

(a) Any person who has been charged with or convicted of the commission of a felony under the laws of this state and has been set at liberty on bail or on his own recognizance upon the condition that he will subsequently appear at a specified time and place commits the offense of felony-bail jumping if, after actual notice to the defendant in open court or notice to the person by mailing to his last known address or otherwise being notified personally in writing by a court official or officer of the court, he fails without sufficient excuse to appear at that time and place. A person convicted of the offense of felony-bail jumping shall be punished by imprisonment for not less than one nor more than five years or by a fine of not more than $5,000.00, or both.

(b) Any person who has been charged with or convicted of the commission of a misdemeanor and has been set at liberty on bail or on his own recognizance upon the condition that he will subsequently appear at a specified time and place commits the offense of misdemeanor-bail jumping if, after actual notice to the defendant in open court or notice to the person by mailing to his last known address or otherwise being notified personally in writing by a court official or officer of the court, he fails without sufficient excuse to appear at that time and place. A person convicted of the offense of misdemeanor-bail jumping shall be guilty of a misdemeanor.

(c)(1) Any person who has been charged with or convicted of the commission of any of the misdemeanors listed in paragraph (2) of this subsection and has been set at liberty on bail or on his or her own recognizance upon the condition that he or she will subsequently appear at a specified time and place and who, after actual notice to the defendant in open court or notice to the defendant by mailing to the defendant's last known address or otherwise being notified personally in writing by a court official or officer of the court, leaves the state to avoid appearing in court at such time commits the offense of out-of-state-bail jumping. A person convicted of the offense of out-of-state-bail jumping shall be guilty of a felony and shall be punished by imprisonment for not less than one year nor more than five years or by a fine of not less than $1,000.00 nor more than $5,000.00, or both.

(2) Paragraph (1) of this subsection shall apply only to the following misdemeanors:

(A) Abandonment, as provided in Code Sections 19–10–1 and 19–10–2;

(B) Simple assault, as provided in Code Section 16–5–20;

(C) Carrying a weapon or long gun in an unauthorized location, as provided in Code Section 16–11–127;

(D) Bad checks, as provided in Code Section 16–9–20;

(E) Simple battery, as provided in Code Section 16–5–23;

(F) Bribery, as provided in Code Section 16–10–3;

(G) Failure to report child abuse, as provided in Code Section 19–7–5;

(H) Criminal trespass, as provided in Code Section 16–7–21;

(I) Contributing to the delinquency of a minor, as provided in Code Section 16–12–1;

(J) Escape, as provided in Code Sections 16–10–52 and 16–10–53;

(K) Tampering with evidence, as provided in Code Section 16–10–94;

(L) Family violence, as provided in Code Section 19–13–6;

(M) Deceptive business practices, as provided in Code Section 16–9–50;

(N) Reserved;

(O) Fraud in obtaining public assistance, food stamps, or Medicaid, as provided in Code Section 49–4–15;

(P) Reckless conduct, as provided in Code Section 16–5–60;

(Q) Any offense under Chapter 8 of this title which is a misdemeanor;

(R) Any offense under Chapter 13 of this title which is a misdemeanor;

(S) Driving under the influence of alcohol or drugs, as provided in Code Section 40–6–391;

(T) Driving without a license in violation of Code Section 40–5–20 or driving while a license is suspended or revoked as provided in Code Section 40–5–121; and

(U) Any offense under Code Section 40–6–10, relating to requirement of the operator or owner of a motor vehicle to have proof of insurance.

(d) Subsections (b) and (c) of this Code section shall not apply to any person who has been charged or convicted of the commission of a misdemeanor under the laws of this state and has been set at liberty after posting a cash bond and fails to appear in court at the specified time and place where such failure to appear, in accordance with the rules of the court having jurisdiction over such misdemeanor, is construed as an admission of guilt and the cash bond is forfeited without the need for any further statutory procedures and the proceeds of the cash bond are applied and distributed as any fine imposed by the court would be.

Laws 1980, p. 387, § 1; Laws 1988, p. 670, § 1; Laws 1989, p. 14, § 16; Laws 1989, p. 623, § 1; Laws 1997, p. 973, § 1; Laws 2010, Act 643, § 2–4, eff. June 4, 2010.

Formerly Code 1933, § 26–2511.

Historical and Statutory Notes

The 2010 amendment by Act 643 rewrote subpar. (c)(2)(C) which had read as follows:

"(C) Carrying deadly weapon to public gathering, as provided in Code Section 16–11–127;"

Laws 2010, Act 643, § 3–1, provides:

"This Act shall become effective upon its approval by the Governor or upon its becoming law without such approval and shall apply to all offenses committed on and after such date. The enactment of this Act shall not affect any prosecutions for acts occurring before the effective date of this Act and shall not act as an abatement of any such prosecutions."

§ 16–10–52. Escape

(a) A person commits the offense of escape when he or she:

(1) Having been convicted of a felony or misdemeanor or of the violation of a municipal ordinance, intentionally escapes from lawful custody or from any place of lawful confinement;

(2) Being in lawful custody or lawful confinement prior to conviction, intentionally escapes from such custody or confinement;

(3) Having been adjudicated of a delinquent or unruly act or a juvenile traffic offense, intentionally escapes from lawful custody or from any place of lawful confinement;

(4) Being in lawful custody or lawful confinement prior to adjudication, intentionally escapes from such custody or confinement; or

(5) Intentionally fails to return as instructed to lawful custody or lawful confinement or to any residential facility operated by the Georgia Department of Corrections after having been released on the condition that he or she will so return; provided, however, such person shall be allowed a grace period of eight hours from the exact time specified for return if such person can prove he or she did not intentionally fail to return.

(a.1) Revocation of probation for conduct in violation of any provision of subsection (a) of this Code section shall not preclude an independent criminal prosecution under this Code section based on the same conduct.

(b)(1) A person who, having been convicted of a felony, is convicted of the offense of escape shall be punished by imprisonment for not less than one nor more than ten years.

(2) Any person charged with a felony who is in lawful confinement prior to conviction or adjudication who is convicted of the offense of escape shall be punished by imprisonment for not less than one nor more than five years.

(3) Notwithstanding paragraphs (1) and (2) of this subsection, a person who commits the offense of escape while armed with a dangerous weapon shall, upon conviction thereof, be punished by imprisonment for not less than one nor more than 20 years.

(4) Any other person convicted of the offense of escape shall be punished as for a misdemeanor.

Laws 1833, Cobb's 1851 Digest, p. 807; Laws 1876, p. 112, § 1; Laws 1882–83, p. 48, § 1; Laws 1884–85, p. 52, § 1; Laws 1953, Nov.-Dec. Sess., p. 187, § 1; Laws 1955, p. 578, § 1; Laws 1961, p. 491, § 1; Laws 1968, p. 1249, § 1; Laws 1983, p. 645, § 1; Laws 1989, p. 329, § 1; Laws 1994, p. 852, § 1; Laws 1997, p. 1064, § 10; Laws 2001, p. 94, § 2.

Formerly Code 1863, § 4378; Code 1868, § 4416; Code 1873, § 4484; Code 1882, §§ 4483a, 4484; Penal Code 1895, §§ 314, 316; Penal Code 1910, §§ 319, 321; Code 1933, §§ 26–4507, 26–4509; Code 1933, § 26–2501.

Historical and Statutory Notes

The 2001 amendment, applicable to offenses of escape committed on or after July 1, 2001, rewrote subsec. (b) which formerly provided:

"A person who, having been convicted of a felony or misdemeanor, is convicted of the offense of escape shall be punished by imprisonment for not less than one nor more than ten years. Any other person convicted of the offense of escape shall be punished as for a misdemeanor, except that a person who commits the offense of escape while armed with a dangerous weapon shall, upon conviction thereof, be punished by imprisonment for not less than one nor more than 20 years."

§ 16–10–53. Aiding escape

(a) A person who knowingly aids another in escaping from lawful custody or from any place of lawful confinement shall, upon conviction thereof, be punished by imprisonment for not less than one nor more than five years.

(b) A peace officer or employee of any place of lawful confinement who recklessly permits any person in his custody to escape is guilty of a misdemeanor.

Laws 1833, Cobb's 1851 Digest, p. 807; Laws 1876, p. 112, § 2; Laws 1955, p. 578, § 2; Laws 1968, p. 1249, § 1.

Formerly Code 1863, §§ 4376, 4377, 4379; Code 1868, §§ 4414, 4415, 4417; Code 1873, §§ 4482, 4483, 4485; Code 1882, §§ 4482, 4483, 4483b, 4485; Penal Code 1895, §§ 312, 313, 315, 317; Penal Code 1910, §§ 317, 318, 320, 322; Code 1933, §§ 26–4505, 26–4506, 26–4508, 26–4510; Code 1933, § 26–2502.

§ 16–10–54. Mutiny in penal institutions

A person in the lawful custody of any penal institution of the state or of a political subdivision of the state who assails, opposes, or resists an officer of the law or of such penal institution or a member of the guard with intent to cause serious bodily injury commits the offense of mutiny and, upon conviction thereof, shall be punished by imprisonment for not less than one nor more than five years.

Laws 1833, Cobb's 1851 Digest, p. 810; Laws 1968, p. 1249, § 1; Laws 1993, p. 808, § 1.

Formerly Code 1863, § 4396; Code 1868, § 4437; Code 1873, § 4510; Code 1882, § 4510; Penal Code 1895, § 329; Penal Code 1910, § 334; Code 1933, § 26–4801; Code 1933, § 26–2507.

§ 16–10–55. Instigating mutiny

A person who persuades, entices, instigates, counsels, aids, or abets a person in the lawful custody of any penal institution to commit the offense of mutiny shall, upon conviction thereof, be punished by imprisonment for not less than one nor more than five years.

Laws 1833, Cobb's 1851 Digest, p. 810; Laws 1968, p. 1249, § 1.

Formerly Code 1863, § 4397; Code 1868, § 4438; Code 1873, § 4511; Code 1882, § 4511; Penal Code 1895, § 330; Penal Code 1910, § 335; Code 1933, § 26–4802; Code 1933, § 26–2508.

§ 16–10–56. Riot in a penal institution

(a) Any person legally confined to any penal institution of this state or of any political subdivision of this state who commits an unlawful act of violence or any other act in a violent or tumultuous manner commits the offense of riot in a penal institution.

(b) Any person who violates subsection (a) of this Code section is guilty of a felony and, upon conviction thereof, shall be punished by imprisonment of not less than one nor more than 20 years.

Laws 1995, p. 137, § 1.1.

Article 4

Perjury and Related Offenses

§ 16–10–70. Perjury

(a) A person to whom a lawful oath or affirmation has been administered commits the offense of perjury when, in a judicial proceeding, he knowingly and willfully makes a false statement material to the issue or point in question.

(b) A person convicted of the offense of perjury shall be punished by a fine of not more than $1,000.00 or by imprisonment for not less than one nor more than ten years, or both. A person convicted of the offense of perjury that was a cause of another's being imprisoned shall be sentenced to a term not to exceed the sentence provided for the crime for which the other person was convicted. A person convicted of the offense of perjury that was a cause of another's being punished by death shall be punished by life imprisonment.

Laws 1833, Cobb's 1851 Digest, pp. 804, 805; Laws 1933, p. 40, § 1; Laws 1968, p. 1249, § 1; Laws 1973, p. 159, § 2.

Formerly Code 1863, §§ 4355, 4356, 4363; Code 1868, §§ 4393, 4394, 4401; Code 1873, §§ 4460, 4461, 4468; Code 1882, §§ 4460, 4461, 4468; Penal Code 1895, §§ 256, 257, 262; Penal Code 1910, §§ 259, 260, 265; Code 1933, §§ 26–4001, 26–4002, 26–4007; Code 1933, § 26–2401.

§ 16–10–71. False swearing

(a) A person to whom a lawful oath or affirmation has been administered or who executes a document knowing that it purports to be an acknowledgment of a lawful oath or affirmation commits the offense of false swearing when, in any matter or thing other than a judicial proceeding, he knowingly and willfully makes a false statement.

(b) A person convicted of the offense of false swearing shall be punished by a fine of not more than $1,000.00 or by imprisonment for not less than one nor more than five years, or both.

Laws 1833, Cobb's 1851 Digest, p. 804; Laws 1968, p. 1249, § 1.

Formerly Code 1863, §§ 4357, 4358; Code 1868, §§ 4395, 4396; Code 1873, §§ 4462, 4463; Code 1882, §§ 4462, 4463; Penal Code 1895, §§ 258, 259; Penal Code 1910, §§ 261, 262; Code 1933, §§ 26–4003, 26–4004; Code 1933, § 26–2402.

§ 16–10–72. Subornation of perjury or false swearing

A person commits the offense of subornation of perjury or false swearing when he procures or induces another to commit the offense of perjury or the offense of false swearing and, upon conviction thereof, shall be punished by a fine of not more than $1,000.00 or by imprisonment for not less than one nor more than ten years, or both.

Laws 1833, Cobb's 1851 Digest, p. 804; Laws 1968, p. 1249, § 1.

Formerly Code 1863, §§ 4359, 4360; Code 1868, §§ 4397, 4398; Code 1873, §§ 4464, 4465; Code 1882, §§ 4464, 4465; Penal Code 1895, §§ 260, 261; Penal Code 1910, §§ 263, 264; Code 1933, §§ 26–4005, 26–4006; Code 1933, § 26–2403.

§ 16–10–73. Impersonating in a legal proceeding

Any person except an attorney of record who shall acknowledge or cause to be acknowledged, in any of the courts of the state or before any authorized officer, any recognizance, bail, or judgment in the name of any person not privy or consenting thereto commits the offense of impersonating in a legal proceeding and, upon conviction thereof, shall be punished by a fine of not more than $1,000.00 or by imprisonment for not less than one nor more than five years, or both.

Laws 1833, Cobb's 1851 Digest, p. 806; Laws 1968, p. 1249, § 1.

Formerly Code 1863, § 4369; Code 1868, § 4407; Code 1873, § 4475; Code 1882, § 4475; Penal Code 1895, § 305; Penal Code 1910, § 310; Code 1933, § 26–4301; Code 1933, § 26–2404.

Article 5

Offenses Related to Judicial and Other Proceedings

§ 16–10–90. Compounding a crime

(a) A person commits the offense of compounding a crime when, after institution of criminal proceedings and without leave of the court or of the prosecuting attorney of the court where the criminal proceedings are pending, he accepts or agrees to accept any benefit in consideration of a promise, express or implied, not to prosecute or aid in the prosecution of a criminal offense.

(b) A person convicted of the offense of compounding a crime which is a felony shall be punished by a fine of not more than $1,000.00 or by imprisonment for not less than one nor more than five years, or both. A person convicted of the offense of compounding a crime which is a misdemeanor is guilty of a misdemeanor.

Laws 1833, Cobb's 1851 Digest, p. 808; Laws 1968, p. 1249, § 1.

Formerly Code 1863, § 4385; Code 1868, § 4423; Code 1873, § 4491; Code 1882, § 4491; Penal Code 1895, § 323; Penal Code 1910, § 328; Code 1933, § 26–4603; Code 1933, § 26–2504.

§ 16–10–91. Embracery

(a) A person commits the offense of embracery when he:

(1) With intent to influence a person summoned or serving as a juror, communicates with him otherwise than is authorized by law in an attempt to influence his action as a juror; or

(2) Summoned as a juror, accepts anything of value offered to him with the understanding that it is given with the intent of influencing his action as a juror.

(b) A person convicted of the offense of embracery shall be punished by a fine of not more than $1,000.00 or by imprisonment for not less than one nor more than five years, or both.

Laws 1833, Cobb's 1851 Digest, p. 809; Laws 1968, p. 1249, § 1.

Formerly Code 1863, § 4390; Code 1868, § 4431; Code 1873, § 4503; Code 1882, § 4503; Penal Code 1895, § 328; Penal Code 1910, § 333; Code 1933, § 26–4702; Code 1933, § 26–2407.

§ 16–10–92. Acceptance by witness of benefit

A person who is or may be a witness at a trial, hearing, or other proceeding before any court or any officer authorized by the law to hear evidence or take testimony and who receives or agrees or offers to receive any benefit, reward, or consideration to which he is not entitled, pursuant to an agreement or understanding that his testimony will be influenced thereby or that he will absent himself from the trial, hearing, or other proceeding, shall, upon conviction thereof, be punished by imprisonment for not less than one nor more than five years.

Laws 1959, p. 34, § 25; Laws 1968, p. 1249, § 1.

Formerly Code 1933, § 26–2312.

§ 16–10–93. Influencing witnesses

(a) A person who, with intent to deter a witness from testifying freely, fully, and truthfully to any matter pending in any court, in any administrative proceeding, or before a grand jury, communicates, directly or indirectly, to such witness any threat of injury or damage to the person, property, or employment of the witness or to the person, property, or employment of any relative or associate of the witness or who offers or delivers any benefit, reward, or consideration to such witness or to a relative or associate of the witness shall, upon conviction thereof, be punished by imprisonment for not less than one nor more than five years.

(b)(1) It shall be unlawful for any person knowingly to use intimidation, physical force, or threats; to persuade another person by means of corruption or to attempt to do so; or to engage in misleading conduct toward another person with intent to:

(A) Influence, delay, or prevent the testimony of any person in an official proceeding;

(B) Cause or induce any person to:

(i) Withhold testimony or a record, document, or other object from an official proceeding;

(ii) Alter, destroy, mutilate, or conceal an object with intent to impair the object's integrity or availability for use in an official proceeding;

(iii) Evade legal process summoning that person to appear as a witness or to produce a record, document, or other object in an official proceeding; or

(iv) Be absent from an official proceeding to which such person has been summoned by legal process; or

(C) Hinder, delay, or prevent the communication to a law enforcement officer, prosecuting attorney, or judge of this state of information relating to the commission or possible commission of a criminal offense or a violation of conditions of probation, parole, or release pending judicial proceedings.

(2) Any person convicted of a violation of this subsection shall be guilty of a felony and, upon conviction thereof, shall be punished by imprisonment for not less than two nor more than ten years or by a fine of not less than $10,000.00 nor more than $20,000.00, or both.

(3)(A) For the purposes of this Code section, the term "official proceeding" means any hearing or trial conducted by a court of this state or its political subdivisions, a grand jury, or an agency of the executive, legislative, or judicial branches of government of this state or its political subdivisions or authorities.

(B) An official proceeding need not be pending or about to be instituted at the time of any offense defined in this subsection.

(C) The testimony, record, document, or other object which is prevented or impeded or attempted to be prevented or impeded in an official proceeding in violation of this Code section need not be admissible in evidence or free of a claim of privilege.

(D) In a prosecution for an offense under this Code section, no state of mind need be proved with respect to the circumstance:

(i) That the official proceeding before a judge, court, magistrate, grand jury, or government agency is before a judge or court of this state, a magistrate, a grand jury, or an agency of state or local government; or

(ii) That the judge is a judge of this state or its political subdivisions or that the law enforcement officer is an officer or employee of the State of Georgia or a political subdivision or authority of the state or a person authorized to act for or on behalf of the State of Georgia or a political subdivision or authority of the state.

(E) A prosecution under this Code section may be brought in the county in which the official proceeding, whether or not pending or about to be instituted, was intended to be affected or in the county in which the conduct constituting the alleged offense occurred.

(c) Any crime committed in violation of subsection (a) or (b) of this Code section shall be considered a separate offense.

Laws 1959, p. 34, § 24; Laws 1975, p. 34, § 1; Laws 1988, p. 316, § 1; Laws 1998, p. 270, § 5.

Formerly Code 1933, § 26–2313.

§ 16–10–94. Tampering with evidence

(a) A person commits the offense of tampering with evidence when, with the intent to prevent the apprehension or cause the wrongful apprehension of any person or to obstruct the prosecution or defense of any person, he knowingly destroys, alters, conceals, or disguises physical evidence or makes, devises, prepares, or plants false evidence.

(b) Nothing in this Code section shall be deemed to abrogate or alter any privilege which any person is entitled to claim under existing laws.

(c) Except as otherwise provided in this subsection, any person who violates subsection (a) of this Code section involving the prosecution or defense of a felony and involving another person shall be guilty of a felony and, upon conviction thereof, shall be punished by imprisonment for not less than one nor more than three years; provided, however, that any person who violates subsection (a) of this Code section involving the prosecution or defense of a serious violent felony as defined in subsection (a) of Code Section 17–10–6.1 and involving another person shall be guilty of a felony and, upon conviction thereof, shall be punished by imprisonment for not less than one nor more than ten years. Except as otherwise provided in this subsection, any person who violates subsection (a) of this Code section involving the prosecution or defense of a misdemeanor shall be guilty of a misdemeanor.

Laws 1974, p. 423, § 1; Laws 2001, p. 982, § 1.

Formerly Code 1933, § 26–2510.

Historical and Statutory Notes

The 2001 amendment rewrote the penal provisions comprising subsec. (c).

§ 16–10–94.1. Destruction, alteration, or falsification of health records

(a) As used in this Code section, the term:

(1) "Patient" means any person who has received health care services from a provider.

(2) "Provider" means all hospitals, including public, private, osteopathic, and tuberculosis hospitals; other special care units, including podiatric facilities, skilled nursing facilities, and kidney disease treatment centers, including freestanding hemodialysis units; intermediate care facilities; ambulatory surgical or obstetrical facilities; health maintenance organizations; and home health agencies. Such term shall also mean any person licensed to practice under Chapter 9, 11, 26, 34, 35, or 39 of Title 43.

(3) "Record" means a patient's health record, including, but not limited to, evaluations, diagnoses, prognoses, laboratory reports, X-rays, prescriptions, and other technical information used in assessing the patient's condition, or the pertinent portion of the record relating to a specific condition or a summary of the record.

(b) Any person who, with intent to conceal any material fact relating to a potential claim or cause of action, knowingly and willfully destroys, alters, or falsifies any record shall be guilty of a misdemeanor.

Laws 1988, p. 412, § 1.

§ 16–10–95. Repealed by Laws 2006, Act 451, § 1, eff. July 1, 2006

Historical and Statutory Notes

The repealed section, relating to the offense of barratry, was derived from Laws 1833, Cobb's 1851 Digest, p. 808; Laws 1895, p. 64, § 1; Laws 1960, p. 1135, § 3; Laws 1968, p. 1249, § 1; Code 1863, §§ 4388, 4389; Code 1868, §§ 4429, 4430; Code 1873, §§ 4501, 4502; Code 1882, §§ 4501, 4502; Penal Code 1895, §§ 325, 327; Penal Code 1910, §§ 330, 332; Code 1933, § 26–4701; Code 1933, § 26–2406. The repealing law also reserved the section designation.

§ 16–10–96. Impersonating another as witness or otherwise, etc.

Any person who shall falsely represent or impersonate another and in such assumed character answer as a witness to interrogatories or do any other act in the course of any action, proceeding, or prosecution or in any other way, matter, or thing, whereby the person so impersonated or represented, or any other person, might suffer damage, loss, or injury shall, upon conviction thereof, be punished by confinement for not less than one year nor more than five years.

Laws 1833, Cobb's 1851 Digest, p. 822.

Formerly Code 1863, § 4464; Code 1868, § 4508; Code 1873, § 4596; Code 1882, § 4596; Penal Code 1895, § 666; Penal Code 1910, § 711; Code 1933, § 38–9901.

§ 16–10–97. Intimidation or obstruction of jurors or court officers

(a) A person who by threat or force or by any threatening letter or communication:

(1) Endeavors to intimidate or impede any grand juror or petit juror or any officer in or of any court of this state or any court of any county or municipality of this state or any officer who may be serving at any proceeding in any such court while in the discharge of such juror's or officer's duties;

(2) Injures any grand juror or petit juror in his or her person or property on account of any indictment or verdict assented to by him or her or on account of his or her being or having been such juror; or

(3) Injures any officer in or of any court of this state or any court of any county or municipality of this state or any officer who may be serving at any proceeding in any such court in his or her person or property on account of the performance of his or her official duties

shall, upon conviction thereof, be punished by a fine of not more than $5,000.00 or by imprisonment for not more than 20 years, or both.

(b) As used in this Code section, the term "any officer in or of any court" means a judge, attorney, clerk of court, deputy clerk of court, court reporter, or probation officer.

Laws 1988, p. 391, § 1; Laws 1989, p. 14, § 16; Laws 1992, p. 6, § 16; Laws 2010, Act 646, § 2, eff. July 1, 2010.

Historical and Statutory Notes

The 2010 amendment by Act 646 designated the introductory clause as subsec. (a); in pars. (2) and (3), inserted "or her" after "him" and "his"; in par. (3), substituted "20 years" for "five years"; and added subsec. (b).

§ 16–10–98. Judge, prosecuting attorney, or law enforcement officer who is witness in criminal case prohibited from receiving remuneration for publishing book or making public appearance

(a) It shall be unlawful for a judge, prosecuting attorney, investigating officer, or law enforcement officer who is a witness in a case to receive or agree to receive remuneration during the period of time between indictment and the completion of direct appeal in any criminal case in which the judge, prosecuting attorney, or law enforcement officer is involved for any of the following activities:

(1) Publishing a book or article concerning the case;

(2) Making a public appearance concerning the case; or

(3) Participating in any commercial activity concerning the case.

(b) A person convicted of a violation of subsection (a) of this Code section shall be guilty of a misdemeanor.

(c) For purposes of this Code section remuneration shall not be deemed to include customary and ordinary salary and benefits of the individual or customary and ordinary expenses paid for public appearances.

Laws 1997, p. 1310, § 1.

CHAPTER 11

OFFENSES AGAINST PUBLIC ORDER AND SAFETY

Article 1

Part 1

Part 2

Article 1

Treason and Other Subversive Activities

Part 1

General Provisions

§ 16–11–1. Treason

(a) A person owing allegiance to the state commits the offense of treason when he knowingly levies war against the state, adheres to her enemies, or gives them aid and comfort. No person shall be convicted of the offense of treason except on the testimony of two witnesses to the same overt act or on confession in open court. When the overt act of treason is committed outside this state, the person charged therewith may be tried in any county in this state.

(b) A person convicted of the offense of treason shall be punished by death or by imprisonment for life or for not less than 15 years.

Laws 1833, Cobb's 1851 Digest, p. 782; Laws 1968, p. 1249, § 1; Laws 1982, p. 3, § 16.

Formerly Code 1863, § 4212; Code 1868, § 4247; Code 1873, § 4313; Code 1882, §§ 4313, 5019; Penal Code 1895, §§ 51, 52, 53; Penal Code 1910, §§ 51, 52, 53; Code 1933, §§ 26–801, 26–802, 26–803; Code 1933, § 26–2201.

§ 16–11–2. Insurrection

(a) A person commits the offense of insurrection when he combines with others to overthrow or attempt to overthrow the representative and constitutional form of government of the state or any political subdivision thereof when the same is manifested by acts of violence.

(b) A person convicted of the offense of insurrection shall be punished by imprisonment for not less than one nor more than ten years. Insurrection shall be bailable only in the discretion of a judge of the superior court.

Laws 1866, p. 152, §§ 1, 3; Laws 1871–72, p. 19, § 1; Laws 1968, p. 1249, § 1; Laws 1981, p. 868, § 1.

Formerly Code 1868, §§ 4249, 4251; Code 1873, §§ 4315, 4317; Code 1882, §§ 4315, 4317; Penal Code 1895, §§ 55, 57; Penal Code 1910, §§ 55, 57; Code 1933, §§ 26–901, 26–903; Code 1933, § 26–2202.

§ 16–11–3. Inciting to insurrection

(a) A person commits the offense of inciting to insurrection when he incites others to overthrow or attempt to overthrow the representative and constitutional form of government of the state or any political subdivision thereof and he or they commit any violent act in furtherance thereof.

(b) A person convicted of the offense of inciting to insurrection shall be punished by imprisonment for not less than one nor more than ten years. Inciting to insurrection shall be bailable only in the discretion of a judge of the superior court.

Laws 1866, p. 152, §§ 2, 4; Laws 1871–72, p. 19, § 1; Laws 1968, p. 1249, § 1; Laws 1969, p. 857, § 10; Laws 1981, p. 868, § 2.

Formerly Code 1868, §§ 4250, 4251; Code 1873, §§ 4316, 4317; Code 1882, §§ 4316, 4317; Penal Code 1895, §§ 56, 57; Penal Code 1910, §§ 56, 57; Code 1933, §§ 26–902, 26–903; Code 1933, § 26–2203.

§ 16–11–4. Advocating overthrow of government

(a) As used in this Code section, the term:

(1) "Organization" means any corporation, company, partnership, association, trust, foundation, fund, club, society, committee, political party, or any group of persons, whether or not incorporated, permanently or temporarily associated together for joint action or advancement of views on any subject.

(2) "Subversive organization" means any organization which engages in or advocates, abets, advises, or teaches, or which has a purpose of engaging in or advocating, abetting, advising, or teaching activities intended to overthrow, to destroy, or to assist in the overthrow or destruction of the government of the state or of any political subdivision thereof by force or violence.

(b) A person commits the offense of advocating the overthrow of the government if he knowingly and willfully commits any of the following acts:

(1) Advocates, abets, advises, or teaches the duty, necessity, desirability, or propriety of overthrowing or destroying the government of the state or any political subdivision thereof by force or violence;

(2) Prints, publishes, edits, issues, circulates, sells, distributes, exhibits, or displays any written or printed matter advocating, advising, or teaching the duty, necessity, desirability, or propriety of overthrowing or destroying the government of the state or of any political subdivision thereof by force or violence;

(3) Assists in the formation, participates in the management, or contributes to the support of any subversive organization, knowing the purpose thereof;

(4) Becomes a member or continues to be a member of a subversive organization, knowing the purpose thereof;

(5) Destroys any books, records, or files or secretes any funds in this state of a subversive organization, knowing the organization to be such; or

(6) Conspires with one or more persons to commit any of the acts prohibited by this Code section.

(c) A person convicted of violating any provision of this Code section shall be punished by a fine of not more than $20,000.00 or by imprisonment for not less than one nor more than 20 years, or both.

Laws 1968, p. 1249, § 1.

Formerly Code 1933, § 26–2204.

Part 2

Sedition and Subversive Activities

§ 16–11–5. Short title

This part may be cited as the "Sedition and Subversive Activities Act of 1953."

Laws 1953, Jan.-Feb. Sess., p. 216, § 12; Laws 1953, Nov.-Dec. Sess., p. 73, § 1.

§ 16–11–6. Definitions

As used in this part, the term:

(1) "Foreign government" means the government of any country, nation, or group of nations other than the government of the United States of America or of one of the states thereof.

(2) "Foreign subversive organizations" means any organization directed, dominated, or controlled directly or indirectly by a foreign government which engages in or advocates, abets, advises, or teaches, or a purpose of which is to engage in or to advocate, abet, advise, or teach activities intended to overthrow, to destroy, or to assist in the overthrow or destruction of the government of the United States or of this state or of any political subdivision of either of them and to establish in place thereof any form of government the direction and control of which is to be vested in, or exercised by or under, the domination or control of any foreign government, organization, or individual.

(3) "Organization" means an organization, corporation, company, partnership, association, trust, foundation, fund, club, society, committee, political party, or any group of persons, whether or not incorporated, permanently or temporarily associated together for joint action or advancement of views on any subject or subjects.

(4) "Subversive organization" means an organization which engages in or advocates, abets, advises, or teaches, or a purpose for which is to engage in or advocate, abet, advise, or teach activities intended to overthrow, to destroy, or to assist in the overthrow or destruction of the government of the United States, government of this state, or of any political subdivision of either of them by revolution, force, or violence.

(5) "Subversive person" means any person who commits, attempts to commit, or aids in the commission or advocates, abets, advises, or teaches by any means any person to commit, attempt to commit, or aid in the commission of any act intended to overthrow, to destroy, or to assist in the overthrow or destruction of the government of the United States or of this state or any political subdivision of either of them by revolution, force, or violence; or who is a knowing member of a subversive organization or a foreign subversive organization.

Laws 1953, Jan.-Feb. Sess., p. 216, § 1; Laws 1953, Nov.-Dec. Sess., p. 73, § 1.

§ 16–11–7. Special assistant Attorney General

The Governor, with the concurrence of the Attorney General, is authorized and directed to appoint a special assistant attorney general for investigating and prosecuting subversive activities, whose responsibility it shall be, under the supervision of the Attorney General, to assemble, arrange, and deliver to the district attorney of any county, together with a list of necessary witnesses for presentation to the next grand jury in the county, all information and evidence of matters within the county which have come to his attention relating in any manner to the acts prohibited by this part and relating generally to the purpose, processes, and activities of communists and any other or related subversive organizations, associations, groups, or persons. Such evidence may be presented by the Attorney General or the special assistant attorney general to the grand jury of any county directly, and he may represent the state on the trial of such a case, should he feel the ends of justice would be best served thereby, and the special assistant attorney general herein provided may testify before any grand jury as to matters referred to in this part as to which he may have information.

Laws 1953, Jan.-Feb. Sess., p. 216, § 6; Laws 1953, Nov.-Dec. Sess., p. 73, § 3.

§ 16–11–8. Obtaining evidence; cooperation of prosecutors; Commissioner of Public Safety, sheriffs and police officers; special enforcement agencies

For the collection of any evidence and information referred to in this part, the Governor and the Attorney General are authorized and directed to call upon all prosecuting attorneys, the commissioner of public safety, sheriffs, and county and municipal police authorities to furnish to the special assistant, provided for in Code Section 16–11–7, such assistance as may from time to time be required. Such police authorities are directed to furnish information and assistance as may be from time to time so requested. The police authorities shall transmit immediately to the special assistant attorney general any information coming to their notice and attention regarding the activities of any subversive persons, subversive organizations, or foreign subversive organizations. The Governor by executive order is authorized to establish within existing departments such special enforcement agencies, designate such personnel, and fix such duties as may from time to time be required to perform any of the functions and duties required by this part.

Laws 1953, Jan.-Feb. Sess., p. 216, § 7; Laws 1953, Nov.-Dec. Sess., p. 73, § 4; Laws 1972, p. 1015, § 1602.

§ 16–11–9. Maintenance of records on subversive activity; secrecy

The Attorney General shall require the special assistant to maintain complete records of all information received by him and all matters handled by him under the requirements of this part. Such records as may reflect on the loyalty of any resident of this state shall not be made public or divulged to any person except with permission of the Governor or the Attorney General to effectuate the purposes of this part. All such records shall be classified as confidential state secrets until declassified by the Governor or the Attorney General.

Laws 1953, Jan.-Feb. Sess., p. 216, § 8; Laws 1953, Nov.-Dec. Sess., p. 73, § 5.

§ 16–11–10. Charge to grand jury with reference to subversive activities

The judge of any court exercising general criminal jurisdiction, when in his discretion it appears appropriate or when informed by the Attorney General or district attorney that there is information or evidence of the character described in Code Section 16–11–7 to be considered by the grand jury, shall charge the grand jury to inquire into violations of this part for the purpose of proper action and further to inquire generally into the purposes, processes, and activities, and any other matters affecting communists or any related or other subversive organizations, associations, groups, or persons.

Laws 1953, Jan.-Feb. Sess., p. 216, § 9.

§ 16–11–11. Subversive organizations forbidden; dissolution; forfeiture of corporate charters; seizure of funds, records and property

It shall be unlawful for any subversive organization or foreign subversive organization to exist or function in this state. Any organization which by a court of competent jurisdiction is found to have violated this Code section shall be dissolved and, if it is a corporation organized and existing under the laws of this state, a finding by a court of competent jurisdiction that it has violated this Code section shall constitute legal cause for forfeiture of its charter and its charter shall be forfeited. All funds, books, records, and files of every kind and all other property of any organization found to have violated this Code section shall be seized by and for this state, the funds to be deposited in the state treasury and the books, records, files, and other property to be turned over to the Attorney General.

Laws 1953, Jan.-Feb. Sess., p. 216, § 5.

§ 16–11–12. Subversive persons prohibited from holding public office or employment

No subversive person shall be eligible for employment in or appointment to any office or any position of trust or profit in the government of this state or in the administration of the business of this state or of any county, municipality, or other political subdivision thereof.

Laws 1953, Jan.-Feb. Sess., p. 216, § 10; Laws 1953, Nov.-Dec. Sess., p. 73, § 6.

§ 16–11–13. Investigation to be conducted on all State employees prior to appointment

(a) Every person and every board, commission, council, department, or other agency of the state or any political subdivision thereof which appoints, employs, or supervises in any manner the appointment or employment of public officials or employees shall establish, by rules, regulations, or otherwise, procedures designated to ascertain before any person, including teachers and other employees of any public educational institution in this state, is appointed or employed, that he is not a subversive person and that there are no reasonable grounds to believe such person is a subversive person. In the event such reasonable grounds exist, he shall not be appointed or employed. In securing any facts necessary to ascertain the information required by this Code section, all applicants and employees shall be required to sign a written statement or questionnaire containing answers to such inquiries as may be material and containing the following questions:

(1) Full name including maiden name, names of former marriages, former names changed legally or otherwise, aliases, and nicknames, and the dates used;

(2) Address;

(3)(A) Are you now or have you been within the last ten years a member of any organization which to your knowledge at the time of membership advocates or has as one of its objectives the overthrow of the government of the United States or of the government of the State of Georgia by force or violence? Yes ____ No ____. If "Yes," state the name of the organization and your past and present membership status including any offices held therein.

(B) If the answer to (A) is "Yes" and the employing authority deems further inquiry necessary, you will be notified of such determination. No action adverse to your application will be taken because of an affirmative answer until after such an inquiry, with notice to you and an opportunity for you to present evidence, and only if the result of such inquiry brings your application within the prohibition within the "Sedition and Subversive Activities Act of 1953."

(4)(A) Have you ever been convicted or are any charges now pending against you by federal, state, or other law enforcement authorities, for any violation of any federal law, state law, county or municipal law, regulation, or ordinance? (Do not include anything that happened before your sixteenth birthday. Do not include minor traffic violations for which a fine of $35.00 or less was imposed. All other convictions must be included even if they were pardoned.) Yes ____ No ____.

(B) If the answer to (A) is "Yes," state the reason convicted, the date convicted, and the place where convicted.

(b) The written statement or questionnaire shall contain notice that it is subject to the penalties of false swearing.

(c) The Governor is authorized to make appropriate orders, rules, and regulations to effectuate the purposes of Code Section 16–11–12, this Code section, and Code Section 16–11–14.

Laws 1953, Jan.-Feb. Sess., p. 216, § 11; Laws 1953, Nov.-Dec. Sess., p. 73, § 7; Laws 1974, p. 411, § 1; Laws 1992, p. 6, § 16.

§ 16–11–14. Penalty provided for false swearing in connection with subversive activities investigation

(a) Every written statement made pursuant to this part by an applicant for appointment or employment or by any employee shall be deemed to have been made under oath if it contains a declaration preceding the signature of the maker to the effect that it is made under the penalties of false swearing. Any person who makes a material misstatement of fact in any such written statement, in any affidavit made pursuant to this part, under oath in any hearing conducted by any agency of this state or of any of its political subdivisions pursuant to this part, or in any written statement by an applicant for appointment or employment or by an employee in any state-aided or private institution of learning in this state intended to determine whether or not such applicant or employee is a subversive person, which statement contains notice that it is subject to the penalties of false swearing, shall be subject to the penalties of false swearing as prescribed in Code Section 16–10–71.

(b) Nothing contained in subsection (a) of this Code section shall be construed to repeal in any way the laws of this state dealing with perjury and false swearing.

Laws 1953, Nov.-Dec. Sess., p. 73, § 9; Laws 1974, p. 411, § 2.

§ 16–11–15. Information required by section 16–11–13 not to require answers to questions concerning relatives of persons investigated

No person giving any information, whether by answering a questionnaire or otherwise, as provided in Code Section 16–11–13 shall be required to give any information or answer any questions relative to the membership in any organization of any relative of such person.

Laws 1956, p. 67, § 1.

§ 16–11–16. Information obtained under section 16–11–13 to be filed at place of employment

Any questionnaires or statements prepared as provided in Code Section 16–11–13 shall be filed at the place of employment rather than with a central state agency.

Laws 1956, p. 67, § 2.

Article 2

Offenses Against Public Order

§ 16–11–30. Riot

(a) Any two or more persons who shall do an unlawful act of violence or any other act in a violent and tumultuous manner commit the offense of riot.

(b) Any persons who violate subsection (a) of this Code section are guilty of a misdemeanor.

Laws 1833, Cobb's 1851 Digest, p. 811; Laws 1865–66, p. 233, § 1; Laws 1968, p. 1249, § 1.

Formerly Code 1863, § 4400; Code 1868, § 4441; Code 1873, § 4514; Code 1882, § 4514; Penal Code 1895, § 354; Penal Code 1910, § 360; Code 1933, § 26–5302; Code 1933, § 26–2601.

§ 16–11–31. Inciting to riot

(a) A person who with intent to riot does an act or engages in conduct which urges, counsels, or advises others to riot, at a time and place and under circumstances which produce a clear and present danger of a riot, commits the offense of inciting to riot.

(b) Any person who violates subsection (a) of this Code section is guilty of a misdemeanor.

Laws 1968, p. 1249, § 1; Laws 1969, p. 857, § 18.

Formerly Code 1933, § 26–2602.

§ 16–11–32. Affray

(a) An affray is the fighting by two or more persons in some public place to the disturbance of the public tranquility.

(b) A person who commits the offense of affray is guilty of a misdemeanor.

Laws 1833, Cobb's 1851 Digest, p. 811; Laws 1865–66, p. 233, § 2; Laws 1968, p. 1249, § 1.

Formerly Code 1863, § 4401; Code 1868, § 4442; Code 1873, § 4515; Code 1882, § 4515; Penal Code 1895, § 355; Penal Code 1910, § 361; Code 1933, § 26–5303; Code 1933, § 26–2603.

§ 16–11–33. Unlawful assembly

A person who knowingly participates in either of the following acts or occurrences is guilty of a misdemeanor:

(1) The assembly of two or more persons for the purpose of committing an unlawful act and the failure to withdraw from the assembly on being lawfully commanded to do so by a peace officer and before any member of the assembly has inflicted injury to the person or property of another; or

(2) The assembly of two or more persons, without authority of law, for the purpose of doing violence to the person or property of one supposed by the accused to have been guilty of a violation of the law, or for the purpose of exercising correctional or regulative powers over any person by violence; provided, however, that it shall be an affirmative defense to a prosecution under this paragraph that the accused withdrew from the assembly on being lawfully commanded to do so by a peace officer or before any member of the assembly had inflicted injury to the person or property of another.

Laws 1833, Cobb's 1851 Digest, p. 810; Laws 1968, p. 1249, § 1; Laws 1989, p. 14, § 16.

Formerly Code 1863, § 4399; Code 1868, § 4440; Code 1873, § 4513; Code 1882, § 4513; Penal Code 1895, § 353; Penal Code 1910, § 359; Code 1933, § 26–5301; Code 1933, § 26–2604.

§ 16–11–34. Disturbance of meeting, gathering or procession

(a) A person who recklessly or knowingly commits any act which may reasonably be expected to prevent or disrupt a lawful meeting, gathering, or procession is guilty of a misdemeanor.

(b) This Code section shall not be construed to affect the powers delegated to counties or to municipal corporations to pass laws to punish disorderly conduct within their respective limits.

Laws 1968, p. 1249, § 1.

Formerly Code 1933, § 26–2605.

Validity

This section has been held unconstitutional in the case of State v. Fielden, 2006, 280 Ga. 444, 629 S.E.2d 252.

§ 16–11–34.1. Disruption of Senate or House of Representatives

(a) It shall be unlawful for any person recklessly or knowingly to commit any act which may reasonably be expected to prevent or disrupt a session or meeting of the Senate or House of Representatives, a joint session thereof, or any meeting of any standing or interim committee, commission, or caucus of members thereof.

(b) It shall be unlawful for any person, other than those persons who are exempt from the provisions of Code Sections 16–11–126 through 16–11–127.2, to enter, occupy, or remain within the state capitol building or any building housing committee offices, committee rooms, or offices of members, officials, or employees of the General Assembly or either house thereof while in the possession of any firearm; knife, as such term is defined in Code Section 16–11–125.1; explosive or incendiary device or compound; bludgeon; knuckles, whether made from metal, thermoplastic, wood, or other similar material; or any other dangerous or deadly weapon, instrument, or device.

(c) It shall be unlawful for any person purposely or recklessly and without authority of law to obstruct any street, sidewalk, hallway, office, or other passageway in that area designated as Capitol Square by Code Section 50–2–28 in such a manner as to render it impassable without unreasonable inconvenience or hazard or to fail or refuse to remove such obstruction after receiving a reasonable official request or the order of a peace officer to do so.

(d) It shall be unlawful for any person willfully and knowingly to enter or to remain upon the floor of the Senate or the floor of the House of Representatives or within any cloakroom, lobby, or anteroom adjacent to such floor unless such person is authorized, pursuant to the rules of the Senate or House of Representatives or pursuant to authorization given by the Senate or House of Representatives, to enter or remain upon the floor or within such area.

(e) It shall be unlawful for any person willfully and knowingly to enter or to remain in the gallery of the Senate or the gallery of the House of Representatives in violation of rules governing admission to such gallery adopted by the Senate or the House of Representatives or pursuant to authorization given by such body.

(f) It shall be unlawful for any person willfully and knowingly to enter or to remain in any room, chamber, office, or hallway within the state capitol building or any building housing committee offices, committee rooms, or offices of members, officials, or employees of the General Assembly or either house thereof with intent to disrupt the orderly conduct of official business or to utter loud, threatening, or abusive language or engage in any disorderly or disruptive conduct in such buildings or areas.

(g) It shall be unlawful for any person to parade, demonstrate, or picket within the state capitol building or any building housing committee offices, committee rooms, or offices of members, officials, or employees of the General Assembly or either house thereof with intent to disrupt the orderly conduct of official business or to utter loud, threatening, or abusive language or engage in any disorderly or disruptive conduct in such buildings or areas.

(h)(1) Any person violating this Code section for the first time shall be guilty of a misdemeanor.

(2) Any person violating this Code section for the second time shall be guilty of a misdemeanor of a high and aggravated nature.

(3) Any person violating this Code section for the third or any subsequent time shall be guilty of a felony and, upon conviction thereof, shall be punished by imprisonment for not less than one nor more than three years.

(i) The enactment of this Code section shall not repeal any other provision of law proscribing or regulating any conduct otherwise prohibited by this Code section.

Laws 1987, p. 614, § 1; Laws 2008, Act 551, § 3, eff. July 1, 2008; Laws 2009, Act 8, § 16, eff. April 14, 2009; Laws 2010, Act 643, § 2–5, eff. June 4, 2010.

Historical and Statutory Notes

The 2008 amendment by Act 551 substituted "knuckles whether made from metal, thermoplastic, wood, or other similar material" for "metal knuckles" and "metal knucks", throughout the section.

The 2009 amendment by Act 8 was a provision contained in a correction bill.

The 2010 amendment by Act 643, in subsec. (b), substituted "16–11–127.2" for "16–11–128", substituted "as such term is defined in Code Section 16–11–125.1;" for "designed for the purpose of offense and defense,", and made nominal changes.

Laws 2010, Act 643, § 3–1, provides:

"This Act shall become effective upon its approval by the Governor or upon its becoming law without such approval and shall apply to all offenses committed on and after such date. The enactment of this Act shall not affect any prosecutions for acts occurring before the effective date of this Act and shall not act as an abatement of any such prosecutions."

§ 16–11–34.2. Disruptive conduct at funerals or memorial services

(a) The General Assembly declares that the interest of persons in planning, participating in, and attending a funeral or memorial service for a deceased relative or loved one without unwanted impediment, disruption, disturbance, or interference is a substantial interest and the General Assembly further recognizes the need to impose content neutral time, place, and manner restrictions on unwanted acts carried out with the intent to impede, disrupt, disturb, or interfere with such funeral or memorial service.

(b) It shall be unlawful to engage in any disorderly or disruptive conduct with the intent to impede, disrupt, disturb, or interfere with the orderly conduct of any funeral or memorial service or with the normal activities and functions carried on in the facilities or buildings where such funeral or memorial service is taking place. Any or all of the following shall constitute such disorderly or disruptive conduct:

(1) Displaying any visual images that convey fighting words or actual or imminent threats of harm directed to any person or property associated with said funeral or memorial service within 500 feet of the ceremonial site or location being used for the funeral or memorial service at any time one hour prior to, during, or one hour after the posted time for said funeral or memorial service;

(2) Uttering loud, threatening, or abusive language or singing, chanting, whistling, or yelling with or without noise amplification including, but not limited to, bullhorns, automobile horns, and microphones, such as would tend to impede, disrupt, disturb, or interfere with a funeral or memorial service within 500 feet of the ceremonial site or location being used for the funeral or memorial service;

(3) Attempting to block or blocking pedestrian or vehicular access to the ceremonial site or location being used for a funeral or memorial service at any time one hour prior to, during, or one hour after the posted time for said funeral or memorial service; or

(4) Conducting a public assembly, parade, demonstration, or other like event, either fixed or processional, within 500 feet of the ceremonial site or location being used for a funeral or memorial service at any time one hour prior to, during, or one hour after the posted time for said funeral or memorial service.

(c) Any person who violates any provision of subsection (b) of this Code section shall be guilty of a misdemeanor.

Laws 2006, Act 530, § 1, eff. July 1, 2006.

Historical and Statutory Notes

Laws 2006, Act 530, § 2, provides:

"This Act shall become effective on July 1, 2006, and shall apply to all offenses committed on or after such date."

§ 16–11–35. Failure to leave campus or facility of unit of university system or public school when directed

(a) As used in this Code section, the term:

(1) "Chief administrative officer," in the case of a public school, means the principal of the school or an officer designated by the superintendent or board of education having jurisdiction of the school to be the officer in charge of the public school.

(2) "Chief administrative officer," in the case of a unit of the university system, means the president of the unit of the university system or the officer designated by the Board of Regents of the University System of Georgia to administer and be the officer in charge of a campus or other facility of a unit of the university system.

(3) "Public school" means any school under the control and management of a county, independent, or area board of education supported by public funds and any school under the control and management of the State Board of Education or department or agency thereof supported by public funds.

(4) "Unit of the university system" means any college or university under the government, control, and management of the Board of Regents of the University System of Georgia.

(b) In any case in which a person who is not a student or officer or employee of a unit of the university system or of a public school and who is not required by his or her employment to be on the campus or any other facility of any such unit or of any public school enters the campus or facility, and it reasonably appears to the chief administrative officer of the campus or facility, or to any officer or employee designated by him or her to maintain order on the campus or facility, that such person is committing any act likely to interfere with the peaceful conduct of the activities of the campus or facility, or has entered the campus or facility for the purpose of committing any such act, the chief administrative officer or the officers or employees designated by him or her to maintain order on the campus or facility may direct the person to leave the campus or facility, and, if the person fails to do so, he or she shall be guilty of a misdemeanor of a high and aggravated nature.

Laws 1972, p. 134, § 1; Laws 1985, p. 149, § 16; Laws 1994, p. 1012, § 10.

Formerly Code 1933, § 26–2615.

§ 16–11–36. Loitering or prowling

(a) A person commits the offense of loitering or prowling when he is in a place at a time or in a manner not usual for law-abiding individuals under circumstances that warrant a justifiable and reasonable alarm or immediate concern for the safety of persons or property in the vicinity.

(b) Among the circumstances which may be considered in determining whether alarm is warranted is the fact that the person takes flight upon the appearance of a law enforcement officer, refuses to identify himself, or manifestly endeavors to conceal himself or any object. Unless flight by the person or other circumstances make it impracticable, a law enforcement officer shall, prior to any arrest for an offense under this Code section, afford the person an opportunity to dispel any alarm or immediate concern which would otherwise be warranted by requesting the person to identify himself and explain his presence and conduct. No person shall be convicted of an offense under this Code section if the law enforcement officer failed to comply with the foregoing procedure or if it appears at trial that the explanation given by the person was true and would have dispelled the alarm or immediate concern.

(c) A person committing the offense of loitering or prowling shall be guilty of a misdemeanor.

(d) This Code section shall not be deemed or construed to affect or limit the powers of counties or municipal corporations to adopt ordinances or resolutions prohibiting loitering or prowling within their respective limits.

Laws 1980, p. 388, § 1.

Formerly Code 1933, § 26–2616.

§ 16–11–37. Terroristic threats and acts

(a) A person commits the offense of a terroristic threat when he or she threatens to commit any crime of violence, to release any hazardous substance, as such term is defined in Code Section 12–8–92, or to burn or damage property with the purpose of terrorizing another or of causing the evacuation of a building, place of assembly, or facility of public transportation or otherwise causing serious public inconvenience or in reckless disregard of the risk of causing such terror or inconvenience. No person shall be convicted under this subsection on the uncorroborated testimony of the party to whom the threat is communicated.

(b) A person commits the offense of a terroristic act when:

(1) He or she uses a burning or flaming cross or other burning or flaming symbol or flambeau with the intent to terrorize another or another's household;

(2) While not in the commission of a lawful act, he or she shoots at or throws an object at a conveyance which is being operated or which is occupied by passengers; or

(3) He or she releases any hazardous substance or any simulated hazardous substance under the guise of a hazardous substance for the purpose of terrorizing another or of causing the evacuation of a building, place of assembly, or facility of public transportation or otherwise causing serious public inconvenience or in reckless disregard of the risk of causing such terror or inconvenience.

(c) A person convicted of the offense of a terroristic threat shall be punished by a fine of not more than $ 1,000.00 or by imprisonment for not less than one nor more than five years, or both. A person convicted of the offense of a terroristic act shall be punished by a fine of not more than $ 5,000.00 or by imprisonment for not less than one nor more than ten years, or both; provided, however, that if any person suffers a serious physical injury as a direct result of an act giving rise to a conviction under this Code section, the person so convicted shall be punished by a fine of not more than $ 250,000.00 or imprisonment for not less than five nor more than 40 years, or both.

(d) A person who commits or attempts to commit a terroristic threat or act with the intent to retaliate against any person for:

(1) Attending a judicial or administrative proceeding as a witness, attorney, judge, clerk of court, deputy clerk of court, court reporter, probation officer, or party or producing any record, document, or other object in a judicial or official proceeding; or

(2) Providing to a law enforcement officer, adult or juvenile probation officer, prosecuting attorney, or judge any information relating to the commission or possible commission of an offense under the laws of this state or of the United States or a violation of conditions of bail, pretrial release, probation, or parole

shall be guilty of the offense of a terroristic threat or act and, upon conviction thereof, shall be punished, for a terroristic threat, by imprisonment for not less than five nor more than ten years or by a fine of not less than $ 50,000.00, or both, and, for a terroristic act, by imprisonment for not less than five nor more than 20 years or by a fine of not less than $ 100,000.00, or both.

Laws 1884–85, p. 131, § 1; Laws 1892, p. 108, § 1; Laws 1893, p. 130, § 1; Laws 1905, p. 86, § 1; Laws 1968, p. 1249, § 1; Laws 1974, p. 1022, § 1; Laws 1998, p. 270, § 6; Laws 2002, p. 1094, § 4; Laws 2010, Act 646, § 3, eff. July 1, 2010.

Formerly Penal Code 1895, §§ 511, 512, 730; Penal Code 1910, §§ 512, 513, 782; Code 1933, §§ 26–1803, 26–7308, 26–7309; Code 1933, § 26–1307; Code 1933, § 26–1307.1.

Historical and Statutory Notes

The 2002 amendment substantially rewrote this section which formerly provided:

"(a) A person commits the offense of a terroristic threat when he threatens to commit any crime of violence or to burn or damage property with the purpose of terrorizing another or of causing the evacuation of a building, place of assembly, or facility of public transportation or otherwise causing serious public inconvenience, or in reckless disregard of the risk of causing such terror or inconvenience. No person shall be convicted under this subsection on the uncorroborated testimony of the party to whom the threat is communicated.

"(b) A person commits the offense of a terroristic act when:

"(1) He uses a burning or flaming cross or other burning or flaming symbol or flambeau with the intent to terrorize another or another's household; or

"(2) While not in the commission of a lawful act, he shoots at or throws an object at a conveyance which is being operated or which is occupied by passengers.

"(c) A person convicted of the offense of a terroristic threat or act shall be punished by a fine of not more than $1,000.00 or by imprisonment for not less than one nor more than five years, or both.

"(d) A person who commits or attempts to commit a terroristic threat or act with the intent to retaliate against any person for:

"(1) Attending a judicial or administrative proceeding as a witness or party or producing any record, document, or other object in a judicial or official proceeding; or

"(2) Providing to a law enforcement officer, adult or juvenile probation officer, prosecuting attorney, or judge any information relating to the commission or possible commission of an offense under the laws of this state or of the United States or a violation of conditions of bail, pretrial release, probation, or parole shall be guilty of the offense of a terroristic threat or act and, upon conviction thereof, shall be punished by imprisonment for not less than five nor more than ten years or by a fine of not less than $50,000.00, or both."

The 2010 amendment by Act 646, in subsec. (d), par. (1), inserted "clerk of court, deputy clerk of court, court reporter, probation officer," after "judge,".

§ 16–11–37.1. Dissemination through computer or computer network of information relating to terroristic acts

It shall be unlawful for any person knowingly to furnish or disseminate through a computer or computer network any picture, photograph, drawing, or similar visual representation or verbal description of any information designed to encourage, solicit, or otherwise promote terroristic acts as defined in Code Section 16–11–37. Any person convicted for violation of this Code section shall be guilty of a misdemeanor of a high and aggravated nature; provided, however, that if such act is in violation of paragraph (1) of subsection (d) of Code Section 16–11–37, the person convicted shall be guilty of a felony and shall be punished by imprisonment for not less than one nor more than ten years or by a fine not to exceed $100,000.00 or both.

Laws 1995, p. 574, § 2; Laws 2010, Act 646, § 4, eff. July 1, 2010.

Historical and Statutory Notes

The 2010 amendment by Act 646, in the first sentence, deleted "or" before "drawing"; in the second sentence, added "provided, however, that if such act is in violation of paragraph (1) of subsection (d) of Code Section 16–11–37, the person convicted shall be guilty of a felony and shall be punished by imprisonment for not less than one nor more than ten years or by a fine not to exceed $100,000.00 or both".

§ 16–11–38. Wearing masks, hoods, etc.

(a) A person is guilty of a misdemeanor when he wears a mask, hood, or device by which any portion of the face is so hidden, concealed, or covered as to conceal the identity of the wearer and is upon any public way or public property or upon the private property of another without the written permission of the owner or occupier of the property to do so.

(b) This Code section shall not apply to:

(1) A person wearing a traditional holiday costume on the occasion of the holiday;

(2) A person lawfully engaged in trade and employment or in a sporting activity where a mask is worn for the purpose of ensuring the physical safety of the wearer, or because of the nature of the occupation, trade, or profession, or sporting activity;

(3) A person using a mask in a theatrical production including use in Mardi gras celebrations and masquerade balls; or

(4) A person wearing a gas mask prescribed in emergency management drills and exercises or emergencies.

Laws 1951, p. 9, §§ 3, 7; Laws 1968, p. 1249, § 1.

Formerly Code 1933, § 26–2913.

§ 16–11–39. Disorderly conduct

(a) A person commits the offense of disorderly conduct when such person commits any of the following:

(1) Acts in a violent or tumultuous manner toward another person whereby such person is placed in reasonable fear of the safety of such person's life, limb, or health;

(2) Acts in a violent or tumultuous manner toward another person whereby the property of such person is placed in danger of being damaged or destroyed;

(3) Without provocation, uses to or of another person in such other person's presence, opprobrious or abusive words which by their very utterance tend to incite to an immediate breach of the peace, that is to say, words which as a matter of common knowledge and under ordinary circumstances will, when used to or of another person in such other person's presence, naturally tend to provoke violent resentment, that is, words commonly called "fighting words"; or

(4) Without provocation, uses obscene and vulgar or profane language in the presence of or by telephone to a person under the age of 14 years which threatens an immediate breach of the peace.

(b) Any person who commits the offense of disorderly conduct shall be guilty of a misdemeanor.

(c) This Code section shall not be deemed or construed to affect or limit the powers of counties or municipal corporations to adopt ordinances or resolutions prohibiting disorderly conduct within their respective limits.

Laws 1865–66, p. 233, § 2; Laws 1872, p. 9, § 1; Laws 1875, p. 25, § 1; Laws 1890–91, p. 83, § 1; Laws 1919, p. 103, § 1; Laws 1963, p. 455, § 1; Laws 1968, p. 1249, § 1; Laws 1974, p. 470, § 1; Laws 1992, p. 6, § 16; Laws 1995, p. 574, § 3.

Formerly Code 1863, § 4271; Code 1868, § 4306; Code 1873, § 4372; Code 1882, § 4372; Penal Code 1895, § 396; Penal Code 1910, § 387; Code 1933, § 26–6303; Code 1933, § 26–2610.

§ 16–11–39.1. Harassing phone calls

(a) A person commits the offense of harassing phone calls if such person telephones another person repeatedly, whether or not conversation ensues, for the purpose of annoying, harassing, or molesting another person or the family of such other person; uses over the telephone language threatening bodily harm; telephones and intentionally fails to hang up or disengage the connection; or knowingly permits any telephone under such person's control to be used for any purpose prohibited by this subsection.

(b) Any person who commits the offense of harassing phone calls shall be guilty of a misdemeanor.

Laws 1995, p. 574, § 3.

§ 16–11–39.2. Unlawful conduct during a 9–1–1 call

(a) As used in this Code section, the term:

(1) "Call" shall have the same meaning as set forth in paragraph (2.1) of Code Section 46–5–122.

(2) "False report" means the fabrication of an incident or crime or of material information relating to an incident or crime which the person making the report knows to be false at the time of making the report.

(3) "Harass" means to knowingly and willingly engage in any conduct directed toward a communications officer that is likely to impede or interfere with such communications officer's duties, that threatens such communication officer or any member of his or her family, or that places any member of the public served or to be served by 9–1–1 service in danger of injury or delayed assistance.

(4) "Harassing" means the willful use of opprobrious and abusive language which has no legitimate purpose in relation to imparting information relevant to an emergency call.

(5) "9–1–1" means a public safety answering point as defined in paragraph (15) of Code Section 46–5–122. The term "9–1–1" also means the digits, address, Internet Protocol address, or other information used to access or initiate a call to a public safety answering point.

(b) A person commits the offense of unlawful conduct during a 9–1–1 telephone call if he or she:

(1) Without provocation, uses obscene, vulgar, or profane language with the intent to intimidate or harass a 9–1–1 communications officer;

(2) Calls or otherwise contacts 9–1–1, whether or not conversation ensues, for the purpose of annoying, harassing, or molesting a 9–1–1 communications officer or for the purpose of interfering with or disrupting emergency telephone service;

(3) Calls or otherwise contacts 9–1–1 and fails to hang up or disengage the connection for the intended purpose of interfering with or disrupting emergency service;

(4) Calls or otherwise contacts 9–1–1 with the intention to harass a communications officer; or

(5) Calls or otherwise contacts 9–1–1 and makes a false report.

(c) Any person who violates subsection (b) of this Code section shall be guilty of a misdemeanor and, upon conviction thereof, shall be punished by a fine of not more than $500.00 or 12 months in jail, or both.

(d) Any violation of subsection (b) of this Code section shall be considered to have been committed in any county where such call to or contact with 9–1–1 originated or in any county where the call to or contact with 9–1–1 was received.

Laws 2007, Act 211, § 1, eff. July 1, 2007.

§ 16–11–40. Criminal defamation

(a) A person commits the offense of criminal defamation when, without a privilege to do so and with intent to defame another, living or dead, he communicates false matter which tends to blacken the memory of one who is dead or which exposes one who is alive to hatred, contempt, or ridicule, and which tends to provoke a breach of the peace.

(b) A person who violates subsection (a) of this Code section is guilty of a misdemeanor.

Laws 1833, Cobb's 1851 Digest, p. 812; Laws 1968, p. 1249, § 1.

Formerly Code 1863, § 4407; Code 1868, § 4448; Code 1873, § 4521; Code 1882, § 4521; Penal Code 1895, § 335; Penal Code 1910, § 340; Code 1933, § 26–2101; Code 1933, § 26–2804.

Validity

This section has been held unconstitutional in the case of Williamson v. State, 1982, 295 S.E.2d 305.

§ 16–11–41. Public drunkenness

(a) A person who shall be and appear in an intoxicated condition in any public place or within the curtilage of any private residence not his own other than by invitation of the owner or lawful occupant, which condition is made manifest by boisterousness, by indecent condition or act, or by vulgar, profane, loud, or unbecoming language, is guilty of a misdemeanor.

(b) This Code section shall not be construed to affect the powers delegated to counties or to municipal corporations to pass laws to punish drunkenness or disorderly conduct within their respective limits.

Laws 1968, p. 1249, § 1.

Formerly Code 1933, § 26–2607.

§ 16–11–42. Refusal to relinquish telephone party line in case of emergency; false statement as to emergency in order to obtain line

(a) A person is guilty of a misdemeanor when he fails to relinquish a telephone party line consisting of subscriber line telephone circuit with two or more main telephone stations connected therewith, each having a distinctive ring or telephone number, after he has been requested to do so to permit another to place a call in an emergency, in which property or human life is in jeopardy and the prompt summoning of aid is essential, to a fire or police department or for medical aid or ambulance service, if the party line at the time of the request is not being used for any such other emergency call. Any person who shall request the use of the party line by falsely stating that the same is needed for any of such purposes, knowing the statement to be false, is guilty of a misdemeanor.

(b) In every telephone directory distributed to the general public in this state, in which is listed the call numbers of any telephones located within this state, except such as are distributed solely for business advertising purposes, commonly known as classified telephone directories, there shall be printed in type not smaller than the smallest type appearing on the same page, a notice setting forth the substance of subsection (a) of this Code section preceded by the word "warning" printed in boldface type.

Laws 1960, p. 915, §§ 1, 2; Laws 1968, p. 1249, § 1.

Formerly Code 1933, § 26–2912.

§ 16–11–43. Obstructing highways

A person who, without authority of law, purposely or recklessly obstructs any highway, street, sidewalk, or other public passage in such a way as to render it impassable without unreasonable inconvenience or hazard and fails or refuses to remove the obstruction after receiving a reasonable official request or the order of a peace officer that he do so, is guilty of a misdemeanor.

Laws 1818, Cobb's 1851 Digest, p. 949; Laws 1859, p. 65, § 1; Laws 1865–66, p. 233, § 2; Laws 1968, p. 1249, § 1.

Formerly Code 1863, § 4481; Code 1868, § 4527; Code 1873, § 4617; Code 1882, § 4617; Penal Code 1895, § 715; Penal Code 1910, § 766; Code 1933, § 26–8106; Code 1933, § 26–2611.

§ 16–11–44. Disorderly house

A person who keeps and maintains, either by himself or others, a common, ill-governed, and disorderly house, to the encouragement of gaming, drinking, or other misbehavior, or to the common disturbance of the neighborhood or orderly citizens, is guilty of a misdemeanor.

Laws 1833, Cobb's 1851 Digest, p. 815; Laws 1865–66, p. 233, § 2; Laws 1968, p. 1249, § 1.

Formerly Code 1863, § 4422; Code 1868, § 4463; Code 1873, § 4537; Code 1882, § 4537; Penal Code 1895, § 392; Penal Code 1910, § 383; Code 1933, § 26–6103; Code 1933, § 26–2614.

Article 3

Invasions of Privacy

Part 1

Wiretapping, Eavesdropping, Surveillance, and Related Offenses

§ 16–11–60. Definitions

As used within this part, the term:

(1) "Device" means an instrument or apparatus used for overhearing, recording, intercepting, or transmitting sounds or for observing, photographing, videotaping, recording, or transmitting visual images and which involves in its operation electricity, electronics, or infrared, laser, or similar beams. Without limiting the generality of the foregoing, the term "device" shall specifically include any camera, photographic equipment, video equipment, or other similar equipment or any electronic, mechanical, or other apparatus which can be used to intercept a wire, oral, or electronic communication other than:

(A) Any telephone or telegraph instrument, equipment, or facility or any component thereof:

(i) Furnished to the subscriber or user by a provider of wire or electronic communication service in the ordinary course of its business and being used by the subscriber or user in the ordinary course of its business or furnished by such subscriber or user for connection to the facilities of such service and used in the ordinary course of its business; or

(ii) Being used by a provider of wire or electronic communication service in the ordinary course of its business or by an investigative or law enforcement officer in the ordinary course of his or her duties; or

(B) A hearing aid or similar device being used to correct subnormal hearing to not better than normal;

(C) Focusing, lighting, or illuminating equipment, optical magnifying equipment; and

(D) A "pen register" or "trap and trace device" as defined in this Code section.

(2) "Pen register" means a device or process which records or decodes dialing, routing, addressing, or signaling information transmitted by an instrument or facility from which a wire or electronic communication is transmitted; provided, however, that such information shall not include the contents of any communication; but such term does not include any device or process used by a provider or customer of a wire or electronic communication service for billing, or recording as an incident to billing, for communications services provided by such provider or any device or process used by a provider or customer of a wire communication service for cost accounting or other like purposes in the ordinary course its business.

(3) "Private place" means a place where one is entitled reasonably to expect to be safe from casual or hostile intrusion or surveillance.

(4) "Trap and trace device" means a device or process which captures the incoming electronic or other impulses which identify the originating number or other dialing, routing, addressing, and signaling information reasonably likely to identify the source of a wire or electronic communication; provided, however, that such information shall not include the contents of any communication.

Laws 1967, p. 844, § 1; Laws 1968, p. 1249, § 1; Laws 1992, p. 6, § 16; Laws 1995, p. 1051, § 2; Laws 2000, p. 875, § 1; Laws 2002, p. 1432, § 2.

Formerly Code 1933, § 26–3009.

Historical and Statutory Notes

The 2000 amendment rewrote subsec. (1) which formerly provided:

"(1) 'Device' means an instrument or apparatus used for overhearing, recording, intercepting, or transmitting sounds or for observing, photographing, recording, or transmitting visual images and which involves in its operation electricity, electronics, infrared, laser or similar beams, but not including merely focusing, lighting, illuminating equipment, optical magnifying equipment, or a device commonly referred to as an 'individual hearing aid,' and not including a 'pen register' or 'trap and trace device' as defined in this Code section."

In 2000, the Code Commission, in the second sentence of par. (1), inserted a comma following "laser", and inserted "or" preceding "illuminating". See § 28–9–5.

The 2002 amendment rewrote the section which, as amended in 2000, provided:

"As used within this part, the term:

"(1) 'Device' means an instrument or apparatus used for overhearing, recording, intercepting, or transmitting sounds or for observing, photographing, videotaping, recording, or transmitting visual images and which involves in its operation electricity, electronics, or infrared, laser, or similar beams. Without limiting the generality of the foregoing, the term 'device' shall specifically include any camera, photographic equipment, video equipment, or other similar equipment but shall not include merely focusing, lighting, or illuminating equipment, optical magnifying equipment, or a device commonly referred to as an 'individual hearing aid,' and not including a 'pen register' or 'trap and trace device' as defined in this Code section.

"(2) 'Pen register' means an instrument or apparatus which records or decodes electronic or other impulses which identify the numbers dialed or otherwise transmitted on the telephone line to which such device is attached, but such term does not include any instrument or apparatus used by a provider or customer of a wire or electronic communication service for billing, or recording as an incident to billing, for communications services provided by such provider or any instrument or apparatus used by a provider or customer of a wire communication service for cost accounting or other like purposes in the ordinary course of its business.

"(3) 'Private place' means a place where one is entitled reasonably to expect to be safe from casual or hostile intrusion or surveillance.

"(4) 'Trap and trace device' means an instrument or apparatus which captures the incoming electronic or other impulses which identify the originating number of an instrument or apparatus from which a wire or electronic communication was transmitted."

§ 16–11–61. "Peeping Tom"

(a) It shall be unlawful for any person to be a "peeping Tom" on or about the premises of another or to go about or upon the premises of another for the purpose of becoming a "peeping Tom."

(b) As used in this Code section, the term "peeping Tom" means a person who peeps through windows or doors, or other like places, on or about the premises of another for the purpose of spying upon or invading the privacy of the persons spied upon and the doing of any other acts of a similar nature which invade the privacy of such persons.

Laws 1919, p. 386, §§ 1, 2; Laws 1967, p. 844, § 1; Laws 1968, p. 1249, § 1.

Formerly Code 1933, §§ 26–2001, 26–2002; Code 1933, § 26–3002.

§ 16–11–62. Unlawful eavesdropping or surveillance

It shall be unlawful for:

(1) Any person in a clandestine manner intentionally to overhear, transmit, or record or attempt to overhear, transmit, or record the private conversation of another which shall originate in any private place;

(2) Any person, through the use of any device, without the consent of all persons observed, to observe, photograph, or record the activities of another which occur in any private place and out of public view; provided, however, that it shall not be unlawful:

(A) To use any device to observe, photograph, or record the activities of persons incarcerated in any jail, correctional institution, or any other facility in which persons who are charged with or who have been convicted of the commission of a crime are incarcerated, provided that such equipment shall not be used while the prisoner is discussing his or her case with his or her attorney;

(B) For an owner or occupier of real property to use for security purposes, crime prevention, or crime detection any device to observe, photograph, or record the activities of persons who are on the property or an approach thereto in areas where there is no reasonable expectation of privacy; or

(C) To use for security purposes, crime prevention, or crime detection any device to observe, photograph, or record the activities of persons who are within the curtilage of the residence of the person using such device. A photograph, videotape, or record made in accordance with this subparagraph, or a copy thereof, may be disclosed by such resident to the district attorney or a law enforcement officer and shall be admissible in a judicial proceeding, without the consent of any person observed, photographed, or recorded;

(3) Any person to go on or about the premises of another or any private place, except as otherwise provided by law, for the purpose of invading the privacy of others by eavesdropping upon their conversations or secretly observing their activities;

(4) Any person intentionally and secretly to intercept by the use of any device, instrument, or apparatus the contents of a message sent by telephone, telegraph, letter, or by any other means of private communication;

(5) Any person to divulge to any unauthorized person or authority the content or substance of any private message intercepted lawfully in the manner provided for in Code Section 16–11–65;

(6) Any person to sell, give, or distribute, without legal authority, to any person or entity any photograph, videotape, or record, or copies thereof, of the activities of another which occur in any private place and out of public view without the consent of all persons observed; or

(7) Any person to commit any other acts of a nature similar to those set out in paragraphs (1) through (6) of this Code section which invade the privacy of another.

Laws 1967, p. 844, § 1; Laws 1968, p. 1249, § 1; Laws 1976, p. 1100, § 1; Laws 1985, p. 149, § 16; Laws 2000, p. 491, § 1; Laws 2000, p. 875, § 2.

Formerly Code 1933, § 26–3001.

Historical and Statutory Notes

Prior to the 2000 amendments to this section, it provided:

"It shall be unlawful for:

"(1) Any person in a clandestine manner intentionally to overhear, transmit, or record or attempt to overhear, transmit, or record the private conversation of another which shall originate in any private place;

"(2) Any person, through the use of any device, without the consent of all persons observed, to observe, photograph, or record the activities of another which occur in any private place and out of public view; provided, however, that it shall not be unlawful:

"(A) To use any device to observe, photograph, or record the activities of persons incarcerated in any jail, correctional institution, or any other facility in which persons who are charged with or who have been convicted of the commission of a crime are incarcerated, provided that such equipment shall not be used while the prisoner is discussing his or her case with his or her attorney; or

"(B) For an owner or occupier of real property to use for security purposes, crime prevention, or crime detection, any device to observe, photograph, or record the activities of persons who are on the property or an approach thereto in areas where there is no reasonable expectation of privacy;

"(3) Any person to go on or about the premises of another or any private place for the purpose of invading the privacy of others by eavesdropping upon their conversations or secretly observing their activities;

"(4) Any person intentionally and secretly to intercept by the use of any device, instrument, or apparatus the contents of a message sent by telephone, telegraph, letter, or by any other means of private communication;

"(5) Any person to divulge to any unauthorized person or authority the content or substance of any private message intercepted lawfully in the manner provided for in Code Section 16–11–65;

"(6) Any person to sell, give, or distribute, without legal authority, to any person or entity any photograph, videotape, or record, or copies thereof, of the activities of another which occur in any private place and out of public view without the consent of all persons observed; or

"(7) Any person to commit any other acts of a nature similar to those set out in paragraphs (1) through (6) of this Code section which invade the privacy of another."

In 2000, the Code Commission, in subpars. (2)(B) and (2)(C), deleted a comma following "detection". See § 28–9–5.

§ 16–11–63. Possession, sale and distribution of eavesdropping devices

(a) Other than law enforcement officers permitted by this part to employ such devices, it shall be unlawful for any person to possess, sell, offer for sale, or distribute any eavesdropping device.

(b) An "eavesdropping device" shall mean any instrument or apparatus which by virtue of its size, design, and method of operation has no normal or customary function or purpose other than to permit the user thereof secretly to intercept, transmit, listen to, or record private conversations of others.

Laws 1967, p. 844, § 1; Laws 1968, p. 1249, § 1; Laws 1982, p. 3, § 16.

Formerly Code 1933, § 26–3003.

§ 16–11–64. Law enforcement officers—exception

(a) *Application of part to law enforcement officers.* Except only as provided in subsection (b) of this Code section, nothing in this part shall apply to a duly constituted law enforcement officer in the performance of his official duties in ferreting out offenders or suspected offenders of the law or in secretly watching a person suspected of violating the laws of the United States or of this state, or any subdivision thereof, for the purpose of apprehending such suspected violator.

(b) When in the course of his or her official duties, a law enforcement officer desiring to make use of any device, but only as such term is defined in Code Section 16–11–60, and such use would otherwise constitute a violation of Code Section 16–11–62, the law enforcement official shall act in compliance with the provisions provided for in this part.

(c) Upon written application, under oath, of the prosecuting attorney having jurisdiction over prosecution of the crime under investigation, or the Attorney General, made before a judge of superior court, said court may issue an investigation warrant permitting the use of such device, as defined in Code Section 16–11–60, for the surveillance of such person or place to the extent the same is consistent with and subject to the terms, conditions, and procedures provided for by Chapter 119 of Title 18 of the United States Code Annotated, as amended.

(d) Evidence obtained in conformity with this part shall be admissible only in the courts of this state having felony and misdemeanor jurisdiction.

(e) *Defenses.* A good faith reliance on a court order or legislative authorization shall constitute a complete defense to any civil or criminal action brought under this part or under any other law.

Laws 1967, p. 844, § 1; Laws 1968, p. 1249, § 1; Laws 1972, p. 615, § 1; Laws 1972, p. 952, § 1; Laws 1979, p. 824, § 1; Laws 1980, p. 326, § 1; Laws 1982, p. 1385, § 7; Laws 1982, p. 2319, § 1; Laws 1983, p. 3, § 13; Laws 1984, p. 22, § 16; Laws 1985, p. 149, § 16; Laws 1992, p. 6, § 16; Laws 2000, p. 491, § 2; Laws 2002, p. 1432, § 3.

Formerly Code 1933, § 26–3004.

Historical and Statutory Notes

The 2000 amendment provided gender neutral language throughout the section, substituted at the end of the introduction to subsec. (b) "part" for "subsection", substituted in subsec. (b)(1) ", or importing, manufacturing, delivering, distributing, dispensing, administering, selling, or possessing with intent to distribute marijuana or any controlled substance, or burglary, prostitution, theft, blackmail, extortion, bribery, gambling, racketeering activity, or any felony involving alcoholic beverage laws or auto thefts, or there is probable cause to believe that a private place is being utilized or has been utilized for the commission of any such crime, then, upon written application, under oath, of the district attorney having jurisdiction over the prosecution of such crime," for ", importation or sale of marijuana or any controlled substance, burglary, prostitution, theft, blackmail, extortion, bribery, gambling, racketeering activity, or any felony involving alcoholic beverage laws or auto thefts or there is probable cause to believe that a private place is being utilized or has been utilized for the commission of any such crime, then, upon written application, under oath, of the district attorney of the circuit wherein the device is to be physically placed", substituted in subsec. (b)(1)(B) for "of the circuit aforesaid" the words "having jurisdiction of such crime", substituted in subsec. (b)(3) "additional 20 day periods" for "an additional 20 day period" in the first sentence and added the second sentence.

The 2002 amendment rewrote subsecs. (b) to (d) which, as last amended in 2000, provided:

"(b) Procedure. When in the course of his or her official duties, a law enforcement officer desiring to make use of any device, but only as such term is specifically defined by Code Section 16–11–60 and such use would otherwise constitute a violation of Code Section 16–11–62, the law enforcement officer shall act in compliance with the procedures provided for in this part:

"(1) When there is probable cause to believe that a person is committing or has committed an act which endangers the national security of the United States or the security of this state or that such person is committing or has committed the crime of treason, insurrection, rebellion, espionage, sabotage, or any felony involving bodily harm, or any crimes involving arson, kidnapping, narcotics, dangerous drugs, or importing, manufacturing, delivering, distributing, dispensing, administering, selling, or possessing with intent to distribute marijuana or any controlled substance, or burglary, prostitution, theft, blackmail, extortion, bribery, gambling, racketeering activity, or any felony involving alcoholic beverage laws or auto thefts, or there is probable cause to believe that a private place is being utilized or has been utilized for the commission of any such crime, then, upon written application, under oath, of the district attorney having jurisdiction over the prosecution of such crime, or the Attorney General, which application affirms that there is probable cause to believe:

"(A) That a person is committing or has committed any of the crimes enumerated in this paragraph; or

"(B) That a private place is being utilized or has been utilized for the commission of any of the crimes enumerated in this paragraph and sets forth specifically the basis of such probable cause and particularly describes the person or place, the crime or crimes, the device or devices to be used, and the specific conversations and activities to be overheard or observed, as the case may be, any judge of the superior court having jurisdiction of such crime may issue an investigation warrant permitting the use of devices, as defined by Code Section 16–11–60, for the surveillance of such person or place, provided that the warrant specifies with particularity the device or devices the use of which is to be permitted thereby; the purpose, duration, and circumstances of use permitted; the crime or crimes allegedly being committed; and the person or persons and place or places to be subject to such surveillance;

"(2) The judge, before issuing such a warrant, shall satisfy himself or herself that the party initiating the application for the warrant is aware of the facts and circumstances through his or her own personal knowledge which are sufficient to lead a person of reasonable caution to believe that the alleged crime set forth in the application has been committed or is being committed or that such person has been informed of such facts and circumstances by a reasonably trustworthy informational source. The judge shall also satisfy himself or herself that there is set forth in the application exigencies adequately supported by facts and circumstances which overcome and override the need for giving of notice of the surveillance to the parties to be overheard or observed by the use of such devices;

"(3) Investigation warrants issued under this Code section shall be valid for no more than 20 days after issuance, unless renewed for additional 20 day periods for good cause shown at the time of written application for each such renewal. An interception authorized pursuant to this Code section may be conducted in whole or in part by law enforcement personnel or by an individual operating under a contract with a law enforcement agency and acting under the supervision of a law enforcement officer authorized to conduct the interception;

"(4) The officer executing the warrant must make a return of the warrant to the judge which shall set forth specifically how the warrant was used and employed and what was obtained thereby. The return shall reflect that the investigation or search in pursuance of the warrant was terminated immediately upon the conversation or activities which were authorized to be overheard, intercepted, or observed were in fact obtained. The return shall set forth with particularity the law enforcement officer or officers or their agents who actually employed the devices used in the execution of the warrant;

"(5) The application for any investigation warrant under this Code section, any supporting evidence in connection therewith, and any entry of the issuance of an investigation warrant as a result thereof shall remain confidential and in the custody of the judge and shall not be released nor information touching same in any manner be disclosed, except upon written order of the judge or except at the time of trial of the case in which such evidence is used or in which evidence derived from such surveillance is used;

"(6) The applicant for the warrant shall return same and report back to the judge issuing same within 30 days of the issuance of the warrant. In the event no evidence of one of the specific crimes set forth in this Code section has been obtained through the use of such device or devices, it shall be the duty of the applicant physically to destroy all evidence obtained by surveillance and to certify that fact in writing to the judge under oath;

"(7) In the event evidence of or information concerning the specific crime set forth in the warrant is obtained through the use of such device or devices, the applicant shall so certify in writing under oath in his or her report under paragraph (6) of this subsection. Upon the return of an indictment or filing of an accusation based in whole or in part on such evidence or information or any part thereof, it shall be the duty of the prosecuting attorney promptly to notify the accused of the existence and substance of such evidence or information and, if the same has been reduced to a permanent form, shall make it available to the accused for inspection and copying; and

"(8) Any publication of the information or evidence obtained under a warrant issued under this Code section other than that necessary and essential to the preparation of and actual prosecution for the crime specified in the warrant shall be an unlawful invasion of privacy under this part and shall cause such evidence and information to be inadmissible in any criminal prosecution.

"(c) Admissibility of evidence. Evidence obtained in conformity with this Code section shall be admissible only in the courts of this state having felony and misdemeanor jurisdiction. When an investigative or law enforcement officer, while engaged in intercepting wire or oral communications or in observation in the manner authorized in this Code section, intercepts wire or oral communications or obtains fruits of observation relating to offenses for which an investigation warrant may issue, other than those specified in the order of authorization, the contents or fruits thereof and evidence derived therefrom may be disclosed or used in the same manner as if a surveillance warrant covering such crimes had initially been used.

"(d) Providing facilities or technical assistance.

"(1) It shall not be unlawful under the provisions of this part for an officer, employee, or agent of any communication common carrier to provide facilities or technical assistance to an investigative or law enforcement officer who, pursuant to this Code section, is authorized by warrant to intercept a wire or oral communication.

"(2) An order authorizing the interception of a wire or oral communication shall, upon request of the applicant, direct that a communication common carrier, landlord, custodian, or other person shall furnish the applicant forthwith with such technical information, facilities, and technical assistance as is necessary to accomplish the interception unobtrusively and with a minimum of interference with the services that the carrier, landlord, custodian, or person is according the person whose communications are to be intercepted. Any communication common carrier, landlord, custodian, or other person furnishing such facilities or technical assistance shall be compensated therefor by the applicant at the prevailing rates."

§ 16–11–64.1. Applications for and orders approving installation and use of pen registers or trap and trace devices

Any district attorney having jurisdiction over the prosecution of the crime under investigation or the Attorney General is authorized to make application for an order or an extension of an order authorizing or approving the installation and use of a pen register or a trap and trace device to a judge of the superior court of the same judicial circuit as the district attorney, or, in the case of the Attorney General, in any judicial circuit; and said court is authorized to enter an order authorizing the use of a pen register or a trap and trace device, to the extent the same is consistent with and permitted by the laws of the United States.

Laws 1995, p. 1051, § 3; Laws 2005, Act 126, § 1, eff. May 2, 2005; Laws 2007, Act 18, § 16, eff. May 11, 2007.

Historical and Statutory Notes

The 2005 amendment by Act 126 rewrote the section, which had read:

"Any district attorney or the Attorney General is authorized to make application for an order or an extension of an order authorizing or approving the installation and use of a pen register or a trap and trace device to a superior court for the circuit wherein the pen register or trap and trace device is to be installed and used, and the superior court for that circuit is authorized to enter an order authorizing the use of a pen register or a trap and trace device, to the extent the same is consistent with and permitted by the laws of the United States."

The 2007 amendment by Act 18 was a provision contained in a correction bill.

§ 16–11–64.2. Emergency installation and use of pen registers or trap and trace devices

Any investigative or law enforcement officer, specially designated in writing for such purpose by the Attorney General or by a district attorney, who reasonably determines that:

(1) An emergency situation exists that involves:

(A) Immediate danger of death or serious bodily injury to any person; or

(B) Conspiratorial activities characteristic of organized crime

that requires the installation and use of a pen register or a trap and trace device before an order authorizing such installation and use can, with due diligence, be obtained; and

(2) There are grounds upon which an order could be entered under the laws of the United States to authorize such installation and use

may have installed and use a pen register or trap and trace device if, within 48 hours of the time the pen register or trap and trace device is installed, an order approving the installation or use is issued in accordance with Code Section 16–11–64.1.

Laws 1995, p. 1051, § 3.

§ 16–11–64.3. Electronic surveillance, interception of communications, or monitoring of persons in emergency situations

(a) Notwithstanding any other provision of this part, in the event that the Attorney General or a district attorney of the judicial circuit having jurisdiction over the emergency situation described herein or where the observation, monitoring, or recording of the activities of any person may occur as provided in this subsection determines that:

(1) An emergency situation exists involving the immediate danger of death or serious physical injury to any person;

(2) The said emergency situation requires the immediate interception of a wire, oral, or electronic communications or the immediate observation, monitoring, or recording of the activities of any person involved in said emergency situation in violation of the provisions of Code Section 16–11–62 before an order authorizing such interception or surveillance can, with due diligence, be obtained; and

(3) There are grounds upon which an investigation warrant pursuant to Code Section 16–11–64 could be issued,

then any investigative or law enforcement officer specifically designated by the prosecuting official making such determination may utilize any device as defined in Code Section 16–11–60 to intercept the wire, oral, or electronic communications or to observe, monitor, or record the activities of the person or persons involved in said emergency situation, provided that an application for an investigation warrant is made pursuant to Code Section 16–11–64 within 48 hours after said interception or surveillance commences.

(b) In the event that an application for an investigation warrant made pursuant to this Code section is granted, then the interception or surveillance shall be conducted in accordance with the provisions of Code Section 16–11–64, except that said interception or surveillance shall continue only so long as the emergency situation exists.

(c) In the event that an application for an investigation warrant made pursuant to this Code section is denied or in any event where the interception or surveillance is terminated without an investigation warrant having been issued, the contents of any intercepted communications or other surveillance effected pursuant to this Code section shall not be admissible in any court of this state except to prove violations of this part. The contents of any such intercepted communications or other surveillance effected pursuant to this Code section without an investigation warrant having been issued shall be confidential and shall not be disclosed except to prove violations of this part.

Laws 2000, p. 491, § 3; Laws 2001, p. 4, § 16.

Historical and Statutory Notes

The 2001 amendment was a correction bill.

§ 16–11–65. Public Service Commission license to intercept telecommunications

(a) Nothing contained within Code Section 16–11–62 shall prohibit the employment and use of any equipment or device which is owned by any person or is furnished by any telephone company authorized to do business in this state under proper tariffs filed with and approved by the Georgia Public Service Commission which may be attached to any telephonic equipment of any user of or subscriber to such equipment which permits the interception of telephonic communications solely for the purposes of business service improvement when the user of or subscriber to such facilities and equipment has duly applied for and obtained from the Georgia Public Service Commission a license for the employment and installation of the equipment. No license shall be issued until the applicant has demonstrated to the commission a clear, apparent, and logically reasonable need for the use of the equipment in connection with a legitimate business activity of the user or subscriber and demonstrated to the satisfaction of the commission that it will be operated by persons of good moral character and that the equipment will be used in a lawful manner and in conformity with the tariffs filed for the equipment. The commission is authorized to establish the necessary procedures to be employed and followed in applying for such permits and to require from the user or subscriber of such equipment the furnishing of any reasonable information required by the commission in regard to the intended and actual use of the equipment.

(b) The Georgia Public Service Commission is authorized to revoke any license and to order any owner of such equipment or any telephone company supplying such equipment to remove from the premises of the licensee the equipment when it is established to the satisfaction of the commission that the equipment is being used in an unlawful manner contrary to the tariff applicable to the equipment or in a manner contrary to the purposes and uses for which the license had been issued. Such licenses may also be revoked by the commission if it is subsequently discovered that a material misrepresentation of fact has been made in applying for the license. The commission is authorized to promulgate such rules and regulations in connection with the licensing and revocation thereof of such users of such equipment as will enable it to carry out the purposes, duties, and responsibilities imposed upon the commission by this Code section. Such rules and regulations shall afford to any aggrieved licensee an opportunity to a full and impartial hearing before the commission. The commission shall further have the authority to adopt any and all appropriate rules and regulations of any sort to ensure the privacy of telephonic and telegraphic communications. A violation of such rules and regulations shall be a violation of this part.

(c) All telephone companies shall have printed in a conspicuously accessible location within their directories a notice to the public that there is available without cost at the business office of the telephone company served by the directory a list of subscribers of such equipment which will be made available to any member of the general public requesting the same from such companies.

(d) The provisions of this part shall not apply to acts by duly authorized employees of any telephone company regulated by the Georgia Public Service Commission, with regard to the reasonable and limited intercepting of telephone communications under circumstances reasonably calculated to assure the privacy of telephone communications when such interception is accomplished solely for the purpose of maintaining the quality of service furnished to the public or for the purpose of preventing the unlawful use of telephone service. All such telephone companies shall adopt regulations and procedures consistent with the requirements of this Code section governing the use of equipment which permits the interception of telephone messages by their employees and file the same with the commission. After being filed with the commission, such regulations and procedures shall be public records.

Laws 1967, p. 844, § 1; Laws 1968, p. 1249, § 1; Laws 1985, p. 149, § 16; Laws 1991, p. 1040, § 1.

Formerly Code 1933, § 26–3005.

§ 16–11–66. Consent; telephonic conversations to which child under age of 18 years is a party

(a) Nothing in Code Section 16–11–62 shall prohibit a person from intercepting a wire, oral, or electronic communication where such person is a party to the communication or one of the parties to the communication has given prior consent to such interception.

(b) After obtaining the consent required by this subsection, the telephonic conversations or electronic communications to which a child under the age of 18 years is a party may be recorded and divulged, and such recording and dissemination may be done by a private citizen, law enforcement agency, or prosecutor's office. Nothing in this subsection shall be construed to require that the recording device be activated by the child. Consent for the recording or divulging of the conversations of a child under the age of 18 years conducted by telephone or electronic communication shall be given only by order of a judge of a superior court upon written application, as provided in subsection (c) of this Code section, or by a parent or guardian of said child as provided in subsection (d) of this Code section. Said recording shall not be used in any prosecution of the child in any delinquency or criminal proceeding. An application to a judge of the superior court made pursuant to this Code section need not comply with the procedures set out in Code Section 16–11–64.

(c) A judge to whom a written application has been made shall issue the order provided by subsection (b) of this Code section only:

(1) Upon finding probable cause that a crime has been committed;

(2) Upon finding that the child understands that the conversation is to be recorded and that such child agrees to participate; and

(3) Upon determining that participation is not harmful to such child.

A true and correct copy of the recording provided for in subsection (b) of this Code section shall be returned to the superior court judge who issued the order and such copy of the recording shall be kept under seal until further order of the court.

(d) The provisions of this article shall not be construed to prohibit a parent or guardian of a child under 18 years of age, with or without the consent of such minor child, from monitoring or intercepting telephonic conversations of such minor child with another person by use of an extension phone located within the family home, or electronic or other communications of such minor child from within the family home, for the purpose of ensuring the welfare of such minor child. If the parent or guardian has a reasonable or good faith belief that such conversation or communication is evidence of criminal conduct involving such child as a victim or an attempt, conspiracy, or solicitation to involve such child in criminal activity affecting the welfare or best interest of such child, the parent or guardian may disclose the content of such telephonic conversation or electronic communication to the district attorney or a law enforcement officer. A recording or other record of any such conversation or communication made by a parent or guardian in accordance with this subsection that contains evidence of criminal conduct involving such child as a victim or an attempt, conspiracy, or solicitation to involve such child in criminal activity shall be admissible in a judicial proceeding except as otherwise provided in subsection (b) of this Code section.

Laws 1967, p. 844, § 1; Laws 1968, p. 1249, § 1; Laws 1993, p. 565, § 1; Laws 1994, p. 97, § 16; Laws 2000, p. 491, § 4.

Formerly Code 1933, § 26–3006.

Historical and Statutory Notes

The 2000 amendment substantially rewrote subsec. (b), substituted at the beginning of subsec. (c) for "The judge" the words "A judge to whom a written application has been made", and added subsec. (d). Prior to amendment subsec. (b) provided:

"(b) After obtaining the consent required by this subsection, the telephonic conversations to which a child under the age of 18 years is a party may be recorded and divulged, and such recording and dissemination may be done by a private citizen, law enforcement agency, or prosecutor's office. Nothing in this subsection shall be construed to require that the recording device be activated by the child. Consent for the recording or divulging of the conversations of a child under the age of 18 years conducted by telephone shall be given only by order of a judge of a superior court upon written application. Said recording shall not be used in any prosecution of the consenting child in any delinquency or criminal proceeding. Such application need not comply with the procedures set out in Code Section 16–11–64."

§ 16–11–66.1. Access to stored wire and electronic communications and transactional records

(a) A law enforcement officer, a prosecuting attorney, or the Attorney General may require the disclosure of stored wire or electronic communications, as well as transactional records pertaining thereto, to the extent and under the procedures and conditions provided for by the laws of the United States.

(b) A provider of electronic communication service or remote computing service shall provide the contents of, and transactional records pertaining to, wire and electronic communications in its possession or reasonably accessible thereto when a requesting law enforcement officer, a prosecuting attorney, or the Attorney General complies with the provisions for access thereto set forth by the laws of the United States.

(c) Search warrants for production of stored wire or electronic communications and transactional records pertaining thereto shall have state-wide application or application as provided by the laws of the United States when issued by a judge with jurisdiction over the criminal offense under investigation and to which such records relate.

(d) A subpoena for the production of stored wire or electronic communications and transactional records pertaining thereto may be issued at any time upon a showing by a law enforcement official, a prosecuting attorney, or the Attorney General that the subpoenaed material relates to a pending criminal investigation.

(e) Violation of this Code section shall be punishable as contempt.

Laws 1993, p. 299, § 1; Laws 1995, p. 1023, § 1; Laws 2002, p. 1432, § 4; Laws 2003, Act 9, § 16, eff. May 14, 2003.

Historical and Statutory Notes

The 2002 amendment rewrote this section which formerly provided:

"(a) As used in this Code section, the term 'cellular radio telephone' means a wireless telephone authorized by the Federal Communications Commission to operate in the frequency bandwidth reserved for cellular radio telephones.

"(b) (1) It shall be unlawful for any person, without the consent of at least one of the parties to the communication, intentionally to intercept, receive, or assist in intercepting or receiving a communication transmitted between cellular radio telephones or between any cellular radio telephone and a landline telephone.

"(2) It shall be unlawful for any person to broadcast, print, or publish the contents of any communication transmitted between cellular radio telephones or between any cellular radio telephone and a landline telephone if the communication has been intercepted in violation of paragraph (1) of this subsection.

"(c) In the following instances, this Code section shall not apply:

"(1) To any public utility engaged in the business of providing communications services and facilities, or to the officers, employees, or agents thereof, where the acts otherwise prohibited are for the purpose of construction, maintenance, conduct, or operation of the services and facilities of the public utility;

"(2) To the use of any instrument, equipment, facility, or service furnished and used pursuant to the tariffs of the public utility;

"(3) To any telephonic communication system used for communication exclusively within a state, county, or municipal correctional institution;

"(4) To the use of equipment, facilities, or services by users licensed by the Public Service Commission pursuant to Code Section 16–11–65; or

"(5) To the interception of wire or oral transmissions by law enforcement officers pursuant to Code Section 16–11–64.

"(d) Any person convicted of violating paragraph (1) or paragraph (2) of subsection (b) of this Code section shall be guilty of a misdemeanor of a high and aggravated nature."

The 2003 amendment by Act 9, in subsec. (e), substituted "punishable as contempt" for "punishable by contempt".

§ 16–11–67. Evidence inadmissible

No evidence obtained in a manner which violates any of the provisions of this part shall be admissible in any court of this state except to prove violations of this part.

Laws 1967, p. 844, § 1; Laws 1968, p. 1249, § 1.

Formerly Code 1933, § 26–3007.

§ 16–11–68. Privileged communications inadmissible

Nothing contained within this part shall permit the introduction into evidence of any communication which is privileged by the laws of this state or by the decisions of the appellate courts thereof.

Laws 1967, p. 844, § 1; Laws 1968, p. 1249, § 1.

Formerly Code 1933, § 26–3008.

§ 16–11–69. Punishment

Except as otherwise provided in subsection (d) of Code Section 16–11–66.1, any person violating any of the provisions of this part shall be guilty of a felony and, upon conviction thereof, shall be punished by imprisonment for not less than one nor more than five years or a fine not to exceed $10,000.00, or both.

Laws 1967, p. 844, § 1; Laws 1968, p. 1249, § 1; Laws 1993, p. 299, § 2.

Formerly Code 1933, § 26–3010.

§ 16–11–70. Acquisition, sale, or release of telephone records by broker prohibited; definitions; violations

(a) As used in this Code section, the term:

(1) "End user" means any person, corporation, partnership, firm, municipality, cooperative, organization, governmental agency, building owner, or other entity provided with a telecommunications service for its own consumption and not for resale.

(2) "Telephone record" means information retained by a telecommunications company that relates to the telephone number dialed by the customer, the number of telephone calls directed to a customer, or other data related to the telephone calls typically contained on a customer telephone bill, such as the time the calls started and ended, the duration of the calls, the time of day the calls were made, and any charges applied. For purposes of this Code section, any information collected and retained by, or on behalf of, customers utilizing caller identification or other similar technology does not constitute a telephone record.

(3) "Telephone records broker" means any person or organization that is neither a telecommunications company nor a vendor or supplier for a telecommunications company obligated by contract to protect the confidentiality of telephone records and that purchases, acquires, sells, or releases the telephone record of any third party with whom it has no prior or existing business relationship or that attempts to purchase, acquire, sell, or release the telephone record of any party with whom it has no prior or existing business relationship.

(b) It is unlawful for any telephone records broker to purchase, acquire, sell, or release the telephone records of any person who is a Georgia resident or to attempt to purchase, acquire, sell, or release the telephone record of any third party who is a Georgia resident. This Code section applies whether the customer's telephone record is obtained by the telephone records broker directly from a telecommunications company or from any other third-party source. For purposes of this Code section, a person is a Georgia resident if the individual has a Georgia billing address.

(c) A violation of any provision of this Code section shall be punishable by a civil fine in an amount not to exceed $10,000.00 for each violation. The prosecuting attorney or the Attorney General shall be authorized to prosecute the civil case. Each telephone record purchased, acquired, sold, or released and each attempt to purchase, acquire, sell, or release a telephone record constitutes a separate violation of this Code section.

(d) Any violation of this Code section shall constitute a tort and shall create a right of action in the person or entity whose telephone records have been purchased, acquired, sold, or released for which damages may be recovered. Special damages may be inferred by the violation. Reasonable attorney's fees shall be awarded to the plaintiff where the plaintiff has prevailed in the underlying action.

(e) No provision of this Code section shall be construed to prevent any action by a law enforcement agency or any officer, employee, or agent of a law enforcement agency to obtain the telephone records or personal identifying information of any third party who is a Georgia resident in connection with the performance of the official duties of the agency, officer, employee, or agent.

Laws 2006, Act 648, § 3, eff. April 28, 2006.

Historical and Statutory Notes

Laws 2006, Act 648, §§ 1 and 2, provide:

"SECTION 1. This Act shall be known and may be cited as the 'Telephone Records Privacy Protection Act.'

"SECTION 2. The General Assembly finds that:

"(1) Telephone records can be of great use to criminals because the information contained in call logs listed in such records include a wealth of personal data;

"(2) Many call logs reveal the names of telephone users' doctors, public and private relationships, business associates, and more;

"(3) Although other personal information such as social security numbers may appear on public documents, which can be accessed by data brokers, the only warehouse of telephone records is located at the telephone companies themselves;

"(4) Telephone records are sometimes accessed without authorization of the customer by:

"(A) An employee of the telephone service provider selling the data; and

"(B) Pretexting, whereby a data broker or other person pretends to be the owner of the telephone and convinces the telephone company's employees to release the data to such person; and

"(5) Telephone companies encourage customers to manage their accounts online with many setting up the online capability in advance, although many customers never access their account online. If someone seeking the information activates the account before the customer, he or she can gain unfettered access to the telephone records and call logs of that customer."

Part 2

Preparation of Federal and State Income Tax Returns

§ 16–11–80. Business of preparing returns defined

For the purposes of this part, a person is engaged in the business of preparing federal or state income tax returns or assisting taxpayers in preparing such returns if he does either of the following:

(1) Advertises or gives publicity to the effect that he prepares or assists others in the preparation of state or federal income tax returns; or

(2) Prepares or assists others in the preparation of state or federal income tax returns for compensation.

Laws 1972, p. 446, § 2.

§ 16–11–81. Disclosure of information obtained in preparing income tax returns; exceptions

It shall be unlawful for any person, including an individual, firm, corporation, association, partnership, joint venture, or any employee or agent thereof, to disclose any information obtained in the business of preparing federal or state income tax returns or assisting taxpayers in preparing such returns unless such disclosure is within any of the following:

(1) Consented to in writing by the taxpayer in a separate document;

(2) Expressly authorized by state or federal law;

(3) Necessary to the preparation of the return;

(4) Pursuant to court order; or

(5) Transmitted to a computer center for preparation.

Laws 1972, p. 446, § 1.

§ 16–11–82. Contacting taxpayer to obtain consent

Contacting a taxpayer to obtain his written consent to disclosure does not constitute a violation of this part.

Laws 1972, p. 446, § 3.

§ 16–11–83. Penalty

Any person violating the provisions of this part shall be guilty of a misdemeanor.

Laws 1972, p. 446, § 4.

Article 4

Dangerous Instrumentalities and Practices

Part 1

General Provisions

§ 16–11–100. Abandonment of containers with snap-locks or motor vehicles which cannot be easily opened

(a) A person is guilty of a misdemeanor when that person leaves in any place accessible to children any abandoned, unattended, or discarded container which has a compartment of more than 1 1/2 cubic feet capacity and a door or lid which locks or fastens automatically when closed and which cannot easily be opened from the inside, without first removing the lid, door, or locking device from such container.

(b) A person is guilty of a misdemeanor when that person leaves in any place accessible to children any abandoned or discarded motor vehicle which does not have at least one door which can easily be opened from the inside or one door or window which has been removed.

Laws 1953, Nov.-Dec. Sess., p. 273, §§ 1, 2; Laws 1968, p. 1249, § 2; Laws 1992, p. 2552, § 1.

Formerly Code 1933, § 26–2911.

§ 16–11–101. Furnishing weapons to persons under 18

A person is guilty of a misdemeanor of a high and aggravated nature when he or she knowingly sells to or furnishes to a person under the age of 18 years knuckles, whether made from metal, thermoplastic, wood, or other similar material, or a knife designed for the purpose of offense and defense.

Laws 1876, p. 112, § 1; Laws 1968, p. 1249, § 1; Laws 1994, p. 1012, § 11; Laws 1995, p. 10, § 16; Laws 2008, Act 551, § 3, eff. July 1, 2008; Laws 2009, Act 8, § 16, eff. April 14, 2009.

Formerly Code 1882, § 4540b; Penal Code 1895, § 344; Penal Code 1910, § 350; Code 1933, § 26–5108; Code 1933, § 26–2905.

Historical and Statutory Notes

The 2008 amendment by Act 551 substituted "knuckles whether made from metal, thermoplastic, wood, or other similar material" for "metal knuckles" and "metal knucks", throughout the section.

The 2009 amendment by Act 8 was a provision contained in a correction bill.

§ 16–11–101.1. Furnishing or permitting minor to possess pistol or revolver

(a) For the purposes of this Code section, the term:

(1) "Minor" means any person under the age of 18 years.

(2) "Pistol or revolver" means a handgun as defined in subsection (a) of Code Section 16–11–125.1.

(b) It shall be unlawful for a person intentionally, knowingly, or recklessly to sell or furnish a pistol or revolver to a minor, except that it shall be lawful for a parent or legal guardian to permit possession of a pistol or revolver by a minor for the purposes specified in subsection (c) of Code Section 16–11–132 unless otherwise expressly limited by subsection (c) of this Code section.

(c)(1) It shall be unlawful for a parent or legal guardian to permit possession of a pistol or revolver by a minor if the parent or legal guardian knows of a minor's conduct which violates the provisions of Code Section 16–11–132 and fails to make reasonable efforts to prevent any such violation of Code Section 16–11–132.

(2) Notwithstanding any provisions of subsection (c) of Code Section 16–11–132 or any other law to the contrary, it shall be unlawful for any parent or legal guardian intentionally, knowingly, or recklessly to furnish to or permit a minor to possess a pistol or revolver if such parent or legal guardian is aware of a substantial risk that such minor will use a pistol or revolver to commit a felony offense or if such parent or legal guardian who is aware of such substantial risk fails to make reasonable efforts to prevent commission of the offense by the minor.

(3) In addition to any other act which violates this subsection, a parent or legal guardian shall be deemed to have

violated this subsection if such parent or legal guardian furnishes to or permits possession of a pistol or revolver by any minor who has been convicted of a forcible felony or forcible misdemeanor, as defined in Code Section 16–1–3, or who has been adjudicated delinquent under the provisions of Article 1 of Chapter 11 of Title 15 for an offense which would constitute a forcible felony or forcible misdemeanor, as defined in Code Section 16–1–3, if such minor were an adult.

(d) Upon conviction of a violation of subsection (b) or (c) of this Code section, a person shall be guilty of a felony and punished by a fine not to exceed $ 5,000.00 or by imprisonment for not less than three nor more than five years, or both.

Laws 1994, p. 1012, § 13; Laws 2000, p. 1630, § 1; Laws 2010, Act 643, § 2–6, eff. June 4, 2010.

Historical and Statutory Notes

The 2000 amendment changed the minimum sentence in subsec. (d) from 2 to 3 years.

The 2010 amendment by Act 643, in par. (a)(2), substituted "handgun" for "pistol or revolver" and "16–11–125.1" for "16–11–132".

Laws 2010, Act 643, § 3–1, provides:

"This Act shall become effective upon its approval by the Governor or upon its becoming law without such approval and shall apply to all offenses committed on and after such date. The enactment of this Act shall not affect any prosecutions for acts occurring before the effective date of this Act and shall not act as an abatement of any such prosecutions."

§ 16–11–102. Pointing gun or pistol at another

A person is guilty of a misdemeanor when he intentionally and without legal justification points or aims a gun or pistol at another, whether the gun or pistol is loaded or unloaded.

Laws 1880–81, p. 151, § 1; Laws 1968, p. 1249, § 1.

Formerly Code 1882, § 4528a; Penal Code 1895, § 343; Penal Code 1910, § 349; Code 1933, § 26–5107; Code 1933, § 26–2908.

§ 16–11–103. Discharge of firearms on or near public highway

A person is guilty of a misdemeanor when, without legal justification, he discharges a gun or pistol on or within 50 yards of a public highway or street.

Laws 1882–83, p. 131, §§ 1, 2; Laws 1968, p. 1249, § 1.

Formerly Penal Code 1895, § 508; Penal Code 1910, § 504; Code 1933, § 26–7301; Code 1933, § 26–2909.

§ 16–11–104. Discharge of firearms on property of another

(a) It shall be unlawful for any person to fire or discharge a firearm on the property of another person, firm, or corporation without having first obtained permission from the owner or lessee of the property. This Code section shall not apply to:

(1) Persons who fire or discharge a firearm in defense of person or property; and

(2) Law enforcement officers.

(b) Any person who violates subsection (a) of this Code section is guilty of a misdemeanor.

Laws 1977, p. 1333, § 1.

Formerly Code 1933, § 26–2909.1.

§ 16–11–105. Repealed by Laws 2005, Act 128, § 1, eff. July 1, 2005

Historical and Statutory Notes

Repealed § 16–11–105, relating to discharging a firearm on Sunday, was derived from Laws 1898, p. 107, §§ 1, 2; Laws 1968, p. 1246, §§ 1, 2; Laws 1976, p. 1437, § 1; Laws 1977, p. 1333, § 2; Laws 1983, p. 448, § 1; Penal Code 1895, § 418; Code 1933, § 26-6907. The repealing law also reserved the section designation.

§ 16–11–106. Possession of firearm or knife during commission of, or attempt to commit, certain crimes

(a) For the purposes of this Code section, the term "firearm" shall include stun guns and tasers. A stun gun or taser is any device that is powered by electrical charging units such as batteries and emits an electrical charge in excess of 20,000 volts or is otherwise capable of incapacitating a person by an electrical charge.

(b) Any person who shall have on or within arm's reach of his or her person a firearm or a knife having a blade of three or more inches in length during the commission of, or the attempt to commit:

(1) Any crime against or involving the person of another;

(2) The unlawful entry into a building or vehicle;

(3) A theft from a building or theft of a vehicle;

(4) Any crime involving the possession, manufacture, delivery, distribution, dispensing, administering, selling, or possession with intent to distribute any controlled substance or marijuana as provided in Code Section 16–13–30, any counterfeit substance as defined in Code Section 16–13–21, or any noncontrolled substance as provided in Code Section 16–13–30.1; or

(5) Any crime involving the trafficking of cocaine, marijuana, or illegal drugs as provided in Code Section 16–13–31,

and which crime is a felony, commits a felony and, upon conviction thereof, shall be punished by confinement for a period of five years, such sentence to run consecutively to any other sentence which the person has received.

(c) Upon the second or subsequent conviction of a person under this Code section, the person shall be punished by confinement for a period of ten years. Notwithstanding any other law to the contrary, the sentence of any person which is imposed for violating this Code section a second or subsequent time shall not be suspended by the court and probationary sentence imposed in lieu thereof.

(d) The punishment prescribed for the violation of subsections (b) and (c) of this Code section shall not be reducible to misdemeanor punishment as is provided by Code Section 17–10–5.

(e) Any crime committed in violation of subsections (b) and (c) of this Code section shall be considered a separate offense.

Laws 1968, p. 982, §§ 1, 2; Laws 1974, p. 385, § 1; Laws 1976, p. 1591, §§ 1, 2; Laws 1985, p. 425, § 1; Laws 1986, p. 1205, § 1; Laws 1987, p. 624, § 1; Laws 2000, p. 1618, § 1; Laws 2001, p. 4, § 16.

Historical and Statutory Notes

The 2000 amendment to subsec. (b)(4) substituted substance "or marijuana as provided in Code Section 16–13–30, any counterfeit substance as defined in Code Section 16–13–21, or noncontrolled substance as provided in Code Section 16–13–30.1" for "substance as provided in Code Section 16–13–30".

The 2001 amendment substituted in subsec. (b)(4) for "or noncontrolled" the words "or any noncontrolled".

§ 16–11–107. Destroying or causing serious or debilitating physical injury to police dog or police horse

(a) As used in this Code section, the term:

(1) "Accelerant detection dog" means a dog trained to detect hydrocarbon substances.

(2) "Bomb detection dog" means a dog trained to locate bombs or explosives by scent.

(3) "Firearms detection dog" means a dog trained to locate firearms by scent.

(4) "Narcotic detection dog" means a dog trained to locate narcotics by scent.

(5) "Narcotics" means any controlled substance as defined in paragraph (4) of Code Section 16–13–21 and shall include marijuana as defined by paragraph (16) of Code Section 16–13–21.

(6) "Patrol dog" means a dog trained to protect a peace officer and to apprehend or hold without excessive force a person in violation of the criminal statutes of this state.

(7) "Police dog" means a bomb detection dog, a firearms detection dog, a narcotic detection dog, a patrol dog, an accelerant detection dog, or a tracking dog used by a law enforcement agency. "Police dog" also means a search and rescue dog.

(8) "Police horse" means a horse trained to transport, carry, or be ridden by a law enforcement officer and used by a law enforcement agency.

(8.1) "Search and rescue dog" means any dog that is owned or the services of which are employed by a fire department or the state fire marshal for the principal purpose of aiding in the detection of missing persons, including but not limited to persons who are lost, who are trapped under debris as a result of a natural or manmade disaster, or who are drowning victims.

(9) "Tracking dog" means a dog trained to track and find a missing person, escaped inmate, or fleeing felon.

(b) Any person who knowingly and intentionally destroys or causes serious or debilitating physical injury to a police dog or police horse, knowing said dog to be a police dog or said horse to be a police horse, shall be guilty of a felony and, upon conviction thereof, shall be punished by imprisonment for not less than one nor more than five years, or a fine not to exceed $10,000.00, or both. This subsection shall not apply to the destruction of a police dog or police horse for humane purposes.

Laws 1983, p. 528, § 1; Laws 1996, p. 370, § 1; Laws 1996, p. 778, § 1; Laws 1998, p. 657, § 1.2.

§ 16–11–107.1. Harassment of assistance dog; penalties

(a) As used in this Code section, the term:

(1) "Assistance dog" means a dog that is or has been trained by a licensed or certified person, organization, or agency to perform physical tasks for a physically challenged person. Assistance dogs include guide or leader dogs that guide individuals who are legally blind; hearing dogs that alert individuals who are deaf or hard of hearing to specific sounds; and service dogs for individuals with disabilities other than blindness or deafness, which are trained to perform a variety of physical tasks, including, but not limited to, pulling a wheelchair, lending balance support, picking up dropped objects, or providing assistance in a medical crisis.

(2) "Harass" means to engage in any conduct directed toward an assistance dog that is knowingly likely to impede or interfere with the assistance dog's performance of its duties or that places the blind, deaf, or physically limited person being served or assisted by the dog in danger of injury.

(3) "Notice" means an oral or otherwise communicated warning proscribing the behavior of another person and a request that the person stop the particular behavior.

(b) Any person who knowingly and intentionally harasses or attempts to harass an assistance dog, knowing the dog to be an assistance dog, shall be guilty of a misdemeanor and, upon conviction thereof, shall be punished by imprisonment for not less than 90 days or a fine not to exceed $500.00, or both.

(c) Any person who has received notice that his or her behavior is interfering with the use of an assistance dog who continues to knowingly and intentionally harass an assistance dog, knowing the dog to be an assistance dog, shall be guilty of a misdemeanor and, upon conviction thereof, shall be punished by imprisonment for not less than 90 days or a fine not to exceed $500.00, or both, provided that any person who is convicted of a second or subsequent violation of this subsection shall be punished as for a misdemeanor of a high and aggravated nature.

(d) Any person who knowingly and intentionally allows his or her dog to harass an assistance dog, knowing the dog to be an assistance dog, shall be guilty of a misdemeanor and, upon conviction thereof, shall be punished by imprisonment for not less than 90 days or a fine not to exceed $500.00, or both, provided that any person who is convicted of a second or subsequent violation of this subsection shall be punished as for a misdemeanor of a high and aggravated nature.

(e) Any person who knowingly and intentionally allows his or her dog to cause death or physical harm to an assistance dog by rendering a part of the assistance dog's body useless or by seriously disfiguring the assistance dog, knowing the dog to be an assistance dog, shall be punished as for a misdemeanor of a high and aggravated nature.

Laws 1996, p. 665, § 1; Laws 2004, Act 722, § 1, eff. July 1, 2004.

Formerly Code 1981 § 30–1–6.

§ 16–11–108. Using firearm or archery tackle in manner to endanger bodily safety of another while hunting wildlife; temporary hunting license

(a) Any person who while hunting wildlife uses a firearm or archery tackle in a manner to endanger the bodily safety of another person by consciously disregarding a substantial and unjustifiable risk that his act or omission will cause harm to or endanger the safety of another person and the disregard constitutes a gross deviation from the standard of care which a reasonable person would exercise in the situation is guilty of a misdemeanor; provided, however, if such conduct results in serious bodily harm to another person, the person engaging in such conduct shall be guilty of a felony and, upon conviction thereof, shall be punished by a fine of not more than $5,000.00 or by imprisonment for not less than one nor more than ten years, or both.

(b) Whenever a person is charged with violating subsection (a) of this Code section, the arresting law enforcement officer shall take the hunting license of the person so charged. The hunting license shall be attached to the court's copy of the citation, warrant, accusation, or indictment and shall be forwarded to the court having jurisdiction of the offense. A copy of the citation, warrant, accusation, or indictment shall be forwarded, within 15 days of its issuance, to the Game and Fish Division of the Department of Natural Resources.

(c) In order to obtain a temporary hunting license, a person charged with violating subsection (a) of this Code section must present to the director of the Game and Fish Division of the Department of Natural Resources a certificate of satisfactory completion, after the date of the incident for which the person was charged and regardless of the person's age or date of birth, of a hunter education course prescribed by the Board of Natural Resources. A temporary hunting license issued under such circumstances shall be valid until the next March 31 or until suspended or revoked under any provision of this title or of Title 27. The director of the Game and Fish Division of the Department of Natural Resources may renew the temporary hunting license during the pendency of charges.

(d)(1) If the person is convicted of violating subsection (a) of this Code section, the court shall, within 15 days of such conviction, forward the person's hunting license and a copy of the record of the disposition of the case to the Game and Fish Division of the Department of Natural Resources. At this time, the court shall also require the person to surrender any temporary hunting licenses issued pursuant to the provisions of subsection (c) of this Code section.

(2) If the person is not convicted of violating subsection (a) of this Code section, the court shall return the hunting license to the person.

Laws 1989, p. 292, § 1.

§ 16–11–109. Unlawful acts during pendency of charges; penalty

(a) It shall be unlawful during the pendency of such charges and any period of license revocation and ineligibility pursuant to Code Section 16–11–110 for any person charged with or convicted of a violation of subsection (a) of Code Section 16–11–108 to either:

(1) Hunt without a license in violation of Code Section 27–2–1; or

(2) Possess a Georgia hunting license other than a temporary hunting license issued by the director of the Game and Fish Division of the Department of Natural Resources pursuant to the provisions of subsection (c) of Code Section 16–11–108.

(b) Any person who violates subsection (a) of this Code section shall be guilty of a felony and, upon conviction thereof, shall be punished by a fine of not more than $5,000.00 or by imprisonment for not less than one nor more than five years, or both.

(c) Upon conviction of a violation of subsection (a) of this Code section, the court shall, within 15 days of such conviction, forward any hunting license found in the possession of the convicted person and a copy of the record of the disposition of the case to the Game and Fish Division of the Department of Natural Resources.

Laws 1989, p. 292, § 1.

§ 16–11–110. Revocation of license

(a) Any hunting license of any person convicted of violating subsection (a) of Code Section 16–11–108 or subsection (a) of Code Section 16–11–109 shall by operation of law be revoked.

(b) Any person convicted of violating subsection (a) of Code Section 16–11–108 or subsection (a) of Code Section 16–11–109 shall be ineligible for a hunting license for a period of five years from the date of conviction.

(c) If a person's hunting license is revoked by operation of law as provided in subsection (a) of this Code section, the fact that the person's hunting license was not surrendered to the law enforcement officer at the time the person was charged with violating subsection (a) of Code Section 16–11–108 or the fact that the person's hunting license was not retained by the court and forwarded to the Game and Fish Division of the Department of Natural Resources as provided in subsection (d) of Code Section 16–11–108 or in subsection (c) of Code Section 16–11–109 shall not affect such revocation.

Laws 1989, p. 292, § 1.

§ 16–11–111. Anhydrous ammonia; unlawful possession; violations

(a)(1) As used in this Code section, the term "anhydrous ammonia" means any substance identified to contain the compound ammonia which is capable of being utilized in the production of methamphetamine or any other controlled substance.

(2) A person commits the crime of unlawful possession of anhydrous ammonia if the person:

(A) Purchases, possesses, transfers, or distributes any amount of anhydrous ammonia knowing that the anhydrous ammonia will be used unlawfully to manufacture a controlled substance;

(B) Possesses, maintains, or transports any quantity of anhydrous ammonia in a container or receptacle other than a tank truck, tank trailer, rail tank car, bulk storage tank, field (nurse) tank, field applicator, or any container approved for anhydrous ammonia by the Department of Agriculture or the United States Department of Transportation; or

(C) Tampers with equipment manufactured to hold, apply, or transport anhydrous ammonia without the express consent of the owner of the equipment.

(3) A person who violates subparagraph (B) of paragraph (2) of this subsection shall be subject to civil penalties in accordance with Code Section 40–16–6.

(b) Any person who violates this Code section shall, upon conviction thereof, be punished by imprisonment for not less than one year nor more than ten years and by a fine not to exceed $100,000.00.

Laws 2003, Act 29, § 2, eff. May 15, 2003.

Historical and Statutory Notes

In 2003, the Code Commission redesignated subsec. (a), par. (3), subpar. (A), as subsec. (a), par. (3) and redesignated subsec. (a), par. (3), subpar. (B) as subsec. (b). See § 28–9–5.

§ 16–11–112. Vehicles containing false or secret compartments; owning or operating prohibited; violations

(a) As used in this Code section, the term:

(1)(A) "False or secret compartment" means any enclosure which is integrated into or attached to a vehicle and the purpose of the compartment is to conceal, hide, or prevent discovery by law enforcement officers of:

(i) A person concealed for an unlawful purpose;

(ii) Controlled substances possessed in violation of Article 2 of Chapter 13 of this title; or

(iii) Other contraband.

(B) Examples of "false or secret compartment" may include, but are not limited to:

(i) False, altered, or modified fuel tanks;

(ii) Original factory equipment on a vehicle that has been modified; or

(iii) Any compartment, space, or box that is added or attached to existing compartments, spaces, or boxes of the vehicle.

(2) "Vehicle" includes, but is not limited to, cars, trucks, buses, motorcycles, bicycles, aircraft, helicopters, boats, ships, yachts, and other vessels.

(b) It may be inferred that the accused intended to use a false or secret compartment if a person knowingly has a false or secret compartment which:

(1) Is concealing a person for an unlawful purpose;

(2) Is concealing a controlled substance in violation of Article 2 of Chapter 13 of this title;

(3) Is concealing other contraband;

(4) Shows evidence of the previous concealment of a person for an unlawful purpose;

(5) Shows evidence of the previous concealment of controlled substances in violation of Article 2 of Chapter 13 of this title; or

(6) Shows evidence of the previous concealment of other contraband.

(c)(1) It is unlawful for any person to knowingly own or operate any vehicle containing a false or secret compartment.

(2) It is unlawful for any person to knowingly install, create, build, or fabricate in any vehicle a false or secret compartment.

(3) It is unlawful for any person to knowingly sell, trade, or otherwise dispose of a vehicle which is in violation of this Code section.

(d) Any person who violates this Code section shall, upon conviction thereof, be punished by imprisonment for not less than one nor more than two years, by a fine not to exceed $10,000.00, or both.

(e) Upon the arrest of a person who owns or is operating a vehicle which is in violation of this Code section, if the vehicle is not otherwise subject to forfeiture under other provisions of law, or not determined to be needed to be held as evidence, the law enforcement officer shall seize the license plate and registration for such vehicle and shall issue a citation for violation of this Code section and a temporary license plate for the vehicle. The temporary license plate shall be on a form as prescribed by the state revenue commissioner. The temporary license plate shall be valid for 30 days or until the owner of the vehicle provides verification that such vehicle has been repaired so as to eliminate any violation of this Code section, whichever occurs first. Such vehicle shall be subject to inspection by law enforcement and if it is determined that such vehicle has been repaired, the license plate and registration shall be returned to the owner at such time.

Laws 2006, Act 469, § 1, eff. April 18, 2006.

§ 16–11–113. Solicitation, persuasion, encouragement, or enticement of dealer to transfer or convey firearm to non-buyer; aiding and abetting; felony violation

Any person who attempts to solicit, persuade, encourage, or entice any dealer to transfer or otherwise convey a firearm other than to the actual buyer, as well as any other person who willfully and intentionally aids or abets such person, shall be guilty of a felony. This Code section shall not apply to a federal law enforcement officer or a peace officer, as defined in Code Section 16–1–3, in the performance of his or her official duties or other person under such officer's direct supervision.

Laws 2008, Act 802, § 2, eff. July 1, 2008.

Part 2

Possession of Dangerous Weapons

§ 16–11–120. Short title

This part shall be known and may be cited as the "Georgia Firearms and Weapons Act."

Laws 1968, p. 983, § 1.

§ 16–11–121. Definitions

As used in this part, the term:

(1) "Dangerous weapon" means any weapon commonly known as a "rocket launcher," "bazooka," or "recoilless rifle" which fires explosive or nonexplosive rockets designed to injure or kill personnel or destroy heavy armor, or similar weapon used for such purpose. The term shall also mean a weapon commonly known as a "mortar" which fires high explosive from a metallic cylinder and which is commonly used by the armed forces as an antipersonnel weapon or similar weapon used for such purpose. The term shall also mean a weapon commonly known as a "hand grenade" or other similar weapon which is designed to explode and injure personnel or similar weapon used for such purpose.

(2) "Machine gun" means any weapon which shoots or is designed to shoot, automatically, more than six shots, without manual reloading, by a single function of the trigger.

(3) "Person" means any individual, partnership, company, association, or corporation.

(4) "Sawed-off rifle" means a weapon designed or redesigned, made or remade, and intended to be fired from the shoulder; and designed or redesigned, made or remade, to use the energy of the explosive in a fixed metallic cartridge to fire only a single projectile through a rifle bore for each single pull of the trigger; and which has a barrel or barrels of less than 16 inches in length or has an overall length of less than 26 inches.

(5) "Sawed-off shotgun" means a shotgun or any weapon made from a shotgun whether by alteration, modification, or otherwise having one or more barrels less than 18 inches in length or if such weapon as modified has an overall length of less than 26 inches.

(6) "Shotgun" means a weapon designed or redesigned, made or remade, and intended to be fired from the shoulder; and designed or redesigned, and made or remade, to use the energy of the explosive in a fixed shotgun shell to fire through a smooth bore either a number of ball shot or a single projectile for each single pull of the trigger.

(7) "Silencer" means any device for silencing or diminishing the report of any portable weapon such as a rifle, carbine, pistol, revolver, machine gun, shotgun, fowling piece, or other device from which a shot, bullet, or projectile may be discharged by an explosive.

Laws 1968, p. 983, § 4; Laws 1974, p. 449, § 1.

§ 16–11–122. Possession of certain types of firearms, dangerous weapons and silencers prohibited

No person shall have in his possession any sawed-off shotgun, sawed-off rifle, machine gun, dangerous weapon, or silencer except as provided in Code Section 16–11–124.

Laws 1968, p. 983, § 2.

§ 16–11–123. Punishment

A person commits the offense of unlawful possession of firearms or weapons when he or she knowingly has in his or her possession any sawed-off shotgun, sawed-off rifle, machine gun, dangerous weapon, or silencer, and, upon conviction thereof, he or she shall be punished by imprisonment for a period of five years.

Laws 1968, p. 983, § 3; Laws 2000, p. 1630, § 2.

Historical and Statutory Notes

The 2000 amendment provided gender neutral language and deleted a minimum sentence of not less than one year.

§ 16–11–124. Exceptions to provisions of law

This part shall not apply to:

(1) A peace officer of any duly authorized police agency of this state or of any political subdivision thereof, or a law enforcement officer of any department or agency of the United States who is regularly employed and paid by the United States, this state, or any such political subdivision, or an employee of the Department of Corrections of this state who is

authorized in writing by the commissioner of corrections to transfer or possess such firearms while in the official performance of his duties;

(2) A member of the National Guard or of the armed forces of the United States to wit: the army, navy, marine corps, air force, or coast guard who, while serving therein, possesses such firearm in the line of duty;

(3) Any sawed-off shotgun, sawed-off rifle, machine gun, dangerous weapon, or silencer which has been modified or changed to the extent that it is inoperative. Examples of the requisite modification include weapons with their barrel or barrels filled with lead, hand grenades filled with sand, or other nonexplosive materials;

(4) Possession of a sawed-off shotgun, sawed-off rifle, machine gun, dangerous weapon, or silencer by a person who is authorized to possess the same because he has registered the sawed-off shotgun, sawed-off rifle, machine gun, dangerous weapon, or silencer in accordance with the dictates of the National Firearms Act, 68A Stat. 725 (26 U.S.C. Sections 5841–5862); and

(5) A security officer employed by a federally licensed nuclear power facility or a licensee of such facility, including a contract security officer, who is trained and qualified under a security plan approved by the United States Nuclear Regulatory Commission or other federal agency authorized to regulate nuclear facility security; provided, however, that this exemption shall apply only while such security officer is acting in connection with his or her official duties on the premises of such nuclear power facility or on properties outside the facility property pursuant to a written agreement entered into with the local law enforcement agency having jurisdiction over the facility. The exemption under this paragraph does not include the possession of silencers.

Laws 1968, p. 983, § 5; Laws 1985, p. 283, § 1; Laws 2006, Act 767, § 1, eff. May 3, 2006.

Historical and Statutory Notes

The 2006 amendment by Act 767 added new par. (5).

§ 16–11–125. Burden of proof of exceptions, etc.

In any complaint, accusation, or indictment and in any action or proceeding brought for the enforcement of this part it shall not be necessary to negative any exception, excuse, proviso, or exemption contained in this part, and the burden of proof of any such exception, excuse, proviso, or exemption shall be upon the defendant.

Laws 1968, p. 983, § 6.

§ 16–11–125.1. Definitions

As used in this part, the term:

(1) "Handgun" means a firearm of any description, loaded or unloaded, from which any shot, bullet, or other missile can be discharged by an action of an explosive where the length of the barrel, not including any revolving, detachable, or magazine breech, does not exceed 12 inches; provided, however, that the term handgun shall not include a gun which discharges a single shot of .46 centimeters or less in diameter.

(2) "Knife" means a cutting instrument designed for the purpose of offense and defense consisting of a blade that is greater than five inches in length which is fastened to a handle.

(3) "License holder" means a person who holds a valid weapons carry license.

(4) "Long gun" means a firearm with a barrel length of at least 18 inches and overall length of at least 26 inches designed or made and intended to be fired from the shoulder and designed or made to use the energy of the explosive in a fixed:

(A) Shotgun shell to fire through a smooth bore either a number of ball shot or a single projectile for each single pull of the trigger or from which any shot, bullet, or other missile can be discharged; or

(B) Metallic cartridge to fire only a single projectile through a rifle bore for each single pull of the trigger;

provided, however, that the term long gun shall not include a gun which discharges a single shot of .46 centimeters or less in diameter.

(5) "Weapon" means a knife or handgun.

(6) "Weapons carry license" or "license" means a license issued pursuant to Code Section 16–11–129.

Laws 2010, Act 643, § 1–1, eff. June 4, 2010.

Historical and Statutory Notes

Laws 2010, Act 643, § 3–1, provides:

"This Act shall become effective upon its approval by the Governor or upon its becoming law without such approval and shall apply to all offenses committed on and after such date. The enactment of this Act shall not affect any prosecutions for acts occurring before the effective date of this Act and shall not act as an abatement of any such prosecutions."

Part 3

Carrying and Possession of Firearms

§ 16–11–126. Possessing or carrying a handgun or long gun

(a) Any person who is not prohibited by law from possessing a handgun or long gun may have or carry on his or her person a weapon or long gun on his or her property or inside his or her home, motor vehicle, or place of business without a valid weapons carry license.

(b) Any person who is not prohibited by law from possessing a handgun or long gun may have or carry on his or her person a long gun without a valid weapons carry license, provided that if the long gun is loaded, it shall only be carried in an open and fully exposed manner.

(c) Any person who is not prohibited by law from possessing a handgun or long gun may have or carry any handgun provided that it is enclosed in a case and unloaded.

(d) Any person who is not prohibited by law from possessing a handgun or long gun who is eligible for a weapons carry license may transport a handgun or long gun in any private passenger motor vehicle; provided, however, that private property owners or persons in legal control of property through a lease, rental agreement, licensing agreement, contract, or any other agreement to control access to such property shall have the right to forbid possession of a weapon or long gun on their property, except as provided in Code Section 16–11–135.

(e) Any person licensed to carry a handgun or weapon in any other state whose laws recognize and give effect to a license issued pursuant to this part shall be authorized to carry a weapon in this state, but only while the licensee is not a resident of this state; provided, however, that such licensee shall carry the weapon in compliance with the laws of this state.

(f) Any person with a valid hunting or fishing license on his or her person, or any person not required by law to have a hunting or fishing license, who is engaged in legal hunting, fishing, or sport shooting when the person has the permission of the owner of the land on which the activities are being conducted may have or carry on his or her person a handgun or long gun without a valid weapons carry license while hunting, fishing, or engaging in sport shooting.

(g) Notwithstanding Code Sections 12–3–10, 27–3–1.1, 27–3–6, and 16–12–122 through 16–12–127, any person with a valid weapons carry license may carry a weapon in all parks, historic sites, or recreational areas, as such term is defined in Code Section 12–3–10, including all publicly owned buildings located in such parks, historic sites, and recreational areas, in wildlife management areas, and on public transportation; provided, however, that a person shall not carry a handgun into a place where it is prohibited by federal law.

(h)(1) No person shall carry a weapon without a valid weapons carry license unless he or she meets one of the exceptions to having such license as provided in subsections (a) through (g) of this Code section.

(2) A person commits the offense of carrying a weapon without a license when he or she violates the provisions of paragraph (1) of this subsection.

(i) Upon conviction of the offense of carrying weapon without a valid weapons carry license, a person shall be punished as follows:

(1) For the first offense, he or she shall be guilty of a misdemeanor; and

(2) For the second offense within five years, as measured from the dates of previous arrests for which convictions were obtained to the date of the current arrest for which a conviction is obtained, and for any subsequent offense, he or she shall be guilty of a felony and, upon conviction thereof, shall be imprisoned for not less than two years and not more than five years.

Laws 1837, Cobb's 1851 Digest, pp. 848, 849; Laws 1851–52, p. 269, §§ 1–3; Laws 1865–66, p. 233, §§ 1, 2; Laws 1882–83, p. 48, § 1; Laws 1898, p. 60, § 1; Laws 1968, p. 1249, § 1; Laws 1976, p. 1430, § 1; Laws 1982, p. 3, § 16; Laws 1992, p. 6, § 16; Laws 1996, p. 108, § 1; Laws 1998, p. 1153, § 1; Laws 2000, p. 1630, § 3; Laws 2007, Act 18, § 16, eff. May 11, 2007; Laws 2008, Act 551, § 3, eff. July 1, 2008; Laws 2008, Act 802, § 3, eff. July 1, 2008; Laws 2009, Act 8, § 16, eff. April 14, 2009; Laws 2010, Act 643, § 1–2, eff. June 4, 2010.

Formerly Code 1863, § 4413; Code 1868, § 4454; Code 1873, § 4527; Code 1882, § 4527; Penal Code 1895, § 341; Penal Code 1910, § 347; Code 1933, § 26–5101; Code 1933, § 26–2901.

Historical and Statutory Notes

The 2000 amendment in subsec. (b)(1) substituted as a minimum sentence two years for one year.

The 2007 amendment by Act 18 was a provision contained in a correction bill.

The 2008 amendment by Act 551 substituted "knuckles whether made from metal, thermoplastic, wood, or other similar material" for "metal knuckles" and "metal knucks", throughout the section.

The 2008 amendment by Act 802 designated subsec. (f) and rewrote subsecs. (c), (d), and (e), which formerly read:

"(c) This Code section shall not permit, outside of his or her home, motor vehicle, or place of business, the concealed carrying of a pistol, revolver, or concealable firearm by any person unless that person has on his or her person a valid license issued under Code Section 16–11–129 and the pistol, revolver, or firearm may only be carried in a shoulder holster, waist belt holster, any other holster, hipgrip, or any other similar device, in which event the weapon may be concealed by the person's clothing, or a handbag, purse, attache case, briefcase, or other closed container. Carrying on the person in a concealed manner other than as provided in this subsection shall not be permitted and shall be a violation of this Code section.

"(d) This Code section shall not forbid the transportation of any firearm by a person who is not among those enumerated as ineligible for a license under Code Section 16–11–129, provided the firearm is enclosed in a case, unloaded, and separated from its ammunition. This Code section shall not forbid any person who is not among those enumerated as ineligible for a license under Code Section 16–11–129 from transporting a loaded firearm in any private passenger motor vehicle in an open manner and fully exposed to view or in the glove compartment, console, or similar compartment of the vehicle; provided, however, that any person in possession of a valid permit issued pursuant to Code Section 16–11–129 may carry a handgun in any location in a motor vehicle.

"(e) On and after October 1, 1996, a person licensed to carry a handgun in any state whose laws recognize and give effect within such state to a license issued pursuant to this part shall be authorized to carry a handgun in this state, but only while the licensee is not a resident of this state; provided, however, that such licenseholder shall carry the handgun in compliance with the laws of this state."

The 2009 amendment by Act 8 was a provision contained in a correction bill.

The 2010 amendment by Act 643 rewrote the section which had read:

"(a) A person commits the offense of carrying a concealed weapon when such person knowingly has or carries about his or her person, unless in an open manner and fully exposed to view, any bludgeon, knuckles, whether made from metal, thermoplastic, wood, or other similar material, firearm, knife designed for the purpose of offense and defense, or any other dangerous or deadly weapon or instrument of like character outside of his or her home or place of business, except as permitted under this Code section.

"(b) Upon conviction of the offense of carrying a concealed weapon, a person shall be punished as follows:

"(1) For the first offense, he or she shall be guilty of a misdemeanor; and

"(2) For the second offense, and for any subsequent offense, he or she shall be guilty of a felony and, upon conviction thereof, shall be imprisoned for not less than two years and not more than five years.

"(c) This Code section shall not permit, outside of his or her home, motor vehicle, or place of business, the concealed carrying of a pistol, revolver, or concealable firearm by any person unless that person has on his or her person a valid license issued under Code Section 16–11–129 and the pistol, revolver, or firearm may only be carried in a shoulder holster, waist belt holster, any other holster, hipgrip, or any other similar device, in which event the weapon may be concealed by the person's clothing, or a handbag, purse, attache case, briefcase, or other closed container. Any person having been issued a license to carry a concealed weapon pursuant to Code Section 16–11–129 shall be permitted to carry such weapon, subject to the limitations of this part, in all parks, historic sites, or recreational areas as defined by Code Section 12–3–10 and in all wildlife management areas.

"(d) This Code section shall not forbid the transportation of any firearm by a person who is not among those enumerated as ineligible for a license under Code Section 16–11–129, provided the firearm is enclosed in a case, unloaded, and separated from its ammunition.

"(e) This Code section shall not forbid any person who is not among those enumerated as ineligible for a license under Code Section 16–11–129 from transporting a loaded firearm in any private passenger motor vehicle.

"(f) On and after October 1, 1996, a person licensed to carry a handgun in any state whose laws recognize and give effect within such state to a license issued pursuant to this part shall be authorized to carry a handgun in this state, but only while the licensee is not a resident of this state; provided, however, that such license holder shall carry the handgun in compliance with the laws of this state."

Laws 2010, Act 643, § 3–1, provides:

"This Act shall become effective upon its approval by the Governor or upon its becoming law without such approval and shall apply to all offenses committed on and after such date. The enactment of this Act shall not affect any prosecutions for acts occurring before the effective date of this Act and shall not act as an abatement of any such prosecutions."

§ 16–11–127. Carrying a weapon in unauthorized locations

(a) As used in this Code section, the term:

(1) "Bar" means an establishment that is devoted to the serving of alcoholic beverages for consumption by guests on the premises and in which the serving of food is only incidental to the consumption of those beverages, including, but not limited to, taverns, nightclubs, cocktail lounges, and cabarets.

(2) "Courthouse" means a building occupied by judicial courts and containing rooms in which judicial proceedings are held.

(3) "Government building" means:

(A) The building in which a government entity is housed;

(B) The building where a government entity meets in its official capacity; provided, however, that if such building is not a publicly owned building, such building shall be considered a government building for the purposes of this Code section only during the time such government entity is meeting at such building; or

(C) The portion of any building that is not a publicly owned building that is occupied by a government entity.

(4) "Government entity" means an office, agency, authority, department, commission, board, body, division, instrumentality, or institution of the state or any county, municipal corporation, consolidated government, or local board of education within this state.

(5) "Parking facility" means real property owned or leased by a government entity, courthouse, jail, prison, place of worship, or bar that has been designated by such government entity, courthouse, jail, prison, place of worship, or bar for the parking of motor vehicles at a government building or at such courthouse, jail, prison, place of worship, or bar.

(b) A person shall be guilty of carrying a weapon or long gun in an unauthorized location and punished as for a misdemeanor when he or she carries a weapon or long gun while:

(1) In a government building;

(2) In a courthouse;

(3) In a jail or prison;

(4) In a place of worship;

(5) In a state mental health facility as defined in Code Section 37–1–1 which admits individuals on an involuntary basis for treatment of mental illness, developmental disability, or addictive disease; provided, however, that carrying a weapon or long gun in such location in a manner in compliance with paragraph (3) of subsection (d) of this Code section shall not constitute a violation of this subsection;

(6) In a bar, unless the owner of the bar permits the carrying of weapons or long guns by license holders;

(7) On the premises of a nuclear power facility, except as provided in Code Section 16–11–127.2, and the punishment provisions of Code Section 16–11–127.2 shall supersede the punishment provisions of this Code section; or

(8) Within 150 feet of any polling place, except as provided in subsection (i) of Code Section 21–2–413.

(c) Except as provided in Code Section 16–11–127.1, a license holder or person recognized under subsection (e) of Code Section 16–11–126 shall be authorized to carry a weapon as provided in Code Section 16–11–135 and in every location in this state not listed in subsection (b) of this Code section; provided, however, that private property owners or persons in legal control of property through a lease, rental agreement, licensing agreement, contract, or any other agreement to control access to such property shall have the right to forbid possession of a weapon or long gun on their property, except as provided in Code Section 16–11–135. A violation of subsection (b) of this Code section shall not create or give rise to a civil action for damages.

(d) Subsection (b) of this Code section shall not apply:

(1) To the use of weapons or long guns as exhibits in a legal proceeding, provided such weapons or long guns are secured and handled as directed by the personnel providing courtroom security or the judge hearing the case;

(2) To a license holder who approaches security or management personnel upon arrival at a location described in subsection (b) of this Code section and notifies such security or management personnel of the presence of the weapon or long gun and explicitly follows the security or management personnel's direction for removing, securing, storing, or temporarily surrendering such weapon or long gun; and

(3) To a weapon or long gun possessed by a license holder which is under the possessor's control in a motor vehicle or is in a locked compartment of a motor vehicle or one which is in a locked container in or a locked firearms rack which is on a motor vehicle and such vehicle is parked in a parking facility.

Laws 1870, p. 421, §§ 1, 2; Laws 1878–79, p. 64, § 1; Laws 1909, p. 90, § 1; Laws 1968, p. 1249, § 1; Laws 1976, p. 1430, § 2; Laws 1986, p. 673, § 1; Laws 1987, p. 358, § 1; Laws 1992, p. 1315, § 1; Laws 1996, p. 748, § 11; Laws 1997, p. 514, § 1; Laws 2003, Act 179, § 1, eff. June 1, 2003; Laws 2008, Act 802, § 4, eff. July 1, 2008; Laws 2010, Act 643, § 1–3, eff. June 4, 2010.

Formerly Code 1882, § 4528; Penal Code 1895, § 342; Penal Code 1910, § 348; Code 1933, § 26–5102; Code 1933, § 26–2902.

Historical and Statutory Notes

The 2003 amendment by Act 179, in subsec. (a), inserted "or she"; and added new subsec. (d).

Laws 2003, Act 179, § 5, provides:

"This Act shall become effective on the first day of the month following the month in which it is approved by the Governor or in which it becomes law without such approval."

The 2008 amendment by Act 802 rewrote this section, which formerly read:

"(a) Except as provided in Code Section 16–11–127.1, a person is guilty of a misdemeanor when he or she carries to or while at a public gathering any explosive compound, firearm, or knife designed for the purpose of offense and defense.

"(b) For the purpose of this Code section, 'public gathering' shall include, but shall not be limited to, athletic or sporting events, churches or church functions, political rallies or functions, publicly owned or operated buildings, or establishments at which alcoholic beverages are sold for consumption on the premises. Nothing in this Code section shall otherwise prohibit the carrying of a firearm in any other public place by a person licensed or permitted to carry such firearm by this part.

"(c) This Code section shall not apply to competitors participating in organized sport shooting events. Law enforcement officers, peace officers retired from state or federal law enforcement agencies, judges, magistrates, solicitors-general, and district attorneys may carry pistols in publicly owned or operated buildings.

"(d) It is an affirmative defense to a violation of this Code section if a person notifies a law enforcement officer or other person employed to provide security for a public gathering of the presence of such item as soon as possible after learning of its presence and surrenders or secures such item as directed by the law enforcement officer or other person employed to provide security for a public gathering."

The 2010 amendment by Act 643 rewrote the section which had read:

"(a) Except as provided in Code Section 16–11–127.1, a person shall be guilty of a misdemeanor when he or she carries to or while at a public gathering any explosive compound, firearm, or knife designed for the purpose of offense and defense.

"(b) For the purpose of this Code section, 'public gathering' shall include, but shall not be limited to, athletic or sporting events, churches or church functions, political rallies or functions, publicly owned or operated buildings, or establishments at which alcoholic beverages are sold for consumption on the premises and which derive less than 50 percent of their total annual gross food and beverage sales from the sale of prepared meals or food. Nothing in this Code section shall otherwise prohibit the carrying of a firearm in any other public place by a person licensed or permitted to carry such firearm by this part.

"(c)(1) This Code section shall not apply to competitors participating in organized sport shooting events.

"(2) Law enforcement officers, peace officers retired from state, local, or federal law enforcement agencies, judges, magistrates, constables, solicitors-general, and district attorneys may carry pistols in publicly owned or operated buildings; provided, however, that a courthouse security plan adopted in accordance with paragraph (10) of subsection (a) of Code Section 15–16–10 may prohibit the carrying of a pistol.

"(d) It shall be an affirmative defense to a violation of this Code section if a person notifies a law enforcement officer or other person employed to provide security for a public gathering of the presence of such item as soon as possible after learning of its presence and surrenders or secures such item as directed by such law enforcement officer or other person employed to provide security for such public gathering.

"(e) A person licensed or permitted to carry a firearm by this part shall be permitted to carry such firearm, subject to the limitations of this part, in all parks, historic sites, and recreational areas, including all publicly owned buildings located in such parks, historic sites, and recreational areas and in wildlife management areas, notwithstanding Code Section 12–3–10, in wildlife management areas notwithstanding Code Section 27–3–1.1 and 27–3–6, and in public transportation notwithstanding Code Sections 16–12–122 through 16–12–127; provided, however, that a person shall not carry a firearm into a place prohibited by federal law.

"(f) A person licensed or permitted to carry a firearm by this part shall not consume alcoholic beverages in a restaurant or other eating establishment while carrying a firearm. Any person violating this subsection shall be guilty of a misdemeanor."

Laws 2010, Act 643, § 3–1, provides:

"This Act shall become effective upon its approval by the Governor or upon its becoming law without such approval and shall apply to all offenses committed on and after such date. The enactment of this Act shall not affect any prosecutions for acts occurring before the effective date of this Act and shall not act as an abatement of any such prosecutions."

§ 16–11–127.1. Weapons on school safety zones, school buildings or grounds or at school functions

(a) As used in this Code section, the term:

(1) "School safety zone" means in or on any real property owned by or leased to any public or private elementary school, secondary school, or school board and used for elementary or secondary education and in or on the campus of any public or private technical school, vocational school, college, university, or institution of postsecondary education.

(2) "Weapon" means and includes any pistol, revolver, or any weapon designed or intended to propel a missile of any kind, or any dirk, bowie knife, switchblade knife, ballistic knife, any other knife having a blade of two or more inches, straight-edge razor, razor blade, spring stick, knuckles, whether made from metal, thermoplastic, wood, or other similar material, blackjack, any bat, club, or other bludgeon-type weapon, or any flailing instrument consisting of two or more rigid parts connected in such a manner as to allow them to swing freely, which may be known as a nun chahka, nun chuck, nunchaku, shuriken, or fighting chain, or any disc, of whatever configuration, having at least two points or pointed blades which is designed to be thrown or propelled and which may be known as a throwing star or oriental dart, or any weapon of like kind, and any stun gun or taser as defined in subsection (a) of Code Section 16–11–106. This paragraph excludes any of these instruments used for classroom work authorized by the teacher.

Subsec. (b), as amended by Laws 2010, Act 465, § 2, eff. May 25, 2010.

(b) Except as otherwise provided in subsection (c) of this Code section, it shall be unlawful for any person to carry to or to possess or have under such person's control while within a school safety zone or at a school building, school function, or school property or on a bus or other transportation furnished by the school any weapon or explosive compound, other than fireworks the possession of which is regulated by Chapter 10 of Title 25. Any person who violates this subsection shall be guilty of a felony and, upon conviction thereof, be punished by a fine of not more than $10,000.00, by imprisonment for not less than two nor more than ten years, or both; provided, however, that upon conviction of a violation of this subsection involving a firearm as defined in paragraph (2) of subsection (a) of Code Section 16–11–131, or a dangerous weapon or machine gun as defined in Code Section 16–11–121, such person shall be punished by a fine of not more than $10,000.00 or by imprisonment for a period of not less than five nor more than ten years, or both. A child who violates this subsection may be subject to the provisions of Code Section 15–11–63.

Subsec. (b), as amended by Laws 2010, Act 643, § 1–4, eff. June 4, 2010.

(b)(1) Except as otherwise provided in subsection (c) of this Code section, it shall be unlawful for any person to carry to or to possess or have under such person's control while within a school safety zone or at a school building, school function, or school property or on a bus or other transportation furnished by the school any weapon or explosive compound, other than fireworks the possession of which is regulated by Chapter 10 of Title 25.

(2) Any license holder who violates this subsection shall be guilty of a misdemeanor. Any person who is not a license holder who violates this subsection shall be guilty of a felony and, upon conviction thereof, be punished by a fine of not more than $10,000.00, by imprisonment for not less than two nor more than ten years, or both

(3) Any person convicted of a violation of this subsection involving a dangerous weapon or machine gun, as such terms are defined in Code Section 16–11–121, shall be punished by a fine of not more than $10,000.00 or by imprisonment for a period of not less than five nor more than ten years, or both.

(4) A child who violates this subsection shall be subject to the provisions of Code Section 15–11–63.

(c) The provisions of this Code section shall not apply to:

(1) Baseball bats, hockey sticks, or other sports equipment possessed by competitors for legitimate athletic purposes;

(2) Participants in organized sport shooting events or firearm training courses;

(3) Persons participating in military training programs conducted by or on behalf of the armed forces of the United States or the Georgia Department of Defense;

(4) Persons participating in law enforcement training conducted by a police academy certified by the Georgia Peace Officer Standards and Training Council or by a law enforcement agency of the state or the United States or any political subdivision thereof;

(5) The following persons, when acting in the performance of their official duties or when en route to or from their official duties:

(A) A peace officer as defined by Code Section 35–8–2;

(B) A law enforcement officer of the United States government;

(C) A prosecuting attorney of this state or of the United States;

(D) An employee of the Georgia Department of Corrections or a correctional facility operated by a political subdivision of this state or the United States who is authorized by the head of such correctional agency or facility to carry a firearm;

(E) A person employed as a campus police officer or school security officer who is authorized to carry a weapon in accordance with Chapter 8 of Title 20; and

(F) Medical examiners, coroners, and their investigators who are employed by the state or any political subdivision thereof;

(6) A person who has been authorized in writing by a duly authorized official of the school to have in such person's possession or use as part of any activity being conducted at a school building, school property, or school function a weapon which would otherwise be prohibited by this Code section. Such authorization shall specify the weapon or weapons which have been authorized and the time period during which the authorization is valid;

(7) A person who is licensed in accordance with Code Section 16–11–129 or issued a permit pursuant to Code Section 43–38–10, when such person carries or picks up a student at a school building, school function, or school property or on a bus or other transportation furnished by the school or a person who is licensed in accordance with Code Section 16–11–129 or issued a permit pursuant to Code Section 43–38–10 when he or she has any weapon legally kept within a vehicle when such vehicle is parked at such school property or is in transit through a designated school zone;

(8) A weapon possessed by a license holder which is under the possessor's control in a motor vehicle or which is in a locked compartment of a motor vehicle or one which is in a locked container in or a locked firearms rack which is on a motor vehicle which is being used by an adult over 21 years of age to bring to or pick up a student at a school building, school function, or school property or on a bus or other transportation furnished by the school, or when such vehicle is used to transport someone to an activity being conducted on school property which has been authorized by a duly authorized official of the school; provided, however, that this exception shall not apply to a student attending such school;

(9) Persons employed in fulfilling defense contracts with the government of the United States or agencies thereof when possession of the weapon is necessary for manufacture, transport, installation, and testing under the requirements of such contract;

(10) Those employees of the State Board of Pardons and Paroles when specifically designated and authorized in writing by the members of the State Board of Pardons and Paroles to carry a weapon;

(11) The Attorney General and those members of his or her staff whom he or she specifically authorizes in writing to carry a weapon;

(12) Probation supervisors employed by and under the authority of the Department of Corrections pursuant to Article 2 of Chapter 8 of Title 42, known as the "State-wide Probation Act," when specifically designated and authorized in writing by the director of the Division of Probation;

(13) Public safety directors of municipal corporations;

(14) State and federal trial and appellate judges;

(15) United States attorneys and assistant United States attorneys;

(16) Clerks of the superior courts;

(17) Teachers and other school personnel who are otherwise authorized to possess or carry weapons, provided that any such weapon is in a locked compartment of a motor vehicle or one which is in a locked container in or a locked firearms rack which is on a motor vehicle; or

(18) Constables of any county of this state.

(d)(1) This Code section shall not prohibit any person who resides or works in a business or is in the ordinary course transacting lawful business or any person who is a visitor of such resident located within a school safety zone from carrying, possessing, or having under such person's control a weapon within a school safety zone; provided, however, it shall be unlawful for any such person to carry, possess, or have under such person's control while at a school building or school function or on school property, a school bus, or other transportation furnished by the school any weapon or explosive compound, other than fireworks the possession of which is regulated by Chapter 10 of Title 25.

(2) Any person who violates this subsection shall be subject to the penalties specified in subsection (b) of this Code section.

(3) This subsection shall not be construed to waive or alter any legal requirement for possession of weapons or firearms otherwise required by law.

(e) It shall be no defense to a prosecution for a violation of this Code section that:

(1) School was or was not in session at the time of the offense;

(2) The real property was being used for other purposes besides school purposes at the time of the offense; or

(3) The offense took place on a school vehicle.

(f) In a prosecution under this Code section, a map produced or reproduced by any municipal or county agency or department for the purpose of depicting the location and boundaries of the area of the real property of a school board or a private or public elementary or secondary school that is used for school purposes or the area of any campus of any public or private technical school, vocational school, college, university, or institution of postsecondary education, or a true copy of the map, shall, if certified as a true copy by the custodian of the record, be admissible and shall constitute prima-facie evidence of the location and boundaries of the area, if the governing body of the municipality or county has approved the map as an official record of the location and boundaries of the area. A map approved under this Code section may be revised from time to time by the governing body of the municipality or county. The original of every map approved or revised under this subsection or a true copy of such original map shall be filed with the municipality or county and shall be maintained as an official record of the municipality or county. This subsection shall not preclude the prosecution from introducing or relying upon any other evidence or testimony to establish any element of this offense. This subsection shall not preclude the use or admissibility of a map or diagram other than the one which has been approved by the municipality or county.

(g) A county school board may adopt regulations requiring the posting of signs designating the areas of school boards and private or public elementary and secondary schools as Weapon-free and Violence-free School Safety Zones.

Laws 1992, p. 1315, § 2; Laws 1994, p. 543, § 1; Laws 1994, p. 547, § 1; Laws 1994, p. 1012, § 4; Laws 1995, p. 10, § 16; Laws 1999, p. 362, § 1; Laws 2000, p. 20, § 6; Laws 2000, p. 1630, § 4; Laws 2003, Act 9, § 16, eff. May 14, 2003; Laws 2008, Act 551, § 3, eff. July 1, 2008; Laws 2008, Act 802, § 5, eff. July 1, 2008; Laws 2009, Act 8, § 16, eff. April 14, 2009; Laws 2010, Act 465, § 2, eff. May 25, 2010; Laws 2010, Act 643, § 1–4, eff. June 4, 2010.

Historical and Statutory Notes

The 2000 amendment by Act 467 rewrote the third sentence of subsec. (b) which formerly provided: "A juvenile who violates this subsection shall be subject to the provisions of Code Section 15–11–37".

The 2000 amendment by Act 924 at the end of the second sentence of subsec. (b) "provided, however, that upon conviction of a violation of this subsection involving a firearm as defined in paragraph (2) of subsection (a) of Code Section 16–11–131, or a dangerous weapon or machine gun as defined in Code Section 16–11–121, such person shall be punished by a fine of not more than $10,000.00 or by imprisonment for a period of not less than five nor more than ten years, or both."

The 2003 amendment by Act 9, in subsec. (c), inserted "Georgia" before "Peace Officer" in par. (4).

The 2008 amendment by Act 551 substituted "knuckles whether made from metal, thermoplastic, wood, or other similar material" for "metal knuckles" and "metal knucks", throughout the section.

The 2008 amendment by Act 802, in subsec. (c), added par. (18), relating to constables.

The 2009 amendment by Act 8 was a provision contained in a correction bill.

The 2010 amendment by Act 465, in subsec (b), replaced "shall" with "may" in the last sentence.

The 2010 amendment by Act 643, in subsec. (a), par. (1), substituted "means in or on any real property" for "means in, on, or within 1,000 feet of any real property" and "secondary education and in or on the campus" for "secondary education and in, on or within 1,000 feet of the campus"; rewrote subsec. (b); in subsec. (c), in par. (7), inserted "a person who is licensed in accordance with Code Section 16–11–129 or issued a permit pursuant to Code Section 43–38–10 when he or she has" and "when such vehicle is parked at such school property or is" and deleted "by any person other than a student" at the end of the paragraph, in par. (8) inserted "possessed by a license holder which is under the possessor's control in a motor vehicle or" ; in subsec. (f), deleted "on or within 1,000 feet" following "location and boundaries of the area" and substituted "the area of any campus" for "within 1,000 feet of any campus"; and in subsec. (g), deleted "within 1,000 feet" preceding "of school boards". Prior to amendment, subsec. (b) had read:

"(b) Except as otherwise provided in subsection (c) of this Code section, it shall be unlawful for any person to carry to or to possess or have under such person's control while within a school safety zone or at a school building, school function, or school property or on a bus or other transportation furnished by the school any weapon or explosive compound, other than fireworks the possession of which is regulated by Chapter 10 of Title 25. Any person who violates this subsection shall be guilty of a felony and, upon conviction thereof, be punished by a fine of not more than $10,000.00, by imprisonment for not less than two nor more than ten years, or both; provided, however, that upon conviction of a violation of this subsection involving a firearm as defined in paragraph (2) of subsection (a) of Code Section 16–11–131, or a dangerous weapon or machine gun as defined in Code Section 16–11–121, such person shall be punished by a fine of not more than $10,000.00 or by imprisonment for a period of not less than five nor more than ten years, or both. A child who violates this subsection may be subject to the provisions of Code Section 15–11–63."

Laws 2010, Act 643, § 3–1, provides:

"This Act shall become effective upon its approval by the Governor or upon its becoming law without such approval and shall apply to all offenses committed on and after such date. The enactment of this Act shall not affect any prosecutions for acts occurring before the effective date of this Act and shall not act as an abatement of any such prosecutions."

§ 16–11–127.2. Possession of weapons on nuclear power facility premises

(a) Except as provided in subsection (c) of this Code section, it shall be unlawful for any person to carry, possess, or have under such person's control while on the premises of a nuclear power facility a weapon or long gun. Any person who violates this subsection shall be guilty of a misdemeanor.

(b) Any person who violates subsection (a) of this Code section with the intent to do bodily harm on the premises of a nuclear power facility shall be guilty of a felony and, upon conviction thereof, shall be punished by a fine of not more than $10,000.00, by imprisonment for not less than two nor more than 20 years, or both.

(c) This Code section shall not apply to a security officer authorized to carry dangerous weapons pursuant to Code Section 16–11–124 who is acting in connection with his or her official duties on the premises of a federally licensed nuclear power facility; nor shall this Code section apply to persons designated in paragraph (3), (4), (5), or (9) of subsection (c) of Code Section 16–11–127.1.

Laws 2006, Act 767, § 2, eff. May 3, 2006; Laws 2007, Act 18, § 16, eff. May 11, 2007; Laws 2010, Act 643, § 1–5, eff. June 4, 2010.

Historical and Statutory Notes

The 2007 amendment by Act 18 was a provision contained in a correction bill.

The 2010 amendment by Act 643, in subsec. (a), deleted "firearm or" following "nuclear power facility".

Laws 2010, Act 643, § 3–1, provides:

"This Act shall become effective upon its approval by the Governor or upon its becoming law without such approval and shall apply to all offenses committed on and after such date. The enactment of this Act shall not affect any prosecutions for acts occurring before the effective date of this Act and shall not act as an abatement of any such prosecutions."

§ 16–11–128. Repealed by Laws 2010, Act 643, § 1–6, eff. June 4, 2010

Historical and Statutory Notes

The repealed section, relating to carrying a pistol without license, was derived from Laws 1910, p. 134, §§ 1, 4; Laws 1968, p. 1249, § 1; Laws 1976, p. 1430, § 3; Laws 1996, p. 108, § 2; Laws 2007, Act 18, § 16; Code 1933, § 26-5103; Code 1933, § 26-2903. The repealing law also reserved the section designation.

§ 16–11–129. License to weapons carry

(a) *Application for weapons carry license or renewal license; term.* The judge of the probate court of each county may, on application under oath and on payment of a fee of $30.00, issue a weapons carry license or renewal license valid for a period of five years to any person whose domicile is in that county or who is on active duty with the United States armed forces and who is not a domiciliary of this state but who either resides in that county or on a military reservation located in whole or in part in that county at the time of such application. Such license or renewal license shall authorize that person to carry any weapon in any county of this state notwithstanding any change in that person's county of residence or state of domicile. Applicants shall submit the application for a weapons carry license or renewal license to the judge of the probate court on forms prescribed and furnished free of charge to persons wishing to apply for the license or renewal license. An applicant who is not a United States citizen shall provide sufficient personal identifying data, including without limitation his or her place of birth and United States issued alien or admission number, as the Georgia Bureau of Investigation may prescribe by rule or regulation. An applicant who is in nonimmigrant status shall provide proof of his or her qualifications for an exception to the federal firearm prohibition pursuant to 18 U.S.C. Section 922(y). Forms shall be designed to elicit information from the applicant pertinent to his or her eligibility under this Code section, including citizenship, but shall not require data which is nonpertinent or irrelevant such as serial numbers or other identification capable of being used as a de facto registration of firearms owned by the applicant. The Department of Public Safety shall furnish application forms and license forms required by this Code section. The forms shall be furnished to each judge of each probate court within the state at no cost.

(b) *Licensing exceptions.*

(1) As used in this subsection, the term:

(A) "Controlled substance" means any drug, substance, or immediate precursor included in the definition of controlled substances in paragraph (4) of Code Section 16–13–21.

(B) "Convicted" means a plea of guilty or a finding of guilt by a court of competent jurisdiction or the acceptance of a plea of nolo contendere, irrespective of the pendency or availability of an appeal or an application for collateral relief.

(C) "Dangerous drug" means any drug defined as such in Code Section 16–13–71.

(2) No weapons carry license shall be issued to:

(A) Any person under 21 years of age;

(B) Any person who has been convicted of a felony by a court of this state or any other state; by a court of the United States including its territories, possessions, and dominions; or by a court of any foreign nation and has not been pardoned for such felony by the President of the United States, the State Board of Pardons and Paroles, or the person or agency empowered to grant pardons under the constitution or laws of such state or nation;

(C) Any person against whom proceedings are pending for any felony;

(D) Any person who is a fugitive from justice;

(E) Any person who is prohibited from possessing or shipping a firearm in interstate commerce pursuant to subsections (g) and (n) of 18 U.S.C. Section 922;

(F) Any person who has been convicted of an offense arising out of the unlawful manufacture or distribution of a controlled substance or other dangerous drug;

(G) Any person who has had his or her weapons carry license revoked pursuant to subsection (e) of this Code section;

(H) Any person who has been convicted of any of the following:

(i) Pointing a gun or a pistol at another in violation of Code Section 16–11–102;

(ii) Carrying a weapon without a weapons carry license in violation of Code Section 16–11–126; or

(iii) Carrying a weapon or long gun in an unauthorized location in violation of Code Section 16–11–127 and has not been free of all restraint or supervision in connection therewith and free of any other conviction for at least five years immediately preceding the date of the application;

(I) Any person who has been convicted of any misdemeanor involving the use or possession of a controlled substance and has not been free of all restraint or supervision in connection therewith or free of:

(i) A second conviction of any misdemeanor involving the use or possession of a controlled substance; or

(ii) Any conviction under subparagraphs (E) through (G) of this paragraph for at least five years immediately preceding the date of the application; or

(J) Any person who has been hospitalized as an inpatient in any mental hospital or alcohol or drug treatment center within the five years immediately preceding the application. The judge of the probate court may require any applicant to sign a waiver authorizing any mental hospital or treatment center to inform the judge whether or not the applicant has been an inpatient in any such facility in the last five years and authorizing the superintendent of such facility to make to the judge a recommendation regarding whether the applicant is a threat to the safety of others and whether a license to carry a weapon should be issued. When such a waiver is required by the judge, the applicant shall pay a fee of $3.00 for reimbursement of the cost of making such a report by the mental health hospital, alcohol or drug treatment center, or the Department of Behavioral Health and Developmental Disabilities, which the judge shall remit to the hospital, center, or department. The judge shall keep any such hospitalization or treatment information confidential. It shall be at the discretion of the judge, considering the circumstances surrounding the hospitalization and the recommendation of the superintendent of the hospital or treatment center where the individual was a patient, to issue the weapons carry license or renewal license.

(3) If first offender treatment without adjudication of guilt for a conviction contained in subparagraph (F) or (I) of paragraph (2) of this subsection was entered and such sentence was successfully completed and such person has not had any other conviction since the completion of such sentence and for at least five years immediately preceding the date of the application, he or she shall be eligible for a weapons carry license provided that no other license exception applies.

(c) *Fingerprinting.*

Following completion of the application for a weapons carry license or the renewal of a license, the judge of the probate court shall require the applicant to proceed to an appropriate law enforcement agency in the county with the completed application. The appropriate local law enforcement agency in each county shall then capture the fingerprints of the applicant for a weapons carry license or renewal license and place the name of the applicant on the blank license form. The appropriate local law enforcement agency shall place the fingerprint on a blank license form which has been furnished to the law enforcement agency by the judge of the probate court if a fingerprint is required to be furnished by subsection (f) of this Code section. The law enforcement agency shall be entitled to a fee of $5. 00 from the applicant for its services in connection with the application.

(d) *Investigation of applicant; issuance of weapons carry license; renewal.*

(1) For both weapons carry license applications and requests for license renewals, the judge of the probate court shall within five days following the receipt of the application or request direct the law enforcement agency to request a fingerprint based criminal history records check from the Georgia Crime Information Center and Federal Bureau of Investigation for purposes of determining the suitability of the applicant and return an appropriate report to the judge of the probate court. Fingerprints shall be in such form and of such quality as prescribed by the Georgia Crime Information Center and under standards adopted by the Federal Bureau of Investigation. The Georgia Bureau of Investigation may charge such fee as is necessary to cover the cost of the records search.

(2) For both weapons carry license applications and requests for license renewals, the judge of the probate court shall within five days following the receipt of the application or request also direct the law enforcement agency to conduct a background check using the Federal Bureau of Investigation's National Instant Criminal Background Check System and return an appropriate report to the probate judge.

(3) When a person who is not a United States citizen applies for a weapons carry license or renewal of a license under this Code section, the judge of the probate court shall direct the law enforcement agency to conduct a search of the records maintained by the United States Bureau of Immigration and Customs Enforcement and return an appropriate report to the probate judge. As a condition to the issuance of a license or the renewal of a license, an applicant who is in nonimmigrant status shall provide proof of his or her qualifications for an exception to the federal firearm prohibition pursuant to 18 U.S.C. Section 922(y).

(4) The law enforcement agency shall report to the judge of the probate court within 30 days, by telephone and in writing, of any findings relating to the applicant which may bear on his or her eligibility for a weapons carry license or renewal license under the terms of this Code section. When no derogatory information is found on the applicant bearing on his or her eligibility to obtain a license or renewal license, a report shall not be required. The law enforcement agency shall return the application and the blank license form with the fingerprint thereon directly to the judge of the probate court within such time period. Not later than ten days after the judge of the probate court receives the report from the law enforcement agency concerning the suitability of the applicant for a license, the judge of the probate court shall issue such applicant a license or renewal license to carry any weapon unless facts establishing ineligibility have been reported or unless the judge determines such applicant has not met all the qualifications, is not of good moral character, or has failed to comply with any of the requirements contained in this Code section. The judge of the probate court shall date stamp the report from the law enforcement agency to show the date on which the report was received by the judge of the probate court.

(e) *Revocation, loss, or damage to license.* If, at any time during the period for which the weapons carry license was issued, the judge of the probate court of the county in which the license was issued shall learn or have brought to his or her attention in any manner any reasonable ground to believe the licensee is not eligible to retain the license, the judge may, after notice and hearing, revoke the license of the person upon a finding that such person is not eligible for a weapons carry license pursuant to subsection (b) of this Code section or an adjudication of falsification of application, mental incompetency, or chronic alcohol or narcotic usage. It shall be unlawful for any person to possess a license which has been revoked, and any person found in possession of any such revoked license, except in the performance of his or her official duties, shall be guilty of a misdemeanor. It shall be required that any license holder under this Code section have in his or her possession his or her valid license whenever he or she is carrying a weapon under the authority granted by this Code section, and his or her failure to do so shall be prima-facie evidence of a violation of Code Section 16–11–126. Loss of any license issued in accordance with this Code section or damage to the license in any manner which shall render it illegible shall be reported to the judge of the probate court of the county in which it was issued within 48 hours of the time the loss or damage becomes known to the license holder. The judge of the probate court shall thereupon issue a replacement for and shall take custody of and destroy a damaged license; and in any case in which a license has been lost, he or she shall issue a cancellation order and notify by telephone and in writing each of the law enforcement agencies whose records were checked before issuance of the original license. The judge shall charge the fee specified in subsection (k) of Code Section 15–9–60 for such services.

(f)(1) *Weapons carry license specifications.* Weapons carry licenses issued as prescribed in this Code section shall be printed on durable but lightweight card stock, and the completed card shall be laminated in plastic to improve its wearing qualities and to inhibit alterations. Measurements shall be 3 1/4 inches long and 2 1/4 inches wide. Each shall be serially numbered within the county of issuance and shall bear the full name, residential address, birth date, weight, height, color of eyes, and sex of the licensee. The license shall show the date of issuance, the expiration date, and the probate court in which issued and shall be signed by the licensee and bear the signature or facsimile thereof of the judge. The seal of the court shall be placed on the face before the license is laminated. Licenses issued on and before December 31, 2011, shall bear a clear print of the licensee's right index finger; however, if the right index fingerprint cannot be secured for any reason, the print of another finger may be used but such print shall be marked to identify the finger from which the print is taken.

(2)(A) On and after January 1, 2012, newly issued or renewal weapons carry licenses shall incorporate overt and covert security features which shall be blended with the personal data printed on the license to form a significant barrier to imitation, replication, and duplication. There shall be a minimum of three different ultraviolet colors used to enhance the security of the license incorporating variable data, color shifting characteristics, and front edge only perimeter visibility. The weapons carry license shall have a color photograph viewable under ambient light on both the front and back of the license. The license shall incorporate custom optical variable devices featuring the great seal of the State of Georgia as well as matching demetalized optical variable devices viewable under ambient light from the front and back of the license incorporating microtext and unique alphanumeric serialization specific to the license holder. The license shall be of similar material, size, and thickness of a credit card and have a holographic laminate to secure and protect the license for the duration of the license period.

(B) Using the physical characteristics of the license set forth in subparagraph (A) of this paragraph, The Council of Probate Court Judges of Georgia shall create specifications for the probate courts so that all weapons carry licenses in this state shall be uniform and so that probate courts can petition the Department of Administrative Services to purchase the equipment and supplies necessary for producing such licenses. The department shall follow the competitive bidding procedure set forth in Code Section 50–5–102.

(g) *Alteration or counterfeiting of license; penalty.* A person who deliberately alters or counterfeits a weapons carry license or who possesses an altered or counterfeit weapons carry license with the intent to misrepresent any information contained in such license shall be guilty of a felony and, upon conviction thereof, shall be punished by imprisonment for a period of not less than one nor more than five years.

(h) *Licenses for former law enforcement officers.* Except as otherwise provided in Code Section 16–11–130, any person who has served as a law enforcement officer for at least ten of the 12 years immediately preceding the retirement of such person as a law enforcement officer shall be entitled to be issued a weapons carry license as provided for in this Code section without the payment of any of the fees provided for in this Code section. Such person shall comply with all the other provisions of this Code section relative to the issuance of such licenses. As used in this subsection, the term "law enforcement officer" means any peace officer who is employed by the United States government or by the State of Georgia or any political subdivision thereof and who is required by the terms of his or her employment, whether by election or appointment, to give his or her full time to the preservation of public order or the protection of life and property or the prevention of crime. Such term shall include conservation rangers.

(i) *Temporary renewal licenses.*

(1) Any person who holds a weapons carry license under this Code section may, at the time he or she applies for a renewal of the license, also apply for a temporary renewal license if less than 90 days remain before expiration of the license he or she then holds or if the previous license has expired within the last 30 days.

(2) Unless the judge of the probate court knows or is made aware of any fact which would make the applicant ineligible for a five-year renewal license, the judge shall at the time of application issue a temporary renewal license to the applicant.

(3) Such a temporary renewal license shall be in the form of a paper receipt indicating the date on which the court received the renewal application and shall show the name, address, sex, age, and race of the applicant and that the temporary renewal license expires 90 days from the date of issue.

(4) During its period of validity the temporary renewal permit, if carried on or about the holder's person together with the holder's previous license, shall be valid in the same manner and for the same purposes as a five-year license.

(5) A $1.00 fee shall be charged by the probate court for issuance of a temporary renewal license.

(6) A temporary renewal license may be revoked in the same manner as a five-year license.

(j) When an eligible applicant fails to receive a license, temporary permit, or renewal license within the time period required by this Code section and the application or request has been properly filed, the applicant may bring an action in mandamus or other legal proceeding in order to obtain a license, temporary license, or renewal license. If such applicant is the prevailing party, he or she shall be entitled to recover his or her costs in such action, including reasonable attorney's fees.

Laws 1910, p. 134, §§ 2, 3; Laws 1960, p. 938, § 1; Laws 1968, p. 1249, § 1; Laws 1976, p. 1430, § 4; Laws 1978, p. 1607, §§ 1, 2; Laws 1981, p. 946, § 1; Laws 1981, p. 1325, § 1; Laws 1983, p. 1431, § 1; Laws 1984, p. 935, § 1; Laws 1984, p. 1388, § 1; Laws 1986, p. 305, § 1; Laws 1986, p. 481, §§ 1, 2; Laws 1990, p. 138, § 1; Laws 1990, p. 2012, § 1; Laws 1992, p. 6, § 16; Laws 1994, p. 351, § 1; Laws 1996, p. 108, §§ 3–5; Laws 1997, p. 514, § 2; Laws 2002, p. 1011, § 2; Laws 2006, Act 534, § 1, eff. July 1, 2006; Laws 2008, Act 802, § 6, eff. July 1, 2008; Laws 2009, Act 102, § 3–2, eff. July 1, 2009; Laws 2010, Act 643, § 1–7, eff. June 4, 2010.

Formerly Code 1933, §§ 26–5104, 26–5105; Code 1933, § 26–2904.

Historical and Statutory Notes

The 2002 amendment inserted gender neutral language in subsecs. (b) and (e), inserted the third sentence in subsec. (b)(4), and substituted at the end of subsec. (e) for "A fee of $3.00 shall be charged by the judge for such services." A sentence providing "The judge shall charge the fee specified in subsection (k) of Code Section 15–9–60for such services."

The 2006 amendment by Act 534 rewrote subsec. (a); in subsecs. (b) and (c), inserted "or renewal license" following "license" throughout; in subsec. (b), redesignated par. (1) as par. (1.1), inserted a new par. (1), added par, (6), and made nonsubstantive changes to pars. (4) and (5); in subsec. (c), deleted the designation for par. (1), inserted "for a license or the renewal of a license", substituted "capture the" for "make two sets of classifiable", and deleted pars. (2) and (3); and rewrote subsec. (d). Prior to amendment, subsec. (a), pars. (c)(2), (c)(3), and subsec. (d) had read:

"(a) *Application for license; term.* The judge of the probate court of each county may, on application under oath and on payment of a fee of $ 15.00, issue a license valid for a period of five years to any person whose domicile is in that county or who is on active duty with the United States armed forces and who is not a domiciliary of this state but who either resides in that county or on a military reservation located in whole or in part in that county at the time of such application, which license shall authorize that person to carry any pistol or revolver in any county of this state notwithstanding any change in that person's county of residence or state of domicile. Applicants shall submit the application for a license to the judge of the probate court on forms prescribed and furnished free of charge to persons wishing to apply for the license. Forms shall be designed to elicit information from the applicant pertinent to his or her eligibility under this Code section but shall not require data which is nonpertinent or irrelevant such as serial numbers or other identification capable of being used as a de facto registration of firearms owned by the applicant. The Department of Public Safety shall furnish application forms and license forms required by this Code section. The forms shall be furnished to each judge of each probate court within the state at no cost."

"[(c)](2) In the case of each applicant who is applying for a license under this Code section for the first time, the judge of the probate court shall direct the law enforcement agency to transmit one set of the applicant's fingerprints to the Georgia Crime Information Center for a search of the Federal Bureau of Investigation records and an appropriate report. In such cases, the applicant shall submit an additional fee in an amount established by the Georgia Bureau of Investigation but not to exceed $ 30.00 for a search of records of the Federal Bureau of Investigation and an appropriate report, payable in such form as the judge may direct, to cover the cost of the records search.

"(3) Applications for renewal of licenses issued under this Code section shall be made to the judge of the probate court of the county in which the applicant is domiciled or, if the applicant is a member of the United States armed forces, the county in which he or she resides or in which the military reservation on which the applicant resides is located in whole or in part at the time of making the renewal application. In the case of an applicant for a renewal of a license, the judge of the probate court may, in his or her discretion, direct that the local county law enforcement agency request a search of the criminal history file and wanted persons file of the Georgia Crime Information Center by computer access from that county in lieu of transmitting the application and forms.

"(d) *Investigation of applicant; issuance of license.* Each law enforcement agency, upon receiving such applications and obtaining such fingerprints, shall promptly conduct a thorough search of its records and records to which it has access and shall notify the judge of the probate court within 50 days, by telephone and in writing, of any findings relating to the applicant which may bear on his eligibility for a license under the terms of this Code section. When no derogatory information is found on the applicant bearing on his eligibility to obtain a license, a report shall not be required. The law enforcement agency shall return the application and the blank license form with the fingerprint thereon directly to the judge of the probate court within such time period. Not later than 60 days after the date of the application the judge of the probate court shall issue the applicant a license to carry any pistol or revolver if no facts establishing ineligibility have been reported and if the judge determines the applicant has met all the qualifications, is of good moral character, and has complied with all the requirements contained in this Code section."

The 2008 amendment by Act 802 rewrote subsec. (d), and added subsec. (j), relating to actions in mandamus to obtain a license. Prior to revision subsec. (d) read:

"(d) *Investigation of applicant; issuance of license; renewal.*

"(1) For both license applications and requests for license renewals, the judge of the probate court shall direct the law enforcement agency to request a fingerprint based criminal history records check from the Georgia Crime Information Center and Federal Bureau of Investigation for purposes of determining the suitability of the applicant and return an appropriate report to the judge of the probate court. Fingerprints shall be in such form and of such quality as prescribed by the Georgia Crime Information Center and under standards adopted by the Federal Bureau of Investigation. The Georgia Bureau of Investigation may charge such fee as is necessary to cover the cost of the records search.

"(2) For both license applications and requests for license renewals, the judge of the probate court shall also direct the law enforcement agency to conduct a background check using the Federal Bureau of Investigation's National Instant Criminal Background Check System and return an appropriate report to the probate judge.

"(3) When a person who is not a United States citizen applies for a license or renewal of a license under this Code section, the judge of the probate court shall direct the law enforcement agency to conduct a search of the records maintained by the United States Bureau of Immigration and Customs Enforcement. As a condition to the issuance of a license or the renewal of a license, an applicant who is in nonimmigrant status shall provide proof of his or her qualifications for an exception to the federal firearm prohibition pursuant to 18 U.S.C. Section 922(y).

"(4) The law enforcement agency shall notify the judge of the probate court within 50 days, by telephone and in writing, of any findings relating to the applicant which may bear on his or her eligibility for a license or renewal license under the terms of this Code section. When no derogatory information is found on the applicant bearing on his or her eligibility to obtain a license or renewal license, a report shall not be required. The law enforcement agency shall return the application and the blank license form with the fingerprint thereon directly to the judge of the probate court within such time period. Not later than 60 days after the date of the application the judge of the probate court shall issue the applicant a license or renewal license to carry any pistol or revolver if no facts establishing ineligibility have been reported and if the judge determines the applicant has met all the qualifications, is of good moral character, and has complied with all the requirements contained in this Code section."

The 2009 amendment by Act 102 substituted "Department of Behavioral Health and Developmental Disabilities" for "Department of Human Resources" throughout the section.

The 2010 amendment by Act 643 rewrote the section which had read:

"(a) *Application for license or renewal license; term.* The judge of the probate court of each county may, on application under oath and on payment of a fee of $15.00, issue a license or renewal license valid for a period of five years to any person whose domicile is in that county or who is on active duty with the United States armed forces and who is not a domiciliary of this state but who either resides in that county or on a military reservation located in whole or in part in that county at the time of such application, which license or renewal license shall authorize that person to carry any pistol or revolver in any county of this state notwithstanding any change in that person's county of residence or state of domicile. Applicants shall submit the application for a license or renewal license to the judge of the probate court on forms prescribed and furnished free of charge to persons wishing to apply for the license or renewal license. An applicant who is not a United States citizen shall provide sufficient personal identifying data, including without limitation his or her place of birth and United States issued alien or admission number, as the Georgia Bureau of Investigation may prescribe by rule or regulation. An applicant who is in nonimmigrant status shall provide proof of his or her qualifications for an exception to the federal firearm prohibition pursuant to 18 U.S.C. Section 922(y). Forms shall be designed to elicit information from the applicant pertinent to his or her eligibility under this Code section, including citizenship, but shall not require data which is nonpertinent or irrelevant such as serial numbers or other identification capable of being used as a de facto registration of firearms owned by the applicant. The Department of Public Safety shall furnish application forms and license forms required by this Code section. The forms shall be furnished to each judge of each probate court within the state at no cost.

"(b) *Licensing exceptions.* No license or renewal license shall be granted to:

"(1) Any person who is prohibited from possessing firearms pursuant to 18 U.S.C. Section 922;

"(1.1) Any person under 21 years of age;

"(2) Any person who is a fugitive from justice or against whom proceedings are pending for any felony, forcible misdemeanor, or violation of Code Section 16–11–126, 16–11–127, or 16–11–128 until such time as the proceedings are adjudicated;

"(3) Any person who has been convicted of a felony by a court of this state or any other state; by a court of the United States including its territories, possessions, and dominions; or by a court of any foreign nation and has not been pardoned for such felony by the President of the United States, the State Board of Pardons and Paroles, or the person or agency empowered to grant pardons under the constitution or laws of such state or nation or any person who has been convicted of a forcible misdemeanor and has not been free of all restraint or supervision in connection therewith for at least five years or any person who has been convicted of a violation of Code Section 16–11–126, 16–11–127, or 16–11–128 and has not been free of all restraint or supervision in connection therewith for at least three years, immediately preceding the date of the application;

"(4) Any individual who has been hospitalized as an inpatient in any mental hospital or alcohol or drug treatment center within five years of the date of his or her application. The probate judge may require any applicant to sign a waiver authorizing any mental hospital or treatment center to inform the judge whether or not the applicant has been an inpatient in any such facility in the last five years and authorizing the superintendent of such facility to make to the judge a recommendation regarding whether a license to carry a pistol or revolver should be issued. When such a waiver is required by the probate judge, the applicant shall pay to the probate judge a fee of $3.00 for reimbursement of the cost of making such a report by the mental health hospital, alcohol or drug treatment center, or the Department of Behavioral Health and Developmental Disabilities, which the probate judge shall remit to the hospital, center, or department. The judge shall keep any such hospitalization or treatment information confidential. It shall be at the discretion of the probate judge, considering the circumstances surrounding the hospitalization and the recommendation of the superintendent of the hospital or treatment center where the individual was a patient, to issue the license or renewal license;

"(5)(A) Any person, the provisions of paragraph (3) of this subsection notwithstanding, who has been convicted of an offense arising out of the unlawful manufacture, distribution, possession, or use of a controlled substance or other dangerous drug.

"(B) As used in this paragraph, the term:

"(i) 'Controlled substance' means any drug, substance, or immediate precursor included in the definition of controlled substances in paragraph (4) of Code Section 16–13–21.

"(ii) 'Convicted' means a plea of guilty, a finding of guilt by a court of competent jurisdiction, the acceptance of a plea of nolo contendere, or the affording of first offender treatment by a court of competent jurisdiction irrespective of the pendency or availability of an appeal or an application for collateral relief.

"(iii) 'Dangerous drug' means any drug defined as such in Code Section 16–13–71; or

"(6) Any person not lawfully present in the United States.

"(c) *Fingerprinting.*

"Following completion of the application for a license or the renewal of a license, the judge of the probate court shall require the applicant to proceed to an appropriate law enforcement agency in the county with the completed application. The appropriate local law enforcement agency in each county shall then capture the fingerprints of the applicant for a license or renewal license to carry a pistol or revolver, place the fingerprint required by subsection (f) of this Code section on a blank license form which has been furnished to the law enforcement agency by the judge of the probate court, and place the name of the applicant on the blank license form. The law enforcement agency shall be entitled to a fee of $5.00 from the applicant for its services in connection with the application.

"(d) *Investigation of applicant; issuance of license; renewal.*

"(1) For both license applications and requests for license renewals, the judge of the probate court shall within two business days following the receipt of the application or request direct the law enforcement agency to request a fingerprint based criminal history records check from the Georgia Crime Information Center and Federal Bureau of Investigation for purposes of determining the suitability of the applicant and return an appropriate report to the judge of the probate court. Fingerprints shall be in such form and of such quality as prescribed by the Georgia Crime Information Center and under standards adopted by the Federal Bureau of Investigation. The Georgia Bureau of Investigation may charge such fee as is necessary to cover the cost of the records search.

"(2) For both license applications and requests for license renewals, the judge of the probate court shall within two business days following the receipt of the application or request also direct the law enforcement agency to conduct a background check using the Federal Bureau of Investigation's National Instant Criminal Background Check System and return an appropriate report to the probate judge.

"(3) When a person who is not a United States citizen applies for a license or renewal of a license under this Code section, the judge of the probate court shall direct the law enforcement agency to conduct a search of the records maintained by the United States Bureau of Immigration and Customs Enforcement. As a condition to the issuance of a license or the renewal of a license, an applicant who is in nonimmigrant status shall provide proof of his or her qualifications for an exception to the federal firearm prohibition pursuant to 18 U.S.C. Section 922(y).

"(4) The law enforcement agency shall report to the judge of the probate court within 30 days, by telephone and in writing, of any findings relating to the applicant which may bear on his or her eligibility for a license or renewal license under the terms of this Code section. When no derogatory information is found on the applicant bearing on his or her eligibility to obtain a license or renewal license, a report shall not be required. The law enforcement agency shall return the application and the blank license form with the fingerprint thereon directly to the judge of the probate court within such time period. Not later than ten days after the judge of the probate court receives the report from the law enforcement agency concerning the suitability of the applicant for a firearms license, the judge of the probate court shall issue such applicant a license or renewal license to carry any pistol or revolver unless facts establishing ineligibility have been reported or unless the judge determines such applicant has not met all the qualifications, is not of good moral character, or has failed to comply with any of the requirements contained in this Code section. The judge of the probate court shall date stamp the report from the law enforcement agency to show the date on which the report was received by the judge of the probate court.

"(e) *Revocation, loss, or damage to license.* If, at any time during the period for which the license was issued, the judge of the probate court of the county in which the license was issued shall learn or have brought to his or her attention in any manner any reasonable ground to believe the licensee is not eligible to retain the license, the judge may, after notice and hearing, revoke the license of the person upon adjudication of falsification of application, mental incompetency, chronic alcohol or narcotic usage, conviction of any felony or forcible misdemeanor, or for violation of Code Section 16–11–126, 16–11–127, or 16–11–128. It shall be unlawful for any person to possess a license which has been revoked, and any person found in possession of any such revoked license, except in the performance of his or her official duties, shall be guilty of a misdemeanor. It shall be required that any license holder under this Code section have in his or her possession his or her valid license whenever he or she is carrying a pistol or revolver under the authority granted by this Code section, and his or her failure to do so shall be prima-facie evidence of a violation of Code Section 16–11–128. Loss of any license issued in accordance with this Code section or damage to the license in any manner which shall render it illegible shall be reported to the judge of the probate court of the county in which it was issued within 48 hours of the time the loss or damage becomes known to the license holder. The judge of the probate court shall thereupon issue a replacement for and shall take custody of and destroy a damaged license; and in any case in which a license has been lost, he or she shall issue a cancellation order and notify by telephone and in writing each of the law enforcement agencies whose records were checked before issuance of the original license. The judge shall charge the fee specified in subsection (k) of Code Section 15–9–60 for such services.

"(f) *License specifications.* Licenses issued as prescribed in this Code section shall be printed on durable but lightweight card stock, and the completed card shall be laminated in plastic to improve its wearing qualities and to inhibit alterations. Measurements shall be 3 1/4 inches long, and 2 1/4 inches wide. Each shall be serially numbered within the county of issuance and shall bear the full name, residential address, birth date, weight, height, color of eyes, sex, and a clear print of the right index finger of the licensee. If the right index fingerprint cannot be secured for any reason, the print of another finger may be used but such print shall be marked to identify the finger from which the print is taken. The license shall show the date of issuance, the expiration date, and the probate court in which issued and shall be signed by the licensee and bear the signature or facsimile thereof of the judge. The seal of the court shall be placed on the face before the license is laminated. The reverse side of the license shall have imprinted thereon in its entirety Code Section 16–11–127.

"(g) *Alteration or counterfeiting of license; penalty.* A person who deliberately alters or counterfeits such a license card commits a felony and, upon conviction thereof, shall be punished by imprisonment for a period of not less than one nor more than five years.

"(h) *Licenses for former law enforcement officers.* Except as otherwise provided in Code Section 16–11–130, any person who has served as a law enforcement officer for at least ten of the 12 years immediately preceding the retirement of such person as a law enforcement officer shall be entitled to be issued a license as provided for in this Code section without the payment of any of the fees provided for in this Code section. Such person must comply with all the other provisions of this Code section relative to the issuance of such licenses. As used in this subsection, the term 'law enforcement officer' means any peace officer who is employed by the United States government or by the State of Georgia or any political subdivision thereof and who is required by the terms of his or her employment, whether by election or appointment, to give his or her full time to the preservation of public order or the protection of life and property or the prevention of crime. Such term shall include conservation rangers.

"(i) *Temporary renewal licenses.*

"(1) Any person who holds a license under this Code section to carry a pistol or revolver may, at the time he applies for a renewal of the license, also apply for a temporary renewal license if less than 90 days remain before expiration of the license he then holds or if his previous license has expired within the last 30 days.

"(2) Unless the judge of the probate court knows or is made aware of any fact which would make the applicant ineligible for a five-year renewal license, the judge shall at the time of application issue a temporary renewal license to the applicant.

"(3) Such a temporary renewal license shall be in the form of a paper receipt indicating the date on which the court received the renewal application and shall show the name, address, sex, age, and race of the applicant and that the temporary renewal license expires 90 days from the date of issue.

"(4) During its period of validity the temporary renewal permit, if carried on or about the holder's person together with the holder's previous license, shall be valid in the same manner and for the same purposes as a five-year license.

"(5) A $ 1.00 fee shall be charged by the probate court for issuance of a temporary renewal license.

"(6) A temporary renewal license may be revoked in the same manner as a five-year license.

"(j) When an eligible applicant who is a United States citizen fails to receive a license, temporary permit, or renewal license within the time period required by this Code section and the application or request has been properly filed, the applicant may bring an action in mandamus or other legal proceeding in order to obtain a license, temporary license, or renewal license, and such applicant shall be entitled to recover his or her costs in such action, including reasonable attorney's fees."

Laws 2010, Act 643, § 3–1, provides:

"This Act shall become effective upon its approval by the Governor or upon its becoming law without such approval and shall apply to all offenses committed on and after such date. The enactment of this Act shall not affect any prosecutions for acts occurring before the effective date of this Act and shall not act as an abatement of any such prosecutions."

§ 16–11–130. Exemptions

(a) Code Sections 16–11–126 through 16–11–127.2 shall not apply to or affect any of the following persons if such persons are employed in the offices listed below or when authorized by federal or state law, regulations, or order:

(1) Peace officers, as such term is defined in paragraph (11) of Code Section 16–1–3, and retired peace officers so long as they remain certified whether employed by the state or a political subdivision of the state or another state or a political subdivision of another state but only if such other state provides a similar privilege for the peace officers of this state;

(2) Wardens, superintendents, and keepers of correctional institutions, jails, or other institutions for the detention of persons accused or convicted of an offense;

(3) Persons in the military service of the state or of the United States;

(4) Persons employed in fulfilling defense contracts with the government of the United States or agencies thereof when possession of the weapon or long gun is necessary for manufacture, transport, installation, and testing under the requirements of such contract;

(5) District attorneys, investigators employed by and assigned to a district attorney's office, assistant district attorneys, attorneys or investigators employed by the Prosecuting Attorneys' Council of the State of Georgia, and any retired district attorney, assistant district attorney, district attorney"s investigator, or attorney or investigator retired from the Prosecuting Attorneys' Council of the State of Georgia, if such employee is retired in good standing and is receiving benefits under Title 47 or is retired in good standing and receiving benefits from a county or municipal retirement system;

(6) State court solicitors-general; investigators employed by and assigned to a state court solicitor-general's office; assistant state court solicitors-general; the corresponding personnel of any city court expressly continued in existence as a city court pursuant to Article VI, Section X, Paragraph I, subparagraph (5) of the Constitution; and the corresponding personnel of any civil court expressly continued as a civil court pursuant to said provision of the Constitution;

(7) Those employees of the State Board of Pardons and Paroles when specifically designated and authorized in writing by the members of the State Board of Pardons and Paroles to carry a weapon or long gun;

(8) The Attorney General and those members of his or her staff whom he or she specifically authorizes in writing to carry a weapon or long gun;

(9) Chief probation officers, probation officers, intensive probation officers, and surveillance officers employed by and under the authority of the Department of Corrections pursuant to Article 2 of Chapter 8 of Title 42, known as the State-wide Probation Act, when specifically designated and authorized in writing by the director of Division of Probation;

(10) Public safety directors of municipal corporations;

(11) Explosive ordnance disposal technicians, as such term is defined by Code Section 16–7–80, and persons certified as provided in Code Section 35–8–13 to handle animals trained to detect explosives, while in the performance of their duties;

(12) State and federal trial and appellate judges, full-time and permanent part-time judges of municipal and city courts, and former state trial and appellate judges retired from their respective offices under state retirement;

(13) United States Attorneys and Assistant United States Attorneys;

(14) County medical examiners and coroners and their sworn officers employed by county government; and

(15) Clerks of the superior courts.

(b) Code Sections 16–11–126 through 16–11–127.2 shall not apply to or affect persons who at the time of their retirement from service with the Department of Corrections were chief probation officers, probation officers, intensive probation officers, or surveillance officers, when specifically designated and authorized in writing by the director of the Division of Probation.

(c) Code Sections 16–11–126 through 16–11–127.2 shall not apply to or affect any:

(1) Sheriff, retired sheriff, deputy sheriff, or retired deputy sheriff if such retired sheriff or deputy sheriff is eligible to receive or is receiving benefits under the Peace Officers' Annuity and Benefit Fund provided under Chapter 17 of Title 47, the Sheriffs' Retirement Fund of Georgia provided under Chapter 16 of Title 47, or any other public retirement system established under the laws of this state for service as a law enforcement officer;

(2) Member of the Georgia State Patrol or agent of the Georgia Bureau of Investigation or retired member of the Georgia State Patrol or agent of the Georgia Bureau of Investigation if such retired member or agent is receiving benefits under the Employees' Retirement System;

(3) Full-time law enforcement chief executive engaging in the management of a county, municipal, state, state authority, or federal law enforcement agency in the State of Georgia, including any college or university law enforcement chief executive that is registered or certified by the Georgia Peace Officer Standards and Training Council; or retired law enforcement chief executive that formerly managed a county, municipal, state, state authority, or federal law enforcement agency in the State of Georgia, including any college or university law enforcement chief executive that was registered or certified at the time of his or her retirement by the Georgia Peace Officer Standards and Training Council, if such retired law enforcement chief executive is receiving benefits under the Peace Officers' Annuity and Benefit Fund provided under Chapter 17 of Title 47 or is retired in good standing and receiving benefits from a county, municipal, State of Georgia, state authority, or federal retirement system; or

(4) Police officer of any county, municipal, state, state authority, or federal law enforcement agency in the State of Georgia, including any college or university police officer that is registered or certified by the Georgia Peace Officer Standards and Training Council, or retired police officer of any county, municipal, state, state authority, or federal law enforcement agency in the State of Georgia, including any college or university police officer that was registered or certified at the time of his or her retirement by the Georgia Peace Officer Standards and Training Council, if such retired employee is receiving benefits under the Peace Officers' Annuity and Benefit Fund provided under Chapter 17 of Title 47 or is retired in

good standing and receiving benefits from a county, municipal, State of Georgia, state authority, or federal retirement system.

In addition, any such sheriff, retired sheriff, deputy sheriff, retired deputy sheriff, active or retired law enforcement chief executive, or other law enforcement officer referred to in this subsection shall be authorized to carry a handgun on or off duty anywhere within the state and the provisions of Code Sections 16–11–126 through 16–11–127.2 shall not apply to the carrying of such firearms.

(d) A prosecution based upon a violation of Code Section 16–11–126 or 16–11–127 need not negative any exemptions.

Laws 1968, p. 1249, § 1; Laws 1974, p. 481, § 1; Laws 1979, p. 1019, § 1; Laws 1982, p. 3, § 16; Laws 1982, p. 789, § 2; Laws 1984, p. 22, § 16; Laws 1985, p. 283, § 1; Laws 1986, p. 1205, § 2; Laws 1988, p. 472, § 1; Laws 1990, p. 558, § 1; Laws 1991, p. 94, § 16; Laws 1993, p. 604, § 1; Laws 1994, p. 547, § 2; Laws 1996, p. 416, § 6; Laws 1996, p. 748, § 12; Laws 1997, p. 514, § 3; Laws 1998, p. 657, §§ 1–3; Laws 2000, p. 843, §§ 1, 2; Laws 2003, Act 9, § 16, eff. May 14, 2003; Laws 2006, Act 623, § 1, eff. July 1, 2006; Laws 2008, Act 564, § 16, eff. July 1, 2008; Laws 2010, Act 643, § 2–7, eff. June 4, 2010.

Formerly Code 1933, § 26–2907.

Historical and Statutory Notes

The 2000 amendment substituted in subsec. (a)(5) "attorneys employed by the Prosecuting Attorneys' Council of Georgia, and any retired district attorney, assistant district attorney, or district attorneys investigator if such retired employee is receiving benefits under Title 47 or is retired in good standing and receiving benefits from a county or municipal retirement system" for and district attorneys emeritus", and in subsec. (a)(12) substituted for "and full-time judges of municipal and city courts" the words ", full-time judges of municipal and city courts, and former state trial and appellate judges retired from their respective offices under state retirement".

The 2003 amendment by Act 9, in subsec. (c), inserted "Georgia" before "Peace Officer" throughout pars. (3) and (4).

The 2006 amendment by Act 623 inserted "and permanent part-time" in par. (a)(12).

The 2008 amendment by Act 564, in subsec. (a), rewrote par. (5), which formerly read:

"(5) District attorneys, investigators employed by and assigned to a district attorney's office, assistant district attorneys, attorneys employed by the Prosecuting Attorneys' Council of Georgia, and any retired district attorney, assistant district attorney, or district attorneys investigator if such retired employee is receiving benefits under Title 47 or is retired in good standing and receiving benefits from a county or municipal retirement system;".

The 2010 amendment by Act 643, in subsec. (a), substituted "16–11–127.2" for "16–11–128" in the introductory paragraph, and substituted "attorney's" for "attorneys" in par. (5); in subsec. (b), substituted "16–11–127.2" for "16–11–128" and inserted "the" preceding "Division of Probation"; in subsec. (c), substituted "16–11–127.2" for "16–11–128" in the introductory paragraph, inserted "sheriff or", "eligible to receive or is", and ", the Sheriffs' Retirement Fund of Georgia provided under Chapter 16 of Title 47, or any other public retirement system established under the laws of this state for service as a law enforcement officer" in par. (1), and substituted "handgun" for "pistol or revolver" and "16–11–127.2" for "16–11–128" in the final undesignated paragraph; and in subsec. (d), substituted "16–11–126 or 16–11–127 " for "16–11–126, 16–11–127, or 16–11–128".

Laws 2010, Act 643, § 3–1, provides:

"This Act shall become effective upon its approval by the Governor or upon its becoming law without such approval and shall apply to all offenses committed on and after such date. The enactment of this Act shall not affect any prosecutions for acts occurring before the effective date of this Act and shall not act as an abatement of any such prosecutions."

§ 16–11–131. Convicted felons, possession of firearms prohibited

(a) As used in this Code section, the term:

(1) "Felony" means any offense punishable by imprisonment for a term of one year or more and includes conviction by a court-martial under the Uniform Code of Military Justice for an offense which would constitute a felony under the laws of the United States.

(2) "Firearm" includes any handgun, rifle, shotgun, or other weapon which will or can be converted to expel a projectile by the action of an explosive or electrical charge.

(b) Any person who is on probation as a felony first offender pursuant to Article 3 of Chapter 8 of Title 42 or who has been convicted of a felony by a court of this state or any other state; by a court of the United States including its territories, possessions, and dominions; or by a court of any foreign nation and who receives, possesses, or transports any firearm commits a felony and, upon conviction thereof, shall be imprisoned for not less than one nor more than five years; provided, however, that if the felony as to which the person is on probation or has been previously convicted is a forcible felony, then upon conviction of receiving, possessing, or transporting a firearm, such person shall be imprisoned for a period of five years.

(b.1) Any person who is prohibited by this Code section from possessing a firearm because of conviction of a forcible felony or because of being on probation as a first offender for a forcible felony pursuant to this Code section and who attempts to purchase or obtain transfer of a firearm shall be guilty of a felony and shall be punished by imprisonment for not less than one nor more than five years.

(c) This Code section shall not apply to any person who has been pardoned for the felony by the President of the United States, the State Board of Pardons and Paroles, or the person or agency empowered to grant pardons under the constitutions or laws of the several states or of a foreign nation and, by the terms of the pardon, has expressly been authorized to receive, possess, or transport a firearm.

(d) A person who has been convicted of a felony, but who has been granted relief from the disabilities imposed by the laws of the United States with respect to the acquisition, receipt, transfer, shipment, or possession of firearms by the secretary of the United States Department of the Treasury pursuant to 18 U.S.C. Section 925, shall, upon presenting to the Board of Public Safety proof that the relief has been granted and it being established from proof submitted by the applicant to the satisfaction of the Board of Public Safety that the circumstances regarding the conviction and the applicant's record and reputation are such that the acquisition, receipt, transfer, shipment, or possession of firearms by the person would not present a threat to the safety of the citizens of Georgia and that the granting of the relief sought would not be contrary to the public interest, be granted relief from the disabilities imposed by this Code section. A person who has been convicted under federal or state law of a felony pertaining to antitrust violations, unfair trade practices, or restraint of trade shall, upon presenting to the Board of Public Safety proof, and it being established from said proof, submitted by the applicant to the satisfaction of the Board of Public Safety that the circumstances regarding the conviction and the applicant's record and reputation are such that the acquisition, receipt, transfer, shipment, or possession of firearms by the person would not present a threat to the safety of the citizens of Georgia and that the granting of the relief sought would not be contrary to the public interest, be granted relief from the disabilities imposed by this Code section. A record that the relief has been granted by the board shall be entered upon the criminal history of the person maintained by the Georgia Crime Information Center and the board shall maintain a list of the names of such persons which shall be open for public inspection.

(e) As used in this Code section, the term "forcible felony" means any felony which involves the use or threat of physical force or violence against any person and further includes, without limitation, murder; felony murder; burglary; robbery; armed robbery; kidnapping; hijacking of an aircraft or motor vehicle; aggravated stalking; rape; aggravated child molestation; aggravated sexual battery; arson in the first degree; the manufacturing, transporting, distribution, or possession of explosives with intent to kill, injure, or intimidate individuals or destroy a public building; terroristic threats; or acts of treason or insurrection.

(f) Any person placed on probation as a first offender pursuant to Article 3 of Chapter 8 of Title 42 and subsequently discharged without court adjudication of guilt pursuant to Code Section 42–8–62 shall, upon such discharge, be relieved from the disabilities imposed by this Code section.

Laws 1980, p. 1509, § 1; Laws 1982, p. 1171, § 2; Laws 1983, p. 945, § 1; Laws 1987, p. 476, §§ 1, 2; Laws 1989, p. 14, § 16; Laws 2000, p. 1630, § 5.

Formerly Code 1933, § 26–2914.

Historical and Statutory Notes

The 2000 amendment inserted "felony" near the beginning of subsec. (b), at the end of subsec. (b) inserted "provided, however, that if the felony as to which the person is on probation or has been previously convicted is a forcible felony, then upon conviction of receiving, possessing, or transporting a firearm, such person shall be imprisoned for a period of five years.", inserted subsec. (b.1), inserted a new subsec. (e), and redesignated former subsec. (e) as subsec. (f).

§ 16–11–132. Possession of handgun by persons under 18

(a) For the purposes of this Code section, a handgun is considered loaded if there is a cartridge in the chamber or cylinder of the handgun.

(b) Notwithstanding any other provisions of this part and except as otherwise provided in this Code section, it shall be unlawful for any person under the age of 18 years to possess or have under such person's control a handgun. A person convicted of a first violation of this subsection shall be guilty of a misdemeanor and shall be punished by a fine not to exceed $1,000.00 or by imprisonment for not more than 12 months, or both. A person convicted of a second or subsequent violation of this subsection shall be guilty of a felony and shall be punished by a fine of $5,000.00 or by imprisonment for a period of three years, or both.

(c) Except as otherwise provided in subsection (d) of this Code section, the provisions of subsection (b) of this Code section shall not apply to:

(1) Any person under the age of 18 years who is:

(A) Attending a hunter education course or a firearms safety course;

(B) Engaging in practice in the use of a firearm or target shooting at an established range authorized by the governing body of the jurisdiction where such range is located;

(C) Engaging in an organized competition involving the use of a firearm or participating in or practicing for a performance by an organized group under 26 U.S.C. Section 501(c)(3) which uses firearms as a part of such performance;

(D) Hunting or fishing pursuant to a valid license if such person has in his or her possession such a valid hunting or fishing license if required; is engaged in legal hunting or fishing; has permission of the owner of the land on which the activities are being conducted; and the handgun, whenever loaded, is carried only in an open and fully exposed manner; or

(E) Traveling to or from any activity described in subparagraphs (A) through (D) of this paragraph if the handgun in such person's possession is not loaded;

(2) Any person under the age of 18 years who is on real property under the control of such person's parent, legal guardian, or grandparent and who has the permission of such person's parent or legal guardian to possess a handgun; or

(3) Any person under the age of 18 years who is at such person's residence and who, with the permission of such person's parent or legal guardian, possesses a handgun for the purpose of exercising the rights authorized in Code Section 16–3–21 or 16–3–23.

(d) Subsection (c) of this Code section shall not apply to any person under the age of 18 years who has been convicted of a forcible felony or forcible misdemeanor, as defined in Code Section 16–1–3, or who has been adjudicated delinquent under the provisions of Article 1 of Chapter 11 of Title 15 for an offense which would constitute a forcible felony or forcible misdemeanor, as defined in Code Section 16–1–3, if such person were an adult.

Laws 1994, p. 1012, § 12; Laws 2000, p. 1630, § 6; Laws 2010, Act 643, § 1–8, eff. June 4, 2010.

Historical and Statutory Notes

The 2000 amendment changed the penalty in the third sentence of subsec. (b).

The 2010 amendment by Act 643 rewrote subsec. (a); and substituted "handgun" for "pistol or revolver" throughout the section. Prior to amendment subsec. (a) had read:

"(a)(1) For the purposes of this Code section, the term 'pistol' or 'revolver' means a firearm of any description, loaded or unloaded, from which any shot, bullet, or other missile can be discharged where the length of the barrel, not including any revolving, detachable, or magazine breech, does not exceed 12 inches; provided, however, that the term pistol or revolver shall not include a gun which discharges shot of .46 centimeters or less in diameter.

"(2) For the purposes of this Code section, a pistol or revolver is considered loaded if:

"(A) There is a cartridge in the chamber or cylinder of the pistol or revolver;

"(B) The person is carrying on his or her body or attached to his or her clothing the pistol or revolver and the ammunition for such pistol or revolver; or

"(C) The pistol or revolver and the ammunition for such pistol or revolver are in such close proximity to such person that such person could readily gain access to the pistol or revolver and the ammunition and load the pistol or revolver."

Laws 2010, Act 643, § 3–1, provides:

"This Act shall become effective upon its approval by the Governor or upon its becoming law without such approval and shall apply to all offenses committed on and after such date. The enactment of this Act shall not affect any prosecutions for acts occurring before the effective date of this Act and shall not act as an abatement of any such prosecutions."

§ 16–11–133. Commission of crime by convicted felon through use of a firearm

(a) As used in this Code section, the term:

(1) "Felony" means any offense punishable by imprisonment for a term of one year or more and includes conviction by a court-martial under the Uniform Code of Military Justice for an offense which would constitute a felony under the laws of the United States.

(2) "Firearm" includes any handgun, rifle, shotgun, stun gun, taser, or other weapon which will or can be converted to expel a projectile by the action of an explosive or electrical charge.

(b) Any person who has previously been convicted of or who has previously entered a guilty plea to the offense of murder, armed robbery, kidnapping, rape, aggravated child molestation, aggravated sodomy, aggravated sexual battery, or any felony involving the use or possession of a firearm and who shall have on or within arm's reach of his or her person a firearm during the commission of, or the attempt to commit:

(1) Any crime against or involving the person of another;

(2) The unlawful entry into a building or vehicle;

(3) A theft from a building or theft of a vehicle;

(4) Any crime involving the possession, manufacture, delivery, distribution, dispensing, administering, selling, or posses-

sion with intent to distribute any controlled substance as provided in Code Section 16–13–30; or

(5) Any crime involving the trafficking of cocaine, marijuana, or illegal drugs as provided in Code Section 16–13–31,

and which crime is a felony, commits a felony and, upon conviction thereof, shall be punished by confinement for a period of 15 years, such sentence to run consecutively to any other sentence which the person has received.

(c) Upon the second or subsequent conviction of a convicted felon under this Code section, such convicted felon shall be punished by confinement for life. Notwithstanding any other law to the contrary, the sentence of any convicted felon which is imposed for violating this Code section a second or subsequent time shall not be suspended by the court and probationary sentence imposed in lieu thereof.

(d) Any crime committed in violation of subsections (b) and (c) of this Code section shall be considered a separate offense.

Laws 1995, p. 137, § 1.

§ 16–11–134. Discharge of firearm while under influence of alcohol, certain drugs, or controlled substances

(a) It shall be unlawful for any person to discharge a firearm while:

(1) Under the influence of alcohol or any drug or any combination of alcohol and any drug to the extent that it is unsafe for the person to discharge such firearm except in the defense of life, health, and property;

(2) The person's alcohol concentration is 0.08 grams or more at any time while discharging such firearm or within three hours after such discharge of such firearm from alcohol consumed before such discharge ended; or

(3) Subject to the provisions of subsection (b) of this Code section, there is any amount of marijuana or a controlled substance, as defined in Code Section 16–13–21, present in the person's blood or urine, or both, including the metabolites and derivatives of each or both without regard to whether or not any alcohol is present in the person's breath or blood.

(b) The fact that any person charged with violating this Code section is or has been legally entitled to use a drug shall not constitute a defense against any charge of violating this Code section; provided, however, that such person shall not be in violation of this Code section unless such person is rendered incapable of possessing or discharging a firearm safely as a result of using a drug other than alcohol which such person is legally entitled to use.

(c) Any person convicted of violating subsection (a) of this Code section shall be guilty of a misdemeanor of a high and aggravated nature.

Laws 1995, p. 139, § 1.

§ 16–11–135. Employer shall not search locked privately owned vehicles; no condition of employment restricting employee from having licensed firearm locked out of sight in vehicle; exceptions; liability

(a) Except as provided in this Code section, no private or public employer, including the state and its political subdivisions, shall establish, maintain, or enforce any policy or rule that has the effect of allowing such employer or its agents to search the locked privately owned vehicles of employees or invited guests on the employer's parking lot and access thereto.

(b) Except as provided in this Code section, no private or public employer, including the state and its political subdivisions, shall condition employment upon any agreement by a prospective employee that prohibits an employee from entering the parking lot and access thereto when the employee's privately owned motor vehicle contains a firearm that is locked out of sight within the trunk, glove box, or other enclosed compartment or area within such privately owned motor vehicle, provided that any applicable employees possess a Georgia weapons carry license.

(c) Subsection (a) of this Code section shall not apply:

(1) To searches by certified law enforcement officers pursuant to valid search warrants or valid warrantless searches based upon probable cause under exigent circumstances;

(2) To vehicles owned or leased by an employer;

(3) To any situation in which a reasonable person would believe that accessing a locked vehicle of an employee is necessary to prevent an immediate threat to human health, life, or safety; or

(4) When an employee consents to a search of his or her locked privately owned vehicle by licensed private security officers for loss prevention purposes based on probable cause that the employee unlawfully possesses employer property.

(d) Subsections (a) and (b) of this Code section shall not apply:

(1) To an employer providing applicable employees with a secure parking area which restricts general public access through the use of a gate, security station, security officers, or other similar means which limit public access into the parking area, provided that any employer policy allowing vehicle searches upon entry shall be applicable to all vehicles entering the property and applied on a uniform and frequent basis;

(2) To any penal institution, correctional institution, detention facility, diversion center, jail, or similar place of confinement or confinement alternative;

(3) To facilities associated with electric generation owned or operated by a public utility;

(4) To any United States Department of Defense contractor, if such contractor operates any facility on or contiguous with a United States military base or installation or within one mile of an airport;

(5) To an employee who is restricted from carrying or possessing a firearm on the employer's premises due to a completed or pending disciplinary action;

(6) Where transport of a firearm on the premises of the employer is prohibited by state or federal law or regulation;

(7) To parking lots contiguous to facilities providing natural gas transmission, liquid petroleum transmission, water storage and supply, and law enforcement services determined to be so vital to the State of Georgia, by a written determination of the Georgia Department of Homeland Security, that the incapacity or destruction of such systems and assets would have a debilitating impact on public health or safety; or

(8) To any area used for parking on a temporary basis.

(e) No employer, property owner, or property owner's agent shall be held liable in any criminal or civil action for damages resulting from or arising out of an occurrence involving the transportation, storage, possession, or use of a firearm, including, but not limited to, the theft of a firearm from an employee's automobile, pursuant to this Code section unless such employer commits a criminal act involving the use of a firearm or unless the employer knew that the person using such firearm would commit such criminal act on the employer's premises. Nothing contained in this Code section shall create a new duty on the part of the employer, property owner, or property owner's agent. An employee at will shall have no greater interest in employment created by this Code section and shall remain an employee at will.

(f) In any action relating to the enforcement of any right or obligation under this Code section, an employer, property owner, or property owner's agent's efforts to comply with other applicable federal, state, or local safety laws, regulations, guidelines, or ordinances shall be a complete defense to any employer, property owner, or property owner's agent's liability.

(g) In any action brought against an employer, employer's agent, property owner, or property owner's agent relating to the criminal use of firearms in the workplace, the plaintiff shall be liable for all legal costs of such employer, employer's agent, property owner, or property owner's agent if such action is concluded in such employer, employer's agent, property owner, or property owner's agent's favor.

(h) This Code section shall not be construed so as to require an employer, property owner, or property owner's agent to implement any additional security measures for the protection of employees, customers, or other persons. Implementation of remedial security measures to provide protection to employees, customers, or other persons shall not be admissible in evidence to show prior negligence or breach of duty of an employer, property owner, or property owner's agent in any action against such employer, its officers or shareholders, or property owners.

(i) All actions brought based upon a violation of subsection (a) of this Code section shall be brought exclusively by the Attorney General.

(j) In the event that subsection (e) of this Code section is declared or adjudged by any court to be invalid or unconstitutional for any reason, the remaining portions of this Code section shall be invalid and of no further force or effect. The General Assembly declares that it would not have enacted the remaining provisions of this Code section if it had known that such portion hereof would be declared or adjudged invalid or unconstitutional.

(k) Nothing in this Code section shall restrict the rights of private property owners or persons in legal control of property through a lease, a rental agreement, a contract, or any other agreement to control access to such property. When a private property owner or person in legal control of property through a lease, a rental agreement, a contract, or any other agreement is also an employer, his or her rights as a private property owner or person in legal control of property shall govern.

Laws 2008, Act 802, § 7, eff. July 1, 2008; Laws 2009, Act 8, § 16, eff. April 14, 2009; Laws 2010, Act 643, § 1–9, eff. June 4, 2010.

Historical and Statutory Notes

The 2009 amendment by Act 8 was a provision contained in a correction bill.

The 2010 amendment by Act 643, in subsec. (b), substituted "weapons carry" for "firearms".

Laws 2010, Act 643, § 3–1, provides:

"This Act shall become effective upon its approval by the Governor or upon its becoming law without such approval and shall apply to all offenses committed on and after such date. The enactment of this Act shall not affect any prosecutions for acts occurring before the effective date of this Act and shall not act as an abatement of any such prosecutions."

Part 4

Antiterroristic Training

§ 16–11–150. Short title

This part shall be known and may be cited as the "Georgia Antiterroristic Training Act."

Laws 1987, p. 866, § 1.

§ 16–11–151. Illegal acts relating to illegal firearms, dangerous weapons, explosives or incendiary devices; punishment

(a) As used in this Code section, the term "dangerous weapon" has the same meaning as found in paragraph (1) of Code Section 16–11–121.

(b) It shall be unlawful for any person to:

(1) Teach, train, or demonstrate to any other person the use, application, or making of any illegal firearm, dangerous weapon, explosive, or incendiary device capable of causing injury or death to persons either directly or through a writing or over or through a computer or computer network if the person teaching, training, or demonstrating knows, has reason to know, or intends that such teaching, training, or demonstrating will be unlawfully employed for use in or in furtherance of a civil disorder, riot, or insurrection; or

(2) Assemble with one or more persons for the purpose of being taught, trained, or instructed in the use of any illegal firearm, dangerous weapon, explosive, or incendiary device capable of causing injury or death to persons if such person so assembling knows, has reason to know, or intends that such teaching, training, or instruction will be unlawfully employed for use in or in furtherance of a civil disorder, riot, or insurrection.

(c) Any person who violates any provision of subsection (b) of this Code section shall be guilty of a felony and, upon conviction thereof, shall be punished by a fine of not more than $5,000.00 or by imprisonment for not less than one nor more than five years, or both.

Laws 1987, p. 866, § 1; Laws 1992, p. 6, § 16; Laws 1995, p. 574, § 4.

§ 16–11–152. Exceptions

This part shall not apply to:

(1) Any act of any peace officer which is performed in the lawful performance of official duties;

(2) Any training for law enforcement officers conducted by or for any police agency of the state or any political subdivision thereof or any agency of the United States;

(3) Any activities of the National Guard or of the armed forces of the United States; or

(4) Any hunter education classes taught under the auspices of the Department of Natural Resources, or other classes intended to teach the safe handling of firearms for hunting, recreation, competition, or self-defense.

Laws 1987, p. 866, § 1.

Part 4A

Enhanced Criminal Penalties

§ 16–11–160. Possession of machine guns, sawed-off rifles, sawed-off shotguns, or firearms equipped with silencers during commission of certain offenses; penalties

(a)(1) It shall be unlawful for any person to possess or to use a machine gun, sawed-off rifle, sawed-off shotgun, or a firearm equipped with a silencer, as those terms are defined in Code Section 16–11–121, during the commission or the attempted commission of any of the following offenses:

(A) Aggravated assault as defined in Code Section 16–5–21;

(B) Aggravated battery as defined in Code Section 16–5–24;

(C) Robbery as defined in Code Section 16–8–40;

(D) Armed robbery as defined in Code Section 16–8–41;

(E) Murder or felony murder as defined in Code Section 16–5–1;

(F) Voluntary manslaughter as defined in Code Section 16–5–2;

(G) Involuntary manslaughter as defined in Code Section 16–5–3;

(H) Sale, possession for sale, transportation, manufacture, offer for sale, or offer to manufacture controlled substances in violation of any provision of Article 2 of Chapter 13 of this title, the "Georgia Controlled Substances Act";

(I) Terroristic threats or acts as defined in Code Section 16–11–37;

(J) Arson as defined in Code Section 16–7–60, 16–7–61, or 16–7–62 or arson of lands as defined in Code Section 16–7–63;

(K) Influencing witnesses as defined in Code Section 16–10–93; and

(L) Participation in criminal gang activity as defined in Code Section 16–15–4.

(2)(A) As used in this paragraph, the term "bulletproof vest" means a bullet–resistant soft body armor providing, as a minimum standard, the level of protection known as "threat level I," which means at least seven layers of bullet–resistant material providing protection from at least three shots of 158–grain lead ammunition fired from a .38 caliber handgun at a velocity of 850 feet per second.

(B) It shall be unlawful for any person to wear a bulletproof vest during the commission or the attempted commission of any of the following offenses:

(i) Any crime against or involving the person of another in violation of any of the provisions of this title for which a sentence of life imprisonment may be imposed;

(ii) Any felony involving the manufacture, delivery, distribution, administering, or selling of controlled substances or marijuana as provided in Code Section 16–13–30; or

(iii) Trafficking in cocaine, illegal drugs, marijuana, or methamphetamine as provided in Code Section 16–13–31.

(b) Any person who violates paragraph (1) of subsection (a) of this Code section shall be guilty of a felony, and, upon conviction thereof, shall be punished by confinement for a period of ten years, such sentence to run consecutively to any other sentence which the person has received. Any person who violates paragraph (2) of subsection (a) of this Code section shall be guilty of a felony, and, upon conviction thereof, shall be punished by confinement for a period of one to five years, such sentence to run consecutively to any other sentence which the person has received.

(c) Upon the second or subsequent conviction of a person under this Code section, the person shall be punished by life imprisonment. Notwithstanding any other law to the contrary, the sentence of any person which is imposed for violating this Code section a second or subsequent time shall not be suspended by a court or a probationary sentence imposed in lieu thereof.

(d) The punishment prescribed for the violation of subsections (a) and (c) of this Code section shall not be probated or suspended as is provided by Code Section 17–10–7.

(e) Any crime committed in violation of this Code section shall be considered a separate offense.

Laws 1996, p. 354, § 1; Laws 2003, Act 39, § 1, eff. July 1, 2003; Laws 2008, Act 530, § 4, eff. July 1, 2008.

Historical and Statutory Notes

The 2003 amendment by Act 39 rewrote subsecs. (a) and (b) which had read as follows:

"(a) It shall be unlawful for any person to possess or to use a machine gun, sawed-off rifle, sawed-off shotgun, or a firearm equipped with a silencer, as those terms are defined in Code Section 16–11–121, during the commission or the attempted commission of any of the following offenses:

"(1) Aggravated assault as defined in Code Section 16–5–21;

"(2) Aggravated battery as defined in Code Section 16–5–24;

"(3) Robbery as defined in Code Section 16–8–40;

"(4) Armed robbery as defined in Code Section 16–8–41;

"(5) Murder or felony murder as defined in Code Section 16–5–1;

"(6) Voluntary manslaughter as defined in Code Section 16–5–2;

"(7) Involuntary manslaughter as defined in Code Section 16–5–3;

"(8) Sale, possession for sale, transportation, manufacture, offer for sale, or offer to manufacture controlled substances in violation of any provision of Article 2 of Chapter 13 of this title, the 'Georgia Controlled Substances Act';

"(9) Terroristic threats or acts as defined in Code Section 16–11–37;

"(10) Arson as defined in Code Sections 16–7–60, 16–7–61, and 16–7–62;

"(11) Influencing witnesses as defined in Code Section 16–10–93; and

"(12) Participation in criminal gang activity as defined in Code Section 16–15–4.

"(b) Any person who violates subsection (a) of this Code section shall be guilty of a felony, and, upon conviction thereof, shall be punished by confinement for a period of ten years, such sentence to run consecutively to any other sentence which the person has received."

The 2008 amendment by Act 530 rewrote subpar. (J) of par. (1) of subsec. (a), which had read as follows:

"(J) Arson as defined in Code Sections 16–7–60, 16–7–61, and 16–7–62;".

§ 16–11–161. Adoption and enforcement of consistent local laws

Nothing in this part shall be construed to prohibit a local governing authority from adopting and enforcing laws consistent with this part relating to gangs and gang violence. Where local laws or ordinances duplicate or supplement this part, this part shall be construed as providing alternative remedies and not as preempting the field.

Laws 1996, p. 354, § 1.

§ 16–11–162. Applicability

This part shall not apply to persons who use force in defense of others as provided by Code Section 16–3–21. This part is intended to supplement not to supplant Code Section 16–11–106.

Laws 1996, p. 354, § 1.

Part 5

Transfer and Purchase of Firearms

§ 16–11–170. Repealed by Laws 2005, Act 118, § 1, eff. July 1, 2005

Historical and Statutory Notes

Repealed § 16–11–170, relating to legislative intent, construction and application of the part, was derived from Laws 1995, p. 139, § 2; 1999, p. 81, § 16; Laws 2000, p. 136, § 16. The repealing law also reserved the section designation.

§ 16–11–171. Definitions

As used in this part, the term:

(1) "Center" means the Georgia Crime Information Center within the Georgia Bureau of Investigation.

(2) "Dealer" means any person licensed as a dealer pursuant to 18 U.S.C. Section 921, et seq., or Chapter 16 of Title 43.

(3) "Firearm" means any weapon that is designed to or may readily be converted to expel a projectile by the action of an explosive or the frame or receiver of any such weapon, any firearm muffler or firearm silencer, or any destructive device as defined in 18 U.S.C. Section 921(a)(3).

(4) "Involuntarily hospitalized" means hospitalized as an inpatient in any mental health facility pursuant to Code Section 37–3–81 or hospitalized as an inpatient in any mental health facility as a result of being adjudicated mentally incompetent to stand trial or being adjudicated not guilty by reason of insanity at the time of the crime pursuant to Part 2 of Article 6 of Title 17.

(5) "NICS" means the National Instant Criminal Background Check System created by the federal "Brady Handgun Violence Prevention Act" (P. L. No. 103–159).

Laws 1995, p. 139, § 2; Laws 2005, Act 118, § 1, eff. July 1, 2005.

Historical and Statutory Notes

The 2005 amendment by Act 118 rewrote the section which had read:

"As used in this part, the term:

"(1) 'Bureau' means the Georgia Bureau of Investigation.

"(2) 'Center' means the Georgia Crime Information Center within the Georgia Bureau of Investigation.

"(3) 'Dealer' means any person licensed as a dealer pursuant to 18 U.S.C. Section 921, et seq., or Chapter 16 of Title 43.

"(4) 'Handgun' means a pistol or revolver or other handgun defined in Code Section 16–11–131 which has a short stock and is designed to be held and fired by the use of a single hand.

"(5) 'Involuntarily hospitalized' means hospitalized as an inpatient in any mental health facility pursuant to Code Section 37–3–81 or hospitalized as an inpatient in any mental health facility as a result of being adjudicated mentally incompetent to stand trial or being adjudicated not guilty by reason of insanity at the time of the crime pursuant to Part 2 of Article 6 of Title 17."

§ 16–11–172. Transfer and purchase of firearms conducted by licensed entity; subject to National Instant Criminal Background Check System

(a) All transfers or purchases of firearms conducted by a licensed importer, licensed manufacturer, or licensed dealer shall be subject to the NICS. To the extent possible, the center shall provide to the NICS all necessary criminal history information and wanted person records in order to complete an NICS check.

(b) The center shall forward to the Federal Bureau of Investigation information concerning persons who have been involuntarily hospitalized as defined in this part for the purpose of completing an NICS check.

(c) Any government official who willfully or intentionally compromises the identity, confidentiality, and security of any records and data pursuant to this part shall be guilty of a felony and fined no less than $5,000.00 and shall be subject to automatic dismissal from his or her employment.

(d) The provisions of this part shall not apply to:

(1) Any firearm, including any handgun with a matchlock, flintlock, percussion cap, or similar type of ignition system, manufactured in or before 1898;

(2) Any replica of any firearm described in paragraph (1) of this subsection if such replica is not designed or redesigned to use rimfire or conventional center–fire fixed ammunition or uses rimfire or conventional center–fire fixed ammunition which is no longer manufactured in the United States and which is not readily available in the ordinary channels of commercial trade; and

(3) Any firearm which is a curio or relic as defined by 27 C.F.R. 178.11.

Laws 2005, Act 118, § 1, eff. July 1, 2005.

Historical and Statutory Notes

Former § 16–11–172, relating to requirements to be complied with by licensed firearms dealers prior to sale or delivery of firearms, derived from Laws 1995, p. 139, § 2; Laws 1997, p. 1411, § 1; Code 1981, § 16–11–172, was repealed by Laws 2005, Act 118, § 1, effective July 1, 2005.

§ 16–11–173. Legislative intent and declaration; authority to bring suit against firearm dealers, etc.; county and municipal corporation firearm regulation

(a)(1) It is declared by the General Assembly that the regulation of firearms is properly an issue of general, state–wide concern.

(2) The General Assembly further declares that the lawful design, marketing, manufacture, and sale of firearms and ammunition to the public is not unreasonably dangerous activity and does not constitute a nuisance per se.

(b)(1) No county or municipal corporation, by zoning or by ordinance, resolution, or other enactment, shall regulate in any manner gun shows; the possession, ownership, transport, carrying, transfer, sale, purchase, licensing, or registration of firearms or components of firearms; firearms dealers; or dealers in firearms components.

(2) The authority to bring suit and right to recover against any firearms or ammunition manufacturer, trade association, or dealer by or on behalf of any governmental unit created by or pursuant to an Act of the General Assembly or the Constitution, or any department, agency, or authority thereof, for damages, abatement, or injunctive relief resulting from or relating to the lawful design, manufacture, marketing, or sale of firearms or ammunition to the public shall be reserved exclusively to the state. This paragraph shall not prohibit a political subdivision or local government authority from bringing an action against a firearms or ammunition manufacturer or dealer for breach of contract or express warranty as to firearms or ammunition purchased by the political subdivision or local government authority.

(c) A county or municipal corporation may regulate the transport, carrying, or possession of firearms by employees of the local unit of government in the course of their employment with such local unit of government.

(d) Nothing contained in this Code section shall prohibit municipalities or counties by ordinance, resolution, or other enactment, from requiring the ownership of guns by heads of households within the political subdivision.

(e) Nothing contained in this Code section shall prohibit municipalities or counties, by ordinance, resolution, or other enactment, from reasonably limiting or prohibiting the discharge of firearms within the boundaries of the municipal corporation or county.

Laws 1995, p. 139, § 2; Laws 1999, p. 2, § 1; Laws 2005, Act 118, § 1, eff. July 1, 2005.

Formerly Code 1981 § 16–11–184.

Historical and Statutory Notes

Former § 16–11–173, relating to the criminal history and involuntary hospitalization records check, derived from Laws 1995, p. 139, § 2; Code 1981, § 16–11–173, was repealed by Laws 2005, Act. 118, § 1, effective July 1, 2005.

§§ 16–11–174 to 16–11–184. Repealed by Laws 2005, Act 118, § 1, eff. July 1, 2005

Historical and Statutory Notes

Section 16–11–174, relating to procedures in event of an emergency causing delay in check, was derived from Laws 1995, p. 139, § 2; Laws 1996, p. 108, § 6.

Section 16–11–175, relating to fees for record checks, was derived from Laws 1995, p. 139, § 2.

Section 16–11–176, prohibiting the bureau from creating a list containing information on potential buyers or transferees unless the person may not lawfully receive or possess handguns, was derived from Laws 1995, p. 139, § 2.

Section 16–11–177, relating to the establishment of a toll-free number for providing information to licensed firearms dealers, was derived from Laws 1995, p. 139, § 2; Laws 1997, p. 1411, § 2.

Section 16–11–178, relating to the correction of records of persons wrongfully denied the right to receive or purchase firearms, was derived from Laws 1995, p. 139, § 2.

Section 16–11–179, relating to confidentiality of records and data, was derived from Laws 1995, p. 139, § 2.

Section 16–11–180, providing that compliance with provisions of the part was a defense to certain claims, was derived from Laws 1995, p. 139, § 2.

Section 16–11–181, relating to applicability and exceptions to the part, was derived from Laws 1995, p. 139, § 2; Laws 1997, p. 1411, § 3; Laws 2000, p. 1418, § 1.

Section 16–11–182, relating to violations, was derived from Laws 1995, p. 139, § 2.

Section 16–11–183, relating to annual reports to the Speaker of the House of Representatives and President of the Senate, was derived from Laws 1995, p. 139, § 2.

Section 16–11–184, relating to authority of political subdivisions with respect to regulation of firearms and limitations thereon, was derived from Laws 1995, p. 139, § 2; Laws 1999, p. 2, § 1. See, now § 16–11–173.

CHAPTER 12

OFFENSES AGAINST PUBLIC HEALTH AND MORALS

Article 1

Article 2

Part 1

Part 2

Article 3

Part 1

Part 2

Part 3

Article 4

Part 1

Article 1

General Provisions

§ 16–12–1. Contributing to delinquency, unruliness, or deprivation of a minor

(a) As used in this Code section, the term:

(1) "Delinquent act" means a delinquent act as defined in Code Section 15–11–2.

(2) "Felony" means any act which constitutes a felony under the laws of this state, the laws of any other state of the United States, or the laws of the United States.

(3) "Minor" means any individual who is under the age of 17 years or any individual under the age of 18 years who is alleged to be a deprived child as such is defined in Code Section 15–11–2, relating to juvenile proceedings.

(4) "Serious injury" means an injury involving a broken bone, the loss of a member of the body, the loss of use of a member of the body, the substantial disfigurement of the body or of a member of the body, an injury which is life threatening, or any sexual abuse of a child under 16 years of age by means of an act described in subparagraph (a)(4)(A), (a)(4)(G), or (a)(4)(I) of Code Section 16–12–100.

(b) A person commits the offense of contributing to the delinquency, unruliness, or deprivation of a minor when such person:

(1) Knowingly and willfully encourages, causes, abets, connives, or aids a minor in committing a delinquent act as such is defined in Code Section 15–11–2, relating to juvenile proceedings;

(2) Knowingly and willfully encourages, causes, abets, connives, or aids a minor in committing an act which would cause such minor to be found to be an unruly child as such is defined in Code Section 15–11–2, relating to juvenile proceedings;

(3) Willfully commits an act or acts or willfully fails to act when such act or omission would cause a minor to be found to be a deprived child as such is defined in Code Section 15–11–2, relating to juvenile proceedings;

(4) Knowingly and willfully hires, solicits, engages, contracts with, conspires with, encourages, abets, or directs any minor to commit any felony which encompasses force or violence as an element of the offense or delinquent act which would constitute a felony which encompasses force or violence as an element of the offense if committed by an adult;

(5) Knowingly and willfully provides to a minor any weapon as defined in paragraph (2) of subsection (a) of Code Section 16–11–127.1 or any weapon as defined in Code Section 16–11–121 to commit any felony which encompasses force or violence as an element of the offense or delinquent act which would constitute a felony which encompasses force or violence as an element of the offense if committed by an adult; or

(6) Knowingly and willfully hires, solicits, engages, contracts with, conspires with, encourages, abets, or directs any minor to commit any smash and grab burglary which would constitute a felony if committed by an adult.

(c) It shall not be a defense to the offense provided for in this Code section that the minor has not been formally adjudged to have committed a delinquent act or has not been found to be unruly or deprived.

(d) A person convicted pursuant to paragraph (1) or (2) of subsection (b) of this Code section shall be punished as follows:

(1) Upon conviction of the first or second offense, the defendant shall be guilty of a misdemeanor and shall be fined not more than $1,000.00 or shall be imprisoned for not more than 12 months, or both fined and imprisoned; and

(2) Upon the conviction of the third or subsequent offense, the defendant shall be guilty of a felony and shall be fined not less than $1,000.00 nor more than $5,000.00 or shall be imprisoned for not less than one year nor more than three years, or both fined and imprisoned.

(d.1) A person convicted pursuant to paragraph (3) of subsection (b) of this Code section shall be punished as follows:

(1) Upon conviction of an offense which resulted in the serious injury or death of a child, without regard to whether such offense was a first, second, third, or subsequent offense, the defendant shall be guilty of a felony and shall be punished as provided in subsection (e) of this Code section;

(2) Upon conviction of an offense which does not result in the serious injury or death of a child and which is the first conviction, the defendant shall be guilty of a misdemeanor and shall be fined not more than $1,000.00 or shall be imprisoned for not more than 12 months, or both fined and imprisoned;

(3) Upon conviction of an offense which does not result in the serious injury or death of a child and which is the second conviction, the defendant shall be guilty of a high and aggravated misdemeanor and shall be fined not less than $1,000.00 nor more than $5,000.00 or shall be imprisoned for not less than one year, or both fined and imprisoned; and

(4) Upon the conviction of an offense which does not result in the serious injury or death of a child and which is the third

or subsequent conviction, the defendant shall be guilty of a felony and shall be fined not less than $10,000.00 or shall be imprisoned for not less than one year nor more than five years, or both fined and imprisoned.

(e) A person convicted pursuant to paragraph (4), (5), or (6) of subsection (b) or paragraph (1) of subsection (d.1) of this Code section shall be guilty of a felony and punished as follows:

(1) Upon conviction of the first offense, the defendant shall be imprisoned for not less than one nor more than ten years; and

(2) Upon conviction of the second or subsequent offense, the defendant shall be imprisoned for not less than three years nor more than 20 years.

Laws 1953, Nov.-Dec. Sess., p. 321, § 1; Laws 1982, p. 968, § 1; Laws 1994, p. 1158, § 1; Laws 1995, p. 10, § 16; Laws 1996, p. 273, § 1; Laws 1999, p. 232, § 1; Laws 2004, Act 439, § 5, eff. July 1, 2004; Laws 2010, Act 674, § 7, eff. July 1, 2010.

Historical and Statutory Notes

The 2004 amendment by Act 439 rewrote subsec. (a)(4) which had read:

"(4) 'Serious injury' means an injury involving a broken bone, the loss of a member of the body, the loss of use of a member of the body, or the substantial disfigurement of the body or of a member of the body or an injury which is life threatening."

Laws 2004, Act 439, § 6, provides:

"This Act shall become effective on July 1, 2004, and shall apply to all crimes which occur on or after that date."

The 2010 amendment by Act 674, in subsec. (b), added par. (6); in subsec. (e), substituted "(4), (5), or (6)" for "(4) or (5)" in the introductory clause, and in par. (1), substituted "ten years" for "five years".

§ 16–12–1.1. Having person reside at, be domiciled at, or be employed at facility which provides care for certain children if such person has been convicted of or has entered plea of guilty or nolo contendere to or has been adjudicated a delinquent for any of certain serious crimes

(a) As used in this Code section the term:

(1) "Facility" means any day-care center, family day-care home, group-care facility, group day-care home, or similar facility at which any child who is not a member of an operator's family is received for pay for supervision and care, without transfer of legal custody, for fewer than 24 hours per day.

(2) "Operator" means any person who applies for or holds a permit or license to operate a facility.

(b) It shall be unlawful for any operator of a facility to knowingly have any person reside at, be domiciled at, or be employed at any such facility if such person has been convicted of or has entered a plea of guilty or nolo contendere to or has been adjudicated a delinquent for:

(1) A violation of Code Section 16–4–1, relating to criminal attempt, when the crime attempted is any of the crimes specified in paragraphs (2) through (10) of this subsection;

(2) A violation of Code Section 16–5–23.1, relating to battery, when the victim at the time of such offense was a minor;

(3) A violation of any provision of Chapter 6 of this title, relating to sexual offenses, when the victim at the time of such offense was a minor;

(4) A violation of Code Section 16–12–1, relating to contributing to the delinquency of a minor;

(5) A violation of Code Section 16–5–1, relating to murder;

(6) A violation of Code Section 16–5–2, relating to voluntary manslaughter;

(7) A violation of Code Section 16–6–2, relating to aggravated sodomy;

(8) A violation of Code Section 16–6–3, relating to rape;

(9) A violation of Code Section 16–6–22.2, relating to aggravated sexual battery; or

(10) A violation of Code Section 16–8–41, relating to armed robbery, if committed with a firearm.

(c) Any person violating subsection (b) of this Code section shall be guilty of a misdemeanor.

Laws 1997, p. 713, § 1.

§ 16–12–2. Smoking in public places prohibited

(a) A person smoking tobacco in violation of Chapter 12A of Title 31 shall be guilty of a misdemeanor and, if convicted, shall be punished by a fine of not less than $100.00 nor more than $500.00.

(b) This Code section shall be cumulative to and shall not prohibit the enactment of any other general and local laws, rules and regulations of state or local agencies, and local ordinances prohibiting smoking which are more restrictive than this Code section.

Laws 1975, p. 45, § 1; Laws 1982, p. 3, § 16; Laws 1994, p. 650, § 3; Laws 2005, Act 19, § 16, eff. April 7, 2005; Laws 2005, Act 368, § 1, eff. July 1, 2005.

Formerly Code 1933, § 26–9910.

Historical and Statutory Notes

The 2005 amendment by Act 19 substituted "Code Section 20–1A–2" for "Code Section 49–5–3" in subsec. (a), par. (4).

The 2005 amendment by Act 368 rewrote the section, which had read:

"(a) A person who smokes tobacco in any form in any of the following public places shall be guilty of a misdemeanor:

"(1) An enclosed elevator which is used by or open to the public and which is clearly designated by a no-smoking sign;

"(2) Any place on a public transportation vehicle which is used by the public and which is clearly designated by a no-smoking sign;

"(3) Any area which is used by or open to the public and which is clearly designated by a no-smoking sign; or

"(4) Any area which is the real property upon which is operated a day-care center, group day-care home, or family day-care home, as defined in Code Section 49–5–3, during the hours of operation of such facility.

"(b) A person convicted of violating subsection (a) of this Code section shall be punished by a fine of not less than $10.00 nor more than $100.00.

"(c) This Code section shall be cumulative to and shall not prohibit the enactment of any other general and local laws, rules and regulations of state or local agencies, and local ordinances prohibiting smoking which are more restrictive than this Code section."

Laws 2005, Act 368, § 3, provides:

"This Act shall become effective upon its approval by the Governor or upon its becoming law without such approval only for purposes of promulgating rules and regulations; for all other purposes, this Act shall become effective on July 1, 2005."

In 2005, the Code Commission, due to irreconcilable conflicts, treated the amendment of this section by Laws 2005, Act 19, § 16, as superseded by Laws 2005, Act 368, § 1. See Butts County v. Strahan, 107 S.E. 163, 151 Ga. 417 (1921).

§ 16–12–3. Suspension of gas or electric service for failure to pay for appliance purchase or repairs prohibited

(a) It shall be unlawful for any gas or electric utility company or electric membership corporation to cut off or suspend gas or electric service in any residence because the resident has failed to pay for or has failed to make timely payments for any appliance purchased from or any appliance repaired by such company or corporation. Payments received from a resident shall be first applied to the service, unless otherwise specified by the resident at the time of payment.

(b) Any company or corporation or any agent or employee thereof acting within the scope of his authority knowingly violating subsection (a) of this Code section shall be guilty of a misdemeanor.

Laws 1975, p. 849, § 1.

§ 16–12–4. Cruelty to animals

(a) As used in this Code section, the term:

(1) "Animal" shall not include any fish nor shall such term include any pest that might be exterminated or removed from a business, residence, or other structure.

(2) "Conviction" shall include pleas of guilty or nolo contendere or probation as a first offender pursuant to Article 3 of Chapter 8 of Title 42 and any conviction, plea of guilty or nolo contendere, or probation as a first offender for an offense under the laws of the United States or any of the several states that would constitute a violation of this Code section if committed in this state.

(3) "Willful neglect" means the intentional withholding of food and water required by an animal to prevent starvation or dehydration.

(b) A person commits the offense of cruelty to animals when he or she causes death or unjustifiable physical pain or suffering to any animal by an act, an omission, or willful neglect. Any person convicted of a violation of this subsection shall be guilty of a misdemeanor; provided, however, that:

(1) Any person who is convicted of a second or subsequent violation of this subsection shall be punished by imprisonment not to exceed 12 months, a fine not to exceed $ 5,000.00, or both; and

(2) Any person who is convicted of a second or subsequent violation of this subsection which results in the death of an animal shall be guilty of a misdemeanor of a high and aggravated nature and shall be punished by imprisonment for not less than three months nor more than 12 months, a fine not to exceed $ 10,000.00, or both, which punishment shall not be suspended, probated, or withheld.

(c) A person commits the offense of aggravated cruelty to animals when he or she knowingly and maliciously causes death or physical harm to an animal by rendering a part of such animal's body useless or by seriously disfiguring such animal. A person convicted of the offense of aggravated cruelty to animals shall be punished by imprisonment for not less than one nor more than five years, a fine not to exceed $ 15,000.00, or both, provided that any person who is convicted of a second or subsequent violation of this subsection shall be punished by imprisonment for not less than one nor more than five years, a fine not to exceed the amount provided by Code Section 17–10–8, or both.

(d) Before sentencing a defendant for any conviction under this Code section, the sentencing judge may require psychological evaluation of the offender and shall consider the entire criminal record of the offender.

(e) The provisions of this Code section shall not be construed as prohibiting conduct which is otherwise permitted under the laws of this state or of the United States, including, but not limited to, agricultural, animal husbandry, butchering, food processing, marketing, scientific, research, medical, zoological, exhibition, competitive, hunting, trapping, fishing, wildlife management, or pest control practices or the authorized practice of veterinary medicine nor to limit in any way the authority or duty of the Department of Agriculture, Department of Natural Resources, any county board of health, any law enforcement officer, dog, animal, or rabies control officer, humane society, veterinarian, or private landowner protecting his or her property.

(f)(1) Nothing in this Code section shall be construed as prohibiting a person from:

(A) Defending his or her person or property, or the person or property of another, from injury or damage being caused by an animal; or

(B) Injuring or killing an animal reasonably believed to constitute a threat for injury or damage to any property, livestock, or poultry.

(2) The method used to injure or kill such animal shall be designed to be as humane as is possible under the circumstances. A person who humanely injures or kills an animal under the circumstances indicated in this subsection shall incur no civil or criminal liability for such injury or death.

Laws 1968, p. 1249, § 1; Laws 1992, p. 1654, § 1; Laws 2000, p. 754, § 12.

Formerly Code 1933, § 26–2802.

Historical and Statutory Notes

The 2000 amendment rewrote this section which formerly provided:

"(a) A person is guilty of a misdemeanor of cruelty to animals in the second degree when his act, omission, or neglect causes unjustifiable physical pain, suffering, or death to any living animal.

" (b) A person is guilty of a misdemeanor of cruelty to animals in the first degree upon a second or subsequent violation of subsection (a) of this Code section and, upon conviction, may be punished by imprisonment not to exceed 12 months or a fine not to exceed $5,000.00 or both.

"(c) This Code section does not apply to the killing of animals raised for the purpose of providing food nor does it apply to any person who hunts wild animals in compliance with the game and fish laws of this state. The killing or injuring of an animal for humane purposes or in the furtherance of medical or scientific research is justifiable."

§ 16–12–5. Tattooing within areas near the eye

(a) As used in this Code section, the term "tattoo" means to mark or color the skin of any person by pricking in, inserting, or implanting pigments, except when performed by a physician licensed as such pursuant to Chapter 34 of Title 43.

(b) It shall be unlawful for any person to tattoo the body of any person within any area within one inch of the nearest part of the eye socket of such person. Any person who violates this Code section shall be guilty of a misdemeanor.

Laws 1990, p. 1866, § 1.

Article 2

Gambling and Related Offenses

Part 1

Gambling

§ 16–12–20. Definitions

As used in this part, the term:

(1) "Bet" means an agreement that, dependent upon chance even though accompanied by some skill, one stands to win or lose something of value. A bet does not include:

(A) Contracts of indemnity or guaranty or life, health, property, or accident insurance; or

(B) An offer of a prize, award, or compensation to the actual contestants in any bona fide contest for the determination of skill, speed, strength, or endurance or to the owners of animals, vehicles, watercraft, or aircraft entered in such contest.

(2) "Gambling device" means:

(A) Any contrivance which for a consideration affords the player an opportunity to obtain money or other thing of value, the award of which is determined by chance even though accompanied by some skill, whether or not the prize is automatically paid by contrivance;

(B) Any slot machine or any simulation or variation thereof;

(C) Any matchup or lineup game machine or device, operated for any consideration, in which two or more numerals, symbols, letters, or icons align in a winning combination on one or more lines vertically, horizontally, diagonally, or otherwise, without assistance by the player. Use of skill stops shall not be considered assistance by the player; or

(D) Any video game machine or device, operated for any consideration, for the play of poker, blackjack, any other card game, or keno or any simulation or variation of any of the foregoing, including, but not limited to, any game in which numerals, numbers, or any pictures, representations, or symbols are used as an equivalent or substitute for cards in the conduct of such game.

Any item described in subparagraph (B), (C), or (D) of this paragraph shall be a prohibited gambling device subject to and prohibited by this part, notwithstanding any inference to the contrary in any other law of this state.

(3) "Gambling place" means any real estate, building, room, tent, vehicle, boat, or other property whatsoever, one of the principal uses of which is the making or settling of bets; the receiving, holding, recording, or forwarding of bets or offers to bet; or the conducting of a lottery or the playing of gambling devices.

(4) "Lottery" means any scheme or procedure whereby one or more prizes are distributed by chance among persons who have paid or promised consideration for a chance to win such prize, whether such scheme or procedure is called a pool, lottery, raffle, gift, gift enterprise, sale, policy game, or by some other name. A lottery shall also include the organization of chain letter or pyramid clubs as provided in Code Section 16–12–38. A lottery shall not mean a:

(A) Promotional giveaway or contest which conforms with the qualifications of a lawful promotion specified in paragraph (16) of subsection (b) of Code Section 10–1–393;

(B) Scheme whereby a business gives away prizes to persons selected by lot if such prizes are made on the following conditions:

(i) Such prizes are conducted as advertising and promotional undertakings in good faith solely for the purpose of advertising the goods, wares, and merchandise of such business; and

(ii) No person to be eligible to receive such prize shall be required to:

(I) Pay any tangible consideration to the operator of such business in the form of money or other property or thing of value;

(II) Purchase any goods, wares, merchandise, or anything of value from such business; or

(III) Be present or be asked to participate in a seminar, sales presentation, or any other presentation, by whatever name denominated, in order to win such prizes; or

(C) Raffle authorized under Code Section 16–12–22.1.

Laws 1968, p. 1249, § 1; Laws 1975, p. 1072, § 2; Laws 1982, p. 1661, § 3; Laws 1985, p. 437, § 1; Laws 1986, p. 1313, § 3; Laws 1987, p. 1386, § 3; Laws 1995, p. 832, § 1; Laws 2001, Ex. Sess., p. 312, § 1.

Formerly Code 1933, § 26–2701.

Historical and Statutory Notes

The 2001 amendment redefined gambling devices so as to prohibit as gambling devices certain video poker games and devices and certain other games and devices.

§ 16–12–21. Gambling

(a) A person commits the offense of gambling when he:

(1) Makes a bet upon the partial or final result of any game or contest or upon the performance of any participant in such game or contest;

(2) Makes a bet upon the result of any political nomination, appointment, or election or upon the degree of success of any nominee, appointee, or candidate; or

(3) Plays and bets for money or other thing of value at any game played with cards, dice, or balls.

(b) A person who commits the offense of gambling shall be guilty of a misdemeanor.

Laws 1847, Cobb's 1851 Digest, pp. 819, 820; Laws 1859, p. 59, § 1; Laws 1865–66, p. 233, § 2; Laws 1968, p. 1249, § 1; Laws 1970, p. 690, § 1.

Formerly Code 1863, § 4425; Code 1868, § 4466; Code 1873, § 4541; Code 1882, § 4541; Penal Code 1895, § 401; Penal Code 1910, § 392; Code 1933, § 26–6404; Code 1933, § 26–2702.

§ 16–12–22. Commercial gambling

(a) A person commits the offense of commercial gambling when he intentionally does any of the following acts:

(1) Operates or participates in the earnings of a gambling place;

(2) Receives, records, or forwards a bet or offer to bet;

(3) For gain, becomes a custodian of anything of value bet or offered to be bet;

(4) Contracts to have or give himself or another the option to buy or sell or contracts to buy or sell at a future time any gain or other commodity whatsoever or any stock or security of any company, when it is at the time of making such contract intended by both parties thereto that the contract to buy or sell, the option whenever exercised or the contract resulting therefrom, shall be settled not by the receipt or delivery of such property but by the payment only of differences in prices thereof;

(5) Sells chances upon the partial or final result of or upon the margin of victory in any game or contest or upon the performance of any participant in any game or contest or upon the result of any political nomination, appointment, or election or upon the degree of success of any nominee, appointee, or candidate;

(6) Sets up or promotes any lottery, sells or offers to sell, or knowingly possesses for transfer or transfers any card, stub, ticket, check, or other device designed to serve as evidence of participation in any lottery; or

(7) Conducts, advertises, operates, sets up, or promotes a bingo game without having a valid license to operate a bingo game as provided by law.

(b) A person who commits the offense of commercial gambling shall be guilty of a felony and, upon conviction thereof, shall be punished by imprisonment for not less than one nor more than five years or by a fine not to exceed $20,000.00, or both.

Laws 1968, p. 1249, § 1; Laws 1970, p. 236, § 6; Laws 1977, p. 747, § 1; Laws 1978, p. 851, § 1.

Formerly Code 1933, § 26–2703.

§ 16–12–22.1. Operation of raffles

(a) It is the intention of the General Assembly that only nonprofit, tax-exempt churches, schools, civic organizations, or related support groups; nonprofit organizations qualified under

Section 501(c) of the Internal Revenue Code, as amended; or bona fide nonprofit organizations approved by the sheriff, which are properly licensed pursuant to this Code section shall be allowed to operate raffles.

(b) As used in this Code section, the term:

(1) "Nonprofit, tax-exempt organization" means churches, schools, civic organizations, or related support groups; nonprofit organizations qualified under Section 501(c) of the Internal Revenue Code, as amended; or bona fide nonprofit organizations approved by the sheriff.

(2) "Operate," "operated," or "operating" means the direction, supervision, management, operation, control, or guidance of activity.

(3) "Raffle" means any scheme or procedure whereby one or more prizes are distributed by chance among persons who have paid or promised consideration for a chance to win such prize. Such term shall also include door prizes which are awarded to persons attending meetings or activities provided that the cost of admission to such meetings or activities does not exceed the usual cost of similar activities where such prizes are not awarded.

(4) "Sheriff" means the sheriff of the county in which the nonprofit tax-exempt organization is located.

(c) Any other law to the contrary notwithstanding, no nonprofit, tax-exempt organization shall be permitted to operate a raffle until the sheriff issues a license to the organization authorizing it to do so. The license described in this subsection is in addition to and not in lieu of any other licenses which may be required by this state or any political subdivision thereof, and no raffle shall be operated until such time as all requisite licenses have been obtained. In the event a nonprofit, tax-exempt organization desires to conduct a raffle in more than one county, such organization shall not be required to obtain a license under this Code section in each county in which such raffle is to be conducted and shall only be required to obtain such license from the sheriff of the county in which the state headquarters of such organization are located.

(d)(1) Any nonprofit, tax-exempt organization desiring to obtain a license to operate raffles shall make application to the sheriff on forms prescribed by the sheriff. The sheriff may require the payment of an annual fee not to exceed $100.00. No license shall be issued to any nonprofit, tax-exempt organization unless the organization has been in existence for 24 months immediately prior to the issuance of the license. The license will expire at 12:00 Midnight on December 31 following the granting of the license. Renewal applications for each calendar year shall be filed with the sheriff prior to January 1 of each year and shall be on a form prescribed by the sheriff.

(2) Each application for a license and each application for renewal of a license shall contain the following information:

(A) The name and home address of the applicant and, if the applicant is a corporation, association, or other similar legal entity, the names and home addresses of each of the officers of the organization as well as the names and addresses of the directors, or other persons similarly situated, of the organization;

(B) The names and home addresses of each of the persons who will be operating, advertising, or promoting the raffle;

(C) The names and home addresses of any persons, organizations, or other legal entities that will act as surety for the applicant or to which the applicant is financially indebted or to which any financial obligation is owed by the applicant;

(D) A determination letter from the Internal Revenue Service certifying that the applicant is an organization exempt under federal tax law;

(E) A statement affirming that the applicant is exempt under the income tax laws of this state under Code Section 48–7–25;

(F) The location at which the applicant will conduct the raffles and, if the premises on which the raffles are to be conducted is to be leased, a copy of the lease or rental agreement; and

(G) A statement showing the convictions, if any, for criminal offenses other than minor traffic offenses of each of the persons listed in subparagraphs (A), (B), and (C) of this paragraph.

(3) The sheriff shall refuse to grant a raffle license to any applicant who fails to provide fully the information required by this Code section.

(4) When a nonprofit, tax-exempt organization which operates or intends to operate raffles for residents and patients of a retirement home, nursing home, or hospital operated by that organization at which gross receipts are or will be limited to $100.00 or less during each raffle and pays or will pay prizes having a value of $100.00 or less during each raffle, then, notwithstanding any other provision of this Code section or any rule or regulation promulgated by the sheriff pursuant to the provisions of subsection (*l*) of this Code section, neither the applicant nor any of the persons whose names and addresses are required under subparagraphs (A) and (B) of paragraph (2) of this subsection shall be required to submit or provide fingerprints or photographs as a condition of being granted a license.

(e)(1) The sheriff shall have the specific authority to suspend or revoke any license for any violation of this Code section. Any licensee accused of violating any provision of this Code section shall be entitled, unless waived, to a hearing on the matter of the alleged violation conducted in accordance with Chapter 13 of Title 50, the "Georgia Administrative Procedure Act."

(2) By making application for a license under this Code section, every applicant consents that the sheriff, as well as any of his agents, together with any prosecuting attorney, as well as any of his agents, may come upon the premises of any licensee or upon any premises on which any licensee is conducting a raffle for the purpose of examining the accounts and records of the licensee to determine if a violation of this Code section has occurred.

(f) The sheriff shall, upon the request of any prosecuting attorney or such prosecuting attorney's designee, certify the status of any organization as to that organization's exemption from payment of state income taxes as a nonprofit organization. The sheriff shall also upon request issue a certificate indicating whether any particular organization holds a currently valid license to operate a raffle. Such certificates properly executed shall be admissible in evidence in any prosecution, and Code Section 48–7–60, relative to the disclosure of income tax information, shall not apply to the furnishing of such certificate.

(g) Notwithstanding the other provisions of this Code section, the sheriff, upon receiving written evidence of the bona fide nonprofit, tax-exempt status of the applicant organization, shall be authorized to issue a special limited license to a nonprofit, tax-exempt organization which will allow it to operate up to three raffles during a calendar year. In such cases, the sheriff shall waive the application and license fee provided for in subsection (d) of this Code section and the annual report provided for in subsection (j) of this Code section.

(h) Raffles shall be operated only on premises owned by the nonprofit, tax-exempt organization operating the raffle, on property leased by the nonprofit, tax-exempt organization and used regularly by that organization for purposes other than the operation of a raffle, or on property leased by the nonprofit, tax-exempt organization operating the raffle from another nonprofit, tax-exempt organization.

(i) No person under the age of 18 years shall be permitted to play any raffle conducted pursuant to any license issued under this Code section unless accompanied by an adult.

(j) On or before April 15 of each year, every nonprofit, tax-exempt organization engaged in operating raffles shall file with the sheriff a report disclosing all receipts and expenditures relating to the operation of raffles in the previous year. The report shall be in addition to all other reports required by law. The report shall be prepared and signed by a certified public accountant competent to prepare such a report and shall be deemed a public record subject to public inspection.

(k)(1) A licensee that conducts or operates a raffle shall maintain the following records for at least three years from the date on which the raffle is conducted:

(A) An itemized list of the gross receipts for each raffle;

(B) An itemized list of all expenses other than prizes that are incurred in the conducting of the raffle as well as the name of each person to whom the expenses are paid and a receipt for all of the expenses;

(C) A list of all prizes awarded during the raffle and the name and address of all persons who are winners of prizes of $50.00 or more in value;

(D) An itemized list of the recipients other than the licensee of the proceeds of the raffle, including the name and address of each recipient to whom such funds are distributed; and

(E) A record of the number of persons who participate in any raffle conducted by the licensee.

(2) A licensee shall:

(A) Own all the equipment used to conduct a raffle or lease such equipment from an organization that is also licensed to conduct a raffle;

(B) Display its raffle license conspicuously at the location where the raffle is conducted;

(C) Conduct raffles only as specified in the licensee's application; and

(D) Not conduct more than one raffle during any one calendar day.

(3) No nonprofit, tax-exempt organization shall enter into any contract with any individual, firm, association, or corporation to have such individual, firm, association, or corporation operate raffles or concessions on behalf of the nonprofit, tax-exempt organization.

(4) A nonprofit, tax-exempt organization shall not lend its name nor allow its identity to be used by any individual, firm, association, or corporation in the operating or advertising of a raffle in which said nonprofit, tax-exempt organization is not directly and solely operating the raffle.

(5) No person shall pay consulting fees to any person for any services performed in relation to the operation or conduct of a raffle.

(6) A person who is a member of more than one nonprofit, tax-exempt organization shall be permitted to participate in the raffle operations of only two organizations of which such person is a member; provided, however, that such person shall not receive more than $30.00 per day for assisting in the conduct of raffles regardless of whether such person assists both organizations in the same day.

(*l*) The sheriff is authorized to promulgate rules and regulations which the sheriff deems necessary for the proper administration and enforcement of this Code section which are not in conflict with any provision of this Code section.

(m) Any person who operates a raffle without a valid license issued by the sheriff as provided in this Code section commits the offense of commercial gambling as defined in Code Section 16–12–22 and, upon conviction thereof, shall be punished accordingly. Any person who knowingly aids, abets, or otherwise assists in the operation of a raffle for which a license has not been obtained as provided in this Code section similarly commits the offense of commercial gambling. Any person who violates any other provision of this Code section shall be guilty of a misdemeanor of a high and aggravated nature. Any person who commits any such violation after having previously been convicted of any violations of this Code section shall be guilty of a felony and, upon conviction thereof, shall be punished by imprisonment for not less than one nor more than five years or by a fine not to exceed $10,000.00, or both.

Laws 1995, p. 832, § 2; Laws 1996, p. 794, §§ 1, 2; Laws 2005, Act 332, § 14, eff. July 1, 2005; Laws 2007, Act 18, § 16, eff. May 11, 2007; Laws 2008, Act 746, § 1, eff. May 14, 2008.

Historical and Statutory Notes

The 2005 amendment by Act 332, in subsec. (j), deleted "or registered" following "signed by a certified".

The 2007 amendment by Act 18 was a provision contained in a correction bill.

Laws 2008, Act 746, § 1, in subsec. (d), par. (2), rewrote subpar. (E), which had formerly read:

"(E) A determination letter from the Georgia Department of Revenue certifying that the applicant is exempt under the tax laws of this state;".

Laws 2008, Act 746, § 13 provides:

"This Act shall become effective upon its approval by the Governor or upon its becoming law without such approval and shall be applicable to all taxable years beginning on or after January 1, 2008."

§ 16–12–23. Keeping a gambling place

(a) A person who knowingly permits any real estate, building, room, tent, vehicle, boat, or other property whatsoever owned by him or under his control to be used as a gambling place or who rents or lets any such property with a view or expectation that it be so used commits the offense of keeping a gambling place.

(b) A person who commits the offense of keeping a gambling place shall be guilty of a misdemeanor of a high and aggravated nature.

Laws 1833, Cobb's 1851 Digest, p. 815; Laws 1865–66, p. 233, § 2; Laws 1884–85, p. 59, § 1; Laws 1968, p. 1249, § 1; Laws 1970, p. 236, § 7.

Formerly Code 1863, § 4423; Code 1868, § 4464; Code 1873, § 4538; Code 1882, § 4538; Penal Code 1895, § 398; Penal Code 1910, §§ 389, 390; Code 1933, §§ 26–6401, 26–6402; Code 1933, § 26–2704.

§ 16–12–24. Ownership, manufacture, transfer, or possession of gambling device or equipment

(a) A person who knowingly owns, manufactures, transfers commercially, or possesses any device which he knows is designed for gambling purposes or anything which he knows is designed as a subassembly or essential part of such device is guilty of a misdemeanor of a high and aggravated nature.

(b)(1) As used in this subsection, the term:

(A) "Antique slot machine" means a coin operated, nonelectronic mechanical gambling device that pays off according to the matching of symbols on wheels spun by a handle and was manufactured in its entirety, except for identical replacement parts, prior to January 1, 1950.

(B) "Conviction" includes a plea of nolo contendere to a felony.

(2) It shall be a defense to any action or prosecution under this Code section for possession of a gambling device that the device is an antique slot machine and that said device was not being used for gambling; provided, however, the defense shall not be available to any person who has been convicted of a felony in this or any other state or under federal law and provided, further, that this defense shall not be available if the antique slot machine is on the premises of a private or public club or in an establishment where alcoholic beverages are sold.

(3) Any antique slot machine seized as a result of a violation of this Code section shall be contraband and subject to seizure and destruction as provided in Code Section 16–12–30. An

antique slot machine seized for a violation of this Code section shall not be destroyed, altered, or sold until the owner has been afforded a reasonable opportunity to present evidence that the device was not operated for unlawful gambling or in violation of this Code section. If the court determines that the device is an antique slot machine and was not operated or possessed in violation of this or any other Code section, such device shall be returned to its owner.

Laws 1968, p. 1249, § 1; Laws 1969, p. 857, §§ 1, 2; Laws 1970, p. 236, § 9; Laws 1985, p. 888, § 1.

Formerly Code 1933, § 26–2707.

§ 16–12–25. Gambling activities on or adjacent to businesses

(a) Any person who solicits another person to commit any of the following acts with the intent to defraud or deceive such person on or adjacent to the premises of any business operated for pecuniary gain shall be guilty of a felony and, upon conviction thereof, shall be punished by imprisonment for not less than one nor more than five years:

(1) Keeps, maintains, employs, or carries on a game for the hazarding of money or other thing of value;

(2) Permits the playing for money or other thing of value of a game or device for the hazarding of money or other thing of value;

(3) Keeps or employs a device or equipment for the purpose of carrying on or operating a game or device for the hazarding of money or other thing of value;

(4) Permits the betting or wagering of money or other thing of value;

(5) Sells or offers to sell to a person a ticket number or combination or chance or anything representing a chance in a lottery or other similar scheme;

(6) Keeps, maintains, employs, or carries on a lottery or scheme or device for the hazarding of money or other thing of value;

(7) Keeps, maintains, or employs a lottery ticket, lottery book, lottery ribbon, or other article used in keeping, maintaining, or carrying on a lottery or other scheme, game, or device for the hazarding of money or other thing of value;

(8) Solicits a person to engage in a game or to operate a device for the hazarding of money or other thing of value; or

(9) Solicits a person to engage in a lottery or other scheme or device for the hazarding of money or other thing of value.

(b) This Code section is cumulative of and supplemental to any laws making any of the activities prohibited by this Code section unlawful and punishable as a misdemeanor; and nothing in this Code section shall be construed to repeal, amend, alter, or supersede any such laws.

Laws 1968, p. 1198, §§ 1, 2.

§ 16–12–26. Advertising commercial gambling

(a) A person who knowingly prints, publishes, or advertises any lottery or other scheme for commercial gambling or who knowingly prints or publishes any lottery ticket, policy ticket, or other similar device designed to serve as evidence of participation in a lottery commits the offense of advertising commercial gambling.

(b) A person who commits the offense of advertising commercial gambling shall be guilty of a misdemeanor of a high and aggravated nature.

Laws 1968, p. 1249, § 1; Laws 1970, p. 236, § 8.

Formerly Code 1933, § 26–2705.

§ 16–12–27. Advertisements; contents

(a) It shall be unlawful for any person, partnership, firm, corporation, or other entity to sell, distribute, televise, broadcast, or disseminate any advertisement, television or radio commercial, or any book, magazine, periodical, newspaper, or other written or printed matter containing an advertisement or solicitation for participation in any lottery declared to be unlawful by the laws of this state unless such advertisement, commercial, or solicitation contains or includes the words "void in Georgia" printed or spoken so as to be clearly legible or audible to persons viewing or hearing such advertisement, commercial, or solicitation.

(b) Any person, partnership, firm, corporation, or other entity violating subsection (a) of this Code section shall be guilty of a misdemeanor.

Laws 1889, p. 187, § 1; Laws 1975, p. 1072, § 1.

Formerly Penal Code 1895, § 410; Penal Code 1910, § 401; Code 1933, § 26–6504; Code 1933, § 26–2705.1.

§ 16–12–28. Communicating gambling information

(a) A person who knowingly communicates information as to bets, betting odds, or changes in betting odds or who knowingly installs or maintains equipment for the transmission or receipt of such information with the intent to further gambling commits the offense of communicating gambling information.

(b) A person who commits the offense of communicating gambling information, upon conviction thereof, shall be punished by imprisonment for not less than one nor more than five years or by a fine not to exceed $5,000.00, or both.

Laws 1968, p. 1249, § 1.

Formerly Code 1933, § 26–2706.

§ 16–12–29. Players competent witnesses

On the trial of any person for violating Code Section 16–12–21, 16–12–22, 16–12–23, or 16–12–24, any other person who may have played and bet at the same time or table shall be a competent witness.

Laws 1833, Cobb's 1851 Digest, pp. 815, 816; Laws 1968, p. 1249, § 1; Laws 1969, p. 857, § 15.

Formerly Code 1863, § 4428; Code 1868, § 4469; Code 1873, § 4545; Code 1882, § 4545; Penal Code 1895, § 404; Penal Code 1910, § 395; Code 1933, § 26–6407; Code 1933, § 26–9907.

§ 16–12–30. Seizure and destruction of gambling devices

(a) Except as provided in subsection (b) of Code Section 16–12–24, every gambling device is declared to be contraband and subject to seizure and confiscation by any state or local authority within whose jurisdiction the same may be found.

(b) At such time as there shall be a final judgment entered in any case or cases in which a seized gambling device is necessary evidence or at such time as the state shall determine that the continued physical existence of the seized gambling device is no longer necessary, the same shall be turned over by that person having custody of the device to the sheriff of the county wherein the device was confiscated. The sheriff shall within ten days after receiving the device destroy the same in the presence of the district attorney of the circuit in which such county is located and shall forward to the state revenue commissioner a certificate so stating which shall include the serial number of the device so destroyed.

Laws 1968, p. 1249, § 1; Laws 1969, p. 857, § 13; Laws 1985, p. 888, § 2.

Formerly Code 1933, § 26–2708.

§ 16–12–31. Repealed by Laws 1982, p. 2325, § 1, eff. November 1, 1982

§ 16–12–32. Seizure of property and vehicles; disposal of forfeited property

(a) As used in this Code section, "property" means any personal property of any type, tangible or intangible, including but not limited to vehicles, conveyances, aircraft, watercraft, funds, other things of value or choses in action or any interest in such property, but shall not include a gambling device subject to seizure and destruction under Code Section 16–12–30.

(b) All property used in, intended for use in, used to facilitate, or derived from or realized through a violation of this article or which is located within any gambling place or within any vehicle or other conveyance used to transport any gambling device, any subassembly or essential part thereof, card, stub, ticket, check, funds, things of value, or other device designed to facilitate participation in any lottery is declared to be contraband and may be seized and forfeited as provided in this Code section.

(c) Any such property shall be seized by any peace officer who, within ten days after the seizure of such property, shall report the same to the district attorney of the superior court having jurisdiction in the county where the seizure was made.

(d) Within 30 days from the date he receives notice of such seizure, the district attorney of said judicial circuit shall cause to be filed in the superior court of the county in which the property was seized an action against the property so seized and any and all persons having an interest in or right affected by the seizure or sale of such property.

(e) A copy of the action shall be served upon the person or persons having custody or possession of such property at the time of seizure, and, if known, upon any owner, lessee, and any person having a duly recorded security interest in or lien upon such property at the time of seizure. If the owner or lessee is unknown or resides out of the state or departs the state or cannot after due diligence be found within the state or conceals himself so as to avoid service, notice of such proceedings shall be published once a week for two consecutive weeks in the newspaper in which sheriff's advertisements are published. Such publication shall be deemed notice to any and all persons having an interest in or right affected by such proceeding and any sale of the property resulting therefrom but shall not constitute notice to any person having a duly recorded security interest in or lien upon such property and required to be served under this subsection unless that person is unknown or resides out of the state or departs the state or cannot after due diligence be found within the state or conceals himself to avoid service.

(f) If no defense is filed within 30 days after the service of a copy of the action or the last publication required under subsection (e) of this Code section, judgment by default shall be entered by the court at chambers, otherwise the case shall proceed as other civil cases in said court.

(g) Should it appear that any person filing a defense in the action knew, or by the exercise of ordinary care should have known, that the property was used in violation of this Code section, the same shall be sold by order of the court after such advertisement as the court shall direct, and such person shall have no claim upon the property or the proceeds from the sale thereof.

(h) Except as otherwise provided in this Code section, property forfeited pursuant to this subsection shall be disposed of by order of the court as follows:

(1) Upon application of the seizing law enforcement agency or any other law enforcement agency of state, county, or municipal government, the court may permit the agency to retain the property for official use in law enforcement work; or

(2) The court may sell that which is not required to be destroyed by law and which is not harmful to the public, and the proceeds of such sale shall be used for payment of all proper expenses of the forfeiture and sale including, but not limited to, the expenses of seizure, maintenance of custody, advertising, and court costs.

The remainder of the proceeds of a sale of forfeited property, after payment of these expenses, shall be paid into the general fund of the county.

Laws 1945, p. 351, § 2; Laws 1968, p. 1249, § 1; Laws 1982, p. 2325, § 1; Laws 1983, p. 3, § 13; Laws 1990, p. 587, § 1.

Formerly Code 1933, §§ 26–2709, 26–2710; Code 1981, § 16–12–31.

§ 16–12–33. Bribery of contestant

A person who gives, offers, or promises any reward, money, or other thing of value to anyone who participates or expects to participate in any amateur or professional athletic contest, sporting event, or exhibition or to any coach, trainer, manager or official in such athletic contest, sporting event, or exhibition with intent to influence such person to lose, try to lose, or cause to be lost or to affect the margin of victory or defeat in such athletic contest, sporting event, or exhibition commits the offense of bribery of a contestant and, upon conviction thereof, shall be punished by a fine of not less than $1,000.00 nor more than $5,000.00 or by imprisonment for not less than one nor more than five years, or both.

Laws 1947, p. 1139, § 2; Laws 1952, p. 303, § 1; Laws 1968, p. 1249, § 1.

Formerly Code 1933, § 26–2711.

§ 16–12–34. Soliciting or accepting a bribe to influence athletic contest

A person participating or expecting to participate or any coach, trainer, manager, or official in any amateur or professional athletic contest, sporting event, or exhibition who solicits or accepts any reward, money, or other thing of value with the intent, understanding, or agreement that it influence him to lose, try to lose, or cause to be lost or to limit the margin of victory or defeat in such athletic contest, sporting event, or exhibition by failing to exert his best efforts or to exercise his best judgment commits the offense of soliciting or accepting a bribe and, upon conviction thereof, shall be punished by a fine of not less than $1,000.00 nor more than $5,000.00 or by imprisonment for not less than one nor more than five years, or both.

Laws 1947, p. 1139, § 3; Laws 1952, p. 303, § 1; Laws 1968, p. 1249, § 1.

Formerly Code 1933, § 26–2712.

§ 16–12–35. Exceptions to gambling law

(a) As used in this Code section, the term "some skill" means any presence of the following factors, alone or in combination with one another:

(1) A learned power of doing a thing competently;

(2) A particular craft, art, ability, strategy, or tactic;

(3) A developed or acquired aptitude or ability;

(4) A coordinated set of actions, including, but not limited to, eye-hand coordination;

(5) Dexterity, fluency, or coordination in the execution of learned physical or mental tasks or both;

(6) Technical proficiency or expertise;

(7) Development or implementation of strategy or tactics in order to achieve a goal; or

(8) Knowledge of the means or methods of accomplishing a task.

The term some skill refers to a particular craft, coordinated effort, art, ability, strategy, or tactic employed by the player to affect in some way the outcome of the game played on a bona fide coin operated amusement machine as defined in paragraph (2) of Code Section 48–17–1. If a player can take no action to affect the outcome of the game, the bona fide coin operated amusement machine does not meet the "some skill" requirement of this Code section.

(b) Nothing in this part shall apply to a coin operated game or device designed and manufactured for bona fide amusement purposes only which may by application of some skill entitle the player to earn replays of the game or device at no additional cost and to discharge the accumulated free replays only by reactivating the game or device for each accumulated free replay or by reactivating the game or device for a portion or all of the accumulated free plays in a single play. This subsection shall not apply, however, to any game or device classified by the United States government as requiring a federal gaming tax stamp under applicable provisions of the Internal Revenue Code or any item described as a gambling device in subparagraph (B), (C), or (D) of paragraph (2) of Code Section 16–12–20.

(c)(1) Nothing in this part shall apply to a crane game machine or device meeting the requirements of paragraph (2) of this subsection.

(2) A crane game machine or device acceptable for the purposes of paragraph (1) of this subsection shall meet the following requirements:

(A) The machine or device must be designed and manufactured only for bona fide amusement purposes and must involve at least some skill in its operation;

(B) The machine or device must reward a winning player exclusively with free replays or merchandise contained within the machine itself and such merchandise must be limited to noncash merchandise, prizes, toys, gift certificates, or novelties, each of which has a wholesale value not exceeding $ 5.00. A player may be rewarded with both free replays and noncash merchandise, prizes, toys, or novelties for a single play of the game or device as provided in this Code section;

(C) The player of the machine or device must be able to control the timing of the use of the claw or grasping device to attempt to pick up or grasp a prize, toy, or novelty;

(D) The player of the machine or device must be made aware of the total time which the machine or device allows during a game for the player to maneuver the claw or grasping device into a position to attempt to pick up or grasp a prize, toy, or novelty;

(E) The claw or grasping device must not be of a size, design, or shape that prohibits picking up or grasping a prize, toy, or novelty contained within the machine or device; and

(F) The machine or device must not be classified by the United States government as requiring a federal gaming stamp under applicable provisions of the Internal Revenue Code.

(d)(1) Nothing in this part shall apply to a coin operated game or device designed and manufactured only for bona fide amusement purposes which involves some skill in its operation if it rewards the player exclusively with:

(A) Free replays;

(B) Merchandise limited to noncash merchandise, prizes, toys, gift certificates, or novelties, each of which has a wholesale value of not more than $ 5.00 received for a single play of the game or device;

(C) Points, tokens, vouchers, tickets, or other evidence of winnings which may be exchanged for rewards set out in subparagraph (A) of this paragraph or subparagraph (B) of this paragraph or a combination of rewards set out in subparagraph (A) and subparagraph (B) of this paragraph; or

(D) Any combination of rewards set out in two or more of subparagraph (A), (B), or (C) of this paragraph.

This subsection shall not apply, however, to any game or device classified by the United States government as requiring a federal gaming stamp under applicable provisions of the Internal Revenue Code or any item described as a gambling device in subparagraph (B), (C), or (D) of paragraph (2) of Code Section 16–12–20.

(2) A player of bona fide coin operated amusement games or devices described in paragraph (1) of this subsection may accumulate winnings for the successful play of such bona fide coin operated amusement games or devices through tokens, vouchers, points, or tickets. Points may be accrued on the machine or device. A player may carry over points on one play to subsequent plays. A player may redeem accumulated tokens, vouchers, or tickets for noncash merchandise, prizes, toys, gift certificates, or novelties so long as the amount of tokens, vouchers, or tickets received does not exceed $ 5.00 for a single play.

(e) Any person who gives to any other person money for free replays on coin operated games or devices described in subsection (b), (c), or (d) of this Code section shall be guilty of a misdemeanor.

(f) Any person owning or possessing an amusement game or device described in subsection (c) or (d) of this Code section or any person employed by or acting on behalf of any such person who gives to any other person money for any noncash merchandise, prize, toy, gift certificate, or novelty received as a reward in playing any such amusement game or device shall be guilty of a misdemeanor.

(g) Any person owning or possessing an amusement game or device described in subsection (b), (c), or (d) of this Code section or any person employed by or acting on behalf of any such person who gives to any other person money as a reward for the successful play or winning of any such amusement game or device shall be guilty of a misdemeanor of a high and aggravated nature.

(h) Any gift certificates, tokens, vouchers, tickets, or other evidence of winnings awarded under subsection (c) or (d) of this Code section must be redeemable only at the premises on which the game or device is located. It shall be unlawful for any person to provide to any other person as a reward for play on any such game or device any gift certificate, token, voucher, ticket, or other evidence of winning which is redeemable or exchangeable for any thing of value at any other premises. It shall be unlawful for any person at any premises other than those on which the game or device is located to give any thing of value to any other person for any gift certificate, token, voucher, ticket, or other evidence of winning received by such other person from play on such game or device. Any person who violates this subsection shall be guilty of a misdemeanor of a high and aggravated nature.

(i) The merchandise, prizes, toys, gift certificates, novelties, or rewards which may be awarded under subsection (c) or (d) of this Code section may not include or be redeemable or exchangeable for any firearms, alcohol, or tobacco or any lottery ticket or other item enabling participation in any lottery. Any person who violates this subsection shall be guilty of a misdemeanor of a high and aggravated nature.

(j) Any other laws to the contrary notwithstanding, this part shall not be applicable to the manufacturing, processing, selling, possessing, or transporting of any printed materials, equipment, devices, or other materials used or designated for use in a legally authorized lottery nor shall it be applicable to the manufacturing, processing, selling, possessing, or transporting of any gaming equipment, devices, or other materials used or designated for use only in jurisdictions in which the use of such items is legal. This part shall in no way prohibit communications between persons in this state and persons involved with such legal lotteries or gaming devices relative to such printed materials, equipment, devices, or other materials or prohibit demonstrations of same within this state.

Laws 1976, p. 1158, § 1; Laws 1978, p. 1779, § 1; Laws 1985, p. 886, § 1; Laws 1991, p. 1398, § 1; Laws 1991, p. 1396, § 1; Laws 1992, p. 1489, § 1; Laws 1996, p. 309, § 1; Laws 1997, p. 689, § 1; Laws 1998, p. 563, § 1; Laws 1999, p. 1224, § 1; Laws 2001, Ex. Sess., p. 312, § 2; Laws 2007, Act 18, § 16, eff. May 11, 2007.

Formerly Code 1933, § 26–2713.

Historical and Statutory Notes

The 2001 amendment provided that certain video poker games and devices and certain other games and devices shall not be permitted under provisions legalizing certain amusement devices; to provide that certificates or other evidence of winning on certain other games and devices must be redeemable only where the game or device is located; to define crimes and declare penalties; and, to provide that the prizes awarded on such other games and devices may not include certain items.

The 2007 amendment by Act 18 was a provision contained in a correction bill.

§ 16–12–36. Promotional contests

(a) A promotional or giveaway contest which conforms with the qualifications of a lawful promotion specified in paragraph (16) of subsection (b) of Code Section 10–1–393 shall not be a lottery.

(b) Except as provided in subsection (a) of this Code section, all promotions or promotional contests involving an element of chance in the distribution of prizes, gifts, awards, or other items which otherwise meet the definition of a "lottery" in this article shall be included within the definition of the term "lottery" for purposes of this article, unless specifically exempted by some other statute or law.

Laws 1982, p. 1661, § 2; Laws 1982, p. 1661, § 4; Laws 1983, p. 3, § 13; Laws 1986, p. 1313, § 4.

Formerly Code 1933, § 26–2714.

§ 16–12–37. Dogfighting

(a) As used in this Code section, the term "dog" means any domestic canine.

(b) Any person who:

(1) Owns, possesses, trains, transports, or sells any dog with the intent that such dog shall be engaged in fighting with another dog;

(2) For amusement or gain, causes any dog to fight with another dog or for amusement or gain, causes any dogs to injure each other;

(3) Wagers money or anything of value on the result of such dogfighting;

(4) Knowingly permits any act in violation of paragraph (1) or (2) of this subsection on any premises under the ownership or control of such person or knowingly aids or abets any such act; or

(5) Knowingly promotes or advertises an exhibition of fighting with another dog

shall be guilty of a felony and, upon the first conviction thereof, shall be punished by imprisonment of not less than one nor more than five years, a fine of not less than $5,000.00, or both such fine and imprisonment. On a second or subsequent conviction, such person shall be punished by imprisonment of not less than one nor more than ten years, a fine of not less than $15,000.00, or both such fine and imprisonment. Each act or omission in violation of this subsection shall constitute a separate offense.

(c) Any person who is knowingly present only as a spectator at any place for the fighting of dogs shall, upon a first conviction thereof, be guilty of a misdemeanor of a high and aggravated nature. On a second conviction, such person shall be guilty of a felony and shall be punished by imprisonment of not less than one nor more than five years, a fine of not less than $5,000.00, or both such fine and imprisonment. On a third or subsequent conviction, such person shall be punished by imprisonment of not less than one nor more than ten years, a fine of not less than $15,000.00, or both such fine and imprisonment. Each act in violation of this subsection shall constitute a separate offense.

(d) Any dog subject to fighting may be impounded pursuant to the provisions of Code Sections 4–11–9.2 through 4–11–9.6.

(e) This Code section shall not prohibit, impede, or otherwise interfere with animal husbandry, training techniques, competition, events, shows, or practices not otherwise specifically prohibited by law and shall not apply to the following activities:

(1) Owning, using, breeding, training, or equipping any animal to pursue, take, hunt, or recover wildlife or any animal lawfully hunted under Title 27 or participating in hunting or fishing in accordance with the provisions of Title 27 and rules and regulations promulgated pursuant thereto as such rules and regulations existed on the date specified in Code Section 27–1–39;

(2) Owning, using, breeding, training, or equipping dogs to work livestock for agricultural purposes in accordance with the rules and regulations of the Commissioner of Agriculture as such rules and regulations existed on January 1, 2008;

(3) Owning, using, breeding, training, or equipping dogs for law enforcement purposes; or

(4) Owning, using, breeding, training, or equipping any animal to control damage from nuisance or pest species in and around structures or agricultural operations.

Laws 1982, p. 2214, § 1; Laws 1982, p. 2214, § 2; Laws 1983, p. 3, § 13; Laws 2008, Act 408, § 1–1, eff. May 6, 2008.

Formerly Code 1933, § 26–2714; Code 1981, § 16–12–36.

Historical and Statutory Notes

The 2008 amendment by Act 408 rewrote the section which had read:

"(a) A person commits the offense of dogfighting when he causes or allows a dog to fight another dog for sport or gaming purposes or maintains or operates any event at which dogs are allowed or encouraged to fight one another.

"(b) A person convicted of the offense of dogfighting shall be punished by a mandatory fine of $5,000.00 or by a mandatory fine of $5,000.00 and imprisonment for not less than one year nor more than five years."

§ 16–12–38. Pyramid promotional scheme.

(a) As used in this Code section, the term:

(1) "Compensation" means a payment of any money, thing of value, or financial benefit.

(2) "Consideration" means the payment of cash or the purchase of goods, services, or intangible property, and does not include the purchase of goods or services furnished at cost to be used in making sales and not for resale, or time and effort spent in pursuit of sales or recruiting activities.

(3) "Inventory" includes both goods and services, including company produced promotional materials, sales aids, and sales kits that the plan or operation requires independent salespersons to purchase.

(4) "Inventory loading" means that the plan or operation requires or encourages its independent salespersons to pur-

chase inventory in an amount which unreasonably exceeds that which the salesperson can expect to resell for ultimate consumption or to use or consume in a reasonable time period.

(5) "Participant" means a person who joins a plan or operation.

(6) "Person" means an individual, a corporation, a partnership, or any association or unincorporated organization.

(7) "Promote" means to contrive, prepare, establish, plan, operate, advertise, or to otherwise induce or attempt to induce another person to be a participant.

(8) "Pyramid promotional scheme" means any plan or operation in which a participant gives consideration for the right to receive compensation that is derived primarily from the recruitment of other persons as participants into the plan or operation rather than from the sale of goods, services, or intangible property to participants or by participants to others.

(b)(1) No person may establish, promote, operate, or participate in any pyramid promotional scheme. A limitation as to the number of persons who may participate or the presence of additional conditions affecting eligibility for the opportunity to receive compensation under the plan does not change the identity of the plan as a pyramid promotional scheme. It is not a defense under this subsection that a person, on giving consideration, obtains goods, services, or intangible property in addition to the right to receive compensation.

(2) Nothing in this Code section may be construed to prohibit a plan or operation, or to define a plan or operation as a pyramid promotional scheme, based on the fact that participants in the plan or operation give consideration in return for the right to receive compensation based upon purchases of goods, services, or intangible property by participants for personal use, consumption, or resale so long as the plan or operation does not promote or induce inventory loading and complies with the cancellation requirements of subsection (d) of Code Section 10–1–415.

(3) Any person who participates in a pyramid promotional scheme shall be guilty of a misdemeanor of a high and aggravated nature. Any person who establishes, promotes, or operates a pyramid promotional scheme shall be guilty of a felony and, upon conviction thereof, shall be punished by imprisonment for not less than one nor more than five years.

(4) Nothing in this Code section shall be construed so as to include a "multilevel distribution company," as defined in paragraph (6) of Code Section 10–1–410, which is operating in compliance with Part 3 of Article 15 of Chapter 1 of Title 10.

Laws 1985, p. 437, § 2; Laws 1988, p. 1868, § 3; Laws 1992, p. 6, § 16; Laws 2005, Act 132, § 1, eff. July 1, 2005.

Historical and Statutory Notes

The 2005 amendment by Act 132 rewrote the section which had read:

"The organization of any chain letter club, pyramid club, or other group organized or brought together under any plan or device whereby fees or dues or anything of material value to be paid or given by members thereof are to be paid or given to any other member thereof, which plan or device includes any provision for the increase in such membership through a chain process of new members securing other new members and thereby advancing themselves in the group to a position where such members in turn receive fees, dues, or things of material value from other members, is declared to be a lottery; and whoever shall participate in any such lottery by becoming a member of, or affiliating with, any such group or organization or whoever shall solicit any person for membership or affiliation in any such group or organization shall be guilty of a misdemeanor of a high and aggravated nature; provided, however, that this Code section shall not include a 'multilevel distribution company,' as defined in paragraph (6) of Code Section 10–1–410, which is operating in compliance with Part 3 of Article 15 of Chapter 1 of Title 10."

Part 2
Bingo

§ 16–12–50. Intent of General Assembly

It is the intention of the General Assembly that, except for recreational bingo, only nonprofit, tax-exempt organizations which are properly licensed pursuant to this part shall be allowed to operate bingo games.

Laws 1977, p. 1164, § 8; Laws 1978, p. 853, § 6; Laws 1993, p. 535, § 1.

§ 16–12–51. Definitions

As used in this part, the term:

(1) "Bingo game" or "nonprofit bingo game" means a game of chance played on cards with numbered squares in which counters or indicators are placed on numbers chosen by lot and won by covering a previously specified number or order of numbered squares. A bingo game may be played manually or with an electronic or computer device that stores the numbers from a player's card or cards, tracks the numbers chosen by lot when such numbers are entered by the player, and notifies the player of a winning combination. Such words, terms, or phrases, as used in this paragraph, shall be strictly construed to include only the series of acts generally defined as bingo and shall exclude all other activity.

(2) "Bingo session" means a time period during which bingo games are played.

(3) "Director" means the director of the Georgia Bureau of Investigation.

(3.1) "Nonprofit, tax-exempt organization" means an organization, association, corporation, or other legal entity which has been determined by the federal Internal Revenue Service to be exempt from taxation under federal tax law and which is exempt from taxation under the income tax laws of this state under Code Section 48–7–25; which is organized or incorporated in this state or authorized to do business in this state; and which uses the proceeds from any bingo games conducted by such organization solely within this state.

(4) "Operate," "operated," or "operating" means the direction, supervision, management, operation, control, or guidance of activity.

(5) "Recreational bingo" means a bingo session operated by any person or entity at no charge to participants in which the prizes for each bingo game during the bingo session shall be noncash prizes and the total of such prizes for each such game shall not exceed the amount established pursuant to regulations established by the director. No such noncash prize awarded in recreational bingo shall be exchanged or redeemed for money or for any other prize with a value in excess of the amount established pursuant to regulations established by the director. Recreational bingo shall also include a bingo session operated by a nonprofit, tax-exempt licensed operator of bingo games at no charge to participants in which the participants are senior citizens attending a function at a facility of the tax-exempt licensed organization or are residents of nursing homes, retirement homes, senior centers, or hospitals and in which the prizes for each bingo game during the bingo session shall be nominal cash prizes not to exceed $5.00 for any single prize and the total of such prizes for each such game shall not exceed the amount established pursuant to regulations established by the director. Recreational bingo shall also include a bingo session operated by an employer with ten or more full-time employees for the purposes of providing a safe workplace incentive and in which the prizes are determined by the employer; provided, however, that no monetary consideration is required by any participant other than the employer and the employer expressly prohibits any monetary consideration from any employee. Recreational bingo shall not be considered a

lottery as defined in paragraph (4) of Code Section 16–12–20 or a form of gambling as defined in Code Section 16–12–21.

Laws 1977, p. 1164, § 1; Laws 1978, p. 853, § 1; Laws 1980, p. 422, § 1; Laws 1993, p. 535, § 2; Laws 1994, p. 490, § 1; Laws 1994, p. 1002, § 1; Laws 2003, Act 171, § 1, eff. July 1, 2003; Laws 2006, Act 551, § 1, eff. July 1, 2006; Laws 2008, Act 746, § 2, eff. May 14, 2008.

Historical and Statutory Notes

The 2003 amendment by Act 171 rewrote par. (1) which had read as follows:

"(1) 'Bingo game' or 'nonprofit bingo game' means a game of chance played on cards with numbered squares in which counters or indicators are placed on numbers chosen by lot and won by covering a previously specified number or order of numbered squares. Such words, terms, or phrases, as used in this paragraph, shall be strictly construed to include only the series of acts generally defined as bingo and shall exclude all other activity."

The 2006 amendment by Act 551 added par. (3.1).

Laws 2008, Act 746, § 2, in par. (3.1) substituted "and which is exempt from taxation under the income tax laws of this state under Code Section 48–7–25" for "and has been determined by the Georgia Department of Revenue to be exempt from taxation under the tax laws of this state".

Laws 2008, Act 746, § 13 provides:

"This Act shall become effective upon its approval by the Governor or upon its becoming law without such approval and shall be applicable to all taxable years beginning on or after January 1, 2008."

§ 16–12–52. Operation of bingo games; license required; exception

(a) Any other law to the contrary notwithstanding except for subsection (b) of this Code section, no nonprofit, tax-exempt organization shall be permitted to operate a bingo game until the director issues a license to the organization authorizing it to do so. In the event of any controversy concerning whether or not certain activity constitutes bingo for which a license may be issued, the decision of the director shall control. The license described in this Code section is in addition to and not in lieu of any other licenses which may be required by this state or any political subdivision thereof, and no bingo game shall be operated until such time as all requisite licenses have been obtained.

(b) Recreational bingo is a nonprofit bingo game or a bingo game operated by an employer with ten or more full-time employees for the purpose of providing a safe workplace incentive and shall not be subject to the licensing requirements and regulations provided in this part applicable to bingo games not considered recreational bingo and operated by nonprofit, tax-exempt organizations.

Laws 1977, p. 1164, § 2; Laws 1980, p. 422, § 2; Laws 1993, p. 535, § 3; Laws 1994, p. 490, § 2; Laws 1994, p. 1002, § 2.

§ 16–12–53. Licensing procedures, applications, fees, renewals

(a) Any nonprofit, tax-exempt organization desiring to obtain a license to operate bingo games shall make application to the director on forms prescribed by the Georgia Bureau of Investigation and shall pay an annual fee of $ 100.00. No license shall be issued to any nonprofit, tax-exempt organization unless the organization has been in existence for 12 months immediately prior to the issuance of the license. The license will expire at 12:00 Midnight on December 31 following the granting of the license. Renewal applications for each calendar year shall be filed with the director prior to January 1 of each year and shall be on a form prescribed by the Georgia Bureau of Investigation.

(b) Each application for a license and each application for renewal of a license shall contain the following information:

(1) The name and home address of the applicant and, if the applicant is a corporation, association, or other similar legal entity, the names and home addresses of each of the officers of the organization as well as the names and addresses of the directors, or other persons similarly situated, of the organization;

(2) The names and home addresses of each of the persons who will be operating, advertising, or promoting the bingo game;

(3) The names and home addresses of any persons, organizations, or other legal entities that will act as surety for the applicant or to which the applicant is financially indebted or to which any financial obligation is owed by the applicant;

(4) A determination letter from the Internal Revenue Service certifying that the applicant is an organization exempt under federal tax law;

(5) A statement affirming that the applicant is exempt under the income tax laws of this state under Code Section 48–7–25;

(6) The location at which the applicant will conduct the bingo games and, if the premises on which the games are to be conducted is to be leased, a copy of the lease or rental agreement;

(7) A statement showing the convictions, if any, for criminal offenses other than minor traffic offenses of each of the persons listed in paragraphs (1), (2), and (3) of this subsection; and

(8) Any other necessary and reasonable information which the director may require.

(c) The director shall refuse to grant a bingo license to any applicant who fails to provide fully the information required by this Code section.

(d) When a nonprofit, tax-exempt organization which operates or intends to operate bingo games for residents and patients of a retirement home, nursing home, or hospital operated by that organization at which gross receipts are or will be limited to $ 100.00 or less during each bingo session and pays or will pay prizes having a value of $ 100.00 or less during each bingo session, then, notwithstanding any other provision of this part or any rule or regulation promulgated by the director pursuant to the provisions of Code Section 16–12–61, neither the applicant nor any of the persons whose names and addresses are required under paragraphs (1) and (2) of subsection (b) of this Code section shall be required to submit or provide fingerprints or photographs as a condition of being granted a license.

(e) If the director determines that an organization has one or more auxiliaries, the members of any such auxiliary may assist in such organization's bingo operations, even if such auxiliary holds a license under this part, and the members of the main organization may assist in the bingo operations of any such licensed auxiliary.

Laws 1977, p. 1164, § 3; Laws 1978, p. 853, § 2; Laws 1980, p. 422, §§ 3, 4; Laws 1985, p. 149, § 16; Laws 1990, p. 1944, § 1; Laws 1991, p. 1113, § 1; Laws 2001, p. 1036, § 1; Laws 2004, Act 581, § 1, eff. July 1, 2004; Laws 2008, Act 746, § 3, eff. May 14, 2008.

Historical and Statutory Notes

The 2001 amendment substituted in the second sentence of subsec. (a) "12" for "24" months.

The 2004 amendment by Act 581 added subsec. (e).

Laws 2008, Act 746, § 3, in subsec. (b), rewrote par. (5), which had formerly read:

"(5) A determination letter from the Georgia Department of Revenue certifying that the applicant is exempt under the tax laws of this state;"

Laws 2008, Act 746, § 13 provides:

"This Act shall become effective upon its approval by the Governor or upon its becoming law without such approval and shall be applicable to all taxable years beginning on or after January 1, 2008."

§ 16–12–54. Revocation of licenses, access to premises by law enforcement agencies

(a) The director shall have the specific authority to suspend or revoke any license for any violation of this part or for any violation of any rule or regulation promulgated under this part. Any licensee accused of violating any provision of this part or of any rule or regulation promulgated hereunder shall be entitled, unless waived, to a hearing on the matter of the alleged violation conducted in accordance with Chapter 13 of Title 50, the "Georgia Administrative Procedure Act."

(b) By making application for a license under this part, every applicant consents that the director, as well as any of his agents, together with any prosecuting attorney, as well as any of his agents, may come upon the premises of any licensee or upon any premises on which any licensee is conducting a bingo game for the purpose of examining the accounts and records of the licensee to determine if a violation of this part has occurred.

Laws 1977, p. 1164, § 2; Laws 1978, p. 853, § 5; Laws 1980, p. 422, §§ 7, 8.

§ 16–12–55. Certificates

The director shall upon the request of any prosecuting attorney or his designee certify the status of any organization as to that organization's exemption from payment of state income taxes as a nonprofit organization. The director shall also upon request issue a certificate indicating whether any particular organization holds a currently valid license to operate a bingo game. Such certificates properly executed shall be admissible in evidence in any prosecution and Code Section 48–7–60, relative to the disclosure of income tax information, shall not apply to the furnishing of such certificate.

Laws 1978, p. 853, § 3; Laws 1980, p. 422, § 5.

§ 16–12–56. One-time license for certain organizations to play bingo

Notwithstanding the other provisions of this part, the director upon receiving written application therefor shall be authorized to issue a one-time license to a nonprofit, tax-exempt school which will allow it to operate a bingo game one day annually. In such cases, the director shall have the power to waive the license fee provided for in Code Section 16–12–53, to waive the annual report provided for in Code Section 16–12–59, and otherwise promulgate rules and regulations to carry out this Code section.

Laws 1977, p. 1164, § 11; Laws 1980, p. 422, § 11.

§ 16–12–57. Operation of bingo games; place where held

Bingo games shall be operated only on premises owned by the nonprofit, tax-exempt organization operating the bingo game, on property leased by the nonprofit, tax-exempt organization and used regularly by that organization for purposes other than the operation of a bingo game, or on property leased by the nonprofit, tax-exempt organization operating the bingo game from another nonprofit, tax-exempt organization.

Laws 1977, p. 1164, § 4.

§ 16–12–58. Age restriction to play or conduct bingo games

No person under the age of 18 years shall be permitted to play any game or games of bingo conducted pursuant to any license issued under this part unless accompanied by an adult. No person under the age of 18 years shall be permitted to conduct or assist in the conducting of any game of bingo conducted pursuant to any license issued under this part.

Laws 1977, p. 1164, § 5.

§ 16–12–59. Annual report to be filed with the director

On or before April 15 of each year, every nonprofit, tax-exempt organization engaged in operating bingo games shall file with the director a report disclosing all receipts and expenditures relating to the operation of bingo games in the previous year. The report shall be in addition to all other reports required by law. The report shall be prepared and signed by a certified public accountant competent to prepare such a report and shall be deemed a public record subject to public inspection.

Laws 1977, p. 1164, § 6; Laws 1980, p. 422, § 6; Laws 2005, Act 332, § 15, eff. July 1, 2005.

Historical and Statutory Notes

The 2005 amendment by Act 332 deleted "or registered" following "signed by a certified".

§ 16–12–60. Duties of licensees; prohibited activities

(a) A licensee that conducts or operates a bingo session shall maintain the following records for at least three years from the date on which the bingo session is conducted:

(1) An itemized list of the gross receipts for each session;

(2) An itemized list of all expenses other than prizes that are incurred in the conducting of the bingo session as well as the name of each person to whom the expenses are paid and a receipt for all of the expenses;

(3) A list of all prizes awarded during the bingo session and the name and address of all persons who are winners of prizes of $ 50.00 or more in value;

(4) An itemized list of the recipients other than the licensee of the proceeds of the bingo game, including the name and address of each recipient to whom such funds are distributed; and

(5) A record of the number of persons who participate in any bingo session conducted by the licensee.

(b) A licensee shall:

(1) Own all the equipment used to conduct a bingo game or lease such equipment;

(2) Display its bingo license conspicuously at the location where the bingo game is conducted;

(3) Conduct bingo games only at the single location specified in the licensee's application; and

(4) Not conduct more than one bingo session during any one calendar day, which session shall not exceed five hours.

(c) No nonprofit, tax-exempt organization shall enter into any contract with any individual, firm, association, or corporation to have such individual, firm, association, or corporation operate bingo games or concessions on behalf of the nonprofit, tax-exempt organization.

(d) A nonprofit, tax-exempt organization shall not lend its name nor allow its identity to be used by any individual, firm, association, or corporation in the operating or advertising of a bingo game in which said nonprofit, tax-exempt organization is not directly and solely operating the bingo game.

(e) It shall be unlawful for two or more nonprofit, tax-exempt organizations which are properly licensed pursuant to this part to operate bingo games jointly or to operate bingo games upon the same premises during any 18 hour period.

(f) It shall be unlawful to award prizes in excess of $1,500.00 in cash or gifts of equivalent value during any calendar day or $3,000.00 in cash or gifts of equivalent value during any calendar week. It shall be unlawful to exceed such limits at any combination of locations operated by a single licensee or such licensee's agents or employees. It shall be unlawful for two or more licensees to pyramid the valuation of prizes in such manner as to exceed the limits contained in this Code section. The term "equivalent value" shall mean the fair market value of the gift on the date the gift is given as the prize in a bingo game.

(g) No person or organization by whatever name or composition thereof shall take any salary, expense money, or fees for the operation of any bingo game, except that not more than $ 30.00 per day may be paid to one or more individuals for assisting in the conduct of such games on such day.

(h) No person shall pay consulting fees to any person for any services performed in relation to the operation or conduct of a bingo game.

(i) A person who is a member of more than one nonprofit, tax-exempt organization shall be permitted to participate in the bingo operations of only two organizations of which such person is a member; provided, however, that such person shall not receive more than $ 30.00 per day for assisting in the conduct of bingo games regardless of whether such person assists both organizations in the same day.

Laws 1977, p. 1164, § 8; Laws 1978, p. 853, §§ 4, 6, 6A, 6B, 7; Laws 1979, p. 1265, § 1; Laws 1986, p. 511, §§ 1, 2; Laws 2001, p. 1036, § 1; Laws 2003, Act 73, § 1, eff. July 1, 2003; Laws 2003, Act 171, § 2, eff. July 1, 2003.

Historical and Statutory Notes

The 2001 amendment in subsec. (f) increased the maximum amounts which may be awarded as prizes.

The 2003 amendment by Act 73, in subsec. (f), substituted "1,500.00" for "1,300.00" and "3,000.00" for "2,600.00".

The 2003 amendment by Act 170 deleted "from an organization that is also licensed to conduct a bingo game" following "such equipment" in subsec. (b), par. (1).

§ 16-12-61. Rules and regulations

The director is authorized to promulgate rules and regulations which he deems necessary for the proper administration and enforcement of this part.

Laws 1977, p. 1164, § 9; Laws 1980, p. 422, § 9.

§ 16-12-62. Violations relating to bingo games

Any person who operates a bingo game for which a license is required without a valid license issued by the director as provided in this part commits the offense of commercial gambling as defined in Code Section 16-12-22 and, upon conviction thereof, shall be punished accordingly. Any person who knowingly aids, abets, or otherwise assists in the operation of a bingo game for which a license is required and has not been obtained as provided in this part similarly commits the offense of commercial gambling. Any person who violates any other provision of this part, including the provisions relating to recreational bingo, shall be guilty of a misdemeanor of a high and aggravated nature. Any person who commits any such violation after having previously been convicted of any violations of this part shall be guilty of a felony and, upon conviction thereof, shall be punished by imprisonment for not less than one nor more than five years or by a fine not to exceed $10,000.00, or both.

Laws 1977, p. 1164, § 10; Laws 1980, p. 422, § 10; Laws 1993, p. 535, § 4.

Article 3

Obscenity and Related Offenses

Part 1

General Provisions

§ 16-12-80. Distributing obscene materials

(a) A person commits the offense of distributing obscene material when he sells, lends, rents, leases, gives, advertises, publishes, exhibits, or otherwise disseminates to any person any obscene material of any description, knowing the obscene nature thereof, or offers to do so, or possesses such material with the intent to do so, provided that the word "knowing," as used in this Code section, shall be deemed to be either actual or constructive knowledge of the obscene contents of the subject matter; and a person has constructive knowledge of the obscene contents if he has knowledge of facts which would put a reasonable and prudent person on notice as to the suspect nature of the material; provided, however, that the character and reputation of the individual charged with an offense under this law, and, if a commercial dissemination of obscene material is involved, the character and reputation of the business establishment involved may be placed in evidence by the defendant on the question of intent to violate this law. Undeveloped photographs, molds, printing plates, and the like shall be deemed obscene notwithstanding that processing or other acts may be required to make the obscenity patent or to disseminate it.

(b) Material is obscene if:

(1) To the average person, applying contemporary community standards, taken as a whole, it predominantly appeals to the prurient interest, that is, a shameful or morbid interest in nudity, sex, or excretion;

(2) The material taken as a whole lacks serious literary, artistic, political, or scientific value; and

(3) The material depicts or describes, in a patently offensive way, sexual conduct specifically defined in subparagraphs (A) through (E) of this paragraph:

(A) Acts of sexual intercourse, heterosexual or homosexual, normal or perverted, actual or simulated;

(B) Acts of masturbation;

(C) Acts involving excretory functions or lewd exhibition of the genitals;

(D) Acts of bestiality or the fondling of sex organs of animals; or

(E) Sexual acts of flagellation, torture, or other violence indicating a sadomasochistic sexual relationship.

(c) Any device designed or marketed as useful primarily for the stimulation of human genital organs is obscene material under this Code section.

(d) Material not otherwise obscene may be obscene under this Code section if the distribution thereof, the offer to do so, or the possession with the intent to do so is a commercial exploitation of erotica solely for the sake of their prurient appeal.

(e) It is an affirmative defense under this Code section that dissemination of the material was restricted to:

(1) A person associated with an institution of higher learning, either as a member of the faculty or a matriculated student, teaching or pursuing a course of study related to such material; or

(2) A person whose receipt of such material was authorized in writing by a licensed medical practitioner or psychiatrist.

(f) A person who commits the offense of distributing obscene material shall be guilty of a misdemeanor of a high and aggravated nature.

Laws 1878–79, p. 163, § 1; Laws 1935, p. 158, § 1; Laws 1941, p. 358, § 1; Laws 1956, p. 801, § 1; Laws 1963, p. 78, § 1; Laws 1968, p. 1249, § 1; Laws 1971, p. 344, § 1; Laws 1975, p. 498, §§ 1, 2; Laws 1992, p. 6, § 16; Laws 1996, p. 6, § 16.

Formerly Code 1882, § 4537a; Penal Code 1895, § 394; Penal Code 1910, § 385; Code 1933, § 26–6301; Code 1933, § 26–2101.

§ 16–12–81. Distributing material depicting nudity or sexual conduct

(a) A person commits the offense of distributing material depicting nudity or sexual conduct when he sends unsolicited through the mail or otherwise unsolicited causes to be delivered material depicting nudity or sexual conduct to any person or residence or office unless there is imprinted upon the envelope or container of such material in not less than eight-point boldface type the following notice:

"Notice—The material contained herein depicts nudity or sexual conduct. If the viewing of such material could be offensive to the addressee, this container should not be opened but returned to the sender."

(b) As used within this Code section, the term:

(1) "Nudity" means the showing of the human male or female genitals, pubic area, or buttocks with less than a full opaque covering or the depiction of covered male genitals in a discernibly turgid state.

(2) "Sexual conduct" means acts of masturbation, homosexuality, sodomy, sexual intercourse, or physical contact with a person's clothed or unclothed genitals, pubic area, buttocks, or, if the person is female, breast.

(c) A person who commits the offense of distributing material depicting nudity or sexual conduct, upon conviction thereof, shall be punished by imprisonment for not less than one nor more than three years or by a fine not to exceed $10,000.00, or both.

Laws 1970, p. 173, § 1.

Formerly Code 1933, § 26–2102.

§ 16–12–82. Use of premises as constituting public nuisance

The use of any premises in violation of any of the provisions of this part shall constitute a public nuisance.

Laws 1971, p. 344, § 2.

Formerly Code 1933, § 26–2103.

§ 16–12–83. Obscene materials declared contraband

Any materials declared to be obscene by this part and advertisements for such materials are declared to be contraband.

Laws 1971, p. 344, § 3.

Formerly Code 1933, § 26–2104.

§ 16–12–84. Repealed by Laws 1981, p. 915, § 1, eff. April 9, 1981

§ 16–12–85. Displaying to theatre audiences scenes from restricted films to be shown at future time

(a) It shall be unlawful for any motion picture theater owner, operator, or projectionist to display to the audience within the theater scenes from a film to be shown at the theater at some future time when the viewing of that film from which the scenes are taken is restricted to adults or requires minors to be accompanied by a parent or guardian. Scenes of such restricted films may be shown within a theater if the audience has been similarly restricted as to viewing age and conditions.

(b) This Code section shall not apply to motion pictures which are not rated as to viewing audience nor to the first display of a preview trailer from any motion picture.

(c) Any person who violates subsection (a) of this Code section shall be guilty of a misdemeanor.

Laws 1973, p. 508, §§ 1–3; Laws 1983, p. 3, § 13.

Part 2

Offenses Related to Minors Generally

§ 16–12–100. Sexual exploitation of children

(a) As used in this Code section, the term:

(1) "Minor" means any person under the age of 18 years.

(2) "Performance" means any play, dance, or exhibit to be shown to or viewed by an audience.

(3) "Producing" means producing, directing, manufacturing, issuing, or publishing.

(4) "Sexually explicit conduct" means actual or simulated:

(A) Sexual intercourse, including genital-genital, oral-genital, anal-genital, or oral-anal, whether between persons of the same or opposite sex;

(B) Bestiality;

(C) Masturbation;

(D) Lewd exhibition of the genitals or pubic area of any person;

(E) Flagellation or torture by or upon a person who is nude;

(F) Condition of being fettered, bound, or otherwise physically restrained on the part of a person who is nude;

(G) Physical contact in an act of apparent sexual stimulation or gratification with any person's unclothed genitals, pubic area, or buttocks or with a female's nude breasts;

(H) Defecation or urination for the purpose of sexual stimulation of the viewer; or

(I) Penetration of the vagina or rectum by any object except when done as part of a recognized medical procedure.

(5) "Visual medium" means any film, photograph, negative, slide, magazine, or other visual medium.

(b)(1) It is unlawful for any person knowingly to employ, use, persuade, induce, entice, or coerce any minor to engage in or assist any other person to engage in any sexually explicit conduct for the purpose of producing any visual medium depicting such conduct.

(2) It is unlawful for any parent, legal guardian, or person having custody or control of a minor knowingly to permit the minor to engage in or to assist any other person to engage in sexually explicit conduct for the purpose of producing any visual medium depicting such conduct.

(3) It is unlawful for any person knowingly to employ, use, persuade, induce, entice, or coerce any minor to engage in or

assist any other person to engage in any sexually explicit conduct for the purpose of any performance.

(4) It is unlawful for any parent, legal guardian, or person having custody or control of a minor knowingly to permit the minor to engage in or to assist any other person to engage in sexually explicit conduct for the purpose of any performance.

(5) It is unlawful for any person knowingly to create, reproduce, publish, promote, sell, distribute, give, exhibit, or possess with intent to sell or distribute any visual medium which depicts a minor or a portion of a minor's body engaged in any sexually explicit conduct.

(6) It is unlawful for any person knowingly to advertise, sell, purchase, barter, or exchange any medium which provides information as to where any visual medium which depicts a minor or a portion of a minor's body engaged in any sexually explicit conduct can be found or purchased.

(7) It is unlawful for any person knowingly to bring or cause to be brought into this state any material which depicts a minor or a portion of a minor's body engaged in any sexually explicit conduct.

(8) It is unlawful for any person knowingly to possess or control any material which depicts a minor or a portion of a minor's body engaged in any sexually explicit conduct.

(c) A person who, in the course of processing or producing visual or printed matter either privately or commercially, has reasonable cause to believe that the visual or printed matter submitted for processing or producing depicts a minor engaged in sexually explicit conduct shall immediately report such incident, or cause a report to be made, to the Georgia Bureau of Investigation or the law enforcement agency for the county in which such matter is submitted. Any person participating in the making of a report or causing a report to be made pursuant to this subsection or participating in any judicial proceeding or any other proceeding resulting therefrom shall in so doing be immune from any civil or criminal liability that might otherwise be incurred or imposed, providing such participation pursuant to this subsection is made in good faith.

(d) The provisions of subsection (b) of this Code section shall not apply to the activities of law enforcement and prosecution agencies in the investigation and prosecution of criminal offenses or to legitimate medical, scientific, or educational activities.

(e)(1) A person who is convicted of an offense under this Code section shall forfeit to the State of Georgia such interest as the person may have in:

(A) Any property constituting or directly derived from gross profits or other proceeds obtained from such offense; and

(B) Any property used, or intended to be used, to commit such offense.

(2) In any action under this Code section, the court may enter such restraining orders or take other appropriate action, including acceptance of performance bonds, in connection with any interest that is subject to forfeiture.

(3) The court shall order forfeiture of property referred to in paragraph (1) of this subsection if the trier of fact determines, beyond a reasonable doubt, that such property is subject to forfeiture.

(4) The provisions of subsection (u) of Code Section 16–13–49 shall apply for the disposition of any property forfeited under this subsection. In any disposition of property under this subsection, a convicted person shall not be permitted to acquire property forfeited by such person.

(f)(1) The following property shall be subject to forfeiture to the State of Georgia:

(A) Any material or equipment used, or intended for use, in producing, reproducing, transporting, shipping, or receiving any visual medium in violation of this Code section;

(B) Any visual medium produced, transported, shipped, or received in violation of this Code section, or any material containing such depiction; provided, however, that any such property so forfeited shall be destroyed by the appropriate law enforcement agency after it is no longer needed in any court proceedings; or

(C) Any property constituting or directly derived from gross profits or other proceeds obtained from a violation of this Code section;

except that no property of any owner shall be forfeited under this paragraph, to the extent of the interest of such owner, by reason of an act or omission established by such owner to have been committed or omitted without knowledge or consent of such owner.

(2) The procedure for forfeiture and disposition of forfeited property under this subsection shall be as provided for forfeitures under Code Section 16–13–49.

(g)(1) Except as otherwise provided in paragraph (2) of this subsection, any person who violates a provision of this Code section shall be guilty of a felony and, upon conviction thereof, shall be punished by imprisonment for not less than five nor more than 20 years and by a fine of not more than $100,000.00. In the event, however, that the person so convicted is a member of the immediate family of the victim, no fine shall be imposed.

(2) Any person who violates subsection (c) of this Code section shall be guilty of a misdemeanor.

Laws 1978, p. 2193, § 1; Laws 1983, p. 1437, § 1; Laws 1987, p. 1164, § 1; Laws 1988, p. 11, §§ 1, 2; Laws 1991, p. 886, § 3; Laws 1995, p. 957, § 6; Laws 1996, p. 6, § 16; Laws 2003, Act 216, § 2, eff. June 2, 2003.

Historical and Statutory Notes

The 2003 amendment by Act 216, in subsec. (b), pars. (5), (6), (7), and (8), inserted "or a portion of a minor's body"; and in subsec. (g), substituted "paragraph (2)" for "paragraphs (2) and (3)" in par. (1), substituted "not less than five" for "not less than five years" in par. (1), deleted par. (2) which read, "Any person who violates paragraph (8) of the subsection (b) of this Code section shall be guilty of a misdemeanor.", and redesignated former par. (3) as (2).

Comparative Laws:

Ala.—Code 1975, §§ 13A–12–190 to 13A–12–198.
Alaska—AS 11.41.455.
Ariz.—A.R.S. § 13–3553.
Ark.—A.C.A. §§ 5–27–301 to 5–27–305.
Cal.—West's Ann.Cal.Penal Code §§ 311 to 311.11.
Colo.—West's C.R.S.A. § 18–6–403.
Conn.—C.G.S.A. §§ 53a–196 to 53a–196b.
Del.—11 Del.C. §§ 1108, 1109.
Fla.—West's F.S.A. § 827.071.
Ga.—O.C.G.A. § 16–12–100.
Hawaii—H R S §§ 707–750, 707–751.
Idaho—I.C. § 44–1306.
Ill.—S.H.A. 720 ILCS 5/11–20.1 to 5/11-20.1A.
Ind.—West's A.I.C. 35–49–1–1 to 35–49–1–10.
Iowa—I.C.A. § 728.12.
Kan.—K.S.A. 21–3516.
Ky.—KRS 531.320, 531.340 to 531.360.
La.—LSA–R.S. 14:81.1.
Md.—Code, Criminal Law, § 11–207.
Mass.—M.G.L.A. c. 272, §§ 29A, 29B.
Mich.—M.C.L.A. § 750.145c.
Minn.—M.S.A. § 617.246.
Miss.—Code 1972, § 97–5–33.
Mo.—V.A.M.S. § 568.060.
Mt.—M.C.A. 45–5–625.
Neb.—R.R.S. 1943, §§ 28–1463.01 to 28-1463.05.
Nev.—N.R.S. 200.700 to 200.760.
N.H.—RSA 650:2.
N.J.—N.J.S.A. 2C:24–4.
N.M.—NMSA 1978, §§ 30–6A–1 to 30–6A–4.
N.C.—G.S. § 14–190.16.
N.D.—NDCC 12.1–27.1–01.
Ohio—R.C. § 2907.32 to 2907.323.
Okl.—21 Okl.St.Ann. § 1021.2.

Ore.—ORS 163.305 et seq.
Pa.—18 Pa.C.S.A. § 6312.
R.I.—Gen.Laws. 1956, § 11–9–1.1.
S.D.—SDCL 22–24A–1, 22–24A–20.
Tenn.—T.C.A. §§ 39–17–911, 39–17–914.
U.S.—18 U.S.C.A. § 2252.
Utah—U.C.A. 1953, 76–5a–1 to 76–5a–4.
Va.—Code 1950, §§ 18.2–374.1 to 18.2–374.1:2.
Wash.—West's RCWA 9.68A.060.
W.Va.—Code, 61–8C–3.
Wis.—W.S.A. 948.05.
Wyo.—Wyo.Stat.Ann. § 27–6–114.

§ 16–12–100.1. Electronically furnishing obscene material to minors

(a) As used in this Code section, the term:

(1) "Bulletin board system" means a computer data and file service that is accessed by telephone line to store and transmit information.

(2) "CD–ROM" means a compact disc with read only memory which has the capacity to store audio, video, and written materials and is used by computers to reveal the above-said material.

(3) "Electronically furnishes" means:

(A) To make available by electronic storage device, including floppy disks and other magnetic storage devices, or by CD–ROM; or

(B) To make available by allowing access to information stored in a computer, including making material available by operating a computer bulletin board.

(4) "Harmful to minors" means that quality of description or representation, in whatever form, of nudity, sexual conduct, sexual excitement, or sadomasochistic abuse, when it:

(A) Taken as a whole, predominantly appeals to the prurient, shameful, or morbid interest of minors;

(B) Is patently offensive to prevailing standards in the adult community as a whole with respect to what is suitable material for minors; and

(C) Is, when taken as a whole, lacking in serious literary, artistic, political, or scientific value for minors.

(5) "Minor" means an unmarried person younger than 18 years of age.

(6) "Sadomasochistic abuse" means flagellation or torture by or upon a person who is nude or clad in undergarments or in revealing or bizarre costume or the condition of being fettered, bound, or otherwise physically restrained on the part of one so clothed.

(7) "Sexual conduct" means human masturbation, sexual intercourse, or any touching of the genitals, pubic areas, or buttocks of the human male or female or the breasts of the female, whether alone or between members of the same or opposite sex or between humans and animals in an act of apparent sexual stimulation or gratification.

(8) "Sexual excitement" means the condition of human male or female genitals or the breasts of the female when in a state of sexual stimulation.

(b) A person commits the crime of electronically furnishing obscene materials to minors if:

(1) Knowing or having good reason to know the character of the material furnished, the person electronically furnishes to an individual whom the person knows or should have known is a minor:

(A) Any picture, photograph, drawing, or similar visual representation or image of a person or portion of a human body which depicts sexually explicit nudity, sexual conduct, or sadomasochistic abuse and which is harmful to minors; or

(B) Any written or aural matter that contains material of the nature described in subparagraph (A) of this paragraph or contains explicit verbal descriptions or narrative accounts of sexual conduct, sexual excitement, or sadomasochistic abuse;

(2) The offensive portions of the material electronically furnished to the minor are not merely an incidental part of an otherwise nonoffending whole;

(3) The material furnished to the minor, taken as a whole, lacks serious literary, artistic, political, or scientific value; and

(4) The material furnished to the minor, taken as a whole, is harmful to minors in that it appeals to and incites prurient interest.

(c) Any person who violates this Code section shall be guilty of a misdemeanor of a high and aggravated nature.

Laws 1993, p. 735, § 1.

§ 16–12–100.2. Computer or Electronic Pornography and Child Exploitation Prevention Act of 2007

(a) This Code section shall be known and may be cited as the "Computer or Electronic Pornography and Child Exploitation Prevention Act of 2007."

(b) As used in this Code section, the term:

(1) "Child" means any person under the age of 16 years.

(2) "Electronic device" means any device used for the purpose of communicating with a child for sexual purposes or any device used to visually depict a child engaged in sexually explicit conduct, store any image or audio of a child engaged in sexually explicit conduct, or transmit any audio or visual image of a child for sexual purposes. Such term may include, but shall not be limited to, a computer, cellular phone, thumb drive, video game system, or any other electronic device that can be used in furtherance of exploiting a child for sexual purposes;

(3) "Identifiable child" means a person:

(A) Who was a child at the time the visual depiction was created, adapted, or modified or whose image as a child was used in creating, adapting, or modifying the visual depiction; and

(B) Who is recognizable as an actual person by the person's face, likeness, or other distinguishing characteristic, such as a unique birthmark or other recognizable feature or by electronic or scientific means as may be available.

The term shall not be construed to require proof of the actual identity of the child.

(4) "Sadomasochistic abuse" has the same meaning as provided in Code Section 16–12–100.1.

(5) "Sexual conduct" has the same meaning as provided in Code Section 16–12–100.1.

(6) "Sexual excitement" has the same meaning as provided in Code Section 16–12–100.1.

(7) "Sexually explicit nudity" has the same meaning as provided in Code Section 16–12–102.

(8) "Visual depiction" means any image and includes undeveloped film and video tape and data stored on computer disk or by electronic means which is capable of conversion into a visual image or which has been created, adapted, or modified to show an identifiable child engaged in sexually explicit conduct.

(c)(1) A person commits the offense of computer or electronic pornography if such person intentionally or willfully:

(A) Compiles, enters into, or transmits by computer or other electronic device;

(B) Makes, prints, publishes, or reproduces by other computer or other electronic device;

(C) Causes or allows to be entered into or transmitted by computer or other electronic device; or

(D) Buys, sells, receives, exchanges, or disseminates

any notice, statement, or advertisement, or any child's name, telephone number, place of residence, physical characteristics, or other descriptive or identifying information for the purpose of offering or soliciting sexual conduct of or with an identifiable child or the visual depiction of such conduct.

(2) Any person convicted of violating paragraph (1) of this subsection shall be punished by a fine of not more than $10,000.00 and by imprisonment for not less than one nor more than 20 years.

(d)(1) It shall be unlawful for any person intentionally or willfully to utilize a computer on-line service or Internet service, including but not limited to a local bulletin board service, Internet chat room, e-mail, on-line messaging service, or other electronic device, to seduce, solicit, lure, or entice, or attempt to seduce, solicit, lure, or entice a child or another person believed by such person to be a child to commit any illegal act described in Code Section 16–6–2, relating to the offense of sodomy or aggravated sodomy; Code Section 16–6–4, relating to the offense of child molestation or aggravated child molestation; Code Section 16–6–5, relating to the offense of enticing a child for indecent purposes; or Code Section 16–6–8, relating to the offense of public indecency or to engage in any conduct that by its nature is an unlawful sexual offense against a child.

(2) Any person who violates paragraph (1) of this subsection shall be guilty of a felony and, upon conviction thereof, shall be punished by imprisonment for not less than one nor more than 20 years and by a fine of not more than $25,000.00; provided, however, that, if at the time of the offense the victim was 14 or 15 years of age and the defendant was no more than three years older than the victim, then the defendant shall be guilty of a misdemeanor of a high and aggravated nature.

(e)(1) A person commits the offense of obscene Internet contact with a child if he or she has contact with someone he or she knows to be a child or with someone he or she believes to be a child via a computer on-line service or Internet service, including but not limited to a local bulletin board service, Internet chat room, e-mail, or on-line messaging service, and the contact involves any matter containing explicit verbal descriptions or narrative accounts of sexually explicit nudity, sexual conduct, sexual excitement, or sadomasochistic abuse that is intended to arouse or satisfy the sexual desire of either the child or the person, provided that no conviction shall be had for a violation of this subsection on the unsupported testimony of a child.

(2) Any person who violates paragraph (1) of this subsection shall be guilty of a felony and, upon conviction thereof, shall be punished by imprisonment for not less than one nor more than ten years or by a fine of not more than $10,000.00; provided, however, that, if at the time of the offense the victim was 14 or 15 years of age and the defendant was no more than three years older than the victim, then the defendant shall be guilty of a misdemeanor of a high and aggravated nature.

(f)(1) It shall be unlawful for any owner or operator of a computer on-line service, Internet service, local bulletin board service, or other electronic device that is in the business of providing a service that may be used to sexually exploit a child to intentionally or willfully to permit a subscriber to utilize the service to commit a violation of this Code section, knowing that such person intended to utilize such service to violate this Code section. No owner or operator of a public computer on-line service, Internet service, local bulletin board service, or other electronic device that is in the business of providing a service that may be used to sexually exploit a child shall be held liable on account of any action taken in good faith in providing the aforementioned services.

(2) Any person who violates paragraph (1) of this subsection shall be guilty of a misdemeanor of a high and aggravated nature.

(g) The sole fact that an undercover operative or law enforcement officer was involved in the detection and investigation of an offense under this Code section shall not constitute a defense to prosecution under this Code section.

(h) A person is subject to prosecution in this state pursuant to Code Section 17–2–1, relating to jurisdiction over crimes and persons charged with commission of crimes generally, for any conduct made unlawful by this Code section which the person engages in while:

(1) Either within or outside of this state if, by such conduct, the person commits a violation of this Code section which involves a child who resides in this state or another person believed by such person to be a child residing in this state; or

(2) Within this state if, by such conduct, the person commits a violation of this Code section which involves a child who resides within or outside this state or another person believed by such person to be a child residing within or outside this state.

(i) Any violation of this Code section shall constitute a separate offense.

Laws 1999, p. 232, § 2; Laws 2003, Act 9, § 16, eff. May 14, 2003; Laws 2003, Act 216, § 3, eff. June 2, 2003; Laws 2007, Act 18, § 16, eff. May 11, 2007; Laws 2007, Act 202, § 2, eff. May 23, 2007.

Historical and Statutory Notes

The 2003 amendment by Act 9, in subsec. (d), substituted "child" for "child," and "indecency" for "indecency;" in par. (1).

The 2003 amendment by Act 216 rewrote the section which had read:

"(a) This Code section shall be known and may be cited as the 'Computer Pornography and Child Exploitation Prevention Act of 1999.'

"(b) As used in this Code section, the term 'child' means any person under the age of 16 years.

"(c)(1) A person commits the offense of computer pornography if such person intentionally or willfully:

"(A) Compiles, enters into, or transmits by means of computer;

"(B) Makes, prints, publishes, or reproduces by other computerized means;

"(C) Causes or allows to be entered into or transmitted by means of computer; or

"(D) Buys, sells, receives, exchanges, or disseminates

"any notice, statement, or advertisement, or any child's name, telephone number, place of residence, physical characteristics, or other descriptive or identifying information for the purpose of offering or soliciting sexual conduct of or with any child or the visual depiction of such conduct.

"(2) Any person convicted of violating paragraph (1) of this subsection shall be punished by a fine of not more than $10,000.00 or by imprisonment for not less than one nor more than 20 years, or both.

"(d)(1) It shall be unlawful for any person intentionally or willfully to utilize a computer on-line service, Internet service, or local bulletin board service to seduce, solicit, lure, or entice, or attempt to seduce, solicit, lure, or entice a child or another person believed by such person to be a child, to commit any illegal act described in Code Section 16–6–2, relating to the offense of sodomy or aggravated sodomy; Code Section 16–6–4, relating to the offense of child molestation or aggravated child molestation; Code Section 16–6–5, relating to the offense of enticing a child for indecent purposes; or Code Section 16–6–8, relating to the offense of public indecency; or to engage in any conduct that by its nature is an unlawful sexual offense against a child.

"(2) Any person who violates paragraph (1) of this subsection shall be guilty of a misdemeanor of a high and aggravated nature.

"(e)(1) It shall be unlawful for any owner or operator of a computer on-line service, Internet service, or local bulletin board service intentionally or willfully to permit a subscriber to utilize the service to commit a violation of this Code section, knowing that such person intended to utilize such service to violate this Code section.

"(2) Any person who violates paragraph (1) of this subsection shall be guilty of a misdemeanor of a high and aggravated nature.

"(f) The sole fact that an undercover operative or law enforcement officer was involved in the detection and investigation of an offense under this Code section shall not constitute a defense to prosecution under this Code section.

"(g) A person is subject to prosecution in this state pursuant to Code Section 17–2–1, relating to jurisdiction over crimes and persons charged with commission of crimes generally, for any conduct made unlawful by this Code section which the person engages in while either within or outside of this state if, by such conduct, the person commits a violation of this Code section which involves a child who resides in this state or another person believed by such person to be a child residing in this state.

"(h) Any violation of this Code section shall constitute a separate offense."

The 2007 amendment by Act 18 was a provision contained in a correction bill.

The 2007 amendment by Act 202 rewrote the section which had read:

"(a) This Code section shall be known and may be cited as the 'Computer Pornography and Child Exploitation Prevention Act of 1999.'

"(b) As used in this Code section, the term:

"(1) 'Child' means any person under the age of 16 years.

"(2) 'Identifiable child' means a person:

"(A) Who was a child at the time the visual depiction was created, adapted, or modified or whose image as a child was used in creating, adapting, or modifying the visual depiction; and

"(B) Who is recognizable as an actual person by the person's face, likeness, or other distinguishing characteristic, such as a unique birthmark or other recognizable feature or by electronic or scientific means as may be available.

"The term shall not be construed to require proof of the actual identity of the child.

"(3) 'Sadomasochistic abuse' has the same meaning as provided in Code Section 16–12–100.1.

"(4) 'Sexual conduct' has the same meaning as provided in Code Section 16–12–100.1.

"(5) 'Sexual excitement' has the same meaning as provided in Code Section 16–12–100.1.

"(6) 'Sexually explicit nudity' has the same meaning as provided in Code Section 16–12–102.

"(7) 'Visual depiction' means any image and includes undeveloped film and video tape and data stored on computer disk or by electronic means which is capable of conversion into a visual image or which has been created, adapted, or modified to show an identifiable child engaged in sexually explicit conduct.

"(c)(1) A person commits the offense of computer pornography if such person intentionally or willfully:

"(A) Compiles, enters into, or transmits by means of computer;

"(B) Makes, prints, publishes, or reproduces by other computerized means;

"(C) Causes or allows to be entered into or transmitted by means of computer; or

"(D) Buys, sells, receives, exchanges, or disseminates any notice, statement, or advertisement, or any child's name, telephone number, place of residence, physical characteristics, or other descriptive or identifying information for the purpose of offering or soliciting sexual conduct of or with an identifiable child or the visual depiction of such conduct.

"(2) Any person convicted of violating paragraph (1) of this subsection shall be punished by a fine of not more than $10,000.00 and by imprisonment for not less than one nor more than 20 years.

"(d)(1) It shall be unlawful for any person intentionally or willfully to utilize a computer on-line service or Internet service, including but not limited to a local bulletin board service, Internet chat room, e-mail, or on-line messaging service, to seduce, solicit, lure, or entice, or attempt to seduce, solicit, lure, or entice a child or another person believed by such person to be a child to commit any illegal act described in Code Section 16–6–2, relating to the offense of sodomy or aggravated sodomy; Code Section 16–6–4, relating to the offense of child molestation or aggravated child molestation; Code Section 16–6–5, relating to the offense of enticing a child for indecent purposes; or Code Section 16–6–8, relating to the offense of public indecency or to engage in any conduct that by its nature is an unlawful sexual offense against a child.

"(2) Any person who violates paragraph (1) of this subsection shall be guilty of a felony and, upon conviction thereof, shall be punished by imprisonment for not less than one nor more than 20 years and by a fine of not more than $25,000.00; provided, however, that, if at the time of the offense the victim was 14 or 15 years of age and the defendant was no more than three years older than the victim, then the defendant shall be guilty of a misdemeanor of a high and aggravated nature.

"(e)(1) A person commits the offense of obscene Internet contact with a child if he or she has contact with someone he or she knows to be a child or with someone he or she believes to be a child via a computer on-line service or Internet service, including but not limited to a local bulletin board service, Internet chat room, e-mail, or on-line messaging service, and the contact involves any matter containing explicit verbal descriptions or narrative accounts of sexually explicit nudity, sexual conduct, sexual excitement, or sadomasochistic abuse that is intended to arouse or satisfy the sexual desire of either the child or the person, provided that no conviction shall be had for a violation of this subsection on the unsupported testimony of a child.

"(2) Any person who violates paragraph (1) of this subsection shall be guilty of a felony and, upon conviction thereof, shall be punished by imprisonment for not less than one nor more than ten years or by a fine of not more than $10,000.00; provided, however, that, if at the time of the offense the victim was 14 or 15 years of age and the defendant was no more than three years older than the victim, then the defendant shall be guilty of a misdemeanor of a high and aggravated nature.

"(f)(1) It shall be unlawful for any owner or operator of a computer on-line service, Internet service, or local bulletin board service intentionally or willfully to permit a subscriber to utilize the service to commit a violation of this Code section, knowing that such person intended to utilize such service to violate this Code section. No owner or operator of a public computer on-line service, Internet service, or local bulletin board service shall be held liable on account of any action taken in good faith in providing the aforementioned services.

"(2) Any person who violates paragraph (1) of this subsection shall be guilty of a misdemeanor of a high and aggravated nature.

"(g) The sole fact that an undercover operative or law enforcement officer was involved in the detection and investigation of an offense under this Code section shall not constitute a defense to prosecution under this Code section.

"(h) A person is subject to prosecution in this state pursuant to Code Section 17–2–1, relating to jurisdiction over crimes and persons charged with commission of crimes generally, for any conduct made unlawful by this Code section which the person engages in while either within or outside of this state if, by such conduct, the person commits a violation of this Code section which involves a child who resides in this state or another person believed by such person to be a child residing in this state.

"(i) Any violation of this Code section shall constitute a separate offense."

§ 16–12–100.3. Obscene telephone contact with a child

(a) As used in this Code section, the terms "sexual conduct," "sexual excitement," and "sadomasochistic abuse" have the same meanings as provided for those terms in Code Section 16–12–100.1, relating to electronically furnishing obscene materials to minors; the term "sexually explicit nudity" has the same meaning as provided for that term in Code Section 16–12–102, relating to distributing harmful materials to minors; and the term "child" means a person under 14 years of age.

(b) A person 17 years of age or over commits the offense of obscene telephone contact with a child if that person has telephone contact with an individual whom that person knows or should have known is a child, and that contact involves any aural matter containing explicit verbal descriptions or narrative accounts of sexually explicit nudity, sexual conduct, sexual excitement, or sadomasochistic abuse which is intended to arouse or satisfy the sexual desire of either the child or the person, provided that no conviction shall be had for this offense on the unsupported testimony of the victim.

(c)(1) Except as otherwise provided in other paragraphs of this subsection, a person convicted of the offense of obscene telephone contact with a child shall be guilty of a misdemeanor of a high and aggravated nature.

(2) Upon the first conviction of the offense of obscene telephone contact with a child:

(A) If the person convicted is less than 21 years of age, such person shall be guilty of a misdemeanor; or

(B) The judge may probate the sentence without regard to the age of the convicted person, and such probation may be upon the special condition that the defendant undergo a mandatory period of counseling administered by a licensed psychiatrist or a licensed psychologist. However, if the judge finds that such probation should not be imposed, the judge shall sentence the defendant to imprisonment; provided, further, that upon a defendant's being incarcerated on a conviction for such first offense, the place of incarceration shall provide counseling to such defendant.

(3) Upon a second or subsequent conviction of such offense, the defendant shall be guilty of a felony and punished by imprisonment for not less than one nor more than five years.

Laws 2000, p. 1237, § 1.

Part 3
Sale or Distribution of Harmful Materials to Minors

§ 16–12–101. Legislative intent

The General Assembly finds that the sale, loan, and exhibition of harmful materials to minors has become a matter of increasingly grave concern to the people of this state. The elimination of such sales, loans, and exhibition and the consequent protection of minors from harmful materials are in the best interest of the morals and general welfare of the citizens of this state in general and of minors in this state in particular. The accomplishment of these ends can best be achieved by providing public prosecutors with an effective power to commence criminal proceedings against persons who engage in the sale, loan, or exhibition of harmful materials to minors.

Laws 1983, p. 1437, § 2.

§ 16–12–102. Definitions

As used in this part, the term:

(1) "Harmful to minors" means that quality of description or representation, in whatever form, of nudity, sexual conduct, sexual excitement, or sadomasochistic abuse, when it:

(A) Taken as a whole, predominantly appeals to the prurient, shameful, or morbid interest of minors;

(B) Is patently offensive to prevailing standards in the adult community as a whole with respect to what is suitable material for minors; and

(C) Is, when taken as a whole, lacking in serious literary, artistic, political, or scientific value for minors.

(2) "Knowingly" means having a general knowledge of, or reason to know, or a belief or ground for belief which warrants further inspection or inquiry of both:

(A) The character and content of any material described in this part which is reasonably susceptible to examination by the defendant; and

(B) The age of the minor; provided, however, that an honest mistake shall constitute an excuse from liability in this part if the defendant made a reasonable, bona fide attempt to ascertain the true age of such minor.

(3) "Minor" means a person less than 18 years of age.

(4) "Sadomasochistic abuse" means actual or simulated flagellation or torture by or upon a person who is nude, clad in undergarments, a mask or bizarre costume, or the condition of being fettered, bound, or otherwise physically restrained by one so clothed or nude.

(5) "Sexual conduct" means actual or simulated acts of masturbation, homosexuality, sexual intercourse, or physical contact in an act of apparent sexual stimulation or gratification with a person's clothed or unclothed genitals, pubic area, buttocks, or, if such person is female, breasts.

(6) "Sexual excitement" means the condition of human male or female genitals when in a state of sexual stimulation or arousal.

(7) "Sexually explicit nudity" means a state of undress so as to expose the human male or female genitals, pubic area, or buttocks with less than a full opaque covering, or the showing of the female breast with less than a fully opaque covering of any portion thereof below the top of the nipple, or the depiction of covered or uncovered male genitals in a discernibly turgid state.

Laws 1983, p. 1437, § 2; Laws 1984, p. 1495, § 3; Laws 1996, p. 6, § 16.

§ 16–12–103. Unlawful disposition of material to minors

(a) It shall be unlawful for any person knowingly to sell or loan for monetary consideration or otherwise furnish or disseminate to a minor:

(1) Any picture, photograph, drawing, sculpture, motion picture film, or similar visual representation or image of a person or portion of the human body which depicts sexually explicit nudity, sexual conduct, or sadomasochistic abuse and which is harmful to minors; or

(2) Any book, pamphlet, magazine, printed matter however reproduced, or sound recording which contains any matter enumerated in paragraph (1) of this subsection, or explicit and detailed verbal descriptions or narrative accounts of sexual excitement, sexual conduct, or sadomasochistic abuse and which, taken as a whole, is harmful to minors.

(b)(1) It shall be unlawful for any person knowingly to sell or furnish to a minor an admission ticket or pass or knowingly to admit a minor to premises whereon there is exhibited a motion picture, show, or other presentation which, in whole or in part, depicts sexually explicit nudity, sexual conduct, or sadomasochistic abuse and which is harmful to minors or exhibit any such motion picture at any such premises which are not designed to prevent viewing from any public way of such motion picture by minors not admitted to any such premises.

(2) It shall be unlawful for any person knowingly to sell or to furnish to a person under the age of 21 an admission ticket or pass or knowingly to admit a person under the age of 21 to premises whereon there is exhibited a show or performance which is harmful to minors and which, in whole or in part, consists of sexually explicit nudity on the part of one or more live performers; sexual conduct on the part of one or more live performers; or sadomasochistic abuse on the part of one or more live performers.

(c) It shall be unlawful for any person to falsely represent his or her age to any person mentioned in subsection (a) or subsection (b) of this Code section or to his or her agent with the intent to unlawfully procure any material set forth in subsection (a) of this Code section or with the intent to unlawfully procure such person's admission to any motion picture, show, or other presentation, as set forth in subsection (b) of this Code section.

(d) It shall be unlawful for any person knowingly to make a false representation to any person mentioned in subsection (a) or subsection (b) of this Code section or to his or her agent that he or she is the parent or guardian of any minor or knowingly to make a false representation with respect to the age of another person with the intent to unlawfully procure for such other person any material set forth in subsection (a) of this Code section or with the intent to unlawfully procure such other person's admission to any motion picture, show, or other presentation, as set forth in subsection (b) of this Code section.

(e) It shall be unlawful for any person knowingly to exhibit, expose, or display in public at newsstands or any other business or commercial establishment or at any other public place frequented by minors or where minors are or may be invited as part of the general public:

(1) Any picture, photograph, drawing, sculpture, motion picture film, or similar visual representation or image of a person or portion of the human body which depicts sexually explicit nudity, sexual conduct, or sadomasochistic abuse and which is harmful to minors; or

(2) Any book, pamphlet, magazine, printed matter however reproduced, or sound recording which contains any matter enumerated in paragraph (1) of this subsection, or explicit and detailed verbal descriptions or narrative accounts of sexual excitement, sexual conduct, or sadomasochistic abuse and which, taken as a whole, is harmful to minors.

(f)(1) As used in this subsection, the term:

(A) "Video game" means an object or device that stores recorded data or instructions, receives data or instructions generated by a person who uses it, and, by processing the data or instructions, creates an interactive game capable of being played, viewed, or experienced on or through a computer, gaming system, console, or other technology.

(B) "Video game retailer" means a person who sells or rents video games to the public.

(2) Every video game retailer shall post a sign providing information to consumers about any video game rating system which appears on a video game offered by such retailer. The sign shall be posted in a conspicuous place within the portion of the establishment dedicated to the display or advertisement of video games. Each video game retailer shall make available to consumers, upon request, written information explaining each such rating system.

(3) A person violating the provisions of this subsection shall be punished with a civil fine in an amount not less than $250.00 and not more than $500.00 for each violation. Each day in violation of this subsection shall constitute a separate offense.

Laws 1983, p. 1437, § 2; Laws 1984, p. 22, § 16; Laws 1984, p. 1495, § 3; Laws 1996, p. 273, § 2; Laws 2005, Act 392, § 1, eff. July 1, 2005.

Formerly Code 1981, § 16–12–104.

Historical and Statutory Notes

The 2005 amendment by Act 392 added subsec. (f).

§ 16–12–104. Exception as to libraries

The provisions of Code Section 16–12–103 shall not apply to any public library operated by the state or any of its political subdivisions nor to any library operated as a part of any school, college, or university.

Laws 1984, p. 1495, § 3.

§ 16–12–105. Punishment

Any person who violates any provision of Code Section 16–12–103 or 16–12–104 shall be guilty of a misdemeanor of a high and aggravated nature.

Laws 1983, p. 1437, § 2.

§§ 16–12–106 to 16–12–108. Repealed by Laws 1981, p. 1578, § 2, eff. July 1, 1981

§ 16–12–109. Reserved designation repealed by Laws 2007, Act 18, § 16, eff. May 11, 2007

§§ 16–12–110 to 16–12–113. Repealed by Laws 1983, p. 1437, § 2, eff. July 1, 1983

Article 4

Offenses against Public Transportation

Part 1

General Provisions

§ 16–12–120. Conduct in public transit buses, rapid rail cars, and rapid rail or intermodal bus stations

(a) A person who commits or attempts to commit any of the following acts in a public transit bus, a rapid rail car, or a rapid rail station or intermodal bus station shall be guilty of a misdemeanor:

(1) Spits, defecates, or urinates;

(2) Discards litter, except into receptacles designated for that purpose;

(3) Smokes tobacco in any form;

(4) Consumes food or beverage or possesses any open food or beverage container, provided that this paragraph shall not apply to resealable beverages in resealable plastic containers, to an operator of a public transit bus at an authorized layover point, or to a person providing food or beverage to any child under age five; provided, further, that nothing in this paragraph shall apply to a rapid rail station or intermodal bus station, unless the public transit system operating such station adopts a policy prohibiting food or beverages in such station; and provided, further, that nothing in this paragraph shall preclude a public transit system operated or funded by a county, municipality, or consolidated government from prohibiting the consumption of any beverage in a public transit bus;

(5) Plays any radio; cassette, cartridge, or tape player; or similar device unless such device is connected to an earphone that limits the sound to the hearing of the individual user;

(6) Carries or possesses any explosives, acids, other dangerous articles, or live animals, except for the following:

(A) A guide dog or service dog as described in Code Section 30–4–2, provided that such guide dog or service dog is accompanied by a physically disabled person, blind person, person with visual disabilities, deaf person, or a person who is responsible for training a guide dog or service dog; and

(B) Small pets confined to rigid pet carriers with locks or latches;

(7) Obstructs, hinders, interferes with, or otherwise disrupts or disturbs the operation, operator, or passengers of a public transit bus or rapid rail car;

(8) Boards any public transit bus through the rear exit door, unless so directed by an employee or agent of the carrier;

(9) Remains aboard any public transit bus or rapid rail car after such vehicle has completed its scheduled route and passengers have been advised to exit the vehicle or remains aboard any public transit bus or rapid rail car after having been warned and after such vehicle has entered a garage or other restricted area not open to the public;

(10) Enters, exits, or passes through any emergency door of any rapid rail car or public transit bus in the absence of a bona fide emergency; or

(11) Enters the operator's cab or driver's seat of any rapid rail car or public transit bus in the absence of a bona fide emergency.

(a.1)(1) It shall be unlawful to solicit money or sell goods or services for a fee to the operator or passengers of a public transit bus or rapid rail car within the confines of such vehicle or within the paid areas of any rapid rail station or intermodal bus station without the express permission or grant of a concession by the public transportation authority or carrier.

(2) It shall be unlawful to deliver or distribute handbills or flyers of a commercial nature to the operator or passengers of a public transit bus or rapid rail car within the confines of such vehicle or within the paid area of any rapid rail station or intermodal bus station.

(3) A person violating the provisions of this subsection shall be guilty of a misdemeanor and, upon conviction thereof, shall be punished by a fine of not less than $50.00 and not more than $100.00. Upon a second or subsequent conviction, a person shall be punished by a fine of not less than $100.00 and not more than $250.00 or by imprisonment for not more than ten days, or both.

(b) Employees of a public transportation authority or carrier while at work performing the duties of their employment shall be exempted from the restrictions of paragraphs (8), (9), (10), and (11) of subsection (a) of this Code section.

(c) A person convicted of a first offense of violating subsection (a) of this Code section shall be punished by a fine of not less than $ 50.00 and not more than $ 100.00. Upon a second or subsequent conviction, a person shall be punished by a fine of not less than $ 100.00 and not more than $ 250.00 or by imprisonment for not more than ten days, or both.

(d) This Code section shall be cumulative to and shall not prohibit the enactment of any other general and local laws, rules, and regulations of state or local authorities or agencies, and local ordinances prohibiting such activities which are more restrictive than this Code section.

Laws 1976, p. 1645, § 1; Laws 1998, p. 890, § 1; Laws 1999, p. 81, § 16; Laws 2001, p. 4, § 16; Laws 2003, Act 77, § 1, eff. July 1, 2003; Laws 2005, Act 365, § 1, eff. July 1, 2005; Laws 2009, Act 153, § 1, eff. July 1, 2009; Laws 2010, Act 624, § 16, eff. June 3, 2010.

Formerly Code 1933, § 26-9911.

Historical and Statutory Notes

The 2003 amendment by Act, subsec. (a), rewrote par. (4) which read:

"(4) Consumes food or beverage or possesses any open food or beverage container, provided that this paragraph shall not apply to an operator of a public transit bus at an authorized layover point or to a person providing food or beverage to any child under age five;"

The 2005 amendment by Act 365 added subsec. (a.1).

Laws 2005, Act 365, § 2, provides:

"This Act shall become effective on July 1, 2005, and shall apply to all offenses occurring on and after such date."

The 2009 amendment by Act 153, in par. (a)(4), deleted "bottled water" preceding "beverages in resealable plastic containers," and inserted "apply to a rapid rail station or intermodal bus station, unless the public transit system operating such station adopts a policy prohibiting food or beverages in such station, and further that nothing in this paragraph shall".

The 2010 amendment by Act 624 was a provision contained in a correction bill.

§ 16-12-120.1. Obtaining entry into bus, rail vehicle, or station by unlawful means

A person who commits or attempts to commit any of the following acts shall be guilty of a misdemeanor if such person:

(1) Sells, makes, or possesses any coin, token, stored value card, transfer, transaction card, ticket, or any other fare medium which has been altered from its original condition contrary to its intended use to enter or gain entry into or on any bus, rail vehicle, or station;

(2) Sells or exchanges any token, stored value card, transfer, transaction card, ticket, fare medium, or similar article which was obtained by fraudulent or illegal means and which is used or to be used as payment for entry into or on any bus, rail vehicle, or terminal without the express consent of the public transit agency owning or operating such vehicles or stations;

(3) Offers entry or provides entry into or on any bus, rapid rail car, or station to any person without the payment of the proper fare to the public transit agency owning or operating such vehicles or stations;

(4) Gains entry into or on any bus, rapid rail car, or station without the payment of the proper fare; or

(5) Gains entry into or on any bus, rapid rail car, or station through the use of a coin, token, transfer, transaction card, ticket, or any other fare medium which is the property of another person when the use of such medium is limited by its terms to a single user. This paragraph shall not apply to stored value cards or similar fare media which deduct the cost of the fare from the value stored on the card or other fare medium each time such card or other fare medium is used.

Laws 1992, p. 985, § 1; Laws 1998, p. 890, § 2; Laws 2006, Act 606, § 1, eff. April 27, 2006.

Historical and Statutory Notes

The 2006 amendment by Act 606 rewrote the section which had read:

"A person who commits or attempts to commit any of the following acts shall be guilty of a misdemeanor:

"(1) Sells, makes, or possesses any coin, note, token, transfer, transaction card, or similar article which has been altered from its original condition contrary to its intended use to enter or gain entry into or on any bus, rail vehicle, or station;

"(2) Sells or exchanges any token, transfer, transaction card, ticket, fare medium, or similar article used or to be used as payment for entry into or on any bus, rail vehicle, or terminal without the express consent of the public transit agency owning or operating such vehicles or stations;

"(3) Offers entry or provides entry into or on any bus, rapid rail car, or station to any person without the payment of the proper fare to the public transit agency owning or operating such vehicles or stations;

"(4) Gains entry into or on any bus, rapid rail car, or station without the payment of the proper fare to the public transit agency owning or operating such vehicles or stations; or

"(5) Gains entry into or on any bus, rapid rail car, or station through the use of a transcard, transaction card, or other similar fare media which is the property of another person."

Part 2

Transportation Passenger Safety

§ 16-12-121. Short title

This part shall be known and may be cited as the "Transportation Passenger Safety Act."

Laws 1978, p. 2238, § 1; Laws 1988, p. 415, § 2; Laws 2002, p. 1094, § 5.

Historical and Statutory Notes

The 2002 amendment rewrote part 2 of article 4. Prior to amendment, § 16-12-121 provided:

"This part shall be known and may be cited as the 'Bus and Rail Vehicle Passenger Safety Act.' "

§ 16-12-122. Definitions

As used in this part, the term:

(1) "Aircraft" means any machine, whether heavier or lighter than air, used or designed for navigation of or flight in the air.

(2) "Avoid a security measure" means to take any action that is intended to result in any person, baggage, container, or item of any type being allowed into a secure area without being subjected to security measures or the assembly of items into an object or substance that is prohibited under the laws of this state or of the United States or any of their agencies, political subdivisions, or authorities after such items have passed through a security measure into a secure area.

(3) "Bus" means any passenger bus or coach or other motor vehicle having a seating capacity of not less than 15 passengers operated by a transportation company for the purpose of carrying passengers or freight for hire.

(4) "Charter" means a group of persons, pursuant to a common purpose and under a single contract and at a fixed charge for the vehicle in accordance with a transportation company's tariff, who have acquired the exclusive use of an aircraft, bus, or rail vehicle to travel together as a group to a specified destination.

(5) "Interfere with a security measure" means to take any action that is intended to defeat, disable, or prevent the full

operation of equipment or procedures designed or intended to detect any object or substance, including, but not limited to, disabling of any device so that it cannot fully function, creation of any diversion intended to defeat a security measure, or packaging of any item or substance so as to avoid detection by a security measure.

(6) "Passenger" means any person served by the transportation company; and, in addition to the ordinary meaning of passenger, the term shall include any person accompanying or meeting another person who is transported by such company, any person shipping or receiving freight, and any person purchasing a ticket or receiving a pass.

(7) "Rail vehicle" means any railroad or rail transit car, carriage, coach, or other vehicle, whether self-propelled or not and designed to be operated upon a rail or rails or other fixed right of way by a transportation company for the purpose of carrying passengers or freight or both for hire.

(8) "Secure area" means any enclosed or unenclosed area within a terminal whereby access is restricted in any manner or the possession of items subject to security measures is prohibited. Access to a secure area may be restricted to persons specifically authorized by law, regulation, or policy of the governing authority or transportation company operating said terminal, and such access into a secure area may be conditioned on passing through security measures, and possession of items may be restricted to designated persons who are acting in the course of their official duties.

(9) "Security measure" means any process or procedure by which employees, agents, passengers, persons accompanying passengers, containers, baggage, freight, or possessions of passengers or persons accompanying passengers are screened, inspected, or examined by any means for the purpose of ensuring the safety and welfare of aircraft, bus, or rail vehicles and the employees, agents, passengers, and freight of any transportation company. The security measures may be operated by or under the authority of any governmental entity, transportation company, or any entity contracting therewith.

(10) "Terminal" means an aircraft, bus, or rail vehicle station, depot, any such transportation facility, or infrastructure relating thereto operated by a transportation company or governmental entity or authority. This term includes a reasonable area immediately adjacent to any designated stop along the route traveled by any coach or rail vehicle operated by a transportation company or governmental entity operating aircraft, bus, or rail vehicle transportation facility and parking lots or parking areas adjacent to a terminal.

(11) "Transportation company" or "company" means any person, group of persons, or corporation providing for-hire transportation to passengers or freight by aircraft, by bus upon the highways in this state, by rail vehicle upon any public or private right of way in this state, or by all, including passengers and freight in interstate or intrastate travel. This term shall also include transportation facilities owned or operated by local public bodies; by municipalities; and by public corporations, authorities, boards, and commissions established under the laws of this state, any of the several states, the United States, or any foreign nation.

Laws 1978, p. 2238, § 2; Laws 1988, p. 415, § 2; Laws 2002, p. 1094, § 5.

Historical and Statutory Notes

The 2002 amendment rewrote part 2 of article 4. Prior to amendment, § 16–12–122 provided:

"As used in this part, the term:

"(1) 'Bus' means any passenger bus or coach or other motor vehicle having a seating capacity of not less than 15 passengers operated by a transportation company for the purpose of carrying passengers or cargo for hire.

"(2) 'Charter' means a group of persons, pursuant to a common purpose and under a single contract and at a fixed charge for the vehicle in accordance with a transportation company's tariff, who have acquired the exclusive use of a bus or rail vehicle to travel together as a group to a specified destination.

"(3) 'Passenger' means any person served by the transportation company; and, in addition to the ordinary meaning of passenger, the term shall include any person accompanying or meeting another person who is transported by such company, any person shipping or receiving cargo, and any person purchasing a ticket or receiving a pass.

"(4) 'Rail vehicle' means any railroad or rail transit car, carriage, coach, or other vehicle, whether self-propelled or pulled or pushed by a locomotive or other vehicle or vehicles, having a seating capacity of not less than 15 passengers, and operated upon a rail or rails or other fixed right of way by a transportation company for the purpose of carrying passengers or cargo for hire.

"(5) 'Terminal' means a bus or rail vehicle station, depot, or any facility operated by a transportation company. This term includes a reasonable area immediately adjacent to any designated stop along the route traveled by any coach or rail vehicle operated by a transportation company and parking lots or parking areas adjacent to a terminal.

"(6) 'Transportation company' or 'company' means any person, group of persons, or corporation providing for-hire transportation to passengers or cargo by bus upon the highways in this state, by rail vehicle upon any public or private right of way in this state, or by both, including passengers and cargo in interstate or intrastate travel. This term shall also include transportation facilities owned or operated by local public bodies; by municipalities; and by public corporations, boards, and commissions established under the laws of the state."

§ 16–12–123. Bus or rail vehicle hijacking; boarding aircraft, bus, or rail vehicle with certain items

(a)(1) A person commits the offense of bus or rail vehicle hijacking when he or she:

(A) Seizes or exercises control by force or violence or threat of force or violence of any bus or rail vehicle within the jurisdiction of this state;

(B) By force or violence or by threat of force or violence seizes or exercises control of any transportation company or all or any part of the transportation facilities owned or operated by any such company; or

(C) By force or violence or by threat of force or violence substantially obstructs, hinders, interferes with, or otherwise disrupts or disturbs the operation of any transportation company or all or any part of a transportation facility.

(2) Any person convicted of the offense of bus or rail hijacking shall be guilty of a felony and, upon conviction thereof, shall be punished by imprisonment for life or by imprisonment for not less than one nor more than 20 years.

(b) Any person who boards or attempts to board an aircraft, bus, or rail vehicle with any explosive, destructive device, or hoax device as such term is defined in Code Section 16–7–80; firearm for which such person does not have on his or her person a valid weapons carry license issued pursuant to Code Section 16–11–129 unless possessing such firearm is prohibited by federal law; hazardous substance as defined by Code Section 12–8–92; or knife or other device designed or modified for the purpose of offense and defense concealed on or about his or her person or property which is or would be accessible to such person while on the aircraft, bus, or rail vehicle shall be guilty of a felony and, upon conviction thereof, shall be sentenced to imprisonment for not less than one nor more than ten years. The prohibition of this subsection shall not apply to any law enforcement officer, peace officer retired from a state or federal law enforcement agency, person in the military service of the state or of the United States, or commercial security personnel employed by the transportation company who is in possession of weapons used within the course and scope of employment; nor shall the prohibition apply to persons transporting weapons contained in baggage which is not accessible to passengers if the presence of such weapons has been declared to the transportation company and such weapons have been secured in a manner prescribed by state or federal law or regulation for the purpose of transportation or shipment. The provisions of this subsection shall not apply to any privately owned aircraft, bus, or rail vehicle if the owner of such aircraft or vehicle has given his or her express permission to board the aircraft or vehicle with the item.

(c) The company may employ reasonable security measures, including any method or device, to detect concealed weapons, explosives, or hazardous material in baggage or freight or upon the person of the passenger. Upon the discovery of any such item or material in the possession of a person, unless the item is a weapon in the possession of a person exempted under subsection (b) of this Code section from the prohibition of that subsection (b), the company shall obtain possession and retain custody of such item or materials until they are transferred to the custody of law enforcement officers.

Laws 1978, p. 2238, § 3; Laws 1982, p. 3, § 16; Laws 1988, p. 415, § 2; Laws 1996, p. 416, § 7; Laws 2002, p. 1094, § 5; Laws 2010, Act 643, § 2–8, eff. June 4, 2010.

Historical and Statutory Notes

The 2002 amendment rewrote part 2 of article 4. Prior to amendment, § 16–12–123 provided:

"(a) The offense of bus or rail vehicle hijacking is the seizure or exercise of control by force or violence or threat of force or violence of any bus or rail vehicle within the jurisdiction of this state. Any person committing the offense of bus or rail vehicle hijacking shall be guilty of a felony and, upon conviction thereof, shall be punished by imprisonment for life or imprisonment for not less than one nor more than 20 years.

"(b) Any person who boards or attempts to board a bus or rail vehicle with a dangerous or deadly weapon concealed on or about his person or his property which is or would be accessible to such person while on the bus or rail vehicle shall be guilty of a felony and, upon conviction thereof, shall be sentenced to imprisonment for not less than one nor more than ten years. The prohibition of this subsection shall not apply to any person who is exempted under Code Section 16–11–130 or commercial security personnel who are in possession of weapons used within the course and scope of their employment; nor shall the prohibition apply to persons who are in the possession of weapons with the consent of the owner of such bus or rail vehicle, his agent, or the lessee or bailee of such bus or rail vehicle; nor shall the prohibition apply to persons transporting weapons contained in baggage which is not accessible to passengers on the bus or rail vehicle if the presence of such weapons has been declared to the transportation company.

"(c) Any person who has on or about his or her person or who has placed, attempted to place, or attempted to have placed aboard such bus or rail vehicle any destructive device, as such term is defined by Code Section 16–7–80, shall be guilty of a felony and, upon conviction thereof, shall be sentenced to imprisonment for not less than one nor more than 20 years.

"(d) Any person who by force or violence or by threat of force or violence seizes or exercises control of any transportation company, or of the transportation facilities owned or operated by any such company, or of any part thereof, or who by force or violence or by threat of force or violence obstructs, hinders, interferes with, or otherwise disrupts or disturbs the operation of any such company or facility, or of any part thereof, shall be guilty of a felony and, upon conviction thereof, shall be punished by imprisonment for life or by imprisonment for not less than one nor more than 20 years.

"(e) The company may employ reasonable means, including mechanical, electronic, or X-ray devices, to detect concealed weapons, explosives, or hazardous material in baggage or upon the person of the passenger. Upon the discovery of any such item or material in the possession of a person, unless the item is a weapon in the possession of a person exempted under subsection (b) of this Code section from the prohibition of that subsection (b), the company shall obtain possession and retain custody of such item or materials until they are transferred to the custody of law enforcement officers."

The 2010 amendment by Act 643, in subsec. (b), inserted "for which such person does not have on his or her person a valid weapons carry license issued pursuant to Code Section 16–11–129 unless possessing such firearm is prohibited by federal law", and deleted "their" following "course and scope".

Laws 2010, Act 643, § 3–1, provides:

"This Act shall become effective upon its approval by the Governor or upon its becoming law without such approval and shall apply to all offenses committed on and after such date. The enactment of this Act shall not affect any prosecutions for acts occurring before the effective date of this Act and shall not act as an abatement of any such prosecutions."

§ 16–12–124. Unlawful to remove baggage, freight, etc., without consent

(a) It shall be unlawful to remove any baggage, freight, container, or other item transported upon an aircraft, bus, or rail vehicle or stored in a terminal without consent of the owner of such property or the company or its duly authorized representative. Any person violating this Code section shall be guilty of a felony and, upon conviction thereof, shall be punished by imprisonment for not less than one nor more than five years.

(b) The actual value of an item removed in violation of this Code section shall not be material to the crime herein defined.

Laws 1978, p. 2238, § 4; Laws 1988, p. 415, § 2; Laws 2002, p. 1094, § 5.

Historical and Statutory Notes

The 2002 amendment rewrote part 2 of article 4. Prior to amendment, § 16–12–124 provided:

"(a) It shall be unlawful to remove any baggage, cargo, or other item transported upon a bus or rail vehicle or stored in a terminal without consent of the owner of such property or the company or its duly authorized representative. Any person violating this Code section shall be guilty of a felony and, upon conviction thereof, shall be punished by imprisonment for not less than one nor more than five years.

"(b) The actual value of an item removed in violation of this Code section shall not be material to the crime herein defined."

§ 16–12–125. Unlawful to avoid or interfere with security measure

(a) Except as otherwise provided in this Code section, it shall be unlawful for any person to avoid or interfere with a properly functioning security measure. Any person convicted of a violation of this Code section shall be guilty of a misdemeanor of a high and aggravated nature; provided, however, that any person who violates this Code section with the intent to commit a felony within the terminal or with regard to any aircraft, bus, or rail vehicle shall be punished by imprisonment for not less than five nor more than 25 years, a fine not to exceed $100,000.00, or both.

(b) Any violation of this Code section shall be considered a separate offense.

(c) This Code section shall not apply to authorized agents of the entity owning or operating such security measure.

Laws 2002, p. 1094, § 5; Laws 2003, Act 179, § 2, eff. June 1, 2003.

Historical and Statutory Notes

The 2002 amendment rewrote part 2 of article 4. Prior to amendment, § 16–12–125 provided:

"This part shall be cumulative and supplemental to any other law of this state. A conviction or acquittal under any of the criminal provisions of Code Section 16–12–123 or 16–12–124 shall not be a bar to any other civil or criminal proceeding."

The 2003 amendment by Act 179, in subsec. (a), substituted "Except as otherwise provided in this Code section, it shall be unlawful for any person to avoid or interfere with a properly functioning security measure" for "It shall be unlawful for any person to avoid or interfere with a security measure"; and added new subsec. (c).

Laws 2003, Act 179, § 5, provides:

"This Act shall become effective on the first day of the month following the month in which it is approved by the Governor or in which it becomes law without such approval."

§ 16–12–126. Unlawful to disable or inhibit operation or effectiveness of safety device or render traffic control device inoperable

(a) Except as otherwise provided in this Code section, it shall be unlawful intentionally to disable or inhibit the operation or effectiveness of any properly functioning safety device of any description or to render any item or substance less safe when said item or substance is in any freight of a transportation company, in baggage or possessions of a passenger, or in a terminal.

(b) Except as otherwise provided in this Code section, it shall be unlawful to intentionally render inoperable or partially inoperable for any period of time any properly functioning device designed or operated for traffic control that is owned, operated, or maintained by or for the benefit of a transportation company.

(c) Any violation of this Code section shall be punished by imprisonment for not less than five nor more than 20 years, a fine not to exceed $100,000.00, or both.

(d) Any violation of this Code section shall be considered a separate offense.

(e) This Code section shall not apply to authorized agents of the entity owning or operating such safety device or device designed or operated for traffic control.

Laws 2002, p. 1094, § 5; Laws 2003, Act 179, § 3, eff. June 1, 2003.

Historical and Statutory Notes

The 2003 amendment by Act 179, in subsec. (a), substituted "Except as otherwise provided in this Code section, it shall be unlawful intentionally to disable or inhibit the operation or effectiveness of any properly functioning safety device" for "It shall be unlawful intentionally to disable or inhibit the operation or effectiveness of any safety device"; in subsec. (b), substituted "Except as otherwise provided in this Code section, it shall be unlawful to intentionally render inoperable or partially inoperable for any period of time any properly functioning device" for "It shall be unlawful to intentionally render inoperable or partially inoperable for any period of time any device"; and added new subsec. (e).

Laws 2003, Act 179, § 5, provides:

"This Act shall become effective on the first day of the month following the month in which it is approved by the Governor or in which it becomes law without such approval."

§ 16–12–127. Unlawful to have certain devices on person or to place them on person or in possession of passengers

(a) It shall be unlawful for any person, with the intention of avoiding or interfering with a security measure or of introducing into a terminal any explosive, destructive device, or hoax device as defined in Code Section 16–7–80; firearm for which such person does not have on his or her person a valid weapons carry license issued pursuant to Code Section 16–11–129 unless possessing such firearm is prohibited by federal law; hazardous substance as defined by Code Section 12–8–92; or knife or other device designed or modified for the purpose of offense and defense, to:

(1) Have any such item on or about his or her person, or

(2) Place or cause to be placed or attempt to place or cause to be placed any such item:

(A) In a container or freight of a transportation company;

(B) In the baggage or possessions of any person or any transportation company without the knowledge of the passenger or transportation company; or

(C) Aboard such aircraft, bus, or rail vehicle.

(b) A person violating the provisions of this Code section shall be guilty of a felony and shall, upon conviction, be sentenced to imprisonment for not less than one year nor more than 20 years, a fine not to exceed $15,000.00, or both. A prosecution under this Code section shall not be barred by the imposition of a civil penalty imposed by any governmental entity.

(c) It is an affirmative defense to a violation of this Code section if a person notifies a law enforcement officer or other person employed to provide security for a transportation company of the presence of such item as soon as possible after learning of its presence and surrenders or secures such item as directed by the law enforcement officer or other person employed to provide security for a transportation company.

Laws 2002, p. 1094, § 5; Laws 2003, Act 179, § 4, eff. June 1, 2003; Laws 2010, Act 643, § 2–9, eff. June 4, 2010.

Historical and Statutory Notes

The 2003 amendment by Act 179 added new subsec. (c).

Laws 2003, Act 179, § 5, provides:

"This Act shall become effective on the first day of the month following the month in which it is approved by the Governor or in which it becomes law without such approval."

The 2010 amendment by Act 643, in subsec. (a), inserted "for which such person does not have on his or her person a valid weapons carry license issued pursuant to Code Section 16–11–129 unless possessing such firearm is prohibited by federal law" in the introductory paragraph.

Laws 2010, Act 643, § 3–1, provides:

"This Act shall become effective upon its approval by the Governor or upon its becoming law without such approval and shall apply to all offenses committed on and after such date. The enactment of this Act shall not affect any prosecutions for acts occurring before the effective date of this Act and shall not act as an abatement of any such prosecutions."

§ 16–12–128. Cumulative and supplemental nature of law; restitution

(a) This part shall be cumulative and supplemental to any other law of this state. A conviction or acquittal under any of the criminal provisions of Code Section 16–12–123, 16–12–124, 16–12–125, or 16–12–126 shall not be a bar to any other civil or criminal proceeding.

(b) In addition to any other penalty imposed by law for a violation of this part, the court may require the defendant to make restitution to any affected public or private entity for the reasonable costs or damages associated with the offense. Restitution made pursuant to this subsection shall not preclude any party from obtaining any other civil or criminal remedy available under any other provision of law. The restitution authorized by this subsection is supplemental and not exclusive.

Laws 1978, p. 2238, § 5; Laws 1982, p. 3, § 16; Laws 1988, p. 415, § 2; Laws 2002, p. 1094, § 5.

Formerly Code 1981, § 16–12–125.

Article 5

Abortion

§ 16–12–140. Criminal abortion

(a) Except as otherwise provided in Code Section 16–12–141, a person commits the offense of criminal abortion when he administers any medicine, drugs, or other substance whatever to any woman or when he uses any instrument or other means whatever upon any woman with intent to produce a miscarriage or abortion.

(b) A person convicted of the offense of criminal abortion shall be punished by imprisonment for not less than one nor more than ten years.

Laws 1876, p. 113, § 2; Laws 1968, p. 1249, § 1; Laws 1973, p. 635, § 1.

Formerly Code 1882, § 4337b; Penal Code 1895, § 81; Penal Code 1910, § 81; Code 1933, § 26-1101; Code 1933, §§ 26-1201, 26-1203; Code 1933, § 26-1204.

§ 16-12-141. When and where procedure authorized; physician authorized to perform procedure

(a) Nothing in this article shall be construed to prohibit an abortion performed by a physician duly licensed to practice medicine and surgery pursuant to Chapter 34 of Title 43, based upon his or her best clinical judgment that an abortion is necessary, except that Code Section 16-12-144 is a prohibition of a particular abortion method which shall apply to both duly licensed physicians and laypersons.

(b)(1) No abortion is authorized or shall be performed after the first trimester unless the abortion is performed in a licensed hospital, in a licensed ambulatory surgical center, or in a health facility licensed as an abortion facility by the Department of Community Health.

(2) An abortion shall only be performed by a physician licensed under Article 2 of Chapter 34 of Title 43.

(c) No abortion is authorized or shall be performed after the second trimester unless the physician and two consulting physicians certify that the abortion is necessary in their best clinical judgment to preserve the life or health of the woman. If the product of the abortion is capable of meaningful or sustained life, medical aid then available must be rendered.

(d) The performing physician shall file with the commissioner of community health within ten days after an abortion procedure is performed a certificate of abortion containing such statistical data as is determined by the Department of Community Health consistent with preserving the privacy of the woman. Hospital or other licensed health facility records shall be available to the district attorney of the judicial circuit in which the hospital or health facility is located.

Laws 1968, p. 1249, § 1; Laws 1973, p. 635, § 1; Laws 1997, p. 142, § 1; Laws 2005, Act 400, § 4, eff. May 10, 2005; Laws 2009, Act 102, §§ 1-4, 1-6, eff. July 1, 2009.

Formerly Code 1933, § 26-1202.

Historical and Statutory Notes

The 2005 amendment by Act 400 designated the existing text of subsec. (b) as par. (1); inserted ", in a licensed ambulatory surgical center," in newly designated par. (1); and added par. (2).

The 2009 amendment by Act 102 substituted "Department of Community Health" for "Department of Human Resources" throughout the section.

The 2009 amendment by Act 102 substituted "commissioner of community health" for "commissioner of human resources" throughout the section.

§ 16-12-141.1. Aborted fetuses; disposal; reporting requirements; forms; violations; public reports; confidentiality

(a)(1) Every hospital and clinic in which abortions are performed or occur spontaneously, and any laboratory to which the aborted fetuses are delivered, shall provide for the disposal of the aborted fetuses by cremation, interment, or other manner approved of by the commissioner of community health. The hospital, clinic, or laboratory may complete any laboratory tests necessary for the health of the woman or her future offspring prior to disposing of the aborted fetus.

(2) Each hospital, clinic, and laboratory shall report, on a form of the type and confidentiality provided for in subsection (d) of Code Section 16-12-141, and provided by the commissioner of community health, the manner in which it disposes of the aborted fetus. Such reports shall be made annually by December 31 and whenever the method of disposal changes. The commissioner of community health shall provide forms for reporting under this Code section.

(b) Any hospital, clinic, or laboratory violating the provisions of subsection (a) of this Code section shall be punished by a fine of not less than $1,000.00 nor more than $5,000.00.

(c) Within 90 days after May 10, 2005, the Department of Human Resources (now known as the Department of Community Health for these purposes) shall prepare a reporting form for physicians which shall include:

(1) The number of females whose parent or guardian was provided the notice required in paragraph (1) of subsection (a) of Code Section 15-11-112 by the physician or such physician's agent; of that number, the number of notices provided personally under subparagraphs (a)(1)(A) and (a)(1)(B) of Code Section 15-11-112 and the number of notices provided by mail under subparagraph (a)(1)(C) of Code Section 15-11-112; and, of each of those numbers, the number of females who, to the best of the reporting physician's information and belief, went on to obtain the abortion;

(2) The number of females upon whom the physician performed an abortion without providing to the parent or guardian of a minor the notice required by subsection (a) of Code Section 15-11-112; and of that number, the number of females for which subsection (b) of Code Section 15-11-112 and Code Section 15-11-116 were applicable;

(3) The number of abortions performed upon a female by the physician after receiving judicial authorization pursuant to subsection (b) of Code Section 15-11-112 and Code Section 15-11-114; and

(4) The same information described in paragraphs (1), (2), and (3) of this subsection with respect to females for whom a guardian or conservator has been appointed.

(d) The Department of Community Health shall ensure that copies of the reporting forms described in subsection (c) of this Code section, together with a reprint of this Code section, are provided:

(1) Within 120 days after May 10, 2005, to all health facilities licensed as an abortion facility by the Department of Human Resources (now known as the Department of Community Health for these purposes) ;

(2) To each physician licensed or who subsequently becomes licensed to practice medicine in this state at the same time as official notification to that physician that the physician is so licensed; and

(3) By December 1 of every year, other than the calendar year in which forms are distributed in accordance with paragraph (1) of this subsection, to all health facilities licensed as an abortion facility by the Department of Community Health.

(e) By February 28 of each year following a calendar year in any part of which this subsection was in effect, each physician who provided, or whose agent provided, the notice described in subsection (a) of Code Section 15-11-112 and any physician who knowingly performed an abortion upon a female or upon a female for whom a guardian or conservator had been appointed because of a finding of incompetency during the previous calendar year shall submit to the Department of Community Health a copy of the form described in subsection (c) of this Code section with the requested data entered accurately and completely.

(f) Reports that are submitted more than 30 days following the due date shall be subject to a late fee of $500.00 for that period and the same fee for each additional 30 day period or portion of a 30 day period in which they remain overdue. Any physician required to report in accordance with this Code section who submits an incomplete report or fails to submit a report for more than one year following the due date may, in an action brought by the Department of Community Health, be directed by a court of competent jurisdiction to submit a complete report within a period stated by court order or be subject to sanctions for civil contempt.

(g) By June 30 of each year, the Department of Community Health shall issue a public report providing statistics for the previous calendar year compiled from all the reports covering that year submitted in accordance with this Code section for each of the items listed in subsection (c) of this Code section. The report shall also include statistics which shall be obtained by the Administrative Office of the Courts giving the total number of petitions or motions filed under subsection (b) of Code Section 15–11–112 and, of that number, the number in which the court appointed a guardian ad litem, the number in which the court appointed counsel, the number in which the judge issued an order authorizing an abortion without notification, the number in which the judge denied such an order, and, of the last, the number of denials from which an appeal was filed, the number of such appeals that resulted in the denials being affirmed, and the number of such appeals that resulted in reversals of such denials. Each report shall also provide the statistics for all previous calendar years for which such a public statistical report was required to be issued, adjusted to reflect any additional information from late or corrected reports. The Department of Community Health shall ensure that none of the information included in the public reports could reasonably lead to the identification of any individual female or of any female for whom a guardian or conservator has been appointed.

(h) The Department of Community Health may by regulation alter the dates established by paragraph (3) of subsection (d) and subsections (e) and (g) of this Code section or consolidate the forms or reports to achieve administrative convenience or fiscal savings or to reduce the burden of reporting requirements so long as reporting forms are sent to all facilities licensed as an abortion facility by the Department of Community Health at least once every year and the report described in subsection (g) of this Code section is issued at least once each year.

(i) The Department of Community Health shall ensure that the names and identities of the physicians filing reports under this Code section shall remain confidential. The names and identities of such physicians shall not be subject to Article 4 of Chapter 18 of Title 50.

Laws 1985, p. 1421, § 1; Laws 2005, Act 400, § 5, eff. May 10, 2005; Laws 2009, Act 102, § 1–6, eff. July 1, 2009.

Historical and Statutory Notes

The 2005 amendment by Act 400 added subsecs. (c) through (i).

In 2005, the Code Commission, in subsec. (c) and par. (1) of subsec. (d), substituted "May 10, 2005" for "the effective date of this subsection". See § 28–9–5.

The 2009 amendment by Act 102 substituted "commissioner of community health" for "commissioner of human resources" throughout the section.

In 2009, the Code Commission substituted "Community Health" for "Human Resources" throughout the section, and inserted "(now known as the Department of Community Health for these purposes)" in the introductory paragraph of subsec. (c) and in par. (d)(1) . See § 28–9–5.

§ 16–12–142. Medical facilities and physicians not required to perform abortions; Provisions for pharmacists to object to filling prescriptions intended to terminate pregnancies; limitations

(a) Nothing in this article shall require a hospital or other medical facility or physician to admit any patient under the provisions of this article for the purpose of performing an abortion. In addition, any person who states in writing an objection to any abortion or all abortions on moral or religious grounds shall not be required to participate in procedures which will result in such abortion; and the refusal of the person to participate therein shall not form the basis of any claim for damages on account of such refusal or for any disciplinary or recriminatory action against the person. The written objection shall remain in effect until the person revokes it or terminates his association with the facility with which it is filed.

(b) Any pharmacist who states in writing an objection to any abortion or all abortions on moral or religious grounds shall not be required to fill a prescription for a drug which purpose is to terminate a pregnancy; and the refusal of the person to fill such prescription shall not form the basis of any claim for damages on account of such refusal or for any disciplinary or recriminatory action against the person; provided, however, that the pharmacist shall make all reasonable efforts to locate another pharmacist who is willing to fill such prescription or shall immediately return the prescription to the prescription holder. The written objection shall remain in effect until the person revokes it or terminates his or her association with the facility with which it is filed. Nothing in this subsection shall be construed to authorize a pharmacist to refuse to fill a prescription for birth control medication, including any process, device, or method to prevent pregnancy and including any drug or device approved by the federal Food and Drug Administration for such purpose.

Laws 1968, p. 1249, § 1; Laws 1973, p. 635, § 1; Laws 2006, Act 468, § 2A, eff. July 1, 2006.

Formerly Code 1933, § 26–1202.

Historical and Statutory Notes

The 2006 amendment by Act 468 added the subsec. (a) designation to the previously existing text; and added subsec. (b).

§ 16–12–143. Failure to file

A person who fails to file or maintain in complete form any of the written reports required in this article within the time set forth is guilty of a misdemeanor.

Laws 1973, p. 635, § 1.

Formerly Code 1933, § 26–1203.

§ 16–12–144. Partial-birth abortion

(a) As used in this Code section, the term:

(1) "Fetus" means the biological offspring of human parents.

(2) "Partial-birth abortion" means an abortion in which the person performing the abortion partially vaginally delivers a living human fetus before ending the life of the fetus and completing the delivery.

(b) Any person who knowingly performs a partial-birth abortion and thereby ends the life of a human fetus shall, upon conviction thereof, be punished by a fine not to exceed $5,000.00, imprisonment for not more than five years, or both. This prohibition shall not apply to a partial-birth abortion that is necessary to save the life of the mother because her life is endangered by a physical disorder, physical illness, or physical injury, including a life-endangering condition caused by or arising from the pregnancy itself, provided that no other medical procedure will suffice to save the mother's life.

(c)(1) The father of the fetus, and the maternal grandparents of the fetus if the mother has not attained the age of 18 years of age at the time of the abortion, may obtain appropriate relief in a civil action, unless the pregnancy resulted from the plaintiff's criminal conduct or the plaintiff consented to the abortion.

(2) Such relief shall include:

(A) Money damages for all injuries, psychological and physical, occasioned by the violation of this Code section; and

(B) Statutory damages equal to three times the cost of the partial-birth abortion.

(d) A woman upon whom a partial-birth abortion is performed may not be prosecuted under this Code section for violating this

Code section or any provision thereof, or for conspiracy or for an attempt to violate this Code section or any provision thereof.

Laws 1997, p. 142, § 2.

Article 6

Human Body Traffic

§ 16–12–160. Unlawful to buy or sell human body; exceptions

(a) It shall be unlawful, except as provided in subsection (b) of this Code section, for any person, firm, or corporation to buy or sell, to offer to buy or sell, or to assist another in buying or selling or offering to buy or sell a human body or any part of a human body or buy or sell a human fetus or any part thereof.

(b) The prohibition contained in subsection (a) of this Code section shall not apply to:

(1) The purchase or sale of whole blood, blood plasma, blood products, blood derivatives, other self-replicating body fluids, or hair;

(2) A gift or donation of a human body or any part of a human body or any procedure connected therewith as provided in Article 6 of Chapter 5 of Title 44 or to the payment of a fee in connection with such gift or donation pursuant to subsection (b) of Code Section 44–5–154 if such fee is paid to a procurement organization, as that term is defined in Code Section 44–5–141;

(3) The reimbursement of actual expenses, including medical costs, lost income, and travel expenses, incurred by a living person in giving or donating a part of the person's body;

(4) The payment of financial assistance under a plan of insurance or other health care coverage;

(5) The purchase or sale of human tissue, organs, or other parts of the human body for health sciences education; or

(6) The payment of reasonable costs associated with the removal, storage, or transportation of a human body or any part of a human body given or donated for medical or scientific purposes.

(c) Any person, firm, or corporation convicted of violating subsection (a) of this Code section shall be guilty of a felony and, upon conviction thereof, shall be punished by a fine not exceeding $5,000.00 or by imprisonment for not less than one year nor more than five years, or both.

Laws 1986, p. 645, § 4; Laws 1989, p. 456, § 1; Laws 1992, p. 2946, § 1; Laws 2008, Act 545, § 2, eff. July 1, 2008.

Historical and Statutory Notes

The 2008 amendment by Act 545, in par. (2) of subsec. (b), substituted "a fee in connection with such gift or donation pursuant to subsection (b) of Code Section 44–5–154 if such fee is paid to a procurement organization, as that term is defined in Code Section 44–5–141" for "a processing fee in connection with such gift or donation if such fee is paid to a bank or storage facility, as those terms are defined in Code Section 44–5–142".

§ 16–12–161. Unlawful to remove human body parts from scene of death or dismemberment; exceptions

(a) It shall be unlawful for any person to remove from the scene of the death or dismemberment of any person any human body part; provided, however, that this Code section shall not apply to a law enforcement officer acting in the lawful discharge of his or her official duties, or to any person acting under the direction of a law enforcement officer, a physician or an emergency medical technician in the course of their professions, or in the absence of any such person to any person who transports such body part directly to a medical facility, law enforcement agency, or licensed funeral home, although all such persons remain obligated to comply with the provisions of Article 2 of Chapter 16 of Title 45 concerning death investigations.

(b) Any person violating the provisions of subsection (a) of this Code section shall be guilty of a misdemeanor of a high and aggravated nature.

Laws 1994, p. 334, § 1.

Article 7

Sale or Distribution to, or Possession by, Minors of Cigarettes and Tobacco Related Objects

§ 16–12–170. Definitions

As used in this article, the term:

(1) "Cigarettes" means any type of tobacco or tobacco product.

(2) "Community service" means a public service which a minor might appropriately be required to perform, as determined by the court, as punishment for certain offenses provided for in this article.

(3) "Minor" means any person who is under the age of 18 years.

(4) "Person" means any natural person or any firm, partnership, company, corporation, or other entity.

(5) "Proper identification" means any document issued by a governmental agency containing a description of the person, such person's photograph, or both, and giving such person's date of birth and includes, without being limited to, a passport, military identification card, driver's license, or an identification card authorized under Code Sections 40–5–100 through 40–5–104. "Proper identification" shall not include a birth certificate.

(6) "Tobacco related objects" means any papers, wrappers, or other products, devices, or substances which are used for the purpose of making cigarettes or tobacco in any form whatsoever.

Laws 1987, p. 945, § 1; Laws 1989, p. 14, § 16; Laws 1993, p. 343, § 1.

§ 16–12–171. Unlawful sales; unlawful purchases; punishment

(a)(1) It shall be unlawful for any person knowingly to:

(A) Sell or barter, directly or indirectly, any cigarettes or tobacco related objects to a minor;

(B) Purchase any cigarettes or tobacco related objects for any minor unless the minor for whom the purchase is made is the child of the purchaser; or

(C) Advise, counsel, or compel any minor to smoke, inhale, chew, or use cigarettes or tobacco related objects.

(2)(A) The prohibition contained in paragraph (1) of this subsection shall not apply with respect to sale of cigarettes, tobacco products, or tobacco related objects by a person when such person has been furnished with proper identification showing that the person to whom the cigarettes, tobacco products, or tobacco related objects are sold is 18 years of age or older.

(B) In any case where a reasonable or prudent person could reasonably be in doubt as to whether or not the person to whom cigarettes or tobacco related objects are to be sold or otherwise furnished is actually 18 years of age or older, it shall be the duty of the person selling or otherwise furnishing such cigarettes or tobacco related objects to request to see and to be furnished with proper identification as provided for in subsection (b) of this Code section in order to verify the age of such person. The failure to make such request and verification in any case where the person to whom the cigarettes or tobacco related objects are sold or otherwise furnished is less than 18 years of age may be considered by the trier of fact in determining whether the person selling or otherwise furnishing such cigarettes or tobacco related objects did so knowingly.

(3) Any person who violates this subsection shall be guilty of a misdemeanor.

(b)(1) It shall be unlawful for any minor to:

(A) Purchase, attempt to purchase, or possess for personal use any cigarettes or tobacco related objects. This subparagraph shall not apply to possession of cigarettes or tobacco related objects by a minor when a parent or guardian of such minor gives the cigarettes or tobacco related objects to the minor and possession is in the home of the parent or guardian and such parent or guardian is present; or

(B) Misrepresent such minor's identity or age or use any false identification for the purpose of purchasing or procuring any cigarettes or tobacco related objects.

(2) A minor who commits an offense provided for in paragraph (1) of this subsection may be punished as follows:

(A) By requiring the performance of community service not exceeding 20 hours;

(B) By requiring attendance at a publicly or privately sponsored lecture or discussion on the health hazards of smoking or tobacco use, provided such lecture or discussion is offered without charge to the minor; or

(C) By a combination of the punishments described in subparagraphs (A) and (B) of this paragraph.

Laws 1987, p. 945, § 1; Laws 1993, p. 343, § 2; Laws 1996, p. 483, § 1; Laws 1999, p. 81, § 16; Laws 2004, Act 464, § 1, eff. July 1, 2004; Laws 2007, Act 252, § 1, eff. July 1, 2007.

Historical and Statutory Notes

The 2004 amendment by Act 464 rewrote subsec. (b), par. (1), which had read:

"(b)(1) It shall be unlawful for any minor to:

"(A) Purchase any cigarettes or tobacco related objects; or

"(B) Misrepresent such minor's identity or age or use any false identification for the purpose of purchasing or procuring any cigarettes or tobacco related objects."

The 2007 amendment by Act 252 inserted ", attempt to purchase," in subpar. (1)(A) of subsec. (b).

§ 16–12–172. Warning signs in businesses

(a) Any person owning or operating a place of business in which cigarettes, tobacco products, or tobacco related objects are sold or offered for sale shall post in a conspicuous place a sign which shall contain the following statement:

"SALE OF CIGARETTES, TOBACCO, TOBACCO PRODUCTS, OR TOBACCO RELATED OBJECTS TO PERSONS UNDER 18 YEARS OF AGE IS PROHIBITED BY LAW."

Such sign shall be printed in letters of at least one-half inch in height.

(b) Any person who fails to comply with the requirements of subsection (a) of this Code section shall be guilty of a misdemeanor.

Laws 1987, p. 945, § 1; Laws 1993, p. 343, § 3.

§ 16–12–173. Warning signs on vending machines

(a)(1) Any person who maintains in such person's place of business a vending machine which dispenses cigarettes, tobacco products, or tobacco related objects shall place or cause to be placed in a conspicuous place on such vending machine a sign containing the following statement:

"THE PURCHASE OF CIGARETTES, TOBACCO PRODUCTS, OR TOBACCO RELATED OBJECTS FROM THIS VENDING MACHINE BY ANY PERSON UNDER 18 YEARS OF AGE IS PROHIBITED BY LAW."

(2) Any person who maintains in such person's place of business a vending machine which dispenses cigarettes, tobacco products, or tobacco related objects shall not dispense any nontobacco product, other than matches, in such vending machine.

(b) Any person who fails to comply with the requirements of subsection (a) of this Code section shall be guilty of a misdemeanor; provided, however, for a first offense, the sentence shall be a fine not to exceed $300.00.

(c) It shall be a violation of subsection (a) of Code Section 16–12–171 for any person knowingly to allow a minor to operate a vending machine which dispenses cigarettes or tobacco related objects.

(d) The offenses provided for by paragraph (1) of subsection (b) of Code Section 16–12–171 shall apply to the operation by a minor of a vending machine which dispenses cigarettes or tobacco related objects.

(e)(1) The sale or offering for sale of cigarettes or tobacco related objects from vending machines shall not be permitted except:

(A) In locations which are not readily accessible to minors, including but not limited to:

(i) Factories, businesses, offices, and other places which are not open to the general public;

(ii) Places open to the general public which do not admit minors; and

(iii) Places where alcoholic beverages are offered for sale;

(B) In areas which are in the immediate vicinity, plain view, and under the continuous supervision of the proprietor of the establishment or an employee who will observe the purchase of cigarettes, tobacco products, and tobacco related objects from the vending machine; and

(C) In rest areas adjacent to roads and highways of the state.

(2) Violation of this subsection shall be punished as provided in subsection (b) of this Code section for violation of subsection (a) of this Code section.

Laws 1987, p. 945, § 1; Laws 1993, p. 343, § 4; Laws 2007, Act 252, § 2, eff. July 1, 2007.

Historical and Statutory Notes

The 2007 amendment by Act 252 designated the existing text of subsec. (a) as par. (1) and added par. (2).

§ 16–12–174. Distribution of tobacco product samples to minors

(a) As used in this Code section, the term "tobacco product sample" means a tobacco product distributed to members of the general public at no cost for purposes of promoting the product.

(b) It shall be unlawful for any person to distribute any tobacco product sample to any person under the age of 18 years.

(c) A person distributing tobacco product samples shall require proof of age from a prospective recipient if an ordinary person would conclude on the basis of appearance that such prospective recipient may be under the age of 18 years.

(d) It shall be unlawful for any person who has not attained the age of 18 years to receive or attempt to receive any tobacco product sample.

(e) No person shall distribute tobacco product samples on any public street, sidewalk, or park within 500 feet of any school or playground when those facilities are being used primarily by persons under the age of 18 years.

(f) Violation of this Code section shall be punished as a misdemeanor.

Laws 1993, p. 343, § 5.

§ 16–12–175. Enforcement of law; inspections; reports

(a) The provisions of this article, inclusive, shall be enforced through actions brought in any court of competent jurisdiction by the prosecuting attorney for the county in which the alleged violation occurred as well as through administrative citations issued by special agents or enforcement officers of the state revenue commissioner. Any fine collected for a violation of said provision shall be paid to the clerk of the court of the jurisdiction in which the violation occurred. Upon receipt of a fine for any violation of said provision, the clerk shall promptly notify the state revenue commissioner of the violation.

(b) The state revenue commissioner, acting through special agents or enforcement officers, shall annually conduct random, unannounced inspections at locations where tobacco products are sold or distributed to ensure compliance with this article. Persons under the age of 18 years may be enlisted to test compliance with this article; provided, however, that such persons may be used to test compliance with this article only if the testing is conducted under the direct supervision of such special agents or enforcement officers, and written parental consent has been provided. Any other use of persons under the age of 18 years to test compliance with this article or any other prohibition of like or similar import shall be unlawful and the person or persons responsible for such use shall be subject to the penalties prescribed in this article. The state revenue commissioner shall prepare annually for submission by the Governor to the secretary of the United States Department of Health and Human Services the report required by section 1926 of subpart I of part B of Title XIX of the federal Public Health Service Act, 42 U.S.C. 300x–26.

Laws 1993, p. 343, § 5; Laws 2000, p. 1343, § 1.

Historical and Statutory Notes

The 2000 amendment rewrote this section which formerly provided:

"(a) The provisions of this article, inclusive, shall be enforced through actions brought in any court of competent jurisdiction by the prosecuting attorney for the county in which the alleged violation occurred. Any fine collected for a violation of said provision shall be paid to the clerk of the court of the jurisdiction in which the violation occurred. Upon receipt of a fine for any violation of said provision, the clerk shall promptly notify the Department of Public Safety of the violation.

"(b) The Department of Public Safety, acting through the sheriffs of the several counties and chiefs of police of the several cities shall annually conduct random, unannounced inspections at locations where tobacco products are sold or distributed to ensure compliance with this article. Persons under the age of 18 years may be enlisted by such sheriffs or chiefs of police, or employees thereof, to test compliance with this article; provided, however, that such persons may be used to test compliance with said article only if the testing is conducted under the direct supervision of said sheriffs or chiefs of police, or employees thereof, and written parental consent has been provided. Any other use of persons under the age of 18 years to test compliance with this article or any other prohibition of like or similar import shall be unlawful and the person or persons responsible for such use shall be subject to the penalties prescribed in this article. The Department of Public Safety shall prepare annually for submission by the Governor to the secretary of the United States Department of Health and Human Services the report required by section 1926 of subpart I of part B of Title XIX of the federal Public Health Service Act, 42 U.S.C. 300x–26."

§ 16–12–176. Administration and enforcement of law by state revenue commissioner

The state revenue commissioner shall administer and enforce this article and may make reasonable rules and regulations for its administration and enforcement. The state revenue commissioner may designate employees of the Department of Revenue for the purpose of administering and enforcing this article and may delegate to employees of such department any of the duties required of the state revenue commissioner pursuant to this article.

Laws 2000, p. 1343, § 1.

CHAPTER 13

CONTROLLED SUBSTANCES

Article 1

Article 2

Article 1

General Provisions

§ 16–13–1. Drug related objects

(a) As used in this Code section, the term:

(1) "Controlled substance" shall have the same meaning as defined in Article 2 of this chapter, relating to controlled substances. For the purposes of this Code section, the term "controlled substance" shall include marijuana as defined by paragraph (16) of Code Section 16–13–21.

(2) "Dangerous drug" shall have the same meaning as defined in Article 3 of this chapter, relating to dangerous drugs.

(3) "Drug related object" means any machine, instrument, tool, equipment, contrivance, or device which an average person would reasonably conclude is intended to be used for one or more of the following purposes:

(A) To introduce into the human body any dangerous drug or controlled substance under circumstances in violation of the laws of this state;

(B) To enhance the effect on the human body of any dangerous drug or controlled substance under circumstances in violation of the laws of this state;

(C) To conceal any quantity of any dangerous drug or controlled substance under circumstances in violation of the laws of this state; or

(D) To test the strength, effectiveness, or purity of any dangerous drug or controlled substance under circumstances in violation of the laws of this state.

(4) "Knowingly" means having general knowledge that a machine, instrument, tool, item of equipment, contrivance, or device is a drug related object or having reasonable grounds to believe that any such object is or may, to an average person, appear to be a drug related object. If any such object has printed thereon or is accompanied by instructions explaining the purpose and use of such object and if following such instructions would cause a person to commit an act involving the use or possession of a dangerous drug or controlled

substance in violation of the laws of this state, then such instructions shall constitute prima-facie evidence of knowledge that the object in question is a drug related object.

(5) "Minor" means any unmarried person under the age of 18 years.

(b) Except as otherwise provided by subsection (d) of this Code section, it shall be unlawful for any person knowingly to sell, deliver, distribute, display for sale, or provide to a minor or knowingly possess with intent to sell, deliver, distribute, display for sale, or provide to a minor any drug related object.

(c) It shall be unlawful for any minor falsely to represent to any person that such minor is 18 years of age or older with the intent to purchase or otherwise obtain any drug related object.

(d) No person shall be guilty of violating subsection (b) of this Code section if:

(1) The person had reasonable cause to believe that the minor involved was 18 years of age or older because the minor exhibited to such person a driver's license, birth certificate, or other official or apparently official document purporting to establish that the minor was 18 years of age or older;

(2) The person made an honest mistake in believing that the minor was 18 years of age or over after making a reasonable bona fide attempt to ascertain the true age of the minor;

(3) The person was the parent or guardian of the minor; or

(4) The person was acting in his capacity as an employee or official of any governmental agency, governmental institution, public school or other public educational institution, any bona fide private school, educational institution, health care facility, or institution; or the person was acting in his capacity as a registered pharmacist or veterinarian or under the direction of a registered pharmacist or veterinarian to sell such object for a legitimate medical purpose.

(e) Any person who violates subsection (b) of this Code section shall be guilty of a misdemeanor for the first offense. For the second or any subsequent offense, a person violating subsection (b) of this Code section shall be guilty of a felony and, upon conviction thereof, shall be punished by imprisonment for not less than one nor more than five years or by a fine of not less than $1,000.00 nor more than $5,000.00, or both. Any person violating subsection (c) of this Code section shall be guilty of a misdemeanor.

Laws 1978, p. 2199, § 1; Laws 1985, p. 149, § 16; Laws 1999, p. 81, § 16.

Formerly Code 1933, § 26–9913.

§ 16–13–2. Conditional discharge for possession as first offense

(a) Whenever any person who has not previously been convicted of any offense under Article 2 or Article 3 of this chapter or of any statute of the United States or of any state relating to narcotic drugs, marijuana, or stimulant, depressant, or hallucinogenic drugs, pleads guilty to or is found guilty of possession of a narcotic drug, marijuana, or stimulant, depressant, or hallucinogenic drug, the court may without entering a judgment of guilt and with the consent of such person defer further proceedings and place him on probation upon such reasonable terms and conditions as the court may require, preferably terms which require the person to undergo a comprehensive rehabilitation program, including, if necessary, medical treatment, not to exceed three years, designed to acquaint him with the ill effects of drug abuse and to provide him with knowledge of the gains and benefits which can be achieved by being a good member of society. Upon violation of a term or condition, the court may enter an adjudication of guilt and proceed accordingly. Upon fulfillment of the terms and conditions, the court shall discharge the person and dismiss the proceedings against him. Discharge and dismissal under this Code section shall be without court adjudication of guilt and shall not be deemed a conviction for purposes of this Code section or for purposes of disqualifications or disabilities imposed by law upon conviction of a crime. Discharge and dismissal under this Code section may occur only once with respect to any person.

(b) Notwithstanding any law to the contrary, any person who is charged with possession of marijuana, which possession is of one ounce or less, shall be guilty of a misdemeanor and punished by imprisonment for a period not to exceed 12 months or a fine not to exceed $1,000.00, or both, or public works not to exceed 12 months.

(c) Persons charged with an offense enumerated in subsection (a) of this Code section and persons charged for the first time with nonviolent property crimes which, in the judgment of the court exercising jurisdiction over such offenses, were related to the accused's addiction to a controlled substance or alcohol who are eligible for any court approved drug treatment program may, in the discretion of the court and with the consent of the accused, be sentenced in accordance with subsection (a) of this Code section. The probated sentence imposed may be for a period of up to five years. No discharge and dismissal without court adjudication of guilt shall be entered under this subsection until the accused has made full restitution to all victims of the charged offenses. Discharge and dismissal under this Code section shall be without court adjudication of guilt and shall not be deemed a conviction for purposes of this Code section or for purposes of disqualifications or disabilities imposed by law upon conviction of a crime. Discharge and dismissal under this Code section may not be used to disqualify a person in any application for employment or appointment to office in either the public or private sector.

Laws 1971, p. 271, § 1; Laws 1973, p. 688, § 1; Laws 1974, p. 221, § 3; Laws 1976, p. 1083, § 1; Laws 1992, p. 6, § 16; Laws 1997, p. 1377, § 2; Laws 2004, Act 526, § 1, eff. May 13, 2004.

Formerly Code 1933, § 79A–9917.

Historical and Statutory Notes

The 2004 amendment by Act 526 added subsec. (c).

§ 16–13–3. Abandonment of certain dangerous drugs, poisons and controlled substances

Any person who shall abandon, in a public place, any dangerous drug, poison, or controlled substance as defined by Article 2 or Article 3 of this chapter shall be guilty of a misdemeanor.

Laws 1977, p. 625, § 9.

Formerly Code 1933, § 79A–9918.

§ 16–13–4. Selling of controlled substances and dangerous drugs

(a) No controlled substance or dangerous drug shall be sold for dispensing unless the controlled substance, as defined in Code Section 16–13–21, or the dangerous drug, as defined in Code Section 16–13–71:

(1) Is approved by the Food and Drug Administration for resale;

(2) Has a new approved drug application number (known as an NDA number) unless excepted by the Food and Drug Administration; or

(3) Has an approved abbreviated new drug application number (known as an ANDA number) unless excepted by the Food and Drug Administration.

(b) Any person who violates subsection (a) of this Code section shall be guilty of a felony and, upon conviction thereof, shall be punished by imprisonment of not less than one year nor more than five years.

Laws 1981, p. 557, § 6; Laws 1985, p. 1219, § 1; Laws 1989, p. 14, § 16.

Article 2

Regulation of Controlled Substances

§ 16–13–20. Short title

This article shall be known and may be cited as the "Georgia Controlled Substances Act."

Laws 1974, p. 221, § 1.

Formerly Code 1933, § 79A–801.

Historical and Statutory Notes

Uniform Law

The Georgia Controlled Substances Act is based upon provisions contained in the Uniform Controlled Substances Act (1970, 1990, and 1994 Acts). See Volume 9, Parts II to IV Uniform Laws Annotated, Master Edition, or ULA Database on Westlaw.

§ 16–13–21. Definitions

As used in this article, the term:

(1) "Administer" means the direct application of a controlled substance, whether by injection, inhalation, ingestion, or by any other means, to the body of a patient or research subject by:

(A) A practitioner or, in his presence, by his authorized agent; or

(B) The patient or research subject at the direction and in the presence of the practitioner.

(2) "Agent" of a manufacturer, distributor, or dispenser means an authorized person who acts on behalf of or at the direction of a manufacturer, distributor, or dispenser. It does not include a common or contract carrier, public warehouseman, or employee of the carrier or warehouseman.

(3) "Bureau" means the Drug Enforcement Administration, United States Department of Justice, or its successor agency.

(4) "Controlled substance" means a drug, substance, or immediate precursor in Schedules I through V of Code Sections 16–13–25 through 16–13–29 and Schedules I through V of 21 C.F.R. Part 1308.

(5) "Conveyance" means any object, including aircraft, vehicle, or vessel, but not including a person, which may be used to carry or transport a substance or object.

(6) "Counterfeit substance" means:

(A) A controlled substance which, or the container or labeling of which, without authorization, bears the trademark, trade name, or other identifying mark, imprint, number, or device, or any likeness thereof, of a manufacturer, distributor, or dispenser other than the person who in fact manufactured, distributed, or dispensed the controlled substance;

(B) A controlled substance or noncontrolled substance, which is held out to be a controlled substance or marijuana, whether in a container or not which does not bear a label which accurately or truthfully identifies the substance contained therein; or

(C) Any substance, whether in a container or not, which bears a label falsely identifying the contents as a controlled substance.

(6.1) "Dangerous drug" means any drug, other than a controlled substance, which cannot be dispensed except upon the issuance of a prescription drug order by a practitioner authorized under this chapter.

(6.2) "DEA" means the United States Drug Enforcement Administration.

(7) "Deliver" or "delivery" means the actual, constructive, or attempted transfer from one person to another of a controlled substance, whether or not there is an agency relationship.

(8) "Dependent," "dependency," "physical dependency," "psychological dependency," or "psychic dependency" means and includes the state of dependence by an individual toward or upon a substance, arising from the use of that substance, being characterized by behavioral and other responses which include the loss of self-control with respect to that substance, or a strong compulsion to use that substance on a continuous basis in order to experience some psychic effect resulting from the use of that substance by that individual, or to avoid any discomfort occurring when the individual does not use that substance.

(9) "Dispense" means to deliver a controlled substance to an ultimate user or research subject by or pursuant to the lawful order of a practitioner, including the prescribing, administering, packaging, labeling, or compounding necessary to prepare the substance for that delivery, or the delivery of a controlled substance by a practitioner, acting in the normal course of his professional practice and in accordance with this article, or to a relative or representative of the person for whom the controlled substance is prescribed.

(10) "Dispenser" means a practitioner who dispenses.

(11) "Distribute" means to deliver a controlled substance, other than by administering or dispensing it.

(12) "Distributor" means a person who distributes.

(12.05) "FDA" means the United States Food and Drug Administration.

(12.1) "Imitation controlled substance" means:

(A) A product specifically designed or manufactured to resemble the physical appearance of a controlled substance, such that a reasonable person of ordinary knowledge would not be able to distinguish the imitation from the controlled substance by outward appearances; or

(B) A product, not a controlled substance, which, by representations made and by dosage unit appearance, including color, shape, size, or markings, would lead a reasonable person to believe that, if ingested, the product would have a stimulant or depressant effect similar to or the same as that of one or more of the controlled substances included in Schedules I through V of Code Sections 16–13–25 through 16–13–29.

(13) "Immediate precursor" means a substance which the State Board of Pharmacy has found to be and by rule identifies as being the principal compound commonly used or produced primarily for use, and which is an immediate chemical intermediary used or likely to be used in the manufacture of a controlled substance, the control of which is necessary to prevent, curtail, or limit manufacture.

(14) "Isomers" means stereoisomers (optical isomers), geometrical isomers, and structural isomers (chain and positional isomers, but shall not include functional isomers).

(15) "Manufacture" means the production, preparation, propagation, compounding, conversion, or processing of a controlled substance, either directly or indirectly by extraction from substances of natural origin, or independently by means of chemical synthesis, and includes any packaging or repackaging of the substance or labeling or relabeling of its container, except that this term does not include the preparation, compounding, packaging, or labeling of a controlled substance:

(A) By a practitioner as an incident to his administering or dispensing of a controlled substance in the course of his professional practice; or

(B) By a practitioner or by his authorized agent under his supervision for the purpose of, or as an incident to, research, teaching, or chemical analysis and not for sale.

(16) "Marijuana" means all parts of the plant of the genus Cannabis, whether growing or not, the seeds thereof, the resin extracted from any part of such plant, and every compound, manufacture, salt, derivative, mixture, or preparation of such plant, its seeds, or resin; but shall not include samples as described in subparagraph (P) of paragraph (3) of Code Section 16–13–25 and shall not include the completely defoliated mature stalks of such plant, fiber produced from such stalks, oil, or cake, or the completely sterilized samples of seeds of the plant which are incapable of germination.

(17) "Narcotic drug" means any of the following, whether produced directly or indirectly by extraction from substances of vegetable origin, or independently by means of chemical synthesis, or by a combination of extraction and chemical synthesis:

(A) Opium and opiate, and any salt, compound, derivative, or preparation of opium or opiate;

(B) Any salt, compound, isomer, derivative, or preparation thereof which is chemically equivalent or identical with any of the substances referred to in subparagraph (A) of this paragraph, but not including the isoquinoline alkaloids of opium;

(C) Opium poppy and poppy straw;

(D) Coca leaves and any salt, compound, derivative, stereoisomers of cocaine, or preparation of coca leaves, and any salt, compound, stereoisomers of cocaine, derivative, or preparation thereof which is chemically equivalent or identical with any of these substances, but not including decocainized coca leaves or extractions of coca leaves which do not contain cocaine or ecgonine.

(18) "Opiate" means any substance having an addiction-forming or addiction-sustaining liability similar to morphine or being capable of conversion into a drug having addiction-forming or addiction-sustaining liability. It does not include, unless specifically designated as controlled under Code Section 16–13–22, the dextrorotatory isomer of 3–methoxy-n-methylmorphinan and its salts (dextromethorphan). It does include its racemic and levorotatory forms.

(19) "Opium poppy" means the plant of the species Papaver somniferum L., except its seeds.

(20) "Person" means an individual, corporation, government, or governmental subdivision or agency, business trust, estate, trust, partnership, or association, or any other legal entity.

(21) "Poppy straw" means all parts, except the seeds, of the opium poppy after mowing.

(22) "Potential for abuse" means and includes a substantial potential for a substance to be used by an individual to the extent of creating hazards to the health of the user or the safety of the public, or the substantial potential of a substance to cause an individual using that substance to become dependent upon that substance.

(23) "Practitioner" means:

(A) A physician, dentist, pharmacist, podiatrist, veterinarian, scientific investigator, or other person licensed, registered, or otherwise authorized under the laws of this state to distribute, dispense, conduct research with respect to, or to administer a controlled substance in the course of professional practice or research in this state;

(B) A pharmacy, hospital, or other institution licensed, registered, or otherwise authorized by law to distribute, dispense, conduct research with respect to, or to administer a controlled substance in the course of professional practice or research in this state;

(C) An advanced practice registered nurse acting pursuant to the authority of Code Section 43–34–25. For purposes of this chapter and Code Section 43–34–25, an advanced practice registered nurse is authorized to register with the federal Drug Enforcement Administration and appropriate state authorities; or

(D) A physician assistant acting pursuant to the authority of subsection (e.1) of Code Section 43–34–103. For purposes of this chapter and subsection (e.1) of Code Section 43–34–103, a physician assistant is authorized to register with the federal Drug Enforcement Administration and appropriate state authorities.

(24) "Production" includes the manufacture, planting, cultivation, growing, or harvesting of a controlled substance.

(25) "Registered" or "register" means registration as required by this article.

(26) "Registrant" means a person who is registered under this article.

(27) "State," when applied to a part of the United States, includes any state, district, commonwealth, territory, insular possession thereof, or any area subject to the legal authority of the United States.

(28) "Ultimate user" means a person who lawfully possesses a controlled substance for his own use, for the use of a member of his household, or for administering to an animal owned by him or by a member of his household or an agent or representative of the person.

(29) "Noncontrolled substance" means any drug or other substance other than a controlled substance as defined by paragraph (4) of this Code section.

Laws 1967, p. 296, § 1; Laws 1974, p. 221, § 1; Laws 1978, p. 2237, § 1; Laws 1979, p. 859, § 4; Laws 1980, p. 1746, § 3; Laws 1982, p. 3, § 16; Laws 1982, p. 1264, §§ 1, 3; Laws 1982, p. 2370, §§ 1, 2; Laws 1982, p. 2403, §§ 10, 15; Laws 1984, p. 22, § 16; Laws 1985, p. 149, § 16; Laws 1986, p. 10, § 16; Laws 1986, p. 1555, §§ 1, 2; Laws 1988, p. 1065, § 1; Laws 1999, p. 643, § 5.1; Laws 2003, Act 80, § 1, eff. May 29, 2003; Laws 2006, Act 463, § 2, eff. July 1, 2006; Laws 2009, Act 243, § 4, eff. July 1, 2009.

Formerly Code 1933, § 79A–802.

Historical and Statutory Notes

The 2003 amendment by Act 80 added pars. (6.1), (6.2), and (12.05).

The 2006 amendment by Act 463 rewrote par. (23) which had read:

"(23) 'Practitioner' means:

"(A) A physician, dentist, pharmacist, podiatrist, veterinarian, scientific investigator, or other person licensed, registered, or otherwise authorized under the laws of this state to distribute, dispense, conduct research with respect to, or to administer a controlled substance in the course of professional practice or research in this state;

"(B) A pharmacy, hospital, or other institution licensed, registered, or otherwise authorized by law to distribute, dispense, conduct research with respect to, or to administer a controlled substance in the course of professional practice or research in this state; or

"(C) A physician's assistant acting pursuant to the authority of subsection (e.1) of Code Section 43–34–103. For purposes of this chapter and subsection (e.1) of Code Section 43–34–103 and notwithstanding the provisions of subsection (g) of Code Section 43–34–26.1, a physician's assistant is authorized to register with the federal Drug Enforcement Administration and appropriate state authorities."

The 2009 amendment by Act 243, in par. (23), twice substituted "Code Section 43–34–25" for "Code Section 43–34–26.3" in subpar. (C), and twice substituted "physician assistant" for "physician's assistant" in subpar. (D).

§ 16–13–22. Authority to control. Standards and schedules

(a) The State Board of Pharmacy shall administer this article and shall add substances to or reschedule all substances enumerated in the schedules in Code Sections 16–13–25 through 16–13–29 pursuant to the procedures of Chapter 13 of Title 50, the "Georgia Administrative Procedure Act." In making a determination or identification regarding a substance, the State Board of Pharmacy shall consider the following factors:

(1) The actual or relative potential for abuse;

(2) The scientific evidence of its pharmacological effect, if known;

(3) The state of current scientific knowledge regarding the substance;

(4) The history and current pattern of abuse;

(5) The scope, duration, and significance of abuse;

(6) The risk to the public health;

(7) The potential of the substance to produce psychic or physiological dependence liability;

(8) Whether the substance is an immediate precursor of a substance already controlled under this article; and

(9) The designation, deletion, or rescheduling of a substance under federal law controlling controlled substances.

(b) After considering the factors enumerated in subsection (a) of this Code section, the State Board of Pharmacy shall make findings with respect thereto and cause the publication of such findings as a rule, in accordance with Chapter 13 of Title 50, the "Georgia Administrative Procedure Act," controlling the substance if it finds the substance has a potential for abuse.

(c) If the State Board of Pharmacy identifies a substance as an immediate precursor, substances which are precursors of the controlled substance shall not be subject to control solely because they are precursors of the controlled substance.

(d) Authority to control under this Code section does not extend to distilled spirits, wine, malt beverages, or tobacco, as those terms are defined or used in Title 3 or 48.

Laws 1974, p. 221, § 1; Laws 1982, p. 3, § 16.

Formerly Code 1933, § 79A–803.

§ 16–13–23. Nomenclature

The controlled substances listed in the schedules in Code Sections 16–13–25 through 16–13–29 are included by whatever official, common, usual, chemical, or trade name designated.

Laws 1974, p. 221, § 1.

Formerly Code 1933, § 79A–804.

§ 16–13–24. Establishment of schedules of controlled substances

(a) There are established five schedules of controlled substances, to be known as Schedules I, II, III, IV, and V. The schedules shall consist of the substances listed in Code Sections 16–13–25 through 16–13–29. The schedules so established shall be updated and republished by the State Board of Pharmacy on an annual basis.

(b) Except in the case of an immediate precursor, a drug or other substance may not be placed in any schedule unless the findings required for such schedule are made with respect to the drug or other substance. The findings for each of the schedules are as follows:

(1) Schedule I:

(A) The drug or other substance has a high potential for abuse;

(B) The drug or other substance has no currently accepted medical use in treatment in the United States; and

(C) There is a lack of accepted safety for use of the drug or other substance under medical supervision.

(2) Schedule II:

(A) The drug or other substance has a high potential for abuse;

(B) The drug or other substance has a currently accepted medical use in treatment in the United States or a currently accepted medical use with severe restrictions; and

(C) Abuse of the drug or other substance may lead to severe psychological or physical dependence.

(3) Schedule III:

(A) The drug or other substance has a potential for abuse less than the drugs or other substances in Schedules I and II;

(B) The drug or other substance has a currently accepted medical use in treatment in the United States; and

(C) Abuse of the drug or other substance may lead to moderate or low physical dependence or high psychological dependence.

(4) Schedule IV:

(A) The drug or other substance has a low potential for abuse relative to the drugs or other substances in Schedule III;

(B) The drug or other substance has a currently accepted medical use in treatment in the United States; and

(C) Abuse of the drug or other substance may lead to limited physical dependence or psychological dependence relative to the drugs or other substances in Schedule III.

(5) Schedule V:

(A) The drug or other substance has a low potential for abuse relative to the drugs or other substances in Schedule IV;

(B) The drug or other substance has a currently accepted medical use in treatment in the United States; and

(C) Abuse of the drug or other substance may lead to limited physical dependence or psychological dependence relative to the drugs or other substances in Schedule IV.

Laws 1974, p. 221, § 1; Laws 1982, p. 3, § 16.

Formerly Code 1933, § 79A–805.

§ 16–13–25. Schedule I

The controlled substances listed in this Code section are included in Schedule I:

(1) Any of the following opiates, including their isomers, esters, ethers, salts, and salts of isomers, esters, and ethers, unless specifically excepted, pursuant to this article, whenever the existence of these isomers, esters, ethers, and salts is possible within the specific chemical designation:

(A) Acetylmethadol;

(B) Allylprodine;

(C) Reserved;

(D) Alphameprodine;

(E) Alphamethadol;

(F) Benzethidine;

(G) Betacetylmethadol;

(H) Betameprodine;

(I) Betamethadol;

(J) Betaprodine;

(K) Clonitazene;

(L) Dextromoramide;

(M) Dextromorphan;
(N) Diampromide;
(O) Diethylthiambutene;
(P) Dimenoxadol;
(Q) Dimetheptanol;
(R) Dimethylthiambutene;
(S) Dioxaphetyl butyrate;
(T) Dipipanone;
(U) Ethylmethylthiambutene;
(V) Etonitazene;
(W) Etoxeridene;
(X) Furethidine;
(Y) Hydroxypethidine;
(Z) Ketobemidone;
(AA) Levomoramide;
(BB) Levophenacylmorphan;
(CC) Morpheridine;
(DD) Noracymethadol;
(EE) Norlevorphanol;
(FF) Normethadone;
(GG) Norpipanone;
(HH) Phenadoxone;
(II) Phenampromide;
(JJ) Phenomorphan;
(KK) Phenoperidine;
(LL) Piritramide;
(MM) Proheptazine;
(NN) Properidine;
(OO) Propiram;
(PP) Racemoramide;
(QQ) Trimeperidine;

(2) Any of the following opium derivatives, their salts, isomers, and salts of isomers, unless specifically excepted, whenever the existence of these salts, isomers, and salts of isomers is possible within the specific chemical designation:
(A) Acetorphine;
(B) Acetyldihydrocodeine;
(C) Benzylmorphine;
(D) Codeine methylbromide;
(E) Codeine–N–Oxide;
(F) Cyprenorphine;
(G) Desomorphine;
(H) Dihydromorphine;
(I) Etorphine;
(J) Heroin;
(K) Hydromorphinol;
(L) Methyldesorphine;
(M) Methyldihydromorphine;
(N) Morphine methylbromide;
(O) Morphine methylsulfonate;
(P) Morphine–N–Oxide;
(Q) Myrophine;
(R) Nicocodeine;
(S) Nicomorphine;
(T) Normorphine;
(U) Pholcodine;
(V) Thebacon;

(3) Any material, compound, mixture, or preparation which contains any quantity of the following hallucinogenic substances, their salts, isomers (whether optical, position, or geometrics), and salts of isomers, unless specifically excepted, whenever the existence of these salts, isomers, and salts of isomers is possible within the specific chemical designation:
(A) 3, 4–methylenedioxyamphetamine;
(B) 5–methoxy–3, 4–methylenedioxyamphetamine;
(C) 3, 4, 5–trimethoxyamphetamine;
(D) Bufotenine;
(E) Diethyltryptamine;
(F) Dimethyltryptamine;
(G) 4–methyl–2, 5–dimethoxyamphetamine;
(H) Ibogaine;
(I) Lysergic acid diethylamide;
(J) Mescaline;
(K) Peyote;
(L) N-ethyl–3–piperidyl benzilate;
(M) N-methyl–3–piperidyl benzilate;
(N) Psilocybin;
(O) Psilocyn (Psilocin);
(P) Tetrahydrocannabinols which shall include, but are not limited to:

(i) All synthetic or naturally produced samples containing more than 15 percent by weight of tetrahydrocannabinols; and

(ii) All synthetic or naturally produced tetrahydrocannabinol samples which do not contain plant material exhibiting the external morphological features of the plant cannabis;

(Q) 2, 5–dimethoxyamphetamine;
(R) 4–bromo–2, 5–dimethoxyamphetamine;
(S) 4–methoxyamphetamine;
(T) Cyanoethylamphetamine;
(U) (1–phenylcyclohexyl) ethylamine;
(V) 1–(1–phenylcyclohexyl) pyrrolidine;
(W) Phencyclidine;
(X) 1–piperidinocyclohexanecarbonitrile;
(Y) 1–phenyl–2–propanone (phenylacetone);
(Z) 3, 4–Methylenedioxymethamphetamine (MDMA);
(AA) 1–methyl–4–phenyl–4–propionoxypiperidine;
(BB) 1–(2–phenylethyl)–4–phenyl–4–acetyloxypiperidine;
(CC) 3–methylfentanyl;
(DD) N-ethyl–3, 4–methylenedioxyamphetamine;
(EE) Para-flurofentanyl;
(FF) 2,5–Dimethoxy–4–Ethylamphetamine;
(GG) Cathinone;
(HH) MPPP (1–Methyl–4–Phenyl–4–Propionoxypiperidine);
(II) PEPAP (1–(2–phenethyl)–4 phenyl–4–acetoxypiperide);
(JJ) Alpha–Methylthiofentanyl;
(KK) Acetyl–Alpha–Methylfentanyl;
(LL) 3–Methylthiofentanyl;
(MM) Beta–Hydroxyfentanyl;
(NN) Thiofentanyl;
(OO) 3,4–Methylenedioxy–N–Ethylamphetamine;
(PP) 4–Methylaminorex;
(QQ) N–Hydroxy–3,4–Methylenedioxyamphetamine;
(RR) Beta–Hydroxy–3–Methylfentanyl;
(SS) Chlorophenylpiperazine (CPP);
(TT) N, N–Dimethylamphetamine;
(UU) 1–(1–(2–thienyl) cyclohexy) pyrrolidine;
(VV) 4–Bromo–2,5–Dimethoxyphenethylamine (DMPE);
(WW) Alpha–Ethyltryptamine;
(XX) Methcathinone;

(YY) Aminorex;

(ZZ) 4–iodo–2,5–dimethoxyamphetamine;

(AAA) 4–chloro–2,5–dimethoxyamphetamine;

(4) Any material, compound, mixture, or preparation which contains any of the following substances having a stimulant effect on the central nervous system, including its salts, isomers, and salts of isomers, unless specifically excepted, whenever the existence of these salts, isomers, and salts of isomers is possible within the specific chemical designation:

(A) Fenethylline;

(B) N-(1–benzyl–4–piperidyl)-N-phenylpropanamide (benzyl-fentanyl);

(C) N-(1–(2–thienyl) methyl–4–piperidyl)-N-phenylpropanamide (thenylfentanyl);

(5) Any material, compound, mixture, or preparation which contains any quantity of the following substances, their salts, isomers (whether optical, position, or geometrics), and salts of isomers, unless specifically excepted, whenever the existence of these substances, their salts, isomers, and salts of isomers is possible within the specific chemical designation:

(A) Gamma hydroxybutyric acid (gamma hydroxy butyrate); provided, however, that this does not include any amount naturally and normally occurring in the human body; and

(B) Sodium oxybate, when the FDA approved form of this drug is not:

(i) In a container labeled in compliance with subsection (a) or (b) of Code Section 26–3–8; and

(ii) In the possession of:

(I) A registrant permitted to dispense the drug;

(II) Any person other than to whom the drug was prescribed; or

(III) Any person who attempts to or does unlawfully possess, sell, distribute, or give this drug to any other person;

(6) Notwithstanding the fact that Schedule I substances have no currently accepted medical use, the General Assembly recognizes certain of these substances which are currently accepted for certain limited medical uses in treatment in the United States but have a high potential for abuse. Accordingly, unless specifically excepted or unless listed in another schedule, any material, compound, mixture, or preparation which contains any quantity of methaqualone, including its salts, isomers, optical isomers, salts of their isomers, and salts of these optical isomers, is included in Schedule I;

(7) 2,5–Dimethoxy–4–(n)–propylthiophenethylamine (2C–T–7);

(8) 1–(3–Trifluoromethylphenyl) Piperazine (TFMPP);

(9) N–Benzylpiperazine (BZP);

(10) 5–Methoxy–N,N–Diisopropyltryptamine (5–MeO–DIPT);

(11) Alpha–Methyltryptamine (AMT);

(12) Any material, compound, mixture, or preparation which contains any quantity of the following substances, their salts, isomers (whether optical, positional, or geometric), homologues, and salts of isomers and homologues, unless specifically excepted, whenever the existence of these salts, isomers, homologues, and salts of isomers and homologues is possible within the specific chemical designation:

(A) 1–pentyl–3–(1–naphthoyl)indole (JWH–018);

(B) 1,1–dimethylheptyl–11–hydroxy–delta–8–tetrahydrocannabinol (HU–210; (6a, 10a)–9–(hydroxymethyl)–6,6–dimethyl–3–(2–methyloctan–2–yl) –6a,7,10,10a–tetrahydrobenzo[c]chromen–1–o1

(C) 2–(3–hydroxycyclohexyl)–5–(2–methyloctan–2–yl)phenol (CP 47,497).

Laws 1974, p. 221, § 1; Laws 1978, p. 1668, § 6; Laws 1979, p. 859, § 5; Laws 1980, p. 1746, § 4; Laws 1981, p. 557, § 3; Laws 1982, p. 2403, §§ 11, 16; Laws 1984, p. 22, § 16; Laws 1984, p. 1019, § 1; Laws 1985, p. 1219, § 2; Laws 1986, p. 1555, § 3; Laws 1987, p. 261, § 1; Laws 1989, p. 233, § 1; Laws 1990, p. 8, § 16; Laws 1990, p. 640, § 1; Laws 1992, p. 1131, § 1; Laws 1994, p. 169, §§ 1–3, 3.1; Laws 1996, p. 356, § 1; Laws 2001, p. 816, § 1; Laws 2002, p. 415, § 16; Laws 2003, Act 80, § 2, eff. May 29, 2003; Laws 2005, Act 330, § 1, eff. May 9, 2005; Laws 2006, Act 516, § 1, eff. April 19, 2006; Laws 2008, Act 433, §§ 1, 2, eff. May 6, 2008; Laws 2010, Act 433, § 1, eff. May 24, 2010; Laws 2010, Act 619, § 1, eff. June 3, 2010.

Formerly Code 1933, § 79A–806.

Historical and Statutory Notes

The 2001 amendment added at the end of par. (5) "provided, however, that this does not include any amount naturally and normally occurring in the human body.

The 2002 amendment correctively deleted the comma following isomers in the phrase "isomers (whether" in the introduction to pars. (3) and (5).

The 2003 amendment by Act 80, in par. (5), designated the existing text as subpar. (A) and added subpar. (B); and added pars. (7), (8), and (9).

The 2005 amendment by Act 330 added pars. (10) and (11).

The 2006 amendment by Act 516, in par. (3), inserted "(Psilocin)" in subpar. (O), inserted "(MDMA)" in subpar. (Z), and deleted subpar. (SS) relating to MDMA and reserved the paragraph designation.

The 2008 amendment by Act 433, in par. (3), added subpars. (ZZ) and (AAA) adding 4-iodo-2,5-dimethoxyamphetamine and 4-chloro-2,5-dimethoxyamphetamine to to the scope of the section; and in par. (8) substituted "1-(3-Trifluoromethylphenyl) Piperazine" for "1-(3-Trifluoromethylphenyl Piperazine".

The 2010 amendment by Act 433 added par. (12).

The 2010 amendment by Act 619, in subpar. (3)(SS), substituted "Chlorophenylpiperazine (CPP)" for "Reserved".

§ 16–13–26. Schedule II

The controlled substances listed in this Code section are included in Schedule II:

(1) Any of the following substances, or salts thereof, except those narcotic drugs specifically exempted or listed in other schedules, whether produced directly or indirectly by extraction from substances of vegetable origin, or independently by extraction from substances of vegetable origin, or independently by means of chemical synthesis, or by combination of extraction and chemical synthesis:

(A) Opium and opiate, and any salt, compound, derivative, or preparation of opium or opiate, excluding naloxone hydrochloride, but including the following:

(i) Raw opium;

(ii) Opium extracts;

(iii) Opium fluid extracts;

(iv) Powdered opium;

(v) Granulated opium;

(vi) Tincture of opium;

(vii) Codeine;

(viii) Ethylmorphine;

(ix) Hydrocodone;

(x) Hydromorphone;

(xi) Metopon;

(xii) Morphine;

(xiii) Oripavine;

(xiv) Oxycodone;

(xv) Oxymorphone;

(xvi) Thebaine;

(B) Any salt, compound, isomer, derivative, or preparation thereof which is chemically equivalent or identical with any of the substances referred to in subparagraph (A) of this paragraph, except that these substances shall not include the isoquinoline alkaloids of opium;

(C) Opium poppy and poppy straw;

(D) Cocaine, coca leaves, any salt, compound, derivative, stereoisomers of cocaine, or preparation of coca leaves, and any salt, compound, derivative, stereoisomers of cocaine, or preparation thereof which is chemically equivalent or identical with any of these substances, but not including decocainized coca leaves or extractions which do not contain cocaine or ecgonine;

(2) Any of the following opiates, including their isomers, esters, ethers, salts, and salts of isomers, whenever the existence of these isomers, esters, ethers, and salts is possible within the specific chemical designation:

(A) Alfentanil;

(A.1) Alphaprodine;

(B) Anileridine;

(C) Bezitramide;

(D) Dihydrocodeine;

(E) Diphenoxylate;

(F) Fentanyl;

(G) Isomethadone;

(G.5) Levo-alphacetylmethadol (some other names: levomethadyl acetate, LAAM);

(H) Levomethorphan;

(I) Levorphanol;

(J) Methazocine;

(K) Methadone;

(L) Methadone–Intermediate, 4–cyano–2–dimethylamino–4, 4–diphenyl butane;

(M) Moramide–Intermediate, 2–methyl–3–morpholino–1, 1–diphenyl-propane-carboxylic acid;

(N) Pethidine (meperidine);

(O) Pethidine–Intermediate–A, 4–cyano–1–methyl–4–phenylpiperidine;

(P) Pethidine–Intermediate–B, ethyl–4–phenylpiperidine–4–carboxylate;

(Q) Pethidine–Intermediate–C, 1–methyl–4–phenylpiperidine–4–carboxylic acid;

(R) Phenazocine;

(S) Piminodine;

(T) Racemethorphan;

(U) Racemorphan;

(U.1) Remifentanil;

(V) Sufentanil;

(V.1) Tapentadol;

(W) 4–anilino-N-phenethyl–4–piperidine (ANPP);

(3) Unless specifically excepted or unless listed in another schedule, any material, compound, mixture, or preparation which contains any quantity of the following substances included as having a stimulant effect on the central nervous system:

(A) Amphetamine, its salts, optical isomers, and salts of its optical isomers;

(B) Any substance which contains any quantity of methamphetamine, including its salts, isomers, and salts of isomers;

(C) Phenmetrazine and its salts;

(D) Methylphenidate, including its salts, isomers, and salts of isomers;

(E) Carfentanil;

(F) Nabilone;

(G) Lisdexamfetamine;

(4) Unless specifically excepted or unless listed in another schedule, any material, compound, mixture, or preparation which contains any of the following substances included as having a depressant effect on the central nervous system, including its salts, isomers, and salts of isomers whenever the existence of such salts, isomers, and salts of isomers is possible within the specific chemical designation:

(A) Amobarbital;

(A.5) Glutethimide;

(B) Secobarbital;

(C) Pentobarbital.

Laws 1974, p. 221, § 1; Laws 1977, p. 625, § 7; Laws 1978, p. 1668, § 7; Laws 1979, p. 859, §§ 6, 7; Laws 1980, p. 1746, § 5; Laws 1982, p. 2403, §§ 12, 17, 17.1; Laws 1985, p. 1219, § 3; Laws 1987, p. 261, §§ 2–4; Laws 1988, p. 420, § 1; Laws 1989, p. 233, § 2; Laws 1992, p. 1131, § 2; Laws 1994, p. 169, § 4; Laws 1997, p. 1311, § 1; Laws 2000, p. 1317, § 1; Laws 2007, Act 331, § 1, eff. May 29, 2007; Laws 2008, Act 433, § 3, eff. May 6, 2008; Laws 2009, Act 43, § 1, eff. Apr. 21, 2009; Laws 2010, Act 619, § 2, eff. June 3, 2010.

Formerly Code 1933, § 79A–807.

Historical and Statutory Notes

The 2000 amendment deleted former par. (5) providing "Dronabinol (synthetie) in sesame oil and encapsulated in a soft gelatin capsule in a U.S. Food and Drug Administration approved drug product."

The 2007 amendment by Act 331 deleted subpar. (G) of par. (3) which had read:

"(3)(G) Dimethylamphetamine;"

The 2008 amendment by Act 433, in par. (3), added subpar. (G).

The 2009 amendment by Act 43, in subpar. (1)(A), redesignated divs. (xiii) through (xv) as (xiv) through (xvi) and inserted new div. (xiii); in par. (2), added subpar. (W); and in subpar. (3)(D), added ", including its salts, isomers, and salts of isomers".

The 2010 amendment by Act 619 added subpar. (2)(V.1).

§ 16–13–27. Schedule III

The controlled substances listed in this Code section are included in Schedule III:

(1) Unless specifically excepted or unless listed in another schedule, any material, compound, mixture, or preparation which contains any quantity of the following substances, included as having a stimulant effect on the central nervous system, including its salts, isomers (whether optical, position, or geometric), and salts of such isomers whenever the existence of such salts, isomers, and salts of isomers is possible within the specific chemical designation:

(A) Those compounds, mixtures, or preparations in dosage unit forms containing any stimulant substances which are listed as excepted compounds by the State Board of Pharmacy pursuant to this article, and any other drug of quantitative composition so excepted or which is the same except that it contains a lesser quantity of controlled substances;

(B) Benzphetamine;

(C) Chlorphentermine;

(D) Clortermine;

(E) Phendimetrazine;

(2) Unless specifically excepted or unless listed in another schedule, any material, compound, mixture, or preparation which contains any quantity of the following substances included as having a depressant effect on the central nervous system:

(A) Any compound, mixture, or preparation containing amobarbital, secobarbital, pentobarbital, or any salts thereof and one or more active medicinal ingredients which are not listed in any schedule;

(B) Any suppository dosage form containing amobarbital, secobarbital, pentobarbital, or any salt of any of these drugs and approved by the State Board of Pharmacy for marketing only as a suppository;

(C) Any substance which contains any quantity of a derivative of barbituric acid or any salt thereof;

(D) Chlorhexadol;

(E) Reserved;

(F) Lysergic acid;

(G) Lysergic acid amide;

(H) Methyprylon;

(I) Sulfondiethylmethane;

(J) Sulfonethylmethane;

(K) Sulfonmethane;

(L) Tiletamine/Zolozepam (Telazol);

(3) Nalorphine;

(4) Unless specifically excepted or unless listed in another schedule, any material, compound, mixture, or preparation containing limited quantities of the following narcotic drugs, or any salts thereof:

(A) Not more than 1.8 grams of codeine, or any of its salts, per 100 milliliters or not more than 90 milligrams per dosage unit, with an equal or greater quantity of an isoquinoline alkaloid of opium;

(B) Not more than 1.8 grams of codeine, or any of its salts, per 100 milliliters or not more than 90 milligrams per dosage unit, with one or more active, nonnarcotic ingredients in recognized therapeutic amounts;

(C) Not more than 300 milligrams of dihydrocodeinone (hydrocodone), or any of its salts, per 100 milliliters or not more than 15 milligrams per dosage unit, with a fourfold or greater quantity of an isoquinoline alkaloid of opium;

(D) Not more than 300 milligrams of dihydrocodeinone (hydrocodone), or any of its salts, per 100 milliliters or not more than 15 milligrams per dosage unit, with one or more active, nonnarcotic ingredients in recognized therapeutic amounts;

(E) Not more than 1.8 grams of dihydrocodeine, or any of its salts, per 100 milliliters or not more than 90 milligrams per dosage unit, with one or more active, nonnarcotic ingredients in recognized therapeutic amounts;

(F) Not more than 300 milligrams of ethylmorphine, or any of its salts, per 100 milliliters or not more than 15 milligrams per dosage unit, with one or more active, nonnarcotic ingredients in recognized therapeutic amounts;

(G) Not more than 500 milligrams of opium per 100 milliliters or per 100 grams, or not more than 25 milligrams per dosage unit, with one or more active, nonnarcotic ingredients in recognized therapeutic amounts;

(H) Not more than 50 milligrams of morphine, or any of its salts, per 100 milliliters or per 100 grams with one or more active, nonnarcotic ingredients in recognized therapeutic amounts;

(5) The State Board of Pharmacy may except by rule any compound, mixture, or preparation containing any stimulant or depressant substance listed in paragraphs (1) and (2) of this Code section from the application of all or any part of this article if the compound, mixture, or preparation contains one or more active, medicinal ingredients not having a stimulant or depressant effect on the central nervous system, and if the admixtures are included therein in combinations, quantity, proportion, or concentration that vitiate the potential for abuse of the substances which have a stimulant or depressant effect on the central nervous system;

(6) Any anabolic steroid or any salt, ester, or isomer of a drug or substance described or listed in this paragraph, if that salt, ester, or isomer promotes muscle growth. Such term does not include an anabolic steroid which is expressly intended for administration through implants to cattle or other nonhuman species and which has been approved by the secretary of health and human services for such administration:

(A) Boldenone;

(A.5) Boldione (Androsta–1,4–diene–3,17–dione);

(B) Chlorotestosterone;

(C) Clostebol;

(D) Dehydrochlormethyltestosterone;

(D.1) Desoxymethyltestosterone (17a–methyl–5a–androst–2–en–17–ol, madol);

(E) Dihydrotestosterone;

(F) Drostanolone;

(G) Ethylestrenol;

(H) Fluoxymesterone;

(I) Formebolone;

(J) Mesterolone;

(K) Methandienone;

(L) Methandranone;

(M) Methandriol;

(N) Methandrostenolone;

(O) Methenolone;

(P) Methyltestosterone;

(Q) Mibolerone;

(R) Nandrolone;

(S) Norethandrolone;

(T) Oxandrolone;

(U) Oxymesterone;

(V) Oxymetholone;

(W) Stanolone;

(X) Stanozolol;

(Y) Testolactone;

(Z) Testosterone;

(AA) Trenbolone;

(BB) 19–nor–4,9(10)–androstadienedione (estra–4,9(10)–diene–3,17–dione);

(7) Ketamine;

(8) Dronabinol (synthetic) in sesame oil and encapsulated in a U.S. Food and Drug Administration approved drug product also known as Marinol;

(9) Sodium oxybate, when the FDA approved form of this drug is in a container labeled in compliance with subsection (a) or (b) of Code Section 26–3–8, in the possession of a registrant permitted to dispense the drug, or in the possession of a person to whom it has been lawfully prescribed;

(10) Buprenorphine;

(11) Embutramide.

Laws 1974, p. 221, § 1; Laws 1978, p. 1668, § 8; Laws 1980, p. 1746, § 6; Laws 1982, p. 3, § 16; Laws 1982, p. 2403, §§ 13, 18; Laws 1989, p. 233, § 3; Laws 1991, p. 312, § 1; Laws 1992, p. 6, § 16; Laws 1992, p. 1131, §§ 3, 4; Laws 1996, p. 356, § 2; Laws 1997, p. 1311, § 2; Laws 1998, p. 778, § 1; Laws 2000, p. 1317, § 2; Laws 2003, Act 80, § 3, eff. May 29, 2003; Laws 2008, Act 433, § 4, eff. May 6, 2008; Laws 2009, Act 43, § 2, eff. Apr. 21, 2009.

Formerly Code 1933, § 79A–808.

Historical and Statutory Notes

The 2000 amendment added par. (8).

The 2003 amendment by Act 80 added pars. (9) and (10).

The 2008 amendment by Act 433, added par. (11).

The 2009 amendment by Act 43, in par. (6), added subpars. (A.5), (BB), and (D.1).

§ 16–13–27.1. Certain anabolic steroids exempted from classification as Schedule III controlled substances

The following anabolic steroid containing compounds, mixtures, or preparations have been exempted as Schedule III Controlled Substances by the United States Drug Enforcement Administration, as listed in 21 C.F.R. 1308.34, and are therefore exempted from paragraph (6) of Code Section 16–13–27:

TABLE OF EXEMPT ANABOLIC STEROID PRODUCTS

Trade Name	Company
Androgen LA	Forest Pharmaceuticals St. Louis, MO
Andro–Estro 90–4	Rugby Labs Rockville Centre, NY
depANDROGYN	Forest Pharmaceuticals St. Louis, MO
DEPO–T.E.	Quality Research Pharm Carmel, IN
depTESTROGEN	Maroca Pharm Phoenix, AZ
Duomone	Winitec Pharm Pacific, MO
DURATESTRIN	W. E. Hauck Alpharetta, GA
DUO–SPAN II	Premedics Labs Gardena, CA
Estratest	Solvay Pharmaceuticals Marietta, GA
Estratest HS	Solvay Pharmaceuticals Marietta, GA
PAN ESTRA TEST	Pan American Labs Covington, LA
Premarin 1.25mg with Methyltestosterone	Ayerst Labs, Inc. New York, NY
Premarin 0.625mg with Methyltestosterone	Ayerst Labs, Inc. New York, NY
TEST–ESTRO Cypionates	Rugby Labs Rockville Centre, NY
Testosterone Cyp 50 Estradiol Cyp 2	I.D.E. Interstate Amityville, NY
Testosterone Cypionate–Estradiol Cypionate Injection	Best Generics N. Miami Beach, FL
Testosterone Cypionate–Estradiol Cypionate Injection	Schein Pharm Port Washington, NY
Testosterone Cypionate–Estradiol Cypionate Injection	Steris Labs, Inc. Phoenix, AZ
Testosterone Cypionate–Estradiol Valerate Injection	Schein Pharm Port Washington, NY
Testosterone Enanthate–Estradiol Valerate Injection	Steris Labs, Inc. Phoenix, AZ

Laws 1993, p. 590, § 1.

§ 16–13–28. Schedule IV

(a) The controlled substances listed in this Code section are included in Schedule IV. Unless specifically excepted or unless listed in another schedule, any material, compound, mixture, or preparation which contains any quantity of the following substances, including its salts, isomers, and salts of isomers whenever the existence of such salts, isomers, and salts of isomers is possible within the specified chemical designation, included as having a stimulant or depressant effect on the central nervous system or a hallucinogenic effect:

(1) Alprazolam;

(1.5) Armodafinil;

(2) Barbital;

(2.1) Bromazepam;

(2.15) Butorphanol;

(2.2) Camazepam;

(2.25) Carisoprodol;

(2.3) Cathine;

(3) Chloral betaine;

(4) Chloral hydrate;

(5) Chlordiazepoxide, but not including librax (chlordiazepoxide hydrochloride and clidinium bromide) or menrium (chlordiazepoxide and water soluble esterified estrogens);

(5.1) Clobazam;

(6) Clonazepam;

(7) Clorazepate;

(7.1) Clotiazepam;

(7.2) Cloxazolam;

(7.3) Delorazepam;

(8) Desmethyldiazepam;

(8.5) Dexfenfluramine;

(9) Reserved;

(10) Diazepam;

(11) Diethylpropion;

(11.05) Difenoxin;

(11.1) Estazolam;

(12) Ethchlorvynol;

(13) Ethinamate;

(13.1) Ethyl loflazepate;

(13.2) Fencamfamin;

(14) Fenfluramine;

(14.1) Flunitrazepam;

(14.2) Fenproporex;

(15) Flurazepam;

(15.3) Fospropofol;

(16) Halazepam;

(16.1) Haloxazolam;

(16.15) Indiplon;

(16.2) Ketazolam;

(16.3) Lometazepam;

(16.4) Loprazolam;

(17) Lorazepam;

(18) Mazindol;

(19) Mebutamate;

(19.1) Medazepam;

(19.2) Mefenorex;

(20) Meprobamate;

(21) Methohexital;

(22) Methylphenobarbital;

(22.1) Midazolam;

(22.15) Modafinil;

(22.2) Nimetazepam;

(22.3) Nitrazepam;

(22.4) Nordiazepam;

(23) Oxazepam;

(23.1) Oxazolam;

(24) Paraldehyde;

(25) Pemoline;

(26) Pentazocine;

(27) Petrichloral;

(28) Phenobarbital;

(29) Phentermine;

(29.1) Pipradrol;

(30) Prazepam;

(30.05) Propoxyphene (including all salts and optical isomers);

(30.1) Quazepam;

(30.2) Sibutramine;

(30.3) SPA (-)–1–dimethylamino–1, 2–diphenylethane;

(31) Temazepam;

(32) Triazolam;

(32.5) Zaleplon;

(33) Zolpidem;

(34) Zopiclone.

(b) The State Board of Pharmacy may except by rule any compound, mixture, or preparation containing any depressant, stimulant, or hallucinogenic substance listed in subsection (a) of this Code section from the application of all or any part of this article if the compound, mixture, or preparation contains one or more active, medicinal ingredients not having a depressant or stimulant effect on the central nervous system, and if the admixtures are included therein in combinations, quantity, proportion, or concentration that vitiate the potential for abuse of the substances which have a depressant or stimulant effect on the central nervous system.

Laws 1974, p. 221, § 1; Laws 1977, p. 1287, § 1; Laws 1979, p. 859, § 8; Laws 1980, p. 1746, § 7; Laws 1981, p. 557, § 4; Laws 1982, p. 3, § 16; Laws 1982, p. 2403, §§ 14, 19; Laws 1984, p. 22, § 16; Laws 1985, p. 1219, § 4; Laws 1986, p. 10, § 16; Laws 1986, p. 1555, § 4; Laws 1987, p. 261, § 5; Laws 1989, p. 233, § 4; Laws 1990, p. 8, § 16; Laws 1993, p. 590, § 2; Laws 1994, p. 169, § 5; Laws 1996, p. 1023, § 1; Laws 1997, p. 1311, § 3; Laws 1998, p. 778, § 2; Laws 1999, p. 643, § 1; Laws 2000, p. 1317, § 3; Laws 2003, Act 80, § 4, eff. May 29, 2003; Laws 2006, Act 516, § 2, eff. April 19, 2006; Laws 2007, Act 18, § 16, eff. May 11, 2007; Laws 2008, Act 433, § 5, eff. May 6, 2008; Laws 2009, Act 43, §§ 3, 4, eff. Apr. 21, 2009; Laws 2010, Act 619, § 3, eff. June 3, 2010.

Formerly Code 1933, § 79A–809.

Historical and Statutory Notes

The 2000 amendment added subsec. (a)(32.5).

The 2003 amendment by Act 80 designated par. (9) as reserved and added par. (30.05). Prior to amendment, par. (9) read: "(9) Dextropropoxyphene;".

The 2006 amendment by Act 516, in subsec. (a), added par. (34) and made a nonsubstantive change to par. (33).

The 2007 amendment by Act 18 was a provision contained in a correction bill.

The 2008 amendment by Act 433, in subsec. (a), added pars. (1.5) and (11.5).

The 2009 amendment by Act 43, in subsec. (a), deleted par. (11.5) which had read "Eszopiclone;" and added par. (11.5).

The 2010 amendment by Act 619 added par. (a)(15.3).

§ 16–13–29. Schedule V

The controlled substances listed in this Code section are included in Schedule V:

(1) Any compound, mixture, or preparation containing limited quantities of any of the following narcotic drugs, or salts thereof, which also contains one or more nonnarcotic, active, medicinal ingredients in sufficient proportion to confer upon the compound, mixture, or preparation valuable medicinal qualities other than those possessed by the narcotic drug alone:

(A) Not more than 200 milligrams of codeine, or any of its salts, per 100 milliliters or per 100 grams;

(B) Not more than 100 milligrams of dihydrocodeine, or any of its salts, per 100 milliliters or per 100 grams;

(C) Not more than 100 milligrams of ethylmorphine, or any of its salts, per 100 milliliters or per 100 grams;

(D) Not more than 2.5 milligrams of diphenoxylate and not less than 25 micrograms of atropine sulfate per dosage unit;

(E) Not more than 100 milligrams of opium per 100 milliliters or per 100 grams;

(2) Lacosamide;

(3) Pregabalin; or

(4) Pyrovalerone.

Laws 1974, p. 221, § 1; Laws 1978, p. 1668, § 9; Laws 1979, p. 859, § 9; Laws 1980, p. 1746, § 8; Laws 1981, p. 557, § 5; Laws 1984, p. 1019, § 2; Laws 1986, p. 1555, § 5; Laws 1989, p. 233, § 5; Laws 1993, p. 590, § 3; Laws 2003, Act 80, § 5, eff. May 29, 2003; Laws 2007, Act 331, § 2, eff. May 29, 2007; Laws 2010, Act 619, § 4, eff. June 3, 2010.

Formerly Code 1933, § 79A–810.

Historical and Statutory Notes

The 2003 amendment by Act 80 designated par. (2) as reserved. Prior to amendment, par. (2) read: "(2) Buprenorphine."

In 2003, the Code Commission substituted a semicolon for a period at the end of par. (2). See § 28–9–5.

The 2007 amendment by Act 331 substituted "Pregabalin" for "Reserved" in par. (3).

The 2010 amendment by Act 619, in par. (2), substituted "Lacosamide" for "Reserved".

§ 16–13–29.1. Nonnarcotic substances excluded from controlled substances schedules

The following nonnarcotic substances which may, under the Federal Food, Drug, and Cosmetic Act (21 U.S.C. 301), be lawfully sold over the counter without a prescription, are excluded from all schedules of controlled substances under this article:

Trade name or designation (Dosage form)	Composition/Potency	Manufacturer or distributor
Amodrine (Tablet)	Phenobarbital/8.00 mg; Aminophylline/100.00 mg; Racephedrine/25.00 mg	Searle, G.D. & Co.
Amodrine E C (Entericcoated tablet)	Phenobarbital/8.00 mg; Aminophylline/100.00 mg; Racephedrine/25.00 mg	Searle, G.D. & Co.

Trade name or designation (Dosage form)	Composition/Potency	Manufacturer or distributor
Anodyne (Ointment)	Chloral hydrate/0.69 g/30 g	Zemmer Co.
Anti–Asthma (Tablet)	Phenobarbital/8.00 mg; Theophylline/130.00 mg; Ephedrine hydrochloride/25.00 mg	Ormont Drug & Chem.
Anti-asthmatic (Tablet)	Phenobarbital/8.10 mg; Ephedrine hydrochloride/24.00 mg; Theophylline/130.00 mg	Zenith Labs., Inc.
Asma–Ese (Tablet)	Phenobarbital/8.10 mg; Theophylline/129.60 mg; Ephedrine hydrochloride/24.30 mg	Parmed Pharm.
Asma–Lief (Tablet)	Phenobarbital/8.10 mg; Ephedrine hydrochloride/24.30 mg; Theophylline/129.60 mg	Columbia Medical Co.
Asma–Lief Pediatric (Suspension)	Phenobarbital/4.00 mg/05 ml; Ephedrine hydrochloride/12.00 mg/05 ml; Theophylline/65.00 mg/05 ml	Columbia Medical Co.
Asma Tuss (Syrup)	Phenobarbital/4.00 mg/05 ml; Glyceryl guaiacolate/50.00 mg/05 ml; Chlorphentramine maleate/1.00 mg/05 ml; Ephedrine sulfate/12.00 mg/05 ml; Theophylline/15.00 mg/05 ml	Halsey Drug Co.
Azma–Aid (Tablet)	Phenobarbital/8.00 mg; Theophylline/129.60 mg Ephedrine hydrochloride/24.30 mg	Rondex Labs.
Azmadrine (Tablet)	Phenobarbital/8.00 mg; Ephedrine hydrochloride/24.00 mg; Theophylline/130.00 mg	U.S. Ethicals.
Benzedrex Inhaler (Inhaler)	Propylhexedrine	Smith Kline Consumer Products.
Bet–U–Lol (Liquid)	Chloral hydrate/0.54 g/30 ml; Methyl salicylate/30.10 g/30 ml; Menthol/0.69 g/30 ml	Huxley Pharm.
Bronkolixir (Elixir)	Phenobarbital/4.00 mg/05 ml; Theophylline/15.00 mg/05 ml; Ephedrine sulfate/12.00 mg/05 ml; Glyceryl guaiacolate/50.00 mg/05 ml	Breon Labs.
Bronkotabs (Tablet)	Phenobarbital/8.00 mg; Theophylline/100.00 mg; Glyceryl guaiacolate/100.00 mg; Ephedrine sulfate/24.00 mg	Breon Labs.
Bronkotabs–Hafs (Tablet)	Phenobarbital/4.00 mg; Glyceryl guaiacolate/50.00 mg; Theophylline/50.00 mg; Ephedrine sulfate/12.00 mg	Breon Labs.
Ceepa (Tablet)	Phenobarbital/8.00 mg; Theophylline/130.00 mg; Ephedrine hydrochloride/24.00 mg	Geneva Drugs.
Chlorasal (Ointment)	Chloral hydrate/648.00 mg/30 g; Menthol/972.00 mg/30 g; Methyl salicylate/4.277 g/30 g	Wisconsin Pharmacal.
Choate's Leg Freeze	Chloral hydrate/7.40 g/30 ml; Ether/10.3 ml/30 ml;	Bickmore, Inc.
(Liquid)	Menthol/6.3 g/30 ml; Camphor/8.7 g/30 ml	
Chlorosalicylate (Ointment)	Chloral hydrate/648.00 mg/30 g; Methyl salicylate/6.66 g/30 g; Menthol/1.13 g/30 g	Kremers–Urban Co.
Menthalgesic (Ointment)	Chloral hydrate/0.45 g/30 g; Menthol/0.45 g/30 g; Methyl salicylate/3.60 g/30 g; Camphor/0.45 g/30 g	Blue Line Chem Co.
Neoasma (Tablet)	Phenobarbital/10.00 mg; Theophylline/130.00 mg; Ephedrine hydrochloride/24.00 mg	Tarmac Products.
P.E.C.T. (Tablet)	Phenobarbital/8.10 mg; Chlorpheniramine maleate/2.00 mg; Ephedrine sulfate/24.30 mg; Theophylline/129.60 mg	Halsom Drug Co.
Primatene (Tablet)	Phenobarbital/8.00 mg; Ephedrine hydrochloride/24.00 mg; Theophylline/130.00 mg	Whitehall Labs.
Rynal (Spray)	dl-methamphetamine hydrochloride/0.11 g/50 ml; Antipyrine/0.14 g/50 ml; Pyriamine maleate/0.005 g/50 ml; Hyamine 2389/0.01 g/50 ml	Blaine Co.
S–K Asthma (Tablet)	Phenobarbital/8.00 mg; Ephedrine hydrochloride/24.30 mg; Theophylline/129.60 mg	S–K Research Labs.
Tedral (Tablet)	Phenobarbital/8.00 mg; Theophylline/130.00 mg; Ephedrine hydrochloride/24.00 mg	Warner–Chilcott.
Tedral Anti H (Tablet)	Phenobarbital/8.00 mg; Chlorpheniramine maleate/2.00 mg; Theophylline/130.00 mg; Ephedrine hydrochloride/24.00 mg	Warner–Chilcott.
Tedral Antiasthmatic (Tablet)	Phenobarbital/8.00 mg; Theophylline/130.00 mg; Ephedrine hydrochloride/24.00 mg	Parke–Davis & Co.
Tedral Elixir (Elixir)	Phenobarbital/2.00 mg/05 ml; Ephedrine hydrochloride/6.00 mg/05 ml; Theophylline/32.50 mg/05 ml	Warner–Chilcott.
Tedral Pediatric (Suspension)	Phenobarbital/4.00 mg/05 ml; Ephedrine hydrochloride/12.00 mg/05 ml; Theophylline/65.00 mg/05 ml	Warner–Chilcott.
Teephen (Tablet)	Phenobarbital/8.00 mg; Ephedrine hydrochloride/24.00 mg; Theophylline/130.00 mg	Robinson Labs.
Teephen Pediatric (Suspension)	Phenobarbital/4.00 mg/05 ml; Ephedrine hydrochloride/12.00 mg/05 ml; Theophylline anhydrous/65.00 mg/05 ml	Robinson Labs.
TEP (Tablet)	Phenobarbital/8.00 mg; Theophylline/130.00 mg; Ephedrine hydrochloride/24.00 mg	Towne, Paulsen & Co., Inc.
T.E.P. Compound (Tablet)	Phenobarbital/8.10 mg; Theophylline/129.60 mg; Ephedrine hydrochloride/24.30 mg	Stanlabs, Inc.

Trade name or designation (Dosage form)	Composition/Potency	Manufacturer or distributor
Thedrizem (Tablet)	Phenobarbital/8.00 mg; Ephedrine hydrochloride/25.00 mg; Theophylline/100.00 mg	Zemmer Co.
Theobal (Tablet)	Phenobarbital/8.00 mg; Ephedrine hydrochloride/24.00 mg; Theophylline/130.00 mg	Halsey Drug Co.
Val–Tep (Tablet)	Phenobarbital/8.00 mg; Ephedrine hydrochloride/24.00 mg; Theophylline/130.00 mg	Vale Chemical Co.
Verequad (Suspension)	Phenobarbital/4.00 mg/05 ml; Ephedrine hydrochloride/12.00 mg/05 ml; Theophylline calcium salicylate/65.00 mg/05 ml; Glyceryl guaiacolate/50.00 mg/05 ml	Knoll Pharm.
Verequad (Tablet)	Phenobarbital/8.00 mg; Ephedrine hydrochloride/24.00 mg; Glyceryl guaiacolate/100.00 mg; Theophylline calcium salicylate/130.00 mg	Knoll Pharm.
Vicks Inhaler (Inhaler)	1–Desoxyephedrine/113.00 mg	Vick Chemical Co.

Laws 1983, p. 349, § 1; Laws 1989, p. 233, § 6; Laws 1990, p. 8, § 16.

§ 16–13–29.2. Exempt Over-The-Counter (OTC) Schedule V controlled substances

The Georgia State Board of Pharmacy shall have the authority to exempt and control the sale of Schedule V controlled substances by rule which shall allow the sale of such substances without the need for issuance of a prescription from a medical practitioner and shall require such substances to be sold only in a pharmacy when such substances are sold without a prescription. Such substances shall be known as Exempt Over-the-Counter (OTC) Schedule V Controlled Substances.

Laws 2003, Act 80, § 6, eff. May 29, 2003.

§ 16–13–30. Possession, manufacturing, etc., of certain controlled substances

(a) Except as authorized by this article, it is unlawful for any person to purchase, possess, or have under his control any controlled substance.

(b) Except as authorized by this article, it is unlawful for any person to manufacture, deliver, distribute, dispense, administer, sell, or possess with intent to distribute any controlled substance.

(c) Except as otherwise provided, any person who violates subsection (a) of this Code section with respect to a controlled substance in Schedule I or a narcotic drug in Schedule II shall be guilty of a felony and, upon conviction thereof, shall be punished by imprisonment for not less than two years nor more than 15 years. Upon conviction of a second or subsequent offense, he shall be imprisoned for not less than five years nor more than 30 years.

(d) Except as otherwise provided, any person who violates subsection (b) of this Code section with respect to a controlled substance in Schedule I or Schedule II shall be guilty of a felony and, upon conviction thereof, shall be punished by imprisonment for not less than five years nor more than 30 years. Upon conviction of a second or subsequent offense, he or she shall be imprisoned for not less than ten years nor more than 40 years or life imprisonment. The provisions of subsection (a) of Code Section 17–10–7 shall not apply to a sentence imposed for a second such offense; provided, however, that the remaining provisions of Code Section 17–10–7 shall apply for any subsequent offense.

(e) Any person who violates subsection (a) of this Code section with respect to a controlled substance in Schedule II, other than a narcotic drug, shall be guilty of a felony and, upon conviction thereof, shall be punished by imprisonment for not less than two years nor more than 15 years. Upon conviction of a second or subsequent offense, he shall be punished by imprisonment for not less than five years nor more than 30 years.

(f) Reserved.

(g) Any person who violates subsection (a) of this Code section with respect to a controlled substance in Schedule III, IV, or V shall be guilty of a felony and, upon conviction thereof, shall be punished by imprisonment for not less than one year nor more than five years. Upon conviction of a second or subsequent offense, he shall be imprisoned for not less than one year nor more than ten years.

(h) Any person who violates subsection (b) of this Code section with respect to a controlled substance in Schedule III, IV, or V shall be guilty of a felony and, upon conviction thereof, shall be punished by imprisonment for not less than one year nor more than ten years.

(i) Except as authorized by this article, it is unlawful for any person to possess, have under his control, manufacture, deliver, distribute, dispense, administer, purchase, sell, or possess with intent to distribute a counterfeit substance. Any person who violates this subsection shall be guilty of a felony and, upon conviction thereof, shall be punished by imprisonment for not less than one year nor more than ten years.

(j)(1) It is unlawful for any person to possess, have under his control, manufacture, deliver, distribute, dispense, administer, purchase, sell, or possess with intent to distribute marijuana.

(2) Except as otherwise provided in subsection (c) of Code Section 16–13–31 or in Code Section 16–13–2, any person who violates this subsection shall be guilty of a felony and, upon conviction thereof, shall be punished by imprisonment for not less than one year nor more than ten years.

(k) It shall be unlawful for any person to hire, solicit, engage, or use an individual under the age of 17 years, in any manner, for the purpose of manufacturing, distributing, or dispensing, on behalf of the solicitor, any controlled substance, counterfeit substance, or marijuana unless the manufacturing, distribution, or dispensing is otherwise allowed by law. Any person who violates this subsection shall be guilty of a felony and, upon conviction thereof, shall be punished by imprisonment for not less than five years nor more than 20 years or by a fine not to exceed $20,000.00, or both.

(*l*)(1) Any person who violates subsection (a) of this Code section with respect to flunitrazepam, a Schedule IV controlled substance, shall be guilty of a felony and, upon conviction thereof, shall be punished by imprisonment for not less than two years nor more than 15 years. Upon conviction of a second or subsequent offense, such person shall be punished by imprisonment for not less than five years nor more than 30 years.

(2) Any person who violates subsection (b) of this Code section with respect to flunitrazepam, a Schedule IV controlled substance, shall be guilty of a felony and, upon conviction thereof, shall be punished by imprisonment for not less than five years nor more than 30 years. Upon conviction of a second or subsequent offense, such person shall be punished by imprisonment for not less than ten years nor more than 40 years or life imprisonment. The provisions of subsection (a) of Code

Section 17–10–7 shall not apply to a sentence imposed for a second such offense, but that subsection and the remaining provisions of Code Section 17–10–7 shall apply for any subsequent offense.

Laws 1974, p. 221, § 1; Laws 1975, p. 1112, § 1; Laws 1979, p. 1258, § 1; Laws 1980, p. 432, § 1; Laws 1985, p. 149, § 16; Laws 1990, p. 992, § 1; Laws 1992, p. 2041, § 1; Laws 1996, p. 1023, §§ 1.1, 2; Laws 1997, p. 1311, § 4.

Formerly Code 1933, § 79A–811.

§ 16–13–30.1. Transactions in noncontrolled substances represented as controlled substances prohibited

(a)(1) It is unlawful for any person knowingly to manufacture, deliver, distribute, dispense, possess with the intent to distribute, or sell a noncontrolled substance upon either:

(A) The express or implied representation that the substance is a narcotic or nonnarcotic controlled substance;

(B) The express or implied representation that the substance is of such nature or appearance that the recipient of said delivery will be able to distribute said substance as a controlled substance; or

(C) The express or implied representation that the substance has essentially the same pharmacological action or effect as a controlled substance.

(2) The definitions of the terms "deliver," "delivery," "distribute," "dispense," and "manufacture" provided in Code Section 16–13–21 shall not be applicable to this Code section; but such terms as used in this Code section shall have the meanings ascribed to them in the ordinary course of business.

(b) An implied representation may be shown by proof of any two of the following:

(1) The manufacture, delivery, distribution, dispensing, or sale included an exchange or a demand for money or other valuable property as consideration for delivery of the substance and the amount of such consideration was substantially in excess of the reasonable value of the noncontrolled substance;

(2) The physical appearance of the finished product containing the substance is substantially identical to a specific controlled substance;

(3) The finished product bears an imprint, identifying mark, number, or device which is substantially identical to the trademark, identifying mark, imprint, number, or device of a manufacturer licensed by the Food and Drug Administration of the United States Department of Health and Human Services.

(c) In any prosecution for unlawful manufacture, delivery, distribution, possession with intent to distribute, dispensing, or sale of a noncontrolled substance, it is no defense that the accused believed the noncontrolled substance to be actually a controlled substance.

(d) The provisions of this Code section shall not prohibit a duly licensed business establishment, acting in the usual course of business, from selling or for a practitioner, acting in the usual course of his professional practice, from dispensing a drug preparation manufactured by a manufacturer licensed by the Food and Drug Administration of the United States Department of Health and Human Services for over-the-counter sale which does not bear a label stating "Federal law prohibits dispensing without a prescription" or similar language meaning that the drug preparation requires a prescription.

(e) The unlawful manufacture, delivery, distribution, dispensing, possession with the intention to distribute, or sale of a noncontrolled substance in violation of this Code section is a felony and, upon conviction thereof, such person shall be punished by imprisonment for not less than one year nor more than ten years or by a fine not to exceed $25,000.00, or both.

(f) All property which would be subject to forfeiture under the provisions of subsection (d) of Code Section 16–13–49 for a violation of this article which is used, or intended for use, to facilitate, or is derived from, a violation of this Code section and any noncontrolled substance which is manufactured, distributed, dispensed, possessed with the intent to distribute, or sold in violation of this Code section are declared to be contraband and there shall be no property interest therein. Any property or noncontrolled substance which is subject to the provisions of this subsection shall be forfeited in accordance with the procedures of Code Section 16–13–49.

Laws 1982, p. 2370, § 3; Laws 1991, p. 886, § 2.

§ 16–13–30.2. Transactions in imitation controlled substances prohibited

(a) Any person who knowingly manufactures, distributes, or possesses with intent to distribute an imitation controlled substance as defined in paragraph (12.1) of Code Section 16–13–21 is guilty of a misdemeanor of a high and aggravated nature.

(b) The provisions of this Code section are cumulative and shall not be construed as restricting any remedy, provisional or otherwise, provided by law for the benefit of any party.

(c) No civil or criminal liability shall be imposed by virtue of this Code section on any person registered under this article who manufactures, distributes, or possesses an imitation controlled substance for use by a practitioner, as defined in paragraph (23) of Code Section 16–13–21, in the course of lawful professional practice or research.

(d) All materials which are manufactured, distributed, or possessed in violation of this Code section are declared to be contraband and shall be forfeited according to the procedure described in Code Section 16–13–49.

Laws 1988, p. 1065, § 2.

§ 16–13–30.3. Ephedrine, pseudoephedrine, and phenylpropanolamine; unlawful possession; violations

(a) As used in this Code section, the term:

(1) "Ephedrine," "pseudoephedrine," or "phenylpropanolamine" means any drug product containing ephedrine, pseudoephedrine, or phenylpropanolamine, or any of their salts, isomers, or salts of isomers, alone or in a mixture.

(2) "Personal use" means the sale in a single transaction to an individual customer for a legitimate medical use of a product containing ephedrine, pseudoephedrine, or phenylpropanolamine in quantities at or below that specified in subsection (b) of this Code section, and includes the sale of those products to employers to be dispensed to employees from first-aid kits or medicine chests.

(3) "Retail distributor" means a grocery store, general merchandise store, drugstore, convenience store, or other related entity, the activities of which involve the distribution of ephedrine, pseudoephedrine, or phenylpropanolamine products.

(b)(1) It is unlawful for any person, other than a person or entity described in paragraph (28), (29), or (33) of Code Section 26–4–5 or a retail distributor, to knowingly possess any product that contains ephedrine, pseudoephedrine, or phenylpropanolamine in an amount which exceeds 300 pills, tablets, gelcaps, capsules, or other individual units or more than 9 grams of ephedrine, pseudoephedrine, or phenylpropanolamine, their salts, isomers, or salts of isomers, or a combination of any of these substances, whichever is smaller.

(2) It shall be unlawful for any person to possess any amount of a substance set forth in this Code section with the intent to manufacture amphetamine or methamphetamine.

(3) Any person who violates the provisions of this Code section shall be guilty of a felony and, upon conviction thereof, shall be punished by imprisonment for not less than one year nor more than ten years.

(b.1)(1) Products whose sole active ingredient is pseudoephedrine may be offered for retail sale only if sold in blister packaging. Such products may not be offered for retail sale by self–service but only from behind a counter or other barrier so that such products are not directly accessible by the public but only by a retail store employee or agent.

(2) No person shall deliver in any single over the counter sale more than three packages of any product containing pseudoephedrine as the sole active ingredient or in combination with other active ingredients or any number of packages that contain a combined total of more than nine grams of pseudoephedrine or its base, salts, optical isomers, or salts of its optical isomers.

(3) It shall be unlawful for a retail distributor to purchase any product containing pseudoephedrine from any person or entity other than a manufacturer or a wholesale distributor licensed by the Georgia State Board of Pharmacy.

(4) This subsection shall not apply to:

(A) Pediatric products labeled pursuant to federal regulation as primarily intended for administration to children under 12 years of age according to label instructions; and

(B) Products that the Georgia State Board of Pharmacy, upon application of a manufacturer, exempts because the product is formulated in such a way as to effectively prevent the conversion of the active ingredient into methamphetamine or its salts or precursors.

(5) This subsection shall preempt all local ordinances or regulations governing the retail sale of over the counter products containing pseudoephedrine by a retail business except such local ordinances or regulations that existed on or before December 31, 2004. Effective January 1, 2006, this subsection shall preempt all local ordinances.

(6)(A) Except as otherwise provided herein, it shall be unlawful for any person knowingly to violate any prohibition contained in paragraph (1), (2), or (3) of this subsection.

(B) Any person convicted of a violation of paragraph (1) or (2) of this subsection shall be guilty of a misdemeanor which, upon the first conviction, shall be punished by a fine of not more than $500.00 and, upon the second or subsequent conviction, shall be punished by not more than six months' imprisonment or a fine of not more than $1,000.00, or both.

(C) Any person convicted of a violation of paragraph (3) of this subsection shall, upon the first conviction, be guilty of a misdemeanor and, upon the second or subsequent conviction, be guilty of a misdemeanor of a high and aggravated nature.

(D) It shall be a defense to a prosecution of a retail business or owner or operator thereof for violation of paragraph (1) or (2) of this subsection that, at the time of the alleged violation, all of the employees of the retail business had completed training under Georgia Meth Watch, the retail business was in compliance with Georgia Meth Watch, and the defendant did not knowingly, willfully, or intentionally violate paragraph (1) or (2) of this subsection. For purposes of this subsection only, the term "Georgia Meth Watch" shall mean that program entitled "Georgia Meth Watch" or similar program which has been promulgated, approved, and distributed by the Georgia Council on Substance Abuse.

(7) Except as otherwise provided in this subsection, the Georgia State Board of Pharmacy may adopt reasonable rules and regulations to effectuate the provisions of this subsection. The board is further authorized to charge reasonable fees to defray expenses incurred in maintaining any records or forms necessitated by this subsection or otherwise administering any other provisions of this subsection.

(c) This Code section shall not apply to:

(1) Pediatric products primarily intended for administration to children under 12 years of age, according to label instructions, either:

(A) In solid dosage form whose recommended dosage, according to label instructions, does not exceed 15 milligrams of ephedrine, pseudoephedrine, or phenylpropanolamine per individual dosage unit; or

(B) In liquid form whose recommended dosage, according to label instructions, does not exceed 15 milligrams of ephedrine, pseudoephedrine, or phenylpropanolamine per five milliliters of liquid product;

(2) Pediatric liquid products primarily intended for administration to children under two years of age for which the recommended dosage does not exceed two milliliters and the total package content does not exceed one fluid ounce; or

(3) Products that the Georgia State Board of Pharmacy, upon application of a manufacturer, exempts by rule from this Code section because the product has been formulated in such a way as to prevent effectively the conversion of the active ingredient into methamphetamine or its salts or precursors.

(d) Except as authorized by this article, it is unlawful for any person to possess, have under his or her control, manufacture, deliver, distribute, dispense, administer, purchase, sell, or possess with intent to distribute any substance containing any amounts of ephedrine, pseudoephedrine, phenylpropanolamine, or any of their salts, optical isomers, or salts of optical isomers which have been altered from their original condition so as to be powdered, liquefied, or crushed. This subsection shall not apply to any of the substances identified within this subsection which are possessed or altered for a legitimate medical purpose. Any person who violates this subsection shall be guilty of a felony and, upon conviction thereof, shall be punished by imprisonment for not less than one year nor more than ten years.

Laws 2003, Act 29, § 3, eff. May 15, 2003; Laws 2005, Act 45, § 1, eff. July 1, 2005; Laws 2006, Act 453, § 16, eff. April 14, 2006; Laws 2007, Act 18, § 16, eff. May 11, 2007.

Historical and Statutory Notes

The 2005 amendment by Act 45 inserted subsec. (b.1).

The 2006 amendment by Act 453 was a provision contained in a correction bill.

The 2007 amendment by Act 18 was a provision contained in a correction bill.

§ 16–13–30.4. Pseudoephedrine; wholesale distributors; license requirements; records; violations

(a) As used in this Code section and unless otherwise specified, the term "board" or "Board of Pharmacy" shall mean the Georgia State board of pharmacy.

(b)(1) A wholesale distributor who sells, transfers, purchases for resale, or otherwise furnishes any product containing pseudoephedrine must first obtain a license from the board of pharmacy; provided, however, that a wholesale distributor that has a valid license as a wholesale distributor under Code Section 26–4–113 shall not be required to obtain an additional license under this Code section.

(2) Wholesale distributors licensed under Code Section 26–4–113 shall be subject to the provisions of this Code section in the same manner as wholesale distributors licensed under this Code section.

(3) Every wholesale distributor licensed as provided in this Code section shall:

(A) Submit reports, upon verbal or written request from the Georgia Drugs and Narcotics Agency, the Georgia Bureau of Investigation, or the sheriff of a county or the police chief of a municipality located in this state, to account for all transactions with persons or firms located within this state; such reportable transactions shall include all sales, distribution, or transactions dealing with products containing pseudoephedrine; and

(B) Within seven days, notify the Georgia Drugs and Narcotics Agency of any purchases of products containing pseudoephedrine from the wholesale distributor which the wholesaler judges to be excessive.

(4) Whenever any firm or person located in this state receives, purchases, or otherwise gains access to products containing pseudoephedrine from any wholesale distributor, whether located in or outside this state, such firm or person shall maintain a copy of such wholesale distributor's license issued by the Georgia State Board of Pharmacy. Such firm or person shall maintain copies of all invoices, receipts, and other records regarding such products containing pseudoephedrine for a minimum of three years from the date of receipt, purchase, or access. Failure to maintain records to verify the presence of any and all products containing pseudoephedrine being held by a firm or person shall subject such products containing pseudoephedrine to being embargoed or seized by proper law enforcement authorities until such time as proof can be shown that such products containing pseudoephedrine were obtained from a Georgia licensed wholesale distributor.

(5) Agents of the Georgia Drugs and Narcotics Agency, agents of the Georgia Bureau of Investigation, and the sheriff of a county or the police chief of a county or municipality in this state in which a firm or person that receives, purchases, or otherwise gains access to products containing pseudoephedrine is located may request to review the receiving records for such products. Failure to provide such records within five business days following such request to account for the presence of such products shall result in the embargo or seizure of such products.

(c) A license or permit obtained pursuant to this Code section shall be denied, suspended, or revoked by the board of pharmacy upon finding that the licensee or permit holder has:

(1) Furnished false or fraudulent material information in any application filed under this Code section;

(2) Been convicted of a crime under any state or federal law relating to any controlled substance;

(3) Had his or her federal registration suspended or revoked to manufacture, distribute, or dispense controlled substances;

(4) Violated the provisions of Chapter 4 of Title 26; or

(5) Failed to maintain effective controls against the diversion of products containing pseudoephedrine to unauthorized persons or entities.

(d) The board of pharmacy may adopt reasonable rules and regulations to effectuate the provisions of this Code section. The board is further authorized to charge reasonable fees to defray expenses incurred in issuing any licenses or permits, maintaining any records or forms required by this Code section, and the administration of the provisions of this Code section.

(e) Notwithstanding any other provision of this Code section to the contrary, no person shall be required to obtain a license or permit for the sale, receipt, transfer, or possession of a product containing pseudoephedrine when:

(1) Such lawful distribution takes place in the usual course of business between agents or employees of a single regulated person or entity; or

(2) A product containing pseudoephedrine is delivered to or by a common or contract carrier for carriage in the lawful and usual course of the business of the common or contract carrier or to or by a warehouseman for storage in the lawful and usual course of the business of the warehouseman.

(f) All products containing pseudoephedrine that have been or that are intended to be sold, transferred, purchased for resale, possessed, or otherwise transferred in violation of a provision of this Code section shall be subject to forfeiture to the state and no property right shall exist in them.

(g)(1) Any person who sells, transfers, receives, or possesses a product containing pseudoephedrine violates this Code section if the person:

(A) Knowingly fails to comply with the reporting requirements of this Code section;

(B) Knowingly makes a false statement in a report or record required by this Code section or the rules adopted thereunder; or

(C) Is required by this Code section to have a license or permit and knowingly or deliberately fails to obtain such a license or permit.

(2) It shall be illegal for a person to possess, sell, transfer, or otherwise furnish a product containing pseudoephedrine if such person possesses, sells, transfers, or furnishes the substance with the knowledge or intent that the substance will be used in the unlawful manufacture of a controlled substance.

(3)(A) A person who violates paragraph (2) of this subsection shall be guilty of a felony and, upon conviction thereof, shall be punished by imprisonment for not less than one nor more than 15 years or by a fine not to exceed $100,000.00, or both.

(B) A person who violates any provision of this Code Section other than paragraph (2) of this subsection shall be guilty of a misdemeanor on the first offense and a misdemeanor of a high and aggravated nature on the second and subsequent offenses.

Laws 2005, Act 45, § 2, eff. July 1, 2005; Laws 2007, Act 18, § 16, eff. May 11, 2007.

Historical and Statutory Notes

The 2007 amendment by Act 18 was a provision contained in a correction bill.

§ 16–13–30.5. Possession of substances with intent to manufacture controlled substances; violations

(a) It shall be illegal for a person to possess, whether acquired through theft or other means, any substance with the intent to:

(1) Use such substance in the manufacture of a Schedule I or Schedule II controlled substance; or

(2) Knowingly convey such substance to another for use in the manufacture of a Schedule I or Schedule II controlled substance.

(b) In determining whether a particular substance is possessed with the intent required to violate subsection (a) of this Code section, the court or other authority making such a determination may, in addition to all other logically relevant factors, consider the following:

(1) Statements by the owner or anyone in control of the substance concerning its use;

(2) Prior convictions, if any, of the owner or of anyone in control of the substance for violation of any state or federal law relating to the sale or manufacture of controlled substances;

(3) Instructions or descriptive materials of any kind accompanying the substance or found in the owner's or controlling person's possession concerning, explaining, or depicting its use;

(4) The manner in which the substance is displayed or offered for sale;

(5) The quantity and location of the substance considered in relation to the existence and scope of legitimate uses for the substance in the community; and

(6) Expert testimony concerning the substance's use.

(c) This Code section shall not apply where possession was by a person authorized by law to dispense, prescribe, manufacture, or possess the substance in question.

(d) A person who violates this Code section shall be guilty of a felony and, upon conviction thereof, shall be punished by imprisonment for not less than one nor more than 15 years or by a fine not to exceed $100,000.00, or both.

Laws 2005, Act 45, § 3, eff. July 1, 2005; Laws 2006, Act 453, § 16, eff. April 14, 2006.

Historical and Statutory Notes

The 2006 amendment by Act 453 was a provision contained in a correction bill.

§ 16–13–30.6. Marijuana flavored products; sale or providing to minors; purchase by minors; violations

(a) As used in this Code section, the term:

(1) "Marijuana flavored product" means any product, including lollipops, gumdrops, or other candy, which is flavored to taste like marijuana or hemp. The term shall include, but is not limited to, "Chronic Candy," "Kronic Kandy," or "Pot Suckers."

(2) "Minor" means any person under the age of 18 years.

(3) "Person" means any natural person, individual, corporation, unincorporated association, proprietorship, firm, partnership, limited liability company, joint venture, joint stock association, or other entity or business organization of any kind.

(b) The General Assembly finds and determines that:

(1) According to the "2004 Monitoring the Future Study" conducted by the University of Michigan, 16.3 percent of eighth graders, 35.1 percent of tenth graders, and 45.7 percent of twelfth graders reported using marijuana at least once during their lifetimes;

(2) According to a 2002 Substance Abuse and Mental Health Service Administration report, "Initiation of Marijuana Use: Trends, Patterns and Implications," the younger children are when they first use marijuana, the more likely they are to use cocaine and heroin and become drug dependent as adults;

(3) Marijuana abuse is associated with many negative health effects, including frequent respiratory infections, impaired memory and learning, increased heart rate, anxiety, and panic attacks;

(4) Marijuana users have many of the same respiratory problems that are associated with tobacco use;

(5) According to the "2001 National Household Survey on Drug Abuse," marijuana is the nation's most commonly used illicit drug, and more than 83,000,000 Americans aged 12 and older have tried marijuana at least once;

(6) Use of marijuana has been shown to lower test scores among high school students, and workers who smoke marijuana are more likely to have problems on their jobs;

(7) Federal, state, and local governments spend millions of dollars annually on programs educating people about the hazards of drugs, and the marketing of marijuana flavored substances would have an adverse impact upon these programs;

(8) The sale of marijuana flavored products, including lollipops and gum drops, which claim "every lick is like taking a hit" is a marketing ploy that perpetuates an unhealthy culture and should not be permitted in the State of Georgia;

(9) Marijuana flavored products are a threat to minors in the State of Georgia because such products give the false impression that marijuana is fun and safe;

(10) Marijuana flavored products packaged as candy or lollipops falling into the hands of unsuspecting minors may serve as a gateway to future use of marijuana and other drugs; and

(11) Merchants who sell marijuana flavored products are promoting marijuana use and creating new customers for drug dealers in the State of Georgia.

Therefore, the purpose of this Code section is to prohibit the purchase and sale of marijuana flavored products to minors in the State of Georgia.

(c) It shall be unlawful for any person knowingly to sell, deliver, distribute, or provide to a minor or knowingly possess with intent to sell, deliver, distribute, or provide to a minor any marijuana flavored product in the State of Georgia.

(d) It shall be unlawful for any minor falsely to represent to any person that such minor is 18 years of age or older with the intent to purchase or otherwise obtain any marijuana flavored product.

(e) Any person who violates subsection (c) of this Code section shall be guilty of a misdemeanor and shall be subject to a fine of $500.00 for each offense. Each sale in violation of this Code section shall constitute a separate offense.

Laws 2008, Act 415, § 1, eff. July 1, 2008; Laws 2009, Act 8, § 16, eff. April 14, 2009.

Historical and Statutory Notes

Laws 2008, Act 415, § 2, provides:

"This Act shall become effective on July 1, 2008, and shall apply to offenses committed on or after that date."

The 2009 amendment by Act 8 was a provision contained in a correction bill.

§ 16–13–31. Sale, manufacture, etc., of certain controlled substances

(a)(1) Any person who knowingly sells, manufactures, delivers, or brings into this state or who is knowingly in possession of 28 grams or more of cocaine or of any mixture with a purity of 10 percent or more of cocaine, as described in Schedule II, in violation of this article commits the felony offense of trafficking in cocaine and, upon conviction thereof, shall be punished as follows:

(A) If the quantity of the cocaine or the mixture involved is 28 grams or more, but less than 200 grams, the person shall be sentenced to a mandatory minimum term of imprisonment of ten years and shall pay a fine of $200,000.00;

(B) If the quantity of the cocaine or the mixture involved is 200 grams or more, but less than 400 grams, the person shall be sentenced to a mandatory minimum term of imprisonment of 15 years and shall pay a fine of $300,000.00; and

(C) If the quantity of the cocaine or the mixture involved is 400 grams or more, the person shall be sentenced to a mandatory minimum term of imprisonment of 25 years and shall pay a fine of $1 million.

(2) Any person who knowingly sells, manufactures, delivers, or brings into this state or who is knowingly in possession of any mixture with a purity of less than 10 percent of cocaine, as described in Schedule II, in violation of this article commits the felony offense of trafficking in cocaine if the total weight of the mixture multiplied by the percentage of cocaine contained in the mixture exceeds any of the quantities of cocaine specified in paragraph (1) of this subsection. Upon conviction thereof, such person shall be punished as provided in paragraph (1) of this subsection depending upon the quantity of cocaine such person is charged with knowingly selling, manufacturing, delivering, or bringing into this state or knowingly possessing.

(b) Any person who knowingly sells, manufactures, delivers, brings into this state, or has possession of 4 grams or more of any morphine or opium or any salt, isomer, or salt of an isomer thereof, including heroin, as described in Schedules I and II, or 4 grams or more of any mixture containing any such substance in violation of this article commits the felony offense of trafficking in illegal drugs and, upon conviction thereof, shall be punished as follows:

(1) If the quantity of such substances involved is 4 grams or more, but less than 14 grams, the person shall be sentenced to a mandatory minimum term of imprisonment of five years and shall pay a fine of $50,000.00;

(2) If the quantity of such substances involved is 14 grams or more, but less than 28 grams, the person shall be sentenced to a mandatory minimum term of imprisonment of ten years and shall pay a fine of $100,000.00; and

(3) If the quantity of such substances involved is 28 grams or more, the person shall be sentenced to a mandatory minimum term of imprisonment of 25 years and shall pay a fine of $500,000.00.

(c) Any person who knowingly sells, manufactures, grows, delivers, brings into this state, or has possession of a quantity of marijuana exceeding 10 pounds commits the offense of trafficking in marijuana and, upon conviction thereof, shall be punished as follows:

(1) If the quantity of marijuana involved is in excess of 10 pounds, but less than 2,000 pounds, the person shall be sentenced to a mandatory minimum term of imprisonment of five years and shall pay a fine of $100,000.00;

(2) If the quantity of marijuana involved is 2,000 pounds or more, but less than 10,000 pounds, the person shall be sentenced to a mandatory minimum term of imprisonment of seven years and shall pay a fine of $250,000.00; and

(3) If the quantity of marijuana involved is 10,000 pounds or more, the person shall be sentenced to a mandatory minimum term of imprisonment of 15 years and shall pay a fine of $1 million.

(d) Any person who knowingly sells, manufactures, delivers, or brings into this state 200 grams or more of methaqualone or of any mixture containing methaqualone, as described in paragraph (6) of Code Section 16–13–25, in violation of this article commits the felony offense of trafficking in methaqualone and, upon conviction thereof, shall be punished as follows:

(1) If the quantity of the methaqualone or the mixture involved is 200 grams or more, but less than 400 grams, the person shall be sentenced to a mandatory minimum term of imprisonment of five years and shall pay a fine of $50,000.00; and

(2) If the quantity of the methaqualone or the mixture involved is 400 grams or more, the person shall be sentenced to a mandatory minimum term of imprisonment of 15 years and shall pay a fine of $250,000.00.

(e) Any person who knowingly sells, delivers, or brings into this state or has possession of 28 grams or more of methamphetamine, amphetamine, or any mixture containing either methamphetamine or amphetamine, as described in Schedule II, in violation of this article commits the felony offense of trafficking in methamphetamine or amphetamine and, upon conviction thereof, shall be punished as follows:

(1) If the quantity of methamphetamine, amphetamine, or a mixture containing either substance involved is 28 grams or more, but less than 200 grams, the person shall be sentenced to a mandatory minimum term of imprisonment of ten years and shall pay a fine of $200,000.00;

(2) If the quantity of methamphetamine, amphetamine, or a mixture containing either substance involved is 200 grams or more, but less than 400 grams, the person shall be sentenced to a mandatory minimum term of imprisonment of 15 years and shall pay a fine of $300,000.00; and

(3) If the quantity of methamphetamine, amphetamine, or a mixture containing either substance involved is 400 grams or more, the person shall be sentenced to a mandatory minimum term of imprisonment of 25 years and shall pay a fine of $1 million.

(f) Any person who knowingly manufactures methamphetamine, amphetamine, or any mixture containing either methamphetamine or amphetamine, as described in Schedule II, in violation of this article commits the felony offense of trafficking methamphetamine or amphetamine and, upon conviction thereof, shall be punished as follows:

(1) If the quantity of methamphetamine, amphetamine, or a mixture containing either substance involved is less than 200 grams, the person shall be sentenced to a mandatory minimum term of imprisonment of ten years and shall pay a fine of $200,000.00;

(2) If the quantity of methamphetamine, amphetamine, or a mixture containing either substance involved is 200 grams or more, but less than 400 grams, the person shall be sentenced to a mandatory minimum term of imprisonment of 15 years and shall pay a fine of $300,000.00; and

(3) If the quantity of methamphetamine, amphetamine, or a mixture containing either substance involved is 400 grams or more, the person shall be sentenced to a mandatory minimum term of imprisonment of 25 years and shall pay a fine of $1 million.

(g)(1) Except as provided in paragraph (2) of this subsection and notwithstanding Code Section 16–13–2, with respect to any person who is found to have violated this Code section, adjudication of guilt or imposition of sentence shall not be suspended, probated, deferred, or withheld prior to serving the mandatory minimum term of imprisonment prescribed by this Code section.

(2) The district attorney may move the sentencing court to impose a reduced or suspended sentence upon any person who is convicted of a violation of this Code section and who provides substantial assistance in the identification, arrest, or conviction of any of his accomplices, accessories, coconspirators, or principals. Upon good cause shown, the motion may be filed and heard in camera. The judge hearing the motion may impose a reduced or suspended sentence if he finds that the defendant has rendered such substantial assistance.

(h) Any person who violates any provision of this Code section in regard to trafficking in cocaine, illegal drugs, marijuana, or methamphetamine shall be punished by imprisonment for not less than five years nor more than 30 years and by a fine not to exceed $1 million.

Laws 1980, p. 432, § 1; Laws 1982, p. 3, § 16; Laws 1982, p. 2215, § 1; Laws 1983, p. 620, § 1; Laws 1985, p. 149, § 16; Laws 1985, p. 552, § 1; Laws 1986, p. 10, § 16; Laws 1986, p. 397, § 1; Laws 1988, p. 420, § 2; Laws 1989, p. 1594, § 1; Laws 1992, p. 2106, § 1; Laws 1994, p. 169, § 5.1; Laws 1997, p. 1311, § 5; Laws 2003, Act 29, § 4, eff. May 15, 2003; Laws 2003, Act 40, § 1, eff. July 1, 2003.

Historical and Statutory Notes

The 2003 amendment by Act 29 made nonsubstantive changes in subsec. (b); deleted "manufactures," following "knowingly sells," in subsec. (e); inserted a new subsec. (f); and redesignated former subsecs. (f) and (g) as subsecs. (g) and (h).

The 2003 amendment by Act 40, in subsec. (c), substituted "10 pounds" for "50 pounds" in the introductory paragraph and in par. (1).

§ 16–13–31.1. Sale, manufacture, possession, etc. of 28 grams or more of certain amphetamines or methamphetamines

Any person who knowingly sells, manufactures, delivers, brings into this state, or has possession of 28 grams or more of 3, 4–methylenedioxyamphetamine or 3, 4–methylenedioxymethamphetamine, or any mixture containing 3,4–methylenedioxyamphetamine or 3, 4–methylenedioxymethamphetamine as described in Schedule I, in violation of this article commits the felony offense of trafficking in 3, 4–methylenedioxyamphetamine or 3, 4–methylenedioxymethamphetamine and, upon conviction thereof, shall be punished as follows:

(1) If the quantity of such substance involved is 28 grams or more, but less than 200 grams, the person shall be sentenced to a mandatory minimum term of imprisonment of three years but not more than 30 years and shall pay a fine of not less than $25,000.00 nor more than $250,000.00;

(2) If the quantity of such substance involved is 200 grams or more, but less than 400 grams, the person shall be sentenced to a mandatory minimum term of imprisonment of five years but not more than 30 years and shall pay a fine of not less than $50,000.00 nor more than $250,000.00; and

(3) If the quantity of such substance involved is 400 grams or more, the person shall be sentenced to a mandatory minimum term of imprisonment of ten years but not more than 30 years and shall pay a fine of not less than $100,000.00 nor more than $250,000.00.

Laws 2004, Act 792, § 1, eff. July 1, 2004; Laws 2007, Act 18, § 16, eff. May 11, 2007.

Historical and Statutory Notes

The 2007 amendment by Act 18 was a provision contained in a correction bill.

§ 16–13–32. Transactions in drug related objects prohibited

(a) As used in this Code section, the term:

(1) "Drug related object" means any instrument, device, or object which is designed or marketed as useful primarily for one or more of the following purposes:

(A) To inject, ingest, inhale, or otherwise introduce marijuana or a controlled substance into the human body;

(B) To enhance the effect of marijuana or a controlled substance on the human body;

(C) To test the strength, effectiveness, or purity of marijuana or a controlled substance;

(D) To process or prepare marijuana or a controlled substance for introduction into the human body;

(E) To conceal any quantity of marijuana or a controlled substance; or

(F) To contain or hold marijuana or a controlled substance while it is being introduced into the human body.

(2) "Knowing" means either actual or constructive knowledge of the drug related nature of the object; and a person or corporation has constructive knowledge of the drug related nature of the object if he or it has knowledge of facts which would put a reasonable and prudent person on notice of the drug related nature of the object.

(b) It shall be unlawful for any person or corporation, knowing the drug related nature of the object, to sell, lend, rent, lease, give, exchange, or otherwise distribute to any person any drug related object. It shall also be unlawful for any person or corporation, knowing the drug related nature of the object, to display for sale, or possess with the intent to distribute any drug related object. Unless stated within the body of the advertisement or notice that the object that is advertised or about which information is disseminated is not available for distribution of any sort in this state, it shall be unlawful for any person or corporation, knowing the drug related nature of the object, to distribute or disseminate in any manner to any person any advertisement of any kind or notice of any kind which gives information, directly or indirectly, on where, how, from whom, or by what means any drug related object may be obtained or made.

(c) It shall be unlawful for any person or corporation, other than a licensed pharmacist, a pharmacy intern or pharmacy extern as defined in Code Section 26–4–5, or a practitioner licensed to dispense dangerous drugs, to sell, lend, rent, lease, give, exchange, or otherwise distribute to any person a hypodermic syringe or needle designed or marketed primarily for human use. It shall be an affirmative defense that the hypodermic syringe or needle was marketed for a legitimate medical purpose.

(d) For a first offense, any person or corporation which violates any provision of this Code section shall be guilty of a misdemeanor. For a second offense, the defendant shall be guilty of a misdemeanor of a high and aggravated nature. For a third or subsequent offense, the defendant shall be guilty of a felony and, upon conviction thereof, shall be imprisoned for not less than one year nor more than five years and shall be fined not more than $5,000.00.

(e) All instruments, devices, and objects which are distributed or possessed in violation of this Code section are declared to be contraband.

(f) After conviction and after all direct appeals from the conviction have been exhausted, any instruments, devices, or objects which are the subject of prosecution under this Code section may be destroyed by the state or any county or municipality thereof without court order.

(g) Any instruments, devices, or objects which are seized after July 1, 1980, on condemnation as being distributed or possessed in violation of this Code section and which are not made the subject of prosecution under this Code section may be destroyed by the state or any county or municipality thereof if within 90 days after such seizures are made, the district attorney or the solicitor-general of any court that has jurisdiction to try misdemeanors in the county where the seizure occurred shall institute condemnation proceedings in the court by petition, a copy of which shall be served upon the owner of the seized items, if known; and if the owner is unknown, notice of such proceedings shall be published once a week for two weeks in the newspaper in which the sheriff's advertisements are published. The petition shall allege that the seized items were distributed or possessed in violation of this Code section; and, if no defense is filed within 30 days from the filing of the petition, judgment by default shall be entered by the court at chambers, and the court shall order the seized items to be destroyed; otherwise, the case shall proceed as other civil cases in the court. Should the state prove, by a preponderance of the evidence, that the seized items were distributed or possessed in violation of this Code section, the court shall order the seized items to be destroyed.

Laws 1978, p. 2237, § 1; Laws 1980, p. 1288, § 1; Laws 1996, p. 748, § 13; Laws 2004, Act 526, § 2, eff. May 13, 2004.

Formerly Code 1933, § 79A–811.1.

Historical and Statutory Notes

The 2004 amendment by Act 526, in subsec. (c), substituted "pharmacist, a pharmacy intern or pharmacy extern as defined in Code Section 26–4–5, or a practitioner licensed to dispense dangerous drugs" for "pharmacist or a practitioner licensed to dispense Legend Drugs".

§ 16–13–32.1. Transactions in drug related objects prohibited

(a) It shall be unlawful for any person or corporation to sell, rent, lease, give, exchange, otherwise distribute, or possess with intent to distribute any object or materials of any kind which such person or corporation intends to be used for the purpose of planting, propagating, cultivating, growing, harvesting, manufacturing, compounding, converting, producing, processing, preparing, testing, analyzing, packaging, repackaging, storing, containing, concealing, injecting, ingesting, inhaling, or otherwise introducing into the human body marijuana or a controlled substance.

(b) Unless stated within the body of the advertisement or notice that the object or materials that are advertised or about which information is disseminated are not available for distribution of any sort in this state, it shall be unlawful for any person or corporation to sell, rent, lease, give, exchange, distribute, or possess with intent to distribute any advertisement of any kind or notice of any kind which gives information, directly or indirectly, on where, how, from whom, or by what means any object or materials may be obtained or made, which object or materials such person or corporation intends to be used for the purpose of planting, propagating, cultivating, growing, harvesting, manufacturing, compounding, converting, producing, processing, preparing, testing, analyzing, packaging, repackaging, storing, containing, concealing, injecting, ingesting, inhaling, or otherwise introducing into the human body marijuana or a controlled substance.

(c) In determining whether any object or materials are intended for any of the purposes listed in subsections (a) and (b) of this Code section, a court or other authority shall consider all logically relevant factors. In a trial under this Code section, any evidence admissible on this question under the rules of evidence shall be admitted. Subject to the rules of evidence, when they are the object of an offer of proof in a court proceeding, the following factors are among those that should be considered by a court or other authority on this question:

(1) Statements by an owner or anyone in control of the object or materials;

(2) Instructions provided with the object or materials;

(3) Descriptive materials accompanying the object or materials;

(4) National and local advertising or promotional materials concerning the object or materials;

(5) The appearance of, and any writing or other representations appearing on, the object or materials;

(6) The manner in which the object or materials are displayed for sale or other distribution;

(7) Expert testimony concerning the object or materials; and

(8) Any written or pictorial materials which are present in the place where the object is located.

(d) For a first offense, any person or corporation which violates any provision of this Code section shall be guilty of a misdemeanor. For a second offense, the defendant shall be guilty of a misdemeanor of a high and aggravated nature. For a third or subsequent offense, the defendant shall be guilty of a felony and, upon conviction thereof, shall be imprisoned for not less than one year nor more than five years and shall be fined not more than $5,000.00.

(e) All objects and materials which are distributed or possessed in violation of this Code section are declared to be contraband and shall be forfeited according to the procedure described in Code Section 16–13–49.

Laws 1981, p. 180, § 1; Laws 1985, p. 149, § 16.

Formerly Code 1933, § 79A–811.2.

§ 16–13–32.2. Possession of drug related objects prohibited

(a) It shall be unlawful for any person to use, or possess with the intent to use, any object or materials of any kind for the purpose of planting, propagating, cultivating, growing, harvesting, manufacturing, compounding, converting, producing, processing, preparing, testing, analyzing, packaging, repackaging, storing, containing, concealing, injecting, ingesting, inhaling, or otherwise introducing into the human body marijuana or a controlled substance.

(b) Any person or corporation which violates any provision of this Code section shall be guilty of a misdemeanor.

Laws 1981, p. 180, § 2.

Formerly Code 1933, § 79A–811.3.

§ 16–13–32.3. Use of communications facilities to violate provisions prohibited

(a) It shall be unlawful for any person knowingly or intentionally to use any communication facility in committing or in causing or facilitating the commission of any act or acts constituting a felony under this chapter. Each separate use of a communication facility shall be a separate offense under this Code section. For purposes of this Code section, the term "communication facility" means any and all public and private instrumentalities used or useful in the transmission of writing, signs, signals, pictures, or sounds of all kinds and includes mail, telephone, wire, radio, computer or computer network, and all other means of communication.

(b) Any person who violates subsection (a) of this Code section shall be punished by a fine of not more than $30,000.00 or by imprisonment for not less than one nor more than four years, or both.

Laws 1982, p. 2359, § 1; Laws 1995, p. 574, § 1.

§ 16–13–32.4. Transactions in controlled substance or marijuana in, on, or within 1,000 feet of real property owned by or leased to public or private school or school board used for elementary or secondary education prohibited

(a) It shall be unlawful for any person to manufacture, distribute, dispense, or possess with intent to distribute a controlled substance or marijuana in, on, or within 1,000 feet of any real property owned by or leased to any public or private elementary school, secondary school, or school board used for elementary or secondary education.

(b) Any person who violates or conspires to violate subsection (a) of this Code section shall be guilty of a felony and upon conviction shall receive the following punishment:

(1) Upon a first conviction, imprisonment for not more than 20 years or a fine of not more than $20,000.00, or both; or

(2) Upon a second or subsequent conviction, imprisonment for not less than five years nor more than 40 years or a fine of not more than $40,000.00, or both. It shall be mandatory for the court to impose a minimum sentence of five years which may not be suspended unless otherwise provided by law.

A sentence imposed under this Code section shall be served consecutively to any other sentence imposed.

(c) A conviction arising under this Code section shall not merge with a conviction arising under any other provision of this article.

(d) It shall be no defense to a prosecution for a violation of this Code section that:

(1) School was or was not in session at the time of the offense;

(2) The real property was being used for other purposes besides school purposes at the time of the offense; or

(3) The offense took place on a school vehicle.

(e) In a prosecution under this Code section, a map produced or reproduced by any municipal or county agency or department for the purpose of depicting the location and boundaries of the area on or within 1,000 feet of the real property of a school board or a private or public elementary or secondary school that is used for school purposes, or a true copy of the map, shall, if certified as a true copy by the custodian of the record, be admissible and shall constitute prima-facie evidence of the location and boundaries of the area, if the governing body of the municipality or county has approved the map as an official record of the location and boundaries of the area. A map approved under this Code section may be revised from time to time by the governing body of the municipality or county. The original of every map approved or revised under this subsection or a true copy of such original map shall be filed with the municipality or county and shall be maintained as an official record of the municipality or county. This subsection shall not preclude the prosecution from introducing or relying upon any other evidence or testimony to establish any element of this offense. This subsection shall not preclude the use or admissibility of a map or diagram other than the one which has been approved by the municipality or county.

(f) A county school board may adopt regulations requiring the posting of signs designating the areas within 1,000 feet of school boards and private or public elementary and secondary schools as "Drug-free School Zones."

(g) It is an affirmative defense to prosecution for a violation of this Code section that the prohibited conduct took place entirely within a private residence, that no person 17 years of age or younger was present in such private residence at any time during the commission of the offense, and that the prohibited conduct was not carried on for purposes of financial gain. Nothing in this subsection shall be construed to establish an affirmative defense with respect to any offense under this chapter other than the offense provided for in subsection (a) of this Code section.

Laws 1990, p. 1097, § 1.

§ 16–13–32.5. Transactions in controlled substance or marijuana in, on, or within 1,000 feet of parks, playgrounds, recreation centers, or housing projects prohibited

(a) It shall be unlawful for any person to manufacture, distribute, dispense, or possess with intent to distribute a controlled substance or marijuana or a counterfeit substance in, on, or within 1,000 feet of any real property which has been dedicated and set apart by the governing authority of any municipality, county, state authority, or the state for use as a park, playground, recreation center, or for any other recreation purposes, unless the manufacture, distribution, or dispensing is otherwise allowed by law.

(b) It shall be unlawful for any person to manufacture, distribute, dispense, or possess with intent to distribute a controlled substance or marijuana or a counterfeit substance in, on, or within 1,000 feet of any real property of any publicly owned or publicly operated housing project, unless the manufacture, distribution, or dispensing is otherwise allowed by law. For the purposes of this Code section, the term "housing project" means any facilities under the jurisdiction of a housing authority which constitute single or multifamily dwelling units occupied by low and moderate-income families pursuant to Chapter 3 of Title 8.

(c) Any person who violates or conspires to violate subsection (a) or (b) of this Code section shall be guilty of a felony and upon conviction shall receive the following punishment:

(1) Upon a first conviction, imprisonment for not more than 20 years or a fine of not more than $ 20,000.00, or both; or

(2) Upon a second or subsequent conviction, imprisonment for not less than five years nor more than 40 years or a fine of not more than $ 40,000.00, or both. It shall be mandatory for the court to impose a minimum sentence of five years which may not be suspended unless otherwise provided by law.

A sentence imposed under this Code section shall be served consecutively to any other sentence imposed.

(d) A conviction arising under this Code section shall not merge with a conviction arising under any other provision of this article.

(e) In a prosecution under this Code section, a map produced or reproduced by any municipal or county agency or department for the purpose of depicting the location and boundaries of the area on or within 1,000 feet of the real property of any publicly owned or publicly operated housing project or the real property set apart for use as a park, playground, recreation center, or for any other recreation purposes, or a true copy of the map, shall, if certified as a true copy by the custodian of the record, be admissible and shall constitute prima-facie evidence of the location and boundaries of the area, if the governing body of the municipality or county has approved the map as an official record of the location and boundaries of the area. A map approved under this Code section may be revised from time to time by the governing body of the municipality or county. The original of every map approved or revised under this subsection or a true copy of such original map shall be filed with the municipality or county and shall be maintained as an official record of the municipality or county. This subsection shall not preclude the prosecution from introducing or relying upon any other evidence or testimony to establish any element of this offense. This subsection shall not preclude the use or admissibility of a map or diagram other than the one which has been approved by the municipality or county.

(f) The governing authority of a municipality or county may adopt regulations requiring the posting of signs designating the areas within 1,000 feet of any lands or buildings set apart for use as parks, playgrounds, recreation centers, or any other recreation purposes as "Drug-free Recreation Zones" and designating the areas within 1,000 feet of the real property of any publicly owned or publicly operated housing project as "Drug-free Residential Zones."

(g) It is an affirmative defense to prosecution for a violation of this Code section that the prohibited conduct took place entirely within a private residence, that no person 17 years of age or younger was present in such private residence at any time during the commission of the offense, and that the prohibited conduct was not carried on for purposes of financial gain. Nothing in this subsection shall be construed to establish an affirmative defense with respect to any offense under this chapter other than the offense provided for in subsections (a) and (b) of this Code section.

Laws 1992, p. 2043, § 1; Laws 2000, p. 1215, § 1; Laws 2008, Act 569, § 1, eff. July 1, 2008.

Historical and Statutory Notes

The 2000 amendment substituted near the beginning of subsec. (c) subsection (a) or (b)" for "subsections (a) and (b)".

The 2008 amendment by Act 569, in subsec. (a), inserted "state authority, or the state" following "set apart by the governing authority of any municipality, county" and made nominal changes.

§ 16–13–32.6. Transactions in controlled substance or marijuana in, on, or within real property designated as drug-free commercial zone

(a) It shall be unlawful for any person to illegally manufacture, distribute, dispense, or possess with intent to distribute a controlled substance or marijuana in, on, or within any real property which has been designated under this Code section as a drug-free commercial zone.

(b)(1) Any person who violates or conspires to violate subsection (a) of this Code section shall be guilty of a felony and upon conviction shall receive the following punishment:

(A) Upon a first conviction, imprisonment for not more than 20 years or a fine of not more than $20,000.00, or both; or

(B) Upon a second or subsequent conviction, imprisonment for not less than five years nor more than 40 years or a fine of not more than $40,000.00, or both.

(2) A sentence imposed under this Code section shall be served consecutively to any other sentence imposed.

(3) Any person convicted of a violation of subsection (a) of this Code section may, as a condition of probation or parole, be required by the sentencing court or State Board of Pardons and Paroles to refrain for a period of not more than 24 months from entering or at any time being within the boundaries of the

drug-free commercial zone wherein such person was arrested for a violation of this Code section. Any person arrested for violation of his or her terms of probation shall be governed by the provisions of Code Section 42–8–38 and any person arrested for a violation of his or her terms of parole shall be governed by the provisions of Article 2 of Chapter 9 of Title 42.

(c) A conviction arising under this Code section shall not merge with a conviction arising under any other provision of this article.

(d) Any municipality or county may designate one or more commercial areas where there is a high rate of drug related crime as drug-free commercial zones. A drug-free commercial zone may include only an area which the municipality or county has previously zoned commercial pursuant to its planning and zoning powers and any residential area contiguous to such commercially zoned area extending not more than one-half mile from the external boundary of any portion of the commercially zoned area. A municipality or county which designates one or more areas as drug-free commercial zones shall be required to make such designations by ordinance and shall be required to post prominent and conspicuous signs on the boundaries of and throughout any such drug-free commercial zone. A municipality or county shall be required to file with the Department of Community Affairs a copy of each ordinance which shall have attached a clearly defined map describing each drug-free commercial zone and a report evidencing all drug related crimes in such drug-free commercial zone area during the 12 months preceding the enactment of such ordinance. A municipality or county shall also be required to file with the Department of Community Affairs, during the period that a drug-free commercial zone is in effect, annual reports evidencing all drug related crimes in such drug-free commercial zone. Such ordinances, maps, and drug crime reports shall be maintained in a permanent register by such department, and copies of such ordinances, maps, and drug crime reports of drug-free commercial zones shall be made available to the public at a reasonable cost. A drug-free commercial zone shall not be effective and valid for the purposes of this Code section until it has been adopted by the General Assembly by general law. After the General Assembly has adopted one or more drug-free commercial zones, the governing authority of each municipality or county which has such a zone or zones designated and adopted shall be required to have a description of each such zone published in the legal organ of the municipality or county at least once a week for three weeks. A drug-free commercial zone adopted by the General Assembly shall remain in effect for five years and shall expire five years from the effective date of such adoption by the General Assembly. An area which has been a drug-free commercial zone may be continued as or again designated as a drug-free commercial zone upon the enactment of an ordinance and adoption thereof by the General Assembly in accordance with the provisions of this subsection. No arrest for a violation of this Code section shall be permissible for a period of 30 days immediately following the effective date of the adoption of such drug-free commercial zone by the General Assembly.

(e) In a prosecution under this Code section, a true copy of a map produced or reproduced by any municipal or county agency or department for the purpose of depicting the location and boundaries of any drug-free commercial zone and filed and on record at the Department of Community Affairs shall, if certified as a true copy by the custodian of such records at such department, be admissible and shall constitute prima-facie evidence of the location and boundaries of such zone. A map approved under this Code section may be revised from time to time by the governing body of the municipality or county; provided, however, that a revised map shall not become effective and the revised area shall not be a drug-free commercial zone until the revised map has been filed with the Department of Community Affairs and adopted by the General Assembly by general law; provided, further, that the revision of a drug-free commercial zone shall not extend the expiration date of such a drug-free commercial zone. The original copy of every map approved or revised under this subsection or a true copy of such original map shall be filed with the Department of Community Affairs and shall be maintained as an official record of the department. This subsection shall not preclude the prosecution from introducing or relying upon any other evidence or testimony to establish any element of this offense.

(f) The General Assembly hereby adopts and incorporates into this Code section all drug-free commercial zones which have been adopted by municipal or county ordinance and entered in the register of the Department of Community Affairs as provided for in subsection (d) of this Code section on or before March 10, 2004.

Laws 1996, p. 1049, § 1; Laws 1999, p. 556, § 1; Laws 2004, Act 792, § 1A, eff. July 1, 2004.

Historical and Statutory Notes

The 2004 amendment by Act 792, in subsec. (f), substituted "March 10, 2004" for "March 22, 1999".

§ 16–13–33. Attempt and conspiracy

Any person who attempts or conspires to commit any offense defined in this article shall be, upon conviction thereof, punished by imprisonment not exceeding the maximum punishment prescribed for the offense, the commission of which was the object of the attempt or conspiracy.

Laws 1974, p. 221, § 1.

Formerly Code 1933, § 79A–812.

§ 16–13–34. Rules

The State Board of Pharmacy may promulgate rules and charge reasonable fees relating to the registration and control of the manufacture, distribution, and dispensing of controlled substances within this state.

Laws 1974, p. 221, § 1; Laws 1982, p. 3, § 16.

Formerly Code 1933, § 79A–813.

§ 16–13–35. Registration requirements

(a) Every person who manufactures, distributes, or dispenses any controlled substances within this state or who proposes to engage in the manufacture, distribution, or dispensing of any controlled substance within this state must obtain annually a registration issued by the State Board of Pharmacy in accordance with its rules.

(b) Persons registered by the State Board of Pharmacy under this article to manufacture, distribute, dispense, or conduct research with controlled substances may possess, manufacture, distribute, dispense, or conduct research with those substances to the extent authorized by their registration and in conformity with this article.

(c) The following persons need not register and may lawfully possess controlled substances under this article:

(1) An agent or employee of any registered manufacturer, distributor, or dispenser of any controlled substance if he is acting in the usual course of his business or employment;

(2) A common or contract carrier or warehouseman, or any employee thereof, whose possession of any controlled substance is in the usual course of his business or employment;

(3) An ultimate user or a person in possession of any controlled substance pursuant to a lawful order of a practitioner or in lawful possession of a Schedule V substance; and

(4) Officers and employees of this state, or of a political subdivision of this state, or of the United States while acting in the course of their official duties.

(d) The State Board of Pharmacy may waive by rule the requirements for registration of certain manufacturers, distributors, or dispensers if it finds it consistent with the public health and safety.

(e) A separate registration is required at each principal place of business or professional practice where the applicant manufactures, distributes, or dispenses controlled substances.

(f) The State Board of Pharmacy, the director of the Georgia Drugs and Narcotics Agency, or other drug agents designated by the State Board of Pharmacy for this purpose may inspect the establishment of a registrant or applicant for registration in accordance with the State Board of Pharmacy rules and the provisions of this article.

(g) The following persons are registered under this article and are exempt from the registration fee and registration application requirements of this article:

(1) Persons licensed by the State Board of Pharmacy as a pharmacist or a pharmacy under Chapter 4 of Title 26;

(2) Persons licensed as a physician, dentist, or veterinarian under the laws of the state to use, mix, prepare, dispense, prescribe, and administer drugs in connection with medical treatment to the extent provided by the laws of this state; and

(3) An employee, agent, or representative of any person described in paragraph (1) or (2) of this subsection acting in the usual course of his employment or occupation and not on his own account, provided that suspension or revocation of licensure as set forth in paragraphs (1) and (2) of this subsection shall nullify the exemption as set forth in this subsection.

Laws 1974, p. 221, § 1; Laws 1982, p. 3, § 16.

Formerly Code 1933, § 79A–814.

§ 16–13–36. Public interest as to registration

(a) The State Board of Pharmacy shall register an applicant to manufacture or distribute controlled substances included in Code Sections 16–13–25 through 16–13–29 unless it determines that the issuance of that registration would be inconsistent with the public interest. In determining the public interest, the State Board of Pharmacy shall consider the following factors:

(1) Maintenance of effective controls against diversion of controlled substances into other than legitimate medical, scientific, or industrial channels;

(2) Compliance with applicable state and local law;

(3) Any convictions of the applicant under any federal or state laws relating to any controlled substance;

(4) Past experience in the manufacture or distribution of controlled substances and the existence in the applicant's establishment of effective controls against illegal diversion of controlled substances;

(5) Furnishing by the applicant of false or fraudulent material in any application filed under this article;

(6) Suspension or revocation of the applicant's federal registration to manufacture, distribute, or dispense controlled substances as authorized by federal law;

(7) Suspension or revocation of the applicant's registration or license to manufacture, distribute, or dispense controlled substances, drugs, or narcotics in this state or any other state of the United States; and

(8) Any other factors relevant to and consistent with the public health and safety.

(b) Registration under subsection (a) of this Code section does not entitle a registrant to manufacture and distribute controlled substances in Schedule I or II other than those specified in the registration.

(c) Practitioners must be registered under state law to dispense any controlled substances or to conduct research with controlled substances in Schedules II through V if they are authorized to dispense or conduct research under the law of this state. The State Board of Pharmacy need not require separate registration under this Code section for practitioners engaging in research with nonnarcotic controlled substances in Schedules II through V where the registrant is already registered under this article in another capacity. Practitioners registered under federal law to conduct research with Schedule I substances may conduct research with Schedule I substances within this state upon furnishing the State Board of Pharmacy satisfactory evidence of that federal registration. Any practitioner conducting research with Schedule I controlled substances must obtain a separate registration with the State Board of Pharmacy.

(d) Compliance by manufacturers and distributors with the provisions of federal law respecting registration (excluding fees) entitles them to be registered under this article.

Laws 1967, p. 296, § 1; Laws 1974, p. 221, § 1; Laws 1977, p. 625, § 8; Laws 1982, p. 3, § 16.

Formerly Code 1933, § 79A–815.

§ 16–13–37. Revocation and suspension of registration

(a) A registration under Code Section 16–13–36 to manufacture, distribute, or dispense a controlled substance may be suspended or revoked by the State Board of Pharmacy upon a finding that the registrant:

(1) Has furnished false or fraudulent material information in any application filed under this article;

(2) Has been convicted of a felony under any state or federal law relating to any controlled substance;

(3) Has had his federal registration to manufacture, distribute, or dispense controlled substances suspended or revoked;

(4) Has violated any provision of this article or the rules and regulations promulgated under this article; or

(5) Has failed to maintain sufficient controls against diversion of controlled substances into other than legitimate medical, scientific, or industrial channels.

(b) The State Board of Pharmacy may limit revocation or suspension of a registration to the particular controlled substance with respect to which grounds for revocation or suspension exist.

(c) If the State Board of Pharmacy suspends or revokes a registration, all controlled substances owned or possessed by the registrant at the time of suspension or the effective date of the revocation order shall be placed under seal. No disposition may be made of substances under seal until the time for taking an appeal has elapsed or until all appeals have been concluded unless a court, upon application therefor, orders the sale of perishable substances and the deposit of the proceeds of the sale with the court. Upon a revocation order becoming final, all controlled substances shall be forfeited to the state.

(d) The State Board of Pharmacy shall promptly notify the bureau of all orders suspending or revoking registration and all forfeitures of controlled substances.

Laws 1967, p. 296, § 1; Laws 1974, p. 221, § 1; Laws 1982, p. 3, § 16; Laws 1992, p. 6, § 16.

Formerly Code 1933, § 79A–816.

§ 16–13–38. Order to show cause

(a) Before denying, suspending, revoking, or limiting registration, or refusing a renewal of registration, the State Board of Pharmacy shall serve upon the applicant or registrant an order to show cause why registration should not be denied, revoked, limited, or suspended, or why the renewal should not be refused. The order to show cause shall contain a statement of the basis therefor and shall call upon the applicant or registrant to appear before the State Board of Pharmacy at a time and place not less than 30 days after the date of service of the order; but in the case of a denial of renewal of registration the show cause order shall be served not later than 30 days before the expiration of the registration. These proceedings shall be conducted in accordance with Chapter 13 of Title 50, the "Georgia Administrative Procedure Act," without regard to any criminal prosecution or other proceeding. Proceedings to refuse renewal or registration shall not abate the existing registration, which shall remain in effect pending the outcome of the administrative hearing.

(b) The State Board of Pharmacy shall suspend, without an order to show cause, any registration simultaneously with the institution of proceedings under Code Section 16–13–37 or where renewal of registration is refused if it finds that there is an imminent danger to the public health or safety which warrants this action. The suspension shall continue in effect until the conclusion of the proceedings, including judicial review thereof, unless sooner withdrawn by the State Board of Pharmacy or dissolved by a court of competent jurisdiction.

Laws 1974, p. 221, § 1; Laws 1982, p. 3, § 16.

Formerly Code 1933, § 79A–817.

§ 16–13–39. Records of registrants

Persons registered to manufacture, distribute, or dispense controlled substances under this article shall keep a complete and accurate record of all controlled substances on hand, received, manufactured, sold, dispensed, or otherwise disposed of and shall maintain such records and inventories in conformance with the record-keeping and inventory requirements of federal law and with any rules issued by the State Board of Pharmacy.

Laws 1967, p. 296, § 1; Laws 1974, p. 221, § 1; Laws 1982, p. 3, § 16.

Formerly Code 1933, § 79A–810; Code 1933, § 79A–818.

§ 16–13–40. Order forms to distribute Schedule I and II substances

Controlled substances in Schedules I and II shall be distributed by a registrant to another registrant only pursuant to an order form. Compliance with federal law respecting order forms shall be deemed compliance with this Code section.

Laws 1974, p. 221, § 1.

Formerly Code 1933, § 79A–819.

§ 16–13–41. Prescriptions

(a) Except when dispensed directly by a registered practitioner, other than a pharmacy or pharmacist, to an ultimate user, no controlled substance in Schedule II may be dispensed without the written prescription of a registered practitioner.

(b) When a practitioner writes a prescription drug order to cause the dispensing of a Schedule II substance, he or she shall include the name and address of the person for whom it is prescribed, the kind and quantity of such Schedule II controlled substance, the directions for taking, the signature, and the name, address, telephone number, and DEA registration number of the prescribing practitioner. Such prescription shall be signed and dated by the practitioner on the date when issued, and the nature of such signature shall be defined in regulations promulgated by the State Board of Pharmacy. Prescription drug orders for Schedule II controlled substances may be transmitted via facsimile machine or other electronic means only in accordance with regulations promulgated by the State Board of Pharmacy in accordance with Code Section 26–4–80 or 26–4–80.1, or in accordance with DEA regulations at 21 C.F.R. 1306.

(c) In emergency situations, as defined by rule of the State Board of Pharmacy, Schedule II drugs may be dispensed upon oral prescription of a registered practitioner, reduced promptly to writing and filed by the pharmacy. Prescriptions shall be retained in conformity with the requirements of Code Section 16–13–39. No prescription for a Schedule II substance may be refilled.

(d)(1) Except when dispensed directly by a practitioner, other than a pharmacy or pharmacist, to an ultimate user, a controlled substance included in Schedule III, IV, or V, which is a prescription drug as determined under any law of this state or the Federal Food, Drug and Cosmetic Act, 21 U.S.C. Section 301, 52 Stat. 1040 (1938), shall not be dispensed without a written or oral prescription of a registered practitioner. The prescription shall not be filled or refilled more than six months after the date on which such prescription was issued or be refilled more than five times.

(2) When a practitioner writes a prescription drug order to cause the dispensing of a Schedule III, IV, or V controlled substance, he or she shall include the name and address of the person for whom it is prescribed, the kind and quantity of such controlled substance, the directions for taking, the signature, and the name, address, telephone number, and DEA registration number of the practitioner. Such prescription shall be signed and dated by the practitioner on the date when issued or may be issued orally, and the nature of the signature of the prescriber shall meet the guidelines set forth in Chapter 4 of Title 26, the regulations promulgated by the State Board of Pharmacy, or both such guidelines and regulations.

(e) A controlled substance included in Schedule V shall not be distributed or dispensed other than for a legitimate medical purpose.

(f) No person shall prescribe or order the dispensing of a controlled substance, except a registered practitioner who is:

(1) Licensed or otherwise authorized by this state to prescribe controlled substances;

(2) Acting in the usual course of his professional practice; and

(3) Prescribing or ordering such controlled substances for a legitimate medical purpose.

(g) No person shall fill or dispense a prescription for a controlled substance except a person who is licensed by this state as a pharmacist or a pharmacy intern acting under the immediate and direct personal supervision of a licensed pharmacist in a pharmacy licensed by the State Board of Pharmacy, provided that this subsection shall not prohibit a registered physician, dentist, veterinarian, or podiatrist authorized by this state to dispense controlled substances as provided in this article if such registered person complies with all record-keeping, labeling, packaging, and storage requirements regarding such controlled substances and imposed upon pharmacists and pharmacies in this chapter and in Chapter 4 of Title 26 and complies with the requirements of Code Section 26–4–130.

(h) It shall be unlawful for any practitioner to issue any prescription document signed in blank. The issuance of such document signed in blank shall be prima-facie evidence of a conspiracy to violate this article. The possession of a prescription document signed in blank by a person other than the person whose signature appears thereon shall be prima-facie evidence of a conspiracy between the possessor and the signer to violate the provisions of this article.

Laws 1974, p. 221, § 1; Laws 1979, p. 859, § 10; Laws 1982, p. 3, § 16; Laws 1983, p. 349, § 2; Laws 1985, p. 149, § 16; Laws 1985, p. 1219, § 5; Laws 1986, p. 1031, § 1; Laws 1999, p. 81, § 16; Laws 2003, Act 80, § 7, eff. May 29, 2003; Laws 2007, Act 18, § 16, eff. May 11, 2007.

Formerly Code 1933, § 79A–820.

Historical and Statutory Notes

The 2003 amendment by Act 80, in subsec. (b), deleted "registered" preceding "practitioner", inserted "drug order", "or she", and "telephone number,", and substituted "DEA registration" for "federal registration" in the first sentence, and deleted "prescribing" preceding "practitioner" and inserted ", and the nature of such signatures shall be defined in regulations promulgated by the State Board of Pharmacy" in the second sentence; and, in subsec. (d), deleted "registered" preceding "practitioner", inserted "drug order", "or she", and "telephone number,", substituted "DEA registration" for "federal registration", and deleted "prescribing" preceding "practitioner" in the first sentence, and rewrote the second sentence which had read: "Such prescriptions shall be signed and dated by the prescribing practitioner on the date when issued."

The 2007 amendment by Act 18 was a provision contained in a correction bill.

§ 16–13–42. Unlawful distribution; failure to keep records or to permit inspection; keeping building or vehicle used by violators

(a) It is unlawful for any person:

(1) Who is subject to the requirements of Code Section 16–13–35 to distribute or dispense a controlled substance in violation of Code Section 16–13–41;

(2) Who is a registrant to manufacture a controlled substance not authorized by his registration or to distribute or dispense a controlled substance not authorized by his registration to another registrant or other authorized person;

(3) To refuse or fail to make, keep, or furnish any record, notification, order form, statement, invoice, or information required under this article;

(4) To refuse an entry into any premises for any inspection authorized by this article; or

(5) Knowingly to keep or maintain any store, shop, warehouse, dwelling, building, vehicle, boat, aircraft, or other structure or place which is resorted to by persons using controlled substances in violation of this article for the purpose of using these substances, or which is used for keeping or selling them in violation of this article.

(b) Any person who violates this Code section is guilty of a felony and, upon conviction thereof, may be imprisoned for not more than five years, fined not more than $25,000.00, or both.

Laws 1974, p. 221, § 1; Laws 1978, p. 1668, § 10.

Formerly Code 1933, § 79A–821.

§ 16–13–43. Distribution without order form; fictitious registration; fraudulently obtaining controlled substance; false reports

(a) It is unlawful for any person:

(1) Who is a registrant to distribute a controlled substance classified in Schedule I or II, except pursuant to an order form as required by Code Section 16–13–40;

(2) To use, in the course of the manufacture or distribution of a controlled substance, a registration number which is fictitious, revoked, suspended, or issued to another person;

(3) To acquire or obtain possession of a controlled substance by misrepresentation, fraud, forgery, deception, subterfuge, or theft;

(4) To furnish false or fraudulent material information in, or omit any material information from, any application, report, or other document or record required to be kept or filed under this article;

(5) To make, distribute, or possess any punch, die, plate, stone, or other thing designed to print, imprint, or reproduce the trademark, trade name, or other identifying mark, imprint, or device of another or any likeness of any of the foregoing, upon any drug or container or labeling thereof so as to render the drug a counterfeit substance; or

(6) To withhold information from a practitioner that such person has obtained a controlled substance of a similar therapeutic use in a concurrent time period from another practitioner.

(b) Any person who violates this Code section is guilty of a felony and, upon conviction thereof, may be imprisoned for not more than eight years or fined not more than $50,000.00, or both.

Laws 1967, p. 296, § 1; Laws 1974, p. 221, § 1; Laws 1978, p. 1668, § 11; Laws 1985, p. 1219, § 6; Laws 1987, p. 261, § 6.

Formerly Code 1933, § 79A–819; Code 1933, § 79A–822.

§ 16–13–44. Penalties under other laws

Any penalty imposed for violation of this article is in addition to, and not in lieu of, any civil or administrative penalty or sanction otherwise authorized by law.

Laws 1974, p. 221, § 1.

Formerly Code 1933, § 79A–823.

§ 16–13–45. Powers of enforcement personnel

Any officer or employee of the State Board of Pharmacy designated by the director of the Georgia Drugs and Narcotics Agency may:

(1) Carry firearms in the performance of his official duties;

(2) Execute and serve search warrants, arrest warrants, administrative inspection warrants, subpoenas, and summonses issued under the authority of this state;

(3) Make arrests without warrant for any offense under this article committed in his presence or if he has probable cause to believe that the person to be arrested has committed or is committing a violation of this article which may constitute a felony;

(4) Make seizures of property pursuant to this article; or

(5) Perform other law enforcement duties as the State Board of Pharmacy or the director of the Georgia Drugs and Narcotics Agency designates.

Laws 1974, p. 221, § 1; Laws 1982, p. 3, § 16.

Formerly Code 1933, § 79A–824.

§ 16–13–46. Administrative inspections and warrants

(a) Issuance and execution of inspection warrants shall be as follows:

(1) A judge of the superior, state, city, or magistrate court, or any municipal officer clothed by law with the powers of a magistrate, upon proper oath or affirmation showing probable cause, may issue warrants for the purpose of conducting inspections authorized by this article, or rules promulgated under this article, and seizures of property appropriate to the inspections. For the purpose of the issuance of inspection warrants, probable cause exists upon showing a valid public interest in the effective enforcement of this article, or rules promulgated under this article, sufficient to justify inspection of the area, premises, building, or conveyance in the circumstances specified in the application for the warrant;

(2) A warrant shall issue only upon an affidavit of a designated officer, drug agent, or employee of the State Board of Pharmacy having knowledge of the facts alleged, sworn to before the judicial officer and establishing the grounds for issuing the warrant. If the judicial officer is satisfied that

grounds for the application exist or that there is probable cause to believe they exist, he shall issue a warrant identifying the area, premises, building, registrant, or conveyance to be inspected, the purpose of the inspection, and, if appropriate, the type of property to be inspected, if any. The warrant shall:

(A) State the grounds for its issuance and the name of each person whose affidavit has been taken in support thereof;

(B) Be directed to persons authorized by Code Section 16–13–45 to execute it;

(C) Command the persons to whom it is directed to inspect the area, premises, building, registrant, or conveyance identified for the purpose specified and, if appropriate, direct the seizure of the property specified;

(D) Identify the item or types of property to be seized, if any; and

(E) Designate the judicial officer to whom it shall be returned;

(3) A warrant issued pursuant to this Code section must be executed and returned within ten days of its date unless, upon a showing of a need for additional time, the court orders otherwise. If property is seized pursuant to a warrant, a copy shall be provided upon request to the person from whom or from whose premises the property is taken, together with a receipt for the property taken. The return of the warrant shall be made promptly, accompanied by a written inventory of any property taken. A copy of the inventory shall be delivered upon request to the person from whom or from whose premises the property was taken and to the applicant for the warrant;

(4) The judicial officer who has issued a warrant shall attach thereto a copy of the return and all papers returnable in connection therewith and file them with the clerk of the superior court for the county in which the inspection was made.

(b) The State Board of Pharmacy, the director of the Georgia Drugs and Narcotics Agency or drug agents may make inspections of controlled premises in accordance with the following provisions:

(1) For purposes of this Code section only, "controlled premises" means:

(A) Places where persons registered or exempted from registration requirements under this article are required to keep records; and

(B) Places, including factories, warehouses, establishments, and conveyances, in which persons registered or exempted from registration requirements under this article are permitted to hold, manufacture, compound, process, sell, deliver, or otherwise dispose of any controlled substance;

(2) When authorized by an inspection warrant issued pursuant to subsection (a) of this Code section, an officer or employee designated by the State Board of Pharmacy or the director of the Georgia Drugs and Narcotics Agency, upon presenting the warrant and appropriate credentials to the owner, operator, or agent in charge, may enter controlled premises for the purpose of conducting an inspection;

(3) When authorized by an inspection warrant, an officer or employee designated by the State Board of Pharmacy or the director of the Georgia Drugs and Narcotics Agency may:

(A) Inspect and copy records required by this article to be kept;

(B) Inspect, within reasonable limits and in a reasonable manner, controlled premises and all pertinent equipment, finished and unfinished material, containers, and labeling found therein, and, except as provided in paragraph (5) of subsection (b) of this Code section, all other things therein, including records, files, papers, processes, controls, and facilities bearing on violation of this article; and

(C) Inventory any stock of any controlled substance therein and obtain samples thereof;

(4) This Code section does not prevent the inspection without a warrant of books and records pursuant to an administrative inspection in accordance with subsection (c) of this Code section, nor does it prevent entries and inspections, including seizures of property, without a warrant:

(A) If the owner, operator, or agent in charge of the controlled premises consents;

(B) In situations presenting imminent danger to health or safety;

(C) In situations involving inspection of conveyance if there is reasonable cause to believe that the mobility of the conveyance makes it impracticable to obtain a warrant;

(D) In any other exceptional or emergency circumstance where time or opportunity to apply for a warrant is lacking; or

(E) In all other situations in which a warrant is not constitutionally required;

(5) An inspection authorized by this Code section shall not extend to financial data, sales data other than shipment data, or pricing data unless the owner, operator, or agent in charge of the controlled premises consents in writing.

(c) The State Board of Pharmacy, its members, or duly authorized agents or drug agents shall have the power to inspect, without a warrant, in a lawful manner at all reasonable hours, any pharmacy or other place licensed by the State Board of Pharmacy pursuant to Chapter 4 of Title 26 for the purpose:

(1) Of determining if any of the provisions of this article or any rule or regulation promulgated under its authority is being violated;

(2) Of securing samples or specimens of any drug or medical supplies, after first paying or offering to pay for such samples or specimens; and

(3) Of securing other such evidence as may be needed for an administrative proceedings action, as provided by this article.

Laws 1974, p. 221, § 1; Laws 1982, p. 3, § 16; Laws 1983, p. 884, § 3–16; Laws 1992, p. 6, § 16; Laws 1999, p. 81, § 16.

Formerly Code 1933, § 79A–825.

§ 16–13–47. Injunctions

(a) The superior courts of this state may exercise jurisdiction to restrain or enjoin violations of this article.

(b) The defendant may demand a trial by jury for an alleged violation of an injunction or restraining order under this Code section.

Laws 1974, p. 221, § 1.

Formerly Code 1933, § 79A–826.

§ 16–13–48. Cooperative arrangements

(a) The State Board of Pharmacy shall cooperate with federal and other state agencies in discharging its responsibilities concerning traffic in controlled substances and in suppressing the abuse of controlled substances. To this end, it may:

(1) Arrange for the exchange of information among governmental officials concerning the use and abuse of controlled substances;

(2) Coordinate and cooperate in training programs concerning controlled substance law enforcement at local and state levels;

(3) Cooperate with the bureau by establishing a centralized unit to accept, catalogue, file, and collect statistics, including records, other than medical treatment records, of drug dependent persons and other controlled substance law offenders

within the state, and make the information available for federal, state, and local law enforcement purposes; and

(4) Conduct or promote programs of eradication aimed at destroying wild or illicit growth of plant species from which controlled substances may be extracted.

(b) Results, information, and evidence received from the bureau relating to the regulatory functions of this article, including results of inspections conducted by it, may be relied and acted upon by the State Board of Pharmacy or drug agents in the exercise of its or their regulatory functions under this article.

Laws 1967, p. 296, § 1; Laws 1974, p. 221, § 1; Laws 1982, p. 3, § 16.

Formerly Code 1933, § 79A–827.

§ 16–13–48.1. Utilization of money, property or proceeds therefrom seized or forfeited by federal law and transferred to state or local law enforcement agency

Money or property seized or forfeited pursuant to federal law regarding controlled substances, marijuana, or dangerous drugs, which money, property, or proceeds therefrom are authorized by that federal law to be transferred to a cooperating law enforcement agency of this state or any political subdivision thereof, shall be utilized by the law enforcement agency or political subdivision to which the money, property, or proceeds are so transferred as provided by such federal law and regulations thereunder. Unless otherwise required by federal law or regulation, such funds shall be received and utilized as provided by Georgia law.

Laws 1987, p. 840, § 1.

§ 16–13–49. Forfeitures

(a) As used in this Code section, the term:

(1) "Controlled substance" shall have the same meaning as provided in paragraph (4) of Code Section 16–13–21 and shall also include marijuana as such term is defined in paragraph (16) of Code Section 16–13–21, notwithstanding any other provisions of this article.

(2) "Costs" means, but is not limited to:

(A) All expenses associated with the seizure, towing, storage, maintenance, custody, preservation, operation, or sale of the property; and

(B) Satisfaction of any security interest or lien not subject to forfeiture under this Code section.

(3) "Court costs" means, but is not limited to:

(A) All court costs, including the costs of advertisement, transcripts, and court reporter fees; and

(B) Payment of receivers, conservators, appraisers, accountants, or trustees appointed by the court pursuant to this Code section.

(4) "Enterprise" means any person, sole proprietorship, partnership, corporation, trust, association, or other legal entity created under the laws of this state, of the United States or any of the several states of the United States, or of any foreign nation or a group of individuals associated in fact although not a legal entity and includes illicit as well as licit enterprises and governmental as well as other entities.

(5) "Governmental agency" means any department, office, council, commission, committee, authority, board, bureau, or division of the executive, judicial, or legislative branch of a state, the United States, or any political subdivision thereof.

(6) "Interest holder" means a secured party within the meaning of Code Section 11–9–102 or the beneficiary of a perfected encumbrance pertaining to an interest in property.

(7) "Owner" means a person, other than an interest holder, who has an interest in property and is in compliance with any statute requiring its recordation or reflection in public records in order to perfect the interest against a bona fide purchaser for value.

(8) "Proceeds" means property derived directly or indirectly from, maintained by, or realized through an act or omission and includes any benefit, interest, or property of any kind without reduction for expenses incurred for acquisition, maintenance, or any other purpose.

(9) "Property" means anything of value and includes any interest in anything of value, including real property and any fixtures thereon, and tangible and intangible personal property, including but not limited to currency, instruments, securities, or any other kind of privilege, interest, claim, or right.

(10) "United States" includes its territories, possessions, and dominions and the District of Columbia.

(b)(1) An action filed pursuant to this Code section shall be filed in the name of the State of Georgia and may be brought:

(A) In the case of an in rem action, by the district attorney for the judicial circuit where the property is located;

(B) In the case of an in personam action, by the district attorney for the judicial circuit in which the defendant resides; or

(C) By the district attorney having jurisdiction over any offense which arose out of the same conduct which made the property subject to forfeiture.

Such district attorney may bring an action pursuant to this Code section in any superior court of this state.

(2) If more than one district attorney has jurisdiction to file an action pursuant to this Code section, the district attorney having primary jurisdiction over a violation of this article shall, in the event of a conflict, have priority over any other district attorney.

(3) Any action brought pursuant to this Code section may be compromised or settled in the same manner as other civil actions.

(c) An action for forfeiture brought pursuant to this Code section shall be tried:

(1) If the action is in rem against real property, in the county where the property is located, except where a single tract is divided by a county line, in which case the superior court of either county shall have jurisdiction;

(2) If the action is in rem against tangible or intangible personal property, in any county where the property is located or will be during the pendency of the action; or

(3) If the action is in personam, as provided by law.

(d) The following are declared to be contraband and no person shall have a property right in them:

(1) All controlled substances, raw materials, or controlled substance analogs that have been manufactured, distributed, dispensed, possessed, or acquired in violation of this article;

(2) All property which is, directly or indirectly, used or intended for use in any manner to facilitate a violation of this article or any proceeds derived or realized therefrom;

(3) All property located in this state which was, directly or indirectly, used or intended for use in any manner to facilitate a violation of this article or of the laws of the United States or any of the several states relating to controlled substances which is punishable by imprisonment for more than one year or any proceeds derived or realized therefrom;

(4) All weapons possessed, used, or available for use in any manner to facilitate a violation of this article or any of the laws of the United States or any of the several states relating to controlled substances which is punishable by imprisonment for more than one year;

(5) Any interest, security, claim, or property or contractual right of any kind affording a source of influence over any enterprise that a person has established, operated, controlled, conducted, or participated in the conduct of in violation of this article or any of the laws of the United States or any of the several states relating to controlled substances which is punishable by imprisonment for more than one year or any proceeds derived or realized therefrom; and

(6) All moneys, negotiable instruments, securities, or other things of value which are found in close proximity to any controlled substance or marijuana or other property which is subject to forfeiture under this subsection.

(e)(1) A property interest shall not be subject to forfeiture under this Code section if the owner of such interest or interest holder establishes that the owner or interest holder:

(A) Is not legally accountable for the conduct giving rise to its forfeiture, did not consent to it, and did not know and could not reasonably have known of the conduct or that it was likely to occur;

(B) Had not acquired and did not stand to acquire substantial proceeds from the conduct giving rise to its forfeiture other than as an interest holder in an arm's length commercial transaction;

(C) With respect to conveyances for transportation only, did not hold the property jointly, in common, or in community with a person whose conduct gave rise to its forfeiture;

(D) Does not hold the property for the benefit of or as nominee for any person whose conduct gave rise to its forfeiture, and, if the owner or interest holder acquired the interest through any such person, the owner or interest holder acquired it as a bona fide purchaser for value without knowingly taking part in an illegal transaction; and

(E) Acquired the interest:

(i) Before the completion of the conduct giving rise to its forfeiture, and the person whose conduct gave rise to its forfeiture did not have the authority to convey the interest to a bona fide purchaser for value at the time of the conduct; or

(ii) After the completion of the conduct giving rise to its forfeiture:

(I) As a bona fide purchaser for value without knowingly taking part in an illegal transaction;

(II) Before the filing of a lien on it and before the effective date of a notice of pending forfeiture relating to it and without notice of its seizure for forfeiture under this article; and

(III) At the time the interest was acquired, was reasonably without cause to believe that the property was subject to forfeiture or likely to become subject to forfeiture under this article.

(2) A property interest shall not be subject to forfeiture under this Code section for a violation involving only one gram or less of a mixture containing cocaine or four ounces or less of marijuana unless said property was used to facilitate a transaction in or a purchase of or sale of a controlled substance or marijuana.

(f) A rented or leased vehicle shall not be subject to forfeiture unless it is established in forfeiture proceedings that the owner of the rented or leased vehicle is legally accountable for the conduct which would otherwise subject the vehicle to forfeiture, consented to the conduct, or knew or reasonably should have known of the conduct or that it was likely to occur. Upon learning of the address or phone number of the company which owns any rented or leased vehicle which is present at the scene of an arrest or other action taken pursuant to this Code section, the duly authorized authorities shall immediately contact the company to inform it that the vehicle is available for the company to take possession.

(g)(1) Property which is subject to forfeiture under this Code section may be seized by the director of the Georgia Drugs and Narcotics Agency or any duly authorized agent or drug agent of this state or by any law enforcement officer of this state or of any political subdivision thereof who has power to make arrests or execute process or a search warrant issued by any court having jurisdiction over the property. A search warrant authorizing seizure of property which is subject to forfeiture pursuant to this Code section may be issued on an affidavit demonstrating that probable cause exists for its forfeiture or that the property has been the subject of a previous final judgment of forfeiture in the courts of this state, any other state, or the United States. The court may order that the property be seized on such terms and conditions as are reasonable.

(2) Property which is subject to forfeiture under this Code section may be seized without process if there is probable cause to believe that the property is subject to forfeiture under this article or the seizure is incident to an arrest or search pursuant to a search warrant or to an inspection under an inspection warrant.

(3) The court's jurisdiction over forfeiture proceedings is not affected by a seizure in violation of the Constitution of Georgia or the United States Constitution made with process or in a good faith belief of probable cause.

(h)(1) When property is seized pursuant to this article, the sheriff, drug agent, or law enforcement officer seizing the same shall report the fact of seizure, in writing, within 20 days thereof to the district attorney of the judicial circuit having jurisdiction in the county where the seizure was made.

(2) Within 60 days from the date of seizure, a complaint for forfeiture shall be initiated as provided for in subsection (n), (*o*), or (p) of this Code section.

(3) If the state fails to initiate forfeiture proceedings against property seized for forfeiture by notice of pending forfeiture within the time limits specified in paragraphs (1) and (2) of this subsection, the property must be released on the request of an owner or interest holder, pending further proceedings pursuant to this Code section, unless the property is being held as evidence.

(i)(1) Seizure of property by a law enforcement officer constitutes notice of such seizure to any person who was present at the time of seizure who may assert an interest in the property.

(2) When property is seized pursuant to this article, the district attorney or the sheriff, drug agent, or law enforcement officer seizing the same shall give notice of the seizure to any owner or interest holder who is not present at the time of seizure by personal service, publication, or the mailing of written notice:

(A) If the owner's or interest holder's name and current address are known, by either personal service or mailing a copy of the notice by certified mail or statutory overnight delivery to that address;

(B) If the owner's or interest holder's name and address are required by law to be on record with a government agency to perfect an interest in the property but the owner's or interest holder's current address is not known, by mailing a copy of the notice by certified mail or statutory overnight delivery, return receipt requested, to any address on the record; or

(C) If the owner's or interest holder's address is not known and is not on record as provided in subparagraph (B) of this paragraph or the owner's or interest holder's interest is not known, by publication in two consecutive issues of a newspaper of general circulation in the county in which the seizure occurs.

(3) Notice of seizure must include a description of the property, the date and place of seizure, the conduct giving rise to forfeiture, and the violation of law alleged.

(j) A district attorney may file, without a filing fee, a lien for forfeiture of property upon the initiation of any civil or criminal proceeding under this article or upon seizure for forfeiture. The filing constitutes notice to any person claiming an interest in the property owned by the named person. The filing shall include the following:

(1) The lien notice must set forth:

(A) The name of the person and, in the discretion of the state, any alias and any corporations, partnerships, trusts, or other entities, including nominees, that are either owned entirely or in part or controlled by the person; and

(B) The description of the property, the criminal or civil proceeding that has been brought under this article, the amount claimed by the state, the name of the court where the proceeding or action has been brought, and the case number of the proceeding or action if known at the time of filing;

(2) A lien under this subsection applies to the described property and to one named person and to any aliases, fictitious names, or other names, including names of corporations, partnerships, trusts, or other entities, that are either owned entirely or in part or controlled by the named person and any interest in real property owned or controlled by the named person. A separate lien for forfeiture of property must be filed for any other person;

(3) The lien creates, upon filing, a lien in favor of the state as it relates to the seized property or to the named person or related entities with respect to said property. The lien secures the amount of potential liability for civil judgment and, if applicable, the fair market value of seized property relating to all proceedings under this article enforcing the lien. The forfeiture lien referred to in this subsection must be filed in accordance with the provisions of the laws in this state pertaining to the type of property that is subject to the lien. The state may amend or release, in whole or in part, a lien filed under this subsection at any time by filing, without a filing fee, an amended lien in accordance with this subsection which identifies the lien amended. The state, as soon as practical after filing a lien, shall furnish to any person named in the lien a notice of the filing of the lien. Failure to furnish notice under this subsection does not invalidate or otherwise affect a lien filed in accordance with this subsection;

(4) Upon entry of judgment in favor of the state, the state may proceed to execute on the lien as in the case of any other judgment;

(5) A trustee, constructive or otherwise, who has notice that a lien for forfeiture of property, a notice of pending forfeiture, or a civil forfeiture proceeding has been filed against the property or against any person or entity for whom the person holds title or appears as the owner of record shall furnish, within ten days, to the district attorney or his designee the following information:

(A) The name and address of the person or entity for whom the property is held;

(B) The names and addresses of all beneficiaries for whose benefit legal title to the seized property, or property of the named person or related entity, is held; and

(C) A copy of the applicable trust agreement or other instrument, if any, under which the trustee or other person holds legal title or appears as the owner of record of the property; and

(6) A trustee, constructive or otherwise, who fails to comply with this subsection shall be guilty of a misdemeanor.

(k) Property taken or detained under this Code section is not subject to replevin, conveyance, sequestration, or attachment. The seizing law enforcement agency or the district attorney may authorize the release of the property if the forfeiture or retention is unnecessary or may transfer the action to another agency or district attorney by discontinuing forfeiture proceedings in favor of forfeiture proceedings initiated by the other law enforcement agency or district attorney. An action under this Code section may be consolidated with any other action or proceeding under this article relating to the same property on motion by an interest holder and must be so consolidated on motion by the district attorney in either proceeding or action. The property is deemed to be in the custody of the State of Georgia subject only to the orders and decrees of the superior court having jurisdiction over the forfeiture proceedings.

(*l*)(1) If property is seized under this article, the district attorney may:

(A) Remove the property to a place designated by the superior court having jurisdiction over the forfeiture proceeding;

(B) Place the property under constructive seizure by posting notice of pending forfeiture, by giving notice of pending forfeiture to its owners and interest holders, or by filing notice of seizure in any appropriate public record relating to the property;

(C) Remove the property to a storage area, within the jurisdiction of the court, for safekeeping or, if the property is a negotiable instrument or money and is not needed for evidentiary purposes, the district attorney may authorize its being deposited in an interest-bearing account in a financial institution in this state. Any accrued interest shall follow the principal in any judgment with respect thereto;

(D) Provide for another governmental agency, a receiver appointed by the court pursuant to Chapter 8 of Title 9, an owner, or an interest holder to take custody of the property and remove it to an appropriate location within the county where the property was seized; or

(E) Require the sheriff or chief of police of the political subdivision where the property was seized to take custody of the property and remove it to an appropriate location for disposition in accordance with law.

(2) If any property which has been attached or seized pursuant to this Code section is perishable or is liable to perish, waste, or be greatly reduced in value by keeping or if the expense of keeping the same is excessive or disproportionate to the value thereof, the court, upon motion of the state, a claimant, or the custodian, may order the property or any portion thereof to be sold upon such terms and conditions as may be prescribed by the court; and the proceeds shall be paid into the registry of the court pending final disposition of the action.

(m) As soon as possible, but not more than 30 days after the seizure of property, the seizing law enforcement agency shall conduct an inventory and estimate the value of the property seized.

(n) If the estimated value of personal property seized is $ 25,000.00 or less, the district attorney may elect to proceed under the provisions of this subsection in the following manner:

(1) Notice of the seizure of such property shall be posted in a prominent location in the courthouse of the county in which the property was seized. Such notice shall include a description of the property, the date and place of seizure, the conduct giving rise to forfeiture, a statement that the owner of such property has 30 days within which a claim must be filed, and the violation of law alleged;

(2) A copy of the notice, which shall include a statement that the owner of such property has 30 days within which a claim must be filed, shall be served upon an owner, interest holder, or person in possession of the property at the time of seizure as provided in subsection (i) of this Code section and shall be published for at least three successive weeks in a newspaper of general circulation in the county where the seizure was made;

(3) The owner or interest holder may file a claim within 30 days after the second publication of the notice of forfeiture by sending the claim to the seizing law enforcement agency and to the district attorney by certified mail or statutory overnight delivery, return receipt requested;

(4) The claim must be signed by the owner or interest holder under penalty of perjury and must set forth:

(A) The caption of the proceedings as set forth on the notice of pending forfeiture and the name of the claimant;

(B) The address at which the claimant will accept mail;

(C) The nature and extent of the claimant's interest in the property;

(D) The date, identity of the transferor, and circumstances of the claimant's acquisition of the interest in the property;

(E) The specific provision of this Code section relied on in asserting that the property is not subject to forfeiture;

(F) All essential facts supporting each assertion; and

(G) The precise relief sought;

(5) If a claim is filed, the district attorney shall file a complaint for forfeiture as provided in subsection (*o*) or (p) of this Code section within 30 days of the actual receipt of the claim. A person who files a claim shall be joined as a party; and

(6) If no claim is filed within 30 days after the second publication of the notice of forfeiture, all right, title, and interest in the property is forfeited to the state and the district attorney shall dispose of the property as provided in subsection (u) of this Code section.

(*o*) In rem proceedings.

(1) In actions in rem, the property which is the subject of the action shall be named as the defendant. The complaint shall be verified on oath or affirmation by a duly authorized agent of the state in a manner required by the laws of this state. Such complaint shall describe the property with reasonable particularity; state that it is located within the county or will be located within the county during the pendency of the action; state its present custodian; state the name of the owner or interest holder, if known; allege the essential elements of the violation which is claimed to exist; state the place of seizure, if the property was seized; and conclude with a prayer of due process to enforce the forfeiture.

(2) A copy of the complaint and summons shall be served on any person known to be an owner or interest holder and any person who is in possession of the property.

(A) Service of the complaint and summons shall be as provided in subsections (a), (b), (c), and (e) of Code Section 9–11–4.

(B) If real property is the subject of the action or the owner or interest holder is unknown or resides out of the state or departs the state or cannot after due diligence be found within the state or conceals himself so as to avoid service, notice of the proceeding shall be published once a week for two successive weeks in the newspaper in which the sheriff's advertisements are published. Such publication shall be deemed notice to any and all persons having an interest in or right affected by such proceeding and from any sale of the property resulting therefrom, but shall not constitute notice to an interest holder unless that person is unknown or resides out of the state or departs the state or cannot after due diligence be found within the state or conceals himself to avoid service.

(C) If tangible property which has not been seized is the subject of the action, the court may order the sheriff or another law enforcement officer to take possession of the property. If the character or situation of the property is such that the taking of actual possession is impracticable, the sheriff shall execute process by affixing a copy of the complaint and summons to the property in a conspicuous place and by leaving another copy of the complaint and summons with the person having possession or his agent. In cases involving a vessel or aircraft, the sheriff or other law enforcement officer is authorized to make a written request with the appropriate governmental agency not to permit the departure of such vessel or aircraft until notified by the sheriff or his deputy that the vessel or aircraft has been released.

(3) An owner of or interest holder in the property may file an answer asserting a claim against the property in the action in rem. Any such answer shall be filed within 30 days after the service of the summons and complaint. Where service is made by publication and personal service has not been made, an owner or interest holder shall file an answer within 30 days of the date of final publication. An answer must be verified by the owner or interest holder under penalty of perjury. In addition to complying with the general rules applicable to an answer in civil actions, the answer must set forth:

(A) The caption of the proceedings as set forth in the complaint and the name of the claimant;

(B) The address at which the claimant will accept mail;

(C) The nature and extent of the claimant's interest in the property;

(D) The date, identity of transferor, and circumstances of the claimant's acquisition of the interest in the property;

(E) The specific provision of this Code section relied on in asserting that the property is not subject to forfeiture;

(F) All essential facts supporting each assertion; and

(G) The precise relief sought.

(4) If at the expiration of the period set forth in paragraph (3) of this subsection no answer has been filed, the court shall order the disposition of the seized property as provided for in this Code section.

(5) If an answer is filed, a hearing must be held within 60 days after service of the complaint unless continued for good cause and must be held by the court without a jury.

(6) An action in rem may be brought by the state in addition to or in lieu of any other in rem or in personam action brought pursuant to this title.

(p) In personam proceedings.

(1) The complaint shall be verified on oath or affirmation by a duly authorized agent of the state in a manner required by the laws of this state. It shall describe with reasonable particularity the property which is sought to be forfeited; state its present custodian; state the name of the owner or interest holder, if known; allege the essential elements of the violation which is claimed to exist; state the place of seizure, if the property was seized; and conclude with a prayer of due process to enforce the forfeiture.

(2) Service of the complaint and summons shall be as follows:

(A) Except as otherwise provided in this subsection, service of the complaint and summons shall be as provided by subsections (a), (b), (c), and (d) of Code Section 9–11–4; and

(B) If the defendant is unknown or resides out of the state or departs the state or cannot after due diligence be found within the state or conceals himself so as to avoid service, notice of the proceedings shall be published once a week for two successive weeks in the newspaper in which the sheriff's advertisements are published. Such publication shall be deemed sufficient notice to any such defendant.

(3) A defendant shall file a verified answer within 30 days after the service of the summons and complaint. Where service is made by publication and personal service has not been made, a defendant shall file such answer within 30 days of the date of final publication. In addition to complying with the general rules applicable to an answer in civil actions, the answer must contain all of the elements set forth in paragraph (3) of subsection (*o*) of this Code section.

(4) Any interest holder or person in possession of the property may join any action brought pursuant to this subsection as provided by Chapter 11 of Title 9, known as the "Georgia Civil Practice Act."

(5) If at the expiration of the period set forth in paragraph (3) of this subsection no answer has been filed, the court shall order the disposition of the seized property as provided for in this Code section.

(6) If an answer is filed, a hearing must be held within 60 days after service of the complaint unless continued for good cause and must be held by the court without a jury.

(7) On a determination of liability of a person for conduct giving rise to forfeiture under this Code section, the court must enter a judgment of forfeiture of the property described in the complaint and must also authorize the district attorney or his agent or any law enforcement officer or peace officer to seize all property ordered to be forfeited which was not previously seized or was not then under seizure. Following the entry of an order declaring the property forfeited, the court, on application of the state, may enter any appropriate order to protect the interest of the state in the property ordered to be forfeited.

(8) Except as provided in this subsection, no person claiming an interest in property subject to forfeiture under this Code section may intervene in a trial or appeal of a criminal action or in an in personam civil action involving the forfeiture of the property.

(q) In conjunction with any civil or criminal action brought pursuant to this article:

(1) The court, on application of the district attorney, may enter any restraining order or injunction; require the execution of satisfactory performance bonds; appoint receivers, conservators, appraisers, accountants, or trustees; or take any action to seize, secure, maintain, or preserve the availability of property subject to forfeiture under this article, including issuing a warrant for its seizure and writ of attachment, whether before or after the filing of a complaint for forfeiture;

(2) A temporary restraining order under this Code section may be entered on application of the district attorney, without notice or an opportunity for a hearing, if the district attorney demonstrates that:

(A) There is probable cause to believe that the property with respect to which the order is sought, in the event of final judgment or conviction, would be subject to forfeiture under this title; and

(B) Provision of notice would jeopardize the availability of the property for forfeiture;

(3) Notice of the entry of a restraining order and an opportunity for a hearing must be afforded to persons known to have an interest in the property. The hearing must be held at the earliest possible date consistent with the date set in subsection (b) of Code Section 9-11-65 and is limited to the issues of whether:

(A) There is a probability that the state will prevail on the issue of forfeiture and that failure to enter the order will result in the property's being destroyed, conveyed, encumbered, removed from the jurisdiction of the court, concealed, or otherwise made unavailable for forfeiture; and

(B) The need to preserve the availability of property through the entry of the requested order outweighs the hardship on any owner or interest holder against whom the order is to be entered;

(4) If property is seized for forfeiture or a forfeiture lien is filed without a previous judicial determination of probable cause or order of forfeiture or a hearing under paragraph (2) of this subsection, the court, on an application filed by an owner of or interest holder in the property within 30 days after notice of its seizure or lien or actual knowledge of such seizure or lien, whichever is earlier, and complying with the requirements for an answer to an in rem complaint, and after five days' notice to the district attorney of the judicial circuit where the property was seized or, in the case of a forfeiture lien, to the district attorney filing such lien, may issue an order to show cause to the seizing law enforcement agency for a hearing on the sole issue of whether probable cause for forfeiture of the property then exists. The hearing must be held within 30 days unless continued for good cause on motion of either party. If the court finds that there is no probable cause for forfeiture of the property, the property must be released pending the outcome of a judicial proceeding which may be filed pursuant to this Code section; and

(5) The court may order property that has been seized for forfeiture to be sold to satisfy a specified interest of any interest holder, on motion of any party, and after notice and a hearing, on the conditions that:

(A) The interest holder has filed a proper claim and:

(i) Is authorized to do business in this state and is under the jurisdiction of a governmental agency of this state or of the United States which regulates financial institutions, securities, insurance, or real estate; or

(ii) Has an interest that the district attorney has stipulated is exempt from forfeiture;

(B) The interest holder must dispose of the property by commercially reasonable public sale and apply the proceeds first to its interest and then to its reasonable expenses incurred in connection with the sale or disposal; and

(C) The balance of the proceeds, if any, must be returned to the actual or constructive custody of the court, in an interest-bearing account, subject to further proceedings under this Code section.

(r) A defendant convicted in any criminal proceeding is precluded from later denying the essential allegations of the criminal offense of which the defendant was convicted in any proceeding pursuant to this Code section, regardless of the pendency of an appeal from that conviction; however, evidence of the pendency of an appeal is admissible. For the purposes of this Code section, a conviction results from a verdict or plea of guilty, including a plea of nolo contendere.

(s) In hearings and determinations pursuant to this Code section:

(1) The court may receive and consider, in making any determination of probable cause or reasonable cause, all evidence admissible in determining probable cause at a preliminary hearing or by a magistrate pursuant to Article 1 of Chapter 5 of Title 17, together with inferences therefrom;

(2) The fact that money or a negotiable instrument was found in proximity to contraband or to an instrumentality of conduct giving rise to forfeiture authorizes the trier of the fact to infer that the money or negotiable instrument was the proceeds of conduct giving rise to forfeiture or was used or intended to be used to facilitate such conduct; and

(3) There is a rebuttable presumption that any property of a person is subject to forfeiture under this Code section if the state establishes probable cause to believe that:

(A) The person has engaged in conduct giving rise to forfeiture;

(B) The property was acquired by the person during the period of the conduct giving rise to forfeiture or within a reasonable time after the period; and

(C) There was no likely source for the property other than the conduct giving rise to forfeiture.

(t)(1) All property declared to be forfeited under this Code section vests in this state at the time of commission of the conduct giving rise to forfeiture together with the proceeds of the property after that time. Any property or proceeds transferred later to any person remain subject to forfeiture and thereafter must be ordered to be forfeited unless the transferee claims and establishes in a hearing under this Code section that the transferee is a bona fide purchaser for value and the transferee's interest is exempt under subsection (e) of this Code section.

(2) On entry of judgment for a person claiming an interest in the property that is subject to proceedings to forfeit property under this Code section, the court shall order that the property or interest in property be released or delivered promptly to that person free of liens and encumbrances, as provided under this article.

(3) The court shall order a claimant who fails to establish that a substantial portion of the claimant's interest is exempt

from forfeiture under subsection (e) of this Code section to pay the reasonable costs relating to the disproving of the claim which were incurred by the state, including costs for investigation, prosecution, and attorneys' fees.

(u)(1) Whenever property is forfeited under this article, any property which is required by law to be destroyed or which is harmful to the public shall, when no longer needed for evidentiary purposes, be destroyed or forwarded to the Division of Forensic Sciences of the Georgia Bureau of Investigation or any other agency of state or local government for destruction or for any medical or scientific use not prohibited under the laws of the United States or this state.

(2) When property, other than money or real property, is forfeited under this article, the court may:

(A) Order the property to be sold, with the proceeds of the sale to be distributed as provided in paragraph (4) of this subsection; or

(B) Provide for the in-kind distribution of the property as provided for in paragraph (4) of this subsection.

(2.1) When real property is forfeited, the court may order that:

(A) The real property be turned over to the state;

(B) The appropriate political subdivision take charge of the property and:

(i) Sell the property with such conditions as the court deems proper, and distribute the proceeds in such manner as the court so orders; or

(ii) Hold the property for use by one or more law enforcement agencies;

(C) The real property be turned over to an appropriate political subdivision without restrictions;

(D) The real property be deeded to a land bank authority as provided in Article 4 of Chapter 4 of Title 48; or

(E) The real property be disposed of in such other manner as the court deems proper.

(3) Where property is to be sold pursuant to this subsection, the court may direct that such property be sold by:

(A) Judicial sale as provided in Article 7 of Chapter 13 of Title 9; provided, however, that the court may establish a minimum acceptable price for such property; or

(B) Any commercially feasible means, including, but not limited to, in the case of real property, listing such property with a licensed real estate broker, selected by the district attorney through competitive bids.

(4) All money and property forfeited in the same forfeiture proceeding shall be pooled together for distribution as follows:

(A) A fair market value shall be assigned to all items of property other than money in such pool; and a total value shall be established for the pool by adding together the fair market value of all such property in the pool and the amount of money in the pool;

(B) All costs, including court costs, shall be paid and the remaining pool shall be distributed pro rata to the state and to local governments, according to the role which their law enforcement agencies played in the seizure of the assets; provided, however, that the amount distributed to the state shall not exceed 25 percent of the amount distributed; county governments are authorized upon request of the district attorney to provide for payment of any and all necessary expenses for the operation of the office from the said forfeiture pool up to 10 percent of the amount distributed, in addition to any other expenses paid by the county to the district attorney's office.

(C) An order of distribution provided for in this subsection shall be submitted by the district attorney to the court for approval; and

(D)(i) Property and money distributed to a local government shall be passed through to the local law enforcement agency until the sum equals 33 ⅓ percent of the amount of local funds appropriated or otherwise made available to such agency for the fiscal year in which such funds are distributed. Proceeds received may be used for any official law enforcement purpose except for the payment of salaries or rewards to law enforcement personnel, at the discretion of the chief officer of the local law enforcement agency, or may be used to fund victim-witness assistance programs or a state law enforcement museum. Such property shall not be used to supplant any other local, state, or federal funds appropriated for staff or operations.

(ii) The local governing authority shall expend any remaining proceeds for any law enforcement purpose; for the representation of indigents in criminal cases; for drug treatment, rehabilitation, prevention, or education or any other program which responds to problems created by drug or substance abuse; for use as matching funds for grant programs related to drug treatment or prevention; to fund victim-witness assistance programs; or for any combination of the foregoing. If real property is distributed to a local government, the local government may transfer the real property to a land bank authority as provided in Article 4 of Chapter 4 of Title 48.

(iii) Any local law enforcement agency receiving property under this subsection shall submit an annual report to the local governing authority. The report shall be submitted with the agency's budget request and shall itemize the property received during the fiscal year and the utilization made thereof.

(iv) Money distributed to the state pursuant to this subsection shall be paid into the general fund of the state treasury, it being the intent of the General Assembly that the same be used, subject to appropriation from the general fund in the manner provided by law for representation of indigents in criminal cases; for funding of the Crime Victims Emergency Fund; for law enforcement and prosecution agency programs and particularly for funding of advanced drug investigation and prosecution training for law enforcement officers and prosecuting attorneys; for drug treatment, rehabilitation, prevention, or education or any other program which responds to problems created by drug or substance abuse; for use as matching funds for grant programs related to drug treatment or prevention; or for financing the judicial system of the state.

(v) Property distributed in kind to the state pursuant to this subsection may be designated by the Attorney General, with the approval of the court, for use by such agency or officer of the state as may be appropriate or, otherwise, shall be turned over to the Department of Administrative Services for such use or disposition as may be determined by the commissioner of the Department of Administrative Services.

(v) An acquittal or dismissal in a criminal proceeding does not preclude civil proceedings under this article.

(w) For good cause shown, the court may stay civil forfeiture proceedings during the criminal trial resulting from a related indictment or information alleging a violation of this article.

(x)(1) The court shall order the forfeiture of any property of a claimant or defendant up to the value of property found by the court to be subject to forfeiture under the provisions of this Code section if any of the forfeited property:

(A) Cannot be located;

(B) Has been transferred or conveyed to, sold to, or deposited with a third party;

(C) Is beyond the jurisdiction of the court;

(D) Has been substantially diminished in value while not in the actual physical custody of the receiver or governmental agency directed to maintain custody of the property; or

(E) Has been commingled with other property that cannot be divided without difficulty.

(2) In addition to any other remedy provided for by law, a district attorney on behalf of the state may institute an action in any court of this state or of the United States or any of the several states against any person acting with knowledge or any person to whom notice of a lien for forfeiture of property has been provided in accordance with subsection (j) of this Code section; to whom notice of seizure has been provided in accordance with subsection (i) of this Code section; or to whom notice of a civil proceeding alleging conduct giving rise to forfeiture under this Code section has been provided, if property subject to forfeiture is conveyed, alienated, disposed of, or otherwise rendered unavailable for forfeiture after the filing of a forfeiture lien notice or notice of seizure or after the filing and notice of a civil proceeding alleging conduct giving rise to forfeiture under this Code section, as the case may be. The state may recover judgment in an amount equal to the value of the lien but not to exceed the fair market value of the property or, if there is no lien, in an amount not to exceed the fair market value of the property, together with reasonable investigative expenses and attorneys' fees. If a civil proceeding is pending, the action must be heard by the court in which the civil proceeding is pending.

(3) A district attorney may file and prosecute in any of the courts of this state or of the United States or of any of the several states such civil actions as may be necessary to enforce any judgment rendered pursuant to this Code section.

(4) No person claiming an interest in property subject to forfeiture under this article may commence or maintain any action against the state concerning the validity of the alleged interest other than as provided in this Code section. Except as specifically authorized by this Code section, no person claiming an interest in such property may file any counterclaim or cross-claim to any action brought pursuant to this Code section.

(5) A civil action under this article must be commenced within five years after the last conduct giving rise to forfeiture or to the claim for relief became known or should have become known, excluding any time during which either the property or defendant is out of the state or in confinement or during which criminal proceedings relating to the same conduct are in progress.

(y) Controlled substances included in Schedule I which are contraband and any controlled substance whose owners are unknown are summarily forfeited to the state. The court may include in any judgment of conviction under this article an order forfeiting any controlled substance involved in the offense to the extent of the defendant's interest.

(z) This Code section must be liberally construed to effectuate its remedial purposes.

Laws 1974, p. 221, § 1; Laws 1975, p. 919, §§ 1, 2; Laws 1979, p. 879, §§ 1–3; Laws 1981, p. 180, § 3; Laws 1982, p. 3, § 16; Laws 1982, p. 2273, § 1; Laws 1982, p. 2325, § 2; Laws 1983, p. 469, § 1; Laws 1986, p. 451, § 1; Laws 1988, p. 958, § 1; Laws 1991, p. 886, § 1; Laws 1992, p. 6, § 16; Laws 1993, p. 1434, § 1; Laws 2000, p. 1225, § 5; Laws 2000, p. 1589, § 3; Laws 2001, p. 362, § 30; Laws 2002, p. 1039, §§ 1A–1C; Laws 2002, p. 1286, § 1; Laws 2003, Act 32, § 7, eff. Dec. 31, 2003; Laws 2004, Act 526, § 3, eff. May 13, 2004.

Formerly Code 1933, § 79A–828.

Historical and Statutory Notes

The 2000 amendment by Act 783 modified the subsection references in subsec. (*o*)(1)(A).

The 2000 amendment by Act 918 in subsecs. (i)(2)(A) and (i)(2)(B) substituted "certified mail or statutory overnight delivery" for "certified mail".

The 2001 amendment modified the statutory reference in subsec. (a)(6).

The 2002 amendment by Act 885 redesignated the subdivisions of subsec. (e) and modified the quantity constituting property interest in the concluding sentence thereof. The sentence formerly provided: "A property interest shall not be subject to forfeiture under this Code section for a violation involving one gram of cocaine or less or four ounces of marijuana or less unless said property was used to facilitate a transaction in or a purchase of or sale of a controlled substance or marijuana."

The 2002 amendment by Act 957 rewrote subsec. (u)(2) which formerly provided:

"(2) When property, other than money, is forfeited under this article, the court may:

"(A) Order the property to be sold, with the proceeds of the sale to be distributed as provided in paragraph (4) of this subsection; or

" (B) Provide for the in-kind distribution of the property as provided for in paragraph (4) of this subsection."

The 2003 amendment by Act 32, in subsec. (u)(4)(D)(iv), deleted ", for funding of Article 2 of Chapter 12 of Title 17, 'The Georgia Indigent Defense Act,' " following "in the manner provided by law".

Laws 2003, Act 32, § 10(b), provides:

"(b) Sections 2 through 8 of this Act shall become effective on December 31, 2003."

The 2004 amendment by Act 526 inserted "or a state law enforcement museum" in subsec. (u), par. (4), subpar. (D)(i).

§ 16–13–50. Burden of proof

(a) It is not necessary for the state to negate any exemption or exception in this article in any complaint, accusation, indictment, or other pleading or in any trial, hearing, or other proceeding under this article. The burden of proof of any exemption or exception is upon the person claiming it.

(b) In the absence of proof that a person is the duly authorized holder of an appropriate registration or order form issued under this article, he is presumed not to be the holder of the registration or form. The burden of proof is upon him to rebut the presumption.

(c) No liability is imposed by this article upon any authorized state, county, or municipal officer engaged in the lawful performance of his duties.

Laws 1974, p. 221, § 1.

Formerly Code 1933, § 79A–829.

§ 16–13–51. Judicial review

All final determinations, findings, and conclusions of the State Board of Pharmacy under this article are final and conclusive decisions of the matters involved. Any person aggrieved by the decision may obtain review of the decision in the Superior Court of Fulton County. Findings of fact by the State Board of Pharmacy, if supported by substantial evidence, are conclusive.

Laws 1974, p. 221, § 1; Laws 1982, p. 3, § 16.

Formerly Code 1933, § 79A–830.

§ 16–13–52. Information and research

(a) The State Board of Pharmacy and the Georgia Drugs and Narcotics Agency shall carry out programs designed to prevent and deter misuse and abuse of controlled substances.

(b) The State Board of Pharmacy and the Georgia Drugs and Narcotics Agency shall encourage research on misuse and abuse of controlled substances. In connection with the research and in furtherance of the enforcement of this article, they may:

(1) Establish methods to assess accurately the effects of controlled substances and identify and characterize those with potential for abuse;

(2) Make studies and undertake programs of research to:

(A) Develop new or improved approaches, techniques, systems, equipment, and devices to strengthen the enforcement of this article;

(B) Determine patterns of misuse and abuse of controlled substances and the social effects thereof;

(C) Improve methods for preventing, predicting, understanding, and dealing with the misuse and abuse of controlled substances; and

(3) Enter into agreements with public agencies, institutions of higher education, and private organizations or individuals for the purpose of conducting research, demonstrations, or special projects which bear directly on misuse and abuse of controlled substances.

(c) The State Board of Pharmacy, in the public interest, may authorize persons engaged in research on the use and effects of controlled substances to withhold the names and other identifying characteristics of individuals who are the subjects of the research. Persons who obtain this authorization are not to be compelled in any civil, criminal, administrative, legislative, or other proceeding to identify the individuals who are the subjects of research for which the authorization was obtained.

(d) The State Board of Pharmacy may authorize the possession and distribution of controlled substances by persons engaged in research. Persons who obtain this authorization are exempt from state prosecution for possession and distribution of controlled substances to the extent of the authorization.

Laws 1974, p. 221, § 1; Laws 1982, p. 3, § 16.

Formerly Code 1933, § 79A–831.

§ 16–13–53. Pending proceedings

(a) Prosecution for any violation of law occurring prior to July 1, 1974, is not affected or abated by this article. If the offense which was being prosecuted is similar to one set out in this article, then the penalties under this article apply if they are less than those under prior law.

(b) Civil seizures or forfeitures and injunctive proceedings commenced prior to July 1, 1974, are not affected by this article.

(c) All administrative proceedings pending under prior laws which were superseded by this article shall be continued and brought to a final determination in accord with the laws and rules in effect prior to July 1, 1974. Any substance controlled under prior law which is not listed within Schedules I through V is automatically controlled without further proceedings and shall be listed in the appropriate schedule.

(d) This article applies to violations of law, seizures, forfeitures, injunctive proceedings, administrative proceedings, and investigations occurring after July 1, 1974.

Laws 1974, p. 221, § 1.

Formerly Code 1933, § 79A–832.

§ 16–13–54. Continuation of rules

Any orders and rules promulgated under any law affected by this article and in effect on July 1, 1974, and not in conflict with it shall continue in effect until modified, superseded, or repealed.

Laws 1974, p. 221, § 1.

Formerly Code 1933, § 79A–833.

§ 16–13–55. Uniformity of interpretation

This article shall be so applied and construed as to effectuate its general purpose to make uniform the law with respect to the subject of this article among those states which enact it.

Laws 1974, p. 221, § 1.

Formerly Code 1933, § 79A–834.

§ 16–13–56. Violations

(a) Unless otherwise specified with respect to a particular offense, any person who violates any provision of this article shall be guilty of a misdemeanor.

(b) In addition to any other penalty imposed by law for a violation of this article, if the sentencing court finds that in committing a violation of this article, the defendant contributed to a release of hazardous waste, a hazardous constituent, or a hazardous substance as such terms are defined by Code Sections 12–8–62 and 12–8–92, the court shall require such defendant to make restitution to the State of Georgia pursuant to subsection (a) of Code Section 12–8–96.1 for the reasonable costs of activities associated with the cleanup of environmental hazards, including legal expenses incurred by the state. Restitution made pursuant to this Code section shall not preclude the State of Georgia from obtaining any other civil or criminal remedy available under any other provision of law. The restitution authorized by this Code section is supplemental and not exclusive.

Laws 1985, p. 1219, § 7; Laws 2001, p. 816, § 2.

Historical and Statutory Notes

The 2001 amendment designated subsec. (a) and added (subsec. (b).

Article 3

Dangerous Drugs

§ 16–13–70. Short title

This article shall be known and may be cited as the "Dangerous Drug Act."

Laws 1967, p. 296, § 1.

Formerly Code 1933, § 79A–701.

§ 16–13–70.1. Definitions

Any term used in this article and not defined in this article but defined in Code Section 16–13–21 shall have the meaning provided for that term in Code Section 16–13–21.

Laws 2001, p. 816, § 3.

§ 16–13–71. Definition of dangerous drug; exceptions; sale of substances with caution label

(a) A "dangerous drug" means any drug other than a drug contained in any schedule of Article 2 of this chapter, which, under the Federal Food, Drug, and Cosmetic Act (52 Stat. 1040 (1938)), 21 U.S.C. Section 301, et seq., as amended, may be dispensed only upon prescription. In any civil or criminal action or other proceedings, a certification from the Food and Drug Administration of the United States Department of Health and Human Services attesting to the fact that a drug other than a drug contained in any schedule of Article 2 of this chapter involved in the action or proceeding is a dangerous drug that federal law prohibits dispensing of without a prescription pursuant to the Federal Food, Drug, and Cosmetic Act shall be admissible as prima-facie proof that such drug is a "dangerous drug."

(b) In addition to subsection (a) of this Code section, a "dangerous drug" means any other drug or substance declared by the General Assembly to be a dangerous drug; to include any of the following drugs, chemicals, or substances; salts, isomers, esters, ethers, or derivatives of such drugs, chemicals, or substances which have essentially the same pharmacological action; all other salts, isomers, esters, ethers, and compounds of such drugs, chemicals, or substances unless specifically exempted and the following devices, identified as "dangerous drugs":

(.03) Abacavir;

(.035) Abarelix;

(.037) Abatacept;

(.04) Abciximab;

(.043) abobotulinumtoxinA;

(.045) Acamprostate;

(.05) Acarbose;

(.1) Acebutolol;

(1) Acecarbromal;

(2) Acenocoumarol;

(3) Acetazolamide;

(3.5) Reserved;

(4) Acetohexamide;

(4.1) Aceto-hydroxamic acid;

(5) Acetophenazine;

(6) Acetosulfone;

(7) Acetyl sulfamethoxypyridazine;

(8) Acetyl sulfisoxazole;

(9) Acetylcarbromal;

(10) Acetylcholine;

(11) Acetylcysteine;

(12) Acetyldigitoxin;

(12.1) Acitretin;

(13) Acrisorcin;

(13.3) Acrivastine;

(13.5) Acyclovir;

(13.53) Adalimumab;

(13.55) Adapalene;

(13.6) Adenosine;

(14) Adenosine 5–monophosphate;

(15) Adenylic acid;

(16) Adiphenine hydrochloride;

(17) Adrenal cortex extracts;

(17.5) Albendazole;

(18) Albumin, normal human serum;

(18.1) Albuterol;

(19) Albutonium;

(19.5) Alclometasone dipropionate;

(19.6) Alendronate;

(19.65) Alfuzosin;

(19.7) Alglucerase;

(19.75) Alglucosidase alfa;

(19.77) Aliskiren;

(19.8) Alitretinoin;

(20) Alkaverir;

(21) Alkavervir;

(21.1) Alkyl nitrites;

(22) Allopurinol;

(22.2) Almotriptan;

(22.5) Alosetron;

(23) Alpha amylase;

(23.1) Alprostadil;

(24) Alseroxylon;

(24.1) Altenodol;

(24.6) Altretamine;

(25) Aluminum nicotinate;

(26) Alverine;

(26.5) Alvimopan;

(27) Amantadine;

(28) Ambenonium chloride;

(28.5) Ambrisentan;

(29) Ambrosiacae follens;

(30) Amcinonide;

(30.1) Amdinocillin;

(30.5) Amifostine;

(31) Amikacin;

(31.1) Amiloride;

(32) Aminacrine;

(33) 4–amino-N-methyl-pteroylglutamic acid;

(34) Amino acid preparations for injection or vaginal use;

(35) Aminocaproic acid;

(36) Aminohippurate;

(36.5) Aminolevulinic acid;

(37) Aminophylline;

(38) Aminosalicylate—See exceptions;

(39) Aminosalicylate calcium—See exceptions;

(40) Aminosalicylate potassium—See exceptions;

(41) Aminosalicylate sodium—See exceptions;

(42) Aminosalicylic acid—See exceptions;

(42.1) Amiodarone;

(43) Amisometradine;

(44) Amitriptyline;

(44.3) Amlexanox;

(44.5) Amlodipine;

(44.6) Ammonia, N–13;

(44.7) Ammonium lactate;

(45) Amodiaquin;

(45.5) Amoxapine;

(46) Amoxicillin;

(47) Amphotericin B;

(48) Ampicillin;

(48.2) Amprenavir;

(48.6) Amrinone;

(49) Amyl nitrite;

(50) Amylolytic enzymes;

(50.1) Anabolic steroids, if listed in Code Section 16–13–27.1 as being exempt as Schedule III controlled substances;

(50.3) Anagrelide;

(50.4) Anakinra;

(50.5) Anastrozole;

(51) Androgens, except those androgens listed in paragraph (6) of Code Section 16–13–27;

(52) Angiotensin amide;

(52.5) Anidulafungin;

(53) Anisindione;

(54) Anisotropine;

(55) Antazoline;

(56) Anterior pituitary hormones;

(57) Anthralin;

(58) Anti-coagulant acid:

(A) Citrate dextrose;
(59) Antigens:
(A) Alternaria tenius;
(B) Aqua ivy;
(C) Ash mix;
(D) Aspergillus fumigatus;
(E) Bacterial, Staphylococcus aureus, Type 1;
(F) Bacterial, Staphylococcus aureus, Type 3;
(G) Bacterial, Undenatured;
(H) Bee;
(I) Beech;
(J) Bermuda grass;
(K) Birch;
(L) California live oak;
(M) Candida albicans;
(N) Careless weed;
(O) Cat epithelia;
(P) Cattle epithelia;
(Q) Coccidioides immitis;
(R) Cottonwood fremont;
(S) Dog epithelia;
(T) Elm mix;
(U) English plantain;
(V) Feather mix;
(W) Gram negative bacterial;
(X) Helminthosporium sativum;
(Y) Hickory;
(Z) Hormodendrum hordei;
(AA) Hornet;
(BB) House dust;
(CC) House dust mix;
(DD) Insects;
(EE) Intradermal or scratching test;
(FF) Johnson grass;
(GG) Kentucky blue grass;
(HH) Kochia;
(II) Lamb quarters;
(JJ) Maple;
(KK) Mesquite;
(LL) Mixed epidermals;
(MM) Mixed grass, ragweeds (spring-fall);
(NN) Mixed grasses (spring);
(OO) Mixed inhalants;
(PP) Mixed molds;
(QQ) Mixed ragweed;
(RR) Mixed ragweed—mixed weeds (fall);
(SS) Mixed weeds;
(TT) Molds;
(UU) Mountain cedar;
(VV) Mugwort common;
(WW) National weed mix;
(XX) Oak mix;
(YY) Olive;
(ZZ) Orchard grass;
(AAA) Pecan;
(BBB) Penicillium notatum;
(CCC) Perennial rye;
(DDD) Poison oak and poison ivy;
(EEE) Pollens;
(FFF) Poplar mix;
(GGG) Prescription;
(HHH) Ragweed mix;
(III) Red top grass;
(JJJ) Respiratory bacterial;
(KKK) Rough pigweed;
(LLL) Russian thistle;
(MMM) Sagebrush common;
(NNN) Scale mix;
(OOO) Short ragweed;
(PPP) Simplified allergy screening set;
(QQQ) Skin bacterial;
(RRR) Southern grass;
(SSS) Staphylococcal;
(TTT) Stinging insect mix;
(UUU) Stinging insects;
(VVV) Sweet vernal;
(WWW) Sycamore;
(XXX) Tall ragweed;
(YYY) Timothy;
(ZZZ) Tree mix;
(AAAA) Trees (early spring);
(BBBB) Walnut;
(CCCC) Wasp;
(DDDD) West ragweed;
(EEEE) West weed mix;
(FFFF) Yellow jacket;
(60) Antihemophilic factor, Human;
(61) Antirabies serum;
(62) Antivenin;
(62.1) Apomorphine;
(62.3) Apraclonidine;
(62.4) Aprepitant;
(62.5) Aprotinin;
(62.7) Ardeparin;
(62.75) Arformoterol tartrate;
(62.8) Argatroban;
(63) Arginine, L-;
(63.5) Aripiprazole;
(64) Arsenic—Preparation for human use;
(64.1) Arsenic trioxide;
(65) Artegraft;
(65.5) Artemether;
(66) Ascorbate sodium—Injection;
(66.5) Asenapine;
(67) Asparaginase;
(67.6) Astemizole;
(67.67) Astenajavol;
(67.72) Atazanavir;
(68.1) Atenolol;
(68.15) Atomoxetine;
(68.2) Atorvastatin;
(68.3) Atovaquone;
(68.4) Atracurium besylate;
(68.5) Atropine—See exceptions;
(68.6) Auranofin;
(69) Aurothioglucose;
(69.5) Azacitidine;
(70) Azapetine;

(71) Azatadine maleate;
(72) Azathioprine;
(72.3) Azelaic acid;
(72.4) Azelastine;
(72.5) Azithromycin;
(72.7) Azlocillin;
(73) Azo-sulfisoxazole;
(73.5) Aztreonam;
(74) Azuresin;
(75) Bacitracin—See exceptions;
(76) Baclofen;
(76.5) Balsalazide;
(77) Barium—See exceptions;
(78) Beclomethasone;
(79) Belladonna;
(80) Belladonna alkaloids;
(81) Belladonna extracts;
(82) Benactyzine;
(82.5) Benazepril;
(82.7) Bendamustine;
(83) Bendroflumethiazide;
(83.1) Benoxaprofen;
(83.2) Bentiromide;
(83.5) Bentoquatam—See exceptions;
(84) Benzestrol;
(85) Benzonatate;
(86) Benzoylpas;
(87) Benzquinamide;
(88) Benzthiazide;
(89) Benztropine;
(90) Benzylpenicilloyl—polylysine;
(91) Bephenium hydroxynaphthoate;
(91.3) Bepotastine;
(91.5) Bepridil;
(91.7) Beractant;
(91.8) Besifloxacin;
(92) Beta-carotene—See exceptions;
(93) Betadine vaginal gel;
(94) Betahistine;
(94.5) Betaine, anhydrous;
(95) Betamethasone;
(95.1) Betaxolol;
(96) Betazole;
(97) Bethanechol;
(97.1) Bethanidine sulfate;
(97.2) Bevacizumab;
(97.3) Bexarotene;
(97.5) Bicalutamide;
(98) Bile extract;
(98.2) Bimatoprost;
(99) Biperiden;
(100) Bisacodyl tannex;
(101) Bishydroxycoumarin;
(101.5) Biskalcitrate;
(102) Bismuth sodium tartrate—See exceptions;
(102.05) Bisoprolol;
(102.1) Bitolterol mesylate;
(102.5) Bivalirudin;
(103) Blastomycine;
(104) Bleomycin;
(105) Boroglycerin glycerite;
(105.3) Bortezomib;
(105.5) Bosentan;
(105.7) Botulinum toxin (B);
(106) Botulism antitoxin;
(107) Bretylium;
(107.3) Briazolamide;
(107.5) Brimonidine;
(108) Bromelains—See exceptions;
(108.5) Bromfenac;
(109) Bromisovalum;
(110) Bromocriptine;
(111) Bromodiphenhydramine;
(112) Brompheniramine—See exceptions;
(113) Brucella antigen;
(114) Brucella protein nucleate;
(115) Buclizine;
(115.3) Budesonide;
(115.5) Bumetanide;
(116) Bupivacaine;
(116.05) Reserved;
(116.1) Bupropion;
(116.5) Buspirone;
(117) Busulfan;
(118) Butacaine;
(119) Butaperazine;
(119.05) Butenafine —See exceptions;
(119.1) Butoconazole—See exceptions;
(120) Reserved;
(121) Butyl nitrite;
(122) Butyrophenone;
(122.5) Cabergoline;
(123) Cadmium sulfide—See exceptions;
(124) Caffeine sodium benzoate;
(124.3) Calcifediol;
(124.7) Calcipotriene;
(125) Calcitonin, Salmon;
(126) Calcitriol;
(127) Calcium disodium edetate—See exceptions;
(128) Calcium gluconogalactogluconate;
(129) Calcium levulinate;
(129.5) Calfactant;
(130) Calusterone;
(130.3) Canakinumab;
(130.5) Candesartan;
(131) Candicidin;
(132) Cantharidin;
(132.5) Capecitabine;
(133) Capreomycin;
(133.05) Capsaicin—see exceptions;
(133.1) Captopril;
(134) Capyodiame;

(135) Caramiphen;
(136) Carbachol;
(137) Carbamazepine;
(138) Carbazochrome;
(139) Carbenicillin;
(140) Carbetapentane;
(141) Carbidopa;
(142) Carbinoxamine;
(142.5) Carboplatin;
(143) Reserved;
(144) Carmustine;
(144.1) Carnitine;
(145) Carphenazine;
(145.6) Carteolol;
(145.8) Carvedilol;
(146) Casein hydrolysate;
(146.6) Caspofungin;
(147) Catarrhalis combined vaccine;
(148) Catarrhalis vaccine mixed;
(149) Cefaclor;
(150) Cefadroxil;
(151) Cefamandole;
(151.3) Cefazolin;
(151.4) Cefdinir;
(151.45) Cefditoren;
(151.5) Cefepime;
(151.6) Cefixime;
(151.7) Cefmetazole;
(151.8) Cefonicid;
(152) Cefoperazone;
(152.1) Ceforanide;
(152.2) Cefotaxime;
(152.3) Cefotetan;
(152.7) Cefotiam;
(152.9) Cefoxitin;
(153.1) Cefpiramide;
(153.2) Cefpodoxime;
(153.3) Cefprozil;
(153.4) Ceftazidime;
(153.5) Ceftibuten;
(153.6) Ceftizoxime;
(153.8) Ceftriaxone;
(153.9) Cefuroxime;
(153.95) Celecoxib;
(154) Cellulose, Oxadized, Regenerated—See exceptions;
(155) Cephalexin;
(156) Cephaloglycin;
(157) Cephaloridine;
(158) Cephalothin;
(159) Cephapirin;
(159.3) Cephradine;
(159.6) Ceretec;
(159.8) Cerivastatin;
(160) Certolizumab;
(160.1) Ceruletide;
(160.15) Cetirizine—See exceptions;
(160.16) Cetrorelix;
(160.165) Cetuximab;
(160.17) Cevimeline;
(160.20) Chenodiol;
(161) Chlophedianol;
(162) Chlorambucil;
(163) Chloramphenicol;
(164) Chloranil—See exceptions;
(165) Chlordantoin;
(166) Chlordiazepoxide in combination with clidinium bromide or water soluble esterified estrogens;
(166.5) Chlorhexidine—See exceptions;
(167) Chlormadinone;
(168) Chlormerodrin;
(169) Chlormezanone;
(170) Chloroacetic acid—See exceptions;
(171) Chlorobutanol—See exceptions;
(172) Chloroform—See exceptions;
(173) Chloroguanide;
(174) Chloroprocaine;
(175) Chloroquine;
(176) Chlorothiazide;
(177) Chlorotrianisene;
(178) Chloroxine;
(179) Chlorphenesin;
(180) Chlorpheniramine—See exceptions;
(181) Chlorphenoxamine;
(182) Chlorpromazine;
(183) Chlorpropamide;
(184) Chlorprothixene;
(185) Chlorquinaldol;
(186) Chlortetracycline;
(187) Chlorthalidone;
(188) Chlorzoxazone;
(189) Cholera vaccine;
(190) Cholestyramine resin;
(191) Chondroitin;
(191.5) Chymopapain;
(192) Chymotrypsin;
(192.02) Ciclesonide;
(192.03) Ciclopirox;
(192.05) Cidofovir;
(192.1) Cilastatin;
(192.4) Cilexetil;
(192.7) Cilostazol;
(193) Cimetidine—See exceptions;
(193.5) Cinacalcet;
(194) Cinoxacin;
(194.5) Ciprofloxacin;
(194.7) Cisapride;
(194.8) Cisatracurium;
(195) Cisplatin;
(195.2) Citalopram;
(195.3) Cladribine;
(195.5) Clarithromycin;
(195.7) Clavulanate;

(196) Clemastine—See exceptions;
(196.5) Clevidipine;
(197) Clidinium bromide;
(198) Clindamycin;
(198.1) Clobetasol propionate;
(199) Clocortolone pivalate;
(200) Clofibrate;
(201) Clomiphene;
(201.5) Clomipramine;
(202) Clonidine;
(203) Clopidogerel;
(204) Clostridiopeptidase;
(205) Clotrimazole—See exceptions;
(206) Cloxacillin;
(206.5) Clozapine;
(207) Coal tar solution topical;
(208) Cobra venom;
(209) Colchicine—See exceptions;
(209.5) Colesevelam;
(210) Colestipol;
(211) Colistimethate;
(212) Colistin;
(213) Collagenase;
(213.3) Conivaptan;
(213.5) Corticorelin;
(214) Corticotropin;
(215) Corticotropin, Respository;
(216) Cortisone;
(217) Cosyntropin;
(217.5) Crixivan;
(218) Cromolyn—See exceptions;
(219) Crotaline antivenin, Polyvalent;
(220) Crotamiton;
(221) Cryptenamine;
(221.5) Cupric chloride—injectable;
(222) Cyanide antidote;
(223) Cyclacillin;
(224) Cyclandelate;
(225) Reserved;
(226) Cyclobenzaprine;
(227) Cyclomethycaine;
(228) Cyclopentamine;
(229) Cyclopentolate;
(230) Cyclophosphamide;
(231) Cycloserine;
(231.5) Cyclosporine;
(232) Cyclothiazide;
(233) Cycrimine;
(234) Cyproheptadine;
(234.5) Cysteamine;
(235) Cytarabine;
(236) Dacarbazine;
(236.6) Daclizumab;
(237) Dactinomycin;
(237.2) Dalfopristin;
(237.5) Dalteparin;
(237.7) Danaparoid;
(238) Danazol;
(239) Dantrolene;
(239.5) Dapiprazole;
(240) Dapsone—See exceptions;
(240.3) Daptomycin;
(240.5) Darbepoetin alfa;
(240.6) Darifenacin;
(240.7) Darunavir;
(240.9) Dasatinib;
(241) Daunorubicin;
(242) Deanol;
(243) Decamethonium;
(243.3) Decitabine;
(243.5) Deferasirox;
(244) Deferoxamine;
(244.4) Degarelix;
(244.5) Delavirdine;
(245) Demecarium;
(246) Demeclocycline;
(247) Demethylchlortetracycline;
(248) Deoxyribonuclease, Pancreatic;
(249) Deserpidine;
(249.5) Desflurane;
(250) Desipramine;
(250.5) Desirudin;
(251) Deslanoside;
(251.5) Desloratadine;
(252) Desmopressin;
(252.5) Desogestrel;
(253) Desonide;
(254) Desoximetasone;
(255) Desoxycorticosterone;
(256) Desoxyribonuclease;
(256.5) Desvenlafaxine;
(257) Dexamethasone;
(258) Dexbrompheniramine—See exceptions;
(259) Dexchlorpheniramine;
(259.5) Dexlansoprazole;
(260) Dexpanthenol;
(260.5) Dexrazoxane;
(261) Dextran;
(262) Reserved;
(263) Dextriferron;
(264) Dextroisoephedrine;
(265) Dextrothyroxine;
(265.5) Dezocine;
(266) Diatrizoate;
(267) Diazoxide;
(268) Dibucaine;
(269) Dichloralphenazone;
(270) Dichlorphenamide;
(270.5) Diclofenac;
(271) Dicloxacillin;
(272) Dicyclomine;
(272.5) Didanosine;

(273) Dienestrol;
(274) Diethylcarbamazine;
(275) Diethylstilbestrol;
(276) Reserved;
(277) Diflorasone diacetate;
(277.5) Diflunisal;
(277.57) Difluprednate;
(278) Digitalis;
(279) Digitoxin;
(280) Digoxin;
(281) Dihydroergocornine;
(282) Dihydroergocristine;
(283) Dihydroergocryptine;
(284) Dihydroergotamine;
(285) Dihydrostreptomycin;
(286) Dihydrotachysterol;
(287) Diiodohydroxyquin;
(287.5) Diltiazem;
(288) Dimenhydrinate—Injection or suppositories;
(289) Dimercaprol;
(290) Dimethindene;
(291) Dimethisterone;
(292) Dimethyl sulfoxide—See exceptions;
(293) Dimethyl tubocurarine;
(293.5) Dimyristoyl;
(294) Dinoprost;
(295) Dinoprostone;
(296) Dioxyline;
(297) Diphemanil;
(298) Diphenadione;
(299) Diphenhydramine—See exceptions;
(300) Diphenidol;
(301) Diphenylhydantoin;
(302) Diphenylpyraline;
(303) Diphtheria antitoxin;
(304) Diphtheria and tetanus toxoids;
(305) Diphtheria and tetanus toxoids and pertussis vaccine;
(306) Diphtheria and tetanus toxoids, Absorbed;
(307) Diphtheria and tetanus toxoids, Pertussis;
(308) Diphtheria toxoid;
(309) Dipivefrin;
(310) Dipyridamole;
(311) Dipyron;
(311.3) Dirithromycin;
(311.5) Disibind;
(312) Disodium edetate—See exceptions;
(313) Disopyramide;
(314) Disulfiram;
(314.5) Divalproex;
(315) Dobutamine;
(315.5) Docetaxel;
(315.7) Docosanol—See exceptions;
(316) Doderlein bacilli;
(316.2) Dofetilide;
(316.3) Dolasetron;
(316.5) Donepezil;
(317) Dopamine;
(317.2) Doripenem;
(317.3) Dornase Alpha;
(317.4) Dorzolamide;
(317.5) Doxacurium;
(318) Doxapram;
(318.5) Doxazosin mesylate;
(319) Doxepin;
(319.5) Doxercalciferol;
(320) Doxorubicin;
(321) Doxycycline;
(322) Doxylamine;
(323) Doxylamine succinate;
(324) Dromostanolone;
(324.5) Dronedarone;
(325) Droperidol;
(325.3) Drospirenone;
(325.4) Drotrecogin alfa;
(325.45) Duloxetine;
(325.5) Dutasteride;
(326) Dyclonine;
(327) Dydrogesterone;
(328) Dyphylline;
(328.5) Ecallantide;
(329) Echothiophate;
(329.5) Econazole;
(330) Ectylurea;
(330.3) Eculizumab;
(330.5) Edetate—See exceptions;
(331) Edrophonium;
(331.03) Efavirenz;
(331.05) Eflornithine;
(331.06) Eltrombopag;
(331.07) Emedastine;
(331.072) Emtricitabine;
(331.1) Enalapril;
(331.6) Enalaprilat;
(332) Enflurane;
(332.2) Enfuvirtide;
(332.5) Enoxacin;
(332.7) Enoxaparin;
(332.8) Entacapone;
(332.85) Entecavir;
(332.9) Epinastine;
(333) Epinephrine;
(334) Epinephryl borate;
(334.3) Epirubicin;
(334.4) Eplerenone;
(334.5) Epoprostenol;
(334.7) Eprosartan;
(334.8) Eptifibatide;
(335) Ergocalciferol—See exceptions;
(335.5) Ergoloid mesylates;
(336) Ergonovine;
(337) Ergotamine;
(338) Ergosine;

(339) Ergocristine;
(340) Ergocryptine;
(341) Ergocornine;
(342) Ergotaminine;
(343) Ergosinine;
(344) Ergocristinine;
(345) Ergocryptinine;
(346) Ergocorninine;
(346.1) Erlotinib;
(346.5) Ertapenem;
(347) Erythrityl tetranitrate;
(348) Erythromycin;
(348.722) Escitalopram;
(349) Eserine;
(349.4) Esmolol;
(349.7) Esomeprazole;
(350) Esterified estrogens;
(351) Estradiol;
(352) Estriol;
(353) Estrogens;
(354) Estrogenic substances;
(355) Estrone;
(355.5) Estropipate;
(356) Ethacrynate;
(357) Ethacrynic acid;
(358) Ethambutol;
(359) Ethamivan;
(359.5) Ethanolamine oleate;
(360) Ethaverine;
(361) Ether—See exceptions;
(361.5) Ethinamate;
(362) Ethinyl estradiol;
(363) Ethiodized oil;
(364) Ethionamide;
(365) Ethisterone;
(366) Ethoheptazine;
(367) Ethopropazine;
(368) Ethosuximide;
(369) Ethotoin;
(370) Ethoxazene—See exceptions;
(371) Ethoxyzolamide;
(372) Ethyl biscoumacetate;
(373) Ethyl chloride—See exceptions;
(374) Ethyl nitrite spirit;
(375) Reserved;
(376) Ethylnorepinephrine;
(377) Ethynodiol diacetate;
(378) Etidocaine;
(379) Etidronate;
(379.05) Etodolac;
(379.07) Etomidate;
(379.09) Etonogestrel;
(379.1) Etoposide;
(379.5) Etravirine;
(380) Eucatropine;
(380.3) Everolimus;
(380.5) Exemestane;
(380.6) Exenatide;
(380.7) Ezetimibe;
(381) Factor IX complex, Human;
(381.1) Famciclovir;
(381.2) Famotidine—See exceptions;
(381.3) Felbamate;
(381.5) Felodipine;
(381.55) Fenfibrate;
(381.6) Fenofenadine;
(381.7) Fenofibrate;
(381.75) Fenofibric acid;
(381.8) Fenoldopam;
(382) Fenoprofen;
(382.25) Febuxostat;
(383) Ferric cacodylate;
(383.15) Ferric Hexacyanoferrate;
(383.3) Ferumoxides;
(383.4) Ferumoxsil;
(383.43) Ferumoxytol;
(383.45) Fesoterodine;
(383.5) Fexofenadine;
(384) Fibrinogen;
(385) Fibrinogen/antihemophilic factor, Human;
(386) Fibrinolysin, Human;
(386.3) Finasteride;
(386.5) Filgrastin;
(387) Flavoxate;
(387.1) Flecainide acetate;
(388) Florantyrone;
(388.5) Flosequinan;
(389) Floxuridine;
(389.5) Fluconazole;
(390) Flucytosine;
(390.5) Fludarabine;
(390.7) Fludeoxyglucose;
(391) Fludrocortisone;
(391.5) Flumazenil;
(392) Flumethasone;
(392.1) Flunisolide;
(393) Fluocinonide;
(394) Fluocinolone;
(395) Fluorescein;
(396) Fluoride—See exceptions;
(396.5) Fluorometholone;
(397) Fluorophosphates;
(398) Fluorouracil;
(399) Fluoxetine;
(399.5) Fluoxymesterone;
(400) Fluphenazine;
(401) Fluprednisolone;
(402) Flurandrenolide;
(402.2) Flurbiprofen;
(402.5) Flutamide;
(402.7) Fluticasone;
(402.8) Fluvastatin;

(402.9) Fluvoxamine;
(403) Folate sodium;
(404) Folic acid—See exceptions;
(404.3) Follitropin;
(404.5) Fomivirsen;
(404.7) Fondaparinux;
(405) Foreign protein;
(406) Formaldehyde—See exceptions;
(406.2) Formoterol;
(406.3) Fosamprenavir;
(406.35) Fosaprepitant;
(406.4) Foscarnet;
(406.5) Fosfomycin;
(406.7) Fosinopril;
(406.9) Fosphenytoin;
(406.93) Fospropofol;
(406.95) Frovatriptan;
(407) Furazolidone;
(408) Furosemide;
(408.2) Gabapentin;
(408.25) Gadobenate;
(408.3) Gadodiamide;
(408.35) Gadofosveset;
(408.4) Gadopentetate dimeglumine;
(408.6) Gadoteridol;
(408.8) Gadoversetamide;
(408.85) Gadoxetate;
(408.9) Galantamine;
(409) Gallamine triethiodide;
(409.3) Gallium citrate;
(409.5) Gallium nitrate;
(409.8) Galsulfase;
(410) Gamma benzene hexachloride;
(411) Gamma globulin;
(411.5) Ganciclovir;
(411.7) Ganirelix;
(412) Gas gangrene polyvalent antitoxin;
(412.03) Gatifloxacin;
(412.04) Gefitinib;
(412.05) Gemcitabine;
(412.1) Gemfibrozil;
(412.2) Gemifloxacin;
(412.3) Gemtuzumab ozogamicin;
(412.5) Genotropin;
(413) Gentamicin;
(414) Gentian violet vaginal suppositories;
(415) Gitalin;
(415.03) Glatiramer;
(415.05) Glimepiride;
(415.1) Glipizide;
(416) Glucagon;
(417) Gluceptate;
(418) Gluconate magnesium;
(419) Gluconate potassium—See exceptions;
(420) Glutamate arginine;
(420.1) Glyburide;
(420.5) Glycine—See exceptions;
(421) Glycobiarsol;
(422) Glycopyrrolate;
(423) Gold sodium thiomalate;
(424) Gold thiosulfate—See exceptions;
(424.4) Golimumab;
(425) Gomenol Solution;
(425.5) Gonadorelin acetate;
(426) Gonadotropin, Chroinic;
(427) Gonadotropin, Chroinic, Anti-human serum;
(428) Gonadotropin, Serum;
(428.5) Goserelin;
(429) Gramicidin;
(430) Gramineae pollens;
(430.3) Gramosetron;
(430.5) Granisetron;
(431) Griseofulvin;
(431.5) Guanabenz;
(432) Guanethidine;
(432.4) Guanadrel;
(432.7) Guanfacine;
(432.9) Guanidine;
(433) Halcinonide;
(433.5) Halobetasol Propionate;
(433.7) Halofantrine;
(434) Haloperidol;
(435) Haloprogin;
(436) Halothane;
(437) Hartman's solution;
(438) Heparin;
(439) Hetacillin;
(440) Hexachlorophene—See exceptions;
(441) Hexafluorenium;
(442) Hexocyclium;
(443) Hexylcaine;
(444) Histamine;
(445) Histoplasmin;
(445.5) Histrelin acetate;
(446) Homatropine;
(446.4) Human secretin;
(446.6) Hyaluronan;
(446.7) Hyaluronic acid;
(447) Hyaluronidase;
(448) Hydralazine;
(449) Hydrocalciferol;
(450) Hydrochlorothiazide;
(451) Hydrocortamate;
(452) Hydrocortisone—See exceptions;
(453) Hydroflumethiazide;
(454) Hydroquinone;
(455) Hydroxocobalamin—See exceptions;
(456) Hydroxyamphetamine;
(457) Hydroxychloroquine;
(458) Hydroxyprogesterone;
(459) Hydroxyurea;
(460) Hydroxyzine;

(461) Hyoscyamine;
(462) Hyoscyamus alkaloids;
(463) Hypophamine;
(463.03) Ibandronate;
(464) Ibuprofen—See exceptions;
(464.05) Ibutilide;
(464.1) Idarubicin;
(464.3) Idoxuridine;
(464.5) Idursulfase;
(464.6) Ifosfamide;
(464.67) Iloperidone;
(464.7) Iloprost;
(464.8) Imatinib;
(465) Imiglucerase;
(465.1) Imipenem/cilastatin;
(466) Imipramine;
(466.5) Imiquimod;
(467) Immune hepatitis B globulin, Human;
(468) Immune poliomyelitis globulin, Human;
(469) Immune serum globulin, Human;
(469.1) Indapamide;
(469.5) Indecainide;
(470) Indigotindisulfonate;
(470.05) Indinavir;
(470.1) Indium IN–III oxyquinolone;
(470.3) Indium IN–III pentetreotide;
(471) Indocyanine green;
(472) Indomethacin;
(472.5) Infliximab;
(473) Influenza virus vaccines;
(474) Injections, All substances for human use—See exceptions;
(474.2) Insulin aspart;
(474.4) Insulin glargine;
(474.45) Insulin glulisine;
(474.5) Interferon;
(475) Intrinsic factor concentrate manufactured for human use;
(475.3) Inulin;
(475.5) Iobenguane;
(476) Iocetamic acid;
(477) Iodamide;
(478) Iodinated I–125 serum albumin;
(479) Iodinated I–131 serum albumin;
(480) Iodinated glycerol-theophylline;
(481) Iodine solution, Strong oral;
(482) Iodipamide;
(482.5) Iodixanol;
(483) Iodized oil;
(484) Iodobenzoic acid—See exceptions;
(485) Iodobrassid;
(485.1) Iodohippurate sodium;
(486) Iodopyracet;
(487) Iodothiouracil;
(487.05) Iofetamine;
(487.08) Iohexol;
(487.1) Iopamidol;
(488) Iopanoic acid—See exceptions;
(489) Iophendylate;
(489.1) Iopromide;
(489.2) Iothalamate;
(489.3) Iothiouracil;
(489.5) Iotrolan;
(489.6) Ioversol;
(490.1) Ioxaglate;
(490.5) Ioxilan;
(491) Ipodate;
(491.5) Ipratropium;
(491.6) Irbesartan;
(491.7) Irinotecan;
(492) Iron cacodylate;
(493) Iron dextran injection;
(494) Iron peptonized;
(495) Iron sorbitex;
(496) Isocarboxazid;
(497) Isoetharine;
(498) Isoflurane;
(499) Isoflurophate;
(500) Isometheptene;
(501) Isoniazid;
(502) Isopropamide;
(503) Isoproterenol;
(504) Isosorbide dinitrate;
(504.05) Isosorbide mononitrate;
(504.1) Isosulfan blue;
(505) Isothipendyl;
(505.5) Isotretinoin;
(506) Isoxsuprine;
(506.5) Isradipine;
(506.7) Itraconazole;
(506.8) Ivermectin;
(506.9) Ixabepilone;
(507) Kanamycin;
(508) Reserved;
(509) Ketocholanic acids;
(509.1) Ketoconazole—See exceptions;
(509.15) Ketoprofen—See exceptions;
(509.17) Ketorolac tromethamine;
(509.18) Ketotifen—See exceptions;
(509.2) Labetalol;
(509.7) Lacosamide;
(510) Lactated ringers solution;
(511) Lactulose;
(511.3) Lamivudine;
(511.5) Lamotrigine;
(512) Lanatoside C;
(512.3) Lanreotide;
(512.5) Lansoprazole—see exceptions;
(512.6) Lanthanum;
(512.67) Lapatinib;
(512.7) Latanoprost;
(513) Latrodectus mactans;

(513.5) Leflunomide;
(513.7) Lenalidomide;
(513.8) Letrozole;
(514) Leucovorin;
(514.1) Leuprolide;
(514.5) Levalbuterol;
(515) Reserved;
(515.5) Levamisole;
(516) Levarterenol;
(516.05) Levetiracetam;
(516.07) Levobetaxolol;
(516.1) Levobunolol;
(516.3) Levobupivacine;
(516.5) Levocabastine;
(516.7) Levocarnitine;
(516.75) Levocetirizine;
(517) Levodopa;
(517.2) Levofloxacin;
(517.25) Levoleucovorin;
(517.3) Levomethadyl;
(517.4) Levonordefrin;
(518) Levopropoxyphene;
(519) Levothyroxine;
(520) Lidocaine—See exceptions;
(521) Lincomycin;
(522) Lindane—See exceptions;
(522.5) Linezolid;
(523) Linolenic acid;
(524) Liothyronine;
(525) Liotrix;
(525.5) Lisinopril;
(526) Lithium carbonate—See exceptions;
(527) Lithium citrate;
(528) Liver extract;
(528.3) Lodoxamide;
(528.5) Lomefloxacin;
(529) Lomustine;
(529.1) Loperamide—See exceptions;
(529.5) Lopinavir;
(529.7) Loracarbef;
(529.9) Loratadine —See exceptions;
(529.95) Losartan;
(529.97) Loteprednol;
(530) Lovastatin;
(530.5) Loxapine;
(530.7) Lubiprostone;
(531) Lugols solution;
(531.5) Lumefantrine;
(532) Lututrin;
(533) Lymphogranuloma venereum antigen;
(534) Lypressin synthetic;
(535) Mafenide;
(536) Magnesium gluconate—See exceptions;
(537) Magnesium salicylate;
(538) Mandelic acid—See exceptions;
(539) Mannitol—See exceptions;
(540) Mannitol hexanitrate;
(540.1) Maprotiline;
(540.3) Maraviroc;
(540.5) Masoprocol;
(541) Measles immune globulin, Human;
(542) Measles virus vaccines;
(543) Mebendazole for human use;
(544) Mecamylamine;
(544.5) Mecasermin;
(545) Mechlorethamine;
(546) Meclizine—See exceptions;
(546.5) Meclocycline;
(547) Meclofenamate;
(548) Medroxyprogesterone;
(549) Medrysone;
(550) Mefenamic acid;
(550.5) Mefloguine;
(551) Megestrol;
(552) Meglumine;
(552.5) Meloxicam;
(553) Melphalan;
(553.5) Memantine;
(554) Menadiol;
(555) Menadione;
(556) Meningococcal polysaccharide vaccine;
(557) Menotropins;
(558) Mepenzolate;
(559) Mephenesin;
(560) Mephentermine;
(561) Mephenytoin;
(562) Meprednisone;
(563) Mepivacaine;
(563.5) Mequinol;
(564) Meralluride;
(565) Mercaptomerin;
(566) Mercaptopurine;
(567) Mercury bichloride—See exceptions;
(567.1) Meropenem;
(567.2) Mersalyl;
(567.3) Mesalamine;
(567.5) Mesna;
(568) Mesoridazine;
(569) Mestranol;
(570) Metaproterenol;
(571) Metaraminol;
(572) Metaxalone;
(572.5) Metformin;
(573) Methacholine;
(574) Methacycline;
(575) Methallenestril;
(576) Reserved;
(577) Reserved;
(578) Methantheline;
(579) Methazolamide;
(580) Methdilazine;
(581) Methenamine hippurate;

(582) Methenamine mandelate;
(583) Methenamine sulfosalicylate;
(584) Methicillin;
(585) Methimazole;
(586) Methiodal;
(587) Methionine;
(588) Methixene;
(589) Methocarbamol;
(590) Methotrexate;
(591) Methotrimeprazine;
(592) Methoxamine;
(593) Methoxsalen;
(594) Methoxyflurane;
(595) Methoxyphenamine;
(595.5) Methoxy polyethylene glycol-epoetin beta;
(596) Methscopolamine;
(597) Methsuximide;
(598) Methyclothiazide;
(599) Methylandrostenediol;
(600) Methylatropine;
(601) Methyldopa;
(602) Methyldopate;
(603) Methylene blue, Oral;
(604) Methylergonovine;
(604.5) Methylnaltrexone;
(605) Methylprednisolone;
(606) Reserved;
(607) Methysergide;
(608) Metoclopramide;
(609) Metocurine iodide injection;
(610) Metolazone;
(611) Metoprolol;
(612) Metrizamide;
(612.5) Metrizoate;
(613) Metronidazole;
(614) Metyrapone;
(615) Metyrosine;
(615.01) Mexiletine;
(615.1) Mezlocillin;
(615.6) Mibefradil;
(615.9) Micafungin;
(616) Miconazole—See exceptions;
(617) Microfibrillar collagen hemostat;
(617.1) Midodrine;
(617.22) Midubosathol;
(617.3) Mifepristone;
(617.4) Miglitol;
(617.44) Miglustat;
(617.47) Milnacipran;
(617.5) Milrinone;
(618) Minocycline;
(619) Minoxidil—See exceptions;
(619.3) Mirtazapine;
(619.5) Misoprostol;
(620) Mithramycin;
(621) Mitomycin;
(622) Mitotane;
(622.3) Mitoxantrone;
(622.5) Mivacurium;
(622.7) Moexipril;
(623) Molindone;
(623.5) Mometasone;
(624) Monobenzone;
(624.1) Monooctanoin;
(624.5) Montelukast;
(624.7) Moricizine;
(625) Morrhuate;
(625.1) Moxalactam;
(625.3) Moxidectin;
(625.5) Moxifloxacin;
(626) Mumps virus vaccines;
(626.5) Mupirocin;
(627) Mushroom spores which, when mature, contain either psilocybin or psilocin;
(627.5) Mycophenolate;
(628) N-acetyl–1–cysteine;
(629) N. cattarhalis antigen;
(629.5) Nabumetone;
(630) Nadolol;
(630.5) Nafarelin;
(631) Nafcillin;
(631.5) Naftifine;
(632) Nalbuphine;
(633) Reserved;
(634) Nalidixic acid;
(634.5) Nalmefene;
(635) Naloxone;
(635.1) Naltrexone;
(636) Reserved;
(637) Naphazoline—See exceptions;
(638) Naproxen—See exceptions;
(638.3) Naratriptan;
(638.4) Natalizumab;
(638.45) Nebivolol;
(638.5) Nedocromil;
(638.7) Nefazodone;
(638.75) Nelarabine;
(638.8) Nelfinavir;
(639) Neomycin—See exceptions;
(640) Neostigmine;
(640.1) Nepafenac;
(640.2) Nesiritide;
(640.3) Netilmicin;
(640.4) Nevirapine;
(640.5) Niacinamide—See exceptions;
(640.7) Nicardipine;
(640.8) Niclosamide;
(641.1) Nicotine resin complex (polacrilex)—See exceptions;
(641.15) Nicotine transdermal system—See exceptions;
(642) Nicotinyl alcohol;
(642.1) Nifedipine;
(643) Nifuroximine;

(644) Nikethamide;
(644.3) Nilotinib;
(644.4) Nilutamide;
(644.5) Nimodipine;
(644.7) Nisoldipine;
(644.72) Nitazoxanide;
(644.8) Nitisinone;
(644.9) Nitric oxide—for use in humans;
(645) Nitrofurantoin;
(646) Nitrofurazone;
(647) Nitroglycerin;
(648) Nitroprusside—See exceptions;
(648.3) Nitrous oxide—See exceptions;
(648.6) Nizatidine—See exceptions;
(649.1) Nomifensine maleate;
(650) Nonoxynol—See exceptions;
(651) Norepinephrine;
(652) Norethindrone;
(653) Norethynodrel;
(653.5) Norfloxacin;
(654) Norgestrel;
(655) Normal serum albumin, Human;
(656) Nortriptyline;
(657) Nositol;
(658) Novobiocin;
(659) Nux vomica;
(660) Nylidrin;
(661) Nystatin;
(661.5) Octreotide acetate;
(661.6) Ofatumumab;
(661.7) Ofloxacin;
(661.8) Olanzapine;
(662) Old tuberculin;
(663) Oleandomycin;
(663.1) Olmesartan;
(663.2) Olopatadine;
(663.3) Olsalazine Sodium;
(663.4) Omega–3–acid;
(663.5) Omeprazole—See exceptions;
(663.7) Ondansetron;
(663.75) Orlistat — See exceptions;
(664) Orphenadrine;
(665) Orthoiodobenzoic acid;
(665.5) Oseltamivir;
(665.7) Ovine hyaluronidase;
(666) Oxacillin;
(666.4) Oxaliplatin;
(666.6) Oxamniquine;
(667) Oxaprozin;
(667.5) Oxcarbazepine;
(668) Oxethazaine;
(668.5) Oxiconazole;
(669) Oxolinic acid;
(669.1) Oxprenolol;
(670) Oxtriphylline;
(671) Oxybutynin;
(672) Oxygen for human use—See exceptions;
(673) Reserved;
(674) Oxyphenbutazone;
(675) Oxyphencyclimine;
(676) Oxyphenisatin;
(677) Oxyphenonium;
(678) Oxyquinoline;
(679) Oxytetracycline;
(680) Oxytocin;
(680.5) Ozogamicin;
(681) P-nitrosulfathiazole;
(681.3) Paclitaxel;
(681.4) Palifermin;
(681.45) Paliperidone;
(681.5) Palonosetron;
(681.7) Pamidronate;
(682) Pancreatin dornase;
(683) Pancreatic enzyme;
(684) Pancrelipase;
(685) Pancuronium;
(685.5) Panidronate;
(685.6) Panitumumab;
(685.7) Pantoprazole;
(686) Papaverine;
(687) Paramethadione;
(688) Paramethasone;
(689) Paranitrosulfathiazole;
(690) Parathyroid injection;
(691) Pargyline;
(691.5) Paricalcitol;
(692) Paromomycin;
(692.2) Paroxetine;
(692.3) Pazopanib;
(692.4) Pegademase bovine;
(692.5) Pegaspargase;
(692.51) Pegfilgrastin;
(692.515) Peginterferon;
(692.52) Pegvisomant;
(692.54) Pemetrexed;
(692.55) Pemirolast;
(692.6) Penbutolol;
(692.8) Penciclovir;
(693) Penicillamine;
(694) Penicillin;
(695) Penicillin G;
(696) Penicillin O;
(697) Penicillin V;
(698) Penicillinase;
(699) Pentaerythritol tetranitrate;
(700) Pentagastrin;
(700.1) Pentamidine isethionate;
(701) Pentapiperide;
(701.5) Pentetate calcium trisodium;
(701.7) Pentetate zinc trisodium;
(702) Penthienate;
(703) Pentolinium;

(703.03) Pentosan;
(703.05) Pentostatin;
(703.1) Pentoxifylline;
(703.4) Pentylenetetrazol;
(703.45) Perflexane;
(703.5) Perflubron;
(703.6) Perfluoroalkylpolyether;
(703.65) Perflutren;
(703.7) Pergolide;
(704) Perindopril;
(704.1) Permethrin—See exceptions;
(705) Perphenazine;
(706) Pertussis immune globulin, Human;
(707) Phenacemide;
(708) Phenaglycodol;
(709) Phenaphthazine;
(710) Phenazopyridine—See exceptions;
(711) Phenelzine;
(712) Phenethicillin;
(713) Phenformin;
(714) Phenindamine;
(715) Phenindione;
(716) Pheniramine—See exceptions;
(717) Phenitramin;
(718) Phenothiazine derivatives;
(719) Phenoxybenzamine;
(720) Phenoxymethyl penicillin;
(721) Phenuprocoumon;
(722) Phensuximide;
(723) Phentolamine;
(724) Phenylbutazone;
(725) Phenylmercuric acetate;
(726) Phenylmercuric nitrate;
(726.5) Phenylpropanolamine;
(727) Phenyltoloxamine dihydrogen citrate;
(727.2) Phenytoin;
(728) Phthalylsulfacetamide;
(729) Phthalylsulfathiazole;
(730) Physostigmine;
(731) Phytonadione;
(731.1) Pimozide;
(732) Pilocarpine;
(732.3) Pinacidil;
(732.7) Pindolol;
(732.8) Pioglitazone;
(732.9) Pimecrolimus;
(733) Pipazethate;
(733.5) Pipecuronium;
(734) Pipenzolate;
(735) Piperacetazine;
(735.1) Piperacillin;
(736) Piperazine;
(737) Piperidolate;
(738) Piperocaine;
(739) Pipobraman;
(740) Pipradrol;
(740.05) Pirbuterol;
(740.1) Piroxicam;
(740.5) Pitavastatin;
(741) Plague vaccine;
(742) Plasma protein fraction;
(742.3) Plerixafor;
(742.5) Plicamycin;
(743) Pneumococcal polyvalent vaccine;
(743.3) Podofilox;
(743.5) Podophyllotoxin;
(744) Poison ivy extract;
(745) Poison ivy oak extract;
(746) Poison ivy oak, sumac extract;
(747) Poldine methylsulfate;
(748) Poliomyelitis vaccine;
(749) Poliovirus vaccine, Live, Oral, All;
(750) Polyestradiol;
(751) Polymyxin B—See exceptions;
(751.5) Polytetrafluoroethylene;
(752) Polythiazide;
(752.2) Poractant alfa;
(752.5) Porfimer;
(752.7) Posaconazole;
(753) Posterior pituitary;
(754) Potassium acetate injection;
(755) Potassium acid phosphate—See exceptions;
(756) Potassium p-aminobenzoate—See exceptions;
(757) Potassium aminosalicylate—See exceptions;
(758) Potassium arsenite—See exceptions;
(759) Potassium bicarbonate—See exceptions;
(760) Potassium carbonate—See exceptions;
(761) Potassium chloride—See exceptions;
(762) Potassium citrate—See exceptions;
(763) Potassium gluconate—See exceptions;
(764) Potassium hetacillin;
(765) Potassium iodide—See exceptions;
(766) Reserved;
(767) Potassium permanganate—See exceptions;
(768) Povidone—Iodine—See exceptions;
(768.8) Pralatrexate;
(769) Pralidoxime;
(769.2) Pramipexole;
(769.3) Pramlintide;
(769.35) Prasugrel;
(769.4) Pravastatin;
(769.7) Praziquantel;
(770) Prazosin;
(770.5) Prednicarbate;
(771) Prednisolone;
(772) Prednisone;
(773) Prilocaine;
(774) Primaquine;
(775) Primidone;
(776) Probenecid;
(777) Probucol;
(778) Procainamide;

(779) Procaine;
(780) Procaine penicillin;
(781) Procaine penicillin G;
(782) Procarbazine;
(783) Prochlorperazine;
(784) Procyclidine;
(785) Progesterone;
(785.5) Proguanil;
(786) Promazine;
(787) Promethazine;
(788) Promethestrol;
(788.5) Propafenone;
(789) Propantheline;
(790) Proparacaine;
(791) Prophenpyridamine—See exceptions;
(792) Propiolactone;
(793) Propiomazine;
(793.5) Propofol;
(794) Propoxycaine;
(795) Propranolol;
(795.5) Propylhexedrine;
(796) Propylparaben;
(797) Propylthiouracil;
(798) Protamine sulfate injection;
(799) Protein hydrolysate injection;
(800) Protein, Foreign injection;
(801) Proteolytic enzyme;
(802) Protirelin;
(803) Protokylol;
(804) Protoveratrine A and B;
(805) Protriptyline;
(805.5) Prussian blue;
(806) Pseudoephedrine—See exceptions;
(807) Pseudomonas polysaccharide complex;
(808) P-ureidobenzenearsonic acid;
(809) Purified protein derivatives of tuberculin;
(810) Pyrantel;
(811) Pyrazinamide;
(812) Pyrazolon;
(813) Pyridostigmine;
(814) Pyrimethamine;
(815) Pyrrobutamine;
(816) Pyrvinium;
(816.5) Quetiapine;
(817) Quinacrine;
(817.5) Quinapril;
(818) Quinestrol;
(819) Quinethazone;
(820) Quinidine;
(821) Quinine hydrochloride;
(822) Quinine and urea hydrochloride;
(822.3) Quinupristin;
(822.5) Rabeprazole;
(823) Rabies anti-serum;
(824) Rabies immune globulin, Human;
(825) Rabies vaccine;
(826) Radio-iodinated compounds;
(827) Radio-iodine;
(828) Radio-iron;
(829) Radioisotopes;
(830) Radiopaque media;
(831) Ragweed pollen extract;
(831.02) Raloxifene;
(831.03) Raltegravir;
(831.04) Ramelteon;
(831.05) Ramipril;
(831.07) Ranibizumab;
(831.1) Ranitidine—See exceptions;
(831.3) Ranolazine;
(831.5) Rapacuronium;
(831.7) Rasagiline;
(832) Rauwolfia serpentina;
(832.2) Reboparhamil;
(832.5) Regadenoson;
(833) Rescinnamine;
(834) Reserpine;
(835) Reserpine alkaloids;
(836) Resorcinol monoacetate—See exceptions;
(836.3) Retapamulin;
(836.5) Retinoic acid, all-trans;
(837) Rhus toxicodendron antigen;
(838) Rh D immune globulin, Human;
(838.5) Ribavirin;
(839) Riboflavin—See exceptions;
(840) Ricinoleic acid;
(840.5) Rifabutin;
(841) Reserved;
(842) Rifampin;
(842.1) Rifapentine;
(842.15) Rifaximin;
(842.17) Rilonacept;
(842.2) Riluzole;
(842.4) Rimantadine;
(842.7) Rimexolone;
(843) Ringer's injection;
(843.2) Risedronate;
(843.3) Risperidone;
(843.7) Ritodrine;
(843.8) Ritonavir;
(843.82) Rituximab;
(843.83) Rivastigmine;
(843.9) Rizatritpan;
(844) Rocky mountain spotted fever vaccine;
(844.5) Rocuronium;
(844.7) Rofecoxib;
(845) Rolitetracycline;
(845.1) Romidepsin;
(845.15) Romiplostim;
(845.3) Ropinirole;
(845.5) Ropivacaine;
(845.7) Rosiglitazone;
(845.8) Rosuvastatin;

(845.9) Rotavirus vaccine;
(845.95) Rotigotine;
(846) Rotoxamine;
(846.5) RSVIGIV;
(847) Rubella and mumps virus vaccine;
(848) Rubella virus vaccine;
(848.5) Rufinamide;
(849) Rutin—See exceptions;
(849.5) Sacrosidase;
(850) Salicylazosulfapyridine;
(850.5) Salmeterol;
(851) Salmonella typhosa, Killed;
(851.02) Salvinorin A;
(851.03) Samarium SM 153 lexidronam;
(851.04) Saneromazile;
(851.045) Sapropterin;
(851.05) Saquinavir;
(851.1) Saralasin acetate;
(851.7) Saxagliptin;
(852) Scopolamine;
(852.1) Secretin;
(852.6) Selegiline;
(853) Selenium sulfide—See exceptions;
(853.5) Selenomethionine;
(854) Senecio cineraria extract ophthalmic solution;
(855) Senega fluid extract;
(855.3) Seractide acetate;
(855.5) Sermorelin Acetate;
(855.6) Sertaconazole;
(855.7) Sertraline;
(855.74) Sevelamer;
(855.8) Sevoflurane;
(855.85) Sildenafil;
(855.9) Silodosin;
(856) Silver nitrate ophthalmic solutions or suspensions;
(857) Silver sulfadiazine cream;
(857.3) Simethicone coated cellulose suspension;
(857.5) Simvastatin;
(858) Sincalide;
(858.3) Sinecatechins;
(858.5) Sirolimus;
(858.7) Sitagliptin;
(859) Sitosterols;
(860) Solutions for injections, All;
(861) Smallpox vaccine;
(862) Sodium acetate injection;
(863) Sodium acetrizoate;
(864) Sodium ascorbate injection;
(865) Sodium biphosphate—See exceptions;
(866) Sodium cacodylate;
(867) Sodium chloride injection;
(868) Sodium dehydrocholate;
(869) Sodium dextrothyroxine;
(870) Sodium estrone;
(871) Sodium fluorescein—See exceptions;
(872) Sodium fluoride—See exceptions;
(873) Sodium iothalamate;
(873.5) Sodium nitroprusside;
(873.7) Sodium phenylbutyrate;
(874) Sodium polystyrene sulfonate;
(875) Sodium propionated vaginal cream;
(876) Sodium sulfacetamide;
(877) Sodium sulfadiazine;
(878) Sodium sulfobromophthalein;
(879) Sodium sulfoxone;
(880) Sodium tetradecyl;
(880.5) Sodium thiosulfate;
(881) Sodium tyropanoate;
(881.05) Solifenacin;
(881.1) Somatrem;
(882) Somatropin;
(882.5) Sorafenib;
(883) Sorbus extract;
(883.5) Sotalol;
(883.8) Sparfloxacin;
(884) Sparteine;
(885) Spectinomycin;
(886) Spirapril;
(887) Spironolactone;
(888) Staphage lysate bacterial antigen;
(889) Staphylococcus and streptococcus vaccine;
(890) Staphylococcus toxoid;
(890.5) Stavudine;
(891) Stibophen;
(892) Stinging insect antigens—Combined;
(893) Stockes expectorant;
(894) Stramonium;
(895) Streptococcus antigen;
(896) Streptokinase-streptodornase;
(897) Streptomycin;
(898) Strontium—See exceptions;
(899) Strophanthin–G;
(900) Strychnine—See exceptions;
(901) Succimer;
(902) Succinylchloline;
(903) Succinylsulfathiazole;
(903.1) Sucralfate;
(903.2) Sulconazole;
(904) Sulfabenzamide vaginal preparations;
(905) Sulfacetamide;
(906) Sulfachlorpyridazine;
(907) Sulfacytine;
(908) Sulfadiazine;
(909) Sulfadimethoxine;
(909.1) Sulfadoxine;
(910) Sulfaethidole;
(911) Sulfaguanidine;
(912) Sulfamerazine;
(913) Sulfameter;
(914) Sulfamethazine;
(915) Sulfamethizole;
(916) Sulfamethoxazole;

(917) Sulfamethoxypyridazine;
(918) Sulfanilamide;
(919) Sulfaphenazole;
(920) Reserved;
(921) Sulfapyridine;
(922) Sulfasalazine;
(922.5) Sulfathiazole;
(923) Sulfinpyrazone;
(924) Sulfisomidine;
(925) Sulfisoxazole;
(926) Sulfur thioglycerol;
(927) Sulindac;
(927.5) Sumatriptan;
(927.7) Sunitinib;
(928) Superinone;
(928.1) Suprofen;
(929) Sutilains;
(930) Syrosingopine;
(930.5) Tacrine;
(930.7) Tacrolimus;
(930.9) Tadalafil;
(931) Tamoxifen;
(931.1) Tamsulosin;
(931.3) Tazarotene;
(931.35) Tazobacam;
(931.5) Technetium;
(931.55) Tegaserod;
(931.555) Telavancin;
(931.56) Telbivudine;
(931.57) Telithromycin;
(931.6) Telmisartan;
(931.7) Temafloxacin;
(931.75) Temozolomide;
(931.77) Temsirolimus;
(931.8) Teniposide;
(931.85) Terazosin;
(931.9) Tenofovir;.
(931.95) Terbinafine—See exceptions;
(932) Terbutaline;
(932.05) Terconazole;
(932.1) Terfenadine;
(932.3) Teriparatide;
(933) Terpin hydrate with codeine;
(934) Reserved;
(935) Reserved;
(936) Tetanus and diphtheria toxoids;
(937) Tetanus antitoxin;
(938) Tetanus immune globulin;
(939) Tetanus toxoids;
(939.5) Tetrabenazine;
(940) Tetracaine;
(941) Tetracycline;
(942) Tetraethylammonium chloride;
(943) Tetrahydrozoline—See exceptions;
(943.5) Thalidomide;
(944) Thallous chloride;
(945) Theobromide;
(945.5) Theobromine;
(946) Theobromine magnesium oleate;
(947) Theophylline—See exceptions;
(948) Theophylline sodium glycinate;
(949) Thiabendazole;
(950) Thiamylal;
(951) Thiethylperazine;
(952) Thiopropazate;
(953) Thioguanine;
(954) Thioridazine;
(955) Thiosalicylate;
(956) Thiotepa;
(957) Thiothixene;
(958) Thiphenamil;
(959) Thrombin;
(960) Thyroglobulin;
(961) Thyroid;
(962) Thyrotropin;
(963) Thyroxine;
(964) Thyroxine fraction;
(964.5) Tiagabine;
(965) Ticarcillin;
(965.5) Ticlopidine;
(966) Ticrynafen;
(966.3) Tigecycline;
(966.6) Tiludronate;
(967) Timolol;
(967.1) Tinidazole;
(967.2) Tinzaparin;
(967.3) Tioconazole—See exceptions;
(967.5) Tiopronin;
(967.55) Tiotropium;
(967.57) Tipranavir;
(967.6) Tirofiban;
(967.7) Tizanidine;
(968) Tobramycin;
(968.1) Tocainide;
(969) Tocamphyl;
(969.6) Tocilizumab;
(970) Tolazamide;
(971) Tolazoline;
(972) Tolbutamide;
(972.5) Tolcapone;
(973) Tolmetin;
(973.05) Tolterodine;
(973.07) Tolvaptan;
(973.1) Topiramate;
(973.3) Topotecan;
(973.4) Toremifene;
(973.5) Torsemide;
(973.7) Tramadol;
(973.8) Trandolapril;
(973.9) Tranexamic acid;
(974) Tranylcypromine;
(974.4) Travoprost;

(974.5) Trazodone;
(974.7) Treprostinil;
(975) Tretinoin;
(976) Triamcinolone;
(977) Triamterene;
(978) Trichlormethiazide;
(979) Trichloroacetic acid—See exceptions;
(980) Trichloroethylene—See exceptions;
(981) Trichlobisonium;
(982) Triclofos;
(983) Tridihexethyl chloride;
(983.1) Trientine;
(984) Triethanolamine polypeptides;
(985) Triethylenethiophosphoramide;
(986) Trifluoperazine;
(987) Triflupromazine;
(988) Trifluridine;
(989) Trihexyphenidyl;
(990) Triiodothyronine;
(990.1) Trilostane;
(991) Trimeprazine;
(992) Trimethadione;
(993) Trimethaphan cansylate;
(994) Trimethobenzamide;
(995) Trimethoprim;
(995.5) Trimetrexate;
(996) Trimipramine;
(997) Triolein;
(998) Trioxsalen;
(999) Tripelennamine—See exceptions;
(1000) Triphenyltetrazolium;
(1001) Triple sulfas;
(1002) Triprolidine —See exceptions;
(1002.5) Triptorelin;
(1003) Trisulfapyrimidines;
(1003.5) Troglitazone;
(1004) Troleandomycin;
(1005) Trolnitrate;
(1006) Tromethamine;
(1007) Tropicamide;
(1007.3) Trospium;.
(1007.5) Trovafloxacin;
(1008) Trypsin;
(1009) Trypsin-chymotrypsin;
(1010) Tuaminoheptane;
(1011) Tuberculin, Purified protein derivatives;
(1012) Tuberculin tine test;
(1013) Tuberculin, Old;
(1014) Tubocurarine;
(1015) Tybamate;
(1016) Typhoid and paratyphoid vaccine;
(1017) Typhus vaccine;
(1018) Tyropanoate;
(1019) Undecoylium;
(1019.5) Unoprostone;
(1020) Uracil;
(1021) Urea—See exceptions;
(1021.3) Urofollitropin;
(1021.5) Ursodiol;
(1021.6) Ustekinumab;
(1021.7) Valacyclovir;
(1021.8) Valdecoxib;
(1022) Valethamate;
(1022.2) Valganciclovir;
(1023) Valproate;
(1024) Valproic acid—See exceptions;
(1024.3) Valrubicin;
(1024.5) Valsartan;
(1025) Vancomycin;
(1025.5) Vardenafil;
(1025.7) Varenicline;
(1026) Vasopressin;
(1027) VDRL antigen;
(1027.1) Vecuronium bromide;
(1027.5) Velnacrine;
(1027.6) Venlafaxine;
(1027.7) Verapamil;
(1028) Veratrum viride;
(1029) Versenate;
(1029.5) Verteporfin;
(1030) Vidarabine;
(1030.3) Vigabatrin;
(1031) Vinblastine;
(1032) Vincristine;
(1032.5) Vinorelbine;
(1033) Vinyl ethyl—See exceptions;
(1034) Viomycin;
(1035) Vitamin K;
(1036) Vitamin B12 injection;
(1037) Vitamine with fluoride;
(1037.5) Voriconazole;
(1037.7) Vorinostat;
(1038) Warfarin;
(1039) Wargarin;
(1039.1) Xylocaine;
(1040) Yellow fever vaccine;
(1041) Yohimbine;
(1042) 4–chloro–3, 5–xylenol—See exceptions;
(1042.01) Zafirlukast;
(1042.02) Zalcitabine;
(1042.03) Zanamivir;
(1042.05) Zidovudine;
(1042.4) Zileuton;
(1042.7) Zinc acetate—See exceptions;
(1042.75) Ziprasidone;
(1042.8) Zoledronic Acid;
(1042.9) Zolmitriptan;
(1042.92) Zonisamide;
(1043) Devices that require a prescription:
(A) Cellulose, Oxadized, Regenerated (surgical absorbable hemostat)—See exceptions;
(B) Diaphragms for vaginal use;

(C) Hemodialysis solutions;

(D) Hemodialysis kits;

(E) Lippes loop intrauterine;

(F) Saf–T–Coil intrauterine device;

(G) Intrauterine devices, All;

(H) Absorbable hemostat;

(I) Gonorrhea test kit.

(c) The following are exceptions to and exemptions from subsection (b) of this Code section:

(1) Atropine sulfate—where the oral dose is less than 1/200 gr. per unit;

(2) Bacitracin cream or ointment for topical use;

(3) Belladonna or belladonna alkaloids when in combination with other drugs and the dosage unit is less than 0.1 mg. of the alkaloids or its equivalent;

(3.5) Bentoquatam—when used with a strength of 5 percent or less in topical preparations;

(4) Beta carotene—all forms occurring in food products or lotions;

(5) Bromelain, pancreatic enzymes, trypsin and bile extract—when labeled properly as digestive aids with appropriate dosage and in compliance with FDA labeling and restrictions;

(6) Brompheniramine—where a single dosage unit is 4 mg. or less but with no more than 3 mg. of the dextrorotary optical isomer of racemic brompheniramine per released dose;

(6.2) Butenafine—when used with a strength of 1 percent or less as a topical preparation;

(6.4) Butoconazole—when used with a strength up to 2 percent in a vaginal preparation;

(6.45) Capsaicin—when in an external analgesic with concentration of 0.25 percent or less;

(6.5) Cetirizine—when a single dosage unit is either 1mg per 1ml or less or 10mg or less;

(6.7) Chlorhexadine—when used with a strength up to 4 percent in a topical skin product;

(7) Chlorpheniramine—where a single dosage unit is 12 mg. or less;

(7.1) Cimetidine—when a single dosage unit is 200 mg. or less;

(7.3) Clemastine—where a single dose is 1.34 mg. or less;

(7.5) Clotrimazole—when a single vaginal insert is 200 mg. or less or with a strength up to 2 percent in a topical skin, topical vaginal, or vaginal product;

(7.8) Cromolyn—when used as cromolyn sodium in a nasal solution of 4 percent or less in strength;

(7.9) Dexbrompheniramine—when a single dosage unit is 6 mg. or less;

(8) Diphenhydramine—up to 12.5 mg. in each 5 cc's when used in cough preparations and up to 50 mg. per single dose when used as a nighttime sleep aid or used as an antihistamine and labeled in compliance with FDA requirements;

(8.5) Docosanol—when used in 10 percent topical preparation to treat fever blisters, cold sores, or fever blisters and cold sores.

(9) Doxylamine succinate—where a single dosage form is 25 mg. or less and when labeled to be used as a nighttime sedative;

(9.3) Edetate—when used in any form other than an oral or parenteral;

(9.5) Famotidine—when a single dosage unit is 20 mg. or less;

(9.7) Fluoride—when used with a strength up to 1,500 parts per million in an oral care or dentifrice product;

(9.8) Glycine—when used with a strength up to 1.5 percent in an irrigation solution, when used in a topical skin product;

(10) Hydrocortisone topical skin preparations up to 1.0 percent in strength;

(11) Hydroxocobalamin, riboflavin, niacinamide, ergocalciferol (maximum of 400 I.U. per day), Folic acid (maximum of 0.4 mg. per day), and magnesium gluconate—when as a source of vitamins and dietary supplement but must bear such labels and adhere to such restrictions of FDA regulations;

(11.1) Ibuprofen—where a single dose is 200 mg. or less;

(11.6) Reserved;

(12) Insulin—all injectable products which do not require a prescription drug order and bear a label which indicates "Rx Use Only" or are otherwise listed under subsection (b) of this Code section; and no injectable insulin product may be sold except by a pharmacy issued a permit by the State Board of Pharmacy or by a medical practitioner authorized to dispense medications;

(12.3) Ketoconazole—when used with a strength of 1 percent or less in topical preparations;

(12.5) Ketoprofen—when a single dosage unit is 12.5 mg. or less;

(12.7) Ketotifen—when used with a strength of 0.025 percent or less in an ophthalmic solution;

(12.9) Lansoprazole—when a single dosage unit is 15 mg. or less;

(13) Lidocaine topical ointment, 25 mg./gm. or less;

(13.5) Loperamide—where a single dose is either 1 mg. per 5 ml. or 2 mg. per dosage unit;

(13.7) Loratadine—when used in a single dose of 10 mg. or less, including doses used in combination with other drugs provided for under this subsection;

(14) Meclizine—25 mg. or less;

(14.1) Miconazole—when used as antifungal powder or cream, or both, and containing not more than 4 percent of miconazole, or when used as a vaginal insert and containing not more than 1,200 mg. of miconazole;

(14.2) Minoxidil—when used with a strength of 5 percent or less in topical preparations;

(14.3) Naphazoline—when used in an ophthalmic solution in a concentration of 0.027 percent or less in combination with a pheniramine concentration of 0.315 percent or less;

(14.5) Naproxen—where a single dosage unit is 220 mg. or less;

(15) Neomycin sulfate ointment or cream for topical use;

(15.5) Nicotine resin complex (polacrilex)—when used as oral chewing gum where a single dose (piece of gum) is 4 mg. or less;

(15.55) Nicotine transdermal system—when used in a strength of 21 mg. or less per transdermal patch (transdermal delivery system);

(16) Nitrous oxide—air products suppliers shall not sell medical grade nitrous oxide to other than licensed practitioners or medical suppliers; industrial grade nitrous oxide shall only be sold when mixed with not less than 100 parts per million of sulfur dioxide and used as a fuel additive for combustion engines or when used in industrial laboratory equipment;

(16.3) Nizatidine—when a single dosage unit is 75 mg. or less;

(16.8) Nonoxynol—when used with a strength up to 12.5 percent or 1 gram per dose in a vaginal product;

(16.9) Omeprazole—when a single dosage unit is 20.6 mg. or less;

(16.95) Orlistat-when a single dosage unit is 60 mg. or less;

(17) Oxygen—compressed oxygen which is not labeled "CAUTION: Federal law prohibits dispensing without prescription" or similar wording;

(17.3) Permethrin—when used as a topical preparation in a strength of 1 percent or less;

(17.5) Phenazopyridine—where a single dose is 100 mg. or less, as approved by the federal Food and Drug Administration;

(18) Pheniramine—when the oral dose is 25 mg. or less, or when used in an ophthalmic solution in a concentration of 0.315 percent or less in combination with a naphazoline concentration of 0.027 percent or less;

(19) Polymyxin B when in combination with other drugs in an ointment or cream for topical use;

(20) Any potassium electrolyte when manufactured for use as a dietary supplement, food additive for industrial, scientific, or commercial use, or when added to other drug products when the product is not intended as a potassium supplement but must bear such labels and adhere to such restrictions of FDA regulations;

(21) Povidone—Iodine solutions and suspensions;

(22) Reserved;

(23) Pseudoephedrine—when a single dosage unit is 60 mg. or less or when manufactured in an extended release form with a dosage unit of 240 mg. or less;

(23.5) Ranitidine—when a single dosage unit is 150 mg. or less;

(24) Rutin—where the dosage unit is less than 60 mg.;

(25) Selenium sulfide suspension 1 percent or less in strength;

(25.1) Strychnine—when used in combination with other active ingredients in a rodent killer, and when not bearing a label containing the words "CAUTION: Federal law prohibits dispensing without prescription" or other similar wording;

(25.5) Terbinafine—when used with a strength of 1 percent or less in a topical antifungal cream;

(26) Tetrahydrozaline for ophthalmic or topical use;

(27) Theophylline preparations alone or in combination with other drugs prepared for and approved for OTC (over the counter) sale by FDA; example—tedral tablets (plain) or oral suspension;

(27.5) Tioconazole—when used with a strength of 1 percent or less in topical preparations or when used with a strength of 6.5 percent or less in vaginal preparations;

(28) Tripelennamine cream or ointment for topical use;

(28.5) Triprolidine—when a single dose is 5 mg. or less when combined in the same preparation as one or more other drug products for use as an antihistamine or decongestant or an antihistamine and decongestant;

(29) Urea—except when the manufacturer's label contains the wording "CAUTION: Federal law prohibits dispensing without prescription" or similar wording;

(29.5) Zinc acetate—when used in topical preparations;

(30) Any drug approved by FDA for animal use and the package does not bear the statement "CAUTION: Federal law prohibits dispensing without prescription" or similar wording; or

(31) Loperamide Oral Liquid (1.00 mg/5.00 ml).

(d) The following list of compounds or preparations may be purchased without a prescription, provided the products are manufactured for industrial, scientific, or commercial sale or use, unless they are intended for human use or contain on the label "CAUTION: Federal law prohibits dispensing without prescription" or similar wording:

(1) Aminosalicylate;

(2) Aminosalicylate calcium;

(3) Aminosalicylate potassium;

(4) Aminosalicylate sodium;

(5) Aminosalicylic acid;

(6) Barium;

(7) Beta-carotene;

(8) Bismuth sodium tartrate;

(9) Cadmium sulfide;

(10) Calcium disodium edetate;

(11) Cellulose, Oxadized, Regenerated;

(12) Chlorabutanol;

(13) Chloranil;

(14) Chloroacetic acid;

(15) Chloroform;

(16) Colchicine;

(17) Dapsone;

(18) Dimethyl sulfoxide;

(19) Disodium edetate;

(20) Edetate disodium;

(21) Ether;

(22) Ethoxazene;

(23) Ethyl chloride;

(24) Fluoride;

(25) Formaldehyde;

(26) Gold thiosulfate;

(27) Hexachlorophene;

(28) Iodobenzoic acid;

(29) Iopanoic acid;

(30) Lindane;

(31) Lithium carbonate;

(32) Mandelic acid;

(33) Mannitol;

(34) Mercury bichloride;

(35) Nitroprusside;

(36) Potassium aminosalicylate;

(37) Potassium p-aminobenzoate;

(37.5) Potassium perchlorate;

(38) Potassium permanganate;

(39) Resorcinol monoacetate;

(40) Selenium sulfide;

(41) Sodium biphosphate;

(42) Sodium fluorescein;

(43) Sodium fluoride;

(44) Strontium;

(45) Trichloroacetic acid;

(46) Trichloroethylene;

(47) Valproic acid;

(48) Vinyl ether;

(49) 4–chloro–3, 5–xylenol.

(e) The State Board of Pharmacy may delete drugs from the dangerous drug list set forth in this Code section. In making such deletions the board shall consider, with respect to each drug, the following factors:

(1) The actual or relative potential for abuse;

(2) The scientific evidence of its pharmacological effect, if known;

(3) The state of current scientific knowledge regarding the drug;

(4) The history and current pattern of abuse, if any;

(5) The scope, duration, and significance of abuse;

(6) Reserved;

(7) The potential of the drug to produce psychic or physiological dependence liability; and

(8) Whether such drug is included under the Federal Food, Drug, and Cosmetic Act, 52 Stat. 1040 (1938), 21 U.S.C. Section 301, et seq., as amended.

Laws 1967, p. 296, § 1; Laws 1972, p. 948, § 1; Laws 1976, p. 631, § 1; Laws 1978, p. 1668, § 5; Laws 1979, p. 859, § 3; Laws 1980, p. 1746, § 2; Laws 1981, p. 557, § 2; Laws 1982, p. 3, § 16; Laws 1982, p. 2403, §§ 3–8, 20; Laws 1983, p. 3, § 13; Laws 1983, p. 349, §§ 3–6; Laws 1984, p. 22, § 16; Laws 1984, p. 1019, §§ 3–5; Laws 1985, p. 1219, §§ 8, 9; Laws 1986, p. 1555, §§ 6, 7; Laws 1987, p. 261, § 7; Laws 1989, p. 233, §§ 7, 8; Laws 1990, p. 640, §§ 2, 3; Laws 1991, p. 312, § 2; Laws 1992, p. 6, § 16; Laws 1992, p. 1131, §§ 5–7; Laws 1993, p. 590, §§ 4–7; Laws 1994, p. 169, §§ 6, 7; Laws 1994, p. 849, § 1; Laws 1996, p. 356, §§ 3–5; Laws 1997, p. 1311, §§ 6–10; Laws 1998, p. 778, §§ 3–6; Laws 1999, p. 81, § 16; Laws 1999, p. 643, §§ 2–5; Laws 2000, p. 1317, §§ 4–6; Laws 2001, p. 816, §§ 4–6; Laws 2003, Act 80, §§ 8 to 11, eff. May 29, 2003; Laws 2004, Act 526, §§ 4 to 7, eff. May 13, 2004; Laws 2005, Act 330, §§ 2, 3, eff. May 9, 2005; Laws 2006, Act 516, §§ 3 to 5, eff. April 19, 2006; Laws 2007, Act 18, § 16, eff. May 11, 2007; Laws 2007, Act 331, §§ 3 to 5, eff. May 29, 2007; Laws 2008, Act 433, §§ 6 to 8, eff. May 6, 2008; Laws 2009, Act 43, § 5, eff. Apr. 21, 2009; Laws 2010, Act 619, §§ 5–7, eff. June 3, 2010; Laws 2010, Act 629, § 1, eff. July 1, 2010.

Formerly Code 1933, § 79A–702.

Historical and Statutory Notes

The 2000 amendment struck the following drugs in subsec. (b) (48.1) Amrinone lactate; (611.5) Metformin; and (931.95) Terbinafine; and, added drugs designated as (19.8) Alitretinoin; (36.5) Aminolevulinic acid; (48.2) Amprenavir; (48.6) Amrinone; (129.5) Calfactant; (151.4) Cefdinir; (153.95) Celecoxib; (237.2) Dalfopristin; (316.2) Dofetilide; (319.5) Doxercalciferol; (332.8) Entacapone; (334.3) Epirubicin; (380.5) Exemestane; (411.7) Ganirelix; (509.18) Ketotifen; (514.5) Levalbuterol; (516.05) Levetiracetam; (516.3) Levobupivacine; (625.5) Moxifloxacin; (641.15) Nicotine transdermal system—See exceptions; (663.75) Orlistat; (665.5) Oseltamivir; (692.55) Pemirolast; (732.8) Pioglitazone; (822.3) Quinupristin; (822.5) Rabeprazole; (831.5) Rapacuronium; (844.7) Rofecoxib; (845.7) Rosiglitazone; (849.5) Sacrosidase; (857.3) Simethicone coated cellulose suspension; (858.5) Sirolimus; (931.35) Tazobacam; (931.75) Temozolomide; (931.95) Terbinafine—See exceptions; (1042.03); and, Zanamivir".The amendment also added in subsec. (c) (15.55) Nicotine transdermal system—when used in a strength of 21 mg. or less per transdermal patch (transdermal delivery system); and, (25.5) Terbinafine—when used with a strength of 1 percent or less in a topical antifungal cream;".

The 2001 amendment struck the following drugs in subsec. (b) (160.2) Chenodiol; (160.15) Cetirizine; and (920) Sulfathiazole; and, added the following drugs (22.5) Alosetron; (62.8) Argatroban; (64.1) Arsenic trioxide; (76.5) Balsalazide; (97.3) Bexarotene; (160.15) Cetirizine; (160.16) Cetrorelix; (160.17) Cevimeline; (160.20) Chenodiol; (192.03) Ciclopirox; (192.4) Cilexetil; (221.5) Cupric chloride—injectable; (315.7) Docosanol—See exceptions; (390.7) Fludeoxyglucose; (404.3) Follitropin; (408.8) Gadoversetamide; (412.03) Gatifloxacin; (412.3) Gemtuzumab ozogamicin; (474.4) Insulin glargine; (516.07) Levobetaxolol; (522.5) Linezolid; (529.5) Lopinavir; (552.5) Meloxicam; (563.5) Mequinol; (622.3) Mitoxantrone; (644.9) Nitric oxide—for use in humans; (667.5) Oxcarbazepine; (680.5) Ozogamicin; (685.7) Pantoprazole; (703.6) Perfluoroalkylpolyether; (726.5) Phenylpropanolamine; (751.5) Polytetrafluoroethylene; (752.2) Poractant Alpha; (785.5) Proguanil; (843.83) Rivastigmine; (920) Reserved; (922.5) Sulfathiazole; (967.2) Tinzaparin; (1002.5) Triptorelin; (1019.5) Unoprostone; (1029.5) Verteporfin; and (1042.92) Zonisamide. In addition the amendment added to subsec. (c) (8.5) Docosanol—when used in 10 percent topical preparation to treat fever blisters, cold sores, or fever blisters and cold sores.

The 2003 amendment by Act 80 struck the following drugs in subsec. (b): (119.05) Butenafine; (349.7) Reserved; (529.9) Loratadine; (623.5) Mometazone; (752.2) Poractant Alpha; (1002) Triprolidine; and added drugs designated as (22.2) Almotriptan; (50.4) Anakinra; (68.15) Atomoxetine; (98.2) Bimatoprost; (102.5) Bivalirudin; (105.5) Bosentan; (105.7) Botulinum toxin (B); (119.05) Butenafine —See exceptions; (146.6) Caspofungin; (151.45) Cefditoren; (240.5) Darbepoetin alfa; (251.5) Desloratadine; (293.5) Dimyristoyl; (325.3) Drospirenone; (325.4) Drotrecogin alfa; (325.5) Dutasteride; (346.5) Ertapenem; (349.7) Esomeprazole; (404.7) Fondaparinux; (406.2) Formoterol; (406.95) Frovatriptan; (408.9) Galantamine; (464.8) Imatinib; (474.2) Insulin aspart; (513.8) Letrozole; (529.9) Loratadine —See exceptions; (623.5) Mometasone; (625.3) Moxidectin; (640.2) Nesiritide; (644.8) Nitisinone; (703.45) Perflexane; (703.65) Perflutren; (732.9) Pimecrolimus; (752.2) Poractant alfa; (930.9) Tadalafil; (931.55) Tegaserod; (931.85) Tenofovir; (932.3) Teriparatide; (974.4) Travoprost; (974.7) Treprostinil; (1002) Triprolidine —See exceptions; (1021.8) Valdecoxib; (1022.2) Valganciclovir; (1037.5) Voriconazole; (1042.75) Ziprasidone; (1042.8) Zoledronic Acid;". The 2003 amendment by Act 80 also, in subsec. (c), struck the following drugs: (12) Insulin, All; and (14.1) Miconazole—when used as antifungal powder, cream, or both, and containing not more than 4 percent of miconazole nitrate, and when used as a vaginal insert of up to 200 mg. in strength; and added drugs designated as (6.2) Butenafine—when used with a strength of 1 percent or less as a topical preparation; (12) Insulin—all injectable products which do not require a prescription drug order and bear a label which indicates "Rx Use Only" or are otherwise listed under subsection (b) of this Code section; and no injectable insulin product may be sold except by a pharmacy issued a permit by the State Board of Pharmacy or by a medical practitioner authorized to dispense medications; (13.7) Loratadine—when used in a single dose of 10 mg. or less, including doses used in combination with other drugs provided for under this subsection; (14.1) Miconazole—when used as antifungal powder or cream, or both, and containing not more than 4 percent of miconazole, or when used as a vaginal insert and containing not more than 1,200 mg. of miconazole; (28.5) Triprolidine—when a single dose is 5 mg. or less when combined in the same preparation as one or more other drug products for use as an antihistamine or decongestant or an antihistimine and decongestant.

The 2004 amendment by Act 526, in subsec. (b), made a punctuation change in par. (509.1), substituted "Methacholine" for "Methachloine" in par. (573), substituted "Nicotine" for "Nicotin" in par. (641.1), inserted "-- See exceptions" in par. (663.5), redesignated par. (931.85) as (931.9) and par. (931.9) as (931.85), and inserted pars. (.035), (19.65), (62.4), (63.5), (67.72), (105.3), (192.7), (240.3), (331.072), (332.2), (332.9), (334.4), (348.722), (380.7), (383.15), (406.3), (412.04), (412.2), (463.03), (553.5), (617.22), (617.44), (644.72), (666.4), (681.5), (692.52), (845.8), (1025.5); and in subsec. (c), inserted par. (16.9), and substituted "or an antihistamine" for "or an antihistimine" in par. (28.5).

The 2005 amendment by Act 330, in subsec. (b), added pars. (.045), (69.5), (97.2), (160.165), (193.5), (230.5), (325.45), (346.1), (408.25), (446.4), (474.45), (512.6), (638.4), (663.1), (663.4), (665.7), (692.54), (701.7), (805.5), (842.15), (851.04), (855.6), (881.05), (931.57), (967.1), (967.55), and (1007.3); and, in subsec. (c), substituted "20 mg." for "10 mg." in par. (9.5) and substituted "150 mg." for "75 mg." in par. (23.5).

The 2006 amendment by Act 516, in subsec. (b), deleted pars. (116.05) and (515) relating to Buprenorphine and Levallorphan respectively and reserved the paragraph designations, substituted "Bupropion" for "Buproprion" in par. (116.1), substituted "Cinacalcet" for "Cinacalet" in par. (193.5), substituted "Olmesartan" for "Olmesartain" in par. (663.1), added " — See exceptions" to par. (663.75), and inserted pars. (13.53), (108.5), (243.5), (332.85), (380.6), (409.8), (464.7), (513.7), (544.5), (616.05), (638.75), (640.1), (681.4), (692.51), (692.515), (769.3), (772.5), (831.04), (843.2), (966.3), and (967.57); and in subsec. (c), inserted par. (16.95).

The 2007 amendment by Act 18 was a provision contained in a corrections bill.

The 2007 amendment by Act 331, in subsec. (b), added "— See exceptions" to par. (509.18), deleted par. (517.5) which read: "(517.5) Levonorgestrel;", deleted par. (772.5) which read: "(772.5) Pregabalin;", and added pars. (.037), (19.75), (52.5), (62.75), (101.5), (192.02), (213.3), (240.7), (240.9), (243.3), (379.09), (464.5), (530.7), (681.45), (685.6), (752.7), (831.07), (831.3), (831.7), (843.82), (845.9), (858.3),(858.7), (882.5), (927.7), (931.56), (1025.7), and (1037.7); and in subsec. (c), added par. (12.7).

In 2007, the Code Commission, in subsec. (b), redesignated par. (616.05) as (615.9); and in subsec. (c), substituted "solution" for "soultion" in par. (12.7). See § 28–9–5.

Laws 2008, Act 433, §§ 6 to 8, in subsec. (b), par. (160.15), inserted "See exceptions", in par. (402.7) deleted "Propionate", added new pars. (19.77), (28.5), (44.6), (67.67), (317.2), (330.3), (506.9), (512.3), (512.67), (516.75), (540.3), (595.5), (638.45), (644.3), (831.03), (836.3), (845.95), (851.045), and (931.77); and in subsec. (c), added par. (6.5).

The 2009 amendment by Act 43, in subsec. (b), added pars. (26.5), (82.7), (160), (196.5), (240.6), (256.5), (277.57), (331.06), (379.5), (381.75), (383.45), (406.35), (406.93), (408.85), (509.7), (517.25), (604.5), (742.3), (832.5), (842.17), (845.15), (848.5), (855.9), (939.5).

The 2010 amendment by Act 619, in subsec. (b), inserted "- see exceptions" to par. (512.5) and added pars. (.043), (65.5), (66.5), (91.3), (91.8), (130.3), (133.05), (209.5), (244.4), (259.5), (324.5), (328.5), (380.3), (382.25), (383.43), (408.35), (424.4), (464.67), (531.5), (617.47), (661.6), (692.3), (740.5), (768.8), (769.35), (845.1), (851.7), (931.555), (969.6), (937.07), (1021.6), and (1030.3); and in subsec. (c), added pars. (6.45) and (12.9).

The 2010 amendment by Act 629, in subsec. (b), added par. (851.02).

§ 16–13–71.1. Repealed by Laws 1991, p. 312, § 3, eff. April 4, 1991

§ 16–13–72. Illegal to sell, give away, barter, exchange, distribute or possess dangerous drugs except under certain conditions

Except as provided for in this article, it shall be unlawful for any person, firm, corporation, or association to sell, give away, barter, exchange, distribute, or possess in this state any dangerous drug, except under the following conditions:

(1) A drug manufacturer, wholesaler, distributor, or supplier holding a license or registration issued in accordance with the Federal Food, Drug, and Cosmetic Act [1] and authorizing the holder to possess dangerous drugs may possess dangerous drugs within this state but may not distribute, sell, exchange, give away, or by any other means supply dangerous drugs without a permit issued by the State Board of Pharmacy. Any drug manufacturer, wholesaler, distributor, or supplier holding a permit issued by the State Board of Pharmacy may sell, give away, exchange, or distribute dangerous drugs within this state, but only to a pharmacy, pharmacist, a practitioner of the healing arts, and educational institutions licensed by the state, or to a drug wholesaler, distributor, or supplier, and only if such distribution is made in the normal course of employment;

(2) A pharmacy may possess dangerous drugs, but the same shall not be sold, given away, bartered, exchanged, or distributed except by a licensed pharmacist in accordance with this article;

(3) A pharmacist may possess dangerous drugs but may sell, give away, barter, exchange, or distribute the same only when he compounds or dispenses the same upon the prescription of a practitioner of the healing arts. No such prescription shall be refilled except upon the authorization of the practitioner who prescribed it;

(4) A practitioner of the healing arts may possess dangerous drugs and may sell, give away, barter, exchange, or distribute the same in accordance with Code Section 16–13–74;

(4.1) A physician in conformity with Code Section 43–34–23 may delegate to a nurse or a physician assistant the authority to possess vaccines and such other drugs as specified by the physician for adverse reactions to those vaccines, and a nurse or physician assistant may possess such drugs pursuant to that delegation; provided, however, that nothing in this paragraph shall be construed to restrict any authority of nurses or physician assistants existing under other provisions of law;

(4.2) A registered professional nurse licensed under Article 1 of Chapter 26 of Title 43 who is employed or engaged by a licensed home health agency may possess sterile saline, sterile water, and diluted heparin for use as intravenous maintenance for use in a home health setting, and such nurse may administer such items to patients of the home health agency upon the order of a licensed physician. The State Board of Pharmacy shall be authorized to adopt regulations governing the storage, quantity, use, and administration of such items; provided, however, nothing in this paragraph or in such regulations shall be construed to restrict any authority of nurses existing under other provisions of law;

(4.3) Possession, planting, cultivation, growing, or harvesting of Salvia divinorum or Salvia divinorum A strictly for aesthetic, landscaping, or decorative purposes;

(5) A manufacturer's sales representative may distribute a dangerous drug as a complimentary sample only upon the written request of a practitioner. The request must be made for each distribution and shall contain the names and addresses of the supplier and the requestor and the name and quantity of the specific dangerous drug requested. The written request shall be preserved by the manufacturer for a period of two years; and

(6) Such person, firm, corporation, or association shall keep a complete and accurate record of all dangerous drugs received, purchased, manufactured, sold, dispensed, or otherwise disposed of and shall maintain such records for at least two years or in conformance with any other state or federal law or rule issued by the Georgia State Board of Pharmacy.

Laws 1967, p. 296, § 1; Laws 1972, p. 948, § 2; Laws 1975, p. 690, § 1; Laws 1982, p. 3, § 16; Laws 1996, p. 356, § 6; Laws 1998, p. 219, § 1; Laws 1999, p. 643, § 5.2; Laws 2003, Act 9, § 16, eff. May 14, 2003; Laws 2009, Act 243, § 5, eff. July 1, 2009; Laws 2010, Act 629, § 2, eff. July 1, 2010.

Formerly Code 1933, § 79A–703.

[1] 21 U.S.C.A. § 301 et seq.

Historical and Statutory Notes

The 2003 amendment by Act 9, in par. 4.2, substituted "sterile water," for "sterile water" and "quantity, use," for "quantity, use".

The 2009 amendment by Act 243, in par. (4.1), substituted "Code Section 43–34–23" for "43–34–26.1", twice substituted "physician assistant" for "physician's assistant" and substituted "physician assistants" for "physician's assistants".

The 2010 amendment by Act 629 added par. (4.3).

§ 16–13–72.1. Revocation or suspension of permit to sell, give away, exchange, or distribute dangerous drugs

(a) A permit issued by the State Board of Pharmacy under paragraph (1) of Code Section 16–13–72 may be suspended or revoked by the State Board of Pharmacy upon a finding that the drug manufacturer, wholesaler, distributor, or supplier:

(1) Has furnished false or fraudulent material information in any application filed under this article;

(2) Has been convicted of a felony under any state or federal law relating to any controlled substance or has been convicted of a felony or misdemeanor under any state or federal law relating to any dangerous drug;

(3) Has violated any provision of this article or the rules and regulations promulgated under this article; or

(4) Has failed to maintain sufficient controls against diversion of dangerous drugs into other than legitimate medical, scientific, or industrial channels.

(b) The State Board of Pharmacy may limit revocation or suspension of a permit to the particular dangerous drug with respect to which grounds for revocation or suspension exist.

(c) Instead of suspending or revoking a permit as authorized by subsection (a) or (b) of this Code section, the State Board of Pharmacy may impose a fine in an amount not to exceed $1,500.00.

(d) If the State Board of Pharmacy suspends or revokes a permit, all dangerous drugs owned or possessed by the permittee at the time of suspension or the effective date of the revocation order shall be placed under seal. No disposition may be made of drugs under seal until the time for taking an appeal has elapsed or until all appeals have been concluded unless a court, upon application therefor, orders the sale of perishable drugs and the deposit of the proceeds of the sale with the court. Upon a revocation order becoming final, all dangerous drugs shall be forfeited to the state.

Laws 1986, p. 421, § 1; Laws 1999, p. 81, § 16.

§ 16–13–73. Labels on containers

(a) Whenever a pharmacist dispenses a dangerous drug, he shall, in each case, place upon the container the following information:

(1) Name of the patient;

(2) Name of the physician prescribing the drug;

(3) The expiration date, if any, of the drug;

(4) Name and address of the pharmacy from which the drug was dispensed; and

(5) The date of the prescription.

(b) Any pharmacist who dispenses a dangerous drug and fails to place the label required by subsection (a) of this Code section upon the container of such drug shall be guilty of a misdemeanor.

Laws 1939, p. 288, § 3; Laws 1967, p. 296, § 1; Laws 1971, p. 406, § 1; Laws 1989, p. 14, § 16.

Formerly Code 1933, §§ 79A–705, 79A–9908.

§ 16–13–74. Information required on prescription drug orders

(a) All written prescription drug orders for dangerous drugs shall be dated as of, and be signed on, the date when issued and shall bear the name and address of the patient, together with the name and strength of the drug, the quantity to be dispensed, complete directions for administration, the printed name, address, and telephone number of the practitioner, and the number of permitted refills. A prescription drug order for a dangerous drug is not required to bear the DEA permit number of the prescribing practitioner. A prescription drug order for a dangerous drug may be prepared by the practitioner or the practitioner's agent. The practitioner's signature must appear on each prescription prepared by the practitioner or the practitioner's agent and the nature of the practitioner's signature must meet the guidelines set forth in Chapter 4 of Title 26, the regulations promulgated by the State Board of Pharmacy, or both such guidelines and regulations. Any practitioner who shall dispense dangerous drugs shall comply with the provisions of Code Section 16–13–73.

(b) Any practitioner of the healing arts who fails to comply with subsection (a) of this Code section shall be guilty of a misdemeanor.

Laws 1939, p. 288, § 4; Laws 1967, p. 296, § 1; Laws 1982, p. 2403, §§ 9, 21; Laws 2003, Act 80, § 12, eff. May 29, 2003.

Formerly Code 1933, §§ 79A–706, 79A–9909.

Historical and Statutory Notes

The 2003 amendment by Act 80 rewrote subsec. (a) which had read:

"(a) All written prescriptions for dangerous drugs shall be dated as of, and be signed on, the date when issued and shall bear the full name and address of the patient, together with complete directions for administration, and the number of permitted refills. A practitioner may sign a prescription as he would sign a check or a legal document. The prescription shall be written with indelible pencil or indelible ink or typewritten and shall be manually signed by the practitioner. The prescription may be prepared by a secretary or other agent, for the signature of the practitioner, but the prescribing practitioner shall be responsible if the prescription does not conform in all essential respects to state and federal laws and regulations. Any practitioner who shall dispense dangerous drugs shall comply with the provisions of Code Section 16–13–73."

§ 16–13–75. Possession legal when drugs in original container

Possession and control of controlled substances or dangerous drugs by anyone other than the individuals specified in Code Section 16–13–35 or 16–13–72 shall be legal only if such drugs are in the original container in which they were dispensed by the pharmacist or the practitioner of the healing arts and are labeled according to Code Section 26–3–8.

Laws 1939, p. 288, § 5; Laws 1967, p. 296, § 1; Laws 1996, p. 356, § 7.

Formerly Code 1933, § 79A–707.

§ 16–13–76. Obtaining drugs by use of fictitious name or false address

No person shall obtain or attempt to obtain any dangerous drug by use of a fictitious name or by the giving of a false address.

Laws 1939, p. 288, § 5; Laws 1967, p. 296, § 1.

Formerly Code 1933, § 79A–708.

§ 16–13–77. Exception from law

Nothing in this article shall be construed to prohibit the administration of dangerous drugs by or under the direction of a practitioner of the healing arts.

Laws 1967, p. 296, § 1.

Formerly Code 1933, § 79A–704.

§ 16–13–78. Obtaining or attempting to obtain regulated drugs by fraud, forgery, concealment of material fact, or use of false name or address

(a) No person shall obtain or attempt to obtain any dangerous drug or attempt to procure the administration of any such drug by:

(1) Fraud, deceit, misrepresentation, or subterfuge;

(2) The forgery or alteration of any prescription or of any written order;

(3) The concealment of a material fact; or

(4) The use of a false name or the giving of a false address.

(b) Any person violating subsection (a) of this Code section shall be guilty of a misdemeanor.

(c) Nothing in this Code section shall apply to drug manufacturers or their agents or employees when such manufacturers or their agents or employees are authorized to engage in and are actually engaged in investigative activities directed toward the safeguarding of the manufacturer's trademark.

Laws 1967, p. 296, § 1; Laws 1970, p. 461, § 1.

Formerly Code 1933, § 79A–9910.

§ 16–13–78.1. Who may prescribe

(a) No person shall prescribe or order the dispensing of a dangerous drug, except a registered practitioner who is:

(1) Licensed or otherwise authorized by this state to prescribe dangerous drugs;

(2) Acting in the usual course of his professional practice; and

(3) Prescribing or ordering such dangerous drug for a legitimate medical purpose.

(b) Any person violating subsection (a) of this Code section shall be guilty of a misdemeanor.

Laws 1985, p. 1219, § 10.

§ 16–13–78.2. Possession, etc., of counterfeit substances

Except as authorized by this article, it is unlawful for any person to possess, have under his control, manufacture, deliver, distribute, dispense, administer, sell, or possess with intent to distribute a counterfeit substance. Any person who violates this Code section shall be guilty of a misdemeanor.

Laws 1985, p. 1219, § 11.

§ 16–13–79. Violations relating to dangerous drugs

(a) Except as provided in subsections (b), (c), and (d) of this Code section, any person who violates this article shall be guilty of a misdemeanor.

(b) Any person who distributes or possesses with the intent to distribute nitrous oxide for any use other than for a medical treatment prescribed by the order of a licensed medical practitioner, except as provided for by paragraph (16) of subsection (c) of Code Section 16–13–71, shall be guilty of a felony and upon conviction thereof shall be punished by imprisonment for not less than one year nor more than three years or by a fine not to exceed $5,000.00 or both.

(c) Any person who distributes or possesses with the intent to distribute to any person under 18 years of age nitrous oxide for any use other than for a medical treatment prescribed by the order of a licensed medical practitioner, except as provided for by paragraph (16) of subsection (c) of Code Section 16–13–71, shall be guilty of a felony and upon conviction thereof shall be punished for not less than two years nor more than six years or by a fine not to exceed $10,000.00 or both.

(d) This article shall not apply to any person who possesses, distributes, sells, or uses nitrous oxide for food preparation in a restaurant, for food service, or in household products.

Laws 1967, p. 296, § 1; Laws 1989, p. 238, § 2; Laws 1991, p. 312, § 4; Laws 1996, p. 356, § 8; Laws 1998, p. 778, § 7; Laws 2008, Act 433, § 9, eff. May 6, 2008.

Formerly Code 1933, § 79A–9907.

Historical and Statutory Notes

The 2008 amendment by Act 433, added subsec. (d), relating to the application of the section.

Article 4

Sale, Possession, Transfer, or Inhalation of Model Glue

§ 16–13–90. "Model glue" defined

As used in this article, the term "model glue" means any glue, cement, solvent, or chemical substance containing one or more of the following chemicals: acetone, amyl chloride (iso-and tertiary), benzene, carbon disulfide, carbon tetrachloride, chloroform, ether, ethyl acetate, ethyl alcohol, ethylene dichloride, isopropyl acetate, isopropyl alcohol, isopropyl ether, methyl acetate, methyl alcohol, propylene dichloride, propylene oxide, trichlorethylene, amyl acetate, amyl alcohol, butyl acetate, butyl alcohol, butyl ether, diethylcarbonate, diethylene oxide (dioxane), dipropyl ketone, ethyl butyrate, ethylene glycol monoethyl ether (cellosolve), ethylene glycol monomethyl ether acetate (methyl cellosolve acetate), isobutyl alcohol, methyl amyl acetate, methyl amyl alcohol, methyl isobutyl ketone, or toluene.

Laws 1968, p. 1194, § 2; Laws 1983, p. 3, § 13.

§ 16–13–91. Intentional inhaling of fumes of model glue

No person shall, for the purpose of causing a condition of intoxication, stupefaction, euphoria, excitement, exhilaration, or dulling of the senses or nervous system, intentionally smell or inhale the fumes from any model glue, provided that this Code section shall not apply to the inhalation of any anesthesia for medical or dental purposes.

Laws 1968, p. 1194, § 1.

§ 16–13–92. Possession, buying, selling or transferring of possession of model glue prohibited

No person shall intentionally possess, buy, sell, transfer possession, or receive possession of any model glue for the purpose of violating or aiding another person to violate this article.

Laws 1968, p. 1194, § 3.

§ 16–13–93. Persons under 18 years of age prohibited from buying model glue without written consent of parent

No person shall sell or transfer possession of any model glue to another person under 18 years of age, nor shall any person under 18 years of age possess or buy any model glue unless the purchase is for model building or other lawful use and the person under 18 years of age has in his possession and exhibits to the seller or transferor the written consent of his parent or legal guardian to make such purchase or take possession of the model glue, provided any minor who shall transfer possession of model glue to another minor for model building or other lawful purpose shall not be held criminally liable for failing to require exhibition of the written consent of the transferee-minor's parents or for failing to keep same available for inspection by law enforcement officials.

Laws 1968, p. 1194, § 4.

§ 16–13–94. Consent of parent to be exhibited when purchasing model glue; records

The person making a sale or transfer of possession of model glue to a person under 18 years of age must require the purchaser to exhibit the written consent of his parent or guardian and the name and address of the consenting parent or guardian. All data required by this Code section shall be kept available by the seller for inspection by law enforcement officials for a period of six months.

Laws 1968, p. 1194, § 5.

§ 16–13–95. Article not to be construed to repeal or limit laws or ordinances of counties or municipalities

No provisions in this article shall be construed to repeal or limit laws or ordinances of the governing authority of any county or municipality regulating, restricting, or prohibiting the sale of model glue to any person under the age of 18, nor shall this article restrict the governing authority of any county or municipality from enacting ordinances or regulations governing the regulation of model glue not inconsistent with this article.

Laws 1968, p. 1194, § 7.

§ 16–13–96. Violations relating to model glue

Any person who violates this article shall be guilty of a misdemeanor. Each violation of this article shall be deemed a separate and distinct offense.

Laws 1968, p. 1194, § 6.

Article 5

Sanctions against Licensed Persons for Offenses Involving Controlled Substances or Marijuana

§ 16–13–110. Definitions

(a) As used in this article, the term:

(1) "Controlled substance" means any drug, substance, or immediate precursor included in the definition of the term "controlled substance" in paragraph (4) of Code Section 16–13–21.

(2) "Convicted" or "conviction" refers to a final conviction in a court of competent jurisdiction, or the acceptance of a plea of guilty or nolo contendere or affording of first offender treatment by a court of competent jurisdiction.

(3) "Licensed individual" means any individual to whom any department, agency, board, bureau, or other entity of state government has issued any license, permit, registration, certification, or other authorization to conduct a licensed occupation.

(4) "Licensed occupation" means any occupation, profession, business, trade, or other commercial activity which requires for its lawful conduct the issuance to an individual of any license, permit, registration, certification, or other authorization by any department, agency, board, bureau, or other entity of state government.

(5) "Licensing authority" means any department, agency, board, bureau, or other entity of state government which issues to individuals any license, permit, registration, certification, or other authorization to conduct a licensed occupation.

(6) "Marijuana" means any substance included in the definition of the term "marijuana" in paragraph (16) of Code Section 16–13–21.

(b) Without limiting the generality of the provisions of subsection (a) of this Code section, the practice of law shall constitute a licensed occupation for purposes of this article and the Supreme Court of Georgia shall be the licensing authority for the practice of law.

Laws 1990, p. 2009, § 1.

§ 16–13–111. Notification to licensing authority of conviction; suspension or revocation of license, etc.; reinstatement

(a) Any licensed individual who is convicted under the laws of this state, the United States, or any other state of any criminal offense involving the manufacture, distribution, trafficking, sale, or possession of a controlled substance or marijuana shall notify the appropriate licensing authority of the conviction within ten days following the conviction.

(b) Upon being notified of a conviction of a licensed individual, the appropriate licensing authority shall suspend or revoke the license, permit, registration, certification, or other authorization to conduct a licensed occupation of such individual as follows:

(1) Upon the first conviction, the licensed individual shall have his or her license, permit, registration, certification, or other authorization to conduct a licensed occupation suspended for a period of not less than three months; provided, however, that in the case of a first conviction for a misdemeanor the licensing authority shall be authorized to impose a lesser sanction or no sanction upon the licensed individual; and

(2) Upon the second or subsequent conviction, the licensed individual shall have his or her license, permit, registration, certification, or other authorization to conduct a licensed occupation revoked.

(c) The failure of a licensed individual to notify the appropriate licensing authority of a conviction as required in subsection (a) of this Code section shall be considered grounds for revocation of his or her license, permit, registration, certification, or other authorization to conduct a licensed occupation.

(d) A licensed individual sanctioned under subsection (b) or (c) of this Code section may be entitled to reinstatement of his or her license, permit, registration, certification, or other authorization to conduct a licensed occupation upon successful completion of a drug abuse treatment and education program approved by the licensing authority.

(e) The suspension and revocation sanctions prescribed in this Code section are intended as minimum sanctions, and nothing in this Code section shall be construed to prohibit any licensing authority from establishing and implementing additional or more stringent sanctions for criminal offenses and other conduct involving the unlawful manufacture, distribution, trafficking, sale, or possession of a controlled substance or marijuana.

Laws 1990, p. 2009, § 1.

§ 16–13–112. Administrative procedures

Administrative procedures for the implementation of this article for each licensed occupation shall be governed by the appropriate provisions applicable to each licensing authority.

Laws 1990, p. 2009, § 1.

§ 16–13–113. Supplemental nature of law

The provisions of this article shall be supplemental to and shall not operate to prohibit any licensing authority from acting pursuant to those provisions of law which may now or hereafter authorize other sanctions and actions for that particular licensing authority.

Laws 1990, p. 2009, § 1.

§ 16–13–114. Applicability of law

This article shall apply only with respect to criminal offenses committed on or after July 1, 1990; provided, however, that nothing in this Code section shall prevent any licensing authority from implementing sanctions additional to or other than those provided for in this article with respect to offenses committed prior to July 1, 1990.

Laws 1990, p. 2009, § 1.

CHAPTER 14

RACKETEER INFLUENCED AND CORRUPT ORGANIZATIONS

Section

§ 16–14–1. Short title

This chapter shall be known and may be cited as the "Georgia RICO (Racketeer Influenced and Corrupt Organizations) Act."

Laws 1980, p. 405, § 1.

Formerly Code 1933, § 26–3401.

§ 16–14–2. Findings and intent

(a) The General Assembly finds that a severe problem is posed in this state by the increasing sophistication of various criminal elements and the increasing extent to which the state and its citizens are harmed as a result of the activities of these elements.

(b) The General Assembly declares that the intent of this chapter is to impose sanctions against those who violate this chapter and to provide compensation to persons injured or aggrieved by such violations. It is not the intent of the General Assembly that isolated incidents of misdemeanor conduct or acts of civil disobedience be prosecuted under this chapter. It is the intent of the General Assembly, however, that this chapter apply to an interrelated pattern of criminal activity motivated by or the effect of which is pecuniary gain or economic or physical threat or injury. This chapter shall be liberally construed to effectuate the remedial purposes embodied in its operative provisions.

Laws 1980, p. 405, § 1; Laws 1997, p. 672, § 1.

Formerly Code 1933, § 26–3401.

§ 16–14–3. Definitions

As used in this chapter, the term:

(1) "Alien corporation" means a corporation organized under laws other than the laws of the United States or the laws of any state of the United States.

(2)(A) "Beneficial interest" means either of the following:

(i) The interest of a person as a beneficiary under any other trust arrangement pursuant to which a trustee holds legal or record title to real property for the benefit of such person; or

(ii) The interest of a person under any other form of express fiduciary arrangement pursuant to which any other person holds legal or record title to real property for the benefit of such person.

(B) "Beneficial interest" does not include the interest of a stockholder in a corporation or the interest of a partner in either a general partnership or limited partnership. A beneficial interest shall be deemed to be located where the real property owned by the trustee is located.

(3) "Civil proceeding" means any civil proceeding commenced by an investigative agency under any provision of this chapter.

(4) "Criminal proceeding" means any criminal proceeding commenced by an investigative agency under any provision of this chapter.

(5) "Documentary material" means any book, paper, document, writing, drawing, graph, chart, photograph, phonorecord, magnetic tape, computer printout, other data compilation from which information can be obtained or from which information can be translated into usable form, or other tangible item.

(6) "Enterprise" means any person, sole proprietorship, partnership, corporation, business trust, union chartered under the laws of this state, or other legal entity; or any unchartered union, association, or group of individuals associated in fact although not a legal entity; and it includes illicit as well as licit enterprises and governmental as well as other entities.

(7) "Investigative agency" means the Department of Law or the office of any district attorney.

(8) "Pattern of racketeering activity" means:

(A) Engaging in at least two acts of racketeering activity in furtherance of one or more incidents, schemes, or transactions that have the same or similar intents, results, accomplices, victims, or methods of commission or otherwise are interrelated by distinguishing characteristics and are not isolated incidents, provided at least one of such acts occurred after July 1, 1980, and that the last of such acts occurred within four years, excluding any periods of imprisonment, after the commission of a prior act of racketeering activity; or

(B) Engaging in any one or more acts of domestic terrorism as described in subsection (a) of Code Section 16–4–10 or any criminal attempt, criminal solicitation, or criminal conspiracy related thereto.

(9)(A) "Racketeering activity" means to commit, to attempt to commit, or to solicit, coerce, or intimidate another person to commit any crime which is chargeable by indictment under the following laws of this state:

(i) Article 2 of Chapter 13 of this title, relating to controlled substances;

(ii) Article 3 of Chapter 13 of this title, known as the "Dangerous Drugs Act";

(iii) Subsection (j) of Code Section 16–13–30, relating to marijuana;

(iv) Article 1 of Chapter 5 of this title, relating to homicide;

(v) Article 2 of Chapter 5 of this title, relating to bodily injury and related offenses;

(vi) Articles 3 and 4 of Chapter 7 of this title, relating to arson and destructive devices, respectively;

(vii) Code Section 16–7–1, relating to burglary, or Code Section 16–7–2, relating to smash and grab burglary;

(viii) Code Section 16–9–1, relating to forgery in the first degree;

(ix) Article 1 of Chapter 8 of this title, relating to theft;

(x) Article 2 of Chapter 8 of this title, relating to robbery;

(xi) Code Sections 16–6–9 through 16–6–12 and 16–6–14, relating to prostitution and pandering;

(xii) Code Section 16–12–80, relating to distributing obscene materials;

(xiii) Code Section 16-10-2, relating to bribery;

(xiv) Code Section 16-10-93, relating to influencing witnesses;

(xv) Article 4 of Chapter 10 of this title and Code Sections 16-10-20, 16-10-23, and 16-10-91, relating to perjury and other falsifications;

(xvi) Code Section 16-10-94, relating to tampering with evidence;

(xvii) Code Section 16-12-22, relating to commercial gambling;

(xviii) Code Section 3-3-27, relating to distilling or making liquors;

(xix) Part 2 of Article 4 of Chapter 11 of this title, known as the "Georgia Firearms and Weapons Act";

(xx) Code Section 16-8-60, relating to unauthorized transfers and reproductions of recorded material;

(xxi) Chapter 5 of Title 10, relating to violations of the Georgia Uniform Securities Act of 2008;

(xxii) Code Section 3-3-27, relating to the unlawful distillation, manufacture, and transportation of alcoholic beverages;

(xxiii) Code Sections 16-9-31, 16-9-32, 16-9-33, and 16-9-34, relating to the unlawful use of financial transaction cards;

(xxiv) Code Section 40-3-90, relating to certain felonies involving certificates of title, security interest, or liens concerning motor vehicles;

(xxv) Code Section 40-4-21, relating to removal or falsification of identification numbers;

(xxvi) Code Section 40-4-22, relating to possession of motor vehicle parts from which the identification has been removed;

(xxvii) Code Section 16-9-70, relating to use of an article with an altered identification mark;

(xxviii) Article 6 of Chapter 9 of this title, known as the "Georgia Computer Systems Protection Act";

(xxix) Any conduct defined as "racketeering activity" under 18 U.S.C. Section 1961 (1)(A), (B), (C), and (D);

(xxx) Article 3 of Chapter 5 of this title, relating to kidnapping, false imprisonment, and related offenses, except for Code Section 16-5-44, relating to aircraft hijacking;

(xxxi) Code Section 16-11-37, relating to terroristic threats and acts;

(xxxii) Code Section 16-5-44.1, relating to motor vehicle hijacking;

(xxxiii) Code Section 16-10-32, relating to tampering with witnesses, victims, or informants;

(xxxiv) Code Section 16-10-97, relating to intimidation of grand or petit juror or court officer;

(xxxv) Article 11 of Chapter 1 of Title 7 and Sections 5311 through 5330 of Title 31 of the United States Code relating to records and reports of currency transactions;

(xxxvi) Article 8 of Chapter 9 of this title, relating to identity fraud, and Section 1028 of Title 18 of the United States Code, relating to fraudulent identification documents and information;

(xxxvii) Code Section 33-1-9, relating to insurance fraud;

(xxxviii) Code Section 16-17-2, relating to payday loans;

(xxxix) Code Section 16-9-101, relating to deceptive commercial e-mail; or

(xxxx) Code Section 16-8-102, relating to residential mortgage fraud.

(B) "Racketeering activity" shall also mean any act or threat involving murder, kidnapping, gambling, arson, robbery, theft, receipt of stolen property, bribery, extortion, obstruction of justice, dealing in narcotic or dangerous drugs, or dealing in securities which is chargeable under the laws of the United States or any of the several states and which is punishable by imprisonment for more than one year.

(10) "Real property" means any real property situated in this state or any interest in such real property, including, but not limited to, any lease of or mortgage upon such real property.

(11) "RICO lien notice" means the notice described in Code Section 16-14-13.

(12)(A) "Trustee" means either of the following:

(i) Any person who holds legal or record title to real property for which any other person has a beneficial interest; or

(ii) Any successor trustee or trustees to any of the foregoing persons.

(B) "Trustee" does not include the following:

(i) Any person appointed or acting as a guardian or conservator under Title 29, relating to guardian and ward, or personal representative under Chapter 6 of Title 53 of the "Pre-1998 Probate Code," relating to the administration of estates, if applicable, or Chapter 6 of Title 53 of the "Revised Probate Code of 1998" and other provisions in such revised probate code relating to the administration of estates; or

(ii) Any person appointed or acting as a trustee of any testamentary trust or as trustee of any indenture of trust under which any bonds are or are to be issued.

Laws 1980, p. 405, § 1; Laws 1982, p. 1385, §§ 2, 8; Laws 1983, p. 3, § 13; Laws 1984, p. 22, § 16; Laws 1989, p. 14, § 16; Laws 1990, p. 8, § 16; Laws 1994, p. 1625, § 4; Laws 1996, p. 416, § 8; Laws 1998, p. 128, § 16, Laws 1998, p. 270, § 7; Laws 1999, p. 81, § 16; Laws 2001, p. 858, § 1; Laws 2002, p. 551, § 3; Laws 2002, p. 1284, § 3; Laws 2003, Act 97, § 1, eff. May 30, 2003; Laws 2004, Act 440, § 2, eff. May 1, 2004; Laws 2004, Act 460, § 4, eff. July 1, 2005; Laws 2005, Act 46, § 5, eff. July 1, 2005; Laws 2005, Act 162, § 3, eff. May 5, 2005; Laws 2006, Act 451, § 2, eff. July 1, 2006; Laws 2008, Act 528, § 9, eff. July 1, 2009; Laws 2010, Act 674, § 8, eff. July 1, 2010.

Formerly Code 1933, § 26-3402.

Historical and Statutory Notes

The 2001 amendment, applicable to racketeering activity occurring on or after July 1, 2001, substantially rewrote par. (8) which formerly provided:

"(8) 'Pattern of racketeering activity' means engaging in at least two incidents of racketeering activity that have the same or similar intents, results, accomplices, victims, or methods of commission or otherwise are interrelated by distinguishing characteristics and are not isolated incidents, provided at least one of such incidents occurred after July 1, 1980, and that the last of such incidents occurred within four years, excluding any periods of imprisonment, after the commission of a prior incident of racketeering activity."

The 2002 amendment by Act 750, applicable to crimes committed after its effective date, added provisions comprising par. (9) (xxxvi) "Article 8 of Chapter 9 of this title, relating to identity fraud, and Section 1028 of Title 18 of the United States Code, relating to fraudulent identification documents and information."

The 2002 amendment by Act 956 rewrote par. (8) which, as amended in 2001, provided:

"(8) 'Pattern of racketeering activity' means engaging in at least two acts of racketeering activity in furtherance of one or more incidents, schemes, or transactions that have the same or similar intents, results, accomplices, victims, or methods of commission or otherwise are interrelated by distinguishing characteristics and are not isolated incidents, provided at least one of such acts occurred after July 1, 1980, and that the last of such acts occurred within four years, excluding any periods of imprisonment, after the commission of a prior act of racketeering activity."

The 2003 amendment by Act 97, in par. (9), added subpar. (A)(xxxvii).

The 2004 amendment by Act 440, in par. (9), added subpar. (A)(xxxviii).

The 2004 amendment by Act 460, in div. (i) of subpar. (B) of par. (12), substituted "guardian or conservator" for "personal representative"; and inserted "personal representative" following "ward, or".

Laws 2004, Act 460, § 16, provides:

"This Act shall become effective on July 1, 2005, and all appointments of guardians of the person or property made pursuant to former Title 29 shall continue in effect and shall thereafter be governed by the provisions of this Act."

The 2005 amendment by Act 46, in subpar. (9)(A), added div. (xxxix).

The 2005 amendment by Act 162, in subpar. (9)(A), added div. (xxxix).

In 2005, the Code Commission, in par. (9), subpar. (A), deleted "or" at the end of div. (xxxviii), substituted "; or" for the period at the end of div. (xxxix), and redesignated div. (xxxix) as added by Laws 2005, Act 162, as div. (xxxx). See § 28–9–5.

The 2006 amendment by Act 451 deleted the reference to § 16–10–95 following the reference to § 16–10–91.

The 2008 amendment by Act 528, rewrote subdiv. (9)(A)(xxi) which had read:

"(xxi) Code Section 10–5–24, relating to violations of the 'Georgia Securities Act of 1973' ".

The 2010 amendment by Act 674, in par. (9), subpar. (A), div. (vii), added "or Code Section 16–7–2, relating to smash and grab burglary".

§ 16–14–4. Prohibited activities

(a) It is unlawful for any person, through a pattern of racketeering activity or proceeds derived therefrom, to acquire or maintain, directly or indirectly, any interest in or control of any enterprise, real property, or personal property of any nature, including money.

(b) It is unlawful for any person employed by or associated with any enterprise to conduct or participate in, directly or indirectly, such enterprise through a pattern of racketeering activity.

(c) It is unlawful for any person to conspire or endeavor to violate any of the provisions of subsection (a) or (b) of this Code section.

Laws 1980, p. 405, § 1; Laws 1982, p. 1385, §§ 3, 9; Laws 1984, p. 22, § 16.

Formerly Code 1933, § 26–3403.

§ 16–14–5. Criminal penalties and alternative fine

(a) Any person convicted of the offense of engaging in activity in violation of Code Section 16–14–4 is guilty of a felony and shall be punished by not less than five nor more than 20 years' imprisonment or the fine specified in subsection (b) of this Code section, or both.

(b) In lieu of any fine otherwise authorized by law, any person convicted of the offense of engaging in conduct in violation of Code Section 16–14–4 may be sentenced to pay a fine that does not exceed the greater of $25,000.00 or three times the amount of any pecuniary value gained by him from such violation.

(c) The court shall hold a hearing to determine the amount of the fine authorized by subsection (b) of this Code section.

(d) For the purposes of subsection (b) of this Code section, "pecuniary value" means:

(1) Anything of value in the form of money, a negotiable instrument, a commercial interest, or anything else, the primary significance of which is economic advantage; or

(2) Any other property or service that has a value in excess of $100.00.

Laws 1980, p. 405, § 1; Laws 1985, p. 149, § 16.

Formerly Code 1933, § 26–3404.

§ 16–14–6. Other civil remedies

(a) Any superior court may, after making due provisions for the rights of innocent persons, enjoin violations of Code Section 16–14–4 by issuing appropriate orders and judgments including, but not limited to:

(1) Ordering any defendant to divest himself of any interest in any enterprise, real property, or personal property;

(2) Imposing reasonable restrictions upon the future activities or investments of any defendant including, but not limited to, prohibiting any defendant from engaging in the same type of endeavor as the enterprise in which he was engaged in violation of Code Section 16–14–4;

(3) Ordering the dissolution or reorganization of any enterprise;

(4) Ordering the suspension or revocation of any license, permit, or prior approval granted to any enterprise by any agency of the state; or

(5) Ordering the forfeiture of the charter of a corporation organized under the laws of this state or the revocation of a certificate authorizing a foreign corporation to conduct business within this state upon a finding that the board of directors or a managerial agent acting on behalf of the corporation, in conducting affairs of the corporation, has authorized or engaged in conduct in violation of Code Section 16–14–4 and that, for the prevention of future criminal activity, the public interest requires that the charter of the corporation be forfeited and that the corporation be dissolved or the certificate be revoked.

(b) Any aggrieved person or the state may institute a proceeding under subsection (a) of this Code section. In such proceeding, relief shall be granted in conformity with the principles that govern the granting of injunctive relief from threatened loss or damage in other civil cases, provided that no showing of special or irreparable damage to the person shall have to be made. Upon the execution of proper bond against damages for an injunction improvidently granted and a showing of immediate danger of significant loss or damage, a temporary restraining order and a preliminary injunction may be issued in any such action before a final determination on the merits.

(c) Any person who is injured by reason of any violation of Code Section 16–14–4 shall have a cause of action for three times the actual damages sustained and, where appropriate, punitive damages. Such person shall also recover attorneys' fees in the trial and appellate courts and costs of investigation and litigation reasonably incurred. The defendant or any injured person may demand a trial by jury in any civil action brought pursuant to this Code section.

(d) Any injured person shall have a right or claim to forfeited property or to the proceeds derived therefrom superior to any right or claim the state or the county (other than for costs) has in the same property or proceeds. To enforce such a claim, the injured person must intervene in the forfeiture proceeding prior to its final disposition.

(e) A conviction in any criminal proceeding under this chapter shall estop the defendant in any subsequent civil action or proceeding as to all matters proved in the criminal proceeding.

Laws 1980, p. 405, § 1.

Formerly Code 1933, § 26–3406.

§ 16–14–7. Forfeiture

(a) All property of every kind used or intended for use in the course of, derived from, or realized through a pattern of racketeering activity is subject to forfeiture to the state. Forfeiture shall be had by a civil procedure known as a RICO forfeiture proceeding under the following rules.

(b) A RICO forfeiture proceeding shall be governed by Chapter 11 of Title 9, the "Georgia Civil Practice Act," except to the extent that special rules of procedure are stated in this chapter.

(c) A RICO forfeiture proceeding shall be an in rem proceeding against the property.

(d) A RICO forfeiture proceeding shall be instituted by complaint and prosecuted by the district attorney of the county in which the property is located or seized. The proceeding may be commenced before or after seizure of the property.

(e) If the complaint is filed before seizure, it shall state what property is sought to be forfeited, that the property is within the jurisdiction of the court, the grounds for forfeiture, and the names of all persons known to have or claim an interest in the property. The court shall determine ex parte whether there is reasonable cause to believe that the property is subject to forfeiture and that notice to those persons having or claiming an interest in the property prior to seizure would cause the loss or destruction of the property. If the court finds that reasonable cause does not exist to believe the property is subject to forfeiture, it shall dismiss the complaint. If the court finds that reasonable cause does exist to believe the property is subject to forfeiture but there is not reasonable cause to believe that prior notice would result in loss or destruction, it shall order service on all persons known to have or claim an interest in the property prior to a further hearing on whether a writ of seizure should issue. If the court finds that there is reasonable cause to believe that the property is subject to forfeiture and to believe that prior notice would cause loss or destruction, it shall without any further hearing or notice issue a writ of seizure directing the sheriff of the county where the property is found to seize it.

(f) Seizure may be effected by a law enforcement officer authorized to enforce the penal laws of this state prior to the filing of the complaint and without a writ of seizure if the seizure is incident to a lawful arrest, search, or inspection and the officer has probable cause to believe the property is subject to forfeiture and will be lost or destroyed if not seized. Within ten days of the date of seizure, the seizure shall be reported by the officer to the district attorney of the circuit in which the seizure is effected; and the district attorney shall, within a reasonable time after receiving notice of seizure, file a complaint for forfeiture. The complaint shall state, in addition to the information required in subsection (e) of this Code section, the date and place of seizure.

(g) After the complaint is filed or the seizure effected, whichever is later, every person known to have or claim an interest in the property shall be served, if not previously served, with a copy of the complaint and a notice of seizure in the manner provided by Chapter 11 of Title 9, the "Georgia Civil Practice Act." Service by publication may be ordered upon any party whose whereabouts cannot be determined.

(h)(1) Any person claiming an interest in the property may become a party to the action at any time prior to judgment whether named in the complaint or not. Any party claiming a substantial interest in the property may upon motion be allowed by the court to take possession of the property upon posting bond with good and sufficient security in double the amount of the property's value conditioned to pay the value of any interest in the property found to be subject to forfeiture or the value of any interest of another not subject to forfeiture. Such a party taking possession shall not remove the property from the territorial jurisdiction of the court without written permission from the court.

(2) The court may, upon such terms and conditions as prescribed by it, order that the property be sold by an innocent party who holds a lien on or security interest in the property at any time during the proceedings. Any proceeds from such sale over and above the amount necessary to satisfy the lien or security interest shall be paid into court pending final judgment in the forfeiture proceeding. No such sale shall be ordered, however, unless the obligation upon which the lien or security interest is based is in default.

(3) Pending final judgment in the forfeiture proceeding, the court may make any other disposition of the property which is in the interest of substantial justice.

(i) After service of process, all further proceedings shall be as provided in Chapter 11 of Title 9, the "Georgia Civil Practice Act," except that any party may bring one motion to dismiss at any time and such motion shall be heard and ruled on within ten days. Any party may demand a jury trial.

(j) The interest of an innocent party in the property shall not be subject to forfeiture. An innocent party is one who did not have actual or constructive knowledge that the property was subject to forfeiture.

(k) Subject to the requirement of protecting the interest of all innocent parties, the court may, after judgment of forfeiture, make any of the following orders for disposition of the property:

(1) Destruction of contraband, the possession of which is illegal;

(2) Retention for official use by any agency of this state or any political subdivision thereof. When such agency or political subdivision no longer has use for such property, it shall be disposed of by judicial sale;

(3) Transfer to the Division of Archives and History of property useful for historical or instructional purposes;

(4) Retention of the property by any innocent party having an interest therein, upon payment or approval of a plan for payment into court of the value of any forfeited interest in the property. The plan may include, in the case of an innocent party who holds a lien on or security interest in the property, the sale of the property by the innocent party under such terms and conditions as may be prescribed by the court and the payment into court of any proceeds from such sale over and above the amount necessary to satisfy the lien or security interest;

(5) Judicial sale of the property;

(6) Transfer of the property to any innocent party having an interest therein equal to or greater than the value of the property; or

(7) Any other disposition of the property which is in the interest of substantial justice and adequately protects innocent parties.

(*l*) The net proceeds of any sale or disposition after satisfaction of the interest of any innocent party, less the greater of one-half thereof or the costs borne by the county in bringing the forfeiture action, shall be paid into the general fund of the state treasury. The costs borne by the county or one-half of the net proceeds of sale or disposition, whichever is greater, shall be paid into the treasury of the county where the forfeiture action is brought. Notwithstanding any other provision in this Code section, the court may, after satisfaction of the interest of any innocent party, make any other division of the proceeds among the state, county, or municipalities or agencies of the state, county, or municipalities, which is commensurate with the proportion of the assistance that each contributed to the underlying criminal action, forfeiture, or criminal action and forfeiture.

(m) In lieu of the provisions of subsections (c) through (g) of this Code section, the state may bring an in personam action for the forfeiture of any property subject to forfeiture under subsection (a) of this Code section.

(n)(1) Upon the entry of a final judgment of forfeiture in favor of the state, the title of the state to the forfeited property shall:

(A) In the case of real property or beneficial interest, relate back to the date of filing of the RICO lien notice in the official records of the county where the real property or beneficial trust is located and, if no RICO lien notice is filed, then to the date of the filing of any notice of lis pendens under Article 9 of Chapter 14 of Title 44 in the official records of the county where the real property or beneficial interest is located and, if no RICO lien notice or notice of lis pendens is so filed, then to the date of recording of the final judgment of forfeiture in the official records of the county where the real property or beneficial interest is located; and

(B) In the case of personal property, relate back to the date the personal property was seized by the investigating agency.

(2) If property subject to forfeiture is conveyed, alienated, disposed of, or otherwise rendered unavailable for forfeiture after the filing of a RICO lien notice or after the filing of a civil proceeding or criminal proceeding, whichever is earlier, the investigative agency may, on behalf of the state, institute an action in the appropriate superior court against the person named in the RICO lien notice or the defendant in the civil proceeding or criminal proceeding; and the court shall enter final judgment against the person named in the RICO lien notice or the defendant in the civil proceeding or criminal proceeding in an amount equal to the fair market value of the property, together with investigative costs and attorney's fees incurred by the investigative agency in the action. If a civil proceeding is pending, such action shall be filed only in the court where such civil proceeding is pending.

Laws 1980, p. 405, § 1; Laws 1982, p. 1385, §§ 4, 5, 10, 11; Laws 1984, p. 22, § 16; Laws 1992, p. 6, § 16; Laws 2000, p. 1114, § 1; Laws 2002, p. 532, § 4.

Formerly Code 1933, § 26-3405.

Validity

This section has been held unconstitutional in the case of Cisco v. State, 2009, 285 Ga 656, 680 S.E.2d 831.

Historical and Statutory Notes

The 2000 amendment added in subsec. (*l*) "Notwithstanding any other provision in this Code section, the court may, after satisfaction of the interest of any innocent party, make any other division of the proceeds among the state, county, or municipalities or agencies of the state, county, or municipalities, which is commensurate with the proportion of the assistance that each contributed to the underlying criminal action, forfeiture, or criminal action and forfeiture."

The 2002 amendment to subsec. (k)(3) substituted following "Transfer to the Division" for "Department".

§ 16-14-8. Limitation of actions

Notwithstanding any other provision of law, a criminal or civil action or proceeding under this chapter may be commenced up until five years after the conduct in violation of a provision of this chapter terminates or the cause of action accrues. If a criminal prosecution or civil action is brought by the state to punish or prevent any violation of this chapter, then the running of this period of limitations, with respect to any cause of action arising under subsection (b) or (c) of Code Section 16-14-6 which is based upon any matter complained of in such prosecution or action by the state, shall be suspended during the pendency of the prosecution or action by the state and for two years thereafter.

Laws 1980, p. 405, § 1.

Formerly Code 1933, § 26-3407.

§ 16-14-9. Supplemental nature of civil remedies

The application of one civil remedy under this chapter shall not preclude the application of any other remedy, civil or criminal, under this chapter or any other provision of law. Civil remedies under this chapter are supplemental and not mutually exclusive.

Laws 1980, p. 405, § 1.

Formerly Code 1933, § 26-3408.

§ 16-14-10. Reciprocity with other jurisdictions

(a) Notwithstanding any other provision of law, a valid judgment rendered by a court of a jurisdiction having a law substantially similar to this chapter will be recognized and enforced by the courts of this state to the extent that a judgment rendered by a court of this state pursuant to this chapter would be enforced in such other jurisdiction.

(b) The Attorney General is authorized to enter into reciprocal agreements with the attorney general or chief prosecuting attorney of any jurisdiction having a law substantially similar to this chapter so as to further the purposes of this chapter.

Laws 1982, p. 1385, § 6; Laws 1982, p. 1385, § 12.

Formerly Code 1933, § 26-3409.

§ 16-14-11. Venue; prior convictions

In any criminal proceeding brought pursuant to this chapter, the crime shall be considered to have been committed in any county in which an incident of racketeering occurred or in which an interest or control of an enterprise or real or personal property is acquired or maintained.

Laws 1982, p. 1385, § 6; Laws 1982, p. 1385, § 12.

Formerly Code 1933, § 26-3410.

§ 16-14-12. Expedition of actions

This state may, in any civil action brought pursuant to this chapter, file with the clerk of the superior court a certificate stating that the case is of special public importance. A copy of that certificate shall be furnished immediately by such clerk to the chief judge or, in his absence, the presiding chief judge of the superior court in which such action is pending; and, upon receipt of such copy, the judge shall immediately designate a judge to hear and determine the action. The judge so designated shall promptly assign such action for hearing, participate in the hearings and determination, and cause the action to be expedited.

Laws 1982, p. 1385, § 6; Laws 1982, p. 1385, § 12.

Formerly Code 1933, § 26-3411.

§ 16-14-13. RICO lien notice

(a) Upon the institution of any civil proceeding, the investigative agency then or at any time during the pendency of the proceeding may file in the official records of any one or more counties a RICO lien notice. No filing fee or other charge shall be required as a condition for filing the RICO lien notice; and the clerk of the superior court shall, upon the presentation of a RICO lien notice, immediately record it in the official records.

(b) The RICO lien notice shall be signed by the Attorney General or his designee or by a district attorney or his designee. The notice shall be in such form as the Attorney General prescribes and shall set forth the following information:

(1) The name of the person against whom the civil proceeding has been brought. In its discretion, the investigative agency may also name in the RICO lien notice any other aliases, names, or fictitious names under which the person may be known. In its discretion, the investigative agency may also name in the RICO lien notice any corporation, partnership, or other entity that is either controlled by or entirely owned by the person;

(2) If known to the investigative agency, the present residence and business addresses of the person named in the RICO lien notice and of the other names set forth in the RICO lien notice;

(3) A reference to the civil proceeding stating that a proceeding under this chapter has been brought against the person named in the RICO lien notice, the name of the county or counties where the proceeding has been brought, and, if known to the investigative agency at the time of filing the RICO lien notice, the case number of the proceeding;

(4) A statement that the notice is being filed pursuant to this chapter; and

(5) The name and address of the investigative agency filing the RICO lien notice and the name of the individual signing the RICO lien notice.

(c) A RICO lien notice shall apply only to one person and, to the extent applicable, any aliases, fictitious names, or other names, including names of corporations, partnerships, or other entities, to the extent permitted in paragraph (1) of subsection (b) of this Code section. A separate RICO lien notice shall be filed for any other person against whom the investigative agency desires to file a RICO lien notice under this Code section.

(d) The investigative agency shall, as soon as practicable after the filing of each RICO lien notice, furnish to the person named in the notice either a copy of the recorded notice or a copy of the notice with a notation thereon of the county or counties in which the notice has been recorded. The failure of the investigative agency to so furnish a copy of the notice under this subsection shall not invalidate or otherwise affect the notice.

(e) The filing of a RICO lien notice creates, from the time of its filing, a lien in favor of the state on the following property of the person named in the notice and against any other names set forth in the notice:

(1) Any real property situated in the county where the notice is filed then or thereafter owned by the person or under any of the names; and

(2) Any beneficial interest situated in the county where the notice is filed then or thereafter owned by the person or under any of the names.

(f) The lien shall commence and attach as of the time of filing of the RICO lien notice and shall continue thereafter until expiration, termination, or release pursuant to Code Section 16-14-14. The lien created in favor of the state shall be superior and prior to the interest of any other person in the real property or beneficial interest if the interest is acquired subsequent to the filing of the notice.

(g) In conjunction with any civil proceedings:

(1) The investigative agency may file without prior court order in any county a lis pendens and, in such case, any person acquiring an interest in the subject real property or beneficial interest, if the real property or beneficial interest is acquired subsequent to the filing of lis pendens, shall take the interest subject to the civil proceeding and any subsequent judgment of forfeiture; and

(2) If a RICO lien notice has been filed, the investigative agency may name as defendants, in addition to the person named in the notice, any persons acquiring an interest in the real property or beneficial interest subsequent to the filing of the notice. If a judgment of forfeiture is entered in the proceeding in favor of the state, the interest of any person in the property that was acquired subsequent to the filing of the notice shall be subject to the notice and judgment of forfeiture.

(h)(1) A trustee who acquires actual knowledge that a RICO lien notice or a civil proceeding or criminal proceeding has been filed against any person for whom he holds legal or record title to real property shall immediately furnish to the investigative agency the following:

(A) The name and address of the person, as known to the trustee;

(B) The name and address, as known to the trustee, of all other persons for whose benefit the trustee holds title to the real property; and

(C) If requested by the investigative agency, a copy of the trust agreement or other instrument pursuant to which the trustee holds legal or record title to the real property.

(2) Any trustee who fails to comply with the provisions of this subsection is guilty of a misdemeanor.

(i) Any trustee who conveys title to real property for which a RICO lien notice has been filed at the time of the conveyance in the county where the real property is situated naming a person who, to the actual knowledge of the trustee, holds a beneficial interest in the trust shall be liable to the state for the greater of:

(1) The amount of proceeds received directly by the person named in the RICO lien notice as a result of the conveyance;

(2) The amount of proceeds received by the trustee as a result of the conveyance and distributed to the person named in the RICO lien notice; or

(3) The fair market value of the interest of the person named in the RICO lien notice in the real property so conveyed; however, if the trustee conveys the real property and holds the proceeds that would otherwise be paid or distributed to the beneficiary or at the direction of the beneficiary or his designee, the trustee's liability shall not exceed the amount of the proceeds so held for so long as the proceeds are held by the trustee.

(j) The filing of a RICO lien notice shall not constitute a lien on the record title to real property as owned by the trustee except to the extent the trustee is named in the RICO lien notice. The investigative agency may bring a civil proceeding in any superior court against the trustee to recover from the trustee the amounts set forth in subsection (i), and the state shall also be entitled to recover investigative costs and attorney's fees incurred by the investigative agency.

(k) The filing of a RICO lien notice shall not affect the use to which real property or a beneficial interest owned by the person named in the RICO lien notice may be put or the right of the person to receive any avails, rents, or other proceeds resulting from the use and ownership, but not the sale, of the property until a judgment of forfeiture is entered.

(*l*)(1) The provisions of this Code section shall not apply to any conveyance by a trustee pursuant to a court order unless such court order is entered in an action between the trustee and the beneficiary.

(2) Unless the trustee has actual knowledge that a person owning a beneficial interest in the trust is named in a RICO lien notice or is otherwise a defendant in a civil proceeding, the provisions of this Code section shall not apply to:

(A) Any conveyance by a trustee required under the terms of any trust agreement, which trust agreement is a matter of public record prior to the filing of any RICO lien notice; or

(B) Any conveyance by a trustee to all of the persons who own a beneficial interest in the trust.

(m) All forfeitures or dispositions under this Code section shall be made with due provision for the rights of innocent persons.

Laws 1982, p. 1385, § 6; Laws 1982, p. 1385, § 12; Laws 1984, p. 22, § 16.

Formerly Code 1933, § 26-3412.

§ 16-14-14. Term

(a) The term of a RICO lien notice shall be for a period of six years from the date of filing unless a renewal RICO lien notice has been filed by the investigative agency; and, in such case, the term of the renewal RICO lien notice shall be for a period of six years from the date of its filing. The investigative agency shall be entitled to only one renewal of the RICO lien notice.

(b) The investigative agency filing the RICO lien notice may release in whole or in part any RICO lien notice or may release any specific real property or beneficial interest from the RICO lien notice upon such terms and conditions as it may determine. Any release of a RICO lien notice executed by the investigative agency may be filed in the official records of any county. No charge or fee shall be imposed for the filing of any release of a RICO lien notice.

(c) If no civil proceeding has been instituted by the investigative agency seeking a forfeiture of any property owned by the person named in the RICO lien notice, the acquittal in the criminal proceeding of the person named in the RICO lien notice or the dismissal of the criminal proceeding shall terminate the RICO lien notice; and, in such case, the filing of the RICO lien notice shall have no effect. In the event the criminal proceeding has been dismissed or the person named in the RICO lien notice has been acquitted in the criminal proceeding, the RICO lien notice shall continue for the duration of the civil proceeding.

(d) If no civil proceeding is then pending against the person named in a RICO lien notice, the person named in a RICO lien notice may institute an action against the investigative agency filing the notice in the county where the notice has been filed seeking a release or extinguishment of the notice; and, in such case:

(1) The court shall, upon the motion of such person, immediately enter an order setting a date for hearing, which date shall be not less than five nor more than ten days after the action has been filed; and the order, along with a copy of the complaint, shall be served on the investigative agency within three days after the institution of the action. At the hearing, the court shall take evidence on the issue of whether any real property or beneficial interest owned by such person is covered by the RICO lien notice or otherwise subject to forfeiture under this chapter; and, if such person shows by the preponderance of the evidence that the RICO lien notice is not applicable to him or that any real property or beneficial interest owned by him is not subject to forfeiture under this chapter, the court shall enter a judgment extinguishing the RICO lien notice or releasing the real property or beneficial interest from the RICO lien notice;

(2) The court shall immediately enter its order releasing from the RICO lien notice any specific real property or beneficial interest if a sale of the real property or beneficial interest is pending and the filing of the notice prevents the sale of the property or interest; however, the proceeds resulting from the sale of the real property or beneficial interest shall be deposited into the registry of the court, subject to the further order of the court; and

(3) At the hearing set forth in paragraph (1), the court may release from the RICO lien notice any real property or beneficial interest upon the posting by such person of such security as is equal to the value of the real property or beneficial interest owned by such person.

(e) In the event a civil proceeding is pending against a person named in a RICO lien notice, the court, upon motion by said person, may grant the relief set forth in this Code section.

Laws 1982, p. 1385, § 6; Laws 1982, p. 1385, § 12; Laws 1996, p. 6, § 16.

Formerly Code 1933, § 26–3413.

§ 16–14–15. Alien corporations

(a) Each alien corporation desiring to acquire of record any real property shall have, prior to acquisition, and shall continuously maintain in this state during any year thereafter in which such real property is owned by the alien corporation:

(1) A registered office; and

(2) A registered agent, which agent may be either:

(A) An individual resident in this state whose business office is identical with such registered office; or

(B) Another corporation authorized to transact business in this state having a business office identical with such registered office.

(b) Each registered agent appointed pursuant to this Code section, on whom process may be served, shall file a statement in writing with the Secretary of State accepting the appointment as registered agent simultaneously with being designated.

(c) Each alien corporation shall file with the Secretary of State an annual registration setting forth:

(1) The name of the alien corporation and the country under whose law it is incorporated;

(2) The mailing address of the principal office of the alien corporation;

(3) The name and mailing address of each officer and each director of the alien corporation;

(4) The name and street address of the registered agent and registered office of the alien corporation; and

(5) The signature of the corporate president, vice-president, secretary, assistant secretary, or treasurer attesting to the accuracy of the report as of the date the annual registration is executed on behalf of the corporation.

(d) The first annual registration must be delivered to the Secretary of State between January 1 and April 1, or such other date as the Secretary of State may specify by rules or regulations, of the year following a calendar year in which an alien corporation filed its initial application pursuant to subsection (a) of this Code section. Subsequent annual registrations must be delivered to the Secretary of State between January 1 and April 1, or such other date as the Secretary of State may specify by rules or regulations, of the following calendar years.

(e) For filing reports required pursuant to this Code section, the Secretary of State shall collect a filing fee as set out in Code Section 14–2–122 for the filing of annual registrations.

(f) If an annual registration does not contain the information required by this Code section, the Secretary of State shall promptly notify the reporting domestic, foreign, or alien corporation in writing and return the report to it for correction. If the report is corrected to contain the information required by this Code section and delivered to the Secretary of State within 30 days after the effective date of notice, it is deemed to be timely filed.

(g) The Secretary of State shall record the status of any alien corporation that fails to comply with the requirements of this Code section.

(h) Each alien corporation that fails to file a report as required by subsection (c) of this Code section or fails to maintain a registered office and a registered agent as required by subsection (a) of this Code section shall not be entitled to own, purchase, or sell any real property and shall not be entitled to bring an action or defend in the courts of the state until such requirements have been complied with.

(i) The filing of a report by a corporation as required by subsection (c) of this Code section shall be solely for the purposes of this chapter and, notwithstanding Code Section 14–2–510 or any other relevant law, shall not be used as a determination of whether the corporation is actually doing business in this state.

Laws 1982, p. 1385, § 6; Laws 1982, p. 1385, § 12; Laws 1984, p. 22, § 16; Laws 1989, p. 946, § 110; Laws 1990, p. 322, § 1.

Formerly Code 1933, § 26–3414.

CHAPTER 15

STREET GANG TERRORISM AND PREVENTION

§ 16–15–1. Short title

This chapter shall be known and may be cited as the "Georgia Street Gang Terrorism and Prevention Act."

Laws 1992, p. 3236, § 1; Laws 1998, p. 270, § 8.

§ 16–15–2. Legislative intent

(a) The General Assembly finds and declares that it is the right of every person to be secure and protected from fear, intimidation, and physical harm caused by the activities of violent groups and individuals. It is not the intent of this chapter to interfere with the exercise of the constitutionally protected rights of freedom of expression and association. The General Assembly recognizes the constitutional right of every citizen to harbor and express beliefs on any lawful subject whatsoever, to associate lawfully with others who share similar beliefs, to petition lawfully constituted authority for a redress of perceived grievances, and to participate in the electoral process.

(b) The General Assembly, however, further finds that the State of Georgia is in a state of crisis which has been caused by violent criminal street gangs whose members threaten, terrorize, and commit a multitude of crimes against the peaceful citizens of their neighborhoods. These activities, both individually and collectively, present a clear and present danger to public order and safety and are not constitutionally protected.

(c) The General Assembly finds that there are criminal street gangs operating in Georgia and that the number of gang related murders is increasing. It is the intent of the General Assembly in enacting this chapter to seek the eradication of criminal activity by criminal street gangs by focusing upon criminal gang activity and upon the organized nature of criminal street gangs which together are the chief source of terror created by criminal street gangs.

(d) The General Assembly further finds that an effective means of punishing and deterring the criminal activities of criminal street gangs is through forfeiture of the profits, proceeds, and instrumentalities acquired, accumulated, or used by criminal street gangs.

Laws 1992, p. 3236, § 1; Laws 1995, p. 933, § 13; Laws 1996, p. 6, § 16; Laws 1998, p. 270, § 8; Laws 2010, Act 406, § 1, eff. July 1, 2010.

Historical and Statutory Notes

The 2010 amendment by Act 406, in subsec. (b), inserted "criminal" preceding "street gangs" in the first sentence; in subsec. (c), inserted "criminal" preceding "street gangs" and deleted "patterns of" preceding "criminal gang activity" in the second sentence; and in subsec. (d), inserted "criminal" before "street gangs" twice.

§ 16–15–3. Definitions

As used in this chapter, the term:

(1) "Criminal gang activity" means the commission, attempted commission, conspiracy to commit, or solicitation, coercion, or intimidation of another person to commit any of the following offenses on or after July 1, 2006:

(A) Any offense defined as racketeering activity by Code Section 16–14–3;

(B) Any offense defined in Article 7 of Chapter 5 of this title, relating to stalking;

(C) Any offense defined in Code Section 16–6–1 as rape, 16–6–2 as aggravated sodomy, 16–6–3 as statutory rape, or 16–6–22.2 as aggravated sexual battery;

(D) Any offense defined in Article 3 of Chapter 10 of this title, relating to escape and other offenses related to confinement;

(E) Any offense defined in Article 4 of Chapter 11 of this title, relating to dangerous instrumentalities and practices;

(F) Any offense defined in Code Section 42–5–15, 42–5–16, 42–5–17, 42–5–18, or 42–5–19, relating to the security of state or county correctional facilities;

(G) Any offense defined in Code Section 49–4A–11, relating to aiding or encouraging a child to escape from custody;

(H) Any offense of criminal trespass or criminal damage to property resulting from any act of gang related painting on, tagging, marking on, writing on, or creating any form of graffiti on the property of another;

(I) Any criminal offense committed in violation of the laws of the United States or its territories, dominions, or possessions, any of the several states, or any foreign nation which, if committed in this state, would be considered criminal gang activity under this Code section; and

(J) Any criminal offense in the State of Georgia, any other state, or the United States that involves violence, possession of a weapon, or use of a weapon, whether designated as a felony or not, and regardless of the maximum sentence that could be imposed or actually was imposed.

(2) "Criminal street gang" means any organization, association, or group of three or more persons associated in fact, whether formal or informal, which engages in criminal gang activity as defined in paragraph (1) of this Code section. The existence of such organization, association, or group of individuals associated in fact may be established by evidence of a common name or common identifying signs, symbols, tattoos, graffiti, or attire or other distinguishing characteristics, including, but not limited to, common activities, customs, or behaviors. Such term shall not include three or more persons, associated in fact, whether formal or informal, who are not engaged in criminal gang activity.

Laws 1992, p. 3236, § 1; Laws 1998, p. 270, § 8; Laws 1999, p. 81, § 16; Laws 2006, Act 616, § 1, eff. July 1, 2006; Laws 2010, Act 406, § 2, eff. July 1, 2010.

Historical and Statutory Notes

The 2006 amendment by Act 616 rewrote the section which had read:

"As used in this chapter, the term:

"(1) 'Criminal street gang' means any organization, association, or group of three or more persons associated in fact, whether formal or informal, which engages in a pattern of criminal gang activity as defined in paragraph (2) of this Code section. The existence of such organization, association, or group of individuals associated in fact may be established by evidence of a common name or common identifying signs, symbols, tattoos, graffiti, or attire or other distinguishing characteristics.

"(2) 'Pattern of criminal gang activity' means the commission, attempted commission, conspiracy to commit, or solicitation, coercion, or intimidation of another person to commit at least two of the following offenses, provided that at least one of these offenses occurred after July 1, 1998, and the last of such offenses occurred within three years, excluding any periods of imprisonment, of prior criminal gang activity:

"(A) Any offense defined as racketeering activity by Code Section 16–14–3;

"(B) Any offense defined in Article 7 of Chapter 5 of this title, relating to stalking;

"(C) Any offense defined in Code Section 16–6–1 as rape, 16–6–2 as aggravated sodomy, 16–6–3 as statutory rape, or 16–6–22.2 as aggravated sexual battery;

"(D) Any offense defined in Article 3 of Chapter 10 of this title, relating to escape and other offenses related to confinement;

"(E) Any offense defined in Article 4 of Chapter 11 of this title, relating to dangerous instrumentalities and practices;

"(F) Any offense defined in Code Section 42–5–15, 42–5–16, 42–5–17, 42–5–18, or 42–5–19, relating to the security of state or county correctional facilities; and

"(G) Any offense defined in Code Section 49–4A–11, relating to aiding or encouraging a child to escape from custody."

Laws 2006, Act 616, § 7, provides:

"This section and Sections 6 and 8 of this Act shall become effective upon their approval by the Governor or upon their becoming law without such approval. The remaining sections of this Act shall become effective on July 1, 2006, and shall apply to all crimes committed on or after such date. Any offense committed before July 1, 2006, shall be punishable as provided by the statute in effect at the time the offense was committed."

The 2010 amendment by Act 406, in par. (2), inserted "including, but not limited to, common activities, customs, or behaviors" following "distinguishing characteristics" in the second sentence.

§ 16–15–4. Unlawful acts; penalties

(a) It shall be unlawful for any person employed by or associated with a criminal street gang to conduct or participate in criminal gang activity through the commission of any offense enumerated in paragraph (1) of Code Section 16–15–3.

(b) It shall be unlawful for any person to commit any offense enumerated in paragraph (1) of Code Section 16–15–3 with the intent to obtain or earn membership or maintain or increase his or her status or position in a criminal street gang.

(c) It shall be unlawful for any person to acquire or maintain, directly or indirectly, through criminal gang activity or proceeds derived therefrom any interest in or control of any real or personal property of any nature, including money.

(d) It shall be unlawful for any person who occupies a position of organizer, supervisory position, or any other position of management or leadership with regard to a criminal street gang to engage in, directly or indirectly, or conspire to engage in criminal gang activity.

(e) It shall be unlawful for any person to cause, encourage, solicit, recruit, or coerce another to become a member or associate of a criminal street gang, to participate in a criminal street gang, or to conduct or participate in criminal gang activity.

(f) It shall be unlawful for any person to communicate, directly or indirectly, with another any threat of injury or damage to the person or property of the other person or of any associate or relative of the other person with the intent to deter such person from assisting a member or associate of a criminal street gang to withdraw from such criminal street gang.

(g) It shall be unlawful for any person to communicate, directly or indirectly, with another any threat of injury or damage to the person or property of the other person or of any associate or relative of the other person with the intent to punish or retaliate against such person for having withdrawn from a criminal street gang.

(h) It shall be unlawful for any person to communicate, directly or indirectly, with another any threat of injury or damage to the person or property of the other person or of any associate or relative of the other person with the intent to punish or retaliate against such person for refusing to or encouraging another to refuse to become or obtain the status of a member or associate of a criminal street gang.

(i) It shall be unlawful for any person to communicate, directly or indirectly, with another any threat of injury or damage to the person or property of the other person or of any associate or relative of the other person with the intent to punish or retaliate against such person for providing statements or testimony against criminal street gangs or any criminal street gang member or associate.

(j) In addition to the prohibitions set forth in Code Section 16–10–93, it shall be unlawful for any person to communicate, directly or indirectly, with another any threat of injury or damage to the person or property of the other person or of any associate or relative of the other person with the intent to intimidate, deter, or prevent such person from communicating to any law enforcement or corrections officer, prosecuting attorney, or judge information relating to criminal street gangs, criminal street gang members or associates, or criminal gang activity.

(k)(1) Any person who violates subsection (a), (b), or (c) of this Code section shall, in addition to any other penalty imposed by law, be punished by imprisonment for not less than five nor more than 15 years or by a fine of not less than $10,000.00 nor more than $15,000. 00, or both.

(2) Any person who violates subsection (d) of this Code section may, in addition to any other penalty provided by law, be punished by imprisonment for an additional ten years which shall be served consecutively to any other sentence imposed on such person by law.

(3) Any person who violates subsection (e), (f), (g), (h), (i) or (j) of this Code section shall, in addition to any other penalty provided by law, be punished by imprisonment for not less than three nor more than ten years.

(*l*) In addition to any other penalty provided by this Code section, all sentences imposed under this Code section shall require as a special condition of the sentence that the person sentenced shall not knowingly have contact of any kind or character with any other member or associate of a criminal street gang, shall not participate in any criminal gang activity, and, in cases involving a victim, shall not knowingly have contact of any kind or character with any such victim or any member of any such victim's family or household.

(m) Any crime committed in violation of this Code section shall be considered a separate offense.

Laws 1992, p. 3236, § 1; Laws 1998, p. 270, § 8; Laws 2006, Act 616, § 2, eff. July 1, 2006; Laws 2010, Act 406, § 3, eff. July 1, 2010.

Historical and Statutory Notes

The 2006 amendment by Act 616, in subsec. (a), substituted "criminal street gang activity through the commission of any offense enumerated in paragraph (1) of Code Section 16–15–3" for "such criminal street gang through a pattern of criminal gang activity"; redesignated former subsecs. (b) to (h) as subsecs. (d) to (j); added new subsecs. (b) and (c); in subsecs. (d) and (e) as redesignated, deleted "a pattern of" preceding "criminal activity"; and, in subsec. (i) as redesignated, substituted "(a), (b), (c), or (d)" for "(a) or (b)", "five" for "three", "$10,0000.00" for "$5,0000.00", and "$15,000.00" for "$10,000.00" in par. (1), substituted "subsection (e)" for "subsection (c)" in par. (2), and substituted "(f), (g), or (h)" for "(d), (e), or (f)", and "three " for "one" in par. (3).

Laws 2006, Act 616, § 7, provides:

"This section and Sections 6 and 8 of this Act shall become effective upon their approval by the Governor or upon their becoming law without such approval. The remaining sections of this Act shall become effective on July 1, 2006, and shall apply to all crimes committed on or after such date. Any offense committed before July 1, 2006, shall be punishable as provided by the statute in effect at the time the offense was committed."

The 2010 amendment by Act 406 rewrote the section which had read:

"(a) It shall be unlawful for any person employed by or associated with a criminal street gang to conduct or participate in criminal street gang activity through the commission of any offense enumerated in paragraph (1) of Code Section 16–15–3.

"(b) It shall be unlawful for any person employed by or associated with a criminal street gang to commit any offense enumerated in paragraph (1) of Code Section 16–15–3 with knowledge that members of such criminal street gang have committed one or more of such offenses.

"(c) It shall be unlawful for any person to commit any offense enumerated in paragraph (1) of Code Section 16–15–3 with the intent to maintain or increase his or her status or position in a criminal street gang.

"(d) It shall be unlawful for any person to acquire or maintain, directly or indirectly, through criminal gang activity or proceeds derived therefrom any interest in or control of any real or personal property of any nature, including money.

"(e) It shall be unlawful for any person who occupies a position of organizer, supervisory position, or any other position of management with regard to a criminal street gang to engage in, directly or indirectly, or conspire to engage in criminal gang activity.

"(f) It shall be unlawful for any person to cause, encourage, solicit, or coerce another to participate in a criminal street gang.

"(g) It shall be unlawful for any person to communicate, directly or indirectly, with another any threat of injury or damage to the person or property of the other person or to any associate or relative of the other person with the intent to deter such person from assisting a member or associate of a criminal street gang to withdraw from such criminal street gang.

"(h) It shall be unlawful for any person to communicate, directly or indirectly, with another any threat of injury or damage to the person or property of the other person or to any associate or relative of the other person with the intent to punish or retaliate against such person for having withdrawn from a criminal street gang.

"(i)(1) Any person who violates subsection (a), (b), (c), or (d) of this Code section shall, in addition to any other penalty imposed by law, be punished by imprisonment for not less than five nor more than 15 years or by a fine of not less than $10,000.00 nor more than $15,000.00, or both.

"(2) Any person who violates subsection (e) of this Code section may, in addition to any other penalty provided by law, be punished by imprisonment for an additional ten years which shall be served consecutively to any other sentence imposed on such person by law.

"(3) Any person who violates subsection (f), (g), or (h) of this Code section shall, in addition to any other penalty provided by law, be punished by imprisonment for not less than three nor more than ten years.

"(j) Any crime committed in violation of this Code section shall be considered a separate offense."

§ 16–15–5. Forfeiture of contraband property

(a) The following are declared to be contraband and no person shall have a property interest in them:

(1) All property which is directly or indirectly used or intended for use in any manner to facilitate a violation of this chapter; and

(2) Any property constituting or derived from gross profits or other proceeds obtained from a violation of this chapter.

(b) In any action under this Code section, the court may enter such restraining orders or take other appropriate action, including acceptance of performance bonds, in connection with any interest that is subject to forfeiture.

(c) Within 60 days of the date of the seizure of contraband pursuant to this Code section, the district attorney shall initiate a forfeiture proceeding as provided in Code Section 16–13–49. An owner or interest holder, as defined by subsection (a) of Code Section 16–13–49, may establish as a defense to the forfeiture of property which is subject to forfeiture under this Code section the applicable provisions of subsection (e) or (f) of Code Section 16–13–49. Property which is forfeited pursuant to this Code section shall be disposed of as provided in Code Section 16–13–49 and the proceeds of such disposition shall be paid to the Criminal Justice Coordinating Council for use in funding gang prevention projects.

Laws 1992, p. 3236, § 1; Laws 1993, p. 91, § 16; Laws 1998, p. 270, § 8.

§ 16–15–6. Applicability with respect to local ordinances

Nothing in this chapter shall prevent a local governing body from adopting and enforcing ordinances relating to gangs and gang violence which are consistent with this chapter. Where local laws duplicate or supplement the provisions of this chapter, this chapter shall be construed as providing alternative remedies and not as preempting the field.

Laws 1992, p. 3236, § 1; Laws 1998, p. 270, § 8.

§ 16–15–7. Abatement of nuisances; actions for damages or injunctions

(a) Any real property which is erected, established, maintained, owned, leased, or used by any criminal street gang for the purpose of conducting criminal gang activity shall constitute a public nuisance and may be abated as provided by Title 41, relating to nuisances.

(b) An action to abate a nuisance pursuant to this Code section may be brought by the district attorney, solicitor-general, prosecuting attorney of a municipal court or city, or county attorney in any superior, state, or municipal court.

(c) Any person who is injured by reason of criminal gang activity shall have a cause of action for three times the actual damages sustained and, where appropriate, punitive damages; provided, however, that no cause of action shall arise under this subsection as a result of an otherwise legitimate commercial transaction between parties to a contract or agreement for the sale of lawful goods or property or the sale of securities regulated by Chapter 5 of Title 10 or by the federal Securities and Exchange Commission. Such person shall also recover attorney's fees in the trial and appellate court and costs of investigation and litigation reasonably incurred. All averments of a cause of action under this subsection shall be stated with particularity. No judgment shall be awarded unless the finder of fact determines that the action is consistent with the intent of the General Assembly as set forth in Code Section 16–15–2.

(d) The state, any political subdivision thereof, or any person aggrieved by a criminal street gang or criminal gang activity may bring an action to enjoin violations of this chapter in the same manner as provided in Code Section 16–14–6.

Laws 1998, p. 270, § 8; Laws 2010, Act 406, § 4, eff. July 1, 2010.

Historical and Statutory Notes

The 2010 amendment by Act 406, in subsec. (d), substituted "criminal street gang or criminal" for "pattern of" preceding "gang activity".

§ 16–15–8. Effect of conviction of criminal gang activity on subsequent civil action

A conviction of an offense defined as criminal gang activity shall estop the defendant in any subsequent civil action or proceeding as to matters proved in the criminal proceeding.

Laws 1998, p. 270, § 8.

§ 16–15–9. Certain offenses admissible as evidence

The commission of any offense enumerated in paragraph (1) of Code Section 16–15–3 by any member or associate of a criminal street gang shall be admissible in any trial or proceeding for the purpose of proving the existence of the criminal street gang and criminal gang activity.

Laws 2006, Act 616, § 3, eff. July 1, 2006; Laws 2010, Act 406, § 5, eff. July 1, 2010.

Historical and Statutory Notes

Laws 2006, Act 616, § 7, provides:

"This section and Sections 6 and 8 of this Act shall become effective upon their approval by the Governor or upon their becoming law without such approval. The remaining sections of this Act shall become effective on July 1, 2006, and shall apply to all crimes committed on or after such date. Any offense committed before July 1, 2006, shall be punishable as provided by the statute in effect at the time the offense was committed."

The 2010 amendment by Act 406, inserted "or associate" after "any member".

§ 16–15–10. Criminal Street Gang Reward Fund

There shall be established as part of the Prosecuting Attorneys' Council of the State of Georgia the Criminal Street Gang Reward Fund. The chief of police, sheriff, or chairperson of any county governing authority may request the posting of up to a $5,000.00 reward for information leading to the arrest and conviction of any person involved in criminal gang activity that leads to the death or maiming of another person or property damage in the amount of $2,500.00 or more.

Laws 2006, Act 616, § 3, eff. July 1, 2006; Laws 2010, Act 406, § 6, eff. July 1, 2010.

Historical and Statutory Notes

Laws 2006, Act 616, § 7, provides:

"This section and Sections 6 and 8 of this Act shall become effective upon their approval by the Governor or upon their becoming law without such approval. The remaining sections of this Act shall become effective on July 1, 2006, and shall apply to all crimes committed on or after such date. Any offense committed before July 1, 2006, shall be punishable as provided by the statute in effect at the time the offense was committed."

The 2010 amendment by Act 406, substituted "Prosecuting Attorneys' Council of the State of Georgia" for "Prosecuting Attorney's Council" and made other nominal changes.

§ 16–15–11. Georgia Criminal Street Gang Database

(a) Subject to funds as may be appropriated by the General Assembly or otherwise available for such purpose, the Georgia Bureau of Investigation shall be authorized to establish, develop, manage, and maintain a state-wide criminal street gang data base, to be known as the Georgia Criminal Street Gang Database, to facilitate the exchange of information between federal, state, county, and municipal law enforcement, prosecution and corrections agencies, offices, and departments. The Georgia Bureau of Investigation shall be authorized to solicit input from law enforcement and prosecuting attorneys in determining useful information for such data base so that information may be used by law enforcement, prosecution and corrections agencies, and other agencies, offices, and departments for investigative, prosecutorial, and corrections purposes.

(b) Once the Georgia Criminal Street Gang Database is created and operational, the Georgia Bureau of Investigation shall be authorized to notify all federal, state, county, and municipal law enforcement, prosecution and corrections agencies, offices, and departments located in this state that information regarding criminal street gangs and their members and associates shall be entered into the Georgia Criminal Street Gang Database.

(c) The Georgia Bureau of Investigation shall be authorized to create and promulgate a uniform reporting format for the entry of pertinent information received from law enforcement, prosecution and corrections agencies, offices, and departments for use in the Georgia Criminal Street Gang Database.

(d) All state, county, and municipal law enforcement, prosecution and corrections agencies, offices, and departments may timely furnish information acquired relating to criminal street gangs and criminal gang activity to the Georgia Bureau of Investigation to be included in the Georgia Criminal Street Gang Database according to the reporting format developed by the Georgia Bureau of Investigation.

(e) Notwithstanding the provisions of Article 4 of Chapter 18 of Title 50, the information and related records associated with the Georgia Criminal Street Gang Database shall not be open to inspection by or made available to the public.

Laws 2010, Act 406, § 7, eff. July 1, 2010.

CHAPTER 16

FORFEITURE OF PROPERTY USED IN BURGLARY OR ARMED ROBBERY

§ 16–16–1. Definitions

As used in this chapter, the term:

(1) "Armed robbery" means the offense defined in subsection (a) of Code Section 16–8–41.

(2) "Burglary" means the offense defined in subsection (a) of Code Section 16–7–1.

Laws 1995, p. 1051, § 4.

§ 16–16–2. Forfeiture of motor vehicles, tools, and weapons used or intended for use in commission of burglary or armed robbery

(a) All motor vehicles, tools, and weapons which are used or intended for use in any manner in the commission of or to facilitate the commission of a burglary or armed robbery are subject to forfeiture under this chapter, but:

(1) No motor vehicle used by any person as a common carrier in the transaction of business as a common carrier is subject to forfeiture under this Code section unless it appears that the owner or other person in charge of the motor vehicle is a consenting party or privy to the commission of a burglary or armed robbery;

(2) No motor vehicle is subject to forfeiture under this Code section by reason of any act or omission established by the owner thereof to have been committed or omitted without his or her knowledge or consent, and any co-owner of a motor vehicle without knowledge of or consent to the act or omission is protected to the extent of the interest of such co-owner; and

(3) A forfeiture of a motor vehicle encumbered by a bona fide security interest is subject to the interest of the secured party if he or she neither had knowledge of or nor consented to the act or omission.

(b) Property subject to forfeiture under this chapter may be seized by any law enforcement officer of this state or any political subdivision thereof who has the power to make arrests upon process issued by any court having jurisdiction over the property. Seizure without process or warrant may be made if:

(1) The seizure is incident to an arrest or a search under a search warrant;

(2) The property subject to seizure has been the subject of a prior judgment in favor of the state in a criminal injunction or forfeiture proceeding based upon this chapter; or

(3) If probable cause exists that the vehicle, tool, or weapon is subject to seizure.

(c) Property taken or detained under this Code section shall not be subject to replevin but is deemed to be in the custody of the superior court wherein the seizure was made or in custody of the superior court where it can be proven that the burglary or armed robbery was committed, subject only to the orders and decrees of the court having jurisdiction over the forfeiture proceedings. When property is seized under this chapter, law enforcement officers seizing such property shall:

(1) Place the property under seal;

(2) Remove the property to a place designated by the judge of the superior court having jurisdiction over the forfeiture as set out in this subsection; or

(3) Deliver such property to the sheriff or police chief of the county in which the seizure occurred, and the sheriff or police chief shall take custody of the property and remove it to an appropriate location for disposition in accordance with law.

(d) When property is seized under this chapter, the sheriff or law enforcement officer seizing the same shall report the fact of seizure, within 20 days thereof, to the district attorney of the judicial circuit having jurisdiction in the county where the seizure was made. Within 60 days from the date he or she receives notice of the seizure, the district attorney of the judicial circuit shall cause to be filed in the superior court of the county in which the property is seized or detained an in rem complaint for forfeiture of such property as provided for in this Code section. The proceedings shall be brought in the name of the state by the district attorney of the circuit in which the property was seized, and the complaint shall be verified by a duly authorized agent of the state in a manner required by the law of this state. The complaint shall describe the property, state its location, state its present custodian, state the name of the owner, if known to the duly authorized agent of the state, allege the essential elements of the violation upon which the forfeiture is based, and shall conclude with a prayer of due process to enforce the forfeiture. Upon the filing of such a complaint, the court shall promptly cause process to issue to the present custodian in possession of the property described in the complaint, commanding him or her to seize the property described in the complaint and to hold that property for further order of the court. A copy of the complaint shall be served on the owner or lessee, if known. A copy of the complaint shall also be served upon any person having a duly recorded security interest in or lien upon that property. If the owner or lessee is unknown or resides out of the state or departs the state or cannot after due diligence be found within the state or conceals himself or herself so as to avoid service, notice of the proceedings shall be published once a week for two weeks in the newspaper in which the sheriff's advertisements are published. Such publication shall be deemed notice to any and all persons having an interest in or right affected by such proceeding and from any sale of the property resulting therefrom but shall not constitute notice to any person having a duly recorded security interest in or lien upon such property and required to be served under this Code section unless that person is unknown or resides out of the state or departs the state or cannot after due diligence be found within the state or conceals himself or herself to avoid service. An owner of or interest holder in the property may file an answer asserting a claim against the property in the action in rem. Any such answer shall be filed within 30 days after the service of the summons and complaint. Where service is made by publication and personal service has not been made, an owner or interest holder shall file an answer within 30 days of the date of final publication. An answer must be verified by the owner or interest holder under penalty of perjury. In addition to complying with the general rules applicable to an answer in civil actions, the answer must set forth:

(1) The caption of the proceedings as set forth in the complaint and the name of the claimant;

(2) The address at which the claimant will accept mail;

(3) The nature and extent of the claimant's interest in the property;

(4) The date, identity of transferor, and circumstances of the claimant's acquisition of the interest in the property;

(5) The specific provision of this Code section relied on in asserting that the property is not subject to forfeiture;

(6) All essential facts supporting each assertion; and

(7) The precise relief sought.

If at the expiration of the period set forth in this subsection no answer has been filed, the court shall order the disposition of the seized property as provided for in this Code section. If an answer is filed, a hearing must be held within 60 days after service of the complaint unless continued for good cause and must be held by the court without a jury. If the court determines that a claimant defending the complaint knew or by the exercise of ordinary care should have known that the property was to be used for an unlawful purpose subjecting it to forfeiture under this chapter, the court shall order the disposition of the seized property as provided in this Code section and that claimant shall have no claim upon the property or proceeds from the sale thereof.

(e) (1) When property is forfeited under this chapter, the judge of the superior court in the county where the seizure was made or in the county in which it can be proven that the burglary or armed robbery was committed may dispose of the property by issuing an order to:

(A) Retain it for official use by any agency of this state or any political subdivision thereof;

(B) Sell that which is not required to be destroyed by law and which is not harmful to the public. The proceeds shall be used for payment of all proper expenses of the proceedings for forfeiture and sale, including but not limited to the expenses of seizure, maintenance of custody, advertising, and court costs; or

(C) Require the sheriff or police chief of the county in which the seizure occurred to take custody of the property and remove it for disposition in accordance with law.

(2) (A) Money, currency, or proceeds which are realized from the sale or disposition of forfeited property shall after satisfaction of the interest of secured parties and after payment of all costs vest in the local political subdivision whose law enforcement officers seized it. If the property was seized by a municipal law enforcement agency then the money, currency, or proceeds realized from the sale or disposition of the property shall vest in that municipality. If the property was seized by a county law enforcement agency, then the money, currency, or proceeds realized from the sale or disposition of the property shall vest in that county. If the property was seized by joint action of a county law enforcement agency and a municipal law enforcement agency, then the money, currency, or proceeds realized from the sale or disposition of the property shall vest in that county and that municipality and shall be divided equally between the county and municipality. If the property was seized by a state law enforcement agency, then the money, currency, or proceeds realized from the sale or disposition of the property shall vest in the county where the condemnation proceedings are filed. Except as otherwise provided in subparagraph (B) of paragraph (1) of this subsection for payment of all costs, the local government in which the money, currency, or proceeds realized from the forfeited property vests shall expend or use such funds or proceeds received for any official law enforcement purpose except for the payment of salaries or rewards to law enforcement personnel, at the discretion of the chief officer of the local law enforcement agency, or to fund

victim-witness assistance programs. Such property shall not be used to supplant any other local, state, or federal funds appropriated for staff or operations.

(B) Any local law enforcement agency receiving property under this subsection shall submit an annual report to the local governing authority. The report shall be submitted with the agency's budget request and shall itemize the property received during the fiscal year and the utilization made thereof.

Laws 1995, p. 1051, § 4.

CHAPTER 17

PAYDAY LENDING

§ 16–17–1. Definition; legislative intent

(a) Without limiting in any manner the scope of this chapter, "payday lending" as used in this chapter encompasses all transactions in which funds are advanced to be repaid at a later date, notwithstanding the fact that the transaction contains one or more other elements and a "payday lender" shall be one who engages in such transactions. This definition of "payday lending" expressly incorporates the exceptions and examples contained in subsections (a) and (b) of Code Section 16–17–2.

(b) Despite the fact that the Attorney General of the State of Georgia has opined in Official Opinion 2002–3 entered on June 27, 2002, that payday lending is in violation of Georgia law and despite the fact that the Industrial Loan Commissioner has issued cease and desist orders against various payday lenders in the State of Georgia, the General Assembly has determined that payday lending continues in the State of Georgia and that there are not sufficient deterrents in the State of Georgia to cause this illegal activity to cease.

(c) The General Assembly has determined that various payday lenders have created certain schemes and methods in order to attempt to disguise these transactions or to cause these transactions to appear to be "loans" made by a national or state bank chartered in another state in which this type of lending is unregulated, even though the majority of the revenues in this lending method are paid to the payday lender. The General Assembly has further determined that payday lending, despite the illegality of such activity, continues to grow in the State of Georgia and is having an adverse effect upon military personnel, the elderly, the economically disadvantaged, and other citizens of the State of Georgia. The General Assembly has further determined that substantial criminal and civil penalties over and above those currently existing under state law are necessary in order to prohibit this activity in the State of Georgia and to cause the cessation of this activity once and for all. The General Assembly further declares that these types of loans are currently illegal and are in violation of Code Section 7–4–2. The General Assembly declares that the use of agency or partnership agreements between in-state entities and out-of-state banks, whereby the in-state agent holds a predominant economic interest in the revenues generated by payday loans made to Georgia residents, is a scheme or contrivance by which the agent seeks to circumvent Chapter 3 of Title 7, the "Georgia Industrial Loan Act," and the usury statutes of this state.

(d) Payday lending involves relatively small loans and does not encompass loans that involve interstate commerce. Certain payday lenders have attempted to use forum selection clauses contained in payday loan documents in order to avoid the courts of the State of Georgia, and the General Assembly has determined that such practices are unconscionable and should be prohibited.

(e) Without limiting in any manner the scope of this chapter, the General Assembly declares that it is the general intent of this chapter to reiterate that in the State of Georgia the practice of engaging in activities commonly referred to as payday lending, deferred presentment services, or advance cash services and other similar activities are currently illegal and to strengthen the penalties for those engaging in such activities.

(f) This chapter in no way impairs or restricts the authority granted to the commissioner of banking and finance, the Industrial Loan Commissioner, or any other regulatory authority with concurrent jurisdiction over the matters stated in this chapter.

Laws 2004, Act 440, § 3, eff. May 1, 2004; Laws 2005, Act 19, § 16, eff. April 7, 2005.

Historical and Statutory Notes

The 2005 amendment by Act 19 was a provision contained in a correction bill.

§ 16–17–2. Violations; exceptions; application; penalties

(a) It shall be unlawful for any person to engage in any business, in whatever form transacted, including, but not limited to, by mail, electronic means, the Internet, or telephonic means, which consists in whole or in part of making, offering, arranging, or acting as an agent in the making of loans of $3,000.00 or less unless:

(1) Such person is engaging in financial transactions permitted pursuant to:

(A) The laws regulating financial institutions as defined under Chapter 1 of Title 7, the "Financial Institutions Code of Georgia";

(B) The laws regulating state and federally chartered credit unions;

(C) Article 13 of Chapter 1 of Title 7, relating to Georgia residential mortgages;

(D) Chapter 3 of Title 7, the "Georgia Industrial Loan Act";

(E) Chapter 4 of Title 7, relating to interest and usury;

(F) Chapter 5 of Title 7, "The Credit Card and Credit Card Bank Act," including financial institutions and their assignees who are not operating in violation of said chapter; or

(G) Paragraph (2) of subsection (a) of Code Section 7–4–2 in which the simple interest rate is not greater than 16 percent per annum;

(2) Such loans are lawful under the terms of:

(A) Article 1 of Chapter 1 of Title 10, "The Retail Installment and Home Solicitation Sales Act";

(B) Article 2 of Chapter 1 of Title 10, the "Motor Vehicle Sales Finance Act"; or

(C) Part 5 of Article 3 of Chapter 12 of Title 44, relating to pawnbrokers;

(3) Subject to the provisions of paragraph (4) of subsection (b) of this Code section, such person is a bank or thrift chartered under the laws of the United States, a bank chartered under the laws of another state and insured by the Federal Deposit Insurance Corporation, or a credit card bank and is not operating in violation of the federal and state laws applicable to its charter; or

(4) Such loan is made as a tax refund anticipation loan. In order to be exempt under this paragraph the tax refund anticipation loan must be issued using a borrower's filed tax return and the loan cannot be for more than the amount of the borrower's anticipated tax refund. Tax returns that are prepared but not filed with the proper government agency will not qualify for a loan exemption under this paragraph.

(b) Subject to the exceptions in subsection (a) of this Code section, this Code section shall apply with respect to all transactions in which funds are advanced to be repaid at a later date, notwithstanding the fact that the transaction contains one or more other elements. Without limiting the generality of the foregoing, the advance of funds to be repaid at a later date shall be subject to this Code section, notwithstanding the fact that the transaction also involves:

(1) The cashing or deferred presentment of a check or other instrument;

(2) The selling or providing of an item, service, or commodity incidental to the advance of funds;

(3) Any other element introduced to disguise the true nature of the transaction as an extension of credit; or

(4) Any arrangement by which a de facto lender purports to act as the agent for an exempt entity. A purported agent shall be considered a de facto lender if the entire circumstances of the transaction show that the purported agent holds, acquires, or maintains a predominant economic interest in the revenues generated by the loan.

(c)(1) A payday lender shall not include in any loan contract made with a resident of this state any provision by which the laws of a state other than Georgia shall govern the terms and enforcement of the contract, nor shall the loan contract designate a court for the resolution of disputes concerning the contract other than a court of competent jurisdiction in and for the county in which the borrower resides or the loan office is located.

(2) An arbitration clause in a payday loan contract shall not be enforceable if the contract is unconscionable. In determining whether the contract is unconscionable, the court shall consider the circumstances of the transaction as a whole, including but not limited to:

(A) The relative bargaining power of the parties;

(B) Whether arbitration would be prohibitively expensive to the borrower in view of the amounts in controversy;

(C) Whether the contract restricts or excludes damages or remedies that would be available to the borrower in court, including the right to participate in a class action;

(D) Whether the arbitration would take place outside the county in which the loan office is located or any other place that would be unduly inconvenient or expensive in view of the amounts in controversy; and

(E) Any other circumstance that might render the contract oppressive.

(d) Any person who violates subsection (a) or (b) of this Code section shall be guilty of a misdemeanor of a high and aggravated nature and upon conviction thereof shall be punished by imprisonment for not more than one year or by a fine not to exceed $5,000.00 or both. Each loan transaction shall be deemed a separate violation of this Code section. Any person who aids or abets such a violation, including any arbiter or arbitration company, shall likewise be guilty of a misdemeanor of a high and aggravated nature and shall be punished as set forth in this subsection. If a person has been convicted of violations of subsection (a) or (b) of this Code section on three prior occasions, then all subsequent convictions shall be considered felonies punishable by a fine of $10,000.00 or five years' imprisonment or both.

Laws 2004, Act 440, § 3, eff. May 1, 2004; Laws 2005, Act 19, § 16, eff. April 7, 2005.

Historical and Statutory Notes

The 2005 amendment by Act 19 was a provision contained in a correction bill.

§ 16–17–3. Transaction void; violator liability to borrower

Any person who violates subsection (a) or (b) of Code Section 16–17–2 shall be barred from the collection of any indebtedness created by said loan transaction and said transaction shall be void ab initio, and any person violating the provisions of subsection (a) or (b) of Code Section 16–17–2 shall in addition be liable to the borrower in each unlawful transaction for three times the amount of any interest or other charges to the borrower. A civil action under Code Section 16–17–2 may be brought on behalf of an individual borrower or on behalf of an ascertainable class of borrowers. In a successful action to enforce the provisions of this chapter, a court shall award a borrower, or class of borrowers, costs including reasonable attorneys' fees.

Laws 2004, Act 440, § 3, eff. May 1, 2004.

§ 16–17–4. Violator liability to state

(a) Any person who violates subsection (a) or (b) of Code Section 16–17–2 shall be liable to the state for a civil penalty equal to three times the amount of any interest or charges to the borrowers in the unlawful transactions.

(b) A civil action under Code Section 16–17–2 may be brought by the Attorney General, any district attorney, or a private party. Where a successful civil action is brought by a district attorney, one-half of the damages recovered on behalf of the state shall be distributed to the office of the district attorney of the judicial circuit of such district attorney to be used by the district attorney in order to fund the budget of that office.

Laws 2004, Act 440, § 3, eff. May 1, 2004; Laws 2005, Act 19, § 16, eff. April 7, 2005.

Historical and Statutory Notes

The 2005 amendment by Act 19 was a provision contained in a correction bill.

§ 16–17–5. State tax on loans in violation

(a) There is imposed a state tax on all loans made in violation of this chapter. Such tax shall be administered and collected in connection with the Georgia income taxation of the person making such loans and shall be in addition to any other tax liability of such person.

(b) The tax imposed by this Code section shall be at the rate of 50 percent of all proceeds received by a person from loans made in violation of this chapter.

(c) A person making loans in violation of this chapter shall declare and return the proceeds subject to taxation under this Code section as a part of such person's Georgia income tax return.

(d) The state revenue commissioner shall retain returns under this Code section apart from all other returns and shall not disclose any part of such a return for any purpose other than the collection of tax owed or a criminal prosecution involving tax matters. In a criminal proceeding under this chapter, a person's return of proceeds under this Code section and any evidence derived as a result of such return shall not be admissible.

Laws 2004, Act 440, § 3, eff. May 1, 2004.

§ 16–17–6. Trial court authority; entity acting as agent

In regard to any loan transaction that is alleged to be in violation of subsection (a) of Code Section 16–17–2, the trial court shall be authorized to review the terms of the transaction in their entirety in order to determine if there has been any contrivance, device, or scheme used by the lender in order to avoid the provisions of subsection (a) of Code Section 16–17–2. The trial court shall not be bound in making such determination by the parol evidence rule or by any written contract but shall be authorized to determine exactly whether the loan transaction includes the use of a scheme, device, or contrivance and whether in reality the loan is in violation of the provisions of subsection (a) of Code Section 16–17–2 based upon the facts and evidence relating to that transaction and similar transactions being made in the State of Georgia. If any entity involved in soliciting or facilitating the making of payday loans purports to be acting as an agent of a bank or thrift, then the court shall be authorized to determine whether the entity claiming to act as agent is in fact the lender. Such entity shall be presumed to be the lender if, under the totality of the circumstances, it holds, acquires, or maintains a predominant economic interest in the revenues generated by the loan. Furthermore, the trial court shall further be authorized to investigate all transactions involving gift cards, telephone cards, the sale of goods or services, computer services, or the like which may be tied to such loan transactions and are an integral part thereof in order to determine whether any such transaction is in fact a contrivance, scheme, or device used by the payday lender in order to evade the provisions of subsection (a) of Code Section 16–17–2.

Laws 2004, Act 440, § 3, eff. May 1, 2004.

§ 16–17–7. Businesses engaged in payday lending; prohibition from obtaining and revocation of existing certificates of authority

All corporations, limited liability companies, and other business entities which are engaged in payday lending in the State of Georgia are prohibited from obtaining any certificate of authority from the Secretary of State or from the Department of Banking and Finance, and engaging in such payday lending activity in the State of Georgia shall result in the revocation of any existing certificate of authority.

Laws 2004, Act 440, § 3, eff. May 1, 2004; Laws 2005, Act 19, § 16, eff. April 7, 2005.

Historical and Statutory Notes

The 2005 amendment by Act 19 was a provision contained in a correction bill.

§ 16–17–8. Payday lending site declared public nuisance

The site or location of a place of business where payday lending takes place in the State of Georgia is declared a public nuisance.

Laws 2004, Act 440, § 3, eff. May 1, 2004.

§ 16–17–9. Military service member or spouse as customer; additional obligations, duties and disclosures

(a) In addition to the other obligations and duties required under this chapter, if the customer is a member of the military services of the United States or a spouse of a member of the military services of the United States, the following duties and obligations apply to any payday lender:

(1) The lender is prohibited from garnishment of any military wages or salaries;

(2) The lender is prohibited from conducting any collection activity against a military customer or his or her spouse when the military member has been deployed to a combat or combat support posting for the duration of the deployment;

(3) The lender is prohibited from contacting the commanding officer of a military customer in an effort to collect on a loan to the military member or his or her spouse;

(4) The lender agrees to be bound by the terms of any repayment agreement that it negotiates through military counselors or third-party credit counselors; and

(5) The lender agrees to honor any statement or proclamation by a military base commander that a specific payday lender branch location has been declared off limits to military personnel and their spouses.

(b) If the customer is a member of the military services of the United States or a spouse of a member of the military services of the United States, the following disclosures shall be made in writing by the payday lender:

(1) A notice that the lender is prohibited from garnishment of any military wages or salaries;

(2) A notice that the lender is prohibited from conducting any collection activity against a military customer or his or her spouse when the military member has been deployed to a combat or combat support posting for the duration of the deployment;

(3) A notice that the lender is prohibited from contacting the commanding officer of a military customer in an effort to collect on a loan to the military member or his or her spouse;

(4) A notice that the lender agrees to be bound by the terms of any repayment agreement that it negotiates through military counselors or third-party credit counselors; and

(5) A notice that the lender agrees to honor any statement or proclamation by a military base commander that a specific payday lending branch location has been declared off limits to military personnel and their spouses.

Laws 2004, Act 440, § 3, eff. May 1, 2004.

§ 16–17–10. Severability of provisions

If any provision of this chapter or the application of such provision is found by a court of competent jurisdiction in the United States to be invalid or is found to be superseded by federal law, then the remaining provisions of this chapter shall not be affected, and this chapter shall continue to apply to any other person or circumstance.

Laws 2004, Act 440, § 3, eff. May 1, 2004.

TITLE 17

CRIMINAL PROCEDURE

CHAPTER 1

GENERAL PROVISIONS

§ 17–1–1. Service and filing of pleadings and other papers

(a) Unless otherwise provided by law or by order of the court, every pleading subsequent to the entry of the initial indictment or accusation upon which the defendant is to be tried; every order not entered in open court; every written motion, unless it is one as to which a hearing ex parte is authorized; and every written notice, demand, and similar paper shall be served upon each party.

(b)(1) Where service is required to be made, the service shall be made upon the party's attorney unless service upon the party himself is ordered by the court. Service upon the attorney or upon a party shall be made by delivering a copy to him or by mailing it to him at his last known address or, if no address is known, by leaving it with the clerk of the court.

(2) As used in this subsection, delivering a copy means:

(A) Handing it to the attorney or to the party;

(B) Leaving it at his office with his clerk or other person in charge thereof; or

(C) If the office is closed or the person to be served has no office, leaving it at his dwelling house or usual place of abode with some person of suitable age and discretion then residing therein.

(3) Service by mail shall be deemed complete upon mailing.

(c) All original papers, copies of which are required to be served upon parties, shall be filed with the court either before service or immediately thereafter.

(d) The filing of pleadings and other papers with the court shall be made by filing them with the clerk of the court unless the judge permits the papers to be filed with him, in which event he shall note thereon the filing date and transmit them to the office of the clerk.

(e)(1) Proof of service may be made by certificate of an attorney or of his employee, written admission, affidavit, or other proof satisfactory to the court. Failure to make proof of service shall not affect the validity of service.

(2) When an attorney executes a certificate, which shall be attached to the original of the paper to be served, certifying as to the service thereof, the certificate shall be taken as prima-facie proof of such service.

(3) The certificate of service provided for in this subsection shall read substantially as follows:

—Certificate of Service—

I do certify that (copy) (copies) hereof have been furnished to (here insert name or names) by (delivery) (mail) this _____ day of _____, _____.

____

Attorney

Laws 1981, Ex. Sess., p. 8; Laws 1999, p. 81, § 17.

§ 17–1–2. Penal action defined; party plaintiff

A "penal action" is an action allowed in pursuance of public justice under particular laws. If no special officer is authorized to be the plaintiff therein, the state, the Governor, the Attorney General, or the prosecuting attorney may be the plaintiff.

Formerly Code 1863, § 3178; Code 1868, § 3189; Code 1873, § 3254; Code 1882, § 3254; Civil Code 1895, § 4933; Civil Code 1910, § 5510; Code 1933, § 3–103.

§ 17–1–3. Mistakes of clerks or ministerial officers

The mistake or misprision of a clerk or other ministerial officer shall in no case work to the injury of a party where by amendment justice may be promoted.

Laws 1799, Cobb's 1851 Digest, p. 480.

Formerly Code 1863, § 3436; Code 1868, § 3456; Code 1873, § 3507; Code 1882, § 3507; Civil Code 1895, § 5125; Civil Code 1910, § 5709; Code 1933, § 81–1205.

§ 17–1–4. Judgments, etc., obtained by perjury

Any judgment, verdict, rule, or order of court which may have been obtained or entered shall be set aside and be of no effect if it appears that the same was entered in consequence of corrupt and willful perjury. It shall be the duty of the court in which the verdict, judgment, rule, or order was obtained or entered to cause the same to be vacated upon motion and notice to the adverse party; but it shall not be lawful for the court to do so unless the person charged with perjury shall have been duly convicted thereof and unless it appears to the court that the verdict, judgment, rule, or order could not have been obtained and entered without the evidence of the perjured person, saving always to third persons innocent of such perjury the rights which they may lawfully have acquired under the verdict, judgment, rule, or order before the same shall have been actually vacated.

Laws 1833, Cobb's 1851 Digest, p. 804.

Formerly Code 1863, § 3510; Code 1868, § 3533; Code 1873, § 3591; Code 1882, § 3591; Civil Code 1895, § 5366; Civil Code 1910, § 5961; Code 1933, § 110–706.

CHAPTER 2

JURISDICTION AND VENUE

§ 17–2–1. Jurisdiction

(a) It is the policy of this state to exercise its jurisdiction over crime and persons charged with the commission of crime to the fullest extent allowable under, and consistent with, the Constitution of this state and the Constitution of the United States.

(b) Pursuant to this policy, a person shall be subject to prosecution in this state for a crime which he commits, while either within or outside the state, by his own conduct or that of another for which he is legally accountable, if:

(1) The crime is committed either wholly or partly within the state;

(2) The conduct outside the state constitutes an attempt to commit a crime within the state; or

(3) The conduct within the state constitutes an attempt to commit in another jurisdiction a crime under the laws of both this state and the other jurisdiction.

(c) A crime is committed partly within this state if either the conduct which is an element of the crime or the result which is such an element occurs within the state. In homicide, the "result" is either the act which causes death or the death itself; and, if the body of a homicide victim is found within this state, the death is presumed to have occurred within the state.

(d) A crime which is based on an omission to perform a duty imposed by the law of this state is committed within the state, regardless of the location of the accused at the time of the omission.

Laws 1968, p. 1249, § 1.

Formerly Code 1933, § 26–301.

§ 17–2–2. Venue

(a) *In general.* Criminal actions shall be tried in the county where the crime was committed, except as otherwise provided by law.

(b) *Crime committed on boundary line of two counties.* If a crime is committed on, or immediately adjacent to, the boundary line between two counties, the crime shall be considered as having been committed in either county.

(c) *Criminal homicide.* Criminal homicide shall be considered as having been committed in the county in which the cause of death was inflicted. If it cannot be determined in which county the cause of death was inflicted, it shall be considered that it was inflicted in the county in which the death occurred. If a dead body is discovered in this state and it cannot be readily determined in what county the cause of death was inflicted, it shall be considered that the cause of death was inflicted in the county in which the dead body was discovered.

(d) *Crime commenced outside the state.* If the commission of a crime under the laws of this state commenced outside the state is consummated within this state, the crime shall be considered as having been committed in the county where it is consummated.

(e) *Crime committed while in transit.* If a crime is committed upon any railroad car, vehicle, watercraft, or aircraft traveling within this state and it cannot readily be determined in which county the crime was committed, the crime shall be considered as having been committed in any county in which the crime could have been committed through which the railroad car, vehicle, watercraft, or aircraft has traveled.

(f) *Crime committed on water boundaries of two counties.* Whenever a stream or body of water is the boundary between two counties, the jurisdiction of each county shall extend to the center of the main channel of the stream or the center of the body of water; and, if a crime is committed on the stream or body of water and it cannot be readily determined in which county the crime was committed, the crime shall be considered as having been committed in either county.

(g) *Crime committed on water boundaries of two states.* Whenever a crime is committed on any river or body of water which forms a boundary between this state and another state, the accused shall be tried in the county of this state which is situated opposite the point where the crime is committed. If it cannot be readily determined on which side of the line a crime was committed between two counties which border the river or body of water, the crime shall be considered as having been committed in either county.

(h) *Crime in more than one county.* If in any case it cannot be determined in what county a crime was committed, it shall be considered to have been committed in any county in which the evidence shows beyond a reasonable doubt that it might have been committed.

(i) *Cumulative effect of Code section.* This Code section is cumulative and shall not supersede venue provisions found in other parts of this Code.

Laws 1833, Cobb's 1851 Digest, p. 840; Laws 1855–56, p. 265, § 1; Laws 1895, p. 70, § 1; Laws 1968, p. 1249, § 1.

Formerly Code 1863, §§ 39, 40, 4556, 4557, 4558; Code 1868, §§ 37, 38, 4576, 4577, 4578; Code 1873, §§ 35, 36, 4570, 4571, 4572, 4686; Code 1882, §§ 35, 36, 4570, 4571, 4572, 4686, 5172; Penal Code 1895, §§ 23, 24, 26, 27, 28, 29; Penal Code 1910, §§ 23, 24, 26, 27, 28, 29; Code 1933, §§ 27–1101, 27–1102, 27–1103, 27–1104, 27–1105, 27–1106; Code 1933, § 26–302.

§ 17–2–3. Boundary lines of the state; determination of question of jurisdiction

This state claims jurisdiction of an offense committed on any of her boundary lines with other states for the county bordering on that part of the line where the offense was committed and, if doubtful as to which of two counties as set forth in subsection (g) of Code Section 17–2–2, for either county, and will proceed to arrest, indict, try, and punish unless the other state makes a demand for the accused person as a fugitive from justice, in which event the progress of the case shall be suspended by order of the Governor until the question of jurisdiction is settled.

Formerly Code 1863, § 41; Code 1868, § 39; Code 1873, § 37; Code 1882, § 37; Penal Code 1895, § 25; Penal Code 1910, § 25; Code 1933, § 27–1107.

§ 17–2–4. Transfer to county where defendant has been arrested, held, or is present to plead guilty, guilty but mentally ill, guilty but mentally retarded, or nolo contendere

(a) A defendant arrested, held, or present in a county other than that in which an indictment or accusation is pending against that defendant may state in writing a wish to plead guilty, guilty but mentally ill, guilty but mentally retarded, or nolo contendere; to waive trial in the county in which the indictment or accusation is pending; and to consent to disposition of the case in the county in which the defendant was arrested, held, or present, subject to the approval of the prosecuting attorney for each county. Upon receipt of the defendant's statement and the written approval of the prosecuting attorney for each county, the clerk of the court in which the indictment or accusation is pending shall transmit the papers in the proceeding or certified copies thereof to the clerk of the court for the county in which the defendant was arrested, held, or present, and the prosecution shall continue in that county.

(b) A defendant arrested, held, or present in a county other than the county in which a complaint or arrest warrant is pending against that defendant may state in writing a wish to plead guilty, guilty but mentally ill, guilty but mentally retarded, or nolo contendere; to waive venue and trial in the county in which the complaint or warrant was issued; and to consent to disposition of the case in the county in which the defendant was arrested, held, or present, subject to the approval of the prosecuting attorney for each county. Upon receipt of the defendant's statement and the written approval of the prosecuting attorney for each county, the clerk of the court in which the complaint or arrest warrant is pending shall transmit the papers in the proceeding or certified copies thereof to the clerk of the court for the county in which the defendant was arrested, held, or present, and the prosecution shall continue in that county.

(c) If after the proceeding has been transferred pursuant to subsection (a) or (b) of this Code section the defendant pleads not guilty or not guilty by reason of insanity, the clerk shall return the papers to the court in which the prosecution was commenced and the proceeding shall be restored to the docket of that court. A defendant's statement that the defendant wishes to plead guilty, guilty but mentally ill, guilty but mentally retarded, or nolo contendere shall not be used against the defendant.

Laws 1995, p. 1250, § 1.

CHAPTER 3

LIMITATIONS ON PROSECUTION

Section

§ 17-3-1. Limitation of prosecutions

(a) A prosecution for murder may be commenced at any time.

(b) Prosecution for other crimes punishable by death or life imprisonment must be commenced within seven years after the commission of the crime except as provided by subsection (c.1) of this Code section; provided, however, that prosecution for the crime of forcible rape must be commenced within 15 years after the commission of the crime.

(c) Prosecution for felonies other than those specified in subsections (a), (b), and (c.1) of this Code section must be commenced within four years after the commission of the crime, provided that prosecution for felonies committed against victims who are at the time of the commission of the offense under the age of 18 years must be commenced within seven years after the commission of the crime.

(c.1) A prosecution for the following offenses may be commenced at any time when deoxyribonucleic acid (DNA) evidence is used to establish the identity of the accused:

(1) Armed robbery, as defined in Code Section 16-8-41;

(2) Kidnapping, as defined in Code Section 16-5-40;

(3) Rape, as defined in Code Section 16-6-1;

(4) Aggravated child molestation, as defined in Code Section 16-6-4;

(5) Aggravated sodomy, as defined in Code Section 16-6-2; or

(6) Aggravated sexual battery, as defined in Code Section 16-6-22.2;

provided, however, that a sufficient portion of the physical evidence tested for DNA is preserved and available for testing by the accused and provided, further, that, if the DNA evidence does not establish the identity of the accused, the limitation on prosecution shall be as provided in subsections (b) and (c) of this Code section.

(d) Prosecution for misdemeanors must be commenced within two years after the commission of the crime.

Laws 1968, p. 1249, § 1; Laws 1987, p. 330, § 1; Laws 1996, p. 1115, § 4; Laws 2002, p. 650, § 1.

Formerly Code 1933, § 26-502.

§ 17-3-2. Periods excluded from limitation

The period within which a prosecution must be commenced under Code Section 17-3-1 or other applicable statute does not include any period in which:

(1) The accused is not usually and publicly a resident within this state;

(2) The person committing the crime is unknown or the crime is unknown;

(3) The accused is a government officer or employee and the crime charged is theft by conversion of public property while such an officer or employee; or

(4) The accused is a guardian or trustee and the crime charged is theft by conversion of property of the ward or beneficiary.

Laws 1968, p. 1249, § 1; Laws 1969, p. 857, § 17.

Formerly Code 1933, § 26-503.

§ 17-3-2.1. Periods excluded from limitation of prosecution for certain offenses

(a) If the victim of a violation of:

(1) Code Section 16-5-70, relating to cruelty to children;

(2) Code Section 16-6-1, relating to rape;

(3) Code Section 16-6-2, relating to sodomy and aggravated sodomy;

(4) Code Section 16-6-3, relating to statutory rape;

(5) Code Section 16-6-4, relating to child molestation and aggravated child molestation;

(6) Code Section 16-6-5, relating to enticing a child for indecent purposes; or

(7) Code Section 16-6-22, relating to incest,

is under 16 years of age on the date of the violation, the applicable period within which a prosecution must be commenced under Code Section 17-3-1 or other applicable statute shall not begin to run until the victim has reached the age of 16 or the violation is reported to a law enforcement agency, prosecuting attorney, or other governmental agency, whichever occurs earlier. Such law enforcement agency or other governmental agency shall promptly report such allegation to the appropriate prosecuting attorney.

(b) This Code section shall apply to any offense designated in paragraphs (1) through (7) of subsection (a) of this Code section occurring on or after July 1, 1992.

Laws 1992, p. 2973, § 1.

§ 17-3-2.2. Periods excluded from limitation of prosecution where victim is 65 years of age or older

In addition to any periods excluded pursuant to Code Section 17-3-2, if the victim is a person who is 65 years of age or older, the applicable period within which a prosecution must be commenced under Code Section 17-3-1 or other applicable statute shall not begin to run until the violation is reported to or discovered by a law enforcement agency, prosecuting attorney, or other governmental agency, whichever occurs earlier. Such law enforcement agency or other governmental agency shall promptly report such allegation to the appropriate prosecuting attorney. Except for prosecutions for crimes for which the law provides a statute of limitations longer than 15 years, prosecution shall not commence more than 15 years after the commission of the crime.

Laws 2000, p. 1085, § 5.

§ 17-3-3. Extended limitations

If an indictment is found within the time provided for in Code Section 17-3-1 or 17-3-2, or other applicable statute, and is quashed or a nolle prosequi entered, the limitation shall be extended six months from the time the first indictment is quashed or the nolle prosequi entered.

Laws 1968, p. 1249, § 1.

Formerly Code 1933, § 26-504.

CHAPTER 4

ARREST OF PERSONS

Article 1

General Provisions

§ 17-4-1. What constitutes an arrest

An actual touching of a person with a hand is not essential to constitute a valid arrest. If the person voluntarily submits to being considered under arrest or yields on condition of being allowed his freedom of locomotion, under the discretion of the officer, the arrest is complete.

Formerly Code 1863, § 4609; Code 1968, § 4631; Code 1873, § 4728; Code 1882, § 4728; Penal Code 1895, § 893; Penal Code 1910, § 914; Code 1933, § 27-201.

§ 17-4-2. Privilege of members of militia and military forces

The members of the organized militia or military forces shall in all cases, except treason, felony, or breach of the peace, be privileged from arrest during their attendance at drills, parades, meetings, encampments, and the election of officers and going to, during, and returning from the performance of any active duty as such members.

Laws 1884-85, p. 74, § 11.

Formerly Penal Code 1895, § 892; Penal Code 1910, § 913; Code 1933, § 27-204.

§ 17–4–3. Breaking open doors

In order to arrest under a warrant charging a crime, the officer may break open the door of any house where the offender is concealed.

Formerly Code 1863, § 4610; Code 1868, § 4632; Code 1873, § 4729; Code 1882, § 4729; Penal Code 1895, § 894; Penal Code 1910, § 915; Code 1933, § 27–205.

Article 2

Arrest by Law Enforcement Officers Generally

§ 17–4–20. Arrest without warrant; use of deadly force; training recommendations; authority of nuclear power facility security officers

(a) An arrest for a crime may be made by a law enforcement officer either under a warrant or without a warrant if the offense is committed in such officer's presence or within such officer's immediate knowledge; if the offender is endeavoring to escape; if the officer has probable cause to believe that an act of family violence, as defined in Code Section 19–13–1, has been committed; if the officer has probable cause to believe that an offense involving physical abuse has been committed against a vulnerable adult, who shall be for the purposes of this subsection a person 18 years old or older who is unable to protect himself or herself from physical or mental abuse because of a physical or mental impairment; or for other cause if there is likely to be failure of justice for want of a judicial officer to issue a warrant.

(b) Sheriffs and peace officers who are appointed or employed in conformity with Chapter 8 of Title 35 may use deadly force to apprehend a suspected felon only when the officer reasonably believes that the suspect possesses a deadly weapon or any object, device, or instrument which, when used offensively against a person, is likely to or actually does result in serious bodily injury; when the officer reasonably believes that the suspect poses an immediate threat of physical violence to the officer or others; or when there is probable cause to believe that the suspect has committed a crime involving the infliction or threatened infliction of serious physical harm. Nothing in this Code section shall be construed so as to restrict such sheriffs or peace officers from the use of such reasonable nondeadly force as may be necessary to apprehend and arrest a suspected felon or misdemeanant.

(c) Nothing in this Code section shall be construed so as to restrict the use of deadly force by employees of state and county correctional institutions, jails, and other places of lawful confinement or by peace officers of any agency in the State of Georgia when reasonably necessary to prevent escapes or apprehend escapees from such institutions.

(d) No law enforcement agency of this state or of any political subdivision of this state shall adopt or promulgate any rule, regulation, or policy which prohibits a peace officer from using that degree of force to apprehend a suspected felon which is allowed by the statutory and case law of this state.

(e) Each peace officer shall be provided with a copy of this Code section. Training regarding elder abuse, abuse of vulnerable adults, and the requirements of this Code section should be offered as part of at least one in-service training program each year conducted by or on behalf of each law enforcement department and agency in this state.

(f) A nuclear power facility security officer, including a contract security officer, employed by a federally licensed nuclear power facility or licensee thereof for the purpose of securing that facility shall have the authority to:

(1) Threaten or use force against another in defense of a federally licensed nuclear power facility and the persons therein as provided for under Code Sections 16–3–21 and 16–3–23;

(2) Search any person on the premises of the nuclear power facility or the properties adjacent to the facility if the facility is under imminent threat or danger pursuant to a written agreement entered into with the local enforcement agency having jurisdiction over the facility for the purpose of determining if such person possesses unauthorized weapons, explosives, or other similarly prohibited material; provided, however, that if such person objects to any search, he or she shall be detained as provided in paragraph (3) of this subsection or shall be required to immediately vacate the premises. Any person refusing to submit to a search and refusing to vacate the premises of a facility upon the request of a security officer as provided for in this Code section shall be guilty of a misdemeanor; and

(3) In accordance with a nuclear security plan approved by the United States Nuclear Regulatory Commission or other federal agency authorized to regulate nuclear facility security, detain any person located on the premises of a nuclear power facility or on the properties adjacent thereto if the facility is under imminent threat or danger pursuant to a written agreement entered into with the local law enforcement agency having jurisdiction over the facility, where there is reasonable suspicion to believe that such person poses a threat to the security of the nuclear power facility, regardless of whether such prohibited act occurred in the officer's presence. In the event of such detention, the law enforcement agency having jurisdiction over the facility shall be immediately contacted. The detention shall not exceed the amount of time reasonably necessary to allow for law enforcement officers to arrive at the facility.

Laws 1975, p. 1209, § 1; Laws 1981, p. 880, § 6; Laws 1981, p. 1393, § 1; Laws 1986, p. 490, § 1; Laws 1986, p. 657, § 1; Laws 1988, p. 1251, § 1; Laws 1991, p. 624, § 1; Laws 1997, p. 700, § 1; Laws 2006, Act 767, § 3, eff. May 3, 2006.

Formerly Code 1863, § 4603; Code 1868, § 4626; Code 1873, § 4723; Code 1882, § 4723; Penal Code 1895, § 896; Penal Code 1910, § 917; Code 1933, § 27–207.

Historical and Statutory Notes

The 2006 amendment by Act 767 added subsec. (f).

§ 17–4–20.1. Investigation of and arrests in incidents of family violence

(a) Whenever a law enforcement officer responds to an incident in which an act of family violence, as defined in Code Section 19–13–1, has been committed, the officer shall not base the decision of whether to arrest and charge a person on the specific consent of the victim or on a request by the victim solely or on consideration of the relationship of the parties. No officer investigating an incident of family violence shall threaten, suggest, or otherwise indicate the arrest of all parties for the purpose of discouraging requests for law enforcement intervention.

(b) Where complaints of family violence are received from two or more opposing parties, the officer shall evaluate each complaint separately to attempt to determine who was the primary aggressor. If the officer determines that one of the parties was the primary physical aggressor, the officer shall not be required to arrest any other person believed to have committed an act of family violence during the incident. In determining whether a person is a primary physical aggressor, an officer shall consider:

(1) Prior family violence involving either party;

(2) The relative severity of the injuries inflicted on each person;

(3) The potential for future injury; and

(4) Whether one of the parties acted in self-defense.

(c) Whenever a law enforcement officer investigates an incident of family violence, whether or not an arrest is made, the officer shall prepare and submit to the supervisor or other designated person a written report of the incident entitled "Family Violence Report." Forms for such reports shall be designed and provided by the Georgia Bureau of Investigation. The report shall include the following:

(1) Name of the parties;

(2) Relationship of the parties;

(3) Sex of the parties;

(4) Date of birth of the parties;

(5) Time, place, and date of the incident;

(6) Whether children were involved or whether the act of family violence was committed in the presence of children;

(7) Type and extent of the alleged abuse;

(8) Existence of substance abuse;

(9) Number and types of weapons involved;

(10) Existence of any prior court orders;

(11) Type of police action taken in disposition of case, the reasons for the officer's determination that one party was the primary physical aggressor, and mitigating circumstances for why an arrest was not made;

(12) Whether the victim was apprised of available remedies and services; and

(13) Any other information that may be pertinent.

(d) The report provided for in subsection (c) of this Code section shall be considered as being made for statistical purposes only and where no arrests are made shall not be subject to the provisions of Article 4 of Chapter 18 of Title 50. However, upon request, a defendant who has been arrested for an act of family violence or the victim shall be entitled to review and copy any report prepared in accordance with this Code section relating to the defendant.

(e) Each police department, including local precincts and county sheriff departments, shall report, according to rules and regulations of the Georgia Crime Information Center, all family violence incidents, both arrests and nonarrests, to the Georgia Bureau of Investigation, which shall compile and analyze statistics of family violence crimes and cause them to be published annually in the Georgia Uniform Crime Reports. An offense shall be counted for each incident reported to the police. A zero shall be reported if no incidents have occurred during the reporting period.

Laws 1991, p. 1778, § 1; Laws 1992, p. 2939, § 1; Laws 1995, p. 1186, § 1.

§ 17–4–21. Taking arrested person before judicial officer; selection of judge to try cause

The arresting officer shall take the arrested person before the most convenient and accessible judicial officer authorized to hear the case unless the arrested person requests otherwise, in which case, if there is no suspicion of improper motive, the arresting officer shall take him before some other judicial officer. An arrested person has no right to select the judicial officer before whom he shall be tried.

Formerly Code 1863, § 4599; Code 1868, § 4621; Code 1873, § 4718; Code 1882, § 4718; Penal Code 1895, § 897; Penal Code 1910, § 918; Code 1933, § 27–208.

§ 17–4–22. Authority of peace officers to make arrests not denied because of race, creed, or national origin

No peace officer of this state or of any political subdivision thereof shall be denied the authority to arrest any person because of the race, creed, or national origin of the peace officer nor because of the race, creed, or national origin of the person who is being arrested.

Laws 1969, p. 732, § 1.

§ 17–4–23. Arrests for motor vehicle violations may be made by citation; warrants for failure to appear

(a) A law enforcement officer may arrest a person accused of violating any law or ordinance governing the operation, licensing, registration, maintenance, or inspection of motor vehicles by the issuance of a citation, provided the offense is committed in his presence or information constituting a basis for arrest concerning the operation of a motor vehicle was received by the arresting officer from a law enforcement officer observing the offense being committed, except that, where the offense results in an accident, an investigating officer may issue citations regardless of whether the offense occurred in the presence of a law enforcement officer. The arresting officer shall issue to such person a citation which shall enumerate the specific charges against the person and the date upon which the person is to appear and answer the charges. Whenever an arresting officer makes an arrest concerning the operation of a motor vehicle based on information received from another law enforcement officer who observed the offense being committed, the citation shall list the name of each officer and each must be present when the charges against the accused person are heard.

(b) If the accused person fails to appear as specified in the citation, the judicial officer having jurisdiction of the offense may issue a warrant ordering the apprehension of the person and commanding that he be brought before the court to answer the charge contained within the citation and the charge of his failure to appear as required. The person shall then be allowed to make a reasonable bond to appear on a given date before the court.

Laws 1969, p. 759, § 1; Laws 1975, p. 874, §§ 1–4.

§ 17–4–24. Execution of penal warrants; summoning of posse

Every law enforcement officer is bound to execute the penal warrants given to him to execute. He may summon to his assistance, either in writing or orally, any of the citizens of the neighborhood or county to assist in the execution of such warrants. The acts of the citizens formed as a posse by such officer shall be subject to the same protection and consequences as official acts.

Laws 1997, p. 143, § 17.

Formerly Code 1863, § 4602; Code 1868, § 4625; Code 1873, § 4722; Code 1882, § 4722; Penal Code 1895, § 895; Penal Code 1910, § 916; Code 1933, § 27–206.

§ 17–4–25. Officer may make arrest in any county. Duty to carry prisoner to county in which offense committed

(a) Under a warrant issued by a judicial officer, an arresting officer may, in any county without regard to the residence of the arresting officer, arrest any person charged with a crime. It is the duty of the arresting officer to take the accused, with the warrant under which he was arrested, to the county in which the offense is alleged to have been committed, for examination before any judicial officer of that county.

(b) The county where the offense is alleged to have been committed shall pay the expenses of the arresting officer in taking the arrested person to the county. The arresting officer may hold or imprison the arrested person in a county other than the county in which the offense is alleged to have been committed long enough to enable him to prepare to take the arrested person to the county in which the offense is alleged to have been committed.

(c) Should the county in which the offense is alleged to have been committed be a member of a regional jail authority created under Article 5 of Chapter 4 of Title 42, known as the "Regional Jail Authorities Act," the arresting officer shall transport the prisoner to the regional jail. The judicial officer of the county in which the offense is alleged to have been committed may conduct the examination of the accused required by subsection (a) of this Code section in the county in which the offense is alleged to have been committed or in facilities available at the regional jail or by audio-visual communication between the two locations and between the accused, the court, the attorneys, and the witnesses.

Laws 1865–66, p. 38, §§ 1, 2; Laws 1895, p. 34, § 1; Laws 1996, p. 742, § 1.

Formerly Code 1863, § 4607; Code 1868, § 4624; Code 1873, § 4721; Code 1882, § 4721; Penal Code 1895, § 898; Penal Code 1910, § 919; Code 1933, § 27–209.

§ 17–4–25.1. Transportation of arrested persons for certain purposes

(a) As provided in subsection (e) of this Code section, a sworn law enforcement officer from a county or municipality in which an offense is alleged to have been committed shall be authorized to transport an arrested person, with the warrant under which such person was arrested, from one jurisdiction to the county or municipality in which the offense is alleged to have been committed for examination before any judicial officer of that county or municipality.

(b) Unless otherwise provided by contract, the agency transporting the arrested person pursuant to subsection (a) of this Code section shall be responsible for all costs associated with the transport. Such officer may hold or imprison the arrested person in a jurisdiction other than where the offense is alleged to have been committed long enough to enable such officer to prepare to take the arrested person to the jurisdiction in which the offense is alleged to have been committed.

(c) A sworn law enforcement officer from a county or municipality shall be authorized to transport a prisoner who is lawfully in the custody of such officer to a medical facility, youth development center, or court appearance outside such county or municipality or to transport such prisoner to a location outside such county or municipality for any lawfully required or necessary purpose.

(d) This Code section shall not be construed to provide any general state-wide police powers or authority for county or municipal law enforcement officers or expand the arrest powers of such officers outside their properly authorized jurisdiction.

(e) Sheriffs and, with the approval of its governing authority, municipal or other law enforcement agency heads are authorized to enter into a contract for the purposes of transporting arrested individuals from the jurisdiction of the arrest to an appropriate detention facility where the alleged crime is to have occurred. In the absence of a written contract between the sheriff and municipal or other law enforcement agency head, the sheriff or his or her designee has the right of first refusal, as evidenced in writing, of transporting persons arrested on a warrant to an appropriate detention facility where the crime is alleged to have occurred. Any responsibility arising as a result of the transportation of an arrested individual as authorized in this Code section shall be that of the agency whose employee is transporting the arrested individual.

Laws 1993, p. 710, § 1.

§ 17–4–26. Arresting officer must bring person before judicial officer within 72 hours of arrest; notice of commitment hearing

Every law enforcement officer arresting under a warrant shall exercise reasonable diligence in bringing the person arrested before the judicial officer authorized to examine, commit, or receive bail and in any event to present the person arrested before a committing judicial officer within 72 hours after arrest. The accused shall be notified as to when and where the commitment hearing is to be held. An arrested person who is not notified before the hearing of the time and place of the commitment hearing shall be released.

Laws 1956, p. 796, § 1; Laws 1995, p. 932, § 1.

Formerly Code 1863, § 4606; Code 1868, § 4629; Code 1873, § 4726; Code 1882, § 4726; Penal Code 1895, § 899; Penal Code 1910, § 920; Code 1933, § 27–210.

§ 17–4–27. Names, addresses and ages of persons arrested to be recorded by sheriffs, police chiefs, and heads of other law enforcement agencies

It shall be the duty of all sheriffs, chiefs of police, and the heads of any other law enforcement agencies of this state to obtain, or cause to be obtained, the name, address, and age of each person arrested by law enforcement officers under the supervision of such sheriffs, chiefs of police, or heads of any other law enforcement agencies of this state, when any such person is charged with an offense against the laws of this state, any other state, or the United States. The information shall be placed on appropriate records which each law enforcement agency shall maintain. The records shall be open for public inspection unless otherwise provided by law.

Laws 1967, p. 839, § 1.

§ 17–4–28. Arresting officer advising dismissal of warrant

Any arresting officer who advises or encourages the dismissal or settlement of any criminal warrant placed in his hands for execution, either before or after an arrest is made on the warrant, or who procures or encourages the dismissal or settlement of such warrants by threats, duress, intimidation, promises, or any other artifice or means shall be guilty of a misdemeanor.

Laws 1897, p. 98, § 1.

Formerly Penal Code 1910, § 923; Code 1933, § 27–9901.

§ 17–4–29. Arresting officer receiving costs before return of warrant

(a) Any arresting officer who collects or receives any costs or other charges of a prosecutor or defendant in a case made on a state's warrant, or of anyone acting in the interest of either of them, before the warrant is returned to the court to which it is made returnable, shall be guilty of a misdemeanor.

(b) Nothing in this Code section or in Code Section 17–4–28 shall be construed as prohibiting arresting officers from receiving from prosecutors sums of money sufficient to defray their expenses in going beyond the limits of the jurisdiction of such arresting officer to search for or to make the arrest of the accused person.

Laws 1897, p. 98, § 2.

Formerly Penal Code 1910, § 924; Code 1933, § 27–9902.

Article 3

Warrants for Arrest

§ 17–4–40. Who may issue warrants for arrest

(a) Any judge of a superior, city, state, or magistrate court or any municipal officer clothed by law with the powers of a magistrate may issue a warrant for the arrest of any offender against the penal laws, based on probable cause either on the judge's or officer's own knowledge or on the information of others given to the judge or officer under oath. Any retired judge or judge emeritus of a state court may likewise issue arrest warrants if authorized in writing to do so by an active judge of the state court of the county wherein the warrants are to be issued.

(b)(1) If application is made for a warrant by a person other than a peace officer or law enforcement officer and the application alleges the commission of an offense against the penal laws, the judge or other officer shall schedule a warrant application hearing as provided in this subsection unless the person accused has been taken into custody by a peace officer or law enforcement officer or except as provided in paragraph (6) of this subsection; provided, however, that a warrant may be denied without the notice required in paragraph (2) of this subsection where the application form and any testimony from the affiant provided at the time of the application do not demonstrate probable cause for issuing a warrant.

(2) Except as otherwise provided in paragraph (6) of this subsection, a warrant application hearing shall be conducted only after attempting to notify the person whose arrest is sought by any means approved by the judge or other officer which is reasonably calculated to apprise such person of the date, time, and location of the hearing.

(3) If the person whose arrest is sought does not appear for the warrant application hearing, the judge or other officer shall proceed to hear the application and shall note on the warrant application that such person is not present.

(4) At the warrant application hearing, the rules regarding admission of evidence at a commitment hearing shall apply. The person seeking the warrant shall have the customary rights of presentation of evidence and cross-examination of witnesses. The person whose arrest is sought may cross-examine the person or persons applying for the warrant and any other witnesses testifying in support of the application at the hearing. The person whose arrest is sought may present evidence that probable cause does not exist for his or her arrest. The judge or other officer shall have the right to limit the presentation of evidence and the cross-examination of witnesses to the issue of probable cause.

(5) At the warrant application hearing, a determination shall be made whether or not probable cause exists for the issuance of a warrant for the arrest of the person whose arrest is sought. If the judge or other officer finds that probable cause exists, the warrant may issue instanter.

(6) Nothing in this subsection shall be construed as prohibiting a judge or other officer from immediately issuing a warrant for the arrest of a person upon application of a person other than a peace officer or law enforcement officer if the judge or other officer determines from the application or other information available to the judge or other officer that:

(A) An immediate or continuing threat exists to the safety or well-being of the affiant or a third party;

(B) The person whose arrest is sought will attempt to evade arrest or otherwise obstruct justice if notice is given;

(C) The person whose arrest is sought is incarcerated or otherwise in the custody of a local, state, or federal law enforcement agency;

(D) The person whose arrest is sought is a fugitive from justice;

(E) The offense for which application for a warrant is made is deposit account fraud under Code Section 16–9–20, and the person whose arrest is sought has previously been served with the ten-day notice as provided in paragraph (2) of subsection (a) of Code Section 16–9–20; or

(F) The offense for which application for the warrant is made consists of an act of family violence as defined in Code Section 19–13–1.

In the event that the judge or officer finds such circumstances justifying dispensing with the requirement of a warrant application hearing, the judge or officer shall note such circumstances on the face of the warrant application.

(7) No warrant shall be quashed nor evidence suppressed because of any irregularity in proceedings conducted pursuant to this subsection not affecting the substantial rights of the accused under the Constitution of this state or of the United States.

(8) Nothing contained in this subsection shall prohibit a judge from denying a warrant based upon the application and testimony heard at the time such application is made without requiring notice to the person whose arrest is sought.

(c) Any warrant for the arrest of a peace officer, law enforcement officer, teacher, or school administrator for any offense alleged to have been committed while in the performance of his or her duties may be issued only by a judge of a superior court, a judge of a state court, or a judge of a probate court.

Laws 1974, p. 1230, § 1; Laws 1983, p. 884, § 3–17; Laws 1985, p. 1105, § 1; Laws 1990, p. 8, § 17; Laws 2000, p. 1702, § 1; Laws 2010, Act 423, § 1, eff. July 1, 2010.

Formerly Code 1863, § 4595; Code 1868, § 4616; Code 1873, § 4713; Code 1882, § 4713; Penal Code 1895, § 882; Penal Code 1910, § 903; Code 1933, § 27–102.

Historical and Statutory Notes

The 2010 amendment by Act 423, in subsec. (b), par. (1), added the final clause beginning "; provided, however", and added par. (8).

§ 17–4–41. What affidavit and warrant for arrest must state

(a) An affidavit made or warrant issued for the arrest of a person who is accused of violating the penal laws of this state shall include, as nearly as practicable, the following facts:

(1) The offense, including the time, date, place of occurrence, against whom the offense was committed, and a statement describing the offense; and

(2) The county in which the offense was committed.

(b) When the offense charged is theft, the affidavit made or warrant issued shall state, in addition to the requirements of subsection (a) of this Code section, the following facts:

(1) Name of the property alleged to have been stolen, with a description thereof, including its value; and

(2) Name of the owner of the property and the person from whose possession such property was taken.

(c) It is the intent of these requirements that the accused person shall be informed of the specific charge against him and of all basic pertinent particulars pertaining thereto.

Laws 1865–66, p. 235, § 1; Laws 1962, p. 668, § 1.

Formerly Code 1868, § 4617; Code 1873, § 4714; Code 1882, § 4714; Penal Code 1895, § 883; Penal Code 1910, § 904; Code 1933, § 27–103; Code 1933, § 27–103.1.

§ 17–4–42. Special warrant for arrest

No judicial officer except a judge of the superior court shall issue a special warrant for arrest returnable only before himself; nor shall any superior court judge issue such warrant outside of his own judicial circuit. If issued outside the judicial circuit, the warrant shall be treated as a general arrest warrant.

Formerly Code 1863, § 4598; Code 1868, § 4620; Code 1873, § 4717; Code 1882, § 4717; Penal Code 1895, § 886; Penal Code 1910, § 907; Code 1933, § 27–106.

§ 17–4–43. Officer may require bond to prosecute

The judicial officer issuing a warrant for arrest upon any sufficient grounds may first require the applicant to file a bond, with sufficient sureties, to prosecute the case in the event of a committal.

Formerly Code 1863, § 4600; Code 1868, § 4622; Code 1873, § 4719; Code 1882, § 4719; Penal Code 1895, § 887; Penal Code 1910, § 908; Code 1933, § 27–107.

§ 17–4–44. Warrant for arrest issued in any county and executed without backing

A warrant for arrest may be issued in any county, though the crime was committed in another county. A warrant, once issued, may be executed in any county without being backed or endorsed by a judicial officer in the county where the warrant is executed.

Laws 1865–66, p. 38, §§ 1, 3.

Formerly Code 1863, § 4601; Code 1868, § 4623; Code 1873, § 4720; Code 1882, § 4720; Penal Code 1895, § 888; Penal Code 1910, § 909; Code 1933, § 27–108.

§ 17–4–45. Form of affidavit for arrest

An affidavit for an arrest warrant substantially complying with the following form shall in all cases be sufficient:

Georgia, _____ County.

Personally came (name of affiant), who on oath says that, to the best of his knowledge and belief, (name of person against whom the warrant is sought) did, on the _____ day of _____, _____, in the county aforesaid, commit the offense of (insert here all information describing offense as required by Code Section 17–4–41) and this affiant makes this affidavit that a warrant may issue for his arrest.

____

(Signature of the affiant)

Sworn to and subscribed before me, this _____ day of _____, _____.

____

Judicial officer

Laws 1982, p. 3, § 17; Laws 1999, p. 81, § 17.

Formerly Code 1863, § 4596; Code 1868, § 4618; Code 1873, § 4715; Code 1882, § 4715; Penal Code 1895, § 884; Penal Code 1910, § 905; Code 1933, § 27–104.

§ 17–4–46. Form of warrant for arrest

An arrest warrant substantially complying with the following form shall in all cases be sufficient:

Georgia, _____ County.

To any sheriff, deputy sheriff, coroner, constable, or marshal of said state—Greetings:

(Name of the affiant) makes oath before me that on the _____ day of _____, in the year _____, in the county aforesaid, (name of person against whom the warrant is sought) did commit the offense of (insert here all information describing offense as required by Code Section 17–4–41). You are therefore commanded to arrest (name of person against whom the warrant is sought) and bring him before me, or some other judicial officer of this state, to be dealt with as the law directs. You will also levy on a sufficiency of the property of (name of person against whom the warrant is sought) to pay the costs in the event of his final conviction. Herein fail not.

____

Judicial officer

Laws 1962, p. 668, § 3; Laws 1999, p. 81, § 17.

Formerly Code 1863, § 4597; Code 1868, § 4619; Code 1873, § 4716; Code 1882, § 4716; Penal Code 1895, § 885; Penal Code 1910, § 906; Code 1933, § 27–105.

§ 17–4–47. Conduct of applications for issuance of arrest warrants by video conference

(a) A judge of any court in this state authorized to issue arrest warrants pursuant to Code Section 17–4–40 may, as an alternative to other laws relating to the issuance of arrest warrants, conduct such applications for the issuance of arrest warrants by video conference.

(b) Arrest warrant applications heard by video conference shall be conducted in a manner to ensure that the judge conducting the hearing has visual and audible contact with all affiants and witnesses giving testimony.

(c) The affiant participating in an arrest warrant application by video conference shall sign the affidavit for an arrest warrant and any related documents by any reasonable means which identifies the affiant, including, but not limited to, his or her typewritten name, signature affixed by electronic stylus, or any other reasonable means which identifies the person signing the affidavit and any related documents. The judge participating in an arrest warrant application by video conference shall sign the affidavit for an arrest warrant, the arrest warrant, and any related documents by any reasonable means which identifies the judge, including, but not limited to, his or her typewritten name, signature affixed by electronic stylus, or any other reasonable means which identifies the judicial officer signing the affidavit and warrant and any related documents. Such authorization shall be deemed to comply with the signature requirements provided for in Code Sections 17–4–45 and 17–4–46.

(d) A judge may also utilize a video conference to conduct hearings relating to the issuance of an initial bond connected with an offense for which an arrest warrant is issued, provided that the setting of such bond is within the jurisdiction of that court.

(e) A judge hearing matters pursuant to this Code section shall administer an oath to any person testifying by means of a video conference.

Laws 1998, p. 872, § 1; Laws 1999, p. 81, § 17; Laws 2008, Act 471, § 17, eff. May 12, 2008.

Historical and Statutory Notes

The 2008 amendment by Act 471 was a provision contained in a correction bill.

Article 4

Arrest by Private Persons

§ 17–4–60. Arrest by private person

A private person may arrest an offender if the offense is committed in his presence or within his immediate knowledge. If the offense is a felony and the offender is escaping or attempting to escape, a private person may arrest him upon reasonable and probable grounds of suspicion.

Formerly Code 1863, § 4604; Code 1868, § 4627; Code 1873, § 4724; Code 1882, § 4724; Penal Code 1895, § 900; Penal Code 1910, § 921; Code 1933, § 27–211.

§ 17–4–61. Procedures subsequent to arrest by private person

(a) A private person who makes an arrest pursuant to Code Section 17–4–60 shall, without any unnecessary delay, take the person arrested before a judicial officer, as provided in Code Section 17–4–62, or deliver the person and all effects removed from him to a peace officer of this state.

(b) A peace officer who takes custody of a person arrested by a private person shall immediately proceed in accordance with Code Section 17–4–62.

(c) A peace officer who in good faith and within the scope of his authority takes custody of a person arrested by a private person pursuant to this Code section shall not be liable at law for false arrest or false imprisonment arising out of the arrest.

Laws 1977, p. 902, § 1.

Formerly Code 1933, § 27–211.1.

§ 17–4–62. Duty of person arresting without warrant

In every case of an arrest without a warrant, the person arresting shall, without delay, convey the offender before the most convenient judicial officer authorized to receive an affidavit and issue a warrant as provided for in Code Section 17–4–40. No such imprisonment shall be legal beyond a reasonable time allowed for this purpose; and any person who is not brought before such judicial officer within 48 hours of arrest shall be released.

Laws 1956, p. 796, § 2.

Formerly Code 1863, § 4605; Code 1868, § 4628; Code 1873, § 4725; Code 1882, § 4725; Penal Code 1895, § 901; Penal Code 1910, § 922; Code 1933, § 27–212.

CHAPTER 5

SEARCHES AND SEIZURES

Article 1

Article 2

Article 3

Article 4

Article 1

Searches without Warrants

§ 17–5–1. Search without warrant

(a) When a lawful arrest is effected a peace officer may reasonably search the person arrested and the area within the person's immediate presence for the purpose of:

(1) Protecting the officer from attack;

(2) Preventing the person from escaping;

(3) Discovering or seizing the fruits of the crime for which the person has been arrested; or

(4) Discovering or seizing any instruments, articles, or things which are being used or which may have been used in the commission of the crime for which the person has been arrested.

(b) When the peace officer is in the process of effecting a lawful search, nothing in this Code section shall be construed to preclude him from discovering or seizing any stolen or embezzled property, any item, substance, object, thing, or matter, the possession of which is unlawful, or any item, substance, object, thing, or matter, other than the private papers of any person, which is tangible evidence of the commission of a crime against the laws of this state.

Laws 1966, p. 567, § 1.

§ 17–5–2. Inventory of things seized

An inventory of all instruments, articles, or things seized in a search without a search warrant shall be given to the person arrested and a copy thereof delivered to the judicial officer before whom the person arrested is taken. If the person arrested is released without a charge being preferred against him, all instruments, articles, or things seized, other than contraband or stolen property, shall be returned to him upon release.

Laws 1966, p. 567, § 2.

Article 2

Searches with Warrants

§ 17–5–20. Application for search warrant

(a) A search warrant may be issued only upon the application of an officer of this state or its political subdivisions charged with the duty of enforcing the criminal laws or a currently certified peace officer engaged in the course of official duty, whether said officer is employed by a law enforcement unit of:

(1) The state or a political subdivision of the state; or

(2) A university, college, or school.

(b) A search warrant shall not be issued upon the application of a private citizen or for his aid in the enforcement of personal, civil, or property rights.

Laws 1966, p. 567, § 14; Laws 1990, p. 1980, § 1.

§ 17–5–21. Grounds for search warrant

(a) Upon the written complaint of any certified peace officer of this state or its political subdivisions charged with the duty of enforcing the criminal laws and otherwise as authorized in Code Section 17–5–20 under oath or affirmation, which states facts sufficient to show probable cause that a crime is being committed or has been committed and which particularly describes the place or person, or both, to be searched and things to be seized, any judicial officer authorized to hold a court of inquiry to examine into an arrest of an offender against the penal laws, referred to in this Code section as "judicial officer," may issue a search warrant for the seizure of the following:

(1) Any instruments, articles, or things, including the private papers of any person, which are designed, intended for use, or which have been used in the commission of the offense in connection with which the warrant is issued;

(2) Any person who has been kidnapped in violation of the laws of this state, who has been kidnapped in another jurisdiction and is now concealed within this state, or any human fetus or human corpse;

(3) Stolen or embezzled property;

(4) Any item, substance, object, thing, or matter, the possession of which is unlawful; or

(5) Any item, substance, object, thing, or matter, other than the private papers of any person, which is tangible evidence of the commission of the crime for which probable cause is shown.

(b) When the peace officer is in the process of effecting a lawful search, nothing in this Code section shall be construed to preclude him from discovering or seizing any stolen or embezzled property, any item, substance, object, thing, or matter, the possession of which is unlawful, or any item, substance, object, thing, or matter, other than the private papers of any person, which is tangible evidence of the commission of a crime against the laws of this state.

(c) Any retired judge or judge emeritus of a state court may issue search warrants as authorized by this Code section if authorized in writing to do so by an active judge of the state court of the county wherein the warrants are to be issued.

(d) Notwithstanding any provisions of Code Section 17–5–20 or other provisions of this Code section to the contrary, with respect to the execution of a search warrant by a certified peace officer employed by a university, college, or school, which search warrant will be executed beyond the arrest jurisdiction of a campus policeman pursuant to Code Section 20–3–72, the execution of such search warrant shall be made jointly by the certified peace officer employed by a university, college, or school and a certified peace officer of a law enforcement unit of the political subdivision wherein the search will be conducted.

Laws 1966, p. 567, § 3; Laws 1985, p. 1105, § 2; Laws 1990, p. 1980, §§ 2, 3.

§ 17–5–21.1. Search warrant application by video conference

(a) A judge of any court in this state authorized to issue search warrants pursuant to Code Section 17–5–21 may, as an alternative to other laws relating to the issuance of search warrants, conduct such applications for the issuance of search warrants by video conference.

(b) Search warrant applications heard by video conference shall be conducted in a manner to ensure that the judge conducting the hearing has visual and audible contact with all affiants and witnesses giving testimony.

(c) The affiant participating in a search warrant application by video conference shall sign the affidavit for a search warrant and any related documents by any reasonable means which identifies the affiant, including, but not limited to, his or her typewritten name, signature affixed by electronic stylus, or any other reasonable means which identifies the person signing the affidavit and any related documents. The judge participating in a search warrant application by video conference shall sign the affidavit for a search warrant, the search warrant, and any related documents by any reasonable means which identifies the judge, including, but not limited to, his or her typewritten name, signature affixed by electronic stylus, or any other reasonable means which identifies the judicial officer signing the affidavit and warrant and any related documents. Such applications shall be deemed to be written within the meaning of Code Section 17–5–21. Such authorization shall be deemed to comply with the issuance requirements provided for in Code Section 17–5–22.

(d) A judge hearing matters pursuant to this Code section shall administer an oath to any person testifying by means of a video conference.

(e) A video recording of the application hearing and any documents submitted in conjunction with the application shall be maintained as part of the record.

Laws 2001, p. 300, § 1.

§ 17–5–22. Issuance of search warrant

All warrants shall state the time and date of issuance and are the warrants of the judicial officer issuing the same and not the warrants of the court in which he is then sitting. Such warrants need not bear the seal of the court or clerk thereof. The warrant, the complaint on which the warrant is issued, the affidavit or affidavits supporting the warrant, and the returns shall be filed with the clerk of the court of the judicial officer issuing the same, or with the court if there is no clerk, at the time the warrant has been executed or has been returned "not executed"; provided, however, the judicial officer shall keep a docket record of all warrants issued by him and upon issuing any warrant he shall immediately record the same, within a reasonable time, on the docket.

Laws 1966, p. 567, § 4; Laws 1992, p. 1328, § 1.

§ 17–5–23. Command of search warrant

The search warrant shall command the officer directed to execute the same to search the place or person particularly described in the warrant and to seize the instruments, articles, or things particularly described in the search warrant.

Laws 1966, p. 567, § 7.

§ 17–5–24. Persons authorized to execute search warrants

The search warrant shall be issued in duplicate and shall be directed for execution to all peace officers of this state. However, the judicial officer may direct the search warrant to be executed by any peace officer named specially therein.

Laws 1966, p. 567, § 5.

§ 17–5–25. Execution of search warrants

The search warrant shall be executed within ten days from the time of issuance. If the warrant is executed, the duplicate copy shall be left with any person from whom any instruments, articles, or things are seized; or, if no person is available, the copy shall be left in a conspicuous place on the premises from which the instruments, articles, or things were seized. Any search warrant not executed within ten days from the time of issuance shall be void and shall be returned to the court of the judicial officer issuing the same as "not executed."

Laws 1966, p. 567, § 6.

§ 17–5–26. When warrant may be executed

The search warrant may be executed at any reasonable time.

Laws 1966, p. 567, § 11.

§ 17–5–27. Use of force in execution of search warrant

All necessary and reasonable force may be used to effect an entry into any building or property or part thereof to execute a search warrant if, after verbal notice or an attempt in good faith to give verbal notice by the officer directed to execute the same of his authority and purpose:

(1) He is refused admittance;

(2) The person or persons within the building or property or part thereof refuse to acknowledge and answer the verbal notice or the presence of the person or persons therein is unknown to the officer; or

(3) The building or property or part thereof is not then occupied by any person.

Laws 1966, p. 567, § 8.

Formerly Code 1863, § 4636; Code 1868, § 4660; Code 1873, § 4758; Code 1882, § 4758; Penal Code 1895, § 1244; Penal Code 1910, § 1326; Code 1933, § 27–301.

§ 17–5–28. Detention and search of persons on premises

In the execution of the search warrant the officer executing the same may reasonably detain or search any person in the place at the time:

(1) To protect himself from attack; or

(2) To prevent the disposal or concealment of any instruments, articles, or things particularly described in the search warrant.

Laws 1966, p. 567, § 9.

§ 17–5–29. Return to court of things seized

A written return of all instruments, articles, or things seized shall be made without unnecessary delay before the judicial officer named in the warrant or before any court of competent jurisdiction. An inventory of any instruments, articles, or things seized shall be filed with the return and signed under oath by the officer executing the warrant. The judicial officer or court shall, upon request, deliver a copy of the inventory to the persons from whom or from whose premises the instruments, articles, or things were taken and to the applicant for the warrant.

Laws 1966, p. 567, § 10.

§ 17–5–30. Motion to suppress evidence illegally seized

(a) A defendant aggrieved by an unlawful search and seizure may move the court for the return of property, the possession of which is not otherwise unlawful, and to suppress as evidence anything so obtained on the grounds that:

(1) The search and seizure without a warrant was illegal; or

(2) The search and seizure with a warrant was illegal because the warrant is insufficient on its face, there was not probable cause for the issuance of the warrant, or the warrant was illegally executed.

(b) The motion shall be in writing and state facts showing that the search and seizure were unlawful. The judge shall receive evidence out of the presence of the jury on any issue of fact necessary to determine the motion; and the burden of proving that the search and seizure were lawful shall be on the state. If the motion is granted the property shall be restored, unless otherwise subject to lawful detention, and it shall not be admissible in evidence against the movant in any trial.

(c) The motion shall be made only before a court with jurisdiction to try the offense. If a criminal accusation is filed or if an indictment or special presentment is returned by a grand jury, the motion shall be made only before the court in which the accusation, indictment, or special presentment is filed and pending.

Laws 1966, p. 567, § 13.

§ 17–5–31. No warrant quashed for technicality

No search warrant shall be quashed or evidence suppressed because of a technical irregularity not affecting the substantial rights of the accused.

Laws 1966, p. 567, § 12; Laws 1990, p. 8, § 17.

§ 17–5–32. Searches and seizures of documentary evidence in possession of an attorney

(a) As used in this Code section, the term "documentary evidence" includes but is not limited to writings, documents, blueprints, drawings, photographs, computer printouts, microfilms, X-rays, files, diagrams, ledgers, books, tapes, audio and video recordings, and papers of any type or description.

(b) Notwithstanding any other provision of law, no search and seizure without a warrant shall be conducted and no search warrant shall be issued for any documentary evidence in the possession of an attorney who is not a criminal suspect, unless the application for the search warrant specifies that the place to be searched is in the possession or custody of an attorney and also shows that there is probable cause to believe that the documentary evidence will be destroyed or secreted in the event a search warrant is not issued. This Code section shall not impair the ability to serve search warrants in cases in which the search is directed against an attorney if there is probable cause to suspect such attorney has committed a crime. This Code section shall not impair the ability to serve subpoenas on nonsuspect attorneys.

(c) In any case in which there is probable cause to believe that documentary evidence will be destroyed or secreted if a search warrant is not issued, no search warrant shall be issued or be executed for any documentary evidence in the possession or custody of an attorney who is not a criminal suspect unless:

(1) At the time the warrant is issued the court shall appoint a special master to accompany the person who will serve the warrant. The special master shall be an attorney who is a member in good standing of the State Bar of Georgia and who has been selected from a list of qualified attorneys maintained by the State Bar of Georgia. Upon service of the warrant, the special master shall inform the party served of the specific items being sought and that the party shall have the opportunity to provide the items requested. If the party, in the judgment of the special master, fails to provide the items requested, the special master shall conduct a search for the items in the areas indicated in the search warrant;

(2) If the party who has been served states that an item or items should not be disclosed, such item or items shall be sealed by the special master and taken to the superior court for a hearing. At the hearing the party whose premises has been searched shall be entitled to raise any issues which may be raised pursuant to Code Section 17-5-30 as well as claims that the item or items are privileged or claims that the item or items are inadmissible because they were obtained in violation of this Code section. Any such hearing shall be held in the superior court;

(3) Any such warrant must, whenever practicable, be served during normal business hours. The law enforcement officer or prosecutor serving the warrant shall not participate in the search but may accompany the special master when the special master is conducting the search;

(4) Any such warrant must be served upon a party who appears to have possession or control of the items sought. If, after reasonable efforts, the party serving the warrant is unable to locate any such person, the special master shall seal and return to the court for determination by the court any items which appear to be privileged;

(5) Any such warrant shall be issued only by the superior court. At the time of applying for such a warrant, the law enforcement officer or prosecutor shall submit a written search plan designed to minimize the intrusiveness of the search. When the warrant is executed, the special master carrying out the search shall have a duty to make reasonable efforts to minimize the intrusiveness of the search.

(d) Notwithstanding any provision of law to the contrary, evidence obtained in violation of this Code section shall be excluded and suppressed from the prosecution's case in chief or in rebuttal, and such evidence shall not be admissible either as substantive evidence or for impeachment purposes.

Laws 1989, p. 1687, § 1.

Article 3

Disposition of Property Seized

§ 17-5-50. Return of articles

(a) The clerk or person having charge of the property section for any police department, sheriff's office, or other law enforcement agency in this state shall enter in a suitable book a description of every article of property alleged to be stolen, embezzled, or otherwise unlawfully obtained and brought into the office or taken from the person of a prisoner and shall attach a number to each article and make a corresponding entry thereof.

(b) (1) Any person claiming ownership of such allegedly stolen, embezzled, or otherwise unlawfully obtained property may make application to the law enforcement agency for the return of such property. Upon such an application being filed, the clerk or person in charge of the property section shall serve upon the person from whom custody of the property was taken a copy of such application. Such person from whom custody of the property was taken shall have a reasonable opportunity to claim ownership of such property and to request a hearing on forms provided by the person in charge of the property section.

(2) If the person from whom custody of the property was taken fails to assert a claim to such property, upon any applicant furnishing satisfactory proof of ownership of such property and presentation of proper personal identification, the person in charge of the property section may deliver such property to the applicant. The person to whom property is delivered shall sign, under penalty of false swearing, a declaration of ownership, which shall be retained by the person in charge of the property section. Such declaration, absent any other proof of ownership, shall be deemed satisfactory proof of ownership for the purposes of this Code section; provided, however, that, in the case of motor vehicles, trailers, tractors, or motorcycles which are required to be registered with the state revenue commissioner, any such stolen vehicle shall be returned to the person evidencing ownership of such vehicle through a certificate of title, tag receipt, bill of sale, or other such evidence. The stolen vehicle shall be returned to the person evidencing ownership within two days after such person makes application for the return of such vehicle unless a hearing on the ownership of such vehicle is required under this Code section or unless law enforcement needs the stolen vehicle for further criminal investigation purposes. Prior to such delivery, such person in charge of the property section shall make and retain a complete photographic record of such property. Such delivery shall be without prejudice to the state or to the person from whom custody of the property was taken or to any other person who may have a claim against the property.

(3) If the person from whom custody of the property was taken asserts a claim to such property and requests a hearing, the court which examines the charge against the person accused of stealing, embezzling, or otherwise unlawfully obtaining the property, or the court before whom the trial is had for stealing, embezzling, or otherwise unlawfully obtaining the property shall conduct the hearing to determine the ownership of such property.

(4) The provisions of this subsection shall not apply to any contraband or property subject to forfeiture under any provision of law.

(c) Photographs, video tapes, or other identification or analysis of the property involved, duly identified in writing by the law enforcement officer originally taking custody of the property as accurately representing such property, shall be admissible at trial in lieu of the original property.

(d) In the case of unknown or unapprehended defendants or defendants willfully absent from the jurisdiction, the court shall have discretion to appoint a guardian ad litem to represent the interest of the unknown or absent defendants.

(e) Statements made by the defendant or a person representing the defendant at a hearing provided for in subsection (b) of this Code section shall not be admissible for use against the defendant at trial.

Laws 1978, p. 2260, § 1; Laws 1979, p. 761, § 1; Laws 1982, p. 2336, § 1; Laws 1986, p. 158, § 1; Laws 2002, p. 415, § 17; Laws 2005, Act 68, § 7-1, eff. July 1, 2005.

Formerly Code 1863, § 4637; Code 1868, § 4661; Code 1873, § 4759; Code 1882, § 4759; Penal Code 1895, § 1245; Penal Code 1910, § 1327; Code 1933, § 27-302.

Historical and Statutory Notes

The 2005 amendment by Act 68 in the third sentence of subsec. (b)(2) substituted "state revenue commissioner" for "commissioner of motor vehicle safety".

§ 17-5-51. Weapons declared contraband; forfeiture; motor vehicles excepted

Any device which is used as a weapon in the commission of any crime against any person or any attempt to commit any crime against any person, any weapon the possession or carrying of which constitutes a crime or delinquent act, and any weapon for which a person has been convicted of violating Code Section 16–11–126 are declared to be contraband and are forfeited. For the purposes of this article, a motor vehicle shall not be deemed to be a weapon or device and shall not be contraband or forfeited under this article; provided, however, this exception shall not be construed to prohibit the seizure, condemnation, and sale of motor vehicles used in the illegal transportation of alcoholic beverages.

Laws 1967, p. 749, § 1; Laws 1977, p. 1131, § 1; Laws 1994, p. 963, § 1; Laws 2010, Act 643, § 2–10, eff. June 4, 2010.

Historical and Statutory Notes

The 2010 amendment by Act 643 substituted "violating Code Section 16–11–126" for "the crime of carrying a concealed weapon, as provided by Code Section 16–11–126,".

Laws 2010, Act 643, § 3–1, provides:

"This Act shall become effective upon its approval by the Governor or upon its becoming law without such approval and shall apply to all offenses committed on and after such date. The enactment of this Act shall not affect any prosecutions for acts occurring before the effective date of this Act and shall not act as an abatement of any such prosecutions."

§ 17–5–52. Sale or destruction of weapons; proceeds of sale; records

(a) When a final judgment is entered finding a defendant guilty of the commission or attempted commission of a crime against any person or guilty of the commission of a crime or delinquent act involving the illegal possession or carrying of a weapon, any device which was used as a weapon in the commission of the crime or delinquent act shall be turned over by the person having custody of the weapon or device to the sheriff, chief of police, or other executive officer of the law enforcement agency that originally confiscated the weapon or device when the weapon or device is no longer needed for evidentiary purposes. Within 90 days after receiving the weapon or device, the sheriff, chief of police, or other executive officer of the law enforcement agency shall retain the weapon or device for use in law enforcement, destroy the same, or sell the weapon or device pursuant to judicial sale as provided in Article 7 of Chapter 13 of Title 9 or by any commercially feasible means, provided that, if the weapon or device used as a weapon in the crime is not the property of the defendant, there shall be no forfeiture of such weapon or device.

(b) The proceeds derived from all sales of such weapons or devices, after deducting the costs of the advertising and the sale, shall be turned in to the treasury of the county or the municipal corporation that sold the weapon or device. The proceeds derived from the sale of such weapons or devices confiscated by a state law enforcement agency shall be paid into the state treasury.

(c) Any law enforcement agency that retains, destroys, or sells any weapon or device pursuant to this Code section shall maintain records that include an accurate description of each weapon or device along with records of whether each weapon or device was retained, sold, or destroyed.

Laws 1967, p. 749, § 3; Laws 1976, p. 167, § 1; Laws 1994, p. 963, § 2; Laws 2008, Act 497, § 1, eff. May 12, 2008.

Historical and Statutory Notes

Laws 2008, Act 497, § 1, rewrote this section, which formerly read:

"(a) When a final judgment is entered finding a defendant guilty of the commission or attempted commission of a crime against any person or guilty of the commission of a crime or delinquent act involving the illegal possession or carrying of a weapon, any device which was used as a weapon in the commission of the crime or delinquent act shall be turned over by the person having custody of the device to the sheriff of the county wherein the device was confiscated when the device is no longer needed for evidentiary purposes. Within 90 days after receiving the device, the sheriff shall retain the device for use in law enforcement, destroy the same, or advertise it for sale in such manner as other sheriff's sales are advertised and shall sell the device to the highest bidder at the next sheriff's sale conducted after the completion of the advertisements, provided that, if the device used as a weapon in the crime is not the property of the defendant, there shall be no forfeiture of such weapon.

"(b) The proceeds derived from all sales of such devices, after deducting the costs of the advertising and the sale, shall be turned in to the treasury of the county wherein the sale is made; provided, however, that if the device was used in the commission of a crime within a municipal corporation, the proceeds derived from the sale of the device, after deducting the costs of the advertising and the sale, shall be turned in to the treasury of the municipality wherein the crime was committed."

§ 17–5–53. Weapons valuable for historical or instructional purposes

(a) After a forfeiture of a device used in a crime, in the event the director of the Division of Archives and History or the commissioner of public safety, in that order or priority, shall desire to receive and retain a device described in Code Section 17–5–51 for historical or instructional purposes of his or her division or department and gives written notice thereof to the sheriff, either prior to the sheriff's advertisement of the device for sale or within ten days thereafter, the sheriff shall forthwith deliver the device to the requesting division or department which shall retain the device for such purposes. A device delivered to either the division or the department in accordance with this Code section shall become the property of the state.

(b) This Code section shall prevail over Code Section 17–5–52.

Laws 1976, p. 749, § 4; Laws 2002, p. 532, § 5.

§ 17–5–54. Disposition of personal property in custody of law enforcement agencies

(a)(1) Except as provided in Code Sections 17–5–55 and 17–5–56 and subsections (d), (e), and (f) of this Code section, when a law enforcement agency assumes custody of any personal property which is the subject of a crime or has been abandoned or is otherwise seized, a disposition of such property shall be made in accordance with the provisions of this Code section. When a final verdict and judgment is entered finding a defendant guilty of the commission of a crime, any personal property used as evidence in the trial shall be returned to the rightful owner of the property. All personal property in the custody of a law enforcement agency, including personal property used as evidence in a criminal trial, which is unclaimed after a period of 90 days following its seizure, or following the final verdict and judgment in the case of property used as evidence, and which is no longer needed in a criminal investigation or for evidentiary purposes in accordance with Code Section 17–5–55 or 17–5–56 shall be subject to disposition by the law enforcement agency. The sheriff, chief of police, or other executive officer of a law enforcement agency shall make application to the superior court for an order to retain, sell, or discard such property. In the application the officer shall state each item of personal property to be retained, sold, or discarded. Upon the superior court's granting an order for the law enforcement agency to retain such property, the law enforcement agency shall retain such property for official use. Upon the superior court's granting an order which authorizes that the property be discarded, the law enforcement agency shall dispose of the property as other salvage or nonserviceable equipment. Upon the superior court's granting an order for the sale of personal property, the officer shall provide for a notice to be placed once a week for four weeks in the legal organ of the county specifically describing each item and advising possible owners of items of the method of contacting the law enforcement agency; provided, however, that miscellaneous items having an estimated fair market value of $75.00 or less may be advertised or sold, or both, in lots. Such notice shall also stipulate a date, time, and place said items will be placed for public sale if not claimed. Such notice shall also stipulate whether said items or groups of items are to be sold in blocks, by lot numbers, by entire list of items, or separately.

(2) Items not claimed by the owners shall be sold at a sale which shall be conducted not less than seven nor more than 15 days after the final advertised notice has been run. The sale shall be to the highest bidder.

(3) If property has not been bid on in two successive sales, the law enforcement agency may retain the property for official use or the property will be considered as salvage and disposed of as other county or municipal salvage or nonserviceable equipment.

(4) With respect to unclaimed perishable personal property or animals or other wildlife, the officer may make application to the superior court for an order authorizing the disposition of such property prior to the expiration of 90 days.

(5) With respect to a seized motor vehicle which is not the subject of forfeiture proceedings, the law enforcement agency shall be required to contact the Georgia Crime Information Center to determine if such motor vehicle has been stolen and to follow generally the procedures of Code Section 40–11–2 to ascertain the registered owner of such vehicle.

(b) Records will be maintained showing the manner in which each item came into possession of the law enforcement agency, a description of the property, all efforts to locate the owner, any case or docket number, the date of publication of any newspaper notices, and the date on which the property was retained by the law enforcement agency, sold, or discarded.

(c) The proceeds from the sale of personal property by the sheriff or other county law enforcement agency pursuant to this Code section shall be paid into the general fund of the county treasury. The proceeds from the sale of personal property by a municipal law enforcement agency pursuant to this Code section shall be paid into the general fund of the municipal treasury.

(d) The provisions of this Code section shall not apply to personal property which is the subject of forfeiture proceedings as otherwise provided by law.

(e) The provisions of this Code section shall not apply to any property which is the subject of a disposition pursuant to Code Sections 17–5–50 through 17–5–53.

(f) The provisions of this Code section shall not apply to any abandoned motor vehicle for which the provisions of Chapter 11 of Title 40 are applicable.

Laws 1991, p. 944, § 1; Laws 1995, p. 909, § 1; Laws 2004, Act 539, § 1, eff. July 1, 2004.

Historical and Statutory Notes

The 2004 amendment by Act 539, in subsec. (a), substituted "Except as provided in Code Sections 17–5–55 and 17–5–56 and subsections (d), (e), and (f) of this Code section" for "Except as otherwise provided in subsections (d) and (e) of this Code section", inserted "verdict and" preceding "judgment" in the second sentence, and substituted "verdict and judgment" for "conviction" and inserted "in accordance with Code Section 17–5–55 or 17–5–56" in the third sentence.

§ 17–5–55. Custody of property; evidence in criminal cases

(a) In all criminal cases, the court shall designate either the clerk of court, the court reporter, or any other officer of the court to be the custodian of any property that is introduced into evidence during the pendency of the case. Property introduced into evidence shall be identified or tagged with an exhibit number. After verdict and judgment has been entered in any criminal case, the person who has custody of the physical evidence introduced in the case shall inventory the evidence and create an evidence log within 30 days of the entry of the judgment. Within 30 days following the creation of the evidence log, physical evidence shall be returned to the rightful owner of the property unless the physical evidence itself is necessary for the appeal of the case, for a new trial, or for purposes of complying with this Code section or Code Section 17–5–56. The evidence log shall contain the case number, style of the case, description of the item, exhibit number, the name of the person creating the evidence log, and the location where the physical evidence is stored. After the evidence log is completed, the judge shall designate the clerk of court, the prosecuting attorney, or the law enforcement agency involved in prosecuting the case to obtain and store the evidence, and a notation shall appear in the evidence log indicating the transfer of evidence. If evidence is transferred to any other party, the evidence log shall be annotated to show the identity of the person or entity receiving the evidence, the date of the transfer, and the location of the evidence. The signature of any person or entity to which physical evidence is transferred shall be captured through electronic means that will be linked to the evidence log or the use of a property transfer form that will be filed with the evidence log. When physical evidence, other than audio or video recordings, is transferred to any person or entity, a photograph or other visual image of the evidence shall be made and placed in the case file.

(b) Physical evidence classified as dangerous or contraband by state or federal law, including, but not limited to, items described by state or federal law as controlled substances, dangerous drugs, explosives, weapons, ammunition, biomedical waste, hazardous substances, or hazardous waste shall be properly secured in a manner authorized by state or federal law. This evidence may be transferred to a government agency authorized to store or dispose of the material.

(c) Documents, photographs, and similar evidence shall be maintained and disposed of in accordance with records retention schedules adopted in accordance with Article 5 of Chapter 18 of Title 50, known as the "Georgia Records Act." Other physical evidence that contains biological material, including, but not limited to, stains, fluids, or hair samples that relate to the identity of the perpetrator of the crime, shall be maintained in accordance with Code Section 17–5–56. A party to an extraordinary motion for new trial or a habeas corpus action in which DNA testing is sought that was filed prior to the expiration of the time prescribed for the preservation of evidence by this Code section may apply to the court in which the defendant was convicted for an order directing that the evidence be preserved beyond the time period prescribed by this Code section and until judgment in the action shall become final.

(d) Except as is otherwise provided in subsections (b) and (c) of this Code section or by law, following the expiration of the period of time set forth in subsections (b) and (c) of this Code section, physical evidence may be disposed of in accordance with the provisions of Article 5 of Chapter 12 of Title 44, known as the "Disposition of Unclaimed Property Act," or, in the case of property of historical or instructional value, as provided in Code Section 17–5–53.

Laws 2003, Act 37, § 3, eff. May 27, 2003; Laws 2004, Act 539, § 2, eff. July 1, 2004.

Historical and Statutory Notes

In 2003, the Code Commission, in subsec. (c), deleted the comma following "evidence by this Code section"; and in subsec. (d), substituted "Title 44" for "Title 50" and inserted a comma following "Unclaimed Property Act". See § 28–9–5.

The 2004 amendment by Act 539, in subsec. (a), inserted the fourth sentence relating to the return of physical evidence to the rightful owner of the property.

§ 17–5–56. Preservation of physical evidence collected at the scene of the crime

(a) Except as otherwise provided in Code Section 17–5–55, on or after May 27, 2003, governmental entities in possession of any physical evidence in a criminal case, including, but not limited to, a law enforcement agency or a prosecuting attorney, shall maintain any physical evidence collected at the time of the crime that contains biological material, including, but not limited to, stains, fluids, or hair samples that relate to the identity of the perpetrator of the crime as provided in this Code section. Biological samples collected directly from any person for use as reference materials for testing or collected for the purpose of drug or alcohol testing shall not be preserved.

(b) In a case in which the death penalty is imposed, the evidence shall be maintained until the sentence in the case has been carried out. In a case that involves the prosecution of a serious violent felony as defined by Code Section 17–10–6.1, a violation of Code Section 16–6–5.1, or sodomy, statutory rape, child molestation, bestiality, incest, or sexual battery as those terms are defined in Chapter 6 of Title 16, the evidence that contains biological material, including, but not limited to, stains, fluids, or hair samples that relate to the identity of the perpetrator of the crime shall be maintained for ten years after judgment in the criminal case becomes final or ten years after May 27, 2003, whichever is later. Evidence in all other felony and misdemeanor cases may be purged.

Laws 2003, Act 37, § 3, eff. May 27, 2003; Laws 2008, Act 539, § 2, eff. May 12, 2008.

Historical and Statutory Notes

In 2003, the Code Commission, in subsecs. (a) and (b), substituted "May 27, 2003" for "the effective date of this Code section". See § 28–9–5.

The 2008 amendment by Act 539 inserted ", a violation of Code Section 16–6–5.1, or sodomy, statutory rape, child molestation, bestiality, incest, or sexual battery as those terms are defined in Chapter 6 of Title 16", and inserted a comma following "including".

Article 4

Investigating Sexual Assault

§ 17–5–70. Definitions

As used in this article, the term:

(1) "Forensic medical examination" means an examination by a health care provider of a person who is a victim of a sexual assault. Such examination shall include a physical examination, documentation of biological and physical findings, and collection of physical evidence from the victim.

(2) "Investigating law enforcement agency" means the law enforcement agency responsible for the investigation of the alleged sexual assault.

(3) "Sexual assault" means rape, sodomy, aggravated sodomy, statutory rape, child molestation, aggravated child molestation, sexual assault against a person in custody, sexual assault against a person detained in a hospital or other institution, sexual assault by a practitioner of psychotherapy against a patient, incest, bestiality, sexual battery, and aggravated sexual battery as those terms and offenses are set forth and defined in Chapter 6 of Title 16.

Laws 2008, Act 539, § 3, eff. May 12, 2008.

§ 17–5–71. Preservation of physical evidence

(a) Except as otherwise provided in subsection (b) of this Code section or Code Section 17–5–55 or 17–5–56, on or after May 12, 2008, the investigating law enforcement agency shall maintain any physical evidence collected as a result of an alleged sexual assault that contains biological material, including, but not limited to, stains, fluids, or hair samples that relate to the identity of the perpetrator of an alleged sexual assault, for ten years after the report of the alleged sexual assault.

(b) If the victim does not cooperate with law enforcement in the investigation or prosecution of an alleged sexual assault, the investigating law enforcement agency shall maintain any physical evidence collected as a result of such alleged sexual assault that contains biological material, including, but not limited to, stains, fluids, or hair samples that relate to the identity of the perpetrator of the alleged sexual assault, for not less than 12 months from the date any such physical evidence is collected.

Laws 2008, Act 539, § 3, eff. May 12, 2008.

Historical and Statutory Notes

In 2008, the Code Commission, in subsec. (a), substituted "May 12, 2008" for "the effective date of this Act". See § 28–9–5.

§ 17–5–72. Forensic medical examinations

A victim shall have the right to have a forensic medical examination regardless of whether the victim participates in the criminal justice system or cooperates with law enforcement in pursuing prosecution of the underlying crime. A victim shall not be required to pay, directly or indirectly, for the cost of a forensic medical examination. The cost of a forensic medical examination shall be paid for by the investigating law enforcement agency.

Laws 2008, Act 539, § 3, eff. May 12, 2008.

§ 17–5–73. Polygraph examinations or other truth-telling devices; refusal to submit

No prosecuting attorney, investigating law enforcement agency, or government official shall ask or require any victim of a sexual assault to submit to a polygraph examination or any other truth-telling device as a condition precedent to investigating such alleged crime. The refusal of a victim to submit to a polygraph examination or any other truth-telling device shall not prevent an investigation or prosecution of any sexual assault.

Laws 2008, Act 539, § 3, eff. May 12, 2008.

CHAPTER 6

BONDS AND RECOGNIZANCES

Article 1

Article 1

General Provisions

§ 17–6–1. Before whom offenses are bailable; when person charged with misdemeanor may be bailed

(a) The following offenses are bailable only before a judge of the superior court:

(1) Treason;

(2) Murder;

(3) Rape;

(4) Aggravated sodomy;

(5) Armed robbery;

(6) Aircraft hijacking and hijacking a motor vehicle;

(7) Aggravated child molestation;

(8) Aggravated sexual battery;

(9) Manufacturing, distributing, delivering, dispensing, administering, or selling any controlled substance classified under Code Section 16–13–25 as Schedule I or under Code Section 16–13–26 as Schedule II;

(10) Violating Code Section 16–13–31 or Code Section 16–13–31.1;

(11) Kidnapping, arson, aggravated assault, or burglary if the person, at the time of the alleged kidnapping, arson, aggravated assault, or burglary, had previously been convicted of, was on probation or parole with respect to, or was on bail for kidnapping, arson, aggravated assault, burglary, or one or more of the offenses listed in paragraphs (1) through (10) of this subsection;

(12) Aggravated stalking; and

(13) Violations of the "Georgia Street Gang Terrorism and Prevention Act."

(b)(1) All offenses not included in subsection (a) of this Code section are bailable by a court of inquiry. Except as provided in subsection (g) of this Code section, at no time, either before a court of inquiry, when indicted or accused, after a motion for new trial is made, or while an appeal is pending, shall any person charged with a misdemeanor be refused bail.

(2) Except as otherwise provided in this chapter:

(A) A person charged with violating Code Section 40–6–391 whose alcohol concentration at the time of arrest, as determined by any method authorized by law, violates that provided in paragraph (5) of subsection (a) of Code Section 40–6–391 may be detained for a period of time up to six hours after booking and prior to being released on bail or on recognizance; and

(B) When an arrest is made by a law enforcement officer without a warrant upon an act of family violence pursuant to Code Section 17–4–20, the person charged with the offense shall not be eligible for bail prior to the arresting officer or some other law enforcement officer taking the arrested person before a judicial officer pursuant to Code Section 17–4–21.

(3)(A) Notwithstanding any other provision of law, a judge of a court of inquiry may, as a condition of bail or other pretrial release of a person who is charged with violating Code Section 16–5–90 or 16–5–91, prohibit the defendant from entering or remaining present at the victim's school, place of employment, or other specified places at times when the victim is present or intentionally following such person.

(B) If the evidence shows that the defendant has previously violated the conditions of pretrial release or probation or parole which arose out of a violation of Code Section 16–5–

90 or 16–5–91, the judge of a court of inquiry may impose such restrictions on the defendant which may be necessary to deter further stalking of the victim, including but not limited to denying bail or pretrial release.

(c)(1) In the event a person is detained in a facility other than a municipal jail for an offense which is bailable only before a judge of the superior court, as provided in subsection (a) of this Code section, and a hearing is held pursuant to Code Section 17–4–26 or 17–4–62, the presiding judicial officer shall notify the superior court in writing within 48 hours that the arrested person is being held without bail. If the detained person has not already petitioned for bail as provided in subsection (d) of this Code section, the superior court shall notify the district attorney and shall set a date for a hearing on the issue of bail within 30 days after receipt of such notice.

(2) In the event a person is detained in a municipal jail for an offense which is bailable only before a judge of the superior court as provided in subsection (a) of this Code section for a period of 30 days, the municipal court shall notify the superior court in writing within 48 hours that the arrested person has been held for such time without bail. If the detained person has not already petitioned for bail as provided in subsection (d) of this Code section, the superior court shall notify the district attorney and set a date for a hearing on the issue of bail within 30 days after receipt of such notice.

(3) Notice sent to the superior court pursuant to paragraph (1) or (2) of this subsection shall include any incident reports and criminal history reports relevant to the detention of such person.

(d) A person charged with any offense which is bailable only before a judge of the superior court as provided in subsection (a) of this Code section may petition the superior court requesting that such person be released on bail. The court shall notify the district attorney and set a date for a hearing within ten days after receipt of such petition.

(e) A court shall be authorized to release a person on bail if the court finds that the person:

(1) Poses no significant risk of fleeing from the jurisdiction of the court or failing to appear in court when required;

(2) Poses no significant threat or danger to any person, to the community, or to any property in the community;

(3) Poses no significant risk of committing any felony pending trial; and

(4) Poses no significant risk of intimidating witnesses or otherwise obstructing the administration of justice.

However, if the person is charged with a serious violent felony and has already been convicted of a serious violent felony, or of an offense under the laws of any other state or of the United States which offense if committed in this state would be a serious violent felony, there shall be a rebuttable presumption that no condition or combination of conditions will reasonably assure the appearance of the person as required or assure the safety of any other person or the community. As used in this subsection, the term "serious violent felony" means a serious violent felony as defined in Code Section 17–10–6.1.

(f)(1) Except as provided in subsection (a) of this Code section or as otherwise provided in this subsection, the judge of any court of inquiry may by written order establish a schedule of bails and unless otherwise ordered by the judge of any court, a person charged with committing any offense shall be released from custody upon posting bail as fixed in the schedule.

(2) For offenses involving an act of family violence, as defined in Code Section 19–13–1, the schedule of bails provided for in paragraph (1) of this subsection shall require increased bail and shall include a listing of specific conditions which shall include, but not be limited to, having no contact of any kind or character with the victim or any member of the victim's family or household, not physically abusing or threatening to physically abuse the victim, the immediate enrollment in and participation in domestic violence counseling, substance abuse therapy, or other therapeutic requirements.

(3) For offenses involving an act of family violence, the judge shall determine whether the schedule of bails and one or more of its specific conditions shall be used, except that any offense involving an act of family violence and serious injury to the victim shall be bailable only before a judge when the judge or the arresting officer is of the opinion that the danger of further violence to or harassment or intimidation of the victim is such as to make it desirable that the consideration of the imposition of additional conditions as authorized in this Code section should be made. Upon setting bail in any case involving family violence, the judge shall give particular consideration to the exigencies of the case at hand and shall impose any specific conditions as he or she may deem necessary. As used in this Code section, the term "serious injury" means bodily harm capable of being perceived by a person other than the victim and may include, but is not limited to, substantially blackened eyes, substantially swollen lips or other facial or body parts, substantial bruises to body parts, fractured bones, or permanent disfigurements and wounds inflicted by deadly weapons or any other objects which, when used offensively against a person, are capable of causing serious bodily injury.

(4) For violations of Code Section 16–15–4, the court shall require increased bail and shall include as a condition of bail or pretrial release that the defendant shall not have contact of any kind or character with any other member or associate of a criminal street gang and, in cases involving a victim, that the defendant shall not have contact of any kind or character with any such victim or any member of any such victim's family or household.

(5) For offenses involving violations of Code Section 40–6–393, bail or other release from custody shall be set by a judge on an individual basis and not a schedule of bails pursuant to this Code section.

(g) No appeal bond shall be granted to any person who has been convicted of murder, rape, aggravated sodomy, armed robbery, aggravated child molestation, child molestation, kidnapping, trafficking in cocaine or marijuana, aggravated stalking, or aircraft hijacking and who has been sentenced to serve a period of incarceration of five years or more. The granting of an appeal bond to a person who has been convicted of any other felony offense or of any misdemeanor offense involving an act of family violence as defined in Code Section 19–13–1, or of any offense delineated as a high and aggravated misdemeanor or of any offense set forth in Code Section 40–6–391, shall be in the discretion of the convicting court. Appeal bonds shall terminate when the right of appeal terminates, and such bonds shall not be effective as to any petition or application for writ of certiorari unless the court in which the petition or application is filed so specifies.

(h) Except in cases in which life imprisonment or the death penalty may be imposed, a judge of the superior court by written order may delegate the authority provided for in this Code section to any judge of any court of inquiry within such superior court judge's circuit. However, such authority may not be exercised outside the county in which said judge of the court of inquiry was appointed or elected. The written order delegating such authority shall be valid for a period of one year, but may be revoked by the superior court judge issuing such order at any time prior to the end of that one-year period.

(i) As used in this Code section, the term bail shall include the releasing of a person on such person's own recognizance, except as limited by the provisions of Code Section 17–6–12.

(j) For all persons who have been authorized by law or the court to be released on bail, sheriffs and constables shall accept such bail; provided, however, that the sureties tendered and offered on the bond are approved by the sheriff of the county in which the offense was committed.

Laws 1922, p. 51, § 1; Laws 1973, p. 454, § 1; Laws 1980, p. 1359, § 1; Laws 1982, p. 910, § 1; Laws 1983, p. 3, § 14; Laws 1983, p. 358, § 1; Laws 1983, p. 452, § 1; Laws 1984, p. 22, § 17; Laws 1984, p. 679, § 1; Laws 1984, p. 760, § 1; Laws 1985, p. 416, § 1; Laws 1986, p. 166, §§ 1, 2; Laws 1988, p. 358, § 1; Laws 1989, p. 1714, § 1; Laws 1990, p. 8, § 17; Laws 1991, p. 416, § 1; Laws 1991, p. 1401, § 1; Laws 1992, p. 1150, § 1; Laws 1992, p. 2527, § 1; Laws 1993, p. 91, § 17; Laws 1993, p. 1534, § 2; Laws 1994, p. 532, § 1; Laws 1994, p. 1270, § .5; Laws 1994, p. 1625, § 5; Laws 1995, p. 379, §§ 1, 2; Laws 1995, p. 989, §§ 1, 2; Laws 1996, p. 1233, § 1; Laws 1996, p. 1624, § 1; Laws 1997, p. 143, § 17; Laws 1998, p. 270, § 9; Laws 1999, p. 391, § 3; Laws 2000, p. 1171, § 1; Laws 2006, Act 571, § 18, eff. July 1, 2006; Laws 2008, Act 717, § 1, eff. July 1, 2008; Laws 2010, Act 404, § 1, eff. July 1, 2010; Laws 2010, Act 406, §§ 8, 9, eff. July 1, 2010.

Formerly Code 1863, § 4625; Code 1868, § 4649; Code 1873, § 4747; Code 1882, § 4747; Penal Code 1895, § 933; Penal Code 1910, § 958; Code 1933, § 27–901.

Historical and Statutory Notes

The 2006 amendment by Act 571, in subsec. (g), added "child molestation," following "aggravated child molestation," and substituted "five years or more" for "seven years or more".

Laws 2006, Act 571, §§ 1 and 30, provide:

"SECTION 1. The General Assembly finds and declares that recidivist sexual offenders, sexual offenders who use physical violence, and sexual offenders who prey on children are sexual predators who present an extreme threat to the public safety. Many sexual offenders are extremely likely to use physical violence and to repeat their offenses; and some sexual offenders commit many offenses, have many more victims than are ever reported, and are prosecuted for only a fraction of their crimes. The General Assembly finds that this makes the cost of sexual offender victimization to society at large, while incalculable, clearly exorbitant. The General Assembly further finds that the high level of threat that a sexual predator presents to the public safety, and the long-term effects suffered by victims of sex offenses, provide the state with sufficient justification to implement a strategy that includes:

"(1) Incarcerating sexual offenders and maintaining adequate facilities to ensure that decisions to release sexual predators into the community are not made on the basis of inadequate space;

"(2) Requiring the registration of sexual offenders, with a requirement that complete and accurate information be maintained and accessible for use by law enforcement authorities, communities, and the public;

"(3) Providing for community and public notification concerning the presence of sexual offenders;

"(4) Collecting data relative to sexual offenses and sexual offenders;

"(5) Requiring sexual predators who are released into the community to wear an electronic monitoring system for the rest of their natural life and to pay for such system; and

"(6) Prohibiting sexual predators from working with children, either for compensation or as a volunteer.

"The General Assembly further finds that the state has a compelling interest in protecting the public from sexual offenders and in protecting children from predatory sexual activity, and there is sufficient justification for requiring sexual offenders to register and for requiring community and public notification of the presence of sexual offenders. The General Assembly declares that in order to protect the public, it is necessary that the sexual offenders be registered and that members of the community and the public be notified of a sexual offender's presence. The designation of a person as a sexual offender is neither a sentence nor a punishment but simply a regulatory mechanism and status resulting from the conviction of certain crimes. Likewise, the designation of a person as a sexual predator is neither a sentence nor a punishment but simply a regulatory mechanism and status resulting from findings by the Sexual Offender Registration Review Board and a court if requested by a sexual offender."

"SECTION 30. (a) This Act shall become effective July 1, 2006.

"(b) Any person required to register pursuant to the provisions of Code Section 42–1–12, relating to the state sexual offender registry, and any person required not to reside within areas where minors congregate, as prohibited by Code Section 42–1–13 [see 42–1–15], shall not be relieved of the obligation to comply with the provisions of said Code sections by the repeal and reenactment of said Code sections.

"(c) The provisions of this Act shall not affect or abate the status as a crime of any such act or omission which occurred prior to the effective date of the Act repealing, repealing and reenacting, or amending such law, nor shall the prosecution of such crime be abated as a result of such repeal, repeal and reenactment, or amendment."

The 2008 amendment by Act 717, in subsec. (a), par. (10), substituted "or Code Section 16–13–31.1" for "relating to trafficking in cocaine, methamphetamine, or marijuana".

The 2010 amendment by Act 404, in subsec. (i), added "except as limited by the provisions of Code Section 17–6–12" to the end of the subsection.

The 2010 amendment by Act 406, in par. (4), substituted "For violations of Code Section 16–15–4" for "If probable cause is shown that the offense charged is in furtherance of a pattern of criminal gang activity as defined by Code Section 16–15–3", inserted "in cases involving a victim" following "member or associate of a criminal street gang", and made nominal changes; and added par. (13).

§ 17–6–1.1. Electronic pretrial release and monitoring program

(a) In addition to other methods of posting bail or as special condition of bond, a defendant may be released from custody pending the trial of his or her case on the condition that the defendant comply with the terms and conditions of an electronic pretrial release and monitoring program which is approved pursuant to subsection (j) of this Code section. The sheriff of a county may enter into agreements with such approved providers. A bonding company, bonding agent, or probation service provider may be a provider of such services.

(b) If it appears to the court that a defendant subject to its jurisdiction is a suitable candidate for electronic pretrial release and monitoring, the court may, in its sole discretion and subject to the eligibility requirements of this Code section, authorize the defendant to be released under the provisions of an electronic pretrial release and monitoring program. A judge may only authorize electronic pretrial release and monitoring if that judge has jurisdiction to set a bond for the offense charged and the defendant is otherwise eligible for bond under subsection (e) of Code Section 17–6–1. When a court of competent jurisdiction has already set bond for a defendant indicating that the defendant is otherwise eligible for release on bail pursuant to subsection (e) of Code Section 17–6–1, in addition to accepting cash in satisfaction of the bond set by a court, the court may instruct the sheriff that the defendant is to be released to an electronic pretrial release and monitoring program.

(c) The court, in its sole discretion, may revoke at any time the eligibility of any defendant to participate in the electronic pretrial release and monitoring program in which event the defendant shall be immediately returned to custody. If the defendant's case has not been assigned to a particular division of the court, the chief judge shall have such authority.

(d) A defendant may not be released to, or remain in, an electronic pretrial release and monitoring program who has any other outstanding warrants, accusations, indictments, holds, or incarceration orders from any other court, law enforcement agency, or probation or parole officer that require the posting of bond or further adjudication.

(e) A defendant released pursuant to an electronic pretrial release and monitoring program shall abide by such conditions as the court may impose relating to such program, including, but not limited to, the following:

(1) Periods of home confinement;

(2) Compliance with all requirements and conditions of the electronic pretrial release and monitoring program provider;

(3) Compliance with any court orders or special conditions of bond which may include an order directing that no contact, direct or indirect, be made with the victim or forbidding entry upon, about, or near certain premises;

(4) An order directing that the accused provide support and maintenance for the person's dependents to the best of his or her ability;

(5) Restrictions on the use of alcoholic beverages and controlled substances;

(6) Curfews;

(7) Limitations on work hours and employment;

(8) An order directing the accused to submit to test of breath, blood, or urine from time to time;

(9) Travel restrictions;

(10) An order directing that electronic pretrial release and monitoring equipment be kept in good working condition;

(11) An order directing that the person refrain from violating the criminal laws of any state, county, or municipality;

(12) An order directing timely payment of all fees connected with the electronic pretrial release and monitoring program;

(13) Payroll deductions to fund electronic pretrial release and monitoring fees;

(14) Provisions to permit reasonable medical treatment;

(15) Provisions for procuring reasonable necessities, such as grocery shopping;

(16) Provisions for attendance in educational, rehabilitative, and treatment programs; and

(17) Such other terms and conditions as the court may deem just and proper.

(f) Under no circumstances shall electronic pretrial release and monitoring equipment be introduced internally or beneath the skin of any person.

(g) In the event that a court of competent jurisdiction finds probable cause, upon oath, affirmation, or sworn affidavit, that a defendant has violated the terms or conditions of his or her electronic pretrial release and monitoring program, other than terms regarding home confinement set forth in paragraph (1) of subsection (e) of this Code section, or finds that the defendant provided false or misleading information concerning his or her qualifications to participate in the electronic pretrial release and monitoring program, including, but not limited to, name, date of birth, address, or other personal identification information, then the defendant's ongoing participation in such program shall be terminated immediately and, upon arrest of the defendant for such violation by any law enforcement officer, the defendant shall be returned to confinement at the county jail or other facility from which the defendant was released.

(h)(1) As an additional condition of electronic pretrial release and monitoring, a defendant authorized to participate in such program by the court shall pay a reasonable, nonrefundable fee for program enrollment, equipment use, and monitoring to the provider of such program. If a bonding company, bonding agent, or probation service provider is the provider, the fees earned in the capacity of being such a provider shall be in addition to the fees allowed in Code Sections 17–6–30, 42–8–34, and 42–8–100.

(2) The fees connected with the electronic pretrial release and monitoring program shall be timely paid by a defendant as a condition of his or her ongoing participation in the electronic pretrial release and monitoring program in accordance with the terms for such programs as approved by the court. Failure to make timely payments shall constitute a violation of the terms of the electronic pretrial release and monitoring program and shall result in the defendant's immediate return to custody.

(3) Defendants who have an extraordinary medical condition requiring ongoing medical treatment or indigent persons, as defined by the court, and who are selected by the court following the indigency standards established by the court may have such electronic pretrial release and monitoring fees paid by the sheriff with the consent of the governing authority.

(i) No defendant released under an electronic pretrial release and monitoring program under this Code section shall be deemed to be an agent, employee, or involuntary servant of the county or the electronic pretrial release and monitoring provider while so released, working, or participating in training or going to and from the defendant's place of employment or training. Neither the electronic pretrial release and monitoring provider nor the sheriff shall be civilly liable for the criminal acts of a defendant released pursuant to this Code section.

(j) Any person or corporation approved by the chief judge of the court and the sheriff in their discretion who meets the following minimum requirements may be approved to provide electronic pretrial release and monitoring services:

(1) The provider shall comply with all applicable federal, state, and local laws and all rules and regulations established by the chief judge and the sheriff in counties where the provider provides electronic pretrial release and monitoring services;

(2) The provider shall provide the chief judge and the sheriff with the name of the provider, the name of an individual who shall serve as the contact person for the provider, and the telephone number of such contact person;

(3) The provider shall promptly, not later than three business days after such change, notify the chief judge and sheriff of any changes in its address, ownership, or qualifications under this Code section;

(4) The provider shall provide simultaneous access to all records regarding all monitoring information, GPS tracking, home confinement, and victim protection regarding each person placed on electronic pretrial release and monitoring; and

(5) The provider shall act as surety for the bond.

(k) The sheriff shall maintain a list of approved providers of electronic pretrial release and monitoring services. The sheriff, in his or her discretion, may temporarily or permanently remove any provider from the list of approved providers should the provider:

(1) Fail to comply with the requirements of this Code section;

(2) Fail to monitor properly any defendant that the provider was required to monitor;

(3) Charge an excessive fee for use and monitoring of electronic monitoring equipment; or

(4) Act or fail to act in such a manner that, in the discretion of the sheriff, constitutes good cause for removal.

Laws 2009, Act 139, § 2, eff. July 1, 2009.

Historical and Statutory Notes

Laws 2009, Act 139, § 1, provides:

"The General Assembly finds that a program of electronic pretrial release, monitoring, and home confinement incorporates modern technology to accomplish the following purposes, including, but not limited to:

"(1) Ensuring proper prioritization of local incarceration resources;

"(2) Improving child support collections by giving nonpayors an opportunity to maintain employment while under electronic surveillance;

"(3) Better protecting crime victims by global positioning satellite (GPS) tracking and monitoring of pretrial release offenders to better ensure ongoing protection of crime victims;

"(4) Permitting defendants with extraordinary health problems to seek appropriate medical care;

"(5) Assisting sheriffs in alleviating jail overcrowding by creating alternative methods of pretrial release and monitoring and home confinement;

"(6) Reducing the costs of pretrial detention to governing authorities of counties as the costs of self-paid, electronic pretrial release and monitoring are substantially less than pretrial incarceration; and

"(7) Creating instant alert capabilities to law enforcement in the event terms of pretrial release are violated."

In 2009, the Code Commission, in par. (h)(3), substituted "condition" for "conditions". See § 28–9–5.

§ 17–6–2. Amount of bail in misdemeanor cases; acceptance by sheriffs and constables

(a) (1) In all cases wherein a licensed driver of this state has been arrested, incarcerated, and charged with a violation of state law and where said violation is a misdemeanor, the sheriff of the county wherein the violation occurred shall be authorized, unless otherwise ordered by a judicial officer, after the individual has been incarcerated for not less than five days, to accept that individual's driver's license as collateral for any bail which has been set in the case, up to and including the amount of $ 1,000.00, provided such license is not under suspension or has not expired or been revoked.

(2) The individual posting a license as collateral pursuant to this subsection shall execute an acknowledgment and agreement between the individual and the State of Georgia as bond wherein the individual agrees to appear in court to answer the charges made against the individual and acknowledges that failure to appear in court when the case is scheduled for hearing, trial, or plea shall result in a forfeiture of the individual's license through suspension by operation of law effective upon the date of the individual's scheduled appearance. The individual shall also be notified that failure to appear in court as required may result in criminal prosecution for bail jumping as provided in Code Section 16–10–51. After execution of the agreement, except as otherwise provided by law, the license shall be returned to the individual and the original agreement shall be delivered to the prosecuting attorney for filing with the accusation, citation, or dismissal. Whenever an individual has been charged with a violation of Code Section 40–6–391, relating to driving under the influence of alcohol or drugs, then the provisions of Code Section 40–5–67 shall apply.

(3) A failure to appear by the individual who has been charged with a misdemeanor offense and who posted that individual's license as bail pursuant to this subsection shall, by operation of law, cause that individual's license to be suspended by the Department of Driver Services effective immediately, and the clerk of the court within five days after that failure to appear shall forward a copy of the agreement to the Department of Driver Services which shall enter the suspension upon the individual's driver history record. The posting of a license as provided in this subsection shall also be considered as bail for the purposes of Code Section 16–10–51. Where the original court date has been continued by the judge, clerk, or other officer of the court and there has been actual notice given to the defendant in open court or in writing by a court official or officer of the court or by mailing such notice to the defendant's last known address, then the provisions of this paragraph shall apply to the new court appearance date.

(4) A license suspended pursuant to this subsection shall only be reinstated when the individual shall pay to the Department of Driver Services a restoration fee of $25.00 together with a certified notice from the clerk of the originating court that the case has either been disposed of or has been rescheduled and a deposit of sufficient collateral approved by the sheriff of the county wherein the charges were made in an amount to satisfy the original bail amount has been paid. The court wherein the charges are pending shall be authorized to require payment of costs by the defendant in an amount not to exceed $100.00 to reschedule the case.

(5) Upon the trial of any individual charged with the offense of driving with a suspended license where such license was suspended as provided in this subsection, a copy of the acknowledgment and agreement executed by the individual together with certification by the clerk of the court of the individual's failure to appear shall be prima-facie evidence of actual notice to the individual that the individual's license was suspended.

(b) In all other misdemeanor cases, sheriffs and constables shall accept bail in such reasonable amount as may be just and fair for any person or persons charged with a misdemeanor, provided that the sureties tendered and offered on the bond are approved by the sheriff in the county where the offense was committed.

Laws 1921, p. 241, § 1; Laws 1966, p. 428, § 1; Laws 1989, p. 448, § 1; Laws 1990, p. 8, § 17; Laws 1991, p. 94, § 17; Laws 2002, p. 415, § 17; Laws 2005, Act 68, § 7–2, eff. July 1, 2005.

Formerly Code 1933, § 27–902.

Historical and Statutory Notes

The 2005 amendment by Act 68, in subsec. (a), substituted "Department of Driver Services" for "Department of Motor Vehicle Safety" twice in par. (3) and once in par. (4).

§ 17–6–3. Amount of bail in misdemeanor cases; recognizance bond for persons in military service

(a) In the case of any person engaged in military service who is charged with a misdemeanor and whose bond has been fixed at not more than $400.00 plus costs, any sheriff shall be allowed to accept, in lieu of bail, a recognizance bond executed and signed by the commanding officer of the person or the officer's lawfully delegated subordinates. Any person so charged may be taken into custody on behalf of the military installation by his commanding officer or by persons designated by the commanding officer of the military installation under the following terms and conditions:

(1) Immediately following his release he will be returned by the military police or other designated authority directly to the military installation and delivered to the duty officer of the command to which he is attached;

(2) He then will be restrained as appropriate in each case. The restraint will be for a minimum of 12 hours in all cases involving consumption of alcoholic beverages. He normally will be restricted to the limits of the military installation until such time as the charges are dismissed or his case has been adjudicated;

(3) He will not be transferred, granted leave, or discharged from the military service without 36 hours' notice to the sheriff or his deputy sheriff;

(4) He will be delivered to the sheriff or his deputy on demand; and

(5) These terms or conditions will be withdrawn only upon his posting the required bond or otherwise being released by the sheriff, his deputy, or the appropriate court.

(b) The recognizance bond shall be of the following type:

In consideration of the release of ____ (name of person charged) charged with ____ (name or description of offense) it is agreed that the aforementioned prisoner will be restrained at the ____ (appropriate military installation) in whatever degree considered to be appropriate by his commanding officer. This restraint will be for a minimum of 12 hours in all cases involving consumption of alcoholic beverages. It is further agreed that he will not be transferred, granted leave, or discharged from the ____ (appropriate service) without notice to the sheriff or his deputy and will be delivered to the sheriff or his deputy upon demand. These terms and conditions will be withdrawn only upon his posting of the required personal bond or upon the release by the sheriff, his deputy, or the appropriate court.

Signed ________________
Official title ________________

Laws 1921, p. 241, § 1; Laws 1966, p. 428, § 1; Laws 1982, p. 3, § 17; Laws 1983, p. 884, § 3–18; Laws 1984, p. 22, § 17.

Formerly Code 1933, § 27–902.

§ 17–6–4. Posting of cash bonds permitted; disposition of unclaimed bonds

(a) Any party, defendant, accused, or other person required or permitted by law to give or post bond (or bail) as surety or security for the happening of any event or act in criminal matters may discharge the requirement by depositing cash in the amount of the bond so required with the appropriate person, official, or other depository.

(b) Any official or other person receiving any such bond shall give a receipt therefor and shall cause the fact of the receipt to be entered and recorded on the docket of the case in which it was given. If bond is given in a matter not appearing as a separate court case on a docket, a docket shall be prepared, maintained, and kept of all such transactions and the name and address of the person giving or making the bond, the date of the receipt of the bond, the name of the person receiving the bond, the amount of the bond, and a description of the cause for giving the bond, together with any and all other information desirable concerning the bond, shall be a part of the record in that separate docket.

(c) In the event that any cash bail posted pursuant to this Code section or Code Section 17-6-5 is not later claimed by the surety on such bond after a period of seven years from the later of either the date on which the defendant was required to appear in court or the date of disposition of the case by the prosecutor or the court, including any appeal of a verdict or sentence, then the cash shall be paid into the general fund of the county having trial venue of the case, as in the case of forfeited cash bonds, provided that the officer who accepted such cash bail shall first have notified the surety, by mailing notice to such surety at the last address given by such surety, that such funds shall be forfeited if they are not claimed within 90 days following the date of mailing of such notice. Any claim by a surety for refund of a cash bail shall include acceptable documentary proof of disposition of the case from the prosecuting official or appropriate court records or such other documentation as may be acceptable to the official holding such cash bail as proof that the case has been settled.

Laws 1969, p. 41, §§ 1, 2; Laws 1991, p. 749, § 1.

§ 17-6-5. Cash bonds in motor vehicle, game, boating violation or litter cases; authorization by court

Any sheriff, deputy sheriff, county peace officer, or other county officer charged with the duty of enforcing the laws of this state relating to (1) traffic or the operation or licensing of motor vehicles or operators; (2) the width, height, or length of vehicles and loads; (3) motor common carriers and motor contract carriers; (4) road taxes on motor carriers as provided in Article 2 of Chapter 9 of Title 48; (5) game and fish; (6) boating; or (7) litter control who makes an arrest outside the corporate limits of any municipality of this state for a violation of said laws and who is authorized, as provided herein by a court of record having jurisdiction over such offenses, to accept cash bonds may accept a cash bond from the person arrested in lieu of a statutory bond or recognizance. No such officer shall accept a cash bond unless he is authorized to receive cash bonds in such cases by an order of the court having jurisdiction over such offenses and unless such order has been entered on the minutes of the court. Any such order may be granted, revoked, or modified by the court at any time.

Laws 1953, Jan.-Feb. Sess., p. 331, § 1; Laws 1962, p. 530, § 1; Laws 1975, p. 845, § 1; Laws 1982, p. 1136, §§ 1, 4.

§ 17-6-6. Receipt book; distribution of copies of receipts

Other laws to the contrary notwithstanding, when an order is passed as provided for in Code Section 17-6-5 authorizing an officer to accept cash bonds, it shall be the duty of the clerk of the court, if there is one, or, if there is no clerk, the judge passing the order to furnish the officer or officers authorized under the order with a book of blank receipts, consecutively numbered in triplicate and readily distinguishable and identifiable. The receipts shall be completed by the officers when making an arrest and accepting a cash bond so as to show the name of the person arrested, date of arrest, nature of the offense, amount of the cash bond given, and the name of the arresting officer. The arresting officer or the person receiving the cash bond shall deliver a copy of the receipt to the person arrested at the time the cash bond is given and shall file the original receipt together with the cash bond with the clerk, or judge, as the case may be, of the court having jurisdiction of the offense not later than the next succeeding business day of such clerk or judge following the date of issuance of the receipt. The remaining copy of the receipt shall be mailed to the commissioner of public safety.

Laws 1953, Jan.-Feb. Sess., p. 331, § 2; Laws 1978, p. 1493, § 1.

§ 17-6-7. Duty of arresting officer to account for receipts; personal liability; contempt of court for failure

All receipts issued to arresting officers and all cash bonds received under Code Sections 17-6-5 and 17-6-6 shall be accounted for by the receiving officers to the court from which the receipts were issued and, in the event that any such officer fails to account for same, he shall be personally liable for any default and may be punished as for contempt by the court, in addition to any other penalties which are provided for by law in such cases.

Laws 1953, Jan.-Feb. Sess., p. 331, § 3.

§ 17-6-8. Forfeiture; distribution of proceeds; subsequent prosecution

If any person arrested for a misdemeanor arising out of a violation of the laws of this state relating to (1) traffic or the operation or licensing of motor vehicles or operators; (2) the width, height, or length of vehicles and loads; (3) motor common carriers and motor contract carriers; (4) road taxes on motor carriers as provided in Article 2 of Chapter 9 of Title 48; (5) game and fish; (6) boating; or (7) litter control gives a cash bond for his appearance as provided in Code Section 17-6-5 and fails to appear on the date, time, and place specified in the citation or summons without legal excuse, the court may order said cash bond forfeited without the necessity of complying with the statutory procedure provided for in the forfeiture of statutory bail bonds. A judgment ordering the case disposed of and settled may be entered by the court and the proceeds shall be applied in the same manner as fines. If the court does not enter a judgment ordering the case disposed of and settled, the forfeiture of the cash bond shall not be a bar to subsequent prosecution of the person charged with the violation of such laws.

Laws 1953, Jan.-Feb. Sess., p. 331, § 4; Laws 1962, p. 530, § 2; Laws 1975, p. 845, § 2; Laws 1982, p. 1136, §§ 2, 5.

§ 17-6-9. Law enforcement officers and officials of political subdivisions authorized to accept cash bonds for violation of litter laws

Any law enforcement officer or official of a political subdivision of this state who is authorized to enforce Part 2 of Article 2 of Chapter 7 of Title 16 and who is authorized by the judge having jurisdiction of the offense to accept cash bonds may accept a cash bond for the personal appearance at trial of the person arrested in lieu of a statutory bond or recognizance. The procedures connected with such cash bonds, including, but not limited to, duties of the arresting officer, forfeiture, distribution of proceeds, and discretion of court as to disposal of the cash bond, shall be the same procedures applicable to arrest by a sheriff for a violation of any litter law.

Laws 1975, p. 845, § 3; Laws 2006, Act 538, § 3-7, eff. July 1, 2006.

Historical and Statutory Notes

The 2006 amendment by Act 538 deleted ", the 'Litter Control Law,' " following "Chapter 7 of Title 16".

Laws 2006, Act 538, § 5–1, provides:

"This Act shall become effective upon its approval by the Governor [April 21, 2006] or upon its becoming law without such approval for purposes of adopting local ordinances to become effective on or after July 1, 2006; and for all other purposes, this Act shall become effective on July 1, 2006."

§ 17–6–10. Offenses against municipalities; cash bonds

(a) All mayors or chief governing officers or their designated official or officials of municipalities are authorized to accept a cash bond for the personal appearance in court of any person charged with a violation of an ordinance or other offense against the municipality. The officer assessing and accepting a cash bond shall issue a receipt for the bond to the person charged with the violation.

(b) When any mayor or chief governing officer of any municipality of this state designates any municipal official to accept cash bonds under subsection (a) of this Code section, the delegation of authority shall be in writing and filed in the records of the municipality.

(c) Any person charged with a violation of an ordinance or other offense against a municipality who gives a cash bond for his personal appearance in court at a designated time and place and who fails to appear at said time and place shall forfeit the cash bond upon the call of the case for trial. It shall not be necessary for the municipality to take any further action to forfeit the cash bond. Forfeiture of a cash bond shall not be a bar to a subsequent prosecution of the accused for the violation.

(d) This Code section shall not apply to municipalities having provisions in their charters with reference to the subject matter of this Code section.

Laws 1952, p. 182, §§ 1–4, 4A.

§ 17–6–11. Display of driver's license in motor vehicle violation apprehensions; suspension of license; organ donations; rules and regulations

(a) Any other laws to the contrary notwithstanding, any person who is apprehended by an officer for the violation of the laws of this state or ordinances relating to: (1) traffic, including any offense under Code Section 40–5–72 or 40–6–10, but excepting any other offense for which a license may be suspended for a first offense by the commissioner of driver services, any offense covered under Code Section 40–5–54, or any offense covered under Article 15 of Chapter 6 of Title 40; (2) the licensing and registration of motor vehicles and operators; (3) the width, height, and length of vehicles and loads; (4) motor common carriers and motor contract carriers; or (5) road taxes on motor carriers as provided in Article 2 of Chapter 9 of Title 48 upon being served with the official summons issued by such apprehending officer, in lieu of being immediately brought before the proper magistrate, recorder, or other judicial officer to enter into a formal recognizance or make direct the deposit of a proper sum of money in lieu of a recognizance ordering incarceration, may display his or her driver's license to the apprehending officer in lieu of bail, in lieu of entering into a recognizance for his or her appearance for trial as set in the aforesaid summons, or in lieu of being incarcerated by the apprehending officer and held for further action by the appropriate judicial officer. The apprehending officer shall note the driver's license number on the official summons. The summons duly served as provided in this Code section shall give the judicial officer jurisdiction to dispose of the matter.

(b) Upon display of the driver's license, the apprehending officer shall release the person so charged for his or her further appearance before the proper judicial officer as required by the summons. The court in which the charges are lodged shall immediately forward to the Department of Driver Services of this state the driver's license number if the person fails to appear and answer to the charge against him or her. The commissioner of driver services shall, upon receipt of a license number forwarded by the court, suspend the driver's license and driving privilege of the defaulting person until notified by the court that the charge against the person has been finally adjudicated. Such person's license shall be reinstated if the person submits proof of payment of the fine from the court of jurisdiction and pays to the Department of Driver Services a restoration fee of $50.00 or $25.00 when such reinstatement is processed by mail.

(b.1) It shall be the duty of a law enforcement officer or emergency medical technician responding to the scene of any motor vehicle accident or other accident involving a fatal injury to examine immediately the driver's license of the victim to determine the victim's wishes concerning organ donation. If the victim has indicated that he or she wishes to be an organ donor, it shall be the duty of such law enforcement officer or emergency medical technician to take appropriate action to ensure, if possible, that the victim's organs shall not be imperiled by delay in verification by the donor's next of kin.

(c) Nothing in this Code section bars any law enforcement officer from arresting or from seizing the driver's license of any individual possessing a fraudulent license or a suspended license or operating a motor vehicle while his or her license is suspended, outside the scope of a driving permit, or without a license.

(d) The commissioner of driver services shall be authorized to promulgate reasonable rules and regulations to carry out the purposes of this Code section and to establish agreements with other states whereby a valid license from that state may be accepted for purposes of this Code section.

Laws 1973, p. 435, §§ 1, 2; Laws 1976, p. 213, § 1; Laws 1979, p. 759, § 1; Laws 1982, p. 1136, §§ 3, 6; Laws 1986, p. 1607, § 1; Laws 1987, p. 542, § 3; Laws 1990, p. 8, § 17; Laws 1991, p. 94, § 17; Laws 1991, p. 1776, § 1; Laws 1996, p. 1624, § 2; Laws 2000, p. 951, § 12–1; Laws 2005, Act 68, § 7–3, eff. July 1, 2005.

Historical and Statutory Notes

The 2005 amendment by Act 68, in subsec. (a), substituted "commissioner of driver services" for "commissioner of motor vehicle safety"; in subsec. (b), substituted "commissioner of driver services" for "commissioner of motor vehicle safety", substituted "Department of Driver Services" for "Department of Motor Vehicle Safety" twice, and substituted "$50.00" for "$35.00"; and in subsec. (d), substituted "commissioner of driver services" for "commissioner of motor vehicle safety".

§ 17–6–12. Release of person charged with crime on his own recognizance only; arrest where person fails to appear for trial

(a) As used in this Code section, the term "bail restricted offense" means the person is charged with:

(1) A serious violent felony as such term is defined in Code Section 17–10–6.1; or

(2) A felony offense of:

(A) Aggravated assault;

(B) Aggravated battery;

(C) Hijacking a motor vehicle

(D) Aggravated stalking;

(E) Child molestation;

(F) Enticing a child for indecent purposes;

(G) Pimping;

(H) Robbery;

(I) Bail jumping;

(J) Escape;

(K) Possession of a firearm or knife during the commission of or attempt to commit certain crimes;

(L) Possession of firearms by convicted felons and first offender probationers;

(M) Trafficking in cocaine, illegal drugs, marijuana, or methamphetamine;

(N) Participating in criminal street gang activity;

(O) Habitual violator; or

(P) Driving under the influence of alcohol, drugs, or other intoxicating substances.

(b) A person charged with a bail restricted offense shall not be released on bail on his or her own recognizance for the purpose of entering a pretrial release program, a pretrial release and diversion program, or a pretrial intervention and diversion program as provided for in Article 4 of Chapter 18 of Title 15, or Article 5 of Chapter 8 of Title 42, or pursuant to Uniform Superior Court Rule 27, unless an elected magistrate, elected state or superior court judge enters a written order to the contrary specifying the reasons why such person should be released upon his or her own recognizance.

(c) Except as provided in subsection (b) of this Code section and in addition to other laws regarding the release of an accused person, the judge of any court having jurisdiction over a person charged with committing an offense against the criminal laws of this state shall have authority, in his or her sound discretion and in appropriate cases, to authorize the release of the person upon his or her own recognizance only.

(d) Upon the failure of a person released on his or her own recognizance only to appear for trial, if the release is not otherwise conditioned by the court, the court may summarily issue an order for his or her arrest which shall be enforced as in cases of forfeited bonds.

Laws 1969, p. 72, §§ 1, 2; Laws 2010, Act 404, § 2, eff. July 1, 2010.

Historical and Statutory Notes

The 2010 amendment by Act 404 added subsecs. (a) and (b), redesignated former subsecs. (a) and (b) as (c) and (d), respectively, and made section general neutral.

§ 17–6–13. Number of times bail may be permitted for same offense

Except as otherwise provided in this chapter, each person who is entitled to bail under this article shall be permitted one bail for the same offense as a matter of right. Subsequent bails shall be in the discretion of the court.

Laws 1832, Cobb's 1851 Digest, p. 862; Laws 1878–79, p. 55, § 1; Laws 1971, p. 408, § 1; Laws 1983, p. 452, § 2.

Formerly Code 1863, § 4625; Code 1868, § 4649; Code 1873, § 4747; Code 1882, § 4747; Penal Code 1895, § 934; Penal Code 1910, § 959; Code 1933, § 27–903.

§ 17–6–14. Preliminary hearing bond valid to insure presence at trial; exception of bail set higher; limitations

(a) When a person posts bail bond prior to a preliminary or commitment hearing and is later bound over to another court for trial, the original bail bond shall not terminate but shall be valid to provide for the person's appearance at the trial of the case unless the amount of the bail is set higher by lawful authority, in which case new bail bond shall be posted.

(b) Nothing contained in subsection (a) of this Code section shall apply to any proceedings in which any federal court or United States commissioner is involved. Subsection (a) of this Code section shall apply only to those instances wherein the person required to post a bail bond shall be bound over to a court or grand jury of the same county wherein the committing court exercised its jurisdiction. Subsection (a) of this Code section shall not apply to those instances where a person is bound over to two or more courts or grand juries.

(c) Nothing contained in subsection (a) of this Code section shall be construed to require an additional bail bond in the event the court to which the person has been committed requires a lesser bail bond than the bond originally posted.

Laws 1971, p. 407, §§ 1, 2.

§ 17–6–15. Bail

(a) After arrest, if bail is tendered and accepted, no regular commitment need be entered, but a simple memorandum of the fact of bail being taken shall be sufficient.

(b)(1) A reasonable opportunity shall be allowed the accused person to give bail; and, even after commitment and imprisonment, the committing court may order the accused person brought before it to receive bail. No person shall be imprisoned under a felony commitment when bail has been fixed, if the person tenders and offers to give bond in the amount fixed, with sureties acceptable to the sheriff of the county in which the alleged offense occurred; provided, however, the sheriff shall publish and make available written rules and regulations defining acceptable sureties and prescribing under what conditions sureties may be accepted. If the sheriff determines that a professional bonding company is an acceptable surety, the rules and regulations shall require, but shall not be limited to, the following:

(A) Complete documentation showing the composition of the company to be an individual, a trust, or a group of individuals, whether or not formed as a partnership or other legal entity, or a corporation or a combination of individuals, trusts, and corporations;

(B) Complete documentation for all employees, agents, or individuals authorized to sign or act on behalf of the bonding company;

(C) Complete documentation showing that the company holds a valid business license in the jurisdiction where bonds will be written;

(D) Fingerprints and background checks of every individual who acts as a professional bondsperson as defined in Code Section 17–6–50 for the professional bonding company seeking approval;

(E) Establishment of a cash escrow account or other form of collateral in a sum and upon terms and conditions approved by the sheriff;

(F) Establishment of application, approval, and reporting procedures for the professional bonding company deemed appropriate by the sheriff which satisfy all rules and regulations required by the laws of this state and the rules and regulations established by the sheriff;

(G) Applicable fees to be paid by the applicant to cover the cost of copying the rules and regulations and processing and investigating all applications and all other costs relating thereto; or

(H) Additional criteria and requirements for approving and regulating bonding companies to be determined at the discretion of the sheriff.

(2) This Code section shall not be construed to require a sheriff to accept a professional bonding company or bondsperson as a surety.

(3) This Code section shall not be construed to prevent the posting of real property bonds and the sheriff may not prohibit the posting of property bonds. Additional requirements for the use of real property may be determined at the discretion of the sheriff. The sheriff shall not prohibit a nonresident of the county from posting a real property bond if such real property is located in the county in which it is offered as bond and if such property has sufficient unencumbered equity to satisfy the sheriff's posted rules and regulations as to acceptable sureties.

(c) This Code section shall not abrogate or repeal the common-law authority of the judge having jurisdiction.

Laws 1977, p. 346, § 1; Laws 1994, p. 532, § 2.

Formerly Code 1863, § 4620; Code 1868, § 4644; Code 1873, § 4742; Code 1882, § 4742; Penal Code 1895, § 922; Penal Code 1910, § 947; Code 1933, § 27–418.

§ 17–6–16. Waiver of hearing; memorandum entered on warrant; supersedeas

If the accused person waives a commitment hearing and tenders bail, a memorandum of these facts shall be entered on the warrant by the person authorized to accept bail; and this waiver may be done by the person charged before arrest and, when done, shall operate as a supersedeas.

Formerly Code 1863, § 4621; Code 1868, § 4645; Code 1873, § 4743; Code 1882, § 4743; Penal Code 1895, § 923; Penal Code 1910, § 948; Code 1933, § 27–419.

§ 17–6–17. Conditions of bail bond and recognizance

In addition to all other requirements prescribed for appearance bonds or recognizances, the appearance bond or recognizance given by a person accused of the commission of a crime shall be conditioned upon the person presenting himself before the court at the time fixed for his arraignment. Upon failure of a person charged with a penal offense to appear before the court at the time fixed for his arraignment, the prosecuting attorney may proceed to forfeit the bond or recognizance.

Laws 1966, p. 430, § 2; Laws 1977, p. 179, § 1.

Formerly Code 1933, § 27–1402.

§ 17–6–18. Amendment of bonds in judicial proceedings

All bonds taken under requisition of law in the course of a judicial proceeding may be amended and new security given if necessary.

Formerly Code 1863, § 3434; Code 1868, § 3454; Code 1873, § 3505; Code 1882, § 3505; Civil Code 1895, § 5123; Civil Code 1910, § 5707; Code 1933, § 81–1204.

Article 2

Sureties

Part 1

General Provisions

§ 17–6–30. Fees of sureties

(a) Sureties on criminal bonds in any court shall not charge or receive more than 12 percent of the face amount of the bond set in the amount of $10,000.00 or less, which amount includes the principal and all applicable surcharges, and shall not charge or receive more than 15 percent of the face amount of the bond set in an amount in excess of $10,000.00, which amount includes the principal and all applicable surcharges, as compensation from defendants or from anyone acting for defendants.

(b) Any person who violates subsection (a) of this Code section shall be guilty of a misdemeanor.

Laws 1921, p. 243, §§ 1, 8; Laws 1958, p. 120, § 1; Laws 1982, p. 1254, § 1; Laws 1999, p. 546, § 1; Laws 2006, Act 581, § 1, eff. July 1, 2006.

Formerly Code 1933, §§ 27–501, 27–9903.

Historical and Statutory Notes

The 2006 amendment by Act 581, in subsec. (a), twice substituted "face amount of the bond" for "principal amount of bonds" and twice inserted ", which amount includes the principal and all applicable surcharges,".

§ 17–6–31. Surety surrendering principal; release of surety from liability

(a) When the court is not in session, a surety on a bond may surrender the surety's principal to the sheriff or to the responsible law enforcement officer of the jurisdiction in which the case is pending in order to be released from liability.

(b) When the court is in session, a surety on a bond may surrender the surety's principal in open court.

(c) The principal shall also be considered surrendered by plea of guilty or nolo contendere to the court or if the principal is present in person when the jury or judge, if tried without a jury, finds the principal guilty or if the judge dead dockets the case prior to entry of judgment and, upon such plea or finding of guilty or dead docketing, the surety shall be released from liability.

(d)(1) Furthermore, the surety shall be released from liability if, prior to entry of judgment, there is:

(A) A deferred sentence;

(B) A presentence investigation;

(C) A court ordered pretrial intervention program;

(D) A court ordered educational and rehabilitation program;

(E) A fine;

(F) A dead docket; or

(G) Death of the principal.

(2) Furthermore, the surety may be released from liability at the discretion of the court if:

(A) The principal used a false name when he or she was bound over and committed to jail or a correctional institution and was subsequently released from such facility unless the surety knew or should have known that the principal used a false name; and

(B) The surety shows to the satisfaction of the court that he or she acted with due diligence and used all practical means to secure the attendance of the principal before the court.

(e) If the prosecuting attorney does not try the charges against a defendant within a period of two years in the case of felonies and one year in the case of misdemeanors after the date of posting bond, then judgment rendered after such period may not be enforced against the surety on the bond and the surety shall thereafter be relieved of liability on the bond. This subsection shall not apply where the prosecuting attorney's failure to try the charges is due to the fault of the principal.

(f) No judgment shall be rendered on any appearance bond if it is shown to the satisfaction of the court that the surety was prevented from returning the principal to the jurisdiction because such principal was on active military duty.

Laws 1943, p. 282, § 1; Laws 1982, p. 1224, § 1; Laws 1986, p. 1588, § 1; Laws 1987, p. 1342, § 1; Laws 1992, p. 2933, § 1; Laws 1997, p. 973, § 2.

Formerly Code 1863, § 4624; Code 1868, § 4648; Code 1873, § 4746; Code 1882, § 4746; Penal Code 1895, § 935; Penal Code 1910, § 960; Code 1933, § 27–904.

Part 2

Professional Bondsmen

§ 17–6–50. Professional bondsmen; definition

(a) Bondsmen or persons who hold themselves out as signers or sureties of bonds for compensation are declared to be professional bondsmen.

(b) A professional bondsperson is one who holds himself or herself out as a signer or surety of bonds for compensation who must meet the following qualifications:

(1) Is 18 years of age or over;

(2) Is a resident of the State of Georgia for at least one year before making application to write bonds;

(3) Is a person of good moral character and has not been convicted of a felony or any crime involving moral turpitude; and

(4) Is approved by the sheriff and remains in good standing with respect to all applicable federal, state, and local laws and all rules and regulations established by the sheriff in the county where the bonding business is conducted.

(c) The sheriff of the county in which the bonding business is conducting business or is seeking approval to conduct business shall initiate a criminal background investigation to ensure that a professional bondsman has not been convicted of a felony or a crime involving moral turpitude in this state or any other jurisdiction. The sheriff shall require the professional bondsman to furnish two full sets of fingerprints which the sheriff shall submit to the Georgia Crime Information Center. The center shall submit a full set of fingerprints to the Federal Bureau of Investigation for a national criminal history record check.

(d) It shall be the duty of each professional bondsman approved by the sheriff in accordance with this part to provide the clerk of each court before which one or more of such professional bondsman's principals are required to appear with the business name, complete address, telephone number, and e-mail address of the chief operating officer or his or her designee of such professional bondsman for the purpose of receiving any notices that may be sent pursuant to Code Section 17–6–71. Each professional bondsman shall have the duty to keep such information current and accurate. It shall be the duty of each clerk of court to keep, maintain, and update such information as provided by a professional bondsman.

Laws 1921, p. 243, § 5; Laws 1994, p. 532, § 3; Laws 2002, p. 942, § A; Laws 2009, Act 137, § 1, eff. May 5, 2009.

Formerly Code 1933, § 27–502.

Historical and Statutory Notes

The 2009 amendment by Act 137 inserted subsec. (d).

§ 17–6–50.1. Continuing education programs for professional bondsmen

(a) The Georgia Association of Professional Bondsmen shall approve continuing education programs offered by professional associations, educational institutions, government agencies, and others as deemed appropriate for professional bondsmen to attend.

(b) The fee for continuing education programs for professional bondsmen shall not exceed $ 125.00 annually.

(c) Professional bondsmen shall be required to obtain eight hours of continuing education annually.

(d) On or before January 31 of each year, each professional bondsman shall submit a certificate of completion of eight hours of approved continuing education to the individual or department which is responsible for issuing bail bonds for each jurisdiction in which he or she is doing business.

Laws 2002, p. 791, § 1.

Historical and Statutory Notes

In 2002, the Code Commission, in subsec. (d), substituted "bondsman" for "bondsmen". See § 28–9–5.

§ 17–6–51. Suggesting employment of attorneys

Professional bondsmen, their agents, or representatives shall not suggest or advise the employment of or name for employment any attorney or attorneys to represent a defendant, during the negotiations for the bondsmen to sign the bond or subsequent thereto.

Laws 1921, p. 243, § 2.

Formerly Code 1933, § 27–503.

§ 17–6–52. Soliciting business by bondsmen and attorneys

Professional bondsmen, their agents, or employees shall not solicit business as bondsmen or loiter about or around jails, places where prisoners are confined, or the courts for the purpose of engaging in or soliciting business as such bondsmen. No state or municipal law enforcement officer or keeper or employee of a penal institution may suggest to or give advice to, in any manner whatsoever, any prisoner regarding the services of a professional bondsman to write a criminal bond for the appearance of a prisoner in any court at any time.

Laws 1921, p. 243, § 3.

Formerly Code 1933, § 27–504.

§ 17–6–53. Participation in defense prohibited

Professional bondsmen, their agents, or employees shall not advise defendants who are principals in bonds signed by them or give any directions in the defense or disposition of the cases in which they sign bonds.

Laws 1921, p. 243, § 4.

Formerly Code 1933, § 27–505.

§ 17–6–54. Payments to and by; forfeiture of bond; surrender of custody of defendant

(a) No professional bondsman or his or her agents or employees who receive compensation for becoming the surety on a criminal bond shall thereafter receive any other sum in the case. If the surety surrenders a defendant into the custody of the court, the sheriff, or another law enforcement officer in the jurisdiction where the bond was made before final disposition of the case, the surety is required to return to the principal the compensation received for signing the bond as surety if such surrender of the defendant is for reasons other than:

(1) The defendant's arrest for a crime other than a traffic violation or misdemeanor;

(2) The defendant's cosigner attests in writing the desire to be released from the bond;

(3) The defendant fails to provide to the court and the surety the defendant's change of address;

(4) The defendant fails to pay any fee due to the surety after being notified by certified mail or statutory overnight delivery that the same is past due;

(5) The defendant fails to notify the court and the surety upon leaving the jurisdiction of the court; or

(6) The defendant provides false information to the surety.

(b) In the event of a forfeiture on the bond by the defendant, the surety shall have the right to surrender into custody the defendant who is the principal on the bond without returning any compensation paid by the defendant for the signing of the bond.

Laws 1921, p. 243, §§ 6, 7; Laws 1996, p. 1233, § 2; Laws 2000, p. 1589, § 3.

Formerly Code 1933, §§ 27–506, 27–507.

§ 17–6–55. Violations relating to sureties on criminal bonds

Any person who violates any Code section in this part shall be guilty of a misdemeanor.

Laws 1921, p. 243, § 8.

Formerly Code 1933, § 27–9903.

§ 17–6–56. Qualifications and registration of bail recovery agents

(a) As used in this Code section and Code Sections 17–6–57 and 17–6–58, the term "bail recovery agent" means any person who performs services or takes action for the purpose of apprehending the principal on a bail bond granted in this state or capturing a fugitive who has escaped from bail in this state for gratuity, benefit, or compensation.

(b) A bail recovery agent must be a United States citizen, 25 years of age or older, and must obtain a license pursuant to Code Section 16–11–129.

(c) Any sheriff of a county shall require any professional bondsman who is a resident of or doing business in the sheriff's county to register his or her bail recovery agents in that county. The professional bondsman must submit to the sheriff, in a form and manner to be determined by the sheriff, a list of all bail recovery agents whose services may be used by such bondsman.

Laws 1999, p. 546, § 1.1.

§ 17–6–56.1. Continuing education programs for bail recovery agents

(a) The Georgia Association of Professional Bondsmen shall approve continuing education programs offered by professional associations, educational institutions, government agencies, and others as deemed appropriate for bail recovery agents to attend.

(b) The fee for continuing education programs for bail recovery agents shall not exceed $ 125.00 annually.

(c) Bail recovery agents shall be required to obtain eight hours of continuing education annually.

(d) On or before January 31 of each year, each bail recovery agent shall submit a certificate of completion of eight hours of approved continuing education to the individual or department which is responsible for issuing bail bonds for each jurisdiction in which he or she is doing business.

Laws 2002, p. 791, § 2.

§ 17–6–57. Notification of sheriff and police chief when action to be taken by bail recovery agent; out-of-state bail recovery agents; uniform identification cards

(a) Any bail recovery agent who enters any local police jurisdiction in pursuit of and for the purpose of apprehending the principal on a bail bond or capturing a fugitive or engaging in surveillance of such principal or fugitive shall, prior to taking any action in his or her capacity as a bail recovery agent in that local police jurisdiction, notify by facsimile transmission or telephone the sheriff and police chief of the local police jurisdiction in which the surveillance, apprehension, or capture is to take place unless it is to take place in public.

(b) An out-of-state bail recovery agent shall submit proof to the sheriff or police chief that he or she is qualified to be a bail recovery agent under the requirements of his or her home state. An out-of-state bail recovery agent shall deliver a certified copy of the bail bond or of the forfeiture or failure to appear to the sheriff or chief of police. Such out-of-state bail recovery agent, if not qualified in his or her home state or if his or her home state does not require bail recovery agents to be qualified, shall employ a Georgia bail recovery agent who is lawfully registered pursuant to this part.

(c) Each professional bondsman shall issue a uniform identification card to each bail recovery agent registered by the professional bondsman which identification card shall include the bail recovery agent's name, height, weight, address, photograph, and signature. The identification card shall also include the signature of the professional bondsman who has registered the bail recovery agent as required in subsection (c) of Code Section 17–6–56. A bail recovery agent shall be required to carry such identification card while acting in the capacity as a bail recovery agent.

Laws 1999, p. 546, § 1.1.

§ 17–6–58. Penalties for bail recovery agents and for bondsmen; civil liability

(a) Any bail recovery agent who fails to register with the local sheriff or who is otherwise unqualified to act as a bail recovery agent but who nonetheless attempts to apprehend or capture a principal on a bail bond or a fugitive or who succeeds in apprehending or capturing such person shall be guilty of a misdemeanor upon conviction for the first violation and shall be guilty of a felony upon conviction for the second and all subsequent violations punishable by imprisonment for not less than one nor more than five years.

(b) Any bondsman or bonding company owner, surety, or agent who hires a bail recovery agent who is not qualified to act as a bail recovery agent pursuant to Code Sections 17–6–56 and 17–6–57 shall be guilty of a misdemeanor upon conviction for the first violation and shall be guilty of a felony upon conviction for the second and all subsequent violations punishable by imprisonment for not less than one nor more than five years, or a fine of not more than $ 10,000.00, or both.

(c) No bail recovery agent shall wear, carry, or display any uniform, badge, shield, card, or other item with any printing, insignia, or emblem that purports to indicate that such bail recovery agent is an employee, officer, or agent of any state or federal government or any political subdivision of any state or federal government. A violation of this subsection shall be punished upon conviction as a felony punishable by imprisonment for not less than one nor more than five years, or a fine of not more than $ 10,000.00, or both.

(d) A bail recovery agent who enters the wrong property, causes damage to said property, or causes injury to anyone thereon is liable for all damages.

Laws 1999, p. 546, § 1.1.

Article 3

Proceedings for Forfeiture of Bonds or Recognizances

§ 17–6–70. Bond forfeiture proceedings

(a) A bond forfeiture occurs at the end of the court day upon the failure of appearance of a principal of any bond or recognizance given for the appearance of that person.

(b) An appearance bond shall not be forfeited unless the clerk of the court gave the surety at least 72 hours' written notice, exclusive of Saturdays, Sundays, and legal holidays, before the time of the required appearance of the principal. Notice shall not be necessary if the time for appearance is within 72 hours from the time of arrest, provided the time for appearance is stated on the bond, or where the principal is given actual notice in open court.

Laws 1831, Cobb's 1851 Digest, p. 861; Laws 1878–79, p. 57, § 1; Laws 1966, p. 430, § 1; Laws 1982, p. 1224, § 2; Laws 1986, p. 1588, § 2; Laws 1987, p. 1342, § 2; Laws 1990, p. 8, § 17; Laws 1992, p. 6, § 17; Laws 1992, p. 2933, § 2.

Formerly Code 1863, § 4584; Code 1868, § 4605; Code 1873, § 4702; Code 1882, § 4702; Penal Code 1895, § 936; Penal Code 1910, § 961; Code 1933, § 27–905.

§ 17–6–70.1. Repealed by Laws 1983, p. 1203, § 1, eff. March 29, 1983

§ 17–6–71. Hearings; notice; orders

(a) The judge shall, at the end of the court day, upon the failure of the principal to appear, forfeit the bond and order an execution hearing not sooner than 120 days but not later than 150 days after such failure to appear. Notice of the execution hearing shall be served by the clerk of the court in which the bond forfeiture occurred within ten days of such failure to appear by certified mail or by electronic means as provided in Code Section 17–6–50 to the surety at the address listed on the bond or by personal service to the surety within ten days of such failure to appear at its home office or to its designated registered agent. Service shall be considered complete upon the mailing of such certified notice. Such ten-day notice shall be adhered to strictly. If notice of the execution hearing is not served as specified in this subsection, the surety shall be relieved of liability on the appearance bond.

(b) If at the execution hearing it is determined that judgment should be entered, the judge shall so order and a writ of fieri facias shall be filed in the office of the clerk of the court where such judgment is entered. The provisions of this subsection shall apply to all bail bonds, whether returnable to superior court, state court, probate court, magistrate court, or municipal court.

Laws 1831, Cobb's 1851 Digest, p. 862; Laws 1943, p. 282, § 2; Laws 1953, Jan.-Feb. Sess., p. 452, § 1; Laws 1982, p. 1224, § 2; Laws 1983, p. 1203, § 2; Laws 1986, p. 1588, § 3; Laws 1987, p. 1342, § 3; Laws 1989, p. 556, § 1; Laws 1990, p. 8, § 17; Laws 1990, p. 2336, § 1; Laws 1992, p. 2933, § 3; Laws 2000, p. 1589, § 3; Laws 2009, Act 137, § 2, eff. May 5, 2009.

Formerly Code 1863, § 4585; Code 1868, § 4606; Code 1873, § 4703; Code 1882, § 4703; Penal Code 1895, § 937; Penal Code 1910, § 962; Code 1933, § 27–906.

Historical and Statutory Notes

The 2009 amendment by Act 137, in subsec. (a), inserted "by the clerk of court in which the bond forfeiture occurred", substituted "by electronic means as provided in Code Section 17–6–50" for "statutory overnight delivery" and added the third sentence.

§ 17–6–72. Forfeiture of appearance bond avoided; avoidance where principal confined in another jurisdiction

(a) No judgment shall be rendered on a forfeiture of any appearance bond if it is shown to the satisfaction of the court by the written statement of a licensed physician that the principal on the bond was prevented from attending by some mental or physical disability.

(b) No judgment shall be rendered on a forfeiture of any appearance bond if it is shown to the satisfaction of the court that the principal on the bond was prevented from attending because he or she was detained by reason of arrest, sentence, or confinement in a penal institution or jail in the State of Georgia, or so detained in another jurisdiction, or because he or she was involuntarily confined or detained pursuant to court order in a mental institution in the State of Georgia or in another jurisdiction. An official written notice of the holding institution in which the principal is being detained or confined shall be considered proof of the principal's detention or confinement and such notice may be sent from the holding institution by mail or delivered by hand or by facsimile machine. Upon the presentation of such written notice to the clerk of the proper court, the prosecuting attorney, and the sheriff or other law enforcement officer having jurisdiction over the case, along with a letter of intent to pay all costs of returning the principal to the jurisdiction of the court, such notice and letter shall serve as the surety's request for a detainer or hold to be placed on the principal. Should there be a failure to place a detainer or hold within 15 days, excluding Saturdays, Sundays, and legal holidays, and after such presentation of such notice and letter of intent to pay costs, the surety shall then be relieved of the liability for the appearance bond without further order of the court.

(c) No judgment shall be rendered on a forfeiture of any appearance bond if it is shown to the satisfaction of the court that prior to the entry of the judgment on the forfeiture the principal on the bond is in the custody of the sheriff or other responsible law enforcement agency. An official written notice of the holding institution in which the principal is being detained or confined shall be considered proof of the principal's detention or confinement and such notice may be sent from the holding institution by mail or delivered by hand or by facsimile machine. Upon presentation of such written notice to the clerk of the proper court, the prosecuting attorney, and the sheriff or other law enforcement officer having jurisdiction over the case along with a letter of intent to pay all costs of returning the principal to the jurisdiction of the court, such notice and letter shall serve as the surety's request for a detainer or hold to be placed against the principal. Should there be a failure to place a detainer or hold within 15 days, excluding Saturdays, Sundays, and legal holidays, and after presentation of such notice and letter of intent to pay costs, the surety shall then be relieved of the liability for the appearance bond without further order of the court.

(c.1) No judgment shall be rendered on a forfeiture of any appearance bond if it is shown to the satisfaction of the court that the principal on the bond was prevented from attending because he or she was deported by federal authorities. An official written notice of such deportation from a federal official shall be considered proof of the principal's deportation.

(d) In cases in which paragraph (3) of this subsection is not applicable, on application filed within 120 days from the payment of judgment, the court shall order remission under the following conditions:

(1) Provided the bond amount has been paid within 120 days after judgment and the delay has not prevented prosecution of the principal and upon application to the court with prior notice to the prosecuting attorney of such application, said court shall direct remission of 95 percent of the bond amount remitted to the surety if the surety locates the principal in the custody of the sheriff in the jurisdiction where the bond was made or in another jurisdiction causing the return of the principal to the jurisdiction where the bond was made, apprehends, surrenders, or produces the principal, if the apprehension or surrender of the principal was substantially procured or caused by the surety, or if the location of the principal by the surety caused the adjudication of the principal in the jurisdiction in which the bond was made. Should the surety, within two years of the principal's failure to appear, locate the principal in the custody of the sheriff in the jurisdiction where the bond was made or in another jurisdiction causing the return of the principal to the jurisdiction where the bond was made, appre-

hend, surrender, or produce the principal, if the apprehension or surrender of the principal is substantially procured or caused by the surety, or if the location of the principal by the surety causes the adjudication of the principal in the jurisdiction in which the bond was made, the surety shall be entitled to a refund of 50 percent of the bond amount. The application for 50 percent remission shall be filed no later than 30 days following the expiration of the two-year period following the date of judgment;

(2) Remission shall be granted upon condition of the payment of court costs and of the expenses of returning the principal to the jurisdiction by the surety; or

(3) If, within 120 days after judgment, the surety surrenders the principal to the sheriff or responsible law enforcement officer, or said surrender has been denied by the sheriff or responsible law enforcement officer, or surety locates the principal in custody in another jurisdiction, the surety shall only be required to pay costs and 5 percent of the face amount of the bond, which amount includes all surcharges. If it is shown to the satisfaction of the court, by the presentation of competent evidence from the sheriff or the holding institution, that said surrender has been made or denied or that the principal is in custody in another jurisdiction or that said surrender has been made and that 5 percent of the face amount of the bond and all costs have been tendered to the sheriff, the court shall direct that the judgment be marked satisfied and that the writ of execution, fi. fa., be canceled.

Laws 1965, p. 266, §§ 1–3; Laws 1982, p. 1224, § 2; Laws 1982, p. 1658, § 2; Laws 1983, p. 3, § 14; Laws 1983, p. 1203, § 3; Laws 1985, p. 982, § 1; Laws 1986, p. 1588, § 4; Laws 1987, p. 1342, § 4; Laws 1989, p. 556, § 2; Laws 1990, p. 2336, § 2; Laws 1992, p. 2933, § 4; Laws 1996, p. 1233, § 3; Laws 2009, Act 137, § 2A, eff. May 5, 2009.

Historical and Statutory Notes

The 2009 amendment by Act 137 inserted subsec. (c.1).

§ 17–6–73. Mailing address of principal and surety

Every bond or recognizance given to secure the appearance of any person in any criminal proceeding shall have entered thereon the mailing address of the principal and each surety.

Laws 1982, p. 1224, § 2.

Article 4

Bonds for Good Behavior and to Keep the Peace

Part 1

Bonds for Good Behavior

§ 17–6–90. Authority to require bond

(a) Any judicial officer authorized to hold a court of inquiry may, upon the information of others under oath or upon his or her own motion, issue a warrant against any person in the county whose conduct is such as to justify the belief that the safety of any one or more persons in the county or the peace or property of the same is in danger of being injured or disturbed thereby. Upon the return of the warrant and upon sufficient cause being shown, the court may require from the person a bond with sureties for such person's good behavior until the next term of the superior court of the county or for a period of up to six months, whichever is greater. Any person against whom a warrant issues must, within 24 hours, be brought for a hearing before the court which issued the warrant or be released on bond by the sheriff, the amount and reasonable conditions of such bond to be set by the court which issued the warrant.

(b) All bonds posted under this Code section shall be returnable in the court which issued the warrant and shall be amendable in the court's discretion. Within seven days after being released on bond by the sheriff, the person shall be entitled to a hearing before the court which issued the warrant. The court may, on its own motion, require a hearing.

(c) If it is determined at a hearing that there was not sufficient cause for the warrant to have been issued, the affiant who caused the warrant to be issued shall pay all court costs.

Laws 1974, p. 322, § 1; Laws 1978, p. 1924, § 1; Laws 1986, p. 1151, § 1; Laws 2007, Act 250, § 1, eff. July 1, 2007.

Formerly Code 1863, § 4627; Code 1868, § 4651; Code 1873, § 4749; Code 1882, § 4749; Penal Code 1895, § 1235; Penal Code 1910, § 1317; Code 1933, § 76–101.

Historical and Statutory Notes

The 2007 amendment by Act 250, in subsec. (a), inserted gender neutral language and substituted "up to six months" for "sixty days".

§ 17–6–91. Spouse may require bond

A person may require a bond for good behavior against the spouse of such person.

Formerly Code 1863, § 4634; Code 1868, § 4658; Code 1873, § 4756; Code 1882, § 4756; Penal Code 1895, § 1242; Penal Code 1910, § 1324; Code 1933, § 76–104.

§ 17–6–92. Suit for breach of bond; disposition of recovery

For a violation of a bond posted pursuant to Code Section 17–6–90, an action may be brought at the instance of any person in the county. The recovery on the bond shall be paid to the person bringing the action.

Laws 1981, p. 622, § 1.

Formerly Code 1863, § 4628; Code 1868, § 4652; Code 1873, § 4750; Code 1882, § 4750; Penal Code 1895, § 1236; Penal Code 1910, § 1318; Code 1933, § 76–102.

§ 17–6–93. Extension from term to term

A bond for good behavior posted pursuant to Code Section 17–6–90 may be extended from term to term by the superior or state court, as the case may be, or for additional 60 day periods by the court which issued the warrant, whichever is greater, in its discretion. The sureties on the bond shall have the privilege of surrendering their principal as in other cases of bail.

Laws 1986, p. 1151, § 2.

Formerly Code 1863, § 4629; Code 1868, § 4653; Code 1873, § 4751; Code 1882, § 4751; Penal Code 1895, § 1237; Penal Code 1910, § 1319; Code 1933, § 76–103.

§ 17–6–94. Contempt proceedings for violation of bonds

Upon oral or written complaint by the injured party or upon motion by the prosecuting attorney, the court may, in its discretion, issue a rule for contempt against a party who violates the bond posted pursuant to Code Section 17–6–90. Upon hearing the rule, if the court finds that there has been a violation of the bond, the court may, in addition to the remedy provided in Code Section 17–6–92, impose a sentence for contempt of court. If it should appear to the court from the evidence and the court finds that the violation of the bond was provoked or brought about by the conduct of the prosecuting witness, the witness may be ruled for contempt of court and sentenced as provided by law.

Laws 1986, p. 1151, § 3.

Part 2

Bonds to Keep the Peace

§ 17–6–110. Authority to require bond

(a) Upon the information of any person, under oath, that he is in fear of bodily harm to himself or his family, or of violent injury to his property, from another person, any judicial officer authorized to hold a court of inquiry may issue his warrant requiring the arrest of such other person. If, after the return of the warrant and upon hearing the evidence of both parties, the court is satisfied that probable cause for such fear exists, the court may require the accused to give bond, with good security, to keep the peace as against the person, family, or property of the affiant. If the accused fails to give bond, the court shall commit him to jail. Any person against whom a warrant issues must, within 24 hours, be brought for a hearing before the court which issued the warrant or be released on bond by the sheriff.

(b) Nothing in this Code section shall prohibit the sheriff from releasing the person at any time prior to the hearing after posting bond. The amount of the bond shall be set by the sheriff but in no event shall the amount set by the sheriff exceed $1,000.00. Such bond shall contain the same conditions as a bond required after a hearing by the court of inquiry, except that, in counties in which a state court is established, all bonds posted under this Code section shall be returnable in the state court rather than in the superior court. Within five days after being released on bond by the sheriff, the person shall be entitled to a hearing before the court of inquiry.

(c) If it is determined at the hearing that there was not sufficient cause for the warrant to have been issued, the affiant who caused the warrant to be issued shall pay all court costs.

(d) A judicial officer shall not be required to issue the warrant provided for in this Code section until the person requesting the issuance of the warrant deposits with the judicial officer a sum, not to exceed $12.00, to be applied against the total cost in the proceedings. At the termination of the proceedings, any part of the deposit remaining because of dismissal or because the costs are assessed against another party shall be refunded to the depositor. If the person requesting the issuance of the warrant is unable to pay any deposit, fee, or other cost which would normally be required in the court and subscribes an affidavit to the effect that because of his indigence he is unable to pay these costs, the person shall be relieved from paying the costs and his rights shall be the same as if he had paid the costs.

Laws 1850, Cobb's 1851 Digest, p. 865; Laws 1962, p. 121, § 1; Laws 1974, p. 322, § 2; Laws 1978, p. 1924, § 2; Laws 1990, p. 8, § 17.

Formerly Code 1863, § 4630; Code 1868, § 4654; Code 1873, § 4752; Code 1882, § 4752; Penal Code 1895, § 1238; Penal Code 1910, § 1320; Code 1933, § 76–201.

§ 17–6–111. Spouse may require bond

A person may require a bond to keep the peace against the spouse of such person.

Formerly Code 1863, § 4634; Code 1868, § 4658; Code 1873, § 4756; Code 1882, § 4756; Penal Code 1895, § 1242; Penal Code 1910, § 1324; Code 1933, § 76–205.

§ 17–6–112. Breach of the peace; right of action

(a) Actual violence, a threat of violence, or any other act intended and calculated to excite alarm or to provoke a breach of the peace shall be a violation of the bond posted pursuant to Code Section 17–6–110. For every such act, the party at whose instance the bond was required shall have a right of action.

(b) In counties having a population of not less than 200,000 nor more than 250,000 according to the United States decennial census of 1950 or any future such census in which there is located a municipal court, upon oral or written complaint by the injured party, the court may in its discretion issue a rule for contempt against the offending defendant. Upon hearing the rule, if the court finds that there has been a violation of the bond, the court may, in addition to the remedy provided in subsection (a) of this Code section, impose a sentence for contempt of court. If it should appear to the court from the evidence and the court finds that the breach of the peace was provoked or brought about by the conduct of the prosecuting witness, the witness may be ruled for contempt of court and sentenced as provided by law.

Laws 1959, p. 3085, § 1; Laws 1982, p. 2107, § 16.

Formerly Code 1863, § 4631; Code 1868, § 4655; Code 1873, § 4753; Code 1882, § 4753; Penal Code 1895, § 1239; Penal Code 1910, § 1321; Code 1933, § 76–202.

§ 17–6–113. Provoking breach of bond; effect

If the person who required the bond provokes a violation thereof by the person who posted the bond, no recovery shall be had.

Formerly Code 1863, § 4632; Code 1868, § 4656; Code 1873, § 4754; Code 1882, § 4754; Penal Code 1895, § 1240; Penal Code 1910, § 1322; Code 1933, § 76–203.

§ 17–6–114. Discharge or extension of bond

The superior or state court, as the case may be, may discharge the bond at any time unless a motion is made to extend it, accompanied by evidence to satisfy the court of the necessity of the extension.

Formerly Code 1863, § 4633; Code 1868, § 4657; Code 1873, § 4755; Code 1882, § 4755; Penal Code 1895, § 1241; Penal Code 1910, § 1323; Code 1933, § 76–204.

CHAPTER 7

PRETRIAL PROCEEDINGS

Article 1

Article 2

Article 1

General Provisions

§ 17-7-1. County sending prisoner to jail in adjoining county liable for fees

When there is no secure jail in a county or when it is deemed necessary by the sheriff, any person committing an offense in the county may be sent to a jail in another county determined to be suitable by the sheriff. The county where the offense is committed shall be primarily liable for jail fees and costs and shall pay the same monthly in advance to the county holding the prisoner. For the purpose of raising funds to pay the costs, the county governing authority may levy and collect an additional tax.

Laws 1865-66, p. 40, §§ 1-3; Laws 1995, p. 291, § 1.

Formerly Code 1868, § 4642; Code 1873, § 4740; Code 1882, § 4740; Penal Code 1895, § 920; Penal Code 1910, § 945; Code 1933, § 27-416.

§ 17-7-2. Receipt of prisoner from another county

The sheriff shall not be bound to receive a prisoner from another county until the jail fees and costs are provided for as set forth in Code Section 17-7-1.

Laws 1865-66, p. 40, § 2.

Formerly Code 1868, § 4643; Code 1873, § 4741; Code 1882, § 4741; Penal Code 1895, § 921; Penal Code 1910, § 946; Code 1933, § 27-417.

§ 17-7-3. Detention facilities required to provide weekly lists of juveniles detained pending trial; information to be included

The official in charge of any facility in which a child is detained pending trial in the superior, state, or juvenile courts, including but not limited to sheriffs, regional jail authorities, and the Department of Juvenile Justice, shall furnish at least once a week a list of all children so detained to the chief judge, or his or her designee, and the prosecuting attorney for the court or courts having jurisdiction to adjudicate the case against the child. The list shall include the following information pertaining to each child:

(1) The child's name;

(2) The date of arrest;

(3) The offense charged or other reason for being held;

(4) The amount of the bond, if known; and

(5) Whether the child is represented by an attorney and, if represented, the name of the attorney.

Laws 2006, Act 475, § 1, eff. July 1, 2006.

Article 2

Commitment Hearings

§ 17-7-20. Who may hold courts of inquiry

Any judge of a superior or state court, judge of the probate court, magistrate, or officer of a municipality who has the criminal jurisdiction of a magistrate may hold a court of inquiry to examine into an accusation against a person legally arrested and brought before him or her. The time and place of the inquiry shall be determined by such judicial officer. Should the county in which the offense is alleged to have been committed be a member of a regional jail authority created under Article 5 of Chapter 4 of Title 42, the "Regional Jail Authorities Act," the judge may order the court of inquiry to be conducted alternatively in the county in which the offense is alleged to have been committed or in facilities available at the regional jail or by audio-visual communication between the two locations and between the accused, the court, the attorneys, and the witnesses.

Laws 1982, p. 493, §§ 1, 2; Laws 1983, p. 884, § 3-19; Laws 1996, p. 742, § 2.

Formerly Code 1863, § 4611; Code 1868, § 4633; Code 1873, § 4730; Code 1882, § 4730; Penal Code 1895, § 906; Penal Code 1910, § 931; Code 1933, § 27-401.

§ 17-7-21. Associates of officer holding court of inquiry

The judicial officer before whom the accused is brought may associate with him, in the investigation, one or more magistrates, in which event a majority shall decide all questions. If there are only two presiding, the original officer shall determine all the questions where the court is not in agreement.

Laws 1984, p. 22, § 17.

Formerly Code 1863, § 4612; Code 1868, § 4634; Code 1873, § 4731; Code 1882, § 4731; Penal Code 1895, § 907; Penal Code 1910, § 932; Code 1933, § 27-402.

§ 17-7-22. Courts of municipal corporations may commit offenders

Any mayor, recorder, or other proper officer presiding in any court of a municipal corporation shall have authority to bind over or commit to jail offenders against any criminal law whenever, in the course of an investigation before such officer, a proper case therefor is made out by the evidence.

Laws 1880-81, p. 176, § 2.

Formerly Code 1882, § 786c; Penal Code 1895, § 927; Penal Code 1910, § 952; Code 1933, § 27-423.

§ 17-7-23. Rule of decision; commitment of accused; limited jurisdiction of certain courts

(a) The duty of a court of inquiry is simply to determine whether there is sufficient reason to suspect the guilt of the accused and to require him to appear and answer before the court competent to try him. Whenever such probable cause exists, it is the duty of the court to commit.

(b) Any court, other than a superior court or a state court, to which any charge of a violation of Code Section 16-11-126 is referred for the determination required by this Code section shall thereafter have and exercise only the jurisdiction of a court of inquiry with respect to the charge and with respect to any other criminal violation arising from the transaction on which the charge was based and shall not thereafter be competent to try the accused for the charge or for any other criminal violation arising from the transaction on which the charge was based, irrespective of the jurisdiction that the court otherwise would have under any other law.

Laws 1980, p. 415, § 1; Laws 2010, Act 643, § 2-11, eff. June 4, 2010.

Formerly Code 1863, § 4618; Code 1868, § 4640; Code 1873, § 4738; Code 1882, § 4738; Penal Code 1895, § 912; Penal Code 1910, § 937; Code 1933, § 27-407.

Historical and Statutory Notes

The 2010 amendment by Act 643, in subsec. (b), deleted "or Code Section 16-11-128" following "Code Section 16-11-126".

Laws 2010, Act 643, § 3-1, provides:

"This Act shall become effective upon its approval by the Governor or upon its becoming law without such approval and shall apply to all offenses committed on and after such date. The enactment of this Act shall not affect any prosecutions for acts occurring before the effective date of this Act and shall not act as an abatement of any such prosecutions."

§ 17-7-24. Time granted parties for preparation of case; bail

A reasonable time shall be given to the defendant and prosecutor for the preparation of the case. In no event shall the defendant be forced to attend the hearing without the aid of counsel if there is a reasonable probability of his securing counsel without too great delay. Where the hearing is postponed to a future day at the instance of either party or the court, it shall not be necessary to commit the defendant to jail pending the hearing; but he shall have the right to give bail for appearance at the hearing before the court of inquiry if the offense is bailable under the authority of the court.

Laws 1865-66, p. 236, § 1.

Formerly Code 1863, § 4613; Code 1868, § 4635; Code 1873, § 4732; Code 1882, § 4732; Penal Code 1895, § 908; Penal Code 1910, § 933; Code 1933, § 27-403.

§ 17-7-25. Attendance of witnesses

A court of inquiry shall have the same power to compel the attendance of witnesses as in other criminal cases, as set forth in and subject to all of the provisions of Chapter 10 of Title 24, at any location where the court shall conduct a hearing, provided that notice is given at least 24 hours prior to the hearing. A court of inquiry may order the arrest of witnesses if required to compel their attendance.

Laws 1996, p. 742, § 3.

Formerly Code 1863, § 4617; Code 1868, § 4639; Code 1873, § 4736; Code 1882, § 4736; Penal Code 1895, § 909; Penal Code 1910, § 934; Code 1933, § 27–404.

§ 17–7–26. Binding over witnesses

In the event of a commitment of the accused person, the court, in its discretion, may require the witnesses, on behalf of the state or others, to give suitable bonds to secure their appearance at court, with or without sureties, as the circumstances seem to demand.

Formerly Code 1863, § 4616; Code 1868, § 4638; Code 1873, § 4735; Code 1882, § 4735; Penal Code 1895, § 915; Penal Code 1910, § 940; Code 1933, § 27–410.

§ 17–7–27. Amount of bonds for appearance of witnesses; sureties

The sheriffs and constables shall accept bond in such reasonable amount as may be just and fair to secure the appearance of any witness to attend the courts, provided the sureties tendered and offered on the bond are approved by a sheriff of any county.

Laws 1921, p. 241, § 1.

Formerly Code 1933, § 27–411.

§ 17–7–28. Evidence; testimony of defendant

The court of inquiry shall hear all legal evidence submitted by either party. If the defendant wishes to testify and announces in open court before the court of inquiry his intention to do so, he may testify in his own behalf. If he so elects, he shall be sworn as any other witness and may be examined and cross-examined as any other witness, except that no evidence of general bad character or prior convictions shall be admissible unless and until the defendant first puts his character into issue. The failure of a defendant to testify shall create no presumption against him, and no comment may be made because of such failure.

Laws 1962, p. 453, § 1; Laws 1973, p. 292, § 1.

Formerly Code 1863, § 4614; Code 1868, § 4636; Code 1873, § 4733; Code 1882, § 4733; Penal Code 1895, § 910; Penal Code 1910, § 935; Code 1933, § 27–405.

§ 17–7–29. Committing for different offense

A court of inquiry may commit the defendant for a different offense than that stated in the warrant if the evidence requires it.

Formerly Code 1863, § 6422; Code 1868, § 4646; Code 1873, § 4744; Code 1882, § 4744; Penal Code 1895, § 913; Penal Code 1910, § 938; Code 1933, § 27–408.

§ 17–7–30. Form of commitment

The following form, or one in substance the same, shall be deemed to be a sufficient commitment:

Georgia, _____ County.

_____ (name of the defendant) having been arrested on a warrant for the offense of _____ and brought before me, after hearing evidence it is ordered that he be committed for trial for the offense of _____. The jailer of said county (or any other county, if necessary) is required to receive and safely keep him until discharged by due process of law.

Witness my hand and seal, this _____ day of _____, _____.

____

Judicial officer (Seal)

Laws 1999, p. 81, § 17.

Formerly Code 1863, § 4619; Code 1868, § 4641; Code 1873, § 4739; Code 1882, § 4739; Penal Code 1895, § 914; Penal Code 1910, § 939; Code 1933, § 27–409.

§ 17–7–31. State's witnesses to be named on warrants

Whenever any judicial officer sitting as a court of inquiry binds over a defendant to appear at an appropriate court to answer any charge, it shall be the duty of the judicial officer to write on the warrant the names of each witness for the state who appeared at the commitment hearing.

Laws 1873, p. 31, § 1.

Formerly Code 1873, § 4737; Code 1882, § 4737; Penal Code 1895, § 916; Penal Code 1910, § 941; Code 1933, § 27–412.

§ 17–7–32. Disposition of papers

The commitment form shall be delivered to the officer in whose charge the accused person is placed, and the officer shall deliver it with the accused person to the sheriff or the other person in charge of the jail. A memorandum of the commitment shall be entered on the warrant by the judicial officer. The warrant and all other papers shall be forwarded to the clerk of the appropriate court having jurisdiction over the offense for delivery to the prosecuting attorney.

Formerly Code 1863, § 4623; Code 1868, § 4647; Code 1873, § 4745; Code 1882, § 4745; Penal Code 1895, § 924; Penal Code 1910, § 949; Code 1933, § 27–420.

§ 17–7–33. Repealed by Laws 1983, p. 884, § 4–2, eff. July 1, 1983

§ 17–7–34. Informality no ground of discharge

No defendant shall be discharged on a writ of habeas corpus because of informality in the commitment or in the proceedings prior thereto, provided there has been substantial compliance with this article.

Cobb's 1851 Digest, p. 856.

Formerly Code 1863, § 4626; Code 1868, § 4650; Code 1873, § 4748; Code 1882, § 4748; Penal Code 1895, § 926; Penal Code 1910, § 951; Code 1933, § 27–422.

Article 3

Indictments

§ 17–7–50. Persons refused bail entitled to grand jury hearing

Any person who is arrested for a crime and who is refused bail shall, within 90 days after the date of confinement, be entitled to have the charge against him or her heard by a grand jury having jurisdiction over the accused person; provided, however, that if the person is arrested for a crime for which the death penalty is being sought, the superior court may, upon motion of the district attorney for an extension and after a hearing and good cause shown, grant one extension to the 90 day period not to exceed 90 additional days; and, provided, further, that if such extension is granted by the court, the person shall not be entitled to have the charge against him or her heard by the grand jury until the expiration of such extended period. In the event no grand jury considers the charges against the accused person within the 90 day period of confinement or within the extended period of confinement where such an extension is granted by the court, the accused shall have bail set upon application to the court.

Laws 1973, p. 291, § 1; Laws 1996, p. 1233, § 4.

Formerly Code 1933, § 27–701.1.

§ 17–7–50.1. Juvenile arrested and subject to the jurisdiction of the superior court entitled to grand jury hearing; failure to return indictment within 180 days; extensions and exceptions

(a) Any child who is charged with a crime that is within the jurisdiction of the superior court, as provided in Code Section 15–11–28 or 15–11–30.2, who is detained shall within 180 days of the date of detention be entitled to have the charge against him or her presented to the grand jury. The superior court shall, upon motion for an extension of time and after a hearing and good cause shown, grant one extension to the original 180 day period, not to exceed 90 additional days.

(b) If the grand jury does not return a true bill against the detained child within the time limitations set forth in subsection (a) of this Code section, the detained child's case shall be transferred to the juvenile court and shall proceed thereafter as provided in Chapter 11 of Title 15.

(c) The provisions of this Code section shall not apply to any case in which the prosecuting attorney files notice with the court that the detained child is a codefendant to a case in which an adult is charged with committing the same offense and the state has filed a notice of its intention to seek the death penalty.

Laws 2006, Act 475, § 2, eff. July 1, 2006.

§ 17–7–51. Presentments treated as indictments; entry upon minutes

All special presentments by the grand jury charging defendants with violations of the penal laws shall be treated as indictments. It shall not be necessary for the clerk of the court to enter the special presentments in full upon the minutes, but only the statement of the case and finding of the grand jury as in cases of indictments. It shall not be necessary for the district attorney to frame bills of indictment on the special presentments, but he may arraign defendants upon the special presentments and put them on trial in like manner as if the presentments were bills of indictment.

Laws 1873, p. 51, § 1.

Formerly Code 1863, § 4520; Code 1868, § 4539; Code 1873, § 4632; Code 1882, § 4632; Penal Code 1895, § 931; Penal Code 1910, § 956; Code 1933, § 27–703.

§ 17–7–52. Indictment against peace officer; procedure

(a) Before an indictment against a present or former peace officer charging the officer with a crime which is alleged to have occurred while he or she was in the performance of his or her duties is returned by a grand jury, the officer shall be notified of the contemplated action by the district attorney of the county wherein the grand jury shall convene and the officer shall be afforded the rights provided in Code Section 45–11–4.

(b) The requirements of subsection (a) of this Code section shall apply to all prosecutions, whether for misdemeanors or felonies, and no such prosecution shall proceed either in state or superior court without a grand jury indictment.

Laws 1975, p. 607, § 1; Laws 1997, p. 879, § 1; Laws 2001, p. 487, § 5.

§ 17–7–53. Two returns of "no bill" as bar to prosecution

Two returns of "no bill" by grand juries on the same charge or allegation shall be a bar to any future prosecution of a person for the same offense under the same or another name; provided, however, that, if the returns have been procured by the fraudulent conduct of the person charged or there is newly discovered evidence, upon proof, the judge may allow a third bill to be presented, found, and prosecuted.

Laws 1850, Cobb's 1851 Digest, p. 864.

Formerly Code 1863, § 4591; Code 1868, § 4612; Code 1873, § 4708; Code 1882, § 4708; Penal Code 1895, § 930; Penal Code 1910, § 955; Code 1933, § 27–702.

§ 17–7–53.1. Quashing of second grand jury indictment or presentment bars further prosecution

If, upon the return of two "true bills" of indictments or presentments by a grand jury on the same offense, charge, or allegation, the indictments or presentments are quashed for the second time, whether by ruling on a motion, demurrer, special plea or exception, or other pleading of the defendant or by the court's own motion, such actions shall be a bar to any future prosecution of such defendant for the offense, charge, or allegation.

Laws 1987, p. 529, § 1.

§ 17–7–54. Form

(a) Every indictment of the grand jury which states the offense in the terms and language of this Code or so plainly that the nature of the offense charged may easily be understood by the jury shall be deemed sufficiently technical and correct. The form of every indictment shall be substantially as follows:

Georgia, _____ County.

The grand jurors selected, chosen, and sworn for the County of _____, to wit: _____, in the name and behalf of the citizens of Georgia, charge and accuse (name of the accused) of the county and state aforesaid with the offense of _____; for that the said (name of the accused) (state with sufficient certainty the offense and the time and place of committing the same), contrary to the laws of said state, the good order, peace, and dignity thereof.

(b) If there should be more than one count, each additional count shall state:

And the jurors aforesaid, in the name and behalf of the citizens of Georgia, further charge and accuse (name of the accused) with having committed the offense of _____; for that the said (name of the accused) (state with sufficient certainty the offense and the time and place of committing the same) contrary to the laws of said state, the good order, peace, and dignity thereof.

Laws 1833, Cobb's 1851 Digest, p. 833.

Formerly Code 1863, § 4516; Code 1868, § 4535; Code 1873, § 4628; Code 1882, § 4628; Penal Code 1895, § 929; Penal Code 1910, § 954; Code 1933, § 27–701.

§ 17–7–55. Concurrent grand juries

In any term of court when the public interest requires it, the court may empanel one or more concurrent grand juries in accordance with Part 1 of Article 4 of Chapter 12 of Title 15.

Laws 2003, Act 26, § 1, eff. May 14, 2003.

Article 4

Accusations

§ 17–7–70. Trial on accusation; waiver of indictment

(a) In all felony cases, other than cases involving capital felonies, in which defendants have been bound over to the superior court, are confined in jail or released on bond pending a commitment hearing, or are in jail having waived a commitment hearing, the district attorney shall have authority to prefer accusations, and such defendants shall be tried on such accusations, provided that defendants going to trial under such accusations shall, in writing, waive indictment by a grand jury.

(b) Judges of the superior court may open their courts at any time without the presence of either a grand jury or a trial jury to receive and act upon pleas of guilty in misdemeanor cases and in felony cases, except those punishable by death or life imprisonment, when the judge and the defendant consent thereto. The judge may try the issues in such cases without a jury upon an accusation filed by the district attorney where the defendant has waived indictment and consented thereto in writing and counsel is present in court representing the defendant either by virtue of his employment or by appointment by the court.

Laws 1915, p. 32, § 1; Laws 1935, p. 116, § 1; Laws 1972, p. 386, § 1; Laws 1972, p. 623, § 1; Laws 1980, p. 452, § 1.

Formerly Code 1933, § 27–704.

§ 17–7–70.1. Trial upon accusation in certain felony cases without necessity of waiving indictment

(a) (1) In felony cases involving violations of the following:

(A) Code Sections 16–8–2, 16–8–14, 16–8–18, 16–9–1, 16–9–2, 16–9–20, 16–9–31, 16–9–33, 16–9–37, 16–10–52, and 40–5–58;

(B) Article 1 of Chapter 8 of Title 16, relating to theft;

(C) Chapter 9 of Title 16, relating to forgery and fraudulent practices;

(D) Article 3 of Chapter 10 of Title 16, relating to escape and other offenses related to confinement; or

(E) Code Section 16–11–131, relating to possession of a firearm by a convicted felon or first offender probationer,

in which defendants have either been bound over to the superior court based on a finding of probable cause pursuant to a commitment hearing under Article 2 of this chapter or have expressly or by operation of law waived a commitment hearing, the district attorney shall have authority to prefer accusations, and the defendants shall be tried on such accusations according to the same rules of substantive and procedural laws relating to defendants who have been indicted by a grand jury.

(2) All laws relating to rights and responsibilities attendant to indicted cases shall be applicable to cases brought by accusations signed by the district attorney.

(3) The accusation need not be supported by an affidavit except in those cases in which the defendant has not been previously arrested in conjunction with the transaction charged in the accusation.

(a.1) The provisions of subsection (a) of this Code section shall apply to violations of Code Section 16–13–30 whenever there has been a finding of probable cause pursuant to a commitment hearing under Article 2 of this chapter or the accused has waived either expressly or by operation of law the right to this hearing.

(b) Judges of the superior court may open their courts at any time without the presence of either a grand jury or a trial jury to receive and act upon pleas of guilty or nolo contendere in felony and misdemeanor cases. The judge of the superior court may try the issues in such cases without a jury upon an indictment or upon an accusation filed by the district attorney where the defendant has waived trial by jury.

(c) An accusation substantially complying with the form provided in subsections (d) and (e) of Code Section 17–7–71 shall in all cases be sufficient.

(d) The district attorney may not bring an accusation pursuant to this Code section in those cases where the grand jury has heard evidence or conducted an investigation or in which a no bill has been returned.

(e) Notwithstanding the above provisions, nothing in this Code section shall affect the rights of police officers and public officials to appear before a grand jury as provided in Code Sections 17–7–52, 45–11–4, and 45–15–11.

Laws 1992, p. 1808, § 1; Laws 1996, p. 678, § 1; Laws 1998, p. 208, § 1.

§ 17–7–71. Trial of misdemeanors upon accusations; form of accusations; amendment

(a) In all misdemeanor cases, the defendant may be tried upon an accusation framed and signed by the prosecuting attorney of the court. The accusation need not be supported by an affidavit except in those cases where the defendant has not been previously arrested in conjunction with the transaction charged in the accusation and where the accusation is to be used as the basis for the issuance of a warrant for the arrest of the defendant.

(b) (1) In all misdemeanor cases arising out of violations of the laws of this state, relating to (A) the operation and licensing of motor vehicles and operators; (B) the width, height, and length of vehicles and loads; (C) motor common carriers and motor contract carriers; or (D) road taxes on motor carriers as provided in Article 2 of Chapter 9 of Title 48, the defendant may be tried upon the uniform traffic citation and complaint provided for in Article 1 of Chapter 13 of Title 40.

(2) In all misdemeanor cases arising out of violations of the laws of this state relating to game, fish, or boating, the defendant may be tried upon the summons provided for in Code Section 27–1–35.

(c) Every accusation which states the offense in the terms and language of the law or so plainly that the nature of the offense charged may be easily understood by the jury shall be deemed sufficiently technical and correct.

(d) An accusation substantially complying with the following form shall in all cases be sufficient:

IN THE ____ COURT OF ____ COUNTY
STATE OF GEORGIA

On behalf of the people of the State of Georgia, the undersigned, as prosecuting attorney for the county and state aforesaid, does hereby charge and accuse (name of accused) with the offense of ____; for that the said (name of accused) (state with sufficient certainty the offense and the time and place it occurred) contrary to the laws of this state, the good order, peace, and dignity thereof.

/s/ ________________________
(District attorney)
(Solicitor-general)

(e) If there should be more than one count, each additional count shall state:

The undersigned, as prosecuting attorney, does further charge and accuse the said (name of accused) with the offense of ____ (the offense as before); for that the said (name of accused) (state with sufficient certainty the offense and the time and place it occurred), contrary to the laws of this state, the good order, peace, and dignity thereof.

(f) Prior to trial, the prosecuting attorney may amend the accusation, summons, or any citation to allege or to change the allegations regarding any offense arising out of the same conduct of the defendant which gave rise to any offense alleged or attempted to be alleged in the original accusation, summons, or citation. A copy of any such amendment shall be served upon the defendant or his or her counsel and the original filed with the clerk of the court. On motion, the court shall grant the defendant a continuance which is reasonably necessitated by an amendment. If any additional charges against the defendant are made the judge shall advise the defendant that he or she has an automatic right to a continuance.

Laws 1980, p. 452, § 2; Laws 1981, p. 828, § 1; Laws 1982, p. 3, § 17; Laws 1996, p. 748, § 14; Laws 2002, p. 627, § 2.

Formerly Code 1933, § 27–705.

§ 17–7–72. Trial of certain misdemeanor cases upon summons or citation in lieu of accusation

In probate courts which have jurisdiction over misdemeanor possession of marijuana in accordance with Code Sections 16–13–2 and 16–13–30 and certain misdemeanor violations of Code Section 3–3–23 pursuant to Code Section 15–9–30.6, the following offenses may be tried upon a summons or citation without an accusation:

(1) Possession of one ounce or less of marijuana, in accordance with Code Sections 16–13–2 and 16–13–30; and

(2) Any violation of paragraph (2) of subsection (a) of Code Section 3–3–23 which is punishable as a misdemeanor, but not violations punishable as high and aggravated misdemeanors.

Laws 1996, p. 1298, § 2.

§ 17–7–73. Violations relating to littering and related environmental offenses that are punishable as misdemeanors; trial upon summons or citation with or without accusation

In probate, magistrate, and municipal courts that have jurisdiction over violations of Part 2, Part 3, or Part 3A of Article 2 of Chapter 7 of Title 16 or Code Section 32–6–51 or 40–6–248.1 that are punishable as misdemeanors in accordance with Code Section 15–9–30.7, 15–10–2.1, or 36–32–10.3 such offenses may be tried upon a summons or citation with or without an accusation.

Laws 2006, Act 538, § 3–8, eff. July 1, 2006.

Historical and Statutory Notes

Laws 2006, Act 538, § 5–1, provides:

"This Act shall become effective upon its approval by the Governor [April 21, 2006] or upon its becoming law without such approval for purposes of adopting local ordinances to become effective on or after July 1, 2006; and for all other purposes, this Act shall become effective on July 1, 2006."

Article 5

Arraignment and Pleas Generally

§ 17–7–90. Bench warrant; definition; execution; who may take bail

A bench warrant is a warrant issued by a judge for the arrest of a person accused of a crime by a grand jury or for the arrest of a person charged with a crime who has failed to appear in court after actual notice to the person in open court or notice to the person by mailing to his or her last known address or otherwise being notified personally in writing by a court official or officer of the court of the time and place to appear or for the arrest of a person charged with a crime upon the filing by the prosecutor of an accusation supported by affidavit. Every officer is bound to execute the warrant within his or her jurisdiction, and every person so arrested must be committed to jail until bail is tendered. Any judicial officer or the sheriff of the county where the charge was returned may receive the bail, fix the amount of the bond, and approve the sureties unless it is a case that is bailable only before some particular judicial officer.

Laws 1989, p. 623, § 2; Laws 2004, Act 564, § 17, eff. May 13, 2004.

Formerly Code 1863, § 4608; Code 1868, § 4630; Code 1873, § 4727; Code 1882, § 4727; Penal Code 1895, § 932; Penal Code 1910, § 957; Code 1933, § 27–801.

Historical and Statutory Notes

The 2004 amendment by Act 564 was a provision contained in a correction bill.

§ 17–7–91. Notice of date of arraignment; time for trial

(a) In all criminal cases the court shall fix a date on which the defendant shall be arraigned. The clerk of the court, at least five days prior to the date set therefor, shall mail to the accused and his attorney of record, if known, notice of the date which has been fixed for arraignment. For such first service of notice, the clerk shall receive the fee prescribed in Code Section 15–6–77. This notice may be served by the sheriff of the county in which the court is situated or his lawful deputies. If the defendant has posted a bond or recognizance, a copy of the notice shall be mailed to each surety on the bond.

(b) On the date fixed by the court the accused shall be arraigned. The court shall receive the plea of the accused and enter the plea as provided for in this chapter. In those cases in which a plea of not guilty is entered, the court shall set the case down for trial at such time as shall be determined by the court.

(c) The appearance and entering of a plea by the accused shall be a waiver of the notice required in this Code section.

Laws 1966, p. 430, § 2; Laws 1977, p. 1098, § 5; Laws 1982, p. 1224, § 3; Laws 1989, p. 223, § 1; Laws 1990, p. 8, § 17.

Formerly Code 1933, § 27–1401.

§ 17–7–92. Service of notice of filing of indictment or presentment against corporation; plea; judgment for fine and costs

Whenever an indictment, special presentment, or accusation against a corporation doing business in this state is returned or filed in any court having jurisdiction over the offense, the clerk of the court shall issue an original and copy notice to the defendant corporation of the filing of the indictment, special presentment, or accusation, which copy notice shall be served by a sheriff upon any officer of the corporation who is found in his county; or, if there is no such officer in his county, then service shall be upon any agent of the corporation. The sheriff serving the copy notice shall make an entry of such service on the original notice and return the same to the court from which it issued. Such service shall be deemed service upon the corporation. Upon the return of the notice, executed as provided for in this Code section, the indictment, special presentment, or accusation shall stand for trial. At the trial, if the defendant corporation fails to appear, or appearing, fails to plead, the judge shall cause a plea of not guilty to be entered, and the trial shall proceed as though the defendant had appeared and pleaded. Upon the conviction of any corporation in any such trial, there shall be rendered against it a judgment for the fine imposed, together with the costs of the prosecution. Upon judgment, an execution shall issue against the property of the defendant.

Laws 1889, p. 120, §§ 1, 2.

Formerly Penal Code 1895, § 938; Penal Code 1910, § 963; Code 1933, § 27-1001.

§ 17-7-93. Form of arraignment; plea of "guilty"; withdrawal of plea; understanding effect on immigration status

(a) Upon the arraignment of a person accused of committing a crime, the indictment or accusation shall be read to him and he shall be required to answer whether he is guilty or not guilty of the offense charged, which answer or plea shall be made orally by the accused person or his counsel.

(b) If the person pleads "guilty," the plea shall be immediately recorded on the minutes of the court by the clerk, together with the arraignment; and the court shall pronounce the judgment of the law upon the person in the same manner as if he had been convicted of the offense by the verdict of a jury. At any time before judgment is pronounced, the accused person may withdraw the plea of "guilty" and plead "not guilty"; and the former plea shall not be admissible as evidence against him at his trial.

(c) In addition to any other inquiry by the court prior to acceptance of a plea of guilty, the court shall determine whether the defendant is freely entering the plea with an understanding that if he or she is not a citizen of the United States, then the plea may have an impact on his or her immigration status. This subsection shall apply with respect to acceptance of any plea of guilty to any state offense in any court of this state or any political subdivision of this state.

Laws 1833, Cobb's 1851 Digest, p. 834; Laws 2000, p. 808, § 1.

Formerly Code 1863, § 4524; Code 1868, § 4543; Code 1873, § 4636; Code 1882, § 4636; Penal Code 1895, § 946; Penal Code 1910, § 971; Code 1933, § 27-1404.

§ 17-7-94. Standing mute or pleading "not guilty"

If the person accused of committing a crime, upon being arraigned, pleads "not guilty" or stands mute, the clerk shall immediately record upon the minutes of the court the plea of "not guilty," together with the arraignment; and the arraignment and plea shall constitute the issue between the accused and the state.

Laws 1833, Cobb's 1851 Digest, p. 834.

Formerly Code 1863, § 4525; Code 1868, § 4544; Code 1873, § 4638; Code 1882, § 4638; Penal Code 1895, § 947; Penal Code 1910, § 972; Code 1933, § 27-1405.

§ 17-7-95. Plea of nolo contendere; right to enter with consent of judge; imposition of sentence; subsequent use against defendant

(a) The defendant in all criminal cases other than capital felonies in any court of this state, whether the offense charged is a felony or a misdemeanor, may, with the consent and approval of the judge of the court, enter a plea of nolo contendere instead of a plea of guilty or not guilty.

(b) Should the judge allow a plea of nolo contendere to be entered, he shall thereupon be authorized to impose such sentence as may be authorized by law as to the offense charged.

(c) Except as otherwise provided by law, a plea of nolo contendere shall not be used against the defendant in any other court or proceedings as an admission of guilt or otherwise or for any purpose; and the plea shall not be deemed a plea of guilty for the purpose of effecting any civil disqualification of the defendant to hold public office, to vote, to serve upon any jury, or any other civil disqualification imposed upon a person convicted of any offense under the laws of this state. The plea shall be deemed and held to put the defendant in jeopardy within the meaning of Article I, Section I, Paragraph XVIII of the Constitution of this state after sentence has been imposed.

Laws 1946, p. 142, §§ 1-3; Laws 1982, p. 3, § 17; Laws 1983, p. 3, § 51.

§ 17-7-96. Arraignment and plea to be entered on the indictment or accusation

The arraignment and plea of the person accused of committing a crime shall be entered on the indictment or accusation by the prosecuting attorney or other person acting as prosecuting officer on the part of the state.

Laws 1833, Cobb's 1851 Digest, p. 835.

Formerly Code 1863, § 4528; Code 1868, § 4547; Code 1873, § 4641; Code 1882, § 4641; Penal Code 1895, § 949; Penal Code 1910, § 974; Code 1933, § 27-1407.

§ 17-7-97. Issue may be recorded afterward

If the clerk of the court shall fail or neglect to record the arraignment and plea of the person accused of committing a crime at the time the arraignment and plea are made, the recordation may be done at any time afterward by order of the court; and this shall cure the error or omission of the clerk.

Laws 1833, Cobb's 1851 Digest, p. 835.

Formerly Code 1863, § 4527; Code 1868, § 4546; Code 1873, § 4640; Code 1882, § 4640; Penal Code 1895, § 948; Penal Code 1910, § 973; Code 1933, § 27-1406.

Article 6

Demurrers, Motions, and Special Pleas and Exceptions

Part 1

General Provisions

§ 17-7-110. Filing of pretrial motions; time limitation

All pretrial motions, including demurrers and special pleas, shall be filed within ten days after the date of arraignment, unless the time for filing is extended by the court.

Laws 2003, Act 26, § 2, eff. May 14, 2003.

Historical and Statutory Notes

Former § 17-7-110 was repealed by Laws 1994, p. 1895, § 1, effective January 1, 1995.

§ 17-7-111. Demurrers and special pleas to be in writing; right to plead "not guilty"

If the defendant, upon being arraigned, demurs to the indictment, pleads to the jurisdiction of the court, pleads in abatement, or enters any other special plea in bar, the demurrer or plea shall be made in writing. If the demurrer or plea is decided against the defendant, he may nevertheless plead and rely on the general issue of "not guilty."

Laws 1833, Cobb's 1851 Digest, p. 834.

Formerly Code 1863, § 4526; Code 1868, § 4545; Code 1873, § 4639; Code 1882, § 4639; Penal Code 1895, § 950; Penal Code 1910, § 975; Code 1933, § 27–1501.

§ 17–7–112. Misnomer, plea of

A plea of misnomer should state the true name of the accused person, that he had never been known by any other name than that, and that he was not known and called by the name which was contained in the indictment or accusation.

Formerly Penal Code 1895, § 954; Penal Code 1910, § 979; Code 1933, § 27–1505.

§ 17–7–113. Time for making exception

All exceptions which go merely to the form of an indictment or accusation shall be made before trial.

Laws 1833, Cobb's 1851 Digest, p. 833.

Formerly Code 1863, § 4517; Code 1868, § 4536; Code 1873, § 4629; Code 1882, § 4629; Penal Code 1895, § 955; Penal Code 1910, § 980; Code 1933, § 27–1601.

Part 2

Insanity and Mental Incompetency

§ 17–7–130. Plea of mental incompetency to stand trial

(a) As used in this Code section, the term:

(1) "Child" means a person under the jurisdiction of the superior court pursuant to Code Section 15–11–28.

(2) "Committing court" means the court which has jurisdiction over the criminal charges against the defendant.

(3) Developmental disability shall have the same meaning as set forth in paragraph (8) of Code Section 37–1–1.

(4) Inpatient shall have the same meaning as in paragraph (9.1) of Code Section 37–3–1; provided, however, that as applied to a child for purposes of this Code section, the term shall mean a child who is mentally ill or has a developmental disability and is in need of involuntary placement.

(5) "Nonviolent offense" means any offense other than:

(A)(i) Murder;

(ii) Rape;

(iii) Aggravated sodomy;

(iv) Armed robbery;

(v) Aggravated assault;

(vi) Hijacking of a motor vehicle or an aircraft;

(vii) Aggravated battery;

(viii) Aggravated sexual battery;

(ix) Aggravated child molestation;

(x) Aggravated stalking;

(xi) Arson in the first degree and in the second degree;

(xii) Stalking;

(xiii) Fleeing and attempting to elude a police officer;

(xiv) Any sexual offense against a minor; or

(xv) Any offense which involves the use of a deadly weapon or destructive device; and

(B) Those felony offenses deemed by the committing court to involve an allegation of actual or potential physical harm to another person.

(6) Outpatient shall have the same meaning as in paragraph (12.1) of Code Section 37–3–1, provided that :

(A) As applied to a child for purposes of this Code section, the term shall mean a child who is mentally ill or has a developmental disability and is in need of involuntary placement; and

(B) The court determines that the defendant meets the criteria for release on bail or other pre-trial release pursuant to Code Section 17–6–1.

(b) Whenever a plea is filed that a defendant in a criminal case is mentally incompetent to stand trial, it shall be the duty of the court to cause the issue of the defendant's mental competency to stand trial to be tried first by a special jury. If the special jury finds the defendant mentally incompetent to stand trial, the court shall retain jurisdiction over the defendant but shall transfer the defendant to the Department of Behavioral Health and Developmental Disabilities and if the defendant is a child, the department shall be authorized to place such defendant in a secure hospital or secure community facility designated by the department; provided, however, that if the defendant is charged with a misdemeanor offense other than as included in subparagraph (a)(5)(A) of this Code section or a nonviolent offense, the court may, in its discretion, retain jurisdiction over the defendant, and may allow evaluation to be done on an outpatient basis by the Department of Behavioral Health and Developmental Disabilities. If the court allows outpatient evaluation and the defendant is in custody, the court may release the defendant in accordance with the provisions of Code Section 17–6–1, et seq.

(c) Within 90 days after the Department of Behavioral Health and Developmental Disabilities has received actual custody of a defendant or, in the case of an outpatient, a court order requiring evaluation of a defendant pursuant to subsection (b) of this Code section, the defendant shall be evaluated and a diagnosis made as to whether the defendant is presently mentally incompetent to stand trial and, if so, whether there is a substantial probability that the defendant will attain mental competency to stand trial in the foreseeable future. If the defendant is found to be mentally competent to stand trial, the department shall immediately report that finding and the reasons therefor to the committing court; and the defendant shall be returned to the court as provided for in subsection (f) of this Code section.

(d) If the defendant is found to be mentally incompetent to stand trial by the Department of Behavioral Health and Developmental Disabilities and there is not a substantial probability that the person will attain competency in the foreseeable future, the department shall return the physical custody of the defendant to a law enforcement officer of the jurisdiction of the court which committed the defendant unless in the opinion of the department's attending physician, and with concurrence of the court, such detention by law enforcement would be detrimental to the well-being of the defendant, in which case the defendant may be held by the department until the date of the defendant's hearing. The department shall report to the committing court the finding regarding competency, the reasons therefor, and its opinion as to whether the defendant currently meets criteria for commitment as an inpatient or as an outpatient pursuant to Chapter 3 or 4 of Title 37. The law enforcement officer of the jurisdiction of the court which committed the defendant shall retain custody of the defendant and the committing court may order an independent evaluation of the defendant by a court appointed licensed clinical psychologist or psychiatrist, who shall report to the court in writing as to the current mental and emotional condition of the defendant. Based on consideration of all evidence and all reports, the committing court may:

(1) If the defendant is not a child, refer the case to the probate court for commitment proceedings pursuant to Chapter 3 or 4 of Title 37, if appropriate and if the charges are dismissed for any reason; or

(2) Retain jurisdiction of the defendant and conduct a hearing at which it shall hear evidence and consider all psychiatric and psychological reports submitted to the court and determine whether the state has proved by clear and convincing evidence that the defendant meets the criteria for involuntary civil commitment as an inpatient or as an outpatient pursuant to Chapter 3 or 4 of Title 37, whichever is applicable. The burden of proof in such hearings shall be upon the state.

(A) If the defendant does not meet the criteria for inpatient or outpatient civil commitment, the defendant shall be released in accordance with the provisions of Code Section 17-6-1 et seq.

(B) If the defendant is found to meet the criteria for involuntary civil commitment as an inpatient or outpatient, the judge may issue an order committing the defendant; provided, however, that if the defendant is a child, the Department of Behavioral Health and Developmental Disabilities shall be authorized to place such defendant in a secure hospital or secure community facility designated by the department.

(i) If the defendant so committed is charged with a misdemeanor offense, the committing court may civilly commit the defendant for a period not to exceed one year. Following the commitment period, the charges against the defendant shall be dismissed by operation of law.

(ii) A defendant who is so committed and is charged with a felony may only be released from that inpatient or outpatient commitment by order of the committing court in accordance with the procedures specified in paragraphs (1) through (3) of subsection (f) of Code Section 17-7-131 except that the burden of proof in such release hearing shall be on the state and if the committed person cannot afford a physician or licensed clinical psychologist of the defendant's choice, the person may petition the court and the court may order such cost to be paid by the county.

The Department of Behavioral Health and Developmental Disabilities shall report annually to the committing court on whether the civilly committed defendant continues to meet criteria for involuntary commitment as an inpatient or an outpatient pursuant to Chapter 3 or 4 of Title 37. The committing court shall review the case and enter an appropriate order, either to renew the inpatient or outpatient civil commitment, to change the commitment either from inpatient to outpatient or from outpatient to inpatient, or in the event charges are dismissed, transfer the jurisdiction of the case to the probate court for further proceedings pursuant to Title 37, if appropriate.

(e) If the defendant is found to be mentally incompetent to stand trial but there is a substantial probability that the person will attain competency in the foreseeable future, by the end of the 90 day period, or at any prior time, the department shall report that finding and the reasons therefor to the committing court and shall retain custody over the defendant for the purpose of continued treatment for an additional period not to exceed nine months; provided, however, that if the defendant is charged with a misdemeanor offense or a nonviolent offense, the court shall retain jurisdiction over the defendant, but may, in its discretion, allow continued treatment to be done on an outpatient basis by the Department of Behavioral Health and Developmental Disabilities. The department shall monitor the defendant's outpatient treatment for an additional period not to exceed nine months. If, by the end of the nine-month period or at any prior time if the defendant's condition warrants, the defendant is still found not to be competent to stand trial, irrespective of the probability of recovery in the foreseeable future, the department shall report that finding and the reasons therefor to the committing court. The committing court shall then follow the procedures in subsection (d) of this Code section for further commitment or release.

(f)(1) If the defendant found to be mentally incompetent to stand trial is at any time found by the Department of Behavioral Health and Developmental Disabilities to be mentally competent to stand trial, the committing court shall be notified. A defendant who is an inpatient and is found by the Department of Behavioral Health and Developmental Disabilities to be mentally competent to stand trial shall be discharged into the custody of a law enforcement officer of the jurisdiction of the court which committed the defendant to the department unless the charges which led to the commitment have been dismissed, in which case the defendant shall be discharged. In the event a law enforcement officer does not appear and take custody of the defendant within 20 days after notice to the appropriate law enforcement official in the jurisdiction of the committing court, the presiding judge of the committing court, and the prosecuting attorney for the court, the department shall itself return the defendant to one of the committing court's detention facilities; and the cost of returning the defendant shall be paid by the county in which the committing court is located. All notifications shall be sent by certified mail or statutory overnight delivery, return receipt requested. With the concurrence of the appropriate court and upon the recommendation of the department's attending physician, any defendant discharged as competent to stand trial may be held by the department instead of at the court's detention facilities whenever, in the attending physician's opinion, such detention in the court's facilities would be detrimental to the well-being of the defendant so committed. Such alternative detention shall continue only until the date of the defendant's trial.

(2) A defendant who is an outpatient and is found by the Department of Behavioral Health and Developmental Disabilities to be mentally competent to stand trial may remain in the community under conditions of bond or other conditions ordered by the committing court, if any, until the date of the person's trial.

(g) Any person found by the Department of Behavioral Health and Developmental Disabilities to be mentally competent to stand trial returned to the court as provided in subsection (f) of this Code section shall again be entitled to file a special plea as provided for in this Code section.

(h) If a defendant is found to be mentally incompetent to stand trial, whether or not committed pursuant to this Code section, the state may file at any time a motion for rehearing on the issue of the defendant's mental competency. The court shall grant said motion upon a showing by the state that there are reasonable grounds to believe that the defendant's mental condition has changed. If this motion is granted, the case shall proceed as provided in subsection (b) of this Code section.

Laws 1977, p. 1293, § 3; Laws 1982, p. 3, § 17; Laws 1995, p. 1250, §§ 1.1, 1.2; Laws 2000, p. 1589, § 3; Laws 2007, Act 348, § 1, eff. July 1, 2007; Laws 2009, Act 102, § 3-2, eff. July 1, 2009; Laws 2010, Act 418, § 12, eff. July 1, 2010.

Formerly Code 1863, § 4195; Code 1868, § 4234; Code 1873, § 4299; Code 1882, § 4299; Penal Code 1895, § 951; Penal Code 1910, § 976; Code 1933, § 27-1502.

Historical and Statutory Notes

The 2007 amendment by Act 348 rewrote the section which had read:

"(a) Whenever a plea is filed that a defendant in a criminal case is mentally incompetent to stand trial, it shall be the duty of the court to cause the issue of the defendant's mental competency to stand trial to be tried first by a special jury. If the special jury finds the defendant mentally incompetent to stand trial, the court shall retain jurisdiction over the defendant but shall transfer the defendant to the Department of Human Resources.

"(b) Within 90 days after the Department of Human Resources has received actual custody of a person pursuant to subsection (a) of this Code section, the person shall be evaluated and a diagnosis made as to whether the person is presently mentally incompetent to stand trial and, if so, whether there is a substantial probability that the person will attain mental competency to stand trial in the foreseeable future. If the person is found to be mentally competent to stand trial, the department shall immediately report that finding and the reasons therefor to the committing court; and the person shall be returned to the court as provided for in subsection (e) of this Code section.

"(c) If the person is found to be mentally incompetent to stand trial by the Department of Human Resources and there is not a substantial probability that the person will attain competency in the foreseeable future, the department shall report that finding and the reasons therefor to the committing court. If the person meets the criteria for civil commitment, he shall thereupon be civilly committed to a state institution pursuant to Chapter 3 or 4 of Title 37, whichever is applicable. If the person does not meet the criteria for civil commitment or if the person after having been committed becomes mentally competent to stand trial, the committing court shall be notified and the person shall be returned to the court as provided for in subsection (e) of this Code section.

"(d) If the person is found to be mentally incompetent to stand trial but there is a substantial probability that the person will attain competency in the foreseeable future, by the end of the 90 day period, or at any prior time, the department shall report that finding and the reasons therefor to the committing court and shall retain custody over the person for the purpose of continued treatment for an additional period not to exceed nine months. If, by the end of the nine-month period or at any prior time if the person's condition warrants, the person is still found not to be competent to stand trial, irrespective of the probability of recovery in the foreseeable future, the department shall report that finding and the reasons therefor to the committing court. If the person meets the criteria for civil commitment, he shall thereupon be civilly committed to a state institution pursuant to Chapter 3 or 4 of Title 37, whichever is applicable. If the person does not meet the criteria for civil commitment or if the person after having been committed becomes mentally competent to stand trial, the committing court shall be notified and the person shall be returned to the court as provided for in subsection (e) of this Code section.

"(e)(1) A person who is found by the Department of Human Resources to be mentally competent to stand trial shall be discharged into the custody of a law enforcement officer of the jurisdiction of the court which committed the person to the department unless the court has dismissed the charges which led to the commitment, in which case the person shall be discharged. In the event a law enforcement officer does not appear and take custody of the person within 20 days after notice to the appropriate law enforcement official in the jurisdiction of the committing court, the presiding judge of the committing court, and the prosecuting attorney for the court, the department shall itself return the person to one of the committing court's detention facilities; and the cost of returning the person shall be paid by the county in which the committing court is located. All notifications shall be sent by certified mail or statutory overnight delivery, return receipt requested. With the concurrence of the appropriate court and upon the recommendation of the attending physician, any person discharged as competent to stand trial may be held by the department instead of at the court's detention facilities whenever, in the attending physician's opinion, such detention in the court's facilities would be detrimental to the well-being of the person so committed. Such alternative detention shall continue only until the date of the person's trial.

"(2) The physical custody of a person who is found by the Department of Human Resources to be mentally incompetent to stand trial and for whom there is no substantial probability that he or she will attain competency in the foreseeable future shall be returned to the committing court. The committing court shall retain custody of the person and may order an independent evaluation of the person by a court appointed licensed clinical psychologist or psychiatrist who shall report to the court in writing as to the current mental and emotional condition of the person. Then the court shall conduct a hearing at which the court shall hear evidence and consider all psychiatric and psychological reports submitted to the court and determine whether the state has proved by clear and convincing evidence that the person meets the criteria for involuntary civil commitment pursuant to Chapter 3 or Chapter 4 of Title 37, whichever is applicable. If the person is found to meet the criteria for involuntary civil commitment, the judge may issue an order committing the person to a state institution. If the person does not meet the criteria for involuntary civil commitment, the person shall be released subject to provisions of bond and other conditions set by the committing court. A person committed under the provisions of this paragraph may only be discharged from that commitment by order of the committing court in accordance with the procedures specified in paragraphs (1) through (3) of subsection (f) of Code Section 17–7–131 except that the burden of proof in such release hearing shall be on the state and if the committed person cannot afford a physician or licensed clinical psychologist of the person's choice, the person may petition the court and the court may order such cost be paid by the county. This paragraph applies to those persons:

"(A) Accused of committing the following crimes:

"(i) Murder;

"(ii) Rape;

"(iii) Aggravated sodomy;

"(iv) Armed robbery;

"(v) Aggravated assault;

"(vi) Hijacking of a motor vehicle or an aircraft;

"(vii) Aggravated battery;

"(viii) Aggravated sexual battery;

"(ix) Aggravated child molestation; or

"(x) Aggravated stalking;

"(B) Who are an obvious threat to society as determined by the Department of Human Resources or the assigned judge; or

"(C) Who have been convicted of or committed for three or more felonies.

"(f) Any person returned to the court as provided in subsection (e) of this Code section shall again be entitled to file a special plea as provided for in this Code section.

"(g) If a person is found to be mentally incompetent to stand trial, whether or not committed to a state institution under this Code section, the state may file at any time a motion for rehearing on the issue of the person's mental competency. The court shall grant said motion upon a showing by the state that there are reasonable grounds to believe that the person's mental condition has changed. If this motion is granted, the case shall proceed as provided in subsection (a) of this Code section."

In 2007, the Code Commission, in subpar. (a)(3)(A), deleted "or" at the end of div. (ix); in subsec. (b) and subpar. (d)(2)(A), substituted "et seq." for "et. seq"; in subsec. (b), substituted "subparagraph (a)(3)(A)" for "subparagraph (A) of paragraph (3) of subsection (a)"; and in subsec. (d), substituted "Chapter 3 or 4 of Title 37" for "Chapters 3 or 4 of Title 37" in the introductory paragraph. See § 28–9–5.

The 2009 amendment by Act 102 substituted "Department of Behavioral Health and Developmental Disabilities" for "Department of Human Resources" throughout the section.

The 2010 amendment by Act 418, in subsec. (a), added par. (1), redesignated former par. (1) as par. (2), added par. (3), redesignated former par. (2) as par. (4) and inserted the proviso relating to application to a child, redesignated former par. (3) as par. (5), redesignated former par. (4) as par. (6), added subpar. (A), and redesignated the former proviso on "release on bail or other pre-trial release" as subpar. (B); in subsec. (b), inserted "and if the defendant is a child, the department shall be authorized to place such defendant in a secure hospital or secure community facility designated by the department" in the second sentence and substituted "(a)(5)(A)" for "(a)(3)(A)"; in subsec. (d), par. (1), inserted "If the defendant is not a child," before "refer"; in par. (2), subpar. (B), added the proviso that "if the defendant is a child, the Department of Behavioral Health and Developmental Disabilities shall be authorized to place such defendant in a secure hospital or secure community facility designated by the department".

§ 17–7–130.1. Evidence of sanity or insanity; appointment of medical witnesses

At the trial of a criminal case in which the defendant intends to interpose the defense of insanity, evidence may be introduced to prove the defendant's sanity or insanity at the time at which he is alleged to have committed the offense charged in the indictment or information. When notice of an insanity defense is filed, the court shall appoint at least one psychiatrist or licensed psychologist to examine the defendant and to testify at the trial. This testimony shall follow the presentation of the evidence for the prosecution and for the defense, including testimony of any medical experts employed by the state or by the defense. The medical witnesses appointed by the court may be cross-examined by both the prosecution and the defense, and each side may introduce evidence in rebuttal to the testimony of such a medical witness.

Laws 1985, p. 637, § 1.

§ 17–7–131. Insanity and incompetency

(a) For purposes of this Code section, the term:

(1) "Insane at the time of the crime" means meeting the criteria of Code Section 16–3–2 or Code Section 16–3–3. However, the term shall not include a mental state manifested only by repeated unlawful or antisocial conduct.

(2) "Mentally ill" means having a disorder of thought or mood which significantly impairs judgment, behavior, capacity to recognize reality, or ability to cope with the ordinary demands of life. However, the term "mental illness" shall not include a mental state manifested only by repeated unlawful or antisocial conduct.

(3) "Mentally retarded" means having significantly subaverage general intellectual functioning resulting in or associated with impairments in adaptive behavior which manifested during the developmental period.

(b)(1) In all cases in which the defense of insanity is interposed, the jury, or the court if tried by it, shall find whether the defendant is:

(A) Guilty;

(B) Not guilty;

(C) Not guilty by reason of insanity at the time of the crime;

(D) Guilty but mentally ill at the time of the crime, but the finding of guilty but mentally ill shall be made only in felony cases; or

(E) Guilty but mentally retarded, but the finding of mental retardation shall be made only in felony cases.

(2) A plea of guilty but mentally ill at the time of the crime or a plea of guilty but mentally retarded shall not be accepted until the defendant has undergone examination by a licensed psychologist or psychiatrist and the court has examined the psychological or psychiatric reports, held a hearing on the issue of the defendant's mental condition, and is satisfied that there is a factual basis that the defendant was mentally ill at the time of the offense or mentally retarded to which the plea is entered.

(2.1) A plea of not guilty by reason of insanity at the time of the crime shall not be accepted and the defendant adjudicated not guilty by reason of insanity by the court without a jury until the defendant has undergone examination by a licensed psychologist or psychiatrist and the court has examined the psychological or psychiatric reports, has held a hearing on the issue of the defendant's mental condition, and the court is satisfied that the defendant was insane at the time of the crime according to the criteria of Code Section 16–3–2 or 16–3–3.

(3) In all cases in which the defense of insanity is interposed, the trial judge shall charge the jury, in addition to other appropriate charges, the following:

(A) I charge you that should you find the defendant not guilty by reason of insanity at the time of the crime, the defendant will be committed to a state mental health facility until such time, if ever, that the court is satisfied that he or she should be released pursuant to law.

(B) I charge you that should you find the defendant guilty but mentally ill at the time of the crime, the defendant will be placed in the custody of the Department of Corrections which will have responsibility for the evaluation and treatment of the mental health needs of the defendant, which may include, at the discretion of the Department of Corrections, referral for temporary hospitalization at a facility operated by the Department of Behavioral Health and Developmental Disabilities.

(C) I charge you that should you find the defendant guilty but mentally retarded, the defendant will be placed in the custody of the Department of Corrections, which will have responsibility for the evaluation and treatment of the mental health needs of the defendant, which may include, at the discretion of the Department of Corrections, referral for temporary hospitalization at a facility operated by the Department of Behavioral Health and Developmental Disabilities.

(c) In all criminal trials in any of the courts of this state wherein an accused shall contend that he was insane or otherwise mentally incompetent under the law at the time the act or acts charged against him were committed, the trial judge shall instruct the jury that they may consider, in addition to verdicts of "guilty" and "not guilty," the additional verdicts of "not guilty by reason of insanity at the time of the crime," "guilty but mentally ill at the time of the crime," and "guilty but mentally retarded."

(1) The defendant may be found "not guilty by reason of insanity at the time of the crime" if he meets the criteria of Code Section 16–3–2 or 16–3–3 at the time of the commission of the crime. If the court or jury should make such finding, it shall so specify in its verdict.

(2) The defendant may be found "guilty but mentally ill at the time of the crime" if the jury, or court acting as trier of facts, finds beyond a reasonable doubt that the defendant is guilty of the crime charged and was mentally ill at the time of the commission of the crime. If the court or jury should make such finding, it shall so specify in its verdict.

(3) The defendant may be found "guilty but mentally retarded" if the jury, or court acting as trier of facts, finds beyond a reasonable doubt that the defendant is guilty of the crime charged and is mentally retarded. If the court or jury should make such finding, it shall so specify in its verdict.

(d) Whenever a defendant is found not guilty by reason of insanity at the time of the crime, the court shall retain jurisdiction over the person so acquitted and shall order such person to be detained in a state mental health facility, to be selected by the Department of Behavioral Health and Developmental Disabilities, for a period not to exceed 30 days from the date of the acquittal order, for evaluation of the defendant's present mental condition. Upon completion of the evaluation, the proper officials of the mental health facility shall send a report of the defendant's present mental condition to the trial judge, the prosecuting attorney, and the defendant's attorney, if any.

(e)(1) After the expiration of the 30 days' evaluation period in the state mental health facility, if the evaluation report from the Department of Behavioral Health and Developmental Disabilities indicates that the defendant does not meet the inpatient commitment criteria of Chapter 3 of Title 37 or Chapter 4 of Title 37, the trial judge may issue an order discharging the defendant from custody without a hearing.

(2) If the defendant is not so discharged, the trial judge shall order a hearing to determine if the defendant meets the inpatient commitment criteria of Chapter 3 of Title 37 or Chapter 4 of Title 37. If such criteria are not met, the defendant must be discharged.

(3) The defendant shall be detained in custody until completion of the hearing. The hearing shall be conducted at the earliest opportunity after the expiration of the 30 days' evaluation period but in any event within 30 days after receipt by the prosecuting attorney of the evaluation report from the mental health facility. The court may take judicial notice of evidence introduced during the trial of the defendant and may call for testimony from any person with knowledge concerning whether the defendant is currently a mentally ill person in need of involuntary treatment or currently mentally retarded and in need of being ordered to receive services, as those terms are defined by paragraph (12) of Code Section 37–3–1 and Code Section 37–4–40. The prosecuting attorney may cross-examine the witnesses called by the court and the defendant's witnesses and present relevant evidence concerning the issues presented at the hearing.

(4) If the judge determines that the defendant meets the inpatient commitment criteria of Chapter 3 of Title 37 or Chapter 4 of Title 37, the judge shall order the defendant to be committed to the Department of Behavioral Health and Developmental Disabilities to receive involuntary treatment under Chapter 3 of Title 37 or to receive services under Chapter 4 of Title 37. The defendant is entitled to the following rights specified below and shall be notified in writing of these rights at the time of his admission for evaluation under subsection (d) of this Code section. Such rights are:

(A) A notice that a hearing will be held and the time and place thereof;

(B) A notice that the defendant has the right to counsel and that the defendant or his representatives may apply immediately to the court to have counsel appointed if the defendant cannot afford counsel and that the court will appoint counsel for the defendant unless he indicates in writing that he does not desire to be represented by counsel;

(C) The right to confront and cross-examine witnesses and to offer evidence;

(D) The right to subpoena witnesses and to require testimony before the court in person or by deposition from any person upon whose evaluation the decision of the court may rest;

(E) Notice of the right to have established an individualized service plan specifically tailored to the person's treatment needs, as such plans are defined in Chapter 3 of Title 37 and Chapter 4 of Title 37; and

(F) A notice that the defendant has the right to be examined by a physician or a licensed clinical psychologist of his own choice at his own expense and to have that physician or psychologist submit a suggested service plan for the patient which conforms with the requirements of Chapter 3 of Title 37 or Chapter 4 of Title 37, whichever is applicable.

(5)(A) If a defendant appears to meet the criteria for outpatient involuntary treatment as defined in Part 3 of Article 3 of Chapter 3 of Title 37, which shall be the criteria for release on a trial basis in the community in preparation for a full release, the court may order a period of conditional release subject to certain conditions set by the court. The court is authorized to appoint an appropriate community service provider to work in conjunction with the Department of Behavioral Health and Developmental Disabilities to monitor the defendant's compliance with these conditions and to make regular reports to the court.

(B) If the defendant successfully completes all requirements during this period of conditional release, the court shall discharge the individual from commitment at the end of that period. Such individuals may be referred for community mental health, mental retardation, or substance abuse services as appropriate. The court may require the individual to participate in outpatient treatment or any other services or programs authorized by Chapter 3, 4, or 7 of Title 37.

(C) If the defendant does not successfully complete any or all requirements of the conditional release period, the court may:

(i) Revoke the period of conditional release and return the defendant to a state hospital for inpatient services; or

(ii) Impose additional or revise existing conditions on the defendant as appropriate and continue the period of conditional release.

(D) For any decision rendered under subparagraph (C) of this paragraph, the defendant may request a review by the court of such decision within 20 days of the order of the court.

(E) The Department of Behavioral Health and Developmental Disabilities and any community services providers, including the employees and agents of both, providing supervision or treatment during a period of conditional release shall not be held criminally or civilly liable for any acts committed by a defendant placed by the committing court on a period of conditional release.

(f) A defendant who has been found not guilty by reason of insanity at the time of the crime and is ordered committed to the Department of Behavioral Health and Developmental Disabilities under subsection (e) of this Code section may only be discharged from that commitment by order of the committing court in accordance with the procedures specified in this subsection:

(1) Application for the release of a defendant who has been committed to the Department of Behavioral Health and Developmental Disabilities under subsection (e) of this Code section upon the ground that he does not meet the civil commitment criteria under Chapter 3 of Title 37 or Chapter 4 of Title 37 may be made to the committing court, either by such defendant or by the superintendent of the state hospital in which the said defendant is detained;

(2) The burden of proof in such release hearing shall be upon the applicant. The defendant shall have the same rights in the release hearing as set forth in subsection (e) of this Code section; and

(3) If the finding of the court is adverse to release in such hearing held pursuant to this subsection on the grounds that such defendant does meet the inpatient civil commitment criteria, a further release application by the defendant shall not be heard by the court until 12 months have elapsed from the date of the hearing upon the last preceding application. The Department of Behavioral Health and Developmental Disabilities shall have the independent right to request a release hearing once every 12 months.

(g)(1) Whenever a defendant is found guilty but mentally ill at the time of a felony or guilty but mentally retarded, or enters a plea to that effect that is accepted by the court, the court shall sentence him or her in the same manner as a defendant found guilty of the offense, except as otherwise provided in subsection (j) of this Code section. A defendant who is found guilty but mentally ill at the time of the felony or guilty but mentally retarded shall be committed to an appropriate penal facility and shall be evaluated then treated, if indicated, within the limits of state funds appropriated therefor, in such manner as is psychiatrically indicated for his or her mental illness or mental retardation.

(2) If at any time following the defendant's conviction as a guilty but mentally ill or guilty but mentally retarded offender it is determined that a temporary transfer to the Department of Behavioral Health and Developmental Disabilities is clinically indicated for his or her mental illness or mental retardation, then the defendant shall be transferred to the Department of Behavioral Health and Developmental Disabilities pursuant to procedures set forth in regulations of the Department of Corrections and the Department of Behavioral Health and Developmental Disabilities. In all such cases, the legal custody of the defendant shall be retained by the Department of Corrections. Upon notification from the Department of Behavioral Health and Developmental Disabilities to the Department of Corrections that hospitalization at a Department of Behavioral Health and Developmental Disabilities facility is no longer clinically indicated for his or her mental illness or mental retardation, the Department of Corrections shall transfer the defendant back to its physical custody and shall place such individual in an appropriate penal institution.

(h) If a defendant who is found guilty but mentally ill at the time of a felony or guilty but mentally retarded is placed on probation under the "State-wide Probation Act," Article 2 of Chapter 8 of Title 42, the court may require that the defendant undergo available outpatient medical or psychiatric treatment or seek similar available voluntary inpatient treatment as a condition of probation. Persons required to receive such services may be charged fees by the provider of the services.

(i) In any case in which the defense of insanity is interposed or a plea of guilty but mentally ill at the time of the felony or a plea of guilty but mentally retarded is made and an examination is made of the defendant pursuant to Code Section 17–7–130.1 or paragraph (2) of subsection (b) of this Code section, upon the defendant's being found guilty or guilty but mentally ill at the time of the crime or guilty but mentally retarded, a copy of any such examination report shall be forwarded to the Department of Corrections with the official sentencing document. The Department of Behavioral Health and Developmental Disabilities shall forward, in addition to its examination report, any records maintained by such department that it deems appropriate pursuant to an agreement with the Department of Corrections, within ten business days of receipt by the Department of Behavioral Health and Developmental Disabilities of the official sentencing document from the Department of Corrections.

(j) In the trial of any case in which the death penalty is sought which commences on or after July 1, 1988, should the judge find in accepting a plea of guilty but mentally retarded or the jury or court find in its verdict that the defendant is guilty of the crime charged but mentally retarded, the death penalty shall not be imposed and the court shall sentence the defendant to imprisonment for life.

Laws 1952, p. 205, § 1; Laws 1972, p. 848, § 1; Laws 1977, p. 1293, § 2; Laws 1982, p. 1476, §§ 1, 2; Laws 1984, p. 22, § 17; Laws 1985, p. 283, § 1; Laws 1985, p. 637, §§ 2–4; Laws 1988, p. 1003, § 1; Laws 1989, p. 14, § 17; Laws 1991, p. 780, §§ 1–3; Laws 1992, p. 1328, §§ 2, 3; Laws 2006, Act 754, § 1, eff. July 1, 2006; Laws 2009, Act 102, § 3–2, eff. July 1, 2009.

Formerly Code 1863, § 1314; Code 1868, § 1395; Code 1873, § 1374; Code 1882, § 1374; Penal Code 1895, § 952; Penal Code 1910, § 977; Code 1933, § 27–1503.

Historical and Statutory Notes

The 2006 amendment by Act 754 rewrote par. (b)(3) and subsec. (g); and inserted the second sentence of subsec. (i). Prior to amendment, par. (b)(3) and subsec. (g) read as follows:

"[(b)](3) In all cases in which the defense of insanity is interposed, the trial judge shall charge the jury, in addition to other appropriate charges, the following:

"(A) I charge you that should you find the defendant not guilty by reason of insanity at the time of the crime, the defendant will be committed to a state mental health facility until such time, if ever, that the court is satisfied that he or she should be released pursuant to law.

"(B) I charge you that should you find the defendant guilty but mentally ill at the time of the crime, the defendant will be given over to the Department of Corrections or the Department of Human Resources, as the mental condition of the defendant may warrant.

"(C) I charge you that should you find the defendant guilty but mentally retarded, the defendant will be given over to the Department of Corrections or the Department of Human Resources, as the mental condition of the defendant may warrant."

"(g)(1) Whenever a defendant is found guilty but mentally ill at the time of a felony or guilty but mentally retarded, or enters a plea to that effect that is accepted by the court, the court shall sentence him in the same manner as a defendant found guilty of the offense, except as otherwise provided in subsection (j) of this Code section. A defendant who is found guilty but mentally ill at the time of the felony or guilty but mentally retarded shall be evaluated by a psychiatrist or a licensed psychologist from the Department of Human Resources after sentencing and prior to transfer to a Department of Corrections facility. The Board of Human Resources shall develop appropriate rules and regulations for the implementation of such procedures.

"(2) If the defendant who is found guilty but mentally ill at the time of the felony or guilty but mentally retarded is not in need of immediate hospitalization, as indicated by the evaluation, then the defendant shall be committed to an appropriate penal facility and shall be further evaluated and then treated, within the limits of state funds appropriated therefor, in such manner as is psychiatrically indicated for his mental illness or mental retardation.

"(3) If at any time following the defendant's transfer to a penal facility it is determined that a transfer to the Department of Human Resources is psychiatrically indicated for his mental illness or mental retardation, then the defendant shall be transferred to the Department of Human Resources pursuant to procedures set forth in regulations of the Department of Corrections and the Department of Human Resources.

"(4) If it is determined by the evaluation that the defendant found guilty but mentally ill at the time of the felony or guilty but mentally retarded is in need of immediate hospitalization, then the defendant shall be transferred by the Department of Corrections to a mental health facility designated by the Department of Human Resources in accordance with rules and regulations of such departments."

The 2009 amendment by Act 102 substituted "Department of Behavioral Health and Developmental Disabilities" for "Department of Human Resources" throughout the section.

Part 3

Change of Venue

§ 17-7-150. When and how venue changed; appeals from denial of change of venue

(a)(1) The defendant, in any criminal case in which a trial by jury is provided, may move in writing for a change of venue, whenever, in the defendant's or defense counsel's judgment, an impartial jury cannot be obtained in the county where the crime is alleged to have been committed. Upon the hearing of the motion it shall not be necessary to examine all persons in the county liable to serve on juries, but the judge shall hear evidence by affidavit or oral testimony in support of or against the motion. If, from the evidence submitted, the judge is satisfied that an impartial jury cannot be obtained to try the case, the judge shall grant a change in venue; the judge shall transfer the case to any county that may be agreed upon by the prosecuting attorney and the defendant or the defense counsel, to be tried in the county agreed upon. The judge has the discretion to reject any county agreed upon; if a county is not thus agreed upon, or if the judge, in the exercise of discretion, rejects a county agreed upon, the judge shall select such county as in the judge's judgment will afford a fair and impartial jury to try the case and have it transferred accordingly.

(2) In the exercise of such discretion, the judge shall consult with the chief superior court judge of the circuit in which a county of transfer lies and consider the following factors:

(A) The existing criminal and civil trial calendars of the transfer county;

(B) The frequency of use as a transfer county;

(C) The estimated length of trial;

(D) The proposed date of trial;

(E) Whether or not the jury is to be sequestered;

(F) Which county shall be responsible for court security, prisoner security, bailiffs, jailers, and clerks of court personnel;

(G) Jury transportation;

(H) Securing hotel accommodations in the event of jury sequestration;

(I) Securing of meals for jurors and other court personnel;

(J) Which county will guarantee and pay vendors for services rendered;

(K) The necessity for deposit or prepayment of expenses by the county of the crime venue; and

(L) All other matters which reasonably may affect the orderly administration of justice in the transfer county. In the event of disagreement between the trial judge and the chief judge of the transfer circuit, the district administrative judge for the proposed transfer of venue shall have final responsibility for resolving the dispute.

(3) Either by the agreement of the defense counsel, the prosecuting attorney, and the judge or by the exercise of discretion by the judge the trial jury may be selected from qualified jurors of the transfer county, although the trial of the criminal case may take place in the county of the venue of the alleged crime. In the exercise of discretion, to select the jury in the transfer county but to try the case in the county of venue of the alleged crime, the judge shall consult with the chief superior court judge of the circuit in which the county of transfer lies and consider all of the factors provided in subparagraphs (A) through (L) of paragraph (2) of this subsection as well as the following factors:

(A) The hardship of sequestration a distance from home on the jurors;

(B) The comparison of court space available;

(C) The comparison of security, jail, clerical, and support staff;

(D) The costs to conduct the trial in each place;

(E) The impact of trial on the orderly administration of justice in each county;

(F) The impact on witnesses;

(G) The availability of hotel accommodations and meals for jurors in each county;

(H) The effect on the prosecuting attorney and defense counsel in each county; and

(I) All other matters which would afford a fair trial and the orderly administration of justice.

In the event of disagreement between the trial judge and the chief judge of the transfer circuit, the district administrative judge for the proposed transfer of venue shall have final responsibility for resolving the dispute.

(b) The judge of the court in whose jurisdiction a crime is alleged to have been committed may change the venue for trial of the case on his own motion whenever, in his judgment, there is danger of violence being committed on the defendant, if carried back to, or allowed to remain in the county where the crime is alleged to have been committed. If a motion is made by the defendant for a change of venue, the judge shall hear the motion at such time and place as the judge may direct. If the evidence submitted shall reasonably show that there is probability or danger of violence, it shall be mandatory on the judge to change the venue to such other county as, in his judgment, will reasonably avoid violence.

(c) Notwithstanding other laws, the denial of a motion to change venue shall be appealable immediately only with a certificate of immediate review. Otherwise, the denial shall be appealed with the merits of the case.

Laws 1895, p. 70, § 2; Laws 1911, p. 74, § 1; Laws 1972, p. 536, § 1; Laws 1995, p. 1292, § 12.

Formerly Penal Code 1895, § 939; Penal Code 1910, § 964; Code 1933, § 27–1201; Code 1933, §§ 27–1201, 27–1202.

§ 17–7–151. Clerk to transmit papers, etc.; subpoenas for witnesses

Whenever a change of venue is made, the clerk of the court from which the case has been transferred shall send to the court to which the case has been transferred a transcript of the order for the change of venue, the evidence before the court of inquiry, a list of all the witnesses subpoenaed in the case, and all other papers connected with the case. The clerk of the court selected to try the case shall issue subpoenas to the witnesses and such others as may be applied for by either party.

Laws 1895, p. 70, § 4; Laws 1972, p. 536, § 1.

Formerly Penal Code 1895, § 940; Penal Code 1910, § 965; Code 1933, § 27–1202; Code 1933, § 27–1203.

§ 17–7–152. Subsequent change of venue

If, on motion, the judge presiding in the court to which a case has been transferred is satisfied that a fair and impartial jury cannot be obtained therein, he shall, in the manner prescribed in subsection (a) of Code Section 17–7–150, transfer the case to some other county where a fair and impartial jury can be obtained.

Laws 1895, p. 70, § 5; Laws 1972, p. 536, § 1.

Formerly Penal Code 1895, § 941; Penal Code 1910, § 966; Code 1933, § 27–1203; Code 1933, § 27–1204.

Article 7

Demand for Trial; Announcement of Readiness for Trial

§ 17–7–170. Demand in noncapital cases

(a) Any defendant against whom a true bill of indictment or an accusation is filed with the clerk for an offense not affecting the defendant's life may enter a demand for speedy trial at the court term at which the indictment or accusation is filed or at the next succeeding regular court term thereafter; or, by special permission of the court, the defendant may at any subsequent court term thereafter demand a speedy trial. In either case, the demand for speedy trial shall be filed with the clerk of court and served upon the prosecutor and upon the judge to whom the case is assigned or, if the case is not assigned, upon the chief judge of the court in which the case is pending. A demand for speedy trial filed pursuant to this Code section shall be filed as a separate, distinct, and individual document and shall not be a part of any other pleading or document. Such demand shall clearly be titled "Demand for Speedy Trial"; reference this Code section within the pleading; and identify the indictment number or accusation number for which such demand is being made. The demand for speedy trial shall be binding only in the court in which the demand for speedy trial is filed, except where the case is transferred from one court to another without a request from the defendant.

(b) If the defendant is not tried when the demand for speedy trial is made or at the next succeeding regular court term thereafter, provided that at both court terms there were juries impaneled and qualified to try the defendant, the defendant shall be absolutely discharged and acquitted of the offense charged in the indictment or accusation. For purposes of computing the term at which a misdemeanor must be tried under this Code section, there shall be excluded any civil term of court in a county in which civil and criminal terms of court are designated; and for purposes of this Code section it shall be as if such civil term was not held.

(c) Any demand for speedy trial filed pursuant to this Code section shall expire at the conclusion of the trial or upon the defendant entering a plea of guilty or nolo contendere.

(d) If a case in which a demand for speedy trial has been filed, as provided in this Code section, is reversed on direct appeal, a new demand for speedy trial shall be filed within the term of court in which the remittitur from the appellate court is received by the clerk of court or at the next succeeding regular court term thereafter.

(e) If the case in which a demand for speedy trial has been filed as provided in this Code section results in a mistrial, the case shall be tried at the next succeeding regular term of court.

Laws 1859, p. 60, § 1; Laws 1985, p. 637, § 5; Laws 1987, p. 841, § 1; Laws 2003, Act 26, § 3, eff. May 14, 2003; Laws 2006, Act 879, § 1, eff. July 1, 2006.

Formerly Code 1863, § 4534; Code 1868, § 4554; Code 1873, § 4648; Code 1882, § 4648; Penal Code 1895, § 958; Penal Code 1910, § 983; Code 1933, § 27–1901.

Historical and Statutory Notes

The 2003 amendment by Act 26 rewrote the section which had read:

"(a) Any person against whom a true bill of indictment or an accusation is filed with the clerk for an offense not affecting his life may enter a demand for trial at the court term at which the indictment or accusation is filed or at the next succeeding regular court term thereafter; or, by special permission of the court, he may at any subsequent court term thereafter demand a trial. In either case, the demand for trial shall be served on the prosecutor and shall be binding only in the court in which the demand is filed, except where the case is transferred from one court to another without a request from the defendant.

"(b) If the person is not tried when the demand is made or at the next succeeding regular court term thereafter, provided at both court terms there were juries impaneled and qualified to try him, he shall be absolutely discharged and acquitted of the offense charged in the indictment or accusation. For purposes of computing the term at which a misdemeanor must be tried under this Code section, there shall be excluded any civil term of court in a county in which civil and criminal terms of court are designated; and for purposes of this Code section it shall be as if such civil term was not held."

The 2006 amendment by Act 879 rewrote subsec. (a); substituted "defendant" for "person" three times in subsec. (b); inserted "for speedy trial" in subsecs. (b) and (c); inserted "speedy" preceding "trial" twice in subsec. (d) and once in subsec. (e); substituted "shall' for "must" in subsec. (d); and made nonsubstantive changes. Prior to amendment, subsec. (a) had read:

"(a) Any person against whom a true bill of indictment or an accusation is filed with the clerk for an offense not affecting the person's life may enter a demand for trial at the court term at which the indictment or accusation is filed or at the next succeeding regular court term thereafter; or, by special permission of the court, he or she may at any subsequent court term thereafter demand a trial. In either case, the demand for trial shall be filed with the clerk of court and served upon the prosecutor and upon the judge to whom the case is assigned or, if the case is not assigned, upon the chief judge of the court in which the case is pending. The demand shall be binding only in the court in which the demand is filed, except where the case is transferred from one court to another without a request from the defendant."

§ 17-7-171. Demand in capital cases

(a) Any person accused of a capital offense may enter a demand for speedy trial at the term of court at which the indictment is found or at the next succeeding regular term thereafter; or, by special permission of the court, the defendant may at any subsequent term thereafter demand a speedy trial. The demand for speedy trial shall be filed with the clerk of court and served upon the prosecutor and upon the judge to whom the case is assigned or, if the case is not assigned, upon the chief judge of the court in which the case is pending. A demand for trial filed pursuant to this Code section shall be filed as a separate, distinct, and individual document and shall not be a part of any other pleading or document. Such demand shall clearly be titled "Demand for Speedy Trial"; reference this Code section within the pleading; and identify the indictment number or accusation number for which such demand is being made. The demand for speedy trial shall be binding only in the court in which such demand is filed, except where the case is transferred from one court to another without a request from the defendant.

(b) If more than two regular terms of court are convened and adjourned after the term at which the demand for speedy trial is filed and the defendant is not given a trial, then the defendant shall be absolutely discharged and acquitted of the offense charged in the indictment, provided that at both terms there were juries impaneled and qualified to try the defendant and provided, further, that the defendant was present in court announcing ready for trial and requesting a trial on the indictment.

(c) In cases involving a capital offense for which the death penalty is sought, if a demand for speedy trial is entered, the counting of terms under subsection (b) of this Code section shall not begin until the convening of the first term following the completion of pretrial review proceedings in the Supreme Court under Code Section 17-10-35.1.

Laws 1952, p. 299, §§ 1, 2; Laws 1983, p. 452, § 3; Laws 1988, p. 1437, § 3; Laws 1990, p. 8, § 17; Laws 2006, Act 879, § 2, eff. July 1, 2006.

Historical and Statutory Notes

The 2006 amendment by Act 879 rewrote subsec. (a); in subsec. (b), inserted "for speedy trial" and substituted "the defendant" for "he"; and inserted "speedy" preceding "trial" in subsec. (c). Prior to amendment, subsec. (a) had read:

"(a) Any person accused of a capital offense may enter a demand for trial at the term of court at which the indictment is found or at the next succeeding regular term thereafter; or, by special permission of the court, he may at any subsequent term thereafter demand a trial."

§ 17-7-172. Announcement by state of ready or not ready for trial

The state shall be required in every case to announce ready or not ready for trial, except in those cases where the defendant is entitled by law to demand a speedy trial, before the defendant shall be called on to make such announcement.

Laws 1862-63, p. 138, § 1; Laws 2006, Act 879, § 3, eff. July 1, 2006.

Formerly Code 1868, § 4613; Code 1873, § 4710; Code 1882, § 4710; Penal Code 1895, § 959; Penal Code 1910, § 984; Code 1933, § 27-1902.

Historical and Statutory Notes

The 2006 amendment by Act 879 inserted "speedy" preceding "trial".

Article 8

Procedure for Securing Attendance of Witnesses at Grand Jury or Trial Proceedings

§ 17-7-190. Attendance of witness before grand jury

When any person accused of a criminal offense before a court of inquiry is bound over or committed for trial in superior court, the judicial officer holding the court of inquiry shall, at the time of the commitment hearing, give a subpoena to all material witnesses examined for the state to appear and testify before the grand jury at the term to which the defendant is committed or bound to appear; and, after the hearing and commitment or binding over, the prosecutor may apply to the clerk of the superior court and obtain a subpoena for any person deemed by him to be a material witness for the state before the grand jury. The subpoenas issued under this Code section shall be effectual in compelling the attendance of the witnesses to appear and give evidence before the grand jury. The judicial officer holding the court of inquiry and the clerk of the superior court shall, on the first day of the term of court to which the defendant is committed or bound to appear, furnish the prosecuting officers with a complete list of all persons so subpoenaed.

Laws 1873, p. 33, §§ 1, 2.

Formerly Code 1873, § 3846; Code 1882, § 3846; Penal Code 1895, § 917; Penal Code 1910, § 942; Code 1933, § 27-413.

§ 17-7-191. Attendance of witnesses for accused

The defendant may, upon application to the committing judicial officer or to the clerk of the court to which he is committed or bound to appear for trial, obtain subpoenas for such witnesses as he deems material for his defense. The judicial officer or the clerk of the court shall issue such subpoenas requiring the witnesses to appear at the term of the court to which the defendant is committed or bound to appear and until his case is ended. The subpoenas so issued shall have the power and authority to compel the attendance of the witnesses at the court but shall not extend to witnesses for the defendant who reside outside the county until a true bill of indictment is found or an accusation is filed against the defendant.

Laws 1873, p. 33, § 3.

Formerly Code 1873, § 3847; Code 1882, § 3847; Penal Code 1895, § 918; Penal Code 1910, § 943; Code 1933, § 27-414.

§ 17-7-192. Continuance for nonattendance of witness refused

A defendant who fails to use the subpoena power provided for in Code Section 17-7-191, when it is within his power to do so, shall not be entitled to a continuance because a witness material to his defense is not in attendance at the term of the court when his case is called for trial, if he is prosecuted for the same criminal act.

Laws 1873, p. 33, § 3.

Formerly Code 1873, § 3848; Code 1882, § 3848; Penal Code 1895, § 919; Penal Code 1910, § 944; Code 1933, § 27–415.

Article 9

Discovery

§§ 17–7–210, 17–7–211. Repealed by Laws 1994, p. 1895, § 1, eff. January 1, 1995

CHAPTER 8

TRIAL

Article 1

General Provisions

§ 17–8–1. Cases called in order in which they stand on docket

The cases on the criminal docket shall be called in the order in which they stand on the docket unless the defendant is in jail or, otherwise, in the sound discretion of the court.

Laws 1862–63, p. 139, § 1.

Formerly Code 1863, § 4592; Code 1868, § 4613; Code 1873, § 4710; Code 1882, § 4710; Penal Code 1895, § 942; Penal Code 1910, § 967; Code 1933, § 27–1301.

§ 17–8–2. Approval of settlement by court

All indictments or special presentments shall be submitted to and passed upon by a jury under the direction of the presiding judge unless there is a settlement of the case between the prosecutor and the defendant, which settlement shall be valid only by the approval and order of the court on examination into the merits of the case.

Laws 1850, Cobb's 1851 Digest, p. 864; Laws 1870, p. 422, § 2.

Formerly Code 1863, § 4588; Code 1868, §§ 4609, 4610; Code 1873, § 4706; Code 1882, § 4706; Penal Code 1895, § 956; Penal Code 1910, § 981; Code 1933, § 27–1701.

§ 17–8–3. Nolle prosequi; when and how allowed; notice to defendant and defendant's attorney

After an examination of the case in open court and before it has been submitted to a jury, the prosecuting attorney may enter a nolle prosequi with the consent of the court. After the case has been submitted to a jury, a nolle prosequi shall not be entered except by the consent of the defendant. The prosecuting attorney shall notify the defendant and the defendant's attorney of record within 30 days of the entry of a nolle prosequi either personally or in writing; such written notice shall be sent by regular mail to the defendant at the defendant's last known address and to the defendant's attorney of record.

Laws 1833, Cobb's 1851 Digest, p. 836; Laws 1870, p. 422, § 1; Laws 1877, p. 108, § 1; Laws 1989, p. 585, § 1.

Formerly Code 1863, § 4535; Code 1868, § 4555; Code 1873, § 4649; Code 1882, § 4649; Penal Code 1895, § 957; Penal Code 1910, § 982; Code 1933, § 27–1801.

§ 17–8–4. Joint or separate trials

(a) When two or more defendants are jointly indicted for a capital offense, any defendant so electing shall be separately tried unless the state shall waive the death penalty. When indicted for a capital felony when the death penalty is waived, or for a felony less than capital, or for a misdemeanor, such defendants may be tried jointly or separately in the discretion of the trial court. In any event, a jointly indicted defendant may testify for another jointly indicted defendant or on behalf of the state. When separate trials are ordered in any case, the defendants shall be tried in the order requested by the state. If the offense requires joint action and concurrence of two or more persons, acquittal or conviction of one defendant shall not operate as acquittal or conviction of others not tried.

(b) When two or more defendants are tried jointly for a crime or offense, such defendants shall be entitled to the same number of strikes as a single defendant if tried separately. The strikes shall be exercised jointly by the defendants or shall be apportioned among the defendants in the manner the court shall direct. In the event two or more defendants are tried jointly, the court, upon request of the defendants, shall allow an equal number of additional strikes to the defendants, not to exceed five each, as the court shall deem necessary, to the ends that justice may prevail. The court may allow the state additional strikes not to exceed the number of additional strikes as are allowed to the defendants.

Laws 1836, Cobb's Digest, p. 841; Laws 1855–56, p. 266, § 1; Laws 1858, p. 99, § 1; Laws 1878–79, p. 59, § 1; Laws 1971, p. 891, § 1; Laws 1972, p. 618, § 1; Laws 2005, Act 8, § 9, eff. July 1, 2005.

Formerly Code 1863, § 4574; Code 1868, § 4595; Code 1873, § 4692; Code 1882, § 4692; Penal Code 1895, § 969; Penal Code 1910, § 995; Code 1933, § 27–2101.

Historical and Statutory Notes

The 2005 amendment by Act 8 added subsection designations; in subsec. (b), substituted "shall allow an equal number" for "acting in its sole discretion, may allow an equal number" and added "The court may allow the state additional strikes not to exceed the number of additional strikes as are allowed to the defendants." at the end of the subsection.

Laws 2005, Act 8, § 17, provides:

"This Act shall apply to all trials which commence on or after July 1, 2005."

§ 17–8–5. Stenographic notes; entry of testimony on minutes of court; transcript or brief

(a) On the trial of all felonies the presiding judge shall have the testimony taken down and, when directed by the judge, the court reporter shall exactly and truly record or take stenographic notes of the testimony and proceedings in the case, except the argument of counsel. In the event of a verdict of guilty, the testimony shall be entered on the minutes of the court or in a book to be kept for that purpose. In the event that a sentence of death is imposed, the transcript of the case shall be prepared within 90 days after the sentence is imposed by the trial court. Upon petition by the court reporter, the Chief Justice of the Supreme Court of Georgia may grant an additional period of time for preparation of the transcript, such period not to exceed 60 days. The requirement that a transcript be prepared within a certain period in cases in which a sentence of death is imposed shall not inure to the benefit of a defendant.

(b) In the event that a mistrial results from any cause in the trial of a defendant charged with the commission of a felony, the presiding judge may, in his discretion, either with or without any application of the defendant or state's counsel, order that a brief or transcript of the testimony in the case be duly filed by the court reporter in the office of the clerk of the superior court in which the mistrial occurred. If the brief or transcript is ordered, it shall be the duty of the judge, in the order, to provide for the compensation of the reporter and for the transcript to be paid for as is provided by law for payment of transcripts in cases in which the law requires the testimony to be transcribed, at a rate not to exceed that provided in felony cases.

Laws 1833, Cobb's 1851 Digest, p. 841; Laws 1876, p. 133, § 1; Laws 1925, p. 101, § 1; Laws 1973, p. 159, § 6; Laws 1976, p. 991, § 1.

Formerly Code 1863, § 4578; Code 1868, § 4599; Code 1873, § 4696; Code 1882, § 4696; Penal Code 1895, § 981; Penal Code 1910, § 1007; Code 1933, § 27–2401.

§ 17–8–6. Municipal court judges authorized to seal criminal records under certain circumstances

(a) Any judge of a municipal court of any municipality of this state or any judge hearing cases for any such court wherein a municipal court is a court of first instance in criminal cases shall have the authority to seal, to all persons except criminal justice officials, all criminal records of the municipality, including, but not limited to, records of arrest, fingerprints, and photographs, whether maintained in the police agency of the municipality or elsewhere in the municipality, related to any individual, upon a finding by such a judge that one of the following conditions exists:

(1) When, upon the call of a case for trial, criminal charges against the individual are dismissed either:

(A) Upon the motion of the arresting officer; or

(B) Because of the lack of prosecution of such charges by the arresting officer or the municipality; or

(2) When criminal charges against the individual are the subject of a pretrial disposition by the municipal prosecutor, provided that the terms and conditions of the pretrial disposition are satisfied.

(b) Any order sealing the records of an individual, as provided for in subsection (a) of this Code section, shall in no way constitute an adjudication of any illegal or wrongful action on the part of the arresting officer or the municipality.

Laws 1980, p. 1683, § 1.

Article 2

Continuances

§ 17–8–20. Diligence required of applicants

In all cases, the party making an application for a continuance must show that he has used due diligence.

Formerly Code 1863, § 3457; Code 1868, § 3477; Code 1873, § 3528; Code 1882, § 3528; Civil Code 1895, § 5135; Penal Code 1895, § 965; Civil Code 1910, § 5721; Penal Code 1910, § 991; Code 1933, § 81–1416.

§ 17–8–21. When showing for continuance is required of state

In all cases in which the defendant cannot, according to law, demand a speedy trial, a continuance shall not be granted to the state, except upon a reasonable showing therefor.

Laws 1862–63, p. 138, § 1; Laws 2006, Act 879, § 4, eff. July 1, 2006.

Formerly Code 1863, § 4592; Code 1868, § 4613; Code 1873, § 4710; Code 1882, § 4710; Penal Code, § 960; Penal Code, § 985; Code 1933, § 27–2001.

Historical and Statutory Notes

The 2006 amendment by Act 879 inserted "speedy" preceding "trial".

§ 17–8–22. Counter-showing and discretion of court

All applications for continuances are addressed to the sound legal discretion of the court and, if not expressly provided for, shall be granted or refused as the ends of justice may require. In all cases the presiding judges may, in their discretion, admit a counter-showing to a motion for a continuance and, after a hearing, may decide whether the motion shall prevail.

Laws 1871–72, p. 49, § 1; Laws 1872, p. 41, § 1.

Formerly Code 1863, § 3460; Code 1868, § 3480; Code 1873, § 3531; Code 1882, § 3531; Civil Code 1895, § 5138; Penal Code 1895, § 966; Civil Code 1910, § 5724; Penal Code 1910, § 992; Code 1933, § 81–1419.

§ 17–8–23. Absence of a party as cause for continuance

If either party is providentially prevented from attending the trial of any case and the counsel of the absent party will state in his place that he cannot go safely to trial without the presence of the absent party, the case shall be continued, provided his continuances are not exhausted.

Formerly Code 1863, § 3453; Code 1868, § 3473; Code 1873, § 3524; Code 1882, § 3524; Civil Code 1895, § 5131; Civil Code 1910, § 5717; Code 1933, § 81–1412.

§ 17–8–24. Absence or illness of counsel as cause for continuance

The illness or absence, from providential cause, of counsel where there is but one, or of the leading counsel where there are more than one, shall be a sufficient ground for continuance, provided that the party making the application will swear that he cannot go safely to trial without the services of the absent counsel, that he expects his services at the next term, and that the application is not made for delay only.

Formerly Code 1863, § 3454; Code 1868, § 3474; Code 1873, § 3525; Code 1882, § 3525; Civil Code 1895, § 5132; Penal Code 1895, § 964; Civil Code 1910, § 5718; Penal Code 1910, § 990; Code 1933, § 81–1413.

§ 17–8–25. Absence of witnesses; showing required

In all applications for continuances upon the ground of the absence of a witness, it shall be shown to the court that the witness is absent; that he has been subpoenaed; that he does not reside more than 100 miles from the place of trial by the nearest practical route; that his testimony is material; that the witness is not absent by the permission, directly or indirectly, of the applicant; that the applicant expects he will be able to procure the testimony of the witness at the next term of the court; that the application is not made for the purpose of delay but to enable the applicant to procure the testimony of the absent witness; and the application must state the facts expected to be proved by the absent witness.

Laws 1959, p. 342, § 1.

Formerly Code 1863, § 3451; Code 1868, § 3471; Code 1873, § 3522; Code 1882, § 3522; Civil Code 1895, § 5129; Penal Code 1895, § 962; Civil Code 1910, § 5715; Penal Code 1910, § 987; Code 1933, § 81–1410.

§ 17–8–26. Membership in General Assembly by party or counsel

(a) A member of the General Assembly who is a party to or the attorney for a party to a case which is pending in any trial or appellate court or before any administrative agency of this state shall be granted a continuance and stay of the case. The continuance and stay shall apply to all aspects of the case, including, but not limited to, the filing and serving of an answer to a complaint, the making of any discovery or motion, or of any response to any subpoena, discovery, or motion, and appearance at any hearing, pretrial appearance, arraignment, plea or motion calendar, trial, or argument. When a case, motion, hearing, or argument is called and is subject to a continuance or stay under this Code section due to the party's attorney's membership in the General Assembly, the party shall not be required to be present at the call of the case, motion, hearing, or argument. Unless a shorter length of time is requested by the member, the continuance and stay shall last the length of any regular or extraordinary session of the General Assembly and during the first three weeks following any recess or adjournment, including an adjournment sine die of any regular or extraordinary session. Notwithstanding any other provision of law, rule of court, or administrative rule or regulation, and to the extent permitted by the Constitutions of the United States and of the State of Georgia, the time for doing any act in the case which is delayed by the continuance or stay provided by this Code section shall be automatically extended by the same length of time as the continuance or stay covered.

(b) A continuance and stay shall also be granted for such other times as the member of the General Assembly or staff member certifies to the court that his or her presence elsewhere is required by his or her duties with the General Assembly.

Laws 1905, p. 93, § 1; Laws 1952, p. 26, § 1; Laws 1973, p. 478, § 1; Laws 1977, p. 760, § 1; Laws 1983, p. 675, § 1; Laws 1996, p. 112, § 2; Laws 2002, p. 403, § 2; Laws 2006, Act 749, § 3, eff. May 3, 2006.

Formerly Civil Code 1910, § 5711; Code 1933, § 81–1402.

Historical and Statutory Notes

The 2006 amendment by Act 749 designated existing text as subsec. (a) and added subsec. (b).

§ 17–8–27. Continuance of case when Attorney General occupied in aid of General Assembly

When any case pending in the courts of this state in which the Attorney General is of counsel is scheduled to be called for any purpose during sessions of the General Assembly or during a period of 15 days preceding or following sessions of the General Assembly, on motion of the Attorney General or an assistant attorney general, it shall be a good ground for continuance that the Attorney General and his staff are occupied in aid of the business of the General Assembly.

Laws 1956, p. 700, § 1.

§ 17–8–28. When witness is in attendance upon General Assembly

(a) Any person summoned to serve as a witness in a criminal case shall be excused by the judge from attendance at the court by reason of his attendance as a legislator at the General Assembly.

(b) In all criminal cases, it shall be the duty of the presiding judge, on motion of either the state or the defendant, to continue the case when it appears that a material witness is absent from the court by reason of his attendance at the General Assembly.

Laws 1905, p. 93, § 3.

Formerly Civil Code 1910, § 5712; Penal Code 1910, § 988; Code 1933, §§ 27–2003, 81–1407.

§ 17–8–29. Absence of party or counsel on meeting of Board of Regents of University System of Georgia or State Board of Education

Should any member of the Board of Regents of the University System of Georgia or any member of the State Board of Education be engaged at the time of any meeting of the board as counsel or party in any case pending in the courts of this state and should the case be called for trial during the regular session of the board, the member's absence from attending the session shall be good ground for a postponement or continuance of the case until the session of the board has ended.

Laws 1931, p. 7, § 56; Laws 1985, p. 1406, § 2; Laws 1997, p. 143, § 17.

Formerly Code 1933, § 81–1404.

§ 17–8–30. Absence of party or counsel on meeting of Board of Human Services

Should any member of the Board of Human Services or the Board of Behavioral Health and Developmental Disabilities be engaged at the time of any meeting of the board as counsel or party in any case pending in the courts of this state and should the case be called for trial during the regular session of the board, the absence of the member to attend the session shall be good ground for a postponement or a continuance of the case until the session of the board has ended.

Laws 1933, p. 7, § 1; Laws 2009, Act 102, § 2–3, eff. July 1, 2009; Laws 2010, Act 418, § 13, eff. July 1, 2010.

Formerly Code 1933, § 81–1405.

Historical and Statutory Notes

The 2009 amendment by Act 102 substituted "Board of Human Services" for "Board of Human Resources" throughout the section.

The 2010 amendment by Act 418 inserted "or the Board of Behavioral Health and Developmental Disabilities" after "Board of Human Services" and substituted "the absence of the member" for "his absence".

§ 17–8–31. Absence of parties or leading attorney by reason of active duty in the armed forces

(a) It shall be the duty of any judge of the courts of this state to continue any case in the court on or without motion when any party thereto or his or her leading attorney is absent from court when the case is reached by reason of his or her attendance on active duty as a member of the National Guard or a reserve or active component of the armed forces of the United States. The case may proceed if the party, in the absence of his or her leading attorney, or the leading attorney, in the absence of the party, announces ready for trial on the call of the case. If counsel is absent, it shall be necessary for his or her client to make oath that he or she cannot safely go to trial without the absent attorney and, if a party is absent, his or her counsel shall state in his or her place that he or she cannot safely go to trial without the client.

(b) It shall be the duty of any judge of the courts of this state to continue any case in the court upon a showing by the state or the defendant that a material and necessary witness is unavailable by reason of being on active duty as a member of the National Guard or as a member of a reserve or active component of the armed forces of the United States.

(c) In cases in which a demand for speedy trial has been filed in accordance with Code Section 17–7–170 or 17–7–171, the court shall grant the continuance if the party moving for a continuance pursuant to subsection (b) of this Code section establishes by testimony, affidavits, or other evidence that:

(1) The witness is material and necessary;

(2) The witness is located outside the territorial limits of the state;

(3) The party has submitted a request to the proper military authorities for the testimony of the witness in accordance with Section 301 of Title 5 of the United States Code and federal regulations or directives issued by the armed forces pursuant thereto; and

(4) The witness will not be available within the time limits prescribed by Code Section 17–7–170 or 17–7–171.

This continuance shall toll the running of the demand for speedy trial and shall continue the trial until the witness is released from active duty or the military makes the witness available to testify. If the witness only becomes available to testify within the last two weeks of the term of court in which the case must be tried, the case may be tried at the next succeeding term of court.

(d) In any case in which the court grants the state a continuance pursuant to subsection (c) of this Code section, the defendant shall have bail set upon application to the court, except in those cases punishable by death or imprisonment for life without parole. In any case in which the defendant is accused of committing a serious violent felony, as defined by subsection (a) of Code Section 17–10–6.1, the court shall consider but shall not be required to set bail.

Laws 1925, p. 149, § 1; Laws 2003, Act 26, § 4, eff. May 14, 2003; Laws 2004, Act 564, 17, eff. May 13, 2004; Laws 2006, Act 879, § 5, eff. July 1, 2006.

Formerly Code 1933, § 81–1406.

Historical and Statutory Notes

The 2003 amendment by Act 26 rewrote the section which had read:

"It shall be the duty of any judge of the courts of this state to continue any case in the court on or without motion when any party thereto or his leading attorney is absent from court when the case is reached by reason of his attendance on active duty as a member of the National Guard. The case may proceed if the party, in the absence of his leading attorney, or the leading attorney, in the absence of the party, announces ready for trial on the call of the case. If counsel is absent, it shall be necessary for his client to make oath that he cannot safely go to trial without the absent attorney and, if a party is absent, his counsel shall state in his place that he cannot safely go to trial without the client."

The 2004 amendment by Act 564 was a provision contained in a correction bill.

The 2006 amendment by Act 879 inserted "speedy" preceding "trial" twice in subsec. (c).

§ 17–8–32. Admission of facts as ground for denial of continuance because of absence of witness

No continuance shall be allowed in any court on account of the absence of a witness or for the purpose of procuring testimony when the opposite party is willing to admit, and does not contest the truth of, the facts expected to be proved; and the court shall order such admission to be reduced to writing.

Laws 1853–54, p. 52, § 1.

Formerly Code 1863, § 3452; Code 1868, § 3472; Code 1873, § 3523; Code 1882, § 3523; Civil Code 1895, § 5130; Penal Code 1895, § 963; Civil Code 1910, § 5716; Penal Code 1910, § 989; Code 1933, § 81–1411.

§ 17–8–33. When case tried and when continued

(a) Every person against whom a true bill of indictment is found or an accusation is made shall be tried at the term of the court at which the indictment is found or the accusation is made unless the absence of a material witness or the principles of justice should require a continuance of the case, in which case the court shall allow a continuance until the next term of the court. The court shall have power to allow the continuance of criminal cases from term to term, as often as the principles of justice may require, upon sufficient cause shown under oath.

(b) No continuance shall be granted over the objection of the adverse party in any court which has a continuous session for 30 days or more where the cause for the continuance can be obviated by a postponement to a later day during the term. Whenever a motion and a proper showing for a continuance is made by either party, the presiding judge, at any time, shall set the case down for a later day during the same term if it shall be practicable thereby to avoid a continuance of the case until the next term.

Laws 1833, Cobb's 1851 Digest, p. 835; Laws 1893, p. 56, § 1.

Formerly Code 1863, § 4533; Code 1868, § 4553; Code 1873, § 4647; Code 1882, § 4647; Penal Code 1895, § 961; Penal Code 1910, § 986; Code 1933, § 27–2002.

§ 17–8–34. Cases sent back from appellate court

When a case is sent back for trial to a superior, state, or city court by the Supreme Court or Court of Appeals, the case shall be in order for trial; and, if the continuances of either party are exhausted, the trial court may grant one continuance to the party, as the ends of justice may require.

Laws 1851–52, p. 214, § 6.

Formerly Code 1863, § 3456; Code 1868, § 3476; Code 1873, § 3527; Code 1882, § 3527; Civil Code 1895, § 5134; Civil Code 1910, § 5720; Code 1933, § 81–1415.

§ 17–8–35. Continuance by codefendant; effect

The continuance of a case by one of several defendants indicted jointly shall not operate as a continuance as to the other defendants objecting thereto.

Laws 1858, p. 99, § 2.

Formerly Code 1863, § 4575; Code 1868, § 4596; Code 1873, § 4693; Code 1882, § 4693; Penal Code 1895, § 967; Penal Code 1910, § 993; Code 1933, § 27–2004.

§ 17–8–36. Public announcement of continuance

The judges of the superior, state, and city courts shall, upon the continuance of any case, enter the date of the continuance upon their dockets opposite the case and in open court make public announcement of the continuance.

Laws 1895, p. 41, § 1; Laws 1983, p. 884, § 3–20.

Formerly Civil Code 1895, § 5140; Penal Code 1895, § 968; Civil Code 1910, § 5726; Penal Code 1910, § 994; Code 1933, § 81–1421.

§ 17–8–37. Length of continuance

When a court grants a continuance of a pending case for whatever cause, the continuance shall extend until the next term of court only.

Laws 1799, Cobb's 1851 Digest, p. 486.

Formerly Code 1863, § 3448; Code 1868, § 3468; Code 1873, § 3519; Code 1882, § 3519; Civil Code 1895, § 5126; Civil Code 1910, § 5710; Code 1933, § 81–1401.

§ 17–8–38. Case not reached at trial term

A case not reached at the trial term stands over as continued.

Formerly Code 1863, § 3455; Code 1868, § 3475; Code 1873, § 3526; Code 1882, § 3526; Civil Code 1895, § 5133; Civil Code 1910, § 5719; Code 1933, § 81–1414.

Article 3

Conduct of Proceedings

§ 17–8–50. Trials for escapees from state or county correctional institutions; witnesses

The trial of inmates escaping from a state or county correctional institution shall take place in the superior court of the county in which the escape occurs, and inmates so escaping shall remain in the correctional institution after their apprehension and shall be treated as are other inmates until the trial takes place. At the trial, the copies of the records transmitted to the superintendent or warden of the state or county correctional institution, relative to the former trials of such inmates, shall be produced and filed of record in the superior court; and any other inmate not included in the same indictment shall be a competent witness.

Laws 1833, Cobb's 1851 Digest, p. 837; Laws 1968, p. 1249, § 1.

Formerly Code 1863, § 4545; Code 1868, § 4565; Code 1873, § 4659; Code 1882, § 4659; Penal Code 1895, § 318; Penal Code 1910, § 323; Code 1933, § 26–4511; Code 1933, § 26–9902.

§ 17–8–51. Convict witnesses on trial for mutiny

At the trial of an inmate of a penal institution for the crime of mutiny, any other inmate not included in the same indictment shall be a competent witness, and the infamy of his character and of the crime of which he has been convicted shall be exceptions to his credit only.

Laws 1833, Cobb's 1851 Digest, p. 840; Laws 1968, p. 1249, § 1.

Formerly Code 1863, § 4563; Code 1868, § 4583; Code 1873, § 4677; Code 1882, § 4677; Penal Code 1895, § 331; Penal Code 1910, § 336; Code 1933, § 26–4803; Code 1933, § 26–9903.

§ 17–8–52. Witnesses' oath in criminal cases

(a) The following oath shall be administered to witnesses in criminal cases:

> "Do you solemnly swear or affirm that the evidence you shall give to the court and jury in the matter now pending before the court shall be the truth, the whole truth, and nothing but the truth? So help you God."

(b) Any oath given that substantially complies with the language in this Code section shall subject the witness to the provisions of Code Section 16–10–70.

Laws 1833, Cobb's 1851 Digest, p. 836; Laws 1997, p. 1499, § 2.

Formerly Code 1863, § 4537; Code 1868, § 4557; Code 1873, § 4651; Code 1882, § 4651; Penal Code 1895, § 980; Penal Code 1910, § 1006; Code 1933, § 38–1702.

§ 17–8–53. Exclusion of public from courtroom when evidence vulgar

During a trial in a court of any case in which the evidence is vulgar and obscene or relates to the improper acts of the sexes, and tends to debauch the morals of the young, the presiding judge shall have the right in his discretion and on his own motion, or on motion of a party or his attorney, to hear and try the case after clearing the courtroom of all or any portion of the audience.

Laws 1890–91, p. 111, § 1; Laws 1895, p. 49, § 1.

Formerly Civil Code 1895, § 5296; Civil Code 1910, § 5885; Code 1933, § 81–1006.

§ 17–8–54. Exclusion of persons from courtroom when person under 16 years of age testifies in sex offense case

In the trial of any criminal case, when any person under the age of 16 is testifying concerning any sex offense, the court shall clear the courtroom of all persons except parties to the cause and their immediate families or guardians, attorneys and their secretaries, officers of the court, jurors, newspaper reporters or broadcasters, and court reporters.

Laws 1985, p. 1190, § 1.

§ 17–8–55. Closed circuit television testimony of sex offense victims under 10 years of age

(a) In all proceedings involving the criminal charges specified in this Code section, the court may order that the testimony of a child ten years of age or younger who has been the victim of any violation of Code Section 16–5–70, Code Section 16–6–1, Code Section 16–6–2, Code Section 16–6–4, or Code Section 16–6–5.1 be taken outside the courtroom and shown in the courtroom by means of a two-way closed circuit television. An order may be granted in such cases only if:

(1) The testimony is taken during the criminal trial proceeding for such violation; and

(2) The judge determines that testimony by the child victim in the courtroom will result in the child's suffering serious emotional distress such that the child cannot reasonably communicate.

(b) Only the prosecuting attorney, the attorney for the defendant, and the judge may question the child who testifies by two-way closed circuit television.

(c) The operators of the two-way closed circuit television shall make every effort to be unobtrusive.

(d) Only the following persons may be in the room with the child when the child testifies by two-way closed circuit television:

(1) The prosecuting attorney;

(2) The attorney for the defendant;

(3) The operators of the two-way closed circuit television equipment;

(4) The judge; and

(5) In the court's discretion, any person whose presence, in the opinion of the court, contributes to the well-being of the child, including a person who has dealt with the child in a therapeutic setting concerning the crime. The defendant and defendant's counsel shall be notified at least 24 hours before the closed circuit testimony as to the prosecution's representatives and any other persons who shall be present in the room with the child victim during the child's testimony.

(e) During the child's testimony by two-way closed circuit television, the defendant shall be in the courtroom.

(f) The defendant shall be allowed to communicate with the persons in the room where the child is testifying by any appropriate electronic method.

(g) The provisions of this Code section do not apply if the defendant is an attorney pro se.

(h) This Code section may not be interpreted to preclude, for purposes of identification of a defendant, the presence of both the child victim and the defendant in the courtroom at the same time.

Laws 1985, p. 1190, § 1; Laws 1990, p. 8, § 17; Laws 1991, p. 1377, § 1.

§ 17–8–56. Judges to write out charges on request when official reporter not present; charges to be filed; certified copies

(a) The judges of the superior, state, and city courts shall, when the counsel for either party requests it before argument begins, write out their charges and read them to the jury; and it shall be error to give any other or additional charge than that so written and read.

(b) The charge so written out and read shall be filed with the clerk of the court in which it was given and shall be accessible to all persons interested in it. The clerk shall give certified copies of the charge to any person applying therefor, upon payment of the usual fee.

(c) This Code section shall not apply when there is an official stenographer or reporter of the court in attendance thereon who takes down in shorthand and writes out the full charge of the trial judge in the case upon the direction of court.

Laws 1860, p. 42, §§ 1, 2; Laws 1877, p. 13, § 1; Laws 1878–79, p. 150, § 1; Laws 1897, p. 41, § 1; Laws 1943, p. 262, § 1; Laws 1983, p. 884, § 3–21; Laws 1985, p. 1190, § 1.

Formerly Code 1863, §§ 240, 241; Code 1868, §§ 234, 235; Code 1873, §§ 244, 245; Code 1882, §§ 244, 245; Civil Code 1895, §§ 4318, 4319; Penal Code 1895, §§ 1030, 1031; Civil Code 1910, §§ 4847, 4848; Penal Code 1910, §§ 1056, 1057; Code 1933, §§ 81–1102, 81–1103.

§ 17–8–57. Expression of opinion on facts, error

It is error for any judge in any criminal case, during its progress or in his charge to the jury, to express or intimate his opinion as to what has or has not been proved or as to the guilt of the accused. Should any judge violate this Code section, the violation shall be held by the Supreme Court or Court of Appeals to be error and the decision in the case reversed, and a new trial granted in the court below with such directions as the Supreme Court or Court of Appeals may lawfully give.

Laws 1850, Cobb's 1851 Digest, p. 462; Laws 1985, p. 1190, § 1.

Formerly Code 1863, § 3172; Code 1868, § 3183; Code 1873, § 3248; Code 1882, § 3248; Civil Code 1895, § 4334; Penal Code 1895, § 1032; Civil Code 1910, § 4863; Penal Code 1910, § 1058; Code 1933, § 81–1104; Code 1981, § 17–8–55.

§ 17–8–58. Objection to charge to jury or failure to charge; failure to object

(a) Any party who objects to any portion of the charge to the jury or the failure to charge the jury shall inform the court of the specific objection and the grounds for such objection before the jury retires to deliberate. Such objections shall be done outside of the jury's hearing and presence.

(b) Failure to object in accordance with subsection (a) of this Code section shall preclude appellate review of such portion of the jury charge, unless such portion of the jury charge constitutes plain error which affects substantial rights of the parties. Such plain error may be considered on appeal even if it was not brought to the court's attention as provided in subsection (a) of this Code section.

Laws 2007, Act 327, § 1, eff. July 1, 2007.

Historical and Statutory Notes

Laws 2007, Act 327, § 5, provides:

"This Act shall become effective on July 1, 2007, and shall apply to all trials which occur on or after July 1, 2007."

Article 4

Conduct and Argument of Counsel

§ 17–8–70. Number of counsel who may argue case

Not more than two counsel shall be permitted to argue any case for each side, except by express leave of the court. In no case shall more than one counsel for each side be heard in conclusion.

Laws 1924, p. 75, § 1.

Formerly Code 1933, § 27–2202.

§ 17–8–71. Order of argument

After the evidence is closed on both sides, the prosecuting attorney shall open and conclude the argument to the jury. The defendant shall be entitled to make a closing argument prior to the concluding argument of the prosecuting attorney.

Laws 1851–52, p. 242, § 1; Laws 2005, Act 8, § 10, eff. July 1, 2005.

Formerly Code 1868, § 4551; Code 1873, § 4645; Code 1882, § 4645; Penal Code 1895, § 1029; Penal Code 1910, § 1055; Code 1933, § 27–2201.

Historical and Statutory Notes

The 2005 amendment by Act 8 substituted "The defendant shall be entitled to make a closing argument prior to the concluding argument of the prosecuting attorney" for "If the defendant introduces no evidence, his counsel shall open and conclude the argument to the jury after the evidence on the part of the state is closed" at the end of the section.

Laws 2005, Act 8, § 17, provides:

"This Act shall apply to all trials which commence on or after July 1, 2005."

§ 17–8–72. Limit of one-half hour in cases below felony

In all misdemeanor cases and cases brought up from inferior judicatories, counsel for either party shall not occupy more than one-half hour in the whole discussion of the case after the evidence is closed without obtaining special leave of the court before the argument is opened.

Laws 1924, p. 75, § 2.

Formerly Code 1933, § 27–2203.

§ 17–8–73. Time limits for closing argument in capital and noncapital felony cases

In felony cases other than those involving capital felonies, counsel shall be limited in their closing arguments to one hour for each side. In cases involving capital felonies, counsel shall be limited to two hours for each side.

Laws 1924, p. 75, § 3.

Formerly Code 1933, § 27–2204.

§ 17–8–74. Extension of time, when allowed

If, before argument begins, counsel on either side applies to the court for an extension of the time prescribed for argument and states in his place or on oath, in the discretion of the court, that he cannot do the case justice within the time prescribed and that it will require for that purpose additional time, stating how much additional time will be necessary, the court shall grant such extension of time as may seem reasonable and proper, provided that the extension of time granted in misdemeanor cases or cases brought up from inferior judicatories shall not exceed 30 minutes.

Laws 1924, p. 75, § 4; Laws 1982, p. 3, § 17.

Formerly Code 1933, § 27–2205.

§ 17–8–75. Improper conduct by counsel; duty of court

Where counsel in the hearing of the jury make statements of prejudicial matters which are not in evidence, it is the duty of the court to interpose and prevent the same. On objection made, the court shall also rebuke the counsel and by all needful and proper instructions to the jury endeavor to remove the improper impression from their minds; or, in his discretion, he may order a mistrial if the prosecuting attorney is the offender.

Formerly Civil Code 1895, § 4419; Civil Code 1910, § 4957; Code 1933, § 81–1009.

§ 17–8–76. Counsel prohibited from arguing possibility of executive clemency; mistrial for violation of rule

(a) No attorney at law in a criminal case shall argue to or in the presence of the jury that a defendant, if convicted, may not be required to suffer the full penalty imposed by the court or jury because pardon, parole, or clemency of any nature may be granted by the Governor, the State Board of Pardons and Paroles, or other proper authority vested with the right to grant clemency.

(b) If counsel for either side in a criminal case argues to or in the presence of the jury as provided in subsection (a) of this Code section, opposing counsel shall have the right immediately to request the court to declare a mistrial, in which case it shall be mandatory upon the court to declare a mistrial. Failure to declare a mistrial shall constitute reversible error.

(c) This Code section shall be construed as setting forth requirements in addition to other requirements of law.

Laws 1955, p. 191, §§ 1–3.

CHAPTER 9

VERDICT AND JUDGMENT GENERALLY

Article 1

Article 1

General Provisions

§ 17–9–1. Direction of verdict of acquittal

(a) Where there is no conflict in the evidence and the evidence introduced with all reasonable deductions and inferences therefrom shall demand a verdict of acquittal or "not guilty" as to the entire offense or to some particular count or offense, the court may direct the verdict of acquittal to which the defendant is entitled under the evidence and may allow the trial to proceed only as to the counts or offenses remaining, if any.

(b) The defendant shall be entitled to move for a directed verdict at the close of the evidence offered by the prosecuting attorney or at the close of the case, even if he fails to introduce any evidence at the trial. A defendant who moves for a directed verdict at the close of the evidence offered by the prosecuting attorney may offer evidence in the event that the motion is not granted, without having reserved the right to do so and to the same extent as if the motion had not been made. A motion for a directed verdict which is not granted shall not be deemed to be a waiver of the right to trial by jury. The order of the court granting a motion for a directed verdict of acquittal is effective without any assent of the jury.

Laws 1971, p. 460, § 1; Laws 1982, p. 3, § 17.

Formerly Code 1933, § 27–1802.

§ 17–9–2. Jury judges of law and facts; general verdict; form and construction of verdicts

The jury shall be the judges of the law and the facts in the trial of all criminal cases and shall give a general verdict of "guilty" or "not guilty." Upon a verdict of "guilty," the sentence shall be imposed by the judge, unless otherwise provided by law. Verdicts are to have a reasonable intendment, are to receive a reasonable construction, and are not to be avoided unless from necessity.

Laws 1833, Cobb's 1851 Digest, p. 835; Laws 1974, p. 352, § 1.

Formerly Code 1863, §§ 3481, 4532; Code 1868, §§ 3503, 4552; Code 1873, §§ 3561, 4646; Code 1882, §§ 3561, 4646; Penal Code 1895, § 1033; Penal Code 1910, § 1059; Code 1933, § 27–2301.

§ 17–9–3. Recommendation for mercy

In all capital cases, other than those of homicide, when the verdict is "guilty," with a recommendation for mercy, it shall be legal and shall mean imprisonment for life. When the verdict is "guilty," without a recommendation for mercy, it shall be legal and shall mean that the convicted person shall be sentenced to death. When it is shown that a person convicted of a capital offense without a recommendation for mercy had not reached his seventeenth birthday at the time of the commission of the offense, the punishment of such person shall not be death but shall be imprisonment for life.

Laws 1875, p. 106, § 2; Laws 1963, p. 122, § 2; Laws 1974, p. 352, § 2.

Formerly Code 1882, § 4646a; Penal Code 1895, § 1034; Penal Code 1910, § 1060; Code 1933, § 27–2302.

§ 17–9–4. Judgments void because of want of jurisdiction of court

The judgment of a court having no jurisdiction of the person or subject matter, or void for any other cause, is a mere nullity and may be so held in any court when it becomes material to the interest of the parties to consider it.

Formerly Code 1863, § 3513; Code 1868, § 3536; Code 1873, § 3594; Code 1882, § 3594; Civil Code 1895, § 5369; Civil Code 1910, § 5964; Code 1933, § 110–709.

Article 2

Rendition and Receipt of Verdict

§ 17–9–20. Juror not to act on private knowledge

A juror shall not act on his private knowledge respecting the facts, witnesses, or parties unless he is sworn and examined as a witness in the case.

Formerly Civil Code 1895, § 5337; Civil Code 1910, § 5932; Code 1933, § 110–108.

§ 17–9–21. Receipt of verdict

Verdicts shall be received only in open court, in the absence of agreement of the parties.

Formerly Code 1863, § 3486; Code 1868, § 3509; Code 1873, § 3567; Code 1882, § 3567; Civil Code 1895, § 5336; Civil Code 1910, § 5931; Code 1933, § 110–107.

§ 17–9–22. Expression in open court of approval or disapproval of verdict or discharge of jury forbidden

(a) No judge of any court shall either directly or indirectly express in open court his approval or disapproval of the verdict of any jury in any case tried before him, except as provided in subsection (c) of this Code section; nor may any judge discharge any jury upon the ground that the verdict rendered in any case does not meet with his approval.

(b) If any judge of any court either directly or indirectly expresses in open court his approval or disapproval of the verdict of the jury in any case tried before him, he shall be disqualified from presiding in the case in the event a new trial is granted.

(c) Nothing in this Code section shall have the effect of prohibiting a judge of any court from approving or disapproving the verdict of a jury in any case tried before him in hearing a motion for a new trial that comes on before him; but the approval or disapproval on the hearing of a motion for new trial shall be expressed in the formal order of the judge in granting or overruling the motion and not otherwise.

Laws 1918, p. 168, §§ 1, 2.

Formerly Code 1933, §§ 110–201, 110–202.

§ 17–9–23. Commending or complimenting jury forbidden

No judge of any court may commend or compliment a jury during the term of any court for discharging its duty if the commendation or compliment has the effect of approving of a verdict.

Laws 1918, p. 168, § 3.

Formerly Code 1933, § 110–203.

Article 3

Amendment and Impeachment of Verdict

§ 17–9–40. Amendment of verdict after dispersion of jury

A verdict may be amended in mere matter of form after the jury have dispersed; but, after it has been received, recorded, and the jury dispersed, it may not be amended in matter of substance, either by what the jurors say they intended to find or otherwise.

Formerly Code 1863, § 3422; Code 1868, § 3442; Code 1873, § 3492; Code 1882, § 3492; Civil Code 1895, § 5111; Civil Code 1910, § 5695; Code 1933, § 110–111.

§ 17–9–41. Jurors may sustain but not impeach verdict

The affidavits of jurors may be taken to sustain but not to impeach their verdict.

Formerly Civil Code 1895, § 5338; Civil Code 1910, § 5933; Code 1933, § 110–109.

Article 4

Motions in Arrest

§ 17–9–60. Motion in arrest of judgment; notice of motion

All motions to arrest a judgment must be made to the court by which the judgment was rendered, and the opposite party must have reasonable notice of such motions.

Formerly Code 1863, § 3511; Code 1868, § 3534; Code 1873, § 3592; Code 1882, § 3592; Civil Code 1895, § 5367; Civil Code 1910, § 5962; Code 1933, § 110–707.

§ 17–9–61. Grounds and time for motion in arrest

(a) When a judgment has been rendered, either party may move in arrest thereof for any defect not amendable which appears on the face of the record or pleadings.

(b) A motion in arrest of judgment must be made during the term at which the judgment was obtained.

Formerly Code 1863, §§ 3506, 3507; Code 1868, §§ 3529, 3530; Code 1873, §§ 3587, 3588; Code 1882, §§ 3587, 3588; Civil Code 1895, §§ 5362, 5363; Civil Code 1910, §§ 5957, 5958; Code 1933, §§ 110–702, 110–703.

§ 17–9–62. Amendable defects not ground for arrest

A judgment may not be arrested for any defect in the pleadings or record that is aided by verdict or amendable as a matter of form.

Formerly Code 1863, § 3509; Code 1868, § 3532; Code 1873, § 3590; Code 1882, § 3590; Civil Code 1895, § 5365; Civil Code 1910, § 5960; Code 1933, § 110–705.

§ 17–9–63. Motion not granted for matters not affecting real merits of offense charged

No motion in arrest of judgment shall be granted for any matter not affecting the real merits of the offense charged in the indictment or accusation.

Laws 1833, Cobb's 1851 Digest, p. 833.

Formerly Code 1863, § 4517; Code 1868, § 4536; Code 1873, § 4629; Code 1882, § 4629; Penal Code 1895, § 955; Penal Code 1910, § 980; Code 1933, § 27–1601.

CHAPTER 10

SENTENCE AND PUNISHMENT

Article 1

Article 1

Procedure for Sentencing and Imposition of Punishment

§ 17–10–1. Determinate sentences

(a)(1) Except in cases in which life imprisonment, life without parole, or the death penalty may be imposed, upon a verdict or plea of guilty in any case involving a misdemeanor or felony, and after a presentence hearing, the judge fixing the sentence shall prescribe a determinate sentence for a specific number of months or years which shall be within the minimum and maximum sentences prescribed by law as the punishment for the crime. The judge imposing the sentence is granted power and authority to suspend or probate all or any part of the entire sentence under such rules and regulations as the judge deems proper, including service of a probated sentence in the sentencing options system, as provided by Article 9 of Chapter 8 of Title 42, and including the authority to revoke the suspension or probation when the defendant has violated any of the rules and regulations prescribed by the court, even before the probationary period has begun, subject to the conditions set out in this subsection; provided, however, that such action shall be subject to the provisions of Code Sections 17–10–6.1 and 17–10–6.2.

(2) Probation supervision shall terminate in all cases no later than two years from the commencement of probation supervision unless specially extended or reinstated by the sentencing court upon notice and hearing and for good cause shown; provided, however, that in those cases involving the collection of fines, restitution, or other funds, the period of supervision shall remain in effect for so long as any such obligation is outstanding, or until termination of the sentence, whichever first occurs, and for those cases involving a conviction under the Georgia Street Gang Terrorism and Prevention Act, the period of supervision shall remain in effect until the termination of the sentence, but shall not exceed five years unless as otherwise provided in this paragraph. Probation supervision shall not be required for defendants sentenced to probation while the defendant is in the legal custody of the Department of Corrections or the State Board of Pardons and Paroles.

(3)(A) Any part of a sentence of probation revoked for a violation other than a subsequent commission of any felony, a violation of a special condition, or a misdemeanor offense involving physical violence resulting in bodily injury to an innocent victim which in the opinion of the trial court constitutes a danger to the community or a serious infraction occurring while the defendant is assigned to an alternative probation confinement facility shall be served in a probation detention center, probation boot camp, diversion center, weekend lock up, or confinement in a local jail or detention facility, or other community correctional alternatives available to the court or provided by the Department of Corrections.

(B) A parolee or probationer charged with a misdemeanor involving physical injury or an attempt to commit physical injury or terroristic threats or with a new felony shall not be entitled to bond pending a hearing on the revocation of his or her parole or probation, except by order of a judge of the superior, state, or magistrate court wherein the alleged new offense occurred after a hearing and upon determination of the superior, state, or magistrate court that the parolee or probationer does not constitute a threat to the community; provided, however, that this subparagraph does not authorize state or magistrate court judges to grant bail for a person charged with any offense listed in subsection (a) of Code Section 17–6–1.

(4) In cases of imprisonment followed by probation, the sentence shall specifically provide that the period of probation shall not begin until the defendant has completed service of the confinement portion of the sentence. No revocation of any part of a probated sentence shall be effective while a defendant is in the legal custody of the State Board of Pardons and Paroles.

(5)(A) Where a defendant has been sentenced to probation, the court shall retain jurisdiction throughout the period of the probated sentence as provided for in subsection (g) of Code Section 42–8–34. Without limiting the generality of the foregoing, the court may shorten the period of probation on motion of the defendant or on its own motion, if the court determines that probation is no longer necessary or appropriate for the ends of justice, the protection of society, and the rehabilitation of the defendant. Prior to entering any order for shortening a period of probation, the court shall afford notice to the victim or victims of all sex related offenses or violent offenses resulting in serious bodily injury or death, and, upon request of the victim or victims so notified, shall afford notice and an opportunity for hearing to the defendant and the prosecuting attorney.

(B) The Department of Corrections shall establish a form document which shall include the elements set forth in this Code section concerning notification of victims and shall make copies of such form available to prosecuting attorneys in the state. When requested by the victim, the form document shall be provided to the victim by the prosecuting attorney. The form shall include the address of the probation office having jurisdiction over the case and contain a statement that the victim must maintain a copy of his or her address with the probation office and must notify the office of any change of address in order to maintain eligibility for notification by the Department of Corrections as required in this Code section.

(6)(A) Except as otherwise authorized by law, no court shall modify, suspend, probate, or alter a previously imposed sentence so as to reduce or eliminate a period of incarceration or probation and impose a financial payment which:

(i) Exceeds the statutorily specified maximum fine, plus all penalties, fees, surcharges, and restitution permitted or authorized by law; or

(ii) Is to be made to an entity which is not authorized by law to receive fines, penalties, fees, surcharges, or restitution.

(B) The prohibitions contained in this paragraph shall apply regardless of whether a defendant consents to the modification, suspension, probation, or alteration of such defendant's sentence and the imposition of such payment.

(C) Nothing in this paragraph shall prohibit or prevent a court from requiring, as a condition of suspension, modification, or probation of a sentence in a criminal case involving child abandonment, that the defendant pay all or a portion of child support which is owed to the custodial parent of a child which is the subject of such case.

(b) The judge, in fixing the sentence as prescribed in subsection (a) of this Code section, may make a determination as to whether the person being sentenced should be considered for parole prior to the completion of any requirement otherwise imposed by law relating to the completion of service of any specified time period before parole eligibility. In the event that the judge so determines, he may specify in the sentence that the person is sentenced under this subsection and may provide that the State Board of Pardons and Paroles, acting in its sole discretion, may consider and may parole any person so sentenced at any time prior to the completion of any minimum requirement otherwise imposed by law, rule, or regulation for the service of sentences or portions thereof. The determination allowed in this subsection shall be applicable to first offenders only.

(c) In any case in which a minor defendant who has not achieved a high school diploma or the equivalent is placed under a probated or suspended sentence, the court may require as a condition of probation or suspension of sentence that the defendant pursue a course of study designed to lead to achieving a high school diploma or the equivalent; and, in any case in which such a condition of probation may be imposed, the court shall give express consideration to whether such a condition should be imposed.

(d) In any case involving a misdemeanor or a felony in which the defendant has been punished in whole or in part by a fine, the sentencing judge shall be authorized to allow the defendant to satisfy such fine through community service as defined in paragraph (2) of Code Section 42–8–70. One hour of community service shall equal the dollar amount of one hour of paid labor at the minimum wage under the federal Fair Labor Standards Act of 1938,[1] as now or hereafter amended, unless otherwise specified by the sentencing judge. A defendant shall be required to serve the number of hours in community service which equals the number derived by dividing the amount of the fine by the federal minimum hourly wage or by the amount specified by the sentencing judge. Prior to or subsequent to sentencing, a defendant may request the court that all or any portion of a fine may be satisfied under this subsection.

(e) In any case involving a felony in which the defendant previously appeared before a juvenile court, the records of the dispositions of the defendant as well as any evidence used in any juvenile court hearing shall be available to the district attorney, the defendant, and the superior court judge in determining sentencing as provided in Code Section 15–11–79.1.

(f) Within one year of the date upon which the sentence is imposed, or within 120 days after receipt by the sentencing court of the remittitur upon affirmance of the judgment after direct appeal, whichever is later, the court imposing the sentence has the jurisdiction, power, and authority to correct or reduce the sentence and to suspend or probate all or any part of the sentence imposed. Prior to entering any order correcting, reducing, or modifying any sentence, the court shall afford notice and an opportunity for a hearing to the prosecuting attorney. Any order modifying a sentence which is entered without notice and an opportunity for a hearing as provided in this subsection shall be void. This subsection shall not limit any other jurisdiction granted to the court in this Code section or as provided for in subsection (g) of Code Section 42–8–34.

(g)(1)(A) In sentencing a defendant convicted of a felony to probated confinement, the sentencing judge may make the defendant's participation in a work release program operated by a county a condition of probation, provided that such program is available and the administrator of such program accepts the inmate.

(B) Any defendant accepted into a county work release program shall thereby be transferred into the legal custody of the administrator of said program; likewise, any defendant not accepted shall remain in the legal custody of the Department of Corrections.

(2) Work release status granted by the court may be revoked for cause by the sentencing court in its discretion or may be revoked by the state or local authority operating the work release program for any reason for which work release status would otherwise be revoked.

(3) The provisions of this subsection shall not limit the authority of the commissioner to authorize work release status pursuant to Code Section 42–5–59 or apply to or affect the authority to authorize work release of county prisoners, which shall be as provided for in Code Sections 42–1–4 and 42–1–9 or as otherwise provided by law.

(4) This subsection shall not apply with respect to any violent felony or any offense for which the work release status is specifically prohibited by law, including but not limited to serious violent felonies as specified in Code Section 17–10–6.1.

Laws 1919, p. 387, § 1; Laws 1950, p. 352, § 3; Laws 1964, p. 483, §§ 2, 4; Laws 1974, p. 352, §§ 3, 4; Laws 1981, p. 1024, § 1; Laws 1982, p. 3, § 17; Laws 1984, p. 894, § 2; Laws 1986, p. 842, § 1; Laws 1988, p. 463, § 1; Laws 1991, p. 310, § 1; Laws 1992, p. 3221, § 1; Laws 1993, p. 1654, § 1; Laws 1994, p. 1959, § 9; Laws 1995, p. 1043, § 1; Laws 1996, p. 1257, § 1; Laws 1998, p. 842, § 6; Laws 2000, p. 20, § 7; Laws 2001, p. 94, § 5; Laws 2001, p. 1030, § 1; Laws 2004, Act 595, § 1, eff. July 1, 2004; Laws 2005, Act 19, § 17, eff. April 7, 2005; Laws 2006, Act 571, § 19, eff. July 1, 2006; Laws 2010, Act 406, § 10, eff. July 1, 2010.

Formerly Code 1933, § 27–2502.

1 29 U.S.C.A. § 201 et seq.

Historical and Statutory Notes

The 2004 amendment by Act 595, in subsec. (a), par. (1), deleted "in conformity with any mandatory minimum sentences required by law or shall be" following "specific number of months or years which shall be", added "sentences" following "minimum and maximum", and added "including service of a probated sentence in the sentencing options system, as provided by Article 9 of Chapter 8 of Title 42, and" in the last sentence.

The 2005 amendment by Act 19 was a provision contained in a correction bill.

The 2006 amendment by Act 571, in subsec. (a), par. (1), substituted "Sections 17–10–6.1 and 17–10–6.2" for "Section 17–10–6.1".

Laws 2006, Act 571, §§ 1 and 30, provide:

"SECTION 1. The General Assembly finds and declares that recidivist sexual offenders, sexual offenders who use physical violence, and sexual offenders who prey on children are sexual predators who present an extreme threat to the public safety. Many sexual offenders are extremely likely to use physical violence and to repeat their offenses; and some sexual offenders commit many offenses, have many more victims than are ever reported, and are prosecuted for only a fraction of their crimes. The General Assembly finds that this makes the cost of sexual offender victimization to society at large, while incalculable, clearly exorbitant. The General Assembly further finds that the high level of threat that a sexual predator presents to the public safety, and the long-term effects suffered by victims of sex offenses, provide the state with sufficient justification to implement a strategy that includes:

"(1) Incarcerating sexual offenders and maintaining adequate facilities to ensure that decisions to release sexual predators into the community are not made on the basis of inadequate space;

"(2) Requiring the registration of sexual offenders, with a requirement that complete and accurate information be maintained and accessible for use by law enforcement authorities, communities, and the public;

"(3) Providing for community and public notification concerning the presence of sexual offenders;

"(4) Collecting data relative to sexual offenses and sexual offenders;

"(5) Requiring sexual predators who are released into the community to wear an electronic monitoring system for the rest of their natural life and to pay for such system; and

"(6) Prohibiting sexual predators from working with children, either for compensation or as a volunteer.

"The General Assembly further finds that the state has a compelling interest in protecting the public from sexual offenders and in protecting children from predatory sexual activity, and there is sufficient justification for requiring sexual offenders to register and for requiring community and public notification of the presence of sexual offenders. The General Assembly declares that in order to protect the public, it is necessary that the sexual offenders be registered and that members of the community and the public be notified of a sexual offender's presence. The designation of a person as a sexual offender is neither a sentence nor a punishment but simply a regulatory mechanism and status resulting from the conviction of certain crimes. Likewise, the designation of a person as a sexual predator is neither a sentence nor a punishment but simply a regulatory mechanism and status resulting from findings by the Sexual Offender Registration Review Board and a court if requested by a sexual offender."

"SECTION 30. (a) This Act shall become effective July 1, 2006.

"(b) Any person required to register pursuant to the provisions of Code Section 42–1–12, relating to the state sexual offender registry, and any person required not to reside within areas where minors congregate, as prohibited by Code Section 42–1–13 [see § 42–1–15], shall not be relieved of the obligation to comply with the provisions of said Code sections by the repeal and reenactment of said Code sections.

"(c) The provisions of this Act shall not affect or abate the status as a crime of any such act or omission which occurred prior to the effective date of the Act repealing, repealing and reenacting, or amending such law, nor shall the prosecution of such crime be abated as a result of such repeal, repeal and reenactment, or amendment."

The 2006 amendment by Act 739 added subsec. (g).

The 2010 amendment by Act 406, in subsec. (a), par. (2), inserted "and for those cases involving a conviction under the 'Georgia Street Gang Terrorism and Prevention Act,' the period of supervision shall remain in effect until the termination of the sentence, but shall not exceed five years unless as otherwise provided in this paragraph" at the end of the first sentence.

§ 17–10–1.1. Victim impact form

(a) A prosecuting attorney bringing charges against a defendant shall notify, where practical, the alleged victim or, when the victim is no longer living, a member of the victim's family of his or her right to submit a victim impact form.

(b)(1) A victim impact form shall identify the victim of the offense and the perpetrator.

(2) A victim impact form may itemize any economic loss suffered by the victim as a result of the offense and may:

(A) Identify any physical injury suffered by the victim as a result of the offense along with its seriousness and permanence;

(B) Describe any change in the victim's personal welfare or familial relationships as a result of the offense; and

(C) Contain any other information related to the impact of the offense upon the victim or the victim's family that the victim wishes to include.

(c) The Prosecuting Attorneys' Council of Georgia shall establish forms which are designed to obtain the information specified by subsection (b) of this Code section. The Prosecuting Attorneys' Council of Georgia shall make copies of such form available to prosecuting attorneys in the state. It shall be the duty of the prosecuting attorney or his or her designee to make such forms available to crime victims.

(d) The victim may complete a victim impact form and submit such form to the appropriate prosecuting attorney charged with the prosecution of the case. If the victim is unable to do so because of such victim's mental, emotional, or physical incapacity, or because of such victim's age, the victim's attorney or a family member may complete the victim impact form on behalf of the victim.

(e)(1) If, prior to trial, the defendant engages in discussion with the prosecuting attorney for the purpose of reaching a plea agreement or other pretrial disposition of his or her case, the prosecuting attorney shall, upon the request of the defendant, provide the defendant with a copy of the victim impact form relating to the defendant's case within a reasonable time prior to such discussions.

(2) If the prosecuting attorney intends to present information from a victim impact form to the court at any hearing at which sentencing or a determination of restitution will be considered by the court, the prosecuting attorney shall furnish a copy of the victim impact form to the defendant not less than five days prior to any such hearing. The defendant shall have the right to rebut the information contained in the victim impact form.

(3) The court shall consider the victim impact form that is presented to the court prior to imposing a sentence or making a determination as to the amount of restitution.

(f) If for any reason a victim was not allowed an opportunity to make a written victim impact statement, the victim may submit a victim impact statement to the State Board of Pardons and Paroles in any case prior to consideration of parole.

(g) No sentence shall be invalidated because of failure to comply with the provisions of this Code section. This Code section shall not be construed to create any cause of action or any right of appeal on behalf of any person.

Laws 1985, p. 739, § 1; Laws 1992, p. 2419, § 2; Laws 1993, p. 1660, § 1; Laws 2005, Act 20, § 3, eff. July 1, 2005.

Historical and Statutory Notes

The 2005 amendment by Act 20 rewrote the section which had read:

"(a)(1) A prosecuting attorney bringing charges against a defendant shall notify, where practical, the alleged victim or, when the victim is no longer living, a member of the victim's family of his or her right under certain circumstances to submit a victim impact statement:

"(A) Where the charge is a felony, if the defendant allegedly caused physical, psychological, or, if restitution is sought, economic injury to the victim; or

"(B) Where the charge is a misdemeanor, if the defendant allegedly caused serious physical injury or death to the victim.

"(2) A victim impact statement submitted by a victim shall be attached to the case file and may be used by the prosecuting attorney or the judge during any stage of the proceedings against the defendant involving predisposition, plea bargaining, sentencing, or determination of restitution.

"(b) A victim impact statement shall:

"(1) Identify the victim of the offense and the perpetrator;

"(2) Itemize any economic loss suffered by the victim as a result of the offense;

"(3) Identify any physical injury suffered by the victim as a result of the offense along with its seriousness and permanence;

"(4) Describe any change in the victim's personal welfare or familial relationships as a result of the offense;

"(5) Identify any request for psychological services initiated by the victim or the victim's family as a result of the offense; and

"(6) Contain any other information related to the impact of the offense upon the victim that the court requires.

"(c) The State Board of Pardons and Paroles shall establish a form document which shall include the elements set forth in subsection (b) of this Code section and shall make copies of such form available to prosecuting attorneys in the state. When requested by the victim, the victim impact statement form document shall be provided to the victim by the prosecuting attorney. The form shall include the address of the State Board of Pardons and Paroles and contain a statement that the victim must maintain a copy of his address with the State Board of Pardons and Paroles and must notify the board of any change of address.

"(d) The victim may complete the victim impact statement form and submit such form to the appropriate prosecuting attorney charged with the prosecution of the case. If the victim is unable to do so because of such victim's mental, emotional, or physical incapacity, or because of such victim's age, the victim's attorney or a family member may complete the victim impact statement form on behalf of the victim. The prosecuting attorney shall file any such written victim impact statement, if in existence at that time, with the court.

"(e) The court shall, in the manner prescribed by rule of court, provide the defendant with a copy of the victim impact statement within a reasonable time prior to any hearing at which it is to be considered and allow the defendant to have the opportunity to rebut the victim's written statements.

"(f) If for any reason a victim was not allowed an opportunity to make a written victim impact statement, the victim may submit a victim impact statement to the State Board of Pardons and Paroles in any case prior to consideration of parole.

"(g) No sentence shall be invalidated because of failure to comply with the provisions of this Code section. This Code section shall not be construed to create any cause of action or any right of appeal on behalf of any person."

§ 17–10–1.2. Admissibility of certain evidence subsequent to adjudication of guilt

(a)(1) In all cases in which the death penalty may be imposed, subsequent to an adjudication of guilt and in conjunction with the procedures in Code Section 17–10–30, the court shall allow evidence from the family of the victim, or such other witness having personal knowledge of the victim's personal characteristics and the emotional impact of the crime on the victim, the victim's family, or the community. Except as provided in paragraph (4) of this subsection, such evidence shall be given in the presence of the defendant and of the jury and shall be subject to cross-examination.

(2) The admissibility of the evidence described in paragraph (1) of this subsection and the number of witnesses other than immediate family who may testify shall be in the sole discretion of the judge and in any event shall be permitted only in such a manner and to such a degree as not to inflame or unduly prejudice the jury. As used in this paragraph, the term "immediate family" means the victim's spouse, child, parent, stepparent, grandparent, grandchild, sibling, stepbrother, stepsister, mother-in-law, father-in-law, sister-in-law, or brother-in-law and the spouses of any such individuals.

(3) In all cases other than those in which the death penalty may be imposed, prior to fixing of the sentence as provided for in Code Section 17–10–1 or the imposing of life imprisonment as mandated by law, and before rendering the appropriate sentence, including any order of restitution, the court shall allow the victim, as such term is defined in Code Section 17–17–3, the family of the victim, or such other witness having personal knowledge of the crime to testify about the impact of the crime on the victim, the family of the victim, or the community. Except as provided in paragraph (4) of this subsection, such evidence shall be given in the presence of the defendant and shall be subject to cross-examination. The admissibility of the testimony and evidence in support of such testimony shall be in the sole discretion of the judge and in any event shall be permitted only in such a manner as to allow for cross-examination by the defendant and to such a degree as not to unduly prejudice the defendant. If the judge excludes the testimony or evidence in support of such testimony, the state shall be allowed to make a proffer of such testimony or evidence.

(4) Upon a finding by the court specific to the case and the witness that the witness would not be able to testify in person without showing undue emotion or that testifying in person will cause the witness severe physical or emotional distress or trauma, evidence presented pursuant to this subsection may be in the form of, but not limited to, a written statement or a prerecorded audio or video statement, provided that such witness is subject to cross-examination and the evidence itself will not be available to the jury during deliberations. Photographs of the victim may be included with any evidence presented pursuant to this subsection.

(5) If the accused has been convicted of a serious violent felony as defined in Code Section 17–10–6.1, attempted murder or attempted kidnapping, or any violation of Code Section 16–5–90, 16–5–91, 16–7–82, 16–7–84, or 16–7–86, and the victim or a representative of the victim is not present at the presentence hearing, it shall be the duty of the court to inquire of the prosecuting attorney whether or not the victim has been notified of the presentence hearing as provided in Code Section 17–17–5. If the court finds that the prosecuting attorney has not made a reasonable attempt to notify the victim, the presentence hearing shall be recessed in order to provide the victim the opportunity to attend prior to sentence being imposed; provided, however, that prior to recessing the presentence hearing, the court shall allow the state or the accused to call any witnesses who were subpoenaed and are present at such presentence hearing. Following any such testimony, the presentence hearing shall be recessed and the victim shall be notified of the date, time, and location when the presentence hearing shall resume.

(b) In presenting such evidence, the victim, the family of the victim, or such other witness having personal knowledge of the impact of the crime on the victim, the victim's family, or the community shall, if applicable:

(1) Describe the nature of the offense;

(2) Itemize any economic loss suffered by the victim or the family of the victim, if restitution is sought;

(3) Identify any physical injury suffered by the victim as a result of the offense along with its seriousness and permanence;

(4) Describe any change in the victim's personal welfare or familial relationships as a result of the offense;

(5) Identify any request for psychological services initiated by the victim or the victim's family as a result of the offense; and

(6) Include any other information related to the impact of the offense upon the victim, the victim's family, or the community that the court inquires of.

(c) The court shall allow the defendant the opportunity to cross-examine and rebut the evidence presented of the victim's personal characteristics and the emotional impact of the crime on the victim, the victim's family, or the community, and such cross-examination and rebuttal evidence shall be subject to the same discretion set forth in paragraph (1) of subsection (a) of this Code section.

(d) No sentence shall be invalidated because of failure to comply with the provisions of this Code section. This Code section shall not be construed to create any cause of action or any right of appeal on behalf of the victim, the state, or the accused; provided, however, that if the court intentionally fails to comply with this Code section, the victim may file a complaint with the Judicial Qualifications Commission.

Laws 1985, p. 739, § 1; Laws 1993, p. 1660, § 2; Laws 2009, Act 55, § 1, eff. July 1, 2009; Laws 2010, Act 403, § 4, eff. July 1, 2010.

Historical and Statutory Notes

The 2009 amendment by Act 55, in subsec. (a), in par. (1), substituted "the court shall" for "the court may" and substituted "Except as provided in paragraph (4) of this subsection, such" for "Such", redesignated par. (2) as par. (3) and inserted a new par. (2), in new par. (2), substituted "the evidence described in paragraph (1) of this subsection and the number of witnesses other than immediate family who may testify" for "such evidence" and added the second sentence, in new par. (3), in the first sentence, substituted "shall" for ", within its discretion, may", substituted "the community. Except as provided in paragraph (4) of this subsection, such" for "community. Such", and added the third sentence, and added par. (4).

The 2010 amendment by Act 403, in subsec. (a), par. (3), deleted "evidence from" after "the court shall allow" and inserted "as such term is defined in Code Section 17–17–3" and "crime to testify about the" in the first sentence, substituted "testimony and evidence in support of such testimony" for "evidence described in this paragraph" in the third sentence, added the fourth sentence and added par. (5); in subsec. (d), replaced "any person" with "the victim, the state, or the accused; provided, however, that if the court intentionally fails to comply with this Code section, the victim may file a complaint with the Judicial Qualifications Commission".

§ 17–10–1.3. Probation or suspension of sentence; inquiry into legality of prisoner's presence in U.S.

(a) In determining whether to probate all or any part of any sentence of confinement in any felony, misdemeanor, or ordinance violation case, the sentencing court shall be authorized to make inquiry into whether the person to be sentenced is lawfully present in the United States under federal law.

(b) If the court determines that the person to be sentenced is not lawfully present in the United States, the court shall be authorized to make inquiry into whether the person to be sentenced would be legally subject to deportation from the United States while serving a probated sentence.

(c) If the court determines that the person to be sentenced would be legally subject to deportation from the United States while serving a probated sentence, the court may:

(1) Consider the interest of the state in securing certain and complete execution of its judicial sentences in criminal and quasi–criminal cases;

(2) Consider the likelihood that deportation may intervene to frustrate that state interest if probation is granted; and

(3) Where appropriate, decline to probate a sentence in furtherance of the state interest in certain and complete execution of sentences.

(d) This Code section shall apply with respect to a judicial determination as to whether to suspend all or any part of a sentence of confinement in the same manner as this Code section applies to determinations with respect to probation.

Laws 2007, Act 13, § 1, eff. May 11, 2007; Laws 2008, Act 471, § 17, eff. May 12, 2008.

Historical and Statutory Notes

Laws 2007, Act 13, § 3, provides:

"The General Assembly finds that this Act states factors for consideration in discretionary decision–making processes within the criminal justice system. The General Assembly finds that such factors could have been considered prior to or without the enactment of this Act. Accordingly, it is the intention of the General Assembly that this Act may be applied with respect to offenses committed prior to its effective date as well as offenses committed on or after its effective date. However, if there should be a judicial determination that retrospective application is prohibited, it is the intention of the General Assembly that retrospective application should be severable."

The 2008 amendment by Act 471 was a provision contained in a correction bill.

§ 17–10–2. Presentence hearings in felony cases

(a)(1) Except in cases in which the death penalty may be imposed, upon the return of a verdict of "guilty" by the jury in any felony case, the judge shall dismiss the jury and shall conduct a presentence hearing at which the only issue shall be the determination of punishment to be imposed. In the hearing the judge shall hear additional evidence in extenuation, mitigation, and aggravation of punishment, including the record of any prior criminal convictions and pleas of guilty or nolo contendere of the accused, or the absence of any prior conviction and pleas.

(2) The judge shall also hear argument by the accused or the accused's counsel and the prosecuting attorney, as provided by law, regarding the punishment to be imposed. Except in cases where the death penalty may be imposed, the prosecuting attorney shall open and conclude the argument. In cases

where the death penalty may be imposed, the prosecuting attorney shall open and the accused or the accused's counsel shall conclude the argument.

(3) Upon the conclusion of the evidence and arguments, the judge shall impose the sentence or shall recess the trial for the purpose of taking the sentence to be imposed under advisement. The judge shall fix a sentence within the limits prescribed by law.

(b) In cases in which the death penalty may be imposed, the judge, when sitting without a jury, in addition to the procedure set forth in subsection (a) of this Code section, shall follow the procedures provided for in Code Section 17-10-30.

(c) In all cases tried by a jury in which the death penalty may be imposed, upon a return of a verdict of "guilty" by the jury, the court shall resume the trial and conduct a presentence hearing before the jury. The hearing shall be conducted in the same manner as presentence hearings conducted before the judge as provided for in subsection (a) of this Code section. Upon the conclusion of the evidence and arguments, the judge shall give the jury appropriate instructions, and the jury shall retire to determine whether any mitigating or aggravating circumstances, as defined in Code Section 17-10-30, exist and whether to recommend mercy for the accused. Upon the findings of the jury, the judge shall fix a sentence within the limits prescribed by law.

(d) If the trial court is reversed on appeal because of error only in the presentence hearing, the new trial which may be ordered shall apply only to the issue of punishment.

Laws 1974, p. 352, § 7; Laws 1990, p. 8, § 17; Laws 1993, p. 1654, § 2; Laws 2005, Act 8, § 11, eff. July 1, 2005; Laws 2009, Act 62, § 2, eff. April 29, 2009.

Formerly Code 1933, § 27-2503.

Historical and Statutory Notes

The 2005 amendment by Act 8, in subsec. (a), designated paragraphs (1), (2), and (3), in par. (1), deleted ", provided that only such evidence in aggravation as the state has made known to the defendant prior to the defendant's trial should be admissible" following "absence of any prior conviction and pleas", in par. (2), substituted "prosecuting attorney" for "district attorney" in the first sentence, substituted "Except in cases where the death penalty may be imposed, the prosecuting attorney shall open and conclude the argument" for "The district attorney shall open and the defendant or the defendant's counsel shall conclude the argument" in the second sentence, and added "In cases where the death penalty may be imposed, the prosecuting attorney shall open and the defendant and the defendant or the defendant's counsel shall conclude the argument." at the end of the paragraph.

Laws 2005, Act 8, § 17, provides:

"This Act shall apply to all trials which commence on or after July 1, 2005."

The 2009 amendment by Act 62, in subsec. (a), in par. (1), deleted "or life without following parole" following "the death penalty" in the first sentence, and substituted "accused" for "defendant" in the second sentence, and in par. (2), substituted "accused" for "defendant" throughout; in subsec. (b), deleted "or life without parole" following "the death penalty" and substituted "Code Section 17-10-30" for "Code Sections 17-10-30 and 17-10-30.1"; and in subsec. (c), deleted "or life without parole" following "the death penalty" in the first sentence, and substituted "accused" for "defendant" in the third sentence.

Laws 2009, Act 62, §§ 8 to 11, provide:

"SECTION 8. Except as provided in this section, the provisions of this Act shall apply only to those offenses committed after the effective date of this Act. With express written consent of the state, an accused whose offense was committed prior to the effective date of this Act may elect in writing to be sentenced under the provisions of this Act, provided that: (1) jeopardy for the offense charged has not attached or (2) the accused has been sentenced to death but the conviction or sentence has been reversed on appeal and the state is not barred from seeking prosecution after the remand.

"SECTION 9. Except as provided in Section 8 of this Act, the amendment or repeal of a Code section by this Act shall not affect any sentence imposed by any court of this state prior to the effective date of this Act.

"SECTION 10. A person may be sentenced to life without parole without the prosecutor seeking the death penalty under the laws of this state.

"SECTION 11.(a) This Act shall become effective upon its approval by the Governor or upon its becoming law without such approval and shall apply to all crimes committed on and after such date, and except as provided in Section 8 of this Act, the law as set forth in Section 2 and in Sections 3 through 7 of this Act as it existed prior to the effective date of this Act shall apply to all offenses committed on and before such date.

"(b) The provisions of this Act shall not affect or abate the status as a crime of any such act or omission which occurred prior to the effective date of the Act repealing, repealing and reenacting, or amending such law, nor shall the prosecution of such crime be abated as a result of such repeal, repeal and reenactment, or amendment."

§ 17-10-3. Misdemeanors, how punished

(a) Except as otherwise provided by law, every crime declared to be a misdemeanor shall be punished as follows:

(1) By a fine not to exceed $ 1,000.00 or by confinement in the county or other jail, county correctional institution, or such other places as counties may provide for maintenance of county inmates, for a total term not to exceed 12 months, or both;

(2) By confinement under the jurisdiction of the Board of Corrections in a state probation detention center or diversion center pursuant to Code Sections 42-8-35.4 and 42-8-35.5, for a determinate term of months which shall not exceed a total term of 12 months; or

(3) If the crime was committed by an inmate within the confines of a state correctional institution, by confinement under the jurisdiction of the Board of Corrections in a state correctional institution or such other institution as the Department of Corrections may direct for a term which shall not exceed 12 months.

(b) Either the punishment provided in paragraph (1) or (2) of subsection (a) of this Code section, but not both, may be imposed in the discretion of the sentencing judge. Misdemeanor punishment imposed under either paragraph may be subject to suspension or probation. The sentencing courts shall retain jurisdiction to amend, modify, alter, suspend, or probate sentences under paragraph (1) of subsection (a) of this Code section at any time, but in no instance shall any sentence under the paragraph be modified in a manner to place a county inmate under the jurisdiction of the Board of Corrections, except as provided in paragraph (2) of subsection (a) of this Code section.

(c) In all misdemeanor cases in which, upon conviction, a six-month sentence or less is imposed, it is within the authority and discretion of the sentencing judge to allow the sentence to be served on weekends by weekend confinement or during the nonworking hours of the defendant. A weekend shall commence and shall end in the discretion of the sentencing judge, and the nonworking hours of the defendant shall be determined in the discretion of the sentencing judge; provided, however, that the judge shall retain plenary control of the defendant at all times during the sentence period. A weekend term shall be counted as serving two days of the full sentence. Confinement during the nonworking hours of a defendant during any day may be counted as serving a full day of the sentence.

(d) In addition to or instead of any other penalty provided for the punishment of a misdemeanor involving a traffic offense, or punishment of a municipal ordinance involving a traffic offense, with the exception of habitual offenders sentenced under Code Section 17-10-7, a judge may impose any one or more of the following sentences:

(1) Reexamination by the Department of Driver Services when the judge has good cause to believe that the convicted licensed driver is incompetent or otherwise not qualified to be licensed;

(2) Attendance at, and satisfactory completion of, a driver improvement course meeting standards approved by the court;

(3) Within the limits of the authority of the charter powers of a municipality or the punishment prescribed by law in other courts, imprisonment at times specified by the court or release from imprisonment upon such conditions and at such times as may be specified; or

(4) Probation or suspension of all or any part of a penalty upon such terms and conditions as may be prescribed by the judge. The conditions may include driving with no further motor vehicle violations during a specified time unless the driving privileges have been or will be otherwise suspended or revoked by law; reporting periodically to the court or a specified agency; and performing, or refraining from performing, such acts as may be ordered by the judge.

(e) Any sentence imposed under subsection (d) of this Code section shall be reported to the Department of Driver Services as prescribed by law.

(f) The Department of Corrections shall lack jurisdiction to supervise misdemeanor offenders, except when the sentence is made concurrent to a probated felony sentence or when the sentence is accepted pursuant to Code Section 42–9–71. Except as provided in this subsection, the Department of Corrections shall lack jurisdiction to confine misdemeanor offenders.

(g) This Code section will have no effect upon any offender convicted of a misdemeanor offense prior January 1, 2001, and sentenced to confinement under the jurisdiction of the Board of Corrections or to the supervision of the Department of Corrections.

Laws 1865–66, p. 233, § 2; Laws 1878–79, p. 54, § 1; Laws 1895, p. 63, § 2; Laws 1908, p. 1119, § 1; Laws 1956, p. 161, § 4; Laws 1957, p. 477, § 5; Laws 1964, p. 485, § 1; Laws 1970, p. 236, § 10; Laws 1972, p. 600, § 1; Laws 1974, p. 361, § 1; Laws 1974, p. 631, § 1; Laws 1976, p. 210, § 1; Laws 1985, p. 283, § 1; Laws 1992, p. 3221, § 2; Laws 1997, p. 1526, § 1; Laws 2000, p. 1643, § 1; Laws 2001, p. 1030, § 2; Laws 2002, p. 415, § 17; Laws 2005, Act 68, § 7–4, eff. July 1, 2005.

Formerly Code 1863, § 4209; Code 1868, §§ 4245, 4608; Code 1873, §§ 4310, 4705; Code 1882, §§ 4310, 4705; Penal Code 1895, § 1039; Penal Code 1910, § 1065; Code 1933, § 27–2506.

Historical and Statutory Notes

The 2005 amendment by Act 68 in subsec. (d) substituted, in par. (1), "Department of Driver Services" for "Department of Motor Vehicle Safety"; and, in subsec. (e), substituted "Department of Driver Services" for "Department of Motor Vehicle Safety".

§ 17–10–3.1. Service of sentence by persons convicted of violating Code Section 40–6–391(k)

(a) In any case where a person is sentenced to a period of imprisonment under Code Section 40–6–391 upon conviction for violating subsection (k) of said Code section, it is within the authority and discretion of the sentencing judge in cases involving the first such violation to allow the sentence to be served on weekends by weekend confinement or during the nonworking hours of the defendant. A weekend shall commence and shall end in the discretion of the sentencing judge, and the nonworking hours of the defendant shall be determined in the discretion of the sentencing judge; provided, however, that the judge shall retain plenary control of the defendant at all times during the sentence period. Confinement during the nonworking hours of a defendant during any day may be counted as serving a full day of the sentence.

(b) Any confinement of a person pursuant to a sentence to a period of imprisonment under Code Section 40–6–391 upon conviction for violating subsection (k) of said Code section shall be served in a county jail, provided that for the first such violation such person shall be kept segregated from all offenders other than those confined for violating subsection (k) of Code Section 40–6–391.

Laws 1997, p. 760, § 2; Laws 1999, p. 391, § 4.

§ 17–10–4. Punishment for misdemeanor of a high and aggravated nature

(a) A person who is convicted of a misdemeanor of a high and aggravated nature shall be punished by a fine not to exceed $ 5,000.00 or by confinement in the county or other jail, county correctional institution, or such other places as counties may provide for maintenance of county inmates, for a term not to exceed 12 months, or both; provided, however, that a person convicted of a misdemeanor of a high and aggravated nature which was committed by an inmate within the confines of a state correctional institution and sentenced to confinement as a result of such offense shall be sentenced to confinement under the jurisdiction of the Board of Corrections in a state correctional institution or such other institution as the Department of Corrections may direct for a term which shall not exceed 12 months. In all cases of a conviction of a misdemeanor of a high and aggravated nature, the sentencing court shall retain jurisdiction to amend, modify, alter, suspend, or probate sentences imposed under this Code section at any time; but in no instance shall a sentence imposed under this Code section be modified in such a manner as to increase the amount of fine or the term of confinement.

(b) Notwithstanding any laws to the contrary, a person sentenced for a misdemeanor of a high and aggravated nature may earn no more than four days per month earned time allowance.

Laws 1970, p. 236, § 11; Laws 1985, p. 283, § 1; Laws 1997, p. 1526, § 2; Laws 2000, p. 1111, § 1.

Formerly Code 1933, § 27–2506.1.

§ 17–10–5. Reducible felonies

When a defendant is found guilty of a felony punishable by imprisonment for a maximum term of ten years or less, the judge may, in his discretion, impose punishment as for a misdemeanor.

Laws 1968, p. 1249, § 1.

Formerly Code 1933, § 26–3101.

§ 17–10–6. Repealed by Laws 2007, Act 327, § 2, eff. July 1, 2007

Historical and Statutory Notes

The repealed section, relating to the right of defendants to have specified sentences reviewed by a panel of three superior court judges to determine whether the sentence imposed was excessively harsh, was derived from Laws 1974, p. 352, § 8; Laws 1977, p. 1098, § 6; Laws 1982, p. 1271, §§ 1, 2; Laws 1993, p. 705, § 1; Laws 1994, p. 1959, § 10; Code 1933, § 27–2511.1. The repealing law reserved the section designation.

Laws 2007, Act 327, § 5, provides:

"This Act shall become effective on July 1, 2007, and shall apply to all trials which occur on or after July 1, 2007."

§ 17–10–6.1. Sentencing of persons convicted of serious violent felonies

(a) As used in this Code section, the term "serious violent felony" means:

(1) Murder or felony murder, as defined in Code Section 16–5–1;

(2) Armed robbery, as defined in Code Section 16–8–41;

(3) Kidnapping, as defined in Code Section 16–5–40;

(4) Rape, as defined in Code Section 16–6–1;

(5) Aggravated child molestation, as defined in subsection (c) of Code Section 16–6–4, unless subject to the provisions of paragraph (2) of subsection (d) of Code Section 16–6–4;

(6) Aggravated sodomy, as defined in Code Section 16–6–2; or

(7) Aggravated sexual battery, as defined in Code Section 16–6–22.2.

(b)(1) Notwithstanding any other provisions of law to the contrary, any person convicted of the serious violent felony of kidnapping involving a victim who is 14 years of age or older or armed robbery shall be sentenced to a mandatory minimum term of imprisonment of ten years and no portion of the mandatory minimum sentence imposed shall be suspended, stayed, probated, deferred, or withheld by the sentencing court and shall not be reduced by any form of pardon, parole, or commutation of sentence by the State Board of Pardons and Paroles.

(2) Notwithstanding any other provisions of law to the contrary, the sentence of any person convicted of the serious violent felony of:

(A) Kidnapping involving a victim who is less than 14 years of age;

(B) Rape;

(C) Aggravated child molestation, as defined in subsection (c) of Code Section 16–6–4, unless subject to the provisions of paragraph (2) of subsection (d) of Code Section 16–6–4;

(D) Aggravated sodomy, as defined in Code Section 16–6–2; or

(E) Aggravated sexual battery, as defined in Code Section 16–6–22.2

shall, unless sentenced to life imprisonment, be a split sentence which shall include a mandatory minimum term of imprisonment of 25 years, followed by probation for life. No portion of the mandatory minimum sentence imposed shall be suspended, stayed, probated, deferred, or withheld by the sentencing court and shall not be reduced by any form of pardon, parole, or commutation of sentence by the State Board of Pardons and Paroles.

(3) No person convicted of a serious violent felony shall be sentenced as a first offender pursuant to Article 3 of Chapter 8 of Title 42, relating to probation for first offenders, or any other provision of Georgia law relating to the sentencing of first offenders. The State of Georgia shall have the right to appeal any sentence which is imposed by the superior court which does not conform to the provisions of this subsection in the same manner as is provided for other appeals by the state in accordance with Chapter 7 of Title 5, relating to appeals or certiorari by the state.

(c)(1) Except as otherwise provided in subsection (c) of Code Section 42–9–39, for a first conviction of a serious violent felony in which the accused has been sentenced to life imprisonment, that person shall not be eligible for any form of parole or early release administered by the State Board of Pardons and Paroles until that person has served a minimum of 30 years in prison. The minimum term of imprisonment shall not be reduced by any earned time, early release, work release, leave, or other sentence-reducing measures under programs administered by the Department of Corrections.

(2) For a first conviction of a serious violent felony in which the accused has been sentenced to death but the sentence of death has been commuted to life imprisonment, that person shall not be eligible for any form of parole or early release administered by the State Board of Pardons and Paroles until that person has served a minimum of 30 years in prison. The minimum term of imprisonment shall not be reduced by any earned time, early release, work release, leave, or other sentence-reducing measures under programs administered by the Department of Corrections.

(3) For a first conviction of a serious violent felony in which the accused has been sentenced to imprisonment for life without parole, that person shall not be eligible for any form of parole or early release administered by the State Board of Pardons and Paroles or for any earned time, early release, work release, leave, or other sentence-reducing measures under programs administered by the Department of Corrections.

(4) Except as otherwise provided in this subsection, any sentence imposed for the first conviction of any serious violent felony shall be served in its entirety as imposed by the sentencing court and shall not be reduced by any form of parole or early release administered by the State Board of Pardons and Paroles or by any earned time, early release, work release, leave, or other sentence-reducing measures under programs administered by the Department of Corrections, the effect of which would be to reduce the period of incarceration ordered by the sentencing court; provided, however, during the final year of incarceration an offender so sentenced shall be eligible to be considered for participation in a department administered transitional center or work release program.

(d) For purposes of this Code section, a first conviction of any serious violent felony means that the person has never been convicted of a serious violent felony under the laws of this state or of an offense under the laws of any other state or of the United States, which offense if committed in this state would be a serious violent felony. Conviction of two or more crimes charged on separate counts of one indictment or accusation, or in two or more indictments or accusations consolidated for trial, shall be deemed to be only one conviction.

Laws 1994, p. 1959, § 11; Laws 1998, p. 180, § 2; Laws 2006, Act 571, § 20, eff. July 1, 2006; Laws 2009, Act 21, § 1, eff. July 1, 2009; Laws 2009, Act 62, § 3, eff. April 29, 2009.

Historical and Statutory Notes

Laws 2003, Act 37, § 5, provides:

"This Act shall become effective upon its approval by the Governor [May 27, 2003] or upon its becoming law without such approval. Notwithstanding the provisions of subsection (b) of Code Section 5–5–41, any person convicted of a serious violent felony as defined in Code Section 17–10–6.1, which conviction was imposed prior to the effective date of this Act, who has, prior to the effective date of this Act, filed an extraordinary motion for new trial, may file an extraordinary motion for new trial pursuant to Section 1 of this Act if the issue of DNA testing was not raised or denied in the prior extraordinary motion for new trial. In any extraordinary motion for new trial allowed pursuant to Section 1 of this Act, the court shall not have jurisdiction to reconsider any other issue raised in the first extraordinary motion for new trial. Notwithstanding the provisions of subparagraph (c)(4)(B) of Code Section 5–5–41, any person convicted of a serious violent felony as defined in Code Section 17–10–6.1, which conviction was imposed prior to the effective date of this Act, who has, prior to the effective date of this Act, previously litigated in a court of this state or the United States the issue of postconviction DNA testing and who was denied DNA testing may file an extraordinary motion for new trial pursuant to Section 1 of this Act."

The 2006 amendment by Act 571, in subsec. (a), par. (5), added "subsection (c) of" following "as defined in" and added "unless subject to the provisions of paragraph (2) of subsection (d) of Code Section 16–6–4" at the end of the paragraph; rewrote subsec. (b); and in subsec. (c), substituted "30 years in prison" for "14 years in prison" in par. (1) and substituted "30 years in prison" for "25 years in prison" in par. (2). Prior to amendment, subsec. (b) had read:

"(b) Notwithstanding any other provisions of law to the contrary, any person convicted of a serious violent felony as defined in paragraphs (2) through (7) of subsection (a) of this Code section shall be sentenced to a mandatory minimum term of imprisonment of ten years and no portion of the mandatory minimum sentence imposed shall be suspended, stayed, probated, deferred, or withheld by the sentencing court and shall not be reduced by any form of pardon, parole, or commutation of sentence by the State Board of Pardons and Paroles. No person convicted of a serious violent felony as defined in subsection (a) of this Code section shall be sentenced as a first offender pursuant to Article 3 of Chapter 8 of Title 42, relating to probation for first offenders, or any other provision of Georgia law relating to the sentencing of first offenders. The State of Georgia shall have the right to appeal any sentence which is imposed by the superior court which does not conform to the provisions of this subsection in the same manner as is provided for other appeals by the state in accordance with Chapter 7 of Title 5, relating to appeals or certiorari by the state."

Laws 2006, Act 571, §§ 1 and 30, provide:

"SECTION 1. The General Assembly finds and declares that recidivist sexual offenders, sexual offenders who use physical violence, and sexual offenders who prey on children are sexual predators who present an extreme threat to the public safety. Many sexual offenders are extremely likely to use physical violence and to repeat their offenses; and some sexual offenders commit many offenses, have many more victims than are ever reported, and are prosecuted for only a fraction of their crimes. The General Assembly finds that this makes the cost of sexual offender victimization to society at large, while incalculable, clearly exorbitant. The General Assembly further finds that the high level of threat that a sexual predator presents to the public safety, and the long-term effects suffered by victims of sex offenses, provide the state with sufficient justification to implement a strategy that includes:

"(1) Incarcerating sexual offenders and maintaining adequate facilities to ensure that decisions to release sexual predators into the community are not made on the basis of inadequate space;

"(2) Requiring the registration of sexual offenders, with a requirement that complete and accurate information be maintained and accessible for use by law enforcement authorities, communities, and the public;

"(3) Providing for community and public notification concerning the presence of sexual offenders;

"(4) Collecting data relative to sexual offenses and sexual offenders;

"(5) Requiring sexual predators who are released into the community to wear an electronic monitoring system for the rest of their natural life and to pay for such system; and

"(6) Prohibiting sexual predators from working with children, either for compensation or as a volunteer.

"The General Assembly further finds that the state has a compelling interest in protecting the public from sexual offenders and in protecting children from predatory sexual activity, and there is sufficient justification for requiring sexual offenders to register and for requiring community and public notification of the presence of sexual offenders. The General Assembly declares that in order to protect the public, it is necessary that the sexual offenders be registered and that members of the community and the public be notified of a sexual offender's presence. The designation of a person as a sexual offender is neither a sentence nor a punishment but simply a regulatory mechanism and status resulting from the conviction of certain crimes. Likewise, the designation of a person as a sexual predator is neither a sentence nor a punishment but simply a regulatory mechanism and status resulting from findings by the Sexual Offender Registration Review Board and a court if requested by a sexual offender."

"SECTION 30. (a) This Act shall become effective July 1, 2006.

"(b) Any person required to register pursuant to the provisions of Code Section 42–1–12, relating to the state sexual offender registry, and any person required not to reside within areas where minors congregate, as prohibited by Code Section 42–1–13 [see § 42–1–15], shall not be relieved of the obligation to comply with the provisions of said Code sections by the repeal and reenactment of said Code sections.

"(c) The provisions of this Act shall not affect or abate the status as a crime of any such act or omission which occurred prior to the effective date of the Act repealing, repealing and reenacting, or amending such law, nor shall the prosecution of such crime be abated as a result of such repeal, repeal and reenactment, or amendment."

The 2009 amendment by Act 21, in subsec. (c), in par. (3), inserted "; provided, however, during the final year of incarceration an offender so sentenced shall be eligible to be considered for participation in a department administered transitional center or work release program".

The 2009 amendment by Act 62 rewrote the subsec. (c) which had read:

"(c)(1) Except as otherwise provided in subsection (c) of Code Section 42–9–39, for a first conviction of a serious violent felony in which the defendant has been sentenced to life imprisonment, that person shall not be eligible for any form of parole or early release administered by the State Board of Pardons and Paroles until that person has served a minimum of 30 years in prison. The minimum term of imprisonment shall not be reduced by any earned time, early release, work release, leave, or other sentence-reducing measures under programs administered by the Department of Corrections.

"(2) For a first conviction of a serious violent felony in which the defendant has been sentenced to death but the sentence of death has been commuted to life imprisonment, that person shall not be eligible for any form of parole or early release administered by the State Board of Pardons and Paroles until that person has served a minimum of 30 years in prison. The minimum term of imprisonment shall not be reduced by any earned time, early release, work release, leave, or other sentence-reducing measures under programs administered by the Department of Corrections.

"(3) Any sentence imposed for the first conviction of any serious violent felony other than a sentence of life imprisonment or life without parole or death shall be served in its entirety as imposed by the sentencing court and shall not be reduced by any form of parole or early release administered by the State Board of Pardons and Paroles or by any earned time, early release, work release, leave, or other sentence-reducing measures under programs administered by the Department of Corrections, the effect of which would be to reduce the period of incarceration ordered by the sentencing court."

Laws 2009, Act 62, §§ 8 to 11, provide:

"SECTION 8. Except as provided in this section, the provisions of this Act shall apply only to those offenses committed after the effective date of this Act. With express written consent of the state, an accused whose offense was committed prior to the effective date of this Act may elect in writing to be sentenced under the provisions of this Act, provided that: (1) jeopardy for the offense charged has not attached or (2) the accused has been sentenced to death but the conviction or sentence has been reversed on appeal and the state is not barred from seeking prosecution after the remand.

"SECTION 9. Except as provided in Section 8 of this Act, the amendment or repeal of a Code section by this Act shall not affect any sentence imposed by any court of this state prior to the effective date of this Act.

"SECTION 10. A person may be sentenced to life without parole without the prosecutor seeking the death penalty under the laws of this state.

"SECTION 11.(a) This Act shall become effective upon its approval by the Governor or upon its becoming law without such approval and shall apply to all crimes committed on and after such date, and except as provided in Section 8 of this Act, the law as set forth in Section 2 and in Sections 3 through 7 of this Act as it existed prior to the effective date of this Act shall apply to all offenses committed on and before such date.

"(b) The provisions of this Act shall not affect or abate the status as a crime of any such act or omission which occurred prior to the effective date of the Act repealing, repealing and reenacting, or amending such law, nor shall the prosecution of such crime be abated as a result of such repeal, repeal and reenactment, or amendment."

§ 17–10–6.2. Sentencing of persons convicted of a sexual offense

(a) As used in this Code section, the term "sexual offense" means:

(1) Aggravated assault with the intent to rape, as defined in Code Section 16–5–21;

(2) False imprisonment, as defined in Code Section 16–5–41, if the victim is not the child of the defendant and the victim is less than 14 years of age;

(3) Sodomy, as defined in Code Section 16–6–2, unless subject to the provisions of subsection (d) of Code Section 16–6–2;

(4) Statutory rape, as defined in Code Section 16–6–3, if the person convicted of the crime is 21 years of age or older;

(5) Child molestation, as defined in subsection (a) of Code Section 16–6–4, unless subject to the provisions of paragraph (2) of subsection (b) of Code Section 16–6–4;

(6) Enticing a child for indecent purposes, as defined in Code Section 16–6–5, unless subject to the provisions of subsection (c) of Code Section 16–6–5;

(7) Sexual assault against persons in custody, as defined in Code Section 16–6–5.1;

(8) Incest, as defined in Code Section 16–6–22;

(9) A second or subsequent conviction for sexual battery, as defined in Code Section 16–6–22.1; or

(10) Sexual exploitation of children, as defined in Code Section 16–12–100.

(b) Except as provided in subsection (c) of this Code section, and notwithstanding any other provisions of law to the contrary, any person convicted of a sexual offense shall be sentenced to a split sentence which shall include the minimum term of imprisonment specified in the Code section applicable to the offense. No portion of the mandatory minimum sentence imposed shall be suspended, stayed, probated, deferred, or withheld by the sentencing court and such sentence shall include, in addition to the mandatory imprisonment, an additional probated sentence of at least one year. No person convicted of a sexual offense shall be sentenced as a first offender pursuant to Article 3 of Chapter 8 of Title 42, relating to probation for first offenders, or any other provision of Georgia law relating to the sentencing of first offenders.

(c)(1) In the court's discretion, the court may deviate from the mandatory minimum sentence as set forth in subsection (b) of this Code section, or any portion thereof, provided that:

(A) The defendant has no prior conviction of an offense prohibited by Chapter 6 of Title 16 or Part 2 of Article 3 of Chapter 12 of Title 16, nor a prior conviction for any offense under federal law or the laws of another state or territory of the United States which consists of the same or similar elements of offenses prohibited by Chapter 6 of Title 16 or Part 2 of Article 3 of Chapter 12 of Title 16;

(B) The defendant did not use a deadly weapon or any object, device, or instrument which when used offensively against a person would be likely to or actually did result in serious bodily injury during the commission of the offense;

(C) The court has not found evidence of a relevant similar transaction;

(D) The victim did not suffer any intentional physical harm during the commission of the offense;

(E) The offense did not involve the transportation of the victim; and

(F) The victim was not physically restrained during the commission of the offense.

(2) If the court deviates in sentencing pursuant to this subsection, the judge shall issue a written order setting forth the judge's reasons. Any such order shall be appealable by the defendant pursuant to Code Section 5-6-34, or by the State of Georgia pursuant to Code Section 5-7-1.

(d) If the court imposes a probated sentence, the defendant shall submit to review by the Sexual Offender Registration Review Board for purposes of risk assessment classification within ten days of being sentenced and shall otherwise comply with Article 2 of Chapter 1 of Title 42.

Laws 2006, Act 571, § 21, eff. July 1, 2006.

Historical and Statutory Notes

Laws 2006, Act 571, §§ 1 and 30, provide:

"SECTION 1. The General Assembly finds and declares that recidivist sexual offenders, sexual offenders who use physical violence, and sexual offenders who prey on children are sexual predators who present an extreme threat to the public safety. Many sexual offenders are extremely likely to use physical violence and to repeat their offenses; and some sexual offenders commit many offenses, have many more victims than are ever reported, and are prosecuted for only a fraction of their crimes. The General Assembly finds that this makes the cost of sexual offender victimization to society at large, while incalculable, clearly exorbitant. The General Assembly further finds that the high level of threat that a sexual predator presents to the public safety, and the long-term effects suffered by victims of sex offenses, provide the state with sufficient justification to implement a strategy that includes:

"(1) Incarcerating sexual offenders and maintaining adequate facilities to ensure that decisions to release sexual predators into the community are not made on the basis of inadequate space;

"(2) Requiring the registration of sexual offenders, with a requirement that complete and accurate information be maintained and accessible for use by law enforcement authorities, communities, and the public;

"(3) Providing for community and public notification concerning the presence of sexual offenders;

"(4) Collecting data relative to sexual offenses and sexual offenders;

"(5) Requiring sexual predators who are released into the community to wear an electronic monitoring system for the rest of their natural life and to pay for such system; and

"(6) Prohibiting sexual predators from working with children, either for compensation or as a volunteer.

"The General Assembly further finds that the state has a compelling interest in protecting the public from sexual offenders and in protecting children from predatory sexual activity, and there is sufficient justification for requiring sexual offenders to register and for requiring community and public notification of the presence of sexual offenders. The General Assembly declares that in order to protect the public, it is necessary that the sexual offenders be registered and that members of the community and the public be notified of a sexual offender's presence. The designation of a person as a sexual offender is neither a sentence nor a punishment but simply a regulatory mechanism and status resulting from the conviction of certain crimes. Likewise, the designation of a person as a sexual predator is neither a sentence nor a punishment but simply a regulatory mechanism and status resulting from findings by the Sexual Offender Registration Review Board and a court if requested by a sexual offender."

"SECTION 30. (a) This Act shall become effective July 1, 2006.

"(b) Any person required to register pursuant to the provisions of Code Section 42-1-12, relating to the state sexual offender registry, and any person required not to reside within areas where minors congregate, as prohibited by Code Section 42-1-13 [see § 42-1-15], shall not be relieved of the obligation to comply with the provisions of said Code sections by the repeal and reenactment of said Code sections.

"(c) The provisions of this Act shall not affect or abate the status as a crime of any such act or omission which occurred prior to the effective date of the Act repealing, repealing and reenacting, or amending such law, nor shall the prosecution of such crime be abated as a result of such repeal, repeal and reenactment, or amendment."

§ 17-10-6.3. Termination of right to review of sentence by three judge panel; disposition of records, equipment, etc.

(a) As used in this Code section, the term "three-judge panel" means the three-judge panel that was created and existed pursuant to the former provisions of Code Section 17-10-6 as it existed on June 30, 2007, which reviewed certain sentences to determine if a sentence was excessively harsh and what relief, if any, should be given.

(b) The right of a defendant to have a sentence reviewed by a three-judge panel shall be terminated for sentences imposed by a trial or appellate court on or after July 1, 2007. No new application for review of a sentence shall be transmitted to the three-judge panel on or after July 1, 2007, except for cases in which a sentence was imposed prior to July 1, 2007.

(c) No new application for review of a sentence shall be accepted by the three-judge panel unless such application has been received by the three-judge panel on or before September 1, 2007. Any sentence that has an application for review with the three-judge panel pending on September 1, 2007, shall have such review completed by the three-judge panel by November 1, 2008.

(d) It shall be the duty of the president of The Council of Superior Court Judges of Georgia to cause all administrative measures which may be necessary to conclude the business of the three-judge panel to be completed no later than January 1, 2009. Such administrative, clerical, or secretarial personnel as may be assigned to provide support for the three-judge panel may continue to be employed for the purpose of providing support to the president of The Council of Superior Court Judges of Georgia until January 1, 2009.

(e) No later than January 1, 2009, all records and documents relating to the activities of the three-judge panels during the period July 1, 1974, through November 1, 2008, shall be transmitted to the Department of Archives and History for retention in accordance with Article 5 of Chapter 18 of Title 50, the "Georgia Records Act." All equipment, supplies, and materials which the president of The Council of Superior Court Judges of Georgia determines are excess or surplus shall be distributed by the president to the judges of the superior courts for use in the performance of their official duties. Any fees or expenses due to any clerk, superior court judge, or other person as a result of the three-judge panel shall be paid out of such funds as are appropriated for the operation of the superior courts during fiscal year 2009.

Laws 2007, Act 327, § 3, eff. July 1, 2007.

Historical and Statutory Notes

Laws 2007, Act 327, § 5, provides:

"This Act shall become effective on July 1, 2007, and shall apply to all trials which occur on or after July 1, 2007."

§ 17–10–7. Repeat offenders

(a) Except as otherwise provided in subsection (b) of this Code section, any person convicted of a felony offense in this state or having been convicted under the laws of any other state or of the United States of a crime which if committed within this state would be a felony and sentenced to confinement in a penal institution, who shall afterwards commit a felony punishable by confinement in a penal institution, shall be sentenced to undergo the longest period of time prescribed for the punishment of the subsequent offense of which he or she stands convicted, provided that, unless otherwise provided by law, the trial judge may, in his or her discretion, probate or suspend the maximum sentence prescribed for the offense.

(b)(1) As used in this subsection, the term "serious violent felony" means a serious violent felony as defined in subsection (a) of Code Section 17–10–6.1.

(2) Any person who has been convicted of a serious violent felony in this state or who has been convicted under the laws of any other state or of the United States of a crime which if committed in this state would be a serious violent felony and who after such first conviction subsequently commits and is convicted of a serious violent felony for which such person is not sentenced to death shall be sentenced to imprisonment for life without parole. Any such sentence of life without parole shall not be suspended, stayed, probated, deferred, or withheld, and any such person sentenced pursuant to this paragraph shall not be eligible for any form of pardon, parole, or early release administered by the State Board of Pardons and Paroles or for any earned time, early release, work release, leave, or any other sentence-reducing measures under programs administered by the Department of Corrections, the effect of which would be to reduce the sentence of life imprisonment without possibility of parole, except as may be authorized by any existing or future provisions of the Constitution.

(c) Except as otherwise provided in subsection (b) of this Code section, any person who, after having been convicted under the laws of this state for three felonies or having been convicted under the laws of any other state or of the United States of three crimes which if committed within this state would be felonies, commits a felony within this state shall, upon conviction for such fourth offense or for subsequent offenses, serve the maximum time provided in the sentence of the judge based upon such conviction and shall not be eligible for parole until the maximum sentence has been served.

(d) For the purpose of this Code section, conviction of two or more crimes charged on separate counts of one indictment or accusation, or in two or more indictments or accusations consolidated for trial, shall be deemed to be only one conviction.

(e) This Code section is supplemental to other provisions relating to recidivous offenders.

Laws 1833, Cobb's 1851 Digest, p. 840; Laws 1953, Nov.-Dec. Sess., p. 289, § 1; Laws 1974, p. 352, § 5; Laws 1983, p. 3, § 14; Laws 1984, p. 760, § 2; Laws 1994, p. 1959, § 12; Laws 2010, Act 498, § 1, eff. July 1, 2010.

Formerly Code 1863, § 4562; Code 1868, § 4582; Code 1873, § 4676; Code 1882, § 4676; Penal Code 1895, § 1042; Penal Code 1910, § 1068; Code 1933, § 27–2511.

Historical and Statutory Notes

The 2010 amendment by Act 498, in subsec. (c), substituted "shall" for "other than a capital felony must".

§ 17–10–8. Payment of fine as condition precedent to probation in felony cases

In any case where the judge may, by any law so authorizing, place on probation a person convicted of a felony, the judge may in his discretion impose a fine on the person so convicted as a condition to such probation. The fine shall not exceed $100,000.00 or the amount of the maximum fine which may be imposed for conviction of such a felony, whichever is greater. In any case where probation is revoked, the defendant shall not be entitled to any rebate or refund of any part of the fine so paid.

Laws 1957, p. 477, § 1; Laws 1964, p. 496, § 1; Laws 1979, p. 848, § 1; Laws 1990, p. 1408, § 1.

§ 17–10–8.1. Payment of legal defense application fee as condition of probation

In any case in which a defendant receives legal defense services pursuant to Chapter 12 of Title 17 where the defendant has not paid the application fee required by Code Section 15–21A–6 and the court has not waived such fee at the time of sentencing, the court shall impose such fee as a condition of probation.

Laws 2006, Act 749, § 2, eff. May 3, 2006.

§ 17–10–9. Time from which sentences run

In the imposition of sentence for violation of the penal laws, it shall be the duty of the judge to specify that the term of service under the sentence shall be computed from the date of sentence if the defendant is confined in jail or otherwise incarcerated and has no appeal or motion for new trial pending. In cases which are appealed to the Georgia Court of Appeals or the Georgia Supreme Court for reversal of the conviction, the sentence shall be computed from the date the remittitur of the appellate court is made the judgment of the court in which the conviction is had, provided the defendant is not at liberty under bond but is incarcerated or in custody of the sheriff of the county where convicted. If a defendant has been convicted and sentenced but, because of his failure or inability to post bond or bail for any reason, he has been incarcerated pending the prosecution of an appeal to any court, the time of the original imposition of his sentence until the time when the remittitur of the appellate court is made the judgment of the court in which the conviction is had shall be counted as time spent under sentence for all purposes.

Laws 1931, p. 165, § 1; Laws 1965, p. 230, § 1.

Formerly Code 1933, § 27–2505.

§ 17–10–9.1. Release of defendants

(a) When a defendant who pleads nolo contendere or guilty or is convicted of an offense against the laws of this state other than:

(1) Treason;

(2) Murder;

(3) Rape;

(4) Aggravated sodomy;

(5) Armed robbery;

(6) Aircraft hijacking and hijacking of a motor vehicle;

(7) Aggravated child molestation;

(8) Manufacturing, distributing, delivering, dispensing, administering, selling, or possessing with intent to distribute any controlled substance classified under Code Section 16–13–25 as Schedule I or under Code Section 16–13–26 as Schedule II;

(9) Violating Code Section 16–13–31, relating to trafficking in cocaine or marijuana;

(10) Kidnapping, arson, or burglary if the person, at the time such person was charged, has previously been convicted of, was

on probation or parole with respect to, or was on bail for kidnapping, arson, aggravated assault, burglary, or one or more of the offenses listed in paragraphs (1) through (9) of this subsection;

(11) Child molestation;

(12) Robbery;

(13) Aggravated assault; or

(14) Voluntary manslaughter

is sentenced to a term of confinement in a county jail or a correctional institution operated by or under the jurisdiction and supervision of the Department of Corrections, the sentencing judge may release the defendant pending the defendant's surrendering to a county jail or to a correctional institution designated by the Department of Corrections as authorized in this Code section. The sentencing court may release the defendant on bond or may release the defendant on the defendant's personal recognizance. This Code section shall not be construed to limit the court's authority in prescribing conditions of probation.

(b) Any defendant who has been released on bond and who has complied with all of the conditions of the bond and any other defendant who, in the opinion of the sentencing judge, is deemed worthy of the procedure to surrender voluntarily, may be eligible to participate in the program. However, the sentencing judge shall be the sole and final arbiter concerning eligibility and the defendant shall have no right to appeal such decision.

(c) When a defendant submits a request to the sentencing judge to be allowed to surrender voluntarily to a county jail or a correctional facility, the judge may consider the request and if, taking into the consideration the crime for which the defendant is being sentenced, the history of the defendant, and any other factors which may aid in the decision, the judge determines that the granting of the request will pose no threat to society, the defendant shall be remanded to the supervision of a probation officer by the judge and ordered to surrender voluntarily to a county jail designated by the court or to a correctional institution as thereafter designated by the Department of Corrections. The surrender date shall be a date thereafter specified as provided in subsection (d) of this Code section. The sentence of any defendant who is released pursuant to this Code section shall not begin to run until such person surrenders to the facility designated by the court or by the department, provided that such person will receive credit toward his sentence for time spent in confinement awaiting trial as provided in Code Section 17–10–11.

(d) In the event the defendant is ordered to surrender voluntarily to a county jail, the court shall designate the date on which the defendant shall surrender, which date shall not be more than 120 days after the date of conviction. When the sentencing judge issues an order requiring a defendant to surrender voluntarily to a correctional institution, the Department of Corrections shall authorize the commitment and designate the correctional institution to which the defendant shall report and the date on which the defendant is to report, which date shall not be more than 120 days after the date of conviction. Upon such designation, the department shall notify the supervising probation officer who shall notify the defendant accordingly. Subsistence and transportation expenses en route to the correctional institution shall be borne by the defendant.

(e) The provisions of this Code section shall not apply to any defendant convicted of a capital felony.

(f) If the defendant fails to surrender voluntarily as directed and required, the defendant may be charged with the offense of bail jumping pursuant to subsection (a) of Code Section 16–10–51 or the offense of escape pursuant to paragraph (3) of subsection (a) of Code Section 16–10–52 and, if convicted of such crimes, shall be punished as provided by law; or may be cited for contempt of court by the sentencing judge and, if convicted of contempt, the defendant shall be punished as provided in Code Section 15–6–8.

(g) The Department of Corrections is authorized and directed to promulgate such rules and regulations as may be necessary to effectuate the purposes of this Code section.

Laws 1989, p. 607, § 1; Laws 1994, p. 1625, § 6.

§ 17–10–10. Sentences, whether concurrent or successive

(a) Where at one term of court a person is convicted on more than one indictment or accusation, or on more than one count thereof, and sentenced to imprisonment, the sentences shall be served concurrently unless otherwise expressly provided therein.

(b) Where a person is convicted on more than one indictment or accusation at separate terms of court, or in different courts, and sentenced to imprisonment, the sentences shall be served concurrently, one with the other, unless otherwise expressly provided therein.

(c) This Code section shall apply alike to felony and misdemeanor offenses.

(d) This Code section shall govern and shall be followed by the Department of Corrections in the computation of time that sentences shall run.

Laws 1833, Cobb's 1851 Digest, p. 836; Laws 1956, p. 161, § 3; Laws 1964, p. 494, §§ 1, 2; Laws 1985, p. 283, § 1.

Formerly Code 1863, § 4539; Code 1868, § 4559; Code 1873, § 4653; Code 1882, § 4653; Penal Code 1895, § 1041; Penal Code 1910, § 1067; Code 1933, § 27–2510.

§ 17–10–11. Credit for time spent awaiting trial or resulting from court order applied to sentence and parole

(a) Each person convicted of a crime in this state shall be given full credit for each day spent in confinement awaiting trial and for each day spent in confinement, in connection with and resulting from a court order entered in the criminal proceedings for which sentence was imposed, in any institution or facility for treatment or examination of a physical or mental disability. The credit or credits shall be applied toward the convicted person's sentence and shall also be considered by parole authorities in determining the eligibility of the person for parole.

(b) This Code section applies to sentences for all crimes, whether classified as violations, misdemeanors, or felonies, and to all courts having criminal jurisdiction located within the boundaries of this state.

Laws 1970, p. 692, §§ 1, 2; Laws 1972, p. 742, § 1; Laws 2010, Act 674, § 9, eff. July 1, 2010.

Historical and Statutory Notes

The 2010 amendment by Act 674, in subsec. (b), deleted "except juvenile courts" after "of this state".

§ 17–10–12. Affidavit of custodian specifying number of days spent in custody

(a) The custodian of the defendant shall be required to make an affidavit specifying the number of days which the defendant has spent in confinement in his custody and furnish the affidavit to the clerk of the court within five days after sentence is imposed if the defendant is convicted. The affidavit of the custodian of the defendant shall be made a part of the official record of the trial.

(b) The clerk of the court shall transmit a copy of the custodian's affidavit to the Department of Corrections when the defendant has been sentenced to the custody of the department. The Department of Corrections shall give the defendant credit for the number of days spent in confinement prior to conviction and sentence, as reflected in the custodian's affidavit, before forwarding the record to the State Board of Pardons and Paroles.

(c) Where the defendant has been sentenced to the custody of an official other than the commissioner of corrections, the clerk of the court shall transmit the custodian's affidavit to the proper authorities who shall give the defendant credit for the number of days spent in custody prior to conviction and sentence.

(d) For service under this Code section, the clerk shall receive the fee prescribed in Code Section 15–6–77 from the funds of the county, except where the clerk is on a salary.

Laws 1970, p. 692, §§ 3, 4; Laws 1972, p. 742, §§ 2, 3; Laws 1977, p. 1098, § 7; Laws 1985, p. 283, § 1; Laws 1990, p. 8, § 17.

§ 17–10–13. Conviction in court having jurisdiction must precede punishment

The punishments prescribed by this Code shall be assessed only after a legal adjudication of guilt in a court having jurisdiction.

Formerly Penal Code 1895, § 20; Penal Code 1910, § 20; Code 1933, § 27–2509.

§ 17–10–14. Sentences of persons under the age of 17 sentenced as adults

(a) Notwithstanding any other provisions of this article and except as otherwise provided in subsections (b) and (c) of this Code section, in any case where a person under the age of 17 years is convicted of a felony and sentenced as an adult to life imprisonment or to a certain term of imprisonment, such person shall be committed to the Department of Juvenile Justice to serve such sentence in a detention center of such department until such person is 17 years of age at which time such person shall be transferred to the Department of Corrections to serve the remainder of the sentence. This Code section shall apply to any person convicted on or after July 1, 1987, and to any person convicted prior to such date who has not been committed to an institution operated by the Department of Corrections.

(b) If a child is transferred to superior court according to subsection (b) of Code Section 15–11–30.2 and convicted of aggravated assault as defined in Chapter 5 of Title 16, the court may sentence such child to the Department of Corrections. Such child shall be housed in a designated youth confinement unit until such person is 17 years of age, at which time such person may be housed in any other unit designated by the Department of Corrections.

(c) In any case where a child 13 to 17 years of age is convicted of a felony provided under subparagraph (b)(2)(A) of Code Section 15–11–28, such child shall be committed to the custody of the Department of Corrections and shall be housed in a designated youth confinement unit until such person is 17 years of age, at which time such person may be housed in any other unit designated by the Department of Corrections.

Laws 1987, p. 1335, § 1; Laws 1990, p. 1930, § 7; Laws 1992, p. 1983, § 19; Laws 1994, p. 1012, § 27; Laws 1997, p. 1453, § 1; Laws 2000, p. 20, § 8.

§ 17–10–15. HIV testing upon arrest, verdict, or plea of guilty or nolo contendere to AIDS transmitting crime; failure or refusal to submit to test; test results

(a) Any term used in this Code section and defined in Code Section 31–22–9.1 shall have the meaning provided for such term in Code Section 31–22–9.1.

(b) A victim or the parent or legal guardian of a minor or incompetent victim of a sexual offense as defined in Code Section 31–22–9.1 or other crime which involves significant exposure as defined by subsection (g) of this Code section may request that the agency responsible for prosecuting the alleged offense request that the person arrested for such offense submit to a test for the human immunodeficiency virus and consent to the release of the test results to the victim. If the person so arrested declines to submit to such a test, the judge of the superior court in which the criminal charge is pending, upon a showing of probable cause that the person arrested for the offense committed the alleged crime and that significant exposure occurred, may order the test to be performed in compliance with the rules adopted by the Department of Community Health. The cost of the test shall be borne by the victim or by the arrested person, in the discretion of the court.

(c) Upon a verdict or plea of guilty or a plea of nolo contendere to any AIDS transmitting crime, the court in which that verdict is returned or plea entered shall require the defendant in such case to submit to an HIV test within 45 days following the date of such verdict or plea. The clerk of the court in such case shall mail, within three days following the date of that verdict or plea, a copy of that verdict or plea to the Department of Community Health.

(d) The Department of Community Health, within 30 days following receipt of the court's order under subsection (b) of this Code section or within 30 days following receipt of the copy of the verdict or plea under subsection (c) of this Code section, shall arrange for the HIV test for the person required to submit thereto.

(e) Any person required under this Code section to submit to the HIV test who fails or refuses to submit to the test arranged pursuant to subsection (d) of this Code section shall be subject to such measures deemed necessary by the court in which the order was entered, verdict was returned, or plea was entered to require involuntary submission to the HIV test, and submission thereto may also be made a condition of suspending or probating any part of that person's sentence for the AIDS transmitting crime.

(f) If a person is required by this Code section to submit to an HIV test and is thereby determined to be infected with HIV, that determination and the name of the person shall be reported to:

(1) The Department of Community Health, which shall disclose the name of the person as necessary to provide counseling to each victim of that person's AIDS transmitting crime if that crime is other than one specified in subparagraph (a)(3)(J) of Code Section 31–22–9.1 or to any parent or guardian of any such victim who is a minor or incompetent person;

(2) The court which ordered the HIV test, which court shall make that report a part of that person's criminal record. That report shall be sealed by the court; and

(3) The officer in charge of any penal institution or other facility in which the person has been confined by order or sentence of the court for purposes of enabling that officer to confine the person separately from those not infected with HIV.

(g) For the purpose of subsection (b) of this Code section, "significant exposure" means contact of the victim's ruptured or broken skin or mucous membranes with the blood or body fluids of the person arrested for such offense, other than tears, saliva, or perspiration, of a magnitude that the Centers for Disease Control have epidemiologically demonstrated can result in transmission of the human immunodeficiency virus.

(h) The state may not use the fact that a medical procedure or test was performed on a person under this Code section or use the results of the procedure or test in any criminal proceeding arising out of the alleged offense.

Laws 1988, p. 1799, § 4; Laws 1991, p. 974, § 1; Laws 2009, Act 102, § 1–4, eff. July 1, 2009.

Historical and Statutory Notes

The 2009 amendment by Act 102 substituted "Department of Community Health" for "Department of Human Resources" throughout the section.

§ 17–10–16. Sentence of death, life imprisonment without parole, or life imprisonment; ineligibility for parole, work release, or leave programs

(a) Notwithstanding any other provision of law, a person who is convicted of an offense committed after May 1, 1993, for which the death penalty may be imposed under the laws of this state may be sentenced to death, imprisonment for life without parole, or life imprisonment as provided in Article 2 of this chapter.

(b) Notwithstanding any other provision of law, any person who is convicted of an offense for which the death penalty may be imposed and who is sentenced to imprisonment for life without parole shall not be eligible for any form of parole during such person's natural life unless the State Board of Pardons and Paroles or a court of this state shall, after notice and public hearing, determine that such person was innocent of the offense for which the sentence of imprisonment for life without parole was imposed. Such person shall not be eligible for any work release program, leave, or any other program administered by the Department of Corrections the effect of which would be to reduce the term of actual imprisonment to which such person was sentenced.

Laws 1993, p. 1654, § 3.

§ 17–10–17. Enhanced sentence where defendant intentionally selected victim or property as object of offense because of bias or prejudice

(a) Subject to the notice requirement provided in Code Section 17–10–18 and in enhancement of the penalty imposed, if the trier of fact determines beyond a reasonable doubt that the defendant intentionally selected any victim or any property of the victim as the object of the offense because of bias or prejudice, the judge imposing sentence shall:

(1) If the offense for which the defendant was convicted is a misdemeanor, increase the sentence and the fine normally imposed by the court through court policy or voluntary sentencing guidelines by 50 percent up to the maximum authorized by law;

(2) If the offense for which the defendant was convicted is a misdemeanor of a high and aggravated nature, increase the sentence and fine normally imposed by the court through court policy or voluntary sentencing guidelines by 50 percent up to the maximum authorized by law; or

(3) If the offense for which the defendant was convicted is a felony, increase the sentence normally imposed by the court through court policy or voluntary sentencing guidelines by up to five years, not to exceed the maximum authorized by law.

(b) The judge shall state when the judge imposes the sentence the amount of the increase of the sentence based on the application of subsection (a) of this Code section.

(c) Any person convicted of a felony and given an enhanced sentence under this Code section shall not be eligible for any form of parole or early release until such person has served at least 90 percent of the sentence imposed by the sentencing court.

Laws 2000, p. 224, § 1.

Validity

This section has been held unconstitutional in the case of Botts v. State, 2004, 278 Ga. 538, 604 S.E.2d 512.

Historical and Statutory Notes

In 2000, the Code Commission, in subsec. (c), substituted "Code section" for "Act" and "90 percent" for "90%". See § 28–9–5.

§ 17–10–18. Notice to defendant of intention to seek enhanced sentence

At any time after the filing of an indictment or accusation but not later than the arraignment, the state shall notify the defendant of its intention to seek the enhanced penalty or penalties authorized by Code Section 17–10–17. The notice shall be in writing and shall allege the specific factor or factors authorizing an enhanced sentence in the case pursuant to Code Section 17–10–17.

Laws 2000, p. 224, § 1.

§ 17–10–19. Procedure for imposing enhanced sentence

(a) In a case where notice has been given pursuant to Code Section 17–10–18, the trier of fact shall initially determine the defendant's guilt on the charge or charges. If the trier of fact finds the defendant guilty of such charge or charges, the trial shall immediately be recommenced to receive evidence as is relevant to determine whether the defendant intentionally selected the victim or the property of the victim as the object of the offense as set forth in the notice given pursuant to Code Section 17–10–18.

(b) If the trier of fact determines beyond a reasonable doubt that the defendant so acted, the judge shall enhance the sentence imposed in accordance with the provisions of Code Section 17–10–17.

Laws 2000, p. 224, § 1.

§ 17–10–20. Fine or restitution as part of sentence

(a) In any case in which a fine or restitution is imposed as part of the sentence, such fine and restitution shall constitute a judgment against the defendant. Upon the request of the prosecuting attorney, it shall be the duty of the clerk of the sentencing court to issue a writ of fieri facias thereon and enter it on the general execution docket of the superior court of the county in which such sentence was imposed. Such fieri facias may also be entered on the general execution docket in any county in which the defendant owns real property.

(b) If, in imposing sentence, the court sets a time certain for such fine or restitution to be paid in full, no execution shall issue upon the writ of fieri facias against the property of the defendant until such time as the time set by the court for payment of the fine or restitution shall have expired.

(c) If the fine or restitution is not paid in full, such judgment may be enforced by instituting any procedure for execution upon the writ of fieri facias through levy, foreclosure, garnishment, and all other actions provided for the enforcement of judgments in the State of Georgia and in other states and foreign nations where such judgment is afforded full faith and credit under the Uniform Foreign Money Judgments Act or domestication thereof.

(d) If the fine is not paid in full by the expiration of the time set by the court for payment of the fine, the governing authority of the county or municipality entitled to such fine may institute procedures to enforce such judgment as provided by subsection (c) of this Code section.

(e) If the restitution is not paid in full by the expiration of the time set by the court for payment of the restitution, the prosecuting attorney or the victim entitled to receive such restitution may institute procedures to enforce such judgment as provided by subsection (c) of this Code section.

(f) Notwithstanding the provisions of Code Section 9–12–60, a judgment entered on the general execution docket pursuant to this Code section shall not become dormant during any period when the defendant is incarcerated and for seven years thereafter. Such judgment shall be subject to revival in the same manner as provided for dormant judgments under Code Section 9–12–60.

(g) No fees, costs, or other charges authorized by law in civil cases shall be charged by a clerk of superior court for entering a judgment arising out of a criminal case on the general execution docket or for any action brought by the state to enforce such judgment.

(h) The provisions of this Code section shall be supplemental to any other provision of law applicable to the collection of fines or restitution in criminal cases.

Laws 2005, Act 20, § 4, eff. July 1, 2005.

Article 2

Death Penalty Generally

§ 17–10–30. Mitigating and aggravating circumstances; death penalty

(a) The death penalty may be imposed for the offenses of aircraft hijacking or treason in any case.

(b) In all cases of other offenses for which the death penalty may be authorized, the judge shall consider, or he shall include in his instructions to the jury for it to consider, any mitigating circumstances or aggravating circumstances otherwise authorized by law and any of the following statutory aggravating circumstances which may be supported by the evidence:

(1) The offense of murder, rape, armed robbery, or kidnapping was committed by a person with a prior record of conviction for a capital felony;

(2) The offense of murder, rape, armed robbery, or kidnapping was committed while the offender was engaged in the commission of another capital felony or aggravated battery, or the offense of murder was committed while the offender was engaged in the commission of burglary or arson in the first degree;

(3) The offender, by his act of murder, armed robbery, or kidnapping, knowingly created a great risk of death to more than one person in a public place by means of a weapon or device which would normally be hazardous to the lives of more than one person;

(4) The offender committed the offense of murder for himself or another, for the purpose of receiving money or any other thing of monetary value;

(5) The murder of a judicial officer, former judicial officer, district attorney or solicitor-general, or former district attorney, solicitor, or solicitor-general was committed during or because of the exercise of his or her official duties;

(6) The offender caused or directed another to commit murder or committed murder as an agent or employee of another person;

(7) The offense of murder, rape, armed robbery, or kidnapping was outrageously or wantonly vile, horrible, or inhuman in that it involved torture, depravity of mind, or an aggravated battery to the victim;

(8) The offense of murder was committed against any peace officer, corrections employee, or firefighter while engaged in the performance of his official duties;

(9) The offense of murder was committed by a person in, or who has escaped from, the lawful custody of a peace officer or place of lawful confinement;

(10) The murder was committed for the purpose of avoiding, interfering with, or preventing a lawful arrest or custody in a place of lawful confinement, of himself or another; or

(11) The offense of murder, rape, or kidnapping was committed by a person previously convicted of rape, aggravated sodomy, aggravated child molestation, or aggravated sexual battery.

(c) The statutory instructions as determined by the trial judge to be warranted by the evidence shall be given in charge and in writing to the jury for its deliberation. The jury, if its verdict is a recommendation of death, shall designate in writing, signed by the foreman of the jury, the aggravating circumstance or circumstances which it found beyond a reasonable doubt. In nonjury cases the judge shall make such designation. Except in cases of treason or aircraft hijacking, unless at least one of the statutory aggravating circumstances enumerated in subsection (b) of this Code section is so found, the death penalty shall not be imposed.

Laws 1973, p. 159, § 3; Laws 1996, p. 748, § 15; Laws 2002, p. 660, § 4; Laws 2002, p. 1259, § 11; Laws 2006, Act 571, § 22, eff. July 1, 2006.

Formerly Code 1933, § 27–2534.1.

Historical and Statutory Notes

The 2006 amendment by Act 571, in subsec. (b), added par. (11).

Laws 2006, Act 571, §§ 1 and 30, provide:

"SECTION 1. The General Assembly finds and declares that recidivist sexual offenders, sexual offenders who use physical violence, and sexual offenders who prey on children are sexual predators who present an extreme threat to the public safety. Many sexual offenders are extremely likely to use physical violence and to repeat their offenses; and some sexual offenders commit many offenses, have many more victims than are ever reported, and are prosecuted for only a fraction of their crimes. The General Assembly finds that this makes the cost of sexual offender victimization to society at large, while incalculable, clearly exorbitant. The General Assembly further finds that the high level of threat that a sexual predator presents to the public safety, and the long-term effects suffered by victims of sex offenses, provide the state with sufficient justification to implement a strategy that includes:

"(1) Incarcerating sexual offenders and maintaining adequate facilities to ensure that decisions to release sexual predators into the community are not made on the basis of inadequate space;

"(2) Requiring the registration of sexual offenders, with a requirement that complete and accurate information be maintained and accessible for use by law enforcement authorities, communities, and the public;

"(3) Providing for community and public notification concerning the presence of sexual offenders;

"(4) Collecting data relative to sexual offenses and sexual offenders;

"(5) Requiring sexual predators who are released into the community to wear an electronic monitoring system for the rest of their natural life and to pay for such system; and

"(6) Prohibiting sexual predators from working with children, either for compensation or as a volunteer.

"The General Assembly further finds that the state has a compelling interest in protecting the public from sexual offenders and in protecting children from predatory sexual activity, and there is sufficient justification for requiring sexual offenders to register and for requiring community and public notification of the presence of sexual offenders. The General Assembly declares that in order to protect the public, it is necessary that the sexual offenders be registered and that members of the community and the public be notified of a sexual offender's presence. The designation of a person as a sexual offender is neither a sentence nor a punishment but simply a regulatory mechanism and status resulting from the conviction of certain crimes. Likewise, the designation of a person as a sexual predator is neither a sentence nor a punishment but simply a regulatory mechanism and status resulting from findings by the Sexual Offender Registration Review Board and a court if requested by a sexual offender."

"SECTION 30. (a) This Act shall become effective July 1, 2006.

"(b) Any person required to register pursuant to the provisions of Code Section 42–1–12, relating to the state sexual offender registry, and any person required not to reside within areas where minors congregate, as prohibited by Code Section 42–1–13 [see § 42–1–15], shall not be relieved of the obligation to comply with the provisions of said Code sections by the repeal and reenactment of said Code sections.

"(c) The provisions of this Act shall not affect or abate the status as a crime of any such act or omission which occurred prior to the effective date of the Act repealing, repealing and reenacting, or amending such law, nor shall the prosecution of such crime be abated as a result of such repeal, repeal and reenactment, or amendment."

In 2006, the Code Commission, in subsec. (b), deleted the period at the end of par. (10). See § 28–9–5.

§ 17–10–30.1. Repealed by Laws 2009, Act 62, § 4, eff. April 29, 2009

Historical and Statutory Notes

The repealed section, relating to a mitigating and aggravating circumstances and sentence of life imprisonment without parole, was derived from Laws 1993, p. 1654, § 4.

§ 17–10–31. Capital felonies; jury verdict and sentence

(a) Where, upon a trial by jury, a person is convicted of an offense which may be punishable by death, a sentence of death shall not be imposed unless the jury verdict includes a finding of at least one statutory aggravating circumstance and a recommendation that such sentence be imposed. Where a statutory aggravating circumstance is found and a recommendation of death is made, the court shall sentence the accused to death. Where a statutory aggravating circumstance is not found or where a statutory circumstance is found but a recommendation of death is not made, the jury shall decide whether to recommend a sentence of life imprisonment without parole or life imprisonment with the possibility of parole. Unless the jury trying the case makes a finding of at least one statutory aggravating circumstance and recommends the death sentence in its verdict, the court shall not sentence the accused to death, provided that no such finding of statutory aggravating circumstance shall be necessary in offenses of treason or aircraft hijacking. This Code section shall not affect a sentence when the case is tried without a jury or when the judge accepts a plea of guilty.

(b) During the sentencing phase before a jury, counsel for the state and the accused may present argument and the trial judge may instruct the jury:

(1) That "life without parole" means that the accused shall be incarcerated for the remainder of his or her natural life and shall not be eligible for parole unless such person is subsequently adjudicated to be not guilty of the offense for which he or she was sentenced; and

(2) That "life imprisonment" means that the accused will be incarcerated for the remainder of his or her natural life but will be eligible for parole during the term of such sentence.

(c) If the jury is unable to reach a unanimous verdict as to sentence, the judge shall dismiss the jury and shall impose a sentence of either life imprisonment or imprisonment for life without parole.

Laws 1968, p. 1249, § 1; Laws 1969, p. 809, § 1; Laws 1973, p. 159, § 7; Laws 2009, Act 62, § 5, eff. April 29, 2009.

Formerly Code 1933, § 26–3102.

Historical and Statutory Notes

The 2009 amendment by Act 62 rewrote the section which had read:

"Where, upon a trial by jury, a person is convicted of an offense which may be punishable by death, a sentence of death shall not be imposed unless the jury verdict includes a finding of at least one statutory aggravating circumstance and a recommendation that such sentence be imposed. Where a statutory aggravating circumstance is found and a recommendation of death is made, the court shall sentence the defendant to death. Where a sentence of death is not recommended by the jury, the court shall sentence the defendant to imprisonment as provided by law. Unless the jury trying the case makes a finding of at least one statutory aggravating circumstance and recommends the death sentence in its verdict, the court shall not sentence the defendant to death, provided that no such finding of statutory aggravating circumstance shall be necessary in offenses of treason or aircraft hijacking. This Code section shall not affect a sentence when the case is tried without a jury or when the judge accepts a plea of guilty."

Laws 2009, Act 62, §§ 8 to 11, provide:

"SECTION 8. Except as provided in this section, the provisions of this Act shall apply only to those offenses committed after the effective date of this Act. With express written consent of the state, an accused whose offense was committed prior to the effective date of this Act may elect in writing to be sentenced under the provisions of this Act, provided that: (1) jeopardy for the offense charged has not attached or (2) the accused has been sentenced to death but the conviction or sentence has been reversed on appeal and the state is not barred from seeking prosecution after the remand.

"SECTION 9. Except as provided in Section 8 of this Act, the amendment or repeal of a Code section by this Act shall not affect any sentence imposed by any court of this state prior to the effective date of this Act.

"SECTION 10. A person may be sentenced to life without parole without the prosecutor seeking the death penalty under the laws of this state.

"SECTION 11.(a) This Act shall become effective upon its approval by the Governor or upon its becoming law without such approval and shall apply to all crimes committed on and after such date, and except as provided in Section 8 of this Act, the law as set forth in Section 2 and in Sections 3 through 7 of this Act as it existed prior to the effective date of this Act shall apply to all offenses committed on and before such date.

"(b) The provisions of this Act shall not affect or abate the status as a crime of any such act or omission which occurred prior to the effective date of the Act repealing, repealing and reenacting, or amending such law, nor shall the prosecution of such crime be abated as a result of such repeal, repeal and reenactment, or amendment."

§ 17–10–31.1. Repealed by Laws 2009, Act 62, § 6, eff. April 29, 2009

Historical and Statutory Notes

The repealed section, relating to a murder conviction and sentence of life imprisonment without parole, was derived from Laws 1993, p. 1654, § 5.

§ 17–10–32. Sentence of life imprisonment or lesser punishment on plea of guilty to an offense punishable by death

Any person who has been indicted for an offense punishable by death may enter a plea of guilty at any time after his indictment, and the judge of the superior court having jurisdiction may, in his discretion, sentence the person to life imprisonment or to any other punishment authorized by law for the offense named in the indictment; provided, however, that the judge must find one of the statutory aggravating circumstances provided in Code Section 17–10–30 before imposing the death penalty, except in cases of treason or aircraft hijacking.

Laws 1956, p. 737, § 1; Laws 1973, p. 159, § 8.

§ 17–10–32.1. Repealed by Laws 2009, Act 62, § 7, eff. April 29, 2009

Historical and Statutory Notes

The repealed section, relating to a sentence of life imprisonment or lesser punishment on plea of guilty to an offense punishable by death or life without parole, was derived from Laws 1993, p. 1654, § 6.

§ 17–10–33. Sentence of death; copy of sentence; time and mode of conveying prisoner to penitentiary; expenses

Upon a judgment of death made by a judge, it shall be the duty of the judge to sentence the defendant to death and to indicate the sentence in writing, which writing shall be filed with the papers in the case against the defendant. A certified copy of the sentence shall be sent by the clerk of the court in which the sentence is pronounced to the defendant's attorney of record, to the Attorney General, and to the superintendent of the state correctional institution where the execution is to take place, not less than ten days prior to the time fixed in the sentence of the court for the execution of the defendant. In all cases it shall be the duty of the sheriff of the county in which the defendant is sentenced, together with one deputy or more if in the sheriff's judgment it is necessary, and provided that in all cases the number of guards shall be approved by the trial judge or, if the trial judge is not available, by the judge of the probate court of the county in which the defendant is sentenced, to convey the defendant to the appropriate state correctional institution, not more than 20 days nor less than two days prior to the time fixed in the judgment for the execution of the defendant, unless otherwise directed by the Governor or unless a stay of execution has been caused by an appeal, granting of a new trial, or other order of a court of competent jurisdiction. The expense for transporting the defendant to the state correctional institution for the purpose of execution of the death sentence shall be paid by the county governing authority of the county in which the defendant was convicted, out of any funds on hand in the treasury of the county.

Laws 1924, p. 195, § 3; Laws 1973, p. 159, § 9; Laws 1983, p. 665, § 1; Laws 2000, p. 947, § 2.

Formerly Code 1933, § 27–2514.

§ 17–10–34. Sentence to specify time period for execution; pregnant females

When a person is sentenced to the punishment of death, the court shall specify the time period for the execution in the sentence. The time period for the execution fixed by the court shall be seven days in duration and shall commence at noon on a specified date and shall end at noon on a specified date. The time period shall commence not less than 20 days nor more than 60 days from the date of sentencing. However, if the person is a female who is pregnant at the time of sentencing, the court shall appoint a time period for execution after the female is no longer pregnant.

Laws 1833, Cobb's 1851 Digest, p. 840; Laws 1985, p. 1463, § 1.

Formerly Code 1863, § 4555; Code 1868, § 4575; Code 1873, § 4669; Code 1882, § 4669; Penal Code 1895, § 1044; Penal Code 1910, § 1070; Code 1933, § 27–2519.

§ 17–10–35. Review of death sentences

(a) Whenever the death penalty is imposed, upon the judgment becoming final in the trial court, the sentence shall be reviewed on the record by the Supreme Court of Georgia. The clerk of the trial court, within ten days after receiving the transcript, shall transmit the entire record and transcript to the Supreme Court together with a notice prepared by the clerk and a report prepared by the trial judge. The notice shall set forth the title and docket number of the case, the name of the defendant and the name and address of his attorney, a narrative statement of the judgment, the offense, and the punishment prescribed. The report shall be in the form of a standard questionnaire prepared and supplied by the Supreme Court.

(b) The Supreme Court shall consider the punishment as well as any errors enumerated by way of appeal.

(c) With regard to the sentence, the court shall determine:

(1) Whether the sentence of death was imposed under the influence of passion, prejudice, or any other arbitrary factor;

(2) Whether, in cases other than treason or aircraft hijacking, the evidence supports the jury's or judge's finding of a statutory aggravating circumstance as enumerated in subsection (b) of Code Section 17–10–30; and

(3) Whether the sentence of death is excessive or disproportionate to the penalty imposed in similar cases, considering both the crime and the defendant.

(d) Both the defendant and the state shall have the right to submit briefs within the time provided by the court and to present oral argument to the court.

(e) The court shall include in its decision a reference to those similar cases which it took into consideration. In addition to its authority regarding correction of errors, the court, with regard to review of death sentences, shall be authorized to:

(1) Affirm the sentence of death; or

(2) Set the sentence aside and remand the case for resentencing by the trial judge based on the record and argument of counsel. The records of those similar cases referred to by the Supreme Court in its decision and the extracts prepared as provided for in subsection (a) of Code Section 17–10–37 shall be provided to the resentencing judge for his consideration.

(f) The sentence review shall be in addition to direct appeal, if taken, and the review and appeal shall be consolidated for consideration. The court shall render its decision on legal errors enumerated, the factual substantiation of the verdict, and the validity of the sentence.

Laws 1973, p. 159, § 4.

Formerly Code 1933, § 27–2537.

§ 17–10–35.1. Review of pretrial proceedings in cases in which death sentence sought

(a) In cases in which the death penalty is sought, there may be a review of all pretrial proceedings by the Supreme Court upon a determination by the trial judge under Code Section 17–10–35.2 that such review is appropriate. The review shall be initiated by the trial judge's filing in the office of the clerk of superior court and delivering to the parties a report certifying that all pretrial proceedings in the case have been completed and that the case stands ready for trial. Within ten days after the filing of the report or the receipt of transcripts of the proceedings, whichever is later, the prosecutor and the defendant may each file with the clerk of superior court and serve upon the opposing party a report identifying all areas of the pretrial proceedings with respect to which reversible error may arguably have occurred. Either party may consolidate with such report an application for appeal with respect to any order, decision, or judgment entered in the case. Any such application for appeal shall be in the form otherwise appropriate under subsection (b) of Code Section 5–6–34, but:

(1) Any such application for appeal shall be filed with the clerk of superior court rather than the clerk of the Supreme Court;

(2) The opposing party shall not be required or permitted to respond to such an application for appeal; and

(3) No certificate of immediate review shall be required for the filing of such application for appeal.

(b) The reports of the trial judge, prosecutor, and defendant under subsection (a) of this Code section shall be in the form of standard questionnaires prepared and supplied by the Supreme Court. Such questionnaires shall be designed to determine whether there is arguably any existence of reversible error with respect to any of the following matters:

(1) Any proceedings with respect to change of venue;

(2) Any proceedings with respect to recusal of the trial judge;

(3) Any challenge to the jury array;

(4) Any motion to suppress evidence;

(5) Any motion for psychiatric or other medical evaluation; and

(6) Any other matter deemed appropriate by the Supreme Court.

(c) Upon the filing of the reports of the parties, the clerk of superior court shall transmit to the Supreme Court the report of the trial judge, the transcripts of proceedings, and the reports of the parties together with any application for appeal consolidated therewith. A copy of all of the foregoing shall also be delivered by the clerk of superior court to the Attorney General.

(d) The Supreme Court shall issue an order granting review of the pretrial proceedings, or portions thereof, or denying review within 45 days of the date on which the case was received. The order of the Supreme Court shall identify the matters which shall be subject to review, and such matters may include, but need not be limited to, any matters called to the court's attention in any of the reports or in any application for appeal. No notice of appeal shall be required to be filed if review of the pretrial proceedings is granted. An order granting review of pretrial proceedings shall specify the period of time within which each party shall file briefs and reply briefs with respect to the matters identified in the Supreme Court's order granting review. The Supreme Court may order oral argument or may render a decision on the record and the briefs.

(e) If requested by the district attorney, the Attorney General shall assist in the review and appeal provided for in this Code section.

(f) Review of any matter under this Code section shall, as to any question passed on in such review, be res judicata as to such question and shall be deemed to be the law of the case.

(g) The procedure under this Code section shall not apply to any ruling or order made, invoked, or sought subsequent to the filing of the report of the trial judge.

(h) The failure of either party to assert the rights given in this Code section, or the failure of the Supreme Court to grant review, shall not waive the right to posttrial review of any question review of which could be sought under this Code section and shall not constitute an adjudication as to such question.

Laws 1988, p. 1437, § 4; Laws 2010, Act 452, § 1, eff. July 1, 2010.

Historical and Statutory Notes

The 2010 amendment by Act 452, in subsec. (d), substituted "45 days" for "20 days".

Laws 2010, Act 452, § 3, provides:

"This Act shall become effective on July 1, 2010, and shall apply to any case docketed on or after such date."

§ 17–10–35.2. Hearing to determine whether interim appellate review of pretrial rulings is appropriate

Prior to the filing of a report by the trial judge under Code Section 17–10–35.1 certifying that pretrial proceedings are complete, the court shall conduct a hearing to determine if an interim appellate review of pretrial rulings is appropriate. The court shall hear from the state and the defense as to whether the delay to be caused by interim appellate review outweighs the need for such review. The court shall order such review and initiate the procedure contained in Code Section 17–10–35.1 unless the court concludes and enters an order to the effect that interim appellate review would not serve the ends of justice in the case. An order obviating interim appellate review shall not be appealable.

Laws 1988, p. 1437, § 4.

§ 17–10–36. Unified review of conviction, sentence, and detention when death sentence imposed; habeas corpus not affected

(a) The Supreme Court of Georgia shall establish, by rules, a new unified review procedure to provide for the presentation to the sentencing court and to the Supreme Court of all possible challenges to the trial, conviction, sentence, and detention of defendants upon whom the sentence of death has been or may be imposed, which challenges before July 1, 1988, have been presented for review by the former unified review procedure under this subsection. Such new unified review procedure shall govern both pretrial and posttrial appellate review of death penalty cases.

(b) The Supreme Court shall establish, by rules, a series of check lists to be utilized by the trial court, the prosecuting attorney, and defense counsel prior to, during, and after the trial of cases in which the death penalty is sought to make certain that all possible matters which could be raised in defense have been considered by the defendant and defense counsel and either asserted in a timely and correct manner or waived in accordance with applicable legal requirements, so that, for purposes of any pretrial review and the trial and posttrial review, the record and transcript of proceedings will be complete for a review by the sentencing court and the Supreme Court of all possible challenges to the trial, conviction, sentence, and detention of the defendant.

(c) Nothing in this Code section or in the rules of the Supreme Court shall limit or restrict the grounds of review or suspend the rights or remedies available through the procedures governing the writ of habeas corpus.

(d) The procedures governing the writ of habeas corpus may be employed to assert rights or seek remedies if the procedures established in the rules of the Supreme Court as applied to the petitioner are inadequate or ineffective in any constitutional sense.

Laws 1980, p. 390, § 1; Laws 1988, p. 1437, § 5.

Formerly Code 1933, § 27–2538.

§ 17–10–37. Review of death sentences; assistant to Supreme Court

(a) There shall be an assistant to the Supreme Court who shall be an attorney appointed by the Chief Justice and who shall serve at the pleasure of the court. The assistant shall assist the Supreme Court in the review of all death sentences.

(b) The court shall be authorized to employ an appropriate staff and such methods to compile such data as are deemed by the Chief Justice to be appropriate and relevant to the statutory questions concerning the validity of the sentence reviewed in accordance with Code Section 17–10–35.

Laws 1973, p. 159, § 4; Laws 2010, Act 452,§ 2 eff. July 1, 2010.

Formerly Code 1933, § 27–2537.

Historical and Statutory Notes

The 2010 amendment by Act 452 rewrote subsec. (a) and deleted subsec. (c) which had read as follows:

"(a) There shall be an assistant to the Supreme Court who shall be an attorney appointed by the Chief Justice and who shall serve at the pleasure of the court. The court shall accumulate the records of all capital felony cases in which sentence was imposed after January 1, 1970, or such earlier date as the court may deem appropriate. The assistant shall provide the court with whatever extracted information it desires with respect thereto, including, but not limited to, a synopsis or brief of the facts in the record concerning the crime and the defendant."

"(c) The office of the assistant shall be attached for administrative purposes to the office of the clerk of the Supreme Court of Georgia."

Laws 2010, Act 452, § 3, provides:

"This Act shall become effective on July 1, 2010, and shall apply to any case docketed on or after such date."

§ 17–10–38. Lethal injection; place of execution; physician not required to participate

(a) All persons who have been convicted of a capital offense and have had imposed upon them a sentence of death shall suffer such punishment by lethal injection. Lethal injection is the continuous intravenous injection of a substance or substances sufficient to cause death into the body of the person sentenced to death until such person is dead.

(b) In all cases in which the defendant is sentenced to death, it shall be the duty of the trial judge in passing sentence to direct that the defendant be delivered to the Department of Corrections for execution of the death sentence at a state correctional institution designated by the department.

(c) Notwithstanding any other provision of law, prescription, preparation, compounding, dispensing, or administration of a lethal injection authorized by a sentence of death by a court of competent jurisdiction shall not constitute the practice of medicine or any other profession relating to health care which is subject by law to regulation, licensure, or certification.

(d) No state agency, department, or official may, through regulation or otherwise, require or compel a physician to participate in the execution of a death sentence. "To participate in the execution of a death sentence" means any of the following actions: selecting injection sites; starting an intravenous line or lines as a port for a lethal injection device; prescribing, preparing, administering, or supervising injection drugs or their doses or types; inspecting, testing, or maintaining lethal injection devices; or consulting with or supervising lethal injection personnel.

Laws 1924, p. 195, § 1; Laws 1937–38, Ex. Sess., p. 330, § 1; Laws 1985, p. 283, § 1; Laws 2000, p. 947, § 3.

Formerly Code 1933, § 27–2512.

§ 17–10–39. Suspension of sentence when defendant is pregnant

After a sentence of death has been imposed, if a female defendant so sentenced is believed to be pregnant, the sheriff of the county in which the defendant is imprisoned, with the concurrence and assistance of the judge of the probate court, shall select one or more physicians who shall conduct an examination. If the female is found to be pregnant, the sheriff shall suspend the execution of the sentence and make a report of the examination and suspension of execution to the presiding judge of the circuit, who shall cause the report and suspension to be entered on the minutes of the superior court of the county where the sentence was imposed. When the defendant is no longer pregnant, the judge shall issue a new order as provided in Code Section 17–10–40 directing the sheriff to execute the sentence at such date and place as the judge may appoint and direct in the order, which the sheriff shall be bound to do accordingly. The judge shall cause the new order and other proceedings in the case to be entered on the minutes of the court in which the sentence was imposed.

Laws 1833, Cobb's 1851 Digest, p. 839; Laws 1874, p. 30.

Formerly Code 1863, § 4553; Code 1868, § 4573; Code 1873, § 4667; Code 1882, § 4667; Penal Code 1895, § 1045; Penal Code 1910, § 1071; Code 1933, § 27–2520.

§ 17–10–40. Fixing of new time period for execution where original time period has passed

(a) Where the time period for the execution of any convicted person in a capital case has passed by reason of a supersedeas incident to appellate review, a stay of execution by the State Board of Pardons and Paroles, or for any other reason, a judge of the superior court of the county where the case was tried shall have the power and authority to pass an order fixing a new time period for the execution of the original sentence without requiring the convicted person to be brought before him by a writ of habeas corpus. The order shall be recorded on the minutes of the court and a certified copy of the order shall be sent immediately to the convicted person's attorney of record, to the Attorney General, and to the superintendent of the state correctional institution at the place of execution.

(b) The new time period for the execution shall be seven days in duration and shall commence at noon on a specified date and shall end at noon on a specified date. The new time period for the execution fixed by the judge shall commence not less than ten nor more than 20 days from the date of the order.

(c) The Department of Corrections shall set the day and time for execution within the time period designated by the judge of the superior court. If the execution is not carried out on the day and at the time originally set by the Department of Corrections, the Department of Corrections is authorized to set new dates and times for execution within the period designated by the judge of the superior court.

Laws 1924, p. 195, § 7; Laws 1983, p. 665, § 2; Laws 1985, p. 1463, § 2.

Formerly Code 1933, § 27–2518.

§ 17–10–41. Who shall be present at execution

There shall be present at the execution of a convicted person the superintendent of the state correctional institution or a deputy superintendent thereof, at least three executioners, two physicians to determine when death supervenes, and other correctional officers, assistants, technicians, and witnesses as determined by the commissioner of corrections. In addition, the convicted person may request the presence of his or her counsel, a member of the clergy, and a reasonable number of relatives and friends, provided that the total number of witnesses appearing at the request of the convicted person shall be determined by the commissioner of corrections.

Laws 1924, p. 195, § 4; Laws 1956, p. 161, § 32; Laws 1988, p. 252, § 1; Laws 2000, p. 947, § 4.

Formerly Code 1933, § 27–2515.

§ 17–10–42. Certificate of execution

The executioner and attending physicians shall certify the fact of the execution to the clerk of the superior court of the county in which the sentence was imposed, which certificate shall be filed by the clerk with the papers in the case.

Laws 1924, p. 195, § 5.

Formerly Code 1933, § 27–2516.

§ 17–10–42.1. Participating physicians or medical professionals not subject to challenge, suspension, or revocation of license

Participation in any execution of any convicted person carried out under this article shall not be the subject of any licensure challenge, suspension, or revocation for any physician or medical professional licensed in the State of Georgia.

Laws 2006, Act 537, § 1, eff. July 1, 2006.

Historical and Statutory Notes

Laws 2006, Act 537, § 2, provides:

"This Act shall become effective on July 1, 2006, and shall apply to executions carried out on or after July 1, 2006."

§ 17–10–43. Disposition of body; expenses of transporting body

The body of an executed person shall be delivered to the relatives of the person if they so desire; and, in case no claim is made by relatives for the body, it shall be disposed of in the same manner as bodies of inmates dying in a state correctional institution. If the nearest relatives of the person executed desire that the body be transported to the former home of the executed person, if in this state, the expenses of transportation shall be paid by the county governing authority of the county where the person was convicted, from any funds on hand in the treasury.

Laws 1924, p. 195, § 6.

Formerly Code 1933, § 27–2517.

§ 17–10–44. Place for execution and apparatus

The Department of Corrections shall provide a place for execution of the death sentence and all necessary apparatus, machinery, and appliances for inflicting the penalty of death.

Laws 1924, p. 195, § 2; Laws 1956, p. 161, § 28; Laws 1985, p. 283, § 1; Laws 2000, p. 947, § 5.

Formerly Code 1933, § 27–2513.

Article 3

Mentally Incompetent to Be Executed

§ 17–10–60. "Mentally incompetent to be executed" defined

As used in this article, the term "mentally incompetent to be executed" means that because of a mental condition the person is presently unable to know why he or she is being punished and understand the nature of the punishment.

Laws 1988, p. 1003, § 2.

§ 17–10–61. When person sentenced to death shall not be executed

A person under sentence of death shall not be executed when it is determined under the provisions of this article that the person is mentally incompetent to be executed as defined in Code Section 17–10–60.

Laws 1988, p. 1003, § 2.

§ 17–10–62. Exclusive procedure

Notwithstanding any other provision of this Code, this article provides the exclusive procedure for challenging mental competency to be executed when such challenge is made subsequent to the time of conviction and sentence.

Laws 1988, p. 1003, § 2.

§ 17–10–63. Filing and contents of application

(a) An application brought under this article must be filed in the superior court of the county in which the applicant is being detained. The named respondent shall be the person having actual custody of the applicant.

(b) An application brought under this article shall identify the proceeding in which the applicant was convicted, give the date of the rendition and the final judgment complained of, set forth the fact that a time period for execution has been set, give the date of the signing of the order and the dates of the designated time period for execution, and shall clearly set forth alleged facts in support of the assertion that the applicant is presently mentally incompetent to be executed. The application shall have attached thereto affidavits, records, or other evidence supporting its allegations or shall state why the same are not attached. The application shall identify any previous proceedings that the applicant may have taken challenging his mental competency to be executed or challenging his mental condition in relation to the conviction and sentence in question. Arguments and citations of authority shall be omitted from the application. The application must be verified with the oath of the applicant or of some other person in his behalf.

Laws 1988, p. 1003, § 2.

§ 17–10–64. Service of application

Service of an application brought under this article shall be made upon the person having custody of the applicant. If the applicant is being detained under the custody of the Department of Corrections, an additional copy of the application shall be served upon the Attorney General. If the applicant is being detained under the custody of some authority other than the Department of Corrections, an additional copy of the petition shall be served upon the district attorney of the county in which the application is filed.

Laws 1988, p. 1003, § 2.

§ 17–10–65. Answer; schedule of case

As soon as possible after the filing and docketing of the application under this article, the respondent shall answer the application. The court may schedule a case for a hearing prior to the filing of responsive pleadings but, in any event, shall schedule the case for a hearing as soon as possible so that the proceedings may move expeditiously.

Laws 1988, p. 1003, § 2.

§ 17–10–66. Examination of applicant for purposes of assessing mental competency to be executed

(a) By filing an application under this article, the applicant specifically consents to submit to a state examination for the purposes of assessing mental competency to be executed.

(b) Simultaneously with the filing of the application, the applicant, if he or she wishes the court to consider any request for appointment of an expert, shall file such a request and shall state specific facts in support of that request so that the court may determine if the applicant's mental competency to be executed is in fact a significant issue. The applicant shall further submit with the motion a specific statement as to the particular expert requested, the nature of the examination to be conducted, the time period within which an examination can be conducted, and an estimate of the expenses to be incurred.

(c) If the applicant has filed a request for an examination as provided in subsection (b) of this Code section and the applicant makes a sufficient showing that his or her mental competency to be executed is a significant issue, the court shall appoint an expert to make an examination of the applicant, with such examination to be conducted as soon as possible. Payment for such expert shall be made by the Department of Corrections unless otherwise designated by the General Assembly.

Laws 1988, p. 1003, § 2.

§ 17–10–67. When application may be filed

An application under this article shall not be filed until completion of direct appeal and until an order has been signed by a judge of the trial court setting a time period for the execution.

Laws 1988, p. 1003, § 2.

§ 17–10–68. Pleadings and evidence; findings

(a) The court may receive proof by depositions, oral testimony, sworn affidavits, or other evidence.

(b) The taking of depositions shall be governed by Code Sections 9–11–26 through 9–11–32 and 9–11–37.

(c) If a sworn affidavit is to be introduced into evidence by either party, the party intending to introduce such an affidavit shall cause it to be served upon the opposing party at least five days in advance of the date set for a hearing in the case or, in the event a hearing is set less than five days from the date of the filing of the application, as soon as possible so that opposing counsel has the opportunity to review the affidavit prior to the hearing. The affidavit so served shall be accompanied by notice of the party's intention to introduce it into evidence. The superior court judge considering the application may resolve disputed issues of fact upon the basis of sworn affidavits standing by themselves.

(d) After reviewing the pleadings and evidence offered at the hearing, the judge of the superior court hearing the case shall make written findings of fact and conclusions of law upon which the judgment is based. The findings of fact and conclusions of law shall be recorded as part of the record in the case.

(e) If the court finds in favor of the applicant by finding that the applicant has proven his or her mental incompetence to be executed by a preponderance of the evidence, the court shall enter an appropriate order with respect to any scheduled execution time period and shall enter such supplementary orders as necessary and proper. If the court denies the application, the court shall direct that immediate telephonic notification be given to the parties and any stay presently entered under this article shall be dissolved instanter.

Laws 1988, p. 1003, § 2.

§ 17–10–69. Prior adjudication of mental competency

If an applicant is determined to have previously filed an application under this article and has previously been determined to be mentally competent to be executed, such prior adjudication shall act as a presumption of mental competency and the applicant shall not be entitled to a new hearing on the question of mental competency to be executed absent the applicant's making a prima-facie showing of a substantial change in circumstances sufficient to raise a significant question as to the applicant's mental competency to be executed at the time of filing of any subsequent applications.

Laws 1988, p. 1003, § 2.

§ 17–10–70. Appeals

(a) Appeals in cases brought under this article shall be governed by Chapter 6 of Title 5 except that as to final orders of the court which are adverse to the applicant, no appeal shall be ordered unless the Supreme Court of this state issues a certificate of probable cause for the appeal.

(b) If an unsuccessful applicant desires to appeal, he or she must file a written application for a certificate of probable cause to appeal with the clerk of the Supreme Court within three days of the entry of the order denying relief. The applicant shall also file within the same period a notice of appeal with the clerk of the concerned superior court. The Supreme Court shall either grant or deny the application within a reasonable time after filing. In order for the Supreme Court to consider fully the request for a certificate, the clerk of the concerned superior court shall forward, as in any other case, the record and transcript, if designated, to the clerk of the Supreme Court when a notice of appeal is filed. The clerk of the concerned superior court need not prepare and retain and the court reporter need not file a copy of the original record and a copy of the original transcript of proceedings. The clerk of the Supreme Court shall return the original record and transcript to the clerk of the concerned superior court upon completion of the appeal if the certificate is granted. If the Supreme Court denies the application for a certificate of probable cause, the clerk of the Supreme Court shall return the original record and transcript and shall notify the clerk of the concerned superior court and the parties to the proceedings below of the determination that probable cause does not exist for appeal.

(c) If the trial court finds in favor of the applicant, no certificate of probable cause need be obtained by the respondent as a condition precedent to appeal. A notice of appeal filed by the respondent shall act as a supersedeas and shall stay the judgment of the superior court until there is a final adjudication by the Supreme Court.

Laws 1988, p. 1003, § 2.

§ 17–10–71. Regaining of mental competency

If a convicted person under sentence of death who is found to be mentally incompetent to be executed under this article regains his or her mental competency, the fact shall be certified at once by the appropriate mental health official to the court initially making the finding of mental incompetency. Upon such certification, that court shall enter an appropriate order noting receipt of certification and vacating any previously entered stay of execution. A copy of such order shall be sent to the sentencing court, at which time the sentencing court shall fix a new time period for execution as provided in Code Section 17–10–40. The judge of the court which made the determination on the issue of mental competency shall cause the new order and other proceedings in the case to be presented on the minutes of the court.

Laws 1988, p. 1003, § 2.

CHAPTER 11

ASSESSMENT AND PAYMENT OF COSTS OF CRIMINAL PROCEEDINGS

Article 1

General Provisions

§ 17–11–1. When defendant shall pay costs

The costs of a prosecution, except the fees of his own witnesses, shall not be demanded of a defendant until after trial and conviction. If convicted, judgment may be entered against the defendant for all costs accruing in the committing and trial courts and by any officer pending the prosecution. The judgment shall be a lien from the date of his arrest on all the property of the defendant. The clerk shall issue an execution on the judgment against the property.

Laws 1816, Cobb's 1851 Digest, p. 857; Laws 1820, Cobb's 1851 Digest, p. 859; Laws 1826, Cobb's 1851 Digest, p. 859; Laws 1830, Cobb's 1851 Digest, p. 860.

Formerly Code 1863, § 4581; Code 1868, § 4602; Code 1873, § 4699; Code 1882, § 4699; Penal Code 1895, § 1078; Penal Code 1910, § 1105; Code 1933, § 27–2801.

§ 17–11–2. Liability of defendant for costs of witnesses

No defendant shall be liable for the costs of any witness of the state, unless such witness was subpoenaed, sworn, and examined during the trial, nor for the costs of more than two witnesses testifying on the same point, unless the court shall certify that the question at issue was of such a character as to require the testimony of more than two witnesses.

Laws 1799, Cobb's 1851 Digest, p. 277.

Formerly Code 1863, § 3608; Code 1868, § 3632; Code 1873, § 3682; Code 1882, § 3682; Penal Code 1895, § 1079; Penal Code 1910, § 1106; Code 1933, § 27–2802.

§ 17–11–3. Cost of inquest when defendant is convicted of murder or manslaughter

Any person convicted of murder or manslaughter in a case where an inquest has been held concerning the cause of death of the victim shall be charged for the costs of the inquest as part of the costs of prosecution.

Formerly Code 1863, § 572; Code 1868, § 636; Code 1873, § 595; Code 1882, § 595; Penal Code 1895, § 1080; Penal Code 1910, § 1107; Code 1933, § 27–2803.

§ 17–11–4. When the prosecutor shall pay costs

(a) The prosecutor's name shall be endorsed on every indictment, and he shall be compelled to pay all costs and jail fees upon the acquittal or discharge of the person accused when:

(1) The grand jury, by its foreman, on returning "no bill," expresses as its opinion that the prosecution was unfounded or malicious;

(2) A jury on the trial of the prosecution finds it to be malicious; or

(3) The prosecution is abandoned before trial. When it is thus abandoned, the officer who issued the warrant shall enter a judgment against the prosecutor for all the costs and enforce it by an execution in the name of the state or by an attachment for contempt.

(b) A magistrate may, in his discretion, assess costs and jail fees against the person who instigated the prosecution when, at a committal hearing, the action is dismissed for want of probable cause and the magistrate finds that the complaint was unfounded and malicious. This subsection shall not apply to law enforcement personnel.

Laws 1833, Cobb's 1851 Digest, p. 833; Laws 1871–72, p. 53, § 1; Laws 1982, p. 3, § 17; Laws 1986, p. 282, § 1.

Formerly Code 1863, § 4518; Code 1868, § 4537; Code 1873, § 4630; Code 1882, § 4630; Penal Code 1895, § 1082; Penal Code 1910, § 1109; Code 1933, § 27–2805.

§ 17–11–5. Payment of costs and expenses when venue is changed

(a) When the venue in a case is changed, the whole costs of the case, jail fees of the person to be tried, and expenses of the trial in the county to which it was transferred shall be paid by the county from which the case was removed.

(b) The entire court costs, including the costs of the sheriff, bailiff, clerks, and jurors, shall also be paid by the county from which the case was removed and shall have the same priority as jail fees. The county in which the case is tried shall be reimbursed after paying the court costs incurred.

Laws 1871–72, p. 49, § 1; Laws 1895, p. 70, § 4.

Formerly Code 1873, § 4689; Code 1882, § 4689; Penal Code 1895, § 1083; Penal Code 1910, § 1110; Code 1933, § 27–2806.

Article 2

Reimbursement of Counties for Expenses of Capital Felony Prosecutions

§ 17–11–20. Short title

This article shall be known and may be cited as the "Capital Felony Expense Act."

Laws 1979, p. 504, § 1.

§ 17–11–21. Definitions

As used in this article, the term:

(1) "Capital felony case" means a criminal case in which the death penalty may be imposed upon the defendant under the laws of this state.

(2) "Capital felony expenses" means expenses incurred by a county and paid from county funds as a direct result of a capital felony case being tried by a superior court. The term includes expenses from the date of the arrest of the defendant to the date of the superior court conviction, expenses from the date of the conviction until the date of the last appellate court affirmance of the conviction, expenses from the last appellate court reversal to any subsequent superior court convictions or retrials, expenses from any retrials to the last appellate court action on the conviction, expenses from the date of the arrest of the defendant to the date of the defendant's release if there is no conviction or if the conviction is reversed and there is no retrial, or expenses during any combination of these periods. The term shall not include the following expenses:

(A) Any expenses reimbursed by or pursuant to state law;

(B) The salaries, compensation, and expenses of all county officers and employees, except for any compensation and expenses of temporary employees employed as a direct result of the capital felony case or extraordinary expenses incurred by county officers and employees as a direct result of the capital felony case; and

(C) County paid supplements to the salaries or compensation of state officers and employees.

(3) "Commissioner" means the commissioner of community affairs.

(4) "County revenue" means the most current available total of adjusted taxes as determined from the annual financial report relating to local government finances filed by the county with the Department of Community Affairs pursuant to Code Section 36–81–8.

Laws 1979, p. 504, § 2; Laws 1983, p. 395, § 1; Laws 1988, p. 1859, § 1.

§ 17–11–22. Basis for reimbursement of capital felony expenses

(a) Each county which is responsible for the costs of a capital felony case will be reimbursed for capital felony expenses as provided in this Code section. With respect to one or more capital felony cases, expenses from the date of arrest will be accumulated. When one or more capital felony cases result in capital felony expenses, the accumulation of which is more than 5 percent of county revenue for the calendar year in which the superior court conviction occurs or in which the defendant is released if not convicted, the county will be reimbursed for all such accumulated capital felony expenses in excess of the 5 percent level. After a county has qualified or been reimbursed for capital felony expenses for any calendar year, the county shall be eligible for any capital felony expenses resulting from such case or cases in subsequent calendar years prior to the appeal of such case or cases. County revenues shall not be applicable in determining the amount of reimbursement for capital felony expenses occurring in such subsequent years prior to the appeal of the case or cases.

(b) If one or more capital felony cases are appealed, expenses from the date of the superior court conviction will be accumulated. When the appeal of one or more capital felony cases results in capital felony expenses, the accumulation of which is more than 5 percent of county revenue for the calendar year in which the last appellate court action on the conviction occurs, the county will be reimbursed for all such capital felony expenses in excess of the 5 percent level. If the county chooses not to seek reimbursement for capital felony expenses from the date of arrest to the date of the superior court conviction and instead seeks reimbursement for its capital felony expenses through the last appellate court action, the county will be reimbursed for all accumulated capital felony expenses in excess of the 5 percent level.

(c) If a capital felony case is appealed and the conviction is reversed, capital felony expenses for any subsequent retrial and appeals will be handled in accordance with the provisions of subsections (a) and (b) of this Code section.

(d) No capital felony expenses for which reimbursement has already been made will again be included in any subsequent calculations or reimbursement requests.

Laws 1979, p. 504, § 3; Laws 1983, p. 395, § 2; Laws 1988, p. 1859, § 2.

§ 17–11–23. Reimbursement payments

(a)(1) Reimbursement payments for eligible capital felony expenses under this article will be made to the governing authority of each county incurring capital felony expenses. The payments will be made during the second quarter of a calendar year for capital felony expenses eligible for reimbursement during the immediately preceding calendar year; provided, however, that, if a county is reimbursed during the second quarter of a calendar year and has additional capital felony expenses eligible for reimbursement during the remainder of such calendar year resulting from the same case or cases, payments will be made during the fourth quarter of such calendar year for the additional capital felony expenses eligible for reimbursement.

(2) Reimbursement payments shall be made from funds appropriated for such purpose pursuant to subsection (a) of Code Section 17–11–24, and no payments are required to be made if funds are not available or have not been appropriated.

(b)(1) In the event that requests for reimbursement exceed the amount appropriated for this article, the commissioner shall have the right to reduce each request proportionally so that the total amount of requests shall not exceed the total amount of funds available for reimbursement payments at the time of the request.

(2) Notwithstanding any other provisions of this Code section, during the first payment cycle of a state fiscal year (fourth quarter of a calendar year) not more than one-half of the funds available for reimbursement will be expended for reimbursement purposes.

Laws 1979, p. 504, § 5; Laws 1983, p. 395, § 3; Laws 1988, p. 1859, § 3.

§ 17–11–24. Administration

(a) The commissioner shall administer this article and shall make payments to counties for the reimbursement of capital felony expenses as provided by this article. The payments shall be made from funds appropriated to the Department of Community Affairs specifically for the purpose of making reimbursements pursuant to this article.

(b) The commissioner shall adopt rules and regulations for the administration of this article. The rules and regulations shall be distributed to the county governing authorities and to the clerks of the superior courts.

(c) The clerks of the superior courts will be the local administrators of this article; and, consistent with rules and regulations promulgated by the commissioner as provided by subsection (b) of this Code section, the clerks will maintain records of capital felony expenses for the purposes of this article. Based on such records, the clerk of each superior court will certify to the commissioner, during the first quarter of each calendar year, capital felony expenses eligible for reimbursement during the preceding calendar year.

Laws 1979, p. 504, § 4; Laws 1983, p. 395, § 4.

CHAPTER 12

LEGAL DEFENSE FOR INDIGENTS

Article 1

Revision of Chapter 12

Laws 2003, Act 32, § 1, amended Title 17 by striking Chapter 12, consisting of Code Sections 17–12–1 to 17–12–97, relating to legal defense of indigents, and adding a new Chapter 12, consisting of Code Sections 17–12–1 to 17–12–128. Section 10(a) of Laws 2003, Act 32, provides: "Section 1 of the Act shall become effective as set forth in said section."

Article 1

Georgia Public Defender Standards Council

Revision of Chapter 12

Laws 2003, Act 32, § 1, added this article effective December 31, 2003. See § 17–12–13.

Former Article 1, Local Indigent Defense Programs Generally, consisting of §§ 17–12–1 to 17–12–14, was repealed by Laws 2003, Act 32, § 1, effective December 31, 2003.

§ 17–12–1. Short title; independent agency of executive branch; responsibility of council

(a) This chapter shall be known and may be cited as the "Georgia Indigent Defense Act of 2003."

(b) The Georgia Public Defender Standards Council shall be an independent agency within the executive branch of state government.

(c) The council shall be responsible for assuring that adequate and effective legal representation is provided, independently of political considerations or private interests, to indigent persons who are entitled to representation under this chapter.

Laws 2003, Act 32, § 1, eff. Dec. 31, 2003; Laws 2007, Act 22, § 1, eff. July 1, 2007.

Historical and Statutory Notes

Laws 2003, Act 32, § 10(a), provides:

"(a) Section 1 of this Act shall become effective as set forth in said section."

The 2007 amendment by Act 22, in subsec. (b), substituted "executive branch" for "judicial branch".

Former § 17–12–1, containing the article short title, derived from Laws 1968, p. 999, § 1, was repealed by Laws 2003, Act 32, § 1, eff. Dec. 31, 2003.

§ 17–12–2. Definitions

As used in this chapter, the term:

(1) "Assistant public defender" means an attorney who is employed by any circuit public defender.

(2) "Circuit public defender" means the head of a public defender office providing indigent defense representation within any given judicial circuit of this state.

(3) "Circuit public defender office" means the office of any of the several circuit public defenders.

(4) "Council" means the Georgia Public Defender Standards Council.

(5) "Director" means the director of the Georgia Public Defender Standards Council.

(6) "Indigent person" or "indigent defendant" means:

(A) A person charged with a misdemeanor, violation of probation, or a municipal or county offense punishable by imprisonment who earns less than 100 percent of the federal poverty guidelines unless there is evidence that the person has other resources that might reasonably be used to employ a lawyer without undue hardship on the person or his or her dependents;

(B) A juvenile charged with a delinquent act or a violation of probation punishable by detention whose parents earn less than 125 percent of the federal poverty guidelines unless there is evidence that the juvenile or his or her parents have other resources that might reasonably be used to employ a lawyer without undue hardship on the juvenile, his or her parents, or the parent's dependents; and

(C) A person charged with a felony who earns or, in the case of a juvenile, whose parents earn, less than 150 percent of the federal poverty guidelines unless there is evidence that the person has other resources that might reasonably be used to employ a lawyer without undue hardship on the person, his or her dependents, or, in the case of a juvenile, his or her parents or the parent's dependents.

In no case shall a person whose maximum income level exceeds 150 percent of the federal poverty level or, in the case of a juvenile, whose household income exceeds 150 percent of the federal poverty level be an indigent person or indigent defendant.

(7) "Legislative oversight committee" means the Legislative Oversight Committee for the Georgia Public Defender Standards Council.

(8) "Public defender" means an attorney who is employed in a circuit public defender office or who represents an indigent person pursuant to this chapter.

Laws 2003, Act 32, § 1, eff. Dec. 31, 2003; Laws 2006, Act 749, § 4, eff. May 3, 2006; Laws 2008, Act 729, § 15, eff. July 1, 2008.

Historical and Statutory Notes

The 2006 amendment by Act 749, redesignated par. (5) as par. (6), and added new par. (5).

The 2008 amendment by Act 729 rewrote this section, which formerly read:

"As used in this chapter, the term:

"(1) 'Assistant public defender' means an attorney who is employed by any circuit public defender or conflict defender office.

"(2) 'Circuit public defender' means the head of a public defender office providing indigent defense representation within any given judicial circuit of this state.

"(3) 'Circuit public defender office' means the office of any of the several circuit public defenders.

"(4) 'Council' means the Georgia Public Defender Standards Council.

"(5) 'Indigent person' or 'indigent defendant' means:

"(A) A person charged with a misdemeanor, violation of probation, or a municipal, county, or juvenile offense punishable by imprisonment who earns or, in the case of a juvenile, whose parents earn, less than 125 percent of the federal poverty guidelines unless there is evidence that the person has other resources that might reasonably be used to employ a lawyer without undue hardship on the person or his or her dependents; and

"(B) A person charged with a felony who earns or, in the case of a juvenile, whose parents earn, less than 150 percent of the federal poverty guidelines unless there is evidence that the person has other resources that might reasonably be used to employ a lawyer without undue hardship on the person or his or her dependents.

"In no case shall a person whose maximum income level exceeds 150 percent of the federal poverty level or, in the case of a juvenile, whose household income exceeds 150 percent of the federal poverty level be an indigent person or indigent defendant.

"(6) 'Public defender' means an attorney who is employed in a circuit public defender office or conflict defender office or who represents an indigent person pursuant to this chapter."

Laws 2008, Act 729, § 43 provides:

"This Act shall become effective on July 1, 2008; provided, however, that for purposes of the appointment of the councilmembers and circuit public defender supervisory panel members, this Act shall become effective upon its approval by the Governor or upon its becoming law without such approval."

Former § 17-12-2, containing definitions, derived from Laws 1968, p. 999, §§ 2, 3; Laws 1974, p. 1100, § 1, was repealed by Laws 2003, Act 32, § 1, eff. Dec. 31, 2003.

§ 17-12-3. Creation of council; appointment of members; effective date

(a) There is created the Georgia Public Defender Standards Council to be composed of 15 members.

(b) Ten members of the council shall be appointed as follows:

(1) Two members shall be appointed by the Governor, the Lieutenant Governor, the Speaker of the House of Representatives, the Chief Justice of the Supreme Court of Georgia, and the Chief Judge of the Georgia Court of Appeals as further set forth in paragraph (2) of this subsection. Except as provided in paragraph (3.1) of this subsection, the members of the council shall be individuals with significant experience working in the criminal justice system or who have demonstrated a strong commitment to the provision of adequate and effective representation of indigent defendants. The members shall serve terms of four years; provided, however, that the members appointed from the even-numbered judicial administration circuits shall serve initial terms of six years and thereafter shall serve terms of four years;

(2) The members appointed pursuant to paragraph (1) of this subsection shall be chosen so that each of the ten judicial administration districts in this state is represented and so that each appointing authority shall rotate the particular judicial administration district for which he or she is responsible for appointing. The appointments shall be as follows:

(A) For the initial appointments:

(i) The Governor shall appoint one person who resides in judicial administration district 1 and one person who resides in judicial administration district 2;

(ii) The Lieutenant Governor shall appoint one person who resides in judicial administration district 3 and one person who resides in judicial administration district 4;

(iii) The Speaker of the House of Representatives shall appoint one person who resides in judicial administration district 5 and one person who resides in judicial administration district 6;

(iv) The Chief Justice of the Supreme Court of Georgia shall appoint one person who resides in judicial administration district 7 and one person who resides in judicial administration district 8, except that on and after July 1, 2008, the Lieutenant Governor shall make such appointments; and

(v) The Chief Judge of the Georgia Court of Appeals shall appoint one person who resides in judicial administration district 9 and one person who resides in judicial administration district 10, except that on and after July 1, 2008, the Speaker of the House of Representatives shall make such appointments;

(B) For the first subsequent council appointments:

(i) The Governor shall appoint one person who resides in judicial administration district 3 and one person who resides in judicial administration district 4;

(ii) The Lieutenant Governor shall appoint one person who resides in judicial administration district 5 and one person who resides in judicial administration district 6;

(iii) The Speaker of the House of Representatives shall appoint one person who resides in judicial administration district 7 and one person who resides in judicial administration district 8;

(iv) The Chief Justice of the Supreme Court of Georgia shall appoint one person who resides in judicial administration district 9 and one person who resides in judicial administration district 10, except that on and after July 1, 2008, the Lieutenant Governor shall make such appointments; and

(v) The Chief Judge of the Georgia Court of Appeals shall appoint one person who resides in judicial administration district 1 and one person who resides in judicial administration district 2, except that on and after July 1, 2008, the Speaker of the House of Representatives shall make such appointments;

(C) For the second subsequent council appointments:

(i) The Governor shall appoint one person who resides in judicial administration district 5 and one person who resides in judicial administration district 6;

(ii) The Lieutenant Governor shall appoint one person who resides in judicial administration district 7 and one person who resides in judicial administration district 8;

(iii) The Speaker of the House of Representatives shall appoint one person who resides in judicial administration district 9 and one person who resides in judicial administration district 10;

(iv) The Chief Justice of the Supreme Court of Georgia shall appoint one person who resides in judicial administration district 1 and one person who resides in judicial administration district 2, except that on and after July 1, 2008, the Lieutenant Governor shall make such appointments; and

(v) The Chief Judge of the Georgia Court of Appeals shall appoint one person who resides in judicial administration district 3 and one person who resides in judicial administration district 4, except that on and after July 1, 2008, the Speaker of the House of Representatives shall make such appointments;

(D) For the third subsequent council appointments:

(i) The Governor shall appoint one person who resides in judicial administration district 7 and one person who resides in judicial administration district 8;

(ii) The Lieutenant Governor shall appoint one person who resides in judicial administration district 9 and one person who resides in judicial administration district 10;

(iii) The Speaker of the House of Representatives shall appoint one person who resides in judicial administration district 1 and one person who resides in judicial administration district 2;

(iv) The Chief Justice of the Supreme Court of Georgia shall appoint one person who resides in judicial administration district 3 and one person who resides in judicial administration district 4, except that on and after July 1, 2008, the Lieutenant Governor shall make such appointments; and

(v) The Chief Judge of the Georgia Court of Appeals shall appoint one person who resides in judicial administration district 5 and one person who resides in judicial administration district 6, except that on and after July 1, 2008, the Speaker of the House of Representatives shall make such appointments; and

(E) For the fourth subsequent council appointments:

(i) The Governor shall appoint one person who resides in judicial administration district 9 and one person who resides in judicial administration district 10;

(ii) The Lieutenant Governor shall appoint one person who resides in judicial administration district 1 and one person who resides in judicial administration district 2;

(iii) The Speaker of the House of Representatives shall appoint one person who resides in judicial administration district 3 and one person who resides in judicial administration district 4;

(iv) The Chief Justice of the Supreme Court of Georgia shall appoint one person who resides in judicial administration district 5 and one person who resides in judicial administration district 6, except that on and after July 1, 2008, the Lieutenant Governor shall make such appointments; and

(v) The Chief Judge of the Georgia Court of Appeals shall appoint one person who resides in judicial administration district 7 and one person who resides in judicial administration district 8, except that on and after July 1, 2008, the Speaker of the House of Representatives shall make such appointments.

All subsequent appointments shall continue on, with the entire cycle starting over again as specified in subparagraph (A) of this paragraph;

(3) The eleventh member shall be one circuit public defender who shall serve on the council. After the initial appointments as set forth in paragraph (4) of this subsection, the circuit public defender to serve on the council shall be elected by a majority vote of all the circuit public defenders. The circuit public defender councilmember shall serve terms of two years;

(3.1) Four members of the council shall be county commissioners who have been elected and are serving as members of a county governing authority in this state. The county commissioner councilmembers shall be appointed by the Governor on or before July 1, 2008, and shall be from different geographic regions of this state. The Governor may solicit recommendations for such appointees from the Association County Commissioners of Georgia. Each county commissioner councilmember shall serve terms of four years; provided, however, that the initial appointments shall be for one, two, three, and four years, respectively, as designated by the Governor for each appointment, and thereafter, such members shall serve terms of four years. A county commission councilmember shall be eligible to serve so long as he or she retains the office by virtue of which he or she is serving on the council;

(4) Except as provided in paragraph (3.1) of this subsection, all initial appointments shall be made to become members of the council on July 1, 2003, and their successors shall become members of the council on July 1 following their appointment. The initial appointees from the even-numbered judicial administration circuits shall serve until June 30, 2009. Notwithstanding the provisions of paragraph (3) of this subsection, the initial member representing the circuit public defenders shall be made by the Supreme Court of Georgia. The person representing the circuit defender position on the initial council shall be engaged on a full-time basis in the provision of criminal defense to the indigent;

(5) Any vacancy for a member appointed pursuant to paragraphs (1), (2), and (3.1) of this subsection shall be filled by the appointing authority, and such appointee shall serve the balance of the vacating member's unexpired term; and

(6) Any vacancy for a member appointed pursuant to paragraph (3) of this subsection shall be the successor to the circuit public defender as set forth in subsection (e) of Code Section 17-12-20.

(c) In making the appointments for ten members of the council as provided in paragraph (2) of subsection (b) of this Code section, the appointing authorities shall seek to identify and appoint persons who represent a diversity of backgrounds and experience and shall solicit suggestions from the State Bar of Georgia, state and local bar associations, the Georgia Association of Criminal Defense Lawyers, the councils representing the various categories of state court judges in Georgia, and the Prosecuting Attorneys' Council of the State of Georgia, as well as from the public and other interested organizations and individuals within this state. The appointing authorities shall not appoint a prosecuting attorney as defined in paragraph (6) of Code Section 19–13–51, any employee of a prosecuting attorney's office, or an employee of the Prosecuting Attorneys' Council of the State of Georgia to serve on the council.

(d) This Code section shall become effective on July 1, 2003, for purposes of making the initial appointments to the council.

Laws 2003, Act 32, § 1, eff. Dec. 31, 2003; Laws 2004, Act 564, § 17, eff. May 13, 2004; Laws 2004, Ex. Sess., Act 4, § 11, eff. June 15, 2004; Laws 2006, Act 749, § 5, eff. May 3, 2006; Laws 2008, Act 729, § 16, eff. July 1, 2008.

Historical and Statutory Notes

In 2003, the Code Commission, in subsec. (b), par. (5), substituted "paragraphs (1) and (2)" for "paragraphs (1) and (3)" and in subsec. (b), par. (6), substituted "paragraph (3)" for "paragraph (2)" and "Section 17–12–20" for "Section 17–12–21". See § 28–9–5.

The 2004 amendment by Act 564 was a provision contained in a correction bill.

The 2004, Ex. Sess., amendment by Act 4, in subsec. (c), added the last sentence relating to the appointment of prosecuting attorneys, etc. to serve on the council.

The 2006 amendment by Act 749, in subsec. (b), substituted "Ten members" for "The membership" in the introductory phrase, added "provided, however, that the members appointed from the even-numbered judicial administration circuits shall serve initial terms of six years and thereafter shall serve terms of four years;" in par. (1), substituted "the eleventh member" for "there" in par. (3), added "The initial appointees from the even-numbered judicial administration circuits shall server until June 30, 2009." in par. (4), and substituted "authority, and such appointee shall serve the balance of the vacating member's unexpired term; and" for "authority; and" in par. (5)

Former § 17–12–3, relating to actions where more than two judges of the superior court in a county or circuit, derived from Laws 1968, p. 999, § 2, was repealed by Laws 2003, Act 32, § 1, eff. Dec. 31, 2003.

The 2008 amendment by Act 729 rewrote this section, which formerly read:

"(a) There is created the Georgia Public Defender Standards Council to be composed of 11 members.

"(b) Ten members of the council shall be appointed as follows:

"(1) Two members shall be appointed by the Governor, the Lieutenant Governor, the Speaker of the House of Representatives, the Chief Justice of the Supreme Court of Georgia, and the Chief Judge of the Georgia Court of Appeals as further set forth in paragraph (2) of this subsection. The members of the council shall be individuals with significant experience working in the criminal justice system or who have demonstrated a strong commitment to the provision of adequate and effective representation of indigent defendants. The members shall serve terms of four years; provided, however, that the members appointed from the even-numbered judicial administration circuits shall serve initial terms of six years and thereafter shall serve terms of four years;

"(2) The members appointed pursuant to paragraph (1) of this subsection shall be chosen so that each of the ten judicial administration districts in the state is represented and so that each appointing authority shall rotate the particular judicial administration district for which he or she is responsible for appointing. The appointments shall be as follows:

"(A) For the initial appointments:

"(i) The Governor shall appoint one person who resides in judicial administration district 1 and one person who resides in judicial administration district 2;

"(ii) The Lieutenant Governor shall appoint one person who resides in judicial administration district 3 and one person who resides in judicial administration district 4;

"(iii) The Speaker of the House of Representatives shall appoint one person who resides in judicial administration district 5 and one person who resides in judicial administration district 6;

"(iv) The Chief Justice of the Supreme Court of Georgia shall appoint one person who resides in judicial administration district 7 and one person who resides in judicial administration district 8; and

"(v) The Chief Judge of the Georgia Court of Appeals shall appoint one person who resides in judicial administration district 9 and one person who resides in judicial administration district 10;

"(B) For the first subsequent council appointments:

"(i) The Governor shall appoint one person who resides in judicial administration district 3 and one person who resides in judicial administration district 4;

"(ii) The Lieutenant Governor shall appoint one person who resides in judicial administration district 5 and one person who resides in judicial administration district 6;

"(iii) The Speaker of the House of Representatives shall appoint one person who resides in judicial administration district 7 and one person who resides in judicial administration district 8;

"(iv) The Chief Justice of the Supreme Court of Georgia shall appoint one person who resides in judicial administration district 9 and one person who resides in judicial administration district 10; and

"(v) The Chief Judge of the Georgia Court of Appeals shall appoint one person who resides in judicial administration district 1 and one person who resides in judicial administration district 2;

"(C) For the second subsequent council appointments:

"(i) The Governor shall appoint one person who resides in judicial administration district 5 and one person who resides in judicial administration district 6;

"(ii) The Lieutenant Governor shall appoint one person who resides in judicial administration district 7 and one person who resides in judicial administration district 8;

"(iii) The Speaker of the House of Representatives shall appoint one person who resides in judicial administration district 9 and one person who resides in judicial administration district 10;

"(iv) The Chief Justice of the Supreme Court of Georgia shall appoint one person who resides in judicial administration district 1 and one person who resides in judicial administration district 2; and

"(v) The Chief Judge of the Georgia Court of Appeals shall appoint one person who resides in judicial administration district 3 and one person who resides in judicial administration district 4;

"(D) For the third subsequent council appointments:

"(i) The Governor shall appoint one person who resides in judicial administration district 7 and one person who resides in judicial administration district 8;

"(ii) The Lieutenant Governor shall appoint one person who resides in judicial administration district 9 and one person who resides in judicial administration district 10;

"(iii) The Speaker of the House of Representatives shall appoint one person who resides in judicial administration district 1 and one person who resides in judicial administration district 2;

"(iv) The Chief Justice of the Supreme Court of Georgia shall appoint one person who resides in judicial administration district 3 and one person who resides in judicial administration district 4; and "(v) The Chief Judge of the Georgia Court of Appeals shall appoint one person who resides in judicial administration district 5 and one person who resides in judicial administration district 6; and

"(E) For the fourth subsequent council appointments:

"(i) The Governor shall appoint one person who resides in judicial administration district 9 and one person who resides in judicial administration district 10;

"(ii) The Lieutenant Governor shall appoint one person who resides in judicial administration district 1 and one person who resides in judicial administration district 2;

"(iii) The Speaker of the House of Representatives shall appoint one person who resides in judicial administration district 3 and one person who resides in judicial administration district 4;

"(iv) The Chief Justice of the Supreme Court of Georgia shall appoint one person who resides in judicial administration district 5 and one person who resides in judicial administration district 6; and

"(v) The Chief Judge of the Georgia Court of Appeals shall appoint one person who resides in judicial administration district 7 and one person who resides in judicial administration district 8.

"All subsequent appointments shall continue on, with the entire cycle starting over again as specified in subparagraph (A) of this paragraph;

"(3) In addition, the eleventh member shall be one circuit public defender who shall serve on the council. After the initial appointments as set forth in paragraph (4) of this subsection, the circuit public defender to serve on the council shall be elected by a majority vote of all the circuit public defenders. The circuit public defender councilmember shall serve terms of two years;

"(4) All initial appointments shall be made to become members of the council on July 1, 2003, and their successors shall become members of the council on July 1 following their appointment. The initial appointees from the even-numbered judicial administration circuits shall serve until June 30, 2009. Notwithstanding the provisions of paragraph (3) of this subsection, the initial member representing the circuit public defenders shall be made by the Supreme Court of Georgia. The person representing the circuit defender position on the initial council shall be engaged on a full-time basis in the provision of criminal defense to the indigent;

"(5) Any vacancy for a member appointed pursuant to paragraphs (1) and (2) of this subsection shall be filled by the appointing authority, and such appointee shall serve the balance of the vacating member's unexpired term; and

"(6) Any vacancy for a member appointed pursuant to paragraph (3) of this subsection shall be the successor to the circuit public defender as set forth in subsection (d) of Code Section 17–12–20.

"(c) In making these appointments, the appointing authorities shall seek to identify and appoint persons who represent a diversity of backgrounds and experience and shall solicit suggestions from the State Bar of Georgia, state and local bar associations, the Georgia Association of Criminal Defense Lawyers, the councils representing the various categories of state court judges in Georgia, and the Prosecuting Attorneys' Council of the State of Georgia, as well as from the public and other interested organizations and individuals within the state. The appointing authorities shall not appoint a prosecuting attorney as defined in paragraph (6) of Code Section 19–13–51, any employee of a prosecuting attorney's office, or an employee of the Prosecuting Attorneys' Council of the State of Georgia to serve on the council.

"(d) This Code section shall become effective on July 1, 2003, for purposes of making the initial appointments to the council."

Laws 2008, Act 729, § 43 provides:

"This Act shall become effective on July 1, 2008; provided, however, that for purposes of the appointment of the councilmembers and circuit public defender supervisory panel members, this Act shall become effective upon its approval by the Governor or upon its becoming law without such approval."

§ 17–12–4. Legal entity; powers

(a) The council:

(1) Shall be a legal entity;

(2) Shall have perpetual existence;

(3) May contract;

(4) May own property;

(5) May accept funds, grants, and gifts from any public or private source, which shall be used to defray the expenses incident to implementing its purposes;

(6) May adopt and use an official seal;

(7) May establish a principal office;

(8) May hire such administrative and clerical personnel as may be necessary and appropriate to fulfill its purposes; and

(9) Shall have such other powers, privileges, and duties as may be reasonable and necessary for the proper fulfillment of its purposes.

(b) The council shall establish auditing procedures as may be required in connection with the handling of public funds. The state auditor shall be authorized and directed to make an annual audit of the transactions of the council and to make a complete report of the same to the General Assembly. The annual audit shall disclose all moneys received by the council and all expenditures made by the council by revenue source, including all programs and special projects itemized in the General Appropriations Act. The annual audit shall include an itemization by revenue source of encumbered and reserved money. Revenue sources shall include each county governing authority's expenditures which are made pursuant to Code Sections 17–12–31 and 17–12–32 and city or county expenditures which are made pursuant to subsection (d) of Code Section 17–12–23. The state auditor shall also make an audit of the affairs of the council at any time when requested to do so by a majority of the council or by the Governor or General Assembly.

(c) The council may not provide compensation from its funds to any administrative or clerical personnel employed by the council if the personnel are then receiving retirement compensation from any retirement or pension fund created by Title 47 to provide compensation for past services as a judicial officer, prosecuting attorney, indigent defense attorney, court officer, or law enforcement officer except for county or municipal retirement funds.

Laws 2003, Act 32, § 1, eff. Dec. 31, 2003; Laws 2008, Act 729, § 17, eff. July 1, 2008.

Historical and Statutory Notes

The 2008 amendment by Act 729, in subsec. (a), deleted par. (8), relating to the appointment of a director and renumbered existing subsec. (9) as (8) and existing subsec. (10) as (9); and rewrote subsec. (b), which formerly read:

"(b) The council shall establish auditing procedures as may be required in connection with the handling of public funds. The state auditor is authorized and directed to make an annual audit of the transactions of the council and to make a complete report of the same to the General Assembly. The report shall disclose all moneys received by the council and all expenditures made by the council, including administrative expense. The state auditor shall also make an audit of the affairs of the council at any time when requested to do so by a majority of the council or by the Chief Justice of the Supreme Court of Georgia."

Laws 2008, Act 729, § 43 provides:

"This Act shall become effective on July 1, 2008; provided, however, that for purposes of the appointment of the councilmembers and circuit public defender supervisory panel members, this Act shall become effective upon its approval by the Governor or upon its becoming law without such approval."

Former § 17–12–4, relating to defender plans for providing representation, derived from Laws 1968, p. 999, § 3; Laws 1974, p.1100, § 1, was repealed by Laws 2003, Act 32, § 1, eff. Dec. 31, 2003.

§ 17–12–5. Director

(a) To be eligible for appointment as the director, a candidate shall be a member in good standing of the State Bar of Georgia with at least seven years' experience in the practice of law. The director shall be selected on the basis of training and experience and such other qualifications as the council deems appropriate. The director shall be appointed by the Governor and shall serve at the pleasure of the Governor.

(b)(1) The director shall work with and provide support services and programs for circuit public defender offices and other attorneys representing indigent persons in criminal or juvenile cases in order to improve the quality and effectiveness of legal representation of such persons and otherwise fulfill the purposes of this chapter. Such services and programs shall include, but shall not be limited to, technical, research, and administrative assistance; educational and training programs for attorneys, investigators, and other staff; assistance with the representation of indigent defendants with mental disabilities; assistance with the representation of juveniles; assistance with death penalty cases; and assistance with appellate advocacy.

(2) The director may establish divisions within the office to administer the services and programs as may be necessary to fulfill the purposes of this chapter. The director shall establish a mental health advocacy division and the Georgia capital defender division.

(3) The director may hire and supervise such staff employees and may contract with outside consultants on behalf of the office as may be necessary to provide the services contemplated by this chapter.

(c) The director shall have and may exercise the following power and authority:

(1) The power and authority to take or cause to be taken any or all action necessary to perform any indigent defense services or otherwise necessary to perform any duties, responsibilities, or functions which the council is authorized by law to perform or to exercise any power or authority which the council is authorized by law to exercise;

(2) The power and authority to make, promulgate, enforce, or otherwise require compliance with any and all rules, regulations, procedures, or directives necessary to perform any indigent defense services, to carry into effect the minimum standards and procedures promulgated by the council, or otherwise necessary to perform any duties, responsibilities, or functions which the council is authorized by law to perform or to exercise any power or authority which the council is authorized by law to exercise; and

(3) The power and authority to assist the council in the performance of its duties, responsibilities, and functions and the exercise of its power and authority.

(d) The director shall:

(1) Prepare and submit to the council a proposed budget for the council. The director shall also prepare and submit an annual report containing pertinent data on the operations, costs, and needs of the council and such other information as the council may require;

(2) Develop such rules, policies, procedures, regulations, and standards as may be necessary to carry out the provisions of this chapter and comply with all applicable laws, standards, and regulations, and submit these to the council for approval;

(3) Administer and coordinate the operations of the council and supervise compliance with rules, policies, procedures, regulations, and standards adopted by the council;

(4) Maintain proper records of all financial transactions related to the operation of the council;

(5) At the director's discretion, solicit and accept on behalf of the council any funds that may become available from any source, including government, nonprofit, or private grants, gifts, or bequests;

(6) Coordinate the services of the council with any federal, county, or private programs established to provide assistance to indigent persons in cases subject to this chapter and consult with professional bodies concerning the implementation and improvement of programs for providing indigent services;

(7) Provide for the training of attorneys and other staff involved in the legal representation of persons subject to this chapter;

(8) Attend all council meetings, except those meetings or portions thereof that address the question of appointment or removal of the director;

(9) Ensure that the expenditures of the council are not greater than the amounts budgeted or available from other revenue sources;

(10) Hire, with the pending approval of the council, a mental health advocate who shall serve as director of the division of the office of mental health advocacy;

(11) Hire, with the pending approval of the council, the capital defender who shall serve as the director of the division of the office of the Georgia capital defender;

(12) Evaluate each circuit public defender's job performance and communicate his or her findings to the council; and

(13) Perform other duties as the council may assign.

Laws 2003, Act 32, § 1, eff. Dec. 31, 2003; Laws 2004, Act 564, § 17, eff. May 13, 2004; Laws 2008, Act 729, § 18, eff. July 1, 2008.

Historical and Statutory Notes

The 2004 amendment by Act 564 was a provision contained in a correction bill.

The 2008 amendment by Act 729 rewrote this section, which formerly read:

"(a) To be eligible for appointment as the council's director, a candidate shall be a member in good standing of the State Bar of Georgia with at least three years' experience in the practice of law. The director shall be selected on the basis of training and experience and such other qualifications as the council deems appropriate. The director shall serve at the pleasure of the council and may be removed by a majority vote of the entire council. The council shall establish the director's salary.

"(b)(1) The director shall work with and provide support services and programs for circuit public defender offices and other attorneys representing indigent persons in criminal or juvenile cases in order to improve the quality and effectiveness of legal representation of such persons and otherwise fulfill the purposes of this chapter. Such services and programs shall include, but shall not be limited to, technical, research, and administrative assistance; educational and training programs for attorneys, investigators, and other staff; assistance with the representation of indigent defendants with mental disabilities; assistance with the representation of juveniles; and assistance with appellate advocacy.

"(2) The director, with the consent of the council, may establish divisions within the office to administer the services and programs as may be necessary to fulfill the purposes of this chapter.

"(3) The director may hire such staff employees and may contract with outside consultants on behalf of the office as may be necessary to provide the services contemplated by this chapter.

"(c) The director shall:

"(1) Prepare and submit to the council a proposed budget for the council. Said budget shall not contain any request for funding for the operation of the circuit public defender offices until the budget submission for Fiscal Year 2005. The director shall also prepare and submit an annual report containing pertinent data on the operations, costs, and needs of the council and such other information as the council may require;

"(2) Develop such rules, policies, procedures, regulations, and standards as may be necessary to carry out the provisions of this chapter and comply with all applicable laws, standards, and regulations, and submit these to the council for approval;

"(3) Administer and coordinate the operations of the council and supervise compliance with rules, policies, procedures, regulations, and standards adopted by the council;

"(4) Maintain proper records of all financial transactions related to the operation of the council;

"(5) At the director's discretion, solicit and accept on behalf of the council any funds that may become available from any source, including government, nonprofit, or private grants, gifts, or bequests;

"(6) Coordinate the services of the council with any federal, county, or private programs established to provide assistance to indigent persons in cases subject to this chapter and consult with professional bodies concerning the implementation and improvement of programs for providing indigent services;

"(7) Provide for the training of attorneys and other staff involved in the legal representation of persons subject to this chapter;

"(8) Attend all council meetings, except those meetings or portions thereof that address the question of appointment or removal of the director;

"(9) Ensure that the expenditures of the council are not greater than the amounts budgeted or available from other revenue sources; and

"(10) Perform other duties as the council may assign."

Laws 2008, Act 729, § 43 provides:

"This Act shall become effective on July 1, 2008; provided, however, that for purposes of the appointment of the councilmembers and circuit public defender supervisory panel members, this Act shall become effective upon its approval by the Governor or upon its becoming law without such approval."

Former § 17–12–5, relating to compensation of assigned counsel, derived from Laws 1968, p. 999, § 4, was repealed by Laws 2003, Act 32, § 1, eff. Dec. 31, 2003.

§ 17–12–6. Assistance to public defenders; fiscal officer; records and statistics

(a) The council shall assist the public defenders throughout the state in their efforts to provide adequate legal defense to the indigent. Assistance may include:

(1) The preparation and distribution of a basic defense manual and other educational materials;

(2) The preparation and distribution of model forms and documents employed in indigent defense;

(3) The promotion of and assistance in the training of indigent defense attorneys;

(4) The provision of legal research assistance to public defenders; and

(5) The provision of such other assistance to public defenders as may be authorized by law.

(b) The council:

(1) Shall be the fiscal officer for the circuit public defender offices and shall account for all moneys received from each governing authority; and

(2) Shall collect, maintain, review, and publish in print or electronically records and statistics for the purpose of evaluating the delivery of indigent defense representation in Georgia.

Laws 2003, Act 32, § 1, eff. Dec. 31, 2003; Laws 2008, Act 729, § 19, eff. July 1, 2008; Laws 2010, Act 615, § 10, eff. June 3, 2010.

Historical and Statutory Notes

The 2008 amendment by Act 729, in subsec. (b), par. (1), inserted "and shall account for all moneys received from each governing authority".

Laws 2008, Act 729, § 43 provides:

"This Act shall become effective on July 1, 2008; provided, however, that for purposes of the appointment of the councilmembers and circuit public defender supervisory panel members, this Act shall become effective upon its approval by the Governor or upon its becoming law without such approval."

Former § 17–12–6, relating to compensation of the legal aid agency, derived from Laws 1968, p. 999, § 5, was repealed by Laws 2003, Act 32, § 1, eff. Dec. 31, 2003.

The 2010 amendment by Act 615, in subsec. (b), par. (2), inserted "in print or electronically" following "publish" throughout the paragraph.

§ 17–12–7. Actions in best interest of indigent defendants; voting; term; quorum; meetings; chairperson; compensation

(a) All members of the council shall at all times act in the best interest of indigent defendants who are receiving legal representation under the provisions of this chapter.

(b) All members of the council shall be entitled to vote on any matter coming before the council unless otherwise provided by law or by rules adopted by the council concerning conflicts of interest.

(c) Each member of the council shall serve until a successor has been appointed. Removal of council members shall be for cause and shall be in accordance with policies and procedures adopted by the council.

(d) Unless otherwise provided in this article, a quorum shall be a majority of the members of the council who are then in office, and decisions of the council shall be by majority vote of the members present, except that a majority of the entire council must approve the appointment or removal of the chairperson or removal of a circuit public defender for cause pursuant to Code Section 17–12–20 and an alternative delivery system pursuant to Code Section 17–12–36 and other matters as set forth in Code Section 17–12–36.

(e) The council shall meet at least quarterly and at such other times and places as it deems necessary or convenient for the performance of its duties.

(f) The council shall elect a chairperson and such officers from the members of the council as it deems necessary and shall adopt such rules for the transaction of its business as it desires. The chairperson and officers shall serve for a term of two years and may be removed without cause by a vote of two-thirds of the members of the entire council and for cause by a majority vote of the entire council. The chairperson shall retain a vote on all matters except those in which the chairperson has a conflict of interest or the removal of the chairperson for cause. The council shall keep and maintain minutes of all council meetings.

(g) The members of the council shall receive no compensation for their services but shall be reimbursed for their actual expenses incurred in the performance of their duties as members of the council. Any expenses incurred by the council shall be paid from the general operating budget of the council.

Laws 2003, Act 32, § 1, eff. Dec. 31, 2003.

Historical and Statutory Notes

Former § 17–12–7, relating to public defenders, generally, derived from Laws 1968, p. 999, § 6; Laws 1982, p. 1181, §§ 1, 2, was repealed by Laws 2003, Act 32, § 1, eff. Dec. 31, 2003.

§ 17–12–8. Approval and implementation of programs, services, rules, procedures, regulations; standards

(a) The council shall approve the development and improvement of programs which provide legal representation to indigent persons and juveniles.

(b) The council shall approve and implement programs, services, rules, policies, procedures, regulations, and standards as may be necessary to fulfill the purposes and provisions of this chapter and to comply with all applicable laws governing the rights of indigent persons accused of violations of criminal law.

(c) All rules, regulations, policies, and standards that are promulgated by the council shall be publicly available for review and shall be posted on the council's website. Each rule, regulation, policy, and standard shall identify the date upon which such rule, regulation, policy, and standard took effect.

Laws 2003, Act 32, § 1, eff. Dec. 31, 2003; Laws 2004, Ex. Sess., Act 4, § 12, eff. June 15, 2004; Laws 2005, Act 19, § 17, eff. April 7, 2005; Laws 2005, Act 281, § 1, eff. May 6, 2005; Laws 2006, Act 749, § 6, eff. May 3, 2006; Laws 2008, Act 729, § 20, eff. July 1, 2008.

Historical and Statutory Notes

The 2004, Ex. Sess., amendment by Act 4, added subsec. (c).

The 2005 amendment by Act 19 was a provision contained in a correction bill.

The 2005 amendment by Act 281 added subsec. (d).

The 2006 amendment by Act 749, in subsec. (b), par. (8), deleted "determining indigence and for assessing and" following "Standards for".

Laws 2006, Act 907, effective May 5, 2006, pursuant to Code Section 17–12–8, ratified and approved the State of Georgia Performance Standards for Criminal Defense Representation in Indigent Criminal Cases.

Laws 2006, Act 912, effective May 5, 2006, pursuant to Code Section 17–12–8, ratified and approved the State of Georgia Performance Standards for Juvenile Defense Representation in Indigent Delinquency and Unruly Cases.

Laws 2006, Act 919, effective May 5, 2006, pursuant to Code Section 17–12–8, ratified and approved the Standard for Removal of a Circuit Public Defender for Cause Pursuant to O.C.G.A. § 17–12–20.

The 2008 amendment by Act 729 rewrote this section, which formerly read:

"(a) The council shall approve the development and improvement of programs which provide legal representation to indigent persons and juveniles.

"(b) The council shall approve and implement programs, services, rules, policies, procedures, regulations, and standards as may be necessary to fulfill the purposes and provisions of this article and to comply with all applicable laws governing the rights of indigent persons accused of violations of criminal law. Standards shall include, but shall not be limited to, the following:

"(1) Standards for maintaining and operating circuit defender offices, including requirements regarding qualifications, training, and size of the legal and supporting staff of such offices;

"(2) Standards prescribing minimum experience, training, and other qualifications for appointed counsel where a conflict of interest arises between the public defender and an indigent person;

"(3) Standards for assistant public defender and appointed counsel caseloads;

"(4) Standards for the performance of assistant public defenders and appointed counsel representing indigent persons;

"(5) Standards and procedures for the appointment of independent, competent, and efficient counsel for representation in both the trial and appellate courts of indigent persons whose cases present conflicts of interest;

"(6) Standards for providing and compensating experts, investigators, and other persons who provide services necessary for the effective representation of indigent persons;

"(7) Standards for qualifications and performance of counsel representing indigent persons in capital cases;

"(8) Standards for collecting the costs of legal representation and related services;

"(9) Standards for compensation of attorneys appointed to represent indigent persons under this article;

"(10) Standards for removing a circuit public defender for cause pursuant to Code Section 17–12–20;

"(11) Standards for a uniform definition of a 'case' for purposes of determining caseload statistics; and

"(12) Standards for accepting contractual indigent defense representation.

"(c) The initial minimum standards promulgated by the council pursuant to this Code section which are determined by the General Oversight Committee for the Georgia Public Defender Standards Council to have a fiscal impact shall be submitted by the council to the General Assembly at the regular session for 2005 and shall become effective only when ratified by joint resolution of the General Assembly and upon the approval of the resolution by the Governor or upon its becoming law without such approval. The power of the council to promulgate such initial minimum standards shall be deemed to be dependent upon such ratification; provided, however, the minimum standards promulgated by the council shall be utilized as a guideline prior to ratification. Any subsequent amendments or additions to the initial minimum standards promulgated by the council pursuant to this Code section which are determined by the General Oversight Committee for the Georgia Public Defender Standards Council to have a fiscal impact shall be ratified at the next regular session of the General Assembly and shall become effective only when ratified by joint resolution of the General Assembly and upon the approval of the resolution by the Governor or upon its becoming law without such approval.

"(d) All standards that are promulgated by the council shall be publicly available for review and shall be posted on the council's website. Each standard shall identify the date upon which the standard took effect, and if the standard is subject to ratification by the General Assembly as provided by subsection (c) of this Code section, the status of the standard with respect to ratification."

Laws 2008, Act 729, § 43 provides:

"This Act shall become effective on July 1, 2008; provided, however, that for purposes of the appointment of the councilmembers and circuit public defender supervisory panel members, this Act shall become effective upon its approval by the Governor or upon its becoming law without such approval."

Former § 17–12–8, relating to the competency to defend, derived from Laws 1968, p. 999, § 7, was repealed by Laws 2003, Act 32, § 1, eff. Dec. 31, 2003.

§ 17–12–9. Legal education and training programs; reimbursement

The council shall be authorized to conduct or approve for credit or reimbursement, or both, basic and continuing legal education courses or other appropriate training programs for the circuit public defenders or their staff members. The council, in accordance with such rules as it shall adopt, shall be authorized to provide reimbursement, in whole or in part, for the actual expenses incurred by any circuit public defender or their staff members in attending any approved course or training program from funds as may be appropriated or otherwise made available to the council. The circuit public defenders or their staff members shall be authorized to receive reimbursement for actual expenses incurred in attending approved courses or training programs. The council shall adopt rules governing the approval of courses and training programs for credit or reimbursement as may be necessary to administer this Code section properly.

Laws 2003, Act 32, § 1, eff. Dec. 31, 2003; Laws 2008, Act 729, § 21, eff. July 1, 2008.

Historical and Statutory Notes

The 2008 amendment by Act 729 deleted "Notwithstanding any other provision of law" in the third sentence, and deleted a sentence regarding reimbursement under § 17–12–9 and 17–12–26.

Laws 2008, Act 729, § 43 provides:

"This Act shall become effective on July 1, 2008; provided, however, that for purposes of the appointment of the councilmembers and circuit public defender supervisory panel members, this Act shall become effective upon its approval by the Governor or upon its becoming law without such approval."

Former § 17–12–9, relating to substitute attorneys, derived from Laws 1968, p. 999, § 8, was repealed by Laws 2003, Act 32, § 1, eff. Dec. 31, 2003.

§ 17–12–10. Report of activities; analysis of grants and funds

(a) The council shall prepare annually a report of its activities in order to provide the General Assembly, the Governor, and the Supreme Court of Georgia with an accurate description and accounting of the preceding year's expenditures and revenue, including moneys received from cities and county governing authorities. Such report shall include a three-year cost projection and anticipated revenues for all programs defined in the General Appropriations Act.

(b) The council shall provide to the General Assembly, the Governor, and the Supreme Court of Georgia a detailed analysis of all grants and funds, whether public or private, applied for or granted, together with how and in what manner the same are to be utilized and expended.

(c) The council shall prepare annually a report in order to provide the General Assembly and the Governor with information on the council's assessment of the delivery of indigent defense services, including, but not limited to, the costs involved in operating each program and each governing authority's indigent person verification system, methodology used, costs expended, and savings realized.

Laws 2003, Act 32, § 1, eff. Dec. 31, 2003; Laws 2008, Act 729, § 22, eff. July 1, 2008.

Historical and Statutory Notes

The 2008 amendment by Act 729, in subsec. (a), substituted "expenditures and revenue, including moneys received from cities and county governing authorities. Such report shall include a three-year cost projection and anticipated revenues for all programs defined in the General Appropriations Act" for "expenditures and accomplishments"; and added subsec. (c), relating to the preparation of an annual report.

Laws 2008, Act 729, § 43 provides:

"This Act shall become effective on July 1, 2008; provided, however, that for purposes of the appointment of the councilmembers and circuit public defender supervisory panel members, this Act shall become effective upon its approval by the Governor or upon its becoming law without such approval."

Former § 17-12-10, relating to the determination of indigency, derived from Laws 1968, p. 999, § 10, was repealed by Laws 2003, Act 32, § 1, eff. Dec. 31, 2003.

§ 17-12-10.1. General Oversight Committee; creation; membership; powers and duties

(a) There is created the Legislative Oversight Committee for the Georgia Public Defender Standards Council which shall be composed of eight persons: three members of the House of Representatives appointed by the Speaker of the House of Representatives, three members of the Senate appointed by the Senate Committee on Assignments or such person or entity as established by Senate rule, and one member of the House of Representatives and one member of the Senate appointed by the Governor. The members of such committee shall be selected within ten days after the convening of the General Assembly in each odd-numbered year and shall serve until their successors are appointed.

(b) The Speaker of the House of Representatives shall appoint a member of such committee to serve as chairperson, and the Senate Committee on Assignments or such person or entity as established by Senate rule shall appoint one member of the committee to serve as vice chairperson during each even-numbered year. The Senate Committee on Assignments or such person or entity as established by Senate rule shall appoint a member of such committee to serve as chairperson, and the Speaker of the House of Representatives shall appoint one member to serve as vice chairperson during each odd-numbered year. Such committee shall meet at least three times each year and, upon the call of the chairperson, at such additional times as deemed necessary by the chairperson.

(c) It shall be the duty of such committee to review and evaluate:

(1) Information on new programs submitted by the council;

(2) Information on rules, regulations, policies, and standards proposed by the council;

(3) The strategic plans for the council;

(4) Program evaluation reports and budget recommendations of the council;

(5) The fiscal impact of fees and fines on counties;

(6) The reports submitted pursuant to Code Section 15-21A-7 in order to identify, among other things, opportunities to reduce or consolidate fees, fines, and surcharges; and

(7) Such other information or reports as deemed necessary by such committee.

(d) The council and director shall cooperate with such committee and provide such information or reports as requested by the committee for the performance of its functions.

(e) The council shall submit its budget estimate to the director of the Office of Planning and Budget in accordance with subsection (a) of Code Section 45-12-78.

(f) The legislative oversight committee shall make an annual report of its activities and findings to the membership of the General Assembly and the Governor within one week of the convening of each regular session of the General Assembly. The chairperson of such committee shall deliver written executive summaries of such report to the members of the General Assembly prior to the adoption of the General Appropriations Act each year.

(g) The members of such committee shall receive the allowances authorized for legislative members of legislative committees. The funds necessary to pay such allowances shall come from funds appropriated to the House of Representatives and the Senate.

(h) The legislative oversight committee shall be authorized to request that a performance audit of the council be conducted.

Laws 2004, Ex. Sess., Act 4, § 13, eff. June 15, 2004; Laws 2007, Act 22, § 2, eff. July 1, 2007; Laws 2008, Act 729, § 23, eff. July 1, 2008.

Historical and Statutory Notes

The 2007 amendment by Act 22 rewrote subsec. (e) which had read:

"(e) Notwithstanding subsection (c) of Code Section 45-12-78, the council shall submit its budget estimate to the director of the Office of Planning and Budget prior to submitting its budget estimate to the Judicial Council of Georgia. The council's budget estimate included in the Governor's budget report as provided in subsection (d) of Code Section 45-12-78 shall be as submitted by the Judicial Council of Georgia; provided, however, that the Governor shall be authorized to analyze the council's budget estimate and include such analysis as a part of the Governor's budget report."

The 2008 amendment by Act 729, in subsec. (a) substituted "the Legislative Oversight Committee" for "the General Oversight Committee"; in subsec. (b), reduced the number of times the committee shall meet from at least 6 times each year to at least 3 times each year; in subsec. (c), par. (2) inserted "rules, regulations, policies, and" following "Information on"; in subsec. (d) substituted "The council and director" for "The council"; and in subsecs. (f) and (h) substituted "The legislative oversight committee" for "The committee".

Laws 2008, Act 729, § 43 provides:

"This Act shall become effective on July 1, 2008; provided, however, that for purposes of the appointment of the councilmembers and circuit public defender supervisory panel members, this Act shall become effective upon its approval by the Governor or upon its becoming law without such approval."

§ 17-12-10.2. Member liability

The members of the council as created by this article, the members of the circuit public defender supervisory panel created by Article 2 of this chapter, and other policy-making or administrative personnel acting in a policy-making or administrative capacity shall not be subject to civil liability resulting from any act or failure to act in the implementation and carrying out of the purposes of this chapter.

Laws 2004, Ex. Sess., Act 4, § 14, eff. June 15, 2004; Laws 2008, Act 729, § 24, eff. July 1, 2008.

Historical and Statutory Notes

The 2008 amendment by Act 729 substituted "public defender supervisory panel" for "public defender selection panel" and removed a reference to this article and Article 2.

Laws 2008, Act 729, § 43 provides:

"This Act shall become effective on July 1, 2008; provided, however, that for purposes of the appointment of the councilmembers and circuit public defender supervisory panel members, this Act shall become effective upon its approval by the Governor or upon its becoming law without such approval."

§ 17–12–11. Mental advocacy division; representation for indigents not guilty by reason of insanity or mental incompetency to stand trial

(a) The mental health advocacy division shall represent in any court in this state indigent persons found not guilty by reason of insanity at the time of the crime or found mentally incompetent to stand trial and shall be the successor to the office of mental health advocacy created by Article 4 of this chapter as it existed on June 30, 2008. Any assets or resources of the office of mental health advocacy shall be transferred to the council. The mental health advocacy division office shall serve all counties of this state.

(b) Whenever any person has been found not guilty by reason of insanity at the time of the crime pursuant to Code Section 17–7–131 or found mentally incompetent to stand trial pursuant to Code Section 17–7–130 and has been determined to be an indigent person, the court in which such case is pending shall notify the mental health advocacy division, and the division may assume the defense and representation of such person in all matters pursuant to Code Sections 17–7–130 and 17–7–131, as applicable, if the resources, funding, and staffing of the division allow; provided, however, that the circuit public defender or other attorney who represented the indigent person at the time of the finding of not guilty by reason of insanity at the time of the crime or the finding of mentally incompetent to stand trial shall have the option to retain responsibility for the representation of any such person.

(c) Nothing in this Code section shall prevent the circuit public defender, the court, or the court appointed attorney from requesting the participation of the mental health advocacy division prior to a finding of not guilty by reason of insanity at the time of the crime or a finding of mentally incompetent to stand trial. The circuit public defender, the court, or the court appointed attorney may request that the mental health advocacy division assist in the case prior to a plea being entered and accepted by the court.

(d) If for any reason the mental health advocacy division is unable to represent any indigent person found not guilty by reason of insanity at the time of the crime or found mentally incompetent to stand trial, such representation shall be provided as otherwise provided by law.

(e) The director shall be responsible for management of the mental health advocacy division; provided, however, that the director may delegate day-to-day operations of the division to the mental health advocate.

Laws 2003, Act 32, § 1, eff. Dec. 31, 2003; Laws 2004, Ex. Sess., Act 4, § 15, eff. June 15, 2004; Laws 2008, Act 729, § 25, eff. July 1, 2008.

Historical and Statutory Notes

In 2003, the Code Commission, in subsec. (a), substituted "Section 17–12–32" for "Section 17–12—31". See § 28–9–5.

The 2004, Ex. Sess., amendment by Act 4, in subsec. (b), inserted "for grants to counties".

Former § 17–12–11, relating to recovery from the defendant, derived from Laws 1968, p. 999, § 11, was repealed by Laws 2003, Act 32, § 1, eff. Dec. 31, 2003.

The 2008 amendment by Act 729 rewrote this section, which formerly read:

"(a) On December 31, 2003, the Georgia Public Defender Standards Council shall assume all powers, duties, and obligations of the Georgia Indigent Defense Council created by former Code Section 17–12–32, and all references in this Code to the Georgia Indigent Defense Council shall be deemed to be references to the Georgia Public Defender Standards Council. Such powers shall include, without limitation, making grants and distributions to the counties.

"(b) At least 90 percent of all state appropriated funds to the former Georgia Indigent Defense Council or the Georgia Public Defender Standards Council for grants to counties shall be distributed to counties for the January 1, 2004, through December 31, 2004, time period, based upon previous year expenditures for the provision of defense services at the local level.

"(c) On December 31, 2003, the employees in good standing, assets, and resources of the Georgia Indigent Defense Council shall be transferred to the Georgia Public Defender Standards Council, and the council shall assume any executory contractual obligations of the Georgia Indigent Defense Council, provided that allocated funding resources for such obligations are also transferred. All full-time employees of the Georgia Public Defender Standards Council shall be state employees in the unclassified service of the State Merit System of Personnel Administration with all of the benefits of appointed state employees provided by law."

Laws 2008, Act 729, § 43 provides:

"This Act shall become effective on July 1, 2008; provided, however, that for purposes of the appointment of the councilmembers and circuit public defender supervisory panel members, this Act shall become effective upon its approval by the Governor or upon its becoming law without such approval."

§ 17–12–12. Georgia capital defender division shall represent indigents charged with capital felony for which death penalty is being sought

(a) The Georgia capital defender division shall represent all indigent persons charged with a capital felony for which the death penalty is being sought in any court in this state and shall be the successor to the Office of the Georgia Capital Defender created by Article 6 of this chapter as it existed on June 30, 2008. Any assets or resources of the Office of the Georgia Capital Defender shall be transferred to the council. The Georgia capital defender division shall serve all counties of this state.

(b) Whenever any person accused of a capital felony for which the death penalty is being sought has been determined to be an indigent person who has requested the assistance of counsel, the court in which the charges are pending shall notify the Georgia capital defender division, and the division shall assume the defense of such person except as provided in Code Section 17–12–12.1.

(c) No person shall be assigned the primary responsibility of representing an indigent person accused of a capital offense for which the death penalty is sought unless such person is authorized to practice law in this state and is otherwise competent to counsel and defend a person charged with a capital felony.

(d) The Georgia capital defender division or appointed counsel's defense of a defendant in a case in which the death penalty is sought shall include all proceedings in the trial court and any appeals to the Supreme Court of Georgia. Neither the Georgia capital defender division nor appointed counsel shall assist with any petition for a writ of habeas corpus in federal court.

(e) The director shall be responsible for management of the Georgia capital defender division; provided, however, that the director may delegate day-to-day operations of the division to the capital defender.

Laws 2003, Act 32, § 1, eff. Dec. 31, 2003; Laws 2008, Act 729, § 26, eff. July 1, 2008.

Historical and Statutory Notes

In 2003, the Code Commission substituted "Article 2" for "Article 1" twice. See § 28–9–5.

The 2008 amendment by Act 729 rewrote this section, which formerly read:

"From January 1, 2005, through December 31, 2005, the Georgia Public Defender Standards Council shall coordinate the transition from the procedures for providing criminal defense to indigent persons in effect on December 31, 2004, in each county to the procedures provided in Article 2 of this chapter. On and after January 1, 2005, the provisions of Article 2 of this chapter shall govern the public provision of criminal defense to indigent persons in the courts of this state."

Laws 2008, Act 729, § 43 provides:

"This Act shall become effective on July 1, 2008; provided, however, that for purposes of the appointment of the councilmembers and circuit public defender supervisory panel members, this Act shall become effective upon its approval by the Governor or upon its becoming law without such approval."

Former § 17-12-12, relating to records and reports, derived from Laws 1968, p. 999, § 12, was repealed by Laws 2003, Act 32, § 1, eff. Dec. 31, 2003.

§ 17-12-12.1. Conflict of interest; appointment of counsel

(a) If there is a conflict of interest such that the Georgia capital defender division is unable to defend any indigent person accused of a capital felony for which the death penalty is being sought, the director shall determine and appoint counsel to represent the defendant. The director shall establish the contractual agreement with the defendant's counsel for payment of representing the defendant, and, when feasible and prudent, a flat fee structure shall be utilized.

(b) A maximum of two attorneys shall be paid by the council pursuant to a contractual agreement or at an hourly rate established by the council with state funds appropriated to the council. State funds shall be appropriated to the council for use by the Georgia capital defender division for the first $150,000.00 paid for each death penalty case. Funding for attorney's fees and expenses between $150,000.01 and $250,000.00 for each death penalty case shall be paid through state appropriations for 75 percent of such attorney's fees and expenses, and the county governing authority where the indictment was returned shall pay 25 percent of such attorney's fees and expenses. Funding for all attorney's fees and expenses in excess of $250,000.00 for each death penalty case shall be paid through state appropriations for 50 percent of such attorney's fees and expenses, and the county governing authority where the indictment was returned shall pay 50 percent of such attorney's fees and expenses.

(c) The council, with the assistance of the Georgia capital defender division, shall establish guidelines for all expense requests for cases in which the death penalty is sought, including, but not limited to, attorney's fees, expert witness fees, investigative fees, travel and accommodation expenses, and copy and transcription costs.

(d) A county governing authority may provide supplemental compensation to counsel appointed pursuant to this Code section.

Laws 2008, Act 729, § 27, eff. July 1, 2008.

Historical and Statutory Notes

Laws 2008, Act 729, § 43 provides:

"This Act shall become effective on July 1, 2008; provided, however, that for purposes of the appointment of the councilmembers and circuit public defender supervisory panel members, this Act shall become effective upon its approval by the Governor or upon its becoming law without such approval."

§ 17-12-13. Effective date of article

This article shall become effective on December 31, 2003, except as specified in Code Section 17-12-3.

Laws 2003, Act 32, § 1, eff. Dec. 31, 2003.

Historical and Statutory Notes

Former § 17-12-13, relating to financing, derived from Laws 1968, p. 999, § 10, was repealed by Laws 2003, Act 32, § 1, eff. Dec. 31, 2003.

§ 17-12-14. Repealed by Laws 2003, Act 32, § 1, eff. Dec. 31, 2003

Historical and Statutory Notes

Section 17-12-14, relating to representation in state and federal courts, was derived from Laws 1968, p. 999, § 13.

Article 1A

Local Indigent Defense Programs [Repealed]

Revision of Chapter 12

Laws 2004, Ex. Sess., Act 4, § 16, added this article effective June 15, 2004, and repealed it effective December 31, 2004.

§§ 17-12-19.1 to 17-12-19.14. Repealed by Laws 2004, Ex. Sess., Act 4, § 16, eff. December 31, 2004 (§ 17-12-19.14)

Historical and Statutory Notes

Section 17-12-19.1, containing definitions, was derived from Laws 2004, Ex. Sess., Act 4, § 16.

Section 17-12-19.2, requiring a majority for actions taken by a court, was derived from Laws 2004, Ex. Sess., Act 4, § 16.

Section 17-12-19.3, requiring courts having jurisdiction of criminal proceedings to provide representation of indigent persons, was derived from Laws 2004, Ex. Sess., Act 4, § 16.

Section 17-12-19.4, relating to arrangements involving assignment of attorneys, was derived from Laws 2004, Ex. Sess., Act 4, § 16.

Section 17-12-19.5, relating to arrangements involving nonprofit legal aid agencies, was derived from Laws 2004, Ex. Sess., Act 4, § 16.

Section 17-12-19.6, relating to the office of public defender, was derived from Laws 2004, Ex. Sess., Act 4, § 16.

Section 17-12-19.7, requiring the person given the primary responsibility of representing an indigent person be authorized to practice law in the state and otherwise competent to counsel and defend, was derived from Laws 2004, Ex. Sess., Act 4, § 16.

Section 17-12-19.8, relating to substitute attorneys, was derived from Laws 2004, Ex. Sess., Act 4, § 16.

Section 17-12-19.9, relating to the standards to govern determination of indigency, was derived from Laws 2004, Ex. Sess., Act 4, § 16.

Section 17-12-19.10, allowing the county, under certain circumstances, to recover payment or reimbursement from a person who received legal assistance, was derived from Laws 2004, Ex. Sess., Act 4, § 16.

Section 17-12-19.11, relating to maintenance of records, was derived from Laws 2004, Ex. Sess., Act 4, § 16.

Section 17-12-19.12, requiring the county governing authority in each county to include costs for implementation of the article in its annual budget, was derived from Laws 2004, Ex. Sess., Act 4, § 16.

Section 17-12-19.13, relating to application of the article, was derived from Laws 2004, Ex. Sess., Act 4, § 16.

Section 17-12-19.14, providing for repeal of the article, was derived from Laws 2004, Ex. Sess., Act 4, § 16.

Article 2

Public Defenders

Revision of Chapter 12

Laws 2003, Act 32, § 1, added this article effective January 1, 2005, and provided that the council and circuit public defender selection panels were authorized to take necessary and appropriate action for phase-in full implementation of this article on or after December 31, 2003. See § 17–12–37.

Former Article 2, State Funded Local Indigent Defense Programs, consisting of §§ 17–12–30 to 17–12–51, was repealed by Laws 2003, Act 32, § 1, effective January 1, 2005.

§ 17–12–20. Circuit public defender selection panel; membership; powers

(a) On and after July 1, 2008, there is created in each judicial circuit in this state a circuit public defender supervisory panel to be composed of seven members. The Lieutenant Governor, the Speaker of the House of Representatives, and the chief judge of the superior court of the circuit shall each appoint one member. The Governor shall appoint four members, two of which shall be members of the governing authority of the counties within the judicial circuit for which such member is appointed to serve. A member of a governing authority shall be eligible to serve so long as he or she retains the office by virtue of which he or she is serving on the panel. Other than the county commissioner, members of the circuit public defender supervisory panel shall be individuals with significant experience working in the criminal justice system or who have demonstrated a strong commitment to the provision of adequate and effective representation of indigent defendants. A prosecuting attorney as defined in paragraph (6) of Code Section 19–13–51, any employee of a prosecuting attorney's office, or an employee of the Prosecuting Attorneys' Council of the State of Georgia shall not serve as a member of the circuit public defender supervisory panel after July 1, 2005. On and after July 1, 2008, no employees of the council shall serve as a member of the circuit public defender supervisory panel. Members of the circuit public defender supervisory panel shall reside in the judicial circuit in which they serve. The circuit public defender supervisory panel members shall serve for a term of five years. Any vacancy for an appointed member shall be filled by the appointing authority.

(b)(1) By majority vote of its membership, the circuit public defender supervisory panel shall annually elect a chairperson and secretary and determine a quorum for the transaction of business. The chairperson shall conduct the meetings and deliberations of the panel and direct all activities. The secretary shall keep accurate records of all the meetings and deliberations and perform such other duties as the chairperson may direct. The panel may be called into session upon the direction of the chairperson or by the council.

(2) By majority vote of its membership, the circuit public defender supervisory panel shall appoint the circuit public defender in the circuit as provided in this article. The first such appointments shall be made to take office on January 1, 2005, for terms of up to four years. The initial appointments shall be for a term of up to four years. A circuit public defender may be appointed for successive terms but shall not be reappointed if he or she was removed pursuant to subsection (c) of this Code section.

(c) A circuit public defender may be removed for cause by a majority vote of the council and may be removed without cause by a vote of two-thirds of the members of the entire council.

(d) A circuit public defender supervisory panel may convene at any time during its circuit public defender's term of office and shall convene at least semiannually for purposes of reviewing the circuit public defender's job performance and the performance of the circuit public defender office. The council and circuit public defender shall be notified at least two weeks in advance of the convening of the circuit public defender supervisory panel. The circuit public defender shall be given the opportunity to appear before the circuit public defender supervisory panel and present evidence and testimony. The chairperson shall determine the agenda for the semiannual review process, but, at a minimum, such review shall include information collected pursuant to subsection (c) of Code Section 17–12–24, usage of state and local funding, expenditures, and budgeting matters. The chairperson shall make an annual report on or before the thirtieth day of September of each year concerning the circuit public defender supervisory panel's findings regarding the job performance of the circuit public defender and his or her office to the council on a form provided to the panel by the council. If at any time the circuit public defender supervisory panel finds that the circuit public defender is performing in a less than satisfactory manner or finds information of specific misconduct, the circuit public defender supervisory panel may by majority vote of its members adopt a resolution seeking review of their findings and remonstrative action by the council. Such resolution shall specify the reason for such request. All evidence presented and the findings of the circuit public defender supervisory panel shall be forwarded to the council within 15 days of the adoption of the resolution. The council shall initiate action on the circuit public defender supervisory panel's resolution at its next regularly scheduled meeting and take final action within 60 days thereafter. The council shall notify the circuit public defender supervisory panel, in writing, of any actions taken pursuant to submission of a resolution under this subsection.

(e) If a vacancy occurs for the position of circuit public defender, the chief judge of the superior court of the circuit shall appoint an interim circuit public defender to serve until the circuit public defender supervisory panel has appointed a replacement. The circuit public defender supervisory panel shall appoint a replacement circuit public defender within three months of the occurring of the vacancy. The replacement circuit public defender shall not be any individual who has been removed by the council pursuant to subsection (c) of this Code section.

Laws 2003, Act 32, § 1, eff. Jan. 1, 2005; Laws 2004, Act 564, § 17, eff. Jan. 1, 2005; Laws 2004, Ex. Sess., Act 4, § 17, eff. Jan. 1, 2005; Laws 2008, Act 729, § 28, eff. July 1, 2008.

Historical and Statutory Notes

The 2004 amendment by Act 564 was a provision contained in a correction bill.

Laws 2004, Act 564, § 55, provides:

"This Act shall become effective upon its approval by the Governor or upon its becoming law without such approval; except that paragraphs (5) through (9) and paragraph (12) of Section 17 of this Act shall become effective January 1, 2005; paragraph (11) of Section 17 of this Act shall become effective 11:58 P.M. on December 31, 2004; and paragraph (1) of Section 25 of this Act shall become effective July 1, 2004."

The 2004, Ex. Sess., amendment by Act 4, in subsec. (a), inserted the fourth sentence relating to the appointment of a prosecuting attorney, etc. to serve on circuit public defender selection panel; and made a gender related change.

Laws 2004, Ex. Sess., Act 4, § 27, subsec. (b), provides:

"(b) Section 17 of this Act shall become effective on January 1, 2005; provided, however, that for purposes of the appointment of the members of the circuit public defender selection panels in conformity with Section 17 of this Act as may be necessary or appropriate to prepare for and phase in full implementation of Article 2 of Chapter 12 of Title 17 of the Official Code of Georgia Annotated as enacted by Ga. L. 2003, p. 191, Section 17 of this Act shall become effective upon approval of this Act by the Governor or upon its becoming law without such approval."

Laws 2006, Act 919, effective May 5, 2006, pursuant to Code Section 17–12–8, ratified and approved the Standard for Removal of a Circuit Public Defender for Cause Pursuant to O.C.G.A. § 17–12–20.

The 2008 amendment by Act 729 rewrote this section, which formerly read:

"(a) There is created in each judicial circuit in the state a circuit public defender selection panel to be composed of five members. The membership shall be composed of one member each appointed by the Governor, the Lieutenant Governor, the Speaker of the House of Representatives, the Chief Justice of the Supreme Court of Georgia, and the chief judge of the superior court of the circuit. Members of the circuit public defender selection panel shall be individuals with significant experience working in the criminal justice system or who have demonstrated a strong commitment to the provision of adequate and effective representation of indigent defendants. A prosecuting attorney as defined in paragraph (6) of Code

Section 19–13–51, any employee of a prosecuting attorney's office, or an employee of the Prosecuting Attorneys' Council of the State of Georgia shall not serve as a member of the circuit public defender selection panel after July 1, 2005. Members of the circuit public defender selection panel shall reside in the judicial circuit in which they serve. The circuit public defender selection panel members shall serve for a term of five years. Any vacancy for an appointed member shall be filled by the appointing authority.

"(b) By majority vote of its membership, the circuit public defender selection panel shall appoint the circuit public defender in the circuit as provided in this article. The first such appointments shall be made to take office on January 1, 2005, for terms of up to four years. The initial appointments shall be for a term of up to four years.

"(c) A circuit public defender may be removed for cause by a majority vote of the council.

"(d) If a vacancy occurs for the position of circuit public defender, the chief judge of the superior court of the circuit shall appoint an interim circuit public defender to serve until the circuit public defender selection panel has appointed a replacement to serve out the unexpired term of office. The circuit public defender selection panel shall appoint a replacement circuit public defender within three months of the occurring of the vacancy."

Laws 2008, Act 729, § 43 provides:

"This Act shall become effective on July 1, 2008; provided, however, that for purposes of the appointment of the councilmembers and circuit public defender supervisory panel members, this Act shall become effective upon its approval by the Governor or upon its becoming law without such approval."

§ 17–12–21. Eligibility

To be eligible to fill the position of circuit public defender, a person must:

(1) Have attained the age of 25 years;

(2) Have been duly admitted and licensed to practice law in the superior courts for at least three years;

(3) Be a member in good standing of the State Bar of Georgia; and

(4) If previously disbarred from the practice of law, have been reinstated as provided by law.

Laws 2003, Act 32, § 1, eff. Jan. 1, 2005.

§ 17–12–22. Conflicts of interest

(a) The council shall establish a procedure for providing legal representation in cases where the circuit public defender office has a conflict of interest. Such procedure may include, but shall not be limited to, the appointment of individual counsel on a case-by-case basis or the utilization of another circuit public defender office. Whatever procedure the council establishes for each circuit's conflict of interest cases shall be adhered to by the circuit public defender office. It is the intent of the General Assembly that the council consider the most efficient and effective system to provide legal representation where the circuit public defender office has a conflict of interest.

(b) The circuit public defender shall establish a method for identifying conflicts of interest at the earliest possible opportunity. If there is a conflict of interest such that the circuit public defender office cannot represent a defendant and an attorney who is not employed by the circuit public defender office is appointed, such attorney shall have a contractual relationship with the council to represent indigent persons in conflict of interest cases, and such relationship may include, but shall not be limited to, a flat fee structure.

(c) Attorneys who seek appointment in conflict cases shall have such experience or training in the defense of criminal cases as is necessary in light of the complexity of the case to which he or she is appointed and shall meet such qualifications, regulations, and standards for the representation of indigent defendants as are established by the council.

Laws 2003, Act 32, § 1, eff. Jan. 1, 2005; Laws 2008, Act 729, § 29, eff. July 1, 2008; Laws 2010, Act 404, § 2A, eff. July 1, 2010.

Historical and Statutory Notes

The 2008 amendment by Act 729 rewrote this section, which formerly read:

"(a) The council shall establish a procedure for providing legal representation in cases where the circuit public defender office has a conflict of interest. This procedure may be by appointment of individual counsel on a case-by-case basis or by the establishment of a conflict defender office in those circuits where the volume of cases may warrant a separate conflict defender office.

"(b) Attorneys who seek appointment in conflict cases must have such experience or training in the defense of criminal cases as is necessary in light of the complexity of the case to which they are appointed and must meet such qualifications and standards for the representation of indigent defendants as are established by the council.

"(c) The circuit public defender shall establish a method for identifying conflicts of interest at the earliest possible opportunity."

Laws 2008, Act 729, § 43 provides:

"This Act shall become effective on July 1, 2008; provided, however, that for purposes of the appointment of the councilmembers and circuit public defender supervisory panel members, this Act shall become effective upon its approval by the Governor or upon its becoming law without such approval."

The 2010 amendment by Act 404, in subsec. (a), deleted "when feasible" following "public defender office" in the second sentence and added the third sentence relating to procedure in conflict of interest cases.

§ 17–12–23. Representation in actions and proceedings; time of entitlement to services; juveniles; contracts with cities or counties

(a) The circuit public defender shall provide representation in the following actions and proceedings:

(1) Any case prosecuted in a superior court under the laws of the State of Georgia in which there is a possibility that a sentence of imprisonment or probation or a suspended sentence of imprisonment may be adjudged;

(2) A hearing on a revocation of probation in a superior court;

(3) Any juvenile court case where the juvenile may face a disposition of confinement, commitment, or probation; and

(4) Any direct appeal of any of the proceedings enumerated in paragraphs (1) through (3) of this subsection.

(b) In each of the actions and proceedings enumerated in subsection (a) of this Code section, entitlement to the services of counsel begins not more than three business days after the indigent person is taken into custody or service is made upon him or her of the charge, petition, notice, or other initiating process and such person makes an application for counsel to be appointed.

(c) Each circuit public defender shall establish a juvenile division within the circuit public defender office to specialize in the defense of juveniles.

(d) A city or county may contract with the circuit public defender office for the provision of criminal defense for indigent persons accused of violating city or county ordinances or state laws. If a city or county does not contract with the circuit public defender office, the city or county shall be subject to all applicable rules, regulation, policies, and standards adopted by the council for representation of indigent persons in this state.

Laws 2003, Act 32, § 1, eff. Jan. 1, 2005; Laws 2006, Act 739, § 5, eff. July 1, 2006; Laws 2008, Act 729, § 30, eff. July 1, 2008.

Historical and Statutory Notes

The 2006 amendment by Act 739, in subsec. (d), substituted "city or county" for "city, county, or consolidated government" throughout the subsection.

The 2008 amendment by Act 729, in subsec. (b), substituted "entitlement to the services of counsel begins not more than three business days after the indigent person is taken into custody or service is made upon him or her of the charge, petition, notice, or other initiating process and such person makes an application for counsel to be appointed" for "entitlement to the services of counsel begins as soon as is feasible and no more than 72 hours after the indigent person is taken into custody or service is made upon him or her of the charge, petition, notice, or other initiating process"; and in subsec. (d) inserted "rules, regulation, policies, and" following "the city or county shall be subject to all applicable".

Laws 2008, Act 729, § 43 provides:

"This Act shall become effective on July 1, 2008; provided, however, that for purposes of the appointment of the councilmembers and circuit public defender supervisory panel members, this Act shall become effective upon its approval by the Governor or upon its becoming law without such approval."

§ 17–12–24. Determination of financial eligibility; administration of operations; records

(a) The circuit public defender, any other person or entity providing indigent defense services, or the system established pursuant to Code Section 17–12–80 shall determine if a person or juvenile arrested, detained, or charged in any manner is an indigent person entitled to representation under this chapter.

(b) The circuit public defenders shall administer and coordinate the day-to-day operations of their respective offices and shall supervise the assistant public defenders and other staff serving in the office.

(c) The circuit public defender shall keep and maintain appropriate records, which shall include the number of persons represented, including cases assigned to other counsel based on conflict of interest; the offenses charged; the outcome of each case; the expenditures made in carrying out the duties imposed by this chapter; and any other information requested by the council.

Laws 2003, Act 32, § 1, eff. Jan. 1, 2005; Laws 2006, Act 749, § 7, eff. May 3, 2006; Laws 2008, Act 729, § 31, eff. July 1, 2008.

Historical and Statutory Notes

The 2006 amendment by Act 749 rewrote subsec. (a) which had read:

"(a) The council shall establish guidelines for determining the financial eligibility of persons claiming indigence, and the circuit public defender and any other person or entity providing indigent defense services shall use the guidelines to determine the financial eligibility of any person or juvenile arrested, detained, or charged in any manner that would entitle him or her to representation under this article."

The 2008 amendment by Act 729 rewrote subsec. (a); and in subsec. (c) deleted a reference to this article and substituted "imposed by this chapter" for "imposed by this article". Prior to revision, subsec. (a) read:

"(a) The circuit public defender and any other person or entity providing indigent defense services shall determine the financial eligibility of any person or juvenile arrested, detained, or charged in any manner in accordance with the definition of an indigent person set forth in Code Section 17–12–2 that would entitle him or her to representation under this chapter."

Laws 2008, Act 729, § 43 provides:

"This Act shall become effective on July 1, 2008; provided, however, that for purposes of the appointment of the councilmembers and circuit public defender supervisory panel members, this Act shall become effective upon its approval by the Governor or upon its becoming law without such approval."

§ 17–12–25. Salary and cost-of-living adjustments; supplementation; private practice of law

(a) Each circuit public defender shall receive an annual salary of $87,593.58, and cost-of-living adjustments may be given by the General Assembly in the General Appropriations Act by a percentage not to exceed the average percentage of the general increase in salary as may from time to time be granted to employees of the executive, judicial, and legislative branches of government; provided, however, that any increase for such circuit public defender shall not include within-grade step increases for which classified employees of the State Personnel Administration are eligible. Any increase granted pursuant to this subsection shall become effective at the same time that funds are made available for the increase for such employees. The Office of Planning and Budget shall calculate the average percentage increase.

(b) The county or counties comprising the judicial circuit may supplement the salary of the circuit public defender in an amount as is or may be authorized by local Act or in an amount as may be determined by the governing authority of the county or counties, whichever is greater.

(c) No circuit public defender shall engage in the private practice of law for profit or serve concurrently in any judicial office.

Laws 2003, Act 32, § 1, eff. Jan. 1, 2005; Laws 2004, Ex. Sess., Act 4, § 18, eff. Jan. 1, 2005; Laws 2008, Act 729, § 32, eff. July 1, 2008; Laws 2009, Act 155, § 1, eff. July 1, 2009.

Historical and Statutory Notes

The 2004, Ex. Sess., amendment by Act 4, in subsec. (a), substituted "salary of $87,593.58 and cost–of–living adjustments as may from time to time be granted to employees of the executive, judicial, and legislative branches of government from state funds" for "salary and cost–of–living adjustments from state funds as prescribed by the council".

Laws 2004, Ex. Sess., Act 4, § 27, subsec. (c), provides:

"(c) Sections 18 through 24 of this Act shall become effective on January 1, 2005."

The 2008 amendment by Act 729 rewrote this section, which formerly read:

"(a) Each circuit public defender shall receive an annual salary of $87,593.58 and cost-of-living adjustments as may from time to time be granted to employees of the executive, judicial, and legislative branches of government from state funds.

"(b) The county or counties comprising the judicial circuit may supplement the salary of the circuit public defender in an amount as is or may be authorized by local Act or in an amount as may be determined by the governing authority of the county or counties, whichever is greater.

"(c) No circuit public defender shall engage in the private practice of law for profit."

Laws 2008, Act 729, § 43 provides:

"This Act shall become effective on July 1, 2008; provided, however, that for purposes of the appointment of the councilmembers and circuit public defender supervisory panel members, this Act shall become effective upon its approval by the Governor or upon its becoming law without such approval."

The 2009 amendment by Act 155 substituted "State Personnel Administration" for "state merit system" throughout the section.

§ 17–12–26. Budget; private or public funds

The council shall prepare and submit to the director of the Office of Planning and Budget its budget estimate necessary for fulfilling the purposes of this chapter in accordance with Code Section 45–12–78. The council shall be authorized to seek, solicit, apply for, and utilize funds from any public or private source to use in fulfilling the purposes of this chapter.

Laws 2003, Act 32, § 1, eff. Jan. 1, 2005; Laws 2004, Ex. Sess., Act 4, § 19, eff. Jan. 1, 2005; Laws 2006, Act 453, § 17, eff. April 14, 2006; Laws 2006, Act 749, § 8, eff. May 3, 2006; Laws 2007, Act 22, § 3, eff. July 1, 2007; Laws 2008, Act 25, § 1–9, eff. Jan. 28, 2008; Laws 2008, Act 729, § 33, eff. July 1, 2008.

Historical and Statutory Notes

The 2004, Ex. Sess., amendment by Act 4, rewrote subsec. (a); deleted subsecs. (c) and (d); and redesignated former subsec. (e) as subsec. (c). Prior to amendment, subsecs. (a), (c) and (d) had read:

"(a) The council shall prepare and submit to the Judicial Council of Georgia an annual proposed budget necessary for fulfilling the purposes of this article in accordance with Code Section 45–12–78. The budget request shall be based on the previous year's expenditures and budget requests submitted by each circuit public defender, the multicounty public defender office or its successor, and the office of the mental health advocate. The council's budget shall not contain any request for funding for the operation of the circuit public defender offices nor any other funding related to funding for this article until the budget submission for Fiscal Year 2005. The council is also authorized to seek, solicit, apply for, and utilize funds from any public or private source to use in fulfilling the purposes of this article."

"(c) The director of the Administrative Office of the Courts shall provide general administrative support, which shall include purchasing, payroll, and similar administrative services, to the council.

"(d) The director of the Administrative Office of the Courts shall not reduce or modify the budget of the council and may not in any manner use funds appropriated to or otherwise designated for the council."

Laws 2004, Ex. Sess., Act 4, § 27, subsec. (c), provides:

"(c) Sections 18 through 24 of this Act shall become effective on January 1, 2005."

The 2006 amendment by Act 453 was a provision contained in a correction bill.

The 2006 amendment by Act 749, in subsec. (b), substituted "Office of the Georgia Capital Defender" for "multicounty public defender office".

The 2007 amendment by Act 22, in subsec. (a), substituted "Office of Planning and Budget" for "Judicial Council of Georgia" in the first sentence, added "; provided, however, that the General Assembly shall not be obligated to appropriate such amount for indigent defense" at the end of the second sentence, and deleted the third sentence which had read: "For fiscal years beginning prior to July 1, 2006, such funds collected for indigent defense may be estimated by the council based on actual monthly collections received prior to the council's budget request submission."

The 2008 amendment by Act 25, in par. (c)(3), substituted "the Senate Budget Office, and the House Budget Office" for "and the legislative budget analyst".

The 2008 amendment by Act 729 rewrote this section, which formerly read:

"(a) The council shall prepare and submit to the Office of Planning and Budget an annual proposed budget necessary for fulfilling the purposes of this article in accordance with Code Section 45–12–78. The budget request shall be based on the previous year's expenditures and budget requests submitted by each circuit public defender, the Office of the Georgia Capital Defender, and the office of the mental health advocate. The council's total budget request for funding for the operations of the circuit public defender offices and the council's programs shall not exceed the amount of funds collected for indigent defense pursuant to Code Sections 15–21–73 and 15–21A–6; provided, however, that the General Assembly shall not be obligated to appropriate such amount for indigent defense. The council is also authorized to seek, solicit, apply for, and utilize funds from any public or private source to use in fulfilling the purposes of this article.

"(b) The budget of the council shall include the budget of all circuit public defenders and other offices and entities, including conflict defender offices and appointed attorneys providing indigent defense representation under the authority of this article and the Office of the Georgia Capital Defender and the office of the mental health advocate.

"(c)(1) Subject to the provisions of paragraphs (3) and (4) of this subsection, expenses paid by the council pursuant to this Code section shall be paid out of funds as may be appropriated by the General Assembly.

"(2) On or before June 1 of each year, the council shall establish and furnish to each circuit public defender and the state auditor the travel budget for each judicial circuit based on the amount appropriated by the General Assembly for travel.

"(3) In determining the travel budget for each judicial circuit, the council shall consider the budget request submitted by the circuit public defender of each judicial circuit, the geographic size and the caseload of each circuit, and other facts as may be relevant. The council is authorized to establish a contingency reserve of not more than 3 percent of the total amount appropriated by the General Assembly in order to meet any expenses which could not be reasonably anticipated. The council shall submit to each circuit public defender, the state auditor, the Senate Budget Office, and the House Budget Office a monthly report showing the budget amount of expenditures made under the travel budget. The council may periodically review and adjust the travel budget as may be necessary to carry out the purposes of this subsection.

"(4) Neither the circuit public defender nor any personnel compensated by the state pursuant to the provisions of this article shall be reimbursed from state funds for any expenses for which the person has been reimbursed from funds other than state funds; provided, however, that the governing authority of the county or counties comprising the judicial circuit are authorized to provide travel advances or to reimburse expenses which may be incurred by the person in the performance of his or her official duties to the extent the expenses are not reimbursed by the state as provided in this Code section."

Laws 2008, Act 729, § 43 provides:

"This Act shall become effective on July 1, 2008; provided, however, that for purposes of the appointment of the councilmembers and circuit public defender supervisory panel members, this Act shall become effective upon its approval by the Governor or upon its becoming law without such approval."

In 2008, the Code Commission, due to irreconcilable conflicts, treated the amendment of this section by Laws 2008, Act 25, § 1–9, as superseded by Laws 2008, Act 729, § 33. See Butts County v. Strahan, 107 S.E. 163, 151 Ga. 417 (1921).

§ 17–12–27. Assistant public defenders

(a) Subject to the provisions of this Code section, the circuit public defender in each judicial circuit is authorized to appoint:

(1) One assistant public defender for each superior court judge authorized for the circuit, excluding the chief judge and senior judges; and

(2) Subject to funds being appropriated by the General Assembly or otherwise available, additional assistant public defenders as may be authorized by the council. In authorizing additional assistant public defenders, the council shall consider the caseload, present staff, and resources available to each circuit public defender and shall make authorizations as will contribute to the efficiency of individual circuit public defenders and the effectiveness of providing adequate legal defense for indigent defendants.

(b) Each assistant public defender appointed pursuant to subsection (a) of this Code section shall be classified based on education, training, and experience. The jobs of assistant public defenders and the minimum qualifications required for appointment or promotion to each job shall be established by the council based on education, training, and experience and in accordance with the provisions of Code Sections 17–12–30 and 17–12–34.

(c) Each assistant public defender appointed pursuant to this Code section shall be compensated based on a salary range established in accordance with subsection (c) of Code Section 17–12–30. The salary range for each job established in accordance with subsection (b) of this Code section shall be as follows:

(1) Assistant public defender I. Not less than $38,124.00 nor more than 65 percent of the compensation of the circuit public defender;

(2) Assistant public defender II. Not less than $40,884.00 nor more than 70 percent of the compensation of the circuit public defender;

(3) Assistant public defender III. Not less than $45,108.00 nor more than 80 percent of the compensation of the circuit public defender; and

(4) Assistant public defender IV. Not less than $52,176.00 nor more than 90 percent of the compensation of the circuit public defender.

(d) All personnel actions involving attorneys appointed pursuant to this Code section shall be made by the circuit public defender in writing in accordance with the provisions of Code Section 17–12–30.

(e)(1) All salary advancements shall be based on quality of work, education, and performance.

(2) The salary of an assistant public defender appointed pursuant to this Code section may be increased at the first of the calendar month following the anniversary of his or her appointment.

(3) The salary of any assistant public defender who, subsequent to his or her appointment pursuant to this Code section, is awarded an LL.M. or S.J.D. degree by a law school recognized by the State Bar of Georgia from which a graduate of or student enrolled therein is permitted to take the bar examination or by a law school accredited by the American Bar Association or the Association of American Law Schools may be increased effective on the first day of the calendar month following the award of the degree, provided that such advancement does not exceed the maximum of the salary range applicable to the attorney's job classification.

(f) Any assistant public defender appointed pursuant to this Code section may be promoted to the next highest job at any time the attorney meets the minimum qualifications for such job, but in order to be eligible for promotion, the attorney shall have served not less than 12 months in the job from which the attorney is to be promoted. When an assistant public defender is promoted to the next highest job, the assistant public defender shall enter the higher job at an annual salary greater than the annual salary the assistant public defender was receiving immediately prior to the promotion.

(g) All full-time state paid employees of the office of the circuit public defender shall be state employees in the unclassified service of the State Personnel Administration with all benefits of such appointed state employees as provided by law. A circuit public defender, assistant public defender, or local public defender may be issued an employee identification card by his or her employing agency; provided, however, no employer of any such public defender shall issue nor shall any public defender display, wear, or carry any badge, shield, card, or other item that is similar to a law enforcement officer's badge or that could be reasonably construed to indicate that the public defender is a peace officer or law enforcement official.

(h) Notwithstanding the provisions of subsection (g) of this Code section, an employee of a local public defender office who was an employee of the office on June 30, 2004, and who becomes a circuit public defender or an employee of a circuit public defender office before July 1, 2005, may elect, with the consent of the former employer and the consent of the council, to remain an employee of the entity for which the employee worked as a local public defender; and such entity shall be his or her employer for all purposes, including, without limitation, compensation and employee benefits. The right to make an election pursuant to this subsection shall expire on July 1, 2005. The council shall reimburse the appropriate entity for compensation, benefits, and employer contributions under the federal Social Security Act, but the total payment from the council to the entity on behalf of the employee shall not exceed the amount otherwise payable to or for the employee under the circumstance where the employee had become a state employee.

Laws 2003, Act 32, § 1, eff. Jan. 1, 2005; Laws 2004, Act 564, § 17, eff. Jan. 1, 2005; Laws 2004, Ex. Sess., Act 4, § 20, eff. Jan. 1, 2005; Laws 2005, Act 19, § 17, eff. April 7, 2005; Laws 2006, Act 749, § 9, eff. May 3, 2006; Laws 2009, Act 155, § 2, eff. July 1, 2009.

Historical and Statutory Notes

The 2004 amendment by Act 564 was a provision contained in a correction bill.

Laws 2004, Act 564, § 55, provides:

"This Act shall become effective upon its approval by the Governor or upon its becoming law without such approval; except that paragraphs (5) through (9) and paragraph (12) of Section 17 of this Act shall become effective January 1, 2005; paragraph (11) of Section 17 of this Act shall become effective 11:58 P.M. on December 31, 2004; and paragraph (1) of Section 25 of this Act shall become effective July 1, 2004."

The 2004, Ex. Sess., amendment by Act 4, substituted the reference to jobs for the reference to classes throughout; substituted "range" for "schedule" in subsec. (c); in subsec. (e), par. (2), substituted "increased" for "advanced one step"; in subsec. (e), par. (3), substituted "The salary of any" for "Any", substituted "increased" for "advanced two salary steps", and substituted "job classification" for "class"; in subsec. (f), substituted "an annual salary greater than the annual salary" for "the salary step which provides an annual salary nearest to, but greater than, the annual salary"; in subsec. (g), inserted "state paid" following "All full-time"; and added subsec. (h).

Laws 2004, Ex. Sess., Act 4, § 27, subsec. (c), provides:

"(c) Sections 18 through 24 of this Act shall become effective on January 1, 2005."

The 2005 amendment by Act 19 was a provision contained in a correction bill.

The 2006 amendment by Act 749, in subsec. (g), added "A circuit public defender, assistant public defender, or local public defender may be issued an employee identification card by his or her employing agency; provided, however, no employer of any such public defender shall issue nor shall any public defender display, wear, or carry any badge, shield, card, or other item that is similar to a law enforcement officer's badge or that could be reasonably construed to indicate that the public defender is a peace officer or law enforcement official."

The 2009 amendment by Act 155 substituted "State Personnel Administration" for "State Merit System of Personnel Administration" throughout the section.

§ 17–12–28. Investigators

(a) Subject to the provisions of this Code section, the circuit public defender in each judicial circuit is authorized to appoint one investigator to assist the circuit public defender in the performance of his or her official duties in the preparation of cases for trial. Subject to funds being appropriated by the General Assembly or otherwise available, the circuit public defender in each judicial circuit may appoint additional investigators as may be authorized by the council. In authorizing additional investigators, the council shall consider the caseload, present staff, and resources available to each circuit public defender and shall make authorizations as will contribute to the efficiency of individual circuit public defenders and the effectiveness of circuit public defenders throughout the state in providing adequate legal defense for indigent defendants.

(b) An investigator appointed pursuant to this Code section shall be not less than 21 years of age and shall serve at the pleasure of the circuit public defender.

(c) An investigator appointed pursuant to this Code section shall:

(1) Assist the attorneys within the office of the circuit public defender in the preparation of cases for preliminary hearings, pretrial hearings, and trial; and

(2) Perform other duties as are required by the circuit public defender.

(d) Each investigator appointed pursuant to this Code section shall be compensated based on a salary range established pursuant to Code Section 17–12–30. The salary range for the investigator appointed pursuant to this Code section shall be not less than $30,828.00 nor more than 70 percent of the compensation of the circuit public defender from state funds.

(e)(1) Except as otherwise provided in this subsection, an investigator appointed pursuant to this Code section shall be appointed initially to the entry grade of the job on the state-wide pay ranges.

(2) Any person who is employed in a nonstate paid investigator's position within the office of the circuit public defender may be transferred to a state paid position. Such transfer shall be to the job and salary range commensurate with the education and experience of the employee.

(3) Any person who is employed as a peace officer by an agency of the executive branch of state government who is appointed as an investigator pursuant to this Code section without a break in service may be appointed to an annual

salary at least equal to the annual salary the person received on the last day of employment immediately preceding said appointment.

(4) Any person who was a certified peace officer employed on a full-time basis by this state, the United States or any of the several states, or a political subdivision or authority thereof may be appointed to the salary that gives the officer credit for experience as a full-time certified peace officer.

(f) Personnel appointed pursuant to this Code section shall be reimbursed for actual expenses incurred in the performance of their official duties.

Laws 2003, Act 32, § 1, eff. Jan. 1, 2005; Laws 2004, Act 564, § 17, eff. Jan. 1, 2005; Laws 2004, Ex. Sess., Act 4, § 21, eff. Jan. 1, 2005; Laws 2008, Act 729, § 34, eff. July 1, 2008.

Historical and Statutory Notes

The 2004 amendment by Act 564 was a provision contained in a correction bill.

Laws 2004, Act 564, § 55, provides:

"This Act shall become effective upon its approval by the Governor or upon its becoming law without such approval; except that paragraphs (5) through (9) and paragraph (12) of Section 17 of this Act shall become effective January 1, 2005; paragraph (11) of Section 17 of this Act shall become effective 11:58 P.M. on December 31, 2004; and paragraph (1) of Section 25 of this Act shall become effective July 1, 2004."

The 2004, Ex. Sess., amendment by Act 4, in subsec. (d), substituted "range" for "schedule"; and rewrote subsec. (e) which had read:

"(e)(1) Except as otherwise provided in this subsection, an investigator appointed pursuant to this Code section shall be appointed initially to the entry grade of the general pay schedule.

"(2) Any person who is employed in a nonstate paid investigator's position within the office of the circuit public defender may be transferred to a state paid position. Such transfer shall be to the salary step which is based on the number of years the person has served in the investigator position as if the person had been initially appointed pursuant to this Code section.

"(3) Any person who is employed as a peace officer by an agency of the executive branch of state government who is appointed as an investigator pursuant to this Code section without a break in service may be appointed to the salary step which is one step above the annual salary the person received on the last day of employment immediately preceding said appointment.

"(4) Any person who was a certified peace officer employed on a full-time basis by this state, the United States or any of the several states, or a political subdivision or authority thereof, may be appointed to the salary step above the entry level based on one step for every three years' experience as a full-time certified peace officer."

Laws 2004, Ex. Sess., Act 4, § 27, subsec. (c), provides:

"(c) Sections 18 through 24 of this Act shall become effective on January 1, 2005."

The 2008 amendment by Act 729, in subsec. (f), deleted a reference to § 17–12–26.

Laws 2008, Act 729, § 43 provides:

"This Act shall become effective on July 1, 2008; provided, however, that for purposes of the appointment of the councilmembers and circuit public defender supervisory panel members, this Act shall become effective upon its approval by the Governor or upon its becoming law without such approval."

§ 17–12–29. Administrative, clerical, and paraprofessional personnel

(a) Each circuit public defender is authorized to employ administrative, clerical, and paraprofessional personnel as may be authorized by the council based on funds appropriated by the General Assembly or otherwise available; provided, however, that each circuit public defender shall be authorized not less than two such personnel. In authorizing administrative, clerical, and paraprofessional personnel, the council shall consider the caseload, present staff, and resources available to each circuit public defender and shall make authorizations as will contribute to the efficiency of individual circuit public defenders in providing effective criminal defense for indigent defendants.

(b) Personnel appointed pursuant to this Code section shall be compensated based on a salary range developed in accordance with Code Section 17–12–30.

(c) All personnel actions involving personnel appointed pursuant to this Code section shall be in accordance with the provisions of Code Section 17–12–30.

Laws 2003, Act 32, § 1, eff. Jan. 1, 2005; Laws 2004, Act 564, § 17, eff. Jan. 1, 2005; Laws 2004, Ex. Sess., Act 4, § 22, eff. Jan. 1, 2005.

Historical and Statutory Notes

The 2004 amendment by Act 564 was a provision contained in a correction bill.

Laws 2004, Act 564, § 55, provides:

"This Act shall become effective upon its approval by the Governor or upon its becoming law without such approval; except that paragraphs (5) through (9) and paragraph (12) of Section 17 of this Act shall become effective January 1, 2005; paragraph (11) of Section 17 of this Act shall become effective 11:58 P.M. on December 31, 2004; and paragraph (1) of Section 25 of this Act shall become effective July 1, 2004."

The 2004, Ex. Sess., amendment by Act 4, in subsec. (b), substituted "range" for "schedule".

Laws 2004, Ex. Sess., Act 4, § 27, subsec. (c), provides:

"(c) Sections 18 through 24 of this Act shall become effective on January 1, 2005."

§ 17–12–30. State paid personnel

(a) All state paid personnel employed by the circuit public defenders pursuant to this article shall be employees of the executive branch of state government and shall be in the unclassified service of the State Personnel Administration.

(b) Personnel employed by the circuit public defenders pursuant to this article shall have the authority, duties, powers, and responsibilities as are authorized by law or as assigned by the circuit public defender and shall serve at the pleasure of the circuit public defender.

(c)(1) The council shall establish salary ranges for each state paid position authorized by this article or any other provision of law. Salary ranges shall be similar to the state-wide and senior executive ranges adopted by the State Personnel Administration and shall provide for minimum, midpoint, and maximum salaries not to exceed the maximum allowable salary. In establishing the salary ranges, all amounts will be rounded off to the nearest whole dollar. The council may, from time to time, revise the salary ranges to include across-the-board increases which the General Assembly may from time to time authorize in the General Appropriations Act.

(2) The circuit public defender shall fix the compensation of each state paid employee appointed pursuant to this article in accordance with the job to which the person is appointed and the appropriate salary range.

(3) All salary advancements shall be based on quality of work, training, and performance. The salary of state paid personnel appointed pursuant to this article may be increased at the first of the calendar month following the annual anniversary of the person's appointment. No employee's salary shall be advanced beyond the maximum established in the applicable pay range.

(4) Any reduction in salary shall be made in accordance with the salary range for the position and the policies, rules, or regulations adopted by the council.

(5) The compensation of state paid personnel appointed pursuant to this article shall be paid in equal installments by the council as provided by this subsection from funds appropriated for such purpose. The council may authorize employees compensated pursuant to this Code section to participate in

voluntary salary deductions as provided by Article 3 of Chapter 7 of Title 45.

(6) The governing authority of the county or counties comprising a judicial circuit may supplement the salary or fringe benefits of any state paid position appointed pursuant to this article.

(7) The governing authority of any municipality within the judicial circuit may, with the approval of the circuit public defender, supplement the salary or fringe benefits of any state paid position appointed pursuant to this article.

Laws 2003, Act 32, § 1, eff. Jan. 1, 2005; Laws 2004, Ex. Sess., Act 4, § 23, eff. Jan. 1, 2005; Laws 2007, Act 22, § 4, eff. July 1, 2007; Laws 2009, Act 155, § 2, eff. July 1, 2009.

Historical and Statutory Notes

The 2004, Ex. Sess., amendment by Act 4, rewrote subsec. (c) which had read:

"(c)(1) The council shall establish salary schedules for each state paid position authorized by this article or any other provision of law. Salary schedules shall be similar to the general and special schedules adopted by the State Merit System of Personnel Administration and shall provide for a minimum entry step and not less than ten additional steps, not to exceed the maximum allowable salary. In establishing the salary schedule, all amounts will be rounded off to the nearest whole dollar. The council may, from time to time, revise the salary schedule to include across-the-board increases which the General Assembly may from time to time authorize in the General Appropriations Act.

"(2) The circuit public defender shall fix the compensation of each state paid employee appointed pursuant to this article in accordance with the class to which the person is appointed and the appropriate step of the salary schedule.

"(3) All salary advancements shall be based on quality of work, training, and performance. The salary of state paid personnel appointed pursuant to this article may be advanced one step at the first of the calendar month following the annual anniversary of the person's appointment. No employee's salary shall be advanced beyond the maximum established in the applicable pay schedule.

"(4) Any reduction in salary shall be made in accordance with the salary schedule for the position and the policies, rules, or regulations adopted by the council.

"(5) The compensation of state paid personnel appointed pursuant to this article shall be paid in equal installments by the Department of Administrative Services as provided by this subsection from funds appropriated for such purpose. The council may, with the consent of the Department of Administrative Services, authorize employees compensated pursuant to this Code section to participate in voluntary salary deductions as provided by Article 3 of Chapter 7 of Title 45.

"(6) The governing authority of the county or counties comprising a judicial circuit may supplement the salary or fringe benefits of any state paid position appointed pursuant to this article.

"(7) The governing authority of any municipality within the judicial circuit may, with the approval of the circuit public defender, supplement the salary or fringe benefits of any state paid position appointed pursuant to this article."

Laws 2004, Ex. Sess., Act 4, § 27, subsec. (c), provides:

"(c) Sections 18 through 24 of this Act shall become effective on January 1, 2005."

The 2007 amendment by Act 22, in subsec. (a), substituted "executive branch" for "judicial branch" and deleted "in accordance with Article VI, Section VIII of the Constitution of Georgia" following branch of state government; and in subsec. (c), par. (5), deleted "the Department of Administrative Services or the Administrative Office of the Courts, as determined by" following "equal installments by", substituted "the council as provided by" for "the council, as provided by" and deleted ", with the consent of the Department of Administrative Services or the Administrative Office of the Courts".

Former § 17–12–30, containing the article short title, derived from Laws 1979, p. 367, § 1, was repealed by Laws 2003, Act 32, § 1, eff. January 1, 2005.

The 2009 amendment by Act 155 substituted "State Personnel Administration" for "State Merit System of Personnel Administration" throughout the section.

§ 17–12–31. Employment of additional assistant or deputy circuit public defenders, other employees, or independent contractors

(a) The circuit public defender in each judicial circuit may employ additional assistant circuit public defenders, deputy circuit public defenders, or other attorneys, investigators, paraprofessionals, clerical assistants, and other employees or independent contractors if the employment of such additional personnel is provided for by local law or if the employment of such additional personnel is specifically authorized and funded by the governing authority of the county or counties comprising the judicial circuit. The circuit public defender shall define the duties and fix the title of any attorney or other employee of the office of the circuit public defender.

(b) Personnel employed by the circuit public defender pursuant to this Code section shall serve at the pleasure of the circuit public defender and shall be compensated by the county or counties comprising the judicial circuit in the manner and in an amount fixed either by local Act or by the circuit public defender with the specific approval of the county or counties comprising the judicial circuit.

Laws 2003, Act 32, § 1, eff. Jan. 1, 2005; Laws 2008, Act 729, § 35, eff. July 1, 2008.

Historical and Statutory Notes

The 2008 amendment by Act 729, in subsec. (a), substituted "or independent contractors if the employment of such additional personnel is provided for by local law or if the employment of such additional personnel is specifically authorized and funded" for "or independent contractors as may be provided for by local law or as may be authorized"; and in subsec. (b), substituted "in the manner and in an amount fixed either by local Act or by the circuit public defender with the specific approval" for "the manner and amount of compensation to be paid to be fixed either by local Act or by the circuit public defender with the approval".

Laws 2008, Act 729, § 43 provides:

"This Act shall become effective on July 1, 2008; provided, however, that for purposes of the appointment of the councilmembers and circuit public defender supervisory panel members, this Act shall become effective upon its approval by the Governor or upon its becoming law without such approval."

Former § 17–12–31, relating to the state policy to provide the constitutional guarantees of the right to counsel and equal access to the courts, derived from Laws 1979, p. 367, § 2, was repealed by Laws 2003, Act 32, § 1, eff. January 1, 2005.

§ 17–12–32. County or city contracts with council to provide additional personnel

The governing authority of any county or municipality within the judicial circuit which provides additional personnel for the office of circuit public defender may contract with the council to provide such additional personnel in the same manner as is provided for state paid personnel in this article. Any such personnel shall be considered state employees and shall be entitled to the same fringe benefits as other state paid personnel employed by the circuit public defender pursuant to this article. The governing authority of such county or municipality shall transfer to the council such funds as may be necessary to cover the compensation, benefits, travel, and other expenses for such personnel.

Laws 2003, Act 32, § 1, eff. Jan. 1, 2005; Laws 2006, Act 749, § 10, eff. May 3, 2006.

Historical and Statutory Notes

The 2006 amendment by Act 749 substituted "council to provide" for "Department of Administrative Services to provide" and substituted "transfer to the council" for "transfer to the department".

Former § 17–12–32, relating to the Georgia Indigent Defense Council, derived from Laws 1979, p. 367, § 4; Laws 1993, p. 308, § 1, was repealed by Laws 2003, Act 32, § 1, eff. January 1, 2005.

§ 17–12–33. Assistant public defenders or other attorneys; private practice of law; admission to practice; powers and duties

(a) Any assistant public defender or other attorney at law employed full time by the circuit public defender who is compensated in whole or in part by state funds shall not engage in the private practice of law for profit or serve concurrently in any judicial office.

(b) Any assistant public defender or any other attorney at law employed by the circuit public defender shall be a member of the State Bar of Georgia and shall be admitted to practice before the appellate courts of this state. The assistant public defender shall serve at the pleasure of the circuit public defender and shall have such authority, powers, and duties as may be assigned by the circuit public defender.

Laws 2003, Act 32, § 1, eff. Jan. 1, 2005; Laws 2004, Act 564, § 17, eff. Jan. 1, 2005; Laws 2008, Act 729, § 36, eff. July 1, 2008.

Historical and Statutory Notes

The 2004 amendment by Act 564 was a provision contained in a correction bill.

Laws 2004, Act 564, § 55, provides:

"This Act shall become effective upon its approval by the Governor or upon its becoming law without such approval; except that paragraphs (5) through (9) and paragraph (12) of Section 17 of this Act shall become effective January 1, 2005; paragraph (11) of Section 17 of this Act shall become effective 11:58 P.M. on December 31, 2004; and paragraph (1) of Section 25 of this Act shall become effective July 1, 2004."

Former § 17–12–33, relating to the purposes and duties of the Georgia Indigent Defense Council, derived from Laws 1979, p. 367, § 5, was repealed by Laws 2003, Act 32, § 1, eff. January 1, 2005.

The 2008 amendment by Act 729, in subsec. (a), at the end of the subsection, added "or serve concurrently in any judicial office".

Laws 2008, Act 729, § 43 provides:

"This Act shall become effective on July 1, 2008; provided, however, that for purposes of the appointment of the councilmembers and circuit public defender supervisory panel members, this Act shall become effective upon its approval by the Governor or upon its becoming law without such approval."

§ 17–12–34. Offices, utilities, telephone expenses, materials, and supplies

The governing authority of the county shall provide, in conjunction and cooperation with the other counties in the judicial circuit and in a pro rata share according to the population of each county, appropriate offices, utilities, telephone expenses, materials, and supplies as may be necessary to equip, maintain, and furnish the office or offices of the circuit public defender in an orderly and efficient manner. The provisions of an office, utilities, telephone expenses, materials, and supplies shall be subject to the budget procedures required by Article 1 of Chapter 81 of Title 36.

Laws 2003, Act 32, § 1, eff. Jan. 1, 2005.

Historical and Statutory Notes

Former § 17–12–34, relating to personnel and facilities, derived from Laws 1979, p. 367, § 6; Laws 1993, p. 308, § 2, was repealed by Laws 2003, Act 32, § 1, eff. January 1, 2005.

§ 17–12–35. Public or private contracts, funds, and grants

A circuit public defender office may contract with and may accept funds and grants from any public or private source.

Laws 2003, Act 32, § 1, eff. Jan. 1, 2005.

Historical and Statutory Notes

Former § 17–12–35, relating to records and reports, derived from Laws 1979, p. 367, § 7, was repealed by Laws 2003, Act 32, § 1, eff. January 1, 2005.

§ 17–12–36. Alternative delivery systems for judicial circuits composed of a single county

(a) The council may permit a judicial circuit composed of a single county to continue in effect an alternative delivery system to the one set forth in this article if:

(1) The delivery system:

(A) Has a full-time director and staff and had been fully operational for at least two years on July 1, 2003; or

(B) Is administered by the county administrative office of the courts or the office of the court administrator of the superior court and had been fully operational for at least two years on July 1, 2003;

(2) The council, by majority vote of the entire council, determines that the delivery system meets or exceeds its rules, regulations, policies, and standards, including, without limitation, caseload standards, as the council adopts;

(3) The governing authority of the county comprising the judicial circuit enacts a resolution expressing its desire to continue its delivery system and transmits a copy of such resolution to the council not later than September 30, 2004; and

(4) The governing authority of the county comprising the judicial circuit enacts a resolution agreeing to fully fund its delivery system.

(b) A judicial circuit composed of a single county may request an alternative delivery system only one time; provided, however, that if such judicial circuit's request for an alternative delivery system was disapproved on or before December 31, 2004, such judicial circuit may make one further request on or before September 1, 2005. The council shall allow such judicial circuit to have a hearing on such judicial circuit's request.

(c) The council shall make a determination with regard to continuation of an alternative delivery system not later than December 1, 2005, and if the council determines that such judicial circuit's alternative delivery system does not meet the standards as established by the council, the council shall notify such judicial circuit of its deficiencies in writing and shall allow such judicial circuit an opportunity to cure such deficiencies. The council shall make a final determination with regard to continuation of an alternative delivery system on or before December 31, 2005. Initial and subsequent approvals of alternative delivery systems shall be by a majority vote of the entire council.

(d) Any circuit whose alternative delivery system is disapproved at any time shall be governed by the provisions of this article other than this Code section.

(e) In the event an alternative delivery system is approved, the council shall annually review the operation of such system and determine whether such system is meeting the standards as established by the council and is eligible to continue operating as an approved alternative delivery system. In the event the council determines that such system is not meeting the standards as established by the council, the council shall provide written notice to such system of the deficiencies and shall provide such system an opportunity to cure such deficiencies.

(f) In the event an alternative delivery system is approved, it shall keep and maintain appropriate records, which shall include the number of persons represented; the offenses charged; the outcome of each case; the expenditures made in providing services; and any other information requested by the council.

(g) In the event the council disapproves an alternative delivery system either in its initial application or annual review, such system may appeal such decision to the Supreme Court of

Georgia under such rules and procedures as shall be prescribed by the Supreme Court.

(h) An approved alternative delivery system shall be paid by the council, from funds available to the council, in an amount equal to the amount that would have been allocated to the judicial circuit for the minimum salary of the circuit public defender, the assistant circuit public defenders, the investigator, and the administrative staff, exclusive of benefits, if the judicial circuit was not operating an alternative delivery system.

Laws 2003, Act 32, § 1, eff. Jan. 1, 2005; Laws 2004, Ex. Sess., Act 4, § 24, eff. Jan. 1, 2005; Laws 2005, Act 281, § 2, eff. May 6, 2005; Laws 2008, Act 729, §§ 37, 38, eff. July 1, 2008.

Historical and Statutory Notes

The 2004, Ex. Sess., amendment by Act 4, rewrote subsec. (a), par. (1), which had read:

"(1) The delivery system has a full-time director and staff and had been fully operational for at least two years on July 1, 2003;".

Laws 2004, Ex. Sess., Act 4, § 27, subsec. (c), provides:

"(c) Sections 18 through 24 of this Act shall become effective on January 1, 2005."

The 2005 amendment by Act 281 rewrote subsecs. (b), (c) and (e); and added subsec. (g). Prior to amendment, subsecs. (b), (c) and (e) had read:

"(b) A judicial circuit composed of a single county may request an alternative delivery system only one time, which request shall be made on or before September 30, 2004.

"(c) The council shall make a final determination with regard to continuation of an alternative delivery system not later than December 31, 2004. Initial and subsequent approvals of alternative delivery systems shall be by a majority vote of the entire council."

"(e) In the event an alternative delivery system is approved, the council shall annually review the operation of such system and determine whether such system is meeting the standards as established by the council and is eligible to continue operating as an approved alternative delivery system."

The 2008 amendment by Act 729, in subsec. (a), par. (2), inserted "rules, regulations, policies, and" following "determines that the delivery system meets or exceeds its" and added subsec. (h).

Laws 2008, Act 729, § 43 provides:

"This Act shall become effective on July 1, 2008; provided, however, that for purposes of the appointment of the councilmembers and circuit public defender supervisory panel members, this Act shall become effective upon its approval by the Governor or upon its becoming law without such approval."

Former § 17-12-36, relating to funding for local indigent defense programs, derived from Laws 1979, p. 367, § 8; Laws 1998, p. 568, § 1, was repealed by Laws 2003, Act 32, § 1, eff. January 1, 2005.

§ 17-12-37. Effective date of article

This article shall become effective on January 1, 2005; provided, however, that the council and the circuit public defender selection panels shall be authorized to take administrative actions as may be necessary or appropriate to prepare for and phase-in full implementation of this article on or after December 31, 2003.

Laws 2003, Act 32, § 1, eff. Jan. 1, 2005.

Historical and Statutory Notes

Former § 17-12-37, relating to notification of availability of funds and to local tripartite governing committees, derived from Laws 1979, p. 367, § 10; Laws 1993, p. 308, § 3, was repealed by Laws 2003, Act 32, § 1, eff. January 1, 2005.

§§ 17-12-38 to 17-12-39. Repealed by Laws 2003, Act 32, § 1, eff. January, 1, 2005

Historical and Statutory Notes

Section 17-12-38, relating to local tripartite governing committees, was derived from Laws 1979, p. 367, § 11.

Section 17-12-38.1, specifying in which cases legal representation would be provided, was derived from Laws 1994, p. 355, § 1.

Section 17-12-39, providing no person could be assigned the primary responsibility of representing an indigent person unless he was authorized to practice law in the state and was otherwise competent to defend a person, was derived from Laws 1979, p. 367, § 14.

Article 3

Assistance by Third-Year Law Student or Staff Instructors

Revision of Chapter 12

Laws 2003, Act 32, § 1, added this article effective January 1, 2005. See § 17-12-45.

Former Article 3, Defense of Indigents in Capital Cases, consisting of §§ 17-12-60 to 17-12-62, was repealed by Laws 2003, Act 32, § 1, effective January 1, 2005.

§ 17-12-40. Definitions

As used in this article, the term:

(1) "Circuit public defender" means any circuit public defender of this state or assistants of such officer.

(2) "Criminal proceeding" means any investigation, trial, juvenile proceeding, adjudicatory hearing, or other legal proceeding by which a person's liability for a crime is investigated or determined, commencing with the investigation and including the final disposition of the case.

(3) "Law school" means a law school within or outside this state which is approved by the American Bar Association or which is authorized to operate under Code Section 20-3-250.8.

(4) "Staff instructor" means a full-time professional staff instructor of a law school in this state who has been admitted to the bar of another state but who has not yet been admitted to the bar of this state.

(5) "Third-year law student" means a student regularly enrolled and in good standing in a law school within or outside this state who has satisfactorily completed at least two-thirds of the requirements for the first professional degree in law (J.D. or its equivalent) in not less than four semesters or six quarters of residence.

Laws 2003, Act 32, § 1, eff. Jan. 1, 2005.

Historical and Statutory Notes

Former § 17-12-40, relating to recovery of payment or reimbursement from defendant, derived from Laws 1979, p. 367, § 12, was repealed by Laws 2003, Act 32, § 1, eff. January 1, 2005.

§ 17-12-41. Assistance in criminal proceedings

An authorized third-year law student or staff instructor, when under the supervision of a circuit public defender, may assist in criminal proceedings within this state as if admitted and licensed to practice law in this state except that all pleadings and other entries of record must be signed by a circuit public defender or by his or her duly appointed assistant and that, in the conduct of a trial or other criminal proceeding, a circuit public defender or his or her duly appointed assistant must be physically present.

Laws 2003, Act 32, § 1, eff. Jan. 1, 2005.

Historical and Statutory Notes

Former § 17-12-41, relating to guidelines for operation of the article, derived from Laws 1979, p. 367, § 9; Laws 1990, p. 8, § 17; Laws 1998, p. 128, § 17, was repealed by Laws 2003, Act 32, § 1, eff. January 1, 2005.

§ 17–12–42. Authorization to assist circuit public defender; certification

A third-year law student or staff instructor may be authorized to assist a circuit public defender in such form and manner as the judge of the court may prescribe, taking care that the requirements of this article and the good moral character of the third-year law student or staff instructor are properly certified by the dean of the law school.

Laws 2003, Act 32, § 1, eff. Jan. 1, 2005.

Historical and Statutory Notes

Former § 17–12–42, providing for immunity from action arising from any acts in relation to implementing the article, derived from Laws 1979, p. 367, § 16, was repealed by Laws 2003, Act 32, § 1, eff. January 1, 2005.

§ 17–12–43. File of certificates, oaths, orders; time of authorization

As to each third-year law student or staff instructor authorized to assist a circuit public defender, there shall be kept on file in the office of the clerk of the court in the county where such authority is to be exercised the dean's certificate, the student's and instructor's oaths, and the judge's order as contemplated under Code Section 17–12–42. The authority to assist a circuit public defender as allowed under this Code section shall extend for no longer than 18 months. If during this period any change occurs in the status of the student or instructor at the law school in which he or she was enrolled or employed, that is, if the student ceases his or her enrollment, is suspended, or is expelled or if the instructor ceases his or her employment or is released by the school, any such authority shall terminate and be revoked.

Laws 2003, Act 32, § 1, eff. Jan. 1, 2005.

Historical and Statutory Notes

Former § 17–12–43, providing for continuation of existing local programs, derived from Laws 1979, p. 367, § 3, was repealed by Laws 2003, Act 32, § 1, eff. January 1, 2005.

§ 17–12–44. Qualifications not required

Any third-year law student or staff instructor authorized to assist a circuit public defender under this article is not required to possess the qualifications for appointment to the office of circuit public defender or appointment as an assistant circuit public defender as provided in Article 1 of this chapter.

Laws 2003, Act 32, § 1, eff. Jan. 1, 2005.

Historical and Statutory Notes

In 2003, the Code Commission substituted "this article" for "this Code section". See § 28–9–5.

Former § 17–12–44, relating to appointment of counsel by the court, derived from Laws 1979, p. 367, § 15, was repealed by Laws 2003, Act 32, § 1, eff. January 1, 2005.

§ 17–12–45. Effective date of article

This article shall become effective on January 1, 2005.

Laws 2003, Act 32, § 1, eff. Jan. 1, 2005.

Historical and Statutory Notes

Former § 17–12–45, relating to creation and purpose of the mental health advocacy division, derived from Laws 1996, p. 1636, § 1; Code 1981, § 17–12–45, was repealed by Laws 2003, Act 32, § 1, eff. January 1, 2005.

§§ 17–12–46 to 17–12–49. Repealed by Laws 2003, Act 32, § 1, eff. January, 1, 2005

Historical and Statutory Notes

Section 17–12–46, providing the mental health advocacy division of the Georgia Indigent Defense Council was a legal entity, was derived from Laws 1996, p. 1636, § 1.

Section 17–12–47, relating to management of the mental health advocacy division, was derived from Laws 1996, p. 1636, § 1.

Section 17–12–48, relating to the budget of the mental health advocacy division, was derived from Laws 1996, p. 1636, § 1.

Section 17–12–49, relating to the mental health advocate, was derived from Laws 1996, p. 1636, § 1.

Article 3A

Reimbursement for Legal Services

§ 17–12–50. Definitions

As used in this article, the term:

(1) "Paid in part" means payment by a county or municipality for a part of the cost of the provision of indigent defense services pursuant to a contract with a circuit public defender office as set forth in subsection (d) of Code Section 17–12–23. The term shall not include payment by a county or municipality for office space and other supplies as set forth in Code Section 17–12–34.

(2) "Public defender" means an attorney employed by a circuit public defender office or any other attorney who is paid from public funds to represent an indigent person in a criminal case.

Laws 2006, Act 739, § 6, eff. July 1, 2006; Laws 2008, Act 729, § 39, eff. July 1, 2008.

Historical and Statutory Notes

The 2008 amendment by Act 729, in par. (1), substituted "shall not" for "does not"; and in par. (2), deleted conflict defender attorneys from the scope of the definition of "public defender".

Laws 2008, Act 729, § 43 provides:

"This Act shall become effective on July 1, 2008; provided, however, that for purposes of the appointment of the councilmembers and circuit public defender supervisory panel members, this Act shall become effective upon its approval by the Governor or upon its becoming law without such approval."

Former § 17–12–50, relating to employment of personnel, derived from Laws 1996, p. 1636, § 1; Code 1981, § 17–12–50, was repealed by Laws 2003, Act 32, § 1, effective July 1, 2005.

§ 17–12–51. Repayment of costs of legal representation as condition of probation; financial hardship

(a) When a defendant who is represented by a public defender, who is paid in part or in whole by a county, enters a plea of nolo contendere, first offender, or guilty or is otherwise convicted, the court may impose as a condition of probation repayment of all or a portion of the cost for providing legal representation and other expenses of the defense if the payment does not impose a financial hardship upon the defendant or the defendant's dependent or dependents. The defendant shall make the payment through the probation department to the county.

(b) When a defendant who is represented by a public defender, who is paid in part or in whole by a municipality, enters a plea of nolo contendere, first offender, or guilty or is otherwise convicted, the court may impose as a condition of probation repayment of all or a portion of the cost for providing legal representation and other expenses of the defense if the payment does not impose a financial hardship upon the defendant or the defendant's dependent or dependents. The defendant shall make the payment through the probation department to the municipality.

(c) If a defendant who is represented by a public defender, who is paid for entirely by the state, enters a plea of nolo contendere, first offender, or guilty or is otherwise convicted, the court may impose as a condition of probation repayment of all or a portion of the cost for providing legal representation and other costs of the defense if the payment does not impose a financial hardship upon such defendant or such defendant's dependent or dependents. Such defendant shall make such payment through the probation department to the Georgia Public Defender Standards Council for payment to the general fund of the state treasury.

(d) In determining whether or not a payment imposed under this Code section imposes a financial hardship upon a defendant or defendant's dependent or dependents and in determining the amount of the payment to impose, the court shall consider the factors set forth in Code Section 17-14-10. The public defender may provide the court with an estimate of the cost for providing to the defendant the legal representation and other expenses of the defense. If requested by the defendant, the court shall hold a hearing to determine the amount to be paid.

(e) This Code section shall not apply to a disposition involving a child pursuant to Chapter 11 of Title 15, relating to juvenile proceedings.

Laws 2006, Act 739, § 6, eff. July 1, 2006; Laws 2008, Act 729, § 40, eff. July 1, 2008.

Historical and Statutory Notes

The 2008 amendment by Act 729, in subsec. (c), substituted "such" for "the" throughout the subsection, and deleted the last sentence relating to the intent of the General Assembly.

Laws 2008, Act 729, § 43 provides:

"This Act shall become effective on July 1, 2008; provided, however, that for purposes of the appointment of the councilmembers and circuit public defender supervisory panel members, this Act shall become effective upon its approval by the Governor or upon its becoming law without such approval."

Former § 17-12-51, relating to representation of persons found not guilty by reason of insanity, derived from Laws 1996, p. 1636, § 1; Code 1981, § 17-12-51, was repealed by Laws 2003, Act 32, § 1, effective July 1, 2005.

§ 17-12-52. Reimbursement to county or municipality for legal assistance

(a) A county or municipality may recover payment or reimbursement from a person who has received legal assistance from a public defender paid in part or in whole by the county or municipality:

(1) If the person was not eligible to receive such legal assistance; or

(2) If the person has been ordered to pay for the legal representation and other expenses of the defense pursuant to Code Section 17-12-51 and has not paid for the legal services.

(b) An action shall be brought within four years after the date on which the legal services were received.

(c) In determining the amount of the payment imposed under this Code section, the court shall consider the factors set forth in Code Section 17-14-10. The public defender may provide the court with an estimate of the cost for providing to the defendant the legal representation and other expenses of the defense.

(d) This Code section shall not apply to proceedings involving a child pursuant to Chapter 11 of Title 15, relating to juvenile proceedings.

Laws 2006, Act 739, § 6, eff. July 1, 2006.

§§ 17-12-60 to 17-12-62. Repealed by Laws 2003, Act 32, § 1, eff. January, 1, 2005

Historical and Statutory Notes

Section 17-12-60, relating to appointment of attorneys in capital cases, was derived from Laws 1953, Nov.-Dec. Sess., p. 478, § 1; Laws 1992, p. 1963, § 1.

Section 17-12-61, appeals in capital cases where defendant is indigent, was derived from Laws 1953, Nov.-Dec. Sess., p. 478, § 2; Laws 1990, p. 8, § 17; Laws 1993, p. 1402, § 18.

Section 17-12-62, relating to attorney compensation, was derived from Laws 1953, Nov.-Dec. Sess., p. 478, § 3.

§ 17-12-70 to 17-12-72. Repealed by Laws 2003, Act. 32, § 1, eff. December 31, 2003

Historical and Statutory Notes

Section 17-12-70, relating to legislative findings, was derived from Laws 1984, p. 495, § 1.

Section 17-12-71, relating to public defender appointments, staff, expenses and funding, and immunity, was derived from Laws 1984, p. 495, § 1.

Section 17-12-72, providing counties were not prevented from establishing indigent defense programs, was derived from Laws 1984, p. 495, § 1; Laws 1990, p. 8, § 17.

Article 4

Mental Health Advocacy for Insane

Revision of Chapter 12

Laws 2003, Act 32, § 1, added this article effective December 31, 2003. See § 17-12-88.

Former Article 4, Public Defenders, consisting of §§ 17-12-70 to 17-12-72, was repealed by Laws 2003, Act 32, § 1, effective December 31, 2003.

§ 17-12-80. Qualification as indigent person; verification

(a) In order to retain funding as provided in Code Sections 15-21-74 and 15-21A-6, a governing authority shall verify that the applicant qualifies as an indigent person. The governing authority shall establish the methodology for verification and fund such process. The governing authority shall produce auditable information to the council to substantiate its verification process as requested by the council or its director.

(b) The council shall establish rules and regulations to determine approval of an indigent person verification system and shall annually provide written notification to the Georgia Superior Court Clerks' Cooperative Authority as to whether or not a governing authority has an approved indigent person verification system.

(c) The governing authority shall advise the circuit public defender, if applicable, or the administrator of the indigent defense system for the jurisdiction of the name of each person who has applied for legal services and provide identifying information for those persons who are financially eligible for services within one business day of such person's application for services.

Laws 2008, Act 729, § 41, eff. July 1, 2008.

Historical and Statutory Notes

Laws 2008, Act 729, § 43 provides:

"This Act shall become effective on July 1, 2008; provided, however, that for purposes of the appointment of the councilmembers and circuit public defender supervisory panel members, this Act shall become effective upon its approval by the Governor or upon its becoming law without such approval."

Former section 17–12–80, providing the definition of the word "office", was repealed by Laws 2008, Act 729, § 41, effective July 1, 2008.

§ 17–12–81 to 17–12–88. Repealed by Laws 2008, Act 729, § 41, eff. July 1, 2008.

Historical and Statutory Notes

Repealed § 17–12–81, relating to the creation of the mental health advocacy office, was derived from Laws 2003, Act 32, § 1.

Repealed § 17–12–82, relating to the powers of the office, was derived from Laws 2003, Act 32, § 1.

Repealed § 17–12–83, relating to management of the office, was derived from Laws 2003, Act 32, § 1.

Repealed § 17–12–84, relating to the office budget, was derived from Laws 2003, Act 32, § 1.

Repealed § 17–12–85, relating to appointment of a mental health advocate, was derived from Laws 2003, Act 32, § 1.

Repealed § 17–12–86, relating to employment of personnel, was derived from Laws 2003, Act 32, § 1.

Repealed § 17–12–87, relating to representation of persons prior to and after a finding of not guilty by reason of insanity, was derived from Laws 2003, Act 32, § 1.

Repealed § 17–12–88, relating to the effective date of the article, was derived from Laws 2003, Act 32, § 1.

§§ 17–12–90 to 17–12–97. Repealed by Laws 2003, Act. 32, § 1, eff. December 31, 2003

Historical and Statutory Notes

Section 17–12–90, containing definitions, was derived from Laws 1992, p. 1963, § 2.

Section 17–12–91, creating the office of the multicounty public defender, was derived from Laws 1992, p. 1963, § 2.

Section 17–12–92, relating to the nature and powers of the office of the multicounty public defender, was derived from Laws 1992, p. 1963, § 2.

Section 17–12–93, relating to management of the office, was derived from Laws 1992, p. 1963, § 2.

Section 17–12–94, relating to the annual budget, was derived from Laws 1992, p. 1963, § 2.

Section 17–12–95, relating to the appointment, qualifications, and compensation of the multicounty public defender, was derived from Laws 1992, p. 1963, § 2.

Section 17–12–96, relating to office staffing and competency of primary counsel, was derived from Laws 1992, p. 1963, § 2.

Section 17–12–97, relating to duties and responsibilities of the office, was derived from Laws 1992, p. 1963, § 2.

Article 5

Office of Multicounty Public Defender [Repealed]

Revision of Chapter 12

Laws 2003, Act 32, § 1, added this article effective December 31, 2003, consisting of §§ 17–12–100 to 17–12–108, and repealed it effective December 31, 2004.

Former Article 5, Office of Multicounty Public Defender, consisting of §§ 17–12–90 to 17–12–97, was repealed by Laws 2003, Act 32, § 1, effective December 31, 2003.

§§ 17–12–100 to 17–12–108. Repealed by Laws 2003, Act 32, § 1, eff. Dec. 31, 2004 (§ 17–12–108)

Historical and Statutory Notes

Section 17–12–100, containing definitions, was derived from Laws 2003, Act 32, § 1.

Section 17–12–101, creating the office of the multicounty public defender, was derived from Laws 2003, Act 32, § 1.

Section 17–12–102, relating to the nature and powers of the office, was derived from Laws 2003, Act 32, § 1.

Section 17–12–103, relating to management of the office, was derived from Laws 2003, Act 32, § 1.

Section 17–12–104, relating to the annual budget, was derived from Laws 2003, Act 32, § 1.

Section 17–12–105, relating to appointment, qualifications, and compensation of the multicounty public defender, was derived from Laws 2003, Act 32, § 1.

Section 17–12–106, relating to office staff, was derived from Laws 2003, Act 32, § 1.

Section 17–12–107, relating to duties and responsibilities of the office, was derived from Laws 2003, Act 32, § 1.

Section 17–12–108, relating to the effective date and the repeal date of the article, was derived from Laws 2003, Act 32, § 1.

Article 6

Georgia Capital Defender [REPEALED]

§§ 17–12–120 to 17–12–128. Repealed by Laws 2008, Act 729, § 42, eff. July 1, 2008.

Historical and Statutory Notes

Repealed § 17–12–120, relating to the definition of the word "office", was derived from Laws 2003, Act 32, § 1.

Repealed § 17–12–121, relating to creation of the Office of the Georgia Capital Defender, was derived from Laws 2003, Act 32, § 1.

Repealed § 17–12–122, relating to powers of the office, was derived from Laws 2003, Act 32, § 1.

Repealed § 17–12–123, relating to management of the office, was derived from Laws 2003, Act 32, § 1; Laws 2004, Act 564, § 17.

Repealed § 17–12–124, relating to an annual budget for the office, was derived from Laws 2003, Act 32, § 1; Laws 2006, Act 749, § 11.

Repealed § 17–12–125, relating to the appointment, qualifications and compensation of a capital defender, was derived from Laws 2003, Act 32, § 1.

Repealed § 17–12–126, relating to staffing of the office, was derived from Laws 2003, Act 32, § 1.

Repealed § 17–12–127, relating to the duties and responsibilities of the office, was derived from Laws 2003, Act 32, § 1; Laws 2007, Act 63, § 2.

Repealed § 17–12–127.1, relating to continuation of representation, was derived from Laws 2003, Act 32, § 1; Laws 2004, Act 564, § 17.

Repealed § 17–12–128, relating to the effective date of the article, was derived from Laws 2003, Act 32, § 1.

CHAPTER 13

CRIMINAL EXTRADITION

Article 1

General Provisions

§ 17-13-1. Rules to be observed by applicants for requisitions

In addition to rules adopted by the Governor, the following rules shall be observed as a condition precedent to obtaining a requisition by him for the extradition of any fugitive from the justice of this state:

(1) The application for a requisition shall be made to the Governor by a district attorney, prosecuting attorney of a state court, judge of a city or state court, or the mayor of any municipal corporation of this state and must show the full name of the fugitive for whom extradition is asked, the crime charged, the state or territory to which he has fled, the full name of the person suggested to act as agent of this state to receive and convey the fugitive to this state, the agent in no case to be the prosecutor; but the Governor may, in his discretion, appoint some other suitable person as agent of this state to receive and convey the fugitive. The application must also show that the ends of public justice require that the fugitive shall be brought back to this state for trial and that the requisition is not wanted for the purpose of enforcing the collection of a debt or for any private purpose whatever but solely for the purpose of a criminal prosecution as provided by law;

(2) The application shall be accompanied by the affidavit of the prosecutor, if any, stating that the requisition is wanted for the sole purpose of punishing the accused and not in any way to collect a debt or money or to enforce the payment thereof;

(3) If the fugitive has been indicted, two certified copies of the indictment or presentment shall be forwarded to the Governor with the application; and

(4) If no indictment has been preferred and an affidavit is the basis of the requisition, the affidavit shall describe the crime committed, with all the particularity required in an indictment, and two certified copies of the affidavit shall accompany the petition for the requisition.

Laws 1884-85, p. 141, § 1; Laws 1983, p. 884, § 3-22.

Formerly Penal Code 1895, § 1275; Penal Code 1910, § 1357; Code 1933, § 44-101.

§ 17-13-2. Duty of Governor

When an application is made as provided in Code Section 17-13-1 and in accordance with other rules adopted by the Governor, he shall make his requisition for the extradition of the fugitive under the seal of the office of the Governor, according to law.

Laws 1884-85, p. 141, § 2; Laws 1983, p. 649, § 1.

Formerly Penal Code 1895, § 1276; Penal Code 1910, § 1358; Code 1933, § 44-102.

§ 17-13-3. Expense authorized by county governing authority

Before any expenses shall be incurred by any officer or duly authorized agent of the state for bringing back to the county where the crime was committed any fugitive from the justice of this state, who may be beyond the limits of the state, so as to become a charge upon any county where the crime was committed, the incurring of any such expense and the amount thereof shall be first authorized by the county governing authority.

Laws 1914, p. 123, § 1.

Formerly Code 1933, § 44-201.

§ 17-13-4. Fugitives from foreign countries

Whenever a fugitive from justice from a foreign country is found within this state, and by the treaty stipulations of the United States the person is to be surrendered to the authorities of the foreign country upon requisition from the proper officers, the Governor, by his warrant, shall cause him to be arrested and delivered over to such authorities.

Formerly Code 1863, § 60; Code 1868, § 56; Code 1873, § 53; Code 1882, § 53; Penal Code 1895, § 1270; Penal Code 1910, § 1352; Code 1933, § 44–301.

§ 17–13–5. Officers must execute warrants for the arrest of fugitives

When the Governor or other officer issues a warrant of arrest, it is the duty of the sheriffs, their deputies, coroners, and constables to execute it when placed in their hands.

Formerly Code 1863, § 64; Code 1868, § 60; Code 1873, § 57; Code 1882, § 57; Penal Code 1895, § 1274; Penal Code 1910, § 1356; Code 1933, § 44–305.

Article 2

Uniform Criminal Extradition Act

§ 17–13–20. Short title

This article shall be known and may be cited as the "Uniform Criminal Extradition Act."

Laws 1951, p. 726, § 32; Laws 2004, Act 564, § 17, eff. May 13, 2004.

Historical and Statutory Notes

The 2004 amendment by Act 564 was a provision contained in a correction bill.

Uniform Law

This section is based upon § 30 of the Uniform Criminal Extradition Act. See 11 Uniform Laws Annotated, Master Edition, or ULA Database on Westlaw.

§ 17–13–21. Definitions

As used in this article, the term:

(1) "Executive authority" includes the Governor and any person performing the functions of governor in a state other than this state.

(2) "Governor" includes any person performing the functions of governor by authority of the laws of this state.

(3) "State," referring to a state other than this state, includes the District of Columbia and any other state or territory, organized or unorganized, of the United States of America.

Laws 1951, p. 726, § 1; Laws 1978, p. 1754, § 1.

Historical and Statutory Notes

Uniform Law

This section is based upon § 1 of the Uniform Criminal Extradition Act. See 11 Uniform Laws Annotated, Master Edition, or ULA Database on Westlaw.

§ 17–13–22. Fugitives from justice; duty of Governor

Subject to this article, the Constitution of the United States, and any and all acts of Congress enacted in pursuance thereof, it is the duty of the Governor of this state to have arrested and delivered up to the executive authority of any other state any person charged in that state with treason, felony, or other crime, who has fled from justice and is found in this state.

Laws 1951, p. 726, § 2.

Historical and Statutory Notes

Uniform Law

This section is based upon § 2 of the Uniform Criminal Extradition Act. See 11 Uniform Laws Annotated, Master Edition, or ULA Database on Westlaw.

§ 17–13–23. Form of demand

No demand for the extradition of a person charged with a crime in another state shall be recognized by the Governor unless in writing, alleging, except in cases arising under Code Section 17–13–25, that the accused was present in the demanding state at the time of the commission of the alleged crime and that thereafter he fled from the state, and accompanied by a copy of an indictment found, or by information supported by affidavit in the state having jurisdiction of the crime, or by a copy of an affidavit made before a magistrate there, together with a copy of any warrant which was issued thereupon, or by a copy of a judgment of conviction or of a sentence imposed in execution thereof, together with a statement by the executive authority of the demanding state that the person claimed has escaped from confinement or has broken the terms of his bail, probation, or parole. The indictment, information, or affidavit made before the magistrate must substantially charge the person demanded with having committed a crime under the law of the state; and the copy of the indictment, information, affidavit, judgment of conviction, or sentence must be authenticated by the executive authority making the demand.

Laws 1951, p. 726, § 3.

Historical and Statutory Notes

Uniform Law

This section is based upon § 3 of the Uniform Criminal Extradition Act. See 11 Uniform Laws Annotated, Master Edition, or ULA Database on Westlaw.

§ 17–13–24. Extradition of person imprisoned or awaiting trial in another state or who has left the demanding state under compulsion

(a) When it is desired to have returned to this state a person charged in this state with a crime, and such person is imprisoned or is held under criminal proceedings then pending against him in another state, the Governor of this state may agree with the executive authority of the other state for the extradition of the person before the conclusion of the proceedings or of his term of sentence in the other state, upon condition that the person be returned to the other state, at the expense of this state, as soon as the prosecution in this state is terminated.

(b) The Governor of this state may also surrender, on demand of the executive authority of any other state, any person in this state who is charged in the manner provided in Code Section 17–13–43 with having violated the laws of the state whose executive authority is making the demand, even though such person left the demanding state involuntarily.

Laws 1951, p. 726, § 5; Laws 1955, p. 587, § 3.

Historical and Statutory Notes

Uniform Law

This section is based upon § 5 of the Uniform Criminal Extradition Act. See 11 Uniform Laws Annotated, Master Edition, or ULA Database on Westlaw.

§ 17–13–25. Extradition of persons not present in demanding state at time of commission of crime

The Governor of this state may also surrender, on demand of the executive authority of any other state, any person in this state charged in such other state in the manner provided in Code

Section 17-13-23 with committing an act in this state, or in a third state, intentionally resulting in a crime in the state whose executive authority is making the demand and the provisions of this article not otherwise inconsistent shall apply to such cases, even though the accused was not in that state at the time of the commission of the crime and has not fled therefrom.

Laws 1951, p. 726, § 6.

Historical and Statutory Notes

Uniform Law

This section is based upon § 6 of the Uniform Criminal Extradition Act. See 11 Uniform Laws Annotated, Master Edition, or ULA Database on Westlaw.

§ 17-13-26. Governor may investigate case

When a demand for the surrender of a person charged with a crime shall be made upon the Governor of this state by the executive authority of another state, the Governor may call upon the Attorney General or any prosecuting officer in this state to investigate or assist in investigating the demand, to report to him the situation and circumstances of the person so demanded, and to advise whether he ought to be surrendered.

Laws 1951, p. 726, § 4.

§ 17-13-27. Warrant of arrest; issuance by Governor

If the Governor decides that the demand should be complied with, he shall sign a warrant of arrest, which shall be sealed with the seal of the office of the Governor and directed to any peace officer or other person whom he may think fit to entrust with the execution thereof. The warrant must substantially recite the facts necessary to the validity of its issuance.

Laws 1951, p. 726, § 7; Laws 1983, p. 649, § 2.

Historical and Statutory Notes

Uniform Law

This section is based upon § 7 of the Uniform Criminal Extradition Act. See 11 Uniform Laws Annotated, Master Edition, or ULA Database on Westlaw.

§ 17-13-28. Manner and place of execution

The warrant shall authorize the peace officer or other person to whom directed to arrest the accused at any time and any place where he may be found within the state, to command the aid of all peace officers or other persons in the execution of the warrant, and to deliver the accused, subject to other provisions of this article, to the duly authorized agent of the demanding state.

Laws 1951, p. 726, § 8.

Historical and Statutory Notes

Uniform Law

This section is based upon § 8 of the Uniform Criminal Extradition Act. See 11 Uniform Laws Annotated, Master Edition, or ULA Database on Westlaw.

§ 17-13-29. Authority of arresting officer

Every peace officer or other person empowered to make the arrest shall have the same authority, in arresting the accused, to command assistance therein as peace officers have by law in the execution of any criminal process directed to them, with like penalties against those who refuse their assistance.

Laws 1951, p. 726, § 9.

Historical and Statutory Notes

Uniform Law

This section is based upon § 9 of the Uniform Criminal Extradition Act. See 11 Uniform Laws Annotated, Master Edition, or ULA Database on Westlaw.

§ 17-13-30. Rights of accused person; application for writ of habeas corpus; penalty

(a) No person arrested upon a warrant shall be delivered over to the agent whom the executive authority demanding him shall have appointed to receive him unless he shall first be taken forthwith before a judge of a court of record in this state, who shall inform him of the demand made for his surrender, of the crime with which he is charged, and that he has the right to demand and procure legal counsel. If the prisoner or his counsel shall state that he or they desire to test the legality of his arrest, the judge of the court of record shall fix a reasonable time to be allowed him within which to apply for a writ of habeas corpus. When the writ is applied for, notice thereof, and of the time and place of hearing thereon, shall be given to the prosecuting officer of the county in which the arrest is made and in which the accused is in custody and to the agent of the demanding state.

(b) Any officer who shall deliver to the agent for extradition of the demanding state a person in his custody under the Governor's warrant, in willful disobedience of subsection (a) of this Code section, shall be guilty of a misdemeanor and, upon conviction, shall be fined not more than $1,000.00 or be imprisoned not more than six months, or both.

Laws 1951, p. 726, §§ 10, 11.

Historical and Statutory Notes

Uniform Law

This section is based upon § 10 of the Uniform Criminal Extradition Act. See 11 Uniform Laws Annotated, Master Edition, or ULA Database on Westlaw.

§ 17-13-31. District attorneys to defend habeas corpus actions

The district attorney shall answer and defend any habeas corpus action brought under this article, which action contests the issuance, execution, or validity of a Governor's warrant of arrest, unless the Governor shall direct the Attorney General to answer and defend the habeas corpus action.

Laws 1979, p. 412, § 1.

§ 17-13-32. Confinement in jail when necessary

(a) The officer or persons executing the Governor's warrant of arrest or the agent of the demanding state to whom the prisoner may have been delivered may, when necessary, confine the prisoner in the jail of any county or city through which he may pass; and the keeper of the jail must receive and safely keep the prisoner until the officer or person having charge of him is ready to proceed on his route, such officer or person being chargeable with the expense of keeping.

(b) The officer or agent of a demanding state to whom a prisoner may have been delivered following extradition proceedings in another state, or to whom a prisoner may have been delivered after waiving extradition in such other state, and who is passing through this state with such a prisoner for the purpose of immediately returning the prisoner to the demanding state may, when necessary, confine the prisoner in the jail of any county or city through which he may pass; and the keeper of the jail must receive and safely keep the prisoner until the officer or agent having charge of him is ready to proceed on his route, the officer or agent, however, being chargeable with the expense of keeping; provided, however, that the officer or agent shall produce and show to the keeper of the jail satisfactory written evidence of the fact that he is actually transporting the prisoner to the demanding state after a requisition by the executive authority of the demanding state. The prisoner shall not be entitled to demand a new requisition while in this state.

Laws 1951, p. 726, § 12.

Historical and Statutory Notes

Uniform Law

This section is based upon § 12 of the Uniform Criminal Extradition Act. See 11 Uniform Laws Annotated, Master Edition, or ULA Database on Westlaw.

§ 17–13–33. Arrest prior to requisition

Whenever any person within this state shall be charged, on the oath of any credible person before any judge or magistrate of this state, with the commission of any crime in any other state and, except in cases arising under Code Section 17–13–25, with having fled from justice, or with having been convicted of a crime in that state and having escaped from confinement, or with having broken the terms of his bail, probation, or parole, or whenever complaint shall have been made before any judge or magistrate in this state setting forth, on the affidavit of any credible person in another state, that a crime has been committed in such other state and that the accused has been charged in such state with the commission of the crime and, except in cases arising under Code Section 17–13–25, has fled from justice, or with having been convicted of a crime in that state and having escaped from confinement, or with having broken the terms of his bail, probation, or parole, and is believed to be in this state, the judge or magistrate shall issue a warrant directed to any peace officer, commanding him to apprehend the person named therein, wherever he may be found in this state, and to bring him before the same or any other judge, magistrate, or court who or which may be available in or convenient of access to the place where the arrest may be made, to answer the charge or complaint and affidavit. A certified copy of the sworn charge or complaint and affidavit upon which the warrant is issued shall be attached to the warrant.

Laws 1951, p. 726, § 13.

Historical and Statutory Notes

Uniform Law

This section is based upon § 13 of the Uniform Criminal Extradition Act. See 11 Uniform Laws Annotated, Master Edition, or ULA Database on Westlaw.

§ 17–13–34. Arrest without a warrant

The arrest of a person may be lawfully made by any peace officer or private person, without a warrant, upon reasonable information that the accused stands charged in the courts of a state with a crime punishable by death or imprisonment for a term exceeding one year, but when so arrested, the accused must be taken before a judge or magistrate with all practicable speed and complaint must be made against him under oath, setting forth the ground for the arrest, as provided in Code Section 17–13–33; and thereafter the answer of the accused shall be heard as if he had been arrested on a warrant.

Laws 1951, p. 726, § 14; Laws 1990, p. 8, § 17.

Historical and Statutory Notes

Uniform Law

This section is based upon § 14 of the Uniform Criminal Extradition Act. See 11 Uniform Laws Annotated, Master Edition, or ULA Database on Westlaw.

§ 17–13–35. Commitment to await requisition; bail

If from the examination before the judge or magistrate it appears that the person held is the person charged with having committed the crime alleged and, except in cases arising under Code Section 17–13–25, that he has fled from justice, the judge or magistrate must, by a warrant reciting the accusation, commit him to the county jail for such a time, not exceeding 30 days and which time must be specified in the warrant, as will enable the arrest of the accused to be made under a warrant of the Governor on a requisition of the executive authority of the state having jurisdiction of the offense, unless the accused gives bail, as provided in Code Section 17–13–36, or until he shall be legally discharged.

Laws 1951, p. 726, § 15.

Historical and Statutory Notes

Uniform Law

This section is based upon § 15 of the Uniform Criminal Extradition Act. See 11 Uniform Laws Annotated, Master Edition, or ULA Database on Westlaw.

§ 17–13–36. Bail; in what cases; conditions of bond

Unless the offense with which the prisoner is charged is shown to be an offense punishable by death or life imprisonment under the laws of the state in which it was committed, a judge or magistrate in this state may admit the prisoner to bail by bond, with sufficient sureties, in such sum as he deems proper, conditioned for the prisoner's appearance before the judge or magistrate at a time specified in such bond and for the prisoner's surrender to be arrested upon the warrant of the Governor of this state.

Laws 1951, p. 726, § 16.

Historical and Statutory Notes

Uniform Law

This section is based upon § 16 of the Uniform Criminal Extradition Act. See 11 Uniform Laws Annotated, Master Edition, or ULA Database on Westlaw.

§ 17–13–37. Extension of time of commitment

If the accused is not arrested under warrant of the Governor by the expiration of the time specified in the warrant or bond, a judge or magistrate may discharge him or may recommit him for a further period not to exceed 60 days, or a judge or magistrate may again take bail for his appearance and surrender as provided for in Code Section 17–13–36, but within a period not to exceed 60 days after the date of such new bond.

Laws 1951, p. 726, § 17.

Historical and Statutory Notes

Uniform Law

This section is based upon § 17 of the Uniform Criminal Extradition Act. See 11 Uniform Laws Annotated, Master Edition, or ULA Database on Westlaw.

§ 17–13–38. Forfeiture of bail

If the prisoner is admitted to bail and fails to appear and surrender himself according to the conditions of his bond, the judge or magistrate, by proper order, shall declare the bond forfeited and order his immediate arrest without warrant if he is within the state. Recovery may be had on the bond in the name of the state as in the case of other bonds given by the accused in criminal proceedings within this state.

Laws 1951, p. 726, § 18.

Historical and Statutory Notes

Uniform Law

This section is based upon § 18 of the Uniform Criminal Extradition Act. See 11 Uniform Laws Annotated, Master Edition, or ULA Database on Westlaw.

§ 17-13-39. Persons under criminal prosecution in this state at time of demand

The Governor may, in his discretion, surrender, upon demand of the executive authority of another state, any person found in this state, notwithstanding the fact that a criminal prosecution or charges under the laws of this state are pending against the person, that the person has already been convicted in this state and is serving a sentence in any jail or penal institution of this state or of any county or municipality thereof, or that the person is serving a suspended or probationary sentence. The Governor may condition the release of the prisoner to the demanding state upon such terms as he may stipulate, including the condition that the prisoner be returned to this state immediately after trial and before commencing the service of sentence, if any, in the demanding state. In no case shall surrender of the prisoner be construed as a complete relinquishment of jurisdiction by this state, but the prisoner shall forthwith be returned to the custody of this state at the expense of the demanding state immediately after trial in the demanding state or the completion of sentence therein, as the case may be, except where the sentence of death has been executed in the demanding state.

Laws 1951, p. 726, § 19; Laws 1955, p. 587, § 2.

Historical and Statutory Notes

Uniform Law

This section is based upon § 19 of the Uniform Criminal Extradition Act. See 11 Uniform Laws Annotated, Master Edition, or ULA Database on Westlaw.

§ 17-13-40. Guilt or innocence of accused; when inquired into

The guilt or innocence of the accused as to the crime of which he is charged may not be inquired into by the Governor or in any proceeding after the demand for extradition accompanied by a charge or crime in legal form as provided for in this article shall have been presented to the Governor, except as it may be involved in identifying the person held as the person charged with the crime.

Laws 1951, p. 726, § 20.

Historical and Statutory Notes

Uniform Law

This section is based upon § 20 of the Uniform Criminal Extradition Act. See 11 Uniform Laws Annotated, Master Edition, or ULA Database on Westlaw.

§ 17-13-41. Governor may recall warrant or issue another warrant

The Governor may recall his warrant of arrest or may issue another warrant whenever he deems proper.

Laws 1951, p. 726, § 21.

Historical and Statutory Notes

Uniform Law

This section is based upon § 21 of the Uniform Criminal Extradition Act. See 11 Uniform Laws Annotated, Master Edition, or ULA Database on Westlaw.

§ 17-13-42. Fugitives from this state; duty of Governor

Whenever the Governor of this state shall demand a person charged with a crime or with escaping from confinement or breaking the terms of his bail, probation, or parole in this state, from the executive authority of any other state, or from the chief justice or an associate justice of the Supreme Court of the District of Columbia authorized to receive such demand under the laws of the United States, he shall issue a warrant under the seal of the office of the Governor to some agent, commanding him to receive the person so charged if delivered to him and convey him to the proper officer of the county in this state in which the offense was committed.

Laws 1951, p. 726, § 22; Laws 1983, p. 649, § 3.

Historical and Statutory Notes

Uniform Law

This section is based upon § 22 of the Uniform Criminal Extradition Act. See 11 Uniform Laws Annotated, Master Edition, or ULA Database on Westlaw.

§ 17-13-43. Application for issuance of demand; by whom made; contents

(a) When the return to this state of a person charged with crime in this state is required, the prosecuting attorney shall present to the Governor his written application, in which application shall be stated the name of the person so charged, the crime charged against him, the approximate time, place, and circumstance of its commission, the state in which he is believed to be, including the location of the accused therein at the time the application is made, and certifying that, in the opinion of the prosecuting attorney, the ends of justice require the arrest and return of the accused to this state for trial and that the proceeding is not instituted to enforce a private claim.

(b) When the return to this state is required of a person who has been convicted of a crime in this state and who has escaped from confinement or broken the terms of his bail, probation, or parole, the prosecuting attorney of the county in which the offense was committed, the State Board of Pardons and Paroles, or the warden of the institution or sheriff of the county from which escape was made shall present to the Governor a written application for a requisition for the return of such person. The application shall state the name of the person, the crime of which he was convicted, the circumstances of his escape from confinement or of the breach of the terms of his bail, probation, or parole and the state in which he is believed to be, including the location of the person therein at the time application is made.

(c) The application shall be verified by affidavit, executed in duplicate, and accompanied by two certified copies of the indictment returned, information and affidavit filed, or of the complaint made to the judge or magistrate, stating the offense with which the accused is charged, or of the judgment of conviction or of the sentence. The prosecuting officer, parole board, warden, or sheriff may also attach such further affidavits and other documents in duplicate as he shall deem proper to be submitted with such application. One copy of the application, with the action of the Governor indicated by endorsement thereon, and one of the certified copies of the indictment, complaint, information and affidavits, or of the judgment of conviction or of the sentence shall be filed in the office of the Governor, to remain of record in that office. The other copies of all papers shall be forwarded with the Governor's requisition.

Laws 1951, p. 726, § 23; Laws 1983, p. 649, § 4.

Historical and Statutory Notes

Uniform Law

This section is based upon § 23 of the Uniform Criminal Extradition Act. See 11 Uniform Laws Annotated, Master Edition, or ULA Database on Westlaw.

§ 17–13–44. Costs and expenses

When the punishment of the crime shall be the confinement of the person in a penal institution, the expenses shall be paid out of the state treasury on the certificate of the Governor and warrant of the state auditor; and in all other cases the expenses shall be paid out of the county treasury in the county wherein the crime is alleged to have been committed. The expenses shall be the fees paid to the officers of the state on whose governor the requisition is made and shall not exceed 8¢ per mile for all necessary travel in returning such prisoner.

Laws 1951, p. 726, § 24.

Historical and Statutory Notes

Uniform Law

This section is based upon § 24 of the Uniform Criminal Extradition Act. See 11 Uniform Laws Annotated, Master Edition, or ULA Database on Westlaw.

§ 17–13–45. Immunity from service of process in certain civil actions

A person brought into this state by or after waiver of extradition based on a criminal charge shall not be subject to service of personal process in civil actions arising out of the same facts as the criminal proceedings to answer which he is being or has been returned until he has been convicted in the criminal proceeding; or, if acquitted, until he has had reasonable opportunity to return to the state from which he was extradited.

Laws 1951, p. 726, § 25.

Historical and Statutory Notes

Uniform Law

This section is based upon § 25 of the Uniform Criminal Extradition Act. See 11 Uniform Laws Annotated, Master Edition, or ULA Database on Westlaw.

§ 17–13–46. Written waiver of extradition proceedings

(a) Any person arrested in this state charged with having committed any crime in another state or alleged to have escaped from confinement, or broken the terms of his bail, probation, or parole, may waive the issuance and service of the warrant provided for in Code Sections 17–13–27 and 17–13–28 and all other procedure incidental to extradition proceedings, by executing or subscribing in the presence of a judge of any court of record within this state a writing which states that he consents to return to the demanding state; provided, however, that before the waiver shall be executed or subscribed by the person it shall be the duty of the judge to inform the person of his rights to the issuance or service of a warrant of extradition and to obtain a writ of habeas corpus as provided in Code Section 17–13–30.

(b) If and when the consent has been duly executed, it shall forthwith be forwarded to the office of the Governor of this state and filed therein. The judge shall direct the officer having the person in custody to deliver forthwith the person to the duly accredited agent or agents of the demanding state and shall deliver or cause to be delivered to the agent or agents a copy of the consent. Nothing in this Code section shall be deemed to limit the rights of the accused person to return voluntarily and without formality to the demanding state; nor shall this waiver procedure be deemed to be an exclusive procedure or to limit the powers, rights, or duties of the officers of the demanding state or of this state.

Laws 1951, p. 726, § 26; Laws 1982, p. 3, § 17.

Historical and Statutory Notes

Uniform Law

This section is based upon § 25–A of the Uniform Criminal Extradition Act. See 11 Uniform Laws Annotated, Master Edition, or ULA Database on Westlaw.

§ 17–13–47. Non-waiver by this state

Nothing in this article contained shall be deemed to constitute a waiver by this state of its right, power, or privilege to try a person demanded for extradition by another state for crimes committed within this state or of its right, power, or privilege to regain custody of the person by extradition proceedings or otherwise for the purpose of trial, sentence, or punishment for any crime committed within this state; nor shall any proceedings had under this article result in, or fail to result in, extradition, be deemed a waiver by this state of any of its rights, privileges, or jurisdiction in any way whatsoever.

Laws 1951, p. 726, § 27.

§ 17–13–48. No immunity from other criminal prosecutions while in this state

After a person has been brought back to this state by, or after waiver of, extradition proceedings, he may be tried in this state for other crimes which he may be charged with having committed here as well as that specified in the requisition for his extradition.

Laws 1951, p. 726, § 28.

§ 17–13–49. Interpretation

This article shall be so interpreted and construed as to effectuate the general purposes to make uniform the laws of those states which enact it.

Laws 1951, p. 726, § 29.

Historical and Statutory Notes

Uniform Law

This section is based upon § 27 of the Uniform Criminal Extradition Act. See 11 Uniform Laws Annotated, Master Edition, or ULA Database on Westlaw.

CHAPTER 14

RESTITUTION AND DISTRIBUTION OF PROFITS TO VICTIMS OF CRIMES

Article 1

Article 1

Restitution

§ 17–14–1. Policy

It is declared to be the policy of this state that restitution to their victims by those found guilty of crimes or adjudicated as having committed delinquent acts is a primary concern of the criminal justice system and the juvenile justice system.

Laws 1980, p. 1382, § 1; Laws 2005, Act 20, § 5, eff. July 1, 2005.

Formerly Code 1933, § 27–3001.

Historical and Statutory Notes

The 2005 amendment by Act 20 added "or adjudicated as having committed delinquent acts" and "and the juvenile justice system".

§ 17–14–2. Definitions

As used in this article, the term:

(1) "Conviction" means an adjudication of guilt of or a plea of guilty or nolo contendere to the commission of an offense against the laws of this state. Such term includes any such conviction or plea, notwithstanding the fact that sentence was imposed pursuant to Article 3 of Chapter 8 of Title 42. Such term also includes the adjudication or plea of a juvenile to the commission of an act which, if committed by an adult, would constitute a crime under the laws of this state.

(2) "Damages" means all special damages which a victim could recover against an offender in a civil action, including a wrongful death action, based on the same act or acts for which the offender is sentenced, except punitive damages and damages for pain and suffering, mental anguish, or loss of consortium. Such special damages shall not be limited by any law which may cap economic damages. Special damages may include the reasonably determined costs of transportation to and from court proceedings related to the prosecution of the crime.

(3) "Offender" means any natural person, firm, partnership, association, public or private corporation, or other legal entity that has been sentenced for any crime or any juvenile who has been adjudged delinquent.

(4) "Ordering authority" means:

(A) A court of competent jurisdiction;

(B) The State Board of Pardons and Paroles;

(C) The Department of Corrections;

(D) The Department of Juvenile Justice; or

(E) Any combination thereof, as is required by the context.

(5) "Parent" means a person who is the legal mother as defined in paragraph (10.2) of Code Section 15–11–2, the legal father as defined in paragraph (10.1) of Code Section 15–11–2, or the legal guardian. Such term shall not include a foster parent.

(6) "Relief" means any parole or other conditional release from incarceration; the awarding of earned time allowances; reduction in security status; or placement in prison rehabilitation programs, including, but not limited to, those in which the offender receives monetary compensation.

(7) "Restitution" means any property, lump sum, or periodic payment ordered to be made by any offender or other person to any victim by any ordering authority. Where the victim is a public corporation or governmental entity or where the offender is a juvenile, restitution may also be in the form of services ordered to be performed by the offender.

(8) "Restitution order" means any order, decree, or judgment of an ordering authority which requires an offender to make restitution.

(9) "Victim" means any:

(A) Natural person or his or her personal representative or, if the victim is deceased, his or her estate; or

(B) Any firm, partnership, association, public or private corporation, or governmental entity

suffering damages caused by an offender's unlawful act; provided, however, that the term "victim" shall not include any person who is concerned in the commission of such unlawful act as defined in Code Section 16–2–20.

Laws 1980, p. 1382, § 1; Laws 1985, p. 283, § 1; Laws 2005, Act 20, § 5, eff. July 1, 2005.

Formerly Code 1933, § 27–3002.

Historical and Statutory Notes

The 2005 amendment by Act 20 rewrote the section which had read:

"As used in this article, the term:

"(1) 'Board' means the State Board of Pardons and Paroles.

"(2) 'Damages' means all damages which a victim could recover against an offender in a civil action, including a wrongful death action, based on the same act or acts for which the offender is sentenced, except punitive damages and damages for pain and suffering, mental anguish, or loss of consortium.

"(3) 'Department' means the Department of Corrections.

"(4) 'Offender' means any natural person who has been placed on probation under Article 3 of Chapter 8 of Title 42 or sentenced for any crime or any juvenile who has been adjudged delinquent or unruly.

"(5) 'Ordering authority' means the court of competent jurisdiction, the State Board of Pardons and Paroles, the Department of Corrections, or any combination thereof, as is required by the context.

"(6) 'Relief' means any suspended or probated sentence, including probation imposed under Article 3 of Chapter 8 of Title 42; any parole or other conditional release from incarceration; the awarding of earned time allowances; reduction in security status; or placement in prison rehabilitation programs, including, but not limited to, those in which the offender receives monetary compensation.

"(7) 'Restitution' means any property, lump sum, or periodic payment ordered to be made by any offender to any victim by any ordering authority. Where the victim is a public corporation or governmental entity or where the offender is a juvenile, restitution may also be in the form of services ordered to be performed by the offender.

"(8) 'Restitution order' means any order, decree, or judgment of an ordering authority which requires an offender to make restitution as a condition or term of any relief granted to an offender.

"(9) 'Victim' means any natural person or his personal representative or any firm, partnership, association, public or private corporation, or governmental entity suffering damages caused by an offender's unlawful act."

§ 17–14–3. Court-ordered restitution

(a) Subject to the provisions of Code Section 17–14–10, notwithstanding the provisions contained in Chapter 11 of Title 15, and in addition to any other penalty imposed by law, a judge of any court of competent jurisdiction shall, in sentencing an offender, make a finding as to the amount of restitution due any victim, and order an offender to make full restitution to such victim.

(b) If the offender is placed on probation, including probation imposed pursuant to Chapter 11 of Title 15 or Article 3 of Chapter 8 of Title 42, or sentence is suspended, deferred, or withheld, restitution ordered under this Code section shall be a condition of that probation, sentence, or order.

(c) If the offender is granted relief by the Department of Juvenile Justice, Department of Corrections, or the State Board of Pardons and Paroles, the terms of any court order requiring the offender to make restitution to a victim shall be a condition of such relief in addition to any other terms or conditions which may apply to such relief.

Laws 1980, p. 1382, § 1; Laws 2005, Act 20, § 5, eff. July 1, 2005; Laws 2010, Act 403, § 5, eff. July 1, 2010.

Formerly Code 1933, § 27–3003.

Historical and Statutory Notes

The 2005 amendment by Act 20 designated the existing text as subsec. (a) and rewrote subsec. (a); and added new subsecs. (b) and (c). Prior to amendment the section had read:

"The judge of any court of competent jurisdiction may order that an adult offender make restitution as a condition of any relief ordered by the court. The board may order that an adult offender make restitution as a condition of any relief ordered by the board. The department may order that an adult offender make restitution as a condition of any relief ordered by the department."

The 2010 amendment by Act 403, in subsec. (a), inserted "in sentencing an offender, make a finding as to the amount of restitution due any victim" after "court of competent jurisdiction shall" and substituted "such victim" for "any victim".

§ 17–14–4. Pardons and paroles

Notwithstanding any provision of Code Section 42–9–45 to the contrary, the State Board of Pardons and Paroles may grant parole prior to the completion of one-third of the sentence if restitution is ordered as a condition of the parole.

Laws 1980, p. 1382, § 1; Laws 2005, Act 20, § 5, eff. July 1, 2005.

Formerly Code 1933, § 27–3004.

Historical and Statutory Notes

The 2005 amendment by Act 20 substituted "State Board of Pardons and Paroles" for "board".

§ 17–14–5. Juveniles

(a) It is declared to be the policy of this state to recognize that restitution is consistent with the goal of rehabilitation of delinquent juveniles and to provide restitution in such cases.

(b) Notwithstanding any provision of Chapter 11 of Title 15, the juvenile courts shall order restitution in any case involving delinquent juveniles in the same manner as is authorized by this article for adult offenders.

(c) For purposes of ensuring compliance with the restitution order, the juvenile courts are authorized to retain jurisdiction over a juvenile subject to such restitution order until the juvenile reaches 21 years of age. If the juvenile court retains jurisdiction of such offender as provided in this Code section and the terms of the restitution order are not completed before the offender's twenty-first birthday, the juvenile court shall transfer the restitution order to the superior court.

(d) As an alternative to subsection (c) of this Code section, the juvenile courts are authorized to transfer to the superior courts, and the superior courts are authorized to accept, jurisdiction over enforcement of restitution orders against juveniles who, since entry of the order, have attained 18 years of age.

(e) If the court determines that a juvenile is or will be unable to pay all of the restitution ordered, after notice to the juvenile's parent or parents and an opportunity for the parent or parents to be heard, the court may order the parent or parents to pay any portion of the restitution ordered that is outstanding where the court or a jury finds by clear and convincing evidence that the parent or parents knew or should have known of the juvenile's propensity to commit such acts and the acts are due to the parent's or parents' negligence or reckless disregard for the juvenile's propensity to commit such acts. Upon the eighteenth birthday of the juvenile, the parental obligation to pay restitution shall be terminated.

(f) If the court orders a parent to pay restitution under subsection (e) of this Code section, the court shall take into account the considerations identified in Code Section 17–14–10. If the parent or parents are required to pay restitution under subsection (e) of this Code section, the court shall provide for payment to be made in specified installments and within a specified period of time.

Laws 1980, p. 1382, § 1; Laws 2005, Act 20, § 5, eff. July 1, 2005.

Formerly Code 1933, § 27–3005.

Historical and Statutory Notes

The 2005 amendment by Act 20 rewrote the section which had read:

"(a) The juvenile courts are expressly directed to consider the strong policy of this state in favor of restitution but are not required to place the goal of restitution by juveniles above the goal of rehabilitation or treatment of delinquent or unruly juveniles. It is, however, declared to be the policy of this state to recognize that the goal of restitution is consistent with the goal of rehabilitation of delinquent or unruly juveniles and to seek to provide restitution in such cases.

"(b) The juvenile courts are expressly authorized to order restitution as a condition or limitation of the probation of delinquent or unruly juveniles in the same manner as is authorized by this article for adult offenders.

"(c) For purposes of ensuring compliance with the order, the juvenile courts are authorized to retain jurisdiction over a juvenile subject to a restitution order for a reasonable period after the juvenile reaches the age of majority.

"(d) As an alternative to subsection (c) of this Code section, the juvenile courts are authorized to transfer to the superior courts, and the superior courts are authorized to accept, jurisdiction over enforcement of restitution orders against juveniles who, since entry of the order, have attained the age of majority."

§ 17–14–6. Past restitution considered

(a) Where an offender has made total or partial restitution to a victim, the ordering authority shall set off any such amounts and reduce the amount payable to the victim.

(b) The ordering authority shall not order restitution to be paid to a victim or victim's estate if the victim or victim's estate has received or is to receive full compensation for that loss from the offender as a result of a civil proceeding.

(c) Any amount paid to a victim or victim's estate under a restitution order shall reduce the amount payable to a victim or a victim's estate by an award from the Georgia Crime Victims Compensation Board made prior to or after a restitution order under this article.

(d) The ordering authority shall order restitution be paid to the Georgia Crime Victims Compensation Board, other governmental entities, or any individuals, partnerships, corporations, associations, or other legal entities acting on behalf of a governmental entity that have compensated the victim or the victim's estate for a loss incurred by the victim to the extent of the compensation paid for that loss. The ordering authority shall also order restitution for the costs of services provided to persons or entities that have provided services to the victim as a result of the crime. Services that are subject to restitution under this subsection include, but are not limited to, shelter, food, clothing, and transportation. However, a restitution order shall require that all restitution to a victim or victim's estate under the restitution order be made before any restitution to any other person or entity under that restitution order is made.

(e) In the event the ordering authority provides for a setoff or priority in terms of payment of restitution, the ordering authority shall state on the record with specificity the reasons for its action.

Laws 1980, p. 1382, § 1; Laws 2005, Act 20, § 5, eff. July 1, 2005; Laws 2006, Act 453, § 17, eff. April 14, 2006.

Formerly Code 1933, § 27–3006.

Historical and Statutory Notes

The 2005 amendment by Act 20 rewrote the section which had read:

"Where an offender has made total or partial restitution to a victim, the ordering authority shall consider the fact of such restitution in considering any case within its power."

The 2006 amendment by Act 453 was a provision contained in a correction bill.

§ 17–14–7. Voluntary restitution plans; restitution hearing; joint liability; multiple victims; waiver of restitution

(a) Any offender may offer a restitution plan to the ordering authority. If a plan is offered, it shall be the duty of the ordering authority to consider the factors stated in Code Section 17–14–10 and to make the plan part of a restitution order if acceptable to the ordering authority.

(b) If the parties have not agreed on the amount of restitution prior to sentencing, the ordering authority shall set a date for a hearing to determine restitution. Any dispute as to the proper amount or type of restitution shall be resolved by the ordering authority by the preponderance of the evidence. The burden of demonstrating the amount of the loss sustained by a victim as a result of the offense shall be on the state. The burden of demonstrating the financial resources of the offender or person being ordered to pay restitution and the financial needs of his or her dependents shall be on the offender or person being ordered to pay restitution. The burden of demonstrating such other matters as the ordering authority deems appropriate shall be upon the party designated by the ordering authority as justice requires.

(c) If the ordering authority finds that more than one offender has contributed to the loss of a victim, the court may make each offender liable for payment of the full amount of restitution or may apportion liability among the offenders to reflect the level of contribution to the victim's loss and economic circumstances of each offender.

(d) If the ordering authority finds that more than one victim has sustained a loss requiring restitution by an offender, the court may provide for a different payment schedule for each victim based on the type and amount of each victim's loss and accounting for the economic circumstances of each victim. In any case in which the state or any of its political subdivisions is a victim and thus is due restitution, the ordering authority shall ensure that any other victim receives full restitution before the state or a political subdivision receives restitution.

(e) A victim may waive his or her right to obtain restitution pursuant to this article. Any such waiver shall be made in writing and filed with the court or ordering authority having jurisdiction over the criminal case. Such waiver shall not affect any other rights or remedies that the victim may have against the offender under the laws of this state or the United States or any of the several states.

Laws 1980, p. 1382, § 1; Laws 2005, Act 20, § 5, eff. July 1, 2005; Laws 2006, Act 453, § 17, eff. April 14, 2006.

Formerly Code 1933, § 27–3007.

Historical and Statutory Notes

The 2005 amendment by Act 20 designated the existing section as subsec. (a) and added new subsecs. (b) through (e).

The 2006 amendment by Act 453 was a provision contained in a correction bill.

§ 17–14–8. Partial payment of restitution; time of payment

(a) In any case in which a court sentences an offender to pay restitution and a fine, if the court permits the offender to pay such restitution and fine in other than a lump sum, the clerk of any superior court of this state, probation officer or parole officer, or other official who receives such partial payments shall apply not less than one-half of each payment to the restitution before paying any portion of such fine or any forfeitures, costs, fees, or surcharges provided for by law to any agency, department, commission, committee, authority, board, or bureau of state or local government.

(b) The clerk of any court of this state, probation officer or parole officer, or other official who receives partial payments for restitution shall pay the restitution amount to the victim as provided in the restitution order not later than the last day of each month, provided that the amount exceeds $100.00. If the amount does not exceed $100.00, the clerk of any court of this state, probation officer or parole officer, or other official may allow the amount of restitution to accumulate until such time as it exceeds $100.00 or until the end of the next calendar quarter, whichever occurs first.

Laws 1980, p. 1382, § 1; Laws 2005, Act 20, § 5, eff. July 1, 2005.

Formerly Code 1933, § 27–3008.

Historical and Statutory Notes

The 2005 amendment by Act 20 rewrote the section which had read:

"(a) In deciding any case subject to this article, before granting any relief the ordering authority shall make a written finding either:

"(1) That there are no victims to whom restitution should be made under the policy of this state;

"(2) That the circumstances of the case are such that no restitution order or plan is reasonably possible;

"(3) That the offender, in cooperation with the ordering authority, has developed and consented to a plan of restitution, which plan shall be made a part of a restitution order; or

"(4) That restitution will be ordered as a condition of the relief.

"(b) The failure to make a finding as required by this Code section, however, shall not invalidate any order or other action of the ordering authority."

§ 17–14–9. Restitution not to exceed damages

The amount of restitution ordered shall not exceed the victim's damages.

Laws 1980, p. 1382, § 1; Laws 2005, Act 20, § 5, eff. July 1, 2005.

Formerly Code 1933, § 27–3009.

Historical and Statutory Notes

The 2005 amendment by Act 20 rewrote the section which had read:

"The amount of restitution ordered may be equal to or less than, but not more than, the victim's damages."

§ 17–14–10. Factors considered

(a) In determining the nature and amount of restitution, the ordering authority shall consider:

(1) The financial resources and other assets of the offender or person ordered to pay restitution including whether any of the assets are jointly controlled;

(2) The earnings and other income of the offender or person ordered to pay restitution;

(3) Any financial obligations of the offender or person ordered to pay restitution, including obligations to dependents;

(4) The amount of damages;

(5) The goal of restitution to the victim and the goal of rehabilitation of the offender;

(6) Any restitution previously made;

(7) The period of time during which the restitution order will be in effect; and

(8) Other factors which the ordering authority deems to be appropriate.

(b) If, subsequent to restitution being ordered pursuant to this article, a victim is convicted of a crime for which restitution is ordered, the ordering authority shall consider the previously ordered restitution as part of the financial resources of such victim.

Laws 1980, p. 1382, § 1; Laws 2005, Act 20, § 5, eff. July 1, 2005.

Formerly Code 1933, § 27-3010.

Historical and Statutory Notes

The 2005 amendment by Act 20 rewrote the section which had read:

"In determining the nature and amount of restitution, the ordering authority shall consider:

"(1) The present financial condition of the offender and his dependents;

"(2) The probable future earning capacity of the offender and his dependents;

"(3) The amount of damages;

"(4) The goal of restitution to the victim and the goal of rehabilitation of the offender;

"(5) Any restitution previously made;

"(6) The period of time during which the restitution order will be in effect; and

"(7) Other appropriate factors which the ordering authority deems to be appropriate."

§ 17-14-11. Civil actions

An order for restitution shall not bar any civil action against the offender. However, any payments made by an offender to a victim under an order for restitution may be a setoff against any judgment awarded to the victim in a civil action based on the same facts for which restitution was ordered. The fact of restitution or a restitution order under this article shall not be placed before the jury on the issue of liability. If the amount of restitution made is in dispute and liability is established, the court shall order further appropriate proceedings to determine the amount of setoff.

Laws 1980, p. 1382, § 1; Laws 2005, Act 20, § 5, eff. July 1, 2005.

Formerly Code 1933, § 27-3011.

Historical and Statutory Notes

The 2005 revision of Article 1 of Chapter 14 by Act 20 reenacted the section without amendment.

§ 17-14-12. Modification

The ordering authority shall retain jurisdiction to modify a restitution order at any time before the expiration of the relief ordered.

Laws 1980, p. 1382, § 1; Laws 2005, Act 20, § 5, eff. July 1, 2005.

Formerly Code 1933, § 27-3012.

Historical and Statutory Notes

The 2005 revision of Article 1 of Chapter 14 by Act 20 reenacted the section without amendment.

§ 17-14-13. Enforcement

(a) A restitution order shall be enforceable as is a civil judgment by execution as provided in Code Section 17-10-20.

(b) If an offender or other person ordered to pay restitution willfully refuses to comply with a restitution order, the order, in the discretion of the court, may be enforced by attachment for contempt, upon the application of the prosecuting attorney or the victim.

(c) Failure to comply with a restitution order may, in the discretion of the ordering authority, be grounds to revoke or cancel the relief at any time the restitution order is in effect. Where the relief is earned time allowances, the Department of Corrections may suspend the offender from earning earned time allowances for a specified period of time.

Laws 1980, p. 1382, § 1; Laws 1982, p. 3, § 17; Laws 1985, p. 231, § 1; Laws 2005, Act 20, § 5, eff. July 1, 2005.

Formerly Code 1933, § 27-3013.

Historical and Statutory Notes

The 2005 amendment by Act 20, in subsec. (a), added "as provided in Code Section 17-10-20", in subsec. (b), added "or other person ordered to pay restitution", in subsec. (c), substituted "Department of Corrections" for "department", and deleted subsec. (d). Prior to amendment, subsec. (d) had read:

"(d) When an inmate offender has been ordered to make restitution for any damage to state property caused by such offender, the department may order the seizure of all moneys in or coming into the monetary account of the inmate offender."

§ 17-14-14. Payments; wage assignment; review of case; interest

(a) Payments pursuant to an order for restitution shall be made to the clerk of the court or to any other person, for the benefit of the victim or victims, as the ordering authority shall order.

(b) In each case in which payment of restitution is ordered as a condition of probation or parole, the ordering authority may require any employed offender to execute a wage assignment to pay the restitution.

(c) Until such time as the restitution has been paid or the sentence has been completed, the clerk of court or the probation or parole officer assigned to the case, whoever is responsible for collecting restitution, shall review the case not less frequently than twice yearly to ensure that restitution is being paid as ordered. If the restitution was ordered to be made within a specific period of time, the case shall be reviewed at the end of the specific period of time to determine if the restitution has been paid in full. The final review shall be conducted before the sentence or probationary or parole period expires. If it is determined at any review that restitution is not being paid as ordered, a written report of the violation shall be filed with the court on a form prescribed by the Council of Superior Court Clerks of Georgia.

(d) If the ordering authority permits the offender to pay restitution in other than a lump sum, the ordering authority may require the offender to pay interest on the amount of restitution due the victim or the victim's estate. Such interest shall be set at the same rate as is provided by Code Section 7-4-12 for judgments.

Laws 1980, p. 1382, § 1; Laws 2005, Act 20, § 5, eff. July 1, 2005.

Formerly Code 1933, § 27-3014.

Historical and Statutory Notes

The 2005 amendment by Act 20 designated existing section as subsec. (a) and added new subsecs. (b) through (d).

§ 17–14–15. Peonage; denial of benefits because of poverty

(a) Nothing in this article shall authorize peonage; and this article shall be construed and diligently administered to prevent peonage.

(b) No offender shall be denied any benefit, relief, or privilege to which he or she might otherwise be entitled or eligible solely because he or she is financially unable and cannot become financially able to make restitution.

Laws 1980, p. 1382, § 1; Laws 2005, Act 20, § 5, eff. July 1, 2005.

Formerly Code 1933, § 27–3016.

Historical and Statutory Notes

The 2005 amendment by Act 20 made the section gender neutral.

§ 17–14–16. Copy of restitution order to department

If an offender who is ordered to pay restitution under this article is remanded to the jurisdiction of the Department of Corrections or the Department of Juvenile Justice, the court shall provide a copy of the restitution order to such department when the offender is remanded to such department's jurisdiction.

Laws 1980, p. 1382, § 1; Laws 2005, Act 20, § 5, eff. July 1, 2005.

Formerly Code 1933, § 27–3015.

Historical and Statutory Notes

The 2005 amendment by Act 20 rewrote the section which had read:

"This article shall not be construed to limit or abrogate any power of any court, agency, or board to place other conditions, limits, terms, rules, or regulations on any relief in the nature of suspension of sentence, probation, parole, pardon, or restoration of rights."

§ 17–14–17. Action pursuant to the Uniform Fraudulent Transfers Act

(a) The state or the victim of a crime may institute an action against an offender pursuant to Article 4 of Chapter 2 of Title 18, the "Uniform Fraudulent Transfers Act," to set aside a transfer of real, personal, or other property made voluntarily by the offender on or after the date of the crime committed by the offender against the victim with the intent to:

(1) Conceal the crime or the fruits of the crime;

(2) Hinder, delay, or defraud any victim; or

(3) Avoid the payment of restitution.

(b) Any such action shall be filed within four years of the date the crime was committed.

Laws 1998, p. 549, § 1; Laws 2005, Act 20, § 5, eff. July 1, 2005.

Historical and Statutory Notes

The 2005 amendment by Act 20 rewrote the section which had read:

"(a) For purposes of this Code section only, the term:

"(1) 'Conviction' means a finding or verdict of guilty or a plea of guilty, regardless of whether an appeal of the conviction has been sought.

"(2) 'Victim' means any natural person against whom a crime specified in Chapter 7 or 8 of Title 16 has been committed.

"(b) Notwithstanding the provisions of Code Section 17–14–3, the judge of any court of competent jurisdiction shall order that an adult offender, upon a conviction of any crime specified in Chapter 7 or 8 of Title 16, make restitution to any victim as a condition of any relief ordered by the court.

"(c) The amount of restitution ordered shall be equal to the unreimbursed or uncompensated portion of the victim's damages.

"(d) For purposes of this Code section only, the court is not required to make any written findings in accordance with Code Section 17–14–8 when ordering restitution; provided, however, that a court may order a restitution plan in accordance with the provisions of Code Sections 17–14–7 and 17–14–10.

"(e) The provisions of Code Sections 17–14–11 to 17–14–16 shall apply to any restitution orders issued in accordance with this Code section."

§ 17–14–18. Deposit of unclaimed restitution in victim's fund

If a person or entity entitled to restitution cannot be located or refuses to claim such restitution within two years after the date on which he or she could have claimed such restitution, the restitution paid to such person or entity shall be deposited in the Crime Victims Emergency Fund created pursuant to Chapter 15 of Title 17 or its successor fund. However, a person or entity entitled to such restitution may claim such restitution any time within five years of the date on which he or she could have claimed such restitution by applying in writing to Georgia Crime Victims Compensation Board. Upon receipt of such application and verification that the person making the claim is in fact entitled to such restitution, the Georgia Crime Victims Compensation Board shall pay such restitution to the person or entity.

Laws 2005, Act 20, § 5, eff. July 1, 2005.

§ 17–14–19. Court, agency, or board power not limited

This article shall not be construed to limit or abrogate any power of any court, agency, or board to place other conditions, limits, terms, rules, or regulations on any relief in the nature of suspension of sentence, probation, parole, pardon, or restoration of rights.

Laws 2005, Act 20, § 5, eff. July 1, 2005.

Article 2

Distribution of Profits of Crimes

§ 17–14–30. Definitions

As used in this article, the term:

(1) "Board" means the Board of Corrections.

(2) "Convicted person" includes a person found not guilty by reason of insanity.

Laws 1979, p. 1262, § 1; Laws 1985, p. 283, § 1.

§ 17–14–31. Distribution of moneys received as a result of the commission of crime

(a)(1) Every person, firm, corporation, partnership, association, or other legal entity contracting with any person or with the representative or assignee of any person who has been accused or convicted of a crime in this state with respect to the reenactment of the crime by way of a movie, book, magazine article, tape recording, phonograph record, radio or television presentation, or live entertainment of any kind or with respect to the expression of the accused or convicted person's thoughts, feelings, opinions, or emotions regarding the crime shall submit a copy of the contract to the board and shall pay over to the board any moneys which would otherwise, by the terms of the contract, be owing to the accused or convicted person or to his representatives.

(2) The board shall deposit such moneys in an escrow account for the benefit of and payable to any victim or the legal representative of any victim of crimes committed by the accused or convicted person.

(3) Payments may be made pursuant to paragraph (2) of this subsection only if the accused person is eventually convicted or enters a plea of guilty of the crime and if the victim, within five years of the date of the establishment of the escrow account, brings a civil action in a court of competent jurisdiction and recovers a money judgment for damages against the convicted or accused person or his representatives.

(4) It shall be the duty of the victim, the victim's attorney, or the victim's representative to notify the board within 30 days of the filing of any claim under this article.

(b) At least once every six months for five years from the date it receives such moneys, the board shall cause to have published a legal notice in newspapers of general circulation in the county in which the crime was committed and in counties contiguous to such county, advising victims of the crime that escrow moneys are available to satisfy money judgments pursuant to this Code section.

(c) Upon dismissal of charges or acquittal of any accused person, the board shall immediately pay over to the accused person the moneys in the escrow account established on behalf of the accused person.

(d) Upon a showing by any convicted person that five years have elapsed from the establishment of the escrow account and that no actions are pending against the convicted person pursuant to this Code section, the board shall immediately pay over any moneys in the escrow account to the person or his legal representatives.

(e) Whenever it is found that a person accused of a crime is unfit to proceed to trial as a result of insanity because the person lacks capacity to understand the proceedings against him or to assist in his own defense, the board shall bring an action of interpleader to determine the disposition of the escrow account.

(f) Any excess which remains in the escrow account or is deposited into the account after all money judgments have been satisfied shall be paid over into the state treasury as compensation for the establishment, administration, and execution of this article.

(g) The board shall make payments from the escrow account to any person accused or convicted of crime, upon the order of a court of competent jurisdiction, after a showing by the person that the moneys shall be used for the exclusive purpose of retaining legal representation at any stage of the proceedings against the person, including the appeals process.

(h) The board shall disburse payments from the escrow account on a pro rata basis of all claims filed, according to the amount of money in the escrow account as compared to the amount of each claim. The sums are not to be disbursed until all pending claims have been settled or reduced to judgment.

(i) Any action taken by a person who is accused or convicted of a crime or who enters a plea of guilty, whether by way of execution of a power of attorney, creation of corporate entities, or otherwise, to defeat the purpose of this Code section shall be null and void as against the public policy of this state.

Laws 1979, p. 1262, § 1.

§ 17–14–32. Penalties

(a) It shall be unlawful for any person, firm, corporation, partnership, association, or other legal entity to fail to comply with this article.

(b) Any person, firm, corporation, partnership, association, or other legal entity violating this article shall be guilty of a misdemeanor.

(c) Each day that a person, firm, corporation, partnership, association, or other legal entity continues in violation of this article shall constitute a separate offense.

Laws 1979, p. 1262, § 1.

CHAPTER 15

VICTIM COMPENSATION

Section

§ 17–15–1. Declaration of purpose

The General Assembly recognizes that many innocent persons suffer personal physical injury, serious mental or emotional trauma, severe financial hardship, or death as a result of criminal acts or attempted criminal acts. The General Assembly finds and determines that there is a need for assistance for such victims of crime. Accordingly, it is the General Assembly's intent that under certain circumstances aid, care, and assistance be provided by the state for such victims of crime.

Laws 1988, p. 591, § 1; Laws 2009, Act 56, § 1, eff. July 1, 2009.

Historical and Statutory Notes

The 2009 amendment by Act 56, inserted "serious mental or emotional trauma" and "or attempted criminal acts".

§ 17–15–2. Definitions

As used in this chapter, the term:

(1) "Board" means the Criminal Justice Coordinating Council.

(2) "Claimant" means any person filing a claim pursuant to this chapter.

(3) "Crime" means:

(A) An act which constitutes hit and run as defined in Code Section 40–6–270, homicide by vehicle as defined in Code Section 40–6–393, serious injury by vehicle as defined in Code Section 40–6–394, or any act which constitutes a violation of Chapter 6 or Part 2 of Article 3 of Chapter 12 of Title 16, a violation of Code Section 16–5–70, or a violent crime as defined by state or federal law which results in physical injury, serious mental or emotional trauma, or death to the victim and which is committed:

(i) In this state;

(ii) In a state which does not have a victims' compensation program, if the victim is a resident of this state; or

(iii) In a state which has compensated the victim in an amount less than the victim would be entitled to pursuant to this chapter, if the victim is a resident of this state;

(B) An act which constitutes international terrorism as defined in 18 U.S.C. Section 2331 which results in physical injury, serious mental or emotional trauma, or death to the victim, if the victim is a resident of this state and is outside the territorial boundaries of the United States when such act is committed; or

(C) An act of mass violence which results in physical injury, serious mental or emotional trauma, or death to the victim, if the victim is a resident of this state and is outside the territorial boundaries of the United States when such act is committed.

(4) "Direct service provider" means a public or nonprofit entity which provides aid, care, and assistance to a victim.

(5) "Director" means the director of the Criminal Justice Coordinating Council.

(6) "Fund" means the Georgia Crime Victims Emergency Fund.

(7) "Investigator" means an investigator of the board.

(8) "Serious mental or emotional trauma" means a nonphysical injury which has been documented by a licensed mental health professional and which meets the specifications promulgated by the board's rules and regulations relating to this type of trauma.

(9) "Victim" means a person who:

(A) Is injured physically, who dies, or who suffers financial hardship as a result of being injured physically as a direct result of a crime;

(B) Suffers a serious mental or emotional trauma as a result of being threatened with a crime which could result in physical injury or death; or

(C) Suffers a serious mental or emotional trauma as a result of being present during the commission of a crime.

Laws 1988, p. 591, § 1; Laws 1990, p. 8, § 17; Laws 1994, p. 1800, § 1; Laws 1997, p. 481, § 1; Laws 2002, p. 843, § 2; Laws 2009, Act 56, § 2, eff. July 1, 2009.

Historical and Statutory Notes

The 2009 amendment by Act 56, in par. (3), in subpar. (A), inserted "violation of Chapter 6 or Part 2 of Article 3 of Chapter 12 of Title 16, a violation of Code Section 16-5-70, or a"; in par. (3), in subpars. (A), (B), and (C), inserted ", serious mental or emotional trauma,"; redesignated par. (8) as par. (9) and inserted new par. (8); in new par. (9) designated subpar. (A) and added subpars. (B) and (C).

§ 17-15-3. Georgia Crime Victims Compensation Board; abolition and recreation

(a) The five-member Georgia Crime Victims Compensation Board in existence on June 30, 1992, is abolished.

(b) There is created the Georgia Crime Victims Compensation Board. The Criminal Justice Coordinating Council created under Chapter 6A of Title 35 shall serve as the Georgia Crime Victims Compensation Board.

(c) The Governor shall appoint the director of the Criminal Justice Coordinating Council to carry out the provisions of this chapter.

Laws 1988, p. 591, § 1; Laws 1992, p. 2426, § 1; Laws 1994, p. 1800, § 2.

§ 17-15-4. Powers and duties of board

(a) The board shall have the following powers and duties:

(1) To promulgate suitable rules and regulations to carry out the provisions and purposes of this chapter;

(2) To request from the Attorney General, the Department of Public Safety, the Georgia Bureau of Investigation, district attorneys, solicitors-general, judges, county and municipal law enforcement agencies, and any other agency or department such assistance and data as will enable the board to determine the needs state wide for victim compensation and whether, and the extent to which, a claimant qualifies for an award. Any person, agency, or department listed in this paragraph is authorized to provide the board with the information requested upon receipt of a request from the board. Any provision of law providing for confidentiality of records does not apply to a request of the board pursuant to this Code section; provided, however, that the board shall preserve the confidentiality of any such records received;

(3) To hear and determine all appeals of denied claims for awards filed with the board pursuant to this chapter and to reinvestigate or reopen cases as the board deems necessary;

(4) To apply for funds from, and to submit all necessary forms to, any federal agency participating in a cooperative program to compensate victims of crime and to receive and administer federal funds for the purposes of this chapter;

(5) To render awards to victims of crimes or to those other persons entitled to receive awards in the manner authorized by this chapter. Victim compensation payments may be made directly to direct service providers who are not the recipients of local, state, federal, or private grant funds awarded for purposes of providing direct services to crime victims. A victim or claimant may be paid directly in the case of lost wages, loss of support, and instances where the victim or claimant has paid the direct service provider and is filing for reimbursement. In all cases where the victim has incurred out-of-pocket expenses, such as lost wages or loss of support or in cases where the victim or claimant has paid the direct service provider directly and is filing for reimbursement, the victim or claimant shall be paid first before any third party;

(6) To carry out programs designed to inform the public of the purposes of this chapter; and

(7) To render each year to the Governor and to the General Assembly a written report of its activities pursuant to this chapter.

(b) The board shall assist applicants with their claims for compensation through educational programs and administrative assistance.

Laws 1988, p. 591, § 1; Laws 1990, p. 8, § 17; Laws 1992, p. 2426, § 2; Laws 1994, p. 1800, § 3; Laws 1996, p. 748, § 16.

§ 17-15-5. Procedures for making claims for awards

(a) A claim may be filed by a person eligible to receive an award, as provided in Code Section 17-15-7, or, if such person is a minor, by his parent or guardian. In any case in which the person entitled to make a claim is mentally incompetent, the claim may be filed on his behalf by his guardian or such other individual authorized to administer his estate.

(b) A claim must be filed by the claimant not later than one year after the occurrence of the crime upon which such claim is based or not later than one year after the death of the victim; provided, however, that, upon good cause shown, the board may extend that time for filing for a period not exceeding three years after such occurrence. Claims shall be filed in the office of the board in person or by mail.

(c) The claim shall be verified and shall contain the following:

(1) A description of the date, nature, and circumstances of the crime;

(2) A complete financial statement, including, but not limited to, the cost of medical care or burial expense, the loss of wages or support the victim has incurred or will incur, any other emergency expenses incurred by the victim, and the extent to which the victim has been or may be indemnified for these expenses from any source;

(3) When appropriate, a statement indicating the extent of any disability resulting from the injury or serious mental or emotional trauma incurred;

(4) An authorization permitting the board to verify the contents of the application; and

(5) Such other information as the board may require.

Laws 1988, p. 591, § 1; Laws 1997, p. 481, § 2; Laws 2005, Act 20, § 6, eff. July 1, 2005; Laws 2009, Act 56, § 3, eff. July 1, 2009.

Historical and Statutory Notes

The 2005 amendment by Act 20, in subsec. (b), substituted "exceeding three years" for "exceeding two years".

The 2009 amendment by Act 56, in subsec. (c), in par. (3), inserted "or serious mental or emotional trauma".

§ 17–15–6. Investigation of claims; decision of director; review of decision by board

(a) A claim, once accepted for filing and completed, shall be assigned to an investigator. The investigator shall examine the papers filed in support of the claim and cause an investigation to be conducted into the validity of the claim. The investigation shall include, but not be limited to, an examination of law enforcement, court, and official records and reports concerning the crime and an examination of medical, psychiatric, counseling, financial, and hospital reports relating to the injury, serious mental or emotional trauma, or loss upon which the claim is based. All claims arising from the death of an individual as a direct result of a crime must be considered together by a single investigator.

(b) Claims must be investigated and determined regardless of whether the alleged criminal has been apprehended, prosecuted, or convicted of any crime based upon the same incident or whether the alleged criminal has been acquitted or found not guilty of the crime in question.

(c) The investigator conducting the investigation shall file with the director a written report setting forth a recommendation and the investigator's reason therefor. The director shall render a decision and furnish the victim or claimant with a copy of the report if so requested. In cases where an investigative report is provided, information deemed confidential in nature shall be excluded.

(d) The claimant may, within 30 days after receipt of the report of the decision of the director, make an application in writing to the director for review of the decision.

(e) Upon receipt of an application for review pursuant to subsection (d) of this Code section, the director shall forward all relevant documents and information to the board. The board shall review the records and affirm or modify the decision of the director. If considered necessary by the board or if requested by the claimant, the board shall order a hearing prior to rendering a decision. At the hearing, any relevant evidence not legally privileged is admissible. The board shall render a decision within 90 days after completion of the investigation. If the director receives no application for review pursuant to subsection (d) of this Code section, the director's decision becomes final.

(f) The board, for purposes of this chapter, may subpoena witnesses, administer or cause to be administered oaths, and examine such parts of the books and records of the parties to proceedings as relate to questions in dispute.

(g) The director shall, within ten days after receipt of the board's final decision, make a report to the claimant including a copy of the final decision and the reasons why the decision was made.

Laws 1988, p. 591, § 1; Laws 1990, p. 8, § 17; Laws 1994, p. 1800, § 4; Laws 2009, Act 56, § 4, eff. July 1, 2009.

Historical and Statutory Notes

The 2009 amendment by Act 56, in subsec. (a), in the first sentence, substituted "shall" for "must", and in the third sentence, inserted "psychiatric, counseling," and ", serious mental or emotional trauma,".

§ 17–15–7. Eligibility for awards

(a) Except as otherwise provided in this Code section, the following persons are eligible for awards pursuant to this chapter:

(1) A victim;

(2) A dependent spouse or child of a victim;

(2.1) For purposes of an award under subsection (k) of Code Section 17–15–8, any member of the immediate family of a victim of homicide by vehicle caused by a violation of Code Section 40–6–391;

(3) Any person who goes to the aid of another and suffers physical injury, serious mental or emotional trauma, or death as a direct result of acting, not recklessly, to prevent the commission of a crime, to apprehend lawfully a person reasonably suspected of having committed a crime, or to aid the victim of a crime or any person who is injured, traumatized, or killed while aiding or attempting to aid a law enforcement officer in the prevention of crime or apprehension of a criminal at the officer's request;

(4) Any person who is a victim of family violence as defined by Code Section 19–13–1 and anyone who is a victim as a result of a violation of Code Section 40–6–391; or

(5) Any person who is not a direct service provider and who assumes the cost of an eligible expense of a victim regardless of such person's relationship to the victim or whether such person is a dependent of the victim.

(b)(1) Victims may be legal residents or nonresidents of this state. A surviving spouse, parent, or child who is legally dependent for his or her principal support upon a deceased victim is entitled to file a claim under this chapter if the deceased victim would have been so entitled, regardless of the residence or nationality of the surviving spouse, parent, or child.

(2) Victims of crimes occurring within this state who are subject to federal jurisdiction shall be compensated on the same basis as resident victims of crime.

(c) No award of any kind shall be made under this chapter to a victim injured while confined in any federal, state, county, or municipal jail, prison, or other correctional facility.

(d) No award of any kind shall be made under this chapter to a victim of a crime which occurred prior to July 1, 1989.

(e) A person who is criminally responsible for the crime upon which a claim is based or is an accomplice of such person shall not be eligible to receive an award with respect to such claim.

(f) There shall be no denial of compensation to a victim based on that victim's familial relationship with the person who is criminally responsible for the crime.

(g) No award of any kind shall be made under this chapter to a victim of a crime for loss of property.

(h) A victim or claimant who has been convicted of a felony involving criminally injurious conduct and who is currently serving a sentence therefor shall not be considered eligible to receive an award under this chapter. For purposes of this subsection, "criminally injurious conduct" means an act which occurs or is attempted in this state that results in physical injury, serious mental or emotional trauma, or death to a victim, which act is punishable by fine, imprisonment, or death. Such term shall not include acts arising out of the operation of motor vehicles, boats, or aircraft unless the acts were committed with the intent to inflict injury, trauma, or death or unless the acts committed were in violation of Code Section 40–6–391. For the purposes of this subsection, a person shall be deemed to have committed criminally injurious conduct notwithstanding that by reason of age, insanity, drunkenness, or other reason, he or she was legally incapable of committing a crime.

Laws 1988, p. 591, § 1; Laws 1992, p. 2426, § 3; Laws 1994, p. 1800, § 5; Laws 1997, p. 481, § 3; Laws 2004, Act 570, § 3, eff. July 1, 2004; Laws 2009, Act 56, § 5, eff. July 1, 2009.

Historical and Statutory Notes

The 2004 amendment by Act 570 inserted par. (2.1) in subsec. (a).

The 2009 amendment by Act 56, in subsec. (a), in par. (3), inserted ", serious mental or emotional trauma," and inserted "traumatized"; in subsec. (h), substituted "physical" for "personal", inserted ", serious mental or emotional trauma," and inserted "trauma".

§ 17–15–8. Limitations on awards; determination of amount of award

(a) No award may be made unless the board or director finds that:

(1) A crime was committed;

(2) The crime directly resulted in the victim's physical injury, serious mental or emotional trauma, or financial hardship as a result of the victim's physical injury, serious mental or emotional trauma, or the victim's death;

(3) Police records, records of an investigating agency, or records created pursuant to a mandatory reporting requirement show that the crime was promptly reported to the proper authorities. In no case may an award be made where the police records, records of an investigating agency, or records created pursuant to a mandatory reporting requirement show that such report was made more than 72 hours after the occurrence of such crime unless the board, for good cause shown, finds the delay to have been justified; and

(4) The applicant has pursued restitution rights against any person who committed the crime unless the board or director determines that such action would not be feasible.

The board, upon finding that any claimant or award recipient has not fully cooperated with all law enforcement agencies, may deny, reduce, or withdraw any award.

(b) Any award made pursuant to this chapter may be in an amount not exceeding actual expenses, including indebtedness reasonably incurred for medical expenses, loss of wages, funeral expenses, mental health counseling, or support for dependents of a deceased victim necessary as a direct result of the injury or hardship upon which the claim is based.

(c)(1) Notwithstanding any other provisions of this chapter, no award made under the provisions of this chapter shall exceed $1,000.00 in the aggregate; provided, however, with respect to any claim filed with the board as a result of a crime occurring on or after July 1, 1994, no award made under the provisions of this chapter payable to a victim and to all other claimants sustaining economic loss because of injury to or death of such victim shall exceed $5,000.00 in the aggregate; provided, further, with respect to any claim filed with the board as a result of a crime occurring on or after July 1, 1995, no award made under the provisions of this chapter payable to a victim and to all other claimants sustaining economic loss because of injury to or death of such victim shall exceed $10,000.00 in the aggregate; provided, further, with respect to any claim filed with the board as a result of a crime occurring on or after July 1, 2002, no award made under the provisions of this chapter payable to a victim and to all other claimants sustaining economic loss because of injury to or death of such victim shall exceed $25,000.00 in the aggregate; provided, further, with respect to any claim filed with the board for serious mental or emotional trauma, no award shall be made for a crime occurring before July 1, 2009.

(2) No award under this chapter for the following losses shall exceed the maximum amount authorized:

Category	Maximum Award
Lost wages	$ 10,000.00
Funeral expenses	3,000.00
Financial hardship or loss of support	10,000.00
Medical	15,000.00
Counseling	3,000.00
Crime scene sanitization	1,500.00

(d) In determining the amount of an award, the director and board shall determine whether because of his or her conduct the victim of such crime contributed to the infliction of his or her injury, serious mental or emotional trauma, or financial hardship, and the director and board may reduce the amount of the award or reject the claim altogether in accordance with such determination.

(e) The director and board may reject an application for an award when the claimant has failed to cooperate in the verification of the information contained in the application.

(f) Any award made pursuant to this chapter may be reduced by or set off by the amount of any payments received or to be received as a result of the injury, serious mental or emotional trauma:

(1) From or on behalf of the person who committed the crime; and

(2) From any other private or public source, including an award of workers' compensation pursuant to the laws of this state,

provided that private sources shall not include contributions received from family members or persons or private organizations making charitable donations to a victim.

(g) No award made pursuant to this chapter is subject to garnishment, execution, or attachment other than for expenses resulting from the injury or serious mental or emotional trauma which is the basis for the claim.

(h) An award made pursuant to this chapter shall not constitute a payment which is treated as ordinary income under either the provisions of Chapter 7 of Title 48 or, to the extent lawful, under the United States Internal Revenue Code.

(i) Notwithstanding any other provisions of this chapter to the contrary, no awards from state funds shall be paid prior to July 1, 1989.

(j) In any case where a crime results in death, the spouse, children, parents, or siblings of such deceased victim may be considered eligible for an award for the cost of psychological counseling which is deemed necessary as a direct result of said criminal incident. The maximum award for said counseling expenses shall not exceed $3,000.00 for each claimant identified in this subsection.

(k)(1) In addition to any other award authorized by this Code section, in any case where a deceased was a victim of homicide by vehicle caused by a violation of Code Section 40–6–391 on any road which is part of the state highway system, upon request of the next of kin of the deceased, an award of compensation in the form of a memorial sign erected by the Department of Transportation as provided by this subsection shall be paid to an eligible claimant.

(2) The provisions of paragraph (4) of subsection (a) of this Code section shall not apply for purposes of eligibility for awards made under this subsection, and the value of any award

paid to a claimant under this subsection shall not apply toward or be subject to any limitation on award amounts paid to any claimant under other provisions of this Code section.

(3) The Department of Transportation, upon receiving payment for the cost of materials and labor from the board, shall upon request of the next of kin of the deceased erect a sign memorializing the deceased on the right of way of such public highway at the location of the accident or as near thereto as safely and reasonably possible and shall maintain such sign for a period of five years from the date the sign is erected unless its earlier removal is requested in writing by the next of kin. Such sign shall be 24 inches wide by 36 inches high and depict a map of the State of Georgia, with a dark blue background and a black outline of the state boundaries. A border of white stars shall be placed on the inside of the state boundaries, and the sign shall contain the words "In Memory of (name), DUI Victim (date of accident)."

(4) In the event of multiple such claims arising out of a single motor vehicle accident, the names of all deceased victims for whom such claims are made and for whom a request has been made by the next of kin of the deceased may be placed on one such sign or, if necessary, on one such sign and a plaque beneath of the same color as the sign. In the event of multiple claims relating to the same deceased victim, no more than one such sign shall be paid for and erected for such victim.

Laws 1988, p. 591, § 1; Laws 1992, p. 2426, §§ 4, 5; Laws 1994, p. 1800, § 6; Laws 1995, p. 385, § 1; Laws 1997, p. 481, § 4; Laws 2002, p. 843, § 3; Laws 2004, Act 564, § 17, eff. May 13, 2004; Laws 2004, Act 570, § 4, eff. July 1, 2004; Laws 2009, Act 56, § 6, eff. July 1, 2009.

Historical and Statutory Notes

The 2004 amendment by Act 564 was a provision contained in a correction bill.

The 2004 amendment by Act 570 added subsec. (k).

In 2004, the Code Commission, in subsec. (k), par. (1), substituted "deceased, an award" for "deceased an award". See § 28–9–5.

The 2009 amendment by Act 56, in subsec. (a), in par. (3), twice inserted ", records of an investigating agency, or records created pursuant to a mandatory reporting requirement"; in subsec. (c), in par. (1), substituted "further" for "however" following $5,000.00 in the aggregate; provided," and inserted "; provided, further, with respect to any claim filed with the board for serious mental or emotional trauma, no award shall be made for a crime occurring before July 1, 2009"; in subsec. (j), substituted "for each claimant identified in this subsection" for "in the aggregate"; in subsec. (k), in par. (3), inserted "(name)" and "(date of accident)"; inserted "or serious mental or emotional trauma" throughout and made other non-substantive changes.

§ 17–15–9. Payment of awards

Notwithstanding any other provision of this chapter to the contrary, where an award under this chapter has been authorized but there are not sufficient funds in the Georgia Crime Victims Emergency Fund to pay or continue paying the award, then the award or the remaining portion thereof must not be paid unless and until sufficient funds become available from the fund and at such time awards which have not been paid must begin to be paid in chronological order with the oldest award being paid first. In the event an award was to be paid in installments and some remaining installments have not been paid due to a lack of funds, then when funds due become available that award must be paid in full when its appropriate time for payment comes on the chronological list before any other postdated award must be paid. Any award under this chapter is specifically not a claim against the state if it cannot be paid due to a lack of funds in the Georgia Crime Victims Emergency Fund.

Laws 1988, p. 591, § 1.

§ 17–15–10. Georgia Crime Victims Emergency Fund; creation; purpose of fund and moneys paid into or disbursed from fund

(a) There is created a fund to be known as the Georgia Crime Victims Emergency Fund. The custodian of the fund shall be the board. The director shall administer the fund and may invest the resources of the fund in the same manner and fashion that an insurer authorized to issue contracts of life insurance is authorized to invest its resources. The board is specifically authorized to contract with any person or organization, public or private, to administer the fund, assume the powers of the director, and carry out the duties of the board relating to the fund.

(b)(1) The fund shall consist of all moneys received pursuant to Article 7 of Chapter 21 of Title 15 from the assessment of additional penalties in cases involving a violation of Code Section 40–6–391, relating to driving under the influence of alcohol or drugs, or a violation of an ordinance of a political subdivision of this state which has adopted by reference Code Section 40–6–391 pursuant to Article 14 of Chapter 6 of Title 40.

(2) The funds placed in the fund shall also consist of all moneys appropriated by the General Assembly, if any, for the purpose of compensating claimants under this chapter and money recovered on behalf of the state pursuant to this chapter by subrogation or other action, recovered by court order, received from the federal government, received from additional court costs, received from specific tax proceeds allocated to the fund, received from other assessments or fines, or received from any other public or private source pursuant to this chapter.

(c) All funds appropriated to or otherwise paid into the fund shall be presumptively concluded to have been committed to the purpose for which they have been appropriated or paid and shall not lapse.

(d) The board is authorized, subject to the limitations contained in this chapter, to pay the appropriate compensation to the persons eligible for compensation under this chapter from the proceeds of the Georgia Crime Victims Emergency Fund.

(e) After determining that an award should be paid and the method of payment, the board or director, within five days, shall be authorized to draw a warrant or warrants upon the Georgia Crime Victims Emergency Fund to pay the amount of the award from such fund.

Laws 1988, p. 591, § 1; Laws 1992, p. 1836, § 2; Laws 1993, p. 91, § 17.

§ 17–15–11. Unlawful to file false claims for awards

Any person who asserts a false claim under the provisions of this chapter shall be guilty of a misdemeanor and, upon conviction thereof, shall be punished as for a misdemeanor and shall further forfeit any benefit received and shall reimburse and repay the state for payments received or paid on his behalf pursuant to any of the provisions of this chapter.

Laws 1988, p. 591, § 1.

§ 17–15–12. Subrogation; pursuit of civil remedies

(a) Acceptance of an award made pursuant to this chapter shall subrogate the state, to the extent of such award, to any right or right of action occurring to the claimant or the victim to recover payments on account of losses resulting from the crime with respect to which the award is made. The board may waive subrogation when the victim or claimant presents documentation and the board verifies that judgment, settlement, or other sources have not fully reimbursed the victim or claimant for expenses compensable under this chapter.

(b) Acceptance of an award made pursuant to this chapter based on damages from a criminal act shall constitute an agreement on the part of the recipient reasonably to pursue any and all civil remedies arising from any right of action against the person or persons responsible for or committing the act.

Laws 1988, p. 591, § 1; Laws 2008, Act 539, § 4, eff. May 12, 2008.

Historical and Statutory Notes

The 2008 amendment by Act 539, in subsec. (a), inserted "The board may waive subrogation when the victim or claimant presents documentation and the board verifies that judgment, settlement, or other sources have not fully reimbursed the victim or claimant for expenses compensable under this chapter."

§ 17-15-13. Restitution from persons convicted of crimes

(a) Any award or payment of benefits to, or on behalf of, a victim or eligible family member under this chapter shall create a debt due and owing to the state by any person found in a court of competent jurisdiction of this state to have committed such criminal act.

(b) A court, when placing on probation any person who owes a debt to the state as a consequence of a criminal act, may set as a condition of probation the payment of the debt or a portion of the debt to the state. The court may also set the schedule or amounts of payments subject to modification based on change of circumstances.

(c) The State Board of Pardons and Paroles shall also have the right to make payment of the debt or a portion of the debt to the state a condition of parole.

(d) When a child is adjudicated delinquent in a juvenile court proceeding involving a crime upon which a claim under this chapter can be made, the juvenile court in its discretion may order that the child pay the debt to the state as an adult would have to pay had an adult committed the crime. Any assessments so ordered may be made a condition of probation as provided in paragraph (2) of subsection (a) of Code Section 15-11-66.

(e) Payments authorized or required under this Code section shall be paid into the Georgia Crime Victims Emergency Fund. The board shall coordinate the development of policies and procedures for the State Board of Pardons and Paroles and the Administrative Office of the Courts to assure that victim restitution programs are administered in an effective manner to increase payments into the fund.

(f) In every case where an individual is serving under active probation supervision and paying a supervision fee, $ 9.00 per month shall be added to any supervision fee collected by any entity authorized to collect such fees and shall be paid into the Georgia Crime Victims Emergency Fund. This subsection shall apply to probationers supervised under either Code Section 42-8-20 or 42-8-100. The probation supervising entity shall collect and forward the $ 9.00 fee to the Georgia Crime Victims Compensation Board by the end of each month.

Laws 1988, p. 591, § 1; Laws 1998, p. 840, § 1; Laws 2000, p. 20, § 9; Laws 2002, p. 843, § 4.

§ 17-15-14. Spending of funds for public information purposes

The board shall be authorized to designate and expend not more than 10 percent of the moneys collected and paid into the fund pursuant to paragraph (1) of subsection (b) of Code Section 17-15-10 and Code Section 17-15-13 to provide funding to victim service providers for the purpose of disseminating materials regarding the availability of compensation for victims of crime and public information purposes regarding the victim compensation program provided in this chapter.

Laws 1994, p. 1800, § 7.

CHAPTER 15A

COMPENSATION FOR CRIMINALLY INFLICTED PROPERTY DAMAGE

Section

§ 17-15A-1. Additional remedy

The provisions of this chapter are enacted pursuant Article III, Section VI, Paragraph VI(f) of the Constitution and are in addition to those provisions for compensation of innocent victims of other crimes under Chapter 15 of this title.

Laws 2003, Act 38, § 1, eff. July 1, 2003.

§ 17-15A-2. Definitions

As used in this chapter, the term "graffiti" means any inscriptions, words, figures, paintings, or other defacements that are written, marked, etched, scratched, sprayed, drawn, painted, or engraved on or otherwise affixed to any surface of real property or improvements thereon without prior authorization of the owner or occupant of the property by means of any aerosol paint container, broad-tipped marker, gum label, paint stick, graffiti stick, etching equipment, brush, or other device capable of scarring or leaving a visible mark on any surface.

Laws 2003, Act 38, § 1, eff. July 1, 2003.

§ 17-15A-3. Declaration of purpose

The General Assembly finds and declares that:

(1) Criminal street gang activity is a serious and continuing public safety concern;

(2) Criminal trespass and criminal damage to property in the second degree caused by graffiti being placed unlawfully upon private property are crimes frequently associated with criminal street gang activity; and

(3) It is in the public interest, not only in the pursuit of justice but also as a means of combating such criminal street gang activity and of contributing to the general public welfare by improving the esthetics of public views, to compensate as provided in this chapter those private property owners who are the innocent victims of such criminal trespass or criminal damage to property in the second degree by using inmate labor to remove or obliterate graffiti unlawfully placed on private properties when such graffiti is visible from public roads or other public property.

Laws 2003, Act 38, § 1, eff. July 1, 2003.

§ 17–15A–4. Powers and duties of Board of Corrections and political subdivisions

(a) In order to provide a form of compensation by the state to innocent victims of criminal trespass in violation of Code Section 16–7–21 or criminal damage to property in the second degree in violation of Code Section 16–7–23, either of which crime involved the unlawful placement of graffiti upon private property by a person who was not the owner of such property, the Board of Corrections or any political subdivision of this state may authorize the use of labor by inmates from any penal institution or jail under its authority to remove or obliterate such unlawfully placed graffiti when such graffiti is visible from any public road or other public property. Any such authorization and related supervision of inmates shall be a discretionary function within the meaning of paragraph (2) of Code Section 50–21–24 for purposes of sovereign immunity, and the sovereign immunity of neither the state nor any political subdivision thereof is waived for any loss arising out of such authorization or related supervision of inmates. The Board of Corrections shall provide rules and regulations governing such use of labor by inmates from institutions under its jurisdiction.

(b) No graffiti removal program operated by any political subdivision of this state shall charge any fee to any property owner or operator for removal of graffiti from such property.

Laws 2003, Act 38, § 1, eff. July 1, 2003.

CHAPTER 16

DISCOVERY

Article 1

Article 2

Article 1

Definitions; Felony Cases

§ 17–16–1. Definitions

As used in this chapter, the term:

(1) "Possession, custody, or control of the state or prosecution" means an item which is within the possession, custody, or control of the prosecuting attorney or any law enforcement agency involved in the investigation of the case being prosecuted.

(2) "Statement of a witness" means:

(A) A written or recorded statement, or copies thereof, made by the witness that is signed or otherwise adopted or approved by the witness;

(B) A substantially verbatim recital of an oral statement made by the witness that is recorded contemporaneously with the making of the oral statement and is contained in a stenographic, mechanical, electrical, or other recording or a transcription thereof; or

(C) A summary of the substance of a statement made by a witness contained in a memorandum, report, or other type of written document but does not include notes or summaries made by counsel.

(3) "Witness" does not include the defendant.

Laws 1994, p. 1895, § 4; Laws 1995, p. 1250, § 2.

§ 17–16–2. Applicability of law

(a) This article shall apply to all criminal cases in which at least one felony offense is charged in the event that at or prior to arraignment, or at such time as the court permits, the defendant provides written notice to the prosecuting attorney that such defendant elects to have this article apply to the defendant's case. When one defendant in a multidefendant case demands discovery under this article, the provisions of this article shall apply to all defendants in the case, unless a severance is granted.

(b) Except as provided in subsection (c) of this Code section, this article shall not apply to juvenile court proceedings.

(c) This article shall be deemed to have been automatically invoked, without the written notice provided for in subsection (a) of this Code section, when a defendant has sought discovery pursuant to Chapter 11 of Title 9, the "Georgia Civil Practice Act," pursuant to Code Section 15–11–75, or pursuant to the Uniform Rules for the Juvenile Courts of Georgia where such discovery material is the same as the discovery material that may be provided under this article when a written notice is filed pursuant to subsection (a) of this Code section.

(d) Except as provided under Code Section 17–16–8, this article is not intended to authorize discovery or inspection of attorney work product.

(e) This article shall apply also to all criminal cases in which at least one felony offense is charged which was docketed, indicted, or in which an accusation was returned prior to January 1, 1995, if both the prosecuting attorney and the defendant agree in writing that the provisions of this article shall apply to the case.

(f) Except as provided in paragraph (3) of subsection (b) of Code Section 17–16–4, if a defendant has elected to have the provisions of this article apply, the provisions of this article shall also apply to sentencing hearings and the sentencing phase of a death penalty trial.

Laws 1994, p. 1895, § 4; Laws 1995, p. 1250, § 2; Laws 2005, Act 8, § 12, eff. July 1, 2005; Laws 2005, Act 79, § 1, eff. July 1, 2005.

Historical and Statutory Notes

The 2005 amendment by Act 8 added new subsec. (e) (redesignated as subsec. (f) by the Code Commission).

Laws 2005, Act 8, § 17, provides:

"This Act shall apply to all trials which commence on or after July 1, 2005."

The 2005 amendment by Act 79, in subsec. (b), substituted "Except as provided in subsection (c) of this Code section, this" for "This"; redesignated former subsecs. (c) and (d) as subsecs. (d) and (e); and added new subsec. (c).

In 2005, the Code Commission redesignated subsec. (e), added by Laws 2005, Act 8, § 12, as subsec. (f). See § 28-9-5.

§ 17-16-3. Copy of indictment or accusation and list of witnesses furnished accused

Prior to arraignment, every person charged with a criminal offense shall be furnished with a copy of the indictment or accusation and a list of witnesses that may be supplemented pursuant to the other provisions of this article.

Laws 1994, p. 1895, § 4; Laws 1995, p. 1250, § 2.

§ 17-16-4. Disclosure of evidence by prosecution and defendants

(a)(1) The prosecuting attorney shall, no later than ten days prior to trial, or at such time as the court orders, disclose to the defendant and make available for inspection, copying, or photographing any relevant written or recorded statements made by the defendant, or copies thereof, within the possession, custody, or control of the state or prosecution and that portion of any written record containing the substance of any relevant oral statement made by the defendant, whether before or after arrest, in response to interrogation by any person then known to the defendant to be a law enforcement officer or member of the prosecuting attorney's staff. The prosecuting attorney shall also disclose to the defendant the substance of any other relevant oral statement made by the defendant, before or after arrest, in response to interrogation by any person then known by the defendant to be a law enforcement officer or member of the prosecuting attorney's staff if the state intends to use that statement at trial. The prosecuting attorney shall also disclose to the defendant the substance of any other relevant written or oral statement made by the defendant while in custody, whether or not in response to interrogation. Statements of coconspirators that are attributable to the defendant and arguably admissible against the defendant at trial also shall be disclosed under this Code section. Where the defendant is a corporation, partnership, association, or labor union, the court may grant the defendant, upon its motion, discovery of any similar such statement of any witness who was:

(A) At the time of the statement, so situated as an officer or employee as to have been legally able to bind the defendant in respect to conduct constituting the offense; or

(B) At the time of the offense, personally involved in the alleged conduct constituting the offense and so situated as an officer or employee as to have been legally able to bind the defendant in respect to that alleged conduct in which the witness was involved.

(2) The prosecuting attorney shall, no later than ten days prior to trial, or as otherwise ordered by the court, furnish to the defendant a copy of the defendant's Georgia Crime Information Center criminal history, if any, as is within the possession, custody, or control of the state or prosecution. Nothing in this Code section shall affect the provisions of Code Section 17-10-2.

(3)(A) Except as provided in subparagraph (B) of this paragraph, the prosecuting attorney shall, no later than ten days prior to trial, or as otherwise ordered by the court, permit the defendant at a time agreed to by the parties or ordered by the court to inspect and copy or photograph books, papers, documents, photographs, tangible objects, audio and visual tapes, films and recordings, or copies or portions thereof and to inspect and photograph buildings or places which are within the possession, custody, or control of the state or prosecution and are intended for use by the prosecuting attorney as evidence in the prosecution's case-in-chief or rebuttal at the trial or were obtained from or belong to the defendant. Evidence that is within the possession, custody, or control of the Forensic Sciences Division of the Georgia Bureau of Investigation or other laboratory for the purpose of testing and analysis may be examined, tested, and analyzed at the facility where the evidence is being held pursuant to reasonable rules and regulations adopted by the Forensic Sciences Division of the Georgia Bureau of Investigation or the laboratory where the evidence is being held.

(B) With respect to any books, papers, documents, photographs, tangible objects, audio and visual tapes, films and recordings, or copies or portions thereof which are within the possession, custody, or control of the state or prosecution and are intended for use by the prosecuting attorney as evidence in the prosecution's case-in-chief or rebuttal at the trial of any violation of Part 2 of Article 3 of Chapter 12 of Title 16, such evidence shall, no later than ten days prior to trial, or as otherwise ordered by the court, be allowed to be inspected by the defendant but shall not be allowed to be copied.

(4) The prosecuting attorney shall, no later than ten days prior to trial, or as otherwise ordered by the court, permit the defendant at a time agreed to by the parties or ordered by the court to inspect and copy or photograph a report of any physical or mental examinations and of scientific tests or experiments, including a summary of the basis for the expert opinion rendered in the report, or copies thereof, if the state intends to introduce in evidence in its case-in-chief or in rebuttal the results of the physical or mental examination or scientific test or experiment. If the report is oral or partially oral, the prosecuting attorney shall reduce all relevant and material oral portions of such report to writing and shall serve opposing counsel with such portions no later than ten days prior to trial. Nothing in this Code section shall require the disclosure of any other material, note, or memorandum relating to the psychiatric or psychological treatment or therapy of any victim or witness.

(5) The prosecuting attorney shall, no later than ten days prior to trial, or at such time as the court orders but in no event later than the beginning of the trial, provide the defendant with notice of any evidence in aggravation of punishment that the state intends to introduce in sentencing.

(b)(1) The defendant within ten days of timely compliance by the prosecuting attorney but no later than five days prior to trial, or as otherwise ordered by the court, shall permit the prosecuting attorney at a time agreed to by the parties or as ordered by the court to inspect and copy or photograph books, papers, documents, photographs, tangible objects, audio and visual tapes, films and recordings, or copies or portions thereof and to inspect and photograph buildings or places, which are within the possession, custody, or control of the defendant and which the defendant intends to introduce as evidence in the defense's case-in-chief or rebuttal at the trial.

(2) The defendant shall within ten days of timely compliance by the prosecuting attorney but no later than five days prior to trial, or as otherwise ordered by the court, permit the prosecuting attorney at a time agreed to by the parties or as ordered by the court to inspect and copy or photograph a report of any physical or mental examinations and of scientific tests or experiments, including a summary of the basis for the expert opinion rendered in the report, or copies thereof, if the defendant intends to introduce in evidence in the defense's case-in-chief or rebuttal the results of the physical or mental examination or scientific test or experiment. If the report is oral or partially oral, the defendant shall reduce all relevant and material oral portions of such report to writing and shall serve opposing counsel with such portions no later than five days prior to trial. Nothing in this Code section shall require the disclosure of any other material, note, or memorandum

relating to the psychiatric or psychological treatment or therapy of any defendant or witness.

(3)(A) The defendant shall, no later than the announcement of the verdict of the jury or if the defendant has waived a jury trial at the time the verdict is published by the court, serve upon the prosecuting attorney all books, papers, documents, photographs, tangible objects, audio and visual tapes, films and recordings, or copies or portions thereof and to inspect and photograph buildings or places which are within the possession, custody, or control of the defendant and which the defendant intends to introduce as evidence in the presentence hearing.

(B) The defendant shall, no later than the announcement of the verdict of the jury or if the defendant has waived a jury trial at the time the verdict is published by the court, serve upon the prosecuting attorney all reports of any physical or mental examinations and scientific tests or experiments, including a summary of the basis for the expert opinions rendered in the reports, or copies thereof, if the defendant intends to introduce in evidence in the presentence hearing the results of the physical or mental examination or scientific test or experiment. If the report is oral or partially oral, the defendant shall reduce all relevant and material oral portions of such report to writing and shall serve opposing counsel with such portions.

(C) The defendant shall, no later than five days before the trial commences, serve upon the prosecuting attorney a list of witnesses that the defendant intends to call as a witness in the presentence hearing. No later than the announcement of the verdict of the jury or if the defendant has waived a jury trial at the time the verdict is published by the court, the defendant shall produce for the opposing party any statement of such witnesses that is in the possession, custody, or control of the defendants or the defendant's counsel that relates to the subject matter of the testimony of such witnesses unless such statement is protected from disclosure by the privilege contained in paragraph (5), (6), (7), or (8) of Code Section 24–9–21.

(c) If prior to or during trial a party discovers additional evidence or material previously requested or ordered which is subject to discovery or inspection under this article, such party shall promptly notify the other party of the existence of the additional evidence or material and make this additional evidence or material available as provided in this article.

(d) Upon a sufficient showing that a discovery required by this article would create a substantial threat of physical or economic harm to a witness, the court may at any time order that the discovery or inspection be denied, restricted, or deferred or make such other order as is appropriate. Upon motion by a party, the court may permit the party to make such showing, in whole or in part, in the form of a written statement to be inspected by the judge alone. If the court enters an order granting relief following such an ex parte showing, the entire text of the party's statement shall be sealed and preserved in the records of the court subject to further order of the court and to be made available to the appellate court in the event of an appeal.

(e) Discovery with respect to alibi witnesses shall be as provided for in Code Section 17–16–5.

Laws 1994, p. 1895, § 4; Laws 1995, p. 1250, § 2; Laws 2003, Act 26, §§ 5, 6, eff. May 14, 2003; Laws 2005, Act 8, § 13, eff. July 1, 2005; Laws 2008, Act 722, § 2, eff. July 1, 2008.

Historical and Statutory Notes

The 2003 amendment by Act 26, in subsec. (a), par. (4) and subsec. (b), par. (2), inserted the second sentence relating to oral or partially oral reports.

The 2005 amendment by Act 8, in subsec. (a), added par. (5); and in subsec. (b), added par. (3).

Laws 2005, Act 8, § 17, provides:

"This Act shall apply to all trials which commence on or after July 1, 2005."

The 2008 amendment by Act 722, in subsec. (a), rewrote par. (3), which formerly read:

"The prosecuting attorney shall, no later than ten days prior to trial, or as otherwise ordered by the court, permit the defendant at a time agreed to by the parties or ordered by the court to inspect and copy or photograph books, papers, documents, photographs, tangible objects, audio and visual tapes, films and recordings, or copies or portions thereof and to inspect and photograph buildings or places which are within the possession, custody, or control of the state or prosecution and are intended for use by the prosecuting attorney as evidence in the prosecution's case-in-chief or rebuttal at the trial or were obtained from or belong to the defendant. Evidence that is within the possession, custody, or control of the Forensic Sciences Division of the Georgia Bureau of Investigation or other laboratory for the purpose of testing and analysis may be examined, tested, and analyzed at the facility where the evidence is being held pursuant to reasonable rules and regulations adopted by the Forensic Sciences Division of the Georgia Bureau of Investigation or the laboratory where the evidence is being held."

§ 17–16–5. Procedure where defendant intends to offer a defense of alibi

(a) Upon written demand by the prosecuting attorney within ten days after arraignment, or at such time as the court permits, stating the time, date, and place at which the alleged offense was committed, the defendant shall serve within ten days of the demand of the prosecuting attorney or ten days prior to trial, whichever is later, or as otherwise ordered by the court, upon the prosecuting attorney a written notice of the defendant's intention to offer a defense of alibi. Such notice by the defendant shall state the specific place or places at which the defendant claims to have been at the time of the alleged offense and the names, addresses, dates of birth, and telephone numbers of the witnesses, if known to the defendant, upon whom the defendant intends to rely to establish such alibi unless previously supplied.

(b) The prosecuting attorney shall serve upon the defendant within five days of the defendant's written notice but no later than five days before trial, whichever is later, a written notice stating the names, addresses, dates of birth, and telephone numbers of the witnesses, if known to the state, upon whom the state intends to rely to rebut the defendant's evidence of alibi unless previously supplied.

(c) If prior to or during trial, a party learns of an additional witness whose identity, if known, should have been included in the information furnished under subsection (a) or (b) of this Code section, the party shall promptly notify the other party of the existence and identity of such additional witness.

(d) Upon a showing that a disclosure required by this Code section would create a substantial threat of physical or economic harm to a witness, the court may grant an exception to any of the requirements of subsections (a) through (c) of this Code section.

(e) If the defendant withdraws the notice of intention to rely upon an alibi defense, the notice and intention to rely upon an alibi defense are not admissible. However the prosecuting attorney may offer any other evidence regarding alibi.

Laws 1994, p. 1895, § 4; Laws 1995, p. 1250, § 2.

§ 17–16–6. Court orders with respect to failure of state or defendant to comply

If at any time during the course of the proceedings it is brought to the attention of the court that the state has failed to comply with the requirements of this article, the court may order the state to permit the discovery or inspection, interview of the witness, grant a continuance, or, upon a showing of prejudice and bad faith, prohibit the state from introducing the evidence not disclosed or presenting the witness not disclosed, or may enter such other order as it deems just under the circumstances. If at any time during the course of the proceedings it is brought to the attention of the court that the defendant has failed to comply with the requirements of this article, the court may order the defendant to permit the discovery or inspection, interview of the witness, grant a continuance, or, upon a showing of prejudice and bad faith, prohibit the defendant from introducing the evidence not disclosed or presenting the witness not disclosed, or may enter such other order as it deems just under the circumstances. The court may specify the time, place, and manner of making the discovery, inspection, and interview and may prescribe such terms and conditions as are just.

Laws 1994, p. 1895, § 4; Laws 1995, p. 1250, § 2.

§ 17–16–7. Production of statements of witnesses

No later than ten days prior to trial or at such time as the court permits, or at the time of any post-indictment pretrial evidentiary hearing other than a bond hearing, the prosecution or the defendant shall produce for the opposing party any statement of any witness that is in the possession, custody, or control of the state or prosecution or in the possession, custody, or control of the defendant or the defendant's counsel that relates to the subject matter concerning the testimony of the witness that the party in possession, custody, or control of the statement intends to call as a witness at trial or at such post-indictment pretrial evidentiary hearing.

Laws 1994, p. 1895, § 4; Laws 1995, p. 1250, § 2.

§ 17–16–8. Furnishing of witness information; certain information regarding law enforcement officers not required

(a) The prosecuting attorney, not later than ten days before trial, and the defendant's attorney, within ten days after compliance by the prosecuting attorney but no later than five days prior to trial, or as otherwise ordered by the court, shall furnish to the opposing counsel as an officer of the court, in confidence, the names, current locations, dates of birth, and telephone numbers of that party's witnesses, unless for good cause the judge allows an exception to this requirement, in which event the counsel shall be afforded an opportunity to interview such witnesses prior to the witnesses being called to testify.

(b) Nothing in this Code section shall be construed to require the prosecuting attorney to furnish the home address, date of birth, or home telephone number of a witness who is a law enforcement officer. Instead, in such cases, the prosecuting attorney shall furnish to the defense attorney the law enforcement officer's current work location and work phone number.

Laws 1994, p. 1895, § 4; Laws 1995, p. 1250, § 2; Laws 1996, p. 1624, § 4.

§ 17–16–9. Reimbursement for costs incurred in providing documents

Any party providing documents or statements to another party under this article shall be reimbursed for the actual cost incurred in providing such documents. If the court has determined the defendant to be indigent, the court shall determine the means of reimbursement.

Laws 1994, p. 1895, § 4; Laws 1995, p. 1250, § 2.

§ 17–16–10. Information previously provided to defendant or prosecuting attorney need not be included in subsequent information furnished

The defendant need not include in materials and information furnished to the prosecuting attorney under this article any material or information which the prosecuting attorney has already furnished to the defendant under this article. The prosecuting attorney need not include in materials and information furnished to the defendant under this article any material or information which that defendant has already furnished to the prosecuting attorney under this article. Either party may call as a witness any person listed on either the prosecuting attorney's or defendant's witness list.

Laws 1995, p. 1250, § 2.

Article 2

Misdemeanor Cases

§ 17–16–20. Applicability of law

The provisions of this article shall apply only to misdemeanor cases or to felony cases docketed, indicted, or in which an accusation was returned prior to January 1, 1995, if the prosecuting attorney and the defendant do not agree in writing that the provisions of Article 1 of this chapter shall apply.

Laws 1994, p. 1895, § 4; Laws 1995, p. 1250, § 3.

§ 17–16–21. Copy of indictment or accusation and list of witnesses furnished accused

Prior to arraignment, every person charged with a criminal offense shall be furnished with a copy of the indictment or accusation and, on demand, with a list of the witnesses on whose testimony the charge against such person is founded. Without the consent of the defendant, no witness shall be permitted to testify for the state whose name does not appear on the list of witnesses as furnished to the defendant unless the prosecuting attorney shall state that the evidence sought to be presented is newly discovered evidence which the state was not aware of at the time of its furnishing the defendant with a list of the witnesses.

Laws 1994, p. 1895, § 4.

§ 17–16–22. Discovery of defendant's statements

(a) At least ten days prior to the trial of the case, the defendant shall be entitled to have a copy of any statement given by the defendant while in police custody. The defendant may make such request for a copy of any such statement, in writing, within any reasonable period of time prior to trial.

(b) If the defendant's statement is oral or partially oral, the prosecution shall furnish, in writing, all relevant and material portions of the defendant's statement.

(c) Failure of the prosecution to comply with a defendant's timely written request for a copy of such defendant's statement, whether written or oral, shall result in such statement being excluded and suppressed from the prosecution's use in its case-in-chief or in rebuttal.

(d) If the defendant's statement is oral, no relevant and material, incriminating or inculpatory, portion of the statement of the defendant may be used against the defendant unless it has been previously furnished to the defendant, if a timely written request for a copy of the statement has been made by the defendant.

(e) This Code section shall not apply to evidence discovered after a request has been filed. If a request has been filed, such evidence shall be produced as soon as possible after it has been discovered.

Laws 1994, p. 1895, § 4.

§ 17–16–23. Discovery of scientific reports

(a) As used in this Code section, the term "written scientific reports" includes, but is not limited to, reports from the Division of Forensic Sciences of the Georgia Bureau of Investigation; an autopsy report by the coroner of a county or by a private pathologist; blood alcohol test results done by a law enforcement agency or a private physician; and similar types of reports that would be used as scientific evidence by the prosecution in its case-in-chief or in rebuttal against the defendant.

(b) In all criminal trials the defendant shall be entitled to have a complete copy of any written scientific reports in the possession of the prosecution which will be introduced in whole or in part against the defendant by the prosecution in its case-in-chief or in rebuttal. The request for a copy of any written scientific reports shall be made by the defendant in writing at arraignment or within any reasonable time prior to trial. If such written request is not made at arraignment, it shall be within the sound discretion of the trial judge to determine in each case what constitutes a reasonable time prior to trial. If the scientific report is in the possession of or available to the prosecuting attorney, the prosecuting attorney must comply with this Code section at least ten days prior to the trial of the case.

(c) Failure by the prosecution to furnish the defendant with a copy of any written scientific report, when a proper and timely written demand has been made by the defendant, shall result in such report being excluded and suppressed from evidence in the prosecution's case-in-chief or in rebuttal.

Laws 1994, p. 1895, § 4.

CHAPTER 17

CRIME VICTIMS' BILL OF RIGHTS

Section

§ 17–17–1. Legislative findings; basic rights

The General Assembly hereby finds and declares it to be the policy of this state that victims of crimes should be accorded certain basic rights just as the accused are accorded certain basic rights. These rights include:

(1) The right to reasonable, accurate, and timely notice of any scheduled court proceedings or any changes to such proceedings;

(2) The right to reasonable, accurate, and timely notice of the arrest, release, or escape of the accused;

(3) The right not to be excluded from any scheduled court proceedings, except as provided in this chapter or as otherwise required by law;

(4) The right to be heard at any scheduled court proceedings involving the release, plea, or sentencing of the accused;

(5) The right to file a written objection in any parole proceedings involving the accused;

(6) The right to confer with the prosecuting attorney in any criminal prosecution related to the victim;

(7) The right to restitution as provided by law;

(8) The right to proceedings free from unreasonable delay; and

(9) The right to be treated fairly and with dignity by all criminal justice agencies involved in the case.

Laws 1995, p. 385, § 2; Laws 2010, Act 403, § 6, eff. July 1, 2010.

Historical and Statutory Notes

The 2010 amendment by Act 403 added "These rights include:" and pars. (1) through (9).

§ 17–17–2. Short title

This chapter shall be known and may be cited as the "Crime Victims' Bill of Rights."

Laws 1995, p. 385, § 2.

§ 17–17–3. Definitions

As used in this chapter, the term:

(1) "Accused" means a person suspected of and subject to arrest for, arrested for, or convicted of a crime against a victim.

(1.1) "Arrest" means an actual custodial restraint of a person or the person's submission to custody and includes the taking of a child into custody.

(2) "Arresting law enforcement agency" means any law enforcement agency, other than the investigating law enforcement agency, which arrests the accused.

(3) "Compensation" means awards granted by the Georgia Crime Victims Compensation Board pursuant to Chapter 15 of this title.

(4) "Crime" means an act committed in this state which constitutes any violation of Chapter 5 of Title 16; Chapter 6 of Title 16; Article 1, 3, or 4 of Chapter 7 of Title 16; Article 1 or 2 of Chapter 8 of Title 16; Chapter 9 of Title 16; Part 3 of

Article 3 of Chapter 12 of Title 16; Code Section 30–5–8; Code Section 40–6–393; Code Section 40–6–393.1; or Code Section 40–6–394.

(4.1) "Criminal justice agency" means an arresting law enforcement agency, custodial authority, investigating law enforcement agency, prosecuting attorney, or the State Board of Pardons and Paroles.

(5) "Custodial authority" means a warden, sheriff, jailer, deputy sheriff, police officer, correctional officer, officer or employee of the Department of Corrections or the Department of Juvenile Justice, or any other law enforcement officer having actual custody of the accused.

(6) "Investigating law enforcement agency" means the law enforcement agency responsible for the investigation of the crime.

(7) "Notice," "notification," or "notify" means a written notice when time permits or, failing such, a documented effort to reach the victim by telephonic or other means.

(8) "Person" means an individual.

(9) "Prompt notice," "prompt notification," or "promptly notify" means notification given to the victim as soon as practically possible so as to provide the victim with a meaningful opportunity to exercise his or her rights pursuant to this chapter.

(10) "Prosecuting attorney" means the district attorney, the solicitor-general of a state court or the solicitor of any other court, the Attorney General, a county attorney opposing an accused in a habeas corpus proceeding, or the designee of any of these.

(11) "Victim" means:

(A) A person against whom a crime has been perpetrated or has allegedly been perpetrated; or

(B) In the event of the death of the crime victim, the following relations if the relation is not either in custody for an offense or the defendant:

(i) The spouse;

(ii) An adult child if division (i) does not apply;

(iii) A parent if divisions (i) and (ii) do not apply;

(iv) A sibling if divisions (i) through (iii) do not apply; or

(v) A grandparent if divisions (i) through (iv) do not apply; or

(C) A parent, guardian, or custodian of a crime victim who is a minor or a legally incapacitated person except if such parent, guardian, or custodian is in custody for an offense or is the defendant.

Laws 1995, p. 385, § 2; Laws 1996, p. 748, § 17; Laws 1997, p. 1453, § 1; Laws 2010, Act 403, § 7, eff. July 1, 2010.

Historical and Statutory Notes

The 2010 amendment by Act 403 added pars. (1.1) and (4.1); rewrote par. (4); and in par. (11), subpar. (A), inserted "or has allegedly been perpetrated" after "has been perpetrated". Prior to amendment par. (4) had read:

"(4) 'Crime' means an act committed in this state which constitutes any violation of Chapter 5 of Title 16, relating to crimes against persons; Chapter 6 of Title 16, relating to sexual offenses; Article 1 or Article 3 of Chapter 7 of Title 16, relating to burglary and arson; Article 1 or Article 2 of Chapter 8 of Title 16, relating to offenses involving theft and armed robbery; Code Section 16–12–100, relating to sexual exploitation of children; Code Section 40–6–393, relating to homicide by vehicle; Code Section 40–6–393.1, relating to feticide by vehicle; or Code Section 40–6–394, relating to serious injury by vehicle."

§ 17–17–4. Designation of persons to act in place of victim during duration of physical disability

If a victim is physically unable to exercise privileges and rights under this chapter, the victim may designate by written instrument his or her spouse, adult child, parent, sibling, or grandparent to act in place of the victim during the duration of the physical disability. During the physical disability, notices to be provided under this chapter to the victim shall continue to be afforded only to the victim.

Laws 1995, p. 385, § 2.

§ 17–17–5. Notice of accused's arrest, release, escape or violation of terms of release

(a) All victims, wherever practicable, shall be entitled to notification of:

(1) The accused's arrest;

(2) The accused's release from custody;

(3) Any judicial proceeding at which the release of the accused will be considered;

(4) An escape by the accused and his or her subsequent rearrest; and

(5) If the accused is released from custody and the terms or conditions of such release require that the accused participate in an electronic release and monitoring program, the accused's violation of the terms or conditions of the electronic release and monitoring program, provided that an arrest warrant has been issued for the accused and the accused is prohibited from contacting the victim.

(b) No such notification shall be required unless the victim provides a current address and telephone number to which such notice can be directed.

(c) The criminal justice agency having knowledge of an event described in subsection (a) of this Code section shall provide notice to the victim of such event. Such agency shall advise the victim of his or her right to notification pursuant to this chapter and of the requirement of the victim's providing a current address and telephone number to which the notification shall be directed. Such victim shall transmit the telephone number described in this subsection to the appropriate criminal justice agency or custodial authority as provided for in this chapter.

Laws 1995, p. 385, § 2; Laws 2010, Act 403, § 8, eff. July 1, 2010.

Historical and Statutory Notes

The 2010 amendment by Act 403 rewrote the section which had read as follows:

"(a) All victims, wherever practicable, shall be entitled to notification as defined by paragraph (7) of Code Section 17-17-3 of the accused's arrest, of the accused's release from custody, and of any judicial proceeding at which the release of the accused will be considered. No such notification shall be required unless the victim provides a landline telephone number other than a pocket pager or electronic communication device number to which such notice can be directed.

"(b) The investigating law enforcement agency, prosecuting attorney, or custodial authority who is required to provide notification pursuant to this chapter shall advise the victim of his or her right to notification and of the requirement of the victim's providing a landline telephone number other than a pocket pager or electronic communication device number to which the notification shall be directed. Such victim shall transmit the telephone number described in this subsection to the appropriate investigating law enforcement agency, prosecuting attorney, or custodial authority as provided for in this chapter."

§ 17–17–5.1. Notice from Department of Behavioral Health and Developmental Disabilities of accused's release, discharge, escape or subsequent readmission

(a) If the accused is committed to the Department of Behavioral Health and Developmental Disabilities pursuant to the provisions of Part 2 of Article 6 of Chapter 7 of this title, the department shall, upon the written request of the victim, mail to the victim at least ten days before the release or discharge of the accused notice of the release or discharge of the accused.

(b) The Department of Behavioral Health and Developmental Disabilities shall mail to the victim immediately after the escape or subsequent readmission of the accused notice of such escape or subsequent readmission of the person who is placed by court order in the custody of the department pursuant to the provisions of Part 2 of Article 6 of Chapter 7 of this title.

Laws 2010, Act 403, § 9, eff. July 1, 2010.

§ 17–17–6. Information to be made available to victim upon initial contact by law enforcement and court personnel

(a) Upon initial contact with a victim, all law enforcement and court personnel shall make available to the victim the following information written in plain language:

(1) The possibility of pretrial release of the accused, the victim's rights and role in the stages of the criminal justice process, and the means by which additional information about these stages can be obtained;

(2) The availability of victim compensation; and

(3) The availability of community based victim service programs.

(b) The Criminal Justice Coordinating Council is designated as the coordinating entity between various law enforcement agencies, the courts, and social service delivery agencies. The Criminal Justice Coordinating Council shall develop and disseminate written information upon which law enforcement personnel may rely in disseminating the information required by this chapter.

Laws 1995, p. 385, § 2.

§ 17–17–7. Notification of victim by investigating law enforcement agency, prosecuting attorney, and custodial authority

(a) Whenever possible, the investigating law enforcement agency shall give to a victim prompt notification as defined in paragraph (9) of Code Section 17–17–3 of the arrest of an accused.

(b) The arresting law enforcement agency shall promptly notify the investigating law enforcement agency of the accused's arrest.

(c) Whenever possible, the prosecuting attorney shall notify the victim prior to any proceeding in which the release of the accused will be considered.

(d) Whenever possible, the prosecuting attorney shall offer the victim the opportunity to express the victim's opinion on the release of the accused pending judicial proceedings.

(e) Whenever possible, the custodial authority shall give prompt notification to a victim of the release of the accused.

(1) Prompt notification of release from a county or municipal jail is effected by placing a telephone call to the telephone number provided by the victim and giving notice to the victim or any person answering the telephone who appears to be sui juris or by leaving an appropriate message on a telephone answering machine.

(2) Notification of release from the custody of the state or any county correctional facility shall be in the manner provided by law.

(f) If the court has granted a pretrial release or supersedeas bond, the victim shall have the right to file a written complaint with the prosecuting attorney asserting acts or threats of physical violence or intimidation by the accused or at the accused's direction against the victim or the victim's immediate family. Based on the victim's written complaint or other evidence, the prosecuting attorney may move the court that the bond or personal recognizance of an accused be revoked.

Laws 1995, p. 385, § 2.

§ 17–17–8. Information to be provided to victim by prosecuting attorney; restitution information

(a) Upon initial contact with a victim, a prosecuting attorney shall give prompt notification to the victim of the following:

(1) The procedural steps in processing a criminal case including the right to restitution;

(2) The rights and procedures of victims under this chapter;

(3) Suggested procedures if the victim is subjected to threats or intimidation;

(4) The names and telephone numbers of contact persons at both the office of the custodial authority and in the prosecuting attorney's office; and

(5) The names and telephone numbers of contact persons at the office of the investigating agency where the victim may make application for the return of any of the victim's property that was taken during the course of the investigation, as provided by Code Section 17–5–50.

(b) If requested in writing by the victim and to the extent possible, the prosecuting attorney shall give prompt advance notification of any scheduled court proceedings and notice of any changes to that schedule. Court proceedings shall include, but not be limited to, pretrial commitment hearings, arraignment, motion hearings, trial, sentencing, restitution hearings, appellate review, and post-conviction relief. The prosecuting attorney shall notify all victims of the requirement to make such request in writing.

(c)(1) In the event the victim seeks restitution, the victim shall provide the prosecuting attorney with his or her legal name, address, phone number, social security number, date of birth, and, if the victim has an e-mail address, his or her e-mail address. The victim shall also provide such information, other than a social security number, to the prosecuting attorney for a secondary contact person in the event the victim cannot be reached after reasonable efforts are made to contact such victim. The prosecuting attorney shall advise the victim of any agency that will receive such information and advise the victim that he or she is responsible for updating such information with the prosecuting attorney while the case involving the victim is pending and that he or she should update the agency with such information after a restitution order has been entered.

(2) The prosecuting attorney shall transmit the information collected in paragraph (1) of this subsection to the Department of Corrections, Department of Juvenile Justice, or the State Board of Pardons and Paroles, as applicable, if an order of restitution is entered.

(3) The information collected pursuant to paragraph (1) of this subsection shall be treated as confidential and shall not be disclosed to any person outside of the disclosure provided by this subsection; such information shall not be subject to Article 4 of Chapter 18 of Title 50, relating to open records, or subject to subpoena, discovery, or introduction into evidence in any civil or criminal proceeding.

Laws 1995, p. 385, § 2; Laws 2010, Act 403, § 10, eff. July 1, 2010.

Historical and Statutory Notes

The 2010 amendment by Act 403, in subsec. (a), added "including the right to restitution" in par. (1) and added par. (5); in subsec. (b), added "restitution hearings" to the second sentence; and added subsec. (c).

§ 17–17–8.1. Victim interviews and contact

(a) A victim shall have the right to refuse to submit to an interview by the accused, the accused's attorney, or an agent of the accused. It shall be the duty of the prosecuting attorney to advise a victim that he or she has the right to agree to such an interview or to refuse such an interview.

(b) If a victim agrees to be interviewed, such victim may set conditions for such interview as he or she desires. Conditions may include, but shall not be limited to, the time, date, and location of the interview, what other persons may be present during the interview, any security arrangements for the interview, and whether or not the interview may be recorded. If requested by a victim, the prosecuting attorney or his or her agent may attend the interview. A victim has the right to terminate the interview at any time or to refuse to answer any question during the interview.

(c) The accused, the accused's attorney, and any agent of the accused shall not contact a victim in an unreasonable manner; and if a victim has clearly expressed to any such party a desire not to be contacted, no contact shall be made. When making any permissible contact with the victim, the accused's attorney or an agent of the accused shall make a clear statement that he or she is contacting the victim on behalf of the accused.

(d) For the purposes of this Code section, a peace officer shall not be considered a victim if the act that would have made the officer a victim occurs while the peace officer is acting within the scope of the officer's official duties.

(e) Except as provided in this Code section, the prosecuting attorney shall not take any action to deny an accused's attorney access to a victim for the purpose of interviewing such victim.

Laws 2010, Act 403, § 11, eff. July 1, 2010.

§ 17–17–9. Victim's right to be present during court proceedings; separation of victims from accused and related parties

(a) A victim has the right to be present at all criminal proceedings in which the accused has the right to be present. A victim or member of the immediate family of a victim shall not be excluded from any portion of any hearing, trial, or proceeding pertaining to the offense based solely on the fact that such person is subpoenaed to testify unless it is established that such victim or family member is a material and necessary witness to such hearing, trial, or proceeding and the court finds that there is a substantial probability that such person's presence would impair the conduct of a fair trial. The provisions of this Code section shall not be construed as impairing the authority of a judge to remove a person from a trial or hearing or any portion thereof for the same causes and in same manner as the rules of court or law provides for the exclusion or removal of the accused. A motion to exclude a victim or family members from the courtroom for any reason other than misconduct shall be made and determined prior to jeopardy attaching.

(b) A victim of a criminal offense who has been or may be subpoenaed to testify at such hearing or trial shall be exempt from the provisions of Code Section 24–9–61 requiring sequestration; provided, however, that the court shall require that the victim be scheduled to testify as early as practical in the proceedings.

(c) If the victim is excluded from the courtroom, the victim shall have the right to wait in an area separate from the accused, from the family and friends of the accused, and from witnesses for the accused during any judicial proceeding involving the accused, provided that such separate area is available and its use in such a manner practical. If such a separate area is not available or practical, the court, upon request of the victim made through the prosecuting attorney, shall attempt to minimize the victim's contact with the accused, the accused's relatives and friends, and witnesses for the accused during any such judicial proceeding.

Laws 1995, p. 385, § 2; Laws 2010, Act 403, § 12, eff. July 1, 2010.

Historical and Statutory Notes

The 2010 amendment by Act 403 added subsecs. (a) and (b); redesignated former section as subsec. (c) and inserted "If the victim is excluded from the courtroom" at the beginning of the subsection.

§ 17–17–9.1. Victim's communications

Communications between a victim, other than a peace officer, and victim assistance personnel appointed by a prosecuting attorney and any notes, memoranda, or other records made by such victim assistance personnel of such communication shall be considered attorney work product of the prosecuting attorney and not subject to disclosure except where such disclosure is required by law. Such work product shall be subject to other exceptions that apply to attorney work product generally.

Laws 2010, Act 403, § 13, eff. July 1, 2010.

§ 17–17–10. Information concerning victim's address, telephone number, or place of employment not to be transmitted to defendant

As a condition of permitting a response to an inquiry as to the victim's current address, telephone number, or place of employment, the court may require counsel or any other officer of the court, including but not limited to counsel for the defendant, not to transmit or permit transmission to the defendant of the victim's current address, telephone number, or place of employment by the counsel or officer of the court or any employee, agent, or other representative of the counsel or officer of the court.

Laws 1995, p. 385, § 2.

§ 17–17–11. Victim's right to express opinion as to disposition of accused's case

The prosecuting attorney shall offer the victim the opportunity to express the victim's opinion on the disposition of an accused's case, including the views of the victim regarding:

(1) Plea or sentence negotiations; and

(2) Participation in pretrial or post-conviction diversion programs.

This provision shall not limit any other right created pursuant to state law.

Laws 1995, p. 385, § 2.

§ 17–17–12. Notification of appellate proceedings by Attorney General

(a) Upon the written request of the victim, the prosecuting attorney shall notify the victim of the following:

(1) That the accused has filed a motion for new trial, an appeal of his or her conviction, or an extraordinary motion for new trial;

(2) Whether the accused has been released on bail or other recognizance pending the disposition of the motion or appeal;

(3) The time and place of any appellate court proceedings relating to the motion or appeal and any changes in the time or place of those proceedings; and

(4) The result of the motion or appeal.

(b) The Attorney General shall notify the prosecuting attorney of the filing of collateral attacks on convictions of this state which are being defended by the Attorney General.

(b.1) In cases in which the accused is convicted of a capital offense and receives the death penalty, the Attorney General shall:

(1) Notify the prosecuting attorney and upon the written request of the victim notify the victim of the filing and disposition of all collateral attacks on such conviction which are being defended by the Attorney General, including, but not limited to, petitions for a writ of habeas corpus, and the time and place of any such proceedings and any changes in the time or place of those proceedings; and

(2) Provide the prosecuting attorney and upon the written request of the victim provide the victim with a report on the status of all pending appeals, collateral attacks, and other litigation concerning such conviction which is being defended by the Attorney General at least every six months until the accused dies or the sentence or conviction is overturned or commuted or otherwise reduced to a sentence other than the death penalty.

(c) In the event the accused is granted a new trial or the conviction is reversed or remanded and the case is returned to the trial court for further proceedings, the victim shall be entitled to request the rights and privileges provided by this chapter.

Laws 1995, p. 385, § 2; Laws 2002, p. 1093, § 1; Laws 2003, Act 37, § 4, eff. May 27, 2003; Laws 2010, Act 403, § 14, eff. July 1, 2010.

Historical and Statutory Notes

The 2003 amendment by Act 37, in subsec. (a), rewrote par. (1) which read:

"(1) That the accused has filed a motion for new trial or an appeal of his or her conviction;"

The 2010 amendment by Act 403 added subsec. (b) and redesignated former subsec. (b) as (b.1); and in subsec. (b.1), pars. (1) and (2), inserted "the prosecuting attorney and upon the written request of the victim" at the beginning of each paragraph.

§ 17-17-12.1. Block of inmate mail

(a) As used in this Code section, the term "mail" means any form of written communication, including, but not limited to, letters, cards, postcards, packages, parcels, and e-mail as defined by Code Section 16-9-100, text messaging, and any other form of electronic communication which is knowingly intended to be delivered to or received by a victim, any member of the victim's family, or any member of the victim's household.

(b)(1) A victim shall have the right to request not to receive mail from an inmate who was convicted of committing a criminal offense against such victim or was adjudicated by the juvenile court of having committed a delinquent act or designed felony against such victim.

(2) A victim's right to request not to receive mail from such inmate shall extend to any member of such victim's family or any member of such victim's household during the term of the sentence imposed or dispositional order for such offense.

(3) As soon as practical following a conviction or adjudication, a victim shall be provided with the instructions for requesting that inmate mail be blocked as provided in subsection (c) of this Code section. If the conviction is from a state or superior court, it shall be the duty of the prosecuting attorney to provide a victim with such instructions. If the adjudication is from the juvenile court, such instructions shall be provided by the juvenile court.

(c) The Department of Corrections and the Department of Juvenile Justice shall develop and provide to the prosecuting attorneys and juvenile courts, respectively, the procedures a victim shall follow in order to block inmate mail. Such procedures may include secure electronic means provided that an alternate, nonelectronic procedure is available for victims without access to a computer. Such departments shall also develop and implement appropriate administrative sanctions which shall be imposed against an inmate violating the provisions of this Code section.

(d) If a victim submits a request to block inmate mail, the Department of Corrections, in the case of an adult, or the Department of Juvenile Justice, in the case of a juvenile, shall:

(1) Notify any other custodial authority having actual custody of the inmate of the names and addresses of such victim and the family or household members denoted by such victim;

(2) Notify the inmate of the request to have mail blocked and advise the inmate that sending mail directly or through any third party to such victim or the family or household members denoted by such victim is prohibited and will result in appropriate sanctions and review of all outgoing mail; and

(3) Institute such procedures to insure that the inmate cannot send mail directly or through any third party to such victim or the family or household members denoted by such victim.

(e) Any custodial authority having actual custody of an inmate with mail restrictions shall not knowingly forward mail addressed to any person who requests not to receive mail pursuant to this Code section.

(f) The imposition of sanctions by a custodial authority pursuant to this Code section shall not preclude the imposition of any other remedies provided by law, nor shall such sanctions bar prosecution of the inmate for any criminal offense which may have been committed in sending such mail.

(g) Notwithstanding the provisions of Article 4 of Chapter 18 of Title 50, information concerning the names and addresses of a victim, and the family or household members denoted by such victim, who requests that inmate mail be blocked shall not be open to inspection by or made available to the public and shall not be subject to discovery in any civil or criminal case or administrative proceeding unless the court, after notice and a hearing, makes a finding of fact that such information is material and relevant to the case and that such information is not available from any other source.

Laws 2010, Act 403, § 15, eff. July 1, 2010.

§ 17-17-13. Notification of victim prior to consideration of pardon, parole, or other clemency by State Board of Pardons and Paroles

The State Board of Pardons and Paroles shall give 20 days' advance notification to a victim whenever it considers making a final decision to grant parole or any other manner of executive clemency action to release a defendant for a period exceeding 60 days; and the board shall provide the victim with an opportunity to file a written objection to such action. No notification need be given unless the victim has expressed objection to release or has expressed a desire for such notification and has provided the State Board of Pardons and Paroles with a current address and telephone number.

Laws 1995, p. 385, § 2.

§ 17-17-14. Responsibility of victim to keep certain persons informed of victim's current address and phone number

(a) It is the right and responsibility of the victim who desires notification under this chapter or under any other notification statute to keep the following informed of the victim's current address and phone number:

(1) The investigating law enforcement agency;

(2) The prosecuting attorney, until final disposition or completion of the appellate and post-conviction process, whichever occurs later; and

(3) As directed by the prosecuting attorney, the sheriff if the accused is in the sheriff's custody for pretrial, trial, or post-conviction proceedings; the Department of Corrections if the accused is in the custody of the state; or any county correctional facility if the defendant is sentenced to serve time in a facility which is not a state facility; and

(4) The State Board of Pardons and Paroles.

(b) Current addresses and telephone numbers of victims and their names provided for the purposes of notification pursuant to this chapter or any other notification statute shall be confidential and used solely for the purposes of this chapter and shall not be subject to disclosure under Article 4 of Chapter 18 of Title 50, relating to inspection of public records.

Laws 1995, p. 385, § 2.

§ 17–17–15. Failure to provide information or notifications

(a) Failure to provide or to timely provide any of the information or notifications required by this chapter shall not subject the person responsible for such notification or that person's employer to any liability for damages.

(b) Failure to provide a victim with any of the rights required by law shall not give an accused a basis for error in either an appellate action or a post-conviction writ of habeas corpus.

(c) This chapter does not confer upon a victim any standing to participate as a party in a criminal proceeding or to contest the disposition of any charge.

(d) The enumeration of these rights shall not be construed to deny or diminish other notification rights granted by state law.

(e) The victim may waive any of the information or notification or other rights provided for by this chapter.

Laws 1995, p. 385, § 2.

§ 17–17–16. Temporary restraining orders and protective orders prohibiting harassment of victims or witnesses

(a) As used in this Code section, the term:

(1) "Course of conduct" spans a series of acts over a period of time, however short, indicating a continuity of purpose.

(2) "Harassment" means a course of conduct directed at a specific person that causes substantial emotional distress in such person.

(b)(1) A superior court, upon application of a prosecuting attorney, shall issue a temporary restraining order prohibiting harassment of a victim or witness in a criminal case if the court finds from specific facts shown by affidavit or by verified complaint that there are reasonable grounds to believe that harassment of an identified victim or witness in a criminal case exists or that such order is necessary to prevent and restrain an offense under Code Section 16–10–32 or 16–10–93.

(2)(A) A temporary restraining order may be issued under this Code section without written or oral notice to the adverse party or such party's attorney in a civil action under this Code section if the court finds, upon written certification of facts by the prosecuting attorney, that such notice should not be required and that there is a reasonable probability that the state will prevail on the merits.

(B) A temporary restraining order issued without notice under this Code section shall be endorsed with the date and hour of issuance and be filed forthwith in the office of the clerk of the court issuing the order.

(C) A temporary restraining order issued under this Code section shall expire at such time, not to exceed ten days from issuance, as the court directs. The court, for good cause shown before expiration of such order, may extend the expiration date of the order for up to ten days or for such longer period agreed to by the adverse party.

(D) When a temporary restraining order is issued without notice, the motion for a protective order shall be set down for hearing at the earliest possible time and takes precedence over all matters except older matters of the same character; and at the hearing, if the prosecuting attorney does not proceed with the application for a protective order, the court shall dissolve the temporary restraining order.

(E) If on two days' notice to the prosecuting attorney or on such shorter notice as the court may prescribe, the adverse party appears and moves to dissolve or modify the temporary restraining order, the court shall proceed to hear and determine such motion as expeditiously as the ends of justice require.

(F) A temporary restraining order shall set forth the reasons for the issuance of such order, be specific in terms, and describe in reasonable detail and not by reference to the complaint or other document the act or acts being restrained.

(c)(1) A superior court, upon motion of the prosecuting attorney, shall issue a protective order prohibiting harassment of a victim or witness in a criminal case if the court, after a hearing, finds by a preponderance of the evidence that harassment of an identified victim or witness in a criminal case exists or that such order is necessary to prevent and restrain an offense under Code Section 16–10–32 or 16–10–93.

(2) At the hearing referred to in paragraph (1) of this subsection, any adverse party named in the complaint shall have the right to present evidence and cross-examine witnesses.

(3) A protective order shall set forth the reasons for the issuance of such order, be specific in terms, and describe in reasonable detail and not by reference to the complaint or other document the act or acts being restrained.

(4) The court shall set the duration of effect of the protective order for such period as the court determines necessary to prevent harassment of the victim or witness but in no case for a period in excess of three years from the date of such order's issuance. The prosecuting attorney may, at any time within 90 days before the expiration of such order, apply for a new protective order under this Code section.

(d) Article 5 of Chapter 11 of Title 9, relating to depositions and discovery, shall not apply to actions brought pursuant to this Code section.

Laws 1998, p. 270, § 10.

CHAPTER 18

WRITTEN STATEMENTS OF INFORMATION TO VICTIMS OF RAPE OR FORCIBLE SODOMY

Section

§ 17–18–1. Certain information to be provided to persons believed to be victims of rape or aggravated sodomy

When any employee of the Department of Human Services, Department of Community Health, Department of Behavioral Health and Developmental Disabilities, a law enforcement agency, or a court has reason to believe that he or she in the course of official duties is speaking to an adult who is or has been a victim of a violation of Code Section 16–6–1, relating to rape, or Code Section 16–6–2, relating to aggravated sodomy, such employee shall offer or provide such adult a written statement of information for victims of rape or aggravated sodomy. Such written statement shall, at a minimum, include the information set out in Code Section 17–18–2 and may include additional information regarding resources available to victims of sexual assault. Information for victims of rape or aggravated sodomy may be provided in any language.

Laws 1996, p. 1115, § 5; Laws 2009, Act 102, § 1–15, eff. July 1, 2009.

Historical and Statutory Notes

The 2009 amendment by Act 102 substituted "Department of Human Services, Department of Community Health, Department of Behavioral Health and Developmental Disabilities," for "Department of Human Resources,".

§ 17–18–2. Information to be provided set out

The following information in substantially the form set out in this Code section shall be provided to adult victims of rape or aggravated sodomy in accordance with Code Section 17–18–1:

—INFORMATION FOR VICTIMS OF RAPE OR FORCIBLE SODOMY—

If you are the victim of rape or forcible sodomy, you have certain rights under the law.

Rape or forcible sodomy by a stranger or a person known to you, including rape or forcible sodomy by a person married to you, is a crime. You can ask the government's lawyer to prosecute a person who has committed a crime. The government pays the cost of prosecuting for crimes.

If you are the victim of rape or forcible sodomy you should contact a local police department or other law enforcement agency immediately. A police officer will come to take a report and collect evidence. You should keep any clothing you were wearing at the time of the crime as well as any other evidence such as bed sheets. Officers will take you to the hospital for a medical examination. You should not shower or douche before the examination. The law requires that the police department or law enforcement agency investigating the crime pay for the medical examination to the extent of the cost for the collection of evidence of the crime.

Laws 1996, p. 1115, § 5.

TITLE 19

DOMESTIC RELATIONS

CHAPTER 7

PARENT AND CHILD RELATIONSHIP GENERALLY

Article 1

General Provisions

§ 19–7–5. Reports by physicians, treating personnel, institutions and others as to child abuse; failure to report suspected child abuse

(a) The purpose of this Code section is to provide for the protection of children whose health and welfare are adversely affected and further threatened by the conduct of those responsible for their care and protection. It is intended that the mandatory reporting of such cases will cause the protective services of the state to be brought to bear on the situation in an effort to prevent further abuses, to protect and enhance the welfare of these children, and to preserve family life wherever possible. This Code section shall be liberally construed so as to carry out the purposes thereof.

(b) As used in this Code section, the term:

(1) "Abused" means subjected to child abuse.

(2) "Child" means any person under 18 years of age.

(3) "Child abuse" means:

(A) Physical injury or death inflicted upon a child by a parent or caretaker thereof by other than accidental means; provided, however, physical forms of discipline may be used as long as there is no physical injury to the child;

(B) Neglect or exploitation of a child by a parent or caretaker thereof;

(C) Sexual abuse of a child; or

(D) Sexual exploitation of a child.

However, no child who in good faith is being treated solely by spiritual means through prayer in accordance with the tenets and practices of a recognized church or religious denomination by a duly accredited practitioner thereof shall, for that reason alone, be considered to be an "abused" child.

(3.1) "Sexual abuse" means a person's employing, using, persuading, inducing, enticing, or coercing any minor who is not that person's spouse to engage in any act which involves:

(A) Sexual intercourse, including genital-genital, oral-genital, anal-genital, or oral-anal, whether between persons of the same or opposite sex;

(B) Bestiality;

(C) Masturbation;

(D) Lewd exhibition of the genitals or pubic area of any person;

(E) Flagellation or torture by or upon a person who is nude;

(F) Condition of being fettered, bound, or otherwise physically restrained on the part of a person who is nude;

(G) Physical contact in an act of apparent sexual stimulation or gratification with any person's clothed or unclothed genitals, pubic area, or buttocks or with a female's clothed or unclothed breasts;

(H) Defecation or urination for the purpose of sexual stimulation; or

(I) Penetration of the vagina or rectum by any object except when done as part of a recognized medical procedure.

"Sexual abuse" shall not include consensual sex acts involving persons of the opposite sex when the sex acts are between minors or between a minor and an adult who is not more than five years older than the minor. This provision shall not be deemed or construed to repeal any law concerning the age or capacity to consent.

(4) "Sexual exploitation" means conduct by any person who allows, permits, encourages, or requires that child to engage in:

(A) Prostitution, as defined in Code Section 16–6–9; or

(B) Sexually explicit conduct for the purpose of producing any visual or print medium depicting such conduct, as defined in Code Section 16–12–100.

(c)(1) The following persons having reasonable cause to believe that a child has been abused shall report or cause reports of that abuse to be made as provided in this Code section:

(A) Physicians licensed to practice medicine, interns, or residents;

(B) Hospital or medical personnel;

(C) Dentists;

(D) Licensed psychologists and persons participating in internships to obtain licensing pursuant to Chapter 39 of Title 43;

(E) Podiatrists;

(F) Registered professional nurses or licensed practical nurses licensed pursuant to Chapter 24 of Title 43;

(G) Professional counselors, social workers, or marriage and family therapists licensed pursuant to Chapter 10A of Title 43;

(H) School teachers;

(I) School administrators;

(J) School guidance counselors, visiting teachers, school social workers, or school psychologists certified pursuant to Chapter 2 of Title 20;

(K) Child welfare agency personnel, as that agency is defined pursuant to Code Section 49–5–12;

(L) Child-counseling personnel;

(M) Child service organization personnel; or

(N) Law enforcement personnel.

(2) If a person is required to report abuse pursuant to this subsection because that person attends to a child pursuant to such person's duties as a member of the staff of a hospital, school, social agency, or similar facility, that person shall notify

the person in charge of the facility, or the designated delegate thereof, and the person so notified shall report or cause a report to be made in accordance with this Code section. A staff member who makes a report to the person designated pursuant to this paragraph shall be deemed to have fully complied with this subsection. Under no circumstances shall any person in charge of such hospital, school, agency, or facility, or the designated delegate thereof, to whom such notification has been made exercise any control, restraint, modification, or make other change to the information provided by the reporter, although each of the aforementioned persons may be consulted prior to the making of a report and may provide any additional, relevant, and necessary information when making the report.

(d) Any other person, other than one specified in subsection (c) of this Code section, who has reasonable cause to believe that a child is abused may report or cause reports to be made as provided in this Code section.

(e) An oral report shall be made immediately, but in no case later than 24 hours from the time there is reasonable cause to believe a child has been abused, by telephone or otherwise and followed by a report in writing, if requested, to a child welfare agency providing protective services, as designated by the Department of Human Services, or, in the absence of such agency, to an appropriate police authority or district attorney. If a report of child abuse is made to the child welfare agency or independently discovered by the agency, and the agency has reasonable cause to believe such report is true or the report contains any allegation or evidence of child abuse, then the agency shall immediately notify the appropriate police authority or district attorney. Such reports shall contain the names and addresses of the child and the child's parents or caretakers, if known, the child's age, the nature and extent of the child's injuries, including any evidence of previous injuries, and any other information that the reporting person believes might be helpful in establishing the cause of the injuries and the identity of the perpetrator. Photographs of the child's injuries to be used as documentation in support of allegations by hospital staff, physicians, law enforcement personnel, school officials, or staff of legally mandated public or private child protective agencies may be taken without the permission of the child's parent or guardian. Such photograph shall be made available as soon as possible to the chief welfare agency providing protective services and to the appropriate police authority.

(f) Any person or persons, partnership, firm, corporation, association, hospital, or other entity participating in the making of a report or causing a report to be made to a child welfare agency providing protective services or to an appropriate police authority pursuant to this Code section or any other law or participating in any judicial proceeding or any other proceeding resulting therefrom shall in so doing be immune from any civil or criminal liability that might otherwise be incurred or imposed, provided such participation pursuant to this Code section or any other law is made in good faith. Any person making a report, whether required by this Code section or not, shall be immune from liability as provided in this subsection.

(g) Suspected child abuse which is required to be reported by any person pursuant to this Code section shall be reported notwithstanding that the reasonable cause to believe such abuse has occurred or is occurring is based in whole or in part upon any communication to that person which is otherwise made privileged or confidential by law.

(h) Any person or official required by subsection (c) of this Code section to report a suspected case of child abuse who knowingly and willfully fails to do so shall be guilty of a misdemeanor.

(i) A report of child abuse or information relating thereto and contained in such report, when provided to a law enforcement agency or district attorney pursuant to subsection (e) of this Code section or pursuant to Code Section 49–5–41, shall not be subject to public inspection under Article 4 of Chapter 18 of Title 50 even though such report or information is contained in or part of closed records compiled for law enforcement or prosecution purposes unless:

(1) There is a criminal or civil court proceeding which has been initiated based in whole or in part upon the facts regarding abuse which are alleged in the child abuse reports and the person or entity seeking to inspect such records provides clear and convincing evidence of such proceeding; or

(2) The superior court in the county in which is located the office of the law enforcement agency or district attorney which compiled the records containing such reports, after application for inspection and a hearing on the issue, shall permit inspection of such records by or release of information from such records to individuals or entities who are engaged in legitimate research for educational, scientific, or public purposes and who comply with the provisions of this paragraph. When those records are located in more than one county, the application may be made to the superior court of any one of such counties. A copy of any application authorized by this paragraph shall be served on the office of the law enforcement agency or district attorney which compiled the records containing such reports. In cases where the location of the records is unknown to the applicant, the application may be made to the Superior Court of Fulton County. The superior court to which an application is made shall not grant the application unless:

(A) The application includes a description of the proposed research project, including a specific statement of the information required, the purpose for which the project requires that information, and a methodology to assure the information is not arbitrarily sought;

(B) The applicant carries the burden of showing the legitimacy of the research project; and

(C) Names and addresses of individuals, other than officials, employees, or agents of agencies receiving or investigating a report of abuse which is the subject of a report, shall be deleted from any information released pursuant to this subsection unless the court determines that having the names and addresses open for review is essential to the research and the child, through his or her representative, gives permission to release the information.

Laws 1965, p. 588, § 1; Laws 1968, p. 1196, § 1; Laws 1973, p. 309, § 1; Laws 1974, p. 438, § 1; Laws 1977, p. 242, §§ 1–3; Laws 1978, p. 2059, §§ 1, 2; Laws 1980, p. 921, § 1; Laws 1981, p. 1034, §§ 1–3; Laws 1988, p. 1624, § 1; Laws 1990, p. 1761, § 1; Laws 1993, p. 1695, §§ 1, 1.1; Laws 1994, p. 97, § 19; Laws 1999, p. 81, § 19; Laws 2006, Act 602, § 1, eff. April 27, 2006; Laws 2009, Act 102, § 2–2, eff. July 1, 2009; Laws 2009, Act 151, § 1, eff. May 5, 2009.

Formerly Code 1933, § 74–111.

Historical and Statutory Notes

The 2006 amendment by Act 602, in par. (2) of subsec. (c), inserted "Under no circumstances shall any person in charge of such hospital, school, agency, or facility, or the designated delegate thereof, to whom such notification has been made exercise any control, restraint, modification, or make other change to the information provided by the reporter, although each of the aforementioned persons may be consulted prior to the making of a report and may provide any additional, relevant, and necessary information when making the report."; and, in subsec. (e), substituted "immediately, but in no case later than 24 hours from the time there is reasonable cause to believe a child has been abused," for "as soon as possible", and deleted "; provided, however, that any photograph taken pursuant to this Code section shall, if reasonably possible, be taken in a manner which shall not reveal the identity of the subject" following "child's parent or guardian".

The 2009 amendment by Act 102 substituted "Department of Human Services" for "Department of Human Resources" throughout the section.

The 2009 amendment by Act 151 rewrote par. (4) of subsec. (b) which had read as follows:

"(4) 'Sexual exploitation' means conduct by a child's parent or caretaker who allows, permits, encourages, or requires that child to engage in:

"(A) Prostitution, as defined in Code Section 16–6–9; or

"(B) Sexually explicit conduct for the purpose of producing any visual or print medium depicting such conduct, as defined in Code Section 16–12–100."

§ 19–7–6. Reporting of child drug abuse

(a) The purpose of this Code section is to provide for the protection of children whose health and welfare are adversely affected and further threatened by the unlawful use and abuse of controlled substances or marijuana. The General Assembly recognizes the need for early intervention, counseling, and treatment as an effective means of addressing the problem of child controlled substance and marijuana abuse. It is intended that the reporting of the unlawful use of any controlled substance or marijuana will cause the protective services of the state to be brought to bear on this situation in an effort to protect and enhance the welfare of children. This Code section shall be liberally construed so as to carry out the purposes thereof.

(b) Any person exercising in loco parentis control over a child under the age of 18 years who has reasonable cause to believe that the child is habitually using in an unlawful manner any controlled substance or marijuana, as defined in Code Section 16–13–21, is encouraged to report such information to the child's parents and a child welfare agency providing protective services, as designated by the Department of Human Services.

(c) When the attendance of the person exercising in loco parentis control over a child is pursuant to the performance of services as a member of the staff of any school, social agency, or similar facility, the reporting person shall notify the person in charge of the facility or his designated delegate; and such person or his delegate shall report or cause reports to be made in accordance with this Code section.

(d) An oral report shall be made as soon as possible by telephone or otherwise and shall be followed by a report in writing, if requested, to the child welfare agency providing protective services, as designated by the Department of Human Services. Such report shall contain the names and addresses of the child and his parents or caretakers, if known, the child's age, and the nature and extent of the child's controlled substance or marijuana abuse history, if known.

(e) No agency or political subdivision of this state shall enact or enforce any disciplinary rule or penalty against an employee of the state or of any political subdivision of the state for failure to make any report referred to in subsection (b), (c), or (d) of this Code section.

(f) Any person or persons, partnership, firm, corporation, association, hospital, or other entity participating in the making of a report or causing a report to be made to a child welfare agency providing protective services pursuant to this Code section or any other law or participating in any judicial proceeding or any other proceeding resulting therefrom shall, in doing so, be immune from any civil or criminal liability that might otherwise be incurred or imposed if such participation, pursuant to this Code section or any other law, is made in good faith. Any person making a report, whether required by this Code section or not, shall be immune from liability as provided in this subsection.

(g) Any person or official required to report under this Code section shall be exempt from reporting any information received from the child during a counseling or treatment program.

(h) The child welfare agency providing protective services, as designated by the Department of Human Services, shall forward a copy of all reports wherein the reporting person or official has actual knowledge that a child under the age of 18 has unlawfully consumed or otherwise used any controlled substance or marijuana to the juvenile court. As used in this subsection, the term "juvenile court" means the court exercising jurisdiction over juvenile matters, as defined under Code Section 15–11–2, in the county where the report was made.

Laws 1987, p. 1000, § 1; Laws 2009, Act 102, § 2–2, eff. July 1, 2009.

Historical and Statutory Notes

The 2009 amendment by Act 102 substituted "Department of Human Services" for "Department of Human Resources" throughout the section.

Article 2

Legitimacy

§ 19–7–21.1. Voluntary acknowledgment of legitimation

(a) As used in this Code section, the term:

(1) "Acknowledgment of legitimation" means a written statement contained in a voluntary acknowledgment of paternity form indicating that a mother and father of a child born out of wedlock have freely agreed and consented that the child may be legitimated.

(2) "Legal father" means a male who:

(A) Has legally adopted a child;

(B) Was married to the biological mother of that child at the time the child was conceived or was born, unless such paternity was disproved by a final order pursuant to Article 3 of this chapter;

(C) Married the legal mother of the child after the child was born and recognized the child as his own, unless such paternity was disproved by a final order pursuant to Article 3 of this chapter;

(D) Has been determined to be the father by a final paternity order pursuant to Article 3 of this chapter;

(E) Has legitimated the child by a final order pursuant to Code Section 19–7–22; or

(F) Has legitimated a child pursuant to this Code section

and who has not surrendered or had terminated his rights to the child.

(b) Prior to the child's first birthday, a father of a child born out of wedlock may render his relationship with the child legitimate when both the mother and father have freely agreed, consented, and signed a voluntary acknowledgment of paternity and an acknowledgment of legitimation which have been made and have not been rescinded pursuant to Code Section 19–7–46.1. The State Office of Vital Records shall provide notice, in writing, of the alternatives to, legal consequences of, and the rights and responsibilities of signing a voluntary acknowledgment of legitimation.

(c) Voluntary acknowledgment of legitimation shall not be recognized if:

(1) The mother was married to another man when the child was born;

(2) The mother was married to another man at any time within the usual period of gestation;

(3) There is another legal father;

(4) The mother has voluntarily and in writing surrendered all of her parental rights pursuant to the provisions of subsection (a) of any of Code Section 19–8–4, 19–8–5, 19–8–6, or 19–8–7 and has not withdrawn her surrender as permitted by the provisions of subsection (b) of Code Section 19–8–9 or the mother's parental rights have been judicially terminated by a court of competent jurisdiction or an action to terminate such rights has been initiated and is pending;

(5) The mother has signed a voluntary acknowledgment of legitimation with another man; or

(6) The child is one year of age or older.

(d) If any of the circumstances described in subsection (c) of this Code section exists, the provisions of Code Section 19–7–22 shall be the only method of legitimation.

(e) Voluntary acknowledgment of legitimation shall not authorize the father to receive custody or visitation until there is a judicial determination of custody or visitation.

(f) It shall be unlawful to make a false statement on a voluntary acknowledgment of legitimation, and the making of a false statement shall be punishable as an act of false statements and writings under Code Section 16–10–20.

(g) Where a voluntary acknowledgment of paternity is timely rescinded and includes a voluntary acknowledgment of legitimation, the legitimation shall also be deemed rescinded.

Laws 2008, Act 580, § 4, eff. July 1, 2008.

§ 19–7–22. Petition to legitimatize child

(a) A father of a child born out of wedlock may render his relationship with the child legitimate by petitioning the superior court of the county of the residence of the child's mother or other party having legal custody or guardianship of the child; provided, however, that if the mother or other party having legal custody or guardianship of the child resides outside the state or cannot, after due diligence, be found within the state, the petition may be filed in the county of the father's residence or the county of the child's residence. If a petition for the adoption of the child is pending, the father shall file the petition for legitimation in the county in which the adoption petition is filed.

(b) The petition shall set forth the name, age, and sex of the child, the name of the mother, and, if the father desires the name of the child to be changed, the new name. If the mother is alive, she shall be named as a party and shall be served and provided an opportunity to be heard as in other civil actions under Chapter 11 of Title 9, the "Georgia Civil Practice Act."

(c) Upon the presentation and filing of the petition, the court may pass an order declaring the father's relationship with the child to be legitimate, and that the father and child shall be capable of inheriting from each other in the same manner as if born in lawful wedlock and specifying the name by which the child shall be known.

(d) A legitimation petition may be filed, pursuant to paragraph (2) of subsection (e) of Code Section 15–11–28, in the juvenile court of the county in which a deprivation proceeding regarding the child is pending.

(e) Except as provided by subsection (f) of this Code section, the court shall upon notice to the mother further establish such duty as the father may have to support the child, considering the facts and circumstances of the mother's obligation of support and the needs of the child as provided under Code Section 19–6–15.

(f) After a petition for legitimation is granted, if a demand for a jury trial as to support has been properly filed by either parent, then the case shall be transferred from juvenile court to superior court for such jury trial.

(f.1) The petition for legitimation may also include claims for visitation, parenting time, or custody. If such claims are raised in the legitimation action, the court may order, in addition to legitimation, visitation, parenting time, or custody based on the best interests of the child standard. In a case involving allegations of family violence, the provisions of paragraph (4) of subsection (a) of Code Section 19–9–3 shall also apply.

(g)(1) In any petition to establish paternity pursuant to paragraph (4) of subsection (a) of Code Section 19–7–43, the alleged father's response may assert a third–party action for the legitimation of the child born out of wedlock. Upon the determination of paternity or if a voluntary acknowledgment of paternity has been made and has not been rescinded pursuant to Code Section 19–7–46.1, the court or trier of fact as a matter of law and pursuant to the provisions of Code Section 19–7–51 may enter an order or decree legitimating a child born out of wedlock, provided that such is in the best interest of the child. Whenever a petition to establish the paternity of a child is brought by the Department of Human Services, issues of name change, visitation, and custody shall not be determined by the court until such time as a separate petition is filed by one of the parents or by the legal guardian of the child, in accordance with Code Section 19–11–8; if the petition is brought by a party other than the Department of Human Services or if the alleged father seeks legitimation, the court may determine issues of name change, visitation, and custody in accordance with subsections (b) and (f.1) of this Code section. Custody of the child shall remain in the mother unless or until a court order is entered addressing the issue of custody.

(2) In any voluntary acknowledgment of paternity which has been made and has not been rescinded pursuant to Code Section 19–7–46.1, when both the mother and father freely agree and consent, the child may be legitimated by the inclusion of a statement indicating a voluntary acknowledgment of legitimation.

Laws 1985, p. 279, § 2; Laws 1988, p. 1720, § 5; Laws 1989, p. 441, § 1; Laws 1997, p. 1613, § 14; Laws 1997, p. 1681, § 5; Laws 2000, p. 20, § 10; Laws 2005, Act 413, § 1, eff. July 1, 2005; Laws 2007, Act 264, § 6, eff. Jan. 1, 2008; Laws 2009, Act 102, § 2–2, eff. July 1, 2009.

Formerly Code 1863, § 1738; Code 1868, § 1778; Code 1873, § 1787; Code 1882, § 1787; Civil Code 1895, § 2494; Civil Code 1910, § 3013; Code 1933, § 74–103.

Historical and Statutory Notes

The 2005 amendment by Act 413 rewrote the section, which had read:

"(a) A father of a child born out of wedlock may render the same legitimate by petitioning the superior court of the county of his residence, the county of residence of the child, or, if a petition for the adoption of the child is pending, the county in which the adoption petition is filed for legitimation of the child.

"(b) The petition shall set forth the name, age, and sex of the child, the name of the mother, and, if the father desires the name of the child to be changed, the new name. If the mother is alive, she shall have notice of the petition for legitimation.

"(c) Upon the presentation and filing of the petition, the court may pass an order declaring the child to be legitimate and to be capable of inheriting from the father in the same manner as if born in lawful wedlock and specifying the name by which the child shall be known.

"(d) A legitimation petition may be filed, pursuant to paragraph (2) of subsection (e) of Code Section 15–11–28, in the juvenile court of the county in which a deprivation proceeding regarding the child is pending.

"(e) Except as provided by subsection (f) of this Code section, the court shall upon notice to the mother further establish such duty as the father may have to support the child, considering the facts and circumstances of the mother's obligation of support and the needs of the child.

"(f) After a petition for legitimation is granted, if a demand for a jury trial as to support has been properly filed by either parent, then the case shall be transferred to superior court for such jury trial.

"(g) Consistent with the purpose of subsection (a) of this Code section, whenever the Department of Human Resources petitions the superior court or other authorized trier of fact to establish paternity, the father may intervene to petition for the legitimation of the child born out of wedlock if the mother of the child consents to the filing of such legitimation petition. Upon the determination of paternity or if a voluntary acknowledgment of paternity has been made and has not been rescinded pursuant to Code Section 19–7–46.1, the court or trier of fact as a matter of law and pursuant to the provisions of Code Section 19–7–51 may enter an order or decree legitimating a child born out of wedlock, provided that such is in the best interest of the child. Issues of name change, visitation, and custody shall not be determined by the court until such time as a separate petition is filed by one of the parents or by the legal guardian of the child. Custody of the child shall remain in the mother until a court order is entered addressing the issue of custody."

The 2007 amendment by Act 264, in subsec. (f.1), inserted ", parenting time," twice, substituted "par. (4)" for "par. (2)", and substituted "19–9–3" for "19–9–1".

Laws 2007, Act 264, § 8, provides:

"This Act shall become effective on January 1, 2008, and shall apply to all child custody proceedings and modifications of child custody filed on or after January 1, 2008."

The 2009 amendment by Act 102 substituted "Department of Human Services" for "Department of Human Resources" throughout the section.

§ 19–7–25. Mother's rights

Only the mother of a child born out of wedlock is entitled to custody of the child, unless the father legitimates the child as provided in Code Section 19–7–21.1 or 19–7–22. Otherwise, the mother may exercise all parental power over the child.

Laws 1988, p. 1720, § 8; Laws 2008, Act 580, § 5, eff. July 1, 2008.

Formerly Code 1863, § 1750; Code 1868, § 1790; Code 1873, § 1799; Code 1882, § 1799; Civil Code 1895, § 2509; Civil Code 1910, § 3028; Code 1933, § 74–203.

Historical and Statutory Notes

The 2008 amendment by Act 580 substituted "is entitled to custody of the child unless the father legitimates the child as provided in Code Section 19–7–21.1 or 19–7–22" for "is entitled to his custody, unless the father legitimates him as provided in Code Section 19–7–22".

CHAPTER 9

CHILD CUSTODY PROCEEDINGS

Article 1

General Provisions

§ 19–9–4. Investigation of home life and home environment of parents in contested child custody proceedings

(a) On motion of either party in any action or proceeding involving determination of the award of child custody between parents of the child, when such motion contains a specific recitation of actual abuse, neglect, or other overt acts which have adversely affected the health and welfare of the child, the judge may direct the appropriate family and children services agency or any other appropriate entity to investigate the home life and home environment of each of the parents. In any action or proceeding involving determination of the award of child custody between parents of the child when during such proceedings a specific recitation of actual abuse, neglect, or other overt acts which have adversely affected the health and welfare of the child has been made the judge shall also have authority on his or her own motion to order such an investigation if in the judge's opinion the investigation would be useful in determining placement or custody of the child. The judge may also direct either party to pay to the agency the reasonable cost, or any portion thereof, of the investigation. The report of the investigation will be made to the judge directing the investigation. Any report made at the direction of the judge shall be made available to either or both parties for a reasonable period of time prior to the proceedings at which any temporary or permanent custody is to be determined. Both parties shall have the right to confront and cross-examine the person or persons who conducted the investigation or compiled the report if adequate and legal notice is given.

(b) This Code section shall apply only with respect to actions or proceedings in which the issue of child custody is contested;

and this Code section is not intended to alter or repeal Code Sections 49–5–40 through 49–5–44.

Laws 1980, p. 1149, §§ 1, 2; Laws 1982, p. 3, § 19; Laws 1982, p. 1189, §§ 1, 2; Laws 2007, Act 264, § 5, eff. Jan. 1, 2008.

Historical and Statutory Notes

The 2007 amendment by Act 264, in subsec. (a), substituted "judge's" for "court's", substituted "his or her" for "its", and substituted "judge" for "court" throughout the subsection.

Laws 2007, Act 264, § 8, provides:

"This Act shall become effective on January 1, 2008, and shall apply to all child custody proceedings and modifications of child custody filed on or after January 1, 2008."

Article 3

Uniform Child Custody Jurisdiction and Enforcement Act

Part 1

General Provisions

§ 19–9–40. Short title

This article may be cited as the "Uniform Child Custody Jurisdiction and Enforcement Act."

Laws 2001, p. 129, § 1.

Historical and Statutory Notes

Uniform Law

This section is based upon § 101 of the Uniform Child Custody Jurisdiction and Enforcement Act. See Vol. 9, Pt. IA, Uniform Laws Annotated, Master Edition, or ULA Database on Westlaw.

§ 19–9–41. Definitions

In this article:

(1) "Abandoned" means left without provision for reasonable and necessary care or supervision.

(2) "Child" means an individual who has not attained 18 years of age.

(3) "Child custody determination" means a judgment, decree, or other order of a court providing for the legal custody, physical custody, or visitation with respect to a child. The term includes a permanent, temporary, initial, and modification order. The term does not include an order relating to child support or other monetary obligations of an individual.

(4) "Child custody proceeding" means a proceeding in which legal custody, physical custody, or visitation with respect to a child is an issue. The term includes a proceeding for divorce, separation, neglect, abuse, dependency, guardianship, paternity, termination of parental rights, and protection from family violence, in which the issue may appear. The term does not include a proceeding involving juvenile delinquency, contractual emancipation, or enforcement under Part 3 of this article.

(5) "Commencement" means the filing of the first pleading in a proceeding.

(6) "Court" means an entity authorized under the law of a state to establish, enforce, or modify a child custody determination.

(7) "Home state" means the state in which a child lived with a parent or a person acting as a parent for at least six consecutive months immediately before the commencement of a child custody proceeding. In the case of a child less than six months of age, the term means the state in which the child lived from birth with any of the persons mentioned. A period of temporary absence of any of the mentioned persons is part of the period.

(8) "Initial determination" means the first child custody determination concerning a particular child.

(9) "Issuing court" means the court that makes a child custody determination for which enforcement is sought under this article.

(10) "Issuing state" means the state in which a child custody determination is made.

(11) "Modification" means a child custody determination that changes, replaces, supersedes, or is otherwise made after a previous determination concerning the same child, whether or not it is made by the court that made the previous determination.

(12) "Person" means an individual, corporation, business trust, estate, trust, partnership, limited liability company, association, joint venture, government; governmental subdivision, agency, or instrumentality; public corporation; or any other legal or commercial entity.

(13) "Person acting as a parent" means a person, other than a parent, who:

(A) Has physical custody of the child or has had physical custody for a period of six consecutive months, including any temporary absence, within one year immediately before the commencement of a child custody proceeding; and

(B) Has been awarded legal custody by a court or claims a right to legal custody under the law of this state.

(14) "Physical custody" means the physical care and supervision of a child.

(15) "State" means a state of the United States, the District of Columbia, Puerto Rico, the United States Virgin Islands, or any territory or insular possession subject to the jurisdiction of the United States.

(16) "Tribe" means an Indian tribe or band or Alaskan Native village which is recognized by federal law or formally acknowledged by a state.

(17) "Warrant" means an order issued by a court authorizing law enforcement officers to take physical custody of a child.

Laws 2001, p. 129, § 1.

Historical and Statutory Notes

Uniform Law

This section is based upon § 102 of the Uniform Child Custody Jurisdiction and Enforcement Act. See Vol. 9, Pt. IA, Uniform Laws Annotated, Master Edition, or ULA Database on Westlaw.

§ 19–9–42. Proceedings governed by other law

This article does not govern an adoption proceeding or a proceeding pertaining to the authorization of emergency medical care for a child.

Laws 2001, p. 129, § 1.

Historical and Statutory Notes

Uniform Law

This section is based upon § 103 of the Uniform Child Custody Jurisdiction and Enforcement Act. See Vol. 9, Pt. IA, Uniform Laws Annotated, Master Edition, or ULA Database on Westlaw.

§ 19–9–43. Application to Indian tribes

(a) A child custody proceeding that pertains to an Indian child as defined in the Indian Child Welfare Act, 25 U.S.C. Section 1901 et seq., is not subject to this article to the extent that it is governed by the Indian Child Welfare Act.

(b) A court of this state shall treat a tribe as if it were a state of the United States for the purpose of applying this part and Part 2 of this article.

(c) A child custody determination made by a tribe under factual circumstances in substantial conformity with the jurisdictional standards of this article must be recognized and enforced under Part 3 of this article.

Laws 2001, p. 129, § 1.

Historical and Statutory Notes

Uniform Law

This section is based upon § 104 of the Uniform Child Custody Jurisdiction and Enforcement Act. See Vol. 9, Pt. IA, Uniform Laws Annotated, Master Edition, or ULA Database on Westlaw.

§ 19–9–44. International application

(a) A court of this state shall treat a foreign country as if it were a state of the United States for the purpose of applying this part and Part 2 of this article.

(b) Except as otherwise provided in subsection (c) of this Code section, a child custody determination made in a foreign country under factual circumstances in substantial conformity with the jurisdictional standards of this article must be recognized and enforced under Part 3 of this article.

(c) A court of this state need not apply this article if the child custody law of a foreign country violates fundamental principles of human rights.

Laws 2001, p. 129, § 1.

Historical and Statutory Notes

Uniform Law

This section is based upon § 105 of the Uniform Child Custody Jurisdiction and Enforcement Act. See Vol. 9, Pt. IA, Uniform Laws Annotated, Master Edition, or ULA Database on Westlaw.

§ 19–9–45. Effect of child custody determination

A child custody determination made by a court of this state that had jurisdiction under this article binds all persons who have been served in accordance with the laws of this state or notified in accordance with Code Section 19–9–47 or who have submitted to the jurisdiction of the court, and who have been given an opportunity to be heard. As to those persons, the determination is conclusive as to all decided issues of law and fact except to the extent the determination is modified.

Laws 2001, p. 129, § 1.

Historical and Statutory Notes

Uniform Law

This section is based upon § 106 of the Uniform Child Custody Jurisdiction and Enforcement Act. See Vol. 9, Pt. IA, Uniform Laws Annotated, Master Edition, or ULA Database on Westlaw.

§ 19–9–46. Priority

If a question of existence or exercise of jurisdiction under this article is raised in a child custody proceeding, the question, upon request of a party, must be given priority on the calendar and handled expeditiously.

Laws 2001, p. 129, § 1.

Historical and Statutory Notes

Uniform Law

This section is based upon § 107 of the Uniform Child Custody Jurisdiction and Enforcement Act. See Vol. 9, Pt. IA, Uniform Laws Annotated, Master Edition, or ULA Database on Westlaw.

§ 19–9–47. Notice to persons outside state

(a) Notice required for the exercise of jurisdiction when a person is outside this state may be given in a manner prescribed by the law of this state for service of process or by the law of the state in which the service is made. Notice must be given in a manner reasonably calculated to give actual notice but may be by publication if other means are not effective.

(b) Proof of service may be made in the manner prescribed by the law of this state or by the law of the state in which the service is made.

(c) Notice is not required for the exercise of jurisdiction with respect to a person who submits to the jurisdiction of the court.

Laws 2001, p. 129, § 1.

Historical and Statutory Notes

Uniform Law

This section is based upon § 108 of the Uniform Child Custody Jurisdiction and Enforcement Act. See Vol. 9, Pt. IA, Uniform Laws Annotated, Master Edition, or ULA Database on Westlaw.

§ 19–9–48. Appearance and limited immunity

(a) A party to a child custody proceeding, including a modification proceeding, or a petitioner or respondent in a proceeding to enforce or register a child custody determination is not subject to personal jurisdiction in this state for another proceeding or purpose solely by reason of having participated, or of having been physically present for the purpose of participating, in the proceeding.

(b) A person who is subject to personal jurisdiction in this state on a basis other than physical presence is not immune from service of process in this state. A party present in this state who is subject to the jurisdiction of another state is not immune from service of process allowable under the laws of that state.

(c) The immunity granted by subsection (a) of this Code section does not extend to civil litigation based on acts unrelated to the participation in a proceeding under this article committed by an individual while present in this state.

Laws 2001, p. 129, § 1.

Historical and Statutory Notes

Uniform Law

This section is based upon § 109 of the Uniform Child Custody Jurisdiction and Enforcement Act. See Vol. 9, Pt. IA, Uniform Laws Annotated, Master Edition, or ULA Database on Westlaw.

§ 19–9–49. Communication between courts

(a) A court of this state may communicate with a court in another state concerning a proceeding arising under this article and concerning any proceeding or court order in another state relating to family violence. A court of this state may consult any state or national registry of court orders relating to family violence with regard to any party.

(b) The court may allow the parties to participate in the communication. If the parties are not able to participate in the communication, they must be given the opportunity to present facts and legal arguments before a decision on jurisdiction is made.

(c) Communication between courts on schedules, calendars, court records, and similar matters may occur without informing the parties. A record need not be made of the communication.

(d) Except as otherwise provided in subsection (c) of this Code section, a record must be made of any communication under this Code section. The parties must be informed promptly of the communication and granted access to the record.

(e) For the purposes of this Code section, "record" means information that is inscribed on a tangible medium or that is stored in an electronic or other medium and is retrievable in perceivable form.

Laws 2001, p. 129, § 1.

Historical and Statutory Notes

Uniform Law

This section is based upon § 110 of the Uniform Child Custody Jurisdiction and Enforcement Act. See Vol. 9, Pt. IA, Uniform Laws Annotated, Master Edition, or ULA Database on Westlaw.

§ 19–9–50. Taking testimony in another state

(a) In addition to other procedures available to a party, a party to a child custody proceeding may offer testimony of witnesses who are located in another state, including testimony of the parties and the child, by deposition or other means allowable in this state for testimony taken in another state. The court on its own motion may order that the testimony of a person be taken in another state and may prescribe the manner in which and the terms upon which the testimony is taken.

(b) A court of this state may permit an individual residing in another state to be deposed or to testify by telephone, audiovisual means, or other electronic means before a designated court or at another location in that state. A court of this state shall cooperate with courts of other states in designating an appropriate location for the deposition or testimony.

(c) Documentary evidence transmitted from another state to a court of this state by technological means that do not produce an original writing may not be excluded from evidence on an objection based on the means of transmission.

Laws 2001, p. 129, § 1.

Historical and Statutory Notes

Uniform Law

This section is based upon § 111 of the Uniform Child Custody Jurisdiction and Enforcement Act. See Vol. 9, Pt. IA, Uniform Laws Annotated, Master Edition, or ULA Database on Westlaw.

§ 19–9–51. Cooperation between courts; preservation of records

(a) A court of this state may request the appropriate court of another state to:

(1) Hold an evidentiary hearing;

(2) Order a person to produce or give evidence pursuant to procedures of that state;

(3) Order that an evaluation be made with respect to the custody of a child involved in a pending proceeding;

(4) Forward to the court of this state a certified copy of the transcript of the record of the hearing, the evidence otherwise presented, and any evaluation prepared in compliance with the request; and

(5) Order a party to a child custody proceeding or any person having physical custody of the child to appear in the proceeding with or without the child.

(b) Upon request of a court of another state, a court of this state may hold a hearing or enter an order described in subsection (a) of this Code section.

(c) Travel and other necessary and reasonable expenses incurred under subsections (a) and (b) of this Code section may be assessed against the parties according to the law of this state.

(d) A court of this state shall preserve the pleadings, orders, decrees, records of hearings, evaluations, and other pertinent records with respect to a child custody proceeding until the child attains 18 years of age. Upon appropriate request by a court or law enforcement official of another state, the court shall forward a certified copy of those records.

Laws 2001, p. 129, § 1.

Historical and Statutory Notes

Uniform Law

This section is based upon § 112 of the Uniform Child Custody Jurisdiction and Enforcement Act. See Vol. 9, Pt. IA, Uniform Laws Annotated, Master Edition, or ULA Database on Westlaw.

§§ 19–9–52 to 19–9–60. Repealed by Laws 2001, p. 129, § 1, eff. April 7, 2001

Part 2

Jurisdiction

§ 19–9–61. Initial child custody jurisdiction

(a) Except as otherwise provided in Code Section 19–9–64, a court of this state has jurisdiction to make an initial child custody determination only if:

(1) This state is the home state of the child on the date of the commencement of the proceeding, or was the home state of the child within six months before the commencement of the proceeding and the child is absent from this state but a parent or person acting as a parent continues to live in this state;

(2) A court of another state does not have jurisdiction under paragraph (1) of this subsection, or a court of the home state of the child has declined to exercise jurisdiction on the ground that this state is the more appropriate forum under Code Section 19–9–67 or 19–9–68 and:

(A) The child and the child's parents, or the child and at least one parent or a person acting as a parent, have a significant connection with this state other than mere physical presence; and

(B) Substantial evidence is available in this state concerning the child's care, protection, training, and personal relationships;

(3) All courts having jurisdiction under paragraph (1) or (2) of this subsection have declined to exercise jurisdiction on the ground that a court of this state is the more appropriate forum to determine the custody of the child under Code Section 19–9–67 or 19–9–68; or

(4) No court of any other state would have jurisdiction under the criteria specified in paragraph (1), (2), or (3) of this subsection.

(b) Subsection (a) of this Code section is the exclusive jurisdictional basis for making a child custody determination by a court of this state.

(c) Physical presence of, or personal jurisdiction over, a party or a child is not necessary or sufficient to make a child custody determination.

Laws 2001, p. 129, § 1.

Historical and Statutory Notes

Uniform Law

This section is based upon § 201 of the Uniform Child Custody Jurisdiction and Enforcement Act. See Vol. 9, Pt. IA, Uniform Laws Annotated, Master Edition, or ULA Database on Westlaw.

§ 19–9–62. Exclusive, continuing jurisdiction

(a) Except as otherwise provided in Code Section 19–9–64, a court of this state which has made a child custody determination consistent with Code Section 19–9–61 or 19–9–63 has exclusive, continuing jurisdiction over the determination until:

(1) A court of this state determines that neither the child nor the child's parents or any person acting as a parent has a significant connection with this state and that substantial evidence is no longer available in this state concerning the child's care, protection, training, and personal relationships; or

(2) A court of this state or a court of another state determines that neither the child nor the child's parents or any person acting as a parent presently resides in this state.

(b) A court of this state which has made a child custody determination and does not have exclusive, continuing jurisdiction under this Code section may modify that determination only if it has jurisdiction to make an initial determination under Code Section 19–9–61.

Laws 2001, p. 129, § 1.

Historical and Statutory Notes

Uniform Law

This section is based upon § 202 of the Uniform Child Custody Jurisdiction and Enforcement Act. See Vol. 9, Pt. IA, Uniform Laws Annotated, Master Edition, or ULA Database on Westlaw.

§ 19–9–63. Jurisdiction to modify determination

Except as otherwise provided in Code Section 19–9–64, a court of this state may not modify a child custody determination made by a court of another state unless a court of this state has jurisdiction to make an initial determination under paragraph (1) or (2) of subsection (a) of Code Section 19–9–61 and:

(1) The court of the other state determines it no longer has exclusive, continuing jurisdiction under Code Section 19–9–62 or that a court of this state would be a more convenient forum under Code Section 19–9–67; or

(2) A court of this state or a court of the other state determines that neither the child nor the child's parents or any person acting as a parent presently resides in the other state.

Laws 2001, p. 129, § 1.

Historical and Statutory Notes

Uniform Law

This section is based upon § 203 of the Uniform Child Custody Jurisdiction and Enforcement Act. See Vol. 9, Pt. IA, Uniform Laws Annotated, Master Edition, or ULA Database on Westlaw.

§ 19–9–64. Temporary emergency jurisdiction

(a) A court of this state has temporary emergency jurisdiction if the child is present in this state and the child has been abandoned or it is necessary in an emergency to protect the child because the child or a sibling or parent of the child is subjected to or threatened with mistreatment or abuse.

(b) If there is no previous child custody determination that is entitled to be enforced under this article and a child custody proceeding has not been commenced in a court of a state having jurisdiction under Code Sections 19–9–61 through 19–9–63, a child custody determination made under this Code section remains in effect until an order is obtained from a court of a state having jurisdiction under Code Sections 19–9–61 through 19–9–63. If a child custody proceeding has not been or is not commenced in a court of a state having jurisdiction under Code Sections 19–9–61 through 19–9–63, a child custody determination made under this Code section becomes a final determination, if it so provides and this state becomes the home state of the child.

(c) If there is a previous child custody determination that is entitled to be enforced under this article, or a child custody proceeding has been commenced in a court of a state having jurisdiction under Code Sections 19–9–61 and 19–9–63, any order issued by a court of this state under this Code section must specify in the order a period that the court considers adequate to allow the person seeking an order to obtain an order from the state having jurisdiction under Code Sections 19–9–61 through 19–9–63. The order issued in this state remains in effect until an order is obtained from the other state within the period specified or the period expires.

(d) A court of this state which has been asked to make a child custody determination under this Code section, upon being informed that a child custody proceeding has been commenced in, or a child custody determination has been made by, a court of a state having jurisdiction under Code Sections 19–9–61 through 19–9–63, shall immediately communicate with the other court. A court of this state which is exercising jurisdiction pursuant to Code Sections 19–9–61 through 19–9–63, upon being informed that a child custody proceeding has been commenced in, or a child custody determination has been made by, a court of another state under a statute similar to this Code section, shall immediately communicate with the court of that state to resolve the emergency, protect the safety of the parties and the child, and determine a period for the duration of the temporary order.

Laws 2001, p. 129, § 1.

Historical and Statutory Notes

Uniform Law

This section is based upon § 204 of the Uniform Child Custody Jurisdiction and Enforcement Act. See Vol. 9, Pt. IA, Uniform Laws Annotated, Master Edition, or ULA Database on Westlaw.

§ 19–9–65. Notice; opportunity to be heard; joinder

(a) Before a child custody determination is made under this article, notice and an opportunity to be heard in accordance with the standards of Code Section 19–9–47 must be given to all persons entitled to notice under the law of this state as in a child custody proceeding between residents of this state, any parent whose parental rights have not been previously terminated, and any person having physical custody of the child.

(b) This article does not govern the enforceability of a child custody determination made without notice or an opportunity to be heard.

(c) The obligation to join a party and the right to intervene as a party in a child custody proceeding under this article are governed by the law of this state as in child custody proceedings between residents of this state.

Laws 2001, p. 129, § 1.

Historical and Statutory Notes

Uniform Law

This section is based upon § 205 of the Uniform Child Custody Jurisdiction and Enforcement Act. See Vol. 9, Pt. IA, Uniform Laws Annotated, Master Edition, or ULA Database on Westlaw.

§ 19–9–66. Simultaneous proceedings

(a) Except as otherwise provided in Code Section 19–9–64, a court of this state may not exercise its jurisdiction under this part if, at the time of the commencement of the proceeding, a proceeding concerning the custody of the child has been commenced in a court of another state having jurisdiction substantially in conformity with this article; unless the proceeding has been terminated or is stayed by the court of the other state because a court of this state is a more convenient forum under Code Section 19–9–67.

(b) Except as otherwise provided in Code Section 19–9–64, a court of this state, before hearing a child custody proceeding, shall examine the court documents and other information supplied by the parties pursuant to Code Section 19–9–69. If the court determines that a child custody proceeding has been commenced in a court in another state having jurisdiction substantially in accordance with this article, the court of this state shall stay its proceeding and communicate with the court of the other state. If the court of the state having jurisdiction substantially in accordance with this article does not determine that the court of this state is a more appropriate forum, the court of this state shall dismiss the proceeding.

(c) In a proceeding to modify a child custody determination, a court of this state shall determine whether a proceeding to enforce the determination has been commenced in another state. If a proceeding to enforce a child custody determination has been commenced in another state, the court may:

(1) Stay the proceeding for modification pending the entry of an order of a court of the other state enforcing, staying, denying, or dismissing the proceeding for enforcement;

(2) Enjoin the parties from continuing with the proceeding for enforcement; or

(3) Proceed with the modification under conditions it considers appropriate.

Laws 2001, p. 129, § 1.

Historical and Statutory Notes

Uniform Law

This section is based upon § 206 of the Uniform Child Custody Jurisdiction and Enforcement Act. See Vol. 9, Pt. IA, Uniform Laws Annotated, Master Edition, or ULA Database on Westlaw.

§ 19–9–67. Inconvenient forum

(a) A court of this state which has jurisdiction under this article to make a child custody determination may decline to exercise its jurisdiction at any time if it determines that it is an inconvenient forum under the circumstances and that a court of another state is a more appropriate forum. The issue of inconvenient forum may be raised upon motion of a party, the court's own motion, or request of another court.

(b) Before determining whether it is an inconvenient forum, a court of this state shall consider whether it is appropriate for a court of another state to exercise jurisdiction. For this purpose, the court shall allow the parties to submit information and shall consider all relevant factors, including:

(1) Whether family violence has occurred and is likely to continue in the future and which state could best protect the parties and the child;

(2) The length of time the child has resided outside this state;

(3) The distance between the court in this state and the court in the state that would assume jurisdiction;

(4) The relative financial circumstances of the parties;

(5) Any agreement of the parties as to which state should assume jurisdiction;

(6) The nature and location of the evidence required to resolve the pending litigation, including testimony of the child;

(7) The ability of the court of each state to decide the issue expeditiously and the procedures necessary to present the evidence; and

(8) The familiarity of the court of each state with the facts and issues in the pending litigation.

(c) If a court of this state determines that it is an inconvenient forum and that a court of another state is a more appropriate forum, it shall stay the proceedings upon condition that a child custody proceeding be promptly commenced in another designated state and may impose any other condition the court considers just and proper.

(d) A court of this state may decline to exercise its jurisdiction under this article if a child custody determination is incidental to an action for divorce or another proceeding while still retaining jurisdiction over the divorce or other proceeding.

Laws 2001, p. 129, § 1.

Historical and Statutory Notes

Uniform Law

This section is based upon § 207 of the Uniform Child Custody Jurisdiction and Enforcement Act. See Vol. 9, Pt. IA, Uniform Laws Annotated, Master Edition, or ULA Database on Westlaw.

§ 19–9–68. Jurisdiction declined by reason of conduct

(a) Except as otherwise provided in Code Section 19–9–64 or by any other law of this state, if a court of this state has jurisdiction under this article because a person seeking to invoke its jurisdiction has engaged in unjustifiable conduct, the court shall decline to exercise its jurisdiction unless:

(1) The parents and all persons acting as parents have acquiesced in the exercise of jurisdiction;

(2) A court of the state otherwise having jurisdiction under Code Sections 19–9–61 through 19–9–63 determines that this state is a more appropriate forum under Code Section 19–9–67; or

(3) No court of any other state would have jurisdiction under the criteria specified in Code Sections 19–9–61 through 19–9–63.

(b) If a court of this state declines to exercise its jurisdiction pursuant to subsection (a) of this Code section, it may fashion an appropriate remedy to ensure the safety of the child and prevent a repetition of the unjustifiable conduct, including staying the proceeding until a child custody proceeding is commenced in a court having jurisdiction under Code Sections 19–9–61 through 19–9–63.

(c) If a court dismisses a petition or stays a proceeding because it declines to exercise its jurisdiction pursuant to subsection (a) of this Code section, it shall assess against the party seeking to invoke its jurisdiction necessary and reasonable expenses including costs, communication expenses, attorney's fees, investigative fees, expenses for witnesses, travel expenses, and child care during the course of the proceedings, unless the party from whom fees are sought establishes that the assessment would be clearly inappropriate. The court may not assess fees, costs, or expenses against this state unless authorized by law other than this article.

Laws 2001, p. 129, § 1.

Historical and Statutory Notes

Uniform Law

This section is based upon § 208 of the Uniform Child Custody Jurisdiction and Enforcement Act. See Vol. 9, Pt. IA, Uniform Laws Annotated, Master Edition, or ULA Database on Westlaw.

§ 19–9–69. Information to be submitted to court

(a) In a child custody proceeding, each party, in its first pleading or in an attached affidavit, shall give information, if reasonably ascertainable, under oath as to the child's present address or whereabouts, the places where the child has lived during the last five years, and the names and present addresses of the persons with whom the child has lived during that period. The pleading or affidavit must state whether the party:

(1) Has participated, as a party or witness or in any other capacity, in any other proceeding concerning the custody of or visitation with the child and, if so, identify the court, the case number, and the date of the child custody determination, if any;

(2) Knows of any proceeding that could affect the current proceeding, including proceedings for enforcement and proceedings relating to family violence, protective orders, termination of parental rights, and adoptions and, if so, identify the court, the case number, and the nature of the proceeding; and

(3) Knows the names and addresses of any person not a party to the proceeding who has physical custody of the child or claims rights of legal custody or physical custody of, or visitation with, the child and, if so, the names and addresses of those persons.

(b) If the information required by subsection (a) of this Code section is not furnished, the court, upon motion of a party or its own motion, may stay the proceeding until the information is furnished.

(c) If the declaration as to any of the items described in paragraphs (1) through (3) of subsection (a) of this Code section is in the affirmative, the declarant shall give additional information under oath as required by the court. The court may examine the parties under oath as to details of the information furnished and other matters pertinent to the court's jurisdiction and the disposition of the case.

(d) Each party has a continuing duty to inform the court of any proceeding in this or any other state that could affect the current proceeding.

(e) If a party alleges in an affidavit or a pleading under oath that the health, safety, or liberty of a party or child would be jeopardized by disclosure of identifying information, the information must be sealed and may not be disclosed to the other party or the public unless the court orders the disclosure to be made after a hearing in which the court takes into consideration the health, safety, or liberty of the party or child and determines that the disclosure is in the interest of justice.

(f) In providing the information required by subsection (a) of this Code section, a party who is disclosing that the child is or has been a resident of a family violence shelter shall provide only the name of the shelter and the state in which the shelter is located to avoid a violation of Code Section 19-13-23. A disclosure of the name of the shelter and the state in which the shelter is located shall be sufficient for the purposes of subsection (a) of this Code section.

Laws 2001, p. 129, § 1.

Historical and Statutory Notes

Uniform Law

This section is based upon § 209 of the Uniform Child Custody Jurisdiction and Enforcement Act. See Vol. 9, Pt. IA, Uniform Laws Annotated, Master Edition, or ULA Database on Westlaw.

§ 19-9-70. Appearance of parties and child

(a) In a child custody proceeding in this state, the court may order a party to the proceeding who is in this state to appear before the court in person with or without the child. The court may order any person who is in this state and who has physical custody or control of the child to appear in person with the child.

(b) If a party to a child custody proceeding whose presence is desired by the court is outside this state, the court may order that a notice given pursuant to Code Section 19-9-47 include a statement directing the party to appear in person with or without the child and informing the party that failure to appear may result in a decision adverse to the party.

(c) The court may enter any orders necessary to ensure the safety of the child and of any person ordered to appear under this Code section.

(d) If a party to a child custody proceeding who is outside this state is directed to appear under subsection (b) of this Code section or desires to appear personally before the court with or without the child, the court may require another party to pay reasonable and necessary travel and other expenses of the party so appearing and of the child.

Laws 2001, p. 129, § 1.

Historical and Statutory Notes

Uniform Law

This section is based upon § 210 of the Uniform Child Custody Jurisdiction and Enforcement Act. See Vol. 9, Pt. IA, Uniform Laws Annotated, Master Edition, or ULA Database on Westlaw.

Part 3

Jurisdiction and Enforcement of Foreign Decrees

§ 19-9-81. Definitions

As used in this part, the term:

(1) "Petitioner" means a person who seeks enforcement of an order for return of a child under the Hague Convention on the Civil Aspects of International Child Abduction or enforcement of a child custody determination.

(2) "Respondent" means a person against whom a proceeding has been commenced for enforcement of an order for return of a child under the Hague Convention on the Civil Aspects of International Child Abduction or enforcement of a child custody determination.

Laws 2001, p. 129, § 1.

Historical and Statutory Notes

Uniform Law

This section is based upon § 301 of the Uniform Child Custody Jurisdiction and Enforcement Act. See Vol. 9, Pt. IA, Uniform Laws Annotated, Master Edition, or ULA Database on Westlaw.

§ 19-9-82. Enforcement under Hague Convention

Under this part a court of this state may enforce an order for the return of the child made under the Hague Convention on the Civil Aspects of International Child Abduction as if it were a child custody determination.

Laws 2001, p. 129, § 1.

Historical and Statutory Notes

Uniform Law

This section is based upon § 302 of the Uniform Child Custody Jurisdiction and Enforcement Act. See Vol. 9, Pt. IA, Uniform Laws Annotated, Master Edition, or ULA Database on Westlaw.

§ 19-9-83. Duty to enforce

(a) A court of this state shall recognize and enforce a child custody determination of a court of another state if the latter court exercised jurisdiction in substantial conformity with this article or the determination was made under factual circumstances meeting the jurisdictional standards of this article and the determination has not been modified in accordance with this article.

(b) A court of this state may utilize any remedy available under other laws of this state to enforce a child custody determination made by a court of another state. The remedies provided in this part are cumulative and do not affect the availability of other remedies to enforce a child custody determination.

Laws 2001, p. 129, § 1.

Historical and Statutory Notes

Uniform Law

This section is based upon § 303 of the Uniform Child Custody Jurisdiction and Enforcement Act. See Vol. 9, Pt. IA, Uniform Laws Annotated, Master Edition, or ULA Database on Westlaw.

§ 19–9–84. Temporary visitation

(a) A court of this state which does not have jurisdiction to modify a child custody determination may issue a temporary order enforcing:

(1) A visitation schedule made by a court of another state; or

(2) The visitation provisions of a child custody determination of another state that does not provide for a specific visitation schedule.

(b) If a court of this state makes an order under paragraph (2) of subsection (a) of this Code section, it shall specify in the order a period that it considers adequate to allow the petitioner to obtain an order from a court having jurisdiction under the criteria specified in Part 2 of this article. The order remains in effect until an order is obtained from the other court or the period expires.

(c) If a court of another state or a court of this state has made a finding of family violence on the part of either parent of the child, in issuing a temporary order enforcing a visitation schedule or the visitation provisions of a child custody determination of another state in accordance with subsection (a) of this Code section, a court of this state may enter any orders necessary to ensure the safety of the child and of any person who has been the victim of family violence, including but not limited to an order for supervised visitation pursuant to Code Section 19–9–7.

Laws 2001, p. 129, § 1.

Historical and Statutory Notes

Uniform Law

This section is based upon § 304 of the Uniform Child Custody Jurisdiction and Enforcement Act. See Vol. 9, Pt. IA, Uniform Laws Annotated, Master Edition, or ULA Database on Westlaw.

§ 19–9–85. Registration of child custody determination

(a) A child custody determination issued by a court of another state may be registered in this state, with or without a simultaneous request for enforcement, by sending to the superior court in the appropriate venue in this state:

(1) A letter or other document requesting registration;

(2) Two copies, including one certified copy, of the determination sought to be registered, and a statement under penalty of perjury that to the best of the knowledge and belief of the person seeking registration the order has not been modified; and

(3) Except as otherwise provided in Code Section 19–9–69, the name and address of the person seeking registration and any parent or person acting as a parent who has been awarded custody or visitation in the child custody determination sought to be registered.

(b) On receipt of the documents required by subsection (a) of this Code section, the registering court shall:

(1) Cause the determination to be filed as a foreign judgment, together with one copy of any accompanying documents and information, regardless of their form; and

(2) Serve notice upon the persons named pursuant to paragraph (3) of subsection (a) of this Code section and provide them with an opportunity to contest the registration in accordance with this Code section.

(c) The notice required by paragraph (2) of subsection (b) of this Code section must state that:

(1) A registered determination is enforceable as of the date of the registration in the same manner as a determination issued by a court of this state;

(2) A hearing to contest the validity of the registered determination must be requested within 20 days after service of notice; and

(3) Failure to contest the registration will result in confirmation of the child custody determination and preclude further contest of that determination with respect to any matter that could have been asserted.

(d) A person seeking to contest the validity of a registered order must request a hearing within 20 days after service of the notice. At that hearing, the court shall confirm the registered order unless the person contesting registration establishes that:

(1) The issuing court did not have jurisdiction under Part 2 of this article;

(2) The child custody determination sought to be registered has been vacated, stayed, or modified by a court having jurisdiction to do so under Part 2 of this article; or

(3) The person contesting registration was entitled to notice, but notice was not given in accordance with the standards of Code Section 19–9–47 in the proceedings before the court that issued the order for which registration is sought.

(e) If a timely request for a hearing to contest the validity of the registration is not made, the registration is confirmed as a matter of law, and the person requesting registration and all persons served must be notified of the confirmation.

(f) Confirmation of a registered order, whether by operation of law or after notice and hearing, precludes further contest of the order with respect to any matter that could have been asserted at the time of registration.

Laws 2001, p. 129, § 1.

Historical and Statutory Notes

Uniform Law

This section is based upon § 305 of the Uniform Child Custody Jurisdiction and Enforcement Act. See Vol. 9, Pt. IA, Uniform Laws Annotated, Master Edition, or ULA Database on Westlaw.

§ 19–9–86. Enforcement of registered determination

(a) A court of this state may grant any relief normally available under the laws of this state to enforce a registered child custody determination made by a court of another state.

(b) A court of this state shall recognize and enforce, but may not modify, except in accordance with Part 2 of this article, a registered child custody determination of a court of another state.

Laws 2001, p. 129, § 1.

Historical and Statutory Notes

Uniform Law

This section is based upon § 306 of the Uniform Child Custody Jurisdiction and Enforcement Act. See Vol. 9, Pt. IA, Uniform Laws Annotated, Master Edition, or ULA Database on Westlaw.

§ 19–9–87. Simultaneous proceedings

If a proceeding for enforcement under this part is commenced in a court of this state and the court determines that a proceeding to modify the determination is pending in a court of another state having jurisdiction to modify the determination under Part 2 of this article, the enforcing court shall immediately communicate with the modifying court. The proceeding for enforcement continues unless the enforcing court, after consultation with the modifying court, stays or dismisses the proceeding.

Laws 2001, p. 129, § 1.

Historical and Statutory Notes

Uniform Law

This section is based upon § 307 of the Uniform Child Custody Jurisdiction and Enforcement Act. See Vol. 9, Pt. IA, Uniform Laws Annotated, Master Edition, or ULA Database on Westlaw.

§ 19–9–88. Expedited enforcement of child custody determination

(a) A petition under this part must be verified. Certified copies of all orders sought to be enforced and of any order confirming registration must be attached to the petition. A copy of a certified copy of an order may be attached instead of the original.

(b) A petition for enforcement of a child custody determination must state:

(1) Whether the court that issued the determination identified the jurisdictional basis it relied upon in exercising jurisdiction and, if so, what the basis was;

(2) Whether the determination for which enforcement is sought has been vacated, stayed, or modified by a court whose decision must be enforced under this article and, if so, identify the court, the case number, and the nature of the proceeding;

(3) Whether any proceeding has been commenced that could affect the current proceeding, including proceedings relating to family violence, protective orders, termination of parental rights, and adoptions and, if so, identify the court, the case number, and the nature of the proceeding;

(4) The present physical address of the child and the respondent, if known, except in cases involving a parent who has been the subject of a finding of family violence by a court of this state or another state;

(5) Whether relief in addition to the immediate physical custody of the child and attorney's fees is sought, including a request for assistance from law enforcement officials and, if so, the relief sought; and

(6) If the child custody determination has been registered and confirmed under Code Section 19–9–85, the date and place of registration.

(c) If a party alleges in an affidavit or pleading under oath that the health, safety, or liberty of a party or child would be jeopardized by disclosure of information required by this Code section, the information must be sealed and may not be disclosed to the other party or the public unless the court orders the disclosure to be made after a hearing in which the court takes into consideration the health, safety, or liberty of the party or child and determines that the disclosure is in the interest of justice.

(d) Upon the filing of a petition, the court shall issue an order directing the respondent to appear in person with or without the child at a hearing and may enter any order necessary to ensure the safety of the parties and the child. The hearing must be held on the next judicial day after service of the order unless that date is impossible. In that event, the court shall hold the hearing on the first judicial day possible. The court may extend the date of hearing at the request of the petitioner.

(e) An order issued under subsection (d) of this Code section must state the time and place of the hearing and advise the respondent that at the hearing the court will order that the petitioner may take immediate physical custody of the child and the payment of fees, costs, and expenses under Code Section 19–9–92, and may schedule a hearing to determine whether further relief is appropriate, unless the respondent appears and establishes that:

(1) The child custody determination has not been registered and confirmed under Code Section 19–9–85 and that:

(A) The issuing court did not have jurisdiction under Part 2 of this article;

(B) The child custody determination for which enforcement is sought has been vacated, stayed, or modified by a court having jurisdiction to do so under Part 2 of this article;

(C) The respondent was entitled to notice, but notice was not given in accordance with the standards of Code Section 19–9–47, in the proceedings before the court that issued the order for which enforcement is sought; or

(2) The child custody determination for which enforcement is sought was registered and confirmed under Code Section 19–9–85, but has been vacated, stayed, or modified by a court of a state having jurisdiction to do so under Part 2 of this article.

Laws 2001, p. 129, § 1.

Historical and Statutory Notes

Uniform Law

This section is based upon § 308 of the Uniform Child Custody Jurisdiction and Enforcement Act. See Vol. 9, Pt. IA, Uniform Laws Annotated, Master Edition, or ULA Database on Westlaw.

§ 19–9–89. Service of petition and order

Except as otherwise provided in Code Section 19–9–91, the petition and order must be served, by any method authorized by the laws of this state, upon respondent and any person who has physical custody of the child.

Laws 2001, p. 129, § 1.

Historical and Statutory Notes

Uniform Law

This section is based upon § 309 of the Uniform Child Custody Jurisdiction and Enforcement Act. See Vol. 9, Pt. IA, Uniform Laws Annotated, Master Edition, or ULA Database on Westlaw.

§ 19–9–90. Hearing and order

(a) Unless the court issues a temporary emergency order pursuant to Code Section 19–9–64, upon a finding that a petitioner is entitled to immediate physical custody of the child, the court shall order that the petitioner may take immediate physical custody of the child unless the respondent establishes that:

(1) The child custody determination has not been registered and confirmed under Code Section 19–9–85 and that:

(A) The issuing court did not have jurisdiction under Part 2 of this article;

(B) The child custody determination for which enforcement is sought has been vacated, stayed, or modified by a court of a state having jurisdiction to do so under Part 2 of this article; or

(C) The respondent was entitled to notice, but notice was not given in accordance with the standards of Code Section 19–9–47, in the proceedings before the court that issued the order for which enforcement is sought; or

(2) The child custody determination for which enforcement is sought was registered and confirmed under Code Section 19–9–85 but has been vacated, stayed, or modified by a court of a state having jurisdiction to do so under Part 2 of this article.

(b) The court shall award the fees, costs, and expenses authorized under Code Section 19–9–92 and may grant additional relief, including a request for the assistance of law enforcement officials, and set a further hearing to determine whether additional relief is appropriate.

(c) If a party called to testify refuses to answer on the ground that the testimony may be self-incriminating, the court may draw an adverse inference from the refusal.

(d) A privilege against disclosure of communications between spouses and a defense of immunity based on the relationship of husband and wife or parent and child may not be invoked in a proceeding under this part.

Laws 2001, p. 129, § 1.

Historical and Statutory Notes

Uniform Law

This section is based upon § 310 of the Uniform Child Custody Jurisdiction and Enforcement Act. See Vol. 9, Pt. IA, Uniform Laws Annotated, Master Edition, or ULA Database on Westlaw.

§ 19–9–91. Warrant to take physical custody of child

(a) Upon the filing of a petition seeking enforcement of a child custody determination, the petitioner may file a verified application for the issuance of a warrant to take physical custody of the child if the child is immediately likely to suffer serious physical harm or be removed from this state.

(b) If the court, upon the testimony of the petitioner or other witness, finds that the child is imminently likely to suffer serious physical harm or be removed from this state, it may issue a warrant to take physical custody of the child. The petition must be heard on the next judicial day after the warrant is executed unless that date is impossible. In that event, the court shall hold the hearing on the first judicial day possible. The application for the warrant must include the statements required by subsection (b) of Code Section 19–9–88.

(c) A warrant to take physical custody of a child must:

(1) Recite the facts upon which a conclusion of imminent serious physical harm or removal from the jurisdiction is based;

(2) Direct law enforcement officers to take physical custody of the child immediately; and

(3) Provide for the placement of the child pending final relief.

(d) The respondent must be served with the petition, warrant, and order immediately after the child is taken into physical custody.

(e) A warrant to take physical custody of a child is enforceable throughout this state. If the court finds on the basis of the testimony of the petitioner or other witness that a less intrusive remedy is not effective, it may authorize law enforcement officers to enter private property to take physical custody of the child. If required by exigent circumstances of the case, the court may authorize law enforcement officers to make a forcible entry at any hour.

(f) The court may impose conditions upon placement of a child to ensure the appearance of the child and the child's custodian.

Laws 2001, p. 129, § 1.

Historical and Statutory Notes

Uniform Law

This section is based upon § 311 of the Uniform Child Custody Jurisdiction and Enforcement Act. See Vol. 9, Pt. IA, Uniform Laws Annotated, Master Edition, or ULA Database on Westlaw.

§ 19–9–92. Costs, fees, and expenses

(a) The court shall award the prevailing party, including a state, necessary and reasonable expenses incurred by or on behalf of the party, including costs, communication expenses, attorney's fees, investigative fees, expenses for witnesses, travel expenses, and child care during the course of the proceedings, unless the party from whom fees or expenses are sought establishes that the award would be clearly inappropriate.

(b) The court may not assess fees, costs, or expenses against a state unless authorized by law other than this article.

Laws 2001, p. 129, § 1.

Historical and Statutory Notes

Uniform Law

This section is based upon § 312 of the Uniform Child Custody Jurisdiction and Enforcement Act. See Vol. 9, Pt. IA, Uniform Laws Annotated, Master Edition, or ULA Database on Westlaw.

§ 19–9–93. Recognition and enforcement

A court of this state shall accord full faith and credit to an order issued by another state and consistent with this article which enforces a child custody determination by a court of another state unless the order has been vacated, stayed, or modified by a court having jurisdiction to do so under Part 2 of this article.

Laws 2001, p. 129, § 1.

Historical and Statutory Notes

Uniform Law

This section is based upon § 313 of the Uniform Child Custody Jurisdiction and Enforcement Act. See Vol. 9, Pt. IA, Uniform Laws Annotated, Master Edition, or ULA Database on Westlaw.

§ 19–9–94. Appeals

An appeal may be taken from a final order in a proceeding under this article in accordance with expedited appellate procedures in other civil cases. Unless the court enters a temporary emergency order under Code Section 19–9–64, the enforcing court may not stay an order enforcing a child custody determination pending appeal.

Laws 2001, p. 129, § 1.

Historical and Statutory Notes

Uniform Law

This section is based upon § 314 of the Uniform Child Custody Jurisdiction and Enforcement Act. See Vol. 9, Pt. IA, Uniform Laws Annotated, Master Edition, or ULA Database on Westlaw.

§ 19–9–95. Powers of district attorney

(a) In a case arising under this article or involving the Hague Convention on the Civil Aspects of International Child Abduction, the district attorney may take any lawful action, including resort to a proceeding under this part or any other available civil proceeding to locate a child, obtain the return of a child, or enforce a child custody determination if there is:

(1) An existing child custody determination;

(2) A request to do so from a court in a pending child custody proceeding;

(3) A reasonable belief that a criminal statute has been violated; or

(4) A reasonable belief that the child has been wrongfully removed or retained in violation of the Hague Convention on the Civil Aspects of International Child Abduction.

(b) A district attorney acting under this Code section acts on behalf of the court and may not represent any party.

Laws 2001, p. 129, § 1.

Historical and Statutory Notes

Uniform Law

This section is based upon § 315 of the Uniform Child Custody Jurisdiction and Enforcement Act. See Vol. 9, Pt. IA, Uniform Laws Annotated, Master Edition, or ULA Database on Westlaw.

§ 19–9–96. Powers of law enforcement officer

At the request of a district attorney acting under Code Section 19–9–95, a law enforcement officer may take any lawful action reasonably necessary to locate a child or a party and assist a district attorney with responsibilities under Code Section 19–9–95.

Laws 2001, p. 129, § 1.

Historical and Statutory Notes

Uniform Law

This section is based upon § 316 of the Uniform Child Custody Jurisdiction and Enforcement Act. See Vol. 9, Pt. IA, Uniform Laws Annotated, Master Edition, or ULA Database on Westlaw.

§ 19–9–97. Costs and expenses

If the respondent is not the prevailing party, the court may assess against the respondent all direct expenses and costs incurred by the district attorney and law enforcement officers under Code Section 19–9–95 or 19–9–96.

Laws 2001, p. 129, § 1.

Historical and Statutory Notes

Uniform Law

This section is based upon § 317 of the Uniform Child Custody Jurisdiction and Enforcement Act. See Vol. 9, Pt. IA, Uniform Laws Annotated, Master Edition, or ULA Database on Westlaw.

Part 4

Construction

§ 19–9–101. Uniformity of construction among states

In applying and construing this uniform Act, consideration must be given to the need to promote uniformity of the law with respect to its subject matter among states that enact it.

Laws 2001, p. 129, § 1.

Historical and Statutory Notes

Uniform Law

This section is based upon § 401 of the Uniform Child Custody Jurisdiction and Enforcement Act. See Vol. 9, Pt. IA, Uniform Laws Annotated, Master Edition, or ULA Database on Westlaw.

§ 19–9–102. Actions commenced before effective date of law

A motion or other request for relief made in a child custody proceeding or to enforce a child custody determination which was commenced before July 1, 2001, is governed by the law in effect at the time the motion or other request was made.

Laws 2001, p. 129, § 1.

Historical and Statutory Notes

In 2001, the Code Commission substituted "July 1, 2001," for "the effective date of this article". See § 28–9–5.

§ 19–9–103. Construction with Code Section 19–13–23

This article shall not be construed to repeal, amend, or impair the provisions of Code Section 19–13–23.

Laws 2001, p. 129, § 1.

§ 19–9–104. Conflict with Georgia Child Custody Intrastate Jurisdiction Act of 1978

In the event of any conflict between this article and Article 2 of this chapter, the "Georgia Child Custody Intrastate Jurisdiction Act of 1978," this article shall apply.

Laws 2001, p. 129, § 1.

CHAPTER 10

ABANDONMENT OF SPOUSE OR CHILD

Section

§ 19–10–1. Child abandonment; defenses and paternity testing; natal expenses and future support; verdicts, sentencing, and punishment

(a) A child abandoned by its father or mother shall be considered to be in a dependent condition when the father or mother does not furnish sufficient food, clothing, or shelter for the needs of the child.

(b) If any father or mother willfully and voluntarily abandons his or her child, either legitimate or born out of wedlock, leaving it in a dependent condition, he or she shall be guilty of a misdemeanor. Moreover, if any father or mother willfully and voluntarily abandons his or her child, either legitimate or born out of wedlock, leaving it in a dependent condition, and leaves this state or if any father or mother willfully and voluntarily abandons his or her child, either legitimate or born out of wedlock, leaving it in a dependent condition, after leaving this state, he or she shall be guilty of a felony punishable by imprisonment for not less than one nor more than three years. The felony shall be reducible to a misdemeanor. Any person, upon conviction of the third offense for violating this Code section, shall be guilty of a felony and shall be imprisoned for not less than one nor more than three years, which felony shall not be reducible to a misdemeanor. The husband and wife shall be competent witnesses in such cases to testify for or against the other.

(c) The offense of abandonment is a continuing offense. Except as provided in subsection (i) of this Code section, former acquittal or conviction of the offense shall not be a bar to further prosecution therefor under this Code section, if it is made to appear that the child in question was in a dependent condition, as defined in this Code section, for a period of 30 days prior to the commencement of prosecution.

(d) In prosecutions under this Code section when the child is born out of wedlock, the venue of the offense shall be in the county in which the child and the mother are domiciled at the time of the swearing out of the arrest warrant; but, if the child and the mother are domiciled in different counties, venue shall be in the county in which the child is domiciled.

(e) Upon the trial of an accused father or mother under this Code section, it shall be no defense that the accused father or mother has never supported the child.

(f) In the trial of any abandonment proceeding in which the question of parentage arises, regardless of any presumptions with respect to parentage, the accused father may request a paternity blood test and agree and arrange to pay for same; and in such cases the court before which the matter is brought, upon pretrial motion of the defendant, shall order that the alleged parent, the known natural parent, and the child submit to any blood tests and comparisons which have been developed and adapted for purposes of establishing or disproving parentage and which are reasonably accessible to the alleged parent, the known natural parent, and the child. The results of those blood tests and comparisons, including the statistical likelihood of the alleged parent's parentage, if available, shall be admitted in evidence when offered by a duly qualified, licensed practicing physician, duly qualified immunologist, duly qualified geneticist, or other duly qualified person. Upon receipt of a motion and the entry of an order under this subsection, the court shall proceed as follows:

(1) Where the issue of parentage is to be decided by a jury, where the results of those blood tests and comparisons are not shown to be inconsistent with the results of any other blood tests and comparisons, and where the results of those blood tests and comparisons indicate that the alleged parent cannot be the natural parent of the child, the jury shall be instructed that if they believe that the witness presenting the results testified truthfully as to those results and if they believe that the tests and comparisons were conducted properly, then it will be their duty to decide that the alleged parent is not the natural parent;

(2) The court shall require the defendant requesting the blood tests and comparisons pursuant to this subsection to be initially responsible for any of the expenses thereof. Upon the entry of a verdict incorporating a finding of parentage or nonparentage, the court shall tax the expenses for blood tests and comparisons, in addition to any fees for expert witnesses whose testimonies supported the admissibility thereof, as costs.

(g) In prosecutions under this Code section, when the child is born out of wedlock and the accused father is convicted, the father may be required by the court to pay the reasonable medical expenses paid by or incurred on behalf of the mother due to the birth of the child.

(h) The accused father and the mother of a child born out of wedlock may enter into a written agreement providing for future support of the child by regular periodic payments to the mother until the child reaches the age of 18 years, marries, or becomes self-supporting; provided, however, that the agreement shall not be binding on either party until it has been approved by the court having jurisdiction to try the pending case.

(i) If, during the trial of any person charged with the offense of abandonment as defined in this Code section, the person contends that he or she is not the father or mother of the child alleged to have been abandoned, in a jury trial the trial judge shall charge the jury that if its verdict is for the acquittal of the person and its reason for so finding is that the person is not the father or mother of the child alleged to have been abandoned, then its verdict shall so state. In a trial before the court without the intervention of the jury, if the court renders a verdict of acquittal based on the contention of the person that he or she is not the father or mother of the child alleged to have been abandoned, the trial judge shall so state this fact in his verdict of acquittal. Where the verdict of the jury or the court is for acquittal of a person on the grounds that the person is not the father or mother of the child alleged to have been abandoned, the person cannot thereafter again be tried for the offense of abandoning the child, and the verdict of acquittal shall be a bar to all civil and criminal proceedings attempting to compel the person to support the child.

(j)(1) In a prosecution for and conviction of the offense of abandonment, the trial court may suspend the service of the sentence imposed in the case, upon such terms and conditions as it may prescribe for the support, by the defendant, of the child or children abandoned during the minority of the child or children. Service of the sentence, when so suspended, shall not begin unless and until ordered by the court having jurisdiction thereof, after a hearing as in cases of revocation or probated sentences, because of the failure or refusal of the defendant to comply with the terms and conditions upon which service of a sentence was suspended.

(2) Service of any sentence suspended in abandonment cases may be ordered by the court having jurisdiction thereof at any time before the child or children reach the age of 18 or become emancipated, after a hearing as provided in paragraph (1) of this subsection and a finding by the court that the defendant has failed or refused to comply with the terms and conditions upon which service of the sentence was suspended by the court having jurisdiction thereof.

(3) Notwithstanding any other provisions of law, in abandonment cases where the suspension of sentence has been revoked and the defendant is serving the sentence, the court may thereafter again suspend the service of sentence under the same terms and conditions as the original suspension. The sentence shall not be considered probated and the defendant shall not be on probation, but the defendant shall again be under a suspended sentence. However, the combined time of incarceration of the defendant during the periods of revocation of suspended sentences shall not exceed the maximum period of punishment for the offense.

(4) Notwithstanding any other provision of law to the contrary, the terms and conditions prescribed by the court as to support by the defendant shall be subject to review and modification by the court, upon notice and hearing to the defendant, as to the ability of the defendant to furnish support and as to the adequacy of the present support payments to the child's or children's needs. The review provided for in this paragraph as to the ability of the defendant to furnish support and as to the adequacy of the present support payments to the child's or children's needs shall not be had in less than two-year intervals and shall authorize the court to increase as well as to decrease the amount of child support to be paid as a term and condition of the suspended sentence. The review as to ability to support and adequacy of support shall not be equivalent to a hearing held in cases of revocation of probated sentences for purposes of service of the suspended sentence; nor shall a modification, if any, be deemed a change in sentence; nor shall a modification, if any, be deemed to change the suspended sentence to a probated sentence.

Laws 1866, p. 151, § 1; Laws 1878–79, p. 66, § 1; Laws 1907, p. 57, § 1; Laws 1941, p. 481, § 2; Laws 1946, p. 63, § 1; Laws 1952, p. 173, § 1; Laws 1956, p. 800, § 1; Laws 1960, p. 952, § 1; Laws 1965, p. 197, § 1; Laws 1967, p. 453, § 1; Laws 1973, p. 697, § 2; Laws 1976, p. 1014, § 1; Laws 1980, p. 1374, § 2; Laws 1988, p. 1720, § 11; Laws 1989, p. 381, § 1; Laws 2006, Act 466, § 6, eff. July 1, 2006.

Formerly Code 1868, § 4307; Code 1873, § 4373; Code 1882, § 4373; Penal Code 1895, § 114; Penal Code 1910, § 116; Code 1933, § 74–9902.

Historical and Statutory Notes

The 2006 amendment by Act 466, in subsec. (j), par. (2), substituted "18 or becomes emancipated" for "majority".

§ 19–10–2. Abandonment of wife while pregnant; wife as witness against her husband; punishment for abandonment

(a) A wife who is pregnant with her husband's child shall be deemed to be in a dependent condition when her husband does not furnish her sufficient food, clothing, or medical treatment to meet her needs, both before and immediately upon the birth of the child.

(b) Any husband who willfully and voluntarily abandons his wife, while she is pregnant with his child, leaving her in a dependent condition, shall be guilty of a misdemeanor.

(c) Any husband who willfully and voluntarily abandons his wife while she is pregnant with his child and leaves the jurisdiction of this state shall be guilty of a felony punishable by imprisonment for not less than one year nor more than three years. The felony shall be reducible to a misdemeanor.

(d) For purposes of this Code section, a husband shall not be deemed to have abandoned his wife willfully and voluntarily unless he has actual knowledge of her pregnant condition.

(e) The offense of abandonment as set forth in this Code section is a continuing offense.

(f) The wife shall be competent to be a witness against her husband in any proceedings or cases brought against the husband for abandonment as set forth in this Code section.

Laws 1964, p. 224, § 1.

Formerly Code 1933, § 74-9903.

CHAPTER 10A

SAFE PLACE FOR NEWBORNS

§ 19-10A-1. Short title

This chapter shall be known and may be cited as the "Safe Place for Newborns Act of 2002."

Laws 2002, p. 1137, § 1.

§ 19-10A-2. Definitions

As used in this chapter, the term "medical facility" shall mean any licensed general or specialized hospital, institutional infirmary, health center operated by a county board of health, or facility where human births occur on a regular and ongoing basis which is classified by the Department of Community Health as a birthing center, but shall not mean physicians' or dentists' private offices.

Laws 2002, p. 1137, § 1; Laws 2008, Act 392, § 2-1, eff. July 1, 2009.

Historical and Statutory Notes

The 2008 amendment by Act 392, substituted "Department of Community Health" for "Department of Human Resources".

Laws 2008, Act 392, § 3-1, provides:

"(a) Except as provided in subsection (b) of this section, this Act shall become effective on July 1, 2008, and shall only apply to applications submitted on or after July 1, 2008.

"(b) Part II of this Act shall become effective on July 1, 2009."

§ 19-10A-3. Legislative intent

It is the express purpose and intent of the General Assembly in enacting this chapter to prevent injuries to and deaths of newborn children that are caused by a mother who abandons the newborn.

Laws 2002, p. 1137, § 1.

§ 19-10A-4. Mother who leaves child with medical facility not to be prosecuted for certain crimes

A mother shall not be prosecuted for the crimes of cruelty to a child, Code Section 16-5-70; contributing to the delinquency, unruliness, or deprivation of a child, Code Section 16-12-1; or abandonment of a dependent child, Code Section 19-10-1, because of the act of leaving her newborn child in the physical custody of an employee, agent, or member of the staff of a medical facility who is on duty, whether there in a paid or volunteer position, provided that the newborn child is no more than one week old and the mother shows proof of her identity, if available, to the person with whom the newborn is left and provides her name and address.

Laws 2002, p. 1137, § 1; Laws 2003, Act 9, § 19, eff. May 14, 2003.

Historical and Statutory Notes

The 2003 amendment by Act 9 substituted "position," for "position;".

§ 19-10A-5. Reports to General Assembly as to children left with medical facility

The Department of Human Services shall investigate and report to the General Assembly as to children left with a medical facility pursuant to Code Section 19-10A-4, including in such report the desirability and cost effectiveness of a dedicated toll-free telephone line for providing information to and answering questions from the public and employees and staff members of medical facilities concerning the acts and consequences thereof contemplated in Code Section 19-10A-4.

Laws 2002, p. 1137, § 1; Laws 2009, Act 102, § 2-2, eff. July 1, 2009.

Historical and Statutory Notes

The 2009 amendment by Act 102 substituted "Department of Human Services" for "Department of Human Resources" throughout the section.

§ 19-10A-6. Reimbursement of medical facility; taking of custody by Department of Human Services

A medical facility which accepts for inpatient admission a child left pursuant to Code Section 19-10A-4 shall be reimbursed by the Department of Human Services for all reasonable medical and other reasonable costs associated with the child prior to the child being placed in the care of the department. A medical facility shall notify the Department of Human Services at such time as the child is left and at the time the child is medically ready for discharge. Upon notification that the child is medically ready for discharge, the Department of Human Services shall take physical custody of the child within six hours. The Department of Human Services upon taking physical custody shall promptly bring the child before the juvenile court as required by Code Section 15-11-47.

Laws 2002, p. 1137, § 1; Laws 2009, Act 102, § 2-2, eff. July 1, 2009.

Historical and Statutory Notes

The 2009 amendment by Act 102 substituted "Department of Human Services" for "Department of Human Resources" throughout the section.

§ 19-10A-7. Immunity from liability

Medical facilities and their employees, agents, and staff members shall not be liable for civil damages or subject to criminal prosecution for failure to discharge the duties provided for in this chapter. The immunity provided in this chapter shall in no way be construed as providing immunity for any acts of negligent treatment of the child taken into custody.

Laws 2002, p. 1137, § 1.

CHAPTER 13

FAMILY VIOLENCE

Article 1

Granting of Relief by Superior Courts

§ 19–13–1. "Family violence" defined

As used in this article, the term "family violence" means the occurrence of one or more of the following acts between past or present spouses, persons who are parents of the same child, parents and children, stepparents and stepchildren, foster parents and foster children, or other persons living or formerly living in the same household:

(1) Any felony; or

(2) Commission of offenses of battery, simple battery, simple assault, assault, stalking, criminal damage to property, unlawful restraint, or criminal trespass.

The term "family violence" shall not be deemed to include reasonable discipline administered by a parent to a child in the form of corporal punishment, restraint, or detention.

Laws 1981, p. 880, § 1; Laws 1988, p. 1251, § 2; Laws 1992, p. 1266, § 3; Laws 1993, p. 1534, § 3.

§ 19–13–2. Jurisdiction

(a) Except for proceedings involving a nonresident respondent, the superior court of the county where the respondent resides shall have jurisdiction over all proceedings under this article.

(b) For proceedings under this article involving a nonresident respondent, the superior court where the petitioner resides or the superior court where an act involving family violence allegedly occurred shall have jurisdiction, where the act involving family violence meets the elements for personal jurisdiction provided for under paragraph (2) or (3) of Code Section 9–10–91.

Laws 1981, p. 880, § 2; Laws 1982, p. 3, § 19; Laws 1997, p. 1543, § 1.

§ 19–13–3. Petition; hearing

(a) A person who is not a minor may seek relief under this article by filing a petition with the superior court alleging one or more acts of family violence. A person who is not a minor may also seek relief on behalf of a minor by filing such a petition.

(b) Upon the filing of a verified petition in which the petitioner alleges with specific facts that probable cause exists to establish that family violence has occurred in the past and may occur in the future, the court may order such temporary relief ex parte as it deems necessary to protect the petitioner or a minor of the household from violence. If the court issues an ex parte order, a copy of the order shall be immediately furnished to the petitioner.

(c) Within ten days of the filing of the petition under this article or as soon as practical thereafter, but in no case later than 30 days after the filing of the petition, a hearing shall be held at which the petitioner must prove the allegations of the petition by a preponderance of the evidence as in other civil cases. In the event a hearing cannot be scheduled within the county where the case is pending within the 30 day period the same shall be scheduled and heard within any other county of that circuit. If a hearing is not held within 30 days, the petition shall stand dismissed unless the parties otherwise agree.

(d) Family violence shelter or social service agency staff members designated by the court may explain to all victims not represented by counsel the procedures for filling out and filing all forms and pleadings necessary for the presentation of their petition to the court. The clerk of the court may provide forms for petitions and pleadings to victims of family violence and to any other person designated by the superior court pursuant to this Code section as authorized to advise victims on filling out and filing such petitions and pleadings. The clerk shall not be required to provide assistance to persons in completing such forms or in presenting their case to the court. Any assistance provided pursuant to this Code section shall be performed without cost to the petitioners. The performance of such assistance shall not constitute the practice of law as defined in Code Section 15–19–51.

Laws 1981, p. 880, § 3; Laws 1982, p. 3, § 19; Laws 1984, p. 542, § 1; Laws 1985, p. 983, § 1; Laws 1988, p. 320, § 3; Laws 1988, p. 1248, § 1; Laws 1994, p. 1270, § 7; Laws 1996, p. 883, § 5.

§ 19–13–4. Protective orders and consent agreements

(a) The court may, upon the filing of a verified petition, grant any protective order or approve any consent agreement to bring about a cessation of acts of family violence. The court shall not have the authority to issue or approve mutual protective orders concerning paragraph (1), (2), (5), (9), or (11) of this subsection, or any combination thereof, unless the respondent has filed a verified petition as a counter petition pursuant to Code Section 19–13–3 no later than three days, not including Saturdays, Sundays, and legal holidays, prior to the hearing and the provisions of Code Section 19–13–3 have been satisfied. The orders or agreements may:

(1) Direct the respondent to refrain from such acts;

(2) Grant to a party possession of the residence or household of the parties and exclude the other party from the residence or household;

(3) Require a party to provide suitable alternate housing for a spouse, former spouse, or parent and the parties' child or children;

(4) Award temporary custody of minor children and establish temporary visitation rights;

(5) Order the eviction of a party from the residence or household and order assistance to the victim in returning to it, or order assistance in retrieving personal property of the victim if the respondent's eviction has not been ordered;

(6) Order either party to make payments for the support of a minor child as required by law;

(7) Order either party to make payments for the support of a spouse as required by law;

(8) Provide for possession of personal property of the parties;

(9) Order the respondent to refrain from harassing or interfering with the victim;

(10) Award costs and attorney's fees to either party; and

(11) Order the respondent to receive appropriate psychiatric or psychological services as a further measure to prevent the recurrence of family violence.

(b) A copy of the order shall be issued by the clerk of the superior court to the sheriff of the county wherein the order was entered and shall be retained by the sheriff as long as that order shall remain in effect.

(c) Any order granted under this Code section shall remain in effect for up to one year; provided, however, that upon the motion of a petitioner and notice to the respondent and after a hearing, the court in its discretion may convert a temporary order granted under this Code section to an order effective for not more than three years or to a permanent order.

(d) A protective order issued pursuant to this Code section shall apply and shall be effective throughout this state. It shall be the duty of every superior court and of every sheriff, every deputy sheriff, and every state, county, or municipal law enforcement officer within this state to enforce and carry out the terms of any valid protective order issued by any court under the provisions of this Code section.

Laws 1981, p. 880, § 4; Laws 1982, p. 2300, §§ 1, 2; Laws 1988, p. 1250, § 1; Laws 1993, p. 788, § 1; Laws 1994, p. 1270, § 8; Laws 2000, p. 1081, § 2; Laws 2003, Act 298, § 2, eff. July 1, 2003.

Historical and Statutory Notes

In 2000, the Code Commission, in the second sentence of the introductory paragraph of subsec. (a), substituted "paragraph" for "paragraphs". See § 28–9–5.

The 2003 amendment by Act 298, in subsec. (c), substituted "order granted under this section shall remain in effect for up to one year" for "such orders granted under this Code section shall not remain in effect for more than six months", and inserted "an order effective for not more than three years or to".

§ 19–13–5. Supplemental nature of law

The remedies provided by this article are not exclusive but are additional to any other remedies provided by law.

Laws 1981, p. 880, § 5.

§ 19–13–6. Violations relating to procedures for prevention of family violence

A violation of an order issued pursuant to this article may be punished by an action for contempt or criminally punished as provided in Article 7 of Chapter 5 of Title 16.

Laws 1985, p. 905, § 1; Laws 1988, p. 1249, § 1; Laws 2003, Act 298, § 3, eff. July 1, 2003.

Historical and Statutory Notes

The 2003 amendment by Act 298 rewrote the section which had read:

"(a) A violation of an order issued pursuant to this article may be punished by an action for contempt.

"(b) Any person who violates the provisions of a domestic violence order which excludes, evicts, or excludes and evicts that person from a residence or household shall be guilty of a misdemeanor."

Article 1A

Family Violence Intervention

Laws 2002, Act 989, § 3, added this article effective July 1, 2002 for certain purposes, and effective July 1, 2003 for other purposes. See the Historical and Statutory Notes following § 19–13–10.

§ 19–13–10. Definitions

As used in this article, the term:

(1) "Commission" means the State Commission on Family Violence.

(2) "Commissioner" means the commissioner of corrections.

(3) "Department" means the Department of Corrections.

(4) "Family or household members" means past or present spouses, persons who are parents of the same child, or other persons living or formerly living in the same household.

(5) "Family violence" means the commission of the offenses of battery, simple battery, simple assault, assault, stalking, criminal damage to property, or criminal trespass between family or household members.

(6) "Family violence intervention program" or "program" means any program that is certified by the Department of Corrections pursuant to Code Section 19–13–14 and designed to rehabilitate family violence offenders. The term includes, but is not limited to, batterer intervention programs, anger management programs, anger counseling, family problem resolution, and violence therapy.

Laws 2002, p. 1435, § 3.

Historical and Statutory Notes

Laws 2002, Act 989, § 7, provides in part:

"Section 3 of this Act [adding §§ 19–13–10 to 19–13–17] shall become effective on July 1, 2002, for the purposes of the development process by the Department of Corrections and the State Commission on Family Violence for certified family violence intervention programs and for the purposes of collecting application fees; for all other purposes, Section 3 of this Act shall become effective on July 1, 2003."

§ 19–13–11. Fee

In carrying out the purpose of this article, the department shall charge a fee for the consideration of applications for certification of family violence intervention programs and instructors. The amount of this fee shall be established by the commission and shall, as best as the commission shall determine, approximate the expense incurred by the department in consideration of an application. These certifications shall be valid for a period of two years unless suspended or revoked prior to the expiration of that time period.

Laws 2002, p. 1435, § 3.

§ 19–13–12. Reserved

§ 19–13–13. Administration of program; rules and regulations

(a) A program certified pursuant to this article shall be administered by the department. The department is authorized to promulgate, adopt, and enforce rules and regulations necessary to carry out this article, including, but not limited to, prescribing the form of applications, visiting program facilities, and investigating complaints.

(b) The department shall be responsible for the approval and certification of programs and staff. This responsibility includes the training for and monitoring of all programs under this article.

Laws 2002, p. 1435, § 3.

§ 19–13–14. Certification of programs

(a) The commission and the department shall establish standards and requirements concerning the content of courses, including, but not limited to, duration of courses, qualifications of instructors, program and certification fees, attendance requirements, and examinations. In order to be certified, a program shall meet the standards established by the commission and the department.

(b) Programs may be operated by any individual, partnership, corporation, association, civic group, club, county, municipality, board of education, school, or college or any public, private, or governmental entity.

(c) No official or employee, or his or her spouse, of the department or the State Board of Pardons or Paroles shall own, operate, instruct at, or be employed by a program except as provided by Code Section 19–13–15.

(d) The department is responsible for establishing requirements for the certification of programs. An applicant must meet the certification requirements promulgated by the department through standards established by the commission and the department. No program shall be approved unless the owner of the program agrees in writing to submit reports as required in the rules and regulations of the department and to allow the examination and audit of the books, records, and financial statements of the program or its authorized agent. No program will be certified unless the owner of the program agrees in writing to pay to the state, for the costs of administration, a fee as established by the commission, provided that nothing in this Code section shall be construed so as to allow the department to retain any funds required by the Constitution of this state to be paid into the state treasury; and provided, further, that the department shall comply with all provisions of Part 1 of Article 4 of Chapter 12 of Title 45, the "Budget Act," except Code Section 45–12–92, prior to expending any such miscellaneous funds. All programs operated by the department and the State Board of Pardons and Paroles shall be exempt from fee provisions relating to obtaining certification.

(e) The department has the authority to deny, suspend, or revoke a certificate under this article or to impose sanctions upon and discipline a program which is not complying with the rules and regulations set forth by the department. The department shall establish criteria to determine noncompliance with its rules and regulations, sanctions for noncompliance, and methods of appeal if certification is denied, suspended, or revoked.

(f) The department shall maintain a list of programs certified pursuant to this article and make the list available to the public and all courts.

Laws 2002, p. 1435, § 3.

§ 19–13–15. Operation of other programs which meet requirements of department

The department and the State Board of Pardons and Paroles may operate family violence intervention programs which meet the requirements of the department. The courts and the State Board of Pardons and Paroles may accept such programs in lieu of certified family violence intervention programs as defined in paragraph (6) of Code Section 19–13–10.

Laws 2002, p. 1435, § 3.

Historical and Statutory Notes

In 2002, the Code Commission, in the second sentence, substituted "paragraph (6)" for "paragraph (1)". See § 28–9–5.

§ 19–13–16. Courts and State Board of Pardons and Paroles to utilize programs; costs

(a) A court, in addition to imposing any penalty provided by law, when sentencing a defendant or revoking a defendant's probation for an offense involving family violence, or when imposing a protective order against family violence, shall order the defendant to participate in a family violence intervention program, whether a certified program pursuant to this article or a program operated pursuant to Code Section 19–13–15, unless the court determines and states on the record why participation in such a program is not appropriate.

(b) The State Board of Pardons and Paroles, for a violation of parole for an offense involving family violence, shall require the conditional releasee to participate in a family violence intervention program, whether a certified program pursuant to this article or a program operated pursuant to Code Section 19–13–15, unless the State Board of Pardons and Paroles determines why participation in such a program is not appropriate.

(c) Unless the defendant is indigent, the cost of the family violence intervention program as provided by this Code section shall be borne by the defendant. If the defendant is indigent, then the cost of the program shall be determined by a sliding scale based upon the defendant's ability to pay.

Laws 2002, p. 1435, § 3.

§ 19–13–17. Enforcement

As an alternative to criminal or other civil enforcement, the commissioner or his or her designee, in order to enforce this article or any orders, rules, or regulations promulgated pursuant to this article, may issue an administrative fine not to exceed $ 1,000.00 for each violation, whenever that commissioner or his or her designee, after a hearing, determines that any person, firm, or corporation has violated any provision of this article or any order, rule, or regulation promulgated pursuant to this article. The hearing and any administrative review thereof shall be conducted in accordance with the procedures for contested cases under Chapter 13 of Title 50, the "Georgia Administrative Procedure Act." Any person, firm, or corporation that has exhausted all administrative remedies available and that is aggrieved or adversely affected by a final order or action of the commissioner or his or her designee shall have the right of judicial review in accordance with Chapter 13 of Title 50. All fines collected or recovered by the commissioner under this Code section shall be remitted to the Office of the State Treasurer to the credit of the general fund of this state. The commissioner or his or her designee may file in the superior court (1) wherein the person under order resides; (2) if such person is a corporation, in the county wherein the corporation maintains its principal place of business; or (3) in the county wherein the violation occurred, a certified copy of a final order of the commissioner or his or her designee, whether unappealed from or affirmed upon appeal, whereupon the court shall render judgment in accordance with the judgment and notify the parties. The judgment shall have the same effect and proceedings in relation thereto shall thereafter be the same as though the judgment had been rendered in an action duly heard and determined by the court. The penalty prescribed in this Code section shall be concurrent, alternative, and cumulative with any and all other civil, criminal, or alternative rights, remedies, forfeitures, or penalties provided, allowed, or available to the commissioner or his or her designee with respect to any violation of this article or any order, rule, or regulation promulgated pursuant to this article.

Laws 2002, p. 1435, § 3; Laws 2010, Act 621, § 2, eff. July 1, 2010.

Historical and Statutory Notes

The 2010 amendment by Act 621 substituted "Office of the State Treasurer" for "Office of Treasury and Fiscal Services" in the fourth sentence.

Article 2

Family Violence Shelters

§ 19-13-20. Definitions

As used in this article, the term:

(1) "Department" means the Department of Human Services.

(2) "Family or household members" means spouses, parents and children, or other persons related by consanguinity or affinity and occupying a common domicile.

(3) "Family violence" means the occurrence of one of the following acts between family or household members who reside together:

(A) Attempting to cause or causing bodily injury or serious bodily injury with or without a deadly weapon; or

(B) By physical menace, placing another in fear of imminent serious bodily injury.

(4) "Family violence program" means any program whose primary stated purpose is to provide services to victims of family violence. A family violence program may be but is not required to be associated with a family violence shelter.

(5) "Family violence shelter" means a facility approved by the department for the purpose of receiving, on a temporary basis, persons who are subject to family violence. Family violence shelters are distinguished from shelters operated for detention or placement of children only, as provided in subsection (a) of Code Section 15-11-48.

Laws 1981, p. 663, § 1; Laws 1983, p. 521, § 1; Laws 1988, p. 13, § 19; Laws 1988, p. 1287, § 1; Laws 1996, p. 819, § 1; Laws 2000, p. 20, § 14; Laws 2009, Act 102, § 2-2, eff. July 1, 2009.

Historical and Statutory Notes

The 2009 amendment by Act 102 substituted "Department of Human Services" for "Department of Human Resources" throughout the section.

§ 19-13-21. Duties and functions of department

(a) It shall be the duty of the department:

(1) To establish minimum standards for an approved family violence shelter to enable such shelter to receive state funds;

(2) To receive applications for the development and establishment of family violence shelters;

(3) To approve or reject each application within 60 days of receipt of the application;

(4) To distribute funds to an approved shelter as funds become available;

(5) To fund other family violence programs as funds become available, provided that such programs meet standards established by the department; and

(6) To evaluate annually each family violence shelter for compliance with the minimum standards.

(b) Without using designated shelter funds, the department may:

(1) Formulate and conduct a research and evaluation program on family violence and cooperate with and assist and participate in programs of other properly qualified agencies, including any agency of the federal government, schools of medicine, hospitals, and clinics, in planning and conducting research on the prevention of family violence and the care, treatment, and rehabilitation of persons engaged in or subject to family violence;

(2) Serve as a clearing-house for information relating to family violence;

(3) Carry on educational programs on family violence for the benefit of the general public, persons engaged in or subject to family violence, professional persons, or others who care for or may be engaged in the care and treatment of persons engaged in or subject to family violence; and

(4) Enlist the assistance of public and voluntary health, education, welfare, and rehabilitation agencies in a concerted effort to prevent family violence and to treat persons engaged in or subject to family violence.

Laws 1981, p. 663, § 2; Laws 1983, p. 521, § 2; Laws 1988, p. 1287, § 2; Laws 1996, p. 819, § 2.

§ 19-13-22. Family violence shelters

(a) In order to be approved and funded under this article, each shelter shall:

(1) Provide a facility which will serve as a shelter to receive or house persons who are family violence victims;

(2) Receive the periodic written endorsement of local law enforcement agencies;

(3) Receive a minimum of 25 percent of its funding from other sources. Contributions in kind, whether materials, commodities, transportation, office space, other types of facilities, or personal services, may be evaluated and counted as part of the required local funding; and

(4) Meet the minimum standards of the department for approving family violence shelters; provided, however, that

facilities not receiving state funds shall not be required to be approved.

(b) The department shall provide procedures whereby local organizations may apply for approval and funding. Any local agency or organization may apply to participate.

(c) Each approved family violence shelter shall be designated to serve as a temporary receiving facility for the admission of persons subject to family violence. Each shelter shall refer such persons and their spouses to any public or private facility, service, or program providing treatment or rehabilitation services, including, but not limited to, the prevention of such violence and the care, treatment, and rehabilitation of persons engaged in or subject to family violence.

(d) Family violence shelters and family violence programs may be established throughout the state as private, local, state, or federal funds are available. Any county or municipality in this state is authorized to make grants of county or municipal funds, respectively, to any family violence center approved as such in accordance with the minimum standards of the department.

(e) The family violence shelters shall establish procedures pursuant to which persons subject to family violence may seek admission to these shelters on a voluntary basis.

(f) Each family violence shelter shall have a board composed of at least three citizens, one of whom shall be a member of a local, municipal, or county law enforcement agency.

Laws 1981, p. 663, § 3; Laws 1983, p. 521, §§ 3–5; Laws 1988, p. 1287, § 3; Laws 1989, p. 1108, § 1; Laws 1996, p. 819, § 3.

§ 19–13–23. Disclosure of location of family violence center

(a) Any person who knowingly publishes, disseminates, or otherwise discloses the location of a family violence shelter is guilty of a misdemeanor.

(b) This Code section shall not apply to:

(1) Confidential communications between a client and his or her attorney; or

(2) Instances when such publication, dissemination, or disclosure is authorized by the director of the shelter.

Laws 1997, p. 1543, § 2.

Article 4

Family Violence and Stalking Protective Order Registry

§ 19–13–50. Short title

This article shall be known and may be cited as the "Family Violence and Stalking Protective Order Registry Act."

Laws 2001, p. 101, § 1.

§ 19–13–51. Definitions

As used in this article, the term:

(1) "Court" means judges in the classes of courts identified in Title 15 and any other person while acting as such a judge pursuant to designation as otherwise authorized by law.

(2) "Foreign court" means a court of competent jurisdiction in any state other than this state or any territory or tribal jurisdiction in the United States.

(3) "Foreign protective order" means any temporary protective order, protective order, restraining order, or injunction that prohibits acts of family violence or stalking or both issued by a court of competent jurisdiction in another state, territory, or tribal jurisdiction in the United States.

(4) "Law enforcement officer" means any agent or officer of this state, or a political subdivision or municipality thereof, who, as a full–time or part–time employee, is vested either expressly by law or by virtue of public employment or service with authority to enforce the criminal or traffic laws and whose duties include the preservation of public order, the protection of life and property, or the prevention, detection, or investigation of crime. Such term also includes the following: state or local officer, sheriff, deputy sheriff, dispatcher, 9–1–1 operator, police officer, prosecuting attorney, member of the State Board of Pardons and Paroles, a hearing officer and parole officer of the State Board of Pardons and Paroles, and a probation officer of the Department of Corrections.

(5) "Modification" means any amendment, dismissal, or continuance of a protective order.

(6) "Prosecuting attorney" means each attorney elected to represent a judicial circuit in this state and any assistant or deputy district attorney, or solicitor, in each judicial circuit in this state.

(7) "Protective order" means any ex parte, temporary, six-month, permanent order, or restraining order issued by a judge in this state pursuant to Code Sections 16–5–90 through 16–5–94 or this chapter and also where appropriate in this context includes a foreign protective order.

(8) "Registry" means the Georgia Protective Order Registry.

Laws 2001, p. 101, § 1; Laws 2005, Act 134, § 2, eff. July 1, 2005.

Historical and Statutory Notes

The 2005 amendment by Act 134, in par. (4), substituted "9–1–1" for "911".

§ 19–13–52. Georgia Protective Order Registry; creation, purpose, maintenance, contents, access, links

(a) The Georgia Protective Order Registry shall be created to serve as a centralized data base for state-wide protective orders issued pursuant to Code Sections 16–5–90 through 16–5–94 and this chapter. The registry is intended to enhance victim safety by providing law enforcement officers, prosecuting attorneys, and the courts access to protective orders issued by the courts of this state and foreign courts 24 hours of the day and seven days of the week. Access to the registry is intended to aid law enforcement officers, prosecuting attorneys, and the courts in the enforcement of protective orders and the protection to victims of stalking and family violence.

(b) The registry shall be maintained by the Georgia Crime Information Center. The Georgia Commission on Family Violence may consult with the Georgia Crime Information Center regarding the effectiveness of the registry in enhancing the safety of victims of domestic violence and stalking.

(c) The registry shall include a complete and systematic record and index of all valid protective orders and modifications thereof. Law enforcement officers and the courts shall have access to the registry.

(d) The registry shall be linked to the National Crime Information Center Network and protective orders entered in the registry shall be immediately transmitted to this network.

Laws 2001, p. 101, § 1; Laws 2003, Act 63, § 1, eff. May 29, 2003.

Historical and Statutory Notes

The 2003 amendment by Act 63, in subsec. (c), deleted the last sentence which read:

"The Georgia Crime Information Center shall implement a daily process of purging protective orders and names of parties from the registry upon expiration or dismissal of protective orders and shall maintain purged protective orders and names in a separate archived file in the registry that shall be available only to the courts."

§ 19–13–53. Standardized form for protective orders; electronic transmittal and maintenance of orders

(a) The courts of this state shall use a standardized form or forms for the issuance of any protective order. The form or forms shall be promulgated by the Uniform Superior Court Rules. The standardized form or forms for protective orders shall be in conformity with the provisions of this Code, shall be subject to the approval of the Georgia Crime Information Center and the Georgia Superior Court Clerks' Cooperative Authority as to form and format, and shall contain, at a minimum, all information required for entry of protective orders into the registry and the National Crime Information Center Protection Order File. The Administrative Office of the Courts shall distribute the forms. A court may modify the standardized form to comply with the court's application of the law and facts to an individual case. The form or forms shall contain, at a minimum, all information that is required for entry of protective orders into the registry and the National Crime Information Center Protection Order file.

(b) The clerk of the issuing court shall electronically transmit a copy of the protective order or modification thereof to the registry as expeditiously as possible but no later than by the end of the next business day after the order is filed with the clerk of court. In the event of electronic failure, the clerk of court shall immediately notify the Georgia Crime Information Center which shall authorize an alternative method of transmitting the protective order or modification thereof to the registry.

(c) The Georgia Crime Information Center shall ensure that any protective order or modification thereof is entered in the registry within 24 hours of receipt of the protective order or modification from the clerk of court. The inability to enter information for all data fields in the registry shall not delay the entry of available information.

(d) The sheriff's department shall be responsible for the validation of all National Crime Information Center protective order entries made on its behalf by the superior court clerk's office in accordance with the validation steps established by the Georgia Crime Information Center and the National Crime Information Center. All registry entries shall be validated in accordance with the file retention schedule established by the National Crime Information Center. The sheriff shall respond to and confirm "HIT" confirmation requests based upon the records maintained in the sheriff's office.

(e) The entry of a protective order in the registry shall not be a prerequisite for enforcement of a valid protective order.

Laws 2001, p. 101, § 1; Laws 2003, Act 63, § 2, eff. May 29, 2003; Laws 2004, Act 564, § 19, eff. May 13, 2004.

Historical and Statutory Notes

The 2003 amendment by Act 63, in subsec. (a), substituted "facts to an individual case. The form or forms shall contain at a minimum, all information that is required for entry of protective orders into the registry and the National Crime Information Center Protection Order file" for "facts to an individual case and shall delete or otherwise make inoperative any provision in the standardized form which is not supported by the evidence of the case"; in subsec. (c), deleted "The Georgia Crime Information Center shall ensure that protective orders that have expired or been terminated are purged from the registry within 24 hours of such expiration or termination." preceding "The inability to enter information"; inserted new subsec. (d); and redesignated former subsec. (d) as (e).

The 2004 amendment by Act 564 was a provision contained in a correction bill.

§ 19–13–54. Foreign protective orders

(a) A petitioner who obtains a valid foreign protective order may file that order by filing a certified copy of the foreign protective order with any clerk of court of the superior court in this state.

(b) Filing shall be without fee or cost.

(c) The clerk of court shall provide the petitioner with a receipt bearing proof of submission of the foreign protective order for entry in the registry.

(d) The clerk of court shall transmit to the registry a copy of the foreign protective order in the same manner as provided in Code Section 19–13–53.

(e) Foreign protective orders shall not be required to be contained on a standardized form or forms in order to be entered in the registry.

(f) Filing and registry of the foreign protective order in the registry shall not be prerequisites for enforcement of the foreign protective order in this state.

Laws 2001, p. 101, § 1.

§ 19–13–55. Confidentiality of information

Any individual, agency, or court which obtains information from the registry shall keep such information or parts thereof confidential, and shall not disseminate or disclose such information, or parts thereof, except as authorized in this article or otherwise by law. Violation of this Code section shall be a misdemeanor.

Laws 2001, p. 101, § 1.

§ 19–13–56. Immunity from civil liability

(a) The state and any local or state law enforcement officer, court official, or official of the registry shall be held harmless for any delay or failure to file a protective order, to transmit information contained in protective orders, or to enter such information in the registry.

(b) The state and any local or state law enforcement officer, court official, or official of the registry shall be held harmless for acting in reliance upon information registered in the registry or information received for the purpose of entry in the registry.

Laws 2001, p. 101, § 1.

CHAPTER 15

CHILD ABUSE

§ 19–15–1. Definitions

As used in this chapter, the term:

(1) "Abused" means subjected to child abuse.

(2) "Child" means any person under 18 years of age.

(3) "Child abuse" means:

(A) Physical injury or death inflicted upon a child by a parent or caretaker thereof by other than accidental means; provided, however, physical forms of discipline may be used as long as there is no physical injury to the child;

(B) Neglect or exploitation of a child by a parent or caretaker thereof;

(C) Sexual abuse of a child; or

(D) Sexual exploitation of a child.

(4) "Child protection professional" means any person who is employed by the state or a political subdivision of the state as a law enforcement officer, school teacher, school administrator, or school counselor or who is employed to render services to children by the Department of Community Health, the Department of Behavioral Health and Developmental Disabilities, or the Department of Human Services or any county board of health, community service board, or county department of family and children services.

(5) "Eligible deaths" means deaths meeting the criteria for review by a county child fatality review committee including deaths resulting from Sudden Infant Death Syndrome, unintentional injuries, intentional injuries, medical conditions when unexpected or when unattended by a physician, or any manner that is suspicious or unusual.

(6) "Investigation" in the context of child death includes all of the following:

(A) A post-mortem examination which may be limited to an external examination or may include an autopsy;

(B) An inquiry by law enforcement agencies having jurisdiction into the circumstances of the death, including a scene investigation and interview with the child's parents, guardian, or caretaker and the person who reported the child's death;

(C) A review of information regarding the child and family from relevant agencies, professionals, and providers of medical care.

(7) "Panel" means the Georgia Child Fatality Review Panel established pursuant to Code Section 19–15–4. The panel oversees the local child fatality review process and reports to the Governor on the incidence of child deaths with recommendations for prevention.

(8) "Protocol committee" means a multidisciplinary, multiagency child abuse protocol committee established for a county pursuant to Code Section 19–15–2. The protocol committee is charged with developing local protocols to investigate and prosecute alleged cases of child abuse.

(9) "Report" means a standardized form designated by the panel which is required for collecting data on child fatalities reviewed by local child fatality review committees.

(10) "Review committee" means a multidisciplinary, multiagency child fatality review committee established for a county or circuit pursuant to Code Section 19–15–3. The review committee is charged with reviewing all eligible child deaths to determine manner and cause of death and if the death was preventable.

(11) "Sexual abuse" means a person's employing, using, persuading, inducing, enticing, or coercing any minor who is not that person's spouse to engage in any act which involves:

(A) Sexual intercourse, including genital-genital, oral-genital, anal-genital, or oral-anal, whether between persons of the same or opposite sex;

(B) Bestiality;

(C) Masturbation;

(D) Lewd exhibition of the genitals or pubic area of any person;

(E) Flagellation or torture by or upon a person who is nude;

(F) Condition of being fettered, bound, or otherwise physically restrained on the part of a person who is nude;

(G) Physical contact in an act of apparent sexual stimulation or gratification with any person's clothed or unclothed genitals, pubic area, or buttocks or with a female's clothed or unclothed breasts;

(H) Defecation or urination for the purpose of sexual stimulation; or

(I) Penetration of the vagina or rectum by any object except when done as part of a recognized medical procedure.

"Sexual abuse" shall not include consensual sex acts involving persons of the opposite sex when the sex acts are between minors or between a minor and an adult who is not more than three years older than the minor. This provision shall not be deemed or construed to repeal any law concerning the age or capacity to consent.

(12) "Sexual exploitation" means conduct by any person who allows, permits, encourages, or requires that child to engage in:

(A) Prostitution, as defined in Code Section 16–6–9; or

(B) Sexually explicit conduct for the purpose of producing any visual or print medium depicting such conduct, as defined in Code Section 16–12–100.

Laws 1990, p. 1785, § 1; Laws 1991, p. 94, § 19; Laws 1993, p. 1695, § 2; Laws 1993, p. 1941, § 1; Laws 2001, p. 1158, § 1; Laws 2009, Act 102, § 2–8, eff. July 1, 2009; Laws 2009, Act 151, § 2, eff. May 5, 2009.

Formerly Code 1981, § 19–1–1.

Historical and Statutory Notes

The 2009 amendment by Act 102 rewrote par. (4) which had read:

"(4) 'Child protection professional' means any person who is employed by the state or a political subdivision of the state as a law enforcement officer, school teacher, school administrator, or school counselor or who is employed to render services to children by the Department of Human Resources or any county board of health or county department of family and children services."

The 2009 amendment by Act 151 rewrote par. (12) which had read:

"(12) 'Sexual exploitation' means conduct by a child's parent or caretaker who allows, permits, encourages, or requires that child to engage in:

"(A) Prostitution, as defined in Code Section 16–6–9; or

"(B) Sexually explicit conduct for the purpose of producing any visual or print medium depicting such conduct, as defined in Code Section 16–12–100."

§ 19–15–2. Child abuse protocol committees; adoption of written child abuse protocol

(a) Each county shall be required to establish a child abuse protocol as provided in this Code section.

(b) The chief superior court judge of the circuit in which the county is located shall establish a child abuse protocol committee as provided in subsection (c) of this Code section and shall appoint an interim chairperson who shall preside over the first meeting and the chief superior court judge shall appoint persons to fill any vacancies on the committee. Thus established, the committee shall thereafter elect a chairperson from its membership.

(c) (1) Each of the following agencies of the county shall designate a representative to serve on the committee:

(A) The office of the sheriff;

(B) The county department of family and children services;

(C) The office of the district attorney;

(D) The juvenile court;

(E) The magistrate court;

(F) The county board of education;

(G) The county mental health organization;

(H) The office of the chief of police of a county in counties which have a county police department;

(I) The office of the chief of police of the largest municipality in the county;

(J) The county board of health, which shall designate a physician to serve on the committee; and

(K) The office of the coroner or county medical examiner.

(2) In addition to the representatives serving on the committee as provided for in paragraph (1) of this subsection, the chief superior court judge shall designate a representative from a local citizen or advocacy group which focuses on child abuse awareness and prevention.

(3) If any designated agency fails to carry out its duties relating to participation on the committee, the chief superior court judge of the circuit may issue an order requiring the participation of such agency. Failure to comply with such order shall be cause for punishment as for contempt of court.

(d) Each protocol committee shall elect or appoint a chairperson who shall be responsible for ensuring that written protocol procedures are followed by all agencies. That person can be independent of agencies listed in paragraph (1) of subsection (c) of this Code section. The child abuse protocol committee thus established may appoint such additional members as necessary and proper to accomplish the purposes of the protocol committee.

(e) The protocol committee shall adopt a written child abuse protocol which shall be filed with the Division of Family and Children Services of the Department of Human Services and the Georgia Child Fatality Review Panel, a copy of which shall be furnished to each agency in the county handling the cases of abused children. The protocol shall be a written document outlining in detail the procedures to be used in investigating and prosecuting cases arising from alleged child abuse and the methods to be used in coordinating treatment programs for the perpetrator, the family, and the child. The protocol shall also outline procedures to be used when child abuse occurs in a household where there is violence between past or present spouses, persons who are parents of the same child, parents and children, stepparents and stepchildren, foster parents and foster children, or other persons living or formerly living in the same household. The protocol adopted shall not be inconsistent with the policies and procedures of the Division of Family and Children Services of the Department of Human Services.

(f) The purpose of the protocol shall be to ensure coordination and cooperation between all agencies involved in a child abuse case so as to increase the efficiency of all agencies handling such cases, to minimize the stress created for the allegedly abused child by the legal and investigatory process, and to ensure that more effective treatment is provided for the perpetrator, the family, and the child, including counseling.

(g) Upon completion of the writing of the child abuse protocol, the protocol committee shall continue in existence and shall meet at least semiannually for the purpose of evaluating the effectiveness of the protocol and appropriately modifying and updating same.

(h) Each protocol committee shall adopt or amend its written child abuse protocol no later than July 1, 2001, to specify the circumstances under which law enforcement officers will and will not be required to accompany child abuse investigators from the county department of family and children services when these investigators investigate reports of child abuse. In determining when law enforcement officers shall and shall not accompany child abuse investigators, the protocol committee shall consider the need to protect the alleged victim and the need to preserve the confidentiality of the report. Each protocol committee shall establish joint work efforts between the law enforcement and child abuse investigative agencies in child abuse investigations. The adoption or amendment of the protocol shall also describe measures which can be taken within the county to prevent child abuse and shall be filed with and furnished to the same entities with or to which an original protocol is required to be filed or furnished. The protocol will be further amended to specify procedures to be adopted by the protocol committee to ensure that written protocol procedures are followed.

(i) The protocol committee shall issue a report no later than the first day of July in 2001 and no later than the first day of July each year thereafter. That report shall evaluate the extent to which child abuse investigations during the 12 months prior to the report have complied with the child abuse protocols of the protocol committee, recommend measures to improve compliance, and describe which measures taken within the county to prevent child abuse have been successful. The report shall be transmitted to the county governing authority, the fall term grand jury of the judicial circuit, the Georgia Child Fatality Review Panel, and the chief superior court judge.

(j) By July 1, 2001, members of each protocol committee shall receive appropriate training. As new members are appointed, they will also receive training within 12 months after their appointment. The Office of the Child Advocate for the Protection of Children shall provide such training.

(k) The protocol committee shall adopt a written sexual abuse and exploitation protocol which shall be filed with the Division of Family and Children Services of the Department of Human Services and the Office of the Child Advocate for the Protection of Children, a copy of which shall be furnished to each agency in the county handling the cases of sexually abused or exploited children. The protocol shall be a written document outlining in detail the procedures to be used in investigating and prosecuting cases arising from alleged child sexual abuse and exploitation and the procedures to be followed concerning the obtainment of and payment for sexual assault examinations. Each protocol committee shall adopt or amend its written sexual abuse and exploitation protocol no later than December 31, 2004. The protocol may incorporate existing sexual abuse and exploitation protocols used within the county. The protocol adopted shall be consistent with the policies and procedures of the Division of Family and Children Services of the Department of Human Services. A failure by an agency to follow the protocol shall not constitute an affirmative or other defense to prosecution of a sexual abuse or exploitation offense, nor shall a failure by an agency to follow the protocol give rise to a civil cause of action.

Laws 1987, p. 1065, § 1; Laws 1988, p. 474, § 1; Laws 1990, p. 1785, § 1; Laws 1991, p. 94, § 19; Laws 1993, p. 1695, § 2; Laws 1993, p. 1941, § 1; Laws 1994, p. 97, § 19; Laws 1998, p. 609, § 1; Laws 1999, p. 81, § 19; Laws 2001, p. 1158, § 1; Laws 2003, Act 105, § .5, eff. July 1, 2003; Laws 2004, Act 519, § 4, eff. July 1, 2004; Laws 2009, Act 102, § 2–2, eff. July 1, 2009; Laws 2010, Act 418, § 14, eff. July 1, 2010.

Formerly Code 1981, § 19–1–1; Code 1981, § 19–1–2.

Historical and Statutory Notes

The 2003 amendment by Act 105 rewrote subsec. (e) which had read as follows:

"(e) The protocol committee shall, by July 1, 2001, adopt a written child abuse protocol which shall be filed with the Division of Family and Children Services of the Department of Human Resources and the Georgia Child Fatality Review Panel, a copy of which shall be furnished to each agency in the county handling the cases of abused children. The protocol shall be a written document outlining in detail the procedures to be used in investigating and prosecuting cases arising from alleged child abuse and the methods to be used in coordinating treatment programs for the perpetrator, the family, and the child. The protocol shall also outline procedures to be used when child abuse occurs in a household where there is violence between past or present spouses, persons who are parents of the same child, parents and children, stepparents and stepchildren, foster parents and foster children, or other persons living or formerly living in the same household."

The 2004 amendment by Act 519 added subsec. (k).

The 2009 amendment by Act 102 substituted "Department of Human Services" for "Department of Human Resources" throughout the section.

The 2010 amendment by Act 418, in subsec. (j), substituted "Office of the Child Advocate for the Protection of Children" for "Department of Human Services".

§ 19–15–3. Child fatality review committees; duties, powers, and reporting requirements

(a)(1) Each county shall establish a local multidisciplinary, multiagency child fatality review committee as provided in this Code section. The chief superior court judge of the circuit in which the county is located shall establish a child fatality review committee composed of, but not limited to, the following members:

(A) The county medical examiner or coroner;

(B) The district attorney or his or her designee;

(C) A county department of family and children services representative;

(D) A local law enforcement representative;

(E) The sheriff or county police chief or his or her designee;

(F) A juvenile court representative;

(G) A county board of health representative; and

(H) A county mental health representative.

(2) The district attorney or his or her designee shall serve as the chairperson to preside over all meetings.

(b) Review committee members shall recommend whether to establish a review committee for that county alone or establish a review committee with and for the counties within that judicial circuit.

(c) The chief superior court judge shall appoint persons to fill any vacancies on the review committee should the membership fail to do so.

(d) If any designated agency fails to carry out its duties relating to participation on the local review committee, the chief superior court judge of the circuit or any superior court judge who is a member of the Georgia Child Fatality Review Panel shall issue an order requiring the participation of such agency. Failure to comply with such order shall be cause for punishment as for contempt of court.

(e) Deaths eligible for review by local review committees are all deaths of children ages birth through 17 as a result of:

(1) Sudden Infant Death Syndrome;

(2) Any unexpected or unexplained conditions;

(3) Unintentional injuries;

(4) Intentional injuries;

(5) Sudden death when the child is in apparent good health;

(6) Any manner that is suspicious or unusual;

(7) Medical conditions when unattended by a physician. For the purpose of this paragraph, no person shall be deemed to have died unattended when the death occurred while the person was a patient of a hospice licensed under Article 9 of Chapter 7 of Title 31; or

(8) Serving as an inmate of a state hospital or a state, county, or city penal institution.

(f) It shall be the duty of any law enforcement officer, medical personnel, or other person having knowledge of the death of a child to immediately notify the coroner or medical examiner of the county wherein the body is found or death occurs.

(g) If the death of a child occurs outside the child's county of residence, it shall be the duty of the medical examiner or coroner in the county where the child died to notify the medical examiner or coroner in the county of the child's residence.

(h) When a county medical examiner or coroner receives a report regarding the death of any child he or she shall within 48 hours of the death notify the chairperson of the child fatality review committee of the county or circuit in which such child resided at the time of death.

(i) The coroner or county medical examiner shall review the findings regarding the cause and manner of death for each child death report received and respond as follows:

(1) If the death does not meet the criteria for review pursuant to subsection (e) of this Code section, the coroner or county medical examiner shall sign the form designated by the panel stating that the death does not meet the criteria for review. He or she shall forward the form and findings, within seven days of the child's death, to the chairperson of the child fatality review committee in the county or circuit of the child's residence; or

(2) If the death meets the criteria for review pursuant to subsection (e) of this Code section, the coroner or county medical examiner shall complete and sign the form designated by the panel stating the death meets the criteria for review. He or she shall forward the form and findings, within seven days of the child's death, to the chairperson of the child fatality review committee in the county or circuit of the child's residence.

(j) When the chairperson of a local child fatality review committee receives a report from the coroner or medical examiner regarding the death of a child, that chairperson shall review the report and findings regarding the cause and manner of the child's death and respond as follows:

(1) If the report indicates the child's death does not meet the criteria for review and the chairperson agrees with this decision, the chairperson shall sign the form designated by the panel stating that the death does not meet the criteria for review. He or she shall forward the form and findings to the panel within seven days of receipt;

(2) If the report indicates the child's death does not meet the criteria for review and the chairperson disagrees with this decision, the chairperson shall follow the procedures for deaths to be reviewed pursuant to subsection (k) of this Code section;

(3) If the report indicates the child's death meets the criteria for review and the chairperson disagrees with this decision, the chairperson shall sign the form designated by the panel stating that the death does not meet the criteria for review. The chairperson shall also attach an explanation for this decision; or

(4) If the report indicates the child's death meets the criteria for review and the chairperson agrees with this decision, the chairperson shall follow the procedures for deaths to be reviewed pursuant to subsection (k) of this Code section.

(k) When a child's death meets the criteria for review, the chairperson shall convene the review committee within 30 days after receipt of the report for a meeting to review and investigate the cause and circumstances of the death. Review committee members shall provide information as specified below, except where otherwise protected by statute:

(1) The providers of medical care and the medical examiner or coroner shall provide pertinent health and medical information regarding a child whose death is being reviewed by the local review committee;

(2) State, county, or local government agencies shall provide all of the following data on forms designated by the panel for reporting child fatalities:

(A) Birth information for children who died at less than one year of age including confidential information collected for medical and health use;

(B) Death information for children who have not reached their eighteenth birthday;

(C) Law enforcement investigative data, medical examiner or coroner investigative data, and parole and probation information and records;

(D) Medical care, including dental, mental, and prenatal health care; and

(E) Pertinent information from any social services agency that provided services to the child or family; and

(3) The review committee may obtain from any superior court judge of the county or circuit for which the review committee was created a subpoena to compel the production of documents or attendance of witnesses when that judge has made a finding that such documents or witnesses are necessary for the review committee's review. However, this Code section shall not modify or impair the privileged communications as provided by law except as otherwise provided in Code Section 19-7-5.

(*l*) The review committee shall complete its review and prepare a report of the child's death within 20 days, weekends and holidays excluded, following the first meeting held after receipt of the county medical examiner or coroner's report. The review committee's report shall:

(1) State the circumstances leading up to death and cause of death;

(2) Detail any agency involvement prior to death, including the beginning and ending dates and kinds of services delivered, the reasons for initial agency activity, and the reasons for any termination of agency activities;

(3) State whether any agency services had been delivered to the family or child prior to the circumstances leading to the child's death;

(4) State whether court intervention had ever been sought;

(5) State whether there have been any acts or reports of violence between past or present spouses, persons who are parents of the same child, parents and children, stepparents and stepchildren, foster parents and foster children, or other persons living or formerly living in the same household;

(6) Conclude whether services or agency activities delivered prior to death were appropriate and whether the child's death could have been prevented;

(7) Make recommendations for possible prevention of future deaths of similar incidents for children who are at risk for such deaths; and

(8) Include other findings as requested by the Georgia Child Fatality Review Panel.

(m) The review committee shall transmit a copy of its report within 15 days of completion to the panel.

(n) The review committee shall transmit a copy of its report within 15 days following its completion to the district attorney of the county or circuit for which the review committee was created if the report concluded that the child named therein died as a result of:

(1) Sudden Infant Death Syndrome when no autopsy was performed to confirm the diagnosis;

(2) Accidental death when it appears that the death could have been prevented through intervention or supervision;

(3) Any sexually transmitted disease;

(4) Medical causes which could have been prevented through intervention by an agency or by seeking medical treatment;

(5) Suicide of a child in custody or known to the Department of Human Services or when the finding of suicide is suspicious;

(6) Suspected or confirmed child abuse;

(7) Trauma to the head or body; or

(8) Homicide.

(*o*) Each local review committee shall issue an annual report no later than the first day of July in 2001 and in each year thereafter. The report shall:

(1) Specify the numbers of reports received by that review committee from a county medical examiner or coroner pursuant to subsection (h) of this Code section for the preceding calendar year;

(2) Specify the number of reports of child fatality reviews prepared by the review committee during such period;

(3) Be published at least once annually in the legal organ of the county or counties for which the review committee was established with the expense of such publication paid each by such county; and

(4) Be transmitted, no later than the fifteenth day of July in 2001 and in each year thereafter, to the Georgia Child Fatality Review Panel.

Laws 1990, p. 1785, § 1; Laws 1991, p. 94, § 19; Laws 1993, p. 1695, § 2; Laws 1993, p. 1941, § 1; Laws 1998, p. 609, § 2; Laws 1999, p. 81, § 19; Laws 2001, p. 1158, § 1; Laws 2003, Act 105, § 1, eff. July 1, 2003; Laws 2008, Act 430, § 1, eff. July 1, 2008; Laws 2009, Act 102, § 2-2, eff. July 1, 2009.

Formerly Code 1981, § 19-1-3.

Historical and Statutory Notes

The 2003 amendment by Act 105 rewrote subsecs. (a), (c), and (d) which had read as follows:

"(a)(1) Each county shall establish a local multidisciplinary, multiagency child fatality review committee as provided in this Code section. The chief superior court judge of the circuit in which the county is located shall establish a child fatality review committee composed of, but not limited to, the following members:

"(A) The county medical examiner or coroner;

"(B) The district attorney or his or her designee;

"(C) A county department of family and children services representative;

"(D) A local law enforcement representative;

"(E) The sheriff or his or her designee;

"(F) A juvenile court representative;

"(G) A county board of health representative; and

"(H) A county mental health representative;

"(2) The chief superior court judge shall appoint an interim chairperson to preside over the first meeting."

"(c) After the local review committee is established, it shall elect a chairperson from its membership. The chief superior court judge shall appoint persons to fill any vacancies on the review committee should the membership fail to do so.

"(d) If any designated agency fails to carry out its duties relating to participation on the local review committee, the chief superior court judge of the circuit shall issue an order requiring the participation of such agency. Failure to comply with such order shall be cause for punishment as for contempt of court."

The 2008 amendment by Act 430, in par. (*o*)(4), deleted "and the Judiciary Committees of the House of Representatives and Senate".

The 2009 amendment by Act 102 substituted "Department of Human Services" for "Department of Human Resources" throughout the section.

§ 19-15-4. Georgia Child Fatality Review Panel; duties, powers, and reporting requirements

(a) There is created the Georgia Child Fatality Review Panel as defined in paragraph (7) of Code Section 19-15-1.

(b) The Office of the Child Advocate for the Protection of Children shall coordinate the work of the panel and shall provide such administrative and staff support to the panel as may be necessary to enable the panel to discharge its duties under this chapter. The panel shall be attached to the Office of Planning and Budget for administrative purposes, and its planning, policy, and budget functions shall be coordinated with those of the Office of the Child Advocate.

(c) The panel shall be composed as follows:

(1) One district attorney appointed by the Governor;

(2) One juvenile court judge appointed by the Governor;

(3) Two citizen members who shall be appointed by the Governor, who are not employed by or officers of the state or any political subdivision thereof and one of whom shall come from each of the following: (A) a state-wide child abuse prevention organization; and (B) a state-wide childhood injury prevention organization;

(4) One forensic pathologist appointed by the Governor;

(5) The chairperson of the Board of Human Services;

(6) The director of the Division of Family and Children Services of the Department of Human Services;

(7) The director of the Georgia Bureau of Investigation;

(8) The chairperson of the Criminal Justice Coordinating Council;

(9) A member of the Georgia Senate appointed by the Lieutenant Governor;

(10) A member of the Georgia House of Representatives appointed by the Speaker of the House of Representatives;

(11) A local law enforcement official appointed by the Governor;

(12) A superior court judge appointed by the Governor;

(13) A coroner appointed by the Governor;

(14) The Child Advocate for the Protection of Children;

(15) The director of the Division of Public Health of the Department of Community Health; and

(16) The commissioner of behavioral health and developmental disabilities.

(d) The Governor shall appoint the chairperson of the panel.

(e) (1) All appointed members shall be appointed for terms of two years beginning on July 1 of the year appointed and shall serve until their respective successors are appointed and qualified.

(2) All ex officio members shall serve during the time such persons hold the offices or positions specified therein.

(3) Members of the General Assembly shall serve for terms of office concurrent with their terms of office as members of the General Assembly.

(4) Vacancies in the membership of the panel so appointed shall be filled in the same manner as the original appointment for the unexpired term of office.

(f) Members of the panel who are members of the General Assembly shall be compensated for service on the panel from legislative funds in the manner provided for service on interim study committees. Those members of the panel who are not state officials or employees shall receive from funds appropriated or otherwise available to the panel for their services on the panel the same daily expense and travel or mileage allowance authorized for members of the General Assembly for service on interim study committees. The members of the panel who are state officials or employees shall receive no additional compensation for their service on the panel but may be reimbursed for reasonable and necessary travel expenses which shall be payable from the department or agency of which such member is an employee or officer.

(g) The panel shall meet quarterly to review the reports of local review committees and shall meet when requested to do so by the Governor.

(h) The purpose of the panel is to recommend measures to decrease the incidence of child death by undertaking all of the following duties:

(1) Identify factors which place a child at risk for death;

(2) Collect and share information among state agencies which provide services to children and families or investigate child deaths;

(3) Make suggestions and recommendations to appropriate participating agencies regarding improving coordination of services and investigations;

(4) Identify trends relevant to unexpected or unexplained child death;

(5) Investigate the relationship, if any, between child deaths and violence between past or present spouses, persons who are parents of the same child, parents and children, stepparents and stepchildren, foster parents and foster children, or other persons living or formerly living in the same household;

(6) Review each report from local child fatality review committees. The chairperson may call a special meeting of the panel to review any report when the chairperson has concluded the report warrants expedited review and has been requested by the submitting local review committee to make such expedited review;

(7) Provide training and written materials to the local review committees to assist them in carrying out their duties. Such written materials shall include model protocols for the operation of the review committees;

(8) Develop a protocol for child fatality investigations and revise the protocol as needed;

(9) Monitor the operations of local review committees to determine training needs and service gaps. If the panel determines that changes to any statute, regulation, or policy is needed to decrease the risk of child death, it shall propose and recommend such changes in its annual report; and

(10) Develop and implement such procedures and policies as are necessary for its own operation.

(i) By January 1 of each calendar year, the panel shall submit a report to the Governor, the Lieutenant Governor, the Speaker of the House of Representatives, and the Judiciary Committees of the Senate and House of Representatives regarding the prevalence and circumstances of child fatalities in the state; recommend measures to reduce such fatalities caused by other than natural causes; and address in the report the following issues:

(1) Whether the deaths could have been prevented;

(2) Whether the children were known to any state or local agency;

(3) The actions, if any, taken by any state or local agency or court;

(4) Whether agency or court intervention could have prevented their deaths;

(5) Whether policy, procedural, regulatory, or statutory changes are called for as a result of these findings; and

(6) Whether any referral should have been made to a law enforcement agency which was not made.

(j) The panel shall also establish procedures for the conduct of reviews by local review committees into deaths of children and may obtain the assistance of child protection professionals in establishing such procedures.

(k) The panel shall have the authority to obtain from any superior court judge of the county or circuit for which the matter is pending a subpoena to compel the production of documents or attendance of witnesses if the county multiagency child fatality review committee has not exercised its authority to subpoena the documents or witnesses as provided in paragraph (3) of subsection (k) of Code Section 19–15–3; provided, however, if a superior court judge has previously ruled that the records or witnesses are not necessary to the fatality review at issue, such finding shall be conclusive on the issuance of the subpoena.

Laws 1990, p. 1785, § 1; Laws 1991, p. 94, § 19; Laws 1993, p. 1695, § 2; Laws 1993, p. 1941, § 1; Laws 1996, p. 803, § 1; Laws 1998, p. 609, § 3; Laws 1999, p. 81, § 19; Laws 2000, p. 243, § 2; Laws 2001, p. 1158, § 1; Laws 2003, Act 105, § 2, eff. July 1, 2003; Laws 2008, Act 430, § 2, eff. July 1, 2008; Laws 2008, Act 562, § 8, eff. July 1, 2008; Laws 2009, Act 102, § 1–19, eff. July 1, 2009.

Formerly Code 1981, § 19–1–4.

Historical and Statutory Notes

The 2003 amendment by Act 105, in subsec. (c), deleted "director of the Office of the" preceding "Child Advocate" in par. (14), and added par. (16); in subsec. (i), substituted "January 1" for "December 1" in the introductory paragraph; and added subsec. (k).

The 2008 amendment by Act 430, in subsec. (i), in the introductory paragraph, inserted ", and the Judiciary Committees of the Senate and House of Representatives".

The 2008 amendment by Act 562 rewrote subsec. (b) which had read:

"(b) The panel shall be attached for administrative purposes only to the Department of Human Resources. Notwithstanding any provision in Code Section 50–4–3 to the contrary, the State Children's Trust Fund Commission shall provide such staff support as may be necessary to enable the panel to discharge its duties under the law."

The 2009 amendment by Act 102, in subsec. (c), substituted "Board of Human Services" for "Board of Human Resources" in par. (5), substituted "Department of Human Services" for "Department of Human Resources" in par. (6), substituted "Department of Community Health" for "Department of Human Resources" in par. (15), and rewrote par. (16). Prior to amendment par. (16) had read:

"The director of the Division of Mental Health, Developmental Disabilities, and Addictive Diseases of the Department of Human Resources."

§ 19–15–5. Open and closed meetings

(a) A protocol committee or review committee in the exercise of its duties shall be closed to the public and shall not be subject to Chapter 14 of Title 50, relating to open meetings.

(b) The panel shall be open to the public as long as information identifying a deceased or abused child, any family member of the child, or alleged or suspected perpetrator of abuse upon the child is not disclosed during such meetings or proceedings, but the panel is authorized to close such meeting to the public when such identifying information is required to be disclosed to members of the panel in order for the panel to carry out its duties.

Laws 1990, p. 1785, § 1; Laws 1991, p. 94, § 19; Laws 1993, p. 1695, § 2; Laws 1993, p. 1941, § 1; Laws 2001, p. 1158, § 1.

Formerly Code 1981, § 19–1–5.

§ 19–15–6. Public records; confidential information

(a) Records and other documents which are made public records pursuant to any other provisions of law shall remain public records notwithstanding their being obtained, considered, or both, by a protocol committee, a review committee, or the panel.

(b) Notwithstanding any other provision of law to the contrary, reports of a review committee made pursuant to Code Section 19–15–3 and reports of the panel made pursuant to Code Section 19–15–4 shall be public records and shall be released to any person making a request therefor but the panel protocol committee or review committee having possession of such records or reports shall only release them after expunging therefrom all information contained therein which would permit identifying the deceased or abused child, any family member of the child, any alleged or suspected perpetrator of abuse upon the child, or any reporter of suspected child abuse.

(c) Statistical compilations of data by a review committee or the panel based upon information received thereby and containing no information which would permit the identification of any person shall be public records.

(d) Members of a protocol committee, a review committee, or of the panel shall not disclose what transpires at any meeting other than one made public by Code Section 19–15–5 nor disclose any information the disclosure of which is prohibited by this Code section, except to carry out the purposes of this chapter. Any person who knowingly violates this subsection shall be guilty of a misdemeanor.

(e) A person who presents information to a protocol committee, a review committee, or the panel or who is a member of any such body shall not be questioned in any civil or criminal proceeding regarding such presentation or regarding opinions formed by or confidential information obtained by such person as a result of serving as a member of any such body. This subsection shall not be construed to prohibit any person from testifying regarding information obtained independently of a protocol committee, a review committee, or the panel. In any proceeding in which testimony of such a member is offered the court shall first determine the source of such witness's knowledge.

(f) Except as otherwise provided in this Code section, information acquired by and records of a protocol committee, a review committee, or the panel shall be confidential, shall not be disclosed, and shall not be subject to Article 4 of Chapter 18 of Title 50, relating to open records, or subject to subpoena, discovery, or introduction into evidence in any civil or criminal proceeding.

(g) A member of a protocol committee, a review committee, or the panel shall not be civilly or criminally liable for any disclosure of information made by such member as authorized by this Code section.

(h) Members of the review committee, persons attending a review committee meeting, and persons who present information to a review committee may release information to such government agencies as is necessary for the purpose of carrying out assigned review committee duties.

(i) Notwithstanding any other provisions of law, information acquired by and documents, records, and reports of the panel and child abuse protocol committees and review committees applicable to a child who at the time of his or her death was in the custody of a state department or agency or foster parent shall not be confidential and shall be subject to Article 4 of Chapter 18 of Title 50, relating to open records.

Laws 1990, p. 1785, § 1; Laws 1991, p. 94, § 19; Laws 1993, p. 1695, § 2; Laws 1993, p. 1941, § 1; Laws 1998, p. 609, § 4; Laws 2001, p. 1158, § 1.

Formerly Code 1981, § 19–1–6.

§ 19–15–7. Construction of law as not to result in loss of federal funds

Nothing in this chapter shall be construed to authorize or require the inspection of any records or the release of any information if that inspection or release would result in the loss of any federal funds to the state.

Laws 1991, p. 94, § 19; Laws 1993, p. 1695, § 2; Laws 1993, p. 1941, § 1.

TITLE 20

EDUCATION

CHAPTER 1

GENERAL PROVISIONS

Article 2

Article 2

Drug–Free Postsecondary Education Act

§ 20–1–20. Short title

This article shall be known and may be cited as the "Drug-free Postsecondary Education Act of 1990."

Laws 1990, p. 2037, § 1.

§ 20–1–21. Legislative findings and intent

The General Assembly finds that the manufacture, distribution, sale, possession, or use of marijuana, controlled substances, or dangerous drugs in an unlawful manner is a serious threat to the public health, safety, and welfare and to the academic achievement of students enrolled in the public and nonpublic colleges, universities, and postsecondary technical institutes of this state. It is declared to be a primary purpose and goal of this state, of all of its agencies and instrumentalities, and of all of its public officials and employees to take all reasonable steps possible to eradicate the unlawful manufacture, distribution, sale, possession, and use of marijuana, controlled substances, and dangerous drugs. With this purpose in mind, the General Assembly declares that the public and nonpublic colleges, universities, and postsecondary technical institutes in this state must be absolutely free of any person who would knowingly manufacture, distribute, sell, possess, or use marijuana, a controlled substance, or a dangerous drug in an unlawful manner. For this reason, the General Assembly enacts this article.

Laws 1990, p. 2037, § 1.

§ 20–1–22. Definitions

As used in this article, the term:

(1) "Authority" means the Georgia Student Finance Authority created pursuant to Code Section 20–3–313.

(2) "Controlled substance" means any drug, substance, or immediate precursor included in the definition of the term "controlled substance" in paragraph (4) of Code Section 16–13–21.

(3) "Convicted" or "conviction" refers to a plea of guilty, a finding of guilty by a court of competent jurisdiction, or the acceptance of a plea of nolo contendere or affording of first offender treatment by a court of competent jurisdiction, irrespective of the pendency or availability of any appeal or application for collateral relief.

(4) "Dangerous drug" means any drug or substance defined as such under Code Section 16–13–71.

(5) "Date of conviction" means the date that the trial court determines guilt and enters judgment thereon or the date on which the court accepts a plea of nolo contendere or formally allows a person to receive first offender treatment.

(6) "Marijuana" shall have the same meaning as such term is defined in paragraph (16) of Code Section 16–13–21.

(7) "Nonpublic educational institution" means any postsecondary educational institution not established, operated, or governed by the State of Georgia.

(8) "Public educational institution" means:

(A) Any two-year college, college, university, or other institution of higher learning under the management and control of the Board of Regents of the University System of Georgia; and

(B) Any postsecondary technical school under the management and control of the State Board of Technical and Adult Education.

(9) "Student" means any person who is enrolled as a student in courses for academic credit on a full-time, part-time, temporary, or intermittent basis in any public or nonpublic educational institution.

Laws 1990, p. 2037, § 1.

§ 20–1–23. Suspension from public educational institutions of students convicted of felony offenses involving marijuana, controlled substances, or dangerous drugs; forfeiture or revocation of academic credit

Any student of a public educational institution who is convicted, under the laws of this state, the United States, or any other state, of any felony offense involving the manufacture, distribution, sale, possession, or use of marijuana, a controlled substance, or a dangerous drug shall as of the date of conviction be suspended from the public educational institution in which such person is enrolled. Except for cases in which the institution has previously taken disciplinary action against a student for the same offense, such suspension shall be effective as of the date of conviction, even though the educational institution may not complete all administrative actions necessary to implement such suspension until a later date. Except for cases in which the institution has already imposed disciplinary sanctions for the same offense, such suspension shall continue through the end of the term, quarter, semester, or other similar period for which the student was enrolled as of the date of conviction. The student shall forfeit any right to any academic credit otherwise earned or earnable for such term, quarter, semester, or other similar period;

and the educational institution shall subsequently revoke any such academic credit which is granted prior to the completion of administrative actions necessary to implement such suspension.

Laws 1990, p. 2037, § 1.

§ 20–1–24. Denial of state funds to students of nonpublic educational institutions convicted of felony offenses involving marijuana, controlled substances, or dangerous drugs

(a) Any student of a nonpublic educational institution who is convicted, under the laws of this state, the United States, or any other state, of any felony offense involving the manufacture, distribution, sale, possession, or use of marijuana, a controlled substance, or a dangerous drug shall as of the date of conviction be denied state funds for any loans, grants, or scholarships administered under the authority of Part 3 of Article 7 of Chapter 3 of this title, the "Georgia Student Finance Authority Act," or similar loans, grants, or scholarships, including but not limited to Georgia Higher Education Loan Program loans, student incentive grants, or tuition equalization grants. The authority is authorized to define such terms and prescribe such rules, regulations, and procedures as may be reasonable and necessary to carry out the purposes of this article.

(b) Such denial of state funds shall be effective as of the first day of the term, quarter, semester, or other similar period for which the student was enrolled immediately following the date of conviction or the date on which the court accepts a plea of nolo contendere or formally allows a student to receive first offender treatment and shall continue through the end of such term, quarter, semester, or other similar period for which the student was enrolled. Any nonpublic educational institution operating within this state that receives state funds shall agree to comply with this article in order to be eligible for its students to receive state funds through scholarships, grants, or loan programs.

Laws 1990, p. 2037, § 1; Laws 1991, p. 94, § 20.

§ 20–1–25. More stringent sanctions not prohibited

The suspension sanctions and sanctions involving denial of state funds as prescribed in this article are intended as minimum sanctions, and nothing in this article shall be construed to prohibit any educational institution from establishing and implementing additional or more stringent sanctions for felony offenses and other conduct involving the unlawful manufacture, distribution, sale, possession, or use of marijuana, a controlled substance, or a dangerous drug.

Laws 1990, p. 2037, § 1.

§ 20–1–26. Administrative procedures

Administrative procedures for the implementation of this article shall be promulgated for the educational institutions under their respective management and control by the Board of Regents of the University System of Georgia and the State Board of Technical and Adult Education or the individual nonpublic educational institutions. Such procedures shall provide for relief from sanctions previously imposed under this article against a person whose conviction is subsequently overturned on appeal or through collateral relief.

Laws 1990, p. 2037, § 1.

§ 20–1–27. Applicability of law

This article shall apply only with respect to felony offenses committed on or after July 1, 1990; provided, however, that nothing in this Code section shall prevent any educational institution from implementing sanctions additional to or other than those provided for in this article with respect to offenses committed prior to July 1, 1990.

Laws 1990, p. 2037, § 1.

CHAPTER 2

ELEMENTARY AND SECONDARY EDUCATION

Article 16

Students

Part 2

Discipline

Subpart 1—Corporal Punishment

§ 20–2–730. Corporal punishment of students

All area, county, and independent boards of education shall be authorized to determine and adopt policies and regulations relating to the use of corporal punishment by school principals and teachers employed by such boards.

Laws 1964, p. 673, § 1.

§ 20–2–731. Method of administering punishment

An area, county, or independent board of education may, upon the adoption of written policies, authorize any principal or teacher employed by the board to administer, in the exercise of his sound discretion, corporal punishment on any pupil or pupils placed under his supervision in order to maintain proper control and discipline. Any such authorization shall be subject to the following requirements:

(1) The corporal punishment shall not be excessive or unduly severe;

(2) Corporal punishment shall never be used as a first line of punishment for misbehavior unless the pupil was informed beforehand that specific misbehavior could occasion its use; provided, however, that corporal punishment may be employed as a first line of punishment for those acts of misconduct which are so antisocial or disruptive in nature as to shock the conscience;

(3) Corporal punishment must be administered in the presence of a principal or assistant principal, or the designee of the principal or assistant principal, employed by the board of education authorizing such punishment, and the other principal or assistant principal, or the designee of the principal or assistant principal, must be informed beforehand and in the presence of the pupil of the reason for the punishment;

(4) The principal or teacher who administered corporal punishment must provide the child's parent, upon request, a written explanation of the reasons for the punishment and the name of the principal or assistant principal, or designee of the principal or assistant principal, who was present; provided, however, that such an explanation shall not be used as evidence in any subsequent civil action brought as a result of the corporal punishment; and

(5) Corporal punishment shall not be administered to a child whose parents or legal guardian has upon the day of enrollment of the pupil filed with the principal of the school a statement from a medical doctor licensed in Georgia stating that it is detrimental to the child's mental or emotional stability.

Laws 1964, p. 673, § 2; Laws 1977, p. 1290, § 1.

§ 20–2–732. Exemption of principals and teachers from legal action

No principal or teacher who shall administer corporal punishment to a pupil or pupils under his care and supervision in conformity with the policies and regulations of the area, county, or independent board of education employing him and in accordance also with this subpart shall be held accountable or liable in any criminal or civil action based upon the administering of corporal punishment where the corporal punishment is administered in good faith and is not excessive or unduly severe.

Laws 1964, p. 673, § 3.

Article 22

School Buses

Part 5

School Buses

§ 20–2–1125. School bus driver mandatory training

All persons employed as school bus drivers by any public school system in this state shall receive annual mandatory training on traffic laws pertaining to the operation of school buses and on school bus operations and safety. The State Board of Education shall establish the content and length of initial driver training and shall determine the qualifications of and certify the instructors who conduct such training. No person employed as a school bus driver by any public school system in this state shall operate a school bus unless such person has completed such training within the preceding 12 month period.

Laws 2004, Act 560, § 6, eff. July 1, 2004.

Historical and Statutory Notes

Laws 2004, Act 560, § 5, provides:

"This part shall be known and may be cited as 'Aleana's Law'. "

§ 20–2–1126. Policy and procedure for student school bus conduct and safety

(a) Each public school system in this state shall promulgate policies and procedures for the operation of school buses and the conduct and safety of those students who ride such buses. Such policies and procedures shall be in writing and available for public inspection. Each person employed as a school bus driver shall acknowledge in writing that he or she has received a copy of and has read and understands such policies and procedures. In the event that such policies and procedures are amended during the school year, such amended policies and procedures shall be provided to all persons employed by the school system as school bus drivers, and each such person shall acknowledge in writing that he or she has received a copy of and has read and understands such amended policies and procedures.

(b) At the beginning of each school year, each public school system in this state shall provide each of its students with a copy of the school system's code of conduct as required by Code Section 20–2–736. In the event such code of conduct is amended during the school year, the school system shall provide copies of such amendments to the students. The receipt of such student code of conduct shall be acknowledged in writing by a parent or guardian of each student.

Laws 2004, Act 560, § 6, eff. July 1, 2004; Laws 2005, Act 19, § 20, eff. April 7, 2005.

§ 20–2–1127. Repealed by Laws 2006, Act 819, § 3.1, eff. July 1, 2006

Historical and Statutory Notes

The repealed section, relating to accessibility of school bus route schedules, was derived from Laws 2004, Act 560, § 1. The repealing law also reserved the section designation.

Article 23

Traffic Safety

§ 20–2–1130. Traffic safety on and around school grounds

The local law enforcement agency charged with the responsibility for law enforcement within the school district attendance area and the board of education of each county and independent school system of this state shall study and evaluate the traffic safety requirements of the school system and the various individual schools therein. The responsible law enforcement agency shall take appropriate action to identify school safety crossings and motor vehicle traffic patterns on and around school grounds. The traffic safety officer of the local law enforcement agency shall advise the school board and the school superintendent relative to compliance by the school system with state laws and policies and regulations of the state agencies requiring safety standards and practices.

Laws 1975, p. 820, § 1.

§ 20–2–1131. Authority of school crossing guards

Any person who is a school-crossing guard designated by a local law enforcement agency shall be authorized to direct and regulate the flow of traffic at school crossings or within a reduced speed school zone during the time when such school-crossing guard is on duty.

Laws 1989, p. 516, § 1.

Article 27

Loitering at or Disrupting Schools

§ 20–2–1180. Remaining on premises or within school safety zone of public or private schools without legitimate cause or need to be present

(a) It shall be unlawful for any person to remain upon the premises or within the school safety zone as defined in paragraph (1) of subsection (a) of Code Section 16–11–127.1 of any public or private school in this state or to remain upon such premises or within such school safety zone when that person does not have a legitimate cause or need to be present thereon. Each principal or designee of each public or private school in this state shall have the authority to exercise such control over the buildings and grounds upon which a school is located so as to prohibit any person who does not have a legitimate need or cause to be present thereon from loitering upon such premises. Each principal or designee of each public or private school in this state shall notify the appropriate law enforcement agency to prohibit any person who does not have a legitimate need or cause to be present therein from loitering within the school safety zone.

(b) Any person who:

(1) Is present upon the premises or within the school safety zone of any public or private school in this state and willfully fails to remove himself or herself from such premises after the principal or designee of such school requests him or her to do so; or

(2) Fails to check in at the designated location as required by subsection (c) of this Code section

shall be guilty of a misdemeanor of a high and aggravated nature.

(c) Upon entering any school building between the official starting time and the official dismissal time, any person who is not a student at such school, an employee of the school or school system, a school board member, an approved volunteer following the established guidelines of the school, or a person who has been invited to or otherwise authorized to be at the school by a principal, teacher, counselor, or other authorized employee of the school shall check in at the designated location as stated on posted signs and provide a reason for his or her presence at the school.

(c.1) Subsections (b) and (c) of this Code section shall not apply to:

(1) Law enforcement officers, firefighters, emergency medical technicians or paramedics, or any public safety or emergency management officials in the performance of an emergency call or to other persons making authorized deliveries to the school;

(2) Any person entering a school on election day, for purposes of voting, when the school serves as an official polling place; or

(3) Any person attending or participating in an academic or athletic event while remaining in the authorized area or a parent, grandparent, or guardian listed on a child's pick-up list who fails to sign-in while delivering school supplies, food, clothing, other legitimate business and who has not previously been sanctioned by school officials for disrupting a school.

(d) A school administrator or his or her designee may ask any visitor to explain his or her presence in the school building at any time when the school is in official session.

(e) If the school posts signs on entrances to the school requiring visitors to check in at the designated location, such signs shall be deemed prima-facie evidence that persons entering the school were on notice of the requirements of this Code section.

(f) Nothing in this Code section shall be construed to prohibit school administrators from prohibiting the admission of any person who has violated school policy or state law.

Laws 1973, p. 719, §§ 1, 2; Laws 1994, p. 1012, § 5; Laws 2002, p. 1078, § 1; Laws 2006, Act 616, § 4, eff. July 1, 2006.

Historical and Statutory Notes

In 2002, the Code Commission, in the last sentence of subsec. (c), substituted "a parent, grandparent, or" for "parent, grandparent or". See § 28–9–5.

The 2006 amendment by Act 616 rewrote subsecs. (b) and (c); and added subsec. (c.1). Prior to amendment, subsecs. (b) and (c) read as follows:

"(b) Any person who shall not have any legitimate cause or need to be present upon the premises or within the school safety zone of any public or private school in this state who shall willfully fail to remove himself or herself from such premises after the principal or designee of such school shall request him or her to do so shall be guilty of a misdemeanor of a high and aggravated nature.

"(c) Upon entering any elementary or secondary school building between the official starting time and the official dismissal time, any person who is not a student at such school, an employee of the school or school system, a school board member, an approved volunteer following the established guidelines of the school, or a person who has been invited to or otherwise authorized to be at the school by a principal, teacher, counselor, or other authorized employee of the school shall check in at the designated location as stated on posted signs and provide a reason for his or her presence at the school. Failure to check in at the designated location as provided in this subsection shall be prima-facie evidence that such person is in violation of subsection (b) of this Code section. This subsection shall not apply to law enforcement officers, firefighters, emergency medical technicians or paramedics, or any public safety or emergency management officials in the performance of an emergency call or to other persons making authorized deliveries to the school. This subsection shall not apply to any person entering a school which serves as an official polling place for the purpose of voting on election day or attending or participating in an academic or athletic event while remaining in the authorized area or a parent, grandparent, or guardian listed on a child's pick-up list who fails to sign-in while delivering school supplies, food, clothing, or other legitimate business and who has not previously been sanctioned by school officials for disrupting a school."

Laws 2006, Act 616, § 7, provides:

"This section and Sections 6 and 8 of this Act shall become effective upon their approval by the Governor or upon their becoming law without such approval. The remaining sections of this Act shall become effective on July 1, 2006, and shall apply to all crimes committed on or after such date. Any offense committed before July 1, 2006, shall be punishable as provided by the statute in effect at the time the offense was committed."

§ 20–2–1181. Disruption or interference with operation of public schools

It shall be unlawful for any person to knowingly, intentionally, or recklessly disrupt or interfere with the operation of any public school, public school bus, or public school bus stop as designated by local school boards of education. Any person violating this Code section shall be guilty of a misdemeanor of a high and aggravated nature.

Laws 1976, p. 480, § 1; Laws 1994, p. 1012, § 6; Laws 2004, Act 560, § 4, eff. July 1, 2004; Laws 2010, Act 471, § 3, eff. May 27, 2010.

Historical and Statutory Notes

The 2004 amendment by Act 560 inserted ", public school bus, or public school bus stop as designated by local school boards of education".

Laws 2004, Act 560, § 9(b), provides:

"Part I of this Act shall become effective on July 1, 2004, and shall apply to offenses committed on or after such date."

The 2010 amendment by Act 471, added the phrase "knowingly, intentionally, or recklessly" prior to "disrupt or interfere".

Laws 2010, Act 471, § 4, provides:

"This Act shall become effective upon its approval by the Governor or upon its becoming law without such approval. This Act shall apply with respect to conduct on or after that date and conduct prior to that date shall continue to be governed by prior law."

§ 20–2–1182. Upbraiding, insulting, or abusing teacher, administrator, or bus driver in presence of pupil while on premises of school or school bus prohibited

Any parent, guardian, or person other than a student at the public school in question who has been advised that minor children are present and who continues to upbraid, insult, or abuse any public school teacher, public school administrator, or public school bus driver in the presence and hearing of a pupil while on the premises of any public school or public school bus may be ordered by any of the above-designated school personnel to leave the school premises or school bus, and upon failure to do so such person shall be guilty of a misdemeanor and, upon conviction thereof, shall be punished by a fine not to exceed $500.00.

Laws 1989, p. 1394, § 1; Laws 2001, p. 4, § 20.

§ 20–2–1183. Possession of electronic communication devices while in school

The possession of an electronic communication device by a student in school shall be permitted or prohibited as specifically prescribed by rule or policy set by the local board of education. If prohibited, the local board of education may provide for exceptions to such prohibition and for disciplinary actions for possession in violation of the prohibition. If possession of an electronic communication device by a student in school is permitted, the local board policy shall not permit the use by a student of any personal electronic communication device during classroom instructional time.

Laws 1989, p. 1394, § 2; Laws 2000, p. 618, § 73; Laws 2003, Act 55, § 1, eff. July 1, 2003.

§ 20–2–1184. School personnel to report certain crimes committed by students upon school property or at school functions; immunity from liability; penalties

(a) Any teacher or other person employed at any public or private elementary or secondary school or any dean or public safety officer employed by a college or university who has reasonable cause to believe that a student at that school has committed any act upon school property or at any school function, which act is prohibited by any of the following:

(1) Code Section 16–5–21, relating to aggravated assault if a firearm is involved;

(2) Code Section 16–5–24, relating to aggravated battery;

(3) Chapter 6 of Title 16, relating to sexual offenses;

(4) Code Section 16–11–127, relating to carrying a weapon or long gun in an unauthorized location;

(5) Code Section 16–11–127.1, relating to carrying weapons at school functions or on school property or within school safety zones;

(6) Code Section 16–11–132, relating to the illegal possession of a handgun by a person under 18 years of age; or

(7) Code Section 16–13–30, relating to possession and other activities regarding marijuana and controlled substances,

shall immediately report the act and the name of the student to the principal or president of that school or the principal's or president's designee.

(b) The principal or designee who receives a report made pursuant to subsection (a) of this Code section who has reasonable cause to believe that the report is valid shall make an oral report thereof immediately by telephone or otherwise to the appropriate school system superintendent and to the appropriate police authority and district attorney.

(c) Any person participating in the making of a report or causing a report to be made as authorized or required pursuant to this Code section or participating in any judicial proceeding or any other proceeding resulting therefrom shall in so doing be immune from any civil or criminal liability that might otherwise be incurred or imposed, providing such participation pursuant to this Code section is made in good faith.

(d) Any person required to make a report pursuant to this Code section who knowingly and willfully fails to do so shall be guilty of a misdemeanor.

Laws 1990, p. 1834, § 1; Laws 1994, p. 1012, § 7; Laws 2010, Act 643, § 2–12, eff. June 4, 2010.

Historical and Statutory Notes

Laws 2010, Act 643, § 3–1, provides:

"This Act shall become effective upon its approval by the Governor or upon its becoming law without such approval and shall apply to all offenses committed on and after such date. The enactment of this Act shall not affect any prosecutions for acts occurring before the effective date of this Act and shall not act as an abatement of any such prosecutions."

§ 20–2–1185. School safety plans

(a) Every public school shall prepare a school safety plan to help curb the growing incidence of violence in schools, to respond effectively to such incidents, and to provide a safe learning environment for Georgia's children, teachers, and other school personnel. Such plan shall also address preparedness for natural disasters, hazardous materials or radiological accidents, acts of violence, and acts of terrorism. School safety plans of public schools shall be prepared with input from students enrolled in that school, parents or legal guardians of such students, teachers in that school, community leaders, other school employees and school district employees, and local law enforcement, fire service, public safety, and emergency management agencies. School safety plans of private schools may be prepared with input from students enrolled in that school, parents or legal guardians of such students, teachers in that school, other school employees, and local law enforcement, fire service, public safety, and emergency management agencies. Such plans shall be reviewed and, if necessary, updated annually. Such plans of public schools shall be submitted to the local emergency management agency.

(b) A public school may request funding assistance from the state for the installation of safety equipment including, but not limited to, video surveillance cameras, metal detectors, and other similar security devices. Funding may be provided to a public school in accordance with a school safety plan prepared by the school and approved by the local board of education, the Department of Education, and the Georgia Emergency Management Agency.

(c) School safety plans prepared by public schools shall address security issues in school safety zones as defined in paragraph (1) of subsection (a) of Code Section 16–11–127.1. School safety plans should also address security issues involving the transportation of pupils to and from school and school functions when such transportation is furnished by the school or school system and school functions held during noninstructional hours.

(d) The Georgia Emergency Management Agency shall provide training and technical assistance to public school systems, and may provide this same training and technical assistance to private school systems, and independent private schools throughout this state in the area of emergency management and safe school operations. This training and technical assistance shall include, but not be limited to, crisis response team development, site surveys and safety audits, crisis management planning, exercise design, safe school planning, emergency operations planning, search and seizure, bomb threat management, and model school safety plans.

Laws 1994, p. 1012, § 3; Laws 1999, p. 379, § 1.

CHAPTER 8

CAMPUS POLICEMEN

Section

§ 20–8–1. Definitions

As used in this chapter, the term:

(1) "Campus" means the grounds and buildings owned or occupied by a college or university or the grounds and buildings of a school or training facility operated by or under the authority of the State Board of Education. The term "campus" shall also include any public or private property within 500 yards of the property of an educational facility and one-quarter mile of any public street or public sidewalk connecting different buildings of the same educational facility when the property or buildings of the educational facility are located within any county in this state having a population of 400,000 or more according to the United States decennial census of 1970 or any future such census.

(2) "Campus policeman" means an employee of an educational facility whose duties include the enforcement of the laws of this state; the preservation of public order; the protection of life and property; the prevention, detection, or investigation of crime; or any combination thereof.

(3) "College or university" means an accredited, nonproprietary, public or private educational institution of higher learning located in this state.

(4) "Educational facility" means a college or university or a school or training facility operated by or under the authority of the State Board of Education.

Laws 1977, p. 1160, § 1; Laws 1979, p. 1323, § 1; Laws 1981, p. 806, § 1; Laws 1984, p. 596, § 1.

§ 20–8–2. Law enforcement powers

On the campus of an educational facility, a campus policeman employed by such educational facility who is certified in accordance with Code Section 20–8–3 and when authorized by the governing body or authority of such educational facility shall have the same law enforcement powers, including the power of arrest, as a law enforcement officer of the local government with police jurisdiction over such campus.

Laws 1977, p. 1160, § 2; Laws 1979, p. 1323, § 1.

§ 20–8–3. Certification

As a condition precedent to the exercise of law enforcement powers pursuant to Code Section 20–8–2, a campus policeman must be certified by the Georgia Peace Officer Standards and Training Council as having met the qualifications and having completed the basic training requirements for a peace officer under Article 2 of Chapter 2 of Title 35. All costs incurred in such certification and training shall be paid by the educational facility employing the campus policeman. This chapter is permissive and shall not require the certification of campus policemen by the Georgia Peace Officer Standards and Training Council. The certification of a campus policeman by the Georgia Peace Officer Standards and Training Council does not require that the campus policeman so certified exercise the powers provided in Code Section 20–8–2.

Laws 1977, p. 1160, § 3; Laws 1979, p. 1323, § 2.

§ 20–8–4. Exemption

A campus policeman exercising the power of arrest pursuant to Code Section 20–3–72 providing campus policemen and other security personnel of the University System of Georgia with arrest powers for offenses committed upon university system property shall be exempt from this chapter.

Laws 1977, p. 1160, § 4.

§ 20–8–5. Law enforcement powers of school security personnel

(a) In each public school system in this state, school security personnel employed by the board of education of a county or an independent board of education of a municipality for the various public schools thereof who are certified pursuant to subsection (b) of this Code section and who are authorized by the board of education of that county or the independent board of education of that municipality shall have the same law enforcement powers on school property, including the power of arrest, as law enforcement officers of that respective county or municipality.

(b) As a condition precedent to the exercise of law enforcement powers pursuant to subsection (a) of this Code section, school security personnel must be certified by the Georgia Peace Officer Standards and Training Council as having met the qualifications and having completed the basic training requirements for a peace officer under Chapter 8 of Title 35. The certification of school security personnel by the Georgia Peace Officer Standards and Training Council does not require that such security personnel exercise the powers provided in subsection (a) of this Code section.

(c) The provisions of this Code section shall not prohibit a board of education of a county or an independent board of education of a municipality from employing school security personnel without law enforcement powers.

(d) School security personnel who are certified by the Georgia Peace Officer Standards and Training Council may be authorized by a local board of education to carry a standard issue firearm or weapon generally used for law enforcement purposes for the purpose of carrying out law enforcement duties.

Laws 1982, p. 515, § 1; Laws 1982, p. 515, § 2; Laws 1983, p. 3, § 16; Laws 1986, p. 1549, § 1; Laws 1988, p. 612, § 16; Laws 1999, p. 362, § 4.

Formerly Code 1933, § 32–913.

§ 20–8–6. Educational institutions employing policemen to report criminal gang activity

Each educational facility which employs campus policemen, including institutions of the University System of Georgia, shall report to the Georgia Bureau of Investigation and to the local law enforcement agency incidents of criminal gang activity as defined by Code Section 16–15–3 which occur on or adjacent to the campus of such educational facility.

Laws 1998, p. 270, § 11.

§ 20–8–7. Law enforcement records: public inspection and copying

Law enforcement records created, received, or maintained by campus policemen that relate to the investigation of criminal conduct and crimes as defined under Georgia law and which are not subject to protection from disclosure by any other Georgia law shall be made available within a reasonable time after request for public inspection and copying.

Laws 2006, Act 616, § 5, eff. July 1, 2006.

Historical and Statutory Notes

Laws 2006, Act 616, § 7, provides:

"This section and Sections 6 and 8 of this Act shall become effective upon their approval by the Governor or upon their becoming law without such approval. The remaining sections of this Act shall become effective on July 1, 2006, and shall apply to all crimes committed on or after such date. Any offense committed before July 1, 2006, shall be punishable as provided by the statute in effect at the time the offense was committed."

TITLE 24

EVIDENCE

CHAPTER 1

GENERAL PROVISIONS

§ 24–1–1. Definitions

As used in this title, the term:

(1) "Competent evidence" means evidence which is admissible.

(2) "Cumulative evidence" means evidence which is additional to other evidence already obtained.

(3) "Direct evidence" means evidence which immediately points to the question at issue.

(4) "Indirect evidence" or "circumstantial evidence" means evidence which only tends to establish the issue by proof of various facts, sustaining by their consistency the hypothesis claimed.

(5) "Preponderance of evidence" means that superior weight of evidence upon the issues involved, which, while not enough to free the mind wholly from a reasonable doubt, is yet sufficient to incline a reasonable and impartial mind to one side of the issue rather than to the other.

(6) "Presumptive evidence" means evidence which consists of inferences drawn by human experience from the connection of cause and effect and from observations of human conduct.

(7) "Sufficient evidence" means evidence which is satisfactory for the purpose.

Formerly Code 1863, § 3671; Code 1868, § 3695; Code 1873, § 3748; Code 1882, § 3748; Civil Code 1895, §§ 5143, 5145; Penal Code 1895, § 983; Civil Code 1910, §§ 5729, 5731; Penal Code 1910, § 1009; Code 1933, §§ 38–102, 38–106.

§ 24–1–2. Object of evidence

The object of all legal investigation is the discovery of truth. The rules of evidence are framed with a view to this prominent end, seeking always for pure sources and the highest evidence.

Formerly Code 1863, § 3670; Code 1868, § 3694; Code 1873, § 3747; Code 1882, § 3747; Civil Code 1895, § 5142; Penal Code 1895, § 982; Civil Code 1910, § 5728; Penal Code 1910, § 1008; Code 1933, § 38–101.

§ 24–1–3. Same rule in all courts and cases

The rules of evidence shall be the same in all courts and in all trials unless otherwise expressly provided by statute.

Formerly Code 1863, § 3673; Code 1868, § 3697; Code 1873, § 3750; Code 1882, § 3750; Civil Code 1895, § 5147; Civil Code 1910, § 5733; Code 1933, § 38–108.

§ 24–1–4. Matters judicially recognized

The existence and territorial extent of states, their forms of government, symbols of nationality, the laws of nations, all laws and resolutions of the General Assembly and the journals of each branch thereof as published by authority, the laws of the United States and of the several states thereof as published by authority, general customs of merchants, the admiralty and maritime courts of the world and their seals, the political constitution and history of our own government as well as the local divisions of our own state, the seals of the several departments of the government of the United States and of the several states of the Union, and all similar matters of public knowledge shall be judicially recognized without the introduction of proof.

Laws 1819, Cobb's 1851 Digest, p. 272.

Formerly Code 1863, §§ 3674, 3738, 3747; Code 1868, §§ 3698, 3762, 3771; Code 1873, §§ 3751, 3815, 3824; Code 1882, §§ 3751, 3815, 3824; Civil Code 1895, §§ 5148, 5210, 5231; Civil Code 1910, §§ 5734, 5797, 5818; Code 1933, § 38–112.

§ 24–1–5. Procedure where hearing impaired persons arrested for violations of criminal laws

In the event a hearing impaired person is arrested for any alleged violation of a criminal law of this state, the arresting officer shall comply with the provisions of Article 5 of Chapter 9 of this title.

Laws 1974, p. 484, § 2; Laws 1983, p. 852, § 1.

CHAPTER 2

RELEVANCY

§ 24–2–1. Evidence must be relevant

Evidence must relate to the questions being tried by the jury and bear upon them either directly or indirectly. Irrelevant matter should be excluded.

Formerly Code 1863, § 3679; Code 1868, § 3703; Code 1873, § 3756; Code 1882, § 3756; Civil Code 1895, § 5158; Civil Code 1910, § 5744; Code 1933, § 38-201.

§ 24-2-2. Character and conduct of parties, relevancy

The general character of the parties and especially their conduct in other transactions are irrelevant matter unless the nature of the action involves such character and renders necessary or proper the investigation of such conduct.

Formerly Code 1863, § 3680; Code 1868, § 3704; Code 1873, § 3757; Code 1882, § 3757; Civil Code 1895, § 5159; Penal Code 1895, § 993; Civil Code 1910, § 5745; Penal Code 1910, § 1019; Code 1933, § 38-202.

§ 24-2-3. Matters not relevant in prosecution for rape

(a) In any prosecution for a violation of Code Section 16-6-1, relating to rape; Code Section 16-6-2, relating to aggravated sodomy; Code Section 16-6-4, relating to aggravated child molestation; or Code Section 16-6-22.2, relating to aggravated sexual battery, evidence relating to the past sexual behavior of the complaining witness shall not be admissible, either as direct evidence or on cross-examination of the complaining witness or other witnesses, except as provided in this Code section. For the purposes of this Code section, evidence of past sexual behavior includes, but is not limited to, evidence of the complaining witness's marital history, mode of dress, general reputation for promiscuity, nonchastity, or sexual mores contrary to the community standards.

(b) In any prosecution for a violation of Code Section 16-6-1, relating to rape; Code Section 16-6-2, relating to aggravated sodomy; Code Section 16-6-4, relating to aggravated child molestation; or Code Section 16-6-22.2, relating to aggravated sexual battery, evidence relating to the past sexual behavior of the complaining witness may be introduced if the court, following the procedure described in subsection (c) of this Code section, finds that the past sexual behavior directly involved the participation of the accused and finds that the evidence expected to be introduced supports an inference that the accused could have reasonably believed that the complaining witness consented to the conduct complained of in the prosecution.

(c) The procedure for introducing evidence as described in subsection (b) of this Code section shall be as follows:

(1) At the time the defense shall seek to introduce evidence which would be covered by subsection (b) of this Code section, the defense shall notify the court of such intent, whereupon the court shall conduct an in camera hearing to examine into the defendant's offer of proof;

(2) At the conclusion of the hearing, if the court finds that any of the evidence introduced at the hearing is admissible under subsection (b) of this Code section or is so highly material that it will substantially support a conclusion that the accused reasonably believed that the complaining witness consented to the conduct complained of and that justice mandates the admission of such evidence, the court shall by order state what evidence may be introduced by the defense at the trial of the case and in what manner the evidence may be introduced; and

(3) The defense may then introduce evidence pursuant to the order of the court.

Laws 1976, p. 741, § 1; Laws 1989, p. 272, § 1; Laws 2005, Act 8, § 13.1, eff. July 1, 2005.

Formerly Code 1933, § 38-202.1.

Historical and Statutory Notes

The 2005 amendment by Act 8, rewrote subsecs. (a) and (b) which had read:

"(a) In any prosecution for rape, evidence relating to the past sexual behavior of the complaining witness shall not be admissible, either as direct evidence or on cross-examination of the complaining witness or other witnesses, except as provided in this Code section. For the purposes of this Code section, evidence of past sexual behavior includes, but is not limited to, evidence of the complaining witness's marital history, mode of dress, general reputation for promiscuity, nonchastity, or sexual mores contrary to the community standards.

"(b) In any prosecution for rape, evidence relating to the past sexual behavior of the complaining witness may be introduced if the court, following the procedure described in subsection (c) of this Code section, finds that the past sexual behavior directly involved the participation of the accused and finds that the evidence expected to be introduced supports an inference that the accused could have reasonably believed that the complaining witness consented to the conduct complained of in the prosecution."

Laws 2005, Act 8, § 17, provides:

"This Act shall apply to all trials which commence on or after July 1, 2005."

§ 24-2-4. Part of paper introduced, balance admissible if relevant

Where either party introduces part of a document or record, the opposite party may read so much of the balance as is relevant.

Formerly Civil Code 1895, § 5241; Civil Code 1910, § 5830; Code 1933, § 38-703.

CHAPTER 3

HEARSAY

Article 1

Article 1

General Provisions

§ 24-3-1. Definition; when and why admitted

(a) Hearsay evidence is that which does not derive its value solely from the credit of the witness but rests mainly on the veracity and competency of other persons.

(b) Hearsay evidence is admitted only in specified cases from necessity.

Formerly Code 1863, § 3693; Code 1868, § 3717; Code 1873, § 3770; Code 1882, § 3770; Civil Code 1895, § 5175; Civil Code 1910, § 5762; Code 1933, § 38-301.

§ 24-3-2. Original evidence, when

When, in a legal investigation, information, conversations, letters and replies, and similar evidence are facts to explain conduct and ascertain motives, they shall be admitted in evidence not as hearsay but as original evidence.

Formerly Code 1863, § 3694; Code 1868, § 3718; Code 1873, § 3771; Code 1882, § 3771; Civil Code 1895, § 5176; Penal Code 1895, § 997; Civil Code 1910, § 5763; Penal Code 1910, § 1023; Code 1933, § 38-302.

§ 24-3-3. Res gestae

Declarations accompanying an act, or so nearly connected therewith in time as to be free from all suspicion of device or afterthought, shall be admissible in evidence as part of the res gestae.

Formerly Code 1863, § 3696; Code 1868, § 3720; Code 1873, § 3773; Code 1882, § 3773; Civil Code 1895, § 5179; Penal Code 1895, § 998; Civil Code 1910, § 5766; Penal Code 1910, § 1024; Code 1933, § 38-305.

§ 24-3-4. Statements for purposes of medical diagnosis or treatment

Statements made for purposes of medical diagnosis or treatment and describing medical history, or past or present symptoms, pain, or sensations, or the inception or general character of the cause or external source thereof insofar as reasonably pertinent to diagnosis or treatment shall be admissible in evidence.

Laws 1977, p. 226, § 1.

Formerly Code 1933, § 38-315.

§ 24-3-5. Declarations by conspirators

After the fact of conspiracy is proved, the declarations by any one of the conspirators during the pendency of the criminal project shall be admissible against all.

Formerly Code 1863, § 3698; Code 1868, § 3722; Code 1873, § 3775; Code 1882, § 3775; Penal Code 1895, § 999; Penal Code 1910, § 1025; Code 1933, § 38-306.

§ 24-3-6. Dying declarations

Declarations by any person in the article of death, who is conscious of his condition, as to the cause of his death and the person who killed him, shall be admissible in evidence in a prosecution for the homicide.

Formerly Code 1863, § 3704; Code 1868, § 3728; Code 1873, § 3781; Code 1882, § 3781; Penal Code 1895, § 1000; Penal Code 1910, § 1026; Code 1933, § 38-307.

§ 24-3-7. Declarations by persons in possession

(a) Declarations by a person in possession of property in disparagement of his own title shall be admissible in evidence in favor of anyone and against privies of the declarant.

(b) Declarations by a person in favor of his own title shall be admissible to prove his adverse possession.

Formerly Code 1863, § 3697; Code 1868, § 3721; Code 1873, § 3774; Code 1882, § 3774; Civil Code 1895, § 5180; Civil Code 1910, § 5767; Code 1933, § 38-308.

§ 24-3-8. Declarations and entries by deceased persons

Declarations and entries made by a person since deceased against his interest and not made with a view to pending litigation shall be admissible in evidence in any case.

Formerly Code 1863, § 3699; Code 1868, § 3723; Code 1873, § 3776; Code 1882, § 3776; Civil Code 1895, § 5181; Civil Code 1910, § 5768; Code 1933, § 38-309.

§ 24-3-9. Matters of public interest; ancient rights

Declarations of deceased persons as to ancient rights made before the litigation arose shall be admissible to prove matters of public interest in which the whole community is supposed to take interest and to have knowledge.

Formerly Code 1863, § 3701; Code 1868, § 3725; Code 1873, § 3778; Code 1882, § 3778; Civil Code 1895, § 5183; Civil Code 1910, § 5770; Code 1933, § 38-311.

§ 24-3-10. Testimony of witness on former trial

The testimony of a witness since deceased, disqualified, or inaccessible for any cause which was given under oath on a former trial upon substantially the same issue and between substantially the same parties may be proved by anyone who heard it and who professes to remember the substance of the entire testimony as to the particular matter about which he testifies.

Formerly Code 1863, § 3705; Code 1868, § 3729; Code 1873, § 3782; Code 1882, § 3782; Civil Code 1895, § 5186; Penal Code 1895, § 1001; Civil Code 1910, § 5773; Penal Code 1910, § 1027; Code 1933, § 38-314.

§ 24-3-11. Ancient documents

Ancient documents purporting to be a part of the transaction to which they relate shall be admissible in evidence.

Formerly Code 1863, § 3702; Code 1868, § 3726; Code 1873, § 3779; Code 1882, § 3779; Civil Code 1895, § 5184; Civil Code 1910, § 5771; Code 1933, § 38-312.

§ 24-3-12. Pedigree, how proved

Pedigree, including descent, relationship, birth, marriage, and death, may be proved by the declarations of deceased persons related by blood or marriage, by general repute in the family, or by genealogies, inscriptions, "family trees," and similar evidence.

Formerly Code 1863, § 3695; Code 1868, § 3719; Code 1873, § 3772; Code 1882, § 3772; Civil Code 1895, § 5177; Civil Code 1910, § 5764; Code 1933, § 38–303.

§ 24–3–13. Ancient boundaries and landmarks

Traditional evidence as to ancient boundaries and landmarks shall be admissible in evidence, the weight to be determined by the jury according to the source from which it comes.

Formerly Code 1863, § 3703; Code 1868, § 3727; Code 1873, § 3780; Code 1882, § 3780; Civil Code 1895, § 5185; Civil Code 1910, § 5772; Code 1933, § 38–313.

§ 24–3–14. Writings, records, entries, and memoranda made in regular course of business

(a) As used in this Code section, the term "business" shall include every kind of business, profession, occupation, calling, or operation of institutions, whether carried on for profit or not.

(b) Any writing or record, whether in the form of an entry in a book or otherwise, made as a memorandum or record of any act, transaction, occurrence, or event shall be admissible in evidence in proof of the act, transaction, occurrence, or event, if the trial judge shall find that it was made in the regular course of any business and that it was the regular course of such business to make the memorandum or record at the time of the act, transaction, occurrence, or event or within a reasonable time thereafter.

(c) All other circumstances of the making of the writing or record, including lack of personal knowledge by the entrant or maker, may be shown to affect its weight; but they shall not affect its admissibility.

(d) This Code section shall be liberally interpreted and applied.

Laws 1952, p. 177, §§ 1, 2, 3.

Historical and Statutory Notes

Comparative Laws:

Cal.—West's Ann.Cal.Evid.Code §§ 1270 to 1272.
Conn.—C.G.S.A. § 52–180.
Ga.—O.C.G.A. § 24–3–14.
Idaho—I.C. §§ 9–413 to 9–416.
Mich.—M.C.L.A. § 600.2146.
Minn.—M.S.A. §§ 600.01 to 600.04.
Mo.—V.A.M.S. §§ 490.660 to 490.690.
N.Y.—McKinney's CPLR Rule 4518.
N.D.—NDCC 31–08–01.
Ohio—R.C. §§ 2317.40, 2317.41.
Pa.—42 PaC.S.A. § 6108.
Vt.—12 V.S.A. § 1700.
Virgin Islands—5 V.I.C. § 932.
Wash.—West's RCWA 5.45.010 to 5.45.920.

§ 24–3–15. Definitions

The term "admissions" usually refers to civil cases. The term "confessions" usually refers to criminal cases.

Formerly Code 1863, § 3706; Code 1868, § 3730; Code 1873, § 3783; Code 1882, § 3783; Civil Code 1895, § 5187; Penal Code 1895, § 1002; Civil Code 1910, § 5774; Penal Code 1910, § 1028; Code 1933, § 38–401.

§ 24–3–16. Statements made by child under age of 14 years describing acts of sexual contact or physical abuse

A statement made by a child under the age of 14 years describing any act of sexual contact or physical abuse performed with or on the child by another or performed with or on another in the presence of the child is admissible in evidence by the testimony of the person or persons to whom made if the child is available to testify in the proceedings and the court finds that the circumstances of the statement provide sufficient indicia of reliability.

Laws 1986, p. 668, § 1; Laws 1995, p. 937, § 1.

Validity

This section has been held unconstitutional in the case of Woodard v. State, 1998, 269 Ga. 317, 496 S.E.2d 896.

§ 24–3–17. Copies of records of Department of Public Safety or comparable agencies in other states

(a) A certified copy of any record of the Department of Public Safety or the Department of Driver Services or comparable agency in any other state is admissible in any judicial proceedings or administrative hearing in the same manner as the original of the record.

(b) Any court may receive and use as evidence in any case information otherwise admissible from the records of the Department of Public Safety or the Department of Driver Services obtained from any terminal lawfully connected to the Georgia Crime Information Center without the need for additional certification of those records.

(c) Any court may receive and use as evidence for the purpose of imposing a sentence in any criminal case information otherwise admissible from the records of the Department of Driver Services obtained from a request made in accordance with a contract with the Georgia Technology Authority for immediate on–line electronic furnishing of information.

Laws 1988, p. 470, § 2; Laws 1989, p. 1080, § 1; Laws 2005, Act 68, § 10A–1, eff. July 1, 2005.

Historical and Statutory Notes

The 2005 amendment by Act 68 rewrote the section, which had read:

"(a) A certified copy of any record of the Department of Public Safety or comparable agency in any other state is admissible in any judicial proceedings or administrative hearing in the same manner as the original of the record.

"(b) Any court may receive and use as evidence in any case information otherwise admissible from the records of the Department of Public Safety obtained from any terminal lawfully connected to the Georgia Crime Information Center without the need for additional certification of those records."

§ 24–3–18. Medical reports

(a) Upon the trial of any civil case involving injury or disease, any medical report in narrative form which has been signed and dated by an examining or treating licensed medical doctor, dentist, orthodontist, podiatrist, physical or occupational therapist, doctor of chiropractic, psychologist, advanced practice nurse, social worker, professional counselor, or marriage and family therapist shall be admissible and received in evidence insofar as it purports to represent the history, examination, diagnosis, treatment, prognosis, or interpretation of tests or examinations, including the basis therefor, by the person signing the report, the same as if that person were present at trial and testifying as a witness; provided, however, that such report and notice of intention to introduce such report must first be provided to the adverse party at least 60 days prior to trial. A statement of the qualifications of the person signing the report may be included as part of the basis for providing the information contained therein, and the opinion of the person signing the report with regard to the etiology of the injury or disease may be included as part of the diagnosis. Any adverse party may object to the admissibility of any portion of the report, other than on the ground that it is hearsay, within 15 days of being provided with the report. Further, any adverse party shall have the right to cross-examine the person signing the report and provide rebuttal testimony. The party tendering the report may also introduce testimony of the person signing the report for the purpose of supplementing the report or otherwise.

(b) The medical narrative shall be presented to the jury as depositions are presented to the jury and shall not go out with the jury as documentary evidence.

Laws 1997, p. 945, § 1.

Article 3

Confessions

§ 24–3–50. Confessions must be voluntary

To make a confession admissible, it must have been made voluntarily, without being induced by another by the slightest hope of benefit or remotest fear of injury.

Formerly Code 1863, § 3716; Code 1868, § 3740; Code 1873, § 3793; Code 1882, § 3793; Penal Code 1895, § 1006; Penal Code 1910, § 1032; Code 1933, § 38–411.

§ 24–3–51. Confessions under spiritual exhortation or promise of secrecy or collateral benefit

The fact that a confession has been made under a spiritual exhortation, a promise of secrecy, or a promise of collateral benefit shall not exclude it.

Formerly Code 1863, § 3717; Code 1868, § 3741; Code 1873, § 3794; Code 1882, § 3794; Penal Code 1895, § 1007; Penal Code 1910, § 1033; Code 1933, § 38–412.

§ 24–3–52. Confession by joint offender or conspirator

The confession of one joint offender or conspirator made after the enterprise is ended shall be admissible only against himself.

Formerly Code 1863, § 3719; Code 1868, § 3743; Code 1873, § 3796; Code 1882, § 3796; Penal Code 1895, § 1009; Penal Code 1910, § 1035; Code 1933, § 38–414.

§ 24–3–53. Weight of admissions or confessions

All admissions shall be scanned with care, and confessions of guilt shall be received with great caution. A confession alone, uncorroborated by any other evidence, shall not justify a conviction.

Formerly Code 1863, § 3715; Code 1868, § 3739; Code 1873, § 3792; Code 1882, § 3792; Civil Code 1895, § 5197; Penal Code 1895, § 1005; Civil Code 1910, § 5784; Penal Code 1910, § 1031; Code 1933, § 38–420.

CHAPTER 4

PROOF GENERALLY

Article 1

Article 1

General Provisions

§ 24–4–1. Burden of proof

The burden of proof generally lies upon the party who is asserting or affirming a fact and to the existence of whose case or defense the proof of such fact is essential. If a negation or negative affirmation is essential to a party's case or defense, the proof of such negation or negative affirmation lies on the party so affirming it.

Formerly Code 1863, § 3681; Code 1868, § 3705; Code 1873, § 3758; Code 1882, § 3758; Civil Code 1895, § 5160; Penal Code 1895, § 994; Civil Code 1910, § 5746; Penal Code 1910, § 1020; Code 1933, § 38–103.

§ 24–4–2. Changing burden of proof

What amount of evidence will change the onus or burden of proof is a question to be decided in each case by the sound discretion of the court.

Formerly Code 1863, § 3682; Code 1868, § 3706; Code 1873, § 3759; Code 1882, § 3759; Civil Code 1895, § 5161; Penal Code 1895, § 995; Civil Code 1910, § 5747; Penal Code 1910, § 1021; Code 1933, § 38–104.

§ 24–4–3. Amount of mental conviction; preponderance of evidence

Moral and reasonable certainty is all that can be expected in legal investigation. In all civil cases a preponderance of evidence is considered sufficient to produce mental conviction. In criminal cases a greater strength of mental conviction is held necessary to justify a verdict of guilty.

Formerly Code 1863, § 3672; Code 1868, § 3696; Code 1873, § 3749; Code 1882, § 3749; Civil Code 1895, § 5144; Penal Code 1895, § 986; Civil Code 1910, § 5730; Penal Code 1910, § 1012; Code 1933, § 38–105.

§ 24–4–4. Determination of where preponderance of evidence lies

In determining where the preponderance of evidence lies, the jury may consider all the facts and circumstances of the case, the witnesses' manner of testifying, their intelligence, their means and opportunity for knowing the facts to which they testified, the nature of the facts to which they testified, the probability or improbability of their testimony, their interest or want of interest, and their personal credibility so far as the same may legitimately appear from the trial. The jury may also consider the number of the witnesses, though the preponderance is not necessarily with the greater number.

Formerly Civil Code 1895, § 5146; Civil Code 1910, § 5732; Code 1933, § 38–107.

§ 24–4–5. When evidence warrants conviction; reasonable doubt

Whether dependent upon direct or circumstantial evidence, the true question in criminal cases is not whether it is possible that the conclusion at which the evidence points may be false, but whether there is sufficient evidence to satisfy the mind and conscience beyond a reasonable doubt.

Formerly Penal Code 1895, § 987; Penal Code 1910, § 1013; Code 1933, § 38–110.

§ 24–4–6. Circumstantial evidence, when sufficient in criminal prosecution

To warrant a conviction on circumstantial evidence, the proved facts shall not only be consistent with the hypothesis of guilt, but shall exclude every other reasonable hypothesis save that of the guilt of the accused.

Formerly Penal Code 1895, § 984; Penal Code 1910, § 1010; Code 1933, § 38–109.

§ 24–4–7. Positive and negative testimony

The existence of a fact testified to by one positive witness is to be believed, rather than that such fact did not exist because many other witnesses who had the same opportunity of observation swear that they did not see or know of its having existed. This rule shall not apply when two parties have equal facilities for seeing or hearing a thing and one swears that it occurred while the other swears that it did not.

Formerly Civil Code 1895, § 5165; Penal Code 1895, § 985; Civil Code 1910, § 5751; Penal Code 1910, § 1011; Code 1933, § 38–111.

§ 24–4–8. Number of witnesses necessary

The testimony of a single witness is generally sufficient to establish a fact. However, in certain cases, including prosecutions for treason, prosecutions for perjury, and felony cases where the only witness is an accomplice, the testimony of a single witness is not sufficient. Nevertheless, corroborating circumstances may dispense with the necessity for the testimony of a second witness, except in prosecutions for treason.

Formerly Code 1863, § 3678; Code 1868, § 3702; Code 1873, § 3755; Code 1882, § 3755; Civil Code 1895, § 5156; Penal Code 1895, § 991; Civil Code 1910, § 5742; Penal Code 1910, § 1017; Code 1933, § 38–121.

§ 24–4–9. Inference of existence of certain facts

In arriving at a verdict, the jury, from facts proved, and sometimes from the absence of counter evidence, may infer the existence of other facts reasonably and logically consequent on those proved.

Formerly Civil Code 1895, § 5157; Civil Code 1910, § 5743; Code 1933, § 38–123.

CHAPTER 5

BEST EVIDENCE RULE

Article 1

Article 1

General Provisions

§ 24–5–1. Primary and secondary evidence defined

(a) Primary evidence is such as in itself does not indicate the existence of other and better proof.

(b) Secondary evidence is such as from necessity in some cases is substituted for stronger and better proof.

Formerly Code 1863, § 3684; Code 1868, § 3708; Code 1873, § 3761; Code 1882, § 3761; Civil Code 1895, § 5164; Civil Code 1910, § 5750; Code 1933, § 38–204.

§ 24–5–2. Secondary evidence admitted when

In order to admit secondary evidence, it shall appear that the primary evidence for some sufficient cause is not accessible to the diligence of the party. This showing shall be made to the court, who shall hear the party himself on the question of diligence and the inaccessibility of the primary evidence.

Formerly Code 1863, § 3690; Code 1868, § 3714; Code 1873, § 3767; Code 1882, § 3767; Civil Code 1895, § 5172; Civil Code 1910, § 5759; Code 1933, § 38–212.

§ 24–5–3. Exceptions to general rule

Cases of necessity or manifest convenience, resting on principles of reason and justice, may be made exceptions to the general rule requiring the production of primary evidence.

Formerly Code 1863, § 3689; Code 1868, § 3713; Code 1873, § 3766; Code 1882, § 3766; Civil Code 1895, § 5171; Civil Code 1910, § 5758; Code 1933, § 38–211.

§ 24–5–4. Best evidence, necessity of producing; written evidence as best evidence

(a) The best evidence which exists of a writing sought to be proved shall be produced, unless its absence shall be satisfactorily accounted for.

(b) Written evidence of a writing is considered of higher proof than oral evidence. In all cases where the parties have reduced their contract, agreement, or stipulation to writing and have assented thereto, such writing is the best evidence of the same.

Formerly Code 1863, §§ 3683, 3685; Code 1868, §§ 3707, 3709; Code 1873, §§ 3760, 3762; Code 1882, §§ 3760, 3762; Civil Code 1895, §§ 5162, 5166; Civil Code 1910, §§ 5748, 5752; Code 1933, §§ 38–203, 38–205.

§ 24–5–5. Degrees in secondary evidence

There are degrees in secondary evidence. The best secondary evidence should always be produced. A duplicate is better than a copy and an examined copy is better than oral evidence.

Formerly Code 1863, § 3691; Code 1868, § 3715; Code 1873, § 3768; Code 1882, § 3768; Civil Code 1895, § 5173; Civil Code 1910, § 5760; Code 1933, § 38–213.

CHAPTER 9

WITNESSES GENERALLY

Article 1

Competency

§ 24–9–1. Competency of witnesses to testify

(a) No person offered as a witness shall be excluded by reason of incapacity, for crime or interest or from being a party, from giving evidence, either in person or by deposition, according to the practice of the court, on the trial of any issue joined, or of any matter or question, or on any inquiry arising in any suit, action, or proceeding, civil or criminal, in any court or before any judge, jury, sheriff, coroner, magistrate, officer, or party having by law or consent of parties authority to hear, receive, and examine evidence; but every person so offered shall be competent and compellable to give evidence on behalf of either or any of the parties to the suit, action, or other proceeding.

(b) This Code section, as revised by an Act approved April 17, 1979 (Ga. L. 1979, p. 1261), shall apply to transactions or occurrences which take place on or after July 1, 1979, and this Code section, as it existed prior to July 1, 1979, shall apply to transactions or occurrences which took place prior to July 1, 1979.

Laws 1866, p. 138, § 1; Laws 1889, p. 85, § 1; Laws 1890–91, p. 107, §§ 1, 2; Laws 1893, p. 53, § 1; Laws 1897, p. 53, § 1; Laws 1900, p. 57, § 1; Laws 1924, p. 62, § 1; Laws 1953, Nov.-Dec. Sess., p. 319, § 1; Laws 1979, p. 1261, §§ 1, 2; Laws 1992, p. 6, § 24.

Formerly Code 1868, § 3798; Code 1873, § 3854; Code 1882, § 3854; Civil Code 1895, §§ 5269, 5270; Civil Code 1910, §§ 5858, 5859; Code 1933, § 38–1603.

§ 24–9–2. Testimony of husband and wife as to adultery of other

In any civil proceeding a husband and wife shall each be competent to testify to the adultery of the other; and a party shall be competent to testify to his or her innocence of adultery in such proceeding.

Laws 1866, p. 138, § 3; Laws 1935, p. 120, § 1; Laws 1951, p. 596, § 1; Laws 1976, p. 1014, § 2; Laws 1982, p. 1187, §§ 1, 2.

Formerly Code 1868, § 3799; Code 1873, § 3855; Code 1882, § 3855; Civil Code 1895, § 5272; Civil Code 1910, § 5861; Code 1933, § 38–1606.

§ 24–9–3. Religious belief

Religious belief shall go only to the credit of a witness.

Laws 1841, p. 144, § 1; Cobb's 1851 Digest, p. 280.

Formerly Code 1863, § 3772; Code 1868, § 3797; Code 1873, § 3853; Code 1882, § 3853; Civil Code 1895, § 5268; Civil Code 1910, § 5857; Code 1933, § 38–1602.

§ 24–9–4. Evidence through interpreter

No physical defect in any of the senses shall incapacitate a witness. An interpreter may explain the evidence of such witness.

Formerly Code 1863, § 3774; Code 1868, § 3802; Code 1873, § 3858; Code 1882, § 3858; Civil Code 1895, § 5275; Penal Code 1895, § 1014; Civil Code 1910, § 5864; Penal Code 1910, § 1040; Code 1933, § 38–1609.

§ 24–9–5. Persons who do not have the use of reason

(a) Except as provided in subsection (b) of this Code section, persons who do not have the use of reason, such as idiots, lunatics during lunacy, and children who do not understand the nature of an oath, shall be incompetent witnesses.

(b) Notwithstanding the provisions of subsection (a) of this Code section, in all cases involving deprivation as defined by Code Section 15–11–2, or in criminal cases involving child molestation, and in all other criminal cases in which a child was a victim of or a witness to any crime, any such child shall be competent to testify, and his credibility shall be determined as provided in Article 4 of this chapter.

Laws 1866, p. 138, § 4; Laws 1989, p. 1639, § 1; Laws 1990, p. 1795, § 1.

Formerly Code 1868, § 3800; Code 1873, § 3856; Code 1882, § 3856; Civil Code 1895, § 5273; Penal Code 1895, § 1012;

Civil Code 1910, § 5862; Penal Code 1910, § 1038; Code 1933, § 38–1607.

§ 24–9–6. Drunkenness

Drunkenness, which dethrones reason and memory, shall incapacitate during its continuance.

Formerly Code 1863, § 3775; Code 1868, § 3801; Code 1873, § 3857; Code 1882, § 3857; Civil Code 1895, § 5274; Penal Code 1895, § 1013; Civil Code 1910, § 5863; Penal Code 1910, § 1039; Code 1933, § 38–1608.

§ 24–9–7. Court decides competency; objections to competency; restoration to competency

(a) The competency of a witness shall be decided by the court. The court shall by examination decide upon the capacity of one alleged to be incompetent from idiocy, lunacy, insanity, drunkenness, or infancy.

(b) If an objection to competency is known, it shall be taken before the witness is examined at all. It may be proved by the witness himself or by other testimony. If proved by other testimony, the witness shall be incompetent to explain it away.

(c) Any fact which in the judgment of the court removes the ground of incompetency shall restore the competency of the witness.

Formerly Code 1863, §§ 3772, 3776, 3784, 3785; Code 1868, §§ 3796, 3803, 3804, 3805; Code 1873, §§ 3852, 3859, 3860, 3861; Code 1882, §§ 3852, 3859, 3860, 3861; Civil Code 1895, §§ 5267, 5276, 5277, 5278; Civil Code 1910, §§ 5856, 5865, 5866, 5867; Code 1933, §§ 38–1601, 38–1610, 38–1611, 38–1612.

Article 2

Privilege

Part 1

General Provisions

§ 24–9–20. Person not compellable to testify for or against self; testimony of defendant in criminal case

(a) No person who is charged in any criminal proceeding with the commission of any indictable offense or any offense punishable on summary conviction shall be compellable to give evidence for or against himself.

(b) If a defendant in a criminal case wishes to testify and announces in open court his or her intention to do so, the defendant may so testify in his or her own behalf. If a defendant testifies, he or she shall be sworn as any other witness and may be examined and cross–examined as any other witness. The failure of a defendant to testify shall create no presumption against him or her, and no comment shall be made because of such failure.

Laws 1866, p. 138, § 2; Laws 1868, p. 24, § 1; Laws 1874, p. 22, § 1; Laws 1878–79, p. 53, § 1; Laws 1962, p. 133, § 2; Laws 1973, p. 292, § 2; Laws 2005, Act 8, § 14, eff. July 1, 2005.

Formerly Code 1868, § 3798; Code 1873, §§ 3854, 4637; Code 1882, §§ 3854, 4637; Penal Code 1895, §§ 1010, 1011; Penal Code 1910, §§ 1036, 1037; Code 1933, §§ 38–415, 38–416.

Historical and Statutory Notes

The 2005 amendment by Act 8, rewrote subsec. (b) and deleted subsec. (c). Prior to amendment, subsecs. (b) and (c) had read:

"(b) If a defendant in a criminal case wishes to testify and announces in open court his intention to do so, he may so testify in his own behalf. If a defendant testifies, he shall be sworn as any other witness and may be examined and cross–examined as any other witness, except that no evidence of general bad character or prior convictions shall be admissible unless and until the defendant shall have first put his character in issue. Evidence of prior felony convictions may be admitted in those cases where the prior felony convictions are alleged in the indictment, as provided by law. The failure of a defendant to testify shall create no presumption against him, and no comment shall be made because of such failure.

"(c) In the event that a defendant elects to be sworn and examined, he shall not lose his right to open and conclude the argument to the jury, if he has not introduced other evidence in the trial."

Laws 2005, Act 8, § 17, provides:

"This Act shall apply to all trials which commence on or after July 1, 2005."

§ 24–9–21. Confidential communications, etc.

There are certain admissions and communications excluded on grounds of public policy. Among these are:

(1) Communications between husband and wife;

(2) Communications between attorney and client;

(3) Communications among grand jurors;

(4) Secrets of state;

(5) Communications between psychiatrist and patient;

(6) Communications between licensed psychologist and patient as provided in Code Section 43–39–16;

(7) Communications between patient and a licensed clinical social worker, clinical nurse specialist in psychiatric/mental health, licensed marriage and family therapist, or licensed professional counselor during the psychotherapeutic relationship; and

(8) Communications between or among any psychiatrist, psychologist, licensed clinical social worker, clinical nurse specialist in psychiatric/mental health, licensed marriage and family therapist, and licensed professional counselor who are rendering psychotherapy or have rendered psychotherapy to a patient, regarding that patient's communications which are otherwise privileged by paragraph (5), (6), or (7) of this Code section.

As used in this Code section, the term "psychotherapeutic relationship" means the relationship which arises between a patient and a licensed clinical social worker, a clinical nurse specialist in psychiatric/mental health, a licensed marriage and family therapist, or a licensed professional counselor using psychotherapeutic techniques as defined in Code Section 43–10A–3 and the term "psychotherapy" means the employment of "psychotherapeutic techniques."

Laws 1959, p. 190, § 1; Laws 1978, p. 1657, § 1; Laws 1995, p. 858, § 1.

Formerly Code 1863, § 3720; Code 1868, § 3744; Code 1873, § 3797; Code 1882, § 3797; Civil Code 1895, § 5198; Civil Code 1910, § 5785; Code 1933, § 38–418.

§ 24–9–22. Communications to ministers, priests and rabbis

Every communication made by any person professing religious faith, seeking spiritual comfort, or seeking counseling to any Protestant minister of the Gospel, any priest of the Roman Catholic faith, any priest of the Greek Orthodox Catholic faith, any Jewish rabbi, or to any Christian or Jewish minister, by whatever name called, shall be deemed privileged. No such minister, priest, or rabbi shall disclose any communications made to him by any such person professing religious faith, seeking spiritual guidance, or seeking counseling, nor shall such minister, priest, or rabbi be competent or compellable to testify with reference to any such communication in any court.

Laws 1951, p. 468, §§ 1, 2; Laws 1986, p. 1277, § 2.

§ 24–9–23. Husband and wife as witnesses for and against each other in criminal proceedings

(a) Husband and wife shall be competent but shall not be compellable to give evidence in any criminal proceeding for or against each other.

(b) The privilege created by subsection (a) of this Code section or by corresponding privileges in paragraph (1) of Code Section 24–9–21 or subsection (a) of Code Section 24–9–27 shall not apply in proceedings in which the husband or wife is charged with a crime against the person of a minor child, but such person shall be compellable to give evidence only on the specific act for which the defendant is charged.

Laws 1866, p. 138, § 2; Laws 1880–81, p. 121, § 1; Laws 1927, p. 145, § 1; Laws 1957, p. 53, § 1; Laws 1987, p. 1155, § 1.

Formerly Code 1868, § 3798; Code 1873, § 3854; Code 1882, § 3854; Penal Code 1895, § 1011; Penal Code 1910, § 1037; Code 1933, § 38–1604.

§ 24–9–24. Communications to attorney by client

Communications to any attorney or to his employee to be transmitted to the attorney pending his employment or in anticipation thereof shall never be heard by the court. The attorney shall not disclose the advice or counsel he may give to his client, nor produce or deliver up title deeds or other papers, except evidences of debt left in his possession by his client. This Code section shall not exclude the attorney as a witness to any facts which may transpire in connection with his employment.

Laws 1850, Cobb's 1851 Digest, p. 280; Laws 1859, p. 18, § 1.

Formerly Code 1863, § 3721; Code 1868, § 3745; Code 1873, § 3798; Code 1882, § 3798; Civil Code 1895, § 5199; Civil Code 1910, § 5786; Code 1933, § 38–419.

§ 24–9–25. Testimony of attorneys as against clients

No attorney shall be competent or compellable to testify for or against his client to any matter or thing, the knowledge of which he may have acquired from his client by virtue of his employment as attorney or by reason of the anticipated employment of him as attorney. However, an attorney shall be both competent and compellable to testify for or against his client as to any matter or thing, the knowledge of which he may have acquired in any other manner.

Laws 1866, p. 138, § 2; Laws 1887, p. 30, § 1.

Formerly Code 1868, § 3798; Code 1873, § 3854; Code 1882, § 3854; Civil Code 1895, § 5271; Penal Code 1895, § 1011; Civil Code 1910, § 5860; Penal Code 1910, § 1037; Code 1933, § 38–1605.

§ 24–9–26. Law enforcement officers testifying in criminal proceedings not compelled to reveal home address

Law enforcement officers testifying before any court in any criminal proceedings shall not be compelled to reveal their home address but may be required to divulge the business address of their employer, except that the court may require any officer to answer questions as to his home address whenever such fact may be material to any issue in the case.

Laws 1973, p. 547, § 1.

§ 24–9–27. Privilege of party or witness

(a) No party or witness shall be required to testify as to any matter which may criminate or tend to criminate himself or which shall tend to bring infamy, disgrace, or public contempt upon himself or any member of his family.

(b) Except in proceedings in which a judgment creditor or his successor in interest seeks postjudgment discovery involving a judgment debtor pursuant to Code Section 9–11–69, no party or witness shall be required to testify as to any matter which shall tend to work a forfeiture of his estate.

(c) No party or witness shall be required to make discovery of the advice of his professional advisers or his consultation with them.

(d) No official persons shall be called on to disclose any state matters of which the policy of the state and the interest of the community require concealment.

Laws 1978, p. 2000, § 1.

Formerly Code 1863, §§ 3035, 3737, 3794; Code 1868, §§ 3047, 3761, 3814; Code 1873, §§ 3102, 3814, 3870; Code 1882, §§ 3102, 3814, 3870; Civil Code 1895, §§ 3947, 3957, 5288; Civil Code 1910, §§ 4544, 4554, 5877; Code 1933, §§ 38–1102, 38–1205, 38–1711.

§ 24–9–28. Immunity from prosecution for persons ordered to testify or produce evidence in criminal prosecutions; contempt

(a) Whenever in the judgment of the Attorney General or any district attorney the testimony of any person or the production of evidence of any kind by any person in any criminal proceeding before a court or grand jury is necessary to the public interest, the Attorney General or the district attorney may request the superior court in writing to order that person to testify or produce the evidence. Upon order of the court that person shall not be excused on the basis of his privilege against self-incrimination from testifying or producing any evidence required; but no testimony or other evidence required under the order or any information directly or indirectly derived from such testimony or evidence may be used against the person in any proceedings or prosecution for a crime or offense concerning which he testified or produced evidence under court order. However, he may nevertheless be prosecuted or subjected to penalty or forfeiture for any perjury, false swearing, or contempt committed in testifying or failing to testify, or in producing or failing to produce evidence in accordance with the order but shall not be required to produce evidence that can be used in any other courts, including federal courts. Any order entered under this Code section shall be entered of record in the minutes of the court so as to afford a permanent record thereof; and any testimony given by a person pursuant to such order shall be transcribed and filed for permanent record in the office of the clerk of the court.

(b) If a person refuses to testify after being granted immunity from prosecution and after being ordered to testify as aforesaid, he may be adjudged in contempt and committed to the county jail until such time as he purges himself of contempt by testifying as ordered without regard to the expiration of the grand jury. If the grand jury before which he was ordered to testify has been dissolved, he may purge himself by testifying before the court.

Laws 1975, p. 727, §§ 1, 2.

§ 24–9–29. Confidential communications; veterinarians

No veterinarian licensed under Chapter 50 of Title 43 shall be required to disclose any information concerning the veterinarian's care of an animal except on written authorization or other waiver by the veterinarian's client or on appropriate court order or subpoena. Any veterinarian releasing information under written authorization or other waiver by the client or under court order or subpoena shall not be liable to the client or any other person. The privilege provided by this Code section shall be waived to the extent that the veterinarian's client or the owner of the animal places the veterinarian's care and treatment of the animal or the nature and extent of injuries to the animal at issue in any civil or criminal proceeding.

Laws 1986, p. 1090, § 1.

§ 24–9–30. Qualified privilege for persons, companies, or other entities engaged in news gathering or dissemination

Any person, company, or other entity engaged in the gathering and dissemination of news for the public through a newspaper, book, magazine, or radio or television broadcast shall have a qualified privilege against disclosure of any information, document, or item obtained or prepared in the gathering or dissemination of news in any proceeding where the one asserting the privilege is not a party, unless it is shown that this privilege has been waived or that what is sought:

(1) Is material and relevant;

(2) Cannot be reasonably obtained by alternative means; and

(3) Is necessary to the proper preparation or presentation of the case of a party seeking the information, document, or item.

Laws 1990, p. 167, § 1.

Article 5

Use of Sign Language and Intermediary Interpreter in Administrative and Judicial Proceedings

§ 24–9–103. Procedures for providing interpreter by arresting law enforcement agency

(a) The arresting law enforcement agency shall provide a qualified interpreter to any hearing impaired person whenever the hearing impaired person is taken into custody for allegedly violating any criminal law or ordinance of the state or any political subdivision thereof.

(b)(1) Except as provided in paragraph (2) of this subsection, the law enforcement agency shall immediately request a qualified interpreter from the department, and the department shall provide a qualified interpreter. No interrogation, warning, informing of rights, taking of statements, or other investigatory procedures shall be undertaken until a qualified interpreter has been provided; and no answer, statement, admission, or other evidence acquired from the hearing impaired person shall be admissible in any criminal or quasi-criminal proceeding unless such was knowingly and voluntarily given through and in the presence of a qualified interpreter. No hearing impaired person who has been taken into custody and who is otherwise eligible for release shall be detained because of the unavailability of a qualified interpreter.

(2) If a qualified interpreter is not available one hour after the hearing impaired person has been taken into custody and a request has been forwarded to the department, the arresting officer may interrogate or take a statement from such person, provided that such interrogation and answers thereto shall be in writing and shall be preserved and turned over to the court in the event such person is tried for the alleged offense.

Laws 1983, p. 852, § 2.

§ 24–9–104. Procedures for providing interpreter by court

(a) A court shall provide a qualified interpreter to any hearing impaired person whenever the hearing impaired person has been provided with a court appointed legal counsel. The court shall request a qualified interpreter from the department, and the department shall provide a qualified interpreter.

(b) The qualified interpreter authorized by this Code section shall be present at all times when the hearing impaired person is consulting with legal counsel.

Laws 1983, p. 852, § 2.

§ 24–9–105. Waiver of right to use of interpreter

Whenever a hearing impaired person shall be authorized a qualified interpreter, such person may waive the right to the use of such interpreter. Any such waiver shall be in writing and shall be approved by the agency, law enforcement agency, or court before which the hearing impaired person is to appear. In no event shall the failure of a hearing impaired person to request an interpreter be deemed to be a waiver.

Laws 1983, p. 852, § 2.

§ 24–9–106. Determination that interpreter is able to communicate with hearing impaired person

(a) Whenever a hearing impaired person shall be authorized a qualified interpreter, the agency, law enforcement agency, or court shall determine whether the qualified interpreter so provided is able to communicate accurately with and translate information to and from the hearing impaired person. If it is determined that the qualified interpreter cannot perform these functions, the agency, law enforcement agency, or court shall request another qualified interpreter from the department or shall appoint an intermediary interpreter to assist the qualified interpreter in communicating with the hearing impaired person.

(b) The department shall prepare and maintain a list of qualified interpreters and qualified intermediary interpreters from which such interpreters shall be provided.

Laws 1983, p. 852, § 2.

TITLE 25

FIRE PROTECTION AND SAFETY

CHAPTER 2

REGULATION OF FIRE AND OTHER HAZARDS TO PERSONS AND PROPERTY GENERALLY

§ 25–2–9. Power of state fire marshal and appointed staff to make arrests

(a) Upon the request of the sheriff of the county, the chief of police of the jurisdiction, the district attorney of the judicial circuit, or a local fire official, the state fire marshal and any employees of such official shall have the authority to investigate the cause and origin of any fire which occurred in said county, jurisdiction, or judicial circuit.

(b) Personnel employed and authorized by the state fire marshal shall have the power to make arrests for criminal violations established as a result of investigations. Such personnel must hold certification as a peace officer from the Georgia Peace Officer Standards and Training Council and shall have the power to execute arrest warrants and search warrants for criminal violations and to arrest, upon probable cause and without warrant, any person found violating any of the provisions of applicable criminal laws. Authorized personnel empowered to make arrests pursuant to this Code section shall be empowered to carry firearms as authorized by the state fire marshal in the performance of their duties. It shall be unlawful for any person to resist an arrest authorized by this Code section or to interfere in any manner, including abetting or assisting such resistance or interference, with personnel employed by the state fire marshal in the duties imposed upon such personnel by law.

Laws 1963, p. 509, § 1; Laws 1972, p. 966, § 1; Laws 2003, Act 70, § 1, eff. May 29, 2003.

TITLE 27

GAME AND FISH

CHAPTER 1

GENERAL PROVISIONS

§ 27–1–18. Powers of conservation rangers

(a) Conservation rangers shall have the power and authority:

(1) To enforce all state laws on all property owned or controlled by the department;

(2) To enforce all state laws pertaining to functions assigned to the department;

(3) To enforce any state law when the violation of that law is committed in conjunction with a violation of a state law pertaining to functions assigned to the department;

(4) To enforce any state law when ordered to do so by the Governor or to protect any life or property when the circumstances demand action; and

(5) At the expense of the department, to assist the Department of Public Safety and the Georgia Bureau of Investigation in carrying out their duties and responsibilities when requested to do so by the Department of Public Safety or the Georgia Bureau of Investigation.

(b) The commissioner may, and in the case of a request by the Governor shall, authorize and direct the department's conservation rangers to cooperate with and render assistance to any law enforcement agency of this state or any municipality, county, or other political subdivision thereof in any criminal case, in the prevention or detection of violations of any law, or in the apprehension or arrest of persons who violate the criminal laws of this state, any other state, or the United States, upon a request by the governing authority or chief law enforcement officer of any municipality, the sheriff of any county, a judge of the superior court of any county, or the Governor.

Laws 1973, p. 1483, § 3; Laws 1977, p. 396, § 1; Laws 1978, p. 816, § 11; Laws 1982, p. 3, § 27; Laws 1990, p. 376, § 1.

Formerly Code 1933, § 45–118.

§ 27–1–19. Power of conservation rangers and deputy conservation rangers to arrest persons

(a) Notwithstanding any other provision of law to the contrary, conservation rangers and deputy conservation rangers, when authorized to do so by the board, may arrest persons accused of violating any law or regulation which such officers are empowered to enforce by the issuance of a citation, provided that the offense is committed in the presence of the officer or information concerning the offense constituting a basis for arrest was received by the arresting officer from a law enforcement officer observing the offense being committed. The arresting officer may issue to the person a citation which shall enumerate the specific charges against the person and the date upon which the person is to appear and answer the charges. Whenever an arrest is made by the arresting officer on the basis of information received from another law enforcement officer observing the offense being committed, the citation shall list the name of each officer, and each must be present when the charges against the offender are heard.

(b) If the person charged shall fail to appear as specified in the citation, the judge having jurisdiction of the offense may issue a warrant ordering the apprehension of the person and commanding that he be brought before the court to answer the charge contained within the citation and the charge of his failure to appear as required. The person shall then be allowed to make a reasonable bond to appear on a given date before the court.

Laws 1976, p. 522, § 2; Laws 1977, p. 396, § 1.

Formerly Code 1933, § 45–119.

§ 27–1–20. Additional powers of conservation rangers

(a) In addition to the powers enumerated in Code Sections 27–1–18 and 27–1–19, conservation rangers shall have all the powers previously vested in any other law enforcement officers within the department including, but not limited to, the following:

(1) To enforce all laws, rules, and regulations pertaining to wildlife and to boating safety and as otherwise provided;

(2) To execute all warrants and search warrants for the violation of the laws, rules, and regulations pertaining to wildlife or to boating safety;

(3) To serve subpoenas issued for the examination, investigation, and trial of all offenses against the laws, rules, and regulations pertaining to wildlife or to boating safety;

(4) To arrest without warrant any person found violating any of the laws, rules, and regulations pertaining to wildlife or to hunting, fishing, or boating;

(5) To seize and take possession of all wildlife or parts thereof taken, caught, killed, captured, possessed, or controlled or which have been shipped or are about to be shipped at any time and in any manner or for any purpose contrary to the laws, rules, and regulations pertaining to wildlife;

(6) To go upon property outside of buildings, posted or otherwise, in the performance of their duties;

(7) To carry firearms while performing duties pertaining to wildlife;

(8) To seize as evidence, without warrant, any device other than a boat, vehicle, or aircraft when they have cause to believe that its possession or use is in violation of any of the provisions of the laws or regulations dealing with wildlife. For the purposes of this Code section, "device" includes any light, hunting apparatus, or fishing or netting gear or tackle;

(9) To enter and inspect any commercial cold storage warehouse, ice house, locker plant, butcher shop, or other plant or building for the purpose of determining whether wildlife is being kept or stored therein in violation of the wildlife laws or regulations; and

(10) To exercise the full authority of peace officers while in the performance of their duties.

(b) Unless inconsistent with this title, whenever any statute pertaining to an agency whose functions are assigned to the department refers to law enforcement personnel of that agency, that reference applies to conservation rangers.

Laws 1911, p. 137, § 4; Laws 1912, p. 113, § 1; Laws 1931, p. 173, §§ 1–3; Laws 1955, p. 483, § 18; Laws 1968, p. 497, § 6; Laws 1970, p. 466, § 1; Laws 1973, p. 1483, § 4; Laws 1977, p. 396, § 1.

Formerly Code 1933, §§ 45–108, 45–126; Code 1933, § 45–120.

CHAPTER 4

FISH

Article 1

Article 1

General Provisions

§ 27–4–2. Unlawful to fish on lands of another without permission; fishing in saltwater creeks, streams or estuaries excepted

It shall be unlawful for any person to fish in the waters or from upon the lands of another without first having obtained permission from the landowner or person in charge of such lands, provided that nothing contained in this Code section shall be construed to apply to the fishing or taking of fish, other than oysters, clams, and other shellfish, in any of the salt-water creeks, streams, or estuaries leading from the Atlantic Ocean or from the sounds, rivers, or bays surrounding the several islands of this state. It shall also be unlawful for any person to obstruct or interfere with the right of any other person to fish in these salt-water creeks, streams, or estuaries leading from the Atlantic Ocean or from the sounds, rivers, or bays surrounding the several islands of this state. Conservation rangers, sheriffs, deputy sheriffs, and all other peace officers of this state or of any county or municipality thereof shall enforce this Code section.

Laws 1911, p. 137, § 7; Laws 1955, p. 483, § 81; Laws 1972, p. 200, § 2; Laws 1977, p. 396, § 1.

Formerly Code 1933, § 45–513; Code 1933, § 45–701.

TITLE 30

HANDICAPPED PERSONS

CHAPTER 5

PROTECTION OF DISABLED ADULTS AND ELDER PERSONS

Section

§ 30–5–1. Short title

This chapter shall be known and may be cited as the "Disabled Adults and Elder Persons Protection Act."

Laws 1981, p. 1320, § 1; Laws 1997, p. 700, § 2.

§ 30–5–2. Legislative purpose

The purpose of this chapter is to provide protective services for abused, neglected, or exploited disabled adults and elder persons. It is not the purpose of this chapter to place restrictions upon the personal liberty of disabled adults or elder persons, but this chapter should be liberally construed to assure the availability of protective services to all disabled adults and elder persons in need of them.

Laws 1981, p. 1320, § 2; Laws 1997, p. 700, § 2.

§ 30–5–3. Definitions

As used in this chapter, the term:

(1) "Abuse" means the willful infliction of physical pain, physical injury, mental anguish, unreasonable confinement, or the willful deprivation of essential services to a disabled adult or elder person.

(2) "Caretaker" means a person who has the responsibility for the care of a disabled adult or elder person as a result of family relationship, contract, voluntary assumption of that responsibility, or by operation of law.

(3) "Court" means the probate court for the county of residence of the disabled adult or elder person or the county in which such person is found. In any case in which the judge of the probate court is unable to hear a case brought under this chapter within the time required for such hearing, such judge shall appoint a person to serve and exercise all the jurisdiction of the probate court in such case. Any person so appointed shall be a member of the State Bar of Georgia and be otherwise qualified for his or her duties by training and experience. Such appointment may be made on a case-by-case basis or by making a standing appointment of one or more persons. Any person receiving such standing appointment shall serve at the pleasure of the judge making the appointment or said judge's successor in office to hear such cases if and when necessary. The compensation of a person so appointed shall be as agreed upon by the judge who makes the appointment and the person appointed, with the approval of the governing authority of the county for which such person is appointed, and shall be paid from the county funds of such county. All fees collected for the services of such appointed person shall be paid into the general funds of the county served.

(4) "Department" means the Department of Human Services.

(5) "Director" means the director of the Division of Aging Services of the Department of Human Services, or the director's designee.

(6) "Disabled adult" means a person 18 years of age or older who is not a resident of a long-term care facility, as defined in Article 4 of Chapter 8 of Title 31, but who is mentally or physically incapacitated or has Alzheimer's disease, as defined in Code Section 31–8–180, or dementia, as defined in Code Section 49–6–72.

(7) "Disabled adult in need of protective services" means a disabled adult who is subject to abuse, neglect, or exploitation as a result of that adult's mental or physical incapacity.

(7.1) "Elder person" means a person 65 years of age or older who is not a resident of a long-term care facility as defined in Article 4 of Chapter 8 of Title 31.

(8) "Essential services" means social, medical, psychiatric, or legal services necessary to safeguard the disabled adult's or elder person's rights and resources and to maintain the physical and mental well-being of such person. These services shall include, but not be limited to, the provision of medical care for physical and mental health needs, assistance in personal hygiene, food, clothing, adequately heated and ventilated shelter, and protection from health and safety hazards but shall not include the taking into physical custody of a disabled adult or elder person without that person's consent.

(9) "Exploitation" means the illegal or improper use of a disabled adult or elder person or that person's resources through undue influence, coercion, harassment, duress, deception, false representation, false pretense, or other similar means for another's profit or advantage.

(10) "Neglect" means the absence or omission of essential services to the degree that it harms or threatens with harm the physical or emotional health of a disabled adult or elder person.

(11) "Protective services" means services necessary to protect a disabled adult or elder person from abuse, neglect, or exploitation. Such services shall include, but not be limited to, evaluation of the need for services and mobilization of essential services on behalf of a disabled adult or elder person.

Laws 1981, p. 1320, § 3; Laws 1997, p. 700, § 2; Laws 2000, p. 136, § 30; Laws 2005, Act 91, § 6, eff. July 1, 2005; Laws 2007, Act 126, § 1, eff. July 1, 2007; Laws 2009, Act 147, § 1, eff. July 1, 2009; Laws 2009, Act 102, § 2–2, eff. July 1, 2009.

§ 30–5–4. Reports of disabled adults or elder persons in need of protective services

(a)(1)(A) Any physician, osteopath, intern, resident, other hospital or medical personnel, dentist, psychologist, chiropractor, podiatrist, pharmacist, physical therapist, occupational therapist, licensed professional counselor, nursing personnel, social work personnel, day-care personnel, coroner, medical examiner, employee of a public or private agency engaged in professional health related services to elder persons or disabled adults, or law enforcement personnel having reasonable cause to believe that a disabled adult or elder person has had a physical injury or injuries inflicted upon such disabled adult or elder person, other than by accidental means, or has been neglected or exploited shall report or cause reports to be made in accordance with the provisions of this Code section.

(B) Except as provided in this paragraph, any employee of a financial institution, as defined in Code Section 7–1–4, having reasonable cause to believe that a disabled adult or elder person has been exploited shall report or cause reports to be made in accordance with the provisions of this Code section; provided, however, that this obligation shall not apply to any employee of a financial institution while that employee is acting as a fiduciary, as defined in Code Section 7–1–4, but only for such assets that the employee is holding or managing in a fiduciary capacity.

(C) When the person having a reasonable cause to believe that a disabled adult or elder person is in need of protective services performs services as a member of the staff of a hospital, social agency, financial institution, or similar facility, such person shall notify the person in charge of the facility and such person or that person's designee shall report or cause reports to be made in accordance with the provisions of this Code section.

(2) Any other person having a reasonable cause to believe that a disabled adult or elder person is in need of protective services, or has been the victim of abuse, neglect, or exploitation may report such information as provided in this Code section.

(b)(1) A report that a disabled adult or elder person who is not a resident of a long-term care facility as defined in Code Section 31–8–80 is in need of protective services or has been the victim of abuse, neglect, or exploitation shall be made to an adult protection agency providing protective services, as designated by the department or, if such agency is unavailable, to an appropriate law enforcement agency or prosecuting attorney. If a report of a disabled adult or elder person abuse is made to an adult protection agency or independently discovered by the agency and the agency has reasonable cause to believe such report is true, then the agency shall immediately notify the appropriate law enforcement agency or prosecuting attorney. If the disabled adult or elder person is a resident of a long-term care facility as defined in Code Section 31–8–80, a report shall be made in accordance with Article 4 of Chapter 8 of Title 31. If a report made in accordance with the provisions of this Code section alleges that the abuse or exploitation occurred within a long-term care facility, such report shall be investigated in accordance with Articles 3 and 4 of Chapter 8 of Title 31.

(2) The report may be made by oral or written communication. The report shall include the name and address of the disabled adult or elder person and should include the name and address of the disabled adult's or elder person's caretaker, the age of the disabled adult or elder person, the nature and extent of the disabled adult's or elder person's injury or condition resulting from abuse, exploitation, or neglect, and other pertinent information. All such reports prepared by a law enforcement agency shall be forwarded to the director within 24 hours.

(c) Anyone who makes a report pursuant to this chapter, who testifies in any judicial proceeding arising from the report, who provides protective services, or who participates in a required investigation under the provisions of this chapter shall be immune from any civil or criminal liability on account of such report or testimony or participation, unless such person acted in bad faith, with a malicious purpose, or was a party to such crime or fraud. Any financial institution, as defined in Code Section 7–1–4, including without limitation officers and directors thereof, that is an employer of anyone who makes a report pursuant to this chapter in his or her capacity as an employee, or who testifies in any judicial proceeding arising from a report made in his or her capacity as an employee, or who participates in a required investigation under the provisions of this chapter in his or her capacity as an employee, shall be immune from any civil or criminal liability on account of such report or testimony or participation of its employee, unless such financial institution knew or should have known that the employee acted in bad faith or with a malicious purpose and failed to take reasonable and available measures to prevent such employee from acting in bad faith or with a malicious purpose. The immunity described in this subsection shall apply not only with respect to the acts of making a report, testifying in a judicial proceeding arising from a report, providing protective services, or participating in a required investigation but also shall apply with respect to the content of the information communicated in such acts.

Laws 1981, p. 1320, § 4; Laws 1984, p. 785, § 1; Laws 1992, p. 6, § 30; Laws 1996, p. 1608, § 1; Laws 1997, p. 700, § 2; Laws 2000, p. 1085, § 6.

§ 30–5–5. Investigation; protective services

(a) When the director receives a report that a disabled adult or elder person is in need of protective services, he or she shall conduct or have conducted a prompt and thorough investigation to determine whether the disabled adult or elder person is in need of protective services and what services are needed. The investigation shall include a visit to the person and consultation with others having knowledge of the facts of the particular case. Within ten days after receipt of the report, the director shall acknowledge receipt of the report, in writing, to the person making the report.

(b) Any person conducting an investigation required by this Code section who is unable to gain access to the disabled adult or elder person as a result of interference by another person may petition the court for an order authorizing the investigation and prohibiting interference therewith, which petition shall allege specific facts in support thereof. A hearing upon such petition and notice thereof shall be carried out pursuant to subsection (f) of this Code section. If as a result of the hearing the court finds probable cause to believe that the person named in the petition is a disabled adult in need of protective services or an elder person needing protective services and that any other person is interfering with the conduct of an investigation required under this Code section, the court may issue an order authorizing that investigation and prohibiting interference therewith by any person.

(c) If as a result of an investigation conducted under this chapter the director determines that a disabled adult or elder person is in need of protective services, the director shall immediately provide or arrange for protective services for any disabled adult or elder person who consents thereto.

(d) Any person providing protective services as authorized by subsection (c) of this Code section who determines that another person is interfering with the provision of such services may petition the court for an order authorizing such services and prohibiting interference therewith. Such petition shall allege specific facts in support thereof, including, but not limited to, the results of any investigation required to be made under this chapter. A hearing upon such petition and notice thereof shall be carried out pursuant to subsection (f) of this Code section. If as a result of the hearing the court finds by clear and convincing evidence that the person named in the petition is a disabled adult in need of protective services or an elder person needing protective services and that any other person is interfering with the provision of such services, the court may issue an order authorizing the provision of such services and prohibiting the interference therewith by any person.

(e) Protective services may not be provided under this chapter to any person who does not consent to such services or who, having consented, withdraws such consent. Nothing in this chapter shall prohibit the department from petitioning for the appointment of a guardian for a disabled adult or elder person pursuant to Chapters 4 and 5 of Title 29.

(f) A hearing on any petition filed under this Code section shall be held no sooner than five and no later than ten days after such petition is filed, unless a continuance is granted. At least three days prior to such hearing, notice thereof shall be served on the petitioner and notice and copy of the petition shall be served on the person alleged to be a disabled adult in need of protective services or an elder person needing protective services and on such person or persons named in the petition as interfering with the investigation or with the provision of protective services, as applicable. Notice shall be served either in person or by first-class mail. Any person willfully violating any order issued pursuant to this Code section shall be in contempt of the court issuing such order and may be punished accordingly by the judge of that court.

(g) The expenses of the court and the hearing officer for any hearing conducted under this Code section shall be the same as those provided in Code Section 37–3–122 and shall be paid as provided therein. A disabled adult or elder person shall be deemed to be a patient under Code Section 37–3–122 only for purposes of determining hearing expenses thereunder. Nothing in this Code section shall authorize the payment of attorney's fees for any hearing conducted under this Code section.

(h) Notwithstanding any other provisions of this Code section, if the director or adult protection agency employee receives a report or gains knowledge that a disabled adult or elder person is in need of protective services and such disabled adult or elder person may be in imminent danger resulting from abuse, exploitation, or neglect, the director or designee of the director may file a petition with the probate or superior court stating the grounds on which the director or designee of the director believes that the disabled adult or elder person may be in imminent danger and seeking immediate access to such person. The judge, in his or her discretion, may issue an ex parte order requiring the caretaker or any other person at the place where the disabled adult or elder person resides to afford an adult protection agency employee immediate access to such person to determine the person's well–being. If the adult protection agency employee is denied access to the disabled adult or elder person, the employee shall contact immediately a law enforcement officer to assist the employee in enforcing such order. Any person willfully violating any order issued pursuant to this subsection shall be in contempt of the court issuing such order and may be punished accordingly by the judge of the court. The adult protection agency employee shall conduct a brief investigation to determine the condition of the disabled adult or elder person.

Laws 1981, p. 1320, § 5; Laws 1984, p. 785, § 2; Laws 1985, p. 149, § 30; Laws 1997, p. 700, § 2; Laws 1999, p. 562, § 6; Laws 2004, Act 460, § 6, eff. July 1, 2005; Laws 2005, Act 91, § 7, eff. July 1, 2005.

Historical and Statutory Notes

The 2004 amendment by Act 460, in subsec. (e), substituted "Chapters 4 and 5" for "Chapter 5".

Laws 2004, Act 460, § 16, provides:

"This Act shall become effective on July 1, 2005, and all appointments of guardians of the person or property made pursuant to former Title 29 shall continue in effect and shall thereafter be governed by the provisions of this Act."

§ 30–5–6. Cooperation of departments and agencies

(a) The staff and physicians of local health departments, mental health clinics, and other public agencies shall cooperate fully with the director in the performance of the director's duties under this chapter.

(b) The director may contract with an agency or private physician for the purpose of providing immediate accessible medical evaluations in the location that the director deems most appropriate.

(c) The Board of Human Services shall adopt regulations to ensure the effective implementation of this chapter.

Laws 1981, p. 1320, § 6; Laws 1997, p. 700, § 2; Laws 2009, Act 102, § 2–3, eff. July 1, 2009.

§ 30–5–7. Records confidential

All records pertaining to the abuse, neglect, or exploitation of disabled adults or elder persons in the custody of the department shall be confidential; and access thereto by persons other than the department, the director, or the district attorney shall only be by valid subpoena or order of any court of competent jurisdiction. Nothing in this Code section shall be construed to deny state agencies participating in joint investigations at the request of and with the department or to deny law enforcement personnel who are conducting an investigation into any criminal offense in which an elder person is a victim from having access to such records.

Laws 1981, p. 1320, § 7; Laws 1997, p. 700, § 2; Laws 1999, p. 562, § 7; Laws 2009, Act 102, § 2–14, eff. July 1, 2009.

§ 30–5–8. Unlawful acts

(a)(1) In addition to any other provision of law, the abuse, neglect, or exploitation of any disabled adult or elder person shall be unlawful.

(2) In addition to any other provision of law, it shall be unlawful for a person to act with the specific intent to abuse, neglect, or commit exploitation of any disabled adult. For purposes of this paragraph only, the term "disabled adult" means a person 18 years of age or older who is:

(A) A resident of a long-term care facility, as defined in Article 4 of Chapter 8 of Title 31; and

(B) Mentally or physically incapacitated or has Alzheimer's disease, as defined in Code Section 31–8–180, or dementia, as defined in Code Section 49–6–72.

An owner, officer, administrator, or board member of a long-term care facility shall not be held criminally liable for the actions of a person who is convicted pursuant to this paragraph. Nothing in this paragraph shall be construed to preempt any other law or to deny to any individual any rights or remedies which are provided under any other law.

(3) Except as otherwise provided in Title 16, any person violating the provisions of this subsection shall be guilty of a felony and, upon conviction, shall be punished by imprisonment for not less than one nor more than five years.

(b)(1) It shall be unlawful for any person or official required by paragraph (1) of subsection (a) of Code Section 30–5–4 to report a case of disabled adult or elder person abuse to fail knowingly and willfully to make such report.

(2) Any person violating the provisions of this subsection shall be guilty of a misdemeanor.

(c) Any violation of this Code section shall constitute a separate offense.

Laws 1984, p. 785, § 3; Laws 1997, p. 700, § 2; Laws 1999, p. 562, § 8; Laws 2001, p. 484, § 1; Laws 2003, Act 50, § 1A, eff. July 1, 2003; Laws 2007, Act 126, § 2, eff. July 1, 2007; Laws 2009, Act 147, § 2, eff. July 1, 2009; Laws 2010, Act 624, § 30, eff. June 3, 2010.

Historical and Statutory Notes

The 2003 amendment by Act 50 substituted "felony and, upon conviction, shall be punished by imprisonment for not less than one not more than five years" for "misdemeanor of a high and aggravated nature" in subsec. (a), par. (2).

The 2007 amendment by Act 126 substituted "the abuse, neglect, or exploitation of any disabled adult or elder person shall be unlawful" for "it shall be unlawful for any person to abuse, neglect, or exploit any disabled adult or elder person" in subsec. (a), par. (1).

The 2009 amendment by Act 147, in subsec. (a), redesignated par. (2) as par. (3) and added new par. (2).

The 2010 amendment by Act 624 was a provision in a corrections bill.

§ 30–5–9. Construction relative to employment of disabled adult or elder person

Nothing in this chapter shall be construed to limit the application of Code Section 34–7–1 to the employment relationship between a disabled adult or elder person and his or her employer or to create a new cause of action as a result of the employment relationship.

Laws 1997, p. 700, § 2.

§ 30–5–10. Development of training programs concerning abuse and exploitation of persons 65 years of age or older

The Department of Human Services, the Georgia Peace Officer Standards and Training Council, the Prosecuting Attorneys' Council of the State of Georgia, and the Institute of Continuing Judicial Education shall develop programs for the education and training of social services, criminal justice, and judicial professionals concerning the abuse and exploitation of persons who are 65 years of age or older. Said agencies, together with any other agency of this state which is involved in the investigation of the abuse or exploitation of persons who are 65 years of age or older, are directed to cooperate in the development of such training programs to the extent allowable under Article I, Section II, Paragraph III of the Constitution of this state.

Laws 2000, p. 1085, § 7; Laws 2009, Act 102, § 2–2, eff. July 1, 2009.

Historical and Statutory Notes

In 2000, the Code Commission, in the first sentence, substituted "Officer" for "Officers". See § 28–9–5.

TITLE 31

HEALTH

CHAPTER 22

CLINICAL LABORATORIES

§ 31–22–9.1. Definitions of AIDS and HIV related terms

(a) As used in this Code section, the term:

(1) "AIDS" means Acquired Immunodeficiency Syndrome or AIDS Related Complex within the reporting criteria of the department.

(2) "AIDS confidential information" means information which discloses that a person:

(A) Has been diagnosed as having AIDS;

(B) Has been or is being treated for AIDS;

(C) Has been determined to be infected with HIV;

(D) Has submitted to an HIV test;

(E) Has had a positive or negative result from an HIV test;

(F) Has sought and received counseling regarding AIDS; or

(G) Has been determined to be a person at risk of being infected with AIDS,

and which permits the identification of that person.

(3) "AIDS transmitting crime" means any of the following offenses specified in Title 16:

(A) Rape;

(B) Sodomy;

(C) Aggravated sodomy;

(D) Child molestation;

(E) Aggravated child molestation;

(F) Prostitution;

(G) Solicitation of sodomy;

(H) Incest;

(I) Statutory rape; or

(J) Any offense involving a violation of Article 2 of Chapter 13 of Title 16, regarding controlled substances, if that offense involves heroin, cocaine, derivatives of either, or any other controlled substance in Schedule I, II, III, IV, or V and that other substance is commonly intravenously injected, as determined by the regulations of the department.

(4) "Body fluids" means blood, semen, or vaginal secretions.

(5) "Confirmed positive HIV test" means the results of at least two separate types of HIV tests, both of which indicate the presence of HIV in the substance tested thereby.

(6) "Counseling" means providing the person with information and explanations medically appropriate for that person which may include all or part of the following: accurate information regarding AIDS and HIV; an explanation of behaviors that reduce the risk of transmitting AIDS and HIV; an explanation of the confidentiality of information relating to AIDS diagnoses and HIV tests; an explanation of information regarding both social and medical implications of HIV tests; and disclosure of commonly recognized treatment or treatments for AIDS and HIV. The Department of Community Health shall develop brochures or other documents which meet the requirements of this paragraph and, upon delivery of such a brochure or document or of another brochure or document approved by the Department of Community Health to the person and referral of that person to the Department of Community Health for further information and explanations, counseling shall be deemed to have been provided within the meaning of this paragraph.

(7) "Determined to be infected with HIV" means having a confirmed positive HIV test or having been clinically diagnosed as having AIDS.

(8) "Health care facility" means any:

(A) Institution or medical facility, as defined in Code Section 31–7–1;

(B) Facility for the mentally ill, developmentally disabled, or alcoholic or drug dependent persons, as defined in Code Sections 37–3–1, 37–4–2, and 37–7–1, respectively;

(C) Medical, dental, osteopathic, or podiatric clinic;

(D) Hospice, as defined in Code Section 31–7–172;

(E) Clinical laboratory, as defined in Code Section 31–22–1; or

(F) Administrative, clerical, or support personnel of any legal entity specified in subparagraphs (A) through (E) of this paragraph.

(9) "Health care provider" means any of the following persons licensed or regulated by the state:

(A) Physician or physician assistant;

(B) Osteopath;

(C) Podiatrist;

(D) Midwife;

(E) Dentist, dental technician, or dental hygienist;

(F) Respiratory care professional, certified respiratory therapy technician, or registered respiratory therapist;

(G) Registered nurse;

(H) Licensed practical nurse;

(I) Emergency medical technician, paramedic, or cardiac technician;

(J) Clinical laboratory director, supervisor, technician, or technologist;

(K) Funeral director or embalmer;

(L) Member of a hospice team, as defined in Code Section 31–7–172;

(M) Nursing home administrator;

(N) Professional counselor, social worker, or marriage and family therapist;

(O) Psychologist;

(P) Administrative, clerical, or support personnel, whether or not they are licensed or regulated by the state, of any person specified in subparagraphs (A) through (O) of this paragraph;

(Q) Trainee, student, or intern, whether or not they are licensed or regulated by the state, of any persons listed in subparagraphs (A) through (O) of this paragraph; or

(R) First responder, as defined in Chapter 11 of this title, although such person is not licensed or regulated by the state.

(10) "HIV" means any type of Human Immunodeficiency Virus, Human T-Cell Lymphotropic Virus Types III or IV,

Lymphadenopathy Associated Virus Types I or II, AIDS Related Virus, or any other identified causative agent of AIDS.

(11) "HIV infected person" means a person who has been determined to be infected with HIV, whether or not that person has AIDS, or who has been clinically diagnosed as having AIDS.

(12) "HIV test" means any antibody, antigen, viral particle, viral culture, or other test to indicate the presence of HIV in the human body, which test has been approved for such purposes by the regulations of the department.

(13) "Institutional care facility" means any:

(A) Health care facility;

(B) Child welfare agency, as defined in Code Section 49–5–12;

(C) Group care facility, as defined in Code Section 49–5–3;

(D) Penal institution; or

(E) Military unit.

(14) "Knowledge of being infected with HIV" means actual knowledge of:

(A) A confirmed positive HIV test; or

(B) A clinical diagnosis of AIDS.

(15) "Law" means federal or state law.

(16) "Legal entity" means a partnership, association, joint venture, trust, governmental entity, public or private corporation, health care facility, institutional care facility, or any other similar entity.

(17) "Military unit" means the smallest organizational unit of the organized militia of the state, as defined in Code Section 38–2–2, or of any branch of the armed forces of the United States, which unit is commanded by a commissioned officer.

(18) "Penal institution" means any jail, correctional institution, or similar facility for the detention of violators of state laws or local ordinances.

(19) "Person" means a natural person.

(20) "Person at risk of being infected with HIV" means any person who may have already come in contact with or who may in the future reasonably be expected to come in contact with the body fluids of an HIV infected person.

(21) "Physician" means any person licensed to practice medicine under Chapter 34 of Title 43.

(22) "Public safety agency" means that governmental unit which directly employs a public safety employee.

(23) "Public safety employee" means an emergency medical technician, firefighter, law enforcement officer, or prison guard, as such terms are defined in Code Section 45–9–81, relating to indemnification of such personnel for death or disability.

(b) Notwithstanding the provisions of Code Section 31–21–10 and Code Section 31–22–11, no person or legal entity, other than an insurer authorized to transact business in this state, shall submit for an HIV test any human body fluid or tissue to any person or legal entity except to:

(1) A clinical laboratory licensed under this chapter;

(2) A clinical laboratory exempt from licensure under Code Section 31–22–9; or

(3) A clinical laboratory licensed as such pursuant to the laws of any other state.

(c) No person or legal entity may sell or offer for sale any HIV test that permits any person or legal entity, including the person whose body fluids are to be tested, to perform that test other than a person or legal entity specified in paragraphs (1) through (3) of subsection (b) of this Code section.

Laws 1988, p. 1799, § 8; Laws 1989, p. 14, § 31; Laws 2002, p. 660, § 4; Laws 2002, p. 1259, § 11; Laws 2009, Act 102, §§ 1–4, 3–5, eff. July 1, 2009; Laws 2009, Act 243, § 3, eff. July 1, 2009.

Historical and Statutory Notes

In 2009, the Code Commission, in subpar. (a)(8)(B), substituted "37–4–2" for "37–4–1". See § 28–9–5.

TITLE 32

HIGHWAYS, BRIDGES, AND FERRIES

CHAPTER 1

GENERAL PROVISIONS

§ 32–1–10. Violations generally; injunctions

(a) Any person who violates any of the provisions of this title for which no specific penalty is provided, whether or not such act or omission is expressly declared elsewhere in this title to be unlawful, or who violates any of the rules and regulations issued under authority of and in accord with the provisions of this title shall be guilty of a misdemeanor; provided, however, that a violation of Code Sections 32–6–26 and 32–6–27 shall not be considered a crime.

(b) In addition to the penalty provided for in subsection (a) of this Code section, the department shall have the right to enjoin any act or omission so punishable as a misdemeanor or punished otherwise as provided elsewhere in this title.

Laws 1973, p. 947, § 1; Laws 1978, p. 1989, § 4.

Formerly Code 1933, § 95A–1101.

CHAPTER 6

REGULATION OF MAINTENANCE AND USE OF PUBLIC ROADS GENERALLY

Article 1

General Provisions

§ 32–6–1. Obstruction of, encroachment on, solicitation on, or material injury to public roads

(a) It shall be unlawful for any person to obstruct, encroach upon, solicit the sale of any merchandise on, or injure materially any part of any public road. For purposes of this Code section, the term "obstruct" shall include without limitation the causing of any buildup of rock, gravel, mud, dirt, chemicals, or other materials by continued ingress or egress of vehicles or of any natural waters dammed or redirected by diversion to an extent which presents a hazard to the traveling public.

(b) Any person who unlawfully obstructs, encroaches upon, or injures said public road shall be responsible for reimbursing the Department of Transportation or the applicable local governing authority in the case of a road which is part of a county road system or municipal street system for the costs of removal of said obstructions or encroachments and the costs of repairs to the public road incurred by such department or local governing authority, including any costs associated with traffic management; provided, however, that such costs shall be limited to those costs which are directly incurred from such damages. Costs incurred for traffic management may include, but not be limited to, costs incurred for flagging, signing, or provision of detours, provided that these activities are directly caused by the obstruction, encroachment, or injury to the public road system. The court may, in addition to any other sentence authorized by law, order a person convicted of violating this Code section to make such restitution for the offense.

(c) Nothing in this Code section shall abridge or limit any authority provided by law for the installation and operation of vending machines at welcome centers, tourist centers, and safety rest areas. Nothing in this Code section shall limit in any way the department's authority to lease property to state or federal agencies, counties, or municipalities as provided for in Code Section 32–7–5, or limit the Department of Transportation's ability to grant a license to any utility or railroad corporation as defined in Code Section 46–1–1.

Laws 1973, p. 947, § 1; Laws 1979, p. 132, § 4; Laws 1988, p. 1431, § 1; Laws 1993, p. 315, § 1; Laws 2002, p. 1126, § 4.

Formerly Code 1933, § 95A–903.

§ 32–6–2. Authority to regulate parking; unattended vehicles on right of way

Notwithstanding Code Section 40–6–200 and Code Sections 40–6–202 through 40–6–204:

(1) The department may regulate and prohibit the parking of any type of vehicle on any public road on the state highway system, including extensions thereof into or through municipalities. Whenever any state or local law enforcement officer finds a vehicle parked in violation of law or the department's regulations, such officer or employee is authorized to move such vehicle or require the driver or other person in charge of the vehicle to move the same. If the vehicle is unattended, such officer is authorized to remove or provide for the removal of such vehicle to the nearest garage or other place of safety at the owner's expense. State or local law enforcement officers and the department are further authorized, with or without the consent of the owner, to remove or have removed any obstruction, cargo, or personal property which is abandoned, unattended, or damaged as a result of a vehicle accident which the department determines to be a threat to public health or safety or to mitigate traffic congestion, and any person or towing service that is removing an obstruction, cargo, or personal property at the location of such obstruction, cargo, or personal property upon instruction by a law enforcement officer, an official of a fire department acting under the authority of paragraph (1) of Code Section 25–3–1 or paragraph (3) of Code Section 25–3–2, or an official of the department shall be liable only for gross negligence;

(2) A county may regulate and control the parking of vehicles on the county road system and to this end the county may place parking meters on or immediately adjacent to any or all such roads, except extensions into a municipality, for the purpose of authorizing timed parking in designated spaces upon the payment of a charge for such privilege. A county may also place such parking meters on or adjacent to any public road on the state highway system located within the county and outside the corporate limits of a municipality when authorized by the department pursuant to paragraph (1) of this Code section;

(3) A municipality may regulate and control the parking of vehicles on its municipal street system and on extensions of a county road system within its corporate limits and to this end may place parking meters on or immediately adjacent to any or all of such roads for the purpose of authorizing timed parking in designated spaces upon the payment of a charge for such privilege. A municipality also may place such parking meters on or adjacent to any public road on the state highway system located within the corporate limits of the municipality when authorized by the department pursuant to paragraph (1) of this Code section; and

(4) It shall be unlawful for any person to park or leave unattended any vehicle upon the right of way of any public road on the state highway system for over 48 hours.

Laws 1973, p. 947, § 1; Laws 1982, p. 3, § 32; Laws 1985, p. 149, § 32; Laws 1993, p. 370, § 1; Laws 2000, p. 951, § 2–3; Laws 2005, Act 68, § 12–1, eff. July 1, 2005; Laws 2007, Act 57, § 1, eff. May 16, 2007.

Formerly Code 1933, § 95A–904.

§ 32–6–3. Repealed by Laws 1999, p. 81, § 32, eff. April 5, 1999

Article 2

Dimensions and Weight of Vehicles and Loads

§ 32–6–20. Dimension or weight of vehicle or load

No vehicle or load shall be operated or moved upon the public roads of Georgia if a dimension or the weight of such vehicle or load exceeds the limitations specified in Code Sections 32–6–22 through 32–6–24 or in Code Section 32–6–26 unless exempted in Code Section 32–6–25 or authorized to do so by a permit issued pursuant to Code Section 32–6–28.

Laws 1927, p. 226, § 15; Laws 1973, p. 947, § 1.

Formerly Code 1933, § 68–401; Code 1933, § 95A–953.

§ 32–6–21. Renumbered § 40–6–248.1 by Laws 2006, Act 538, § 3–9, eff. July 1, 2006

Historical and Statutory Notes

Laws 2006, Act 538, § 4–1, reserved the section designation.

§ 32–6–22. Height of vehicles and loads; automobile carriers

(a) Except as authorized in subsection (b) of this Code section and except when so authorized by a permit issued pursuant to Code Section 32–6–28, no vehicle unladen or with a load shall exceed a height of 13 feet, six inches.

(b) On highways which constitute a part of The Dwight D. Eisenhower System of Interstate and Defense Highways as such term is used in 23 U.S.C. Section 127 and ramps or service streets which provide reasonable access thereto, no vehicle transporting motor vehicles (commonly known as automobile carriers) unladen or with a load shall exceed a height of 14 feet.

Laws 1927, p. 226, § 15; Laws 1941, p. 449, § 1; Laws 1956, p. 83, § 2; Laws 1959, p. 27, § 1; Laws 1964, p. 83, § 1; Laws 1968, p. 30, § 1; Laws 1973, p. 947, § 1; Laws 1996, p. 1010, § 1; Laws 2000, p. 136, § 32.

Formerly Code 1933, § 68–401; Code 1933, § 95A–956.

§ 32–6–23. Width of vehicles and loads

Unless otherwise provided in this Code section or exempted in Code Section 32–6–25 or so authorized by a permit issued pursuant to Code Section 32–6–28, no vehicle shall exceed a total outside width, including any load thereon, of 102 inches, exclusive of mirrors and accessories attached thereto, when operated on any street, road, or highway.

Laws 1927, p. 226, § 15; Laws 1941, p. 449, § 1; Laws 1951, p. 772, § 1; Laws 1956, p. 83, § 2; Laws 1959, p. 27, § 1; Laws 1964, p. 83, § 1; Laws 1968, p. 30, § 1; Laws 1973, p. 947, § 1; Laws 1979, p. 439, § 1; Laws 1983, p. 1798, § 1; Laws 1984, p. 22, § 32; Laws 1984, p. 621, § 1; Laws 1999, p. 567, § 1.

Formerly Code 1933, § 68–401; Code 1933, § 95A–957.

§ 32–6–24. Length of vehicles and load

(a) As used in this article, the term:

(1) "Bimodal semitrailer" means a detachable load-carrying unit designed to be attached to a coupling on the rear of a truck tractor by which it is partly supported during movement

over the highway and designed either with retractable flanged wheels or to attach to a detachable flanged wheel assembly for movement on the rails.

(2) "Combination of vehicles" means a semitrailer pulled by a truck tractor or a semitrailer and trailer pulled by a truck tractor operating in a truck tractor-semitrailer-trailer combination.

(3) "Extendable semitrailer" means a semitrailer that has been manufactured for the purpose of extending the frame to increase the overall length for the purpose of transporting single-piece loads.

(4) "NHS" means the National Highway System.

(5) "Semitrailer" means a detachable load-carrying unit designed to be attached to a coupling on the rear of a truck tractor by which it is partly supported.

(6) "Trailer" means a detachable load-carrying unit designed to be attached to a coupling at the rear of a semitrailer and capable of support in operation without the truck tractor.

(7) "Truck tractor" means the noncargo-carrying power unit that operates in combination with a semitrailer or trailer, except that a truck tractor and semitrailer engaged in the transportation of automobiles may transport motor vehicles on part of the power unit.

(b) Unless exempted in Code Section 32–6–25 or so authorized by a permit issued pursuant to Code Section 32–6–28, the following length limits shall apply:

(1) Trailer and semitrailer lengths:

(A) Truck tractor-semitrailer-trailer combinations shall have trailers and semitrailers that do not exceed 28 feet in length;

(B) Truck tractor-semitrailer combinations shall have semitrailers that do not exceed 53 feet in length, unless signs are posted that indicate semitrailer length restrictions;

(C) On interstate and NHS routes, single-piece loads may be transported on an extendable semitrailer that exceeds 53 feet, provided that no pieces will be loaded end to end and the semitrailer does not exceed 75 feet in length; on roads other than the interstate and NHS routes, the foregoing provisions of this subparagraph shall also apply, except that the overall length shall not exceed 100 feet. Empty extendable semitrailers or extendable semitrailers transporting a single-piece load of 53 feet or less shall be required to maintain a semitrailer length of 53 feet or less. When the semitrailer is extended as described in this subparagraph, the rear extremity of each extendable semitrailer or load shall be marked with a four-inch multidirectional amber strobe light and with 18 inch bright red or orange warning flags on the rearmost of the load or semitrailer;

(D) Maxi-cube combinations shall have a cargo box that does not exceed 34 feet, provided that the pair of cargo boxes together does not exceed 60 feet and the overall length, including the power unit, does not exceed 65 feet; and

(E) Trailer and semitrailer length requirements in this paragraph shall not apply to automobile and boat transporters; however, no unit of the vehicle shall exceed 56 feet in length; and

(2) Overall truck tractor-semitrailer or truck tractor-semitrailer-trailer lengths:

(A) Maxi-cube combinations shall have an overall length that does not exceed 65 feet;

(B) Saddlemount and saddlemount with fullmount combinations shall have an overall length that does not exceed 97 feet; and

(C) All other combinations of truck tractor-semitrailer or truck tractor-semitrailer-trailer operated on roads other than interstate or the NHS shall have an overall length that does not exceed 100 feet, unless signs are posted that indicate length restrictions. This maximum length shall include the federal allowance for automobile and boat transporter loads to overhang up to three feet over the front of the vehicle and overhang up to four feet over the rear of the vehicle.

Laws 1927, p. 226, § 15; Laws 1956, p. 83, § 2; Laws 1959, p. 27, § 1; Laws 1964, p. 83, § 1; Laws 1968, p. 30, § 1; Laws 1973, p. 947, § 1; Laws 1974, p. 1422, §§ 35, 36; Laws 1979, p. 439, § 2; Laws 1980, p. 576, §§ 1–3; Laws 1981, p. 133, § 1; Laws 1983, p. 1798, § 2; Laws 1985, p. 1002, § 1; Laws 1987, p. 414, § 1; Laws 1987, p. 1030, § 1; Laws 1989, p. 1569, § 1; Laws 1989, p. 693, § 1; Laws 1990, p. 255, § 1; Laws 1991, p. 94, § 32; Laws 1992, p. 2467, § 1; Laws 1993, p. 786, § 1; Laws 1995, p. 990, § 1; Laws 1996, p. 1010, § 2; Laws 1999, p. 567, § 2; Laws 1999, p. 828, § 1; Laws 2000, p. 136, § 32; Laws 2000, p. 1654, § 1; Laws 2001, p. 4, § 32; Laws 2010, Act 460, § 1, eff. July 1, 2010.

Formerly Code 1933, § 68–401; Code 1933, § 95A–958.

§ 32–6–25. Exemptions for farming, agricultural, and forest management equipment

The limitations of Code Section 32–6–23 as to width and of Code Section 32–6–24 as to length shall not apply to the following loads and vehicles, which may exceed such limitation without a permit: farming or agricultural equipment or forest management equipment, whether self-propelled or being hauled, when such vehicle or equipment is being operated during daylight hours upon a public road not part of The Dwight D. Eisenhower System of Interstate and Defense Highways by dealers or by the owner thereof or his agent within a radius of 40 miles of the property of the dealer or owner. The foregoing exemptions do not apply to vehicles hauling or transporting forest products.

Laws 1965, p. 206, § 1; Laws 1968, p. 30, § 1; Laws 1973, p. 947, § 1; Laws 1974, p. 532, § 1; Laws 2000, p. 136, § 32.

Formerly Code 1933, § 95A–954.

§ 32–6–25.1. Exemptions for vehicles or equipment used within or within radius of ten miles of port facility

The limitations of Code Section 32–6–23 as to width and of Code Section 32–6–24 as to length shall not apply to the following loads and vehicles, which may exceed such limitation without a permit: Any vehicle or equipment used for transporting cargo or containers between and within wharves, storage areas, or terminals within the facilities of any port under the jurisdiction of the Georgia Ports Authority when such vehicle or equipment is being operated upon any public road not part of The Dwight D. Eisenhower System of Interstate and Defense Highways by the owner thereof or his or her agent within a radius of ten miles of the port facility of origin and accompanied by an escort vehicle equipped with one or more operating amber flashing lights that are visible from a distance of 500 feet.

Laws 1999, p. 784, § 2; Laws 2000, p. 136, § 32.

§ 32–6–26. Weight of vehicle and load

(a) As used in this Code section, the term:

(1) "Federal bridge formula" means:

$$W = 500 \left(\frac{LN}{N-1} + 12N + 36 \right)$$

Where W = the overall gross weight on any group of two or more consecutive axles to the nearest 500 pounds, L = the distance in feet between the extreme of any group of two or more consecutive axles, and N = the number of axles in the group under consideration.

(2) "Lift axle" means any axle on any vehicle manufactured after July 1, 1978, which axle may be raised or lowered with respect to the horizontal plane of the vehicle.

(3) "Single axle" means all the wheels whose centers may be included between two parallel transverse vertical planes 40 inches apart.

(4) "State bridge formula" means:

$$W = 500 \left(\frac{LN}{N-1} + 12N + 36 \right)$$

Where W = the maximum allowable gross weight of the vehicle or combination of vehicles to the nearest 500 pounds, L = the distance in feet between the first and last axles of the vehicle or combination of vehicles, and N = the number of axles on the vehicle or combination of vehicles.

(5) "Tandem axle" means two or more consecutive axles, excluding the steering axle, which extend across the full width of the vehicle and whose centers may be included between parallel vertical planes spaced more than 40 inches apart but not more than 216 inches apart.

(b) Except when authorized by a permit issued pursuant to Code Section 32–6–28 and except as otherwise provided in this Code section:

(1) No vehicle equipped with high pressure pneumatic, solid rubber, or cushion tires and operated upon any public road of this state shall carry a load on any wheel which exceeds 8,000 pounds by more than 13 percent or a load on any single axle which exceeds 16,000 pounds by more than 13 percent; and

(2) No vehicle equipped with low pressure pneumatic tires and operated upon any public road of this state shall carry a load on any wheel which exceeds 9,000 pounds by more than 13 percent or a load on any single axle which exceeds 18,000 pounds by more than 13 percent.

(c)(1)(A) On all highways within this state which are not interstate highways, the maximum total gross weight authorized for any vehicle and load shall not exceed 80,000 pounds; the maximum load authorized on any single axle shall be as provided in subsection (b) of this Code section; the maximum load on any tandem axle shall be 40,680 pounds; and subject to subparagraph (B) and subparagraph (C) of this paragraph, the maximum total gross weight authorized for any vehicle and load shall be the maximum load authorized on any single axle multiplied by the number of axles with which the vehicle is equipped.

(B) For vehicles and loads with an actual total gross weight between 73,280 pounds and 80,000 pounds, the maximum total gross weight authorized for the vehicle and load shall be determined by applying the state bridge formula.

(C) For any vehicle equipped with four axles, the maximum total gross weight authorized for the vehicle and load shall be 70,000 pounds.

(2) Reserved.

(3) No lift axle may be used in computing the maximum total gross weight authorized for any vehicle or load.

(d)(1)(A) On all highways within this state which are interstate highways, the maximum total gross weight authorized for any vehicle and load shall not exceed 80,000 pounds; the maximum load authorized on any single axle shall be as provided in subsection (b) of this Code section; and, except as provided in subparagraph (B) of this paragraph, the maximum overall gross weight in pounds on a group of two or more consecutive axles shall be determined by applying the federal bridge formula. In applying the formula, no lift axle shall be counted as an individual or additional axle when determining the maximum overall gross weight.

(B) Notwithstanding the provisions of subparagraph (A) of this paragraph, the maximum load authorized on any tandem axle shall be 34,000 pounds, and any two consecutive sets of tandem axles may carry a gross load of 34,000 pounds each if the overall distance between the first and last axles of such consecutive sets of tandem axles is 36 feet or more; however, except for vehicles and combinations of vehicles exceeding 55 feet in length, the maximum gross weight authorized on a tandem axle for a vehicle or combination of vehicles carrying a gross weight of less than 73,280 pounds shall be 40,680 pounds.

(2) If at any time federal law authorizes any weight greater than that authorized by this subsection, such greater weight under federal law shall be authorized on the interstate highways within this state.

(e) Subject to the provisions of this article, the department shall be authorized, on behalf of the state, to enter into agreements with the United States Secretary of Transportation as provided in Section 127 of Title 23 of the United States Code, relating to the control of vehicle weight and width limitations, which agreements shall exempt certain vehicles from the requirements of subsection (d) of this Code section. The department shall be authorized to take action in the name of the state to comply with the terms of any such agreement and to promulgate any rules and regulations necessary to ensure the department's compliance with federal laws and to provide for the issuance of the special permits required by this Code section.

(f) On any public road of a county road system, the maximum total gross weight of a vehicle and load shall not exceed 56,000 pounds unless the vehicle is making a pickup or delivery on such road; except that if a county road is constructed to the same standards as those highways of this state which are interstate highways and is authorized as a designated local truck route pursuant to official resolution of the county and approval of the commissioner, the maximum weight limits for such designated local truck route shall be the same as those for highways in this state which are not interstate highways as provided by paragraph (1) of subsection (c) of this Code section.

(g)(1) The weight limitations provided for in this Code section, except the limitation in subsections (f) and (h) of this Code section, may be exceeded on any public road within this state which is not an interstate highway, or when making a pickup or delivery on any public road of a county road system, without a permit only when the load on any single axle does not exceed 23,000 pounds, the load on any tandem axle does not exceed 46,000 pounds, and the maximum total gross weight of the vehicle and load does not exceed 80,000 pounds when:

(A) Hauling forest products from the forest where cut to the first point of marketing or processing;

(B) Hauling live poultry or cotton from a farm to a processing plant;

(C) Hauling feed from a feed mill to a farm;

(D) Hauling granite, either block or sawed, or any other naturally occurring raw ore or mineral for further processing, from the quarry or stockpile area to a processing plant located in the same or an adjoining county and construction aggregates hauled to any point, unless otherwise prohibited;

(E) Hauling solid waste or recovered materials from points of generation to a solid waste handling facility or other processing facility; or

(F) Hauling concrete that is in a freshly mixed and unhardened state for delivery to a customer.

No lift axle may be used in computing the maximum total gross weight authorized for any vehicle or load under this paragraph.

(2) A vehicle which is hauling the products listed in subparagraph (A) or (B) of paragraph (1) of this subsection or which is hauling any other agricultural or farm product from a farm to the first point of marketing or processing shall be permitted a 5 percent variance from the weight limitations in paragraph (1) of this subsection within a 100 mile radius of the farm or point of origin. Any person who violates the load limitations provided for in this paragraph by exceeding the 5 percent variance per single axle, tandem axle, or maximum total gross weight shall be fined on the basis of the weight limitations of paragraph (1) of this subsection, including the variance allowed by this paragraph.

(3) A vehicle which is hauling the products listed in subparagraph (C), (D), or (F) of paragraph (1) of this subsection shall be permitted a 5 percent variance from the weight limitations in paragraph (1) of this subsection within a 100 mile radius of the farm or point of origin. Any person who violates the load limitations provided for in this paragraph by exceeding the 5 percent variance per single axle, tandem axle, or maximum total gross weight shall be fined on the basis of the weight limitations of paragraph (1) of this subsection and not on the basis of the variance allowed by this paragraph.

(4) Any vehicle carrying a load as authorized in this subsection at night shall be equipped with lights clearly visible for a distance of not less than 300 feet from the front and rear of the vehicle.

(h) Notwithstanding any provision of this Code section to the contrary, no vehicle or combination of vehicles shall be operated over any bridge with a posted limit which is less than the total gross weight of the vehicle and its load.

(i)(1) Any vehicle which can be made to comply with the requirements of this Code section by shifting the load and which is then loaded to comply with this Code section shall not be held to be in violation of this Code section.

(2) On all highways within this state which are not interstate highways:

(A) Except as provided in subparagraph (B) of this paragraph, for all vehicles, fines for violations of the total gross weight limitations provided for in subsection (c) of this Code section shall be based on the amount by which the actual weight of the vehicle and load exceeds the allowable maximum weight determined under subsection (c) of this Code section.

(B) For vehicles equipped with four axles, fines for violations of the total gross weight limitations provided for in subsection (c) of this Code section shall be based on the amount by which the actual weight of the vehicle and load exceeds 70,000 pounds.

(j) Except as provided in subsections (f) and (h) of this Code section, weight limits and axle definitions for any bimodal semitrailer, semitrailers, and trailers operated on highways and public roads within this state shall be weight limits and axle definitions authorized by federal law governing interstate highways.

Laws 1927, p. 226, § 16; Laws 1931, Ex. Sess., p. 114, § 2; Laws 1941, p. 449, §§ 1–3; Laws 1955, p. 392, §§ 1, 2; Laws 1956, p. 83, § 2; Laws 1964, p. 83, § 1; Laws 1968, p. 30, §§ 1, 2; Laws 1973, p. 947, § 1; Laws 1974, p. 1111, § 1; Laws 1975, p. 68, § 1; Laws 1978, p. 1965, § 1; Laws 1978, p. 1989, § 1; Laws 1980, p. 576, § 4; Laws 1983, p. 3, § 23; Laws 1983, p. 1798, §§ 3, 4; Laws 1984, p. 621, § 2; Laws 1987, p. 414, § 2; Laws 1989, p. 693, §§ 2, 3; Laws 1995, p. 862, § 1; Laws 1996, p. 1512, §§ 2, 3; Laws 1998, p. 1206, § 3; Laws 2000, p. 136, § 32; Laws 2002, p. 1484, § 1; Laws 2004, Act 479, § 22, eff. July 1, 2004; Laws 2005, Act 115, § 2, eff. July 1, 2005; Laws 2005, Act 158, § 1, eff. July 1, 2005; Laws 2006, Act 453, § 32, eff. April 14, 2006; Laws 2006, Act 540, § 1, eff. July 1, 2006; Laws 2007, Act 133, § 1, eff. July 1, 2007; Laws 2008, Act 425, § 1, eff. July 1, 2008.

Formerly Code 1933, §§ 68–402, 68–702; Code 1933, § 95A–959.

§ 32–6–27. Enforcement of load limitations

(a) Any person who violates the load limitation provisions of Code Section 32–6–26 shall be conclusively presumed to have damaged the public roads, including bridges, of this state by reason of such overloading and shall recompense the state for such damage in accordance with the following schedule:

(1) Five cents per pound for all excess weight over the allowed weight limitations, including any applicable variances;

(2) For the following vehicles, damages for excess weight shall be assessed at 125 percent times the rate imposed on offending vehicles operating without a permit:

(A) Where a vehicle is authorized to exceed the weight limitations of Code Section 32–6–26 by a permit issued pursuant to Code Section 32–6–28, the term "excess weight" means that weight which exceeds the weight allowed by such permit; and

(B) Where a vehicle is authorized to exceed the weight limitations of Code Section 32–6–26 by a permit issued pursuant to Code Section 32–6–28 as a superload permit or superload plus permit, the term "excess weight" means:

(i) Any single axle weight which exceeds any single axle weight allowed by such permit; and

(ii) All weight greater than 150,000 pounds when the gross weight of the vehicle and load exceeds the gross weight allowed by such permit or when any axle spacing is less than that specified by such permit; or

(3) Any vehicle that utilizes idle reduction technology shall have any penalty for violating Code Section 32–6–26, except for subsections (f) and (h), calculated by reducing from the actual gross weight, single axle weight, tandem axle weight, or the allowed weight on any group of two or more axles the manufacturer's certified weight of the idle reducing technology or 400 pounds, whichever is less. The operator of the vehicle shall present written certification from the manufacturer specifying the weight of the idle reducing technology and demonstrate that the idle reducing technology is fully functional at all times when so requested by any law enforcement officer or employee of the Department of Public Safety.

(a.1)(1)(A) The Department of Public Safety is authorized to issue a citation to the owner or operator of any vehicle in violation of a maximum weight limit on a county road which is a designated local truck route under subsection (f) of Code Section 32–6–26 and for which signs have been placed and maintained as required under paragraph (2) of subsection (c) of Code Section 32–6–50.

(B) The Department of Public Safety is authorized to issue a warning to the owner or operator of any vehicle in violation of a maximum weight limit on a county road which is a designated local truck route under subsection (f) of Code Section 32–6–26 but for which signs have not been placed or maintained as required under paragraph (2) of subsection (c) of Code Section 32–6–50 upon the first such violation and to issue a citation to such owner or operator for a subsequent such violation.

(2)(A) The Department of Public Safety is authorized to issue a citation to the owner or operator of any vehicle in violation of a maximum weight limit on a bridge for which signs have been placed and maintained as required under paragraph (3) of Code Section 32–4–41 or subsection (a.1) of Code Section 32–4–91.

(B) The Department of Public Safety is authorized to issue a warning to the owner or operator of any vehicle in violation of a maximum weight limit on a bridge but for which signs have not been placed or maintained as required under paragraph (3) of Code Section 32–4–41 or subsection (a.1) of Code Section 32–4–91 upon the first such violation and to issue a citation to such owner or operator for a subsequent such violation.

(b) The schedules listed in paragraphs (1) and (2) of subsection (a) of this Code section shall apply separately to:

(1) The excess weight of the gross load; and

(2) The sum of the excess weight or weights of any axle or axles; provided, however, that where both gross load and axle weight limits are exceeded, the owner or operator shall be required to recompense the state only for the largest of the money damages imposed under paragraphs (1) and (2) of this subsection.

(c)(1) Within 30 days after the issuance of the citation, the owner or operator of any offending vehicle shall pay the amount of the assessment to the Department of Public Safety or request an administrative determination of the amount and validity of the assessment.

(2) The right to an administrative determination of the amount and validity of the assessment shall be granted only to the owner or operator of an offending vehicle.

(3) The party requesting an administrative determination of the amount and validity of the assessment shall deposit the amount of the assessment with the Department of Public Safety, within the time permitted to request such determination, before the determination will be granted. In the event the assessment is determined to be erroneous, the Department of Public Safety shall make prompt refund of any overpayment after receipt of a final decision making such determination.

(4) If an administrative hearing is requested, it shall be held in accordance with Chapter 13 of Title 50, the "Georgia Administrative Procedure Act," and the rules and regulations of the Department of Public Safety. The scope of any such hearing shall be limited to a determination of:

(A) The weight of the offending vehicle;

(B) The maximum weight allowed by law on the roadway upon which the offending vehicle was operated; and

(C) Whether the operator had in his or her actual possession a valid oversize or overweight permit issued by the Department of Transportation allowing the vehicle to operate in excess of the maximum weight otherwise allowed by law on the roadway upon which the offending vehicle was operated.

(5) Any person who has exhausted all administrative remedies available within the Department of Public Safety and who is aggrieved by a final order of the Department of Public Safety is entitled to judicial review in accordance with Chapter 13 of Title 50.

(6) If a party requests an administrative determination of the amount and validity of the assessment and fails to appear without first obtaining permission from the administrative law judge or does not withdraw the request in writing no less than five days in advance of a scheduled hearing, the party shall be deemed in default and the citation shall be affirmed by operation of law. The party shall be deemed to owe the sum of $75.00 in addition to the amount due on the citation, which sum shall represent hearing costs.

(d) All moneys collected in accordance with this Code section shall be disposed of as follows:

(1) All moneys collected for violations of the weight limitations imposed by this article shall be remitted to the general fund of the state treasury;

(2) All moneys collected for violations of the height, width, or length limitations imposed by this article, after the appropriate statutory deductions, shall be retained by the governing authority of the county wherein the violation occurred for deposit in the general treasury of said county;

(3) Hearing costs imposed pursuant to paragraph (6) of subsection (c) of this Code section shall be retained by the Department of Public Safety;

(4) Reissuance fees imposed pursuant to paragraph (4) of subsection (g) of this Code section shall be retained by the Department of Revenue; and

(5) Restoration fees imposed pursuant to paragraph (1) of subsection (i) of this Code section shall be retained by the Department of Revenue.

(e) Any owner or operator of a vehicle which is operated on the public roads of this state in violation of the weight limitations provided in this article shall be required, in addition to paying the moneys provided in subsection (a) of this Code section, to unload all gross weight in excess of 6,000 pounds over the legal weight limit before being allowed to move the vehicle.

(f) Any person authorized by law to enforce this article may seize the offending vehicle of an owner who fails or whose operator fails to pay the moneys prescribed in subsection (a) of this Code section and hold such vehicle until the prescribed moneys are paid. If the offending vehicle is not registered in this state, any person authorized by law to enforce this article may seize any vehicle owned or operated by an owner who fails or whose operator fails to pay the moneys prescribed in subsection (a) of this Code section and hold such vehicle until the prescribed moneys are paid. Any person seizing a vehicle under this subsection or subsection (e) of this Code section may, when necessary, store the vehicle; and the owner thereof shall be responsible for all reasonable storage charges thereon. When any vehicle is seized, held, unloaded, or partially unloaded under these subsections, the load or any part thereof shall be removed or cared for by the owner or operator of the vehicle without any liability on the part of the authorized person or of the state or any political subdivision because of damage to or loss of such load or any part thereof.

(g)(1) Whenever any person, firm, or corporation violates this article and becomes indebted to the Department of Public Safety because of such violations and fails within 30 days of the date of issuance of the overweight assessment citation either to pay the assessment or appeal to the Department of Public Safety for administrative review, as provided for in subsection (c) of this Code section, such assessment shall become a lien upon the overweight motor vehicle so found to be in violation, which lien shall be superior to all liens except liens for taxes or perfected security interests established before the debt to the Department of Public Safety was created.

(2) Whenever any person, firm, or corporation requests an administrative review, it shall be held in accordance with Chapter 13 of Title 50, the "Georgia Administrative Procedure Act." In the event that the administrative law judge finds in favor of the Department of Public Safety, the person, firm, or corporation shall pay the assessment within 30 days after that decision becomes final or, if judicial review is had in accordance with Chapter 13 of Title 50, then within 30 days after final judicial review is terminated. If the person, firm, or corporation fails to pay the assessment within 30 days, such assessment shall become a lien as provided for under paragraph (1) of this subsection.

(3) The Department of Public Safety shall perfect the lien created under this subsection by sending notice thereof on a notice designated by the commissioner of public safety, by first–class mail or by statutory overnight delivery, to the owner and all holders of liens and security interests shown on the records of the Department of Revenue maintained pursuant to Chapter 3 of Title 40. Upon receipt of notice from the Department of Public Safety, the holder of the certificate of title shall surrender same to the state revenue commissioner for issuance of a replacement certificate of title bearing the lien of the department unless the assessment is paid within 30 days of the receipt of notice. The Department of Revenue may append the lien to its records, notwithstanding the failure of the holder of the certificate of title to surrender said certificate as required by this paragraph.

(4) Upon issuance of a title bearing the lien of the Department of Public Safety, or the appending of the lien to the records of the Department of Revenue, the owner of the vehicle or the holder of any security interest or lien shown in the records of the Department of Revenue may satisfy such lien by payment of the amount of the assessment, including hearing costs, if any, and payment of a reissuance fee of $100.00. Upon receipt of such amount, the Department of Public Safety shall release its lien and the Department of Revenue shall issue a new title without the lien.

(h)(1) The Department of Public Safety, in seeking to foreclose its lien on the motor vehicle arising out of an overweight motor vehicle citation assessed under this article, may seek an immediate writ of possession from the court before whom the petition is filed, if the petition contains a statement of facts, under oath, by the Department of Public Safety, its agents, its officers, or attorney setting forth the basis of the petitioner's claim and sufficient grounds for issuance of an immediate writ of possession.

(2) The Department of Public Safety shall allege under oath specific facts sufficient to show that it is within the power of the defendant to conceal, encumber, convert, convey, or remove from the jurisdiction of the court the property which is the subject matter of the petition.

(3) The court before whom the petition is pending shall issue a writ for immediate possession, upon finding that the petitioner has complied with paragraphs (1) and (2) of this subsection. If the petitioner is found not to have made sufficient showing to obtain an immediate writ of possession, the court may, nevertheless, treat the petition as one being filed under Code Section 44–14–231 and proceed accordingly.

(4) When an immediate writ of possession has been granted, the Department of Public Safety shall proceed against the defendant in the same manner as provided for in Code Sections 44–14–265 through 44–14–269.

(i)(1) Whenever any person, firm, or corporation violates this article and fails within 30 days of the date of issuance of the overweight assessment citation either to pay the assessment or appeal to the Department of Public Safety for an administrative review as provided for under Chapter 13 of Title 50, the "Georgia Administrative Procedure Act," the Department of Revenue may act to suspend the motor vehicle registration of the vehicle involved. However, if the person, firm, or corporation requests an administrative review, the Department of Revenue shall act to suspend the registration only after the issuance of a final decision favorable to the Department of Public Safety and the requisite failure of the person, firm, or corporation to pay the assessment. Upon such failure to pay the assessment, the Department of Revenue shall send a letter to the owner of such motor vehicle notifying the owner of the suspension of the motor vehicle registration issued to the motor vehicle involved in the overweight assessment citation. Upon complying with this subsection by paying the overdue assessment and upon submitting proof of compliance and paying a $10.00 restoration fee to the Department of Revenue, the state revenue commissioner shall reinstate any motor vehicle registration suspended under this subsection. In cases where the motor vehicle registration has been suspended under this subsection for a second or subsequent time during any two-year period, the Department of Revenue shall suspend the motor vehicle registration for a period of 60 days and thereafter until the owner submits proof of compliance with this subsection and pays the $150.00 restoration fee to the Department of Revenue.

(2) Unless otherwise provided for in this Code section, notice of the effective date of the suspension of a motor vehicle registration occurs when the owner has actual knowledge or legal notice thereof, whichever first occurs. For the purposes of making any determination relating to the restoration of a suspended motor vehicle registration, no period of suspension shall be deemed to have begun until ten days after the mailing of the notice required in paragraph (1) of this subsection.

(3) For the purposes of this subsection, except where otherwise provided, the mailing of a notice to a person at the name and address shown in records of the Department of Revenue maintained under Chapter 3 of Title 40 shall, with respect to the holders of liens and security interests, be presumptive evidence that such person received the required notice.

(4) For the purposes of this subsection, except where otherwise provided, the mailing of a notice to a person or firm at the name and address shown on the overweight assessment citation shall, with respect to owners and operators of vehicles involved in an overweight assessment, be presumptive evidence that such person received the required notice.

(5) The state revenue commissioner may suspend the motor vehicle registration of any offending vehicle for which payment of an overweight assessment is made by a check that is returned for any reason.

(6) For the purposes of this subsection, where any provisions require the Department of Public Safety or the Department of Revenue to give notice to a person, which notice affects such person's motor vehicle license plate, the mailing of such notice and the name and address shown on the notice of overdue assessment citation supplied by the Department of Public Safety, as required by this subsection, shall be presumptive evidence that such person received the required notice.

Laws 1956, p. 83, § 3; Laws 1973, p. 947, § 1; Laws 1974, p. 1422, § 37; Laws 1978, p. 1989, § 2; Laws 1981, p. 998, § 1; Laws 1982, p. 3, § 32; Laws 1983, p. 3, § 23; Laws 1985, p. 149, § 32; Laws 1992, p. 1236, § 2; Laws 1998, p. 1206, § 4; Laws 2000, p. 951, §§ 2–4, 2–5; Laws 2002, p. 415, § 32; Laws 2003, Act 191, § 1, eff. July 1, 2003; Law 2005, Act 68, § 12–2, eff. July 1, 2005; Laws 2005, Act 158, § 2, eff. July 1, 2005; Laws 2006, Act 453, § 32, eff. April 14, 2006; Laws 2007, Act 133, § 2, eff. July 1, 2007; Laws 2010, Act 460, § 2, eff. July 1, 2010.

Formerly Code 1933, § 95A–960.

Historical and Statutory Notes

The 2003 amendment by Act 191 rewrote the section which had read:

"(a) Any person who violates the load limitation provisions of Code Section 32–6–26 shall be conclusively presumed to have damaged the public roads, including bridges, of this state by reason of such overloading and shall recompense the state for such damage in accordance with the following schedule:

"(1) For the first 1,000 pounds of excess weight, 0.8¢ per pound; plus 1.5¢ per pound for the next 2,000 pounds of excess weight; plus 3¢ per pound for the next 2,000 pounds of excess weight; plus 4¢ per pound for the next 3,000 pounds of excess weight; plus 5¢ per pound for all excess weight over 8,000 pounds;

"(2) Where a vehicle is authorized to exceed the weight limitations of Code Section 32–6–26 by a permit issued pursuant to Code Section 32–6–28, the term 'excess weight' means that weight which exceeds the weight allowed by such permit. For such vehicles, damages for excess weight shall be assessed according to the following schedule: 125 percent times, in each category of excess weights, the rate imposed on offending vehicles operating without a permit.

"(a.1)(1)(A) The Department of Motor Vehicle Safety is authorized to issue a citation to the owner or operator of any vehicle in violation of a maximum weight limit on a county road which is a designated local truck route under subsection (f) of Code Section 32–6–26 and for which signs have been placed and maintained as required under paragraph (2) of subsection (c) of Code Section 32–6–50.

"(B) The Department of Motor Vehicle Safety is authorized to issue a warning to the owner or operator of any vehicle in violation of a maximum weight limit on a county road which is a designated local truck route under subsection (f) of Code Section 32–6–26 but for which signs have not been placed or maintained as required under paragraph (2) of subsection (c) of Code Section 32–6–50 upon the first such violation and to issue a citation to such owner or operator for a subsequent such violation.

"(2)(A) The Department of Motor Vehicle Safety is authorized to issue a citation to the owner or operator of any vehicle in violation of a maximum weight limit on a bridge for which signs have been placed and maintained as required under paragraph (3) of Code Section 32–4–41 or subsection (a.1) of Code Section 32–4–91.

"(B) The Department of Motor Vehicle Safety is authorized to issue a warning to the owner or operator of any vehicle in violation of a maximum weight limit on a bridge but for which signs have not been placed or maintained as required under paragraph (3) of Code Section 32–4–41 or subsection (a.1) of Code Section 32–4–91 upon the first such violation and to issue a citation to such owner or operator for a subsequent such violation.

"(b) The schedules listed in paragraphs (1) and (2) of subsection (a) of this Code section shall apply separately to (1) the excess weight of the gross load and (2) the sum of the excess weight or weights of any axle or axles, provided that where both gross load and axle weight limits are exceeded, the owner or operator shall be required to recompense the state only for the largest of the money damages imposed under items (1) and (2) of this subsection.

"(c) Within 15 days after the issuance of the citation, the owner or operator of any offending vehicle shall pay the amount of the assessment to the Department of Motor Vehicle Safety or request an administrative determination of the amount and validity of the assessment. If an administrative hearing is requested, it shall be held in accordance with Chapter 13 of Title 50, the 'Georgia Administrative Procedure Act,' and the rules and regulations of the Department of Motor Vehicle Safety. Any person who has exhausted all administrative remedies available within the Department of Motor Vehicle Safety and who is aggrieved by a final order of the Department of Motor Vehicle Safety is entitled to judicial review in accordance with Chapter 13 of Title 50.

"(d) All moneys collected in accordance with this Code section shall be transmitted to the Department of Motor Vehicle Safety, thereafter to be disposed of as follows:

"(1) All moneys collected for violations of the weight limitations imposed by this article shall be remitted to the general fund of the state treasury; and

"(2) All moneys collected for violations of the height, width, or length limitations imposed by this article, after the appropriate statutory deductions, shall be retained by the governing authority of the county wherein the violation occurred for deposit in the general treasury of said county.

"(e) Any owner or operator of a vehicle which is operated on the public roads of this state in violation of the weight limitations provided in this article shall be required, in addition to paying the moneys provided in subsection (a) of this Code section, to unload all gross weight in excess of 6,000 pounds over the legal weight limit before being allowed to move the vehicle.

"(f) Any person authorized by law to enforce this article may seize the offending vehicle of an owner who fails or whose operator has failed to pay the moneys prescribed in subsection (a) of this Code section and hold such vehicle until the prescribed moneys are paid. Any person seizing such vehicle under this subsection or subsection (e) of this Code section may, when necessary, store the vehicle; and the owner thereof shall be responsible for all reasonable storage charges thereon. When any vehicle is seized, held, unloaded, or partially unloaded under these subsections, the load or any part thereof shall be removed or cared for by the owner or operator of the vehicle without any liability on the part of the authorized person or of the state or any political subdivision because of damage to or loss of such load or any part thereof.

"(g)(1) Whenever any person, firm, or corporation violates this article and becomes indebted to the Department of Motor Vehicle Safety because of such violations and fails within 15 days of the date of issuance of the overweight assessment citation either to pay the assessment or appeal to the Department of Motor Vehicle Safety for administrative review, as provided for in subsection (c) of this Code section, such assessment shall become a lien upon the overweight motor vehicle so found to be in violation, which lien shall be superior to all liens except liens for taxes or perfected security interests established before the debt to the Department of Motor Vehicle Safety was created.

"(2) Whenever any person, firm, or corporation requests an administrative review, it shall be held in accordance with Chapter 13 of Title 50, the 'Georgia Administrative Procedure Act.' In the event that the administrative law judge finds in favor of the Department of Motor Vehicle Safety, the person, firm, or corporation shall pay the assessment within 30 days after the issuance of a final decision by the administrative law judge or, if judicial review is had in accordance with Chapter 13 of Title 50, then within 30 days after final judicial review is terminated. If the person, firm, or corporation fails to pay the assessment within 30 days, such assessment shall become a lien as provided for under paragraph (1) of this subsection.

"(3) The Department of Motor Vehicle Safety shall perfect the lien created under this subsection in the same manner as is provided for in subsection (b) of Code Section 40–3–50 and Code Section 40–3–53.

"(h)(1) The Department of Motor Vehicle Safety, in seeking to foreclose its lien on the motor vehicle arising out of an overweight motor vehicle citation assessed under this article, may seek an immediate writ of possession from the court before whom the petition is filed, if the petition contains a statement of facts, under oath, by the Department of Motor Vehicle Safety, its agents, its officers, or attorney setting forth the basis of the petitioner's claim and sufficient grounds for issuance of an immediate writ of possession.

"(2) The Department of Motor Vehicle Safety shall allege under oath specific facts sufficient to show that it is within the power of the defendant to conceal, encumber, convert, convey, or remove from the jurisdiction of the court the property which is the subject matter of the petition.

"(3) The court before whom the petition is pending shall issue a writ for immediate possession, upon finding that the petitioner has complied with paragraphs (1) and (2) of this subsection. If the petitioner is found not to have made sufficient showing to obtain an immediate writ of possession, the court may, nevertheless, treat the petition as one being filed under Code Section 44–14–231 and proceed accordingly.

"(4) When an immediate writ of possession has been granted, the Department of Motor Vehicle Safety shall proceed against the defendant in the same manner as provided for in Code Sections 44–14–265 to 44–14–269.

"(i)(1) Whenever any person, firm, or corporation violates this article and fails within 15 days of the date of issuance of the overweight assessment citation either to pay the assessment or appeal to the Department of Motor Vehicle Safety for an administrative review as provided for under Chapter 13 of Title 50, the 'Georgia Administrative Procedure Act,' the Department of Motor Vehicle Safety may act to suspend the motor vehicle license plate of the vehicle involved. However, if the person, firm, or corporation requests an administrative review, the Department of Motor Vehicle Safety shall act to suspend the license plate only after the issuance of a final decision favorable to the Department of Motor Vehicle Safety and the requisite failure of the person, firm, or corporation to pay the assessment. Upon such failure to pay the assessment, the Department of Motor Vehicle Safety shall send a letter to the owner of such motor vehicle stating the fact of such overdue assessment. Upon receipt of such letter from the Department of Motor Vehicle Safety, it shall be the duty of the owner of such vehicle to notify the Department of Motor Vehicle Safety, within 15 days of the date on which notification was mailed by the Department of Motor Vehicle Safety, as to whether the assessment has been paid. If such information is not received by the Department of Motor Vehicle Safety within the specified time period or if the assessment has not in fact been paid, the Department of Motor Vehicle Safety shall suspend the motor vehicle license plate issued to the motor vehicle involved in the overweight assessment citation and shall notify the owner of the motor vehicle that he or she must forward the motor vehicle license plate issued to such motor vehicle to the Department of Motor Vehicle Safety. Upon complying with this subsection by paying the overdue assessment and upon submitting proof of compliance and paying a $ 10.00 restoration fee to the Department of Motor Vehicle Safety, the commissioner of motor vehicle safety shall return any motor vehicle license plate suspended under this subsection to the owner of such motor vehicle. In cases where the motor vehicle license plate has been suspended under this subsection for a second or subsequent time during any two-year period, the Department of Motor Vehicle Safety shall suspend the motor vehicle license plate for a period of 60 days and thereafter until the owner submits proof of compliance with this subsection and pays the $ 25.00 restoration fee to the Department of Motor Vehicle Safety.

"(2) The Department of Motor Vehicle Safety, upon suspending the motor vehicle license plate, as provided for in this subsection, shall require that such plate be surrendered to the Department of Motor Vehicle Safety immediately following the effective date of suspension; and it is the duty of the owner, immediately upon receipt of notice from the Department of Motor Vehicle Safety, to forward the license plate to the Department of Motor Vehicle Safety.

"(3) If such motor vehicle license plate is not received by the Department of Motor Vehicle Safety within ten days following the effective date of suspension, the commissioner of motor vehicle safety shall forthwith direct any peace officer to secure possession of such plate and return the same to the commissioner of motor vehicle safety.

"(4) Unless otherwise provided for in this subsection, notice of the effective date of suspension shall occur when the driver receives actual knowledge or legal notice thereof, whichever occurs first. For the purposes of making any determination under this article relating to the return of a suspended motor vehicle license plate, no period of suspension under this subsection shall begin until the plate is surrendered to the Department of Motor Vehicle Safety or to a court of competent jurisdiction under this subsection, whichever shall occur first. If the motor vehicle license plate is lost or for any other reason surrender to the Department of Motor Vehicle Safety is impossible, the period of suspension shall begin on the date an affidavit setting forth the reasons for such impossibility is received by the department.

"(5) It shall be unlawful to refuse to deliver upon a legal demand any motor vehicle license plate.

"(6) Any person violating the provisions of paragraph (2) of this subsection shall be guilty of a misdemeanor and, upon conviction thereof, shall be subject to a fine of not more than $ 1,000.00 or imprisonment for not more than 90 days.

"(7) For the purposes of this subsection, where any provisions require the Department of Motor Vehicle Safety to give notice to a person, which notice affects such person's motor vehicle license plate, the mailing of such notice and the name and address shown on the notice of overdue assessment citation supplied by the Department of Motor Vehicle Safety, as required by this subsection, shall be presumptive evidence that such person received the required notice."

The 2005 amendment by Act 68 rewrote the section, which had read:

"(a) Any person who violates the load limitation provisions of Code Section 32–6–26 shall be conclusively presumed to have damaged the public roads, including bridges, of this state by reason of such overloading and shall recompense the state for such damage in accordance with the following schedule:

"(1) For the first 1,000 pounds of excess weight, 0.8¢ per pound; plus 1.5¢ per pound for the next 2,000 pounds of excess weight; plus 3¢ per pound for the next 2,000 pounds of excess weight; plus 4¢ per pound for the next 3,000 pounds of excess weight; plus 5¢ per pound for all excess weight over 8,000 pounds;

"(2) Where a vehicle is authorized to exceed the weight limitations of Code Section 32–6–26 by a permit issued pursuant to Code Section 32–6–28, the term "excess weight" means that weight which exceeds the weight allowed by such permit. For such vehicles, damages for excess weight shall be assessed according to the following schedule: 125 percent times, in each category of excess weights, the rate imposed on offending vehicles operating without a permit.

"(a.1)(1)(A) The Department of Motor Vehicle Safety is authorized to issue a citation to the owner or operator of any vehicle in violation of a maximum weight limit on a county road which is a designated local truck route under subsection (f) of Code Section 32–6–26 and for which signs have been placed and maintained as required under paragraph (2) of subsection (c) of Code Section 32–6–50.

"(B) The Department of Motor Vehicle Safety is authorized to issue a warning to the owner or operator of any vehicle in violation of a maximum weight limit on a county road which is a designated local truck route under subsection (f) of Code Section 32–6–26 but for which signs have not been placed or maintained as required under paragraph (2) of subsection (c) of Code Section 32–6–50 upon the first such violation and to issue a citation to such owner or operator for a subsequent such violation.

"(2)(A) The Department of Motor Vehicle Safety is authorized to issue a citation to the owner or operator of any vehicle in violation of a maximum weight limit on a bridge for which signs have been placed and maintained as required under paragraph (3) of Code Section 32–4–41 or subsection (a.1) of Code Section 32–4–91.

"(B) The Department of Motor Vehicle Safety is authorized to issue a warning to the owner or operator of any vehicle in violation of a maximum weight limit on a bridge but for which signs have not been placed or maintained as required under paragraph (3) of Code Section 32–4–41 or subsection (a.1) of Code Section 32–4–91 upon the first such violation and to issue a citation to such owner or operator for a subsequent such violation.

"(b) The schedules listed in paragraphs (1) and (2) of subsection (a) of this Code section shall apply separately to (1) the excess weight of the gross load and (2) the sum of the excess weight or weights of any axle or axles, provided that where both gross load and axle weight limits are exceeded, the owner or operator shall be required to recompense the state only for the largest of the money damages imposed under items (1) and (2) of this subsection.

"(c)(1) Within 30 days after the issuance of the citation, the owner or operator of any offending vehicle shall pay the amount of the assessment to the Department of Motor Vehicle Safety or request an administrative determination of the amount and validity of the assessment.

"(2) The right to an administrative determination of the amount and validity of the assessment shall be granted only to the owner or operator of an offending vehicle.

"(3) The party requesting an administrative determination of the amount and validity of the assessment shall deposit the amount of the assessment with the Department of Motor Vehicle Safety, within the time permitted to request such determination, before the determination will be granted. In the event the assessment is determined to be erroneous, the Department of Motor Vehicle Safety shall make prompt refund of any overpayment after receipt of a final decision making such determination.

"(4) If an administrative hearing is requested, it shall be held in accordance with Chapter 13 of Title 50, the "Georgia Administrative Procedure Act," and the rules and regulations of the Department of Motor Vehicle Safety. The scope of any such hearing shall be limited to a determination of:

"(A) The weight of the offending vehicle;

"(B) The maximum weight allowed by law on the roadway upon which the offending vehicle was operated; and

"(C) Whether the operator had in his or her actual possession a valid oversize or overweight permit issued by the Department of Transportation allowing the vehicle to operate in excess of the maximum weight otherwise allowed by law on the roadway upon which the offending vehicle was operated.

"(5) Any person who has exhausted all administrative remedies available within the Department of Motor Vehicle Safety and who is aggrieved by a final order of the Department of Motor Vehicle Safety is entitled to judicial review in accordance with Chapter 13 of Title 50.

"(6) If a party requests an administrative determination of the amount and validity of the assessment and fails to appear without first obtaining permission from the administrative law judge or does not withdraw the request in writing no less than five days in advance of a scheduled hearing, the party shall be deemed in default and the citation shall be affirmed by operation of law. The party shall be deemed to owe the sum of $75.00 in addition to the amount due on the citation, which sum shall represent hearing costs.

"(d) All moneys collected in accordance with this Code section shall be transmitted to the Department of Motor Vehicle Safety, thereafter to be disposed of as follows:

"(1) All moneys collected for violations of the weight limitations imposed by this article shall be remitted to the general fund of the state treasury;

"(2) All moneys collected for violations of the height, width, or length limitations imposed by this article, after the appropriate statutory deductions, shall be retained by the governing authority of the county wherein the violation occurred for deposit in the general treasury of said county;

"(3) Hearing costs imposed pursuant to paragraph (6) of subsection (c) of this Code section shall be retained by the Department of Motor Vehicle Safety;

"(4) Reissuance fees imposed pursuant to paragraph (4) of subsection (g) of this Code section shall be retained by the Department of Motor Vehicle Safety; and

"(5) Restoration fees imposed pursuant to paragraph (1) of subsection (i) of this Code section shall be retained by the Department of Motor Vehicle Safety.

"(e) Any owner or operator of a vehicle which is operated on the public roads of this state in violation of the weight limitations provided in this article shall be required, in addition to paying the moneys provided in subsection (a) of this Code section, to unload all gross weight in excess of 6,000 pounds over the legal weight limit before being allowed to move the vehicle.

"(f) Any person authorized by law to enforce this article may seize the offending vehicle of an owner who fails or whose operator fails to pay the moneys prescribed in subsection (a) of this Code section and hold such vehicle until the prescribed moneys are paid. If the offending vehicle is not registered in this state, any person authorized by law to enforce this article may seize any vehicle owned or operated by an owner who fails or whose operator fails to pay the moneys prescribed in subsection (a) of this Code section and hold such vehicle until the prescribed moneys are paid. Any person seizing a vehicle under this subsection or subsection (e) of this Code section may, when necessary, store the vehicle; and the owner thereof shall be responsible for all reasonable storage charges thereon. When any vehicle is seized, held, unloaded, or partially unloaded under these subsections, the load or any part thereof shall be removed or cared for by the owner or operator of the vehicle without any liability on the part of the authorized person or of the state or any political subdivision because of damage to or loss of such load or any part thereof.

"(g)(1) Whenever any person, firm, or corporation violates this article and becomes indebted to the Department of Motor Vehicle Safety because of such violations and fails within 30 days of the date of issuance of the overweight assessment citation either to pay the assessment or appeal to the Department of Motor Vehicle Safety for administrative review, as provided for in subsection (c) of this Code section, such assessment shall become a lien upon the overweight motor vehicle so found to be in violation, which lien shall be superior to all liens except liens for taxes or perfected security interests established before the debt to the Department of Motor Vehicle Safety was created.

"(2) Whenever any person, firm, or corporation requests an administrative review, it shall be held in accordance with Chapter 13 of Title 50, the "Georgia Administrative Procedure Act." In the event that the administrative law judge finds in favor of the Department of Motor Vehicle Safety, the person, firm, or corporation shall pay the assessment within 30 days after that decision becomes final or, if judicial review is had in accordance with Chapter 13 of Title 50, then within 30 days after final judicial review is terminated. If the person, firm, or corporation fails to pay the assessment within 30 days, such assessment shall become a lien as provided for under paragraph (1) of this subsection.

"(3) The Department of Motor Vehicle Safety shall perfect the lien created under this subsection by sending notice thereof on a notice designated by the commissioner of motor vehicle safety, by first-class mail or by statutory overnight delivery, to the owner and all holders of liens and security interests shown on the records of the Department of Motor Vehicle Safety maintained pursuant to Chapter 3 of Title 40. Upon receipt of notice from the Department of Motor Vehicle Safety, the holder of the certificate of title shall surrender same to the commissioner of motor vehicle safety for issuance of a replacement certificate of title bearing the lien of the department unless the assessment is paid within 30 days of the receipt of notice. The Department of Motor Vehicle Safety may append its lien to its records, notwithstanding the failure of the holder of the certificate of title to surrender said certificate as required by this paragraph.

"(4) Upon issuance of a title bearing the lien of the Department of Motor Vehicle Safety, or the appending of the lien to the records of the Department of Motor Vehicle Safety, the owner of the vehicle or the holder of any security interest or lien shown in the records of the department may satisfy such lien by payment of the amount of the assessment, including hearing costs, if any, and payment of a reissuance fee of $100.00. Upon receipt of such amount, the Department of Motor Vehicle Safety shall release its lien.

"(h)(1) The Department of Motor Vehicle Safety, in seeking to foreclose its lien on the motor vehicle arising out of an overweight motor vehicle citation assessed under this article, may seek an immediate writ of possession from the court before whom the petition is filed, if the petition contains a statement of facts, under oath, by the Department of Motor Vehicle Safety, its agents, its officers, or attorney setting forth the basis of the petitioner's claim and sufficient grounds for issuance of an immediate writ of possession.

"(2) The Department of Motor Vehicle Safety shall allege under oath specific facts sufficient to show that it is within the power of the defendant to conceal, encumber, convert, convey, or remove from the jurisdiction of the court the property which is the subject matter of the petition.

"(3) The court before whom the petition is pending shall issue a writ for immediate possession, upon finding that the petitioner has complied with paragraphs (1) and (2) of this subsection. If the petitioner is found not to have made sufficient showing to obtain an immediate writ of possession, the court may, nevertheless, treat the petition as one being filed under Code Section 44–14–231 and proceed accordingly.

"(4) When an immediate writ of possession has been granted, the Department of Motor Vehicle Safety shall proceed against the defendant in the same manner as provided for in Code Sections 44–14–265 through 44–14–269.

"(i)(1) Whenever any person, firm, or corporation violates this article and fails within 30 days of the date of issuance of the overweight assessment citation either to pay the assessment or appeal to the Department of Motor Vehicle Safety for an administrative review as provided for under Chapter 13 of Title 50, the "Georgia Administrative Procedure Act," the Department of Motor Vehicle Safety may act to suspend the motor vehicle registration of the vehicle involved. However, if the person, firm, or corporation requests an administrative review, the Department of Motor Vehicle Safety shall act to suspend the registration only after the issuance of a final decision favorable to the Department of Motor Vehicle Safety and the requisite failure of the person, firm, or corporation to pay the assessment. Upon such failure to pay the assessment, the Department of Motor Vehicle Safety shall send a letter to the owner of such motor vehicle notifying the owner of the suspension of the motor vehicle registration issued to the motor vehicle involved in the overweight assessment citation. Upon complying with this subsection by paying the overdue assessment and upon submitting proof of compliance and paying a $10.00 restoration fee to the Department of Motor Vehicle Safety, the commissioner of motor vehicle safety shall reinstate any motor vehicle registration suspended under this subsection. In cases where the motor vehicle registration has been suspended under this subsection for a second or subsequent time during any two-year period, the Department of Motor Vehicle Safety shall suspend the motor vehicle registration for a period of 60 days and thereafter until the owner submits proof of compliance with this subsection and pays the $150.00 restoration fee to the Department of Motor Vehicle Safety.

"(2) Unless otherwise provided for in this Code section, notice of the effective date of the suspension of a motor vehicle registration occurs when the owner has actual knowledge or legal notice thereof, whichever first occurs. For the purposes of making any determination relating to the restoration of a suspended motor vehicle registration, no period of suspension shall be deemed to have begun until ten days after the mailing of the notice required in paragraph (1) of this subsection.

"(3) For the purposes of this subsection, except where otherwise provided, the mailing of a notice to a person at the name and address shown in records of the Department of Motor Vehicle Safety maintained under Chapter 3 of Title 40 shall, with respect to the holders of liens and security interests, be presumptive evidence that such person received the required notice.

"(4) For the purposes of this subsection, except where otherwise provided, the mailing of a notice to a person or firm at the name and address shown on the overweight assessment citation shall, with respect to owners and operators of vehicles involved in an overweight assessment, be presumptive evidence that such person received the required notice.

"(5) The commissioner of motor vehicle safety may suspend the motor vehicle registration of any offending vehicle for which payment of an overweight assessment is made by a check that is returned for any reason.

"(6) For the purposes of this subsection, where any provisions require the Department of Motor Vehicle Safety to give notice to a person, which notice affects such person's motor vehicle license plate, the mailing of such notice and the name and address shown on the notice of overdue assessment citation supplied by the Department of Motor Vehicle Safety, as required by this subsection, shall be presumptive evidence that such person received the required notice."

The 2005 amendment by Act 158 rewrote subsec. (a), par. (1), which had read:

"(a)(1) For the first 1,000 pounds of excess weight, 0.8¢ per pound; plus 1.5¢ per pound for the next 2,000 pounds of excess weight; plus 3¢ per pound for the next 2,000 pounds of excess weight; plus 4¢ per pound for the next 3,000 pounds of excess weight; plus 5¢ per pound for all excess weight over 8,000 pounds;"

The 2006 amendments by Act 453 were provisions contained in a correction bill.

The 2007 amendment by Act 133 inserted ", including any applicable variances" in par. (1) of subsec. (a).

The 2010 amendment by Act 460 rewrote subsec. (a) which had read:

"(a) Any person who violates the load limitation provisions of Code Section 32–6–26 shall be conclusively presumed to have damaged the public roads, including bridges, of this state by reason of such overloading and shall recompense the state for such damage in accordance with the following schedule:

"(1) Five cents per pound for all excess weight over the allowed weight limitations, including any applicable variances; or

"(2) Where a vehicle is authorized to exceed the weight limitations of Code Section 32–6–26 by a permit issued pursuant to Code Section 32–6–28, the term 'excess weight' means that weight which exceeds the weight allowed by such permit. For such vehicles, damages for excess weight shall be assessed according to the following schedule: 125 percent times the rate imposed on offending vehicles operating without a permit."

§ 32–6–28. Permits for excess weight and dimensions

(a) *Generally.*

(1)(A) The commissioner or an official of the department designated by the commissioner may, in his or her discretion, upon application in writing and good cause being shown therefor, issue a permit in writing authorizing the applicant to operate or move upon the state's public roads a motor vehicle or combination of vehicles and loads whose weight, width, length, or height, or combination thereof, exceeds the maximum limit specified by law, provided that the load transported by such vehicle or vehicles is of such nature that it is a unit which cannot be readily dismantled or separated; and provided, further, that no permit shall be issued to any vehicle whose operation upon the public roads of this state threatens to unduly damage a road or any appurtenance thereto, except that the dismantling limitation specified in this Code section shall not apply to loads which consist of cotton, tobacco, concrete pipe, and plywood that do not exceed a width of nine feet or of round bales of hay that do not exceed a width of 11 feet and which are not moved on part of The Dwight D. Eisenhower System of Interstate and Defense Highways. However, vehicles transporting portable buildings and vehicles not exceeding 65 feet in length transporting boats on roads not a part of The Dwight D. Eisenhower System of Interstate and Defense Highways, regardless of whether the nature of such buildings or boats is such that they can be readily dismantled or separated, may exceed the lengths and widths established in this article, provided that a special permit for such purposes has been issued as provided in this Code section, but no such special permit shall be issued for a load exceeding 12 feet in width when such load may be readily dismantled or separated. A truck tractor and low boy type trailer may, after depositing its permitted load, return to its point of origin on the authorization of its original permit.

(B) Notwithstanding the provisions of subparagraph (A) of this paragraph, the commissioner or an official of the department designated by the commissioner may, in his or her discretion, upon application in writing and good cause being shown therefor, issue to a specific tow vehicle a permit in writing authorizing the applicant to operate or move upon the state's public roads a motor vehicle or combination of vehicles and loads for transporting not more than two modular housing units or sectional housing units if the total weight, width, length, and height of the vehicle or combination of vehicles, including the load, does not exceed the limits specified in Code Section 32–6–22 and Code Section 32–6–26. Permission to transport two modular housing units is only authorized when the modular unit transporter meets the minimum specifications contained in subparagraph (C) of this paragraph. No permit shall be issued to any vehicle or combination of vehicles whose operation upon the public roads of this state threatens the safety of others or threatens to damage unduly a road or any appurtenance thereto.

(C) A modular unit transporter shall meet all requirements of the Federal Motor Carrier Safety Administration and all state safety requirements, rules, and regulations. The modular unit transporter shall be properly registered and have a proper, current license plate. At a minimum, the modular unit transporter shall:

(i) Be constructed of 12 inch steel I beams doubled and welded together;

(ii) Have all axles equipped with brakes;

(iii) Have every floor joist on each modular section securely attached to the beams with lag bolts and washers, or lag bolts, washers, and cable winches; and

(iv) Have an overall length not to exceed 80 feet including the hitch.

(2) Permits may be issued, on application to the department, to persons, firms, or corporations without specifying license plate numbers in order that such permits which are issued on an annual basis may be interchanged from vehicle to vehicle. The department is authorized to promulgate reasonable rules and regulations which are necessary or desirable to govern the issuance of such permits, provided that such rules and regulations are not in conflict with this title or other provisions of law.

(3) Every such permit shall be carried in the vehicle or combination of vehicles to which it refers and shall be open to inspection by any police officer, state trooper, or authorized agent of the department.

(4) The application for any such permit shall specifically describe the type of permit applied for, as said types of permits are described in subsection (c) of this Code section. In addition, the application for a single-trip permit shall describe the points of departure and destination.

(5) The commissioner or an official of the department designated by the commissioner is authorized to withhold such permit or, if such permit is issued, to establish seasonal or other time limitations within which the vehicles described may be operated on the public road indicated, or otherwise to limit or prescribe conditions of operation of such vehicles when necessary to ensure against undue damage to the road foundation, surfaces, or bridge structures, and to require such undertaking or other security as may be deemed necessary to compensate the state for any injury to any roadway or bridge structure.

(6) For just cause, including, but not limited to, repeated and consistent past violations, the commissioner or an official of the department designated by the commissioner may refuse to issue or may cancel, suspend, or revoke the permit and any permit privileges of an applicant or permittee. The specific period of time of any suspension shall be determined by the department. In addition, any time the restrictions or conditions within which a permitted vehicle must be operated are violated, the permit may be immediately declared null and void.

(7) The department is authorized to promulgate rules and regulations necessary to enforce the suspension of permits authorized in this Code section.

(8) The department shall issue rules to establish a driver training and certification program for drivers of vehicles escorting oversize/overweight loads. Any driver operating a vehicle escorting an oversize/overweight load shall meet the training requirements and obtain certification under the rules issued by the department pursuant to this Code section. The rules may provide for reciprocity with other states having a similar program for escort certification. Certification credentials of the driver of an escort vehicle shall be carried in the escort vehicle and be readily available for inspection by law enforcement personnel or an authorized employee of the department. The department shall implement the vehicle escort driver training and certification program on or before July 1, 2010, and the requirements for training and certification shall be enforced beginning on January 1, 2011.

(9) Permit holders shall be required to meet the following minimum insurance standards:

(A) For loads where the gross vehicle weight is less than or equal to 10,000 pounds:

(i) For bodily injury a limit of $50,000.00 per person for injury or death as a result of any one occurrence; and

(ii) For property damage a limit of $50,000.00 for damage to property of others in any one occurrence; or

(B) For commercial motor carriers where the gross vehicle weight is greater than 10,000 pounds:

(i) For bodily injury a minimum of $300,000.00 for each person and $1 million for multiple persons for injury or death as a result of any one occurrence; and

(ii) For property damage a minimum of $1 million for damage to property of others in any one occurrence.

(b) *Duration and limits of permits.*

(1) ANNUAL PERMIT. The commissioner or an official of the department designated by the commissioner may, pursuant to this Code section, issue an annual permit which shall permit a vehicle to be operated on the public roads of this state for 12 months from the date the permit is issued even though the vehicle or its load exceeds the maximum limits specified in this article. However, except as specified in paragraph (2) of this subsection, an annual permit shall not authorize the operation of a vehicle:

(A) Whose total gross weight exceeds 100,000 pounds;

(B) Whose single axle weight exceeds 25,000 pounds;

(C) Whose total load length exceeds 100 feet;

(D) Whose total width exceeds 102 inches or whose load width exceeds 144 inches; or

(E) Whose height exceeds 14 feet and six inches.

(2) ANNUAL PERMIT PLUS. Vehicles and loads that meet the requirements for an annual permit may apply for a special annual permit to carry wider loads on the NHS. The wider load limits shall be a maximum of 14 feet wide from the base of the load to a point 10 feet above the pavement and 14 feet and eight inches for the upper portion of the load.

(2.1) SIX-MONTH PERMIT. Six-month permits may be issued for loads of tobacco or unginned cotton the widths of which do not exceed nine feet, provided that such loads shall not be operated on The Dwight D. Eisenhower System of Interstate and Defense Highways.

(3) SINGLE TRIP. Pursuant to this Code section, the commissioner may issue a single-trip permit to any vehicle or load allowed by federal law.

(c) *Fees.* The department may promulgate rules and regulations concerning the issuance of permits and charge a fee for the issuance thereof as follows:

(1) ANNUAL. Charges for the issuance of annual permits shall be $150.00 per permit.

(2) ANNUAL PERMIT PLUS. Charges for the issuance of annual permits plus shall be $500.00 per permit.

(3) SIX MONTHS. The charges for the issuance of six-month permits for loads of tobacco or unginned cotton shall be $25.00 per permit.

(4) SINGLE TRIP. Charges for the issuance of single-trip permits shall be as follows:

(A) Any load not greater than 16 feet wide, not greater than 16 feet high, and not weighing more than 150,000 pounds or any load greater than 100 feet long which does not exceed the maximum width, height, and weight limits specified by this subparagraph	$ 30.00
(B) Superload permit—Any load having a width, height, or weight exceeding the maximum limit therefor specified in subparagraph (A) of this paragraph and not weighing more than 180,000 pounds	125.00
(C) Superload plus permit—Any load having a weight exceeding the maximum limit therefor specified in subparagraph (B) of this paragraph	500.00

(d) Notwithstanding any provision of Code Section 48–2–17 to the contrary, all fees collected in accordance with this Code section shall be paid to the treasurer of the department to help defray the expenses of enforcing the limitations set forth in this article and may also be used for public road maintenance purposes in addition to any sums appropriated therefor to the department.

Laws 1968, p. 30, § 1; Laws 1969, p. 637, § 1; Laws 1971, p. 43, § 1; Laws 1971, p. 462, §§ 2, 3; Laws 1972, p. 356, §§ 1, 2; Laws 1973, p. 947, § 1; Laws 1974, p. 1422, § 38; Laws 1975, p. 400, § 1; Laws 1979, p. 439, § 4; Laws 1980, p. 576, § 7; Laws 1982, p. 3, § 32; Laws 1983, p. 1798, § 5; Laws 1986, p. 471, §§ 1–3; Laws 1986, p. 655, § 1; Laws 1987, p. 846, § 1; Laws 1992, p. 987, § 1; Laws 1992, p. 2467, §§ 2–4; Laws 1993, p. 348, § 1; Laws 1995, p. 10, § 32; Laws 1995, p. 155, § 1; Laws 1996, p. 1010, § 3; Laws 1996, p. 1512, § 3A; Laws 1999, p. 567, § 3; Laws 2000, p. 136, § 32; Laws 2000, p. 1654, § 2; Laws 2002, p. 1126, §§ 5, 6; Laws 2010, Act 460, § 3, eff. July 1, 2010.

Formerly Code 1933, § 95A–961.

§ 32–6–29. Police powers of department

(a) The Department of Transportation shall be responsible for rules and regulations relating to size and weight limits and issuance of permits under this article.

(b) The Department of Transportation shall not, however, employ any law enforcement officers or agents except as may be specifically authorized by other laws. Law enforcement responsibility for enforcement of this article shall be in the Department of Public Safety.

Laws 1960, p. 1122, § 1; Laws 1968, p. 193, § 2; Laws 1973, p. 947, § 1; Laws 1974, p. 1422, § 40; Laws 1976, p. 1500, § 1; Laws 1978, p. 1989, § 3; Laws 1979, p. 814, § 1; Laws 1982, p. 3, § 32; Laws 1993, p. 91, § 32; Laws 1993, p. 366, § 1; Laws 2000, p. 951, § 2–6; Laws 2000, p. 1199, § 1; Laws 2005, Act 68, § 12–3, eff. July 1, 2005.

Formerly Code 1933, § 95A–962.

Historical and Statutory Notes

The Code Commission redesignated subsec. (e), added to this section by Laws 2000, p. 1199, § 1, as subsec. (d) of § 40–16–2, effective when § 40–16–2 becomes effective. See § 28–9–5.

§ 32–6–30. General authority of law enforcement officers; penalty for failure to stop for examination; report of violation; consent to stop

(a) Any law enforcement officer or employee of the Department of Public Safety to whom law enforcement authority has been designated who observes a motor vehicle being operated upon a public road of the state and who has reason to believe that:

(1) Any provision of this article is being violated;

(2) The vehicle is improperly licensed in violation of Code Sections 40–2–150 through 40–2–162; or

(3) A fuel tax registration card is not being carried or that a proper distinguishing identification marker is not affixed to the vehicle in violation of Code Section 48–9–39 is authorized to stop such vehicle and weigh, measure, or inspect the same.

Violations of such licensing or fuel tax registration and identification requirements shall be reported to the Department of Revenue.

(b)(1) If the operator of the vehicle shall refuse to stop upon proper order as directed by a person authorized by subsection (a) of this Code section to stop, weigh, measure, or inspect the vehicle or its load, the operator shall be guilty of a misdemeanor and, upon conviction thereof, shall be punished by a fine not to exceed $200.00. The operator shall have the right to post an appropriate bond, which shall not exceed $400.00, when any law enforcement officer or employee of the Department of Public Safety authorized to enforce this article apprehends said operator for any violation of this article.

(2) In addition, the operator's driver's license or nonresident's driving privilege may be suspended for a period of not more than 90 days by the Department of Driver Services upon satisfactory proof of said refusal to stop or drive the vehicle upon the scales. Each person who shall apply for a Georgia driver's license, or for nonresident driving privileges, or for a renewal of same thereby consents to stop such vehicle for inspection or to drive such vehicle upon scales whenever so ordered by a law enforcement official or authorized employee of the Department of Public Safety.

Laws 1960, p. 1122, § 2; Laws 1968, p. 193, §§ 1, 3; Laws 1973, p. 947, § 1; Laws 1982, p. 3, § 32; Laws 2000, p. 951, § 2–7; Laws 2002, p. 1074, § 5; Laws 2005, Act 68, § 12–4, eff. July 1, 2005; Laws 2007, Act 18, § 32, eff. May 11, 2007.

Formerly Code 1933, § 95A–963.

Historical and Statutory Notes

In 2002, the Code Commission, in par. (a)(2), substituted "Code Sections 40-2-150 through 40-2-162" for "Code Section 40-2-150 through Code Section 40-2-162". See § 28–9–5.

The 2005 amendment by Act 68, in subsec. (a), substituted "Department of Public Safety" for "Department of Motor Vehicle Safety" in the first sentence and "Department of Revenue" for "Department of Motor Vehicle Safety or the Department of Revenue as appropriate" following "shall be reported to the" in the last sentence; and in subsec. (b), in par. (1) substituted "Department of Public Safety" for "Department of Motor Vehicle Safety", and in par. (2) substituted "Department of Driver Services" prior to "upon satisfactory proof" in the first sentence, and "Department of Public Safety" for "Department of Motor Vehicle Safety" at the end of the last sentence.

The 2007 amendment by Act 18 was a provision contained in a corrections bill.

§ 32–6–31. Effect on other laws

The provisions of Code Sections 32–1–10, 32–6–26, 32–6–27, and 32–6–29 shall not, and shall not be construed to, modify, change, or diminish any power or duty held by any other law enforcement unit, enforcement officer, or peace officer.

Laws 1978, p. 1989, § 5; Laws 1982, p. 3, § 32; Laws 2000, p. 136, § 32; Laws 2002, p. 415, § 32.

Article 3

Control of Signs and Signals

Part 2

State Highway System

§ 32–6–91. Penalty for erecting and maintaining sign without a permit

Any person who erects or maintains any sign for which a permit is required by this part without a valid permit or renewal of such permit issued by the department shall be guilty of a misdemeanor. Each day or fraction thereof during which a sign is unlawfully maintained shall constitute a separate offense. The commissioner and officials or employees of said department designated by the commissioner are authorized to take such actions as may be necessary or appropriate to procure the prosecution and conviction of any person, firm, or corporation violating this Code section.

Laws 1971, Ex. Sess., p. 5, § 15; Laws 1973, p. 947, § 1.

Formerly Code 1933, § 95A–927.

§ 32–6–92. Penalty for maintaining unauthorized sign

Any person who maintains any sign not authorized by this part and which was not lawfully in existence on October 6, 1971, shall be guilty of a misdemeanor. Each day or fraction thereof during which a sign is unlawfully maintained shall constitute a separate offense. The commissioner and officials or employees of the department designated by the commissioner are authorized to take such actions as may be necessary or appropriate to procure the prosecution and conviction of any person, firm, or corporation violating this Code section.

Laws 1971, Ex. Sess., p. 5, § 16; Laws 1973, p. 947, § 1.

Formerly Code 1933, § 95A–928.

TITLE 33

INSURANCE

CHAPTER 1

GENERAL PROVISIONS

§ 33–1–9. Fraudulent insurance claims

(a) Any natural person who knowingly or willfully:

(1) Makes or aids in the making of any false or fraudulent statement or representation of any material fact or thing:

(A) In any written statement or certificate;

(B) In the filing of a claim;

(C) In the making of an application for a policy of insurance;

(D) In the receiving of such an application for a policy of insurance; or

(E) In the receiving of money for such application for a policy of insurance for the purpose of procuring or attempting to procure the payment of any false or fraudulent claim or other benefit by an insurer;

(2) Receives money for the purpose of purchasing insurance and converts such money to such person's own benefit;

(3) Issues fake or counterfeit insurance policies, certificates of insurance, insurance identification cards, or insurance binders; or

(4) Makes any false or fraudulent representation as to the death or disability of a policy or certificate holder in any written statement or certificate for the purpose of fraudulently obtaining money or benefit from an insurer

commits the crime of insurance fraud.

(b) Any natural person who knowingly and willfully or with reckless disregard engages in the following activities, either directly or indirectly, as an agent for, as a representative of, or on behalf of an insurer not authorized to transact insurance in this state commits the crime of insurance fraud:

(1) Soliciting, negotiating, procuring, or effectuating insurance or annuity contracts or renewals thereof;

(2) Soliciting, negotiating, procuring, or effectuating any contract relating to benefits or services;

(3) Disseminating information as to coverage or rates;

(4) Forwarding applications;

(5) Delivering policies or contracts;

(6) Inspecting or assessing risk;

(7) Fixing of rates;

(8) Investigating or adjusting claims or losses;

(9) Collecting or forwarding of premiums; or

(10) In any other manner representing or assisting such an insurer in the transaction of insurance with respect to subjects of insurance resident, located, or to be performed in this state.

(c) Any natural person who knowingly and willfully with intent to defraud subscribes, makes, or concurs in making any annual or other statement required by law to be filed with the Commissioner containing any material statement which is false commits the crime of insurance fraud.

(d) In any prosecution under this Code section, the crime shall be considered as having been committed in the county of the purported loss, in the county in which the insurer or the insurer's agent received the fraudulent or false claim or application, in the county in which money was received for the fraudulent application, or in any county where any act in furtherance of the criminal scheme was committed.

(e) A natural person convicted of a violation of this Code section shall be guilty of a felony and shall be punished by imprisonment for not less than two nor more than ten years, or by a fine of not more than $10,000.00, or both.

(f) Subsection (b) of this Code section shall not apply to a contract of insurance entered into in accordance with Article 2 of Chapter 5 of this title.

Laws 1960, p. 289, § 1; Laws 1985, p. 723, § 1; Laws 1991, p. 1608, § 1.1; Laws 1997, p. 1296, § 1; Laws 1998, p. 1064, § 1; Laws 2003, Act 97, § 1.2, eff. May 30, 2003; Laws 2003, Act 276, § 1, eff. June 3, 2003; Laws 2004, Act 583, § 1A, eff. May 13, 2004.

Formerly Code 1933, § 56–9910.

Historical and Statutory Notes

The 2003 amendment by Act 97, in subsec. (c) (redesignated as subsec. (e) by Laws 2003, Act 276, § 1), inserted "natural" before "person".

The 2003 amendment by Act 276 inserted new subsecs. (b), (c), and (f), and redesignated former subsecs. (b) and (c) as (d) and (e).

In 2003, the Code Commission, in subsec. (c), substituted "Commissioner" for "commissioner". See § 28–9–5.

The 2004 amendment by Act 583 deleted "subsection (a) of" following "violation of" in subsec. (e).

TITLE 35

LAW ENFORCEMENT OFFICERS AND AGENCIES

CHAPTER 1

GENERAL PROVISIONS

§ 35–1–1. Definitions

As used in this title, the term:

(1) "Board" means the Board of Public Safety.

(2) "Commissioner" means the commissioner of public safety.

(3) "Department" means the Department of Public Safety.

§ 35–1–2. Repealed by Laws 2007, Act 42, § 1, eff. July 1, 2007

Historical and Statutory Notes

The repealed section, relating to the motor vehicle furnished to the state prison warden, was derived from Laws 1937, p. 322, art. 2, § 13; Laws 1952, p. 3, § 1. The repealing law also reserved the section designation.

§ 35–1–3. Subsistence allowances for sheriffs, deputies, policemen and other law enforcement officers; pension systems unaffected

(a) The governing authorities of the several counties, municipal corporations, and other political subdivisions of this state are authorized to designate and set apart a portion of the compensation, whether payable on a salary or fee basis, to sheriffs, deputy sheriffs, patrolmen, policemen, and other law enforcement officers, as a subsistence allowance, which allowance shall not exceed $5.00 for each day actually spent by such sheriff or other law enforcement officer in the performance of his duties.

(b) Nothing in this Code section shall affect any pension system which was being operated by any county, municipal corporation, or political subdivision of this state on March 9, 1956, nor shall this Code section affect any rights of any person under any pension system which was being operated by any county, municipal corporation, or political subdivision on March 9, 1956.

Laws 1956, p. 741, §§ 1, 3.

§ 35–1–4. Stolen or recovered motor vehicles or license plates; rules and regulations for submission of reports; intentional failure to report

(a) As used in this Code section, the term:

(1) "Recovering agency" means the law enforcement agency which recovers a motor vehicle which has previously been reported stolen.

(2) "Reporting agency" means the law enforcement agency which receives a report that a motor vehicle has been stolen or lost and which reports such theft or loss to the Georgia Crime Information Center.

(b) It shall be the duty of every law enforcement officer who receives a report based on reliable information that any motor vehicle has been stolen or that the license plate for such vehicle has been stolen or lost to report the theft or loss to the Georgia Crime Information Center immediately after receiving such information, unless prior thereto information has been received of the recovery of the vehicle or plate. It shall be the duty of any person who reports the theft of a motor vehicle to provide the law enforcement agency to which the report of theft was made and the Georgia Crime Information Center with a means of contacting the owner of the stolen motor vehicle or the successor in interest to such owner in the event of the recovery of the motor vehicle. Any law enforcement officer, upon receiving information of the recovery of any motor vehicle or license plate which has previously been reported as stolen or lost, shall immediately report the recovery of the motor vehicle or plate directly to the Georgia Crime Information Center. It shall be the duty of the reporting law enforcement agency, the agency to which the vehicle was first reported stolen, to notify the owner or the successor in interest to the owner within 72 hours when a previously reported stolen motor vehicle has been recovered, or within 72 hours after the reporting agency has received notification of recovery if recovery is by another agency. The owner or successor in interest shall not be charged or otherwise incur any storage fee on the recovered stolen motor vehicle until the expiration of at least 24 hours immediately following such notification to the owner or the successor in interest. In the event the reporting agency is different from the recovering agency, the recovering agency shall contact the reporting agency and provide all information required by the guidelines established by the Georgia Crime Information Center and any other relevant information. In all cases, it shall remain the responsibility of the reporting agency to notify the owner or the successor in interest to the owner. This requirement shall be included in the rules and regulations of the board promulgated pursuant to subsection (c) of this Code section. If, after a reasonable attempt, the reporting law enforcement agency is unable to contact the owner or the successor in interest to the owner, a record of such fact shall be made and filed with the incident reports and posted in the record required to be maintained by Code Section 17–5–50.

(c) The board is authorized and directed to promulgate rules and regulations pertaining to the submissions of the reports provided for in subsection (b) of this Code section. Such rules and regulations shall include time limits for the submission of the reports and the forms upon which the reports shall be submitted.

(d) The intentional failure of any law enforcement officer to submit reports as prescribed in subsection (b) of this Code section or the failure to do so through wanton neglect shall constitute cause for removal from office, if the officer is elected, or shall be grounds for dismissal if the officer is a nonelected employee.

(e) The provisions of this Code section shall not be construed to affect the responsibilities of the Georgia Crime Information Center as provided by paragraph (14) of Code Section 35–3–33.

Laws 1966, p. 733, §§ 2–4; Laws 1984, p. 632, §§ 1, 2; Laws 1987, p. 3, § 35; Laws 1991, p. 723, § 1; Laws 1993, p. 91, § 35; Laws 1993, p. 762, § 1.

§ 35–1–5. Radio interference; penalty

(a) It shall be a misdemeanor for any person, firm, or corporation to use the same wavelength of the radio system adopted by the department without the prior written authorization of the commissioner or to do any act interfering with the proper receipt or transmission of information relating to the department or any division thereof.

(b) It shall be a misdemeanor for any person, firm, or corporation to use the same wavelength of the radio system adopted by the Georgia Bureau of Investigation without the prior written authorization of the director or to do any act interfering with the proper receipt or transmission of information relating to the Georgia Bureau of Investigation.

Laws 1937, p. 322, art. 3, § 1; Laws 1960, p. 995, § 1.

§ 35–1–6. Commissioner of Public Safety to appoint investigators; powers, duties and compensation of investigators

(a) The commissioner is authorized to appoint five nonuniformed investigators who shall be certified peace officers pursuant to Chapter 8 of this title, the "Georgia Peace Officer Standards and Training Act." The commissioner shall determine the salaries of such investigators. The investigators shall be in the unclassified service of the State Personnel Administration and therefore shall not be governed by any rules of position, classification, appointment, promotion, demotion, transfer, dismissal, qualification, compensation, seniority privileges, tenure, or other such matters concerning their employment as may now or hereafter be established by the State Personnel Board, the State Personnel Administration, or any successor boards or agencies. The investigators shall be assigned to the Internal Affairs Section of the Department of Public Safety in the office of the commissioner at the department's headquarters complex.

(b) The investigators shall have full arrest powers in cases involving internal affairs and in such cases shall be authorized:

(1) To investigate crimes committed anywhere in the state;

(2) To arrest any person violating the criminal laws of this state;

(3) To serve and execute warrants after notifying the law enforcement agency of the local jurisdiction of the intent to serve such warrant or warrants;

(4) To enforce in general the criminal laws of this state; and

(5) To carry firearms while performing their duties.

Laws 1981, p. 1450, § 2; Laws 1992, p. 3131, § 1; Laws 2009, Act 155, §§ 1, 2, eff. July 1, 2009.

§ 35–1–7. Law enforcement officers, limitation of liability

A law enforcement officer shall not be liable at law for any action or actions done while performing any duty at the scene of an emergency except for gross negligence, willful or wanton misconduct, or malfeasance. As used in this Code section, the term "law enforcement officer" means any peace officer who is employed by this state or any political subdivision thereof and who is required by the terms of his employment, whether by election or appointment, to give his full time to the preservation of public order or the protection of life and property or the prevention of crime. Such term shall include sheriffs and deputy sheriffs.

Laws 1981, p. 655, § 1.

Formerly Code 1933, § 3–1004.3.

§ 35–1–8. Collection, classification and preservation of information for identification of deceased individuals or location of missing persons

(a) It shall be the duty of every law enforcement agency to:

(1) Acquire, collect, classify, and preserve any information which would assist in the identification of any deceased individual who has not been identified after the discovery of such deceased individual;

(2) Acquire, collect, classify, and preserve immediately any information which would assist in the location of any missing person, including any minor, and provide confirmation as to any entry for such a person to the parent, legal guardian, or next of kin of that person and the agency shall acquire, collect, classify, and preserve such information from such parent, guardian, or next of kin;

(3) Exchange such records and information as provided in paragraphs (1) and (2) of this subsection with other law enforcement agencies of this state, any other state, or the United States. With respect to missing minors, such information shall be transmitted immediately to other law enforcement agencies; and

(4) Report any case of an unusual illness, health condition, or death, or an unusual cluster of such events, or any other suspicious health related event to the Department of Community Health and the appropriate county board of health.

(b)(1) For purposes of this subsection, "facility" means a facility pursuant to Chapter 3, 4, or 7 of Title 37, relating to treatment of mentally ill, developmentally disabled, and alcoholic or drug dependent persons, or an institution classified as a nursing home pursuant to Code Section 31–7–1.

(2) A person hospitalized or resident in a facility shall be considered to be a missing person at the time such person's unaccounted for absence from that facility is reported by that facility, either by telephone or in writing, to a law enforcement agency.

(c) Any law enforcement agency which receives a report that a person who has Alzheimer's disease or other mental illness involving dementia is missing shall immediately open an investigation for the purpose of determining such person's whereabouts; and no policy for applying any waiting period prior to initiation of a missing persons investigation shall apply in the case of a person who has Alzheimer's disease or other mental illnesses involving dementia.

Laws 1984, p. 690, § 1; Laws 1985, p. 1128, § 1; Laws 1992, p. 6, § 35; Laws 1997, p. 1504, § 1; Laws 2002, p. 1386, § 10; Laws 2009, Act 102, §§ 1–4, 3–5, eff. July 1, 2009.

§ 35–1–9. Repealed by Laws 1999, p. 809, § 2, eff. July 1, 1999

§ 35–1–10. Training in investigation of family violence incidents

(a) The Georgia Peace Officer Standards and Training Council and the Georgia Public Safety Training Center shall establish guidelines and procedures for the incorporation of training materials and information in:

(1) Methods for identifying, combating, and reporting family violence incidents; and

(2) Methods for identifying and reporting sexual offenses and assisting victims of sexual offenses.

(b) The guidelines and procedures listed in subsection (a) of this Code section shall be for use by law enforcement training centers monitored by the Georgia Peace Officer Standards and Training Council and monitored and funded by the Georgia Public Safety Training Center in all courses for which they have responsibility and oversight.

Laws 1992, p. 2939, § 2; Laws 1993, p. 91, § 35; Laws 1997, p. 1488, § 1; Laws 2004, Act 780, § 1, eff. July 1, 2004.

§ 35–1–11. Designation, equipment, and training of police volunteers in area of traffic control; authority to direct traffic in emergencies

A police chief of a local law enforcement agency with the approval of the local governing authority shall be authorized to designate and equip police volunteers and to provide training to such police volunteers in the area and manner of traffic control. With the approval of the police chief of a local law enforcement agency or fire chief of a local fire department, a police volunteer shall be authorized to direct and regulate the flow of traffic in the event of a fire, explosion, hurricane, tornado, or other emergency situation. A police volunteer shall not have the power of arrest provided to peace officers.

Laws 1999, p. 654, § 1.

§ 35–1–12. Head of law enforcement agency of county, municipality, etc., required to be certified police officer

Any county, municipality, or other public subdivision of this state which has a law enforcement agency shall declare a chief of police or a law enforcement head for such law enforcement agency who is required to be a certified peace officer pursuant to the provisions of Chapter 8 of this title, known as the "Georgia Peace Officer Standards and Training Act." The provisions of this Code section shall not apply to sheriffs.

Laws 1999, p. 777, § 1.

§ 35–1–13. Reports of identity fraud

Notwithstanding any other provision of law, any law enforcement agency that receives a report from a resident of this state that such person has been the victim of identity fraud shall prepare an incident report and transmit the same to the Governor's Office of Consumer Affairs identity fraud repository, as provided in Code Section 16–9–123, notwithstanding the fact that such person's identity may have been used solely to commit one or more criminal offenses beyond the jurisdiction of this state. Copies of such incident reports shall be referred from the Governor's Office of Consumer Affairs to the Georgia Crime Information Center as provided in Chapter 3 of this title and to any jurisdiction in which such identity has been used.

Laws 2002, p. 551, § 4.

§ 35–1–14. Adoption of pursuit policies by law enforcement agencies

On and after January 1, 2004, each state, county, and local law enforcement agency that conducts emergency response and vehicular pursuits shall adopt written policies that set forth the manner in which these operations shall be conducted. Each law enforcement agency may create its own such policies or adopt an existing model. All pursuit policies created or adopted by any law enforcement agency must address situations in which police pursuits cross over into other jurisdictions. Law enforcement agencies which do not comply with the requirements of this Code section are subject to the withholding of any state funding or state administered federal funding.

Laws 2003, Act 395, § 1, eff. July 1, 2003; Laws 2006, Act 453, § 35, eff. April 14, 2006.

§ 35–1–15. Authority of out-of-state law enforcement officer entering state in fresh pursuit; arrest and custody; hearings

(a) As used in this Code section, the term:

(1) "Fresh pursuit" means pursuit by a law enforcement officer of a person who is in immediate and continuous flight from the commission of a criminal offense.

(2) "Law enforcement officer" means a person employed or appointed by a state or political subdivision who is granted, by state law, the authority to enforce criminal, traffic, or penal laws of his or her respective state and who possesses the power to effect arrests.

(b) A law enforcement officer from Alabama, Florida, North Carolina, South Carolina, or Tennessee who enters this state in fresh pursuit of a person shall have the same authority to arrest and hold in custody such person within this state as that of a law enforcement officer of this state; provided, however, that the authority granted by this Code section shall be limited to criminal offenses of the pursuing state that also are criminal offenses under the laws of this state and that are punishable by death or imprisonment in excess of one year under the laws of the pursuing state.

(c)(1) When an arrest is made in this state by a law enforcement officer of another state pursuant to this Code section, the law enforcement officer shall, without unnecessary delay, take the person arrested before a judicial officer of this state.

(2) The judicial officer shall conduct a hearing for the limited purpose of determining whether such arrest meets the requirements of this Code section unless the person arrested executes a written waiver of his or her right to a hearing under this Code section. If the judicial officer determines that such arrest was unlawful, he or she shall discharge such person arrested. If the judicial officer determines that such arrest was lawful, he or she shall commit such person arrested to imprisonment as provided in Code Section 17–13–35. Once such person is imprisoned pursuant to this Code section, the provisions of Chapter 13 of Title 17 shall govern the extradition and return of such person to the state in which the criminal offense was committed.

(d) This Code section shall apply only to a law enforcement officer from Alabama, Florida, North Carolina, South Carolina, or Tennessee where the state in which the law enforcement officer is employed or appointed has enacted a provision similar to this Code section relating to the arrest and custody of a person pursued into a neighboring state.

Laws 2008, Act 426, § 1, eff. May 6, 2008; Laws 2009, Act 8, § 35, eff. April 14, 2009.

Historical and Statutory Notes

The 2009 amendment by Act 8 was a provision contained in a correction bill.

CHAPTER 2

DEPARTMENT OF PUBLIC SAFETY

Article 1

General Provisions

§ 35–2–1. Board of Public Safety; membership

Section effective until January 20, 2011. See also, section effective January 20, 2011.

(a) There is created a Board of Public Safety which shall establish the general policy to be followed by the Department of Public Safety.

(b) The board shall consist of 15 members:

(1) The following three members serve as follows:

(A) The Governor, ex officio, who shall be chairperson of the board;

(B) An appointee of the Governor who shall not be the Attorney General; and

(C) The official in charge of the Department of Corrections, ex officio.

(2) Four members shall be selected as follows:

(A) A representative appointed by the Governor by and with the advice and consent of the Senate from the membership of the Georgia Sheriffs Association; the first representative shall serve an initial term ending on January 20, 1975, each subsequent term being three years;

(B) A representative appointed by the Governor by and with the advice and consent of the Senate from the membership of the Georgia Association of Chiefs of Police; the first representative shall serve an initial term ending on January 20, 1974, each subsequent term being three years;

(C) A representative appointed by the Governor by and with the advice and consent of the Senate from the membership of the District Attorneys Association of Georgia; the first representative shall serve an initial term ending on January 20, 1973, each subsequent term being three years; and

(D) A representative appointed by the Governor by and with the advice and consent of the Senate from the membership of the Georgia State Firemen's Association; the first representative shall serve an initial term ending on January 20, 1984. Each subsequent term shall be for three years.

(3) Five members shall be selected as follows:

(A) Three members appointed by the Governor. The first appointees shall serve an initial term ending on January 20, 2002. Each subsequent term shall be for three years;

(B) One member appointed by the Lieutenant Governor. The first appointee shall serve an initial term ending on January 20, 2002. Each subsequent term shall be for three years; and

(C) One member appointed by the Speaker of the House of Representatives. The first appointee shall serve an initial term ending on January 20, 2002. Each subsequent term shall be for three years.

(4) By majority vote the board shall appoint three members from the state at large; no person so appointed shall be an officer or employee of any state or local governmental entity at the time of his or her appointment to or during his or her membership on the board. All terms of the three at-large members shall be four years. Any vacancy in the at-large membership shall be filled by the board for the unexpired term.

(c) Appointments made pursuant to paragraph (2) of subsection (b) of this Code section at times when the Senate is not in session shall be effective ad interim.

Laws 1972, p. 1015, §§ 18, 1609; Laws 1981, p. 814, § 1; Laws 1985, p. 283, § 1; Laws 1988, p. 426, § 1; Laws 1999, p. 1211, § 1.

§ 35–2–1. Board of Public Safety; membership

Section effective January 20, 2011. See also, section effective until January 20, 2011.

(a) There is created a Board of Public Safety which shall establish the general policy to be followed by the Department of Public Safety.

(b) The board shall consist of 15 members:

(1) The following three members serve as follows:

(A) The Governor, ex officio, who shall be chairperson of the board;

(B) An appointee of the Governor who shall not be the Attorney General; and

(C) The official in charge of the Department of Corrections, ex officio.

(2) Five members shall be selected as follows:

(A) A representative appointed by the Governor by and with the advice and consent of the Senate from the membership of the Georgia Sheriffs Association; the first representative shall serve an initial term ending on January 20, 1975, each subsequent term being three years;

(B) A representative appointed by the Governor by and with the advice and consent of the Senate from the membership of the Georgia Association of Chiefs of Police; the first representative shall serve an initial term ending on January 20, 1974, each subsequent term being three years;

(C) A representative appointed by the Governor by and with the advice and consent of the Senate from the membership of the District Attorneys Association of Georgia; the first representative shall serve an initial term ending on January 20, 1973, each subsequent term being three years;

(D) A representative appointed by the Governor by and with the advice and consent of the Senate from the membership of the Georgia State Firemen's Association; the first representative shall serve an initial term ending on January 20, 1984. Each subsequent term shall be for three years; and

(E) A representative appointed by the Governor by and with the advice and consent of the Senate from the membership of the Georgia Association of Fire Chiefs; the first representative shall serve an initial term beginning on January 21, 2011. Each term shall be for three years.

(3) Four members shall be selected as follows:

(A) Two members appointed by the Governor. The first appointees shall serve an initial term ending on January 20, 2002. Each subsequent term shall be for three years;

(B) One member appointed by the Lieutenant Governor. The first appointee shall serve an initial term ending on January 20, 2002. Each subsequent term shall be for three years; and

(C) One member appointed by the Speaker of the House of Representatives. The first appointee shall serve an initial term ending on January 20, 2002. Each subsequent term shall be for three years.

(4) By majority vote the board shall appoint three members from the state at large; no person so appointed shall be an officer or employee of any state or local governmental entity at the time of his or her appointment to or during his or her membership on the board. All terms of the three at-large members shall be four years. Any vacancy in the at-large membership shall be filled by the board for the unexpired term.

(c) Appointments made pursuant to paragraph (2) of subsection (b) of this Code section at times when the Senate is not in session shall be effective ad interim.

Laws 1972, p. 1015, §§ 18, 1609; Laws 1981, p. 814, § 1; Laws 1985, p. 283, § 1; Laws 1988, p. 426, § 1; Laws 1999, p. 1211, § 1; Laws 2009, Act 178, § 1, eff. Jan. 20, 2011.

§ 35–2–2. Department of Public Safety; created

There is created a Department of Public Safety.

Laws 1937, p. 322, art. 1, § 1; Laws 1972, p. 1015, § 1601.

§ 35–2–3. Commissioner of public safety; created

(a) There is created the position of commissioner of public safety. The commissioner shall be the chief administrative officer and shall be both appointed and removed by the board with the approval of the Governor. Except as otherwise provided by law and subject to the general policy established by the board, the commissioner shall supervise, direct, account for, organize, plan, administer, and execute the functions vested in the department by law.

(b) The commissioner shall be authorized to promulgate rules and regulations as necessary to carry out his or her official duties.

Laws 1972, p. 1015, § 1602; Laws 1996, p. 271, § 1.

§ 35–2–4. Commissioner of Public Safety member of Uniform Division

The commissioner may be a member of the Uniform Division of the department and upon removal from such office without prejudice he shall revert to his original rank in the Uniform Division which he held when he was appointed to office.

Laws 1949, p. 70, § 1.

§ 35–2–5. Rank

As prescribed by the board, the commissioner may rank as senior colonel in the Uniform Division and may be the chief officer thereof or the board may appoint a colonel in the Uniform Division as the chief officer thereof.

Laws 1937, p. 322, art. 1, § 4; Laws 1949, p. 70, § 2; Laws 2000, p. 951, § 12–3.

§ 35–2–6. Expert assistance; pay

In perfecting the organization of the department or any division thereof, the commissioner shall be authorized with approval of the board to employ and provide compensation for such expert temporary assistance as may be necessary.

Laws 1937, p. 322, art. 2, § 8.

§ 35–2–7. Deputy commissioner; appointment; duties; oath

(a) The commissioner is vested with authority to appoint a deputy commissioner of public safety, who shall have the rank of lieutenant colonel in the Uniform Division of the department.

(b) The deputy commissioner may be a member of the Uniform Division of the department and upon removal from office without prejudice he shall revert to the original rank in the Uniform Division which he held when he was appointed to office.

(c) His appointment shall be subject to confirmation by the board.

(d) The deputy commissioner shall perform such duties as he may be charged with by the commissioner, and in case of a vacancy shall act as commissioner until an appointment is made to fill the vacancy.

(e) The deputy commissioner shall take the same oath as that required of the commissioner, which oath shall be administered by the commissioner.

Laws 1937, p. 332, art. 1, § 5; Laws 1943, p. 196, § 3; Laws 1949, p. 70, § 3; Laws 1958, p. 296, § 2; Laws 1967, p. 98, § 2; Laws 1969, p. 145, § 1; Laws 1972, p. 409, § 1; Laws 1989, p. 1285, § 1.

§ 35–2–8. Comptroller

The commissioner shall appoint a comptroller to ensure the proper receipt, accounting, and disbursement of funds of the department. The comptroller shall not be a member of the Uniform Division of the department. The comptroller shall give a good and sufficient surety bond in the amount of $100,000.00, payable to the Governor and his successors in office and to be approved by the commissioner, conditioned for the faithful discharge of his duties and the faithful accounting of all funds received by him.

Laws 1977, p. 228, § 2.

§ 35–2–9. Payment of medical, surgical, and similar expenses of personnel injured in line of duty

The department is authorized to pay all medical, surgical, hospital, nursing, and other similar expenses incurred by any member of the Georgia State Patrol as a result of injuries received in the line of duty. The department is authorized to make such payments in addition to any award made by the State Board of Workers' Compensation based on such injuries. Such payments shall only be made upon proper presentation of bills to the comptroller of the department. The comptroller and the injured party shall together ascertain the correctness of all bills presented. No payments shall be made without the approval of the commissioner.

Laws 1953, Nov.-Dec. Sess., p. 392, § 1.

§ 35–2–10. Awards to employees for outstanding service, heroism and other exemplary acts; costs

(a) The department shall have the authority to make awards to employees of the department on behalf of the department or the state in recognition of outstanding service, heroism, or other exemplary acts arising out of the performance of their duties. All expenditures incurred in making such awards shall be defrayed from the department's regular operating budget and shall not exceed $100.00 per award.

(b) The board shall promulgate rules and regulations in connection with the granting of the awards provided for in this Code section.

Laws 1977, p. 246, §§ 1, 2.

§ 35–2–11. Lectures and demonstrations

The commissioner is authorized to furnish one or more lecturers to conduct lectures and demonstrations relating to public safety in the public schools in cooperation with school authorities. The commissioner may furnish such lecturers with appropriate literature and equipment.

Laws 1937, p. 322, art. 3, § 1.

§ 35–2–12. Political activity of employees

No person in the employ of the department shall, either directly or indirectly, contribute any money or any other thing of value to any person, organization, or committee for political campaign or election in county or state primaries or general elections.

Laws 1949, p. 70, § 4; Laws 1956, p. 573, § 1; Laws 1957, p. 103, § 1; Laws 1958, p. 296, § 3; Laws 1994, p. 1921, § 1.

§ 35–2–13. Headquarters

The department is authorized to provide comfortable and accessible headquarters for the commissioner and deputy commissioner of public safety and for the various divisions thereof. The department is authorized and empowered to provide such quarters and offices by purchase, lease, or construction, any contract made or title acquired to be made in the name of and on behalf of the State of Georgia.

Laws 1937, p. 322, § 10.

§ 35–2–14. Memorandum of understanding concerning enforcement of federal immigration and custom laws; training of peace officers to enforce immigration laws

(a) As used in this Code section, the term "peace officer" means peace officer as defined in subparagraph (A) of paragraph (8) of Code Section 35–8–2, as amended.

(b) The commissioner is authorized and directed to negotiate the terms of a memorandum of understanding between the State of Georgia and the United States Department of Justice or Department of Homeland Security concerning the enforcement of federal immigration and customs laws, detention and removals, and investigations in the State of Georgia.

(c) The memorandum of understanding negotiated pursuant to subsection (b) of this Code section shall be signed on behalf of the state by the commissioner and the Governor or as otherwise required by the appropriate federal agency.

(d) The commissioner shall designate appropriate peace officers to be trained pursuant to the memorandum of understanding provided for in subsections (b) and (c) of this Code section. Such training shall be funded pursuant to the federal Homeland Security Appropriation Act of 2006, Public Law 109–90, or any subsequent source of federal funding. The provisions of this subsection shall become effective upon such funding.

(e) A peace officer certified as trained in accordance with the memorandum of understanding as provided in this Code section is authorized to enforce federal immigration and customs laws while performing within the scope of his or her authorized duties.

Laws 2006, Act 457, § 4, eff. July 1, 2007.

Historical and Statutory Notes

In 2006, the Code Commission, in subsec. (b), substituted "customs" for "custom". See § 28–9–5.

Article 2

Georgia State Patrol

§ 35–2–30. Creation

There is created and established a division of the Department of Public Safety to be known as the Uniform Division, the members of which shall be known and designated as the "Georgia State Patrol."

Laws 1937, p. 322, art. 2, § 1.

§ 35–2–31. Component parts

The Uniform Division of the Department of Public Safety shall consist of:

(1) The officers, noncommissioned officers, and troopers of the headquarters staff;

(2) The officers, noncommissioned officers, and troopers of one battalion.

Laws 1937, p. 322, art. 2, § 2; Laws 1949, p. 70, § 4; Laws 1952, p. 129, § 1; Laws 1955, p. 298, § 1; Laws 1956, p. 573, § 1; Laws 1957, p. 103, § 1; Laws 1958, p. 296, §§ 3, 4; Laws 1960, p. 132, § 1; Laws 1975, p. 1115, § 1.

§ 35–2–32. Jurisdiction and duties of Uniform Division

(a) The Uniform Division of the department shall have jurisdiction throughout this state with such duties and powers as are prescribed by law.

(b) It shall be the primary duty of the Uniform Division to patrol the public roads and highways of this state, including interstate and state maintained highways, and to safeguard the lives and property of the public; and such duty shall also include accident investigation and traffic enforcement. The Uniform Division shall prevent, detect, and investigate violations of the criminal laws of this state, any other state, or the United States which are committed upon these public roads and highways or upon property appertaining thereto and shall apprehend and arrest those persons who violate such criminal laws.

(c) Without limiting the generality of any other provisions of this article, it is specifically provided that the Uniform Division shall have jurisdiction to patrol safety rest areas and welcome centers located on or adjacent to the state highway system for the purposes of: (1) enforcing the laws of this state relating to the use, ownership, control, licensing, and registration of motor vehicles; (2) enforcing the criminal laws of this state; and (3) enforcing the laws of this state and the regulations of the Department of Transportation with respect to the use of such safety rest areas and welcome centers. The limitations of paragraph (5) of subsection (a) of Code Section 35–2–33 shall not apply with respect to enforcement in safety rest areas and welcome centers.

Laws 1937, p. 322, art. 2, § 14; Laws 1950, p. 77, § 1; Laws 1970, p. 577, § 1; Laws 1981, p. 1450, § 1; Laws 1990, p. 1329, § 1.

§ 35–2–33. Additional duties of Uniform Division

(a) It shall be the duty of the Uniform Division:

(1) To enforce the laws of this state relating to the use, ownership, control, licensing, and registration of motor vehicles and Code Sections 32–9–4 and 40–6–54, relating to designation of restricted travel lanes;

(2) On property owned by this state or any agency thereof:

(A) To enforce the criminal laws of this state;

(B) To apprehend and arrest any person who violates the criminal laws of this state; and

(C) To serve and execute warrants;

(3) To apprehend and arrest any person who is a fugitive from justice;

(4) To suppress riots, labor strikes, or picketing, as provided by law, at the direction of the Governor on request made by the chief of police of any municipality or the sheriff of any county; and

(5)(A) To make initial inquiries into any situation which occurs off the public roads and highways and which occurs under circumstances where it has reasonable grounds to believe a criminal law has been, is being, or is about to be violated. The Uniform Division shall further have the duty to make arrests in connection with such initial inquiries.

(B) Any initial inquiry or arrest which is made pursuant to subparagraph (A) of this paragraph shall be initiated only if a local law enforcement officer is not readily available and the member of the Uniform Division reasonably believes that his failure to act could result in the commission of a criminal act or the escape of a person who has committed a criminal act. In any action taken by the Uniform Division under subparagraph (A) of this paragraph, the Uniform Division shall relinquish jurisdiction to the local law enforcement agency as soon as possible under the circumstances.

(b) The Uniform Division shall cooperate with all law enforcement agencies of this state or any municipality, county, or other political subdivision thereof in enforcing the laws of this state, any other state, or the United States relating to the operation of motor vehicles. The commissioner may, and in the case of a request by the Governor shall, authorize and direct the Uniform Division to cooperate with and render assistance to any law enforcement agency of this state or any municipality, county, or other political subdivision thereof in any criminal case, in the prevention or detection of violations of any law, or in the apprehension or arrest of persons who violate the criminal laws of this state, any other state, or the United States, upon a request by the governing authority or chief law enforcement officer of any municipality, the sheriff of any county, a judge of the superior court of any county, or the Governor.

(c) The commissioner may, and in the case of a request by the Governor shall, authorize and direct the Uniform Division to:

(1) Provide security protection services, or transportation or escort services, or both to coaches, players, and referees and other officials in connection with collegiate athletic events involving an institution of the University System of Georgia which offers four-year postsecondary degrees when such security protection services, or transportation or escort services, or both are necessary or appropriate to deter actual or potential threats to the safety of such individuals;

(2) Provide services which are necessary or appropriate to promote the safety of the collegiate athletic teams of such institutions of the University System of Georgia which offer four-year postsecondary degrees or the general public or both or to facilitate travel by such collegiate athletic teams or the general public or both;

(3) Allow personnel of the Uniform Division, while on duty and in uniform, to accompany collegiate athletic teams of such institutions of the University System of Georgia which offer four-year postsecondary degrees traveling to athletic events inside or outside the state and to make use of department vehicles for this purpose, provided that the department shall be reimbursed by such affected institution of the University System of Georgia for any expenses incurred by such personnel of the Uniform Division while carrying out such duties; and

(4) Allow personnel of the Uniform Division, while on duty and in uniform, to provide security at special events at any location, whether or not the event takes place on state property.

(d) In no case where the Uniform Division is exercising any power or performing any duty authorized by this Code section shall it usurp any of the duties or authority of any sheriff of any county, any chief of police of any municipality, or any chief of police of any county police force.

(e) The duties and powers of the Uniform Division, as provided for in this Code section, shall be in addition to any other duties or powers provided by law.

Laws 1937, p. 322, art. 2, §§ 14, 15; Laws 1950, p. 77, § 1; Laws 1956, p. 495, § 1; Laws 1970, p. 577, § 1; Laws 1974, p. 447, § 1; Laws 1978, p. 254, § 1; Laws 1981, p. 1450, § 1; Laws 1988, p. 1982, § 1; Laws 1989, p. 14, § 35; Laws 1996, p. 1507, § 1; Laws 2005, Act 68, § 13A–1, eff. July 1, 2005.

§ 35–2–34. Headquarters staff; personnel

The headquarters staff shall be composed of the commissioner, deputy commissioner, and such other commissioned and noncommissioned officers, troopers, and clerical personnel as the commissioner deems necessary for use at headquarters.

Laws 1937, p. 322, art. 2, § 2; Laws 1946, p. 39, § 1; Laws 1952, p. 129, § 1; Laws 1955, p. 298, § 1; Laws 1956, p. 573, § 1; Laws 1957, p. 103, § 1; Laws 1958, p. 296, § 3; Laws 1960, p. 132, § 1; Laws 1975, p. 1115, § 1; Laws 1977, p. 228, § 1.

§ 35–2–35. Clerical duties

The clerical duties at headquarters shall be performed by the headquarters staff. The commissioner, in his discretion, may transfer any member of the headquarters staff to any other division or district for any other duty.

Laws 1937, p. 322, art. 2, § 2; Laws 1946, p. 39, § 1; Laws 1952, p. 129, § 1; Laws 1955, p. 298, § 1; Laws 1956, p. 573, § 1; Laws 1957, p. 103, § 1; Laws 1958, p. 296, § 3; Laws 1960, p. 132, § 1; Laws 1975, p. 1115, § 1; Laws 1977, p. 228, § 1.

§ 35–2–36. Battalion; members; recruits

(a) The battalion of the Uniform Division shall consist of such personnel as the commissioner, with the approval of the board, may deem necessary within the limits set by available appropriations.

(b) The personnel of the battalion shall be ranked according to a semimilitary structure with such ranks as the board shall deem appropriate, including, but not restricted to, the following:

(1) Major;

(2) Captain;

(3) First lieutenant;

(4) Sergeant first class;

(5) Sergeant;

(6) Corporal;

(7) Trooper first class;

(8) Trooper;

(9) Trooper cadets; and

(10) Process servers.

(c) Within the limits set by available appropriations, the commissioner, with the approval of the board, is authorized to employ such recruits or cadets as may be deemed necessary, who may become members of the Uniform Division but who shall not be members of the Uniform Division so long as they remain recruits or cadets; provided, however, that such recruits or cadets are designated as "peace officers" as such term is defined in paragraph (11) of Code Section 16–1–3 and shall have the authority of a peace officer.

(d) The commissioner shall prescribe rules and regulations governing the enlistment and training of recruits or cadets subject to the approval of the board.

Laws 1937, p. 322, art. 2, § 2; Laws 1939, p. 135, § 2; Laws 1946, p. 39, § 2; Laws 1947, p. 1159, § 2; Laws 1949, p. 70, § 4; Laws 1951, p. 635, §§ 1, 1A; Laws 1952, p. 129, § 1; Laws 1955, p. 298, § 1; Laws 1956, p. 573, § 1; Laws 1957, p. 103, § 1; Laws 1958, p. 296, §§ 3, 4; Laws 1960, p. 132, § 1; Laws 1965, p. 125, § 1; Laws 1967, p. 84, § 1; Laws 1969, p. 147, § 1; Laws 1970, p. 117, § 1; Laws 1971, p. 306, § 1; Laws 1971, p. 309, § 1; Laws 1972, p. 354, § 2; Laws 1973, p. 449, §§ 1, 2; Laws 1974, p. 1007, § 1; Laws 1974, p. 1122, § 1; Laws 1975, p. 1115, § 1; Laws 1977, p. 228, § 2; Laws 1982, p. 3, § 35; Laws 1986, p. 452, § 1; Laws 1988, p. 312, § 1; Laws 1992, p. 3131, § 2.

§ 35–2–36.1. Auxiliary Service

(a) There is created within the Uniform Division, a special service known as the Auxiliary Service. The members of the Auxiliary Service of the Uniform Division shall be appointed by the commissioner on a part-time basis and shall serve at the pleasure of the commissioner. The members shall have such rank as assigned by the commissioner. The members of the Auxiliary Service shall be paid on an hourly basis and, with the exception of workers' compensation medical coverage and any benefits mandated by federal law, shall not be entitled to any employee benefits based on their employment in the Auxiliary Service.

(b) Members of the Auxiliary Service shall have the same authority and powers as other members of the Uniform Division.

(c) The commissioner is authorized to furnish the members of the Auxiliary Service with such equipment, uniforms, and badges as the commissioner deems necessary for the duties of such members.

(d) No person shall be eligible for appointment in the Auxiliary Service unless that person has, prior to such appointment, successfully completed trooper school, served in the Uniform Division, and voluntarily left the Uniform Division in good standing through retirement, resignation, or otherwise. Persons appointed to the Auxiliary Service must complete the annual training required under Code Section 35–8–21 for certified law enforcement officers, provided that such persons may serve up to six months without having such training. The Department of Public Safety is authorized to provide or to pay for such training in the same fashion that it provides or pays for such training for members of the Uniform Division.

Laws 1996, p. 1507, § 2.

§ 35–2–37. Communications officers; license examiners

To support the battalion, the commissioner, with the approval of the board, is authorized to employ such communications officers as may be necessary, within the limits set by available appropriations. Such personnel shall not be considered members of the Uniform Division. Communications officers may be divided into such ranks or categories as the commissioner, with the approval of the board, deems appropriate.

Laws 1937, p. 322, art. 2, § 2; Laws 1939, p. 135, § 2; Laws 1946, p. 39, § 2; Laws 1947, p. 1159, § 2; Laws 1949, p. 70, § 4; Laws 1951, p. 635, §§ 1, 1A; Laws 1952, p. 129, § 1; Laws 1955, p. 298, § 1; Laws 1956, p. 573, § 1; Laws 1957, p. 103, § 1; Laws 1958, p. 296, §§ 3, 4; Laws 1960, p. 132, § 1; Laws 1965, p. 125, § 1; Laws 1967, p. 84, § 1; Laws 1969, p. 147, § 1; Laws 1970, p. 117, § 1; Laws 1971, p. 306, § 1; Laws 1971, p. 309, § 1; Laws 1972, p. 354, § 2; Laws 1973, p. 449, §§ 1, 2; Laws 1974, p. 1007, § 1; Laws 1974, p. 1122, § 1; Laws 1975, p. 1115, § 1; Laws 1977, p. 228, § 2; Laws 2000, p. 951, § 12–4.

§ 35–2–38. Districts or divisions of the state

The commissioner, with the approval of the board, is authorized to divide the state into districts or divisions as may be necessary for the purpose of effectually patrolling the public roads and highways of the state and of the counties thereof and for combating, detecting, and preventing crime.

Laws 1937, p. 322, art. 2, § 11; Laws 1946, p. 39, § 3.

§ 35–2–39. Barracks

The commissioner is authorized, with the approval of the board, to provide comfortable barracks and quarters for the officers and troopers of the Uniform Division.

Laws 1937, p. 322, art. 2, § 11; Laws 1946, p. 39, § 3.

§ 35–2–40. Lease or purchase of quarters and equipment; donations

In the event any district or division headquarters is established by the commissioner, he shall be authorized, with the approval of the board, to purchase, lease, or construct proper quarters or barracks for the men and equipment at such district or division, and to this end may contract with municipalities, persons, or corporations in the name of the state. Subject to the provisions of Code Section 50–16–38 and Code Section 35–2–41.1, the board is authorized to accept in the name and on behalf of the state any property, equipment, or service that may be donated for use at headquarters or any division or district thereof which may be of value to any division of the department.

Laws 1937, p. 322, art. 2, § 12; Laws 1985, p. 486, § 1.

§ 35–2–41. County or municipal grants

Subject to the provisions of Code Section 35–2–41.1, any municipality or county of this state is authorized to purchase and convey property by deed, gift, rent, or lease for the use of the department for division or district headquarters. If the deed from the municipality or county to the property to be used for such headquarters contains a reversionary clause to the effect that the property shall revert to the municipality or county in the event it ceases to be used for the headquarters, the commissioner shall not be authorized to enter into any contract or agreement relative to the construction of quarters, barracks, or other facilities for such headquarters which shall, in any manner whatsoever, obligate the department to pay for more than one-half the costs of construction of the quarters, barracks, or other facilities. Any such contract or agreement must be approved by the board.

Laws 1937, p. 322, art. 2, § 12; Laws 1964, p. 144, § 1; Laws 1985, p. 486, § 2.

§ 35–2–41.1. Procedure for making and accepting grants

(a) Any offer to donate or convey by deed, gift, rent, lease, or other means any property, equipment, or services to the department shall be made in writing through command channels to the commissioner. If the commissioner approves the offer, he or she shall submit a written proposal of the offer to the board for its approval. A copy of the formal proposal shall be forwarded by the commissioner to the Office of Planning and Budget, the Senate Budget Office, and the House Budget Office, any of which may comment on the proposal.

(b) Title to real property shall be in the State of Georgia for the use of the Department of Public Safety. No member of the department shall be authorized to accept any donation or conveyance of property, equipment, or services unless the provisions of this Code section have been complied with and until the board has approved the donation or conveyance.

Laws 1985, p. 486, § 3; Laws 2008, Act 25, § 1–16, eff. Jan. 28, 2008.

§ 35–2–42. Compensation and expenses

(a) All members of the Uniform Division, all communications officers, and all recruits or cadets shall be governed by rules and regulations as now or hereafter established under Chapter 20 of Title 45.

(b) The board shall be authorized to provide for a subsistence and per diem allowance for commissioned officers, noncommissioned officers, and troopers of the Uniform Division.

(c) The board shall be authorized to pay to sworn members of the Department of Public Safety additional compensation to be paid upon retirement in the form of the badge and the duty weapon issued by the department to such member.

(d) The board shall be authorized to grant incentive pay to those members of the Uniform Division of the Department of Public Safety and those members of the Georgia Bureau of Investigation who have obtained degrees or certificates from an accredited member of the Federation of Regional Accrediting Commissions of Higher Education or who have obtained a degree or certificate of completion from some other educational institution with respect to a course of instruction related to law enforcement, so long as both the course of instruction and the institution are specifically approved by the board. Any such incentive pay shall be paid according to the following schedule:

(1) Completion of at least one year of degree-creditable college study consisting of the equivalent of 30 semester hours or 45 quarter hours of education: $200.00 per year;

(2) Obtaining of associate or two-year degree or certificate of completion of 60 semester hours or 90 quarter hours of education: $400.00 per year;

(3) Obtaining of a bachelor's or four-year degree: $800.00 per year.

(e) This Code section is not intended to repeal existing law concerning the following:

(1) The authority of the board to pay certain medical expenses incurred by any member of the Georgia State Patrol or the Georgia Bureau of Investigation;

(2) The authority of the commissioner to provide uniforms and supplies to members of the Uniform Division;

(3) The requirement that board and quarters be furnished to every member of the Uniform Division on active duty; or

(4) The authorization for officers and troopers to receive a legal award offered for the apprehension of any criminal.

Laws 1937, p. 322, art. 2, § 2; Laws 1939, p. 135, § 2; Laws 1946, p. 39, § 2; Laws 1947, p. 1159, § 2; Laws 1949, p. 70, § 4; Laws 1951, p. 635, §§ 1, 1A; Laws 1952, p. 129, § 1; Laws 1955, p. 298, § 1; Laws 1956, p. 573, § 1; Laws 1957, p. 103, § 1; Laws 1958, p. 296, §§ 3, 4; Laws 1960, p. 132, § 1; Laws 1965, p. 125, § 1; Laws 1967, p. 84, § 1; Laws 1969, p. 147, § 1; Laws 1970, p. 117, § 1; Laws 1971, p. 306, § 1; Laws 1971, p. 309, § 1; Laws 1972, p. 354, § 2; Laws 1973, p. 449, §§ 1, 2; Laws 1974, p. 1007, § 1; Laws 1974, p. 1122, § 1; Laws 1975, p. 1115, §§ 1, 2; Laws 1977, p. 228, § 2; Laws 1982, p. 3, § 35; Laws 1987, p. 3, § 35; Laws 1992, p. 3131, § 3; Laws 2000, p. 951, § 12-5; Laws 2006, Act 936, § 1, eff. May 5, 2006.

§ 35-2-43. Repealed by Laws 1998, p. 852, § 1, eff. April 10, 1998

§ 35-2-44. Enlistment; examination; training

It shall be the duty of the commissioner, subject to the laws of this state, to arrange for the enlistment and examination of applicants for service as troopers or officers of the Uniform Division of the Department of Public Safety, to provide the necessary preliminary training and subsequent instruction of troopers and recruits as peace officers of this state, and to make all necessary rules and regulations for the discipline, conduct, and control of all officers, troopers, and other employees of the department.

Laws 1937, p. 322, art. 2, § 8.

§ 35-2-45. Promotions

(a) Any trooper first class of the Uniform Division of the Department of Public Safety shall be eligible for promotion to the rank of corporal, provided he has served a period of 12 months in the Georgia State Patrol including the period of probation.

(b) Any noncommissioned or commissioned officer shall be eligible for promotion to a higher rank, provided he has served at least one year in the preceding rank.

(c) Promotions to ranks of corporal through lieutenant shall be made in accordance with the Georgia State Patrol Promotion System.

Laws 1937, p. 322, art. 2, § 4; Laws 1939, p. 135, § 4; Laws 1949, p. 70, § 6; Laws 1975, p. 1115, § 2; Laws 1987, p. 3, § 35; Laws 1992, p. 3131, § 4.

§ 35-2-46. Dismissal from employment

All officers, troopers, and communications officers who are in the classified service of the State Personnel Administration may be dismissed from their employment with the department only in accordance with Chapter 20 of Title 45 and the rules and regulations promulgated thereunder.

Laws 1937, p. 322, art. 2, § 5; Laws 1949, p. 70, § 7; Laws 1976, p. 465, § 1; Laws 1992, p. 3131, § 5; Laws 1997, p. 880, § 1; Laws 2000, p. 951, § 12-6; Laws 2009, Act 155, § 1, eff. July 1, 2009.

§ 35-2-47. Suspension

All officers, troopers, and communications officers who are in the classified service of the State Personnel Administration may be suspended pending their dismissal from employment with the department as provided in Chapter 20 of Title 45 or the rules and regulations promulgated thereunder.

Laws 1937, p. 322, art. 2, § 5; Laws 1949, p. 70, § 7; Laws 1976, p. 465, § 1; Laws 1992, p. 3131, § 6; Laws 1997, p. 880, § 2; Laws 2000, p. 951, § 12-6; Laws 2009, Act 155, § 1, eff. July 1, 2009.

§ 35-2-48. Repealed by Laws 1992, p. 3131, § 7, eff. July 1, 1992

§ 35-2-49. Uniforms, outfits, and supplies

The commissioner shall, within the limit of the appropriation, provide the sworn members of the Department of Public Safety with proper uniforms, suitable to the season, and also with emergency and first-aid outfits, weapons, motor vehicles with radio equipment, and all other necessary supplies and equipment for the purpose of carrying out this article, the same to remain the property of the state; provided, however, that after a sworn member has accumulated 15 years of service with the Department of Public Safety, including prior service with the Department of Motor Vehicle Safety, Georgia Public Service Commission, Georgia Department of Transportation, or Georgia Building Authority, upon leaving the department under honorable conditions, or upon leaving the department as a result of a disability arising in the line of duty regardless of the number of years of service, such member shall be entitled, as part of his or her compensation, to retain his or her weapon and badge pursuant to regulations promulgated by the commissioner. The commissioner shall also, within the limit of the appropriation, provide proper uniforms and equipment to radio operators. After a radio operator has accumulated 15 years of service with the department, including prior service with the Georgia Department of Motor Vehicle Safety, Georgia Public Service Commission, Georgia Department of Transportation, or Georgia Building Authority, upon leaving the department under honorable conditions, such radio operator shall be entitled, as part of his or her compensation, to retain his or her badge pursuant to regulations promulgated by the commissioner.

Laws 1937, p. 322, art. 2, § 9; Laws 1949, p. 70, § 8; Laws 1975, p. 1175, § 7; Laws 1979, p. 1072, § 1; Laws 1996, p. 271, § 3; Laws 2000, p. 951, § 12-6; Laws 2006, Act 936, § 2, eff. May 5, 2006.

§ 35-2-49.1. Disability arising in the line of duty; retention of weapon and badge

(a) As used in this Code section, the term "disability" means a disability that prevents an individual from working as a law enforcement officer.

(b) When a member of the Uniform Division of the Department of Public Safety leaves the Uniform Division as a result of a disability arising in the line of duty, such member of the Uniform Division shall be entitled as part of such officer's compensation to retain his or her weapon and badge in accordance with regulations promulgated by the commissioner.

Laws 2004, Act 784, § 3, eff. July 1, 2004; Laws 2005, Act 19, § 35, eff. April 7, 2005.

§ 35–2–50. Purchases; advertisements; bids

(a) The uniforms, supplies, and equipment authorized by Code Section 35–2–49 shall be purchased by the Department of Administrative Services, with the consent and approval of the Department of Public Safety, by bid let to the lowest and best bidder and in accordance with specifications named in the advertisement of bid.

(b) The advertisement of the letting of contracts for the purchase of uniforms, supplies, or equipment shall be published in at least two issues of some public journal of the state published daily and having a state-wide circulation for not less than 15 days before the time bids for the contracts are opened. The Department of Administrative Services shall have the right to reject any and all bids.

Laws 1937, p. 322, art. 2, § 9; Laws 1949, p. 70, § 8; Laws 1979, p. 1072, § 1.

§ 35–2–51. Storerooms; custodian

(a) The commissioner shall provide a storeroom or rooms where all excess supplies of clothing, equipment, and other articles shall be stored and shall insure the same against loss by fire.

(b) All old and worn equipment must be delivered to the custodian or custodians of such storeroom or rooms, who need not be members of the Uniform Division of the Department of Public Safety nor subject to age limitations, to be properly receipted before new equipment shall be issued.

Laws 1937, p. 322, art. 2, § 9; Laws 1949, p. 70, § 8.

§ 35–2–52. Clothing allowance

The commissioner, at his discretion and subject to available funds, shall be authorized to pay to members of the Uniform Division a clothing allowance when the members are permanently assigned to personal security or special duty assignments which necessitate those members wearing clothing other than the uniform of the Uniform Division. The commissioner, subject to the approval of the Board of Public Safety, shall establish the amount of clothing allowance to be paid each year.

Laws 1937, p. 322, art. 2, § 9; Laws 1949, p. 70, § 8; Laws 1975, p. 1175, § 7; Laws 1979, p. 1072, § 1; Laws 1986, p. 452, § 2.

§ 35–2–53. No emoluments or costs

No member of the Uniform Division of the Department of Public Safety shall receive any costs, emoluments, or other compensation other than his salary and any additional compensation provided by or through federal funding to which he may be entitled, except a legal reward as otherwise stated in this article. All fines and costs shall be paid into the treasury of the tribunal having jurisdiction of the offense and distributed according to law.

Laws 1937, p. 322, art. 2, §§ 6, 15; Laws 1973, p. 449, § 3.

§ 35–2–54. Purchase of insurance

(a) The commissioner, with the approval of the board, is authorized to purchase group life, group accident, and group hospitalization insurance contracts, policies, or certificates issued to the members of the Uniform Division, provided that such contracts of insurance shall be approved by the board as to the amount of insurance, amount of premiums, and company issuing or writing them; provided, further, that the premiums for such contracts, policies, or certificates of insurance shall be paid by the members of the Uniform Division desiring to participate therein; and this purchase shall be in no way considered as incurring a liability on the part of the state to pay for such insurance.

(b) The contracts, policies, or certificates of insurance, as provided for in subsection (a) of this Code section, may be made payable to the beneficiary designated by the member of the Uniform Division to whom the contracts, policies, or certificates are issued.

Laws 1941, p. 277, § 1; Laws 1987, p. 3, § 35.

§ 35–2–55. Compensatory time

The commissioner is authorized and directed to arrange the work schedules of members of the Uniform Division in such a manner that each member shall be given compensatory time off for each day which he is required to work and which is also a legal state holiday. Such compensatory time off shall be given within 90 days of the holiday involved, except where the day of compensatory time off coincides with an emergency situation, in which case the granting of compensatory time off shall be postponed until such time as the emergency no longer exists.

Laws 1970, p. 849.

§ 35–2–56. Use of motor vehicles and other equipment

(a) Except as otherwise provided in subsection (b) of this Code section, no department motor vehicles shall be used by any member of the Uniform Division except in discharge of official duties. Any other equipment shall be used only with the express written approval of the commissioner. The commissioner shall adopt rules and regulations governing the use of equipment subject to approval of the Board of Public Safety.

(b)(1) Members of the Uniform Division may use a department motor vehicle while working an approved off-duty job, provided that:

(A) The off-duty employment is of a general nature that is the subject of a contract between the off-duty employer and the Department of Public Safety and is service in which the use of the department motor vehicle is a benefit to the department or is in furtherance of the department's mission;

(B) The off-duty employer agrees to pay and does pay to the department an amount determined by the commissioner to be sufficient to reimburse the department for the use of the vehicle and to pay the off-duty employee sufficient compensation. Pursuant to such contract, the department shall pay the employee of the department the compensation earned on off-duty employment whenever such employee performs such service in a department motor vehicle; and

(C) The commissioner has specifically approved, in writing, the individual use of the vehicle by the employee.

(2) At no time will an off-duty employee be allowed use of a department motor vehicle at any political function of any kind.

Laws 1937, p. 322, art. 2, § 13; Laws 1952, p. 3, § 1; Laws 1992, p. 1310, § 1; Laws 1999, p. 560, § 1.

§ 35–2–57. Certain unmarked pursuit vehicles to be made available to Georgia Public Safety Training Center

When an unmarked pursuit vehicle used by the Georgia State Patrol for the purpose of enforcing the traffic laws of this state is first removed from the field and will no longer be used on a regular basis for pursuit purposes, the commissioner of public safety shall notify the administrator of the Georgia Public Safety Training Center and shall make such pursuit vehicle available to such center for the purpose of training public safety officers pursuant to Chapter 5 of this title. Upon notification by the commissioner, the administrator of the Georgia Public Safety Training Center shall be authorized to take immediate possession of any such pursuit vehicle.

Laws 1987, p. 317, § 1.

Article 3

Security Guard Division

§ 35–2–70. Establishment

The commissioner is authorized, with the approval of the board, to establish a Security Guard Division within the department.

Laws 1968, p. 475, § 1.

§ 35–2–71. Powers and duties

(a) While in the performance of their duties, such security guards shall have the same powers of arrest and the same powers to enforce law and order as the sheriff of the county and the chief of police of the municipality in this state in which any such security guards are performing their duties.

(b) While in the performance of their duties, such security guards shall also be authorized to exercise such powers and duties as are authorized by law for members of the Uniform Division of the department.

Laws 1968, p. 475, § 4; Laws 1987, p. 3, § 35.

§ 35–2–72. Compensation, uniforms and equipment

All persons employed as security guards shall be compensated in an amount to be prescribed by the commissioner and shall be furnished with and shall wear such distinctive uniforms and equipment as may be prescribed by the commissioner.

Laws 1968, p. 475, § 3.

§ 35–2–73. Employment of security guards

(a) The commissioner shall be authorized to employ such number of security guards as may be necessary to keep watch over and protect the Governor and members of his immediate family, the Lieutenant Governor and members of his immediate family, the Speaker of the House of Representatives and members of his immediate family, the executive department at the state capitol or at any other place as the executive department may be moved, the executive center or other residence of the Governor, the residences and offices of the Lieutenant Governor and the Speaker of the House of Representatives, and such other state property and individuals as may be directed by the Governor.

(b) Members of the Governor's family, the Lieutenant Governor's family, and the Speaker's family for whom protection is provided by the Security Guard Division, when traveling with the Governor, the Lieutenant Governor, or the Speaker, as the case may be, when traveling on state related business at the request of the Governor, the Lieutenant Governor, or the Speaker, as the case may be, or when in the judgment of the commissioner security considerations so dictate, may be transported by means of state owned transportation facilities, when appropriate, or at state expense by private carrier, when the use of such state owned facilities are not practical or appropriate.

Laws 1968, p. 475, § 1; Laws 1979, p. 143, § 2; Laws 1981, p. 684, § 1; Laws 1982, p. 3, § 35; Laws 1987, p. 3, § 35; Laws 1992, p. 6, § 35.

§ 35–2–74. Employees to be covered by State Merit System if authorized by Governor

(a) The Governor is authorized, in his discretion, to direct by executive order that the employees of the Security Guard Division shall be covered by the State Personnel Administration and in such order shall specify the date on which the system shall become applicable to such personnel.

(b) The application of the State Personnel Administration to employees of the Security Guard Division shall not affect any other personnel of the Department of Public Safety.

Laws 1968, p. 475, § 6; Laws 2009, Act 155, § 2, eff. July 1, 2009.

Historical and Statutory Notes

In 2009, the Code Commission, in subsec. (b), substituted "State Personnel Administration" for "state merit system". See § 28–9–5.

§ 35–2–75. Rules, regulations and orders

The board shall be authorized to promulgate and adopt such rules, regulations, and orders in regard to security guards as in its judgment public service may demand.

Laws 1968, p. 475, § 5.

Article 4

Department of Public Safety Nomenclature

§ 35–2–80. Short title

This article shall be known and may be cited as the "Department of Public Safety Nomenclature Act of 1995."

Laws 1995, p. 925, § 2.

§ 35–2–81. Definitions

As used in this article, the term:

(1) "Badge" means any official badge used by members of the Department of Public Safety, either in the past or currently.

(2) "Commissioner" means the commissioner of public safety.

(3) "Department" means the Department of Public Safety.

(4) "Emblem" means any official patch or other emblem worn currently or formerly or used by the department to identify the department or its employees.

(5) "Person" means any person, corporation, organization, or political subdivision of the State of Georgia.

(6) "Willful violator" means any person who knowingly violates the provisions of this article. Any person who violates this article after being advised in writing by the commissioner that such person's activity is in violation of this article shall be considered a willful violator and shall be considered in willful violation of this article. Any person whose agent or representative is a willful violator and who has knowledge of the violation by the agent or representative shall also be considered a willful violator and in willful violation of this article unless, upon learning of the violation, he or she immediately terminates the agency or other relationship with such violator.

Laws 1995, p. 925, § 2.

§ 35–2–82. Unauthorized use of nomenclature prohibited

Whoever, except with the written permission of the commissioner, knowingly uses the words "Georgia Department of Public Safety," "State Patrol," "State Police," "State Highway Patrol," "State Trooper," or "State Patrolman" in connection with any advertisement, circular, book, pamphlet, or other publication, play, motion picture, broadcast, telecast, or other production in a manner reasonably calculated to convey the impression that such advertisement, circular, book, pamphlet, or other publication, play, motion picture, broadcast, telecast, or other production is approved, endorsed, or authorized by or associated with the department shall be in violation of this article.

Laws 1995, p. 925, § 2.

§ 35–2–83. Unauthorized use of symbols prohibited

Any person who uses or displays any symbol, including any emblem, seal, or badge, current or historical, used by the department without written permission from the commissioner shall be in violation of this article.

Laws 1995, p. 925, § 2.

§ 35–2–84. Procedure for seeking permission to use nomenclature or symbols; grant or denial of permission; appeals

Any person wishing permission to use either department nomenclature or symbols may request such permission in writing to the commissioner. The commissioner shall serve notice on the requesting party within 15 calendar days after receipt of the request of his or her decision on whether the person may use the nomenclature or the symbol. If the commissioner does not respond within the 15 day time period, then the request is presumed to have been denied. The grant of permission under Code Section 35–2–82 or 35–2–83 shall be in the discretion of the commissioner under such conditions as the commissioner may impose. If the commissioner denies such request and the person making such request reasonably believes that the commissioner has acted in bad faith or based on an illegal motive, then the person may, within 15 days after the person's request was denied or granted on limited terms, file an appeal with the Board of Public Safety. The matter will then be considered before the board, but the burden will be with the person making the request to show that the request was improperly denied or limited.

Laws 1995, p. 925, § 2.

§ 35–2–85. Injunctive relief to restrain violations

Whenever there shall be an actual or threatened violation of Code Section 35–2–82 or 35–2–83, the commissioner shall have the right to apply to the Superior Court of Fulton County or to the superior court of the county of residence of the violator for an injunction to restrain the violation.

Laws 1995, p. 925, § 2.

§ 35–2–86. Civil sanctions

In addition to any other relief or sanction for a violation of Code Section 35–2–82 or 35–2–83, where the violation is willful, the commissioner shall be entitled to collect a civil penalty in the amount of $500.00 for each violation. Further, when there is a finding of willful violation, the commissioner shall be entitled to recover reasonable attorney's fees for bringing any action against the violator. The commissioner shall be entitled to seek civil sanctions in the Superior Court of Fulton County or in the county of residence of the violator.

Laws 1995, p. 925, § 2.

§ 35–2–87. Damages

Any person who has given money or any other item of value to another person due in part to such person's use of department nomenclature or symbols in violation of this article may maintain a suit for damages against the violator. Where it is proven that the violation was willful, the victim shall be entitled to recover treble damages, punitive damages, and reasonable attorney's fees.

Laws 1995, p. 925, § 2.

§ 35–2–88. Criminal penalties

Any person who violates the provisions of this article shall be guilty of a felony and upon conviction thereof shall be subject to a fine of not less than $1,000.00 nor more than $5,000.00 or to imprisonment for not less than one and not more than five years, or both. Each violation shall constitute a separate offense.

Laws 1995, p. 925, § 2.

Article 5

Motor Carrier Compliance Division

§ 35–2–100. Creation

There is created and established a division of the Department of Public Safety to be known as the Motor Carrier Compliance Division. Except as provided in Code Section 35–2–102, the members of the Motor Carrier Compliance Division shall be known and designated as "law enforcement officers."

Laws 2005, Act 68, § 13A–2, eff. July 1, 2005; Laws 2009, Act 41, § 1, eff. April 21, 2009.

§ 35–2–101. Jurisdiction; powers and duties

(a) The Motor Carrier Compliance Division of the department shall have jurisdiction throughout this state with such duties and powers as are prescribed by law.

(b) The primary duties of the Motor Carrier Compliance Division shall be as follows:

(1) Enforcement of laws and regulations relating to the size and the weights of motor vehicles, trailers, and loads as provided for in Article 2 of Chapter 6 of Title 32;

(2) Enforcement of laws and regulations relating to licensing and fuel tax registration requirements and the reporting of violations thereof to the Department of Revenue;

(3) Enforcement of safety standards for motor vehicles and motor vehicle components;

(4) Enforcement of laws relating to hazardous materials carriers;

(5) Enforcement of all state laws on the following properties owned or controlled by the Department of Transportation or the State Road and Tollway Authority: rest areas, truck–weighing stations or checkpoints, wayside parks, parking facilities, toll facilities, and any buildings and grounds for public equipment and personnel used for or engaged in administration, construction, or maintenance of the public roads or research pertaining thereto;

(6) Enforcement of Code Section 16–10–24, relating to obstructing or hindering law enforcement officers;

(7) Directing and controlling traffic on any public road which is part of the state highway system but only in areas where maintenance and construction activities are being performed and at scenes of accidents and emergencies until local police officers or Georgia State Patrol officers arrive and have the situation under control;

(8) Enforcement of Code Sections 32–9–4 and 40–6–54, relating to designation of restricted travel lanes;

(9) Enforcement of Code Section 16–11–43, relating to obstructing highways, streets, sidewalks, or other public passages, on any public road which is part of the state highway system;

(10) Enforcement of Code Section 16–7–43, relating to littering public or private property or waters, on any public road which is part of the state highway system;

(11) Enforcement of Code Section 16–7–24, relating to interference with government property, on any public road which is part of the state highway system; and

(12) Enforcement of any state law when ordered to do so by the commissioner.

(c) In performance of the duties specified in subsection (b) of this Code section, certified law enforcement officers employed by the department or designated by the commissioner shall:

(1) Be authorized to carry firearms;

(2) Exercise arrest powers;

(3) Have the power to stop, enter upon, and inspect all motor vehicles using the public highways for purposes of determining whether such vehicles have complied with and are complying with laws, the administration or enforcement of which is the responsibility of the department;

(4) Have the power to examine the facilities where motor vehicles are housed or maintained and the books and records of motor carriers for purposes of determining compliance with laws, the administration or enforcement of which is the responsibility of the department; and

(5) Exercise the powers generally authorized for law enforcement officers in the performance of their duties or otherwise to the extent needed to protect any life or property when the circumstances demand action.

(d) The commissioner shall authorize law enforcement officers of the Motor Carrier Compliance Division to make use of dogs trained for the purpose of detection of drugs and controlled substances while such officers are engaged in the performance of their authorized duties. If such authorized use of such a dog indicates probable cause to indicate the presence of contraband, the officer or officers shall in those circumstances have the full authority of peace officers to enforce the provisions of Article 2 of Chapter 13 of Title 16, the "Georgia Controlled Substances Act," and Article 3 of Chapter 13 of Title 16, the "Dangerous Drug Act"; provided, however, that the department must immediately notify the local law enforcement agency and district attorney of the jurisdiction where a seizure is made.

(e)(1) Certified law enforcement officers employed by the Motor Carrier Compliance Division may use a department motor vehicle while working an approved off–duty job, provided that:

(A) The off–duty employment is of a general nature that is the subject of a contract between the off–duty employer and the department and is service in which the use of the department motor vehicle is a benefit to the department or is in furtherance of the department's mission;

(B) The off–duty employer agrees to pay and does pay to the department an amount determined by the commissioner to be sufficient to reimburse the department for the use of the vehicle and to pay the off–duty employee sufficient compensation. Pursuant to such contract, the department shall pay the employee of the department the compensation earned on off–duty employment whenever such employee performs such service in a department motor vehicle; and

(C) The commissioner has specifically approved, in writing, the individual use of the vehicle by the employee.

(2) At no time will an off–duty employee be allowed use of a department motor vehicle at any political function of any kind.

Laws 2005, Act 68, § 13A–2, eff. July 1, 2005.

§ 35–2–102. Weight inspectors

(a) The commissioner is authorized to establish a position to be known as "weight inspector" within the Motor Carrier Compliance Division of the Department of Public Safety. Weight inspectors shall be assigned to fixed scales facilities and shall not be authorized to operate outside such facilities. The number of such positions shall be determined by the commissioner within the limits set by available appropriations. Weight inspectors may be divided into such ranks as the commissioner deems appropriate.

(b) The commissioner shall ensure that a weight inspector is properly trained regarding laws governing commercial motor vehicle weight, registration, size, and load, including, but not limited to, commercial motor vehicle provisions in Article 2 of Chapter 6 of Title 32 and safety standards for commercial motor vehicles and such motor vehicle components. The training required in the areas required by this subsection shall be equivalent to training provided to certified officers in the Motor Carrier Compliance Division.

(c) A weight inspector, at the fixed scales facility, shall be authorized to:

(1) Enforce noncriminal provisions relating to commercial motor vehicle weight, registration, size, and load and assess a civil penalty for a violation of such provisions; and

(2) Detain a commercial motor vehicle that:

(A) Has a safety defect which is critical to the continued safe operation of the vehicle;

(B) Is being operated in violation of any criminal law; or

(C) Is being operated in violation of an out-of-service order as reported on the federal Safety and Fitness Electronic Records data base.

The detention authorized by this paragraph shall be for the purpose of contacting a certified member of the Motor Carrier Compliance Division or Georgia State Patrol. A certified officer shall report to the scene of a detained vehicle and take any further action deemed appropriate including completing the inspection and investigation, making an arrest, or bringing criminal or civil charges.

(d) A weight inspector is not a peace officer and shall not be authorized to carry a firearm or exercise any power of arrest other than a citizen's arrest in accordance with Code Sections 17–4–60 and 17–4–61. At all times while a weight inspector is on duty, there shall be a supervisor over the weight inspector also on duty who shall be a certified peace officer.

Laws 2009, Act 41, § 2, eff. April 21, 2009.

Article 6

Capitol Police Division

§ 35–2–120. Definitions

As used in this article, the term:

(1) "Capitol Square" means that area designated as such by Code Section 50–2–28.

(2) "Commissioner" means the commissioner of public safety.

(3) "Department" means the Department of Public Safety.

(4) "Division" means the Capitol Police Division of the department created by this article.

Laws 2010, Act 379, § 1, eff. July 1, 2010.

§ 35–2–121. Establishment and staffing

There is created and established a division of the Department of Public Safety to be known as the Capitol Police Division. The department shall staff such division with certified law enforcement officers, who shall be designated capitol police officers, security personnel under the employment of or contract with the department, and any other certified peace officer employed by the department.

Laws 2010, Act 379, § 1, eff. July 1, 2010.

§ 35–2–122. Jurisdiction and duties

(a) The division shall have jurisdiction and the primary duty to enforce all laws in Capitol Square and the property and buildings owned by the Georgia Building Authority within a five-mile radius of Capitol Square.

(b) The division shall have the following additional duties:

(1) To maintain peace and order and enforce the laws and regulations relating to controlling access to any building or property under the control or operation of the Georgia Building Authority;

(2) To maintain peace and order and enforce the laws and regulations relating to controlling access to Capitol Square;

(3) To enforce parking and traffic laws and to investigate accidents within Capitol Square;

(4) To enforce state law when ordered to do so by the commissioner; and

(5) To exercise the powers of a law enforcement officer to protect life and property.

(c) In the performance of their duties, certified law enforcement officers shall be authorized to carry firearms and exercise the power of arrest.

Laws 2010, Act 379, § 1, eff. July 1, 2010.

§ 35–2–123. Use of official vehicles

(a) Certified law enforcement officers employed by the division shall be authorized to use official vehicles while engaging in approved off-duty employment, provided that:

(1) The off-duty employment is related to a contract between the off-duty employer and the department and is service in which the use of the official vehicle is a benefit to the department or is in furtherance of the department's mission;

(2) The off-duty employer pays to the department an amount determined by the commissioner to be sufficient to reimburse the department for the use of the official vehicle; and

(3) The commissioner has approved, in writing, the individual use of the official vehicle by the law enforcement officer.

(b) At no time shall an off-duty law enforcement officer be allowed the use of an official vehicle at a political function of any kind.

Laws 2010, Act 379, § 1, eff. July 1, 2010.

§ 35–2–124. Reimbursement of costs

The Georgia Building Authority shall reimburse the department for the costs to the department of performing police and security duties within Capitol Square in accordance with an intergovernmental agreement by and between the department and the Georgia Building Authority. Such agreement shall set forth the amount to be paid by the Georgia Building Authority to the department for each fiscal year and shall be executed prior to the budget submission deadline set by the Governor's Office of Planning and Budget.

Laws 2010, Act 379, § 1, eff. July 1, 2010.

CHAPTER 3

GEORGIA BUREAU OF INVESTIGATION

Article 1

Article 2

Article 1

General Provisions

§ 35–3–1. Definitions

As used in this chapter, the term:

(1) "Bureau" means the Georgia Bureau of Investigation.

(2) "Director" means the director of the Georgia Bureau of Investigation.

Laws 2005, Act 114, § 1, eff. July 1, 2005.

§ 35–3–2. Creation

There is created a Georgia Bureau of Investigation which shall be a separate department and agency of state government.

Laws 1937, p. 322, art. 3, § 1; Laws 1972, p. 1015, §§ 1608, 1608.1; Laws 1974, p. 109, § 2.

§ 35–3–3. Divisions

The Georgia Bureau of Investigation shall be composed of the Investigations Division, the Forensic Sciences Division, the Georgia Crime Information Center Division, and such other divisions as may be created by the board.

Laws 1974, p. 109, § 2; Laws 1980, p. 497, § 1.

§ 35–3–4. Duties; fingerprints; photographs, etc.

(a) It shall be the duty of the bureau to:

(1) Take, receive, and forward fingerprints, photographs, descriptions, and measurements of persons in cooperation with the bureaus and departments of other states and of the United States;

(2) Exchange information relating to crime and criminals;

(3) Keep permanent files and records of such information procured or received;

(4) Provide for the scientific investigation of articles used in committing crimes or articles, fingerprints, or bloodstains found at the scene of a crime;

(5) Provide for the testing and identification of weapons and projectiles fired therefrom;

(6) Acquire, collect, classify, and preserve any information which would assist in the identification of any deceased individual who has not been identified after the discovery of such deceased individual;

(7) Acquire, collect, classify, and preserve immediately any information which would assist in the location of any missing person, including any minor, and provide confirmation as to any entry for such a person to the parent, legal guardian, or next of kin of that person and the bureau shall acquire, collect, classify, and preserve such information from such parent, guardian, or next of kin;

(8) Exchange such records and information as provided in paragraphs (6) and (7) of this subsection with, and for the official use of, authorized officials of the federal government, the states, cities, counties, and penal and other institutions. With respect to missing minors, such information shall be transmitted immediately to other law enforcement agencies;

(9) Identify and investigate violations of Article 4 of Chapter 7 of Title 16;

(10) Identify and investigate violations of Part 2 of Article 3 of Chapter 12 of Title 16, relating to offenses related to minors;

(11) Identify and investigate violations of Article 8 of Chapter 9 of Title 16; or

(12) Identify and investigate violations of Article 5 of Chapter 8 of Title 16.

(b) In addition to the duties provided in subsection (a) of this Code section, the members of the bureau shall have and are vested with the same authority, powers, and duties as are possessed by the members of the Uniform Division of the Department of Public Safety under this title.

Laws 1937, p. 322, art. 3, § 1; Laws 1941, p. 277, § 4; Laws 1974, p. 109, § 2; Laws 1977, p. 752, § 1; Laws 1982, p. 3, § 35; Laws 1984, p. 690, § 2; Laws 1985, p. 149, § 35; Laws 1996, p. 416, § 9; Laws 2007, Act 202, § 3, eff. May 23, 2007; Laws 2008, Act 570, § 2, eff. May 13, 2008; Laws 2010, Act 678, § 2, eff. July 1, 2010.

§ 35–3–4.1. Subpoena authority for electronic communication service or remote communication service records

(a)(1) In any investigation of a violation of Code Section 16–12–100, 16–12–100.1, or 16–12–100.2 involving the use of a computer or an electronic device in furtherance of an act related to a minor, or any investigation of a violation of Article 8 of Chapter 9 of Title 16, the director, assistant director, or deputy director for investigations shall be authorized to issue a subpoena, with the consent of the Attorney General, to compel the production of electronic communication service or remote communication service records or other information pertaining to a subscriber or customer of such service, exclusive of contents of communications.

(2) A provider of electronic communication service or remote computing service shall disclose to the bureau the:

(A) Name;

(B) Address;

(C) Local and long distance telephone connection records, or records of session times and durations;

(D) Length of service, including the start date, and types of service utilized;

(E) Telephone or instrument number or other subscriber number or identity, including any temporarily assigned network address; and

(F) Means and source of payment for such service, including any credit card or bank account number of a subscriber to or customer of such service.

(b) Upon failure of a person without lawful excuse to obey a subpoena, the director, assistant director, or the deputy director for investigations, through the Attorney General or district attorney, may apply to a superior court having jurisdiction for an order compelling compliance. Such person may object to the subpoena on grounds that it fails to comply with this Code section or upon any constitutional or other legal right or privilege of such person. The court may issue an order modifying or setting aside such subpoena or directing compliance with the original subpoena.

(c) The Attorney General may request that a natural person who refuses to produce relevant matter on the ground that the production of records may incriminate such person be ordered by the court to provide such records. With the exception of a prosecution for perjury, a natural person who complies with the court order to provide such records asserting a privilege against self-incrimination to which he or she is entitled by law shall not be prosecuted or subjected to any penalty or forfeiture for or on account of any transaction, matter, or thing concerning which he or she may testify or produce evidence, documentary or otherwise.

(d)(1) Information obtained pursuant to a subpoena enforced by this Code section shall not be made public or, except as authorized in paragraph (2) of this subsection, disclosed by the director, assistant director, deputy director for investigations, or the director's employees beyond the extent necessary for the enforcement of this Code section.

(2) The director, assistant director, deputy director for investigations, or the director's employees shall be authorized to provide to any federal, state, or local law enforcement agency any information acquired under this Code section in furtherance of a criminal investigation in violation of Code Section 16–12–100, 16–12–100.1, or 16–12–100.2.

(e) As used in this Code section, the terms "electronic communication service" and "remote communication service" shall have the same meaning as set forth in Code Section 16–9–92.

Laws 2007, Act 202, § 4, eff. May 23, 2007; Laws 2008, Act 570, § 3, eff. May 13, 2008.

Historical and Statutory Notes

The 2008 amendment by Act 570, in par. (1) of subsec. (a), inserted ", or any investigation of a violation of Article 8 of Chapter 9 of Title 16,".

§ 35–3–4.2. Subpoena authority for computer or other electronic device

(a) In any investigation of a violation of Article 5 of Chapter 8 of Title 16 or other criminal violations involving fraudulent real estate transactions, the director, assistant director, or deputy director for investigations shall be authorized to issue a subpoena, with the consent of the Attorney General, to compel the production of books, papers, documents, or other tangible things, including records and documents contained within, or generated by, a computer or any other electronic device.

(b) Upon the failure of a person without lawful excuse to obey a subpoena, the director, assistant director, or the deputy director for investigations, through the Attorney General or district attorney, may apply to a superior court having jurisdiction for an order compelling compliance. Such person may object to the subpoena on grounds that it fails to comply with this Code section or upon any constitutional or other legal right or privilege of such person. The court may issue an order modifying or setting aside such subpoena or directing compliance with the original subpoena. Failure to obey a subpoena issued under this Code section may be punished by the court as contempt of court.

Laws 2010, Act 678, § 3, eff. July 1, 2010.

§ 35–3–5. Director of Investigation

(a) There is created the position of director.

(b) The director shall be the chief administrative officer and shall be both appointed and removed by the Board of Public Safety with the approval of the Governor.

(c) Except as otherwise provided by this chapter, and subject to the general policy established by the board, the director shall supervise, direct, account for, organize, plan, administer, and execute the functions vested in the bureau by this chapter.

Laws 1974, p. 109, § 2; Laws 2005, Act 114, § 2, eff. July 1, 2005.

§ 35–3–6. Compensation of the director

The director shall be in the unclassified service of the State Personnel Administration and his compensation shall be fixed by the board.

Laws 1974, p. 109, § 2; Laws 2009, Act 155, § 2, eff. July 1, 2009.

§ 35–3–7. Authorization to enter into agreements

The director and the commissioner of public safety are authorized to enter into agreements, subject to approval of the Board of Public Safety, for the provision of such services, material, or combination thereof as may be useful in the performance of the official duties of the bureau or the department.

Laws 1974, p. 109, § 2; Laws 1987, p. 3, § 35; Laws 2005, Act 114, § 3, eff. July 1, 2005.

§ 35–3–8. Agents to have powers concurrent with Department of Revenue to enforce criminal statutes pertaining to manufacture, transportation, distribution, sale, or possession of liquor, wine, beer, alcoholic beverages, cigars, cigarettes, cheroots, stogies, and loose or smokeless tobacco

(a) All properly appointed agents of the bureau shall have the powers, including the power of making arrests and appearing in court, for the enforcement of all criminal statutes pertaining to the manufacture, transportation, distribution, sale, or possession of liquor, wine, beer, alcoholic beverages, cigars, cigarettes, little cigars, cheroots, stogies, and loose or smokeless tobacco and shall concurrently with agents and enforcement officers appointed by the state revenue commissioner have the authority throughout the state to:

(1) Obtain and execute warrants for the arrest of persons charged with violations of such laws;

(2) Obtain and execute search warrants in the enforcement of such laws;

(3) Arrest without warrant any person found in violation of such laws, or endeavoring to escape, or if for other cause there is likely to be a failure of enforcement of such laws for want of an officer to issue a warrant;

(4) Make investigations in the enforcement of such laws and in connection therewith to go upon any property outside of buildings, posted or otherwise, in the performance of such duties;

(5) Seize and take possession of all property which is declared contraband under such laws; and

(6) Carry firearms while performing their duties.

(b) The enforcement powers conferred in this Code section upon agents of the bureau shall relate only to the enforcement of the criminal provisions relating to the manufacture, transportation, distribution, sale, or possession of liquor, wine, beer, alcoholic beverages, cigars, cigarettes, little cigars, cheroots, stogies, and loose or smokeless tobacco and shall not extend to regulatory matters with respect to such products under the jurisdiction of the state revenue commissioner.

Laws 1980, p. 420, § 1; Laws 1982, p. 3, § 35; Laws 2003, Act 343, § 42, eff. July 1, 2003.

§ 35–3–8.1. Assistance to municipal and county authorities

Upon request of the governing authority or chief law enforcement officer of any municipality, the sheriff of any county, the chief of the county police force of any county having a population of more than 100,000 according to the United States decennial census of 1970 or any future such census, the judge of the superior court of any county of this state, or the Governor, the director, in unusual circumstances, may, and in the case of a request by the Governor, shall, direct the bureau to render assistance in any criminal case, in the prevention or detection of violations of law, or in the detection or apprehension of persons violating the criminal laws of this state, any other state, or the United States.

Laws 1982, p. 3, § 35; Laws 1987, p. 3, § 35.

§ 35–3–9. Retention of narcotics agents to support local law enforcement in combating drug abuse

(a) The director is authorized to retain on a contractual basis such persons as he shall deem necessary to detect and apprehend violators of the criminal statutes of this state pertaining to the possession, sale, or use of narcotics or other dangerous drugs.

(b) Those persons contracting with the director pursuant to subsection (a) of this Code section shall be known as narcotics agents.

(c) The investigative services provided for in this Code section shall be designed to support local law enforcement efforts. The director shall, with the advice and consent of the board, appoint a three-member priority committee comprised of a representative from the Georgia Sheriffs Association, the Georgia Association of Chiefs of Police, and the District Attorneys Association. The committee shall establish priorities for use of investigative resources and determine the bona fide nature of requests for assistance. The recommendations of the committee shall be followed by the director except where otherwise expressly authorized by the board.

(d) Narcotics agents shall have all powers necessary and incidental to the fulfillment of their contractual obligations, including the power of arrest when authorized by the director.

(e) No person shall be a narcotics agent unless he is at least 18 years of age.

(f) The director shall conduct a background investigation of all potential narcotics agents. If the background investigation discloses a criminal record, the applicant shall not be retained without the express approval of the board.

(g) Any matters pertaining to narcotics agents shall be exempt from Chapter 14 of Title 50, relating to meetings open to the public.

(h) Persons retained as narcotics agents shall be considered persons in the service of the bureau under a contract of hire with that agency whose employment of those persons as narcotics agents shall be considered an employment in the usual course of the business of that agency. Persons retained by the bureau as narcotics agents shall have all the rights and privileges of other employees of the bureau; provided, however, that such persons shall be in the unclassified service of the State Personnel Administration and therefore shall not be governed by any rules of position, classification, appointment, promotion, demotion, transfer, dismissal, qualification, compensation, seniority privileges, tenure, or other such matters concerning their employment established by the State Personnel Board, the State Personnel Administration, or any successor boards or agencies.

(i) The director shall have all powers necessary and incidental to the effective operation of this Code section.

Laws 1973, p. 544, § 1; Laws 1976, p. 392, § 1; Laws 1978, p. 1646, § 1; Laws 1987, p. 3, § 35; Laws 1990, p. 540, § 2; Laws 2001, p. 1058, § 1; Laws 2009, Act 155, § 2, eff. July 1, 2009.

§ 35–3–9.1. Repealed by Laws 1985, p. 552, § 2, eff. June 30, 1990

§ 35–3–9.2. Repealed by Laws 2005, Act 114, § 4, eff. July 1, 2005

Historical and Statutory Notes

Repealed § 35–3–9.2, relating to the mobile cocaine education van, was derived from Laws 1985, p. 552, § 3.

Laws 2006, Act 453, § 35(2), struck the reserved designation from Code Section 35–3–9.2.

§ 35–3–10. Retirement benefits

All personnel and the director of the bureau are authorized to be members of the Employees' Retirement System of Georgia, as established by Chapter 2 of Title 47. All rights, credits, and funds in the retirement system which are possessed by any personnel of the bureau, including the director, at the time of employment in the bureau are continued; and it is the intention of the General Assembly that such personnel and the director shall not lose any rights, credits, or funds to which they were entitled prior to being employed with the bureau.

Laws 1974, p. 109, § 2; Laws 2001, p. 1058, § 2.

§ 35–3–11. Agents under merit system

(a) All agents of the bureau shall be governed by such rules of position, classification, appointment, promotion, demotion, transfer, dismissal, qualification, compensation, seniority privileges, tenure, and other employment standards as may now or hereafter be established under such merit system controls as may be authorized by Chapter 20 of Title 45, relating to the State Personnel Board and the State Personnel Administration.

(b) This Code section shall not apply to narcotics agents as provided for in Code Section 35–3–9.

(c) As used in this subsection, the term "disability" means a disability that prevents an individual from working as a law enforcement officer. When an agent of the bureau leaves the bureau as a result of a disability arising in the line of duty, such agent shall be entitled as part of such agent's compensation to retain his or her weapon and badge pursuant to regulations promulgated by the director.

Laws 1974, p. 109, § 2; Laws 2004, Act 784, § 4, eff. July 1, 2004; Laws 2009, Act 155, § 2, eff. July 1, 2009.

§ 35–3–12. Payment of medical, surgical, and similar expenses of personnel injured in line of duty

The bureau is authorized to pay all medical, surgical, hospital, nursing, and other similar expenses incurred by any member of the bureau as a result of injuries received in the line of duty. The bureau is authorized to make such payments in addition to any award made by the State Board of Workers' Compensation based on such injuries. Such payments shall be made only upon proper presentation of bills to the bureau. The bureau and the injured party shall together ascertain the correctness of all bills presented. No payments shall be made without the approval of the bureau.

Laws 1953, Nov.-Dec. Sess., p. 392, § 1.

§ 35–3–13. Requests for assistance; access to records

(a) Any district attorney of this state may request the assistance of the bureau to conduct and exercise its lawful powers and authorities in the investigation of any criminal matter.

(b) Any head of a municipal or county fire department may request the assistance of the bureau to conduct and exercise its lawful powers and authorities in the investigation of any crime related fires.

(c) In the event the bureau acts in cooperation with a municipality or other political subdivision of the state, the services and records of such municipality or other subdivision shall be accessible and available to the bureau at all times.

Laws 1937, p. 322, art. 3, § 1; Laws 1941, p. 277, § 4; Laws 1977, p. 752, § 1; Laws 1978, p. 254, § 2.

§§ 35–3–14 to 35–3–16. Repealed by Laws 1997, p. 1421, § 2, eff. May 1, 1997

Article 2

Georgia Crime Information Center

§ 35–3–30. Definitions

As used in this article, the term:

(1) "Career criminal" means any person who has been previously convicted three times under the laws of this state of felonies or under the laws of any other state or the United States of crimes which would be felonies if committed within this state.

(1.1) "Center" means the Georgia Crime Information Center.

(2) "Council" means the Georgia Crime Information Center Council.

(3) "Criminal justice agencies" means those public agencies at all levels of government which perform as their principal function activities relating to the apprehension, prosecution, adjudication, or rehabilitation of criminal offenders.

(4) "Criminal justice information" means the following classes of information:

(A) "Criminal history record information" means information collected by criminal justice agencies on individuals consisting of identifiable descriptions and notations of arrests, detentions, indictments, accusations, information, or other formal charges, and any disposition arising therefrom, sentencing, correctional supervision, and release. Such term also includes the age and sex of each victim as provided by criminal justice agencies. The term does not include identification information, such as fingerprint records, to the extent that such information does not indicate involvement of the individual in the criminal justice system.

(B) "Restricted data" means data which contains information relating to data-gathering techniques, distribution methods, manuals, and forms.

(C) "Secret data" means data which includes information dealing with those operational and programming elements which prevent unlawful intrusion into the Georgia Crime Information Center/Criminal Justice Information System computer system, the communications network, and satellite computer systems handling criminal justice information.

(D) "Sensitive data" means data which contains statistical information in the form of reports, lists, and documentation, which information may identify a group characteristic. It may apply to groups of persons, articles, vehicles, etc., such as white males or stolen guns.

(5) "Criminal justice information system" means all those agencies, procedures, mechanisms, media, and forms, as well as the information itself, which are or which become involved in the origination, transmittal, storage, retrieval, and dissemination of information related to reported offenses, offenders, and the subsequent actions related to such events or persons.

(6) "Law enforcement agency" means a governmental unit of one or more persons employed full time or part time by the state, a state agency or department, or a political subdivision of the state for the purpose of preventing and detecting crime and enforcing state laws or local ordinances, employees of which unit are authorized to make arrests for crimes while acting within the scope of their authority.

(7) "Offense" means an act which is a felony, a misdemeanor, or a violation of a county or municipal ordinance.

Laws 1973, p. 1301, § 1; Laws 1976, p. 617, § 1; Laws 1982, p. 952, §§ 1, 3; Laws 1984, p. 22, § 35; Laws 1985, p. 149, § 35; Laws 2006, Act 571, § 23, eff. July 1, 2006.

Historical and Statutory Notes

Laws 2006, Act 571, §§ 1 and 30, provide:

"SECTION 1. The General Assembly finds and declares that recidivist sexual offenders, sexual offenders who use physical violence, and sexual offenders who prey on children are sexual predators who present an extreme threat to the public safety. Many sexual offenders are extremely likely to use physical violence and to repeat their offenses; and some sexual offenders commit many offenses, have many more victims than are ever reported, and are prosecuted for only a fraction of their crimes. The General Assembly finds that this makes the cost of sexual offender victimization to society at large, while incalculable, clearly exorbitant. The General Assembly further finds that the high level of threat that a sexual predator presents to the public safety, and the long-term effects suffered by victims of sex offenses, provide the state with sufficient justification to implement a strategy that includes:

"(1) Incarcerating sexual offenders and maintaining adequate facilities to ensure that decisions to release sexual predators into the community are not made on the basis of inadequate space;

"(2) Requiring the registration of sexual offenders, with a requirement that complete and accurate information be maintained and accessible for use by law enforcement authorities, communities, and the public;

"(3) Providing for community and public notification concerning the presence of sexual offenders;

"(4) Collecting data relative to sexual offenses and sexual offenders;

"(5) Requiring sexual predators who are released into the community to wear an electronic monitoring system for the rest of their natural life and to pay for such system; and

"(6) Prohibiting sexual predators from working with children, either for compensation or as a volunteer.

"The General Assembly further finds that the state has a compelling interest in protecting the public from sexual offenders and in protecting children from predatory sexual activity, and there is sufficient justification for requiring sexual offenders to register and for requiring community and public notification of the presence of sexual offenders. The General Assembly declares that in order to protect the public, it is necessary that the sexual offenders be registered and that members of the community and the public be notified of a sexual offender's presence. The designation of a person as a sexual offender is neither a sentence nor a punishment but simply a regulatory mechanism and status resulting from the conviction of certain crimes. Likewise, the designation of a person as a sexual predator is neither a sentence nor a punishment but simply a regulatory mechanism and status resulting from findings by the Sexual Offender Registration Review Board and a court if requested by a sexual offender."

"SECTION 30. (a) This Act shall become effective July 1, 2006.

"(b) Any person required to register pursuant to the provisions of Code Section 42–1–12, relating to the state sexual offender registry, and any person required not to reside within areas where minors congregate, as prohibited by Code Section 42–1–13 [see § 42–1–15], shall not be relieved of the obligation to comply with the provisions of said Code sections by the repeal and reenactment of said Code sections.

"(c) The provisions of this Act shall not affect or abate the status as a crime of any such act or omission which occurred prior to the effective date of the Act repealing, repealing and reenacting, or amending such law, nor shall the prosecution of such crime be abated as a result of such repeal, repeal and reenactment, or amendment."

§ 35–3–31. Establishment

(a) There is established for the state, within the Georgia Bureau of Investigation, a system for the intrastate communication of vital information relating to crimes, criminals, and criminal activity, to be known as the Georgia Crime Information Center.

(b) Central responsibility for the development, maintenance, and operation of the center shall be vested with the director of the center with the assistance and guidance of the Georgia Crime Information Council, the establishment of which is provided for in Code Section 35–3–32.

(c) The director of the center shall maintain the necessary staff along with support services to be procured within the Georgia state government, such as computer services from the Department of Administrative Services, physical space and logistic support from the Department of Public Safety, and other services or sources as necessary, to enable the effective and efficient performance of the duties and responsibilities ascribed to the center in this article.

(d) All personnel of the center shall be administered according to appropriate special and standard schedules by the State Personnel Administration with due recognition to be given by the latter to the special qualifications and availability of the types of individuals required in such an agency.

Laws 1973, p. 1301, § 2; Laws 1974, p. 109, § 2; Laws 1976, p. 617, § 2; Laws 1982, p. 3, § 35; Laws 2009, Act 155, § 2, eff. July 1, 2009.

§ 35–3–32. Georgia Crime Information Center Council

(a) There is created the Georgia Crime Information Center Council.

(b) The duties and responsibilities of the council are to:

(1) Advise and assist in the establishment of policies under which the center is to be operated;

(2) Ensure that the information obtained pursuant to this article shall be restricted to the items specified in this article and ensure that the center is administered so as not to accumulate any information or distribute any information that is not specifically approved in this article;

(3) Ensure that adequate security safeguards are incorporated so that the data available through this system is used only by properly authorized persons and agencies;

(4) Establish appropriate disciplinary measures to be taken by the center in the instance of violations of data reporting or dissemination of laws, rules, and regulations by criminal justice agencies or members thereof covered by this article; and

(5) Establish other policies which provide for the efficient and effective use and operation of the center under the limitations imposed by the terms of this article.

(c) The members of the board shall serve ex officio as members of the council and shall constitute the council.

Laws 1973, p. 1301, § 5; Laws 1976, p. 617, § 7; Laws 1979, p. 613, § 1; Laws 1987, p. 3, § 35.

§ 35–3–33. Functions

(a) The center shall:

(1) Obtain and file fingerprints, descriptions, photographs, and any other pertinent identifying data on persons who:

(A) Have been or are hereafter arrested or taken into custody in this state:

(i) For an offense which is a felony;

(ii) For an offense which is a misdemeanor or a violation of an ordinance involving burglary tools, commercial gambling, dealing in gambling devices, contributing to the delinquency of a child, dealing in stolen property, dangerous drugs, marijuana, narcotics, firearms, dangerous weapons, explosives, pandering, prostitution, sex offenses where children are victims, or worthless checks;

(iii) For an offense charged as disorderly conduct but which relates to an act connected with one or more of the offenses under division (ii) of this subparagraph;

(iv) As a fugitive from justice; or

(v) For any other offense designated by the Attorney General;

(B) Are or become career criminals, well-known offenders, or habitual offenders;

(C) Are currently or become confined to any prison, penitentiary, or other penal institution;

(D) Are unidentified human corpses found in this state; or

(E) Are children who are charged with an offense that if committed by an adult would be a felony or are children whose cases are transferred from a juvenile court to another court for prosecution;

(2) Compare all fingerprint and other identifying data received with those already on file and, whether or not a criminal record is found for a person, at once inform the requesting agency or arresting officer of such facts as may be disseminated consistent with applicable security and privacy laws and regulations. A log shall be maintained of all disseminations made of each individual criminal history including at least the date and recipient of such information;

(3) Provide a uniform crime reporting system for the periodic collection, analysis, and reporting of crimes reported to and otherwise processed by any and all law enforcement agencies within the state, as defined and provided for in this article;

(4) Periodically conduct audits of crime reporting practices of criminal justice agencies to ensure compliance with the standards of national and state uniform crime reporting systems and to ensure reporting of criminal arrests, dispositions, and custodial information;

(5) Develop, operate, and maintain an information system which will support the collection, storage, retrieval, and dissemination of all crime and offender data described in this article consistent with those principles of scope, security, and responsiveness prescribed by this article;

(6) Cooperate with all criminal justice agencies within the state in providing those forms, procedures, standards, and related training assistance necessary for the uniform operation of the center;

(7) Offer assistance and, when practicable, instruction to all criminal justice agencies in establishing efficient local records systems;

(8) Compile statistics on the nature and extent of crime in the state and compile other data related to planning for and operating criminal justice agencies, provided that such statistics do not identify persons, and make available all such statistical information obtained to the Governor, the General Assembly, and any other governmental agencies whose primary responsibilities include the planning, development, or execution of crime reduction programs. Access to such information by the latter governmental agencies will be on an individual, written request basis wherein must be demonstrated a need to know, the intent of any analyses, dissemination of such analyses, and any security provisions deemed necessary by the center;

(9) Periodically publish in print or electronically statistics, no less frequently than annually, that do not identify persons and report such information to the Governor, the General Assembly, state and local criminal justice agencies, and the general public. Such information shall accurately reflect the level and nature of crime in the state and the operations in general of the different types of agencies within the criminal justice system;

(10) Make available, upon request, to all local and state criminal justice agencies, all federal criminal justice agencies,

and criminal justice agencies in other states any information in the files of the center which will aid these agencies in the performance of their official duties. For this purpose the center shall operate on a 24 hour basis, seven days a week. Such information when authorized by the council may also be made available to any other agency of the state or political subdivision of the state and to any other federal agency upon assurance by the agency concerned that the information is to be used for official purposes only in the prevention or detection of crime or the apprehension of criminal offenders;

(11) Cooperate with other agencies of the state, the crime information agencies of other states, and the Uniform Crime Reports and National Crime Information Center systems of the Federal Bureau of Investigation in developing and conducting an interstate, national, and international system of criminal identification, records, and statistics;

(12) Provide the administrative mechanisms and procedures necessary to respond to those individuals who file requests to view their own records as provided for in this article and to cooperate in the correction of the central center records and those of contributing agencies when their accuracy has been successfully challenged either through the related contributing agencies or by court order issued on behalf of the individual;

(13) Institute the necessary measures in the design, implementation, and continued operation of the criminal justice information system to ensure the privacy and security of the system. This will include establishing complete control over use and access of the system and restricting its integral resources and facilities to those either possessed or procured and controlled by criminal justice agencies as defined in this article. Such security measures must meet standards to be set by the council as well as those set by the nationally operated systems for interstate sharing of information;

(14) Provide availability, by means of data processing, to files listing motor vehicle drivers' license numbers, motor vehicle registration numbers, wanted and stolen motor vehicles, outstanding warrants, identifiable stolen property, and such other files as may be of general assistance to criminal justice agencies; and

(15) Receive and process fingerprints from the Supreme Court of Georgia Office of Bar Admissions for the purpose of determining whether or not an applicant for admission to the State Bar of Georgia has a criminal record. The processing shall include submission of fingerprints to the Georgia Bureau of Investigation and the Federal Bureau of Investigation for comparison to each of their respective files and data bases.

(b) Criminal justice agencies shall furnish upon written request and without charge to any local fire department in this state a copy, processed under purpose code "E", of the criminal history record information of an applicant for employment.

(c) The provisions of this article notwithstanding, information and records of children shall only be inspected and disclosed as provided in Code Sections 15–11–82 and 15–11–83. Such records and information shall be destroyed according to the procedures outlined in Code Sections 15–11–79.2 and 15–11–81.

Laws 1973, p. 1301, § 3; Laws 1976, p. 617, § 5; Laws 1980, p. 394, § 1; Laws 1982, p. 3, § 35; Laws 1982, p. 952, §§ 2, 4; Laws 1984, p. 22, § 35; Laws 1986, p. 513, § 1; Laws 1992, p. 6, § 35; Laws 1998, p. 842, § 7; Laws 2000, p. 20, § 21; Laws 2000, p. 1549, § 1; Laws 2003, Act 72, § 2, eff. May 29, 2003; Laws 2007, Act 16, § 1, eff. May 11, 2007; Laws 2010, Act 615, § 10, eff. June 3, 2010.

§ 35–3–34. Dissemination of records and information to private persons and businesses

(a) The center shall be authorized to:

(1) Make criminal history records maintained by the center available to private persons and businesses under the following conditions:

(A) Private individuals and businesses requesting criminal history records shall, at the time of the request, provide the fingerprints of the person whose records are requested or provide a signed consent of the person whose records are requested on a form prescribed by the center which shall include such person's full name, address, social security number, and date of birth;

(B) The center may not provide records of arrests, charges, and sentences for crimes relating to first offenders pursuant to Article 3 of Chapter 8 of Title 42 in cases where offenders have been exonerated and discharged without court adjudications of guilt, except as specifically authorized by Code Section 35–3–34.1 or other law; and

(C) When the identifying information provided is sufficient to identify persons whose records are requested electronically, the center may disseminate electronically criminal history records of in-state felony convictions, pleas, and sentences without:

(i) Fingerprint comparison; or

(ii) Consent of the person whose records are requested; or

(2) Make criminal history records of the defendant or witnesses in a criminal action available to counsel for the defendant upon receipt of a written request from the defendant's counsel under the following conditions:

(A) Such request shall contain the style of the case and the name and identifying information for each person whose records are requested. Such request shall be submitted to the center;

(B) In cases where the court has determined the defendant to be indigent, any fees authorized by law shall be waived; and

(C) Disclosure of criminal history information to the defendant's counsel as provided in this paragraph shall be solely in such counsel's capacity as an officer of the court. Any use of such information in a manner not authorized by law or the court in which such action is pending where the records were disclosed shall constitute a violation of Code Section 35–3–38; and

(3) Charge fees for disseminating records pursuant to this Code section which will raise an amount of revenue which approximates, as nearly as practicable, the direct and indirect costs to the state for providing such disseminations.

(b) In the event that an employment decision is made adverse to a person whose record was obtained pursuant to this Code section, the person will be informed by the business or person making the adverse employment decision of all information pertinent to that decision. This disclosure shall include information that a record was obtained from the center, the specific contents of the record, and the effect the record had upon the decision. Failure to provide all such information to the person subject to the adverse decision shall be a misdemeanor.

(c) Neither the center, its employees, nor any agency or employee of the state shall be responsible for the accuracy of information nor have any liability for defamation, invasion of privacy, negligence, or any other claim in connection with the dissemination pursuant to this Code section and shall be immune from suit based upon any such claims.

(d) Local criminal justice agencies may disseminate criminal history records, without fingerprint comparison or prior contact with the center, to private individuals and businesses under the same conditions as set forth in paragraph (1) of subsection (a) of this Code section and may charge fees as needed to reimburse such agencies for their direct and indirect costs related to the providing of such disseminations.

(d.1) Reserved.

(d.2) When identifying information provided is sufficient to identify persons whose records are requested, local criminal justice agencies may disseminate criminal history records of in-state felony convictions, pleas, and sentences without:

(1) Fingerprint comparison;

(2) Prior contact with the center; or

(3) Consent of the person whose records are requested.

Such information may be disseminated to private individuals and businesses under the conditions specified in subparagraph (a)(1)(B) of this Code section upon payment of the fee for the request and when the request is made upon a form prescribed by the center. Such agencies may charge and retain fees as needed to reimburse such agencies for the direct and indirect costs of providing such information and shall have the same immunity therefor as provided in subsection (c) of this Code section.

(d.3) No fee charged pursuant to this Code section may exceed $20.00 per person whose criminal history record is requested or be charged to any person or entity authorized prior to January 1, 1995, to obtain information pursuant to this Code section without payment of such fee.

(d.4) The center shall place a high priority on inquiries from any nuclear power facility requesting a criminal history and shall respond to such requests as expeditiously as possible, but in no event shall a response be made more than two business days following receipt of the request.

(e)(1) The Georgia Crime Information Center shall be authorized to provide criminal history records, wanted person records, and involuntary hospitalization records information to the Federal Bureau of Investigation in conjunction with the National Instant Criminal Background Check System in accordance with the federal Brady Handgun Violence Prevention Act, 18 U.S.C. Section 921, et seq.

(2) The records of the Georgia Crime Information Center shall include information as to whether a person has been involuntarily hospitalized. Notwithstanding any other provisions of law and in order to carry out the provisions of this Code section and Code Section 16–11–172, the Georgia Crime Information Center shall be provided such information and no other mental health information from the involuntary hospitalization records of the probate courts concerning persons involuntarily hospitalized after March 22, 1995, in a manner agreed upon by the Probate Judges Training Council and the Georgia Bureau of Investigation to preserve the confidentiality of patients' rights in all other respects. Further, notwithstanding any other provisions of law and in order to carry out the provisions of this Code section and Code Section 16–11–172, the center shall be provided information as to whether a person has been adjudicated mentally incompetent to stand trial or not guilty by reason of insanity at the time of the crime, has been involuntarily hospitalized, or both from the records of the clerks of the superior courts concerning persons involuntarily hospitalized after March 22, 1995, in a manner agreed upon by The Council of Superior Court Clerks of Georgia and the Georgia Bureau of Investigation to preserve the confidentiality of patients' rights in all other respects. After five years have elapsed from the date that a person's involuntary hospitalization information has been received by the Georgia Crime Information Center, the center shall purge its records of such information as soon as practicable and in any event purge such records within 30 days after the expiration of such five–year period.

(f) The council is empowered to adopt rules, regulations, and forms necessary to implement this Code section. The council shall promulgate regulations to ensure the identity, confidentiality, and security of all records and data provided in accordance with this Code section.

Laws 1973, p. 1301, § 3; Laws 1976, p. 1401, § 2; Laws 1977, p. 1243, § 1; Laws 1978, p. 1981, § 1; Laws 1982, p. 3, § 35; Laws 1988, p. 203, § 1; Laws 1989, p. 1080, § 2; Laws 1994, p. 1895, § 12; Laws 1995, p. 139, § 3; Laws 1995, p. 633, §§ 1, 2; Laws 1996, p. 6, § 35; Laws 2000, p. 1206, § 1; Laws 2003, Act 375, § 1, eff. July 1, 2004; Laws 2005, Act 118, § 2, eff. July 1, 2005; Laws 2006, Act 453, § 35, eff. April 14, 2006; Laws 2006, Act 767, § 4, eff. May 3, 2006.

Historical and Statutory Notes

The 2003 amendment by Act 375, in subsec. (a)(1)(B), substituted "except as specifically authorized by Code Section 35–3–34.1 or other law" for "except as specifically authorized by law".

Laws 2003, Act 375, § 6, provides:

"This Act shall become effective on July 1, 2004, except that Section 3A shall become effective on July 1, 2003."

The 2005 amendment by Act 118 deleted and reserved subsec. (d.1); inserted a new subsec. (e); redesignated former subsec. (e) as subsec. (f); and added the last sentence to newly designated subsec. (f). Prior to amendment, subsecs. (d.1) and (e) had read:

"(d.1)(1) The center shall be authorized and directed to review its criminal history records and involuntary hospitalization records information and to report to each dealer as provided in Code Section 16–11–173 as to whether a named potential buyer or transferee of a handgun is prohibited from purchasing or possessing a handgun by state or federal law pursuant to the requirements of Part 5 of Article 4 of Chapter 11 of Title 16. The director of the center shall establish with adequate staff and adequate telephone lines a toll-free telephone number as required in Code Section 16–11–177.

"(2) The records of the Georgia Crime Information Center shall include information as to whether a person has been involuntarily hospitalized. Notwithstanding any other provisions of law and in order to carry out the provisions of this Code section and Code Sections 16–11–173 and 16–11–174, the Georgia Crime Information Center shall be provided such information and no other mental health information from the involuntary hospitalization records of the probate courts concerning persons involuntarily hospitalized after March 22, 1995, in a manner agreed upon by the Probate Judges Training Council and the Georgia Bureau of Investigation to meet the requirements of this Code section and Code Sections 16–11–173 and 16–11–174 and to preserve the confidentiality of patients' rights in all other respects. Further, notwithstanding any other provisions of law and in order to carry out the provisions of this Code section and Code Sections 16–11–172 and 16–11–173, the center shall be provided information as to whether a person has been adjudicated mentally incompetent to stand trial or not guilty by reason of insanity at the time of the crime and has been involuntarily hospitalized from the records of the clerks of the superior courts concerning persons involuntarily hospitalized after March 22, 1995, in a manner agreed upon by The Council of Superior Court Clerks of Georgia and the Georgia Bureau of Investigation to meet the requirements of this Code section and Code Sections 16–11–172 and 16–11–173 and to preserve the confidentiality of patients' rights in all other respects. After five years have elapsed from the date that a person's involuntary hospitalization information has been received by the Georgia Crime Information Center, the center shall purge its records of such information as soon as practicable and in any event purge such records within 30 days after the expiration of such five-year period."

"(e) The council is empowered to adopt rules, regulations, and forms necessary to implement this Code section."

The 2006 amendment by Act 453 were provisions contained in a correction bill.

The 2006 amendment by Act 767 added subsec. (d.4).

§ 35–3–34.1. Offenders exonerated and discharged without court adjudication of guilt

(a) Where an offender has been exonerated and discharged without court adjudication of guilt pursuant to Article 3 of Chapter 8 of Title 42, the center is authorized to provide the first offender's record of arrests, charges, or sentences if the offender was exonerated and discharged without a court adjudication of guilt on or after July 1, 2004, and either:

(1) The request for information is an inquiry about a person who has applied for employment with a public school, private school, child welfare agency, or a person or entity that provides day care for minor children or after school care for minor children and the person who is the subject of the inquiry to the center was prosecuted for the offense of child molestation, sexual battery, enticing a child for indecent purposes, sexual exploitation of a child, pimping, pandering, or incest;

(2) The request for information is an inquiry about a person who has applied for employment with a nursing home, personal care home, or a person or entity that offers day care for elderly persons and the person who is the subject of the inquiry to the

center was prosecuted for the offense of sexual battery, incest, pimping, pandering, or a violation of Code Section 30–5–8; or

(3) The request for information is an inquiry about a person who has applied for employment with a facility as defined in Code Section 37–3–1 or 37–4–2 that provides services to persons who are mentally ill as defined in Code Section 37–1–1 or developmentally disabled as defined in Code Section 37–1–1, and the person who is the subject of the inquiry to the center was prosecuted for the offense of sexual battery, incest, pimping, or pandering.

(b) First offender records including records of arrests, charges, or sentences may be released to any law enforcement unit and the Georgia Peace Officer Standards and Training Council where the request for information is an inquiry about a person who has applied for employment in a certified position or a person who is an applicant, candidate, or peace officer as defined in Code Section 35–8–2.

Laws 2003, Act 375, § 3, eff. July 1, 2004; Laws 2006, Act 453, § 35(4), eff. April 14, 2006; Laws 2006, Act 473, § 1, eff. April 18, 2006; Laws 2009, Act 102, § 3–10, eff. July 1, 2009.

Historical and Statutory Notes

Laws 2003, Act 375, § 6, provides:

"This Act shall become effective on July 1, 2004, except that Section 3A shall become effective on July 1, 2003."

The 2006 amendment by Act 453 was a provision contained in a correction bill.

The 2006 amendment by Act 473 designated the existing text as subsec. (a) and added subsec. (b).

§ 35–3–34.2. National criminal history background checks; authorized care providers

(a) It is the purpose of this Code section to authorize and facilitate, but not require, the exchange of national criminal history background checks with authorized agencies on behalf of qualified entities as authorized under federal law.

(b) As used in this Code section, the term:

(1) "Authorized agency" means any local government agency designated to report, receive, or disseminate information under the NCPA and the VCA.

(2) "Care" means the provision of care, treatment, education, training, instruction, supervision, or recreation to children, the elderly, or individuals with disabilities.

(3) "FBI" means the Federal Bureau of Investigation.

(4) "National criminal history background check" means a fingerprint based check of state and national criminal history files based on submission of a set of classifiable fingerprints and records fee.

(5) "NCPA" means the National Child Protection Act of 1993, 42 U.S.C. Sections 3759, 5101 note, 5119, and 5119a through 5119c.

(6) "ORI" means an originating agency identifier.

(7) "Provider" means:

(A) A person who:

(i) Is employed by or volunteers with a qualified entity;

(ii) Owns or operates a qualified entity; or

(iii) Has or may have unsupervised access to a person to whom the qualified entity provides care; and

(B) A person who:

(i) Seeks to be employed by or volunteer with a qualified entity;

(ii) Seeks to own or operate a qualified entity; or

(iii) Seeks to have or may have unsupervised access to a person to whom the qualified entity provides care.

(8) "Qualified entity" means a business or organization, whether public, private, for profit, not for profit, or voluntary, that provides care or care placement services, including a business or organization that licenses or certifies others to provide care or care placement services.

(9) "VCA" means the Volunteers for Children Act, 42 U.S.C. Sections 5101 note, 5119a, and 5119b.

(c) An authorized agency is responsible for the designation of qualified entities within its local jurisdiction and for the submission of national criminal history background checks as authorized under the NCPA and the VCA.

(d) An authorized agency, other than a criminal justice agency as defined in Code Section 35–3–30, must request an ORI from the FBI for the express purpose of submitting national criminal history background checks under this Code section. Requests shall be made in writing to the FBI through the center.

(e) National criminal history background checks shall be submitted directly to the center for a state records check; fingerprint cards shall then be forwarded to the FBI for a national check. The responses from both the state and national criminal history background checks shall be returned to the authorized agency.

(f) The authorized agency may provide directly to the qualified entity the state criminal history record provided as part of the national criminal history background check.

(g) An authorized agency shall be responsible for review of the national criminal history record provided as part of the national criminal history background check to determine whether the provider has been convicted of or is under indictment for a crime that bears upon the provider's fitness to have responsibility for the safety and well–being of children, the elderly, or individuals with disabilities and to convey that determination to the qualified entity.

(h) The qualified entity must obtain the fingerprints of the provider, communicate the fitness determination of the authorized agency to the provider, and notify the provider of his or her right to challenge the accuracy and completeness of any information contained in the national criminal history background check.

(i) Fees charged for a national criminal history background check shall be determined based on reasonable costs as allowed under federal law.

(j) The provisions of this Code section shall be supplementary to and not in place of any other law of this state which authorizes or requires background checks.

(k) Any person, authorized agency, or qualified entity, or any person who is an employee of an authorized agency or qualified entity, shall not disseminate any criminal history or any information concerning any criminal history except the determination of fitness which such person obtains pursuant to this Code section.

Laws 2005, Act 373, § 1, eff. May 10, 2005.

Historical and Statutory Notes

In 2005, the Code Commission, in subsec. (b), par. (5), deleted the quotation marks from "National Child Protection Act of 1993", and inserted "and" following "5119,"; and, in subsec. (b), par. (9), deleted the quotation marks from "Volunteers for Children Act" and substituted "5119a, and 5119b" for "5119(a) and 5119(b)". See § 28–9–5.

§ 35–3–35. Dissemination of information to public agencies, political subdivisions, authorities, and instrumentalities

(a) The center shall be authorized to:

(1) Make criminal history records maintained by the center available to public agencies, political subdivisions, authorities, and instrumentalities, including state or federal licensing and regulatory agencies or their designated representatives, under the following conditions:

(A) Public agencies or political subdivisions shall, at the time of the request, provide the fingerprints of the person whose records are requested in such manner prescribed by the center, which may include the electronic imaging of a person's fingerprints, or provide a signed consent of the person whose records are requested on a form prescribed by the center which shall include such person's full name, address, social security number, and date of birth; provided, however, that the provisions of this paragraph shall supersede any other provision relating to the submission of fingerprints to the center;

(B) The center may not provide records of arrests, charges, or sentences for crimes relating to first offenders pursuant to Article 3 of Chapter 8 of Title 42 in cases where offenders have been exonerated and discharged without court adjudications of guilt, except as specifically authorized by Code Section 35–3–34.1 or other law; and

(C) When the identifying information provided is sufficient to identify persons whose records are requested electronically, the center may disseminate electronically criminal history records of in-state felony convictions, pleas, and sentences without:

(i) Fingerprint comparison; or

(ii) Consent of the person whose records are requested;

(1.1) Make criminal history records maintained by the center available to any county board of registrars or county board of registration and election. The making of an application for voter registration shall be deemed to be consent of the person making the application to release such records to the county board of registrars or county board of registration and election. Such records shall be requested for the sole purpose of verification of information provided on voter registration cards by registration applicants;

(1.2) Make criminal history records maintained by the center and national criminal history records maintained by the Federal Bureau of Investigation, obtained by the center, available to the governing authority of any county or municipality, for any applicant or licensee in a specified occupation for which such local governing authority has adopted an ordinance or resolution requiring such applicants or licensees in a particular occupation or profession regulated by the governing authority to be fingerprinted as a condition of submitting an application or obtaining or renewing a license. The center shall establish a uniform method of obtaining criminal history records required under this paragraph. Such uniform method shall require the submission to the center of two complete sets of fingerprints and the records search fee. Upon receipt thereof, the center shall promptly transmit one set of fingerprints to the Federal Bureau of Investigation for a search of bureau records and an appropriate report and shall retain the other set and promptly conduct a search of its own records and records to which it has access. After receiving the fingerprints and fee, the center shall notify the requesting local government authority in writing of any derogatory finding, including, but not limited to, any criminal record data regarding the fingerprint records check or if there is no such finding. Nothing in this paragraph shall prevent the local governing authority from obtaining national criminal history records directly from the Federal Bureau of Investigation, if an ordinance or resolution requiring the fingerprints of an applicant or licensee of a particular occupation or profession regulated by the local governing authority has been adopted by such governing authority of the county or municipality; and

(2) Charge fees for disseminating records pursuant to this Code section which will raise an amount of revenue which approximates, as nearly as practicable, the direct and indirect costs to the state for providing such disseminations.

(b) In the event an employment or licensing decision is made adverse to a person whose record was obtained pursuant to this Code section, the person will be informed by the public agency, political subdivision, authority or instrumentality, or licensing or regulatory agency making the adverse employment decision of all information pertinent to that decision. This disclosure shall include information that a record was obtained from the center, the specific contents of the record, and the effect the record had upon the decision. Failure to provide all such information to the person subject to the adverse decision shall be a misdemeanor.

(c) Neither the center, its employees, nor any agency or employee of the state shall be responsible for the accuracy of information disseminated nor have any liability for defamation, invasion of privacy, negligence, nor any other claim in connection with any dissemination pursuant to this Code section and shall be immune from suit based upon such claims.

(d) Local criminal justice agencies may disseminate criminal history records to public agencies, political subdivisions, authorities, and instrumentalities, including state or federal licensing and regulatory agencies under the same conditions as set forth in paragraph (1) of subsection (a) of this Code section and may charge fees as necessary to reimburse such agencies for their direct and indirect costs associated with providing such disseminations.

(d.1) When identifying information provided is sufficient to identify persons whose records are requested, local criminal justice agencies may disseminate criminal history records of in-state felony convictions, pleas, and sentences without:

(1) Fingerprint comparison;

(2) Prior contact with the center; or

(3) Consent of the person whose records are requested.

Such information may be disseminated to entities to which such records may be made available under subsection (d) of this Code section under the conditions specified in subparagraph (a)(1)(B) of this Code section upon payment of the fee for the request and when the request is made upon a form prescribed by the center. Such agencies may charge and retain fees as needed to reimburse such agencies for the direct and indirect costs of providing such information and shall have the same immunity therefor as provided in subsection (c) of this Code section.

(d.2) No fee charged pursuant to this Code section may exceed $20.00 per person whose criminal history record is requested or be charged to any person or entity authorized prior to January 1, 1995, to obtain information pursuant to this Code section without payment of such fee.

(e) The council is empowered to adopt rules, regulations, and forms necessary to implement this Code section.

Laws 1978, p. 1981, § 1; Laws 1988, p. 203, § 2; Laws 1990, p. 1831, § 1; Laws 1992, p. 1009, § 1; Laws 1995, p. 633, §§ 3, 4; Laws 2000, p. 1206, § 2; Laws 2003, Act 375, § 2, eff. July 1, 2004; Laws 2007, Act 16, §§ 2, 3, eff. May 11, 2007.

Historical and Statutory Notes

The 2003 amendment by Act 375, in subsec. (a)(1)(B), substituted "except as specifically authorized by Code Section 35–3–34.1 or other law" for "except as specifically authorized by law".

Laws 2003, Act 375, § 6, provides:

"This Act shall become effective on July 1, 2004, except that Section 3A shall become effective on July 1, 2003."

The 2007 amendment by Act 16, in subsec. (a), added "in such manner prescribed by the center, which may include the electronic imaging of a person's fingerprints," and "provided, however, that the provisions of this paragraph shall supersede any other provision relating to the submission of fingerprints to the center;" in subpar. (1)(A), deleted "and" at the end of par. (1.1), and added par. (1.2).

§ 35–3–35.1. Exchange of national criminal history background checks [Superseded]

Historical and Statutory Notes

In 2005, the Code Commission, due to irreconcilable conflicts, treated the addition of this section by Laws 2005, Act 323 § 1, as superseded by the addition of § 35–3–34.2, by Laws 2005, Act 373, § 1. See Butts County v. Strahan, 107 S.E. 163, 151 Ga. 417 (1921).

§ 35–3–36. Duties of criminal justice agencies

(a) All criminal justice agencies within the state shall submit to the center fingerprints, descriptions, photographs when specifically requested, and other identifying data on persons who have been lawfully arrested or taken into custody in the state for all felonies and for the misdemeanors and violations designated in subparagraph (A) of paragraph (1) of Code Section 35–3–33 and for persons in the categories enumerated in subparagraphs (B), (C), and (D) of paragraph (1) of Code Section 35–3–33.

(b) It shall be the duty of all chiefs of police, sheriffs, prosecuting attorneys, courts, judges, parole and probation officers, wardens, or other persons in charge of penal and correctional institutions in this state to furnish the center with any other data deemed necessary by the center to carry out its responsibilities under this article.

(c) All persons in charge of law enforcement agencies shall obtain or cause to be obtained fingerprints in accordance with the fingerprint system of identification established by the director of the Federal Bureau of Investigation, full-face and profile photographs if photo equipment is available, and other available identifying data of each person arrested or taken into custody for an offense of a type designated in paragraph (1) of Code Section 35–3–33, of all persons arrested or taken into custody as fugitives from justice, and of all unidentified human corpses in their jurisdictions; but photographs need not be taken if it is known that photographs of the type listed taken within the previous year are on file. Fingerprints and other identifying data of persons arrested or taken into custody for offenses other than those designated may be taken at the discretion of the law enforcement agency concerned. Any person arrested or taken into custody and subsequently released without charge or cleared of the offense through court proceedings shall have any fingerprint record taken in connection therewith returned if required by statute or upon court order and any such dispositions must also be reported to the center.

(d) Fingerprints and other identifying data required to be taken under subsection (c) of this Code section shall be forwarded within 24 hours after taking for filing and classification, but the period of 24 hours may be extended to cover any intervening holiday or weekend. Photographs taken shall be forwarded at the discretion of the agency concerned; but, if not forwarded, the fingerprint record shall be marked "Photo available" and the photographs shall be forwarded subsequently if the center so requests.

(e) All persons in charge of law enforcement agencies shall submit to the center detailed descriptions of arrest warrants and related identifying data for all felonies and for the misdemeanors and violations designated in subparagraph (a)(1)(A) of Code Section 35–3–33 immediately upon determination of the fact that the warrant cannot be served for the reasons stated. If any such warrant is subsequently served or withdrawn, the law enforcement agency concerned must immediately notify the center of the service or withdrawal. In addition, the agency concerned must annually, no later than January 31 of each year, and at other times if requested by the center confirm to the center all such arrest warrants of this type which continue to be outstanding.

(f) All persons in charge of state penal and correctional institutions shall obtain fingerprints in accordance with the fingerprint system of identification established by the director of the Federal Bureau of Investigation or as otherwise directed by the center and full-face and profile photographs of all persons received on commitment to these institutions. The prints and photographs so taken shall be forwarded to the center together with any other identifying data requested within ten days after the arrival at the institution of the person committed. At the time of release of any person committed to a correctional institution, the institution shall again obtain fingerprints as provided for in this subsection and forward them to the center within ten days along with any other related information requested by the center. Immediately upon release, the institution shall notify the center of the release of the person.

(g) All persons in charge of law enforcement agencies, all clerks of court, all municipal judges where they have no clerks, all magistrates, and all persons in charge of state and county probation and parole offices shall supply the center with the information described in Code Section 35–3–33 on the basis of the forms and instructions to be supplied by the center.

(h) All persons in charge of law enforcement agencies in this state shall furnish the center with any other identifying data required in accordance with guidelines established by the center. All law enforcement agencies and penal and correctional institutions in this state having criminal identification files shall cooperate in providing to the center copies of identifying data, as required in accordance with center guidelines, in those files as will aid in establishing the nucleus of the state criminal identification file.

(i) All criminal justice agencies within the state shall submit to the center, periodically at a time and in such form as prescribed by the center, information regarding only the cases within its jurisdiction and in which it is or has been actively engaged. Such report shall be known as the "uniform crime report" and shall contain crimes reported and otherwise processed during the period preceding the period of report, including the number and nature of offenses committed, the disposition of such offenses, and such other information as the center shall specify, relating to the method, frequency, cause, and prevention of crime. The incident/complaint report forms used by criminal justice agencies shall, when applicable, include the identification of any victim who is a student and the name of the school attended by any such student.

(j) Any governmental agency which is not included within the description of those departments and agencies required to submit the uniform crime report provided for in subsection (i) of this Code section but which desires to submit a report shall be furnished with the proper forms by the center. When a report is received by the center from a governmental agency not required to make a report, the information contained therein shall be included within the periodic compilation provided for in paragraph (9) of Code Section 35–3–33.

(k) Upon the request of the center, local law enforcement agencies shall periodically provide for audit samples of incident reports for the preceding reporting period so that the center may help ensure agency compliance with national and state uniform crime reporting requirements.

(*l*) All law enforcement agencies within the state shall report to the center, in a manner prescribed by the center, all persons wanted by and all vehicles and identifiable property stolen from their jurisdictions. The report shall be made as soon as practicable after the investigating department or agency either ascertains that a vehicle or identifiable property has been stolen or obtains a warrant for an individual's arrest or determines that there are reasonable grounds to believe that the individual has committed the crime. In no event shall this time exceed 12 hours after the investigating department or agency determines that it has grounds to believe that a vehicle or property was stolen or that the wanted person should be arrested.

(m) If at any time after making a report as required by subsection (l) of this Code section it is determined by the reporting department or agency that a person is no longer wanted due to his apprehension or any other factor or when a vehicle or property stolen is recovered, the law enforcement agency shall immediately notify the center of such status. Furthermore, if the agency making the apprehension or recovery is other than the one which made the original wanted or stolen report, then it shall immediately notify the originating agency of the full particulars relating to the apprehension or recovery.

(n) Neither the center nor its employees shall be responsible for the accuracy of information contained in records representing wanted persons, missing persons, and stolen serial numbered property established in computerized files on the Georgia Criminal Justice Information System (CJIS) network or in computerized files maintained by the Federal Bureau of Investigation National Crime Information Center (NCIC). Criminal justice agencies establishing such records bear all responsibilities for entry, update, and removal as dictated by actions of criminal justice employees and officials.

Laws 1973, p. 1301, § 4; Laws 1976, p. 617, § 6; Laws 1980, p. 396, § 2; Laws 1982, p. 3, § 35; Laws 1983, p. 884, § 4–1; Laws 1984, p. 22, § 35; Laws 1985, p. 149, § 35; Laws 1992, p. 1022, § 1; Laws 2001, p. 1024, § 1; Laws 2002, p. 415, § 35; Laws 2003, Act 74, § 1, eff. July 1, 2003; Laws 2003, Act 375, § 3A, eff. July 1, 2003.

Historical and Statutory Notes

The introductory language of Laws 2003, Act 375, § 3A, identified § 33–3–36 as the section being amended. The amendment was to § 35–3–36.

§ 35–3–37. Inspection of records; correction

(a) Nothing in this article shall be construed so as to authorize any person, agency, corporation, or other legal entity to invade the privacy of any citizen as defined by the General Assembly or the courts other than to the extent provided in this article.

(b) The center shall make a person's criminal records available for inspection by such person or his or her attorney upon written application to the center. Should the person or his or her attorney contest the accuracy of any portion of the records, it shall be mandatory upon the center to make available to the person or such person's attorney a copy of the contested record upon written application identifying the portion of the record contested and showing the reason for the contest of accuracy. Forms, procedures, identification, and other related aspects pertinent to access to records may be prescribed by the center.

(c) If an individual believes his or her criminal records to be inaccurate or incomplete, he or she may request the original agency having custody or control of the detail records to purge, modify, or supplement them and to notify the center of such changes. Should the agency decline to act or should the individual believe the agency's decision to be unsatisfactory, the individual or his or her attorney may, within 30 days of such decision, enter an appeal to the superior court of the county of his or her residence or to the court in the county where the agency exists, with notice to the agency, to acquire an order by the court that the subject information be expunged, modified, or supplemented by the agency of record. The court shall conduct a de novo hearing and may order such relief as it finds to be required by law. Such appeals shall be entered in the same manner as appeals are entered from the probate court, except that the appellant shall not be required to post bond or pay the costs in advance. If the aggrieved person desires, the appeal may be heard by the judge at the first term or in chambers. A notice sent by registered or certified mail or statutory overnight delivery shall be sufficient service on the agency having custody or control of disputed record that such appeal has been entered. Should the record in question be found to be inaccurate, incomplete, or misleading as set forth in paragraph (3) of subsection (d) of this Code section, the court shall order it to be appropriately expunged, modified, or supplemented by an explanatory notation. Each agency or individual in the state with custody, possession, or control of any such record shall promptly cause each and every copy thereof in his or her custody, possession, or control to be altered in accordance with the court's order. Notification of each such deletion, amendment, and supplementary notation shall be promptly disseminated to any individuals or agencies, including the center, to which the records in question have been communicated, as well as to the individual whose records have been ordered so altered.

(d)(1) An individual who was:

(A) Arrested for an offense under the laws of this state but subsequent to such arrest is released by the arresting agency without such offense being referred to the prosecuting attorney for prosecution; or

(B) After such offense referred to the proper prosecuting attorney, and the prosecuting attorney dismisses the charges without seeking an indictment or filing an accusation

may request the original agency in writing to expunge the records of such arrest, including any fingerprints or photographs of the individual taken in conjunction with such arrest, from the agency files. Such request shall be in such form as the center shall prescribe. Reasonable fees shall be charged by the original agency and the center for the actual costs of the purging of such records, provided that such fees shall not exceed $50.00.

(2) Upon receipt of such written request, the agency shall provide a copy of the request to the proper prosecuting attorney. Upon receipt of a copy of the request to expunge a criminal record, the prosecuting attorney shall promptly review the request to determine if it meets the criteria for expungement set forth in paragraph (3) of this subsection. If the request meets those criteria, the prosecuting attorney shall review the records of the arrest to determine if any of the material contained therein must be preserved in order to protect the constitutional rights of an accused under *Brady v. Maryland.*

(3) An individual has the right to have his or her record of such arrest expunged, including any fingerprints or photographs of the individual taken in conjunction with such arrest, if the prosecuting attorney determines that the following criteria have been satisfied:

(A) The charge was dismissed under the conditions set forth in paragraph (1) of this subsection;

(B) No other criminal charges are pending against the individual; and

(C) The individual has not been previously convicted of the same or similar offense under the laws of this state, the United States, or any other state within the last five years, excluding any period of incarceration.

(4) The agency shall expunge the record by destroying the fingerprint cards, photographs, and documents relating exclusively to such person. Any material which cannot be physically destroyed or which the prosecuting attorney determines must be preserved under *Brady v. Maryland* shall be restricted by the agency and shall not be subject to disclosure to any person except by direction of the prosecuting attorney or as ordered by a court of record of this state.

(5) It shall be the duty of the agency to notify promptly the center of any records which are expunged pursuant to this subsection. Upon receipt of notice from an agency that a record has been expunged, the center shall, within a reasonable time, restrict access to the criminal history of such person relating to such charge. Records for which access is restricted pursuant to this subsection shall be made available only to criminal justice officials upon written application for official judicial law enforcement or criminal investigative purposes.

(6) If the agency declines to expunge such arrest record, the individual may file an action in the superior court where the agency is located as provided in Code Section 50–13–19. A decision of the agency shall be upheld only if it is determined by clear and convincing evidence that the individual did not meet the criteria set forth in paragraph (3) of this subsection or subparagraphs (A) through (G) of paragraph (7) of this subsection. The court in its discretion may award reasonable court costs including attorney's fees to the individual if he or she prevails in the appellate process. Any such action shall be served upon the agency, the center, the prosecuting attorney having jurisdiction over the offense sought to be expunged, and the Attorney General who may become parties to the action.

(7) After the filing of an indictment or an accusation, a record shall not be expunged if the prosecuting attorney shows that the charges were nolle prossed, dead docketed, or otherwise dismissed because:

(A) Of a plea agreement resulting in a conviction for an offense arising out of the same underlying transaction or occurrence as the conviction;

(B) The government was barred from introducing material evidence against the individual on legal grounds including but not limited to the grant of a motion to suppress or motion in limine;

(C) A material witness refused to testify or was unavailable to testify against the individual unless such witness refused to testify based on his or her statutory right to do so;

(D) The individual was incarcerated on other criminal charges and the prosecuting attorney elected not to prosecute for reasons of judicial economy;

(E) The individual successfully completed a pretrial diversion program, the terms of which did not specifically provide for expungement of the arrest record;

(F) The conduct which resulted in the arrest of the individual was part of a pattern of criminal activity which was prosecuted in another court of this state, the United States, another state, or foreign nation; or

(G) The individual had diplomatic, consular, or similar immunity or inviolability from arrest or prosecution.

(8) If the prosecuting attorney having jurisdiction determines that the records should not be expunged because the criteria set forth in paragraph (3) or subparagraphs (A) through (G) of paragraph (7) of this subsection were not met, and the agency or center fails to follow the prosecuting attorney's recommendation, the prosecuting attorney having jurisdiction over the offense sought to be expunged or the Attorney General may appeal a decision by the agency or center to expunge a criminal history as provided in Code Section 50–13–19.

(9) An individual who has been indicted or charged by accusation that was subsequently dismissed, dead docketed, or nolle prossed may request an expungement as provided by paragraphs (1) through (3) of this subsection; provided, however, that if the prosecuting attorney objects to the expungement request within 60 days after receiving a copy of said request from the agency, the agency shall decline to expunge and the individual shall have the right to appeal as provided by paragraph (6) of this subsection.

(10) Nothing in this subsection shall be construed as requiring the destruction of incident reports or other records that a crime was committed or reported to law enforcement. Further, nothing in this subsection shall be construed to apply to custodial records maintained by county or municipal jail or detention centers. It shall be the duty of the agency to take such action as may be reasonable to prevent disclosure of information to the public which would identify such person whose records were expunged.

(e) Agencies, including the center, at which criminal offender records are sought to be inspected may prescribe reasonable hours and places of inspection and may impose such additional procedures, fees not to exceed $3.00, or restrictions including fingerprinting as are reasonably necessary to assure the records' security, to verify the identities of those who seek to inspect them, and to maintain an orderly and efficient mechanism for inspection of records.

(f) The provisions of Chapter 13 of Title 50, the "Georgia Administrative Procedure Act," shall not apply to proceedings under this Code section.

(g) If the center has notified a firearms dealer that a person is prohibited from purchasing or possessing a handgun pursuant to Part 5 of Article 4 of Chapter 11 of Title 16 and if the prohibition is the result of such person's being involuntarily hospitalized within the immediately preceding five years, upon such person or his or her attorney making an application to inspect his or her records, the center shall provide the record of involuntary hospitalization and also inform the person or attorney of his or her right to a hearing before the judge of the probate court or superior court relative to such person's eligibility to possess or transport a handgun.

Laws 1973, p. 1301, § 6; Laws 1995, p. 139, § 4; Laws 1997, p. 1345, § 1; Laws 2000, p. 1589, § 3.

§ 35–3–38. Violations relating to criminal justice information systems

(a) Any person who knowingly requests, obtains, or attempts to obtain criminal history record information under false pretenses, or who knowingly communicates or attempts to communicate criminal history record information to any agency or person except in accordance with this article, or any member, officer, employee or agent of the center, the council, or any participating agency who knowingly falsifies criminal history record information or any records relating thereto shall for each such offense, upon conviction thereof, be fined not more than $5,000.00, or imprisoned for not more than two years, or both.

(b) Any person who communicates or attempts to communicate criminal history record information in a negligent manner not in accordance with this article shall for each such offense, upon conviction thereof, be fined not more than $100.00, or imprisoned not more than ten days, or both.

(c) Any person who knowingly discloses or attempts to disclose the techniques or methods employed to ensure the security and privacy of information or data contained in criminal justice information systems except in accordance with this article shall for each such offense, upon conviction thereof, be fined not more than $5,000.00, or imprisoned not more than two years, or both.

(d) Any person who discloses or attempts to disclose the techniques or methods employed to ensure the security and privacy of information or data contained in criminal justice information systems in a manner not permitted by this article shall for each such offense, upon conviction thereof, be fined not more than $100.00, or imprisoned not more than ten days, or both.

Laws 1973, p. 1301, § 7; Laws 1976, p. 617, § 8; Laws 1982, p. 3, § 35.

§ 35–3–39. Neglect or refusal by officers to do any required act

Any officer or official mentioned in this article who shall neglect or refuse to make any report or to do any act required by any provision of this article shall be deemed guilty of nonfeasance in office and subject to removal therefrom.

Laws 1973, p. 1301, § 8.

§ 35–3–39.1. Ratification and administration of National Crime Prevention and Privacy Compact

(a) As used in this Code section, the term:

(1) "Compact" means the National Crime Prevention and Privacy Compact established by Section 217 of the federal law.

(2) "Compact council" means the compact council established by Article VI of the compact.

(3) "Director" means the director of the Georgia Crime Information Center.

(4) "Federal law" means the National Crime Prevention and Privacy Compact Act of 1998 contained in Public Law 92–544, 42 U.S.C. Section 14616.

(5) "Interstate Identification Index System" or "III System" means the cooperative federal-state system for the exchange of criminal history records as provided for in the compact.

(b) The National Crime Prevention and Privacy Compact established by federal law is ratified, enacted, and entered into by the State of Georgia. The compact shall become operative immediately upon approval of this state's participation by the United States Attorney General.

(c) The director shall be the compact officer and shall be responsible for:

(1) Administering the compact within this state;

(2) Ensuring that compact provisions and rules, procedures, and standards established by the compact council are complied with in this state; and

(3) Regulating the in-state use of records received from the Federal Bureau of Investigation or other states party to the compact.

(d) The center shall establish and maintain a criminal history record repository to provide:

(1) Information and records for the National Identification Index and the National Fingerprint File; and

(2) This state's III System-indexed criminal history records for noncriminal justice purposes described in Article IV of the compact.

(e) This state shall comply with III System rules, procedures, and standards established pursuant to the compact concerning record dissemination and use, response times, data quality, system security, accuracy, privacy protection, and other aspects of the III System operation.

(f) Use of the III System by the center for noncriminal justice purposes authorized in the compact shall be managed so as not to diminish the level of services provided in support of criminal justice purposes.

(g) Administration of the compact provisions shall not reduce the level of services available to noncriminal justice users on the effective date of the compact with this state.

(h) The center shall provide criminal history records, excluding sealed records, to criminal justice agencies and other governmental and nongovernmental agencies for noncriminal justice purposes as required by the compact.

(i) Records obtained under the compact may be used only for the official purposes for which the records were requested and under such procedures established by the director in conformity with rules, procedures, and standards established pursuant to Article IV of the compact.

(j) Notwithstanding any other law to the contrary, fingerprints or other forms of positive identification, as provided for in the compact, shall be submitted with all requests for criminal history record checks for noncriminal justice purposes authorized under the compact. Such records checks made pursuant to any other law of this state shall comply with this Code section, the compact, and federal law.

Laws 1999, p. 574, § 1; Laws 2000, p. 136, § 35; Laws 2000, p. 1549, § 2.

Historical and Statutory Notes

Complementary Legislation:

Alaska—AS § 12.64.010.
Arizona—A.R.S. § 41–1750.01.
Colo.—West's C.R.S.A. §§ 24–60–2701, 24–60–2702.
Conn.—C.G.S.A. § 29–164f.
Fla.—West's F.S.A. § 943.0543.
Ga.—O.C.G.A. § 35–3–39.1.
Idaho—I.C. §§ 67–3012.
Iowa—I.C.A. §§ 692B.1 to 692B.3.
Kan.—K.S.A. § 22–5001.
Maine—25 M.R.S.A. §§ 1701 to 1711.
Md.—Code, Criminal Procedure, §§ 10–237 to 10–250.
Minn.—M.S.A. §§ 299C.57 to 299C.582.
Mo.—V.A.M.S. § 43.542.
Mt.—M.C.A. 44–5–601, 44–5–602.
Nev.—N.R.S. 179A.800.
N.H.—RSA § 106–B:14.
N.J.—N.J.S.A. 53:1–32.
N.C.—G.S. § 114–19.50.
Ohio—R.C. § 109.571.
Okl.—74 Okl.St.Ann. § 150.9b.
Ore.—ORS 181.036.
S.C.—Code 1976 § 23–3–1010.
Tenn.—T.C.A. § 38–14–101.
U.S.—42 U.S.C.A. §§ 14601 et seq.

§ 35–3–40. Supersedeas of existing laws; records of juvenile offenders exempted

(a) In the event of conflict, this article shall to the extent of the conflict supersede all existing statutes which regulate, control, or otherwise relate, directly or by implication, to the collection, storage, and dissemination or usage of fingerprint identification, offender criminal history, uniform crime reporting, and criminal justice activity data records or any existing statutes which relate directly or by implication to any other provisions of this article.

(b) Notwithstanding subsection (a) of this Code section, this article shall not be understood to alter, amend, or supersede the statutes and rules of law governing the collection, storage, dissemination, or usage of records concerning individual juvenile offenders in which they are individually identified by name or by other means.

Laws 1973, p. 1301, § 9.

CHAPTER 8

EMPLOYMENT AND TRAINING OF PEACE OFFICERS

§ 35–8–1. Short title

This chapter shall be known and may be cited as the "Georgia Peace Officer Standards and Training Act."

Laws 1970, p. 208, § 1.

§ 35–8–2. Definitions

As used in this chapter, the term:

(1) "Applicant" means a prospective peace officer who has not commenced employment or service with a law enforcement unit.

(2) "Candidate" means a peace officer who, having satisfied preemployment requirements, has commenced employment with a law enforcement unit but who has not satisfied the training requirement provided for in this chapter.

(3) "Council" means the Georgia Peace Officer Standards and Training Council.

(4) "Department head" means the chief executive or head of a state department or agency, a county, a municipality, or a railroad who is a peace officer and whose responsibilities include the supervision and assignment of one or more employees or the performance of administrative and managerial duties of a police agency or law enforcement unit. Such term does not include the Attorney General, the director of the Georgia Drugs and Narcotics Agency, a district attorney, a solicitor general, a county or municipal fire chief, or peace officers employed exclusively as investigators of any such offices who do not exercise any law enforcement supervisory or managerial duties. The provisions of this paragraph shall not apply to any sheriff or to any head of any law enforcement unit within the office of sheriff.

(4.1) "Detention facility" means a municipal or county jail used for the detention of persons charged with or convicted of a felony, a misdemeanor, or a municipal or county ordinance, but shall not include a facility customarily used to hold one or more persons for a period not to exceed eight hours while any such person awaits processing, booking, court appearance, or release.

(5) "Emergency peace officers" means any peace officers who are employed or appointed to act as peace officers during an emergency or disaster which has been so declared by the chief executive officer of the state and whose status as peace officers is intended to be temporary and for that limited purpose.

(5.1) "Jail officer" means any person who is employed or appointed by a county or a municipality and who has the responsibility of supervising inmates who are confined in a municipal or county detention facility.

(5.2) "Juvenile correctional facility" means a facility operated by the Department of Juvenile Justice and used for the detention of youth who are delinquent or who are alleged to be delinquent or a facility operated by the Department of Juvenile Justice used for the care, treatment, and rehabilitation of juvenile offenders.

(5.3) "Juvenile correctional officer" means any person employed or appointed by the Department of Juvenile Justice who has the primary responsibility for the supervision and control of youth confined in its programs and facilities.

(6) "Law enforcement support personnel" means persons, other than peace officers, whose primary employment with a law enforcement unit consists of performing functions directly related to the prevention, detection, or investigation of crime.

(7) "Law enforcement unit" means:

(A) Any agency, organ, or department of this state, a subdivision or municipality thereof, or a railroad whose primary functions include the enforcement of criminal or traffic laws, the preservation of public order, the protection of life and property, or the prevention, detection, or investigation of crime;

(B) The Office of Permits and Enforcement of the Department of Transportation, the Department of Juvenile Justice and its institutions and facilities for the purpose of personnel who are authorized to exercise the power of arrest and who are employed or appointed by said department or institutions, and the office or section in the Department of Juvenile Justice in which persons are assigned who have been designated by the commissioner to investigate and apprehend unruly and delinquent children; and

(C) The Department of Corrections, the State Board of Pardons and Paroles, municipal correctional institutions employing 300 or more correctional officers, and county correctional institutions for the purpose of personnel who are authorized to exercise the power of arrest and who are employed or appointed by said department, board, or institutions.

(8) "Peace officer" means, for purposes of this chapter only:

(A) An agent, operative, or officer of this state, a subdivision or municipality thereof, or a railroad who, as an employee for hire or as a volunteer, is vested either expressly by law or by virtue of public employment or service with authority to enforce the criminal or traffic laws through the power of arrest and whose duties include the preservation of public order, the protection of life and property, and the prevention, detection, or investigation of crime;

(B) An enforcement officer who is employed by the Department of Transportation in its Office of Permits and Enforcement and any person employed by the Department of Juvenile Justice who is designated by the commissioner to investigate and apprehend unruly and delinquent children;

(B.1) Personnel who are authorized to exercise the power of arrest, who are employed or appointed by the Department of Juvenile Justice, and whose full-time duties include the preservation of public order, the protection of life and property, the detection of crime, or the supervision of delinquent and unruly children in the department's institutions, facilities, or programs;

(C) Personnel who are authorized to exercise the power of arrest and who are employed or appointed by the Department of Corrections, the State Board of Pardons and Paroles, municipal correctional institutions employing 300 or more correctional officers, county probation systems, and county correctional institutions; and

(D) An administrative investigator who is an agent, operative, investigator, or officer of this state whose duties include the prevention, detection, and investigation of violations of law and the enforcement of administrative, regulatory, licensing, or certification requirements of his or her respective employing agency.

Law enforcement support personnel are not peace officers within the meaning of this chapter, but they may be certified upon voluntarily complying with the certification provisions of this chapter.

(9) "Retired peace officer" means a retired law enforcement officer who, prior to his or her retirement from service with the state or a subdivision or municipality thereof, was a peace officer within the meaning of such term as defined in paragraph (8) of this Code section. A retired peace officer may be certified or registered upon voluntarily complying with the certification or registration provisions of this chapter. Such term shall also mean a retired law enforcement officer who retired from service with the United States who meets all criteria as specified by the council for such classification; provided, however, that such classification shall not exempt such officer from satisfying the minimum employment and training requirements of this chapter if such officer is appointed or employed as a peace officer by the state or a subdivision or municipality thereof.

(10) "School" means any school, college, university, academy, or training program approved by the council which offers basic law enforcement training and which consists of a combination of a course curriculum, instructors, and facilities.

(11) "Speed detection device" means that particular device designed to measure the speed or velocity of a motor vehicle and marketed under the name "Vascar," any device designed to measure the speed or velocity of motor vehicles using the Doppler principle of radio detection and ranging and commonly marketed under the name "radar," or any similar device, including but not limited to laser, operating under the same or similar principle, which device is approved by the Department of Public Safety for the measurement of speed, including any device for the measurement of speed or velocity based upon the Doppler principle of radar or speed timing principle of laser.

Laws 1970, p. 208, §§ 2, 14; Laws 1975, p. 1165, §§ 2, 3, 10; Laws 1976, p. 395, §§ 1–5; Laws 1978, p. 992, §§ 1, 2; Laws 1978, p. 2299, § 1; Laws 1980, p. 979, § 1; Laws 1981, p. 778, § 1; Laws 1982, p. 3, § 35; Laws 1982, p. 2478, §§ 1, 2, 5, 6; Laws 1985, p. 283, § 1; Laws 1987, p. 1141, § 1; Laws 1989, p. 568, § 1; Laws 1993, p. 91, § 35; Laws 1993, p. 966, §§ 1, 2; Laws 1995, p. 880, § 1; Laws 1995, p. 1238, § 1; Laws 1996, p. 1281, § 1; Laws 1997, p. 582, §§ 1, 2; Laws 1997, p. 1453, § 1; Laws 1997, p. 1488, §§ 2A, 2B, 7A, 7B; Laws 1998, p. 128, § 35; Laws 1998, p. 224, § 2; Laws 1999, p. 777, §§ 2, 3.

§ 35–8–3. Georgia Peace Officer Standards and Training Council; establishment; membership

(a) The Georgia Peace Officer Standards and Training Council is established. The council shall consist of 19 voting members and five advisory members.

(b) The voting members shall consist of:

(1) An appointee of the Governor who is not the Attorney General, the commissioner of public safety or his or her designee, the director of investigation of the Georgia Bureau of Investigation or his or her designee, the president of the Georgia Association of Chiefs of Police or his or her designee, the president of the Georgia Sheriffs Association or his or her designee, the president of the Georgia Municipal Association or his or her designee, the president of the Association of County Commissioners of Georgia or his or her designee, the president of the Peace Officers' Association of Georgia or his or her designee, the commissioner of corrections or his or her designee, the chairperson of the State Board of Pardons and Paroles or his or her designee, and the president of the Georgia Prison Wardens Association or his or her designee, who shall be ex officio members of the council;

(2) Six members who shall be appointed by the Governor for terms of four years, their initial appointments, however, being two for four-year terms, two for three-year terms, and two for two-year terms. Appointments shall be made so that there are always on the council the following persons who are appointed by the Governor: one chief of police; two municipal police officers other than a chief of police; one county sheriff; one city manager or mayor; and one county commissioner. No person shall serve beyond the time he or she holds the office or employment by reason of which he or she was initially eligible for appointment. Vacancies shall be filled in the same manner as the original appointment and successors shall serve for the unexpired term. Any member may be appointed for additional terms; and

(3) Two members who are peace officers and who shall be appointed by the Governor for terms of four years. Neither person shall serve beyond the time he or she is actively employed or serves as a peace officer. Vacancies shall be filled in the same manner as the original appointment and successors shall serve for the unexpired term.

(c) Five advisory members shall be appointed by the council to serve on the council in an advisory capacity only without voting privileges.

(d) Membership on the council does not constitute public office and no member shall be disqualified from holding public office by reason of his or her membership.

(e) The council is assigned to the Department of Public Safety for administrative purposes only, as prescribed in Code Section 50–4–3.

Laws 1970, p. 208, § 3; Laws 1972, p. 866, § 1; Laws 1972, p. 1015, § 1606; Laws 1975, p. 1165, § 1; Laws 1976, p. 395, § 6; Laws 1976, p. 1684, §§ 1, 2; Laws 1977, p. 717, §§ 2–4; Laws 1982, p. 3, § 35; Laws 1982, p. 2478, §§ 3, 7, 8; Laws 1983, p. 3, § 26; Laws 1985, p. 283, § 1; Laws 1988, p. 426, § 1; Laws 1997, p. 1488, § 3.

§ 35–8–4. Officers; quorum; minutes; reports

The business of the council shall be conducted in the following manner:

(1) The officers of the council, who shall consist of a chairman, vice-chairman, and secretary-treasurer, shall be elected at the first meeting of each calendar year.

(2) Seven members of the council shall constitute a quorum for the transaction of business.

(3) The council shall maintain minutes of its meetings and such other records as it deems necessary.

(4) The council shall report at least annually to the Governor and to the General Assembly as to its activities.

Laws 1970, p. 208, § 4.

§ 35–8–5. Compensation

The members of the council shall receive no salary but shall be reimbursed for their reasonable and necessary expenses actually incurred in the performance of their duties.

Laws 1970, p. 208, § 5.

§ 35–8–6. Executive director; investigators and other personnel; direct appropriations to council

(a) The council may appoint an executive director who shall serve at the pleasure of the council. The council shall establish the compensation for the executive director.

(b) The executive director may contract for such services as may be necessary and authorized in order to carry out the provisions of this chapter and may employ such other professional, technical, and clerical personnel deemed necessary to carry out the purposes of this chapter.

(c) The executive director is authorized to appoint certain investigators for the purpose of carrying out the provisions of this chapter. The executive director and persons so appointed shall meet all employment and training requirements of this chapter as for all other peace officers and shall have all of the powers of other peace officers. Any investigator of the council shall have access to and may examine any writing, document, or other material which is deemed by the chairman of the council to be related to the fitness of any peace officer or applicant to practice as a peace officer. The chairman or executive director of the council may issue subpoenas to compel such access. When a subpoena is disobeyed, the council may apply to the superior court of the county where the person to whom the subpoena is issued resides for an order requiring obedience. Failure to comply with such order shall be punishable as for contempt of court.

(d) The funds necessary to carry out this chapter shall come from the funds appropriated to and available to the council and from any other available funds.

(e) The council is authorized to accept and use gifts, grants, donations, property, both real and personal, and services for the purpose of carrying out this chapter.

(f) Any funds, property, or services received as gifts, grants, or donations shall be kept separate and apart from any funds appropriated to the council; and the funds, property, or services so received by gifts, grants, or donations shall be the property and funds of the council and, as such, shall not lapse at the end of each fiscal year but shall remain under the control of and subject to the direction of the council for carrying out this chapter.

Laws 1970, p. 208, § 7; Laws 1975, p. 1165, § 5; Laws 1988, p. 483, § 1; Laws 1989, p. 514, § 1.

§ 35-8-7. Functions and powers

The council is vested with the following powers and duties:

(1) To meet at such times and places as it may deem necessary;

(2) To contract with other agencies, public or private, or persons as it deems necessary for the rendering and affording of such services, facilities, studies, and reports to the council as will best assist it to carry out its duties and responsibilities;

(3) To cooperate with and secure the cooperation of every department, agency, or instrumentality in the state government or its political subdivisions in the furtherance of the purposes of this chapter;

(4) To establish criteria to be used in certifying schools authorized to conduct training required by this chapter;

(5) To certify schools as authorized to conduct training required by this chapter;

(6) To prescribe minimum qualifications for directors of schools certified to conduct training required by this chapter;

(7) To certify such school directors;

(8) To establish minimum qualifications for instructors at schools certified to conduct training required by this chapter;

(9) To certify instructors authorized to conduct training required by this chapter;

(10) To reevaluate certified schools annually to determine if such schools shall continue to be certified;

(11) To withdraw or suspend certification of schools, school directors, and instructors who fail to continue to meet or maintain, at any given time, the criteria and qualifications required for school, school director, or instructor certification;

(12) To determine whether a candidate has met the requirements of this chapter and is qualified to be employed as a peace officer and to issue a certificate to those so qualified;

(13) To certify to designated law enforcement units a candidate's successful completion of the course;

(14) To refuse to grant a certificate to or to discipline a certified peace officer or an exempt peace officer under this chapter or any antecedent law;

(15) To establish and modify the curriculum, including the methods of instruction, composing the basic training courses and to set the minimum number of hours therefor;

(16) To establish and recommend curricula for such advanced, in-service, and specialized training courses as the council shall deem advisable and to recognize the completion of such courses by the issuance of certificates;

(17) To provide technical assistance as requested by law enforcement units;

(18) To provide for and administer the registration of all exempt peace officers;

(19) To research, plan, and establish policy relative to peace officer training and to develop and coordinate the delivery of peace officer training programs through such agencies and institutions as the council may deem appropriate;

(20) To establish as part of the curriculum for basic and in-service training courses for all peace officers training on organized criminal activity and criminal street gangs;

(21) To develop, adopt, and issue advanced or professional peace officer certificates based upon the attainment of specified education, advanced or specialized training, and experience as the council may determine;

(22) To provide and administer the certification of persons qualified to operate radar speed detection devices and to withdraw or suspend such certificates as provided for in this chapter;

(23) To impose administrative fees, as determined by the council, for services provided pursuant to the provisions of this chapter;

(24) To adopt in accordance with Chapter 13 of Title 50, the "Georgia Administrative Procedure Act," such rules and regulations as are necessary to carry out the purposes of this chapter; and.

(25) To do any and all things necessary or convenient to enable it to perform wholly and adequately its duties and to exercise the power granted to it.

Laws 1970, p. 208, § 6; Laws 1975, p. 1165, § 4; Laws 1976, p. 395, § 7; Laws 1977, p. 713, §§ 1, 2; Laws 1977, p. 717, § 1; Laws 1978, p. 1680, § 1; Laws 1980, p. 979, § 2; Laws 1985, p. 539, § 1; Laws 1987, p. 3, § 35; Laws 1997, p. 1488, § 4; Laws 1998, p. 270, § 12; Laws 2010, Act 401, § 1, eff. May 20, 2010.

Historical and Statutory Notes

Laws 2010, Act 401, § 2, provides:

"Nothing contained in this Act shall be construed so as to suggest that any administrative fees that may have been collected by the Georgia Peace Officer Standards and Training Council prior to this Act's enactment were collected without authority. Nor shall this Act be construed so as to create in any person paying administrative fees prior to the effective date of this Act a cause of action for the payment of such fees."

§ 35-8-7.1. Authority of council to refuse to grant certificate or to discipline peace officer; restoration and reissuance of certificates

(a) The council shall have authority to refuse to grant a certificate to an applicant or to discipline a certified peace officer or exempt peace officer under this chapter or any antecedent law upon a determination by the council that the applicant or certified peace officer or exempt peace officer has:

(1) Failed to demonstrate the qualifications or standards for a certificate provided in this chapter or in the rules and regulations of the council. It shall be incumbent upon the applicant to demonstrate to the satisfaction of the council that he meets all requirements for the issuance of a certificate;

(2) Knowingly made misleading, deceptive, untrue, or fraudulent representations in the practice of being a peace officer or in any document connected therewith or practiced fraud or deceit or intentionally made any false statement in obtaining a certificate to practice as a peace officer;

(3) Been convicted of a felony in the courts of this state or any other state, territory, country, or of the United States. As used in this paragraph, the term "conviction of a felony" shall include a conviction of an offense which if committed in this state would be deemed a felony under either state or federal law without regard to its designation elsewhere. As used in this paragraph, the term "conviction" shall include a finding or a verdict of guilt, a plea of guilty, or a plea of nolo contendere in a criminal proceeding, regardless of whether the adjudication of guilt or sentence is withheld or not entered thereon. However, the council may not deny a certificate to an applicant with a conviction if the adjudication of guilt or sentence is withheld or not entered thereon;

(4) Committed a crime involving moral turpitude, without regard to conviction. The conviction of a crime involving moral turpitude shall be conclusive of the commission of such crime. As used in this paragraph, the term "conviction" shall have the meaning prescribed in paragraph (3) of this subsection;

(5) Had his certificate or license to practice as a peace officer revoked, suspended, or annulled by any lawful certifying or licensing authority; or had other disciplinary action taken against him by any lawful certifying or licensing authority; or was denied a certificate or license by any lawful certifying or licensing authority;

(6) Engaged in any unprofessional, unethical, deceptive, or deleterious conduct or practice harmful to the public, which conduct or practice need not have resulted in actual injury to any person. As used in this paragraph, the term "unprofessional conduct" shall include any departure from, or failure to conform to, the minimal standards of acceptable and prevailing practice of a peace officer;

(7) Violated or attempted to violate a law, rule, or regulation of this state, any other state, the council, the United States, or any other lawful authority without regard to whether the violation is criminally punishable, which law, rule, or regulation relates to or in part regulates the practice of a peace officer;

(8) Committed any act or omission which is indicative of bad moral character or untrustworthiness;

(9) Been adjudged mentally incompetent by a court of competent jurisdiction, within or outside this state;

(10) Become unable to perform as a peace officer with reasonable skill and safety to citizens by reason of illness or use of alcohol, drugs, narcotics, chemicals, or any other type of material or as a result of any mental or physical condition; or

(11) Been suspended or discharged by the peace officer's employing law enforcement unit for disciplinary reasons.

(b)(1) When the council finds that any person is unqualified to be granted a certificate or finds that any person should be disciplined pursuant to subsection (a) of this Code section, the council may take any one or more of the following actions:

(A) Refuse to grant a certificate to an applicant;

(B) Administer a public or private reprimand, provided that a private reprimand shall not be disclosed to any person except the peace officer;

(C) Suspend any certificate for a definite period;

(D) Limit or restrict any certificate;

(E) Revoke any certificate; or

(F) Condition the penalty, or withhold formal disposition, upon the peace officer's completing such care, counseling, or treatment, as directed by the council.

(2) In addition to and in conjunction with the foregoing actions, the council may make a finding adverse to the applicant or peace officer but withhold imposition of judgment and penalty or it may impose the judgment and penalty but suspend enforcement thereof and place the peace officer on probation, which probation may be vacated upon noncompliance with such reasonable terms as the council may impose.

(c) In its discretion, the council may restore and reissue a certificate issued under this chapter or any antecedent law to a peace officer and, as a condition thereof, may impose any disciplinary or corrective measure provided in this chapter.

(d) Upon arrest or indictment of a peace officer for any crime which is punishable as a felony, the executive director of the council shall order the emergency suspension of such officer's certification upon the executive director's determination that the suspension is in the best interest of the health, safety, or welfare of the public. The order of emergency suspension shall be made in writing and shall specify the basis for the executive director's determination. Following the issuance of an emergency suspension order, proceedings of the council in the exercise of its authority to discipline any peace officer shall be promptly scheduled as provided for in Code Section 35–8–7.2. The emergency suspension order of the executive director shall continue in effect until issuance of the final decision of the council or such order is withdrawn by the executive director.

Laws 1985, p. 539, § 2; Laws 1987, p. 3, § 35; Laws 1993, p. 91, § 35; Laws 2008, Act 446, § 1, eff. May 6, 2008.

§ 35–8–7.2. Proceedings to issue certificate or discipline peace officer

(a) Except as otherwise provided in subsection (b) of this Code section, proceedings of the council in the exercise of its authority to issue any certificate or discipline any peace officer under the terms of this chapter shall be conducted in accordance with Chapter 13 of Title 50, the "Georgia Administrative Procedure Act." In all such proceedings the council shall have authority to compel the attendance of witnesses and the production of any book, writing, or document upon the issuance of a subpoena therefor. In any hearing in which the fitness of a peace officer or applicant is in question, the council may exclude all persons from its deliberation of the appropriate action and may, when it deems necessary, speak to the peace officer or applicant in private. All final determinations, findings, and conclusions of the council under this chapter are final and conclusive decisions of the matters involved.

(b) Proceedings for review of a final decision of the council shall be instituted by filing a petition within 30 days after the service of the final decision of the council or, if a rehearing is requested, within 30 days after the decision thereon. The petition shall be filed in the superior court of the county of residence of the petitioner.

Laws 1985, p. 539, § 2.

§ 35–8–8. Qualifications for peace officers

(a) Any person employed or certified as a peace officer shall:

(1) Be at least 18 years of age;

(2) Be a citizen of the United States;

(3) Have a high school diploma or its recognized equivalent;

(4) Not have been convicted by any state or by the federal government of any crime the punishment for which could have been imprisonment in the federal or state prison or institution nor have been convicted of sufficient misdemeanors to establish a pattern of disregard for the law, provided that, for

purposes of this paragraph, violations of traffic laws and other offenses involving the operation of motor vehicles when the applicant has received a pardon shall not be considered;

(5) Be fingerprinted for the purpose of conducting a fingerprint based search at the Georgia Bureau of Investigation and the Federal Bureau of Investigation to determine the existence of any criminal record;

(6) Possess good moral character as determined by investigation under procedure established by the council;

(7) Be found, after examination by a licensed physician or surgeon, to be free from any physical, emotional, or mental conditions which might adversely affect his or her exercising the powers or duties of a peace officer; and

(8) Successfully complete a job related academy entrance examination provided for and administered by the council in conformity with state and federal law. Such examination shall be administered prior to entrance to the basic course provided for in Code Sections 35–8–9 and 35–8–11. The council may change or modify such examination and shall establish the criteria for determining satisfactory performance on such examination. Peace officers who do not perform satisfactorily on the examination shall be ineligible to retake such examination for a period of six months after an unsuccessful attempt. The provisions of this paragraph establish only the minimum requirements of academy entrance examinations for peace officer candidates in this state; each law enforcement unit is encouraged to provide such additional requirements and any preemployment examination as it deems necessary and appropriate.

(b) Any person authorized to attend the basic training course prior to employment as a peace officer shall meet the requirements of this Code section.

Laws 1970, p. 208, § 8; Laws 1973, p. 539, § 1; Laws 1976, p. 1563, § 1; Laws 1976, p. 1684, §§ 3, 4; Laws 1977, p. 712, § 1; Laws 1977, p. 1180, §§ 1, 2; Laws 1982, p. 3, § 35; Laws 1987, p. 3, § 35; Laws 2004, Act 780, § 2, eff. July 1, 2004; Laws 2008, Act 446, § 2, eff. May 6, 2008.

§ 35–8–9. Basic course of instruction

(a) In addition to complying with the preemployment standards as set forth in Code Section 35–8–8, each and every candidate shall satisfactorily complete a basic training course prior to his or her appointment as a peace officer.

(b) The council shall have the authority to recognize instruction received by a candidate if, in the determination of the council, such instruction is at least equivalent to that required by this chapter. If such instruction is recognized, then it shall be in lieu of part or parts of the minimum hours of instruction required for certification by this chapter.

(c) Should any candidate fail to complete successfully the basic training requirements specified in this Code section, he or she shall not perform any of the duties of a peace officer involving the power of arrest until such training shall have been successfully completed.

(d) A municipal correctional institution covered under the provisions of subparagraph (C) of paragraph (7) and subparagraph (C) of paragraph (8) of Code Section 35–8–2 shall not be permitted to have more than ten correctional officers in any 12 month period take the basic training course necessary to become a certified peace officer.

Laws 1970, p. 208, § 9; Laws 1975, p. 1165, § 6; Laws 1992, p. 1004, § 1; Laws 1994, p. 1355, § 1; Laws 1997, p. 1488, § 4A.

§ 35–8–10. Persons subject to certification provisions; exceptions

(a) No person required to comply with the certification provisions of this chapter shall be employed or appointed by any law enforcement unit without certification from the council that the applicant has met the preemployment requirements established in this chapter, and no candidate shall perform any of the duties of a peace officer involving the power of arrest until such training shall have been successfully completed.

(b) Peace officers commencing any employment or service on any terms with the Department of Public Safety, counties, municipalities, the Georgia Bureau of Investigation, the Department of Natural Resources, the Department of Revenue, Alcohol and Tobacco Tax Unit, the Secretary of State's investigative section, the Office of the Commissioner of Insurance and Safety Fire Commissioner, or a railroad after July 1, 1975, are required to comply with the certification provisions of this chapter. Peace officers commencing such employment or service prior to July 1, 1975, and whose employment continues on July 1, 1975, are exempt and excused from compliance with the certification provisions of this chapter except as provided in this Code section so long as the registration provided for in subsections (d) and (e) of this Code section remains in effect. Any peace officer otherwise exempt from the certification provisions of this chapter must meet the qualifications and requirements specified in paragraphs (2), (4), (5), and (8) of subsection (a) of Code Section 35–8–8.

(c) If, after July 1, 1975, any other employment or service is conditioned on compliance with this chapter, persons so employed or serving shall be required to comply with the certification provisions established in this chapter, except that persons so employed or serving whose employment or service commenced prior to and continues upon the effective date of the peace officer's law enforcement unit becoming subject to the provisions of this chapter shall be exempt and excused from compliance so long as registration provided for in subsections (d) and (e) of this Code section remains in effect. Notwithstanding this subsection, the effective date of requirements for certification or registration shall be determined by the council based upon identification of the applicability of this chapter to particular peace officers. Nothing in this subsection shall be deemed to grant an exemption to persons required to be certified by subsections (a) and (b) of this Code section.

(d) Peace officers exempt from the certification provisions of this chapter are required to register with the council. The registration shall remain in effect for the period of time said person is employed as a peace officer.

(e) Any registration granted in this Code section shall not terminate upon a subsequent employment or appointment as a peace officer, provided that subsequent employment or appointment as a peace officer is recognized by the council to be substantially the same or similar to the employment or appointment by virtue of which said peace officer was exempted and registered as such; provided, further, that such subsequent employment or appointment is commenced within 12 months of such prior termination as a peace officer.

(f) Except as otherwise provided by subsection (b) of this Code section, nothing in this subsection or in subsection (d) shall be deemed to require any exempt peace officer to comply with Code Sections 35–8–8 and 35–8–9 for the period of time the registration shall remain in effect.

(g) A peace officer excused from mandatory compliance with this chapter by this Code section may choose to be certified under this chapter. If so, the council shall have the authority to recognize instruction received by such a peace officer as equivalent to all or part of the instruction required for certification under this chapter.

(h) Any person who was serving as a sheriff on July 1, 1970, and who subsequently becomes a peace officer shall not be required to comply with this chapter.

(i) A retired peace officer may be voluntarily registered by the council as an exempt peace officer without meeting the qualifications and requirements specified in paragraphs (2), (4), (5), and (8) of subsection (a) of Code Section 35–8–8. Such registration of a retired peace officer shall not terminate, as provided for in subsection (e) of this Code section. Nothing in this subsection shall be deemed to grant an exemption to persons required to be certified or registered by this chapter.

Laws 1970, p. 208, § 13; Laws 1975, p. 1165, § 9; Laws 1976, p. 395, § 8; Laws 1977, p. 713, §§ 3–7; Laws 1978, p. 1680, § 2; Laws 1978, p. 2299, §§ 2–6; Laws 1981, p. 778, §§ 2, 3; Laws 1994, p. 1355, § 2; Laws 2003, Act 70, § 2, eff. May 29, 2003.

§ 35–8–11. Schools where basic course to be completed

The basic course provided for in Code Section 35–8–9 shall be completed at any school certified by the council which provides the course requirements and methods of instruction established by the council.

Laws 1970, p. 208, § 10; Laws 1975, p. 567, § 5; Laws 1975, p. 1165, § 7.

§ 35–8–12. Certification of persons operating speed detection devices; training course; withdrawal or suspension of certificate

(a) Persons employed or appointed by any agency, organ, or department of this state or a subdivision or municipality thereof authorized to use speed detection devices shall be required to be certified by the council as qualified speed detection device operators. Each person operating radar speed or laser detection devices shall satisfactorily complete a course of instruction in the theory and application of speed detection device operation as a condition for certification. The council shall establish and modify the curriculum for the course of instruction, including a minimum number of hours. Persons authorized and qualified to conduct the course of instruction required by this Code section shall be certified by the council as speed detection device operator instructors upon complying with requirements prescribed by the council. The council shall have the authority to recognize instruction received by persons subject to the requirements of this Code section if, in the determination of the council, the instruction is at least equivalent to that required by this chapter. If the instruction is recognized, then it shall be accepted in lieu of part or parts of the minimum hours of instruction required for speed detection device certification by this chapter. Should any person fail to complete successfully the training requirements for operation of speed detection devices, he or she shall not perform any functions related to the use of the devices until such training shall have been successfully completed and until such time as the council shall issue appropriate certification. All persons certified to use speed detection devices shall complete an update or refresher training course of such duration and at such time as may be prescribed by the council in order for their speed detection device operators' certifications to remain in force and effect. The council is authorized to withdraw or suspend the certification of any person for failure to meet the update or refresher requirements specified in this Code section or for violation of any portion of this chapter relating to conditions which may lead to the withdrawal or suspension of peace officer certification to operate radar or laser speed detection devices.

(b) Upon the withdrawal or suspension of any certificate to operate speed detection devices for the reasons set forth in this Code section, the executive director of the council shall notify the commissioner. The notification shall contain the officer's name and employing law enforcement agency.

(c) Upon receipt from the commissioner that a speed detection device permit has been suspended or revoked pursuant to Code Section 40–14–11, the council shall withdraw or suspend the certification to operate speed detection devices for every certified operator employed by the agency whose permit has been suspended or revoked. The period of withdrawal or suspension shall be consistent with the action taken by the department.

Laws 1980, p. 979, § 3; Laws 1996, p. 1281, § 2.

§ 35–8–13. Training program and standards for certification of police chaplains

(a) In addition to the other powers vested in the council, the council may develop a training program and standards for certification of police chaplains. The council shall issue certificates to qualified police chaplains who desire to be certified and who meet the standards and complete the training program.

(b) The council may suspend or revoke the certification of any police chaplain who commits an offense or act set forth in paragraph (4) of Code Section 35–8–7.1.

(c) This Code section shall be optional for police chaplains and a person who is not certified pursuant to this Code section may serve as a police chaplain.

Laws 1980, p. 1127, § 1; Laws 1991, p. 94, § 35.

§ 35–8–13.1. Training and certification of municipal probation officers

(a) Any person employed or appointed as a municipal probation officer on or after January 1, 1999, shall not be authorized to serve as a municipal probation officer unless such person has successfully completed a training course and received certification for municipal probation officers approved by the Georgia Peace Officer Standards and Training Council.

(b) Persons applying for certification and persons certified by the council under this Code section shall be subject to the powers and authority of the Georgia Peace Officer Standards and Training Council applicable to peace officers as defined in this chapter and shall be required to fulfill all of the requirements of a peace officer, except peace officer training requirements applicable to peace officers only. Such persons shall be required to register with the council. Such registration shall remain in effect for the period of time such person is employed as a municipal probation officer.

(c) Any person who registers with the council pursuant to this Code section shall not have such registration invalidated upon termination of employment or appointment as a municipal probation officer if subsequent employment or appointment as a municipal probation officer is commenced within 12 months of such prior termination of employment or appointment as a municipal probation officer.

(d) Any municipal probation officer exempted from mandatory compliance with this Code section may choose to be certified under this Code section. If so, the council shall have the authority to recognize instruction received by such municipal probation officer as equivalent to all or part of the instruction required for certification under this Code section.

(e) The term "municipal probation officer" as used in this Code section means only municipal probation officers employed directly by a municipality or consolidated government and shall not include employees of private probation providers which contract with municipalities or consolidated governments in accordance with the provisions of Article 6 of Chapter 8 of Title 42; provided, however, that the term "municipal probation officer" shall not include probation officers of any municipal corporation which conducts a training course for such officers if such training course is approved by the Georgia Peace Officer Standards and Training Council.

(f) Any person who has completed the peace officer basic training course and is certified as a peace officer by the Georgia Peace Officer Standards and Training Council may serve as a municipal probation officer without obtaining the municipal probation officer training and certification required by this Code section.

Laws 1998, p. 192, § 1.

§ 35–8–14. Repealed by Laws 1982, p. 2478, § 9, eff. November 1, 1982

§ 35–8–15. Employment records

(a) Each law enforcement unit shall prepare duplicate records on any candidate or peace officer employed under this chapter as may be prescribed by the rules and regulations of the council. One copy of the records shall be maintained in the headquarters of the law enforcement unit; the second copy shall be forwarded to the council and shall be maintained by the council.

(b) The contents of the records provided for in subsection (a) of this Code section, except for court proceedings, shall be considered as confidential and shall be released only to the candidate or peace officer to whom they pertain or to a law enforcement unit considering the candidate or peace officer for employment.

Laws 1970, p. 208, § 12; Laws 1975, p. 1165, § 1.

§ 35–8–16. Additional training requirements

This chapter establishes only the minimum qualification standards and training requirements for peace officers in this state; each law enforcement unit is encouraged to prescribe such additional requirements as it deems necessary and appropriate.

Laws 1970, p. 208, § 11.

§ 35–8–17. Effect of failure to comply with law

(a) Any peace officer so employed who does not comply with this chapter shall not be authorized to exercise the powers of a law enforcement officer generally and particularly shall not be authorized to exercise the power of arrest.

(b) The council is authorized to bring a civil action against any peace officer who does not comply with this chapter to enjoin the peace officer from performing any and all functions of a peace officer, including the power of arrest, until the officer shall meet the certification or registration requirements of this chapter.

(c) The council is authorized to bring a civil action against any law enforcement unit which employs or appoints any peace officer who fails to meet the certification or registration requirements of this chapter to enjoin the law enforcement unit from allowing the peace officer to perform any and all peace officer functions, including exercising the power of arrest, until such time as the peace officer shall comply with the certification or registration requirements of this chapter.

Laws 1970, p. 208, § 15; Laws 1975, p. 1165, § 11; Laws 1977, p. 713, § 8; Laws 1977, p. 1180, § 3.

§ 35–8–18. Chapter not applicable to emergency peace officers

This chapter shall not apply to emergency peace officers.

Laws 1970, p. 208, § 14; Laws 1975, p. 1165, § 10.

§ 35–8–19. Appointment of nonresident peace officers in certain cities

In each city of this state adjacent to the State of Georgia boundary line, the sheriff, mayor, or other person authorized to appoint peace officers may appoint as special deputy, special constable, marshal, policeman, or other peace officer a person who is not a citizen of Georgia but who is a citizen of an adjoining state, provided such appointed person is otherwise qualified to serve as a peace officer.

Laws 1982, p. 2107, § 29; Laws 1992, p. 1325, § 1.

§ 35–8–20. Training of chief of police or department head of each law enforcement unit and wardens of state institutions

(a) During calendar year 1985 and during each calendar year thereafter, the chief of police or department head of each law enforcement unit and wardens of state institutions shall complete 20 hours of training as provided in this Code section.

(b) The training required by subsection (a) of this Code section shall be completed in sessions as selected and provided or approved by the Georgia Association of Chiefs of Police or the Georgia Prison Wardens Association and which have been recognized by the Georgia Peace Officer Standards and Training Council.

(c) The salary and travel expenses of a chief of police or department head of a law enforcement unit or a warden of a state institution taking the required training shall be paid by the law enforcement unit by which he or she is employed.

(d) Any chief of police or department head of a law enforcement unit or a warden of a state institution who does not fulfill the training requirement of this Code section shall lose his or her power of arrest.

(e) A waiver of the requirement of training provided in this Code section may be granted by the Georgia Peace Officer Standards and Training Council, in its discretion, upon the presentation of evidence by a chief of police or department head of a law enforcement unit or a warden of a state institution that he or she was unable to complete such training due to medical disability, providential cause, or other reason deemed sufficient by the council.

Laws 1984, p. 1210, § 1; Laws 1985, p. 149, § 35; Laws 1993, p. 91, § 35; Laws 1997, p. 542, § 1; Laws 1997, p. 1488, § 5.

§ 35–8–20.1. Newly appointed chiefs of police and heads of law enforcement units required to attend law enforcement chief executive training class; waiver of requirement

(a) Any newly appointed chief of police or department head of a law enforcement unit whose term of employment commences after June 30, 1999, shall successfully complete a minimum of 60 hours of law enforcement chief executive training at the next scheduled law enforcement chief executive training class sponsored by the Georgia Association of Chiefs of Police following his or her appointment. Such training shall be in addition to the basic training required of peace officers in Code Section 35–8–9. A sworn employee acting in the capacity of a department head of a law enforcement unit for more than 60 days shall be required to attend training specified under this Code section and Code Section 35–8–20. The provisions of this subsection shall not apply to any sheriff or to any head of any law enforcement unit within the office of sheriff.

(b) The training required by subsection (a) of this Code section shall be completed in sessions as selected and provided by the Georgia Association of Chiefs of Police which have been recognized by the Georgia Peace Officer Standards and Training Council.

(c) Reserved.

(d) The salary and travel expenses of a chief of police or department head of a law enforcement unit taking the required training shall be paid by the law enforcement unit by which he is employed.

(e) Any newly appointed chief of police or department head of a law enforcement unit who does not fulfill the training requirement of this Code section shall lose his power of arrest.

(f) Any newly appointed chief of police or department head of a law enforcement unit who satisfactorily completes the training required by subsection (a) of this Code section shall be exempted for the year in which he completes such training from the training required by subsection (a) of Code Section 35–8–20.

(g) A chief of police or head of a law enforcement department who successfully completes the training required by subsection (a) of this Code section will not be required to repeat such training if he terminates an appointment and is subsequently reappointed to the same or another department.

(h) A waiver of the requirement of training provided in this Code section may be granted by the Georgia Peace Officer Standards and Training Council, in its discretion, upon the presentation of evidence by a newly appointed chief of police or department head of a law enforcement unit that he or she has served as an appointed chief of police or head of a law enforcement unit since December 31, 1992, without more than a 60 day break in service, that he or she has satisfactorily completed training or education deemed by the council to be equivalent to the training required by this Code section, or that he or she was unable to complete such training due to medical disability, providential cause, or other reason deemed sufficient by the council.

(i) Any chief of police or department head of a law enforcement unit who is exempted from the training required by subsection (a) of this Code section may choose to attend such training in lieu of the training required by Code Section 35–8–20 for any year.

Laws 1989, p. 1637, § 1; Laws 1993, p. 1780, § 1; Laws 1997, p. 542, § 2; Laws 1997, p. 1488, § 6; Laws 1999, p. 777, § 4.

§ 35–8–21. Annual training requirements

(a) During calendar year 1999 and during each calendar year thereafter, any person employed or appointed as a peace officer shall complete 20 hours of training as provided in this Code section; provided, however, that any peace officer serving with the Department of Public Safety who is a commissioned officer shall receive annual training as specified by the commissioner of public safety.

(b) The training required by subsection (a) of this Code section shall be completed in sessions approved or recognized by the Georgia Peace Officer Standards and Training Council.

(c) Peace officers who satisfactorily complete the basic course of training in accordance with the provisions of this chapter after April 1 in any calendar year shall be excused from the minimum annual training requirement for the calendar year during which the basic course is completed.

(d) Any peace officer who does not fulfill the training requirements of this Code section shall lose his power of arrest.

(e) A waiver of the requirement of training provided in this Code section may be granted by the Georgia Peace Officer Standards and Training Council, in its discretion, upon the presentation of evidence by a peace officer that he was unable to complete such training due to medical disability, providential cause, or other reason deemed sufficient by the council.

(f) Any person who is registered or certified with the council as a retired peace officer is excused and exempt from compliance with this Code section. A retired peace officer may voluntarily comply with the requirements of this Code section and, in that event, such retired peace officer shall receive such minimal annual training without payment of any fees or costs, but only if sufficient class space is available. Nothing in this subsection shall be deemed to grant an exemption to persons required to complete the annual training requirement of this Code section.

Laws 1988, p. 1063, § 1; Laws 1999, p. 777, § 5; Laws 2004, Act 780, § 2A, eff. July 1, 2004.

§ 35–8–22. Reimbursement for peace officer's mandated or formalized training

(a) Unless otherwise provided by an employment contract to the contrary, if the State of Georgia or any county or municipality thereof employs a peace officer and said peace officer is hired by another agency within 15 months after completing mandated or formalized training requirements, then the total expense of training, including salary paid during training, shall be reimbursed by the hiring agency to the State of Georgia or any county or municipality thereof which initially paid for such training. If said officer is hired by another agency during a period of 15 to 24 months after mandated or formalized training requirements are completed, then one-half of the total expense of training, including salary paid during training, shall be reimbursed by the hiring agency to the State of Georgia or any county or municipality thereof which initially paid for such training. The council shall set standards for reimbursement by hiring agencies based upon actual expenses incurred in mandated or formalized training by individual departments.

(b) The State of Georgia or any county or municipality thereof which initially paid for the training of a peace officer shall submit an itemized, sworn statement to the new employer of the peace officer and shall demand payment thereof and may enforce collection of such obligation through civil remedies and procedures.

(c) Effective July 1, 2003, in order for the State of Georgia or any county or municipality thereof to demand reimbursement, the demanding governmental unit must be able to document that the peace officer in question signed an acknowledgment of the terms of this Code section or an employment contract specifying the provisions of this Code section prior to such peace officer's employment with the demanding governmental unit. Otherwise, this Code section shall not apply to such demand for reimbursement.

Laws 1992, p. 1325, § 2; Laws 2003, Act 66, § 1, eff. July 1, 2003.

§ 35–8–23. Training for communications officers

(a) As used in this Code section, the term "communications officer" means and includes any person employed by a local governmental agency to receive, process, or transmit public safety information and dispatch law enforcement officers, firefighters, medical personnel, or emergency management personnel.

(b) Any person employed on or after July 1, 1995, as a communications officer shall satisfactorily complete a basic training course approved by the council. Persons who are employed on July 1, 1994, shall register with the council and may be certified by voluntarily complying with the certification process. Any person who fails to comply with the registration or certification process of the council shall not perform any duties of a communications officer and may have his or her certificate sanctioned or revoked.

(c) The council shall conduct administrative compliance reviews with respect to the requirements of this Code section. The council shall be authorized to promulgate rules and regulations to facilitate the administration and coordination of standards, certification, and compliance reviews consistent with the provisions of this Code section.

(d) On and after July 1, 1998, the basic training course for communications officers shall include training in the use of telecommunications devices for the deaf (TDD's), and no person shall on or after that date be certified by the council under this

Code section unless such person has satisfactorily completed such training.

Laws 1994, p. 1355, § 2.1; Laws 1997, p. 1488, § 7; Laws 1998, p. 540, § 1.

§ 35–8–24. Training of jail officers and juvenile correctional officers

(a)(1) Any person employed or appointed as a jail officer six months after January 1, 1999, shall not be authorized to serve as a jail officer in any detention facility after a certain date as provided in subsection (b) of this Code section unless such person has successfully completed a training course for jail officers approved by the Georgia Peace Officer Standards and Training Council.

(2) Any person employed or appointed as a juvenile correctional officer six months after January 1, 1999, shall not be authorized to serve as a juvenile correctional officer in any juvenile correctional facility after a certain date as provided in subsection (b) of this Code section unless such person has successfully completed a training course for juvenile correctional officers approved by the Georgia Peace Officer Standards and Training Council.

(b) Any person employed or appointed as a jail officer or juvenile correctional officer six months after January 1, 1999, shall have a period of six months from the date of initial employment to complete the required training course successfully. Any person who fails to complete such training course successfully within six months of the date of initial employment or appointment as a jail officer or as a juvenile correctional officer shall be prohibited from working as a jail officer in a detention facility or as a juvenile correctional officer in a juvenile correctional facility.

(c) Applicants and persons certified under this Code section shall be subject to the powers and authority of the Georgia Peace Officer Standards and Training Council applicable to peace officers as defined in this chapter and shall be required to fulfill all requirements of a peace officer, except the requirements of paragraph(8) of subsection (a) of Code Section 35–8–8 and peace officer training requirements applicable to peace officers only.

(d) Persons employed or serving as jail officers or juvenile correctional officers whose employment or service commences prior to and continues on January 1, 1999, are exempt and excused from compliance with the certification provisions of this Code section.

(e) Jail officers or juvenile correctional officers exempt from the certification provisions of this Code section are required to register with the council. The registration shall remain in effect for the period of time said person is employed as a jail officer or as a juvenile correctional officer.

(f) Any registration granted in this Code section shall not become invalid upon termination of employment or appointment as a jail officer or juvenile correctional officer if subsequent employment or appointment as a jail officer or juvenile correctional officer is commenced within 12 months of such prior termination as a jail officer or a juvenile correctional officer.

(g) Any jail officer or juvenile correctional officer exempted from mandatory compliance with this Code section may choose to be certified under this Code section. If so, the council shall have the authority to recognize instruction received by such jail officer or juvenile correctional officer as equivalent to all or part of the instruction required for certification under this Code section.

Laws 1995, p. 880, § 2; Laws 2008, Act 446, § 3, eff. May 6, 2008.

§ 35–8–25. Training and certification of bomb technicians, explosive ordnance disposal technicians, and animal handlers; intergovernmental assistance agreements; materials exempted from public disclosure

(a)(1) Any person who is employed by an agency or authority of this state or an agency or authority of a political subdivision of this state as a bomb technician, explosive ordnance disposal technician, handler of an animal trained to detect explosives, or any person who is assigned to such duties shall be required to complete successfully a training program prescribed by the council which shall consist of an initial training program, an apprenticeship, and annual recertification.

(2) The council is authorized to award a distinctive device to any person certified as an explosive ordnance disposal technician or as a handler of an animal trained to detect explosives upon completion of the initial training program and apprenticeship period. The council may also establish and award distinctive devices for certified explosive ordnance disposal technicians who qualify as senior or master explosive ordnance disposal technicians. Such devices may be worn on any law enforcement officer's or fire official's uniform.

(b)(1) The head of any agency which employs one or more certified bomb technicians, explosive ordnance disposal technicians, handlers of animals trained to detect explosives, or emergency medical technicians or emergency medical professionals who provide medical support of explosive ordnance disposal operations may establish a mutual aid agreement with any other agency for the purpose of assisting with the detection, rendering safe, and disposal of destructive devices as such term is defined by Code Section 16–7–80. Any such mutual aid agreement shall be subject to approval of the governing authority of such agency.

(2) A political subdivision which is aided pursuant to this subsection shall reimburse the political subdivision providing the aid for any loss or damage to equipment other than fair wear and tear and shall pay any expenses incurred in the operation and maintenance of such equipment; provided, however, that no such claim shall be allowed unless, within 60 days after the same is sustained or incurred, the political subdivision providing the aid provides to the chief financial officer of the political subdivision receiving the aid an itemized notice of the claim made under oath. The political subdivision which received the aid shall also pay and reimburse the political subdivision furnishing the aid for any overtime compensation paid to any employee furnished under this Code section during the time of the rendering of the aid and shall defray the actual traveling and maintenance expenses of any employee while such employee was engaged in rendering the aid. Such reimbursement shall include any amounts paid or due for compensation due to personal injury or death while such employee was engaged in rendering the aid.

(3) Unless otherwise expressly provided by its terms, a mutual aid agreement established pursuant to this subsection shall not be construed as superseding or amending any mutual aid agreement adopted pursuant to Chapter 6 of Title 25, Chapter 69 of Title 36, or Chapter 3 of Title 38 which applies to emergencies involving explosives or destructive devices.

(c)(1) Whenever a bomb technician, explosive ordnance disposal technician, handler of an animal trained to detect explosive devices, or an emergency medical technician or emergency medical professional who provides medical support of explosive ordnance disposal operations employed by an agency or authority of local government provides assistance at the request of a state agency or authority, such person shall be considered an employee of this state for the purposes of Code Section 50–21–22, paragraph (3) of Code Section 34–9–1, and Code Section 45–9–3. Such person shall also be entitled to reimbursement by the requesting agency or authority for actual expenses incurred in the same manner as other employees of the agency or authority.

(2) A state agency or authority receiving assistance from an agency or authority of a local government shall reimburse such political subdivision for any loss or damage, other than fair wear and tear, to any equipment owned by such political subdivision. No claim for the loss, damage, or expense shall be allowed unless, within 60 days after the same is sustained or incurred, the local government submits an itemized notice of the claim under oath to the fiscal officer of the state agency or authority.

(3) A state agency or authority which receives aid from a local government shall also pay and reimburse such political subdivision for any overtime compensation paid to an employee furnished under this Code section during the time of the rendering of the aid. Such reimbursement shall include any amounts paid or due for compensation due to personal injury or death while such employee was engaged in rendering the aid.

(d) An employee of a political subdivision or agency or authority thereof who is engaged in the rendering of outside aid pursuant to a mutual aid agreement adopted pursuant to this Code section shall have the same powers, duties, rights, privileges, and immunities as if such employee was engaged in the performing of his or her duties in the political subdivisions in which he or she is normally employed.

(e) Any other provision of law to the contrary notwithstanding, any records, books, or documents, as such terms are defined by subsection (e) of Code Section 45–11–1, which are prepared for use in any training program conducted pursuant to the provisions of this Code section and any rules or regulations relating to such training which contain or may disclose techniques and procedures for the manufacture or rendering safe of any destructive device, as such term is defined by Code Section 16–7–80, or would disclose guidelines for law enforcement investigations or prosecutions of violations of the laws of this state or of the United States relating to destructive devices, explosives, or chemical, biological, or nuclear materials shall not be subject to public disclosure pursuant to Article 5 of Chapter 11 of Title 9 or Chapter 16 of Title 17 or Article 4 of Chapter 18 of Title 50 unless the request for disclosure is served on the Attorney General as provided by Code Section 9–10–2 and a judge of the superior court finds that such disclosure is required to prevent a manifest injustice and that the information is not available from any other source. Any such order requiring disclosure shall impose such restrictions on access or copying of the material as will ensure that such material is not disclosed beyond that required to preserve the rights of the parties. Any order requiring disclosure of such material may be appealed by the district attorney of the circuit in which such order is entered or by the Attorney General.

Laws 1996, p. 416, § 10; Laws 1997, p. 160, § 1.

§ 35–8–26. TASER and electronic control weapons

Section effective January 1, 2007 except certain provisions, see Laws 2006, Act 692, § 2

(a) This Code section shall be known and may be cited as the "TASER and Electronic Control Weapons Act."

(b) It is the intent and purpose of the Georgia General Assembly to establish legal requirements for the official use of electronic control weapons and similar devices by law enforcement officers, including those officers employed in detention facilities, which requirements shall be consistent with generally accepted industry practices. It is the further intent of the General Assembly to require that such devices, commonly referred to as TASERS or stun-guns, which disrupt the central nervous system of the human body, be used for law enforcement purposes in a manner consistent with established standards and with federal and state constitutional provisions.

(c) A law enforcement unit authorizing the use of electronic control weapons or similar devices shall establish lawful written policies and directives providing for the use and deployment of such weapons and devices that are consistent with the training requirements established by the Georgia Peace Officer Standards and Training Council. The policies and directives required by this subsection shall be issued prior to the issuance of such devices.

(d) Prior to the official use of electronic control weapons or similar devices, peace officers authorized by the officer's law enforcement unit to use such devices shall be required to satisfactorily complete a course of instruction and certification requirements approved by the council. All persons certified to use electronic control weapons shall complete an update or refresher training course of such duration and at such time as may be prescribed by the council in order for their electronic control weapons certification to remain in force and effect.

(e) A department head authorizing the use of an electronic control weapon or similar device or a peace officer using an electronic control weapon or similar device in violation of this Code section shall be subject to disciplinary action as provided for in this chapter. The council is authorized to withdraw or suspend the certification to operate an electronic control weapon of any person for failure to meet the update or refresher requirements specified in this Code section or for violation of any portion of this chapter relating to conditions which may lead to the withdrawal, suspension, or probation of a peace officer's certification.

(f) The Georgia Public Safety Training Center shall provide council approved training to peace officers for the use of electronic control weapons and similar devices.

Laws 2006, Act 692, § 1, eff. Jan. 1, 2007.

Historical and Statutory Notes

Laws 2006, Act 692, § 2, provides:

"This Act shall become effective on January 1, 2007, excepting that provisions applying to council certification and provisions for training offered by the Georgia Public Safety Training Center shall become effective six months after the effective date of an appropriations Act containing a specific appropriation to fund certification by the council and training by the center."

Funds were not appropriated for this purpose.

TITLE 37

MENTAL HEALTH

CHAPTER 3

EXAMINATION, TREATMENT, ETC., FOR MENTAL ILLNESS

Article 1

General Provisions

§ 37–3–4. Liability for violations

Any physician, psychologist, peace officer, attorney, or health official, or any hospital official, agent, or other person employed by a private hospital or at a facility operated by the state, by a political subdivision of the state, or by a hospital authority created pursuant to Article 4 of Chapter 7 of Title 31, who acts in good faith in compliance with the admission and discharge provisions of this chapter shall be immune from civil or criminal liability for his actions in connection with the admission of a patient to a facility or the discharge of a patient from a facility.

Laws 1969, p. 505, § 1; Laws 1978, p. 1789, § 1; Laws 1981, p. 996, § 3.

Formerly Code 1933, § 88–502.18; Code 1933, § 88–502.23.

§ 37–3–5. Unauthorized leave from a facility

If, during the period of involuntary hospitalization pursuant to any valid physician's certificate, court order, or order by the hearing examiner authorized by this chapter, a patient escapes or otherwise leaves a facility without permission, the facility may advise any peace officer that the patient has escaped or otherwise left the facility without permission; and the peace officer shall be authorized to take the patient into custody and return him to such facility.

Laws 1979, p. 723, § 10.

Formerly Code 1933, § 88–507.9.

§ 37–3–7. Abandoning or leaving patients on grounds of psychiatric hospital

Any person who abandons or leaves any patient on the grounds of any state owned or state operated psychiatric hospital without the permission of the regional state hospital administrator of the hospital commits the offense of criminal trespass.

Laws 1918, p. 274, § 1; Laws 1964, p. 499, § 1; Laws 2002, p. 1324, § 1–18.

Formerly Code 1933, § 35–9901; Code 1933, § 88–2715.

Historical and Statutory Notes

The 2002 amendment substituted for "superintendent" the words "regional state hospital administrator".

§ 37–3–8. Loitering or trespassing, driving or riding, on ground of psychiatric hospital

Any person who loiters about or trespasses on the property of any state owned or state operated psychiatric hospital or drives or rides over the grounds or roads of such hospital property with horses, automobiles, bicycles, motorcycles, or other vehicles, except in accordance with such rules and regulations as may be posted under the authority of the board, commits the offense of criminal trespass.

Laws 1918, p. 274, § 1; Laws 1964, p. 499, § 1.

Formerly Code 1933, § 35–9902; Code 1933, § 88–2716.

Article 3

Examination, Hospitalization, and Treatment of Involuntary Patients

Part 1

Emergency Receiving Facilities for Examination of Persons Apprehended Pursuant to Physician's Certificate, Court Order, etc.

§ 37–3–41. Admission to an emergency receiving facility

(a) Any physician within this state may execute a certificate stating that he has personally examined a person within the preceding 48 hours and found that, based upon observations set forth in the certificate, the person appears to be a mentally ill person requiring involuntary treatment. A physician's certificate shall expire seven days after it is executed. Any peace officer, within 72 hours after receiving such certificate, shall make diligent efforts to take into custody the person named in the certificate and to deliver him forthwith to the nearest available emergency receiving facility serving the county in which the patient is found, where he shall be received for examination.

(b) The appropriate court of the county in which a person may be found may issue an order commanding any peace officer to take such person into custody and deliver him forthwith for examination, either to the nearest available emergency receiving facility serving the county in which the patient is found, where such person shall be received for examination, or to a physician who has agreed to examine such patient and who will provide, where appropriate, a certificate pursuant to subsection (a) of this Code section to permit delivery of such patient to an emergency receiving facility pursuant to subsection (a) of this Code section. Such order may only be issued if based either upon an unexpired physician's certificate, as provided in subsection (a) of this Code section, or upon the affidavits of at least two persons who attest that, within the preceding 48 hours, they have seen the person to be taken into custody and that, based upon observations contained in their affidavit, they have reason to believe such person is a mentally ill person requiring involuntary treatment. The court order shall expire seven days after it is executed.

(c) Any peace officer taking into custody and delivering for examination a person, as authorized by subsection (a) or (b) of this Code section, shall execute a written report detailing the circumstances under which such person was taken into custody. The report and either the physician's certificate or court order authorizing such taking into custody shall be made a part of the patient's clinical record.

(d) Any psychologist, clinical social worker, or clinical nurse specialist in psychiatric/mental health may perform any act specified by this Code section to be performed by a physician. Any reference in any part of this chapter to a physician acting under this Code section shall be deemed to refer equally to a psychologist, a clinical social worker, or a clinical nurse specialist in psychiatric/mental health acting under this Code section. For purposes of this subsection, the term "psychologist" means any person authorized under the laws of this state to practice as a licensed psychologist, the term "clinical social worker" means any person authorized under the laws of this state to practice as a licensed clinical social worker, and the term "clinical nurse specialist in psychiatric/mental health" means any person authorized under the laws of this state to practice as a registered professional nurse and who is recognized by the Georgia Board of Nursing to be engaged in advanced nursing practice as a clinical nurse specialist in psychiatric/mental health.

Laws 1969, p. 505, § 1; Laws 1971, p. 796, § 1; Laws 1978, p. 1789, § 1; Laws 1981, p. 996, § 4; Laws 1987, p. 3, § 37; Laws 1992, p. 2531, § 1.1; Laws 1994, p. 1249, § 1.

Formerly Code 1933, § 88–504.2.

§ 37–3–42. Examination by physician; psychologist performing acts of physician

(a) A peace officer may take any person to a physician within the county or an adjoining county for emergency examination by the physician, as provided in Code Section 37–3–41, or directly to an emergency receiving facility if (1) the person is committing a penal offense, and (2) the peace officer has probable cause for believing that the person is a mentally ill person requiring involuntary treatment. The peace officer need not formally tender charges against the individual prior to taking the individual to a physician or an emergency receiving facility under this Code section. The peace officer shall execute a written report detailing the circumstances under which the person was taken into custody; and this report shall be made a part of the patient's clinical record.

(b) Any psychologist may perform any act specified by this Code section to be performed by a physician. Any reference in any part of this chapter to a physician acting under this Code section shall be deemed to refer equally to a psychologist acting under this Code section. For purposes of this subsection, the term "psychologist" means any person authorized under the laws of this state to practice as a licensed psychologist.

Laws 1969, p. 505, § 1; Laws 1978, p. 1789, § 1; Laws 1981, p. 996, § 4; Laws 1987, p. 3, § 37.

Formerly Code 1933, § 88–504.3.

§ 37–3–43. Procedure in emergency receiving facility; notice of proposed discharge

(a) A patient who is admitted to an emergency receiving facility shall be examined by a physician as soon thereafter as possible but in any event within 48 hours and may be given such emergency treatment as is indicated by good medical practice. The patient must be discharged within 48 hours of his admission unless:

(1) An examining physician or psychologist concludes that there is reason to believe that the patient may be a mentally ill person requiring involuntary treatment and executes a certificate to that effect within such time; or

(2) The patient is under criminal charges, notice of which has been given in writing to the facility, in which case the provisions of Code Section 37–3–95 shall apply.

Nothing in this chapter shall be construed to prohibit a physician or psychologist who previously executed a certificate authorized by the provisions of this chapter from executing any other certificate provided for in this chapter for the same or any other patient.

(b) Within 24 hours of the execution of the certificate under paragraph (1) of subsection (a) of this Code section, the patient shall be transported, as provided in Code Section 37–3–101, to an evaluating facility where he shall be received pursuant to Code Section 37–3–63 unless the patient has been determined and certified to meet all of the outpatient treatment requirements of paragraphs (1) and (2) of subsection (c) of Code Section 37–3–90, in which event the patient shall be discharged under the conditions provided in Code Section 37–3–91, except that if the patient is under criminal charges, notice of which has been given in writing to the facility, the provisions of Code Section 37–3–95 shall apply.

(c) Notice of any proposed discharge shall be given to the patient and his representatives; if the patient was admitted to the facility under subsection (a) of Code Section 37–3–41, to the physician or psychologist who executed the certificate; if the patient was admitted to the facility under subsection (b) of Code Section 37–3–41, to the court which issued the order; and, if the patient was under criminal charges, written notice of which had been given to the facility, by certified mail or statutory overnight delivery to the law enforcement agency originally having custody of the patient.

Laws 1958, p. 697, § 9; Laws 1960, p. 837, § 9; Laws 1964, p. 499, § 1; Laws 1969, p. 505, § 1; Laws 1977, p. 1293, § 8; Laws 1978, p. 1789, § 1; Laws 1982, p. 3, § 37; Laws 1982, p. 937, §§ 5, 7; Laws 1985, p. 1024, § 1; Laws 1986, p. 1098, § 2; Laws 1991, p. 1059, § 11; Laws 1992, p. 1902, § 3; Laws 1996, p. 6, § 37; Laws 2000, p. 1589, § 3.

Formerly Code 1933, § 88–509; Code 1933, §§ 88–504.4, 88–504.5.

Historical and Statutory Notes

The 2000 amendment provided statutory overnight delivery as an alternative to certified mail in subsec. (c).

Part 4

Involuntary Outpatient Care

§ 37–3–95. Discharge of patients under criminal charges

Notwithstanding any other provisions of any part of this article, a patient under criminal charges, notice of which has been given in writing to the facility, may only be discharged from the physical custody of a facility if the facility, by certified mail or statutory overnight delivery, provides written notification of the proposed discharge to the law enforcement agency originally having custody of the patient and the patient is discharged into the physical custody of a peace officer from that agency. That agency shall be required to assume such physical custody within five days after receipt in writing of the notification of proposed discharge.

Laws 1986, p. 1098, § 5; Laws 2000, p. 1589, § 3.

Historical and Statutory Notes

The 2000 amendment provided statutory overnight delivery as an alternative to certified mail in the first sentence.

Article 4

Placement, Transfer, and Transportation of Patients Generally

§ 37–3–101. Transportation

(a) The governing authority of the county where the patient is found or located shall arrange for initial emergency transport of a patient to an emergency receiving facility. Except as otherwise authorized under subsection (b) of this Code section, the governing authority of the county of the patient's residence shall arrange for all required transportation for mental health purposes subsequent to the initial transport. The type of vehicle employed shall be in the discretion of the governing authority of the county, provided that, whenever possible, marked vehicles normally used for the transportation of criminals or those accused of crimes shall not be used for the transportation of patients. The court shall, upon the request of the community mental health center, order the sheriff to transport the patient in such manner as the patient's condition demands. At any time the community mental health center is satisfied that the patient can be transported safely by family members or friends, such private transportation shall be encouraged and authorized. In nonemergency situations, no female patient shall be transported at any time without another female in attendance who is not a patient, unless such female patient is accompanied by her husband, father, adult brother, or adult son.

(b) Notwithstanding the provisions of subsection (a) of this Code section, when a patient is under the care of a facility, the facility shall have the discretion to determine the type of vehicle to safely transport the patient and to arrange for such transportation without the need to obtain the prior approval of the governing authority of the county of the patient's residence, the court, or the community mental health center. This subsection shall not prevent the facility from requesting and receiving transportation services from the governing authority of the county of the patient's residence and shall not relieve the county sheriff of the duty of providing transportation. Persons providing transportation are authorized to transport a patient from a sending facility to a receiving facility but shall not release the patient under any circumstances except into the custody of the receiving facility. The use of physical restraints to ensure the safe transport of the patient shall comply with the requirements of Code Section 37–3–165. When transportation is not provided by the county sheriff, the expense of such transportation shall not be billed to the county governing authority but may be billed to the patient and, unless agreed to in writing by the facility, shall not be billed to or considered an obligation of the facility.

Laws 1958, p. 697, § 8; Laws 1960, p. 837, § 8; Laws 1964, p. 499, § 1; Laws 1969, p. 505, § 1; Laws 1978, p. 1789, § 1; Laws 1993, p. 1445, § 17.3; Laws 2002, p. 1067, § 1.

Formerly Code 1933, § 88–508; Code 1933, § 88–502.14; Code 1933, § 88–502.17.

Historical and Statutory Notes

The 2002 amendment rewrote this section which formerly provided:

"The governing authority of the county of the patient's residence shall arrange for all required transportation of the patient. The type of vehicle employed shall be in the discretion of the governing authority of the county, provided that, whenever possible, marked vehicles normally used for the transportation of criminals or those accused of crimes shall not be used for the transportation of patients. The court shall, upon the request of the community mental health center, order the sheriff to transport the patient in such manner as the patient's condition demands. At any time the community mental health center is satisfied that the patient can be transported safely by family members or friends, such private transportation shall be encouraged and authorized. No female patient shall be transported at any time without another female in attendance who is not a patient, unless such female patient is accompanied by her husband, father, adult brother, or adult son."

§ 37–3–102. Hospitalization by an agency of the United States; jurisdiction over patient

(a) If a patient ordered to be hospitalized pursuant to this chapter is eligible for hospital care or treatment by the United States Department of Veterans Affairs or any other federal agency, the department shall transfer the patient to the custody of the nearest such agency with available bed space for diagnosis, care, or treatment. When any such patient is admitted under this Code section to any such hospital or institution within or outside the state, he shall be subject to the rules and regulations of such agency. Upon notification from the superintendent or the chief medical officer of the United States Department of Veterans Affairs Medical Center for those patients therein who may require involuntary treatment pursuant to this chapter, the patient will be evaluated, while remaining in the physical custody of the United States Department of Veterans Affairs Medical Center, by the nearest emergency receiving facility. The superintendent and chief medical officer of any hospital or institution operated by such agency in which the individual is so hospitalized shall, with respect to such individual, be vested with the same powers and duties as the superintendent and chief medical officer of facilities within this state with respect to all matters under this chapter. Jurisdiction is retained in the appropriate courts of this state at any time to inquire into the mental condition of an individual so hospitalized to determine the necessity for continuance of his hospitalization and to order his release; and every transfer of a patient by the department pursuant to this Code section is so conditioned.

(b) An order of a court of competent jurisdiction of another state, territory, or possession or of the District of Columbia authorizing hospitalization of a patient by any agency of the United States shall have the same force and effect as to the patient while in this state as in the jurisdiction in which is situated the court entering the order; and the courts of the state, territory, possession, or district issuing such order shall be deemed to have retained jurisdiction of the patient so hospitalized for the purpose of inquiring into his mental condition and determining the necessity for continuance of his hospitalization, as is provided in subsection (a) of this Code section with respect to patients ordered hospitalized by the courts of this state. Consent is given for the application of the law of the state, territory, possession, or district in which is located the court issuing the order for hospitalization with respect to the authority of the chief medical officer of any hospital or institution operated in this state by the United States Department of Veterans Affairs or any other federal agency to retain custody, transfer, furlough, or discharge the patient therein hospitalized.

Laws 1958, p. 697, §§ 7, 10; Laws 1960, p. 837, §§ 7, 10; Laws 1964, p. 499, § 1; Laws 1969, p. 505, § 1; Laws 1978, p. 1789, § 1; Laws 1984, p. 756, § 1; Laws 1990, p. 45, § 1.

Formerly Code 1933, §§ 88–507, 88–510; Code 1933, § 88–508.5; Code 1933, § 88–507.4.

Article 6

Rights and Privileges of Patients, Their Representatives, Etc., Generally

Part 2

Rights and Privileges as to Manner of Care and Treatment and as to Maintenance and Release of Clinical Records

§ 37–3–160. Dignity of patients to be respected

The patient's dignity as an individual shall be respected at all times and upon all occasions, including any occasion wherein the patient is taken into custody, detained, or transported. Mentally ill patients or those suspected of being mentally ill shall, to the maximum extent reasonably possible, be treated at all times as medical patients. All patients shall be treated by a physician or psychologist acting within the scope of his or her license. Except where required under conditions of extreme urgency, those procedures, facilities, vehicles, and restraining devices normally utilized for criminals or those accused of crime shall not be used in connection with the mentally ill.

Laws 1969, p. 505, § 1; Laws 1978, p. 1789, § 1; Laws 1992, p. 1902, § 12.

Formerly Code 1933, § 88–502.1; Code 1933, § 88–502.2.

§ 37–3–166. Confidentiality

(a) A clinical record for each patient shall be maintained. Authorized release of the record shall include but not be limited to examination of the original record, copies of all or any portion of the record, or disclosure of information from the record, except for matters privileged under the laws of this state. Such examination shall be conducted on hospital premises at reasonable times determined by the facility. The clinical record shall not be a public record and no part of it shall be released except:

(1) When the chief medical officer of the facility where the record is kept deems it essential for continued treatment, a copy of the record or parts thereof may be released to physicians or psychologists when and as necessary for the treatment of the patient;

(2) A copy of the record may be released to any person or entity designated in writing by the patient or, if appropriate, the parent of a minor, the legal guardian of an adult or minor, or a person to whom legal custody of a minor patient has been given by order of a court;

(2.1) A copy of the record of a deceased patient or deceased former patient may be released to or in response to a valid subpoena of a coroner or medical examiner under Chapter 16 of Title 45, except for matters privileged under the laws of this state;

(3) When a patient is admitted to a facility, a copy of the record or information contained in the record from another facility, community mental health center, or private practitioner may be released to the admitting facility. When the service plan of a patient involves transfer of that patient to another facility, community mental health center, or private practitioner, a copy of the record or information contained in the record may be released to that facility, community mental health center, or private practitioner;

(4) A copy of the record or any part thereof may be disclosed to any employee or staff member of the facility when it is necessary for the proper treatment of the patient;

(5) A copy of the record shall be released to the patient's attorney if the attorney so requests and the patient, or the patient's legal guardian, consents to the release;

(6) In a bona fide medical emergency, as determined by a physician treating the patient, the chief medical officer may release a copy of the record to the treating physician or to the patient's psychologist;

(7) At the request of the patient, the patient's legal guardian, or the patient's attorney, the record shall be produced by the entity having custody thereof at any hearing held under this chapter;

(8) A copy of the record shall be produced in response to a valid subpoena or order of any court of competent jurisdiction, except for matters privileged under the laws of this state;

(8.1) A copy of the record may be released to the legal representative of a deceased patient's estate, except for matters privileged under the laws of this state;

(9) Notwithstanding any other provision of law to the contrary, a law enforcement officer in the course of a criminal investigation may be informed as to whether a person is or has been a patient in a state facility, as well as the patient's current address, if known; and

(10) Notwithstanding any other provision of law to the contrary, a law enforcement officer in the course of investigating the commission of a crime on the premises of a facility covered by this chapter or against facility personnel or a threat to commit such a crime may be informed as to the circumstances of the incident, including whether the individual allegedly committing or threatening to commit a crime is or has been a patient in the facility, and the name, address, and last known whereabouts of any alleged patient perpetrator.

(b) In connection with any hearing held under this chapter, any physician, including any psychiatrist, or any psychologist who is treating or who has treated the patient shall be authorized to give evidence as to any matter concerning the patient, including evidence as to communications otherwise privileged under Code Section 24–9–21, 24–9–40, or 43–39–16.

(c) Any disclosure authorized by this Code section or any unauthorized disclosure of confidential or privileged patient information or communications shall not in any way abridge or destroy the confidential or privileged character thereof, except for the purpose for which such authorized disclosure is made. Any person making a disclosure authorized by this Code section shall not be liable to the patient or any other person, notwithstanding any contrary provision of Code Section 24–9–21, 24–9–40, or 43–39–16.

(d) When a sheriff transports an adult involuntary patient to a facility, that sheriff may request in writing that a notice of such patient's discharge be given to the sheriff; and such notice shall be provided if such patient or the patient's guardian consents in writing to the disclosure or if, in its discretion, the court ordering the involuntary treatment provides for such notice in the order issued pursuant to Code Section 37–3–81.1.

Laws 1958, p. 697, § 19; Laws 1960, p. 837, § 18; Laws 1964, p. 499, § 1; Laws 1969, p. 505, § 1; Laws 1978, p. 1789, § 1; Laws 1979, p. 723, §§ 4, 5; Laws 1981, p. 985, § 1; Laws 1987, p. 3, § 37; Laws 1991, p. 1059, §§ 21, 22; Laws 1994, p. 1072, § 2.

Formerly Code 1933, § 88–518; Code 1933, § 88–502.10; Code 1933, § 88–502.12.

TITLE 40

MOTOR VEHICLES AND TRAFFIC

CHAPTER 1

GENERAL PROVISIONS

§ 40–1–1. Definitions

As used in this title, the term:

(1) "Alcohol concentration" means grams of alcohol per 100 milliliters of blood or grams of alcohol per 210 liters of breath.

(2) "Alley" means a street or highway intended to provide access to the rear or side of lots or buildings in urban districts and not intended for the purpose of through vehicular traffic.

(3) "All-terrain vehicle" means any motorized vehicle designed for off-road use which is equipped with three or more low pressure tires and with a seat to be straddled by the operator and with handlebars for steering control.

(4) "Arterial street" means any U.S. or state numbered route, controlled-access highway, or other major radial or circumferential street or highway designated by local authorities within their respective jurisdictions as part of a major arterial system of streets or highways.

(5) "Authorized emergency vehicle" means a motor vehicle belonging to a public utility corporation or operated by the Department of Transportation and designated as an emergency vehicle by the Department of Public Safety; a motor vehicle belonging to a fire department or a certified private vehicle belonging to a volunteer firefighter or a fire-fighting association, partnership, or corporation; an ambulance; or a motor vehicle belonging to a federal, state, or local law enforcement agency, provided such vehicle is in use as an emergency vehicle by one authorized to use it for that purpose.

(6) "Bicycle" means every device propelled by human power upon which any person may ride, having only two wheels which are in tandem and either of which is more than 13 inches in diameter.

(6.1) "Bicycle path" means a right of way under the jurisdiction and control of this state or a local political subdivision thereof designated for use by bicycle riders.

(6.2) "Bicycle trailer" means every device pulled by a bicycle and designed by the manufacturer of such device to carry human passengers.

(7) "Bus" means every motor vehicle designed for carrying more than ten passengers and used for the transportation of persons and every motor vehicle, other than a taxicab, designed and used for the transportation of persons for compensation.

(8) "Business district" means the territory contiguous to and including a highway when within any 600 feet along such highway there are buildings in use for business or industrial purposes, including but not limited to hotels, banks, office buildings, railroad stations, and public buildings which occupy at least 300 feet of frontage on one side or 300 feet collectively on both sides of the highway.

(8.1) "Class I all-terrain vehicle" means a motorized, off-highway recreational vehicle 50 inches or less in width with a dry weight of 1,000 pounds or less that travels on three or more low-pressure tires, has a saddle or seat for the operator, and is designed for or capable of cross-country travel on or immediately over land, water, sand, snow, ice, marsh, swampland, or other natural terrain.

(8.2) "Class II all-terrain vehicle" means any motor vehicle that:

(A) Weighs more than a class I all-terrain vehicle and less than 8,000 pounds;

(B) Is designed for or capable of cross-country travel on or immediately over land, water, sand, snow, ice, marsh, swampland, or other natural terrain; and

(C) Is actually being operated off a highway.

(8.3) "Commercial motor vehicle" means any self–propelled or towed motor vehicle used on a highway in intrastate and interstate commerce to transport passengers or property when the vehicle:

(A) Has a gross vehicle weight rating, gross combination weight rating, gross vehicle weight, or gross combination weight of 4,537 kg (10,001 lbs.) or more;

(B) Is designed or used to transport more than eight passengers, including the driver, for compensation;

(C) Is designed or used to transport more than 15 passengers, including the driver, and is not used to transport passengers for compensation; or

(D) Is used to transport material determined to be hazardous by the secretary of the United States Department of Transportation under 49 U.S.C. Section 5103 and transported in a quantity that requires placards under regulations prescribed under 49 C.F.R., Subtitle B, Chapter I, Subchapter C.

(9) "Controlled-access highway" means every highway, street, or roadway in respect to which owners or occupants of abutting lands and other persons have no legal right of access to or from the same except only at such points and in such manner as may be determined by the public authority having jurisdiction over such highway, street, or roadway.

(10) "Crosswalk" means:

(A) That part of a roadway at an intersection included within the connections of the lateral lines of the sidewalks on opposite sides of the highway measured from the curbs or in the absence of curbs, from the edges of the traversable roadway; or

(B) Any portion of a roadway at an intersection or elsewhere distinctly indicated for pedestrian crossing by lines or other markings on the surface.

(11) "Dealer" means a person engaged in the business of buying, selling, or exchanging vehicles who has an established place of business in this state.

(12) "Demonstrator" means any motor vehicle which has not been the subject of a sale at retail to the general public but which has been operated on the roads of this state in the course of a motor vehicle dealer's business.

(13) "Divided highway" means a highway divided into two or more roadways by leaving an intervening space or by a physical barrier or by a clearly indicated dividing section so constructed as to impede vehicular traffic.

(14) "Driver" means every person who drives or is in actual physical control of a vehicle.

(15) "Driver's license" means any license to operate a motor vehicle issued under the laws of this state.

(15.5) "Electric assisted bicycle" means a device with two or three wheels which has a saddle and fully operative pedals for human propulsion and also has an electric motor. For such a device to be considered an electric assisted bicycle, it shall meet the requirements of the Federal Motor Vehicle Safety Standards, as set forth in 49 C.F.R. Section 571, et seq., and shall operate in such a manner that the electric motor disengages or ceases to function when the brakes are applied. The electric motor in an electric assisted bicycle shall:

(A) Have a power output of not more than 1,000 watts;

(B) Be incapable of propelling the device at a speed of more than 20 miles per hour on level ground; and

(C) Be incapable of further increasing the speed of the device when human power alone is used to propel the device at or more than 20 miles per hour.

(15.6) "Electric personal assistive mobility device" or "EPAMD" means a self-balancing, two nontandem wheeled device designed to transport only one person and having an electric propulsion system with average power of 750 watts (1 horsepower) and a maximum speed of less than 20 miles per hour on a paved level surface when powered solely by such propulsion system and ridden by an operator who weighs 170 pounds.

(16) "Explosives" means any chemical compound or mechanical mixture that is commonly used or intended for the purpose of producing an explosion and which contains any oxidizing and combustive units or other ingredients in such proportions, quantities, or packing that an ignition by fire, by friction, by concussion, by percussion, or by detonator of any part of the compound or mixture may cause such a sudden generation of highly heated gases that the resultant gaseous pressures are capable of producing destructive effects on contiguous objects or of destroying life or limb.

(17) "Flammable liquid" means any liquid which has a flash point of 141 degrees Fahrenheit or less.

(18) "Gross weight" means the weight of a vehicle without load plus the weight of any load thereon.

(19) "Highway" means the entire width between the boundary lines of every way publicly maintained when any part thereof is open to the use of the public for purposes of vehicular travel.

(20) "House trailer" means:

(A) A trailer or semitrailer which is designed, constructed, and equipped as a dwelling place or living abode (either permanently or temporarily) and is equipped for use as a conveyance on streets and highways; or

(B) A trailer or a semitrailer whose chassis and exterior shell is designed and constructed for use as a house trailer, as defined in subparagraph (A) of this paragraph, but which is used instead permanently or temporarily for the advertising, sales, display, or promotion of merchandise or services, or for any other commercial purpose except the transportation of property for hire or the transportation of property for distribution by a private carrier.

(21) "Implement of husbandry" means a vehicle designed and adapted exclusively for agricultural, horticultural, or livestock-raising operations or for lifting or carrying an implement of husbandry and in either case not subject to registration if used upon the highways.

(21.1) "Infant sling" means every device which is designed by the manufacturer to be worn by a person for the purpose of carrying an infant either on the chest or back of the wearer.

(22)(A) "Intersection" means the area embraced within the prolongation or connection of the lateral curb lines, or, if none, then the lateral boundary lines of the roadways of two highways which join one another at, or approximately at, right angles, or the area within which vehicles traveling upon different highways joining at any other angle may come in conflict.

(B) Where a highway includes two roadways 30 feet or more apart, then every crossing of each roadway of such divided highway by an intersecting highway shall be regarded as a separate intersection. In the event such intersecting highway also includes two roadways 30 feet or more apart, then every crossing of two roadways of such highways shall be regarded as a separate intersection.

(C) The junction of an alley with a street or highway shall not constitute an intersection.

(23) "Laned roadway" means a roadway which is divided into two or more clearly marked lanes for vehicular traffic.

(24) "License" or "license to operate a motor vehicle" means any driver's license or any other license or permit to operate a motor vehicle issued under, or granted by, the laws of this state, including:

(A) Any temporary license or instruction permit;

(B) The privilege of any person to drive a motor vehicle whether or not such person holds a valid license; and

(C) Any nonresident's operating privilege as defined in this Code section.

(24.1) "Limousine" has the same meaning as provided in paragraph (4) of Code Section 46–7–85.1.

(25) "Local authorities" means every county, municipal, and other local board or body having authority to enact laws relating to traffic under the Constitution and laws of this state.

(25.1) "Low-speed vehicle" means any four-wheeled electric vehicle whose top speed attainable in one mile is greater than 20 miles per hour but not greater than 25 miles per hour on a paved level surface and which is manufactured in compliance with those federal motor vehicle safety standards for low-speed vehicles set forth in 49 C.F.R. Section 571.500 and in effect on January 1, 2001.

(26) "Manufacturer" means a person engaged in the manufacture of vehicles and who has an established place of business in this state.

(27) "Metal tire" means every tire of which the surface in contact with the highway is wholly or partly of metal or other hard, nonresilient material. A vehicle shall be considered equipped with metal tires when metal tires are used on two or more wheels.

(28) "Moped" means a motor driven cycle equipped with two or three wheels, with or without foot pedals to permit muscular propulsion, and an independent power source providing a maximum of two brake horsepower. If a combustion engine is used, the maximum piston or rotor displacement shall be 3.05 cubic inches (50 cubic centimeters) regardless of the number of chambers in such power source. The power source shall be capable of propelling the vehicle, unassisted, at a speed not to exceed 30 miles per hour (48.28 kilometers per hour) on level road surface and shall be equipped with a power drive system that functions directly or automatically only, not requiring clutching or shifting by the operator after the drive system is engaged.

(29) "Motorcycle" means every motor vehicle having a seat or saddle for the use of the rider and designed to travel on not more than three wheels in contact with the ground, but excluding a tractor, all-terrain vehicle, and moped.

(30) "Motor driven cycle" means every motorcycle, including every motor scooter, with a motor which produces not to exceed five brake horsepower, every bicycle with a motor attached, and every moped.

(31) "Motor home" means every motor vehicle designed, used, or maintained primarily as a mobile dwelling, office, or commercial space.

(32) "Motorized cart" means every motor vehicle having no less than three wheels and an unladen weight of 1,300 pounds or less and which cannot operate at more than 20 miles per hour.

(33) "Motor vehicle" means every vehicle which is self-propelled other than an electric personal assistive mobility device (EPAMD).

(34) "New motor vehicle" means any motor vehicle which is not a demonstrator and has never been the subject of a sale at retail to the general public.

(35) "Nonresident" means every person who is not a resident of this state.

(36) "Nonresident's operating privilege" means the privilege conferred upon a nonresident by the laws of this state pertaining to the operation by such person of a motor vehicle or the use of a vehicle owned by such person in this state.

(37) "Official traffic-control devices" means all signs, signals, markings, and devices not inconsistent with this title which are placed or erected by authority of a public body or official having jurisdiction for the purpose of regulating, warning, or guiding traffic.

(38) "Operator" means any person who drives or is in actual physical control of a motor vehicle.

(39) "Owner" means a person, other than a lienholder or security interest holder, having the property in or title to a vehicle. The term includes a person entitled to the use and possession of a vehicle subject to a security interest in or lien by another person but excludes a lessee under a lease not intended as security except as otherwise specifically provided in this title.

(40) "Park" or "parking" means the standing of a vehicle, whether occupied or not, otherwise than temporarily for the purpose of and while actually engaged in loading or unloading property or passengers.

(41) "Passenger car" means every motor vehicle, except motorcycles, motor driven cycles, and low-speed vehicles, designed for carrying ten passengers or less and used for the transportation of persons.

(42) "Pedestrian" means any person afoot.

(42.1) "Pedestrian hybrid beacon" means a special type of hybrid beacon used to warn and control traffic at locations without a traffic-control signal to assist pedestrians in crossing a street or highway at a marked crosswalk.

(43) "Person" means every natural person, firm, partnership, association, corporation, or trust.

(44) "Pneumatic tire" means every tire in which compressed air is designed to support the load. A vehicle shall be considered equipped with pneumatic tires when pneumatic tires are used on all wheels.

(45) "Pole trailer" means every vehicle without motive power designed to be drawn by another vehicle and attached to the towing vehicle by means of a reach or pole, or by being boomed or otherwise secured to the towing vehicle, and ordinarily used for transporting long or irregularly shaped loads such as poles, pipes, or structural members capable, generally, of sustaining themselves as beams between the supporting connections.

(46) "Police officer" means every officer authorized to direct or regulate traffic or to make arrests for violations of traffic regulations.

(47) "Private road or driveway" means every way or place in private ownership and used for vehicular traffic by the owner and those having express or implied permission from the owner, but not by other persons.

(48) "Railroad" means a carrier of persons or property upon cars operated upon stationary rails.

(49) "Railroad sign or signal" means any sign, signal, or device erected by authority of a public body or official or by a railroad and intended to give notice of the presence of railroad tracks or the approach of a railroad train.

(50) "Railroad train" means a steam engine or electric engine or other motor, with or without cars coupled thereto, operated upon rails.

(51) "Residence district" means the territory contiguous to and including a highway not comprising a business district, when the property on such highway for a distance of 300 feet or more is in the main improved with residences or residences and buildings in use for business.

(52) "Right of way" means the right of one vehicle or pedestrian to proceed in a lawful manner in preference to another vehicle or pedestrian approaching under such circumstances of direction, speed, and proximity as to give rise to danger of collision unless one grants precedence to the other.

(53) "Roadway" means that portion of a highway improved, designed, or ordinarily used for vehicular travel, exclusive of the berm or shoulder. In the event a highway includes two or more separate roadways, the term "roadway" shall refer to any such roadway separately, but not to all such roadways collectively.

(54) "Safety zone" means the area or space officially set apart within a roadway for the exclusive use of pedestrians and which is protected or is so marked or indicated by adequate signs as to be plainly visible at all times while set apart as a safety zone.

(55) "School bus" means:

(A) A motor vehicle operated for the transportation of school children to and from school or school activities or for the transportation of children to and from church or church activities. Such term shall not include a motor vehicle with a capacity of 15 persons or less operated for the transportation of school children to and from school activities or for the transportation of children to and from church or church activities if such motor vehicle is not being used for the transportation of school children to and from school; or

(B) A motor vehicle operated by a local transit system which meets the equipment and identification requirements of Code Section 40–8–115; provided, however, that such vehicle shall be a school bus only while transporting school children and no other passengers to or from school.

(56) "Semitrailer" means every vehicle with or without motive power, other than a pole trailer, designed for carrying persons or property and for being drawn by a motor vehicle and so constructed that some part of its weight and that of its load rests upon or is carried by another vehicle.

(57) "Sidewalk" means that portion of a street between the curb lines, or the lateral lines of a railway, and the adjacent property lines, intended for use by pedestrians.

(58) "Solid tires" means tires of rubber or similarly elastic material that do not depend on confined air for the support of the load. A vehicle shall be considered equipped with solid tires when solid tires are used on two or more wheels.

(59) "Special mobile equipment" means every vehicle not designed or used primarily for the transportation of persons or property and only incidentally operated or moved over a highway, including but not limited to: ditch-digging apparatus, well-boring apparatus, and road construction and maintenance machinery such as asphalt spreaders, bituminous mixers, bucket loaders, tractors other than truck tractors, ditchers, leveling graders, finishing machines, motor graders, road rollers, scarifiers, earth-moving carryalls and scrapers, power shovels and drag lines, and self-propelled cranes and earth-moving equipment. The term does not include house trailers, dump trucks, truck mounted transit mixers, cranes or shovels, or other

vehicles designed for the transportation of persons or property to which machinery has been attached.

(60) "Stand" or "standing" means the halting of a vehicle, whether occupied or not, otherwise than temporarily for the purpose of and while actually engaged in receiving or discharging passengers.

(61) "State" means a state, territory, or possession of the United States, the District of Columbia, the Commonwealth of Puerto Rico, or a province of Canada.

(62) "Stop" or "stopping":

(A) When required, means complete cessation from movement; or

(B) When prohibited, means any halting, even momentarily, of a vehicle, whether occupied or not, except when necessary to avoid conflict with other traffic or in compliance with the directions of a police officer or traffic-control sign or signal.

(63) "Street" means the entire width between boundary lines of every way publicly maintained when any part thereof is open to the use of the public for purposes of vehicular travel.

(63.1) "Taxicab" means a motor vehicle for hire which conveys passengers between locations of their choice and is a mode of public transportation for a single passenger or small group for a fee. Such term shall also mean taxi or cab, but not a bus or school bus, limousine, passenger car, or commercial motor vehicle.

(64) "Through highway" means every highway or portion thereof on which vehicular traffic is given preferential right of way and at the entrances to which vehicular traffic from intersecting highways is required by law to yield the right of way to vehicles on such through highway in obedience to a stop sign, yield sign, or other official traffic-control device, when such signs or devices are erected as provided in this title.

(65) "Tractor" means any self-propelled vehicle designed for use as a traveling power plant or for drawing other vehicles but having no provision for carrying loads independently.

(66) "Traffic" means pedestrians, ridden or herded animals, vehicles, and other conveyances either singly or together while using any highway for purposes of travel.

(67) "Traffic-control signal" means any device, whether manually, electrically, or mechanically operated, by which traffic is alternately directed to stop and permitted to proceed.

(68) "Trailer" means every vehicle with or without motive power, other than a pole trailer, designed for carrying persons or property and for being drawn by a motor vehicle and so constructed that no part of its weight rests upon the towing vehicle.

(69) "Tripper service" means regularly scheduled mass transportation service which is open to the fare-paying public but which is also designed or modified to accommodate the needs of elementary or secondary school students and school personnel.

(70) "Truck" means every motor vehicle designed, used, or maintained primarily for the transportation of property.

(71) "Truck camper" means any structure designed, used, or maintained primarily to be loaded on or affixed to a motor vehicle to provide a mobile dwelling, sleeping place, office, or commercial space.

(72) "Truck tractor" means every motor vehicle designed and used primarily for drawing other vehicles and not so constructed as to carry a load other than a part of the weight of the vehicle and load so drawn.

(73) "Urban district" means the territory contiguous to and including any street which is built up with structures devoted to business, industry, or dwelling houses situated at intervals of less than 100 feet for a distance of a quarter of a mile or more.

(74) "Used motor vehicle" means any motor vehicle which has been the subject of a sale at retail to the general public.

(75) "Vehicle" means every device in, upon, or by which any person or property is or may be transported or drawn upon a highway, excepting devices used exclusively upon stationary rails or tracks.

Laws 1927, p. 226, § 2; Laws 1953, Nov.-Dec. Sess., p. 556, §§ 1–9, 11, 13–21; Laws 1966, p. 183, § 1; Laws 1970, p. 586, § 1; Laws 1973, p. 595, § 1; Laws 1973, p. 598, § 1; Laws 1974, p. 633, § 1; Laws 1978, p. 1483, § 1; Laws 1978, p. 2241, §§ 1, 3, 4; Laws 1982, p. 3, § 40; Laws 1983, p. 633, § 1; Laws 1988, p. 691, §§ 1, 2; Laws 1988, p. 1893, § 1; Laws 1989, p. 1792, § 1; Laws 1990, p. 2048, § 1; Laws 1993, p. 518, § 1; Laws 1994, p. 97, § 40; Laws 1996, p. 236, § 1; Laws 1997, p. 419, § 1; Laws 1999, p. 334, § 1; Laws 2001, p. 4, § 40; Laws 2002, p. 506, § 2; Laws 2002, p. 512, §§ 2, 3; Laws 2002, p. 660, § 4; Laws 2002, p. 1259, § 11; Laws 2002, p. 1378, § 1; Laws 2003, Act 56, §§ 1 to 3, eff. May 29, 2003; Laws 2004, Act 442, § 1, eff. April 22, 2004; Laws 2004, Act 580, § 1, eff. May 13, 2004; Laws 2006, Act 579, § 1, eff. July 1, 2006; Laws 2007, Act 346, § 1, eff. Jan. 1, 2008; Laws 2010, Act 381, § 1, eff. May 20, 2010; Laws 2010, Act 460, § 4, eff. July 1, 2010.

Formerly Code 1933, § 68–101; Code 1933, § 68A–101.

Historical and Statutory Notes

Laws 2007, Act 346, § 14, provides:

"Sections 2, 3, 4, 5, and 13 through 15 of this Act shall become effective July 1, 2007. Sections 1, 6, 7, and 12 of this Act shall become effective January 1, 2008. Sections 8, 9, 10, and 11 of this Act shall become effective July 1, 2008."

§ 40–1–2. How horsepower determined

The Society of Automotive Engineers horsepower rating formula is adopted as the standard for determining the horsepower of passenger-carrying vehicles.

Laws 1927, p. 226, § 2; Laws 1990, p. 2048, § 1.

Formerly Code 1933, § 68–102.

§ 40–1–3. Offenses by persons owning or controlling vehicles

It is unlawful for the owner or any other person employing or otherwise directing the driver of any vehicle to require or knowingly permit the operation of such vehicle upon a highway in any manner contrary to law.

Laws 1953, Nov.-Dec. Sess., p. 556, § 122; Laws 1990, p. 2048, § 1.

§ 40–1–4. Attachment of stickers, decals, etc., containing profane or lewd words, etc., prohibited

No person owning, operating, or using a motor vehicle in this state shall knowingly affix or attach to any part of such motor vehicle any sticker, decal, emblem, or other device containing profane or lewd words describing sexual acts, excretory functions, or parts of the human body. Any person who violates any part of this Code section shall be guilty of a misdemeanor and shall be punished by a fine not to exceed $100.00.

Laws 1988, p. 1561, § 1; Laws 1990, p. 2048, § 1.

Validity

This section has been held unconstitutional in the case of Cunningham v. State, 1991, 260 Ga. 827, 400 S.E.2d 916.

§ 40–1–5. Disclosure of damage to new motor vehicles

(a) As used in this Code section, the terms "dealer," "distributor," "manufacturer," and "new motor vehicle" shall have the same meaning as set forth in Code Section 40–2–39.

(b) Except as provided in this subsection and in subsection (c) of this Code section, prior to the sale of a new motor vehicle, a dealer must disclose to the buyer any damage which has occurred to the vehicle of which the dealer has actual knowledge and which costs more than 5 percent of the manufacturer's suggested retail price to repair. Prior to the sale of a new motor vehicle, a dealer must also disclose to the buyer any damage which has occurred to the paint of which the dealer has actual knowledge and which costs more than $500.00 to repair. Damages shall be calculated at the actual cost of such repair.

(c) Notwithstanding anything to the contrary in subsection (b) of this Code section, in calculating the amount of damage for purposes of disclosure under subsection (b) of this Code section, a dealer shall not be required to take into account nor shall a dealer be required to disclose damage to glass, tires, wheels, bumpers, radio, or in-dash audio equipment, regardless of cost, so long as the item is replaced with original or reasonably comparable equipment.

(d) Prior to the delivery of a new motor vehicle, each manufacturer, distributor, carrier, or motor vehicle importer must disclose to the dealer any damage which has occurred to the vehicle of which the manufacturer, distributor, carrier, or importer has actual knowledge and which is required to be disclosed to a buyer under subsections (b) and (c) of this Code section. If a manufacturer, distributor, carrier, or motor vehicle importer fails to make any disclosure required by this subsection, then such shall be liable to the dealer for any liability imposed on such dealer for a failure on the part of the dealer to comply with the requirements of this Code section.

(e) Prior to the delivery of a new motor vehicle, each manufacturer, carrier, or motor vehicle importer must disclose to the distributor any damage which has occurred to the vehicle of which the manufacturer, carrier, or importer has actual knowledge and which is required to be disclosed to a buyer under subsections (b) and (c) of this Code section. If a manufacturer, carrier, or motor vehicle importer fails to make any disclosure required by this subsection, then such shall be liable to the distributor for any liability imposed on such distributor for a failure on the part of the distributor to comply with the requirements of this Code section.

(f) If disclosure is not required under this Code section, a buyer may not revoke or rescind a sales contract, and relief may not be sought under this or any other provision of this Code, including Part 2 of Article 15 of Chapter 1 of Title 10 due to the fact that the new motor vehicle was damaged and repaired prior to the sale.

(g) A violation of this Code section shall be a per se violation of Code Section 10–1–393, and the penalties, procedures, and remedies applicable to violations of Code Section 10–1–393 shall be applicable to a violation of this Code section.

Laws 1990, p. 1657, § 1; Laws 1994, p. 97, § 40.

§ 40–1–6. Uniforms of law enforcement officers assigned to traffic law enforcement or special operations activities

Uniformed law enforcement officers of an agency who are assigned routinely or primarily to traffic law enforcement or other traffic safety duties on the roadways or highways of this state shall wear the same type uniform as other members of the assigned division of such officers' respective agencies. Officers assigned to special operations activities may wear other identifiable uniforms or other clothing appropriate to an operation upon approval of the sheriff, chief of police, or other agency head. An otherwise lawful arrest shall not be invalidated or in any manner affected by failure to comply with this Code section.

Laws 2000, p. 1313, § 1.

§ 40–1–7. Placement of blue light on roof of law enforcement vehicle required when pursuing person for traffic offense; exceptions

Whenever pursuing a person in violation of a traffic related offense, a uniformed law enforcement officer who is assigned routinely or primarily to traffic law enforcement or other traffic safety duties on the roadways or highways of this state must place a visible blue light on the roof of his or her vehicle if such vehicle is not equipped with permanent exterior mounted roof blue lights; provided, however, that the provisions of this Code section shall not apply to law enforcement officers operating vehicles manufactured prior to 2001. This Code section shall not apply to any officer assigned to special operations activities or responding to an immediate threat to public safety as a result of an accident or other emergency. This Code section shall not apply to vehicles of the Georgia State Patrol or of a sheriff's office or police department which office or police department provides law enforcement services by certified peace officers 24 hours a day, seven days a week where the vehicles are marked in accordance with Code Section 40–8–91, with flashing or revolving colored lights visible under normal atmospheric conditions for a distance of 500 feet from the front and rear of such vehicle, and which also has an illuminating agency identifier reasonably visible to a driver of a vehicle subject to a traffic stop; provided, however, that the Georgia State Patrol shall not be permitted to have more than two vehicles per post without such exterior mounted roof lights; and provided, further, that a sheriff's office or police department shall not be permitted to have more than one vehicle per agency without such exterior mounted roof lights. An otherwise lawful arrest shall not be invalidated or in any manner affected by failure to comply with this Code section.

Laws 2000, p. 1313, § 1; Laws 2006, Act 522, § 1, eff. April 20, 2006; Laws 2007, Act 18, § 40, eff. May 11, 2007.

CHAPTER 2

REGISTRATION AND LICENSING OF MOTOR VEHICLES

Article 1

Article 2

Article 2A

Article 3

Article 1

General Provisions

§ 40–2–1. Definitions

As used in this chapter, the term:

(1) "Cancellation of vehicle registration" means the annulment or termination by formal action of the department of a person's vehicle registration because of an error or defect in the registration or because the person is no longer entitled to such registration. The cancellation of registration is without prejudice and application for a new registration may be made at any time after such cancellation.

(2) "Commissioner" means the state revenue commissioner.

(3) "Department" means the Department of Revenue.

(4) "Motor carrier" means:

(A) Any entity subject to the terms of the Unified Carrier Registration Agreement pursuant to 49 U.S.C. Section 14504a whether engaged in interstate or intrastate commerce, or both; or

(B) Any entity defined by the commissioner, commissioner of public safety, or Public Service Commission who operates or controls commercial motor vehicles as defined in 49 C.F.R. Section 390.5, Title 46, or this chapter whether operated in interstate or intrastate commerce, or both.

(5) "Operating authority" means the registration required by 49 U.S.C. Section 13902, 49 C.F.R. Part 365, 49 C.F.R. Part 368, and 49 C.F.R. Section 392.9a.

(6) "Regulatory compliance inspection" means the examination of facilities, property, buildings, vehicles, drivers, employees, cargo, packages, records, books, or supporting documentation kept or required to be kept in the normal course of motor carrier business or enterprise operations.

(7) "Resident" means a person who has a permanent home or domicile in Georgia and to which, having been absent, he or she has the intention of returning. For the purposes of this chapter, there is a rebuttable presumption that any person who, except for infrequent, brief absences, has been present in the state for 30 or more days is a resident.

(8) "Revocation of vehicle registration" means the termination by formal action of the department of a vehicle registration, which registration shall not be subject to renewal or reinstatement, except that an application for a new registration may be presented and acted upon by the department after the expiration of the applicable period of time prescribed by law.

(9) "Suspension of vehicle registration" means the temporary withdrawal by formal action of the department of a vehicle registration, which temporary withdrawal shall be for a period specifically designated by the department.

Laws 1990, p. 2048, § 2; Laws 1991, p. 327, § 1; Laws 2000, p. 951, § 3–1; Laws 2002, p. 1024, § 1; Laws 2005, Act 68, § 14–1, eff. July 1, 2005; Laws 2009, Act 114, § 1, eff. May 4, 2009.

§ 40–2–2. Violations

Except as otherwise provided in this chapter, any person who violates any provision of this chapter shall be guilty of a misdemeanor.

Laws 1925, p. 315, § 2; Laws 1927, p. 226, § 26; Laws 1931, p. 7, § 84; Laws 1953, Jan.-Feb. Sess., p. 366, § 5; Laws 1990, p. 2048, § 2.

Formerly Code 1933, §§ 68–9902, 68–9908.

§ 40–2–3. False statement in connection with registering and licensing motor vehicles

Any person who shall make any false statement in any application for the registration of any vehicle, or in transferring any certificate of registration, or in applying for a new certificate of registration, shall be guilty of false swearing, whether or not an oath is actually administered to him, if such statement shall purport to be under oath. On conviction of such offense, such person shall be punished as provided by Code Section 16–10–71.

Laws 1925, p. 315, § 2; Laws 1931, p. 7, § 84; Laws 1953, Jan.-Feb. Sess., p. 366, § 5; Laws 1990, p. 2048, § 2.

Formerly Code 1933, § 68–9902.

§ 40–2–4. Manufacture of license plates and revalidation decals prohibited

(a) It shall be unlawful for any person, firm, or corporation to make, sell, or issue any license plate or revalidation decal.

(b) Any person, firm, or corporation violating subsection (a) of this Code section shall be guilty of a misdemeanor.

Laws 1921, p. 255, § 11; Laws 1990, p. 2048, § 2.

Formerly Code 1933, §§ 68–216, 68–9905.

§ 40–2–5. Acquiring license plate for purpose of concealing identity of vehicle; penalties

(a) Except as otherwise provided in this chapter, it shall be unlawful:

(1) To remove or transfer a license plate from the motor vehicle for which such license plate was issued;

(2) To sell or otherwise transfer or dispose of a license plate upon or for use on any motor vehicle other than the vehicle for which such license plate was issued;

(3) To buy, receive, use, or possess for use on a motor vehicle any license plate not issued for use on such motor vehicle; or

(4) To operate a motor vehicle bearing a license plate which was improperly removed or transferred from another vehicle.

(b) Any person who shall knowingly violate any provision of subsection (a) of this Code section shall be guilty of a misdemeanor of a high and aggravated nature and, upon conviction thereof, shall be punished by a fine of not less than $500.00 or by confinement for not more than 12 months, or both.

(c) It shall not be unlawful for any person to place an expired prestige license plate on the front of a motor vehicle provided that such vehicle also bears a current valid license plate on the rear of such vehicle.

Laws 1918, p. 264, §§ 1, 2; Laws 1966, p. 10, § 1; Laws 1990, p. 1657, § 2; Laws 1990, p. 2048, § 2.

Formerly Code 1933, § 68–9916.

§ 40–2–6. Mutilation or alteration of license plates; operation of vehicle with improper license plates

Except as otherwise provided in this chapter, any person who shall willfully mutilate, obliterate, deface, alter, change, or conceal any numeral, letter, character, county designation, or other marking of any license plate issued under the motor vehicle registration laws of this state; who shall knowingly operate a vehicle bearing a license plate on which any numeral, letter, character, county designation, or other marking has been willfully mutilated, obliterated, defaced, altered, changed, or concealed; or who shall knowingly operate a vehicle bearing a license plate issued for another vehicle and not properly transferred as provided by law shall be guilty of a misdemeanor.

Laws 1957, p. 626, § 1; Laws 1985, p. 149, § 40; Laws 1990, p. 2048, § 2; Laws 1991, p. 1145, § 1; Laws 1997, p. 419, § 2.

Formerly Code 1933, § 68–9929.

§ 40–2–6.1. Covering plate; penalty

Any person who willfully covers any license plate with plastic, other material, or any part of his or her body in order to prevent or impede the ability of surveillance equipment to clearly photograph or otherwise obtain a clear image of the license plate is guilty of a misdemeanor and shall be punished by a fine not to exceed $1,000.00.

Laws 2005, Act 138, § 1, eff. July 1, 2005.

§ 40–2–7. Removing or affixing license plate for purpose of concealing identity of vehicle

A person who removes a license plate from a vehicle or affixes to a vehicle a license plate not authorized by law for use on it, in either case with intent to conceal or misrepresent the identity of the vehicle or its owner, is guilty of a misdemeanor. As used in this Code section, "remove" includes deface or destroy.

Laws 1961, p. 68, § 34; Laws 1990, p. 8, § 40; Laws 1990, p. 2048, § 2.

§ 40–2–8. Operating motor vehicle without registration or valid license plate

Section effective until January 1, 2011. See also, section effective January 1, 2011.

(a) Any person owning or operating any vehicle described in Code Section 40–2–20 on any public highway or street without complying with that Code section shall be guilty of a misdemeanor, provided that a person shall register his or her motor vehicle within 30 days after becoming a resident of this state. Any person renting, leasing, or loaning any vehicle described in Code Section 40–2–20 which is being used on any public highway or street without complying with that Code section shall be guilty of a misdemeanor and, upon conviction thereof, shall be punished by a fine of $ 100.00 for each violation; and each day that such vehicle is operated in violation of Code Section 40–2–20 shall be deemed to be a separate and distinct offense.

(b)(1) Any vehicle operated in the State of Georgia which is required to be registered and which does not have attached to the rear thereof a numbered license plate and current revalidation decal affixed to a corner or corners of the license plate as designated by the commissioner, if required, shall be stored at the owner's risk and expense by any law enforcement officer of the State of Georgia, unless such operation is otherwise permitted by this chapter.

Subpar. (A) effective until January 1, 2011

(2)(A) It shall be a misdemeanor to operate any vehicle required to be registered in the State of Georgia without a valid numbered license plate properly validated, unless such operation is otherwise permitted under this chapter; and provided, further, that the purchaser of a new vehicle or a used vehicle may operate such vehicle on the public highways and streets of this state without a current valid license plate during the period within which the purchaser is required by Code Section 40–2–20 to register such vehicle; but the purchaser of any vehicle from a dealer of new or used motor vehicles shall display a temporary plate issued as provided by subparagraph (B) of this paragraph on the rear of such vehicle in the space provided for a license plate when such vehicle is operated on the public highways and streets of this state during such period prior to registration, unless such purchaser has made application to transfer to such vehicle in accordance with this chapter a valid license plate issued to him or her, in which event the license plate to be transferred shall be displayed on the vehicle during the period prior to registration, or unless such vehicle is to be registered under the International Registration Plan.

Subpar. (A) effective January 1, 2011

(2)(A) It shall be a misdemeanor to operate any vehicle required to be registered in the State of Georgia without a valid numbered license plate properly validated, unless such operation is otherwise permitted under this chapter; and provided, further, that the purchaser of a new vehicle or a used vehicle may operate such vehicle on the public highways and streets of this state without a current valid license plate during the period within which the purchaser is required by Code Section 40–2–20 to register such vehicle as provided for in Code Section 40–2–29; but the purchaser of any vehicle from a dealer of new or used motor vehicles shall display a temporary plate issued as provided by subparagraph (B) of this paragraph on the rear of such vehicle in the space provided for a license plate when such vehicle is operated on the public highways and streets of this state during such period prior to registration, unless such purchaser has made application to transfer to such vehicle in accordance with this chapter a valid license plate issued to him or her, in which event the license plate to be transferred shall be displayed on the vehicle during the period prior to registration, or unless such vehicle is to be registered under the International Registration Plan.

(B)(i) Any dealer of new or used motor vehicles shall issue to the purchaser of a vehicle at the time of sale thereof, unless at such time the purchaser makes application to transfer to such vehicle in accordance with this chapter a valid license plate issued to him or her or unless such vehicle is to be registered under the International Registration Plan, a temporary plate which may bear the dealer's name and location and shall bear, in characters not less than one-quarter of an inch wide and one and one-half inches high, the expiration date of the period within which the purchaser is required by Code Section 40–2–20 to register such vehicle. Such temporary plates shall be made of heavy stock paper, inscribed with indelible ink, and designed to resist deterioration or fading due to exposure to the elements during the period for which display is required. The expiration date, the vehicle identification number, and the year, make, and model of the vehicle shall be handprinted on the plate at the time of issuance by use of an indelible ink marker, with contrasting ink, provided that the month of expiration shall be indicated by complete word or by three-letter abbreviation thereof. The expiration date of such a temporary plate may be revised and extended by the county tag agent only if an extension of the purchaser's initial registration period has been granted as provided by Code Section 40–2–20. Such temporary plate shall not resemble a license plate issued by this state and shall be issued without charge or fee therefor. Such temporary plate shall be surrendered to the tag agent at the time the vehicle is registered, and the tag agent shall destroy such temporary plate. The requirements of this subparagraph do not apply to a dealer whose primary business is the sale of salvage motor vehicles and other vehicles on which total loss claims have been paid by insurers.

(ii) All temporary plates issued by dealers to purchasers of vehicles shall be of a standard design prescribed by regulation promulgated by the department in accordance with the requirements of this subparagraph. All temporary plates shall be required to have a holographic security image and a write-resistant overlay with security features such that any attempt to change or modify the expiration date on the temporary plate will show immediate signs of tampering. All holographic security images required under this division and manufactured on or after July 1, 2005, shall be numbered with a separate and distinct number at the point of manufacture. All holographic security images affixed to temporary plates on or after January 1, 2006, shall be numbered as required by this division.

(3) All sellers and distributors of holographic strips must register with the department and shall be assigned a distinct identifier by the department. Such identifier shall precede the numbers required under division (b)(2)(B)(ii) of this Code section. All sellers and distributors of holographic security images must maintain an inventory record of holographic security images by number and purchaser.

(4) The purchaser and operator of a vehicle shall not be subject to the penalties set forth in this Code section during the period allowed for the registration. If the owner of such vehicle presents evidence that such owner has properly applied for the registration of such vehicle, but that the license plate or revalidation decal has not been delivered to such owner, then the owner shall not be subject to the above penalties.

(c) It shall be unlawful and punishable as for a misdemeanor to operate any vehicle required to be registered in the State of Georgia without a valid county decal designating the county where the vehicle was last registered, unless such operation is otherwise permitted under this chapter. Any person convicted of such offense shall be punished by a fine of $ 25.00 for a first offense and $ 100.00 for a second or subsequent such offense. However, a county name decal shall not be required if there is no space provided for a county name decal on the current license plate.

Laws 1927, p. 226, § 8; Laws 1931, p. 7, § 84; Laws 1931, p. 213, § 2; Laws 1943, p. 341, § 4; Laws 1953, Nov.-Dec. Sess., p. 343, Part 1, § 1; Laws 1969, p. 266, § 3; Laws 1977, p. 1039, § 1; Laws 1980, p. 746, § 1; Laws 1981, p. 714, § 4; Laws 1982, p. 1584, §§ 2, 5; Laws 1986, p. 1053, § 1; Laws 1990, p. 2048, § 2; Laws 1992, p. 2785, § 1.3; Laws 1993, p. 1260, § 1; Laws 1995, p. 809, § 1; Laws 1996, p. 1118, § 1; Laws 1997, p. 419, § 3; Laws 1998, p. 1179, § 3; Laws 2000, p. 523, § 1; Laws 2001, p. 1173, § 1–1; Laws 2002, p. 415, § 40; Laws 2004, Act 564, § 40, eff. May 13, 2004; Laws 2005, Act 65, § 1, eff. July 1, 2005; Laws 2005, Act 68, § 14–2, eff. July 1, 2005; Laws 2010, Act 381, § 2, eff. Jan. 1, 2011.

Formerly Code 1933, §§ 68–214, 68–9901.

Historical and Statutory Notes

The 2004 amendment by Act 564, in subpar. (b)(2)(A), twice substituted "registration," for "registration:".

The 2005 amendment by Act 65, in subsec. (b), par. (2)(B), substituted "expiration date, the vehicle identification number, and the year, make, and model of the vehicle shall be handprinted" for "expiration date may be handprinted" in div. (i), and, in div. (ii), deleted "on or after January 1, 2001," following "purchasers of vehicles", deleted "Temporary plates issued by dealers to purchasers prior to such date may be of any design if such plates meet the requirements of this subparagraph." following "requirements of this subparagraph.", and added "All temporary plates shall be required to have a holographic security image and a write-resistant overlay with security features such that any attempt to change or modify the expiration date on the temporary plate will show immediate signs of tampering. All holographic security images required under this division and manufactured on or after July 1, 2005, shall be numbered with a separate and distinct number at the point of manufacture. All holographic security images affixed to temporary plates on or after January 1, 2006, shall be numbered as required by this division."; redesignated former par. (b)(3) as par. (b)(4); and added new par. (b)(3).

The 2005 amendment by Act 68 in subsec. (b)(2)(B)(ii) substituted "department" for "Department of Motor Vehicle Safety" following "promulgated by the" in the first sentence.

The 2010 amendment by Act 381, in subpar. (b)(2)(A), inserted "as provided for in Code Section 40–2–29" following "Code Section 40–2–20 to register such vehicle".

§ 40–2–8.1. Operating motor vehicle without having required revalidation decal affixed to license plate

Notwithstanding Code Section 40–2–8 or any other provision of law, a person who operates a vehicle which is required to be registered in this state and which has attached to the rear thereof a valid numbered license plate without having the required revalidation decal affixed upon that plate, which person is otherwise guilty of a misdemeanor for not having such decal affixed to the plate, shall be subject for that offense only to a fine not to exceed $25.00 if that person shows to the court having jurisdiction of the offense that the proper revalidation decal had been obtained prior to the time of the offense.

Laws 1993, p. 698, § 1.

§ 40–2–9. Provisions relative to county name decals applicable to special, distinctive, or prestige license plates

Effective until January 1, 2011. See also section effective January 1, 2011.

Any special, distinctive, or prestige license plate, except those provided for in Code Sections 40–2–61, 40–2–62, 40–2–74, 40–2–82, and 40–2–85.1 or as otherwise expressly provided in this chapter, shall contain a space for a county name decal. The provisions of this chapter relative to county name decals shall be applicable to all such license plates.

Laws 1985, p. 261, § 8; Laws 1986, p. 1333, § 5; Laws 1989, p. 1186, § 4; Laws 1990, p. 2048, § 2; Laws 2001, p. 479, § 3; Laws 2008, Act 727, § 1, eff. May 14, 2008; Laws 2010, Act 360, § 1–64, eff. May 12, 2010.

Formerly Code 1981, § 40–2–77; Code 1981, § 40–2–81.

§ 40–2–9. Provisions relative to county name decals applicable to special, distinctive, or prestige license plates

Section effective January 1, 2011. See also section effective until January 1, 2011.

(a) Any metal special, distinctive, or prestige license plate, except those provided for in Code Sections 40–2–61, 40–2–62, 40–2–74, 40–2–82, and 40–2–85.1 or as otherwise expressly provided in this chapter, shall contain a space for a county name decal. The provisions of this chapter relative to county name decals shall be applicable to all such license plates.

(b) The department shall make available to all license plates recipients a decal with the same dimensions as the county name decal that contains the words, In God We Trust. The department shall charge any person requesting such decal no more than the cost to the department for the manufacture and distribution of such decal. Such decal may be displayed in the space reserved for the county name decal in lieu of the county name decal.

Laws 1985, p. 261, § 8; Laws 1986, p. 1333, § 5; Laws 1989, p. 1186, § 4; Laws 1990, p. 2048, § 2; Laws 2001, p. 479, § 3; Laws 2008, Act 727, § 1, eff. May 14, 2008; Laws 2010, Act 360, § 1–64, eff. May 12, 2010; Laws 2010, Act 381, § 2.1, eff. Jan. 1, 2011.

Formerly Code 1981, § 40–2–77; Code 1981, § 40–2–81.

§ 40–2–10. Voluntary cancellation of vehicle registration

A vehicle registrant may voluntarily cancel the registration on a vehicle when such vehicle is not in use for any reason, including without limitation if the vehicle is stolen, repossessed but not redeemed by the registrant, junked, inoperable, in storage, used seasonally for agricultural or other purposes, or if the owner is on active duty in the armed forces of the United States and is transferred to a duty station away from the location of the vehicle or is on active sea duty. A registration that has been voluntarily cancelled may be reinstated upon payment of all accrued ad valorem taxes and license fees, if any.

Laws 2003, Act 44, § 1, eff. May 28, 2003.

§ 40–2–11. Commissioner duties and authority; employees

(a) The commissioner shall be responsible for the administration of this chapter and may employ such clerical assistants and agents as may be necessary from time to time to enable the commissioner to speedily and efficiently perform the duties conferred on the commissioner in this chapter. The commissioner shall be authorized to delegate any administrative responsibility for retention of applications, certificates of registration, and any other forms or documents relating to the application and registration process to the appropriate authorized tag agent for the county in which the application is made or the registration is issued.

(b) The commissioner shall prescribe and provide suitable forms of applications and all other notices and forms necessary to administer this chapter.

(c) The commissioner may:

(1) Perform any investigation necessary to procure information required to carry out this chapter; and

(2) Adopt and enforce reasonable rules and regulations to administer this chapter.

Laws 2008, Act 727, § 2, eff. May 14, 2008.

Article 2

Registration and Licensing Generally

§ 40–2–20. Registration and license of motor vehicles; exceptions

Text of section effective until January 1, 2011. See also, section effective January 1, 2011.

(a)(1)(A) Except as provided in subsection (b) of this Code section and subsection (a) of Code Section 40–2–47, every owner of a motor vehicle, including a tractor or motorcycle, and every owner of a trailer shall, during the owner's registration period in each year, register such vehicle as provided in this chapter and obtain a license to operate it for the 12 month period until such person's next registration period.

(B)(i) The purchaser or other transferee owner of every new or used motor vehicle, including tractors and motorcycles, or trailer shall, within the initial registration period of such vehicle, register such vehicle as provided in this chapter and obtain or transfer as provided in this chapter a license to operate it for the period remaining until such person's next registration period which immediately follows such initial registration period, without regard to whether such next registration period occurs in the same calendar year as the initial registration period or how soon such next registration period follows the initial registration period; provided, however, that this registration and licensing requirement does not apply to a dealer which acquires a new or used motor vehicle and holds it for resale. The commissioner may provide by rule or regulation for one 30 day extension of such initial registration period which may be granted by the county tag agent to a purchaser or other transferee owner if the transferor has not provided such purchaser or other transferee owner with a title to the motor vehicle more than five business days prior to the expiration of such initial registration period.

(ii) No person, company, or corporation, including, but not limited to, used motor vehicle dealers and auto auctions, shall sell or transfer a motor vehicle without providing to the purchaser or transferee of such motor vehicle the last certificate of registration on such vehicle at the time of such sale or transfer; provided, however, that in the case of a salvage motor vehicle or a motor vehicle which is stolen but subsequently recovered by the insurance company after payment of a total loss claim, the salvage dealer or insurer, respectively, shall not be required to provide the certificate of registration for such vehicle; and provided, further, that in the case of a repossessed motor vehicle or a court ordered sale or other involuntary transfer, the lienholder or the transferor shall not be required to provide the certificate of registration for such vehicle but shall, prior to the sale of such vehicle, surrender the license plate of such vehicle to the commissioner or the county tag agent by personal delivery or by certified mail or statutory overnight delivery for cancellation.

(2) An application for the registration of a motor vehicle may not be submitted separately from the application for a certificate of title for such motor vehicle, unless a certificate of title has been issued in the owner's name, has been applied for in the owner's name, or the motor vehicle is not required to be titled. An application for a certificate of title for a motor vehicle may be submitted separately from the application for the registration of such motor vehicle.

(b) Subsection (a) of this Code section shall not apply:

(1) To any motor vehicle or trailer owned by the state or any municipality or other political subdivision of this state and used exclusively for governmental functions except to the extent provided by Code Section 40–2–37;

(2) To any tractor or three-wheeled motorcycle used only for agricultural purposes;

(2.1) To any vehicle or equipment used for transporting cargo or containers between and within wharves, storage areas, or terminals within the facilities of any port under the jurisdiction of the Georgia Ports Authority when such vehicle or equipment is being operated upon any public road not part of The Dwight D. Eisenhower System of Interstate and Defense Highways by the owner thereof or his or her agent within a radius of ten miles of the port facility of origin and accompanied by an escort vehicle equipped with one or more operating amber flashing lights that are visible from a distance of 500 feet;

(3) To any trailer which has no springs and which is being employed in hauling unprocessed farm products to their first market destination;

(4) To any trailer which has no springs, which is pulled from a tongue, and which is used primarily to transport fertilizer to a farm;

(5) To any motorized cart; or

(6) To any moped.

(c) Any person who fails to register a new or used motor vehicle as required in subsection (a) of this Code section shall be guilty of a misdemeanor and, upon conviction thereof, shall be punished by a fine not exceeding $ 100.00.

Laws 1927, p. 226, § 3; Laws 1931, p. 7, § 84; Laws 1931, p. 213, § 1; Laws 1943, p. 341, § 2; Laws 1953, Jan.-Feb. Sess., p. 392, § 2; Laws 1957, p. 590, § 1; Laws 1960, p. 777, § 1; Laws 1966, p. 252, § 1; Laws 1969, p. 266, § 1; Laws 1973, p. 595, § 2; Laws 1973, p. 781, § 1; Laws 1974, p. 414, § 1; Laws 1974, p. 451, § 1; Laws 1978, p. 2241, § 2; Laws 1984, p. 603, § 1; Laws 1984, p. 1329, § 1; Laws 1985, p. 149, § 40; Laws 1986, p. 1053, § 2; Laws 1987, p. 949, § 1; Laws 1990, p. 1657, § 3; Laws 1990, p. 2048, § 2; Laws 1993, p. 1260, § 2; Laws 1994, p. 352, § 1; Laws 1995, p. 809, § 2; Laws 1996, p. 1118, § 2; Laws 1997, p. 419, § 4; Laws 1998, p. 1179, § 4; Laws 1999, p. 81, § 40; Laws 1999, p. 784, § 1; Laws 2000, p. 136, § 40; Laws 2000, p. 1589, § 3; Laws 2001, p. 1173, § 1–2; Laws 2002, p. 506, § 3; Laws 2002, p. 512, § 4; Laws 2009, Act 101, § 1, eff. Jan. 1, 2010.

Formerly Code 1933, § 68–201.

§ 40–2–20. Registration and license of motor vehicles; exceptions

Text of section effective January 1, 2011. See also, section effective until January 1, 2011.

(a)(1)(A) Except as provided in subsection (b) of this Code section and subsection (a) of Code Section 40–2–47, every owner of a motor vehicle, including a tractor or motorcycle, and every owner of a trailer shall, during the owner's registration period in each year, register such vehicle as provided in this chapter and obtain a license to operate it for the 12 month period until such person's next registration period.

(B)(i) The purchaser or other transferee owner of every new or used motor vehicle, including tractors and motorcycles, or trailer shall register such vehicle as provided in Code Section 40–2–8 and obtain or transfer as provided in this chapter a license to operate it for the period remaining until such person's next registration period which immediately follows such initial registration period, without regard to whether such next registration period occurs in the same calendar year as the initial registration period or how soon such next registration period follows the initial registration period; provided, however, that this registration and licensing requirement does not apply to a dealer which acquires a new or used motor vehicle and holds it for resale. The commissioner may provide by rule or regulation for one 30 day extension of such initial registration period which may be granted by the county tag agent to a purchaser or other transferee owner if the transferor has not provided such purchaser or other transferee owner with a title to the motor vehicle more than five business days prior to the expiration of such initial registration period.

(ii) No person, company, or corporation, including, but not limited to, used motor vehicle dealers and auto auctions, shall sell or transfer a motor vehicle without providing to the purchaser or transferee of such motor vehicle the last certificate of registration on such vehicle at the time of such sale or transfer; provided, however, that in the case of a salvage motor vehicle or a motor vehicle which is stolen but subsequently recovered by the insurance company after payment of a total loss claim, the salvage dealer or insurer, respectively, shall not be required to provide the certificate of registration for such vehicle; and provided, further, that in the case of a repossessed motor vehicle or a court ordered sale or other involuntary transfer, the lienholder or the transferor shall not be required to provide the certificate of registration for such vehicle but shall, prior to the sale of such vehicle, surrender the license plate of such vehicle to the commissioner or the county tag agent by personal delivery or by certified mail or statutory overnight delivery for cancellation.

(2) An application for the registration of a motor vehicle may not be submitted separately from the application for a certificate of title for such motor vehicle, unless a certificate of title has been issued in the owner's name, has been applied for in the owner's name, or the motor vehicle is not required to be titled. An application for a certificate of title for a motor vehicle may be submitted separately from the application for the registration of such motor vehicle.

(b) Subsection (a) of this Code section shall not apply:

(1) To any motor vehicle or trailer owned by the state or any municipality or other political subdivision of this state and used exclusively for governmental functions except to the extent provided by Code Section 40–2–37;

(2) To any tractor or three-wheeled motorcycle used only for agricultural purposes;

(2.1) To any vehicle or equipment used for transporting cargo or containers between and within wharves, storage areas, or terminals within the facilities of any port under the jurisdiction of the Georgia Ports Authority when such vehicle or equipment is being operated upon any public road not part of The Dwight D. Eisenhower System of Interstate and Defense Highways by the owner thereof or his or her agent within a radius of ten miles of the port facility of origin and accompanied by an escort vehicle equipped with one or more operating amber flashing lights that are visible from a distance of 500 feet;

(3) To any trailer which has no springs and which is being employed in hauling unprocessed farm products to their first market destination;

(4) To any trailer which has no springs, which is pulled from a tongue, and which is used primarily to transport fertilizer to a farm;

(5) To any motorized cart; or

(6) To any moped.

(c) Any person who fails to register a new or used motor vehicle as required in subsection (a) of this Code section shall be guilty of a misdemeanor and, upon conviction thereof, shall be punished by a fine not exceeding $ 100.00.

Laws 1927, p. 226, § 3; Laws 1931, p. 7, § 84; Laws 1931, p. 213, § 1; Laws 1943, p. 341, § 2; Laws 1953, Jan.-Feb. Sess., p. 392, § 2; Laws 1957, p. 590, § 1; Laws 1960, p. 777, § 1; Laws 1966, p. 252, § 1; Laws 1969, p. 266, § 1; Laws 1973, p. 595, § 2; Laws 1973, p. 781, § 1; Laws 1974, p. 414, § 1; Laws 1974, p. 451, § 1; Laws 1978, p. 2241, § 2; Laws 1984, p. 603, § 1; Laws 1984, p. 1329, § 1; Laws 1985, p. 149, § 40; Laws 1986, p. 1053, § 2; Laws 1987, p. 949, § 1; Laws 1990, p. 1657, § 3; Laws 1990, p. 2048, § 2; Laws 1993, p. 1260, § 2; Laws 1994, p. 352, § 1; Laws 1995, p. 809, § 2; Laws 1996, p. 1118, § 2; Laws 1997, p. 419, § 4; Laws 1998, p. 1179, § 4; Laws 1999, p. 81, § 40; Laws 1999, p. 784, § 1; Laws 2000, p. 136, § 40; Laws 2000, p. 1589, § 3; Laws 2001, p. 1173, § 1–2; Laws 2002, p. 506, § 3; Laws 2002, p. 512, § 4; Laws 2009, Act 101, § 1, eff. Jan. 1, 2010; Laws 2010, Act 381, § 3, eff. Jan. 1, 2011.

Formerly Code 1933, § 68–201.

Historical and Statutory Notes

Laws 2009, Act 101, § 4 provided:

"Section 3A of this Act shall become effective upon its approval by the Governor or upon its becoming law without such approval. The remaining sections of this Act shall become effective on January 1, 2010, and shall apply to registration and licensing of trailers on and after such date."

§ 40–2–20.1. Repealed by Laws 1990, p. 2048, § 2, eff. July 1, 1990

§ 40–2–21. Designated registration periods

(a) As used in this chapter, the term:

(.1) "Initial registration period" means the 30 day period immediately following the date of purchase or other acquisition of a new or used motor vehicle, including tractors and motorcycles, or trailer.

(.2) "Owner" has the meaning provided by paragraph (39) of Code Section 40–1–1 except that such term shall mean a lessee of a vehicle when the vehicle is operated under a lease agreement.

(1) "Registration period" means:

(A) In all counties except those for which a local Act has been enacted pursuant to this Code section:

(i) For natural persons, the 30 day period ending at midnight on the birthday of the owner whose surname appears first on the certificate of title or other record of ownership; or

(ii) For entities other than natural persons:

(I) The month of January for the owner whose name begins with the letter A or B;

(II) The month of February for the owner whose name begins with the letter C or D;

(III) The month of March for the owner whose name begins with the letter E or F;

(IV) The month of April for the owner whose name begins with the letter G or H;

(V) The month of May for the owner whose name begins with the letter I or J;

(VI) The month of June for the owner whose name begins with the letter K or L;

(VII) The month of July for the owner whose name begins with the letter M or N;

(VIII) The month of August for the owner whose name begins with the letter O or P;

(IX) The month of September for the owner whose name begins with the letter Q or R;

(X) The month of October for the owner whose name begins with the letter S or T;

(XI) The month of November for the owner whose name begins with the letter U, V, or W; and

(XII) The month of December for the owner whose name begins with the letter X, Y, or Z; or

(iii) The provisions of divisions (i) and (ii) of this subparagraph notwithstanding, December 1 through February 15 for vehicles in excess of 26,000 pounds which are not being registered under the International Registration Plan and are owned by natural persons or entities other than natural persons; or

(B) In those counties which are authorized by a local Act enacted pursuant to this Code section to have a four-month staggered registration period:

(i) For natural persons:

(I) The month of January for the owner whose surname appears first on the certificate of title or other record of ownership and whose birthday is in the month of January, February, or March;

(II) The month of February for the owner whose surname appears first on the certificate of title or other record of ownership and whose birthday is in the month of April, May, or June;

(III) The month of March for the owner whose surname appears first on the certificate of title or other record of ownership and whose birthday is in the month of July, August, or September; and

(IV) The month of April for the owner whose surname appears first on the certificate of title or other record of ownership and whose birthday is in the month of October, November, or December; or

(ii) For entities other than natural persons:

(I) The month of January for the owner whose name begins with the letter A, B, C, or D;

(II) The month of February for the owner whose name begins with the letter E, F, G, H, I, J, or K;

(III) The month of March for the owner whose name begins with the letter L, M, N, O, P, Q, or R; and

(IV) The month of April for the owner whose name begins with the letter S, T, U, V, W, X, Y, or Z; or

(iii) The provisions of divisions (i) and (ii) of this subparagraph notwithstanding, December 1 through February 15 for vehicles in excess of 26,000 pounds which are not being registered under the International Registration Plan and are owned by natural persons or entities other than natural persons; or

(C)(i) In those counties which are authorized by a local Act enacted pursuant to this Code section not to have staggered registration periods, January 1 through April 30.

(ii) The provisions of division (i) of this subparagraph notwithstanding, December 1 through February 15 for vehicles in excess of 26,000 pounds which are not being registered under the International Registration Plan and are owned by natural persons or entities other than natural persons.

For purposes of determining the registration period of an owner which is an entity other than a natural person in subparagraphs (A) and (B) of this paragraph, the owner shall be deemed to be the owner whose name appears first on the certificate of title or other record of ownership. Any other provision of this paragraph notwithstanding, registration of vehicles under the International Registration Plan shall be as provided by Code Section 40–2–88, and registration of vehicles under the fleet registration plan shall be as provided by Article 2A of this chapter.

(2) "Vehicle" means every motor vehicle, including a tractor or motorcycle, and every trailer required to be registered and licensed under Code Section 40–2–20.

(b) The owner of every vehicle registered in the previous calendar year shall register and obtain a license to operate such vehicle not later than the last day of the owner's registration period.

(c) The owner of any vehicle registered in the previous calendar year who moves his or her residence from a county which does not have staggered registration to a county which has a four-month or 12 month staggered registration period or who moves his or her residence from a county which has a 12 month staggered registration period to a county which has a four-month staggered registration period or to a county which does not have staggered registration shall register and obtain a license to operate such vehicle prior to the last day of such new registration period or, if such registration period has passed for that year at the time of the change of residence, not later than 30 days following the date of the change of residence.

(d) The transferee owner of a new or used vehicle shall register and obtain or transfer a license to operate such vehicle as provided in subsection (a) of Code Section 40–2–20.

(e) Any local law enacted pursuant to this Code section shall specify either a staggered registration period of four months or a nonstaggered registration period of four months. If such local law is conditioned upon approval in a referendum, the results of such referendum shall be verified to the commissioner.

(f) On and after January 1, 2000, no local Act shall be enacted pursuant to this Code section authorizing a staggered system of motor vehicle registration. This subsection shall not apply to any county in which such a local Act has been enacted prior to January 1, 2000.

Laws 1986, p. 1053, § 3; Laws 1987, p. 1, §§ 1, 2; Laws 1988, p. 380, § 1; Laws 1990, p. 2048, § 2; Laws 1995, p. 809, § 3; Laws 1996, p. 1118, § 3; Laws 1997, p. 419, § 5; Laws 1998, p. 1179, § 4A; Laws 1999, p. 667, § 1; Laws 1999, p. 741, § 1; Laws 2000, p. 951, § 3–2.

Formerly Code 1981, § 40–2–20.1.

Historical and Statutory Notes

In 2001, the Code Commission, in div. (a)(1)(A)(iii), substituted "the" for "hte". See § 28–9–5.

§ 40–2–22. Issuance of tags to be only upon application to local tag agent

License plates and revalidation decals shall be issued only upon applications made to the local tag agent or the commissioner in accordance with the terms of this chapter.

Laws 1955, p. 659, § 6; Laws 1957, p. 197, § 4; Laws 1966, p. 508, § 6; Laws 1990, p. 2048, § 2; Laws 2010, Act 360, § 1–65, eff. May 12, 2010.

Formerly Code 1981, § 40–2–21.

§ 40–2–23. Tax collectors or commissioners as agents to receive applications for registration of motor vehicles and to collect sales and use tax on casual sale or use

(a) The tax collectors of the various counties of this state and the tax commissioners of those counties in which the duties of the tax collector are performed by a tax commissioner shall be designated as tag agents of the commissioner for the purpose of accepting applications for the registration of vehicles. The commissioner is authorized to promulgate rules and regulations for the purpose of delegating to such tag agents the custodial responsibility for properly receiving, processing, issuing, and storing motor vehicle titles or registrations, or both.

(b) The state revenue commissioner is authorized to further designate each such tag agent as a sales tax agent for the purpose of collecting sales and use tax with respect to the casual sale or casual use of a motor vehicle. For purposes of this Code section, "casual sale" or "casual use" means the sale of a motor vehicle by a person who is not regularly or systematically engaged in making retail sales of motor vehicles and the first use, consumption, distribution, or storage for use or consumption of such motor vehicle purchased through a casual sale. As personal compensation for services rendered to the Department of Revenue with respect to the collection of such sales and use tax, each such designated tag agent shall be authorized to retain from such collection a fee of $200.00 per month. In any month in which an insufficient amount of such tax is collected to pay such fee, the amount of any such unpaid fee may be deferred until such month as sufficient collections are made. Such compensation shall be in addition to any other compensation to which such tax collector or tax commissioner is entitled.

(c) The duties and responsibilities of agents of the commissioner designated under this Code section shall be a part of the official duties and responsibilities of the county tax collectors and tax commissioners.

Laws 1955, p. 659, § 1; Laws 1957, p. 197, § 1; Laws 1965, p. 5, § 1; Laws 1966, p. 508, § 1; Laws 1990, p. 2048, § 2; Laws 1993, p. 1815, § 1; Laws 1997, p. 739, § 1; Laws 2000, p. 951, § 3–3.

Formerly Code 1981, § 40–2–22.

§ 40–2–24. Bond of tag agent

Each tag agent shall give bond conditioned as the commissioner may require, and in such amount as the commissioner may deem necessary and proper, not exceeding $250,000.00, to protect the state adequately. Such bond shall be executed by a surety corporation licensed to do business in the State of Georgia, as surety, and the premiums shall be paid by the department. The bond shall run to the Governor and his or her successors in office and shall be approved as to conditions, form, and sufficiency by the commissioner.

Laws 1955, p. 645, § 4; Laws 1957, p. 197, § 3; Laws 1966, p. 508, § 5; Laws 1990, p. 2048, § 2; Laws 2000, p. 951, § 3–4; Laws 2005, Act 68, § 14–3, eff. July 1, 2005.

Formerly Code 1981, § 40–2–23.

§ 40–2–25. Processing of applications of registration of motor vehicles by private persons

(a) The commissioner is authorized and directed to promulgate rules and regulations governing the processing by private persons, in any manner whatsoever, of applications for the registration of vehicles.

(b)(1) The tax commissioner of each county shall be authorized to require any private person processing applications for the registration of vehicles pursuant to subsection (a) of this Code section to give an annual fidelity bond in the amount of $ 50,000.00 with good and sufficient surety or sureties licensed to do business in this state payable to, in favor of, and for the protection of either the payee, taxpayer, or the tax commissioner of the county in which such person processes such applications. Such bond shall be posted prior to the beginning of business operations each year and satisfactory proof of such bond shall be filed in the office of the tax commissioner requiring such bond prior to the beginning of business operations each year.

(2) Any person who violates any provision of paragraph (1) of this subsection shall be guilty of a misdemeanor.

Laws 1977, p. 697, § 1; Laws 1988, p. 892, § 1; Laws 1989, p. 1403, § 1; Laws 1990, p. 2048, § 2; Laws 2002, p. 838, § 1.

Formerly Code 1981, § 40–2–24.

§ 40–2–25.1. Renumbered as § 40–2–27 by Laws 1990, p. 2048, § 2, eff. July 1, 1990

§ 40–2–26. Application for registration; blanks; contents; proof of payment of heavy vehicle tax

(a) All applicants to register a vehicle shall apply to the tag agent of the county wherein such vehicle is required to be returned for ad valorem taxation.

(b) Application shall be made by the owner of the vehicle upon blanks prepared by the commissioner for such purposes. The application shall contain a statement of the name, place of residence, and address of the applicant; a brief description of the vehicle to be registered, including its name and model, the name of the manufacturer, the manufacturer's vehicle identification number, and its shipping weight and carrying capacity; from whom, where, and when the vehicle was purchased; the total amount of all liens, if any, thereon, with the name and address of the lienholder; and such other information as the commissioner may require.

(c)(1) As used in this subsection, the term "heavy vehicle tax" means that tax imposed by Subchapter D of Chapter 36 of the Internal Revenue Code.

(2) On or after September 30, 1984, no vehicle registration or renewal thereof shall be issued to any motor vehicle subject to the heavy vehicle tax unless the owner of the motor vehicle provides satisfactory proof that the heavy vehicle tax has been paid for the federal tax year during which the application for registration or renewal thereof is made or that a heavy motor vehicle tax return has been filed with the United States Internal Revenue Service for the federal tax year during which the application for registration or renewal thereof is made.

(3) The commissioner is authorized to promulgate rules and regulations consistent with paragraph (2) of this subsection which are necessary to ensure that the state complies with the requirements of the Surface Transportation Assistance Act of 1982, Section 143, 23 U.S.C. Section 141d.

(4) The requirements of this subsection are in addition to any requirements of this Code relative to the registration of motor vehicles.

(d)(1) As used in this subsection, for the purpose of issuing or renewing motor vehicle registration, the term "satisfactory proof" means:

(A) Any type of proof that is satisfactory or sufficient proof of the owner's insurance coverage under subsection (a) of Code Section 40–6–10;

(B) Information obtained from the records or data base of the department regarding the owner's insurance coverage which information is derived from notice provided to the department pursuant to Code Section 40–2–137; or

(C) Such other type of proof of the owner's insurance coverage as may be approved for purposes of this Code section by rule or regulation of the department.

(2) No vehicle registration or renewal thereof shall be issued to any motor vehicle unless the tag agent receives satisfactory proof that the motor vehicle is subject to a policy of insurance that provides the minimum motor vehicle insurance coverage required by Chapter 34 of Title 33 or an approved self-insurance plan and, in the case of a private passenger vehicle, that such coverage was initially issued for a minimum term of six months; provided, however, that the owner's inability to register or renew the registration of any motor vehicle due to lack of proof of insurance shall not excuse or defer the timely payment of ad valorem taxes due and payable upon said vehicle.

Laws 1927, p. 226, § 3; Laws 1931, p. 7, § 84; Laws 1953, Jan.-Feb. Sess., p. 366, § 1; Laws 1957, p. 452, § 1; Laws 1966, p. 508, § 3; Laws 1984, p. 609, § 2; Laws 1985, p. 149, § 40; Laws 1987, p. 191, § 9; Laws 1990, p. 2048, § 2; Laws 2002, p. 1024, § 2; Laws 2003, Act 44, § 2, eff. May 28, 2003; Laws 2010, Act 381, § 3.1, eff. May 20, 2010.

Formerly Code 1933, § 68–202; Code 1981, § 40–2–25.

§ 40–2–27. Certificates of registration and title not to be issued to motor vehicles not manufactured to comply with federal emission and safety standards

(a) No application shall be accepted and no certificate of registration shall be issued to any motor vehicle which was not manufactured to comply with applicable federal emission standards issued pursuant to 42 U.S.C.A. Section 7401 through Section 7642, known as the Clean Air Act, as amended, and applicable federal motor vehicle safety standards issued pursuant to 49 U.S.C.A. Section 30101, et seq., unless and until the United States Customs Service or the United States Department of Transportation has certified that the motor vehicle complies with such applicable federal standards and unless all documents required by the commissioner for processing an application for a certificate of registration or title are printed and filled out in the English language or are accompanied by an English translation.

(b) The provisions of subsection (a) of this Code section shall only apply to applications for certificates of registration for such motor vehicles first registered in Georgia after July 1, 1985. Certification of compliance shall only be required at the time of application for the issuance of the initial Georgia certificate of registration.

(c) Applications for registration of such motor vehicles shall be accompanied by a Georgia certificate of title, proof that an application for a Georgia certificate of title has been properly submitted, or such other information and documentation of ownership as the commissioner shall deem proper.

(d) Before a certificate of registration is issued for an assembled motor vehicle or motorcycle, such assembled motor vehicle or motorcycle shall have been issued a certificate of title in Georgia and shall comply with the provisions of Code Section 40–3–30.1.

Laws 1985, p. 693, § 1; Laws 1990, p. 2048, § 2; Laws 1994, p. 97, § 40; Laws 2000, p. 951, § 3–5; Laws 2002, p. 512, § 5; Laws 2002, p. 1378, § 2; Laws 2008, Act 727, § 3, eff. May 14, 2008.

Formerly Code 1981, § 40–2–25.1.

§ 40–2–28. Registration of motor vehicles; applications; ownership; vehicles registered in other states

(a) Initial applications for registration shall contain such information of ownership as the commissioner shall deem proper, and no vehicle shall be registered unless the commissioner shall be satisfied that the applicant for registration is entitled to have the vehicle registered in his name. Proof of purchase at a judicial sale or previous registration in this state by the applicant may be accepted as evidence of ownership by the commissioner.

(b) Applications for registration of vehicles brought into this state and previously registered in other states shall be accompanied by an affidavit from the motor vehicle registering official of that state, or other satisfactory evidence indicating that the applicant is the lawful owner of the vehicle, including the date, name, and address of the person from whom it was purchased.

Laws 1925, p. 315, § 1; Laws 1931, p. 7, § 84; Laws 1953, Jan.-Feb. Sess., p. 366, § 2; Laws 1955, p. 424, § 1; Laws 1973, p. 455, § 1; Laws 1990, p. 2048, § 2.

Formerly Code 1933, § 68–205; Code 1981, § 40–2–26.

§ 40–2–29. License fee to accompany application for registration; temporary permits

Text of section effective until January 1, 2011. See also, section effective January 1, 2011.

An application for registration shall be accompanied by check; cash; certified or cashier's check; bank, postal, or express money order; or other similar bankable paper, for the amount of the license fee required by law. A money order receipt or other evidence of the purchase and remittance of such bankable paper for the proper amount, dated prior to any delinquency by the proper authority of the issuer, and showing the office of the commissioner or the office of the county tag agent as the payee and the owner of the vehicle sought to be licensed and registered as the remitter shall serve as a temporary permit to operate such vehicle for a period of 15 days from the date of such remittance.

Laws 1925, p. 315, § 1; Laws 1927, p. 226, § 6; Laws 1931, p. 7, § 84; Laws 1960, p. 943, § 1; Laws 1985, p. 149, § 40; Laws 1985, p. 537, § 2; Laws 1990, p. 2048, § 2.

Formerly Code 1933, §§ 68–208, 68–212; Code 1981, § 40–2–27.

§ 40–2–29. Registration for license plate to operate vehicle; License fee to accompany registration; temporary permits; penalties

Section effective January 1, 2011. See also, section effective until January 1, 2011.

(a) Except as otherwise provided in this chapter, any person purchasing or acquiring a vehicle shall register and obtain, or transfer, a license plate to operate such vehicle from the county tag agent in their county of residence no later than seven business days after the date of purchase or acquisition of the vehicle by presenting to the county tag agent the following:

(1) A motor vehicle certificate of title as provided in Chapter 3 of this title;

(2) Satisfactory proof of owner's insurance coverage as provided for in subsection (d) of Code Section 40–2–26;

(3) If applicable, satisfactory proof of compliance with the Article 2 of Chapter 9 of Title 12, the Georgia Motor Vehicle Emission Inspection and Maintenance Act; and

(4) Satisfactory proof that all fees, permits, and taxes have been paid.

(b) An application for registration shall be accompanied by check; cash; certified or cashier's check; bank, postal, or express money order; or other similar bankable paper for the amount of the license plate or temporary permit fee or any taxes required by law.

(c) A person unable to fully comply with the requirements of subsection (a) of this Code section shall register such vehicle and receive a temporary operating permit that will be valid until the end of the initial registration period as provided for in paragraph (1) of subsection (a) of Code Section 40–2–21.

(d) A conviction for displaying a license plate or temporary license plate not provided for in this chapter shall be punished as a misdemeanor.

Laws 1925, p. 315, § 1; Laws 1927, p. 226, § 6; Laws 1931, p. 7, § 84; Laws 1960, p. 943, § 1; Laws 1985, p. 149, § 40; Laws 1985, p. 537, § 2; Laws 1990, p. 2048, § 2; Laws 2010, Act 381, § 4, eff. Jan. 1, 2011.

Formerly Code 1933, §§ 68–208, 68–212; Code 1981, § 40–2–27.

§ 40–2–29.21. Renumbered as § 40–2–32 by Laws 1990, p. 2048, § 2, eff. July 1, 1990

§ 40–2–30. Purchase of tag by mail

An applicant may purchase a vehicle license plate or revalidation decal by mail, by mailing a properly completed application form to the tag agent of the county of his or her residence along with a bank check or money order in the amount of the license fee and all ad valorem taxes due thereon plus an additional fee of $1.00.

Laws 1957, p. 454, § 1; Laws 1966, p. 508, § 4; Laws 1968, p. 1386, § 1; Laws 1982, p. 964, § 1; Laws 1987, p. 655, § 1; Laws 1990, p. 2048, § 2; Laws 2010, Act 360, § 1–66, eff. May 12, 2010.

Formerly Code 1981, § 40–2–28.

§ 40–2–31. Five-year license plates; description; revalidation stickers; county name decals

(a) If the applicant meets the requirements set forth in this chapter, the commissioner shall issue to the applicant a license plate bearing a distinctive number.

(b) Such license plates shall be at least six inches wide and not less than 12 inches in length, except motorcycle license plates which shall be at least four inches wide and not less than seven inches in length, and shall show in boldface characters the month and year of expiration, the serial number, and either the full name or the abbreviation of the name of the state, shall designate the county from which the license plate was issued unless specifically stated otherwise in this chapter, and shall show such other distinctive markings as in the judgment of the commissioner may be deemed advisable, so as to indicate the class of weight of the vehicle for which the license plate was issued; and any license plate for a low-speed vehicle shall designate the vehicle as such. Such plates may also bear such figures, characters, letters, or combinations thereof as in the judgment of the commissioner will to the best advantage advertise, popularize, and otherwise promote Georgia as the Peach State. The license plate shall be of such strength and quality that the plate shall provide a minimum service period of at least five years. The commissioner shall adopt rules and regulations, pursuant to the provisions of Chapter 13 of Title 50, the Georgia Administrative Procedure Act, for the design and issuance of new license plates and to implement the other provisions of this Code section.

(b.1) . Notwithstanding the provisions of Code Sections 40–2–131 and 48–2–17, the commissioner shall retain the costs of manufacturing and delivery of license plates, revalidation decals, and county name decals from the registration fee as set forth in Code Section 40–2–151.

(c) The face of the license plate to be displayed shall be treated completely with a retroreflective material which will increase the nighttime visibility and legibility of the plate. The department shall prepare the specifications which such retroreflective material shall meet.

(d) In those years in which a new license plate is not issued, a revalidation decal with a distinctive serial number shall be issued and affixed in the space provided on the license plate issued to the applicant which shall indicate the year and month through which the registration of the vehicle shall be valid; provided, however, that if the commissioner determines that it is necessary, two revalidation decals shall be issued for each license plate to reflect the required information. When an applicant is issued a revalidation decal and such applicant registered the vehicle in another county the previous year, the applicant shall also be issued a new county decal which shall be properly affixed to the license plate and shall replace the other county decal.

(e) The commissioner shall furnish without cost to each tag agent reflective adhesive decals in sufficient number, upon which there shall be printed the name of the agent's county. Such a decal shall be issued with each metal license plate and shall be affixed in the space provided on the license plate without obscuring any number or other information required to be present on the plate.

(f) A county tag agent shall issue a county name decal for the agent's county only if:

(1) The applicant is a resident of or a business located in the county named on the decal;

(2) The applicant is registering a new vehicle in such county, is renewing a current vehicle registration, or is transferring registration of a vehicle to the county named on the decal; and

(3) The application for registration of the vehicle is being made in the county named on the decal.

Laws 1927, p. 226, § 8; Laws 1931, p. 7, § 84; Laws 1939, p. 182, § 2; Laws 1943, p. 341, § 3; Laws 1953, Nov.-Dec. Sess., p. 343, Part 1, § 1; Laws 1955, p. 659, § 7C; Laws 1969, p. 266, §§ 2, 3; Laws 1979, p. 615, § 1; Laws 1981, p. 714, §§ 1, 2; Laws 1982, p. 1584, §§ 2A, 5A; Laws 1986, p. 1333, § 1; Laws 1987, p. 949, § 2; Laws 1988, p. 380, § 3; Laws 1990, p. 2048, § 2; Laws 1995, p. 809, § 4; Laws 1996, p. 1118, § 4; Laws 1997, p. 419, § 6; Laws 2001, p. 4, § 40; Laws 2002, p. 512, § 6; Laws 2006, Act 585, § 1, eff. July 1, 2006; Laws 2010, Act 360, § 1–67, eff. May 12, 2010.

Formerly Code 1933, § 68–214; Code 1981, § 40–2–29.

§ 40–2–32. Repealed by Laws 2010, Act 360, § 1–74, eff. May 12, 2010

Historical and Statutory Notes

The repealed section, relating to the procedure for issuance of special license plates commemorating colleges or universities, was derived from Laws 1987, p. 658, § 1A; Laws 1989, p. 921, § 1; Laws 1990, p. 2048, § 2; Laws 1992, p. 779, § 1; Laws 1997, p. 419, § 7; Code 1981, § 40–2–29.21. The repealing law also reserved the section designation.

§ 40–2–32.1. Repealed by Laws 2010, § 1–75, eff. May 12, 2010

Historical and Statutory Notes

The repealed section, relating to the commissioner being authorized to enter into agreements promoting sale of commemorative license plates and the issuance of plates was derived from Laws 1997, p. 739, § 2; Laws 1998, p. 1179, § 5; Laws 2006, Act 947, § 1.

§ 40–2–33. Issuance of tags; procedure where tag is not in inventory; compensation

(a)(1) Upon compliance with the provisions of this chapter and the payment of the license fee required by law, the tag agent shall accept the application for registration and, except as otherwise provided for in this chapter, if the license plate or revalidation decal applied for is in such tag agent's inventory, he shall issue the appropriate plate or revalidation decal.

(2) The commissioner may provide for the issuance of a temporary license plate for any low-speed vehicle, to be displayed until such time as a license plate of the design required by Code Section 40–2–31 has been issued to the registrant as a replacement for such temporary license plate; provided, however, that any such temporary license plate shall designate the low-speed vehicle as such; and provided, further, that the commissioner shall make available for issuance low-speed vehicle license plates of the design required by Code Section 40–2–31 not later than September 1, 2002.

(3) If the license plate applied for is not in inventory, the application shall be approved and forwarded to the commissioner, who, upon receipt of a proper and approved application, shall issue the license plate applied for by mailing or delivering the plate to the applicant. Until the license plate is received by the applicant from the commissioner, the applicant may operate the vehicle without a license plate therefor upon the receipt issued to him by the tag agent.

(b) Except as provided for in Code Section 40–2–22, the amount of commission permitted as compensation to tag agents under this Code section shall be $1.00 per license plate or revalidation decal issued during any calendar year. Twenty-five cents for each license plate or revalidation decal sold in excess of 4,000 during any one calendar year shall become the property of the county and shall be turned over to the fiscal authorities of the county by the tag agent. The remaining portion of such commissions shall be disposed of as provided in Code Section 40–2–34.

(c)(1) Any other provisions of any law of this state, whether general, special, or local, to the contrary notwithstanding, and except as provided in subsection (b) of this Code section and paragraph (2) of this subsection, the fees prescribed in subsection (b) of this Code section shall be retained by the tag agent appointed by the commissioner under this chapter and shall be his or her own personal compensation for the services rendered in the administration of this chapter, regardless of whether such agent may otherwise be an elected or appointed official of the county, and regardless of whether as such county officer he or she is compensated for the performance of the duties of such office on a fee basis or salary basis, or combination thereof. It shall be his or her duty, however, as agent for the commissioner in the administration of the purposes of this chapter, to compensate any additional personnel which may be necessary to enable said agent to effectuate the provisions of this chapter and the rules and regulations promulgated under this chapter by the commissioner.

(2) If such tag agent shall be a salaried employee of the county and at a salary in excess of $ 7,999.00 per annum, the amount of such fees so collected shall go into the general treasury of the county. In such cases, it shall be the duty of the governing authorities of the county to furnish to the tag agent such additional clerical help as is necessary to carry out the provisions of this chapter.

(d) The initial issuance of any tag, on or after July 1, 2007, shall not be made unless the applicant presents at the time of application a valid Georgia driver's license or Georgia identification card. This subsection shall not apply to those applicants expressly exempted in Code Section 40–5–21.

Laws 1955, p. 659, § 3; Laws 1957, p. 197, § 2; Laws 1966, p. 508, § 3; Laws 1970, p. 728, § 1; Laws 1982, p. 3, § 40; Laws 1985, p. 149, § 40; Laws 1988, p. 377, § 1; Laws 1989, p. 857, § 1; Laws 1990, p. 159, § 1; Laws 1990, p. 2048, § 2; Laws 1992, p. 779, § 2; Laws 1997, p. 419, § 8; Laws 2000, p. 951, § 3–6; Laws 2002, p. 512, § 7; Laws 2007, Act 257, § 1, eff. July 1, 2007; Laws 2010, Act 360, § 1–68, eff. May 12, 2010.

Formerly Code 1981, § 40–2–30.

§ 40–2–34. Submission of reports and moneys to commissioner

(a) All county tag agents accepting license applications shall endeavor to submit to the commissioner on at least a weekly basis reports of license applications handled and remit with such reports related sums of money to which the state is entitled. All tag reports of license applications handled and related sums of money to which the state is entitled must be submitted to the commissioner within seven calendar days from the close of the business week during which the aforementioned license applications were handled and related sums of money received. The term "business week" shall mean Monday through Friday (or Saturday if applicable).

(b) Funds received as a result of the handling of license applications shall be considered trust funds in the hands of such tag agents until such time as paid over to the commissioner.

(c) Failure to submit the reports or remit the funds within the period required by this Code section shall result in the penalties imposed by Code Section 48–2–44.

(d) Before the expiration of the time period within which a tag report is required to be filed with the commissioner or related funds remitted to the commissioner, application may be made to the commissioner for an extension. The commissioner shall be authorized, upon a showing of justifiable cause, to grant up to a 30 day extension from the deadline provided for the performance of the above duties. Only one such extension may be granted with regard to any reports or funds due the commissioner for a specific business week.

(e) Proof of mailing within the appropriate time periods provided for in this Code section, as evidenced by a United States Postal Service postmark, shall be prima-facie proof that the county tag agent has complied in a timely manner with the duties enumerated by this Code section.

(f) All funds derived from motor vehicle registrations or the sale of any license plates and remitted to the state shall be deposited in the general fund of the state treasury unless otherwise specifically authorized by the Constitution and provided for in this chapter.

Laws 1980, p. 1050, § 2; Laws 1985, p. 149, § 40; Laws 1990, p. 2048, § 2; Laws 1995, p. 809, § 5; Laws 2000, p. 951, § 3–7; Laws 2001, p. 1173, §§ 2–1, 3–1; Laws 2006, Act 947, § 2, eff. Jan. 1, 2007.

Formerly Code 1981, § 40–2–31.

Historical and Statutory Notes

Laws 2006, Act 947, § 13, provides:

"(a) This Act [adding subsec. (f)] shall become effective on January 1, 2007, except as otherwise provided in subsection (b) of this section.

"(b) If an amendment to the Constitution of the State of Georgia authorizing the dedication of revenue from sales of special license plates to agencies, funds, or nonprofit corporations designated by the General Assembly is not ratified at the general election in 2006, this Act shall be repealed in its entirety on January 1, 2007, and no such motor vehicle license plates shall be issued pursuant to this Act."

An amendment to Article III, § IX, Par. VI, of the Georgia constitution, authorizing such a dedication, was approved by the electorate at the general election held on November 7, 2006.

§ 40-2-35. Commissioner to have license plates by December 1

The commissioner shall have in his possession on or before December 1 of each year, for distribution, the license plates and revalidation decals provided for in this chapter.

Laws 1931, p. 7, § 84; Laws 1931, p. 213, § 3; Laws 1990, p. 2048, § 2.

Formerly Code 1933, § 68-209; Code 1981, § 40-2-32.

§ 40-2-36. License plates and decals furnished by commissioner; inventory of plates; rules and regulations

(a) The commissioner shall furnish to each tag agent such number of motor vehicle license plates, revalidation decals, and decals as he may deem necessary for issuance by such agent, together with such forms and other supplies as are necessary to enable such agent to perform the duties required of him by this chapter.

(b) The county tag agent shall, immediately upon receipt of the motor vehicle license plates from the commissioner, take a full and complete inventory of the arriving shipment of license plates for motor vehicles over 26,000 pounds. The affidavit of lost or missing plates which the county tag agents are required to file with the commissioner shall be filed within ten days of the county tag agents' receipt of the license plates for motor vehicles over 26,000 pounds in weight. Failure to submit the required affidavit within ten days shall result in a denial of credit for any lost or missing license plates and the receiving county shall be responsible for full payment of said license plates.

(c) The county is responsible for providing a secure storage area for all license plates and revalidation decals.

(d) Notwithstanding any other provision of law, should a county desire to maintain an inventory of license plates for vehicles weighing in excess of 26,000 pounds and sell said license plates for vehicles weighing in excess of 26,000 pounds, the county shall first request permission in writing from the commissioner. Permission shall be granted at the discretion of the commissioner and, once granted, the permission may be revoked should the county fail to file tag and title reports with the commissioner in a timely and proper manner and fail to remit to the commissioner in a timely manner sums of money collected.

(e) The commissioner shall prescribe such reasonable rules and regulations as in his discretion may be necessary to effectuate the purposes of this Code section.

Laws 1955, p. 659, § 2; Laws 1966, p. 508, § 2; Laws 1980, p. 1050, § 1; Laws 1990, p. 1883, § 1; Laws 1990, p. 2048, § 2.

Formerly Code 1981, § 40-2-33.

§ 40-2-36.1. Renumbered as § 40-2-39 by Laws 1990, p. 2048, § 2, eff. July 1, 1990

§ 40-2-37. License plates and registration for vehicles of state and political subdivisions

(a) All vehicles of the type required to be registered by Code Section 40-2-20 owned by the State of Georgia or any municipality or other political subdivision of this state and used exclusively for governmental functions, except those employed in secret investigatory police functions to which regular Georgia license plates are issued, and except for those assigned for the transportation of employees of the Georgia Lottery Corporation to which regular Georgia license plates are issued, shall be registered with the commissioner by the fiscal officers or other proper officials of the respective departments and agencies of the state, municipality, or political subdivision to which such vehicles belong prior to operation and use thereof. Such registration shall be made upon forms prescribed and prepared by the commissioner for such purpose and shall contain a brief description of the vehicle to be registered; its name and model; the name of the manufacturer; the manufacturer's vehicle identification number; the department, agency, political subdivision, or branch thereof to which such vehicle is to be registered; and such other information as to use and identity as the commissioner may require. Upon the filing of the properly executed application for registration, the commissioner, upon being satisfied that such vehicle is bona fide owned by the state or a municipality or political subdivision thereof and is to be used exclusively for governmental functions, shall issue, upon payment by such applicant of a license fee of $3.00, a license plate which shall be displayed upon such vehicle in the same manner as provided for private vehicles. The license fee, less the actual manufacturing cost of the plates which will be retained by the department, shall be deposited in the general fund of the state treasury. Such license plates shall be replaced at such time as other license plates issued for private vehicles are required to be replaced.

(b) For all vehicles owned by the State of Georgia or any municipality or other political subdivision of this state, except those vehicles employed in covert or secret investigatory police functions to which regular Georgia license plates are issued, those assigned for the transportation of employees of the Georgia Lottery Corporation to which regular Georgia license plates are issued, and those vehicles owned by the Department of Public Safety, the commissioner shall provide for registration and issuance of regular license plates for such vehicles. The license plates issued pursuant to this subsection shall be identical in appearance to regular license plates issued for private vehicles, except that such license plates shall not display any registration expiration. Such license plates may be transferred as provided for in subsection (d) of this Code section. Such license plates shall be issued at the time the vehicle is purchased by the state.

(c) All license plates issued to government vehicles pursuant to this Code section shall be marked in such a manner as to indicate the specific type of governmental unit operating the vehicle. These markings shall be prominently displayed and shall consist of one of the following appropriate legends: "STATE," "CITY," "COUNTY," "AUTHORITY," or "BOARD." In addition, each such license plate shall bear a county identification strip indicating the county in which the vehicle is based except that vehicles owned by the state shall not be required to bear such county identification strip.

(d) Any such license plates shall remain displayed and affixed upon such vehicle so long as such vehicle continues to be owned by the state or such municipality or political subdivision and used exclusively for governmental functions. Upon cessation of either such ownership or use, the license plate shall be removed from such vehicle and returned to the commissioner or the county tag agent for destruction. In the event of a transfer of a vehicle to a department or agency, or branch thereof, other than the specific one to which such vehicle is registered, the commissioner shall be notified in writing by the department or agency from which the same is being transferred upon a form prepared and furnished for such purpose by the commissioner. On due proof of loss of any such license plate, or of mutilation due to accidental or natural causes, another license plate may be issued upon application of the fiscal officer or other proper official of the department, agency, or political subdivision to which any such lost plate is registered.

(e) No person, firm, or corporation owning or operating any such vehicle shall display upon the motor vehicle any license plate provided for in this Code section unless at the time of such ownership or operation such vehicle is properly registered under this Code section and is owned by the state or a municipality or political subdivision of this state and is being used exclusively for governmental purposes. Any person who violates this subsection shall be guilty of a misdemeanor.

(f) This Code section shall apply to all vehicle license plates issued for governmental vehicles on and after January 1, 2007.

Laws 1960, p. 777, §§ 3, 4; Laws 1971, p. 667, § 1; Laws 1980, p. 357, §§ 1, 2; Laws 1990, p. 2048, § 2; Laws 1995, p. 1302, § 5; Laws 2000, p. 951, § 3–8; Laws 2001, p. 1173, §§ 2–2, 3–2; Laws 2006, Act 585, § 2, eff. July 1, 2006; Laws 2007, Act 346, § 2, eff. July 1, 2007.

Formerly Code 1981, § 40–2–35.

Historical and Statutory Notes

Prior to the 2006 amendment by Act 585, the section had read:

"(a) All vehicles of the type required to be registered by Code Section 40–2–20 owned by the State of Georgia or any municipality or other political subdivision of this state and used exclusively for governmental functions, except those employed in secret investigatory police functions to which regular Georgia license plates are issued, shall be registered with the commissioner by the fiscal officers or other proper officials of the respective departments and agencies of the state, municipality, or political subdivision to which such vehicles belong prior to operation and use thereof. Such registration shall be made upon forms prescribed and prepared by the commissioner for such purpose and shall contain a brief description of the vehicle to be registered; its name and model; the name of the manufacturer; the manufacturer's vehicle identification number; the department, agency, political subdivision, or branch thereof to which such vehicle is to be registered; and such other information as to use and identity as the commissioner may require. Upon the filing of the properly executed application for registration, the commissioner, upon being satisfied that such vehicle is bona fide owned by the state or a municipality or political subdivision thereof and is to be used exclusively for governmental functions, shall issue, upon payment by such applicant of a license fee of $1.00, a license plate which shall be displayed upon such vehicle in the same manner as provided for private vehicles. Such license plates shall be replaced at such time as other license plates issued for private vehicles are required to be replaced.

"(b) For all vehicles owned by the State of Georgia or any municipality or other political subdivision of this state, except those vehicles employed in covert or secret investigatory police functions to which regular Georgia license plates are issued and those vehicles owned by the Department of Public Safety, the commissioner shall provide for five-year registration and issuance of regular license plates for such vehicles. The five-year license plates issued pursuant to this subsection shall be identical in appearance to regular license plates issued for private vehicles, except that such five-year license plates shall not display any year of registration or registration expiration. Such license plates may be transferred as provided for in subsection (d) of this Code section. Such five-year license plates shall be issued at the beginning of a five-year license period as for private vehicles or shall be issued at the time the vehicle is purchased by the state, and all such license plates shall expire at the same time as regular license plates.

"(c) All license plates issued to government vehicles pursuant to this Code section shall be marked in such a manner as to indicate the specific type of governmental unit operating the vehicle. These markings shall be prominently displayed and shall consist of one of the following appropriate legends: "STATE," "CITY," "COUNTY," "AUTHORITY," or "BOARD." In addition, each such license plate shall bear a county identification strip indicating the county in which the vehicle is based except that vehicles owned by the state shall not be required to bear such county identification strip.

"(d) Any such license plates shall remain displayed and affixed upon such vehicle so long as such vehicle continues to be owned by the state or such municipality or political subdivision and used exclusively for governmental functions. Upon cessation of either such ownership or use, the license plate shall be removed from such vehicle and either destroyed by such agency or returned to the commissioner for destruction. If a license plate has been destroyed by the agency, certification of such destruction shall be provided by the agency to the commissioner upon a form prepared and furnished for such purpose by the commissioner. In the event of a transfer of a vehicle to a department or agency, or branch thereof, other than the specific one to which such vehicle is registered, the commissioner shall be notified in writing by the department or agency from which the same is being transferred upon a form prepared and furnished for such purpose by the commissioner. Such transfer shall be recorded on the registration lists maintained by the commissioner. On due proof of loss of any such license plate, or of mutilation due to accidental or natural causes, another license plate may be issued upon application of the fiscal officer or other proper official of the department, agency, or political subdivision to which any such lost plate is registered.

"(e) No person, firm, or corporation owning or operating any such vehicle shall display upon the motor vehicle any license plate provided for in this Code section unless at the time of such ownership or operation such vehicle is properly registered under this Code section and is owned by the state or a municipality or political subdivision of this state and is being used exclusively for governmental purposes. Any person who violates this subsection shall be guilty of a misdemeanor.

"(f) This Code section shall apply to all vehicle license plates issued for governmental vehicles on and after January 1, 1996."

The 2007 amendment, by Act 346, in subsec. (a), added "and except for those assigned for the transportation of employees of the Georgia Lottery Corporation to which regular Georgia license plates are issued,"; and in subsec. (b), added ", those assigned for the transportation of employees of the Georgia Lottery Corporation to which regular Georgia license plates are issued,".

§ 40–2–38. Registration and license of manufacturers, distributors, dealers, and transporters of vehicles; revocation of plates; lost plates; expiration of plates; rules and regulations

(a)(1) Manufacturers, distributors, and dealers engaged in the manufacture, sale, or leasing of vehicles required to be registered under Code Section 40–2–20 shall register with the commissioner, making application for a distinguishing dealer's number, specifying the name and make of motor vehicle, tractor, or trailer manufactured, sold, or leased by them, upon forms prepared by the commissioner for such purposes, and pay therefor a fee of $62.00, which shall accompany such application. Upon payment of such fee by a dealer, the commissioner shall furnish to the dealer one master number plate to expire each year in accordance with subsection (f) of this Code section, to be known as a dealer's number and to be distinguished from the number plates provided for in this chapter by different and distinguishing colors to be determined by the commissioner. The dealer plate for a franchise motor vehicle dealer shall be distinguishable from the dealer plate for a used car dealer and from the dealer plate for a motor vehicle wholesaler. A dealer's number plate is for the purpose of demonstrating or transporting dealer's vehicles or trailers for sale or lease. Persons engaged in the business of transporting vehicles for a dealer under a vehicle's own power shall be permitted to use such dealer's plate for the purpose of transporting a vehicle.

(2) No dealer may use or permit to be used a dealer's number for private use or on cars for hire, for lease, or other manner not provided for in this Code section. A dealer may use or permit to be used a dealer's number for private use on vehicles owned by the dealership, regardless of whether such vehicle has been issued a certificate of title or registered, when such vehicles are operated by an employee or corporate officer of the dealer which has been issued such number. A distinguishing dealer's number used by an employee or officer for private use shall authorize such person to operate the vehicle to which the number is attached on the public highways and streets. For purposes of this paragraph, "employee" means a person who works a minimum of 36 hours per week at the dealership.

(3) The manufacturer's or distributor's license plate is limited to no longer than six months' use per vehicle. Upon payment of such a fee by a manufacturer or distributor, the commissioner shall issue to manufacturers and distributors number plates with the word "Manufacturer" or "Distributor" on such plates. Nothing in this subsection shall preclude a manufacturer or distributor from using a "Manufacturer" or "Distributor" number plate on motor vehicles it owns when such vehicles are used for evaluation or demonstration purposes, notwithstanding incidental personal use by a manufacturer or distributor. A dealer may apply for one or more distinguishing dealer's numbers. In the event the dealers, distributors, or manufacturers desire more than one tag, they shall so state on the application, and, in addition to the fee of $62.00 provided in this Code section, shall pay $12.00 for each and every additional number plate furnished.

(b) Dealer plates shall be issued in the following manner:

(1) Dealers shall be issued a master plate and two additional plates, for a total of three initial plates; and

(2) In addition to the three dealer plates issued in accordance with paragraph (1) of this subsection, each dealer may also be issued one additional dealer plate for every 20 units sold in a calendar year.

In order to determine the additional number and classification of plates to be issued to a dealer, a dealer shall be required to certify by affidavit to the department the number of retail and wholesale units sold in the prior calendar year using the past motor vehicle sales history of the dealer as identified by department records of documentation approved by the department. If no sales history is available, the department shall issue a number of plates based on an estimated number of sales for the coming calendar year. The department may, in its discretion, request documentation supporting sales history and may increase or decrease the number and classification of plates issued based on actual sales.

(c) This Code section shall not apply in any manner to mopeds as such term is defined in Code Section 40–1–1.

(d) The license plates issued pursuant to this Code section shall be revoked and confiscated upon a determination after a hearing that such dealer, distributor, or manufacturer has unlawfully used such license plates in violation of this Code section.

(e) If a license plate issued pursuant to this Code section is lost or stolen, the dealer, manufacturer, distributor, or other party to whom the license plate was issued must immediately report the lost or stolen plate to local law enforcement agencies. If a replacement license plate is sought, the dealer, manufacturer, distributor, or other party to whom the license plate was issued shall file a notarized affidavit with the department requesting a replacement plate. Such affidavit shall certify under penalty of perjury that the license plate has been lost or stolen and that the loss has been reported to a local law enforcement agency.

(f)(1) The expiration of a license plate issued pursuant to this Code section shall be the last day of the registration period as provided in division (a)(1)(A)(ii) of Code Section 40–2–21, except that for the purposes of this subsection, the registration period shall be determined by the first letter of the legal name of the business listed on the application for registration or renewal of registration. An application for renewal of registration shall not be submitted earlier than 90 days prior to the last day of the registration period. A penalty of 25 percent of the total registration fees due shall be assessed any person registering pursuant to this Code section who, prior to the expiration of such person's registration period, fails to apply for renewal or if having applied fails to pay the required fees.

(2) A transition period shall commence on October 1, 2007, and conclude on December 31, 2007, for all existing registrations and any new registration applications presented prior to January 1, 2008. On or after January 1, 2008, new applications for registration shall be submitted and remain valid until the expiration of such registration as specified in paragraph (1) of this subsection.

(g) The commissioner shall adopt rules and regulations for the implementation of this Code section.

Laws 1927, p. 226, § 7; Laws 1931, p. 7, § 84; Laws 1963, p. 529, § 1; Laws 1977, p. 591, § 1; Laws 1978, p. 2241, § 2A; Laws 1982, p. 3, § 40; Laws 1985, p. 149, § 40; Laws 1990, p. 2048, § 2; Laws 1992, p. 2978, § 1; Laws 1993, p. 296, § 1; Laws 1997, p. 1559, § 1; Laws 2004, Act 564, § 40, eff. May 13, 2004; Laws 2005, Act 65, § 2, eff. Jan. 1, 2006; Laws 2006, Act 592, § 1, eff. April 27, 2006; Laws 2007, Act 346, §§ 3, 4, eff. July 1, 2007.

Formerly Code 1933, § 68–213; Code 1981, § 40–2–36.

Historical and Statutory Notes

The 2004 amendment by Act 564, in subsec. (a), substituted "it owns" for "they own".

The 2005 amendment by Act 65 rewrote the section which had read:

"(a) Manufacturers, distributors, and dealers engaged in the manufacture, sale, or leasing of vehicles required to be registered under Code Section 40–2–20 shall register with the commissioner, making application for a distinguishing dealer's number, specifying the name and make of motor vehicle, tractor, or trailer manufactured, sold, or leased by them, upon forms prepared by the commissioner for such purposes, and pay therefor a fee of $62.00, which shall accompany such application. Upon payment of such fee by a dealer, the commissioner shall furnish to the dealer one number plate to expire December 31 of odd-numbered years, to be known as a dealer's number, and to be distinguished from the number plates provided for in this chapter by a different and distinguishing color to be determined by the commissioner, with the word "Dealer" on same; a dealer's number plate to be for the purpose of demonstrating or transporting dealer's vehicles or trailers for sale or lease. No dealer may use or permit to be used a dealer's number for private use or on cars for hire, for lease, or other manner not provided for in this Code section. A dealer may use or permit to be used a dealer's number for private use on vehicles owned by the dealership, regardless of whether such vehicle has been issued a certificate of title or registered, when such vehicles are operated by an employee or corporate officer of the dealer which has been issued such number. A distinguishing dealer's number used by an employee or officer shall authorize such person to operate the vehicle to which the number is attached on the public highways and streets. A dealer may apply for one or more distinguishing dealer's numbers. The manufacturer's or distributor's license plate is limited to no longer than six months' use per vehicle. Upon payment of such a fee by a manufacturer or distributor, the commissioner shall issue to manufacturers and distributors number plates with the word "Manufacturer" or "Distributor" on such plates. Nothing in this subsection shall preclude a manufacturer or distributor from using a "Manufacturer" or "Distributor" number plate on motor vehicles it owns when such vehicles are used for evaluation or demonstration purposes, notwithstanding incidental personal use by a manufacturer or distributor. In the event the dealers, distributors, or manufacturers desire more than one tag, they shall so state on the application, and, in addition to the fee of $62.00 provided in this Code section, shall pay $12.00 for each and every additional number plate furnished. Persons engaged in the business of transporting vehicles for others under such vehicle's own power shall likewise be entitled to obtain license plates under this Code section, but such plates shall be used only on vehicles being transported.

"(b) Persons engaged in the business of transporting mobile homes and house trailers for others shall likewise be entitled to obtain license plates under this Code section. The commissioner is authorized to promulgate rules and regulations covering the issuance of plates to such persons; provided, however, this Code section shall not apply in any manner to farm tractors.

"(c) This Code section shall not apply in any manner to mopeds as such term is defined in Code Section 40–1–1.

"(d) The license plates issued pursuant to this Code section shall be revoked and confiscated upon a determination after a hearing that such dealer, distributor, manufacturer, or person engaged in transporting mobile homes and house trailers has unlawfully used such license plates in violation of this Code section."

The 2006 amendment by Act 592, in subsec. (a), designated the existing introductory text as par. (1) and redesignated former pars. (1) and (2) as pars. (2) and (3); in subsec. (b), deleted "retail" following "20" in par. (2), and rewrote the last undesignated paragraph; deleted subsec. (c); redesignated former subsecs. (d) through (f) as subsecs (c) through (e); and in newly designated subsec. (d) (former subsec. (e)), substituted "or manufacturer" for "manufacturer, or person engaged in transporting mobile homes and house trailers". Prior to the 2006 amendment, the last paragraph of subsec. (b) and subsec. (c) had read:

"In order to determine the additional number of plates to be issued to a dealer, a dealer shall be required to certify to the department the number of retail units sold in the prior calendar year using the past motor vehicle sales history of the dealer. If no sales history is available, the department shall issue a number of plates based on an estimated number of sales for the coming calendar year. The department may, in its discretion, increase or decrease the number of plates issued based on actual sales.

"(c) Persons engaged in the business of transporting mobile homes and house trailers for others shall likewise be entitled to obtain license plates under this Code section. The commissioner is authorized to promulgate rules and regulations covering the issuance of plates to such persons; provided, however, this Code section shall not apply in any manner to farm tractors."

The 2007 amendment by Act 346, in subsec. (a), substituted "expire each year in accordance with subsection (f) of this Code section" for "expire December 31 of each year" in par. (1); and added subsecs. (f) and (g).

§ 40–2–38.1. Transporter plates

(a) A person engaged in the business of the limited operation of a motor vehicle for any of the following purposes may obtain a transporter plate authorizing the movement of the vehicle for the specific purpose:

(1) To facilitate the delivery of new or used motor vehicles, trucks, or buses between manufacturers, distributors, dealers, sellers, or purchasers;

(2) To move a mobile office, a mobile classroom, a mobile or manufactured home, or a house trailer;

(3) To drive a motor vehicle that is part of the inventory of a dealer to and from a motor vehicle trade show or exhibition or to, during, and from a parade in which the motor vehicle is used; or

(4) To drive special mobile equipment in any of the following circumstances:

(A) From the manufacturer of the equipment to a facility of a dealer; or

(B) From one facility of a dealer to another facility of a dealer.

(b) This Code section shall not be construed to require a motor vehicle dealer to obtain transporter plates in order to transport vehicles for sale or lease.

(c) A person may obtain a transporter plate by filing an application with the Department of Revenue and paying the required fee. The fee for an initial transporter plate shall be $62.00 and the fee for all additional plates shall be $12.00. An application for a transporter plate must be on a form provided by the department and must contain the information required by the department. The department is authorized to promulgate regulations consistent with this Code section.

(d) Transporter plates issued under this Code section shall be distinguishable from dealer, wholesaler, manufacturer, or distributor plates, as provided for in Code Section 40–2–38.

(e) During the year for which it is issued, a person may transfer a transporter plate from one vehicle to another so long as the vehicle is driven only for a purpose authorized by subsection (a) of this Code section. In order to obtain a transporter plate, an applicant must demonstrate to the department compliance with all applicable federal and state laws.

(f) The license plates issued pursuant to this Code section shall be revoked and confiscated upon a determination after a hearing that an applicant has unlawfully used such license plates for purposes other than those expressly permitted by this Code section.

(g) If a license plate issued pursuant to this Code section is lost or stolen, the dealer, manufacturer, distributor, or other party to whom the license plate was issued must immediately report the lost or stolen plate to local law enforcement agencies. If a replacement license plate is sought, the dealer, manufacturer, distributor, or other party to whom the license plate was issued shall file a notarized affidavit with the department requesting a replacement plate. Such affidavit shall certify under penalty of perjury that the license plate has been lost or stolen and that the loss has been reported to a local law enforcement agency.

(h) This Code section shall not in any way apply to farm tractors.

(i)(1) The expiration of a license plate issued pursuant to this Code section shall be the last day of the registration period as provided in division (a)(1)(A)(ii) of Code Section 40–2–21, except that for the purposes of this subsection, the registration period shall be determined by the first letter of the legal name of the business listed on the application for registration or renewal of registration. An application for renewal of registration shall not be submitted earlier than 90 days prior to the last day of the registration period. A penalty of 25 percent of the total registration fees due shall be assessed any person registering pursuant to this Code section who, prior to the expiration of such person's registration period, fails to apply for renewal or if having applied fails to pay the required fees.

(2) A transition period shall commence on October 1, 2007, and conclude on December 31, 2007, for all existing registrations and any new registration applications presented prior to January 1, 2008. On or after January 1, 2008, new applications for registration shall be submitted and remain valid until the expiration of such registration as specified in paragraph (1) of this subsection.

(j) The commissioner shall adopt rules and regulations for the implementation of this Code section.

Laws 2006, Act 592, § 2, eff. April 27, 2006; Laws 2007, Act 346, § 5, eff. July 1, 2007.

§ 40–2–39. Requirements for engaging in activity as new motor vehicle dealer

(a) As used in this Code section, the term:

(1) "Dealer" means any person engaged in the business of selling or leasing or offering to sell or lease new motor vehicles and who is licensed or otherwise authorized to utilize trademarks or service marks associated with one or more makes of motor vehicles in connection with such sales or leases. The term "dealer" shall not mean any person engaged solely in the business of selling used motor vehicles and shall not mean any person engaged in the solicitation, advertising, or financing of the sale of new motor vehicles and shall not mean any person engaged solely in activities as a manufacturer or distributor of new motor vehicles.

(2) "Distributor" means any person who, pursuant to a contract with a manufacturer, sells or offers to sell new motor vehicles to new motor vehicle dealers.

(3) "Established place of business" means a permanent salesroom or sales office of a new motor vehicle dealer, which permanent salesroom or sales office is located in a permanent building on an open lot and which is marked by an appropriate sign and at which a permanent business of bartering, trading, or selling of new motor vehicles is carried on in good faith.

(4) "Manufacturer" means any person who makes or assembles new motor vehicles.

(5) "Motor vehicle" means every self–propelled vehicle intended primarily for use and operation on the public highways, except farm tractors and other machines and tools used in the production, harvesting, and care of farm products and except construction equipment.

(6) "New motor vehicle" means a motor vehicle which has been sold to a dealer and on which the original motor vehicle title has not been issued.

(7) "Person" means every natural person, partnership, corporation, association, trust, estate, or any other legal entity.

(8) "Temporary site" means a location at which new or used motor vehicles are sold or offered for sale for which a temporary site permit has been issued by the department in accordance with paragraph (4) of subsection (b) of this Code Section and which location is:

(A) Used for a period not to exceed 96 hours in any 30 day period of time;

(B) Used not more than three times in any calendar year; and

(C) Located in the county in which the established place of business of the new motor vehicle dealer using the temporary site is located or an adjoining county.

(9) "Trade shows" means the display or solicitation for sale of new motor vehicles at a location other than the established place of business at which the sales transaction is accomplished or at which delivery of the new motor vehicle is completed.

(b)(1) It shall be unlawful for any person to engage in any activity as a new motor vehicle dealer unless and until such person has registered with the commissioner and obtained a dealer's number license plate under Code Section 40–2–38 for each established place of business at which the person engages in such activity. The commissioner shall not accept such application for registration and shall not issue a dealer's number license plate unless and until the applicant establishes to the satisfaction of the commissioner, under criteria established by rules or regulations promulgated by the commissioner, that the applicant shall not engage in any activity of a new motor vehicle dealer except at an established place of business, a temporary site, or a properly licensed auto auction or licensed facility. This paragraph shall not be construed to prohibit a new motor vehicle dealer from delivering a vehicle off site if the transaction is initiated at an established place of business under this chapter.

(2) It shall be unlawful for any person to engage in any activity as a new motor vehicle dealer except at an established place of business which has been registered as such under this Code section and Code Section 40–2–38 or at a temporary site.

(3) This subsection shall not apply to new motor vehicle trade shows and shall not be construed to prohibit new motor vehicle trade shows or properly licensed auctions.

(4)(A) At least 60 days prior to the opening of a sale at a temporary site, a new motor vehicle dealer must make application to the department for a temporary site permit.

(B) To be eligible for a temporary site permit, a new motor vehicle dealer must be registered with the department as required by Code Section 40–2–38. In order to obtain a temporary site permit, a new motor vehicle dealer must provide, on a form promulgated by the department, the following:

(i) The address, including county, of the new motor vehicle dealer's established place of business;

(ii) The address, including county, of the temporary site location;

(iii) The dates and hours of the temporary site sale;

(iv) The number of temporary site sales already conducted by the new motor vehicle dealer during the calendar year in which the requested temporary site sale is to occur; and

(v) The name, address, and contact person of any sponsors, promoters, and lending institutions involved in or to be represented at the temporary site sale.

(C) As part of the application, a new motor vehicle dealer must submit written documentation demonstrating that the new motor vehicle dealer has complied with any licensing requirements applicable in the local jurisdiction in which the temporary site sale will occur and a copy of a written agreement with the owner of the real property where the sale is to occur.

(D) A temporary site permit issued pursuant to this paragraph shall be valid only for the dates and hours of the sale as indicated in the application submitted to the department and must be prominently displayed at the temporary site at all times during the sale. No new motor vehicle dealer may purchase more than three temporary site permits within a calendar year. A temporary site permit is not transferable to any other dealer or location.

(E) The filing fee for each application for a temporary site permit shall be $100.00.

(c) As an alternative to criminal or other civil enforcement, the commissioner, in order to enforce this Code section or any orders, rules, and regulations promulgated pursuant thereto, may issue an administrative fine not to exceed $1,000.00 for each violation, whenever the commissioner, after a hearing, determines that any person has violated any provisions of this Code section or any regulations or orders promulgated thereunder. If, after a hearing, the commissioner determines that any person has violated this Code section more than once, the commissioner may suspend a dealer's registration for a period not to exceed ten days. Any hearing and any administrative review held pursuant to this Code section shall be conducted in accordance with the procedure for contested cases under Chapter 13 of Title 50, the "Georgia Administrative Procedure Act." Any person who has exhausted all administrative remedies available and who is aggrieved or adversely affected by a final order or action of the commissioner shall have the right of judicial review thereof in accordance with Chapter 13 of Title 50. All fines recovered under this subsection shall be paid into the state treasury. The commissioner may file, in the superior court (1) wherein the person under order resides; (2) if such person is a corporation, in the county wherein the corporation maintains its established place of business; or (3) in the county wherein the violation occurred, a certified copy of a final order of the commissioner, whether unappealed from or affirmed upon appeal, whereupon the court shall render judgment in accordance therewith and notify the parties. Such judgment shall have the same effect and proceedings in relation thereto shall thereafter be the same as though the judgment had been rendered in an action duly heard and determined by the court. The penalty prescribed in this Code section shall be concurrent, alternative, and cumulative with any and all other civil, criminal, or alternative rights, remedies, forfeitures, or penalties provided, allowed, or available to the commissioner with respect to any violation of this Code section or any order, rules, or regulations promulgated pursuant thereto. For purposes of this subsection, the sale of each motor vehicle while not in compliance with temporary site permit requirements shall constitute a separate violation.

(d) Any person who violates any provision of this Code section shall be guilty of a misdemeanor and, upon conviction thereof, shall be subject to a fine not to exceed $1,000.00 or imprisonment for a period not to exceed 12 months, or both.

Laws 1988, p. 854, § 1; Laws 1990, p. 2048, § 2; Laws 1998, p. 1179, § 6; Laws 2005, Act 65, § 3, eff. July 1, 2005; Laws 2006, Act 453, § 40, eff. April 14, 2006.

Formerly Code 1981, § 40–2–36.1.

Historical and Statutory Notes

The 2005 amendment by Act 65 rewrote the section which had read:

"(a) As used in this Code section, the term:

"(1) 'Dealer' means any person engaged in the business of selling or leasing or offering to sell or lease new motor vehicles and who is licensed or otherwise authorized to utilize trademarks or service marks associated with one or more makes of motor vehicles in connection with such sales or leases. The term "dealer" shall not mean any person engaged solely in the business of selling used motor vehicles and shall not mean any person engaged in the solicitation, advertising, or financing of the sale of new motor vehicles and shall not mean any person engaged solely in activities as a manufacturer or distributor of new motor vehicles.

"(2) 'Distributor' means any person who, pursuant to a contract with a manufacturer, sells or offers to sell new motor vehicles to new motor vehicle dealers.

"(3) 'Established place of business' means a permanent salesroom or sales office of a new motor vehicle dealer, which permanent salesroom or sales office is located in a permanent building on an open lot and which is marked by an appropriate sign and at which a permanent business of bartering, trading, or selling of new motor vehicles is carried on in good faith.

"(4) 'Manufacturer' means any person who makes or assembles new motor vehicles.

"(5) 'Motor vehicle' means every self-propelled vehicle intended primarily for use and operation on the public highways, except farm tractors and other machines and tools used in the production, harvesting, and care of farm products and except construction equipment.

"(6) 'New motor vehicle' means a motor vehicle which has been sold to a dealer and on which the original motor vehicle title has not been issued.

"(7) 'Person' means every natural person, partnership, corporation, association, trust, estate, or any other legal entity.

"(8) 'Temporary site' means a location at which new motor vehicles are sold or offered for sale which location is:

"(A) Used for a period not to exceed 96 hours in any one-month period of time;

"(B) Used not more than three times in any calendar year; and

"(C) Located in the county which is within two counties of the county in which the established place of business of the new motor vehicle dealer using the temporary site is located.

"(9) 'Trade shows' means the display or solicitation for sale of new motor vehicles at a location other than the established place of business at which the sales transaction is accomplished or at which delivery of the new motor vehicle is completed.

"(b)(1) It shall be unlawful for any person to engage in any activity as a new motor vehicle dealer unless and until such person has registered with the commissioner and obtained a dealer's number license plate under Code Section 40–2–38 for each established place of business at which the person engages in such activity. The commissioner shall not accept such application for registration and shall not issue a dealer's number license plate unless and until the applicant establishes to the satisfaction of the commissioner, under criteria established by rules or regulations promulgated by the commissioner, that the applicant shall not engage in any activity of a new motor vehicle dealer except at an established place of business or at a temporary site.

"(2) It shall be unlawful for any person to engage in any activity as a new motor vehicle dealer except at an established place of business which has been registered as such under this Code section and Code Section 40–2–38 or at a temporary site.

"(3) This subsection shall not be construed to prohibit new motor vehicle trade shows.

"(c) As an alternative to criminal or other civil enforcement, the commissioner, in order to enforce this Code section or any orders, rules, and regulations promulgated pursuant thereto, may issue an administrative fine not to exceed $1,000.00 for each violation, whenever the commissioner, after a hearing, determines that any person has violated any provisions of this Code section or any regulations or orders promulgated thereunder. The hearing and any administrative review thereof shall be conducted in accordance with the procedure for contested cases under Chapter 13 of Title 50, the "Georgia Administrative Procedure Act." Any person who has exhausted all administrative remedies available and who is aggrieved or adversely affected by a final order or action of the commissioner shall have the right of judicial review thereof in accordance with Chapter 13 of Title 50. All fines recovered under this subsection shall be paid into the state treasury. The commissioner may file, in the superior court (1) wherein the person under order resides; (2) if such person is a corporation, in the county wherein the corporation maintains its established place of business; or (3) in the county wherein the violation occurred, a certified copy of a final order of the commissioner, whether unappealed from or affirmed upon appeal, whereupon the court shall render judgment in accordance therewith and notify the parties. Such judgment shall have the same effect and proceedings in relation thereto shall thereafter be the same as though the judgment had been rendered in an action duly heard and determined by the court. The penalty prescribed in this Code section shall be concurrent, alternative, and cumulative with any and all other civil, criminal, or alternative rights, remedies, forfeitures, or penalties provided, allowed, or available to the commissioner with respect to any violation of this Code section or any order, rules, or regulations promulgated pursuant thereto.

"(d) Any person who violates any provision of this Code section shall be guilty of a misdemeanor."

In 2005, the Code Commission, in subsec. (a), par. (8) and in subpar. (A) of subsec. (b), par. (4), substituted "the department" for "the Department of Motor Vehicle Safety". See § 28–9–5.

The 2006 amendment by Act 453 was a provision contained in a correction bill.

§ 40–2–39.1. Displaying or parking used motor vehicles on property for purpose of selling or advertising sale of such vehicles; violations

(a)(1) An owner or lessee of any real property shall not authorize more than five used motor vehicles within any 12 month period displayed or parked on such real property for the purpose of selling or advertising the sale of such used motor vehicles by the owner or lessee of such vehicles.

(2) An owner or lessee of any real property shall not authorize more than two used motor vehicles at the same time displayed or parked on such real property for the purpose of selling or advertising the sale of such used motor vehicles by the owner or lessee of such vehicles.

(3) An owner or lessee of any used motor vehicle shall not display or park such used motor vehicle on the real property of another for the purpose of selling or advertising the sale of such used motor vehicle if the display or parking of such vehicle will cause the owner or lessee of the real property to be in violation of paragraph (1) or (2) of this subsection.

(4) An owner or lessee of any used motor vehicle shall not display or park such used motor vehicle on the real property of another for the purpose of selling or advertising the sale of such used motor vehicle unless the owner or lessee of such vehicle has the prior permission of the owner or lessee of the real property.

(b) The provisions of subsection (a) of this Code section shall not apply:

(1) If the owner or lessee of the vehicle displayed or parked is employed by the owner or lessee of the real property on which the vehicle is displayed or parked;

(2) If the owner or lessee of the vehicle displayed or parked is conducting business with the owner or lessee of the real property on which the vehicle is parked or displayed at the time such vehicle is displayed or parked; or

(3) If the real property on which a vehicle is parked is a parking lot for which a fee is charged for the use of such parking lot, the owner or lessee of the parked vehicle has paid the fee for the use of such parking lot, and such vehicle is legitimately parked on the property for purposes other than displaying, selling, or advertising the sale of such vehicle.

(c)(1) An owner or lessee of any real property shall not authorize any used motor vehicle to be displayed or parked on such real property for the purpose of selling or advertising the sale of such used motor vehicle if such vehicle is not lawfully titled and registered in the name of the individual or entity offering such vehicle for sale in accordance with the applicable provisions of this chapter and Chapter 3 of this title.

(2) A person shall not advertise, display, sell, or offer for sale any used motor vehicle unless such vehicle is lawfully titled and registered in such person's name in accordance with the applicable provisions of this chapter and Chapter 3 of this title.

(d) Any law enforcement officer or agency, the board, or the owner or lessee of any real property upon which a vehicle is displayed or parked in violation of subsection (a) or (c) of this Code section for longer than 24 consecutive hours may have any such vehicle towed from such real property and stored at the expense of the owner or lessee of such vehicle and may then dispose of said vehicle in accordance with Chapter 11 of this title.

(e) A violation of this Code section shall constitute an unfair or deceptive act or practice and shall be a violation of Part 2 of Article 15 of Chapter 1 of Title 10, the "Fair Business Practices Act of 1975." A violation of this Code section may be penalized as provided in Code Section 43–47–21 or any other applicable provision of this Code, including, but not limited to, the "Fair Business Practices Act of 1975."

(f) This Code section shall not apply to any person licensed under Chapter 47 of Title 43 or to any franchised motor vehicle dealer or any subsidiary wholly owned or controlled by such dealer. This Code section shall not eliminate or change the requirement for any person to obtain a license under Chapter 47 of Title 43 if such person engages in any conduct or activity for which a license is required under Chapter 47 of Title 43.

(g) Any person who violates this Code section shall be guilty of a misdemeanor and, upon conviction thereof, shall be subject to a fine not to exceed $1,000.00 for each violation or imprisonment for a period not to exceed 12 months, or both.

Laws 2007, Act 124, § 2, eff. July 1, 2007.

Historical and Statutory Notes

Laws 2007, Act 124, § 4, provides:

"This Act shall be effective on July 1, 2007. Prosecutions for or cases involving any violation of law occurring prior to the effective date of this Act shall not be affected by the repeals or amendments made by it or abated by reason thereof."

§ 40-2-40. Registration of vehicle after owner's registration period; penalties

(a) The owner of a vehicle required to be registered under Code Section 40-2-20 which was registered for the previous year, who has failed to comply with Code Section 40-2-20 for the current year shall be deemed and held to be a delinquent under this Code section; and the registration of such vehicle shall, after the expiration of the owner's registration period, be subject to a penalty of 25 percent of the registration fee for such vehicle in addition to the fee provided by law, provided that such penalty shall in no event be levied prior to the expiration of the owner's registration period, notwithstanding that the owner failed to register such vehicle within an initial registration period.

(b) All applications for the registration of a delinquent vehicle shall, before being accepted by a tag agent, be first endorsed by a sheriff or a deputy sheriff, a chief of police or his or her designated representative, a state law enforcement officer, a tax commissioner, or a tax collector. The officer endorsing the delinquent application shall indicate, with his or her endorsement on the application, the total amount of the prescribed registration fee together with the 25 percent penalty provided in this Code section, and the full total of such amount shall be paid to the tag agent before any license plate or revalidation decal as provided for in this chapter shall be assigned to the applicant.

(c) All penalties assessed under this Code section shall be accredited in the office of the tag agent when received in the name of the officer making the endorsement, without regard to the residence of the applicant, whether such penalty is received through the exercise of such officer's authority as an arresting officer or through appearance of the applicant at his office for proper endorsement on an application.

(d) Between the first and fifth days of each calendar month, the tag agent shall remit to the respective fiscal authorities of the counties or cities employing the endorsing officers the full amount of such penalties accredited to such officers during and for the preceding calendar month. All sums accredited to state law enforcement officers shall be paid to the fiscal authorities of the county where the vehicle is registered.

Laws 1931, p. 7, § 84; Laws 1931, p. 213, § 1; Laws 1943, p. 341, § 2; Laws 1953, Jan.-Feb. Sess., p. 392, § 2; Laws 1959, p. 351, § 1; Laws 1969, p. 266, § 1; Laws 1973, p. 595, § 2; Laws 1973, p. 781, § 1; Laws 1974, p. 414, § 1; Laws 1986, p. 1053, § 4; Laws 1990, p. 2048, § 2; Laws 1995, p. 809, § 6; Laws 1996, p. 1118, § 5; Laws 1997, p. 419, § 9; Laws 2000, p. 523, § 2; Laws 2001, p. 4, § 40; Laws 2005, Act 68, § 14-3.1, eff. July 1, 2005.

Formerly Code 1933, § 68-201; Code 1981, § 40-2-37.

Historical and Statutory Notes

In 2001, the Code Commission, in subsec. (d), substituted "state patrolmen" for "state patrolman". See § 28-9-5.

The 2005 amendment by Act 68, in the first sentence of subsec. (b), substituted "a state law enforcement officer," for "a state patrolman, a state revenue special agent or enforcement officer, a Department of Transportation enforcement officer,"; and, in the second sentence of subsec. (d), substituted "state law enforcement officers" for "state patrolmen, state revenue special agents or enforcement officers, or Department of Transportation enforcement officers".

§ 40-2-41. Display of license plates

Unless otherwise permitted under this chapter, every vehicle required to be registered under this chapter, which is in use upon the highways, shall at all times display the license plate issued to the owner for such vehicle, and the plate shall be fastened to the rear of the vehicle in a position so as not to swing and shall be at all times plainly visible. No person shall display on the rear of a motor vehicle any temporary or permanent plate or tag not issued by the State of Georgia which is intended to resemble a license plate which is issued by the State of Georgia. The commissioner is authorized to adopt rules and regulations so as to permit the display of a license plate on the front of certain vehicles. It shall be the duty of the operator of any vehicle to keep the license plate legible at all times. No license plate shall be covered with any material unless the material is colorless and transparent. No apparatus that obstructs or hinders the clear display and legibility of a license plate shall be attached to the rear of any motor vehicle required to be registered in the state. Any person who violates any provision of this Code section shall be guilty of a misdemeanor.

Laws 1927, p. 226, § 8; Laws 1977, p. 596, § 1; Laws 1982, p. 1584, §§ 3, 6; Laws 1990, p. 2048, § 2; Laws 1991, p. 779, § 1; Laws 1992, p. 6, § 40; Laws 1997, p. 419, § 10; Laws 2000, p. 523, § 3.

Formerly Code 1933, § 68-215; Code 1981, § 40-2-38.

§ 40-2-41.1. Display of authentic historical Georgia license plates

(a) As used in this Code section, the term "authentic historical Georgia license plate" means a license plate originally issued in the year 1970 or earlier and originally required to be displayed on motor vehicles operated upon the streets and highways of this state in the year 1970 or earlier pursuant to former motor vehicle registration laws of this state.

(b) The owner of any antique motor vehicle manufactured in 1970 or earlier shall be authorized to display in lieu of and in the same manner as the license plate otherwise required under Code Section 40-2-41 an authentic historical Georgia license plate which clearly represents the model year of any such antique motor vehicle, provided that the owner has properly registered such antique motor vehicle for the current year as otherwise required under this chapter and has obtained a current Georgia license plate or revalidation decal for such antique motor vehicle. Such currently valid Georgia license plate shall be kept in such antique motor vehicle at all times but need not be displayed in a manner to be visible from outside the vehicle.

(c) For purposes of this Code section, the authentic historical Georgia license plate shall be furnished by the owner of any such antique motor vehicle.

(d) No later than January 1, 2006, the commissioner shall have installed within the department's computer information system applicable to the registration of motor vehicles the necessary program which will include in the information relating to the current Georgia license plate or revalidation decal issued for an antique motor vehicle the information relating to the authentic historical Georgia license plate authorized to be displayed on such antique motor vehicle.

Laws 1999, p. 791, § 2; Laws 2001, p. 1021, § 2; Laws 2002, p. 415, § 40; Laws 2005, Act 110, § 1, eff. July 1, 2005.

§ 40–2–42. Transferring license plates and decals

(a) A license plate or revalidation decal, when issued, shall be transferred from one vehicle to another vehicle of the same class acquired by the same person as provided in this chapter. Any use of a license plate or revalidation decal by any other person or persons in any manner not provided for in this chapter shall be a violation of this chapter.

(b) The commissioner shall provide by rules and regulations appropriate procedures whereby, upon the payment of a fee of $5.00, and, upon preparation and filing of an appropriate application therefor, currently valid annual and five-year license plates and revalidation decals shall be transferred from one vehicle to another vehicle of the same class of which ownership is acquired following that person's or those persons' ceasing to own or operate on the public roads the vehicle for which such plate was originally issued and during the initial registration period for the acquired vehicle. If such acquired vehicle is of a different class than the vehicle no longer owned or operated by such person, he or she shall submit the license plate currently issued to him or her for cancellation and, upon payment of any additional fee for registering such acquired vehicle, the commissioner shall issue a new license plate to such person for use on such acquired vehicle. License plates and revalidation decals may be transferred in accordance with the provisions of this subsection at any time after issuance or renewal thereof and until the expiration of the period for which issued.

(c) The commissioner shall provide appropriate procedures whereby, when the registered owner of a jointly owned motor vehicle is deceased, the license plate issued for the motor vehicle may, upon appropriate application and payment of fees, be transferred to the surviving owner's name, provided that the surviving owner acquires a new certificate of title under subsection (d) or paragraph (1) of subsection (e) of Code Section 40–3–34 and makes the payment of appropriate ad valorem taxes.

Laws 1927, p. 226, § 8; Laws 1931, p. 7, § 84; Laws 1939, p. 182, § 2; Laws 1969, p. 266, § 3; Laws 1972, p. 178, § 1; Laws 1979, p. 615, § 2; Laws 1981, p. 714, § 3; Laws 1990, p. 8, § 40; Laws 1990, p. 2048, § 2; Laws 1992, p. 779, § 3; Laws 1997, p. 419, § 11; Laws 1998, p. 1179, § 7.

Formerly Code 1933, § 68–214; Code 1981, § 40–2–39.

§ 40–2–43. Certificate of registration; duplicate registration certificates; fee

(a) Upon an applicant's compliance with all laws relevant to the registration of his vehicle, the appropriate licensing authority shall issue to such applicant a certificate of registration for his vehicle. If a registration certificate issued under this chapter is lost, stolen, mutilated, or destroyed or becomes illegible, the registered owner shall promptly make application for a duplicate registration certificate to the commissioner. The commissioner, upon receipt of an application and a fee of $1.00, shall issue the registered owner a duplicate registration certificate. If the application for a duplicate registration certificate is submitted to the same county that issued the current certificate of registration, the county tag agent may issue the duplicate registration certificate and may retain the application fee as compensation for issuing such duplicate certificate of registration.

(b) Any dealer or owner of a vehicle may apply to the commissioner or any county tag agent for a duplicate of the last registration certificate issued to the previous or current owner for that vehicle. The commissioner or county tag agent, upon receipt of an application and a fee of $1.00, shall provide the duplicate registration certificate.

Laws 1925, p. 315, § 1; Laws 1931, p. 7, § 84; Laws 1978, p. 901, § 1; Laws 1985, p. 149, § 40; Laws 1985, p. 1276, § 1; Laws 1986, p. 1333, § 2; Laws 1990, p. 2048, § 2; Laws 1997, p. 419, § 11A; Laws 1998, p. 1179, § 8.

Formerly Code 1933, § 68–206; Code 1981, § 40–2–41.

§ 40–2–44. Report of theft, loss, or mutilation of license plate or revalidation decal; duplicate license plate or revalidation decal

(a) Except as provided in subsection (b) of this Code section, the owner of a motor vehicle shall immediately report the theft, loss, or mutilation of a license plate or revalidation decal to the appropriate law enforcement agency or official, including but not limited to a municipal or county police department or officer, the county sheriff, the Department of Public Safety, or the Georgia State Patrol. Said owner shall obtain a copy of the police report and shall submit such copy to the commissioner with a fee of $8.00 to obtain a duplicate license plate or revalidation decal. Alternatively, the copy of the police report may be submitted to the applicant's county tag agent with a fee of $8.00 in which case the county tag agent is authorized to issue a replacement license plate or decal. In those instances in which a vehicle owner is unable to obtain a police report of such theft, loss, or mutilation of a license plate or revalidation decal, the owner shall be authorized to submit to the appropriate law enforcement agency or official and to either the commissioner or to the county tag agent a sworn affidavit as to such theft, loss, or mutilation in lieu of a police report and obtain a replacement license plate or decal. The county tag agent shall be entitled to retain as compensation for issuance of a replacement license plate or decal the same commission as provided for issuance of a new license plate or decal under the terms and conditions provided in subsection (b) of Code Section 40–2–33.

(b) If the license plate or revalidation decal is mutilated but still legible and if such license plate or revalidation decal is surrendered with the application for the duplicate, the requirements of subsection (a) of this Code section, relating to reporting the theft, loss, or mutilation of a license plate or decal and submitting a copy of a police report, shall not apply.

(c) A duplicate county decal when the original has been lost, defaced, or destroyed may be obtained from the commissioner at no cost. A replacement license plate or revalidation decal when the original has been lost in the mail prior to receipt by the registered owner shall be issued by the commissioner without charge upon application and completion of the form and affidavit prescribed by the commissioner setting forth the circumstances of nonreceipt of the license plate or decal. The owner shall report the nonreceipt or loss of the license plate or decal to the appropriate law enforcement agency or official, including, but not limited to, a municipal or county police department or officer, the county sheriff, or the Department of Public Safety. Said owner shall obtain a copy of the police report on which the license plate or decal number is listed and shall submit such copy to the commissioner. The owner shall not be charged a fee by the Department of Public Safety or the local law enforcement agency or official for a copy of such police report.

(d) The commissioner is authorized to establish procedures and promulgate rules and regulations for carrying out this Code section.

Laws 1927, p. 226, § 8; Laws 1931, p. 7, § 84; Laws 1939, p. 182, § 2; Laws 1969, p. 266, § 3; Laws 1974, p. 397, § 1; Laws 1979, p. 615, § 2; Laws 1981, p. 714, § 3; Laws 1982, p. 1584, §§ 1, 4; Laws 1983, p. 676, § 1; Laws 1985, p. 1278, § 1; Laws 1988, p. 380, § 2; Laws 1990, p. 2048, § 2; Laws 1992, p. 2978, § 2; Laws 1993, p. 91, § 40; Laws 1994, p. 1851, § 1; Laws 1995, p. 742, § 1; Laws 2000, p. 951, § 3–9.

Formerly Code 1933, § 68–214; Code 1981, § 40–2–40; Code 1981, § 40–2–42.

§ 40–2–45. Transferring license plates and decals to and from salvage or rebuilt motor vehicles

(a) No person shall transfer a license plate or decal from one vehicle to any other motor vehicle which is a "salvage" or "rebuilt" motor vehicle as provided in Chapter 3 of this title unless the owner of such vehicle submits satisfactory proof to the commissioner that the motor vehicle inspection required by Code Section 40–3–37 has been performed and such vehicle has been determined to be in full compliance with the law.

(b) Notwithstanding subsection (a) of this Code section, if a vehicle is damaged, scrapped, dismantled, or demolished and transferred to an insurance company or licensed rebuilder and the transferor of such vehicle has a current, unexpired license plate and registration issued therefor, such license plate shall be transferred to another vehicle acquired by such transferor according to the provisions of Code Section 40–2–42 or 40–2–80, as applicable.

Laws 1989, p. 1186, § 1; Laws 1990, p. 2048, § 2; Laws 1997, p. 419, § 12; Laws 1998, p. 1179, § 9.

Formerly Code 1981, § 40–2–43.

§ 40–2–46. Repealed by Laws 1998, p. 128, § 40, eff. March 27, 1998, and Laws 1998, p. 1179, § 10, eff. May 1, 1998

§ 40–2–47. Permanent license plates for certain trailers

(a) Notwithstanding any other provision of this chapter to the contrary, the owner of any trailer, including:

(1) Any leased or rented trailer and including single pole and twin-beam trailers and other trailers used in commercial logging or commercial trailers used for the hauling of unprocessed farm products used as or in connection with a motor vehicle, truck, or tractor used as a common or contract carrier for hire, a private carrier, or a motor carrier of property; or

(2) Any boat trailer, utility trailer, or noncommercial cattle and livestock trailer, shall have the option of obtaining a permanent registration and license plate for such trailer, in lieu of an annual registration and license plate, upon the payment of the one-time fee specified in Code Section 40–2–151 and compliance with the provisions of this Code section.

(b) The certificate of registration and license plate issued for a specific trailer under this Code section shall continue to be valid for the duration of the owner's interest in such trailer. No registration or license plate issued for any trailer under this Code section shall be transferred for any reason and a new registration and license plate shall be required when ownership of the trailer is transferred to a new owner. The payment of the fee for a permanent registration and license plate shall be in addition to and not in lieu of the payment of annual ad valorem taxes on such trailer during the period of December 1 to February 15.

(c) As used in this Code section, the term "leased or rented trailer" means any utility trailer that is owned by and leased or rented out by a person, firm, or corporation in the business of leasing or renting out such trailers.

Laws 1994, p. 1373, § 1; Laws 1995, p. 742, § 2; Laws 1997, p. 419, § 12A; Laws 2002, p. 1074, § 5; Laws 2009, Act 101, § 2, eff. Jan. 1, 2010.

Historical and Statutory Notes

Laws 2009, Act 101, § 4 provided:

"Section 3A of this Act shall become effective upon its approval by the Governor or upon its becoming law without such approval. The remaining sections of this Act shall become effective on January 1, 2010, and shall apply to registration and licensing of trailers on and after such date."

§ 40–2–48. Repealed by Laws 2006, Act 947, § 3, eff. January 1, 2007

Historical and Statutory Notes

The repealed section, relating to special license plates to support United States Disabled Athletes Fund, was derived from Laws 1995, p. 238, § 1; Laws 1997, p. 1415, § 1; Laws 1998, p. 1179, § 11. The repealing law also reserved the section designation.

Laws 2006, Act 947, § 13, provides:

"(a) This Act [repealing and reserving this section] shall become effective on January 1, 2007, except as otherwise provided in subsection (b) of this section.

"(b) If an amendment to the Constitution of the State of Georgia authorizing the dedication of revenue from sales of special license plates to agencies, funds, or nonprofit corporations designated by the General Assembly is not ratified at the general election in 2006, this Act shall be repealed in its entirety on January 1, 2007, and no such motor vehicle license plates shall be issued pursuant to this Act."

An amendment to Article III, § IX, Par. VI, of the Georgia constitution, authorizing such a dedication, was approved by the electorate at the general election held on November 7, 2006.

Laws 2010, Act 360, § 1–75, repealed the reserved designation, effective May 12, 2010.

§ 40–2–49. Repealed by Laws 2006, Act 947, § 4, eff. January 1, 2007

Historical and Statutory Notes

The repealed section, relating to the special license plates to promote the wildlife conservation fund, was derived from Laws 1995, p. 1021, § 1; Laws 1997, p. 419, § 13; Laws 1998, p. 1179, § 12. The repealing law also reserved the section designation.

Laws 2006, Act 947, § 13, provides:

"(a) This Act [repealing and reserving this section] shall become effective on January 1, 2007, except as otherwise provided in subsection (b) of this section.

"(b) If an amendment to the Constitution of the State of Georgia authorizing the dedication of revenue from sales of special license plates to agencies, funds, or nonprofit corporations designated by the General Assembly is not ratified at the general election in 2006, this Act shall be repealed in its entirety on January 1, 2007, and no such motor vehicle license plates shall be issued pursuant to this Act."

An amendment to Article III, § IX, Par. VI, of the Georgia constitution, authorizing such a dedication, was approved by the electorate at the general election held on November 7, 2006.

Laws 2010, Act 360, § 1–75 repealed the reserved designation, effective May 12, 2010.

§ 40–2–49.1. Repealed by Laws 2006, Act 947, § 5, eff. January 1, 2007

Historical and Statutory Notes

The repealed section, relating to special license plates to promote the restoration and enhancement of the bobwhite quail population, was derived from Laws 1999, p. 791, § 1. The repealing law also reserved the section designation.

Laws 2006, Act 947, § 13, provides:

"(a) This Act [repealing and reserving this section] shall become effective on January 1, 2007, except as otherwise provided in subsection (b) of this section.

"(b) If an amendment to the Constitution of the State of Georgia authorizing the dedication of revenue from sales of special license plates to agencies, funds, or nonprofit corporations designated by the General Assembly is not ratified at the general election in 2006, this Act shall be repealed in its entirety on January 1, 2007, and no such motor vehicle license plates shall be issued pursuant to this Act."

An amendment to Article III, § IX, Par. VI, of the Georgia constitution, authorizing such a dedication, was approved by the electorate at the general election held on November 7, 2006.

Laws 2010, Act 360, § 1–75 repealed the reserved designation, effective May 12, 2010.

§ 40–2–49.2. Repealed by Laws 2010, Act 360, § 1–75, eff. May 12, 2010

Historical and Statutory Notes

The repealed section, relating to special license plates to promote roadside enhancement and beautification projects and programs, was derived from Laws 2001, p. 1021, § 3.

§ 40–2–49.3. Repealed by Laws 2010, Act 360, § 1–75, eff. May 12, 2010

Historical and Statutory Notes

The repealed section, relating to special license plates promoting dog and cat reproductive sterilization support programs, was derived from Laws 2002, p. 1215, § 2.

Article 2A

Fleet Vehicles

§ 40–2–50. Definitions

As used in this article, the term:

(1) "Fleet" means 1,000 or more motor vehicles.

(2) "Fleet registration plan" means the method of registering the motor vehicles of a fleet as provided in this article.

Laws 1998, p. 1179, § 12A.

§ 40–2–51. Enrollment

(a)(1) A corporation or firm which has an established place of business in this state or which is controlled by a parent corporation which has an established place of business in this state and which owns or operates under a lease agreement a fleet which is not required to be registered under the International Registration Plan in accordance with Article 3A of this chapter may enroll in the fleet registration plan and register and obtain licenses to operate the motor vehicles in such fleet as provided in this article.

(2) The provisions of this article for fleet enrollment, registration, and licensing shall not apply to any corporation or firm which leases or rents motor vehicles to other persons for use thereby.

(b)(1) Applications for enrollment of a fleet under the fleet registration plan may be submitted to the department in the form and manner prescribed thereby during the period of December 1 of the prior registration year to February 15 of the year for which the license plates are to be issued. Motor vehicles of a fleet shall be enrolled separately by classes and by counties where the vehicles are to be registered.

(2)(A) An applicant for enrollment of a fleet under the fleet registration plan shall pay a fleet enrollment fee of $200.00 for initial enrollment of the fleet.

(B) If the applicant for enrollment of a fleet or the parent corporation or firm thereof has not had an established place of business in this state for a period of ten consecutive years or more, the applicant shall post a $25,000.00 surety bond at the time of applying for enrollment.

(3) If the department determines that the applicant is eligible for fleet registration and proper application has been made, the department shall enroll the fleet, indicate the amount of license fees due for the fleet, validate the enrollment form or forms for the applicable county or counties, and mail the validated original enrollment form or forms with fees indicated to the applicant. Such enrollment shall be valid for a period which is concurrent with that period for which regular license plates are issued for use under Code Section 40–2–31. Thereafter, the department shall, prior to December 1 of each year of the enrollment period, mail the enrollee a statement of the amount of license fees due and payable during the forthcoming registration period for such fleet.

Laws 1998, p. 1179, § 12A.

§ 40–2–52. Registering and licensing of vehicles

(a) After receipt of a validated fleet enrollment form, the owner or operator of the enrolled fleet shall register and obtain licenses to operate the motor vehicles thereof during the period of December 1 of the prior registration year to February 15 of the year for which the license plates are to be issued.

(b) An applicant for registration of a vehicle of an enrolled fleet shall submit a validated original fleet enrollment form to the county tag agent in each county in which vehicles enrolled under the fleet registration plan are to be registered.

(c) The provisions of Article 2 of this chapter for registering and licensing motor vehicles generally which are not inconsistent with the provisions of this article shall apply to the registration and licensing of each vehicle of an enrolled fleet.

Laws 1998, p. 1179, § 12A.

§ 40–2–53. Issuance of license plates; renewal; transfer

(a)(1) Upon submission by the applicant of a validated original fleet enrollment form and compliance with all applicable requirements for registration and licensing of motor vehicles, the county tag agent shall issue to the applicant a fleet motor vehicle license plate for each vehicle of the fleet to be registered and licensed in such county.

(2) The county tag agent shall mark the validated original fleet enrollment form as "taxes paid" or "tax exempt," as applicable, and return such form to the registrant.

(3) The registrant shall submit to the department the validated original fleet enrollment form which has been marked as provided in paragraph (2) of this subsection.

(b) Fleet motor vehicle license plates shall be similar in design to and issued for the same period as regular license plates issued under Code Section 40–2–31, except that such fleet motor vehicle license plates shall contain such words or symbols, in addition to the numbers and letters otherwise prescribed by law, so as to distinctively identify the motor vehicles on which they are placed as fleet motor vehicles. It shall be a requirement that a county name decal shall be affixed and displayed on license plates issued under this Code section.

(c)(1) License plates issued under this Code section shall be renewed annually with a generic fleet revalidation decal.

(2) The bond required under subsection (b) of Code Section 40–2–51 shall be required at the time of any renewal of such license plates if at the time of such renewal the registrant or the parent corporation or firm thereof has not had an established place of business in this state for a period of ten consecutive years or more.

(d) License plates issued under this Code section shall be transferred between vehicles in the same manner as provided by Code Section 40–2–80 for special license plates issued under Article 3 of this chapter.

Laws 1998, p. 1179, § 12A.

§ 40–2–54. Audits of fleet registrants

(a) If a fleet registrant or the parent corporation or firm thereof has not had an established place of business in this state for a period of ten consecutive years or more, the department or its designated agent shall annually conduct an audit of such fleet registrant to ensure compliance with the requirements of this article which may include, without limitation, examination of records of all vehicles in a fleet, additions to or deletions from a fleet since the most recent such audit, and proof of proper payment of or exemption from ad valorem taxes on fleet vehicles. The fleet registrant shall bear the cost of or reimburse the department for the expenses of any audit required by this subsection.

(b) The department or its designated agent may perform an audit of any fleet registrant to ensure compliance with the requirements of this article which may include, without limitation, examination of records of all vehicles in a fleet, additions to or deletions from a fleet since the most recent such audit, and proof of proper payment of or exemption from ad valorem taxes on fleet vehicles.

Laws 1998, p. 1179, § 12A.

§ 40–2–55. Termination of enrollment

An enrollment of a fleet in the fleet registration plan shall be terminated by the department in the event:

(1) The department determines on the basis of an audit that fees for registration and licensing are not paid as required for 20 percent or more of the vehicles in any class of vehicles in the fleet or of those vehicles of the fleet registered in a county;

(2) The department determines on the basis of an audit that fees for registration and licensing are not paid as required for 5 percent or more of the total vehicles in the fleet;

(3) Of the conviction of the fleet registrant for any unlawful use of any license plate issued for a fleet vehicle;

(4) Of the failure of the fleet registrant to pay ad valorem taxes as required for any fleet vehicle;

(5) Of the failure of the fleet registrant to pay enrollment fees as required; or

(6) Of the forfeiture of the surety bond required under Code Section 40–2–52 or 40–2–53.

Laws 1998, p. 1179, § 12A.

Article 3

Prestige License Plates and Special Plates for Certain Persons and Vehicles

§ 40–2–60. Prestige license plates; fee

(a) Motor vehicle owners who are residents of Georgia, upon complying with the motor vehicle laws relating to registration and licensing of motor vehicles and, except as provided in subsection (c) of this Code section, upon the payment of a fee of $35.00 in addition to the regular motor vehicle registration fee, shall be issued special personalized prestige license plates by the commissioner. Special personalized license plates issued pursuant to this Code section shall be subject to an additional annual registration fee of $35.00 as a condition of obtaining an annual revalidation decal for such license plate which fee shall be collected by the county tag agent at the time of collection of other registration fees and shall be remitted to the state as provided in Code Section 40–2–34.

(b) For the purpose of this Code section, a license plate with a low number or special number may also be considered as a prestige or personalized plate.

(c) Additional fees for special or distinctive license plates issued pursuant to this article shall be as prescribed in the Code section authorizing such plate, and, when no additional fee is specified, no additional fee shall be required.

(d) The commissioner is authorized to establish procedures and promulgate rules and regulations for carrying out this Code section.

Laws 1968, p. 1404, §§ 2, 3, 5; Laws 1985, p. 261, § 1; Laws 1990, p. 2048, § 2; Laws 1992, p. 779, § 4; Laws 2010, Act 360, § 1–69, eff. May 12, 2010.

§ 40–2–60.1. Rules and regulations for issuance of special license plates

(a) The General Assembly finds that in recent years numerous laws were enacted providing for the issuance of special license plates for certain persons and vehicles. The General Assembly finds that there exists a need for a standardized administrative process to provide for the authorization of issuance of such special license plates and that the public interest will be best served by such a standardized administrative process. While recognizing that the legislature may not abridge or delegate its powers, the General Assembly declares that it is in the public interest of this state for future proposals for special license plates to be governed by the administrative process established by this Code section rather than by the legislative process.

(b)(1) The General Assembly determines that the issuance of special license plates to support an agency, fund, or program beneficial to the people of this state that is administered by a nonprofit corporation organized under Section 501(c)(3) of Title 26 of the Internal Revenue Code and the dedication of a portion of the funds raised from the issuance of these special license plates is in the best interests of the people of this state and is authorized by Article III, Section IX, Paragraph VI(n) of the Constitution.

(2) The commissioner is authorized to adopt rules and regulations for the issuance of special license plates for groups of individuals and vehicles. All special license plates issued pursuant to this paragraph shall not be subject to the provisions of subsection (e) of this Code section.

(c) As used in this Code section, the term:

(1) "Manufacturing fee" means a $25.00 fee paid at the time an application is submitted or upon the issuance of a special license plate.

(2) "Registration fee" means the fees as set forth in Code Section 40–2–151.

(3) "Special license plate" means a license plate that is authorized under this Code section that commemorates an event or supports an agency, fund, or program beneficial to the people of this state or is specifically authorized by the General Assembly for certain persons or vehicles.

(4) "Special license plate fee" means a $35. 00 fee paid at the time a special license plate is issued.

(5) "Special license plate renewal fee" means a $35.00 fee paid at the time a special license plate is renewed and a revalidation decal is issued.

(c.1) Any special license plate issued under the provisions of this Code section shall be subject to the manufacturing fee, special license plate fee, and special license plate renewal fee provided for in this Code section.

(d) The agency, fund, or nonprofit corporation sponsoring a special license plate, in cooperation with the commissioner, shall design a special distinctive license plate appropriate to promote the program benefited by the issuance of the special license plate. Special license plates for groups of individuals and vehicles shall be readily recognizable by the insertion of an appropriate logo or graphic identifying the special nature of the license plate. All special license plates must be of the same size as general issue motor vehicle license plates and shall include a unique design and identifying number, whereby the total number of characters does not exceed an amount to be determined by the commissioner. No two recipients shall receive identically numbered plates. . Spaces for county name labels are required for license plates authorized under this Code section unless expressly eliminated by the request of the agency, fund, or nonprofit corporation sponsoring a special license plate at the time the license plate is designed.

(e) Before the department disburses to the agency, fund, or nonprofit corporation funds from the issuance of special license plates, the agency, fund, or nonprofit corporation must provide a written statement stating the manner in which such funds will be utilized. In addition, a nonprofit corporation must provide the department with documentation of its nonprofit status under Section 501(c)(3) of Title 26 of the Internal Revenue Code. The agency, fund, or nonprofit corporation shall periodically provide to the commissioner an audit of the use of the funds or other evidence of use of the funds satisfactory to the commissioner. If it is determined that the funds are not being used for the purposes set forth in the statement provided by the agency, fund, or nonprofit corporation, the department shall withhold payment of such funds until such noncompliance issues are resolved.

(f) Notwithstanding the other provisions of this Code section, no special license plate shall be produced until such time as the State of Georgia has, through a licensing agreement or otherwise, received such licenses or other permissions as may be required to produce the special license plate. The department shall not utilize any graphic that is copyrighted unless a sponsoring organization has secured for the state the authority to utilize the copyrighted design at no cost to the state and the sponsoring organization has agreed to hold the state harmless against any related claim of copyright violation or infringement. The design of the initial edition of any special license plate, as well as the design of subsequent editions and excepting only any part or parts of the designs owned by others and licensed to the state, shall be owned solely by the State of Georgia for its exclusive use and control, except as authorized by the commissioner. The commissioner may take such steps as may be necessary to give notice of and protect such right, including the copyright or copyrights. However, such steps shall be cumulative of the ownership and exclusive use and control established by this subsection as a matter of law, and no person shall reproduce or otherwise use such design or designs, except as authorized by the commissioner.

(g) Any Georgia resident who is the owner of a motor vehicle, except a commercial vehicle as defined in 49 C.F.R. Section 390.5, upon complying with the motor vehicle laws relating to registration and licensing of motor vehicles and payment of the appropriate fees as set forth in this Code section in addition to the required motor vehicle registration fee, shall be able to apply for a special license plate as provided in this Code section.

(h) Any party requesting a special license plate not previously authorized by this chapter shall make application with the department. The application shall include a design of the proposed license plate and a bond of $50,000.00 to serve as surety for moneys collected from applicants by the sponsor. The commissioner shall review and approve or disapprove all applications within 30 days of receipt by the department. Upon approval of the design by the commissioner, the special license plate authorized pursuant to this subsection shall not be issued except upon the receipt by the department of at least 1,000 prepaid applications together with the manufacturing fees within two years after the date of approval by the commissioner. After such time if the minimum number of applications is not met, the department shall not continue to accept the manufacturing fees, and all fees held by the department and the sponsor shall be refunded to applicants; provided, however, that once the department has received 1,000 prepaid applications along with the manufacturing fees, the sponsor shall not be entitled to a refund.

(i) Upon the receipt of 1,000 applications together with manufacturing fees, the commissioner shall provide a letter of certification to the sponsor verifying that the sponsor has satisfied the requirements of the provisions of this Code section. Upon receipt of the letter of certification, the sponsor, if necessary, shall seek enactment of the appropriate legislation required to authorize manufacture of the special license plate.

(j) The department shall not be required to continue to manufacture a special license plate or accept renewals and applications if the number of active registrations falls below 500 registrations at any time during a calendar year. A current registrant may continue to renew such special license plate during his or her annual registration period. The department may continue to issue such special license plates that it has in its inventory to assist in achieving the minimum number of registrations. If the number of active registrations for the special license plate falls below 500 at any time during a calendar year, the sponsoring agency, fund, or nonprofit corporation shall be required to obtain 1,000 applications accompanied by the manufacturing fee to continue to manufacture the special license plate.

(k) Special license plates shall be transferred from one vehicle to another vehicle in accordance with the provisions of Code Section 40–2–80.

(*l*) Special license plates shall be issued within 30 days of application once the requirements of this Code section have been met.

(m) The commissioner is authorized and directed to establish procedures and promulgate rules and regulations to effectuate the purposes of this Code section. The rules and regulations to be promulgated by the commissioner may provide for exceptions whereby a special license plate will not be issued if the issuance of the plate would adversely affect public safety.

Laws 1997, p. 1559, § 2; Laws 1998, p. 1179, § 12B; Laws 2000, p. 951, § 3–10; Laws 2002, p. 1215, § 3; Laws 2005, Act 363, § 1, eff. Jan. 1, 2006; Laws 2006, Act 453, § 40(2), eff. April 14, 2006; Laws 2007, Act 62, § 1, eff. July 1, 2007; Laws 2010, Act 360, § 1–70, eff. May 12, 2010.

§ 40–2–61. Distinctive license plates for certain elected officials

The commissioner shall design and issue distinctive license plates to each United States Senator and Congressman elected from the State of Georgia, the Governor, the Lieutenant Governor, the Speaker of the House of Representatives, and each Justice of the Supreme Court and each Judge of the Court of Appeals to be placed on such official's personal motor vehicle. Each such distinctive license plate shall indicate the individual's elected office and no county name decal need be affixed to such plate. The special license plate authorized by this Code section shall be issued to such elected official upon application and payment of a manufacturing fee of $25.00 and upon compliance with the state laws relating to registration and licensing of motor vehicles and shall be transferred as provided in Code Section 40–2–80. Distinctive license plates issued pursuant to this Code section shall be renewed annually, and revalidation decals shall be issued upon compliance with the laws relating to registration and licensing and upon payment of an additional registration fee of $35.00 which shall be collected by the county tag agent at the time for collection of other registration fees and shall be remitted to the state as provided in Code Section 40–2–34.

Laws 1989, p. 1186, § 2; Laws 1990, p. 1902, § 1; Laws 1990, p. 2048, § 2; Laws 1992, p. 779, § 4.1; Laws 1997, p. 419, § 14; Laws 2010, Act 360, § 1–71, eff. May 12, 2010.

Formerly Code 1981, § 40–2–60.1.

§ 40–2–62. Special and distinctive license plates for members of General Assembly

The commissioner shall mail special and distinctive license plates printed for members of the General Assembly to the local tag agent in the counties wherein such members reside on or before the owner's registration period each year. Such special and distinctive license plates shall be issued only upon applications made to the local tag agent and payment of a $25.00 manufacturing fee. License plates may be issued by the local tag agent upon a proper application and in accordance with the terms of this chapter. License plates issued pursuant to this Code section need not contain a place for the county name decal, and no county name decal need be affixed to a license plate issued pursuant to this Code section. Special and distinctive license plates issued pursuant to this Code section shall be renewed annually, and revalidation decals shall be issued upon compliance with the laws relating to registration and licensing and upon payment of an additional registration fee of $35.00 which shall be collected by the county tag agent at the time for collection of other registration fees and shall be remitted to the state as provided in Code Section 40–2–34. The special license plates issued pursuant to this Code section shall be transferred to another vehicle as provided in Code Section 40–2–80.

Laws 1968, p. 1216, § 1; Laws 1986, p. 1333, § 3; Laws 1990, p. 2048, § 2; Laws 1992, p. 779, § 4.1; Laws 1995, p. 809, § 7; Laws 1997, p. 419, § 15; Laws 2010, Act 360, § 1–72, eff. May 12, 2010.

Formerly Code 1981, § 40–2–61.

§ 40–2–63. Special and distinctive license plates for elected sheriffs

The commissioner shall mail to the local tag agents special and distinctive license plates for the elected sheriffs in the counties of this state on or before the owner's registration period of each sheriff. The sheriffs shall make application with the local tag agent and shall pay a fee of $25.00. Special sheriffs' license plates issued pursuant to this Code section shall be renewed annually, and revalidation decals shall be issued upon compliance with the laws relating to registration and licensing and upon payment of an additional registration fee of $25.00 which shall be collected by the county tag agent at the time of collection of other registration fees and shall be remitted to the state as provided in Code Section 40–2–34. License plates shall be issued by the local tag agents upon proper application and in accordance with the terms of Article 2 of this chapter. Only one special and distinctive license plate shall be issued to each elected sheriff; however, a sheriff may choose to use the sheriff's distinctive license plate either on the law enforcement vehicle assigned to such sheriff or on his or her personal vehicle.

Laws 1978, p. 1530, § 1; Laws 1985, p. 261, § 2; Laws 1990, p. 159, § 2; Laws 1990, p. 2048, § 2; Laws 1992, p. 779, § 5; Laws 1995, p. 809, § 8.

Formerly Code 1981, § 40–2–62.

§ 40–2–64. Consular corps license plates

(a) Honorary consuls, upon application and compliance with the state motor vehicle laws relative to the registration and licensing of motor vehicles, payment of the regular license fees for license plates as provided by law, payment of a manufacturing fee of $25.00, and payment of an additional annual registration fee of $25.00 which fee shall be collected by the county tag agent at the time of collection of other registration fees and shall be remitted as provided in Code Section 40–2–34, shall be issued license plates as prescribed in Code Section 40–2–31 in duplicate for use on their official or private passenger automobiles. Such license plates shall be fastened to both the front and the rear of the vehicle. No more than two sets of honorary consular corps license plates shall be issued to any country. Such plates shall not be used by any person after his or her appointment has ended.

(b) License plates issued under this Code section shall not be transferred so as to be used by any person other than the person to whom such plate was originally issued but shall be transferred to another vehicle as provided in Code Section 40–2–80.

(c) The commissioner is authorized to establish procedures and promulgate rules and regulations for carrying out this Code section.

Laws 1976, p. 215, §§ 2–4; Laws 1985, p. 261, § 3; Laws 1990, p. 2048, § 2; Laws 1998, p. 1179, § 13.

Formerly Code 1981, § 40–2–63.

§ 40–2–64.1. Foreign organization license plates

(a) In accordance with the Taiwan Relations Act as provided for in Code Section 50–1–2, the commissioner shall design a distinctive Foreign Organization license plate.

(b) Upon application and compliance with the state motor vehicle laws relating to the registration and licensing of motor vehicles and the payment of any registration fees, including the $25.00 manufacturing fee and the $35.00 special license plate fee or the $35.00 special license plate renewal fee, as applicable, official representatives of the Taipei Economic and Cultural Representatives Office in the United States who maintain a presence in Georgia shall be issued Foreign Organization license plates as prescribed in Code Section 40–2–31 in duplicate. Such license plates shall be fastened to both the front and the rear of the vehicle.

(c) Official representatives of the Taipei Economic and Cultural Representatives Office in Atlanta accredited by the Georgia Department of Economic Development shall be entitled to Foreign Organization license plates for the representative's privately owned motor vehicle. Such license plates shall not be used by any representative after his or her presence in Georgia has terminated.

(d) License plates issued under this Code section shall not be transferred so as to be used by any person other than the person to whom such plates were originally issued but shall be transferred to another vehicle as provided in Code Section 40–2–80.

(e) The commissioner is authorized to establish procedures and promulgate rules and regulations for implementing this Code section.

Laws 2005, Act 68, § 14–4, eff. July 1, 2005; Laws 2010, Act 360, § 1–73, eff. May 12, 2010.

§ 40–2–65. Special license plates for members of active reserve components of the United States

(a)(1) Motor vehicle owners who are assigned or attached members of troop program units of any branch of the active reserve components of the United States inside or outside the State of Georgia shall be eligible to receive free motor vehicle license plates for private passenger cars, motorcycles, or trucks used for personal transportation. Motor vehicle owners who are members of any National Guard unit in a state adjoining the State of Georgia and for whom there is no National Guard unit in the county of their residence shall be eligible to receive free motor vehicle plates for private passenger cars, motorcycles, or trucks used for personal transportation to identify such vehicle owner as a reservist. Such license plates shall be issued in compliance with the state motor vehicle laws relating to registration and licensing of motor vehicles as prescribed in Article 2 of this chapter. No person shall be entitled to more than one free motor vehicle license plate for any calendar year; provided, however, that, upon payment of the regular license fee provided for in Code Section 40–2–151 and a manufacturing fee of $ 25.00, a reservist shall be entitled to receive one additional such license plate. For each additional license plate for which an initial $ 25.00 fee was required, there shall be an additional annual registration fee of $ 25.00, which fee shall be collected by the county tag agent at the time of collection of other registration fees and shall be remitted to the state as provided in Code Section 40–2–34. Additional words or symbols in addition to numbers and letters prescribed by law shall be inscribed upon such license plates so as to identify distinctively the owner as a member of one of the following branches of the United States military reserve: Army, Navy, Marines, Air Force, or Coast Guard. The commanding officer of each active reserve component program unit or the adjutant general of the National Guard unit of each neighboring state shall, upon request of any reserve member or National Guard member of that unit, respectively, furnish to that member approved documentation supporting the member's current membership in the respective reserve or National Guard unit. This documentation shall be presented annually to the tax commissioner of the county in which the reserve member or National Guard member applies for the special license plate under this Code section and upon subsequent reregistration for each succeeding year.

(2) Motor vehicle owners who are retired from any branch of the active reserve components whose active reservists are eligible to obtain free motor vehicle license plates under paragraph (1) of this subsection, upon application for license plates and upon compliance with the state motor vehicle laws relating to registration and licensing of motor vehicles as prescribed under Article 2 of this chapter, shall be issued, free of charge, a license plate as prescribed in that article for private passenger cars, motorcycles, or trucks used for personal transportation. Each such retired member shall be entitled to no more than one such free plate for any calendar year; provided, however, that, upon payment of the regular license fee provided for in Code Section 40–2–151 and a manufacturing fee of $ 25.00, a retired member shall be entitled to receive one additional such license plate. For each additional license plate for which an initial $ 25.00 fee was required, there shall be an additional annual registration fee of $ 25.00, which fee shall be collected by the county tag agent at the time of collection of other registration fees and shall be remitted to the state as provided in Code Section 40–2–34. The license plates issued pursuant to this paragraph shall, in addition to the numbers and letters prescribed by law, be identical to those issued pursuant to paragraph (1) of this subsection to members of the branch of the active reserve component from which that person retired. The commanding officer of each active reserve component program unit shall, upon request of any retired reserve member from that unit, furnish to that retired member approved documentation supporting the retired member's current retired membership status from that reserve unit. This documentation shall be presented to the tax commissioner of the county in which the retired reserve member applies for the special license plate under this Code section.

(b)(1) Upon transfer of the ownership of a private passenger vehicle upon which there is a license plate distinctively identifying the owner thereof as a member of one of the components of the United States military reserve, whether the owner is an active or retired reservist, and acquisition by the reservist of another motor vehicle, the license plate issued pursuant to this Code section shall be placed on such newly acquired motor vehicle, and such reservist shall notify the commissioner of such transfer of the license plate to such newly acquired motor vehicle in such manner as the commissioner may prescribe by regulation. No transfer or cancellation fee shall be charged for the transfer of free reservist license plates. There shall be a transfer and cancellation fee of $ 5.00 for the transfer of any other reservist license plate.

(2) Should an active reservist who has been issued a license plate or license plates be discharged or otherwise separated, except by retirement, from his or her reserve unit, the immediate commanding officer of such active reservist shall obtain the discharged member's license plate or license plates at the time of the discharge and shall forward same to the commissioner along with a certificate to the effect that such person has been discharged, and thereupon the commissioner shall issue a regular license plate, at no additional charge, to such former reservist to replace the reservist plate or plates. Should an active reservist enlist or be commissioned after purchasing a regular license plate for his or her current registration period, the commanding officer of the unit in which such person enlists or is commissioned shall likewise secure the regular license plate of such person and return same to the commissioner, along with a certificate to the effect that such person has been enlisted or commissioned in a troop program unit of the reserve components, and the effective date thereof, whereupon the commissioner shall issue a reservist license plate, at no extra charge, to such new member to replace the returned regular plate. Upon such request for a change in plate for a discharged reservist or a newly enlisted reservist, the commanding officer shall furnish such member with a copy of the commanding officer's letter to the commissioner requesting the appropriate change in plate, which copy of such letter may be used by such member pending the issuance of the new plate.

(c) The commissioner shall promulgate such rules and regulations as may be necessary to enforce compliance with all state license laws relating to the use and operation of private passenger cars, motorcycles and trucks before issuing these plates in lieu of the regular Georgia license plates, and all applications for such plates shall be made to the commissioner. The commissioner is specifically authorized to promulgate all rules and regulations necessary to ensure compliance in instances where such vehicles have been transferred or sold. Except as provided in subsection (b) of this Code section, such plates shall be nontransferable.

(d) The spouse of a member of the active reserve of the United States military who is killed while serving in a combat arena shall continue to be eligible to be issued a distinctive license plate as provided in this Code section so long as such spouse does not remarry.

Laws 1978, p. 2205, §§ 1–3; Laws 1989, p. 14, § 40; Laws 1990, p. 2048, § 2; Laws 1992, p. 779, § 6; Laws 1992, p. 2785, § 1; Laws 1992, p. 3311, § 1; Laws 1995, p. 809, § 9; Laws 1996, p. 1118, § 6; Laws 1997, p. 419, § 16; Laws 2000, p. 830, § 1; Laws 2002, p. 838, § 2; Laws 2002, p. 1074, § 5; Laws 2006, Act 765, § 2, eff. July 1, 2006.

Formerly Code 1981, § 40–2–64.

Historical and Statutory Notes

In 2001, the Code Commission, in the second sentence of par. (a)(1) and in the first sentence of par. (a)(2), inserted a comma following "motorcycles". See § 28–9–5.

§ 40–2–66. Special licenses for members of Georgia National Guard

(a)(1) Motor vehicle owners who are members of the Georgia National Guard, upon application for license plates and upon compliance with the state motor vehicle laws relating to registration and licensing of motor vehicles as prescribed under Article 2 of this chapter, shall be issued, free of charge, a license plate, as prescribed in that article for private passenger cars, motorcycles, or trucks used for personal transportation. Each member of the Georgia National Guard shall be entitled to no more than one such free plate at a time; provided, however, that, upon payment of the regular license fee provided for in Code Section 48–10–2 and a manufacturing fee of $25.00, a member shall be entitled to one additional such license plate. For each additional license plate for which an initial $25.00 fee was required, there shall be an additional annual registration fee of $25.00 which fee shall be collected by the county tag agent at the time of collection of other registration fees and shall be remitted to the state as provided in Code Section 40–2–34. Additional words or symbols, in addition to the numbers and letters prescribed by law, shall be inscribed upon such license plates so as to identify distinctively the owner as a member of the Georgia National Guard. The adjutant general of Georgia shall, upon request of any member of that National Guard unit, furnish to that member approved documentation supporting the member's current membership in that National Guard unit. This documentation shall be presented annually to the tax commissioner of the county in which the National Guard member applies for the special license plate under this Code section and upon subsequent reregistration for each succeeding year.

(2) Motor vehicle owners who are retired members of the Georgia National Guard, upon application for license plates and upon compliance with the state motor vehicle laws relating to registration and licensing of motor vehicles as prescribed under Article 2 of this chapter, shall be issued, free of charge, a license plate as prescribed in that article for private passenger cars, motorcycles, or trucks used for personal transportation. Each retired member of the Georgia National Guard shall be entitled to no more than one such free plate at a time; provided, however, that, upon payment of the regular license fee provided for in Code Section 48–10–2 and a manufacturing fee of $25.00, a member shall be entitled to one additional such license plate. For each additional license plate for which an initial $25.00 fee was required, there shall be an additional annual registration fee of $25.00 which fee shall be collected by the county tag agent at the time of collection of other registration fees and shall be remitted to the state as provided in Code Section 40–2–34. The license plates issued pursuant to this paragraph shall, in addition to the numbers and letters prescribed by law, be identical to those issued pursuant to paragraph (1) of this subsection. The adjutant general of Georgia shall, upon request of any member retired from that National Guard unit, furnish to that retired member approved documentation supporting the member's retired membership status in that National Guard unit. This documentation shall be presented annually to the tax commissioner of the county in which the retired National Guard member applies for the special license plate under this Code section and upon subsequent reregistration for each succeeding year.

(b) Upon transfer of the ownership of a private passenger vehicle upon which there is a license plate bearing the words "National Guard" and acquisition by the member or retired member of the National Guard of another motor vehicle, the license plate issued pursuant to this Code section shall be placed on such newly acquired motor vehicle and such member or retired member shall notify the commissioner of such transfer of the license plate to such newly acquired motor vehicle in such manner as the commissioner may prescribe by regulation and shall pay a transfer and cancellation fee of $5.00 and shall also pay license fees in an amount, if any, that the license fee for the newly acquired vehicle exceeds the license fee of the original vehicle. No transfer or cancellation fee shall be charged for the transfer of free National Guard license plates. There shall be a transfer and cancellation fee of $5.00 for the transfer of any other National Guard license plate. Should a member of the National Guard who has been issued a National Guard license plate be discharged or otherwise separated except by retirement from the National Guard, the immediate commanding officer of such member shall obtain the discharged member's National Guard license plate or plates at the time of the discharge and shall forward same to the commissioner along with a certificate to the effect that such member has been discharged, and thereupon the commissioner shall issue a regular license plate or plates, at no additional charge, to such former National Guard member to replace the National Guard plate. Should a member of the National Guard enlist or be commissioned in the National Guard after purchasing a regular license plate for the current year, the commanding officer of the unit in which such member enlists or is commissioned shall likewise secure the regular license plate of such new member and return same to the commissioner, along with a certificate to the effect that such new member has been enlisted or commissioned in the National Guard and the effective date thereof, whereupon the commissioner shall issue a National Guard license plate, at no extra charge, to such new member to replace the returned regular plate. Upon such request for a change in plate for a discharged member of the National Guard or a newly enlisted member of the National Guard, the commanding officer shall furnish such member with a copy of the commanding officer's letter to the commissioner requesting the appropriate change in plate, which copy of such letter may be used by such member pending the issuance of the new plate.

(c) The commissioner shall furnish to the sheriff of each county in the state an alphabetical arrangement of the list of names, addresses, and license plate letters of each person to whom a license plate is issued under this Code section, and it shall be the duty of the sheriffs of the state to maintain and to keep current such lists for public information and inquiry.

(d) The commissioner shall make such rules and regulations as necessary to enforce compliance with all state license laws relating to the use and operation of a private passenger car before issuing National Guard plates in lieu of the regular Georgia license plates, and all applications for such plates shall be made to the commissioner. The commissioner is specifically authorized to make all rules and regulations necessary to make adequate provision for instances where such vehicles have been transferred or sold. Except as provided in subsection (b) of this Code section, such plates shall be nontransferable.

(e) The spouse of a member of the National Guard who is killed while serving in a combat arena shall continue to be eligible to be issued a distinctive license plate as provided in this Code section so long as such spouse does not remarry.

Laws 1953, Nov.-Dec. Sess., p. 57, §§ 1–4; Laws 1958, p. 642, § 2; Laws 1973, p. 457, § 1; Laws 1977, p. 593, § 1; Laws 1985, p. 149, § 40; Laws 1988, p. 854, § 2; Laws 1989, p. 14, § 40; Laws 1990, p. 2048, § 2; Laws 1992, p. 779, § 7; Laws 1993, p. 1260, § 3; Laws 1994, p. 1848, § 1; Laws 1995, p. 809, § 10; Laws 1996, p. 1118, § 7; Laws 1997, p. 419, § 17; Laws 2000, p. 830, § 2; Laws 2006, Act 765, § 3, eff. July 1, 2006.

Formerly Code 1981, § 40–2–65.

§ 40–2–67. Special license plates for veterans' organization commanders

(a) The state commanders of nationally chartered veterans' organizations, upon application and compliance with the state motor vehicle laws relative to the registration and licensing of motor vehicles, upon payment of the regular license fees for license plates as provided by law, and upon the payment of an additional initial fee of $25.00 and an additional annual registration fee of $25.00 which fee shall be collected by the county tag agent at the time of collection of other registration fees and shall be remitted as provided in Code Section 40–2–34, shall be issued license plates as prescribed in Code Section 40–2–31 for use on their official or private passenger automobiles, upon which, in lieu of the numbers prescribed by said Code section, shall be such figures or symbols indicative of the office held by such individuals as may be prescribed by the commissioner.

(b) License plates issued under this Code section may not be transferred so as to be used by any person other than the person to whom such plate was originally issued but shall be transferred to another vehicle as provided in Code Section 40–2–80, except that such plates shall not be used by any person after vacating the office of commander of any of the organizations enumerated in this Code section.

Laws 1960, p. 3; Laws 1985, p. 261, § 4; Laws 1990, p. 2048, § 2; Laws 1992, p. 779, § 8; Laws 1994, p. 413, § 1; Laws 1996, p. 1118, § 8; Laws 1997, p. 419, § 18.

Formerly Code 1981, § 40–2–66.

§ 40–2–68. Special license plates for Medal of Honor recipients

(a) Motor vehicle owners who have been awarded the Medal of Honor and who are residents of this state, upon complying with the motor vehicle laws relating to registration and licensing of motor vehicles, shall be issued two distinctive personalized license plates free of charge. Such license plates shall be fastened to both the front and the rear of the vehicle. Such license plates shall be transferred to another vehicle as provided in Code Section 40– 2–80. In the event of the death of the person who received the special license plates pursuant to this Code section, upon complying with the motor vehicle laws relating to registration and licensing of motor vehicles, his or her surviving spouse may retain the special license plates and continue to display such plates on the vehicle.

(b) The commissioner may begin issuing distinctive personalized license plates to such Medal of Honor winners for the year 1980 and thereafter.

(c) The commissioner is authorized and directed to design the license plate, establish procedures, and promulgate rules and regulations to effectuate the purposes of this Code section.

Laws 1979, p. 887, §§ 2–4; Laws 1985, p. 149, § 40; Laws 1990, p. 2048, § 2; Laws 1996, p. 1118, § 9; Laws 1997, p. 419, § 19; Laws 1998, p. 1179, § 14; Laws 2005, Act 363, § 2, eff. Jan. 1, 2006.

Formerly Code 1981, § 40–2–67.

§ 40–2–69. Free special license plates for disabled veterans; continued use by surviving spouse

(a) Any veteran who was discharged under honorable conditions and who served on active duty in the armed forces of the United States or on active duty in a reserve component of the United States, including the National Guard, shall, upon application therefor, be issued a free motor vehicle license plate upon presentation of proof that such veteran is receiving or that he or she is entitled to receive a statutory award from the United States Department of Veterans Affairs for:

(1) Loss or permanent loss of use of one or both feet;

(2) Loss or permanent loss of use of one or both hands;

(3) Loss of sight in one or both eyes; or

(4) Permanent impairment of vision of both eyes of the following status: central visual acuity of 20/200 or less in the better eye, with corrective glasses, or central visual acuity of more than 20/200 if there is a field defect in which the peripheral field has contracted to such an extent that the widest diameter of visual field subtends on angular distance no greater than 20 degrees in the better eye.

(b) Any veteran who was discharged under honorable conditions and who has been adjudicated by the United States Department of Veterans Affairs as being 100 percent totally disabled and entitled to receive service connected benefits shall, upon application therefor, be issued a free motor vehicle license plate upon presentation of proof that he or she is receiving or that he or she is entitled to receive benefits for a 100 percent service connected disability, as long as he or she is 100 percent disabled. A veteran who claims that such 100 percent total disability is permanent shall furnish proof of such permanent disability through a letter from the United States Department of Veterans Affairs.

(c)(1) Once a veteran has established his or her eligibility to receive free motor vehicle license plates as a result of being permanently disabled, he or she shall be entitled to receive free plates or free revalidation decals in succeeding years on any automobile, private passenger pickup truck, motorcycle, station wagon, or van type vehicle of three-quarter tons or less that he or she may own or jointly with his or her spouse own or acquire in the future.

(2) Once a veteran has established his or her eligibility to receive free motor vehicle license plates as a result of having a 100 percent total disability which has not been determined to be a permanent disability, he or she shall be entitled to receive free plates or free revalidation decals in succeeding years upon furnishing, on an annual basis, proof of such 100 percent disability through a letter from the United States Department of Veterans Affairs. Such free plates or free revalidation decals shall apply to any automobile, private passenger pickup truck, motorcycle, station wagon, or van type vehicle of three-quarter tons or less that he or she may own or jointly with his or her spouse own or acquire in the future.

(3)(A) Two license plates or revalidation decals each year shall be furnished for vehicles other than motorcycles to veterans qualifying under this Code section unless the originals are lost. Such plates shall be fastened to both the front and the rear of the vehicle.

(B) One license plate or revalidation decal each year shall be furnished for motorcycles to veterans qualifying under this Code section unless the original is lost. Such plate shall be fastened to the rear of the vehicle.

(4) In the event of the death of the person who received the special license plates pursuant to this Code section, upon complying with the motor vehicle laws relating to registration and licensing of motor vehicles, his or her surviving spouse may continue to receive the free special license plates and revalidation decals until the death of the surviving spouse.

Laws 1956, p. 336, § 1; Laws 1957, p. 69, § 1; Laws 1959, p. 349, § 1; Laws 1961, p. 554, § 1; Laws 1965, p. 325, § 1; Laws 1968, p. 1211, § 1; Laws 1970, p. 315, § 1; Laws 1970, p. 316, § 1; Laws 1975, p. 720, § 1; Laws 1985, p. 149, § 40; Laws 1990, p. 45, § 1; Laws 1990, p. 2048, § 2; Laws 1992, p. 1498, § 1; Laws 1994, p. 393, §§ 1, 2; Laws 1997, p. 1559, § 3; Laws 2007, Act 351, § 1, eff. May 29, 2007.

Formerly Code 1981, § 40–2–68.

§ 40–2–70. Special license plates for disabled veterans unable to qualify for free tags

Any citizen and resident of the State of Georgia who has been discharged from the armed forces under conditions other than dishonorable, who is disabled to any degree specified and enumerated in Code Section 40–2–69, and who is the owner of a private passenger motor vehicle, but who cannot qualify under Code Section 40–2–69, shall be entitled to a special and distinctive automobile license plate. Such license plate shall be transferred to another vehicle acquired by such veteran or jointly by such veteran and his or her spouse as provided in Code Section 40–2–80. Such veteran shall be entitled to such plate regardless of whether he or she is suffering from a service connected or nonservice connected disability. Such veteran must apply for such license plate and, upon compliance with the state motor vehicle laws for licensing of motor vehicles and payment of the regular license fee for plates as prescribed under Article 7 of this chapter, such veteran shall be issued similar license plates as prescribed in Code Section 40–2–71 for private passenger cars. There shall be no charge for the additional plate issued such veteran under this Code section. If a veteran has not been certified as disabled by the United States Department of Veterans Affairs, such veteran may submit to the Department of Veterans Service such veteran's discharge papers and a certified statement from a physician, licensed under Chapter 34 of Title 43, certifying that in the opinion of such physician such veteran is disabled to a degree enumerated in Code Section 40–2–69. If the certificate from the physician indicates the qualifying disabilities which meet the standards of the United States Department of Veterans Affairs, the commissioner of veterans service shall submit a letter to the state revenue commissioner indicating that the veteran meets the requirements of this Code section and qualifies for a special license plate as provided in this Code section.

Laws 1967, p. 539, § 1; Laws 1985, p. 149, § 40; Laws 1990, p. 2048, § 2; Laws 1993, p. 467, § 1; Laws 1996, p. 1118, § 10; Laws 1997, p. 419, § 20; Laws 1998, p. 1179, § 15; Laws 2000, p. 951, § 3–11; Laws 2002, p. 1074, § 6; Laws 2005, Act 68, § 14–5, eff. July 1, 2005.

Formerly Code 1981, § 40–2–69.

§ 40–2–71. Issuance, form and description of license plates for disabled veterans

(a) The commissioner is directed to furnish the license plates provided for in Code Sections 40–2–69 and 40–2–70. Such plates shall be printed in three colors: red, white, and blue. The commissioner is authorized and directed to design the license plate. Each plate shall contain, in bold characters, the name of the state, or abbreviation thereof, the year, the serial number, and either the words "Disabled Veteran" or "Disabled Vet."

(b) Such license plates so issued shall be transferred to another vehicle as provided in Code Section 40–2–80.

(c) No disabled veteran shall be entitled to own or operate more than one vehicle with the free license plates provided by Code Sections 40–2–69, 40–2–70, and this Code section.

Laws 1956, p. 336, §§ 2, 3, 5; Laws 1957, p. 69, § 2; Laws 1959, p. 349, § 2; Laws 1990, p. 1476, § 1; Laws 1990, p. 2048, § 2; Laws 1996, p. 6, § 40; Laws 1996, p. 1118, § 11; Laws 1997, p. 419, § 21; Laws 1998, p. 1179, § 16.

Formerly Code 1981, § 40–2–70.

§ 40–2–71.1. Renumbered as § 40–2–73 by Laws 1990, p. 2048, § 2, eff. July 1, 1990

§ 40–2–72. Penalty for violations relating to free license tags for veterans

Any person evading or violating any provision of Code Sections 40–2–69 through 40–2–71 or attempting to secure benefits under those Code sections to which he is not entitled shall be guilty of a felony and, upon conviction thereof, shall be punished by imprisonment for not less than two nor more than five years.

Laws 1956, p. 336, § 6; Laws 1957, p. 69, § 6; Laws 1990, p. 2048, § 2.

Formerly Code 1981, § 40–2–71.

§ 40–2–73. Special license plates for former prisoners of war

(a) As used in this Code section, the term "prisoners of war" means those veterans of the armed forces of the United States who were discharged under honorable conditions and who were captured and held prisoner by forces hostile to the United States while serving in the armed forces of the United States in World War I, World War II, the Korean War, or the Vietnam War.

(b) Owners of motor vehicles who are veterans of the armed forces of the United States, who have been prisoners of war, who were discharged under honorable conditions, and who are residents of this state, upon complying with the motor vehicle laws relating to registration and licensing of motor vehicles, shall be issued one distinctive personalized license plate free of charge and, upon the payment of the appropriate taxes and registration fees, shall be issued additional distinctive personalized license plates. Such license plates shall be transferred to another vehicle acquired by such person individually or jointly with his or her spouse as provided in Code Section 40–2–80. Such license plates shall be fastened to the rear of the vehicles.

(c) The spouse of a deceased former prisoner of war shall continue to be eligible to be issued a distinctive personalized license plate as provided in this Code section so long as such person does not remarry.

(d) The commissioner is authorized and directed to design the license plate, establish procedures, and promulgate rules and regulations to effectuate the purposes of this Code section.

(e) The commissioner may begin issuing distinctive personalized license plates to such prisoners of war for the year 1982 and thereafter.

Laws 1981, p. 516, §§ 1–5; Laws 1984, p. 423, § 1; Laws 1985, p. 1278, § 2; Laws 1986, p. 626, § 1; Laws 1990, p. 2048, § 2; Laws 1996, p. 1118, § 12; Laws 1997, p. 419, § 22; Laws 1998, p. 1179, § 17.

Formerly Code 1981, § 40–2–71.1.

§ 40–2–74. Persons with disabilities; special license plates

(a) Any owner of a private passenger motor vehicle who is a resident of Georgia, upon complying with the motor vehicle laws relating to registration, licensing, and payment of fees and upon submitting an affidavit of a practitioner of the healing arts stating that the owner or his or her spouse, child, or ward is a person with disabilities, as defined in paragraph (5) of Code Section 40–6–221, whose disability or incapacity can be expected to last for more than 180 days and stating the specific disability that limits or impairs the ability to walk, shall be issued a specially designated disabled person's license plate from the commissioner. As used in this Code section, the term "practitioner of the healing arts" means a person holding a license to practice medicine, podiatric medicine, or chiropractic issued pursuant to Article 2 of Chapter 34 of Title 43, Chapter 35 of Title 43, or Chapter 9 of Title 43, respectively.

(a.1) Any business registered in Georgia that is a sole proprietorship, a Subchapter "S" Corporation under Subchapter S of Chapter 1 of the Internal Revenue Code, or a single principal limited liability corporation or limited liability partnership which assigns or makes available a passenger motor vehicle for the use of an employee of such business, upon complying with the motor vehicle laws relating to registration, licensing, and payment of fees and upon submitting an affidavit of a practitioner of the healing arts stating that such employee is a person with disabilities, as defined in paragraph (5) of Code Section 40–6–221, whose disability or incapacity can be expected to last for more than 180 days and stating the specific disability that limits or impairs the ability to walk, shall be issued a specially designated disabled person's license plate from the commissioner. The affidavit shall also state that such business vehicle shall be used only or primarily by such disabled employee. If such disabled employee leaves the employment of the company, the company shall surrender the plate to the commissioner within 60 days. In the event that an employee or other person that is not a disabled person uses a business vehicle which has been issued a special plate pursuant to this subsection, he or she shall not avail himself or herself of the privileges afforded under this title to a disabled person with a special plate. Any person who is not a disabled person as prescribed by this Code section and who willfully and falsely avails himself or herself of the privileges afforded to such special plate under this title shall be guilty of a misdemeanor. Any business to which one or more special plates are issued pursuant to this subsection which is determined by the commissioner to have repeated violations of this subsection by an employee or employees or other person or persons that are not disabled as prescribed by this Code section shall be subject to revocation of such special plate or plates.

(b) A hearing impaired person otherwise qualified under this subsection shall be eligible to have issued to him or her a specially designated disabled person's license plate in accordance with this Code section. As used in this Code section, "hearing impaired person" shall have the same meaning as defined in Code Section 24–9–101, except that the term "hearing impaired person" shall not include any person who is not qualified for a driver's license pursuant to Code Section 40–5–35, relating to reports by physicians and vision specialists in connection with the issuance or revocation of drivers' licenses, as now or hereafter amended. For purposes of this subsection, presentation of an identification card for persons with disabilities issued pursuant to

Article 8 of Chapter 5 of this title shall constitute proof of hearing impairment.

(c) Upon complying with the motor vehicle laws relating to registration, licensing, and payment of fees and upon submission of proof of disability as provided in subsection (a) of this Code section, as applicable:

(1) Any resident person who is the joint owner of a motor vehicle with a disabled person as prescribed in this Code section shall be authorized to obtain such specialized plates for such jointly owned vehicle; and

(2) Any resident motor vehicle owner who is the spouse, parent, or legal guardian of a person who is disabled as prescribed in this Code section shall be authorized to obtain such specialized plates for such vehicle.

Upon the death of the disabled person or if the joint ownership of such vehicle ceases for any reason, the specialized license plate shall be canceled and the owner of such motor vehicle shall be issued a regular license plate for such vehicle.

(d) The commissioner is directed to furnish such license plates as provided for in this Code section, which shall bear the official international wheelchair symbol or a reasonable facsimile thereof, or such other symbols as the commissioner may deem appropriate.

(e) Any license plate issued pursuant to the provisions of this Code section shall be transferred to another vehicle as provided in Code Section 40–2–80.

(f) Any person who is not a disabled person as prescribed in this Code section or a person otherwise entitled to obtain such special license plates and who willfully and falsely represents himself or herself as having the qualifications to obtain the special plates prescribed by this Code section shall be guilty of a misdemeanor.

(g) Any practitioner of the healing arts who knowingly and willfully makes a false or misleading statement in his or her affidavit stating that an applicant is a disabled person as prescribed in this Code section shall be guilty of a misdemeanor.

(h) Any person owning a vehicle bearing the special plates and not entitled to do so under this Code section shall be guilty of a misdemeanor.

Laws 1973, p. 576, §§ 2–5; Laws 1978, p. 1653, § 1; Laws 1984, p. 22, § 40; Laws 1985, p. 149, § 40; Laws 1989, p. 1186, § 3; Laws 1990, p. 2048, § 2; Laws 1994, p. 413, §§ 2, 3; Laws 1995, p. 1302, § 6; Laws 1996, p. 1118, § 13; Laws 1997, p. 419, § 23; Laws 1998, p. 1179, § 18; Laws 2000, p. 1182, § 1; Laws 2005, Act 363, § 3, eff. Jan. 1, 2006; Laws 2008, Act 459, § 1, eff. July 1, 2008.

Historical and Statutory Notes

In 2008, the Code Commission, in subsec. (a.1), deleted "person" following "that are not disabled" in the last sentence. See § 28–9–5.

§ 40–2–74.1. Parking permits for persons with disabilities; no fee

(a) The department shall issue parking permits for persons with disabilities and may delegate to county tag agents the responsibility for issuance of such permits to residents of the county served by the tag agent. The department shall receive applications for and issue parking permits by mail to persons with disabilities upon presentation of an affidavit of a licensed doctor of medicine, licensed doctor of osteopathic medicine, licensed doctor of podiatric medicine, licensed optometrist, or licensed chiropractor stating that such person is a disabled person, the specific disability that limits or impairs the person's ability to walk, and that he or she is a person with disabilities as specified in paragraph (5) of Code Section 40–6–221. Permits shall be in such form as the department prescribes but shall be of sufficient size and sufficiently distinctively marked to be easily visible when placed on or affixed to the driver's side of the dashboard or hung from the rearview mirror of the parked vehicle. Permits shall be made of plastic or heavyweight cardboard and shall be of sufficient quality to ensure that the coloring of the permit and the ink used thereon will resist fading for a period of at least four years. The front and back surfaces of the permit shall be laminated to prevent alteration of the information printed underneath on the permit. Permits shall be issued to individuals, and the name of the individual and an identification number shall appear on the permit. The individual to whom a permit is issued may use the permit for any vehicle he or she is operating or in which he or she is a passenger. Permits shall also be issued to institutions when the primary purpose of a vehicle operated by the institution is to transport individuals with disabilities. The name of the institution, the license number of the particular vehicle, and an identification number shall appear on the permit. The institution shall use such permit only for a vehicle which is operated by the institution and which is used primarily to transport individuals with disabilities.

(b) The department shall issue a temporary permit to any temporarily disabled person upon presentation of an affidavit of a licensed doctor of medicine, licensed doctor of osteopathic medicine, licensed doctor of podiatric medicine, licensed optometrist, or licensed chiropractor stating that such person is a temporarily disabled person, the specific disability that limits or impairs the person's ability to walk, that he or she is a person with disabilities as specified in paragraph (5) of Code Section 40–6–221, and a date until which such person is likely to remain disabled. The temporary permit shall vary in color from one period to the next renewal period and shall show prominently on its face an expiration date the same as the date specified by such doctor for the likely termination of the disability, which date shall not be more than 180 days after the date the permit is issued. The expiration date shall be machine printed, not handwritten, in boldface type of sufficient size to be legible when the permit is displayed on the driver's side of the dashboard or hung from the rearview mirror.

(c) The department shall issue a permanent permit to any permanently disabled person upon presentation of an affidavit of a licensed doctor of medicine, licensed doctor of osteopathic medicine, licensed doctor of podiatric medicine, licensed optometrist, or licensed chiropractor stating that such person is a permanently disabled person. The affidavit shall further state the specific disability that limits or impairs the person's ability to walk or that he or she is a person with disabilities as specified in paragraph (5) of Code Section 40–6–221. The department shall also issue a permanent permit to an institution which operates vehicles used primarily for the transportation of individuals with disabilities upon presentation of a certification from the institution regarding use of its vehicles. The institution shall receive permits only for the number of vehicles so used and shall affix the permits to the driver's side of the dashboards of such vehicles. The permanent permit shall be predominantly blue in color and shall show prominently on its face an expiration date four years from the date it is issued. The expiration date shall be machine printed, not handwritten, in boldface type of sufficient size to be legible when the permit is displayed on the driver's side of the dashboard or hung from the rearview mirror.

(d) Any individual to whom a specially designated disabled veteran's license plate has been issued pursuant to Code Sections 40–2–69 through 40–2–72 and any individual to whom a specially designated disabled person's license plate has been issued pursuant to Code Section 40–2–74 shall be authorized to park the passenger motor vehicle on which the specially designated license plate is attached in a parking place for persons with disabilities without the necessity of obtaining a parking permit for persons with disabilities pursuant to this Code section.

(e) The department shall issue a special permanent permit to any person who:

(1) Because of a physical disability drives a motor vehicle which has been equipped with hand controls for the operation of the vehicle's brakes and accelerator; or

(2) Is physically disabled due to the loss of, or loss of use of, both upper extremities.

This special permanent permit shall be gold in color and shall show prominently on its face an expiration date four years from the date it is issued. The expiration date shall be printed in a size of print that is legible when the permit is displayed on the driver's side of the dashboard or hung from the rearview mirror. Such a special permit shall be used in the same manner as, and shall be subject to the provisions of this Code section relating to, other permanent parking permits for persons with disabilities and shall also be used as provided in Code Section 10–1–164.1. In addition to any other required printing, the following shall be printed upon this special gold permit:

"Code Section 10–1–164.1 of the Official Code of Georgia Annotated requires that any owner or operator of a gasoline station that sells full-service gasoline at one price and self-service at a lower price shall provide the service of dispensing gasoline at the self-service price for the holder of this special permit when such holder requests such service and is the operator of the vehicle and is not accompanied by another person 16 years of age or older who is not mobility impaired or blind."

(f) The department and county tag agents shall not charge or collect any fee for issuing parking permits for persons with disabilities under this Code section.

(g) Any special disabled person decal issued under the former provisions of this Code section shall be valid until its expiration date but shall not be reissued.

(h) For purposes of this Code section, an active duty military physician shall be entitled to submit an affidavit in support of the application of active duty or retired military personnel for parking permits for persons with disabilities whether or not such physician is licensed to practice in Georgia. Such affidavit shall state that the applicant is in active military service and is stationed in Georgia pursuant to military orders or is retired from the military and is a resident of Georgia and that such person is a disabled person, the specific disability that limits or impairs the person's ability to walk, and that he or she is a person with disabilities as specified in paragraph (5) of Code Section 40–6–221.

Laws 2005, Act 363, § 4, eff. Jan. 1, 2006; Laws 2006, Act 674, § 1, eff. May 1, 2006; Laws 2008, Act 422, § 1, eff. July 1, 2008; Laws 2008, Act 524, § 1, eff. July 1, 2008.

Historical and Statutory Notes

In 2006, the Code Commission, in subsec. (c), deleted "person who is" preceding "permanently disabled person upon presentation" in the first sentence. See § 28–9–5.

§ 40–2–75. Repealed by Laws 2010, Act 360, § 1–74, eff. May 12, 2010

Historical and Statutory Notes

The repealed section, relating to special license plates for amateur radio station operators , was derived from Laws 1951, p. 653, §§ 1-4; Laws 1970, p. 699, § 1; Laws 1982, p. 1075, §§ 1, 2; Laws 1983, p. 3, § 29; Laws 1984, p. 433, § 1; Laws 1985, p. 261, § 5; Laws 1986, p. 1333, § 4; Laws 1990, p. 2048, § 2; Laws 1992, p. 779, § 9; Laws 1994, p. 1848, § 2; Laws 1995, p. 809, § 11; Laws 1996, p. 1118, § 14; Laws 1997, p. 419, § 24; Laws 1998, p. 1179, § 19; Code 1981, § 40–2–73. The repealing law also reserved the section designation.

§ 40–2–75.1. Renumbered as § 40–2–78 by Laws 1990, p. 2048, § 2, eff. July l, 1990

§ 40–2–75.2. Renumbered as § 40–2–79 by Laws 1990, p. 2048, § 2, eff. July 1, 1990

§§ 40–2–76 to 40–2–78. Repealed by Laws 2010, Act 360, § 1–74, eff. May 12, 2010

Historical and Statutory Notes

Repealed § 40–2–76, relating to special license plates for alternatively fueled vehicles, was derived from Laws 1997, p. 1589, § 2; Laws 1998, p. 1179, § 20; Laws 2000, p. 951, § 3-12; Laws 2003, Act 191, § 3.

Repealed § 40–2–77, relating to special license plates for antique or hobby or special interest vehicles, was derived from Laws 1958, p. 302, §§ 1-5; Laws 1977, p. 596, § 1; Laws 1982, p. 2298, §§ 1-4; Laws 1983, p. 3, § 29; Laws 1985, p. 261, § 7; Laws 1990, p. 8, § 40; Laws 1990, p. 2048, § 2; Laws 1992, p. 779, § 10; Laws 1993, p. 1678, § 1; Laws 1994, p. 97, § 40; Laws 1997, p. 419, § 25; Laws 1998, p. 1179, § 21; Code 1981, 40–2–75.

Repealed § 40–2–78, relating to special license plates for certified firefighters, was derived from Laws 1986, p. 427, § 1; Laws 1989, p. 921, § 3; Laws 1990, p. 2048, § 2; Laws 1992, p. 779, § 11; Laws 1994, p. 1853, § 1; Laws 1995, p. 809, § 12; Laws 1997, p. 419, § 26; Laws 1998, p. 1179, § 22; Laws 1999, p. 791, § 3; Laws 2008, Act 725, § 1; Code 1981, 40–2–75.1.

§ 40–2–79. Repealed by Laws 1997, p. 419, § 26a, eff. May 1, 1997

§ 40–2–80. Rules for transfer of special license plates

Except as otherwise provided by law, the commissioner shall provide by rules and regulations appropriate procedures whereby, upon the payment of the fee prescribed in Code Section 40–2–42 for transfer of license plates and revalidation decals, currently valid special and distinctive license plates and special personalized prestige license plates authorized by this article shall be transferred from one vehicle to another vehicle of the same class of which ownership is acquired following that person's or those persons' ceasing to own or operate on the public roads the vehicle for which such plate was originally issued and during the initial registration period for the acquired vehicle. If the vehicle acquired by such person is of a different class than the vehicle no longer owned or operated by such person, then upon payment by such person of any additional fee for registering such acquired vehicle, the commissioner shall issue a new license plate to such person for use on such vehicle. Special license plates and revalidation decals for such plates may be transferred in accordance with the provisions of this Code section at any time after issuance or renewal thereof and until the expiration of the period for which issued.

Laws 1969, p. 266, § 3; Laws 1990, p. 2048, § 2; Laws 1992, p. 779, § 12; Laws 1997, p. 419, § 27; Laws 1998, p. 1179, § 23.

Formerly Code 1981, § 40–2–76.

§ 40–2–81. Renumbered as § 40–2–9 by Laws 2001, p. 479, § 3, eff. January 1, 2002

§ 40–2–82. Distinctive license plates to be used on vehicles operated by Georgia State Patrol troopers or Motor Carrier Compliance Division law enforcement officers

The commissioner of public safety shall be issued distinctive license plates to be used on motor vehicles assigned to the Department of Public Safety and operated by troopers of the Georgia State Patrol or law enforcement officers of the Motor Carrier Compliance Division. The distinctive plates shall be issued free of charge in accordance with procedures agreed upon by the commissioner of public safety and the state revenue commissioner. License plates issued pursuant to this Code section need not contain a place for the county name decal and no county name decal need be affixed to a license plate issued pursuant to this Code section.

Laws 1989, p. 1186, § 5; Laws 1990, p. 2048, § 2; Laws 2000, p. 951, § 3–13; Laws 2005, Act 68, § 14–6, eff. July 1, 2005.

Formerly Code 1981, § 40–2–78.

§ 40–2–83. Special or prestige license plates for jointly owned vehicles

(a) Notwithstanding any other provision of law, any resident person who is authorized to obtain a special or prestige license plate pursuant to this article may, upon complying with the motor vehicle laws relating to licensing, registration, and fees, obtain such special or prestige license plate in his or her own name and the name of any other person with whom he or she jointly owns a motor vehicle.

(b) Special or prestige license plates issued pursuant to this article to joint owners shall be transferred to another vehicle having the same joint owners as provided by Code Section 40–2–80.

(c) If any resident person who is authorized to obtain a special or prestige license plate and who has been issued a special or prestige plate for a jointly owned vehicle dies or for any other reason is no longer a joint owner of such vehicle, the surviving owner of such vehicle shall surrender the license plate to the commissioner and shall obtain a regular license plate or some other type of special or prestige license plate upon complying with the motor vehicle laws relating to registration, licensing, and fees.

Laws 1990, p. 2048, § 2; Laws 1992, p. 2978, § 2.1; Laws 1997, p. 419, § 28; Laws 1998, p. 1179, § 24.

§ 40–2–84. Special and distinctive license plates for veterans of the United States armed forces who have been awarded the Purple Heart

(a) Motor vehicle or motorcycle owners who are veterans of the armed forces of the United States who have been awarded the Purple Heart citation shall be eligible to receive a special and distinctive vehicle license plate for a private passenger car, motorcycle, or truck used for personal transportation, provided that the requisite number of applications are received by the commissioner as provided in subsection (b) of this Code section. Such license plate shall be issued in compliance with the state motor vehicle laws relating to registration and licensing of motor vehicles as prescribed in Article 2 of this chapter.

(b) A veteran who qualifies for the special and distinctive license plate pursuant to subsection (a) of this Code section shall make application therefor with the commissioner and include the requisite fee. Said applicant may apply for and be limited to not more than one free license plate at a time; provided, however, that upon payment of the regular license fee provided for in Code Section 40–2–151 and payment of the manufacturing fee provided for in this Code section, a veteran may obtain an additional such license plate. The commissioner shall retain all applications received for such special and distinctive license plate until a minimum of 250 applications have been received. After receipt of 250 applications for such distinctive license plate, the commissioner shall design a distinctive license plate as provided in subsection (c) of this Code section and issue the distinctive license plates to present and future qualifying applicants. If the commissioner does not receive the required minimum 250 applications no later than July 31 of the year preceding the year of issuance of such plates, the commissioner shall not accept any applications for nor issue such distinctive license plates and all fees shall be refunded to applicants. The commissioner shall promulgate such rules and regulations as may be necessary to enforce compliance with all state license laws relating to the use and operation of private passenger cars, motorcycles, and trucks before issuing these license plates in lieu of the regular Georgia license plates. The manufacturing fee for each additional special and distinctive license plate shall be $25.00. The commissioner is specifically authorized to promulgate all rules and regulations necessary to ensure compliance in instances where such vehicles have been transferred or sold. Except as provided in subsection (d) of this Code section, such plates shall be nontransferable.

(c) The special and distinctive vehicle license plates shall be as prescribed in Article 2 of this chapter for private passenger cars, motorcycles, or trucks used for personal transportation. Additional words or symbols, in addition to the numbers and letters prescribed by law, shall be inscribed upon such license plates so as to identify distinctively the owner as a Purple Heart recipient. For any redesigned plates issued on or after January 1, 2006, such inscription shall include the designation "Combat Wounded."

(d) The license plate issued pursuant to this Code section shall be transferred between vehicles as provided in Code Section 40–2–80. The spouse of a deceased veteran of the armed forces of the United States who was awarded the Purple Heart citation shall continue to be eligible to be issued a distinctive personalized license plate as provided in this Code section for any vehicle owned by such veteran ownership of which is transferred to the surviving spouse or for any other vehicle owned by such surviving spouse either at the time of the qualifying veteran's death or acquired thereafter, so long as such person does not remarry.

(e) For each additional special license plate issued under this Code section there shall be an additional $25.00 annual registration fee which fee shall be collected by the county tag agent at the time of collection of other registration fees and shall be remitted to the state as provided in Code Section 40–2–34.

Laws 1990, p. 1316, § 1; Laws 1991, p. 1145, § 2; Laws 1992, p. 6, § 40; Laws 1992, p. 779, § 13; Laws 1993, p. 1793, § 1; Laws 1994, p. 97, § 40; Laws 1994, p. 564, § 1; Laws 1997, p. 419, § 29; Laws 1998, p. 1179, § 25; Laws 2000, p. 830, § 3; Laws 2002, p. 1074, § 5; Laws 2005, Act 363, § 5, eff. Jan. 1, 2006.

§ 40–2–85. Special and distinctive license plates for veterans of the United States armed forces who survived the Japanese attack on Pearl Harbor

(a) Motor vehicle owners who are veterans of the armed forces of the United States who survived the Japanese attack on Pearl Harbor on December 7, 1941, shall be eligible to receive special and distinctive vehicle license plates for private passenger cars, trucks, or recreational vehicles used for personal transportation, provided that the requisite number of applications are received by the commissioner as provided in subsection (b) of this Code section. Such license plates shall be issued in compliance with the state motor vehicle laws relating to registration and licensing of motor vehicles as prescribed in Article 2 of this chapter.

(b) A veteran who qualifies for the special and distinctive license plate pursuant to subsection (a) of this Code section shall make application therefor with the commissioner and include the requisite fee. The commissioner shall design a distinctive license plate as provided in subsection (c) of this Code section and issue the distinctive license plates to present and future qualifying applicants. There shall be no minimum required number of applicants for such distinctive license plate. The commissioner shall promulgate such rules and regulations as may be necessary to enforce compliance with all state license laws relating to the use and operation of private passenger cars and trucks before issuing these license plates in lieu of the regular Georgia license plates. The manufacturing fee for such special and distinctive license plates shall be $25.00. The commissioner is specifically authorized to promulgate all rules and regulations necessary to ensure compliance in instances where such vehicles have been transferred or sold. Except as provided in subsection (d) of this Code section, such plates shall be nontransferable.

(c) The special and distinctive vehicle license plates shall be as prescribed in Article 2 of this chapter for private passenger cars or trucks used for personal transportation. Additional words or symbols, in addition to the numbers and letters prescribed by law, shall be inscribed upon such license plates so as to identify distinctively the owner as a survivor of the Japanese attack on Pearl Harbor on December 7, 1941.

(d) The license plate issued pursuant to this Code section shall be transferred between vehicles as provided in Code Section 40–2–80. The spouse of a deceased survivor of the Japanese attack on Pearl Harbor on December 7, 1941, shall continue to be eligible to be issued a distinctive personalized license plate as provided in this Code section for any vehicle owned by such veteran ownership of which is transferred to the surviving spouse or for any other vehicle owned by such surviving spouse either at the time of the qualifying veteran's death or acquired thereafter, so long as such person does not remarry.

(e) Special license plates issued under this Code section shall be renewed annually with a revalidation decal as provided in Code Section 40–2–31. It shall be a requirement that a county name decal shall be affixed and displayed on license plates issued under this Code section.

(f) Any resident motor vehicle owner who is the spouse or legal guardian of a person who is disabled as prescribed in this Code section shall be authorized to obtain such specialized plates for such vehicle.

Laws 1990, p. 797, § 1; Laws 1992, p. 779, § 14; Laws 1994, p. 558, § 1; Laws 1994, p. 564, § 2; Laws 1996, p. 1259, § 1; Laws 1997, p. 419, § 30; Laws 1997, p. 1515, § 1; Laws 1998, p. 1179, § 26.

§ 40–2–85.1. Special and distinctive license plates for retired veterans of the armed forces of the United States and persons who served during World War I, World War II, the Korean War, the Vietnam War, or Operation Desert Storm

(a)(1) Motor vehicle owners who are retired veterans of the armed forces of the United States or persons who served during World War I, World War II, the Korean War, the Vietnam War, or Operation Desert Storm shall be eligible to receive special and distinctive vehicle license plates for private passenger cars, trucks, or recreational vehicles used for personal transportation. Such license plates shall be issued in compliance with the state motor vehicle laws relating to registration and licensing of motor vehicles as prescribed in Article 2 of this chapter.

(2)(A) Motor vehicle owners who retired from active duty with the armed forces of the United States shall be issued upon application for and upon compliance with the state motor vehicle laws relating to registration and licensing of motor vehicles a retired veteran's license plate. One such retired veteran's license plate shall be issued without the requisite registration fee, manufacturing fee, or annual registration fee.

(B) Each retired member of the armed forces shall be entitled to no more than one such free license plate at a time; provided, however, that upon payment of a manufacturing fee of $25.00, a member shall be entitled to one additional such license plate. For each additional license plate for which a $25.00 manufacturing fee is required, there shall be an additional annual registration fee of $25.00 which fee shall be collected by the county tag agent at the time of collection of other registration fees and shall be remitted to the state as provided in Code Section 40–2–34.

(b) The commissioner shall design a retired veteran's license plate or a distinctive license plate to commemorate service by the United States armed forces in wars listed in subsection (a) of this Code section. The commissioner shall promulgate such rules and regulations as may be necessary to enforce compliance with all state license laws relating to the use and operation of private passenger cars and trucks before issuing these license plates in lieu of the regular Georgia license plates. The manufacturing fee for such special and distinctive license plates shall be $25.00. The commissioner is specifically authorized to promulgate all rules and regulations necessary to ensure compliance in instances where such vehicles have been transferred or sold. Except as provided in subsection (d) of this Code section, such plates shall be nontransferable.

(c) The special and distinctive vehicle license plates shall be as prescribed in Article 2 of this chapter for private passenger cars or trucks used for personal transportation. Such plates shall contain such words or symbols, in addition to the numbers and letters prescribed by law, so as to identify distinctively the owners as retired veterans of the armed forces of the United States or persons who served during World War I, World War II, the Korean War, the Vietnam War, or Operation Desert Storm and shall additionally, for such plates manufactured after July 1, 2001, identify distinctly the owner as a veteran of one of the following branches of the armed forces: Army, Navy, Marines, Air Force, or Coast Guard.

(d) The license plate issued pursuant to this Code section shall be transferred between vehicles as provided in Code Section 40–2–80. The spouse of a deceased retired veteran of the armed forces of the United States or of a deceased person who served during World War I, World War II, the Korean War, the Vietnam War, or Operation Desert Storm shall continue to be eligible to be issued a distinctive personalized license plate as provided in this Code section for any vehicle owned by such veteran ownership of which is transferred to the surviving spouse or for any other vehicle owned by such surviving spouse either at the time of the qualifying veteran's death or acquired thereafter, so long as such person does not remarry.

(e) Special license plates issued under this Code section, except as provided in subparagraph (a)(2)(A) of this Code section, shall be renewed annually with a revalidation decal as provided in Code Section 40–2–31 without payment of an additional $25.00 annual registration fee. It shall be a requirement that a county name decal shall be affixed and displayed on license plates issued under this Code section.

Laws 1991, p. 1036, § 1; Laws 1992, p. 779, § 15; Laws 1992, p. 2785, § 1.1; Laws 1994, p. 413, § 4; Laws 1994, p. 564, § 3; Laws 1997, p. 419, § 31; Laws 1998, p. 1179, § 27; Laws 2001, p. 479, § 1; Laws 2007, Act 351, § 2, eff. May 29, 2007.

§ 40–2–85.2. Special and distinctive license plates for United States armed forces veterans of the Chosin Reservoir Campaign of 1950 in North Korea

(a) On and after January 1, 1999, motor vehicle owners who are United States armed forces veterans of the Chosin Reservoir Campaign of 1950 in North Korea shall be eligible to receive special and distinctive vehicle license plates for private passenger cars, trucks under 14,000 pounds gross vehicle weight, or recreational vehicles used for personal transportation. Such license plates shall be issued in compliance with the state motor vehicle laws relating to registration and licensing of motor vehicles as prescribed in Article 2 of this chapter.

(b) A veteran who qualifies for the special and distinctive license plate pursuant to subsection (a) of this Code section shall make application therefor with the commissioner and include the requisite fee. The commissioner shall design a distinctive license plate as provided in subsection (c) of this Code section and issue the distinctive license plates to qualifying applicants. There shall be no minimum required number of applicants for such distinctive license plate. The commissioner shall promulgate such rules and regulations as may be necessary to enforce compliance with all state license laws relating to the use and operation of private passenger cars and trucks before issuing these license plates in lieu of the regular Georgia license plates. The additional manufacturing fee for such special and distinctive license plates shall be $25.00. The commissioner is specifically authorized to promulgate all rules and regulations necessary to ensure compliance in instances where such vehicles have been transferred or sold.

(c) The special and distinctive vehicle license plates shall be as prescribed in Article 2 of this chapter for private passenger cars or trucks used for personal transportation, except that the word "CHOSIN" and no other letters shall be placed horizontally immediately to the left of the numbers on the license plate so as to distinctively identify the owner as a veteran of the Chosin Reservoir Campaign of 1950 in North Korea.

(d) The license plate issued pursuant to this Code section shall be transferred between vehicles as provided in Code Section 40–2–80. The spouse of a deceased veteran of the Chosin Reservoir Campaign of 1950 in North Korea shall continue to be eligible to be issued a distinctive personalized license plate as provided in this Code section for any vehicle owned by such veteran ownership of which is transferred to the surviving spouse or for any other vehicle owned by such surviving spouse either at the time of the qualifying veteran's death or acquired thereafter, so long as such person does not remarry.

(e) Special license plates issued under this Code section shall be renewed annually with a revalidation decal, as provided in Code Section 40–2–31, without payment of an additional $25.00 annual registration fee. Special license plates issued under this Code section shall be transferred between vehicles as provided in Code Section 40–2–80.

Laws 1998, p. 1179, § 27A; Laws 2007, Act 351, § 3, eff. May 29, 2007.

§ 40–2–85.3. Gold Star license plates

(a) Special license plates honoring the family members of service members who have been killed in action while serving in the armed forces of the United States shall be issued in this state. The license plate shall be officially designated as the Gold Star license plate.

(b) The commissioner, in cooperation with supporters of this license plate, shall design a special license plate for the family members of service members who have been killed in action while serving in the armed forces of the United States. The license plates must be of the same size as general issue motor vehicle license plates and shall include a unique design and identifying number, whereby the total number of characters does not exceed an amount to be determined by the commissioner. The license plate shall bear in a conspicuous place a gold star with blue fringe on a white background with a red border. This is the symbol for a fallen service member. In the indented area normally used for the county of residence decal, the words Gold Star Family shall be displayed.

(c) Notwithstanding the provisions of subsections (a) and (b) of this Code section, this Code section shall not be implemented until such time as the State of Georgia has, through a licensing agreement or otherwise, received such license or other permission as may be required to implement this Code section. The design of the initial edition of such special license plate, as well as the design of subsequent editions and excepting only any part or parts of the designs owned by others and licensed to the state, shall be owned solely by the State of Georgia for its exclusive use and control, except as authorized by the commissioner. The commissioner may take such steps as may be necessary to give notice of and protect such right, including the copyright or copyrights. However, such steps shall be cumulative of the ownership and exclusive use and control established by this subsection as a matter of law, and no person shall reproduce or otherwise use such design or designs, except as authorized by the commissioner.

(d) Any motor vehicle owner who is a resident of Georgia, other than one registering under the International Registration Plan, upon complying with state laws relating to registration and licensing of motor vehicles shall be issued such a special license plate upon application therefor. Special license plates issued under this Code section shall be renewed annually with a revalidation decal as provided in Code Section 40–2–31. Upon payment of all ad valorem taxes and other fees due at registration of a motor vehicle an eligible family member may apply for a Gold Star license plate. In order to qualify as an eligible family member, the person must be directly related to the fallen service member as a spouse, mother, father, sibling, child, or step-parent. One free license plate shall be allowed for the spouse, mother, and father, and they may purchase additional license plates for each motor vehicle they register in this state. Siblings, children, or step-parents may purchase Gold Star license plates for motor vehicles registered in this state. The cost of a Gold Star license plate shall be established by the department, but shall not exceed the cost of other specialty license plates. If a Gold Star license plate is lost, damaged, or stolen, the eligible family member must pay the reasonable cost, to be established by the department, but not to exceed the cost of other specialty license plates, to replace the Gold Star license plate.

(e) Whether a service member is deemed to have been killed in action shall be determined by the classification of death as listed by the United States Department of Defense and may be verified from documentation directly from the Department of Defense.

(f) A free Gold Star license plate shall be issued only to the spouse, mother, and father of service members who resided in Georgia at the time of the death of the service member. However, an eligible family member, except for nonresident siblings, who was not a resident of Georgia at the time of the death of the service member may purchase a Gold Star license plate, at a cost to be established by the department, not to exceed the cost of other specialty license plates.

(g) Renewal decals shall be issued at no cost to any person that received a free license plate under the provisions of this Code section upon the payment of ad valorem taxes and other registration fees, provided that the renewal is applied for on or within 30 days prior to the renewal date of the eligible person. If the eligible person fails to renew within such time, he or she shall pay a standard renewal fee and be subject to the standard penalties for late payment of ad valorem taxes due on the motor vehicle.

(h) An eligible family member may request a Gold Star license plate at any time during his or her registration period. If such a license plate is to replace a current valid license plate, the license plate shall be issued with appropriate renewal decals attached.

(i) License plates issued pursuant to this Code section shall not be transferred between vehicles as provided in Code Section 40–2–42, unless the transfer is to another motor vehicle owned by the eligible family member.

(j) Gold Star license plates shall be issued within 30 days of application.

(k) The commissioner is authorized and directed to establish procedures and promulgate rules and regulations to effectuate the purposes of this Code section.

Laws 2006, Act 746, § 1, eff. Jan. 1, 2007; Laws 2010, Act 360, § 1–76, eff. May 12, 2010; Laws 2010, Act 380, § 1, eff. July 1, 2010.

Formerly Code 1981, § 40–2–86.18

Historical and Statutory Notes

In 2006, the Code Commission, redesignated § 40–2–86.18, which was enacted by Laws 2006, Act 764, § 1, as § 40–2–86.19; redesignated § 40–2–86.18, which was enacted by Laws 2006, Act 765, § 1, as § 40–2–86.20; and redesignated § 40–2–86.18, which was enacted by Laws 2006, Act 947, § 12, as § 40–2–86.21. See § 28–9–5.

In 2006, the Code Commission, due to irreconcilable conflicts, treated the enactment of § 40–2–86.18 by Laws 2006, Act 946, § 1, as superseded by Laws 2006, Act 947, § 12. See Butts County v. Strahan, 107 S.E. 163, 151 Ga. 417 (1921).

The 2010 amendment by Act 380 purported to amended § 40–2–86.18, which was renumbered § 40-2-85.3 by Laws 2010, Act 360, § 1–76, effective May 12, 2010.

Former § 40–2–86.18 was renumbered by Laws 2010, Act 360, § 1–76, effective May 12, 2010.

§ 40–2–86. Special license plates supporting beneficial agencies, funds, or programs administered by nonprofit corporations; funds dedicated

(a)(1) As used in this Code section, the term:

(A) "Manufacturing fee" means a $25.00 fee paid at the time a special license plate is issued.

(B) "Special license plate fee" means a $35.00 fee paid at the time a special license plate is issued.

(C) "Special license plate renewal fee" means a $35.00 fee paid at the time a revalidation decal is issued for a special license plate.

(2) In accordance with Article III, Section IX, Paragraph VI(n) of the Constitution, the General Assembly has determined that the issuance of special license plates to support an agency or fund or a program beneficial to the people of this state that is administered by a nonprofit corporation organized under Section 501(c)(3) of Title 26 of the Internal Revenue Code and dedicating a portion of the funds raised from the sale of these special license plates is in the best interests of the people of this state. . Any new special license plates adopted on or after July 1, 2010, that share a portion of the revenue raised with any agency, fund, nonprofit organization, or other similar entity shall allocate the revenue in accordance with the formula contained in subsection (*l*) of this Code section.

(b) The agency, fund, or nonprofit corporation sponsoring the special license plate, in cooperation with the commissioner, shall design special distinctive license plates appropriate to promote the program benefited by the sale of the special license plate. The special license plates must be of the same size as general issue motor vehicle license plates and shall include a unique design and identifying number, whereby the total number of characters does not exceed an amount to be determined by the commissioner. No two recipients shall receive identically numbered plates. The agency, fund, or nonprofit corporation sponsoring the license plate may request the assignment of the first of 100 in a series of license plates upon payment of an additional initial registration fee of $25. 00 for each license plate requested.

(c) Notwithstanding the provisions of subsection (b) of this Code section, no special license plate shall be produced until such time as the State of Georgia has, through a licensing agreement or otherwise, received such licenses or other permissions as may be required to produce the special license plate. The design of the initial edition of any special license plate, as well as the design of subsequent editions and excepting only any part or parts of the designs owned by others and licensed to the state, shall be owned solely by the State of Georgia for its exclusive use and control, except as authorized by the commissioner. The commissioner may take such steps as may be necessary to give notice of and protect such right, including the copyright or copyrights. However, such steps shall be cumulative of the ownership and exclusive use and control established by this subsection as a matter of law, and no person shall reproduce or otherwise use such design or designs, except as authorized by the commissioner.

(d) Any Georgia resident who is the owner of a motor vehicle, except a vehicle registered under the International Registration Plan, upon complying with the motor vehicle laws relating to registration and licensing of motor vehicles and upon the payment of the appropriate fees in addition to the regular motor vehicle registration fee shall be able to apply for a special license plate listed in this Code section. Revalidation decals shall be issued for special license plates in the same manner as provided for general issue license plates.

(e) Before the department disburses to the agency, fund, or nonprofit corporation funds from the sale of special license plates, the agency, fund, or nonprofit corporation must provide a written statement stating the manner in which such funds shall be utilized. In addition, a nonprofit corporation must provide the department with documentation of its nonprofit status under Section 501(c)(3) of Title 26 of the Internal Revenue Code. The purposes for which the funds shall be utilized must be the same as those specified in this Code section authorizing the dedication to the agency, fund, or nonprofit corporation of revenue from the sale of special license plates. The agency, fund, or nonprofit corporation shall periodically provide to the commissioner an audit of the use of the funds or other evidence of use of the funds satisfactory to the commissioner. If it is determined that the funds are not being used for the purposes set forth in the statement provided by the agency, fund, or nonprofit corporation, the department shall withhold payment of such funds until such noncompliance issues are resolved.

(f) An applicant may request a special license plate any time during the applicant's registration period. If such a license plate is to replace a current valid license plate, the special license plate shall be issued with appropriate decals attached upon payment of the manufacturing fee and the special license plate renewal fee.

(g) On or after July 1, 2010, no special license plate authorized pursuant to subsection (*l*) of this Code section shall be issued except upon the receipt by the department of at least 1,000 prepaid applications along with the manufacturing fees. The special license plate shall have an application period of two years after the date on which the application period becomes effective for payment of the manufacturing fee. After such time if the minimum number of applications is not met, the department shall not continue to accept the manufacturing fees, and all fees shall be refunded to applicants; provided, however, that once the department has received 1,000 prepaid applications along with the manufacturing fees, the sponsor shall not be entitled to a refund.

(h) The department shall not be required to continue to manufacture the special license plate if the number of active registrations falls below 500 registrations at any time during the period provided for in subsection (b) of Code Section 40–2–31. A current registrant may continue to renew such special license plate during his or her annual registration period upon payment of the special license plate renewal fee which shall be collected by the county tag agent at the time of collection of other registration fees and shall be remitted to the state as provided in Code Section 40–2–34. The department may continue to issue such special license plates that it has in its inventory to assist in achieving the minimum number of registrations. If the special license plate falls below 500 active registrations at any time during the period provided for in subsection (b) of Code Section 40–2–31, the sponsoring agency, fund, or nonprofit corporation shall be required again to obtain 1,000 prepaid applications accompanied by the manufacturing fees to continue to manufacture the special license plate.

(i) Special license plates shall be transferred from one vehicle to another vehicle in accordance with the provisions of Code Section 40–2–80.

(j) Special license plates shall be issued within 30 days of application once the requirements of this Code section have been met.

(k) The commissioner is authorized and directed to establish procedures and promulgate rules and regulations to effectuate the purposes of this Code section.

(*l*)(1) The General Assembly has determined that special license plates supporting the agencies, funds, or nonprofit corporations listed in this subsection shall be issued for the purposes indicated. The special license plates listed in this subsection shall be subject to a manufacturing fee, a special license plate fee, and a special license plate renewal fee. The revenue disbursement for the special license plates listed in this subsection shall be as follows:

(A) Manufacturing fee—$25.00 of which $24.00 is to be deposited into the general fund and $1.00 to be paid to the local county tag agent;

(B) Special license plate fee—$35.00 of which $25.00 is to be deposited into the general fund and $10.00 is to be dedicated to the sponsoring agency, fund, or nonprofit corporation as permitted by Article III, Section IX, Paragraph VI(n) of the Constitution; and

(C) Special license plate renewal fee—$35.00 of which $25.00 is to be deposited into the general fund and $10.00 is to be dedicated to the sponsoring agency, fund, or nonprofit corporation as permitted by Article III, Section IX, Paragraph VI(n) of the Constitution.

(2) Special license plates promoting the Nongame–Endangered Wildlife Program of the Georgia Department of Natural Resources. The funds raised by the sale of these special license plates shall be disbursed to the Nongame Wildlife Conservation and Wildlife Habitat Acquisition Fund of the Georgia Department of Natural Resources for the purposes enumerated in subsection (b) of Code Section 12–3–602. Such license plates shall not include a space for a county name decal but shall instead bear the legend Give Wildlife a Chance in lieu of the name of the county of issuance.

(3) A special license plate promoting conservation and enhancement of trout populations. The funds raised by the sale of this special license plate shall be disbursed to the Wildlife Resources Division of the Department of Natural Resources to supplement trout restoration and management programs.

(4) A special license plate supporting the Bobwhite Quail Restoration Initiative. The funds raised by the sale of this special license plate shall be disbursed to the Wildlife Resources Division of the Department of Natural Resources to conduct programs designed to enhance the bobwhite quail population in this state. Such programs may include the creation of habitat demonstration areas on state managed wildlife lands, education programs, technical assistance to private landowners in the creation and maintenance of bobwhite quail habitats on their lands, and projects to encourage public support for the license plate and the activities it funds. The Department of Natural Resources may enter into such contractual agreements as may be appropriate to further the objectives of the Bobwhite Quail Restoration Initiative, including entering into contractual agreements whereby private landowners, public agencies, or corporate entities create, preserve, or enhance habitat for bobwhite quail in return for the payment of incentives. Such license plate shall not include a space for a county decal but shall instead bear the legend Support Wildlife in lieu of the name of the county of issuance.

(5) Special license plates promoting the conservation of wildflowers within this state. The funds raised by the sale of these special license plates shall be disbursed to the Department of Transportation to be deposited in the Roadside Enhancement and Beautification Fund established by Code Section 32–6–75.2 and shall be expended only for the purposes enumerated in Code Section 32–6–75.2 and Article III, Section IX, Paragraph VI(*l*) of the Constitution of the State of Georgia.

(6) Special license plates promoting the dog and cat reproductive sterilization support program of the Georgia Department of Agriculture. The funds raised by the sale of these special license plates shall be disbursed to the Georgia Department of Agriculture and shall be deposited in the special fund for support of the dog and cat reproductive sterilization support program created by Code Section 4–15–1 and Article III, Section IX, Paragraph VI(m) of the Constitution of the State of Georgia.

(7) Special license plates to honor Georgia educators. The funds raised by the sale of these special license plates shall be disbursed to a charitable foundation designated by the State School Superintendent and used to fund educational programs, grants to teachers, and scholarships. The license plates shall display the phrase Georgia Educators Make A Difference and a ripe Red Delicious apple shall be depicted to the left of the identifying number of each plate.

(8)(A) The commissioner in cooperation with a college or university may design a special license plate to be issued commemorating that college or university, which license plate shall be similar in design to the license plate issued to all other residents of the state except that the logo or emblem of the college or university shall be placed on the license plate along with the letters and numbers on the license plate. The name of the college or university shall be imprinted on such special license plate in lieu of the county name decal.

(B) Any college or university that enters into an agreement with the commissioner pursuant to this paragraph shall waive any royalty fees to which it might otherwise be entitled for use of its seal, symbol, emblem, or logotype as provided in this paragraph.

(C) Each college or university located in Georgia that enters into an agreement with the commissioner pursuant to this paragraph shall designate a charitable foundation which shall annually receive an allocation from the special license plate and special license plate renewal fees collected as provided in paragraph (1) of this subsection. Special license plates issued under this paragraph shall be transferred between vehicles as provided in Code Section 40–2–42.

(D) The funds allocated for colleges and universities located in Georgia shall be delivered by the department to the charitable foundation designated by the particular college or university to support needs based, academic, financial aid scholarships for eligible undergraduate students enrolled in the college or university. The funds otherwise allocated for colleges and universities located outside the State of Georgia shall be placed into the general fund.

(E) Each college or university shall review and approve plans for the implementation of these scholarship programs by the applicable charitable foundation. These plans shall include, but need not be limited to, criteria for the awarding of the scholarships and procedures for determining the recipients.

(9) A special license plate for the Georgia Center for the Book to support the purchase of books for public libraries in Georgia. The funds raised by the sale of this special license plate shall be disbursed to the Georgia Center for the Book.

(10) A special license plate for Children's Healthcare of Atlanta to support the work this pediatric hospital system does in the State of Georgia. The funds raised by the sale of this special license plate shall be disbursed to Children's Healthcare of Atlanta.

(11) A special license plate for the Georgia War Veterans Nursing Home to support the implementation and operation of the Georgia War Veterans Nursing Home. The funds raised by the sale of this special license plate shall be disbursed to the Department of Veterans Service for use in operating the Georgia War Veterans Nursing Home.

(12) A special license plate for the Georgia Automobile Racing Hall of Fame Association to promote the Georgia Automobile Racing Hall of Fame Association, which is devoted to preserving the history of automobile racing in Georgia. The funds raised by the sale of this special license plate shall be disbursed to the Georgia Automobile Racing Hall of Fame Association.

(13) A special license plate for the Alzheimer's Association, Georgia Chapter, to help eliminate Alzheimer's disease through the advancement of research and to enhance care and support for individuals, their families, and caregivers. The funds raised by the sale of this special license plate shall be disbursed to the Alzheimer's Association, Georgia Chapter.

(14) A special license plate for the school health and physical education program to help fund school health and physical education programs. The funds raised by the sale of this special license plate shall be disbursed to the Department of Education.

(15) A special license plate for stroke awareness, treatment, and prevention to support programs aiding stroke victims in Georgia. Such license plate shall not include a space for a county name decal but shall instead bear the legend Stroke Awareness in lieu of the name of the county of issuance. The

funds raised by the sale of this special license plate shall be disbursed to the Center for Telehealth of the Medical College of Georgia.

(16) A special license plate for Project Lifesaver promoting the establishment of a Project Lifesaver or similar type of program by local law enforcement agencies. Project Lifesaver's mission is to use state of the art technology in assisting those who care for victims of Alzheimer's disease and other related mental dysfunction disorders and victims who become lost. The funds raised by the sale of this special license plate shall be disbursed to the Department of Public Safety or a nonprofit corporation organized exclusively for the purpose of establishing a Project Lifesaver or similar type of program by local law enforcement agencies.

(17) A special license plate for pediatric cancer to raise funds to support the treatment of pediatric cancer. Such license plate shall not include a space for a county name decal but shall instead bear the legend Cure Kids' Cancer in lieu of the name of the county of issuance. The funds raised by the sale of this special license plate shall be disbursed to the Department of Community Health to be deposited in the Indigent Care Trust Fund created by Code Section 31–8–152 to fund pediatric cancer screening and treatment related programs for those children who are medically indigent and may have cancer.

(18) A special license plate for the child care industry to promote the child care industry by encouraging higher educational standards and providing for professional camaraderie for child care providers. Such license plate shall not include a space for a county name decal but shall instead bear the legend Support Improved Child Care in lieu of the name of the county of issuance. The funds raised by the sale of this special license plate shall be disbursed to the Minority Alliance for Child Care Development Advocates, Inc., for the development of programs to help improve child care.

(19) A special license plate to display the motto, In God We Trust. The funds raised by the sale of this special license plate shall be disbursed to the Boy Scouts of America for the development of scouting programs.

(20) A special license plate for child abuse prevention. Such license plate shall not include a space for a county name decal but shall instead bear the legend Prevent Child Abuse in lieu of the name of the county of issuance. The funds raised by the sale of this special license plate shall be disbursed to the Foster Family Foundation of Georgia for the development of programs to help victims of child abuse.

(21) A special license plate for the Thanks Mom and Dad Fund. The funds raised by the sale of this special license plate shall be disbursed to the Department of Human Services to address the key needs of the state's older population or a nonprofit corporation organized to serve the needs of the state's older population.

(22) A special license plate for pediatric cancer research. The funds raised by the sale of this special license plate shall be disbursed to the Joanna McAfee Childhood Cancer Foundation for support of pediatric cancer research. The design of the special license plate provided for in this paragraph shall include the words Joanna McAfee Childhood Cancer Foundation horizontally across the bottom of the plate in lieu of the county name.

(23) A special license plate for supporting beautification projects in Cobb County. The funds raised by the sale of this special license plate shall be disbursed to Keep Cobb Beautiful, Inc., for support of beautification projects in Cobb County.

(24) A special license plate for the AIDS Survival Project. The funds raised by the sale of this special license plate shall be disbursed to the AIDS Survival Project which is committed to providing people living with HIV the information and support they need to live healthy and productive lives.

(25) A special license endorsing Support Our Troops. The funds raised by the sale of this special license plate shall be disbursed to the Georgia National Guard Family Support Foundation, Incorporated.

(26) A special license plate for the Sons of Confederate Veterans. The funds raised by the sale of this special license plate shall be disbursed to Georgia Sons of Confederate Veterans.

(27) A special license plate for amyotrophic lateral sclerosis (ALS), also known as Lou Gehrig's disease, to support research and education on amyotrophic lateral sclerosis. The funds raised by the sale of this special license plate shall be disbursed to the ALS Association of Georgia.

(28) A special license plate for foster parents to support programs for foster parents in Georgia. The funds raised by the sale of this special license plate shall be disbursed to The Adoptive and Foster Parent Association of Georgia, Inc., for support of foster parents in Georgia.

(29) A special license plate for the Atlanta Braves Foundation to assist the charities supported by the foundation. The funds raised by the sale of this special license plate shall be disbursed to the Department of Community Affairs or such other public agency or nonprofit corporation as may be designated.

(30) A special license plate for the Atlanta Falcons Youth Foundation to assist the charities supported by the foundation. The funds raised by the sale of this special license plate shall be disbursed to the Atlanta Falcons Youth Foundation. Such license plate shall not include a space for a county name decal but shall instead bear the legend Atlanta Falcons in lieu of the name of the county of issuance.

(31) A special license plate for supporting beautification projects in Georgia. The funds raised by the sale of this special license plate shall be disbursed to Keep Georgia Beautiful Foundation, Inc., for support of beautification projects in Georgia.

(32) A special license plate displaying the logo of Choose Life, Inc. The words Choose Life must appear at the bottom. The funds raised by the sale of this special license plate shall be disbursed to Choose Life of Georgia, Inc., to be distributed among nonprofit corporations in Georgia that counsel women to consider adoption.

(33) A special license plate supporting education on the maritime history of Georgia's coast. The funds raised by the sale of this special license plate shall be disbursed to The Georgia Maritime Foundation, Inc., for use in programs supporting education on the maritime history of Georgia.

(34) A special license plate supporting programs for persons with brain related disorders and disabilities. The funds raised by the sale of this special license plate shall be disbursed to Pilot International for support of programs for persons with brain related disorders in Georgia.

(35) A special license plate supporting agriculture in Georgia. The funds raised by the sale of this special license plate shall be evenly split between Georgia 4–H and the Georgia Association of Future Farmers of America to fund projects promoting agriculture in Georgia.

(36) A special license plate promoting the Georgia equine industry. The funds raised by the sale of this special license plate shall be disbursed to the Agricultural Commodity Commission for Equines.

(37) A special license plate promoting African American history and tourism in Georgia. The funds raised by the sale of this special license plate shall be disbursed to organizations dedicated to the preservation of African American history in Georgia.

(38) A special license plate honoring veterans who have been awarded the Bronze Star. The funds raised by the sale of this special license plate shall be disbursed to the National Guard Family Foundation.

(39) A special license plate promoting the arts in Georgia. The funds raised by the sale of this special license plate shall be disbursed to the Georgia Council for the Arts.

(40) A special license plate supporting programs for the treatment of autism. The funds raised by the sale of this special license plate shall be disbursed to the Department of Behavioral Health and Developmental Disabilities for the support of programs for the treatment of autism in Georgia.

(41) A special license plate honoring the work of The Garden Club of Georgia, Inc. The funds raised by the sale of this special license plate shall be disbursed to The Garden Club of Georgia, Inc., and used to fund scholarships that are awarded by the club.

(42) A special license plate promoting the Georgia Junior Golf Foundation. The funds raised by the sale of this special license plate shall be disbursed to the Georgia Junior Golf Foundation.

(43) A special license plate commemorating 100 years of scouting in the United States. The funds raised by the sale of this special license plate shall be disbursed to the Boy Scouts of America for the development of scouting programs.

(44) A special license plate supporting Cobb County Public Schools. The funds raised by the sale of this special license plate shall be disbursed to the Cobb County Public Schools Educational Foundation and used to fund educational programs, grants to teachers, and scholarships in the Cobb County Public School System.

(45) A special license plate supporting the Georgia Sea Turtle Center. The funds raised by the sale of this special license plate shall be charged and disbursed to the Nongame Wildlife Conservation and Wildlife Habitat Acquisition Fund and used to fund nongame wildlife conservation and education programs. The design of the license plate provided for in this paragraph shall include the words Jekyll Island—Georgia's Jewel horizontally across the bottom of the plate in lieu of the county name, with a diamond jewel symbol in place of the dash.

(46) A special license plate commemorating and supporting the sport of soccer in Georgia. The funds raised by the sale of this special license plate shall be disbursed to the Georgia State Soccer Association, Inc., for the development and promotion of soccer programs in the State of Georgia. Such license plate shall not include a space for a county decal but shall instead bear the legend gasoccer.org.

(47) A special license plate for the Georgia Aquarium to support its mission as an entertaining, educational, and scientific institution and to promote the conservation of aquatic biodiversity throughout the world. The funds raised by the sale of this special plate shall be disbursed to Georgia Aquarium, Inc. Such license plate shall not include a space for a county name decal but shall instead bear the legend Georgia Aquarium in lieu of the name of the county of issuance.

(m)(1) The General Assembly has determined that the following special license plates supporting the agencies, funds, or nonprofit corporations listed in this subsection shall be issued for the purposes indicated. The special license plates listed in this subsection shall be subject to a manufacturing fee, a special license plate fee, and a special license plate renewal fee. The revenue disbursement for the special license plates listed in this subsection shall be as follows:

(A) Manufacturing fee—$25.00 of which $24.00 is to be deposited into the general fund and $1.00 to be paid to the local county tag agent;

(B) Special license plate fee—$35.00 of which $13.00 is to be deposited into the general fund and $22.00 is to be dedicated to the sponsoring agency, fund, or nonprofit corporation; and

(C) Special license plate renewal fee—$35.00 of which $13.00 is to be deposited into the general fund and $22.00 is to be dedicated to the sponsoring agency, fund, or nonprofit corporation.

(2) A special license plate promoting the United States Disabled Athletes Fund, for the support of disabled athletes. The funds raised by the sale of this special license plate shall be disbursed as provided in paragraph (1) of this subsection to the United States Disabled Athletes Fund.

(3) A special license plate commemorating Civil War battlefields and historic sites. The funds raised by the sale of this special license plate shall be disbursed as provided in paragraph (1) of this subsection to the Civil War Commission for the acquisition of Civil War battlefields and associated Civil War historic sites in this state and for the maintenance, protection, and interpretation of the same as provided by Article 5 of Chapter 7 of Title 50.

(4) A special license plate promoting historic preservation efforts. The funds raised by the sale of this special license plate shall be disbursed as provided in paragraph (1) of this subsection to the Department of Natural Resources for use by the Historic Preservation Division to fund historic preservation programs in the state through the Georgia historic preservation grant program as otherwise authorized by law.

(5) A special license plate promoting bicycle safety. The funds raised by the sale of this special license plate shall be disbursed as provided in paragraph (1) of this subsection to the Governor's Highway Safety Program administered by the Office of Highway Safety in the Department of Public Safety.

(6) A special license plate honoring families with a member serving in the military. The funds raised by the sale of this special license plate shall be disbursed as provided in paragraph (1) of this subsection to the Department of Veterans Service for use by the National Guard Foundation in carrying out such programs and purposes as may be contractually agreed upon by the department and the foundation.

(7) A special license plate promoting Support Georgia Troops. The funds raised by the sale of this special license plate shall be disbursed as provided in paragraph (1) of this subsection to the Department of Veterans Service for use by the National Guard Foundation in carrying out such programs and purposes as may be contractually agreed upon by the department and the foundation.

(8) A special license plate promoting NASCAR. The provisions of paragraph (1) of this subsection notwithstanding, from the additional $35.00 special license plate renewal fee charged for the issuance and renewal of the NASCAR license plates authorized under this paragraph, $10.25 shall be used by the department for purchasing plates from the supplier of the plates, as designated by NASCAR, and royalty costs, $10.00 shall be deposited in the general fund, and $14.75 shall be disbursed to the Governor's Highway Safety Program administered by the Office of Highway Safety in the Department of Public Safety.

(9) A special license plate to support breast cancer related programs for the medically indigent. The provisions of paragraph (1) of this subsection notwithstanding, from the additional $35.00 special license plate fee or special license plate renewal fee charged for the issuance and renewal of breast cancer license plates authorized under this paragraph, $12. 95 shall be deposited in the general fund and $22.05 shall be deposited in the Indigent Care Trust Fund created by Code Section 31–8–152 to fund cancer screening and treatment related to programs for those persons who are medically indigent and may have breast cancer. To the extent consistent with Article III, Section IX, Paragraph VI(i) of the Constitution and Article 6 of Chapter 8 of Title 31, such programs may include education, breast cancer screening, grants-in-aid to breast cancer victims, pharmacy assistance programs for breast cancer victims, and other projects to encourage public support for the special license plate and the activities which it funds. Such design shall include a logo the same as the United States postal stamp supporting breast cancer research and bearing the

slogan Fund the Fight. Find A Cure. over the sketch of a woman and the breast cancer awareness pink ribbon symbol.

Laws 2006, Act 947, § 12, eff. Jan. 1, 2007; Laws 2007, Act 18, § 40, eff. May 11, 2007; Laws 2007, Act 351, §§ 4 to 6, eff. May 29, 2007; Laws 2008, Act 725, §§ 2, 3, eff. May 14, 2008; Laws 2008, Act 800, § 1, eff. July 1, 2008; Laws 2009, Act 102, § 2–18, eff. July 1, 2009; Laws 2009, Act 179, § 1, eff. July 1, 2009; Laws 2010, Act 360, § 1–77, eff. May 12, 2010.

Formerly Code 1981, § 40–2–86.21

Historical and Statutory Notes

Laws 2006, Act 947, § 13, provides:

"(a) This Act [adding this section] shall become effective on January 1, 2007, except as otherwise provided in subsection (b) of this section.

"(b) If an amendment to the Constitution of the State of Georgia authorizing the dedication of revenue from sales of special license plates to agencies, funds, or nonprofit corporations designated by the General Assembly is not ratified at the general election in 2006, this Act shall be repealed in its entirety on January 1, 2007, and no such motor vehicle license plates shall be issued pursuant to this Act."

An amendment to Article III, § IX, Par. VI, of the Georgia constitution, authorizing such a dedication, was approved by the electorate at the general election held on November 7, 2006.

In 2006, the Code Commission redesignated § 40–2–86.18, which was enacted by Laws 2006, Act 947, § 12, as § 40–2–86.21. See § 28–9–5.

In 2006, the Code Commission, due to irreconcilable conflicts, treated the enactment of § 40–2–8.18 by Laws 2006, Act 946, § 1, as superseded by Laws 2006, Act 947, § 12. See Butts County v. Strahan, 107 S.E. 163, 151 Ga. 417 (1921).

In 2007, the Code Commission, due to irreconcilable conflicts, treated the amendment of this section by Laws 2007, Act 18, § 40, as superseded by Laws 2007, Act 351, §§ 4 to 6. See Butts County v. Strahan, 107 S.E. 163, 151 Ga. 417 (1921).

In 2007, the Code Commission, in subsec. (n), substituted "Article 5 of Chapter 7 of Title 50" for "Ga. L. 1993, p. 1952" in the last sentence of par. (3). See § 28–9–5.

In 2008, the Code Commission redesignated par. (*o*)(38), which was added by Laws 2008, Act 524, § 1, as par. (*o*)(39). See § 28–9–5.

This section, added as § 40–2–86.21, was renumbered by Laws 2010, Act 360, § 1–77, effective May 12, 2010.

Former § 40–2–86 was repealed by Laws 1998, p. 1179, § 28, eff. May 1, 1998

§ 40–2–86.1. Repealed by Laws 2010, Act 360, § 1–75, eff. May 12, 2010

Historical and Statutory Notes

The repealed section, relating to special license plates commemorating square and round dancers, was derived from Laws 1997, p. 1559, § 4.

§ 40–2–86.1. Special license plates to support beneficial agencies, funds, or programs administered by nonprofit corporations; revenue deposited in general fund

(a) The General Assembly has determined that the issuance of special license plates to support an agency or fund or a program beneficial to the people of this state that is administered by a nonprofit corporation organized under Section 501(c)(3) of Title 26 of the Internal Revenue Code and, subject to the appropriation process of the General Assembly, appropriating a portion of the funds raised from the sale of these special license plates is in the best interests of the people of this state. Therefore, the license plates listed in subsection (*l*) of this Code section shall be issued by the department beginning on January 1, 2007, if all of the requirements of subsections (b) through (k) of this Code section have been satisfied.

(b) The commissioner, in cooperation with the agency, fund, or nonprofit corporation sponsoring the special license plate, shall design special distinctive license plates intended to promote the program benefited by the sale of the special license plate. The special license plates must be of the same size as general issue motor vehicle license plates and shall include a unique design and identifying number, whereby the total number of characters does not exceed six. No two recipients shall receive identically numbered plates. The graphic on the special license plate shall be placed to the left of the alphanumeric characters and shall be no larger than three inches by three inches. The agency, fund, or nonprofit corporation sponsoring the license plate may request the assignment of the first of 100 in a series of license plates upon payment of an additional initial registration fee of $25.00 for each license plate requested.

(c) Notwithstanding the provisions of subsection (b) of this Code section, no special license plate shall be produced until such time as the State of Georgia has, through a licensing agreement or otherwise, received such licenses or other permissions as may be required to produce the special license plate. The design of the initial edition of any special license plate, as well as the design of subsequent editions and excepting only any part or parts of the designs owned by others and licensed to the state, shall be owned solely by the State of Georgia for its exclusive use and control, except as authorized by the commissioner. The commissioner may take such steps as may be necessary to give notice of and protect such right, including the copyright or copyrights. However, such steps shall be cumulative of the ownership and exclusive use and control established by this subsection as a matter of law, and no person shall reproduce or otherwise use such design or designs, except as authorized by the commissioner.

(d) Beginning on January 1, 2007, any Georgia resident who is the owner of a motor vehicle, except a vehicle registered under the International Registration Plan, upon complying with the motor vehicle laws relating to registration and licensing of motor vehicles and upon the payment of a manufacturing fee of $25.00 in addition to the regular motor vehicle registration fee shall be able to apply for a special license plate listed in subsection (*l*) of this Code section. Revalidation decals shall be issued for special license plates in the same manner as provided for general issue license plates.

(e) The manufacturing fee derived from the sale of special license plates shall be deposited into the general fund. The sponsoring agency, fund, or nonprofit corporation, subject to the appropriation process of the General Assembly, may request that the funds derived from the sale of special license plates be appropriated to the department for disbursement to such agency, fund, or nonprofit corporation.

(f) Before the department disburses to the agency, fund, or nonprofit corporation funds from the sale of special license plates, the agency, fund, or nonprofit corporation must provide a written statement stating the manner in which such funds shall be utilized. In addition, a nonprofit corporation must provide the department with documentation of its nonprofit status under Section 501(c)(3) of Title 26 of the Internal Revenue Code. The purposes for which the funds shall be utilized must be the same as those specified in subsection (*l*) of this Code section authorizing the potential appropriation to the agency, fund, or nonprofit corporation of revenue from the sale of special license plates. The agency, fund, or nonprofit corporation shall periodically provide to the commissioner an audit of the use of the funds or other evidence of use of the funds satisfactory to the commissioner. If it is determined that the funds are not being used for the purposes set forth in the statement provided by the agency, fund, or nonprofit corporation, the department shall withhold payment of such funds until such noncompliance issues are resolved.

(g) An applicant may request a special license plate any time during the applicant's registration period. If such a license plate is to replace a current valid license plate, the special license plate shall be issued with appropriate decals attached.

(h) No special license plate authorized pursuant to subsection (*l*) of this Code section shall be issued except upon the receipt by the department of at least 1,000 applications. The special license plate shall have an application period of two years after January 1, 2007, for payment of the manufacturing fee. After such time if the minimum number of applications is not met, the department shall not continue to accept the manufacturing fee, and all fees shall be refunded to applicants.

(i) The department shall not be required to continue to manufacture the special license plate if the number of active registrations falls below 500 registrations at any time during the period provided for in subsection (b) of Code Section 40–2–31. A current registrant may continue to renew such special license plate during his or her annual registration period upon payment of an additional $25.00 annual special tag fee, which fee shall be collected by the county tag agent at the time of collection of other registration fees and shall be remitted to the state as provided in Code Section 40–2–34. The department may continue to issue such special license plates that it has in its inventory to assist in achieving the minimum number of registrations. If the special license plate falls below 500 active registrations at any time during the period provided for in subsection (b) of Code Section 40–2–31, the sponsoring agency, fund, or nonprofit corporation shall be required again to obtain 1,000 applications accompanied by the manufacturing fee to continue to manufacture the special license plate.

(j) Special license plates shall be transferred from one vehicle to another vehicle in accordance with the provisions of Code Section 40–2–80.

(k) Special license plates shall be issued within 30 days of application once the requirements of this Code section have been met.

(*l*)(1) The General Assembly has determined that license plates promoting the agencies, funds, or nonprofit corporations listed in this subsection shall be issued for the purposes indicated and the revenue shall be deposited in the general fund, subject to the appropriation process of the General Assembly.

(2) A special license plate identifying persons with diabetes. The main purpose of the special license plate is that law enforcement officers and emergency personnel will be alerted to the potential for special needs before they approach the driver of a vehicle, especially if the vehicle has been involved in an accident. The funds raised by the sale of this special license plate shall be deposited in the general fund.

(3) A special license plate honoring all veterans who have served in the armed services of the United States. All of these men and women have sacrificed a portion of their lives in order to serve their country and protect our freedom. The funds raised by the sale of this special license plate shall be deposited in the general fund.

(4) A special license plate honoring the Georgia Association of Realtors. The Association is being honored for its longstanding support of housing opportunities for all citizens of this state, private property rights, and all organizations that assist people in achieving the American dream of home ownership. The funds raised by the sale of this special license plate shall be deposited in the general fund.

(5) A special license plate honoring Georgia municipal clerks. The municipal clerk's office provides the professional link connecting citizens with their local governing bodies and agencies of government at other levels. The funds raised by the sale of this license plate shall be deposited in the general fund.

Laws 2006, Act 576, § 1, eff. July 1, 2006; Laws 2007, Act 351, § 7, eff. May 29, 2007.

Historical and Statutory Notes

In 2006, the Code Commission redesignated § 40–2–86.19, which was enacted by Laws 2006, Act 576, § 1, as § 40–2–86.22. See § 28–9–5.

In 2006, the Code Commission, in subsec. (i), inserted "period" following "any time during the" in the first sentence. See § 28–9–5.

The amending language of Laws 2007, Act 351, § 7, purports to add pars. (5) and (6) to subsec. (*l*). The section contained only par. (5).

§ 40–2–86.2. Repealed by Laws 2010, Act 360, § 1–75, eff. May 12, 2010

Historical and Statutory Notes

The repealed section, relating to special license plates to honor and support Shrine hospitals for children, was derived from Laws 1997, p. 1559, § 4.

§ 40–2–86.3. Repealed by Laws 2006, Act 947, § 6, eff. January 1, 2007

Historical and Statutory Notes

The repealed section, relating to special license plates commemorating Civil War battlefields and historic sites, was derived from Laws 1997, p. 1559, § 4; Laws 1998, p. 1179, § 29. The repealing law also reserved the section designation.

Laws 2006, Act 947, § 13, provides:

"(a) This Act [repealing and reserving this section] shall become effective on January 1, 2007, except as otherwise provided in subsection (b) of this section.

"(b) If an amendment to the Constitution of the State of Georgia authorizing the dedication of revenue from sales of special license plates to agencies, funds, or nonprofit corporations designated by the General Assembly is not ratified at the general election in 2006, this Act shall be repealed in its entirety on January 1, 2007, and no such motor vehicle license plates shall be issued pursuant to this Act."

An amendment to Article III, § IX, Par. VI, of the Georgia constitution, authorizing such a dedication, was approved by the electorate at the general election held on November 7, 2006.

Laws 2010, Act 360, § 1–75, repealed the reserved designation, effective May 12, 2010.

§ 40–2–86.4. Repealed by Laws 2010, Act 360, § 1–75, eff. May 12, 2010

Historical and Statutory Notes

The repealed section, relating to special license plates bearing the words "Supporting Public Schools", was derived from Laws 1997, p. 1559, § 4; Laws 1998, p. 1179, § 30.

§ 40–2–86.5. Repealed by Laws 2010, Act 360, 1–75, eff. May 12, 2010

Historical and Statutory Notes

The repealed section, relating to special license plates bearing the words "Georgia Educators Make a Difference", was derived from Laws 2000, p. 768, § 1.

§ 40–2–86.6. Repealed by Laws 2006, Act 947, § 7, eff. January 1, 2007

Historical and Statutory Notes

The repealed section, relating to special license plates recognizing Trout Unlimited of Georgia, was derived from Laws 2001, p. 479, § 2. The repealing law also reserved the section designation.

Laws 2006, Act 947, § 13, provides:

"(a) This Act [repealing and reserving this section] shall become effective on January 1, 2007, except as otherwise provided in subsection (b) of this section.

"(b) If an amendment to the Constitution of the State of Georgia authorizing the dedication of revenue from sales of special license plates to agencies, funds, or nonprofit corporations designated by the General Assembly is not ratified at the general election in 2006, this Act shall be repealed in its entirety on January 1, 2007, and no such motor vehicle license plates shall be issued pursuant to this Act."

An amendment to Article III, § IX, Par. VI, of the Georgia constitution, authorizing such a dedication, was approved by the electorate at the general election held on November 7, 2006.

Laws 2010, Act 360, § 1–75, repealed the reserve designation, effective May 12, 2010.

§ 40–2–86.7. Repealed by Laws 2010, Act 360, 1–75, eff. May 12, 2010

Historical and Statutory Notes

The repealed section, relating to special license plates supporting the National Rifle Association, was derived from Laws 2002, p. 1019, § 1.

§ 40–2–86.8. Repealed by Laws 2010, Act 360, § 1–75, eff. May 12, 2010

Historical and Statutory Notes

The repealed section, relating to special license plates to support breast cancer related programs for the medically indigent, was derived from Laws 2002, p. 1090, § 1; Laws 2006, Act 691, § 1.

Laws 2002, p. 1090, § 1; Laws 2006, Act 691, § 1, eff. July 1, 2006.

§ 40–2–86.9. Repealed by Laws 2010, Act 360, § 1–75, eff. May 12, 2010

Historical and Statutory Notes

The repealed section, relating to special license plates supporting Rotary International, was derived from Laws 2004, Act 585, § 1.

§ 40–2–86.10. Repealed by Laws 2010, Act 360, § 1–75, eff. May 12, 2010

Historical and Statutory Notes

The repealed section, relating to special license plates for wounded police officers , was derived from Laws 2005, Act 363, § 6; Laws 2006, Act 453, § 40.

§ 40–2–86.11. Repealed by Laws 2010, Act 360, § 1–75, eff. May 12, 2010.

Historical and Statutory Notes

The repealed section, relating to special license plates to honor the Benevolent and Protective Order of Elks, was derived from Laws 2005, Act 363, § 6, eff. Jan. 1, 2006; Laws 2006, Act 453, § 40.

§ 40–2–86.12. Repealed by Laws 2010, Act 360, § 1–75, eff. May 12, 2010

Historical and Statutory Notes

The repealed section, relating to special license plates displaying the EMS Star of Life Symbol, was derived from Laws 2005, Act 363, § 6.

§ 40–2–86.13. Repealed by Laws 2006, Act 947, § 8, eff. January 1, 2007

Historical and Statutory Notes

The repealed section, relating to special license plates promoting historic preservation efforts, was derived from laws 2005, Act 363, § 6. The repealing law also reserved the section designation.

Laws 2006, Act 947, § 13, provides:

"(a) This Act [repealing and reserving this section] shall become effective on January 1, 2007, except as otherwise provided in subsection (b) of this section.

"(b) If an amendment to the Constitution of the State of Georgia authorizing the dedication of revenue from sales of special license plates to agencies, funds, or nonprofit corporations designated by the General Assembly is not ratified at the general election in 2006, this Act shall be repealed in its entirety on January 1, 2007, and no such motor vehicle license plates shall be issued pursuant to this Act."

An amendment to Article III, § IX, Par. VI, of the Georgia constitution, authorizing such a dedication, was approved by the electorate at the general election held on November 7, 2006.

Laws 2010, Act 360, § 1–75, repealed the reserved designation, effective May 12, 2010.

§ 40–2–86.14. Repealed by Laws 2010, Act 360, § 1–75, eff. May 12, 2010

Historical and Statutory Notes

The repealed section, relating to special license plates identifying Georgia physicians, was derived from Laws 2005, Act 363, § 6.

§ 40–2–86.15 to 40–2–86.17. Repealed by Laws 2006, Act 947, §§ 9 to 11, eff. January 1, 2007

Historical and Statutory Notes

Section 40–2–86.15, relating to special license plates bearing the NASCAR logo promoting the Governor's Highway Safety Program, was derived from Laws 2005, Act 363, § 6. The repealing law also reserved the section designation.

Section 40–2–86.16, relating to special license plates honoring families with a member serving in the military, was derived from Laws 2005, Act 404, § 1. The repealing law also reserved the section designation.

Section 40–2–86.17, relating to special plates identifying persons supporting Georgia troops, was derived from Laws 2005, Act 407, § 1. The repealing law also reserved the section designation.

Laws 2006, Act 947, § 13, provides:

"(a) This Act [repealing and reserving these sections] shall become effective on January 1, 2007, except as otherwise provided in subsection (b) of this section.

"(b) If an amendment to the Constitution of the State of Georgia authorizing the dedication of revenue from sales of special license plates to agencies, funds, or nonprofit corporations designated by the General Assembly is not ratified at the general election in 2006, this Act shall be repealed in its entirety on January 1, 2007, and no such motor vehicle license plates shall be issued pursuant to this Act."

An amendment to Article III, § IX, Par. VI, of the Georgia constitution, authorizing such a dedication, was approved by the electorate at the general election held on November 7, 2006.

Laws 2010, Act 360, § 1–75, repealed the reserved designations, effective May 12, 2010.

§ 40–2–86.18. Renumbered as § 40–2–85.3 by Laws 2010, Act 360, § 1–76, eff. May 12, 2010

§ 40–2–86.19. Repealed by Laws 2010, Act 360, § 1–75, eff. May 12, 2010

Historical and Statutory Notes

The repealed section, relating to special plates supporting the Global War on Terrorism and Operation Enduring Freedom, was derived from Laws 2006, Act 764, § 1.

§ 40–2–86.20. Repealed by Laws 2010, Act 360, § 1–75, eff. May 12, 2010

Historical and Statutory Notes

The repealed section, relating to special plates supporting the Global War on Terrorism and Iraqi freedom, was derived from Laws 2006, Act 765, § 1.

§ 40–2–86.21. Special license plates supporting beneficial agencies, funds, or programs administered by nonprofit corporations; funds dedicated

(a)(1) As used in this Code section, the term:

(A) "Manufacturing fee" means a $25.00 fee paid at the time a metal special license plate is issued.

(B) "Special tag renewal fee" means a $25.00 fee paid at the time a revalidation decal is issued for a special license plate.

(2) The General Assembly has determined that the issuance of special license plates to support an agency or fund or a program beneficial to the people of this state that is administered by a nonprofit corporation organized under Section 501(c)(3) of Title 26 of the Internal Revenue Code and dedicating a portion of the funds raised from the sale of these special license plates is in the best interests of the people of this state. Therefore, the special license plates listed in subsection (*o*) of this Code section shall be issued by the department beginning on July 1, 2007, if all of the requirements of subsections (b) through (k) of this Code section have been satisfied. The license plates listed in subsections (m) and (n) of this Code section shall continue to be issued so long as they meet the requirements of subsections (b), (c), (f), (g), (i), (j), and (k) of this Code section.

(b) The agency, fund, or nonprofit corporation sponsoring the special license plate, in cooperation with the commissioner, shall design special distinctive license plates appropriate to promote the program benefited by the sale of the special license plate. The special license plates must be of the same size as general issue motor vehicle license plates and shall include a unique design and identifying number, whereby the total number of characters does not exceed six. No two recipients shall receive identically numbered plates. The graphic on the special license plate shall be placed to the left of the alphanumeric characters and shall be no larger than three inches by three inches. The agency, fund, or nonprofit corporation sponsoring the license plate may request the assignment of the first of 100 in a series of license plates upon payment of an additional initial registration fee of $25.00 for each license plate requested.

(c) Notwithstanding the provisions of subsection (b) of this Code section, no special license plate shall be produced until such time as the State of Georgia has, through a licensing agreement or otherwise, received such licenses or other permissions as may be required to produce the special license plate. The design of the initial edition of any special license plate, as well as the design of subsequent editions and excepting only any part or parts of the designs owned by others and licensed to the state, shall be owned solely by the State of Georgia for its exclusive use and control, except as authorized by the commissioner. The commissioner may take such steps as may be necessary to give notice of and protect such right, including the copyright or copyrights. However, such steps shall be cumulative of the ownership and exclusive use and control established by this subsection as a matter of law, and no person shall reproduce or otherwise use such design or designs, except as authorized by the commissioner.

(d) Beginning on January 1, 2007, any Georgia resident who is the owner of a motor vehicle, except a vehicle registered under the International Registration Plan, upon complying with the motor vehicle laws relating to registration and licensing of motor vehicles and upon the payment of the manufacturing fee and the special tag renewal fee in addition to the regular motor vehicle registration fee shall be able to apply for a special license plate listed in subsection (*o*) of this Code section. Revalidation decals shall be issued for special license plates in the same manner as provided for general issue license plates.

(e) The manufacturing fee and the special tag renewal fee derived from the sale of special license plates listed in subsection (*o*) of this Code section shall be apportioned as follows: $1.00 to the county tag agent, $2.00 to the department, $12.00 to be deposited into the general fund, and $10.00 to be dedicated to the sponsoring agency, fund, or nonprofit corporation as permitted by Article III, Section IX, Paragraph VI(n) of the Constitution.

(f) Before the department disburses to the agency, fund, or nonprofit corporation funds from the sale of special license plates, the agency, fund, or nonprofit corporation must provide a written statement stating the manner in which such funds shall be utilized. In addition, a nonprofit corporation must provide the department with documentation of its nonprofit status under Section 501(c)(3) of Title 26 of the Internal Revenue Code. The purposes for which the funds shall be utilized must be the same as those specified in subsections (m) and (n) of this Code section authorizing the dedication to the agency, fund, or nonprofit corporation of revenue from the sale of special license plates. The agency, fund, or nonprofit corporation shall periodically provide to the commissioner an audit of the use of the funds or other evidence of use of the funds satisfactory to the commissioner. If it is determined that the funds are not being used for the purposes set forth in the statement provided by the agency, fund, or nonprofit corporation, the department shall withhold payment of such funds until such noncompliance issues are resolved.

(g) An applicant may request a special license plate any time during the applicant's registration period. If such a license plate is to replace a current valid license plate, the special license plate if issued under subsection (m) of this Code section shall be issued with appropriate decals attached upon payment of the manufacturing fee but without payment of the special tag renewal fee. However, special license plates issued under subsections (n) and (*o*) of this Code section shall be issued with appropriate decals attached upon payment of the manufacturing fee and the special tag renewal fee.

(h) No special license plate authorized pursuant to subsection (*o*) of this Code section shall be issued except upon the receipt by the department of at least 1,000 applications. The special license plate shall have an application period of two years after the date on which the application period becomes effective for payment of the manufacturing fee. After such time if the minimum number of applications is not met, the department shall not continue to accept the manufacturing fee, and all fees shall be refunded to applicants.

(i) The department shall not be required to continue to manufacture the special license plate if the number of active registrations falls below 500 registrations at any time during the period provided for in subsection (b) of Code Section 40–2–31. A current registrant may continue to renew such special license plate during his or her annual registration period upon payment of the special tag renewal fee, if applicable, which shall be collected by the county tag agent at the time of collection of other registration fees and shall be remitted to the state as provided in Code Section 40–2–34. The department may continue to issue such special license plates that it has in its inventory to assist in achieving the minimum number of registrations. If the special license plate falls below 500 active registrations at any time during the period provided for in subsection (b) of Code Section 40–2–31, the sponsoring agency, fund, or nonprofit corporation shall be required again to obtain 1,000 applications accompanied by the manufacturing fee to continue to manufacture the special license plate.

(j) Special license plates shall be transferred from one vehicle to another vehicle in accordance with the provisions of Code Section 40–2–80.

(k) Special license plates shall be issued within 30 days of application once the requirements of this Code section have been met.

(*l*) The commissioner is authorized and directed to establish procedures and promulgate rules and regulations to effectuate the purposes of this Code section.

(m)(1) The General Assembly has determined that the following existing special license plates supporting the agencies, funds, or nonprofit corporations listed in this subsection shall continue to be issued for the purposes indicated and that all of the funds raised from the manufacturing fee, less a $1.00 fee to be paid to the county tag agent and a $2.00 manufacturing fee to be paid to the department, shall be disbursed to the agency, fund, or nonprofit corporation indicated in this subsection. The special license plates listed in this subsection shall not be subject to a special tag renewal fee.

(2) Special license plates promoting the Nongame–Endangered Wildlife Program of the Georgia Department of Natural Resources. The funds raised by the sale of these special

license plates shall be disbursed to the Nongame Wildlife Conservation and Wildlife Habitat Acquisition Fund of the Georgia Department of Natural Resources for the purposes enumerated in subsection (b) of Code Section 12–3–602. Such license plates shall not include a space for a county name decal but shall instead bear the legend "Give Wildlife a Chance" in lieu of the name of the county of issuance.

(3) A special license plate promoting conservation and enhancement of trout populations. The funds raised by the sale of this special license plate shall be disbursed to the Wildlife Resources Division of the Department of Natural Resources to supplement trout restoration and management programs.

(4) A special license plate supporting the Bobwhite Quail Restoration Initiative. The funds raised by the sale of this special license plate shall be disbursed to the Wildlife Resources Division of the Department of Natural Resources to conduct programs designed to enhance the bobwhite quail population in this state. Such programs may include the creation of habitat demonstration areas on state managed wildlife lands, education programs, technical assistance to private landowners in the creation and maintenance of bobwhite quail habitats on their lands, and projects to encourage public support for the license plate and the activities it funds. The Department of Natural Resources may enter into such contractual agreements as may be appropriate to further the objectives of the Bobwhite Quail Restoration Initiative, including entering into contractual agreements whereby private landowners, public agencies, or corporate entities create, preserve, or enhance habitat for bobwhite quail in return for the payment of incentives. Such license plate shall not include a space for a county decal but shall instead bear the legend "Support Wildlife" in lieu of the name of the county of issuance.

(n)(1) The General Assembly has determined that the following special license plates supporting the agencies, funds, or nonprofit corporations listed in this subsection shall be issued for the purposes indicated and that all of the funds raised from the manufacturing fee and the special tag renewal fee, less a $1.00 fee to be paid to the county tag agent and a $2.00 manufacturing fee to be paid to the department, shall be disbursed to the agency, fund, or nonprofit corporation indicated in this subsection. The special license plates listed in this subsection shall be subject to a special tag renewal fee.

(2) A special license plate promoting the United States Disabled Athletes Fund, for the support of disabled athletes. The funds raised by the sale of this special license plate shall be disbursed to the United States Disabled Athletes Fund.

(3) A special license plate commemorating Civil War battlefields and historic sites. The funds raised by the sale of this special license plate shall be disbursed to the Civil War Commission for the acquisition of Civil War battlefields and associated Civil War historic sites in this state and for the maintenance, protection, and interpretation of the same as provided by Article 5 of Chapter 7 of Title 50.

(4) A special license plate promoting historic preservation efforts. The funds raised by the sale of this special license plate shall be disbursed to the Department of Natural Resources for use by the Historic Preservation Division to fund historic preservation programs in the state through the Georgia historic preservation grant program as otherwise authorized by law.

(5) A special license plate promoting bicycle safety. The funds raised by the sale of this special license plate shall be disbursed to the Governor's Highway Safety Program administered by the Office of Highway Safety in the Department of Public Safety.

(6) A special license plate honoring families with a member serving in the military. The funds raised by the sale of this special license plate shall be disbursed to the Department of Veterans Service for use by the National Guard Foundation in carrying out such programs and purposes as may be contractually agreed upon by the department and the foundation.

(7) A special license plate promoting "Support Georgia Troops." The funds raised by the sale of this special license plate shall be disbursed to the Department of Veterans Service for use by the National Guard Foundation in carrying out such programs and purposes as may be contractually agreed upon by the department and the foundation.

(8) A special license plate promoting NASCAR. The provisions of paragraph (1) of this subsection notwithstanding, from the additional $25.00 fee charged for the issuance and renewal of the NASCAR license plates authorized under this paragraph, $10.25 shall be used by the department for purchasing plates from the supplier of the plates, as designated by NASCAR, and royalty costs, and $14.75 shall be disbursed to the Governor's Highway Safety Program administered by the Office of Highway Safety in the Department of Public Safety.

(*o*)(1) The General Assembly has determined that license plates supporting the agencies, funds, or nonprofit corporations listed in this subsection shall be issued for the purposes indicated and with a portion of the revenue being disbursed to the agency, fund, or nonprofit corporation indicated in this subsection. The revenue disbursement for the special license plates in this subsection shall be as described in subsection (e) of this Code section.

(2) A special license plate for the Georgia Center for the Book to support the purchase of books for public libraries in Georgia. The funds raised by the sale of this special license plate shall be disbursed to the Georgia Center for the Book.

(3) A special license plate for Children's Healthcare of Atlanta to support the work this pediatric hospital system does in the State of Georgia. The funds raised by the sale of this special license plate shall be disbursed to Children's Healthcare of Atlanta.

(4) A special license plate for the Georgia War Veterans Nursing Home to support the implementation and operation of the Georgia War Veterans Nursing Home. The funds raised by the sale of this special license plate shall be disbursed to the Department of Veterans Service for use in operating the Georgia War Veterans Nursing Home.

(5) A special license plate for the Georgia Automobile Racing Hall of Fame Association to promote the Georgia Automobile Racing Hall of Fame Association, which is devoted to preserving the history of automobile racing in Georgia. The funds raised by the sale of this special license plate shall be disbursed to the Georgia Automobile Racing Hall of Fame Association.

(6) A special license plate for the Alzheimer's Association, Georgia Chapter, to help eliminate Alzheimer's disease through the advancement of research and to enhance care and support for individuals, their families, and caregivers. The funds raised by the sale of this special license plate shall be disbursed to the Alzheimer's Association, Georgia Chapter.

(7) A special license plate for the school health and physical education program to help fund school health and physical education programs. The funds raised by the sale of this special license plate shall be disbursed to the Department of Education.

(8) A special license plate for stroke awareness, treatment, and prevention to support programs aiding stroke victims in Georgia. Such license plate shall not include a space for a county name decal but shall instead bear the legend "Stroke Awareness" in lieu of the name of the county of issuance. The funds raised by the sale of this special license plate shall be disbursed to the Center for Telehealth of the Medical College of Georgia.

(9) A special license plate for Project Lifesaver promoting the establishment of a Project Lifesaver or similar type of program by local law enforcement agencies. Project Lifesaver's mission is to use state of the art technology in assisting those who care for victims of Alzheimer's disease and other related mental dysfunction disorders and victims who become lost. The funds raised by the sale of this special license plate

shall be disbursed to the Department of Public Safety or a nonprofit corporation organized exclusively for the purpose of establishing a Project Lifesaver or similar type of program by local law enforcement agencies.

(10) A special license plate for pediatric cancer to raise funds to support the treatment of pediatric cancer. Such license plate shall not include a space for a county name decal but shall instead bear the legend "Cure Kids' Cancer" in lieu of the name of the county of issuance. The funds raised by the sale of this special license plate shall be disbursed to the Department of Community Health to be deposited in the Indigent Care Trust Fund created by Code Section 31–8–152 to fund pediatric cancer screening and treatment related programs for those children who are medically indigent and may have cancer.

(11) A special license plate for the child care industry to promote the child care industry by encouraging higher educational standards and providing for professional camaraderie for child care providers. Such license plate shall not include a space for a county name decal but shall instead bear the legend "Support Improved Child Care" in lieu of the name of the county of issuance. The funds raised by the sale of this special license plate shall be disbursed to the Minority Alliance for Child Care Development Advocates, Inc., for the development of programs to help improve child care.

(12) A special license plate to display the motto, "In God We Trust." The funds raised by the sale of this special license plate shall be disbursed to the Boy Scouts of America for the development of scouting programs.

(13) A special license plate for child abuse prevention. Such license plate shall not include a space for a county name decal but shall instead bear the legend "Prevent Child Abuse" in lieu of the name of the county of issuance. The funds raised by the sale of this special license plate shall be disbursed to the Foster Family Foundation of Georgia for the development of programs to help victims of child abuse.

(14) A special license plate for the Thanks Mom and Dad Fund. The funds raised by the sale of this special license plate shall be disbursed to the Department of Human Services to address the key needs of the state's older population or a nonprofit corporation organized to serve the needs of the state's older population.

(15) A special license plate for pediatric cancer research. The funds raised by the sale of this special license plate shall be disbursed to the Joanna McAfee Childhood Cancer Foundation for support of pediatric cancer research. The design of the special license plate provided for in this paragraph shall include the words "Joanna McAfee Childhood Cancer Foundation" horizontally across the bottom of the plate in lieu of the county name.

(16) A special license plate for supporting beautification projects in Cobb County. The funds raised by the sale of this special license plate shall be disbursed to Keep Cobb Beautiful, Inc., for support of beautification projects in Cobb County.

(17) A special license plate for the AIDS Survival Project. The funds raised by the sale of this special license plate shall be disbursed to the AIDS Survival Project which is committed to providing people living with HIV the information and support they need to live healthy and productive lives.

(18) A special license endorsing "Support Our Troops." The funds raised by the sale of this special license plate shall be disbursed to the Georgia National Guard Family Support Foundation, Incorporated.

(19) A special license plate for the Sons of Confederate Veterans. The funds raised by the sale of this special license plate shall be disbursed to Georgia Sons of Confederate Veterans.

(20) A special license plate for amyotrophic lateral sclerosis (ALS), also known as "Lou Gehrig's disease," to support research and education on amyotrophic lateral sclerosis. The funds raised by the sale of this special license plate shall be disbursed to the ALS Association of Georgia.

(21) A special license plate for foster parents to support programs for foster parents in Georgia. The funds raised by the sale of this special license plate shall be disbursed to The Adoptive and Foster Parent Association of Georgia, Inc., for support of foster parents in Georgia.

(22) A special license plate for the Atlanta Braves Foundation to assist the charities supported by the foundation. The funds raised by the sale of this special license plate shall be disbursed to the Department of Community Affairs or such other public agency or nonprofit corporation as may be designated.

(23) A special license plate for the Atlanta Falcons Youth Foundation to assist the charities supported by the foundation. The funds raised by the sale of this special license plate shall be disbursed to the Atlanta Falcons Youth Foundation. Such license plate shall not include a space for a county name decal but shall instead bear the legend "Atlanta Falcons" in lieu of the name of the county of issuance.

(24) A special license plate for supporting beautification projects in Georgia. The funds raised by the sale of this special license plate shall be disbursed to Keep Georgia Beautiful Foundation, Inc., for support of beautification projects in Georgia.

(25) A special license plate displaying the logo of Choose Life, Inc. The words "Choose Life" must appear at the bottom. The funds raised by the sale of this special license plate shall be disbursed to Choose Life of Georgia, Inc., to be distributed among nonprofit corporations in Georgia that counsel women to consider adoption.

(26) A special license plate supporting education on the maritime history of Georgia's coast. The funds raised by the sale of this special license plate shall be disbursed to The Georgia Maritime Foundation, Inc., for use in programs supporting education on the maritime history of Georgia.

(27) A special license plate supporting programs for persons with brain-related disorders and disabilities. The funds raised by the sale of this special license plate shall be disbursed to Pilot International, for support of programs for persons with brain-related disorders in Georgia.

(28) A special license plate supporting agriculture in Georgia. The funds raised by the sale of this special license plate shall be evenly split between Georgia 4–H and the Georgia Association of Future Farmers of America to fund projects promoting agriculture in Georgia.

(29) A special license plate promoting the Georgia equine industry. The funds raised by the sale of this special license plate shall be disbursed to the Agricultural Commodity Commission for Equines.

(30) A special license plate promoting African American history and tourism in Georgia. The funds raised by the sale of this special license plate shall be disbursed to organizations dedicated to the preservation of African American history in Georgia.

(31) A special license plate honoring veterans who have been awarded the Bronze Star. The funds raised by the sale of this special license plate shall be disbursed to the National Guard Family Foundation.

(32) A special license plate promoting the arts in Georgia. The funds raised by the sale of this special license plate shall be disbursed to the Georgia Council for the Arts.

(33) A special license plate supporting programs for the treatment of autism. The funds raised by the sale of this special license plate shall be disbursed to the Department of Behavioral Health and Developmental Disabilities for the support of programs for the treatment of autism in Georgia.

(34) A special license plate honoring the work of The Garden Club of Georgia, Inc. The funds raised by the sale of

this special license plate shall be disbursed to The Garden Club of Georgia, Inc., and used to fund scholarships that are awarded by the club.

(35) A special license plate promoting the Georgia Junior Golf Foundation. The funds raised by the sale of this special license plate shall be disbursed to the Georgia Junior Golf Foundation.

(36) A special license plate commemorating 100 years of scouting in the United States. The funds raised by the sale of this special license plate shall be disbursed to the Boy Scouts of America for the development of scouting programs.

(37) A special license plate supporting Cobb County Public Schools. The funds raised by the sale of this special license plate shall be disbursed to the Cobb County Public Schools Educational Foundation and used to fund educational programs, grants to teachers, and scholarships in the Cobb County Public School System.

(38) A special license plate supporting the Georgia Sea Turtle Center. The funds raised by the sale of this special license plate shall be charged and disbursed to the Nongame Wildlife Conservation and Wildlife Habitat Acquisition Fund and used to fund nongame wildlife conservation and education programs. The design of the license plate provided for in this paragraph shall include the words "Jekyll Island—Georgia's Jewel" horizontally across the bottom of the plate in lieu of the county name, with a diamond jewel symbol in place of the dash.

(39) A special license plate commemorating and supporting the sport of soccer in Georgia. The funds raised by the sale of this special license plate shall be disbursed to the Georgia State Soccer Association, Inc., for the development and promotion of soccer programs in the State of Georgia. Such license plate shall not include a space for a county decal but shall instead bear the legend "gasoccer.org".

(40) A special license plate for the Georgia Aquarium to support its mission as an entertaining, educational, and scientific institution and to promote the conservation of aquatic biodiversity throughout the world. The funds raised by the sale of this special plate shall be disbursed to Georgia Aquarium, Inc. Such license plate shall not include a space for a county name decal but shall instead bear the legend "Georgia Aquarium" in lieu of the name of the county of issuance.

(41) A special license plate for Zoo Atlanta to support its mission to inspire the citizens of Atlanta and Georgia and all visitors to the zoo to value wildlife on Earth; to help safeguard existing species through conservation by providing for an informative, educational, and engaging experience to all visitors; to carry out the responsible stewardship of the animals and the zoo facility; and to engage in related conservation activities and research. The funds raised by the sale of this special plate shall be disbursed to the Atlanta–Fulton County Zoo, Inc. Such license plate shall not include a space for a county name decal but shall instead bear the legend Protect Wildlife in lieu of the name of the county of issuance.

Laws 2006, Act 947, § 12, eff. Jan. 1, 2007; Laws 2007, Act 18, § 40, eff. May 11, 2007; Laws 2007, Act 351, §§ 4 to 6, eff. May 29, 2007; Laws 2008, Act 725, §§ 2, 3, eff. May 14, 2008; Laws 2008, Act 800, § 1, eff. July 1, 2008; Laws 2009, Act 102, § 2–18, eff. July 1, 2009; Laws 2009, Act 179, § 1, eff. July 1, 2009; Laws 2010, Act 381, § 4.1, eff. May 20, 2010.

Historical and Statutory Notes

Laws 2006, Act 947, § 13, provides:

"(a) This Act [adding this section] shall become effective on January 1, 2007, except as otherwise provided in subsection (b) of this section.

"(b) If an amendment to the Constitution of the State of Georgia authorizing the dedication of revenue from sales of special license plates to agencies, funds, or nonprofit corporations designated by the General Assembly is not ratified at the general election in 2006, this Act shall be repealed in its entirety on January 1, 2007, and no such motor vehicle license plates shall be issued pursuant to this Act."

An amendment to Article III, § IX, Par. VI, of the Georgia constitution, authorizing such a dedication, was approved by the electorate at the general election held on November 7, 2006.

In 2006, the Code Commission redesignated § 40–2–86.18, which was enacted by Laws 2006, Act 947, § 12, as § 40–2–86.21. See § 28–9–5.

In 2006, the Code Commission, due to irreconcilable conflicts, treated the enactment of § 40–2–8.18 by Laws 2006, Act 946, § 1, as superseded by Laws 2006, Act 947, § 12. See Butts County v. Strahan, 107 S.E. 163, 151 Ga. 417 (1921).

In 2007, the Code Commission, due to irreconcilable conflicts, treated the amendment of this section by Laws 2007, Act 18, § 40, as superseded by Laws 2007, Act 351, §§ 4 to 6. See Butts County v. Strahan, 107 S.E. 163, 151 Ga. 417 (1921).

In 2007, the Code Commission, in subsec. (n), substituted "Article 5 of Chapter 7 of Title 50" for "Ga. L. 1993, p. 1952" in the last sentence of par. (3). See § 28–9–5.

In 2008, the Code Commission redesignated par. (*o*)(38), which was added by Laws 2008, Act 524, § 1, as par. (*o*)(39). See § 28–9–5.

§ 40–2–86.21. Renumbered as § 40–2–86 by Laws 2010, Act 360, § 1–77, eff. May 21, 2010

§ 40–2–86.22. Renumbered § 40–2–86.1 by Laws 2010, Act 360, § 1–77, eff. May 11, 2010

Article 3A

Reciprocal Agreements for Registration of Commercial Vehicles

§ 40–2–87. Definitions

As used in this article, the term:

(1) "Allocated vehicle" means a vehicle to which a particular jurisdiction's basic registration plate or apportioned registration plate is attached upon payment of the jurisdiction's full basic registration fee. A portion of each fleet of one-way vehicles is allocated to each jurisdiction into or through which the fleet travels although each vehicle of the fleet need not enter every jurisdiction.

(2) "Apportionable fee" means any periodic recurring fee required for licensing or registering vehicles, including, but not limited to, registration fees, license fees, or weight fees.

(3) "Apportionable vehicle" means any vehicle, except recreational vehicles, vehicles displaying restricted plates, city pickup and delivery vehicles, buses used in transportation of chartered parties, and government owned vehicles, used or intended for use in two or more member jurisdictions that allocate or proportionally register vehicles and used for the transportation of persons for hire or designed, used, or maintained primarily for the transportation of property and which is:

(A) A power unit having a gross vehicle weight in excess of 26,000 pounds;

(B) A power unit having three or more axles, regardless of weight; or

(C) Used in combination, when the weight of such combination exceeds 26,000 pounds gross vehicle weight.

Vehicles or combinations thereof having a gross vehicle weight of 26,000 pounds or less and two-axle vehicles and buses used in transportation of chartered parties may be proportionally registered at the option of the registrant.

(4) "Auxiliary axle" means an auxiliary undercarriage assembly with a fifth wheel and tow bar used to convert a semitrailer to a full trailer.

(5) "Axle" means an assembly of a vehicle consisting of two or more wheels whose centers are in one horizontal plane, by

means of which a portion of the weight of a vehicle and its load, if any, is continually transmitted to the roadway. For purposes of registration under the International Registration Plan, an axle is any such assembly whether or not it is load-bearing only part of the time. For example, a single-unit truck with a steering axle and two axles in a rear-axle assembly is an apportionable vehicle even though one of the rear axles is a so-called dummy, drag, tag, or pusher type axle.

(6) "Base jurisdiction" means, for purposes of fleet registration, the jurisdiction where the registrant has an established place of business, where mileage is accrued by the fleet, and where operational records of such fleet are maintained or can be made available in accordance with the provisions of this article.

(7) "Base plate" means the plate issued by the base jurisdiction and shall be the only registration identification plate issued for the vehicle by any member jurisdiction. Base plates shall be identified by having the word "apportioned" or "PRP" and the jurisdiction's name on the plate. The numbering system and color shall be determined by the issuing jurisdiction.

(8) "Chartered party" means a group of persons who, pursuant to a common purpose and under a single contract and at a fixed charge for the vehicle in accordance with the carrier's tariff, lawfully on file with the Interstate Commerce Commission, have acquired the exclusive use of a passenger-carrying motor vehicle to travel together as a group to a specified destination or for a particular itinerary, either agreed upon in advance or modified by the chartered group after having left the place of origin.

(9) "Commissioner" means the jurisdiction official in charge of registration of vehicles and means, for the State of Georgia, the state revenue commissioner.

(10) "Established place of business" means a physical structure owned, leased, or rented by the fleet registrant. The physical structure shall be designated by a street number or road location, be open during normal business hours, and have located within it:

(A) A telephone or telephones publicly listed in the name of the fleet registrant;

(B) A person or persons conducting the fleet registrant's business; and

(C) The operational records of the fleet, unless such records can be made available in accordance with the provisions of this article.

(11) "Fleet" means one or more apportionable vehicles.

(12) "In-jurisdiction miles" means the total number of operating miles accrued by a fleet of apportioned vehicles in a jurisdiction during the preceding year. In those cases where the registrant operated a fleet of apportioned vehicles in jurisdictions that require no apportionment and grant reciprocity, the base jurisdiction may add such miles to the in-jurisdiction miles.

(13) "Interjurisdictional movement" means vehicle movement between or through two or more jurisdictions.

(14) "Intrajurisdictional movement" means vehicle movement from one point within a jurisdiction to another point within the same jurisdiction.

(15) "Jurisdiction" means a state, territory, or possession of the United States, the District of Columbia, or a state, province, or territory of another country.

(16) "Long term" means any period of time exceeding 29 days.

(17) "Motor carrier audit" means a physical examination of a motor carrier's operational records including source documentation to verify fleet mileage and accuracy of a carrier's record-keeping system.

(18) "Operational records" means documents supporting miles traveled in each jurisdiction and total miles traveled such as fuel reports, trip sheets, and drivers' logs.

(19) "Owner-operator" means an equipment lessor who leases his vehicular equipment with driver to a carrier.

(20) "Pool fleet" means a fleet of rental company trailers and semitrailers having a gross weight in excess of 26,000 pounds and used solely in pool operation with no permanent base.

(21) "Preceding year" means the period of 12 consecutive months immediately prior to July 1 of the year immediately preceding the commencement of the registration or license year for which apportioned registration is sought.

(22) "Reciprocity" means that an apportionable vehicle properly registered under this article shall be exempt from further registration by any other member jurisdiction.

(23) "Reciprocity agreement" means an agreement, arrangement, or understanding governing the reciprocal grant of rights and privileges to vehicles which are based in and properly registered under the applicable laws of the jurisdictions which are parties to such an agreement, arrangement, or understanding.

(24) "Recreational vehicle" means as used in this article a vehicle used for personal pleasure or travel by an individual or his family.

(25) "Registrant" means a person, firm, or corporation in whose name or names a vehicle is properly registered.

(26) "Registration year" means the 12 month period during which the registration plates issued by the base jurisdiction are valid according to the laws of the base jurisdiction.

(27) "Restricted plate" means a license plate that has time (less than a registration year), geographic area, mileage, or commodity restrictions.

(28) "Service representative" means a person who furnishes facilities and services including sales, warehousing, motorized equipment, and drivers under contract or other arrangements to a carrier for transportation of property by a household goods carrier.

(29) "Total distance" means the total number of miles or kilometers traveled by a fleet of apportioned vehicles in all jurisdictions during the preceding year. For purposes of motor bus apportionment, total distance shall be calculated as provided for fleets.

(30) "Trip-lease" means a lease of vehicular equipment to a carrier or lessee for a single interjurisdictional movement. The term may also include a similar intrajurisdictional movement where such movement is authorized under the laws of the jurisdiction.

Laws 1990, p. 1883, § 2; Laws 1994, p. 97, § 40; Laws 2000, p. 951, § 3–14; Laws 2005, Act 68, § 14–7, eff. July 1, 2005; Laws 2006, Act 453, § 40, eff. April 14, 2006.

§ 40–2–88. Applicability and procedures

(a) In addition to and regardless of the provisions of Article 3 of this chapter or any other provisions of law relating to the operation of motor vehicles over the public highways of this state, the commissioner is authorized to enter into reciprocal agreements or plans on behalf of the State of Georgia with the appropriate authorities of any of the states of the United States, the District of Columbia, a state or province of any foreign country, or a territory or possession of the United States or any foreign country providing for the registration of commercial vehicles on an apportionment basis and may, in the exercise of this authority, enter and become a member of the International Registration Plan developed by the American Association of Motor Vehicle Administrators. Any such reciprocal agreement or plan may provide for but shall not be limited to the following provisions: (1) full reciprocity in accordance with such agreement or plan for commercial vehicles not based in Georgia, which vehicles are operated in interstate commerce or a combination of interstate and intrastate commerce and are of specified types or weights, in exchange for equivalent reciprocity for Georgia based commercial vehicles; (2) reciprocal exchange of audits of records of the owners of such commercial vehicles by the states participating in any such agreement or plan; and (3) any other matters which would facilitate the administration of such agreement or plan, including exchange of information for audits enforcement activities and collection and disbursement of proportional registration fees for other jurisdictions in the case of Georgia based commercial vehicles.

(b) Any reciprocity agreement, arrangement, or declaration relating to commercial vehicles in effect between this state and any jurisdiction not a party to such reciprocal agreement or plan or which relates to any matters not covered in such reciprocal agreement or plan shall continue in force and effect until specifically revoked or amended as provided by law.

(c)(1)(A) Applications for registration or renewal of registration under the International Registration Plan may be submitted during the period of December 1, 2001, to February 15, 2002, for registration under such plan which shall be valid for a period beginning January 1, 2002, and ending at the conclusion of the applicable registration period specified in division (a)(1)(A)(ii) of Code Section 40–2–21 which occurs between July 1, 2002, and June 30, 2003.

(B) On and after July 1, 2002, applications for annual registration or renewal of registration under the International Registration Plan shall be submitted during the applicable registration period specified in division (a)(1)(A)(ii) of Code Section 40–2–21.

(2) Any owner of a vehicle required to be registered under the International Registration Plan who does not apply for registration on or before the first day of the registration period for such vehicle as prescribed in paragraph (1) of this subsection, in addition to any other penalty which may be imposed if such vehicle is not timely registered in accordance with paragraph (1) of this subsection, shall be subject to a late application penalty of 10 percent of the total registration fees due this state. Additionally, the owner of a vehicle required to be registered under the International Registration Plan who does not pay to the commissioner the registration fees due this state on or before the last day of the registration period shall be subject to a late payment penalty in accordance with Code Section 40–2–40. The commissioner may provide by rule or regulation for waiver of penalties provided by this paragraph in cases where failure to timely make application or timely pay fees is due to force majeure.

(d) The provisions of Code Sections 40–2–9, 40–2–22, 40–2–23, 40–2–24, and 40–2–26 shall not apply to vehicles registered under this Code section, except that:

(1) Registration under the International Registration Plan shall not relieve a registrant from any other taxes due and registration shall be denied any such vehicle if any Georgia ad valorem property taxes due upon such vehicle are unpaid;

(2) No vehicle registration or renewal thereof shall be issued to any motor vehicle subject to the heavy vehicle tax unless the owner of the motor vehicle provides satisfactory proof that the heavy vehicle tax imposed by Subchapter D of Chapter 36 of the Internal Revenue Code has been paid for the federal tax year during which the application for registration or renewal thereof is made or that a heavy motor vehicle tax return has been filed with the Internal Revenue Service for the federal tax year during which the application for registration or renewal thereof is made; and

(3) No vehicle registration or renewal thereof shall be issued without the commissioner's having first received certification that the vehicle sought to be licensed is insured in compliance with the mandatory provisions of Chapter 34 of Title 33, the "Georgia Motor Vehicle Accident Reparations Act."

(e) In the event of conflict between the provisions of this Code section or any agreement entered into under the provisions of this Code section and any other law or provision on this subject, the provisions of this Code section or any agreement entered into under the provisions of this Code section shall prevail.

(f) Each motor carrier registered under the International Registration Plan shall maintain and keep, for the current year and the three preceding years, such pertinent records and papers as may be required by the commissioner for the reasonable administration of this chapter. If a registrant fails to make records available to the commissioner upon proper request or if any registrant fails to maintain records from which its true liability may be determined, the commissioner may, 30 days after written demand for production of or access to the records or notification of insufficient records, impose an assessment of liability based on the commissioner's estimate of the true liability of such registrant as determined from information furnished by the registrant, information gathered by the commissioner at his or her own instance, information available to the commissioner concerning operations by similar registrants, and such other pertinent information as may be available to the commissioner.

(g) The commissioner or any authorized agent of the commissioner is authorized to examine the records, books, papers, and equipment of any motor carrier that are deemed necessary to verify the truth and accuracy of any statement or report and ascertain whether the tax imposed by Code Section 40–2–152 and the International Registration Plan has been properly paid. The duties and powers of the commissioner as specified in Code Sections 48–2–7 through 48–2–11 are expressly made applicable to this Code section.

(h) In lieu of full registration under the International Registration Plan, trip permit registration may be issued for any vehicle or combination of vehicles which could be lawfully operated in the state if full registration or apportioned registration were obtained. A person desiring a trip permit shall make application therefor as prescribed by the commissioner. A trip permit shall be issued for the sum of $ 30.00. Any vehicle or combination of vehicles for which a trip permit has been issued may be operated in interstate or intrastate commerce in Georgia for a period of 72 hours from the time of issuance.

(i) The department is authorized and empowered to promulgate and to enforce such rules and regulations, including without limitation rules and regulations providing for appointment and regulation of private tag agents and use of electronic and direct registration methods, and to publish such forms as may be necessary to carry out the provisions of the International Registration Plan or any other agreement entered into under the authority set forth in this Code section.

(j) Any person who violates any provision of this Code section shall, in addition to any other penalties provided by any other law, be punished by a fine of not less than $ 100.00 and not more than $ 250.00.

Laws 1990, p. 1883, § 2; Laws 1992, p. 2978, § 3; Laws 1999, p. 741, § 2; Laws 2000, p. 951, § 3–15; Laws 2001, p. 1173, § 1–3; Laws 2002, p. 415, § 40; Laws 2004, Act 564, § 40, eff. May 13, 2004.

§ 40–2–88.1. Electronic filing system for registration of commercial vehicles

The department shall commence to initiate an electronic filing system for registration of commercial vehicles under the International Registration Plan by January 1, 2008, including temporary operating permits valid for any length of time; provided, however, that in no event shall the total number of days of all temporary operating permits issued for a vehicle exceed 60 days from the registration application filing date.

Laws 2007, Act 341, § 1, eff. July 1, 2007.

Historical and Statutory Notes

In 2007, the Code Commission, designated Laws 2007, Act 341, § 1, as § 40–2–88.1, and deleted the subsec. (d) designation. See § 28–9–5.

§ 40–2–89. Noneligibility for registration of vehicles prohibited from operating in interstate commerce

Any vehicle which is prohibited by any federal agency acting pursuant to federal law, rule, or regulation from being operated in interstate commerce shall not be eligible for registration under this article, and the commissioner shall suspend or revoke such registration for any vehicle so prohibited from operating.

Laws 2001, p. 1173, § 1–4; Laws 2005, Act 68, § 14–8, eff. July 1, 2005.

Article 4

Vehicles of Nonresidents

§ 40–2–90. Nonresidents and visitors; registration required when

(a) For purposes of this Code section:

(1) "Nonresident" means any person who does not reside in the State of Georgia but who accepts employment or engages in any trade, profession, or occupation in the state or enters his children in the public schools of this state.

(2) "Visitor" means any person who does not reside in the State of Georgia and who is not a nonresident as defined in this subsection.

(b)(1) Motor vehicles owned by nonresidents may be used and operated on the public streets and highways for a period of 30 days without registering said motor vehicles in the State of Georgia.

(2) Motor vehicles owned by visitors may be used and operated on the public streets and highways, for pleasure purposes only, for a period of 90 days without registering said motor vehicles in the State of Georgia.

(3) To be eligible for the exemptions provided for in paragraph (1) or (2) of this subsection, a nonresident or visitor shall have fully complied with the laws relating to the registration of motor vehicles of the state or territory wherein he resides, and the registration number and initial letter of such state or territory shall be displayed and plainly visible on such motor vehicles.

(4) No resident of Georgia shall be entitled to the exemptions provided for in paragraph (1) or (2) of this subsection.

(c) Notwithstanding subsection (a) of this Code section, a nonresident student who is a resident of a state which is a member of the Multistate Reciprocity Agreement shall be exempt from the requirement of registering his motor vehicle in this state in accordance with the provisions of said Multistate Reciprocity Agreement.

Laws 1927, p. 226, § 10; Laws 1973, p. 342, § 1; Laws 1978, p. 927, § 1; Laws 1982, p. 720, § 1; Laws 1983, p. 638, § 1; Laws 1985, p. 149, § 40; Laws 1990, p. 2048, § 2.

Formerly Code 1933, § 68–221.

§ 40–2–91. Reciprocal agreements with other states as to privileges, etc.

The commissioner is directed to negotiate with the proper authorities of adjoining states and consummate, as speedily as is practicable, reciprocal agreements, whereby residents of such states operating motor vehicles licensed in their respective states may have such privileges and exemptions in the operation of such motor vehicles as residents of this state may have and enjoy in such adjoining states in the operation of motor vehicles duly licensed in this state. In the making of such agreements, the commissioner shall have due regard for the advantage and convenience of the motor vehicle owners and other citizens of this state and particularly those who reside near the borders of adjoining states.

Laws 1931, p. 7, § 84; Laws 1931, p. 216, §§ 1, 2; Laws 1990, p. 2048, § 2.

Formerly Code 1933, § 68–217.

§ 40–2–92. Agreements subject to confirmation by General Assembly

Any and all reciprocal agreements entered into by the commissioner shall be subject to confirmation by Act or resolution of the General Assembly and shall not be of force or effect until the passage of such Act or resolution and its approval by the Governor except such agreement or agreements as may be entered into while the General Assembly is not in session.

Laws 1931, p. 7, § 84; Laws 1931, p. 216, § 3; Laws 1990, p. 2048, § 2.

Formerly Code 1933, § 68–218.

§ 40–2–93. Agreements while General Assembly not in session

All reciprocal agreements entered into by the commissioner while the General Assembly is not in session shall be approved by the Governor. Such agreements shall be submitted by the commissioner to the General Assembly not later than the tenth day of its next session, whereupon the General Assembly may confirm or reject such agreement or agreements by appropriate Act or resolution approved by the Governor. Pending passage and approval of such Act or resolution of confirmation or rejection, the agreement or agreements made during the adjournment of the General Assembly shall be of full force and effect according to their terms.

Laws 1931, p. 7, § 84; Laws 1931, p. 216, §§ 3, 5; Laws 1990, p. 2048, § 2.

Formerly Code 1933, §§ 68–218, 68–220.

§ 40–2–94. Publication enforcement, and effect of reciprocal agreements

The commissioner shall give proper publicity to the terms of every agreement entered into pursuant to Code Sections 40–2–91 through 40–2–93 and is authorized and empowered to promulgate rules and regulations for the observance and enforcement of the terms of such agreement, which rules and regulations shall have the force and effect of law.

Laws 1931, p. 7, § 84; Laws 1931, p. 216, § 4; Laws 1990, p. 2048, § 2.

Formerly Code 1933, § 68–219.

§ 40–2–95. Reciprocal agreements; vehicles for hire excepted

No reciprocal agreement shall be made or approved under Code Sections 40–2–91 through 40–2–93 which relate to motor vehicles operated for hire, nor shall Code Sections 40–2–91 through 40–2–93 apply to such vehicles.

Laws 1931, p. 7, § 84; Laws 1931, p. 216, § 5; Laws 1990, p. 2048, § 2.

Formerly Code 1933, § 68–220.

Article 5

Unregistered Motor Trucks

§ 40–2–110. Definition of motor truck

As used in this article, the term "motor truck" means any motor vehicle having a gross weight of 18,000 pounds or over which is designed and used for the transportation of merchandise or freight.

Laws 1953, Nov.-Dec. Sess., p. 343, Part 2, § 5; Laws 1990, p. 2048, § 2.

§ 40–2–111. Permit to operate unregistered truck; application; fee; identification tag

In addition to any other provision of law relating to registration of motor vehicles or fees paid therefor, a person owning or operating a motor truck, as defined in Code Section 40–2–110, upon the highways of this state, which is not registered in this state, shall apply to the commissioner for a highway use permit for each such motor truck to be so operated. Application shall be made upon a form prescribed by the commissioner and shall set forth such information as the commissioner may require. The application shall be accompanied by a permit fee of not more than $200.00, as determined under the rules and regulations of the commissioner, using a comparison of such fees charged by the state or province of registration of the motor truck, for each motor truck listed in the application. The commissioner shall issue a permit and an identification tag, plate, or decal for each such motor truck, which tag, plate, or decal shall be of such size and design and contain such information as the commissioner shall prescribe. Any such permit and tag, plate, or decal shall be valid for the same period of time as provided by law for license plates issued to motor vehicles in Georgia. Such permits shall be carried in the motor truck and the tag, plate, or decal shall be affixed to the motor truck and at all times be visible and legible.

Laws 1953, Nov.-Dec. Sess., p. 343, Part 2, § 1; Laws 1984, p. 1199, § 1; Laws 1990, p. 2048, § 2.

§ 40–2–112. Fee where foreign state or province imposes tax on Georgia vehicles

In addition to the permit fee provided in Code Section 40–2–111, a person operating a motor truck on the highways of this state, which truck is registered in a state or province which imposes upon motor trucks registered in this state a tax, fee, or toll for the privilege of operating such truck upon the highways of such state or province, which is in addition to any tax, fee, or toll imposed upon gasoline or other motor fuel purchased within such state or province, or registration fee, shall pay a fee of not more than $25.00, as determined under the rules and regulations of the commissioner, using a comparison of such taxes, fees, or tolls charged by the state or province of registration of the motor truck, for each round trip into this state in lieu of a tax computed and applied in the same manner as the tax, fee, or toll of such other state or province so long as such tax, fee, or toll imposed by such other state or province shall remain in force.

Laws 1953, Nov.-Dec. Sess., p. 343, Part 2, § 2; Laws 1984, p. 1199, § 2; Laws 1990, p. 2048, § 2.

§ 40–2–113. Collection of taxes and fees by commissioner

The commissioner shall collect the taxes and fees imposed by this article and he is authorized to make such rules and regulations and prescribe such forms as are necessary to carry out this article.

Laws 1953, Nov.-Dec. Sess., p. 343, Part 2, § 3; Laws 1990, p. 2048, § 2.

§ 40–2–114. Penalties for violations

(a) It shall be unlawful for any person:

(1) To operate a motor truck subject to this article upon any public highway in this state without first obtaining the permit required under Code Section 40–2–111;

(2) To violate any regulation issued by the commissioner pursuant to the authority granted under this article;

(3) To fail to file any return or report required by the commissioner;

(4) To make a false return or fail to keep records of operations as may be required by the commissioner; or

(5) To make knowingly any false statement in any application for registration.

(b) Any person who violates any provision of this Code section, upon first conviction, shall be punished by a fine of not less than $100.00 nor more than $250.00; and upon a second or subsequent conviction, by a fine of not less than $250.00 nor more than $500.00, or by imprisonment for not more than 30 days, or both.

Laws 1953, Nov.-Dec. Sess., p. 343, Part 2, § 6; Laws 1985, p. 149, § 40; Laws 1987, p. 949, § 4; Laws 1990, p. 2048, § 2.

Article 6

Administration and Enforcement of Chapter

§ 40–2–130. Records of certificates of registration

(a) A record of certificates of registration shall be maintained by the commissioner or the commissioner's duly authorized county tag agent. All certificates of registration shall be issued:

(1) Under a distinctive tag registration number assigned to the vehicle;

(2) Under the identifying number of the vehicle;

(3) Alphabetically, under the name of the owner;

(4) Under the vehicle title number; and

(5) In the discretion of the commissioner, in any other method the commissioner determines.

(b) The commissioner is authorized and empowered to provide for photographic and photostatic recording of certificate of registration records in such manner as he may deem expedient. The photographic or photostatic copies authorized in this subsection shall be admitted in evidence in all actions and proceedings to the same extent that the originals would have been admitted.

(c) The motor vehicle registration records which the commissioner is required to maintain under this Code section or any other provision are exempt from the provisions of any law of this state requiring that such records be open for public inspection; provided, however, that, subject to subsection (d) of this Code section, the records may be disclosed for use as provided in the federal Driver's Privacy Protection Act of 1994, 18 U.S.C. Chapter 123, and by the following:

(1) Any licensed dealer of new or used motor vehicles;

(2) Any tax collector, tax receiver, or tax commissioner;

(3) The director of the Environmental Protection Division of the Department of Natural Resources or his or her designee;

(4) Any private person who has met the requirements of Code Section 40–2–25, provided that the information shall be used for the sole purpose of effectuating the registration or renewal of motor vehicles by electronic or similar means and that the private person requesting the information has entered into an agreement to provide electronic services to the commissioner or a county tag agent; provided, further, that the information made available pursuant to this paragraph for such purpose shall be limited to the vehicle identification number, the license tag number, the date of expiration of registration, and the amount of tax owed; and

(5) A person or entity authorized by the commissioner for use in providing notice to the owners of towed or impounded vehicles.

(d) Except as otherwise required in the federal Driver's Privacy Protection Act of 1994, 18 U.S.C. Chapter 123, personal information furnished under paragraphs (1) through (5) of subsection (c) of this Code section shall be limited to the natural person's name, address, and driver identification number. The personal information obtained by a business under this Code section shall not be resold or redisclosed for any purposes other than those permitted under the federal Driver's Privacy Protection Act of 1994, 18 U.S.C. Chapter 123, without the written consent of the individual. Furnishing of information to a business under this Code section shall be pursuant to a contract entered into by such business and the state which specifies the consideration to be paid by such business to the state for such information and the frequency of updates.

Laws 1990, p. 2048, § 2; Laws 1996, p. 336, § 13; Laws 1997, p. 739, § 3; Laws 1999, p. 334, § 2; Laws 2000, p. 136, § 40; Laws 2000, p. 951, § 3–16; Laws 2003, Act 200, § 1, eff. Oct. 1, 2003; Laws 2003, Act 246, § 1, eff. July 1, 2003; Laws 2004, Act 521, § 8, eff. July 1, 2004; Laws 2008, Act 711, § 1, eff. July 1, 2008.

Historical and Statutory Notes

Laws 2003, Act 200, § 15 provides:

"This Act shall become effective on October 1, 2003."

§ 40–2–131. Fees to be turned over to state treasury

Except as provided in Code Section 40–2–33 and Code Section 40–2–88, the full amount of the fees collected under this chapter shall be turned over to the state treasury by the commissioner within 30 days after collection in such manner as the state treasurer may prescribe.

Laws 1927, p. 226, § 21; Laws 1931, p. 7, § 84; Laws 1990, p. 1883, § 3; Laws 1990, p. 2048, § 2; Laws 1993, p. 1402, § 18; Laws 2010, Act 621, § 3, eff. July 1, 2010.

Formerly Code 1933, § 68–104; Code 1981, § 40–2–130.

§ 40–2–132. Destruction of records

The commissioner, in his discretion, may destroy all motor vehicle records required to be maintained under this chapter, except those of the current year and the two years immediately preceding.

Laws 1925, p. 315, § 1; Laws 1931, p. 7, § 84; Laws 1953, Jan.-Feb. Sess., p. 366, § 2; Laws 1955, p. 424, § 1; Laws 1973, p. 455, § 1; Laws 1990, p. 2048, § 2.

Formerly Code 1933, § 68–205; Code 1981, § 40–2–131.

§ 40–2–133. Duty of arresting officers

It is the duty of every arresting officer, county, municipal, and state, to enforce this chapter.

Laws 1927, p. 226, § 26; Laws 1985, p. 149, § 40; Laws 1990, p. 2048, § 2.

Formerly Code 1933, § 68–109; Code 1981, § 40–2–132.

§ 40–2–134. Special agents or enforcement officers of Department of Revenue authorized to enforce laws relating to licensing and registration of motor vehicles

Certified law enforcement officers appointed by the commissioner are authorized to enforce the laws of this state relating to the licensing and registration of motor vehicles and are endowed with all the powers of a police officer of this state when engaged in the enforcement of said laws.

Laws 1976, p. 1093, § 1; Laws 1990, p. 2048, § 2; Laws 2000, p. 951, § 3–17.

Formerly Code 1981, § 40–2–133.

§ 40–2–135. Revocation of regular, prestige, special, or distinctive license plates; suspension or revocation of permanent registration and license plates for certain trailers

(a) The commissioner shall revoke any regular, prestige, special, or distinctive license plate which the commissioner determines was issued in error and shall revoke the special and distinctive license plate issued to a member of the General Assembly at such time as the holder ceases to hold such public office. The commissioner or his or her designated agent may revoke any license plate purchased with a check which was returned for any reason. The commissioner shall notify the holder of such regular, prestige, special, or distinctive license plate or of such other license plate of such revocation. The holder of such revoked license plate shall return the license plate to the commissioner or the commissioner's designated agent and register his or her vehicle as otherwise required by this chapter.

(b) The commissioner shall suspend or revoke any permanent registration and license plate issued in accordance with Code Section 40–2–47 when the owner has not complied with the annual requirement of the payment of ad valorem taxes and is delinquent for more than 12 months from the last date of ad valorem tax payment.

(c) Any state or county law enforcement officer or any special agent or enforcement officer appointed under Code Section 40–2–134 may, upon the direction or request of the commissioner, go upon public or private property to seize a license plate or renewal decal which has been revoked as provided in subsection (a) of this Code section.

Laws 1988, p. 376, § 1; Laws 1990, p. 2048, § 2; Laws 1993, p. 972, § 1.5; Laws 2005, Act 68, § 14–9, eff. July 1, 2005.

Formerly Code 1981, § 40–2–134.

§ 40–2–135.1. Suspension of motor vehicle registration for failure to pay tolls

As provided in subsection (c) of Code Section 32–10–64, the motor vehicle registration of any owner who has failed to pay, within 30 days of the date of notice thereof, the amount determined by the Office of State Administrative Hearings as due and payable for one or more violations of such subsection, shall be immediately suspended by operation of law.

Laws 2006, Act 543, § 2, eff. Jan. 1, 2007.

§ 40–2–136. Surrender of license plates of certain habitual violators; special license plates; conveyances of motor vehicles

(a) Upon any person's second or subsequent conviction of violating Code Section 40–6–391 within five years, as measured from the dates of previous arrests for which convictions were obtained to the date of the current arrest for which a conviction is obtained, the court shall issue an order requiring that the license plates of all motor vehicles registered in such person's name be surrendered to the court. The court shall notify the commissioner within ten days after issuing any such order, and the commissioner shall revoke each such license plate upon receiving such notice. The court shall issue a receipt for the surrendered license plate or plates. The court shall forward the surrendered license plate or plates to the local tag agent immediately upon receipt. For purposes of this subsection, a plea of nolo contendere shall constitute a conviction.

(b) Except as provided in subsection (c) of this Code section, no new license plate or plates may be issued to a person subject to a court order issued pursuant to subsection (a) of this Code section until such person has been issued a limited driving permit or probationary driver's license in accordance with Code Section 42–8–112 or the driver's license of such person has been reissued or reinstated, whichever first occurs; and, except as provided in this subsection or subsection (c) of this Code section, it shall be a misdemeanor for such person to obtain a new license plate or plates.

(c)(1) A person who is subject to a court order issued pursuant to subsection (a) of this Code section may apply to the commissioner for authorization to obtain a new license plate or plates bearing a special series of numbers and letters so as to be identifiable by law enforcement officers. Such license plate shall not, in and of itself, constitute probable cause to authorize a traffic stop, search of a motor vehicle, or seizure. The commissioner shall authorize the issuance of such a special license plate only if he or she determines that there is another member of such person's household who possesses a valid driver's license and that a co-owner of the vehicle or a member of the offender's family, other than the offender, is completely dependent upon the motor vehicle for the necessities of life and would be subjected to undue hardship without such special license plate; in no event shall such decision take more than five business days. A local tag agent shall not issue any plates except on written approval of the commissioner, payment of a $ 20.00 fee for each vehicle for which a special plate is issued, and compliance by the applicant with all applicable state laws. The written authorization from the commissioner shall specify the maximum number of license plates a person may obtain.

(2) A motor vehicle owned or leased by a person subject to a court order issued pursuant to subsection (a) of this Code section or for which a license plate has been issued subject to paragraph (1) of this subsection may not be sold or conveyed unless the commissioner determines, upon receipt of proper application, that the proposed sale or conveyance is in good faith, that the person subject to such court order will be deprived of custody or control of the motor vehicle, and that the sale or conveyance is not for the purpose of circumventing the provisions of this Code section. Upon making such determination, the commissioner shall transfer the certificate of title to such vehicle and issue a new certificate of registration and license plate.

(3) If the title to a motor vehicle owned by a person subject to a court order issued pursuant to subsection (a) of this Code section or for which a license plate has been issued pursuant to paragraph (1) of this subsection is transferred by the foreclosure, cancellation of a conditional sales contract, sale upon execution, or order of a court of competent jurisdiction, the commissioner shall transfer the certificate of title as provided in Code Section 40–3–34 and issue a new license plate to the new registered owner.

(4) Upon full restoration of the driving privileges of a person subject to a court order under subsection (a) of this Code section, the commissioner shall authorize the person to apply for a regular issue license plate. The fee for a regular issue license plate shall be as provided by Code Section 40–2–151. As a condition of obtaining any regular issue license plate, the person shall surrender his or her special issue license plate to the local tag agent.

(5) Nothing in this Code section shall be deemed to waive any lawful requirement for the issuance of a license plate including, but not limited to, proof of financial responsibility.

(6) Display of a license plate issued pursuant to paragraph (1) of this subsection shall not constitute probable cause for stopping or detaining a vehicle.

(7) Any person aggrieved by a decision of the commissioner pursuant to paragraph (1) of this subsection may make a request in writing to the Office of State Administrative Hearings for a hearing. Such hearing shall follow the procedures required by Chapter 13 of Title 50, the "Georgia Administrative Procedure Act."

Laws 1997, p. 760, § 7; Laws 2000, p. 951, § 3–18; Laws 2001, p. 208, §§ 2–1, 3–1; Laws 2002, p. 1074, § 5.

§ 40–2–137. Minimum motor vehicle liability insurance; notice of issue, renewal, or consolidations; records; proof of insurance; lapse of coverage; fees; suspension

(a) As used in this Code section, the term:

(1) "Commercial vehicle policy" means a policy of motor vehicle liability insurance insuring a motor vehicle that is rated or insured as a business use or commercial use vehicle or is licensed by the state as a commercial vehicle.

(2) "Fleet policy" means a commercial vehicle policy that insures two or more vehicles that are not identified individually by vehicle identification number on the policy or a commercial policy that is subject to adjustment by audit for vehicle changes at the end of the policy period.

(3) "Lapse" means one or more days upon which the records of the department do not reflect that a motor vehicle was covered by a policy of minimum motor vehicle insurance coverage.

(4) "Minimum motor vehicle insurance coverage" means minimum coverage as specified in Chapter 34 of Title 33.

(5) "Proof of minimum insurance coverage" means the receipt from an insurer by the department of notice of such insurance coverage by electronic transmission or other means approved by the department.

(6) "Terminate" or "termination" means actual cessation of insurance coverage after the date upon which coverage will not be restored for any reason, including without limitation cancellation, nonrenewal, and nonpayment of premium and without regard to whether such cessation was preceded by any extension or grace period allowed by the insurer.

(b)(1)(A) For purposes of aiding in the enforcement of the requirement of minimum motor vehicle liability insurance, any insurer issuing or renewing in this state any policy of motor vehicle liability insurance required by Chapter 34 of Title 33 other than a fleet policy shall within 30 days after the date the insurance agent binds the coverage or on the date such coverage was renewed, whichever is applicable, provide notice of such insurance coverage by electronic transmission to the department; except that once coverage data has been electronically transmitted to the department, there shall be no requirement to report on subsequent renewals of that coverage. Insurance coverage information included in such notice of issue or renewal shall be limited exclusively to name of insurer; vehicle identification number; the make and year of the insured motor vehicle; and policy effective date. The department shall not require the policy limits to be disclosed for purposes of this subparagraph. For the purposes of this Code section, the vehicle identification number shall be the vehicle identification number as that number is shown in the records of the department. For the purposes of this Code section, the Commissioner of Insurance shall furnish such notices to the department upon issuance of a certificate of self-insurance.

(B) In cases in which the minimum motor vehicle insurance coverage required by Chapter 34 of Title 33 terminates, the insurer shall by electronic transmission notify the department of such coverage termination on or before the date coverage ends or, if termination is at the request of the insured, then on the date such request is processed by the insurer. Insurance coverage termination information included in such notice shall include vehicle identification number and the date of coverage termination. For the purposes of this Code section, the Commissioner of Insurance shall furnish such notices to the department upon termination of a certificate of self-insurance.

(C) The commissioner shall notify the Commissioner of Insurance quarterly of any and all violations of the notice requirements of this paragraph by any insurer, and the Commissioner of Insurance may take appropriate action against such insurer the same as is authorized by Code Section 33–2–24 for violations of Title 33; provided, however, that there shall be no private cause of action against an insurer or the department for civil damages for providing information, failing to provide information, or erroneously providing information pursuant to this Code section. No insurer shall utilize the costs of any audit or examination conducted by the Insurance Department pursuant to this paragraph as a cost of business in the insurer's rate base. The department shall commence the reports provided for in this Code section beginning July 1, 2010.

(D) The reports required of insurers and the Commissioner of Insurance shall not apply to any vehicle for which the vehicle coverage is provided by a fleet policy.

(2) The department shall prescribe the form and manner of electronic transmission for the purposes of insurers sending the notices required by this Code section which shall in no way be construed as modifying the provisions of Code Section 33–24–45.

(3) Notwithstanding the provisions of paragraph (1) of this subsection, any irregularities in the notice to the department required by paragraph (1) of this subsection shall not invalidate an otherwise valid termination.

(4) The minimum liability insurance records which the department is required to maintain under this Code section or any other provision are exempt from the provisions of any law of this state requiring that such records be open for public inspection; provided, however, that the records of any particular motor vehicle may be available for inspection by any law enforcement officer for official law enforcement investigations, the insurer of record, and the owner of the vehicle in the manner prescribed by the commissioner.

(c)(1) The department shall monitor the reporting by insurers of the issuance of new and renewal policies and the termination of coverage.

(2)(A) A match is based upon the vehicle identification number as recorded on the department's motor vehicle records. When the vehicle identification number does not match the department's motor vehicle records, the department shall notify the insurer and the insurer shall, within 30 days from receipt of the returned error, correct the vehicle identification number and resubmit the transaction.

(B) After receipt of the department's notice, if the insurer determines that the vehicle identification number that it submitted to the department is in fact the accurate number on the insured vehicle, then the insurer shall so notify the department and the owner of the vehicle.

(C) Upon notification, the owner shall, in a manner prescribed by the commissioner, make a correction of such number at the appropriate county tag office.

(d)(1)(A) Upon notification of coverage termination by the insurer, the department shall send a notice to the owner of the motor vehicle stating that the department has been informed of the fact that coverage has been terminated and provide an explanation of the penalties provided for by law.

(B) The department shall send such notice to the address of the owner of the motor vehicle shown on the records of the department.

(C) The mailing of such notice by the department shall be deemed notice of such owner's duty to maintain the required minimum insurance coverage and the possible penalties and consequences for failing to do so and shall be deemed to satisfy all notice requirements of law.

(2) It shall be the duty of the owner of such motor vehicle to obtain minimum motor vehicle insurance coverage and it shall be the duty of the owner's insurer to provide proof of such coverage to the department within 30 days of the date of such notice, pursuant to the requirements of subparagraph (b)(1)(A) of this Code section.

(3) If the vehicle is covered by a fleet policy, the owner's insurer shall not be required to provide such proof electronically to the department.

(e)(1) When proof of minimum motor vehicle insurance coverage is provided within the time period specified in this Code section, but there has been a lapse of coverage for a period of more than ten days, the owner shall remit a $25.00 lapse fee to the department. Failure to remit the lapse fee to the department within 30 days of the date of such notice will result in the suspension of the owner's motor vehicle registration by operation of law. If any lapse fee provided for in this Code section is paid to the county tax commissioner, the county shall retain $5.00 thereof as a collection fee.

(2) If proof is not provided within the time period specified in this Code section that minimum motor vehicle insurance coverage is in effect, the owner's motor vehicle registration shall be suspended immediately by operation of law by the department. When such proof is provided and the owner pays a $25.00 lapse fee and pays a $60.00 restoration fee, the suspension shall terminate; provided, however, that the commissioner may waive the lapse fee and restoration fee for any owner whose vehicle registration has been suspended pursuant to this paragraph who provides proof of continuous minimum motor vehicle insurance coverage. If any restoration fee provided for in this Code section is paid to the county tax commissioner, the county shall retain $10.00 thereof as a collection fee.

(3) In the event of a second suspension of the owner's registration under this Code section, within a five-year period of a prior suspension, the department by operation of law shall suspend the motor vehicle registration. When proof is provided that minimum motor vehicle insurance coverage is in effect and the owner pays a $25.00 lapse fee and pays a $60.00 restoration fee, the suspension shall terminate.

(4) In the event of a third or subsequent suspension of the owner's registration under this Code section, within the previous five-year period from the date of the third or subsequent suspension, the department by operation of law shall revoke the motor vehicle registration. When proof is provided that minimum motor vehicle insurance coverage is in effect and the owner pays a $25.00 lapse fee and pays a $160.00 restoration fee, the owner may apply for registration of the motor vehicle.

(f)(1) The commissioner may waive the lapse fee for any owner whose vehicle registration has been voluntarily canceled pursuant to Code Section 40–2–10.

(2) Upon being presented with a copy of official orders or other satisfactory proof of ordered duty as approved by rule or regulation of the commissioner showing that an owner of a

motor vehicle was deployed outside the continental United States on active military duty in the armed forces of the United States at the time his or her minimum motor vehicle insurance coverage for such vehicle terminated, the county tag agent shall waive the lapse fee and restoration fee, suspension of the owner's motor vehicle registration under this Code section shall terminate, and application for registration of the vehicle which otherwise satisfies requirements provided by law may be accepted without delay.

(g) The county tax commissioner shall have the authority to waive a lapse fee if sufficient proof is provided that no actual lapse in coverage occurred. Such proof shall be retained by the county tax commissioner for audit purposes.

(h) Notwithstanding any provision of law to the contrary, a person on active military duty in the armed forces of the United States whose motor vehicle is registered in this state and has license plates from this state and who, as a result of his or her military duties or assignment, is required to reside in another state may meet the requirements for minimum motor vehicle liability coverage by purchasing such coverage in amounts equal to or greater than the minimum coverages required by Georgia law and providing proof of such coverage to the department. In such cases, the motor vehicle shall continue to be registered and licensed in this state as long as it otherwise meets the requirements of law.

Laws 2002, p. 1024, § 3; Laws 2003, Act 44, § 3, eff. May 28, 2003; Laws 2004, Act 564, § 40, eff. May 13, 2004; Laws 2004, Act 582, § 1, eff. July 1, 2004; Laws 2005, Act 68, § 14–10, eff. July 1, 2005; Laws 2006, Act 752, § 1, eff. July 1, 2006; Laws 2010, Act 381, § 5, eff. May 20, 2010.

§ 40–2–138. Vehicles prohibited by federal law

Any vehicle which is prohibited by any federal agency acting pursuant to federal law, rule, or regulation from being operated in intrastate commerce shall not be eligible for registration under this article, and the commissioner shall suspend or revoke such registration for any vehicle so prohibited from operating.

Laws 2007, Act 346, § 6, eff. Jan. 1, 2008.

Historical and Statutory Notes

Laws 2007, Act 346, § 14, provides:

"Sections 2, 3, 4, 5, and 13 through 15 of this Act shall become effective July 1, 2007. Sections 1, 6, 7, and 12 of this Act shall become effective January 1, 2008. Sections 8, 9, 10, and 11 of this Act shall become effective July 1, 2008."

Article 6A

Unified Carrier Registration Agreement

§ 40–2–140. Administration of Unified Carrier Registration Agreement

(a) The Department of Revenue shall be the state agency responsible for the administration of the federal Unified Carrier Registration Act of 2005, which includes participating in the development, implementation, and administration of the Unified Carrier Registration Agreement.

(b) Every foreign or domestic motor carrier, leasing company leasing to a motor carrier, broker, or freight forwarder that engages in interstate commerce in this state shall register with the commissioner or a base state and pay all fees as required by the federal Unified Carrier Registration Act of 2005.

(c)(1) Any motor carrier, leasing company leasing to a motor carrier, broker, or freight forwarder that engages in intrastate commerce and operates a motor vehicle on or over any public highway of this state shall register with the commissioner and pay a fee determined by the commissioner.

(2) No motor carrier shall be issued a registration unless there is filed with the commissioner or the Federal Motor Carrier Safety Administration or any successor agency a certificate of insurance for such applicant or holder, on forms prescribed by the commissioner, evidencing a policy of indemnity insurance by an insurance company licensed to do business in this state. Such policy shall provide for the protection of passengers in passenger vehicles and the protection of the public against the negligence of such motor carrier, and its servants or agents, when it is determined to be the proximate cause of any injury. The commissioner shall determine and fix the amounts of such indemnity insurance and shall prescribe the provisions and limitations thereof. The insurer shall file such certificate. Failure to file any form required by the commissioner shall not diminish the rights of any person to pursue an action directly against a motor carrier's insurer. The insurer may file its certificate of insurance electronically with the commissioner.

(3) The commissioner shall have the power to permit self-insurance in lieu of a policy of indemnity insurance whenever in his or her opinion the financial ability of the motor carrier so warrants.

(4) Any person having a cause of action, whether arising in tort or contract, under this Code section may join in the same cause of action the motor carrier and its insurance carrier.

(d) Before any motor carrier engaged in exempt passenger intrastate commerce shall operate any motor vehicle on or over any public highway of this state, the motor carrier shall register with the commissioner and pay a fee determined by the commissioner.

(e) In addition to any requirements under the federal Unified Carrier Registration Act of 2005, motor carriers required to have operating authority shall fulfill all applicable requirements for obtaining operating authority prior to any operation of a motor vehicle to which such requirements apply.

(f) The commissioner shall collect the fees imposed by this Code section and may establish rules and regulations and prescribe such forms as are necessary to administer this Code section and the federal Unified Carrier Registration Act of 2005. Notwithstanding the provisions of Code Sections 40–2–131 and 48–2–17, the commissioner shall retain and utilize such fees for motor carrier safety programs and enforcement and administration of this article.

(g) The commissioner of public safety, and persons he or she designates pursuant to Chapter 2 of Title 35, shall have the authority to perform regulatory compliance inspections under the provisions of Article 5 of Chapter 2 of Title 35 for purposes of determining compliance with laws and regulations, the enforcement and administration of which is the responsibility of the Department of Public Safety.

(h) Every officer, agent, or employee of any corporation and every person who fails to comply with this article and any order, rule, or regulation of the Public Service Commission, Department of Public Safety, or Department of Revenue, or who procures, aids, or abets therein, shall be guilty of a misdemeanor. Misdemeanor violations of this article may be prosecuted, handled, and disposed of in the manner provided for in Chapter 13 of this title.

Laws 2009, Act 114, §2, eff. May 4, 2009.

Article 7

Motor Vehicle License Fees And Classes

§ 40–2–150. Definitions

As used in this article, the term:

(.1) "Agricultural field use vehicle" means a commercial truck designed specifically for field applications of fertilizers, poultry litter, and crop protection chemicals which is owned and operated by a farmer or business engaged in the sale and application of fertilizers, poultry litter, and crop protection chemicals and is operated primarily off the highway.

(1) "Farm truck" or "farm trailer" means a truck or trailer for which the owner submits a sworn statement as a part of the registration application to the effect that the vehicle is used primarily on and is domiciled upon a farm primarily for the carriage of unprocessed products of the farm.

(2) "Farm vehicle" means a vehicle or combination of vehicles owned by a farmer or rancher, which are operated over public highways and used exclusively to transport unprocessed agricultural or livestock products raised, owned, and grown by the owner of the vehicle to market or a place of storage; and shall include the transportation by the farmer or rancher of any equipment, supplies, or products purchased by that farmer or rancher for his own use and used in the farming or ranching operation or used by a farmer or rancher partly in transporting agricultural products or livestock from the farm or ranch of another farmer or rancher that were originally grown or raised on that farm or ranch or when used partly in transporting agricultural supplies, equipment, materials, or livestock to the farm or ranch of another farmer or rancher for use or consumption on that farm or ranch but not transported for hire.

(3) "Motor bus" means any passenger-carrying motor vehicle operated for hire and having a passenger seating capacity of eight or more persons exclusive of the driver.

(4) "Owner declared gross vehicle weight" means the empty weight of the truck or truck-trailer fully equipped and fueled and ready for operation on the road and, in the case of combinations, means the weight when ready for operation on the road of the heaviest trailer or semitrailer with which the power unit will be placed in combination, plus the heaviest load which will be carried within the licensed period.

(5) "Private truck" or "private trailer" means a truck or trailer other than a farm truck, a farm trailer, farm vehicle, or a truck or trailer operated for hire by a common or contract carrier.

(6) "Trailer" means any vehicle operated over the public roads of this state without motive power when the vehicle is designed for carrying persons or property, either partially or wholly, on its own structure and is designed for being drawn by a self-propelled vehicle.

Laws 1937–38, Ex. Sess., p. 259, § 3; Laws 1960, p. 998, § 1; Laws 1978, p. 309, § 2; Laws 1990, p. 1883, § 4; Laws 1998, p. 1580, § 3; Laws 2000, p. 951, § 11–2; Laws 2002, p. 1074, §§ 1, 4; Laws 2005, Act 68, § 14–11, eff. July 1, 2005.

Formerly Code 1933, § 91A–5301; Code 1981, § 48–10–1.

§ 40–2–151. Annual license fees for operating motor vehicles; optional one time fee for registration and license plate for certain trailers

(a) The annual fees for the licensing of the operation of vehicles shall be as follows for each vehicle registered:

(1) For each passenger motor vehicle not operated as a common or contract carrier for hire — $ 20.00

(2) For each motorcycle — 20.00

(3)(A) For each private commercial motor vehicle in accordance with the owner declared gross vehicle weight rating, as follows:

(i)	Less than 18,001 lbs.	25.00
(ii)	18,001 to 26,000 lbs.	38.00
(iii)	26,001 to 30,000 lbs.	45.00
(iv)	30,001 to 36,000 lbs.	70.00
(v)	36,001 to 44,000 lbs.	115.00
(vi)	44,001 to 54,999 lbs.	190.00
(vii)	55,000 to 63,280 lbs.	300.00
(viii)	63,281 lbs. to maximum permitted	400.00

(B) Subparagraph (A) of this paragraph notwithstanding:

(i) A straight truck which is not a truck–tractor shall not be classified higher than $75.00;

(ii) A straight truck hauling fertilizer or agricultural products shall not be classified higher than $31.00; and

(iii) A truck–tractor hauling fertilizer, milk, or crops as defined in paragraph (7.1) of Code Section 1–3–3 shall not be classified higher than $ 220.00;

(4) For each farm truck — 20.00

(5) Except as otherwise specifically provided in this Code section, for each private trailer — 20.00

(6)(A) For each farm trailer including, but not limited to, horse and cattle trailers, the maximum fee shall be $12.00.

(B) There shall be no fee for trailers:

(i) Used exclusively to haul agricultural products from one place on the farm to another or from one farm or field to another;

(ii) With no springs which are being employed in hauling unprocessed farm products to their market destination; and

(iii) With no springs which are pulled from a tongue and used primarily to transport fertilizer to the farm;

(7) For house trailers, auto trailers, and boat trailers, whether pulled by a private automobile or a private truck, and not used as or in connection with a motor vehicle, truck, or tractor used as a common or contract carrier for hire — 12.00

(8) For trailers used as or in connection with a motor vehicle, truck, or tractor used as a common or contract carrier for hire 12.00

(9) For each motor bus or van–type vehicle used as a common or contract carrier for hire in public transportation transporting passengers, the following:

(A) Weighing 10,000 pounds or less, $1.90 per 100 pounds factory weight or fractional part of 100 pounds factory weight;

(B) Weighing more than 10,000 pounds and not over 15,000 pounds factory weight, $2.75 for each 100 pounds or fractional part of 100 pounds factory weight;

(C) Weighing more than 15,000 pounds and not more than 20,000 pounds factory weight, $3.45 for each 100 pounds or fractional part of 100 pounds factory weight; and

(D) Weighing more than 20,000 pounds factory weight, $3.75 for each 100 pounds or fractional part of 100 pounds factory weight. No motor bus license fee shall exceed $875.00;

(10)(A) For each commercial motor vehicle operated as a common or contract carrier for hire in accordance with owner declared gross vehicle weight rating, as follows:

(i)	Less than 18,001 lbs.	25.00
(ii)	18,001 to 26,000 lbs.	38.00
(iii)	26,001 to 30,000 lbs.	85.00
(iv)	30,001 to 36,000 lbs.	130.00
(v)	36,001 to 44,000 lbs.	215.00
(vi)	44,001 to 54,999 lbs.	365.00
(vii)	55,000 to 63,280 lbs.	575.00
(viii)	63,281 lbs. to maximum permitted	725.00

(B) Subparagraph (A) of this paragraph notwithstanding, a straight truck which is not a truck–tractor shall not be classified higher than $150.00;

(11) For each commercial motor vehicle leased to a common or contract carrier without regard to the duration of the lease and in accordance with the gross vehicle weight rating, the same license fees as required under paragraph (10) of this subsection;

(12) For each motor driven hearse or ambulance 20.00

(13) For each school bus operated exclusively in the transportation of pupils and teachers to and from schools or school activities or in the transportation of the owner and the members of his immediate family, the sum of $ 20.00. A bus owned by a church or owned in common with other churches and used and operated exclusively for the church in transporting members and patrons to and from church or church activities, when no part of the proceeds of the operation of the bus inures to the benefit of any private person, shall be licensed for the sum of $ 20.00 in the same manner as school buses when the bus complies with the laws applicable to school buses;

(14) For each motor vehicle owned by the state or by a political subdivision or municipality of the state and used exclusively for governmental functions 1.00

(15) For each motor vehicle used by carriers and operated under special franchise granted by the United States Department of Defense over a route of not more than 20 miles in length which is solely between a point in this state and a point within a United States military reservation in this state 20.00

(16) Heavy earth-moving machinery, fertilizer application equipment, and crop protection chemical application equipment, not including trucks, which are used primarily off the highway shall not be required to be licensed under this article;

(17)(A) Trucks transporting logs, pulpwood, or other forest products shall be licensed in accordance with the following annual fees:

(i) Straight trucks and truck-tractors pulling a single pole trailer hauling logs from the woods to the sawmill 38.00

(ii) Other truck-tractors 220.00

(B) Skidders, tractors, and loaders used only in the woods shall not be required to be licensed. Trucks and truck-tractors specified in subparagraph (A) of this paragraph shall be licensed in accordance with this paragraph even though the trucks or truck-tractors are also used to transport skidders, tractors, loaders, and other logging equipment. Trucks and truck-tractors specified in subparagraph (A) of this paragraph shall not be required to pay additional fees or obtain additional license plates in order to transport logging equipment owned by the owner of the trucks or truck-tractors;

(18) For each agricultural field use vehicle 31.00

(b) In lieu of the annual fee provided in paragraphs (6), (7) or (8) of subsection (a) of this Code section, the optional one-time fee for a permanent registration and license plate for:

(1) Any trailer used as or in connection with a motor vehicle, truck, or tractor used as a common or contract carrier for hire, a private carrier, or a motor carrier of property; or

(2) Any boat trailer, utility trailer, or noncommercial cattle and livestock trailer authorized to obtain a permanent registration and license plate under the provisions of Code Section 40–2–47 shall be $48.00.

Laws 1937–38, Ex. Sess., p. 259, § 4; Laws 1946, p. 77, § 1; Laws 1953, Nov.-Dec. Sess., p. 371, § 1; Laws 1955, p. 303, § 1; Laws 1955, Ex. Sess., p. 38, § 1; Laws 1957, p. 376, § 2; Laws 1960, p. 777, § 2; Laws 1960, p. 998, § 2; Laws 1962, p. 450, § 1; Laws 1964, p. 80, §§ 1, 2; Laws 1966, p. 132, §§ 1, 2; Laws 1966, p. 252, §§ 2, 3; Laws 1974, p. 451, §§ 2–4; Laws 1976, p. 694, § 1; Laws 1978, p. 309, § 2; Laws 1978, p. 2210, § 1; Laws 1979, p. 5, § 106; Laws 1979, p. 1038, §§ 1–3; Laws 1982, p. 3, § 48; Laws 1983, p. 3, § 37; Laws 1984, p. 22, § 48; Laws 1984, p. 896, § 1; Laws 1985, p. 1, §§ 1, 2; Laws 1987, p. 348, § 1; Laws 1990, p. 1883, § 5; Laws 1991, p. 434, § 1; Laws 1992, p. 6, § 48; Laws 1992, p. 779, § 27; Laws 1994, p. 1373, § 2; Laws 1995, p. 10, § 48; Laws 1995, p. 742, § 3; Laws 1998, p. 1580, §§ 4, 5; Laws 2002, p. 1074, §§ 1, 4; Laws 2004, Act 789, § 1, eff. July 1, 2004; Laws 2007, Act 346, § 7, eff. Jan. 1, 2008; Laws 2008, Act 471, § 40, eff. May 12, 2008; Laws 2008, Act 727, § 4, eff. Jan. 1, 2009; Laws 2009, Act 101, § 3, eff. Jan. 1, 2010.

Formerly Code 1933, § 91A–5302; Code 1981, § 48–10–2.

Historical and Statutory Notes

Laws 2007, Act 346, § 14, provides:

"Sections 2, 3, 4, 5, and 13 through 15 of this Act shall become effective July 1, 2007. Sections 1, 6, 7, and 12 of this Act shall become effective January 1, 2008. Sections 8, 9, 10, and 11 of this Act shall become effective July 1, 2008."

In 2007, the Code Commission, in subsec. (a), substituted "subsection" for "Code section" at the end of par. (11). See § 28–9–5.

Laws 2008, Act 727, § 9, provides:

"Sections 4 and 5 of this Act shall become effective January 1, 2009. Section 7 of this Act shall become effective July 1, 2009. The remaining sections of this Act shall become effective upon this Act's approval by the Governor or upon this Act becoming law without such approval."

In 2008, the Code Commission, due to irreconcilable conflicts, treated the amendment of this section by Laws 2008, Act 471, § 40, as superseded by Laws 2008, Act 727, § 4. See Butts County v. Strahan, 107 S.E. 163, 151 Ga. 417 (1921).

Laws 2009, Act 101, § 4 provided:

"Section 3A of this Act shall become effective upon its approval by the Governor or upon its becoming law without such approval. The remaining sections of this Act shall become effective on January 1, 2010, and shall apply to registration and licensing of trailers on and after such date."

§ 40–2–152. Annual license fees for apportionable vehicles

(a) Except as otherwise provided for in this Code section, the annual fee for all apportionable vehicles not operated as a common or contract carrier for hire in accordance with owner declared gross vehicle weight or combined vehicle gross weight shall be as follows:

(1)	Less than 30,001 lbs.	$ 45.00
(2)	30,001 to 36,000 lbs.	70.00
(3)	36,001 to 44,000 lbs.	115.00
(4)	44,001 to 54,999 lbs.	190.00
(5)	55,000 to 63,280 lbs.	300.00
(6)	63,281 lbs. to maximum permitted	400.00

(b) Except as otherwise provided for in this Code section, the annual fee for all apportionable vehicles operated as a common or contract carrier for hire in accordance with owner declared gross vehicle weight or combined vehicle gross weight shall be as follows:

(1)	Less than 30,001 lbs.	$ 85.00
(2)	30,001 to 36,000 lbs.	130.00
(3)	36,001 to 44,000 lbs.	215.00
(4)	44,001 to 54,999 lbs.	365.00
(5)	55,000 to 63,280 lbs.	575.00
(6)	63,281 lbs. to maximum permitted	725.00

(c) For each apportionable motor bus or van-type vehicle the fee is $ 3.75 for each 100 pounds or fractional part of 100 pounds factory weight. No motor bus license fee shall exceed $ 875.00.

(d) Trucks transporting logs, pulpwood, or other forest products shall be issued restricted license plates and the fees shall be as enumerated in Code Section 40–2–151.

(e) Each school bus operated exclusively in the transportation of pupils and teachers to and from schools or school activities or in the transportation of the owner and his immediate family shall be issued a restricted license plate for the sum of $ 5.00. A bus owned by a church or owned in common with other churches and used and operated exclusively for the church in transporting members and patrons to and from church or church activities, when no part of the proceeds of the operation of the bus inures to the benefit of any private person, shall be issued a restricted license plate for the sum of $ 5.00 in the same manner as school buses when the bus complies with the laws applicable to school buses.

(f) A truck or a truck-tractor hauling fertilizer, milk, or crops as defined in paragraph (7.1) of Code Section 1–3–3 shall be issued a restricted license plate with the fee computed in accordance with Code Section 40–2–151.

(g) A farm vehicle shall be issued a restricted license plate with the fee computed in accordance with Code Section 40–2–151.

Laws 1990, p. 1883, § 6; Laws 1992, p. 771, § 28; Laws 2002, p. 1074, §§ 1, 5; Laws 2004, Act 789, § 2, eff. July 1, 2004; Laws 2008, Act 727, § 5, eff. Jan. 1, 2009.

Formerly Code 1981, § 48–10–2.1.

Historical and Statutory Notes

Laws 2008, Act 7270, § 9, provides:

"Sections 4 and 5 of this Act shall become effective January 1, 2009. Section 7 of this Act shall become effective July 1, 2009. The remaining sections of this Act shall become effective upon this Act's approval by the Governor or upon this Act becoming law without such approval."

§ 40–2–153. Repealed by Laws 2005, Act 65, § 4, eff. July 1, 2005

Historical and Statutory Notes

Repealed § 40–2–153, relating to registration and licensure of makers and dealers, was derived from Laws 1937–38, Ex. Sess., p. 259, § 4; Laws 1955, Ex. Sess., p. 38, § 2; Laws 1959, p. 232, § 1; Laws 1969, p. 135, § 1; Laws 1978, p. 309, § 2; Laws 1982, p. 3, § 48; Laws 1992, p. 771, § 29; Laws 1992, p. 2978, § 12; Laws 2002, p. 1074, § 1; Code 1933, § 91A–5303; Code 1981, § 48–10–3. The repealing law also reserved the section designation.

§ 40–2–154. License plates for different classes

The commissioner may provide a different license plate for each different class of vehicles specified in this article and may distinguish the plate furnished to each class of vehicles by a different letter or lettering or other symbols or markings on the plates.

Laws 1937–38, Ex. Sess., p. 259, § 4; Laws 1955, p. 447, § 1; Laws 1978, p. 309, § 2; Laws 2002, p. 1074, §§ 1, 4.

Formerly Code 1933, § 91A–5304; Code 1981, § 48–10–4.

§ 40–2–155. Transfers of licenses and plates to another vehicle

The annual license and plate issued for the operation of a vehicle described in paragraph (3), (9), or (10) of subsection (a) of Code Section 40–2–151, except those named in divisions (a)(3)(A)(i), (a)(3)(A)(ii), (a)(3)(A)(iii), (a)(10)(A)(i), (a)(10)(A)(ii), and (a)(10)(A)(iii) of Code Section 40–2–151, may be transferred with the approval of the commissioner from a destroyed or retired motor vehicle to another vehicle upon payment of a transfer fee of $ 5.00 and upon presentation of an appropriate application for transfer. If the substituted vehicle normally calls for a higher-priced plate than the vehicle displaced, a proportionate additional fee shall be paid for the remainder of the taxable year.

Laws 1937–38, Ex. Sess., p. 259, § 4; Laws 1977, p. 595, § 1; Laws 1978, p. 309, § 2; Laws 1991, p. 94, § 48; Laws 1992, p. 771, § 30; Laws 1995, p. 10, § 48; Laws 2002, p. 1074, §§ 1, 5.

Formerly Code 1933, § 91A–5306; Code 1981, § 48–10–6.

§ 40–2–156. Rate of license fee for part of year

Any person registering any of the vehicles named in paragraph (3), (9), or (10) of subsection (a) of Code Section 40–2–151, except those named in divisions (a)(3)(A)(i), (a)(3)(A)(ii), (a)(3)(A)(iii), (a)(10)(A)(i), (a)(10)(A)(ii), and (a)(10)(A)(iii) of Code Section 40–2–151 between the dates of:

(1) March 1 and May 31 of any year shall pay three-fourths of the annual license fee provided in this article;

(2) June 1 and August 31 of any year shall pay one-half of the annual license fee provided in this article; or

(3) September 1 and November 30 of any year shall pay one-fourth of the annual license fee provided in this article.

Laws 1937–38, Ex. Sess., p. 259, § 5; Laws 1960, p. 1031, § 1; Laws 1963, p. 606, § 1; Laws 1978, p. 309, § 2; Laws 1986, p. 1053, § 6; Laws 1991, p. 94, § 48; Laws 1995, p. 10, § 48; Laws 1997, p. 419, § 40; Laws 2002, p. 1074, §§ 1, 4, 5.

Formerly Code 1933, § 91A–5307; Code 1981, § 48–10–7.

§ 40–2–157. Rate of license fee for part of year; registration under section 40–2–152(a), (b), or (c)

Any person initially registering under the International Registration Plan any of the vehicles named in subsection (a), (b), or (c) of Code Section 40–2–152 and whose next registration period ends less than 12 months from the date of application or first date of service of such vehicle shall pay a license fee in an amount equal to one-twelfth of the annual license fee provided by this article multiplied by the number of months remaining until the end of such next registration period.

Laws 1999, p. 741, § 3; Laws 2001, p. 1173, § 1–7; Laws 2002, p. 1074, §§ 1, 4.

Formerly Code 1981, § 48–10–7.1.

Historical and Statutory Notes

In 2002, the Code Commission substituted "40–2–152" for "48–10–2.1". See § 28–9–5.

§ 40–2–158. Rate of license fee for part of year; registration under section 40–2–88(c)(1)(A)

For purposes of registration of any vehicle under subparagraph (c)(1)(A) of Code Section 40–2–88 only, registrants shall be assessed fees equivalent to one-twelfth of the annual fee otherwise provided by law multiplied by the number of months remaining until the end of the applicable registration period.

Laws 1999, p. 741, § 3; Laws 2001, p. 1173, § 1–8; Laws 2002, p. 1074, § 1.

Formerly Code 1981, § 48–10–7.2.

§ 40–2–159. Time of application for license plate

Each person subject to a license fee as provided in this article shall apply for and obtain the required license plate on or before the expiration of the owner's registration period each year. Payment for the license plate shall be made to the commissioner, a duly authorized agent, or any other person specified by law.

Laws 1937–38, Ex. Sess., p. 259, § 7; Laws 1943, p. 341, § 1; Laws 1960, p. 1031, § 2; Laws 1963, p. 606, § 2; Laws 1978, p. 309, § 2; Laws 1986, p. 1053, § 7; Laws 1995, p. 809, § 20; Laws 2002, p. 1074, §§ 1, 4.

Formerly Code 1933, § 91A–5308; Code 1981, § 48–10–8.

§ 40–2–160. Nonresidents and residents; when taxable

(a) Each resident and nonresident person shall be liable for and shall pay the taxes and fees required by law for the operation of motor vehicles in this state.

(b) With respect to motor vehicles used solely for the purpose of hauling seasonal agricultural products grown in this state, the fees required by this article may be prorated on a daily basis in accordance with the owner declared gross vehicle weight. The commissioner may issue a special plate or other means of identification to indicate compliance with this subsection. No motor vehicle to which this subsection is applicable shall be operated in violation of this article.

Laws 1937–38, Ex. Sess., p. 259, § 8; Laws 1960, p. 248, § 1; Laws 1964, p. 242, § 1; Laws 1978, p. 309, § 2; Laws 2002, p. 1074, §§ 1, 4.

Formerly Code 1933, § 91A–5309; Code 1981, § 48–10–9.

§ 40–2–161. Carriers of passengers

If a vehicle described in this article is operated as a carrier of passengers, the rate of annual license fee shall be one-half of the amount specified in this article when the vehicle is operated over a route of 50 miles or less.

Laws 1937–38, Ex. Sess., p. 259, § 8B; Laws 1969, p. 981, § 1; Laws 1978, p. 309, § 2; Laws 2002, p. 1074, §§ 1, 4.

Formerly Code 1933, § 91A–5310; Code 1981, § 48–10–10.

§ 40–2–162. Apportionment of fees of motor buses to motor carriers of passengers for hire operated partially beyond state; rules

(a) The commissioner shall apportion the cost of the annual fees for the licensing of motor buses to motor common carriers of passengers for hire operating a fleet of two or more motor buses either interstate, or both interstate and intrastate, under the authority of the Interstate Commerce Commission or under authority of both the Interstate Commerce Commission and the Public Service Commission of this state. The apportionment shall be done so that the total cost of the fees shall bear the same proportion to the annual fees for motor buses as the total number of miles traveled by the fleet of the carrier in this state in both interstate and intrastate operations during the preceding year bears to the total number of miles traveled by the fleet during the year in both interstate and intrastate operations.

(b) The commissioner shall promulgate rules for the apportionment required by this Code section. The rules shall provide that the apportionment apply as nearly as practicable to each class of vehicle operated by the motor common carrier of passengers for hire.

Laws 1957, p. 653, § 1; Laws 1978, p. 309, § 2; Laws 2002, p. 1074, § 1.

Formerly Code 1933, § 91A–5312; Code 1981, § 48–10–12.

§ 40–2–163. Up-rating of licenses

A vehicle owner may voluntarily increase the allowable gross weight for which his vehicle is licensed by purchasing the appropriate weight license plate for his truck or tractor and paying the difference between the fee charged for the license which is surrendered and the fee charged for the new license, as calculated pursuant to Code Section 40–2–151.

Laws 1960, p. 998, § 3; Laws 1978, p. 309, § 2; Laws 2002, p. 1074, §§ 1, 5.

Formerly Code 1933, § 92–2918; Code 1933, § 91A–5313; Code 1981, § 48–10–13.

§ 40–2–164. Down-rating of licenses

The allowable maximum weight (license class) for which a truck or tractor is registered may be decreased only once a year, at the beginning of a new license year. Trucks classified in divisions (a)(3)(A)(i), (a)(3)(A)(ii), (a)(3)(A)(iii), (a)(10)(A)(i), (a)(10)(A)(ii), and (a)(10)(A)(iii) of Code Section 40–2–151 shall not be entitled to any partial year license.

Laws 1960, p. 998, § 4; Laws 1978, p. 309, § 2; Laws 1991, p. 94, § 48; Laws 1995, p. 10, § 48; Laws 2002, p. 1074, §§ 1, 5.

Formerly Code 1933, § 92–2919; Code 1933, § 91A–5314; Code 1981, § 48–10–14.

§ 40–2–165. Under-licensing of trucks

If upon inspection a truck licensed under Code Section 40–2–151 is found to weigh, together with its loaded trailer, more than is permitted by the license plate which it carries, the owner shall be required to purchase immediately a new license plate for the weight of the truck so inspected. One-half credit shall be given for the surrendered underrated license plate.

Laws 1960, p. 998, § 5; Laws 1978, p. 309, § 2; Laws 2002, p. 1074, §§ 1, 5.

Formerly Code 1933, § 92–2920; Code 1933, § 91A–5315; Code 1981, § 48–10–15.

§ 40–2–166. Violation of law taxing the operation of motor vehicles

(a) It shall be unlawful for any person to violate any provision of this article.

(b) Any person who violates any provision of this article shall be guilty of a misdemeanor.

Laws 1937–38, Ex. Sess., p. 259, § 10; Laws 1978, p. 309, § 2; Laws 2002, p. 1074, §§ 1, 4.

Formerly Code 1933, § 91A–9927; Code 1981, § 48–10–16.

§ 40–2–167. Motor vehicle rental companies; recoverable facility charges; recoverable fees and taxes

(a) As used in this Code section, the term:

(1) "Motor vehicle rental company" means an individual or business entity whose business activity is renting motor vehicles to consumers under rental agreements for periods of 90 days or less or renting "heavy-duty equipment motor vehicles" as such term is defined in Code Section 48–5–505.

(2) "Recoverable facility charges" means governmental and private concession fees, including airport concession fees, consolidated facility charges, and the fees and charges incurred thereon, actually paid by a motor vehicle rental company.

(3) "Recoverable fees and taxes" means costs incurred by a motor vehicle rental company to license, title, register, plate, and inspect rental motor vehicles and ad valorem taxes imposed in connection with the registration of rental motor vehicles or a 1 ½ percent property tax recovery fee on "heavy-duty equipment motor vehicles" as such term is defined in Code Section 48–5–505.

(4) "Rental agreement" means an agreement under which a rental motor vehicle is rented or leased.

(5) "Rental motor vehicle" means a motor vehicle that is rented or leased without a driver.

(b) Pursuant to a written rental agreement between a motor vehicle rental company and a rental customer, a motor vehicle rental company may include separately stated fees in a rental agreement, which may include, but shall not be limited to, recoverable facility charges and recoverable fees and taxes, as provided in this Code section.

(c) If a motor vehicle rental company includes a charge for recoverable fees and taxes as a separately stated fee in a rental transaction disclosed on the rental agreement, the amount of the charge shall represent the motor vehicle rental company's good faith estimate of the motor vehicle rental company's daily charge as calculated by the motor vehicle rental company to recover its actual total annual recoverable fees and taxes on its rental motor vehicle fleet for the corresponding calendar year.

(d) If the total amount of the recoverable fees and taxes collected by a motor vehicle rental company under this Code section in any calendar year exceeds the motor vehicle rental company's actual recoverable fees and taxes for that calendar year, the motor vehicle rental company shall:

(1) Retain the excess amount; and

(2) Adjust the estimated average per vehicle fee for recoverable fees and taxes for the following calendar year by a corresponding amount.

Nothing herein shall prevent a motor vehicle rental company from making adjustments to the per vehicle recoverable fees and taxes charge during the calendar year to reflect interim developments affecting the motor vehicle rental company's prior estimated per vehicle fee for such calendar year.

(e) The property tax recovery fee may be assessed if the motor vehicle rental company includes the fee as a separately stated fee on its rental agreement.

(f) The recovery fee authorized by this Code section for recoverable fees and taxes shall be subject to state and local sales and use tax in the manner and to the same extent as the fee charged for the lease or rental of the rental motor vehicle.

Laws 2008, Act 575, § 1, eff. May 13, 2008.

§ 40–2–168. License plate registration of taxicabs or limousines

Owners of a taxicab or limousine, prior to commencing operation in this state, shall, upon complying with the motor vehicle laws relating to registration and licensing of motor vehicles, and the payment of an annual registration fee of $25.00, be issued a distinctive license plate by the commissioner. Such distinctive license plate shall be designed by the commissioner and displayed on the vehicle as provided in Code Section 40–2–41. The certificate of registration shall be kept in the vehicle. Revalidation decals shall be issued, upon payment of fees required by law, in the same manner as provided for general issue license plates. Such license plates shall be transferred from one vehicle to another vehicle of the same class and acquired by the same person as provided in Code Section 40–2–42. The transition period shall commence upon the effective date of this Code section and conclude no later than December 31, 2010, for all existing registrations. For all existing registrations, except during the owner's registration period as provided in Code Section 40–2–21, the commissioner shall exchange and replace any current and valid registration and license plate at no charge to the owner.

Laws 2010, Act 381, § 6, eff. May 20, 2010.

CHAPTER 3

CERTIFICATES OF TITLE, SECURITY INTERESTS, AND LIENS

Article 1

General Provisions

§ 40–3–1. Short title

This chapter shall be known and may be cited as the "Motor Vehicle Certificate of Title Act."

Laws 1961, p. 68, § 1; Laws 1990, p. 2048, § 3.

§ 40–3–2. Definitions

As used in this chapter, the term:

(1) "Boat trailer" means any vehicle without motive power designed for carrying boats, either partially or wholly on its own structure, which is being drawn by a self–propelled vehicle and operated over the public roads of this state.

(2) "Commissioner" means the state revenue commissioner.

(3) "Dealer" means a "dealer" as defined in Code Section 40–1–1 to whom current dealer registration plates have been issued by the commissioner.

(3.1) "Department" means the Department of Revenue.

(4) "Homemade trailer" means a vehicle without motive power, designed for carrying persons or property either partially or wholly on its own structure and for being drawn by a self–propelled vehicle other than a self–propelled vehicle running exclusively on tracks, which trailer has been manufactured and constructed from component parts for personal use and not for the purpose of commercial resale.

(5) "Identifying number" means the numbers and letters, if any, on a vehicle designated by the commissioner for the purpose of identifying the vehicle.

(6) "Lien" means any lien created by operation of law and not by contract or agreement with respect to a vehicle and includes all liens mentioned in Code Section 44–14–320, other than that in paragraph (5) thereof, and all liens for taxes due the United States of America, constructive notice of which is given by filing notice thereof in the office designated by state law.

(7) "Lienholder" means a person holding a lien created by operation of law on a motor vehicle.

(8) To "mail" means to deposit in the United States mail properly addressed and with postage paid.

(9) "Major component part" means any one of the following subassemblies of a motor vehicle:

(A) Front clip assembly (fenders, hood, and bumper);

(B) Rear clip assembly (quarter panels, floor panel assembly, and roof assembly, excluding a soft top);

(C) Engine and transmission;

(D) Frame; or

(E) Complete side (fenders, door, and quarter panel).

(9.1) "Natural person" means an individual human being and does not include any firm, partnership, association, corporation, or trust.

(10) "Rebuilt motor vehicle" means any motor vehicle which has been damaged and subsequently restored to an operable condition by the replacement of two or more major component parts.

(11) "Salvage motor vehicle" means any motor vehicle:

(A) Which has been damaged to the extent that its restoration to an operable condition would require the replacement of two or more major component parts;

(B) For which an insurance company has paid a total loss claim and the vehicle has not been repaired, regardless of the extent of damage to such vehicle or the number of major component parts required to repair such vehicle, but shall not mean or include any stolen motor vehicle which has been recovered with the public manufacturer's vehicle identification number plate intact and the vehicle:

(i) Is undamaged;

(ii) Has only cosmetic damage; or

(iii) Has been damaged but only to the extent that its restoration to an operable condition will not require the replacement of two or more major component parts;

(C) Which is an imported motor vehicle which has been damaged in shipment and disclaimed by the manufacturer as a result of the damage, has never been the subject of a retail sale to a consumer, and has never been issued a certificate of title.

The term salvage motor vehicle shall not include any motor vehicle for which a total loss claim has been paid which vehicle has sustained only cosmetic damage from causes other than fire or flood.

(12) "Security agreement" means a written agreement which reserves or creates a security interest.

(13) "Security interest" means an interest in a vehicle reserved or created by agreement which secures the payment or performance of an obligation, such as a conditional sales contract, chattel mortgage, bill of sale to secure debt, deed of trust, and the like. This term includes the interest of a lessor under a lease intended as security.

(14) "Security interest holder" means the holder of an interest in a vehicle reserved or created by agreement and which secures payment or performance of an obligation.

Laws 1961, p. 68, § 2; Laws 1962, p. 79, § 1; Laws 1964, p. 178, § 1; Laws 1980, p. 518, § 1; Laws 1981, p. 644, § 1; Laws 1982, p. 3, § 40; Laws 1982, p. 152, §§ 1, 2; Laws 1984, p. 781, §§ 1, 2; Laws 1989, p. 1186, § 6; Laws 1990, p. 1657, § 4; Laws 1990, p. 2048, § 3; Laws 1993, p. 1260, § 4; Laws 2000, p. 951, § 4–1; Laws 2001, p. 1173, § 1–5; Laws 2004, Act 514, § 1, eff. July 1, 2004; Laws 2005, Act 68, § 15–1, eff. July 1, 2005; Laws 2007, Act 340, § 1, eff. July 1, 2007.

Historical and Statutory Notes

In 2007, the Code Commission, in par. (3), deleted a comma following "Code Section 40–1–1". See § 28–9–5.

§ 40–3–3. Powers of commissioner

(a) The commissioner is responsible for the administration of this chapter and may employ such clerical assistants and agents as may be necessary from time to time to enable the commissioner speedily, completely, and efficiently to perform the duties conferred on the commissioner in this chapter. The commissioner shall be authorized to delegate any administrative responsibility for retention of applications, certificates of title, notices of security interest, and any other forms or documents relating to the application and registration process to the appropriate authorized tag agent for the county in which the application is made or the registration is issued.

(b) The commissioner shall prescribe and provide suitable forms of applications, certificates of title, notices of security interest, and all other notices and forms necessary to carry out this chapter.

(c) The commissioner may:

(1) Make necessary investigation to procure information required to carry out this chapter;

(2) Adopt and enforce reasonable rules and regulations to carry out this chapter; and

(3) Assign a new identifying number to a vehicle if it has none, or its identifying number is destroyed or obliterated, and shall either issue a new certificate of title showing the new identifying number or make an appropriate endorsement on the original certificate.

Laws 1961, p. 68, § 3; Laws 1990, p. 2048, § 3; Laws 1992, p. 2978, § 5; Laws 1997, p. 739, § 4.

§ 40–3–4. Exclusions

No certificate of title shall be obtained for:

(1) A vehicle owned by the United States unless it is registered in this state;

(2) A vehicle owned by a manufacturer of or dealer in vehicles and held for sale, even though incidentally used on the highway or used for purpose of testing or demonstration; a vehicle owned by a dealer in vehicles but used by any Georgia public or private school for driver education purposes; or a

vehicle used by a manufacturer solely for testing; except that all dealers acquiring new vehicles after July 1, 1962, from a manufacturer for resale shall obtain such evidence of origin of title from the manufacturer as the commissioner shall by rule and regulation prescribe;

(3) A vehicle owned by a nonresident of this state and not required by law to be registered in this state;

(4) A vehicle regularly engaged in the interstate transportation of persons or property for which a currently effective certificate of title has been issued in another state;

(5) A vehicle moved solely by human or animal power;

(6) An implement of husbandry;

(7) Special mobile equipment;

(8) A self-propelled wheelchair or invalid tricycle;

(9) A pole trailer;

(10) Motor buses used for the transportation of persons by a street railroad or other company engaged in the operation of an urban transit system over fixed routes;

(11) A boat trailer;

(12) A homemade trailer;

(13) A device used exclusively upon stationary rails or tracks or which obtains motive power from fixed overhead electric wires;

(14)(A) A vehicle, other than a mobile home or crane, the model year of which is prior to 1986.

(B) The owner of any vehicle which has a valid certificate of title and which becomes subject to the exclusion provided in subparagraph (A) of this paragraph may retain the certificate of title. Each subsequent transferee of any vehicle covered by subparagraph (A) of this paragraph, for which the certificate of title has been retained, may obtain a certificate of title by complying with Code Section 40–3–32. However, the failure of any subsequent transferee to comply with Code Section 40–3–32 shall preclude transferees subsequent to that transferee from obtaining a certificate of title. The department shall maintain such records as may be necessary to allow owners to obtain a certificate of title under this subparagraph. No certificate of title authorized to be issued under this subparagraph shall be issued under Code Section 40–3–28.

(C)(i) A security interest in or lien against a vehicle which is subject to the exclusion provided for in subparagraph (A) of this paragraph and which arises after such vehicle becomes subject to the operation of subparagraph (A) of this paragraph may be perfected in the same manner as such security interests and liens are perfected on vehicles required by this chapter to have certificates of title.

(ii) The transferee of any vehicle which is subject to the exclusion provided for in subparagraph (A) of this paragraph, regardless of whether that vehicle has a certificate of title issued pursuant to subparagraph (B) of this paragraph, shall take such vehicle subject to any security interest or lien perfected under this paragraph;

(15)(A) Except as provided in subparagraph (B) of this paragraph, a trailer with an unladen gross weight of 2,000 pounds or less.

(B) The exclusion provided in subparagraph (A) of this paragraph shall not apply to a travel trailer or camper, regardless of its unladen gross weight;

(16) A vehicle which is not sold for the purpose of lawful highway use;

(17) A vehicle with a model year prior to 1963; or

(18) A moped.

Laws 1961, p. 68, § 4; Laws 1962, p. 79, § 2; Laws 1964, p. 178, § 2; Laws 1980, p. 518, § 2; Laws 1981, p. 617, § 1; Laws 1985, p. 1271, § 1; Laws 1987, p. 655, § 2; Laws 1990, p. 2048, § 3; Laws 1993, p. 1260, § 5; Laws 1994, p. 97, § 40; Laws 1994, p. 741, § 1; Laws 1997, p. 143, § 40; Laws 1997, p. 1515, § 1; Laws 1998, p. 1179, §§ 31, 32; Laws 1999, p. 334, § 3; Laws 2000, p. 951, § 4–2; Laws 2002, p. 506, § 4; Laws 2002, p. 512, § 8.

§ 40–3–5. Stolen, converted, recovered and unclaimed vehicles

(a) *Duties of peace officers.* A peace officer who learns of the theft of a vehicle not since recovered shall report the theft to the commissioner. A peace officer who learns of the recovery of a vehicle whose theft or conversion he knows or has reason to believe has been reported to the commissioner shall forthwith report the recovery to the commissioner.

(b) *Owner's, security holder's, or lienholder's report.* An owner or a security interest holder or lienholder shall report the theft of a vehicle, or its conversion if a crime, to the commissioner. A person who has so reported the theft or conversion of a vehicle shall, after learning of its recovery, immediately report the recovery to the commissioner.

(c) *Records to be kept by commissioner; distribution.* The commissioner shall maintain appropriately indexed weekly and cumulative public records of stolen, converted, and recovered vehicles reported to him pursuant to this Code section. The commissioner may make and distribute copies of the weekly records so maintained to peace officers upon request without fee and to others for the fee, if any, the commissioner prescribes.

(d) *Action by commissioner.* The commissioner may suspend the registration of a vehicle whose theft or conversion is reported to him pursuant to this Code section, and until the commissioner learns of its recovery or that the report of its theft or conversion was erroneous he shall not issue a certificate of title for the vehicle.

Laws 1961, p. 68, § 32; Laws 1980, p. 995, § 9; Laws 1990, p. 2048, § 3.

§ 40–3–6. Hearings; review of proceedings

(a) A person aggrieved by an act or omission to act of the department under this chapter is entitled, upon request, to a hearing. The commissioner shall establish a board to hear complaints of persons aggrieved by an act or omission to act of the commissioner or any employee of the department pertaining to the administration of this chapter. The procedure established in this chapter for the handling of complaints and grievances shall be exclusive and these procedures shall apply to all such complaints and grievances. The commissioner shall promulgate rules and regulations governing the membership of the board and the organization thereof.

(b) Hearings conducted under subsection (a) of this Code section shall be conducted under the terms and conditions of Chapter 13 of Title 50, the "Georgia Administrative Procedure Act," and court review of such hearings shall be as provided by that chapter.

Laws 1961, p. 68, §§ 29, 30; Laws 1963, p. 32, § 2; Laws 1965, p. 304, § 10; Laws 1984, p. 1194, § 1; Laws 1985, p. 149, § 40; Laws 1990, p. 2048, § 3; Laws 2000, p. 951, § 4–3.

Article 2

Certificates of Title

§ 40–3–20. Certificate of title required

(a) Except as provided in Code Section 40–3–4, every owner of a vehicle which is required by law to be registered in this state and for which no certificate of title has been issued by the commissioner may make application to the commissioner or to the tag agent in the county wherein the owner resides for a certificate of title to the vehicle according to the model of the vehicle. If a vehicle is owned by and used in connection with an established business, application may be made to the commissioner or to the tag agent in the county in which the business is located. Such application shall be made in the following manner: All 1963 model vehicles and all successive model vehicles thereafter shall have a certificate of title. However, once a vehicle comes within the exclusion provided by paragraph (14) of Code Section 40–3–4, a certificate of title shall no longer be required.

(b) The commissioner may by rule or regulation exempt from the requirements of this chapter vehicles owned by nonresident individuals or corporations that are properly titled in the state of such owner's residence where the vehicle is required to be registered in this state because:

(1) Georgia has no reciprocity agreement on registration and licensing of motor vehicles with the owner's state; or

(2) The vehicle is used in both interstate and intrastate transportation.

(c) When the owner of a vehicle is required to have a certificate of title, the tag agent or the commissioner shall not register or renew the registration of such vehicle until a certificate of title has been issued or applied for.

(d) No application for a certificate of title for a vehicle purchased outside the State of Georgia shall be accepted or processed unless the applicant shows, by a valid bill of sale or contract of purchase or by such other documentation satisfactory to the commissioner, that state and local sales and use tax has been paid or is not due. If state and local sales and use tax is owed on such vehicle but has not been paid, the local tag agent shall return the unprocessed application to the applicant informing him or her of the requirements of this Code section.

Laws 1961, p. 68, § 6; Laws 1962, p. 79, § 4; Laws 1963, p. 32, § 1; Laws 1964, p. 436, § 1; Laws 1967, p. 451, § 1; Laws 1981, p. 617, § 2; Laws 1990, p. 2048, § 3; Laws 2005, Act 358, § 1, eff. Jan. 1, 2006.

Historical and Statutory Notes

Laws 2005, Act 358, § 2, provides:

"This Act shall become effective on January 1, 2006."

§ 40–3–21. Application for first certificate of title

(a) The application for the first certificate of title of a vehicle in this state shall be made by the owner to the commissioner or the commissioner's duly authorized county tag agent on the prescribed form. Except as provided in subsection (b) of this Code section, the application must be submitted to the commissioner or the appropriate authorized county tag agent by the owner of the vehicle within 30 days from the date of purchase of the vehicle or from the date the owner is otherwise required by law to register the vehicle in this state. If the owner does not submit the application within that time, the owner of the vehicle shall be required to pay a penalty of $10.00 in addition to the ordinary title fee provided for by this chapter. If the documents submitted in support of the title application are rejected, the party submitting the documents shall have 60 days from the date of rejection to resubmit the documents required by the commissioner or the authorized county tag agent for the issuance of a certificate of title. Should the documents not be properly resubmitted within the 60 day period, there shall be an additional $10.00 penalty assessed, and the owner of the vehicle shall be required to remove immediately the license plate of the vehicle and return same to the commissioner or the authorized county tag agent. The license plate shall be deemed to have expired at 12:00 Midnight of the sixtieth day following the initial rejection of the documents submitted, if the documents have not been resubmitted as required under this subsection. Such application shall contain:

(1) The full legal name, driver's license number, residence, and mailing address of the owner;

(2) A description of the vehicle, including, so far as the following data exist: its make, model, identifying number, type of body, the number of cylinders, and whether new, used, or a demonstrator and, for a manufactured home, the manufacturer's statement or certificate of origin and the full serial number for all manufactured homes sold in this state on or after July 1, 1994;

(3) The date of purchase by the applicant and, except as provided in paragraph (2) of subsection (c) of this Code section, the name and address of the person from whom the vehicle was acquired and the names and addresses of the holders of all security interests and liens in order of their priority; and

(4) Any further information the commissioner reasonably requires to identify the vehicle and to enable the commissioner or the authorized county tag agent to determine whether the owner is entitled to a certificate of title and the existence or nonexistence of security interests in the vehicle and liens on the vehicle.

(b)(1) As used in this subsection, the term "digital signature" means a digital or electronic method executed or adopted by a party with the intent to be bound by or to authenticate a record, which is unique to the person using it, is capable of verification, is under the sole control of the person using it, and is linked to data in such a manner that if the data are changed the digital or electronic signature is invalidated.

(2) If the application refers to a vehicle purchased from a dealer, it shall contain the name and address of the holder of any security interest created or reserved at the time of the sale by the dealer. The application shall be signed by the owner and, unless the dealer's signature appears on the certificate of title or manufacturer's statement of origin submitted in support of the title application, the dealer, provided that as an alternative to a handwritten signature, the commissioner may authorize use of a digital signature as long as appropriate security measures are implemented which assure security and verification of the digital signature process, in accordance with regulations promulgated by the commissioner. The dealer shall promptly mail or deliver the application to the commissioner or the county tag agent of the county in which the seller is located, of the county in which the sale takes place, of the county in which the vehicle is delivered, or of the county wherein the vehicle owner resides so as to have the application submitted to the commissioner or such authorized county tag agent within 30 days from the date of the sale of the vehicle. If the application is not submitted within that time, the dealer, or in nondealer sales the transferee, shall be required to pay a penalty of $10.00 in addition to the ordinary title fee paid by the transferee provided for in this chapter. If the documents submitted in support of the title application are rejected, the dealer submitting the documents shall have 60 days from the date of initial rejection to resubmit the documents required by the commissioner or authorized county tag agent for the issuance of a certificate of title. Should the documents not be properly resubmitted within 60 days, there shall be an additional penalty of $10.00 assessed against the dealer. The willful failure of a dealer to obtain a certificate of title for a purchaser shall be grounds for suspension or revocation of the dealer's state issued license and registration for the sale of motor vehicles.

(c)(1) If the application refers to a vehicle last previously registered in another state or country, the application shall contain or be accompanied by:

(A) Any certificate of title issued by the other state or country; and

(B) Any other information and documents the commissioner or authorized county tag agent reasonably requires to establish the ownership of the vehicle and the existence or nonexistence of security interests in it and liens against it.

(2) If the application refers to a vehicle last previously registered in another state and if the applicant is the last previously registered owner in such state, the application need not contain the name and address of the person from whom the vehicle was acquired.

Laws 1961, p. 68, § 8; Laws 1962, p. 79, § 6; Laws 1964, p. 436, § 2; Laws 1981, p. 883, §§ 1, 2; Laws 1982, p. 3, § 40; Laws 1985, p. 149, § 40; Laws 1985, p. 1271, § 2; Laws 1986, p. 438, § 1; Laws 1990, p. 2048, § 3; Laws 1994, p. 741, § 2; Laws 1995, p. 809, § 13; Laws 1997, p. 739, § 5; Laws 2003, Act 205, § 1, eff. July 1, 2003; Laws 2007, Act 346, § 8, eff. July 1, 2008.

Formerly Code 1981, § 40–3–22.

Historical and Statutory Notes

Laws 2007, Act 346, § 14, provides:

"Sections 2, 3, 4, 5, and 13 through 15 of this Act shall become effective July 1, 2007. Sections 1, 6, 7, and 12 of this Act shall become effective January 1, 2008. Sections 8, 9, 10, and 11 of this Act shall become effective July 1, 2008."

§ 40–3–21.1. Repealed by Laws 1996, p. 5, § 1, eff. February 9, 1996

§ 40–3–22. Examination of records

(a) The commissioner or the commissioner's duly authorized county tag agent, upon receiving application for a first certificate of title, shall check the identifying number of the vehicle shown in the application against the records of vehicles required to be maintained by Code Section 40–3–23 and against the record of stolen and converted vehicles required to be maintained by Code Section 40–3–5.

(b) Subsection (a) of this Code section shall not be applicable to an application for the first certificate of title of a new car or a demonstrator when such application is accompanied by a manufacturer's certificate of origin.

Laws 1961, p. 68, § 9; Laws 1990, p. 2048, § 3; Laws 1997, p. 739, § 6.

Formerly Code 1981, § 40–3–23.

§ 40–3–23. Issuance and records

(a) The commissioner or the commissioner's duly authorized county tag agent shall file each application received and, when satisfied as to its genuineness and regularity and that the applicant is entitled to the issuance of a certificate of title, shall issue a certificate of title of the vehicle.

(b) The commissioner or the commissioner's duly authorized county tag agent shall maintain a record of all certificates of title issued:

(1) Under a distinctive title number assigned to the vehicle;

(2) Under the identifying number of the vehicle;

(3) Alphabetically, under the name of the owner;

(4) Under the vehicle tag registration number; and

(5) In the discretion of the commissioner, in any other method the commissioner determines.

(c) The commissioner or the commissioner's duly authorized county tag agent is authorized and empowered to provide for photographic and photostatic recording of certificate of title records in such manner as the commissioner or the commissioner's duly authorized county tag agent may deem expedient. The photographic or photostatic copies authorized in this subsection shall be sufficient as evidence in tracing of titles of the motor vehicles designated therein and shall also be admitted in evidence in all actions and proceedings to the same extent that the originals would have been admitted.

(d) The motor vehicle records which the commissioner or the commissioner's duly authorized county tag agent is required to maintain under this Code section or any other provision are exempt from the provisions of any law of this state requiring that such records be open for public inspection; provided, however, that, subject to subsection (f) of this Code section, the records may be disclosed for use as provided in the federal Driver's Privacy Protection Act of 1994, 18 U.S.C. Chapter 123, and by the following:

(1) Any licensed dealer of new or used motor vehicles;

(2) Any tax collector, tax receiver, or tax commissioner; and

(3) A person or entity authorized by the commissioner for use in providing notice to the owners of towed or impounded vehicles.

(e) In addition to any public inspection of records authorized under subsection (d) of this Code section, motor vehicle records consisting of vehicle description, title status, title brands, last recorded mileage, recorded liens, or recorded security interests which the commissioner or the commissioner's duly authorized county tag agent is required to maintain under this Code section shall, in such manner and under such conditions as prescribed by the commissioner, be furnished individually or in bulk to any person upon payment of a reasonable fee, for any purpose not otherwise prohibited by law, including without limitation for the purpose of providing information to allow for informed motor vehicle purchase and safety decisions. Records furnished in accordance with this subsection may be subsequently transferred to third parties. Personal information of any registrant, including name, address, date of birth, or driver's license or social security number, shall not be furnished or transferred by or to any person pursuant to this subsection.

(f) Except as otherwise required in the federal Driver's Privacy Protection Act of 1994, 18 U.S.C. Chapter 123, personal information furnished under paragraphs (1), (2), and (3) of subsection (d) of this Code section shall be limited to the natural person's name, address, and driver identification number. The personal information obtained by a business under this Code section shall not be resold or redisclosed for any purposes other than those permitted under the federal Driver's Privacy Protection Act of 1994, 18 U.S.C. Chapter 123, without the written consent of the individual. Furnishing of information to a business under this Code section shall be pursuant to a contract entered into by such business and the state which specifies the consideration to be paid by such business to the state for such information and the frequency of updates.

Laws 1961, p. 68, § 10; Laws 1962, p. 79, § 7; Laws 1969, p. 92, § 1; Laws 1981, p. 473, § 1; Laws 1982, p. 1784, §§ 1, 2; Laws 1990, p. 2048, § 3; Laws 1997, p. 739, § 7; Laws 2000, p. 951, § 4–4; Laws 2001, p. 1173, § 1–6; Laws 2003, Act 200, § 2, eff. Oct. 1, 2003; Laws 2004, Act 521, § 9, eff. July 1, 2004; Laws 2008, Act 711, § 2, eff. July 1, 2008.

Formerly Code 1981, § 40–3–24.

Historical and Statutory Notes

Laws 2003, Act 200, § 15 provides:

"This Act shall become effective on October 1, 2003."

§ 40–3–24. Contents and effect; not subject to judicial process

(a) Each certificate of title issued by the commissioner or the commissioner's duly authorized county tag agent shall contain:

(1) The date issued;

(2) The name and address of the owner;

(3) The names and addresses of the holders of any security interest and of any lien as shown on the application or, if the

application is based on a certificate of title, as shown on the certificate;

(4) The title number assigned to the vehicle;

(5) A description of the vehicle including, so far as the following data exist: its make, model, identifying number, type of body, number of cylinders, whether new, used, or a demonstrator and, if a new vehicle or a demonstrator, the date of the first sale of the vehicle for use; and

(6) Any other data the commissioner prescribes.

(b) The certificate of title shall contain forms for assignment and warranty of title by the owner, and for assignment and warranty of title by a dealer, and may contain forms for applications for a certificate of title by a transferee or naming of a security interest holder and of a lienholder and the assignment or release of the security interest and lien.

(c) A certificate of title issued by the commissioner or the commissioner's duly authorized county tag agent is prima-facie evidence of the facts appearing on it.

(d) A certificate of title for a vehicle is not subject to garnishment, attachment, execution, or other judicial process, but this subsection does not prevent a lawful levy upon the vehicle.

Laws 1961, p. 68, § 11; Laws 1962, p. 79, § 8; Laws 1989, p. 1186, § 7; Laws 1990, p. 2048, § 3; Laws 1997, p. 739, § 8.

Formerly Code 1981, § 40–3–25.

§ 40–3–25. Odometer readings

In addition to the information required by Code Section 40–3–24, each certificate of title issued by the commissioner or the commissioner's duly authorized county tag agent shall contain spaces thereon for the entry of the mileage of the motor vehicle as shown on the odometer of such motor vehicle at the time of its sale or transfer. When a demonstrator or a new motor vehicle is sold by a dealer, it shall be the duty of the dealer to insert on the application for the certificate of title and on the manufacturer's statement of origin where assigned to the first retail purchaser the mileage of such motor vehicle as shown on its odometer on the day of the sale. When the owner of a motor vehicle sells or transfers such motor vehicle, such owner shall enter on the certificate of title the mileage as shown on the odometer of such motor vehicle at the time such owner executes the assignment and warranty of title. When a new certificate of title is issued for a previously titled motor vehicle, the odometer reading as recorded on the old certificate of title shall be shown on the new certificate of title. When a replacement certificate of title is issued to the owner of a lost, stolen, mutilated, or destroyed certificate of title, the mileage as shown on the odometer on the day application is made for the replacement certificate of title shall be shown on the replacement certificate of title. Notwithstanding any other provision of this Code section, the odometer reading of any motor vehicle which is more than ten model years old shall not be required to be recorded on the certificate of title for such vehicle. However, vehicles having a gross vehicle weight rating of more than 16,000 pounds shall be exempt from the requirement of disclosure of the odometer mileage on certificates of title. The commissioner is authorized and directed to provide by regulation for the implementation of this Code section.

Laws 1981, p. 517, § 1; Laws 1988, p. 1340, § 2; Laws 1989, p. 1186, § 8; Laws 1990, p. 2048, § 3; Laws 1997, p. 739, § 9.

Formerly Code 1981, § 40–3–25.1.

§ 40–3–25.1. Renumbered as § 40–3–25 by Laws 1990, p. 2048, § 3, eff. July 1, 1990

§ 40–3–26. Delivery; notice to security interest holders and lienholders; satisfaction of lien or security interest

(a)(1) The certificate of title shall be mailed or delivered to the holder of the first security interest or lien named in it. In the event there is no security interest holder or lienholder named in such certificate, the certificate of title shall be mailed or delivered directly to the owner.

(2) The commissioner may enter into agreements with any such security interest holder or lienholder to provide a means of delivery by secure electronic measures of a notice of the recording of such security interest or lien. Such security interest or lien shall remain on the official records of the department until such time as the security interest or lien is released by secure electronic measures or affidavit of lien or security interest release; after which release, or at the request of the lienholder or security interest holder, the certificate of title may be printed and mailed or delivered to the next lienholder or security interest holder or as otherwise provided by paragraph (1) of this subsection without payment of any fee provided by Code Section 40–3–38.

(3) If the certificate of title has not been electronically delivered as provided for in paragraph (2) of this subsection, in lieu of delivering a certificate of title, the commissioner may deliver to any security interest holder or lienholder a confirmation form stating the certificate of title is available for printing:

(A) When such confirmation is presented to the commissioner's duly authorized county tag agent or to the commissioner requesting delivery of the title in accordance with this Code section;

(B) When the security interest or lien is satisfied and the confirmation form is delivered to the owner stating the security interest or lien is satisfied and released. The owner may then present the confirmation letter to the commissioner's duly authorized county tag agent or the commissioner for printing in accordance with this Code section; or

(C) When the security interest holder or lienholder delivers the confirmation form to the commissioner's duly authorized county tag agent or the commissioner stating the security interest or lien is satisfied and released and provides an alternate delivery address to include any subsequent security interest holder, lienholder, vehicle dealer, or other business with an interest in such vehicle.

(4) In the event the confirmation form is lost or stolen, the security interest holder or lienholder shall file an affidavit stating the circumstances under which the confirmation form was lost or stolen. Upon receipt, the commissioner shall deliver a certificate of title in accordance with this Code section.

(b) If the certificate of title is mailed to a security interest holder or lienholder, such person shall notify by mail all other lien or security interest holders that such person has received the certificate of title. The notice shall inform the security interest holder or lienholder of the contents and information reflected on such certificate of title. Such mailing or delivery shall be within five days, exclusive of holidays, after the receipt of the certificate by the holder of any security interest or lien.

(c) The security interest holder or lienholder may retain custody of the certificate of title until such security interest holder's or lienholder's claim has been satisfied. The security interest holder or lienholder having custody of a certificate of title must deliver the certificate of title to the next lienholder or security interest holder within ten days after such custodial security interest holder's or lienholder's lien or security interest has been satisfied and, if there is no other security interest holder or lienholder, such custodial security interest holder or lienholder must deliver the certificate of title to the owner.

(d) If a lien or security interest has been electronically recorded, the release of such lien or security interest will require the lienholder to notify the commissioner and the owner of the vehicle, on a form prescribed by the commissioner, or by electronic means approved by the commissioner, of the release of the lien or security interest. Such notice will inform the owner that such owner may request a title free of lien, upon verification of such owner's current mailing address, from the commissioner as provided in Code Section 40–3–56.

Laws 1961, p. 68, § 12; Laws 1962, p. 79, § 9; Laws 1964, p. 436, § 3; Laws 1965, p. 304, § 1; Laws 1974, p. 594, § 1; Laws 1985, p. 149, § 40; Laws 1990, p. 2048, § 3; Laws 1997, p. 739, § 10; Laws 2000, p. 951, § 4–5; Laws 2010, Act 381, § 7, eff. May 20, 2010.

§ 40–3–27. Subsequent transactions

(a) Whenever the certificate of title is in the possession of a security interest holder or lienholder as allowed by this chapter and some other person, including the owner, who has an interest in a transaction concerning a security interest or lien shown on the certificate of title desires to have that transaction reflected on the certificate of title, such security interest holder or lienholder may execute a notice of that transaction in the form prescribed by the commissioner, setting forth the details of the transaction such security interest holder or lienholder desires to be reflected on the certificate of title. The notice, a fee as provided by Code Section 40–3–38, and the title application shall be mailed by certified mail or statutory overnight delivery, return receipt requested, by the person desiring the change to the first security interest holder or lienholder having possession of the certificate of title. The notice shall contain on its face instructions to the security interest holder or lienholder having custody of the certificate of title directing such security interest holder or lienholder within ten days to forward the notice, the fee, the title application, and the certificate of title to the commissioner or the commissioner's duly authorized county tag agent. The first security interest holder or lienholder having possession of the certificate of title shall comply with the instructions contained in the notice. The commissioner or the authorized county tag agent, upon receipt of such a notice and title application, together with the fee and certificate of title, shall enter the transaction shown on the notice on such commissioner's or authorized county tag agent's records and on the certificate of title or issue a new certificate of title and shall then deliver the certificate of title as provided for in this chapter. The person desiring the change shall retain the return certified mail or statutory overnight delivery receipt as proof of such person's compliance with this Code section.

(b) In the event the first security interest holder or lienholder holding the certificate of title fails, refuses, or neglects to forward the title application, notice, fee, and original certificate of title to the commissioner or the commissioner's duly authorized county tag agent, as required by this Code section, the person desiring the change may, on a form prescribed by the commissioner, make direct application to the commissioner or the authorized county tag agent. Such direct application to the commissioner or the authorized county tag agent shall have attached to it the return registered or certified mail or statutory overnight delivery receipt showing the previous mailing of the title application, fee, and notice to the first security interest holder or lienholder. Upon receipt of such a direct application, the commissioner or the authorized county tag agent shall order the first security interest holder or lienholder having custody of the certificate of title to forward the certificate of title to the commissioner or the authorized county tag agent for the purpose of having the subsequent transaction entered thereon or a new certificate of title issued. If, after a direct application to the commissioner or the authorized county tag agent and the order of the commissioner or authorized county tag agent, the first security interest holder or lienholder continues to fail, refuse, or neglect to forward the certificate of title as provided in this Code section, the commissioner or authorized county tag agent may cancel the outstanding certificate of title and issue a new certificate of title reflecting all security interests and liens, including the subsequent security interest, and this new certificate of title shall be delivered as provided for in this chapter.

(c) As an alternative to mailing notices of transactions concerning a security interest or lien on the certificate of title to the commissioner or the commissioner's appropriate authorized county tag agent in accordance with this Code section, the commissioner shall be authorized to permit the transaction to be made by electronic means in accordance with regulations promulgated by the commissioner.

(d) Any first security interest holder or lienholder having possession of a certificate of title shall not have the validity of such first security interest holder's or lienholder's security interest or lien affected by surrendering the certificate of title as provided by this Code section.

Laws 1965, p. 304, § 2; Laws 1981, p. 883, § 4; Laws 1986, p. 438, § 2; Laws 1990, p. 2048, § 3; Laws 1997, p. 739, § 11; Laws 1998, p. 1179, § 33; Laws 2000, p. 1589, § 3.

§ 40–3–28. Issuance where commissioner not satisfied as to ownership of vehicle

If the commissioner or the commissioner's duly authorized county tag agent is not satisfied as to the ownership of the vehicle or that there are no undisclosed security interests in it, the commissioner or authorized county tag agent may register the vehicle, but shall either: (1) withhold issuance of a certificate of title until the applicant presents documents reasonably sufficient to satisfy the commissioner or authorized county tag agent as to the applicant's ownership of the vehicle and that there are no undisclosed security interests in it; or (2) as a condition of issuing a certificate of title, require the applicant to file with the commissioner or authorized county tag agent a bond in the form prescribed by the commissioner and executed by the applicant and by a bonding, surety, or insurance company licensed to do business in Georgia. The bond shall be in an amount equal to the value of the vehicle as determined by the commissioner or authorized county tag agent and payable to the commissioner for the benefit of any prior owner, lienholder, or security interest holder, and any subsequent purchaser of the vehicle or person acquiring any security interest or lien on it, and their respective successors in interest, against any expense, loss, or damage, by reason of the issuance of the certificate of title of the vehicle or on account of any defect in or undisclosed security interest upon the right, title, and interest of the applicant in and to the vehicle. The commissioner shall have a right of action to recover on the bond for any breach of its conditions, but the aggregate liability of the surety to all persons shall not exceed the amount of the bond. The bond shall expire at the end of four years unless the commissioner or authorized county tag agent has been notified of a breach of a condition of the bond.

Laws 1967, p. 450, § 1; Laws 1973, p. 712, § 1; Laws 1976, p. 319, § 1; Laws 1990, p. 2048, § 3; Laws 1997, p. 739, § 12; Laws 2002, p. 838, § 3.

§ 40–3–29. Refusing certificate of title

(a) The commissioner or the commissioner's duly authorized county tag agent shall refuse issuance of a certificate of title only if any required fee is not paid or if the commissioner or the commissioner's duly authorized county tag agent has reasonable grounds to believe that:

(1) The applicant is not the owner of the vehicle;

(2) The application contains a false or fraudulent statement;

(3) The applicant fails to furnish required information or documents or any additional information the commissioner or authorized county tag agent reasonably requires; or

(4) The registration of the vehicle stands suspended or revoked for any reason as provided in the motor vehicle laws of this state.

(b) If the application for first certificate of title is rejected, the application shall be returned to the holder of the first security interest or lien named in the application or to the owner if there is no security interest holder or lienholder.

Laws 1961, p. 68, § 13; Laws 1982, p. 403, §§ 1, 3; Laws 1990, p. 2048, § 3; Laws 1997, p. 739, § 13.

§ 40–3–29.1. Renumbered as § 40–3–30 by Laws 1990, p. 2048, § 3, eff. July 1, 1990

§ 40–3–30. Certificates of title not to be issued to vehicles not manufactured to comply with federal emission and safety standards

(a) In addition to the reasons set forth in Code Section 40–3–29, no application shall be accepted and no certificate of title shall be issued to any motor vehicle which was not manufactured to comply with applicable federal motor vehicle safety standards issued pursuant to 49 U.S.C.A. Section 30101, et seq., unless and until the United States Customs Service or the United States Department of Transportation has certified that the motor vehicle complies with such applicable federal standards and unless all documents required by the commissioner for processing an application for a certificate of registration or title are printed and filled out in the English language or are accompanied by an English translation.

(b) The provisions of subsection (a) of this Code section shall only apply to applications for certificates of title for such motor vehicles first titled in Georgia after July 1, 1985. Certification of compliance shall only be required at the time of application for the issuance of the initial Georgia certificate of title.

Laws 1985, p. 693, § 2; Laws 1990, p. 8, § 40; Laws 1990, p. 2048, § 3; Laws 1994, p. 97, § 40; Laws 2000, p. 951, § 4–6; Laws 2002, p. 512, § 9; Laws 2002, p. 1378, § 3.

Formerly Code 1981, § 40–3–29.1.

§ 40–3–30.1. Inspection of assembled motor vehicle or motorcycle

(a) As used in this Code section and in Code Section 40–2–27, the term:

(1) "Assembled motor vehicle or motorcycle" or "kit motor vehicle or motorcycle" means any motor vehicle or motorcycle that is:

(A) Manufactured from a manufacturer's kit or manufacturer's fabricated parts, including replicas and original designs:

(i) By an owner;

(ii) At the request of the owner by a third-party manufacturer of motor vehicles or motorcycles; and

(iii) Such manufacturer is not manufacturing and testing in accordance with federal safety standards issued pursuant to 49 U.S.C.A. Section 30101, et seq., unless and until the United States Customs Service or the United States Department of Transportation has certified that the motor vehicle complies with such applicable federal standards;

(B) A new vehicle and consists of a prefabricated body, chassis, and drive train;

(C) Handmade and not mass produced by any manufacturer for retail sale; or

(D) Not otherwise excluded from emission requirements and is in compliance with Chapter 8 of Title 40, relating to equipment and inspection of motor vehicles.

(2) "Unconventional motor vehicle or motorcycle" means any motor vehicle or motorcycle that is manufactured, including, but not limited to, all-terrain vehicles, off-road vehicles, motorized carts, motor driven cycles, and mopeds, and that is not in compliance with the following:

(A) Chapter 8 of Title 40, relating to equipment and inspection of motor vehicles;

(B) Applicable federal motor vehicle safety standards issued pursuant to 49 U.S.C.A. Section 30101, et seq., unless and until the United States Customs Service or the United States Department of Transportation has certified that the motor vehicle complies with such applicable federal standards; or

(C) Applicable federal emission standards issued pursuant to 42 U.S.C.A. Section 7401 through Section 7642, the "Clean Air Act," as amended.

(b) In addition to the requirements contained in Code Section 40–3–30, prior to the issuance of a certificate of title to the owner of an assembled motor vehicle or motorcycle, the owner shall cause such assembled motor vehicle or motorcycle to be inspected in order to establish:

(1) The existence of a verifiable Manufacturer's Certificate of Origin (MCO) or other verifiable documentation of purchase of all major components; and

(2) That such assembled motor vehicle or motorcycle complies with:

(A) Chapter 8 of Title 40, relating to equipment and inspection of motor vehicles; and

(B) If applicable, federal emission standards issued pursuant to 42 U.S.C.A. Section 7401 through Section 7642, the "Clean Air Act," as amended.

(c) The inspection conducted under subsection (b) of this Code section shall only be for the purpose of establishing that such assembled motor vehicle or motorcycle is eligible to receive a certificate of title.

(d) The department shall be authorized to charge an inspection fee.

(e) Unconventional motor vehicles or motorcycles shall not be titled or registered.

Laws 2008, Act 727, § 6, eff. May 14, 2008.

§ 40–3–31. Lost, stolen or mutilated certificates

If a certificate of title is lost, stolen, mutilated, or destroyed or becomes illegible, the owner or the legal representative of the owner named in the certificate, as shown by the records of the commissioner or the commissioner's duly authorized county tag agent, shall promptly make application for and may obtain a replacement, upon furnishing information satisfactory to the commissioner or authorized county tag agent. The replacement shall be issued on the following terms and conditions:

(1) If the replacement title is issued to the owner named in the lost, stolen, mutilated, or destroyed certificate, as shown by the records of the commissioner or authorized county tag agent, the replacement certificate of title shall contain the legend:

"This is a replacement certificate and may be subject to the rights of a person under the original certificate.";

(2) When the vehicle for which a replacement certificate of title has been issued is transferred to a new owner, the certificate of title issued to the transferee shall continue to contain the legend:

"This is a replacement certificate and may be subject to the rights of a person under the original certificate."

After a replacement certificate has been issued and the records of the commissioner or authorized county tag agent show that the owner has held record title continuously for a period of not less than six calendar months and the record title of the owner has not been challenged, the commissioner or authorized county tag agent may, upon proper application, issue a replacement title, which shall simply contain the legend "Replacement Title";

(3) A person recovering an original certificate of title for which a replacement has been issued shall promptly surrender

the original certificate to the commissioner or authorized county tag agent. Where the owner named in a replacement certificate of title, or a transferee, recovers the original certificate such owner or transferee may surrender the original certificate together with the replacement title and if such owner or transferee is otherwise entitled to a certificate the commissioner or authorized county tag agent may issue such owner or transferee a new certificate of title with no legend thereon;

(4) If two or more innocent persons are the victims of the fraud or mistake of another and none of the victims could have reasonably taken steps to detect or prevent the fraud or mistake, the victim who first acquired an interest in a vehicle through any certificate of title shall have such victim's interest protected; and

(5) A replacement title when the original has been lost in the mail prior to receipt by the registered owner shall be issued by the commissioner without charge upon application and completion of the form and affidavit prescribed by the commissioner setting forth the circumstances of nonreceipt of the title. The owner shall report the nonreceipt or loss and apply for replacement of the title to the commissioner within 60 days of the issuance of such title by the commissioner. An applicant shall provide an affidavit of nonreceipt and verify his or her current mailing address.

Laws 1961, p. 68, § 14; Laws 1965, p. 304, § 3; Laws 1974, p. 593, § 1; Laws 1977, p. 252, §§ 1, 2; Laws 1985, p. 149, § 40; Laws 1986, p. 438, § 3; Laws 1990, p. 2048, § 3; Laws 1994, p. 97, § 40; Laws 1997, p. 739, § 14; Laws 1998, p. 1179, § 34.

Formerly Code 1981, § 40–3–30.

§ 40–3–31.1. Repealed by Laws 2003, Act 184, § 2, eff. May 31, 2003

Historical and Statutory Notes

The repealed section, relating to replacement certificates of title for mobile homes, was derived from Laws 1994, p. 741, § 3; Laws 1997, p. 739, § 15; Code 1981, §40–3–31.1.

§ 40–3–32. Transfer of title

(a) If an owner transfers his interest in a vehicle other than by the creation of a security interest, he shall, at the time of delivery of the vehicle, execute an assignment and warranty of title to the transferee in the space provided therefor on the certificate of title or as the commissioner prescribes and cause the certificate and assignment to be delivered to the transferee. If the transferor willfully fails to deliver the properly assigned certificate of title to the transferee, the transferor shall be guilty of a misdemeanor. In addition, the transferor shall be civilly liable to the transferee for all damages, including reasonable attorney's fees, occasioned by the transferor's failure to comply with this subsection.

(b) Except as provided in Code Section 40–3–33, the transferee, promptly after delivery to him of the vehicle and certificate of title, shall execute the application for a new certificate of title on the form the commissioner prescribes and cause the application and the certificate of title to be mailed or delivered to the commissioner or his appropriate authorized county tag agent together with the application for change of registration for the vehicle, so that the title application shall be received within 30 days from the date of the transfer of the vehicle. If the title application is not received within that time, the owner shall be required to pay a penalty of $10.00 in addition to the ordinary title fee provided for by this chapter. If the documents submitted in support of the title application are rejected, the party submitting the documents shall have 60 days from the date of initial rejection to resubmit the documents required by the commissioner for the issuance of title. If the documents are not properly resubmitted within 60 days, there shall be an additional $10.00 penalty assessed, and the owner of the vehicle shall be required to remove immediately the license plate of the vehicle and return same to the commissioner. The license plate shall be deemed to have expired at 12:00 Midnight of the sixtieth day following the initial rejection of the documents, if the documents have not been resubmitted as required under this subsection.

(c) If a security interest is reserved or created at the time of the transfer, the certificate of title shall be retained by or delivered to the person who becomes the lienholder, and the parties shall comply with Code Section 40–3–51.

(d) Except as provided in Code Section 40–3–33 and as between the parties, a transfer by an owner is not effective until this Code section and Code Section 40–3–33 have been complied with; and no purchaser or transferee shall acquire any right, title, or interest in and to a vehicle purchased by him unless and until he shall obtain from the transferor the certificate of title thereto, duly transferred in accordance with this Code section.

(e) The commissioner shall promulgate procedures and provide forms whereby a prospective purchaser may, if such prospective purchaser desires, have the commissioner's or the commissioner's duly authorized county tag agent's records searched for undisclosed certificates of title and security interests.

Laws 1961, p. 68, § 15; Laws 1981, p. 883, § 5; Laws 1986, p. 438, § 4; Laws 1990, p. 2048, § 3; Laws 1997, p. 739, § 16; Laws 2007, Act 346, § 9, eff. July 1, 2008.

Formerly Code 1981, § 40–3–31.

Historical and Statutory Notes

Laws 2007, Act 346, § 14, provides:

"Sections 2, 3, 4, 5, and 13 through 15 of this Act shall become effective July 1, 2007. Sections 1, 6, 7, and 12 of this Act shall become effective January 1, 2008. Sections 8, 9, 10, and 11 of this Act shall become effective July 1, 2008."

§ 40–3–32.1. Application for transfer or certificate of title to manufactured home to indicate serial number and certification of payment of ad valorem taxes

In addition to any other requirements imposed by this chapter for the transfer of a certificate of title, the purchaser of a manufactured home shall submit an application for a transfer of title to the local tag agent in the county in which the manufactured home is to be installed, which application shall indicate the full serial number for such manufactured home and shall be accompanied by a certificate of the tax commissioner or tax collector of the county in which the manufactured home was previously installed, if different, stating that all ad valorem taxes assessed against such manufactured home have been paid. No new certificate of title shall be issued for a manufactured home unless all ad valorem taxes on such home have been paid.

Laws 1994, p. 741, § 4.

§ 40–3–33. Transfer to or from dealer

(a)(1) Except as provided in paragraph (2) of this subsection, a dealer who buys a vehicle and holds it for resale need not apply to the commissioner for a new certificate of title but may retain the certificate delivered to him. Upon transferring the vehicle to another person other than by the creation of a security interest, such dealer shall promptly execute the assignment and warranty of title by a dealer. Such assignment and warranty shall show the names and addresses of the transferee and any holder of a security interest created or reserved at the time of the resale and the date of his security agreement, in the spaces provided therefor on the certificate or as the commissioner prescribes. Transfers of vehicles under this Code section shall otherwise conform with Code Section 40–3–32. A dealer selling a previously registered vehicle which under this chapter need not have a certificate of title need not furnish a purchaser of such a vehicle a certificate of title. After a previously registered vehicle has been brought under the terms of this chapter, a dealer, when selling that vehicle, shall conform to all provisions of this chapter.

(2)(A) As used in this paragraph, the term "franchise dealer" means a dealer who under a contract or franchise agreement with a manufacturer, distributor, wholesaler, or importer is authorized to sell new motor vehicles of or for such manufacturer, distributor, wholesaler, or importer and who is authorized to use trademarks or service marks associated with one or more makes of motor vehicles in connection with such sales.

(B) A dealer who is not a franchise dealer who acquires a vehicle for which the original certificate of title has not been issued and who holds such vehicle for resale shall not be exempt from the requirement to obtain a certificate of title in such dealer's name as provided in paragraph (1) of this subsection. Such dealer shall, as provided in Code Section 40–3–32, obtain a certificate of title in such dealer's name prior to selling or otherwise transferring said vehicle to any other person or dealer.

(b) Every dealer shall maintain a record, in the form the commissioner prescribes, of every vehicle bought, sold, or exchanged by him, or received by him for sale or exchange. Such record shall be kept for three years and shall be open to inspection by a representative of the commissioner during reasonable business hours.

(c) Except as otherwise provided for in subsection (c) of Code Section 40–3–32, the dealer shall submit a properly completed certificate of title application and proper supporting documents to the commissioner or to the appropriate authorized county tag agent so that the application and supporting documents shall be submitted to the commissioner or the appropriate authorized county tag agent within 30 days from the date of the transfer of the vehicle. If the application and supporting documents are not submitted within that time, the dealer shall be required to pay a penalty of $10.00 in addition to the ordinary title fee as provided by this chapter. If the documents submitted in support of the title application are rejected, the dealer submitting the documents shall have 60 days from the date of initial rejection to resubmit the documents required by the commissioner for the issuance of title. If the documents are not properly resubmitted within 60 days, there shall be an additional penalty of $10.00 assessed against the dealer. The willful failure of a dealer to obtain a certificate of title for a purchaser shall be grounds for suspension or revocation of the dealer's state issued license and registration for the sale of motor vehicles.

Laws 1961, p. 68, § 16; Laws 1965, p. 304, § 4; Laws 1981, p. 883, § 6; Laws 1985, p. 149, § 40; Laws 1986, p. 438, § 5; Laws 1990, p. 2048, § 3; Laws 1992, p. 2785, § 2; Laws 2007, Act 346, § 10, eff. July 1, 2008.

Formerly Code 1981, § 40–3–32.

Historical and Statutory Notes

Laws 2007, Act 346, § 14, provides:

"Sections 2, 3, 4, 5, and 13 through 15 of this Act shall become effective July 1, 2007. Sections 1, 6, 7, and 12 of this Act shall become effective January 1, 2008. Sections 8, 9, 10, and 11 of this Act shall become effective July 1, 2008."

§ 40–3–34. Transfer by operation of law

(a) If the interest of an owner in a vehicle passes to another other than by voluntary transfer, the transferee shall, except as provided in subsection (b) of this Code section, mail or deliver to the commissioner or his appropriate authorized county tag agent the last certificate of title, if available; proof of the transfer; and his application for a new certificate in the form the commissioner prescribes, together with the application for change of registration for the vehicle so that the title application and other documents shall be received by the commissioner or his appropriate authorized county tag agent no later than 30 days from the date that the transferee acquired the interest in the vehicle. If the title application and other documents are not received within that time, the transferee shall be required to pay a penalty of $10.00 in addition to the ordinary title fee provided for by this chapter. If the documents submitted in support of the title application are rejected, the party submitting the documents shall have 60 days from the date of initial rejection to resubmit the documents required by the commissioner for the issuance of title. Should the documents not be properly resubmitted within the 60 day period, there shall be an additional $10.00 penalty assessed, and the owner of the vehicle shall be required to remove immediately the license plate of the vehicle and return same to the commissioner. The license plate shall be deemed to have expired at 12:00 Midnight of the sixtieth day following the initial rejection of the documents, if the documents have not been resubmitted as required in this subsection. If the last certificate of title is not available for transfer under this Code section, then the transferee shall forward such proof of transfer as the commissioner may by regulation prescribe.

(b) If the interest of the owner is terminated, whether the vehicle is sold pursuant to a power contained in a security agreement or by legal process at the instance of the holder either of a security interest or a lien, the transferee shall promptly mail or deliver to the commissioner or his appropriate authorized county tag agent the last certificate of title, if available; proof of transfer; his application for a new certificate, in the form prescribed by the commissioner; and an affidavit made by or on behalf of the holder of a security interest in or lien on the vehicle with respect to the termination of the interest of the owner, so as to have the application and supporting documents submitted to the commissioner or his appropriate authorized county tag agent within 30 days from the date the transferee acquired the interest in the vehicle. If the application and supporting documents are not submitted within that time, the transferee shall be required to pay a penalty of $10.00 in addition to the ordinary title fee prescribed by this chapter. If the documents submitted in support of the title application are rejected, the transferee submitting the documents shall have 60 days from the date of initial rejection to resubmit the documents required by the commissioner for the issuance of title. If the documents are not properly resubmitted within 60 days, there shall be an additional $10.00 penalty assessed, and the owner of the vehicle shall be required to remove immediately the license plate of the vehicle and return same to the commissioner. The license plate shall be deemed to have expired at 12:00 Midnight of the sixtieth day following the initial rejection of the documents, if the documents have not been resubmitted as required under this subsection. If the holder of a security interest or lien succeeds to the interest of the owner and holds the vehicle for resale, he need not secure a new certificate of title but, upon transfer, shall promptly deliver to the transferee the last certificate of title, if available, and such other documents as the commissioner may require by rule or regulation.

(c) A person holding a certificate of title whose interest in the vehicle has been extinguished or transferred other than by voluntary transfer shall mail or deliver the certificate to the commissioner or the commissioner's duly authorized county tag agent upon request of the commissioner or authorized county tag agent. The delivery of the certificate pursuant to the request of the commissioner or authorized tag agent does not affect the rights of the person surrendering the certificate; and the action of the commissioner or authorized tag agent in issuing a new certificate of title as provided in this article is not conclusive upon the rights of an owner or lienholder named in the old certificate.

(d) In the event of transfer as upon inheritance, devise, or bequest, upon receipt of an application for a new certificate of title with the required fee, the last certificate of title, if available, and a certified copy of a will or letters of administration or, if no administration is to be had on the estate, an affidavit by the applicant to the effect that the estate is not indebted and the surviving spouse, if any, and the heirs, if any, have amicably agreed among themselves upon a division of the estate or a certificate from the judge of the probate court showing that the motor vehicle registered in the name of the decedent owner has been assigned to the decedent's survivors as part of their year's support, the commissioner shall issue to the person or persons shown by such evidence to be entitled thereto the certificate of title for the vehicle.

(e)(1) In the event of transfer under a will when the motor vehicle was the decedent's only asset, upon receipt of an application for a new certificate of title accompanied by the required fee, the last certificate of title, if available, and an affidavit by the applicant to the effect that the motor vehicle was owned by the decedent and was the decedent's only asset and was not encumbered, that under the will the applicant is entitled to receive title to such motor vehicle, that no application for the administration of the estate of the deceased or the probate of such will is to be had, and that the estate is not indebted and the surviving spouse, if any, and the heirs, if any, are sui juris and have amicably agreed that title to said vehicle be issued to the applicant, the commissioner shall issue to the person or persons shown by such evidence to be entitled thereto the certificate of title for the vehicle.

(2) The commissioner shall prescribe the form of the affidavit to be used in paragraph (1) of this subsection.

(f) A joint interest in a vehicle with survivorship in two or more persons may be created in the manner provided by subsection (a) of Code Section 44–6–190; and, if a certificate of title has been issued to two or more persons having such a joint interest with survivorship, then, in the event of the death of such a joint owner, the surviving such owner or owners, if any, need not secure a new certificate of title.

Laws 1961, p. 68, § 17; Laws 1962, p. 79, § 10; Laws 1981, p. 883, § 7; Laws 1985, p. 149, § 40; Laws 1986, p. 281, § 1; Laws 1990, p. 2048, § 3; Laws 1997, p. 739, § 17; Laws 1998, p. 510, § 1; Laws 2007, Act 346, § 11, eff. July 1, 2008.

Formerly Code 1981, § 40–3–33.

Historical and Statutory Notes

Laws 2007, Act 346, § 14, provides:

"Sections 2, 3, 4, 5, and 13 through 15 of this Act shall become effective July 1, 2007. Sections 1, 6, 7, and 12 of this Act shall become effective January 1, 2008. Sections 8, 9, 10, and 11 of this Act shall become effective July 1, 2008."

§ 40–3–35. When commissioner to issue new certificate

(a) The commissioner or the commissioner's duly authorized county tag agent, upon receipt of a properly assigned certificate of title, with an application for a new certificate of title, the required fee, and any other documents required by law, shall issue a new certificate of title in the name of the transferee as owner and mail the certificate to the first lienholder named in the application or, if none, to the owner.

(b) The commissioner or the commissioner's duly authorized county tag agent, upon receipt of an application for a new certificate of title by a transferee other than by voluntary transfer, with proof of the transfer, the required fee, and any other documents required by law, shall issue a new certificate of title in the name of the transferee as owner. If the outstanding certificate of title is not delivered to the commissioner or the authorized county tag agent, the commissioner or authorized county tag agent shall make demand therefor from the holder thereof.

(c) The commissioner or the commissioner's duly authorized county tag agent shall file and retain for five years every surrendered certificate of title, the file to be maintained so as to permit the tracing of title of the vehicle designated therein.

Laws 1961, p. 68, § 19; Laws 1990, p. 2048, § 3; Laws 1997, p. 739, § 18.

Formerly Code 1981, § 40–3–34.

§ 40–3–35.1. Renumbered as § 40–3–37 by Laws 1990, p. 2048, § 3, eff. July 1, 1990

§ 40–3–35.2. Repealed by Laws 1987, p. 626, § 2, eff. July 1, 1987

§ 40–3–36. Cancellation of certificates of title for scrapped, dismantled, or demolished motor vehicles; certificate of title for salvage motor vehicles

(a)(1) Any registered owner or authorized agent of a registered owner who in any manner sells or disposes of any vehicle as scrap metal or parts only or who scraps, dismantles, or demolishes a vehicle shall within 72 hours mail or deliver the certificate of title to the commissioner for cancellation.

(2) Notwithstanding any other provision of this article to the contrary, if the owner or authorized agent of the owner has not obtained a title in his or her name for the vehicle to be transferred, or has lost the title for the vehicle to be transferred, he or she may sign a statement swearing that, in addition to the foregoing conditions, the vehicle is worth $750.00 or less and is at least 12 model years old. The statement described in this paragraph may be used only to transfer such a vehicle to a licensed used motor vehicle parts dealer under Code Section 43–47–7 or scrap metal processor under Code Section 43–43–1. The department shall promulgate a form for the statement which shall include, but not be limited to:

(A) A statement that the vehicle shall never be titled again; it must be dismantled or scrapped;

(B) A description of the vehicle including the year, make, model, vehicle identification number, and color;

(C) The name, address, and driver's license number of the owner;

(D) A certification that the owner:

(i) Never obtained a title to the vehicle in his or her name; or

(ii) Was issued a title for the vehicle, but the title was lost or stolen;

(E) A certification that the vehicle:

(i) Is worth $750.00 or less;

(ii) Is at least 12 model years old; and

(iii) Is not subject to any secured interest or lien.

(F) An acknowledgment that the owner realizes this form will be filed with the department and that it is a felony, punishable by imprisonment for not fewer than one nor more than three years or a fine of not less than $1,000.00 nor more than $5,000.00, or both, to knowingly falsify any information on this statement;

(G) The owner's signature and the date of the transaction;

(H) The name and address of the business acquiring the vehicle;

(I) A certification by the business that $750.00 or less was paid to acquire the vehicle; and

(J) The business agent's signature and date along with a printed name and title if the agent is signing on behalf of a corporation.

(3) The used motor vehicle parts dealer or scrap metal processor shall mail or otherwise deliver the statement required under paragraph (2) of this subsection to the department within 72 hours of the completion of the transaction, requesting that the department cancel the Georgia certificate of title and registration.

(4)(A) The registered owner of any motor vehicle which is damaged to the extent that its restoration to an operable condition would require the replacement of the front clip assembly, which includes the fenders, hood, and bumper; the rear clip assembly, which includes the quarter panels, the floor panel assembly, and the roof assembly, excluding a soft top; the frame; and a complete side, which includes the fenders, door, and quarter panel shall mail or deliver the certificate of title to the commissioner for cancellation.

(B) A motor vehicle owner who retains possession of a damaged vehicle which is a salvage motor vehicle as defined in paragraph (11) of Code Section 40–3–2 shall surrender the license plates and registration for such vehicle, shall not operate such vehicle upon the roads of this state, and shall not sell, trade, or otherwise dispose of such vehicle prior to obtaining a salvage certificate of title for such vehicle.

(C) Any insurance company which acquires a damaged motor vehicle by virtue of having paid a total loss claim shall mail or deliver the certificate of title to the commissioner for cancellation. In every case in which a total loss claim is paid and the insurance company does not acquire such damaged motor vehicle, the insurance company paying such total loss claim, the vehicle owner, and the lienholder or security interest holder, as applicable, shall take the following steps to secure a salvage certificate of title for such motor vehicle:

(i) If the vehicle owner is in possession of the certificate of title, the owner shall deliver the certificate of title to the insurance company prior to any payment of the claim, and the insurance company shall mail or deliver the certificate of title, an application for a salvage certificate of title, and the form provided by the commissioner for issuance of a salvage certificate of title;

(ii) If the certificate of title has been lost, destroyed, or misplaced, the vehicle owner shall, prior to payment of the claim on such vehicle, complete an application for a replacement title on the form provided by the commissioner and deliver such application and form to the insurance company and the insurance company shall mail or deliver such application and form to the commissioner for issuance of a replacement original title marked salvage;

(iii) If the lienholder or security interest holder has possession of the certificate of title, the vehicle owner shall complete an application for a replacement title on a form provided by the commissioner and shall deliver the completed form to the insurance company prior to the payment of the claim; the insurance company shall thereafter mail or deliver the application to the commissioner with notice of the payment of the total loss claim and the name and address of the lienholder or security interest holder in possession of the title. The commissioner shall mail notice to the lienholder or security interest holder that a total loss claim has been paid on the vehicle and that the title to such vehicle has been canceled, and the commissioner shall provide to the lienholder or security interest holder a salvage certificate of title for such vehicle, provided that the validity of the security interest shall not be affected by issuance of a salvage certificate of title. The lienholder or security interest holder shall, within ten days after receipt of such notice of total loss claim and cancellation of the original certificate of title, mail or deliver the canceled original certificate of title to the commissioner; or

(iv) For the sole purpose of payment of a total loss claim, for any vehicle ten years of age or older for which neither the vehicle owner nor the lienholder or security interest holder, if any, possesses a certificate of title, the vehicle owner shall deliver the vehicle license plate and certificate of registration for such vehicle to the insurance company prior to payment of any claim and the insurance company shall mail or deliver the license plate and certificate of registration to the commissioner with a completed form provided by the commissioner; provided, however, that the vehicle owner shall not operate such vehicle and the owner shall obtain a certificate of title for such vehicle as provided by law, which certificate of title shall then be subject to cancellation as provided in this paragraph.

(D) The department shall give priority to the title submissions provided for in subparagraph (C) of this paragraph and shall issue a salvage certificate of title for such vehicles within seven days of receipt of such submissions by an insurance company.

(a.1) In the case of a motor vehicle which is subject to more than one perfected security interest or lien which motor vehicle is a total loss, if the insurer is to acquire title to the damaged motor vehicle, the holder of the senior security interest or lien, upon receipt of the settlement proceeds of the insurance policy in accordance with Code Section 33–34–9, shall apply for a new certificate of title for a transferee other than by voluntary transfer in accordance with subsection (b) of Code Section 40–3–35, naming the insurer only as transferee.

(b) Except as provided in subsection (a) of this Code section, any person, firm, or corporation which purchases or otherwise acquires a salvage motor vehicle shall apply to the commissioner for a salvage certificate of title for such motor vehicle within 30 days of the purchase or acquisition of the motor vehicle or within 30 days of the payment of a total loss claim as provided in paragraph (4) of subsection (a) of this Code section to the registered owner of the salvage motor vehicle, if the person, firm, or corporation intends to operate or to sell, convey, or transfer the motor vehicle; and no such person, firm, or corporation shall sell, transfer, or convey a salvage motor vehicle until such person, firm, or corporation has applied for and obtained a salvage certificate of title.

(c) The application for a salvage certificate of title shall be made in a manner to be prescribed by the commissioner.

(d) Any certificate of title which is issued to a salvage motor vehicle, as provided for in this Code section, shall contain the word "salvage" on the face of the certificate in such a manner as the commissioner may prescribe, so as to indicate clearly that the motor vehicle described is a salvage motor vehicle. The legend "rebuilt" in no larger than 12 point font shall be placed on a certificate of title to a vehicle which was declared a salvage vehicle and subsequently repaired with less than two major component parts to restore the vehicle to an operable condition.

(e) Notwithstanding this subsection and subsections (c) and (d) of Code Section 40–3–37, the legend "rebuilt" shall only be required to be placed on the certificate of title to a vehicle which was declared a salvage vehicle on or after July 1, 2004, and which was subsequently rebuilt.

(f) As an alternative to criminal or other civil enforcement, the commissioner, in order to enforce this Code section or any orders, rules, and regulations promulgated pursuant to this Code section, may issue an administrative fine not to exceed $ 1,000.00 for each violation, whenever the commissioner, after a hearing, determines that any person has violated any provisions of this Code section or any regulations or orders promulgated under this Code section. The hearing and any administrative review thereof shall be conducted in accordance with the procedure for contested cases under Chapter 13 of Title 50, the "Georgia Administrative Procedure Act." Any person who has exhausted all administrative remedies available and who is aggrieved or adversely affected by a final order or action of the commissioner shall have the right of judicial review thereof in accordance with Chapter 13 of Title 50. All fines recovered under this subsection shall be paid into the state treasury. The commissioner may file, in the superior court (1) wherein the person under order resides; (2) if such person is a corporation, in the county wherein the corporation maintains its principal place of business; or (3) in the county wherein the violation occurred, a certified copy of a final order of the commissioner, whether unappealed from or affirmed upon appeal, whereupon the court shall render judgment in accordance therewith and notify the parties. Such judgment shall have the same effect and proceedings in relation thereto shall thereafter be the same as though the judgment had been rendered in an action duly heard and determined by the court. The penalty prescribed in this Code section shall be concurrent, alternative, and cumulative with any and all other civil, criminal, or alternative rights, remedies, forfeitures, or penalties provided, allowed, or available to the commissioner with respect to any violation of this Code section or any order, rules, or regulations promulgated pursuant thereto.

(g) The Commissioner of Insurance is authorized to enforce the provisions of this Code section to the extent such provisions are applicable to insurers which are under the jurisdiction of the Insurance Department. The Commissioner of Insurance is also authorized to cooperate with the commissioner in enforcing this Code section and to provide the commissioner with any information acquired by the Commissioner of Insurance during any investigation or proceeding involving this Code section. Nothing in this subsection shall be construed to limit the powers and duties of the commissioner to enforce the provisions of this Code section as such provisions apply to insurers.

(h) It shall be unlawful for any person, firm, or corporation to violate the provisions of subsection (a), (b), or (c) of this Code section; and any person, firm, or corporation convicted of violating such provisions shall be guilty of a misdemeanor. Any owner of a salvage motor vehicle who transfers or attempts to transfer such vehicle without obtaining a salvage certificate of title for such vehicle shall be guilty of a misdemeanor of a high and aggravated nature, punishable by a fine not to exceed $ 5,000.00. Any lienholder or security interest holder who, after notice by the commissioner of payment of a total loss claim and cancellation of the title of a vehicle, fails or refuses to return the title to the commissioner or who surrenders the title to anyone other than the commissioner shall be guilty of a misdemeanor of a high and aggravated nature, punishable by a fine not to exceed $ 5,000.00.

(i) The registered owner who retains possession of a salvage motor vehicle to whom a total loss claim has been paid shall promptly remove the license plate from such vehicle and return such plate to the commissioner for cancellation. An insurer which pays a total loss claim shall, on a form prescribed by the commissioner, notify the owner of the duty to remove and return such license plate for cancellation and of all inspection requirements for rebuilding or restoring such vehicle.

Laws 1961, p. 68, § 20; Laws 1965, p. 264, § 1; Laws 1966, p. 139, § 1; Laws 1970, p. 185, § 1; Laws 1975, p. 1596, § 1; Laws 1979, p. 1108, § 1; Laws 1981, p. 644, §§ 2, 4; Laws 1985, p. 1227, § 1; Laws 1990, p. 8, § 40; Laws 1990, p. 1657, § 5; Laws 1990, p. 2048, § 3; Laws 1992, p. 2978, §§ 6, 7; Laws 1993, p. 1260, § 7; Laws 1998, p. 1179, § 35; Laws 2000, p. 951, § 4–7; Laws 2002, p. 848, § 2; Laws 2004, Act 514, § 2, eff. July 1, 2004; Laws 2007, Act 323, § 1, eff. July 1, 2007; Laws 2007, Act 340, § 2, eff. July 1, 2007; Laws 2007, Act 346, § 12, eff. Jan. 1, 2008.

Formerly Code 1981, § 40–3–35.

Historical and Statutory Notes

In 2004, the Code Commission, in subsec. (d), added "to a vehicle" preceding "which was declared". See § 28–9–5.

The 2007 amendment by Act 323, in subsec. (a), inserted new pars. (2) and (3) and redesignated former par. (2) as par. (4); and in subsec. (b), substituted "paragraph (4)" for "paragraph (2)".

The 2007 amendment by Act 340 substituted "legend 'rebuilt' in no larger than 12 point font" for "legend 'salvaged–repaired' " in subsec. (d) and deleted "or 'salvage' or 'salvaged–repaired' " following "the legend 'rebuilt' " in subsec. (e).

The 2007 amendment by Act 346, in par. (1) of subsec. (a), deleted "motor" preceding "vehicle" twice.

Laws 2007, Act 346, § 14, provides:

"Sections 2, 3, 4, 5, and 13 through 15 of this Act shall become effective July 1, 2007. Sections 1, 6, 7, and 12 of this Act shall become effective January 1, 2008. Sections 8, 9, 10, and 11 of this Act shall become effective July 1, 2008."

§ 40–3–36.1. Designation of flood damaged or fire damaged motor vehicles; indication of designation on certificate of title

For any salvage motor vehicle which, after inspection, it is determined that repair to an operable condition does not require replacement of two or more major component parts but it is determined that the damage to the vehicle is a result of flood or fire shall be designated as flood damaged or fire damaged by the commissioner and such designation shall be indicated on the face of the certificate of title for such vehicle.

Laws 1993, p. 1260, § 8.

§ 40–3–37. Certificate of title for salvaged or rebuilt motor vehicle

(a) As used in this Code section, the term:

(1) "Application for a certificate of title on a recovered stolen motor vehicle" means an application for a certificate of title for a motor vehicle for which an insurance company has paid a total loss claim, has obtained a title marked "unrecovered stolen motor vehicle," and which has subsequently been recovered.

(2) "Application for a certificate of title on a salvaged or rebuilt motor vehicle" means:

(A) An application for a certificate of title for a motor vehicle for which a current Georgia certificate of title is marked "salvage" pursuant to subsection (e) of Code Section 40–3–36 and which has been repaired;

(B) An application for a certificate of title for a motor vehicle for which a current out-of-state certificate of title is marked "salvage," "rebuilt," or "restored" or any similar such phrase; or

(C) An application for a certificate of title for a motor vehicle for which a current Georgia certificate of title is marked "salvage" pursuant to subsection (e) of Code Section 40–3–36 and for which the transferee is anyone other than a licensed dealer as defined in Code Section 43–48–2.

(b)(1) Upon receipt of an application for a certificate of title on a salvaged or rebuilt motor vehicle, the commissioner shall promptly conduct an initial inspection on each such motor vehicle prior to the issuance of a certificate of title for the motor vehicle. Upon receipt of an application for a certificate of title on a recovered stolen motor vehicle which has been stripped of:

(A) Substantially all its interior parts;

(B) Engine;

(C) Transmission;

(D) All doors;

(E) Complete soft top assembly including roof mechanism;

(F) Front clip assembly (fenders, hood, and bumper); or

(G) Cab and bed of a pick-up truck,

the commissioner shall promptly conduct an initial inspection on each such motor vehicle prior to the issuance of a certificate of title for the motor vehicle. The initial inspection shall include, but shall not be limited to, verification of the vehicle identification number, verification of the bills of sale or title for the major components, verification in regard to rebuilt vehicles that the word "rebuilt" is permanently affixed as required by subsection (d) of this Code section, verification that the vehicle was rebuilt in the State of Georgia, and, if the vehicle has been repaired, verification that the motor vehicle conforms to all safety equipment standards required by law. The commissioner shall be authorized to charge a fee of $100.00 for each initial inspection of each motor vehicle. In the event a motor vehicle fails an inspection, a fee of $100.00 shall be charged for each subsequent reinspection. The commissioner may conduct any such initial inspection and any required reinspections even though the motor vehicle may have been previously inspected under this Code section.

(2) If, upon inspection under paragraph (1) of this subsection, it is determined that the motor vehicle is not in full compliance with the law, the commissioner shall refuse to issue a certificate of title until compliance is reached. The commissioner may order additional, corrective repairs to such vehicle as a condition of issuance of a certificate of title.

(c) All applications submitted pursuant to this Code section shall be accompanied by one or more photographs of the motor vehicle in its salvaged condition before any repairs have been made to such vehicle, which photographs shall be used by the commissioner in his or her inspections of the vehicle pursuant to this Code section. Any person who rebuilds or repairs a salvage motor vehicle shall submit an application for a certificate of title and obtain an inspection of such vehicle prior to the painting of such vehicle.

(d)(1)(A) Upon inspection under subsection (b) of this Code section, if it is determined that the motor vehicle has been restored to an operable condition by the replacement of two or more major component parts, a certificate of title may be issued for such motor vehicle which shall contain the word "rebuilt" on its face in no larger than 12 point font. This requirement will indicate to all subsequent owners of the motor vehicle that such is a rebuilt motor vehicle. If any such inspection determines that the motor vehicle shall require the replacement of less than two major component parts in order to restore the motor vehicle to an operable condition, a certificate of title shall be issued for such motor vehicle which shall contain the word "rebuilt" on its face in such manner as the commissioner shall prescribe. This requirement will indicate to all subsequent owners of the motor vehicle that such is a rebuilt motor vehicle.

(B) If it is determined that the motor vehicle required or shall require the replacement of two or more major component parts in order to restore the motor vehicle to an operable condition, the department shall cause the word "rebuilt" to be affixed to said motor vehicle at the time of inspection by the commissioner. The word "rebuilt" shall be affixed in a clear and conspicuous manner to the door post or such other location as the commissioner may prescribe. The word "rebuilt" shall be stamped on a certificate and shall be affixed to the motor vehicle in such manner as the commissioner may prescribe. The requirement of this subparagraph shall only apply to motor vehicles restored after November 1, 1982.

(2) Upon inspection by the commissioner and compliance with paragraph (2) of subsection (b) of this Code section, if it is determined that the motor vehicle does not require the replacement of two or more major components or has not had two or more major components changed, a certificate of title shall be issued and shall contain the word "rebuilt" on its face.

(3) If, after the initial inspection, the commissioner determines that the damage is so extensive that returning such vehicle to a safe, operable condition is impossible, the salvage certificate shall be revoked and such vehicle may only be used for scrap or parts. A vehicle for which such a determination is made shall not be issued a title under any circumstances or conditions including but not limited to obtaining of a surety bond.

(e) Any person, firm, or corporation who rebuilds or repairs a motor vehicle whose current certificate of title is marked "salvage" shall make application for and obtain a certificate of title as provided in this Code section prior to the sale or transfer of said motor vehicle. If, under the laws of any other state, a vehicle has been declared to be nonrebuildable, the commissioner shall not issue any certificate of title for such vehicle and the vehicle shall not be used for any purpose except parts.

(f)(1) Motorcycles which are over 25 years old shall be exempt from the salvage laws of this state.

(2) Motor vehicles which have been altered by the installation of a glider kit shall be issued a certificate of title containing the word "rebuilt."

Laws 1981, p. 644, §§ 3, 4; Laws 1982, p. 403, §§ 2, 4; Laws 1982, p. 1676, §§ 1, 2; Laws 1983, p. 3, § 29; Laws 1985, p. 1227, § 2; Laws 1987, p. 626, § 1; Laws 1990, p. 2048, § 3; Laws 1992, p. 2978, § 8; Laws 1993, p. 91, § 40; Laws 1993, p. 1260, § 9; Laws 1998, p. 1179, § 36; Laws 2004, Act 514, § 3, eff. July 1, 2004; Laws 2007, Act 340, § 3, eff. July 1, 2007.

Formerly Code 1981, § 40–3–35.1.

§ 40–3–38. Fees

(a) An application for a certificate of title shall be accompanied by the required fee when mailed or delivered to the commissioner or a designated agent.

(b) An application for the naming of a lienholder on a certificate of title shall be accompanied by the required fee when mailed or delivered to the commissioner or a designated agent.

(c) The commissioner shall be paid a fee of $18.00 for the filing of an application for any certificate of title and for the filing of the notice of a security interest or a lien on vehicles not required by law to be titled in this state. The commissioner may, by appropriate regulation, provide for additional fees not to exceed $18.00 for the special handling of applications for certificates of title and related documents. The commissioner shall be paid a fee of $8.00 for the filing of an application for a replacement certificate of title. The fee for issuance of a replacement certificate of title shall be the same whether mailed or delivered to the commissioner or an agent.

(d) The above fees shall be required of all applicants except the State of Georgia and the United States of America.

Laws 1961, p. 68, § 18; Laws 1969, p. 92, §§ 2, 3; Laws 1981, p. 883, § 8; Laws 1984, p. 1194, § 2; Laws 1985, p. 485, § 1; Laws 1990, p. 2048, § 3; Laws 1992, p. 779, § 17; Laws 1994, p. 1851, § 2.

Formerly Code 1981, § 40–3–36.

§ 40–3–39. Utilization of county tag agents; fee of; mailing applications

The commissioner is authorized to utilize the services of persons appointed as county tag agents under Code Section 40–2–23 and to allow such county tag agents to retain a fee therefor not in excess of 50¢ for each application handled, such fee to be disposed of as other tag fees retained by him or her as tag agent are disposed of in his or her county. Any applicant for a title shall have the right to mail the application directly to the department.

Laws 1961, p. 68, § 18; Laws 1985, p. 485, § 2; Laws 1990, p. 2048, § 3; Laws 1994, p. 97, § 40; Laws 2000, p. 951, § 4–8.

Formerly Code 1981, § 40–3–37.

§ 40–3–40. Time period within which county tag agents must submit reports on title applications

(a) All county tag agents accepting and handling title applications shall endeavor to submit such applications and related sums of money to which the department is entitled to the commissioner on a daily basis. All reports of title applications handled and related sums of money collected to which the department is entitled must be submitted to the commissioner within seven calendar days from the close of the business day during which such applications were handled and related sums of money collected.

(b) Funds received as a result of handling title applications shall be considered trust funds in the hands of the tag agents until such time as they are paid over to the commissioner.

(c) Failure to submit the reports or remit the funds within the seven-calendar-day period from the close of the business day as required by this Code section shall result in the penalties imposed by Code Section 48–2–44.

(d) Before the expiration of the time period within which a title report is required to be filed with the commissioner or funds remitted to the commissioner, application may be made to the commissioner for an extension. The commissioner is authorized, upon a showing of justifiable cause, to grant up to a ten-day extension from the deadline provided for the performance of the above duties. Only one such extension may be granted with regard to any reports or funds due the commissioner for a specific business day.

(e) Proof of mailing within the appropriate time period provided for in this Code section, as evidenced by a United States Postal Service postmark, shall be prima-facie proof that the county tag agent has complied in a timely manner with his duties as enumerated by this Code section.

Laws 1980, p. 1038, § 1; Laws 1985, p. 149, § 40; Laws 1990, p. 2048, § 3; Laws 2005, Act 19, § 40, eff. April 7, 2005; Laws 2005, Act 68, § 15–2, eff. July 1, 2005.

Formerly Code 1981, § 40–3–38.

§ 40–3–41. Suspension or revocation of certificates

(a) The commissioner shall suspend or revoke a certificate of title, upon notice and reasonable opportunity to be heard in accordance with Code Section 40–3–6, when authorized by any other provision of law or if he finds:

(1) The certificate of title was fraudulently procured or erroneously issued; or

(2) The vehicle has been scrapped, dismantled, or destroyed.

(b) Suspension or revocation of a certificate of title does not, in itself, affect the validity of a security interest noted on it.

(c) When the commissioner suspends or revokes a certificate of title, the owner or person in possession of it shall, immediately upon receiving notice of the suspension or revocation, mail or deliver the certificate to the commissioner.

(d) The commissioner may seize and impound any certificate of title which has been suspended or revoked.

Laws 1961, p. 68, § 28; Laws 1990, p. 2048, § 3.

Formerly Code 1981, § 40–3–39.

§ 40–3–42. United States Postal Service postmark as proof of timely submission of documents

In instances when an application for title is required to be submitted within a certain time period, proof of mailing within the designated period allowed for submission of the documents, as evidenced by a United States Postal Service postmark, shall be prima-facie proof that the application was timely submitted. Additionally, when the law provides for a penalty for the untimely submission of a title application, the responsibility for the collection of such penalty shall be that of the department.

Laws 1981, p. 883, § 3; Laws 1990, p. 2048, § 3; Laws 2000, p. 951, § 4–9.

Formerly Code 1981, § 40–3–40.

§ 40–3–43. Transfer of certificate of title on stolen vehicle upon payment of total loss claim

(a) Any person, firm, or corporation which pays a total loss claim on a vehicle as a result of such vehicle's being stolen shall within 15 days of the payment of such total loss claim apply to the commissioner for a transfer of the certificate of title into such person's, firm's, or corporation's name. No person, firm, or corporation shall sell, transfer, or convey such vehicle until the requirements of this Code section have been met.

(b) As an alternative to criminal or other civil enforcement, the commissioner, in order to enforce this Code section or any orders, rules, and regulations promulgated pursuant to this Code section, may issue an administrative fine not to exceed $1,000.00 for each violation, whenever the commissioner, after a hearing, determines that any person has violated any provisions of this Code section or any regulations or orders promulgated under this Code section. The hearing and any administrative review thereof shall be conducted in accordance with the procedure for contested cases under Chapter 13 of Title 50, the "Georgia Administrative Procedure Act." Any person who has exhausted all administrative remedies available and who is aggrieved or adversely affected by a final order or action of the commissioner shall have the right of judicial review thereof in accordance with Chapter 13 of Title 50. All fines recovered under this subsection shall be paid into the state treasury. The commissioner may file, in the superior court (1) wherein the person under order resides; (2) if such person is a corporation, in the county wherein the corporation maintains its principal place of business; or (3) in the county wherein the violation occurred, a certified copy of a final order of the commissioner, whether unappealed from or affirmed upon appeal, whereupon the court shall render judgment in accordance therewith and notify the parties. Such judgment shall have the same effect and proceedings in relation thereto shall thereafter be the same as though the judgment had been rendered in an action duly heard and determined by the court. The penalty prescribed in this Code section shall be concurrent, alternative, and cumulative with any and all other civil, criminal, or alternative rights, remedies, forfeitures, or penalties provided, allowed, or available to the commissioner with respect to any violation of this Code section or any order, rules, or regulations promulgated pursuant thereto.

(c) The Commissioner of Insurance is authorized to enforce the provisions of this Code section to the extent such provisions are applicable to insurers which are under the jurisdiction of the Insurance Department. The Commissioner of Insurance is also authorized to cooperate with the commissioner in enforcing this Code section and to provide the commissioner with any information acquired by the Commissioner of Insurance during any investigation or proceeding involving this Code section. Nothing in this subsection shall be construed to limit the powers and duties of the commissioner to enforce the provisions of this Code section as such provisions apply to insurers.

Laws 1988, p. 1340, § 1; Laws 1990, p. 2048, § 3.

Formerly Code 1981, § 40–3–41.

Article 3

Security Interests in and Liens on Motor Vehicles

§ 40–3–50. Perfection of security interest on a vehicle

(a) Except as provided in Code Sections 11–9–303, 11–9–316, and 11–9–337, the security interest in a vehicle of the type for which a certificate of title is required shall be perfected and shall be valid against subsequent creditors of the owner, subsequent transferees, and the holders of security interests and liens on the vehicle by compliance with this chapter.

(b)(1) A security interest is perfected by delivery to the commissioner or to the county tag agent of the county in which the seller is located, of the county in which the sale takes place, of the county in which the vehicle is delivered, or of the county wherein the vehicle owner resides, of the required fee and:

(A) The existing certificate of title, if any, and an application for a certificate of title containing the name and address of the holder of a security interest; or

(B) A notice of security interest on forms prescribed by the commissioner.

(2) The security interest is perfected as of the time of its creation if the initial delivery of the application or notice to the commissioner or local tag agent is completed within 20 days thereafter, regardless of any subsequent rejection of the application or notice for errors; otherwise, as of the date of the delivery to the commissioner or local tag agent. The local tag agent shall issue a receipt or other evidence of the date of filing of such application or notice. When the security interest is perfected as provided for in this subsection, it shall constitute notice to everybody of the security interest of the holder.

Laws 1961, p. 68, § 21; Laws 1962, p. 79, § 11; Laws 1978, p. 1081, § 9; Laws 1981, p. 883, § 9; Laws 1990, p. 2048, § 3; Laws 1994, p. 352, § 2; Laws 1995, p. 809, § 14; Laws 2000, p. 227, § 1; Laws 2001, p. 362, § 32.

§ 40–3–51. Security interest created by owner

If the owner creates a security interest in a vehicle:

(1) The owner shall immediately execute the application in the space provided therefor on the certificate of title or on a separate form that the commissioner prescribes, naming the holder of the security interest on the certificate and showing the name and address of the security interest holder, and shall cause the certificate, the application, and the required fee to be delivered to the security interest holder;

(2) The security interest holder shall immediately cause the certificate of title and application and the required fee to be mailed or delivered to the commissioner or the commissioner's appropriate authorized county tag agent within 30 days of the date of creation of the security interest or lien. If the certificate of title and application and the required fee are not mailed or delivered within such time, the lien or security interest holder shall be required to pay a $10.00 penalty in addition to the ordinary title fee provided for by this chapter. If the documents submitted in support of the title application are rejected, the party submitting the documents shall have 60 days from the date of initial rejection to resubmit the documents required by the commissioner or the authorized county tag agent for the issuance of title. If the documents are not properly resubmitted within the 60 day period, there shall be an additional $10.00 penalty assessed, and the owner of the vehicle shall be required to remove immediately the license plate of the vehicle and return same to the commissioner or authorized county tag agent. The license plate shall be deemed to have expired at 12:00 Midnight of the sixtieth day following the initial rejection of the documents, if the documents have not been resubmitted as required under this paragraph; and

(3) Upon receipt of the certificate of title, the application, and the required fee, the commissioner or the commissioner's duly authorized county tag agent shall issue a new certificate containing the name and address of the holder of the security interest and of holders of previous unreleased security interests and liens, if any, and shall mail the certificate to the first holder on it. If more than one holder is named on the certificate, the first holder shall comply with subsection (b) of Code Section 40–3–26 in regard to notifying other holders of the content of the certificate.

Laws 1961, p. 68, § 22; Laws 1962, p. 79, § 12; Laws 1964, p. 436, § 4; Laws 1965, p. 304, § 6; Laws 1969, p. 92, § 5; Laws 1981, p. 883, § 11; Laws 1990, p. 8, § 40; Laws 1990, p. 2048, § 3; Laws 1997, p. 739, § 19; Laws 2008, Act 727, § 7, eff. July 1, 2009.

Historical and Statutory Notes

Laws 2008, Act 7270, § 9, provides:

"Sections 4 and 5 of this Act shall become effective January 1, 2009. Section 7 of this Act shall become effective July 1, 2009. The remaining sections of this Act shall become effective upon this Act's approval by the Governor or upon this Act becoming law without such approval."

§ 40–3–52. Perfection of second or subsequent security interest

(a) If the owner of a motor vehicle desires to place a second or subsequent security interest against the vehicle and the certificate of title on that vehicle is being held by a security interest holder or lienholder, the owner shall, on the form prescribed by the commissioner, execute a title application and a notice of the second or subsequent security interest; and the holder of the second or subsequent security interest shall forward such notice and title application, together with a fee as provided by Code Section 40–3–38, by certified mail or statutory overnight delivery, return receipt requested, to the first holder of a security interest or lien who has custody of the certificate of title. The notice of such second or subsequent security interest shall contain on its face instructions to the security interest holder or lienholder having custody of the certificate of title directing such custodial security interest holder or lienholder within ten days to forward the notice, title application, and fee, together with the certificate of title, to the commissioner or the commissioner's duly authorized county tag agent in order that the commissioner or authorized county tag agent may issue a new certificate of title and reflect on the certificate of title the subsequent security interest. The first security interest holder or lienholder having possession of the certificate of title shall comply with the instructions contained in the notice. The commissioner or authorized county tag agent, upon receipt of a properly executed application notice, the fee, and the original certificate of title, shall enter the subsequent security interest on such commissioner's or authorized county tag agent's records and shall issue a new certificate of title and shall then deliver the certificate of title as provided for in this chapter.

(b) If the holder of the second or subsequent security interest forwards by registered or certified mail or statutory overnight delivery the title application, notice of the second or subsequent security interest, and fee to the first security interest holder or lienholder who has custody of the certificate of title within ten days of the execution of that second or subsequent security interest, it shall be perfected as of the date it was executed; otherwise, as of the date the notice was forwarded to the first security interest holder or lienholder holding the certificate of title. The second or subsequent security interest holder shall retain the return registered or certified mail or statutory overnight delivery receipt as proof of perfection of his security interest under this Code section.

(c) In the event the first security interest holder or lienholder holding the certificate of the title fails, refuses, or neglects to forward the title application, notice, fee, and original certificate of title to the commissioner or the commissioner's duly authorized county tag agent as required by this Code section, the holder of the second or subsequent security interest may, on a form prescribed by the commissioner, make direct application to the commissioner or authorized county tag agent. Such direct application to the commissioner or authorized county tag agent shall have attached to it the return registered or certified mail or statutory overnight delivery receipt showing the previous mailing of the title application, fee, and notice to the first security interest holder or lienholder. Upon receipt of such a direct application, the commissioner or authorized county tag agent shall order the first security interest holder or lienholder having custody of the certificate of title to forward the certificate of title to the commissioner or the authorized county tag agent for the purpose of having the second or subsequent security interest entered and a new certificate of title issued. If after a direct application of the commissioner or authorized county tag agent and the order of the commissioner or authorized county tag agent the first security interest holder or lienholder continues to fail, refuse, or neglect to forward the certificate of title as provided in this Code section, the commissioner or authorized county tag agent may cancel the outstanding certificate of title and issue a new certificate of title reflecting all security interests and liens, including the second or subsequent security interest, and this new certificate of title shall be delivered as provided for in this chapter.

(d) As an alternative to mailing notices concerning a second or subsequent security interest to the commissioner or the commissioner's duly authorized county tag agent in accordance with this Code section, the commissioner shall be authorized to permit the transaction to be made by electronic means in accordance with regulations promulgated by the commissioner.

(e) No first security interest holder or lienholder having possession of the certificate of title shall have the validity of that security interest or lien affected by surrendering the certificate of title as provided for by this Code section.

Laws 1965, p. 304, § 5; Laws 1978, p. 1081, § 9; Laws 1981, p. 883, § 10; Laws 1982, p. 3, § 40; Laws 1990, p. 2048, § 3; Laws 1997, p. 739, § 20; Laws 1998, p. 1179, § 37; Laws 2000, p. 1589, § 3.

§ 40–3–53. Perfection of lien on a vehicle; enforcement

(a) If the holder of any lien as defined in paragraph (7) of Code Section 40–3–2, except the holder of a mechanic's lien, perfection of which is prescribed in Code Section 40–3–54, desires to perfect such lien against a vehicle, the lienholder shall, on the form prescribed by the commissioner, execute a title application and a notice of lien stating the type of lien and the specific vehicle against which the lien is claimed and shall forward such notice and title application, together with a fee as provided by Code Section 40–3–38, either personally or by certified mail or statutory overnight delivery, return receipt requested, to the person who has custody of the current certificate of title at the address shown on such certificate of title. If someone other than the owner is holding the certificate of title, a copy of the notice shall also be forwarded to the owner. The lien claimant shall retain the certified mail or statutory overnight delivery receipt as proof of compliance with this Code section.

(b) After receipt of the notice of lien, as specified in this Code section, neither the owner nor any other person shall take any action affecting the title other than as provided in this Code section. After receipt of the notice of lien, the person holding the certificate of title shall hold the notice of lien and attachments and the title for ten days. If, during the ten-day period following receipt of the notice, the claimed lien is satisfied, the lien claimant shall, on the form prescribed by the commissioner, notify the owner and the person holding the certificate of title of such satisfaction. The notice of satisfaction shall serve as a release and withdrawal of the pending notice of lien. If the owner or person holding the certificate of title chooses to contest the claimed lien, such owner or person holding the certificate of title shall so indicate on the notice of lien form and shall notify the other interested parties. If the notice contesting the lien is given, or if ten days have elapsed without the lien being satisfied, the person holding the certificate of title shall forward the certificate of title together with the notice of lien and attachments thereto to the commissioner or the commissioner's duly authorized county tag agent in order that the commissioner or authorized county tag agent may issue a new certificate of title and reflect on the new certificate of title the lien on the vehicle. The owner or the person who has custody of the current certificate of title shall comply with the instructions contained in the notice, and in the event such owner or person having custody of the current title cannot do so such owner or person having custody of the current title shall notify the lien claimant. The commissioner or authorized county tag agent, upon receipt of a properly executed title application, notice, fee, and the current certificate of title, shall enter the lien on the commissioner's or authorized county tag agent's records and shall issue a new certificate of title reflecting the lien and shall then deliver the certificate of title as provided for in this chapter. The lien shall be perfected at the time the lien notice, application for title, fee, and current certificate of title are received by the commissioner or authorized county tag agent.

(c) In the event that the person who has custody of the current certificate of title fails, refuses, or neglects to forward the title application, notice, fee, and current certificate of title to the commissioner or the commissioner's duly authorized county tag agent as required in this Code section, the lien claimant may, if such lien claimant's lien has not been satisfied, on a form prescribed by the commissioner, make direct application to the commissioner or authorized county tag agent. Such direct application to the commissioner or authorized county tag agent shall have attached to it the return registered or certified mail or statutory overnight delivery receipt showing the previous mailing of the title application, fee, and notice to the person who has custody of the current certificate of title. Upon receipt of such a direct application, the commissioner or authorized county tag agent shall order the person who has custody of the current certificate of title to forward the certificate of title to the commissioner or authorized county tag agent for the purpose of having the lien entered and a new certificate of title reflecting the lien issued. If, after a direct application to the commissioner or authorized county tag agent and after the order of the commissioner or authorized county tag agent, the person who has custody of the current certificate of title continues to fail, refuse, or neglect to forward the certificate of title as provided in this Code section, the commissioner or authorized county tag agent may cancel the current certificate of title and issue a new certificate of title reflecting all security interests and liens, and this new certificate of title shall be delivered as provided for in this chapter. In the event a direct application is made, the lien shall be perfected as of the date the outstanding certificate of title is canceled.

(d) No security interest holder or lienholder having custody of the certificate of title shall have the validity of such security interest holder's or lienholder's security interest or lien affected by surrendering the certificate of title as provided by this Code section. The first security interest holder or lienholder shall have the responsibility to advise a prospective transferee or security interest holder, upon inquiry, that a notice of subsequent lien has been received. Upon the issuing of a new certificate of title, the commissioner or the commissioner's duly authorized county tag agent shall cancel the old certificate of title.

(e) A lien perfected under this Code section shall be a lien only against the specific vehicle identified in the application for a new certificate.

(f) A lien on a vehicle for which a certificate of title is required shall be perfected and shall be valid against subsequent transferees and holders of security interests and liens only by compliance with this Code section. The procedure contained in this chapter shall be the exclusive method for the perfection of liens on vehicles, and no lien shall be effective as to a vehicle unless so perfected.

Laws 1961, p. 68, § 21; Laws 1962, p. 79, § 11; Laws 1969, p. 92, § 4; Laws 1978, p. 1081, § 9; Laws 1985, p. 149, § 40; Laws 1990, p. 2048, § 3; Laws 1997, p. 739, § 21; Laws 1998, p. 1179, § 38; Laws 2000, p. 1589, § 3.

§ 40–3–54. Mechanics' liens

(a) All mechanics of every sort shall have a special lien on any vehicle required to have a certificate of title by Code Section 40–3–20 for work done, or for work done and materials furnished, or for materials furnished in repairing or servicing such vehicle. Perfection of the lien by recording shall be as provided in Code Section 40–3–53. The lien may be asserted by retention of the vehicle, and all contracts for repairs or service to vehicles shall be deemed to incorporate a right of retention by the mechanic to protect this lien until it is paid or satisfied through foreclosure as provided in this Code section. The lien may also be asserted by surrendering the vehicle, giving credit, and foreclosing the lien claim in the manner provided in this Code section. If he surrenders possession of the vehicle to the debtor, the mechanic shall record his claim of lien as provided in Code Section 40–3–53. Such special lien shall be superior to all liens except for taxes and such other liens and security interests of which the mechanic had actual or constructive notice before the work was done or material furnished. The validity of the lien against third parties shall be determined in accordance with this chapter.

(b) If possession is retained or the lien recorded, the owner-debtor may contest the validity of the amount claimed to be due by making written demand upon the lienholder. If upon receipt of such demand the lienholder fails to institute foreclosure proceedings within ten days where possession has been retained, or within 30 days where possession has been surrendered, the lien is forfeited.

(c) The lien shall be foreclosed in the following manner:

(1) A person asserting the lien, either for himself or as a guardian, administrator, executor, or trustee, may move to foreclose it by making an affidavit to a court of competent jurisdiction showing all the facts necessary to constitute a lien under this Code section and the amount claimed to be due;

(2) Upon such affidavit being filed, the clerk or a judge of the court shall serve notice upon the owner, the recorded lienholders and security interest holders, and the lessee, if any, of the vehicle of a right to a hearing to determine if reasonable cause exists to believe that a valid debt exists, and that such hearing must be petitioned for within five days after receipt of the notice and that, if no petition for such hearing is filed within the time allowed, the lien will conclusively be deemed a valid one and foreclosure thereof allowed;

(3) If a petition for a hearing is filed within the time allowed, the court shall set a probable cause hearing within ten days of the filing of the petition. If, at the probable cause hearing, the court determines that reasonable cause exists to believe that a valid debt exists, the mechanic shall be given possession of the vehicle or the court shall obtain possession of the vehicle, as ordered by the court. The owner-debtor may retain possession of the vehicle by giving bond and security in the amount determined to be probably due and the costs of the action;

(4) Within five days of the probable cause hearing, a defendant must petition the court for a full hearing on the validity of the debt if a further determination of the validity of the debt is desired. If no such petition is filed, the lien on the amount determined reasonably due shall be conclusively deemed a valid one and foreclosure thereof allowed. If such a petition is filed, the court shall set a full hearing thereon within 30 days of the filing of the petition. Upon the filing of such petition by the defendant, neither the prosecuting mechanic nor the court may sell the vehicle, although possession of the vehicle may be retained;

(5) If, after a full hearing, the court finds that a valid debt exists, then the court shall authorize foreclosure upon and sale of the vehicle subject to the lien to satisfy the debt if the debt is not otherwise immediately paid;

(6) If the court finds the actions of the mechanic in retaining or seeking possession of the vehicle were not taken in good faith, the court, in its discretion, may award damages to the owner, the lessee, or any person deprived of the rightful use of the vehicle due to the deprivation of the use of the vehicle;

(7) Any proceeding to foreclose a mechanic's lien on a vehicle must be instituted within one year from the time the lien is recorded or is asserted by retention.

Laws 1961, p. 68, § 23; Laws 1962, p. 79, § 13; Laws 1969, p. 92, § 6; Laws 1975, p. 489, § 1; Laws 1985, p. 149, § 40; Laws 1990, p. 2048, § 3.

§ 40–3–55. Assignment by security interest holder or lienholder

(a) The holder of any security interest in or lien on a vehicle may assign, absolutely or otherwise, such holder's security interest or lien to a person other than the owner without affecting the interest of the owner or the validity of the security interest or lien, but any person without notice of the assignment is protected in dealing with the holder of the security interest or lien, and the holder of the security interest or lien remains liable for any obligations as such holder until the assignee is named as the holder of the security interest or lien on the certificate of title.

(b) The assignee may, but need not to perfect the assignment, have the certificate of title endorsed or issued with the assignee named as holder of a security interest or lien, upon delivering to the commissioner or the commissioner's duly authorized county tag agent the certificate and assignment by the holder of a security interest or lien named in the certificate in the form the commissioner prescribes, provided that as an alternative to a handwritten signature, the commissioner may authorize use of a digital signature as long as appropriate security measures are implemented which assure security and verification of the digital signature process, in accordance with regulations promulgated by the commissioner. If the assignment refers to a security interest or lien which is reflected on the certificate of title and the certificate of title is in the possession of the first security interest holder or lienholder as provided by this chapter, the assignee may, but need not to perfect the assignment, have the certificate of title endorsed, or a new certificate of title issued, by complying with Code Section 40–3–27.

Laws 1961, p. 68, § 24; Laws 1962, p. 79, § 14; Laws 1965, p. 304, § 7; Laws 1990, p. 2048, § 3; Laws 1997, p. 739, § 22.

§ 40–3–56. Release of security interest or lien

(a)(1) If any security interest or lien listed on a certificate of title is satisfied, the holder thereof shall, within ten days after demand, execute a release in the form the commissioner prescribes and mail or deliver the release to the owner, provided that as an alternative to a handwritten signature, the commissioner may authorize use of a digital signature as long as appropriate security measures are implemented which assure security and verification of the digital signature process, in accordance with regulations promulgated by the commissioner. For the purposes of the release of a security interest or lien the "holder" of the lien or security interest is the parent bank or other lending institution and any branch or office of the parent institution may execute such release.

(2) If the commissioner has entered into an agreement with such a security interest holder or lienholder to provide a means of delivery by secure electronic measures of a notice of the recording of such security interest or lien, at such time as the security interest or lien is released, by secure electronic measures, the certificate of title may be printed and mailed or delivered to the next lienholder or security interest holder or, if there is no other security interest holder or lienholder, to the owner without payment of any fee provided by Code Section 40–3–38.

(b) The owner may then forward the certificate of title, the release, the properly executed title application, and title application fee to the commissioner or the commissioner's duly authorized county tag agent, and the commissioner or authorized county tag agent shall release the security interest or lien on the certificate or issue a new certificate and mail or deliver the certificate to the owner. If the satisfied security interest or lien is one reflected on the certificate of title but the certificate of title is in the custody of the first security interest holder or lienholder as provided by this chapter, the release may be handled as provided in Code Section 40–3–27, and Code Section 40–3–26 shall otherwise be complied with. In the event that the lienholder or security interest holder is no longer in business, an individual shall not be required to submit a release to secure a new certificate of title. The owner shall be required to present to the commissioner or authorized county tag agent certification from the appropriate regulatory agency that such lienholder or security interest holder is no longer in business.

(c) Except for liens and security interests listed on certificates of title for mobile homes, cranes, or vehicles which weigh more than 10,000 pounds gross vehicle weight, which shall be satisfied only in conformity with subsections (a) and (b) of this Code section, any lien or security interest shall be considered satisfied and release shall not be required after ten years from the date of issuance of a title on which such lien or security interest is listed. None of the provisions of this Code section shall preclude the perfection of a new lien or security agreement, or the perfection of an extension of a lien or security agreement beyond a period of ten years, by application for a new certificate of title on which such lien or security agreement is listed. In order to provide for the continuous perfection of a lien or security interest originally entered into for a period of more than ten years for a vehicle other than a mobile home, crane, or vehicle which weighs more than 10,000 pounds gross vehicle weight, an application for a second title on which the lien or security interest is listed must be submitted to the commissioner or the commissioner's duly authorized tag agent before ten years from the date of the original title on which such lien or security interest is listed. Otherwise the lien or security interest shall be perfected as of the date of receipt of the application by the commissioner or the commissioner's duly authorized county tag agent.

Laws 1961, p. 68, § 25; Laws 1962, p. 79, § 15; Laws 1965, p. 304, § 8; Laws 1985, p. 149, § 40; Laws 1990, p. 2048, § 3; Laws 1992, p. 2978, § 9; Laws 1993, p. 1260, § 10; Laws 1997, p. 739, § 23.

§ 40–3–57. Disclosure requirements

The holder of any security interest or of any lien named in a certificate of title shall, on written request of the owner, or of another holder of any security interest or lien named in the certificate, or of an interested third party, or of the commissioner, disclose any pertinent information as to the security interest, the security agreement, and the debt secured thereby, and the lien and the amount for which it is claimed.

Laws 1961, p. 68, § 26; Laws 1962, p. 79, § 16; Laws 1990, p. 2048, § 3.

§ 40–3–58. Exclusiveness of procedure

The method provided in this chapter of perfecting and giving notice of security interests and liens with respect to motor vehicles as to which certificates of title need be obtained under this chapter is exclusive, and such security interests and liens are exempt from the provisions of law which otherwise require or relate to the recording or filing of security interests or liens, claims of lien executions, and other like instruments with respect to such vehicles.

Laws 1961, p. 68, § 27; Laws 1962, p. 79, § 17; Laws 1990, p. 2048, § 3.

§ 40–3–59. Exception as to certain security interests

This chapter does not apply to or affect a security interest in a vehicle created by a manufacturer or dealer who holds the vehicle for sale. A buyer in the ordinary course of trade from the manufacturer or dealer takes free of such security interest.

Laws 1961, p. 68, § 5; Laws 1962, p. 79, § 3; Laws 1990, p. 2048, § 3.

§ 40–3–60. Certain transactions not create sales or security interest in motor vehicle or trailer

Notwithstanding any other provision of law, in the case of a motor vehicle or trailer, a transaction does not create a sales or security interest merely because it provides that the rental price is permitted or required to be adjusted under the agreement either upward or downward by reference to the amount realized upon sale or other disposition of the motor vehicle or trailer.

Laws 1995, p. 739, § 1.

§ 40–3–61. Procedure on total loss of vehicle subject to more than one perfected security interest or lien

Notwithstanding any other provision of law to the contrary, in any claim involving the total loss of a vehicle which is subject to more than one perfected security interest or lien as recorded on the title of the vehicle, the proceeds of the insurance policy shall be first applied to the debt owed to the first lienholder. In the event that there are proceeds remaining after satisfying the first lienholder, the proceeds shall be then applied to the debt owed to the second and subsequent lienholders in order of priority and any proceeds remaining after the satisfaction of all such recorded liens shall be paid to the insured. If the amount of debt secured by such security interests or liens or the seniority of such security interests or liens is in doubt, any remaining funds shall be deposited with the court and a complaint for interpleader shall be filed in accordance with Code Section 9–11–22.

Laws 2002, p. 848, § 3.

Historical and Statutory Notes

In 2002, the Code Commission, in the second sentence, deleted a comma following "In the event". See § 28–9–5.

Article 4

Offenses

§§ 40–3–70 to 40–3–76. Repealed by Laws 1990, p. 2048, § 3, eff. July 1, 1990

§ 40–3–90. Felonies

A person who, with fraudulent intent:

(1) Alters, forges, or counterfeits a certificate of title;

(2) Alters or forges an assignment of a certificate of title or an assignment or release of a security interest on a certificate of title or a form the commissioner prescribed;

(3) Has possession of or uses a certificate of title knowing it to have been altered, forged, or counterfeited;

(4) Uses a false or fictitious name or address or makes a material false statement, or fails to disclose a security interest, or conceals any other material fact in an application for a certificate of title;

(5) Alters or forges a notice of a transaction concerning a security interest or lien reflected on the certificate of title as provided by Code Section 40–3–27; or

(6) Willfully violates any other provision of this chapter after having previously violated the same or any other provision of this chapter and having been convicted of that act in a court of competent jurisdiction shall be guilty of a felony.

Laws 1961, p. 68, § 31; Laws 1965, p. 304, § 9; Laws 1975, p. 1596, § 2; Laws 1985, p. 149, § 40; Laws 1990, p. 2048, § 3.

§ 40–3–91. Misdemeanors

(a) A person who:

(1) With fraudulent intent, permits another, not entitled thereto, to use or have possession of a certificate of title;

(2) Willfully fails to mail or deliver a certificate of title to the commissioner or to the purchaser of the motor vehicle or a release of security interest or lien to the owner within ten days of the time required by this chapter, except as provided in Code Section 40–3–90;

(3) Willfully fails or refuses to mail or deliver the certificate of title to the commissioner within ten days after having received a notice, as provided for in Code Section 40–3–27 or 40–3–52; or

(4) Willfully violates any other provision of this chapter

shall be guilty of a misdemeanor.

(b) Any person, firm, or corporation which knowingly makes any false statement in any title application as to the date a vehicle was sold or acquired or as to the date of creation of a security interest or lien shall be guilty of a misdemeanor and, upon conviction thereof, shall be fined not more than $100.00 or imprisoned for a period not to exceed 30 days.

(c) Any person, firm, or corporation which delivers or accepts a certificate of title assigned in blank shall be guilty of a misdemeanor and, upon conviction thereof, shall be fined not more than $100.00 or imprisoned for a period not to exceed 30 days for the acceptance or delivery of each certificate of title assigned in blank.

Laws 1961, p. 68, § 31; Laws 1965, p. 304, § 9; Laws 1969, p. 92, § 7; Laws 1975, p. 1596, § 2; Laws 1981, p. 883, § 12; Laws 1990, p. 2048, § 3.

§ 40–3–92. False report of theft or conversion

A person who knowingly makes a false report to a peace officer or the commissioner of the theft or conversion of a vehicle shall be guilty of a misdemeanor of a high and aggravated nature.

Laws 1961, p. 68, § 33; Laws 1990, p. 2048, § 3; Laws 1991, p. 969, § 1.

§ 40–3–93. Evidence of criminal intent or knowledge

In a prosecution for a crime specified in this chapter, evidence that the defendant has committed a prior act or acts of the same kind is admissible to prove criminal intent or knowledge.

Laws 1961, p. 68, § 35; Laws 1990, p. 2048, § 3.

§ 40–3–94. Violations relating to Motor Vehicle Certificate of Title Act

Unless another penalty is provided in this chapter:

(1) A person convicted of a felony for the violation of a provision of this chapter shall be punished by a fine of not less than $500.00 nor more than $5,000.00, or by imprisonment for not less than one year nor more than five years, or by both such fine and imprisonment;

(2) A person convicted of a misdemeanor for the violation of a provision of this chapter shall be punished as provided in Code Section 17–10–3.

Laws 1961, p. 68, § 36; Laws 1990, p. 2048, § 3.

§ 40–3–95. Supplementary nature

The penal provisions of this chapter in no way repeal or modify any existing provision of criminal law but are additional and supplementary thereto.

Laws 1961, p. 68, § 37; Laws 1990, p. 2048, § 3.

CHAPTER 4

IDENTIFICATION OF AND PURCHASE AND RESALE OF MOTOR VEHICLES AND PARTS

Article 1

Article 2

Article 3

Article 1

Identification of Passenger Cars, Truck Chassis, and Components

§ 40–4–1. Definitions

As used in this article, the term:

(1) "Component" means a passenger car engine or a passenger car transmission.

(2) "New passenger car" means any passenger car which has never been the subject of a sale at retail to the general public.

(3) "Passenger car" means every motor vehicle designed for carrying ten passengers or less except trackless trolleys or vehicles used exclusively upon streetcar rails or tracks or overhead trolley wires.

(4) "Used passenger car" means any passenger car which has been the subject of a sale at retail to the general public.

Laws 1966, p. 188, § 3; Laws 1967, p. 113, § 3; Laws 1996, p. 336, § 13A.

§ 40–4–2. Application

(a) The provisions of this article requiring vehicle identification numbers on passenger cars and truck chassis with features designed for specialized requirements of a wrecker shall apply only to such items manufactured after January 1, 1967, and designated by the manufacturer as a 1968 or subsequent model.

(b) This article shall not apply to motorcycles, motor driven cycles, school buses, farm tractors, buses, truck tractors, road tractors, trucks, trailers, semitrailers, pole trailers, streetcars, or go-carts or to any vehicle whether self-propelled or not which is not required to be issued a license plate under the laws of this state.

(c) This article shall not apply to the following special purpose vehicles:

Type 1. Truck chassis with body (other than station wagon or bus body) designed primarily for the transportation of persons;

Type 2. Truck chassis with other features designed for a specialized requirement other than a wrecker, including but not limited to fire fighting or snowplow features;

Type 3. Truck chassis with station wagon body;

Type 4. Passenger car chassis with body designed for the commercial transportation of persons;

Type 5. Bus chassis with other features designed for a specialized requirement, including but not limited to mobile laboratory, office, post office, classroom, studio, rescue unit, or library features;

Type 6. Utility vehicle, being a motor vehicle with a removable top, designed for carrying passengers or cargo and with particular features for operation both on highway and cross-country.

(d) This article shall not apply to the components of any vehicle excluded by subsection (b) or (c) of this Code section.

Laws 1966, p. 188, § 6; Laws 1967, p. 113, § 6; Laws 1992, p. 6, § 40; Laws 1993, p. 91, § 40; Laws 1996, p. 336, § 13A; Laws 1997, p. 143, § 40.

§ 40–4–3. Required identification numbers

(a) *New passenger cars and components manufactured within state.* After January 1, 1997, new passenger cars, truck chassis with features designed for specialized requirements of wreckers, passenger car engines, and transmissions, as specified in this article, manufactured within this state and intended for sale to the general public within this state, shall be required to have placed upon them vehicle identification numbers and component identification numbers. The vehicle identification number shall not be the same as the vehicle identification number of any other passenger car or truck chassis manufactured by the same manufacturer. The component identification number shall not be the same as the component identification number for any other like component manufactured by the same manufacturer but may be the same as the vehicle identification number if the component is installed as original equipment in the passenger car or truck chassis.

(b) *New passenger cars sold within state.* After January 1, 1997, no new passenger car or truck chassis with features designed for specialized requirements of a wrecker shall be sold to the general public in this state unless such passenger car shall bear a vehicle identification number, which shall not be the same as the vehicle identification number of any other passenger car made by the same manufacturer.

(c) *New components sold within state.* After January 1, 1967, no new passenger car engine or passenger car transmission shall be sold to the general public in this state unless it shall bear an identification number. The component identification number shall not be the same as the identification number for any other like passenger car component made by the same manufacturer but may be the same as the vehicle identification number if the particular component has been installed as original equipment in the passenger car prior to its sale to the general public.

Laws 1966, p. 188, § 1; Laws 1967, p. 113, § 1; Laws 1996, p. 336, § 13A.

§ 40–4–4. Specifications for and installation of identification numbers

(a) The identification numbers required by Code Section 40–4–3 shall be placed upon the passenger car, truck chassis, and component parts by the manufacturer thereof.

(b) The identification numbers shall be placed upon the passenger car, truck chassis, and components in such a manner that any attempt to remove, alter, deface, obliterate, or destroy them will be ascertainable. The numbers may be affixed by any suitable manufacturing process that will result in the numbers becoming a permanent part of the passenger car or component.

(c) The identification numbers shall be of a height and width easily readable by the naked eye. They may consist of letters, digits, or any combination of them.

(d) The identification numbers may be in accordance with recommended practices approved by the Society of Automotive Engineers as to material, lettering, manufacturing, and installation.

(e) Vehicle identification numbers shall be easily accessible for inspection.

Laws 1966, p. 188, §§ 1, 2; Laws 1967, p. 113, §§ 1, 2; Laws 1996, p. 336, § 13A.

§ 40–4–5. Vehicle identification number for truck chassis with features designed for specialized requirements of a wrecker

Truck chassis with features designed for specialized requirements of a wrecker manufactured after January 1, 1967, but before January 1, 1997, shall, at the time the vehicle is first registered on or after January 1, 1997, pursuant to Code Section 40–2–21, be issued by the Department of Revenue a unique vehicle identification number which shall be affixed to and maintained upon the chassis by the owner in a manner consistent with the requirements of subsections (b) and (e) of Code Section 40–4–4.

Laws 1996, p. 336, § 13A; Laws 2002, p. 415, § 40; Laws 2005, Act 68, § 16–1, eff. July 1, 2005.

§ 40–4–6. Records to be kept

Any person who purchases or sells or offers for sale any used passenger car, truck chassis, engine, or transmission required to be numbered by this article shall keep a permanent record of such transactions. Such record shall include: the item and its identification number or numbers; the name and address of the person from whom the item was purchased; and the name and address of the person to whom the item was sold. Such record shall be kept for three years from the date of the transaction and shall be available to all law enforcement officers for inspection at any reasonable time during business hours without prior notice or the necessity of obtaining a search warrant.

Laws 1966, p. 188, § 4; Laws 1967, p. 113, § 4; Laws 1996, p. 336, § 13A.

§ 40–4–7. Violations

(a) *Sale, shipment, or manufacture of unnumbered passenger car or component.* Any person who sells or offers for sale in this state, ships or causes to be shipped into this state, or manufactures with the intention that it shall be sold at retail in this state a passenger car, truck chassis, passenger car engine, or passenger car transmission that does not bear an identification number or numbers as required by this article shall be guilty of a misdemeanor.

(b) *Failure to keep records.* Any person who purchases, sells, or offers for sale any passenger car, truck chassis, passenger car engine, or passenger car transmission that is required by this article to bear an identification number when intended to be sold at wholesale or retail within this state and who willfully fails to keep the records required by Code Section 40–4–6 shall be guilty of a misdemeanor for each such failure.

Laws 1966, p. 188, § 5; Laws 1967, p. 113, § 5; Laws 1985, p. 149, § 40; Laws 1994, p. 97, § 40; Laws 1996, p. 336, § 13A.

Article 2

Alteration or Removal of Identification Numbers

§ 40–4–20. Definitions of vehicle or engine

As used in this article, the term:

(1) "Falsify" includes alter or forge.

(2) "Identification number" means an identifying number, serial number, engine number, or other distinguishing number or mark placed on a vehicle or engine by its manufacturer or by authority of the commissioner or in accordance with the laws of another state or country.

(3) "Remove" includes deface or destroy.

Laws 1961, p. 68, § 34; Laws 1985, p. 149, § 40; Laws 1992, p. 6, § 40.

§ 40–4–21. Removed, falsified or unauthorized identification number of vehicle or engine

(a) A person who willfully removes, except in conformance with Code Section 40–3–35, or falsifies an identification number of a vehicle or an engine for a vehicle is guilty of a misdemeanor.

(b) A person who, willfully and with intent to misrepresent the identity of a vehicle or engine, removes or falsifies an identification number of the vehicle or engine with intent to convert or defraud is guilty of a felony. A person convicted of a felony under this subsection shall be punished by a fine of not less than $500.00 nor more than $5,000.00, or by imprisonment for not less than one year nor more than five years, or by both such fine and imprisonment.

Laws 1961, p. 68, § 34; Laws 1984, p. 22, § 40.

§ 40–4–22. Removal or falsification of identifying numbers with intent to conceal identity of vehicle; penalties

(a) It shall be unlawful to buy, sell, receive, dispose of, conceal, use, or possess any motor vehicle, or any part thereof, from which the manufacturer's serial numbers or other distinguishing numbers or identifying marks have been removed, defaced, covered, altered, or destroyed for the purpose of concealing or misrepresenting the identity of such motor vehicle.

(b) Any person who knowingly violates any provisions of subsection (a) of this Code section is guilty of a felony and, upon conviction, shall be punished by confinement in the penitentiary for not less than one nor more than five years.

Laws 1918, p. 264, § 1; Laws 1966, p. 10, § 1; Laws 1982, p. 3, § 40.

Formerly Code 1933, § 68–9916.

§ 40–4–23. Identification number placed on vehicle or engine by manufacturer not falsified

An identification number may be placed on a vehicle or engine by its manufacturer in the regular course of business or placed or restored on a vehicle or engine by authority of the commissioner without violating this article. An identification number so placed or restored is not falsified.

Laws 1961, p. 68, § 34.

Article 3

Purchase and Resale of Used Motor Vehicles, Used Parts, and Farm Tractors

§ 40–4–40. Records to be kept by purchasers of used motor vehicles or used automotive parts

Any person who purchases a used motor vehicle or any used part comprising a component part of any motor vehicle for resale shall keep an accurate record of the date of purchase, the price paid, and the name and address of the person from whom the vehicle or part is purchased. Such information shall be maintained in permanent records for a period of not less than one year and shall be open to inspection by appropriate law enforcement officers.

Laws 1963, p. 436, § 1.

§ 40–4–41. Reports of purchases where identification markings removed

Any person who purchases for resale a motor vehicle or used part from which the identification markings or plates have been removed, altered, mutilated, or destroyed shall immediately report such purchase to the sheriff of the county in which such person conducts his business.

Laws 1963, p. 436, § 4.

§ 40–4–42. Evidentiary effect of possession of motor vehicles and parts

The possession of the motor vehicles and parts covered by Code Sections 40–4–40, 40–4–41, this Code section, 40–4–43, and 40–4–44 shall be prima–facie evidence that they were purchased for the purpose of resale.

Laws 1963, p. 436, § 5.

§ 40–4–43. Penalty for failure to keep records and file reports relating to used motor vehicles and parts

Any person who fails to comply with any provision of Code Section 40–4–40 or 40–4–41 shall be guilty of a misdemeanor.

Laws 1963, p. 436, § 6.

§ 40–4–44. Exception as to certain parts

Code Sections 40–4–40 through 40–4–43 shall not apply to the purchase of any motor vehicle part which may be removed from a motor vehicle by an individual possessing the ordinary skill and dexterity of an ordinary motor vehicle owner.

Laws 1963, p. 436, § 3.

§ 40–4–45. Sale of farm tractors

(a) As used in this Code section, the term:

(1) "Certificate of origin" means the evidence of origin of title of a farm tractor from the manufacturer. It shall show the following information:

(A) The name and the address of the manufacturer;

(B) The serial number of the farm tractor; and

(C) The year, make, and model of the farm tractor.

(2) "Dealer" means a person engaged in buying, selling, trading, or exchanging farm tractors who has an established place of business in this state.

(3) "Farm tractor" means any self-propelled vehicle having more than 15 horsepower designed and used primarily as a farm implement for drawing plows, mowing machines, and other implements of husbandry.

(4) "Person" means a natural person, firm, partnership, association, or corporation.

(5) "Serial number" means the number or letters, or both, placed on a farm tractor by stamping thereon or by affixing a plate thereto by the manufacturer for the purpose of identifying the tractor.

(b) It shall be unlawful for any dealer to sell, trade, or exchange any farm tractor in this state which was manufactured after July 1, 1970, unless:

(1) The original serial number is stamped upon or affixed to the farm tractor; and

(2) The certificate of origin is presented to the purchaser, or to the person who otherwise receives the farm tractor through an exchange or trade with the dealer, at the time the sale, trade, or exchange is completed.

(c) Any person violating any provision of this Code section shall be guilty of a misdemeanor.

Laws 1970, p. 242, §§ 1–3; Laws 1994, p. 97, § 40.

CHAPTER 5

DRIVERS' LICENSES

Article 1

Article 2

Article 1

General Provisions

§ 40–5–1. Definitions

As used in this chapter, the term:

(1) "Assessment component" means the standard screening instrument or instruments designated by the Department of Driver Services which are used to screen for the extent of an individual's alcohol or drug use and its impact on driving.

(2) Reserved.

(3) "Cancellation of driver's license" means the annulment or termination by formal action of the department of a person's license because of some error or defect in the license or because the licensee is no longer entitled to such license. The cancellation of a license is without prejudice, and application for a new license may be made at any time after such cancellation.

(3.1) "Clinical evaluation" means an evaluation under Chapter 7 of Title 37 at a facility to diagnose an individual's substance abuse or dependence and, if indicated, to refer the individual to appropriate treatment.

(4) "Code Section 40–6–391" means Code Section 40–6–391 of the Official Code of Georgia Annotated, as now or hereafter amended, any federal law or regulation substantially conforming to or parallel with the offense covered under Code Section 40–6–391, any local ordinance adopted pursuant to Article 14 of Chapter 6 of this title, which ordinance adopts the provisions of Code Section 40–6–391, or any previously existing or existing law of this or any other state, which law was or is substantially conforming to or parallel with Code Section 40–6–391.

(5) "Commissioner" means the commissioner of driver services.

(6) "Conviction" means a forfeiture of bail or collateral deposited to secure a defendant's appearance in court, the payment of a fine, a plea of guilty, or a finding of guilt on a traffic violation charge, regardless of whether the sentence is suspended, probated, or rebated.

(7) "Department" means the Department of Driver Services.

(8) "Disqualification of driver's license" means a prohibition against driving a commercial motor vehicle.

(9) "DUI Alcohol or Drug Use Risk Reduction Program" means a program certified by the Department of Driver Services which consists of two components: assessment and intervention. In the case of a conviction or plea of nolo contendere to a violation of Code Section 40–6–391 or in any other instance in which a person may be referred to a DUI Alcohol or Drug Use Risk Reduction Program, the program administers the assessment component and refers such offender to the intervention component.

(10) "Intervention component" means a program which delivers therapeutic education about alcohol and drug use and driving and peer group counseling concerning alcohol and drug use over a period of 20 hours utilizing a methodology and curriculum approved and certified by the Department of Driver Services for the DUI Alcohol or Drug Use Risk Reduction Programs under subsection (e) of Code Section 40–5–83.

(11) Reserved.

(12) "Mail" means to deposit in the United States mail properly addressed and with postage prepaid. For purposes of payment of a reinstatement or restoration fee for a driver's license suspension or revocation, "mail" shall also mean payment via means other than personal appearance.

(13) "Owner" means a person other than a lienholder or security interest holder having the property in or title to a vehicle. The term includes a person entitled to the use and possession of a vehicle subject to a lien or security interest in another person, but excludes a lessee under a lease not intended as security.

(13.5) "Personal information" means any information that identifies a person, including but not limited to an individual's fingerprint, photograph, or computerized image, social security number, driver identification number, name, address (other than five-digit ZIP Code), telephone number, and medical or disability information.

(14) "Present and future minimum motor vehicle insurance coverage" means minimum coverage as specified in Chapter 34 of Title 33, which coverage cannot be canceled except for a subsequent conviction of an offense enumerated in Code Section 40–5–54 and after giving the commissioner 20 days' written notice prior to the effective date of the cancellation.

(15) "Resident" means a person who has a permanent home or abode in Georgia to which, whenever such person is absent, he or she has the intention of returning. For the purposes of this chapter, there is a rebuttable presumption that the following person is a resident:

(A) Any person who accepts employment or engages in any trade, profession, or occupation in Georgia or enters his or her children to be educated in the private or public schools of Georgia within ten days after the commencement of such employment or education; or

(B) Any person who, except for infrequent, brief absences, has been present in the state for 30 or more days;

provided, however, that no person shall be considered a resident for purposes of this chapter unless such person is either a United States citizen or an alien with legal authorization from the U.S. Immigration and Naturalization Service.

(16) "Revocation of driver's license" means the termination by formal action of the department of a person's license or privilege to operate a motor vehicle on the public highways, which license shall not be subject to renewal or restoration, except that an application for a new license may be presented and acted upon by the department after the expiration of the applicable period of time prescribed in this chapter.

(16.1) "Singularly or in combination" means that the department, in determining whether or not a person's license or privilege to operate a motor vehicle on the public highways is to be revoked as a habitual violator, is to treat each charge for which a conviction was obtained as a separate transaction when determining whether or not a person has the requisite convictions which mandate such a revocation.

(16.2) "Substance abuse treatment program" means a program of treatment under Chapter 7 of Title 37 at a facility authorized to provide services designed to meet an individual's substance abuse treatment needs based upon the results of a clinical evaluation performed by a provider other than the provider of the treatment program for such individual.

(17) "Suspension of driver's license" means the temporary withdrawal by formal action of the department of a person's license or privilege to operate a motor vehicle on the public highways, which temporary withdrawal shall be for a period specifically designated by the department.

Laws 1975, p. 1008, § 1; Laws 1989, p. 519, § 2; Laws 1990, p. 1154, § 1; Laws 1990, p. 2048, § 4; Laws 1991, p. 1886, § 1; Laws 1994, p. 97, § 40; Laws 1994, p. 514, § 1; Laws 1995, p. 920, § 1; Laws 1996, p. 1250, § 1; Laws 1997, p. 143, § 40; Laws 1997, p. 760, § 8; Laws 1997, p. 1446, § 1; Laws 1999, p. 731, § 1; Laws 2000, p. 951, § 5–1; Laws 2005, Act 68, § 17–1, eff. July 1, 2005; Laws 2010, Act 360, § 1–78, eff. May 12, 2010; Laws 2010, Act 633, § 1, eff. July 1, 2010.

Formerly Code 1933, § 68B–101.

Historical and Statutory Notes

The 2005 amendment by Act 68 in par. (1), substituted "Department of Driver Services" for "Department of Human Resources"; in par. (3), substituted "department" for "Department of Motor Vehicle Safety" following "formal action of the" in the first sentence; in par. (5), substituted "commissioner of driver services" for "commissioner of motor vehicle safety"; in par. (7), substituted "Department of Driver Services" for "Department of Motor Vehicle Safety"; in par. (9), substituted "Department of Driver Services" for "Department of Human Resources"; and in par. (10), substituted "Department of Driver Services" for "Department of Human Resources".

The 2010 amendment by Act 360, in par. (12), added the last sentence relating to the purpose of payment.

The 2010 amendment by Act 633, in par. (12), added the second sentence which was the same sentence added by Laws 2010, Act 360.

§ 40–5–2. Records to be kept by the department

(a) The department shall maintain records regarding the drivers' licenses and permits issued by the department under this chapter. The drivers' records maintained by the department shall include:

(1) A record of every application for a license received by it and suitable indexes containing:

(A) All applications granted; and

(B) The name of every licensee whose license has been canceled, suspended, or revoked by the department and after each such name shall note the reasons for such action;

(2) Drivers' records received from other jurisdictions. Upon receipt of such driver's record, it shall become a part of such driver's record in this state and shall have the same force and effect as though entered on the driver's record in this state in the original instance; and

(3) Records of all accident reports and abstracts of court records of convictions of any offense listed in subsection (a) of Code Section 40–5–20, subsection (a) of Code Section 40–5–54, Code Section 40–6–10, driving on a suspended license in violation of Code Section 40–5–121, administrative license suspension pursuant to Code Sections 40–5–67 through 40–5–67.2, Code Section 40–5–75, Chapter 9 of this title, the "Motor Vehicle Safety Responsibility Act," and Chapter 34 of Title 33, the "Georgia Motor Vehicle Accident Reparations Act," any felony offense under this title, any offense committed while operating a commercial motor vehicle, serious traffic offenses, or other offenses requiring the assessment of points on the driving record that are received by it under the laws of this state and in connection therewith maintain convenient records or make suitable notations in order that an individual record of each licensee or individual showing the convictions of such licensee or individual and the traffic accidents in which such licensee or individual has been involved shall be readily ascertainable and available for the consideration of the department upon any application for, or application for renewal of license and at other suitable times. For purposes of issuing a driver's operating record to the public as provided in this Code section, the period of calculation for compilation of such report shall be determined by the date of arrest.

(b) The records maintained by the department on individual drivers are exempt from any law of this state requiring that such records be open for public inspection; provided, however, that initial arrest reports, incident reports, and the records pertaining to investigations or prosecutions of criminal or unlawful activity shall be subject to disclosure pursuant to paragraph (4) of subsection (a) of Code Section 50–18–72 and related provisions. Georgia Uniform Motor Vehicle Accident Reports shall be subject to disclosure pursuant to paragraph (4.1) of subsection (a) of Code Section 50–18–72. The department shall not make records or personal information available on any driver except as otherwise provided in this Code section or as otherwise specifically required by 18 U.S.C. Section 2721.

(c)(1) The driver's record provided by the department shall include an enumeration of any accidents in which the individual was convicted of a moving traffic violation, such moving traffic violation convictions, and information pertaining to financial responsibility. The department shall furnish a driver's operating record or personal information from a driver's record under the following circumstances:

(A) With the written instructions and consent of the driver upon whom the operating record has been made and compiled; such instructions and consent shall be signed by the driver but shall not be required to be notarized;

(B)(i) Pursuant to a written request or a request made in accordance with a contract with the Georgia Technology Authority for immediate on-line electronic furnishing of information, for use by any insurer or insurance support organization, or by a self-insured entity, or its agents, employees, or contractors, in connection with claims investigation activities, antifraud activities, rating, or underwriting involving the driver; provided, however, that notwithstanding the definition of personal information under Code Section 40–5–1, personal information furnished under this division shall be limited to name, address, driver identification number, and medical or disability information. The person who makes a request for a driver's operating record shall identify himself or herself and shall have certified or affirmed that the information contained in the record will be used only for the purpose specified in the request. Further, the person making the request shall certify or affirm that he or she has on file an application for insurance or for the renewal or amendment thereof involving the driver or drivers; or

(ii) For the purpose of ascertaining necessary rating information by an insurance agent pursuant to an insurer's contract with the Georgia Technology Authority for the immediate on-line electronic furnishing of limited rating information to such insurer's agents. Limited rating information furnished under this division shall include only the number of violations of Code Section 40–6–391, relating to driving under the influence of alcohol, drugs, or other intoxicating substances, and the number and type of other moving traffic violations which were committed by the proposed insured driver or drivers within the immediately preceding three or five years, which period shall be specified by the person making the request. The provisions of division (i) of this subparagraph notwithstanding, no other information concerning a driver's operating record shall be released to such agents for purposes of rating;

(B.1) The department shall implement a pilot program for 12 months to determine the revenue feasibility of supplying limited rating information to agents, insurers, and insurance support organizations. The department shall report the results of such pilot program to the Office of Planning and Budget. Unless the Office of Planning and Budget determines that the pilot program is not successful, the department shall continue the program on a year-to-year basis and furnish limited rating information to insurance support organizations for the same purposes as provided in division (ii) of subparagraph (B) of this paragraph, pursuant to a contract with the Georgia Technology Authority, provided that all other necessary requirements of this subsection have been met;

(C) In accordance with Article 7 of this chapter, the "Georgia Uniform Commercial Driver's License Act";

(D) To a judge, prosecuting official, or law enforcement agency for use in investigations or prosecutions of alleged criminal or unlawful activity, or to the driver's licensing agency of another state;

(E) Pursuant to a request from a public or private school system concerning any person currently employed or an applicant for employment as a school bus driver who agrees in writing to allow the department to release the information;

(F) With the written release of the driver, to a rental car company for use in the normal course of its business; provided, however, that notwithstanding the definition of personal information under Code Section 40–5–1, personal information furnished under this subparagraph shall be limited to name, address, driver identification number, and medical or disability information. Such access shall be provided and funded through the GeorgiaNet Division of the Georgia Technology Authority, and the department shall bear no costs associated with such access; and

(G) For use in the normal course of business by a legitimate business or its agents, employees, or contractors, but only:

(i) To verify the accuracy of personal information submitted by the individual to the business or its agents, employees, or contractors; and

(ii) If such information as so submitted is not correct or is no longer correct, to obtain the correct information, but only for the purposes of preventing fraud by, pursuing legal remedies against, or recovering on a debt or security interest against, the individual;

provided, however, that notwithstanding the definition of personal information under Code Section 40–5–1, personal information furnished under this subparagraph shall be limited to name, address, and driver identification number and shall not include photographs, fingerprints, computer images, or medical or disability information. The personal information obtained by a business under this subparagraph shall not be resold or redisclosed for any other purpose without the written consent of the individual. Furnishing of information to a business under this subparagraph shall be pursuant to a contract entered into by such business and the state which specifies, without limitation, the consideration to be paid by such business to the state for such information and the frequency of updates.

(2) Nothing in this Code section shall preclude the department from confirming or verifying the status of a driver's license or permit.

(d)(1) The commissioner shall designate members of the department to be the official custodians of the records of the department. No disclosure or release of operating records or personal information shall be made without the signed written approval of a designated custodian; except that such approval shall not be required for any release or disclosure through the GeorgiaNet Division of the Georgia Technology Authority pursuant to the signed written consent of the driver, provided that any such signed written consent shall be retained for a period of not less than four years by the party requesting the information; and except that such approval shall not be required for any release or disclosure of information made electronically through the GeorgiaNet Division of the Georgia Technology Authority in accordance with a contract authorized by subparagraph (c)(1)(B) of this Code section. The custodians may certify copies or compilations, including extracts thereof, of the records of the department. When so certified, such records shall be admissible as evidence in any civil or criminal proceeding as proof of the contents thereof.

(2) In response to a subpoena or upon the request of any judicial official, the department shall provide a duly authenticated copy of any record or other document. This authenticated copy may consist of a photocopy or computer printout of the requested document certified by the commissioner or the commissioner's duly authorized representative.

(e) Upon written request, the department may provide copies of any record or personal information from any driver's record for use by any appropriate governmental official, entity, or agency for the purposes of carrying out official governmental functions or legitimate governmental duties; provided, however, that notwithstanding the definition of personal information under Code Section 40–5–1, personal information furnished under this subsection shall be limited to name, address, driver identification number, and medical or disability information.

(f) The department is specifically authorized to disseminate the following records and information:

(1) To the United States Selective Service System and the Georgia Crime Information Center, compilations of the names, most current addresses, license or identification card numbers, and dates of birth of licensees or applicants for licenses or applicants for or holders of identification cards issued under this chapter, or, in the case of the United States Selective Service System, any other information from the license or identification card application as necessary for purposes of registration of persons therewith. Such information shall only be used in the fulfillment of the legitimate governmental duties of the United States Selective Service System and the Georgia Crime Information Center and shall not be further disseminated to any person. Information transmitted to the United States Selective Service System pursuant to this paragraph shall be provided in an electronic format;

(2) To the military branches of the United States Department of Defense, compilations of the names, dates of birth, sex, and most current addresses of licensees between the ages of 16 and 24 for the sole purpose of mailing recruiting and job opportunity information, provided that the department shall not be required to provide such a compilation more than once every two months;

(3) To the Department of Human Services, compilations of the names, dates of birth, and most current addresses of licensees or applicants for licenses. Any information provided pursuant to this subsection shall only be used by the Department of Human Services in connection with the recovery of delinquent child support payments under Article 1 of Chapter 11 of Title 19, known as the "Child Support Recovery Act";

(4) To a local fire or law enforcement department, a copy of the abstract of the driving record of any applicant for employment or any current employee and to the Georgia Bureau of Investigation for the purpose of providing a local fire or law enforcement department with the abstract through the Criminal Justice Information System. It shall be unlawful for any person who receives an abstract of the driving record of an individual under this subsection to disclose any information pertaining to such abstract or to make any use thereof except in the performance of official duties with the local fire or law enforcement department;

(5) The information required to be made available to organ procurement organizations pursuant to subsection (d) of Code Section 40–5–25 and for the purposes set forth in such Code section;

(6)(A) The information required to be made available regarding voter registration pursuant to Code Section 21–2–221 and for the purposes set forth in such Code section; and

(B) Information sufficient for use in verifying a registered voter's identity by the Secretary of State, the county election superintendent, or the county registrar, including name, address, date of birth, gender, driver identification number, photograph, and signature; and

(7) The lists required to be made available to boards of jury commissioners and the Administrative Office of the Courts pursuant to Code Section 15–12–40 regarding county residents who are the holders of drivers' licenses or personal identification cards issued pursuant to this chapter. Such lists shall identify each such person by name, address, date of birth, and gender, and, whenever racial and ethnic information is collected by the department for purposes of voter registration pursuant to Code Section 21–2–221, the department shall also provide such information. The department shall also provide the address, effective date, document issue date, and document expiration date and shall indicate whether the document is a driver's license or a personal identification card.

(g) The drivers' records and personal information disseminated by the department pursuant to this Code section may be used only by the authorized recipient and only for the authorized purpose. It shall be unlawful to disclose, distribute, or sell such records or information to an unauthorized recipient or for an unauthorized purpose. It shall be a violation of this Code section to make a misrepresentation or false statement in order to obtain access to or information from the department's records. Any person who knowingly and willfully violates the provisions of this Code section shall be guilty of a misdemeanor of a high and aggravated nature and, upon conviction thereof, shall be punished as provided in Code Section 17–10–4.

(h) The department shall maintain for four years a record of each release of a driver's operating record or personal information, including the name and address of the requesting party, the date of the release, and the provision of law authorizing the release. Such record of releases shall be reported to the affected driver upon written application by the driver, except that the department shall not report any information about the existence of a release made in connection with a criminal investigation which is ongoing and which involves, though not necessarily focuses upon, such driver. Upon receipt of an application from a driver for such record of releases, the department shall have three business days to determine whether an ongoing criminal investigation is involved, and such determination shall be in the discretion of the commissioner. Where a release is not reported to a driver because the underlying release involved an ongoing criminal investigation, the records concerning the underlying release shall be maintained for four years after the criminal investigation is closed and such records shall during such period after closure of the investigation be subject to disclosure upon application by the driver.

(i) The provisions of this Code section shall apply, where relevant, to the maintenance and disclosure of the department's records regarding state identification cards issued under Article 5 of this chapter.

(j) The commissioner is authorized to promulgate any rules, regulations, or policies as are necessary to carry out the provisions of this Code section, including the promulgation of regulations limiting the retention of conviction and withdrawal information on a driving record. Notwithstanding the foregoing, any regulation relating to the retention of conviction and withdrawal information on a driving record shall apply the same retention schedule to both commercial and noncommercial drivers. In accordance with paragraph (6) of subsection (a) of Code Section 50–25–4, reasonable fees shall be assessed for furnishing information from records or data bases pursuant to provisions of this Code section; provided, however, that the fee for furnishing an abstract of a driver's record shall not exceed $10.00.

(k)(1) The department, pursuant to rules and regulations promulgated by the commissioner, may periodically review all records maintained pursuant to this Code section and shall correct those records which contain known improper, false, fraudulent, or invalid information.

(2) Not later than July 31, 2006, the department shall destroy all records of fingerprints obtained on and after April 15, 1996, and prior to July 1, 2006, from applicants for drivers' licenses, identification cards, and identification cards for persons with disabilities issued by the department and shall compile and make available for public inspection a list of all persons or entities to whom the department provided such fingerprint records. Notwithstanding the provisions of this paragraph, fingerprint images electronically stored on existing drivers' licenses will be destroyed upon application for a renewal of the driver's license.

(*l*) In any case in which the release or transmittal of one or more driver's records is authorized under this Code section or any other provision of law, the commissioner may determine the method of release or transmittal of the record or records, including without limitation release or transmittal by mail or by means of the Internet or other electronic means.

Laws 1937, p. 322, art. 4, § 13; Laws 1939, p. 135, § 12; Laws 1975, p. 1008, § 1; Laws 1978, p. 920, § 1; Laws 1979, p. 142, § 1; Laws 1980, p. 917, §§ 1, 2; Laws 1985, p. 149, § 40; Laws 1985, p. 1182, § 1; Laws 1985, p. 1339, § 1; Laws 1986, p. 156, § 1; Laws 1986, p. 514, § 1; Laws 1988, p. 470, § 1; Laws 1988, p. 687, § 1; Laws 1989, p. 519, § 3; Laws 1990, p. 8, § 40; Laws 1990, p. 2048, § 4; Laws 1991, p. 1870, § 1; Laws 1992, p. 6, § 40; Laws 1995, p. 917, § 1; Laws 1996, p. 6, § 40; Laws 1996, p. 1061, § 1; Laws 1996, p. 1624, § 5; Laws 1997, p. 1446, § 2; Laws 1999, p. 809, § 3; Laws 2000, p. 249, § 2; Laws 2000, p. 429, § 3; Laws 2000, p. 951, § 5–2; Laws 2001, p. 294, § 2; Laws 2001, Ex. Sess., p. 318, § 1–2; Laws 2002, p. 415, § 40; Laws 2004, Act 582, § 2, eff. July 1, 2004; Laws 2005, Act 19, § 40, eff. April 7, 2005; Laws 2005, Act 68, § 17–2, eff. July 1, 2005; Laws 2005, Act 72, § 1, eff. May 2, 2005; Laws 2005, Act 355, § 1, eff. July 1, 2006; Laws 2006, Act 583, §§ 1, 2, eff. July 1, 2006; Laws 2006, Act 590, § 1, eff. July 1, 2006; Laws 2006, Act 880, § 2, eff. July 1, 2006; Laws 2008, Act 434, § 1, eff. Jan. 1, 2009; Laws 2008, Act 778, § 1, eff. July 1, 2008; Laws 2009, Act 86, § 2, eff. April 30, 2009; Laws 2009, Act 102, § 2–2, eff. July 1, 2009; Laws 2010, Act 633, § 1.1, eff. July 1, 2010.

Formerly Code 1933, § 68B–215.

Historical and Statutory Notes

The 2004 amendment by Act 582 added new subpar. (c)(1)(B.1).

The 2005 amendment by Act 19 was a provision contained in a correction bill.

The 2005 amendment by Act 68 rewrote subsec. (j); and added a new subsec. l. Prior to amendment, subsec. (j) had read:

"(j) The commissioner is authorized to promulgate any rules, regulations, or policies as are necessary to carry out the provisions of this Code section. The department and the Georgia Technology Authority are each authorized to charge reasonable fees to defray costs incurred in affording access to or disseminating information from records or data bases pursuant to provisions of this Code section; provided, however, that the fee for furnishing an abstract of a driver's record shall not exceed $ 10.00; and provided, further, that the fee for furnishing the limited information provided for purposes of insurance rating pursuant to division (c)(1)(B)(ii) of this Code section shall not exceed 20 percent of the fee for furnishing the abstract of a driver's record."

The 2005 amendment by Act 72, rewrote subpar. (c)(1)(B.1) which had read:

"(B.1) The department shall implement a pilot program of up to six months to determine the revenue feasibility of supplying limited rating information to agents, insurers, and insurance support organizations. The department shall report the results of such pilot program to the Office of Planning and Budget. If the Office of Planning and Budget determines that the pilot program is successful, then the department shall also furnish limited rating information to insurance support organizations for the same purposes as provided in division (c)(1)(B)(ii) of this Code section, pursuant to a contract with the Georgia Technology Authority, provided that all other necessary requirements of subsection (c) of this Code section have been met;"

The 2005 amendment by Act 355 designated the existing text of subsec. (k) as par. (1) and added par. (2).

Laws 2005, Act 355, § 6, provides:

"This Act shall become effective on July 1, 2006."

In 2005, the Code Commission, in subsec. (k), substituted "July 31, 2006" for "30 days after the effective date of this paragraph" and substituted "July 1, 2006," for "the effective date of this paragraph". See § 28–9–5.

The 2006 amendment by Act 583, in subsec. (c), par. (1), subpar. (A), added "; such instructions and consent shall be signed by the driver but shall not be required to be notarized"; and in subsec. (f), par. (4), added "and to the Georgia Bureau of Investigation for the purpose of providing a local fire or law enforcement department with the abstract through the Criminal Justice Information System".

The 2006 amendment by Act 590, in subsec. (c), par. (1), subpar. (D), deleted "provided, however, that notwithstanding the definition of personal information under Code Section 40–5–1, personal information furnished to the driver's licensing agency of another state shall be limited to name, address, driver identification number, and medical or disability information;" at the end of the subparagraph.

The 2006 amendment by Act 880 inserted "and the Administrative Office of the Courts" in subsec. (f), par. (7).

The 2008 amendment by Act 434, in subsec. (f), par. (6), designated existing paragraph as subpar. (A) and added subpar. (B).

The 2008 amendment by Act 778, in subsec. (a), par. (3), inserted a reference to § 40–5–20, inserted "or individual" following "licensee" throughout the paragraph, and inserted "or application for" following ", upon any application for".

The 2009 amendment by Act 86, in subsec. (f), par. (7), substituted "and gender, and," for "gender, driver's license or personal identification card number issued pursuant to the provisions of this chapter, and", substituted "the department shall also provide such information" for "by racial or ethnic group", and added the third sentence.

The 2009 amendment by Act 102 substituted "Department of Human Services" for "Department of Human Resources" throughout the section.

The 2010 amendment by Act 633, in subsec. (j), added "including the promulgation of regulations limiting the retention of conviction and withdrawal information on a driving record" to the first second and added the second sentence.

§ 40–5–3. Appointment of notaries public

The commissioner shall cause designated employees of the department to be appointed as notaries public, in accordance with Chapter 17 of Title 45, for the purpose of performing the notarial acts required by this chapter, free of charge to applicants.

Laws 1975, p. 1008, § 1; Laws 1990, p. 2048, § 4.

Formerly Code 1933, § 68B–207.

§ 40–5–4. Regulatory authority of board

(a) The commissioner is authorized to implement any and all provisions of this chapter by the promulgation of necessary rules and regulations. An express grant of authority to the commissioner in any Code section to promulgate regulations shall not be construed as excluding such authority in any other Code section.

(b) When duly promulgated and adopted, all regulations issued pursuant to this chapter shall have the force of law.

Laws 1937, p. 322, art. 4, § 10; Laws 1943, p. 196, § 5; Laws 1951, p. 598, § 7; Laws 1975, p. 1008, § 1; Laws 1990, p. 2048, § 4; Laws 2000, p. 951, § 5–3.

Formerly Code 1933, § 68B–501.

§ 40–5–4.1. Delay of compliance with provisions of federal Real ID Act

The Governor of the State of Georgia, or his or her designee, is authorized to delay compliance with certain provisions of the federal Real ID Act, H.R. 1268, P.L. 109–13[1], enacted by Congress in 2005, until it is expressly guaranteed by the Department of Homeland Security, through adequately defined safeguards, that implementation of the Real ID Act will not compromise the economic privacy or biological sanctity of any citizen or resident of the State of Georgia. This Code section shall not be interpreted as limiting the Governor's discretion or authority to delay compliance with certain provisions of the Real ID Act for any other reason.

Laws 2007, Act 11, § 2, eff. July 1, 2007.

1 9 USCA § 1778.

Historical and Statutory Notes

Laws 2007, Act 11, § 1, provides:

"The General Assembly of Georgia finds that the Real ID Act, H.R. 1268, P.L. 109–13, enacted by Congress in 2005, established standards that state–issued drivers' licenses and identification cards must meet by May 11, 2008, if the licenses or identification cards are to be accepted as valid identification by the federal government. After May 11, 2008, federal agencies are scheduled to accept only drivers' licenses or identification cards that meet Real ID standards. Noncompliant cards will not be accepted for federal purposes such as boarding a domestic flight, opening a bank account, or any other service or activity over which the federal government claims jurisdiction. Each state will also be required to share data from their drivers' licenses or identification cards data base with other states. The exact requirements of the Real ID Act have yet to be defined. The Department of Homeland Security was originally going to promulgate regulations by November, 2005. That date was changed to November, 2006. Currently, regulations are scheduled for January, 2007, but many parties feel this deadline may also pass without the regulations being issued.

"Because the Real ID Act was attached to a vital supplemental spending bill for defense and tsunami relief, there was no opportunity for a full examination of the consequences of the proposal. While everyone recognizes the need to make identifying documents as secure as is humanly possible, the one–size–fits–all approach required by the Real ID Act may actually increase the documents' vulnerability to counterfeiting. If criminals are able to invade one state's system, they may have access to all states' systems. On another front, a report from the National Conference of State Legislatures, the National Governors Association, and the American Association of Motor Vehicle Administrators suggests that the new requirements of the Real ID Act will cost states at least $11 billion over the first five years of the program. Despite this massive price tag, there has been no money appropriated to help states meet the law's demands.

"The Real ID Act gives the Department of Homeland Security the power to set federal standards and determine whether state drivers' licenses and other identification cards meet these standards. There is no provision in the Real ID Act that requires or even mentions information privacy or data security. The federal and state governments must ensure that the data needed to verify the identity of driver's license applicants is maintained securely and not used for other unrelated purposes. The Department of Homeland Security must include privacy protections for personal driver data as they promulgate regulations spelling out what states need to do to implement the federal law. Success of the Real ID Act depends on the Department of Homeland Security and the states collaborating to find a way of implementing its requirements in a fiscally responsible and risk adjusted manner. Therefore, the Georgia Department of Driver Services is directed to withhold any legislation designed to implement the Real ID Act in Georgia until such time as the Department of Homeland Security has enacted regulations that define the exact type of information that is to be required on a state driver's license. Furthermore, before the Real ID Act is implemented in Georgia, the Governor of Georgia is entitled to review the regulations promulgated by the Department of Homeland Security and determine if they adequately safeguard and restrict use of the information in order to protect the privacy rights of the citizens of Georgia.

"The citizens of Georgia also recognize the importance of ensuring that drivers' licenses are issued only to persons legally present in this state. Therefore, the use of secure and verifiable identification will be required in this state in order to obtain a driver's license. This requirement is in harmony with the intent of the Real ID Act to secure identification processes in this country. The Department of Driver Services is instructed to take the necessary steps to become a participant in the SAVE Program (Systematic Alien Verification for Entitlements). This program, administered by the United States Bureau of Citizenship and Immigration Services, is designed to verify the immigration status of noncitizens."

§ 40–5–5. Authority of Governor or his designees to negotiate reciprocal agreements

(a) The Governor is authorized and directed to negotiate and consummate, with the proper authorities of the several states of the United States, the District of Columbia, and the territories and possessions of the United States, valid and binding reciprocal agreements whereby residents of such states, the District of Columbia, and the territories and possessions of the United States operating motor vehicles properly licensed and registered in their respective jurisdictions may have the same or substantially the same privileges or exemptions in the operation of their motor vehicles in this state as residents of this state may have and enjoy in the operation in such other jurisdictions of their motor vehicles properly licensed and registered in this state. Notwithstanding any provision of law to the contrary, the Governor may likewise negotiate and consummate valid and binding reciprocal agreements with the proper authorities of said jurisdictions relating to the suspension, revocation, cancellation, and reinstatement of motor vehicle drivers' licenses. In the making of such agreements, due regard shall be had for the benefit and convenience of the motor vehicle owners and other citizens of this state. The Governor may adopt and promulgate such rules and regulations as shall be necessary to effectuate and administer the provisions of this Code section.

(b) The Governor or a commission appointed by him shall give proper publicity to the terms of every reciprocal agreement entered into by him pursuant to this chapter; and he is authorized and empowered to promulgate rules and regulations for observance and enforcement of the terms of such agreement, which rules and regulations shall have the force and effect of law.

Laws 1937–38, Ex. Sess., p. 617, §§ 1, 5; Laws 1941, p. 361, §§ 2, 5; Laws 1959, p. 25, § 1; Laws 1973, p. 559, § 1; Laws 1976, p. 198, § 1; Laws 1979, p. 1015, § 1; Laws 1985, p. 149, § 40; Laws 1990, p. 2048, § 4.

§ 40–5–6. Forms for gift of person's body to be furnished; notation on driver's license

(a) Whenever any person applies for or requests the issuance, reissuance, or renewal of any class of driver's license, the department shall furnish that person with a form, sufficient under Article 6 of Chapter 5 of Title 44, the "Georgia Revised Uniform Anatomical Gift Act," for the gift of all or part of the donor's body conditioned upon the donor's death. If any such person, legally authorized to execute such a gift, desires to execute a gift, the department shall provide that person with appropriate assistance and the presence of the legally required number of witnesses.

(b) A notation shall be affixed to or made a part of every driver's license issued in this state indicating whether or not the licensee has executed, under Article 6 of Chapter 5 of Title 44, the "Georgia Revised Uniform Anatomical Gift Act," a gift, by will or otherwise, of all or part of his body conditioned upon the donor's death.

Laws 1974, p. 1117, §§ 1, 2; Laws 1990, p. 2048, § 4; Laws 2008, Act 545, § 4, eff. July 1, 2008.

Formerly Code 1981, § 40–5–7.

§ 40–5–7. Repealed by Laws 2001, p. 208, § 10, eff. Dec. 31, 2002

Historical and Statutory Notes

In 2003, the Code Commission reserved this section. See § 28–9–5.

§ 40–5–8. Application for driving permit or identification card by male under 26 years of age constitutes consent to be registered with Selective Service System

(a) Any male United States citizen or immigrant who applies for any driver's license or identification card issued under this chapter, including without limitation any instruction permit, limited driving permit, provisional driver's license, or commercial driver's license, or for renewal thereof, and who is less than 26 years of age shall be registered in compliance with the requirements of Section 3 of the Military Selective Service Act, 50 App. U.S.C.A. Section 451, et seq., as amended.

(b) The signature of any applicant described in subsection (a) of this Code section submitted to the department in application for such license or identification card issuance or renewal shall serve as an indication that the applicant either has registered already with the United States Selective Service System or that he is authorizing the department to forward to the United States Selective Service System the necessary information for such registration. The department shall notify the applicant at the time of application that his signature constitutes consent to be registered with the United States Selective Service System if he is not already so registered. The department shall, as soon as practical following such application and in accordance with paragraph (1) of subsection (f) of Code Section 40–5–2, forward the necessary personal information of the applicant to the United States Selective Service System for purposes of registration therewith at such time as required by federal law.

Laws 2001, p. 294, § 3.

Historical and Statutory Notes

In 2001, the Code Commission redesignated § 40–5–7, which was enacted by Laws 2001, p. 294, § 3, as § 40–5–8. See § 28–9–5.

Article 2

Issuance, Expiration, and Renewal of Licenses

§ 40–5–20. Drivers must be licensed; prior licenses surrendered; local licenses forbidden

(a) No person, except those expressly exempted in this chapter, shall drive any motor vehicle upon a highway in this state unless such person has a valid driver's license under this chapter for the type or class of vehicle being driven. Any person who is a resident of this state for 30 days shall obtain a Georgia driver's license before operating a motor vehicle in this state. Any violation of this subsection shall be punished as provided in Code Section 40–5–121, except the violation of driving with an expired license, or a violation of Code Section 40–5–29 or if such person produces in court a valid driver's license issued by this state to such person, he or she shall not be guilty of such offenses. Any court having jurisdiction over traffic offenses in this state shall report to the department the name and other identifying information of any individual convicted of driving without a license.

(b) No person, except those expressly exempted in this chapter, shall steer or, while within the passenger compartment of such vehicle, exercise any degree of physical control of a vehicle being towed by a motor vehicle upon a highway in this state unless such person has a valid driver's license under this chapter for the type or class of vehicle being towed.

(c)(1) Except as provided in paragraph (2) of this subsection and in Code Section 40–5–32, no person shall receive a driver's license unless and until such person surrenders to the department all valid licenses in such person's possession issued to him or her by this or any other jurisdiction. All surrendered licenses issued by another jurisdiction shall be destroyed. The license information shall be forwarded to the previous jurisdiction. No person shall be permitted to have more than one valid driver's license at any time.

(2) Any noncitizen who is eligible for issuance of a driver's license pursuant to the requirements of this chapter may be issued a driver's license without surrendering any driver's license previously issued to him or her by any foreign jurisdiction. This exemption shall not apply to a person who is applying for a commercial driver's license or who is required to terminate any previously issued driver's license pursuant to federal law. The department shall make a notation on the driving record of any person who retains a foreign driver's license, and this information shall be made available to law enforcement officers and agencies on such person's driving record through the Georgia Crime Information Center.

(d) Any person licensed as a driver under this chapter may exercise the privilege thereby granted upon all streets and highways in this state and shall not be required to obtain any other license to exercise such privilege by any county, municipality, or local board or body having authority to adopt local police regulations.

Laws 1975, p. 1008, § 1; Laws 1990, p. 2048, § 4; Laws 1996, p. 1250, § 2; Laws 2002, p. 1045, § 1; Laws 2008, Act 778, § 2, eff. July 1, 2008; Laws 2008, Act 787, § 1, eff. Jan. 1, 2009; Laws 2009, Act 22, § 1, eff. July 1, 2009.

Formerly Code 1933, § 68B–201.

Historical and Statutory Notes

The 2008 amendment by Act 778, in subsec. (a), at the end of the subsection, added two sentences relating to penalties for violation of the subsection.

The 2008 amendment by Act 787 rewrote subsec. (c) which had read:

"(c) No person shall receive a driver's license unless and until such person surrenders to the department all valid licenses in such person's possession issued to him or her by this or any other jurisdiction, except as otherwise provided by Code Section 40–5–32. All surrendered licenses issued by another jurisdiction shall be destroyed. The license information shall be forwarded to the previous jurisdiction. No person shall be permitted to have more than one valid driver's license at any time."

The 2009 amendment by Act 22, in subsec. (a), inserted "shall be punished as provided in Code Section 40–5–121" and substituted "valid driver's license issued by this state to such person, he or she shall not be guilty of such offenses" for "license issued to such person and valid at the time of such person's arrest, shall be punished as provided in Code Section 40–5–121".

§ 40–5–21. Persons exempt from licensing requirement; exemptions for nonresidents

(a) Except as provided in Article 7 of this chapter, the "Uniform Commercial Driver's License Act," the following persons are exempt from licenses under this chapter:

(1) Any employee of the United States government while operating a motor vehicle owned by or leased to the United States government and which is being operated on official business, unless such employee is required by the United States government or any agency thereof to have a state driver's license;

(2) A nonresident who has in his or her immediate possession a valid driver's license issued to him or her in his or her home state or country; provided, however, that such person would otherwise satisfy all requirements to receive a Georgia driver's license and, if such nonresident driver's license is in a language other than English, the nonresident also has in his or her immediate possession a valid international driving permit which conforms to and has been issued in accordance with the provisions of the Convention on Road Traffic, 3 U.S.T. 3008, TIAS 2487, or any similar such treaty, international agreement, or reciprocal agreement between the United States and a foreign nation concerning driving privileges of nonresidents;

(3) A nonresident on active duty in the armed forces of the United States who has a valid license issued by his or her home state, and such nonresident's spouse or dependent son or daughter who has a valid license issued by such person's home state;

(4) Any person on active duty in the armed forces of the United States who has in his or her immediate possession a valid license issued in a foreign country by the armed forces of the United States, for a period of not more than 45 days from the date of his or her return to the United States;

(5) Any inmate or resident patient of a state, county, or municipally owned institution who drives a vehicle while on the grounds of such institution and while accompanied by and under the direct personal supervision of a qualified driving instructor or of some other person duly authorized in writing to so accompany and supervise such inmate or resident patient;

(6) Any person driving or operating a farm tractor or farm implement temporarily operated on a highway for the purpose of conducting farm business;

(7) Any inmate of a state, county, or municipal prison, correctional institution, or jail while operating a motor vehicle owned by or leased to the state, county, or municipality and being operated with the written approval of the warden or superintendent and in such manner and for such purpose as may be specified by the warden or superintendent, provided that such inmate, within the 60 day period prior to the grant of written authority, has passed the vision, written, and driving tests required for licensing a citizen to operate such motor vehicle. The department shall give such tests and issue a certificate, without charge therefor, to any inmate passing such tests;

(8) A member of the reserve components of the armed forces of the United States while operating a motor vehicle owned by or leased to the United States government and being operated in accordance with the duties of such member as a member of the reserve components of the armed forces;

(9) Any person seeking to obtain a driver's license while taking the driving examination for such license accompanied by a driver license examiner of the department or a certified examining agent of the department;

(10) Any migrant farm worker who works in this state less than 90 days in any calendar year and who possesses a valid driver's license issued by another state;

(11) Any resident who is 15 years of age or over while taking actual in–car training in a training vehicle other than a commercial motor vehicle under the direct personal supervision of a driving instructor when such driving instructor and training vehicle are licensed by the department in accordance with the provisions of Chapter 13 of Title 43, "The Driver Training School License Act." As used in the previous sentence, the term "commercial motor vehicle" shall have the meaning specified in Code Section 40–5–142. All vehicles utilized for the in–car training authorized under this paragraph shall be equipped with dual controlled brakes and shall be marked with signs in accordance with the rules of the department clearly identifying such vehicles as training cars belonging to a licensed driving school. A driving instructor shall test the eyesight of any unlicensed person who will be receiving actual in-car training prior to commencement of such training, and no unlicensed driver shall receive in–car training unless such person has at least the visual acuity and horizontal field of vision as is required for issuance of a driver's license in subsection (c) of Code Section 40–5–27; and

(12) Any person while operating a motorized cart:

(A) On any way publicly maintained for the use of motorized carts by the public and no other types of motor vehicles in accordance with a local ordinance adopted pursuant to subsection (a) of Code Section 40–6–331; or

(B) When crossing a street or highway used by other types of motor vehicles at a location designated for such crossing pursuant to subsection (d) of Code Section 40–6–331.

(b) Notwithstanding any contrary provisions of Code Section 40–5–20 or subsection (a) of this Code section, a nonresident of this state who is attending a school in this state shall be exempt from the driver's licensing requirements of this chapter if and only if:

(1) He or she is at least 16 years of age and has in his or her immediate possession a valid license issued to him or her in his or her home state or country; provided, however, that any restrictions which would apply to a Georgia driver's license as a matter of law would apply to the privilege afforded to the out-of-state license; and

(2) He or she is currently enrolled or was enrolled during the immediately preceding period of enrollment in a school in this state, has paid for the current period of enrollment or paid for the immediately preceding period of enrollment the tuition charged by the school to nonresidents of Georgia, and has in his or her possession proof of payment of such tuition for such current or immediately preceding period of enrollment.

Laws 1937, p. 322, art. 4, § 1; Laws 1939, p. 135, § 9; Laws 1975, p. 1008, § 1; Laws 1977, p. 307, § 1; Laws 1978, p. 931, § 1; Laws 1978, p. 2189, § 1; Laws 1983, p. 638, § 2; Laws 1989, p. 519, § 5; Laws 1990, p. 2048, § 4; Laws 1992, p. 2785, § 4; Laws 1994, p. 478, § 1; Laws 1996, p. 1624, § 6; Laws 1997, p. 760, § 9; Laws 2000, p. 951, § 5–4; Laws 2001, p. 184, §§ 2–1, 3–1; Laws 2004, Act 442, § 2, eff. April 22, 2004; Laws 2005, Act 68, § 17–3, eff. July 1, 2005; Laws 2008, Act 566, § .1, eff. July 1, 2008; Laws 2008, Act 787, § 2, eff. Jan. 1, 2009.

Formerly Code 1933, § 68B–202; Code 1981, § 40–5–21.1.

Historical and Statutory Notes

In 2001, the Code Commission, in the introductory portion of subsec. (a), deleted "Georgia" preceding "Uniform Commercial Driver's License Act". See § 28–9–5.

The 2004 amendment by Act 442 added subsec. (a), par. (12).

The 2005 amendment by Act 68 in subsec. (a)(11) substituted "rules of the department" for "Department of Motor Vehicle Safety rules" following "in accordance with" in the third sentence.

The 2008 amendment by Act 566, in subsec. (b), par. (2), inserted "or was enrolled during the immediately preceding period of enrollment", "or paid for the immediately preceding period of enrollment", and "or immediately preceding".

The 2008 amendment by Act 787 rewrote the par. (a)(2) which had read:

"(2) A nonresident who is at least 16 years of age and who has in his or her immediate possession a valid license issued to him or her in his or her home state or country; provided, however, that any restrictions which would apply to a Georgia driver's license as a matter of law would apply to the privilege afforded to the out–of–state license;"

§ 40–5–21.1. Temporary license, permit, or special identification card; driver's licenses issued to persons not lawfully present in the United States

(a) Notwithstanding any other provision of this title, an applicant who presents in person valid documentary evidence of:

(1) Admission to the United States in a valid, unexpired nonimmigrant status;

(2) A pending or approved application for asylum in the United States;

(3) Admission into the United States in refugee status;

(4) An approved application for temporary protected status in the United States;

(5) Approved deferred action status;

(6) Other federal documentation verified by the United States Department of Homeland Security to be valid documentary evidence of lawful presence in the United States under federal immigration law; or

(7) Verification of lawful presence as provided by Code Section 40–5–21.2 may be issued a temporary license, permit, or special identification card. Such temporary license, permit, or special identification card shall be valid only during the period of time of the applicant's authorized stay in the United States or five years, whichever occurs first.

(b) A driver's license or identification card issued by any state or territory which, on or after July 1, 2006, authorized such driver's license or identification card to be issued to persons not lawfully present in the United States may not be accepted as evidence of legal presence in the United States.

Laws 2005, Act 355, § 2, eff. July 1, 2006; Laws 2006, Act 453, § 40, eff. July 1, 2006; Laws 2008, Act 787, § 3, eff. Jan. 1, 2009; Laws 2010, Act 633, § 2, eff. July 1, 2010.

Historical and Statutory Notes

Laws 2005, Act 355, § 6, provides:

"This Act shall become effective on July 1, 2006."

The 2006 amendment by Act 453 was a provision contained in a correction bill.

Laws 2006, Act 453, § 55, provides in part:

"[b](3) Paragraph (6) of Section 40 of this Act shall become effective on July 1, 2006."

Former § 40–5–21.1 was repealed by Laws 1990, p. 2048, § 4, eff. January 1, 1991.

The 2008 amendment by Act 787 rewrote par. (a)(6), including designating the latter half of the paragraph as par. (a)(7). Prior to the amendment par. (a)(6) had read:

"(6) Other federal documentation verified by the United States Department of Homeland Security to be valid documentary evidence of lawful presence in the United States under federal immigration law

"may be issued a temporary license, permit or special identification card. Such temporary license, permit, or special identification card shall be valid only during the period of time of the applicant's authorized stay in the United States."

The 2010 amendment by Act 633, in subsec. (a), par. (7), substituted "five years" for "three years".

§ 40–5–21.2. SAVE Program; issuance of official document to noncitizen applicant; application and effective date of provisions

(a) As used in this Code section, the term:

(1) "Department" means the Georgia Department of Driver Services.

(2) "SAVE Program" means the Systematic Alien Verification for Entitlements (SAVE) Program established by the United States Bureau of Citizenship and Immigration Services.

(b) The department shall utilize the following procedures in this subsection before issuing an identification card, license, permit, or other official document to an applicant who is a noncitizen:

(1) The department shall attempt to confirm through the SAVE program that the applicant is lawfully present in the United States; and

(2) If the SAVE program does not provide sufficient information to the department to make a determination, the department shall be authorized to accept verbal or e-mail confirmation of the legal status of the applicant from the Department of Homeland Security.

(c) This Code section shall not apply to instances when a federal law mandates acceptance of a document.

(d) Subsection (b) of this Code section shall become effective upon the department's full implementation of the SAVE Program but not later than January 1, 2008.

Laws 2007, Act 11, § 3, eff. July 1, 2007; Laws 2008, Act 787, § 4, eff. Jan. 1, 2009; Laws 2010, Act 633, § 3, eff. July 1, 2010.

Historical and Statutory Notes

Laws 2007, Act 11, § 1, provides:

"The General Assembly of Georgia finds that the Real ID Act, H.R. 1268, P.L. 109-13, enacted by Congress in 2005, established standards that state-issued drivers' licenses and identification cards must meet by May 11, 2008, if the licenses or identification cards are to be accepted as valid identification by the federal government. After May 11, 2008, federal agencies are scheduled to accept only drivers' licenses or identification cards that meet Real ID standards. Noncompliant cards will not be accepted for federal purposes such as boarding a domestic flight, opening a bank account, or any other service or activity over which the federal government claims jurisdiction. Each state will also be required to share data from their drivers' licenses or identification cards data base with other states. The exact requirements of the Real ID Act have yet to be defined. The Department of Homeland Security was originally going to promulgate regulations by November, 2005. That date was changed to November, 2006. Currently, regulations are scheduled for January, 2007, but many parties feel this deadline may also pass without the regulations being issued.

"Because the Real ID Act was attached to a vital supplemental spending bill for defense and tsunami relief, there was no opportunity for a full examination of the consequences of the proposal. While everyone recognizes the need to make identifying documents as secure as is humanly possible, the one-size-fits-all approach required by the Real ID Act may actually increase the documents' vulnerability to counterfeiting. If criminals are able to invade one state's system, they may have access to all states' systems. On another front, a report from the National Conference of State Legislatures, the National Governors Association, and the American Association of Motor Vehicle Administrators suggests that the new requirements of the Real ID Act will cost states at least $11 billion over the first five years of the program. Despite this massive price tag, there has been no money appropriated to help states meet the law's demands.

"The Real ID Act gives the Department of Homeland Security the power to set federal standards and determine whether state drivers' licenses and other identification cards meet these standards. There is no provision in the Real ID Act that requires or even mentions information privacy or data security. The federal and state governments must ensure that the data needed to verify the identity of driver's license applicants is maintained securely and not used for other unrelated purposes. The Department of Homeland Security must include privacy protections for personal driver data as they promulgate regulations spelling out what states need to do to implement the federal law. Success of the Real ID Act depends on the Department of Homeland Security and the states collaborating to find a way of implementing its requirements in a fiscally responsible and risk adjusted manner. Therefore, the Georgia Department of Driver Services is directed to withhold any legislation designed to implement the Real ID Act in Georgia until such time as the Department of Homeland Security has enacted regulations that define the exact type of information that is to be required on a state driver's license. Furthermore, before the Real ID Act is implemented in Georgia, the Governor of Georgia is entitled to review the regulations promulgated by the Department of Homeland Security and determine if they adequately safeguard and restrict use of the information in order to protect the privacy rights of the citizens of Georgia.

"The citizens of Georgia also recognize the importance of ensuring that drivers' licenses are issued only to persons legally present in this state. Therefore, the use of secure and verifiable identification will be required in this state in order to obtain a driver's license. This requirement is in harmony with the intent of the Real ID Act to secure identification processes in this country. The Department of Driver Services is instructed to take the necessary steps to become a participant in the SAVE Program (Systematic Alien Verification for Entitlements). This program, administered by the United States Bureau of Citizenship and Immigration Services, is designed to verify the immigration status of noncitizens."

In 2007, the Code Commission, in subsec. (b), deleted a comma following "noncitizen". See § 28-9-5.

The 2008 amendment by Act 787 rewrote subsec. (b) which had read:

"(b) The department shall not issue an identification card, license, permit, or other official document to an applicant who is a noncitizen until the applicant has been confirmed through the SAVE Program to be lawfully present in the United States."

The 2010 amendment by Act 633, in subsec. (b), par. (2), inserted "not" after "SAVE program does".

§ 40-5-22. Persons not to be licensed

(a) Except as otherwise provided in this Code section, the department shall not issue any Class C driver's license to any person who is under 18 years of age or Class M driver's license to any person who is under the age of 17 years, except that the department may, under subsection (a) of Code Section 40-5-24, issue a Class P instruction permit permitting the operation of a noncommercial Class C vehicle to any person who is at least 15 years of age, and may, under subsection (b) of Code Section 40-5-24, issue a Class D driver's license permitting the operation of a noncommercial Class C vehicle to any person who is at least 17 years of age. On and after January 1, 1985, the department shall not issue any driver's license to any person under 18 years of age unless such person presents a certificate or other evidence acceptable to the department which indicates satisfactory completion of an alcohol and drug course as prescribed in subsection (b) of Code Section 20-2-142; provided, however, that a person under 18 years of age who becomes a resident of this state and who has in his or her immediate possession a valid license issued to him or her in another state or country shall not be required to take or complete the alcohol and drug course. The department shall not issue a driver's license or a Class P instruction permit for the operation of a Class A or B vehicle or any commercial driver's license to any person who is under the age of 18 years.

(a.1)(1) The department shall not issue an instruction permit or driver's license to a person who is younger than 18 years of age unless at the time such minor submits an application for an instruction permit or driver's license the applicant presents acceptable proof that he or she has received a high school diploma, a general educational development (GED) diploma, a special diploma, or a certificate of high school completion or has terminated his or her secondary education and is enrolled in a postsecondary school, is pursuing a general educational development (GED) diploma, or the records of the department indicate that said applicant:

(A) Is enrolled in and not under expulsion from a public or private school and has satisfied relevant attendance requirements as set forth in paragraph (2) of this subsection for a period of one academic year prior to application for an instruction permit or driver's license; or

(B) Is enrolled in a home education program that satisfies the reporting requirements of all state laws governing such program.

The department shall notify such minor of his or her ineligibility for an instruction permit or driver's license at the time of such application.

(2) The department shall forthwith notify by certified mail or statutory overnight delivery, return receipt requested, any minor issued an instruction permit or driver's license in accordance with this subsection other than a minor who has terminated his or her secondary education and is enrolled in a postsecondary school or who is pursuing a general educational development (GED) diploma that such minor's instruction permit or driver's license is suspended subject to review as provided for in this subsection if the department receives notice that indicates that such minor:

(A) Has dropped out of school without graduating and has remained out of school for ten consecutive school days;

(B) Has ten or more school days of unexcused absences in the current academic year or ten or more school days of unexcused absences in the previous academic year; or

(C) Has been found in violation by a hearing officer, panel, or tribunal of one of the following offenses, has received a change in placement for committing one of the following offenses, or has waived his or her right to a hearing and pleaded guilty to one of the following offenses:

(i) Threatening, striking, or causing bodily harm to a teacher or other school personnel;

(ii) Possession or sale of drugs or alcohol on school property or at a school sponsored event;

(iii) Possession or use of a weapon on school property or at a school sponsored event. For purposes of this division, the term weapon shall have the same meaning as in Code Section 16-11-127.1 but shall not include any part of an archeological or cultural exhibit brought to school in connection with a school project;

(iv) Any sexual offense prohibited under Chapter 6 of Title 16; or

(v) Causing substantial physical or visible bodily harm to or seriously disfiguring another person, including another student.

Notice given by certified mail or statutory overnight delivery with return receipt requested mailed to the person's last known address shall be prima-facie evidence that such person received the required notice. Such notice shall include instructions to the minor to return immediately the instruction permit or driver's license to the department and information summarizing the minor's right to request an exemption from the provisions of this subsection. The minor so notified may request in writing a hearing within ten business days from the date of receipt of notice. Within 30 days after receiving a written request for a hearing, the department shall hold a hearing as provided for in Chapter 13 of Title 50, the Georgia Administrative Procedure Act. After such hearing, the department shall sustain its order of suspension or rescind such order. The department shall be authorized to grant an exemption from the provisions of this subsection to a minor, upon such minor's petition, if there is clear and convincing evidence that the enforcement of the provisions of this subsection upon such minor would create an undue hardship upon the minor or the minor's family or if there is clear and convincing evidence that the enforcement of the provisions of this subsection would act as a detriment to the health or welfare of the minor. Appeal from such hearing shall be in accordance with said chapter. If no hearing is requested within the ten business days specified above, the right to a hearing shall have been waived and the instruction permit or driver's license of the minor shall remain suspended. The suspension provided for in this paragraph shall be for a period of one year or shall end upon the date of such minor's eighteenth birthday or, if the suspension was imposed pursuant to subparagraph (A) of this paragraph, upon receipt of satisfactory proof that the minor is pursuing or has received a general educational development (GED) diploma, a high school diploma, a special diploma, a certificate of high school completion, or has terminated his or her secondary education and is enrolled in a postsecondary school, whichever comes first.

(3) The State Board of Education and the commissioner of driver services are authorized to promulgate rules and regulations to implement the provisions of this subsection.

(4) The Technical College System of Georgia shall be responsible for compliance and noncompliance data for students pursuing a general educational development (GED) diploma.

(a.2)(1) On and after January 1, 2002, the department shall not issue any initial Class D driver's license or, in the case of a person who has never been issued a Class D driver's license by the department or the equivalent thereof by any other jurisdiction, any initial Class C driver's license unless such person:

(A) Is at least 16 years of age and has completed an approved driver education course in a licensed private or public driver training school and in addition a cumulative total of at least 40 hours of other supervised driving experience including at least six hours at night, all of which is verified in writing signed before a person authorized to administer oaths by a parent or guardian of the applicant or by the applicant if such person is at least 18 years of age; or

(B) Is at least 17 years of age and has completed a cumulative total of at least 40 hours of supervised driving experience including at least six hours at night, and the same is verified in writing signed before a person authorized to administer oaths by a parent or guardian of the applicant or by the applicant if such person is at least 18 years of age; provided, however, that a person 17 years of age or older who becomes a resident of this state, who meets all of the qualifications for issuance of a Class C license with the exception of the completion of an approved driver education training course and at least 40 hours of supervised driving experience as required by this subsection, and who has in his or her immediate possession a valid license equivalent to a Class C license issued to him or her in another state or country shall be entitled to receive a Class C license.

(2) The commissioner shall by rule or regulation establish standards for approval of any driver education course for purposes of subparagraph (A) of paragraph (1) of this subsection, provided that such course shall be designed to educate young drivers about safe driving practices and the traffic laws of this state and to train young drivers in the safe operation of motor vehicles.

(3) For purposes of supervised driving experience under paragraph (1) of this subsection, supervision shall be provided by a person at least 21 years of age who is licensed as a driver for a commercial or noncommercial Class C vehicle, who is fit and capable of exercising control over the vehicle, and who is occupying a seat beside the driver.

(4) For the purposes of this Code section, the term "approved driver education training course" shall include those driver education training courses approved by the Department of Driver Services.

(5) For purposes of this Code section, the term approved driver education training course shall include instruction given in the course of a home education program that satisfies the reporting requirements of all state laws governing such programs, provided that such instruction utilizes a curriculum approved by the department.

(b)(1) Notwithstanding the provisions of subsection (a) of this Code section, any person 14 years of age who has a parent or guardian who is medically incapable of being licensed to operate a motor vehicle due to visual impairment may apply for and, subject to the approval of the commissioner, may be issued a restricted noncommercial Class P instruction permit for the operation of a noncommercial Class C vehicle. Any person permitted pursuant to this subsection shall be accompanied by such visually impaired parent or guardian whenever operating a motor vehicle.

(2) Notwithstanding the provisions of subsection (a) of this Code section, any person 15 years of age or older who has a parent or guardian who is medically incapable of being licensed to operate a motor vehicle due to physical impairment and has been issued an identification card containing the international handicapped symbol pursuant to Article 8 of this chapter may apply for and, subject to the approval of the commissioner, may be issued a restricted noncommercial Class P instruction permit for the operation of a noncommercial Class C vehicle. Any person permitted pursuant to this paragraph shall be accompanied whenever operating a motor vehicle by such physically impaired parent or guardian or by a person at least 21 years of age who is licensed as a driver for a commercial or noncommercial Class C vehicle, who is fit and capable of exercising control over the vehicle, and who is occupying a seat beside the driver. The department shall require satisfactory proof that the physically impaired parent or guardian previously held a valid driver's license in the State of Georgia, another state, or the District of Columbia before issuing an instructional permit pursuant to this paragraph.

(c) The department shall not issue any driver's license to nor renew the driver's license of any person:

(1) Whose license has been suspended during such suspension, or whose license has been revoked, except as otherwise provided in this chapter;

(2) Whose license is currently under suspension or revocation in any other jurisdiction upon grounds which would authorize the suspension or revocation of a license under this chapter;

(3) Who is a habitual user of alcohol or any drug to a degree rendering him or her incapable of safely driving a motor vehicle;

(4) Who has previously been adjudged to be afflicted with or suffering from any mental disability or disease and who has not at the time of application been restored to competency by the methods provided by law;

(5) Who is required by this chapter to take an examination, unless such person shall have successfully passed such examination;

(6) Who the commissioner has good cause to believe would not, by reason of physical or mental disability, be able to operate a motor vehicle with safety upon the highway; or

(7) Whose license issued by any other jurisdiction is suspended or revoked by such other jurisdiction during the period such license is suspended or revoked by such other jurisdiction.

Laws 1937, p. 322, art. 4, § 2; Laws 1966, p. 12, § 1; Laws 1975, p. 1008, § 1; Laws 1983, p. 745, § 2; Laws 1984, p. 22, § 40; Laws 1986, p. 839, § 1; Laws 1989, p. 519, § 6; Laws 1990, p. 2048, § 4; Laws 1991, p. 321, § 1; Laws 1994, p. 97, § 40; Laws 1997, p. 760, § 10; Laws 2000, p. 951, § 5–5; Laws 2000, p. 1589, § 3; Laws 2001, p. 184, § 1–1; Laws 2004, Act 449, § 21B, eff. May 4, 2004; Laws 2005, Act 19, § 40, eff. April 7, 2005; Laws 2005, Act 68, § 17–4, eff. July 1, 2005; Laws 2005, Act 155, § 22, eff. July 1, 2005; Laws 2005, Act 401, § 3, eff. Jan. 1, 2007; Laws 2006, Act 453, § 40, eff. April 14, 2006; Laws 2006, Act 553, § 3, eff. Jan. 1, 2007; Laws 2006, Act 590, § 2, eff. July 1, 2006; Laws 2008, Act 434, § 2, eff. Jan. 1, 2009; Laws 2008, Act 472, § 6, eff. July 1, 2008; Laws 2008, Act 566, § 1, eff. July 1, 2008; Laws 2010, Act 394, § 1, eff. July 1, 2010.

Formerly Code 1933, § 68B–203.

Historical and Statutory Notes

The 2004 amendment by Act 449 rewrote subsec. (a.1) which had read:

"(a.1)(1) The department shall not issue an instruction permit or driver's license to a person who is younger than 18 years of age unless at the time such minor submits an application for an instruction permit or driver's license the applicant presents acceptable proof that he or she has received a high school diploma, a general educational development (GED) equivalency diploma, a special diploma, or a certificate of high school completion, has permission of his or her parent or guardian to withdraw from school, or has terminated his or her secondary education and is enrolled in a postsecondary school or the records of the department indicate that said applicant:

"(A) Is enrolled in and not under suspension from a public or private school and satisfies relevant attendance requirements as set forth in paragraph (2) of this subsection; or

"(B) Is enrolled in a home education program that satisfies the requirements of all state laws governing such courses.

"(2) The department shall forthwith notify by certified mail or statutory overnight delivery, return receipt requested, any minor issued an instruction permit or driver's license in accordance with this subsection other than a minor who has terminated his or her secondary education and is enrolled in a postsecondary school or who has permission of his or her parent or guardian to withdraw from school that such minor's instruction permit or driver's license is suspended subject to review as provided for in this subsection if the records of the department indicate that such minor:

"(A) Has dropped out of school without graduating and has remained out of school for ten consecutive school days;

"(B) Has more than ten consecutive school days of unexcused absences in any semester or combination of two consecutive quarters; or

"(C) Has been suspended from school for:

"(i) Threatening, striking, or causing bodily harm to a teacher or other school personnel;

"(ii) Possession or sale of drugs or alcohol on school property; or

"(iii) Possession or use of a weapon on school property. For purposes of this subparagraph, the term 'weapon' shall not include any part of an archeological or cultural exhibit brought to school in connection with a school project.

"Notice given by certified mail or statutory overnight delivery with return receipt requested mailed to the person's last known address shall be prima-facie evidence that such person received the required notice. The minor so notified may request in writing a hearing within ten business days from the date of receipt of notice. Within 30 days after receiving a written request for a hearing, the department shall hold a hearing as provided for in Chapter 13 of Title 50, the 'Georgia Administrative Procedure Act.' After such hearing, the department shall sustain its order of suspension or rescind such order. Appeal from such hearing shall be in accordance with said chapter. If no hearing is requested within the ten business days specified above, the right to a hearing shall have been waived and the instruction permit or driver's license of the minor shall remain suspended. The suspension provided for in this paragraph shall be for a period to end upon the date of such minor's eighteenth birthday, but such minor's instruction permit or driver's license shall be reinstated if the minor submits evidence satisfactory to the department that he or she has resumed regular studies as determined by the State Board of Education and qualifies for an instruction permit or driver's license under the provisions of this subsection, upon payment of a restoration fee of $50.00; provided, however, that any instruction permit or driver's license suspended pursuant to subparagraph (C) of this paragraph shall not be reinstated until 90 days after the effective date of the suspension of such permit or license.

"(3) The State Board of Education and the commissioner of motor vehicle safety are authorized to promulgate rules and regulations to implement the provisions of this subsection."

In 2004, the Code Commission, in subsec. (a.1), par. (2), subpar. (C), div. (iii), added quotations around weapon. See § 28–9–5.

The 2005 amendment by Act 19 was a provision contained in a correction bill.

The 2005 amendment by Act 68 in subsec. (a.1)(3) substituted "commissioner of driver services" for "commissioner of motor vehicle safety" prior to "are authorized".

The 2005 amendment by Act 155 rewrote subsec. (a.1) which had read:

"(a.1)(1) The department shall not issue an instruction permit or driver's license to a person who is younger than 18 years of age unless at the time such minor submits an application for an instruction permit or driver's license the applicant presents acceptable proof that he or she has received a high school diploma, a general educational development (GED) diploma, a special diploma, or a certificate of high school completion, or has terminated his or her secondary education and is enrolled in a postsecondary school or the records of the department indicate that said applicant:

"(A) Is enrolled in and not under suspension from a public or private school and has satisfied relevant attendance requirements as set forth in paragraph (2) of this subsection for a period of one academic year prior to application for an instruction permit or driver's license; or

"(B) Is enrolled in a home education program that satisfies the requirements of all state laws governing such courses.

"The department shall notify such minor of his or her ineligibility for an instruction permit or driver's license at the time of such application.

"(2) The department shall forthwith notify by certified mail or statutory overnight delivery, return receipt requested, any minor issued an instruction permit or driver's license in accordance with this subsection other than a minor who has terminated his or her secondary education and is enrolled in a postsecondary school that such minor's instruction permit or driver's license is suspended subject to review as provided for in this subsection if the department receives notice pursuant to Code Section 20–2–701 that indicates that such minor:

"(A) Has dropped out of school without graduating and has remained out of school for ten consecutive school days;

"(B) Has more than ten school days of unexcused absences in any semester or combination of two consecutive quarters; or

"(C) Has been suspended from school for:

"(i) Threatening, striking, or causing bodily harm to a teacher or other school personnel;

"(ii) Possession or sale of drugs or alcohol on school property;

"(iii) Possession or use of a weapon on school property. For purposes of this subparagraph, the term "weapon" shall be defined in accordance with Code Section 16–11–127.1 but shall not include any part of an archeological or cultural exhibit brought to school in connection with a school project;

"(iv) Any sexual offense prohibited under Chapter 6 of Title 16; or

"(v) Causing substantial physical or visible bodily harm to or seriously disfiguring another person, including another student.

"Notice given by certified mail or statutory overnight delivery with return receipt requested mailed to the person's last known address shall be prima-facie evidence that such person received the required notice. Such notice shall include instructions to the minor to return immediately the instruction permit or driver's license to the department and information summarizing the minor's right to request an exemption from the provisions of this subsection. The minor so notified may request in writing a hearing within ten business days from the date of receipt of notice. Within 30 days after receiving a written request for a hearing, the department shall hold a hearing as provided for in Chapter 13 of Title 50, the "Georgia Administrative Procedure Act." After such hearing, the department shall sustain its order of suspension or rescind such order. The department shall be authorized to grant an exemption from the provisions of this subsection to a minor, upon such minor's petition, if there is clear and convincing evidence that the enforcement of the provisions of this subsection upon such minor would create an undue hardship upon the minor or the minor's family or if there is clear and convincing evidence that the enforcement of the provisions of this subsection would act as a detriment to the health or welfare of the minor. Appeal from such hearing shall be in accordance with said chapter. If no hearing is requested within the ten business days specified above, the right to a hearing shall have been waived and the instruction permit or driver's license of the minor shall remain suspended. The suspension provided for in this paragraph shall be for a period of one year or shall end upon the date of such minor's eighteenth birthday, whichever comes first.

"(3) The State Board of Education and the commissioner of motor vehicle safety are authorized to promulgate rules and regulations to implement the provisions of this subsection."

The 2005 amendment by Act 401, in subsec. (a), substituted "Except as otherwise provided in this Code section, the" for "The" and twice substituted "17 years" for "16 years"; and in subsec. (a.2), par. (1), substituted "Is at least 16 years of age and has" for "Has" and substituted "40 hours" for "20 hours" in subpar. (A), and substituted "Is at least 17 years of age and has" for "Has" and added "; provided, however, that a person 17 years of age or older who becomes a resident of this state, who meets all of the qualifications for issuance of a Class C license with the exception of the completion of an approved driver's training course and at least 40 hours of supervised driving experience as required by this subsection, and who has in his or her immediate possession a valid license equivalent to a Class C license issued to him or her in another state or country shall be entitled to receive a Class C license" in subpar. (B).

Laws 2005, Act 401, § 3, which amended § 40–5–22, effective January 1, 2007 contingent on funding, was amended by Laws 2006, Act 553, § 3. See amendment note, post.

Laws 2005, Act 401, § 6, provides:

"The provisions of this Act shall not apply to or otherwise affect any valid license or instructional permit which has been issued to any person by this state and which is in effect on the effective date of this Act. On and after the effective date of this Act, no new license or instructional permit shall be issued except in compliance with the provisions of this Act."

Laws 2005, Act 401, § 7, provides:

"Section 2 of this Act shall become effective upon its approval by the Governor or upon its becoming law without such approval and shall apply to all traffic offenses committed on and after such date. The remaining sections of this Act shall become effective on January 1, 2007, subject to available funds."

Funds were appropriated at the 2006 session for the purposes of Laws 2005, Act 401, § 7.

The 2006 amendment by Act 453 was a provision contained in a correction bill.

The 2006 amendment to Laws 2005, Act 401 (p. 1461), § 3 (effective January 1, 2007 subject to available funds), by Act 553, in subsec. (a.1), substituted "development (GED) diploma" for "developmental (GED) diploma" in the introductory phrase of par. (1), substituted "educational development (GED)" for "education development (GED)" in the introductory phrase of par. (2), added "a high school diploma, a special diploma, a certificate of high school completion, or has terminated his or her secondary education and is enrolled in a postsecondary school," in the undesignated paragraph following div. (2)(C)(v), and substituted "educational development (GED) diploma" for "education development (GED) diploma" in par. (4); and in subsec. (a.2), substituted "driver education" for "driver's education" in subpar. (1)(B), and added new par. (4).

The 2006 amendment by Act 590, in div. (a.1)(2)(C), added "a high school diploma, a special diploma, a certificate of high school completion, or has terminated his or her secondary education and is enrolled in a postsecondary school," in the last sentence.

The 2008 amendment by Act 434, in par. (a.1)(2), deleted "pursuant to Code Section 20–2–701" following "if the department receives notice" in the introductory paragraph, substituted "division, the term 'weapon' shall have the same meaning as in Code Section 16–11–127.1" for "subparagraph, the term 'weapon' shall be defined in accordance with Code Section 16–11–127.1" in div. (C)(iii), and inserted ", if the suspension was imposed pursuant to subparagraph (A) of this paragraph," in the last sentence of the undesignated paragraph following div. (C)(v).

The 2008 amendment by Act 472, in subsec. (a.1), par. (4), substituted "Technical College System of Georgia" for "Department of Technical and Adult Education".

The 2008 amendment by Act 566 added par. (5) to subsec. (a.2).

The 2010 amendment by Act 394, in subsec. (b), designated existing subsec. as par. (1) and added par. (2).

§ 40–5–22.1. Suspension and delay of issuance of driver's license to children under age of sixteen; adjudications or convictions of driving under the influence or of specified drug offenses

Notwithstanding any other provision of law, if a child under 16 years of age is adjudicated delinquent of driving under the influence of alcohol or drugs or of possession of marijuana or a controlled substance in violation of Code Section 16–13–30 or of the unlawful possession of a dangerous drug in violation of Code Section 16–13–72 or convicted in any other court of such offenses, the court shall order that the privilege of such child to apply for and be issued a driver's license or learner's permit shall be suspended and delayed until such child is 17 years of age for a first conviction and until such child is 18 years of age for a second or subsequent such conviction. Upon reaching the required age, such license privilege shall be reinstated if the child submits proof of completion of a DUI Alcohol or Drug Use Risk Reduction Program or an assessment and intervention program approved by the juvenile court and pays a reinstatement fee to the Department of Driver Services. The reinstatement fee for a first such conviction shall be $210.00 or $200.00 if paid by mail. The reinstatement fee for a second such conviction shall be $310.00 or $300.00 if paid by mail. The reinstatement fee for a third or subsequent such conviction shall be $410.00 or $400.00 if paid by mail. The court shall notify the department of its order delaying the issuance of such child's license within 15 days of the date of such order. The department shall not issue a driver's license or learner's permit to any person contrary to a court order issued pursuant to this Code section.

Laws 1990, p. 1148, § 1; Laws 1992, p. 2785, § 5; Laws 2000, p. 951, § 5–6; Laws 2005, Act 68, § 17–5, eff. July 1, 2005; Laws 2009, Act 135, § 1, eff. July 1, 2009.

Historical and Statutory Notes

The 2005 amendment by Act 68 in the second sentence deleted "approved by the Department of Human Resources" following "Drug Use Risk Reduction Program" and substituted "Department of Driver Services" for "Department of Motor Vehicle Safety", and in the third and fourth sentences substituted "department" for "Department of Motor Vehicle Safety".

The 2009 amendment by Act 135 substituted "pays a reinstatement fee to the Department of Driver Services" for "pays a fee of $210.00 to the Department of Driver Services or $200.00 when such application is processed by mail"; and added "The reinstatement fee for a first such conviction shall be $210.00 or $200.00 if paid by mail. The reinstatement fee for a second such conviction shall be $310.00 or $300.00 if paid by mail. The reinstatement fee for a third or subsequent such conviction shall be $410.00 or $400.00 if paid by mail."

§ 40–5–23. Classes of licenses

(a) The department upon issuing a driver's license shall indicate thereon the type or general class of vehicles that the licensee may drive.

(b) Subject to this chapter, the commissioner shall establish by rules and regulations such qualifications, including but not limited to, training, experience, or educational prerequisites, as he or she believes are necessary for the safe operation of the various types, sizes, or combinations of vehicles and shall appropriately examine each applicant to determine his or her qualification according to the type or general class of license applied for.

(c) The noncommercial classes of motor vehicles for which operators may be licensed shall be as follows:

Class C—Any single vehicle with a gross vehicle weight rating not in excess of 26,000 pounds, any such vehicle towing a vehicle with a gross vehicle weight rating not in excess of 10,000 pounds, any such vehicle towing a vehicle with a gross vehicle weight rating in excess of 10,000 pounds, provided that the combination of vehicles has a gross combined vehicle weight rating not in excess of 26,000 pounds, and any self-propelled or towed vehicle that is equipped to serve as temporary living quarters for recreational, camping, or travel purposes and is used solely as a family or personal conveyance; except that any combination of vehicles with a gross vehicle weight rating not in excess of 26,000 pounds may be operated under such class of license if such combination of vehicles are controlled and operated by a farmer, used to transport agricultural products, livestock, farm machinery, or farm supplies to or from a farm, and are not used in the operations of a common or contract carrier;

Class D—Provisional license applicable to noncommercial Class C vehicles for which an applicant desires a driver's license but is not presently licensed to drive;

Class E—Any combination of vehicles with a gross vehicle weight rating of 26,001 pounds or more, provided the gross vehicle weight rating of the vehicle or vehicles being towed is in excess of 10,000 pounds, and all vehicles included within Class F and Class C;

Class F—Any single vehicle with a gross vehicle weight rating of 26,001 pounds or more, any such vehicle towing a vehicle with a gross vehicle weight rating not in excess of 10,000 pounds, and all vehicles included within Class C;

Class M—Motorcycles, motor driven cycles, and three-wheeled motorcycles;

Class P—Instruction permit applicable to all types of vehicles for which an applicant desires a driver's license but is not presently licensed to drive.

Any applicant for a Class E or Class F license must possess a valid Georgia driver's license for Class C vehicles. A license issued pursuant to this Code section shall not be a commercial driver's license.

Laws 1975, p. 1008, § 1; Laws 1984, p. 1329, § 1A; Laws 1989, p. 519, § 7; Laws 1990, p. 2048, § 4; Laws 1997, p. 760, § 11; Laws 2000, p. 951, § 5–7; Laws 2005, Act 164, § 1, eff. July 1, 2005; Laws 2006, Act 614, § 1, eff. July 1, 2006; Laws 2007, Act 18, § 40, eff. May 11, 2007; Laws 2010, Act 633, § 5, eff. July 1, 2010.

Formerly Code 1933, § 68B–204.

Historical and Statutory Notes

The 2005 amendment by Act 164, in subsec. (c), substituted "excess of 26,000 pounds," for "excess of 26,000 pounds or", and added ", any such vehicle towing a vehicle with a gross vehicle weight rating in excess of 10,000 pounds, provided that the combination of vehicles has a gross combined vehicle weight rating not in excess of 26,000 pounds," in the paragraph relating to Class C licenses.

Laws 2005, Act 164, § 3, provides:

"This Act shall become effective on July 1, 2005, and will apply to offenses occurring on or after that date."

The 2006 amendment by Act 614, in subsec. (c), added "except that any combination of vehicles with a gross vehicle weight rating not in excess of 26,000 pounds may be operated under such class of license if such combination of vehicles are controlled and operated by a farmer, used to transport agricultural products, livestock, farm machinery, or farm supplies to or from a farm, and are not used in the operations of a common or contract carrier;" to the paragraph designated "Class C—".

The 2007 amendment by Act 18 was a provision contained in a correction bill.

The 2010 amendment by Act 633, in subsec. (c), substituted "Class E" for "Class A" and substituted "Class F" for "Class B" in each place they appeared.

§ 40–5–24. Instruction permits, provisional licenses, and temporary licenses

(a)(1)(A) Any resident of this state who is at least 15 years of age may apply to the department for an instruction permit to operate a noncommercial Class C vehicle. The department shall, after the applicant has successfully passed all parts of the examination referred to in Code Section 40–5–27 other than the driving test, issue to the applicant an instruction permit which shall entitle the applicant, while having such permit in his or her immediate possession, to drive a Class C vehicle upon the public highways for a period of two years when accompanied by a person at least 21 years of age who is licensed as a driver for a commercial or noncommercial Class C vehicle, who is fit and capable of exercising control over the vehicle, and who is occupying a seat beside the driver.

(B) Notwithstanding the provisions of subparagraph (A) of this paragraph, any person holding a valid Class C instructional permit may drive a Class C motor vehicle when accompanied by a disabled parent or guardian who has been issued an identification card containing the international handicapped symbol pursuant to Article 8 of this chapter.

(2) A person who has been issued an instruction permit under this subsection and has never been issued a Class D driver's license under subsection (b) of this Code section will become eligible for a Class D driver's license under subsection (b) of this Code section only if such person is at least 17 years of age, has a valid instruction permit which is not under suspension, and, for a period of not less than 12 consecutive months prior to making application for a Class D driver's license, has not been convicted of a violation of Code Section 40–6–391, hit and run or leaving the scene of an accident in violation of Code Section 40–6–270, racing on highways or streets, using a motor vehicle in fleeing or attempting to elude an officer, reckless driving, or convicted of any offense for which four or more points are assessable under subsection (c) of Code Section 40–5–57; provided, however, that a person who is at least 16 years of age and meets all of the other qualifications of this paragraph except for age who has completed an approved driver education training course as provided in subsection (a.2) of Code Section 40–5–22 will be eligible for a Class D driver's license.

(3) This subsection does not apply to instruction permits for the operation of motorcycles.

(b)(1) Any resident of this state who is at least 17 years of age and who, for a period of at least 12 months, had a valid instruction permit issued under subsection (a) of this Code section may apply to the department for a Class D driver's license to operate a noncommercial Class C vehicle if such resident has otherwise complied with all prerequisites for the issuance of such Class D driver's license as provided in subsection (a) of this Code section, provided that a resident at least 17 years of age who has at any age surrendered to the department a valid instruction permit or driver's license issued by another state or the District of Columbia or who has submitted to the department proof, to the satisfaction of the department, of a valid instruction permit or driver's license issued by another state or the District of Columbia may apply his or her driving record under such previously issued permit or driver's license toward meeting the eligibility requirements for a Class D driver's license the same as if such previously issued permit or driver's license were an instruction permit issued under subsection (a) of this Code section; provided, however, that a person who is at least 16 years of age and meets all of the other qualifications of this paragraph except for age who has completed an approved driver education training course as provided in subsection (a.2) of Code Section 40–5–22 may apply for a Class D driver's license.

(2) The department shall, after all applicable requirements have been met, issue to the applicant a Class D driver's license which shall entitle the applicant, while having such license in his or her immediate possession, to drive a Class C vehicle upon the public highways of this state under the following conditions:

(A) Any Class D license holder shall not drive a Class C motor vehicle on the public roads, streets, or highways of this state between the hours of 12:00 Midnight and 6:00 A.M. eastern standard time or eastern daylight time, whichever is applicable; and

(B)(i) Any Class D license holder shall not drive a Class C motor vehicle upon the public roads, streets, or highways of this state when more than three other passengers in the vehicle who are not members of the driver's immediate family are less than 21 years of age.

(ii) During the six-month period immediately following issuance of such license, any Class D license holder shall not drive a Class C motor vehicle upon the public roads, streets, or highways of this state when any other passenger in the vehicle is not a member of the driver's immediate family.

(iii) Notwithstanding the provisions of division (i) of this subparagraph, during the second six-month period immediately following issuance of such license, any Class D license holder shall not drive a Class C motor vehicle upon the public roads, streets, or highways of this state when more than one other passenger in the vehicle who is not a member of the driver's immediate family is less than 21 years of age;

provided, however, that a Class D license holder shall not be charged with a violation of this paragraph alone but may be charged with violating this paragraph in addition to any other traffic offense.

(3) A person who has been issued a Class D driver's license under this subsection and has never been issued a Class C driver's license under this chapter will become eligible for a Class C driver's license under this chapter only if such person has a valid Class D driver's license which is not under suspension and, for a period of not less than 12 consecutive months prior to making application for a Class C driver's license, has not been convicted of a violation of Code Section 40–6–391, hit and run or leaving the scene of an accident in violation of Code Section 40–6–270, racing on highways or streets, using a motor vehicle in fleeing or attempting to elude an officer, reckless driving, or convicted of any offense for which four or more points are assessable under subsection (c) of Code Section 40–5–57 and is at least 18 years of age.

(c) Any resident of this state who is at least 17 years of age may apply to the department for a noncommercial Class M motorcycle instruction permit. The department shall, after the applicant has successfully passed all parts of the examination other than the driving test, issue to the applicant an instruction permit which shall entitle the applicant, while having such permit in his or her immediate possession, to drive a motorcycle or a motor driven cycle upon the public highways for a period of six months; provided, however, that a person who is at least 16 years of age and meets all of the other qualifications of this subsection except for age who has completed an approved driver education training course as provided in subsection (a.2) of Code Section 40–5–22 may apply for a Class M motorcycle instruction permit. A motorcycle instruction permit shall not be valid when carrying passengers, on a limited access highway, or at night.

(d) Any resident of this state who is at least 18 years of age may apply to the department for an instruction permit to operate noncommercial vehicles in Classes E and F. Such permits may be issued only to persons with valid commercial or noncommercial Class C licenses or persons who have passed all required tests for a commercial or noncommercial Class C license. The department shall, after the applicant has successfully passed all parts of the appropriate examination other than the skill and driving test, issue to the applicant an instruction permit which shall entitle the applicant, while having the permit in his or her immediate possession, to operate a vehicle of the appropriate noncommercial class upon the public highways for a period of 12 months when accompanied by a licensed driver, qualified in the vehicle being operated, who is fit and capable of exercising control over the vehicle, and who is occupying a seat beside the driver as an instructor. Prior to being issued a driver's license for Classes E and F, the applicant shall pass a knowledge and skill test for driving a Class E or F vehicle as provided by the commissioner.

(e) The department shall issue a temporary driver's permit to an applicant for a driver's license permitting him or her to operate a specified type or class of motor vehicle while the department is completing its investigation and determination of all facts relative to such applicant's eligibility to receive a driver's license. Such permit must be in his or her immediate possession while operating a motor vehicle, and it shall be invalid when the applicant's license has been issued or for good cause has been refused. Such permit shall be valid for no more than 45 days. When a license has been refused, the permit shall be returned to the department within ten days of receipt of written notice of refusal.

(f) For the purposes of this Code section, the term "approved driver education training course" shall include those driver education training courses approved by the Department of Driver Services.

Laws 1937, p. 322, art. 4, § 3; Laws 1943, p. 196, § 5; Laws 1951, p. 598, § 2; Laws 1957, p. 103, § 3; Laws 1958, p. 268, § 1; Laws 1959, p. 318, § 1; Laws 1975, p. 1008, § 1; Laws 1985, p. 149, § 40; Laws 1989, p. 519, § 8; Laws 1990, p. 1241, § 1; Laws 1990, p. 2048, § 4; Laws 1994, p. 514, § 2; Laws 1997, p. 760, § 12; Laws 1998, p. 3, § 1; Laws 2001, p. 184, § 1–2; Laws 2005, Act 401, § 4, eff. Jan. 1, 2007; Laws 2006, Act 553, § 3, eff. Jan. 1, 2007; Laws 2010, Act 394, § 2, eff. July 1, 2010; Laws 2010, Act 633, § 6, eff. July 1, 2010.

Formerly Code 1933, § 68B–205.

Historical and Statutory Notes

In 2001, the Code Commission, in subpar. (b)(2)(A), substituted "; and" for a period at the end; and in div. (b)(2)(B)(i), substituted a period for "; and" at the end. See § 28–9–5.

The 2005 amendment by Act 401, in subsec. (a), par. (2), substituted "17 years" for "16 years" and added "; provided, however, that a person who is at least 16 years of age and meets all of the other qualifications of this paragraph except for age who has completed an approved driver education training course as provided in subsection (a.2) of Code Section 40–5–22 will be eligible for a Class D driver's license"; in subsec. (b), twice substituted "17 years" for "16 years" and added "; provided, however, that a person who is at least 16 years of age and meets all of the other qualifications of this paragraph except for age who has completed an approved driver education training course as provided in subsection (a.2) of Code Section 40–5–22 will be eligible for a Class D driver's license" in par. (1), and added new div. (iii) in subpar. (2)(B); in subsec. (c), added "; provided, however, that a person who is at least 16 years of age and meets all of the other qualifications of this paragraph except for age who has completed an approved driver education training course as provided in subsection (a.2) of Code Section 40–5–22 may apply for a Class M motorcycle instruction permit".

Laws 2005, Act 401, § 4, which amended § 40–5–24, effective January 1, 2007 contingent on funding, was amended by Laws 2006, Act 553, § 3. See amendment note, post.

Laws 2005, Act 401, § 6, provides:

"The provisions of this Act shall not apply to or otherwise affect any valid license or instructional permit which has been issued to any person by this state and which is in effect on the effective date of this Act. On and after the effective date of this Act, no new license or instructional permit shall be issued except in compliance with the provisions of this Act."

Laws 2005, Act 401, § 7, provides:

"Section 2 of this Act shall become effective upon its approval by the Governor or upon its becoming law without such approval and shall apply to all traffic offenses committed on and after such date. The remaining sections of this Act shall become effective on January 1, 2007, subject to available funds."

Funds were appropriated at the 2006 session.

The 2006 amendment to Laws 2005, Act 401 (p. 1461), § 4 (effective January 1, 2007), by Act 533 added subsec. (f).

The 2010 amendment by Act 394, in subsec. (a), designated existing par. (1) as subpar. (A) and added subpar. (B).

The 2010 amendment by Act 633, in subsec. (d), substituted "Classes E and F" for "Classes A and B" in the first and fourth sentences.

§ 40–5–25. Application for license or instruction permit; disclosure of organ donor information; voluntary contributions for preventing blindness

(a) Every application for an instruction permit or for a driver's license shall be made upon a form furnished by the department. Every application shall be accompanied by the proper license fee. The fees shall be as established by the Board of Driver Services, not to exceed:

(1)	For instruction permits for Classes C, E, F, and M driver's licenses and for Class D drivers' licenses	$ 10.00
(2)	For five-year Classes C, E, F, and M noncommercial drivers' licenses	20.00
(2.1)	For eight-year Classes C, E, F, and M noncommercial drivers' licenses	32.00
(3)	For Classes A, B, C, and M commercial drivers' licenses	20.00
(4)	For application for Classes A, B, C, and M commercial drivers' licenses or a Class P commercial driver's instruction permit	35.00
(5)	For Class P commercial drivers' instruction permits for Classes A, B, C, and M commercial drivers' licenses	10.00
(6)	For Classes A, B, C, and M commercial drivers' licenses, initial issuance requiring a road test	70.00
(7)	For Classes A, B, C, and M commercial drivers' licenses, initial issuance not requiring a road test	20.00
(8)	For renewal of Classes A, B, C, and M commercial drivers' licenses	20.00
(8.1)	For renewal of five-year Classes C, E, F, and M noncommercial drivers' licenses	20.00
(8.2)	For renewal of eight-year Classes C, E, F, and M noncommercial drivers' licenses	32.00
(9)	Initial issuance of Classes A, B, C, and M commercial drivers' licenses and Class P commercial drivers' instruction permits shall include all endorsement fees within the license fee. Each endorsement added after initial licensing	5.00

The commissioner may by rule provide incentive discounts in otherwise applicable fees reflecting cost savings to the department where a license is renewed by means other than personal appearance. The discount for renewal of a Class C or Class M license and any other discounts shall be as determined by the commissioner. Except as provided in Code Section 40–5–36, relating to veterans' licenses, and Code Section 40–5–149, relating to application fees for public school bus drivers, there shall be no exceptions to the fee requirements for a commercial driver's license or a commercial driver's license permit. Notwithstanding any other provision of this Code section, there shall be no fee whatsoever for replacement of any driver's license solely due to a change of the licensee's name or address, provided that such replacement license shall be valid only for the remaining period of such original license; and provided, further, that only one such free replacement license may be obtained within the period for which the license was originally issued. Any application for the replacement of a lost license pursuant to Code Section 40–5–31 or due to a change in the licensee's name or address submitted within 150 days of the expiration of said license shall be treated as an application for renewal subject to the applicable license fees as set forth in this subsection. The maximum period for which any driver's license shall be issued is eight years.

(b)(1) Each person applying for a Class P commercial or noncommercial instruction permit for a Class A, B, C, E, F, or M driver's license shall pay the applicable license fee prior to attempting the knowledge test for the instruction permit sought. If said person fails to achieve a passing score on the knowledge test, the license fee paid shall be considered a testing fee and retained by the department. Any person failing to achieve a passing score on the knowledge test for an instructional permit shall pay the applicable license fee on each subsequent attempt until successful, at which time said fee shall be his or her license fee.

(2) Each person applying for a Class A, B, or C commercial driver's license shall pay the applicable license fee at the time that he or she schedules his or her appointment for said skills test. If said person fails to appear for his or her scheduled skills test appointment or fails to achieve a passing score on the skills test, the license fee paid shall be considered a testing fee and retained by the department. The person shall pay the applicable license fee on each subsequent attempt until successful, at which time said fee shall be his or her license fee. All fees retained by the department pursuant to this Code section shall be remitted to the general fund.

(c) Every such application shall state the full legal name, date of birth, sex, and residence address of the applicant; shall briefly describe the applicant; shall state whether the applicant has theretofore been licensed as a driver and, if so, when and by what state or country, and whether any such license has ever been suspended, revoked, or refused, and, if so, the date of and reason for such suspension, revocation, or refusal; and shall state such other information as the commissioner may require to determine the applicant's identity, competence, and eligibility. The application shall include any other information as required by paragraph (1) of subsection (a.1) of Code Section 19–11–9.1. The department shall not issue a license until a complete examination of the applicant's record has been completed. The commissioner may issue such rules and regulations as shall be necessary for the orderly processing of license applications.

(d)(1) The General Assembly finds that it is in the best interest of the state to encourage improved public education and awareness regarding anatomical gifts of human organs and tissues and to address the ever increasing need for donations of anatomical gifts for the benefit of the citizens of Georgia.

(2) The department shall make available to those federally designated organ procurement organizations the name, license number, date of birth, and most recent address of any person who obtains an organ donor driver's license. Information so obtained by such organizations shall be used for the purpose of establishing a state-wide organ donor registry accessible to organ tissue and eye banks authorized to function as such in this state and shall not be further disseminated.

(e)(1) The General Assembly finds that it is in the best interests of the state to encourage improved public education and awareness regarding blindness and to address the need for blindness prevention screenings and treatments for the benefit of the citizens of Georgia.

(2) Each application form for issuance, reissuance, or renewal of a driver's license under subsection (a) of this Code section shall include language permitting the applicant to make a voluntary contribution of $ 1.00 to be used for purposes of preventing blindness and preserving the sight of residents of this state. Any such voluntary contribution shall be made at the discretion of the applicant at the time of application in addition to payment of the license fee required under this Code section.

(3) Voluntary contributions made pursuant to this subsection shall be transmitted to the Department of Community Health for use thereby in providing the blindness education, screening, and treatment program provided by Code Section 31–1–23.

(4) This subsection shall become effective on January 1, 2000.

Laws 1937, p. 322, art. 4, § 5; Laws 1943, p. 196, § 5; Laws 1947, p. 294, § 1; Laws 1951, p. 157, § 7; Laws 1955, p. 662, § 1; Laws 1955, Ex. Sess., p. 35, § 1; Laws 1961, p. 136, § 2; Laws 1961, p. 433, § 1; Laws 1964, p. 171, § 1; Laws 1975, p. 1008, § 1; Laws 1983, p. 819, § 1; Laws 1989, p. 519, § 9; Laws 1990, p. 8, § 40; Laws 1990, p. 2048, § 4; Laws 1992, p. 6, § 40; Laws 1992, p. 779, § 18; Laws 1993, p. 615, § 1; Laws 1994, p. 1390, § 1; Laws 1994, p. 1876, § 1; Laws 1996, p. 228, § 1; Laws 1997, p. 760, § 13; Laws 1999, p. 537, § 2; Laws 2000, p. 951, §§ 5–8, 5–9; Laws 2002, p. 1045, § 3; Laws 2003, Act 175, § 9, eff. July 1, 2003; Laws 2005, Act 68, § 17–6, eff. July 1, 2005; Laws 2006, Act 453, § 40, eff. April 14, 2006; Laws 2008, Act 434, § 3, eff. Jan. 1, 2009; Laws 2009, Act 102, § 1–4, eff. July 1, 2009; Laws 2010, Act 360, § 1–79, eff. May 12, 2010; Laws 2010, Act 633, § 7, eff. July 1, 2010.

Formerly Code 1933, § 68B–206.

Historical and Statutory Notes

The 2003 amendment by Act 175, in subsec. (c), inserted "The application shall include any other information as required by paragraph (1) of subsection (a.1) of Code Section 19–11–9.1."

The 2005 amendment by Act 68 rewrote the section, which had read:

"(a) Every application for an instruction permit or for a driver's license shall be made upon a form furnished by the department. Every application shall be accompanied by the proper license fee. The fees shall be as established by the commissioner, not to exceed:

(1) For instruction permits for Classes A, B, C, and M drivers' licenses and for Class D drivers' licenses	$ 10.00
(2) For Classes C and M drivers' licenses	15.00
(3) For Classes A and B drivers' licenses	15.00
(4) For application for Classes A, B, C, and M commercial drivers' licenses or a Class P commercial driver's instruction permit ...	35.00
(5) For Class P commercial drivers' instruction permits for Classes A, B, C, and M commercial drivers' licenses	10.00
(6) For Classes A, B, C, and M commercial drivers' licenses, initial issuance requiring a road test	65.00
(7) For Classes A, B, C, and M commercial drivers' licenses, initial issuance not requiring a road test	15.00
(8) For renewal of Classes A, B, C, and M commercial drivers' licenses.........	15.00
(9) Initial issuance of Classes A, B, C, and M commercial drivers' licenses and Class P commercial drivers' instruction permits shall include all endorsement fees within the license fee. Each endorsement added after initial licensing...............	5.00

"Except as provided in Code Section 40–5–36, relating to veterans' licenses, and Code Section 40–5–149, relating to application fees for public school bus drivers, there shall be no exceptions to the fee requirements for a commercial driver's license or a commercial driver's license permit. Notwithstanding any other provision of this Code section, there shall be no fee whatsoever for replacement of any driver's license solely due to a change of the licensee's name or address, provided that such replacement license shall be valid only for the remaining period of such original license; and provided, further, that only one such free replacement license may be obtained within any four-year period for which the license was originally issued.

"(b) Notwithstanding the provisions of subsection (a) of this Code section, any Class 1 or 2 license issued prior to April 3, 1989, shall remain valid until its expiration unless otherwise lost, destroyed, suspended, or revoked prior to its expiration. A Class 3, 4, or 5 license shall remain valid unless lost, destroyed, suspended, revoked, or canceled, until its expiration or its earlier replacement under Article 7 of this chapter, the 'Uniform Commercial Driver's License Act.'

"(c) Every such application shall state the full name, date of birth, sex, and residence address of the applicant; shall briefly describe the applicant; and shall state whether the applicant has theretofore been licensed as a driver and, if so, when and by what state or country, and whether any such license has ever been suspended, revoked, or refused, and, if so, the date of and reason for such suspension, revocation, or refusal; and shall state such other information as the commissioner may require to determine the applicant's identity, competence, and eligibility. The application shall include any other information as required by paragraph (1) of subsection (a.1) of Code Section 19–11–9.1. The department shall not issue a license until a complete examination of the applicant's record has been completed. The commissioner may issue such rules and regulations as shall be necessary for the orderly processing of license applications.

"(d)(1) The General Assembly finds that it is in the best interest of the state to encourage improved public education and awareness regarding anatomical gifts of human organs and tissues and to address the ever increasing need for donations of anatomical gifts for the benefit of the citizens of Georgia.

"(2) Notwithstanding the provisions of paragraph (2) or (3) of subsection (a) of this Code section, each applicant for the issuance, reissuance, or renewal of a Class C, M, A, or B driver's license under paragraph (2) or (3) of subsection (a) of this Code section shall accompany such application with a license fee as established by the commissioner, not to exceed $ 8.00, if such applicant executes an anatomical gift pursuant to Code Section 40–5–6.

"(3) The department shall make available to those federally designated organ procurement organizations the name, license number, date of birth, and most recent address of any person who obtains a driver's license with the reduced fee provided for in paragraph (2) of this subsection. Information so obtained by such organizations shall be used for the purpose of establishing a state-wide organ donor registry accessible to organ tissue and eye banks authorized to function as such in this state and shall not be further disseminated.

"(e)(1) The General Assembly finds that it is in the best interests of the state to encourage improved public education and awareness regarding blindness and to address the need for blindness prevention screenings and treatments for the benefit of the citizens of Georgia.

"(2) Each application form for issuance, reissuance, or renewal of a driver's license under subsection (a) of this Code section shall include language permitting the applicant to make a voluntary contribution of $ 1.00 to be used for purposes of preventing blindness and preserving the sight of residents of this state. Any such voluntary contribution shall be made at the discretion of the applicant at the time of application in addition to payment of the license fee required under this Code section.

"(3) Voluntary contributions made pursuant to this subsection shall be transmitted to the Department of Human Resources for use thereby in providing the blindness education, screening, and treatment program provided by Code Section 31–1–23.

"(4) This subsection shall become effective on January 1, 2000."

The 2006 amendment by Act 453 was a provision contained in a correction bill.

The 2008 amendment by Act 434 added subsec. (b) which had formerly been reserved.

The 2009 amendment by Act 102 substituted "Department of Community Health" for "Department of Human Resources" throughout the section.

The 2010 amendment by Act 360, in subsec. (a), in the introductory paragraph, substituted "Board of Driver Services" for "commissioner"; in par. (2.1), substituted "eight-year" for "ten-year" and "32.00" for "35.00"; in par. (8.2), substituted "eight-year" for "ten-year" and "32.00" for "35.00"; and in the final undesignated paragraph, deleted "shall be $5.00" following "Class C or Class M license" in the second sentence, and added the last sentence "The maximum period for which any driver's license shall be issued is eight years."

The 2010 amendment by Act 633, in subsec. (a), pars. (1), (2), (2.1), (8.1) and (8.2), deleted "A, B," and inserted "E, F," after "C"; in pars. (2.1) and (8.2), substituted "eight-year" for "ten-year"; in subsec. (b), par. (1), inserted "E, F," after "C," and in par. (2), substituted "A, B, or C" for "A or B".

§ 40–5–26. Application of minors; distinctive licenses for persons under 21 years of age

(a)(1) The application of any person under the age of 18 years for an instruction permit or driver's license shall be:

(A) Signed and verified by the father, mother, or guardian of the applicant before a person authorized to administer oaths or, in the event there is no parent or guardian, by another responsible adult; or

(B) Signed and verified by a licensed driver training instructor before a person authorized to administer oaths when such instructor is acting as an agent for such purposes on behalf of the father, mother, or guardian of the applicant and such agency is evidenced by permission of such parent or guardian which has been granted in writing and signed and verified by such parent or guardian before a person authorized to administer oaths and on such form as shall be prescribed by rule or regulation of the department.

(2)(A) A person who signed and verified a minor's successful application for an instruction permit or driver's license may subsequently during such minority request revocation of the minor's instruction permit or driver's license by written notice to the department on such form as specified thereby, signed and verified before a person authorized to administer oaths. If the request for revocation is submitted by a licensed driver training instructor acting as an agent on behalf of the father, mother, or guardian of the applicant, such agency must be evidenced by permission for the revocation of such parent or guardian which has been granted in writing and signed and verified by such parent or guardian before a person authorized to administer oaths. Upon receipt of such request and payment of a fee in an amount equivalent to that which was required for issuance of the instruction permit or driver's license, and after a mandatory three business day waiting period, during which the request for revocation may be withdrawn but the fee shall not be returned, the department shall revoke the minor's instruction permit or driver's license.

(B) A minor whose instruction permit or driver's license has been revoked under this paragraph shall not be eligible for issuance of another instruction permit or driver's license until he or she reaches 18 years of age, unless consent for issuance of an instruction permit or driver's license has been granted as provided by subparagraphs (A) and (B) of paragraph (1) of this subsection upon application of the minor made not sooner than three months after the effective date of revocation.

(C) The provisions of Code Section 40–5–62 shall not apply to a person whose instruction permit or driver's license has been revoked under this paragraph.

(D) A revocation of a minor's instruction permit or driver's license under this paragraph shall not be deemed a revocation for purposes of any increase in insurance rates or cancellation of any policy of motor vehicle insurance for which the minor is not the sole named insured, but such a policy may be amended so as to remove such minor from the list of named insureds under such policy.

(b) The department shall, by rule and regulation, provide that all licenses issued to applicants under 21 years of age shall be so designed as to be readily distinguishable from all other licenses issued to other applicants. After having attained 21 years of age, the holder of any such distinctive license may obtain a new license which shall not be distinctive. Such new license shall be obtained in the same manner and under the same conditions and limitations as are provided in Code Section 40–5–32, relating to renewals of licenses.

Laws 1937, p. 322, art. 4, § 3; Laws 1951, p. 597, § 2; Laws 1953, Nov.-Dec. Sess., p. 339, §§ 1–3; Laws 1957, p. 103, § 3; Laws 1975, p. 1008, § 1; Laws 1976, p. 1421, § 1; Laws 1982, p. 1862, § 1; Laws 1983, p. 819, § 2; Laws 1984, p. 1070, § 1; Laws 1985, p. 758, § 1; Laws 1990, p. 2048, § 4; Laws 2004, Act 582, § 3, eff. July 1, 2004; Laws 2005, Act 401, § 5, eff. Jan. 1, 2007.

Formerly Code 1933, § 68B–207.

Historical and Statutory Notes

The 2004 amendment by Act 582 rewrote subsec. (a) which had read:

"(a) The application of any person under the age of 18 years for an instruction permit or driver's license shall be signed and verified by the father, mother, or guardian of the applicant before a person authorized to administer oaths or, in the event there is no parent or guardian, by another responsible adult."

The 2005 amendment by Act 401, in subsec. (a), designated existing introductory paragraph as par. (1), designated existing pars. (1) and (2) as subpars. (1)(A) and (1)(B) respectively, and added new par. (2).

Laws 2005, Act 401, § 6, provides:

"The provisions of this Act shall not apply to or otherwise affect any valid license or instructional permit which has been issued to any person by this state and which is in effect on the effective date of this Act. On and after the effective date of this Act, no new license or instructional permit shall be issued except in compliance with the provisions of this Act."

Laws 2005, Act 401, § 7, provides:

"Section 2 of this Act shall become effective upon its approval by the Governor or upon its becoming law without such approval and shall apply to all traffic offenses committed on and after such date. The remaining sections of this Act shall become effective on January 1, 2007, subject to available funds."

Funds were appropriated at the 2006 session for the purposes of Laws 2005, Act 401, § 7.

§ 40–5–27. Examination of applicants

(a) The department shall examine every applicant for a driver's license, except as otherwise provided by subsection (d) of this Code section. Such examination shall include a test of the applicant's eyesight, his or her ability to understand official traffic–control devices, and his or her knowledge of safe driving practices and the traffic laws of this state and shall also include a comprehensive on–the–road driving test during which the applicant shall be required to fully demonstrate his or her ability to exercise ordinary and reasonable control in the operation of a motor vehicle of the type or general class of vehicles he or she desires a license to drive; provided, however, that the on–the–road driving test requirement shall not apply to any applicant for a Class C driver's license who holds a Class D driver's license issued on or after January 1, 2002. An applicant 18 years of age and older with a valid and current license, or a license that has been expired for less than two years, issued by another state of the United States or the District of Columbia who surrenders his or her previous license to obtain a Georgia license shall be exempt from taking such tests. The examination may also include such further physical and mental examination as the department finds necessary to determine the applicant's fitness to operate a motor vehicle safely upon the highways. The commissioner may establish by rules and regulations the type of tests or demonstrations to be made by applicants for any class of license.

(b) The department shall make provision for giving an examination either in the county where the applicant resides or at another place reasonably convenient to the applicant. The examination, with the exception of those required for a commercial driver's license, commercial driver's license permit, or noncommercial Class A, B, or M license, shall be given at least once each month in each county of the state.

(c)(1) Except as provided in paragraphs (2), (3), and (4) of this subsection, no driver's license shall be issued to any person who does not have a visual acuity of 20/60, corrected or uncorrected, in at least one eye or better and a horizontal field of vision with both eyes open of at least 140 degrees or, in the event that one eye only has usable vision, horizontal field of vision must be at least 70 degrees temporally and 50 degrees nasally.

(2) A person whose visual acuity is less than 20/60 but better than 20/200 using spectacles, contact lenses, or the carrier portion of bioptic spectacles shall be considered eligible for a driver's license if the person is not otherwise disqualified from having a driver's license under the provisions of this article and if:

(A) The person can attain a visual acuity of at least 20/60 through utilizing bioptic telescopes;

(B) The telescopes are prescribed by a licensed optometrist or ophthalmologist;

(C) The person presents documentation of having satisfactorily completed training in the use of the bioptic telescope as certified by the prescribing doctor;

(D) The person presents documentation of an on-the-road evaluation and having satisfactorily completed any recommended training in driving while using bioptic telescopes from a certified driver's license examiner;

(E) The person completes a standard driver's education course while using the bioptic telescopes subsequent to completing evaluation or training with a driver's license examiner; and

(F) The person presents said documentation to a department operated test site and passes a driver's test examination administered by the department.

(3) A person who is licensed to drive using bioptic telescopes shall be subject to possible restrictions placed on his or her license as determined and recommended by the prescribing optometrist or ophthalmologist or the driver's license examiner. Any recommended restrictions shall be reported to the department in writing at the time the person presents himself or herself for a driver's test examination. Restrictions may include daylight driving only, outside rear-view mirrors, certain area and time restrictions, no interstate driving, yearly reevaluations by an optometrist or ophthalmologist, and other such restrictions. Any restrictions shall be eligible for review and reconsideration after one year by completing all of the steps described in subparagraphs (A) through (F) of paragraph (2) of this subsection, including completing any additional possible testing under special conditions, as determined by the optometrist or ophthalmologist.

(4) The user of a bioptic telescope shall require renewal of his or her license every four years. However, the person must be reevaluated at least biennially by an optometrist or ophthalmologist. A certification by the optometrist or ophthalmologist that the user's visual acuity, visual field, and eye health remain stable shall be presented to the department at the time of the biennial eye examination. In the event that changes in vision are determined, the person's license shall expire and the person must successfully repeat all of the steps described in subparagraphs (A) through (F) of paragraph (2) of this subsection in order to have his or her license reinstated. If no significant changes occur in the user's vision at the second biennial examination in a license renewal cycle, the user's license shall be renewed without the necessity of a road test examination or any further eyesight examination.

(d) The department shall authorize licensed driver training schools to conduct on–the–road driving tests and other tests required for issuance of a driver's license as provided in this subsection. The department may authorize licensed driver training schools to issue driver's licenses to successful applicants as provided in this subsection. The department shall, prior to approving a licensed driver training school to conduct tests or issue licenses or both as provided in this subsection, make a determination that the school has been licensed for a minimum of two years and has conducted driver education courses on a full–time basis for such two–year period and that such school meets all other standards which the department may establish as a condition for approval to conduct such tests or issue licenses or both. The department shall authorize a driver training school licensed pursuant to Chapter 13 of Title 43 and approved by the department to administer the testing provided for in this Code section, provided that the applicant has successfully completed a driver training course which includes a minimum of 30 class hours of instruction and six hours of private in–car training. The department may establish by rules and regulations the type of tests or demonstrations to be made by applicants for any Class C or Class D driver's license under this Code section.

Laws 1937, p. 322, art. 4, § 4; Laws 1951, p. 598, § 3; Laws 1975, p. 1008, § 1; Laws 1989, p. 519, § 10; Laws 1990, p. 2048, § 4; Laws 1992, p. 3311, § 2; Laws 1996, p. 1250, § 3; Laws 1997, p. 760, § 14; Laws 2001, p. 184, § 1–3; Laws 2004, Act 582, § 4, eff. July 1, 2004; Laws 2005, Act 68, § 17–7, eff. July 1, 2005; Laws 2005, Act 68 § 17–7, eff. July 1, 2005; Laws 2005, Act 94, § 1, eff. July 1, 2005.

Formerly Code 1933, § 68B–208.

Historical and Statutory Notes

In 2001, the Code Commission, in the second sentence of subsec. (a), substituted "January 1, 2002" for "the effective date of such requirement". See § 28–9–5.

The 2004 amendment by Act 582, in the first sentence of subsec. (a), inserted ", except as otherwise provided by subsection (d) of this code section" following "a driver's license"; and added subsecs. (d) and (e).

The 2005 amendment by Act 68 in the third sentence of subsec. (a) substituted "An applicant 18 years of age and older with a valid and current license, or a license that has been expired for less than two years, issued by another state of the United States or the District of Columbia who surrenders his or her previous license to obtain a Georgia license shall be exempt from taking such tests" for "Applicants 18 years of age and older with valid and current licenses issued by another state of the United States or the District of Columbia who surrender their previous licenses to obtain a Georgia license shall be exempt from taking such tests other than tests of eyesight"; rewrote subsec. (d); and deleted subsec. (e). Prior to amendment, subsecs. (d) and (e) had read:

"(d) The department shall implement a six-month pilot program to determine licensing requirements for licensed driver training schools to conduct on-the-road driving tests as provided in subsection (e) of this Code section. The department shall report the results of such pilot program to the House Committee on Motor Vehicles.

"(e) If the department determines that the pilot program provided for in subsection (d) of this Code section is successful, it shall authorize licensed driver training schools to conduct on-the-road driving tests as provided in this subsection. The department shall, prior to approving a licensed driver training school to conduct on-the-road driving tests as provided in this subsection, make a determination that the school has been licensed for a minimum of one year and has conducted driver education and adult education courses on a full-time basis for such one-year period and that such school meets all other standards which the department may establish as a condition for approval to conduct such tests. The department shall authorize a driver training school licensed pursuant to Chapter 13 of Title 43 and approved by the department to administer the testing provided for in this Code section, provided that the applicant has successfully completed a driver training course which includes a minimum of 30 class hours of instruction and six hours of private in-car training. The department may establish by rules and regulations the type of tests or demonstrations to be made by applicants for any Class C or Class D driver's license under this Code section."

The 2005 amendment by Act 94 rewrote subsec. (c), par. (4), which had read:

"(4) The user of a bioptic telescope shall require renewal of his or her license biennially. The person must be reevaluated at least biennially by an optometrist or ophthalmologist and must biennially pass the driver's road test examination administered by the department. A certification by the optometrist or ophthalmologist that the user's visual acuity, visual field, and eye health remain stable shall be presented to the department at the time of the biennial road test examination. In the event that changes in vision are determined, the person's license shall expire and the person must successfully repeat all of the steps described in subparagraphs (A) through (F) of paragraph (2) of this subsection in order to have his or her license reinstated."

§ 40–5–28. Licenses issued to drivers

(a) The department shall, upon payment of the required fee, issue to every applicant qualifying therefor a driver's license indicating the type or general class of vehicles the licensee may drive, which license shall be upon a form prescribed by the department and which shall bear thereon a distinguishing number assigned to the licensee, a color photograph of the licensee, the licensee's full legal name, either a facsimile of the signature of the licensee or a space upon which the licensee shall write his or her usual signature with a pen and ink immediately upon receipt of the license, and such other information or identification as is required by the department. No license shall be valid until it has been so signed by the licensee. The department shall not require applicants to submit or otherwise obtain from applicants any fingerprints or any other biological characteristic or information which uniquely identifies an individual, including without limitation deoxyribonucleic acid (DNA) and retinal scan identification characteristics but not including a photograph, by any means upon application.

(b) The commissioner may determine the location and manner of issuance of drivers' licenses. Without limiting the generality of the foregoing, it is specifically provided that the commissioner may designate county tag agents, if they so agree, as agents of the department for this purpose and may authorize the issuance of drivers' licenses by county tag agents. No county tag agent shall be required to issue or renew drivers' licenses unless such county tag agent agrees in writing to perform such functions. No county tag agent shall be required to issue or renew drivers' licenses for residents of any county other than the residents of the county for which he or she serves as tax commissioner.

Laws 1975, p. 1008, § 1; Laws 1990, p. 2048, § 4; Laws 1996, p. 1250, § 4; Laws 2005, Act 68, § 17–8, eff. July 1, 2005; Laws 2005, Act 355, § 3, eff. July 1, 2006; Laws 2010, Act 633, § 8, eff. July 1, 2010.

Formerly Code 1933, § 68B–209.

Historical and Statutory Notes

The 2005 amendment by Act 68 designated the existing text as subsec. (a), and added subsec. (b) relating to location and manner of issuance of drivers' licenses.

The 2005 amendment by Act 355 substituted "The department shall not require applicants to submit or otherwise obtain from applicants any fingerprints or any other biological characteristic or information which uniquely identifies an individual, including without limitation, deoxyribonucleic acid (DNA) and retinal scan identification characteristics but not including a photograph by any means upon application." for "Specifically but without limitation, the department may require applicants to submit fingerprints by means of an inkless fingerprint scanning device upon application."

Laws 2005, Act 355, § 6, provides:

"This Act shall become effective on July 1, 2006."

In 2005, the Code Commission, in the last sentence of subsec. (a), deleted the comma following "including without limitation" and inserted a comma following "including a photograph". See § 28–9–5.

The 2010 amendment by Act 633, in subsec. (a), inserted "legal" before "name" in the first sentence.

§ 40–5–28.1. Use of social security numbers on licenses and permits prohibited unless specifically requested

No license or permit issued or renewed on or after January 1, 2007, pursuant to this article shall contain the social security number of the licensee or permit holder.

Laws 1997, p. 1443, § 1; Laws 2006, Act 590, § 3, eff. July 1, 2006.

Historical and Statutory Notes

The 2006 amendment by Act 590 substituted "January 1, 2007" for "July 1, 1997" and deleted "unless such person specifically requests the use of such number" following "license or permit holder".

§ 40–5–29. License to be carried and exhibited on demand

(a) Every licensee shall have his driver's license in his immediate possession at all times when operating a motor vehicle.

(b) Every licensee shall display his license upon the demand of a law enforcement officer. A refusal to comply with such demand not only shall constitute a violation of this subsection but shall also give rise to a presumption of a violation of subsection (a) of this Code section and of Code Section 40–5–20.

(c) A person convicted of a violation of subsection (a) of this Code section shall be fined no more than $10.00 if he produces in court a license theretofore issued to him and valid at the time of his arrest.

Laws 1937, p. 322, art. 4, § 7; Laws 1951, p. 598, § 4; Laws 1975, p. 1008, § 1; Laws 1990, p. 2048, § 4.

Formerly Code 1933, § 68B–210.

§ 40–5–30. Restricted licenses

(a) Upon issuing a driver's license, the department shall have authority, whenever good cause appears, to impose restrictions suitable to the licensee's driving ability with respect to special mechanical control devices required on a motor vehicle which the licensee may operate or such other restrictions applicable to the licensee as the department may determine to be appropriate to assure the safe operation of a motor vehicle by the licensee. The commissioner may promulgate such rules and regulations as are necessary to implement this Code section.

(b) The department may either issue a special restricted license or set forth such restrictions upon the usual license form.

Subsecs. (c) and (d) as added by Laws 2010, Act 623, 1.

(c) No person shall operate a motor vehicle in any manner in violation of the restrictions imposed in a restricted license issued to him or her.

(d) Upon a person being convicted of a violation of this Code section, the court may order the department to suspend such person's license for a period not to exceed six months. The court shall determine the length of such suspension and shall report such suspension and the length thereof to the department. The department shall reinstate the license at the end of the suspension period upon receipt of a reinstatement fee of $210.00 or $200. 00 if paid by mail.

Subsecs. (c) and (d) as added by Laws 2010, Act 625, § 1.

(c) The department, upon receiving satisfactory evidence of any violation of the restrictions of such license, may suspend the license for a period of six months. The department shall reinstate the license at the end of six months upon receipt of a reinstatement fee of $210.00 or $200.00 if paid by mail.

(d) No person shall operate a motor vehicle in any manner in violation of the restrictions imposed in a restricted license issued to him or her; provided, however, that at the time of the hearing on such offense, if such person was charged with driving in violation of a restriction requiring that he or she wear eyeglasses or contact lenses, such person shall not be guilty of such offense if he or she presents the trial court with admissible medical or other evidence sufficient to demonstrate to the satisfaction of the trial court that he or she no longer suffers from the vision condition that resulted in the imposition of such restriction.

Laws 1975, p. 1008, § 1; Laws 1990, p. 2048, § 4; Laws 2000, p. 951, § 5–10; Laws 2006, Act 590, § 4, eff. July 1, 2006; Laws 2009, Act 135, § 2, eff. July 1, 2009; Laws 2010, Act 623, § 1, eff. July 1, 2010; Laws 2010, Act 625, § 1, eff. July 1, 2010.

Formerly Code 1933, § 68B–211.

Historical and Statutory Notes

The 2006 amendment by Act 590, in subsec. (c), substituted "suspend the license for a period of six months" for "revoke the license, but the licensee shall be entitled to a hearing as upon a revocation under subsection (c) of Code Section 40–5–59" and added "or her" at the end of the subsection.

The 2009 amendment by Act 135, in subsec. (c), inserted "The department shall reinstate the license at the end of six months upon receipt of a reinstatement fee of $210.00 or $200.00 if paid by mail."

The 2010 amendment by Act 623, in subsec. (c), deleted "The department, upon receiving satisfactory evidence of any violation of the restrictions of such license, may suspend the license for a period of six months. The department shall reinstate the license at the end of six months upon receipt of a reinstatement fee of $210.00 or $200.00 if paid by mail." at the beginning of the subsection; and added subsec. (d).

The 2010 amendment by Act 625, redesignated the last sentence of subsec. (c) as subsec. (d), and added "; provided, however, that at the time of the hearing on such offense, if such person was charged with driving in violation of a restriction requiring that he or she wear eyeglasses or contact lenses, such person shall not be guilty of such offense if he or she presents the trial court with admissible medical or other evidence sufficient to demonstrate to the satisfaction of the trial court that he or she no longer suffers from the vision condition that resulted in the imposition of such restriction" at the end of newly designated subsec. (d).

§ 40–5–31. Duplicate permit or license

(a) In the event that an instruction permit or a driver's license issued under this chapter is lost or destroyed, the person to whom the same was issued may upon payment of the required fee and upon furnishing proof satisfactory to the department that such permit has been lost or destroyed:

(1) Obtain a new permit or license; or

(2) Obtain a replacement permit or license.

A new permit obtained under this Code section shall be obtained in the same manner and under the same conditions and limitations as provided in Code Section 40–5–24. A new license obtained under this Code section shall be obtained in the same manner and under the same conditions and limitations as provided in Code Section 40–5–32, relating to renewals of licenses. A replacement permit or license obtained under this Code section shall be issued only for the remaining period for which the original permit or license was issued for a fee of $5.00, and no examination or eyesight test shall be required to obtain such replacement permit.

(b) The department shall issue a temporary permit or driver's license to each individual who has lost by misplacement, and not by revocation or suspension, his or her instruction permit or driver's license and who has made application under oath on a form furnished by the department which states that the applicant presently has a valid permit or license which has been lost or misplaced. In lieu of the applicant's signature on a form, any application for the issuance of a replacement license submitted electronically shall contain an acknowledgment and attestation under penalty of perjury that he or she meets each requirement of this Code section.

(c) A temporary permit or license issued pursuant to this Code section shall be valid for 30 days but may be renewed in the event the applicant's new permit or license has not been received within such time.

(d) Any person who falsely swears or falsely makes the oath provided for in subsection (b) of this Code section shall be guilty of a misdemeanor.

Laws 1969, p. 991, § 1; Laws 1975, p. 1008, § 1; Laws 1983, p. 819, § 3; Laws 1989, p. 519, § 11; Laws 1990, p. 2048, § 4; Laws 1996, p. 1250, § 5; Laws 2000, p. 469, § 1; Laws 2005, Act 68, § 17–9, eff. July 1, 2005.

Formerly Code 1933, § 68B–212.

Historical and Statutory Notes

The 2005 amendment by Act 68 in subsec. (b) made a change in a gender reference in the first sentence and added the second sentence relating to applications submitted electronically.

§ 40–5–32. Expiration and renewal of licenses; reexamination requirements

(a)(1) Except as otherwise provided in this Code section, every driver's license shall expire on the licensee's birthday in the fifth year following the issuance of such license. Notwithstanding the foregoing, any commercial license that contains an H or X endorsement as defined in subsection (c) of Code Section 40–5–150 shall expire on the date of expiration of the licensee's security threat assessment conducted by the Transportation Security Administration of the United States Department of Homeland Security. An applicant for a Class C, E, F, or M noncommercial driver's license who is under age 60 shall at the applicant's option apply for a license which shall expire on the licensee's birthday in the fifth or eighth year following the issuance of such license. Every such license shall be renewed on or before its expiration upon application, payment of the required fee, and, if applicable, satisfactory completion of the examination required or authorized by subsection (c) of this Code section.

(2) Except as otherwise provided by subsection (c) of this Code section, every veteran's or honorary license shall expire on the licensee's birthday in the eighth year following the issuance thereof until the holder reaches age 65 and shall thereafter be subject to renewal pursuant to paragraph (1) of this subsection on or before his or her birthday every five years. The department may allow a veteran or honorary license holder to retain his or her expired veteran's or honorary license as a souvenir.

(3) The commissioner shall issue such rules and regulations as are required to enforce this subsection.

(b) An application for driver's license renewal may be submitted by means of:

(1) Personal appearance before the department; or

(2) Subject to rules or regulations of the department which shall be consistent with considerations of public safety and efficiency of service to licensees, means other than such personal appearance which may include without limitation by mail or electronically. The department may by such rules or regulations exempt persons renewing drivers' licenses under this paragraph from the license surrender requirement of subsection (c) of Code Section 40–5–20.

(c)(1) The department shall require every person who is age 64 or older applying for renewal of a driver's license to take and pass successfully such test of his or her eyesight as the department shall prescribe.

(2) The commissioner may issue such rules and regulations as are necessary to implement this subsection.

Laws 1937, p. 322, art. 4, § 5; Laws 1943, p. 196, § 5; Laws 1947, p. 294, § 1; Laws 1951, p. 157, § 7; Laws 1955, p. 662, § 1; Laws 1955, Ex. Sess., p. 35, § 1; Laws 1961, p. 136, § 2; Laws 1961, p. 433, § 1; Laws 1975, p. 1008, § 1; Laws 1977, p. 307, § 2; Laws 1977, p. 576, § 1; Laws 1989, p. 519, § 12; Laws 1990, p. 2048, § 4; Laws 2000, p. 951, § 5–11; Laws 2002, p. 1045, § 2; Laws 2004, Act 582, § 5, eff. July 1, 2004; Laws 2005, Act 68, § 17–10, eff. July 1, 2005; Laws 2010, Act 633, § 9, eff. July 1, 2010.

Formerly Code 1933, § 68B–213.

Historical and Statutory Notes

The 2004 amendment by Act 582, in subsec. (c), deleted par. (2) which had read "(2) At the time of the renewal, the department shall issue a pamphlet containing information pertaining to new traffic laws and to traffic laws most frequently violated" and redesignated former par. (3) as new par. (2).

The 2005 amendment by Act 68 rewrote subsec. (a) and par. (1) of subsec. (c). Prior to amendment, subsecs. (a) and (c)(1) had read:

"(a)(1) Every driver's license shall expire on the licensee's birthday in the fourth year following the issuance of such license. Every such license shall be renewed on or before its expiration upon application, payment of the required fee, and, if applicable, satisfactory completion of the examination required or authorized by subsection (c) of this Code section.

"(2) Except as otherwise provided by subsection (c) of this Code section, every holder of a veteran's or honorary license shall meet the requirements of subsection (c) of this Code section on or before his or her birthday every four years, beginning from the date on which the holder was last required to take an examination under former Ga. L. 1972, p. 1076, as amended by Ga. L. 1973, pp. 916, 917. The department may allow a veteran or honorary license holder to retain his or her expired veteran's or honorary license as a souvenir.

"(3) The commissioner shall issue such rules and regulations as are required to enforce this subsection."

"(c)(1) The department shall require every person applying for renewal of a driver's license to take and pass successfully such test of his or her eyesight as the department shall prescribe, unless otherwise provided by rule or regulation for purposes of paragraph (2) of subsection (b) of this Code section."

The 2010 amendment by Act 633, in subsec. (a), par. (1), deleted "A, B," inserted "E, F," after "C" and substituted "eighth" for "tenth" in the third sentence; in par. (2), substituted "expire on the licensee's birthday in the eighth year following the issuance thereof" for "be valid" after "honorary license shall" in the first sentence.

§ 40–5–33. Change of address or name

Whenever any person, after applying for or receiving a driver's license, shall move from the address named in such application or in the license issued to him or her or when the name of a licensee is changed by marriage or otherwise, such person shall apply to the department for a license showing the correct name or address within 60 days. Failure to change the name or address shall not deem the license invalid. The commissioner may determine the locations at which applications shall be accepted for applications due to change of name or address. Without limiting the generality of the foregoing, it is specifically provided that the commissioner may designate county tag agents, if they so agree, as agents of the department for this purpose.

Laws 1975, p. 1008, § 1; Laws 1985, p. 149, § 40; Laws 1989, p. 519, § 13; Laws 1990, p. 2048, § 4; Laws 1994, p. 1876, § 2; Laws 1995, p. 920, § 2; Laws 2005, Act 68, § 17–11, eff. July 1, 2005.

Formerly Code 1933, § 68B–214.

Historical and Statutory Notes

The 2005 amendment by Act 68 added the provisions at the end of the section authorizing the commissioner to determine the locations at which applications shall be accepted and to designate county tag agents.

§ 40–5–34. Driver License Advisory Board

(a) The commissioner is authorized to appoint a Driver License Advisory Board.

(b) The Driver License Advisory Board shall advise the commissioner on medical criteria and vision standards relating to the licensing of drivers under this chapter.

(c) If the department has cause to believe that a licensed driver or applicant may not be physically or mentally qualified to be licensed, it may obtain the advice of the Driver License Advisory Board. The Driver License Advisory Board may formulate its advice from records and reports or may cause an examination and report to be made by one or more members of the Driver License Advisory Board or any other qualified person it may designate. The licensed driver or applicant may cause a written report to be forwarded to the Driver License Advisory Board by a person of his choice who is licensed under Chapter 30 of Title 43 and Article 2 of Chapter 34 of Title 43 to diagnose and treat disorders of humans. Such report shall be given due consideration by the Driver License Advisory Board.

(d) Members of the Driver License Advisory Board and other persons making examinations shall not be held liable for their opinions and recommendations presented pursuant to subsection (c) of this Code section.

(e) Reports received or made by the Driver License Advisory Board or its members for the purpose of assisting the department in determining whether a person is qualified to be licensed are for the confidential use of the Driver License Advisory Board or the department and may not be divulged to any person or used as evidence in any trial except that the reports may be admitted in proceedings under subsection (c) of Code Section 40–5–59 and Code Section 40–5–66, and any person conducting an examination pursuant to subsection (c) of this Code section may be compelled to testify concerning his observations and findings in such proceedings.

Laws 1975, p. 1008, § 1; Laws 1990, p. 2048, § 4.

Formerly Code 1933, § 68B–216.

§ 40–5–35. Reports by physicians and vision specialists

(a) The Driver License Advisory Board appointed by the department shall define disorders characterized by lapses of consciousness or other mental or physical disabilities affecting the ability of a person to drive safely for the purpose of the reports required by this Code section, and the commissioner may use these definitions to promulgate regulations making such disorders and disabilities disqualifications, under certain conditions, for obtaining or keeping a driver's license for any class or classes of vehicles; provided, however, that a person shall not be disqualified from obtaining a noncommercial Class C driver's license for having had an episode of lapsed or altered consciousness due to epilepsy unless such an episode occurred within the immediately preceding six-month period.

(b) All physicians licensed under Article 2 of Chapter 34 of Title 43 to diagnose and treat disorders and disabilities defined by the commissioner may report to the department the full name, date of birth, and address of any person with a disability which would render such person incapable of operating a motor vehicle safely.

(c) All other persons licensed under Chapter 30 of Title 43 to diagnose and treat disorders defined by the commissioner may report to the department the full name, date of birth, and address of any person with a disability which would render such person incapable of operating a motor vehicle safely.

(d) The reports required by this Code section shall be confidential and shall be used solely for the purpose of determining the qualifications of any person to drive a motor vehicle on the highways of this state. No civil or criminal action may be brought against any person or agency for providing the information required in this Code section. The reports, or any reference to the reports, shall not be included in any abstract prepared pursuant to Code Section 40–5–2.

(e) Reports received or made by the Driver License Advisory Board or its members for the purpose of assisting the department in determining whether a person is qualified to be licensed are for the confidential use of the Driver License Advisory Board or the department and may not be divulged to any person or used as evidence in any civil or criminal trial, except that the reports may be admitted in proceedings conducted pursuant to this Code section and Code Section 40–5–66.

(f) Whenever the department shall determine that a person is unqualified to be licensed, the department shall inform such person in writing and give him an opportunity to request a hearing, in writing, within 15 days. If no hearing is requested within the 15 day period as specified in this subsection, the right to this hearing shall be waived and the license of the person shall be revoked. The person may request an opinion of the Driver License Advisory Board as provided in subsection (c) of Code Section 40–5–34. The department may not grant any exceptions to any regulations issued pursuant to subsection (a) of this Code section. The scope of the hearing shall determine, upon evidence and testimony submitted, if the driver is competent to drive a motor vehicle as defined in this title. No driving privileges shall be revoked unless the department shows that the driver had disorders characterized by lapses of consciousness or other mental or physical disabilities affecting his ability to drive safely. The hearing shall be informal and an appeal shall be as provided for in Code Section 40–5–66.

Laws 1975, p. 1008, § 1; Laws 1977, p. 890, § 1; Laws 1990, p. 2048, § 4; Laws 1995, p. 1302, § 13; Laws 2000, p. 951, § 5–12; Laws 2000, p. 1313, § 2.

Formerly Code 1933, § 68B–217.

§ 40–5–36. Veterans', honorary, and distinctive licenses

(a) Except as specifically provided in this chapter, no part of this chapter shall be interpreted as affecting the rights and privileges of a person holding a veteran's, honorary, or distinctive license, and nothing in this chapter shall be construed so as to authorize the department to impose any charge or fee of any type whatsoever for the issuance or renewal of a veteran's, honorary, or distinctive license; provided, however, that the commissioner may issue regulations on types and classes of vehicles which may be operated by the holder of such license.

(b) The commissioner shall establish by rules and regulations the proof required to be produced by an applicant for a veteran's, honorary, or distinctive license. The contents of such license shall be the same as for any other license. The forms upon which such licenses are issued shall be such that the licenses are of a permanent nature, provided that nothing in this subsection shall authorize the department to require any person holding a veteran's or honorary license before January 1, 1976, to surrender such license. Veterans', honorary, and distinctive licenses shall not be subject to any fees.

(c) Veterans' licenses may be issued to:

(1) Veterans who were residents of Georgia at the time of enlistment or commissioning and are residents at the time of application for the license, or who have been residents of Georgia for at least two years immediately preceding the date of application for the license, who served on active duty in the armed forces of the United States or on active duty in a reserve component of the armed forces of the United States, including the National Guard, during wartime or any conflict when personnel were committed by the President of the United States, whether or not such veteran was assigned to a unit or division which directly participated in such war or conflict, except for periodic transfer from reserve status to active duty status for training purposes, and who were discharged or separated under honorable conditions; and

(2) All members or former members of the National Guard or reserve forces who have 20 or more years' creditable service therein.

(d) Honorary licenses may be issued to:

(1) A resident of Georgia who is the surviving spouse of a veteran as defined by paragraph (1) of subsection (c) of this Code section. Any license to such spouse shall be valid only as long as that person remains unmarried; or

(2) A resident of Georgia who is the spouse of a veteran who would be qualified to receive a veteran's license but who is disabled to the extent that he or she cannot operate a motor vehicle.

(e) A distinctive license may be issued to any member of the Georgia National Guard in good standing who has completed at least one year of satisfactory service. The department shall have the authority to cancel the distinctive license of any person upon receipt of written notice from the adjutant general who shall notify the department that the person is no longer a member of the Georgia National Guard in good standing.

Laws 1949, p. 1152, §§ 2–5; Laws 1966, p. 546, §§ 3–7, 12; Laws 1966, p. 553, § 2; Laws 1975, p. 1008, § 1; Laws 1978, p. 2191, § 1; Laws 1990, p. 2048, § 4; Laws 1992, p. 1496, § 1; Laws 1994, p. 393, § 3; Laws 2000, p. 951, § 5–13; Laws 2004, Act 521, § 10, eff. July 1, 2004.

Formerly Code 1933, § 68B–218.

Historical and Statutory Notes

The 2004 amendment by Act 521, in subsec. (c), par. (1), substituted "two years" for "five years".

§ 40–5–37. Expired license; exception to violation; active duty service members

(a) As used in this Code section, the term "service member" means an active duty member of the regular or reserve component of the United States armed forces, the United States Coast Guard, the Georgia National Guard, or the Georgia Air National Guard who is on ordered federal duty for a period of 90 days or longer.

(b) Any service member whose Georgia driver's license expired while such service member was serving on active duty outside the state shall be permitted to operate a motor vehicle in accordance with such expired license and shall not be charged with a violation of Code Section 40–5–20 for a period of six months from the date of his or her discharge from active duty or reassignment to a location within the state. The service member must present to the department either a copy of the official military orders or a written verification signed by the service member's commanding officer to waive charges.

Laws 2005, Act 48, § 5, eff. July 1, 2005.

§ 40–5–38. Notation of post traumatic stress disorder

(a) Members of the armed services and veterans who have been diagnosed with post traumatic stress disorder may request to have a notation of such diagnosis placed on his or her driver's license. Such applicant shall present the department with a sworn statement from a person licensed to practice medicine or psychology in this state verifying such diagnosis.

(b) The commissioner shall by rules and regulations establish procedures necessary to carry out the provisions of this Code section including, without limitation, application forms to include a waiver of liability for the release of any medical information and an appropriate symbol to be placed on the drivers' licenses.

Laws 2010, Act 649, § 1, eff. July 1, 2010.

Article 3

Cancellation, Suspension, and Revocation of Licenses

§ 40–5–50. Authority of department to cancel license or personal identification card

The department is authorized to cancel any driver's license or personal identification card issued by the department pursuant to

Code Section 40–5–100 upon determining that the holder of such license or identification card was not entitled to the issuance thereof under this chapter or failed to give the required or correct information in the application for such license or identification card.

Laws 1975, p. 1008, § 1; Laws 1990, p. 2048, § 4; Laws 1995, p. 920, § 3; Laws 2000, p. 951, § 5–14.

Formerly Code 1933, § 68B–301.

§ 40–5–51. Suspending or revoking privileges of nonresidents; reporting convictions, suspensions and revocations

(a) The privilege of driving a motor vehicle on the highways of this state given to a nonresident under this chapter shall be subject to suspension or revocation by the department only when suspension or revocation is required by law for the violation. No points shall be assessed as provided in Code Section 40–5–57 for any violation committed by a nonresident.

(b) The department is required, upon receiving a record of the conviction in this state of a nonresident driver of a motor vehicle of any offense, to forward a certified copy of such record to the motor vehicle administrator in the state wherein the person so convicted is a resident.

(c) When a nonresident's operating privilege is suspended or revoked, the department shall forward a certified copy of the record of such action to the motor vehicle administrator in the state wherein such person resides.

Laws 1975, p. 1008, § 1; Laws 1990, p. 2048, § 4; Laws 2004, Act 582, § 6, eff. July 1, 2004.

Formerly Code 1933, § 68B–302.

Historical and Statutory Notes

The 2004 amendment by Act 582, subsec. (a), substituted "only when suspension or revocation is required by law for the violation. No points shall be assessed as provided in Code Section 40–5–57 for any violation committed by a nonresident" for "in like manner and for like cause as a driver's license issued under this chapter may be suspended or revoked".

§ 40–5–52. Suspending resident's license based upon conduct in another state

(a) The department shall suspend, as provided in Code Section 40–5–63, the license of any resident of this state and may suspend a nonresident's operating privilege, upon receiving notice of a conviction in another state of an offense described in Code Section 40–5–54 or Code Section 40–6–391 or any drug related offense.

(b) The department is authorized to suspend or revoke the license of any resident or the operating privilege of any nonresident upon receiving notice of the conviction of such person in another state of an offense other than those described in Code Section 40–5–54 or Code Section 40–6–391 which, if committed in this state, would be grounds for the suspension or revocation of a driver's license.

(c) The department may give such effect to the conduct of a resident in another state as is provided by the laws of this state had such conduct occurred in this state.

(d) Whenever the department has suspended the license of a Georgia resident or refused to issue a driver's license to any person for conduct that occurred in another state, it shall review the suspension at least once every five years and shall reinstate the license if the department determines that the suspension is no longer warranted and the person would otherwise be eligible for a license.

Laws 1975, p. 1008, § 1; Laws 1984, p. 614, § 1; Laws 1990, p. 2048, § 4; Laws 1994, p. 730, § 1; Laws 2010, Act 633, § 4, eff. July 1, 2010.

Formerly Code 1933, § 68B–303.

Historical and Statutory Notes

The 2010 amendment by Act 633 added subsec. (d).

§ 40–5–53. Surrender of license to court upon conviction; destruction of suspended or revoked licenses, permits, or identification cards; issuance of new license, permit, or identification card; transmittal of conviction reports

(a) Whenever any person is convicted of any offense for which this chapter makes mandatory the suspension of the license of such person by the department, the court in which such conviction is had shall require the surrender to it of any driver's license then held by the person so convicted and the court shall thereupon forward the same to the department, together with the uniform citation form authorized by Article 1 of Chapter 13 of this title, within ten days after the conviction. Notwithstanding any other provision of this title, the department shall destroy any suspended or revoked drivers' licenses, permits, or identification cards forwarded to it under this or any other provision of law. The department shall issue a new driver's license, permit, or identification card upon satisfaction of the applicable reinstatement requirement, including but not limited to the payment of the applicable reinstatement fee. No additional fee shall be required for the issuance of a replacement driver's license, permit, or identification card.

(b) Every court in each county of this state having jurisdiction over offenses committed under this chapter and Chapter 6 of this title or any other law of this state or ordinance adopted by a local authority regulating the operation of motor vehicles on highways shall forward to the department, within ten days after the conviction of any person in such court for a violation of any such law other than regulations governing speeding in a noncommercial motor vehicle for which no points are assigned under Code Section 40–5–57, standing, or parking, a uniform citation form authorized by Article 1 of Chapter 13 of this title. Notwithstanding any other provision of this title, in satisfaction of the reporting requirement of this subsection, the courts of this state shall transmit the information contained on the uniform citation form by electronic means, using the electronic reporting method approved by the department. Subject to appropriations by the General Assembly, the department shall pay to the clerk of the court forwarding the required report 40¢ for each report transmitted electronically in a timely manner as required in this subsection; and notwithstanding any general or local law to the contrary, the clerk shall pay such fees over to the general fund of the city or county operating the court.

Laws 1937, p. 322, art. 4, § 13; Laws 1939, p. 135, § 12; Laws 1968, p. 430, § 6; Laws 1975, p. 1008, § 1; Laws 1985, p. 149, § 40; Laws 1986, p. 1002, § 9; Laws 1987, p. 392, § 1; Laws 1990, p. 1913, § 1; Laws 1990, p. 2048, § 4; Laws 1992, p. 1118, § 1; Laws 1992, p. 2785, § 6; Laws 1993, p. 1665, § 1; Laws 1995, p. 917, § 2; Laws 2000, p. 951, § 5–15; Laws 2003, Act 238, § 1, eff. July 1, 2003; Laws 2004, Act 521, § 1, eff. July 1, 2004; Laws 2005, Act 68, § 17–12, eff. July 1, 2005; Laws 2006, Act 590, § 5, eff. July 1, 2006; Laws 2010, Act 633, § 10, eff. July 1, 2010.

Formerly Code 1933, § 68B–304.

Historical and Statutory Notes

The 2003 amendment by Act 238, in subsec. (b), deleted "having a population of 550,000 or more according to the United States decennial census of 1980 or any future such census and" following "Every court in each county of this state" and substituted "The department shall pay to the clerk of the court forwarding the required report 40¢ for each report transmitted electronically and 10¢ for each report transmitted otherwise; and notwithstanding any general or local law to the contrary, the clerk shall pay such fees over to the general fund of the city or county operating the court" for "The department shall pay to the clerk of the court forwarding the report 25¢ for each report required to be forwarded; and notwithstanding any general or local law to the contrary, the clerk shall retain such 25¢ fee as additional compensation"; and deleted subsec. (c) which had read:

"(c) Every court in each county of this state having a population of less than 550,000 according to the United States decennial census of 1980 or any future such census and having jurisdiction over offenses committed under this chapter or Chapter 6 of this title or any other law of this state or ordinance adopted by a local authority regulating the operation of motor vehicles on highways shall forward to the department, within ten days after the conviction of any person in such court for a violation of any such law other than regulations governing speeding in a noncommercial vehicle for which no points are assigned under Code Section 40–5–57, standing or parking, a uniform citation form authorized by Article 1 of Chapter 13 of this title. Notwithstanding any other provision of this title, in satisfaction of the reporting requirement of this subsection, the courts of this state may transmit the information contained on the uniform citation form by electronic means, provided that the department has first given approval to the reporting court for the electronic reporting method utilized. The department shall pay to the clerk of the court forwarding the report 25¢ for each report required to be forwarded; and in those cases where the clerk receiving such 25¢ fee is compensated solely on a fee basis, the clerk shall retain such 25¢ fee as additional compensation. In those cases where the clerk receiving such 25¢ fee is compensated in whole or in part on a salary basis, such fee shall be the property of and shall be paid over to the city or county operating the court, unless expressly provided otherwise in a local law relating to the compensation of such clerk."

The 2004 amendment by Act 521 rewrote subsec. (a) which had read:

"(a) Whenever any person is convicted of any offense for which this chapter makes mandatory the suspension of the license of such person by the department, the court in which such conviction is had shall require the surrender to it of any driver's license then held by the person so convicted and the court shall thereupon forward the same to the department, together with the uniform citation form authorized by Article 1 of Chapter 13 of this title, within ten days after the conviction. Notwithstanding any other provision of this title, the department shall retain possession of any suspended drivers' licenses forwarded to it under this or any other provision of law if the license's expiration date, as shown on the driver's license, is one year or more away. The department shall return the driver's original license upon payment of the applicable reinstatement fee if such driver applies for and is granted reinstatement while the original license is in the possession of the department. No additional fee shall be required for the return of such original license. The department may destroy a suspended license if the license's expiration date, as shown on the license, is less than one year away."

The 2005 amendment by Act 68 rewrote subsec. (b), which had read:

"(b) Every court in each county of this state having jurisdiction over offenses committed under this chapter and Chapter 6 of this title or any other law of this state or ordinance adopted by a local authority regulating the operation of motor vehicles on highways shall forward to the department, within ten days after the conviction of any person in such court for a violation of any such law other than regulations governing speeding in a noncommercial motor vehicle for which no points are assigned under Code Section 40–5–57, standing, or parking, a uniform citation form authorized by Article 1 of Chapter 13 of this title. Notwithstanding any other provision of this title, in satisfaction of the reporting requirement of this subsection, the courts of this state may transmit the information contained on the uniform citation form by electronic means, provided that the department has first given approval to the reporting court for the electronic reporting method utilized. The department shall pay to the clerk of the court forwarding the required report 40¢ for each report transmitted electronically and 10¢ for each report transmitted otherwise; and notwithstanding any general or local law to the contrary, the clerk shall pay such fees over to the general fund of the city or county operating the court."

The 2006 amendment by Act 590, in subsec. (b), deleted "Where a court has not implemented transmittal by electronic means, the commissioner may require such court or courts to submit by electronic means no later than a future date to be determined by the commissioner." at the end of the subsection.

The 2010 amendment by Act 633, in subsec. (b), inserted "Subject to appropriations by the General Assembly," at the beginning of the third sentence.

§ 40–5–54. Mandatory suspension of license by department

(a) The department shall forthwith suspend, as provided in Code Section 40–5–63, the license of any driver upon receiving a record of such driver's conviction of the following offenses, whether charged as a violation of state law or of a local ordinance adopted pursuant to Article 14 of Chapter 6 of this title:

(1) Homicide by vehicle, as defined by Code Section 40–6–393;

(2) Any felony in the commission of which a motor vehicle is used;

(3) Hit and run or leaving the scene of an accident in violation of Code Section 40–6–270;

(4) Racing on highways and streets;

(5) Using a motor vehicle in fleeing or attempting to elude an officer;

(6) Fraudulent or fictitious use of or application for a license as provided in Code Section 40–5–120 or 40–5–125; or

(7) Operating a motor vehicle with a revoked, canceled, or suspended registration in violation of Code Section 40–6–15.

(b) All judges of all courts having jurisdiction of the offenses set forth in subsection (a) of this Code section shall, at the time of sentencing, give notice to the defendant on forms prescribed by the department of the suspension of the defendant's driver's license. The period of suspension shall be determined by the department for the term authorized by law. The court shall forward the notice of suspension and the defendant's driver's license to the department within ten days from the date of conviction. The department shall notify the defendant of the period of suspension at the address provided by the defendant.

Laws 1939, p. 135, § 10; Laws 1943, p. 196, § 5; Laws 1951, p. 565, § 7A; Laws 1956, p. 543, § 15; Laws 1957, p. 124, § 4; Laws 1964, p. 225, § 3; Laws 1968, p. 430, § 8; Laws 1971, p. 249, § 1; Laws 1975, p. 1008, § 1; Laws 1976, p. 1073, § 1; Laws 1983, p. 1000, § 2; Laws 1987, p. 1082, § 1; Laws 1988, p. 897, § 1; Laws 1990, p. 2048, § 4; Laws 1992, p. 1284, § 1; Laws 1993, p. 940, § 1; Laws 2000, p. 951, § 5–16; Laws 2002, p. 1024, § 4; Laws 2004, Act 582, § 7, eff. July 1, 2004.

Formerly Code 1933, § 68B–305.

Historical and Statutory Notes

The 2004 amendment by Act 582, in subsec. (b), substituted "prescribed" for "provided".

§ 40–5–54.1. Suspension or denial of license for failure to comply with order of child support

(a) As used in this Code section, the term:

(1) "Agency" means the agency within the Department of Human Services which is responsible for enforcing orders for child support pursuant to this article.

(2) "Compliance with an order for child support" means, as set forth in a court order, administrative order, or contempt order for child support, the obligor is not more than 60 calendar days in arrears in making payments in full for current support, periodic payments on a support arrearage, or periodic payments on a reimbursement for public assistance.

(3) "Proof of compliance" means the notice of release issued by the agency or court of competent jurisdiction stating that the delinquent obligor is in compliance with an order for child support.

(b) The department shall suspend, as provided in Code Sections 19–6–28.1 and 19–11–9.3, the license of any driver upon receiving a record from the agency or a court of competent jurisdiction stating that such driver is not in compliance with an order for child support. The department shall send notice of any suspension imposed pursuant to this Code section. Such notice shall be sent via certified mail to the address reflected on its records as the driver's mailing address. The mailing of such notice by the department shall be deemed conclusively to be notice to such driver of the suspension of his or her driver's license and shall be deemed to satisfy all notice requirements of law, and no further notice to the driver shall be required for the suspensions provided for in this Code section.

(c) The suspension or denial of an application for issuance or renewal of a license shall be for an indefinite period and until such person shall provide proof of compliance with an order for child support. Such person's license shall be reinstated if the person submits proof of compliance with an order for child support from the agency or court of competent jurisdiction and pays a restoration fee of $35.00 or $25.00 when such reinstatement is processed by mail for the return of his or her license.

(d) Any person who receives notice from the agency that his or her registration is subject to denial or suspension may request a hearing and appeal as provided for in Code Section 19–6–28.1 or 19–11–9.3. Notwithstanding any provisions of law to the contrary, the hearings and appeal procedures provided for in such Code sections shall be the only such procedures required for purposes of this Code section.

Laws 1996, p. 453, § 11; Laws 2000, p. 951, § 5–17; Laws 2008, Act 434, § 4, eff. Jan. 1, 2010; Laws 2009, Act 102, § 2–2, eff. July 1, 2009.

Historical and Statutory Notes

The 2008 amendment by Act 434, in subsec. (b) added "The department shall send notice of any suspension imposed pursuant to this Code section. Such notice shall be sent via certified mail to the address reflected on its records as the driver's mailing address. The mailing of such notice by the department shall be deemed conclusively to be notice to such driver of the suspension of his or her driver's license and shall be deemed to satisfy all notice requirements of law, and no further notice to the driver shall be required for the suspensions provided for in this Code section."; and deleted subsec. (e) which had read "A person whose driver's license has been suspended pursuant to this Code section may apply to the department for a restricted driving permit as provided in Code Section 40–5–71."

The 2009 amendment by Act 102 substituted "Department of Human Services" for "Department of Human Resources" throughout the section.

§ 40–5–55. Implied consent to tests to determine presence of alcohol or other drugs

(a) The State of Georgia considers that any person who drives or is in actual physical control of any moving vehicle in violation of any provision of Code Section 40–6–391 constitutes a direct and immediate threat to the welfare and safety of the general public. Therefore, any person who operates a motor vehicle upon the highways or elsewhere throughout this state shall be deemed to have given consent, subject to Code Section 40–6–392, to a chemical test or tests of his or her blood, breath, urine, or other bodily substances for the purpose of determining the presence of alcohol or any other drug, if arrested for any offense arising out of acts alleged to have been committed in violation of Code Section 40–6–391 or if such person is involved in any traffic accident resulting in serious injuries or fatalities. The test or tests shall be administered at the request of a law enforcement officer having reasonable grounds to believe that the person has been driving or was in actual physical control of a moving motor vehicle upon the highways or elsewhere throughout this state in violation of Code Section 40–6–391. The test or tests shall be administered as soon as possible to any person who operates a motor vehicle upon the highways or elsewhere throughout this state who is involved in any traffic accident resulting in serious injuries or fatalities. Subject to Code Section 40–6–392, the requesting law enforcement officer shall designate which of the test or tests shall be administered, provided a blood test with drug screen may be administered to any person operating a motor vehicle involved in a traffic accident resulting in serious injuries or fatalities.

(b) Any person who is dead, unconscious, or otherwise in a condition rendering such person incapable of refusal shall be deemed not to have withdrawn the consent provided by subsection (a) of this Code section, and the test or tests may be administered, subject to Code Section 40–6–392.

(c) As used in this Code section, the term "traffic accident resulting in serious injuries or fatalities" means any motor vehicle accident in which a person was killed or in which one or more persons suffered a fractured bone, severe burns, disfigurement, dismemberment, partial or total loss of sight or hearing, or loss of consciousness.

Laws 1968, p. 448, § 2; Laws 1974, p. 562, § 2; Laws 1974, p. 633, § 3; Laws 1975, p. 1008, § 1; Laws 1983, p. 1000, § 3; Laws 1985, p. 630, § 1; Laws 1985, p. 758, § 2; Laws 1987, p. 1489, § 1; Laws 1989, p. 1698, § 1; Laws 1990, p. 2048, § 4; Laws 1991, p. 1886, § 2; Laws 1992, p. 912, § 1; Laws 1992, p. 2564, § 1; Laws 1993, p. 940, § 2; Laws 2001, p. 208, § 1–1.

Formerly Code 1933, § 68B–306.

Validity

This section has been held unconstitutional, in part, in the case of Cooper v. State, 2003, 277 Ga. 282, 587 S.E.2d 605.

§ 40–5–56. Suspension of license for failure to respond to citation

(a) Notwithstanding any other provisions of this chapter or any other law to the contrary, the department shall suspend the driver's license or privilege to operate a motor vehicle in this state of any person who has failed to respond to a citation to appear before a court of competent jurisdiction in this state or in any other state for a traffic violation other than a parking violation. The department shall include language in the uniform traffic citation stating that failure to appear and respond to such citation shall result in the suspension of the violator's driver's license or nonresident driving privilege. The language reflected on a uniform traffic citation issued in this state shall be sufficient notice of said suspension to support a conviction for a violation of Code Section 40–5–121 if such person drives subsequent to the imposition of such a suspension following his or her failure to appear. Notwithstanding the foregoing, the department shall send notice of any suspension imposed pursuant to this Code section. Such notice shall be sent via certified mail to the address reflected on its records as the person's mailing address. Proof of receipt of said notice shall be admissible to support a conviction for a violation of Code Section 40–5–121 if such person drives subsequent to the imposition of such a suspension following his or her failure to appear.

(b) The suspension provided for in this Code section shall be for an indefinite period until such person shall respond and pay any fines and penalties imposed. Such person's license shall be reinstated if the person submits proof of payment of the fine from the court of jurisdiction and pays a restoration fee of $100.00 or $90.00 when such reinstatement is processed by mail to the department. Such suspension shall be in addition to any other suspension or revocation provided for in this chapter.

Laws 1978, p. 1452, § 1; Laws 1979, p. 1049, § 2; Laws 1983, p. 1000, § 4; Laws 1984, p. 22, § 40; Laws 1986, p. 184, § 1; Laws 1988, p. 897, § 2; Laws 1990, p. 2048, § 4; Laws 1994, p. 97, § 40; Laws 2000, p. 951, § 5–18; Laws 2000, p. 1589, § 4; Laws 2006, Act 590, § 6, eff. July 1, 2006; Laws 2008, Act 434, § 5, eff. Jan. 1, 2010; Laws 2009, Act 135, § 3, eff. July 1, 2009; Laws 2010, Act 633, § 12, eff. July 1, 2010.

Formerly Code 1933, § 68B–316.

Historical and Statutory Notes

The 2006 amendment by Act 590, in subsec. (a), substituted "jurisdiction in this state or in any" for "jurisdiction of this state or of any" and deleted "The department shall forthwith notify such person that his license is to be suspended subject to review as provided for in this chapter." at the end of the subsection; deleted subsec. (b); and redesignated existing subsec. (c) as subsec. (b). Prior to amendment subsec. (b) had read:

"(b) The person so notified may request a hearing within ten days from the date of receipt of notice sent by registered mail or statutory overnight delivery. Within 30 days after receiving a written request for a hearing, the department shall hold a hearing as provided for in Chapter 13 of Title 50, the 'Georgia Administrative Procedure Act.' After such hearing, the department shall sustain its order of suspension or rescind such order. If no hearing is requested within the ten days specified above, the right to a hearing shall have been waived and the license of the driver shall be suspended."

The 2008 amendment by Act 434, in subsec. (a), added "The department shall include language in the uniform traffic citation stating that failure to appear and respond to such citation shall result in the suspension of the violator's driver's license or nonresident driving privilege. The language reflected on a uniform traffic citation issued in this state shall be sufficient notice of said suspension to support a conviction for a violation of Code Section 40–5–121 if such person drives subsequent to the imposition of such a suspension following his or her failure to appear. Notwithstanding the foregoing, the department shall send notice of any suspension imposed pursuant to this Code section. Such notice shall be sent via certified mail to the address reflected on its records as the person's mailing address. The mailing of such notice by the department shall be deemed conclusively to be notice to such person of the suspension of his or her driver's license and shall be deemed to satisfy all notice requirements of law, and no further notice to the owner shall be required for the suspension provided for in this Code section." at the end of the subsection.

The 2009 amendment by Act 135, in subsec. (b), substituted "\$100.00 or \$90.00" for "\$35.00 or \$25.00".

The 2010 amendment by Act 633, in subsec. (a), substituted the sentence beginning with "Proof of receipt of said notice" for "The mailing of such notice by the department shall be deemed conclusively to be notice to such person of the suspension of his or her driver's license and shall be deemed to satisfy all notice requirements of law, and no further notice to the owner shall be required for the suspension provided in this Code section."

§ 40–5–57. Suspension of license of habitually dangerous or negligent driver; assessment of points; periods of suspension; reinstatement

(a) The State of Georgia considers dangerous and negligent drivers to be a direct and immediate threat to the welfare and safety of the general public, and it is in the best interests of the citizens of Georgia immediately to remove such drivers from the highways of this state. Therefore, the department is authorized to suspend the license of a driver without a preliminary hearing upon a showing by the records of the department or other sufficient evidence that the licensee is a habitually dangerous or negligent driver of a motor vehicle, such fact being established by the point system in subsection (b) of this Code section.

(b) For the purpose of identifying habitually dangerous or negligent drivers and habitual or frequent violators of traffic regulations governing the movement of vehicles, the department shall assess points, as provided in subsection (c) of this Code section, for convictions of violations of the provisions of Chapter 6 of this title, of violations of lawful ordinances adopted by local authorities regulating the operation of motor vehicles, and of offenses committed in other states which if committed in this state would be grounds for such assessment. Notice of each assessment of points may be given, but the absence of notice shall not affect any suspension made pursuant to this Code section. No points shall be assessed for violating a provision of state law or municipal ordinance regulating standing, parking, equipment, size, and weight. The department is required to suspend the license of a driver, without preliminary hearing, when his driving record identifies him as a habitually dangerous or negligent driver or as a habitual or frequent violator under this subsection.

(c)(1)(A) Except as provided in subparagraph (C) of this paragraph, the points to be assessed for each offense shall be as provided in the following schedule:

Aggressive driving	6 points
Reckless driving	4 points
Unlawful passing of a school bus	6 points
Improper passing on a hill or a curve	4 points
Exceeding the speed limit by more than 14 miles per hour but less than 19 miles per hour	2 points
Exceeding the speed limit by 19 miles per hour or more but less than 24 miles per hour	3 points
Exceeding the speed limit by 24 miles per hour or more but less than 34 miles per hour	4 points
Exceeding the speed limit by 34 miles per hour or more	6 points
Disobedience of any traffic-control device or traffic officer	3 points
Too fast for conditions	0 points
Possessing an open container of an alcoholic beverage while driving	2 points
Failure to adequately secure a load, except fresh farm produce, resulting in loss of such load onto the roadway which results in an accident	2 points
Violation of child safety restraint requirements, first offense	1 point
Violation of child safety restraint requirements, second or subsequent offense	2 points
Violation of usage of wireless telecommunications device requirements	1 point
Operating a vehicle while text messaging	1 point
All other moving traffic violations which are not speed limit violations	3 points

(B) The commissioner shall suspend the driver's license of any person who has accumulated a violation point count of 15 or more points in any consecutive 24 month period, as measured from the dates of previous arrests for which convictions were obtained to the date of the most current arrest for which a conviction is obtained. A second or subsequent plea of nolo contendere, within the preceding five years, as measured from the dates of previous arrests for which pleas of nolo contendere were accepted to the date of the most current arrest for which a plea of nolo contendere is accepted, to a charge of committing an offense listed in this subsection shall be considered a conviction for the purposes of this Code section. At the end of the period of suspension, the violation point count shall be reduced to zero points.

(C) A court may order a person to attend a driver improvement course for any violation for which points are assessed against a driver's license under this subsection or may accept the attendance by a person at a driver improvement clinic after the issuance of a citation for such offense and prior to such person's appearance before the court, in which event the court shall reduce the fine assessed against such person by 20 percent, and no points shall be assessed by the department against such driver. The disposition and court order shall be reported to the department and shall be placed on the motor vehicle record with a zero point count. This plea may be accepted by the court once every five years as measured from date of arrest to date of arrest.

(2) Any points assessed against an individual for exceeding the speed limit shall be deducted from that individual's accumulated violation point count and the uniform traffic citation issued therefor shall be removed from the individual's record if:

(A) The points were assessed based on the use of a radar speed detection device by a county or municipality during a period of time when the commissioner has determined that such county or municipality was operating a radar speed detection device in violation of Chapter 14 of this title, relating to the use of radar speed detection devices; and

(B) The commissioner has suspended or revoked the radar speed detection device permit of such county or municipality pursuant to Code Section 40–14–11.

(d) Any person who has such points assessed against him as to require the suspension of his license pursuant to subsection (a) or (b) of this Code section shall have his license suspended as follows:

(1) Upon a first assessment of the requisite points, the period of suspension shall be one year, provided that at any time after completion of the requirements set forth in Code Section 40–5–84, such person may apply to the department for the return of his license;

(2) For a second assessment of the requisite points within five years, as measured from the dates of previous arrests for which convictions were obtained to the date of the most current arrest for which a conviction is obtained, the period of suspension shall be three years, provided that at any time after completion of the requirements set forth in Code Section 40–5–84, such person may apply to the department for the return of his license; and

(3) For a third assessment of requisite points within five years, as measured from the dates of previous arrests for which convictions were obtained to the date of the most current arrest for which a conviction is obtained, such person shall have his license suspended for a period of two years. Such person shall not be eligible for early return of his license or for a limited driving permit as provided in Code Section 40–5–64 during such two-year period.

(e) The periods of suspension provided for in this Code section shall begin on the date the license is surrendered to and received by the department, from the date a license is surrendered to a court under any provision of this chapter, or on the date that the department processes the citation or conviction, whichever date shall first occur. If the license cannot be surrendered to the department, the period of suspension may begin on the date set forth in a sworn affidavit setting forth the date and reasons for such impossibility, if the department shall have sufficient evidence to believe that the date set forth in such affidavit is true; in the absence of such evidence, the date of receipt of such affidavit shall be controlling.

(f) In all cases in which the department may return a license to a driver prior to the termination of the full period of suspension, the department may require such tests of driving skill and knowledge as it determines to be proper, and the department's discretion shall be guided by the driver's past driving record and performance, and the driver shall pay the fee provided for in Code Section 40–5–84 for the return of his or her license.

Laws 1968, p. 430, §§ 1–5; Laws 1975, p. 1008, § 1; Laws 1977, p. 1235, § 1; Laws 1978, p. 1655, § 1; Laws 1980, p. 691, § 1; Laws 1982, p. 1633, §§ 1, 2; Laws 1983, p. 3, § 29; Laws 1985, p. 758, § 3; Laws 1985, p. 758, § 4; Laws 1989, p. 555, § 1; Laws 1990, p. 2048, § 4; Laws 1991, p. 1587, § 1; Laws 1992, p. 1967, § 1; Laws 1992, p. 2755, § 1; Laws 1992, p. 2785, § 7; Laws 1995, p. 917, § 3; Laws 1996, p. 469, § 1; Laws 1999, p. 515, § 1; Laws 2000, p. 951, § 5–19; Laws 2001, p. 208, § 1–2; Laws 2004, Act 521, § 2, eff. July 1, 2004; Laws 2006, Act 538, § 3–12, eff. July 1, 2006; Laws 2010, Act 676, § 1, eff. July 1, 2010; Laws 2010, Act 677, § 2, eff. July 1, 2010.

Formerly Code 1933, § 68B–307; Code 1981, § 40–5–57.1.

Historical and Statutory Notes

The 2004 amendment by Act 521, in subsec. (e), deleted "or" preceding "from the date a license is surrendered", and added "or on the date that the department processes the citation or conviction," preceding "whichever date shall first occur".

The 2006 amendment by Act 538 amended the section without change.

Laws 2006, Act 538, § 5–1, provides:

"This Act shall become effective upon its approval by the Governor [April 21, 2006] or upon its becoming law without such approval for purposes of adopting local ordinances to become effective on or after July 1, 2006; and for all other purposes, this Act shall become effective on July 1, 2006."

The 2010 amendment by Act 676, in subsec. (c), par. (1), subpar. (A), added "Violation of usage of wireless telecommunications device requirements ... 1 point".

Laws 2010, Act 676, § 4, provides:

"This Act shall become effective on July 1, 2010, and shall apply to offenses committed on or after such date."

The 2010 amendment by Act 677, in subsec. (c), par. (1), subpar. (A), added "Operating a vehicle while text messaging ... 1 point".

Laws 2010, Act 677, § 6, provides:

"This Act shall become effective on July 1, 2010, and shall apply to offenses committed on or after such date."

§ 40–5–57.1. Revocation of drivers' licenses of persons under 21 years of age; issuance of new licenses

(a) Notwithstanding any other provision of this chapter, the driver's license of any person under 21 years of age convicted of hit and run or leaving the scene of an accident in violation of Code Section 40–6–270, racing on highways or streets, using a motor vehicle in fleeing or attempting to elude an officer, reckless driving, any offense for which four or more points are assessable under subsection (c) of Code Section 40–5–57, purchasing an alcoholic beverage in violation of paragraph (2) of subsection (a) of Code Section 3–3–23, or violation of paragraph (3) or (5) of subsection (a) of Code Section 3–3–23, or violation of Code Section 40–6–391 shall be suspended by the department as provided by this Code section; and the driver's license of any person under 18 years of age who has accumulated a violation point count of four or more points under Code Section 40–5–57 in any consecutive 12 month period shall be suspended by the department as provided by this Code section. A plea of nolo contendere shall be considered a conviction for purposes of this subsection. Notice of suspension shall be given by certified mail or statutory overnight delivery, return receipt requested; or, in lieu thereof, notice may be given by personal service upon such person. Such license shall be surrendered within ten days of notification of such suspension. Notice given by certified mail or statutory overnight delivery, return receipt requested, mailed to the person's last known address shall be prima-facie evidence that such person received the required notice.

(b) A person whose driver's license has been suspended under subsection (a) of this Code section shall:

(1) Subject to the requirements of subsection (c) of this Code section and except as otherwise provided by paragraph (2) of this subsection:

(A) Upon a first such suspension, be eligible to apply for license reinstatement and, subject to payment of required fees, have his or her driver's license reinstated after six months; and

(B) Upon a second or subsequent such suspension, be eligible to apply for license reinstatement and, subject to payment of required fees, have his or her driver's license reinstated after 12 months; or

(2)(A) If the driver's license was suspended upon conviction for violation of Code Section 40–6–391, be subject to the provisions of Code Section 40–5–63.

(B) If such driver was convicted of driving under the influence of alcohol or of having an unlawful alcohol concentration and is otherwise subject to the provisions of paragraph (1) of subsection (a) of Code Section 40–5–63, then such person shall not be eligible for a limited driving permit under Code Section 40–5–64, and:

(i) If the driver's alcohol concentration at the time of the offense was less than 0.08 grams, he or she shall not be eligible for license reinstatement until the end of six months; or

(ii) If the driver's alcohol concentration at the time of the offense was 0.08 grams or more, he or she shall not be eligible for license reinstatement until the end of 12 months.

(b.1) In any case where a person's driver's license was administratively suspended as a result of the offense for which the person's driver's license has been suspended pursuant to this

Code section, the administrative license suspension period and the license suspension period provided by this Code section may run concurrently, and any completed portion of such administrative license suspension period shall apply toward completion of the license suspension period provided by this Code section.

(c)(1) Any driver's license suspended under subsection (a) of this Code section for commission of any offense other than violation of Code Section 40–6–391 shall not become valid and shall remain suspended until such person submits proof of completion of a defensive driving program approved by the department and pays the applicable reinstatement fee.

(2) The reinstatement fee for a first such conviction shall be $210.00 or $200.00 if paid by mail. The reinstatement fee for a second or subsequent such conviction shall be $310.00 or $300.00 if paid by mail.

(d) A suspension provided for in this Code section shall be imposed based on the person's age on the date of the conviction giving rise to the suspension.

Laws 1997, p. 760, § 15; Laws 2000, p. 951, § 5–20; Laws 2000, p. 1457, § 1; Laws 2000, p. 1589, § 3; Laws 2001, p. 184, §§ 2–2, 3–2; Laws 2001, p. 208, §§ 2–2, 3–2; Laws 2002, p. 415, § 40; Laws 2004, Act 521, § 3, eff. July 1, 2004; Laws 2005, Act 68, §§ 17–13, 17–14, eff. July 1, 2005; Laws 2009, Act 135, § 4, eff. July 1, 2009.

Historical and Statutory Notes

The 2004 amendment by Act 521 rewrote subsec. (b), par. (1), which had read:

"(1) Subject to the requirements of subsection (c) of this Code section and except as otherwise provided by paragraph (2) of this subsection:

"(A) Upon a first such suspension, be eligible to apply for license reinstatement and, subject to successful recompletion of the examination requirements of Code Section 40–5–27 and payment of required fees, have his or her driver's license reinstated six months from the date on which the suspended license was surrendered to and received by the department; and

"(B) Upon a second or subsequent such suspension, be eligible to apply for license reinstatement and, subject to successful recompletion of the examination requirements of Code Section 40–5–27 and payment of required fees, have his or her driver's license reinstated 12 months from the date on which the suspended license was surrendered to and received by the department; or".

The 2005 amendment by Act 68 in subsec. (b), in subpars. (A) and (B) of par. (1) deleted "successful recompletion of the examination requirements of Code Section 40–5–27 and" following "subject to", in par. (2) deleted subpar. (C); and added subsec. (d). Prior to amendment, subpar. (b)(1)(C) had read:

"(C) Any driver subject to the provisions of this paragraph shall, as an additional prerequisite for license reinstatement, be required to successfully recomplete the examination requirements of Code Section 40–5–27."

The 2009 amendment by Act 135 rewrote subsec. (c) which had read as follows:

"(c) Any driver's license suspended under subsection (a) of this Code section for commission of any offense other than violation of Code Section 40–6–391 shall not become valid and shall remain suspended until such person submits proof of completion of a defensive driving program approved by the department and pays a fee equivalent to that required for restoration of a suspended driver's license under paragraph (1) of subsection (a) of Code Section 40–5–63; provided, however, that such fee shall not be required under this subsection if such person's driver's license was administratively suspended as a result of the offense for which the person's driver's license has been suspended pursuant to this Code section and the restoration fee was paid for such administratively suspended driver's license."

§ 40–5–57.2. Suspension of license for driving off without payment or charge having been made for gasoline dispensed into vehicle

(a) The driver's license of any person convicted for a second or subsequent offense of violating Code Section 40–6–255 shall be suspended as provided in this Code section. The person shall submit the driver's license to the court upon conviction and the court shall forward the driver's license to the department.

(b)(1) A first suspension of a driver's license under this Code section shall be for a period of six months.

(2) A second or subsequent suspension of a driver's license under this Code section shall be for a period of one year.

(c) After the suspension period and when the person pays a restoration fee of $60.00 or, when processed by mail, $50.00, the suspension shall terminate and the department shall return the person's driver's license to such person.

Laws 1998, p. 1658, § 1.

§ 40–5–57.3. License suspension for second offenses

(a) The driver's license of any person who is convicted for a second or subsequent offense of violating Code Section 40–6–77 within a five-year period of time, as measured from the dates of previous arrests for which convictions were obtained or pleas of nolo contendere were accepted to the date of the current arrest for which a conviction is obtained or a plea of nolo contendere is accepted, shall be suspended for 30 days. The person shall submit his or her driver's license to the court upon conviction and the court shall forward the driver's license to the department.

(b) After the suspension period and the person pays a restoration fee of $60.00 or, when processed by mail, $50.00, the suspension shall terminate and the department shall return the person's driver's license to such person.

Laws 2009, Act 22, § 2, eff. July 1, 2009.

§ 40–5–58. Determination of habitual violators; revocation of license; probationary license

(a) As used in this Code section, "habitual violator" means any person who has been arrested and convicted within the United States three or more times within a five-year period of time, as measured from the dates of previous arrests for which convictions were obtained to the date of the most recent arrest for which a conviction was obtained, of:

(1) Committing any offense covered under Code Section 40–5–54 or Code Sections 40–6–391 through 40–6–395 or violating a federal law or regulation or the law of any state or a valid municipal or county ordinance substantially conforming to any offense covered under Code Section 40–5–54 or Code Sections 40–6–391 through 40–6–395; or

(2) Singularly or in combination, any of the offenses described in paragraph (1) of this subsection.

(b) When the records of the department disclose that any person has been arrested and convicted of a violation of Chapter 6 of this title, or of a valid local ordinance adopted pursuant thereto, of an offense occurring on or after January 1, 1976, which record of arrest and conviction, when taken with and added to previous arrests and convictions of such person as contained in the files of the department, reveals that such person is a habitual violator as defined in subsection (a) of this Code section, the department shall forthwith notify such person that upon the date of notification such person has been declared by the department to be a habitual violator, and that henceforth it shall be unlawful for such habitual violator to operate a motor vehicle in this state unless otherwise provided in this Code section. Notice shall be given by certified mail or statutory overnight delivery, with return receipt requested; or, in lieu thereof, notice may be given by personal service upon such person. In the event that at the time of determination the habitual violator had been issued a driver's license, such license shall be revoked by such notice and shall be surrendered to the department within ten days of notification of such determination. For the purposes of this chapter, notice given by certified mail or statutory overnight delivery with return receipt requested mailed to the person's last known address shall be prima-facie evidence that such person received the required notice. In addition to the procedure set forth in this subsection, the sentencing judge or prosecutor in a conviction which conviction classifies the defendant as a habitual violator may, at the time of sentencing, declare such defendant to be a habitual violator. The judge or prosecutor shall, when declaring a defendant to be a habitual violator, then give personal notice to such defendant on forms provided by the department that henceforth it shall be unlawful for such habitual violator to operate a motor vehicle in this state unless otherwise provided in this Code section. The judge or prosecutor, as the case may be, shall within three days forward to the department the order declaring that the defendant is a habitual violator, the notice of service, with the defendant's driver's license or a sworn affidavit of the defendant declaring that the driver's license has been lost, and the department's copy of the uniform citation or the official notice of conviction attached thereto.

(c)(1) Except as provided in paragraph (2) of this subsection or in subsection (e) of this Code section, it shall be unlawful for any person to operate any motor vehicle in this state after such person has received notice that his or her driver's license has been revoked as provided in subsection (b) of this Code section, if such person has not thereafter obtained a valid driver's license. Any person declared to be a habitual violator and whose driver's license has been revoked under this Code section and who is thereafter convicted of operating a motor vehicle before the department has issued such person a driver's license or before the expiration of five years from such revocation, whichever occurs first, shall be punished by a fine of not less than $750.00 or by imprisonment in the penitentiary for not less than one nor more than five years, or both. Any person declared to be a habitual violator and whose driver's license has been revoked and who is convicted of operating a motor vehicle after the expiration of five years from such revocation but before the department has issued such person a driver's license shall be guilty of a misdemeanor.

(2) Any person declared to be a habitual violator as a result of three or more convictions of violations of Code Section 40–6–391 within a five-year period of time, as measured from the dates of previous arrests for which convictions were obtained to the date of the most recent arrest for which a conviction was obtained, and who is thereafter convicted of operating a motor vehicle during such period of revocation, prior to the issuance of a probationary license under subsection (e) of this Code section or before the expiration of five years, shall be guilty of the felony of habitual impaired driving and shall be punished by a fine of not less than $1,000.00 or by imprisonment in the penitentiary for not less than one nor more than five years, or both.

(d) Notwithstanding any contrary provisions of Code Section 17–7–95, for the purposes of this Code section, any plea of nolo contendere entered and accepted after January 1, 1976, shall be considered a conviction.

(e)(1) Notwithstanding any contrary provisions of this Code section or any other Code section of this chapter, any person who has been declared a habitual violator and who has had his driver's license revoked under subsection (b) of this Code section for a period of five years and two years have expired since the date on which such person's license was surrendered or an affidavit was accepted as provided in subsection (e) of Code Section 40–5–61, such person may be issued a probationary driver's license for a period of time not to exceed three years upon compliance with the following conditions:

(A) Such person has not been convicted, or pleaded nolo contendere to a charge, of violating any provision of this chapter, Chapter 6 of this title, or any local ordinance relating to the movement of vehicles for a period of two years immediately preceding the application for a probationary driver's license;

(B) Such person has not been convicted, or pleaded nolo contendere to a charge, of a violation of any provision of this chapter which resulted in the death or injury of any individual;

(C) Such person has successfully completed, prior to the issuance of the probationary driver's license, a defensive driving course or a DUI Alcohol or Drug Use Risk Reduction Program as designated by the department;

(D) Such person has not been convicted, or pleaded nolo contendere to a charge, of violating any provision of Title 3, relating to alcoholic beverages, or of violating any provision of Chapter 13 of Title 16, relating to controlled substances;

(E) Such person shall submit a sworn affidavit that such person does not excessively use alcoholic beverages and does not illegally use controlled substances or marijuana. It shall be a misdemeanor to falsely swear on such affidavit and, upon conviction, the probationary license shall be revoked. No probationary license shall be issued during the remainder of the revocation period, and no driver's license shall be issued for the remainder of the original revocation period or for a period of two years from the date of conviction under this subparagraph;

(F) Such person submits proof of financial responsibility as provided in Chapter 9 of this title; and

(G) Refusal to issue a probationary driver's license would cause extreme hardship to the applicant. For the purposes of this subsection, the term "extreme hardship" means that the applicant cannot reasonably obtain other transportation, and, therefore, the applicant would be prohibited from:

(i) Going to his place of employment or performing the normal duties of his occupation;

(ii) Receiving scheduled medical care or obtaining prescription drugs;

(iii) Attending a college or school at which he is regularly enrolled as a student;

(iv) Attending regularly scheduled sessions or meetings of support organizations for persons who have addiction or abuse problems related to alcohol or other drugs, which organizations are recognized by the commissioner; or

(v) Attending under court order any driver education or improvement school or alcohol or drug treatment program or course approved by the court which entered the judgment of conviction resulting in revocation of his driver's license or by the commissioner.

(2) Application for a probationary driver's license shall be made upon such forms as the commissioner may prescribe. Such forms shall require such information as is necessary for the department to determine the need for such license. All applications shall be signed by the applicant before a person authorized to administer oaths.

(3) Upon compliance with the above conditions and the payment of a fee of $210.00 or $200.00 when processed by mail, such person may be issued a probationary driver's license by the department. Upon payment of a fee in an amount the same as that provided by Code Section 40–5–25 for issuance of a Class C driver's license, a person may be issued a replacement for a lost or destroyed probationary driver's license issued to him or her.

(4) A probationary driver's license shall be endorsed with such conditions as the commissioner deems necessary to ensure that such license will be used by the licensee only to avoid the conditions of extreme hardship. Such conditions may include the following restrictions:

(A) Specific places between which the licensee may be allowed to operate a motor vehicle;

(B) Routes to be followed by the licensee;

(C) Times of travel;

(D) The specific vehicles which the licensee may operate; and

(E) Such other restrictions as the department may require.

(5) A probationary driver's license issued pursuant to this Code section shall become invalid upon the expiration of the period of the suspension or revocation of the driver's license of such person.

(6)(A)(i) Any probationary licensee violating the provisions of paragraph (4) of this subsection or operating a vehicle in violation of any conditions specified in this subsection shall be guilty of a misdemeanor.

(ii) Except as provided in division (iii) of this subparagraph, any probationary licensee violating any state law or local ordinance involving an offense listed in Code Section 40–5–54 or Code Section 40–6–391 shall be guilty of a felony and shall be punished by a fine of not less than $1,000.00 or by imprisonment in the penitentiary for not less than one nor more than five years, or both.

(iii) Any probationary licensee violating any state law or local ordinance involving a felony offense listed in Code Section 40–5–54 shall be guilty of a felony and shall be punished as is provided for conviction of such felony.

(B) Any probationary licensee who is convicted of violating, or who pleads nolo contendere to a charge of violating, any state law or local ordinance involving an offense listed in Code Section 40–5–54 or Code Section 40–6–391 or any probationary licensee who is convicted of violating, or who pleads nolo contendere to a charge of violating, the conditions endorsed on his license, shall have his license revoked by the department. Any court in which such conviction is had or in which said nolo contendere plea is accepted shall require the licensee to surrender the license to the court. The court shall forward the license to the department within ten days after the conviction or acceptance of the plea, with a copy of the conviction. Any person whose probationary license is revoked for committing an offense listed in Code Section 40–5–54 or Code Section 40–6–391 shall not be eligible to apply for a regular driver's license until the expiration of the original five-year revocation period during which the probationary license was originally issued or for a period of two years following the conviction, whichever is greater.

(C) If the commissioner has reason to believe or makes a preliminary finding that the requirements of the public safety or welfare outweigh the individual needs of a person for a probationary license, the commissioner, in his discretion, after affording the person notice and an opportunity to be heard, may refuse to issue the license under this subsection.

(D) Any person whose probationary driver's license has been revoked shall not be eligible to apply for a subsequent probationary license under this Code section for a period of five years.

(7) Any person whose probationary license has been revoked or who has been refused a probationary license by the department may make a request in writing for a hearing to be provided by the department. Such hearing shall be provided by the department within 30 days after the receipt of such request and shall follow the procedures required by Chapter 13 of Title 50, the "Georgia Administrative Procedure Act." Appeal from such hearing shall be in accordance with Chapter 13 of Title 50.

(f) If a person's license was revoked for a violation of Code Section 40–6–391 resulting from a motor vehicle collision in which any person lost his life, the person whose license was revoked shall not be entitled to a probationary license as set forth in this Code section.

Laws 1975, p. 1008, § 1; Laws 1977, p. 307, § 3; Laws 1978, p. 225, § 1; Laws 1980, p. 691, §§ 2, 3; Laws 1982, p. 3, § 40; Laws 1982, p. 867, § 1; Laws 1982, p. 1862, § 2; Laws 1983, p. 3, § 29; Laws 1983, p. 1000, § 5; Laws 1984, p. 22, § 40; Laws 1984, p. 797, §§ 1, 2; Laws 1985, p. 758, §§ 5, 6; Laws 1987, p. 1082, §§ 2, 3; Laws 1988, p. 385, § 1; Laws 1988, p. 897, § 3; Laws 1988, p. 1893, § 1A; Laws 1989, p. 14, § 40; Laws 1990, p. 1154, § 2; Laws 1990, p. 2048, § 4; Laws 1992, p. 779, § 19; Laws 1992, p. 2556, § 1; Laws 1992, p. 2785, § 8; Laws 1994, p. 745, § 1; Laws 2000, p. 951, §§ 5–21, 5–22; Laws 2000, p. 1204, § 1; Laws 2000, p. 1589, § 3; Laws 2006, Act 590, § 7, eff. July 1, 2006.

Formerly Code 1933, § 68B–308.

Historical and Statutory Notes

The 2006 amendment by Act 590, in subpar. (e)(1)(A), added ", Chapter 6 of this title,".

§ 40–5–59. Department may require a reexamination; revocation of license on showing licensee is incompetent to operate motor vehicle; confidentiality of report

(a) The department, having good cause to believe that a licensed driver is incompetent or otherwise not qualified to be licensed, shall require him to submit to an examination at the nearest license examining facility within ten days of receipt of written notice from the department. Upon the conclusion of such examination, the department shall take action as may be appropriate and may revoke the license of such person or permit him to retain such license or may issue a license subject to restrictions as permitted under Code Section 40–5–30 or restrictions as to the type or class of vehicles that may be driven. Refusal or neglect of the licensee to submit to such examination shall be grounds for revocation of his license.

(b) Notwithstanding the provisions of subsection (a) of this Code section, the department is authorized to revoke the license of a driver without a preliminary examination or hearing upon a recommendation by a court or prosecutor or upon a showing by the records of the department that the licensee is incapacitated by reason of disease, mental or physical disability, or addiction to alcohol or drugs to the extent that such person is incompetent to operate a motor vehicle.

(c) Any person whose license is revoked pursuant to subsection (b) of this Code section thereafter shall be entitled to a hearing before the department upon receipt by the department of a written request therefor. Such hearing shall be held within 30 days of the receipt of such request. The person may request an opinion of the Driver License Advisory Board as provided for in subsection (c) of Code Section 40–5–34. The department may not grant any exceptions to any regulations issued pursuant to subsection (a) of Code Section 40–5–35. The scope of the hearing shall be to determine if the driver is competent to drive a motor vehicle. The hearing shall be informal and appeal shall be as provided for in Code Section 40–5–66.

(d) The reports required by this Code section shall be confidential and shall be used solely for the purpose of determining the qualifications of any person to drive a motor vehicle on the highways of this state. No civil or criminal action may be brought against any person or agency for providing the information to the department for the purposes of this Code section. The reports, or any reference to the reports, shall not be included in any abstract prepared pursuant to Code Section 40–5–2.

Laws 1975, p. 1008, § 1; Laws 1990, p. 2048, § 4; Laws 2006, Act 590, § 8, eff. July 1, 2006.

Formerly Code 1933, § 68B–309.

Historical and Statutory Notes

The 2006 amendment by Act 590 added subsec. (d).

§ 40–5–60. Effective date of revocation or suspension

All revocations and suspensions provided for in this chapter shall be effective on the day the driver receives actual knowledge or legal notice thereof, whichever occurs first. Notice of suspension by operation of law shall be considered legal notice. Any license suspension or revocation mandated in this chapter following a person's conviction for any offense, including suspensions due to the accumulation of points pursuant to Code Section 40–5–57, shall be by operation of law.

Laws 1976, p. 1668, § 1; Laws 1990, p. 2048, § 4; Laws 2008, Act 434, § 6, eff. Jan. 1, 2009.

Historical and Statutory Notes

The 2008 amendment by Act 434 added "Any license suspension or revocation mandated in this chapter following a person's conviction for any offense, including suspensions due to the accumulation of points pursuant to Code Section 40–5–57, shall be by operation of law." at the end of the section.

§ 40–5–61. Surrender and return of license

(a) The department, upon canceling, suspending, or revoking a license, shall require that such license shall be surrendered to the department and be processed in accordance with the rules and regulations of the department.

(b) Any person whose license has been canceled, suspended, or revoked shall immediately return his license to the department.

(c) It shall be unlawful to refuse to deliver upon a legal demand any driver's license which has been canceled, suspended, or revoked.

(d) Except as provided in Code Section 40–5–62, when the revocation period expires, the department shall reinstate the license to the driver within 30 days.

(e) For the purpose of making any determination under this Code section relating to the return of revoked or suspended licenses to drivers, the period of revocation or suspension shall begin on the date the license is surrendered to the department or a court of competent jurisdiction under any provision of this chapter or on the date that the department processes the citation or conviction, whichever date shall first occur. If the license is lost, or for any other reason surrender to the department is impossible, the period of revocation or suspension may begin on the date set forth in a sworn affidavit setting forth the date and reasons for such impossibility, if the department shall have sufficient evidence to believe that the date set forth in such affidavit is true; in the absence of such evidence, the date of receipt of such affidavit by the department shall be controlling.

Laws 1975, p. 1008, § 1; Laws 1976, p. 1668, § 1; Laws 1989, p. 628, § 2; Laws 1990, p. 2048, § 4; Laws 1993, p. 940, § 3; Laws 2000, p. 951, § 5–23; Laws 2004, Act 521, § 4, eff. July 1, 2004.

Formerly Code 1933, § 68B–313.

Historical and Statutory Notes

The 2004 amendment by Act 521, in subsec. (e), substituted "the period of revocation or suspension shall begin on the date the license is surrendered to the department or a court of competent jurisdiction under any provision of this chapter or on the date that the department processes the citation or conviction" for "no period of revocation or suspension shall begin until the license is surrendered to the department or a court of competent jurisdiction under any provision of this chapter".

§ 40–5–62. Period of revocation

(a) Unless the revocation was for a cause which has been removed, any person whose license or privilege to drive a motor vehicle on the public highways has been revoked shall not be eligible to apply for a new license nor restoration of his nonresident's operating privilege until:

(1) Five years from the date on which the revoked license was surrendered to and received by the department pursuant to a person's having been declared a habitual violator under Code Section 40–5–58 or from the date on which the department processed the citation or conviction, reduced by a period of time equal to that period of time which elapses between the date the person surrenders his driver's license to the court after conviction for the offense for which the person is declared a habitual violator and the date the department receives such license from the court; or

(2) Such time as any cause for revocation under subsection (b) of Code Section 40–5–59 has been removed.

(b) The department shall not issue a new license nor restore a person's suspended license or nonresident's operating privilege unless and until it is satisfied after investigation of the character, habits, and driving ability of such person that it will be safe to grant the privilege of driving a motor vehicle on the public highways. Notwithstanding subsection (a) of this Code section or any other provision of this title, the department shall not issue a new license to any person whose license was revoked as a habitual violator for three violations of Code Section 40–6–391 within a five-year period unless and until such person submits proof of completion of an approved DUI Alcohol or Drug Use Risk Reduction Program. The department may issue rules and regulations providing for reinstatement hearings. In the case of a revocation pursuant to Code Section 40–5–58, the department shall charge a fee of $410.00 or $400.00 if processed by mail in addition to the fee prescribed by Code Section 40–5–25 to issue a new driver's license to a person whose driver's license has been revoked.

Laws 1975, p. 1008, § 1; Laws 1983, p. 487, § 1; Laws 1984, p. 22, § 40; Laws 1985, p. 758, § 8; Laws 1990, p. 2048, § 4; Laws 1992, p. 779, § 19.1; Laws 1993, p. 940, § 4; Laws 2004, Act 521, § 5, eff. July 1, 2004; Laws 2009, Act 135, § 5, eff. July 1, 2009.

Formerly Code 1933, § 68B–310.

Historical and Statutory Notes

The 2004 amendment by Act 521, in subsec. (a), par. (1), added "or from the date on which the department processed the citation or conviction" following "Code Section 40–5–58".

The 2009 amendment by Act 135, in subsec. (b), substituted "$410.00 or $400.00" for "$210.00 or $200.00".

§ 40–5–63. Period, terms and conditions of suspension

(a) The driver's license of any person convicted of an offense listed in Code Section 40–5–54 or of violating Code Section 40–6–391, unless the driver's license has been previously suspended pursuant to Code Sections 40–5–67.1 and 40–5–67.2, shall by operation of law be suspended and such suspension shall be subject to the following terms and conditions; provided, however, that any person convicted of a drug related offense pursuant to Code Section 40–6–391 shall be governed by the suspension requirements of Code Section 40–5–75; and further provided that each charge for which a conviction was obtained shall be treated as a separate transaction for the purpose of imposing a license suspension hereunder, even if said convictions arise from a single incident; and further provided that the department shall treat each conviction received in the order in which said convictions are processed even if it is not the order in which said offenses occurred:

(1) Upon the first conviction of any such offense, with no arrest and conviction of and no plea of nolo contendere

accepted to such offense within the previous five years, as measured from the dates of previous arrests for which convictions were obtained to the date of the current arrest for which a conviction is obtained, the period of suspension shall be for 12 months. At the end of 120 days, the person may apply to the department for reinstatement of said driver's license. Such license shall be reinstated if such person submits proof of completion of a DUI Alcohol or Drug Use Risk Reduction Program and pays a restoration fee of $210.00 or $200.00 when such reinstatement is processed by mail unless such conviction was a recidivist conviction in which case the restoration fee shall be $510.00 or $500.00 when such reinstatement is processed by mail, provided that, if such license was suspended as a result of a conviction of an offense listed in Code Section 40–5–54, such license shall be reinstated if such person submits proof of completion of either a defensive driving program approved by the department or a DUI Alcohol or Drug Use Risk Reduction Program and pays the prescribed restoration fee. A driver's license suspended as a result of a conviction of a violation of Code Section 40–6–391 shall not become valid and shall remain suspended until such person submits proof of completion of a DUI Alcohol or Drug Use Risk Reduction Program and pays the prescribed restoration fee. For purposes of this paragraph, an accepted plea of nolo contendere to an offense listed in Code Section 40–5–54 by a person who is under 18 years of age at the time of arrest shall constitute a conviction. For the purposes of this paragraph only, an accepted plea of nolo contendere by a person 21 years of age or older, with no conviction of and no plea of nolo contendere accepted to a charge of violating Code Section 40–6–391 within the previous five years, as measured from the dates of previous arrests for which convictions were obtained or pleas of nolo contendere accepted to the date of the current arrest for which a plea of nolo contendere is accepted, shall be considered a conviction, and the court having jurisdiction shall forward, as provided in Code Section 40–6–391.1, the record of such disposition of the case to the department and the record of such disposition shall be kept on file for the purpose of considering and counting such accepted plea of nolo contendere as a conviction under paragraphs (2) and (3) of this subsection;

(2) Upon the second conviction of any such offense within five years, as measured from the dates of previous arrests for which convictions were obtained to the date of the current arrest for which a conviction is obtained, the period of suspension shall be for three years. At the end of 120 days, the person may apply to the department for reinstatement of said driver's license; except that if such license was suspended as a result of a second conviction of a violation of Code Section 40–6–391 within five years, the person shall not be eligible to apply for license reinstatement until the end of 18 months. Such license shall be reinstated if such person submits proof of completion of a DUI Alcohol or Drug Use Risk Reduction Program and pays a restoration fee of $210.00 or $200.00 when such reinstatement is processed by mail unless such conviction was a recidivist conviction in which case the restoration fee shall be $510.00 or $500.00 when processed by mail, provided that, if such license was suspended as a result of a conviction of an offense listed in Code Section 40–5–54, such license shall be reinstated if such person submits proof of completion of either a defensive driving program approved by the department or a DUI Alcohol or Drug Use Risk Reduction Program and pays the prescribed restoration fee. A driver's license suspended as a result of a conviction of a violation of Code Section 40–6–391 shall not become valid and shall remain suspended until such person submits proof of completion of a DUI Alcohol or Drug Use Risk Reduction Program and pays the prescribed restoration fee. For purposes of this paragraph, a plea of nolo contendere and all previous accepted pleas of nolo contendere to an offense listed in Code Section 40–5–54 within such five–year period of time shall constitute a conviction. For the purposes of this paragraph, a plea of nolo contendere to a charge of violating Code Section 40–6–391 and all prior accepted pleas of nolo contendere within five years, as measured from the dates of previous arrests for which convictions were obtained or pleas of nolo contendere were accepted to the date of the current arrest for which a plea of nolo contendere is accepted, shall be considered and counted as convictions; or

(3) Upon the third conviction of any such offense within five years, as measured from the dates of previous arrests for which convictions were obtained to the date of the current arrest for which a conviction is obtained, such person shall be considered a habitual violator, and said license shall be revoked as provided for in paragraph (1) of subsection (a) of Code Section 40–5–62. For purposes of this paragraph, a plea of nolo contendere and all previous accepted pleas of nolo contendere to an offense listed in Code Section 40–5–54 within such five–year period shall constitute a conviction. For the purposes of this paragraph, a plea of nolo contendere and all prior accepted pleas of nolo contendere to a charge of violating Code Section 40–6–391 within five years, as measured from the dates of previous arrests for which convictions were obtained or pleas of nolo contendere were accepted to the date of the current arrest for which a plea of nolo contendere is accepted, shall be considered and counted as convictions.

(b) The periods of suspension provided for in this Code section shall begin on the date the person is convicted of an offense listed in Code Section 40–5–54 or of violating Code Section 40–6–391.

(c) In all cases in which the department may return a license to a driver prior to the termination of the full period of suspension, the department may require such tests of driving skill and knowledge as it determines to be proper, and the department's discretion shall be guided by the driver's past driving record and performance, and the driver shall pay the applicable restoration fee. In addition to any other requirement the department may impose, a driver's license suspended as a result of a conviction of a violation of Code Section 40–6–391 shall not become valid, shall remain suspended, and shall not be returned to such driver or otherwise reinstated until such person submits proof of completion of a DUI Alcohol or Drug Use Risk Reduction Program.

(d)(1) Any person convicted of violating subsection (a) of Code Section 40–6–393, relating to homicide by vehicle, or Code Section 40–6–394, relating to serious injury by vehicle, shall have his or her license suspended for a period of three years. Such person shall not be eligible for early reinstatement of said driver's license as provided in this Code section or in Article 4 of this chapter and shall not be eligible for a limited driving permit as provided in Code Section 40–5–64.

(2) For purposes of this chapter, an accepted plea of nolo contendere to any violation of Code Section 40–6–393 or 40–6–394 shall constitute a conviction.

(e) The driver's license of any person under 21 years of age who is convicted of unlawful possession of alcoholic beverages in violation of Code Section 3–3–23 while operating a motor vehicle may be suspended for a period of not less than 120 days. At the end of 120 days, the person may apply to the department for reinstatement of said driver's license. Such license shall be reinstated only if the person submits proof of completion of an approved DUI Alcohol or Drug Use Risk Reduction Program and pays a restoration fee of $35.00 or $25.00 when processed by mail. For purposes of this subsection, a sentence under subsection (c) of Code Section 3–3–23.1 shall not be considered a conviction, and the driver's license of such person shall not be suspended, provided that such person completes a DUI Alcohol or Drug Use Risk Reduction Program within 120 days after sentencing.

(f) The driver's license of any person who is convicted of attempting to purchase an alcoholic beverage in violation of paragraph (2) of subsection (a) of Code Section 3–3–23 upon the first conviction shall be suspended for a period of six months and upon the second or subsequent conviction shall be suspended for a period of one year. At the end of the period of suspension, the person may apply to the department for reinstatement of his or her driver's license. Such license shall be reinstated upon payment of a restoration fee of $35.00 or $25.00 when processed by mail. For purposes of this subsection, a sentence under subsection (c) of Code Section 3–3–23.1 shall not be considered a conviction, and the driver's license of such person shall not be suspended.

Laws 1975, p. 1008, § 1; Laws 1976, p. 1670, § 1; Laws 1978, p. 225, § 4; Laws 1982, p. 3, § 40; Laws 1982, p. 1601, §§ 1, 2; Laws 1983, p. 3, § 29; Laws 1983, p. 487, § 2; Laws 1983, p. 1000, § 6; Laws 1985, p. 149, § 40; Laws 1985, p. 758, § 7; Laws 1987, p. 1082, § 4; Laws 1989, p. 1698, § 2; Laws 1989, p. 14, § 40; Laws 1990, p. 2048, § 4; Laws 1991, p. 1886, § 3; Laws 1992, p. 779, § 20; Laws 1992, p. 2564, § 2; Laws 1992, p. 2746, § 2; Laws 1992, p. 2785, §§ 9, 10; Laws 1993, p. 940, § 5; Laws 1994, p. 730, § 2; Laws 1997, p. 760, § 16; Laws 1997, p. 1085, § 3; Laws 2000, p. 951, §§ 5–24, 5–25; Laws 2000, p. 1457, § 2; Laws 2001, p. 208, §§ 2–3, 3–3; Laws 2005, Act 68, § 17–15, eff. July 1, 2005; Laws 2006, Act 590, § 9, eff. July 1, 2006; Laws 2007, Act 18, § 40, eff. May 11, 2007; Laws 2010, Act 633, § 13, eff. July 1, 2010.

Formerly Code 1933, § 68B–312.

Historical and Statutory Notes

The 2005 amendment by Act 68, throughout subsec. (a), deleted "approved by the Department of Human Resources" following "DUI Alcohol or Drug Use Risk Reduction Program" and in the third sentence of par. (1) substituted "department" for "Department of Motor Vehicle Safety" following "either a defensive driving program approved by the"; at the end of subsec. (c) deleted "approved by the Department of Human Resources" following "DUI Alcohol or Drug Use Risk Reduction Program"; and, in subsec. (e), in the second sentence deleted "prescribed by the Department of Human Resources" following "DUI Alcohol or Drug Use Risk Reduction Program".

The 2006 amendment by Act 590, in the introductory language of subsec. (a), added "; and further provided that each charge for which a conviction was obtained shall be treated as a separate transaction for the purpose of imposing a license suspension hereunder, even if said convictions arise from a single incident" at the end of the subsection; and in subsec. (d), added paragraph designations, and in newly designated par. (2), substituted "chapter" for "subsection" and substituted "any violation of Code Section 40–6–393 or 40–6–394" for "homicide by vehicle in the first degree or serious injury by vehicle".

The 2007 amendment by Act 18 was a provision contained in a correction bill.

The 2010 amendment by Act 633, in subsec. (a), inserted "; and further provided that the department shall treat each conviction received in the order in which said convictions are processed even if it is not the order in which said offenses occurred" at the end of the subsection.

§ 40–5–63.1. Clinical evaluation and substance abuse treatment program as condition of license reinstatement, issuance, or restoration

In addition to any and all other conditions of license reinstatement, issuance, or restoration under Code Section 40–5–58, 40–5–62, or 40–5–63, any person with two or more convictions for violating Code Section 40–6–391 within ten years, as measured from the dates of previous arrests for which convictions were obtained to the date of the current arrest for which a conviction is obtained, shall be required to undergo a clinical evaluation and, if recommended as a part of such evaluation, shall complete a substance abuse treatment program prior to such license reinstatement, issuance, or restoration; provided, however, that such evaluation and treatment shall be at such person's expense except as otherwise provided by Code Section 37–7–120. Acceptable proof of completion of such a program shall be submitted to the department prior to license reinstatement, issuance, or restoration. For purposes of this Code section, a plea of nolo contendere to a charge of violating Code Section 40–6–391 and all prior accepted pleas of nolo contendere within ten years, as measured from the dates of previous arrests for which convictions were obtained or pleas of nolo contendere were accepted to the date of the current arrest for which a plea of nolo contendere is accepted, shall be considered and counted as convictions.

Laws 1997, p. 760, § 17; Laws 2000, p. 951, § 5–26; Laws 2000, p. 1457, § 3; Laws 2008, Act 544, § 1, eff. July 1, 2008.

Historical and Statutory Notes

The 2008 amendment by Act 544 substituted "for violating" for "of violation of"; substituted "ten years" for "five years" twice; substituted "recommended as a part of such evaluation, shall complete a substance abuse treatment program prior to such license reinstatement, issuance, or restoration; provided, however," for "indicated by such evaluation, must complete a substance abuse treatment program, provided"; and substituted "program shall" for "program must".

Laws 2008, Act 544, § 5, provides:

"This Act shall become effective on July 1, 2008, and shall be applied to offenses occurring on or after July 1, 2008; provided, however, that for purposes of determining the number of prior convictions or pleas of nolo contendere pursuant to the felony provisions of paragraph (4) of subsection (c) of Code Section 40–6–391, only those offenses for which a conviction or a plea of nolo contendere is obtained on or after July 1, 2008, shall be considered."

§ 40–5–64. Limited permits for particular offenders

(a) *To whom issued.*

(1) Notwithstanding any contrary provision of Code Section 40–5–57 or 40–5–63 or any other Code section of this chapter, any person who has not been previously convicted or adjudicated delinquent for a violation of Code Section 40–6–391 within five years, as measured from the dates of previous arrests for which convictions were obtained or pleas of nolo contendere were accepted to the date of the current arrest for which a conviction is obtained or a plea of nolo contendere is accepted, may apply for a limited driving permit when and only when that person's driver's license has been suspended in accordance with paragraph (2) of subsection (a.1) of Code Section 40–5–22, subsection (d) of Code Section 40–5–57, paragraph (1) of subsection (a) of Code Section 40–5–63, paragraph (1) of subsection (a) of Code Section 40–5–67.2, or subsection (a) of Code Section 40–5–57.1, when the person is 18 or over and his or her license was suspended for exceeding the speed limit by 24 miles per hour or more but less than 34 miles per hour, and the sentencing judge, in his or her discretion, decides it is reasonable to issue a limited driving permit.

(2) Any person whose driver's license has been suspended and who is subject to a court order for installation and use of an ignition interlock device as a condition of probation pursuant to the provisions Article 7 of Chapter 8 of Title 42 may apply for a limited driving permit.

(b) *Application form.* Applications for limited driving permits shall be made upon such forms as the commissioner may prescribe. Such forms shall require such information as is necessary for the department to determine the need for such permit. All applications shall be signed by the applicant before a person authorized to administer oaths.

(c) *Standards for approval.* The department shall issue a limited driving permit if the application indicates that refusal to issue such permit would cause extreme hardship to the applicant. Except as otherwise provided by subsection (c.1) of this Code section, for the purposes of this Code section, "extreme hardship" means that the applicant cannot reasonably obtain other transportation, and therefore the applicant would be prohibited from:

(1) Going to his or her place of employment or performing the normal duties of his or her occupation;

(2) Receiving scheduled medical care or obtaining prescription drugs;

(3) Attending a college or school at which he or she is regularly enrolled as a student;

(4) Attending regularly scheduled sessions or meetings of support organizations for persons who have addiction or abuse problems related to alcohol or other drugs, which organizations are recognized by the commissioner; or

(5) Attending under court order any driver education or improvement school or alcohol or drug program or course approved by the court which entered the judgment of conviction resulting in suspension of his or her driver's license or by the commissioner.

(c.1) *Exception to standards for approval.* The provisions of paragraphs (2), (3), (4), and (5) of subsection (c) of this Code section shall not apply and shall not be considered for purposes of granting a limited driving permit or imposing conditions thereon under this Code section in the case of a driver's license suspension under paragraph (2) of subsection (a.1) of Code Section 40–5–22.

(d) *Conditions attached.* A limited driving permit shall be endorsed with such conditions as the commissioner deems necessary to ensure that such permit will be used by the permittee only to avoid the conditions of extreme hardship. Such conditions may include the following restrictions:

(1) Specific places between which the permittee may be allowed to operate a motor vehicle;

(2) Routes to be followed by the permittee;

(3) Times of travel;

(4) The specific vehicles which the permittee may operate;

(4.1) The installation and use of an ignition interlock device in accordance with Article 7 of Chapter 8 of Title 42, which shall be required for any permittee who is applying for an ignition interlock limited driving permit; and

(5) Such other restrictions as the department may require.

(e) *Fees, duration, renewal, and replacement of permit.* A permit issued pursuant to this Code section shall be $25.00 and shall become invalid upon the driver's eighteenth birthday in the case of a suspension under paragraph (2) of subsection (a.1) of Code Section 40–5–22, upon the expiration of one year following issuance thereof in the case of a suspension for an offense listed in Code Section 40–5–54 or a suspension under Code Section 40–5–57, or a suspension in accordance with paragraph (1) of subsection (a) of Code Section 40–5–63 for a violation of Code Section 40–6–391, upon the expiration of 30 days in the case of an administrative license suspension in accordance with paragraph (1) of subsection (a) of Code Section 40–5–67.2, or upon the expiration of six months following proof of installation of an ignition interlock device in the case of a limited driving permit issued to a person subject to a court order for installation and use of such a device pursuant to Article 7 of Chapter 8 of Title 42; except that such limited driving permit shall expire upon any earlier reinstatement of the driver's license. A person may apply to the department for a limited driving permit immediately following such conviction if he or she has surrendered his or her driver's license to the court in which the conviction was adjudged or to the department if the department has processed the citation or conviction. Upon the applicant's execution of an affidavit attesting to such facts and to the fact that the court had not imposed a suspension or revocation of his or her driver's license or driving privileges inconsistent with the driving privileges to be conferred by the limited driving permit applied for, the department may issue such person a limited driving permit. Permits issued pursuant to this Code section are renewable upon payment of a renewal fee of $5.00. Permits may be renewed until the person has his or her license reinstated for the violation that was the basis of the issuance of the permit. Upon payment of a fee in an amount the same as that provided by Code Section 40–5–25 for issuance of a Class C driver's license, a person may be issued a replacement for a lost or destroyed limited driving permit issued to him or her.

(f) *Liability of issuing officer.* No official or employee of the department shall be criminally or civilly liable or subject to being held in contempt of court for issuing a limited driving permit in reliance on the truth of the affidavits required by this Code section.

(g) *Revocation of permit.*

(1)(A) Any permittee who is convicted of violating any state law or local ordinance relating to the movement of vehicles or any permittee who is convicted of violating the conditions endorsed on his or her permit shall have his or her permit revoked by the department. Any court in which such conviction is had shall require the permittee to surrender the permit to the court, and the court shall forward it to the department within ten days after the conviction, with a copy of the conviction.

(B) Upon receipt of notice from the Department of Behavioral Health and Developmental Disabilities that a permittee who is required to complete a substance abuse treatment program pursuant to Code Section 40–5–63.1 enrolled in but failed to attend or complete such program as scheduled, the department shall revoke such person's limited driving permit and, by regular mail to his or her last known address, notify such person of such revocation. Such notice of revocation shall inform the person of the grounds for and effective date of the revocation and of the right to review. The notice of revocation shall be deemed received three days after mailing.

(C) Upon receipt of notice from a provider center for ignition interlock devices that an ignition interlock device which a permittee is required to use has been tampered with or the permittee has failed to report for monitoring of such device as required by law, the department shall revoke such permittee's limited driving permit and, by regular mail to his or her last known address, notify such person of such revocation. Such notice of revocation shall inform the person of the grounds for and effective date of the revocation and of the right to review. The notice of revocation shall be deemed received three days after mailing.

(2) Any person whose limited driving permit has been revoked shall not be eligible to apply for a driver's license until six months from the date such permit was surrendered to the department. In any case of revocation of a limited driving permit pursuant to subparagraph (A) of paragraph (1) of this subsection, the department may impose an additional period of suspension for the conviction upon which revocation of the permit was based.

(h) *Hearings.* Any person whose permit has been revoked or who has been refused a permit by the department may make a request in writing for a hearing to be provided by the department. Such hearing shall be provided by the department within 30 days after the receipt of such request and shall follow the procedures required by Chapter 13 of Title 50, the "Georgia Administrative Procedure Act." Appeal from such hearing shall be in accordance with said chapter.

(i) *Rules and regulations.* The commissioner may promulgate such rules and regulations as are necessary to implement this Code section.

(j) *Penalty.* Any permittee who operates a motor vehicle in violation of any condition specified on the permit shall be guilty of a misdemeanor.

Laws 1975, p. 1008, § 1; Laws 1977, p. 648, § 1; Laws 1978, p. 225, § 3; Laws 1983, p. 1000, § 7; Laws 1985, p. 149, § 40; Laws 1985, p. 758, § 9; Laws 1990, p. 2048, § 4; Laws 1992, p. 779, § 21; Laws 1992, p. 2564, § 3; Laws 1992, p. 2785, § 11; Laws 1994, p. 1600, § 1; Laws 1997, p. 760, § 18; Laws 1999, p. 391, § 5; Laws 2000, p. 951, § 5–27; Laws 2000, p. 1457, § 4; Laws 2002, p. 1324, § 1–20; Laws 2003, Act 353, § 1, eff. Jan. 1, 2004; Laws 2004, Act 521, § 6, eff. July 1, 2004; Laws 2006, Act 590, § 10, eff. July 1, 2006; Laws 2008, Act 434, § 7, eff. Jan. 1, 2009; Laws 2009, Act 102, § 3–4, eff. July 1, 2009; Laws 2010, Act 394, § 3, eff. July 1, 2010; Laws 2010, Act 633, § 14, eff. July 1, 2010.

Formerly Code 1933, § 68B–311.

Historical and Statutory Notes

The 2003 amendment by Act 353, in subsec. (g), par. (1), added new subpar. (C).

Laws 2003, Act 353, § 19, provides in part:

"(a) Section 1 of this Act shall become effective January 1, 2004."

The 2004 amendment by Act 521 rewrote subsec. (e) which had read:

"(e) *Duration of permit.* A permit issued pursuant to this Code section shall be $ 25.00 and shall be nonrenewable and shall become invalid upon the driver's eighteenth birthday in the case of a suspension under paragraph (2) of subsection (a.1) of Code Section 40–5–22, upon the expiration of one year following the effective date of suspension of the applicant's driver's license in the case of a suspension for an offense listed in Code Section 40–5–54 or a suspension under Code Section 40–5–57, upon the expiration of 120 days following conviction in the case of a suspension in accordance with paragraph (1) of subsection (a) of Code Section 40–5–63 for a violation of Code Section 40–6–391, upon the expiration of 30 days in the case of an administrative license suspension in accordance with paragraph (1) of subsection (a) of Code Section 40–5–67.2, or upon the expiration of six months following proof of installation of an ignition interlock device in the case of a limited driving permit issued to a person subject to a court order for installation and use of such a device pursuant to Article 7 of Chapter 8 of Title 42; except that such limited driving permit shall expire upon any earlier reinstatement of the driver's license. A person convicted of such offense whose driver's license had been surrendered to the court in which such conviction was adjudged may apply to the department for a limited driving permit immediately following such conviction. Upon the applicant's execution of an affidavit attesting to such facts and to the fact that the court had not imposed a suspension or revocation of his or her driver's license or driving privileges inconsistent with the driving privileges to be conferred by the limited driving permit applied for, the department may issue such person a limited driving permit. A person convicted of such offense whose driver's license had not been surrendered to such court immediately following such conviction may apply to the department for a permit. Upon the applicant's surrender to the department of his or her driver's license and the execution of a similar affidavit, or if the driver's license has been lost, upon execution of an additional affidavit to that effect, the department may issue such person a limited driving permit."

In 2004, the Code Commission, in subsec. (e), substituted "adjudged or to the department if" for "adjudged, to the department, or if". See § 28–9–5.

The 2006 amendment by Act 590, in subsec. (e), substituted "issuance thereof in the case of a suspension" for "the effective date of suspension of the applicant's driver's license in the case of a suspension" and substituted "Code Section 40–5–57, or" for "Code Section 40–5–57, upon the expiration of 120 days following conviction in the case of".

The 2008 amendment by Act 434, in subsec. (e), substituted "Fees, duration, renewal, and replacement of permit." for "Duration of permit" in the introductory sentence, deleted "and shall be nonrenewable" following "shall be $25.00" in the second sentence, and added "Permits issued pursuant to this Code section are renewable upon payment of a renewal fee of $5.00. Permits may be renewed until the person has his or her license reinstated for the violation that was the basis of the issuance of the permit. Upon payment of a fee in an amount the same as that provided by Code Section 40–5–25 for issuance of a Class C driver's license, a person may be issued a replacement for a lost or destroyed probationary driver's license issued to him or her." at the end of the subsection.

The 2009 amendment by Act 102 substituted "Department of Behavioral Health and Developmental Disabilities" for "Division of Mental Health, Developmental Disabilities, and Addictive Diseases of the Department of Human Resources" throughout the section.

The 2010 amendment by Act 394, in subsec. (a), par. (1), inserted "or subsection (a) of Code Section 40–5–57.1, when the person is 18 or over and his or her license was suspended for exceeding the speed limit by 24 miles per hour or more but less than 34 miles per hour, and the sentencing judge, in his or her discretion, decides it is reasonable to issue a limited driving permit" after "Code Section 40–5–67.2".

The 2010 amendment by Act 633, in subsec. (d), par. (4.1), inserted "which shall be required for any permittee who is applying for an ignition interlock limited driving permit" after "Title 42"; in subsec. (e), substituted "limited driving permit" for "probationary driver's license" in the last sentence.

§ 40–5–65. No operation under foreign license during suspension or revocation in this state

Any resident or nonresident whose driver's license or privilege to operate a motor vehicle in this state has been suspended or revoked as provided in this chapter shall not operate a motor vehicle in this state under a license or permit issued by any other jurisdiction or otherwise during such suspension or after such revocation until the license is restored when and as permitted under this chapter.

Laws 1975, p. 1008, § 1; Laws 1990, p. 2048, § 4.

Formerly Code 1933, § 68B–314.

§ 40–5–66. Right of appeal to superior court

(a) Except as provided in subsection (h) of Code Section 40–5–67.1 and subsection (h) of Code Section 40–5–64, any decision rendered by the department shall be final unless the aggrieved person shall desire an appeal. In such case, such person shall have the right to enter an appeal in the superior court of the county of his residence or in the Superior Court of Fulton County. Such appeal shall name the commissioner as defendant and must be filed within 30 days from the date the department enters its decision or order. The person filing the appeal shall not be required to post any bond nor to pay the costs in advance.

(b) If the person so desires, the appeal may be heard by the judge at term or in chambers or by a jury at the first term. The hearing on the appeal shall be de novo, but no appeal shall act as a supersedeas of any orders or acts of the department. No person shall be allowed to operate any vehicle in violation of any suspension or revocation by the department while any such appeal is pending.

Laws 1937, p. 322, art. 4, § 11; Laws 1943, p. 196, § 5; Laws 1951, p. 598, § 8; Laws 1975, p. 1008, § 1; Laws 1989, p. 14, § 40; Laws 1990, p. 2048, § 4; Laws 1992, p. 2564, § 4.

Formerly Code 1933, § 68B–315.

§ 40–5–67. Persons charged with driving under the influence; taking of driver's license; issuance of temporary permit; procedure upon conviction or acquittal

(a) Whenever any resident or nonresident person is charged with violating Code Section 40–6–391, the law enforcement officer shall take the driver's license of the person so charged. The driver's license shall be attached to the court's copy of the uniform traffic citation and complaint form and shall be forwarded to the court having jurisdiction of the offense. A copy of the uniform traffic citation and complaint form shall be forwarded, within ten days of issue, to the department. Taking the driver's license as required in this Code section shall not prohibit any law enforcement officer or agency from requiring any cash bond authorized by Article 1 of Chapter 6 of Title 17.

(b) At the time the law enforcement officer takes the driver's license, the officer shall issue a temporary driving permit to the person as follows:

(1) If the driver refuses to submit to a test or tests to determine the presence of alcohol or drugs as required in Code Section 40–5–55, the officer shall issue a 30 day temporary driving permit;

(2) If the driver's license is required to be suspended under Code Section 40–5–67.1, the officer shall issue a 30 day temporary driving permit; or

(3) If the test or tests administered pursuant to Code Section 40–5–55 indicate an alcohol concentration in violation of Code Section 40–6–391 but less than the level for an administrative suspension of the license under subsection (c) of Code

Section 40–5–67.1, the officer shall issue a 180 day temporary driving permit.

This temporary driving permit shall be valid for the stated period or until the person's driving privilege is suspended or revoked under any provision of this title. The department, at its sole discretion, may delay the expiration date of the temporary driving permit, but in no event shall this delay extend beyond the date when such person's driving privilege is suspended or revoked under any provision of this title. The department shall by rules and regulations establish the conditions under which the expiration of the temporary permit may be delayed.

(c)(1) If the person is convicted of violating or enters a plea of nolo contendere to a charge of violating Code Section 40–6–391, the court shall, within ten days, forward the person's driver's license and the record of the disposition of the case to the department. At this time, the court shall also require the person to surrender the temporary driving permit issued pursuant to subsection (b) of this Code section.

(2) If the person is not convicted of violating and does not enter a plea of nolo contendere to a charge of violating Code Section 40–6–391, and the court is in possession of the driver's license, the court shall return the driver's license to the person unless the license is in suspension for any other offense, in which case the court shall forward the license to the department for disposition.

Laws 1983, p. 1000, § 1; Laws 1990, p. 2048, § 4; Laws 1992, p. 2564, § 5; Laws 1994, p. 1600, § 2; Laws 1997, p. 760, § 19; Laws 2000, p. 951, § 5–28.

Formerly Code 1981, § 40–5–69.

§ 40–5–67.1. Tests to determine presence of alcohol or other drugs; implied consent notice; suspension of license; refusal to submit to testing; hearing; judicial review; attendance of law enforcement officers at implied consent hearings; certification of breath-testing instruments

(a) The test or tests required under Code Section 40–5–55 shall be administered as soon as possible at the request of a law enforcement officer having reasonable grounds to believe that the person has been driving or was in actual physical control of a moving motor vehicle upon the highways or elsewhere throughout this state in violation of Code Section 40–6–391 and the officer has arrested such person for a violation of Code Section 40–6–391, any federal law in conformity with Code Section 40–6–391, or any local ordinance which adopts Code Section 40–6–391 by reference or the person has been involved in a traffic accident resulting in serious injuries or fatalities. Subject to Code Section 40–6–392, the requesting law enforcement officer shall designate which test or tests shall be administered initially and may subsequently require a test or tests of any substances not initially tested.

(b) At the time a chemical test or tests are requested, the arresting officer shall select and read to the person the appropriate implied consent notice from the following:

(1) Implied consent notice for suspects under age 21:

"Georgia law requires you to submit to state administered chemical tests of your blood, breath, urine, or other bodily substances for the purpose of determining if you are under the influence of alcohol or drugs. If you refuse this testing, your Georgia driver's license or privilege to drive on the highways of this state will be suspended for a minimum period of one year. Your refusal to submit to the required testing may be offered into evidence against you at trial. If you submit to testing and the results indicate an alcohol concentration of 0.02 grams or more, your Georgia driver's license or privilege to drive on the highways of this state may be suspended for a minimum period of one year. After first submitting to the required state tests, you are entitled to additional chemical tests of your blood, breath, urine, or other bodily substances at your own expense and from qualified personnel of your own choosing. Will you submit to the state administered chemical tests of your (designate which tests) under the implied consent law?"

(2) Implied consent notice for suspects age 21 or over:

"Georgia law requires you to submit to state administered chemical tests of your blood, breath, urine, or other bodily substances for the purpose of determining if you are under the influence of alcohol or drugs. If you refuse this testing, your Georgia driver's license or privilege to drive on the highways of this state will be suspended for a minimum period of one year. Your refusal to submit to the required testing may be offered into evidence against you at trial. If you submit to testing and the results indicate an alcohol concentration of 0.08 grams or more, your Georgia driver's license or privilege to drive on the highways of this state may be suspended for a minimum period of one year. After first submitting to the required state tests, you are entitled to additional chemical tests of your blood, breath, urine, or other bodily substances at your own expense and from qualified personnel of your own choosing. Will you submit to the state administered chemical tests of your (designate which tests) under the implied consent law?"

(3) Implied consent notice for commercial motor vehicle driver suspects:

"Georgia law requires you to submit to state administered chemical tests of your blood, breath, urine, or other bodily substances for the purpose of determining if you are under the influence of alcohol or drugs. If you refuse this testing, you will be disqualified from operating a commercial motor vehicle for a minimum period of one year. Your refusal to submit to the required testing may be offered into evidence against you at trial. If you submit to testing and the results indicate the presence of any alcohol, you will be issued an out-of-service order and will be prohibited from operating a motor vehicle for 24 hours. If the results indicate an alcohol concentration of 0.04 grams or more, you will be disqualified from operating a commercial motor vehicle for a minimum period of one year. After first submitting to the required state tests, you are entitled to additional chemical tests of your blood, breath, urine, or other bodily substances at your own expense and from qualified personnel of your own choosing. Will you submit to the state administered chemical tests of your (designate which tests) under the implied consent law?"

If any such notice is used by a law enforcement officer to advise a person of his or her rights regarding the administration of chemical testing, such person shall be deemed to have been properly advised of his or her rights under this Code section and under Code Section 40–6–392 and the results of any chemical test, or the refusal to submit to a test, shall be admitted into evidence against such person. Such notice shall be read in its entirety but need not be read exactly so long as the substance of the notice remains unchanged.

(c) If a person under arrest or a person who was involved in any traffic accident resulting in serious injuries or fatalities submits to a chemical test upon the request of a law enforcement officer and the test results indicate that a suspension or disqualification is required under this Code section, the results shall be reported to the department. Upon the receipt of a sworn report of the law enforcement officer that the officer had reasonable grounds to believe the arrested person had been driving or was in actual physical control of a moving motor vehicle upon the highways or elsewhere throughout this state in violation of Code Section 40–6–391 or that such person had been driving or was in actual physical control of a moving motor vehicle upon the highways or elsewhere throughout this state and was involved in a traffic accident involving serious injuries or fatalities and that the person submitted to a chemical test at the request of the law enforcement officer and the test results indicate either an alcohol concentration of 0.08 grams or more or, for a person under the age of 21, an alcohol concentration of 0.02 grams or more, the department shall suspend the person's driver's license, permit, or nonresident operating privilege pursuant to Code Section 40–5–67.2, subject to review as provided for in this chapter. Upon the receipt of a sworn report of the law enforcement officer that the arrested person had been operating or was in actual physical control of a moving commercial motor vehicle and the test results indicate an alcohol concentration of 0.04 grams or more, the department shall disqualify the person from operating a motor vehicle for a minimum period of one year.

(d) If a person under arrest or a person who was involved in any traffic accident resulting in serious injuries or fatalities refuses, upon the request of a law enforcement officer, to submit to a chemical test designated by the law enforcement officer as provided in subsection (a) of this Code section, no test shall be given; but the law enforcement officer shall report the refusal to the department. Upon the receipt of a sworn report of the law enforcement officer that the officer had reasonable grounds to believe the arrested person had been driving or was in actual physical control of a moving motor vehicle upon the highways or elsewhere throughout this state in violation of Code Section 40–6–391 or that such person had been driving or was in actual physical control of a moving motor vehicle upon the highways or elsewhere throughout this state and was involved in a traffic accident which resulted in serious injuries or fatalities and that the person had refused to submit to the test upon the request of the law enforcement officer, the department shall suspend the person's driver's license, permit, or nonresident operating privilege for a period of one year or if the person was operating or in actual physical control of a commercial motor vehicle, the department shall disqualify the person from operating a commercial motor vehicle and shall suspend the person's driver's license, permit, or nonresident operating privilege, subject to review as provided for in this chapter.

(d.1) Nothing in this Code section shall be deemed to preclude the acquisition or admission of evidence of a violation of Code Section 40–6–391 if obtained by voluntary consent or a search warrant as authorized by the Constitution or laws of this state or the United States.

(e) If the person is a resident without a driver's license, commercial driver's license, or permit to operate a motor vehicle in this state, the department shall deny issuance of a license or permit to such person for the same period provided in subsection (c) or (d) of this Code section, whichever is applicable, for suspension of a license or permit or disqualification to operate a commercial motor vehicle subject to review as provided for in this chapter.

(f)(1) The law enforcement officer, acting on behalf of the department, shall personally serve the notice of intention to suspend or disqualify the license of the arrested person or other person refusing such test on such person at the time of the person's refusal to submit to a test or at the time at which such a test indicates that suspension or disqualification is required under this Code section. The law enforcement officer shall take possession of any driver's license or permit held by any person whose license is subject to suspension pursuant to subsection (c) or (d) of this Code section, if any, and shall issue a 30 day temporary permit. The officer shall forward the person's driver's license to the department along with the notice of intent to suspend or disqualify and the sworn report required by subsection (c) or (d) of this Code section within ten calendar days after the date of the arrest of such person. This paragraph shall not apply to any person issued a 180 day temporary permit pursuant to subsection (b) of Code Section 40–5–67. The failure of the officer to transmit the sworn report required by this Code section within ten calendar days shall not prevent the department from accepting such report and utilizing it in the suspension of a driver's license as provided in this Code section.

(2) If notice has not been given by the arresting officer, the department, upon receipt of the sworn report of such officer, shall suspend the person's driver's license, permit, or nonresident operating privilege or disqualify such person from operating a motor vehicle and, by regular mail, at the last known address, notify such person of such suspension or disqualification. The notice shall inform the person of the grounds of suspension or disqualification, the effective date of the suspension or disqualification, and the right to review. The notice shall be deemed received three days after mailing.

(g)(1) A person whose driver's license is suspended or who is disqualified from operating a commercial motor vehicle pursuant to this Code section shall remit to the department a $150.00 filing fee together with a request, in writing, for a hearing within ten business days from the date of personal notice or receipt of notice sent by certified mail or statutory overnight delivery, return receipt requested, or the right to said hearing shall be deemed waived. Within 30 days after receiving a written request for a hearing, the department shall hold a hearing as is provided in Chapter 13 of Title 50, the Georgia Administrative Procedure Act. The hearing shall be recorded.

(2) The scope of the hearing shall be limited to the following issues:

(A)(i) Whether the law enforcement officer had reasonable grounds to believe the person was driving or in actual physical control of a moving motor vehicle while under the influence of alcohol or a controlled substance and was lawfully placed under arrest for violating Code Section 40–6–391; or

(ii) Whether the person was involved in a motor vehicle accident or collision resulting in serious injury or fatality; and

(B) Whether at the time of the request for the test or tests the officer informed the person of the person's implied consent rights and the consequence of submitting or refusing to submit to such test; and

(C)(i) Whether the person refused the test; or

(ii) Whether a test or tests were administered and the results indicated an alcohol concentration of 0.08 grams or more or, for a person under the age of 21, an alcohol concentration of 0.02 grams or more or, for a person operating or having actual physical control of a commercial motor vehicle, an alcohol concentration of 0.04 grams or more; and

(D) Whether the test or tests were properly administered by an individual possessing a valid permit issued by the Division of Forensic Sciences of the Georgia Bureau of Investigation on an instrument approved by the Division of Forensic Sciences or a test conducted by the Division of Forensic Sciences, including whether the machine at the time of the test was operated with all its electronic and operating components prescribed by its manufacturer properly attached and in good working order, which shall be required. A copy of the operator's permit showing that the operator has been trained on the particular type of instrument used and one of the original copies of the test results or, where the test is performed by the Division of Forensic Sciences, a copy of the crime lab report shall satisfy the requirements of this subparagraph.

(3) The hearing officer shall, within five calendar days after such hearing, forward a decision to the department to rescind or sustain the driver's license suspension or disqualification. If no hearing is requested within the ten business days specified above, and the failure to request such hearing is due in whole or in part to the reasonably avoidable fault of the person, the right to a hearing shall have been waived. The request for a hearing shall not stay the suspension of the driver's license; provided, however, that if the hearing is timely requested and is not held before the expiration of the temporary permit and the delay is not due in whole or in part to the reasonably avoidable fault of the person, the suspension shall be stayed until such

time as the hearing is held and the hearing officer's decision is made.

(4) In the event the person is acquitted of a violation of Code Section 40–6–391 or such charge is initially disposed of other than by a conviction or plea of nolo contendere, then the suspension shall be terminated and deleted from the driver's license record. An accepted plea of nolo contendere shall be entered on the driver's license record and shall be considered and counted as a conviction for purposes of any future violations of Code Section 40–6–391. In the event of an acquittal or other disposition other than by a conviction or plea of nolo contendere, the driver's license restoration fee shall be promptly returned by the department to the licensee.

(h) If the suspension is sustained after such a hearing, the person whose license has been suspended under this Code section shall have a right to file for a judicial review of the department's final decision, as provided for in Chapter 13 of Title 50, the "Georgia Administrative Procedure Act"; while such appeal is pending, the order of the department shall not be stayed.

(i) Subject to the limitations of this subsection, any law enforcement officer who attends a hearing provided for by subsection (g) of this Code section for the purpose of giving testimony relative to the subject of such hearing shall be compensated in the amount of $20.00 for each day's attendance at such hearing. In the event a law enforcement officer gives testimony at two or more different hearings on the same day, such officer shall receive only $20.00 for attendance at all hearings. The compensation provided for in this subsection shall not be paid to any law enforcement officer who is on regular duty or who is on a lunch or other break from regular duty at the time the officer attends any such hearing. The compensation provided for by this subsection shall be paid to the law enforcement officer by the department from department funds at such time and in such manner as the commissioner shall provide by rules or regulations. The commissioner shall also require verification of a law enforcement officer's qualifying to receive the payment authorized by this subsection by requiring the completion of an appropriate document in substantially the following form:

IMPLIED CONSENT HEARING
ATTENDANCE RECORD

OFFICER: ____________ S.S. No. ____________

ADDRESS: ________________________________
Street City State ZIP Code

DATE: __________ TIME: __________ A.M.
P.M.

CASE: ________________________________

This is to certify that the police officer named above attended an implied consent hearing as a witness or complainant on the date and time shown above.

HEARING OFFICER: _____ TITLE: __________

I certify that I appeared at the implied consent hearing described above on the date and time shown above and that I was not on regular duty at the time of attending the hearing and that I have not received and will not receive compensation from my regular employer for attending the hearing.

Signature of officer: ______________

APPROVED FOR PAYMENT: ______________
Comptroller

(j) Each time an approved breath-testing instrument is inspected, the inspector shall prepare a certificate which shall be signed under oath by the inspector and which shall include the following language:

"This breath-testing instrument (serial no. _____) was thoroughly inspected, tested, and standardized by the undersigned on (date _____) and all of its electronic and operating components prescribed by its manufacturer are properly attached and are in good working order."

When properly prepared and executed, as prescribed in this subsection, the certificate shall, notwithstanding any other provision of law, be self-authenticating, shall be admissible in any court of law, and shall satisfy the pertinent requirements of paragraph (1) of subsection (a) of Code Section 40–6–392 and subparagraph (g)(2)(F) of this Code section.

Laws 1992, p. 2564, § 6; Laws 1994, p. 472, § 1; Laws 1994, p. 1600, § 3–6; Laws 1995, p. 1160, §§ 1–3; Laws 1995, Ex. Sess., p. 5, § 1; Laws 1997, p. 143, § 40; Laws 1997, p. 760, § 20; Laws 1998, p. 210, § 2; Laws 2000, p. 951, §§ 5–29—5–32; Laws 2000, p. 1589, § 3; Laws 2001, p. 208, § 1–3; Laws 2006, Act 545, § 2, eff. July 1, 2006; Laws 2007, Act 18, § 40, eff. May 11, 2007; Laws 2010, Act 360, § 1–80, eff. May 12, 2010.

Historical and Statutory Notes

The 2006 amendment by Act 545 added subsec. (d.1).

The 2007 amendment by Act 18 was a provision contained in a correction bill.

The 2010 amendment by Act 360, in par. (g)(1), substituted "shall remit to the department a $150.00 filing fee together with a request, in writing, for a hearing" for "shall request, in writing, a hearing".

§ 40–5–67.2. Terms and conditions for suspension of license; return of license

(a) Any driver's license required to be suspended under subsection (c) of Code Section 40–5–67.1 shall be suspended subject to the following terms and conditions:

(1) Upon the first suspension pursuant to subsection (c) of Code Section 40–5–67.1 within the previous five years, as measured from the dates of previous arrests for which a suspension was obtained to the date of the current arrest for which a suspension is obtained, the period of suspension shall be for one year. Not sooner than 30 days following the effective date of suspension, the person may apply to the department for reinstatement of his or her driver's license. Such license shall be reinstated if such person submits proof of completion of a DUI Alcohol or Drug Use Risk Reduction Program and pays a restoration fee of $210.00 or $200.00 when such reinstatement is processed by mail unless such conviction was a recidivist conviction in which case the restoration fee shall be $510.00 or $500.00 when processed by mail. A driver's license suspended pursuant to Code Section 40–5–67.1 shall not become valid and shall remain suspended until such person submits proof of completion of a DUI Alcohol or Drug Use Risk Reduction Program and pays the prescribed restoration fee.

(2) Upon the second suspension pursuant to subsection (c) of Code Section 40–5–67.1 within five years, as measured from the dates of previous arrests for which suspensions were obtained to the date of the current arrest for which a suspension is obtained, the period of suspension shall be for three years. The person shall be eligible to apply to the department for license reinstatement not sooner than 18 months following the effective date of suspension. Such license shall be reinstated if such person submits proof of completion of a DUI Alcohol or Drug Use Risk Reduction Program and pays a restoration fee of $210.00 or $200.00 when such reinstatement is processed by mail unless such conviction was a recidivist conviction in which case the restoration fee shall be $510.00 or $500.00 when processed by mail. A driver's license suspended pursuant to Code Section 40–5–67.1 shall not become valid and shall remain suspended until such person submits proof of completion of a DUI Alcohol or Drug Use Risk Reduction Program and pays the prescribed restoration fee.

(3) Upon the third or subsequent suspension pursuant to subsection (c) of Code Section 40–5–67.1 within five years, as

measured from the dates of previous arrests for which suspensions were obtained to the date of the current arrest for which a suspension is obtained, the period of suspension shall be for five years. A driver's license suspended pursuant to Code Section 40–5–67.1 shall not become valid and shall remain suspended until such person submits proof of completion of a DUI Alcohol or Drug Use Risk Reduction Program and pays the prescribed restoration fee. The driver may apply for a probationary license pursuant to Code Section 40–5–58 after the expiration of two years from the effective date of suspension.

(b) An administrative license suspension pursuant to Code Section 40–5–67.1 shall be counted toward fulfillment of any period of suspension subsequently imposed as a result of a conviction of violating Code Section 40–6–391 which arises out of the same violation for which the administrative license suspension was imposed. An administrative license suspension pursuant to Code Section 40–5–67.1 shall run concurrently with any revocation of such driver's license pursuant to a subsequent determination that such person is a habitual violator.

(c) In all cases in which the department may return a license to a driver prior to the termination of the full period of suspension, the department may require such tests of driving skill and knowledge as it determines to be proper, and the department's discretion shall be guided by the driver's past driving record and performance, and the driver shall pay a restoration fee of $210.00 or $200.00 when processed by mail.

(d) Any other provision of law to the contrary notwithstanding, a driver with no previous conviction for a violation of Code Section 40–6–391 within the previous five years, as measured from the dates of previous arrests for which convictions were obtained to the date of the current arrest, during the period of administrative suspension contemplated under this chapter, shall be entitled to a limited driving permit as provided in Code Section 40–5–64.

Laws 1992, p. 2564, § 6; Laws 1994, p. 1600, § 7; Laws 2000, p. 951, § 5–33; Laws 2000, p. 1457, § 5; Laws 2001, p. 208, §§ 2–4, 3–4; Laws 2005, Act 68, § 17–15.1, eff. July 1, 2005; Laws 2007, Act 18, § 40, eff. May 11, 2007.

Historical and Statutory Notes

The 2005 amendment by Act 68 deleted "approved by the Department of Human Resources" following "DUI Alcohol or Drug Use Risk Reduction Program" throughout subsec. (a).

The 2007 amendment by Act 18 was a provision contained in a correction bill.

§ 40–5–68. Repealed by Laws 1997, p. 760, § 21, eff. July 1, 1997

§ 40–5–69. Suspension not affected by fact that license not surrendered or not retained by court and forwarded to Department of Public Safety

If a person's driver's license is suspended by operation of law as provided in Code Section 40–5–63, 40–5–67.1, or 40–5–67.2, the fact that the person's driver's license was not physically surrendered to the law enforcement officer at the time the person was charged with violating Code Section 40–6–391 or that the person's driver's license was not retained by the court and forwarded to the department as provided in Code Section 40–5–67 or that the person's driver's license was not forwarded as provided in Code Section 40–5–72 shall not affect such suspension.

Laws 1983, p. 1000, § 1; Laws 1990, p. 2048, § 4; Laws 1992, p. 2564, § 8; Laws 1997, p. 760, § 22; Laws 2000, p. 951, § 5–34.

Formerly Code 1981, § 40–5–73.

§ 40–5–70. Suspension of driver's license on failure to have minimum insurance

(a) In addition to any other punishment, the driver's license of a person convicted under subsection (a), (b), or (c) of Code Section 40–6–10 shall be suspended for a period of 60 days. The person shall submit the driver's license to the court upon conviction, and the court shall forward the driver's license to the department. After the 60 day suspension period and when the person provides proof of having prepaid a six-month minimum insurance policy and pays a restoration fee of $210.00 or $200.00 when processed by mail to the department, the suspension shall terminate and the department shall return the person's driver's license to such person. For a second or subsequent offense within a five-year period, the suspension period shall be increased to 90 days, and, in addition to the driver's license, such person's license tag and tag registration shall also be suspended for a period of 90 days. The restoration fee for a second or subsequent offense within a five-year period shall be $310.00 or $300.00 if paid by mail. The procedures for submission of drivers' licenses to the court and the forwarding of such licenses to the department shall also apply to license tags and tag registrations.

(b) A hearing of contempt of court shall be scheduled for any person refusing to deliver his motor vehicle driver's license and, where applicable, motor vehicle license tag and tag registration to the court after a conviction under subsection (a), (b), or (c) of Code Section 40–6–10 and a warrant shall issue for the arrest of such person.

(c) For the purposes of mandatory suspension of a driver's license for a first violation of subsection (a), (b), or (c) of Code Section 40–6–10, a forfeiture of bail or collateral used to seek a defendant's appearance in court, the payment of a fine, a plea of guilty, or a finding of guilty shall be considered a conviction regardless of whether the sentence is suspended, probated, rebated, or revoked. A plea of nolo contendere shall not be considered a conviction under this subsection, but a record of the disposition of the case shall be forwarded by the court to the department for the purposes of counting the plea of nolo contendere as a conviction under subsection (d) of this Code section.

(d) For the purposes of mandatory suspension of a driver's license, license tag, and tag registration for a second or subsequent violation within a five-year period, as measured from the dates of previous arrests for which convictions were obtained to the date of the current arrest for which a conviction was obtained, of subsection (a), (b), or (c) of Code Section 40–6–10, a forfeiture of bail or collateral used to seek a defendant's appearance in court, the payment of a fine, a plea of guilty, a plea of nolo contendere, a plea of nolo contendere to a previous violation of subsection (a), (b), or (c) of Code Section 40–6–10, or a finding of guilty shall be considered a conviction regardless of whether the sentence is suspended, probated, rebated, or revoked.

Laws 1990, p. 2048, § 4; Laws 1992, p. 6, § 40; Laws 1992, p. 779, § 23; Laws 2009, Act 135, § 6, eff. July 1, 2009.

Historical and Statutory Notes

The 2009 amendment by Act 135, in subsec. (a), inserted commas following "conviction" and "90 days", substituted "$210.00 or $200.00" for "$60.00 or $50.00", substituted "shall be increased" for "will be increased", and inserted "The restoration fee for a second or subsequent offense within a five-year period shall be $310.00 or $300.00 if paid by mail."

§ 40–5–71. Repealed by Laws 2010, Act 381, 8, eff. May, 20, 2010

Historical and Statutory Notes

The repealed section, relating to the procedure upon termination of minimum insurance, was derived from Laws 1990, p. 2048, § 4; Laws 1992, p. 6, § 40; Laws 1992, p. 779, § 24; Laws 1992, p. 2785, § 12; Laws 1993, p. 91, § 40; Laws 1993, p. 936, §§ 1, 2; Laws 1994, p. 97, § 40; Laws

1996, p. 453, § 12; Laws 2000, p. 429, § 4; Laws 2000, p. 951, §§ 5-35--5-37; Laws 2002, p. 1024, § 5; Laws 2003, Act 44, § 4. The repealing law also reserved the statute designation.

§ 40–5–72. Procedure upon suspension of driver's license, license tag, and tag registration for failure to have minimum insurance

(a) It is the duty of any person who has his or her driver's license and, where applicable, license tag and tag registration suspended under the provisions of Code Section 40–5–70 or 40–2–137 immediately upon suspension and demand of the department to forward such items to the department.

(b) If such driver's license and, where applicable, license tag and tag registration are not received by the department within ten days following the effective date of suspension, the commissioner shall immediately direct any peace officer to secure possession of the driver's license and, where applicable, license tag and tag registration and return the same to the department. The person whose driver's license and, where applicable, license tag and tag registration have been suspended shall surrender such items to any peace officer upon demand.

(c) Unless otherwise provided in this Code section, notice of the effective date of suspension shall occur when the driver receives actual knowledge or legal notice of the suspension, whichever occurs first. For the purposes of making any determination relating to the return of a suspended motor vehicle driver's license and, where applicable, license tag and tag registration, a period of suspension under Code Section 40–5–70 or 40–2–137 or this Code section shall begin upon the date of conviction adjudicated by the court having jurisdiction.

(d) Any person violating subsection (a) or (b) of this Code section shall be guilty of a misdemeanor and, upon conviction thereof, shall be subject to a fine of not less than $200.00 nor more than $1,000.00 or imprisonment for not more than 30 days.

Laws 1990, p. 2048, § 4; Laws 2000, p. 951, § 5–38; Laws 2010, Act 381, § 9, eff. May 20, 2010.

Historical and Statutory Notes

The 2010 amendment by Act 381, in subsec. (a) and subsec. (c), substituted "or 40–2–137" for "or 4§–5–71".

§ 40–5–73. Exemptions from law

The provisions of Code Sections 40–5–70, 40–6–10, and 40–6–11 shall not be applicable to persons operating vehicles which are not required to be registered or licensed in this state.

Laws 1990, p. 2048, § 4.

§ 40–5–74. Stapling, defacing, or altering of license which has been seized by law enforcement officer

Whenever a person is charged with a violation of the law relating to the operation of motor vehicles resulting in the person's driver's license being seized by a law enforcement officer and forwarded to the court having jurisdiction of the offense or whenever a person is convicted of any offense resulting in the person's driver's license being suspended and forwarded to the department, such driver's license shall not be stapled to any document or in any manner defaced or altered so as to indicate at any time in the future such previous seizure and processing of the license.

Laws 1996, p. 1250, § 6.

Article 3A

Suspension of License for Certain Drug Offenses

§ 40–5–75. Persons convicted of possession of controlled substance or marijuana; suspension of license

(a) The driver's license of any person convicted of any violation of the Georgia Controlled Substances Act, including, but not limited to, possession, distribution, manufacture, cultivation, sale, transfer of, trafficking in, the attempt or conspiracy to possess, distribute, manufacture, cultivate, sell, transfer or traffic in a controlled substance or marijuana, or the law of any other jurisdiction, shall by operation of law be suspended, and such suspension shall be subject to the following terms and conditions:

(1) Upon the first conviction of any such offense, with no arrest and conviction of and no plea of nolo contendere accepted to such offense within the previous five years, as measured from the dates of previous arrests for which convictions were obtained to the date of the current arrest for which a conviction is obtained, the period of suspension shall be for not less than 180 days. At the end of 180 days, the person may apply to the department for reinstatement of his or her driver's license. Such license shall be reinstated only if the person submits proof of completion of a DUI Alcohol or Drug Use Risk Reduction Program and pays to the Department of Driver Services a restoration fee of $210.00 or $200.00 when such reinstatement is processed by mail. For purposes of this paragraph, a plea of nolo contendere by a person to a charge of any drug related offense listed in this subsection shall, except as provided in subsection (c) of this Code section, constitute a conviction;

(2) Upon the second conviction of any such offense within five years, as measured from the dates of previous arrests for which convictions were obtained to the date of the current arrest for which a conviction is obtained, the period of suspension shall be for three years, provided that after one year from the date of the conviction, the person may apply to the department for reinstatement of his or her driver's license by submitting proof of completion of a DUI Alcohol or Drug Use Risk Reduction Program and paying to the Department of Driver Services a restoration fee of $310.00 or $300.00 when such reinstatement is processed by mail. For purposes of this paragraph, a plea of nolo contendere and all previous pleas of nolo contendere within such five-year period of time shall constitute a conviction; and

(3) Upon the third conviction of any such offense within five years, as measured from the dates of previous arrests for which convictions were obtained to the date of the current arrest for which a conviction is obtained, such person's license shall be suspended for a period of five years. At the end of two years, the person may apply to the department for a three-year driving permit upon compliance with the following conditions:

(A) Such person has not been convicted or pleaded nolo contendere to any drug related offense, including driving under the influence, for a period of two years immediately preceding the application for such permit;

(B) Such person submits proof of completion of a licensed drug treatment program. Such proof shall be submitted within two years of the license suspension and prior to the issuance of the permit. Such licensed drug treatment program shall be paid for by the offender. The offender shall pay a permit fee of $25.00 to the department;

(C) Such person submits proof of financial responsibility as provided in Chapter 9 of this title; and

(D) Refusal to issue such permit would cause extreme hardship to the applicant. For the purposes of this subparagraph, the term "extreme hardship" means that the applicant cannot reasonably obtain other transportation, and, therefore, the applicant would be prohibited from:

(i) Going to his or her place of employment or performing the normal duties of his or her occupation;

(ii) Receiving scheduled medical care or obtaining prescription drugs;

(iii) Attending a college or school at which he or she is regularly enrolled as a student; or

(iv) Attending regularly scheduled sessions or meetings of support organizations for persons who have addiction or abuse problems related to alcohol or other drugs, which organizations are recognized by the commissioner.

At the end of five years from the date on which the license was suspended, the person may apply to the department for reinstatement of his or her driver's license by submitting proof of completion of a DUI Alcohol or Drug Use Risk Reduction Program and paying to the Department of Driver Services a restoration fee of $410.00 or $400.00 when such reinstatement is processed by mail. For purposes of this paragraph, a plea of nolo contendere and all previous pleas of nolo contendere within such five-year period of time shall constitute a conviction.

(a.1) Any permittee who is convicted of violating any state law or local ordinance relating to the movement of vehicles or any permittee who is convicted of violating the conditions endorsed on his or her permit shall have his or her permit revoked by the department. Any court in which such conviction is had shall require the permittee to surrender the permit to the court, and the court shall forward it to the department within ten days after the conviction, with a copy of the conviction. Any person whose limited driving permit has been revoked shall not be eligible to apply for a driver's license until six months from the date such permit was surrendered to the department.

(b) Whenever a person is convicted of possession, distribution, manufacture, cultivation, sale, transfer of, the attempt or conspiracy to possess, distribute, manufacture, cultivate, sell, or transfer a controlled substance or marijuana, or driving or being in actual physical control of any moving vehicle while under the influence of such substance in violation of subsection (b) of Code Section 16–13–2, subsection (a), (b), or (j) of Code Section 16–13–30, or Code Section 16–13–33; paragraph (2), (4), or (6) of subsection (a) of Code Section 40–6–391; or the law of any other jurisdiction, the court in which such conviction is had shall require the surrender to it of any driver's license then held by the person so convicted and the court shall thereupon forward such license and a copy of its order to the department within ten days after the conviction. The periods of suspension provided for in this Code section shall begin on the date of surrender of the driver's license or on the date that the department processes the conviction or citation, whichever shall first occur.

(c)(1) The decision to accept a plea of nolo contendere to a misdemeanor charge of unlawful possession of less than one ounce of marijuana shall be at the sole discretion of the judge. If a plea of nolo contendere is accepted as provided in this subsection, the judge shall, as a part of the disposition of the case, order the defendant to attend and complete a DUI Alcohol or Drug Use Risk Reduction Program. The order shall stipulate that the defendant shall complete such program within 120 days and that the defendant shall submit evidence of such completion to the department. The judge shall also notify the defendant that, if he or she fails to complete such program by the date specified in the court's order, his or her driver's license shall be suspended, by operation of law, as provided in this Code section. The record of the disposition of the case shall be forwarded to the department.

(2) If a plea of nolo contendere is accepted and the defendant's driver's license has not been suspended under any other provision of this title and if the defendant has not been convicted of or has not had a plea of nolo contendere accepted to a charge of violating this Code section within the previous five years, the court shall, subject to paragraph (1) of this subsection, return the driver's license to the person; otherwise, such driver's license shall be forwarded to the department.

(d) Application for reinstatement of a driver's license under paragraph (1) or (2) of subsection (a) of this Code section shall be made on such forms as the commissioner may prescribe and shall be accompanied by proof of completion of a DUI Alcohol or Drug Use Risk Reduction Program and a restoration fee of $210.00 or $200.00 when such reinstatement is processed by mail. Application for a three-year driving permit under paragraph (3) of subsection (a) of this Code section shall be made on such form as the commissioner may prescribe and shall be accompanied by proof of completion of an approved residential drug treatment program and a fee of $25.00 for such permit.

(e) Notwithstanding any other provision of this Code section or any other provision of this chapter, any person whose license is suspended pursuant to this Code section shall not be eligible for early reinstatement of his license and shall not be eligible for a limited driving permit, but such person's license shall be reinstated only as provided in this Code section.

(f) Except as provided in subsection (a) of this Code section, it shall be unlawful for any person to operate any motor vehicle in this state after such person's license has been suspended pursuant to this Code section if such person has not thereafter obtained a valid license. Any person who is convicted of operating a motor vehicle before the department has reinstated such person's license or issued such person a three-year driving permit shall be punished by a fine of not less than $750.00 nor more than $5,000.00 or by imprisonment in the penitentiary for not more than 12 months, or both.

(g) Notwithstanding the provisions of Code Section 15–11–72 and except as provided in subsection (c) of this Code section, an adjudication of a minor child as a delinquent child or an unruly child for any offense listed in subsection (a) of this Code section shall be deemed a conviction for purposes of this Code section.

(h) Notwithstanding the provisions of subsection (a) of this Code section, licensed drivers who are 16 years of age who are adjudicated in a juvenile court pursuant to this Code section may, at their option, complete a DUI Alcohol or Drug Use Risk Reduction Program or an assessment and intervention program approved by the juvenile court.

(i) Notwithstanding any other provision of this chapter to the contrary, the suspension imposed pursuant to this Code section shall be in addition to and run consecutively to any other suspension imposed by the department at the time of the conviction that results in said suspension. If the person has never been issued a driver's license in the State of Georgia or holds a driver's license issued by another state, the person shall not be eligible for a driver's license for the applicable period of suspension following his or her submission of an application for issuance thereof.

Laws 1990, p. 1149, § 1; Laws 1990, p. 1097, § 1.5; Laws 1991, p. 1767, § 1; Laws 1992, p. 779, § 25; Laws 1992, p. 2785, § 13; Laws 1994, p. 97, § 40; Laws 1994, p. 730, §§ 3–5; Laws 1997, p. 143, § 40; Laws 2000, p. 20, § 23; Laws 2000, p. 951, § 5–39; Laws 2004, Act 521, § 7, eff. July 1, 2004; Laws 2005, Act 68, § 17–16, eff. July 1, 2005; Laws 2006, Act 590, § 11, eff. July 1, 2006; Laws 2007, Act 18, § 40, eff. May 11, 2007; Laws 2007, Act 44, § 1, eff. Jan. 1, 2008; Laws 2009, Act 135, § 7, eff. July 1, 2009; Laws 2010, Act 633, § 15, eff. July 1, 2010.

Historical and Statutory Notes

The 2004 amendment by Act 521 rewrote subsec. (b) which had read:

"(b) Whenever a person is convicted of possession, distribution, manufacture, cultivation, sale, transfer of, the attempt or conspiracy to possess, distribute, manufacture, cultivate, sell, or transfer a controlled substance or marijuana, or driving or being in actual physical control of any moving vehicle while under the influence of such substance in violation of subsection (b) of Code Section 16–13–2, subsection (a), (b), or (j) of Code Section 16–13–30, or Code Section 16–13–33; paragraph (2), (4), or (6) of subsection (a) of Code Section 40–6–391; or the law of any other jurisdiction, the court in which such conviction is had shall require the surrender to it of any driver's license then held by the person so convicted and the court shall thereupon forward such license and a copy of its order to the department within ten days after the conviction. The periods of suspension provided for in this Code section shall begin on the date of such person's conviction for the offense resulting in such suspension; provided, however, that, effective July 1, 1994, if, at the time of conviction of any offense listed in subsection (a) of this Code section, the person does not have a driver's license or the person's driver's license has been previously suspended, the periods of suspension specified by this Code section shall not commence until the person applies for the issuance or reinstatement of a driver's license."

The 2005 amendment by Act 68 in subsec. (a) substituted "and pays to the Department of Driver Services" for "approved by the Department of Human Resources and pays to the Department of Motor Vehicle Safety" following "DUI Alcohol or Drug Use Risk Reduction Program" in par. 1 and substituted "and paying to the Department of Driver Services" for "approved by the Department of Human Resources and pays to the Department of Motor Vehicle Safety" following "DUI Alcohol or Drug Use Risk Reduction Program" in par. 2; and in subsec. (h) deleted "approved by the Department of Human Resources" following "DUI Alcohol or Drug Use Risk Reduction Program".

The 2006 amendment by Act 590, in subsec. (a), rewrote the introductory paragraph which had read:

"(a) The driver's license of any person convicted of possession, distribution, manufacture, cultivation, sale, transfer of, the attempt or conspiracy to possess, distribute, manufacture, cultivate, sell, or transfer a controlled substance or marijuana, or driving or being in actual physical control of any moving vehicle while under the influence of such a substance in violation of subsection (b) of Code Section 16–13–2, subsection (a), (b), or (j) of Code Section 16–13–30, or Code Section 16–13–33; paragraph (2), (4), or (6) of subsection (a) of Code Section 40–6–391; or the law of any other jurisdiction shall by operation of law be suspended and such suspension shall be subject to the following terms and conditions:".

The 2007 amendment by Act 18 was a provision contained in a correction bill.

The 2007 amendment by Act 44 added subsec. (i).

Laws 2007, Act 44, § 8, provides:

"This Act shall become effective on January 1, 2008."

The 2009 amendment by Act 135, in pars. (1) and (2) of subsec. (a), deleted "unless such conviction was a recidivist conviction in which case the restoration fee shall be $510.00 or $500.00 when such reinstatement is processed by mail" following "processed by mail"; in par. (2) of subsec. (a), inserted a comma following "conviction", and substituted "$310.00 or $300.00" for "$210.00 or $200.00"; in subpar. (B) of par. (3) of subsec. (a), substituted "shall pay" for "must pay"; and inserted the undesignated paragraph at the end of subsec. (b).

The 2010 amendment by Act 633, added subsec. (a.1); in subsec. (i), inserted "in the State of Georgia or holds a driver's license issued by another state" after "issued a driver's license" in the second sentence.

Article 4

Restoration of Licenses to Persons Completing Defensive Driving Course or Alcohol or Drug Program

§ 40–5–80. Georgia Driver Improvement Act; purpose; duties of Department

The purpose of this article, the "Georgia Driver Improvement Act," is to improve and promote greater safety upon the highways and streets of this state; to improve the attitude and driving habits of drivers who accumulate traffic accident and motor vehicle conviction records; and to provide uniform DUI Alcohol or Drug Use Risk Reduction Programs for the rehabilitation of persons identified as reckless or negligent drivers and frequent violators. In carrying out this purpose, the Department of Driver Services shall:

(1) Charge a fee for the consideration of applications for approval of driver improvement clinics and instructors. The amount of this fee shall be established by the commissioner and shall, as best as the commissioner shall determine, approximate the expense incurred by the department in consideration of an application. These licenses and each renewal thereof shall be valid for a period of four years unless suspended or revoked prior to the expiration of that time period; and

(2) Require, in addition to the criteria established by the commissioner for approval of driver improvement clinics and DUI Alcohol or Drug Use Risk Reduction Programs, as provided in subsections (a) and (e) of Code Section 40–5–83, that every driver improvement clinic and DUI Alcohol or Drug Use Risk Reduction Program shall, as a condition of approval, provide a continuous surety company bond for the protection of the contractual rights of students in such form as will meet with the approval of the department, and written by a company authorized to do business in this state. The principal sum of the bond shall be established by the commissioner; however, in no event shall this amount be less than $10,000.00 per location, and a single bond at such rate may be submitted for all locations under the same ownership. If at any time said bond is not valid and in force, the license of the clinic or program shall be deemed suspended by operation of law until a valid surety company bond is again in force.

Laws 1978, p. 2302, § 1; Laws 1990, p. 1154, § 5; Laws 1990, p. 2048, § 4; Laws 1992, p. 2785, § 14; Laws 1994, p. 1066, § 1; Laws 1997, p. 143, § 40; Laws 2000, p. 951, § 5–40; Laws 2003, Act 353, § 2, eff. July 1, 2003; Laws 2005, Act 68, § 17–17, eff. July 1, 2005.

Formerly Code 1933, § 68D–101.

Historical and Statutory Notes

The 2003 amendment by Act 353, in par. (1), inserted "and each renewal thereof" following "These licenses" and substituted "four years" for "two years"; and in par. (2), inserted "per location, and a single bond at such rate may be submitted for all locations under the same ownership".

The 2005 amendment by Act 68 at the end of the introductory paragraph substituted "the Department of Driver Services shall:" for "the Department of Motor Vehicle Safety and the Department of Human Resources, as applicable, shall:"; and rewrote pars. (1) and (2), which had read:

"(1) Charge a fee for the consideration of applications for approval of driver improvement clinics and instructors. The amount of this fee shall be established by the commissioner of motor vehicle safety and shall, as best as the commissioner shall determine, approximate the expense incurred by the Department of Motor Vehicle Safety in consideration of an application. These licenses and each renewal thereof shall be valid for a period of four years unless suspended or revoked prior to the expiration of that time period; and

"(2) Require, in addition to the criteria for approval of driver improvement clinics established by the commissioner of motor vehicle safety and DUI Alcohol or Drug Use Risk Reduction Programs established by the Department of Human Resources, as provided in subsections (a) and (e) of Code Section 40–5–83, respectively, that every driver improvement clinic and DUI Alcohol or Drug Use Risk Reduction Program shall, as a condition of approval, provide a continuous surety company bond for the protection of the contractual rights of students in such form as will meet with the approval of the Department of Motor Vehicle Safety or the Department of Human Resources, as applicable, and written by a company authorized to do business in this state. The principal sum of the bond shall be established by the commissioner of motor vehicle safety or the Board of Human Resources, as applicable; however, in no event shall this amount be less than $2,500.00 per location, and a single bond at such rate may be submitted for all locations under the same ownership. If at any time said bond is not valid and in force, the license of the clinic or program shall be deemed suspended by operation of law until a valid surety company bond is again in force."

§ 40–5–81. Persons authorized to attend any certified driver improvement clinic or DUI Alcohol or Drug Use Risk Reduction Program

(a) Any driver improvement program at which attendance is required by court order shall conform to the requirements of this article.

(b) Whenever any person is authorized or required to attend a driver improvement clinic or DUI Alcohol or Drug Use Risk Reduction Program as a condition of any sentence imposed under this title or any ordinance enacted pursuant to this title or as a condition of the retention or restoration of the person's driving privilege, such person, in complying with such condition, shall be authorized to attend any driver improvement clinic or DUI Alcohol or Drug Use Risk Reduction Program certified under this article; and no judicial officer, probation officer, law enforcement officer, or other officer or employee of a court or person who owns, operates, or is employed by a private company which has contracted to provide private probation services for misdemeanor cases shall specify, directly or indirectly, a particular driver improvement clinic or DUI Alcohol or Drug Use Risk Reduction Program which the person may or shall attend. This Code section shall not prohibit any judicial officer, probation officer, law enforcement officer, or other officer or employee of a court or owner, operator, or employee of a private company which has contracted to provide probation services for misdemeanor offenders from furnishing any person, upon request, the names of certified driver improvement clinics or DUI Alcohol or Drug Use Risk Reduction Programs.

(c) It shall be unlawful for the owner, agent, servant, or employee of any driver improvement clinic or DUI Alcohol or Drug Use Risk Reduction Program licensed by the department to directly or indirectly solicit business by personal solicitation on public property, by phone, or by mail. A violation of this subsection shall be a misdemeanor. Advertising in any mass media, including, but not limited to, newspapers, radio, television, magazines, or telephone directories by a driver improvement clinic or DUI Alcohol or Drug Use Risk Reduction Program shall not be considered a violation of this subsection.

Laws 1978, p. 2302, § 1; Laws 1985, p. 758, § 20; Laws 1990, p. 2048, § 4; Laws 1992, p. 2564, § 9; Laws 1992, p. 2785, § 15; Laws 1992, p. 2978, § 9.1; Laws 1993, p. 454, § 1; Laws 2000, p. 951, § 5–41; Laws 2003, Act 353, § 3, eff. July 1, 2003; Laws 2004, Act 564, § 40, eff. May 13, 2004; Laws 2005, Act 68, § 17–18, eff. July 1, 2005.

Formerly Code 1933, § 68D–102; Code 1981, § 40–5–85.2.

Historical and Statutory Notes

The 2003 amendment by Act 353 rewrote subsec. (a) which had read:

"(a) This article shall not affect the power of any court to require attendance at any course or driver improvement program to which the court could otherwise require attendance."

The 2004 amendment by Act 564 was a provision contained in a correction bill.

The 2005 amendment by Act 68 in subsec. (c) substituted "department" for "Department of Motor Vehicle Safety or the Department of Human Resources" and ", or by mail" for "or mail" following "on public property, by phone" in the first sentence.

§ 40–5–82. Program administration

(a) The Driver Improvement Program created by this article shall be administered by the commissioner. The commissioner is authorized to promulgate and adopt rules and regulations necessary to carry out this article.

(b) For the purpose of generating greater interest in highway safety, the commissioner may solicit the assistance of local governmental authorities, associations, societies, clubs, schools, colleges, and other organizations or persons knowledgeable in highway safety driving standards to participate in conjunction with the department in the development of local driver improvement programs and in conducting driver improvement classes.

(c) The department is designated as the agency responsible for the approval and certification of DUI Alcohol or Drug Use Risk Reduction Programs and staff. This responsibility includes selection of the assessment instrument, development of the intervention curricula, training of program staff, and monitoring of all DUI Alcohol or Drug Use Risk Reduction Programs under this article.

(d) All DUI Alcohol or Drug Use Risk Reduction Program records including, but not limited to, assessment results and other components attended shall be confidential and shall not be released without the written consent of the DUI offender, except that such records shall be made available to the Department of Behavioral Health and Developmental Disabilities and the Department of Driver Services. The provision of assessments to the Department of Behavioral Health and Developmental Disabilities shall be according to an interagency agreement between the Department of Driver Services and the Department of Behavioral Health and Developmental Disabilities, and the agreement may provide for assessment fees to be transmitted to the Department of Behavioral Health and Developmental Disabilities.

(e) The department shall conduct a records check for any applicant for certification as an operator, director, or instructor of a DUI Alcohol or Drug Use Risk Reduction Program. Each applicant shall submit at least one set of classifiable fingerprints to the department in accordance with the fingerprint system of identification established by the director of the Federal Bureau of Investigation. The department shall transmit the fingerprints to the Georgia Crime Information Center, which shall submit the fingerprints to the Federal Bureau of Investigation for a search of bureau records and an appropriate report and shall promptly conduct a search of state records based upon the fingerprints. After receiving the report from the Georgia Crime Information Center and the Federal Bureau of Investigation, the department shall determine whether the applicant may be certified. No applicant shall be certified who has previously been convicted of a felony. The department shall promulgate rules and regulations regarding certification requirements, including restrictions regarding misdemeanor convictions. No applicant shall be certified unless he or she is a United States citizen, or if not a citizen, he or she presents federal documentation verified by the United States Department of Homeland Security to be valid documentary evidence of lawful presence in the United States under federal immigration law.

Laws 1978, p. 2302, § 1; Laws 1985, p. 149, § 40; Laws 1990, p. 1154, § 6; Laws 1990, p. 2048, § 4; Laws 1991, p. 1140, § 1; Laws 1997, p. 143, § 40; Laws 1999, p. 731, § 2; Laws 2000, p. 951, § 5–42; Laws 2005, Act 68, § 17–19, eff. July 1, 2005; Laws 2009, Act 102, § 3–2, eff. July 1, 2009; Laws 2010, Act 633, § 16, eff. July 1, 2010.

Formerly Code 1933, § 68D–103.

Historical and Statutory Notes

The 2005 amendment by Act 68, in subsec. (a), substituted "commissioner" for "commissioner of motor vehicle safety" at the end of the first sentence; in subsec. (c), substituted "department" for "Department of Human Resources" in the first sentence; in subsec. (d), substituted "Department of Driver Services" for "Department of Motor Vehicle Safety" and added the second sentence relating to provision of assessments to the Human Resources Department; and in subsec. (e), substituted "department" for "Department of Human Resources" in the first sentence.

The 2009 amendment by Act 102 substituted "Department of Behavioral Health and Developmental Disabilities" for "Department of Human Resources" throughout the section.

The 2010 amendment by Act 633, in subsec. (e), inserted ", director" after "operator" in the first sentence, substituted "at least one set" for "two sets" and inserted "in accordance with the fingerprint system of identification established by the director of the Federal Bureau of Investigation" in the second sentence, substituted "the" for "both sets of" and "one set of", deleted "retain one set and" before "promptly conduct" and added "based upon the fingerprints" after "state records" in the third sentence, and added the seventh sentence relating to verification by the Department of Homeland Security.

§ 40–5–83. Driver improvement clinics; DUI alcohol or drug use risk reduction programs

(a)(1) The commissioner shall establish criteria for the approval of driver improvement clinics. To be approved, a clinic shall provide and operate either a defensive driving course, an advanced defensive driving course, or a professional defensive driving course or any combination thereof. Clinics shall be composed of uniform education and training programs consisting of six hours of instruction designed for the rehabilitation of problem drivers. The commissioner shall establish standards and requirements concerning the contents of courses, qualifications of instructors, attendance requirements for students, and examinations. Approved clinics shall charge a fee of $75.00 for a defensive driving course, an advanced defensive driving course, or a professional defensive driving course; except that such clinics may charge different fees of their own choosing if the person is not enrolling in such course pursuant to court order or department requirement. No clinic shall be approved unless such clinic agrees in writing to allow the examination and audit of the books, records, and financial statements of such clinic. Clinics may be operated by any individual, partnership, corporation, association, civic group, club, county, municipality, board of education, school, or college.

(1.1)(A) No driver improvement clinic shall be permitted to use, adopt, or conduct any business under any name that is like or deceptively similar to any name used by any other driver improvement clinic, Georgia company, or Georgia corporation registered with the Secretary of State. This subparagraph shall not prohibit the franchising or licensing of any part or all of the name of a driver improvement clinic by the owner or the rights thereof to another licensed driver improvement clinic.

(B) This paragraph shall not prohibit the franchising or licensing of any part or all of the name of a clinic by the owner of the rights therein to another licensed driver improvement clinic.

(2) The commissioner may issue a special license to the instructor of any commercial driver training school authorizing such instructor to teach a defensive driving course, advanced defensive driving course, or professional defensive driving course of a driver improvement clinic provided pursuant to this Code section if such instructor is qualified to teach a teen-age driver education course which consists of a minimum of 30 hours of classroom and six hours of behind-the-wheel training and such instructor certifies to the commissioner that he or she has provided at least 250 hours of behind-the-wheel training in a teen-age driver education course.

(b)(1) The commissioner shall be authorized to accept certificates of completion from all defensive driving, driving under the influence, and alcohol and drug programs, clinics, and courses approved by any other state, the District of Columbia, and territories and possessions of the United States, including military reservations, whereby driver improvement clinics, programs, and courses shall be approved for use by residents of this state, other states, the District of Columbia, and territories and possessions of the United States.

(2) Driver improvement clinics, programs, and courses outside of the State of Georgia shall not be required to comply with the provisions of subsection (a) of this Code section.

(3) Driving under the influence and alcohol and drug programs, clinics, and courses outside of the State of Georgia shall not be required to comply with the provisions of subsection (e) of this Code section; provided, however, that the department shall not accept certificates of completion from any such program, clinic, or course unless said program, clinic, or course has been certified by the department as substantially conforming, with respect to course content, with the standards and requirements promulgated by the department under subsection (e) of this Code section. Certificates of completion from an out–of–state program, clinic, or course not so certified by the department may be accepted only for the purpose of permitting persons who are not residents of the State of Georgia to reinstate nonresident operating privileges.

(c) The commissioner shall be authorized to issue a special license to the instructor of any driver improvement clinic who is qualified to teach the alcohol and drug course prescribed in subsection (b) of Code Section 20–2–142. A driver improvement clinic shall offer such alcohol and drug course only through a qualified instructor and shall not charge a fee for such course of more than $25.00. The commissioner shall be authorized to issue a special license to the instructor of any commercial driver training school to teach the alcohol and drug course prescribed in subsection (b) of Code Section 20–2–142 who is qualified to teach a teen-age driver education course, which course consists of a minimum of 30 hours of classroom and six hours of behind-the-wheel training. The alcohol and drug program may be included in the 30 hours of classroom training as part of a curriculum approved by the department. Any fee authorized by law for such a drug and alcohol course may be included in the tuition charge for a teen-age driver education course. Any text or workbook provided or required by the Department of Public Safety for such alcohol and drug course shall be provided by the department at the same fee as currently charged by the department to any public or private school, contractor, or appropriate representative currently teaching the program.

(d) Notwithstanding the provisions of any law or rule or regulation which prohibits any individual who is a probation officer or other official or employee of the probation division of the Department of Corrections or a spouse of such individual from owning, operating, instructing at, or being employed by a driver improvement clinic, any individual who is a probation officer or other official or employee of the probation division of the Department of Corrections or a spouse of such individual who owns, operates, instructs at, or is employed by a driver improvement clinic on June 1, 1985, and who in all respects is and remains qualified to own, operate, instruct at, or be employed by a driver improvement clinic is expressly authorized to continue on and after June 1, 1985, to engage in such activities. No person who owns, operates, or is employed by a private company which has contracted to provide probation services for misdemeanor cases shall be authorized to own, operate, be an instructor at, or be employed by a driver improvement clinic or a DUI Alcohol or Drug Use Risk Reduction Program.

(e) The department is designated as the agency responsible for establishing criteria for the approval of DUI Alcohol or Drug Use Risk Reduction Programs. An applicant shall meet the certification criteria promulgated by the department through its standards and shall provide the following services: (1) the assessment component and (2) the intervention component. The department is designated as the agency responsible for establishing rules and regulations concerning the contents and duration of the components of DUI Alcohol or Drug Use Risk Reduction Programs, qualifications of instructors, attendance requirements for students, examinations, and program evaluations. Qualified instructors shall be certified for periods of four years each, which may be renewed. Approved DUI Alcohol or Drug Use Risk Reduction Programs shall charge a fee of $82.00 for the assessment component and $190.00 for the intervention component. An additional fee for required student program materials shall be established by the department in such an amount as is reasonable and necessary to cover the cost of such materials. No DUI Alcohol or Drug Use Risk Reduction Program shall be approved unless such clinic agrees in writing to submit reports as required in the rules and regulations of the department and to allow the examination and audit of the books, records, and financial statements of such DUI Alcohol or Drug Use Risk Reduction Program by the department or its authorized agent. DUI Alcohol or Drug Use Risk Reduction Programs may be operated by any public, private, or governmental entity; provided, however, that, except as otherwise provided in this subsection, in any political subdivision in which a DUI Alcohol or Drug Use Risk Reduction Program is operated by a private entity, whether for profit or nonprofit, neither the local county board of health nor any other governmental entity shall fund any new programs in that area. Programs currently in existence which are operated by local county boards of health or any other governmental entities shall be authorized to continue operation. New programs may be started in areas where no private DUI Alcohol or Drug Use Risk Reduction Programs have been made available to said community. The Department of Corrections is authorized to operate DUI Alcohol or Drug Use Risk Reduction Programs in its facilities where offenders are not authorized to participate in such programs in the community, provided that such programs meet the certification criteria promulgated by the Department of Driver Services. All such programs operated by the Department of Corrections shall be exempt from all fee provisions established in this subsection specifically including the rebate of any fee for the costs of administration. No DUI Alcohol or Drug Use Risk Reduction Program shall be approved unless such clinic agrees in writing to pay to the state, for the costs of administration, a fee of $22.00, for each offender assessed or each offender attending for points reduction, provided that nothing in this Code section shall be construed so as to allow the department to retain any funds required by the Constitution of Georgia to be paid into the state treasury; and provided, further, that the department shall comply with all provisions of Part 1 of Article 4 of Chapter 12 of Title 45, the "Budget Act," except Code Section 45–12–92, prior to expending any such miscellaneous funds.

(f)(1) Each applicant for certification to own or operate a driver improvement clinic shall submit at least one set of classifiable electronically recorded fingerprints to the department in accordance with the fingerprint system of identification established by the director of the Federal Bureau of Investigation. The department shall transmit the fingerprints to the Georgia Crime Information Center, which shall submit the fingerprints to the Federal Bureau of Investigation for a search of bureau records and an appropriate report and promptly conduct a search of state records based upon the fingerprints. After receiving the report from the Georgia Crime Information Center and the Federal Bureau of Investigation, the department shall determine whether the applicant may be certified.

(2) No applicant shall be certified unless he or she is a United States citizen, or if not a citizen, he or she presents federal documentation verified by the United States Department of Homeland Security to be valid documentary evidence of lawful presence in the United States under federal immigration law.

Laws 1978, p. 2302, § 1; Laws 1983, p. 745, § 3; Laws 1985, p. 409, § 1; Laws 1985, p. 758, § 12; Laws 1985, p. 758, § 20; Laws 1986, p. 839, § 2; Laws 1987, p. 431, § 1; Laws 1990, p. 1154, § 7; Laws 1990, p. 2048, § 4; Laws 1991, p. 1140, § 2; Laws 1992, p. 913, § 1; Laws 1992, p. 2785, § 16; Laws 1993, p. 91, § 40; Laws 1993, p. 454, § 2; Laws 1994, p. 1066, § 2; Laws 1997, p. 143, § 40; Laws 1999, p. 731, § 3; Laws 2000, p. 951, § 5–43; Laws 2003, Act 353, § 4, eff. July 1, 2003; Laws 2005, Act 68, § 17–20, eff. July 1, 2005; Laws 2009, Act 22, § 6, eff. July 1, 2009; Laws 2010, Act 633, § 17, eff. July 1, 2010.

Formerly Code 1933, § 68D–104; Code 1981, § 40–5–83.1; Code 1981, § 40–5–85.1.

Historical and Statutory Notes

The 2003 amendment by Act 353 rewrote subsec. (a); in subsec. (b), added new par. (3); , in subsec. (c) added "Any text or workbook provided or required by the Department of Public Safety for such alcohol and drug course shall be provided by the department at the same fee as currently charged by department to any public or private school, contractor, or appropriate representative currently teaching the program"; and in subsec. (e), inserted "Qualified instructors shall be certified for periods of four years each, which may be renewed." Prior to amendment, subsec. (a) had read:

"(a)(1) The commissioner of motor vehicle safety shall establish criteria for the approval of driver improvement clinics. To be approved, a clinic shall provide and operate a defensive driving course, an advanced defensive driving course, or a professional defensive driving course or any combination thereof. Clinics shall be composed of uniform education and training programs designed for the rehabilitation of problem drivers. The commissioner shall establish standards and requirements concerning the contents of courses, duration of courses, qualifications of instructors, fees, attendance requirements for students, and examinations. Approved clinics may charge a fee of not more than $60.00 for a defensive driving course, an advanced defensive driving course, or a professional defensive driving course. No clinic shall be approved unless such clinic agrees in writing to allow the examination and audit of the books, records, and financial statements of such clinic. Clinics may be operated by any individual, partnership, corporation, association, civic group, club, county, municipality, board of education, school, or college."

"(2) The commissioner may issue a special license to the instructor of any commercial driver training school authorizing such instructor to teach a defensive driving course, advanced defensive driving course, or professional defensive driving course of a driver improvement clinic provided pursuant to this Code section if such instructor is qualified to teach a teen-age driver education course which consists of a minimum of 30 hours of classroom and six hours of behind-the-wheel training and such instructor certifies to the commissioner that he or she has provided at least 250 hours of behind-the-wheel training in a teen-age driver education course."

The 2005 amendment by Act 68 in subsec. (a) deleted "of motor vehicle safety" following "commissioner" in the first sentence of par. (1) and in par. (3) substituted "department" for "Department of Human Resources" three times; and rewrote subsec. (e), which had read:

"(e) The Department of Human Resources is designated as the agency responsible for establishing criteria for the approval of DUI Alcohol or Drug Use Risk Reduction Programs. An applicant must meet the certification criteria promulgated by the Department of Human Resources through its standards and must provide the following services: (1) the assessment component and (2) the intervention component. The Department of Human Resources is designated as the agency responsible for establishing rules and regulations concerning the contents and duration of the components of DUI Alcohol or Drug Use Risk Reduction Programs, qualifications of instructors, attendance requirements for students, examinations, and program evaluations. Qualified instructors shall be certified for periods of four years each, which may be renewed. Approved DUI Alcohol or Drug Use Risk Reduction Programs shall charge a fee of $75.00 for the assessment component and $190.00 for the intervention component. An additional fee for required student program materials shall be established by the Department of Human Resources in such an amount as is reasonable and necessary to cover the cost of such materials. No DUI Alcohol or Drug Use Risk Reduction Program shall be approved unless such clinic agrees in writing to submit reports as required in the rules and regulations of the Department of Human Resources and to allow the examination and audit of the books, records, and financial statements of such DUI Alcohol or Drug Use Risk Reduction Program by the Department of Human Resources or its authorized agent. DUI Alcohol or Drug Use Risk Reduction Programs may be operated by any public, private, or governmental entity; provided, however, that, except as otherwise provided in this subsection, in any political subdivision in which a DUI Alcohol or Drug Use Risk Reduction Program is operated by a private entity, whether for profit or nonprofit, neither the local county board of health nor any other governmental entity shall fund any new programs in that area. Programs currently in existence which are operated by local county boards of health or any other governmental entities shall be authorized to continue operation. New programs may be started in areas where no private DUI Alcohol or Drug Use Risk Reduction Programs have been made available to said community. The Department of Corrections is authorized to operate DUI Alcohol or Drug Use Risk Reduction Programs in its facilities where offenders are not authorized to participate in such programs in the community, provided that such programs meet the certification criteria promulgated by the Department of Human Resources. All such programs operated by the Department of Corrections shall be exempt from all fee provisions established in this subsection specifically including the rebate of any fee for the costs of administration. No DUI Alcohol or Drug Use Risk Reduction Program will be approved unless such clinic agrees in writing to pay to the state, for the costs of administration, a fee of $15.00, for each offender assessed or each offender attending for points reduction, provided that nothing in this Code section shall be construed so as to allow the Department of Human Resources to retain any funds required by the Constitution of Georgia to be paid into the state treasury; and provided, further, that the Department of Human Resources shall comply with all provisions of Part 1 of Article 4 of Chapter 12 of Title 45, the 'Budget Act,' except Code Section 45–12–92, prior to expending any such miscellaneous funds."

The 2009 amendment by Act 22, in subsec. (e), in the second sentence, twice substituted "shall" for "must", in the fifth sentence, substituted "$82.00" for "$75.00", and in the last sentence, substituted "shall" for "will" following "Program" and substituted "$22.00" for "$15.00".

The 2010 amendment by Act 633 added subsec. (f).

§ 40–5–83.1. Repealed by Laws 1990, p. 2048, § 4, eff. January 1, 1991

§ 40–5–84. Reinstatement of licenses

(a) Except as otherwise provided, the license of any person whose license is suspended for the first time as a result of the conviction of an offense listed in Code Section 40–5–54 shall, at the expiration of 120 days following the date the license is suspended, be reinstated by the department upon receipt by the department of a certificate of completion of an approved defensive driving course and the payment of a restoration fee of $210.00 or $200.00 when such reinstatement is processed by mail.

(b) The license of any person whose license is suspended for the second time as a result of the conviction of an offense listed in Code Section 40–5–54 shall, at the expiration of 120 days following the date the license is suspended, be reinstated by the department upon receipt by the department of a certificate of completion of an advanced defensive driving course and the payment of a restoration fee of $310.00 or $300. 00 when such reinstatement is processed by mail.

(c) The license of any person whose license is suspended for the first time within a five-year period as a result of the assessment of points pursuant to Code Section 40–5–57 shall be reinstated by the department immediately upon receipt by the department of a certificate of completion of an approved defensive driving course and the payment of a restoration fee of $210.00 or $200.00 when such reinstatement is processed by mail.

(d) The license of any person whose license is suspended for the second time within a five-year period as a result of the assessment of points pursuant to Code Section 40–5–57 shall be reinstated by the department immediately upon receipt by the department of a certificate of completion of an advanced defensive driving course and the payment of a restoration fee of $310.00 or $300.00 when such reinstatement is processed by mail.

(e) The license of any person whose license is suspended for the third or subsequent time within a five-year period as a result of the assessment of points pursuant to Code Section 40–5–57 shall be reinstated by the department upon receipt by the department of a certificate of completion of an advanced defensive driving course and the payment of a restoration fee of $410.00 or $400.00 when such reinstatement is processed by mail.

Laws 1978, p. 2302, § 1; Laws 1983, p. 1000, § 8; Laws 1984, p. 22, § 40; Laws 1985, p. 149, § 40; Laws 1985, p. 758, § 13; Laws 1990, p. 2048, § 4; Laws 1992, p. 2785, § 17; Laws 2003, Act 353, § 5, eff. July 1, 2003; Laws 2009, Act 135, § 8, eff. July 1, 2009.

Formerly Code 1933, § 68D–105.

Historical and Statutory Notes

The 2003 amendment by Act 353, in subsecs. (a) through (d), deleted "or an approved DUI Alcohol or Drug Use Risk Reduction Program" following "defensive driving course".

The 2009 amendment by Act 135, in subsecs. (b) and (d) of subsec. (a), substituted "$310.00 or $300.00" for "$210.00 or $200.00"; in subsecs. (c) and (d), inserted "within a five-year period"; and added subsec. (e).

§ 40–5–85. Reinstatement of licenses; marker on license of person convicted for second time of driving under the influence

Notwithstanding any other provision of this chapter, any person convicted within five years of his or her first conviction as measured in paragraph (2) of subsection (c) of Code Section 40–6–391 for a second time of the offense of driving under the influence of alcohol or drugs in violation of Code Section 40–6–391 shall, upon compliance with all other requirements for reinstatement of his or her license as provided for in this chapter, be issued a driver's license which may bear a red stripe thereon. After seven years with no additional convictions for driving under the influence of alcohol or drugs any such person shall be issued a regular driver's license without such red stripe provided that he or she is otherwise entitled to such license under the laws of this state.

Laws 1996, p. 1624, § 8.

§ 40–5–85.1. Repealed by Laws 1990, p. 2048, § 4, eff. January 1, 1991

§ 40–5–85.2. Repealed by Laws 1990, p. 2048, § 4, eff. January 1, 1991

§ 40–5–86. Point count; reduction

Upon the accumulation of points pursuant to Code Section 40–5–57, the total number of points accumulated by any driver shall be reduced by seven points, but to not less than zero points, upon the satisfactory completion by such driver of an approved defensive driving course and the submission of a certificate by such driver to the department. The provisions of this Code section shall be available one time only to each driver in any five-year period.

Laws 1978, p. 2302, § 1; Laws 1987, p. 1082, § 5; Laws 1990, p. 2048, § 4; Laws 1992, p. 2105, § 1; Laws 1992, p. 2785, § 18; Laws 2003, Act 353, § 6, eff. July 1, 2003.

Formerly Code 1933, § 68D–107.

Historical and Statutory Notes

The 2003 amendment by Act 353 deleted "or a DUI Alcohol or Drug Use Risk Reduction Program" following "approved defensive driving course".

§ 40–5–87. Requirements for restoration of license or issuance of limited driving permit exclusive

The requirements and conditions of this article and the rules and regulations adopted pursuant to this article shall be the exclusive requirements for restoration of a license under this article or the issuance of a limited driving permit under this article.

Laws 1978, p. 2302, § 1; Laws 1990, p. 2048, § 4.

Formerly Code 1933, § 68D–108.

§ 40–5–88. Administrative fines

(a) As an alternative to criminal or other civil enforcement, the commissioner of driver services in order to enforce this article or any orders, rules, or regulations promulgated pursuant to this article, may issue an administrative fine not to exceed $1,000.00 for each violation, whenever the commissioner, after a hearing, determines that any person, firm, or corporation has violated any provisions of this article or any regulations or orders promulgated under this article. Notwithstanding the foregoing, violations that are minor in nature and committed by a person, firm, or corporation shall be punished only by a written reprimand unless the person, firm, or corporation fails to remedy the violation within 30 days, in which case an administrative fine, not to exceed $250.00, may be issued.

(b) The hearing and any administrative review thereof shall be conducted in accordance with the procedure for contested cases under Chapter 13 of Title 50, the "Georgia Administrative Procedure Act." Any person, firm, or corporation who has exhausted all administrative remedies available and who is aggrieved or adversely affected by a final order or action of the commissioner of driver services shall have the right of judicial review thereof in accordance with Chapter 13 of Title 50. All fines recovered under this Code section shall be paid into the state treasury. The commissioner of driver services may file, in the superior court (1) wherein the person under order resides; (2) if such person is a corporation, in the county wherein the corporation maintains its principal place of business; or (3) in the county wherein the violation occurred, a certified copy of a final order of the commissioner, whether unappealed from or affirmed upon appeal, whereupon the court shall render judgment in accordance therewith and notify the parties. Such judgment shall have the same effect and proceedings in relation thereto shall thereafter be the same as though the judgment had been rendered in an action duly heard and determined by the court. The penalty prescribed in this Code section shall be concurrent, alternative, and cumulative with any and all other civil, criminal, or alternative rights, remedies, forfeitures, or penalties provided, allowed, or available to such commissioner with respect to any violation of this article or any order, rules, or regulations promulgated pursuant to this article.

Laws 1985, p. 758, § 14; Laws 1990, p. 2048, § 4; Laws 1992, p. 2785, § 19; Laws 2000, p. 951, § 5–44; Laws 2003, Act 353, § 7, eff. July 1, 2003; Laws 2005, Act 68, § 17–21, eff. July 1, 2005.

Historical and Statutory Notes

The 2003 amendment by Act 353, divided the former section into new subsecs. (a) and (b), and in subsec. (a), added "Notwithstanding the foregoing, violations that are minor in nature and committed by a person, firm, or corporation shall be punished only by a written reprimand unless the person, firm, or corporation fails to remedy the violation within 30 days, in which case an administrative fine, not to exceed $250.00, may be issued".

The 2005 amendment by Act 68, in subsec. (a), substituted "commissioner of driver services" for "commissioner of motor vehicle safety or the commissioner of human resources, whichever is applicable," prior to "in order to enforce" and made a nonsubstantive change; and in subsec. (b) substituted "the commissioner of driver services" for "either the commissioner of motor vehicle safety or the commissioner of human resources" prior to "shall have the right of judicial review" in the second sentence and "commissioner of driver services" for "commissioner of motor vehicle safety or the commissioner of human resources, as appropriate" prior to "may file, in the superior court" in the fourth sentence, and made a nonsubstantive change.

Article 5

Identification Cards for Persons without Drivers' Licenses

§ 40–5–100. Issuance and form of cards

(a) The department shall issue personal identification cards to all residents as defined in Code Section 40–5–1 who make application to the department in accordance with rules and regulations prescribed by the commissioner. Cards issued to applicants under 21 years of age shall contain the distinctive characteristics of drivers' licenses issued pursuant to Code Section 40–5–26. The identification card shall be similar in form but distinguishable in color from motor vehicle drivers' licenses and may contain a recent color photograph of the applicant and include the following information:

(1) Full legal name;

(2) Address of residence;

(3) Birth date;

(4) Date identification card was issued;

(5) Sex;

(6) Height;

(7) Weight;

(8) Eye color;

(9) Location where the identification card was issued;

(10) Signature of person identified or facsimile thereof; and

(11) Such other information or identification as required by the department; provided, however, that the department shall not require an applicant to submit or otherwise obtain from an applicant any fingerprints or any other biological characteristic or information which uniquely identifies an individual, including without limitation deoxyribonucleic acid (DNA) and retinal scan identification characteristics but not including a photograph, by any means upon application.

(b) The identification card shall be valid for a period of five or eight years, at the option of the applicant, and shall bear the signatures of the commissioner and the Governor and shall bear an identification card number which shall not be the same as the social security number.

(c)(1) No person may possess more than one identification card issued pursuant to this Code section; provided, however, that this subsection shall not be construed to prevent a resident of this state who possesses a driver's license from also possessing an identification card issued under this article.

(2) Except as provided in paragraph (3) of this subsection, each applicant for an identification card shall surrender any identification card or driver's license previously issued by any other state and any identification card previously issued by this state.

(3)(A) Any noncitizen who is eligible for issuance of an identification card pursuant to the requirements of this chapter may be issued an identification card without surrendering any driver's license or identification card previously issued to him or her by any foreign jurisdiction. This exemption shall not apply to a person who is required to terminate any previously issued identification card pursuant to federal law.

(B) The department shall make a notation on the driving record of any person who retains a foreign identification card or driver's license, and this information shall be made available to law enforcement officers and agencies on such person's driving record through the Georgia Crime Information Center.

(4) Willful failure to surrender any such previous driver's license or personal identification card upon application for a new personal identification card will be considered an act of fraud and upon conviction be punished as provided for in Code Section 40–5–125.

(d) An application for identification card renewal may be submitted by:

(1) Personal appearance before the department; or

(2) Subject to rules or regulations of the department which shall be consistent with considerations of public safety and efficiency of service to customers, means other than such personal appearance which may include without limitation by mail or electronically. The department may by such rules or regulations exempt persons renewing identification cards under this paragraph from the surrender requirement in this Code section.

Laws 1973, p. 807, § 1; Laws 1976, p. 1421, § 2; Laws 1984, p. 1674, § 1; Laws 1986, p. 395, § 1; Laws 1988, p. 897, § 4; Laws 1990, p. 1913, § 2; Laws 1990, p. 2048, § 4; Laws 1992, p. 2785, § 20; Laws 1995, p. 920, § 4; Laws 1996, p. 1250, § 7; Laws 1997, p. 1443, § 2; Laws 2000, p. 951, §§ 5–45, 5–46; Laws 2004, Act 564, § 40, eff. May 13, 2004; Laws 2005, Act 68, § 17–23, eff. July 1, 2005; Laws 2005, Act 355, § 4, eff. July 1, 2006; Laws 2008, Act 787, § 5, eff. Jan. 1, 2009; Laws 2010, Act 633, § 18, eff. July 1, 2010.

Historical and Statutory Notes

The 2004 amendment by Act 564 was a provision contained in a correction bill.

The 2005 amendment by Act 68 rewrote subsec. (b) which had read:

"(b) The identification card shall be valid for four years and shall bear the signatures of the commissioner and the Governor and shall bear an identification card number which shall not be the same as the social security number, unless the person specifically requests that the social security number be used, or, in the case of an individual who is not a citizen of the United States, the passport number of the person identified or any number the department deems necessary to implement this Code section."

The 2005 amendment by Act 355, in subsec. (a), deleted par. (11), redesignated former par. (12) as par. (11), and rewrote the paragraph. Prior to amendment, pars. (11) and (12) had read:

"(11) Fingerprint of the person identified; and

"(12) Such other information or identification as required by the department."

Laws 2005, Act 355, § 6, provides:

"This Act shall become effective on July 1, 2006."

In 2005, the Code Commission, in subsec. (a), par. (11), deleted the comma following "including without limitation" and inserted a comma following "including a photograph". See § 28–9–5.

The 2008 amendment by Act 787 rewrote the subsec. (c) and added subsec. (d). Prior to amendment subsec. (c) had read:

"(c) No person may possess more than one identification card issued pursuant to this Code section; provided, however, that this subsection shall not be construed to prevent a resident of this state who possesses a driver's license from also possessing an identification card issued under this article. Each applicant for an identification card shall surrender any identification card or driver's license previously issued by any other state and any identification card previously issued by this state. Willful failure to surrender any such previous driver's license or personal identification card upon application for a new personal identification card will be considered an act of fraud and upon conviction be punished as provided for in Code Section 40–5–125."

The 2010 amendment by Act 633, in subsec. (b), substituted "eight years" for "ten years".

§ 40–5–101. Rules and regulations

The commissioner shall promulgate rules and regulations under which this article shall be implemented and administered.

Laws 1973, p. 807, § 2; Laws 1990, p. 2048, § 4; Laws 2000, p. 951, § 5–47.

§ 40–5–102. Birth certificate required

The department shall require an applicant for an identification card to furnish a birth certificate or other verifiable evidence stating the applicant's birth date.

Laws 1973, p. 807, § 4; Laws 1990, p. 2048, § 4.

§ 40–5–103. Fee; renewal; replacement

(a) Except as provided in Code Section 40–5–21.1 and subsections (b) and (c) of this Code section, the department shall collect a fee of $20.00 for a five-year card and a fee of $35.00 for an eight-year card, which fee shall be deposited in the state treasury in the same manner as other motor vehicle driver's license fees.

(a.1) The maximum period for which any identification card shall be issued is eight years.

(b) The department shall collect a fee of $5.00 for the identification card for all persons who are referred by a nonprofit organization which organization has entered into an agreement with the department whereby such organization verifies that the individual applying for such identification card is indigent. The department shall enter into such agreements and shall adopt rules and regulations to govern such agreements.

(c) The department shall not be authorized to collect a fee for an identification card from those persons who are entitled to a free veterans' driver's license under the provisions of Code Section 40–5–36.

(d) The department shall not be authorized to collect a fee for an identification card from any person:

(1) Who swears under oath that he or she desires an identification card in order to vote in a primary or election in Georgia and that he or she does not have any other form of identification that is acceptable under Code Section 21–2–417 for identification at the polls in order to vote; and

(2) Who produces evidence that he or she is registered to vote in Georgia.

This subsection shall not apply to a person who has been issued a driver's license in this state.

(e) The commissioner may by rule authorize incentive discounts where identification cards are renewed by Internet, telephone, or mail.

(f)(1) Every identification card shall be renewed on or before its expiration upon application, payment of the required fee, and, if applicable, satisfactory completion of any other requirements imposed by law.

(2) An application for renewal of an identification card may be submitted by:

(A) Personal appearance before the department; or

(B) Subject to rules or regulations of the department consistent with considerations of public safety and efficiency of service to identification card holders, means other than personal appearance which may include, without limitation, by mail or electronically. The department may by such rules or regulations exempt persons renewing identification cards under this paragraph from any surrender requirement imposed under Georgia law.

(3) Notwithstanding any other provision of this Code section, there shall be no fee whatsoever for replacement of any identification card solely due to a change of the identification card holder's name or address, provided that such replacement identification card shall be valid only for the remaining period of such original term; and provided, further, that only one such free replacement identification card may be obtained within the period for which the identification card was originally issued. Any application for the replacement of a lost identification card or due to a change in the identification card holder's name or address submitted within 150 days of the expiration of said identification card shall be treated as an application for renewal subject to the applicable fees as set forth in this Code section.

Laws 1973, p. 807, § 3; Laws 1983, p. 461, § 1; Laws 1990, p. 2048, § 4; Laws 1992, p. 779, § 26; Laws 2000, p. 951, § 5–48; Laws 2005, Act 53, § 66, eff. July 1, 2005; Laws 2005, Act 68, § 17–24, eff. July 1, 2005; Laws 2006, Act 432, § 3, eff. Jan. 26, 2006; Laws 2008, Act 434, § 8, eff. Jan. 1, 2009; Laws 2010, Act 360, § 1–81, eff. May 12, 2010; Laws 2010, Act 633, § 19, eff. July 1, 2010.

Historical and Statutory Notes

The 2005 amendment by Act 53 added subsec. (d).

Laws 2005, Act 53, § 67, provides:

"In the event any Code section, subsection, paragraph, subparagraph, item, sentence, clause, phrase, or word of this Act is declared or adjudged to be invalid or unconstitutional, such declaration or adjudication shall not affect the remaining portions of this Act, which shall remain of full force and effect as if such portion so declared or adjudged invalid or unconstitutional were not originally a part of this Act. The General Assembly declares that it would have enacted the remaining parts of this Act if it had known that such portion thereof would be declared or adjudged invalid or unconstitutional."

The 2005 amendment by Act 68 in subsec. (a) substituted "$20.00 for a five-year card and a fee of $35.00 for a ten-year card" for "$10.00 for the identification card" following "collect a fee of"; and added subsec. (d) relating to authorization of incentive discounts for renewals by Internet, telephone, or mail.

In 2005, the Code Commission redesignated subsec. (d), which was added by Laws 2005, Act 68, § 17, as subsec. (e). See § 28–9–5.

The 2006 amendment by Act 432, in subsec. (d), par. (1), deleted "is indigent and cannot pay the fee for an identification card, that he or she" following "swears under oath that he or she", and made a nonsubstantive change.

The 2008 amendment by Act 434 added subsec. (f).

The 2010 amendment by Act 360, in par. (a), substituted "an eight-year card" for "a ten-year card", and added par. (a.1).

The 2010 amendment by Act 633, in subsec. (a), inserted "Code Section 40–5–21.1 and" after "Except as provided in" and substituted "an eight-year" for "a ten-year".

§ 40–5–104. Violations relating to identification cards for persons not having driver's licenses

Any person who knowingly makes any false statement in an application for an identification card provided for by this article shall be guilty of a violation of Code Section 16–10–20.

Laws 1973, p. 807, § 5; Laws 1990, p. 2048, § 4; Laws 2002, p. 551, § 5.

Historical and Statutory Notes

The 2002 amendment by Act 750 substituted "violation of Code Section 16–10–20" for "misdemeanor".

§ 40–5–105. Maintenance and disclosure of department records

The provisions of Code Section 40–5–2 regarding the maintenance and disclosure of department records shall apply, where relevant, to those records maintained or received by the department in connection with identification cards issued under this article.

Laws 1997, p. 1446, § 3.

Article 6

Miscellaneous Offenses and Jurisdiction of Offenses

§ 40–5–120. Unlawful use of license or personal identification card

It is a misdemeanor for any person to:

(1) Display or cause or permit to be displayed or have in his or her possession any canceled, revoked, or suspended driver's license or personal identification card issued pursuant to Code Section 40–5–100;

(2) Fail or refuse to surrender to the department upon lawful demand any driver's license or personal identification card issued pursuant to Code Section 40–5–100 which has been suspended, revoked, disqualified, or canceled;

(3) Permit any unlawful use of a driver's license or personal identification card issued pursuant to Code Section 40–5–100 issued to such person;

(4) Do any act forbidden or fail to perform any act required by this chapter for which a criminal sanction is not provided elsewhere in this chapter; or

(5) Scan another person's driver's license, permit, or identification card without the person's prior knowledge and consent. If a person consents to the scanning of his or her driver's license, permit, or identification card, the information collected may be stored and used for any legitimate purpose. Each unlawful act of storage, disclosure, or usage in violation of this paragraph shall be considered a separate violation of this Code section. This prohibition shall not apply to law enforcement officers or any governmental entity that scans a driver's license, permit, or identification card to verify the contents thereof or to gather information for use for any governmental purpose.

Laws 1975, p. 1008, § 1; Laws 1989, p. 519, § 14; Laws 1990, p. 2048, § 4; Laws 1995, p. 920, § 5; Laws 2010, Act 633, § 20, eff. July 1, 2010.

Formerly Code 1933, § 68B–401.

Historical and Statutory Notes

The 2010 amendment by Act 633 added par. (5).

§ 40–5–121. Driving while license suspended or revoked

(a) Except when a license has been revoked under Code Section 40–5–58 as a habitual violator, any person who drives a motor vehicle on any public highway of this state without being licensed as required by subsection (a) of Code Section 40–5–20 or at a time when his or her privilege to so drive is suspended, disqualified, or revoked shall be guilty of a misdemeanor for a first conviction thereof and, upon a first conviction thereof or plea of nolo contendere within five years, as measured from the dates of previous arrests for which convictions were obtained to the date of the current arrest for which a conviction is obtained or a plea of nolo contendere is accepted, shall be fingerprinted and shall be punished by imprisonment for not less than two days nor more than 12 months, and there may be imposed in addition thereto a fine of not less than $500.00 nor more than $1,000.00. Such fingerprints, taken upon conviction, shall be forwarded to the Georgia Crime Information Center where an identification number shall be assigned to the individual for the purpose of tracking any future violations by the same offender. For the second and third conviction within five years, as measured from the dates of previous arrests for which convictions were obtained or pleas of nolo contendere were accepted to the date of the current arrest for which a conviction is obtained or a plea of nolo contendere is accepted, such person shall be guilty of a high and aggravated misdemeanor and shall be punished by imprisonment for not less than ten days nor more than 12 months, and there may be imposed in addition thereto a fine of not less than $1,000.00 nor more than $2,500.00. For the fourth or subsequent conviction within five years, as measured from the dates of previous arrests for which convictions were obtained or pleas of nolo contendere were accepted to the date of the current arrest for which a conviction is obtained or a plea of nolo contendere is accepted, such person shall be guilty of a felony and shall be punished by imprisonment for not less than one year nor more than five years, and there may be imposed in addition thereto a fine of not less than $2,500.00 nor more than $5,000.00.

(b)(1) The department, upon receiving a record of the conviction of any person under this Code section upon a charge of driving a vehicle while the license of such person was suspended, disqualified, or revoked, including suspensions under subsection (f) of Code Section 40–5–75, shall extend the period of suspension or disqualification by six months. Upon the expiration of six months from the date on which the suspension or disqualification is extended and payment of the applicable reinstatement fee, the department shall reinstate the license. The reinstatement fee for a first such conviction within a five-year period shall be $210.00 or $200.00 if paid by mail. The reinstatement fee for a second such conviction within a five-year period shall be $310.00 or $300.00 if paid by mail. The reinstatement fee for a third or subsequent such conviction within a five-year period shall be $410.00 or $400.00 if paid by mail.

(2) The court shall be required to confiscate the license, if applicable, and attach it to the uniform citation and forward it to the department within ten days of conviction. The period of suspension or disqualification provided for in this Code section shall begin on the date the person is convicted of violating this Code section.

(c) For purposes of pleading nolo contendere, only one nolo contendere plea will be accepted to a charge of driving without being licensed or with a suspended or disqualified license within a five-year period as measured from date of arrest to date of arrest. All other nolo contendere pleas in this period will be considered convictions. For the purpose of imposing a sentence under this subsection, a plea of nolo contendere shall constitute a conviction. There shall be no limited driving permit available for a suspension or disqualification under this Code section.

(d) Notwithstanding the limits set forth in Code Section 40–5–124 and in any municipal charter, any municipal court of any municipality shall be authorized to impose the punishment for a misdemeanor or misdemeanor of a high and aggravated nature as applicable and provided for in this Code section upon a conviction of a nonfelony charge of violating this Code section or upon conviction of violating any ordinance adopting the provisions of this Code section.

Laws 1975, p. 1008, § 1; Laws 1979, p. 1049, § 1; Laws 1983, p. 1000, § 10; Laws 1984, p. 22, § 40; Laws 1988, p. 897, § 5; Laws 1989, p. 350, § 1; Laws 1989, p. 519, § 15; Laws 1990, p. 2048, § 4; Laws 1991, p. 1886, § 5; Laws 1992, p. 1128, § 1; Laws 1999, p. 391, § 6; Laws 2000, p. 951, § 5-49; Laws 2004, Act 564, § 40, eff. May 13, 2004; Laws 2006, Act 590, § 12, eff. July 1, 2006; Laws 2008, Act 778, § 3, eff. July 1, 2008; Laws 2009, Act 22, § 3, eff. July 1, 2009; Laws 2009, Act 135, § 9, eff. July 1, 2009.

Formerly Code 1933, § 68B-402.

Historical and Statutory Notes

The 2004 amendment by Act 564 was a provision contained in a correction bill.

The 2006 amendment by Act 590 rewrote subsec. (b) which had read:

"(b)(1) The charge of driving with a suspended or disqualified license shall not be made where the suspension is a result of a failure to respond under Code Section 40-5-56 or an insurance cancellation unless the arresting officer has verified a service date and such date is placed on the uniform citation. If the suspension or disqualification is verified and the driver possesses a driver's license, the license shall be confiscated and mailed to the department. If the suspension or disqualification is not verified, the arresting officer shall serve the driver and attach the driver's license, if available, to the copy of service and send it to the department.

"(2) The department, upon receiving a record of the conviction of any person under this Code section upon a charge of driving a vehicle while the license of such person was suspended, disqualified, or revoked, shall extend the period of suspension or disqualification for six months. The court shall be required to confiscate the license, if applicable, and attach it to the uniform citation and forward it to the department within ten days of conviction. The period of suspension or disqualification provided for in this Code section shall begin on the date the person is convicted of violating this Code section."

The 2008 amendment by Act 778 rewrote this section, which formerly read:

"(a) Except when a license has been revoked under Code Section 40-5-58 as a habitual violator, any person who drives a motor vehicle on any public highway of this state at a time when his privilege to do so is suspended, disqualified, or revoked shall be guilty of a misdemeanor for a first conviction thereof and, upon a first conviction thereof or plea of nolo contendere within five years, as measured from the dates of previous arrests for which convictions were obtained to the date of the current arrest for which a conviction is obtained, shall be punished by imprisonment for not less than two days nor more than 12 months, and there may be imposed in addition thereto a fine of not less than $500.00 nor more than $1,000.00. For the second or subsequent conviction within five years, as measured from the dates of previous arrests for which convictions were obtained or pleas of nolo contendere were accepted to the date of the current arrest for which a conviction is obtained or a plea of nolo contendere is accepted, such person shall be guilty of a high and aggravated misdemeanor and shall be punished by imprisonment for not less than ten days nor more than 12 months and there may be imposed in addition thereto a fine of not less than $1,000.00 nor more than $2,500.00.

"(b) The department, upon receiving a record of the conviction of any person under this Code section upon a charge of driving a vehicle while the license of such person was suspended, disqualified, or revoked, including suspensions under subsection (f) of Code Section 40-5-75, shall extend the period of suspension or disqualification for six months. The court shall be required to confiscate the license, if applicable, and attach it to the uniform citation and forward it to the department within ten days of conviction. The period of suspension or disqualification provided for in this Code section shall begin on the date the person is convicted of violating this Code section.

"(c) For purposes of pleading nolo contendere, only one nolo contendere plea will be accepted to a charge of driving with suspended or disqualified license within a five-year period as measured from date of arrest to date of arrest. All other nolo contendere pleas in this period will be considered convictions. For the purpose of imposing a sentence under this subsection, a plea of nolo contendere shall constitute a conviction. There shall be no limited driving permit available for a suspension or disqualification under this Code section.

"(d) Notwithstanding the limits set forth in Code Section 40-5-124 and in any municipal charter, any municipal court of any municipality shall be authorized to impose the punishment provided for in this Code section upon a conviction of violating this Code section or upon conviction of violating any ordinance adopting the provisions of this Code section."

The 2009 amendment by Act 22, in subsec. (a), deleted "; provided, however, that at the time of the hearing such person shall not be guilty of such offense if he or she presents the court with proof of a valid driver's license issued by this state" following "$500.00 nor more than $1,000.00".

The 2009 amendment by Act 135 rewrote subsec. (b) which had read:

"(b) The department, upon receiving a record of the conviction of any person under this Code section upon a charge of driving a vehicle while the license of such person was suspended, disqualified, or revoked, including suspensions under subsection (f) of Code Section 40-5-75, shall extend the period of suspension or disqualification for six months. The court shall be required to confiscate the license, if applicable, and attach it to the uniform citation and forward it to the department within ten days of conviction. The period of suspension or disqualification provided for in this Code section shall begin on the date the person is convicted of violating this Code section."

§ 40-5-122. Permitting unlicensed person to drive

No person shall knowingly authorize or permit a motor vehicle owned by him or under his control to be driven upon any highway by any person who is not authorized under this chapter or who is not licensed for the type or class of vehicles to be driven or in violation of any of the provisions of this chapter.

Laws 1975, p. 1008, § 1; Laws 1990, p. 2048, § 4.

Formerly Code 1933, § 68B-404.

§ 40-5-123. Permitting unauthorized minor to drive

No person shall cause or knowingly permit his child or ward under the age of 18 years to drive a motor vehicle upon any highway when such minor is not authorized under this chapter or in violation of any of the provisions of this chapter. This Code section shall not apply to any vehicle not required to be registered by the laws of this state.

Laws 1975, p. 1008, § 1; Laws 1990, p. 2048, § 4.

Formerly Code 1933, § 68B-403.

§ 40-5-124. Offenses triable in municipal court

(a) Any person charged with an offense under this chapter may be tried in any municipal court of any municipality if the offense occurred within the corporate limits of such municipality. Such courts are granted the jurisdiction to try and dispose of such cases. The jurisdiction of such courts shall be concurrent with the jurisdiction of any other courts within the county having jurisdiction to try and dispose of such cases. Any fines and forfeitures arising from the prosecution of such cases shall be retained by the municipality and shall be paid into the treasury of such municipality. Any person charged with an offense under this chapter shall be entitled to request to have the case against him transferred to the court having general misdemeanor jurisdiction in the county wherein the alleged offense occurred.

(b) Nothing in this Code section shall be construed to give any municipality the right to impose a fine or punish by imprisonment in excess of the limits as set forth in the municipality's charter.

Laws 1977, p. 1038, § 1; Laws 1987, p. 3, § 40; Laws 1990, p. 2048, § 4.

Formerly Code 1933, § 68B-405.

§ 40–5–125. Violations relating to application for and use of driver's license

(a) It is a misdemeanor for any person to:

(1) Lend his or her driver's license or identification card to any other person or permit knowingly the use thereof by another person; or

(2) Display or represent as his or her own any driver's license or identification card not issued to him or her.

(b) Any person who knowingly makes any false statement in an application for a driver's license provided for by this chapter shall be guilty of a violation of Code Section 16–10–20.

Laws 1989, p. 519, § 16; Laws 1990, p. 2048, § 4; Laws 1996, p. 1250, § 8; Laws 2000, p. 951, § 5–50; Laws 2002, p. 551, § 6.

Article 7

Commercial Drivers' Licenses

§ 40–5–140. Short title

This article shall be known and may be cited as the "Uniform Commercial Driver's License Act."

Laws 1989, p. 519, § 1; Laws 1990, p. 2048, § 4.

§ 40–5–141. Purpose

The purpose of this article is to implement the federal Commercial Motor Vehicle Safety Act of 1986, Title XII of Public Law 99–570, and reduce or prevent commercial motor vehicle accidents, fatalities, and injuries by permitting commercial drivers to hold only one license; disqualifying commercial drivers who have committed certain criminal or other offenses or serious traffic violations; and strengthening commercial driver licensing and testing standards. This article is a remedial law and shall be liberally construed to promote the public health, safety, and welfare. To the extent that this article conflicts with general driver licensing provisions, this article shall prevail. Where this article is silent, the general driver licensing provisions shall apply.

Laws 1989, p. 519, § 1; Laws 1990, p. 2048, § 4.

§ 40–5–142. Definitions

As used in this article, the term:

(1) "Alcohol" means:

(A) Beer, ale, port, or stout and other similar fermented beverages, including sake or similar products, of any name or description containing one–half of 1 percent or more of alcohol by volume, brewed or produced from malt, wholly or in part, or from any substitute therefor;

(B) Wine of not less than one–half of 1 percent of alcohol by volume;

(C) Distilled spirits which means that substance known as ethyl alcohol, ethanol, or spirits of wine in any form, including all dilutions and mixtures thereof from whatever source or by whatever process produced; or

(D) Any substance containing any form of alcohol, including, but not limited to, ethanol, methanol, propanol, and isopropanol.

(2) "Alcohol concentration" means:

(A) The number of grams of alcohol per 100 milliliters of blood;

(B) The number of grams of alcohol per 210 liters of breath; or

(C) The number of grams of alcohol per 67 milliliters of urine.

(3) "Commerce" means:

(A) Trade, traffic, and transportation within the jurisdiction of the United States between locations in a state and between a location in a state and a location outside such state including a location outside the United States; and

(B) Trade, traffic, and transportation in the United States which affects any trade, traffic, and transportation described in subparagraph (A) of this paragraph.

(4) "Commercial Driver License Information System" (CDLIS) means the information system established pursuant to the Commercial Motor Vehicle Safety Act of 1986, Title XII, Public Law 99–570, to serve as a clearing–house for locating information related to the licensing and identification of commercial motor vehicle drivers.

(5) "Commercial driver's instruction permit" means a permit issued pursuant to subsection (c) of Code Section 40–5–147.

(6) "Commercial driver's license" (CDL) means a license issued in accordance with the requirements of this article to an individual which authorizes the individual to drive a class of commercial motor vehicle.

(7) "Commercial motor vehicle" means a motor vehicle designed or used to transport passengers or property:

(A) If the vehicle has a gross vehicle weight rating of 26,001 or more pounds or such lesser rating as determined by federal regulation;

(B) If the vehicle is designed to transport 16 or more passengers, including the driver; or

(C) If the vehicle is transporting hazardous materials as designated under 49 U.S.C. Section 5103 and is required to be placarded in accordance with the Motor Carrier Safety Rules prescribed by the United States Department of Transportation, Title 49 C.F.R. Part 172, subpart F or is transporting any quantity of a material listed as a select agent or toxin in Title 42 C.F.R. Part 73;

provided, however, that for the purposes of this article, no agricultural vehicle, commercial vehicle operated by military personnel for military purposes, recreational vehicle, or fire–fighting or emergency equipment vehicle shall be considered a commercial motor vehicle. As used in this paragraph, the term "fire–fighting or emergency equipment vehicle" means an authorized emergency vehicle as defined in paragraph (5) of Code Section 40–1–1; provided, however, that the vehicle must be equipped with audible and visible signals and shall be subject to traffic regulations in accordance with the requirements of Code Section 40–6–6. As used in this paragraph, the term "agricultural vehicle" means a farm vehicle which is controlled and operated by a farmer, including operation by employees or family members; used to transport agricultural products, farm machinery, or farm supplies to or from a farm; and operated within 150 miles of such person's farm; which vehicle is not used in the operations of a common or contract carrier. Any other waiver by the Federal Motor Carrier Safety Administration pursuant to Federal Law 49 C.F.R. Parts 383 and 384 of the United States Department of Transportation shall supersede state law in authorizing the Department of Driver Services to exempt said classes.

(8) "Controlled substance" means any substance so defined under Code Section 16–13–21 and includes all substances listed in Schedules I through V of 21 C.F.R. Part 1308, as they may be revised from time to time.

(9) "Conviction" means an unvacated adjudication of guilt, or a determination that a person has violated or failed to comply with the law in a court of original jurisdiction or by an authorized administrative tribunal, an unvacated forfeiture of bail or collateral deposited to secure the person's appearance in court, a plea of guilty or nolo contendere accepted by the court, the payment of a fine or court cost, or violation of a condition of release without bail, regardless of whether the penalty is rebated, suspended, or probated.

(10) "Disqualification" means any of the following:

(A) The suspension, revocation, or cancellation of a commercial driver's license by any state or jurisdiction of issuance;

(B) The withdrawal of a person's privilege to drive a commercial motor vehicle by any state or by any other jurisdiction as the result of a violation of any state or local law relating to motor vehicle traffic control, other than parking, vehicle weight, or vehicle defect violations; or

(C) A determination by the Federal Motor Carrier Safety Administration that a person is not qualified to operate a commercial motor vehicle.

(11) "Drive" means to operate or be in actual physical control of a motor vehicle in any place open to the general public for purposes of vehicular traffic. For purposes of Code Sections 40–5–151 and 40–5–152, "drive" includes operation or actual physical control of a motor vehicle anywhere in this state, in any other state, or in any foreign jurisdiction.

(12) "Driver" means any person who drives, operates, or is in actual physical control of a commercial motor vehicle in any place open to the general public for purposes of vehicular traffic or who is required to hold a commercial driver's license.

(13) "Driver's license" means a license issued by a state to any individual which authorizes the individual to drive a motor vehicle.

(13.1) "Driving a vehicle under the influence" means committing any one or more of the following acts while a person is driving or in actual physical control of a moving commercial or noncommercial vehicle:

(A) Driving under the influence, as prescribed by Code Section 40–6–391 or any law or ordinance equivalent thereto in this state, in any other state, or in any foreign jurisdiction; or

(B) Refusal to submit to state administered chemical testing when requested to do so by a law enforcement officer.

(14) "Employer" means any person, including the United States, a state, or a political subdivision of a state, who owns or leases a commercial motor vehicle or assigns a person to drive a commercial motor vehicle on its behalf.

(14.1) "Fatality" means the death of a person as a result of a motor vehicle crash.

(15) "Felony" means any offense under state or federal law that is punishable by death, by imprisonment for life, or by imprisonment for more than 12 months.

(16) "Foreign jurisdiction" means any jurisdiction other than a state of the United States.

(17) "Gross vehicle weight rating" (GVWR) means the value specified by the manufacturer or manufacturers as the maximum loaded weight of a single or a combination (articulated) vehicle, or registered gross weight, whichever is greater. The gross vehicle weight rating of a combination (articulated) vehicle, commonly referred to as the "gross combination weight rating" (GCWR), is the gross vehicle weight rating of the power unit plus the gross vehicle weight rating of the towed unit or units. In the absence of a value specified for the towed unit or units by the manufacturer or manufacturers, the gross vehicle weight rating of a combination (articulated) vehicle is the gross vehicle weight rating of the power unit plus the total weight of the towed unit or units, including the loads on them.

(18) "Hazardous materials" means any material that has been designated as hazardous under 49 U.S.C. Section 5103 and is required to be placarded in accordance with the Motor Carrier Safety Rules prescribed by the United States Department of Transportation, Title 49 C.F.R. Part 172, subpart F or any quantity of a material listed as a select agent or toxin in Title 42 C.F.R. Part 73.

(18.1) "Imminent hazard" means the existence of a condition that presents a substantial likelihood that death, serious illness, severe personal injury, or a substantial endangerment to health, property, or the environment may occur before the reasonably foreseeable completion date of a formal proceeding begun to lessen the risk of that death, illness, injury, or endangerment.

(18.2) "Major traffic violation" means a conviction of any of the following offenses or a conviction of any law or ordinance equivalent thereto in this state, in any other state, or in any foreign jurisdiction, when operating either a commercial motor vehicle or, unless otherwise specified, a noncommercial motor vehicle:

(A) Driving a vehicle under the influence in violation of Code Section 40–6–391;

(B) Hit and run or leaving the scene of an accident in violation of Code Section 40–6–270, failure to report striking an unattended vehicle in violation of Code Section 40–6–271, failure to report striking a fixed object in violation of Code Section 40–6–272, or failure to report an accident in violation of Code Section 40–6–273;

(C) Except as provided in subsection (b) of Code Section 40–5–151, any felony in the commission of which a motor vehicle is used;

(D) Driving a commercial motor vehicle while the person's commercial driver's license or commercial driving privilege is revoked, suspended, canceled, or disqualified;

(E) Homicide by vehicle in violation of Code Section 40–6–393;

(F) Racing on highways or streets in violation of Code Section 40–6–186;

(G) Using a motor vehicle in fleeing or attempting to elude an officer in violation of Code Section 40–6–395;

(H) Fraudulent or fictitious use of or application for a license as provided in Code Section 40–5–120 or 40–5–125;

(I) Operating a motor vehicle with a revoked, canceled, or suspended registration in violation of Code Section 40–6–15;

(J) Violating Code Sections 16–8–2 through 16–8–9, if the property that was the subject of the theft was a vehicle engaged in commercial transportation of cargo or any appurtenance thereto or the cargo being transported therein or thereon, as set forth in paragraph (8) of subsection (a) of Code Section 16–8–12; or

(K) Refusing to submit to a state administered chemical test requested by a law enforcement officer pursuant to Code Section 40–5–55.

(19) "Motor vehicle" means a vehicle, machine, tractor, trailer, or semitrailer propelled or drawn by mechanical power used on highways, or any other vehicle required to be registered under the laws of this state, but does not include any vehicle, machine, tractor, trailer, or semitrailer operated exclusively on a rail.

(19.1) "Noncommercial motor vehicle" means a motor vehicle or combination of vehicles not defined by the term "commercial motor vehicle" in this Code section or in the regulations of the department for the purpose of licensure.

(20) "Nonresident commercial driver's license" means a commercial driver's license issued by a state to any individual who resides in a foreign jurisdiction.

(21) "Out–of–service order" means a temporary prohibition against driving a commercial motor vehicle.

(21.1) "School bus" means a commercial motor vehicle used to transport pre–primary, primary, or secondary school students from home to school, from school to home, or to and from school sponsored events. The term does not include a bus used as a common carrier.

(22) "Serious traffic violation" means conviction of any of the following offenses or a conviction of any law or ordinance equivalent thereto in this state, in any other state, or in any foreign jurisdiction, when operating either a commercial motor vehicle or, unless otherwise specified, a noncommercial motor vehicle:

(A) Speeding 15 or more miles per hour above the posted speed limit;

(B) Reckless driving;

(C) Following another vehicle too closely;

(D) Improper or erratic lane change, including failure to signal a lane change;

(E) A violation, arising in connection with a fatal crash, of state law or a local ordinance, relating to motor vehicle traffic control, excluding parking, weight, length, height, and vehicle defect violations, and excluding homicide by vehicle as defined in Code Section 40–6–393;

(F) A railroad grade crossing violation in a noncommercial motor vehicle;

(G) Driving a commercial motor vehicle without obtaining a commercial driver's license;

(H) Driving a commercial motor vehicle without a commercial driver's license in the driver's immediate possession, and excluding such violations when the person's commercial driver's license or commercial driving privilege is suspended, revoked, canceled, or disqualified; or

(I) Driving a commercial motor vehicle without a commercial driver's license of the proper class and endorsements for the specific vehicle being operated or for the passengers or type of cargo transported.

(23) "State" means a state of the United States and the District of Columbia.

(24) "Tank vehicle" means any commercial motor vehicle designed to transport any liquid or gaseous materials within a tank that is either permanently or temporarily attached to the vehicle or the chassis. Such vehicles include, but are not limited to, cargo tanks and portable tanks as defined by federal law. However, the term "tank vehicle" shall not include a portable tank having a rated capacity under 1,000 gallons.

(25) "United States" means the 50 states and the District of Columbia.

Laws 1989, p. 519, § 1; Laws 1990, p. 8, § 40; Laws 1990, p. 2048, § 4; Laws 1991, p. 618, § 1; Laws 1992, p. 6, § 40; Laws 1994, p. 1058, § 1; Laws 2000, p. 951, § 5–51; Laws 2002, p. 1378, § 4; Laws 2003, Act 200, § 3, eff. Oct. 1, 2003; Laws 2004, Act 564, § 40, eff. May 13, 2004; Laws 2005, Act 68, § 17–22, eff. July 1, 2005; Laws 2006, Act 590, § 13, eff. July 1, 2006; Laws 2007, Act 44, § 2, eff. Jan. 1, 2008; Laws 2008, Act 471, § 40, eff. May 12, 2008.

Historical and Statutory Notes

The 2003 amendment by Act 200, redesignated par. (4) as par. (6); redesignated par. (5) as par. (4); redesignated par. (6) as par. (5); rewrote par. (10); added pars. (13.1), (14.1), (18.1), (19.1), and (21.1); in par. (22), substituted "crash" for "accident" in subpar. (E) and added new subpars. (G), (H), and (I). Prior to amendment, par. (10) had read:

"(10) 'Disqualification' means a prohibition against driving a commercial motor vehicle."

Laws 2003, Act 200, § 15 provides:

"This Act shall become effective on October 1, 2003."

The 2004 amendment by Act 564 was a provision contained in a correction bill.

The 2005 amendment by Act 68 in par. (7) substituted "motor carrier" for "common or contract carrier" in provisions defining the term "agricultural vehicle" and substituted "Department of Driver Services" for "Department of Motor Vehicle Safety" prior to "to exempt said classes" at the end of the paragraph.

The 2006 amendment by Act 590, in par. (7), rewrote subpar. (C) and the undesignated paragraph; rewrote par. (9); and in par. (22), added "conviction of any of the following offenses when operating a commercial motor vehicle or a noncommercial motor vehicle" to the introductory phrase. Prior to amendment, subpar. (7)(C), the undesignated subpar. of par. (7), and par. (9) had read:

"[(7)](C) If the vehicle is transporting hazardous materials and is required to be placarded in accordance with the Motor Carrier Safety Rules prescribed by the United States Department of Transportation, Title 49 C.F.R. Part 172, subpart F;

"provided, however, that for the purposes of this article, no agricultural vehicle, military vehicle operated by military personnel, recreational vehicle, or fire–fighting or emergency equipment vehicle shall be considered a commercial vehicle. As used in this paragraph, the term 'agricultural vehicle' means a farm vehicle which is controlled and operated by a farmer; used to transport agricultural products, farm machinery, or farm supplies to or from a farm; and operated within 150 miles of such person's farm; which vehicle is not used in the operations of a motor carrier. Any other waiver by the Federal Highway Administration pursuant to Federal Law 49 C.F.R. Parts 383, 391, RIN 2125–AB 68, of the United States Department of Transportation shall supersede state law in authorizing the Department of Driver Services to exempt said classes."

"(9) 'Conviction' means a forfeiture of bail or collateral deposited to secure the person's appearance in court, a plea of guilty or nolo contendere accepted by the court, a finding of guilt, or the payment of a fine or court cost, regardless of whether the penalty is rebated, suspended, or probated."

The 2007 amendment by Act 44, in the last paragraph of par. (7), inserted the sentence defining the term fire–fighting or emergency equipment vehicle; in par. (11), inserted ", in any other state, or in any foreign jurisdiction"; rewrote pars. (13.1) and (18); inserted par. (18.2); made a nonsubstantive change in par. (21); and rewrote par. (22). Prior to amendment, pars. (13.1), (18), and (22) had read:

"(13.1) 'Driving a commercial vehicle while under the influence of alcohol' means committing any one or more of the following acts while a person is driving or in actual physical control of a moving commercial motor vehicle:

"(A) Driving while the person's alcohol concentration is 0.04 percent or more by weight of alcohol in his or her blood, breath, or urine;

"(B) Driving under the influence of alcohol, as prescribed by Code Section 40–6–391; or

"(C) Refusal to submit to state-administered chemical testing when requested to do so by a law enforcement officer."

"(18) 'Hazardous materials' has the meaning the term has under 49 U.S.C.A. Section 5101, et seq."

"(22) 'Serious traffic violation' means conviction of any of the following offenses when operating a commercial motor vehicle or a noncommercial motor vehicle:

"(A) Speeding 15 or more miles per hour above the posted speed limit;

"(B) Reckless driving, as defined under state or local law;

"(C) Following another vehicle too closely, as defined under state or local law;

"(D) Improper or erratic lane change which presents a risk to any other vehicle, but not including failure to signal a lane change;

"(E) A violation, arising in connection with a fatal crash, of state law or a local ordinance, relating to motor vehicle traffic control, excluding parking, weight, length, height, and vehicle defect violations;

"(F) A railroad grade crossing violation as defined under state law or local ordinance;

"(G) Driving a commercial motor vehicle without obtaining a commercial driver's license;

"(H) Driving a commercial motor vehicle without a valid commercial driver's license in the driver's immediate possession; or

"(I) Driving a commercial motor vehicle without a commercial driver's license of the proper class and/or endorsements for the specific vehicle being operated or for the passengers or type of cargo transported."

Laws 2007, Act 44, § 8, provides:

"This Act shall become effective on January 1, 2008."

In 2007, the Code Commission, in subpar. (13.1)(B), substituted "state administered" for "state–administered". See § 28–9–5.

The 2008 amendment by Act 471 was a provision contained in a correction bill.

§ 40–5–143. Persons not to have more than one driver's license

No person who drives a commercial motor vehicle shall have more than one driver's license.

Laws 1989, p. 519, § 1; Laws 1990, p. 2048, § 4.

§ 40–5–144. Notice of motor vehicle traffic violations, suspensions, revocations, and cancellations; notice to employers of previous commercial driver employment

(a) Any driver of a commercial motor vehicle holding a license issued by this state who is convicted of violating any state law or local ordinance relating to motor vehicle traffic control in any other state or any federal, provincial, territorial, or municipal laws of Canada relating to motor vehicle traffic control, other than parking violations, shall notify the department in the manner specified by the department within 30 days of the date of conviction. If the court notifies the department of such conviction, the responsibility of the driver to notify the department shall be waived.

(b) Any driver of a commercial motor vehicle holding a license issued by this state who is convicted of violating any state law or local ordinance relating to motor vehicle traffic control in this or any other state or any federal, provincial, territorial, or municipal laws of Canada relating to motor vehicle traffic control, other than parking violations, shall notify his or her employer in writing of the conviction within 30 days of the date of conviction.

(c) Each driver whose driver's license is suspended, revoked, or canceled by any state; who loses the privilege to drive a commercial motor vehicle in any state for any period; or who is disqualified from driving a commercial motor vehicle for any period shall notify his or her employer of that fact before the end of the business day following the day the driver received notice of that fact.

(d) Each person who applies to be a commercial motor vehicle driver shall, at the time of the application, provide the employer with the following information for the ten years preceding the date of application:

(1) A list of the names and addresses of the applicant's previous employers for which the applicant was a driver of a commercial motor vehicle;

(2) The dates between which the applicant drove for each employer; and

(3) The reason for leaving that employer.

The applicant shall certify that all information furnished is true and complete. An employer may require an applicant to provide additional information.

Laws 1989, p. 519, § 1; Laws 1990, p. 2048, § 4; Laws 2000, p. 951, § 5–52.

§ 40–5–145. Employer responsibilities

(a) Each employer shall require every commercial motor vehicle driver applicant to provide the information specified in subsection (d) of Code Section 40–5–144.

(b) No employer may knowingly allow, require, permit, or authorize a driver to drive a commercial motor vehicle during any period:

(1) In which the driver has a driver's license suspended, revoked, or canceled by a state; has lost the privilege to drive a commercial motor vehicle in a state; or has been disqualified from driving a commercial motor vehicle;

(2) In which the driver has more than one driver's license;

(3) In which the driver, or the commercial motor vehicle that he or she is driving, or the motor carrier operation, is subject to an out of service order; or

(4) In violation of a federal, state, or local law or regulation pertaining to railroad-highway grade crossings.

Laws 1989, p. 519, § 1; Laws 1990, p. 2048, § 4; Laws 2003, Act 200, § 4, eff. Oct. 1, 2003.

Historical and Statutory Notes

The 2003 amendment by Act 200, in subsec. (b), inserted "require," in the introductory sentence, deleted "or" at the end of par. (1), and added pars. (3) and (4).

Laws 2003, Act 200, § 15 provides:

"This Act shall become effective on October 1, 2003."

In 2003, the Code Commission, in subsec. (b), par. (3), substituted "subject" for "subect". See § 28–9–5.

§ 40–5–146. Commercial driver's license required for operation of commercial motor vehicle

(a) Except when driving under a commercial driver's instruction permit and accompanied by the holder of a commercial driver's license valid for the vehicle being driven, no person may operate a commercial motor vehicle unless the person has been issued and is in immediate possession of a commercial driver's license valid for the vehicle he or she is driving.

(b)(1) No person may drive a commercial motor vehicle while his or her driving privilege is suspended, revoked, or canceled, or while subject to a disqualification.

(2) No person may drive a commercial motor vehicle in violation of an out of service order.

Laws 1989, p. 519, § 1; Laws 1990, p. 2048, § 4; Laws 2006, Act 590, § 14, eff. July 1, 2006.

Historical and Statutory Notes

The 2006 amendment by Act 590, in subsec. (b), added paragraph designations; in newly designated par. (1), substituted "or while subject to a disqualification." for "while subject to a disqualification," and in newly designated par. (2), substituted "No person may drive a commercial motor vehicle in violation" for "or in violation".

§ 40–5–147. Qualifications and standards; testing; commercial driver's instruction permit

(a)(1) Except as provided in Code Section 40–5–148, no person may be issued a commercial driver's license unless that person is a resident of this state, is at least 18 years of age, has passed a knowledge and skills test for driving a commercial motor vehicle which complies with minimum federal standards established by federal regulations enumerated in 49 C.F.R. Part 383, subparts G and H, and has satisfied all other requirements of the Commercial Motor Vehicle Safety Act of 1986, Title XII of Public Law 99–570, in addition to any other requirements imposed by state law or federal regulation. The tests shall be prescribed and conducted by the department in English only.

(2) The department may authorize a person, including an agency of this or another state, an employer, a private driver training facility, or other private institution or a department, agency, or instrumentality of a local government, to administer the skills test specified by this Code section, provided that:

(A) The test is the same which would otherwise be administered by the state;

(B) The third party has entered into an agreement with the state which complies with the requirements set forth in 49 C.F.R. Part 383.75; and

(C) The third party complies with all other requirements set by the department by regulations.

(b) The department may waive the skills test specified in this Code section for a commercial driver's license applicant who meets the requirements of 49 C.F.R. Part 383.77.

(c)(1) A commercial driver's instruction permit may be issued to any individual who holds a valid noncommercial Class C license or has passed all required tests for the operation of a noncommercial Class C vehicle and is 18 years of age.

(2) An applicant for the commercial driver's instruction permit must pass the vision test and all knowledge tests for the type of vehicle he intends to operate along with any knowledge test required for any desired endorsements.

(3) The commercial driver's instruction permit may not be issued for a period to exceed one year. The holder of a commercial driver's instruction permit may drive a commercial motor vehicle on a highway only when accompanied by the holder of a commercial driver's license valid for the type of vehicle driven who occupies a seat beside the individual for the purpose of giving instruction in driving the commercial motor vehicle.

(d)(1) A commercial driver's license or commercial driver's instruction permit shall not be issued to a person while the person is subject to a disqualification from driving a commercial motor vehicle or while the person's driver's license or driving privilege is suspended, revoked, or canceled in this or any other licensing jurisdiction; nor may a driver's license be issued to a person who has a commercial driver's license issued by any other state unless the person first surrenders all driver's licenses issued by any other state, which license or licenses shall be returned to the issuing state or states for cancellation.

(2) The department shall obtain the driving record of any person who applies for a commercial driver's license from any other states in which he or she has been licensed or convicted. Upon receipt of conviction information for such a person, said convictions shall become part of the person's driving record in the State of Georgia as provided in Code Section 40–5–2. The department shall review each such person's prior driving record and impose any commercial driving disqualification to which such person is subject that was not imposed by another jurisdiction as required under federal law.

(e) The department is authorized to promulgate rules necessary to grant a waiver or exemption of the physical requirements for a commercial driver's license or a commercial driver's instruction permit in 49 C.F.R. Part 391, Subpart E; provided, however, that the person who is applying for a commercial driver's license or a commercial driver's instruction permit or who has previously been issued a commercial driver's license and who is granted the waiver or exemption shall only be authorized to drive a commercial motor vehicle in this state. Notwithstanding this subsection, the department shall not grant any type of waiver or exemption of said physical requirements unless such type of waiver or exemption has previously been granted by the Federal Motor Carrier Safety Administration.

Laws 1989, p. 519, § 1; Laws 1990, p. 2048, § 4; Laws 1991, p. 618, § 2; Laws 2000, p. 951, § 5–53; Laws 2006, Act 590, § 15, eff. July 1, 2006; Laws 2007, Act 44, § 3, eff. Jan. 1, 2008; Laws 2008, Act 434, § 9, eff. Jan. 1, 2009.

Historical and Statutory Notes

The 2006 amendment by Act 590, in subsec. (a), par. (1), added "has completed the Highway Watch safety and security training program or its federally designated successor program and is properly registered with the same,".

The 2007 amendment by Act 44, in subsec. (a), par. (1), deleted "has completed the Highway Watch safety and security training program or its federally designated successor program and is properly registered with the same," following "subparts G and H"; and added subsec. (e).

Laws 2007, Act 44, § 8, provides:

"This Act shall become effective on January 1, 2008."

In 2007, the Code Commission, in subsec. (a), deleted a second comma following "subparts G and H," in par. (1). See § 28–9–5.

The 2008 amendment by Act 434, in subsec. (d), designated existing subsection as par. (1), substituted "shall" for "may" in newly designated par. (1), and added par. (2)

§ 40–5–148. Nonresident commercial driver's license

The department may issue a nonresident commercial driver's license to a resident of a foreign jurisdiction if the United States Secretary of Transportation has determined that the commercial motor vehicle testing and licensing standards of the foreign jurisdiction do not meet the testing standards established in 49 C.F.R. Part 383. The word "nonresident" must appear on the face of the nonresident commercial driver's license. An applicant must surrender any nonresident commercial driver's license issued by another state. Prior to issuing a nonresident commercial driver's license, the department must establish the practical capability of revoking, suspending, and canceling the nonresident commercial driver's license and disqualifying that person from driving a commercial motor vehicle under the same conditions applicable to the commercial driver's license issued to a resident of this state.

Laws 1989, p. 519, § 1; Laws 1990, p. 2048, § 4; Laws 2000, p. 951, § 5–54.

§ 40–5–148.1. Restricted commercial driver's license

(a) Pursuant to a waiver of the United States Secretary of Transportation, issued April 17, 1992, the department is authorized to issue Class B or Class C restricted commercial drivers' licenses to certain persons employed in the agricultural industry. Such restricted licenses shall be issued annually but shall not be valid for more than a total of 180 days in a 12 month period.

(b) A person shall not be required to pass a knowledge or skills test for issuance of a restricted commercial driver's license, except that such person shall possess a valid noncommercial driver's license, have at least one year's driving experience, submit an application for and submit proof of all information required for a commercial driver's license except for the testing requirements, and not be subject to any other disqualification from driving a commercial motor vehicle or be under any suspension or revocation of such person's regular driver's license.

(c) The holder of a restricted commercial driver's license issued pursuant to this Code section may operate a commercial motor vehicle only within 150 miles of the place of business at which such person is employed and only during such seasonal periods as indicated on such person's restricted driver's license. The holder of a restricted commercial driver's license shall be authorized to transport only the following hazardous materials requiring placarding: diesel fuel in quantities of 1,000 gallons or less; liquid fertilizers in vehicles with total capacities of 3,000 gallons or less, including anhydrous ammonia and other types of liquid fertilizers in vehicles or implements of husbandry with total capacities of 3,000 gallons or less; and solid fertilizers not mixed with any organic substance.

(d) All holders of restricted commercial drivers' licenses shall be subject to disqualifications and penalties under Code Sections 40–5–151 through 40–5–153 and shall be subject to all notices, verifications, and license checks otherwise required under this article.

(e) The department shall promulgate rules and regulations as necessary to implement this Code section by September 1, 1993.

Laws 1993, p. 797, § 1; Laws 2000, p. 951, § 5–55.

§ 40–5–148.2. Nonresident from state that prohibits issuing commercial drivers' licenses

If an individual is a resident of another state while that other state is prohibited from issuing commercial drivers' licenses pursuant to 49 C.F.R. Section 384.405, that individual is eligible to obtain a nonresident commercial driver's license. The individual shall provide the information specified in Code Section 40–5–149. The department shall promulgate rules and regulations as necessary to implement this Code section within 90 days of being notified that a state will be prohibited from issuing commercial drivers' licenses.

Laws 2006, Act 590, § 16, eff. July 1, 2006.

§ 40–5–149. Applications for commercial driver's license or commercial driver's instruction permit; fees

(a) The application for a commercial driver's license or commercial driver's instruction permit shall include the following:

(1) The full legal name and current mailing and residential address of the person;

(2) A physical description of the person including sex, height, weight, and eye color;

(3) Full date of birth;

(4) Reserved;

(5) The person's signature;

(6) The person's current photograph;

(7) Certifications, including those required by 49 C.F.R. Part 383.71(a);

(8) Any other information required by the department; and

(9) Consent to release driving record information to the Commercial Driver License Information System clearing-house and whatever agent or agency the Commercial Driver License Information System deems necessary by federal requirements.

Each application shall be accompanied by an application fee of $35.00, except for those who operate or are applying to operate a public school bus and inmates of state or county correctional institutions who operate or are applying to operate commercial motor vehicles under the supervision of such institutions during the period of such inmates' confinement, in which cases there shall be no application fee.

(b) When a licensee changes his or her name, mailing address, or residence, an application for a new license shall be made within 30 days of such change. The fee for such new license shall be as provided in Code Section 40–5–25.

(c) No person who has been a resident of this state for 30 days or longer may drive a commercial motor vehicle under the authority of a commercial driver's license issued by another jurisdiction. It shall be the responsibility of the employer to notify the employee of the license issuance law of this state.

(d) Except as provided in Code Section 40–5–36, relating to veterans' licenses and except as provided in this Code section for public school bus drivers, there shall be no exceptions to the application and licenses fees required for issuance of a commercial driver's license or a commercial driver's instruction permit.

Laws 1989, p. 519, § 1; Laws 1990, p. 2048, § 4; Laws 1992, p. 1284, § 2; Laws 1997, p. 1443, § 3; Laws 2000, p. 951, § 5–56; Laws 2008, Act 434, § 10, eff. Jan. 1, 2009.

Historical and Statutory Notes

The 2008 amendment by Act in subsec. (a), par. (1), inserted "legal" following "The full".

§ 40–5–150. Content of commercial driver's license; classifications, endorsements, and restrictions; hazardous materials endorsement

(a) The commercial driver's license shall be marked Commercial Driver's License or CDL and shall be, to the maximum extent practicable, tamperproof, and shall include, but not be limited to, the following information:

(1) The full legal name and residential address of the person;

(2) The person's color photograph;

(3) A physical description of the person, including sex, height, weight, and eye color;

(4) Full date of birth;

(5) The license number or identifier assigned by the department;

(6) The person's signature;

(7) The class or type of commercial motor vehicle or vehicles which the person is authorized to drive, together with any endorsements or restrictions;

(8) The name of this state;

(9) The dates between which the license is valid; and

(10) The license fee and fees for any endorsements.

(b) Commercial driver's licenses may be issued with the following classifications:

(1) Class A—Any combination of vehicles with a gross vehicle weight rating of 26,001 pounds or more, provided the gross vehicle weight rating of the vehicle or vehicles being towed is in excess of 10,000 pounds;

(2) Class B—Any single vehicle with a gross vehicle weight rating of 26,001 pounds or more, or any such vehicle towing a vehicle not in excess of 10,000 pounds gross vehicle weight rating;

(3) Class C—Any single vehicle with a gross vehicle weight rating of less than 26,001 pounds, any such vehicle towing a vehicle with a gross vehicle weight rating not in excess of 10,000 pounds, or any such vehicle towing a vehicle with a gross vehicle weight rating in excess of 10,000 pounds, provided that the combination of vehicles has a gross combined vehicle weight rating less than 26,001 pounds. This classification shall apply to vehicles designed to transport 16 or more passengers, including the driver, and vehicles used in the transportation of hazardous materials which require the vehicles to be placarded under 49 C.F.R. Part 172, subpart F;

(4) Class M—A motorcycle as defined in Code Section 40–1–1; and

(5) Class P—A commercial driver's instruction permit used in conjunction with the commercial driver's instruction permit vehicle classification.

(c) Commercial driver's licenses may be issued with the following endorsements and restrictions:

(1) "H" —Authorizes the driver to drive a vehicle transporting hazardous materials;

(2) "L" —Restricts the driver to vehicles not equipped with air brakes;

(3) "T" —Authorizes driving double and triple trailers;

(4) "P" —Authorizes driving vehicles carrying 16 or more passengers, including the driver, but does not authorize the driver to drive a school bus;

(5) "N" —Authorizes driving tank vehicles;

(5.1) "S" —Authorizes the driver to drive a school bus; and

(6) "X" —Represents a combination of hazardous materials and tank vehicle endorsements.

The fee for Classes A, B, C, M, and P licenses and for the endorsements and restrictions shall be as provided in Code Section 40–5–25.

(d) The holder of a valid commercial driver's license may drive all vehicles in the class for which that license is issued and all lesser classes of vehicles except motorcycles. No person shall drive a vehicle which requires an endorsement unless the proper endorsement appears on the driver's license.

(e) Before issuing a commercial driver's license, the department shall obtain driving record information through the Commercial Driver License Information System, through the National Driver Register (NDR), and from each state in which the applicant has been licensed.

(f) Within ten days after issuing a commercial driver's license, the department shall notify the Commercial Driver License Information System of that fact and provide all information required to ensure identification of the licensee.

(g) Except as provided for in Code Section 40–5–21.1, the commercial driver's license shall expire on the licensee's birthdate in the fifth year following the issuance of such license.

(h) When applying for renewal of a commercial driver's license, the applicant shall complete the application form required by subsection (a) of Code Section 40–5–149, providing updated information and required medical certifications. If the applicant wishes to retain a hazardous materials endorsement, the written test for a hazardous materials endorsement must be taken and passed.

(i)(1) Before issuing, renewing, upgrading, or transferring a commercial driver's license with a hazardous materials endorsement, the department shall obtain a Transportation Security Administration determination that the individual does not pose a security risk warranting denial of the endorsement. The department shall promulgate rules and regulations as necessary to implement this subsection.

(2) If, after issuing a commercial driver's license bearing a hazardous materials endorsement, the department receives notification that the Transportation Security Administration has determined that the holder thereof poses a security risk, it shall cancel the commercial driver's license. The department may issue a new commercial driver's license without a hazardous materials endorsement to said licensee upon surrender of the license bearing the cancelled endorsement.

(3) If a person to whom the department previously issued a commercial driver's license with a hazardous materials endorsement has provided all of the required information to the Transportation Security Administration for the completion of a security threat assessment, but the Transportation Security Administration has not provided a Determination of No Security Threat or a Final Determination of Threat Assessment before the expiration date of said commercial driver's license, the department may renew the commercial driver's license for a period of 90 days if the licensee wishes to retain the hazardous materials endorsement. Notwithstanding the foregoing, the person's commercial driver's license may be renewed for the full renewal period if the licensee wishes to drop the hazardous materials endorsement.

(4) If a person to whom another state previously issued a commercial driver's license with a hazardous materials endorsement applies prior to the expiration thereof to transfer said license, the department may issue a temporary commercial driver's license with a hazardous materials endorsement valid for a period of 90 days upon the person's successful completion of all other statutory requirements. It shall be a prerequisite to the issuance of such a temporary license that the person has provided all of the required information to the Transportation Security Administration for the completion of a security threat assessment, but the Transportation Security Administration has not provided a Determination of No Security Threat or a Final Determination of Threat Assessment prior to the expiration date of the person's commercial driver's license issued by the previous state.

Laws 1989, p. 519, § 1; Laws 1990, p. 2048, § 4; Laws 1994, p. 97, § 40; Laws 1996, p. 1250, § 9; Laws 1997, p. 1443, § 4; Laws 2000, p. 951, §§ 5–57, 5–58; Laws 2003, Act 200, § 5, eff. Oct. 1, 2003; Laws 2005, Act 164, § 2, eff. July 1, 2005; Laws 2006, Act 590, §§ 17, 18, eff. July 1, 2006; Laws 2007, Act 44, § 4, eff. Jan. 1, 2008; Laws 2008, Act 434, § 11, eff. Jan. 1, 2009.

Historical and Statutory Notes

The 2003 amendment by Act 200, in subsec. (c), inserted ", but does not authorize the driver to drive a school bus", deleted "and" at the end of par. (5), and inserted new par. (5.1); and in subsec. (e), deleted "within the past five years" following "applicant has been licensed".

Laws 2003, Act 200, § 15 provides:

"This Act shall become effective on October 1, 2003."

The 2005 amendment by Act 164, in subsec. (b), par. (3), substituted "less than 26,001 pounds," for "less than 26,011 pounds or", and added ", or any such vehicle towing a vehicle with a gross vehicle weight rating in excess of 10,000 pounds, provided that the combination of vehicles has a gross combined vehicle weight rating less than 26,001 pounds".

Laws 2005, Act 164, § 3, provides:

"This Act shall become effective on July 1, 2005, and will apply to offenses occurring on or after that date."

The 2006 amendment by Act 590, in subsec. (h), added ", and provide evidence the applicant has completed the Highway Watch safety and security training program or its federally designated successor program and is properly registered with the same"; and added subsec. (i).

The 2007 amendment by Act 44, in subsec. (g), substituted "Except as provided for in code Section 40–5–21.1, the" for "The", and substituted "fifth year" for "fourth year"; and in subsec. (h), deleted ", and provide evidence the applicant has completed the Highway Watch safety and security training program or its federally designated successor program and is properly registered with the same" following "required medical certifications".

Laws 2007, Act 44, § 8, provides:

"This Act shall become effective on January 1, 2008."

The 2008 amendment by Act 434, in subsec. (a), inserted "full legal" in par. (1), and rewrote par. (5). Prior to amendment par. (5) had read:

"(5) The person's social security number if such person has requested the use of such social security number on such license or another number or identifier deemed appropriate by the department;"

§ 40–5–151. Disqualification and cancellation of commercial driver's license

(a) Any person is disqualified from driving a commercial motor vehicle for a period of not less than one year if convicted of a first violation of a major traffic violation as defined in paragraph (18.2) of Code Section 40–5–142.

(b) Any person is disqualified from driving a commercial motor vehicle for a period of three years if convicted of a first violation of using a commercial motor vehicle in the commission of a felony or a major traffic violation as defined in paragraph (18.2) of Code Section 40–5–142, provided that the vehicle being operated or used in connection with such violation or commission of such felony is transporting a hazardous material required to be placarded under Section 105 of the Hazardous Materials Transportation Act, 49 U.S.C. app. 1804.

(c) Any person is disqualified from driving a commercial motor vehicle for life if convicted of a second or subsequent major traffic violation as defined in paragraph (18.2) of Code Section 40–5–142 or any combination of such violations arising from two or more separate incidents.

(d) The department may issue regulations establishing guidelines, including conditions, under which a disqualification for life under subsection (c) of this Code section may be reduced to a period of not less than ten years. The department is not authorized to make any other reduction in a term of disqualification or to issue a limited or other permit or license that would allow the operation of a commercial motor vehicle during the term of disqualification mandated by this Code section.

(e) Notwithstanding the provisions of subsection (d) of this Code section, any person is disqualified from driving a commercial motor vehicle for life who knowingly uses a motor vehicle in the commission of any felony involving the manufacture, distribution, cultivation, sale, transfer of, trafficking in, or dispensing of a controlled substance or marijuana, or possession with intent to manufacture, distribute, cultivate, sell, transfer, traffic in, or dispense a controlled substance or marijuana.

(f) Any person is disqualified from driving a commercial motor vehicle for a period of:

(1) Not less than 60 days if convicted of two serious traffic violations as defined in paragraph (22) of Code Section 40–5–142 arising from separate incidents occurring within a three–year period as measured from the dates of arrests for which convictions were obtained; or

(2) Not less than 120 days if convicted of a third or subsequent serious traffic violation as defined in paragraph (22) of Code Section 40–5–142 arising from separate incidents occurring within a three–year period as measured from the dates of arrests for which convictions were obtained.

(g)(1) Any person is disqualified from driving a commercial motor vehicle based on the following violations of out–of–service orders:

(A) First violation—a driver who is convicted of a first violation of an out-of-service order is disqualified for a period of not less than 180 days and not more than one year;

(B) Second violation—a driver who is convicted of two violations of out-of-service orders in separate incidents is disqualified for a period of not less than two years and not more than five years; and

(C) Third or subsequent violation——a driver who is convicted of three or more violations of out–of–service orders in separate incidents is disqualified for a period of not less than three years and not more than five years.

(2) Whenever the operator of a commercial motor vehicle is issued an out–of–service order, a copy of such order shall be issued to the operator of the commercial motor vehicle, the operator of the commercial motor vehicle's employer, and a copy or notice of such out–of–service order shall be provided to the department. The form of such out–of–service order, the procedures for notifying the department upon the issuance of such an order, and other matters relative to the issuance of out–of–service orders and violations thereof shall be provided in rules and regulations promulgated by the commissioner.

(3) Any person is disqualified for a period of not less than 180 days nor more than two years if the driver is convicted of a first violation of an out–of–service order while transporting hazardous materials required to be placarded under Section 105 of the Hazardous Materials Transportation Act, 49 U.S.C. app. 1804, or while operating commercial motor vehicles designed to transport more than 15 passengers, including the driver. A driver is disqualified for a period of not less than three years nor more than five years if, during any ten–year period, the driver is convicted of any subsequent violations of out–of–service orders, in separate incidents, while transporting hazardous materials required to be placarded under Section 105 of the Hazardous Materials Transportation Act, 49 U.S.C. app. 1804, or while operating commercial motor vehicles designed to transport more than 15 passengers, including the driver.

(4) In addition to any other penalty imposed pursuant to this article, any driver who is convicted of violating an out-of-service order shall be subject to a civil penalty of not less than $2,500.00 for a first offense and not less than $5,000.00 for a second or subsequent offense.

(h) After suspending, revoking, or canceling a commercial driver's license, the department shall update its records to reflect that action within ten days. After suspending, revoking, or canceling a nonresident commercial driver's privileges, the department shall notify the licensing authority of the state which issued the commercial driver's license within ten days.

(i) Any person is disqualified from driving a commercial motor vehicle for a period of not less than 60 days if it is determined, in a check of an applicant's license status and record prior to issuing a commercial driver's license or at any time after the commercial driver's license is issued, that the applicant has falsified information on his or her application or any related filing.

(j)(1) Any person is disqualified from driving a commercial vehicle for a period of not less than 30 days if the department receives notification from the Federal Motor Carrier Safety Administration that the person poses an imminent hazard.

(2) If the Federal Motor Carrier Safety Administration notifies the department that a person's driving constitutes an imminent hazard and imposes a disqualification greater than 30 days, the person shall be disqualified from driving a commercial vehicle for the period designated by the Federal Motor Carrier Safety Administration, not to exceed one year.

(k)(1) Any person is disqualified from operating a commercial motor vehicle if convicted of any of the following railroad grade crossing offenses while operating a commercial motor vehicle:

(A) Failing to slow down and check the tracks are clear of an approaching train before proceeding;

(B) Failing to stop before reaching the crossing if the tracks are not clear;

(C) Failing to stop before driving onto the crossing;

(D) Failing to leave sufficient space to drive completely through a railroad crossing without stopping;

(E) Failing to obey a traffic–control device or the directions of an enforcement official at a railroad crossing; or

(F) Failing to negotiate a crossing because of insufficient undercarriage clearance.

(2)(A) Upon a first conviction for an offense listed in paragraph (1) of this subsection, the period of disqualification shall be 60 days.

(B) Upon a second conviction within a three–year period for an offense listed in paragraph (1) of this subsection arising from a separate incident within a three–year period, the period of disqualification shall be 120 days.

(C) Upon a third or subsequent conviction within a three–year period for an offense listed in paragraph (1) of this subsection arising from a separate incident, the period of disqualification shall be one year.

(*l*)(1) All disqualifications as provided for in subsection (f) of this Code section shall become effective upon the date that the department processes the citation or conviction, provided that no such disqualification is in effect; if such disqualification is in effect the subsequent disqualification shall not take effect until the current disqualification expires.

(2) Notwithstanding paragraph (1) of this subsection, any other disqualification as provided for in this Code section shall become effective upon the date that the department processes the citation or conviction and may run concurrently to any other disqualifications in effect.

(m) All disqualifications provided for in this Code section shall be imposed based on offenses in state law or on offenses of any laws or ordinances equivalent thereto in this state, in any other state, or in any foreign jurisdiction.

Laws 1989, p. 519, § 1; Laws 1990, p. 2048, § 4; Laws 1991, p. 618, § 3; Laws 1992, p. 2785, § 21; Laws 1995, p. 229, § 5; Laws 2000, p. 951, § 5–59; Laws 2002, p. 1378, § 5; Laws 2003, Act 200, § 6, eff. Oct. 1, 2003; Laws 2004, Act 564, § 40, eff. May 13, 2004; Laws 2006, Act 545, § 3, eff. July 1, 2006; Laws 2006, Act 590, § 19, eff. July 1, 2006; Laws 2007, Act 18, § 40, eff. May 11, 2007; Laws 2007, Act 44, § 5, eff. Jan. 1, 2008; Laws 2008, Act 434, § 12, eff. Jan. 1, 2009; Laws 2008, Act 471, § 40, eff. May 12, 2008.

Historical and Statutory Notes

The 2002 amendment by Act 972 rewrote subsec. (f) which had read:

"(f) Any person is disqualified from driving a commercial motor vehicle for a period of not less than 60 days if convicted of two serious traffic violations or 120 days if convicted of three serious traffic violations committed in a commercial motor vehicle or a noncommercial motor vehicle arising from separate incidents occurring within a three-year period as measured from the dates of arrests for which convictions were obtained."

The 2003 amendment by Act 200, in subsec. (a), par. (1), substituted "or a moving noncommercial vehicle;" for "; or" in subpar. (A), and added subpar. (C); in subsec. (a), par. (2), substituted "Code Section 40-5-55" for "paragraph (1) of subsection (a) of Code Section 40-6-392", and added "or a noncommercial motor vehicle"; in subsec. (c), substituted ", the refusal to submit to state-administered chemical testing as prescribed by Code Section 40-5-55" for "or 40-6-392", and inserted "or refusals"; in subsec. (d), added the last sentence; and in subsec. (f), par. (1), inserted "or a noncommercial motor vehicle".

Laws 2003, Act 200, § 15 provides:

"This Act shall become effective on October 1, 2003."

The 2004 amendment by Act 564 was a provision contained in a correction bill.

The 2006 amendment by Act 545, in subsec. (a), par. (1), deleted "or" at the end of subpar. (B), and added subpar. (D).

The 2006 amendment by Act 590, in subsec. (b), deleted "paragraph (1) of" prior to "subsection (a) of this Code section"; in subsec. (c), added ", paragraph (1) of subsection (b) of Code Section 40-5-146,"; in subsec. (g), added pars. (3) and (4); and added subsecs. (i) and (j).

The 2007 amendment by Act 18 was a provision contained in a correction bill.

The 2007 amendment by Act 44 rewrote the section which had read:

"(a) Any person is disqualified from driving a commercial motor vehicle for a period of not less than one year:

"(1) If convicted of a first violation of:

"(A) Any offense specified in Code Section 40-5-54 that occurs while the person is driving or being in actual physical control of a moving commercial motor vehicle or a moving noncommercial vehicle;

"(B) Driving or being in actual physical control of a moving commercial motor vehicle while there is 0.04 percent or more by weight of alcohol in his or her blood, breath, or urine;

"(C) Driving or being in actual physical control of a moving noncommercial vehicle in violation of Code Section 40-6-391; or

"(D) Code Sections 16-8-2 through 16-8-9, if the property that was the subject of the theft was a vehicle engaged in commercial transportation as set forth in paragraph (8) of subsection (a) of Code Section 16-8-12; or

"(2) For refusal to submit to a test as prescribed in Code Section 40-5-55 to determine the driver's alcohol concentration while driving a commercial motor vehicle or a noncommercial motor vehicle.

"(b) Any person is disqualified from driving a commercial motor vehicle for a period of not less than three years if convicted of a first violation of using a commercial motor vehicle in the commission of a felony or for offenses specified in subsection (a) of this Code section, provided that the vehicle being operated or used in connection with such violation or commission of such felony is transporting a hazardous material required to be placarded under Section 105 of the Hazardous Materials Transportation Act, 49 U.S.C. app. 1804.

"(c) Any person is disqualified from driving a commercial motor vehicle for life if convicted of two or more violations of any of the offenses specified in subsection (a) of Code Section 40-5-54, paragraph (1) of subsection (b) of Code Section 40-5-146, or Code Section 40-6-391, the refusal to submit to state administered chemical testing as prescribed by Code Section 40-5-55, or any combination of those offenses or refusals, arising from two or more separate incidents.

"(d) The department may issue regulations establishing guidelines, including conditions, under which a disqualification for life under subsection (c) of this Code section may be reduced to a period of not less than ten years. The department is not authorized to make any other reduction in a term of disqualification or to issue a limited or other permit or license that would allow the operation of a commercial motor vehicle during the term of disqualification mandated by this Code section.

"(e) Any person is disqualified from driving a commercial motor vehicle for life who knowingly uses a commercial motor vehicle in the commission of any felony involving the manufacture, distribution, or dispensing of a controlled substance, or possession with intent to manufacture, distribute, or dispense a controlled substance.

"(f)(1) Except as otherwise provided by paragraph (2) of this subsection, any person is disqualified from driving a commercial motor vehicle for a period of not less than 60 days if convicted of two serious traffic violations or 120 days if convicted of three serious traffic violations committed in a commercial motor vehicle or a noncommercial motor vehicle arising from separate incidents occurring within a three-year period as measured from the dates of arrests for which convictions were obtained.

"(2) If the serious traffic violation committed in a commercial motor vehicle is a railroad grade crossing violation, the person shall be disqualified from driving a commercial motor vehicle for a period of not less than 60 days upon the first conviction within a three-year period as measured from the dates of arrests for which convictions were obtained, for not less than 120 days if convicted of two railroad grade crossing violations arising from separate incidents within a three-year period as measured from the dates of arrests for which convictions were obtained, or for not less than one year if convicted of three railroad grade crossing violations arising from separate incidents within a three-year period as measured from the dates of arrests for which convictions were obtained.

"(g)(1) Any person is disqualified from driving a commercial motor vehicle based on the following violations of out-of-service orders:

"(A) First violation—a driver who is convicted of a first violation of an out-of-service order is disqualified for a period of not less than 90 days and not more than one year;

"(B) Second violation—a driver who is convicted of two violations of out-of-service orders in separate incidents is disqualified for a period of not less than one year and not more than five years; and

"(C) Third or subsequent violation—a driver who is convicted of three or more violations of out-of-service orders in separate incidents is disqualified for a period of not less than three years and not more than five years.

"(2) Whenever the operator of a commercial motor vehicle is issued an out-of-service order, a copy of such order shall be issued to the operator of the commercial motor vehicle, the operator of the commercial motor vehicle's employer, and a copy or notice of such out-of-service order shall be provided to the department. The form of such out-of-service order, the procedures for notifying the department upon the issuance of such an order, and other matters relative to the issuance of out-of-service orders and violations thereof shall be provided in rules and regulations promulgated by the commissioner.

"(3) Any person is disqualified for a period of not less than 180 days nor more than two years if the driver is convicted of a first violation of an out-of-service order while transporting hazardous materials required to be placarded under Section 105 of the Hazardous Materials Transportation Act, or while operating commercial motor vehicles designed to transport more than 15 passengers, including the driver. A driver is disqualified for a period of not less than three years nor more than five years if, during any ten-year period, the driver is convicted of any subsequent violations of out-of-service orders, in separate incidents, while transporting hazardous materials required to be placarded under Section 105 of the Hazardous Materials Transportation Act, or while operating commercial motor vehicles designed to transport more than 15 passengers, including the driver.

"(4) In addition to any other penalty imposed pursuant to this article, any driver who is convicted of a railroad grade crossing violation in a commercial vehicle shall be subject to a civil penalty of not less than $1,100.00 and not to exceed $2,750.00.

"(h) After suspending, revoking, or canceling a commercial driver's license, the department shall update its records to reflect that action within ten days. After suspending, revoking, or canceling a nonresident commercial driver's privileges, the department shall notify the licensing authority of the state which issued the commercial driver's license within ten days.

"(i) Any person is disqualified from driving a commercial motor vehicle for a period of not less than 60 days if it is determined, in a check of an applicant's license status and record prior to issuing a commercial driver's license or at any time after the commercial driver's license is issued, that the applicant has falsified information on his or her application or any related filing.

"(j)(1) Any person is disqualified from driving a commercial vehicle for a period of not less than 30 days if the department receives notification from the Federal Motor Carrier Safety Administration that the person poses an imminent hazard.

"(2) If the Federal Motor Carrier Safety Administration notifies the department that a person's driving constitutes an imminent hazard and imposes a disqualification greater than 30 days, the person shall be disqualified from driving a commercial vehicle for the period designated by the Federal Motor Carrier Safety Administration, not to exceed one year."

Laws 2007, Act 44, § 8, provides:

"This Act shall become effective on January 1, 2008."

The 2008 amendment by Act 434, in subsec. (g), substituted "180" for "90" in subpar. (1)(A), substituted "two years" for "one year" in subpar. (1)(B), and substituted "$2,500.00 for a first offense and not less than $5,000.00 for a second or subsequent offense" for "$1,000.00 and not to exceed $2,750.00" in par. (4).

The 2008 amendment by Act 471 was a provision contained in a correction bill.

§ 40–5–152. Operation of commercial motor vehicle with any measurable alcohol in driver's system prohibited

(a) Notwithstanding any other provision of this article, a person may not drive, operate, or be in physical control of a commercial motor vehicle while having any measurable alcohol in his or her system.

(b) A person who drives, operates, or is in physical control of a commercial motor vehicle while having any measurable alcohol in his or her system or who refuses to take a test prescribed by Code Section 40–5–55 to determine his or her alcohol content must be placed out of service for 24 hours.

Laws 1989, p. 519, § 1; Laws 1990, p. 2048, § 4; Laws 2003, Act 200, § 7, eff. Oct. 1, 2003.

Historical and Statutory Notes

The 2003 amendment by Act 200, in subsec. (b), substituted "prescribed by Code Section 40–5–55" for "under paragraph (1) of subsection (a) of Code Section 40–6–392".

Laws 2003, Act 200, § 15 provides:

"This Act shall become effective on October 1, 2003."

§ 40–5–153. Implied consent to alcohol and drug testing

(a) Any person who drives a commercial motor vehicle anywhere in the state shall be deemed to have given consent, subject to the provisions of Code Sections 40–5–55 and 40–6–392, to a test or tests of that person's blood, breath, or urine for the purpose of determining that person's alcohol concentration or the presence of other drugs.

(b) A test or tests may be administered at the direction of a law enforcement officer who, after stopping or detaining the commercial motor vehicle driver, has probable cause to believe that driver was driving a commercial motor vehicle while having any measurable alcohol in his or her system.

(c) A person requested to submit to a test as provided in subsection (a) of this Code section must be warned by the law enforcement officer requesting the test that a refusal to submit to the test will result in that person's being disqualified from operating a commercial motor vehicle for one year under Code Section 40–5–151 and from operating a private motor vehicle as provided in Code Section 40–5–67.1.

(d) If the person refuses testing, the law enforcement officer must submit an affidavit to the department within ten days of such refusal certifying that the test was requested pursuant to subsection (a) of this Code section and that the person refused to submit to testing.

(e) Upon receipt of the affidavit submitted by a law enforcement officer under subsection (d) of this Code section, the department must disqualify the driver from driving a commercial motor vehicle for a period of one year as provided under Code Section 40–5–151 and, if the driver refused testing, from operating a private motor vehicle as provided under Code Section 40–5–67.1. If the driver is in possession of a driver's license, the officer shall take possession of the license and attach it to the affidavit.

Laws 1989, p. 519, § 1; Laws 1990, p. 2048, § 4; Laws 1992, p. 2564, § 11; Laws 2000, p. 951, § 5–60.

§ 40–5–154. Notification to licensing state of conviction of nonresident holder of commercial driver's license for violations relating to motor vehicle traffic control

Within ten days after receiving a report of the conviction of any nonresident holder of a commercial driver's license for any violation of state law or local ordinance relating to motor vehicle traffic control, other than parking violations, committed in a commercial motor vehicle, the department shall notify the licensing state of such conviction.

Laws 1989, p. 519, § 1; Laws 1990, p. 2048, § 4; Laws 2000, p. 951, § 5–61.

§ 40–5–155. Release of driving records to certain persons

Notwithstanding any other provision of law to the contrary, the department shall furnish full information regarding the driving record of any person to:

(1) The driver's license administrator of any other state or of any province or territory of Canada requesting that information;

(2) Any employer or prospective employer upon the request of such employer and the payment of a fee of not more than $10.00; and

(3) Insurers upon request and payment of a fee of not more than $10.00.

Laws 1989, p. 519, § 1; Laws 1990, p. 2048, § 4; Laws 2000, p. 951, § 5–62.

§ 40–5–156. Rules and regulations

The commissioner may adopt any rules and regulations necessary to carry out the provisions of this article.

Laws 1989, p. 519, § 1; Laws 1990, p. 2048, § 4; Laws 2000, p. 951, § 5–63.

§ 40–5–157. Commissioner authorized to enter into agreements to implement law

The commissioner or his or her designee may enter into or make agreements, arrangements, or declarations to carry out the provisions of this article.

Laws 1989, p. 519, § 1; Laws 1990, p. 2048, § 4; Laws 2000, p. 951, § 5–64.

§ 40–5–158. Reciprocity

Notwithstanding any other law to the contrary, a person may drive a commercial motor vehicle if the person has a commercial driver's license issued by any state or any province or territory of Canada in accordance with the minimum federal standards for the issuance of commercial motor vehicle driver's licenses; if the person's license is not suspended, revoked, or canceled; and if the person is not disqualified from driving a commercial motor vehicle or subject to an out of service order.

Laws 1989, p. 519, § 1; Laws 1990, p. 2048, § 4.

§ 40–5–159. Penalties

(a) Any person who drives a commercial motor vehicle while in violation of the provisions of Code Section 40–5–143 or any employer who knowingly allows, requires, permits, or authorizes a driver to drive a commercial motor vehicle in violation of the provisions of subsection (b) of Code Section 40–5–145 shall be guilty of a felony and, upon conviction thereof, shall be punished as follows:

(1) Except as provided for in subsections (d) and (e) of this Code section, by a civil penalty of $2,500.00 for each offense; and

(2) By a fine of $5,000.00, imprisonment for not more than 90 days, or both, for each offense.

(b) Any employer who reports fraudulent information to the department regarding an employee's employment or experience as required under 49 C.F.R. Part 383 shall be guilty of a misdemeanor and, upon conviction thereof, shall be fined not less than $500.00.

(c) Any person who drives a commercial motor vehicle while in violation of the provisions mandated under Code Section 40–5–146 shall be guilty of a misdemeanor and, upon conviction thereof, shall be fined not less than $500.00.

(d) Any employer who knowingly allows, requires, permits, or authorizes a driver to drive a commercial motor vehicle in violation of any federal, state, or local law or regulation pertaining to an out-of-service order shall be subject to a civil penalty in an amount not less than $2,750.00 and not to exceed $25,000.00.

(e) Any employer who knowingly allows, requires, permits, or authorizes a driver to drive a commercial motor vehicle in violation of any federal, state, or local law or regulation pertaining to railroad grade crossings shall be subject to a civil penalty not to exceed $10,000.00.

Laws 1989, p. 519, § 1; Laws 1990, p. 2048, § 4; Laws 2000, p. 951, § 5–65; Laws 2003, Act 200, § 8, eff. Oct. 1, 2003; Laws 2006, Act 590, § 20, eff. July 1, 2006; Laws 2007, Act 44, § 6, eff. Jan. 1, 2008; Laws 2008, Act 434, § 13, eff. Jan. 1, 2009.

Historical and Statutory Notes

The 2003 amendment by Act 200 inserted "requires," in the first paragraph of subsec. (a); and added subsec. (d).

Laws 2003, Act 200, § 15 provides:

"This Act shall become effective on October 1, 2003."

The 2006 amendment by Act 590, rewrote subsec. (c); and in subsec. (d), added "less than $2,750.00 and not" and substituted "$11,000.00" for "$10,000.00". Prior to amendment subsec. (c) had read:

"(c) Any person who drives a commercial motor vehicle while in violation of the provisions mandated under Code Section 40–5–146 shall be guilty of a misdemeanor and, upon conviction thereof, shall be fined not less than $500.00. The department shall suspend the commercial driver's license or commercial driving privilege of such driver for a period of six months."

The 2007 amendment by Act 44, in subsec. (a), par. (1), substituted "Except as provided for in subsections (d) and (e) of this Code section, by" for "By"; rewrote subsec. (c); in subsec. (d), substituted "an out–of–service order" for "railroad grade crossings"; and added subsec. (e). Prior to amendment, subsec. (c) had read:

"(c)(1) Any person who drives a commercial motor vehicle while in violation of the provisions mandated under Code Section 40–5–146 shall be guilty of a misdemeanor and, upon conviction thereof, shall be fined not less than $500.00. The department shall suspend the commercial driver's license or commercial driving privilege of any driver convicted of violating subsection (a) or paragraph (1) of subsection (b) of Code Section 40–5–146 for a period of six months.

"(2) The department shall suspend the commercial driver's license or commercial driving privilege of any person who is convicted of violating Code Section 40–5–29 in a commercial vehicle for a period of six months."

Laws 2007, Act 44, § 8, provides:

"This Act shall become effective on January 1, 2008."

The 2008 amendment by Act 434, in subsec. (d), substituted "$25,-000.00" for "$11,000.00" at the end of the subsection.

Article 8

Identification Cards for Persons with Disabilities

§ 40–5–170. Definitions

As used in this article, the term:

(1) "Disability" means any physical, mental, or neurological impairment which severely restricts a person's mobility, manual dexterity, or ability to climb stairs; substantial loss of sight or hearing; loss of one or more limbs or use thereof; or significantly diminished reasoning capacity.

(2) "Identification card for persons with disabilities" means an identification card issued as provided in this article.

(3) "Permanent disability" means any disability which is permanent in nature or which is expected to continue for a period of at least five years.

(4) "Person with disabilities" means any person with a permanent or temporary disability.

(5) "Temporary disability" means any disability which is expected to continue for at least six months but less than five years.

Laws 1989, p. 628, § 1; Laws 1990, p. 2048, § 4; Laws 1995, p. 1302, § 7.

§ 40–5–171. Information to be contained on card

(a) The department shall issue personal identification cards to persons with disabilities who make application to the department in accordance with rules and regulations prescribed by the commissioner. The identification card for persons with disabilities shall contain a recent color photograph of the applicant and the following information:

(1) Full legal name;

(2) Address of residence;

(3) Birth date;

(4) Date identification card was issued;

(5) Date identification card expires;

(6) Sex;

(7) Height;

(8) Weight;

(9) Eye color;

(10) Signature of person identified or facsimile thereof; and

(11) Such other information as required by the department; provided, however, that the department shall not require an applicant to submit or otherwise obtain from an applicant any fingerprints or any other biological characteristic or information which uniquely identifies an individual, including without limitation deoxyribonucleic acid (DNA) and retinal scan identification characteristics but not including a photograph, by any means upon application.

(b) The identification card for persons with disabilities shall bear the signatures of the commissioner and the Governor and shall bear an identification card number which shall not be the same as the applicant's social security number.

(c) In addition to the information required in subsection (a) of this Code section, identification cards issued to persons with disabilities shall display the international handicapped symbol on a location designated by the department. The department may display the international handicapped symbol on any driver's license or identification card issued pursuant to the provisions of this chapter upon receipt of the required documentation from the person requesting its inclusion.

Laws 1989, p. 628, § 1; Laws 1990, p. 2048, § 4; Laws 1995, p. 1302, § 7; Laws 1996, p. 1250, § 10; Laws 1997, p. 1443, § 5; Laws 2000, p. 951, § 5–66. Laws 2005, Act 355, § 5, eff. July 1, 2006; Laws 2008, Act 434, § 14, eff. Jan. 1, 2009; Laws 2010, Act 633, § 21, eff. July 1, 2010.

Historical and Statutory Notes

The 2005 amendment by Act 355, in subsec. (a), deleted par. (12), redesignated former par. (13) as par. (12), and rewrote the paragraph. Prior to amendment, pars. (12) and (13) had read:

"(12) Fingerprint of person identified; and

"(13) Such other information as required by the department."

Laws 2005, Act 355, § 6, provides:

"This Act shall become effective on July 1, 2006."

In 2005, the Code Commission, in subsec. (a), par. (12), deleted the comma following "including without limitation" and inserted a comma following "including a photograph". See § 28–9–5.

The 2008 amendment by Act 434, in subsec. (b), deleted ", unless the person specifically requests that the social security number be used, or, in the case of an individual who is not a citizen of the United States, the passport number of the person identified or any number the department deems necessary to implement this Code section" at the end of the subsection.

The 2010 amendment by Act 633, in subsec. (a), deleted "prominently display the international handicapped symbol and, in addition to any other information required by this article, may" after "persons with disabilities shall" in the second sentence, deleted former par. (10) and redesignated former pars. (11) and (12) as pars. (10) and (11); added subsec. (c).

§ 40–5–172. Issuance and renewal of cards

(a) The identification card for persons with disabilities shall be issued to a person with a permanent disability for a period of four years and shall be renewable on the applicant's birthday in the fourth year following such issuance. Such identification cards shall be issued to persons:

(1) With obvious permanent disabilities without further verification of disability; and

(2) With disabilities which are not obvious upon presentation of the current sworn affidavit of at least one medical doctor attesting to such permanent disability. A current affidavit shall be presented at each request for renewal.

(b) The identification card for persons with disabilities shall be issued to a person with a temporary disability upon presentation of a sworn affidavit of at least one medical doctor attesting to such disability and estimating the duration of such disability. Such identification cards shall be issued for periods of six months. A current affidavit of a medical doctor attesting to the continuance of such disability shall be presented at each request for renewal thereafter.

Laws 1989, p. 628, § 1; Laws 1990, p. 2048, § 4; Laws 1995, p. 1302, § 7.

§ 40–5–173. Medical information to be entered on card

The face of the identification card for persons with disabilities shall prominently bear wording selected by the department that is indicative of the presence of urgent medical information on the reverse of the card. On the reverse side of the identification card shall be a space within which the department shall enter such medical information as the applicant may request. The department may print the urgent medical indicator and wording on the reverse of any driver's license or identification card upon receipt of the required documentation from the person requesting its inclusion.

Laws 1989, p. 628, § 1; Laws 1990, p. 2048, § 4; Laws 1995, p. 1302, § 7; Laws 2010, Act 633, § 22, eff. July 1, 2010.

Historical and Statutory Notes

The 2010 amendment by Act 633 rewrote the section which had read as follows:

"The face of the identification card for persons with disabilities shall prominently bear the words "URGENT MEDICAL INFORMATION ON REVERSE." On the reverse side of the identification card shall be a space within which the issuer of the card shall enter such medical information as the applicant may request."

§ 40–5–174. Need for special transportation services for persons with disabilities to be indicated on card

The face of the identification card for persons with disabilities shall bear the word TRANSPORTATION with a box or blank space adjacent thereto. The department shall place an X in such box or blank space if the applicant's disability creates mobility limitations which prevent him or her from climbing stairs or otherwise from entering normally designed buses or other vehicles normally used for public transportation. When so marked, the identification card for persons with disabilities shall serve as sufficient proof of the need for special transportation services for persons with disabilities provided by any entity in this state. The department may print the transportation indicator on any driver's license or identification card upon receipt of the required documentation from the person requesting its inclusion.

Laws 1989, p. 628, § 1; Laws 1990, p. 2048, § 4; Laws 1995, p. 1302, § 7; Laws 2010, Act 633, § 23, eff. July 1, 2010.

Historical and Statutory Notes

The 2010 amendment by Act 633 substituted "department" for "issuer of the card" in the second sentence and added the fourth sentence.

§ 40–5–175. Need for seating for persons with disabilities at public events to be indicated on card

The identification card for persons with disabilities shall bear the word "SEATING" with a box or blank space adjacent thereto. The department shall place an X in such box or blank space if the applicant's disability creates mobility or health limitations which prevent him or her from climbing stairs or steep inclines. When so marked, the identification card for persons with disabilities shall be sufficient to admit the holder to seating for persons with disabilities at public events in this state. The department may print the priority seating indicator on any driver's license or identification card upon receipt of the required documentation from the person requesting its inclusion.

Laws 1989, p. 628, § 1; Laws 1990, p. 2048, § 4; Laws 1995, p. 1302, § 7; Laws 2010, Act 633, § 24, eff. July 1, 2010.

Historical and Statutory Notes

The 2010 amendment by Act 633 substituted "department" for "issuer of the card" in the second sentence and added the fourth sentence.

§ 40–5–176. Rules and regulations

The commissioner shall promulgate rules and regulations under which this article shall be implemented.

Laws 1989, p. 628, § 1; Laws 1990, p. 2048, § 4; Laws 1995, p. 1302, § 7; Laws 2000, p. 951, § 5–67.

§ 40–5–177. Applicants to furnish proof of birth date

The department shall require an applicant for an identification card for persons with disabilities to furnish a birth certificate or other verifiable evidence stating the applicant's birth date.

Laws 1989, p. 628, § 1; Laws 1990, p. 2048, § 4; Laws 1995, p. 1302, § 7.

§ 40–5–178. Fees

(a) The department shall collect a fee of $5.00 for an identification card for persons with disabilities, which fee shall be deposited in the state treasury in the same manner as motor vehicle driver's license fees.

(b) The department shall not be authorized to collect a fee for an identification card for persons with disabilities from those persons who meet the qualifications for a veteran's driver's license under the provisions of Code Section 40–5–36.

Laws 1989, p. 628, § 1; Laws 1990, p. 2048, § 4; Laws 1995, p. 1302, § 7.

§ 40–5–179. Violations

It is a misdemeanor for any person:

(1) To lend his or her identification card for persons with disabilities to any other person or knowingly to permit the use thereof by another; and

(2) To display or represent as his or her own any identification card for persons with disabilities not issued to him or her.

Laws 1989, p. 628, § 1; Laws 1990, p. 2048, § 4; Laws 1995, p. 1302, § 7; Laws 2002, p. 551, § 7.

Historical and Statutory Notes

The 2002 amendment by Act 750 rewrote the section which had read:

"It is a misdemeanor for any person:

"(1) To use false or fictitious name in any application for an identification card for persons with disabilities or knowingly to make a false statement or conceal a material fact or otherwise commit a fraud in any such application;

"(2) To display or cause to be displayed or have in his or her possession any fictitious or fraudulently altered identification card for persons with disabilities;

"(3) To lend his or her identification card for persons with disabilities to any other person or knowingly to permit the use thereof by another; and

"(4) To display or represent as his or her own any identification card for persons with disabilities not issued to him or her."

CHAPTER 6

UNIFORM RULES OF THE ROAD

Article 1

Article 2

Article 3

Article 4

Article 1

General Provisions

§ 40–6–1. Required obedience to traffic laws; maximum fines for violating speed limits

(a) It is unlawful and, unless otherwise declared in this chapter with respect to particular offenses, it is a misdemeanor for any person to do any act forbidden or fail to perform any act required in this chapter.

(b) Unless a different maximum fine or greater minimum fine is specifically provided in this chapter for a particular violation, the maximum fine which may be imposed as punishment for a first offense of violating any lawful speed limit established by or pursuant to the provisions of Article 9 of this chapter by exceeding a maximum lawful speed limit:

(1) By five miles per hour or less shall be no dollars;

(2) By more than five but not more than ten miles per hour shall not exceed $25.00;

(3) By more than ten but not more than 14 miles per hour shall not exceed $100.00;

(4) By more than 14 but less than 19 miles per hour shall not exceed $125.00;

(5) By 19 or more but less than 24 miles per hour shall not exceed $150.00; or

(6) By 24 or more but less than 34 miles per hour shall not exceed $500.00.

Laws 1953, Nov.-Dec. Sess., p. 556, § 23; Laws 1974, p. 633, § 1; Laws 1990, p. 2048, § 5; Laws 2001, p. 770, § 1.

Formerly Code 1933, § 68A–102.

Historical and Statutory Notes

The 2001 amendment designated subsec. (a) and added subsec. (b).

§ 40–6–2. Obedience to authorized persons directing traffic

No person shall fail or refuse to comply with any lawful order or direction of any police officer, firefighter, police volunteer authorized under Code Section 35–1–11, or school-crossing guard designated by a local law enforcement agency invested by law with authority to direct, control, or regulate traffic.

Laws 1953, Nov.-Dec. Sess., p. 556, § 24; Laws 1974, p. 633, § 1; Laws 1989, p. 516, § 2; Laws 1990, p. 2048, § 5; Laws 1999, p. 654, § 2; Laws 2002, p. 660, § 4; Laws 2002, p. 1259, § 11.

Formerly Code 1933, § 68A–104.

Historical and Statutory Notes

The 2002 amendments by Acts 787 and 952 substituted references to the the terms "fireman" and "firemen" with "firefighter" and "firefighters".

§ 40–6–3. Provisions refer to vehicles upon the highways—exceptions

(a) The provisions of this chapter relating to the operation of vehicles refer to the operation of vehicles upon highways except:

(1) Where a different place is specifically referred to in a given Code section;

(2) The provisions of this chapter shall apply to a vehicle operated at shopping centers or parking lots or similar areas which although privately owned are customarily used by the public as through streets or connector streets;

(3) The provisions of this chapter relating to reckless driving, driving in violation of Code Section 40–6–391, and homicide by vehicle shall apply to vehicles operated upon highways and elsewhere throughout the state;

(4) The provisions of Code Sections 40–6–270, 40–6–271, and 40–6–272 shall apply upon the highways of this state, in all parking areas, and in all areas which are customarily open to the public and within 200 feet of all such highways, parking areas, and areas customarily open to the public;

(5)(A) The provisions of this chapter shall apply to a vehicle operated on any private property of this state which fronts on coastal marshlands or estuarine area as defined in Code Section 12–5–282, provided the owner of the private property files with the local law enforcement agency having primary jurisdiction to enforce the uniform rules of the road in such area:

(i) A petition requesting such local law enforcement agency to enforce the uniform rules of the road on such private property; and

(ii) Simultaneously files a plat with the petition delineating the location of the roads, streets, and common areas on such private property.

(B) The local law enforcement agency having primary jurisdiction to enforce the uniform rules of the road in such area shall enforce the uniform rules of the road on said private property at no cost to the owner of the private property or enter into a contractual agreement with the owner of the private property whereby the owner of the private property consents to pay part or all of the law enforcement expenses to such law enforcement agency.

(C) All persons operating vehicles on said roads, streets, and common areas shall be subject to all state and local traffic laws and regulations the same as if said private roads and streets were public roads and streets.

(D) Any state or local law enforcement agency empowered to enforce the uniform rules of the road in such area shall have concurrent jurisdiction with the primary local law enforcement agency to enforce the rules of the road on said private property.

(E) At least 30 days' prior notice shall be given to users of said private roads, streets, and common areas by publication in the newspapers of general circulation in the area and by posting signs along the private roads and streets specifying that state and local law enforcement agencies will be enforcing the uniform rules of the road on said private roads, streets, and common areas; and

(6)(A) Subject to the approval of the governing authority of the county or municipality, the provisions of this chapter shall apply to a vehicle operated within a privately owned residential area located within the corporate boundaries of a municipality or located within the boundaries of a county, provided the owner of the privately owned residential area files with the governing authority of such county or municipality:

(i) A petition signed by 50 percent of the property owners located in said subdivision requesting the law enforcement agency of the county or municipality to enforce the uniform rules of the road within such privately owned residential area; and

(ii) A plat delineating the location of roads, streets, and common areas within the privately owned residential area.

(B) Upon approval by the governing authority of the county or municipality, the law enforcement agency of such county or municipality shall enforce the uniform rules of the road within said privately owned residential area.

(C) All persons operating vehicles on the roads, streets, and common areas of said privately owned residential property shall be subject to all state and local traffic laws and regulations the same as if such private roads, streets, and common areas were public roads and streets.

(D) At least 30 days' prior notice shall be given to users of said private roads, streets, and common areas by publication in a newspaper of general circulation in the area and by posting signs along the private road, streets, and common areas specifying that the county law enforcement agency or municipal law enforcement agency will be enforcing the uniform rules of the roads on said private roads, streets, and common areas.

(b) Notwithstanding the provisions of subsection (a) of this Code section, any law enforcement officer shall be authorized to write an accident report regarding any motor vehicle accident occurring on private property.

Laws 1953, Nov.-Dec. Sess., p. 556, § 22; Laws 1974, p. 633, § 1; Laws 1983, p. 1000, § 11; Laws 1985, p. 758, § 15; Laws 1986, p. 834, § 1; Laws 1990, p. 2048, § 5; Laws 1991, p. 1000, § 1; Laws 1992, p. 2294, § 2.

Formerly Code 1933, § 68A–103.

§ 40–6–4. Persons riding animals or driving animal drawn vehicles

Every person riding an animal or driving an animal drawn vehicle upon a roadway shall be granted all of the rights and shall be subject to all of the duties applicable to the driver of a vehicle by this chapter, except those provisions of this chapter which by their very nature can have no application.

Laws 1953, Nov.-Dec. Sess., p. 556, § 27; Laws 1974, p. 633, § 1; Laws 1990, p. 2048, § 5.

Formerly Code 1933, § 68A–105.

§ 40–6–5. Persons working on highways—exceptions

Unless specifically made applicable, the provisions of this chapter, except those contained in Article 15 of this chapter, shall not apply to authorized persons, teams, motor vehicles, and other equipment while actually engaged in work upon a highway but shall apply to such persons and vehicles when traveling to or from such work.

Laws 1953, Nov.-Dec. Sess., p. 556, § 25; Laws 1974, p. 633, § 1; Laws 1982, p. 3, § 40; Laws 1990, p. 2048, § 5.

Formerly Code 1933, § 68A–106.

§ 40–6–6. Authorized emergency vehicles

(a) The driver of an authorized emergency vehicle or law enforcement vehicle, when responding to an emergency call, when in the pursuit of an actual or suspected violator of the law, or when responding to but not upon returning from a fire alarm, may exercise the privileges set forth in this Code section.

(b) The driver of an authorized emergency vehicle or law enforcement vehicle may:

(1) Park or stand, irrespective of the provisions of this chapter;

(2) Proceed past a red or stop signal or stop sign, but only after slowing down as may be necessary for safe operation;

(3) Exceed the maximum speed limits so long as he or she does not endanger life or property; and

(4) Disregard regulations governing direction of movement or turning in specified directions.

(c) The exceptions granted by this Code section to an authorized emergency vehicle shall apply only when such vehicle is making use of an audible signal and use of a flashing or revolving red light visible under normal atmospheric conditions from a distance of 500 feet to the front of such vehicle, except that a vehicle belonging to a federal, state, or local law enforcement agency and operated as such shall be making use of an audible signal and a flashing or revolving blue light with the same visibility to the front of the vehicle.

(d)(1) The foregoing provisions shall not relieve the driver of an authorized emergency vehicle from the duty to drive with due regard for the safety of all persons.

(2) When a law enforcement officer in a law enforcement vehicle is pursuing a fleeing suspect in another vehicle and the fleeing suspect damages any property or injures or kills any person during the pursuit, the law enforcement officer's pursuit shall not be the proximate cause or a contributing proximate cause of the damage, injury, or death caused by the fleeing suspect unless the law enforcement officer acted with reckless disregard for proper law enforcement procedures in the officer's decision to initiate or continue the pursuit. Where such reckless disregard exists, the pursuit may be found to constitute a proximate cause of the damage, injury, or death caused by the fleeing suspect, but the existence of such reckless disregard shall not in and of itself establish causation.

(3) The provisions of this subsection shall apply only to issues of causation and duty and shall not affect the existence or absence of immunity which shall be determined as otherwise provided by law.

(4) Claims arising out of this subsection which are brought against local government entities, their officers, agents, servants, attorneys, and employees shall be subject to the procedures and limitations contained in Chapter 92 of Title 36.

(e) It shall be unlawful for any person to operate an authorized emergency vehicle with flashing lights other than as authorized by subsection (c) of this Code section.

Laws 1953, Nov.-Dec. Sess., p. 556, § 26; Laws 1974, p. 633, § 1; Laws 1990, p. 2048, § 5; Laws 1995, p. 855, § 1; Laws 2002, p. 579, § 4.

Formerly Code 1933, § 68A–107.

Historical and Statutory Notes

The 2002 amendment added par. (d)(4).

Laws 2002, Act 763, § 5, provides:

"This act [adding par. (d)(4)] shall become effective on January 1, 2005."

§ 40–6–7. Operation of motor vehicles and motorcycles in parades

Notwithstanding any other provisions of law, it shall be lawful to operate motor vehicles and motorcycles in parades although such motor vehicles and motorcycles and their operators and passengers do not meet the necessary requirements of law, especially with respect to flashing lights, sirens, and safety equipment. This Code section shall be applicable only in the event that the local authority which has the power to issue parade permits, at its discretion, authorizes the operation of such motor vehicles and motorcycles after it has been determined that the operation of such motor vehicles and motorcycles will not endanger the lives, safety, or property of other participants in the parade, bystanders, or other persons. The authorization for vehicles to be operated in parades as exceptions to otherwise required provisions of law shall extend to only such time as the vehicles are actually engaged in the parade and in the return to the marshaling area. At all times, such vehicles shall be operated by a person properly licensed to operate such vehicles. Such motor vehicles and motorcycles covered under this Code section shall be operated in accordance with all provisions of law when traveling to and from a parade site and at all other times when not directly participating in a parade.

Laws 1974, p. 446, § 1; Laws 1990, p. 2048, § 5.

§ 40–6–8. Law not to interfere with rights of owners of real property with reference thereto

Nothing in this chapter shall be construed to prevent the owner of real property used by the public for purposes of vehicular travel by permission of the owner, and not as matter of right, from prohibiting such use, or from requiring other or different or additional conditions than those specified in this chapter, or from otherwise regulating such use as may seem best to such owner.

Laws 1953, Nov.-Dec. Sess., p. 556, § 30; Laws 1990, p. 2048, § 5.

§ 40–6–9. When local authorities may alter lawful speed limits

(a) As used in this Code section, the term "speed limits" shall be construed to refer to and include stop lights, stop signs, slow signs, yield signs, and any and every other light, device, or sign which may be used to impede, slow, stop, or regulate the speed of motor vehicles on the public highways.

(b) Any provisions of this chapter to the contrary notwithstanding, whenever any complaint is made to the Governor that any speed limit established by any county or municipal authority is arbitrary or unreasonable, or upon any complaint being made to the Governor that any speed limit established by the state or by any county or municipal governing authority is being enforced primarily for the collection of revenue rather than for purposes of public safety, the Governor may, in his discretion, direct that an investigation and any necessary studies be commenced by the commissioner of public safety or his delegate who shall make a report thereon together with his recommendations as to whether the state should suspend the authority of the applicable local county or municipal governing authorities to enforce speed limits upon any state and federal highways lying within the jurisdiction of such authorities. Upon receipt of a report accompanied by recommendations that the power to enforce speed limits be restricted, the Governor shall furnish a copy of such report to the local authorities affected thereby, together with notice of hearing on the allegations of the report made by the commissioner of public safety or his delegate. Such hearing may be held at such time and such place as may be determined by the Governor but shall not be held less than ten days after notice to the local governing authorities. Such hearing shall be conducted before a board to be composed of the Governor, the Secretary of State, and an appointee of the Governor who is not the Attorney General who shall be reimbursed for the actual and necessary expenses pertaining to their services on the board but who shall receive no other additional compensation for their services thereon. Upon determination by the board that the speed limits established by the county or municipal governing authorities against whom complaint has been brought are either unreasonable or that speed limits are being primarily enforced for the collection of revenue rather than for purposes of public safety, the Governor shall issue his executive order suspending the power of such local governing authority to enforce speed limits on state or federal highways lying within its jurisdiction or on any particular such highway. In the event that this power is suspended, the Governor shall direct the commissioner of public safety to enforce the speed limits on such highways.

(c) At intervals of not less than six months, any governing authority affected by subsection (b) of this Code section and by an executive order issued in accordance with subsection (b) of this Code section may, upon a change of circumstances being shown to the Governor, petition the Governor for reconsideration, whereupon the Governor, in his discretion, may direct the commissioner of public safety or his delegate to inquire into such change of circumstances and report the same to him together with any recommendations for modification of the Governor's previous order; and the Governor, in his discretion, may order a new hearing on the matter before the board or may, without hearing, modify or revoke his previous executive order.

(d) Any provisions of this chapter to the contrary notwithstanding, when any complaint is made to the Governor that any traffic law, ordinance, or regulation, other than speed regulations for which provision has been made in subsection (b) of this Code section, established by any county or municipal authority is arbitrary or unreasonable, or upon any complaint being made to the Governor that any traffic law, ordinance, or regulation established by the state or by any county or municipal governing authority, other than speed regulations for which provision has been made in subsection (b) of this Code section, is being enforced primarily for the collection of revenue rather than for purposes of public safety, the Governor may, in his discretion, direct that an investigation and any necessary studies be commenced by the commissioner of public safety or his delegate who shall make a report thereon together with his recommendations as to whether the state should suspend the authority of the applicable local county or municipal governing authorities to enforce traffic laws, ordinances, or regulations upon any state and federal highways lying within the jurisdiction of such authorities. Upon receipt of a report accompanied by recommendations that the power to enforce traffic laws, ordinances, and regulations be restricted, the Governor shall furnish a copy of such report to the local authorities affected thereby, together with notice of a hearing on the allegations of the report made by the commissioner of public safety or his delegate. Such hearing may be held at such time and at such place as may be determined by the Governor but shall not be less than ten days after notice to the local governing authorities. This hearing shall be conducted before a board to be composed of the Governor, the Secretary of State, and an appointee of the Governor who is not the Attorney General who shall be reimbursed for the actual and necessary expenses pertaining to their services on the board but who shall receive no other additional compensation for their services thereon. Upon the determination by the board either that traffic laws, ordinances, or regulations, other than speed regulations for which provision has been made in subsection (b) of this Code section, established by the county or municipal governing authority against whom complaint has been brought are unreasonable or that traffic laws, ordinances, or regulations established by the state or by any county or municipal governing authority are being primarily enforced for the collection of revenue rather than for purposes of public safety, the Governor shall issue his executive order suspending the power of such local governing authority to enforce traffic laws, ordinances, and regulations on state or federal highways lying within its jurisdiction or on any particular such highway. In the event that this power is suspended, the Governor shall direct the commissioner of public safety to enforce the traffic laws and regulations on such highways.

(e) At intervals of not less than six months, any governing authority affected by subsection (d) of this Code section and by an executive order issued in accordance with subsection (d) of this Code section may, upon a change of circumstances being shown to the Governor, petition the Governor for reconsideration, whereupon the Governor, in his discretion, may direct the commissioner of public safety or his delegate to inquire into such change of circumstances and report the same to him together with any recommendations for modification of the Governor's previous executive order; and the Governor, in his discretion, may order a new hearing on the matter before the board or may, without hearing, modify or revoke his previous executive order.

Laws 1953, Nov.-Dec. Sess., p. 556, § 50; Laws 1963, p. 461, § 1; Laws 1968, p. 1422, § 1; Laws 1975, p. 1582, § 4; Laws 1985, p. 149, § 40; Laws 1988, p. 426, § 1; Laws 1990, p. 2048, § 5.

§ 40-6-10. Proof of minimum insurance; penalties

(a)(1) The owner or operator of a motor vehicle for which minimum motor vehicle liability insurance coverage is required under Chapter 34 of Title 33 shall keep proof or evidence of required minimum insurance coverage in the vehicle at all times during the operation of the vehicle. The owner of a motor vehicle shall provide to any operator of such vehicle proof or evidence of required minimum insurance coverage for the purposes of compliance with this subsection.

(2) The following shall be acceptable proof of insurance on a temporary basis:

(A) If the policy providing such coverage was applied for within the last 30 days, a current written binder for such coverage for a period not exceeding 30 days from the date such binder was issued shall be considered satisfactory proof or evidence of required minimum insurance coverage;

(B) If the vehicle is operated under a rental agreement, a duly executed vehicle rental agreement shall be considered satisfactory proof or evidence of required minimum insurance coverage; and

(C) If the owner acquired ownership of the vehicle within the past 30 days, if the type of proof described in subparagraph (A) of this paragraph is not applicable but the vehicle is currently effectively provided with required minimum insurance coverage under the terms of a policy providing required minimum insurance coverage for another motor vehicle, then a copy of the insurer's declaration of coverage under the policy providing such required minimum insurance coverage for such other vehicle shall be considered satisfactory proof or evidence of required minimum insurance coverage for the vehicle, but only if accompanied by proof or evidence that the owner acquired ownership of the vehicle within the past 30 days.

(2.1) If the vehicle is insured under a fleet policy as defined in Code Section 40-2-137 providing the required minimum insurance coverage or if the vehicle is engaged in interstate commerce and registered under the provisions of Article 3A of

Chapter 2 of this title, the insurance information card issued by the insurer shall be considered satisfactory proof of required minimum insurance coverage for the vehicle.

(2.2) If the vehicle is insured under a certificate of self-insurance issued by the Commissioner of Insurance providing the required minimum insurance coverage under which the vehicle owner did not report the vehicle identification number to the Commissioner of Insurance, the insurance information card issued by the Commissioner of Insurance shall be considered satisfactory proof of required minimum insurance coverage for the vehicle, but only if accompanied by a copy of the certificate issued by the Commissioner of Insurance.

(3) The requirement under this Code section that proof or evidence of minimum liability insurance be maintained in a motor vehicle at all times during the operation of the vehicle shall not apply to the owner or operator of any vehicle for which the records or data base of the Department of Revenue indicates that required minimum insurance coverage is currently effective.

(4) Except as otherwise provided in paragraph (7) of this subsection, any person who fails to comply with the requirements of this subsection shall be guilty of a misdemeanor and, upon conviction thereof, shall be subject to a fine of not less than $200.00 nor more than $1,000.00 or imprisonment for not more than 12 months, or both.

(5) Every law enforcement officer in this state shall determine if the operator of a motor vehicle subject to the provisions of this Code section has the required minimum insurance coverage every time the law enforcement officer stops the vehicle or requests the presentation of the driver's license of the operator of the vehicle.

(6) If a law enforcement officer of this state determines that the owner or operator of a motor vehicle subject to the provisions of this Code section does not have proof or evidence of required minimum insurance coverage, the arresting officer shall issue a uniform traffic citation for operating a motor vehicle without proof of insurance. If the court or arresting officer determines that the operator is not the owner, then a uniform traffic citation may be issued to the owner for authorizing the operation of a motor vehicle without proof of insurance.

(7) If the person receiving a citation under this subsection shows to the court having jurisdiction of the case that required minimum insurance coverage was in effect at the time the citation was issued, the court may impose a fine not to exceed $25.00. The court shall not in this case forward a record of the disposition of the case to the department and the driver's license of such person shall not be suspended.

(8)(A) For purposes of this Code section a valid insurance card shall be sufficient proof of insurance only for any vehicle covered under a fleet policy as defined in Code Section 40–2–137. The insurance card for a fleet policy shall contain at least the name of the insurer, policy number, policy issue or effective date, policy expiration date, and the name of the insured and may, but shall not be required to, include the year, make, model, and vehicle identification number of the vehicle insured. If the operator of any vehicle covered under a fleet policy as defined in Code Section 40–2–137 presents a valid insurance card for a fleet policy to any law enforcement officer or agency, and the officer or agency does not recognize the insurance card as valid proof of insurance and impounds or tows such vehicle for lack of proof of insurance, the law enforcement agency or political subdivision shall be liable for and limited to the fees of the wrongful impoundment or towing of the vehicle, which in no way waives or diminishes any sovereign immunity of such governmental entity.

(B) For any vehicle covered under a policy of motor vehicle liability insurance that is not a fleet policy as defined in Code Section 40–2–137, the insurer shall issue a policy information card which shall contain at least the name of the insurer, policy number, policy issue or effective date, policy expiration date, name of the insured, and year, make, model, and vehicle identification number of each vehicle insured; the owner or operator of the motor vehicle shall keep such policy information card in the vehicle at all times during operation of the vehicle for purposes of Code Section 40–6–273.1, but any such policy information card shall not be sufficient proof of insurance for any purposes of this Code section except as otherwise provided in this Code section.

(b) An owner or any other person who knowingly operates or knowingly authorizes another to operate a motor vehicle without effective insurance on such vehicle or without an approved plan of self-insurance shall be guilty of a misdemeanor and, upon conviction thereof, shall be subject to a fine of not less than $200.00 nor more than $1,000.00 or imprisonment for not more than 12 months, or both. An operator of a motor vehicle shall not be guilty of a violation of this Code section if such operator maintains a policy of motor vehicle insurance which extends coverage to any vehicle the operator may drive. An owner or operator of a motor vehicle shall not be issued a citation by a law enforcement officer for a violation of this Code section if the sole basis for issuance of such a citation is that the law enforcement officer is unable to obtain insurance coverage information from the records of the department.

(c) Any person who knowingly makes a false statement or certification under Code Section 40–5–71 or this Code section shall be guilty of a misdemeanor and, upon conviction thereof, shall be subject to a fine of not less than $200.00 nor more than $1,000.00 or imprisonment for not more than 12 months, or both.

(d) Except for vehicles insured under a fleet policy as defined in Code Section 40–2–137 or under a plan of self-insurance approved by the Commissioner of Insurance, insurance coverage information from records of the department shall be prima-facie evidence of the facts stated therein and shall be admissible as evidence in accordance with Code Section 24–3–17 for the purposes of this Code section.

Laws 1990, p. 2048, § 5; Laws 1996, p. 1079, § 1; Laws 2000, p. 429, §§ 5, 5A; Laws 2001, p. 1228, § 2A; Laws 2002, p. 1, § 1; Laws 2003, Act 44, § 5, eff. May 28, 2003; Laws 2005, Act 68, § 18–1, eff. July 1, 2005; Laws 2008, Act 437, § 1, eff. July 1, 2008; Laws 2010, Act 381, § 10, eff. May 20, 2010.

Historical and Statutory Notes

The 2000 amendment rewrote subsec. (a) and added the third sentence to subsec. (b).

The 2001 amendment modified the dates in subsec. (a)(5).

The 2002 amendment rewrote this section which, as amended in 2001 provided:

"(a)(1) The owner or operator of a motor vehicle for which minimum motor vehicle liability insurance coverage is required under Chapter 34 of Title 33 shall keep proof or evidence of required minimum insurance coverage in the vehicle at all times during the operation of the vehicle if:

"(A) The policy providing such coverage was applied for within the last 30 days, in which case a current written binder for such coverage for a period not exceeding 30 days from the date such binder was issued shall be considered satisfactory proof or evidence of required minimum insurance coverage;

"(B) The vehicle is operated under a rental agreement, in which case a duly executed vehicle rental agreement shall be considered satisfactory proof or evidence of required minimum insurance coverage; or

"(C) The owner acquired ownership of the motor vehicle in question within the past 20 days, in which case if the type of proof described in subparagraph (A) of this paragraph is not applicable but the vehicle is currently effectively provided with required minimum insurance coverage under the terms of a policy providing required minimum insurance coverage for another motor vehicle, then a copy of the insurer's declaration of coverage under the policy providing such required minimum insurance coverage for such other vehicle shall be considered satisfactory proof or evidence of required minimum insurance coverage for the vehicle in question, but only if accompanied by proof or evidence that the owner acquired ownership of the vehicle in question within the past 20 days;provided, however, that the requirements of this paragraph shall not apply to the owner or operator of any vehicle for which the records of the

Department of Public Safety indicate that required minimum insurance coverage is currently effective. The owner of a motor vehicle shall provide to any operator of such vehicle proof or evidence of required minimum insurance coverage for the purposes of compliance with this subsection. Except as otherwise provided in paragraph (4) of this subsection, any person who fails to comply with the requirements of this subsection shall be guilty of a misdemeanor and, upon conviction thereof, shall be subject to a fine of not less than $200.00 nor more than $1,000.00 or imprisonment for not more than 12 months, or both.

"(2)(A) Insurance coverage information from records of the department shall be prima-facie evidence of the facts stated therein and shall be admissible as evidence in accordance with Code Section 24–3–17.

"(B) Every law enforcement officer in this state shall request the operator of a motor vehicle subject to the provisions of paragraph (1) of this subsection to produce proof or evidence of required minimum insurance coverage every time the law enforcement officer requests the presentation of the driver's license of the operator of the vehicle.

"(3) If the owner or operator of a motor vehicle subject to the provisions of paragraph (1) of this subsection fails to show proof or evidence of required minimum insurance, the arresting officer shall issue a uniform traffic citation for operating a motor vehicle without proof of insurance and shall take possession of the driver's license and forward it to a court of competent jurisdiction. If the court or arresting officer determines that the operator is not the owner, then a uniform traffic citation may be issued to the owner for authorizing the operation of a motor vehicle without proof of insurance.

"(4) If the person receiving a citation under this subsection shows to the court having jurisdiction of the case that required minimum insurance coverage was in effect at the time the citation was issued, the court shall return the driver's license upon payment of a fine not to exceed $25.00. The court shall not in this case forward a record of the disposition of the case to the department and the driver's license of such person shall not be suspended.

"(5)(A) For purposes of this Code section up to and including December 31, 2001, a valid insurance card shall be sufficient proof of insurance for any vehicle.

"(B) For purposes of this Code section on and after January 1, 2002, a valid insurance card shall be sufficient proof of insurance only for any vehicle covered under a commercial vehicle policy as defined in Code Section 40–5–71.

"(C) For any vehicle covered under a policy of motor vehicle liability insurance that is not a commercial vehicle policy as defined in Code Section 40–5–71, the insurer shall issue a policy information identification card which shall contain at least the name of the insurer, policy number, policy issue or effective date, policy expiration date, name of the insured, and year, make, model, and vehicle identification number of each vehicle insured; provided, however, that on and after January 1, 2002, any such policy information identification card shall not be sufficient proof of insurance for any purposes of this Code section.

"(b) An owner or any other person who knowingly operates or knowingly authorizes another to operate a motor vehicle without effective insurance on such vehicle or without an approved plan of self-insurance shall be guilty of a misdemeanor and, upon conviction thereof, shall be subject to a fine of not less than $200.00 nor more than $1,000.00 or imprisonment for not more than 12 months, or both. An operator of a motor vehicle shall not be guilty of a violation of this Code section if such operator maintains a policy of motor vehicle insurance which extends coverage to any vehicle the operator may drive. An owner or operator of a motor vehicle shall not be issued a citation by a law enforcement officer for a violation of this Code section if the sole basis for issuance of such a citation is that the law enforcement officer is unable to obtain insurance coverage information from the records of the department.

"(c) Any person who knowingly makes a false statement or certification under Code Section 40–5–71 or this Code section shall be guilty of a misdemeanor and, upon conviction thereof, shall be subject to a fine of not less than $200.00 nor more than $1,000.00 or imprisonment for not more than 12 months, or both."

In 2002, the Code Commission, in par. (a)(3) and subsec. (e), substituted "data base" for "database". See § 28–9–5.

The 2003 amendment by Act 44 rewrote the section which had read:

"(a)(1) Until January 31, 2003, the owner or operator of a motor vehicle for which minimum motor vehicle liability insurance coverage is required under Chapter 34 of Title 33 shall keep proof or evidence of required minimum insurance coverage in the vehicle at all times during the operation of the vehicle. The owner of a motor vehicle shall provide to any operator of such vehicle proof or evidence of required minimum insurance coverage for the purposes of compliance with this subsection.

"(2) The following shall be acceptable proof of insurance on a temporary basis:

"(A) If the policy providing such coverage was applied for within the last 30 days, a current written binder for such coverage for a period not exceeding 30 days from the date such binder was issued shall be considered satisfactory proof or evidence of required minimum insurance coverage;

"(B) If the vehicle is operated under a rental agreement, a duly executed vehicle rental agreement shall be considered satisfactory proof or evidence of required minimum insurance coverage; and

"(C) If the owner acquired ownership of the motor vehicle in question within the past 20 days, if the type of proof described in subparagraph (A) of this paragraph is not applicable but the vehicle is currently effectively provided with required minimum insurance coverage under the terms of a policy providing required minimum insurance coverage for another motor vehicle, then a copy of the insurer's declaration of coverage under the policy providing such required minimum insurance coverage for such other vehicle shall be considered satisfactory proof or evidence of required minimum insurance coverage for the vehicle in question, but only if accompanied by proof or evidence that the owner acquired ownership of the vehicle in question within the past 20 days.

"(3) On and after February 1, 2003, the requirement under this Code section that proof or evidence of minimum liability insurance be maintained in a motor vehicle at all times during the operation of the vehicle shall not apply to the owner or operator of any vehicle for which the records or data base of the Department of Motor Vehicle Safety indicate that required minimum insurance coverage is currently effective.

"(4) Except as otherwise provided in paragraph (7) of this subsection, any person who fails to comply with the requirements of this subsection shall be guilty of a misdemeanor and, upon conviction thereof, shall be subject to a fine of not less than $ 200.00 nor more than $ 1,000.00 or imprisonment for not more than 12 months, or both.

"(5) Every law enforcement officer in this state shall determine if the operator of a motor vehicle subject to the provisions of this Code section has the required minimum insurance coverage every time the law enforcement officer requests the presentation of the driver's license of the operator of the vehicle.

"(6) If a law enforcement officer of this state determines that the owner or operator of a motor vehicle subject to the provisions of this Code section does not have proof or evidence of required minimum insurance coverage, the arresting officer shall issue a uniform traffic citation for operating a motor vehicle without proof of insurance and shall take possession of the driver's license and forward it to a court of competent jurisdiction. If the court or arresting officer determines that the operator is not the owner, then a uniform traffic citation may be issued to the owner for authorizing the operation of a motor vehicle without proof of insurance.

"(7) If the person receiving a citation under this subsection shows to the court having jurisdiction of the case that required minimum insurance coverage was in effect at the time the citation was issued, the court shall return the driver's license upon payment of a fine not to exceed $ 25.00. The court shall not in this case forward a record of the disposition of the case to the department and the driver's license of such person shall not be suspended.

"(8)(A) For purposes of this Code section up to and including January 31, 2003, a valid insurance card shall be sufficient proof of insurance for any vehicle.

"(B) For purposes of this Code section on and after February 1, 2003, a valid insurance card shall be sufficient proof of insurance only for any vehicle covered under a commercial vehicle policy as defined in Code Section 40–5–71.

"(C) For any vehicle covered under a policy of motor vehicle liability insurance that is not a commercial vehicle policy as defined in Code Section 40–5–71, the insurer shall issue a policy information identification card which shall contain at least the name of the insurer, policy number, policy issue or effective date, policy expiration date, name of the insured, and year, make, model, and vehicle identification number of each vehicle insured; provided, however, that on and after February 1, 2003, any such policy information identification card shall not be sufficient proof of insurance for any purposes of this Code section.

"(b) An owner or any other person who knowingly operates or knowingly authorizes another to operate a motor vehicle without effective insurance on such vehicle or without an approved plan of self-insurance shall be guilty of a misdemeanor and, upon conviction thereof, shall be subject to a fine of not less than $ 200.00 nor more than $ 1,000.00 or imprisonment for not more than 12 months, or both. An operator of a motor vehicle shall not be guilty of a violation of this Code section if such operator maintains a policy of motor vehicle insurance which extends coverage to any vehicle the operator may drive. An owner or operator of a motor vehicle shall not be issued a citation by a law enforcement officer for a violation of this Code section if the sole basis for issuance of such a citation is that the law enforcement officer is unable to obtain insurance coverage information from the records of the department.

"(c) Any person who knowingly makes a false statement or certification under Code Section 40–5–71 or this Code section shall be guilty of a misdemeanor and, upon conviction thereof, shall be subject to a fine of not less than $ 200.00 nor more than $ 1,000.00 or imprisonment for not more than 12 months, or both.

"(d) Insurance coverage information from records of the department shall be prima-facie evidence of the facts stated therein and shall be admissible as evidence in accordance with Code Section 24–3–17.

"(e) The minimum liability insurance data base of the department shall be operational for the purposes of testing, evaluation, verification of data, and validation of accuracy not later than November 1, 2002, and shall be fully operational not later than February 1, 2003."

The 2005 amendment by Act 68 in par. (3) of subsec. (a) substituted "July 1, 2005" for "January 1, 2004" prior to ", the requirement under this Code section" and "Department of Revenue" for "Department of Motor Vehicle Safety" following "the records or data base of the".

The 2008 amendment by Act 437, in subsec. (a), par. (8), subpar. (B), added a sentence to the end of the subparagraph relating to liability for fees for wrongful impoundment or towing of fleet vehicles.

The 2010 amendment by Act 381, in subsec. (a), substituted "The owner or operator" for "Until December 31, 2003, the owner or operator" in par. (1); substituted "The requirement" for "On and after July 1, 2005, the requirement" in par. (3); rewrote par. (8); and deleted subsec. (e). Prior to amendment par. (a)(8) and subsec. (e) had read:

"[(a)](8)(A) For purposes of this Code section up to and including December 31, 2003, a valid insurance card shall be sufficient proof of insurance for any vehicle.

"(B) For purposes of this Code section on and after January 1, 2004, a valid insurance card shall be sufficient proof of insurance only for any vehicle covered under a fleet policy as defined in Code Section 40–5–71. The insurance card for a fleet policy shall contain at least the name of the insurer, policy number, policy issue or effective date, policy expiration date, and the name of the insured and may, but shall not be required to, include the year, make, model, and vehicle identification number of the vehicle insured. If the operator of any vehicle covered under a fleet policy as defined in Code Section 40–5–71 presents a valid insurance card for a fleet policy to any law enforcement officer or agency, and the officer or agency does not recognize the insurance card as valid proof of insurance and impounds or tows such vehicle for lack of proof of insurance, the law enforcement agency or political subdivision shall be liable for and limited to the fees of the wrongful impoundment or towing of the vehicle, which in no way waives or diminishes any sovereign immunity of such governmental entity.

"(C) For any vehicle covered under a policy of motor vehicle liability insurance that is not a fleet policy as defined in Code Section 40–5–71, the insurer shall issue a policy information card which shall contain at least the name of the insurer, policy number, policy issue or effective date, policy expiration date, name of the insured, and year, make, model, and vehicle identification number of each vehicle insured; and on and after January 1, 2004, the owner or operator of the motor vehicle shall keep such policy information card in the vehicle at all times during operation of the vehicle for purposes of Code Section 40–6–273.1, but any such policy information card shall not be sufficient proof of insurance for any purposes of this Code section except as otherwise provided in this Code section."

"(e) The minimum liability insurance data base of the department shall be operational for the purposes of testing, evaluation, verification of data, and validation of accuracy not later than November 1, 2002, and shall be fully operational not later than January 1, 2004."

§ 40–6–11. Liability insurance required for motorcycle operation; proof of minimum insurance

(a) For the purposes of this Code section, "motorcycle" means any motor vehicle traveling on public streets or highways having a seat or saddle for the use of the rider and designed to travel on not more than three wheels in contact with the ground but excluding a tractor and a moped.

(b) No owner of a motorcycle or any other person, other than a self-insurer as defined in Chapter 34 of Title 33, shall operate or authorize any other person to operate the motorcycle unless the owner has liability insurance on the motorcycle equivalent to that required as evidence of security for bodily injury and property damage liability under Code Section 40–9–37. Any person who violates this subsection shall be guilty of a misdemeanor.

(c) The operator of a motorcycle shall keep proof or evidence of the minimum insurance coverage required by this Code section in his or her immediate possession or on the motorcycle at all times when such person is operating the motorcycle but only under the same circumstances and of the same type as prescribed for operators of other motor vehicles in Code Section 40–6–10. Any person who violates this subsection shall be subject to a fine not to exceed $25.00; however, there shall be no suspension of the person's operator's license or motor vehicle license tag for a violation of this subsection.

(d)(1) Insurance coverage information from records of the department shall be prima-facie evidence of the facts stated therein and shall be admissible as evidence in accordance with Code Section 24–3–17 for the purposes of this Code section.

(2) Every law enforcement officer in this state shall request the operator of a motorcycle subject to the provisions of subsection (c) of this Code section to produce proof or evidence of minimum insurance coverage required by this Code section at any time the law enforcement officer stops the motorcycle or requests the presentation of the driver's license of such operator.

(e) An owner or operator of a motorcycle shall not be issued a citation by a law enforcement officer for a violation of this Code section if the sole basis for issuance of such a citation is that the law enforcement officer is unable to obtain insurance coverage information from the records of the department.

Laws 1990, p. 2048, § 5; Laws 1992, p. 2785, § 22; Laws 2000, p. 429, §§ 6, 6A; Laws 2003, Act 44, § 6, eff. May 28, 2003.

Historical and Statutory Notes

The 2000 amendment substantially rewrote this section which prior thereto provided:

"(a) For the purposes of this Code section, 'motorcycle' means any motor vehicle traveling on public streets or highways having a seat or saddle for the use of the rider and designed to travel on not more than three wheels in contact with the ground but excluding a tractor and a moped.

" (b) No owner of a motorcycle or any other person, other than a self-insurer as defined in Chapter 34 of Title 33, shall operate or authorize any other person to operate the motorcycle unless the owner has liability insurance on the motorcycle equivalent to that required as evidence of security for bodily injury and property damage liability under Code Section 40–9–37. Any person who violates this subsection shall be guilty of a misdemeanor.

"(c) The operator of a motorcycle shall keep proof or evidence of the minimum insurance coverage required by this Code section in his immediate possession or on the motorcycle at all times when such person is operating the motorcycle. Any person who violates this subsection shall be subject to a fine not to exceed $25.00; however, there shall be no suspension of the person's operator's license or motor vehicle license tag for a violation of this subsection.

"(d) Every law enforcement officer in this state shall request the operator of a motorcycle to produce proof or evidence of minimum insurance coverage required by this Code section at any time the law enforcement officer requests the presentation of the driver's license of such operator."

The 2003 amendment by Act 44, in subsec. (c), deleted "paragraph (1) of subsection (a) of" preceding "Code Section 40–6–10"; and in subsec. (d), added "for the purposes of this Code section" in par. (1) and added "stops the motorcycle or" in par. (2).

§ 40–6–12. Persons convicted of certain violations to file and maintain proof of financial responsibility for period of three years

(a) Any person convicted of a second or subsequent violation of Code Section 40–6–10 within a five–year period, as measured from date of arrest to date of arrest, shall be required to file with the Department of Driver Services and maintain for a period of three years from the date of conviction proof of financial responsibility, as such term is defined in paragraph (5) of Code Section 40–9–2, in addition to any other punishment.

(b) If the proof of financial responsibility filed in accordance with subsection (a) of this Code section is based upon a policy issued by an insurance company, such insurer may not cancel the policy until the Department of Driver Services is given at least 30 days' prior written notice of such cancellation.

Laws 1990, p. 2048, § 5; Laws 2000, p. 951, § 5A–1; Laws 2005, Act 68, § 18–2, eff. July 1, 2005.

Historical and Statutory Notes

The 2000 amendment inserted the department name in lieu of "department" in subsecs. (a) and (b).

The 2005 amendment by Act 68 in subsecs. (a) and (b) substituted "Department of Driver Services" for " Department of Motor Vehicle Safety".

§ 40–6–13. Jurisdiction of offenses

Any court having jurisdiction to try and dispose of traffic offenses shall have jurisdiction to try and dispose of the misdemeanor offenses provided for in Code Sections 40–6–10 and 40–6–11. Such jurisdiction shall be concurrent with the jurisdiction of any other court within the county having jurisdiction to try and dispose of such offenses.

Laws 1990, p. 2048, § 5.

§ 40–6–14. Operation of radio, etc., from motor vehicle at level audible at distance of 100 feet or more prohibited; penalties

(a) It is unlawful for any person operating or occupying a motor vehicle on a street or highway to operate or amplify the sound produced by a radio, tape player, or other mechanical sound-making device or instrument from within the motor vehicle so that the sound is plainly audible at a distance of 100 feet or more from the motor vehicle.

(b) The provisions of this Code section shall not apply to any law enforcement motor vehicle equipped with any communication device necessary in the performance of law enforcement duties or to any emergency vehicle equipped with any communication device necessary in the performance of any emergency procedures.

(c) The provisions of this Code section do not apply to motor vehicles used for business or political purposes, which in the normal course of conducting such business use sound-making devices. The provisions of this subsection shall not be deemed to prevent local authorities, with respect to streets and highways under their jurisdiction and within the reasonable exercise of the police power, from regulating the time and manner in which such business may be operated.

(d) The provisions of this Code section do not apply to the noise made by a horn or other warning device required or permitted by Code Section 40–8–70. The Department of Public Safety shall promulgate rules defining "plainly audible" and establish standards regarding the measurement of sound by law enforcement personnel.

(e) A violation of this Code section shall be a misdemeanor.

Laws 1991, p. 417, § 1.

§ 40–6–15. Operating motor vehicle while registration of such vehicle is suspended, canceled or revoked

(a) Any person who knowingly drives a motor vehicle on any public road or highway of this state at a time when the vehicle registration of such vehicle is suspended, canceled, or revoked shall be guilty of a misdemeanor.

(b) Upon a first conviction thereof or a plea of nolo contendere, such person shall be punished by imprisonment for not more than 12 months and there may be imposed in addition thereto a fine of not less than $ 500.00 nor more than $ 1,000.00, at the discretion of the court.

(c) For a second or subsequent conviction within five years as measured from the dates of previous arrests for which convictions were obtained or pleas of nolo contendere were accepted to the date of the current arrest for which a conviction is obtained or a plea of nolo contendere accepted, such person shall be guilty of a high and aggravated misdemeanor and shall be punished by imprisonment for not less than ten days nor more than 12 months and there may be imposed in addition thereto a fine of not less than $ 1,000.00 nor more than $ 2,500.00.

(d) The department, upon receiving a record of the conviction of any person under this Code section upon a charge of driving a vehicle while the registration of such vehicle was suspended or revoked, shall extend the period of suspension or revocation for six months. The department may reinstate the suspended or revoked vehicle registration following the expiration of the original suspension or revocation period, the additional six-month suspension imposed pursuant to this subsection, and upon payment of a restoration fee of $ 210.00, or $ 200.00 when such reinstatement is processed by mail.

(e) For all purposes under this Code section, a plea of nolo contendere shall be considered as a conviction.

(f) Notwithstanding the limits set forth in Article 14 of this chapter and in any municipal charter, any municipal court of any municipality in this state shall be authorized to impose the punishment provided for in this Code section upon a conviction of violating this Code section or upon conviction of violating any ordinance adopting the provisions of this Code section.

Laws 2002, p. 1024, § 6.

Historical and Statutory Notes

In 2002, the Code Commission, in the last sentence of subsec. (d), substituted "six-month suspension" for "six month suspension". See § 28–9–5.

§ 40–6–16. Operating motor vehicle approaching emergency vehicle; violations

(a) The operator of a motor vehicle approaching a stationary authorized emergency vehicle that is displaying flashing yellow, amber, white, red, or blue lights shall approach the authorized emergency vehicle with due caution and shall, absent any other direction by a peace officer, proceed as follows:

(1) Make a lane change into a lane not adjacent to the authorized emergency vehicle if possible in the existing safety and traffic conditions; or

(2) If a lane change under paragraph (1) of this subsection would be impossible, prohibited by law, or unsafe, reduce the speed of the motor vehicle to a reasonable and proper speed for the existing road and traffic conditions, which speed shall be less than the posted speed limit, and be prepared to stop.

(b) The operator of a motor vehicle approaching a stationary towing or recovery vehicle or a stationary highway maintenance vehicle that is displaying flashing yellow, amber, or red lights shall approach the vehicle with due caution and shall, absent any other direction by a peace officer, proceed as follows:

(1) Make a lane change into a lane not adjacent to the towing, recovery, or highway maintenance vehicle if possible in the existing safety and traffic conditions; or

(2) If a lane change under paragraph (1) of this subsection would be impossible, prohibited by law, or unsafe, reduce the speed of the motor vehicle to a reasonable and proper speed for the existing road and traffic conditions, which speed shall be less than the posted speed limit, and be prepared to stop.

(c) Violation of subsection (a) or (b) of this Code section shall be punished by a fine of not more than $500.00.

Laws 2003, Act 181, § 1, eff. July 1, 2003; Laws 2006, Act 522, § 2, eff. April 20, 2006.

Historical and Statutory Notes

The 2006 amendment by Act 522 inserted "not more than" in subsec. (c).

§ 40–6–17. Traffic–control device preemption emitter

(a) As used in this Code section, the term "traffic-control device preemption emitter" means a mobile infrared transmitter or any other similar device which transmits an infrared beam, radio wave, or other signal used for the purpose of changing, altering, disabling, or disrupting the normal signal sequence of a traffic-control device.

(b) It shall be unlawful for any person other than law enforcement, fire department, or emergency personnel to use, possess with the ability to use, sell, or purchase a traffic-control device preemption emitter.

(c) Any person who violates subsection (b) of this Code section shall be guilty of a misdemeanor.

Laws 2004, Act 803, § 1, eff. May 17, 2004.

Article 2

Traffic Signs, Signals, and Markings

§ 40–6–20. Obedience to and required traffic-control devices; use of traffic-control signal monitoring devices

(a) The driver of any vehicle shall obey the instructions of an official traffic-control device applicable thereto, placed in accordance with this chapter, unless otherwise directed by a police officer, subject to the exceptions granted the driver of an authorized emergency vehicle in this chapter. A violation of this subsection shall be a misdemeanor, except as otherwise provided by subsection (f) of this Code section.

(b) No provisions of this chapter which require official traffic-control devices shall be enforced against an alleged violator if at the time and place of the alleged violation an official device was not in proper position and sufficiently legible to be seen by an ordinarily observant person. Whenever a particular Code section does not state that official traffic-control devices are required, such Code section shall be effective even though no devices are erected or in place.

(c) Whenever official traffic-control devices are placed in position approximately conforming to the requirements of this chapter, such devices shall be presumed to have been so placed by the official act or direction of lawful authority, unless the contrary shall be established by competent evidence.

(d) Any official traffic-control device placed pursuant to this chapter and purporting to conform to the lawful requirements pertaining to such devices shall be presumed to comply with the requirements of this chapter, unless the contrary shall be established by competent evidence.

(e) The disregard or disobedience of the instructions of any official traffic-control device or signal placed in accordance with the provisions of this chapter by the driver of a vehicle shall be deemed prima-facie evidence of a violation of law, without requiring proof of who and by what authority such sign or device has been erected.

(f)(1) As used in this subsection, the term:

(A) "Owner" means the registrant of a motor vehicle, except that such term shall not include a motor vehicle rental company when a motor vehicle registered by such company is being operated by another person under a rental agreement with such company.

(B) "Recorded images" means images recorded by a traffic-control signal monitoring device:

(i) On:

(I) Two or more photographs;

(II) Two or more microphotographs;

(III) Two or more electronic images; or

(IV) Videotape; and

(ii) Showing a traffic-control signal displaying a CIRCULAR RED or RED ARROW signal along with the rear of a motor vehicle apparently operated in disregard or disobedience of such signal and, on at least one image or portion of tape, clearly revealing the number or other identifying designation of the license plate displayed on the motor vehicle.

(C) "Traffic-control signal monitoring device" means a device with one or more motor vehicle sensors working in conjunction with a traffic-control signal to produce recorded images of motor vehicles being operated in disregard or disobedience of a CIRCULAR RED or RED ARROW signal.

(2) Subsection (a) of this Code section may be enforced as provided in this subsection pursuant to the use of traffic-control signal monitoring devices in accordance with Article 3 of Chapter 14 of this title.

(3) For the purpose of enforcement pursuant to this subsection:

(A) The driver of a motor vehicle shall be liable for a civil monetary penalty of not more than $70.00 if such vehicle is found, as evidenced by recorded images produced by a traffic-control signal monitoring device, to have been operated in disregard or disobedience of a CIRCULAR RED or RED ARROW signal in violation of subsection (a) of this Code section and such disregard or disobedience was not otherwise authorized by law;

(B) The law enforcement agency authorized to enforce the provisions of this Code section shall send by regular mail addressed to the owner of the motor vehicle postmarked not later than ten days after the date of the alleged violation:

(i) A citation for the alleged violation, which shall include the date and time of the violation, the location of the intersection, the amount of the civil monetary penalty imposed, and the date by which the civil monetary penalty shall be paid;

(ii) A copy of the recorded image;

(iii) A copy of a certificate sworn to or affirmed by a certified peace officer employed by a law enforcement agency authorized to enforce this Code section and stating that, based upon inspection of recorded images, the owner's motor vehicle was operated in disregard or disobedience of a CIRCULAR RED or RED ARROW signal in violation of subsection (a) of this Code section and that such disregard or disobedience was not otherwise authorized by law;

(iv) A statement of the inference provided by subparagraph (D) of this paragraph and of the means specified therein by which such inference may be rebutted;

(v) Information advising the owner of the motor vehicle of the manner and time in which liability as alleged in the citation may be contested in court; and

(vi) Warning that failure to pay the civil monetary penalty or to contest liability in a timely manner shall waive any right to contest liability and result in a civil monetary penalty;

provided, however, that only warning notices and not citations for violations shall be sent during the 30 day period commencing with the installation of a traffic-control signal monitoring device at such location;

(C) Proof that a motor vehicle was operated in disregard or disobedience of a CIRCULAR RED or RED ARROW signal in violation of subsection (a) of this Code section shall be evidenced by recorded images produced by a traffic-control signal monitoring device authorized pursuant to Article 3 of Chapter 14 of this title. A copy of a certificate sworn to or affirmed by a certified peace officer employed by a law enforcement agency and stating that, based upon inspection of recorded images, a motor vehicle was operated in disregard or disobedience of a CIRCULAR RED or RED ARROW signal in violation of subsection (a) of this Code section and that such disregard or disobedience was not otherwise authorized by law shall be prima-facie evidence of the facts contained therein; and

(D) Liability under this subsection shall be determined based upon preponderance of the evidence. Prima-facie evidence that the vehicle described in the citation issued pursuant to this subsection was operated in violation of subsection (a) of this Code section, together with proof that the defendant was at the time of such violation the registered owner of the vehicle, shall permit the trier of fact in its discretion to infer that such owner of the vehicle was the driver of the vehicle at the time of the alleged violation. Such an inference may be rebutted if the owner of the vehicle:

(i) Testifies under oath in open court or submits to the court a sworn notarized statement that he or she was not the operator of the vehicle at the time of the alleged violation;

(ii) Presents to the court a certified copy of a police report showing that the vehicle had been reported to the police as stolen prior to the time of the alleged violation; or

(iii) Submits to the court a sworn notarized statement identifying the name of the operator of the vehicle at the time of the alleged violation.

(4) A violation for which a civil penalty is imposed pursuant to this subsection shall not be considered a moving traffic violation, for the purpose of points assessment under Code Section 40–5–57. Such violation shall be deemed noncriminal, and imposition of a civil penalty pursuant to this subsection shall not be deemed a conviction and shall not be made a part of the operating record of the person upon whom such liability is imposed, nor shall it be used for any insurance purposes in the provision of motor vehicle insurance coverage.

(5) If a person summoned by regular mail fails to appear on the date of return set out in the citation and has not paid the penalty for the violation or filed a police report or notarized statement pursuant to subparagraph (D) of paragraph (3) of this subsection, the person shall then be summoned a second time by certified mail with a return receipt requested. The second summons shall include all information required in subparagraph (B) of paragraph (3) of this subsection for the initial summons and shall include a new date of return. If a person summoned by certified mail again fails to appear on the date of return set out in the second citation and has failed to pay the penalty or file an appropriate document for rebuttal, the person summoned shall have waived the right to contest the violation and shall be liable for a civil monetary penalty of not more than $70.00.

(6) Any court having jurisdiction over violations of subsection (a) of this Code section or any ordinance adopting the provisions of said subsection pursuant to Code Section 40–6–372 shall have jurisdiction over cases arising under this subsection and shall be authorized to impose the civil monetary penalty provided by this subsection. Except as otherwise provided in this subsection, the provisions of law governing jurisdiction, procedure, defenses, adjudication, appeal, and payment and distribution of penalties otherwise applicable to violations of subsection (a) of this Code section shall apply to enforcement under this subsection; provided, however, that any appeal from superior or state court shall be by application in the same manner as that provided by Code Section 5–6–35.

(7) Recorded images made for purposes of this subsection shall not be a public record for purposes of Article 4 of Chapter 18 of Title 50.

(8) A governing authority shall not impose a civil penalty under this subsection on the owner of a motor vehicle if the operator of the vehicle was arrested or issued a citation and notice to appear by a peace officer for the same violation that is recorded by a traffic-control signal monitoring device.

Laws 1953, Nov.-Dec. Sess., p. 556, §§ 32, 34; Laws 1974, p. 633, § 1; Laws 1990, p. 2048, § 5; Laws 2001, p. 770, § 2; Laws 2003, Act 246, § 2, eff. July 1, 2003; Laws 2008, Act 799, §§ 1 to 2, eff. December 31, 2008.

Formerly Code 1933, § 68A–201.

Historical and Statutory Notes

The 2001 amendment added the second sentence of subsec. (a) and added subsec. (f).

The 2003 amendment by Act 246, in subsec. (f), deleted "uniform traffic" preceding "citation for the violation" in subpar. (B)(i), substituted "citation" for "summons" in par. (5), and inserted "Any court having jurisdiction over violations of subsection (a) of this Code section or any ordinance adopting the provisions of said subsection pursuant to Code Section 40–6–372 shall have jurisdiction over cases arising under this subsection and shall be authorized to impose the civil monetary penalty provided by this subsection." in par. (6).

The 2008 amendment by Act 799, in subpar. (f)(3)(B), substituted "authorized to enforce the provisions of this Code section shall send by regular mail" for "for which such device is permitted shall send by first-class mail" in the introductory paragraph, inserted "alleged" prior to "violation," in div. (i), and substituted "certified peace officer employed by a law enforcement agency authorized to enforce this Code section" for "trained law enforcement officer or a technician employed by a law enforcement agency for which such device is authorized" in div. (iii); in subpar. (f)(3)(C), substituted "certified peace officer employed by a law enforcement agency" for "trained law enforcement officer or a technician employed by a law enforcement agency for which such device is authorized"; in subpar. (f)(3)(D), inserted "or submits to the court a sworn notarized statement" in div. (i); and rewrote pars. (f)(5) and (f)(8), which had read as follows:

"(5) If a person summoned by first-class mail fails to appear on the date of return set out in the citation and has not paid the penalty for the violation or filed a police report or affidavit pursuant to division (3)(D)(ii) or (3)(D)(iii) of this subsection, the person summoned shall have waived the right to contest the violation and shall be liable for a civil monetary penalty of not more than $70.00."

"(8) The provisions of this subsection shall not limit law enforcement agencies to the use of traffic-control signal monitoring devices in enforcing subsection (a) of this Code section; and, when there is evidence obtained from another source or sources which constitutes a prima-facie case of a violation of subsection (a) of this Code section, such violation may be prosecuted as otherwise provided by law in lieu of, but not in addition to, enforcement under this subsection."

In 2008, the Code Commission, in subsec. (f), added the par. (8) designation to the last paragraph. See § 28–9–5.

§ 40–6–21. Meaning of traffic signal indications

(a) The following meanings shall be given to highway traffic signal indications, except those on pedestrian signals:

(1) Green indications shall have the following meanings:

(A) Traffic, except pedestrians, facing a CIRCULAR GREEN signal may proceed straight through or turn right or left unless a sign at such place prohibits either such turn. Vehicular traffic turning shall yield the right of way to approaching vehicles. Vehicular traffic must stop and remain stopped to allow a pedestrian to cross the roadway within a crosswalk when the pedestrian lawfully within the intersection or an adjacent crosswalk at the time such signal is exhibited is upon the half of the roadway upon which the vehicle is traveling, or when the pedestrian is approaching and is within one lane of the half of the roadway on which the vehicle is traveling or onto which it is turning. For the purposes of this subparagraph, "half of the roadway" means all traffic lanes carrying traffic in one direction of travel;

(B) Traffic, except pedestrians, facing a GREEN ARROW signal, shown alone or in combination with another indication, may cautiously enter the intersection only to make the movement indicated by such arrow or such other movement as is permitted by other indications shown at the same time. Such vehicular traffic shall stop and remain stopped to allow a pedestrian lawfully within an adjacent crosswalk to cross the roadway within a crosswalk when the pedestrian is upon the half of the roadway upon which the vehicle is traveling, or when the pedestrian is approaching and is within one lane of the half of the roadway on which the vehicle is traveling or onto which it is turning. For the purposes of this subparagraph, "half of the roadway" means all traffic lanes carrying traffic in one direction of travel. Vehicular traffic shall yield the right of way to other traffic lawfully using the intersection; and

(C) Unless otherwise directed by a pedestrian signal, pedestrians facing any green indication, except when the sole green indication is a turn arrow, may proceed across the roadway within any marked or unmarked crosswalk;

(2) Steady yellow indications shall have the following meanings:

(A) Traffic, except pedestrians, facing a steady CIRCULAR YELLOW or YELLOW ARROW signal is thereby warned that the related green movement is being terminated or that a red indication will be exhibited immediately thereafter when vehicular traffic shall not enter the intersection; and

(B) Pedestrians facing a steady CIRCULAR YELLOW or YELLOW ARROW signal, unless otherwise directed by a pedestrian signal, are thereby advised that there is insufficient time to cross the roadway before a red indication is shown, and no pedestrian shall then start to cross the roadway; and

(3) Steady red indications shall have the following meanings:

(A) Traffic, except pedestrians, facing a steady CIRCULAR RED signal alone shall stop at a clearly marked stop line or, if there is no stop line, before entering the crosswalk on the near side of the intersection or, if there is no crosswalk, before entering the intersection, and shall remain standing until an indication to proceed is shown, except as provided in subparagraphs (B), (C), and (D) of this paragraph;

(B) Vehicular traffic facing a steady CIRCULAR RED signal may cautiously enter the intersection to make a right turn after stopping as provided in subparagraph (A) of this paragraph. Such vehicular traffic shall stop and remain stopped to allow a pedestrian to cross the roadway within a crosswalk when the pedestrian is upon the half of the roadway upon which the vehicle is traveling, or when the pedestrian is approaching and is within one lane of the half of the roadway on which the vehicle is traveling or onto which it is turning. For the purposes of this subparagraph, "half of the roadway" means all traffic lanes carrying traffic in one direction of travel. Vehicular traffic shall yield the right of way to other traffic lawfully using the intersection;

(C) Traffic, except pedestrians, facing a steady CIRCULAR RED signal, after stopping as provided in subparagraph (A) of this paragraph, may make a right turn but shall stop and remain stopped for pedestrians and yield the right of way to other traffic proceeding as directed by the signal at such intersection. Such vehicular traffic shall not make a right turn against a steady CIRCULAR RED signal at any intersection where a sign is erected prohibiting such right turn;

(D) Traffic, except pedestrians, facing a steady CIRCULAR RED signal, after stopping as provided in subparagraph (A) of this paragraph, may make a left turn from the left-hand lane of a one-way street onto a one-way street on which the traffic moves toward the driver's left but shall stop and remain stopped for pedestrians and yield the right of way to other traffic proceeding as directed by the signal at such intersection. Such vehicular traffic shall not make a left turn against a steady CIRCULAR RED signal at any intersection where a sign is erected prohibiting such left turn;

(E) Unless otherwise directed by a pedestrian signal, pedestrians facing a steady CIRCULAR RED signal alone shall not enter the roadway;

(F) Traffic, except pedestrians, facing a steady RED ARROW signal indication may not enter the intersection to make the movement indicated by such arrow and, unless entering the intersection to make such other movement as is permitted by other indications shown at the same time, shall stop at a clearly marked stop line or, if there is no stop line, before entering the crosswalk on the near side of the intersection or, if there is no crosswalk, before entering the intersection, and shall remain standing until an indication to make the movement indicated by such arrow is shown; and

(G) Unless otherwise directed by a pedestrian signal, pedestrians facing a steady RED ARROW signal indication shall not enter the roadway.

(b) In the event an official traffic-control device signal is erected and maintained at a place other than an intersection, the provisions of this Code section shall be applicable except as to those provisions which by their nature can have no application. Any stop required shall be made at a sign or marking on the pavement indicating where the stop shall be made, but, in the absence of any such sign or marking, the stop shall be made at the signal.

Laws 1953, Nov.-Dec. Sess., p. 556, § 35; Laws 1973, p. 474, § 1; Laws 1974, p. 633, § 1; Laws 1975, p. 496, § 1; Laws 1977, p. 278, § 1; Laws 1985, p. 149, § 40; Laws 1990, p. 8, § 40; Laws 1990, p. 2048, § 5; Laws 1995, p. 229, § 1; Laws 1997, p. 143, § 40.

Formerly Code 1933, § 68A–202.

§ 40–6–22. Pedestrian-control signals

Whenever special pedestrian-control signals exhibiting the words WALK or DON'T WALK or symbols so directing a pedestrian are in place, such signals shall indicate as follows:

(1) Word or symbol message *WALK*—Pedestrians facing such signal may proceed across the roadway in the direction of the signal. Every driver of a vehicle shall stop and remain stopped for such pedestrians; and

(2) Flashing or steady *DON'T WALK*—No pedestrian shall start to cross the roadway in the direction of such signal, but

any pedestrian who has partially completed his crossing on the WALK signal shall proceed to sidewalk or safety island while the DON'T WALK signal is showing.

Laws 1953, Nov.-Dec. Sess., p. 556, § 36; Laws 1974, p. 633, § 1; Laws 1990, p. 2048, § 5; Laws 1995, p. 229, § 2.

Formerly Code 1933, § 68A–203.

§ 40–6–23. Flashing red and yellow signals

Flashing signal indications shall have the following meanings:

(1) FLASHING RED (STOP SIGNAL)—When a red lens is illuminated with rapid intermittent flashes, drivers of vehicles shall stop at a clearly marked stop line or, if there is no stop line, before entering the crosswalk on the near side of the intersection or, if there is no crosswalk, at the point nearest the intersecting roadway where the driver has a view of approaching traffic on the intersecting roadway before entering the intersection, and the right to proceed shall be subject to the rules applicable after making a stop at a stop sign;

(2) FLASHING YELLOW (CAUTION SIGNAL)—When a yellow lens is illuminated with rapid intermittent flashes, drivers of vehicles may proceed through the intersection or past such signal only with caution.

Laws 1953, Nov.-Dec. Sess., p. 556, § 37; Laws 1974, p. 633, § 1; Laws 1990, p. 2048, § 5.

Formerly Code 1933, § 68A–204.

§ 40–6–24. Lane direction control signals

When lane direction control signals are placed over the individual lanes of a street or road, vehicular traffic may travel in any lane over which a green signal is shown but shall not enter or travel in any lane over which a red signal is shown, provided that a vehicle may enter a lane over which a yellow or amber signal is shown for purposes of making a left turn only.

Laws 1966, p. 183, § 3; Laws 1974, p. 633, § 1; Laws 1985, p. 149, § 40; Laws 1990, p. 2048, § 5.

Formerly Code 1933, § 68A–204.1.

§ 40–6–25. Display of unauthorized signs, signals or markings

(a) No person shall place, maintain, or display upon or in view of any highway any sign, signal, marking, or device which purports to be or is an imitation of or resembles an official traffic-control device or railroad sign or signal or which attempts to direct the movement of traffic or which hides from view or interferes with the effectiveness of an official traffic-control device or any railroad sign or signal.

(b) No person shall maintain or place nor shall any public authority permit upon any highway any traffic sign or signal bearing thereon any commercial advertising.

(c) This Code section shall not be deemed to prohibit the erection upon private property adjacent to highways of signs giving useful directional information and of a type that cannot be mistaken for official signs.

(d) Every such prohibited sign, signal, or marking is declared to be a public nuisance, and the authority having jurisdiction over the highway is empowered to remove it or cause it to be removed without notice.

Laws 1953, Nov.-Dec. Sess., p. 556, § 38; Laws 1974, p. 633, § 1; Laws 1990, p. 2048, § 5.

Formerly Code 1933, § 68A–205.

§ 40–6–26. Interference with official traffic-control devices or railroad signs or signals

(a) No person shall, without lawful authority, attempt to or in fact alter, deface, injure, knock down, or remove any official traffic-control device or any railroad sign or signal or any inscription, shield, or insignia thereon or any other part thereof.

(b) No person shall, without lawful authority, drive around or through or ignore any official traffic-control device so as to go onto an officially closed highway or road or onto a section of highway or road before it has been officially opened to the public. This Code section shall not apply to police officers in the performance of their duties, to individuals domiciled or making their livelihood within the affected area, or to any person authorized to be in the affected area by the appropriate municipal, county, or state officer.

Laws 1953, Nov.-Dec. Sess., p. 556, § 39; Laws 1974, p. 633, § 1; Laws 1990, p. 2048, § 5.

Formerly Code 1933, § 68A–206.

§ 40–6–27. Placement of blue retroreflective raised pavement markers

It shall be unlawful for any person to place or install any blue retroreflective raised pavement marker on any public highway, road, or street, provided that such marker may be placed or installed by the state or any county, municipality, fire department, or employee or agent thereof solely for the purpose of marking the location of fire hydrants.

Laws 1991, p. 943, § 1.

Article 3

Driving on Right Side of Roadway, Overtaking and Passing, Following Too Closely

§ 40–6–40. Driving on right side of roadway—exceptions

(a) Upon all roadways of sufficient width, a vehicle shall be driven upon the right half of the roadway, except as follows:

(1) When overtaking and passing another vehicle proceeding in the same direction under the rules governing such movement;

(2) When an obstruction exists making it necessary to drive to the left of the center of the highway, provided that any person so doing shall yield the right of way to all vehicles traveling in the proper direction upon the unobstructed portion of the highway within such a distance as to constitute an immediate hazard;

(3) Upon a roadway divided into three marked lanes for traffic under the rules applicable thereon; or

(4) Upon a roadway restricted to one-way traffic.

(b) Upon all roadways, any vehicle proceeding at less than the normal speed of traffic at the time and place and under the conditions then existing shall be driven in the right-hand lane then available for traffic, or as close as practicable to the right-hand curb or edge of the roadway, except when overtaking and passing another vehicle proceeding in the same direction or when preparing for a left turn at an intersection or into a private road or driveway.

(c) Upon any roadway having four or more lanes for moving traffic and providing for two-way movement of traffic, no vehicle shall be driven to the left of the center of the roadway except when authorized by official traffic-control devices designating certain lanes to the left of the center of the roadway for use by traffic not otherwise permitted to use such lanes or except as permitted under paragraph (2) of subsection (a) of this Code section. However, this subsection shall not be construed as prohibiting the crossing of the center of the roadway in making a left turn into or from an alley, private road, or driveway.

(d) No two vehicles shall impede the normal flow of traffic by traveling side by side at the same time while in adjacent lanes, provided that this Code section shall not be construed to prevent vehicles traveling side by side in adjacent lanes because of congested traffic conditions.

Laws 1953, Nov.-Dec. Sess., p. 556, § 55; Laws 1967, p. 542, § 1; Laws 1968, p. 1065, § 1; Laws 1974, p. 633, § 1; Laws 1990, p. 2048, § 5.

Formerly Code 1933, § 68A–301.

§ 40–6–41. Passing vehicles proceeding in opposite directions

Drivers of vehicles proceeding in opposite directions shall pass each other to the right, and, upon roadways having width for not more than one lane of traffic in each direction, each driver shall give to the other at least one-half of the main traveled portion of the roadway or as nearly one-half as possible.

Laws 1953, Nov.-Dec. Sess., p. 556, § 56; Laws 1974, p. 633, § 1; Laws 1985, p. 149, § 40; Laws 1990, p. 2048, § 5.

Formerly Code 1933, § 68A–302.

§ 40–6–42. Overtaking a vehicle on the left

The following rules shall govern the overtaking and passing of vehicles proceeding in the same direction, subject to those limitations, exceptions, and special rules stated in this article:

(1) The driver of a vehicle overtaking another vehicle proceeding in the same direction shall pass to the left thereof at a safe distance and shall not again drive to the right side of the roadway until safely clear of the overtaken vehicle; and

(2) Except when overtaking and passing on the right is permitted, the driver of an overtaken vehicle shall give way to the right in favor of the overtaking vehicle and shall not increase the speed of his vehicle until completely passed by the overtaking vehicle.

Laws 1953, Nov.-Dec. Sess., p. 556, § 57; Laws 1974, p. 633, § 1; Laws 1989, p. 14, § 40; Laws 1990, p. 2048, § 5.

Formerly Code 1933, § 68A–303.

§ 40–6–43. When overtaking on the right is permitted

(a) The driver of a vehicle may overtake and pass upon the right of another vehicle only under the following conditions:

(1) When the vehicle overtaken is making or about to make a left turn; or

(2) Upon a street or highway with unobstructed pavement of sufficient width for two or more lanes of moving vehicles in the direction being traveled by the overtaking vehicle.

(b) If otherwise authorized, the driver of a vehicle may overtake and pass another vehicle upon the right only under conditions permitting such movement in safety. Such movement shall not be made by driving off the roadway.

Laws 1953, Nov.-Dec. Sess., p. 556, § 58; Laws 1974, p. 633, § 1; Laws 1990, p. 2048, § 5.

Formerly Code 1933, § 68A–304.

§ 40–6–44. Limitations on overtaking on the left

No vehicle shall be driven to the left side of the center of the roadway in overtaking and passing another vehicle proceeding in the same direction unless such left side is clearly visible and is free of oncoming traffic for a sufficient distance ahead to permit such overtaking and passing to be completely made without interfering with the operation of any vehicle approaching from the opposite direction or any vehicle overtaken. In every event, the overtaking vehicle shall return to an authorized lane of travel as soon as practicable and, in the event the passing movement involves the use of a lane authorized for vehicles approaching from the opposite direction, before coming within 200 feet of any approaching vehicle.

Laws 1953, Nov.-Dec. Sess., p. 556, § 58A; Laws 1974, p. 633, § 1; Laws 1990, p. 2048, § 5.

Formerly Code 1933, § 68A–305.

§ 40–6–45. Further limitations on driving on left of center of roadway

(a) No vehicle shall be driven on the left side of a roadway designed and authorized for traffic traveling in opposite directions under the following conditions:

(1) When approaching or upon the crest of a grade or a curve in the highway where the driver's view is obstructed within such distance as to create a hazard in the event another vehicle might approach from the opposite direction;

(2) When traversing any:

(A) Intersection which is clearly marked by a solid barrier line placed on the right-hand element of a combination stripe along the center or lane line or by a solid double yellow line; or

(B) Railroad grade crossing; or

(3) When the view is obstructed upon approaching within 100 feet of any bridge, viaduct, or tunnel.

(b) The foregoing limitations shall not apply upon a one-way roadway nor under the conditions described in paragraph (2) of subsection (a) of Code Section 40–6–40 nor to the driver of a vehicle turning left into or from an alley, private road, driveway, or roadway.

Laws 1953, Nov.-Dec. Sess., p. 556, § 59; Laws 1974, p. 633, § 1; Laws 1990, p. 2048, § 5; Laws 2000, p. 1313, § 3.

Formerly Code 1933, § 68A–306.

Historical and Statutory Notes

The 2000 amendment rewrote par. (2) which formerly provided:

"(2) When approaching within 100 feet of or traversing any intersection or railroad grade crossing; or".

§ 40–6–46. No-passing zones

(a) The Department of Transportation and local authorities are authorized to determine those portions of any highway under their respective jurisdictions where overtaking and passing or driving to the left side of the roadway would be especially hazardous and may, by appropriate signs or markings on the roadway, indicate the beginning and end of such zones and, when such signs or markings are in place and clearly visible to an ordinarily observant person, every driver of a vehicle shall obey the directions thereof. Such no-passing zones shall be clearly marked by a solid barrier line placed on the right-hand element of a combination stripe along the center or lane line or by a solid double yellow line.

(b) Where signs or markings are in place to define a no-passing zone as set forth in subsection (a) of this Code section, no driver shall at any time drive on the left side of the roadway within such no-passing zone or on the left side of any pavement striping designed to mark such no-passing zone throughout its length.

(c) This Code section does not apply under the conditions described in paragraph (2) of subsection (a) of Code Section 40–6–40 nor to the driver of a vehicle turning left into or from an alley, private road, or driveway.

Laws 1953, Nov.-Dec. Sess., p. 556, § 60; Laws 1959, p. 144, § 1; Laws 1974, p. 633, § 1; Laws 1990, p. 2048, § 5.

Formerly Code 1933, § 68A–307.

§ 40–6–47. One-way roadways and rotary traffic islands

(a) The Department of Transportation and local authorities with respect to highways under their respective jurisdictions may designate any highway, roadway, part of a roadway, or specific lanes upon which vehicular traffic shall proceed in one direction at all of such times as shall be indicated by official traffic-control devices.

(b) Upon a roadway so designated for one-way traffic, a vehicle shall be driven only in the direction designated at all or such times as shall be indicated by official traffic-control devices.

(c) A vehicle passing around a rotary traffic island shall be driven only to the right of such island.

Laws 1953, Nov.-Dec. Sess., p. 556, § 61; Laws 1974, p. 633, § 1; Laws 1990, p. 2048, § 5.

Formerly Code 1933, § 68A–308.

§ 40–6–48. Driving on roadway laned for traffic

Whenever any roadway has been divided into two or more clearly marked lanes for traffic, the following rules, in addition to all others consistent with this Code section, shall apply:

(1) A vehicle shall be driven as nearly as practicable entirely within a single lane and shall not be moved from such lane until the driver has first ascertained that such movement can be made with safety;

(2) Upon a roadway which is divided into three lanes, and provides for two-way movement of traffic, with two lanes in one direction, a vehicle being driven in a continuous or center lane shall have the right of way when overtaking and passing another vehicle traveling in the same direction;

(3) Upon a roadway which is divided into three lanes and provides for two-way movement of traffic, a vehicle shall not be driven in the center lane except when overtaking and passing another vehicle traveling in the same direction when such center lane is clear of traffic within a safe distance, or in preparation for making a left turn, or where such center lane is at the time allocated exclusively to traffic moving in the same direction that the vehicle is proceeding and such allocation is designated by official traffic-control devices or road striping;

(4) Official traffic-control devices may be erected directing specified traffic, including but not limited to buses or trucks, to use a designated lane or designating those lanes to be used by traffic moving in a particular direction regardless of the center of the roadway, and drivers of vehicles shall obey the directions of every such device; and

(5) Official traffic-control devices may be installed prohibiting the changing of lanes on sections of roadway, and drivers of vehicles shall obey the directions of every such device.

Laws 1953, Nov.-Dec. Sess., p. 556, § 62; Laws 1967, p. 542, §§ 2, 3; Laws 1974, p. 633, § 1; Laws 1990, p. 2048, § 5.

Formerly Code 1933, § 68A–309.

§ 40–6–49. Following too closely

(a) The driver of a motor vehicle shall not follow another vehicle more closely than is reasonable and prudent, having due regard for the speed of such vehicles and the traffic upon and the condition of the highway.

(b) The driver of any motor vehicle which is drawing another vehicle when traveling upon a roadway outside of a business or residential district and which is following another motor truck or motor vehicle drawing another vehicle shall, whenever conditions permit, leave sufficient space so that an overtaking vehicle may enter and occupy such space without danger, except that this shall not prevent a motor truck or motor vehicle drawing another vehicle from overtaking and passing any like vehicle or other vehicle.

(c) Motor vehicles being driven upon any roadway outside of a business or residential district in a caravan or motorcade whether or not towing other vehicles shall be so operated as to allow sufficient space between each such vehicle or combination of vehicles so as to enable any other vehicle to enter and occupy such space without danger. This subsection shall not apply to funeral processions, parades, or other groups of vehicles if such groups of vehicles are under the supervision and control of a law enforcement agency.

(d) Vehicles which approach from the rear any other vehicle or vehicles stopped or slowed to make a lawful turn shall be deemed to be following for purposes of this Code section.

Laws 1953, Nov.-Dec. Sess., p. 556, § 63; Laws 1974, p. 633, § 1; Laws 1990, p. 2048, § 5.

Formerly Code 1933, § 68A–310.

§ 40–6–50. Driving on divided highways; transit bus use of emergency lanes

(a) As used in this Code section, the term "gore" means the area of convergence between two lanes of traffic.

(b) Every vehicle driven on a divided highway shall be driven only upon the right-hand roadway unless directed or permitted to use another roadway by official traffic-control devices or police officers. No vehicle shall be driven over, across, or within any dividing space, barrier, gore, paved shoulder, or section separating the roadways of a divided highway; except that a vehicle may be driven through an opening in such physical barrier or dividing space or at an established crossover or intersection unless specifically prohibited by an official sign, signal, or control device. No person shall drive a vehicle onto or from any controlled-access roadway except at such entrances and exits as are established by public authority. Except as provided for in subsection (c) of this Code section, no vehicle shall be driven in an emergency lane except in the event of an actual emergency.

(c) For purposes of this subsection, "transit bus" means a bus used for the transportation of passengers within a system which is operated by or under contract to the state, a public agency or authority, or a county or municipality of this state. If the commissioner of transportation permits the use of emergency lanes of a controlled-access roadway by transit buses in the metropolitan Atlanta nonattainment area, the commissioner shall designate on which controlled-access roadways the use of emergency lanes by transit buses may be allowed and upon such designation the commissioner shall only permit the use on that emergency lane of a transit bus with a seating capacity of 33 passengers or more. Transit buses authorized to use the emergency lanes under this subsection may be operated on the emergency lane only when main lane traffic speeds are less than 35 miles per hour. Drivers of transit buses being operated on the emergency lanes may not exceed the speed of the main lane traffic by more than 15 miles per hour and may never exceed 35 miles per hour. Drivers of transit buses being operated on the emergency lanes must yield to merging, entering, and exiting traffic and must yield to other vehicles on the emergency lanes. Transit buses operating on the emergency lanes must be registered with the Department of Transportation.

(d) Nothing in this Code section shall prohibit the use of a FlexAuto lane in the manner permitted under Code Section 32–9–4.1.

Laws 1953, Nov.-Dec. Sess., p. 556, § 64; Laws 1963, p. 254, § 4; Laws 1974, p. 633, § 1; Laws 1990, p. 2048, § 5; Laws 2003, Act 68, § 1, eff. July 1, 2003; Laws 2005, Act 135, § 3, eff. May 3, 2005.

Formerly Code 1933, §§ 68A–311, 68A–312; Code 1981, § 40–6–51.

Historical and Statutory Notes

The 2003 amendment by Act 68, in subsec. (b) substituted "Except as provided for in subsection (c) of this Code section, no vehicle shall be driven in an emergency lane except in the event of an actual emergency." for "No vehicle shall be driven in an emergency lane except in the event of an actual emergency"; and added new subsec. (c).

The 2005 amendment by Act 135 added subsec. (d).

§ 40–6–51. Restrictions on use of controlled access highway

(a) The Department of Transportation by order and local authorities by ordinance may regulate or prohibit the use of any controlled-access roadway within their respective jurisdictions by any class or kind of traffic which is found to be incompatible with the normal and safe movement of traffic.

(b) The Department of Transportation or the local authority adopting any such prohibition shall erect and maintain official traffic-control devices on the controlled-access highway on which such prohibitions are applicable, and when such devices are in place no person shall disobey the restrictions stated thereon.

(c) For purposes of this Code section, roadways within the jurisdiction of the Department of Transportation and roadways within the jurisdiction of local authorities shall be as set forth in Code Section 32–4–1.

Laws 1953, Nov.-Dec. Sess., p. 556, § 65; Laws 1963, p. 254, § 3; Laws 1974, p. 633, § 1; Laws 1990, p. 2048, § 5.

Formerly Code 1933, § 68A–313; Code 1981, § 40–6–52.

§ 40–6–52. Unlawful for trucks with more than six wheels to operate in certain lanes

(a) As used in this Code section, the term "truck" means any vehicle equipped with more than six wheels, except buses and motorcoaches.

(b) On roads, streets, or highways with three or more lanes allowing for movement in the same direction, it shall be unlawful for any truck to operate in any lanes other than the two most right-hand lanes, except when the truck is preparing for a left turn or as otherwise provided by subsection (d) of this Code section.

(c) On roads, streets, or highways with two lanes allowing for movement in the same direction, it shall be unlawful for any truck to operate in the left-hand lane, except when the truck is actually overtaking and passing another vehicle, preparing for a left turn, or as otherwise provided by subsection (d) of this Code section.

(d) On interstate highways with four or more lanes allowing for movement in the same direction, the Department of Transportation may designate specific lanes that either prohibit or allow trucks. Where truck usage has been so designated and indicated as such by signs erected by the Department of Transportation, it shall be unlawful for any truck to operate in any lanes other than as designated.

Laws 1987, p. 361, § 1; Laws 1990, p. 2048, § 5; Laws 2001, p. 1050, § 1; Laws 2004, Act 580, § 2, eff. May 13, 2004.

Formerly Code 1981, § 40–6–53.

Historical and Statutory Notes

The 2001 amendment in subsecs. (b) and (c) added "or as otherwise provided by subsection (d) of this Code section" and added subsec. (d).

The 2004 amendment by Act 580, in subsec. (a), added ", except buses and motorcoaches".

§ 40–6–53. Buses or motorcoaches to operate in specified lanes

(a) On roads, streets, or highways with three or more lanes allowing for movement in the same direction, it shall be unlawful for any bus or motorcoach to operate in any lanes other than the two most right-hand lanes, except when the bus or motorcoach is preparing for a left turn, is moving to or from an HOV lane, or as otherwise provided by subsection (c) of this Code section.

(b) On roads, streets, or highways with two lanes allowing for movement in the same direction, it shall be unlawful for any bus or motorcoach to operate in the left-hand lane, except when the bus or motorcoach is actually overtaking and passing another vehicle, preparing for a left turn, or as otherwise provided by subsection (c) of this Code section.

(c) On interstate highways with four or more lanes allowing for movement in the same direction, the Department of Transportation may designate specific lanes that either prohibit or allow buses or motorcoaches. Where such usage has been so designated and indicated by signs erected by the Department of Transportation, it shall be unlawful for any bus or motorcoach to operate in any lanes other than those designated for its use except when moving to or from an HOV lane.

(d) When moving to or from an HOV lane, a bus or motorcoach shall move to the proper lanes of travel expeditiously and in the shortest distance possible under the circumstances.

Laws 2004, Act 580, § 3, eff. May 13, 2004.

Historical and Statutory Notes

Former § 40–6–53 was renumbered as § 40–6–52 by Laws 1990, p. 2048, § 5.

§ 40–6–54. Designation and use of travel lanes; penalties for violations

(a) The Department of Transportation may designate travel lanes on any road in the state highway system for the exclusive use of certain vehicles, as provided in Code Section 32–9–4; provided, however, that where such designation has been made, the road shall be appropriately marked with signs or other roadway markers or markings to inform the traveling public of the restrictions imposed.

(b) Any person who violates subsection (b) of Code Section 32–9–4 shall be guilty of a misdemeanor and, upon conviction thereof, shall be punished by a fine:

(1) Not to exceed $75.00 for the first such offense;

(2) Not to exceed $100.00 for the second such offense;

(3) Not to exceed $150.00 for the third such offense; and

(4) Not to exceed $150.00 plus one point on such person's driver's license as provided for under Code Section 40–5–57 for the fourth or subsequent offense.

(c) In the prosecution of an offense committed in the presence of or witnessed by a law enforcement officer whether by direct observation or as recorded through means of video surveillance, either by magnetic imaging or photographic copy, of failure to obey a road sign restricting a highway or portion thereof to the use of high occupancy vehicles (HOV), proof that the vehicle described in the HOV violation summons was operated in violation of this Code section, together with proof that the defendant was at the time of such violation the registered owner of the vehicle, shall constitute evidence as a rebuttable presumption that such registered owner of the vehicle was the person committing the violation. Notwithstanding any other provision of this subsection to the contrary, said rebuttable presumption shall be overcome if the owner of said vehicle states, under oath, in open court, that he or she was not the operator of the vehicle at the time the alleged offense occurred.

(d) The General Assembly finds and declares that the development, improvement, and use of exclusive or preferential high occupancy vehicle lanes, emergency vehicle lanes, and truck lanes or routes should be undertaken in order to relieve congestion and increase the efficiency of the federal-aid highway system. The Department of Transportation in cooperation with the State Road and Tollway Authority is hereby authorized to implement high occupancy toll (HOT) lanes where appropriate in qualifying HOV lanes. A "HOT lane" is a designated lane which allows single occupancy vehicles to gain access to HOV lanes by paying a toll set by the State Road and Tollway Authority. The department may design and develop a system of HOT lanes which uses value pricing and lane management. "Value pricing" recognizes the need to vary the road user charge according to the levels of congestion and time of day; and "lane management" restricts access to the designated HOT lanes based on occupancy, vehicle type, or other objective which would maximize the efficiency of the federal-aid highway system.

Laws 1993, p. 363, § 2; Laws 2004, Act 580, § 4, eff. May 13, 2004.

Historical and Statutory Notes

The 2004 amendment by Act 580 added subsec. (d).

Article 4

Right of Way

§ 40–6–70. Vehicle approaching or entering intersection

(a) When two vehicles approach or enter an intersection from different highways at approximately the same time, the driver of the vehicle on the left shall yield the right of way to the vehicle on the right, provided that when a vehicle approaches or enters an intersection with no stop signs or other traffic-control devices from a highway that terminates at the intersection, the driver of that vehicle shall yield the right of way to the other vehicle, whether the latter vehicle be on such driver's right or left. When two vehicles approach or enter an intersection with an inoperative traffic light, the driver of each vehicle shall be required to stop in the same manner as if a stop sign were facing in each direction at the intersection. Drivers shall not be required to stop if the traffic signal is properly signed as a pedestrian hybrid beacon and operating in the unactivated dark mode. When a flashing indication is given, the driver shall stop for the flashing red signal and exhibit caution while passing through a flashing yellow indication.

(b) The right of way rule declared in subsection (a) of this Code section is modified at through highways and otherwise as stated in this chapter.

Laws 1953, Nov.-Dec. Sess., p. 556, § 72; Laws 1966, p. 183, § 5; Laws 1974, p. 633, § 1; Laws 1982, p. 3, § 40; Laws 1990, p. 2048, § 5; Laws 1999, p. 904, § 1; Laws 2010, Act 460, § 5, eff. July 1, 2010.

Formerly Code 1933, § 68A–401.

Historical and Statutory Notes

The 2010 amendment by Act 460, in subsec. (a), added "Drivers shall not be required to stop if the traffic signal is properly signed as a pedestrian hybrid beacon and operating in the unactivated dark mode." as the third sentence.

§ 40–6–71. Vehicle turning left

The driver of a vehicle intending to turn to the left within an intersection or into an alley, private road, or driveway shall yield the right of way to any vehicle approaching from the opposite direction which is within the intersection or so close thereto as to constitute an immediate hazard.

Laws 1953, Nov.-Dec. Sess., p. 556, § 73; Laws 1974, p. 633, § 1; Laws 1990, p. 2048, § 5.

Formerly Code 1933, § 68A–402.

§ 40–6–72. Stop signs and yield signs

(a) Preferential right of way may be indicated by stop signs or yield signs as authorized in Code Section 32–6–50.

(b) Except when directed to proceed by a police officer, every driver of a vehicle approaching a stop sign shall stop at a clearly marked stop line or, if there is no stop line, before entering the crosswalk on the near side of the intersection or, if there is no crosswalk, at the point nearest the intersecting roadway where the driver has a view of approaching traffic on the intersecting roadway before entering it. After stopping, the driver shall yield the right of way to any vehicle in the intersection or approaching on another roadway so closely as to constitute an immediate hazard during the time when such driver is moving across or within the intersection or junction of roadways.

(c) The driver of a vehicle approaching a yield sign shall, in obedience to such sign, slow down to a speed reasonable for the existing conditions and, if required for safety to stop, shall stop at a clearly marked stop line or, if there is no stop line, before entering the crosswalk on the near side of the intersection or, if there is no crosswalk, at the point nearest the intersecting roadway where the driver has a view of approaching traffic on the intersecting roadway before entering it. After slowing or stopping, the driver shall yield the right of way to any vehicle in the intersection or approaching on another roadway so closely as to constitute an immediate hazard during the time such driver is moving across or within the intersection or junction of roadways. If such a driver is involved in a collision with a vehicle in the intersection after driving past a yield sign without stopping, such collision shall be deemed prima-facie evidence of his failure to yield the right of way.

Laws 1953, Nov.-Dec. Sess., p. 556, § 74; Laws 1974, p. 633, § 1; Laws 1990, p. 2048, § 5.

Formerly Code 1933, § 68A–403.

§ 40–6–73. Vehicle entering roadway

The driver of a vehicle about to enter or cross a roadway from any place other than another roadway shall yield the right of way to all vehicles approaching on the roadway to be entered or crossed.

Laws 1953, Nov.-Dec. Sess., p. 556, § 75; Laws 1974, p. 633, § 1; Laws 1990, p. 2048, § 5.

Formerly Code 1933, § 68A–404.

§ 40–6–74. Operation of vehicles on approach of authorized emergency vehicles

(a) Upon the immediate approach of an authorized emergency vehicle or a vehicle belonging to a federal, state, or local law enforcement agency making use of an audible signal and visual signals meeting the requirements of Code Section 40–6–6, the driver of every other vehicle shall yield the right of way and shall immediately drive to a position parallel to, and as close as possible to, the right-hand edge or curb of the roadway clear of any intersection and shall stop and remain in such position until the authorized emergency vehicle or law enforcement vehicle has passed, except when otherwise directed by a police officer.

(b) This Code section shall not operate to relieve the driver of any authorized emergency vehicle from the duty to drive with due regard for the safety of all persons using the highway.

Laws 1953, Nov.-Dec. Sess., p. 556, § 76; Laws 1974, p. 633, § 1; Laws 1990, p. 2048, § 5.

Formerly Code 1933, § 68A–405.

§ 40–6–75. Highway construction and maintenance vehicles

(a) The driver of a vehicle shall yield the right of way to any authorized vehicle or pedestrian actually engaged in work upon a highway within any highway construction or maintenance area indicated by official traffic-control devices.

(b) The driver of a vehicle shall yield the right of way to an authorized vehicle actually engaged in work upon a highway whenever such vehicle displays flashing or revolving amber lights and has a permit to use such amber lights.

Laws 1974, p. 633, § 1; Laws 1990, p. 2048, § 5.

Formerly Code 1933, § 68A–406.

§ 40–6–76. Funeral processions

(a) As used in this Code section, a "funeral procession" means an array of motor vehicles in which the lead vehicle displays a sign, pennant, flag, or other insignia furnished by a funeral home indicating a funeral procession unless led by a state or local law enforcement vehicle and each vehicle participating in the funeral procession is operating its headlights.

(b) Funeral processions shall have the right of way at intersections subject to the following conditions and exceptions:

(1) Operators of vehicles in a funeral procession shall yield the right of way upon the approach of an authorized emergency vehicle or law enforcement vehicle giving an audible and visual signal; and

(2) Operators of vehicles in a funeral procession shall yield the right of way when directed to do so by a traffic officer.

(c) Funeral processions escorted by the police, a sheriff, or a sheriff's deputy shall have the right of way in any street or highway through which they may pass. Local governments may, by ordinance, provide for such escort service and provide for the imposition of reasonable fees to defray the cost of such service.

(d) The operator of a vehicle not in a funeral procession shall not interrupt a funeral procession except when authorized to do so by a traffic officer or when such vehicle is an authorized emergency vehicle or law enforcement vehicle giving an audible and visual signal.

(e) Operators of vehicles not a part of a funeral procession shall not join a funeral procession by operating their headlights for the purpose of securing the right of way granted by this Code section to funeral processions.

(f) The operator of a vehicle not in a funeral procession shall not attempt to pass vehicles in a funeral procession on a two-lane highway.

(g) Any person violating subsection (d), (e), or (f) of this Code section shall be guilty of a misdemeanor and, upon conviction thereof, shall be punished by a fine not to exceed $100.00.

(h) Any law enforcement officer who is directing or escorting a funeral procession in this state, whether such service is provided while on duty or not, shall enjoy the same immunities from liability as the officer possesses while in the performance of other official duties.

Laws 1989, p. 1803, § 1; Laws 1990, p. 1319, § 2; Laws 1990, p. 2048, § 5.

§ 40–6–77. Violations

(a) For purposes of this Code section, "serious injury" shall include, but shall not be limited to, causing bodily harm to another by depriving him or her of a member of his or her body, by rendering a member of his or her body useless, by seriously disfiguring his or her head or body or a member thereof, or by causing organic brain damage which renders the body or any member thereof useless.

(b) Any person who causes a serious injury to another person as a result of a collision with a motorcyclist, bicyclist, pedestrian, or farmer operating any vehicle used to transport agricultural products, livestock, farm machinery, or farm supplies by committing any right of way violation under this chapter when such motorcyclist, bicyclist, pedestrian, or farmer operating any vehicle used to transport agricultural products, livestock, farm machinery, or farm supplies is abiding by the provisions of this title shall be guilty of a misdemeanor and shall be punished:

(1) For a first offense, by a fine of not less than $250.00 in addition to any other penalties stipulated by law and the court shall report such conviction to the Department of Driver Services; and

(2) For a second or subsequent offense within a five-year period of time, as measured from the dates of previous arrests for which convictions were obtained or pleas of nolo contendere were accepted to the date of the current arrest for which a conviction is obtained or a plea of nolo contendere is accepted, by a fine of not less than $500.00 nor more than $1,000.00 and imprisonment for not less than ten days nor more than 12 months. Any fine imposed under this paragraph shall be mandatory and shall not be suspended or waived or conditioned upon the completion of any course or sentence. The court imposing punishment under this subsection shall forward a record of the disposition of the case to the Department of Driver Services.

Laws 2006, Act 614, § 2, eff. July 1, 2006; Laws 2009, Act 22, § 4, eff. July 1, 2009.

Historical and Statutory Notes

The 2009 amendment by Act 22 rewrote the section which had read:

"Any person who causes a serious injury to another person as a result of a collision with a motorcyclist, bicyclist, pedestrian, or farmer operating any vehicle used to transport agricultural products, livestock, farm machinery, or farm supplies by committing any right of way violation under this chapter when such motorcyclist, bicyclist, pedestrian, or farmer operating any vehicle used to transport agricultural products, livestock, farm machinery, or farm supplies is abiding by the provisions of this title shall be guilty of a misdemeanor and shall be punished by a fine of not less than $250.00 in addition to any other penalties stipulated by law. For purposes of this Code section, serious injury shall include, but shall not be limited to, causing bodily harm to another by depriving him or her of a member of his or her body, by rendering a member of his or her body useless, by seriously disfiguring his or her body or a member thereof, or by causing organic brain damage which renders the body or any member thereof useless."

Article 5

Rights and Duties of Pedestrians

§ 40–6–90. Pedestrian obedience to traffic-control devices and traffic regulations

(a) A pedestrian shall obey the instructions of any official traffic-control device specifically applicable to him, unless otherwise directed by a police officer.

(b) Pedestrians shall be subject to traffic and pedestrian control signals as provided in Code Sections 40–6–21 and 40–6–22.

(c) At all other places, pedestrians shall be accorded the privileges and shall be subject to the restrictions stated in this chapter.

Laws 1953, Nov.-Dec. Sess., p. 556, § 77; Laws 1974, p. 633, § 1; Laws 1990, p. 2048, § 5.

Formerly Code 1933, § 68A–501.

§ 40–6–91. Pedestrians' right of way in cross walks

(a) The driver of a vehicle shall stop and remain stopped to allow a pedestrian to cross the roadway within a crosswalk when the pedestrian is upon the half of the roadway upon which the vehicle is traveling, or when the pedestrian is approaching and is within one lane of the half of the roadway on which the vehicle is traveling or onto which it is turning. For the purposes of this subsection, "half of the roadway" means all traffic lanes carrying traffic in one direction of travel.

(b) No pedestrian shall suddenly leave a curb or other place of safety and walk or run into the path of a vehicle which is so close that it is impractical for the driver to yield.

(c) Subsection (a) of this Code section shall not apply under the conditions stated in subsection (b) of Code Section 40–6–92.

(d) Whenever any vehicle is stopped at a marked crosswalk or at any unmarked crosswalk at an intersection to permit a pedestrian to cross the roadway, the driver of any other vehicle approaching from the rear shall not overtake and pass such stopped vehicle.

Laws 1953, Nov.-Dec. Sess., p. 556, § 78; Laws 1974, p. 633, § 1; Laws 1990, p. 2048, § 5; Laws 1995, p. 229, § 3.

Formerly Code 1933, § 68A–502.

§ 40–6–92. Crossing at other than crosswalks

(a) Every pedestrian crossing a roadway at any point other than within a marked crosswalk or within an unmarked crosswalk at an intersection shall yield the right of way to all vehicles upon the roadway unless he has already, and under safe conditions, entered the roadway.

(b) Any pedestrian crossing a roadway at a point where a pedestrian tunnel or overhead pedestrian crossing has been provided shall yield the right of way to all vehicles upon the roadway if he uses the roadway instead of such tunnel or crossing.

(c) Between adjacent intersections at which traffic-control signals are in operation, pedestrians shall not cross at any place except in a marked crosswalk.

(d) No pedestrian shall cross a roadway intersection diagonally unless authorized by official traffic-control devices. When authorized to cross diagonally, pedestrians shall cross only in accordance with the official traffic-control devices pertaining to such crossing movements.

Laws 1953, Nov.-Dec. Sess., p. 556, § 79; Laws 1967, p. 542, § 4; Laws 1974, p. 633, § 1; Laws 1990, p. 2048, § 5.

Formerly Code 1933, § 68A–503.

§ 40–6–93. Drivers to exercise due care

Notwithstanding other provisions of this chapter, every driver of a vehicle shall exercise due care to avoid colliding with any pedestrian upon any roadway, shall give warning by sounding his horn when necessary, and shall exercise proper precautions upon observing any child or any obviously confused, incapacitated, or intoxicated person.

Laws 1953, Nov.-Dec. Sess., p. 556, § 80; Laws 1974, p. 633, § 1; Laws 1990, p. 2048, § 5.

Formerly Code 1933, § 68A–504.

§ 40–6–94. Blind pedestrian right of way

The driver of every vehicle shall yield the right of way to any blind pedestrian who is carrying a walking cane or stick white in color or white tipped with red or who is accompanied by a guide dog.

Laws 1953, Nov.-Dec. Sess., p. 556, § 80; Laws 1974, p. 633, § 1; Laws 1990, p. 2048, § 5.

Formerly Code 1933, § 68A–504.1.

§ 40–6–95. Pedestrians under the influence

A person who is under the influence of intoxicating liquor or any drug to a degree which renders him a hazard shall not walk or be upon any roadway or the shoulder of any roadway. Violation of this Code section is a misdemeanor and is punishable upon conviction by a fine not to exceed $500.00.

Laws 1974, p. 633, § 1; Laws 1990, p. 2048, § 5.

Formerly Code 1933, § 68A–505.1; Code 1981, § 40–6–96.

§ 40–6–96. Pedestrians on highways

(a) As used in this Code section, the term "pedestrian" means any person afoot and shall include, without limitation, persons standing, walking, jogging, running, or otherwise on foot.

(b) Where a sidewalk is provided, it shall be unlawful for any pedestrian to stand or stride along and upon an adjacent roadway unless there is no motor vehicle traveling within 1,000 feet of such pedestrian on such roadway or the available sidewalk presents an imminent threat of bodily injury to such pedestrian.

(c) Where a sidewalk is not provided but a shoulder is available, any pedestrian standing or striding along and upon a highway shall stand or stride only on the shoulder, as far as practicable from the edge of the roadway.

(d) Where neither a sidewalk nor a shoulder is available, any pedestrian standing or striding along and upon a highway shall stand or stride as near as practicable to an outside edge of the roadway, and, if on a two-lane roadway, shall stand or stride only on the left side of the roadway.

(e) Except as otherwise provided in this chapter, any pedestrian upon a roadway shall yield the right of way to all vehicles upon the roadway.

(f) No pedestrian shall enter or remain upon any bridge or approach thereto beyond the bridge signal, gate, or barrier after a bridge operation signal indication has been given.

(g) No pedestrian shall pass through, around, over, or under any crossing gate or barrier at a railroad grade crossing or bridge while such gate or barrier is closed or is being opened or closed.

Laws 1953, Nov.-Dec. Sess., p. 556, § 82; Laws 1974, p. 633, § 1; Laws 1990, p. 2048, § 5; Laws 2009, Act 22, § 5, eff. July 1, 2009.

Formerly Code 1933, § 68A–506; Code 1981, § 40–6–97.

Historical and Statutory Notes

The 2009 amendment by Act 22, redesignated subsecs. (a) to (f) as subsecs. (b) to (g); inserted a new subsec. (a); in new subsec. (b), substituted "stand or stride" for "walk" and inserted "unless there is no motor vehicle traveling within 1,000 feet of such pedestrian on such roadway or the available sidewalk presents an imminent threat of bodily injury to such pedestrian"; in new subsecs. (c) and (d), substituted "standing or striding" for "walking" and substituted "stand or stride" for "walk".

§ 40–6–97. Pedestrians soliciting rides or business

(a) No person shall stand in a roadway for the purpose of soliciting a ride.

(b) Except as provided in Code Section 40–6–97.1, no person shall stand on a highway for the purpose of soliciting employment, business, or contributions from the occupant of any vehicle.

(c) No person shall stand on or in proximity to a street or highway for the purpose of soliciting the watching or guarding of any vehicle while parked or about to be parked on a street or highway.

Laws 1953, Nov.-Dec. Sess., p. 556, § 82; Laws 1974, p. 633, § 1; Laws 1990, p. 2048, § 5; Laws 1996, p. 737, § 1.

Formerly Code 1933, § 68A–507; Code 1981, § 40–6–98.

§ 40–6–97.1. Municipal and county ordinances for issuance of permits to charitable organizations for solicitation of contributions on streets and highways

Municipal or county governments are authorized to adopt ordinances for the issuance of permits for the solicitation of contributions on streets and highways within the geographic jurisdiction of such governments to charitable organizations registered in accordance with Code Section 43–17–5 and to charitable organizations exempt from such registration in accordance with Code Section 43–17–9.

Laws 1996, p. 737, § 1; Laws 2001, p. 4, § 40.

§ 40–6–98. Driving through safety zone prohibited

No vehicle shall at any time be driven through or within a safety zone.

Laws 1974, p. 633, § 1; Laws 1990, p. 2048, § 5.

Formerly Code 1933, § 68A–508; Code 1981, § 40–6–99.

§ 40–6–99. Pedestrians yield to authorized emergency vehicles

(a) Upon the immediate approach of an authorized emergency vehicle making use of an audible signal meeting the requirements of Code Section 40–8–94, and visual and audible signals meeting the requirements of Code Section 40–6–6 or a vehicle belonging to a federal, state, or local law enforcement agency making use of visual and audible signals meeting the requirements of Code Section 40–6–6, every pedestrian shall yield the right of way to the authorized emergency vehicle or law enforcement vehicle.

(b) This Code section shall not operate to relieve the driver of an authorized emergency vehicle from the duty to drive with due regard for the safety of all persons using the highway nor from the duty to exercise due care to avoid colliding with any pedestrian.

Laws 1974, p. 633, § 1; Laws 1990, p. 2048, § 5.

Formerly Code 1933, § 68A–510; Code 1981, § 40–6–101.

§ 40–6–100. Repealed by Laws 1990, p. 2048, § 5, eff. January 1, 1991

§ 40–6–101. Renumbered as § 40–6–99 by Laws 1990, p. 2048, § 5

Article 6

Turning, Starting, Signaling

§ 40–6–120. Required position and methods of turning at intersections

The driver of a vehicle intending to turn at an intersection shall do so as follows:

(1) RIGHT TURN. Both the approach for a right turn and a right turn shall be made as close as practicable to the right-hand curb or edge of the roadway;

(2) LEFT TURN. (A) As used in this paragraph, the term "extreme left-hand lane" means the lane furthest to the left that is lawfully available to traffic moving in the same direction as the turning vehicle. In the event of multiple lanes, the second extreme left-hand lane shall be the lane to the right of the extreme left-hand lane that is lawfully available to traffic moving in the same direction as the turning vehicle. The third extreme left-hand lane shall be the lane to the right of the second extreme left-hand lane and so forth.

(B) The driver of a vehicle intending to turn left shall approach the turn in the extreme left-hand lane lawfully available to traffic moving in the direction of travel of the turning vehicle. Whenever practicable, the left turn shall be made to the left of the center of the intersection and so as to exit the intersection or other location in the extreme left-hand lane lawfully available to traffic moving in the same direction as the turning vehicle on the roadway being entered.

(C) In the event of multiple left turn lanes, the driver of a vehicle turning left shall exit the intersection in the same relative travel lane as the vehicle entered the intersection. If the vehicle is in the second extreme left-hand lane entering the intersection the vehicle shall exit the intersection in the second extreme left-hand lane. Where there are multiple lanes of travel in the same direction safe for travel, a vehicle shall not be permitted to make a lane change once the intersection has been entered.

Laws 1953, Nov.-Dec. Sess., p. 556, § 66; Laws 1974, p. 633, § 1; Laws 1990, p. 2048, § 5; Laws 2010, Act 412, § 1, eff. July 1, 2010.

Formerly Code 1933, § 68A–601.

Validity

This section has been held unconstitutional in the case of McNair v. State, 2009, 285 Ga. 514, 678 S.E.2d 69.

Historical and Statutory Notes

The 2010 amendment by Act 412 rewrote the section which had read:

"(a) The driver of a vehicle intending to turn at an intersection shall do so as follows:

"(1) Right turn. Both the approach for a right turn and a right turn shall be made as close as practicable to the right-hand curb or edge of the roadway;

"(2) Left turn. The driver of a vehicle intending to turn left shall approach the turn in the extreme left-hand lane lawfully available to traffic moving in the direction of travel of such vehicle. Whenever practicable, the left turn shall be made to the left of the center of the intersection and so as to leave the intersection or other location in the extreme left-hand lane lawfully available to traffic moving in the same direction as such vehicle on the roadway being entered.

"(b) The Department of Transportation and local authorities in their respective jurisdictions may cause official traffic-control devices to be placed within or adjacent to intersections or other locations and thereby require and direct that a different course from that specified in this Code section be traveled by turning vehicles, and when such devices are so placed, no driver of a vehicle shall turn a vehicle other than as directed and required by such devices."

Laws 2010, Act 410, § 3, provides:

"This Act shall become effective on July 1, 2010, and be applicable to all offenses committed on or after that date."

§ 40–6–121. U-turns, when prohibited

No vehicle shall be turned so as to proceed in the opposite direction:

(1) Upon any curve;

(2) Upon the approach to or near the crest of a grade where such vehicle cannot be seen by the driver of another vehicle approaching from either direction;

(3) Where such turn cannot be made in safety and without interfering with other traffic; or

(4) Where a prohibition is posted.

Laws 1953, Nov.-Dec. Sess., p. 556, § 67; Laws 1974, p. 633, § 1; Laws 1990, p. 2048, § 5.

Formerly Code 1933, § 68A–602.

§ 40–6–122. Starting parked vehicle

No person shall start a vehicle which is stopped, standing, or parked unless and until such movement can be made with reasonable safety.

Laws 1953, Nov.-Dec. Sess., p. 556, § 68; Laws 1974, p. 633, § 1; Laws 1990, p. 2048, § 5.

Formerly Code 1933, § 68A–603.

§ 40–6–123. Turning movements and required signals

(a) No person shall turn a vehicle at an intersection unless the vehicle is in proper position upon the roadway as required in Code Section 40–6–120 or turn a vehicle to enter a private road or driveway or otherwise turn a vehicle from a direct course or change lanes or move right or left upon a roadway unless and until such movement can be made with reasonable safety. No person shall so turn any vehicle without giving an appropriate and timely signal in the manner provided in this Code section.

(b) A signal of intention to turn right or left or change lanes when required shall be given continuously for a time sufficient to alert the driver of a vehicle proceeding from the rear in the same direction or a driver of a vehicle approaching from the opposite direction.

(c) No person shall stop or suddenly decrease the speed of a vehicle without first giving an appropriate signal in the manner provided in this Code section to the driver of any vehicle immediately to the rear when there is an opportunity to give such signal.

(d) The signals provided for in subsection (b) of Code Section 40–6–124 shall be used to indicate an intention to turn, change lanes, or start from a parked position and shall not be flashed on one side only on a parked or disabled vehicle or flashed as a courtesy or "do pass" signal to operators of other vehicles approaching from the rear.

Laws 1953, Nov.-Dec. Sess., p. 556, § 69; Laws 1974, p. 633, § 1; Laws 1985, p. 149, § 40; Laws 1990, p. 2048, § 5.

Formerly Code 1933, § 68A–604.

§ 40–6–124. Signals by hand and arm or signal lights

(a) Any stop or turn signal when required in this chapter shall be given either by means of the hand and arm or by signal lights, except as otherwise provided in subsection (b) of this Code section.

(b) Any motor vehicle in use on a highway shall be equipped with, and a required signal shall be given by, signal lights when the distance from the center of the top of the steering post to the left outside limit of the body, cab, or load of such motor vehicle exceeds 24 inches or when the distance from the center of the top of the steering post to the rear limits of the body or load thereof exceeds 14 feet. The latter measurement shall apply to any single vehicle and also to any combination of vehicles.

Laws 1953, Nov.-Dec. Sess., p. 556, § 70; Laws 1974, p. 633, § 1; Laws 1985, p. 149, § 40; Laws 1990, p. 2048, § 5.

Formerly Code 1933, § 68A–605.

§ 40–6–125. Method of giving hand and arm signals

All signals required by this article when given by hand and arm shall be given from the left side of the vehicle in the following manner and shall indicate as follows:

(1) Left turn, hand and arm extended horizontally;

(2) Right turn, hand and arm extended upward;

(3) Stop or decrease speed, hand and arm extended downward.

Laws 1953, Nov.-Dec. Sess., p. 556, § 71; Laws 1974, p. 633, § 1; Laws 1990, p. 2048, § 5.

Formerly Code 1933, § 68A–606.

§ 40–6–126. Restrictions on use of central lane of highway

Whenever a highway or roadway has a central lane in which traffic may enter from either direction for the purposes of making a left turn, no vehicle shall be driven into such central lane except for the purpose of making a left turn, and no vehicle shall enter into such central lane at a location which is more than 300 feet from the location where the vehicle will turn left across one or more lanes of oncoming traffic. No vehicle which has been driven into such a central lane shall be operated in such central lane for more than 300 feet.

Laws 1997, p. 866, § 1.

Article 7

Negotiating Railroad Crossings, Entering Highways from Private Driveways

§ 40–6–140. Obedience to signal indicating approach of train

(a) Whenever any person driving a vehicle approaches a railroad grade crossing, such driver shall stop within 50 feet but not less than 15 feet from the nearest rail of such railroad and shall not proceed until he can do so safely, when:

(1) A clearly visible electric or mechanical signal device gives warning of the immediate approach of a train;

(2) A crossing gate is lowered or a human flagman gives or continues to give a signal of the approach of the passage of a train; or

(3) An approaching train is plainly visible and is in hazardous proximity to such crossing.

(b) No person shall drive any vehicle through, around, or under any crossing gate or barrier at a railroad crossing while such gate or barrier is closed or is being opened or closed.

(c) If no electric or mechanical signal device is giving warning of the immediate approach of a train, no crossing gate or barrier is closed, there is no stop sign at the crossing, and there is no human flagman giving warning, all drivers shall slow to a reasonable and prudent speed and verify that there is no approaching train prior to proceeding. For the purposes of this subsection, "a reasonable and prudent speed" means a speed slow enough to enable the driver to safely stop the vehicle prior to reaching the nearest rail of such crossing.

(d) No person shall drive a vehicle over a railroad grade crossing when a train is approaching.

(e) No person shall drive a vehicle over a railroad grade crossing if there is insufficient space to drive completely through the crossing without stopping.

(f) No person shall drive a vehicle over a railroad grade crossing if there is insufficient undercarriage clearance for the vehicle to negotiate the crossing.

Laws 1953, Nov.-Dec. Sess., p. 556, § 83; Laws 1974, p. 633, § 1; Laws 1990, p. 2048, § 5; Laws 2003, Act 200, § 9, eff. Oct. 1, 2003.

Formerly Code 1933, § 68A–701.

Historical and Statutory Notes

The 2003 amendment by Act 200 added new subsecs. (c), (d), (e), and (f).

Laws 2003, Act 200, § 15 provides:

"This Act shall become effective on October 1, 2003."

§ 40–6–141. All vehicles must stop at certain railroad grade crossings

The Department of Transportation and local authorities with the approval of the department are authorized to designate particularly dangerous highway grade crossings of railroads and to erect stop signs thereat. When such stop signs are erected, the driver of any vehicle shall stop within 50 feet but not less than 15 feet from the nearest rail of such railroad and shall proceed only upon exercising due care.

Laws 1953, Nov.-Dec. Sess., p. 556, § 84; Laws 1973, p. 947, § 2; Laws 1974, p. 633, § 1; Laws 1990, p. 2048, § 5.

Formerly Code 1933, § 68A–702.

§ 40–6–142. Certain vehicles must stop at all railroad crossings

(a) Except as provided in subsection (b) of this Code section, the driver of any motor vehicle carrying passengers for hire, any bus, whether or not operated for hire, or of any school bus, whether carrying any school children or empty, or of any vehicle carrying any hazardous material listed in Section 392.10 of Title 49 of the Code of Federal Regulations as those regulations currently exist or as they may in the future be amended or in regulations adopted by the commissioner of public safety, before crossing at grade any track or tracks of a railroad, shall stop such vehicle within 50 feet but not less than 15 feet from the nearest rail of such railroad and while so stopped shall listen and look in both directions along such track for any approaching train and for signals indicating the approach of a train and shall not proceed until he or she can do so safely. After stopping as required in this Code section and upon proceeding when it is safe to do so, the driver of any such vehicle shall cross only in such gear of the vehicle that there will be no necessity for changing gears while traversing such crossing, and the driver shall not shift gears while crossing the track or tracks.

(b) No stop need be made at any such crossing where:

(1) Traffic is directed to proceed by a police officer, a firefighter, or a railroad flagman;

(2) A traffic-control signal directs traffic to proceed;

(3) The highway crosses an abandoned railroad track which is marked with a sign indicating its abandoned status, where such signs are erected by or under the direction of the local or state authority having jurisdiction over the highway; or

(4) The highway crosses an industrial siding or spur track marked "exempt," where such signs are erected by or under the direction of the local or state authority having jurisdiction over the highway.

Laws 1953, Nov.-Dec. Sess., p. 556, § 85; Laws 1974, p. 633, § 1; Laws 1990, p. 2048, § 5; Laws 1991, p. 1004, § 1; Laws 2003, Act 200, § 10, eff. Oct. 1, 2003; Laws 2004, Act 564, § 40, eff. May 13, 2004; Laws 2005, Act 68, § 18–3, eff. July 1, 2005.

Formerly Code 1933, § 68A–703.

Historical and Statutory Notes

The 2003 amendment by Act 200, in subsec. (a), inserted ", any bus, whether or not operated for hire," and substituted "any hazardous material listed in Section 392.10 of Title 49 of the Code of Federal Regulations, as those regulations currently exist or as they may in the future be amended or in regulations adopted by the commissioner of motor vehicle safety" for "explosive substances, flammable liquids, hazardous waste or constituents, or hazardous acidic liquids as cargo or part of a cargo"; and rewrote subsec. (b) which had read:

"(b) No stop need be made at any such crossing where a police officer or a traffic-control signal directs traffic to proceed."

Laws 2003, Act 200, § 15 provides:

"This Act shall become effective on October 1, 2003."

The 2004 amendment by Act 564 was a provision contained in a correction bill.

The 2005 amendment by Act 68 in subsec. (a) substituted "commissioner of public safety" for "commissioner of motor vehicle safety" following "in regulations adopted by" and made a gender neutral change.

§ 40–6–143. Moving heavy equipment at railroad grade crossings

(a) No person shall operate or move a crawler-type tractor, steam shovel, derrick, roller, or any equipment or structure having a normal operating speed of ten miles per hour or less or a vertical body or load clearance of less than one-half inch per foot of the distance between any two adjacent axles or in any event of less than nine inches, measured above the level surface of a roadway, upon or across any tracks at a railroad grade crossing without first complying with this Code section.

(b) Notice of any such intended crossing shall be given to a station agency of such railroad and a reasonable time shall be given to such railroad to provide proper protection at such crossing.

(c) Before making any such crossing, the person operating or moving any such vehicle or equipment shall first stop it not less than 15 feet nor more than 50 feet from the nearest rail of such railroad and while so stopped shall listen and look in both directions along such track for any approaching train and for signals indicating the approach of a train and shall not proceed until the crossing can be made safely.

(d) No such crossing shall be made when warning is given by automatic signal or crossing gates or a flagman or otherwise of the immediate approach of a railroad train or car. If a flagman is provided by the railroad, movement over the crossing shall be under his direction.

Laws 1953, Nov.-Dec. Sess., p. 556, § 86; Laws 1974, p. 633, § 1; Laws 1990, p. 2048, § 5.

Formerly Code 1933, § 68A–704.

§ 40–6–144. Emerging from alley, building, private road, or driveway

The driver of a vehicle emerging from an alley, building, private road, or driveway within a business or residential district shall stop such vehicle immediately prior to driving onto a sidewalk or onto the sidewalk area extending across such alley, building entrance, road, or driveway or, in the event there is no sidewalk area, shall stop at the point nearest the street to be entered where the driver has a view of approaching traffic thereon. The driver of a vehicle shall yield the right of way to any pedestrian on a sidewalk. Except as provided by resolution or ordinance of a local government for sidewalks within the jurisdiction of such local government authorizing the operation of bicycles on sidewalks by persons 12 years of age or younger, no person shall drive any vehicle upon a sidewalk or sidewalk area except upon a permanent or duly authorized driveway.

Laws 1953, Nov.-Dec. Sess., p. 556, § 88; Laws 1974, p. 633, § 1; Laws 1990, p. 2048, § 5; Laws 2009, Act 22, § 7, eff. July 1, 2009.

Formerly Code 1933, §§ 68A–509, 68A–705.

Historical and Statutory Notes

The 2009 amendment by Act 22, substituted "Except as provided by resolution or ordinance of a local government for sidewalks within the jurisdiction of such local government authorizing the operation of bicycles on sidewalks by persons 12 years of age or younger, no" for "No".

Article 8

School Buses

§ 40–6–160. Speed of school bus

(a) Except as otherwise provided in subsection (b) of this Code section, it shall be unlawful to operate:

(1) A school bus transporting school children to and from school or to and from school activities at a speed greater than 40 miles per hour on a public road other than one which is a part of The Dwight D. Eisenhower System of Interstate and Defense Highways; or

(2) A school bus transporting school children to and from school or to and from school activities on a public road which is a part of The Dwight D. Eisenhower System of Interstate and Defense Highways at a speed greater than 55 miles per hour.

(b) When a school bus is transporting school children to or from an event or school activity or an express bus transporting students from one school to another school and is not loading or unloading children during such transportation, the speed limit shall be 55 miles per hour on other public roads as well as on those public roads which are a part of The Dwight D. Eisenhower System of Interstate and Defense Highways.

Laws 1974, p. 633, § 1; Laws 1978, p. 2065, § 1; Laws 1988, p. 540, § 1; Laws 1989, p. 14, § 40; Laws 1990, p. 8, § 40; Laws 1990, p. 2048, § 5; Laws 1992, p. 2785, § 23; Laws 2000, p. 136, § 40.

Formerly Code 1933, § 68A–706.

Historical and Statutory Notes

The 2000 amendment substituted for references to the "National System of Interstate and Defense Highways" references to "The Dwight D. Eisenhower System of Interstate and

Defense Highways".

§ 40–6–161. Headlights illuminated; communications equipment of driver

(a) It shall be unlawful to operate any school bus which is transporting children unless the headlights on such school bus are illuminated.

(b) It shall be unlawful to operate any school bus which is transporting children unless the driver of the bus is equipped with one or more devices to allow live communication between the driver and school officials or public safety officials or both. Such communication may be provided by two-way radio, cellular telephone, or any other device which provides similar communications capability.

Laws 1964, p. 338, § 1; Laws 1974, p. 633, § 1; Laws 1990, p. 2048, § 5; Laws 2000, p. 1629, § 1.

Formerly Code 1933, § 68A–706.

Historical and Statutory Notes

The 2000 amendment designated the existing provision as subsec. (a) and added subsec. (b).

§ 40–6–162. Visual signals

A school bus driver shall actuate the visual signals required by Code Sections 40–8–111 and 40–8–115 whenever, but only whenever, the school bus is stopped on the highway for the purpose of receiving or discharging school children. A school bus driver shall not actuate the visual signals:

(1) At intersections or other places where traffic is controlled by traffic-control signals or police officers; or

(2) In designated school bus loading areas where the bus is entirely off the roadway.

Laws 1953, Nov.-Dec. Sess., p. 556, § 89; Laws 1974, p. 633, § 1; Laws 1990, p. 8, § 40; Laws 1990, p. 2048, § 5.

Formerly Code 1933, § 68A–706.

§ 40–6–163. Overtaking and passing school bus

(a) Except as provided in subsection (b) of this Code section, the driver of a vehicle meeting or overtaking from either direction any school bus stopped on the highway shall stop before reaching such school bus when there are in operation on the school bus the visual signals as specified in Code Sections 40–8–111 and 40–8–115, and such driver shall not proceed until the school bus resumes motion or the visual signals are no longer actuated.

(b) The driver of a vehicle upon a highway with separate roadways need not stop upon meeting or passing a school bus which is on a different roadway, or upon a controlled-access highway when the school bus is stopped in a loading zone which is a part of or adjacent to such highway and where pedestrians are not permitted to cross the roadway.

(c) Every school bus driver who observes a violation of subsection (a) of this Code section is authorized and directed to record specifically the vehicle description, license number of the offending vehicle, and time and place of occurrence on forms furnished by the Department of Public Safety. Such report shall be submitted within 15 days of the occurrence of the violation to the local law enforcement agency which has law enforcement jurisdiction where the alleged offense occurred.

Laws 1953, Nov.-Dec. Sess., p. 556, § 89; Laws 1974, p. 633, § 1; Laws 1985, p. 1175, § 1; Laws 1986, p. 819, § 1; Laws 1990, p. 2048, § 5.

Formerly Code 1933, § 68A–706.

§ 40–6–164. School bus driver to wait until all children have crossed roadway

After stopping to allow children to disembark from the bus, it shall be unlawful for the driver of the school bus to proceed until all children who need to cross the roadway have done so safely. Any driver willfully violating this Code section shall be guilty of a misdemeanor.

Laws 1976, p. 479, § 1; Laws 1990, p. 8, § 40; Laws 1990, p. 2048, § 5.

§ 40–6–165. School bus driver safety procedures

(a) Prior to moving a school bus from a stop at which passengers have been loaded or unloaded, the driver of the bus shall check all mirrors to ensure that it is safe to place the bus in motion.

(b) Prior to loading or unloading passengers from a school bus, the driver shall engage the parking brakes of the bus and shall not release such brakes until each passenger boarding the bus is on board and until each passenger disembarking from the bus is off the roadway and safely on the pedestrian areas of the roadway.

(c) Prior to loading or unloading passengers from a school bus, the driver shall display the stop arm on the bus and shall not retract the stop arm until each passenger boarding the bus is on board and until each passenger disembarking from the bus is off the roadway and safely on the pedestrian areas of the roadway.

(d) The driver of a school bus shall not use or operate a cellular telephone or two-way radio while loading or unloading passengers.

(e) The driver of a school bus shall not use or operate a cellular telephone while the bus is in motion.

(f) The driver of a school bus shall instruct all passengers exiting the bus of the proper procedures of crossing the roadway in front of the bus only.

(g) The driver of a school bus shall ensure that the red flasher lights on the bus remain illuminated and flashing until all passengers have boarded or have exited the bus and have safely crossed the roadway and are safely on the pedestrian areas of the roadway.

(h) The driver of a school bus shall extend the extension arm or gate on the front of the bus until all passengers have boarded or have exited the bus and have safely crossed the roadway and are safely on the pedestrian areas of the roadway.

Laws 2004, Act 560, § 7, eff. July 1, 2004.

Article 9

Speed Restrictions

§ 40–6–180. Basic rules

No person shall drive a vehicle at a speed greater than is reasonable and prudent under the conditions and having regard for the actual and potential hazards then existing. Consistently with the foregoing, every person shall drive at a reasonable and prudent speed when approaching and crossing an intersection or railroad grade crossing, when approaching and going around a curve, when approaching and traversing a hill crest, when traveling upon any narrow or winding roadway, and when special hazards exist with respect to pedestrians or other traffic or by reason of weather or highway conditions.

Laws 1953, Nov.-Dec. Sess., p. 556, § 48; Laws 1975, p. 1582, § 1; Laws 1990, p. 2048, § 5.

Formerly Code 1933, § 68A–801.

§ 40–6–181. Maximum limits

(a) The limits specified in this Code section or established as authorized in this article shall be the maximum lawful vehicle speeds, except when a special hazard exists that requires a lower speed for compliance with Code Section 40–6–180.

(b) Consistent with the provision of engineering and traffic investigations regarding maximum speed limits as provided in Code Section 40–6–182, no person shall drive a vehicle at a speed in excess of the following maximum limits:

(1) Thirty miles per hour in any urban or residential district;

(1.1) Thirty-five miles per hour on an unpaved county road unless designated otherwise by appropriate signs;

(2) Seventy miles per hour on a highway on the federal interstate system and on physically divided highways with full control of access which are outside of an urbanized area of 50,000 population or more, provided that such speed limit is designated by appropriate signs;

(3) Sixty-five miles per hour on a highway on the federal interstate system which is inside of an urbanized area of 50,000 population or more, provided that such speed limit is designated by appropriate signs;

(4) Sixty-five miles per hour on those sections of physically divided highways without full access control on the state highway system, provided that such speed limit is designated by appropriate signs; and

(5) Fifty-five miles per hour in other locations.

(c) The maximum speed limits set forth in this Code section may be altered as authorized in Code Sections 40–6–182, 40–6–183, and 40–6–188.

Laws 1953, Nov.-Dec. Sess., p. 556, § 48; Laws 1963, p. 26, § 1; Laws 1974, p. 11, § 1; Laws 1975, p. 1582, § 1; Laws 1982, p. 1290, §§ 1, 2; Laws 1983, p. 3, § 29; Laws 1984, p. 22, § 40; Laws 1988, p. 30, § 1; Laws 1990, p. 2048, § 5; Laws 1995, p. 759, § 1.1; Laws 1996, p. 469, § 1.1.

Formerly Code 1933, § 68A–802.

§ 40–6–182. Establishment of state speed zones

Whenever the commissioner of public safety or the commissioner of transportation shall determine upon the basis of an engineering and traffic investigation that any maximum speed set forth in this article is greater or less than is reasonable or safe under the conditions found to exist at any intersection or other place or upon any part of the state highway system, they may jointly determine and declare a reasonable and safe maximum speed limit at such place, which shall be effective when appropriate signs giving notice thereof are erected. Such a maximum speed limit may be declared to be effective at all times as are indicated upon such signs; and differing limits may be established for different times of day, different varying weather conditions, and other factors bearing on safe speeds, which shall be effective when posted upon appropriate fixed or variable signs. In no case shall the maximum speed limit for any highway be established at higher than the maximum speed limits set forth in Code Section 40–6–181 for that type of highway.

Laws 1953, Nov.-Dec. Sess., p. 556, § 49; Laws 1957, p. 419, § 1; Laws 1963, p. 254, § 2; Laws 1975, p. 1582, § 1; Laws 1990, p. 2048, § 5.

Formerly Code 1933, § 68A–803.

§ 40–6–183. When local authorities may and shall alter maximum speed limits

(a) Whenever the governing authority of an incorporated municipality or county, in its respective jurisdiction, determines on the basis of an engineering and traffic investigation that the maximum vehicle speed permitted under this chapter is greater than is reasonable and safe under the conditions found to exist upon a highway or part of a highway under its jurisdiction, such authority may determine and declare a reasonable and safe maximum vehicle speed limit thereon which:

(1) Decreases the limit at intersections;

(2) Decreases the limit outside an urban or residential district, but not to less than 30 miles per hour;

(3) Decreases the limit within an urban or residential district, but not to less than 25 miles per hour; or

(4) Decreases any speed limit where a special hazard or condition exists that requires lower speed for compliance with Code Section 40–6–180.

(b) Such an authority in its respective jurisdiction shall determine by an engineering and traffic investigation the proper maximum speed for all arterial streets and shall declare a reasonable and safe maximum speed limit thereon which may be greater or less than the maximum speed permitted under this chapter for an urban district, but in no case shall the maximum be established at higher than 55 miles per hour.

(c) Any altered limit established as authorized in this Code section shall be effective at all times or during hours of darkness or at other times as may be determined when appropriate signs giving notice thereof are erected upon such street or highway.

(d) Not more than six alterations as authorized in this Code section shall be made per mile along a street or highway, except in the case of reduced limits at intersections. The difference between adjacent limits shall not be more than ten miles per hour, except for reductions for school speed zones, which may be not more than 20 miles per hour when a warning sign is placed 700 feet in advance of the point at which the speed reduction is required.

Laws 1953, Nov.-Dec. Sess., p. 556, § 50; Laws 1975, p. 1582, § 1; Laws 1978, p. 1967, § 1; Laws 1990, p. 2048, § 5.

Formerly Code 1933, § 68A–804.

§ 40–6–184. Minimum speed regulation

(a)(1) No person shall drive a motor vehicle at such a slow speed as to impede the normal and reasonable movement of traffic, except when reduced speed is necessary for safe operation.

(2) On roads, streets, or highways with two or more lanes allowing for movement in the same direction, no person shall continue to operate a motor vehicle in the most left-hand lane at less than the maximum lawful speed limit once such person knows or should reasonably know that he is being overtaken in such lane from the rear by a motor vehicle traveling at a higher rate of speed, except when such motor vehicle is preparing for a left turn.

(b) Whenever the commissioner of public safety or the commissioner of transportation or local authorities determine on the basis of any engineering and traffic investigation that slow speeds on any part of a road under their respective jurisdictions impede the normal and reasonable movement of traffic, such commissioners jointly, or such local authorities, may determine and declare a minimum speed limit below which no person shall drive a vehicle except when necessary for safe operation, and that limit shall be effective when posted upon fixed or variable signs.

Laws 1953, Nov.-Dec. Sess., p. 556, § 51; Laws 1975, p. 1582, § 1; Laws 1987, p. 361, § 2; Laws 1990, p. 2048, § 5.

Formerly Code 1933, § 68A–805.

§ 40–6–185. Special speed limitations

(a) No person shall drive a vehicle over any bridge or other elevated structure constituting a part of a highway at a speed which is greater than the maximum speed which can be maintained with safety to such bridge or structure, when such structure is posted as provided in this Code section.

(b) The Department of Transportation may conduct an investigation of any bridge or other elevated structure constituting a part of a highway, and, if it shall thereupon find that such structure cannot, with safety to itself, withstand vehicles traveling at the speed otherwise permissible under this chapter, the department shall determine and declare the maximum speed of vehicles which such structure can safely withstand and shall cause or permit suitable signs stating such maximum speed to be erected and maintained before each end of such structure.

(c) Upon the trial of any person charged with a violation of subsection (a) of this Code section, proof of determination of the maximum speed by the department and the existence of such signs shall constitute conclusive evidence of the maximum speed which can be maintained with safety to such bridge or structure.

Laws 1953, Nov.-Dec. Sess., p. 556, § 53; Laws 1975, p. 1582, § 1; Laws 1990, p. 2048, § 5.

Formerly Code 1933, § 68A–806.

§ 40–6–186. Racing on highways and streets

(a) As used in this Code section, the term:

(1) "Drag race" means the operation of two or more vehicles from a point side by side at accelerated speeds in a competitive attempt to outdistance each other or the operation of one or more vehicles over a common selected course from the same point to the same point for the purpose of comparing the relative speeds or power of acceleration of such vehicle or vehicles within a certain distance or time limit.

(2) "Racing" means the use of one or more vehicles in an attempt to outgain, outdistance, or prevent another vehicle from passing, to arrive at a given destination ahead of another vehicle or vehicles, or to test the physical stamina or endurance of drivers over long-distance driving routes.

(b) No person shall drive any vehicle on a highway in this state in any race, speed competition or contest, drag race or acceleration contest, test of physical endurance, exhibition of speed or acceleration, or for the purpose of making a speed record, and no person shall in any manner participate in any such race, competition of speed, contest of speed, or test or exhibition of speed.

(c) Any person convicted of violating subsection (b) of this Code section shall be guilty of a misdemeanor.

Laws 1959, p. 303, § 1; Laws 1961, p. 438, §§ 1–4; Laws 1975, p. 1582, § 1; Laws 1990, p. 2048, § 5; Laws 2006, Act 590, § 21, eff. July 1, 2006.

Formerly Code 1933, § 68A–808.

Historical and Statutory Notes

The 2006 amendment by Act 590, in subsec. (c), deleted the second sentence which had read "In addition to the punishment prescribed by law, the Department of Public Safety shall suspend for 12 months the license of any person convicted of such violation."

§ 40–6–187. Charging violations

(a) In every charge of violation of any speed regulation in this chapter, the summons, uniform traffic citation, official charging instrument, or notice to appear shall specify the speed at which the defendant is alleged to have driven, the maximum speed applicable within the district or at the location, and whether the violation occurred on a two-lane road or highway. For purposes of this Code section, the term "two-lane road or highway" means a road or highway with two lanes for through-traffic movement exclusive of any portion of the road or highway adjoining the traveled way for parking, speed change, turning, weaving, truck climbing, or other purposes supplementary to through-traffic movement.

(b) For the purpose of imposing points pursuant to Code Section 40–5–57, every sentence for a violation of any speed regulation in this chapter shall state the specific amount by which the person convicted exceeded the speed limit.

Laws 1953, Nov.-Dec. Sess., p. 556, § 54; Laws 1975, p. 1582, § 1; Laws 1985, p. 149, § 40; Laws 1990, p. 2048, § 5; Laws 2006, Act 590, § 22, eff. July 1, 2006; Laws 2009, Act 135, § 10, eff. Jan. 1, 2010.

Formerly Code 1933, § 68A–807.

Historical and Statutory Notes

The 2006 amendment by Act 590 designated the existing text as subsec. (a) and added subsec. (b).

The 2009 amendment by Act 135 rewrote subsec. (a) which read:

"(a) In every charge of violation of any speed regulation in this chapter, the summons or notice to appear shall specify the speed at which the defendant is alleged to have driven and also the maximum speed applicable within the district or at the location."

§ 40–6–188. Reduction of maximum speed limits in highway work zones

(a) As used in this Code section, the term:

(1) "Highway work zone" means a segment of any highway, road, or street where the Department of Transportation, a county, a municipality, or any contractor for any of the foregoing is engaged in constructing, reconstructing, or maintaining the physical structure of the roadway or its shoulders or features adjacent to the roadway, including without limitation underground or overhead utilities or highway appurtenances, or any other type of work related thereto.

(2) "Work zone personnel" means employees of the Department of Transportation, a county, a municipality, or any contractor for any of the foregoing.

(b)(1) The Department of Transportation, any county, or any municipality may designate any segment of a highway, road, or street under its jurisdiction as a highway work zone.

(2) Whenever a highway work zone is designated pursuant to paragraph (1) of this subsection, there shall be erected or posted signage of adequate size at the beginning point of such highway work zone designating the zone and warning the traveling public that increased penalties for speeding violations are in effect for the highway work zone, and there shall be erected or posted at the end of such highway work zone adequate signage indicating the end of such zone and that increased penalties for speeding violations are no longer in effect.

(c)(1) The Department of Transportation or the governing authority of any county or municipal corporation is authorized to establish a temporary reduction in the maximum speed limit through any highway work zone located on or adjacent to any street or highway under its respective jurisdiction. The commissioner of transportation or the local governing authority shall not be required to conduct any engineering and traffic investigation in order to establish a reduced speed limit in a highway work zone pursuant to this paragraph.

(2) Whenever reduced speed zones are established pursuant to paragraph (1) of this subsection, there shall be erected or posted signage of adequate size at the beginning point of such speed zone designating the zone and the speed limit to be observed therein, and there shall be erected or posted at the end of such speed zone adequate signage indicating the end of such speed zone, which signage shall also indicate such different speed limit as may then be observed. Signs indicating such reduced speed limit shall be spaced not further than one mile apart throughout the highway work zone. Where the speed limit established pursuant to paragraph (1) of this subsection is at least ten miles per hour less than the established speed limit on the street or highway, there shall be erected at least 600 feet in advance of the beginning of the speed zone a sign of adequate size which shall bear the legend "Reduced Speed Ahead." Whenever any signage is required by this paragraph, the same shall be in addition to the signage requirements of paragraph (2) of subsection (b) of this Code section.

(d)(1) Any signage required by this Code section shall conform to applicable provisions of the Manual on Uniform Traffic Control Devices; provided, however, that nothing in this Code section shall prohibit the use of movable or portable speed limit signs in highway work zones.

(2) Any existing regulatory signage conflicting with signage erected or posted pursuant to this Code section shall be removed, covered, folded, or turned so as not to be readable by oncoming motorists.

(e)(1) In order for a person to be cited or convicted for exceeding a speed limit, reduced or otherwise, in any highway work zone as provided in paragraph (2) of this subsection, there must be present in the highway work zone at the time of the offense the signage required by this Code section and either:

(A) Work zone personnel; or

(B) Barriers, on-site work vehicles, or shoulder or pavement drop offs that constitute a hazard to the traveling public.

(2) A person convicted of exceeding the speed limit, reduced or otherwise, in any highway work zone designated pursuant to this Code section shall be guilty of a misdemeanor of a high and aggravated nature and shall be punished by a fine of not less than $100.00 nor more than $2,000.00 or by imprisonment for a term not to exceed 12 months, or both.

(f) Whenever the Department of Transportation finds it necessary to designate a highway work zone within a county or municipality, the Department of Transportation shall be required to notify the county or municipality of the work activity; provided, however, that the failure of the Department of Transportation to give such notice shall not be a defense to any charge of violating the speed limit in any highway work zone.

Laws 1995, p. 759, § 2; Laws 1997, p. 143, § 40; Laws 1997, p. 866, § 2; Laws 2000, p. 1313, § 4; Laws 2003, Act 191, § 4, eff. July 1, 2003.

Historical and Statutory Notes

The 2000 amendment rewrote this section which formerly provided:

"(a) The Department of Transportation or the governing authority of any county or municipal corporation is authorized to establish a maximum speed limit through any construction site located on or adjacent to any street or highway under its respective jurisdiction.

"(b) Whenever speed zones are established pursuant to subsection (a) of this Code section, there shall be erected or posted signage of adequate size at the beginning point of such speed zone designating the zone and the speed limit to be observed therein, and there shall be erected or posted at the end of such speed zone adequate signage indicating the end of such speed zone, which signage shall also indicate such different speed limit as may then be observed. Where the speed limit established pursuant to subsection (a) of this Code section is at least ten miles per hour less than the established speed limit on the street or highway, there shall be erected at least 600 feet in advance of the beginning of the speed zone a sign of adequate size which shall bear the legend 'Reduce Speed Ahead.'

"(c) A person convicted of exceeding the speed limit in any speed zone established pursuant to subsection (a) of this Code section shall be guilty of a misdemeanor of a high and aggravated nature and shall be punished by a fine of not less than $100.00 nor more than $2,000.00 or by imprisonment for a term not to exceed 12 months, or both."

The 2003 amendment by Act 191 rewrote subsec. (e) which had read:

"(e) A person convicted of exceeding the speed limit, reduced or otherwise, in any highway work zone designated pursuant to this Code section and identified at the time of the violation by such signage at the beginning of the highway work zone as required herein and, if such speed limit was reduced as provided by this Code section, by such signage at the beginning and in advance of such reduced speed zone to the extent required herein shall be guilty of a misdemeanor of a high and aggravated nature and shall be punished by a fine of not less than $100.00 nor more than $2,000.00 or by imprisonment for a term not to exceed 12 months, or both. The provisions of this subsection shall apply without regard to whether work zone personnel were present in the highway work zone when the violation occurred."

§ 40–6–189. Super speeder; fees

(a) As used in this Code section, the term "department" means the Department of Driver Services.

(b) In addition to any other fines or penalties imposed by any local jurisdiction or the department, the department shall administer and collect a fee of $200.00 from any driver who is convicted of driving at a speed of 85 miles per hour or more on any road or highway or 75 miles per hour or more on any two-lane road or highway, as defined in Code Section 40–6–187. Such a driver, upon conviction, shall be classified as a "super speeder."

(c) The department shall notify offenders of the imposition of a fee under this Code section within 30 days after receipt of a qualifying ticket and notice of conviction. Failure to pay the fee imposed by this Code section within 90 days after receipt of the notice shall result in the suspension of the driver's license or driving privileges of the offender, and, in addition to the existing fees and penalties, a fee of $50.00 shall be assessed, payable upon the application for reinstatement of the driver's license or driving privileges. Notice shall be provided by the department to the offender by first-class mail to the address shown on the records of the department. Such mailed notice shall be adequate notification of the fee imposed by this Code section and of the offender's ability to avoid a driver's license suspension by paying the fee prior to the effective date of the suspension. No other notice shall be required to make the driver's license suspension effective.

(d) The department shall be authorized to promulgate rules and regulations to implement the provisions of this Code section.

(e) All fees collected under the provisions of this Code section shall be deposited in the general fund of this state with the intent that these moneys be used to fund a trauma care system in Georgia and the direct and indirect costs associated with the administration of this Code section. The Office of Treasury and Fiscal Services shall separately account for all of the moneys received under the provisions of this Code section.

Laws 2009, Act 135, § 11, eff. Jan. 1, 2010.

Article 10

Stopping, Standing, and Parking

Part 1

General Provisions

§ 40–6–200. Parking procedure

(a) Except as otherwise provided in this Code section, every vehicle stopped or parked upon a two-way roadway shall be stopped or parked with the right-hand wheels parallel to and within 12 inches of the right-hand curb or as close as practicable to the right edge of the right-hand shoulder.

(b) Except when otherwise provided by local ordinance, every vehicle stopped or parked upon a one-way roadway shall be stopped or parked parallel to the curb or edge of the roadway, in the direction of authorized traffic movement, with its right-hand wheels within 12 inches of the right-hand curb or as close as practicable to the right edge of the right-hand shoulder or with its left-hand wheels within 12 inches of the left-hand curb or as close as practicable to the left edge of the left-hand shoulder.

(c) Local authorities may by ordinance permit angle parking on any roadway, except that angle parking shall not be permitted on any federal-aid or state highway unless the Department of Transportation has determined that the roadway is of sufficient width to permit angle parking without interfering with the free movement of traffic.

(d) The department, with respect to highways under its jurisdiction, may place signs prohibiting, restricting, or limiting the stopping, standing, or parking of vehicles on any highway where, in its opinion, as evidenced by resolution or order entered in its minutes, such stopping, standing, or parking is dangerous to those using the highway or where the stopping, standing, or parking of vehicles would unduly interfere with the free movement of traffic thereon. Such signs shall be official signs, and no person shall stop, stand, or park any vehicle in violation of the restrictions on such signs.

Laws 1953, Nov.-Dec. Sess., p. 556, § 93; Laws 1963, p. 254, § 6; Laws 1974, p. 633, § 1; Laws 1990, p. 2048, § 5.

Formerly Code 1933, § 68A–1004.

§ 40–6–201. Repealed by Laws 2007, Act 124, § 3, eff. July 1, 2007

Historical and Statutory Notes

The repealed section, relating to precautions to be taken before leaving a motor vehicle unattended, was derived from Laws 1974, p. 633, § 1; Laws 1990, p. 2048, § 5; Code 1933, § 68A–1101; Code 1981, § 40–6–201. The repealing law also reserved the section designation.

Laws 2007, Act 124, § 4, provides:

"This Act shall be effective on July 1, 2007. Prosecutions for or cases involving any violation of law occurring prior to the effective date of this Act shall not be affected by the repeals or amendments made by it or abated by reason thereof."

§ 40–6–202. Stopping, standing or parking outside of business or residence districts

Outside of a business or residential district, no person shall stop, park, or leave standing any vehicle, whether attended or unattended, upon the roadway when it is practicable to stop, park, or so leave such vehicle off the roadway; but in every event, an unobstructed width of the highway opposite a standing vehicle shall be left for the free passage of other vehicles, and a clear view of the stopped vehicle shall be available from a distance of 200 feet in each direction upon the highway.

Laws 1953, Nov.-Dec. Sess., p. 556, § 90; Laws 1974, p. 633, § 1; Laws 1990, p. 2048, § 5.

Formerly Code 1933, § 68A–1001.

§ 40–6–203. Stopping, standing or parking prohibited in specified places

(a) Except when necessary to avoid conflict with other traffic, or in compliance with law or the directions of a police officer or official traffic-control device, no person shall:

(1) Stop, stand, or park a vehicle:

(A) On the roadway side of any vehicle stopped or parked at the edge of a curb of a street;

(B) On a sidewalk;

(C) Within an intersection;

(D) On a crosswalk;

(E) Between a safety zone and the adjacent curb or within 30 feet of points on the curb immediately opposite the ends of a safety zone, unless a different length is indicated by signs or markings;

(F) Alongside or opposite any street excavation or obstruction when stopping, standing, or parking would obstruct traffic;

(G) Upon any bridge or other elevated structure upon a highway or within a highway tunnel;

(H) On any railroad tracks;

(I) On any controlled-access highway;

(J) In the area between roadways of a divided highway, including crossovers; or

(K) At any place where official signs prohibit stopping;

(2) Stand or park a vehicle, whether occupied or not, except momentarily to pick up or discharge a passenger or passengers:

(A) In front of a public or private driveway;

(B) Within 15 feet of a fire hydrant;

(C) Within 20 feet of a crosswalk at an intersection;

(D) Within 30 feet upon the approach to any flashing signal, stop sign, yield sign, or traffic-control signal located at the side of a roadway;

(E) Within 20 feet of the driveway entrance to any fire station or on the side of a street opposite the entrance to any fire station within 75 feet of such entrance (when properly posted); or

(F) At any place where official signs prohibit standing; or

(3) Park a vehicle, whether occupied or not, except temporarily for the purpose of and while actually engaged in loading or unloading property or passengers:

(A) Within 50 feet of the nearest rail of a railroad crossing; or

(B) At any place where official signs prohibit parking.

(b) No person shall move a vehicle not lawfully under his control into any prohibited area or to such a distance away from the curb as is unlawful.

(c) Notwithstanding any other provision of law, any vehicle used solely for the purpose of collecting municipal solid waste or recovered materials as defined in Code Section 12–8–22 may stop or stand on the road, street, or highway for the sole purpose of collecting such waste or materials; provided, however, that such vehicle shall maintain flashing hazard lights at all times that it is engaged in stopping or standing for the purpose of waste or materials collection.

Laws 1953, Nov.-Dec. Sess., p. 556, § 92; Laws 1974, p. 633, § 1; Laws 1989, p. 14, § 40; Laws 1990, p. 2048, § 5; Laws 1994, p. 639, § 1.

Formerly Code 1933, § 68A–1003.

§ 40–6–204. Disabled vehicles

Code Sections 40–6–200, 40–6–202, and 40–6–203 shall not apply to the driver of any vehicle which is disabled while on the roadway in such a manner and to such extent that it is impossible to avoid stopping and temporarily leaving such disabled vehicle in such position.

Laws 1953, Nov.-Dec. Sess., p. 556, § 90; Laws 1974, p. 633, § 1; Laws 1990, p. 2048, § 5.

Formerly Code 1933, § 68A–1001.

§ 40–6–205. Obstructing an intersection

No driver shall enter an intersection unless there is sufficient space on the other side of the intersection to accommodate the vehicle he is operating without obstructing the passage of other vehicles or pedestrians, notwithstanding any traffic-control signal indication to proceed.

Laws 1974, p. 633, § 1; Laws 1990, p. 2048, § 5.

Formerly Code 1933, § 68A–1005.

§ 40–6–206. Officers authorized to remove vehicles

(a) Whenever any police officer finds a vehicle in violation of any of the provisions of Code Section 40–6–202, such officer is authorized to move such vehicle or require the driver or other person in charge of the vehicle to move it to a position off the roadway.

(b) Any police officer is authorized to remove or cause to be removed to a place of safety any unattended vehicle illegally left standing upon any highway, bridge, or causeway or in any tunnel.

(c) Any police officer is authorized to remove or cause to be removed to the nearest garage or other place of safety any vehicle found upon a highway when:

(1) Report has been made that such vehicle has been stolen or taken without the consent of its owner;

(2) The person or persons in charge of such vehicle are unable to provide for its custody or removal;

(3) The person driving or in control of such vehicle is arrested for an alleged offense for which the officer is required by law to take the person arrested before a proper magistrate without unnecessary delay;

(4) Any such vehicle has been left unattended for 24 hours or more; or

(5) Such vehicle is stopped, except when traffic congestion makes movement impossible, on a controlled-access highway which is part of The Dwight D. Eisenhower System of Interstate and Defense Highways for more than eight hours, unless such vehicle constitutes a traffic hazard, in which case it may be removed immediately.

(d) Because uninsured vehicles pose a threat to the public safety and health, any law enforcement officer is authorized to remove or cause to be removed to the nearest garage or other place of safety the vehicle of a person who is charged under subsection (a) or (b) of Code Section 40–6–10 if such person admits to the law enforcement officer that there is no insurance in effect on the vehicle or if the law enforcement officer verifies that the proof of insurance provided by such person is fraudulent.

Laws 1953, Nov.-Dec. Sess., p. 556, § 91; Laws 1974, p. 633, § 1; Laws 1975, p. 1286, § 1; Laws 1985, p. 149, § 40; Laws 1987, p. 542, § 5; Laws 1990, p. 2048, § 5; Laws 2000, p. 136, § 40.

Formerly Code 1933, § 68A–1002.

Historical and Statutory Notes

The 2000 amendment substituted for reference to the "National System of Interstate and Defense Highways" reference to "The Dwight D. Eisenhower System of Interstate and Defense Highways".

In 2001, the Code Commission, in par. (c)(5), deleted a comma following "Defense Highways". See § 28–9–5.

§ 40–6–207. Liability for parking violations

(a) The owner of any motor vehicle leased to another shall not be liable for a state, county, or municipal traffic or parking violation occurring while such leased vehicle was not in the owner's possession or control, if upon notice of the violation the owner notifies the clerk of the court in which the case is pending of the name and address of the lessee of the vehicle on the date the violation occurred. If the owner fails to submit the notice, the court in which the case is heard may find the owner of the motor vehicle liable for the violation.

(b) After providing the name and address of the lessee, the owner shall not be required to attend a hearing on the offense, unless notified that the offense occurred through a mechanical failure of the vehicle which resulted from the owner's failure to maintain the vehicle.

(c) The owner of any leased vehicle shall be liable for any violation which was caused by the owner's failure to maintain the vehicle properly. The lessee claiming the violation resulted from the owner's failure to maintain the vehicle properly shall notify the clerk of the court in which the case is pending along with the owner of the vehicle of the claim within seven days after receiving notice of the violation or at least ten days prior to the date the case will be heard by the court, whichever is later.

Laws 1981, p. 1004, § 1; Laws 1990, p. 2048, § 5.

Formerly Code 1933, § 68A–1005.1.

§ 40–6–208. Acts prohibited in parking lots, parking decks, and other such facilities owned or operated by public transit authority

(a) In all parking lots, parking decks, and other such facilities owned or operated by any public transit authority or established for the exclusive purpose of providing parking for passengers of rapid rail or public transit buses, it shall be unlawful to:

(1) Stop, stand, or park a vehicle other than in marked spaces designed for that purpose;

(2) Stop, stand, or park a vehicle on any yellow curb;

(3) Stop, stand, or park a vehicle in any location which results in impeding ingress or egress to said facility or which results in impeding the free passage of any other vehicle;

(4) Leave any vehicle unattended in areas designated as "kiss-ride" or designated as "attended vehicles only";

(5) Stop, stand, or park any taxicab or other vehicle for hire, whether attended or unattended, in any area not specifically designated for such vehicles;

(6) Stop, stand, or park any vehicle for the purpose of loading or unloading passengers, except in areas specifically designated for that use, such as "kiss-ride" or "passenger drop-off" areas;

(7) Stop, stand, or park any vehicle for a period in excess of 24 hours unless such parking area is designated "overnight" or "long-term" parking;

(8) Stop, stand, or park any vehicle for any purpose other than to board the rapid rail car or public transit bus serving such parking lot; or

(9) Create or maintain any fire or flame, including fires or flames for cooking or grilling, or to fail to extinguish said fire or flame and to remove from such public transit parking facility all debris and residue associated with the creation and maintenance of said fire or flame.

(b) Any person violating subsection (a) of this Code section shall be subject to a fine levied by the municipality or, in the case of properties located outside the boundaries of a municipality, by the county in which the offense occurs. Such offense shall be cited by the issuance of a written citation which shall be left on the violator's vehicle and which shall contain, at a minimum:

(1) The nature of the violation;

(2) The amount of the fine which will be levied for such violation;

(3) That the cited individual has the right to contest the citation and be given an opportunity to be heard;

(4) The location of the court in which the cited individual must appear within five days of the date of the citation to contest same; and

(5) The location at which fines may be paid.

(c) Nothing in this Code section shall be construed to limit the enforcement of any other provision of state law which may be applicable, including, but not limited to, Part 2 of this article, the "Parking Law For Persons With Disabilities," and the uniform rules of the road.

Laws 1998, p. 890, § 3.

Part 2

Parking for Persons with Disabilities

§ 40–6–220. Short title

This part shall be known and may be cited as the "Parking Law for Persons with Disabilities."

Laws 1980, p. 1334, § 3; Laws 1990, p. 2048, § 5; Laws 1995, p. 1302, § 8.

Formerly Code 1933, § 68A–1020.

§ 40–6–221. Definitions

As used in this part, the term:

(1) "Counterfeit" means any copy of any kind of parking permit for persons with disabilities which is not authorized by and does not carry the official seal of the Department of Revenue.

(2) "Institution" means an institution for which a permit or conditional permit may be issued under Article 1 of Chapter 7 of Title 31.

(3) "Parking place for persons with disabilities" means any area on public or private property which has been designated as reserved for use of persons with disabilities as follows:

(A) By a blue metal reflective sign which is at least 12 inches in width and 18 inches in length and is erected at a height of seven feet from the bottom of the sign to its ground surface and in such manner that it will not be obscured by a vehicle parked in the space and bearing the following words: "Permit Parking Only," "Tow–Away Zone," and the international symbol for accessibility. The warnings required in this subparagraph shall be centered on the sign, printed in white, and shall occupy not less than 75 percent of the surface area of the sign. The sign required by this subparagraph shall be the official authorized sign for parking place designations for persons with disabilities in this state. In addition, parking spaces which are required by Code Section 30–3–6 shall be designated as "For Disabled Persons With Ambulatory Assistive Devices Only"; or

(B) Where the parking place is on private property, is constructed solely from concrete, was used by the public or finished prior to July 1, 1987, and which is designated by having imprinted and maintained in reflective paint upon each such place the words "Tow–Away Zone" or "Parking Only for Persons with Disabilities" or the universal symbol of accessibility, that designation shall be deemed to meet the requirements of subparagraph (A) of this paragraph until such time as that concrete lot is renovated, repaired, or remodeled, at which time a sign shall be erected which shall comply with the requirements of subparagraph (A) of this paragraph.

(4) "Permanently disabled person" means a person with disabilities whose disability or incapacity can be expected to last for more than 180 days.

(5) "Person with disabilities" means a person who:

(A) Is so ambulatorily disabled that he or she cannot walk 200 feet without stopping to rest;

(B) Cannot walk without the use of or assistance from a brace, a cane, a crutch, another person, a prosthetic device, a wheelchair, or other assistive device;

(C) Is restricted by lung disease to such an extent that his or her forced respiratory volume for one second, when measured by spirometry, is less than one liter, or when at rest, his or her arterial oxygen tension is less than 60 millimeters of mercury on room air;

(D) Uses portable oxygen;

(E) Has a cardiac condition to the extent that his or her functional limitations are classified in severity as Class III or Class IV according to standards set by the American Heart Association;

(F) Is severely limited in his or her ability to walk due to an arthritic, neurological, or orthopedic condition or complications due to pregnancy; or

(G) Is a blind individual whose central visual acuity does not exceed 20/200 in the better eye with correcting lenses or whose visual acuity, if better than 20/200, is accompanied by a limit to the field of vision in the better eye to such a degree that its widest diameter subtends an angle of no greater than 20 degrees.

(5.1) "Practitioner of the healing arts" means a person holding a license to practice medicine, podiatric medicine, or chiropractic issued pursuant to Article 2 of Chapter 34 of Title 43, Chapter 35 of Title 43, or Chapter 9 of Title 43, respectively.

(6) "Ramp" shall mean, in addition to any other specified meanings:

(A) Any ramp or curb ramp as defined in ANSI A117.1–1986 by Chapter 3 of Title 30; and

(B) Any vehicle mounted lift used by handicapped persons for the purpose of access to and from the vehicle upon which it is mounted.

(7) "Temporarily disabled person" means a person with disabilities whose disability or incapacity can be expected to last for not more than 180 days and shall include, but not be limited to, any woman who is pregnant and who presents a sworn affidavit of a medical doctor attesting to a medical need for access to parking for persons with disabilities.

Laws 1980, p. 1334, § 3; Laws 1981, p. 677, § 1; Laws 1984, p. 1263, § 1; Laws 1987, p. 1439, § 1; Laws 1988, p. 1460, § 1; Laws 1990, p. 2048, § 5; Laws 1992, p. 1394, § 1; Laws 1995, p. 1302, § 8; Laws 2000, p. 951, § 5A–2; Laws 2000, p. 1182, § 2; Laws 2004, Act 559, § 1, eff. July 1, 2004; Laws 2005, Act 68, § 18–4, eff. July 1, 2005.

Formerly Code 1933, § 68A–1021.

Historical and Statutory Notes

The 2000 amendment by Act 737 substituted in par. (1) for Department of "Public Safety" the Department of "Motor Vehicle Safety".

The 2000 amendment by Act 765 substantially rewrote this section which formerly provided:

"As used in this part, the term:

"(1) 'Counterfeit' means any copy of any kind of parking permit for persons with disabilities which is not authorized by and does not carry the official seal of the Department of Public Safety.

"(2) 'Institution' means an institution for which a permit or conditional permit may be issued under Article 1 of Chapter 7 of Title 31.

"(3) 'Parking place for persons with disabilities' means any area on public or private property which has been designated as reserved for use of handicapped persons as follows:

"(A) By a blue metal reflective sign which is at least 12 inches in width and 18 inches in length and is erected at such height or in such manner that it will not be obscured by a vehicle parked in the space and bearing the following words: 'Permit Parking Only,' 'Tow–Away Zone,' or the international symbol for accessibility. The warnings required in this subparagraph shall be centered on the sign, printed in white, and shall occupy not less than 75 percent of the surface area of the sign. The sign required by this subparagraph shall be the official authorized sign for parking place designations for persons with disabilities in this state; or

"(B) Where the parking place is on private property, is constructed solely from concrete, was used by the public or finished prior to July 1, 1987, and which is designated by having imprinted and maintained in reflective paint upon each such place the words 'Tow–Away Zone' or 'Parking Only for Persons with Disabilities' or the universal symbol of accessibility, that designation shall be deemed to meet the requirements of subparagraph (A) of this paragraph until such time as that concrete lot is renovated, repaired, or remodeled, at which time a sign shall be erected which shall comply with the requirements of subparagraph (A) of this paragraph.

"(4) 'Permanently disabled person' means a person with disabilities whose disability or incapacity can be expected to last for more than 180 days.

"(5) 'Person with disabilities' means a person who by reason of illness, injury, age, congenital malfunction, or other incapacity or disability has a significant loss or impairment of mobility.

"(6) 'Ramp' shall mean, in addition to any other specified meanings:

"(A) Any ramp or curb ramp as defined in ANSI A117.1–1986 by Chapter 3 of

Title 30; and

"(B) Any vehicle mounted lift used by handicapped persons for the purpose of

access to and from the vehicle upon which it is mounted.

"(7) 'Temporarily disabled person' means a person with disabilities whose disability or incapacity can be expected to last for not more than 180 days and shall include, but not be limited to, any woman who is pregnant and who presents a sworn affidavit of a medical doctor attesting to a medical need for access to parking for persons with disabilities."

The 2004 amendment by Act 559 added par. (5), subpar. (G).

The 2005 amendment by Act 68 in par. (1), defining "counterfeit", substituted "Department of Revenue" for "Department of Motor Vehicle Safety".

§ 40–6–222. Repealed by Laws 2006, Act 674, § 2, eff. May 1, 2006

Historical and Statutory Notes

The repealed section, relating to parking permits for persons with disabilities, was derived from Laws 1980, p. 1334, § 3; Laws 1981, p. 624, § 1; Laws 1981, p. 677, § 2; Laws 1985, p. 149, § 40; Laws 1987, p. 1464, § 2; Laws 1988, p. 1460, § 2; Laws 1990, p. 2048, § 5; Laws 1995, p. 1302, § 8; Laws 2000, p. 951, § 5A–3; Laws 2000, p. 1182, § 3; Laws 2004, Act 559, § 2; Laws 2005, Act 68, § 18–5; Laws 2005, Act 127, § 1; Code 1933, § 68A–1022. The repealing law also reserved the section designation.

For continuation of subject matter, see § 40–2–74.1.

In 2006, the Code Commission, due to irreconcilable conflicts, treated the amendment of this section by Laws 2006, Act 627, § 2, as superseded by Laws 2006, Act 674, § 2. See Butts County v. Strahan, 107 S.E. 163, 151 Ga. 417 (1921).

§ 40–6–223. Repealed by Laws 2006, Act 674, § 3, eff. May 1, 2006

Historical and Statutory Notes

The repealed section, relating to fees for handicapped parking permits, was derived from Laws 1980, p. 1334, § 3; Laws 1981, p. 677, § 3; Laws 1990, p. 2048, § 5; Laws 1995, p. 1302, § 8; Laws 2000, p. 951, § 5A–4; Laws 2005, Act 68, § 18–6; Code 1933, § 68A–1023. The repealing law also reserved the section designation.

For continuation of subject matter, see § 40–2–74.1.

§ 40–6–224. Out-of-state handicapped license plates and persons with disabilities license plates honored

State and local authorities shall honor visitors' out-of-state handicapped license plates or persons with disabilities license plates and similar special parking permits on the same basis as license plates for persons with disabilities and special parking permits issued within this state.

Laws 1980, p. 1334, § 3; Laws 1981, p. 677, § 4; Laws 1990, p. 2048, § 5; Laws 1995, p. 1302, § 8.

Formerly Code 1933, § 68A–1024.

§ 40–6–224.1. Repealed by Laws 1990, p. 2048, § 5, eff. January 1, 1991

§ 40–6–225. Parking places for persons with disabilities for the nonambulatory

Any business entity may elect to designate parking places for persons with disabilities for the nonambulatory. Such parking places for the nonambulatory shall be in addition to any parking places for persons with disabilities required by Chapter 3 of Title 30. Such parking places for the nonambulatory shall be clearly marked by a sign bearing the words "Parking for Persons with Disabilities—nonambulatory persons only." Such parking places for the nonambulatory shall be utilized only for the purpose of allowing a nonambulatory permanently disabled person to enter or exit a vehicle while in such parking place. A vehicle in a parking place for the nonambulatory shall be required to have a valid unexpired parking permit for persons with disabilities or a specially designated license plate for disabled persons authorized under Code Section 40–2–74 or 40–2–74.1. For the purposes of this Code section, the term "nonambulatory permanently disabled person" means a person who is permanently disabled as a result of the loss or loss of use of one or both legs and who is dependent upon crutches, a walker, or a wheelchair for locomotion.

Laws 1989, p. 572, § 1; Laws 1990, p. 2048, § 5; Laws 1995, p. 1302, § 8; Laws 2006, Act 674, § 4, eff. May 1, 2006; Laws 2007, Act 18, § 40, eff. May 11, 2007.

Formerly Code 1981, § 40–6–224.1.

Historical and Statutory Notes

The 2006 amendment by Act 674 substituted "persons authorized under Code Section 40–2–74 or 40–2–74.1" for "persons authorized under subsection (d) of Code Section 40–6–222".

The 2007 amendment by Act 18 was a provision contained in a correction bill.

§ 40–6–226. Penalties

(a) It shall be unlawful for any person to stop, stand, or park any vehicle in a parking place for persons with disabilities unless there is displayed on the driver's side of the dashboard or hung from the rearview mirror of the parked vehicle a valid unexpired parking permit for persons with disabilities or unless there is attached to the vehicle a specially designated license plate for disabled veterans or other disabled persons authorized under Code Section 40–2–74 or 40–2–74.1 and unless such person is the person to whom such permit or license plate was issued; the person to whom such permit or license plate was issued is a passenger in the vehicle; or such vehicle is being used for the transportation of disabled passengers on behalf of the institution to which such permit was issued.

(a.1) It shall be unlawful for any person to stop, stand, or park any vehicle in a parking place for persons with disabilities which is designated "For Persons With Disabled Ambulatory Assistive Devices Only" unless:

(1) There is displayed on the driver's side of the dashboard or hung from the rearview mirror of the parked vehicle a valid unexpired parking permit for persons with disabilities or unless there is attached to the vehicle a specially designated license plate for disabled veterans or other disabled persons authorized under Code Section 40–2–74 or 40–2–74.1; and

(2) A person with disabilities who is using a wheelchair, crutches, walker, or other ambulatory assistive device is the driver of or a passenger in such vehicle.

(b)(1) It shall be unlawful for any person to stop, stand, or park any vehicle in a parking place for persons with disabilities except for the purpose of allowing a disabled person to enter or get out of such vehicle while in such parking place. However, nothing in this paragraph shall prevent an ambulance or emergency vehicle from stopping in a parking place for persons with disabilities.

(2) It shall be unlawful for any person to stop, stand, or park any vehicle in a parking place for the nonambulatory as provided by a business pursuant to the provisions of Code Section 40–6–225 except for the purpose of allowing a nonambulatory permanently disabled person to enter or get out of such vehicle while in such parking place. However, nothing in this paragraph shall prevent an ambulance or emergency vehicle from stopping in a parking place for the nonambulatory.

(3) It shall be unlawful for any person to stop, stand, or park any vehicle in any area directly connecting with a parking place for persons with disabilities which area is clearly designed and designated for access to such parking place for persons with disabilities.

(c) It shall be unlawful for any person to obtain by fraud or counterfeit a parking permit for persons with disabilities.

(c.1) It shall be unlawful for any person to knowingly and willfully make a false or misleading statement in an application for a parking permit for persons with disabilities or in the affidavit of a practitioner of the healing arts stating that an applicant is a disabled person.

(d) It shall be unlawful for any person or institution, other than the one to whom a parking permit for persons with disabilities or specially designated license plate for the disabled person is issued, to make use of a parking permit for persons with disabilities or specially designated license plate for a disabled person unless the person to whom such permit or license plate was issued is a passenger in such vehicle. It shall be unlawful for any person to use a parking permit for persons with disabilities for any institutional vehicle other than the vehicle for which the permit has been issued. It shall be unlawful for any person to use a parking permit for persons with disabilities issued to an institution for any purpose other than to transport disabled persons.

(e) No person shall park a vehicle so as to block any entrance or exit ramp used by persons with disabilities on public or private property.

(f)(1) Any person violating subsection (c) or (c.1) of this Code section shall be guilty of a misdemeanor.

(2) Any person violating subsection (a), (a.1), (b), (d), or (e) of this Code section shall be subject to a fine of not less than $100.00 and not more than $500.00.

(g) In addition to the penalties provided for in subsection (f) of this Code section, any vehicle which is illegally parked in a parking place for persons with disabilities which is marked by a sign bearing the words "Tow–Away Zone" as described in paragraph (3) of Code Section 40–6–221 on public or private property may be towed away or caused to be towed away by a proper law enforcement agency or the official security agency of said property at the expense of the owner of the vehicle or, if the vehicle is leased or rented, at the expense of the person responsible for payment on the lease or rental agreement.

(h) A property owner who is required to provide parking places for persons with disabilities shall designate each such place with a sign meeting the applicable requirements specified therefor by paragraph (3) of Code Section 40–6–221 and upon failure so to designate each such parking place for persons with disabilities shall be subject to a fine of $150.00 for each place which is not so designated; provided, however, that the fine will be waived if the required designation is made within 14 days from the date of citation. If that property owner fails or refuses to designate properly the parking places for persons with disabilities within such 14 days, the property owner shall, on the fifteenth day after receiving the citation, be subject to the $150.00 fine for each place and an additional $5.00 fine for each place for each day that the owner fails to comply with provisions of this subsection until the places are properly designated. All fines assessed under this subsection shall be paid into the treasury of the city or county issuing the citation against the owner.

Laws 1980, p. 1334, § 3; Laws 1981, p. 677, § 4; Laws 1984, p. 1263, § 2; Laws 1985, p. 558, § 1; Laws 1987, p. 1439, §§ 2, 3; Laws 1989, p. 572, § 2; Laws 1990, p. 8, § 40; Laws 1990, p. 2048, § 5; Laws 1993, p. 707, § 1; Laws 1994, p. 97, § 40; Laws 1995, p. 1302, § 8; Laws 2000, p. 1182, § 4; Laws 2005, Act 127, § 2, eff. July 1, 2005; Laws 2006, Act 674, § 5, eff. May 1, 2006.

Formerly Code 1933, § 68A–1024; Code 1981, § 40–6–225.

Historical and Statutory Notes

The 2000 amendment substantially rewrote this section which formerly provided:

"(a) It shall be unlawful for any person to stop, stand, or park any vehicle in a parking place for persons with disabilities unless there is displayed on the dashboard or hung from the rearview mirror of the parked vehicle a valid unexpired parking permit for persons with disabilities or unless there is attached to the vehicle a specially designated license plate for disabled veterans or other disabled persons authorized under subsection (d) of Code Section 40–6–222.

"(b)(1) It shall be unlawful for any person to stop, stand, or park any vehicle in a parking place for persons with disabilities except for the purpose of allowing a disabled person to enter or get out of such vehicle while in such parking place. However, nothing in this paragraph shall prevent an ambulance or emergency vehicle from stopping in a parking place for persons with disabilities.

"(2) It shall be unlawful for any person to stop, stand, or park any vehicle in a parking place for the nonambulatory as provided by a business pursuant to the provisions of Code Section 40–6–225 except for the purpose of allowing a nonambulatory permanently disabled person to enter or get out of such vehicle while in such parking place. However, nothing in this paragraph shall prevent an ambulance or emergency vehicle from stopping in a parking place for the nonambulatory.

"(3) It shall be unlawful for any person to stop, stand, or park any vehicle in any area directly connecting with a parking place for persons with disabilities which area is clearly designed and designated for access to such parking place for persons with disabilities.

" (c) It shall be unlawful for any person to obtain by fraud or counterfeit a parking permit for persons with disabilities.

"(d) It shall be unlawful for any person or institution, other than the one to whom a parking permit for persons with disabilities or specially designated license plate for the disabled person is issued, to make use of a parking permit for persons with disabilities or specially designated license plate for a disabled person. It shall be unlawful for any person to use a parking permit for persons with disabilities for any institutional vehicle other than the vehicle for which the permit has been issued.

"(e) No person shall park a vehicle so as to block any entrance or exit ramp used by persons with disabilities on public or private property.

"(f)(1) Any person violating subsection (c) of this Code section shall be guilty of a misdemeanor.

"(2) Any person violating subsection (a), (b), (d), or (e) of this Code section shall be subject to a fine of not less than $100.00 and not more than $500.00.

"(g) In addition to the penalties provided for in subsection (f) of this Code section, any vehicle which is illegally parked in a parking place for persons with disabilities which is marked by a sign bearing the words 'Tow–Away Zone' as described in paragraph (3) of Code Section 40–6–221 on public or private property may be towed away or caused to be towed away by a proper law enforcement agency or the official security agency of said property at the expense of the owner of the vehicle or, if the vehicle is leased or rented, at the expense of the person responsible for payment on the lease or rental agreement.

"(h) A property owner who is required to provide parking places for persons with disabilities shall designate each such place with a sign meeting the applicable requirements specified therefor by paragraph (3) of Code Section 40–6–221 and upon failure so to designate each such parking place for persons with disabilities shall be subject to a fine of $150.00 for each place which is not so designated; provided, however, that the fine will be waived if the required designation is made within 14 days from the date of citation. If that property owner fails or refuses to designate properly the parking places for persons with disabilities within such 14 days, the property owner shall, on the fifteenth day after receiving the citation, be subject to the $150.00 fine for each place and an additional $5.00 fine for each place for each day that the owner fails to comply with provisions of this subsection until the places are properly designated. All fines assessed under this subsection shall be paid into the treasury of the city or county issuing the citation against the owner."

The 2005 amendment by Act 127 rewrote subsecs. (a) and (d), which had read:

"(a) It shall be unlawful for any person to stop, stand, or park any vehicle in a parking place for persons with disabilities unless there is displayed on the driver's side of the dashboard or hung from the rearview mirror of the parked vehicle a valid unexpired parking permit for persons with disabilities or unless there is attached to the vehicle a specially designated license plate for disabled veterans or other disabled persons authorized under subsection (d) of Code Section 40–6–222."

"(d) It shall be unlawful for any person or institution, other than the one to whom a parking permit for persons with disabilities or specially designated license plate for the disabled person is issued, to make use of a parking permit for persons with disabilities or specially designated license plate for a disabled person. It shall be unlawful for any person to use a parking permit for persons with disabilities for any institutional vehicle other than the vehicle for which the permit has been issued."

The 2006 amendment by Act 674 substituted "persons authorized under Code Section 40–2–74 or 40–2–74.1" for "persons authorized under subsection (d) of Code Section 40-6-222" in subsec. (a) and par. (a.1)(1).

§ 40–6–227. Applicability and enforcement

The provisions of this part are applicable to both public and private property; and all law enforcement officers of this state and its political subdivisions are expressly authorized to enforce the provisions of this part on private property as well as on public property.

Laws 1984, p. 1263, § 3; Laws 1990, p. 2048, § 5; Laws 1995, p. 1302, § 8.

Formerly Code 1981, § 40–6–226.

§ 40–6–228. Appointment of persons with disabilities to enforce Parking Law for Persons with Disabilities

(a) Any county or municipal law enforcement agency of the state which is empowered to enforce the provisions of this part may, in its discretion, appoint any person who is a citizen of the United States, is of good moral character, and has not previously been convicted of a felony to enforce the provisions of Code Section 40–6–226 within the county or municipality in which the appointing law enforcement agency exercises jurisdiction. Each person appointed pursuant to this Code section shall take and subscribe an oath of office as prescribed by the appointing authority. Any person appointed and sworn pursuant to this subsection shall be authorized to enforce the provisions of this part in the same manner as any law enforcement officer of the state or any county or municipality of the state subject to the limitations provided in subsections (b) and (c) of this Code section.

(b) No person appointed pursuant to subsection (a) of this Code section shall be deemed a peace officer under the laws of this state or:

(1) Be deemed an employee of or receive any compensation from the state, county, municipality, or appointing law enforcement agency, but the appointing law enforcement agency shall provide any person so appointed with a uniform consisting of a pith helmet and a windbreaker jacket which shall remain the property of the appointing law enforcement agency;

(2) Be required to complete any training or be certified pursuant to the requirements of Chapter 8 of Title 35;

(3) Have the power or duty to enforce any other traffic or criminal laws of the state, county, or municipality;

(4) Have the power to possess and carry firearms and other weapons for the purpose of enforcing the parking laws for persons with disabilities; provided, however, that a person who possesses a valid weapons carry license issued under Code Section 16–11–129 and who carries such weapon in a manner permitted under Code Section 16–11–126 shall not be in violation of this paragraph; or

(5) Be entitled to any indemnification from the state, county, or municipality for any injury or property damage sustained by such person as a result of attempting to enforce the parking laws of the state for persons with disabilities.

(c) Neither the state nor any county, municipality, or other political subdivision of the state or any department, agency, board, or officer of the state or any county, municipality, or political subdivision of the state shall be liable or accountable for or on account of any act or omission of any person appointed pursuant to this Code section in connection with such person's enforcement of the provisions of Code Section 40–6–226. No person appointed pursuant to this Code section shall be liable on account of any act or omission in connection with such person's enforcement of the provisions of Code Section 40–6–226.

(d) It shall be unlawful for any person willfully to obstruct, resist, impede, or interfere with any person appointed pursuant to this Code section in connection with such person's enforcement of Code Section 40–6–226 or to retaliate or discriminate in any manner against such person as a reprisal for any act or omission of such person. Any violation of this subsection shall be punishable as a misdemeanor.

Laws 1988, p. 389, § 1; Laws 1990, p. 2048, § 5; Laws 1994, p. 504, § 1; Laws 1995, p. 1302, § 8; Laws 1997, p. 521, § 1; Laws 2010, Act 643, § 2–16, eff. June 4, 2010; Laws 2010, Act 482, § 1, eff. July 1, 2010.

Formerly Code 1981, § 40–6–227.

Historical and Statutory Notes

The 2010 amendment by Act 482, in subsec. (a), deleted ", and is a person with disabilities as defined in paragraph (5) of Code Section 40–6–221" after "felony" and made nominal changes; and in subsec. (c), added "No person appointed pursuant to this Code section shall be liable on account of any act or omission in connection with such person's enforcement of the provisions of Code Section 40–6–226." as the second sentence.

The 2010 amendment by Act 643, in par. (b)(4), substituted "valid weapons carry license issued" for "valid license to carry a pistol or revolver issued".

Laws 2010, Act 643, § 3–1, provides:

"This Act shall become effective upon its approval by the Governor or upon its becoming law without such approval and shall apply to all offenses committed on and after such date. The enactment of this Act shall not affect any prosecutions for acts occurring before the effective date of this Act and shall not act as an abatement of any such prosecutions."

Article 11

Miscellaneous Provisions

§ 40–6–240. Limitations on backing

(a) A driver shall not back a vehicle unless such movement can be made with safety and without interfering with other traffic.

(b) A driver of a vehicle shall not back a vehicle upon any shoulder or roadway of any controlled-access highway.

Laws 1953, Nov.-Dec. Sess., p. 556, § 94; Laws 1974, p. 633, § 1; Laws 1990, p. 2048, § 5.

Formerly Code 1933, § 68A–1102.

§ 40–6–241. Driver to use due care; proper use of radio or mobile telephone not violate section

A driver shall exercise due care in operating a motor vehicle on the highways of this state and shall not engage in any actions which shall distract such driver from the safe operation of such vehicle, provided that, except as prohibited by Code Section 40–6–241.1, the proper use of a radio, citizens band radio, mobile telephone, or amateur or ham radio shall not be a violation of this Code section.

Laws 1974, p. 633, § 1; Laws 1990, p. 2048, § 5; Laws 2010, Act 676, § 2, eff. July 1, 2010; Laws 2010, Act 677, § 3, eff. July 1, 2010.

Formerly Code 1933, § 68A–1103.

Historical and Statutory Notes

The 2010 amendment by Act 676 inserted ", except as prohibited by Code Section 40–6–241.1," after "provided that", deleted "or" before "mobile telephone", and inserted ", or amateur or ham radio" after "mobile telephone".

Laws 2010, Act 676, § 4, provides:

"This Act shall become effective on July 1, 2010, and shall apply to offenses committed on or after such date."

The 2010 amendment by Act 677 made the same changes as those made by Laws 2010, Act 676.

Laws 2010, Act 677, § 6, provides:

"This Act shall become effective on July 1, 2010, and shall apply to offenses committed on or after such date."

§ 40–6–241.1. Wireless telecommunications device use prohibited

Section as added by Laws 2010, Act 676, § 3. See also, section as added by Laws 2010, Act 677, § 4.

(a) As used in the Code section, the term:

(1) "Engage in a wireless communication" means talking, writing, sending, or reading a text-based communication, or listening on a wireless telecommunications device.

(2) "Wireless telecommunications device" means a cellular telephone, a text-messaging device, a personal digital assistant, a stand alone computer, or any other substantially similar wireless device that is used to initiate or receive a wireless communication with another person. It does not include citizens band radios, citizens band radio hybrids, commercial two-way radio communication devices, subscription-based emergency communications, in-vehicle security, navigation, and remote diagnostics systems or amateur or ham radio devices.

(b) Except in a driver emergency and as provided in subsection (c) of this Code section, no person who has an instruction permit or a Class D license and is under 18 years of age shall operate a motor vehicle on any public road or highway of this state while engaging in a wireless communication using a wireless telecommunications device.

(c) The provisions of this Code section shall not apply to a person who has an instruction permit or a Class D license and is under 18 years of age who engages in a wireless communication using a wireless telecommunications device to do any of the following:

(1) Report a traffic accident, medical emergency, or serious road hazard;

(2) Report a situation in which the person believes his or her personal safety is in jeopardy;

(3) Report or avert the perpetration or potential perpetration of a criminal act against the driver or another person; or

(4) Engage in a wireless communication while the motor vehicle is lawfully parked.

(d)(1) Any conviction for a violation of the provisions of this Code section shall be punishable by a fine of $150.00. The provisions of Chapter 11 of Title 17 and any other provision of law to the contrary notwithstanding, the costs of such prosecution shall not be taxed nor shall any additional penalty, fee, or surcharge to a fine for such offense be assessed against a person for conviction thereof. The court imposing such fine shall forward a record of the disposition of the case of unlawfully operating a motor vehicle while using a wireless telecommunications device to the Department of Driver Services.

(2) If the operator of the moving motor vehicle is involved in an accident at the time of a violation of this Code section, then the fine shall be equal to double the amount of the fine imposed in paragraph (1) of this subsection. The law enforcement officer investigating the accident shall indicate on the written accident form whether such operator was engaging in a wireless communication at the time of the accident.

(e) Each violation of this Code section shall constitute a separate offense.

Laws 2010, Act 676, § 3, eff. July 1, 2010.

Historical and Statutory Notes

Laws 2010, Act 676, § 4, provides:

"This Act shall become effective July 1, 2010, and shall apply to offenses committed on or after such date."

§ 40–6–241.1. Wireless telecommunications device use prohibited

Section as added by Laws 2010, Act 677, § 4. See also, section as added by Laws 2010, Act 676, § 3.

(a) As used in the Code section, the term "wireless telecommunications device" means a cellular telephone, a text messaging device, a personal digital assistant, a stand alone computer, or any other substantially similar wireless device that is used to initiate or receive a wireless communication with another person. It does not include citizens band radios, citizens band radio hybrids, commercial two-way radio communication devices, subscription based emergency communications, in-vehicle security, navigation devices, and remote diagnostics systems, or amateur or ham radio devices.

(b) No person who is 18 years of age or older or who has a Class C license shall operate a motor vehicle on any public road or highway of this state while using a wireless telecommunications device to write, send, or read any text based communication, including but not limited to a text message, instant message, e-mail, or Internet data.

(c) The provisions of this Code section shall not apply to:

(1) A person reporting a traffic accident, medical emergency, fire, serious road hazard, or a situation in which the person reasonably believes a person's health or safety is in immediate jeopardy;

(2) A person reporting the perpetration or potential perpetration of a crime;

(3) A public utility employee or contractor acting within the scope of his or her employment when responding to a public utility emergency;

(4) A law enforcement officer, firefighter, emergency medical services personnel, ambulance driver, or other similarly employed public safety first responder during the performance of his or her official duties; or

(5) A person engaging in wireless communication while in a motor vehicle which is lawfully parked.

(d) Any conviction for a violation of the provisions of this Code section shall be a misdemeanor punishable by a fine of $150.00. The provisions of Chapter 11 of Title 17 and any other provision of law to the contrary notwithstanding, the costs of such prosecution shall not be taxed nor shall any additional penalty, fee, or surcharge to a fine for such offense be assessed against a person for conviction thereof. The court imposing such fine shall forward a record of the disposition to the Department of Driver Services. Any violation of this Code section shall constitute a separate offense.

Laws 2010, Act 677, § 4, eff. July 1, 2010.

Historical and Statutory Notes

Laws 2010, Act 677, § 6, provides:

"This Act shall become effective July 1, 2010, and shall apply to offenses committed on or after such date."

§ 40–6–242. Obstruction of driver's view or control of vehicle

(a) No person shall drive a vehicle when it is so loaded or when there are in the front seat such a number of persons, exceeding three, as to obstruct the view of the driver to the front or sides of the vehicle or as to interfere with the driver's control over the driving mechanism of the vehicle.

(b) No passenger in a vehicle shall ride in such position or commit any act as to interfere with the driver's view ahead or to the sides or to interfere with his control over the driving mechanism of the vehicle.

Laws 1953, Nov.-Dec. Sess., p. 556, § 96; Laws 1974, p. 633, § 1; Laws 1990, p. 2048, § 5.

Formerly Code 1933, § 68A–1104.

§ 40–6–243. Opening and closing vehicle doors

No person shall open the door of a motor vehicle on the side available to moving traffic unless and until it is reasonably safe to do so and can be done without interfering with the movement of other traffic, nor shall any person leave a door open on the side of a vehicle available to moving traffic for a period of time longer than necessary to load or unload passengers.

Laws 1967, p. 542, § 5; Laws 1974, p. 633, § 1; Laws 1990, p. 2048, § 5.

Formerly Code 1933, § 68A–1105.

§ 40–6–244. Riding in house trailers

No driver of a motor vehicle shall allow a person or persons to occupy a towed house trailer while it is being towed by a motor vehicle upon a public highway.

Laws 1974, p. 633, § 1; Laws 1975, p. 1202, § 1; Laws 1990, p. 2048, § 5.

Formerly Code 1933, § 68A–1106.

§ 40–6–245. Driving on mountain highways

The driver of a vehicle traveling through a defile or canyon or on a mountain highway shall hold such vehicle under control and as near the right-hand edge of the highway as reasonably possible and, except when driving entirely to the right of the center of the roadway, shall give audible warning with the horn of such vehicle upon approaching any curve where the view is obstructed within a distance of 200 feet along the highway.

Laws 1953, Nov.-Dec. Sess., p. 556, § 97; Laws 1974, p. 633, § 1; Laws 1978, p. 1483, § 3; Laws 1985, p. 149, § 40; Laws 1990, p. 2048, § 5.

Formerly Code 1933, § 68A–1107.

§ 40–6–246. Coasting prohibited

(a) The driver of any motor vehicle when traveling upon a down grade shall not coast with the gears or transmission of such vehicle in neutral.

(b) The driver of a truck or bus when traveling upon a down grade shall not coast with the clutch disengaged.

Laws 1953, Nov.-Dec. Sess., p. 556, § 98; Laws 1974, p. 633, § 1; Laws 1990, p. 2048, § 5.

Formerly Code 1933, § 68A–1108.

§ 40–6–247. Following emergency vehicles prohibited

The driver of any vehicle other than one on official business shall not follow any fire apparatus traveling in response to a fire alarm or any other emergency vehicle closer than 200 feet and shall not park such vehicle within 500 feet of any fire apparatus stopped in answer to a fire alarm.

Laws 1953, Nov.-Dec. Sess., p. 556, § 99; Laws 1974, p. 633, § 1; Laws 1990, p. 2048, § 5.

Formerly Code 1933, § 68A–1109.

§ 40–6–248. Crossing fire hose

No vehicle shall be driven over any unprotected hose of a fire department when laid down on any street, private road, or driveway to be used at any fire or alarm of fire, without consent of the fire department official in command.

Laws 1953, Nov.-Dec. Sess., p. 556, § 100; Laws 1974, p. 633, § 1; Laws 1990, p. 2048, § 5.

Formerly Code 1933, § 68A–1110.

§ 40–6–248.1. Securing loads on vehicles

(a) As used in this Code section, the term "litter" has the meaning provided by paragraph (1) of Code Section 16–7–42.

(a.1) No vehicle shall be driven or moved on any public road unless such vehicle is constructed or loaded or covered so as to prevent any of its load from dropping, escaping, or shifting in such a manner as to:

(1) Create a safety hazard; or

(2) Deposit litter on public or private property while such vehicle is on a public road. However, this Code section shall not prohibit the necessary spreading of any substance in public road maintenance or construction operations.

(b) No person shall operate or load for operation, on any public road, any vehicle with any load unless such load and any covering thereon is securely fastened so as to prevent said covering or load from:

(1) Becoming loose, detached, or in any manner becoming a hazard to other users of the public road; or

(2) Depositing litter on public or private property while such vehicle is on a public road.

(c) Nothing in this Code section nor any regulations based thereon shall conflict with federal, Georgia Public Service Commission, or Georgia Board of Public Safety regulations applying to the securing of loads on motor vehicles.

(d) The provisions of paragraph (2) of subsection (a) and paragraph (2) of subsection (b) of this Code section and regulations based thereon shall not apply to organic debris that escapes during the transportation of silage from field or farm to storage and storage to feedlot or during the transportation of agricultural or farm products or silvicultural products from farm or forest to a processing plant or point of sale or use.

Laws 1973, p. 947, § 1; Laws 1981, p. 705, § 1; Laws 2002, p. 1270, § 1; Laws 2006, Act 538, § 3–9, eff. July 1, 2006.

Formerly Code 1933, § 95A–955; Code 1981, § 32–6–21.

Historical and Statutory Notes

This section, added as § 32–6–21, was renumbered as § 40–6–248.1 and amended by Laws 2006, Act 538, § 3–9. Prior to being amended, the section had read:

"(a) No vehicle shall be driven or moved on any public road unless such vehicle is constructed or loaded or covered so as to prevent any of its load from dropping, escaping, or shifting in such a manner as to create a safety hazard. However, this Code section shall not prohibit the necessary spreading of any substance in public road maintenance or construction operations.

"(b) No person shall operate or load for operation, on any public road, any vehicle with any load unless such load and any covering thereon is securely fastened so as to prevent said covering or load from becoming loose, detached, or in any manner becoming a hazard to other users of the public road.

"(c) Nothing in this Code section nor any regulations based thereon shall conflict with federal, Georgia Public Service Commission, or Georgia Board of Public Safety regulations applying to the securing of loads on motor vehicles.

"(d) The provisions of subsection (b) of this Code section and regulations based thereon shall not apply to vehicles carrying silage from field to storage and storage to feedlot or vehicles or equipment carrying unginned cotton."

Laws 2006, Act 538, § 5–1, provides:

"This Act shall become effective upon its approval by the Governor [April 21, 2006] or upon its becoming law without such approval for purposes of adopting local ordinances to become effective on or after July 1, 2006; and for all other purposes, this Act shall become effective on July 1, 2006."

§ 40–6–249. Littering; vehicles with unsecured loads; violations

Any person littering a highway in violation of Part 2 of Article 2 of Chapter 7 of Title 16 or driving, moving, or loading for operation a vehicle in violation of Code Section 40–6–248.1 shall be guilty of a misdemeanor and, upon conviction thereof, shall be punished as provided in Code Section 16–7–43.

Laws 1953, Nov.-Dec. Sess., p. 556, § 101; Laws 1974, p. 633, § 1; Laws 1990, p. 2048, § 5; Laws 2006, Act 538, § 3–13, eff. July 1, 2006.

Formerly Code 1933, § 68A–1111.

Historical and Statutory Notes

The 2006 amendment by Act 538 rewrote the section which had read:

"A person littering a highway in violation of Part 2 of Article 2 of Chapter 7 of Title 16, the 'Litter Control Law,' shall be guilty of a misdemeanor and, upon conviction thereof, shall be punished as provided in Code Section 16–7–43."

Laws 2006, Act 538, § 5–1, provides:

"This Act shall become effective upon its approval by the Governor [April 21, 2006] or upon its becoming law without such approval for purposes of adopting local ordinances to become effective on or after July 1, 2006; and for all other purposes, this Act shall become effective on July 1, 2006."

§ 40–6–250. Wearing headsets or headphones prohibited

No person shall operate a motor vehicle while wearing a headset or headphone which would impair such person's ability to hear, nor shall any person while operating a motor vehicle wear any device which impairs such person's vision; provided, however, that a person may wear a headset or headphone for communication purposes.

Laws 1974, p. 1137, § 1; Laws 1978, p. 1601, § 1; Laws 1989, p. 1399, § 1; Laws 1990, p. 2048, § 5; Laws 1995, p. 759, § 1; Laws 2010, Act 677, § 5, eff. July 1, 2010.

Formerly Code 1933, § 68A–1112.

Historical and Statutory Notes

The 2010 amendment by Act 677 deleted "only while operating a motorcycle. This Code section shall not apply to hearing aids or instruments for the improvement of defective human hearing, eyeglasses, or sunglasses. This Code section shall not apply to any law enforcement officer or firefighter equipped with any communications device necessary in the performance of such person's duties." after "communication purposes."

Laws 2010, Act 677, § 6, provides:

"This Act shall become effective on July 1, 2010, and shall apply to offenses committed on or after such date."

§ 40–6–251. Intentional operation of motor vehicles to create danger to persons or property; "laying drags"

(a) No driver of any motor vehicle shall operate the vehicle upon the public streets, highways, public or private driveways, airport runways, or parking lots in such a manner as to create a danger to persons or property by intentionally and unnecessarily causing the vehicle to move in a zigzag or circular course or to gyrate or spin around, except to avoid a collision or injury or damage.

(b) The offenses described in this Code section shall be sufficiently identified on any traffic ticket, warrant, accusation, or indictment when referred to as "laying drags."

(c) This Code section shall not apply to drivers operating vehicles in or on any raceway, drag strip, or similar place customarily and lawfully used for such purposes.

(d) Any person violating subsection (a) of this Code section shall be guilty of a misdemeanor.

Laws 1970, p. 549, §§ 1–4; Laws 1990, p. 2048, § 5.

§ 40–6–252. Parking or repeatedly driving motor vehicle through parking area located on privately owned property after request not to do so

(a) No person shall, after having been requested not to do so by a law enforcement officer or an authorized agent of the owner, park or stand an occupied or unoccupied motor vehicle in or repeatedly drive a motor vehicle through or within a parking area located on privately owned property and provided by a merchant, group of merchants, or shopping center or other facility for customers if:

(1) The parking area is identified by at least one sign as specified in this paragraph, and if the parking area contains more than 150 parking spaces then by at least one such sign at each entrance to the parking area, each such sign containing the following information in easy-to-read printing:

(A) Notice of this Code section;

(B) Identification of the property which is reserved for customers' use only;

(C) Identification of the merchant, group of merchants, or shopping center or other similar facility providing the parking area; and

(D) Warning that violators will be prosecuted; and

(2) The motor vehicle is parked, is standing, or is being operated other than for the purpose of:

(A) Transporting some person to or from the interior of the place of business of a merchant identified by the sign or signs in the parking area or to or from the interior of the shopping center or other facility so identified;

(B) Making use of a telephone, vending machine, automatic teller machine, or other similar facility located in the parking area;

(C) Meeting the requirements of a situation in which it has unexpectedly become impossible or impractical for the motor vehicle to continue to travel on the public roads; or

(D) Carrying out an activity for which express permission has been given by the owner of the parking area or an authorized representative of the owner.

(b) Any person who violates subsection (a) of this Code section shall be guilty of a misdemeanor and, upon conviction thereof, shall be punished by a fine:

(1) Not to exceed $50.00 for the first such offense;

(2) Not to exceed $100.00 for the second such offense; and

(3) Not to exceed $150.00 for the third or subsequent such offense.

(c) The governing authority of any municipal corporation by ordinance may adopt by reference the provisions of subsection (a) of this Code section without publishing or posting in full the provisions thereof. Any person violating any such ordinance shall be subject to a monetary fine:

(1) Not to exceed $50.00 for the first such violation;

(2) Not to exceed $100.00 for the second such violation; and

(3) Not to exceed $150.00 for the third or subsequent such violation.

Laws 1990, p. 2048, § 5; Laws 1992, p. 2785, § 24; Laws 1993, p. 91, § 40.

§ 40–6–253. Consuming alcoholic beverage or possessing open alcoholic beverage container while in passenger area of motor vehicle

(a) As used in this Code section, the term:

(1) "Alcoholic beverage" means:

(A) Beer, ale, porter, stout, and other similar fermented beverages, including sake or similar products, of any name or description containing one-half of 1 percent or more of alcohol by volume, brewed or produced from malt, wholly or in part, or from any substitute therefor;

(B) Wine of not less than one-half of 1 percent of alcohol by volume; or

(C) Distilled spirits which is that substance known as ethyl alcohol, ethanol, or spirits of wine in any form, including all dilutions and mixtures thereof from whatever source or by whatever process produced.

(2) "Open alcoholic beverage container" means any bottle, can, or other receptacle that:

(A) Contains any amount of alcoholic beverage; and

(B)(i) Is open or has a broken seal; or

(ii) The contents of which are partially removed.

A bottle of wine that has been resealed pursuant to Code Section 3–6–4 shall not constitute an open alcoholic beverage container for purposes of this Code section.

(3) "Passenger area" means the area designed to seat the driver and passengers while a motor vehicle is in operation and any area that is readily accessible to the driver or a passenger while in his or her seating position; provided, however, that such term does not include any locked glove compartment or, in a passenger car not equipped with a trunk, any area behind the rearmost upright seat or not normally occupied by the driver or passengers.

(b)(1) A person shall not:

(A) Consume any alcoholic beverage; or

(B) Possess any open alcoholic beverage container

in the passenger area of any motor vehicle which is on the roadway or shoulder of any public highway.

(2) The provisions of paragraph (1) of this subsection shall not apply to any passenger in the passenger area of a motor vehicle designed, maintained, or used primarily for the transportation of persons for compensation or in the living quarters of a motor home or house trailer.

(3) Only a person who consumes an alcoholic beverage or possesses an open alcoholic beverage container in violation of this Code section shall be charged with such offense; provided, however, that an operator of a motor vehicle who is alone in the passenger area of such motor vehicle shall be deemed to be in possession of any open alcoholic beverage container in such passenger area.

(c) Any person who violates this Code section is subject to a fine not to exceed $200.00.

Laws 1991, p. 1587, § 2; Laws 2001, p. 208, § 1-4; Laws 2008, Act 726, § 2, eff. July 1, 2008.

Historical and Statutory Notes

The 2001 amendment rewrote this section which as enacted provided:

"(a) As used in this Code section, 'open container' means any container which is immediately capable of being consumed from or the seal of which has been broken.

"(b) No person shall possess an open container of any alcoholic beverage while operating a vehicle in this state. For the purposes of this Code section, an open container shall be considered to be in the possession of the operator of a vehicle if the container is not in the possession of a passenger and is not located in a locked glove compartment, locked trunk, or other locked nonpassenger area of the vehicle.

"(c) Any person who violates this Code section is subject to a fine not to exceed $200.00.

"(d) A county or municipal corporation ordinance which imposes more stringent restrictions on the possession of alcoholic beverages in vehicles than those imposed by this Code section shall not be preempted by this Code section."

The 2008 amendment by Act 726, in subsec. (a), par. (2), added a sentence to the end of the paragraph relating to resealed bottles of wine.

§ 40-6-253.1. Marking of vehicles transporting medical waste, infectious substance, or etiologic agents

(a) As used in this Code section, the terms "infectious substance" and "regulated medical waste" have the same meaning as given to those terms under the federal Hazardous Materials Regulations published in Title 49 of the Code of Federal Regulations as those regulations currently exist or may in the future be amended. The terms "etiologic agent" and "infectious substance" are synonymous.

(b) The transportation of infectious substances and regulated medical waste, including but not limited to the marking of packages and marking or placarding of vehicles with appropriate warnings, shall comply with the requirements of the federal Hazardous Material Regulations published in Title 49 of the Code of Federal Regulations as those regulations currently exist or may in the future be amended and with compatible regulations adopted or promulgated by the commissioner of public safety.

(c) Nurses, physicians, and other health care professionals may utilize all applicable exceptions contained in federal regulations and in the regulations of the Department of Public Safety when transporting infectious substances.

(d) Violation of the provisions of this Code section shall constitute a misdemeanor.

Laws 1991, p. 1058, § 1; Laws 1992, p. 982, § 1; Laws 2003, Act 200, § 11, eff. Oct. 1, 2003; Laws 2005, Act 68, § 18-7, eff. July 1, 2005.

Historical and Statutory Notes

The 2003 amendment by Act 200 rewrote the section which had read:

"(a) As used in this Code section, the term 'etiologic agent' means any tissue, body fluid, or any other biological material which has the potential to transmit illness or disease or other harm upon contact, ingestion, or inhalation.

"(b) Except as provided in subsection (c) of this Code section, any vehicle while transporting any etiologic agent or any biomedical waste as such term is defined in Code Section 12-8-22 in this state shall be clearly marked on both sides and on the back with a sign or placard bearing the internationally recognized symbol designated for use in this state by the Environmental Protection Division of the Department of Natural Resources denoting biohazardous material, not less than 12 inches in height and red in color on a white background, and the words 'BIOHAZARDOUS MATERIAL' in capital block letters not less than two inches in height and red in color on a white background.

"(c) Any nurse who under the orders of a physician transports in accordance with the containment procedures established in the rules of the Department of Natural Resources for transportation of biomedical products or waste less than 100cc of any body fluid shall be exempt from the placarding requirements of subsection (b) of this Code section.

"(d) Violation of the provisions of this Code section shall constitute a misdemeanor."

Laws 2003, Act 200, § 15 provides:

"This Act shall become effective on October 1, 2003."

The 2005 amendment by Act 68 in subsec. (b) substituted "the commissioner of public safety" for "the commissioner of motor vehicle safety" following "regulations adopted or promulgated by"; and in subsec. (c) substituted "Department of Public Safety" for "Department of Motor Vehicle Safety".

§ 40-6-254. Placing load on or in vehicle which is not adequately secured prohibited

No person shall operate any motor vehicle with a load on or in such vehicle unless the load on or in such vehicle is adequately secured to prevent the dropping or shifting of such load onto the roadway in such a manner as to create a safety hazard. Any person who operates a vehicle in violation of this Code section shall be guilty of a misdemeanor.

Laws 1992, p. 1967, § 2; Laws 2002, p. 1270, § 2.

Historical and Statutory Notes

The 2002 amendment added at the end of the first sentence "in such a manner as to create a safety hazard."

§ 40-6-255. Driving off without payment or charge having been made for gasoline dispensed into vehicle

(a) No person shall drive a motor vehicle so as to cause it to leave the premises of an establishment at which gasoline offered for retail sale was dispensed into the fuel tank of such motor vehicle unless due payment or authorized charge for the gasoline so dispensed has been made.

(b) Any person who violates subsection (a) of this Code section shall be guilty of a misdemeanor and, upon conviction thereof, shall be punished by a fine not to exceed $100.00 or by confinement in the county or other jail, county correctional institution, or such other places as counties may provide for maintenance of county inmates for a term not to exceed 60 days, or both.

Laws 1998, p. 1658, § 2.

Article 12

Accidents

§ 40-6-270. Duty in accidents involving personal injury to or death of person or damage to vehicle

(a) The driver of any vehicle involved in an accident resulting in injury to or the death of any person or in damage to a vehicle which is driven or attended by any person shall immediately stop such vehicle at the scene of the accident or shall stop as close thereto as possible and forthwith return to the scene of the accident and shall:

(1) Give his or her name and address and the registration number of the vehicle he or she is driving;

(2) Upon request and if it is available, exhibit his or her operator's license to the person struck or the driver or occupant of or person attending any vehicle collided with;

(3) Render to any person injured in such accident reasonable assistance, including the transporting, or the making of arrangements for the transporting, of such person to a physician, surgeon, or hospital for medical or surgical treatment if it is apparent that such treatment is necessary or if such transporting is requested by the injured person; and

(4) Where a person injured in such accident is unconscious, appears deceased, or is otherwise unable to communicate, make every reasonable effort to ensure that emergency medical services and local law enforcement are contacted for the purpose of reporting the accident and making a request for assistance.

The driver shall in every event remain at the scene of the accident until fulfilling the requirements of this subsection. Every such stop shall be made without obstructing traffic more than is necessary.

(b) If such accident is the proximate cause of death or a serious injury, any person knowingly failing to stop and comply with the requirements of subsection (a) of this Code section shall be guilty of a felony and, upon conviction thereof, shall be punished by imprisonment for not less than one nor more than five years.

(c)(1) If such accident is the proximate cause of an injury other than a serious injury or if such accident resulted in damage to a vehicle which is driven or attended by any person, any person knowingly failing to stop or comply with the requirements of this Code section shall be guilty of a misdemeanor and:

(A) Upon conviction shall be fined not less than $300.00 nor more than $1,000.00, which fine shall not be subject to suspension, stay, or probation, or imprisoned for up to 12 months, or both;

(B) Upon the second conviction within a five-year period of time, as measured from the dates of previous arrests for which convictions were obtained to the date of the current arrest for which a conviction is obtained, shall be fined not less than $600.00 nor more than $1,000.00, which fine shall not be subject to suspension, stay, or probation, or imprisoned for up to 12 months, or both; and for purposes of this subparagraph, previous pleas of nolo contendere accepted within such five-year period shall constitute convictions; and

(C) Upon the third or subsequent conviction within a five-year period of time, as measured from the dates of previous arrests for which convictions were obtained to the date of the current arrest for which a conviction is obtained, shall be fined $1,000.00, which fine shall not be subject to suspension, stay, or probation, or imprisoned for up to 12 months, or both; and for purposes of this subparagraph, previous pleas of nolo contendere accepted within such five-year period shall constitute convictions.

(2) For the purpose of imposing a sentence under this subsection, a plea of nolo contendere shall constitute a conviction.

(3) If the payment of the fine required under this subsection will impose an economic hardship on the defendant, the judge, at his sole discretion, may order the defendant to pay such fine in installments and such order may be enforced through a contempt proceeding or a revocation of any probation otherwise authorized by this Code section.

(d) Notwithstanding the limits set forth in any municipal charter, any municipal court of any municipality shall be authorized to impose the punishments provided for in this Code section upon a conviction of violating this Code section or upon conviction of violating any ordinance adopting the provisions of this Code section.

Laws 1953, Nov.-Dec. Sess., p. 556, §§ 40, 41; Laws 1985, p. 758, § 16; Laws 1987, p. 3, § 40; Laws 1988, p. 1499, § 1; Laws 1988, p. 1893, § 6; Laws 1989, p. 14, § 40; Laws 1990, p. 8, § 40; Laws 1990, p. 2048, § 5; Laws 1991, p. 1608, § 2.1; Laws 2008, Act 793, § 1, eff. July 1, 2008.

Historical and Statutory Notes

The 2008 amendment by Act 793, in subsec. (a), made gender neutral changes throughout the subsection, and added par. (4) relating to the contacting of emergency services for injured persons.

Laws 2008, Act 793, § 6, provides:

"This Act shall become effective on July 1, 2008, and shall apply to all offenses committed on or after such date."

§ 40–6–271. Duty upon striking unattended vehicle

(a) The driver of any vehicle which collides with any vehicle which is unattended shall immediately stop and shall then and there either locate and notify the operator or owner of such vehicle of the name and address of the driver and owner of the vehicle striking the unattended vehicle or shall leave in a conspicuous place on the vehicle struck a written notice giving the name and address of the driver and the owner of the vehicle doing the striking.

(b) Any person who fails to comply with the requirements of subsection (a) of this Code section shall be guilty of a misdemeanor.

Laws 1953, Nov.-Dec. Sess., p. 556, § 43; Laws 1980, p. 1059, § 1; Laws 1990, p. 2048, § 5.

Formerly Code 1981, § 40–6–272.

§ 40–6–272. Duty upon striking fixtures upon highway

The driver of any vehicle involved in an accident resulting only in damage to a fixture legally upon or adjacent to a highway shall take reasonable steps to locate and notify the owner or person in charge of such property of such fact and of his name and address and of the registration number of the vehicle he is driving and shall, upon request and if available, exhibit his operator's license.

Laws 1953, Nov.-Dec. Sess., p. 556, § 44; Laws 1990, p. 2048, § 5.

Formerly Code 1981, § 40–6–273.

§ 40–6–273. Duty to make immediate reports of accidents

The driver of a vehicle involved in an accident resulting in injury to or death of any person or property damage to an apparent extent of $500.00 or more shall immediately, by the quickest means of communication, give notice of such accident to the local police department if such accident occurs within a municipality. If such accident occurs outside a municipality, such notice shall be given to the office of the county sheriff or to the nearest office of the state patrol.

Laws 1953, Nov.-Dec. Sess., p. 556, § 45; Laws 1978, p. 1494, § 1; Laws 1990, p. 2048, § 5; Laws 1994, p. 97, § 40; Laws 1994, p. 363, § 1.

Formerly Code 1981, § 40–6–274.

§ 40–6–273.1. Law enforcement officer at scene of accident to instruct drivers to provide certain information to other parties

The law enforcement officer at the scene of an accident required to be reported in accordance with the provisions of Code Section 40–6–273 shall instruct the driver of each motor vehicle involved in the accident to report the following to all other parties suffering injury or property damage as an apparent result of the accident:

(1) The name and address of the owner and the driver of the motor vehicle;

(2) The license number of the motor vehicle; and

(3) The name of the liability insurance carrier for the motor vehicle or the fact that such driver has a certificate of self-insurance issued pursuant to Code Section 33–34–5.1.

Laws 1994, p. 831, § 1; Laws 2000, p. 1246, § 17.

Historical and Statutory Notes

The 2000 amendment changed the statutory reference at the end of par. (3).

§ 40–6–274. No duty to stop or make immediate report of certain accidents

Any other provision of this article or any other law to the contrary notwithstanding, the driver of any vehicle involved in a traffic accident in which there is no personal injury or in which no second party and no property of a second party is involved shall not have the duty to stop or immediately report such accident, and no such driver shall be prosecuted for his failure to stop or immediately to report such accident. This Code section shall not abrogate or affect a driver's duty to file any written report which may be required by the local law enforcement agency.

Laws 1972, p. 819, § 1; Laws 1990, p. 2048, § 5; Laws 1994, p. 97, § 40.

Formerly Code 1981, § 40–6–275.

§ 40–6–275. Duty to remove vehicles involved in traffic accidents on expressways and multilane highways of state

(a) Any other provision of this article or any other law to the contrary notwithstanding, motor vehicles involved in traffic accidents and the drivers of such motor vehicles shall be subject to the provisions of this Code section.

(b) This Code section shall apply to motor vehicle traffic accidents which occur on the public roads of this state as defined in paragraph (24) of Code Section 32–1–3. Any violation of this Code section shall be punishable as a misdemeanor pursuant to Code Section 40–6–1.

(c) When a motor vehicle traffic accident occurs with no apparent serious personal injury or death, it shall be the duty of the drivers of the motor vehicles involved in such traffic accident, or any other occupant of any such motor vehicle who possesses a valid driver's license, to remove said vehicles from the immediate confines of the roadway into a safe refuge on the shoulder, emergency lane, or median or to a place otherwise removed from the roadway whenever such moving of a vehicle can be done safely and the vehicle is capable of being normally and safely driven, does not require towing, and can be operated under its own power in its customary manner without further damage or hazard to itself, to the traffic elements, or to the roadway. The driver of any such motor vehicle may request any person who possesses a valid driver's license to remove any such motor vehicle as provided in this Code section, and any such person so requested shall be authorized to comply with such request.

(d) The driver or any other person who has removed a motor vehicle from the main traveled way of the road as provided in subsection (c) of this Code section before the arrival of a police officer shall not be considered liable or at fault regarding the cause of the accident solely by reason of moving the vehicle pursuant to this Code section.

(e) This Code section shall not abrogate or affect a driver's duty to file any written report which may be required by a local law enforcement agency, but compliance with the requirements of this Code section shall not allow a driver to be prosecuted for his or her failure to stop and immediately report a traffic accident.

(f) This Code section shall not abrogate or affect a driver's duty to stop and give information in accordance with law, nor shall it relieve a police officer of his or her duty to render a report in accordance with law.

(g) Employees of the Department of Transportation, in the exercise of the management, control, and maintenance of the state highways, may require and assist in the removal from the main traveled way of roads on the state highway system of all vehicles incapacitated from any cause other than having been involved in a motor vehicle accident and of all vehicles incapacitated as a result of motor vehicle traffic accidents and of debris caused thereby when such motor vehicle accidents occur with no apparent serious personal injury or death, where such move can be accomplished safely by the drivers of the vehicles involved or with the assistance of a towing or recovery vehicle and will result in the improved safety or convenience of travel upon the road. However, a vehicle incapacitated as a result of a motor vehicle traffic accident with apparent serious personal injury or death may not be moved until the enforcement officer has made the necessary measurements and diagrams required for the initial accident investigation.

Laws 1974, p. 969, § 1; Laws 1977, p. 742, §§ 1, 2; Laws 1990, p. 2048, § 5; Laws 1993, p. 370, § 2; Laws 1994, p. 97, § 40; Laws 1999, p. 904, § 2; Laws 2004, Act 615, § 1, eff. July 1, 2004.

Formerly Code 1981, § 40–6–276.

Historical and Statutory Notes

The 2004 amendment by Act 615 rewrote subsec. (b) which had read:

"(b) This Code section shall apply to motor vehicle traffic accidents which occur on the expressways and multilane highways of this state."

§ 40–6–276. Driver of wrecker truck to remove parts and glass from scene of wreck

(a) The driver of each wrecker truck towing away any vehicle from the scene of a wreck shall also take away all parts belonging to the vehicle which he is towing away, or, if they consist of small parts or broken glass, he shall clear the streets of said small parts or glass, unless the driver is ordered not to do so by the investigating police officer due to circumstances at the scene of the accident.

(b) Any person violating subsection (a) of this Code section shall be guilty of a misdemeanor and, upon conviction thereof, shall be punished by a fine not to exceed $100.00.

Laws 1970, p. 445, §§ 1, 2; Laws 1982, p. 3, § 40; Laws 1990, p. 2048, § 5.

Formerly Code 1981, § 40–6–277.

§ 40–6–277. Sheriffs to report upon deaths caused by accidents

Every sheriff and chief executive officer of a law enforcement agency other than a sheriff shall, on or before the tenth day of each month, report in writing to the Department of Transportation the death of any person within their jurisdiction during the preceding calendar month as the result of a traffic accident known to them, giving the time and place of the accident and the circumstances relating thereto, in the manner specified by the commissioner of transportation.

Laws 1953, Nov.-Dec. Sess., p. 556, § 46; Laws 1990, p. 2048, § 5; Laws 2000, p. 951, § 5A–5; Laws 2003, Act 200, § 12, eff. Oct. 1, 2003; Laws 2005, Act 68, § 18–8, eff. July 1, 2005.

Formerly Code 1981, § 40–6–278.

Historical and Statutory Notes

The 2003 amendment by Act 200 inserted "and chief executive officer of a law enforcement agency other than a sheriff" and ", in the manner specified by the commissioner of motor vehicle safety", substituted "their jurisdiction" for "his or her jurisdiction", and substituted "known to them" for "known to him or her".

Laws 2003, Act 200, § 15 provides:

"This Act shall become effective on October 1, 2003."

The 2005 amendment by Act 68 substituted "Department of Transportation" for "Department of Motor Vehicle Safety" and "commissioner of transportation" for "commissioner of motor vehicle safety".

§ 40–6–278. Uniform reports and procedures

The commissioner of transportation shall prescribe, by rule, uniform motor vehicle accident reports and reporting procedures which shall be used by all police officers, whether state, county, or municipal. The rules shall be adopted in accordance with Chapter 13 of Title 50, the "Georgia Administrative Procedure Act." The rules may require one type of report and reporting procedure for motor vehicle accidents in which property damage alone is involved and another type of report and reporting procedure for motor vehicle accidents involving personal injury or death. The commissioner may, by rule, require additional investigation or reports in case of serious bodily injury or death.

Laws 1973, p. 443, § 1; Laws 1990, p. 2048, § 5; Laws 2000, p. 951, § 5A–6; Laws 2005, Act 68, § 18–9, eff. July 1, 2005.

Formerly Code 1981, § 40–6–279.

Historical and Statutory Notes

The 2000 amendment provided gender neutral language and substituted for Department of "Public Safety" the Department of "Motor Vehicle Safety".

The 2005 amendment by Act 68 in the first sentence substituted "commissioner of transportation" for "commissioner of motor vehicle safety".

§ 40–6–279. Renumbered as § 40–6–278 by Laws 1990, p. 2048, § 5

Article 13

Special Provisions for Certain Vehicles

Part 1

Bicycles and Play Vehicles

§ 40–6–290. Effect of regulations

The provisions of this part applicable to bicycles shall apply whenever a bicycle is operated upon a highway or upon any path set aside for the exclusive use of bicycles, subject to those exceptions stated in this part.

Laws 1974, p. 633, § 1; Laws 1990, p. 2048, § 5.

Formerly Code 1933, § 68A–1201.

§ 40–6–291. Traffic laws apply to persons riding bicycles

The provisions of this chapter that apply to vehicles, but not exclusively to motor vehicles, shall apply to bicycles, except that the penalties prescribed in subsection (b) of Code Section 40–6–390, subsection (c) of Code Section 40–6–391, and subsection (a) of Code Section 40–6–393 shall not apply to persons riding bicycles.

Laws 1973, p. 471, § 3; Laws 1974, p. 633, § 1; Laws 1978, p. 1483, § 4; Laws 1988, p. 13, § 40; Laws 1990, p. 2048, § 5.

Formerly Code 1933, § 68A–1202.

§ 40–6–292. Riding on bicycles

(a) A person propelling a bicycle shall not ride other than upon or astride a permanent and regular seat attached thereto and shall allow no person to ride upon the handlebars.

(b) No bicycle shall be used to carry more persons at one time than the number for which it is designed and equipped.

(c) No person shall transport a child under the age of one year as a passenger on a bicycle on a highway, roadway, bicycle path, or sidewalk; provided, however, that a child under the age of one year may be transported on a bicycle trailer or in an infant sling so long as such child is seated in the bicycle trailer or carried in an infant sling according to the bicycle trailer's or infant sling's manufacturer's instructions, and the bicycle trailer is properly affixed to the bicycle according to the bicycle trailer's manufacturer's instructions or the infant sling is properly worn by the rider of the bicycle according to the infant sling's manufacturer's instructions and such child transported in a bicycle trailer or infant sling is wearing a bicycle helmet as required under paragraph (1) of subsection (e) of Code Section 40–6–296.

(d) No child between the ages of one year and four years shall ride as a passenger on a bicycle or bicycle trailer or be transported in an infant sling unless the child is securely seated in a child passenger bicycle seat, bicycle trailer, or infant sling according to the child passenger bicycle seat's, bicycle trailer's, or infant sling's manufacturer's instructions and the child passenger seat or bicycle trailer is properly affixed to the bicycle according to the child passenger bicycle seat's or bicycle trailer's manufacturer's instructions or the infant sling is worn according to the infant sling's manufacturer's instructions.

(e) Violation of subsections (c) and (d) of this Code section shall not constitute negligence per se nor contributory negligence per se or be considered evidence of negligence or liability.

(f) No person under the age of 16 years failing to comply with subsections (c) and (d) of this Code section may be fined or imprisoned.

Laws 1973, p. 471, § 8; Laws 1974, p. 633, § 1; Laws 1990, p. 2048, § 5; Laws 1993, p. 518, § 2.

Formerly Code 1933, § 68A–1203.

§ 40–6–293. Clinging to vehicles

No person riding upon any bicycle, coaster, roller skates, sled, or toy vehicle shall attach the same or himself to any vehicle upon a roadway.

Laws 1973, p. 471, § 7; Laws 1974, p. 633, § 1; Laws 1990, p. 2048, § 5.

Formerly Code 1933, § 68A–1204.

§ 40–6–294. Riding on roadways and bicycle paths

(a) Every person operating a bicycle upon a roadway shall ride as near to the right side of the roadway as practicable, except when turning left or avoiding hazards to safe cycling, when the lane is too narrow to share safely with a motor vehicle, when traveling at the same speed as traffic, or while exercising due care when passing a standing vehicle or one proceeding in the same direction; provided, however, that every person operating a bicycle away from the right side of the roadway shall exercise reasonable care and shall give due consideration to the other applicable rules of the road. As used in this subsection, the term "hazards to safe cycling" includes, but is not limited to, surface debris, rough pavement, drain grates which are parallel to the side of the roadway, parked or stopped vehicles, potentially opening car doors, or any other objects which threaten the safety of a person operating a bicycle.

(b) Persons riding bicycles upon a roadway shall not ride more than two abreast except on paths or parts of roadways set aside for the exclusive use of bicycles.

(c) Whenever a usable path has been provided adjacent to a roadway and designated for the exclusive use of bicycle riders, then the appropriate governing authority may require that bicycle riders use such path and not use those sections of the roadway so specified by such local governing authority. The governing authority may be petitioned to remove restrictions upon demonstration that the path has become inadequate due to capacity, maintenance, or other causes.

(d) Paths subject to the provisions of subsection (c) of this Code section shall at a minimum be required to meet accepted guidelines, recommendations, and criteria with respect to planning, design, operation, and maintenance as set forth by the American Association of State Highway and Transportation Officials, and such paths shall provide accessibility to destinations equivalent to the use of the roadway.

(e) Electric assisted bicycles as defined in Code Section 40–1–1 may be operated on bicycle paths.

Laws 1973, p. 471, § 6; Laws 1974, p. 633, § 1; Laws 1990, p. 2048, § 5; Laws 1992, p. 1546, §§ 1, 2; Laws 1995, p. 271, § 1; Laws 1996, p. 236, § 2.

Formerly Code 1933, § 68A–1205.

§ 40–6–295. Carrying articles

No person operating a bicycle shall carry any package, bundle, or other article which prevents him from keeping at least one hand upon the handlebars.

Laws 1973, p. 471, § 9; Laws 1974, p. 633, § 1; Laws 1990, p. 2048, § 5.

Formerly Code 1933, § 68A–1206.

§ 40–6–296. Lights and other equipment on bicycles; helmets by persons under 16 years of age

(a) Every bicycle when in use at nighttime shall be equipped with a light on the front which shall emit a white light visible from a distance of 300 feet to the front and with a red reflector on the rear of a type approved by the Department of Public Safety which shall be visible from a distance of 300 feet to the rear when directly in front of lawful upper beams of headlights on a motor vehicle. A light emitting a red light visible from a distance of 300 feet to the rear may be used in addition to the red reflector.

(b) Every bicycle sold or operated shall be equipped with a brake which will enable the operator to make the braked wheels skid on dry, level pavement.

(c) No bicycle shall be equipped or operated while equipped with a set of handlebars so raised that the operator must elevate his hands above his shoulders in order to grasp the normal steering grip area.

(d) No bicycle shall be equipped, modified, or altered in such a way as to cause the pedal in its lowermost position to be more than 12 inches above the ground, nor shall any bicycle be operated if so equipped.

(e)(1) No person under the age of 16 years shall operate or be a passenger on a bicycle on a highway, bicycle path, or sidewalk under the jurisdiction or control of this state or any local political subdivision thereof without wearing a bicycle helmet.

(2) For the purposes of this subsection, the term "bicycle helmet" means a piece of protective headgear which meets or exceeds the impact standards for bicycle helmets set by the American National Standards Institute (ANSI) or the Snell Memorial Foundation.

(3) For the purposes of this subsection, a person shall be deemed to wear a helmet only if a helmet of good fit is fastened securely upon the head with the straps of the helmet.

(4) No bicycle without an accompanying protective bicycle helmet shall be rented or leased to or for the use of any person under the age of 16 years unless that person is in possession of a bicycle helmet at the time of the rental or lease.

(5) Violation of any provision of this subsection shall not constitute negligence per se nor contributory negligence per se or be considered evidence of negligence or liability.

(6) No person under the age of 16 failing to comply with any provision of this subsection may be fined or imprisoned.

Laws 1973, p. 471, § 5; Laws 1974, p. 633, § 1; Laws 1990, p. 2048, § 5; Laws 1993, p. 518, § 3; Laws 2000, p. 951, § 5A–7; Laws 2005, Act 68, § 18–10, eff. July 1, 2005.

Formerly Code 1933, § 68A–1207.

Historical and Statutory Notes

The 2000 amendment in the first sentence of subsec. (a) substituted for Department of "Public Safety" the Department of "Motor Vehicle Safety".

The 2005 amendment by Act 68 in subsec. (a) substituted "the Department of Public Safety" for "the Department of Motor Vehicle" following "of a type approved by".

§ 40–6–297. Reflectors on pedals

(a) It shall be unlawful for any person to sell a new bicycle or a pedal for use on a bicycle unless the pedals on such bicycle or such pedals are equipped with reflectors of a type approved by the Department of Public Safety. The reflector on each pedal shall be so designed and situated as to be visible from the front and rear of the bicycle during darkness from a distance of 200 feet. The commissioner of public safety is authorized to promulgate rules and regulations and establish standards for such reflectors.

(b) This Code section shall not apply to any bicycle purchased prior to July 1, 1972, by a retailer for the purpose of resale.

Laws 1972, p. 547, §§ 1, 2; Laws 1973, p. 471, § 4; Laws 1974, p. 633, § 1; Laws 1990, p. 2048, § 5.

Formerly Code 1933, § 68A–1208.

§ 40–6–298. Violations

(a) It is a misdemeanor for any person to do any act forbidden or fail to perform any act required in this part.

(b) The parent of any child and the guardian of any ward shall not authorize or knowingly permit such child or ward to violate any of the provisions of this part.

Laws 1974, p. 633, § 1; Laws 1990, p. 2048, § 5.

Formerly Code 1933, § 68A–1201.

§ 40–6–299. Promulgation of rules and regulations

The Board of Public Safety is authorized to promulgate rules and regulations to carry this part into effect and is authorized to establish regulations for any additional safety equipment or standards it shall require for bicycles.

Laws 1973, p. 471, § 12; Laws 1974, p. 633, § 1; Laws 1990, p. 2048, § 5.

Formerly Code 1933, § 68A–1209.

Part 2

Motorcycles

§ 40–6–310. Traffic laws apply to persons operating motorcycles

Every person operating a motorcycle shall be granted all of the rights and shall be subject to all of the duties applicable to the driver of any other vehicle under this chapter except as to special regulations in this part and except as to those provisions of this chapter which by their nature can have no application.

Laws 1974, p. 633, § 1; Laws 1990, p. 2048, § 5.

Formerly Code 1933, § 68A–1301.

§ 40–6–311. Riding on motorcycles

(a) A person operating a motorcycle shall ride only upon the permanent and regular seat attached thereto; and such operator shall not carry any other person nor shall any other person ride on a motorcycle unless such motorcycle is designed to carry more than one person, in which event a passenger may ride upon the permanent and regular seat if designed for two persons or upon another seat firmly attached to the motorcycle at the rear or side of the operator.

(b) A person shall ride upon a motorcycle only while sitting astride the seat, facing forward, with one leg on either side of the motorcycle.

(c) No person shall operate a motorcycle while carrying any package, bundle, or other article which prevents him from keeping both hands on the handlebars.

(d) No operator shall carry any person, nor shall any person ride, in a position that will interfere with the operation or control of the motorcycle or the view of the operator.

(e) No person shall operate or ride upon a motorcycle unless he shall wear some type of footwear in addition to or other than socks.

Laws 1953, Nov.-Dec. Sess., p. 556, § 95; Laws 1962, p. 716, § 1; Laws 1969, p. 732, § 1; Laws 1972, p. 475, § 1; Laws 1974, p. 633, § 1; Laws 1985, p. 149, § 40; Laws 1990, p. 2048, § 5.

Formerly Code 1933, § 68A–1302.

§ 40–6–312. Operating motorcycles on roadways laned for traffic

(a) All motorcycles are entitled to full use of a lane, and no motor vehicle shall be driven in such a manner as to deprive any motorcycle of the full use of a lane. This subsection shall not apply to motorcycles operated two abreast in a single lane.

(b) The operator of a motorcycle shall not overtake and pass in the same lane occupied by the vehicle being overtaken.

(c) No person shall operate a motorcycle between lanes of traffic or between adjacent lines or rows of vehicles.

(d) Motorcycles shall not be operated more than two abreast in a single lane.

(e) A person operating a motorcycle shall at all times keep his headlights and taillights illuminated.

(f) Subsections (b) and (c) of this Code section shall not apply to police officers in the performance of their official duties.

Laws 1974, p. 633, § 1; Laws 1990, p. 2048, § 5.

Formerly Code 1933, § 68A–1303.

§ 40–6–313. Clinging to other vehicles

No person riding upon a motorcycle shall attach himself or the motorcycle to any other vehicle on a roadway.

Laws 1974, p. 633, § 1; Laws 1990, p. 2048, § 5.

Formerly Code 1933, § 68A–1304.

§ 40–6–314. Footrests and handlebars

(a) Any motorcycle carrying a passenger, other than in a sidecar or enclosed cab, shall be equipped with footrests for such passenger.

(b) No person shall operate any motorcycle with handlebars more than 15 inches in height above that portion of the seat occupied by the operator or with a backrest more commonly known as a sissy bar that is designed in such a way as to create a sharp point at its apex.

Laws 1969, p. 732, § 2; Laws 1972, p. 475, § 2; Laws 1974, p. 633, § 1; Laws 1990, p. 2048, § 5.

Formerly Code 1933, § 68A–1305.

§ 40–6–315. Equipment for motorcycle riders

(a) No person shall operate or ride upon a motorcycle unless he or she is wearing protective headgear which complies with standards established by the commissioner of public safety.

(b) No person shall operate or ride upon a motorcycle if the motorcycle is not equipped with a windshield unless he or she is wearing an eye-protective device of a type approved by the commissioner of public safety.

(c) This Code section shall not apply to persons riding within an enclosed cab or motorized cart. This Code section shall not apply to a person operating a three–wheeled motorcycle used only for agricultural purposes.

(d) The commissioner of public safety is authorized to approve or disapprove protective headgear and eye–protective devices required in this Code section and to issue and enforce regulations establishing standards and specifications for the approval thereof. The commissioner shall publish in print or electronically lists of all protective headgear and eye-protective devices by name and type which have been approved.

Laws 1969, p. 732, § 3; Laws 1974, p. 633, § 1; Laws 1984, p. 1329, § 2; Laws 1990, p. 2048, § 5; Laws 2000, p. 951, § 5A–8; Laws 2005, Act 68, § 18–11, eff. July 1, 2005; Laws 2010, Act 615, § 10, eff. June 3, 2010.

Formerly Code 1933, § 68A–1306.

Historical and Statutory Notes

The 2000 amendment substituted for Department or Board of "Public Safety" the commissioner or Department of "Motor Vehicle Safety".

The 2005 amendment by Act 68 in subsecs. (a), (b) and (d) substituted "commissioner of public safety" for "commissioner of motor vehicle safety", and at the end of subsec. (d) deleted "by it" following "which have been approved".

The 2010 amendment by Act 615, in subsec. (d), inserted "in print or electronically" following "publish" throughout the subsection.

§ 40–6–316. Rules and regulations

The commissioner of public safety is authorized to promulgate rules and regulations to carry this part into effect and to establish regulations for safety standards for the operation of motorcycles.

Laws 1974, p. 633, § 1; Laws 1985, p. 149, § 40; Laws 1990, p. 2048, § 5; Laws 2000, p. 951, § 5A–8; Laws 2005, Act 68, § 18–12, eff. July 1, 2005.

Formerly Code 1933, § 68A–1306.

Historical and Statutory Notes

The 2000 amendment substituted for Board of "Public Safety" the commissioner of "Motor Vehicle Safety".

In 2000, the Code Commission substituted "motor vehicle" for "motor vehicles". See § 28–9–5.

The 2005 amendment by Act 68 substituted "commissioner of public safety" for "commissioner of motor vehicle safety".

Part 2A

Personal Assistive Mobility Devices

§ 40–6–320. Operation of vehicle on highway, roadway, or sidewalk; direction of travel

(a) Electric personal assistive mobility devices may be operated on highways and on sidewalks where a 48 inch clear path is maintained for access for persons with disabilities, provided that any person operating such a device shall have the same rights and duties as prescribed for pedestrians in Article 5 of this chapter and except as otherwise provided in this part.

(b) No person shall operate any electric personal assistive mobility device on the roadway of any highway unless:

(1) The maximum speed limit of the roadway is 35 miles per hour or less; or

(2) The roadway has a separately striped bicycle lane and the device is operated within the bicycle lane.

(c) When traveling on any roadway of a highway, a person operating an electric personal assistive mobility device shall travel in the same direction authorized for motor vehicle traffic on such roadway.

Laws 2003, Act 56, § 4, eff. May 29, 2003.

§ 40–6–321. Obedience to laws and local ordinances; exercise of due care

Any person operating an electric personal assistive mobility device on a sidewalk or roadway shall comply with the requirements of this part or any local ordinance regulating the use of such devices pursuant to Code Section 40–6–371 and shall exercise due care to avoid colliding with, and shall yield the right of way to, persons traveling on foot.

Laws 2003, Act 56, § 4, eff. May 29, 2003.

§ 40–6–322. Maximum speed of operation

No person shall operate an electric personal assistive mobility device at a speed greater than seven miles per hour when traveling on any sidewalk or 15 miles per hour elsewhere; provided, however, that a county or municipal governing authority or the commissioner of transportation may further restrict the speed of such devices in locations where pedestrian traffic is congested and there is a significant speed differential between pedestrians and operators of such devices.

Laws 2003, Act 56, § 4, eff. May 29, 2003.

§ 40–6–323. Parking regulations and restrictions

(a) An electric personal assistive mobility device may be parked on a sidewalk unless otherwise prohibited or restricted by an official traffic control device or local ordinance; provided, however, that in no case shall an electric personal assistive mobility device be parked on any sidewalk in such a manner as to prevent the movement of a wheelchair.

(b) An electric personal assistive mobility device shall not be parked on any roadway in such a manner as to prevent the movement of a legally parked motor vehicle.

(c) Except as otherwise provided in this Code section, any person operating an electric personal assistive mobility device shall be subject to the same parking restrictions as provided for motor vehicles under Part 1 of Article 10 of this chapter. All violations of parking restrictions shall be deemed the responsibility of the owner of such device; and, for purposes of parking restrictions, the owner shall be deemed to be in control of the device at the time of a parking violation involving such device, and no evidence of actual control by such owner need be proven as an element of the offense.

Laws 2003, Act 56, § 4, eff. May 29, 2003.

§ 40–6–324. Hazardous materials, transport prohibited

No person shall carry or transport any hazardous materials on an electric personal assistive mobility device. Oxygen carried for personal medical reasons shall not be deemed a hazardous material for purposes of this Code section.

Laws 2003, Act 56, § 4, eff. May 29, 2003.

§ 40–6–325. Use of reflectors; minimum age of operation

(a) Any electric personal assistive mobility device, when operated on any highway or sidewalk, shall be equipped with front, rear, and side reflectors which shall be visible from a distance of 300 feet when directly in front of lawful upper beams of headlights on a motor vehicle; a system that when employed will enable the operator to bring the device to a controlled stop; and, if the device is operated between one-half hour after sunset and one-half hour before sunrise, a lamp emitting a white light which, while the device is in motion, illuminates the area in front of the operator for a distance of 300 feet.

(b) No person under the age of 16 years shall operate an electric assistive personal mobility device on any highway; provided, however, that a person under the age of 16 years may operate an electric assistive personal mobility device on any sidewalk if such person is wearing protective headgear which meets or exceeds the impact standards for bicycle helmets required by Code Section 40–6–296.

Laws 2003, Act 56, § 4, eff. May 29, 2003.

§ 40–6–326. Operating under the influence of drugs or alcohol, violation and penalties

Any person who is under the influence of any intoxicating liquor or any drug to a degree which renders him or her a hazard shall not operate any electric personal assistive mobility device on any highway or sidewalk. Violation of this Code section shall be a misdemeanor, punishable upon conviction by a fine not to exceed $500.00.

Laws 2003, Act 56, § 4, eff. May 29, 2003.

§ 40–6–327. Violations of part; penalties

Any person who violates any provision of this part other than Code Section 40–6–326 shall not be guilty of a criminal offense or a moving traffic violation for purposes of Code Section 40–5–57 but shall be subject to a civil penalty not to exceed $500.00.

Laws 2003, Act 56, § 4, eff. May 29, 2003.

Part 3

Motorized Carts

§ 40–6–330. Daylight operation

Motorized carts may be operated on streets only during daylight hours unless they comply with the equipment regulations promulgated by the commissioner of public safety.

Laws 1973, p. 598, § 2; Laws 1974, p. 633, § 1; Laws 1990, p. 2048, § 5; Laws 2000, p. 951, § 5A–9; Laws 2002, p. 506, § 5; Laws 2002, p. 512, § 10; Laws 2005, Act 68, § 18–13, eff. July 1, 2005.

Formerly Code 1933, § 68A–1401.

Historical and Statutory Notes

The 2000 amendment substituted for Department of "Public Safety" the Department of "Motor Vehicle Safety".

The 2002 amendment by Act 500 inserted "and low-speed vehicles".

The 2002 amendment by Act 501 reinstated the text as it read prior to the other 2002 amendment.

In 2002, the Code Commission, due to irreconcilable conflicts, treated the amendment of this section by Laws 2002, p. 506, § 5 [Act 500], as superseded by Laws 2002, p. 512, § 10 [Act 501]. See *Butts County v. Strahan*, 107 S.E. 163, 151 Ga. 417 (1921).

The 2005 amendment by Act 68 substituted "commissioner of public safety" for "commissioner of motor vehicle safety".

§ 40–6–331. Authority to operate on streets granted by ordinance

(a) A local governing authority may, by ordinance, designate certain public streets or portions thereof that are under its regulation and control for the combined use of motorized carts and regular vehicular traffic or the use of motorized carts and no other types of motor vehicles and establish the conditions under which motorized carts may be operated upon such streets or portions thereof, including without limitation the conditions under which a person may operate motorized carts on such designated streets or portions thereof without a driver's license.

(b) Such ordinances may establish operating standards but shall not require motorized carts to meet any requirements of general law as to registration, inspection, or licensing; provided, however, that a local governing authority may, by ordinance, require the local registration and licensing of such carts operated within its boundaries for a fee not to exceed $15.00, the license to remain permanently with such cart unless such cart is sold or the license is destroyed. The provisions of this subsection and the authority granted by this subsection shall not apply to motorized carts owned by golf courses, country clubs, or other such organized entities which own such carts and make them available to members or the public on a rental basis, provided that such motorized carts are used only on the premises of such golf courses, country clubs, or other such organized entities.

(c) Ordinances establishing operating standards shall not be effective unless appropriate signs giving notice are posted along the public streets affected.

(d)(1) Motorized carts may cross streets and highways that are part of the state highway system only at crossings or intersections designated for that purpose by the Department of Transportation.

(2) Motorized carts may cross streets and highways that are part of a municipal street system or county road system and used by other types of motor vehicles only at crossings or intersections designated for that purpose by the local governing authority having jurisdiction over such system.

Laws 1973, p. 598, § 2; Laws 1974, p. 633, § 1; Laws 1990, p. 1241, § 2; Laws 1990, p. 2048, § 5; Laws 2002, p. 506, § 6; Laws 2002, p. 512, § 11; Laws 2004, Act 442, § 3, eff. April 22, 2004.

Formerly Code 1933, § 68A–1402.

Historical and Statutory Notes

The 2002 amendment by Act 500 inserted "and low-speed vehicles" and references thereto throughout the section.

The 2002 amendment by Act 501 reinstated the text as it read prior to the other 2002 amendment.

In 2002, the Code Commission, due to irreconcilable conflicts, treated the amendment of this section by Laws 2002, p. 506, § 6 [Act 500], as superseded by Laws 2002, p. 512, § 11 [Act 501]. See *Butts County v. Strahan*, 107 S.E. 163, 151 Ga. 417 (1921).

The 2004 amendment by Act 442 rewrote the section which had read:

"(a) A local governing authority may, by ordinance, designate certain public streets or portions thereof for the combined use of motorized carts and regular vehicular traffic and establish the conditions under which motorized carts may be operated upon such streets or portions thereof.

"(b) Such ordinances may establish operating standards but shall not require motorized carts to meet any requirements of general law as to registration, inspection, or licensing; provided, however, that a local governing authority may, by ordinance, require the registration and licensing of such carts operated within its boundaries for a fee not to exceed $ 15.00, the license to remain permanently with such cart unless such cart is sold or the license is destroyed. The provisions of this subsection and the authority granted by this subsection shall not apply to motorized carts owned by golf courses, country clubs, or other such organized entities which own such carts and make them available to members or the public on a rental basis.

"(c) Ordinances establishing operating standards shall not be effective unless appropriate signs giving notice are posted along the public streets affected.

"(d) Motorized carts may cross streets and highways under the jurisdiction of the Department of Transportation only at crossings or intersections designated for that purpose by the department."

Part 4

Mopeds

§ 40–6–350. Traffic laws apply to operation of mopeds

Every person operating a moped shall be granted all the rights and shall be subject to all the duties applicable to the driver of any other vehicle under this chapter except as to special regulations in this part and except as to those provisions of this chapter which by their nature can have no application. However, the operator of a moped shall not be required to comply with subsection (e) of Code Section 40–6–312, relating to headlights and taillights, or subsection (b) of Code Section 40–6–315, relating to windshields and eye-protective devices.

Laws 1978, p. 2241, § 5; Laws 1990, p. 2048, § 5.

Formerly Code 1933, § 68A–1112.

§ 40–6–351. Persons under 15 prohibited from operating moped or electric assisted bicycle; license or permit required for operation of moped

No person under 15 years of age shall operate a moped or an electric assisted bicycle upon the public roads and highways of this state. No person shall operate a moped upon the public roads and highways of this state unless he or she shall have in his or her possession a valid driver's license, instruction permit, or limited permit issued to him or her pursuant to Chapter 5 of this title; provided, however, that all classes of licenses, instruction permits, or limited permits issued pursuant to Chapter 5 of this title shall be valid for the purposes of operating mopeds upon the public roads and highways of this state. No license or permit shall be required for the operation of an electric assisted bicycle.

Laws 1978, p. 2241, § 5; Laws 1990, p. 2048, § 5; Laws 1996, p. 236, § 3; Laws 2007, Act 18, § 40, eff. May 11, 2007.

Formerly Code 1933, § 68A–1112.

Historical and Statutory Notes

The 2007 amendment by Act 18 was a provision contained in a correction bill.

§ 40–6–352. Protective headgear

(a) No person shall operate or ride as a passenger upon a moped unless he or she is wearing protective headgear which complies with standards established by the commissioner of public safety. The commissioner in determining such standards shall consider the size, speed, and operational characteristics of the moped. Such standards need not necessarily be the same as for motorcyclists; however, any moped operator wearing an approved motorcycle helmet shall be deemed in compliance with this subsection. Operators of electric assisted bicycles may wear a properly fitted and fastened bicycle helmet which meets the standards of the American National Standards Institute or the Snell Memorial Foundation's Standards for Protective Headgear for Use in Bicycling, rather than a motorcycle helmet.

(b) The commissioner of public safety is authorized to approve or disapprove protective headgear for moped operators and to issue and enforce regulations establishing standards and specifications for the approval thereof. He or she shall publish in print or electronically lists by name and type of all protective headgear which have been approved by him or her.

Laws 1978, p. 2241, § 5; Laws 1990, p. 2048, § 5; Laws 1996, p. 236, § 4; Laws 2000, p. 951, § 5A–10; Laws 2005, Act 68, § 18–14, eff. July 1, 2005; Laws 2010, Act 615, § 10, eff. June 3, 2010.

Formerly Code 1933, § 68A–1112.

Historical and Statutory Notes

The 2000 amendment provided gender neutral language and substituted for Department of "Public Safety" the Department of "Motor Vehicle Safety".

The 2005 amendment by Act 68 in subsecs. (a) and (b) substituted "commissioner of public safety" for "commissioner of motor vehicle safety".

The 2010 amendment by Act 615, in subsec. (b), inserted "in print or electronically" following "publish" throughout the subsection.

§ 40–6–353. Jurisdiction over operation

The commissioner of transportation or local governing authorities having jurisdiction over public roads and highways may prohibit the operation of mopeds on public roads and highways within their jurisdiction if it is determined that such operation endangers the safety of the traveling public.

Laws 1978, p. 2241, § 5; Laws 1990, p. 2048, § 5.

Formerly Code 1933, § 68A–1112.

§ 40–6–354. Rules and regulations

The commissioner of public safety is authorized to promulgate rules and regulations to carry this part into effect and is authorized to establish regulations for safety equipment or standards for the operation of mopeds.

Laws 1978, p. 2241, § 5; Laws 1990, p. 2048, § 5; Laws 2000, p. 951, § 5A–11; Laws 2005, Act 68, § 18–15, eff. July 1, 2005.

Formerly Code 1933, § 68A–1112.

Historical and Statutory Notes

The 2000 amendment substituted for Department of "Public Safety" the Department of "Motor Vehicle Safety".

The 2005 amendment by Act 68 substituted "commissioner of public safety" for "commissioner of motor vehicle safety".

Part 5

Low–Speed Vehicles

§ 40–6–360. Traffic laws apply to persons operating low-speed vehicles

Every person operating a low-speed vehicle shall be granted all the rights and shall be subject to all the duties applicable to the driver of any other vehicle under this chapter except as to special regulations in this part and except as to those provisions of this chapter which by their nature can have no application.

Laws 2002, p. 512, § 12.

§ 40–6–361. Operating low-speed vehicles on roadways laned for traffic

(a) All low-speed vehicles are entitled to full use of a lane, and no motor vehicle shall be driven in such a manner as to deprive any low-speed vehicle of the full use of a lane.

(b) The operator of a low-speed vehicle shall not overtake and pass in the same lane occupied by the vehicle being overtaken.

(c) No person shall operate a low-speed vehicle between lanes of traffic or between adjacent lines or rows of vehicles.

(d) Low-speed vehicles shall not be operated two or more abreast in a single lane.

Laws 2002, p. 512, § 12.

§ 40–6–362. Operation on highway where speed limit exceeds 35 miles per hour prohibited

Low-speed vehicles shall be operated only on any highway where the posted speed limit does not exceed 35 miles per hour. The operator of a low-speed vehicle shall not operate such vehicle on any highway where the posted speed limit exceeds 35 miles per hour.

Laws 2002, p. 512, § 12.

Article 14

Effect of Chapter on Powers of Local Authorities

§ 40–6–370. Provisions uniform throughout the state

The provisions of this chapter and the definitions contained in Code Section 40–1–1 shall be applicable and uniform throughout this state and in all counties and municipalities therein, and no local authority shall enact or enforce any ordinance on a matter covered by the provisions of this chapter except as expressly authorized in Code Sections 40–6–371 and 40–6–372.

Laws 1974, p. 633, § 1; Laws 1984, p. 22, § 40; Laws 1990, p. 2048, § 5.

Formerly Code 1933, § 68A–1501.

§ 40–6–371. Powers of local authorities

(a) This chapter shall not be deemed to prevent local authorities with respect to streets and highways under their jurisdiction and within the reasonable exercise of the police power from:

(1) Regulating or prohibiting stopping, standing, or parking;

(2) Regulating traffic by means of police officers or official traffic-control devices;

(3) Regulating or prohibiting processions or assemblages on the highways;

(4) Designating particular highways or roadways for use by traffic moving in one direction as authorized in Code Section 40–6–47;

(5) Establishing speed limits for vehicles in public parks, notwithstanding any provisions of law establishing a minimum speed limit for an area outside an urban or residential district;

(6) Designating any highway as a through highway or designating any intersection or junction of roadway as a stop or yield intersection or junction;

(7) Requiring the registration and inspection of bicycles, including the requirement of a registration fee;

(8) Designating any highway intersection as a "yield right of way" intersection and requiring vehicles facing a "yield right of way" sign to yield the right of way to other vehicles;

(9) Regulating or prohibiting the turning of vehicles or specified types of vehicles;

(10) Altering or establishing speed limits as authorized by law;

(11) Designating no-passing zones as authorized in Code Section 40–6–46;

(12) Prohibiting or regulating the use of controlled-access roadways by any class or kind of traffic as authorized in Code Section 40–6–51;

(13) Prohibiting or regulating the use of heavily traveled streets by any class or kind of traffic found to be incompatible with the normal and safe movement of traffic;

(14) Establishing minimum speed limits as authorized by law;

(15) Designating hazardous railroad grade crossings as authorized in Code Section 40–6–141;

(16) Designating and regulating traffic on play streets;

(17) Regulating persons propelling push carts;

(18) Regulating persons upon skates, coasters, sleds, and other toy vehicles;

(18.1) Regulating the operation of electric personal assistive mobility devices, provided that such regulations are no less restrictive than those imposed by Part 2A of Article 13 of this chapter;

(19) Adopting and enforcing such temporary or experimental regulations as may be necessary to cover emergencies or special conditions; or

(20) Adopting such other traffic regulations as are specifically authorized by this chapter.

(a.1) No fine imposed by a local authority for violation of an ordinance or regulation for conduct which constitutes a violation of a provision of this chapter shall exceed any maximum fine specified by this chapter for such violation.

(b) No local authority shall erect or maintain any official traffic-control device at any location so as to require the traffic on any state highway to stop before entering or crossing any intersecting highway unless approval in writing has first been obtained from the Department of Transportation of the State of Georgia. If this issue is on trial in a civil or criminal action, the proper authority shall be presumed.

(c) No ordinance or regulation enacted under paragraph (4), (5), (6), (8), (9), (10), (11), (12), (13), (14), (15), (16), (17), or (18) of subsection (a) of this Code section shall be effective until official traffic-control devices giving notice of such local traffic regulations are erected upon or at the entrances to the highway or the part thereof affected as may be most appropriate.

Laws 1955, p. 736, § 1; Laws 1973, p. 98, § 1; Laws 1974, p. 633, § 1; Laws 1975, p. 1582, § 4; Laws 1990, p. 2048, § 5; Laws 2001, p. 770, § 3; Laws 2003, Act 56, § 5, eff. May 29, 2003.

Formerly Code 1933, § 68A–1502.

Historical and Statutory Notes

The 2001 amendment inserted subsec. (a.1).

The 2003 amendment by Act 56, in subsec. (a), inserted par. (18.1).

§ 40–6–372. Adoption by reference

Local authorities by ordinance may adopt by reference any or all provisions of this chapter or of Code Section 40–1–1 without publishing or posting in full the provisions thereof.

Laws 1955, p. 736, § 1; Laws 1973, p. 98, § 1; Laws 1974, p. 633, § 1; Laws 1975, p. 1582, § 4; Laws 1984, p. 22, § 40; Laws 1990, p. 2048, § 5.

Formerly Code 1933, § 68A–1503.

§ 40–6–373. Adoption of future changes

A future amendment or repeal of a provision of this chapter or of Code Section 40–1–1 shall so amend or repeal the pertinent provision, if any, of the original ordinance adopted by a local authority pursuant to the authority of Code Section 40–6–372 without any action by such local authority being required.

Laws 1974, p. 633, § 1; Laws 1984, p. 22, § 40; Laws 1990, p. 2048, § 5.

Formerly Code 1933, § 68A–1504.

§ 40–6–374. Form of enacting ordinance

Local authorities shall use the following wording or similar wording in adopting by reference the provisions of this chapter or the definitions contained in Code Section 40–1–1:

(Municipality or County) of _____

Ordinance _____ number

An ordinance adopting the Georgia Uniform Rules of the Road, Code Sections [_____ to _____ (except for Code Sections _____)] of Chapter 6 of Title 40 of the Official Code of Georgia Annotated, to regulate traffic upon the public streets of the (Municipality or County) of _____ and repealing ordinance number _____ and all other ordinances and sections of ordinances in conflict herewith.

It is ordained by _____ as follows:

Section 1. Adoption by reference. Pursuant to Chapter 6 of Title 40 of the Official Code of Georgia Annotated, Code Sections 40–6–372 through 40–6–376, Code Sections [_____ to _____ (except for Code Sections _____)] of that chapter known as the Uniform Rules of the Road and the definitions contained in Code Section 40–1–1 are hereby adopted as and for the traffic regulations of this (Municipality or County) with like effect as if recited herein.

Section 2. Penalties. Unless another penalty is expressly provided by law, every person convicted of a violation of any provision of this ordinance shall be punished by a fine of not more than _____ dollars or by imprisonment for not more than _____ days or by both such fine and imprisonment.

Section 3. Repeal. The (existing ordinances covering the same matters as embraced in this ordinance) are hereby repealed and all ordinances or parts of ordinances inconsistent with the provisions of this ordinance are hereby repealed.

Section 4. Effective date. This ordinance shall take effect from and after the ____ day of ____, ____.

Laws 1974, p. 633, § 1; Laws 1983, p. 3, § 29; Laws 1984, p. 22, § 40; Laws 1990, p. 2048, § 5; Laws 1999, p. 81, § 40.

Formerly Code 1933, § 68A–1505.

§ 40–6–375. Citations for violations

It shall be sufficient in citing a violation of a provision of this chapter to refer to the ordinance number of the enacting ordinance, provided that the citation form used is the one developed by the commissioner of public safety under the authority of Code Section 40–13–1.

Laws 1974, p. 633, § 1; Laws 1990, p. 2048, § 5.

Formerly Code 1933, § 68A–1506.

§ 40–6–376. Option to treat as state or local offense; right of defendant to have case treated as state offense; double jeopardy

(a) Any offense, except a violation of subsection (b) of Code Section 40–6–270 or a violation of Code Section 40–6–393, which is a violation of a provision of this chapter and of a local ordinance may, at the discretion of the local law enforcement officer or prosecutor, be charged as a violation of the state statute or of the local ordinance. A violation of subsection (b) of Code Section 40–6–270 or a violation of Code Section 40–6–393 shall be charged as a state violation.

(b) If the offense charged under an ordinance constitutes a violation of any provision of this chapter, the defendant may request transfer of the charge to the appropriate state tribunal. If the defendant so requests, the recorder or city judge, after conducting a commitment hearing in which probable cause for arrest is found, or upon obtaining a waiver of commitment hearing, shall summarily fix the defendant's bond and bind his case over to the appropriate state tribunal.

(c) No person tried in any court for a violation of this chapter or any ordinance adopted pursuant thereto shall thereafter be tried in any court for the same offense. A conviction for the violation of an ordinance adopted pursuant to this chapter shall be considered a prior conviction for all purposes under this chapter and under Chapter 13 of this title.

(d) No court, other than a court having jurisdiction to try a person charged with a violation of Code Section 40–6–393, shall have jurisdiction over any offense arising under the laws of this state or the ordinances of any political subdivision thereof, which offense arose out of the same conduct which led to said person's being charged with a violation of Code Section 40–6–393 and any judgment rendered by such court shall be null and void.

Laws 1955, p. 736, §§ 1, 2; Laws 1974, p. 633, § 1; Laws 1975, p. 1582, § 4; Laws 1982, p. 1694, §§ 2, 4; Laws 1988, p. 1499, § 2; Laws 1989, p. 14, § 40; Laws 1990, p. 2048, § 5.

Formerly Code 1933, § 68A–1507.

Article 15

Serious Traffic Offenses

§ 40–6–390. Reckless driving

(a) Any person who drives any vehicle in reckless disregard for the safety of persons or property commits the offense of reckless driving.

(b) Every person convicted of reckless driving shall be guilty of a misdemeanor and, upon conviction thereof, shall be punished by a fine not to exceed $1,000.00 or imprisonment not to exceed 12 months, or by both such fine and imprisonment, provided that no provision of this Code section shall be construed so as to deprive the court imposing the sentence of the power given by law to stay or suspend the execution of such sentence or to place the defendant on probation.

Laws 1974, p. 633, § 1; Laws 1989, p. 350, § 2; Laws 1990, p. 2048, § 5.

Formerly Code 1933, § 68A–901.

§ 40–6–391. Drivers with ability impaired by alcohol, drugs, or toxic vapor

(a) A person shall not drive or be in actual physical control of any moving vehicle while:

(1) Under the influence of alcohol to the extent that it is less safe for the person to drive;

(2) Under the influence of any drug to the extent that it is less safe for the person to drive;

(3) Under the intentional influence of any glue, aerosol, or other toxic vapor to the extent that it is less safe for the person to drive;

(4) Under the combined influence of any two or more of the substances specified in paragraphs (1) through (3) of this subsection to the extent that it is less safe for the person to drive;

(5) The person's alcohol concentration is 0.08 grams or more at any time within three hours after such driving or being in actual physical control from alcohol consumed before such driving or being in actual physical control ended; or

(6) Subject to the provisions of subsection (b) of this Code section, there is any amount of marijuana or a controlled substance, as defined in Code Section 16–13–21, present in the person's blood or urine, or both, including the metabolites and derivatives of each or both without regard to whether or not any alcohol is present in the person's breath or blood.

(b) The fact that any person charged with violating this Code section is or has been legally entitled to use a drug shall not constitute a defense against any charge of violating this Code section; provided, however, that such person shall not be in violation of this Code section unless such person is rendered incapable of driving safely as a result of using a drug other than alcohol which such person is legally entitled to use.

(c) Every person convicted of violating this Code section shall, upon a first or second conviction thereof, be guilty of a misdemeanor, upon a third conviction thereof, be guilty of a high and aggravated misdemeanor, and upon a fourth or subsequent conviction thereof, be guilty of a felony except as otherwise provided in paragraph (4) of this subsection and shall be punished as follows:

(1) First conviction with no conviction of and no plea of nolo contendere accepted to a charge of violating this Code section within the previous ten years, as measured from the dates of previous arrests for which convictions were obtained or pleas of nolo contendere were accepted to the date of the current arrest for which a conviction is obtained or a plea of nolo contendere is accepted:

(A) A fine of not less than $300.00 and not more than $1,000. 00, which fine shall not, except as provided in subsection (g) of this Code section, be subject to suspension, stay, or probation;

(B) A period of imprisonment of not fewer than ten days nor more than 12 months, which period of imprisonment may, at the sole discretion of the judge, be suspended, stayed, or probated, except that if the offender's alcohol concentration at the time of the offense was 0.08 grams or more, the judge may suspend, stay, or probate all but 24 hours of any term of imprisonment imposed under this subparagraph;

(C) Not fewer than 40 hours of community service, except that for a conviction for violation of subsection (k) of this Code section where the person's alcohol concentration at the time of the offense was less than 0.08 grams, the period of community service shall be not fewer than 20 hours;

(D) Completion of a DUI Alcohol or Drug Use Risk Reduction Program. The sponsor of any such program shall provide written notice of the department's approval of the program to the person upon enrollment in the program;

(E) A clinical evaluation as defined in Code Section 40–5–1 and, if recommended as a part of such evaluation, completion of a substance abuse treatment program as defined in Code Section 40–5–1; provided, however, that in the court's discretion such evaluation may be waived; and

(F) If the person is sentenced to a period of imprisonment for fewer than 12 months, a period of probation of 12 months less any days during which the person is actually incarcerated;

(2) For the second conviction within a ten-year period of time, as measured from the dates of previous arrests for which convictions were obtained or pleas of nolo contendere were accepted to the date of the current arrest for which a conviction is obtained or a plea of nolo contendere is accepted:

(A) A fine of not less than $600.00 and not more than $1,000.00, which fine shall not, except as provided in subsection (g) of this Code section, be subject to suspension, stay, or probation;

(B) A period of imprisonment of not fewer than 90 days and not more than 12 months. The judge shall probate at least a portion of such term of imprisonment, in accordance with subparagraph (F) of this paragraph, thereby subjecting the offender to the provisions of Article 7 of Chapter 8 of Title 42 and to such other terms and conditions as the judge may impose; provided, however, that the offender shall be required to serve not fewer than 72 hours of actual incarceration;

(C) Not fewer than 30 days of community service;

(D) Completion of a DUI Alcohol or Drug Use Risk Reduction Program. The sponsor of any such program shall provide written notice of the department's approval of the program to the person upon enrollment in the program;

(E) A clinical evaluation as defined in Code Section 40–5–1 and, if recommended as a part of such evaluation, completion of a substance abuse treatment program as defined in Code Section 40–5–1; and

(F) A period of probation of 12 months less any days during which the person is actually incarcerated;

(3) For the third conviction within a ten-year period of time, as measured from the dates of previous arrests for which convictions were obtained or pleas of nolo contendere were accepted to the date of the current arrest for which a conviction is obtained or a plea of nolo contendere is accepted:

(A) A fine of not less than $1,000.00 and not more than $5,000.00, which fine shall not, except as provided in subsection (g) of this Code section, be subject to suspension, stay, or probation;

(B) A mandatory period of imprisonment of not fewer than 120 days and not more than 12 months. The judge shall probate at least a portion of such term of imprisonment, in accordance with subparagraph (F) of this paragraph, thereby subjecting the offender to the provisions of Article 7 of Chapter 8 of Title 42 and to such other terms and conditions as the judge may impose; provided, however, that the offender shall be required to serve not fewer than 15 days of actual incarceration;

(C) Not fewer than 30 days of community service;

(D) Completion of a DUI Alcohol or Drug Use Risk Reduction Program. The sponsor of any such program shall provide written notice of the department's approval of the program to the person upon enrollment in the program;

(E) A clinical evaluation as defined in Code Section 40–5–1 and, if recommended as a part of such evaluation, completion of a substance abuse treatment program as defined in Code Section 40–5–1; and

(F) A period of probation of 12 months less any days during which the person is actually incarcerated;

(4) For the fourth or subsequent conviction within a ten-year period of time, as measured from the dates of previous arrests for which convictions were obtained or pleas of nolo contendere were accepted to the date of the current arrest for which a conviction is obtained or a plea of nolo contendere is accepted:

(A) A fine of not less than $1,000.00 and not more than $5,000.00, which fine shall not, except as provided in subsection (g) of this Code section, be subject to suspension, stay, or probation;

(B) A period of imprisonment of not less than one year and not more than five years; provided, however, that the judge may suspend, stay, or probate all but 90 days of any term of imprisonment imposed under this paragraph. The judge shall probate at least a portion of such term of imprisonment, in accordance with subparagraph (F) of this paragraph, thereby subjecting the offender to the provisions of Article 7 of Chapter 8 of Title 42 and to such other terms and conditions as the judge may impose;

(C) Not fewer than 60 days of community service; provided, however, that if a defendant is sentenced to serve three years of actual imprisonment, the judge may suspend the community service;

(D) Completion of a DUI Alcohol or Drug Use Risk Reduction Program. The sponsor of any such program shall provide written notice of the department's approval of the program to the person upon enrollment in the program;

(E) A clinical evaluation as defined in Code Section 40–5–1 and, if recommended as a part of such evaluation, completion of a substance abuse treatment program as defined in Code Section 40–5–1; and

(F) A period of probation of five years less any days during which the person is actually imprisoned;

provided, however, that if the ten-year period of time as measured in this paragraph commenced prior to July 1, 2008, then such fourth or subsequent conviction shall be a misdemeanor of a high and aggravated nature and punished as provided in paragraph (3) of this subsection;

(5) If a person has been convicted of violating subsection (k) of this Code section premised on a refusal to submit to required testing or where such person's alcohol concentration at the time of the offense was 0.08 grams or more, and such person is subsequently convicted of violating subsection (a) of this Code section, such person shall be punished by applying the applicable level or grade of conviction specified in this subsection such that the previous conviction of violating subsection (k) of this Code section shall be considered a previous conviction of violating subsection (a) of this Code section;

(6) For the purpose of imposing a sentence under this subsection, a plea of nolo contendere based on a violation of this Code section shall constitute a conviction; and

(7) For purposes of determining the number of prior convictions or pleas of nolo contendere pursuant to the felony provisions of paragraph (4) of this subsection, only those offenses for which a conviction is obtained or a plea of nolo contendere is accepted on or after July 1, 2008, shall be considered; provided, however, that nothing in this subsection shall be construed as limiting or modifying in any way administrative proceedings or sentence enhancement provisions under Georgia law, including, but not limited to, provisions relating to punishment of recidivist offenders pursuant to Title 17.

(d)(1) Notwithstanding the limits set forth in any municipal charter, any municipal court of any municipality shall be authorized to impose the misdemeanor or high and aggravated misdemeanor punishments provided for in this Code section upon a conviction of violating this Code section or upon a conviction of violating any ordinance adopting the provisions of this Code section.

(2) Notwithstanding any provision of this Code section to the contrary, any court authorized to hear misdemeanor or high and aggravated misdemeanor cases involving violations of this Code section shall be authorized to exercise the power to probate, suspend, or stay any sentence imposed. Such power shall, however, be limited to the conditions and limitations imposed by subsection (c) of this Code section.

(e) The foregoing limitations on punishment also shall apply when a defendant has been convicted of violating, by a single transaction, more than one of the four provisions of subsection (a) of this Code section.

(f) The provisions of Code Section 17–10–3, relating to general punishment for misdemeanors including traffic offenses, and the provisions of Article 3 of Chapter 8 of Title 42, relating to probation of first offenders, shall not apply to any person convicted of violating any provision of this Code section.

(g)(1) If the payment of the fine required under subsection (c) of this Code section will impose an economic hardship on the defendant, the judge, at his or her sole discretion, may order the defendant to pay such fine in installments and such order may be enforced through a contempt proceeding or a revocation of any probation otherwise authorized by this Code section.

(2) In the sole discretion of the judge, he or she may suspend up to one-half of the fine imposed under subsection (c) of this Code section conditioned upon the defendant's undergoing treatment in a substance abuse treatment program as defined in Code Section 40–5–1.

(h) For purposes of determining under this chapter prior convictions of or pleas of nolo contendere to violating this Code section, in addition to the offense prohibited by this Code section, a conviction of or plea of nolo contendere to any of the following offenses shall be deemed to be a violation of this Code section:

(1) Any federal law substantially conforming to or parallel with the offense covered under this Code section;

(2) Any local ordinance adopted pursuant to Article 14 of this chapter, which ordinance adopts the provisions of this Code section; or

(3) Any previously or currently existing law of this or any other state, which law was or is substantially conforming to or parallel with this Code section.

(i) A person shall not drive or be in actual physical control of any moving commercial motor vehicle while there is 0.04 percent or more by weight of alcohol in such person's blood, breath, or urine. Every person convicted of violating this subsection shall be guilty of a misdemeanor and, in addition to any disqualification resulting under Article 7 of Chapter 5 of this title, the "Uniform Commercial Driver's License Act," shall be fined as provided in subsection (c) of this Code section.

(j)(1) The clerk of the court in which a person is convicted a second or subsequent time under subsection (c) of this Code section within five years, as measured from the dates of previous arrests for which convictions were obtained or pleas of nolo contendere were accepted to the date of the current arrest for which a conviction is obtained or a plea of nolo contendere is accepted, shall cause to be published a notice of conviction for each such person convicted. Such notices of conviction shall be published in the manner of legal notices in the legal organ of the county in which such person resides or, in the case of nonresidents, in the legal organ of the county in which the person was convicted. Such notice of conviction shall be one column wide by two inches long and shall contain the photograph taken by the arresting law enforcement agency at the time of arrest, the name of the convicted person, the city, county, and zip code of the convicted person's residential address, and the date, time, place of arrest, and disposition of the case and shall be published once in the legal organ of the appropriate county in the second week following such conviction or as soon thereafter as publication may be made.

(2) The convicted person for which a notice of conviction is published pursuant to this subsection shall be assessed $25.00 for the cost of publication of such notice and such assessment shall be imposed at the time of conviction in addition to any other fine imposed pursuant to this Code section.

(3) The clerk of the court, the publisher of any legal organ which publishes a notice of conviction, and any other person involved in the publication of an erroneous notice of conviction shall be immune from civil or criminal liability for such erroneous publication, provided such publication was made in good faith.

(k)(1) A person under the age of 21 shall not drive or be in actual physical control of any moving vehicle while the person's alcohol concentration is 0.02 grams or more at any time within three hours after such driving or being in physical control from alcohol consumed before such driving or being in actual physical control ended.

(2) Every person convicted of violating this subsection shall be guilty of a misdemeanor for the first and second convictions and upon a third or subsequent conviction thereof be guilty of a high and aggravated misdemeanor and shall be punished and fined as provided in subsection (c) of this Code section, provided that any term of imprisonment served shall be subject to the provisions of Code Section 17–10–3.1, and any period of community service imposed on such person shall be required to be completed within 60 days of the date of sentencing.

(3) No plea of nolo contendere shall be accepted for any person under the age of 21 charged with a violation of this Code section.

(*l*) A person who violates this Code section while transporting in a motor vehicle a child under the age of 14 years is guilty of the separate offense of endangering a child by driving under the influence of alcohol or drugs. The offense of endangering a child by driving under the influence of alcohol or drugs shall not be merged with the offense of driving under the influence of alcohol or drugs for the purposes of prosecution and sentencing. An offender who is convicted of a violation of this subsection shall be punished in accordance with the provisions of subsection (d) of Code Section 16–12–1, relating to the offense of contributing to the delinquency, unruliness, or deprivation of a child.

Laws 1953, Nov.-Dec. Sess., p. 556, § 47; Laws 1968, p. 448, § 1; Laws 1974, p. 633, § 1; Laws 1983, p. 1000, § 12; Laws 1984, p. 22, § 40; Laws 1985, p. 149, § 40; Laws 1985, p. 758, § 17; Laws 1987, p. 3, § 40; Laws 1987, p. 904, § 1; Laws 1988, p. 1893, § 2; Laws 1989, p. 14, § 40; Laws 1990, p. 2048, § 5; Laws 1991, p. 1886, §§ 6–8; Laws 1992, p. 2556, § 2; Laws 1994, p. 1600, § 8; Laws 1996, p. 1413, § 1; Laws 1997, p. 760, § 23; Laws 1999, p. 293, §§ 1, 2; Laws 1999, p. 391, §§ 7, 8; Laws 2001, p. 208, § 1–5; Laws 2005, Act 68, § 18–15.1, eff. July 1, 2005; Laws 2007, Act 18, § 40, eff. May 11, 2007; Laws 2008, Act 544, §§ 2 to 4, eff. July 1, 2008; Laws 2009, Act 8, § 40, eff. April 14, 2009; Laws 2010, Act 454, § 1, eff. July 1, 2010.

Formerly Code 1933, § 68A–902.

Historical and Statutory Notes

The 2001 amendment changed the alcohol concentration in subsec. (a)(5) from 0.10 to 0.08 grams; in subsec. (c)(2) (B) substituted for "At the sole discretion and under such terms and conditions as the judge shall impose, the judge may suspend, stay, or probate all but 48 hours of any term of imprisonment imposed under this subparagraph" the words "The judge shall probate at least a portion of such term of imprisonment, in accordance with subparagraph (F) of this paragraph, thereby subjecting the offender to the provisions of Article 7 of Chapter 8 of Title 42 and to such other terms and conditions as the judge may impose; provided, however, that the offender shall be required to serve not less than 72 hours of actual incarceration"; substituted in subsec. (c)(2)(C) "30 days of community service" for "80 hours of community service, except that for a second conviction for violation of subsection (k) of this Code section where the person's alcohol concentration at the time of the offense was less than 0.08 grams, the period of community service shall be not less than 40 hours"; deleted at the beginning of subsec. (c)(2)(F) "If the defendant is sentenced to a period of imprisonment for less than 12 months,"; substituted in subsec. (c)(3)(B) for "At the sole discretion and under such terms and conditions as the judge shall impose, the judge may suspend, stay, or probate all but ten days of any term of imprisonment imposed under this Subparagraph" the words "The judge shall probate at least a portion of such term of imprisonment, in accordance with subparagraph (F) of this paragraph, thereby subjecting the offender to the provisions of Article 7 of Chapter 8 of Title 42 and to such other terms and conditions as the judge may impose; provided, however, that the offender shall be required to serve not less than 15 days of actual incarceration"; substituted in subsec. (c)(3)(C) "30 days of community service" for "20 days of community service, except that for a third or subsequent conviction for violation of subsection (k) of this Code section where the person's alcohol concentration at the time of the offense was less than 0.08 grams, the period of community service shall be not less than 40 hours"; deleted at the beginning of subsec. (c)(3)(F) "If the defendant is sentenced to a period of imprisonment for less than 12 months"; and deleted subsec. (k)(4) which provided:

"(4) The driver's license of any person convicted of violating this subsection shall be revoked as provided by Code Section 40–5–57.1."

The 2005 amendment by Act 68 in subpars. (c)(1)(D), (c)(2)(D), and (c)(3)(D) substituted "the Department of Driver Services" for "the Department of Human Resources".

The 2007 amendment by Act 18 was a provision contained in a correction bill.

The 2008 amendment by Act 544 rewrote subsec. (c); in subsec. (d), inserted "misdemeanor or high and aggravated misdemeanor" in pars. (1) and (2) and made a nonsubstantive change; in subsec. (g), par. (2), substituted "subsection (c) of this Code section" for "paragraph (2) or (3) of subsection (c) of this Code section for a second or subsequent conviction". Prior to amendment, subsec. (c) had read:

"(c) Every person convicted of violating this Code section shall, upon a first or second conviction thereof, be guilty of a misdemeanor and, upon a third or subsequent conviction thereof, be guilty of a high and aggravated misdemeanor and shall be punished as follows:

"(1) First conviction with no conviction of and no plea of nolo contendere accepted to a charge of violating this Code section within the previous five years, as measured from the dates of previous arrests for which convictions were obtained or pleas of nolo contendere were accepted to the date of the current arrest for which a conviction is obtained or a plea of nolo contendere is accepted:

"(A) A fine of not less than $300.00 nor more than $1,000.00, which fine shall not, except as provided in subsection (g) of this Code section, be subject to suspension, stay, or probation;

"(B) A period of imprisonment of not less than ten days nor more than 12 months, which period of imprisonment may, at the sole discretion of the judge, be suspended, stayed, or probated, except that if the offender's alcohol concentration at the time of the offense was 0.08 grams or more, the judge may suspend, stay, or probate all but 24 hours of any term of imprisonment imposed under this subparagraph;

"(C) Not less than 40 hours of community service, except that for a conviction for violation of subsection (k) of this Code section where the person's alcohol concentration at the time of the offense was less than 0.08 grams, the period of community service shall be not less than 20 hours;

"(D) Completion of a DUI Alcohol or Drug Use Risk Reduction Program approved by the Department of Driver Services. The sponsor of any such program shall provide written notice of such approval to the person upon enrollment in the program; and

"(E) If the defendant is sentenced to a period of imprisonment for less than 12 months, a period of probation of 12 months less any days during which the defendant is actually incarcerated;

"(2) For the second conviction within a five-year period of time, as measured from the dates of previous arrests for which convictions were obtained or pleas of nolo contendere were accepted to the date of the current arrest for which a conviction is obtained or a plea of nolo contendere is accepted:

"(A) A fine of not less than $600.00 nor more than $1,000.00, which fine shall not, except as provided in subsection (g) of this Code section, be subject to suspension, stay, or probation;

"(B) A period of imprisonment of not less than 90 days nor more than 12 months. The judge shall probate at least a portion of such term of imprisonment, in accordance with subparagraph (F) of this paragraph, thereby subjecting the offender to the provisions of Article 7 of Chapter 8 of Title 42 and to such other terms and conditions as the judge may impose; provided, however, that the offender shall be required to serve not less than 72 hours of actual incarceration;

"(C) Not less than 30 days of community service;

"(D) Completion of a DUI Alcohol or Drug Use Risk Reduction Program approved by the Department of Driver Services. The sponsor of any such program shall provide written notice of such approval to the person upon enrollment in the program;

"(E) Undergoing a clinical evaluation as defined in Code Section 40–5–1 and, if indicated by such evaluation, completion of a substance abuse treatment program as defined in Code Section 40–5–1; and

"(F) A period of probation of 12 months less any days during which the defendant is actually incarcerated; or

"(3) For the third or subsequent conviction within a five-year period of time, as measured from the dates of previous arrests for which convictions were obtained or pleas of nolo contendere were accepted to the date of the current arrest for which a conviction is obtained or a plea of nolo contendere is accepted:

"(A) A fine of not less than $1,000.00 and not more than $5,000.00, which fine shall not, except as provided in subsection (g) of this Code section, be subject to suspension, stay, or probation;

"(B) A mandatory period of imprisonment of not less than 120 days nor more than 12 months. The judge shall probate at least a portion of such term of imprisonment, in accordance with subparagraph (F) of this paragraph, thereby subjecting the offender to the provisions of Article 7 of Chapter 8 of Title 42 and to such other terms and conditions as the judge may impose; provided, however, that the offender shall be required to serve not less than 15 days of actual incarceration;

"(C) Not less than 30 days of community service;

"(D) Completion of a DUI Alcohol or Drug Use Risk Reduction Program approved by the Department of Driver Services. The sponsor of any such program shall provide written notice of such approval to the person upon enrollment in the program;

"(E) Undergoing a clinical evaluation as defined in Code Section 40–5–1 and, if indicated by such evaluation, completion of a substance abuse treatment program as defined in Code Section 40–5–1; and

"(F) A period of probation of 12 months less any days during which the defendant is actually incarcerated.

"For the purpose of imposing a sentence under this subsection, a plea of nolo contendere or an adjudication of delinquency based on a violation of this Code section shall constitute a conviction."

Laws 2008, Act 544, § 5, provides:

"This Act shall become effective on July 1, 2008, and shall be applied to offenses occurring on or after July 1, 2008; provided, however, that for purposes of determining the number of prior convictions or pleas of nolo contendere pursuant to the felony provisions of paragraph (4) of subsection (c) of Code Section 40–6–391, only those offenses for which a conviction or a plea of nolo contendere is obtained on or after July 1, 2008, shall be considered."

The 2009 amendment by Act 8 was a provision contained in a correction bill.

The 2010 amendment by Act 454, in subsec. (j), par. (1), substituted "the name of the convicted person, the city, county, and zip code of the convicted person's residential address" for "name and address of the convicted person".

§ 40–6–391.1. Plea of nolo contendere by persons charged with driving under the influence of alcohol or drugs

(a) The decision to accept a plea of nolo contendere to a charge of violating Code Section 40–6–391 shall be at the sole discretion of the judge but, if such plea is accepted, the penalties provided for in subsection (c) of Code Section 40–6–391 shall be imposed; provided, however, that no such plea of nolo contendere shall be accepted if the person charged with violating Code Section 40–6–391 had an alcohol concentration of more than 0.15 at any time within three hours after driving or being in control of any moving vehicle from alcohol consumed before such driving or being in control ended.

(b) If the defendant has not been convicted of or had a plea of nolo contendere accepted to a charge of violating Code Section 40–6–391 within the previous five years and if the plea of nolo contendere shall be used as provided in paragraph (1) of subsection (a) of Code Section 40–5–63, no such plea shall be accepted unless, at a minimum, the following conditions are met:

(1) The defendant has filed a verified petition with the court requesting that such plea be accepted and setting forth the facts and special circumstances necessary to enable the judge to determine that accepting such plea is in the best interest of justice; and

(2) The judge has reviewed the defendant's driving records that are on file with the Department of Driver Services.

(c) The judge, as part of the record of the disposition of the charge, shall set forth, under seal of the court, his or her reasons for accepting the plea of nolo contendere.

(d) The record of the disposition of the case, including the ruling required in subsection (c) of this Code section, shall be forwarded to the Department of Driver Services within ten days after disposition.

(e) If a plea of nolo contendere is accepted under the conditions set forth in subsection (b) of this Code section, the defendant's driver's license shall be forwarded to the Department of Driver Services as provided in subsection (c) of Code Section 40–5–67.

Laws 1983, p. 1000, § 13; Laws 1984, p. 22, § 40; Laws 1990, p. 1154, § 8; Laws 1990, p. 2048, § 5; Laws 1991, p. 1886, § 9; Laws 1992, p. 2564, § 12; Laws 1992, p. 2785, § 25; Laws 1994, p. 831, § 2; Laws 1994, p. 1600, § 9; Laws 1997, p. 760, § 24; Laws 2000, p. 951, § 5A–12; Laws 2005, Act 68, § 18–16, eff. July 1, 2005.

Historical and Statutory Notes

The 2000 amendment inserted gender neutral language and substituted for Department of "Public Safety" the Department of "Motor Vehicle Safety".

The 2005 amendment by Act 68, in subsecs. (b)(2), (d), and (e), substituted "Department of Driver Services" for "Department of Motor Vehicle Safety".

§ 40–6–391.2. Forfeiture of motor vehicle operated by person who has been declared habitual violator and whose license has been revoked and who has been arrested for driving under the influence

(a) Except as provided in this Code section, any motor vehicle operated by a person who has been declared a habitual violator for three violations of Code Section 40–6–391 and whose license has been revoked and who is arrested and charged with a violation of Code Section 40–6–391, is declared to be contraband and subject to forfeiture to the state, as provided in this Code section, provided that said forfeiture shall not be absolute unless the defendant is finally convicted of such offense.

(b) Any motor vehicle subject to forfeiture under subsection (a) of this Code section shall be seized immediately upon discovery by any law enforcement officer, peace officer, or law enforcement agency of this state or any political subdivision thereof who has the power to make arrests and whose duty it is to enforce this article, that said motor vehicle has been declared contraband. Said motor vehicle shall be delivered within 20 days to the district attorney whose circuit includes the county in which a seizure is made or to his duly authorized agent. At any time subsequent to the seizure, the chief officer of the seizing agency, his designee, or the district attorney may release the vehicle upon bond being posted in like manner as authorized in subsection (e) of this Code section.

(c) Within 60 days from the date of the seizure, the district attorney of the judicial circuit, or the director on his behalf, shall cause to be filed in the superior court of the county in which the motor vehicle is seized or detained an action for condemnation of such motor vehicle. The proceedings shall be brought in the name of the state by the district attorney of the circuit in which the motor vehicle was seized, and the action shall be verified by a duly authorized agent of the state in a manner required by the law of this state. The action shall describe the motor vehicle and state its location, present custodian, and the name of the owner, if known, to the duly authorized agent of the state; allege the essential elements of the violation which is claimed to exist; and conclude with a prayer of due process to enforce the forfeiture. Upon the filing of such an action, the court shall promptly cause process to issue to the present custodian in possession of the motor vehicle described in the action, commanding him to seize the motor vehicle in the action and to hold that motor vehicle for further order of the court. The owner, lessee, or any person having a duly recorded security interest in or lien on such motor vehicle shall be notified by any means of service provided for in Title 9 or by delivery of a copy of the complaint and summons by certified mail or statutory overnight delivery to said owner or lienholder or a person of suitable age or discretion having charge of said owner's premises. For purposes of this subsection, where forfeiture of a motor vehicle titled or registered in Georgia is sought, notice to the titleholder shall be deemed adequate if a copy of the complaint and summons is mailed by certified mail or statutory overnight delivery to the titleholder at the address set out in the title and an additional copy is mailed by certified mail or statutory overnight delivery to the firm, person, or corporation which holds the current registration for said motor vehicle, who shall be deemed agent for service for said titleholder, and said complaint is advertised once a week for two weeks as set out in this subsection. If the owner, lessee, or person having a duly recorded security interest in or lien on the contraband motor vehicle is unknown or resides out of the state or departs the state or cannot after due diligence be found within the state or conceals himself so as to avoid notice, notice of the proceedings shall be published once a week for two weeks in the newspaper in which the sheriff's advertisements are published. Such publication shall be deemed notice to any and all persons having an interest in or right affected by such proceeding and any sale of the motor vehicle resulting therefrom, but shall not constitute notice to any person having a duly recorded security interest in or lien upon such motor vehicle and required to be served under this Code section unless that person is unknown or resides out of the state or departs the state or cannot after due diligence be found within the state or conceals himself to avoid notice.

(d)(1) Any party at interest may appear, by answer under oath, and file an intervention or defense within 30 days from the date of service on the condemnee of the action for condemnation. The owner, lessee, security interest holder, or lienholder shall be permitted to defend by showing that the motor vehicle seized was not subject to forfeiture under this Code section.

(2) A rented or leased vehicle shall not be subject to forfeiture unless it is established in the forfeiture proceedings that the owner of the rented or leased vehicle knew or should have

known of or consented to the operation of such motor vehicle in a manner which would subject the vehicle to forfeiture. Upon learning of the address or phone number of the rental or leasing company which owns such vehicle, the district attorney shall immediately contact the company to inform it that the vehicle is available for the company to take possession.

(e) The court to which any such petition for condemnation may be referred may, in its discretion, allow any party at interest, after making said defense under subsection (d) of this Code section, to give bond and take possession of the motor vehicle seized. Such motor vehicle shall not be sold or leased without prior approval of the court. In the event the court approves such sale or lease, the proceeds arising therefrom shall be deposited in the registry of the court, pending final adjudication of the forfeiture proceeding. The court shall determine whether the bond shall be a forthcoming bond or an eventual condemnation money bond and shall also determine the amount of the bond. The enforcement of any bond so given shall be regulated by the general law applicable to such cases.

(f) If no defense or intervention is filed within 30 days from the date of service on the condemnee of the petition, judgment shall be entered by the court and the motor vehicle shall be sold. The court may direct that such property be sold by:

(1) Judicial sale as provided in Article 7 of Chapter 13 of Title 9; provided, however, that the court may establish a minimum acceptable price for such property; or

(2) Any commercially feasible means.

(g) The proceeds arising from such sale shall be deposited into the general treasury of the state or any other governmental unit whose law enforcement agency it was that originally seized the motor vehicle. It is the intent of the General Assembly that, where possible, proceeds deposited into the state treasury should be used and that proceeds vested in any local governmental unit shall be applied to fund alcohol or drug treatment, rehabilitation, and prevention and education programs, after making the necessary expenditures for:

(1) Any costs incurred in the seizure;

(2) The costs of the court and its officers; and

(3) Any cost incurred in the storage, advertisement, maintenance, or care of the motor vehicle.

(h) The interest of an owner, lessee, security interest holder, or lienholder shall not be subject to forfeiture unless the condemnor shows by a preponderance of evidence that such person knew or reasonably should have known that the operator was a habitual violator as set forth in subsection (a) of this Code section and knew or reasonably should have known that such person would operate or was operating the vehicle while in violation of Code Section 40–6–391.

(i) In any case where a vehicle which is the only family vehicle is determined to be subject to forfeiture, the court may, if it determines that the financial hardship to the family as a result of the forfeiture and sale outweighs the benefit to the state from such forfeiture, order the title to the vehicle transferred to such other family member who is a duly licensed operator and who requires the use of such vehicle for employment or family transportation purposes. Such transfer shall be subject to any valid liens and shall be granted only once.

Laws 1991, p. 1896, § 1; Laws 2000, p. 1589, § 3.

Historical and Statutory Notes

The 2000 amendment substituted in two instances in subsec. (c) "certified mail or statutory overnight delivery" for "certified mail".

§ 40–6–391.3. Punishment for school bus driver convicted of driving under influence of alcohol or drugs while driving school bus

A school bus driver licensed pursuant to Article 7 of Chapter 5 of this title shall upon a conviction of a violation of Code Section 40–6–391 while driving a school bus be punished by imprisonment for a period of not less than one year nor more than five years or by a fine of not less than $1,000.00 nor more than $5,000.00, or both.

Laws 1991, p. 1140, § 3.

§ 40–6–392. Chemical tests

(a) Upon the trial of any civil or criminal action or proceeding arising out of acts alleged to have been committed by any person in violation of Code Section 40–6–391, evidence of the amount of alcohol or drug in a person's blood, urine, breath, or other bodily substance at the alleged time, as determined by a chemical analysis of the person's blood, urine, breath, or other bodily substance shall be admissible. Where such a chemical test is made, the following provisions shall apply:

(1)(A) Chemical analysis of the person's blood, urine, breath, or other bodily substance, to be considered valid under this Code section, shall have been performed according to methods approved by the Division of Forensic Sciences of the Georgia Bureau of Investigation on a machine which was operated with all its electronic and operating components prescribed by its manufacturer properly attached and in good working order and by an individual possessing a valid permit issued by the Division of Forensic Sciences for this purpose. The Division of Forensic Sciences of the Georgia Bureau of Investigation shall approve satisfactory techniques or methods to ascertain the qualifications and competence of individuals to conduct analyses and to issue permits, along with requirements for properly operating and maintaining any testing instruments, and to issue certificates certifying that instruments have met those requirements, which certificates and permits shall be subject to termination or revocation at the discretion of the Division of Forensic Sciences.

(B) In all cases where the arrest is made on or after January 1, 1995, and the state selects breath testing, two sequential breath samples shall be requested for the testing of alcohol concentration. For either or both of these sequential samples to be admissible in the state's or plaintiff's case-in-chief, the readings shall not differ from each other by an alcohol concentration of greater than 0.020 grams and the lower of the two results shall be determinative for accusation and indictment purposes and administrative license suspension purposes. No more than two sequential series of a total of two adequate breath samples each shall be requested by the state; provided, however, that after an initial test in which the instrument indicates an adequate breath sample was given for analysis, any subsequent refusal to give additional breath samples shall not be construed as a refusal for purposes of suspension of a driver's license under Code Sections 40–5–55 and 40–5–67.1. Notwithstanding the above, a refusal to give an adequate sample or samples on any subsequent breath, blood, urine, or other bodily substance test shall not affect the admissibility of the results of any prior samples. An adequate breath sample shall mean a breath sample sufficient to cause the breath-testing instrument to produce a printed alcohol concentration analysis.

(2) When a person shall undergo a chemical test at the request of a law enforcement officer, only a physician, registered nurse, laboratory technician, emergency medical technician, or other qualified person may withdraw blood for the purpose of determining the alcoholic content therein, provided that this limitation shall not apply to the taking of breath or urine specimens. No physician, registered nurse, or other qualified person or employer thereof shall incur any civil or criminal liability as a result of the medically proper obtaining of such blood specimens when requested in writing by a law enforcement officer;

(3) The person tested may have a physician or a qualified technician, chemist, registered nurse, or other qualified person of his own choosing administer a chemical test or tests in

addition to any administered at the direction of a law enforcement officer. The justifiable failure or inability to obtain an additional test shall not preclude the admission of evidence relating to the test or tests taken at the direction of a law enforcement officer; and

(4) Upon the request of the person who shall submit to a chemical test or tests at the request of a law enforcement officer, full information concerning the test or tests shall be made available to him or his attorney. The arresting officer at the time of arrest shall advise the person arrested of his rights to a chemical test or tests according to this Code section.

(b) Except as provided in subsection (c) of this Code section, upon the trial of any civil or criminal action or proceeding arising out of acts alleged to have been committed by any person in violation of Code Section 40–6–391, the amount of alcohol in the person's blood at the time alleged, as shown by chemical analysis of the person's blood, urine, breath, or other bodily substance, may give rise to inferences as follows:

(1) If there was at that time an alcohol concentration of 0.05 grams or less, the trier of fact in its discretion may infer therefrom that the person was not under the influence of alcohol, as prohibited by paragraphs (1) and (4) of subsection (a) of Code Section 40–6–391; or

(2) If there was at that time an alcohol concentration in excess of 0.05 grams but less than 0.08 grams, such fact shall not give rise to any inference that the person was or was not under the influence of alcohol, as prohibited by paragraphs (1) and (4) of subsection (a) of Code Section 40–6–391, but such fact may be considered by the trier of fact with other competent evidence in determining whether the person was under the influence of alcohol, as prohibited by paragraphs (1) and (4) of subsection (a) of Code Section 40–6–391.

(c)(1) In any civil or criminal action or proceeding arising out of acts alleged to have been committed in violation of paragraph (5) of subsection (a) of Code Section 40–6–391, if there was at that time or within three hours after driving or being in actual physical control of a moving vehicle from alcohol consumed before such driving or being in actual physical control ended an alcohol concentration of 0.08 or more grams in the person's blood, breath, or urine, the person shall be in violation of paragraph (5) of subsection (a) of Code Section 40–6–391.

(2) In any civil or criminal action or proceeding arising out of acts alleged to have been committed by any person in violation of subsection (i) of Code Section 40–6–391, if there was at that time or within three hours after driving or being in actual physical control of a moving vehicle from alcohol consumed before such driving or being in actual physical control ended an alcohol concentration of 0.04 grams or more in the person's blood, breath, or urine, the person shall be in violation of subsection (i) of Code Section 40–6–391.

(3) In any civil or criminal action or proceeding arising out of acts alleged to have been committed by any person in violation of subsection (k) of Code Section 40–6–391, if there was at that time or within three hours after driving or being in actual physical control of a moving vehicle from alcohol consumed before such driving or being in actual physical control ended an alcohol concentration of 0.02 grams or more in the person's blood, breath, or urine, the person shall be in violation of subsection (k) of Code Section 40–6–391.

(d) In any criminal trial, the refusal of the defendant to permit a chemical analysis to be made of his blood, breath, urine, or other bodily substance at the time of his arrest shall be admissible in evidence against him.

(e)(1) A certification by the office of the Secretary of State or by the Department of Community Health that a person who drew blood was a licensed or certified physician, physician assistant, registered nurse, practical nurse, medical technologist, medical laboratory technician, or phlebotomist at the time the blood was drawn;

(2) Testimony, under oath, of the blood drawer; or

(3) Testimony, under oath, of the blood drawer's supervisor or medical records custodian that the blood drawer was properly trained and authorized to draw blood as an employee of the medical facility or employer

shall be admissible into evidence for the purpose of establishing that such person was qualified to draw blood as required by this Code section.

(f) Each time an approved breath-testing instrument is inspected, the inspector shall prepare a certificate which shall be signed under oath by the inspector and which shall include the following language:

"This breath-testing instrument (serial no. _____) was thoroughly inspected, tested, and standardized by the undersigned on (date _____) and all of its electronic and operating components prescribed by its manufacturer are properly attached and are in good working order."

When properly prepared and executed, as prescribed in this subsection, the certificate shall, notwithstanding any other provision of law, be self-authenticating, shall be admissible in any court of law, and shall satisfy the pertinent requirements of paragraph (1) of subsection (a) of this Code section and subparagraph (g)(2)(F) of Code Section 40–5–67.1.

Laws 1953, Nov.-Dec. Sess., p. 556, § 47; Laws 1968, p. 448, §§ 1, 2; Laws 1974, p. 562, §§ 1, 2; Laws 1974, p. 633, § 1; Laws 1975, p. 1008, § 3; Laws 1977, p. 1036, § 1; Laws 1983, p. 1000, § 14; Laws 1988, p. 1893, §§ 3, 5; Laws 1990, p. 2048, § 5; Laws 1991, p. 1886, § 10; Laws 1992, p. 2564, § 13; Laws 1994, p. 1600, § 10; Laws 1995, p. 1160, § 4; Laws 1997, p. 143, § 40; Laws 1997, p. 760, § 25; Laws 2001, p. 208, § 1–6; Laws 2009, Act 102, § 1–4, eff. July 1, 2009; Laws 2009, Act 243, § 3, eff. July 1, 2009.

FormerlyCode 1933, § 68A–902.1.

Historical and Statutory Notes

The 2001 amendment rewrote subsecs. (b), (c), and (e) which formerly provided:

"(b) Except as provided in subsection (c) of this Code section, upon the trial of any civil or criminal action or proceeding arising out of acts alleged to have been committed by any person in violation of Code Section 40–6–391, the amount of alcohol in the person's blood at the time alleged, as shown by chemical analysis of the person's blood, urine, breath, or other bodily substance, shall give rise to the following presumptions:

"(1) If there was at that time an alcohol concentration of 0.05 grams or less, it shall be presumed that the person was not under the influence of alcohol, as prohibited by paragraphs (1), (2), and (4) of subsection (a) of Code Section 40–6–391;

"(2) If there was at that time an alcohol concentration in excess of 0.05 grams but less than 0.08 grams, such fact shall not give rise to any presumption that the person was or was not under the influence of alcohol, as prohibited by paragraphs (1), (2), and (4) of subsection (a) of Code Section 40–6–391, but such fact may be considered with other competent evidence in determining whether the person was under the influence of alcohol, as prohibited by paragraphs (1), (2), and (4) of subsection (a) of Code Section 40–6–391;

"(3) If there was at that time an alcohol concentration of 0.08 grams or more, it shall be presumed that the person was under the influence of alcohol, as prohibited by paragraphs (1), (2), and (4) of subsection (a) of Code Section 40–6–391; and

"(4) If there was at that time or within three hours after driving or being in actual physical control of a moving vehicle from alcohol consumed before such driving or being in actual physical control ended an alcohol concentration of 0.10 or more grams, the person shall be in violation of paragraph (5) of subsection (a) of Code Section 40–6–391.

"(c)(1) In any civil or criminal action or proceeding arising out of acts alleged to have been committed by any person in violation of subsection (i) of Code Section 40–6–391, if there was at that time or within three hours after driving or being in actual physical control of a moving vehicle from alcohol consumed before such driving or being in actual physical control ended an alcohol concentration of 0.04 grams or more in the person's blood, breath, or urine, the person shall be in violation of subsection (i) of Code Section 40–6–391.

"(2) In any civil or criminal action or proceeding arising out of acts alleged to have been committed by any person in violation of subsection (k) of Code Section 40–6–391, if there was at that time or within three hours after driving or being in actual physical control of a moving vehicle from alcohol consumed before such driving or being in actual physical control ended an alcohol concentration of 0.02 grams or more in the person's blood, breath, or urine, the person shall be in violation of subsection (k) of Code Section 40–6–391.

"(e) A certification by the office of the Secretary of State or by the Department of Human Resources that a person was a licensed or certified physician, physician's assistant, registered nurse, practical nurse, medical technologist, medical laboratory technician, or phlebotomist at the time the blood was drawn shall be admissible into evidence for the purpose of establishing that such person was qualified to draw blood as required by this Code section."

The 2009 amendment by Act 102 substituted "Department of Community Health" for "Department of Human Resources" throughout the section.

The 2009 amendment by Act 243, in subsec. (e)(1), substituted "physician assistant" for "physician's assistant"'.

§ 40–6–393. Homicide by vehicle

(a) Any person who, without malice aforethought, causes the death of another person through the violation of subsection (a) of Code Section 40–6–163, Code Section 40–6–390 or 40–6–391, or subsection (a) of Code Section 40–6–395 commits the offense of homicide by vehicle in the first degree and, upon conviction thereof, shall be punished by imprisonment for not less than three years nor more than 15 years.

(b) Any driver of a motor vehicle who, without malice aforethought, causes an accident which causes the death of another person and leaves the scene of the accident in violation of subsection (b) of Code Section 40–6–270 commits the offense of homicide by vehicle in the first degree and, upon conviction thereof, shall be punished by imprisonment for not less than three years nor more than 15 years.

(c) Any person who causes the death of another person, without an intention to do so, by violating any provision of this title other than subsection (a) of Code Section 40–6–163, subsection (b) of Code Section 40–6–270, Code Section 40–6–390 or 40–6–391, or subsection (a) of Code Section 40–6–395 commits the offense of homicide by vehicle in the second degree when such violation is the cause of said death and, upon conviction thereof, shall be punished as provided in Code Section 17–10–3.

(d) Any person who, after being declared a habitual violator as determined under Code Section 40–5–58 and while such person's license is in revocation, causes the death of another person, without malice aforethought, by operation of a motor vehicle, commits the offense of homicide by vehicle in the first degree and, upon conviction thereof, shall be punished by imprisonment for not less than five years nor more than 20 years, and adjudication of guilt or imposition of such sentence for a person so convicted may be suspended, probated, deferred, or withheld but only after such person shall have served at least one year in the penitentiary.

Laws 1974, p. 633, § 1; Laws 1976, p. 977, § 1; Laws 1982, p. 1694, §§ 1, 3; Laws 1983, p. 1000, § 15; Laws 1990, p. 2048, § 5; Laws 1992, p. 2093, § 1; Laws 1999, p. 391, § 9; Laws 2008, Act 793, § 2, eff. July 1, 2008.

Formerly Code 1933, § 68A–903.

Historical and Statutory Notes

The 2008 amendment by Act 793 rewrote this section, which formerly read:

"(a) Any person who, without malice aforethought, causes the death of another person through the violation of subsection (a) of Code Section 40–6–163 or subsection (b) of Code Section 40–6–270 or Code Section 40–6–390 or 40–6–391 or subsection (a) of Code Section 40–6–395 commits the offense of homicide by vehicle in the first degree and, upon conviction thereof, shall be punished by imprisonment for not less than three years nor more than 15 years.

"(b) Any person who causes the death of another person, without an intention to do so, by violating any provision of this title other than subsection (a) of Code Section 40–6–163 or subsection (b) of Code Section 40–6–270 or Code Section 40–6–390 or 40–6–391 or subsection (a) of Code Section 40–6–395 commits the offense of homicide by vehicle in the second degree when such violation is the cause of said death and, upon conviction thereof, shall be punished as provided in Code Section 17–10–3.

"(c) Any person who, after being declared a habitual violator as determined under Code Section 40–5–58 and while such person's license is in revocation, causes the death of another person, without malice aforethought, by operation of a motor vehicle, commits the offense of homicide by vehicle in the first degree and, upon conviction thereof, shall be punished by imprisonment for not less than five years nor more than 20 years, and adjudication of guilt or imposition of such sentence for a person so convicted may be suspended, probated, deferred, or withheld but only after such person shall have served at least one year in the penitentiary."

Laws 2008, Act 793, § 6, provides:

"This Act shall become effective on July 1, 2008, and shall apply to all offenses committed on or after such date."

§ 40–6–393.1. Feticide by vehicle in the first degree

(a) For the purposes of this Code section, the term "unborn child" means a member of the species homo sapiens at any stage of development who is carried in the womb.

(b)(1) A person commits the offense of feticide by vehicle in the first degree if he or she causes the death of an unborn child by any injury to the mother of such child which would be homicide by vehicle in the first degree as provided in subsection (a), (b), or (d) of Code Section 40–6–393 if it resulted in the death of such mother.

(2) A person convicted of the offense of feticide by vehicle in the first degree shall be punished by imprisonment for not less than three years nor more than 15 years.

(c)(1) A person commits the offense of feticide by vehicle in the second degree if he or she causes the death of an unborn child by any injury to the mother of such child by violating any provision of this title other than Code Section 40–6–390 or 40–6–391, which would be homicide by vehicle in the second degree as provided in subsection (c) of Code Section 40–6–393 if it resulted in the death of such mother.

(2) A person convicted of the offense of feticide by vehicle in the second degree shall be punished as provided in Code Section 17–10–3.

Laws 1991, p. 1109, § 1; Laws 2006, Act 654, § 3, eff. July 1, 2006; Laws 2008, Act 793, § 3, eff. July 1, 2008.

Historical and Statutory Notes

The 2006 amendment by Act 654 rewrote the section which had read:

"(a)(1) A person commits the offense of feticide by vehicle in the first degree if he causes the death of an unborn child so far developed as to be ordinarily called 'quick' by any injury to the mother of such child through the violation of Code Section 40–6–390 or 40–6–391, which would be homicide by vehicle in the first degree as provided in subsection (a) or (c) of Code Section 40–6–393 if it resulted in the death of such mother.

"(2) A person convicted of the offense of feticide by vehicle in the first degree shall be punished by imprisonment for not less than two years nor more than 15 years.

"(b)(1) A person commits the offense of feticide by vehicle in the second degree if he causes the death of an unborn child so far developed as to be ordinarily called 'quick' by any injury to the mother of such child by violating any provision of this title other than Code Section 40–6–390 or 40–6–391, which would be homicide by vehicle in the second degree as provided in subsection (b) of Code Section 40–6–393 if it resulted in the death of such mother.

"(2) A person convicted of the offense of feticide by vehicle in the second degree shall be punished as provided in Code Section 17–10–3."

Laws 2006, Act 654, § 5, provides:

"This Act shall become effective on July 1, 2006, and shall apply to all offenses committed on or after such date."

The 2008 amendment by Act 793, in subsec. (b), par. (2), increased the minimum length of imprisonment from not less than 2 years to not less than 3 years, and corrected internal references throughout the rest of the section.

Laws 2008, Act 793, § 6, provides:

"This Act shall become effective on July 1, 2008, and shall apply to all offenses committed on or after such date."

§ 40–6–394. Serious injury by vehicle

Whoever, without malice, shall cause bodily harm to another by depriving him of a member of his body, by rendering a member of his body useless, by seriously disfiguring his body or a member thereof, or by causing organic brain damage which renders the body or any member thereof useless through the violation of Code Section 40–6–390 or 40–6–391 shall be guilty of the crime of serious injury by vehicle. A person convicted under this Code section shall be guilty of a felony and shall be punished by imprisonment for not less than one year nor more than 15 years.

Laws 1979, p. 768, § 1; Laws 1985, p. 758, § 18; Laws 1989, p. 232, § 1; Laws 1990, p. 2048, § 5; Laws 1999, p. 391, § 10.

Formerly Code 1933, § 68A–903.1.

§ 40–6–395. Fleeing or attempting to elude a police officer; impersonation of a law enforcement officer

(a) It shall be unlawful for any driver of a vehicle willfully to fail or refuse to bring his or her vehicle to a stop or otherwise to flee or attempt to elude a pursuing police vehicle or police officer when given a visual or an audible signal to bring the vehicle to a stop. The signal given by the police officer may be by hand, voice, emergency light, or siren. The officer giving such signal shall be in uniform prominently displaying his or her badge of office, and his or her vehicle shall be appropriately marked showing it to be an official police vehicle.

(b)(1) Any person violating the provisions of subsection (a) of this Code section shall be guilty of a high and aggravated misdemeanor and:

(A) Upon conviction shall be fined not less than $500.00 nor more than $5,000.00, which fine shall not be subject to suspension, stay, or probation and imprisoned for not less than ten days nor more than 12 months. Any period of such imprisonment in excess of ten days may, in the sole discretion of the judge, be suspended, stayed, or probated;

(B) Upon the second conviction within a ten-year period of time, as measured from the dates of previous arrests for which convictions were obtained to the date of the current arrest for which a conviction is obtained, shall be fined not less than $1,000.00 nor more than $5,000.00, which fine shall not be subject to suspension, stay, or probation and imprisoned for not less than 30 days nor more than 12 months. Any period of such imprisonment in excess of 30 days may, in the sole discretion of the judge, be suspended, stayed, or probated; and for purposes of this paragraph, previous pleas of nolo contendere accepted within such ten-year period shall constitute convictions; and

(C) Upon the third or subsequent conviction within a ten-year period of time, as measured from the dates of previous arrests for which convictions were obtained to the date of the current arrest for which a conviction is obtained, shall be fined not less than $2,500.00 nor more than $5,000.00, which fine shall not be subject to suspension, stay, or probation and imprisoned for not less than 90 days nor more than 12 months. Any period of such imprisonment in excess of 90 days may, in the sole discretion of the judge, be suspended, stayed, or probated; and for purposes of this paragraph, previous pleas of nolo contendere accepted within such ten-year period shall constitute convictions.

(2) For the purpose of imposing a sentence under this subsection, a plea of nolo contendere shall constitute a conviction.

(3) If the payment of the fine required under paragraph (1) of this subsection will impose an economic hardship on the defendant, the judge, at his or her sole discretion, may order the defendant to pay such fine in installments and such order may be enforced through a contempt proceeding or a revocation of any probation otherwise authorized by this subsection.

(4) Notwithstanding the limits set forth in any municipal charter, any municipal court of any municipality shall be authorized to impose the punishments provided for in this subsection upon a conviction of violating this subsection or upon conviction of violating any ordinance adopting the provisions of this subsection.

(5)(A) Any person violating the provisions of subsection (a) of this Code section who, while fleeing or attempting to elude a pursuing police vehicle or police officer in an attempt to escape arrest for any offense, other than a violation of this chapter not expressly provided for in this paragraph:

(i) Operates his or her vehicle in excess of 20 miles an hour above the posted speed limit;

(ii) Strikes or collides with another vehicle or a pedestrian;

(iii) Flees in traffic conditions which place the general public at risk of receiving serious injuries;

(iv) Commits a violation of paragraph (5) of subsection (a) of Code Section 40–6–391; or

(v) Leaves the state

shall be guilty of a felony punishable by a fine of $5,000.00 or imprisonment for not less than one year nor more than five years or both.

(B) Following adjudication of guilt or imposition of sentence for a violation of subparagraph (A) of this paragraph, the sentence shall not be suspended, probated, deferred, or withheld, and the charge shall not be reduced to a lesser offense, merged with any other offense, or served concurrently with any other offense.

(c) It shall be unlawful for a person:

(1) To impersonate a sheriff, deputy sheriff, state trooper, agent of the Georgia Bureau of Investigation, agent of the Federal Bureau of Investigation, police officer, or any other authorized law enforcement officer by using a motor vehicle or motorcycle designed, equipped, or marked so as to resemble a motor vehicle or motorcycle belonging to any federal, state, or local law enforcement agency; or

(2) Otherwise to impersonate any such law enforcement officer in order to direct, stop, or otherwise control traffic.

Laws 1974, p. 633, § 1; Laws 1978, p. 1483, § 2; Laws 1983, p. 836, § 1; Laws 1985, p. 758, § 19; Laws 1987, p. 3, § 40; Laws 1990, p. 585, § 1; Laws 1990, p. 2048, § 5; Laws 1992, p. 6, § 40; Laws 1994, p. 831, § 3; Laws 1995, p. 855, § 2; Laws 2004, Act 512, § 1, eff. July 1, 2004; Laws 2010, Act 412, § 2, eff. July 1, 2010.

Formerly Code 1933, § 68A–904.

Historical and Statutory Notes

The 2004 amendment by Act 512, in subsec. (b), par. (5)(A), substituted "arrest for any offense" for "arrest for a felony offense", substituted "or imprisonment" for "and imprisonment", and added "or both" following "five years".

The 2010 amendment by Act 412 rewrote subsec. (b), par. (5), subpar. (A) which had read as follows:

"Any person violating the provisions of subsection (a) of this Code section who, while fleeing or attempting to elude a pursuing police vehicle or police officer in an attempt to escape arrest for any offense other than a violation of this chapter, operates his or her vehicle in excess of 30 miles an hour above the posted speed limit, strikes or collides with another vehicle or a pedestrian, flees in traffic conditions which place the general public at risk of receiving serious injuries, or leaves the state shall be guilty of a felony punishable by a fine of $5,000.00 or imprisonment for not less than one year nor more than five years or both."

Laws 2010, Act 412, § 3, provides:

"This Act shall become effective on July 1, 2010, and be applicable to all offenses committed on or after that date."

§ 40–6–396. Homicide or serious injury by interference with traffic-control device or railroad sign or signal

(a) Any person who, without malice aforethought, causes the death of another person through the violation of subsection (a) of Code Section 40–6–26 commits the offense of homicide by interference with an official traffic-control device or railroad sign or signal and, upon conviction thereof, shall be punished by imprisonment for not less than two nor more than 15 years.

(b) Any person who, without malice aforethought, causes bodily harm to another by depriving such other person of a member of his or her body, by rendering a member of his or her body useless, by seriously disfiguring his or her body or a member thereof, or by causing organic brain damage which renders the body or any member thereof useless through the violation of subsection (a) of Code Section 40–6–26 commits the offense of serious injury by interference with an official traffic-control device or railroad sign or signal and, upon conviction thereof, shall be punished by imprisonment for not less than one nor more than five years.

Laws 1996, p. 1281, § 3.

§ 40–6–397. Aggressive driving

(a) A person commits the offense of aggressive driving when he or she operates any motor vehicle with the intent to annoy, harass, molest, intimidate, injure, or obstruct another person, including without limitation violating Code Section 40–6–42, 40–6–48, 40–6–49, 40–6–123, 40–6–184, 40–6–312, or 40–6–390 with such intent.

(b) Any person convicted of aggressive driving shall be guilty of a misdemeanor of a high and aggravated nature.

Laws 2001, p. 208, § 1–7.

CHAPTER 7

OFF–ROAD VEHICLES

§ 40–7–1. Short title

This chapter shall be known and may be cited as the "Off–Road Vehicle Act of 1975."

Laws 1976, p. 330, § 1.

§ 40–7–2. Declaration of policy

The rapid increase in the use of off-road vehicles and their growing impact upon aspects of the public interest are matters of concern to the General Assembly and to the people of this state. Therefore, in order to promote the safe use of off-road vehicles, to protect the wildlife and natural resources of the state, and to guarantee the availability of various forms of recreation to all citizens in an environment of diversity and quality, this chapter is enacted.

Laws 1976, p. 330, § 2; Laws 1985, p. 149, § 40.

§ 40–7–3. Definitions

As used in this chapter, the term "off-road vehicle" means any motorized vehicle designed for or capable of cross-country travel on or immediately over land, water, snow, ice, marsh, swampland, or other natural terrain and not intended for use predominantly on public roads. It includes, but is not limited to, four-wheel drive or low-pressure tire vehicles, two-wheel vehicles, amphibious machines, ground effect or air cushion vehicles, and any other means of transportation deriving power from any source other than muscle or wind, except that such term shall exclude any motorboat; any military, fire, law enforcement, or other government vehicle being used for official purposes; any vehicles used exclusively on airports; all farm machinery, farm tractors, and other vehicles used exclusively for agricultural purposes; any self-propelled equipment for harvesting and transportation of forest products, for clearing land for planting, for utility services and maintenance, for earth moving, construction, or mining; and self-propelled lawnmowers, snowblowers, garden or lawn tractors, or golf carts, while such vehicles are being used exclusively for their designed purposes.

Laws 1976, p. 330, § 3; Laws 2010, Act 365, § 1–1, eff. July 1, 2010.

§ 40–7–4. Operating restrictions

Any person operating an off-road vehicle under any of the following conditions shall be deemed to be in violation of this chapter and subject to the penalties provided in Code Section 40–7–6:

(1) Without operative brakes or without mufflers or other silencing equipment;

(2) On any private property without the express written permission of the owner of the property or his or her agent; or

(3) Within any perennial stream, except when directly crossing such stream. As used in this paragraph, the term "perennial stream" means a stream:

(A) That under normal circumstances has water flowing year round;

(B) That has the channel located below the ground-water table most of the year;

(C) For which ground water is the primary source of water; and

(D) For which runoff from rainfall is a supplemental source of water flow.

Laws 1976, p. 330, § 4; Laws 1994, p. 97, § 40; Laws 2010, Act 365, § 1–2, eff. July 1, 2010.

Historical and Statutory Notes

The 2010 amendment by Act 365 added subsec. (3) and made the section gender neutral.

§ 40–7–5. Authority to regulate time periods and to establish zones of use

(a) Incorporated towns and municipalities and counties shall have the authority to adopt ordinances consistent with state laws or regulations to regulate time periods and zones of use for off-road vehicles.

(b) Agencies of state government shall have the authority to adopt rules and regulations to regulate time periods and zones for use for off-road vehicles on property under their jurisdiction or management.

Laws 1976, p. 330, § 5.

§ 40–7–6. Enforcement

All peace officers shall enforce the provisions of this chapter. Any person who violates any provision of this chapter shall not thereby be guilty of a criminal act but shall be subject to a civil penalty of not less than $25.00.

Laws 1976, p. 330, § 6; Laws 2010, Act 365, § 1–3, eff. July 1, 2010.

Historical and Statutory Notes

The 2010 amendment by Act 365 rewrote the second sentence which had read as follows:

"Any person who violates any provision of this chapter shall be guilty of a misdemeanor and, upon conviction thereof, shall be punished by a fine not to exceed $25.00."

CHAPTER 8

EQUIPMENT AND INSPECTION OF MOTOR VEHICLES

Article 1

Part 1

Article 1

Equipment Generally

Part 1

General Provisions

§ 40–8–1. Exceptions; additional parts and accessories not prohibited

(a) This article shall not apply to implements of husbandry, road machinery, road rollers, farm tractors, or three-wheeled motorcycles used only for agricultural purposes, except when expressly made applicable. This article shall not apply to motorized carts.

(b) Nothing in this article shall be construed to prohibit the use of additional parts and accessories on any vehicle, which use is not inconsistent with the provisions of this article.

Laws 1953, Nov.-Dec. Sess., p. 556, § 102; Laws 1973, p. 598, § 3; Laws 1982, p. 165, § 4; Laws 1982, p. 165, § 10; Laws 1984, p. 1329, § 3; Laws 1992, p. 6, § 40.

Formerly Code 1933, § 68E–101.

§ 40–8–2. Rules and regulations as to motor vehicles within jurisdiction of Department of Public Safety

In addition to the requirements of this article, the commissioner of public safety, as to the motor vehicles within the jurisdiction of the Department of Public Safety, shall have the authority to promulgate rules designed to promote safety pursuant to the provisions of Chapter 16 of this title and Chapter 7 of Title 46. Any such rules promulgated or deemed necessary by the commissioner shall include the following: every motor unit and all parts thereof shall be maintained in a safe condition at all times. The lights, brakes, and equipment shall meet such safety requirements as the commissioner shall promulgate from time to time.

Laws 1953, Nov.-Dec. Sess., p. 556, § 102; Laws 1973, p. 598, § 3; Laws 1982, p. 165, § 4; Laws 1982, p. 165, § 10; Laws 2000, p. 951, § 5B–1; Laws 2005, Act 68, § 19–1, eff. July 1, 2005.

Formerly Code 1933, § 68E–102.

§ 40–8–3. Certain vehicles and loads prohibited

No vehicle or load any portion of which drags or slides on the surface of the roadway shall be used or transported on the highways. No vehicle shall be used or transported on the highways the wheels of which, while being used or transported, either from construction or otherwise, cause pounding on the road surface.

Laws 1927, p. 226, § 17; Laws 1970, p. 628, § 1; Laws 1982, p. 165, § 4; Laws 1982, p. 165, § 10.

Formerly Code 1933, § 68–404; Code 1933, § 68E–103.

§ 40–8–4. Slow-moving vehicles and three-wheeled motorcycles used only for agricultural purposes; emblem required

(a) It shall be unlawful for any person to operate upon the public roads of this state any slow-moving vehicle or equipment, any farm trailer or semitrailer which is used for agricultural purposes and which would otherwise be exempt from this article as an implement of husbandry under Code Section 40–8–1, any animal drawn vehicle, or any machinery designed for use and generally operated at speeds less than 25 miles per hour, including all road construction or maintenance equipment and machinery except when engaged in actual construction or maintenance procedures and all other construction equipment and machinery, unless there is displayed on the rear thereof an emblem which shall comply with subsection (b) of this Code section. It shall also be unlawful to operate upon the public roads of this state without such an emblem any three-wheeled motorcycle used only for agricultural purposes unless such three-wheeled motorcycle is licensed as required by Chapter 2 of this title and is in compliance with all other requirements of this chapter.

(b) The emblem required by subsection (a) of this Code section shall conform with those standards and specifications adopted for slow-moving vehicles by the American Society of Agricultural Engineers in December, 1966, and contained within such society's standard ASAE S276.1, or shall be an emblem of the same shape and size painted on such vehicle in a bright and conspicuous retroreflective red orange paint. Such emblem shall be mounted on the rear of such vehicles, in the approximate horizontal geometric center of the vehicle, at a height of three to five feet above the roadway, and shall be maintained at all times in a clean and reflective condition.

(c) Any person violating this Code section shall be guilty of a misdemeanor.

(d) Nothing in this Code section shall apply to any self-propelled, two-wheeled vehicle.

Laws 1970, p. 229, §§ 1–4; Laws 1982, p. 165, § 4; Laws 1982, p. 165, § 10; Laws 1984, p. 1329, § 4; Laws 1989, p. 298, § 1.

Formerly Code 1933, § 68E–104.

§ 40–8–5. Tampering with, adjusting, altering, etc., odometer to reflect lower mileage; penalty for violation

(a) It shall be unlawful for any person knowingly to tamper with, adjust, alter, change, set back, disconnect, or fail to connect an odometer of a motor vehicle, or to cause any of the foregoing to occur to an odometer of a motor vehicle, so as to reflect a lower mileage than the motor vehicle has actually been driven, except as provided in this Code section.

(b) It shall be unlawful for any person knowingly to bring into this state a motor vehicle which reflects a lower mileage than the motor vehicle actually has been driven due to any illegal acts outlined in subsection (a) of this Code section.

(c) It shall be unlawful for any person knowingly to sell or attempt to sell a motor vehicle which reflects a lower mileage than the motor vehicle actually has been driven due to any illegal acts outlined in subsection (a) of this Code section.

(d) Subsections (a), (b), and (c) of this Code section shall not apply to the disconnection of the odometer used for registering the mileage or use of new motor vehicles being tested by the manufacturer prior to delivery to a franchised dealer.

(e) It shall be unlawful for any person to advertise for sale, to sell, to use, to install, or to have installed any device which causes an odometer to register any mileage other than the actual mileage driven. For the purposes of this subsection, the actual mileage driven is that mileage driven by the vehicle as registered by the odometer within the manufacturer's designed tolerance.

(f) It shall be unlawful for any person to conspire with any other person to violate this Code section.

(g)(1) In addition to any other penalty provided by law, any person who, with intent to defraud, violates this Code section shall be liable in an amount equal to the sum of:

(A) Three times the amount of actual damages sustained or $1,500.00, whichever is greater; and

(B) In the case of any successful action to enforce the foregoing liability, the costs of the action, together with reasonable attorney's fees, as determined by the court.

(2) Any action to enforce any liability created under this subsection may be brought in any superior court or state court having proper jurisdiction, within two years from the date on which the liability arises.

(h)(1) If any person violates any provision of this Code section, the Attorney General, any district attorney in this state, or any solicitor-general in this state may bring an action in any superior court or state court having jurisdiction to restrain such violation.

(2) Any action arising under paragraph (1) of this subsection may be brought within two years from the date of the violation.

(i) Any person violating this Code section shall be guilty of a misdemeanor.

Laws 1975, p. 754, §§ 1, 2; Laws 1977, p. 1227, § 1; Laws 1981, p. 649, § 1; Laws 1982, p. 165, § 4; Laws 1982, p. 165, § 10; Laws 1985, p. 149, § 40; Laws 1996, p. 748, § 20.

Formerly Code 1933, § 68E–105.

§ 40–8–6. Alteration of suspension system; operation of vehicle with altered suspension system; penalty for violation

(a) It shall be unlawful to alter the suspension system of any private passenger motor vehicle which may be operated on any public street or highway more than two inches above or below the factory recommendation for any such vehicle.

(b) It shall be unlawful to operate any private passenger motor vehicle upon any highway, roadway, or street if the suspension system of such vehicle has been altered more than two inches above or below the factory recommendation for such vehicle.

(c) It shall be unlawful to operate any motor vehicle upon any highway, roadway, or street if the springs relative to the suspension system are broken.

(d) Any person violating this Code section shall be guilty of a misdemeanor.

Laws 1973, p. 458, §§ 1, 2; Laws 1975, p. 763, § 1; Laws 1982, p. 165, § 4; Laws 1982, p. 165, § 10.

Formerly Code 1933, § 68E–106.

§ 40–8–6.1. Alteration of suspension system of trucks; operation of truck with altered suspension; penalty for violation

(a) As used in this Code section, the term:

(1) "Frame" means the main longitudinal structural members of the chassis of a truck.

(2) "Frame height" means the vertical distance between a level surface and the lowest point on the frame of a truck, measured when the truck is upon such level surface without a load.

(3) "Gross vehicle weight rating" means the manufacturer's gross vehicle weight rating whether or not the vehicle is modified by use of parts not originally installed by the manufacturer.

(b) It shall be unlawful to alter the suspension system of any truck with a gross vehicle weight rating of 4,500 pounds or less, which may be operated on any public street or highway, so as to exceed 27 inches as measured from the surface of the street to the lowest point on the frame of the truck.

(c) It shall be unlawful to alter the suspension system of any truck with a gross vehicle weight rating of not less than 4,501 pounds and not more than 7,500 pounds, which may be operated on any public street or highway, so as to exceed 30 inches as measured from the surface of the street to the lowest point on the frame of the truck.

(d) It shall be unlawful to alter the suspension system of any truck with a gross vehicle weight rating of not less than 7,501 pounds and not more than 14,000 pounds, which may be operated on any public street or highway, so as to exceed 31 inches as measured from the surface of the street to the lowest point on the frame of the truck.

(e) It shall be unlawful to operate any truck upon any highway, roadway, or street if the suspension system has been altered in excess of the limitations provided for in this Code section.

(f) Any person violating this Code section shall be guilty of a misdemeanor.

Laws 1986, p. 1210, § 1; Laws 1992, p. 6, § 40.

§ 40–8–7. Equipment; inspection by law enforcement officers; penalty for violation

(a) No person shall drive or move on any highway any motor vehicle, trailer, semitrailer, or pole trailer, or any combination thereof, unless the equipment upon any and every such vehicle is in good working order and adjustment as required in this chapter and the vehicle is in such safe mechanical condition as not to endanger the driver or other occupant or any person upon the highway.

(b) It is a misdemeanor for any person to drive or move, or for the owner to cause or knowingly permit to be driven or moved, on any street or highway any vehicle or combination of vehicles:

(1) Which is in such unsafe condition as to endanger any person;

(2) Which does not contain those parts or is not at all times equipped with such lights and other equipment in proper condition and adjustment as required in this chapter; or

(3) Which is equipped in any manner in violation of this chapter.

(c) It is also a misdemeanor for any person to do any act forbidden or fail to perform any act required under this chapter.

(d) Any vehicle suspected of being operated in violation of this article may be the subject of an inspection conducted by any law enforcement officer who has reason to believe such violation is occurring, without the necessity of obtaining a warrant to permit such inspection.

Laws 1953, Nov.-Dec. Sess., p. 556, §§ 102, 123; Laws 1963, p. 333, § 1; Laws 1982, p. 165, § 4; Laws 1982, p. 165, § 10; Laws 1994, p. 97, § 40.

Formerly Code 1933, § 68E–107.

§ 40–8–8. Speedometer

Every motor vehicle operated upon a public street or highway shall be equipped with a speedometer in good working order.

Laws 1982, p. 165, § 4; Laws 1982, p. 165, § 10.

Formerly Code 1933, § 68E–108.

§ 40–8–9. Name display requirements for trucks having gross weight of 43,000 or more pounds

It shall be unlawful to operate in this state any truck or truck tractor having a gross weight of 43,000 or more pounds which does not comply with the vehicle identification rules of the commissioner promulgated pursuant to Chapter 7 of Title 46 and Chapter 16 of this title or the vehicle identification rules of the United States Department of Transportation.

Laws 1986, p. 946, § 1; Laws 2000, p. 951, § 5B–2; Laws 2002, p. 415, § 40; Laws 2002, p. 1378, § 6; Laws 2004, Act 582, § 8, eff. July 1, 2004.

Historical and Statutory Notes

In 2002, the Code Commission, due to irreconcilable conflicts, treated the amendment of this section by Laws 2002, p. 415, § 40, as superseded by Laws 2002, p. 1378, § 6. See *Butts County v. Strahan*, 107 S.E. 163, 151 Ga. 417 (1921).

§ 40–8–10. Driving passenger car which supplies motor vehicle's combustion engine with nitrous oxide

(a) It shall be unlawful for any person on a public road to drive a passenger car, excluding a motor home, which supplies the motor vehicle's combustion engine with nitrous oxide unless the system supplying nitrous oxide is made inoperative by disconnecting the line feeding nitrous oxide to the engine or by removing the container or containers of nitrous oxide from the vehicle.

(b) Any person who violates subsection (a) of this Code section shall be guilty of a misdemeanor.

Laws 2002, p. 1080, § 1.

Part 2

Lighting Equipment

§ 40–8–20. When lighted lights and headlights required

Every vehicle upon a highway within this state at any time from a half-hour after sunset to a half-hour before sunrise and at any time when it is raining in the driving zone and at any other time when there is not sufficient visibility to render clearly discernible persons and vehicles on the highway at a distance of 500 feet ahead shall display lights, including headlights, and illuminating devices as required in this part for different classes of vehicles, subject to exceptions with respect to parked vehicles as stated in this part.

Laws 1953, Nov.-Dec. Sess., p. 556, § 103; Laws 1973, p. 434, § 1; Laws 1977, p. 667, § 1; Laws 1982, p. 165, § 4; Laws 1982, p. 165, § 10.

Formerly Code 1933, § 68E–201.

§ 40–8–21. Standards applicable to visibility distance and mounted height of lights

(a) Whenever this article declares the required distance from which certain lights and devices shall render objects visible or within which such lights or devices shall be visible, such provisions shall apply during the times stated in Code Section 40–8–20 in respect to a vehicle without load when upon a straight, level, unlighted highway under normal atmospheric conditions, unless a different time or condition is expressly stated.

(b) Except as provided in subsection (c) of this Code section, whenever this article declares the required mounted height of lights or devices, it shall mean the distance from the center of such light or device to the level ground upon which the vehicle stands when such vehicle is without a load.

(c)(1) As used in this subsection, the term "wrecker" means any vehicle designed to tow other vehicles.

(2) Except as provided in paragraph (3) of this subsection, the taillights required by Code Section 40–8–23, the brake lights required by Code Section 40–8–26, and the rear turn signal devices required by Code Section 40–8–26 shall be permanently mounted on a wrecker so as to be visible above any vehicle being towed by such wrecker by the drivers of vehicles following such wrecker.

(3) If a wrecker is not permanently equipped with lights as required by paragraph (2) of this subsection, then whenever a wrecker is towing another vehicle temporary taillights, brake lights, and rear turn signals which function so as to signal the actions of the wrecker shall be attached to the vehicle being towed so as to be visible by the drivers of vehicles following such wrecker.

Laws 1953, Nov.-Dec. Sess., p. 556, § 104; Laws 1982, p. 165, § 4; Laws 1982, p. 165, § 10; Laws 1986, p. 1185, § 1.

Formerly Code 1933, § 68E–202.

§ 40–8–22. Headlights

(a) Every motor vehicle other than a motorcycle or motor driven cycle shall be equipped with at least two but not more than four headlights, with at least one on each side of the front of the motor vehicle, which headlights shall comply with the requirements and limitations set forth in this article.

(b) Every motorcycle and every motor driven cycle shall be equipped with at least one and not more than two headlights, which shall comply with the requirements and limitations of this article.

(c) Every headlight upon every motor vehicle, including every motorcycle and motor driven cycle, shall be located at a height measured from the center of the headlight of not more than 54 inches nor less than 24 inches, to be measured as set forth in subsection (b) of Code Section 40–8–21.

(d) The headlights required by this Code section shall be maintained in proper working condition and shall not be covered by any type of material, provided that the covering restriction shall not apply to any vehicle on which the original factory headlights were covered.

(e) It shall be unlawful to operate a motor vehicle unless such motor vehicle is equipped with aiming pads on each headlight.

Laws 1953, Nov.-Dec. Sess., p. 556, § 105; Laws 1957, p. 616, § 1; Laws 1982, p. 165, § 4; Laws 1982, p. 165, § 10; Laws 1992, p. 2785, § 26.

Formerly Code 1933, § 68E–203.

§ 40–8–23. Taillights

(a) Every motor vehicle, trailer, semitrailer, and pole trailer manufactured prior to January 1, 1954, shall be equipped with at least one taillight mounted on the rear, which when lighted as required in this article shall emit a red light plainly visible from a distance of 500 feet to the rear.

(b) Every motor vehicle, trailer, semitrailer, and pole trailer manufactured after January 1, 1954, shall be equipped with two taillights which meet the specifications provided in this Code section.

(c) Every taillight upon every vehicle shall be located at a height of not more than 60 inches nor less than 20 inches, to be measured as set forth in subsection (b) of Code Section 40–8–21.

(d) Either a taillight or a separate light shall be so constructed and placed as to illuminate with a white light the rear registration plate and render it clearly legible from a distance of 50 feet to the rear. Any taillight or taillights, together with any separate light for illuminating the rear registration plate, shall be so wired as to be lighted whenever the headlights or auxiliary driving lights are lighted.

(e) All lenses on taillights shall be maintained in good repair and shall meet manufacturers' specifications.

Laws 1953, Nov.-Dec. Sess., p. 556, § 106; Laws 1982, p. 165, § 4; Laws 1982, p. 165, § 10.

Formerly Code 1933, § 68E–204.

§ 40–8–24. Reflectors

(a) Every motor vehicle manufactured after March 12, 1954, and operated upon a highway, other than a truck tractor, motorcycle, or motor driven cycle, shall carry on the rear, either as a part of the taillights or separately, two red reflectors, and every motorcycle and every motor driven cycle shall carry on the rear at least one red reflector, meeting the requirements of this Code section.

(b) Every such reflector shall be mounted on the vehicle at a height not less than 20 inches nor more than 60 inches measured as set forth in subsection (b) of Code Section 40–8–21 and shall be of such size and characteristics and so mounted as to be visible at night from all distances within 300 feet to 50 feet from the rear of such vehicle except that visibility from the greater distance is hereinafter required of reflectors on certain types of vehicles.

(c) When operated, towed, or parked upon a highway, roadway, or street at any time, every trailer and semitrailer which would otherwise be exempt from this article as an implement of husbandry under Code Section 40–8–1 shall carry on the rear, either as a part of the taillights or separately, two red reflectors and shall carry on the front two red reflectors. The reflectors carried on the rear shall meet the requirements of subsection (b) of this Code section. The reflectors carried on the front of such trailer or semitrailer shall be mounted thereon at a height of not less than 20 inches nor more than 60 inches measured as set forth in subsection (b) of Code Section 40–8–21 and shall be of such size and characteristics and so mounted as to be visible at night from all distances within 300 feet to 50 feet from the front of such trailer or semitrailer.

Laws 1953, Nov.-Dec. Sess., p. 556, § 107; Laws 1982, p. 165, § 4; Laws 1982, p. 165, § 10; Laws 1989, p. 298, § 2.

Formerly Code 1933, § 68E–205.

§ 40–8–25. Brake lights and turn signals

(a) It shall be unlawful for any person to sell any motor vehicle manufactured after January 1, 1954, including any motorcycle or motor driven cycle manufactured after January 1, 1954, in this state or for any person to drive such vehicle on the highways unless it is equipped with at least one brake light meeting the requirements of Code Section 40–8–26.

(b) If a motor vehicle is manufactured with two brake lights, both must be operational.

(c) No person shall sell or offer for sale or operate on the highways any motor vehicle, trailer, or semitrailer registered in this state and manufactured or assembled after January 1, 1954, unless it is equipped with mechanical or electrical turn signals meeting the requirements of Code Section 40–8–26. This subsection shall not apply to any motorcycle or motor driven cycle manufactured prior to January 1, 1972.

Laws 1953, Nov.-Dec. Sess., p. 556, § 108; Laws 1982, p. 165, § 4; Laws 1982, p. 165, § 10.

Formerly Code 1933, § 68E–206.

§ 40–8–26. Standards for signal lights and devices

(a) Any motor vehicle may be equipped and when required under this article shall be equipped with the following signal lights or devices:

(1) A brake light on the rear which shall emit a red light and which shall be actuated upon application of the service (foot) brake and which may but need not be incorporated with a taillight; and

(2) A light or lights or mechanical signal device capable of clearly indicating any intention to turn either to the right or to the left and which shall be visible from both the front and the rear.

(b) Every brake light shall be plainly visible and understandable from a distance of 300 feet to the rear both during normal sunlight and at nighttime, and every signal light or lights indicating intention to turn shall be visible and understandable during daytime and nighttime from a distance of 300 feet from both the front and the rear. When a vehicle is equipped with a brake light or other signal lights, such light or lights shall at all times be maintained in good working condition. No brake light or signal light shall project a glaring or dazzling light.

(c) All mechanical signal devices shall be self-illuminated when in use at the times mentioned in Code Section 40–8–20.

(d) All lenses on brake lights and signal devices shall be maintained in good repair and shall meet manufacturers' specifications.

Laws 1953, Nov.-Dec. Sess., p. 556, § 112; Laws 1982, p. 165, § 4; Laws 1982, p. 165, § 10.

Formerly Code 1933, § 68E–207.

§ 40–8–27. Light or flag on projecting load

(a) Except as provided in subsection (b) of this Code section, whenever the load upon any vehicle extends to the rear four feet or more beyond the bed or body of such vehicle, there shall be displayed at the extreme rear end of the load, at the times specified in Code Section 40–8–20, a red light plainly visible from a distance of at least 500 feet to the sides and rear. The red light required under this Code section shall be in addition to the red rear light required upon every vehicle. At any other time there shall be displayed at the extreme rear end of such load a flag as described in subsection (c) of this Code section not less than 12 inches square and so hung that the entire area is visible to the driver of a vehicle approaching from the rear.

(b) Any motor vehicle or trailer transporting a load of logs, long pulpwood, poles, or posts which extend more than four feet beyond the rear of the body or bed of such vehicle shall have securely affixed as close as practical to the end of any such projection one amber strobe type lamp equipped with a multidirectional type lens so mounted as to be visible from the rear and both sides of the projecting load. If the mounting of one strobe lamp cannot be accomplished so that it is visible from the rear and both sides of the projecting load, multiple strobe lights shall be utilized so as to meet the visibility requirements of this subsection. The strobe lamp shall flash at a rate of at least 60 flashes per minute and shall be plainly visible from a distance of at least 500 feet to the rear and sides of the projecting load any time of the day or night. The lamp shall be operating at any time of the day or night when the vehicle is operated on any highway or parked on the shoulder or immediately adjacent to the traveled portion of any public roadway. The projecting load shall also be marked with a flag as described in subsection (c) of this Code section. An emergency light permit as provided for in Code Section 40–8–92 is not required on a vehicle utilizing an amber strobe light to comply with the provisions of this Code section.

(b.1) In lieu of the strobe type lamp or lamps provided for in subsection (b) of this Code section, any motor vehicle or trailer transporting a load of logs, long pulpwood, poles, or posts which extend more than four feet beyond the rear of the body or bed of such vehicle shall have securely affixed as close as practical to the end of any such projection, one light-emitting diode (LED) light equipped with a multidirectional type lens, mounted so as to be visible from the rear and from both sides of the projecting load. If the mounting of one light-emitting diode (LED) light cannot be accomplished so that it is visible from the rear and from both sides of the projecting load, multiple light-emitting diode (LED) lights shall be utilized so as to meet the visibility requirements of this subsection. The light-emitting diode (LED) light shall flash at a rate of at least 60 flashes per minute and shall be plainly visible from a distance of at least 500 feet from the rear and sides at a radius of 180 degrees of the projecting load at any time of the day or night. Any light-emitting diode (LED) light shall be constructed of durable, weather resistant material and may be powered by the vehicle's electrical system or by an independent battery system, or both. If the light-emitting diode (LED) light is powered by an independent battery system, the driver of the vehicle shall have in his or her immediate possession charged, spare batteries for use in case of battery failure. Any solid state light-emitting diode (LED) lighting that consists of multiple light-emitting diode (LED) lights shall not have less than 85 percent of the light-emitting diode (LED) lights in operable condition. The lights shall remain in operation at any time of the day or night when the vehicle is operated on any highway or parked on the shoulder or immediately adjacent to the traveled portion of any public roadway. The projecting load shall also be marked with a flag as described in subsection (c) of this Code section. An emergency light permit as provided for in Code Section 40–8–92 is not required on a vehicle utilizing a light-emitting diode (LED) light to comply with the provisions of this Code section.

(c) The flag as required by subsection (a) or (b) of this Code section shall be of a bright red or orange color not less than 12 inches square which is clearly visible and shall be displayed in such a manner that the entire area of the flag is visible from the rear of the vehicle.

Laws 1953, Nov.-Dec. Sess., p. 556, § 109; Laws 1982, p. 165, § 4; Laws 1982, p. 165, § 10; Laws 1999, p. 828, § 2; Laws 2008, Act 434, § 15, eff. Jan. 1, 2009.

Formerly Code 1933, § 68E–208.

§ 40–8–28. Lights on parked vehicles

(a) When a vehicle is lawfully parked upon a street or highway during the hours between a half-hour after sunset and a half-hour before sunrise, and there is sufficient light to reveal any person or object within a distance of 500 feet upon such street or highway, no lights need be displayed upon such parked vehicle.

(b) When a vehicle is parked or stopped upon a roadway or shoulder adjacent thereto, whether attended or unattended, during the hours between a half-hour after sunset and a half-hour before sunrise and there is not sufficient light to reveal any person or object within a distance of 500 feet upon such highway, such vehicle so parked or stopped shall be equipped with one or more lights meeting the following requirements: at least one light shall display a white or amber light visible from a distance of 500 feet to the front of the vehicle, and the same light or at least one other light shall display a red light visible from a distance of 500 feet to the rear of the vehicle; and the location of such light or lights shall always be such that at least one light or combination of lights meeting the requirements of this Code section is installed as near as practicable to the side of the vehicle which is closest to passing traffic. This subsection shall not apply to a motor driven cycle.

(c) If a vehicle is manufactured with two lights meeting the requirements of subsection (b) of this Code section, both such lights shall be maintained in good working order.

(d) Any lighted headlights upon a parked vehicle shall be depressed or dimmed.

Laws 1953, Nov.-Dec. Sess., p. 556, § 110; Laws 1982, p. 165, § 4; Laws 1982, p. 165, § 10.

Formerly Code 1933, § 68E–209.

§ 40–8–29. Spotlights and auxiliary lights

(a) Any motor vehicle may be equipped with not to exceed one spotlight, and no lighted spotlight shall be aimed and used upon any approaching vehicle. It shall be unlawful for any person except law enforcement officers and persons licensed under Chapter 38 of Title 43 to operate a spotlight from any moving vehicle on any highway or public roadway.

(b) Any motor vehicle may be equipped with not to exceed two foglights mounted on the front at a height not less than 12 inches nor more than 30 inches above the level surface upon which the vehicle stands and so aimed that when the vehicle is not loaded none of the high intensity portion of the light to the left of the center of the vehicle shall at a distance of 25 feet ahead project higher than a level of four inches below the level of the center of the light from which it comes.

(c) Any motor vehicle may be equipped with not to exceed one auxiliary passing light mounted on the front at a height not less than 24 inches nor more than 42 inches above the level surface upon which the vehicle stands, and every such auxiliary passing light shall meet the requirements and limitations set forth in this article.

(d) Any motor vehicle may be equipped with not to exceed one auxiliary driving light mounted on the front at a height not less than 16 inches nor more than 42 inches above the level surface upon which the vehicle stands, and every such auxiliary driving light shall meet the requirements and limitations set forth in this article.

Laws 1953, Nov.-Dec. Sess., p. 556, § 111; Laws 1982, p. 165, § 4; Laws 1982, p. 165, § 10; Laws 1983, p. 3, § 29; Laws 1992, p. 6, § 40.

Formerly Code 1933, § 68E–210.

§ 40–8–30. Multiple-beam road-lighting equipment

Except as hereinafter provided in this part, the headlights or the auxiliary driving light or the auxiliary passing light or combination thereof on motor vehicles other than motorcycles or motor driven cycles shall be so arranged that the driver may select at will between distributions of light projected to different elevations, and such lights may, in addition, be so arranged that such selection can be made automatically, subject to the following limitations:

(1) There shall be an uppermost distribution of light, or composite beam, so aimed and of such intensity as to reveal persons and vehicles at a distance of at least 350 feet ahead for all conditions of loading;

(2) There shall be a lowermost distribution of light, or composite beam, so aimed and of sufficient intensity to reveal persons and vehicles at a distance of at least 100 feet ahead; and on a straight level road under any condition of loading none of the high intensity portion of the beam shall be directed to strike the eyes of an approaching driver;

(3) Every new motor vehicle other than a motorcycle or a motor driven cycle registered in this state which has multiple-beam road lighting equipment shall be equipped with a beam indicator which shall be lighted whenever the uppermost distribution of light from the headlights is in use and shall not otherwise be lighted. Such indicator shall be so designed and located that when lighted it will be readily visible without glare to the driver of the vehicle so equipped.

Laws 1953, Nov.-Dec. Sess., p. 556, § 113; Laws 1955, Ex. Sess., p. 25, § 1; Laws 1982, p. 165, § 4; Laws 1982, p. 165, § 10.

Formerly Code 1933, § 68E–211.

§ 40–8–31. Use of multiple-beam road-lighting equipment

Whenever a motor vehicle is being operated on a roadway or shoulder adjacent thereto during the times specified in Code Section 40–8–20, the driver shall use a distribution of light, or composite beam, directed high enough and of sufficient intensity to reveal persons and vehicles at a safe distance in advance of the vehicle, subject to the following requirements and limitations:

(1) Whenever a driver of a vehicle approaches an oncoming vehicle within 500 feet, such driver shall use a distribution of light, or composite beam, so aimed that the glaring rays are not projected into the eyes of the oncoming driver. The lowermost distribution of light, or composite beam, specified in paragraph (2) of Code Section 40–8–30 shall be deemed to avoid glare at all times, regardless of road contour and loading; and

(2) Whenever the driver of a vehicle follows another vehicle within 200 feet to the rear, except when engaged in the act of overtaking and passing, such driver shall use a distribution of light permissible under this chapter other than the uppermost distribution of light specified in paragraph (1) of Code Section 40–8–30.

Laws 1953, Nov.-Dec. Sess., p. 556, § 114; Laws 1955, Ex. Sess., p. 25, § 1; Laws 1982, p. 165, § 4; Laws 1982, p. 165, § 10; Laws 1989, p. 14, § 40.

Formerly Code 1933, § 68E–212.

§ 40–8–32. Amber lights on automobiles of rural mail carriers

Any automobile operated by a rural mail carrier for the purpose of delivering mail shall be authorized to display two amber colored lights so as to warn approaching travelers to decrease their speed because of the danger of colliding with such mail carrier as he stops and starts along the edge of the highway. Such amber lights should be visible under normal atmospheric conditions from a distance of 500 feet to the front of such vehicle.

Laws 1961, p. 202, § 1; Laws 1982, p. 165, § 4; Laws 1982, p. 165, § 10; Laws 1997, p. 143, § 40.

Formerly Code 1933, § 68E–213.

§ 40–8–33. Farm tractors and three-wheeled motorcycles used only for agricultural purposes

(a) Every farm tractor and every three-wheeled motorcycle used only for agricultural purposes equipped with an electric lighting system shall at all times mentioned in Code Section 40–8–20 display a red taillight and either multiple-beam or single-beam road lighting equipment meeting the requirements of Code Sections 40–8–23 and 40–8–30, respectively.

(b) When operated or towed upon a highway, roadway, or street at any time from a half-hour after sunset to a half-hour before sunrise and at any time when it is raining in the driving zone and at any other time when there is not sufficient visibility to render clearly discernible persons and vehicles on the highway, roadway, or street at a distance of 500 feet to the rear, every trailer and semitrailer which would otherwise be exempt from this article as an implement of husbandry under Code Section 40–8–1 either shall comply with Code Section 40–8–23, relating to taillights, or shall be equipped with an operating red flashing light which is plainly visible from a distance of 500 feet to the rear and which is either permanently or temporarily fixed to the rear of such trailer or semitrailer or shall be accompanied by an escort vehicle which is equipped with one or more operating red or amber flashing lights that are visible from a distance of 500 feet and which shall follow such trailer or semitrailer.

(c) Nothing in this Code section shall be construed to impose a duty on a manufacturer of an implement of husbandry under Code Section 40–8–1 to install an electric lighting system, taillights, or red flashing lights or otherwise equip implements of husbandry to be in compliance with the provisions of this Code section at the time of manufacture or sale; it being the intent of this Code section to place a duty on operators of the equipment only under specified circumstances and conditions, and not on manufacturers.

Laws 1953, Nov.-Dec. Sess., p. 556, § 102; Laws 1973, p. 598, § 3; Laws 1982, p. 165, § 4; Laws 1982, p. 165, § 10; Laws 1984, p. 1329, § 5; Laws 1989, p. 298, § 3.

Formerly Code 1933, § 68E–214.

§ 40–8–34. Color of lighting equipment

The color in all lighting equipment covered in this title shall be in accordance with Society of Automotive Engineers (SAE) Standard J578, April, 1965, as thereafter revised or amended.

Laws 1974, p. 633, § 1; Laws 1982, p. 165, § 4; Laws 1982, p. 165, § 10.

Formerly Code 1933, § 68E–215.

§ 40–8–35. Amber strobe lights on low-speed vehicles

Any low-speed vehicle operated on the highways of this state shall display an amber strobe light so as to warn approaching travelers to decrease their speed because of the danger of colliding with such vehicle. Such amber strobe light shall be mounted in a manner so as to be visible under normal atmospheric conditions from a distance of 500 feet from the front and rear of such vehicle.

Laws 2002, p. 512, § 13.

Part 3

Brakes

§ 40–8–50. Equipment required

(a) As used in this Code section, the term:

(1) "Gross combination weight rating (GCWR)" means the combined gross vehicle weight ratings of all vehicles in a combination of vehicles.

(2) "Gross vehicle weight rating (GVWR)" means the value specified by the manufacturer or manufacturers as the maximum loaded weight of a single or a combination (articulated) vehicle, the actual gross weight, or registered gross weight, whichever is greater.

(3) "Hazardous material" has the meaning provided by Chapter 51 of Title 49 of the United States Code Annotated.

(4) "Surge brakes" means a self-contained, permanently closed hydraulic brake system for trailers that relies on inertial forces, developed in response to the braking action of the towing vehicle, applied to a hydraulic device mounted on or connected to the tongue of the trailer to slow down or stop the towed vehicle.

(b) Every motor vehicle, other than a motorcycle or motor driven cycle, when operated upon a highway shall be equipped with brakes adequate to control the movement of and to stop and hold such vehicle, including two separate means of applying the brakes, each of which means shall be effective to apply the brakes to at least two wheels. If these two separate means of applying the brakes are connected in any way, they shall be so constructed that failure on any one part of the operating mechanism shall not leave the motor vehicle without brakes on at least two wheels.

(c) Every motorcycle and motor driven cycle manufactured after January 1, 1974, when operated upon a highway, shall be equipped with at least two brakes which may be operated by hand or foot.

(d) Except as otherwise provided in subsection (e) of this Code section, every trailer or semitrailer of 3,000 pounds gross weight or more shall be equipped with brakes on all wheels. Any farm trailer with two or more wheels, pulled from a tongue, used in or operated for farm purposes, including transporting fertilizer and agricultural materials to the farm, shall not be required to have an independent braking system thereon, provided such farm trailer shall not weigh over 4,000 pounds when empty.

(e) Any trailer or semitrailer may utilize surge brakes, subject to the following conditions and limitations:

(1) The gross vehicle weight rating or the actual gross weight of any surge brake equipped trailer or semitrailer does not exceed 20,000 pounds;

(2) For trailers and semitrailers with a gross vehicle weight rating of 12,000 pounds or less, the gross vehicle weight rating of any such trailer shall not exceed 1.75 times the gross vehicle weight rating of the towing vehicle;

(3) For trailers and semitrailers with a gross vehicle weight rating greater than 12,000 pounds, but less than 20,001 pounds, the gross vehicle weight rating of any such trailer shall not exceed 1.25 times the gross vehicle weight rating of the towing vehicle;

(4) The actual gross weight of the trailer or semitrailer and load does not exceed the manufacturer's gross vehicle weight rating;

(5) The trailer or semitrailer brakes must be designed and connected in such a manner that in case of accidental breakaway of the towed vehicle the brakes shall apply automatically; and

(6) For vehicles used for commercial purposes, the vehicle or combination of vehicles complies in all other respects with licensing, insurance, registration, identification, driver and vehicle safety, and hazardous materials regulations of the Department of Public Safety and United States Department of Transportation applicable to such vehicles or combination of vehicles.

(f) Where there is no manufacturer's gross vehicle weight rating or the manufacturer's gross vehicle weight rating is exceeded in violation of paragraph (4) of subsection (e) of this Code section, then the actual gross weight of the trailer or semitrailer shall be used to determine compliance with paragraphs (2) and (3) of subsection (e) of this Code section.

Laws 1953, Nov.-Dec. Sess., p. 556, § 115; Laws 1965, p. 406, § 1; Laws 1970, p. 438, § 1; Laws 1974, p. 422, § 1; Laws 1982, p. 165, § 4; Laws 1982, p. 165, § 10; Laws 2000, p. 809, § 1; Laws 2002, p. 415, § 40; Laws 2005, Act 68, § 19–2, eff. July 1, 2005; Laws 2009, Act 101, § 3A, eff. May 1, 2009.

Formerly Code 1933, § 68E–301.

Historical and Statutory Notes

Laws 2009, Act 101, § 4 provided:

"Section 3A of this Act shall become effective upon its approval by the Governor or upon its becoming law without such approval. The remaining sections of this Act shall become effective on January 1, 2010, and shall apply to registration and licensing of trailers on and after such date."

§ 40–8–51. Mechanical connection from operating lever to brake shoes or bands

(a) One of the means of brake operation shall consist of a mechanical connection from the operating lever to the brake shoes or bands, and this brake shall be capable of holding the vehicle or combination of vehicles stationary under any condition of loading on any upgrade or downgrade upon which it is operated.

(b) The brake shoes operating within or upon the drums on the vehicle wheels of any motor vehicle may be used for both service and hand operation.

Laws 1953, Nov.-Dec. Sess., p. 556, § 115; Laws 1982, p. 165, § 4; Laws 1982, p. 165, § 10.

Formerly Code 1933, § 68E–302.

§ 40–8–52. Parking brakes

Every 1966 model motor vehicle and all subsequent model motor vehicles shall be equipped with parking brakes adequate to hold the vehicle on any grade on which it is operated, under all conditions of loading, on a surface free from snow, ice, or loose material. The parking brakes shall be capable of being applied in conformance with the foregoing requirements by the driver's muscular effort or by spring action or by equivalent means. Their operation may be assisted by the service brakes or other source of power, provided that failure of the service brake actuation system or other power assisting mechanism will not prevent the parking brakes from being applied in conformance with the foregoing requirements. The parking brakes shall be so designed that when once applied they shall remain applied with the required effectiveness despite exhaustion of any source of energy or leakage of any kind. The same brake drums, brake shoes and lining assemblies, brake shoe anchors, and mechanical brake shoe actuation mechanism normally associated with the wheel brake assemblies may be used for both the service brakes and the parking brakes. If the means of applying the parking brakes and the service brakes are connected in any way, they shall be so constructed that failure of any one part shall not leave the vehicle without operative brakes.

Laws 1970, p. 438, § 2; Laws 1971, p. 515, § 1; Laws 1982, p. 165, § 4; Laws 1982, p. 165, § 10.

Formerly Code 1933, § 68E–303.

§ 40–8–53. Performance ability of brakes

Every motor vehicle or combination of motor drawn vehicles shall be capable at all times and under all conditions of loading of being stopped on a dry, smooth, level road free from loose material, upon application of the service (foot) brake within the distances specified in this Code section or shall be capable of being decelerated at a sustained rate corresponding to these distances.

	Feet to Stop From 20 Miles Per Hour	Deceleration in Feet Per Second
Vehicles or combinations of vehicles having brakes on all wheels	30	14
Vehicles or combinations of vehicles not having brakes on all wheels	40	10.7

Laws 1953, Nov.-Dec. Sess., p. 556, § 115; Laws 1982, p. 3, § 40; Laws 1982, p. 165, § 4; Laws 1982, p. 165, § 10; Laws 1994, p. 97, § 40.

Formerly Code 1933, § 68E–304.

§ 40–8–54. Maintenance of brakes

All brakes shall be maintained in good working order and shall be so adjusted as to operate as equally as practicable with respect to the wheels on opposite sides of the vehicle.

Laws 1953, Nov.-Dec. Sess., p. 556, § 115; Laws 1982, p. 165, § 4; Laws 1982, p. 165, § 10.

Formerly Code 1933, § 68E–305.

Part 4

Horns, Exhaust Systems, Mirrors, Windshields, Tires, Safety Belts, Energy Absorption Systems

§ 40–8–70. Horns and warning devices

(a) Every motor vehicle when operated upon a highway shall be equipped with a horn in good working order and capable of emitting sound audible under normal conditions from a distance of not less than 200 feet, but no horn or other warning device shall emit an unreasonably loud or harsh sound or a whistle. The driver of a motor vehicle shall, when it is reasonably necessary to ensure safe operation, give audible warning with his or her horn but shall not otherwise use such horn when upon a highway.

(b) No vehicle shall be equipped with nor shall any person use upon a vehicle any siren, whistle, or bell except as otherwise permitted in this Code section and Code Section 40–8–94.

(c) No vehicle shall be equipped with a theft alarm signal device which is so arranged that it can be used by the driver as an ordinary warning signal.

Laws 1953, Nov.-Dec. Sess., p. 556, § 116; Laws 1982, p. 165, § 4; Laws 1982, p. 165, § 10; Laws 2001, p. 4, § 40.

Formerly Code 1933, § 68E–401.

§ 40–8–71. Exhaust systems; penalty for violation

(a) Every motor vehicle shall at all times be equipped with an exhaust system, in good working order and in constant operation, meeting the following specifications:

(1) The exhaust system shall include the piping leading from the flange of the exhaust manifold to and including the muffler or mufflers and tail pipes;

(2) The use of flexible pipe shall be prohibited except on diesel tractors or according to manufacturers' original specifications;

(3) The exhaust emission point shall extend beyond the rear or outside of the passenger compartment. The trunk shall be considered as part of the passenger compartment;

(4) The exhaust system and its elements shall be securely fastened, including the consideration of missing or broken hangers; and

(5) There shall be no part of the exhaust system passing through the passenger compartment or any exposed stack so located that any individual entering or leaving the vehicle may be burned.

(b) The engine and power mechanism of every motor vehicle shall be so equipped and adjusted as to prevent the escape of excessive fumes or smoke.

(c) It shall be unlawful for any person to sell or offer for sale any muffler which causes excessive or unusual noise or annoying smoke or any muffler cutout, bypass, or similar device for use on a motor vehicle or for any person to use, to sell, or to offer for sale any motor vehicle equipped with any such muffler, muffler cutout, bypass, or similar device. Any person violating this subsection shall be guilty of a misdemeanor.

Laws 1953, Nov.-Dec. Sess., p. 556, § 117; Laws 1962, p. 653, § 1; Laws 1971, p. 779, § 1; Laws 1982, p. 165, § 4; Laws 1982, p. 165, § 10; Laws 1994, p. 97, § 40.

Formerly Code 1933, § 68E–402.

§ 40–8–72. Mirrors

Every motor vehicle which is so constructed or loaded as to obstruct the driver's view to the rear thereof from the driver's position shall be equipped with a mirror so located as to reflect to the driver a view of the highway for a distance of at least 200 feet to the rear of such vehicle.

Laws 1953, Nov.-Dec. Sess., p. 556, § 118; Laws 1982, p. 165, § 4; Laws 1982, p. 165, § 10.

Formerly Code 1933, § 68E–403.

§ 40–8–73. Windshield and windshield wipers

(a) No person shall drive any motor vehicle with any sign, poster, or other nontransparent material upon the front windshield, side windows, or rear windows of such vehicle which obstructs the driver's clear view of the highway or any intersecting highway.

(b) The windshield of every motor vehicle shall be equipped with a device for cleaning rain, snow, or other moisture therefrom, which device shall be so constructed as to be controlled or operated by the driver of the vehicle.

(c) Every windshield wiper upon a motor vehicle shall be maintained in good working order.

(d) No opaque or solid material including, but not limited to, cardboard, plastic, and taped glass shall be employed in lieu of a glass windshield or window.

(e) No motor vehicle shall be operated with a windshield or rear window having a starburst or spider webbing effect greater than three inches by three inches.

Laws 1953, Nov.-Dec. Sess., p. 556, § 119; Laws 1982, p. 165, § 4; Laws 1982, p. 165, § 10.

Formerly Code 1933, § 68E–404.

§ 40–8–73.1. Material affixed to front windshield or front door windows which obstructs vision into vehicle; penalty for violation

(a) As used in this Code section, the term:

(1) "Light reflectance" means the ratio of the amount of total light that is reflected outward by a product or material to the amount of total light falling on the product or material.

(2) "Light transmission" means the ratio of the amount of total light, expressed in percentages, which is allowed to pass through a surface to the amount of light falling on the surface.

(3) "Manufacturer" means a person who produces or assembles a vehicle glass–coating material or who fabricates, laminates, or tempers a safety-glazing material, which material reduces light transmission.

(4) "Material" means any transparent product or substance which reduces light transmission.

(5) "Multipurpose passenger vehicle" means a motor vehicle designed to carry ten persons or less which is constructed on a truck chassis or with special features for occasional off-road operation.

(b) Except as provided in this Code section, it shall be unlawful for any person to operate a motor vehicle in this state:

(1) Which has material and glazing applied or affixed to the front windshield, which material and glazing when so applied or affixed reduce light transmission through the windshield; or

(2) Which has material and glazing applied or affixed to the rear windshield or the side or door windows, which material and glazing when so applied or affixed reduce light transmission through the windshield or window to less than 32 percent, plus or minus 3 percent, or increase light reflectance to more than 20 percent.

(c) The provisions of subsection (b) of this Code section shall not apply to:

(1) Adjustable sun visors which are mounted forward of the side windows and are not attached to the glass;

(2) Signs, stickers, or other matter which is displayed in a seven-inch square in the lower corner of the windshield farthest removed from the driver or signs, stickers, or other matter which is displayed in a five-inch square in the lower corner of the windshield nearest the driver;

(3) Direction, destination, or termination signs upon a passenger common carrier motor vehicle if the signs do not interfere with the driver's clear view of approaching traffic;

(4) Any transparent item which is not red or amber in color which is placed on the uppermost six inches of the windshield;

(5) Any federal, state, or local sticker or certificate which is required by law to be placed on any windshield or window;

(6) The rear windshield or the side or door windows, except those windows to the right and left of the driver of:

(A) A multipurpose passenger vehicle;

(B) A school bus, any other bus used for public transportation, and any bus or van owned or leased by any religious or any nonprofit organization duly incorporated under the laws of this state;

(C) Any limousine owned or leased by a public or private entity; or

(D) Any other vehicle, the windows or windshields of which have been tinted or darkened before factory delivery or permitted by federal law or regulation;

(7) Any law enforcement vehicle;

(8) Any vehicle that displays a valid special license plate issued to a government official under Code Section 40–2–61, 40–2–63, or 40–2–64;

(9) Any vehicle owned or operated by the state or a political subdivision thereof and that displays a valid license plate issued pursuant to Code Section 40–2–37; or

(10) Any vehicle operated in the course of business by a person licensed or registered under Chapter 38 of Title 43, relating to private detective and private security businesses.

(d) The Department of Public Safety may, upon application from a person required for medical reasons to be shielded from the direct rays of the sun and only if such application is supported by written attestation of such fact from a person licensed to practice medicine under Chapter 34 of Title 43 or a person certified as an optometrist under Chapter 30 of Title 43, issue an exemption from the provisions of this Code section for any motor vehicle owned by such person or in which such person is a habitual passenger. The exemption shall be issued with such conditions and limitations as may be prescribed by the Department of Public Safety.

(e) No person shall install any material upon the windshields or windows of any motor vehicle, the installation of which would result in a reduction of light transmission or an increase in light reflectance in violation of subsection (b) of this Code section.

(f) The Department of Public Safety is authorized to promulgate such rules and regulations as may be necessary to carry out the provisions of this Code section.

(g) Any person who violates subsection (b) or (e) of this Code section shall be guilty of a misdemeanor.

Laws 1983, p. 1300, § 1; Laws 1984, p. 1211, § 1; Laws 1984, p. 22, § 40; Laws 1985, p. 149, § 40; Laws 1989, p. 896, § 1; Laws 1992, p. 2785, § 27; Laws 2000, p. 951, § 5B–3; Laws 2005, Act 67, § 1, eff. May 2, 2005; Laws 2005, Act 68, § 19–3, eff. July 1, 2005; Laws 2006, Act 761, § 1, eff. July 1, 2006; Laws 2007, Act 119, § 1, eff. May 18, 2007.

Historical and Statutory Notes

The 2005 amendment by Act 67, in subsec. (b), deleted "from and after January 1, 1990," following "in this Code section," and deleted "resident" preceding "person" in the introductory paragraph, and added ", plus or minus 3 percent," in par. (2); in subsec. (c), added "; or" at the end of subpar. (6)(D), deleted par. (7) which had read "Any motor vehicle not registered in this state; or", and designated existing par. (8) as new par. (7); rewrote subsec. (e); deleted subsec. (f); designated existing subsecs. (g) and (h) as new subsecs. (f) and (g); and in newly designated subsec. (f), substituted "Motor Vehicle Safety" for "Public Safety". Prior to amendment subsec. (e) had read:

"(e) From and after January 1, 1990, each manufacturer of material designed to be affixed or applied to the windows or windshields of a motor vehicle shall, before shipping such material into this state, apply to the commissioner of public safety for approval and registration of its material and the label for identification and certification of compliance. No material shall be approved by the commissioner unless the manufacturer demonstrates that such material, when applied or affixed to a window, shall not reduce light transmission or increase light reflectance in violation of subsection (b) of this Code section. The manufacturer of any material shipped into this state on or after January 1, 1990, shall provide labels of a size and type approved by the commissioner, written instructions for the placement of such labels, and a notice that the improper installation of material to a window or windshield or the failure to display a label as provided in this subsection is a violation of state law. It shall be unlawful for any person to alter or reproduce any label approved by the commissioner or to knowingly use any approved label except as authorized by this Code section."

The 2005 amendment by Act 68 in subsec. (d) substituted "Department of Public Safety" for "Department of Motor Vehicle Safety" twice.

In 2005, the Code Commission, due to irreconcilable conflicts, treated the amendment of this section by Laws 2005, Act 67, § 1, as superseded by Laws 2005, Act 68, § 19. See Butts County v. Strahan, 107 S.E. 163, 151 Ga. 417 (1921). Also, the Code Commission substituted "Department of Public Safety" for "Department of Motor Vehicle Safety" in subsec. (f).

The 2006 amendment by Act 761, in subsec. (d), inserted "a person certified as an optometrist under Chapter 30 of Title 43" preceding "issue an exemption from the provisions of this Code section".

The 2007 amendment by Act 119, in subsec. (c), added pars. (8) through (10).

§ 40–8–74. Tires

(a) No vehicle equipped with solid rubber tires shall be used or transported on the highways, unless every solid rubber tire on such vehicle shall have rubber on its entire traction surface at least one inch thick above the edge of the flange on the entire periphery.

(b) No person shall operate or move on any highway any motor vehicle, trailer, or semitrailer having any metal tire in contact with the roadway.

(c) No tire on a vehicle moved on a highway shall have on its periphery any block, stud, flange, cleat, or spike or any other protuberance of any material other than rubber which projects beyond the tread of the traction surface of the tire, except that it shall be permissible to use:

(1) Farm machinery with tires having protuberances which will not injure the highway; and

(2) Tire chains of reasonable proportions or tires equipped with safety metal spike studs upon any vehicle when required for safety because of snow, ice, or other conditions tending to cause a vehicle to skid.

(d) The transportation board and local authorities in their respective jurisdictions may in their discretion issue special permits authorizing the operation upon a highway of traction engines or tractors having movable tracks with transverse corrugations upon the periphery of such movable tracks, or of farm tractors or other farm machinery, the operation of which upon a highway would otherwise be prohibited under this Code section.

(e) All tires:

(1) Shall have not less than 2/32 inch tread measurable in all major grooves with the exception of school buses which shall have not less than 4/32 inch tread measurable in all major grooves on the front tires and not less than 2/32 inch tread measurable in all major grooves on the rear tires when there are at least four tires on the rear otherwise the tread on the rear tires shall be not less than 4/32 inch;

(2) Shall be free from any cuts, breaks, or snags on tread and sidewall deep enough to expose body cord; and

(3) Shall be free from bumps, bulges, or separations.

(f) No motor vehicle shall be operated on a public street or highway with tires that have been marked "not for highway use," "for racing purposes only," or "unsafe for highway use."

(g) Retreaded tires shall not be used upon the front wheels of buses.

Laws 1927, p. 226, § 17; Laws 1953, Nov.-Dec. Sess., p. 556, § 120; Laws 1970, p. 628, § 1; Laws 1982, p. 165, § 4; Laws 1982, p. 3, § 40; Laws 1982, p. 165, § 10; Laws 1992, p. 2785, § 28; Laws 1993, p. 727, § 1.

Formerly Code 1933, § 68–404; Code 1933, § 68E–405.

§ 40–8–75. Tire covers

Every bus, truck, full trailer, semitrailer, and pole trailer, with the exception of local haul pulpwood trucks and local haul waste collection dumping trailers, shall be equipped with suitable metal protectors or substantial flexible flaps on the rearmost wheels to prevent, as far as practicable, such wheels from throwing dirt, gravel, rocks, water, or other materials on the windshields of following vehicles. Such protectors or flaps shall have a ground clearance of not more than one-half of the distance from the center of the rearmost axle to the center of the protector or flap under any conditions of loading of the vehicle and shall be at least as wide as the tires they are covering; provided, however, that if any such bus, truck, full trailer, semitrailer, or pole trailer is so designed and constructed that the foregoing requirements are accomplished by means of fenders, body construction, or other enclosures, then the protectors or flaps provided for in this Code section shall not be required.

Laws 1979, p. 906, § 2; Laws 1982, p. 165, § 4; Laws 1982, p. 165, § 10.

Formerly Code 1933, § 68E–406.

§ 40–8–76. Safety belts; child passenger restraining systems; penalty for violation

(a) No new private passenger automobile manufactured after January 1, 1964, shall be sold to the general public in this state unless such automobile shall be equipped with two sets of safety belts for the front seat thereof. The safety belts may be installed by the manufacturer prior to delivery to the dealer, or they may be installed by the dealer.

(b)(1) Every driver who transports a child under six years of age in a passenger automobile, van, or pickup truck, other than a taxicab as defined by Code Section 33–34–5.1 or a public transit vehicle as defined by Code Section 16–5–20, shall, while such motor vehicle is in motion and operated on a public road, street, or highway of this state, provide for the proper restraint of such child in a child passenger restraining system appropriate for such child's height and weight and approved by the United States Department of Transportation under provisions of Federal Motor Vehicle Safety Standard 213 in effect on January 1, 1983, or at the time of manufacture, subject to the following specific requirements and exceptions:

(A) Any such child weighing at least 40 pounds may be secured by a lap belt when:

(i) The vehicle is not equipped with both lap and shoulder belts; or

(ii) Not including the driver's seat, the vehicle is equipped with one or more lap and shoulder belts that are all being used to properly restrain other children;

(B) Any such child shall be properly restrained in a rear seat of the motor vehicle consistent with the requirements of this paragraph. If the vehicle has no rear seating position appropriate for correctly restraining a child or all appropriate rear seating positions are occupied by other children, any such child may be properly restrained in a front seat consistent with the requirements of this paragraph;

(C) A driver shall not be deemed to be complying with the provisions of this paragraph unless any child passenger restraining system required by this paragraph is installed and being used in accordance with the manufacturer's directions for such system; and

(D) The provisions of this paragraph shall not apply when the child's parent or guardian either obtains a physician's written statement that a physical or medical condition of the child prevents placing or restraining him or her in the manner required by this paragraph. If the parent or guardian can show the child's height is over 4 feet and 9 inches, such child shall be restrained in a safety belt as required in Code Section 40–8–76.1.

(2) Upon a first conviction of an offense under this subsection, the defendant shall be punished by a fine of not more than $50.00, except in the case of a child who is five years of age, if the defendant shows to the court having jurisdiction of the case that a child passenger restraining system meeting the applicable requirements of this subsection has been purchased by him or her after the time of the offense and prior to the court appearance, the court may waive or suspend the fine for such first conviction. This exception shall apply until January 1, 2005. Upon a second or subsequent conviction of an offense under this subsection, the defendant shall be punished by a fine of not more than $100.00. No court shall impose any additional fees or surcharges to a fine for such a violation. The court imposing a fine for any violation of this Code section shall forward a record of the disposition of the cases annually to the Department of Public Safety for the sole purpose of data collection on a county by county basis.

(c) Violation of this Code section shall not constitute negligence per se nor contributory negligence per se. Violation of subsection (b) of this Code section shall not be the basis for cancellation of coverage or increase in insurance rates.

(d) The provisions of this Code section shall not apply to buses, as defined in paragraph (7) of Code Section 40–1–1, used in the transport of children over four years of age until July 1, 2007, provided that the bus is operated by a licensed or commissioned child care facility, has a current annual transportation safety inspection certificate as required by the appropriate licensing body, and has evidence of being inspected for use by a child care facility. If the bus is not a school bus, as defined in paragraph (55) of Code Section 40–1–1, or a multifunction school activities bus, as defined in 49 C.F.R. 571.3(B), each child over four years of age and under six years of age shall be properly restrained by a safety belt. Multifunction school activities buses, as defined in 49 C.F.R. 571.3(B), shall not be required to transport children five years of age in a child passenger restraining system.

Laws 1963, p. 366, § 2; Laws 1964, p. 168, § 1; Laws 1982, p. 165, § 4; Laws 1982, p. 165, § 10; Laws 1983, p. 1464, § 1; Laws 1984, p. 22, § 40; Laws 1985, p. 149, § 40; Laws 1988, p. 480, § 1; Laws 1996, p. 469, § 2; Laws 2000, p. 1246, § 17; Laws 2001, p. 740, § 1; Laws 2004, Act 572, § 1, eff. July 1, 2004.

Formerly Code 1933, § 68E–407.

Historical and Statutory Notes

The 2004 amendment by Act 572 rewrote the section which had read:

"(a) No new private passenger automobile manufactured after January 1, 1964, shall be sold to the general public in this state unless such automobile shall be equipped with two sets of safety belts for the front seat thereof. The safety belts may be installed by the manufacturer prior to delivery to the dealer, or they may be installed by the dealer.

"(b)(1) On and after July 1, 1984, every driver who transports a child four years of age or younger in a passenger automobile, van, or pickup truck, other than a taxicab as defined by Code Section 33–34–5.1 or a public transit vehicle as defined by Code Section 16–5–20, shall, while such motor vehicle is in motion and operated on a public road, street, or highway of this state, provide for the protection of such child in a child passenger restraining system approved by the United States Department of Transportation under Federal Motor Vehicle Safety Standard 213 in effect on January 1, 1983. A driver shall not be deemed to be complying with the provisions of this subsection unless the child passenger restraining system is installed and being used in accordance with the manufacturer's directions for such system. The provisions of this subsection shall not apply when the child's parent or guardian obtains a physician's written statement that a physical or medical condition of the child prevents placing or restraining him or her in any such child passenger restraining system.

"(2) Upon a first conviction of an offense under this subsection, the defendant shall be punished by a fine of not more than $50.00. Upon a second or subsequent conviction of an offense under this subsection, the defendant shall be punished by a fine of not more than $100.00. No court shall impose any additional fees or surcharges to a fine for such a violation. The court imposing a fine for any violation of this Code section shall forward a record of the disposition of the cases annually to the Department of Public Safety for the sole purpose of data collection on a county by county basis.

"(c) It shall be the duty of the Governor's Office of Highway Safety to implement and coordinate a program to inform parents and other citizens of Georgia of the reasons for the enactment of subsection (b) of this Code section. Such program shall be carried out prior to January 1, 1997. The Governor's Office of Highway Safety shall solicit the cooperation and assistance of the Georgia State Patrol, the Georgia Sheriffs Association, the Georgia Association of Chiefs of Police, Incorporated, the Peace Officers' Association of Georgia, the Medical College of Georgia, the Georgia Hospital Association, the Georgia Association of Educators, the Georgia Parent–Teacher Association, and other appropriate organizations in educating the citizens of the state and in implementing, coordinating, and carrying out the program provided for herein.

"(d) Violation of this Code section shall not constitute negligence per se nor contributory negligence per se. Violation of child safety restraint requirements shall not be the basis for cancellation of coverage or increase in insurance rates."

Laws 2004, Act 572, § 3, provides:

"It shall be the duty of the Governor's Office of Highway Safety to implement and coordinate a program to inform parents and other citizens of Georgia of the provisions of subsection (b) of Code Section 40–8–76 and paragraph (3) of subsection (e) of Code Section 40–8–76.1 as amended by this Act. Such program shall be carried out prior to January 1, 2005. The Governor's Office of Highway Safety shall solicit the cooperation and assistance of the Georgia State Patrol, Department of Motor Vehicle Safety, Georgia Sheriffs Association, Georgia Association of Chiefs of Police, Incorporated, Peace Officers' Association of Georgia, Medical College of Georgia, Georgia Hospital Association, Georgia Association of Educators, Professional Association of Georgia Educators, Georgia Parent–Teacher Association, and other appropriate organizations in educating the citizens of the state and in implementing, coordinating, and carrying out such provisions."

In 2004, the Code Commission, in subsec. (d), substituted "C.F.R." for "CFR" twice. See § 28–9–5.

§ 40–8–76.1. Safety belts; required usage

(a) As used in this Code section, the term "passenger vehicle" means every motor vehicle, including, but not limited to, pickup trucks, vans, and sport utility vehicles, designed to carry ten passengers or fewer and used for the transportation of persons; provided, however, that such term shall not include motorcycles; motor driven cycles; or off-road vehicles or pickup trucks being used by an owner, driver, or occupant 18 years of age or older in connection with agricultural pursuits that are usual and normal to the user's farming operation.

(b) Each occupant of the front seat of a passenger vehicle shall, while such passenger vehicle is being operated on a public road, street, or highway of this state, be restrained by a seat safety belt approved under Federal Motor Vehicle Safety Standard 208.

(c) The requirement of subsection (b) of this Code section shall not apply to:

(1) A driver or passenger frequently stopping and leaving the vehicle or delivering property from the vehicle, if the speed of the vehicle between stops does not exceed 15 miles per hour;

(2) A driver or passenger possessing a written statement from a physician that such person is unable, for medical or physical reasons, to wear a seat safety belt;

(3) A driver or passenger possessing an official certificate or license endorsement issued by the appropriate agency in another state or country indicating that the driver is unable for medical, physical, or other valid reasons to wear a seat safety belt;

(4) A driver operating a passenger vehicle in reverse;

(5) A passenger vehicle with a model year prior to 1965;

(6) A passenger vehicle which is not required to be equipped with seat safety belts under federal law;

(7) A passenger vehicle operated by a rural letter carrier of the United States Postal Service while performing duties as a rural letter carrier;

(8) A passenger vehicle from which a person is delivering newspapers; or

(9) A passenger vehicle performing an emergency service.

(d) The failure of an occupant of a motor vehicle to wear a seat safety belt in any seat of a motor vehicle which has a seat safety belt or belts shall not be considered evidence of negligence or causation, shall not otherwise be considered by the finder of fact on any question of liability of any person, corporation, or insurer, shall not be any basis for cancellation of coverage or increase in insurance rates, and shall not be evidence used to diminish any recovery for damages arising out of the ownership, maintenance, occupancy, or operation of a motor vehicle.

(e)(1) Except as otherwise provided in paragraphs (2) and (3) of this subsection, a person failing to comply with the requirements of subsection (b) of this Code section shall not be guilty of any criminal act and shall not be guilty of violating any ordinance. A violation of this Code section shall not be a moving traffic violation for purposes of Code Section 40–5–57.

(2) A person failing to comply with the requirements of subsection (b) of this Code section shall be guilty of the offense of failure to wear a seat safety belt and, upon conviction thereof, may be fined not more than $15.00; but, the provisions of Chapter 11 of Title 17 and any other provision of law to the contrary notwithstanding, the costs of such prosecution shall not be taxed nor shall any additional penalty, fee, or surcharge to a fine for such offense be assessed against a person for conviction thereof. The court imposing such fine shall forward a record of the disposition of the case of failure to wear a seat safety belt to the Department of Driver Services.

(3) Each minor six years of age or older who is an occupant of a passenger vehicle shall, while such passenger vehicle is being operated on a public road, street, or highway of this state, be restrained by a seat safety belt approved under Federal Motor Vehicle Safety Standard 208. In any case where a minor passenger six years of age or older fails to comply with the requirements of this paragraph, the driver of the passenger vehicle shall be guilty of the offense of failure to secure a seat safety belt on a minor and, upon conviction thereof, may be fined not more than $25.00. The court imposing such a fine shall forward a record of the court disposition of the case of failure to secure a seat safety belt on a minor to the Department of Driver Services.

(f) Probable cause for violation of this Code section shall be based solely upon a law enforcement officer's clear and unobstructed view of a person not restrained as required by this Code section. Noncompliance with the restraint requirements of this Code section shall not constitute probable cause for violation of any other Code section.

Laws 1988, p. 31, § 1; Laws 1990, p. 588, § 1; Laws 1993, p. 516, § 1; Laws 1994, p. 1005, § 1; Laws 1996, p. 469, § 3; Laws 1997, p. 143, § 40; Laws 1998, p. 1579, § 1; Laws 1999, p. 276, § 1; Laws 2000, p. 862, § 1; Laws 2000, p. 951, § 5B–4; Laws 2004, Act 572, § 2, eff. July 1, 2004; Laws 2005, Act 68, § 19–4, eff. July 1, 2005; Laws 2010, Act 609, § 1, eff. June 3, 2010.

Historical and Statutory Notes

The 2004 amendment by Act 572, in subsec. (e), par. (3), twice substituted "six years of age or older" for "over four years of age".

Laws 2004, Act 572, § 3, provides:

"It shall be the duty of the Governor's Office of Highway Safety to implement and coordinate a program to inform parents and other citizens of Georgia of the provisions of subsection (b) of Code Section 40–8–76 and paragraph (3) of subsection (e) of Code Section 40–8–76.1 as amended by this Act. Such program shall be carried out prior to January 1, 2005. The Governor's Office of Highway Safety shall solicit the cooperation and assistance of the Georgia State Patrol, Department of Motor Vehicle Safety, Georgia Sheriffs Association, Georgia Association of Chiefs of Police, Incorporated, Peace Officers' Association of Georgia, Medical College of Georgia, Georgia Hospital Association, Georgia Association of Educators, Professional Association of Georgia Educators, Georgia Parent–Teacher Association, and other appropriate organizations in educating the citizens of the state and in implementing, coordinating, and carrying out such provisions."

The 2005 amendment by Act 68 in pars. (2) and (3) of subsec. (e) substituted "Department of Driver Services" for "Department of Motor Vehicle Safety".

The 2010 amendment by Act 609 rewrote subsec. (a) which had read as follows:

"(a) As used in this Code section, the term "passenger vehicle" means every motor vehicle designed to carry ten passengers or less and used for the transportation of persons but shall not mean pickup trucks, motorcycles, motor driven cycles, or vehicles equipped for off-road use, provided that the term "passenger vehicle" includes any sport utility vehicle and also includes pickup trucks for any occupant who is under 18 years of age."

§ 40–8–77. Warranty as to energy absorption system

(a) As used in this Code section, the term "private passenger automobile" shall mean a four-wheel motor vehicle designed for carrying ten passengers or less, not for hire, for use on public roads and highways, and not designed for use as a dwelling or for camping, provided that the term "private passenger automobile" shall not include a multipurpose vehicle, which is, for the purposes of this Code section, defined as a motor vehicle, except a trailer, designed to carry ten passengers or less and constructed either on a truck chassis or with special features for occasional off-road operation.

(b) Every new private passenger automobile manufactured on and after August 1, 1973, which is sold or licensed in this state shall be sold subject to the manufacturer's warranty that it is equipped with an appropriate energy absorption system conforming to all federal motor vehicle safety standards applicable to such automobile on the date of manufacture. The warranty may be given by means of the federal safety standard certification label affixed to the automobile.

Laws 1971, p. 373, §§ 1–3; Laws 1974, p. 8, § 1; Laws 1976, p. 1413, § 1; Laws 1982, p. 165, § 4; Laws 1982, p. 165, § 10; Laws 1992, p. 2785, § 28.

Formerly Code 1933, § 68E–408.

§ 40–8–78. Safety glazing material

(a) No person shall sell any motor vehicle manufactured after January 1, 1954, nor shall any such motor vehicle be registered unless such vehicle is equipped with safety glazing materials of a type approved by the commissioner of public safety wherever glazing materials are used in doors, windows, and windshields. The provisions of this Code section shall apply to all passenger–type motor vehicles, including passenger buses and school buses, but in respect to trucks, including truck tractors, the requirements as to safety glazing materials shall apply to all glazing materials used in doors, windows, and windshields in the drivers' compartments of such vehicles.

(b) The term "safety glazing materials" means glazing materials so constructed, treated, or combined with other materials as to reduce substantially, in comparison with ordinary sheet glass or plate glass, the likelihood of injury to persons by objects from exterior sources or by these safety glazing materials when they may be cracked or broken.

(c) Any person engaged in the business of replacing windshields or any side or rear windows of motor vehicles, which are subject to the provisions of this Code section, shall not replace such windshields or side or rear windows with any glazing materials other than safety glazing materials approved by the commissioner.

(d) The commissioner of public safety shall compile and publish in print or electronically a list of types of glazing materials by name approved by him or her as meeting the requirements of this Code section and the commissioner shall not register any motor vehicle which is subject to the provisions of this Code section unless it is equipped with an approved type of safety glazing materials, and he or she shall thereafter suspend the registration of any motor vehicle so subject to this Code section which he or she finds is not so equipped until it is made to conform to the requirements of this Code section.

(e) This Code section shall not be construed to require that side or rear windows of motor vehicles which were replaced or installed prior to January 1, 1954, must be replaced with safety glazing materials as provided in this Code section.

Laws 1982, p. 165, § 4; Laws 1982, p. 165, § 10; Laws 1994, p. 97, § 40; Laws 2000, p. 951, § 5B–5; Laws 2005, Act 68, § 19–5, eff. July 1, 2005; Laws 2010, Act 615, § 10, eff. June 3, 2010.

Formerly Code 1933, § 68E–409.

§ 40–8–79. Unlawful for person under 18 years of age to ride as passenger in uncovered bed of pickup truck

It shall be unlawful for any person under the age of 18 to ride as a passenger in the uncovered bed of a pickup truck on any interstate highway in this state. The driver of any vehicle in violation of this Code section shall be guilty of a misdemeanor.

Laws 1990, p. 588, § 2.

Part 5

Equipment of Law Enforcement and Emergency Vehicles

§ 40–8–90. Authorized use of blue lights; violations

(a)(1) Except as provided in this paragraph and subsection (b) of this Code section, it shall be unlawful for any person, firm, or corporation to operate any motor vehicle equipped with or containing a device capable of producing any blue lights, whether flashing, blinking, revolving, or stationary, except:

(A) Motor vehicles owned or leased by any federal, state, or local law enforcement agency;

(B) Motor vehicles with a permit granted by a state agency to bear such lights; or

(C) Antique, hobby, and special interest vehicles, as defined in paragraph (8) of subsection (*l*) of Code Section 40–2–86.1, which may display a blue light or lights of up to one inch in diameter as part of any such vehicle's rear stop lamps, rear turning indicator, rear hazard lamps, and rear reflectors.

(2) Any person who violates paragraph (1) of this subsection shall be guilty of a misdemeanor.

(b) The prohibition contained in subsection (a) of this Code section shall not apply to any elected sheriff who, pursuant to an agreement between the sheriff and the county governing authority, is using his or her personal motor vehicle in a law enforcement activity, provided such vehicle is marked as provided in Code Section 40–8–91.

(c) It shall be unlawful for any person to use any motor vehicle equipped with flashing, blinking, revolving, or stationary blue lights in the commission of a felony, and, upon conviction of a violation of this subsection, the punishment shall be a fine of not less than $1,000.00 or imprisonment of not less than one year, or both.

Laws 1966, p. 208, § 1; Laws 1971, p. 781, § 1; Laws 1972, p. 1092, § 1; Laws 1977, p. 1012, § 1; Laws 1984, p. 1193, § 1; Laws 1985, p. 149, § 40; Laws 1992, p. 1287, § 1; Laws 2005, Act 327, § 1, eff. July 1, 2005; Laws 2010, Act 360, § 1–82, eff. May 12, 2010.

Historical and Statutory Notes

The 2005 amendment by Act 327, rewrote subsec. (a); in subsec. (b), added "or her"; and in subsec. (c), substituted "flashing, blinking, revolving, or stationary blue lights" for "flashing or revolving blue lights". Prior to amendment subsec. (a) had read:

"(a) Except as provided in subsection (b) of this Code section, it shall be unlawful for any person, firm, or corporation to operate any motor vehicle equipped with or containing a device capable of producing flashing or revolving blue lights except motor vehicles owned or leased by any federal, state, or local law enforcement agency."

Laws 2005, Act 327, § 2, provides:

"This Act shall become effective on July 1, 2005, and shall be applied to offenses occurring on or after such date."

The 2010 amendment by Act 360, in par. (a)(1), substituted "paragraph (8) of subsection (*l*) of Code Section 40–2–86.1" for "subsection (a) of Code Section 40–2–77" in subpar. (C).

§ 40–8–91. Marking of official vehicles; unauthorized use of specially marked vehicles; violations; traffic stops; continuation by motorist to safe stopping location

(a) Except as provided in subsection (b) of this Code section, any motor vehicle which is used on official business by any person authorized to make arrests for traffic violations in this state, or any municipality or county thereof, shall be distinctly marked on each side and the back with the name of the agency responsible therefor, in letters not less than four inches in height.

Subsec. (b) effective until June 30, 2013.

(b) Any motor vehicle, except as hereinafter provided in this subsection, used by any employee of the Georgia State Patrol for the purpose of enforcing the traffic laws of this state shall be distinctly painted, marked, and equipped in such manner as shall be prescribed by the commissioner of public safety pursuant to this Code section. The commissioner in prescribing the manner in which such vehicles shall be painted, marked, or equipped shall:

(1) Require that all such motor vehicles be painted in a two-toned uniform color or a solid color. For vehicles painted in a two-toned color, the hood, top, and the top area not to exceed 12 inches below the bottom of the window opening thereof shall be a light gray color and the remaining portion of said motor vehicle shall be painted a dark blue color;

(2) Require that any such motor vehicle be equipped with at least one lamp which when lighted shall display a flashing or revolving colored light visible under normal atmospheric conditions for a distance of 500 feet from the front and rear of such vehicle; and

(3) Require that any such motor vehicle shall be distinctly marked on each side and the back thereof with the wording State Patrol in letters not less than six inches in height of a contrasting color from the background color of the motor vehicle.

Subsec. (b) effective June 30, 2013.

(b) Any motor vehicle, except as hereinafter provided in this subsection, used by any employee of the Georgia State Patrol for the purpose of enforcing the traffic laws of this state shall be distinctly painted, marked, and equipped in such manner as shall be prescribed by the commissioner of public safety pursuant to this Code section. The commissioner in prescribing the manner in which such vehicles shall be painted, marked, or equipped shall:

(1) Require that all such motor vehicles be painted in a two-toned uniform color. The hood, top, and the top area not to exceed 12 inches below the bottom of the window opening thereof shall be a light gray color and the remaining portion of said motor vehicle shall be painted a dark blue color;

(2) Require that any such motor vehicle be equipped with at least one lamp which when lighted shall display a flashing or

revolving colored light visible under normal atmospheric conditions for a distance of 500 feet from the front and rear of such vehicle; and

(3) Require that any such motor vehicle shall be distinctly marked on each side and the back thereof with the wording "State Patrol" in letters not less than six inches in height of a contrasting color from the background color of the motor vehicle.

Notwithstanding the above provisions, it shall be permissible for the commissioner to allow not more than five motor vehicles per State Patrol post to be employed in traffic law enforcement which are painted any solid color designated by the commissioner and marked with "State Patrol" in six inch high letters of a contrasting color.

(c) It shall be unlawful for any person, except persons lawfully entitled to own vehicles for law enforcement purposes, to paint, mark, or equip any motor vehicle in the same manner prescribed by this Code section or by the commissioner for law enforcement vehicles.

(d) When a law enforcement vehicle is disposed of, or is not in use for law enforcement, the lettering and colored lights must be removed. Any person using such vehicle for personal use prior to removing colored lights and lettering shall be guilty of a misdemeanor.

(e) Whenever a motorist driving on the roadways of this state is directed to stop by a law enforcement officer in a law enforcement vehicle marked as required under this Code section, the motorist may continue to drive until a reasonably safe location for stopping is reached. Such motorist shall indicate to the officer his or her intent to proceed to a safe location by displaying the vehicle's flashing lights or turn signal. In proceeding to a safe location, the motorist shall observe the posted maximum speed limit.

(f) An otherwise lawful arrest shall not be invalidated or in any manner affected by failure to comply with this Code section.

Laws 1953, Nov.-Dec. Sess., p. 556, § 107A; Laws 1966, p. 166, § 1; Laws 1976, p. 208, § 1; Laws 1986, p. 802, §§ 1–3; Laws 1987, p. 3, § 405; Laws 2006, Act 522, § 3, eff. April 20, 2006; Laws 2006, Act 529, § 1, eff. July 1, 2006; Laws 2010, Act 368, § 1-1, eff. July 1, 2010.

Historical and Statutory Notes

The 2010 amendment by Act 368, Part III, § 3-1, provided:

"SECTION 3-1. This Act shall become effective on July 1, 2010, and Part I of this Act shall stand repealed on June 30, 2013."

§ 40–8–91.1. All-terrain vehicles

(a) As used in this Code section, the term "all-terrain vehicle" means any motorized vehicle designed for off-road use which is equipped with at least a 500 cubic centimeter engine, four or more low pressure tires, a seat to be straddled by the operator, and handlebars for steering control.

(b) Every all-terrain vehicle must comply with the equipment and marking specifications set forth in this article before such vehicle can be used by law enforcement agencies and officers upon the public roads of this state. All provisions of law relating to safe operation of law enforcement or emergency vehicles shall be applied to the operation of such all-terrain vehicles.

(c) Any all-terrain vehicle which is operated by law enforcement agencies and officers upon the public roads of this state shall be registered and licensed in accordance with the provisions of Code Section 40–2–37.

Laws 2006, Act 695, § 1, eff. July 1, 2006.

§ 40–8–92. Emergency vehicles; flashing or revolving lights

(a) All emergency vehicles shall be designated as such by the commissioner of public safety. The commissioner shall so designate each vehicle by issuing to such vehicle a permit to operate flashing or revolving emergency lights of the appropriate color. Such permit shall be valid for one year from the date of issuance; provided, however, that permits for vehicles belonging to federal, state, county, or municipal governmental agencies shall be valid for five years from the date of issuance. Any and all officially marked law enforcement vehicles as specified in Code Section 40–8–91 shall not be required to have a permit for the use of a blue light. Any and all fire department vehicles which are distinctly marked on each side shall not be required to have a permit for the use of a red light. Any and all ambulances, as defined in Code Section 31–11–2, licensed by this state shall not be required to have a permit for the use of a red light.

(b) The commissioner shall authorize the use of red or amber flashing or revolving lights only when the person or governmental agency shall demonstrate to the commissioner a proven need for equipping a vehicle with emergency lights. The fee for such lights shall be $2.00, provided that no federal, state, county, or municipal governmental agency or an ambulance provider, as defined in Code Section 31–11–2, shall be required to pay such fee.

(c) Nothing contained in this Code section shall prohibit the commissioner from issuing a single special use permit to cover more than one vehicle, provided each vehicle covered under such special use permit shall pay the fee specified in subsection (b) of this Code section.

(d) Except as provided in this subsection, it shall be unlawful for any person, firm, or corporation to operate any motor vehicle or to park any motor vehicle on public property with flashing or revolving green lights. This subsection shall not apply to any motor vehicle being used by any law enforcement agency, fire department, emergency management agency, or other governmental entity to designate the location of the command post for such agency, department, or entity at the site of an emergency.

Laws 1971, p. 781, § 2; Laws 1972, p. 1092, §§ 3, 4; Laws 1977, p. 1012, § 4; Laws 1983, p. 447, § 1; Laws 1988, p. 582, § 1; Laws 1991, p. 1145, § 3; Laws 2000, p. 951, § 5B–6; Laws 2005, Act 68, § 19–6, eff. July 1, 2005; Laws 2010, Act 363, § 1, eff. July 1, 2010.

§ 40–8–93. Exceptions

Nothing contained in Code Sections 40–8–90 and 40–8–92 shall be deemed to apply to nor construed to prohibit blinking or flashing parking or brake lights or directional signals on any motor vehicle.

Laws 1972, p. 1092, § 6; Laws 1977, p. 1012, § 5.

§ 40–8–94. Sirens, whistles or bells

Any authorized emergency vehicle may be equipped with a siren, whistle, or bell capable of emitting sound audible under normal conditions from a distance of not less than 500 feet, but such siren shall not be used except when such vehicle is operated in response to an emergency call or in the immediate pursuit of an actual or suspected violator of the law, in which latter event the driver of such vehicle shall sound the siren when necessary to warn pedestrians and other drivers of the approach thereof.

Laws 1953, Nov.-Dec. Sess., p. 556, § 116.

§ 40–8–95. Rules and regulations

The commissioner of public safety shall implement any and all provisions of Code Sections 40–8–90, 40–8–92, and 40–8–93 by the promulgation of necessary rules and regulations.

Laws 1977, p. 1012, § 6; Laws 2000, p. 951, § 5B–7; Laws 2005, Act 68, § 19–7, eff. July 1, 2005.

§ 40–8–96. Violations relating to the use of flashing or revolving lights

Any person violating Code Sections 40–8–90 and 40–8–92 shall be guilty of a misdemeanor.

Laws 1972, p. 1092, § 5; Laws 1977, p. 1012, § 7.

Part 6

Equipment of School Buses

§ 40–8–110. Marking and color

(a) Every bus used for the transportation of school children shall bear upon the front and rear thereof a plainly visible sign containing the words "SCHOOL BUS" in letters not less than eight inches in height.

(b) On and after January 1, 1971, every new school bus purchased for the transportation of school children shall be painted National School Bus Chrome Yellow.

Laws 1953, Nov.-Dec. Sess., p. 556, § 89; Laws 1970, p. 586, § 2.

§ 40–8–111. Equipment, standards, requirements, and specifications for school buses

(a) Each school bus used for the transportation of school children in the State of Georgia shall be in compliance with the State Board of Education bus specifications for the model year of such school bus.

(b) Each public school system shall be required to maintain each of its school buses in good working condition, including all safety equipment required in accordance with the specifications established pursuant to subsection (a) of this Code section.

(c) Nothing in subsection (a) of this Code section shall apply to motor vehicles operated by a local transit system which transport school children to and from school on regular or scheduled routes of a transit vehicle with regular fare-paying passengers.

Laws 1970, p. 586, § 2; Laws 1978, p. 1367, §§ 1, 2; Laws 1982, p. 3, § 40; Laws 1986, p. 501, § 1; Laws 1992, p. 2963, § 1; Laws 2004, Act 560, § 8, eff. July 1, 2004.

§ 40–8–112. State Board Bus Specifications

Every school bus used to transport children to and from school shall comply with the State Board Bus Specifications prescribed by the State Board of Education.

Laws 1970, p. 586, § 2.

§ 40–8–113. Applicability of identification and equipment standards

The identification and equipment standards provided in this part shall apply to all school buses as defined in paragraph (55) of Code Section 40–1–1 regardless of size or capacity.

Laws 1974, p. 633, § 1; Laws 1992, p. 6, § 40.

§ 40–8–114. Operation by churches, private schools and local transit systems

(a) Notwithstanding any other provision of this title to the contrary, churches, private schools, or local transit systems may operate school buses meeting the equipment, color, and marking requirements of Code Sections 40–8–110 through 40–8–112 and 40–8–115 and drivers of such vehicles shall be required to stop as set forth in Code Section 40–6–163. For purposes of this subsection, only churches and private schools are authorized to comply with Code Sections 40–8–110 through 40–8–112, and only local transit systems are authorized to comply with Code Section 40–8–115.

(b) Notwithstanding any other provision of this title to the contrary, the requirements relating to buses used for the transportation of school children, which requirements are contained in the following Code sections:

(1) Code Section 40–6–160, relating to speed limits;

(2) Code Section 40–6–161, relating to headlamps;

(3) Code Section 40–6–162, relating to use of visual signals;

(4) Code Section 40–6–163, relating to meeting or passing school buses;

(5) Code Section 40–8–110, relating to identification and color;

(6) Code Section 40–8–111, relating to equipment generally;

(7) Code Section 40–8–112, relating to compliance with certain State Board of Education specifications;

(8) Code Section 40–8–115, relating to identification and equipment of certain school buses; and

(9) Code Section 40–8–220, relating to inspection of school buses,

shall not apply to any bus which is owned or operated by a publicly owned and operated transit system and which either transports school children to and from school on regular or scheduled routes with regular fare-paying passengers or which engages in tripper service.

Laws 1974, p. 633, § 1; Laws 1983, p. 633, § 2.

§ 40–8–115. Special school route service; identification and equipment standards

This part shall not prohibit the use of a school bus as defined in paragraph (55) of Code Section 40–1–1 for special school route service, provided it shall meet the following identification and equipment requirements:

(1) The bus need not be painted yellow or black;

(2) The bus shall be equipped with four hooded or recessed red flasher lights, or four red flasher lights and four amber flasher lights mounted on the same horizontal centerline as the red lights and nearer the centerline. Such amber lights shall be at least two and one-half times brighter than the red lights. The system shall be wired so that the amber signal lights are activated only by manual or foot operation and if activated are automatically deactivated and the red signal lights activated when the bus entrance door is opened; and

(3) While transporting children to or from school, the bus shall be equipped with the following temporary signs, located conspicuously on the front and back of such vehicle:

(A) The sign on the front shall have the words "SCHOOL BUS" printed in black letters not less than six inches high, on a background of National School Bus Glossy Yellow; and

(B) The sign on the rear shall be at least ten square feet in size and shall be painted National School Bus Glossy Yellow and have the words "SCHOOL BUS" printed in black letters not less than eight inches high.

Laws 1974, p. 633, § 1; Laws 1992, p. 6, § 40.

§ 40–8–116. Unlawful operation

It shall be unlawful to operate:

(1) Any vehicle displaying the words "SCHOOL BUS" unless it meets the color, identification, and equipment requirements set forth in Code Section 40–8–113 or 40–8–115;

(2) A vehicle without the words "SCHOOL BUS" but which is of a color and exhibits some equipment or identification which reasonably could cause a motorist to confuse it with a properly colored, identified, and equipped school bus;

(3) Any school bus for any purpose other than the transportation of school children to or from school or school activities without concealing or covering all markings thereon indicating "SCHOOL BUS"; or

(4) A vehicle which has been permanently converted from the purpose of transporting students to or from school or school activities without first having painted such vehicle some color other than the yellow required in subsection (b) of Code Section 40–8–110 and without having removed the stop arms, if any, and any other equipment required by Code Section 40–8–111.

Laws 1974, p. 633, § 1.

Article 2

Control of Vehicle Emissions

Part 1

Emission Control Devices Generally

§ 40–8–130. Devices controlling or abating atmospheric emissions

(a) It shall be unlawful for the owner of any motor vehicle to operate or permit the operation of such vehicle on which any device controlling or abating atmospheric emissions which is placed on a motor vehicle by the manufacturer pursuant to regulations promulgated by the United States secretary of health and human services in accordance with the provisions of Title II, the National Emissions Standards Act, of the Air Quality Act of 1967, Public Law 90–148 has been rendered unserviceable by removal, alteration, or other interference with its operation.

(b) Any person violating subsection (a) of this Code section shall be guilty of a misdemeanor.

(c) Subsection (a) of this Code section shall not apply to any person repairing any such device described in that subsection or to the removal of any such device by any person for the purpose of repairing or replacing such device.

(d) Subsection (a) of this Code section shall not apply to any person removing any such device for the purpose of converting any motor vehicle to operate on natural or liquefied petroleum gas or make any other modifications which would reduce atmospheric emissions.

Laws 1971, p. 188, § 1; Laws 1982, p. 3, § 40; Laws 1997, p. 143, § 40.

§ 40–8–131. Inspection without warrant

Any vehicle suspected of being operated in violation of this part may be the subject of an inspection conducted by an officer of the Georgia State Patrol who has reason to believe such violation is occurring, without the necessity of obtaining a warrant to permit such inspection.

Laws 1971, p. 188, § 1.

§ 40–8–132. Repealed by Laws 1982, p. 165, §§ 1, 6, eff. November 1, 1982

Part 2

Establishment of Emission Standards; Inspection of Motor Vehicles for Compliance with Standards

§§ 40–8–150 to 40–8–163. Repealed by Laws 1992, p. 918, § 1, eff. July 1, 1992

Part 3

Visible Emissions

§ 40–8–180. Short title

This part shall be known and may be cited as the "Vehicular Visible Emission Control Act."

Laws 1971, p. 186, § 1; Laws 1994, p. 97, § 40.

§ 40–8–181. Visible emissions from vehicles on public roadways

(a) It shall be unlawful for any person to operate on a public roadway of this state a diesel powered vehicle which discharges into the atmosphere visible emissions resulting in a decrease of light transmission beyond 30 percent, whether emitted from the crankcase, the exhaust system, or from any part of the power system; provided, however, that the light obscuring limitations prescribed in this subsection may be exceeded during periods of acceleration and deceleration not to exceed ten continuous seconds or 1,000 feet.

(b) It shall be unlawful for any person to operate on a public roadway of this state a gasoline powered vehicle which discharges into the atmosphere visible emissions resulting in a decrease of light transmission, whether emitted from the crankcase, the exhaust system, or from any part of the power system; provided, however, that the light obscuring limitation prescribed in this subsection may be exceeded for periods not to exceed ten continuous seconds or 1,000 feet.

(c) Subsections (a) and (b) of this Code section shall not apply to the normal discharge of condensed water vapor.

Laws 1971, p. 186, § 2.

§ 40–8–182. Enforcement of law; traffic violation citations

(a) This part shall be enforced by the duly authorized traffic control agency of this state or of any political subdivision thereof. The Air Quality Control Agency of this state shall produce and furnish to such traffic control agency appropriate light transmission gauges to be used in the enforcement of this part.

(b) A traffic violation citation shall be issued to the operator of a vehicle in violation of any provision of this part on and after January 1, 1973.

Laws 1971, p. 186, § 2.

§ 40–8–183. Violations relating to Vehicular Visible Emission Control Act

Any person who violates any provision of this part shall be guilty of a misdemeanor and, upon conviction thereof, shall be punished by a fine of not less than $10.00 nor more than $25.00.

Laws 1971, p. 186, § 3.

§ 40–8–184. Municipal and county regulation prohibited

No subdivision of this state shall enact any ordinance or issue any rules and regulations pertaining to the discharging into the atmosphere of visible emissions from diesel powered vehicles or gasoline powered vehicles.

Laws 1971, p. 186, § 4.

§ 40–8–185. Vehicles excepted

This part shall not apply to off-highway farm, forest, and construction equipment being moved from one work location to another.

Laws 1971, p. 186, § 5.

Article 3

Inspections by Officers of Department of Public Safety

§ 40–8–200. Inspections by officers of the Department of Public Safety

(a) The commissioner of public safety and members of the Department of Public Safety, and such other officers and employees of the department as the commissioner may designate, may at any time, upon reasonable cause to believe that a vehicle is unsafe or not equipped as required by law or that its equipment is not in proper adjustment or repair, require the driver of such vehicle to stop and submit such vehicle to an inspection and such tests with reference thereto as may be appropriate.

(b) In the event such vehicle and its equipment are found to be in safe condition and in full compliance with the law, the officer making such an inspection shall issue to the driver an official certificate of inspection and approval of such vehicle specifying those parts or equipment so inspected and approved.

(c) In the event such vehicle is found to be in unsafe condition or any required part or equipment is not present or is not in proper repair and adjustment, the officer shall give a written notice to the driver and shall send a copy to the department. Such notice shall require that such vehicle be placed in safe condition and its equipment in proper repair and adjustment specifying the particulars with reference thereto and shall require that a certificate of inspection and approval be obtained within 30 days.

Laws 1953, Nov.-Dec. Sess., p. 556, § 124; Laws 1960, p. 950, § 1; Laws 1963, p. 333, § 1; Laws 1965, p. 188, § 2.

§ 40–8–201. Owners and drivers to comply with inspection laws

(a) No person driving a vehicle shall refuse to submit such vehicle to an inspection and test when required to do so by the commissioner of public safety or an authorized officer of the Department of Public Safety.

(b) Every owner or driver, upon receiving a notice as provided in Code Section 40–8–200, shall comply therewith and shall within 30 days secure an official certificate of inspection and approval, which shall be issued in duplicate, one copy to be retained by the owner or driver and the other copy to be forwarded to the Department of Public Safety. In lieu of compliance with this subsection, the vehicle shall not be operated, except as provided in subsection (c) of this Code section.

(c) No person shall operate any vehicle after receiving a notice with reference thereto as provided in Code Section 40–8–200 except as may be necessary to return such vehicle to the residence or place of business of the owner or driver, or to a garage, until such vehicle and its equipment have been placed in proper repair and adjustment and otherwise made to conform to the requirements of this article. A certificate of inspection and approval shall be obtained as promptly as possible thereafter.

(d) In the event repair or adjustment of any vehicle or its equipment is found necessary upon inspection, the owner of such vehicle may obtain such repair or adjustment at any place he may choose, but in every event an official certificate of inspection and approval must be obtained; otherwise, such vehicle shall not be operated upon the highways of this state.

Laws 1953, Nov.-Dec. Sess., p. 556, § 125; Laws 1963, p. 333, § 1; Laws 1965, p. 188, § 3.

Article 4

Inspection of Public School Buses

§ 40–8–220. School bus inspection

(a) Every school bus which is defined by paragraph (55) of Code Section 40–1–1 which is owned or operated by a state, county, or municipal government or under contract by any independent school system shall be inspected annually, or more frequently at the discretion of the commissioner of public safety, under the supervision of an employee of the Department of Public Safety.

(b) The employee of the department shall supervise the inspection of such vehicle to determine if such vehicle possesses in safe operating condition the equipment which is applicable to school buses required by Parts 1 through 4 of Article 1 of this chapter and the equipment required by Part 6 of Article 1 of this chapter.

(c) If such vehicle is found to meet the equipment and safety requirements specified in subsection (b) of this Code section, then the employee of the department making the inspection shall issue a school bus certificate of safety inspection to the vehicle.

(d) If such vehicle does not meet the equipment and safety requirements specified in subsection (b) of this Code section, then that vehicle shall not be operated on the streets and highways of this state, and no school bus certificate of safety inspection shall be issued to such vehicle.

(e) All public school buses shall be made available for the inspection required under this Code section, and no person shall conceal any bus required to be inspected under this Code section.

(f) The commissioner of public safety is authorized to implement any and all provisions of this Code section by the promulgation of necessary rules and regulations. When duly promulgated and adopted, all rules and regulations issued pursuant to this Code section shall have the force of law.

Laws 1979, p. 906, § 1; Laws 1982, p. 165, § 4; Laws 1982, p. 165, § 9; Laws 1992, p. 6, § 40; Laws 2000, p. 951, § 5B–8; Laws 2005, Act 68, § 19–8, eff. July 1, 2005.

Formerly Code 1933, § 68E–208; Code 1933, § 68E–501; Code 1981, § 40–8–249.

§ 40–8–221. Penalties

Any person who violates any provision of this article shall be guilty of a misdemeanor.

Laws 1982, p. 165, § 9.

§§ 40–8–222 to 40–8–264. Repealed by Laws 1982, p. 165, § 9, eff. November 1, 1982

Article 5

Vehicle Equipment Safety Compact

§§ 40–8–280 to 40–8–291. Repealed by Laws 1983, p. 691, § 1, eff. March 16, 1983

CHAPTER 9

REPORTING ACCIDENTS; GIVING PROOF OF FINANCIAL RESPONSIBILITY

Article 1

General Provisions

§ 40–9–1. Short title

This chapter shall be known and may be cited as the "Motor Vehicle Safety Responsibility Act."

Laws 1977, p. 1014, § 1; Laws 2005, Act 68, § 20–1, eff. July 1, 2005.

Historical and Statutory Notes

The 2005 revision of Article 1 by Act 68 reenacted the section without amendment.

§ 40–9–2. Definitions

As used in this chapter, the term:

(1) "Accident" means the collision of any motor vehicle with another vehicle or with any object or fixture, or involvement of a motor vehicle in any manner in which any person is killed or injured or in which damage to the property of any one person to an extent of $500.00 or more is sustained.

(2) "Commissioner" means the commissioner of driver services.

(3) "Department" means the Department of Driver Services.

(4) "Operator" means every person who drives or is in actual physical control of a motor vehicle upon a highway or who is exercising control over or steering a vehicle being towed by a motor vehicle.

(5) "Proof of financial responsibility" means proof of ability to respond in damages for liability on account of accidents occurring subsequent to the effective date of said proof in the amounts specified in subparagraph (a)(1)(A) of Code Section 33–7–11.

(6) "Suspension of driver's license" means the temporary withdrawal by formal action of the department of a resident's

license or nonresident's privilege to operate a motor vehicle on the public highways.

Laws 1951, p. 565, § 1; Laws 1956, p. 543, §§ 2–5; Laws 1977, p. 1014, § 1; Laws 1978, p. 1494, § 2; Laws 1982, p. 1751, § 1; Laws 1983, p. 3, § 29; Laws 1983, p. 938, § 2; Laws 1990, p. 649, § 1; Laws 1991, p. 1608, § 2.2; Laws 1994, p. 363, § 2; Laws 2000, p. 951, § 6–1; Laws 2000, p. 1516, § 2; Laws 2005, Act 68, § 20–1, eff. July 1, 2005.

Formerly Code 1933, § 68C–101.

Historical and Statutory Notes

The 2000 amendment by Act 737 substituted for Department or Board of "Public Safety" the commissioner or Department of "Motor Vehicle Safety".

The 2000 amendment by Act 898 redefined proof of financial responsibility.

The 2005 amendment by Act 68 in par. (2) substituted "commissioner of driver services" for "commissioner of motor vehicle safety"; in par. (3) substituted "Department of Driver Services" for "Department of Motor Vehicle Safety"; and rewrote par. (6), which formerly read:

"(6) 'Registration' means the registration certificates and registration plates issued under the laws of this state pertaining to the registration of vehicles."

§ 40–9–3. Commissioner to administer; rules and regulations; hearings; judicial review

(a) The commissioner shall administer and enforce this chapter and is authorized to adopt and enforce rules and regulations necessary for its administration. The commissioner shall prescribe suitable forms requisite or deemed necessary for the purposes of this chapter.

(b) The commissioner shall provide for hearings upon request of persons aggrieved by orders or acts of the commissioner under this chapter. Such hearings shall not be subject to the procedural provisions of Chapter 13 of Title 50, the "Georgia Administrative Procedure Act."

(c) The commissioner is authorized to adopt and enforce rules and regulations necessary for the administration of such hearings, including but not limited to, hearings provided in Code Section 40–9–32. Except as provided in Code Section 40–9–32, a request for a hearing under this chapter shall not operate as a stay of any order or act of the commissioner.

(d) The commissioner's decision as rendered at such hearing shall be final unless the aggrieved person shall desire an appeal, in which case he or she shall have the right to enter an appeal to the superior court of the county of his or her residence or the Superior Court of Fulton County by filing a complaint in the superior court, naming the commissioner as defendant, within 30 days from the date the commissioner enters his or her decision or order. The appellant shall not be required to post any bond nor pay the costs in advance. If the aggrieved person desires, the appeal may be heard by the judge at term or in chambers or before a jury at the first term. The hearing on the appeal shall be de novo. However, such appeal shall not act as a supersedeas of any order or acts of the commissioner, nor shall the appellant be allowed to operate or permit a motor vehicle to be operated in violation of any suspension or revocation by the commissioner while such appeal is pending.

Laws 1951, p. 565, § 2; Laws 1956, p. 543, § 6; Laws 1973, p. 509, § 1; Laws 1977, p. 1014, § 1; Laws 2000, p. 951, § 6–2; Laws 2003, Act 200, § 13, eff. Oct. 1, 2003; Laws 2004, Act 582, § 9, eff. July 1, 2004; Laws 2005, Act 68, § 20–1, eff. July 1, 2005.

Formerly Code 1933, § 68C–201.

Historical and Statutory Notes

The 2003 amendment by Act 200, in subsec. (a), deleted ", except that the form for accident reports shall be prescribed by the commissioner of public safety" following "purposes of this chapter".

Laws 2003, Act 200, § 15 provides:

"This Act shall become effective on October 1, 2003."

The 2004 amendment by Act 582, in subsec. (a), deleted "and provide" following "The commissioner shall prescribe".

The 2005 amendment by Act 68 in subsec. (d) made changes in gender references throughout.

§ 40–9–4. Exceptions to application of chapter

This chapter shall not apply with respect to any motor vehicle owned by the United States, the State of Georgia, any political subdivision of this state, or any municipality therein, or any motor carrier required by any other law to file evidence of insurance or other surety. Code Sections 40–9–81, 40–9–7, 40–9–8, and 40–9–12 shall apply as to the operator of such motor vehicles. All provisions of this chapter shall apply to the operator of such motor vehicles while on unofficial business.

Laws 1951, p. 565, § 15; Laws 1956, p. 543, § 19; Laws 1963, p. 593, § 10; Laws 1977, p. 1014, § 1; Laws 1994, p. 97, § 40; Laws 2005, Act 68, § 20–1, eff. July 1, 2005.

Formerly Code 1933, § 68C–603.

Historical and Statutory Notes

The 2005 amendment by Act 68 substituted "40–9–81, 40–9–7, 40–9–8, and 40–9–12" for "40–9–81, 40–9–6 through 40–9–8, and 40–9–12".

§ 40–9–5. Application to nonresidents, unlicensed drivers, and accidents in other states

(a) If the operator or the owner of a vehicle involved in an accident in this state has no license, such operator shall not be allowed a license until he or she has complied with the requirements of this chapter to the same extent that would be necessary if, at the time of the accident, he or she had held a license in this state.

(b) When a nonresident's operating privilege is suspended pursuant to Code Section 40–9–33 or 40–9–61, the department shall transmit a certified copy of the record of such action to the official in charge of the issuance of licenses and registration certificates in the state in which such nonresident resides, if the law of such other state provides for action in relation thereto similar to that provided for in subsection (c) of this Code section.

(c) Upon receipt of a certification that the operating privilege of a resident of this state has been suspended in another state pursuant to a law providing for its suspension for failure to deposit security for the payment of judgments arising out of a motor vehicle accident, under circumstances which would require the department to suspend a nonresident's operating privilege had the accident occurred in this state, the department shall suspend the license of such resident. Such suspension shall continue until such resident furnishes evidence of his or her compliance with the laws of such other state relating to the showing of proof of financial responsibility or reinstatement of operating privilege.

Laws 1951, p. 565, § 8; Laws 1956, p. 543, § 16; Laws 1958, p. 694, § 4; Laws 1977, p. 1014, § 1; Laws 1982, p. 3, § 40; Laws 2005, Act 68, § 20–1, eff. July 1, 2005.

Formerly Code 1933, § 68C–306.

Historical and Statutory Notes

The 2005 amendment by Act 68 rewrote subsec. (a) and (c). Prior to amendment, subsecs. (a) and (c) had read:

"(a) If the operator or the owner of a vehicle involved in an accident in this state has no license or registration, such operator shall not be allowed a license nor shall such owner be allowed to register any vehicle until he has complied with the requirements of this chapter to the same extent that would be necessary if, at the time of the accident, he had held a license or been the owner of a vehicle registered in this state."

"(c) Upon receipt of a certification that the operating privilege of a resident of this state has been suspended in another state pursuant to a law providing for its suspension for failure to deposit security for the payment of judgments arising out of a motor vehicle accident, under circumstances which would require the department to suspend a nonresident's operating privilege had the accident occurred in this state, the department shall suspend the license of such resident and such resident's vehicle registration if he was the owner or operator of a motor vehicle involved in the accident. Such suspension shall continue until such resident furnishes evidence of his compliance with the laws of such other state relating to the showing of proof of financial responsibility, or reinstatement of operating or registration privilege."

§ 40–9–6. Repealed by Laws 2005, Act 68, § 20–1, eff. July 1, 2005

Historical and Statutory Notes

Repealed § 40–9–6, relating to prohibitions on transfers of registration to defeat purpose of reporting accidents and giving proof of financial responsibility, was derived from Laws 1951, p. 565, § 12; Laws 1977, p. 1014, § 1; Code 1933, § 68C-701. The repealing law also reserved the section designation.

§ 40–9–7. Surrender and return of license following suspension

(a) Any person whose driver's license shall have been suspended under any provision of this chapter shall immediately return his or her license to the department. If any person shall fail to return such license to the department, the department shall direct any peace officer to secure possession thereof and to return it to the department.

(b) Any person willfully failing to return his or her driver's license as required in subsection (a) of this Code section shall be guilty of a misdemeanor and, upon conviction thereof, shall be punished by a fine not to exceed $500.00 or by imprisonment for not more than 30 days, or by both such fine and imprisonment.

Laws 1951, p. 565, § 14; Laws 1977, p. 1014, § 1; Laws 2005, Act 68, § 20–1, eff. July 1, 2005.

Formerly Code 1933, § 68C–702.

Historical and Statutory Notes

The 2005 amendment by Act 68 in subsec. (a) deleted "or vehicle registration" following "whose driver's license", substituted "his or her license" for "his license and registration" prior to "to the department" in the first sentence, and deleted "or registration" prior to "to the department" in the second sentence; and in subsec. (b) substituted "his or her driver's license" for "his driver's license or registration" following "failing to return".

§ 40–9–8. Vehicle operation during suspension prohibited; penalty

Any person whose driver's license or nonresident's operating privilege has been suspended under this chapter and who, during such suspension, drives any motor vehicle upon any highway, except where permitted under this chapter, shall be guilty of a misdemeanor and, upon conviction thereof, shall be punished by imprisonment for not less than five days nor more than six months and there may be imposed in addition thereto a fine of not more than $500.00.

Laws 1951, p. 565, § 14; Laws 1969, p. 819, § 5; Laws 1977, p. 1014, § 1; Laws 2005, Act 68, § 20–1, eff. July 1, 2005.

Formerly Code 1933, § 68C–704.

Historical and Statutory Notes

The 2005 amendment by Act 68 rewrote the section, which had read:

"Any person whose driver's license, vehicle registration, or nonresident's operating privilege has been suspended under this chapter and who, during such suspension, drives any motor vehicle upon any highway or knowingly permits any motor vehicle owned by such person to be operated by another upon any highway, except where permitted under this chapter, shall be guilty of a misdemeanor and, upon conviction thereof, shall be punished by imprisonment for not less than five days nor more than six months and there may be imposed in addition thereto a fine of not more than $500.00."

§ 40–9–9. Reinstatement of licenses; fee

Whenever a driver's license is suspended under any provisions of this chapter and the filing of proof of financial responsibility is made a prerequisite to reinstatement of such license, no such license shall be reinstated unless the driver or owner, in addition to complying with the other provisions of this chapter, pays to the department a fee of $25.00. Only one such fee shall be paid by any one person irrespective of the number of licenses to be reinstated. The fees paid pursuant to this Code section shall be expendable receipts to be used only by the department toward the cost of administration of this chapter.

Laws 1963, p. 593, § 9; Laws 1969, p. 819, § 6; Laws 1977, p. 1014, § 1; Laws 1983, p. 487, § 3; Laws 2005, Act 68, § 20–1, eff. July 1, 2005.

Formerly Code 1933, § 68C–605.

Historical and Statutory Notes

The 2005 amendment by Act 68 substituted "driver's license" for "driver's license or vehicle registration" prior to "is suspended", and "reinstatement of such license, no such license shall be reinstated" for "reinstatement of such license or registration or both, no such license or registration shall be reinstated" in the first sentence, and substituted "licenses" for "licenses and registrations" following "irrespective of the number of" in the second sentence.

§ 40–9–10. Chapter supplemental to motor vehicle laws

This chapter shall in no respect be considered as a repeal of the state motor vehicle laws but shall be construed as supplemental thereto.

Laws 1951, p. 565, § 18; Laws 1963, p. 593, § 10; Laws 1977, p. 1014, § 1; Laws 1985, p. 149, § 40; Laws 2005, Act 68, § 20–1, eff. July 1, 2005.

Formerly Code 1933, § 68C–606.

Historical and Statutory Notes

The 2005 revision of Article 1 by Act 68 reenacted the section without amendment.

§ 40–9–11. Chapter not to prevent other process

Nothing in this chapter shall be construed as preventing the plaintiff in any action at law from relying for relief upon the other processes provided by law.

Laws 1951, p. 565, § 20; Laws 1963, p. 593, § 10; Laws 1977, p. 1014, § 1; Laws 2005, Act 68, § 20–1, eff. July 1, 2005.

Formerly Code 1933, § 68C–607.

Historical and Statutory Notes

The 2005 revision of Article 1 by Act 68 reenacted the section without amendment.

§ 40–9–12. Penalty for other violations

Any person who shall violate any provision of this chapter for which no penalty is otherwise provided shall be guilty of a misdemeanor.

Laws 1951, p. 565, § 14; Laws 1977, p. 1014, § 1; Laws 2005, Act 68, § 20–1, eff. July 1, 2005.

Formerly Code 1933, § 68C–705.

Historical and Statutory Notes

The 2005 revision of Article 1 by Act 68 reenacted the section without amendment.

Article 2

Reporting Accidents; Giving Security for Damages

§ 40–9–30. Fee for accident report

The Department of Transportation shall charge a fee of $5.00 for each copy of any accident report received and maintained by that department pursuant to Code Section 40–6–273.

Laws 1991, p. 309, § 1; Laws 2005, Act 68, § 20–2, eff. July 1, 2005.

Historical and Statutory Notes

The 2005 amendment by Act 68 substituted "Department of Transportation" for "department" and made a nonsubstantive change.

§ 40–9–31. Submission of copy of accident report to Department of Transportation

Each state and local law enforcement agency shall submit to the Department of Transportation the original document of any accident report prepared by such law enforcement agency or submitted to such agency by a member of the public. If the Department of Driver Services receives a claim requesting determination of security, the Department of Transportation shall provide a copy or an electronic copy of any relevant accident reports to the Department of Driver Services. A law enforcement agency may transmit the information contained on the accident report form by electronic means, provided that the Department of Transportation has first given approval to the reporting agency for the electronic reporting method utilized. The law enforcement agency shall retain a copy of each accident report. All such reports shall be submitted to the Department of Transportation not more than 15 days following the end of the month in which such report was prepared or received by such law enforcement agency.

Laws 1994, p. 362, § 1; Laws 1999, p. 871, § 1; Laws 2000, p. 951, § 6–3; Laws 2002, p. 415, § 40; Laws 2005, Act 68, § 20–2, eff. July 1, 2005.

Historical and Statutory Notes

The 2000 amendment rewrote this section which formerly provided:

"Each local law enforcement agency shall submit to the Department of Public Safety the original document of any accident report prepared by such local law enforcement agency or submitted to such agency by a member of the public. A local law enforcement agency may transmit the information contained on the accident report form by electronic means, provided that the department has first given approval to the reporting agency for the electronic reporting method utilized. The local law enforcement agency shall retain a copy of each accident report. All such reports shall be submitted to the department not more than 15 days following the end of the month in which such report was prepared or received by such local law enforcement agency."

The 2002 amendment deleted "the Department of Public Safety and" preceding "and the Department of Motor Vehicle Safety".

The 2005 amendment by Act 68 rewrote the section, which had read:

"Each state and local law enforcement agency shall submit to the Department of Motor Vehicle Safety the original document of any accident report prepared by such law enforcement agency or submitted to such agency by a member of the public. A law enforcement agency may transmit the information contained on the accident report form by electronic means, provided that the department has first given approval to the reporting agency for the electronic reporting method utilized. The law enforcement agency shall retain a copy of each accident report. All such reports shall be submitted to the department not more than 15 days following the end of the month in which such report was prepared or received by such law enforcement agency."

§ 40–9–32. Department to determine amount of security required; hearing; judicial review

(a) The department, not less than 30 days after receipt of an accident report or notice of an accident with respect to which a person claims under oath to have suffered damages and requests determination of security, shall determine the amount of security sufficient in its judgment to satisfy any judgment or judgments for damages resulting from such accident that may be recovered against each operator and owner. Such determination shall be made on the basis of the reports or other information submitted. Notwithstanding any other provisions of this chapter, the department shall not consider or take any action with respect to an accident report, notice of accident, or any claim filed under this Code section which is received more than six months after the date of the accident.

(b) The department, upon determining the amount of security required, shall give written notice to each operator and owner of the amount of security required to be deposited by him or her. Such notice shall state that each operator's license shall be suspended on the thirtieth day from the date of mailing of notice unless within that time the required security is deposited and such owner or operator shall give proof of financial responsibility for the future. The license of the one depositing the security will not then be suspended.

(c)(1) Any person so notified may, within ten days after receipt of such notification, make a written request to the department for a hearing. Such request shall operate as a stay of any suspension pending the outcome of such hearing. The scope of such hearing, for the purposes of this Code section, shall cover the issues of whether there is a reasonable possibility that a judgment could be rendered against such person in an action arising out of the accident and whether such person is exempt from the requirement of depositing security under Code Section 40–9–34. The department may also consider at such hearing the amount of security required. The requirements of depositing security under this Code section shall not apply to any person against whom the department has found that there is not a reasonable possibility of a judgment being rendered.

(2) For the purposes of this Code section, a hearing may consist of a department determination of such issues, such determination to be based solely on written reports submitted by the operator or owner and by investigatory officers, provided that the owner or operator in his or her request to the department for a hearing has expressly consented to this type of hearing and that the department has also consented thereto.

(d) Any person required to give security after a hearing as provided in subsection (c) of this Code section may petition for judicial review of the decision of the department, but suspension of such person's driver's license or operating privilege shall not be stayed while such appeal is pending. The superior court upon such appeal may consider the written reports considered by the department at the hearing as authorized by subsection (c) of this Code section.

Laws 1951, p. 565, §§ 9, 11; Laws 1963, p. 593, §§ 2, 3; Laws 1964, p. 225, § 2; Laws 1969, p. 819, § 2; Laws 1977, p. 1014, § 1; Laws 1985, p. 1647, §§ 1, 2; Laws 1986, p. 10, § 40; Laws 1994, p. 859, § 1; Laws 2005, Act 68, § 20–2, eff. July 1, 2005.

Formerly Code 1933, §§ 68C–302, 68C–310.

Historical and Statutory Notes

The 2005 amendment by Act 68 in subsec. (a) inserted "with respect to which a person claims under oath to have suffered damages and requests determination of security" prior to "shall determine" in the first sentence; in subsec. (b) made a change in a gender reference and substituted "each operator's license" for "each operator's and owner's license and vehicle registration" prior to "shall be suspended" in the second sentence; in par. (2) of subsec. (c) made a change in a gender reference; and, in subsec. (d) substituted "such person's driver's license or operating privilege" for "such person's driver's license, operating privilege, or vehicle registration".

§ 40–9–33. Failure to deposit security; suspension; duration

(a) In the event that any person required to deposit security fails to deposit such security within 30 days from the date of mailing of notice as provided in Code Section 40–9–32 and such person does not make a timely request for a hearing, or in the event any person fails to deposit security after the department has determined that there exists a reasonable possibility of a judgment being rendered against such person, the department shall thereupon suspend:

(1) The driver's license of such person; and

(2) If such person is a nonresident, the privilege of operating or permitting the operation of a vehicle within this state.

(b) The license or nonresident's operating privilege shall remain so suspended and shall not be restored, nor shall any such license be issued to such person, nor shall such nonresident's operating privilege be restored, until:

(1) Such person shall deposit or there shall be deposited on his or her behalf the security and proof of financial responsibility for the future as required by this chapter;

(2) One year shall have elapsed following the date of such suspension and evidence satisfactory to the department has been filed with it that during the period of suspension no action for damages arising out of the accident has been instituted; or

(3) Evidence satisfactory to the commissioner has been filed with him or her of a release from liability or a final adjudication of nonliability.

Laws 1951, p. 565, §§ 5, 7; Laws 1956, p. 543, § 9; Laws 1963, p. 593, § 4; Laws 1977, p. 1014, § 1; Laws 2005, Act 68, § 20–2, eff. July 1, 2005.

Formerly Code 1933, § 68C–303.

Historical and Statutory Notes

The 2005 amendment by Act 68 rewrote the section, which had read:

"(a) In the event that any person required to deposit security fails to deposit such security within 30 days from the date of mailing of notice as provided in Code Section 40–9–32 and such person does not make a timely request for a hearing, or in the event any person fails to deposit security after the department has determined that there exists a reasonable possibility of a judgment being rendered against such person, the department shall thereupon suspend:

"(1) The driver's license of such person;

"(2) The registration of all vehicles owned by such person which are subject to registration under the laws of this state; and

"(3) If such person is a nonresident, the privilege of operating or permitting the operation of a vehicle within this state.

"(b) The license and registration or nonresident's operating privilege shall remain so suspended and shall not be restored, nor shall any such license and registration be issued to such person, nor shall such nonresident's operating privilege be restored, until:

"(1) Such person shall deposit or there shall be deposited on his behalf the security and proof of financial responsibility for the future as required by this chapter;

"(2) One year shall have elapsed following the date of such suspension and evidence satisfactory to the department has been filed with it that during the period of suspension no action for damages arising out of the accident has been instituted; or

"(3) Evidence satisfactory to the commissioner has been filed with him of a release from liability or a final adjudication of nonliability."

§ 40–9–34. Exceptions to requirement of security

The requirements as to security and suspension provided in Code Sections 40–9–32 and 40–9–33 shall not apply:

(1) To the operator or owner of the vehicle involved in the accident if the owner had in effect at the time of the accident an automobile liability policy with respect to the vehicle involved in the accident, except that a driver shall not be so exempt if at the time of the accident the vehicle was being operated without the owner's permission, express or implied;

(2) To the operator, if he is not the owner of the vehicle involved in the accident but there was in effect at the time of the accident an automobile liability policy with respect to his driving of vehicles not owned by him which provided him with liability coverage in the operation of the motor vehicle involved in such accident;

(3) To an operator or owner whose liability for damages resulting from the accident is, in the judgment of the department, covered by any other form of liability insurance policy;

(4) To any person qualifying as a self-insurer under Code Section 33–34–5.1 or to any person operating a vehicle for such self-insurer;

(5) To the operator or the owner of a vehicle involved in an accident wherein no injury or damage was caused to the person or property of anyone other than such driver or owner;

(6) To the operator or the owner of a motor vehicle legally parked at the time of the accident;

(7) To the owner of a vehicle if at the time of the accident the vehicle was being operated without his permission, express or implied, or was parked by a person who had been operating such vehicle without such permission;

(8) To a resident of this state involved in an accident with a nonresident of this state when the damage is less than $300.00, except upon the written request of any party in interest;

(9) If, prior to the date that the department would otherwise suspend a license and registration or a nonresident's operating privilege under Code Section 40–9–33, there shall be filed with the department evidence satisfactory to it that the person who would otherwise have to file security has been released from liability or finally adjudicated not to be liable.

Laws 1951, p. 565, §§ 5, 6; Laws 1956, p. 543, §§ 9, 11; Laws 1977, p. 1014, § 1; Laws 2000, p. 1246, § 17.

Formerly Code 1933, § 68C–304.

Historical and Statutory Notes

The 2000 amendment modified the statutory reference in par. (4).

§ 40–9–35. Agreements for payments of damages

(a) Any two or more of the persons involved in or affected by an accident may enter into a written agreement for the payment of an agreed amount with respect to all claims of any of such persons because of bodily injury to or death or property damage arising from such accident, which agreement may provide for payment in installments, and may file a signed copy thereof with the department.

(b) The department, to the extent provided by any such written agreement filed with it, shall not require the deposit of security and shall terminate any prior order of suspension or, if security has previously been deposited, the department shall immediately return such security to the depositor or his personal representative.

Laws 1951, p. 565, § 6; Laws 1977, p. 1014, § 1.

Formerly Code 1933, § 68C–305.

§ 40–9–36. Amount of security; departmental action

(a) The security under this chapter shall be in such amount as the department may require, but in no case in excess of the limits specified in subsection (a) of Code Section 40–9–37. Every depositor of security shall designate in writing every person on whose behalf the deposit is made and may at any time change such designation, in writing, to include an additional person or persons; provided, however, that a single deposit of security shall be applicable only on behalf of persons required to furnish security because of the same accident.

(b) The department may, upon written notice to all parties involved, reduce or increase the amount of security ordered in any case within six months after the date of the accident if in its judgment the amount ordered is excessive or inadequate. In case the security originally ordered has been deposited, the excess deposit over the reduced amount ordered shall be returned to the depositor or his personal representative.

Laws 1951, p. 565, § 9; Laws 1956, p. 543, § 17; Laws 1963, p. 593, § 6; Laws 1977, p. 1014, § 1.

Formerly Code 1933, § 68C–307.

§ 40–9–37. Requirements as to liability insurance policy

(a) No liability insurance policy shall be effective under Code Section 40–9–34 unless issued by an insurance company authorized to do business in this state, except as provided in subsection (b) of this Code section, and unless such policy or bond is subject to limits, exclusive of interest and costs, of not less than the amounts specified in subparagraph (a)(1)(A) of Code Section 33–7–11.

(b) No policy shall be effective under Code Section 40–9–34 with respect to any vehicle which was not registered in this state or which was registered elsewhere than in this state at the effective date of the policy or the most recent renewal thereof unless the insurance company issuing such policy is authorized to do business in this state, or if such company is not authorized to do business in this state, unless it shall execute a power of attorney authorizing the commissioner to accept service on its behalf of notice or process in any action upon such policy arising out of such accident.

(c) Whenever erroneous information is given to the department with respect to the matters set forth in paragraph (1), (2), or (3) of Code Section 40–9–34, the department shall take appropriate action as provided in Code Section 40–9–32 after receipt of correct information with respect to such matters.

Laws 1951, p. 565, §§ 5, 9; Laws 1956, p. 543, § 10; Laws 1957, p. 124, §§ 1, 5; Laws 1958, p. 694, §§ 1, 5; Laws 1964, p. 225, § 5; Laws 1977, p. 1014, § 1; Laws 1982, p. 1751, § 2; Laws 1983, p. 3, § 29; Laws 1983, p. 938, § 3; Laws 2000, p. 1516, § 3.

Formerly Code 1933, § 68C–307.

Historical and Statutory Notes

The 2000 amendment rewrote subsec. (a).

§ 40–9–38. Surety bonds and real property bonds; requirements; increase or decrease of security; actions; departmental action

(a) Security under this chapter may also be provided for by a surety bond executed by the person and by a surety company duly authorized to transact business in this state or by the person giving proof of his ownership of real property and by one or more individual sureties owning real property within this state and having an equity therein in at least the amount of the bond. The commissioner may not accept any real property bond unless the real property is scheduled in an affidavit attached thereto setting forth a description of such property and the title thereto, including any liens and encumbrances and amounts thereof, market value and value of such sureties' interest therein, executed by the owner or owners of such interest, and such bond and affidavit shows thereon that a duplicate original of such bond and affidavit has been recorded in the office of the clerk of the superior court where deeds are admitted to record in the county where the real property is located. The clerk shall provide a separate book for such purpose. The bond shall be approved by the clerk in the same manner as a supersedeas bond is approved. The fee of the clerk for recording and approving such affidavit and bond shall be $2.50.

(b) The commissioner shall not accept any such bond unless it is conditioned for payments in amounts requested by the commissioner, subject to the maximum amounts of security as specified under this chapter.

(c) No such bond shall be canceled unless 20 days' prior written notice of cancellation is given the commissioner, and cancellation of the bond shall not prevent recovery thereon with respect to any cause of action which necessitated the filing of such bond.

(d) A bond with individual sureties shall constitute a lien upon the real property of the principal and any individual surety in favor of the Governor of Georgia for the use of any holder of any final judgment arising out of the cause of action which necessitated the filing of the bond, against the principal on account of damage to property or injury to or death of any person or persons, upon the recording of the bond in the office of the clerk of the court where deeds are admitted to record in the county where the real property is located.

(e) When a bond with individual sureties filed with the commissioner is no longer required under this chapter, the commissioner shall, upon request, cancel it as to liability for damage to property or injury to or death of any person or persons; and, when a bond has been canceled by the commissioner, he shall, upon request, furnish a certificate of cancellation with the seal of the department thereon. The certificate, notwithstanding any other provision of law, may be recorded in the office of the clerk of the court in which the bond was admitted to record.

(f) When the certificate of cancellation with the seal of the department thereon has been filed in the office of the clerk of the superior court in which the bond was admitted to record, and when there are no claims or judgments against the principal in the bond on account of damage to property or injury to or death of any person or persons resulting from the ownership or operation of a motor vehicle by the principal arising out of the cause of action which necessitated the filing of the bond, the clerk of the superior court of the county in which the bond was admitted to record shall thereupon record the certificate of cancellation, which shall discharge the lien of the bond on the real property of the sureties. The cost of such recording shall be upon such sureties.

(g) If a final judgment rendered against the principal on the bond filed with the commissioner is not satisfied within 30 days after its rendition, the judgment creditor may, for his own use and benefit and at his sole expense, bring an action on the bond in the name of the state against the company or persons issuing the bond.

(h) When the sureties on the bond are individuals, the judgment creditor may proceed against any or all parties to the bond at law for a judgment or in equity for a decree and foreclosure of the lien on the real property of the sureties. The proceeding whether at law or in equity may be against one, all, or any intermediate number of parties to the bond; and, when less than all are joined, another or others may be impleaded in the same proceeding; and, after final judgment or decree, other proceedings may be instituted until full satisfaction is obtained.

(i) The department may, upon written notice to all parties involved, reduce or increase the amount of security ordered in any case within six months after the date of the accident if in its judgment the amount ordered is excessive or inadequate. In case the security originally ordered has been deposited, the excess deposit over the reduced amount ordered shall be returned to the depositor or his personal representative.

(j) Whenever erroneous information is given the department with respect to the matters set forth in paragraph (1), (2), or (3) of Code Section 40–9–34, the department shall take appropriate action as provided in Code Section 40–9–32 after receipt of correct information with respect to such matters.

Laws 1951, p. 565, §§ 5, 9; Laws 1956, p. 543, § 12; Laws 1959, p. 341, § 1; Laws 1978, p. 1527, § 1; Laws 1985, p. 149, § 40; Laws 1989, p. 14, § 40.

Formerly Code 1933, § 68C–307.1.

§ 40–9–39. Custody, disposition, and return of deposit

(a) The department shall place any security deposited with it under this chapter in the general fund of the state treasury. Such security shall be applicable and available only:

(1) For the payment of any settlement agreement covering any claim arising out of the accident upon instruction of the person who made the deposit; or

(2) For the payment of a judgment or judgments for damages arising out of the accident rendered against the person required to make the deposit in an action at law begun not later than one year after the deposit of such security or within one year after the date of deposit of any security following failure to make payments under an agreement to pay.

(b) Upon the expiration of one year from the date of any deposit of security, any security remaining on deposit shall be returned to the person who made such deposit or to his legal representative, if evidence satisfactory to the department has been filed with it:

(1) That no action for damages arising out of the accident for which deposit was made is pending against any person on whose behalf the deposit was made; and

(2) That there does not exist any unpaid judgment rendered against any such person in any such action.

In any case where the depositor shall die while security is on deposit with the department, the commissioner is authorized to return such security to the executor or administrator of the estate of the deceased depositor, or, if there is no executor or administrator and the amount on deposit is $1,000.00 or less, the commissioner is authorized to pay over such deposit to the surviving spouse or heirs at law of the deceased depositor. In any event, no deposit shall be returned unless and until satisfactory evidence has been filed by the person seeking such return, under the same conditions as provided in paragraph (1) of this subsection for the filing of such evidence by the depositor.

(c) In any case where, after the expiration of one year from the date of any deposit of security, the commissioner is unable to contact the depositor by mail or receives no response from the depositor, the commissioner shall have a notice printed in the local newspaper in which legal notices are usually printed, in the county of the last known address of the depositor, once each week for four consecutive weeks. Such notice shall specify that the depositor is eligible for the return of the security subject to the provisions of this Code section and shall further specify that, if no response is received from the notice within one year from the date on which the last notice is printed, the security will be deposited in the general fund of the state treasury. If no response to the notice is received by the commissioner, the commissioner shall dispose of the security as provided in this subsection. The cost of the publication shall be deducted from the security on deposit, regardless of whether the security is returned to the depositor or his legal representative or deposited in the state treasury. After such security is deposited in the general fund of the state treasury, the state treasurer is authorized to return such security to the proper person as provided in this Code section as a refund, in the event proof is furnished to the commissioner that such person is the proper person to whom such security should be refunded. The state treasurer shall make no such refund without a certification by the commissioner of the name of the person to whom the refund should be made.

(d) Upon receiving a certificate from the clerk of any court wherein a judgment has been obtained against the person in whose behalf the deposit was made, which certificate shall set forth the parties to the litigation, the time, place, and date of the accident, and the fact that the judgment is unsatisfied of record and that the time for appeal has expired, it shall be the duty of the commissioner to transmit immediately to the clerk of such court any cash security held by the department, to be applied to the satisfaction of the judgment and any accrued interest and court costs. Any additional security over and above the amount required to satisfy the foregoing shall be returned by the department to the depositor.

Laws 1951, p. 565, § 10; Laws 1956, p. 543, § 18; Laws 1963, p. 593, § 7; Laws 1965, p. 456, § 1; Laws 1969, p. 819, § 4; Laws 1971, p. 654, § 1; Laws 1972, p. 412, § 1; Laws 1977, p. 1014, § 1; Laws 1985, p. 149, § 40; Laws 1993, p. 1402, § 18; Laws 2010, Act 621, § 3, eff. July 1, 2010.

Formerly Code 1933, § 68C–308.

Historical and Statutory Notes

The 2010 amendment by Act 621, in subsec. (c), substituted "state treasurer" for "director of the Office of Treasury and Fiscal Services" in the fifth and sixth sentences.

§ 40–9–40. Court record; pending action; unsatisfied judgment; certificate by clerk

At the end of the expiration of one year from the date of the accident or one year from the date of the suspension under this chapter, the clerk, or the judge if there is no clerk, of any court of this state having jurisdiction over civil cases shall, upon request of an operator or owner or an authorized representative of either, check the records of such court and furnish such operator or owner or authorized representative with a certificate showing whether or not there is an action at law pending or an unsatisfied judgment on file against such operator or owner arising out of the accident which necessitated the depositing of security or on which the suspension was based. The fee for providing such certificate shall be as provided in Code Section 15–6–77 and shall be paid by the party requesting the certificate.

Laws 1951, p. 565, § 3; Laws 1956, p. 543, §§ 7, 14; Laws 1977, p. 1014, § 1; Laws 1981, p. 1396, § 7; Laws 1991, p. 1324, § 7.

Formerly Code 1933, § 68C–309.

§ 40–9–41. Matters not to be evidence in civil suits

Neither any accident report filed with the Department of Transportation, the action taken by the Department of Driver Services pursuant to this chapter, the findings, if any, of the department upon which such action is based, nor the security filed as provided in this chapter shall be referred to in any way, nor shall they be any evidence of the negligence or due care of either party, at the trial of any action at law to recover damages.

Laws 1951, p. 565, § 11; Laws 1977, p. 1014, § 1; Laws 1994, p. 97, § 40; Laws 2005, Act 68, § 20–3, eff. July 1, 2005.

Formerly Code 1933, § 68C–310.

Historical and Statutory Notes

The 2005 amendment by Act 68 substituted "Department of Transportation, the action taken by the Department of Driver Services" for "department, the action taken by the department" prior to "pursuant to this chapter.

Article 3

Unsatisfied Judgments

§ 40–9–60. When courts, department, to report nonpayment of judgments

(a) Whenever any person fails within 30 days to satisfy any judgment rendered in an action at law arising out of a motor vehicle accident, to which no appeal has been entered or motion for a new trial entered, then upon the request of the judgment creditor or his attorney it shall be the duty of the court in which such judgment is rendered within this state to forward to the department immediately after the expiration of said 30 days a certified copy of such judgment. The court shall be entitled to a fee as required by paragraphs (4) and (5) of subsection (g) of Code Section 15–6–77. In the event a certificate of pending or unsatisfied judgment is requested, the court shall be entitled to a fee as required by paragraph (8) of subsection (g) of Code Section 15–6–77.

(b) If the defendant named in any certified copy of a judgment reported to the department is a nonresident, the department shall transmit a certified copy of the judgment to the official in charge of the issuance of licenses and registrations of the state of which the defendant is a resident.

Laws 1956, p. 543, § 13; Laws 1977, p. 1014, § 1; Laws 1981, p. 1396, § 8; Laws 1992, p. 6, § 40.

Formerly Code 1933, § 68C–401.

§ 40–9–61. Suspension of license for nonpayment of judgment

(a) The department, upon receipt of a certified copy of an unsatisfied judgment, shall suspend the driver's license or nonresident's operating privilege of the person against whom such judgment was rendered except as provided in subsections (b) and (c) of this Code section.

(b) If the judgment creditor consents, in writing, in such form as the department may prescribe, the department, in its discretion, may allow the judgment debtor to retain his or her license or nonresident's operating privilege for six months from the date of such consent and thereafter until such consent is revoked in writing, notwithstanding default in the payment of such judgment or of any installments as provided in Code Section 40–9–63.

(c) The department shall take no action pursuant to subsection (a) of this Code section if it shall find that an insurer was obligated to pay the judgment upon which suspension is based, at least to the extent and for the amounts required in this article, but has not paid such judgment for any reason. Such finding shall not be binding upon such insurer and shall have no legal effect whatever except for the purposes of administering this Code section. Whenever, in any judicial proceedings, it shall be determined by any final judgment, decree, or order that an insurer is not obligated to pay any such judgment, the department, notwithstanding any contrary finding theretofore made by it, shall forthwith suspend the license or nonresident's operating privilege of any person against whom such judgment was rendered.

Laws 1956, p. 543, § 13; Laws 1977, p. 1014, § 1; Laws 1985, p. 149, § 40; Laws 2005, Act 68, § 20–4, eff. July 1, 2005.

Formerly Code 1933, § 68C–402.

Historical and Statutory Notes

The 2005 amendment by Act 68, in subsec. (a), deleted "and vehicle registration" following "suspend the driver's license"; in subsec. (b), substituted "retain his or her license or nonresident's operating privilege" for "retain his license and registration or nonresident's operating privilege"; and in third sentence of subsec. (c), substituted "suspend the license or nonresident's operating privilege" for "suspend the license and registration and any nonresident's operating privilege" following "shall forthwith".

§ 40–9–62. Suspension to continue until judgments paid

(a) A driver's license or nonresident's operating privilege suspended pursuant to Code Section 40–9–61 shall remain so suspended and shall not be renewed, nor shall any such license or registration be thereafter issued in the name of the judgment debtor, whether or not he or she was previously licensed, unless and until every such judgment is stayed, or satisfied in full or to the extent provided in subsection (b) of this Code section, subject to the exceptions provided in this article.

(b) Judgment referred to in this article, which is based upon an accident which occurred on or after January 1, 2001, shall, for the purpose of this chapter only, be deemed satisfied:

(1) When $25,000.00 has been credited upon any judgment or judgments rendered in excess of that amount because of bodily injury to or death of one person as the result of any one accident;

(2) When, subject to such limit of $25,000.00 because of bodily injury to or death of one person, $50,000.00 has been credited upon any judgment or judgments rendered in excess of that amount because of bodily injury to or death of two or more persons as the result of any one accident; or

(3) When $25,000.00 has been credited upon any judgment or judgments rendered in excess of that amount because of injury to or destruction of property of others as a result of any one accident.

(c) Reserved.

(d) Payments made in settlement of any claims because of bodily injury, death, or property damage arising from the accident shall be credited in reduction of the amounts provided for in this Code section.

Laws 1956, p. 543, § 13; Laws 1957, p. 124, §§ 2, 3; Laws 1958, p. 694, § 2; Laws 1977, p. 1014, § 1; Laws 1983, p. 938, § 4; Laws 1984, p. 22, § 40; Laws 2000, p. 1516, § 4; Laws 2005, Act 68, § 20–4, eff. July 1, 2005.

Formerly Code 1933, § 68C–403.

Historical and Statutory Notes

The 2000 amendment inserted gender neutral language in subsec. (a), inserted in subsec. (b) ", which is based upon an accident which occurred on or after January 1, 2001," changed the limit from $10,000 to $25,000 in subsec. (b), and deleted former subsec. (c) pertaining to accidents which occurred prior to January 1, 1984.

The 2005 amendment by Act 68 in subsec. (a) deleted ", vehicle registration," prior to "or nonresident's operating privilege suspended pursuant".

§ 40–9–63. Installment payment of judgments; default

(a) A judgment debtor, upon due notice to the judgment creditor, may apply to the court in which such judgment was rendered for the privilege of paying such judgment in installments, and the court, in its discretion and without prejudice to any other legal remedies which the judgment creditor may have, may so order and fix the amounts and times of payment of the installments.

(b) The department shall not suspend a license or nonresident's operating privilege and shall restore any license or nonresident's operating privilege suspended following nonpayment of a judgment, when the judgment debtor obtains such an order permitting the payment of any such judgment in installments, and while the payment of any such installments is not in default.

Laws 1956, p. 543, § 13; Laws 1977, p. 1014, § 1; Laws 1994, p. 97, § 40; Laws 2005, Act 68, § 20–4, eff. July 1, 2005.

Formerly Code 1933, § 68C–404.

Historical and Statutory Notes

The 2005 amendment by Act 68 in subsec. (b) deleted ", registration," prior to "or nonresident's operating privilege" twice.

Article 4

Giving Proof of Financial Responsibility for the Future

§ 40–9–80. Duration of proof; methods of giving proof

(a) In all those situations under this chapter in which proof of financial responsibility for the future is required, such proof may be given by filing with the department:

(1) A written certificate of any insurance carrier certifying that there is in effect a liability policy as to that vehicle meeting the requirements of subsections (a) and (b) of Code Section 40–9–37; or

(2) A plan of self-insurance, accepted by the commissioner, as provided in Code Section 33–34–5.1.

(b) Such proof must be maintained for a one-year period.

Laws 1964, p. 225, § 6; Laws 1969, p. 819, § 7; Laws 1977, p. 1014, § 1; Laws 2000, p. 1246, § 17.

Formerly Code 1933, § 68C–501.

Historical and Statutory Notes

The 2000 amendment modified the statutory reference in subsec. (a)(2).

§ 40–9–81. Proof upon conviction of certain offenses

(a) Whenever any person is convicted of any offense making mandatory the suspension of such person's driver's license, the department shall not restore the license to such person until permitted under the motor vehicle laws of this state, and not then unless and until such person shall give and thereafter maintain proof of financial responsibility for the future.

(b) If such person does not have the required proof at any time during the one-year period following the date of restoration of his driver's license, the department shall immediately revoke the license.

Laws 1951, p. 565, § 7A; Laws 1956, p. 543, § 15; Laws 1957, p. 124, § 4; Laws 1958, p. 694, § 3; Laws 1963, p. 593, § 8; Laws 1964, p. 225, § 3; Laws 1971, p. 249, § 1; Laws 1977, p. 1014, § 1.

Formerly Code 1933, § 68C–502.

§ 40–9–82. Insurance cancellation offenses

Any insurance company filing a certification with the department in order for the operator to show the proof required in this article shall not cancel such certification within 12 months from its effective date except for a subsequent conviction of any offense requiring the mandatory suspension of such operator's license, and the department shall be given at least 20 days' prior written notice of such cancellation. The commissioner may, in his discretion, permit the cancellation of such certificate for other cause made known to and approved by him.

Laws 1977, p. 1014, § 1.

Formerly Code 1933, § 68C–502.

Article 5

Assigned Risk Plans, "Spot" Insurance, and Cooperation by Insured

§ 40–9–100. Assigned risk plans; review of decision of insurance commissioner

(a) After consultation with insurance companies authorized to issue automobile policies in this state, the Commissioner of Insurance shall approve a reasonable plan or plans for the equitable apportionment among such companies of applicants for motor vehicle liability policies and other automobile policies who are in good faith entitled to but are unable to procure such policies through ordinary methods. When any such plan has been approved, all such insurance companies shall subscribe thereto and participate therein.

(b) Any applicant for a policy to be issued under any such plan, any person insured under any such plan, and any insurance company affected may appeal to the Commissioner of Insurance from any ruling or decision of the manager or committee designated to operate such plan. Any person aggrieved by any order or act of the Commissioner of Insurance under this Code section may, within ten days after notice of such order or act, file a petition in the superior court of the county of his residence for a review thereof. The court will summarily hear his petition and may make any appropriate order or decree.

(c) A person who has committed no traffic offenses for the prior three years and has had no claims based on fault against an insurer for the prior three years shall not be eligible for a policy to be issued under the plan created by this Code section unless such person's application or the subsequent investigation on the application discloses reasons for which the person would not be able to procure a policy through ordinary methods.

Laws 1951, p. 565, § 17; Laws 1963, p. 593, § 10; Laws 1977, p. 1014, § 1; Laws 1990, p. 738, § 1; Laws 1994, p. 97, § 40.

Formerly Code 1933, § 68C–601.

§ 40–9–101. Renumbered as § 33–34–5.1 by Laws 2000, p. 1246, §§ 15 and 16, eff. July 1, 2000

Historical and Statutory Notes

In 2000, the Code Commission reserved this section. See § 28–9–5.

§ 40–9–102. Insurance for U-drive-it operator

Any person who rents motor vehicles from a U-drive-it owner is required to provide his own insurance, and insurance companies authorized to issue automobile policies in this state shall be required by the Commissioner of Insurance to provide "spot" insurance, which shall be purchased by such person before the U-drive-it owner shall be authorized to turn a motor vehicle over to such person. If a U-drive-it owner turns over any motor vehicle to any person without first ascertaining that such "spot" insurance has been obtained, the U-drive-it owner shall not, as to that particular rental transaction, be exempted from the provisions of this chapter as provided in Code Section 40–9–4.

Laws 1951, p. 565, § 23; Laws 1963, p. 593, § 10; Laws 1977, p. 1014, § 1; Laws 1994, p. 97, § 40.

Formerly Code 1933, § 68C–604.

§ 40–9–103. Liability insurance policies to contain provisions requiring insured to send insurer copies of summons or other process

(a) No motor vehicle liability insurance policy covering a motor vehicle principally garaged or principally used in this state shall be issued, delivered or issued for delivery, or renewed in this state unless such policy contains provisions or has an endorsement thereto which specifically requires the insured to send his insurer, as soon as practicable after the receipt thereof, a copy of every summons or other process relating to the coverage under the policy and to cooperate otherwise with the insurer in connection with the defense of any action or threatened action covered under the policy.

(b)(1) Noncompliance by the insured with this required provision or endorsement shall constitute a breach of the insurance contract which, if prejudicial to the insurer, shall relieve the insurer of its obligation to defend its insureds under the policy and of any liability to pay any judgment or other sum on behalf of its insureds.

(2) In the event the insurer denies coverage and it is determined by declaratory judgment or other civil process that there is in fact coverage, the insurer shall be liable to the insured for legal costs and attorney's fees as may be awarded by the court.

(c) Subsections (a) and (b) of this Code section shall not operate to deny coverage for failure to send a copy of a summons or other process relating to policy coverage if such documents are sent by a third party to the insurer or to the insurer's agent by certified mail or statutory overnight delivery within ten days of the filing of such documents with the clerk of the court. If the name of the insurer or the insurer's agent is unknown, the third party shall have a period of 30 days from the date the insurer or agent becomes known in which to send these required documents. Such documents must be sent to the insurer or agent at least 30 days prior to the entry of any judgment against the insured.

Laws 1982, p. 1624, § 2; Laws 1982, p. 1624, § 4; Laws 1984, p. 22, § 40; Laws 1989, p. 14, § 40; Laws 2000, p. 1589, § 3.

Formerly Code 1933, § 68C–608.

Historical and Statutory Notes

The 2000 amendment substituted in subsec. (c) "certified mail or statutory overnight delivery" for "certified mail".

CHAPTER 10

FORMULATION AND COORDINATION OF STATE AND LOCAL HIGHWAY SAFETY PROGRAMS

§ 40–10–1. Short title

This chapter shall be known and may be cited as the "Highway Safety Coordination Act of 1967."

Laws 1967, p. 708, § 1.

§ 40–10–2. Public policy; Governor as chief administrator

It is the public policy of this state in every way possible to reduce the number of traffic accidents, deaths, injuries, and property damage through the formulation of comprehensive highway safety programs. The Governor, as the chief executive and highest elected official of this state, is vested with the power and authority to act as the chief administrator in the formulation of such programs of highway safety.

Laws 1967, p. 708, § 2.

§ 40–10–3. Definitions

As used in this chapter, the term:

(1) "Director" means the director of the Office of Highway Safety in the Department of Public Safety.

(2) "National Highway Safety Act of 1966" means the National Highway Safety Act of 1966, Pub. Law 89–564, 23 U.S.C. Section 401, et seq., and all amendments thereto.

(3) "Office" means the Office of Highway Safety in the Department of Public Safety.

Laws 1985, p. 149, § 40; Laws 1997, p. 143, § 40.

§ 40–10–4. Office of Highway Safety; created; assigned

There is created within the executive department the Office of Highway Safety. The Office of Highway Safety is assigned to the Department of Public Safety for administrative purposes only as provided in Code Section 50–4–3. The director of the Office of Highway Safety is designated the Governor's highway safety representative and shall be appointed by the Governor and serve at his pleasure. The Office of Highway Safety is charged and empowered to carry out the responsibilities established by the National Highway Safety Act of 1966.

Laws 1972, p. 1015, § 1605; Laws 1973, p. 466, § 1.

§ 40–10–5. Office of Highway Safety; appointment of director and duties

The director shall advise with and assist the Governor in the formulation, coordination, and supervision of comprehensive state and local highway safety programs to reduce traffic accidents, deaths, injuries, and property damage within this state. The director, acting under the direction and supervision of the Governor, shall also advise with and assist the various departments and agencies of state government concerned with highway safety programs. He shall coordinate and review, cooperatively, the programs developed by the various local political subdivisions, for the purpose of assisting them in the preparation of their highway safety programs to ensure that they meet the criteria established for such programs by the appropriate state and federal authorities.

Laws 1967, p. 708, § 3.

§ 40–10–6. Office space, staff and supplies

The Governor is authorized to provide and designate for the use of the director such space as shall be necessary to quarter the director and his staff. The director is authorized to employ and secure the necessary staff, supplies, and materials to carry out this chapter, subject to the approval of the Governor.

Laws 1967, p. 708, § 4.

§ 40–10–7. Powers of Governor

Notwithstanding the provisions of Code Section 50–5–143, the Governor is authorized and granted the power to contract and to exercise any other powers which may be necessary in order to ensure that all departments of the state government and local political subdivisions participate to the fullest extent possible in the benefits available under the National Highway Safety Act of 1966 and similar federal programs of highway safety. The Governor shall formulate standards for highway safety programs for political subdivisions to assure that they meet the criteria of the National Highway Safety Agency and shall institute a reporting system for the local political subdivisions to report the status of their programs to the state.

Laws 1967, p. 708, § 5; Laws 2008, Act 566, § 2, eff. July 1, 2008.

§ 40–10–8. Participation in programs of federal, state, local, public and private agencies

The Governor, acting for and in behalf of the State of Georgia, is authorized to cooperate with, and participate in, the programs of all federal, state, local, public, and private agencies and organizations in order to effectuate the purposes of this chapter.

Laws 1967, p. 708, § 6.

§ 40–10–9. Powers of governing authorities of counties and municipalities

The governing authorities of the various counties and municipalities are empowered to contract with the state, federal, and other local public and private agencies and organizations and exercise other necessary powers to participate to the fullest extent possible in the highway safety programs of this state, the National Highway Safety Act of 1966, and similar federal programs of highway safety.

Laws 1967, p. 708, § 7; Laws 1985, p. 149, § 40.

§ 40–10–10. Funds

The Governor is designated the appropriate state official to accept and administer any funds which shall be made available to the State of Georgia and its various political subdivisions for the purpose of carrying out a comprehensive highway safety program.

Laws 1967, p. 708, § 8.

CHAPTER 11

ABANDONED MOTOR VEHICLES

Article 1

Article 2

Article 1

General Provisions

§ 40–11–1. Definitions

As used in this article, the term:

(1) "Abandoned motor vehicle" means a motor vehicle or trailer:

(A) Which has been left by the owner or some person acting for the owner with an automobile dealer, repairman, or wrecker service for repair or for some other reason and has not been called for by such owner or other person within a period of 30 days after the time agreed upon; or within 30 days after such vehicle is turned over to such dealer, repairman, or wrecker service when no time is agreed upon; or within 30 days after the completion of necessary repairs;

(B) Which is left unattended on a public street, road, or highway or other public property for a period of at least five days and when it reasonably appears to a law enforcement officer that the individual who left such motor vehicle unattended does not intend to return and remove such motor vehicle. However, on the state highway system, any law enforcement officer may authorize the immediate removal of vehicles posing a threat to public health or safety or to mitigate congestion;

(C) Which has been lawfully towed onto the property of another at the request of a law enforcement officer and left there for a period of not less than 30 days without anyone having paid all reasonable current charges for such towing and storage;

(D) Which has been lawfully towed onto the property of another at the request of a property owner on whose property the vehicle was abandoned and left there for a period of not less than 30 days without anyone having paid all reasonable current charges for such towing and storage; or

(E) Which has been left unattended on private property for a period of not less than 30 days.

(2) "Motor vehicle" or "vehicle" means motor vehicle or trailer.

(3) "Owner" or "owners" means the registered owner, the owner as recorded on the title, lessor, lessee, security interest holders, and all lienholders as shown on the records of the Department of Revenue.

Laws 1972, p. 342, § 1; Laws 1977, p. 253, § 1; Laws 1980, p. 995, § 1; Laws 1981, p. 469, § 1; Laws 1984, p. 548, § 1; Laws 1985, p. 1265, § 1; Laws 1993, p. 370, § 3; Laws 2000, p. 951, § 7–1; Laws 2002, p. 415, § 40; Laws 2002, p. 563, § 1; Laws 2005, Act 68, § 21–1, eff. July 1, 2005.

Historical and Statutory Notes

The 2005 amendment by Act 68 in par. (1)(B) deleted "or employee of the Department of Motor Vehicle Safety to whom enforcement authority has been designated pursuant to Code Section 40–16–4" prior to "may authorize the immediate removal" in the second sentence; and in par. (3) substituted "Department of Revenue" for "Department of Motor Vehicle Safety".

§ 40–11–2. Duty of person who removes or stores a motor vehicle

(a) Any person who removes a motor vehicle from public property at the request of a law enforcement officer or stores such vehicle shall, if the owner of the vehicle or some person acting for the owner is not present, seek the identity of and address of all known owners of such vehicle from the law enforcement officer requesting removal of such, from such officer's agency, from a local law enforcement agency for the jurisdiction in which the remover's or storer's place of business is located, or from the State of Georgia by direct electronic access as provided through its agencies and authorities within three business days of removal. The local law enforcement agency shall furnish such information to the person removing such vehicle within three business days after receipt of such request.

(b) Any person who removes a motor vehicle from private property at the request of the property owner or stores such vehicle shall, if the owner of the vehicle or some person acting for the owner is not present, notify in writing a local law enforcement agency of the location of the vehicle, the manufacturer's vehicle identification number, license number, model, year, and make of the vehicle within three business days of the removal of such vehicle and shall seek from the local law enforcement agency or from the State of Georgia by direct electronic access as provided through its agencies and authorities the identity and address of all known owners of such vehicle and any information indicating that such vehicle is a stolen motor vehicle. The local law enforcement agency shall furnish such information to the person removing such vehicle within three business days after receipt of such request.

(c) If any motor vehicle removed under conditions set forth in subsection (a) or (b) of this Code section is determined to be a stolen motor vehicle, the local law enforcement officer or agency shall notify the Georgia Crime Information Center of the location of such motor vehicle within 72 hours after receiving notice that such motor vehicle is a stolen vehicle.

(d) If any motor vehicle removed under conditions set forth in subsection (a) or (b) of this Code section is determined not to be a stolen vehicle or is not a vehicle being repaired by a repair facility or is not being stored by an insurance company providing insurance to cover damages to the vehicle, the person removing or storing such motor vehicle shall, within seven calendar days of the day such motor vehicle was removed or one business day after the information is furnished to the remover or storer pursuant to subsection (a) or (b) of this Code section, whichever is later, notify all owners, if known, by written acknowledgment signed thereby or by certified or registered mail or statutory overnight delivery, of the location of such motor vehicle, the fees connected with removal and storage of such motor vehicle, and the fact that such motor vehicle will be deemed abandoned under this chapter unless the owner, security interest holder, or lienholder redeems such motor vehicle within 30 days of the day such vehicle was removed.

(e) If none of the owners redeems such motor vehicle as described in subsection (d) of this Code section, or if a vehicle being repaired by a repair facility or being stored by an insurance company providing insurance to cover damages to the vehicle becomes abandoned, the person removing or storing such motor vehicle shall, within seven calendar days of the day such vehicle became an abandoned motor vehicle, give notice by electronic means as provided by the State of Georgia through its agencies and authorities, in writing, or by sworn statement, on the form prescribed by the state revenue commissioner, to the Department of Revenue with a research fee as fixed by rule or regulation payable to the Department of Revenue, stating the manufacturer's vehicle identification number, the license number, the fact that such vehicle is an abandoned motor vehicle, the model, year, and make of the vehicle, the date the vehicle became an abandoned motor vehicle, the date the vehicle was removed, and the present location of such vehicle and requesting the name and address of all owners of such vehicle. If the form submitted is rejected because of inaccurate or missing information, the person removing or storing the vehicle shall resubmit, within seven calendar days of the date of the rejection, a corrected notice form together with an additional research fee as fixed by rule or regulation payable to the Department of Revenue. Each subsequent corrected notice, if required, shall be submitted with an additional research fee as fixed by rule or regulation payable to the Department of Revenue. If a person removing or storing the vehicle has knowledge of facts which reasonably indicate that the vehicle is registered or titled in a certain other state, such person shall check the motor vehicle records of that other state in the attempt to ascertain the identity of the owner of the vehicle. Research requests may be submitted and research fees made payable to the office of the tax commissioner and deposited in the general fund for the county in which the remover's or storer's place of business is located in lieu of the Department of Revenue, but in like manner, if such office processes motor vehicle records of the Department of Revenue.

(f) Upon ascertaining the owners of such motor vehicle, the person removing or storing such vehicle shall, within five calendar days, by certified or registered mail or statutory overnight delivery, notify all known owners of the vehicle of the location of such vehicle and of the fact that such vehicle is deemed abandoned and shall be disposed of if not redeemed.

(g) If the identity of the owners of such motor vehicle cannot be ascertained, the person removing or storing such vehicle shall place an advertisement in a newspaper of general circulation in the county where such vehicle was obtained or, if there is no newspaper in such county, shall post such advertisement at the county courthouse in such place where other public notices are posted. Such advertisement shall run in the newspaper once a week for two consecutive weeks or shall remain posted at the courthouse for two consecutive weeks. The advertisement shall contain a complete description of the motor vehicle, its license and manufacturer's vehicle identification numbers, the location from where such vehicle was initially removed, the present location of such vehicle, and the fact that such vehicle is deemed abandoned and shall be disposed of if not redeemed.

(h) The Department of Revenue shall provide to the Georgia Crime Information Center all relevant information from sworn statements described in subsection (e) of this Code section for a determination of whether the vehicles removed have been entered into the criminal justice information system as stolen vehicles. The results of the determination shall be provided electronically to the Department of Revenue.

(i) Any person storing a vehicle under the provisions of this Code section shall notify the Department of Revenue if the vehicle is recovered, is claimed by the owner, is determined to be stolen, or for any reason is no longer an abandoned motor vehicle. Such notice shall be provided within seven calendar days of such event.

(j) If vehicle information on the abandoned motor vehicle is not in the files of the Department of Revenue, the department may require such other information or confirmation as it determines is necessary or appropriate to determine the identity of the vehicle.

(k) Any person who does not provide the notice and information required by this Code section shall be guilty of a misdemeanor and, upon conviction thereof, shall be punished as for a misdemeanor, shall not be entitled to any storage fees, shall not be eligible to contract with or serve on a rotation list providing wrecker services for this state or any political subdivision thereof, and shall not be licensed by any municipal authority to provide removal of improperly parked cars under Code Section 44–1–13.

(*l*) Any person who knowingly provides false or misleading information when providing any notice or information as required by this Code section shall be guilty of a misdemeanor and, upon conviction thereof, shall be punished as for a misdemeanor.

Laws 1972, p. 342, § 2; Laws 1977, p. 253, § 2; Laws 1980, p. 995, § 2; Laws 1981, p. 469, § 2; Laws 1982, p. 3, § 40; Laws 1985, p. 1265, § 2; Laws 1988, p. 1750, § 1; Laws 1990, p. 1657, § 6; Laws 1992, p. 2978, § 10; Laws 1993, p. 772, § 1; Laws 1995, p. 663, § 1; Laws 1996, p. 6, § 40; Laws 1998, p. 1305, § 1; Laws 2000, p. 951, § 7–1; Laws 2000, p. 1589, § 4; Laws 2002, p. 563, § 2; Laws 2005, Act 68, § 21–2, eff. July 1, 2005; Laws 2008, Act 711, § 3, eff. July 1, 2008.

Historical and Statutory Notes

The 2005 amendment by Act 68 rewrote subsec. (e); and in subsecs. (h), (i) and (j) substituted "Department of Revenue" for "Department of Motor Vehicle Safety". Prior to amendment, subsec. (e) had read:

"(e) If none of the owners redeems such motor vehicle as described in subsection (d) of this Code section, or if a vehicle being repaired by a repair facility or being stored by an insurance company providing insurance to cover damages to the vehicle becomes abandoned, the person removing or storing such motor vehicle shall, within seven calendar days of the day such vehicle became an abandoned motor vehicle, give notice in writing, by sworn statement, on the form prescribed by the commissioner, to the Department of Motor Vehicle Safety with a research fee of $ 2.00 payable to the Department of Motor Vehicle Safety, stating the manufacturer's vehicle identification number, the license number, the fact that such vehicle is an abandoned motor vehicle, the model, year, and make of the vehicle, the date the vehicle became an abandoned motor vehicle, the date the vehicle was removed, and the present location of such vehicle and requesting the name and address of all owners of such vehicle. If the form submitted is rejected because of inaccurate or missing information, the person removing or storing the vehicle shall resubmit, within seven calendar days of the date of the rejection, a corrected notice form together with an additional research fee of $ 2.00 payable to the Department of Motor Vehicle Safety. Each subsequent corrected notice, if required, shall be submitted with an additional research fee of $ 2.00 payable to the Department of Motor Vehicle Safety. If a person removing or storing the vehicle has knowledge of facts which reasonably indicate that the vehicle is registered or titled in a certain other state, such person shall check the motor vehicle records of that other state in the attempt to ascertain the identity of the owner of the vehicle. Research requests may be submitted and research fees made payable to the office of the tax commissioner and deposited in the general fund for the county in which the remover's or storer's place of business is located in lieu of the Department of Motor Vehicle Safety, but in like manner, if such office processes motor vehicle records of the Department of Motor Vehicle Safety."

The 2008 amendment by Act 711, in subsecs. (a) and (b), inserted "or from the State of Georgia by direct electronic access as provided through its agencies and authorities"; and, in subsec. (e), inserted "by electronic means as provided by the State of Georgia through its agencies and authorities".

§ 40–11–3. Peace officers authorized to remove vehicles from public property; liability for gross negligence; notification of removal

(a) Any peace officer who finds a motor vehicle which has been left unattended on a public street, road, or highway or other public property for a period of at least five days shall be authorized to cause such motor vehicle to be removed to a garage or other place of safety, if such peace officer reasonably believes that the person who left such motor vehicle unattended does not intend to return and remove such motor vehicle.

(b) Any law enforcement officer who finds a motor vehicle which has been left unattended on the state highway system shall be authorized to cause such motor vehicle to be removed immediately to a garage or other place of safety when such motor vehicle poses a threat to public health or safety or to mitigate congestion. Any peace officer who finds a motor vehicle which has been left unattended on a public street, road, or highway or other public property, other than the state highway system, shall be authorized immediately to cause such motor vehicle to be removed immediately to a garage or other place of safety when such motor vehicle poses a threat to public health or safety or to mitigate congestion.

(c) Any peace officer who, under this Code section, causes any motor vehicle to be removed to a garage or other place of safety shall be liable for gross negligence only.

(d)(1) Any peace officer or the law enforcement agency which causes a motor vehicle to be removed to a garage or other place of safety or which is notified of the removal of a motor vehicle from private property shall within 72 hours from the time of removal or notice and if the owner is unknown attempt to determine vehicle ownership through official inquiries to the Department of Revenue vehicle registration and vehicle title files. These inquiries shall be made from authorized criminal justice information system network terminals.

(2) If the name and address of the last known registered owner of the motor vehicle is obtained from the Georgia Crime Information Center, the peace officer who causes the motor vehicle to be removed shall, within three calendar days, make available to the person removing such motor vehicle the name and address of the last known registered owner of such motor vehicle, the owner of the motor vehicle as recorded on the title of such vehicle, and all security interest holders or lienholders. If such information is not available, the peace officer shall, within three calendar days, notify the person removing or storing such vehicle of such fact.

(3) Law enforcement agencies shall make record entries in Georgia criminal justice information system files through authorized criminal justice information system network terminals after an unsuccessful attempt to obtain vehicle ownership information and shall remove the record entries when ownership is determined.

Laws 1972, p. 342, § 3; Laws 1980, p. 995, § 3; Laws 1984, p. 548, § 2; Laws 1988, p. 1750, § 2; Laws 1990, p. 1657, § 7; Laws 1993, p. 370, § 4; Laws 1995, p. 663, § 2; Laws 1996, p. 6, § 40; Laws 1997, p. 143, § 40; Laws 2000, p. 951, § 7–1; Laws 2002, p. 415, § 40; Laws 2005, Act 68, § 21–3, eff. July 1, 2005.

Historical and Statutory Notes

The 2005 amendment by Act 68 in subsec. (b) deleted "or employee of the Department of Motor Vehicle Safety to whom law enforcement authority has been designated pursuant to Code Section 40–16–4" prior to "who finds a motor vehicle" in the first sentence; and in subsec. (d)(1) substituted "Department of Revenue" for "Department of Motor Vehicle Safety".

§ 40–11–3.1. Peace officers authorized to perform unattended vehicle check on unattended vehicles

(a) It shall be the duty of any peace officer who discovers a motor vehicle which has been left unattended on a public street, road, or highway or other public property to immediately perform an unattended vehicle check on such motor vehicle, unless there is displayed on such motor vehicle an unattended vehicle check card indicating that another peace officer has already performed such an unattended vehicle check. For purposes of this Code section, an unattended vehicle check shall consist of such actions as are reasonably necessary to determine that the unattended vehicle does not contain an injured or incapacitated person and to determine that the unattended vehicle does not pose a threat to public health or safety.

(b) A peace officer completing an unattended vehicle check shall complete and attach to the vehicle an unattended vehicle check card. Unattended vehicle check cards shall be in such form, and shall be attached to vehicles in such manner, as may be specified by rule or regulation of the Department of Public Safety; and to the extent that sufficient funds are available to the department, the department may distribute such forms free of charge to law enforcement agencies in this state. Unattended vehicle check cards shall be serially numbered; shall be of a distinctive color and shape, so as to be readily visible to passing motorists; and shall contain spaces for the investigating police officer to indicate the location of the vehicle, the date and time of the completion of the unattended vehicle check, and the name of such peace officer's law enforcement agency. A detachable stub, which shall be filed with the investigating peace officer's law enforcement agency, shall bear the same serial number and shall contain the same information, together with the identity of the investigating peace officer and the license plate number and other pertinent identifying information relating to the abandoned vehicle.

(c) Nothing in the Code section shall limit the otherwise applicable authority of a peace officer to have an unattended motor vehicle removed to a garage or other place of safety.

(d) It shall be unlawful for any person other than a peace officer to attach a genuine or counterfeit unattended motor vehicle check card to a motor vehicle; and any person convicted of violating this subsection shall be guilty of a misdemeanor.

Laws 1988, p. 688, § 1; Laws 2000, p. 951, § 7–1.

§ 40–11–3.2. Unlawful to remove motor vehicle from certain paid private parking lots between midnight and noon of following day

(a) It shall be unlawful for the owner or operator of a paid private parking lot or paid private parking facility located within 500 feet of an establishment which serves alcoholic beverages for consumption on the premises to remove, tow, or immobilize or cause to be removed, towed, or immobilized a motor vehicle left in such lot or facility between midnight and noon of the following day. Nothing in this Code section shall prohibit the owner of such a parking lot or facility from charging a penalty not to exceed $ 25.00 in excess of normal parking fees for vehicles which remain on the property during such period without authorization. No owner or operator of such a parking lot or facility shall be liable for any damages to any motor vehicle remaining on the property during such period without authorization. Nothing in this Code section shall prohibit a resident or a business owner from towing or removing or causing to be towed or removed a motor vehicle left on private property. For purposes of this subsection, the terms "paid private parking lot" and "paid private parking facility" mean private parking lots where the owner or operator of a motor vehicle pays a valuable consideration for the right to park in such parking lot or parking facility.

(b) Any person violating the provisions of subsection (a) of this Code section shall be guilty of a misdemeanor.

Laws 2002, p. 563, § 3.

§ 40–11–4. Fees and liens for removal or storage; jurisdiction

(a) Any person who removes or stores any motor vehicle which is or becomes an abandoned motor vehicle shall have a lien on such vehicle for the reasonable fees connected with such removal or storage plus the cost of any notification or advertisement. Such lien shall exist if the person moving or storing such vehicle is in compliance with Code Section 40–11–2.

(b) The lien acquired under subsection (a) of this Code section may be foreclosed in any court which is competent to hear civil cases, including, but not limited to, magistrate courts. Liens shall be foreclosed in magistrate courts only when the amount of the lien does not exceed the jurisdictional limits established by law for such courts.

Laws 1972, p. 342, § 3; Laws 1980, p. 995, § 4; Laws 1981, p. 469, § 3; Laws 1983, p. 884, § 3–28; Laws 1984, p. 22, § 40; Laws 1998, p. 1305, § 2; Laws 2000, p. 951, § 7–1.

§ 40–11–5. Foreclosure of lien

All liens acquired under Code Section 40–11–4 shall be foreclosed as follows:

(1) Any proceeding to foreclose a lien on an abandoned motor vehicle must be instituted within one year from the time the lien is recorded or is asserted by retention;

(2) The person desiring to foreclose a lien on an abandoned motor vehicle shall, by certified or registered mail or statutory overnight delivery, make a demand upon the owners for the payment of the reasonable fees for removal and storage plus the costs of any notification or advertisement. Such written demand shall include an itemized statement of all charges and may be made concurrent with the notice required by subsection (f) of Code Section 40–11–2. Such demand shall be made on a form prescribed by rule or regulation of the Department of Revenue and shall notify the owner of his or her right to a judicial hearing to determine the validity of the lien. The demand shall further state that failure to return the written demand to the lien claimant, file with a court of competent jurisdiction a petition for a judicial hearing, and provide the lien claimant with a copy of such petition, all within ten days of delivery of the lien claimant's written demand, shall effect a waiver of the owner's right to such a hearing prior to sale. The form shall also provide the suspected owner with the option of disclaiming any ownership of the vehicle, and his or her affidavit to that effect shall control over anything contrary in the records of the Department of Revenue. No such written demand shall be required if the identity of the owner cannot be ascertained and the notice requirements of subsection (g) of Code Section 40–11–2 have been complied with;

(3)(A) If, within ten days of delivery to the appropriate address of the written demand required by paragraph (2) of this Code section, the owner of the abandoned motor vehicle fails to pay or file with the court a petition for a judicial hearing with a copy to the lien claimant in accordance with the notice provided pursuant to paragraph (2) of this Code section, or if the owner of the abandoned motor vehicle cannot be ascertained, the person removing or storing the abandoned motor vehicle may foreclose such lien. The person asserting such lien may move to foreclose by making an affidavit to a court of competent jurisdiction, on a form prescribed by rule or regulation of the Department of Revenue, showing all facts necessary to constitute such lien and the amount claimed to be due. Such affidavit shall aver that the notice requirements of Code Section 40–11–2 have been complied with, and such affidavit shall also aver that a demand for payment in accordance with paragraph (2) of this Code section has been made without satisfaction or without a timely filing of a petition for a judicial hearing or that the identity of the owner cannot be ascertained. The person foreclosing shall verify the statement by oath or affirmation and shall affix his or her signature thereto.

(B) Regardless of the court in which the affidavit required by this paragraph is filed, the fee for filing such affidavit shall be $10.00 per motor vehicle upon which a lien is asserted;

(4) If no timely petition for a hearing has been filed with a court of competent jurisdiction, then, upon such affidavit's being filed by the lien claimant pursuant to paragraph (3) of this Code section, the lien will conclusively be deemed a valid one and foreclosure thereof allowed;

(5) If a petition for a hearing is filed with a court of competent jurisdiction within ten days after delivery of the lien claimant's demand, a copy of which demand shall be attached to the petition, the court shall set such a hearing within ten days of filing of the petition;

(6) Upon the filing of such petition by an owner, neither the lien claimant nor the court may sell the motor vehicle, although possession of the motor vehicle may be retained by the lien claimant or obtained by the court in accordance with the order of the court which sets the date for the hearing;

(7) If, after a full hearing, the court finds that a valid debt exists, then the court shall authorize foreclosure upon and sale of the motor vehicle subject to the lien to satisfy the debt if such debt is not otherwise immediately paid;

(8) If the court finds the actions of the person asserting the lien in retaining possession of the motor vehicle were not taken in good faith, then the court, in its discretion, may award damages to the owner, any party which has been deprived of the rightful use of the vehicle, or the lessee due to the deprivation of the use of the motor vehicle; and

(9) If an affidavit meeting the requirements of paragraph (3) of this Code section is filed and no petition for a hearing is timely filed, or if, after a full hearing, the court determines that a valid debt exists, the court shall issue an order authorizing the sale of such motor vehicle. However, the holder of a security interest in or a lien on the vehicle, other than the holder of a lien created by Code Section 40–11–4, shall have the right, in the order of priority of such security interest or lien, to pay the debt and court costs. If the holder of a security interest or lien does so pay the debt and court costs, he or she shall have the right to possession of the vehicle, and his or her security interest in or lien on such vehicle shall be increased by the amount so paid. A court order shall be issued to this effect, and in this instance there shall not be a sale of the vehicle.

Laws 1980, p. 995, § 5; Laws 1982, p. 1650, §§ 1, 2; Laws 1983, p. 3, § 29; Laws 1984, p. 22, § 40; Laws 1985, p. 1265, § 3; Laws 1988, p. 1750, § 3; Laws 1998, p. 1305, § 3; Laws 2000, p. 951, § 7–1; Laws 2000, p. 1589, §§ 3, 4; Laws 2002, p. 563, § 4; Laws 2005, Act 68, § 21–4, eff. July 1, 2005.

Historical and Statutory Notes

In 2002, the Code Commission, twice in subpar. (3)(A), and in pars. (4) and (9), substituted "Code section" for "subsection". See § 28–9–5.

The 2005 amendment by Act 68, in pars. (2) and (3)(A) substituted "Department of Revenue" for "Department of Motor Vehicle Safety" throughout.

§ 40–11–6. Sale of motor vehicle; proceeds of sale

(a) Upon order of the court, the person holding the lien on the abandoned motor vehicle shall be authorized to sell such motor vehicle at public sale, as defined by Code Section 11–1–201.

(b) After satisfaction of the lien, the person selling such motor vehicle shall, not later than 30 days after the date of such sale, provide the clerk of the court with a copy of the bill of sale as provided to the purchaser and turn the remaining proceeds of such sale, if any, over to the clerk of the court. Any person who fails to comply with the requirements of this subsection shall be guilty of a misdemeanor and, upon conviction thereof, shall be punished as for a misdemeanor.

Laws 1980, p. 995, § 6; Laws 1998, p. 1305, § 4; Laws 2000, p. 951, § 7–1.

§ 40–11–7. Certificate of title

The purchaser at a sale as authorized in this article shall receive a certified copy of the court order authorizing such sale. Any such purchaser may obtain a certificate of title to such motor vehicle by filing the required application, paying the required fees, and filing a certified copy of the order of the court with the Department of Revenue. The Department of Revenue shall then issue a certificate of title, which shall be free and clear of all liens and encumbrances.

Laws 1972, p. 342, § 4; Laws 1975, p. 913, § 1; Laws 1977, p. 253, § 3; Laws 1980, p. 995, § 7; Laws 2000, p. 951, § 7–1; Laws 2005, Act 68, § 21–5, eff. July 1, 2005.

Historical and Statutory Notes

The 2005 amendment by Act 68 substituted "Department of Revenue" for "Department of Motor Vehicle Safety" twice.

§ 40–11–8. Proceeds of sale, disposition of

The clerk of the court shall retain the remaining balance of the proceeds of a sale under Code Section 40–11–6, after satisfaction of liens, security interests, and debts, for a period of 12 months; and, if no claim has been filed against such proceeds by the owner of the abandoned motor vehicle or any interested party, then he or she shall pay such remaining balance as follows:

(1) If the abandoned motor vehicle came into the possession of the person creating the lien other than at the request of a peace officer, the proceeds of the sale shall be divided equally and paid into the general fund of the county in which the sale was made and into the general fund of the municipality, if any, in which the sale was made;

(2) If the abandoned motor vehicle came into the possession of the person creating the lien at the request of a police officer of a municipality, the proceeds of the sale shall be paid into the general fund of the municipality;

(3) If the abandoned motor vehicle came into the possession of the person creating the lien at the request of a county sheriff, deputy sheriff, or county police officer, the proceeds of the sale shall be paid into the general fund of the county in which the sale was made;

(4) If the abandoned motor vehicle came into the possession of the person creating the lien at the request of a member of the Georgia State Patrol or other employee of the State of Georgia, the proceeds of the sale shall be paid into the general fund of the county in which the sale was made.

Laws 1972, p. 342, § 8; Laws 1977, p. 253, § 5; Laws 1980, p. 995, § 8; Laws 2000, p. 951, § 7–1.

§ 40–11–9. Procedures for determination that vehicle is a derelict motor vehicle; disposition of derelict motor vehicles

(a) If a motor vehicle has been left unattended on private property for not less than two days or on public property for not less than three days without the owner or driver making any attempt to recover such vehicle or to leave a conspicuously placed note that such owner or driver intends to return for such vehicle; or, if a conspicuous note was left, if the motor vehicle has been left unattended for not less than five days and if because of damage, vandalism, theft, or fire the vehicle is damaged to the extent that its restoration to an operable condition would require the replacement of one or more major component parts or involves any structural damage that would affect the safety of the vehicle; or if there is evidence that the vehicle was inoperable due to major mechanical breakdown at the time it was left on the property, such as the engine, transmission, or wheels missing, no coolant in the cooling system, no oil in the engine, or burned fluid in the transmission; or if the vehicle is seven or more years old; or if the vehicle is not currently tagged or is not verifiable by the state as to who is the current owner or lienholder of the vehicle; or if the vehicle has been abandoned to a wrecker service by an insurance company and the owner following the insurance company's making a total loss payment, then any person removing such vehicle shall within 72 hours of removing such vehicle obtain the identity of and address of the last known registered owner of the vehicle, the owner of the vehicle as recorded on the certificate of title of such vehicle, and any security interest holder or lienholder on such vehicle from the local law enforcement agency of the jurisdiction in which the vehicle was located. If the law enforcement agency shows no information on the vehicle, then a request for such information shall be sent to the Department of Revenue. Within 72 hours after obtaining such information, the person removing such vehicle shall, by certified mail or statutory overnight delivery, return receipt requested, notify the registered owner, title owner, and security interest holder or lienholder of the vehicle that such vehicle will be declared a derelict vehicle and the title to such vehicle will be canceled by the Department of Revenue if such person or persons fail to respond within ten days of receipt of such notice. The state revenue commissioner shall prescribe the form and content of such notice. If the registered owner, title owner, or security interest holder or lienholder fails to respond within 30 days from the date of such notice by certified mail or statutory overnight delivery, and if the vehicle is appraised as having a total value of less than $300.00, the vehicle shall be considered to be a derelict vehicle. The value of the vehicle shall be determined as 50 percent of the wholesale value of a similar car in the rough section of the *National Auto Research Black Book, Georgia Edition,* or if a similar vehicle is not listed in such book or, regardless of the model year or book value of the vehicle, if the vehicle is completely destroyed by fire, flood, or vandalism or is otherwise damaged to the extent that restoration of the vehicle to a safe operable condition would require replacement of more than 50 percent of its major component parts, the person shall obtain an appraisal of the motor vehicle from the local law enforcement agency's auto theft section with jurisdiction in the county or municipality where such vehicle is located. Any person removing a vehicle shall complete a form, to be provided by the Department of Revenue, indicating that the vehicle meets at least four of the above–stated eight conditions for being a derelict vehicle and shall file such form with the Department of Revenue and the law enforcement agency with jurisdiction from which such vehicle was removed.

(b) Upon determination that a vehicle is a derelict motor vehicle as provided in subsection (a) of this Code section, it may be disposed of by sale to a person who scraps, dismantles, or demolishes motor vehicles, provided that such vehicle may be sold for scrap or parts only and shall in no event be rebuilt or sold to the general public. Any person disposing of a derelict motor vehicle shall, prior to disposing of such vehicle, photograph such vehicle and retain with such photograph the appraisal required in subsection (a) of this Code section and the notice to the Department of Revenue required in this subsection for a period of three years after its disposition. Such person shall also notify the Department of Revenue of the disposition of such vehicle in such manner as may be prescribed by the state revenue commissioner. The Department of Revenue shall cancel the certificate of title for such vehicle and shall not issue a rebuilt or salvage title for such vehicle.

(c) For purposes of this Code section, the term "derelict vehicle" shall not include a vehicle which does not bear a manufacturer's vehicle identification number plate or a vehicle identification number plate assigned by a state jurisdiction.

(d) Any person who abandons a derelict motor vehicle on public or private property shall be guilty of a misdemeanor and upon conviction shall be fined not more than $500.00 and shall pay all costs of having such derelict motor vehicle removed, stored, and sold as provided for in this Code section. Notwithstanding any other provision of law to the contrary, such fines shall be disposed as follows:

(1) If the abandoned motor vehicle was removed other than at the request of a peace officer, the moneys arising from the fine shall be divided equally and paid into the general fund of the county in which the offense was committed and into the general fund of the municipality, if any, in which the offense was committed;

(2) If the abandoned motor vehicle was removed at the request of a police officer of a municipality, the moneys arising from the fine shall be paid into the general fund of the municipality;

(3) If the abandoned motor vehicle was removed at the request of a county sheriff, deputy sheriff, or county police officer, the moneys arising from the fine shall be paid into the general fund of the county in which the offense was committed; and

(4) If the abandoned motor vehicle was removed at the request of a member of the Georgia State Patrol or other employee of the State of Georgia, the moneys arising from the fine shall be paid into the general fund of the county in which the offense was committed.

(e) Any person removing a derelict motor vehicle who fails to comply with the requirements of this Code section or who knowingly provides false or misleading information when providing any notice or information required by this Code section shall be guilty of a misdemeanor.

(f) Neither the State of Georgia nor any state agency nor the person removing, storing, and processing the vehicle unless recklessly or grossly negligent shall be liable to the owner of a vehicle declared to be a derelict motor vehicle pursuant to this Code section or an abandoned motor vehicle.

Laws 1993, p. 772, § 2; Laws 1994, p. 97, § 40; Laws 1998, p. 1305, § 5; Laws 2000, p. 951, § 7–1; Laws 2000, p. 1589, § 3; Laws 2005, Act 68, § 21–6, eff. July 1, 2005.

Historical and Statutory Notes

The 2005 amendment by Act 68 throughout subsecs. (a) and (b) substituted "Department of Revenue" for "Department of Motor Vehicle Safety" and "state revenue commissioner" for "commissioner of motor vehicle safety".

Article 2

Forfeiture of Vehicles and Components

§ 40–11–20. Items declared to be contraband

The following items are declared to be contraband and are subject to forfeiture:

(1) Any motor vehicle the manufacturer's vehicle identification number of which has been removed, altered, defaced, falsified, or destroyed; and

(2) Any component part of a motor vehicle the manufacturer's identification number of which has been removed, altered, defaced, falsified, or destroyed.

Laws 1988, p. 1948, § 1; Laws 2000, p. 951, § 7–1.

§ 40–11–21. Property deemed to be in custody of superior court of county wherein property is located

Property subject to forfeiture under Code Section 40–11–20 and in the possession of any state or local law enforcement agency shall not be subject to replevin but is deemed to be in the custody of the superior court of the county wherein the property is located subject only to the orders and decrees of the court having jurisdiction over the forfeiture proceedings.

Laws 1988, p. 1948, § 1; Laws 2000, p. 951, § 7–1.

§ 40–11–22. Proceedings for forfeiting property

The law enforcement agency having possession of any property subject to forfeiture under Code Section 40–11–20 shall report such fact, within ten days of taking possession, to the district attorney of the judicial circuit having jurisdiction in the county where the property is located. Within 30 days from the date he or she receives such notice, the district attorney of the judicial circuit shall file in the superior court of the county in which the property is located an action for condemnation of the property. The proceedings shall be brought in the name of the state, and the action shall be verified by a duly authorized agent of the state in the manner required by law. The action shall describe the property, state its location, state its present custodian, state the name of the owner, if known, to the duly authorized agent of the state, allege the essential elements which are claimed to exist, and shall conclude with a prayer of due process to enforce the forfeiture. Upon the filing of such an action, the court shall promptly cause process to issue to the present custodian in possession of the property described in the action, commanding him or her to seize the property described in the action and to hold that property for further order of the court. A copy of the action shall be served on the owner, if known. If the owner is known, a copy of the action shall also be served upon any person having a duly recorded security interest in or lien upon that property. If the owner is unknown or resides out of the state or departs the state or cannot after due diligence be found within the state or conceals himself or herself so as to avoid service, notice of the proceedings shall be published once a week for two weeks in the newspaper in which the sheriff's advertisements are published. Such publication shall be deemed notice to any and all persons having an interest in or right affected by such proceeding and from any sale of the property resulting therefrom but shall not constitute notice to any person having a duly recorded security interest in or lien upon such property and required to be served under this Code section unless that person is unknown or resides out of the state or departs the state or cannot after due diligence be found within the state or conceals himself or herself to avoid service. At the expiration of 30 days after such filing, if no claimant has appeared to defend the action, the court shall order the disposition of the seized property as provided for in this Code section. If the owner of the property appears and defends the action and can show that he or she was unaware of the fact that the identification number had been removed, altered, defaced, falsified, or destroyed, the court shall order the property returned to the owner upon the owner's paying proper expenses relating to proceedings for forfeiture, including the expenses of the maintenance of custody, advertising, and court costs and upon the property's being assigned a new identification number as provided in this article.

Laws 1988, p. 1948, § 1; Laws 2000, p. 951, § 7–1.

§ 40–11–23. Order of court

Except as otherwise provided in this article, when property is forfeited under this article, the court may:

(1) Order that the property be retained by the law enforcement agency or the county in which the property is located; or

(2) Order that the property be disposed of by sale, the proceeds of which shall be used to pay the proper expenses relating to the proceedings for forfeiture, including the expenses of maintenance of custody, advertising, and court costs, with the remaining funds to be paid into the general fund of the county.

Laws 1988, p. 1948, § 1; Laws 2000, p. 951, § 7–1.

§ 40–11–24. Assignment of new identification number

Prior to the property's being sold or returned to the owner or otherwise disposed of, the Department of Revenue shall assign it a new identification number.

Laws 1988, p. 1948, § 1; Laws 2000, p. 951, § 7–1; Laws 2005, Act 68, § 21–7, eff. July 1, 2005.

Historical and Statutory Notes

The 2005 amendment by Act 68 substituted "Department of Revenue" for "Department of Motor Vehicle Safety".

CHAPTER 12

ACTIONS AGAINST NONRESIDENTS

§ 40–12–1. Operation of vehicle within state deemed appointment of Secretary of State as attorney for service of process; service upon minors

(a) The acceptance by any nonresident of this state, whether a person, firm, or corporation, of the rights and privileges conferred by the laws now or hereafter enforced in this state permitting the operation of motor vehicles, as evidenced by the operation of a motor vehicle by any such nonresident anywhere within the territorial limits of this state, shall be deemed equivalent to the appointment by such nonresident of the Secretary of State of Georgia, or his successor in office, to be his true and lawful attorney in fact upon whom may be served all summonses or other lawful processes in any action or proceeding against any such nonresident growing out of any accident or collision in which any such nonresident may be involved by reason of the operation by him, for him, or under his control or direction, express or implied, of a motor vehicle anywhere within the territorial limits of the State of Georgia, and said acceptance or operation shall be a signification of his agreement that any such process against him shall be of the same legal force and validity as if served upon him personally.

(b) If such nonresident motorist is a minor, then the minor and his parents or guardians shall be deemed to have assented to the appointment by such nonresident minor and his parents or guardians of the Secretary of State of Georgia, or his successor in office, to be the true and lawful attorney in fact for such minor and his parents or guardians, upon whom may be served any summons or other lawful process in any action or proceeding against such nonresident minor, his parents, or guardians growing out of any accident or collision in which any such nonresident minor may be involved by reason of the operation by him, for him, or under his control or direction, express or implied, of a motor vehicle anywhere within the territorial limits of the State of Georgia, and such acceptance or operation shall be a signification of his agreement or an agreement for him by his parents or guardians that any such process against him or them shall be of the same legal force and validity as if served upon him or them personally; and in this respect, the court wherein such action shall have been filed shall be authorized to appoint, upon motion duly made, a guardian ad litem for such minor for the purposes of defending such suit.

Laws 1937, p. 732, § 1; Laws 1964, p. 299, § 1; Laws 1967, p. 800, § 1.

§ 40–12–2. Service of process on Secretary of State

Service of process upon a nonresident pursuant to Code Section 40–12–1 shall be made by serving a copy of the complaint or other pleading with summons attached thereto on the Secretary of State, his duly authorized agent, or his successor in office, along with a copy of the affidavit to be submitted to the court pursuant to this Code section. Such service shall be sufficient service upon any such nonresident, provided that notice of such service and a copy of the complaint and process are forthwith sent by registered or certified mail or statutory overnight delivery by the plaintiff to the defendant, if his address is known, and the defendant's return receipt and the plaintiff's affidavit of compliance with this Code section are appended to the summons or other process and filed with the summons, complaint, and other papers in the case in the court wherein the action is pending. The Secretary of State shall charge and collect a fee as set out in Code Section 45–13–26 for service of process on him under this Code section.

Laws 1937, p. 732, § 2; Laws 1959, p. 113, § 1; Laws 1965, p. 231, § 1; Laws 1983, p. 1474, § 2; Laws 1984, p. 22, § 40; Laws 1989, p. 364, § 2; Laws 2000, p. 1589, § 3.

§ 40–12–3. Venue of actions; joint defendants

All actions brought under this chapter relating to the use of the highways of this state by nonresident motorists shall be brought in the county in which the accident or injury occurred or the cause of action originated, or in the county of the residence of the plaintiff, as the plaintiff in such action may elect, if the plaintiff in such action is a resident of the State of Georgia; and, if the plaintiff in such action is a nonresident of the State of Georgia, the action shall be brought in the county in this state in which the accident or injury occurred or the cause of action originated; and the courts in such counties having jurisdiction of tort actions shall have jurisdiction of all such nonresident users in actions arising under this chapter. Where an action for damages is brought against a resident of this state, any nonresident involved in the same accident or collision and who is suable under this chapter may be joined as a defendant in the county wherein the resident defendant is suable, and the jurisdiction of the court of and over such nonresident joint defendant shall not be affected or lost by reason of the fact that the jury returns a verdict in favor of such resident joint defendant although the accident, injury, or cause of action did not originate in the county wherein the action is brought.

Laws 1937, p. 732, § 3; Laws 1947, p. 305, § 2; Laws 1955, p. 650, § 1; Laws 1959, p. 120, § 1.

§ 40–12–4. Record of process and service

The Secretary of State or his successor in office shall keep a record of all processes, which record shall show the day and hour of service upon him. When the return receipt for any such registered notice shall be returned to the Secretary of State, he shall deliver it to the plaintiff on request and keep a record of the date of its receipt by him and of its delivery to the plaintiff.

Laws 1937, p. 732, § 5.

§ 40–12–5. Certificate of service to be filed; time to answer

The Secretary of State or his successor in office, within three days from the date of the service upon him of the summons or process provided for in this chapter, shall certify to the court in which the action is pending that the summons or process has been filed in his office as provided for in this chapter. Upon receipt of such certification by the clerk of the court in which the action is pending, the complaint shall be answered within 30 days after service of the summons and complaint upon him, unless the time for the appearance of the defendant shall be extended by an order of the court in order to allow the defendant ample opportunity to be heard.

Laws 1937, p. 732, § 6.

§ 40–12–6. Continuances

The court in which an action brought against a nonresident pursuant to this chapter is pending shall cause any such action to be continued as long as may be necessary to afford the defendant reasonable opportunity to defend the action.

Laws 1937, p. 732, § 4.

§ 40–12–7. Designation by Secretary of State of employee to accept service

The Secretary of State is authorized and empowered to designate such of his employees as he deems necessary for the purposes of accepting service as provided in this chapter and performing all other duties and functions as provided in this chapter for the Secretary of State. Such designation shall be in writing, and all actions by any such person designated shall be as valid and binding as though performed by the Secretary of State himself. The power and authority of any such person so designated shall cease immediately upon such person's ceasing to be an employee of the Secretary of State.

Laws 1957, p. 65, § 1.

§ 40–12–8. Service upon nonresident personal representatives

If any person upon whom service of process is authorized by this chapter shall die, or be or become insane, or shall not be sui juris, service shall be made upon his administrator, executor, guardian, or other personal representative in the manner prescribed in this chapter, if such administrator, executor, guardian, or personal representative is not a resident of this state.

Laws 1957, p. 649, § 3.

CHAPTER 13

PROSECUTION OF TRAFFIC OFFENSES

Article 1

Uniform Traffic Citation and Complaint Form

§ 40–13–1. Authorization for development of form; contents; identifying number

The commissioner of driver services shall develop a uniform traffic citation and complaint form for use by all law enforcement officers who are empowered to enforce the traffic laws and ordinances in effect in this state. Such form shall serve as the citation, summons, accusation, or other instrument of prosecution of the offense or offenses for which the accused is charged, and as the record of the disposition of the matter by the court before which the accused is brought, and shall contain such other matter as the commissioner shall provide. Each such form shall have a unique identifying number which shall serve as the docket number for the court having jurisdiction of the accused.

Laws 1972, p. 1148, § 1; Laws 1985, p. 149, § 40; Laws 2005, Act 68, § 22–1, eff. July 1, 2005.

Historical and Statutory Notes

The 2005 amendment by Act 68 substituted "commissioner of driver services" for "commissioner of public safety".

§ 40–13–2. Rules and regulations

The Board of Public Safety, by rule and regulation, shall establish a system of accountability for all traffic citations and complaints, and it shall also provide the procedures governing the use and issuance of such citations and complaints.

Laws 1972, p. 1148, § 3.

§ 40–13–2.1. Traffic citation signature requirements

(a) A person who is issued a citation as provided in this chapter or Code Section 17–6–11, relating to display of driver's license in lieu of bail, shall sign the citation to acknowledge receipt of the citation and of his or her obligation to appear for trial. The officer shall advise the person that signing the citation is not an admission of guilt and that failure to sign will result in the person having to post a cash bond. If the person refuses to sign the citation, it shall constitute reasonable cause to believe that the person will not appear at trial and the officer may bring the person before a judicial officer or traffic violations bureau to post a bond as is otherwise provided by law.

(b) The provisions of subsection (a) of Code Section 17–6–11 shall not apply to a person in possession of a driver's license issued by a state or foreign country that has not entered into a reciprocal agreement regarding the operation of motor vehicles with this state as provided in Chapter 5 of Title 40, which provides for the suspension of a driver's license by the other state or foreign country of a person who fails to appear for trial of a traffic offense committed in this state.

(c) The signature of any person to whom a citation is issued may be captured electronically.

Laws 2000, p. 1313, § 5; Laws 2010, Act 633, § 25, eff. July 1, 2010.

Historical and Statutory Notes

The 2010 amendment by Act 633 added subsec. (c).

§ 40–13–3. Indictment or accusation unnecessary to bring accused to trial, when; report of disposition of case

Except for offenses tried in the superior courts, all other courts having jurisdiction of the offense may proceed with the adjudication of the offenses contained within the complaint without the necessity of filing an indictment or other accusation in order to bring the accused to trial. The judge or clerk of each court before whom a person accused of such an offense is brought shall promptly report the final disposition of the case to the Department of Driver Services. Notwithstanding the reporting requirements of this Code section, the Department of Driver Services may by rule or regulation relieve the judge or clerk of each such court of the responsibility of reporting those offenses which do not result in convictions or adjudications of guilt or pleas of nolo contendere.

Laws 1972, p. 1148, §§ 2, 4; Laws 1992, p. 1118, § 2; Laws 1992, p. 2785, § 29; Laws 2000, p. 951, § 7A–1; Laws 2005, Act 68, § 22–2, eff. July 1, 2005.

Historical and Statutory Notes

The 2000 amendment substituted for Department or Board of "Public Safety" the commissioner or Department of "Motor Vehicle Safety".

The 2005 amendment by Act 68 substituted "Department of Driver Services" for "Department of Motor Vehicle Safety" twice.

§ 40–13–4. Fees not precluded

Nothing contained in this article shall be construed to prohibit or to deny to any officer or official of any court any fees prescribed for his duties and services in connection with the offenses provided for in this article.

Laws 1972, p. 1148, § 4.

Article 2

Arrests, Trials, and Appeals

§ 40–13–20. Municipal courts defined

As used in this article, the term "municipal courts" shall be construed to include municipal courts of the incorporated municipalities of this state.

Laws 1937–38, Ex. Sess., p. 558, § 3; Laws 1987, p. 3, § 40; Laws 1994, p. 604, § 1.

§ 40–13–21. Jurisdiction of probate courts and municipal courts

(a) The probate courts and municipal courts of the incorporated towns and cities of this state, acting by and through the judges or presiding officers thereof, shall have the right and power to conduct trials, receive pleas of guilty, and impose sentence, in the manner required by law, upon defendants violating any and all criminal laws of this state relating to traffic upon the public roads, streets, and highways of this state where the penalty for the offense does not exceed that of the grade of misdemeanor.

(b) The probate court shall have jurisdiction to issue warrants, try cases, and impose sentence thereon in all misdemeanor cases arising under the traffic laws of this state in all counties of this state in which there is no city, county, or state court, provided the defendant waives a jury trial. Notwithstanding any provision of law to the contrary, all municipal courts are granted jurisdiction to try and dispose of misdemeanor traffic offenses arising under state law except violations of Code Section 40–6–393 and to impose any punishment authorized for such offenses under general state law, whether or not there is a city, county, or state court in such county, if the defendant waives a jury trial and the offense arises within the territorial limits of the respective jurisdictions as now or hereafter fixed by law.

(c) In any traffic misdemeanor trial, a judge of the probate court, upon his or her own motion, may request the assistance of the district attorney of the circuit in which the court is located or solicitor-general of the state court of the county to conduct the trial on behalf of the state. If, for any reason, the district attorney or solicitor-general is unable to assist, the district attorney or solicitor-general may designate a member of his or her staff to conduct the trial on behalf of the state.

Laws 1937–38, Ex. Sess., p. 558, §§ 1–3; Laws 1953, Nov.-Dec. Sess., p. 83, § 2; Laws 1962, p. 3146, § 2; Laws 1971, p. 2299, § 1; Laws 1982, p. 2107, § 44; Laws 1987, p. 3, § 40; Laws 1989, p. 354, § 1; Laws 1989, p. 604, § 1; Laws 1992, p. 909, § 1; Laws 1992, p. 980, § 1; Laws 1996, p. 748, § 21.

§ 40–13–22. Operating motor vehicle without license

(a) Notwithstanding any provision of the law to the contrary, any person, firm, or corporation charged with an offense under Code Section 40–2–8 may be tried in any municipal court of any municipality if the offense occurred within the corporate limits of such municipality. Such courts are granted the jurisdiction to try and dispose of such cases. The jurisdiction of such courts shall be concurrent with the jurisdiction of any other courts within the county having jurisdiction to try and dispose of such cases. Any fines and forfeitures arising from the prosecution of such cases shall be retained by the municipality and shall be paid into the treasury of such municipality. Any person, firm, or corporation charged with any offense under this Code section shall be entitled to request to have the case against him transferred to the court having general misdemeanor jurisdiction in the county wherein the alleged offense occurred.

(b) Nothing in this Code section shall be construed to give any municipality the right to impose a fine or punish by imprisonment in excess of the limits as set forth in the municipality's charter.

Laws 1931, p. 213, § 2; Laws 1977, p. 1039, § 1; Laws 1987, p. 3, § 40.

Formerly Code 1933, § 68–9901.

§ 40–13–23. Waiver of jury trial necessary

(a) No court defined in this article shall have the power to dispose of traffic misdemeanor cases as provided in this article unless the defendant shall first waive in writing a trial by jury. If the defendant wishes a trial by jury, he shall notify the court and, if reasonable cause exists, he shall be immediately bound over to the court in the county having jurisdiction to try the offense, wherein a jury may be impaneled. Where a cash bond, property bond, or driver's license in lieu of bond has been posted, the bond shall be transferred to the court assuming jurisdiction, and the defendant shall not be required to post a new bond by the court assuming jurisdiction.

(b) No waiver of a trial by jury may be withdrawn when such waiver has been interposed for the purpose of delay. Except with approval of the court, no waiver of a trial by jury may be withdrawn after the commencement of the trial or the filing of motions on behalf of the defendant, whichever comes first.

Laws 1937–38, Ex. Sess., p. 558, § 4; Laws 1985, p. 149, § 40; Laws 1987, p. 329, § 1; Laws 1992, p. 2785, § 29; Laws 1996, p. 1279, § 1.

§ 40–13–24. Citation and complaint; dockets

An indictment or accusation shall not be required against a defendant under this article, but a citation and complaint specifically setting out the charge shall be issued. The court shall keep a docket on which shall be plainly kept the name and address of the defendant, the nature of the offense in brief, the date when brought before the court, and the final disposition of the case with the date thereof. Such docket shall be the same in each probate court handling traffic misdemeanor cases and shall be on a form to be prescribed by the Department of Law. Such docket shall be paid for from the treasury of the county in which such court is located. Municipal courts may use the dockets ordinarily in use by them in the trial of other cases or, in the discretion of the court, may adopt the docket provided in this Code section for probate courts.

Laws 1937–38, Ex. Sess., p. 558, § 6; Laws 1987, p. 3, § 40.

§ 40–13–25. Costs

The costs in any case disposed of under this article shall be as provided in Code Section 15–9–60. In case a defendant refuses to waive a trial by jury and is bound over to another court, the costs shall await the final disposition of the case.

Laws 1937–38, Ex. Sess., p. 558, § 5.

§ 40–13–26. Sentences, costs, fines, fees; urban interstate system violations

(a) Defendants who plead guilty or who are convicted under this article shall be required to serve their sentences in such manner as is provided for by law in misdemeanor cases. In case a fine is imposed and paid, the officers of court, where on fee basis, shall first be paid their costs arising in such case. After the payment of all costs, the remainder of such fine shall be paid into the county treasury in the event the case is disposed of by the probate court; if the case is disposed of by the municipal court of an incorporated municipality, the remainder of such fine or fines shall be paid into the treasury of the municipality where the court is located, except that where such courts have jurisdiction beyond the corporate limits of a municipality, and the offense occurs outside the municipality, the fine shall be paid into the county treasury; provided, however, that in any case where a fine was imposed for violation of any traffic offense provided in or authorized by Chapter 6 of this title on any "urban interstate system" if the arrest or citation in such case was made or issued by a member of the Uniform Division of the Department of Public Safety's motorcycle enforcement unit, the remainder of such fine shall be remitted to the Department of Public Safety for the maintenance and enhancement of the Department's motorcycle program. The judge of the probate court or the person presiding over the municipal court must pay into the county treasury, municipal treasury, or Department of Public Safety by the fifteenth day of each month the remainder of all fines for the preceding month. Such payment must be accompanied by a list showing the name of the defendant in each case, the fine imposed in each case, the costs in each case and to whom paid, and the balance which is being paid into the treasury. The official making such payment must be given a written receipt by the person receiving the payment. No officer receiving a salary will receive any fees for arresting or attending court in any case arising under this article, but the usual fees must be assessed, and, if the arresting officer is not entitled to the costs, they must go to the county or city to which the fine is paid or Department of Public Safety as required by this Code section.

(b) As used in this Code section, the term "urban interstate system" means a portion of the national system of interstate and defense highways which:

(1) Is located entirely within any part of this state; and

(2) Includes a single numbered interstate highway which forms a closed loop or perimeter.

Where these conditions exist, the urban interstate system shall consist of the interstate highway constituting the closed loop or perimeter and all interstate highways or portions thereof located within such loop or perimeter, not including any portion of any interstate highway outside of the loop or perimeter.

Laws 1937–38, Ex. Sess., p. 558, § 7; Laws 1953, Jan.-Feb. Sess., p. 416, § 1; Laws 1953, Nov.-Dec. Sess., p. 207, § 1; Laws 1985, p. 149, § 40; Laws 1987, p. 3, § 40; Laws 2006, Act 470, § 2, eff. July 1, 2006.

Historical and Statutory Notes

The 2006 amendment by Act 470 rewrote the section which had read:

"Defendants who plead guilty or who are convicted under this article shall be required to serve their sentences in such manner as is provided for by law in misdemeanor cases. In case a fine is imposed and paid, the officers of court, where on fee basis, shall first be paid their costs arising in such case. After the payment of all costs, the remainder of such fine shall be paid into the county treasury in the event the case is disposed of by the probate court; if the case is disposed of by the municipal court of an incorporated municipality, the remainder of such fine or fines shall be paid into the treasury of the municipality where the court is located, except that where such courts have jurisdiction beyond the corporate limits of a municipality, and the offense occurs outside the municipality, the fine shall be paid into the county treasury. The judge of the probate court or the person presiding over the municipal court must pay into the county treasury or municipal treasury by the fifteenth day of each month the remainder of all fines for the preceding month. Such payment must be accompanied by a list showing the name of the defendant in each case, the fine imposed in each case, the costs in each case and to whom paid, and the balance which is being paid into the treasury. The official making such payment must be given a written receipt by the person receiving the payment. No officer receiving a salary will receive any fees for arresting or attending court in any case arising under this article, but the usual fees must be assessed, and, if the arresting officer is not entitled to the costs, they must go to the county or city to which the fine is paid."

Laws 2006, Act 470, § 3, as amended by Laws 2007, Act 18, § 15A; Laws 2010, Act 368, 2–1, provides:

"This Act [amending this section] shall become effective on July 1, 2006, and shall stand repealed June 30, 2011, unless renewed, and shall apply with respect to fines collected and forfeitures forfeited on or after July 1, 2006."

Laws 2010, Act 368, § 2–1, removed the self-repeal language, "and shall stand repealed June 30, 2011, unless renewed, and shall apply with respect to fines collected and forfeitures forfeited on or after July 1, 2006."

In 2006, the Code Commission, in subsec. (b), substituted "Code section" for "subsection" in the introductory paragraph. See § 28–9–5.

§ 40–13–27. Record to be kept for public inspection

A written record is required to be kept of every case made or disposed of under this article. Such record shall be accessible at all times for public inspection and official audit and shall be kept and remain as a part of the permanent records of the court.

Laws 1937–38, Ex. Sess., p. 558, § 8.

§ 40–13–28. Appeals to superior court; bail; hearing

Any defendant convicted under this article shall have the right of appeal to the superior court. The provisions of Code Sections 5–3–29 and 5–3–30 shall not apply to appeals under this Code section. Otherwise, the appeal shall be entered as appeals are entered from the probate court to the superior court, provided that the defendant shall be entitled to bail and shall be released from custody upon giving the bond as is provided for appearances in criminal cases in the courts of this state. Such bond shall have the same conditions as appearance bonds in criminal cases. The appeal to the superior court shall not be a de novo investigation before a jury but shall be on the record of the hearing as certified by the judge of that court who presided at the hearing below.

Laws 1937–38, Ex. Sess., p. 558, § 10; Laws 1986, p. 982, § 15.

§ 40–13–29. Jurisdiction, when exclusive

In all counties except those having city, county, or state courts, the judge of the probate court shall have exclusive jurisdiction of all traffic misdemeanor cases originating in the county outside of municipal corporations, and the judge of the municipal court in each municipal corporation shall have exclusive jurisdiction of traffic misdemeanor cases originating inside the corporate limits of municipalities.

Laws 1937–38, Ex. Sess., p. 558, § 11; Laws 1987, p. 3, § 40; Laws 1992, p. 2785, § 29.

§ 40–13–30. Arrests by Officers of the Georgia State Patrol or any arresting officer

Officers of the Georgia State Patrol and any other officer of this state or of any county or municipality thereof having authority to arrest for a criminal offense of the grade of misdemeanor shall have authority to prefer charges and bring offenders to trial under this article, provided that officers of an incorporated municipality shall have no power to make arrests beyond the corporate limits of such municipality unless such jurisdiction is given by local or other law.

Laws 1937–38, Ex. Sess., p. 558, § 9; Laws 1992, p. 2785, § 29.

§ 40–13–31. Sheriffs entitled to arresting fees for arrests

The sheriffs of the several counties of this state are entitled to an arresting fee, as provided by law, in every case in which the sheriff or his lawful deputy arrests, assists in arresting, or takes custody of any person charged with a crime who has been apprehended by an officer of the Georgia State Patrol and delivered to the sheriff or his lawful deputy. If the sheriff is upon a salary, the fee shall be paid into the county treasury.

Laws 1943, p. 571, § 1; Laws 1992, p. 2785, § 29.

§ 40–13–32. Procedures for modifying sentences or judgments

(a) No court having jurisdiction over cases arising out of the traffic laws of this state or the traffic laws of any county or municipal government shall change or modify a traffic law sentence or judgment rendered pursuant to a conviction, plea of guilty, or plea of nolo contendere after 90 days from the date of judgment, except for the purpose of correcting clerical errors therein, unless there is strict compliance with all of the following requirements:

(1) A motion to change or modify the sentence or judgment is made by the defendant to the court rendering the judgment;

(2) Notice, including a copy of the motion and rule nisi, is given to the prosecuting official who brought the original charge at least ten days prior to the motion hearing; and

(3) A hearing is held with opportunity for the state to be heard.

(b) If the original judgment is changed or modified pursuant to this Code section, the judge shall certify to the Department of Driver Services that such change or modification is a true and correct copy of the change or modification and that the requirements set forth in paragraphs (1) through (3) of subsection (a) of this Code section have been met.

(c) Except for orders correcting clerical errors, the Department of Driver Services shall not recognize as valid any change or modification order nor make any changes to a driver's history unless such change or modification as submitted to the department is in strict compliance with the requirements set forth in subsections (a) and (b) of this Code section.

(d) In the case of municipal courts, notice to the city attorney, or to the solicitor in those cases where the municipal court has a solicitor, shall be deemed to be notice as provided for in this Code section.

(e) In all cases wherein notice is required in this Code section, same shall be deemed sufficient if sent by certified mail or statutory overnight delivery, return receipt requested, with adequate postage thereon, to the correct address of the prosecuting official.

(f) Notwithstanding other laws and specifically notwithstanding Code Section 17–7–93, a motion to change or modify a traffic law sentence or judgment may, at any time prior to the expiration of the term of court following the term at which judgment and sentence were pronounced or within 90 days of the time judgment and sentence were pronounced, whichever time period is greater, be made by the defendant and accepted by the court as provided in this Code section.

Laws 1984, p. 1144, § 1; Laws 1985, p. 149, § 40; Laws 1988, p. 1893, § 4; Laws 1989, p. 14, § 40; Laws 2000, p. 951, § 7A–2; Laws 2000, p. 1589, § 3; Laws 2005, Act 68, § 22–3, eff. July 1, 2005.

Historical and Statutory Notes

The 2000 amendment by Act 737 substituted for Department or Board of "Public Safety" the commissioner or Department of "Motor Vehicle Safety".

The 2000 amendment by Act 918 substituted in subsec. (c) "certified mail or statutory overnight delivery" for "certified mail".

The 2005 amendment by Act 68 in subsec. (b) and (c) substituted "Department of Driver Services" for "Department of Motor Vehicle Safety".

§ 40–13–33. Challenges to misdemeanor convictions of traffic laws

(a) Any challenge to a misdemeanor conviction of any of the traffic laws of this state or the traffic laws of any county or municipal government which may be brought pursuant to Chapter 14 of Title 9 must be filed within 180 days of the date the conviction becomes final.

(b) Any challenge to a conviction specified in subsection (a) of this Code section which became final before March 28, 1986, must be filed within 180 days following March 28, 1986.

(c) When the commissioner of driver services is named as the respondent, all such petitions must be brought in the Superior Court of Fulton County.

(d) Failure to file the challenge within the time prescribed in this Code section shall divest the court of jurisdiction.

Laws 1986, p. 444, § 1; Laws 1992, p. 2785, § 29; Laws 2000, p. 951, § 7A–3; Laws 2005, Act 68, § 22–4, eff. July 1, 2005.

Historical and Statutory Notes

The 2000 amendment substituted for Department or Board of "Public Safety" the commissioner or Department of "Motor Vehicle Safety".

The 2005 amendment by Act 68 substituted "commissioner of driver services" for "commissioner of motor vehicle safety".

Article 3

Traffic Violations Bureaus

§ 40–13–50. Power of judges to establish traffic violations bureau

In every court of this state having jurisdiction over the violation of traffic laws or traffic ordinances, the judge, or the judges where there is more than one judge, may provide by written order for the establishment of a traffic violations bureau for the handling or disposition of certain traffic cases in substantial compliance with this article. The court shall promulgate and provide to the clerk of the traffic violations bureau a list of the traffic offenses which shall be handled and disposed of by the traffic violations bureau. However, nothing in this article shall authorize the judge of such court to employ any person or persons to administer this article.

Laws 1966, p. 381, § 1; Laws 1992, p. 2785, § 29.

§ 40–13–51. Clerk appointed to receive money; bond

(a) The court may appoint a clerk or deputy clerk or deputy clerks, who shall be named in the order establishing the traffic violations bureau, for the purpose of receiving money as provided in this article. Any deputy clerk so appointed shall be under the direct supervision of and attached to the office of the clerk of the court.

(b) Such person or persons, except where such person is the clerk of the court and is already under bond, shall be bonded in the sum of $2,500.00.

Laws 1966, p. 381, § 2.

§ 40–13–52. Traffic offense cards; contents

The court may, in its order, provide that there shall be maintained in the office of the traffic violations bureau cards known as "traffic offense cards." Upon each traffic offense card shall appear: the name and address of the person charged with a traffic offense; the date of the birth of such person; the sex of such person; and his driver's license number. The card shall be numbered so that it may show any previous traffic offense, giving the date of the offense, the trial date, the citation number, the disposition of the case, and the amount of any fine paid.

Laws 1966, p. 381, § 5.

§ 40–13–53. Release of offenders upon citation and complaint; excepted offenses

(a) Subject to the exceptions set out in subsection (b) of this Code section, any officer who arrests any person for the violation of a traffic law or traffic ordinance alleged to have been committed outside the corporate limits of any municipality shall permit such person to be released upon being served with a citation and complaint and agreeing to appear, as provided in this article. If such officer has reasonable and probable grounds to believe that the person will not obey such citation and agreement to appear, the officer may require such person to surrender his driver's license in accordance with Code Section 17–6–11.

(b) The following offenses shall not be handled or disposed of by a traffic violations bureau:

(1) Any offense for which a driver's license may be suspended by the commissioner of driver services;

(2) Any motor vehicle registration violation;

(3) A violation of Code Section 40–5–20;

(4) Speeding in excess of 30 miles per hour over the posted speed limit; or

(5) Any offense which would otherwise be a traffic violations bureau offense but which arose out of the same conduct or occurred in conjunction with an offense which is excluded from the jurisdiction of the traffic violations bureau. Any such offense shall be subject to the maximum punishment set by law.

Laws 1966, p. 381, § 3; Laws 1983, p. 1000, § 16; Laws 1992, p. 2785, § 29; Laws 2000, p. 951, § 7A–4; Laws 2005, Act 68, § 22–5, eff. July 1, 2005.

Historical and Statutory Notes

The 2000 amendment substituted for Department or Board of "Public Safety" the commissioner or Department of "Motor Vehicle Safety".

The 2005 amendment by Act 68 in subsec. (b)(1) substituted "commissioner of driver services" for "commissioner of motor vehicle safety".

§ 40–13–54. Disposition of original and copies of citations

The original citation and complaint shall be sent by the officer issuing it to the traffic violations bureau of the court within 24 hours of the arrest. The defendant named in the citation shall be given the second copy. The officer issuing the citation and complaint shall retain one copy for himself or herself, and the court may, by order, provide that an additional copy shall be made for the use of any municipality in the county or the Department of Driver Services.

Laws 1966, p. 381, §§ 7, 8; Laws 2000, p. 951, § 7A–5; Laws 2005, Act 68, § 22–6, eff. July 1, 2005.

Historical and Statutory Notes

The 2000 amendment inserted gender neutral language and substituted for Department or Board of "Public Safety" the commissioner or Department of "Motor Vehicle Safety".

The 2005 amendment by Act 68 at the end of the third sentence substituted "Department of Driver Services" for "Department of Motor Vehicle Safety".

§ 40–13–55. Cash bonds to be accepted

Any person cited for any traffic offense under the jurisdiction of the traffic violations bureau of the court shall be permitted to give a cash bond for his appearance under the terms and conditions as set forth upon the citation and complaint given to him at the time he is cited by the arresting officer for a traffic violation.

Laws 1966, p. 381, § 10.

§ 40–13–56. Officers prohibited from accepting cash bonds

No officer giving a citation and complaint to a defendant for a traffic violation shall accept a cash bond himself.

Laws 1966, p. 381, § 11.

§ 40–13–57. Discretion of arresting officer to bring offender before bureau; cash bond

In the event an officer has authority to issue citation and complaint as set forth in Code Section 40–13–53 but declines to do so because of his belief that such person will not obey the citation and agreement to appear, such officer may bring such person to the traffic violations bureau and such person may be allowed to post a cash bond for his appearance in accordance with the schedule established by the court.

Laws 1966, p. 381, § 4; Laws 1992, p. 2785, § 29.

§ 40–13–58. Cash bonds; effect of forfeiture

Where a defendant cited for a traffic violation posts a cash bond according to the schedule set up by court order and fails to appear in court at the term of court and on the day set in the original citation and complaint, then and in that event, such failure shall be construed as an admission of guilt and the cash bond may be forfeited without the necessity for the statutory procedure provided for the forfeiture of statutory bail bonds. A judgment of guilty may be entered accordingly, ordering the case disposed of and settled. The proceeds of the cash bond shall be applied and distributed as any fine imposed by said court would be. Nothing in this Code section shall be construed as preventing the judge from ordering the defendant to appear and stand trial.

Laws 1966, p. 381, § 10.

§ 40–13–59. Information to be recorded on summons and driver history cards; filing citation and complaint; recording of forfeiture order

(a) The traffic violations bureau of the court shall record on the prescribed form, as set out in Code Section 40–13–52, the driving record of the defendant. If there is no previous record of the driver's history, the citation appearing on the original citation and complaint shall be entered on the driver's traffic offense card; and each traffic offense thereafter shall be entered thereon, with the disposition thereof, up to a period of four years.

(b) All the pending cases which appear on the citation and complaint issued by the arresting officer, as provided for in this article, shall be filed at the cashier's desk in the traffic violations bureau of the court and shall be retained there up until 72 hours, or such other period of time as the judge shall fix by order, prior to the time the case is set for trial in the court. If cash bond is posted according to the schedules prescribed by order of the judge at any time up to 72 hours, or such other period of time as the judge shall fix by order, prior to the date of the court appearance, as specified in the citation and complaint, the same shall be entered on the driver's traffic offense card and an entry shall be made thereon that the driver has posted a cash bond.

(c) Within 72 hours after the date set for a hearing in the court on the citation and complaint given, where the defendant has posted a cash bond and has failed to appear for the hearing, the court shall enter an order that the cash bond has been forfeited in accordance with this article. Such order shall be recorded on the back of the citation and complaint which is maintained in the traffic violations bureau of the court and shall also be recorded on the defendant's traffic offense card.

Laws 1966, p. 381, § 11.

§ 40–13–60. Traffic violations distinguished from misdemeanors; handling of cases

Any traffic violation under the jurisdiction of the traffic violations bureau shall be characterized and classified as a traffic violation and shall not be considered as a misdemeanor. Whenever any traffic violation is transferred from another court to a court which has a traffic violations bureau, if such offense is classified as a traffic violation on the traffic violations bureau schedule of the receiving court, such violation shall be handled and disposed of by such traffic violations bureau. Where a defendant demands a trial on a traffic violation, it shall be tried before a judge of the court which established the traffic violations bureau. The request for a trial shall not result in a loss of jurisdiction by the traffic violations bureau.

Laws 1966, p. 381, § 12; Laws 1992, p. 2785, § 29.

Validity

This section has been held unconstitutional in the case of Geng v. State, 2003, 276 Ga. 428, 578 S.E.2d 115.

§ 40–13–61. Maintenance of records; accusations not entered on misdemeanor docket; failure to post bond or appear as grounds for accusation

All records other than those excepted in this article shall be maintained at the traffic violations bureau of the court. No accusation of an offense for which citation and complaint may be issued shall be entered on the misdemeanor docket maintained by the clerk of the court. No accusation for any offense coming under the jurisdiction of the traffic violations bureau of the court shall be taken by the prosecuting attorney of the court or maintained in his office unless said person to whom the said summons was issued fails to post a cash bond as defined in this article or fails to appear on the date specified in the summons to answer said complaint.

Laws 1966, p. 381, § 9; Laws 1985, p. 149, § 40.

§ 40–13–62. Procedure on failure of person cited to appear

When any person cited for a traffic violation pursuant to this article fails to appear in court on the date specified in the citation and in accordance with his written promise to appear, unless such person has posted a cash bond as provided in this article, the traffic violations bureau thereupon loses jurisdiction and the citation shall be forwarded to the prosecuting attorney of the court who shall have an accusation issued against such person. Upon motion of the prosecuting attorney, a bench warrant shall issue based on the accusation for the arrest of the defendant. The defendant's case shall be docketed by the clerk of the court and handled as all other misdemeanors.

Laws 1966, p. 381, § 12; Laws 1992, p. 2785, § 29.

§ 40–13–63. Penalty for failure of person cited to appear

The willful failure of any person to appear in accordance with the written promise contained on the citation and complaint and served upon such person shall constitute an offense which shall be punishable by fine in an amount not to exceed $200.00 or by confinement in jail for a period not to exceed three days.

Laws 1966, p. 381, § 13; Laws 1999, p. 334, § 4.

§ 40–13–64. Bureau to have charge of suspended sentence division of court

The court may provide that its traffic violations bureau, in addition to the duties set out in this article, shall have charge of what shall be called and designated in the court as the "Suspended Sentence Division of the ____ Court." This division of the court shall be responsible for collecting fines imposed upon persons convicted in the court, where the sentence is suspended upon the payment of a fine. The person or persons in the division shall be authorized, where the judge imposing the sentence stipulates the same therein, to permit such persons receiving suspended sentences, in addition to the other conditions imposed in the suspended sentence, to pay the suspended sentence fine in installments. The person or persons responsible for the administration of the suspended sentence division shall be responsible for collecting the suspended sentence fine by installments and shall also be responsible for the arrest of persons who fail in this respect to comply with the conditions of the suspended sentence.

Laws 1966, p. 381, § 14.

CHAPTER 14

USE OF SPEED DETECTION AND TRAFFIC–CONTROL SIGNAL MONITORING DEVICES

Article 1

General Provisions

§ 40–14–1. Definitions

As used in this chapter, the term:

(1) "Campus" means the grounds owned or occupied by a college or university.

(2) "Campus law enforcement agency" means the campus agency charged with the enforcement of the laws of this state.

(3) "College or university" means an accredited public or private educational institution of higher learning.

(4) "Speed detection device" means, unless otherwise indicated, that particular device designed to measure the speed or velocity of a motor vehicle and marketed under the name "Vascar" or any similar device operating under the same or similar principle and any devices for the measurement of speed or velocity based upon the Doppler principle of radar or the speed timing principle of laser. All such devices must meet or exceed the minimum performance specifications established by the Department of Public Safety.

Laws 1968, p. 425, § 3; Laws 1970, p. 435, § 3; Laws 1984, p. 502, § 1; Laws 1989, p. 586, § 1; Laws 1996, p. 1281, §§ 4, 5.

Article 2

Speed Detection Devices

§ 40–14–2. Approval of governing authority or president of college or university; use prohibited when arresting officer or court officials paid by fee system; use by certified peace officers

(a) The law enforcement officers of the various counties, municipalities, colleges, and universities may use speed detection devices only if the sheriffs of such counties, or the governing authorities of such counties, or the governing authorities of such municipalities, or the president of such college or university shall approve of and desire the use of such devices and shall apply to the Department of Public Safety for a permit to use such devices in accordance with this chapter.

(b) No county sheriff, county or municipal governing authority, college, or university shall be authorized to use speed detection devices where any arresting officer or official of the court having jurisdiction of traffic cases is paid on a fee system. This subsection shall not apply to any official receiving a recording fee.

(c) A permit shall not be issued by the Department of Public Safety to an applicant under this Code section unless the applicant provides law enforcement services by certified peace officers 24 hours a day, seven days a week on call or on duty or allows only peace officers employed full time by the applicant to operate speed detection devices. Speed detection devices can only be operated by registered or certified peace officers of the county sheriff, county, municipality, college, or university to which the permit is applicable. Persons operating the speed detection devices must be registered or certified by the Georgia Peace Officer Standards and Training Council as peace officers and certified by the Georgia Peace Officer Standards and Training Council as operators of speed detection devices.

Laws 1968, p. 425, § 1; Laws 1978, p. 2254, § 1; Laws 1979, p. 771, § 1; Laws 1989, p. 586, § 1; Laws 1996, p. 1281, § 6; Laws 1997, p. 956, § 1; Laws 1999, p. 1227, § 1.

§ 40–14–3. Applications for permits

(a) A county sheriff, county or municipal governing authority, or the president of a college or university may apply to the Department of Public Safety for a permit to authorize the use of speed detection devices for purposes of traffic control within such counties, municipalities, colleges, or universities on streets, roads, and highways, provided that such application shall name the street or road on which the device is to be used and the speed limits on such street or road shall have been approved by the Office of Traffic Operations of the Department of Transportation. Law enforcement agencies are authorized to use speed detection devices on streets and roads for which an application is pending as long as all other requirements for the use of speed detection devices are met. Nothing in this subsection shall be construed to affect the provisions of Code Section 40–14–9.

(b) The Department of Public Safety is authorized to prescribe by appropriate rules and regulations the manner and procedure in which applications shall be made for such permits and to prescribe the required information to be submitted by the applicants. The Department of Public Safety may deny the application or suspend the speed detection device permit for failure to provide information or documentation at the department's request.

Laws 1968, p. 425, §§ 2, 4; Laws 1970, p. 435, § 2; Laws 1989, p. 586, § 1; Laws 1995, p. 713, § 1; Laws 1996, p. 1281, § 7; Laws 1999, p. 1227, § 2; Laws 2004, Act 564, § 40, eff. May 13, 2004.

§ 40–14–4. Federal Communications Commission license required to use

No state, county, municipal, or campus law enforcement agency may use speed detection devices unless the agency possesses a license in compliance with Federal Communications Commission rules, and unless each device, before being placed in service and annually after being placed in service, is certified for compliance by a technician possessing a certification as required by the Department of Public Safety.

Laws 1978, p. 2254, § 1; Laws 1979, p. 771, § 1; Laws 1988, p. 308, § 1; Laws 1989, p. 586, § 1.

§ 40–14–5. Testing device for accuracy

(a) Each state, county, municipal, or campus law enforcement officer using a radar device shall test the device for accuracy and record and maintain the results of the test at the beginning and end of each duty tour. Each such test shall be made in accordance with the manufacturer's recommended procedure. Any radar unit not meeting the manufacturer's minimum accuracy requirements shall be removed from service and thereafter shall not be used by the state, county, municipal, or campus law enforcement agency until it has been serviced, calibrated, and recertified by a technician with the qualifications specified in Code Section 40–14–4.

(b) Each county, municipal, or campus law enforcement officer using a radar device shall notify each person against whom the officer intends to make a case based on the use of the radar device that the person has a right to request the officer to test the radar device for accuracy. The notice shall be given prior to the time a citation and complaint or ticket is issued against the person and, if requested to make a test, the officer shall test the radar device for accuracy. In the event the radar device does not meet the minimum accuracy requirements, the citation and complaint or ticket shall not be issued against the person, and the radar device shall be removed from service and thereafter shall not be used by the county, municipal, or campus law enforcement agency until it has been serviced, calibrated, and recertified by a technician with the qualifications specified in Code Section 40–14–4.

Laws 1978, p. 2254, § 1; Laws 1979, p. 771, § 1; Laws 1989, p. 586, § 1; Laws 1996, p. 1281, § 8.

§ 40–14–6. Warning signs

(a) Each county, municipality, college, and university using speed detection devices shall erect signs on every highway which comprises a part of the state highway system at that point on the highway which intersects the corporate limits of the municipality, the county boundary, or the boundary of the college or university campus. Such signs shall be at least 24 by 30 inches in area and shall warn approaching motorists that speed detection devices are being employed. No such devices shall be used within 500 feet of any such warning sign erected pursuant to this subsection.

(b) In addition to the signs required under subsection (a) of this Code section, each county, municipality, college, and university using speed detection devices shall erect speed limit warning signs on every highway which comprises a part of the state highway system at that point on the highway which intersects the corporate limits of the municipality, the county boundary, or the boundary of the college or university campus. Such signs shall be at least 24 by 30 inches in area, shall warn approaching motorists of changes in the speed limit, shall be visible plainly from every lane of traffic, shall be viewable in any traffic conditions, and shall not be placed in such a manner that the view of such sign is subject to being obstructed by any other vehicle on such highway. No such devices shall be used within 500 feet of any such warning sign erected pursuant to this subsection.

Laws 1968, p. 425, § 5; Laws 1970, p. 435, § 4; Laws 1989, p. 586, § 1; Laws 1996, p. 1281, § 9; Laws 2003, Act 191, § 5, eff. July 1, 2003.

§ 40–14–7. Visibility to approaching motorists

No stationary speed detection device shall be employed by county, municipal, college, or university law enforcement officers where the vehicle from which the device is operated is obstructed from the view of approaching motorists or is otherwise not visible for a distance of at least 500 feet.

Laws 1968, p. 425, § 7; Laws 1978, p. 1968, § 1; Laws 1989, p. 586, § 1; Laws 1992, p. 2785, § 30.

§ 40–14–8. Use in school and residential districts

(a) No county, city, or campus officer shall be allowed to make a case based on the use of any speed detection device, unless the speed of the vehicle exceeds the posted speed limit by more than ten miles per hour and no conviction shall be had thereon unless such speed is more than ten miles per hour above the posted speed limit.

(b) The limitations contained in subsection (a) of this Code section shall not apply in properly marked school zones one hour before, during, and one hour after the normal hours of school operation, in properly marked historic districts, and in properly marked residential zones. For purposes of this chapter, thoroughfares with speed limits of 35 miles per hour or more shall not be considered residential districts. For purposes of this Code section, the term "historic district" means a historic district as defined in paragraph (5) of Code Section 44–10–22 and which is listed on the Georgia Register of Historic Places or as defined by ordinance adopted pursuant to a local constitutional amendment.

Laws 1968, p. 425, § 1; Laws 1970, p. 435, § 1; Laws 1978, p. 2254, § 1; Laws 1979, p. 771, § 1; Laws 1989, p. 586, § 1; Laws 1992, p. 2785, § 30; Laws 2000, p. 1257, § 1.

§ 40–14–9. Where use permitted; evidence

Evidence obtained by county or municipal law enforcement officers in using speed detection devices within 300 feet of a reduction of a speed limit inside an incorporated municipality or within 600 feet of a reduction of a speed limit outside an incorporated municipality or consolidated city-county government shall be inadmissible in the prosecution of a violation of any municipal ordinance, county ordinance, or state law regulating speed; nor shall such evidence be admissible in the prosecution of a violation as aforesaid when such violation has occurred within 30 days following a reduction of the speed limit in the area where the violation took place, except that this 30 day limitation shall not apply to a speeding violation within a highway work zone, as defined in Code Section 40–6–188, or in an area with variable speed limits, as defined in Code Section 40–6–182. No speed detection device shall be employed by county, municipal, or campus law enforcement officers on any portion of any highway which has a grade in excess of 7 percent.

Laws 1968, p. 425, § 6; Laws 1970, p. 435, § 5; Laws 1978, p. 2256, § 1; Laws 1979, p. 771, § 2; Laws 1989, p. 586, § 1; Laws 2003, Act 191, § 6, eff. July 1, 2003; Laws 2010, Act 460, § 6, eff. July 1, 2010.

§ 40–14–10. Use without permit or where permit has been suspended or revoked

It shall be unlawful for speed detection devices to be used in any county or municipality or on any campus for which a permit authorizing such use has not been issued or for which a permit authorizing such use has been suspended or revoked and not reissued. It shall be unlawful for any official of such county, municipality, college, or university to order such speed detection devices to be used. It shall be unlawful for any law enforcement officer of any such county, municipality, college, or university to use any such speed detection devices. Any such official or law enforcement officer violating this Code section shall be guilty of a misdemeanor.

Laws 1977, p. 800, § 4; Laws 1985, p. 149, § 40; Laws 1989, p. 586, § 1; Laws 1996, p. 1281, § 10.

§ 40–14–11. Revocation of permits; investigation

(a) Upon a complaint being made to the commissioner of public safety that any county, municipality, college, or university is employing speed detection devices for purposes other than the promotion of the public health, welfare, and safety or in a manner which violates this chapter or violates its speed detection device permit, the commissioner or the commissioner's designee is authorized and empowered to conduct an investigation into the acts and practices of such county, municipality, college, or university with respect to speed detection devices. If, as a result of this investigation, the commissioner or the commissioner's designee finds that there is probable cause to suspend or revoke the speed detection device permit of such county, municipality, college, or university, he or she shall issue an order to that effect.

(b) Upon the suspension or revocation of any speed detection device permit for the reasons set forth in this Code section, the commissioner of public safety shall notify the executive director of the Georgia Peace Officer Standards and Training Council of the action taken.

(c) Upon receipt from the executive director of the Georgia Peace Officer Standards and Training Council that an officer's certification to operate speed detection devices has been withdrawn or suspended pursuant to Code Section 35–8–12, the commissioner of public safety or the commissioner's designee shall suspend the speed detection device permit for the employing agency. The period of suspension or revocation shall be consistent with the action taken by the Georgia Peace Officer Standards and Training Council.

(d) There shall be a rebuttable presumption that a law enforcement agency is employing speed detection devices for purposes other than the promotion of the public health, welfare, and safety if the fines levied based on the use of speed detection devices for speeding offenses are equal to or greater than 40 percent of that law enforcement agency's budget; provided, however, that fines for speeding violations exceeding 17 miles per hour over the established speed limit shall not be considered when calculating total speeding fine revenue for the agency.

Laws 1968, p. 425, § 8; Laws 1977, p. 800, § 1; Laws 1989, p. 586, § 1; Laws 1996, p. 1281, § 11; Laws 1999, p. 1227, § 3.

§ 40–14–12. Revocation of permits; hearing

Upon issuance by the commissioner of public safety of an order suspending or revoking the speed detection device permit of any county, municipality, college, or university, the county, municipality, college, or university affected shall be afforded a hearing, to be held within ten days of the effective date of the order. The hearing shall be held before the commissioner or deputy commissioner of public safety, and, following the hearing, the county, municipality, college, or university affected shall be served with a written decision announcing whether the permit shall remain revoked or whether it shall be reinstated.

Laws 1968, p. 425, § 9; Laws 1977, p. 800, § 2; Laws 1989, p. 586, § 1; Laws 1996, p. 1281, § 12.

§ 40–14–13. Revocation of permits; appeal

Any county, municipality, college, or university aggrieved by a decision of the commissioner or deputy commissioner of public safety suspending or revoking its speed detection device permit may appeal that decision within 30 days of its effective date to the Board of Public Safety, which shall schedule a hearing with respect thereto before the board. Following a hearing before the board, the county, municipality, college, or university affected shall be served with a written decision announcing whether the permit shall remain revoked or whether it shall be reinstated. An adverse decision of the board may be appealed by the county, municipality, college, or university to the superior court with appropriate jurisdiction, but the municipality, county, college, or university shall be denied the use of the speed detection device until after such appeal is decided by the court.

Laws 1968, p. 425, § 10; Laws 1977, p. 800, § 3; Laws 1989, p. 586, § 1; Laws 1996, p. 1281, § 13.

§ 40–14–14. Revocation of permits; reconsideration of revocation

At the expiration of six months following the suspension or revocation of a speed detection device permit by the Board of Public Safety or, if no appeal was taken, by the commissioner or deputy commissioner of public safety, the governing authority of any such county or municipality or the president of any such college or university may, upon a change of circumstances being shown to the commissioner, petition the commissioner for a reconsideration of whether such county, municipality, college, or university should be permitted to use speed detection devices within their respective jurisdictions.

Laws 1968, p. 425, § 11; Laws 1977, p. 800, § 5; Laws 1989, p. 586, § 1; Laws 1996, p. 1281, § 14.

§ 40–14–15. Change of circumstances; hearing; application for rehearing

The Governor, in his discretion, may direct the commissioner of public safety, or his delegate, to inquire into such change of circumstances and report the same to him together with any recommendations he might have. The Governor, in his discretion, may order a new hearing on the matter before the Board of Public Safety or may, without hearing, issue his order directing the commissioner to grant a permit to such a county, municipality, college, or university to use speed detection devices. If a county, municipality, college, or university shall not be granted a permit to use such devices, it shall not apply for a rehearing until the expiration of six months.

Laws 1968, p. 425, § 12; Laws 1989, p. 586, § 1.

§ 40–14–16. Revocation of drivers' licenses

No speeding violation of less than ten miles per hour above the legal speed limit in the county or municipality or on a college or university campus in which a person is given a speeding ticket shall be used by the Department of Driver Services for the purpose of suspending or revoking the driver's license of the violator. No speeding violation report by a county, municipality, or college or university campus to the Department of Driver Services which fails to specify the speed of the violator shall be used by the Department of Driver Services to revoke the driver's license of a violator.

Laws 1968, p. 425, § 13; Laws 1989, p. 586, § 1; Laws 2002, p. 415, § 40; Laws 2005, Act 68, § 23–1, eff. July 1, 2005.

Historical and Statutory Notes

The 2005 amendment by Act 68 substituted "Department of Driver Services" for "Department of Motor Vehicle Safety" three times.

§ 40–14–17. Laser speed detection devices; admissibility of results

Evidence of speed based on a speed detection device using the speed timing principle of laser which is of a model that has been approved by the Department of Public Safety shall be considered scientifically acceptable and reliable as a speed detection device and shall be admissible for all purposes in any court, judicial, or administrative proceedings in this state. A certified copy of the Department of Public Safety list of approved models of such laser devices shall be self-authenticating and shall be admissible for all purposes in any court, judicial, or administrative proceedings in this state.

Laws 1999, p. 5, § 1.

Article 3

Traffic–Control Signal Monitoring Devices

§ 40–14–20. Definitions

As used in this article, the term:

(1) "Governing authority" means any county, municipality, or consolidated government.

(2) "Recorded images" has the meaning provided in subparagraph (f)(1)(B) of Code Section 40–6–20.

(3) "Traffic-control signal monitoring device" has the meaning provided in subparagraph (f)(1)(C) of Code Section 40–6–20.

Laws 2001, p. 770, § 4.; Laws 2008, Act 799, § 3, eff. Dec. 31, 2008.

§ 40–14–21. Permit to operate traffic-control signal monitoring system; public hearing; rules and regulations; application process; conditions of use; amendment; review; fees

(a) A governing authority must obtain an operating permit from the Department of Transportation prior to using any traffic-control signal monitoring device. The governing authority shall not use traffic-control signal monitoring devices unless the chief law enforcement officer of such governing authority desires the use of such devices and such use is approved by a properly adopted resolution of the governing authority.

(b) The governing authority shall also conduct a public hearing on the proposed use of such devices prior to entering any contract on or after July 1, 2001, for the use or purchase of such devices.

(c) The Department of Transportation is authorized to prescribe by appropriate rules and regulations the manner and procedure in which applications shall be made for traffic-control signal monitoring device permits and to prescribe the required information to be submitted by an applicant consistent with the requirements of this title. The Department of Transportation may deny an application or suspend or revoke a permit for failure of the governing authority to provide requested information or documentation or for any other violation of this article or violation of the rules and regulations of the department.

(d) An application for the operation of a traffic-control signal monitoring device by a governing authority shall name the intersection at which the device is to be used and provide demonstrable evidence that there is a genuine safety need for the use of such device at the designated intersection. The documented safety need for each designated intersection shall be approved by the Department of Transportation in accordance with nationally recognized safety standards. For each designated intersection, the governing authority shall conduct a traffic engineering study to determine whether, in addition to or as an alternative to the traffic-control signal monitoring device, there are other possible design or operational changes likely to reduce the number of accidents or red light violations at that intersection. This report shall be submitted with the application for an operation permit required under these provisions and any request to amend the operation permit to include an additional intersection.

(e) The revenue generated by the use of a traffic-control signal monitoring device shall not be considered when determining whether to issue a permit for the operation of such devices at a designated intersection. The only consideration shall be the increased life-saving safety value by the use of such a device at the designated intersection.

(f) Permits shall be issued by the Department of Transportation within three months of receiving a completed permit application from a governing authority where such governing authority is otherwise in compliance with the provisions of this article. An application for amendment to an existing permit and an application for a renewal permit following a suspension or revocation of a permit shall also be processed within three months of receipt of such application, provided that the application is complete and complies with the provisions of this article. A permit shall authorize use of a traffic-control signal monitoring device for only those designated intersections approved as having a documented life-saving safety need by the Department of Transportation.

(g) No governing authority shall be authorized to use traffic-control signal monitoring devices where any arresting officer or official of the court having jurisdiction of traffic cases is paid on a fee system. This subsection shall not apply to any official receiving a recording fee.

(h) If a governing authority elects to use traffic-control signal monitoring devices, no portion of any civil monetary penalty collected through the use of such devices may be paid to the manufacturer or vendor of the traffic-control signal monitoring devices. The compensation paid by the governing authority for such devices shall be based on the value of such equipment and shall not be based on the number of citations issued or the revenue generated by such devices.

(i) Charges for violations based on evidence obtained from a traffic-control signal monitoring device shall not be made by a law enforcement agency unless the law enforcement agency employs at least one full-time certified peace officer.

(j) A traffic-control signal monitoring device shall not be used to produce any photograph, microphotograph, electronic image, or videotape showing the identity of any person in a motor vehicle.

(k) A governing authority utilizing traffic-control signal monitoring devices shall at all times cooperate fully with the Department of Transportation. The department is authorized, at any time, to inspect traffic-control signal monitoring devices used by a governing authority and any records pertaining to revenues collected from the use of such devices.

(*l*) A permit may be amended at any time by amended application submitted by a governing authority. The request to amend an application and to add a new intersection to the list of authorized intersections for the operation of a traffic-control signal monitoring device shall be considered by the department in the same manner as original permit applications.

(m) A permit shall be reviewed by the Department of Transportation once every three years from the date of issuance or date of the most recent extension unless the permit has been revoked or suspended by the department. The review shall be conducted in the same manner as the original permit application.

(n) The department is authorized to set reasonable application fees to compensate the department for necessary costs in issuing, amending, or reviewing a permit to operate traffic-control signal monitoring devices.

(*o*) Any governing authority operating a traffic-control signal monitoring device on December 31, 2008, shall have until January 1, 2010, to obtain a permit for the operation of such device as required by this Code section.

Laws 2001, p. 770, § 4; Laws 2003, Act 246, § 3, eff. July 1, 2003; Laws 2004, Act 530, § 2, eff. July 1, 2004; Laws 2008, Act 799, § 4, eff. Dec. 31, 2008.

§ 40–14–22. Timing of signal testing of devices for accuracy

The timing of any traffic-control signal which is being monitored by a traffic-control signal monitoring device shall conform to regulations promulgated by the Department of Transportation pursuant to Code Section 32–6–50. The duration of the yellow or red light of any traffic-control device at which a traffic-control signal monitoring device is installed shall not be decreased prior to the installation of a device or during the time for which the device is operated. The Department of Transportation shall establish minimal yellow light change interval times for traffic-control devices at intersections where a traffic-control signal monitoring device is utilized. The minimal yellow light change interval time shall be established in accordance with nationally recognized engineering standards, and any such established time shall not be less than the recognized national standard plus one additional second. Each governing authority using a traffic-control signal monitoring device shall at its own expense test the device for accuracy at regular intervals and record and maintain the results of each test. Such test results shall be public records subject to inspection as provided by Article 4 of Chapter 18 of Title 50. Each such test shall be made in accordance with the manufacturer's recommended procedure. Any such device not meeting the manufacturer's minimum accuracy requirements shall be removed from service and thereafter shall not be used by the governing authority, nor shall any charges for violations based on evidence from such device be made by a law enforcement agency, until such device has been serviced and calibrated at the expense of the governing authority by a qualified technician.

Laws 2001, p. 770, § 4; Laws 2008, Act 799, § 5, eff. Dec. 31, 2008.

§ 40–14–23. Warning signs that traffic-control signal monitoring devices are being employed

Each governing authority using traffic-control signal monitoring devices shall erect signs on every highway which comprises a part of the state highway system at that point on the highway which intersects the jurisdictional limits of the governing authority. A sign shall be erected also by such entity on each public road on the approach to the next traffic-control signal for such road when a traffic-control signal monitoring device is monitoring such next signal for such road and signs shall also be erected at any other location required by the Department of Transportation. Such signs shall be of a design specified by the Department of Transportation in accordance with nationally recognized standards.

Laws 2001, p. 770, § 4; Laws 2008, Act 799, § 6, eff. Dec. 31, 2008.

§ 40–14–24. Reports on use of devices

(a) Each governing authority using any traffic-control signal monitoring device shall submit not later than February 1 of each year a report on such use during the preceding calendar year to the Department of Transportation. Such report shall include, without limitation:

(1) A description of the locations where traffic-control signal monitoring devices were used;

(2) The number of violations recorded at each location and in the aggregate on a monthly basis;

(3) The total number of citations issued;

(4) The number of civil monetary penalties and total amount of such penalties paid after citation without contest;

(5) The number of violations adjudicated and results of such adjudications, including a breakdown of dispositions made;

(6) The total amount of civil monetary penalties paid; and

(7) The quality of the adjudication process and its results.

(b) If any governing authority fails to provide the report provided for in subsection (a) of this Code section all revenues generated from the operation of any traffic-control signal monitoring device from the date the report was due shall be forwarded to the general fund of the state. The governing authority shall not be entitled to retain any revenue until the annual report is filed and accepted by the Department of Transportation.

(c) The Department of Transportation shall forward copies of all reports to the offices of the Governor, Lieutenant Governor, and the Speaker of the House by March 1 of each year. The department shall also forward to the offices of the Governor, Lieutenant Governor, and the Speaker of the House a complete list of all traffic-control signal monitoring devices currently in use.

Laws 2001, p. 770, § 4; Laws 2003, Act 246, § 4, eff. July 1, 2003; Laws 2008, Act 799, § 7, eff. Dec. 31, 2008.

§ 40–14–25. Complaints; presumptions; violations by governing authorities

(a) Complaints surrounding the use and operation of traffic-control signal monitoring devices by governing authorities, including the use by a governing authority for any purpose other than the promotion of the public health, welfare, and safety or in a manner which violates this article or violates its operating permit, may be made to the commissioner of transportation. The commissioner or the commissioner's designee is authorized to conduct an investigation into the acts and practices of the governing authority with respect to the use of traffic-control signal monitoring devices. If, as a result of this investigation, there is evidence to substantiate a violation of this article or the rules and regulations of the Department of Transportation, the department may take any action deemed necessary to prevent further misconduct or violations, including denying an application for a permit or suspension or revocation of a permit.

(b) There shall be a rebuttable presumption that a governing authority is using traffic-control signal monitoring devices for purposes other than the promotion of the public health, welfare, and safety if such devices are used by a governing authority without a valid permit issued by the Department of Transportation or in violation of any requirement of this article or the rules and regulations of the department.

(c) Where a violation of this article by a governing authority or any law enforcement agency enforcing the use of traffic-control signal monitoring devices on behalf of such governing authority is substantiated, the Department of Transportation may order that revenues generated from the use of traffic-control signal monitoring devices during the time of such violation or misconduct shall be remitted to the state's general fund. The department's order to remit funds shall be a continuous order until the violation is corrected by the governing authority as determined by the department. Any governing authority failing to abide by such order shall be liable for interest and costs, including reasonable attorney fees, incurred in the enforcement of the order. Jurisdiction for enforcing the department's order shall be in the Superior Court of Fulton County.

Laws 2008, Act 799, § 8, eff. Dec. 31, 2008; Laws 2009, Act 8, § 40, eff. April 14, 2009.

§ 40–14–26. Denial or revocation of permit; reconsideration of revoked permit

(a) Upon issuance by the commissioner of transportation of an order denying an application for or suspending or revoking a traffic-control signal monitoring device permit, the governing authority affected shall be afforded a hearing, to be held within 30 days of the effective date of the order. The hearing shall be held before the commissioner of the department or his or her designee, and, within 30 days following the hearing, the governing authority affected shall be served with a written decision announcing whether the permit shall remain denied, suspended, or revoked or whether it shall be granted or reinstated.

(b) Only after the expiration of three years following the revocation of a traffic-control signal monitoring device permit shall the governing authority make application, upon a change of circumstances being shown, to the commissioner of transportation for a reconsideration of whether the governing authority should be permitted to use traffic-control signal monitoring devices.

Laws 2008, Act 799, § 8, eff. Dec. 31, 2008; Laws 2009, Act 8, § 40, eff. April 14, 2009.

CHAPTER 15

MOTORCYCLE OPERATOR SAFETY TRAINING PROGRAM

Section

§ 40–15–1. Definitions

As used in this chapter, the term:

(1) "Board" means the Board of Driver Services.

(2) "Commissioner" means the commissioner of driver services.

(3) "Coordinator" means the state–wide motorcycle safety coordinator provided for in Code Section 40–15–4.

(4) "Department" means the Department of Driver Services.

(5) "Motorcycle" means every motor vehicle having a seat or saddle for the use of the rider and designed to travel on not more than three wheels in contact with the ground, but excluding a tractor and a moped.

(6) "Operator" means any person who drives or is in actual physical control of a motorcycle.

(7) "Program" means a motorcycle operator safety training program provided for in Code Section 40–15–2.

Laws 1984, p. 644, § 1; Laws 1986, p. 181, § 1; Laws 1997, p. 143, § 40; Laws 1997, p. 1505, § 1; Laws 2000, p. 951, § 8–1; Laws 2005, Act 68, § 23–2, eff. July 1, 2005.

§ 40–15–2. Establishment and operation of program

(a)(1) The department is authorized to set up, establish, and operate a motorcycle operator safety training program for the purpose of assisting motorcycle operators to meet the requirements for licensed driving of motorcycles in this state.

(2) The coordinator, with the approval of the commissioner, shall be authorized to set up, establish, and operate additional motorcycle operator safety training programs.

(b) Any such programs shall provide courses on motorcycle operator safety. The programs shall be based on the Motorcycle Safety Foundation Motorcycle Rider Course or its equivalent in quality, utility, and merit.

(c) The department shall issue a certificate of completion to each person who satisfactorily completes the motorcycle operator safety training program.

Laws 1984, p. 644, § 1; Laws 1986, p. 181, § 1; Laws 1992, p. 6, § 40; Laws 1997, p. 1505, § 2.

§ 40–15–3. Rules and regulations

The board is authorized to adopt, promulgate, and establish rules and regulations for the operation of any motorcycle operator safety training program; to provide for the entrance and enrollment of students; to prescribe fees for the course; and to prescribe the ages, requirements, and conditions under which students may be received for instruction in any such program.

Laws 1984, p. 644, § 1; Laws 1986, p. 181, § 1.

§ 40–15–4. Motorcycle safety coordinator

(a) The commissioner shall appoint a state-wide motorcycle safety coordinator who shall carry out and enforce the provisions of this chapter and the rules and regulations of the department. The coordinator shall be placed in the unclassified service of the State Personnel Administration and shall serve at the pleasure of the commissioner.

(b) The coordinator shall also be authorized to:

(1) Promote motorcycle safety throughout the state;

(2) Provide consultation to the various departments of state government and local political subdivisions relating to motorcycle safety; and

(3) Do any other thing deemed necessary by the commissioner to promote motorcycle safety in the state.

Laws 1984, p. 644, § 1; Laws 1986, p. 181, § 1; Laws 1994, p. 97, § 40; Laws 1997, p. 143, § 40; Laws 1997, p. 1505, § 3; Laws 2009, Act 155, § 1, eff. July 1, 2009.

§ 40–15–5. Instructors, qualifications

Every person who desires to qualify as an instructor in a motorcycle operator safety training program shall meet the following requirements:

(1) Be of good moral character;

(2) Give satisfactory performance on a written, oral, performance, or combination examination administered by the coordinator testing both knowledge of the field of motorcycle operator education and skills necessary to instruct and impart motorcycle driving skills and safety to students. The instructor training program shall provide for a course of instruction based on the Motorcycle Safety Foundation's Instructor Course or its equivalent in quality, utility, and merit. This course of instruction shall be held periodically based on the applications received and the need for instructors, and an examination fee prescribed by the coordinator shall be charged;

(3) Be physically able to operate safely a motorcycle and to instruct others in the operation of motorcycles; and

(4) Hold a valid Class M driver's license.

Laws 1984, p. 644, § 1; Laws 1986, p. 181, § 1; Laws 1994, p. 97, § 40.

CHAPTER 16

DEPARTMENT OF DRIVER SERVICES

§ 40–16–1. Definitions

As used in this chapter, the term:

(1) "Board" means the Board of Driver Services.

(2) "Commissioner" means the commissioner of driver services.

(3) "Department" means the Department of Driver Services.

Laws 2000, p. 951, § 1–1; Laws 2005, Act 68, § 1–1, eff. July 1, 2005.

§ 40–16–2. Creation of Department; powers and duties

(a) There is created the Department of Driver Services. The Department of Driver Services shall be a successor agency to and continuation of the former Department of Motor Vehicle Safety. The department shall be the agency primarily responsible for:

(1) Administration of the laws and regulations relating to drivers' licenses, as provided for in Chapter 5 of this title;

(2) Administration of the laws and regulations relating to proof of financial responsibility, as provided for in Chapter 9 of this title;

(3) Administration of laws relating to ignition interlock devices for use by driving under the influence offenders;

(4) Administration of laws relating to driver training schools, driver improvement clinics, DUI Alcohol or Drug Use Risk Reduction Programs, and commercial driving schools;

(5) Administration of laws relating to motorcycle safety programs;

(6) Administration of laws and regulations relating to issuance of limousine chauffeur permits; and

(7) Administration of any other laws specifically providing for their administration by the department.

(b) Responsibility for the following functions formerly exercised by the Department of Motor Vehicle Safety is transferred as follows:

(1) Promulgation of regulations relating to the size and the weights of motor vehicles, trailers, and loads as provided for in Article 2 of Chapter 6 of Title 32 shall be vested in the Department of Transportation; and administrative enforcement of such regulations and the law enforcement function of apprehending and citing violators of such laws and regulations are transferred to the Department of Public Safety, as well as the function of promulgating regulations relative to its enforcement function;

(2) Enforcement of laws and regulations relating to licensing and fuel tax registration requirements is transferred to the Department of Public Safety;

(3) Administration of laws and regulations relating to certification of motor carriers and limousine carriers is transferred to the Public Service Commission and administration of laws and regulations relating to carrier registration and registration and titling of vehicles is transferred to the Department of Revenue;

(4) Administration of laws relating to motor vehicle franchise practices is transferred to the Department of Revenue;

(5) Administration of laws relating to handicapped parking permits is transferred to the Department of Revenue;

(6) Responsibility for establishment of safety standards for motor vehicles and motor vehicle components is generally transferred to the Department of Public Safety except as may be specifically otherwise provided by law;

(7) Administration of laws relating to hazardous materials carriers is transferred to the Department of Public Safety;

(8) Enforcement of all state laws on the following properties owned or controlled by the Department of Transportation or the State Road and Tollway Authority is transferred to the Department of Public Safety: rest areas, truck-weighing stations or checkpoints, wayside parks, parking facilities, toll facilities, and any buildings and grounds for public equipment and personnel used for or engaged in administration, construction, or maintenance of the public roads or research pertaining thereto;

(9) Enforcement of Code Section 16–10–24, relating to obstructing or hindering law enforcement officers is transferred to the Department of Public Safety;

(10) Enforcement of Code Sections 32–9–4 and 40–6–54, relating to designation of restricted travel lanes is transferred to the Department of Public Safety;

(11) Enforcement of Code Section 16–11–43, relating to obstructing highways, streets, sidewalks, or other public passages, on any public road which is part of the state highway system is transferred to the Department of Public Safety;

(12) Enforcement of Code Section 16–7–43, relating to littering public or private property or waters, on any public road which is part of the state highway system is transferred to the Department of Public Safety; and

(13) Enforcement of Code Section 16–7–24, relating to interference with government property, on any public road which is part of the state highway system is transferred to the Department of Public Safety.

(c) In the performance of its duties, the department shall be required to comply with all applicable federal laws and rules and regulations and shall certify that the state is in compliance with all provisions and requirements of all applicable federal–aid acts and programs.

Laws 2000, p. 951, § 1–1; Laws 2000, p. 1199, § 1; Laws 2001, p. 1251, § 2–1; Laws 2003, Act 200, § 14, eff. Oct. 1, 2003; Laws 2005, Act 68, § 1–1, eff. July 1, 2005.

Historical and Statutory Notes

The Code Commission redesignated subsec. (e) of § 32–6–29, added by Laws 2000, p. 1199, § 1, as subsec. (d) of this section, effective when this section becomes effective. See § 28–9–5.

The 2003 amendment by Act 200, in subsec. (b), inserted "or designated by the commissioner".

Laws 2003, Act 200, § 15 provides:

"This Act shall become effective on October 1, 2003."

In 2005, the Code Commission redesignated the second subsec. (b) as subsec. (c). See § 28–9–5.

§ 40–16–2.1. Reports to General Assembly; reorganization of Department and other activities

Annual reports shall be provided to the General Assembly by the affected departments with respect to the reorganization provided for in Code Section 40–16–2 and with respect to other activities of the departments as follows:

(1) The Department of Driver Services shall provide an annual report which shall include, together with other information deemed pertinent by the department, service metrics clearly indicating the department's ability to meet public demand for its services; and

(2) The Department of Public Safety shall provide an annual report which shall include, together with other information deemed pertinent by the department, the records of the department with respect to safety inspections and citations issued.

Laws 2005, Act 68, § 1–1, eff. July 1, 2005.

§ 40–16–3. Board of Drivers Services and commissioner of driver services

(a) The department shall be under the direction, control, and management of the Board of Driver Services and the commissioner of driver services. The commissioner shall be appointed by and serve at the pleasure of the board.

(b)(1) The Board of Driver Services shall be a successor to and continuation of the Board of Motor Vehicle Safety and shall consist of nine members. Five members shall be appointed by the Governor and their terms shall expire as follows: two members on June 30, 2003, and June 30 of each sixth year thereafter; two members on June 30, 2005, and June 30 of each sixth year thereafter; and one member on June 30, 2007, and June 30 of each sixth year thereafter. Two members shall be appointed by the Lieutenant Governor and their terms shall expire as follows: one member on June 30, 2003, and June 30 of each sixth year thereafter and one member on June 30, 2006, and June 30 of each sixth year thereafter. Two members shall be appointed by the Speaker of the House and their terms shall expire as follows: one member on June 30, 2003, and June 30 of each sixth year thereafter and one member on June 30, 2006, and June 30 of each sixth year thereafter. All members except for the initial appointees shall serve for terms of six years and until their successors are appointed and qualified.

(2) All members serving on the Board of Motor Vehicle Safety as of May 2, 2005, shall continue to serve as members of the Board of Driver Services for the remainder of their original terms of office and shall if necessary hold over beyond the end of those terms until successors are appointed and qualified.

(c) The Governor shall designate a member to serve as chairperson of the board. The chairperson's term as chairperson shall expire on June 30, 2003, and June 30 of each second year thereafter. The board may elect other officers from among its membership and may establish bylaws for the conduct of its business.

(d) The members of the board shall receive no salary for their service on the board but any member who is not otherwise a state officer or employee shall receive a per diem expense allowance as provided in subsection (b) of Code Section 45–7–21.

(e) The board shall be the general policy-making body for the Department of Driver Services; and the commissioner shall be the chief executive officer of the department, subject to the policies established by the board. All rules and regulations promulgated by the commissioner must be approved by the board before they take effect.

(f) The commissioner shall receive an annual salary to be set by the board which shall be his or her total compensation for services as commissioner. The commissioner shall be reimbursed for all actual and necessary expenses incurred by him or her in carrying out his or her official duties.

(g) The commissioner shall take and subscribe before the board an oath to discharge faithfully and impartially the duties of such office, which oath shall be in addition to the oath required of all civil officers.

Laws 2000, p. 951, § 1–1; Laws 2002, p. 837, § 1; Laws 2005, Act 68, § 1–1; Laws 2006, Act 453, § 40, eff. April 14, 2006.

Historical and Statutory Notes

Laws 2005, Act 68, § 32–1, provides:

"This Act shall become effective July 1, 2005, except that the provisions of paragraph (2) of subsection (b) of Code Section 40–16–3 shall become effective upon the approval of this Act by the Governor or upon its becoming law without such approval."

§ 40–16–4. Officers and employees of department

(a) The commissioner shall establish such units within the department as he or she deems proper for its administration and shall designate persons to be directors and assistant directors of such units to exercise such authority as he or she may delegate to them in writing.

(b) The commissioner shall have the authority to employ as many persons as he or she deems necessary for the administration of the department and for the discharge of the duties of his or her office. He or she shall issue all necessary directions, instructions, orders, and rules applicable to such persons. He or she shall have authority, as he or she deems proper, to employ, assign, compensate, and discharge employees of the department within the limitations of the department's appropriation and the restrictions set forth by law.

(c) All employees of the department shall be compensated upon a fixed salary basis and no person shall be compensated for services to the department on a commission or contingent fee basis.

(d) Neither the commissioner nor any officer or employee of the department shall be given or receive any fee, compensation, loan, gift, or other thing of value in addition to the compensation and expense allowance provided by law for any service or pretended service either rendered or to be rendered as commissioner or as an officer or employee of the department.

(e)(1) The commissioner shall have the authority to appoint and employ 30 investigators who shall be certified peace officers pursuant to the provisions of Chapter 8 of Title 35, the "Georgia Peace Officer Standards and Training Act."

(2) The investigators of the department shall have jurisdiction throughout this state with such duties and powers as are prescribed by law.

(f) The department shall have the authority to contract and make cooperative and rental agreements with the United States government; any county, municipality, or local government, or any combination thereof; any public or private corporation or firm; or any public authority, agency, commission, or institution, including agencies of state government, for the purpose of obtaining goods, materials, and services needed to perform any of the duties, responsibilities, or functions vested in the department.

Laws 2000, p. 951, § 1–1; Laws 2005, Act 68, § 1–1, eff. July 1, 2005; Laws 2007, Act 44, § 7, eff. Jan. 1, 2008; Laws 2010, Act 633, § 26, eff. July 1, 2010.

Historical and Statutory Notes

Laws 2007, Act 44, § 8, provides:

"This Act shall become effective on January 1, 2008."

§ 40–16–5. Rules and regulations; forms

(a) Subject to approval by the board, the commissioner shall have the power to make and publish in print or electronically reasonable rules and regulations not inconsistent with this title or other laws or with the Constitution of this state or of the United States for the administration of this chapter or any law which it is his or her duty to administer.

(b) The commissioner may prescribe forms as he or she deems necessary for the administration and enforcement of this chapter or any law which it is his or her duty to administer.

(c) The authority granted to the commissioner pursuant to this Code section shall be exercised at all times in conformity with Chapter 13 of Title 50, the "Georgia Administrative Procedure Act"; provided, however, that regulations governing commercial driver licensing may be adopted by administrative order referencing compatible federal regulations or standards without compliance with the procedural requirements of Chapter 13 of Title 50; provided, further, that such compatible federal regulations or standards shall be maintained on file by the department and made available for inspection and copying by the public, by means including but limited to posting on the department's computer Internet site.

(d) Rules and regulations previously adopted which relate to functions performed by the Department of Driver Services shall remain of full force and effect as rules and regulations of the Department of Driver Services until amended, repealed, or superseded by rules or regulations adopted by the commissioner of driver services. The following rules and regulations shall remain of full force and effect as rules and regulations of the referenced department until amended, repealed, or superseded by rules or regulations adopted by the referenced department:

(1) All rules and regulations previously adopted which relate to functions transferred under this chapter to the Department of Transportation from the Department of Motor Vehicle Safety;

(2) All rules and regulations previously adopted which relate to functions transferred under this chapter to the Public Service Commission from the Department of Motor Vehicle Safety;

(3) All rules and regulations previously adopted which relate to functions transferred under this chapter to the Department of Public Safety from the Department of Motor Vehicle Safety;

(4) All rules and regulations previously adopted which relate to functions transferred under this chapter to the Department of Revenue from the Department of Motor Vehicle Safety; and

(5) All rules and regulations previously adopted which relate to functions transferred under this chapter from the Department of Human Resources (now known as the Department of Behavioral Health and Developmental Disabilities for these purposes) to the Department of Driver Services.

(e) All valid licenses, permits, certificates, and similar authorizations previously issued by any department or agency with respect to any function transferred as provided in this chapter shall continue in effect until the same expire by their terms unless they are suspended, revoked, or otherwise made ineffective as provided by law.

Laws 2000, p. 951, § 1–1; Laws 2002, p. 1378, § 7; Laws 2005, Act 68, § 1–1, eff. July 1, 2005; Laws 2009, Act 102, § 3–22, eff. July 1, 2009; Laws 2010, Act 615, § 10, eff. June 3, 2010.

§ 40–16–5.1. Use of department motor vehicles and other equipment by off-duty employees

(a) Except as otherwise provided in this Code section, no department motor vehicles shall be used by any investigators employed by the department except in the discharge of official duties. Any other equipment shall be used only with the express written approval of the commissioner.

(b) The commissioner may adopt rules and regulations governing the use of equipment. The commissioner may adopt rules and regulations pursuant to which investigators employed by the department may use a department motor vehicle while working an approved off–duty job, provided that any such use shall comply with such conditions as may be imposed by the commissioner, which conditions shall include but shall not be limited to a finding of public benefit and reimbursement to the department by the employer or employee for use of the vehicle.

(c) At no time will an off–duty employee be allowed use of a department motor vehicle at any political function of any kind.

Laws 2002, p. 838, § 4; Laws 2005, Act 68, § 1–1, eff. July 1, 2005.

§ 40–16–6. Civil monetary penalties

(a) To the extent specifically authorized by law, the commissioner may pursuant to rule or regulation specify and impose civil monetary penalties for violations of laws, rules, and regulations administered by the commissioner. Except as may be hereafter authorized by law, the maximum amount of any such monetary penalty shall not exceed the maximum penalty authorized by law or rule or regulation for the same violation immediately prior to July 1, 2005.

(b) All proceedings for the imposition of civil monetary penalties by the commissioner and other contested cases to be decided by or under authority of the commissioner shall be subject to Chapter 13 of Title 50, the "Georgia Administrative Procedure Act." All such administrative proceedings which are pending on July 1, 2005, under laws the administration of which is transferred from the commissioner of motor vehicle safety to another enforcement agency shall be transferred to the jurisdiction of such other enforcement agency as of July 1, 2005.

(c) The amendment of this chapter and the Act by which it is amended shall not affect or abate the status as a crime of any act or omission which occurred prior to July 1, 2005, nor shall the prosecution of such crime be abated as a result of such amendment.

Laws 2000, p. 951, § 1–1; Laws 2002, p. 415, § 40; Laws 2003, Act 29, § 5, eff. May 15, 2003; Laws 2005, Act 68, § 1–1, eff. July 1, 2005.

Historical and Statutory Notes

The 2003 amendment by Act 29 added subsec. (d).

The 2005 amendment by Act 68, rewrote the section which had read:

"(a) The commissioner may pursuant to rule or regulation specify and impose civil monetary penalties for violations of laws, rules, and regulations administered by the commissioner. Except as may be hereafter authorized by law, the maximum amount of any such monetary penalty shall not exceed the maximum penalty authorized by law or rule or regulation for the same violation immediately prior to July 1, 2001.

"(b) All proceedings for the imposition of civil monetary penalties by the commissioner and other contested cases to be decided by or under authority of the commissioner shall be subject to Chapter 13 of Title 50, the 'Georgia Administrative Procedure Act.' All such administrative proceedings which are pending on July 1, 2001, under laws the administration of which is transferred to the commissioner shall be transferred to the jurisdiction of the commissioner as of July 1, 2001.

"(c) The enactment of this chapter and the Act by which it is enacted shall not affect or abate the status as a crime of any act or omission which occurred prior to July 1, 2001, nor shall the prosecution of such crime be abated as a result of such enactment.

"(d)(1) As used in this subsection, the term 'anhydrous ammonia' means any substance identified to contain the compound ammonia which is capable of being utilized in the production of methamphetamine or any other controlled substance.

"(2) Any person, firm, or corporation transporting methamphetamine, amphetamine, any mixture containing either methamphetamine or amphetamine, anhydrous ammonia, or any mixture containing anhydrous ammonia shall be subject to all rules and regulations promulgated by the commissioner pursuant to Code Section 46–7–26 governing the safe operation of motor vehicles and drivers and the safe transportation of hazardous materials.

"(3) Notwithstanding the provisions of subsection (a) of this Code section, the commissioner may impose civil monetary penalties in an amount not to exceed $25,000.00 for each violation of any rules and regulations promulgated pursuant to Code Section 46–7–26 with respect to persons transporting methamphetamine, amphetamine, any mixture containing either methamphetamine or amphetamine, anhydrous ammonia, or any mixture containing anhydrous ammonia."

§ 40–16–7. Appropriations of funds; disposition of fines and forfeitures

(a) The department shall be a budget unit to which funds may be appropriated as provided in the "Budget Act," Part 1 of Article 4 of Chapter 12 of Title 45. The department shall be an independent and distinct department of state government. The duties of the department shall be performed by that department and not by any other agency of state government, and the department shall not perform the duties of any other agency of state government. The position of commissioner of driver services shall be a separate and distinct position from any other position in state government. The duties of the commissioner shall be performed by the commissioner and not by any other officer of state government, and the commissioner shall not perform the duties of any other officer of state government.

(b) Appropriations for functions transferred to and from the Department of Motor Vehicle Safety and other departments may be transferred to and from such departments as provided for in Code Section 45–12–90, relating to disposition of appropriations for duties, purposes, and objects which have been transferred. Personnel, equipment, and facilities previously employed for such transferred functions shall likewise be transferred to the appropriate departments. Contracts relating to functions transferred to and from the Department of Motor Vehicle Safety and other departments, and any rights of renewal under such contracts, shall also be transferred to the appropriate departments. Any disagreement between such departments as to any such transfers shall be determined by the Governor.

(c) Except as specifically provided otherwise by law, all fines and forfeitures collected for criminal violations cited by the department's investigators shall, after deduction from the total fine or forfeiture of the amounts due the Peace Officers' Annuity and Benefit Fund and the Sheriffs' Retirement Fund of Georgia and any other deductions specified by law, be paid by the clerk of the court into the fine and forfeiture fund of the county treasurer in the same manner and subject to the same rules of distribution as other fines and forfeitures.

Laws 2000, p. 951, § 1–1; Laws 2005, Act 68, § 1–1, eff. July 1, 2005.

§ 40–16–8. Governor's Commercial Transportation Advisory Committee

(a) There shall be established, within the department, the Governor's Commercial Transportation Advisory Committee. The purpose of this committee is to advise the Governor on all laws, regulations, rules, and other matters related to the operation within this state of motor carriers, including private carriers, as defined in Code Section 46–1–1. The committee shall also serve as a forum for representatives of the motor carrier industry to meet with representatives of the various state agencies responsible for the oversight, enforcement, taxation, and regulation of the commercial transportation industry.

(b) The committee shall consist of the following members:

(1) The commissioner of driver services or his or her designee;

(2) The commissioner of public safety or his or her designee;

(3) The commissioner of transportation or his or her designee;

(4) The state revenue commissioner or his or her designee;

(5) The Speaker of the House or his or her designee;

(6) The chairperson of the House Transportation Committee, who shall chair the committee;

(7) The President Pro Tempore of the Senate or his or her designee;

(8) The chairperson of the Senate Transportation Committee;

(9) The president of the Georgia Motor Trucking Association or his or her designee;

(10) Five industry representatives appointed by the Governor; and

(11) The Governor or his or her designee who shall serve ex officio.

(c) Each member of the committee shall serve until replaced. All members of the committee shall have equal voting privileges on all matters brought before the committee. The committee shall meet at least three times per year at a date and time set by the chairperson. The chairperson shall prepare an agenda for each meeting and shall distribute the agenda for each meeting at least 20 days prior to the date of the meeting.

Laws 2005, Act 66, § 1, eff. May 2, 2005; Laws 2006, Act 453, § 40, eff. April 14, 2006.

TITLE 42

PENAL INSTITUTIONS

CHAPTER 1

GENERAL PROVISIONS

§ 42–1–12. Registration of sex offenders

(a) As used in this article, the term:

(1) "Address" means the street or route address of the sexual offender's residence. For purposes of this Code section, the term shall not mean a post office box.

(2) "Appropriate official" means:

(A) With respect to a sexual offender who is sentenced to probation without any sentence of incarceration in the state prison system or who is sentenced pursuant to Article 3 of Chapter 8 of this title, relating to first offenders, the Division of Probation of the Department of Corrections;

(B) With respect to a sexual offender who is sentenced to a period of incarceration in a prison under the jurisdiction of the Department of Corrections and who is subsequently released from prison or placed on probation, the commissioner of corrections or his or her designee;

(C) With respect to a sexual offender who is placed on parole, the chairperson of the State Board of Pardons and Paroles or his or her designee; and

(D) With respect to a sexual offender who is placed on probation through a private probation agency, the director of the private probation agency or his or her designee.

(3) "Area where minors congregate" shall include all public and private parks and recreation facilities, playgrounds, skating rinks, neighborhood centers, gymnasiums, school bus stops, public libraries, and public and community swimming pools.

(4) "Assessment criteria" means the tests that the board members use to determine the likelihood that a sexual offender will commit another criminal offense against a victim who is a minor or commit a dangerous sexual offense.

(5) "Board" means the Sexual Offender Registration Review Board.

(6) "Child care facility" means all public and private pre-kindergarten facilities, day-care centers, child care learning centers, preschool facilities, and long-term care facilities for children.

(7) "Church" means a place of public religious worship.

(8) "Conviction" includes a final judgment of conviction entered upon a verdict or finding of guilty of a crime, a plea of guilty, or a plea of nolo contendere. A defendant who is discharged without adjudication of guilt and who is not considered to have a criminal conviction pursuant to Article 3 of Chapter 8 of this title, relating to first offenders, shall be subject to the registration requirements of this Code section for the period of time prior to the defendant's discharge after completion of his or her sentence or upon the defendant being adjudicated guilty. Unless otherwise required by federal law, a defendant who is discharged without adjudication of guilt and who is not considered to have a criminal conviction pursuant to Article 3 of Chapter 8 of this title, relating to first offenders, shall not be subject to the registration requirements of this Code section upon the defendant's discharge.

(9)(A) "Criminal offense against a victim who is a minor" with respect to convictions occurring on or before June 30, 2001, means any criminal offense under Title 16 or any offense under federal law or the laws of another state or territory of the United States which consists of:

(i) Kidnapping of a minor, except by a parent;

(ii) False imprisonment of a minor, except by a parent;

(iii) Criminal sexual conduct toward a minor;

(iv) Solicitation of a minor to engage in sexual conduct;

(v) Use of a minor in a sexual performance;

(vi) Solicitation of a minor to practice prostitution; or

(vii) Any conviction resulting from an underlying sexual offense against a victim who is a minor.

(B) "Criminal offense against a victim who is a minor" with respect to convictions occurring after June 30, 2001, means any criminal offense under Title 16 or any offense under federal law or the laws of another state or territory of the United States which consists of:

(i) Kidnapping of a minor, except by a parent;

(ii) False imprisonment of a minor, except by a parent;

(iii) Criminal sexual conduct toward a minor;

(iv) Solicitation of a minor to engage in sexual conduct;

(v) Use of a minor in a sexual performance;

(vi) Solicitation of a minor to practice prostitution;

(vii) Use of a minor to engage in any sexually explicit conduct to produce any visual medium depicting such conduct;

(viii) Creating, publishing, selling, distributing, or possessing any material depicting a minor or a portion of a minor's body engaged in sexually explicit conduct;

(ix) Transmitting, making, selling, buying, or disseminating by means of a computer any descriptive or identifying information regarding a child for the purpose of offering or soliciting sexual conduct of or with a child or the visual depicting of such conduct;

(x) Conspiracy to transport, ship, receive, or distribute visual depictions of minors engaged in sexually explicit conduct; or

(xi) Any conduct which, by its nature, is a sexual offense against a victim who is a minor.

(C) For purposes of this paragraph, a conviction for a misdemeanor shall not be considered a criminal offense against a victim who is a minor, and conduct which is adjudicated in juvenile court shall not be considered a criminal offense against a victim who is a minor.

(10)(A) "Dangerous sexual offense" with respect to convictions occurring on or before June 30, 2006, means any criminal offense, or the attempt to commit any criminal offense, under Title 16 as specified in this paragraph or any offense under federal law or the laws of another state or territory of the United States which consists of the same or similar elements of the following offenses:

(i) Aggravated assault with the intent to rape in violation of Code Section 16–5–21;

(ii) Rape in violation of Code Section 16–6–1;

(iii) Aggravated sodomy in violation of Code Section 16–6–2;

(iv) Aggravated child molestation in violation of Code Section 16–6–4; or

(v) Aggravated sexual battery in violation of Code Section 16–6–22.2.

(B) "Dangerous sexual offense" with respect to convictions occurring after June 30, 2006, means any criminal offense, or the attempt to commit any criminal offense, under Title 16 as specified in this paragraph or any offense under federal law or the laws of another state or territory of the United States which consists of the same or similar elements of the following offenses:

(i) Aggravated assault with the intent to rape in violation of Code Section 16–5–21;

(ii) Kidnapping in violation of Code Section 16–5–40 which involves a victim who is less than 14 years of age, except by a parent;

(iii) False imprisonment in violation of Code Section 16–5–41 which involves a victim who is less than 14 years of age, except by a parent;

(iv) Rape in violation of Code Section 16–6–1;

(v) Sodomy in violation of Code Section 16–6–2;

(vi) Aggravated sodomy in violation of Code Section 16–6–2;

(vii) Statutory rape in violation of Code Section 16–6–3, if the individual convicted of the offense is 21 years of age or older;

(viii) Child molestation in violation of Code Section 16–6–4;

(ix) Aggravated child molestation in violation of Code Section 16–6–4, unless the person was convicted of a misdemeanor offense;

(x) Enticing a child for indecent purposes in violation of Code Section 16–6–5;

(xi) Sexual assault against persons in custody in violation of Code Section 16–6–5.1;

(xii) Incest in violation of Code Section 16–6–22;

(xiii) A second conviction for sexual battery in violation of Code Section 16–6–22.1;

(xiv) Aggravated sexual battery in violation of Code Section 16–6–22.2;

(xv) Sexual exploitation of children in violation of Code Section 16–12–100;

(xvi) Electronically furnishing obscene material to minors in violation of Code Section 16–12–100.1;

(xvii) Computer pornography and child exploitation prevention in violation of Code Section 16–12–100.2;

(xviii) Obscene telephone contact in violation of Code Section 16–12–100. 3; or

(xix) Any conduct which, by its nature, is a sexual offense against a victim who is a minor or an attempt to commit a sexual offense against a victim who is a minor.

(C) For purposes of this paragraph, a conviction for a misdemeanor shall not be considered a dangerous sexual offense, and conduct which is adjudicated in juvenile court shall not be considered a dangerous sexual offense.

(10.1) "Day-care center" shall have the same meaning as set forth in paragraph (4) of Code Section 20–1A–2.

(11) "Institution of higher education" means a private or public community college, state university, state college, or independent postsecondary institution.

(12) "Level I risk assessment classification" means the sexual offender is a low sex offense risk and low recidivism risk for future sexual offenses.

(13) "Level II risk assessment classification" means the sexual offender is an intermediate sex offense risk and intermediate recidivism risk for future sexual offenses and includes all sexual offenders who do not meet the criteria for classification either as a sexually dangerous predator or for Level I risk assessment.

(14) "Minor" means any individual under the age of 18 years and any individual that the sexual offender believed at the time of the offense was under the age of 18 years if such individual was the victim of an offense.

(15) "Public and community swimming pools" includes municipal, school, hotel, motel, or any pool to which access is granted in exchange for payment of a daily fee. The term includes apartment complex pools, country club pools, or subdivision pools which are open only to residents of the subdivision and their guests. This term does not include a private pool or hot tub serving a single-family dwelling and used only by the residents of the dwelling and their guests.

(16) "Required registration information" means:

(A) Name; social security number; age; race; sex; date of birth; height; weight; hair color; eye color; fingerprints; and photograph;

(B) Address, within this state or out of state, and, if applicable in addition to the address, a rural route address and a post office box;

(C) If the place of residence is a motor vehicle or trailer, the vehicle identification number, the license tag number, and a description, including color scheme, of the motor vehicle or trailer;

(D) If the place of residence is a mobile home, the mobile home location permit number; the name and address of the owner of the home; a description, including the color scheme of the mobile home; and, if applicable, a description of where the mobile home is located on the property;

(E) If the place of residence is a manufactured home, the name and address of the owner of the home; a description, including the color scheme of the manufactured home; and, if applicable, a description of where the manufactured home is located on the property;

(F) If the place of residence is a vessel, live-aboard vessel, or houseboat, the hull identification number; the manufacturer's serial number; the name of the vessel, live-aboard vessel, or houseboat; the registration number; and a description, including color scheme, of the vessel, live-aboard vessel, or houseboat;

(F.1) If the place of residence is the status of homelessness, information as provided under paragraph (2.1) of subsection (f) of this Code section;

(G) Date of employment, place of any employment, and address of employer;

(H) Place of vocation and address of the place of vocation;

(I) Vehicle make, model, color, and license tag number;

(J) If enrolled, employed, or carrying on a vocation at an institution of higher education in this state, the name, address, and county of each institution, including each campus attended, and enrollment or employment status; and

(K) The name of the crime or crimes for which the sexual offender is registering and the date released from prison or placed on probation, parole, or supervised release.

(17) "Risk assessment classification" means the notification level into which a sexual offender is placed based on the board's assessment.

(18) "School" means all public and private kindergarten, elementary, and secondary schools.

(19) "School bus stop" means a school bus stop as designated by local school boards of education or by a private school.

(20) "Sexual offender" means any individual:

(A) Who has been convicted of a criminal offense against a victim who is a minor or any dangerous sexual offense;

(B) Who has been convicted under the laws of another state or territory, under the laws of the United States, under the Uniform Code of Military Justice, or in a tribal court of a criminal offense against a victim who is a minor or a dangerous sexual offense; or

(C) Who is required to register pursuant to subsection (e) of this Code section.

(21) "Sexually dangerous predator" means a sexual offender:

(A) Who was designated as a sexually violent predator between July 1, 1996, and June 30, 2006; or

(B) Who is determined by the Sexual Offender Registration Review Board to be at risk of perpetrating any future dangerous sexual offense.

(22) "Vocation" means any full-time, part-time, or volunteer employment with or without compensation exceeding 14 consecutive days or for an aggregate period of time exceeding 30 days during any calendar year.

(b) Before a sexual offender who is required to register under this Code section is released from prison or placed on parole, supervised release, or probation, the appropriate official shall:

(1) Inform the sexual offender of the obligation to register, the amount of the registration fee, and how to maintain registration;

(2) Obtain the information necessary for the required registration information;

(3) Inform the sexual offender that, if the sexual offender changes any of the required registration information, other than residence address, the sexual offender shall give the new information to the sheriff of the county with whom the sexual offender is registered within 72 hours of the change of information; if the information is the sexual offender's new residence address, the sexual offender shall give the information to the sheriff of the county with whom the sexual offender last registered within 72 hours prior to moving and to the sheriff of the county to which the sexual offender is moving within 72 hours prior to moving;

(4) Inform the sexual offender that he or she shall also register in any state where he or she is employed, carries on a vocation, or is a student;

(5) Inform the sexual offender that, if he or she changes residence to another state, the sexual offender shall register the new address with the sheriff of the county with whom the sexual offender last registered and that the sexual offender shall also register with a designated law enforcement agency in the new state within 72 hours after establishing residence in the new state;

(6) Obtain fingerprints and a current photograph of the sexual offender;

(7) Require the sexual offender to read and sign a form stating that the obligations of the sexual offender have been explained;

(8) Obtain and forward any information obtained from the clerk of court pursuant to Code Section 42–5–50 to the sheriff's office of the county in which the sexual offender will reside; and

(9) If required by Code Section 42–1–14, place any required electronic monitoring system on the sexually dangerous predator and explain its operation and cost.

(c) The Department of Corrections shall:

(1) Forward to the Georgia Bureau of Investigation a copy of the form stating that the obligations of the sexual offender have been explained;

(2) Forward any required registration information to the Georgia Bureau of Investigation;

(3) Forward the sexual offender's fingerprints and photograph to the sheriff's office of the county where the sexual offender is going to reside;

(4) Inform the board and the prosecuting attorney for the jurisdiction in which a sexual offender was convicted of the impending release of a sexual offender at least eight months prior to such release so as to facilitate compliance with Code Section 42–1–14; and

(5) Keep all records of sexual offenders in a secure facility until official proof of death of a registered sexual offender; thereafter, the records shall be destroyed in accordance with Code Sections 15–1–10, 15–6–62, and 15–6–62.1.

(d) No sexual offender shall be released from prison or placed on parole, supervised release, or probation until:

(1) The appropriate official has provided the Georgia Bureau of Investigation and the sheriff's office in the county where the sexual offender will be residing with the sexual offender's required registration information and risk assessment classification level; and

(2) The sexual offender's name has been added to the list of sexual offenders maintained by the Georgia Bureau of Investigation and the sheriff's office as required by this Code section.

(e) Registration pursuant to this Code section shall be required by any individual who:

(1) Is convicted on or after July 1, 1996, of a criminal offense against a victim who is a minor;

(2) Is convicted on or after July 1, 1996, of a dangerous sexual offense;

(3) Has previously been convicted of a criminal offense against a victim who is a minor and may be released from prison or placed on parole, supervised release, or probation on or after July 1, 1996;

(4) Has previously been convicted of a sexually violent offense or dangerous sexual offense and may be released from prison or placed on parole, supervised release, or probation on or after July 1, 1996;

(5) Is a resident of Georgia who intends to reside in this state and who is convicted under the laws of another state or the United States, under the Uniform Code of Military Justice, or in a tribal court of a sexually violent offense, a criminal offense against a victim who is a minor on or after July 1, 1999, or a dangerous sexual offense on or after July 1, 1996;

(6) Is a nonresident who changes residence from another state or territory of the United States or any other place to Georgia who is required to register as a sexual offender under federal law, military law, tribal law, or the laws of another state or territory or who has been convicted in this state of a criminal offense against a victim who is a minor or any dangerous sexual offense;

(7) Is a nonresident sexual offender who enters this state for the purpose of employment or any other reason for a period exceeding 14 consecutive days or for an aggregate period of time exceeding 30 days during any calendar year regardless of whether such sexual offender is required to register under federal law, military law, tribal law, or the laws of another state or territory; or

(8) Is a nonresident sexual offender who enters this state for the purpose of attending school as a full-time or part-time student regardless of whether such sexual offender is required to register under federal law, military law, tribal law, or the laws of another state or territory.

(f) Any sexual offender required to register under this Code section shall:

(1) Provide the required registration information to the appropriate official before being released from prison or placed on parole, supervised release, or probation;

(2) Register in person with the sheriff of the county in which the sexual offender resides within 72 hours after the sexual offender's release from prison or placement on parole, supervised release, probation, or entry into this state;

(2.1) In the case of a sexual offender whose place of residence is the status of homelessness, in lieu of the requirements of paragraph (2) of this subsection, register in person with the sheriff of the county in which the sexual offender sleeps within 72 hours after the sexual offender's release from prison or placement on parole, supervised release, probation, or entry into this state and provide the location where he or she sleeps;

(3) Maintain the required registration information with the sheriff of each county in which the sexual offender resides or sleeps;

(4) Renew the required registration information with the sheriff of the county in which the sexual offender resides or sleeps by reporting in person to the sheriff within 72 hours prior to such offender's birthday each year to be photographed and fingerprinted;

(5) Update the required registration information with the sheriff of the county in which the sexual offender resides within 72 hours of any change to the required registration information, other than where he or she resides or sleeps if such person is homeless. If the information is the sexual offender's new address, the sexual offender shall give the information regarding the sexual offender's new address to the sheriff of the county in which the sexual offender last registered within 72 hours prior to any change of address and to the sheriff of the county to which the sexual offender is moving within 72 hours prior to establishing such new address. If the sexual offender is homeless and the information is the sexual offender's new sleeping location, within 72 hours of changing sleeping locations, the sexual offender shall give the information regarding the sexual offender's new sleeping location to the sheriff of the county in which the sexual offender last registered, and if the county has changed, to the sheriff of the county to which the sexual offender has moved; and

(6) Continue to comply with the registration requirements of this Code section for the entire life of the sexual offender, excluding ensuing periods of incarceration.

(g) A sexual offender required to register under this Code section may petition to be released from the registration requirements and from the residency or employment restrictions of this Code section in accordance with the provisions of Code Section 42-1-19.

(h)(1) The appropriate official or sheriff shall, within 72 hours after receipt of the required registration information, forward such information to the Georgia Bureau of Investigation. Once the data is entered into the Criminal Justice Information System by the appropriate official or sheriff, the Georgia Crime Information Center shall notify the sheriff of the sexual offender's county of residence, either permanent or temporary, the sheriff of the county of employment, and the sheriff of the county where the sexual offender attends an institution of higher education within 24 hours of entering the data or any change to the data.

(2) The Georgia Bureau of Investigation shall:

(A) Transmit all information, including the conviction data and fingerprints, to the Federal Bureau of Investigation within 24 hours of entering the data;

(B) Establish operating policies and procedures concerning record ownership, quality, verification, modification, and cancellation; and

(C) Perform mail out and verification duties as follows:

(i) Send each month Criminal Justice Information System network messages to sheriffs listing sexual offenders due for verification;

(ii) Create a photo image file from original entries and provide such entries to sheriffs to assist in sexual offender identification and verification;

(iii) Mail a nonforwardable verification form to the last reported address of the sexual offender within ten days prior to the sexual offender's birthday;

(iv) If the sexual offender changes residence to another state, notify the law enforcement agency with which the sexual offender shall register in the new state; and

(v) Maintain records required under this Code section.

(i) The sheriff's office in each county shall:

(1) Prepare and maintain a list of all sexual offenders and sexually dangerous predators residing in each county. Such list shall include the sexual offender's name; age; physical description; address; crime of conviction, including conviction date and the jurisdiction of the conviction; photograph; and the risk assessment classification level provided by the board, and an explanation of how the board classifies sexual offenders and sexually dangerous predators;

(2) Electronically submit and update all information provided by the sexual offender within two business days to the Georgia Bureau of Investigation in a manner prescribed by the Georgia Bureau of Investigation;

(3) Maintain and provide a list, manually or electronically, of every sexual offender residing in each county so that it may be available for inspection:

(A) In the sheriff's office;

(B) In any county administrative building;

(C) In the main administrative building for any municipal corporation;

(D) In the office of the clerk of the superior court so that such list is available to the public; and

(E) On a website maintained by the sheriff of the county for the posting of general information;

(4) Update the public notices required by paragraph (3) of this Code section within two business days of the receipt of such information;

(5) Inform the public of the presence of sexual offenders in each community;

(6) Update the list of sexual offenders residing in the county upon receipt of new information affecting the residence address of a sexual offender or upon the registration of a sexual offender moving into the county by virtue of release from prison, relocation from another county, conviction in another state, federal court, military tribunal, or tribal court. Such list, and any additions to such list, shall be delivered, within 72 hours of updating the list of sexual offenders residing in the county, to all schools or institutions of higher education located in the county;

(7) Within 72 hours of the receipt of changed required registration information, notify the Georgia Bureau of Investigation through the Criminal Justice Information System of each change of information;

(8) Retain the verification form stating that the sexual offender still resides at the address last reported;

(9) Enforce the criminal provisions of this Code section. The sheriff may request the assistance of the Georgia Bureau of Investigation to enforce the provisions of this Code section;

(10) Cooperate and communicate with other sheriffs' offices in this state and in the United States to maintain current data on the location of sexual offenders;

(11) Determine the appropriate time of day for reporting by sexual offenders, which shall be consistent with the reporting requirements of this Code section;

(12) If required by Code Section 42-1-14, place any electronic monitoring system on the sexually dangerous predator and explain its operation and cost;

(13) Provide current information on names and addresses of all registered sexual offenders to campus police with jurisdiction for the campus of an institution of higher education if the campus is within the sheriff's jurisdiction; and

(14) Collect the annual $250.00 registration fee from the sexual offender and transmit such fees to the state for deposit into the general fund.

(j)(1) The sheriff of the county where the sexual offender resides or last registered shall be the primary law enforcement official charged with communicating the whereabouts of the sexual offender and any changes in required registration information to the sheriff's office of the county or counties where the sexual offender is employed, volunteers, attends an institution of higher education, or moves.

(2) The sheriff's office may post the list of sexual offenders in any public building in addition to those locations enumerated in subsection (h) of this Code section.

(k) The Georgia Crime Information Center shall create the Criminal Justice Information System network transaction screens by which appropriate officials shall enter original data required by this Code section. Screens shall also be created for sheriffs' offices for the entry of record confirmation data; employment; changes of residence, institutions of higher education, or employment; or other pertinent data to assist in sexual offender identification.

(*l*)(1) On at least an annual basis, the Department of Education shall obtain from the Georgia Bureau of Investigation a complete list of the names and addresses of all registered sexual offenders and shall provide access to such information, accompanied by a hold harmless provision, to each school in this state. In addition, the Department of Education shall provide information to each school in this state on accessing and retrieving from the Georgia Bureau of Investigation's website a list of the names and addresses of all registered sexual offenders.

(2) On at least an annual basis, the Department of Early Care and Learning shall provide current information to all child care programs regulated pursuant to Code Section 20–1A–10 and to all child care learning centers, day-care, group day-care, and family day-care programs regulated pursuant to Code Section 49–5–12 on accessing and retrieving from the Georgia Bureau of Investigation's website a list of the names and addresses of all registered sexual offenders and shall include, on a continuing basis, such information with each application for licensure, commissioning, or registration for early care and education programs.

(3) On at least an annual basis, the Department of Human Services shall provide current information to all long-term care facilities for children on accessing and retrieving from the Georgia Bureau of Investigation's website a list of the names and addresses of all registered sexual offenders.

(m) Within ten days of the filing of a defendant's discharge and exoneration of guilt pursuant to Article 3 of Chapter 8 of this title, the clerk of court shall transmit the order of discharge and exoneration to the Georgia Bureau of Investigation and any sheriff maintaining records required under this Code section.

(n) Any individual who:

(1) Is required to register under this Code section and who fails to comply with the requirements of this Code section;

(2) Provides false information; or

(3) Fails to respond directly to the sheriff of the county where he or she resides or sleeps within 72 hours prior to such individual's birthday shall be guilty of a felony and shall be punished by imprisonment for not less than one nor more than 30 years; provided, however, that upon the conviction of the second offense under this subsection, the defendant shall be punished by imprisonment for not less than five nor more than 30 years.

(*o*) The information collected pursuant to this Code section shall be treated as private data except that:

(1) Such information may be disclosed to law enforcement agencies for law enforcement purposes;

(2) Such information may be disclosed to government agencies conducting confidential background checks; and

(3) The Georgia Bureau of Investigation or any sheriff maintaining records required under this Code section shall, in addition to the requirements of this Code section to inform the public of the presence of sexual offenders in each community, release such other relevant information collected under this Code section that is necessary to protect the public concerning sexual offenders required to register under this Code section, except that the identity of a victim of an offense that requires registration under this Code section shall not be released.

(p) The Board of Public Safety is authorized to promulgate rules and regulations necessary for the Georgia Bureau of Investigation and the Georgia Crime Information Center to implement and carry out the provisions of this Code section.

(q) Law enforcement agencies, employees of law enforcement agencies, and state officials shall be immune from liability for good faith conduct under this article.

Laws 1996, p. 1520, § 1; Laws 1997, p. 143, § 42; Laws 1997, p. 380, § 1; Laws 1998, p. 831, § 1; Laws 1999, p. 81, § 42; Laws 1999, p. 837, § 1; Laws 2001, p. 1004, § 1; Laws 2002, p. 571, § 1; Laws 2002, p. 1400, §§ 1, 2; Laws 2003, Act 9, § 42, eff. May 14, 2003; Laws 2003, Act 47, § 1, eff. May 28, 2003; Laws 2004, Act 565, § 5, eff. Oct. 1, 2004; Laws 2004, Act 790, §§ 1, 2, eff. July 1, 2004; Laws 2005, Act 71, § 1, eff. July 1, 2005; Laws 2006, Act 453, § 42, eff. April 14, 2006; Laws 2006, Act 571, § 24, eff. July 1, 2006; Laws 2008, Act 582, §§ 2, 3, eff. July 1, 2008; Laws 2008, Act 715, §§ 3, 4, eff. Jan. 1, 2009; Laws 2009, Act 8, § 42, eff. April 14, 2009; Laws 2009, Act 102, § 2–2, eff. July 1, 2009; Laws 2010, Act 388, § 1, eff. July 1, 2010; Laws 2010, Act 389, §§ 5 to 11, eff. May 20, 2010.

Validity

This section has been held unconstitutional, in part, in the case of White v. Baker, 2010, ___ F.Supp.2d ___, 2010 WL 1009758.

Historical and Statutory Notes

The 2003 amendment by Act 9, in subsec. (b), substituted "Criminal Justice Information System" for "criminal justice information system" in subpar. (3)(B); in subsec. (c), substituted "Criminal Justice Information System" for "criminal justice information system" in par. (1); in subsec. (c), substituted "U.S.C. Section" for "U.S.C." throughout par. (3), and substituted "Internet website" for "Web page" in par. (3); and in subsec. (c.1), substituted "one-time" for "one time" in pars. (2) and (3).

The 2003 amendment by Act 47, in subsec. (a), par. (4), substituted "distributing, or possessing any material depicting a minor or a portion of a minor's body" for "or distributing any material depicting a minor" in subpar. (B)(viii), inserted a new subpar. (B)(x), and redesignated former (B)(x) as (B)(xi); in subsec. (b), substituted "new address, employment, and vocation" for "new address and employment" in par. (3)(D), inserted "and status" following "permanent address in the person's state of residence, employment and vocation address" in par. (3)(E), and inserted new par. (4); in subsec. (c), substituted "The requirements of this paragraph" for "This paragraph" in par. (2), and substituted "Internet website" for "Web page" in par. (3); in subsec. (d), par. (1), substituted "Upon receipt of the verification form the person shall be required to report in person to the sheriff of the person's county of residence within ten days of the anniversary date" for "The person shall be required as a condition of parole or probation to respond directly to the sheriff within ten days after receipt of the form" in subpar. (B), inserted a new subpar. (D), and redesignated former subpar. (D) as (E); in subsec. (g), inserted ", during which time all registration requirements shall be stayed. Upon release from incarceration, the person shall report to the sheriff of the person's county of residence within ten days from the date of release from incarceration"; added new subsec. (m); and made nonsubstantive changes throughout.

The 2004 amendment by Act 565 rewrote subsec. (c.1), par, (3) which had read:

"[(c.1)] (3) The Department of Human Resources shall provide, on a one-time basis, information to all day care and group day care programs regulated pursuant to Code Section 49–5–12 on how to access and retrieve from the Georgia Bureau of Investigation's Internet website a list of the names and addresses of all registered sexual offenders and shall include, on a continuing basis, such information with each application for licensure."

The 2004 amendment by Act 790, in subsec. (a), rewrote par. (3) and added par. (4), subpar. (D); and added subsec. (n). Prior to amendment, subsec. (a), par. (3), had read:

"[(a)] (3) 'Conviction' includes a final judgment of conviction entered upon a verdict or finding of guilty of a crime, a plea of guilty, or a plea of nolo contendere. Unless otherwise required by federal law, a defendant who is discharged without adjudication of guilt and who is not considered to have a criminal conviction pursuant to Article 3 of Chapter 8 of this title, relating to first offenders, shall not be subject to the registration requirements of this Code section."

Laws 2004, Act 790, § 3, provides:

"This Act shall become effective on July 1, 2004, and shall apply to sentences imposed on or after July 1, 2004."

The 2005 amendment by Act 71, in subsec. (a), added new par. (.1), substituted "Appropriate official" for "Appropriate state official" and added new subpar. (D) in par. (1), in par. (4), deleted subpar. (D) which had read "For purposes of this paragraph, 'criminal offense against a victim who is a minor' shall not include conduct which, by its nature, is a sexual offense against a victim who is 13 years of age or older when the defendant enters a first offender plea pursuant to Article 3 of Chapter 8 of this title.", added new par. (5.1), substituted "or Code Section 16–5–21, relating to aggravated assault with intent to rape" for "or an offense that has as its element engaging in physical contact with another person with intent to commit such and offense" in par. (7); in subsec. (b), added "as a sex offender" in division (1)(A)(i), substituted "Sexual Offender Registration Review Board" for "Sexual Offender Review Board" in the introductory portion of subpar. (2)(C), and rewrote subpar. (3)(D). Prior to amendment subpar. (b)(3)(D) had read:

"(D) Any person changing residence from another state or territory of the United States to Georgia who is required to register under federal law or the laws of another state, territory, or tribal authority or who has been convicted of an offense in another state, territory, or tribal authority which would require registration under this Code section if committed in this state shall comply with the registration requirements of this Code section. Such person shall register the new address, employment, and vocation information with the appropriate sheriff of the county as specified in subsection (c) of this Code section not later than ten days after the date of establishing residency in this state. Upon the person's registration with the sheriff of the county of new residence, the sheriff or his or her designee shall forward the registration information to the Georgia Bureau of Investigation. The sheriff or his or her designee shall obtain any needed information concerning the registrant, including fingerprints and a photograph of the person if such fingerprints and photograph have not previously been obtained within the State of Georgia. In addition, the sheriff or his or her designee shall inform the person of the duty to report any change of address as otherwise required in this Code section. The Georgia Bureau of Investigation shall forward such information in the manner described in subsection (c) of this Code section."

In 2005, the Code Commission, in subpar. (b)(3)(E), a comma was inserted prior to "not later than ten days" and "register with the sheriff" in the first sentence of the undesignated paragraph. See § 28–9–5.

The 2006 amendment by Act 453, a provision contained in a correction bill, substituted "appropriate official" for "appropriate state official" throughout subsecs. (b) and (c); substituted "appropriate officials" for "appropriate state officials" in subsec. (b); and, in subsec. (c.1), par. (2), substituted "The Department of Early Care and Learning" for "The Office of School Readiness", and substituted "pursuant to Code Section 20–1A–8" for "pursuant to Code Section 20–1A–5".

The 2006 amendment by Act 571 rewrote the section which, as it had been amended by Laws 2005, Act 71, had read:

"(a) As used in this Code section, the term:

"(.1) 'Address' means the street or route address of the person's residence. For purposes of this Code section, the term does not mean a post office box.

"(1) 'Appropriate official' means:

"(A) With respect to an offender who is sentenced to probation without any sentence of incarceration in the state prison system or who is sentenced pursuant to Article 3 of Chapter 8 of this title, relating to first offenders, the Division of Probation of the Department of Corrections;

"(B) With respect to an offender who is sentenced to a period of incarceration in a prison under the jurisdiction of the Department of Corrections and who is subsequently released from prison or placed on probation, the commissioner of corrections or his or her designee;

"(C) With respect to an offender who is placed on parole, the chairperson of the State Board of Pardons and Paroles or his or her designee; and

"(D) With respect to an offender who is placed on probation through a private probation agency, the director of the private probation agency or his or her designee.

"(2) 'Board' means the Sexual Offender Registration Review Board.

"(2.1) 'Change in enrollment status' or 'change in employment status' means the commencement or termination of enrollment or employment.

"(2.2) 'Change in vocation status' means the commencement or termination of a vocation.

"(3) 'Conviction' includes a final judgment of conviction entered upon a verdict or finding of guilty of a crime, a plea of guilty, or a plea of nolo contendere. A defendant who is discharged without adjudication of guilt and who is not considered to have a criminal conviction pursuant to Article 3 of Chapter 8 of this title, relating to first offenders, shall be subject to the registration requirements of this Code section for the period of time prior to the defendant's discharge after completion of his or her sentence or upon the defendant being adjudicated guilty. Unless otherwise required by federal law, a defendant who is discharged without adjudication of guilt and who is not considered to have a criminal conviction pursuant to Article 3 of Chapter 8 of this title, relating to first offenders, shall not be subject to the registration requirements of this Code section upon the defendant's discharge.

"(4)(A) 'Criminal offense against a victim who is a minor' with respect to convictions occurring on or before June 30, 2001, means any criminal offense under Title 16 or any offense under federal law or the laws of another state or territory of the United States which consists of:

"(i) Kidnapping of a minor, except by a parent;

"(ii) False imprisonment of a minor, except by a parent;

"(iii) Criminal sexual conduct toward a minor;

"(iv) Solicitation of a minor to engage in sexual conduct;

"(v) Use of a minor in a sexual performance;

"(vi) Solicitation of a minor to practice prostitution; or

"(vii) Any conviction resulting from an underlying sexual offense against a victim who is a minor.

(B) 'Criminal offense against a victim who is a minor' with respect to convictions occurring after June 30, 2001, means any criminal offense under Title 16 or any offense under federal law or the laws of another state or territory of the United States which consists of:

"(i) Kidnapping of a minor, except by a parent;

"(ii) False imprisonment of a minor, except by a parent;

"(iii) Criminal sexual conduct toward a minor;

"(iv) Solicitation of a minor to engage in sexual conduct;

"(v) Use of a minor in a sexual performance;

"(vi) Solicitation of a minor to practice prostitution;

"(vii) Use of a minor to engage in any sexually explicit conduct to produce any visual medium depicting such conduct;

"(viii) Creating, publishing, selling, distributing, or possessing any material depicting a minor or a portion of a minor's body engaged in sexually explicit conduct;

"(ix) Transmitting, making, selling, buying, or disseminating by means of a computer any descriptive or identifying information regarding a child for the purpose of offering or soliciting sexual conduct of or with a child or the visual depicting of such conduct;

"(x) Conspiracy to transport, ship, receive, or distribute visual depictions of minors engaged in sexually explicit conduct; or

"(xi) Any conduct which, by its nature, is a sexual offense against a minor.

"(C) For purposes of this paragraph, conduct which is criminal only because of the age of the victim shall not be considered a criminal offense if the perpetrator is 18 years of age or younger.

"(4.1) 'Institution of higher education' means a community college, state university, state college, or independent postsecondary institution.

"(5) 'Mental abnormality' means a congenital or acquired condition of a person that affects the emotional or volitional capacity of the person in a manner that predisposes that person to the commission of criminal sexual acts to a degree that makes the person a menace to the health and safety of other persons.

"(5.1) 'Minor' means any person under the age of 18 years and any person that the offender believed at the time of the offense was under the age of 18 years if such person was the victim of an offense.

"(6) 'Predatory' means an act directed at a stranger or a person with whom a relationship has been established or promoted for the primary purpose of victimization.

"(7) 'Sexually violent offense' means a conviction for violation of Code Section 16–6–1, relating to rape; Code Section 16–6–2, relating to aggravated sodomy; Code Section 16–6–4, relating to aggravated child molestation; Code Section 16–6–22.2, relating to aggravated sexual battery; or Code Section 16–5–21, relating to aggravated assault with intent to rape; or a conviction in a federal court, military court, tribal court, or court of another state or territory for any offense which under the laws of this state would be classified as a violation of a Code section listed in this paragraph.

"(8) 'Sexually violent predator' means a person who has been convicted on or after July 1, 1996, of a sexually violent offense and who suffers from a mental abnormality or personality disorder or attitude that places the person at risk of perpetrating any future predatory sexually violent offenses.

"(9) 'Vocation' means any sort of full-time, part-time, or volunteer employment with or without compensation exceeding 14 consecutive days or for an aggregate period of time exceeding 30 days during any calendar year.

"(b)(1)(A)(i) On and after July 1, 1996, a person who is convicted of a criminal offense against a victim who is a minor or who is convicted of a sexually violent offense shall register as a sex offender within ten days after his or her release from prison or placement on parole, supervised release, or probation his or her name and current address; place of employment and vocation, if any; the crime of which convicted; school name and address, if any; and the date released from prison or placed on parole, supervised release, or probation with the appropriate sheriff's office as specified in subsection (c) of this Code section in the county where such person will reside for the time period specified in subsection (g) of this Code section.

"(ii) A person who has previously been convicted of a criminal offense against a victim who is a minor or who has previously been convicted of a sexually violent offense and who is released from prison or placed on parole, supervised release, or probation on or after July 1, 1996, shall register within ten days after such release or placement his or her name and current address; place of employment and vocation, if any; the crime of which convicted; school name and address, if any; and the date released from prison or placed on parole, supervised release, or probation with the appropriate sheriff's office as specified in subsection (c) of this Code section in the county where such person will reside for the time period specified in subsection (g) of this Code section.

"(iii) On and after July 1, 1999, any resident of Georgia who is convicted under the laws of another state or territory, under the laws of the United States, under the Uniform Code of Military Justice, or in a tribal court of a sexually violent offense or a criminal offense against a victim who is a minor shall register within ten days after his or her release from prison or placement on parole, supervised release, or probation. The information such an offender is required to register shall include his or her name and current address; place of employment and vocation, if any; the crime of which convicted; school name and address, if any; and the date released from prison or placed on parole, supervised release, or probation. Such an offender shall register with the appropriate sheriff's office as specified in subsection (c) of this Code section in the county where such person will reside for the time period specified in subsection (g) of this Code section.

"(B) A person who is a sexually violent predator shall register within ten days after his or her release from prison or placement on parole, supervised release, or probation the information required under subparagraph (A) of this paragraph with the appropriate sheriff's office as specified in subsection (c) of this Code section in the county where such person will reside. The sheriff may prepare a list of such sexual predators providing each person's name, address, and photograph. The sheriff shall update the list periodically and may post such list in a prominent and visible location in the sheriff's office and each city hall or primary administration building of every incorporated municipality within the county. Such list shall also be made available upon request to any public or private elementary, secondary, or postsecondary school or educational institution located in the county.

"(2)(A) Upon a determination that an offender is guilty of a sexually violent offense, the court may request a report from the Sexual Offender Registration Review Board as to the likelihood that the offender suffers from a mental abnormality or personality disorder that would make the person likely to engage in a predatory sexually violent offense. The report shall be requested as a matter of course for any offender with a history of sexually violent offenses. The court shall provide the Sexual Offender Registration Review Board with any information available to assist the board in rendering an opinion. The board shall have 60 days from receipt of the court's request to respond with its report. After receiving a recommendation from the Sexual Offender Registration Review Board that a convicted sexually violent offender be classified as a sexually violent predator, the sentencing court shall so inform the offender and shall set a date to conduct a hearing affording the offender the opportunity to present testimony or evidence relevant to the recommended classification. After the hearing and within 60 days of receiving the report, the court shall issue a ruling as to whether or not the offender shall be classified as a sexually violent predator. If the court determines the offender to be a sexually violent predator, such fact shall be communicated in writing to the appropriate state official and to the Georgia Bureau of Investigation.

"(B) The Sexual Offender Registration Review Board shall be composed of three professionals licensed under Title 43 and knowledgeable in the field of the behavior and treatment of sexual offenders; at least one representative from a victims' rights advocacy group or agency; and at least two representatives from law enforcement, each of whom is either employed by a law enforcement agency as a certified peace officer under Title 35 or retired from such employment. The members of such board shall be appointed by the commissioner of human resources for terms of four years. Members of the board shall take office on the first day of September immediately following the expired term of that office and shall serve for a term of four years and until the appointment of their respective successors. No member shall serve on the board more than two consecutive terms. Vacancies occurring on the board, other than those caused by expiration of a term of office, shall be filled in the same manner as the original appointment to the position vacated for the remainder of the unexpired term and until a successor is appointed. Members shall be entitled to an expense allowance and travel cost reimbursement the same as members of certain other boards and commissions as provided in Code Section 45–7–21.

"(C) The Sexual Offender Registration Review Board shall be attached to the Department of Human Resources for administrative purposes and provided there is adequate funding provided shall:

"(i) Exercise its quasi–judicial, rule–making, or policy–making functions independently of the department and without approval or control of the department;

"(ii) Prepare its budget, if any, and submit its budgetary requests, if any, through the department; and

"(iii) Hire its own personnel if authorized by the Constitution of this state or by statute or if the General Assembly provides or authorizes the expenditure of funds therefor.

"(3)(A) If a person who is required to register under this Code section is released from prison or placed on parole, supervised release, or probation, the appropriate state official shall:

"(i) Inform the person of the duty to register and obtain the information required under subparagraph (A) of paragraph (1) of this subsection for such registration;

"(ii) Inform the person that, if the person changes residence address, employment address, vocation address, school name, school address, or enrollment status, the person shall give the new information to the sheriff or sheriffs with whom the person last registered and the sheriff or sheriffs of the county to which the person is changing residence address, employment address, vocation address, school name, school address, or enrollment status, not later than ten days after the change of information. Following such notification, the sheriff's office shall notify immediately the Georgia Bureau of Investigation through the Criminal Justice Information System (CJIS) of each change of information;

"(iii) Inform the person that the person must register in any state where the person is employed or carries on a vocation or is a student;

"(iv) Inform the person that, if the person changes residence to another state, the person shall register the new address with the sheriff or sheriffs with whom the person last registered, and that the person shall also register with a designated law enforcement agency in the new state not later than ten days after establishing residence in the new state;

"(v) Obtain fingerprints and a photograph of the person if such fingerprints and photograph have not already been obtained in connection with the offense that triggered the initial registration; and

"(vi) Require the person to read and sign a form stating that the duty of the person to register under this Code section has been explained. A copy of this form and any other registration information furnished by the Department of Corrections shall be forwarded to the Georgia Bureau of Investigation.

"(B) In addition to the requirements of subparagraph (A) of this paragraph, for a person required to register under subparagraph (B) of paragraph (1) of this subsection, the appropriate state official shall obtain the name of the person; descriptive physical and behavioral information to assist law enforcement personnel in identifying the person; known current or proposed residence addresses of the person; place of employment, if any; offense history of the person; and documentation of any treatment received for any mental abnormality or personality disorder of the person; provided, however, that the appropriate state official shall not be required to obtain any information already on the Criminal Justice Information System of the Georgia Crime Information Center.

"(C) The Georgia Crime Information Center shall create the Criminal Justice Information System network transaction screens by which appropriate state officials shall enter original data required by this Code section including residence address, school name, school address, enrollment status, and employment and vocation address and status. Screens shall also be created for sheriffs' offices for the entry of record confirmation data; employment; changes of residence, school, or employment; or other pertinent data and to assist in offender identification.

"(D) Any person changing residence from another state or territory of the United States to Georgia shall be subject to the following registration requirements:

"(i) Any person changing residence from another state or territory of the United States to Georgia who is required to register under federal law or the laws of another state, territory, or tribal authority shall comply with the registration requirements of this Code section and register in this state regardless of when the conviction occurred.

"(ii) Any person changing residence from another state or territory of the United States to Georgia who has been convicted of an offense in another state, territory, or tribal authority which would require registration under this Code section if committed in this state shall comply with the registration requirements of this Code section regardless of when the conviction occurred.

"(iii) Any person who is subject to the registration requirements of this Code section shall register the new address, employment, and vocation information with the appropriate sheriff of the county as specified in subsection (c) of this Code section not later than ten days after the date of establishing residency in this state.

"(iv) Upon the person's registration with the sheriff of the county of new residence, the sheriff or the sheriff's designee shall forward the registration information to the Georgia Bureau of Investigation. The sheriff or the sheriff's designee shall obtain any needed information concerning the registrant, including fingerprints and a photograph of the person if such fingerprints and photograph have not previously been obtained within the State of Georgia. In addition, the sheriff or the sheriff's designee shall inform the person of the duty to report any change of address as otherwise required in this Code section. The Georgia Bureau of Investigation shall forward such information in the manner described in subsection (c) of this Code section.

"(v) Any person who is subject to the registration requirements of this Code section shall be required to register in Georgia for the remaining period of time established by the state of last registration, or for the period of time as set forth in subsection (g) of this Code section, whichever is longer.

"(vi) Any person who is designated in another state as a sexually violent predator and changes residency to Georgia shall also be designated as a sexually violent predator in this state and subject to subsection (g) of this Code section.

"(E) The following persons are also required to register:

"(i) Any nonresident who enters this state for the purpose of employment for a period exceeding 14 consecutive days or for an aggregate period of time exceeding 30 days during any calendar year and who is required to register under federal law, military law, tribal law, or the laws of another state or territory, which, based on an act, would require registration under this Code section; or

"(ii) Any nonresident who enters this state for the purpose of attending school as a full–time or part–time student and who is required to register under federal law, military law, tribal law, or the laws of another state or territory, which, based on an act, would require registration under this Code section.

"Any person required to register by this subparagraph shall, not later than ten days after the person enters the state, register with the sheriff of the county of his or her temporary address, with the sheriff of the county of his or her employment, and with the sheriff of the county in which the person is attending school. The information registered shall include the person's temporary address, permanent address in the person's state of residence, employment and vocation address and status, and school name, school address, and enrollment status. Upon the person's registration, the sheriff or the sheriff's designee shall forward the registration information to the Georgia Bureau of Investigation. The sheriff or the sheriff's designee shall obtain the fingerprints and photograph of the person, if the person's fingerprints and photograph have not previously been obtained in Georgia. The sheriff or the sheriff's designee shall inform the person of his or her duty to report any change in temporary residence, permanent residence, employment and vocation address and status, school name, school address, or enrollment status.

"(4) A person who is required to register under any provision of this Code section shall:

"(A) Report in person within ten days of release from prison, placement on probation, parole, or supervised release to the appropriate sheriff's office of the county or counties where the person resides, is employed, or attends school. A person who is so required to register must provide his or her street address to the sheriff of the person's county of residence;

"(B) Report in person within ten days to the appropriate sheriff or sheriffs if the person changes residence address, employment address, vocation address, school name, school address, or enrollment status;

"(C) In the event of a move to a new state, advise the sheriff of the county where the person last registered of his or her impending move within ten days of moving. He or she shall also report to the designated law enforcement agency in the new state of residence within ten days of arrival at the new residence;

"(D) Read and sign the offender registration notification form at the time of registration; and

"(E) Report in person to the sheriff of the person's county of residence within ten days of the anniversary date of the original registration with the offender's verification form from the Georgia Bureau of Investigation.

"(c)(1) The appropriate state official shall, within three days after receipt of information described in paragraph (3) of subsection (b) of this Code section, forward such information to the Georgia Bureau of Investigation. Once the data is entered into the Criminal Justice Information System by the appropriate state official or sheriff, the Georgia Crime Information Center, where appropriate, shall immediately notify the sheriff of the person's county of residence, either permanent or temporary, the sheriff of the county of employment, and the sheriff of the county where the person attends school. The Georgia Bureau of Investigation shall also immediately transmit the conviction data and fingerprints to the Federal Bureau of Investigation. It shall be the duty of the sheriff of each county within this state to maintain a register of the names and addresses of all registered offenders within the sheriff's jurisdiction whose names have been provided by the Georgia Bureau of Investigation to the sheriff under this Code section. The Georgia Bureau of Investigation shall establish operating policies and procedures concerning record ownership, quality, verification, modification, and cancellation and shall perform mail out and verification duties on a quarterly basis. The Georgia Bureau of Investigation shall send each month Criminal Justice Information System network messages to sheriffs listing offenders due for verification. The bureau shall also create a photo image file from original entries and provide such entries to sheriffs to assist in offender identification and verification.

"(2) Any person who is required to register under this Code section and who is enrolled, employed, or carries on a vocation at an institution of higher education in this state shall provide the name, address, and county of each institution including each campus attended and the person's position or enrollment status, as well as any change in enrollment, employment, or vocation status. The requirements of this paragraph shall be accomplished in a manner specified in subparagraphs (b)(1)(A), (b)(1)(B), (b)(3)(A), (b)(3)(D), and (b)(3)(E) of this Code section.

"(3) The Georgia Bureau of Investigation shall establish operating policies and procedures in order to provide prompt notice of offender registration and any change in status information contained in paragraph (2) of this subsection to any law enforcement agency having jurisdiction where an institution of higher education is located and to include notification to the campus police if appropriate for the institution of higher education. The law enforcement agency or agencies having jurisdiction where an institution of higher education is located shall provide a statement advising the campus community where law enforcement agency information may be obtained as provided by the state under 20 U.S.C. Section 1092 (f)(1) and 42 U.S.C. Section 1407 (j), concerning registered sex offenders. This information may be obtained at the law enforcement office of the institution, a local law enforcement agency with jurisdiction for the campus, or via the Georgia Bureau of Investigation's Internet website.

"(c.1)(1) On an annual basis, the Department of Education shall obtain from the Georgia Bureau of Investigation a complete list of the names and addresses of all registered sexual offenders and shall send such list, accompanied by a hold harmless provision, to each public elementary and secondary school in this state. In addition, the Department of Education shall provide information to each public elementary and secondary school in this state on how to access and retrieve from the Georgia Bureau of Investigation's Internet website a list of the names and addresses of all registered sexual offenders. The Department of Education shall make such information available to any private school upon request.

"(2) The Office of School Readiness shall provide, on a one–time basis, information to all child care programs regulated pursuant to Code Section 20–1A–5 on how to access and retrieve from the Georgia Bureau of Investigation's Internet website a list of the names and addresses of all registered sexual offenders and shall include, on a continuing basis, such information with each application for licensure.

"(3) The Department of Human Resources shall provide, on a one-time basis, information to all day-care, group day-care, and family day-care programs regulated on how to access and retrieve from the Georgia Bureau of Investigation's Internet website a list of the names and addresses of all registered sexual offenders. On and after October 1, 2004, the Department of Early Care and Learning shall include, on a continuing basis, such information with each application for licensure, commissioning, or registration for early care and education programs.

"(d)(1) For a person required to register under subparagraph (b)(1)(A) of this Code section, on each anniversary of the person's initial registration date during the period in which the person is required to register under this Code section, the following applies:

"(A) The Georgia Bureau of Investigation shall mail a nonforwardable verification form to the last reported address of the person;

"(B) Upon receipt of the verification form the person shall be required to report in person to the sheriff of the person's county of residence within ten days of the anniversary date;

"(C) The verification form stating that the person still resides at the address last reported to the Georgia Bureau of Investigation shall be signed by the person and retained by the sheriff;

"(D) The person shall report to the sheriff of the person's county of residence to be photographed every year within ten days of the anniversary date of the original registration; and

"(E) If the person fails to respond directly to the sheriff within ten days after receipt of the form, the person shall be in violation of this Code section.

"(2) The provisions of paragraph (1) of this subsection shall be applied to a person required to register under subparagraph (b)(1)(B) of this Code section, except that such person must verify the registration every 90 days after the date of the initial release on probation by the court or the initial release by the Department of Corrections or commencement of parole.

"(e) A change of address by a person required to register under this Code section reported to the Georgia Bureau of Investigation shall be immediately reported to the sheriff of the county where the person resides as set forth in subparagraph (b)(3)(E) of this Code section. The Georgia Bureau of Investigation shall, if the person changes residence to another state, notify the law enforcement agency with which the person must register in the new state.

"(f) A person who has been convicted of an offense which requires registration under this Code section shall register the new address with a designated law enforcement agency in another state to which the person moves not later than ten days after such person establishes residence in the new state if the new state has a registration requirement.

"(g) A person required to register under subparagraph (b)(1)(A) of this Code section shall continue to comply with this Code section, except during ensuing periods of incarceration, during which time all registration requirements shall be stayed. Upon release from incarceration, the person shall report to the sheriff of the person's county of residence within ten days from the date of release from incarceration, until:

"(1) Ten years have elapsed since the person was released from prison or placed on parole, supervised release, or probation; or

"(2) For the life of that person if that person:

"(A) Has one or more prior convictions for an offense described in subparagraph (a)(4)(A) and paragraph (7) of subsection (a) of this Code section;

"(B) Has been convicted of an aggravated offense described in paragraph (7) of subsection (a) of this Code section; or

"(C) Has been determined to be a sexually violent predator pursuant to subparagraph (b)(2)(A) of this Code section.

"(h) Any person who is required to register under this Code section and who fails to comply with the requirements of this Code section or who provides false information shall be guilty of a felony and shall be punished by imprisonment for not less than one nor more than three years; provided, however, that upon the conviction of the second or subsequent offense under this subsection, the defendant shall be punished by imprisonment for not less than one nor more than three years or by a fine in an amount of up to $100,000.00, or both.

"(i) The information collected under the state registration program shall be treated as private data except that:

"(1) Such information may be disclosed to law enforcement agencies for law enforcement purposes;

"(2) Such information may be disclosed to government agencies conducting confidential background checks;

"(3) The Georgia Bureau of Investigation or any sheriff maintaining records required under this Code section shall release relevant information collected under this Code section that is necessary to protect the public concerning those persons required to register under this Code section, except that the identity of a victim of an offense that requires registration under this Code section shall not be released. In addition to any other notice that may be necessary to protect the public, nothing in this Code section shall prevent any sheriff from posting this information in any public building in addition to those locations enumerated in subparagraph (b)(1)(B) of this Code section; and

"(4) It shall be the responsibility of the sheriff maintaining records required under this Code section to enforce the criminal provisions of this Code section. The sheriff may request the assistance of the Georgia Bureau of Investigation upon his or her discretion.

"(j) Law enforcement agencies, employees of law enforcement agencies, members of the Sexual Offender Registration Review Board, and state officials shall be immune from liability for good faith conduct under this Code section.

"(k) The provisions of this Code section shall be in addition to and not in lieu of the provisions of Code Section 42–9–44.1, relating to conditions for parole of sexual offenders.

"(*l*) The Board of Public Safety is authorized to promulgate rules and regulations necessary for the Georgia Bureau of Investigation and the Georgia Crime Information Center to implement and carry out the provisions of this Code section.

"(m) No cause of action shall arise against any real estate broker or any affiliated licensee of the broker or any person or entity or its employees which own property or any person or entity or its employees who provide property management services as defined in paragraph (7) of Code Section 43–40–1 for the failure to disclose in any real estate transaction any information which is provided or maintained or required to be provided or maintained in accordance with this Code section. No cause of action shall arise against any real estate broker or any affiliated licensee of the broker or any person or entity or its employees which own property or any person or entity or its employees who provide property management services as defined in paragraph (7) of Code Section 43–40–1 for revealing any information provided or maintained or required to be provided or maintained in accordance with this Code section.

"(n) Within ten days of the filing of a defendant's discharge and exoneration of guilt pursuant to Article 3 of Chapter 8 of this title, the clerk of court shall transmit the order of discharge and exoneration to the Georgia Bureau of Investigation and any sheriff maintaining records required under this Code section."

Laws 2006, Act 571, §§ 1 and 30, provide:

"SECTION 1. The General Assembly finds and declares that recidivist sexual offenders, sexual offenders who use physical violence, and sexual offenders who prey on children are sexual predators who present an extreme threat to the public safety. Many sexual offenders are extremely likely to use physical violence and to repeat their offenses; and some sexual offenders commit many offenses, have many more victims than are ever reported, and are prosecuted for only a fraction of their crimes. The General Assembly finds that this makes the cost of sexual offender victimization to society at large, while incalculable, clearly exorbitant. The General Assembly further finds that the high level of threat that a sexual predator presents to the public safety, and the long-term effects suffered by victims of sex offenses, provide the state with sufficient justification to implement a strategy that includes:

"(1) Incarcerating sexual offenders and maintaining adequate facilities to ensure that decisions to release sexual predators into the community are not made on the basis of inadequate space;

"(2) Requiring the registration of sexual offenders, with a requirement that complete and accurate information be maintained and accessible for use by law enforcement authorities, communities, and the public;

"(3) Providing for community and public notification concerning the presence of sexual offenders;

"(4) Collecting data relative to sexual offenses and sexual offenders;

"(5) Requiring sexual predators who are released into the community to wear an electronic monitoring system for the rest of their natural life and to pay for such system; and

"(6) Prohibiting sexual predators from working with children, either for compensation or as a volunteer.

"The General Assembly further finds that the state has a compelling interest in protecting the public from sexual offenders and in protecting children from predatory sexual activity, and there is sufficient justification for requiring sexual offenders to register and for requiring community and public notification of the presence of sexual offenders. The General Assembly declares that in order to protect the public, it is necessary that the sexual offenders be registered and that members of the community and the public be notified of a sexual offender's presence. The designation of a person as a sexual offender is neither a sentence nor a punishment but simply a regulatory mechanism and status resulting from the conviction of certain crimes. Likewise, the designation of a person as a sexual predator is neither a sentence nor a punishment but simply a regulatory mechanism and status resulting from findings by the Sexual Offender Registration Review Board and a court if requested by a sexual offender."

"SECTION 30. (a) This Act shall become effective July 1, 2006.

"(b) Any person required to register pursuant to the provisions of Code Section 42–1–12, relating to the state sexual offender registry, and any person required not to reside within areas where minors congregate, as prohibited by Code Section 42–1–13 [see § 42–1–15], shall not be relieved of the obligation to comply with the provisions of said Code sections by the repeal and reenactment of said Code sections.

"(c) The provisions of this Act shall not affect or abate the status as a crime of any such act or omission which occurred prior to the effective date of the Act repealing, repealing and reenacting, or amending such law, nor shall the prosecution of such crime be abated as a result of such repeal, repeal and reenactment, or amendment."

In 2006, the Code Commission, due to irreconcilable conflicts, treated the amendment of this section by Laws 2006, Act 453, § 42, as superseded by Laws 2006, Act 571, § 24. See Butts County v. Strahan, 107 S.E. 163, 151 Ga. 417 (1921).

In 2007, the Code Commission, in subsec. (g), substituted "subsection" for "Code section" preceding "may petition" in the first sentence of par. (1). See § 28–9–5.

The 2008 amendment by Act 582, in subsec. (a), par. (3), inserted "public libraries,".

The 2008 amendment by Act 715, in subsec. (a), redesignated subpar. (K) as subpar. (L) and added a new subpar. (K) in par. (16), and added pars. (21.1) and (21.2).

The 2009 amendment by Act 8 was a provision contained in a correction bill.

The 2010 amendment by Act 389, in subsec. (a), rewrote pars. (1), (9), (10), (16), (20), and deleted pars. (21.1) and (21.2); in subsec. (b), substituted "prior to moving" for "after the change of information" at the end of par. (3); in subsec. (e), substituted "1996" for "2006" in par. (2), inserted "victim who is a" preceding "minor" in par. (3), inserted "or dangerous sexual offense" and "on or after July 1, 1996" in par. (4), substituted "1996" for "2006" in par. (5), and rewrote par. (6); rewrote subsecs. (f) and (g); in subsec. (i), substituted "business" for "working" in par. (2), substituted "provide list, manually or electronically," for "post a list" and inserted "so that it may be available for inspection" in par. (3), and substituted "business days of the receipt of such information" for "working days" in par. (4); and in subsec. (n), substituted "of the county where he or she resides or sleeps within 72 hours prior to" for "within 72 hours of", substituted "not less than one nor more than 30 years" for "not less than ten not more than 30 years" and substituted """imprisonment for not less than five nor more than 30 years" for "imprisonment for life" in par. (3). Prior to amendment, pars. (a)(1), (a)(9), (a)(10), (a)(16), (a)(20), (a)(21.1), (a)(21.2), (e)(6), and subsecs. (f) and (g) had read:

"[(a)](1) 'Address' means the street or route address of the sexual offender's residence. For purposes of this Code section, the term does not mean a post office box, and homeless does not constitute an address."

"[(a)](9)(A) Criminal offense against a victim who is a minor" with respect to convictions occurring on or before June 30, 2001, means any criminal offense under Title 16 or any offense under federal law or the laws of another state or territory of the United States which consists of:

"(i) Kidnapping of a minor, except by a parent;

"(ii) False imprisonment of a minor, except by a parent;

"(iii) Criminal sexual conduct toward a minor;

"(iv) Solicitation of a minor to engage in sexual conduct;

"(v) Use of a minor in a sexual performance;

"(vi) Solicitation of a minor to practice prostitution; or

"(vii) Any conviction resulting from an underlying sexual offense against a victim who is a minor.

"(B) "Criminal offense against a victim who is a minor" with respect to convictions occurring after June 30, 2001, means any criminal offense under Title 16 or any offense under federal law or the laws of another state or territory of the United States which consists of:

"(i) Kidnapping of a minor, except by a parent;

"(ii) False imprisonment of a minor, except by a parent;

"(iii) Criminal sexual conduct toward a minor;

"(iv) Solicitation of a minor to engage in sexual conduct;

"(v) Use of a minor in a sexual performance;

"(vi) Solicitation of a minor to practice prostitution;

"(vii) Use of a minor to engage in any sexually explicit conduct to produce any visual medium depicting such conduct;

"(viii) Creating, publishing, selling, distributing, or possessing any material depicting a minor or a portion of a minor's body engaged in sexually explicit conduct;

"(ix) Transmitting, making, selling, buying, or disseminating by means of a computer any descriptive or identifying information regarding a child for the purpose of offering or soliciting sexual conduct of or with a child or the visual depicting of such conduct;

"(x) Conspiracy to transport, ship, receive, or distribute visual depictions of minors engaged in sexually explicit conduct; or

"(xi) Any conduct which, by its nature, is a sexual offense against a minor.

"(C) For purposes of subparagraph (a)(9)(B) of this Code section, conduct which is punished as for a misdemeanor or which is prosecuted in juvenile court shall not be considered a criminal offense against a victim who is a minor.

"[(a)](10)(A) "Dangerous sexual offense" with respect to convictions occurring after June 30, 2006, means any criminal offense under Title 16 as specified in this paragraph or any offense under federal law or the laws of another state or territory of the United States which consists of the same or similar elements of the following offenses:

"(i) Aggravated assault with the intent to rape in violation of Code Section 16-5-2;

"(ii) Kidnapping in violation of Code Section 16-5-40 which involves a victim who is less than 14 years of age, except by a parent;

"(iii) False imprisonment in violation of Code Section 16-5-41 which involves a victim who is less than 14 years of age, except by a parent;

"(iv) Rape in violation of Code Section 16-6-1;

"(v) Sodomy in violation of Code Section 16-6-2;

"(vi) Aggravated sodomy in violation of Code Section 16-6-2;

"(vii) Statutory rape in violation of Code Section 16-6-3, if the individual convicted of the offense is 21 years of age or older;

"(viii) Child molestation in violation of Code Section 16-6-4;

"(ix) Aggravated child molestation in violation of Code Section 16-6-4, unless the person was convicted of a misdemeanor offense;

"(x) Enticing a child for indecent purposes in violation of Code Section 16-6-5;

"(xi) Sexual assault against persons in custody in violation of Code Section 16-6-5.1;

"(xii) Incest in violation of Code Section 16-6-22;

"(xiii) A second conviction for sexual battery in violation of Code Section 16-6-22.1;

"(xiv) Aggravated sexual battery in violation of Code Section 16-6-23;

"(xv) Sexual exploitation of children in violation of Code Section 16-12-100;

"(xvi) Electronically furnishing obscene material to minors in violation of Code Section 16-12-100.1;

"(xvii) Computer pornography and child exploitation prevention in violation of Code Section 16-12-100.2;

"(xviii) Obscene telephone contact in violation of Code Section 16-12-100.3; or

"(xix) Any conduct which, by its nature, is a sexual offense against a minor or an attempt to commit a sexual offense against a minor.

"(B) For purposes of this paragraph, conduct which is punished as for a misdemeanor or which is prosecuted in juvenile court shall not be considered a dangerous sexual offense."

"(16) Required registration information" means:

"(A) Name; social security number; age; race; sex; date of birth; height; weight; hair color; eye color; fingerprints; and photograph;

"(B) Address of any permanent residence and address of any current temporary residence, within the state or out of state, and, if applicable in addition to the address, a rural route address and a post office box;

"(C) If the place of residence is a motor vehicle or trailer, the vehicle identification number, the license tag number, and a description, including color scheme, of the motor vehicle or trailer;

"(D) If the place of residence is a mobile home, the mobile home location permit number; the name and address of the owner of the home; a description, including the color scheme of the mobile home; and, if applicable, a description of where the mobile home is located on the property;

"(E) If the place of residence is a manufactured home, the name and address of the owner of the home; a description, including the color scheme of the manufactured home; and, if applicable, a description of where the manufactured home is located on the property;

"(F) If the place of residence is a vessel, live-aboard vessel, or houseboat, the hull identification number; the manufacturer's serial number; the name of the vessel, live-aboard vessel, or houseboat; the registration number; and a description, including color scheme, of the vessel, live-aboard vessel, or houseboat;

"(G) Date of employment, place of any employment, and address of employer;

"(H) Place of vocation and address of the place of vocation;

"(I) Vehicle make, model, color, and license tag number;

"(J) If enrolled, employed, or carrying on a vocation at an institution of higher education in this state, the name, address, and county of each institution, including each campus attended, and enrollment or employment status;

"(K) E-mail addresses, usernames, and user passwords; and

"(L) The name of the crime or crimes for which the sexual offender is registering and the date released from prison or placed on probation, parole, or supervised release."

"(20) 'Sexual offender' means any individual:

"(A) Who has been convicted of a criminal offense against a victim who is a minor or any dangerous sexual offense; or

"(B) Who has been convicted under the laws of another state or territory, under the laws of the United States, under the Uniform Code of Military Justice, or in a tribal court of a criminal offense against a victim who is a minor or a dangerous sexual offense."

"[(a)](21.1) 'Username' means a string of characters chosen to uniquely identify an individual who uses a computer or other device with Internet capability to communicate with other individuals through the exchange of e-mail or instant messages or by participating in interactive online forums.

"[(a)](21.2) 'User password' means a string of characters that enables an individual who uses a computer or other device with Internet capability to gain access to e-mail messages and interactive online forums."

"[(e)](6) Is a nonresident sexual offender who changes residence from another state or territory of the United States to Georgia who is required to register as a sexual offender under federal law, military law, tribal law, or the laws of another state or territory, regardless of when the conviction occurred;"

"(f) Any sexual offender required to register under this Code section shall:

"(1) Provide the required registration information to the appropriate official before being released from prison or placed on parole, supervised release, or probation;

"(2) Register with the sheriff of the county in which the sexual offender resides within 72 hours after the sexual offender's release from prison or placement on parole, supervised release, probation, or entry into this state;

"(3) Maintain the required registration information with the sheriff of the county in which the sexual offender resides;

"(4) Renew the required registration information with the sheriff of the county in which the sexual offender resides by reporting to the sheriff within 72 hours prior to such offender's birthday each year to be photographed and fingerprinted;

"(5) Update the required registration information with the sheriff of the county in which the sexual offender resides within 72 hours of any change to the required registration information, other than residence address; if the information is the sexual offender's new residence address, the sexual offender shall give the information to the sheriff of the county with whom the sexual offender last registered within 72 hours prior to any change of residence address and to the sheriff of the county to which the sexual offender is moving within 72 hours after establishing the new residence;

"(6) If convicted of a dangerous sexual offense on or after July 1, 2006, pay to the sheriff of the county where the sexual offender resides an annual registration fee of $250.00 upon each anniversary of such registration; and

"(7) Continue to comply with the registration requirements of this Code section for the entire life of the sexual offender, including ensuing periods of incarceration.

"(g)(1) Any sexual offender required to register under this Code section who meets the criteria set forth in paragraph (2) of this subsection may petition the superior court of the jurisdiction in which the sexual offender is registered to be released from the registration requirements of this Code section. The court may issue an order releasing the sexual offender from further registration if the court finds that the sexual offender does not pose a substantial risk of perpetrating any future dangerous sexual offense.

"(2) In order to petition the court pursuant to paragraph (1) of this subsection, the sexual offender shall:

"(A) Have been sentenced pursuant to subsection (c) of Code Section 17-10-6.2; and

"(B) Have had ten years elapse since his or her release from prison, parole, supervised release, or probation."

CHAPTER 4

JAILS

Article 1

Article 1

General Provisions

§ 42–4–1. Sheriffs as jailers; authority to appoint jailers

(a) By virtue of their offices, sheriffs are jailers of the counties and have the authority to appoint other jailers, subject to the supervision of the county governing authority, as prescribed by law.

(b) By virtue of their offices, chiefs of police are the jailers of the municipal corporations and have the authority to appoint other jailers, subject to the supervision of the municipal governing authority, as prescribed by law. Each jailer of a municipal corporation shall maintain the records required of sheriffs by subsection (a) of Code Section 42-4-7.

Laws 1988, p. 266, § 1.

Formerly Code 1863, § 331; Code 1868, § 392; Code 1873, § 356; Code 1882, § 356; Penal Code 1895, § 1120; Penal Code 1910, § 1149; Code 1933, § 77-101.

§ 42-4-2. Oath and bond

Before commencing to carry out the duties of their office, jailers must give to the sheriff a bond and surety for the sum of $1,000.00, conditioned for the faithful performance of their duties as jailers, and shall take and subscribe before the sheriff of their respective counties, to be filed in and entered into the records of the sheriff's office, the following oath:

> "I do swear that I will well and truly do and perform, all and singular, the duties of jailer for the County of _____; and that I will humanely treat prisoners who may be brought to the jail of which I am keeper and not suffer them to escape by any negligence or inattention of mine. So help me God."

Laws 1811, Cobb's 1851 Digest, pp. 201, 202; Laws 1987, p. 342, § 1.

Formerly Code 1863, § 332; Code 1868, § 393; Code 1873, § 357; Code 1882, § 357; Penal Code 1895, § 1121; Penal Code 1910, § 1150; Code 1933, § 77-102.

§ 42-4-3. When coroner is keeper of the jail

The county coroner shall be keeper of the jail when the sheriff is imprisoned or absent from the county leaving no deputy.

Formerly Code 1863, § 564; Code 1868, § 628; Code 1873, § 587; Code 1882, § 587; Penal Code 1895, § 1122; Penal Code 1910, § 1151; Code 1933, § 77-105.

§ 42-4-4. Duties of the sheriff; failure to comply with section

(a) It shall be the duty of the sheriff:

(1) To take from the outgoing sheriff custody of the jail and the bodies of such persons as are confined therein, along with the warrant or cause of commitment;

(2) To furnish persons confined in the jail with medical aid, heat, and blankets, to be reimbursed if necessary from the county treasury, for neglect of which he shall be liable to suffer the penalty prescribed in this Code section; provided, however, that, with respect to an inmate covered under Article 3 of this chapter, the officer in charge will provide such person access to medical aid and may arrange for the person's health insurance carrier to pay the health care provider for the aid rendered; and

(3) To take all persons arrested or in execution under any criminal or civil process to the jail of an adjoining county, or to the jail of some other county if the latter is more accessible, if the jail of his county is in an unsafe condition, under such rules as are prescribed in this chapter.

(b) Subject to the provisions of this subsection and except as provided by law or as directed by a court of competent jurisdiction, a sheriff shall not release a prisoner from his custody prior to the lawful completion of his sentence including any lawful credits under a trusty system. The provision shall not, however, preclude a sheriff from designating an inmate as a trusty and utilizing him in a lawful manner and, furthermore, this provision shall not preclude a sheriff from transferring a prisoner to another jail in another county if the sheriff concludes that such transfer is in the best interest of the prisoner or that such transfer is necessary for the orderly administration of the jail.

(c) Any sheriff or deputy who fails to comply with this Code section shall be fined for contempt, as is the clerk of the superior court in similar cases. The sheriff or deputy shall also be subject to removal from office as prescribed in Code Section 15-6-82.

Laws 1799, Cobb's 1851 Digest, p. 574; Laws 1810, Cobb's 1851 Digest, p. 577; Laws 1818, Cobb's 1851 Digest, p. 858; Laws 1820, Cobb's 1851 Digest, p. 480; Laws 1823, Cobb's 1851 Digest, p. 512; Laws 1865-66, p. 64, § 15; Laws 1990, p. 1443, § 1; Laws 1992, p. 2125, § 1.

Formerly Code 1863, §§ 336, 340; Code 1868, §§ 397, 401; Code 1873, §§ 361, 366; Code 1882, §§ 361, 366; Penal Code 1895, §§ 1127, 1128; Penal Code 1910, §§ 1156, 1157; Code 1933, §§ 77-110, 77-111.

§ 42-4-5. Cruelty by jailers prohibited

(a) No jailer, by duress or other cruel treatment, shall make or induce an inmate to accuse or give evidence against another; nor shall he be guilty of willful inhumanity or oppression to any inmate under his care and custody.

(b) Any jailer who violates subsection (a) of this Code section shall be punished by removal from office and imprisonment for not less than one year nor longer than three years.

Cobb's 1851 Digest, p. 805.

Formerly Code 1863, § 4367; Code 1868, § 4405; Code 1873, § 4473; Code 1882, § 4473; Penal Code 1895, § 282; Penal Code 1910, § 286; Code 1933, §§ 77-104, 77-9901.

§ 42-4-6. Disposition of tubercular prisoners

(a) When any person confined in the common jail who is awaiting trial for any offense against the penal laws of this state or who has been convicted of an offense or who is serving any jail sentence imposed upon him by authority or who has been committed for any civil or criminal contempt or who is serving any misdemeanor sentence under county jurisdiction in a county correctional institution or other institution for the maintenance of county inmates is afflicted with tuberculosis, the judge of the superior court may order the person's delivery by the sheriff to an institution as may be approved and supported by the Department of Community Health for the care of tubercular patients; thereupon, he shall be so delivered and received in such institution and shall be securely confined, kept, and cared for.

(b) The period of time a person is kept and confined in a hospital or institution pursuant to subsection (a) of this Code section shall be credited upon any jail sentence being served by him, in the same manner as though he had remained in jail. Any person committed for any civil or criminal contempt shall remain for all purposes under the orders, jurisdiction, and authority of the court committing him for contempt while in the hospital or institution, in the same manner as though he had remained in the common jail.

Laws 1960, p. 769, § 2; Laws 1964, p. 365, § 1; Laws 1994, p. 97, § 42; Laws 2009, Act 102, § 1-4, eff. July 1, 2009.

§ 42-4-7. Record of inmates to be kept; earned allowances

(a) The sheriff shall keep a record of all persons committed to the jail of the county of which he or she is sheriff. This record shall contain the name of the person committed, such person's age, sex, race, under what process such person was committed and from what court the process issued, the crime with which the person was charged, the date of such person's commitment to jail, the day of such person's discharge, under what order such person was discharged, and the court from which the order issued. This record shall be subject to examination by any person in accordance with the provisions of Article 4 of Chapter 18 of Title 50, relating to the inspection of public records.

(b)(1) The sheriff, chief jailer, warden, or other officer designated by the county as custodian of inmates confined as county inmates for probation violations of felony offenses or as provided in subsection (a) of Code Section 17–10–3 may award earned time allowances to such inmates based on institutional behavior. Earned time allowances shall not be awarded which exceed one-half of the period of confinement imposed, except that the sheriff or other custodian may authorize the award of not more than four days' credit for each day on which an inmate does work on an authorized work detail; provided, however, that such increased credit for performance on a work detail shall not apply to an inmate who is incarcerated for:

(A) A second or subsequent offense of driving under the influence under Code Section 40–6–391 within a five-year period of time, as measured from the date of any previous arrest for which a conviction was obtained or a plea of nolo contendere was accepted to the date of the current arrest for which a conviction is obtained or a plea of nolo contendere is accepted;

(B) A misdemeanor of a high and aggravated nature; or

(C) A crime committed against a family member as defined in Code Section 19–13–1.

(2) While an inmate sentenced to confinement as a county inmate is in custody as a county inmate, the custodian of such inmate may award an earned time allowance consistent with this subsection and subsection (b) of Code Section 17–10–4 based on the institutional behavior of such inmate while in custody as a county inmate.

(3) An inmate sentenced to confinement as a county inmate shall be released at the expiration of his or her sentence less the time deducted for earned time allowances.

(c) Commencing January 1, 1984, those provisions of subsection (b) of this Code section which provide for good-time allowances to be awarded to inmates sentenced to confinement as county inmates as provided in subsection (a) of Code Section 17–10–3 shall apply to all such inmates in confinement on December 31, 1983, and all inmates who commit crimes on or after January 1, 1984, and are subsequently convicted and sentenced to confinement as county inmates. Conversion of the computation of the sentences of county inmates in confinement on December 31, 1983, from earned time governed sentences to good-time governed sentences shall be made by the sheriff or other custodian of such inmates. Commencing July 1, 1994, those provisions of subsection (b) of this Code section which provide for good-time allowances to be awarded to inmates sentenced to confinement as county inmates for probation violations of felony offenses shall apply to all such inmates in confinement on June 30, 1994, and all inmates whose probation is revoked or who commit crimes on or after July 1, 1994, and are subsequently sentenced to confinement as county inmates. Commencing July 1, 2000, the award of earned time allowances pursuant to subsection (b) of this Code section for persons who commit crimes on or after July 1, 2000, and are subsequently convicted and sentenced to confinement as county inmates and inmates whose probation is revoked on or after July 1, 2000, or who commit crimes on or after July 1, 2000, and are subsequently sentenced to confinement as county inmates is not automatic or mandatory but shall be based upon institutional behavior.

Laws 1877, p. 111, § 1; Laws 1983, p. 1340, § 1; Laws 1993, p. 632, § 1; Laws 1994, p. 1955, § 1; Laws 2000, p. 1111, § 2; Laws 2004, Act 457, § 1, eff. July 1, 2004.

Formerly Code 1882, § 366a; Penal Code 1895, § 1125; Penal Code 1910, § 1154; Code 1933, § 77–108.

§ 42–4–8. Grand jury to inquire into record; contempt by sheriff

It shall be the duty of the grand jury, at each term of the superior court held in the county, to inquire into the contents of the record kept by the sheriff as required by Code Section 42–4–7. If the record is not kept or is incorrectly kept, the grand jury shall so report to the court. Upon the report's being made, the judge presiding shall cause the district attorney to have the sheriff served with a rule requiring him to show cause why he should not be punished for contempt. The judge shall inquire into the facts and, if he finds that Code Section 42–4–7 has not been complied with, he shall impose a fine of not less than $25.00 nor more than $50.00 for the first offense and not more than $100.00 and not less than $50.00 for each subsequent offense. The fines shall be enforced and collected by attachment, as in other cases of attachments against sheriffs.

Laws 1877, p. 111, § 2; Laws 1994, p. 97, § 42.

Formerly Code 1882, § 366b; Penal Code 1895, § 1126; Penal Code 1910, § 1155; Code 1933, § 77–109.

§ 42–4–9. United States prisoners, receiving, etc.

The keeper of a county jail may decline to receive a person from the custody of anyone acting under the authority of the United States government. He may receive the person if the consent of the authority having control of county matters is first obtained. If the keeper receives the person he shall have the same duties and responsibilities toward him as in the case of inmates committed under the authority of this state.

Laws 1889, p. 47, § 2.

Formerly Code 1863, § 334; Code 1868, § 395; Code 1873, § 359; Code 1882, § 359; Penal Code 1895, § 1123; Penal Code 1910, § 1152; Code 1933, § 77–106.

§ 42–4–10. When notice of refusal to receive United States prisoners shall be given

If the keeper of the jail consents to receive a person from the custody of federal authorities, as provided in Code Section 42–4–9, neither the jailer nor the county authorities shall refuse to receive any other person so committed by the authority of the United States government unless 20 days' prior written notice of the sheriff's refusal to receive any more persons committed by the federal authorities is given by him to the United States marshal or other federal officers charged with the custody of such persons.

Laws 1889, p. 47, § 3.

Formerly Penal Code 1895, § 1124; Penal Code 1910, § 1153; Code 1933, § 77–107.

§ 42–4–11. Duty of officers when venue is changed

In all cases in which a change of venue is made, the sheriff of the county from which a person in custody is to be moved shall carry the person to the county to which the change of venue was directed and deliver him to the sheriff of such county, who shall then take charge of the person as in other cases. The sheriff of the county from which the person is to be moved shall carry with him and deliver to the sheriff the warrant under which the person was arrested or the commitment.

Laws 1868, p. 133, § 1.

Formerly Code 1873, § 4688; Code 1882, § 4688; Penal Code 1895, § 1129; Penal Code 1910, § 1158; Code 1933, § 77–112.

§ 42–4–12. Refusing to receive prisoner; penalty

Except as otherwise provided in this Code section, any sheriff, constable, keeper of a jail, or other officer whose duty it is to receive persons charged with or guilty of an indictable offense who refuses to receive and take charge of such a person shall, upon conviction thereof, be guilty of a misdemeanor and shall be punished by a fine of not more than $1,000.00. A sheriff, constable, keeper of a jail, or other officer whose duty it is to receive persons charged with or guilty of an indictable offense shall be authorized to refuse acceptance of any person who has not received medical treatment for obvious physical injuries or conditions of an emergency nature. Upon such refusal, it shall be the responsibility of the arresting agency to take the individual to a health care facility or health care provider in order to secure a medical release. Upon medical release by the health care facility or health care provider, the sheriff, constable, or keeper of the jail must assume custody of the individual; provided, however, that in all cases the sheriff, constable, or keeper of the jail must assume custody where no health care facility is located in the county in which the arrest occurred and, in such instances, the governing authority of the arresting agency shall pay all costs related to the medical release.

Cobb's 1851 Digest, p. 807; Laws 1996, p. 1638, § 1.

Formerly Code 1863, § 4380; Code 1868, § 4418; Code 1873, § 4486; Code 1882, § 4486; Penal Code 1895, § 285; Penal Code 1910, § 289; Code 1933, § 77–9902.

§ 42–4–13. Possession by, delivery to inmate of, or bringing within guard lines drugs, weapons, alcohol, or other prohibited articles

(a) As used in this Code section, the term:

(1) "Alcoholic beverage" means and includes all alcohol, distilled spirits, beer, malt beverage, wine, or fortified wine.

(2) "Controlled substance" means a drug, substance, or immediate precursor as defined in Code Section 16–13–21.

(3) "Dangerous drug" has the same meaning as defined by Code Section 16–13–71.

(4) "Jail" means any county jail, municipal jail, or any jail or detention facility operated by a county, municipality, or a regional jail authority as authorized under Article 5 of this chapter.

(5) "Jailer" means the sheriff in the case of any county jail, or the chief of police if the jail is under the supervision of the chief of police of a municipality, or the warden, captain, administrator, superintendent, or other officer having supervision of any other jail, or the designee of such officer.

(b)(1) It shall be unlawful for an inmate of a jail to possess any controlled substance, dangerous drug, gun, pistol, or other dangerous weapon or marijuana.

(2) Any person who violates paragraph (1) of this subsection shall be guilty of a felony and, upon conviction thereof, shall be imprisoned for not less than one nor more than five years.

(3) Notwithstanding the provisions of this subsection, possession of a controlled substance, a dangerous drug, or marijuana shall be punished as provided in Chapter 13 of Title 16; provided, however, that the provisions of Code Section 16–13–2 shall not apply to a violation of paragraph (1) of this subsection.

(4) The provisions of this subsection shall not prohibit the lawful use or dispensing of a controlled substance or dangerous drug to an inmate with the knowledge and consent of the jailer when such use or dispensing is lawful under the provisions of Chapter 13 of Title 16.

(c)(1) Unless otherwise authorized by law, it shall be unlawful for an inmate of a jail to possess any alcoholic beverage.

(2) Any person who violates paragraph (1) of this subsection shall be guilty of a misdemeanor.

(d)(1)(A) It shall be unlawful for any person to come inside the guard lines established at any jail with, or to give or have delivered to an inmate of a jail, any controlled substance, dangerous drug, marijuana, or any gun, pistol, or other dangerous weapon without the knowledge and consent of the jailer or a law enforcement officer.

(B) It shall be unlawful for any person to come inside the guard lines established at any jail with, or to give or have delivered to an inmate of a jail, any alcoholic beverage without the knowledge and consent of the jailer or a law enforcement officer; provided, however, that the provisions of this subsection shall not apply to nor prohibit the use of an alcoholic beverage by a clergyman or priest in sacramental services only.

(2) Except as otherwise provided in paragraph (3) of this subsection, any person who violates subparagraph (A) of paragraph (1) of this subsection shall be guilty of a felony and, upon conviction thereof, shall be imprisoned for not less than one nor more than five years. Any person who violates subparagraph (B) of paragraph (1) of this subsection shall be guilty of a misdemeanor.

(3) Notwithstanding the provisions of paragraph (2) of this subsection, the possession, possession with intent to distribute, trafficking, or distribution of a controlled substance or marijuana shall be punished as provided in Chapter 13 of Title 16; provided, however, that the provisions of Code Section 16–13–2 shall not apply to a violation of subparagraph (A) of paragraph (1) of this subsection.

(e) It shall be unlawful for any person to obtain, to procure for, or to give to an inmate, or to bring within the guard lines, any other article or item without the knowledge and consent of the jailer or a law enforcement officer. Any person violating this subsection shall be guilty of a misdemeanor.

(f)(1) It shall be unlawful for any person to come inside the guard lines or be within any jail while under the influence of a controlled substance, dangerous drug, or marijuana without the knowledge and consent of the jailer or a law enforcement officer unless such person has a valid prescription for such controlled substance or dangerous drug issued by a person licensed under Chapter 11 or 34 of Title 43 and such prescribed substance is consumed only as authorized by the prescription. Any person convicted of a violation of this subsection shall be punished by imprisonment for not less than one nor more than four years.

(2) It shall be unlawful for any person to come inside the guard lines or be within any jail while under the influence of alcohol without the knowledge and consent of the jailer or a law enforcement officer. Any person violating this subsection shall be guilty of a misdemeanor.

(g) It shall be unlawful for any person to loiter where inmates are assigned after having been ordered by the jailer or a law enforcement officer to desist therefrom. Any person violating this subsection shall be guilty of a misdemeanor.

(h) It shall be unlawful for any person to attempt, conspire, or solicit another to commit any offense defined by this Code section and, upon conviction thereof, shall be punished by imprisonment not exceeding the maximum punishment prescribed for the offense, the commission of which was the object of the attempt, conspiracy, or solicitation.

(i) Any violation of this Code section shall constitute a separate offense.

(j) Perimeter guard lines shall be established at every jail by the jailer thereof. Such guard lines shall be clearly marked by signs on which shall be plainly stamped or written: "Guard line of ______." Signs shall also be placed at all entrances and exits for vehicles and pedestrians at the jail and at such intervals along the guard lines as will reasonably place all persons approaching the guard lines on notice of the location of the jail.

Laws 1987, p. 611, § 1; Laws 1993, p. 630, § 1; Laws 1999, p. 648, § 1; Laws 2000, p. 136, § 42.

§ 42–4–14. Nationality of confined person to be determined; verification of lawful status

(a) When any person is confined, for any period, in the jail of a county or municipality or a jail operated by a regional jail authority in compliance with Article 36 of the Vienna Convention on Consular Relations, a reasonable effort shall be made to determine the nationality of the person so confined.

(b) If the prisoner is a foreign national charged with a felony, driving under the influence pursuant to Code Section 40–6–391, driving without being licensed pursuant to subsection (a) of Code Section 40–5–20, or with a misdemeanor of a high and aggravated nature, the keeper of the jail or other officer shall make a reasonable effort to verify that the prisoner has been lawfully admitted to the United States and if lawfully admitted, that such lawful status has not expired. If verification of lawful status can not be made from documents in the possession of the prisoner, verification shall be made within 48 hours through a query to the Law Enforcement Support Center (LESC) of the United States Department of Homeland Security or other office or agency designated for that purpose by the United States Department of Homeland Security. If the prisoner is determined not to be lawfully admitted to the United States, the keeper of the jail or other officer shall notify the United States Department of Homeland Security.

(c) Nothing in this Code section shall be construed to deny a person bond or from being released from confinement when such person is otherwise eligible for release.

(d) The Georgia Sheriffs Association shall prepare and issue guidelines and procedures used to comply with the provisions of this Code section.

Laws 2006, Act 457, § 5, eff. July 1, 2007; Laws 2008, Act 778, § 4, eff. July 1, 2008; Laws 2009, Act 8, § 42, eff. April 14, 2009; Laws 2009, Act 339, § 2, eff. Jan. 1, 2010.

Historical and Statutory Notes

The 2008 amendment by Act 778, in subsec. (a), inserted "or convicted of driving without being licensed in violation of subsection (a) of Code Section 40–5–20" following the citation to § 40–6–391.

The 2009 amendment by Act 8 was a provision contained in a correction bill.

In 2009, the Code Commission, due to irreconcilable conflicts, treated the amendment of this section by Laws 2009, Act 8, § 42, as superseded by Laws 2009, Act 339, § 2. See Butts County v. Strahan, 107 S.E. 163, 151 Ga. 417 (1921).

CHAPTER 8

PROBATION

Article 3

Probation of First Offenders

§ 42–8–60. When applicable; violation of probation

(a) Upon a verdict or plea of guilty or a plea of nolo contendere, but before an adjudication of guilt, in the case of a defendant who has not been previously convicted of a felony, the court may, without entering a judgment of guilt and with the consent of the defendant:

(1) Defer further proceeding and place the defendant on probation as provided by law; or

(2) Sentence the defendant to a term of confinement as provided by law.

(b) Upon violation by the defendant of the terms of probation, upon a conviction for another crime during the period of probation, or upon the court determining that the defendant is or was not eligible for sentencing under this article, the court may enter an adjudication of guilt and proceed as otherwise provided by law. No person may avail himself or herself of this article on more than one occasion.

(c) The court shall not sentence a defendant under the provisions of this article and, if sentenced under the provisions of this article, shall not discharge the defendant upon completion of the sentence unless the court has reviewed the defendant's criminal record as such is on file with the Georgia Crime Information Center.

(d) The court shall not sentence a defendant under the provisions of this article who has been found guilty of or entered a plea of guilty or a plea of nolo contendere for:

(1) A serious violent felony as such term is defined in Code Section 17–10–6.1;

(2) A sexual offense as such term is defined in Code Section 17–10–6.2;

(3) Sexual exploitation of a minor as defined in Code Section 16–12–100;

(4) Electronically furnishing obscene material to a minor as defined in Code Section 16–12–100.1; or

(5) Computer pornography and child exploitation, as defined in Code Section 16–12–100.2.

Laws 1968, p. 324, § 1; Laws 1982, p. 1807, § 1; Laws 1985, p. 380, § 1; Laws 1986, p. 218, § 1; Laws 2006, Act 571, § 26, eff. July 1, 2006.

Historical and Statutory Notes

The 2006 amendment by Act 571, in subsec. (b), added "or herself" in the last sentence; and added subsec. (d).

Laws 2006, Act 571, §§ 1 and 30, provide:

"SECTION 1. The General Assembly finds and declares that recidivist sexual offenders, sexual offenders who use physical violence, and sexual offenders who prey on children are sexual predators who present an extreme threat to the public safety. Many sexual offenders are extremely likely to use physical violence and to repeat their offenses; and some sexual offenders commit many offenses, have many more victims than are ever reported, and are prosecuted for only a fraction of their crimes. The General Assembly finds that this makes the cost of sexual offender victimization to society at large, while incalculable, clearly exorbitant. The General Assembly further finds that the high level of threat that a sexual predator presents to the public safety, and the long-term effects suffered by victims of sex offenses, provide the state with sufficient justification to implement a strategy that includes:

"(1) Incarcerating sexual offenders and maintaining adequate facilities to ensure that decisions to release sexual predators into the community are not made on the basis of inadequate space;

"(2) Requiring the registration of sexual offenders, with a requirement that complete and accurate information be maintained and accessible for use by law enforcement authorities, communities, and the public;

"(3) Providing for community and public notification concerning the presence of sexual offenders;

"(4) Collecting data relative to sexual offenses and sexual offenders;

"(5) Requiring sexual predators who are released into the community to wear an electronic monitoring system for the rest of their natural life and to pay for such system; and

"(6) Prohibiting sexual predators from working with children, either for compensation or as a volunteer.

"The General Assembly further finds that the state has a compelling interest in protecting the public from sexual offenders and in protecting children from predatory sexual activity, and there is sufficient justification for requiring sexual offenders to register and for requiring community and public notification of the presence of sexual offenders. The General Assembly declares that in order to protect the public, it is necessary that the sexual offenders be registered and that members of the community and the public be notified of a sexual offender's presence. The designation of a person as a sexual offender is neither a sentence nor a punishment but simply a regulatory mechanism and status resulting from the conviction of certain crimes. Likewise, the designation of a person as a sexual predator is neither a sentence nor a punishment but simply a regulatory mechanism and status resulting from findings by the Sexual Offender Registration Review Board and a court if requested by a sexual offender."

"SECTION 30. (a) This Act shall become effective July 1, 2006.

"(b) Any person required to register pursuant to the provisions of Code Section 42–1–12, relating to the state sexual offender registry, and any person required not to reside within areas where minors congregate, as prohibited by Code Section 42–1–13 [see § 42–1–15], shall not be relieved of the obligation to comply with the provisions of said Code sections by the repeal and reenactment of said Code sections.

"(c) The provisions of this Act shall not affect or abate the status as a crime of any such act or omission which occurred prior to the effective date of the Act repealing, repealing and reenacting, or amending such law, nor shall the prosecution of such crime be abated as a result of such repeal, repeal and reenactment, or amendment."

In 2006, the Code Commission, in subsec. (d), substituted "plea of guilty or" for "plea of guilty of" in the introductory paragraph. See § 28–9–5.

§ 42–8–61. Defendant to be informed of terms of law

The defendant shall be informed of the terms of this article at the time of imposition of sentence.

Laws 1968, p. 324, § 3; Laws 1982, p. 1807, § 2.

§ 42–8–62. Discharged defendant not to be considered to have criminal conviction; exception; records of probation

(a) Upon fulfillment of the terms of probation, upon release by the court prior to the termination of the period thereof, or upon release from confinement, the defendant shall be discharged without court adjudication of guilt. Except for the registration requirements under the state sexual offender registry and except as otherwise provided in Code Section 42–8–63.1, the discharge shall completely exonerate the defendant of any criminal purpose and shall not affect any of his or her civil rights or liberties; and the defendant shall not be considered to have a criminal conviction. It shall be the duty of the clerk of court to enter on the criminal docket and all other records of the court pertaining thereto the following:

> "Discharge filed completely exonerates the defendant of any criminal purpose and shall not affect any of his or her civil rights or liberties, except for registration requirements under the state sexual offender registry and except with regard to employment providing care for minor children or elderly persons as specified in Code Section 42–8–63.1; and the defendant shall not be considered to have a criminal conviction. O.C.G.A. 42–8–62."

Such entry shall be written or stamped in red ink, dated, and signed by the person making such entry or, if the docket or record is maintained using computer print-outs, microfilm, or similar means, such entry shall be underscored, boldface, or made in a similar conspicuous manner and shall be dated and include the name of the person making such entry. The criminal file, docket books, criminal minutes and final record, and all other records of the court relating to the offense of a defendant who has been discharged without court adjudication of guilt pursuant to this subsection shall not be altered as a result of that discharge, except for the entry of discharge thereon required by this subsection, nor shall the contents thereof be expunged or destroyed as a result of that discharge.

(b) Should a person be placed under probation or in confinement under this article, a record of the same shall be forwarded to the Georgia Crime Information Center. Without request of the defendant a record of discharge and exoneration, as provided in this Code section, shall in every case be forwarded to the Georgia Crime Information Center. In every case in which the record of probation or confinement shall have been previously forwarded to the Department of Corrections, to the Georgia Crime Information Center, and to the Identification Division of the Federal Bureau of Investigation and a record of a subsequent discharge and exoneration of the defendant has not been forwarded as provided in this Code section, upon request of the defendant or his attorney or representative, the record of the same shall be forwarded by the clerk of court so as to reflect the discharge and exoneration.

Laws 1968, p. 324, § 2; Laws 1978, p. 1621, § 1; Laws 1982, p. 1807, § 3; Laws 1985, p. 283, § 1; Laws 1986, p. 442, § 1; Laws 1990, p. 735, § 1; Laws 2001, p. 1004, § 2; Laws 2003, Act 375, § 4, eff. July 1, 2004.

Historical and Statutory Notes

The 2001 amendment to subsec. (a) inserted at the beginning of the second sentence of the first paragraph "Except for the registration requirements under the state sexual offender registry," inserted in the second paragraph "except for registration requirements under the state sexual offender registry;" and inserted gender neutral language.

The 2003 amendment by Act 375, in subsec. (a), inserted "and except as otherwise provided in Code Section 42–8–63.1" and "and except with regard to employment providing care for minor children or elderly persons as specified in Code Section 42–8–63.1".

Laws 2003, Act 375, § 6, provides:

"This Act shall become effective on July 1, 2004, except that Section 3A shall become effective on July 1, 2003."

§ 42–8–63. Discharge not to be used to disqualify person for employment or appointment to office

Except as otherwise provided in this article, a discharge under this article is not a conviction of a crime under the laws of this state and may not be used to disqualify a person in any application for employment or appointment to office in either the public or private sector.

Laws 1978, p. 1621, § 2.

§ 42–8–63.1. Discharge used to disqualify person for employment

(a) A discharge under this article may be used to disqualify a person for employment if:

(1) The offender was discharged under this article on or after July 1, 2004; and either

(2) The employment is with a public school, private school, child welfare agency, or a person or entity that provides day care for minor children or after school care for minor children and the defendant was discharged under this article after prosecution for the offense of child molestation, sexual battery, enticing a child for indecent purposes, sexual exploitation of a child, pimping, pandering, or incest;

(3) The employment is with a nursing home, personal care home, or a person or entity that offers day care for elderly persons and the defendant was discharged under this article after prosecution for the offense of sexual battery, incest, pimping, pandering, or a violation of Code Section 30–5–8; or

(4) The request for information is an inquiry about a person who has applied for employment with a facility as defined in Code Section 37–3–1 or 37–4–2 that provides services to persons who are mentally ill as defined in Code Section 37–1–1 or developmentally disabled as defined in Code Section 37–1–1, and the person who is the subject of the inquiry to the center was prosecuted for the offense of sexual battery, incest, pimping, or pandering.

(b) Any discharge under this article may be used to disqualify a person from acquiring or maintaining a peace officer certification as provided for in Chapter 8 of Article 35 and also may disqualify a person from employment in a certified position with a law enforcement unit where the discharge under this article pertained to a felony offense or a crime involving moral turpitude.

Laws 2003, Act 375, § 5, eff. July 1, 2004; Laws 2006, Act 473, § 2, eff. April 18, 2006; Laws 2009, Act 102, § 3–25, eff. July 1, 2009.

Historical and Statutory Notes

Laws 2003, Act 375, § 6, provides:

"This Act shall become effective on July 1, 2004, except that Section 3A shall become effective on July 1, 2003."

The 2006 amendment by Act 473, designated the existing statute as subsec. (a) and added subsec. (b).

The 2009 amendment by Act 102, in subsec. (a), par. (4), substituted "Code Section 37–1–1 or developmentally disabled as defined in Code Section 37–1–1" for "Code Section 37–3–1 or mentally retarded as defined in Code Section 37–4–2".

§ 42–8–64. Right to appeal

A defendant sentenced pursuant to this article shall have the right to appeal in the same manner and with the same scope and same effect as if a judgment of conviction had been entered and appealed from.

Laws 1968, p. 324, § 5.

§ 42–8–65. Pleading and proof of finding of guilt on subsequent prosecutions; release of records

(a) If otherwise allowable by law in any subsequent prosecution of the defendant for any other offense, a prior finding of guilt may be pleaded and proven as if an adjudication of guilt had been entered and relief had not been granted pursuant to this article.

(b) The records of the Georgia Crime Information Center shall be modified, without a court order, to show a conviction in lieu of treatment as a first offender under this article whenever the conviction of a person for another crime during the term of probation is reported to the Georgia Crime Information Center. If a report is made showing that such person has been afforded first offender treatment under this article on more than one occasion, the Georgia Crime Information Center may report information on first offender treatments subsequent to the first such first offender treatment as if they were convictions. Such records may be disseminated by the Georgia Crime Information Center in the same manner and subject to the same restrictions as any other records of convictions.

(c) Notwithstanding any other provision of this article, any person who is sentenced to a term of confinement pursuant to paragraph (2) of subsection (a) of Code Section 42–8–60 shall be deemed to have been convicted of the offense during such term of confinement for all purposes except that records thereof shall be treated as any other records of first offenders under this article and except that such presumption shall not continue after completion of such person's confinement sentence. Upon completion of the confinement sentence, such person shall be treated in the same manner and the procedures to be followed by the court shall be the same as in the case of a person placed on probation under this article.

Laws 1968, p. 324, § 4; Laws 1978, p. 1621, § 3; Laws 1982, p. 1807, § 4; Laws 1983, p. 3, § 31; Laws 1985, p. 283, § 1; Laws 1985, p. 380, § 2; Laws 1990, p. 735, § 2; Laws 1994, p. 97, § 42.

§ 42–8–66. Not applicable to persons convicted of serious violent felonies

The provisions of this article shall not apply to any person who is convicted of a serious violent felony as defined in subsection (a) of Code Section 17–10–6.1.

Laws 1998, p. 180, § 3.

Article 7

Ignition Interlock Devices as Probation Condition

§ 42–8–110. Definitions; applicability of law; charges and fees; use by indigent persons

(a) As used in this article, the term "ignition interlock device" means a constant monitoring device certified by the commissioner of driver services which prevents a motor vehicle from being started at any time without first determining the equivalent blood alcohol concentration of the operator through the taking of a deep lung breath sample. The system shall be calibrated so that the motor vehicle may not be started if the blood alcohol concentration of the operator, as measured by the device, exceeds 0.02 grams or if the sample is not a sample of human breath.

(b) As used in this article, the term "provider center" means a facility established for the purpose of providing and installing ignition interlock devices when their use is required by or as a result of an order of a court.

(c) Ignition interlock devices for provider centers may be purchased or leased by counties, municipalities, or private entities.

(d) A provider center shall be authorized to charge the person whose vehicle is to be equipped with an ignition interlock device such installation, deinstallation, and user fees as are approved by the Department of Driver Services. A provider center may also require such person to make a security deposit for the safe return of the ignition interlock device. Payment of any or all of such fees and deposits may be made a condition of probation under this order.

(e) If a county, municipality, or other political subdivision of this state purchases or leases ignition interlock devices from a private entity, such county or municipality shall allow persons who are found by the court to be indigent and unable to pay the fees or deposits for such an ignition interlock device to participate in the ignition interlock program.

Laws 1993, p. 568, § 1; Laws 1997, p. 760, § 26; Laws 1999, p. 391, § 11; Laws 2000, p. 1457, § 6; Laws 2002, p. 415, § 42; Laws 2005, Act 68, § 24–3, eff. July 1, 2005.

Historical and Statutory Notes

The 2005 amendment by Act 68 in subsec. (a) substituted "commissioner of driver services" for "commissioner of motor vehicle safety"; and in subsec. (d) substituted "Department of Driver Services" for "Department of Motor Vehicle Safety".

§ 42–8–111. Condition of probation; DUI Alcohol or Drug Use Risk Reduction Program; Department records; driver's license fee

(a) In addition to any other provision of probation, upon a second or subsequent conviction of a resident of this state for violating Code Section 40–6–391 within five years, as measured from the dates of previous arrests for which convictions were obtained to the date of the current arrest for which a conviction is obtained, for which such person is granted probation, the court shall order as conditions of probation that:

(1) Such person shall have installed and shall maintain in each motor vehicle registered in such person's name throughout the applicable six-month period prescribed by subsection (b) of Code Section 42–8–112 a functioning, certified ignition interlock device, unless the court exempts the person from the requirements of this paragraph based upon the court's determination that such requirements would subject the person to undue financial hardship; and

(2) Such person shall have installed and shall maintain in any other motor vehicle to be driven by such person during the applicable six-month period prescribed by subsection (b) of Code Section 42–8–112 a functioning, certified ignition interlock device, and such person shall not during such six-month period drive any motor vehicle whatsoever that is not so equipped.

For the purposes of this subsection, a plea of nolo contendere shall constitute a conviction; and a conviction of any offense under the law of another state or territory substantially conforming to any offense under Code Section 40–6–391 shall be deemed a conviction of violating said Code section.

(b) Any resident of this state who is ordered to use an ignition interlock device, as a condition of probation, shall complete the DUI Alcohol or Drug Use Risk Reduction Program and submit to the court or probation department a certificate of completion of the DUI Alcohol or Drug Use Risk Reduction Program and certification of installation of a certified ignition interlock device to the extent required by subsection (a) of this Code section.

(c) In the case of any person subject to the provisions of subsection (a) of this Code section, the court shall include in the record of conviction or violation submitted to the Department of Driver Services notice of the requirement for, and the period of the requirement for, the use of a certified ignition interlock device. Such notice shall specify any exemption from the installation requirements of paragraph (1) of subsection (a) of this Code section and any vehicles subject to the installation requirements of paragraph (2) of said subsection. The records of the Department of Driver Services shall contain a record reflecting mandatory use of such device and the person's driver's license or limited driving permit shall contain a notation that the person may only operate a motor vehicle equipped with a functioning, certified ignition interlock device.

(d) Except as provided in Code Section 42–8–112, no provision of this article shall be deemed to reduce any period of driver's license suspension or revocation otherwise imposed by law.

(e) The fee for issuance of any driver's license indicating that use of an ignition interlock device is required shall be as prescribed for a regular driver's license in Code Section 40–5–25, and the fee for issuance of any limited driving permit indicating that use of an ignition interlock device is required shall be as prescribed for a limited driving permit in Code Section 40–5–64; except that, for habitual violators required to use an ignition interlock device as a condition of a probationary license, the fee shall be as prescribed for a probationary license in Code Section 40–5–58.

Laws 1993, p. 568, § 1; Laws 1999, p. 391, § 12; Laws 2000, p. 1457, § 6; Laws 2001, p. 208, § 1–8; Laws 2002, p. 415, § 42; Laws 2003, Act 9, § 42, eff. May 14, 2003; Laws 2005, Act 68, § 24–4, eff. July 1, 2005.

Historical and Statutory Notes

In 2001, the Code Commission added a period at the end of par. (a)(2). See § 28–9–5.

The 2003 amendment by Act 9, in subsec. (c), deleted "or its successor agency" each time it appeared.

The 2005 amendment by Act 68 in subsec. (c) substituted "Department of Driver Services" for "Department of Motor Vehicle Safety" twice.

§ 42–8–112. Restricted driving license; proof of compliance

(a) In any case where the court imposes the use of an ignition interlock device as a condition of probation on a resident of this state whose driving privilege is not suspended or revoked, the court shall require the person to surrender his or her driver's license to the court immediately and provide proof of compliance with such order to the court or the probation officer and obtain an ignition interlock device restricted driving license within 30 days. Upon expiration of the period of time for which such person is required to use an ignition interlock device, the person may apply for and receive a regular driver's license upon payment of the fee provided for in Code Section 40–5–25. If such person fails to provide proof of installation to the extent required by subsection (a) of Code Section 42–8–111 and receipt of the restricted driving license within such period, absent a finding by the court of good cause for that failure, which finding is entered in the court's record, the court shall revoke or terminate the probation.

(b)(1) In any case where the court imposes the use of an ignition interlock device as a condition of probation on a resident of this state whose driving privilege is suspended or revoked, the court shall require the person to provide proof of compliance with such order to the court or the probation officer and the Department of Driver Services not later than ten days after the date on which such person first becomes eligible to apply for an ignition interlock device limited driving permit in accordance with paragraph (2) of this subsection or a habitual violator's probationary license in accordance with paragraph (3) of this subsection, whichever is applicable. If such person fails to provide proof of installation to the extent required by subsection (a) of Code Section 42–8–111 within the period required by this subsection, absent a finding by the court of good cause for that failure, which finding is entered on the court's record, the court shall revoke or terminate the probation if such is still applicable.

(2) If the person subject to court ordered use of an ignition interlock device as a condition of probation is authorized under Code Section 40–5–63 or 40–5–67.2 to apply for reinstatement of his or her driver's license during the period of suspension, such person shall, prior to applying for reinstatement of the license, have an ignition interlock device installed and shall maintain such ignition interlock device in a motor vehicle or vehicles to the extent required by subsection (a) of Code Section 42–8–111 for a period of six months running concurrently with that of an ignition interlock device limited driving permit, which permit shall not be issued until such person submits to the department proof of completion of a DUI Alcohol or Drug Use Risk Reduction Program, proof of having undergone any clinical evaluation and of having enrolled in any substance abuse treatment program required by Code Section 40–5–63.1, and proof of installation of an ignition interlock device on a vehicle or vehicles to the extent required by subsection (a) of Code Section 42–8–111. Such a person may apply for and be issued an ignition interlock device limited driving permit at the end of 12 months after the suspension of the driver's license. At the expiration of such six-month ignition interlock device limited driving permit, the driver may, if otherwise qualified, apply for reinstatement of a regular driver's license upon payment of the fee provided in Code Section 40–5–25.

(3) If the person subject to court ordered use of an ignition interlock device as a condition of probation is authorized under Code Section 40–5–58 or under Code Section 40–5–67.2 to obtain a habitual violator's probationary license, such person shall, if such person is a habitual violator as a result of two or more convictions for driving under the influence of alcohol or drugs, have an ignition interlock device installed and maintained in a motor vehicle or vehicles to the extent required by subsection (a) of Code Section 42–8–111 for a period of six months following issuance of the probationary license, and such person shall not during such six-month period drive any motor vehicle that is not so equipped, all as conditions of such probationary license. Following expiration of such six-month period with no violation of the conditions of the probationary license, the person may apply for a habitual violator probationary license without such ignition interlock device condition.

(4) In any case where installation of an ignition interlock device is required, failure to show proof of such device shall be grounds for refusal of reinstatement of such license or issuance of such habitual violator's probationary license or the immediate suspension or revocation of such license.

(c) Each resident of this state who is required to have an ignition interlock device installed pursuant to this article shall report to the provider center every 30 days for the purpose of monitoring the operation of each required ignition interlock device. If at any time it is determined that a person has tampered with the device, the Department of Driver Services shall be given written notice within five days by the probation officer, the court ordering the use of such device, or the interlock provider. If an ignition interlock device is found to be malfunctioning, it shall be replaced or repaired, as ordered by the court or the Department of Driver Services, at the expense of the provider.

(d)(1) If a person required to report to an ignition interlock provider as required by subsection (c) of this Code section fails to report to the provider as required or receives an unsatisfactory report from the provider at any time during the six-month period, the Department of Driver Services shall revoke such person's ignition interlock device limited driving permit immediately upon notification from the provider of the failure to report or failure to receive a satisfactory report. Except as provided in paragraph (2) of this subsection, within 30 days after such revocation, the person may make a written request for a hearing and remit to the department a payment of $250.00 for the cost of the hearing. Within 30 days after receiving a written request for a hearing and a payment of $250.00, the Department of Driver Services shall hold a hearing as provided in Chapter 13 of Title 50, the "Georgia Administrative Procedure Act." The hearing shall be recorded.

(2) Any person whose ignition interlock device limited driving permit was revoked on or before July 1, 2004, for failure to report or failure to receive a satisfactory report may make a written request for a hearing and remit to the department a payment of $250.00 for the cost of the hearing. Within 30 days after receiving a written request for a hearing and a payment of $250.00, the Department of Driver Services shall hold a hearing as provided in Chapter 13 of Title 50, the "Georgia Administrative Procedure Act." The hearing shall be recorded.

(3) If the hearing officer determines that the person failed to report to the ignition interlock provider for any of the reasons specified below, the Department of Driver Services shall issue a new ignition interlock device limited driving permit that shall be valid for a period of six months to such person. Such reasons shall be for providential cause and include, but not be limited to, the following:

(A) Medical necessity, as evidenced by a written statement from a medical doctor;

(B) The person was incarcerated;

(C) The person was required to be on the job at his or her place of employment, with proof that the person would be terminated if he or she was not at work; or

(D) The vehicle with the installed interlock device was rendered inoperable by reason of collision, fire, or a major mechanical failure.

(4) If the hearing officer determines that the person failed to report to the ignition interlock provider for any reason other than those specified in paragraph (3) of this subsection, or if the person received an unsatisfactory report from the provider, after the expiration of 120 days the person may apply to the department and the department shall issue a new ignition interlock device limited driving permit to such person.

(5) This subsection shall not apply to any person convicted of violating Code Section 42–8–118.

Laws 1993, p. 568, § 1; Laws 2000, p. 1457, § 6; Laws 2001, p. 208, § 1–9; Laws 2002, p. 415, § 42; Laws 2003, Act 353, § 8, eff. July 1, 2003; Laws 2004, Act 555, § 1, eff. July 1, 2004; Laws 2005, Act 19, § 42, eff. April 7, 2005; Laws 2005, Act 68, § 24–5, eff. July 1, 2005.

Historical and Statutory Notes

The 2004 amendment by Act 555 added subsec. (d).

The 2005 amendment by Act 19 was a provision contained in a correction bill.

The 2005 amendment by Act 68 substituted "Department of Driver Services" for "Department of Motor Vehicle Safety" throughout the section.

§ 42–8–113. Rental, lease, or loan of motor vehicle

(a) No person shall knowingly rent, lease, or lend a motor vehicle to a person known to have had his or her driving privilege restricted as a condition of probation as provided in this article, unless the vehicle is equipped with a functioning, certified ignition interlock device. Any person whose driving privilege is restricted as a condition of probation as provided in this article shall notify any other person who rents, leases, or loans a motor vehicle to him or her of such driving restriction.

(b) Any person convicted of a violation of subsection (a) of this Code section shall be guilty of a misdemeanor.

Laws 1993, p. 568, § 1.

§ 42–8–114. Particular provider not to be specified when use of ignition interlock device specified

(a) No judicial officer, probation officer, law enforcement officer, or other officer or employee of a court; person who owns, operates, or is employed by a private company which has contracted to provide private probation services for misdemeanor cases; or professional bondsman or agent or employee thereof shall specify, directly or indirectly, a particular provider center which the person may or shall utilize when use of an ignition interlock device is required. This subsection shall not prohibit any judicial officer, probation officer, law enforcement officer, or other officer or employee of a court; owner, operator, or employee of a private company which has contracted to provide probation services for misdemeanor cases; or professional bondsman or agent or employee thereof from furnishing any person, upon request, the names of certified provider centers.

(b) No person who owns, operates, or is employed by a private company which has contracted to provide probation services for misdemeanor cases or professional bondsman or agent or employee thereof shall be authorized to own, operate, or be employed by a provider center.

Laws 1993, p. 568, § 1; Laws 2000, p. 1457, § 6.

§ 42–8–115. Certification of devices

(a) The commissioner of driver services or the commissioner's designee shall certify ignition interlock devices required by this article and the providers of such devices and shall promulgate rules and regulations for the certification of said devices and providers. The standards for certification of such devices shall include, but not be limited to, those standards for such devices promulgated by the National Highway Traffic Safety Administration and adopted by rule or regulation of the Department of Driver Services.

(b) The commissioner of driver services may utilize information from an independent agency to certify ignition interlock devices on or off the premises of the manufacturer in accordance with rules and regulations promulgated pursuant to this article. The cost of certification shall be borne by the manufacturers of ignition interlock devices.

(c) The commissioner of driver services shall adopt rules and regulations for determining the accuracy of and proper use of the ignition interlock devices in full compliance with this article. No model of ignition interlock device shall be certified unless it meets the accuracy requirements specified by such rules and regulations.

Laws 1993, p. 568, § 1; Laws 2000, p. 1457, § 6; Laws 2002, p. 415, § 42; Laws 2005, Act 68, § 24–6, eff. July 1, 2005.

Historical and Statutory Notes

The 2005 amendment by Act 68 in subsec. (a) substituted "commissioner of driver services" for "commissioner of motor vehicle safety" and "Department of Driver Services" for "Department of Motor Vehicle Safety"; and in subsecs. (b) and (c) substituted "commissioner of driver services" for "commissioner of motor vehicle safety".

§ 42–8–116. Warning labels

The providers certified by the Department of Driver Services shall design and adopt pursuant to regulations of the department a warning label which shall be affixed to each ignition interlock device upon installation. The label shall contain a warning that any person tampering, circumventing, or otherwise misusing the device is guilty of a misdemeanor and may be subject to civil liability.

Laws 1993, p. 568, § 1; Laws 2000, p. 1457, § 6; Laws 2002, p. 415, § 42; Laws 2005, Act 68, § 24–7, eff. July 1, 2005.

Historical and Statutory Notes

The 2005 amendment by Act 68 substituted "Department of Driver Services" for "Department of Motor Vehicle Safety".

§ 42–8–116.1. Effect of failure to install ignition interlock device or lack of certification prior to effective date of Code section

Any other or former provision of this article notwithstanding:

(1) The failure to install an ignition interlock device pursuant to an order of probation granted on or after May 1, 1999, but prior to May 1, 2000, shall not be ground for suspension or revocation of driving privileges, revocation of probation, refusal to issue a probationary driver's license, or refusal to reinstate a driver's license for the person granted such probation unless the order granting such probation unequivocally conditioned probation upon the installation of an ignition interlock device; and

(2) In the case of any person who had installed and maintained an ignition interlock device in a motor vehicle for a period of six months pursuant to any order of probation granted on or after May 1, 1999, but prior to May 1, 2000, any lack of certification of such ignition interlock device or of the provider center for such device or lack of a limited driving permit for the period of use of such device shall not be ground for suspension or revocation of driving privileges, revocation of probation, refusal to issue a probationary driver's license, or refusal to reinstate a driver's license for the person subject to such order if such installation and the monitoring required by this article for the required period of maintenance is confirmed in writing by the provider center for such device.

Laws 2000, p. 1457, § 6; Laws 2001, p. 4, § 42.

Historical and Statutory Notes

In 2000 and 2001, the Code Commission, in pars. (1) and (2), substituted "May 1, 2000" for "the effective date of this Code section". See § 28–9–5.

§ 42–8–117. Revocation of probation and revocation of driving privilege

(a)(1) In the event the sentencing court finds that a person has violated the terms of probation imposed pursuant to subsection (a) of Code Section 42–8–111, the Department of Driver Services shall revoke that person's driving privilege for one year from the date the court revokes that person's probation. The court shall report such probation revocation to the Department of Driver Services by court order.

(2) This subsection shall not apply to any person whose limited driving permit has been revoked under subsection (d) of Code Section 42–8–112.

(b) In the event the sentencing court finds that a person has twice violated the terms of probation imposed pursuant to subsection (a) of Code Section 42–8–111 during the same period of probation, the Department of Driver Services shall revoke that person's driving privilege for five years from the date the court revokes that person's probation for a second time. The court shall report such probation revocation to the Department of Driver Services by court order.

Laws 1993, p. 568, § 1; Laws 2000, p. 1457, § 6; Laws 2002, p. 415, § 42; Laws 2004, Act 555, § 2, eff. July 1, 2004; Laws 2005, Act 68, § 24–8, eff. July 1, 2005.

Historical and Statutory Notes

The 2004 amendment by Act 555 redesignated former subsec. (a) as par. (a)(1) and added par. (a)(2).

The 2005 amendment by Act 68 substituted "Department of Driver Services" for "Department of Motor Vehicle Safety" throughout the section.

§ 42–8–118. Violations and penalties

(a) It is unlawful for any person whose driving privilege is restricted pursuant to subsection (a) of Code Section 42–8–111 to request or solicit any other person to blow into an ignition interlock device or to start a motor vehicle equipped with the device for the purpose of providing the person so restricted with an operable motor vehicle.

(b) It is unlawful for any person to blow into an ignition interlock device or to start a motor vehicle equipped with the device for the purpose of providing an operable motor vehicle to a person whose driving privilege is restricted pursuant to subsection (a) of Code Section 42–8–111.

(c) It is unlawful to tamper with, or circumvent the operation of, an ignition interlock device.

(d) Any person violating any provision of this Code section shall be guilty of a misdemeanor.

Laws 1993, p. 568, § 1.

Article 9

Probation Management

§ 42–8–150. Short title

This article shall be known and may be cited as the "Probation Management Act."

Laws 2009, Act 11, § 1, eff. April 21, 2009.

Historical and Statutory Notes

Former § 42–8–150, relating to the short title of the Probation Management Act of 2004, derived from Laws 2004, Act 595, § 7, was repealed by Laws 2004, Act 595, § 7; Laws 2006, Act 577, § 2, eff. June 30, 2008.

§ 42–8–151. Definitions

For purposes of this article, the term:

(1) "Chief probation officer" means the highest ranking field probation officer in each judicial circuit.

(2) "Commissioner" means the commissioner of corrections.

(3) "Department" means the Department of Corrections.

(4) "Electronic monitoring" means supervising, mapping, or tracking the location of a probationer by means including electronic surveillance, voice recognition, facial recognition, fingerprinting or biometric scan, automated kiosk, automobile ignition interlock device, or global positioning systems which may coordinate data with crime scene information.

(5) "Hearing officer" means an impartial department employee or representative who has been selected and appointed to hear alleged cases regarding violations of probation for administrative sanctioning.

(6) "Initial sanction" means the sanction set by the judge upon initial sentencing.

(7) "Intensive probation" means a level of probation supervision which includes, but is not limited to, curfews, community service, drug testing, program participation, special conditions of probation, and general conditions of probation as set forth in Code Section 42–8–35.

(8) "Options system day reporting center" means a state facility providing supervision of probationers which includes, but is not limited to, mandatory reporting, program participation, drug testing, community service, all special conditions of probation, and general conditions of probation as set forth in Code Section 42–8–35.

(9) "Options system probationer" means a probationer who has been sentenced to the sentencing options system.

(10) "Probation supervision" means a level of probation supervision which includes, but is not limited to, general conditions of probation as set forth in Code Section 42–8–35 and all special conditions of probation.

(11) "Residential substance abuse treatment facility" means a state correctional facility that provides inpatient treatment for alcohol and drug abuse.

(12) "Sentencing options system" means a continuum of sanctions for probationers that includes the sanctions set forth in subsection (c) of Code Section 42–8–153.

Laws 2009, Act 11, § 1, eff. April 21, 2009; Laws 2010, Act 624, § 42, eff. June 3, 2010.

Historical and Statutory Notes

Former § 42–8–151, relating to definitions for the Probation Management Act of 2004, derived from Laws 2004, Act 595, § 7, was repealed by Laws 2004, Act 595, § 7; Laws 2006, Act 577, § 2, eff. June 30, 2008.

The 2010 amendment by Act 624 was a provision contained in a correction bill.

§ 42–8–152. Sentencing options system; jurisdiction

(a) In addition to any other terms or conditions of probation provided for under this chapter, the trial judge may require that defendants who are sentenced to probation pursuant to subsection (c) of Code Section 42–8–34 be ordered to the sentencing options system.

(b) Where a defendant has been ordered to the sentencing options system, the court shall retain jurisdiction throughout the period of the probated sentence as provided in subsection (g) of Code Section 42–8–34, and may modify or revoke any part of a probated sentence as provided in Code Section 42–8–34.1 and subsection (c) of Code Section 42–8–38.

Laws 2009, Act 11, § 1, eff. April 21, 2009.

Historical and Statutory Notes

Former § 42–8–152, relating to sentencing options system and jurisdiction, derived from Laws 2004, Act 595, § 7; Laws 2005, Act 19, § 42, was repealed by Laws 2004, Act 595, § 7; Laws 2006, Act 577, § 2, eff. June 30, 2008.

§ 42–8–153. Authorization to establish Administrative sanctions

(a) The department is authorized to establish by rules and regulations a system of administrative sanctions as an alternative to judicial modifications or revocations for probationers who violate the terms and conditions of the sentencing options system established under this article. The department may not, however, sanction probationers for violations of special conditions of probation or general conditions of probation for which the sentencing judge has expressed an intention that such violations be heard by the court pursuant to Code Section 42–8–34.1.

(b) The department shall only impose restrictions which are equal to or less restrictive than the sanction cap set by the sentencing judge.

(c) The administrative sanctions which may be imposed by the department are as follows, from most restrictive to least restrictive:

(1) Probation detention center or residential substance abuse treatment facility;

(2) Probation boot camp;

(3) Department of Corrections day reporting center;

(4) Intensive probation;

(5) Electronic monitoring;

(6) Community service; or

(7) Probation supervision.

(d) The department may order offenders sanctioned pursuant to paragraphs (1) through (3) of subsection (c) of this Code section to be held in the local jail until transported to a designated facility.

Laws 2009, Act 11, § 1, eff. April 21, 2009.

Historical and Statutory Notes

Former § 42–8–153, relating to authorization to establish administrative sanctions, derived from Laws 2004, Act 595, § 7, was repealed by Laws 2004, Act 595, § 7; Laws 2006, Act 577, § 2, eff. June 30, 2008.

§ 42–8–154. Preliminary hearings for violations

(a) Whenever an options system probationer is arrested on a warrant for an alleged violation of probation, an informal preliminary hearing shall be held within a reasonable time not to exceed 15 days.

(b) A preliminary hearing shall not be required when:

(1) The probationer is not under arrest on a warrant;

(2) The probationer signed a waiver of a preliminary hearing; or

(3) The administrative hearing referred to in Code Section 42–8–155 will be held within 15 days of arrest.

Laws 2009, Act 11, § 1, eff. April 21, 2009.

Historical and Statutory Notes

Former § 42–8–154, relating to preliminary hearings for violations, derived from Laws 2004, Act 595, § 7; Laws 2005, Act 19, § 42, was repealed by Laws 2004, Act 595, § 7; Laws 2006, Act 577, § 2, eff. June 30, 2008.

§ 42–8–155. Imposition of administrative sanctions and hearings

(a) If an options system probationer violates the conditions of probation, the department may impose administrative sanctions as an alternative to judicial modification or revocation of probation.

(b) Upon issuance of a petition outlining the alleged probation violations, the chief probation officer, or his or her designee, may conduct a hearing to determine whether an options system probationer has violated a condition of probation. If the chief probation officer determines that the probationer has violated a condition of probation, the chief probation officer is authorized to impose sanctions consistent with paragraphs (4) through (7) of subsection (c) of Code Section 42–8–153. The failure of an options system probationer to comply with a sanction imposed by the chief probation officer shall constitute a violation of probation.

(c)(1) Upon issuance of a petition outlining the alleged probation violations, the hearing officer may initiate an administrative proceeding to determine whether an options system probationer has violated a condition of probation. If the hearing officer determines by a preponderance of the evidence that the probationer has violated a condition of probation, the hearing officer may impose sanctions consistent with Code Section 42–8–153.

(2) The administrative proceeding provided for under this subsection shall be commenced within 15 days, but not less than 48 hours after notice of the administrative proceeding has been served on the probationer. The administrative proceeding may be conducted electronically.

(d) The failure of a probationer to comply with the sanction or sanctions imposed by the chief probation officer or hearing officer shall constitute a violation of probation.

(e) An options system probationer may at any time waive a hearing and voluntarily accept the sanctions proposed by the department.

Laws 2009, Act 11, § 1, eff. April 21, 2009.

Historical and Statutory Notes

Former § 42–8–155, relating to imposition of administrative sanctions and hearings, derived from Laws 2004, Act 595, § 7; Laws 2005, Act 19, § 42, was repealed by Laws 2004, Act 595, § 7; Laws 2006, Act 577, § 2, eff. June 30, 2008.

§ 42–8–156. Appeal and review

(a) The hearing officer's decision shall be final unless the options system probationer files a request for review with the senior hearing officer. A request for review must be filed within 15 days of the issuance of the department's decision. Such request shall not stay the department's decision. The senior hearing officer shall issue a response within seven days of receipt of the review request.

(b) The senior hearing officer's decision shall be final unless the options system probationer files an appeal in the sentencing court. Such appeal shall name the commissioner as defendant and shall be filed within 30 days of the issuance of the decision by the senior hearing officer.

(c) This appeal shall first be reviewed by the judge upon the record. At the judge's discretion, a de novo hearing may be held on the decision. The filing of the appeal shall not stay the department's decision.

(d) Where the sentencing judge does not act on the appeal within 30 days of the date of the filing of the appeal, the department's decision shall be affirmed by operation of law.

Laws 2009, Act 11, § 1, eff. April 21, 2009.

Historical and Statutory Notes

Former § 42–8–156, relating to appeal and review, derived from Laws 2004, Act 595, § 7, was repealed by Laws 2004, Act 595, § 7; Laws 2006, Act 577, § 2, eff. June 30, 2008.

§ 42–8–157. Effect of law on powers of the court

Nothing contained in this article shall be construed as repealing any power given to any court of this state to place offenders on probation or to supervise offenders.

Laws 2009, Act 11, § 1, eff. April 21, 2009.

Historical and Statutory Notes

Former § 42–8–157, relating to the effect of law on powers of the court, derived from Laws 2004, Act 595, § 7, was repealed by Laws 2004, Act 595, § 7; Laws 2006, Act 577, § 2, eff. June 30, 2008.

§ 42–8–158. Scope of article

This article shall only apply in judicial circuits where the department has allocated certified hearing officers.

Laws 2009, Act 11, § 1, eff. April 21, 2009.

Historical and Statutory Notes

Former § 42–8–158, relating to scope of article, derived from Laws 2004, Act 595, § 7, was repealed by Laws 2004, Act 595, § 7; Laws 2006, Act 577, § 2, eff. June 30, 2008.

§ 42–8–159. Liberal construction of article

This article shall be liberally construed so that its purposes may be achieved.

Laws 2009, Act 11, § 1, eff. April 21, 2009.

Historical and Statutory Notes

Former § 42–8–159, relating to liberal construction of article, derived from Laws 2004, Act 595, § 7, was repealed by Laws 2004, Act 595, § 7; Laws 2006, Act 577, § 2, eff. June 30, 2008.

§§ 42–8–160. Repealed by Laws 2004, Act 595, § 7; Laws 2006, Act 577, § 2, eff. June 30, 2008

Historical and Statutory Notes

Repealed § 42–8–160, relating to the repeal of the article, was derived from Laws 2004, Act 595, § 7; Laws 2006, Act 577, § 2.

TITLE 43

PROFESSIONS AND BUSINESSES

CHAPTER 4B

GEORGIA ATHLETIC AND ENTERTAINMENT COMMISSION

Article 3

Article 3

Ticket Brokers

§ 43–4B–25. Persons other than ticket brokers prohibited from reselling or offering for sale tickets to athletic contest or entertainment event for price exceeding face value of ticket; service charge

(a) Except as otherwise provided in Code Section 43–4B–29, it shall be unlawful for any person other than a ticket broker to resell or offer for resale any ticket of admission or other evidence of the right of entry to any athletic contest, concert, theater performance, amusement, exhibition, or other entertainment event to which the general public is admitted for a price in excess of the face value of the ticket. Notwithstanding any other provision of this article to the contrary, a service charge not to exceed $ 3.00 may be charged when tickets or other evidences of the right of entry are sold by an authorized ticket agent through places of established business licensed to do business by the municipality or county, where applicable, in which such places of business are located. Notwithstanding any other provision of this article to the contrary, the owner, operator, lessee, or tenant of the property on which such athletic contest or entertainment event is to be held or is being held or the sponsor of such contest or event may charge or may authorize, in writing, any person to charge a service charge for the sale of such ticket, privilege, or license of admission in addition to the face value of the ticket. Such writing granting authority to another shall specify the amount of the service charge to be charged for the sale of each ticket, privilege, or license of admission.

(b) Notwithstanding any other provision of this article to the contrary, in the case of any athletic contest or entertainment event that is described in Code Section 43–4B–30, a sponsor of such a contest or event may contractually restrict the resale of a ticket to such contest or event by giving notice of such restriction on the back of the ticket. Notwithstanding any other provision of this article to the contrary, in the case of any athletic contest or entertainment event, an owner, operator, lessee, or tenant of the property on which such contest or event is to be held or is being held may contractually restrict the resale of the right of occupancy of any specific suite, seat, or seating area by giving notice in writing of such restriction.

Laws 2001, p. 752, § 2.

§ 43–4B–26. Requirements for ticket brokers

In order to engage in the practice or business of a ticket broker a person shall be required to:

(1) Maintain a permanent office or place of business in this state, excluding a post office box, for the purpose of engaging in the business of a ticket broker;

(2) Apply to the commission for a ticket broker's license on a form designated by the commission, pay an annual license fee of $500.00, and renew the license annually;

(3) Pay any local tax required by a local government; and

(4) Register for sales and use tax purposes pursuant to Article 1 of Chapter 8 of Title 48.

Laws 2001, p. 752, § 2; Laws 2003, Act 347, § 29, eff. June 4, 2003; Laws 2005, Act 325, § 7, eff. July 1, 2005.

§ 43–4B–27. Convicted felons prohibited from engaging in business of ticket broker

No person shall engage in the practice or business of a ticket broker, or be employed as general manager for a person engaged in the practice or business of a ticket broker, who has been convicted of a felony and who has not been pardoned or had his or her civil rights restored.

Laws 2001, p. 752, § 2.

§ 43–4B–28. Disclosures by ticket brokers; prohibited practices

(a) The ticket broker shall be required to:

(1) Post at its established place of business the terms of the purchaser's right to cancel the purchase of a ticket from a ticket broker;

(2) Disclose to the purchaser the refund policy of the ticket broker should an athletic contest or entertainment event be canceled;

(3) Disclose to the purchaser in writing the difference between the face value of the ticket and the amount which the ticket broker is charging for such ticket; and

(4) Sell tickets only at its permanent office, place of business, or through the Internet; provided, however, that delivery of one or more tickets after the transaction is completed to a place other than the ticket broker's office or place of business shall not violate this paragraph.

(b)(1) A ticket broker shall be prohibited from employing any agent or employee for the purpose of making future purchases of tickets from the owner, operator, lessee, or tenant of the property on which an athletic contest or entertainment event is to be held.

(2) Each ticket broker, including any affiliated group of ticket brokers, shall be prohibited from acquiring and reselling

in excess of 1 percent of the total tickets allocated for any contest or event.

(3) Unless otherwise provided in a written agreement between a ticket broker and the purchaser, a ticket broker shall be required to refund any payment received for the purchase of a ticket under this article if the purchaser returns the ticket and requests a cancellation of the sale thereof within 36 hours from the time of purchase of the ticket and if such return is made more than 72 hours preceding the athletic contest or entertainment event.

(4) A ticket broker shall be required to refund any payment received for the purchase of a ticket under this article if the athletic contest or entertainment event is canceled and not rescheduled.

(5) If a ticket broker guarantees in writing delivery of a ticket or tickets to an athletic contest or entertainment event as provided under this article to a purchaser and fails to complete such delivery, the ticket broker shall be required to provide within 15 days a full refund of any amount paid by the purchaser and, in addition, shall pay the purchaser a refund fee of three times the amount paid by the purchaser for each such ticket.

(c)(1) For all venues which seat or admit less than 15,000 persons, a ticket broker and its employees, agents, and assigns are criminally prohibited from reselling or offering for resale any ticket within 1,500 feet from the venue where an event or contest is to be held or is being held.

(2) For all venues which seat or admit 15,000 or more persons, a ticket broker and its employees, agents, and assigns are criminally prohibited from reselling or offering for resale any ticket within 2,700 feet from the venue where an event or contest is to be held or is being held.

(d) Any ticket broker offering to resell tickets to an athletic contest or entertainment event through any printed, broadcast, or Internet advertising shall include in such advertising the license number of such ticket broker offering such tickets for resale.

Laws 2001, p. 752, § 2; Laws 2003, Act 347, § 30, eff. June 4, 2003; Laws 2005, Act 325, § 8, eff. July 1, 2005.

Historical and Statutory Notes

The 2005 amendment by Act 325 rewrote subsecs. (a) and (c), which had read:

"(a) The ticket broker shall be required to:

"(1) Disclose the terms of the purchaser's right to cancel the purchase of a ticket from a ticket broker;

"(2) Disclose to the purchaser the refund policy of the ticket broker should an athletic contest or entertainment event be canceled; and

"(3) Disclose to the purchaser in writing the difference between the face value of the ticket and the amount which the ticket broker is charging for such ticket."

"(c) A ticket broker and its employees, agents, and assigns are criminally prohibited from reselling or offering for resale any ticket within 1,500 feet from the venue where an event or contest is to be held or is being held."

§ 43–4B–29. Original purchaser for personal use may sell tickets at any price; charitable organizations exempted from provisions regulating ticket sales

(a) No provision of this article or any other provision of law shall criminally prohibit any person who is the original purchaser for personal use of one or more tickets to an athletic contest or entertainment event covered under this article from reselling or offering for resale any of such tickets for any price, provided that such person does not sell or offer to sell such tickets within 2,700 feet of a venue which seats or admits 15,000 or more persons for such a contest or event or a public entrance to such a contest or event.

(b) Charitable organizations and their employees and volunteers shall not be subject to the provisions of this article when offering for sale any tickets of admission in a raffle, auction, or similar fundraising activity for the benefit of the organization's charitable purposes.

Laws 2001, p. 752, § 2; Laws 2002, p. 415, § 43; Laws 2005, Act 325, § 9, eff. July 1, 2005.

§ 43–4B–29.1. Ticket resale; when authorized

(a) Notwithstanding subsection (c) of Code Section 43–4B–28 and subsection (b) of Code Section 43–4B–30, no provision of this article or any other provision of law shall provide a criminal penalty for or prohibit the resale or offering for resale of a ticket or tickets to an athletic contest or entertainment event covered under this article by a ticket broker or a ticket broker's employees, agents, and assigns in a zone or zones within the area where such resale or offering for resale is prohibited by such subsections, if such activity is authorized by the organizer of the contest or event and the owner or operator of the venue where such contest or event is being held or to be held.

(b) Notwithstanding subsection (a) of Code Section 43–4B–29 and subsection (b) of Code Section 43–4B–30, no provision of this article or any other provision of law shall provide a criminal penalty for or prohibit the resale or offering for resale of a ticket or tickets purchased by any person who is the original purchaser for personal use of such ticket or tickets to an athletic contest or entertainment event covered under this article in a zone or zones within the area where such resale or offering for resale is prohibited by such subsections, if such activity is authorized by the organizer of the contest or event and the owner or operator of the venue where such contest or event is being held or to be held.

Laws 2005, Act 325, § 10, eff. July 1, 2005.

Historical and Statutory Notes

In 2005, the Code Commission, in subsec. (a), deleted a comma following "Code Section 43–4B–28". See § 28–9–5.

§ 43–4B–30. More restrictive regulation by local government authorized in certain circumstances

(a) With regard to any single athletic contest or entertainment event which occurs no more often than once annually and with regard to any series of athletic contests which occur no more often than once annually and which occur within a time period not exceeding ten days, the municipal corporation in which such contest, event, or series of contests is to be held, or if the contest, event, or series of contests is to be held in an unincorporated area, the county of such unincorporated area, is authorized to enact by ordinance regulations governing ticket brokers for such contest, event, or series of contests which are more restrictive than the provisions of this article.

(b) The municipal corporation in which an athletic contest or entertainment event is to be held, or if the contest or entertainment event is to be held in an unincorporated area, the county of such unincorporated area, is authorized to enact an ordinance prohibiting the resale or offering for resale of one or more tickets by a ticket broker or by a person who is the original purchaser for personal use of one or more tickets within 2,700 feet of a venue which seats or admits 15,000 or more persons.

Laws 2001, p. 752, § 2; Laws 2003, Act 347, § 31, eff. June 4, 2003; Laws 2005, Act 325, § 11, eff. July 1, 2005.

§ 43–4B–31. Criminal penalty for violation of this article

Any person who violates this article is guilty of a misdemeanor of a high and aggravated nature.

Laws 2001, p. 752, § 2.

§ 43–4B–32. Rules and regulations

(a) In addition to the powers and duties set out in Code Section 43–4B–3, the commission is authorized to promulgate rules and regulations to accomplish the purposes of this article in accordance with Chapter 13 of Title 50, the "Georgia Administrative Procedure Act." The commission shall enforce the provisions of this article. The enforcement powers of the commission set out in this Code section shall be in addition to the criminal penalty provided by Code Section 43–4B–31.

(b) Whenever it may appear to the commission that any person is violating or has violated any provision of this article and that proceedings would be in the public interest:

(1) Subject to notice and opportunity for hearing in accordance with Chapter 13 of Title 50, the "Georgia Administrative Procedure Act," unless the right to notice is waived by the person against whom the sanction is imposed, the commission may:

(A) Issue a cease and desist order prohibiting any violation of this article;

(B) Issue an order against a person who violates this article, imposing a civil penalty up to a maximum of $ 1,000.00 per violation; or

(C) Issue an order suspending or revoking the ticket broker's license; or

(2) Upon a showing by the commission in any superior court of competent jurisdiction that a person has violated or is about to violate this article, a rule promulgated under this article, or an order of the commission, the court may enter or grant any or all of the following relief:

(A) A temporary restraining order or a temporary or permanent injunction;

(B) A civil penalty up to a maximum of $ 2,000.00 per violation of this article;

(C) A declaratory judgment;

(D) Restitution to any person or persons adversely affected by a defendant's action in violation of this article; or

(E) Other relief as the court deems just or reasonable.

(c) Unless the commission determines that a person subject to this article intends to depart quickly from this state or to remove his or her property from this state or to conceal his or her person or property in this state or that there is immediate danger of harm to citizens of this state or another state, the commission shall give notice in writing that such proceedings are contemplated and allow such person a reasonable opportunity to appear before the commission and execute an assurance of voluntary compliance. The determination of the commission under this subsection shall be final and not subject to review.

(d) Procedures relating to hearings, notice, counsel, subpoenas, records, enforcement powers, intervention, rules of evidence, decisions, exceptions, review of initial decisions, final decisions, and judicial review of decisions shall be governed by Chapter 13 of Title 50, the "Georgia Administrative Procedure Act," unless the provisions of such chapter are contrary to the express provisions of this article.

Laws 2001, p. 752, § 2.

CHAPTER 38

OPERATORS OF PRIVATE DETECTIVE BUSINESSES AND PRIVATE SECURITY BUSINESSES

§ 43–38–1. Short title

This chapter shall be known and may be cited as the "Georgia Private Detective and Security Agencies Act."

Laws 1973, p. 40, § 1; Laws 1981, p. 1828, § 1.

§ 43–38–2. Purpose

This chapter is enacted for the purpose of safeguarding the citizens of this state by regulation of the private detective and private security businesses. The regulation of such businesses is declared to be in the public interest; and this chapter shall be liberally construed so as to accomplish the foregoing purpose.

Laws 1981, p. 1828, § 1.

§ 43–38–3. Definitions

As used in this chapter, the term:

(1) "Board" means the Georgia Board of Private Detective and Security Agencies, a professional licensing board.

(2) "Law enforcement agency" means an agency responsible for ensuring compliance with the laws and ordinances enacted by federal, state, and local governing authorities.

(3) "Private detective business" means the business of obtaining or furnishing, or accepting employment to obtain or to furnish, information with reference to:

(A) Crimes or wrongs done or threatened against the United States of America or any state or territory thereof;

(B) The background, identity, habits, conduct, business, employment, occupation, assets, honesty, integrity, credibility, knowledge, trustworthiness, efficiency, loyalty, activity, movement, whereabouts, affiliations, associations, transactions, acts, reputation, or character of any person;

(C) The location, disposition, or recovery of lost or stolen property;

(D) The cause or responsibility for fires, libels, losses, accidents, damage, or injury to persons or property;

(E) The securing of evidence in the course of the private detective business to be used before any court, board, officer, or investigating committee; or

(F) The protection of individuals from serious bodily harm or death.

(4) "Private security business" means engaging in the business of, or accepting employment to provide, any or all of the following:

(A) Private patrol service;

(B) Watchman service;

(C) Guard service;

(D) Armored car service; or

(E) The protection of persons from death or serious bodily harm.

Laws 1973, p. 40, § 2; Laws 1981, p. 1828, § 2; Laws 2000, p. 1161, § 1; Laws 2000, p. 1706, § 15.

§ 43–38–4. Board; composition; expenses; secretary; powers and duties

(a) There is created the Georgia Board of Private Detective and Security Agencies. The board shall consist of seven members, each of whom shall be appointed by the Governor. Each member shall serve for a term of four years. Four members shall be engaged in the contract private detective or contract private security business and shall have at least four years of experience in such business immediately preceding their appointment; provided, however, that on and after October 1, 1987, at least two members shall be engaged in the contract private security business. Two members shall be engaged in state, county, or municipal law enforcement and shall have at least four years of experience in governmental law enforcement immediately preceding their appointment. One member shall be appointed from the public at large. At the first meeting of the board held each year, the members shall elect a chairman to serve for one year. The Governor may remove any member of the board for neglect of duty, incompetence, or other unethical or dishonorable conduct. After such removal or after the creation of a vacancy due to death, resignation, or ineligibility, the Governor shall appoint a successor to serve the unexpired term. Appointees to the board shall, immediately after their appointment, take and subscribe to a written oath or affirmation required by law for all public officers.

(b) The members of the board shall be reimbursed as provided for in subsection (f) of Code Section 43–1–2.

(c) The division director shall be the secretary of the board and shall perform such administrative duties as may be prescribed by the board. All official records of the board or affidavits by the division director as to the content of such records shall be prima-facie evidence of all matters required to be kept therein.

(d) In addition to any authority otherwise granted by this chapter and subject to the laws relating to the division director, the board shall have the following powers and duties:

(1) To determine the qualifications of applicants for licenses or registration under this chapter;

(2) To investigate alleged violations of this chapter or any rules and regulations adopted by the board, including the power to conduct inspections of a licensee's employee lists and training records;

(3) To promulgate all rules and regulations necessary to carry out this chapter;

(4) To establish and enforce standards governing the conduct of persons licensed and registered under this chapter;

(5) To maintain in its name an action for injunctive or other appropriate legal or equitable relief to remedy violations of this chapter. In pursuing equitable remedies, it shall not be necessary that the board allege or prove that it has no adequate remedy at law. It is declared that violations of this chapter are a menace and a nuisance and are dangerous to the public health, safety, and welfare;

(6) To recommend to the division director the employment or appointment of such personnel, including, but not limited to, inspectors, as may be necessary to assist the board in exercising and performing any and all the powers, duties, and obligations set forth in this chapter;

(7) To require a licensee to maintain and keep such records as are subject to inspection under this chapter;

(8) To issue, renew, deny, suspend, or revoke licenses, certificates, registrations, or permits in a manner consistent with this chapter;

(9) To hold hearings on all matters properly brought before it and, in connection therewith, to administer oaths, receive evidence, make the necessary determinations, and enter orders consistent with the findings; and

(10) To develop and apply such techniques which may include examinations as may be deemed necessary to assure that applicants licensed, registered, or issued weapons permits have the requisite skills and qualifications.

Laws 1973, p. 40, § 3; Laws 1981, p. 1828, § 3; Laws 1987, p. 1400, § 1; Laws 1994, p. 97, § 43; Laws 2000, p. 1706, § 19.

§ 43–38–5. Repealed by Laws 1987, p. 1400, § 2, eff. July 1, 1987

§ 43–38–6. Licenses; application; qualifications; bond; fees; display; suspension; persons licensed in other states

(a) Any individual, firm, association, company, partnership, limited liability company, or corporation desiring to engage in the private detective or private security business in this state shall make a verified application to the division director for a license therefor. If the applicant is a firm, association, company, partnership, limited liability company, or corporation, the person filing the application on behalf of such firm, association, company, partnership, limited liability company, or corporation shall be a corporate officer of such corporation or an officer of such firm, association, partnership, or limited liability company; and such individual shall meet the qualifications set out in this Code section.

(b) Upon being satisfied of the good character, competency, and integrity of an applicant for licensure under this chapter or, if the applicant is a firm, association, company, partnership, limited liability company, or corporation, upon being satisfied of the good character, competency, and integrity of the corporate officer of such corporation or officer of such firm, association, partnership, or limited liability company, the board may grant a license to conduct a private detective or private security business to such individual, firm, association, company, partnership, limited liability company, or corporation if:

(1) The applicant is at least 18 years of age;

(2) The applicant is a citizen of the United States or a registered resident alien;

(3) The applicant is of good moral character;

(4) The applicant has not been convicted of a felony or any crime involving the illegal use, carrying, or possession of a dangerous weapon or any crime involving moral turpitude; provided, however, that, if the applicant has been convicted of such crime, or has entered a plea of nolo contendere, or has entered a plea pursuant to Article 3 of Chapter 8 of Title 42 or otherwise been granted first offender treatment, the board may inquire into the nature of the crime, the date of conviction or plea, and other underlying facts and circumstances surrounding such criminal proceedings and, in its discretion, may grant a license to such applicant;

(5) The applicant has not committed an act constituting dishonesty or fraud;

(6) The applicant has satisfied the board that his or her private detective or private security business has a competent training officer and adequate training program with a curriculum approved by the board or that adequate training will be obtained from such other source as the board may approve;

(7) The applicant for a private detective company license has had at least two years' experience as an agent registered with a licensed detective agency, or has had at least two years' experience in law enforcement, or has a four-year degree in criminal justice or a related field from an accredited university or college; and the applicant for a security company license has had at least two years' experience as a supervisor or administrator in in-house security operations or with a licensed security agency, or has had at least two years' experience in law enforcement, or has a four-year degree in criminal justice or a related field from an accredited university or college;

(8) The applicants for private detective company licenses and security company licenses may be required to pass successfully a written examination as the board may prescribe; and

(9) The applicant meets such other qualifications as the board may prescribe by rule.

(c) The application for a license shall be made under oath on a form to be furnished by the division director. The application shall state the applicant's full name, age, date and place of birth; residences and employment within the past five years, with the names and addresses of employers; present occupation; date and place of conviction or arrest for any crime, including the plea of nolo contendere or a plea entered pursuant to Article 3 of Chapter 8 of Title 42 or other first offender treatment; and such additional information as the board may require to investigate the qualifications, character, competency, and integrity of the applicant. Each applicant shall submit with the application two complete sets of fingerprints on forms specified and furnished by the board and one photograph, two inches wide by three inches high, full face, taken within six months prior to the application; provided, however, that the board may waive the submission of fingerprints and photograph for any employee who has been employed by a person licensed under this chapter within the previous 12 months. The application shall contain such additional documentation as the board may prescribe by rule. The board shall have the discretion to deny a license to an applicant who fails to provide the information and supporting documentation required by this subsection.

(d)(1) In addition to the requirements enumerated in this Code section, each applicant for a license under this chapter shall provide satisfactory evidence to the board that the prospective licensee has posted or has made provision for the posting of a bond. The required bond shall be executed in favor of the state, in the amount of $ 25,000.00, with a surety company authorized to do business in this state and conditioned to pay damages not to exceed the amount of such bond to any person aggrieved by any act of the principal named in such bond, which act is in violation of this chapter and would be grounds for denial, suspension, or revocation of a license under Code Section 43–38–11. Immediately upon the granting of a license, such bond shall be filed with the division director by the licensee and shall be approved by the division director as to form and as to the solvency of the surety. The prospective licensee may file the required bond with the division director prior to the granting of a license for the division director's approval as provided in this Code section. In lieu of the required bond, a prospective licensee may submit to the board evidence of a policy of liability insurance in an amount of not less than $ 1 million insuring such prospective licensee against personal liability for damages arising out of acts of the insured or his employees. No licensee shall cancel or cause to be canceled a bond or liability insurance policy issued pursuant to this Code section unless the board is so informed in writing by certified mail or statutory overnight delivery at least 30 days prior to the proposed cancellation. In lieu of the required bond or liability insurance policy, the prospective licensee may submit a net worth affidavit, prepared using standard accounting procedures, which affidavit indicates that the prospective licensee has a net worth of more than $ 50,000.00. The board, in its discretion, may accept a financial affidavit in lieu of the bond or liability insurance policy required by this subsection. The board, in its discretion, may require licensees under this Code section to submit periodic financial updates to ensure continued financial responsibility. If the surety or licensee fails to submit, within ten days of the effective date of cancellation, a new bond or liability insurance policy or a net worth statement as outlined in this subsection, the board shall have the authority to revoke any license issued under this chapter.

(2) Licensees who have previously posted bonds or submitted net worth affidavits to comply with the provisions of this subsection may hereafter prove continued financial responsibility through the use of liability insurance policies in accordance with paragraph (1) of this subsection.

(e) Immediately upon receipt of a license certificate issued by the board pursuant to this chapter, the licensee shall post and at all times display such license in a conspicuous place at his place of business. A copy of the duplicate of the license certificate shall be conspicuously posted at each branch office.

(f) Notwithstanding any other provisions of this Code section, an applicant for a license shall agree that if such applicant makes a false statement in the application or if such applicant has been found to have been convicted of a felony and has not had all his or her civil rights restored pursuant to law, then the board shall be authorized to suspend any license granted to such applicant without a prior hearing as required in Code Section 43–38–11. Upon request, any such person shall be entitled to a hearing on such matter subsequent to the suspension.

(g) The board may grant a license provided in this Code section to a person who is licensed in another state or territory of the United States which has licensing requirements substantially similar to the licensing requirements provided in this Code section.

(h) The board may issue a temporary permit for not longer than 30 days to any person who is licensed in another state or territory of the United States which has licensing requirements substantially similar to the licensing requirements provided in this Code section if such person, in the course of an investigation which arose in the state in which he or she is licensed, finds it necessary to conduct an investigation in this state. Such temporary permit shall be limited to the scope of such investigation. No more than one temporary permit shall be issued in any 12 month period.

(i) The board may, in its discretion and in accordance with regulations adopted by the board, enter into limited license recognition agreements with any other state or the District of Columbia having licensure requirements substantially equal to the requirements provided by this chapter pursuant to which a person so licensed in such state or district may conduct an investigation in this state directly related to an investigation which was initiated outside of this state; provided, however, that such privilege shall be limited to 30 days for each agency for each such investigation.

Laws 1973, p. 40, §§ 5–7; Laws 1981, p. 1828, § 5; Laws 1984, p. 1338, § 1; Laws 1986, p. 751, § 2; Laws 1987, p. 3, § 43; Laws 1987, p. 1400, §§ 3–5; Laws 1988, p. 13, § 43; Laws 1991, p. 1027, § 1; Laws 1993, p. 123, § 43; Laws 1994, p. 291, § 1; Laws 2000, p. 1161, §§ 2, 3; Laws 2000, p. 1589, § 3; Laws 2000, p. 1706, § 19; Laws 2001, p. 1075, § 1; Laws 2010, Act 417, § 39, eff. May 20, 2010.

§ 43–38–7. Registration of employees; application; qualifications; fees

(a) Any employer may employ as many agents, guards, watchmen, or patrolmen as he or she deems necessary for the conduct of his or her business, provided that such employees meet the requirements and qualifications for licensure under this chapter.

(b)(1) Except as provided in paragraph (2) of this subsection, within 180 days of completing board mandated prelicensure training, potential licensees shall make application to be licensed with the board.

(2) Any guard, watchman, or patrolman who will be unarmed and who will be employed in the private security business shall not be required to be licensed by the board but shall be governed by Code Section 43–38–7.1.

(c)(1) Except as otherwise provided in paragraph (2) of subsection (b) of this Code section, upon being satisfied of the applicant"s character, competency, and eligibility for licensure, the board may license such applicant if her or she:

(A) Is at least 18 years of age;

(B) Is a citizen of the United States or a registered resident alien;

(C) Is of good moral character;

(D) Has not been convicted of a felony or any crime involving the illegal use, carrying, or possession of a dangerous weapon or any crime involving moral turpitude; provided, however, that, if the applicant has been convicted of such crime, or has entered a plea of nolo contendere to such crime, or has entered a plea pursuant to Article 3 of Chapter 8 of Title 42 or otherwise been granted first offender treatment, the board may inquire into the nature of the crime, the date of conviction or plea, and other underlying facts and circumstances surrounding such criminal proceedings and, in its discretion, may allow the applicant to be licensed;

(E) Has not committed an act constituting dishonesty or fraud; and

(F) Meets such other qualifications as the board may prescribe by rule.

(2) The board shall be authorized to require continuing education as a condition of renewal for all persons required to be licensed or registered with the board under this chapter. The board shall be authorized to promulgate rules and regulations addressing the requirement for continuing education and circumstances for which a waiver of this requirement may be granted.

(d) The license application shall be made under oath and on a form to be furnished by the division director. The application shall state the applicant"s full name, age, and date and place of birth; residences and employment within the past five years; experience in the position applied for or held; the date and place of conviction or arrest for any crime, including the entry of a plea of nolo contendere or the entry of a plea entered pursuant to Article 3 of Chapter 8 of Title 42 or other first offender treatment; and such other information as the board may require. The license application shall be accompanied by two sets of fingerprints of the applicant and one photograph of the applicant, two inches wide by three inches high, full face, and taken within six months prior to the application. The board shall have discretion to deny a license to any individual when the information and supporting documentation required by this subsection are not provided.

(e) Upon granting a license pursuant to this Code section, the board shall so notify the licensee. An employer shall notify the board within 30 days of the hiring or termination of employment of any employee licensed under this Code section.

(f) Upon receipt of a license card issued by the board pursuant to this chapter, the licensee shall maintain said card on his person at all times while on his post or at his place of employment and at all times when the licensee wears a uniform in the course of his employment in the private detective or private security business.

(g) Notwithstanding any other provisions of this Code section, any person who is to be licensed under this Code section shall agree that if such person makes a false statement in the application or if such person is found to have been convicted of a felony and has not had all his or her civil rights restored pursuant to law, then the board shall be authorized to suspend any license granted to such person without a prior hearing as required in Code Section 43–38–11. Upon request, any such person shall be entitled to a hearing on such matter subsequent to the suspension.

Laws 1973, p. 40, § 8; Laws 1981, p. 1828, § 6; Laws 1987, p. 1400, § 6; Laws 1988, p. 13, § 43; Laws 2000, p. 1161, § 4; Laws 2000, p. 1706, § 19; Laws 2005, Act 147, § 1, eff. July 1, 2005; Laws 2008, Act 471, § 43, eff. May 12, 2008; Laws 2010, Act 417, § 40, eff. May 20, 2010; Laws 2010, Act 438, § 2, eff. May 24, 2010.

Historical and Statutory Notes

In 2005, the Code Commission, in subsec. (c), redesignated existing the introductory par. as par. (c)(1), redesignated existing pars. (c)(1) through (c)(6) as subpars. (c)(1)(A) through (c)(1)(F), redesignated par. (c)(7) as (c)(2), and substituted a period for "; and" at the end of new subpar. (c)(1)(F). See § 28–9–5.

§ 43–38–7.1. Registration of unarmed employees; training; criminal records check

(a) Any individual, firm, association, company, partnership, limited liability company, or corporation engaged in the private security business and licensed pursuant to Code Section 43–38–6 shall be required to maintain registration records of all guards, watchmen, or patrolmen who are unarmed pursuant to rules and regulations of the board. A licensee shall not be required to register such unarmed employees with the board. Unarmed employees shall be required to complete a certain number of hours of training as prescribed by the board, and a record of such training shall be maintained with the registration records of such employees.

(b) The licensee shall forward fingerprints received from each prospective registrant to the Georgia Crime Information Center of the Georgia Bureau of Investigation for the purpose of criminal identification through the fingerprint system of identification established by the Georgia Bureau of Investigation and the fingerprint system of investigation established by the Federal Bureau of Investigation.

(c) It shall be the duty of the licensee to keep a record of all information received from the Georgia Bureau of Investigation and the Federal Bureau of Investigation with respect to criminal identification and to cooperate with the Georgia Bureau of Investigation, similar departments in other states, and the United States Department of Justice in any criminal identification system.

(d) At such times as the board may require, fingerprint cards of registrants may be periodically reprocessed by a licensee to identify criminal convictions subsequent to registration.

Laws 1987, p. 1400, § 7; Laws 1993, p. 123, § 44.

§ 43–38–8. Temporary employees

Notwithstanding any other provisions of this chapter, any person or corporation may use temporary employees for special events, provided that such temporary employment does not exceed 30 days in a calendar year and such employees do not carry firearms in connection with such employment.

Laws 1973, p. 40, § 9; Laws 1981, p. 1828, § 7A; Laws 1987, p. 1400, § 8.

§ 43–38–9. Fingerprints; criminal identification

(a) The board shall forward the necessary fingerprints received from each prospective licensee and registrant required to be licensed or registered by the board under this chapter to the Georgia Crime Information Center or the Georgia Bureau of Investigation for the purpose of criminal identification through the fingerprint system of identification established by such bureau and the fingerprint system of investigation established by the Federal Bureau of Investigation.

(b) It shall be the duty of the division director to keep a record of all information received from the Georgia Bureau of Investigation and the Federal Bureau of Investigation with respect to criminal identification and to cooperate with the Georgia Bureau of Investigation, similar departments in other states, and the United States Department of Justice in any criminal identification system.

(c) At such times as the board may require, fingerprint cards of licensees and registrants may be periodically reprocessed to identify criminal convictions subsequent to licensure or registration.

Laws 1973, p. 40, § 11; Laws 1981, p. 1828, § 8; Laws 1984, p. 1338, § 2; Laws 1987, p. 1400, § 9; Laws 2000, p. 1706, § 19.

§ 43–38–10. Permits to carry firearms; fees; training; exemptions; denials; sanctions

(a) The board may grant a permit to carry a pistol, revolver, or other firearm to any person who is at least 21 years of age and who is licensed or registered in accordance with this chapter and who meets the qualifications and training requirements set forth in this Code section and such other qualifications and training requirements as the board by rule may establish. The board shall have the authority to establish limits on type and caliber of such weapons by rule. Application for such permit and for renewal thereof shall be made on forms provided by the division director. No weapons permit issued under this Code section shall be transferable to another individual.

(b) No permit under this Code section shall be issued or renewed until the applicant has presented proof to the board that he is proficient in the use of firearms. The board shall have the authority to require periodic recertification of proficiency in the use of firearms and to refuse to renew a permit upon failure to comply with such requirement. The applicant shall present proof to the board that:

(1) He has demonstrated on the firearms range proficiency in the use of firearms by meeting such minimum qualifications on pistol and shotgun (if so armed) courses as the board may prescribe by rule; and

(2) He has received such other training and instruction in the use of firearms as the board may require by rule.

(c) All licensees and registrants under this chapter shall be required to obtain from the board a weapons permit under this Code section if a firearm is carried, or is to be carried, by such licensee or registrant while at or en route directly to and from his post or place of employment.

(d) Any licensee or registrant under this chapter meeting the qualifications and training requirements set out in this Code section may be issued an exposed weapons permit in accordance with this Code section and shall be authorized to carry such firearm in an open and fully exposed manner. Such carrying of a firearm shall be limited to the time the licensee or registrant is on duty or en route directly to and from his post or place of employment. No stopover en route to and from such post or place of employment is permitted under the terms of this Code section.

(e) Licensees or registrants under this chapter may apply to the board for a concealed weapons permit. Qualifications and training requirements for such permits and restrictions on such permits shall be established by appropriate rules of the board. The board shall, in its discretion, consider and approve each application for a concealed weapons permit on an individual basis.

(f) An individual issued a permit in accordance with this Code section shall be exempt from the following laws of this state:

(1) Code Section 16–11–126, relating to carrying a weapon;

(2) Code Section 16–11–127, relating to carrying a weapon or long gun in an unauthorized location; and

(3) Code Section 16–11–129, relating to licenses to carry weapons generally.

(g) The board shall have the power to deny a weapons permit to any applicant who fails to provide the information and supporting documentation required by this Code section or to refuse to renew a permit upon failure to comply with such weapons proficiency recertification requirements as the board may prescribe.

(h) The board shall have the authority to order the summary suspension of any weapons permit issued under this Code section, pending proceedings for revocation or other sanction, upon finding that the public health, safety, or welfare imperatively requires such emergency action, which finding shall be incorporated in its order.

(i) The board shall have the same power and authority to deny and sanction weapons permits under this Code section as that enumerated in Code Section 43–38–11, based on the same grounds as those enumerated in that Code section.

(j) A weapons permit issued under this Code section to any person whose license is suspended pursuant to subsection (f) of Code Section 43–38–6 or whose registration is suspended pursuant to subsection (g) of Code Section 43–38–7 shall be suspended at the same time as the suspension of the license or registration without a prior hearing as required in Code Section 43–38–11. A weapons permit shall be restored to a person upon the restoration of the person's license or registration.

Laws 1973, p. 40, § 12; Laws 1981, p. 1828, § 10; Laws 1982, p. 3, § 43; Laws 1987, p. 1400, § 10; Laws 2000, p. 1161, § 5; Laws 2000, p. 1706, § 19; Laws 2010, Act 643, § 2–19, eff. June 4, 2010.

Historical and Statutory Notes

Laws 2010, Act 643, § 3–1, provides:

"This Act shall become effective upon its approval by the Governor or upon its becoming law without such approval and shall apply to all offenses committed on and after such date. The enactment of this Act shall not affect any prosecutions for acts occurring before the effective date of this Act and shall not act as an abatement of any such prosecutions."

§ 43–38–10.1. Training instructors and training programs

(a) The board shall provide by rule and regulation for the registration of all training instructors or training programs so as to regulate all training requirements for licensure, registration, or weapons permits required by this chapter.

(b) The board shall have the authority to promulgate rules and regulations governing minimum training standards for licensure, registration, or weapons permits. Such training shall be conducted by a board registered training instructor or through a board approved training program.

(c) Any board registered training instructor or board approved training program shall be required to submit to appropriate inspection of facilities and review of curriculum.

(d) The board may suspend, revoke, or deny any application for registration for any training instructor or suspend, revoke, or deny approval of any training program as provided in Code Section 43–38–11.

Laws 1987, p. 1400, § 11.

§ 43–38–11. Denial or sanction of licenses and registrations; hearings

(a) The board shall have the authority to refuse to grant a license or registration to an applicant therefor or to revoke the license or registration of a person licensed or registered by the board or to discipline a person licensed or registered by the board upon a finding by a majority of the entire board that the licensee, registrant, or applicant has:

(1) Failed to demonstrate the qualifications or standards for a license or registration contained in this chapter or the rules or regulations under which licensure is sought or held. It shall be incumbent upon the applicant to demonstrate to the satisfaction of the board that he meets all the requirements for the issuance of a license or registration and, if the board is not satisfied as to the applicant's qualifications, it may deny a license or registration without a prior hearing; provided, however, that the applicant shall be allowed to appear before the board if he so desires;

(2) Made any false statement or given any false information in connection with an application for license or registration, including an application for renewal or reinstatement thereof;

(3) Knowingly violated this chapter or violated any rule or regulation promulgated by the board pursuant to the authority contained in this chapter;

(4) Been convicted, in the courts of this state or of the United States, or in the courts of any other state, territory, or country, of a felony, or any crime involving the illegal use, carrying, or possession of a dangerous weapon, or any crime involving moral turpitude. As used in this subsection, the term "felony" shall include any offense which if committed in this state would be deemed a felony, without regard to its designation elsewhere. For purposes of this subsection, a "conviction" shall be deemed to include a finding or verdict of guilty or plea of guilty, regardless of whether an appeal of the conviction has been sought;

(5) Been arrested, charged, and sentenced for the commission of a felony, any crime involving the illegal use, carrying, or possession of a dangerous weapon, or any crime involving moral turpitude, where:

(A) A plea of nolo contendere was entered to the charge;

(B) First offender treatment was granted without adjudication of guilt pursuant to the charge; or

(C) An adjudication or sentence was otherwise withheld or not entered on the charge.

The plea of nolo contendere or the order entered pursuant to Article 3 of Chapter 8 of Title 42 or other first offender treatment shall be conclusive evidence of arrest and sentencing for such crime;

(6) Become unable to engage in the private detective or private security business with reasonable skill and safety to the public by reason of illness; use of alcohol, drugs, narcotics, chemicals, or any other type of material; or any other mental or physical condition. The board may, however, after investigation of the circumstances surrounding each application, approve for licensure and registration these individuals who produce certified medical evidence of having been successfully treated and cured of alcoholism, drug addiction, or mental illness;

(7) Committed any act in the practice of the private detective or private security business constituting dishonesty or fraud;

(8) Been convicted of impersonating, or permitting or aiding and abetting any other person to impersonate, a law enforcement officer or employee of the United States or of this state or of any political subdivision thereof in the practice of the private detective or private security business;

(9) Engaged in, or permitted any employee to engage in, the private detective or private security business without a valid license or registration issued under this chapter;

(10) Willfully failed or refused to render a service or to tender a report to a client in connection with the private detective or private security business as agreed between the parties and for which compensation was paid or tendered in accordance with the agreement of the parties;

(11) Committed a felony, any crime involving the illegal use, carrying, or possession of a dangerous weapon, or any crime involving moral turpitude;

(12) Knowingly violated, or advised, encouraged, or assisted in the violation of, any court order or injunction in the course of the private detective or private security business or knowingly advised, encouraged, or assisted in the violation of any lawful order issued by the board;

(13) Failed to renew a canceled bond or liability insurance policy in accordance with subsection (d) of Code Section 43–38–6 or failed to supply the financial affidavit required in lieu thereof;

(14) Undertaken to give legal advice or counsel; misrepresented that he is representing an attorney or is appearing or will appear in any legal proceeding; issued, delivered, or uttered any simulation of process of any nature which might lead a person to believe that such simulation, whether written, printed, or typed, may be a summons, warrant, writ, or other court process or pleading in any court proceeding;

(15) Failed to demonstrate the qualifications or standards for licensure or registration contained in this chapter or in the rules and regulations of the board. It shall be incumbent upon the applicant to demonstrate to the satisfaction of the board that he meets all the requirements for licensure or registration; and, if the board is not satisfied as to the applicant's qualifications, it shall have the power to deny such licensure or registration; or

(16) Purchased, acquired, sold, or released the telephone records, as such term is defined in Code Section 46–5–210, of any third party who is a Georgia resident.

(b)(1) If the board finds that any applicant for licensure or any prospective registrant is unqualified to be granted such license or to be registered, the board may:

(A) Deny the application for licensure or registration; or

(B) Limit or restrict any license or registration for a definite period of time.

(2) If, after notice and hearing, the board finds that the license or registration of any holder thereof should be revoked or otherwise sanctioned, the board may take any one or more of the following actions:

(A) Administer a public reprimand;

(B) Suspend any license or registration for a definite period of time;

(C) Limit or restrict any license or registration for a definite period of time;

(D) Revoke or suspend a license or registration;

(E) Fine any licensee or registrant in an amount not to exceed $ 500.00 for each violation of a law or rule or regulation; or

(F) Place a licensee or registrant on probation for a definite period of time and impose such conditions of probation as will adequately protect the public during that period.

In its discretion, the board may restore or reinstate a license or registration which has been sanctioned and, in conjunction therewith, may impose any disciplinary or corrective action provided for in this chapter.

(c) Initial judicial review of a final decision of the board shall be had solely in the superior court of the county of domicile of the board.

Laws 1973, p. 40, § 14; Laws 1981, p. 1828, § 9; Laws 1982, p. 3, § 43; Laws 1984, p. 1338, § 3; Laws 1986, p. 751, § 3; Laws 1987, p. 3, § 43; Laws 1987, p. 1400, § 12; Laws 1992, p. 6, § 43; Laws 2000, p. 1161, § 6; Laws 2000, p. 1706, § 18; Laws 2006, Act 648, § 4, eff. April 28, 2006.

Historical and Statutory Notes

The 2006 amendment by Act 648 made nonsubstantive changes to pars. (14) and (15); and added par. (16)

Laws 2006, Act 648, §§ 1 and 2, provide:

"SECTION 1. This Act shall be known and may be cited as the 'Telephone Records Privacy Protection Act.'

"SECTION 2. The General Assembly finds that:

"(1) Telephone records can be of great use to criminals because the information contained in call logs listed in such records include a wealth of personal data;

"(2) Many call logs reveal the names of telephone users' doctors, public and private relationships, business associates, and more;

"(3) Although other personal information such as social security numbers may appear on public documents, which can be accessed by data brokers, the only warehouse of telephone records is located at the telephone companies themselves;

"(4) Telephone records are sometimes accessed without authorization of the customer by:

"(A) An employee of the telephone service provider selling the data; and

"(B) Pretexting, whereby a data broker or other person pretends to be the owner of the telephone and convinces the telephone company's employees to release the data to such person; and

"(5) Telephone companies encourage customers to manage their accounts online with many setting up the online capability in advance, although many customers never access their account online. If someone seeking the information activates the account before the customer, he or she can gain unfettered access to the telephone records and call logs of that customer."

§ 43-38-11.1. Suspension of license, registration, or weapons permit without prior hearing

(a) After proper notification, the board may suspend the license, registration, or weapons permit of any licensee, registrant, or weapons permit holder without a prior hearing as required in Code Section 43-38-11, provided that said licensee, registrant, or weapons permit holder is determined by the board to present a clear and present danger to the public safety on the grounds outlined in Code Section 43-38-11, is found to have had a prior felony conviction, or is currently under a first offender sentence for a felony crime that was not reported on the application for licensure or registration.

(b) After proper notification the board may suspend without a prior hearing as required in Code Section 43-38-11 the license of any licensee pursuant to subsection (f) of Code Section 43-38-6 or the registration of any registrant pursuant to subsection (g) of Code Section 43-38-7 or the weapons permit of any weapons permit holder pursuant to subsection (j) of Code Section 43-38-10.

Laws 1983, p. 489, § 1; Laws 1987, p. 1400, § 13; Laws 1988, p. 13, § 43; Laws 1991, p. 1027, § 2.

§ 43-38-12. Hearings

All hearings required to be conducted by the board shall be conducted in accordance with Chapter 13 of Title 50, the "Georgia Administrative Procedure Act"; and all rules and regulations of the board shall be adopted and promulgated in accordance with Chapter 13 of Title 50.

Laws 1981, p. 1828, § 13.

§ 43-38-13. Arrest powers

Licensees or registrants under this chapter shall have the same power of arrest as that granted to a private person by Code Section 17-4-60.

Laws 1973, p. 40, § 13; Laws 1981, p. 1828, § 11.

§ 43-38-14. Exceptions

(a) This chapter shall not apply to:

(1) An officer or employee of the United States of America or of this state or a political subdivision thereof while the employee or officer is engaged in the performance of official duties;

(2) A person engaged in the business of furnishing information in connection with credit or marketing and a person or firm engaged as a consumer reporting agency, as defined by the federal Fair Credit Reporting Act;[1]

(3) An attorney at law or a bona fide legal assistant in performing his or her duties;

(4) Admitted insurers, agents, and insurance brokers licensed by the state while performing duties in connection with insurance transacted by them;

(5) A peace officer employed on a full-time basis by a federal, state, county, or local law enforcement agency who contracts directly with an employer to work during his or her off-duty hours and whose off-duty employment is conducted on an independent contractor basis with another employer other than a peace officer engaged in the private detective or private security business or a private detective or private security agency, subject to Code Section 16-10-3, relating to the receipt of funds by state officers or employees for the enforcement of penal laws;

(6) A firm engaged in the business of independent insurance claims adjusting whose employees hold a valid Georgia adjuster's license; or

(7) The employees of a firm mentioned in paragraph (6) of this subsection.

(b) This chapter does not apply to any person covered by Chapter 8 of Title 35, the "Georgia Peace Officer Standards and Training Act."

(c) This chapter shall not prevent the local authorities of any municipality or county, by ordinance and within the exercise of the police power of such municipality or county, from imposing local regulations upon any street patrol, special officer, or person furnishing street patrol service, including regulations requiring registration with an agency to be designated by such municipality or county.

(d) This chapter shall not apply to a person or corporation which employs persons who do private security work in connection with the affairs of such employer only and who have an employer-employee relationship with such employer. Neither such persons or corporations nor their employees shall be required to register or be licensed under this chapter, although such persons or corporations or their employees may elect to be licensed under this chapter.

Laws 1973, p. 40, § 15; Laws 1975, p. 785, § 1; Laws 1978, p. 1515, § 2; Laws 1981, p. 1828, § 12; Laws 1982, p. 3, § 43; Laws 1991, p. 1027, § 3; Laws 2000, p. 1161, § 7.

1 15 U.S.C.A. § 1681 et seq.

§ 43-38-14.1. Action to be taken on application before license granted

(a) No municipality, county, or other political subdivision of this state shall grant a business license to any person required to be licensed under this chapter until such person has made bona fide application to the board to be licensed under this chapter and the board has taken action under the application other than refusal, cancellation, revocation, or failure to renew the applicant's license.

(b) As used in this Code section, the term "person" shall mean any individual, firm, association, partnership, limited liability company, or corporation.

Laws 1984, p. 1338, § 4; Laws 1993, p. 123, § 45.

§ 43-38-15. Application

No individual, firm, association, company, partnership, limited liability company, or corporation shall engage in any activity covered by this chapter unless such individual, firm, association, company, partnership, limited liability company, or corporation is in compliance with this chapter.

Laws 1981, p. 1828, § 14; Laws 1993, p. 123, § 46.

§ 43-38-16. Penalties relating to private detective, etc., businesses

Any person who engages in the private detective business or private security business or offers, pretends, or holds himself out as eligible to engage in the private detective business or private security business and who is not legally licensed or registered under this chapter shall be guilty of a misdemeanor. Each day or fraction of a day that he practices in violation of this chapter shall constitute a separate offense.

Laws 1973, p. 40, § 16; Laws 1981, p. 1828, § 15; Laws 1984, p. 1338, § 5.

§ 43-38-17. Repealed by Laws 1992, p. 3137, § 30, eff. July 1, 1992

TITLE 45

PUBLIC OFFICERS AND EMPLOYEES

CHAPTER 11

MISCELLANEOUS OFFENSES CONCERNING PUBLIC OFFICERS AND EMPLOYEES

§ 45–11–1. Stealing, altering, etc., of public documents

(a) If any public officer or other person shall steal, embezzle, alter, corrupt, withdraw, falsify, or avoid any record, process, charter, gift, grant, conveyance, or contract; or shall knowingly and willfully take off, discharge, or conceal any issue, forfeited recognizance, or other forfeiture; or shall forge, deface, or falsify any document or instrument recorded or any registry, acknowledgment, or certificate; or shall alter, deface, or falsify any minutes, document, book, or any proceeding whatever of or belonging to any public office within this state; or if any person shall cause or procure any of these offenses to be committed, or to be in any manner concerned therein, he shall be guilty of a felony and, upon conviction thereof, shall be punished by imprisonment and labor in the penitentiary for not less than two years nor more than ten years.

(b) Whosoever, without authority and with the intention of converting to his own or another's use, willfully conceals any record, book, or document while on the premises of any public office or willfully removes any book, document, record, or other property from any such office shall be guilty of stealing such property. Proof of the concealment of such record or other office property while still on the premises shall be prima-facie evidence of intent to steal.

(c) A public officer or employee may detain and question any person whose conduct causes reasonable ground for suspicion that such person is engaging in stealing or criminal damage to the records in a public office.

(d) A public officer or employee causing the arrest or detention of any person pursuant to this Code section shall not be held civilly liable for slander, malicious prosecution, false imprisonment, malicious arrest, assault and battery of the person, physical injuries and mental suffering, or any other suit for damages arising from such arrest, whether such arrest takes place on the public property or after close pursuit from such premises by such officer; provided, however, that, in causing the arrest of such person, the officer or employee had probable cause at the time of such arrest to believe that the person was committing unlawful acts relating to public documents and the arrest and detention were under reasonable circumstances.

(e) Upon presentation of affirmative proof, the Secretary of State or his or her designee may initiate action through the Attorney General or other appropriate jurisdiction to prevent the sale, transfer, conveyance, destruction, or alienation of any records, books, documents, or other office property which has been unlawfully removed from any public office or public officer or employee. Upon request of the Secretary of State or his or her designee, the Attorney General or other appropriate jurisdiction shall have the authority to enjoin, recover, and replevin such records, books, documents, or other office property.

(f) As used in this Code section, the term:

(1) "Records, books, documents, or other office property" means, but is not limited to, all books, plates, pictures, photographs, films, engravings, paintings, drawings, maps, newspapers, magazines, pamphlets, broadsides, personal papers, organization records, documents, letters, public records, microforms, sound recordings, audiovisual materials in any format, magnetic or other tapes, electronic data processing records, artifacts, or other documentary, written, or printed material, regardless of physical form or characteristics, belonging to, on loan to, or otherwise in the custody of any public office;

(2) "Public office" means any office held, used, or controlled for public purposes by any department, agency, board, or branch of state, county, or municipal government without reference to the ownership of the building or of the realty on which it is situated. Such term includes any archives, library, or records storage area maintained by such governments;

(3) "Avoid" means to annul, cancel, make void, destroy the efficacy of, or destroy without authority any record, book, document, or other office property;

(4) "Public officer or employee" means any officer or employee having custody of or responsibility for any records, books, documents, or other office property referred to in this Code section.

Laws 1833, Cobb's 1851 Digest, p. 805; Laws 1977, p. 568, § 1; Laws 2004, Act 549, § 1, eff. July 1, 2004.

Formerly Code 1863, § 4366; Code 1868, § 4404; Code 1873, § 4471; Code 1882, § 4471; Penal Code 1895, § 280; Penal Code 1910, § 284; Code 1933, § 89–9903.

Historical and Statutory Notes

The 2004 amendment by Act 549 inserted a new subsec. (e) and redesignated former subsec. (e) as subsec. (f).

§ 45–11–2. Selling office or dividing profits thereof

If any person who has been elected to any office shall sell or farm out said office; or if any person shall purchase or agree to give any money or other thing of value to a person elected for the privilege of exercising the duties of said office; or if any person shall promise or agree to divide the profits, fees, or emoluments of said office with the person so elected, he shall be guilty of a felony and, upon conviction thereof, shall be punished by confinement and labor in the penitentiary for not less than one year nor more than three years.

Laws 1871–72, p. 285, §§ 1, 2.

Formerly Code 1873, § 4472; Code 1882, § 4472; Penal Code 1895, § 281; Penal Code 1910, § 285; Code 1933, § 89–9904.

§ 45–11–3. Assault under color of office

Any officer of this state who shall assault or beat any individual under color of his office or commission without a lawful justification to do so shall be guilty of a misdemeanor.

Laws 1833, Cobb's 1851 Digest, p. 806.

Formerly Code 1863, § 4371; Code 1868, § 4409; Code 1873, § 4477; Code 1882, § 4477; Penal Code 1895, § 284; Penal Code 1910, § 288; Code 1933, § 89–9906.

§ 45–11–4. Malpractice, oppression, tyrannical partiality, etc.

(a) As used in this Code section, the term:

(1) "County officer" shall mean any elected county officer, including the judge of the probate court, clerk of the superior court, tax receiver, tax collector, and tax commissioner where such office has replaced the tax receiver and tax collector, and any county commissioner.

(2) "Municipal officer" shall mean any mayor or elected member of any municipal governing authority.

(3) "Public officer" shall mean a county officer, a municipal officer, and state officials as provided in Code Section 45–15–11.

(b) A public officer may be charged under this Code section for:

(1) Malpractice, misfeasance, or malfeasance in office;

(2) Using oppression or tyrannical partiality in the administration or under the color of his or her office;

(3) When required by law, willfully refusing or failing to preside in or hold his or her court at the regular terms thereof, or when it is his or her duty under the law to do so;

(4) Using any other deliberate means to delay or avoid the due course or proceeding of law; or

(5) Willfully and knowingly demanding more cost than he or she is entitled to by law in the administration and under color of his or her office.

(c) A conviction for violating subsection (b) of this Code section shall be punished as for a misdemeanor and, upon conviction in a court of competent jurisdiction, the accused shall be removed from office.

(d) This Code section shall only apply to a public officer charged under subsection (b) of this Code section. This Code section shall not apply when a public officer is charged with any other crime alleged to have occurred while such official was in the performance of an official duty.

(e) This Code section shall only apply to a public officer holding office at the time of indictment and not to former office holders.

(f) Any indictment brought pursuant to subsection (b) of this Code section shall specially set forth the merits of the complaint against the accused public officer. A copy of the proposed bill of indictment shall be served on the accused public officer at least 15 days before it is presented to the grand jury.

(g) The accused shall have the right to appear before the grand jury to make such sworn statement as he or she shall desire at the conclusion of the presentation of the state's evidence. The accused shall not be subject to examination, either direct or cross, and shall not have the right individually or through his or her counsel to examine the state's witnesses. The accused and his or her counsel shall have the right to be present during the presentation of all evidence and alleged statements of the accused on the proposed indictment, presentment, or accusation, after which the accused and his or her counsel shall retire instanter from the grand jury room to permit the grand jury to deliberate upon the indictment.

(h) At any time during the presentation of evidence or during deliberations, the grand jury may amend the indictment or instruct the district attorney to cause a new indictment to be drawn as in any other case. In such case, a copy of the amendment or new indictment, if it relates to the accused public official, shall be provided to the accused public official and his or her counsel.

(i) If a true bill is returned by the grand jury, the indictment shall, as in other cases, be published in open court and shall be placed on the superior court criminal docket of cases to be tried by a petit jury.

Laws 1833, Cobb's 1851 Digest, pp. 644, 809; Laws 1865–66, p. 233, § 1; Laws 1873, p. 23, § 1; Laws 1895, p. 63, § 1; Laws 1967, p. 858, § 1; Laws 1975, p. 1325, § 1; Laws 1983, p. 884, § 3–33; Laws 1984, p. 22, § 45; Laws 1988, p. 298, § 1; Laws 1990, p. 1969, § 1; Laws 2001, p. 487, § 3.

Formerly Code 1863, § 4391; Code 1868, § 4432; Code 1873, § 4504; Code 1882, § 4504; Penal Code 1895, §§ 291, 292; Penal Code 1910, §§ 295, 296; Code 1933, §§ 89–9907, 89–9908.

Historical and Statutory Notes

The 2001 amendment rewrote this section which formerly provided:

"Any elected county officer, including the judge of the probate court, clerk of the superior court, tax receiver, tax collector, and tax commissioner, where the office has replaced the tax receiver and tax collector, any member of any board of commissioners, or any mayor or member of any municipal governing authority, presently or formerly holding such office, who shall be charged with malpractice, misfeasance, or malfeasance in office; or with using oppression or tyrannical partiality in the administration or under the color of his office; or, when required by law, with willfully refusing or failing to preside in or hold his court at the regular terms thereof, or when it is his duty under the law to do so; or with using any other deliberate or illegal means to delay or avoid the due course or proceeding of law; or with any other illegal conduct in the performance or administration of the office which is unbecoming the character of a public officer; or who shall willfully and knowingly demand more cost than he is entitled to by law in the administration and under color of his office may be indicted. The indictment shall specially set forth the merits of the complaint against the accused public officer. A copy of the indictment shall be served on the accused public officer at least 15 days before it is presented to the grand jury. The accused shall have the right to appear before the grand jury to make such sworn statement as he shall desire at the conclusion of the presentation of the state's evidence. The accused shall not be subject to examination, either direct or cross, and shall not have the right individually or through his counsel to examine the state's witnesses. The accused and his counsel shall have the right to be present during the presentation of all evidence and alleged statements of the accused on the proposed indictment, presentment, or accusation, after which he and his counsel shall retire instanter from the grand jury room to permit the grand jury to deliberate upon the indictment. If a true bill is returned by the grand jury, the indictment shall, as in other cases, be published in open court and shall be placed on the superior court criminal docket of cases to be tried by a petit jury. If the accused is convicted, he shall be punished by a fine or by imprisonment, or both, at the discretion of the court; and, if still in office, he shall be removed from office."

§ 45–11–5. Extortion

(a) As used in this Code section, the term "extortion" means an unlawful taking by a public officer, under color of his office, from any person of any money or thing of value that is not due to him or more than is due to him.

(b) Any public officer who shall by himself, his deputy, his agent, or other person employed by him be guilty of extortion in demanding or receiving other and greater fees than by law are allowed him shall be guilty of a misdemeanor and shall be dismissed from office.

Laws 1833, Cobb's 1851 Digest, p. 809; Laws 1990, p. 8, § 45.

Formerly Code 1863, §§ 4393, 4394; Code 1868, §§ 4434, 4435; Code 1873, §§ 4507, 4508; Code 1882, §§ 4507, 4508; Penal Code 1895, §§ 298, 299; Penal Code 1910, §§ 302, 303; Code 1933, §§ 89–9909, 89–9910.

§ 45–11–6. Penalty for demanding more than legal rate for advertising

Any judge of the probate court, sheriff, coroner, clerk, marshal, or other officer who shall receive, collect, or demand other and greater fees for any legal advertising than are provided by law shall be guilty of extortion as defined in Code Section 45–11–5 and shall be punished as provided in that Code section.

Laws 1878–79, p. 81, § 2; Laws 1990, p. 8, § 45.

Formerly Code 1863, § 3634; Code 1868, § 3659; Code 1882, § 3704b; Penal Code 1895, § 303; Penal Code 1910, § 307; Code 1933, § 89–9911.

§ 45–11–7. Retaining part of advertising fee

If any officer shall directly or indirectly demand or retain as a commission any part of the compensation allowed by law to publishers for publishing legal advertisements, he shall be guilty of extortion as defined in Code Section 45–11–5 and shall be punished as provided in that Code section.

Laws 1878–79, p. 81, § 14.

Formerly Code 1882, § 3704d; Penal Code 1895, § 304; Penal Code 1910, § 308; Code 1933, § 89–9912.

§ 45–11–8. Elected officials, etc., engaging in bail bond business

(a) It shall be unlawful for any elected official, officer of the court, law enforcement officer, or attorney in this state to engage either directly or indirectly in the bail bond business. For purposes of this Code section, "elected official" shall not include a person who is elected to the local school board.

(b) Any person who violates this Code section shall be guilty of a misdemeanor.

Laws 1972, p. 403, §§ 1, 2; Laws 1986, p. 303, § 1; Laws 2004, Act 550, § 1, eff. July 1, 2004; Laws 2010, Act 458, § 1, eff. July 1, 2010.

Historical and Statutory Notes

The 2004 amendment by Act 550, in subsec. (a), added the second sentence relating to persons elected to local school boards.

In 2004, the Code Commission, in subsec. (a), substituted "a person who is elected" for "persons who are elected". See § 28–9–5.

The 2010 amendment by Act 458, in subsec. (a), deleted "; provided, however, that any such person shall not be allowed to participate in the operation of a bail bond business within the jurisdiction of the office to which he or she is elected" from the end of the second sentence

§ 45–11–9. Discrimination against optometrists or physicians in recommendations for visual care; referrals

(a) It shall be unlawful for any state board, body, agency, or institution or any public official to discriminate against optometrists licensed under Chapter 30 of Title 43 or against physicians licensed under Chapter 34 of Title 43 in the suggestion or recommendation for visual care which is within the scope of the practice licensed by those chapters.

(b) Nothing contained in this Code section shall be construed to prevent a person having custodial care of another person from referring such person to the practitioner of his choice.

(c) Nothing contained in this Code section shall be construed to prevent a physician from referring patients to any practitioner of his choice.

Laws 1976, p. 474, §§ 1–3.

§ 45–11–10. Coercion of any other state or political subdivision officer or employee to pay, lend or contribute any part of his salary, kick back any sum of money, or anything else of value to any party, etc., for political purposes

(a) It shall be unlawful for any officer or employee of this state to coerce or attempt to coerce or command directly or indirectly any other state officer or employee to pay, lend, or contribute any part of his salary or to kick back any sum of money or anything else of value to any party, committee, organization, agency, or person for political purposes.

(b) It shall be unlawful for any officer or employee of any county, municipal corporation, school district, or other political subdivision to coerce or attempt to coerce or command directly or indirectly any other officer or employee of such political subdivision to pay, lend, or contribute any part of his salary or to kick back any sum of money or anything else of value to any party, committee, organization, agency, or person for political purposes.

(c) Any person who violates any provision of this Code section shall be guilty of a misdemeanor.

Laws 1977, p. 1035, §§ 1, 2; Laws 1985, p. 617, § 1.

CHAPTER 16

CORONERS

Article 1

Article 1

General Provisions

§ 45–16–1. How elected, commissioned, qualified, and removed

(a) Coroners are elected, commissioned, and removed as are clerks of the superior courts; and coroners shall hold their offices for four years.

(b)(1) No person shall be eligible to offer for election to or to hold the office of coroner unless he or she:

(A) Is a citizen of the United States;

(B) Is a resident of the county in which he or she seeks the office of coroner for at least two years prior to his or her qualifying for the election to the office and remains a resident of such county during his or her term of office;

(C) Is a registered voter;

(D) Has attained the age of 25 years prior to the date of the general primary in the year he or she qualifies for election to the office;

(E) Has obtained a high school diploma or its recognized equivalent. This subparagraph shall not apply to any person serving as a coroner on July 1, 1980;

(F) Has not been convicted of a felony offense or any offense involving moral turpitude contrary to the laws of this state, any other state, or the United States; and

(G) Has successfully completed the next scheduled class no longer than 180 days after such person's election or appointment a basic training course provided by the Georgia Police Academy, but the affidavit required by paragraph (2) of this subsection shall not be required to affirm that the requirements of this subparagraph have been met at the time of qualifying for the office of coroner.

(2) Each person offering his or her candidacy for the office of coroner shall file an affidavit with the officer before whom such person has qualified to seek the office of coroner prior to or at the time for qualifying, which affidavit shall affirm that he or she meets all of the qualifications required pursuant to paragraph (1) of this subsection.

(c) Notwithstanding any other provision of law, any person holding office as the mayor of a municipality with a population of 5,000 or less according to the United States decennial census of 1980 or any future such census is specifically authorized to serve simultaneously as coroner; and any person holding the office of coroner is specifically authorized to serve simultaneously as mayor of a municipality with a population of 5,000 or less according to the United States decennial census of 1980 or any future such census.

Laws 1914, p. 43, § 1; Laws 1985, p. 843, § 1; Laws 1986, p. 10, § 45; Laws 1987, p. 630, § 1; Laws 1988, p. 13, § 45; Laws 1989, p. 1091, § 6; Laws 1990, p. 1735, § 2; Laws 1992, p. 1436, § 1; Laws 1999, p. 869, § 1.

Formerly Code 1863, § 559; Code 1868, § 623; Code 1873, § 582; Code 1882, § 582; Civil Code 1895, § 491; Civil Code 1910, § 609; Code 1933, § 21–101.

§ 45–16–2. Appointment by judges of the probate courts

(a) Whenever an election fails to fill the office of coroner, the judge of the probate court shall appoint a person to serve as the coroner until a successor is duly elected in a special election which shall be held at the time of the next general election to serve out the remainder of the unexpired term of office.

(b) In the event a vacancy occurs in the office of coroner, the judge of the probate court shall appoint a person to serve out the unexpired term of office and until his successor shall be duly elected and qualified.

(c) No appointment or election under subsection (a) or (b) of this Code section shall be of any effect until proper bond and security is given and the oath of office is taken.

Laws 1988, p. 586, § 4.

Formerly Code 1863, § 560; Code 1868, § 624; Code 1873, § 583; Code 1882, § 583; Civil Code 1895, § 492; Civil Code 1910, § 610; Code 1933, § 21–102.

§ 45–16–3. Oath of office; form

Before beginning the duties of the office of coroner, a coroner shall take the oath required of all civil officers and shall take the following oath:

"I swear that I will well and truly serve the State of Georgia in said office and faithfully and truly execute all writs and precepts to me directed or which I may lawfully execute, when placed in my charge, and return the same according to the best of my knowledge, skill, and judgment; that I will in no case knowingly use or exercise my office illegally, corruptly, or unjustly and that I will not, under any pretense, take, accept, or enjoy any fee or reward pertaining to my office other than such as are allowed by law; but that I will, in all things touching the duties of my office, demean myself honestly, fairly, and impartially according to the best of my ability, so help me God."

Laws 1823, Cobb's 1851 Digest, p. 536.

Formerly Code 1863, § 561; Code 1868, § 625; Code 1873, § 584; Code 1882, § 584; Civil Code 1895, § 493; Civil Code 1910, § 611; Code 1933, § 21–103.

§ 45–16–4. Bond. Liability for moneys collected and failure of duty

A coroner shall give bond and surety in the sum of $ 12,500.00 at the same time as he takes the oath provided for in Code Section 45–16–3. He is liable for retaining moneys collected or for otherwise failing to do his duty as sheriffs are and is subject to the same proceedings.

Laws 1823, Cobb's 1851 Digest, p. 539; Laws 1985, p. 843, § 2.

Formerly Code 1863, § 562; Code 1868, § 626; Code 1873, § 585; Code 1882, § 585; Civil Code 1895, § 494; Civil Code 1910, § 612; Code 1933, § 21–104.

§ 45–16–5. Additional bond when acting in place of sheriff

When a coroner is required to act in the place of a sheriff, generally or specially, the judge of the probate court may require of him an additional bond in such sum and with such sureties as the judge, in his discretion, may think sufficient to meet the contingency.

Formerly Code 1863, § 563; Code 1868, § 627; Code 1873, § 586; Code 1882, § 586; Civil Code 1895, § 495; Civil Code 1910, § 613; Code 1933, § 21–107.

§ 45–16–6. Training course

During every calendar year they are in office, every coroner and deputy coroner shall be required, as a condition of continuing to serve as coroner, to take a training course approved by the Georgia Coroner's Training Council pursuant to Code Section 45–16–66. Any coroner or deputy coroner taking the approved training course provided by the Georgia Police Academy shall receive the same expense allowance per day as that received by a member of the General Assembly, plus reimbursement of actual transportation costs while traveling by public carrier or the legal mileage rate for the use of a personal automobile and registration fees for such training course. Such expense allowance and reimbursements shall be paid by the county governing authority from county funds. In the event, however, that a coroner or deputy is prevented in any calendar year from taking such training by sickness or other providential cause, the requirement of training for that year may be waived by the Georgia Coroner's Training Council.

Laws 1980, p. 543, § 3; Laws 1985, p. 843, § 3; Laws 1988, p. 1539, § 1; Laws 1990, p. 333, § 1; Laws 1992, p. 1436, § 2; Laws 1994, p. 356, § 1.

Formerly Code 1933, § 21–108; Code 1981, § 45–16–8.

§ 45–16–7. Deputies

(a) As soon as practicable after July 1, 1980, and at the beginning of each term of the coroner thereafter, the coroner of each county shall appoint a deputy coroner or coroners as provided in this Code section. A deputy coroner shall be appointed for each county, and one or more additional deputy coroners may be appointed for any county, in the discretion of the coroner. Each deputy coroner shall serve at the pleasure of the coroner and may be replaced by the coroner at any time. Each deputy coroner shall take the same oath, give the same bond, be entitled to the same fees, and have the same powers as the coroner; but a deputy coroner shall act as coroner only when the coroner is himself unable to act.

(b) No person shall be eligible to hold the office of deputy coroner unless he or she holds a high school diploma or its recognized equivalent. Any deputy coroner who is in office on July 1, 1980, however, shall without limitation be eligible to serve as deputy coroner at any time after said date without regard to whether he or she meets the requirements of this subsection.

(c) Notwithstanding any law to the contrary, there shall be appointed only one deputy coroner, and, on and after July 1, 1999, there shall only be one deputy coroner in each such county unless otherwise approved by the local governing authority of the county.

Laws 1980, p. 543, §§ 1, 3; Laws 1985, p. 843, § 3; Laws 1999, p. 869, § 2.

Formerly Code 1933, §§ 21–102.1, 21–108; Code 1981, § 45–16–8.

§ 45–16–8. Shall serve process, when by the judge of the probate court.

If any person makes an affidavit stating (1) that a sheriff is disqualified from acting in any proceeding, which disqualification was not apparent at the outset of the proceeding, or (2) that a sheriff or his deputy refuses to serve a writ or other process, then the clerk of the court from which the process issues shall place the process in the hands of the coroner for execution. The clerk may compel the sheriff to return the writ or other process to the clerk's office in order to allow for execution by the coroner.

Laws 1985, p. 843, § 3.

Formerly Code 1863, § 565; Code 1868, § 629; Code 1873, § 588; Code 1882, § 588; Civil Code 1895, § 496; Civil Code 1910, § 614; Code 1933, § 21–106; Code 1981, § 45–16–9.

§ 45–16–9. Fees when performing duties of sheriff

(a) When performing the duties of a sheriff, the coroner's fees are the same as a sheriff's.

(b) This Code section shall not be construed to repeal or preempt any local Act or general Act of local application which places any coroner upon an annual salary or authorizes any coroner to receive fees in excess of those specified in this Code section.

Laws 1792, Cobb's 1851 Digest, p. 352; Laws 1859, p. 25, § 1; Laws 1878–79, p. 73, § 1; Laws 1953, Jan.-Feb. Sess., p. 210, § 1; Laws 1980, p. 543, § 2; Laws 1985, p. 843, § 3.

Formerly Code 1863, § 3625; Code 1868, § 3650; Code 1873, § 3701; Code 1882, § 3701; Penal Code 1895, § 1112; Penal Code 1910, § 1141; Code 1933, § 21–105; Code 1981, § 45–16–6.

§ 45–16–10. Release of records of death to coroners of other states under certain circumstances

Records, papers, or reports concerning the death of a person on file at any hospital, nursing home, or other medical facility in this state shall be available to a coroner of another state if such person was injured in, a resident of, or buried in the county of such coroner in such other state or if such records, papers, or reports are the subject of a subpoena issued by the coroner of another state. The release of such records to the coroner of another state shall not be prohibited by Article 4 of Chapter 18 of Title 50.

Laws 1986, p. 1594, § 1; Laws 1987, p. 559, § 1.

§ 45–16–11. Additional compensation

(a)(1) Any other law to the contrary notwithstanding, the minimum annual salary of each coroner in any of the counties in this state in the following population brackets shall be fixed according to the population of the county in which he or she serves, as determined by the United States decennial census of 1990 or any future such census. Except as otherwise provided in paragraph (2) of this subsection, each such coroner shall receive an annual salary, payable in equal monthly installments from the funds of the coroner's county, of not less than the amount fixed in the following schedule:

Population	Minimum Salary
0—11,889	$ 1,200.00
11,890—19,999	2,400.00
20,000—34,999	3,600.00

(2) On and after July 1, 2001, whenever the employees in the classified service of the State Personnel Administration receive a cost-of-living increase or general performance based increase of a certain percentage or a certain amount, the amounts fixed in the minimum salary schedule in paragraph (1) of this subsection, and in Code Section 45–16–11.1, or the amounts derived by increasing each of said amounts through the application of longevity increases pursuant to subsection (b) of this Code section, where applicable, shall be increased by the same percentage or same amount applicable to such state employees. If the cost-of-living increase or general performance based increase received by state employees is in different percentages or different amounts as to certain categories of employees, the amounts fixed in the minimum salary schedule in paragraph (1) of this subsection, and in Code Section 45–16–11.1, or the amounts derived through the application of longevity increases, shall be increased by a percentage or an amount not to exceed the average percentage or average amount of the general increase in salary granted to the state employees. The Office of Planning and Budget shall calculate the average percentage increase or average amount increase when necessary. The periodic changes in the amounts fixed in the minimum salary schedule in paragraph (1) of this subsection, and in Code Section 45–16–11.1, or the amounts derived through the application of longevity increases, as authorized by this paragraph shall become effective on the first day of January following the date that the cost-of-living increases received by state employees become effective; provided, however, that if the cost-of-living increases or general performance based increases received by state employees become effective on January 1, such periodic changes in the amounts fixed in the minimum salary schedule in paragraph (1) of this subsection, and in Code Section 45–16–11.1, or the amounts derived through the application of longevity increases, as authorized by this paragraph shall become effective on the same date that the cost-of-living increases or general performance based increases received by state employees become effective.

(3) The county governing authority may supplement the minimum annual salary of the coroner in such amount as it may fix from time to time; but no coroner's compensation supplement shall be decreased during any term of office. Any prior expenditure of county funds to supplement the coroner's salary in the manner authorized by this paragraph is ratified and confirmed. Nothing contained in this paragraph shall prohibit the General Assembly by local law from supplementing the annual salary of the coroner.

(b) The amounts provided in paragraph (1) of subsection (a) of this Code section and Code Section 45–16–11.1, as increased by paragraph (2) of subsection (a) of this Code section, shall be increased by multiplying said amounts by the percentage which equals 5 percent times the number of completed four-year terms of office served by any coroner after December 31, 2000, effective the first day of January following the completion of each such period of service.

(c) The minimum salaries provided for under this Code section shall be in addition to any fees paid by the county governing authority to the coroner on a per-call basis and in addition to any expenses.

(d) The minimum salaries provided for in this Code section shall be considered as salary only. Expenses for deputies, equipment, supplies, copying equipment, and other necessary and reasonable expenses for the operation of a coroner's office shall come from funds other than the funds specified as salary in this Code section.

(e) This Code section shall not be construed to reduce the salary of any coroner in office on July 1, 2001; provided, however, that successors to such coroners in office on July 1, 2001, shall be governed by the provisions of this Code section. All local legislation in effect on July 1, 2001, or enacted thereafter affecting compensation for coroners of the various counties shall be of full force and effect except where the same provides for a salary lower than provided in this Code section, in which event this Code section shall prevail.

Laws 2001, p. 902, § 18A; Laws 2009, Act 155, § 1, eff. July 1, 2009.

§ 45–16–11.1. Additional compensation

In addition to the minimum salary provided for in Code Section 45–16–11, in any county which is the site of more than one state correctional institution or prison for adults or juveniles and which compensates the county coroner by salary, the state shall compensate the county coroner in the amount of $ 110.00 for each state inmate death in such county. The county coroner of such a county is authorized to accept the compensation provided in accordance with this Code section despite any local Act which requires such a coroner to send fees to the county treasury or the county governing authority.

Laws 1998, p. 1159, § 17; Laws 2001, p. 902, § 18A.

Formerly Code 1981, § 45–16–11.

§ 45–16–11.2. Monthly expense allowance

In addition to any salary, fees, or expenses now or hereafter provided by law, the governing authority of each of the counties in this state in the following population bracket is authorized to provide as contingent expenses for the operation of the office of coroner, and payable from county funds, a monthly expense allowance of not less than the amount fixed in the following schedule:

Population	Minimum Salary
0—34,999	$ 50.00

Laws 2001, p. 902, § 18A.

Article 2

Death Investigations

§ 45–16–20. Short title

This article shall be known and may be cited as the "Georgia Death Investigation Act."

Laws 1953, Jan.-Feb. Sess., p. 602, § 1; Laws 1990, p. 1735, § 3.

§ 45–16–21. Definitions

As used in this article, the term:

(1) "Autopsy" means the dissection of a dead body and the examination of bone, tissue, organs, and foreign objects for the purpose of determining the cause of death and circumstances surrounding the same, which procedure shall include as a minimum an external examination and the examination of the brain, neck and thoracic organs, and abdominal organs.

(1.1) "Chief medical examiner" means the chief medical examiner appointed pursuant to Code Section 35–3–153.

(2) "County medical examiner" means that office established in lieu of the office of coroner pursuant to Code Section 45–16–80 or any amendment to the Constitution continued pursuant to the authority of Article XI, Section I, Paragraph IV of the Constitution.

(3) "Division" means the Division of Forensic Sciences of the Georgia Bureau of Investigation.

(4) "External examination" means an external examination of a dead body but shall not include dissection of the body for any purpose except dissection which is necessary for and limited to procurement of blood or body fluids for toxicological or other analysis.

(5) "Forensic consultant" means a person meeting the requirements and authorized to perform the duties specified in subsection (c) of Code Section 45–16–23.

(6) "Inquest" means an official judicial inquiry before a coroner and coroner's jury for the purpose of determining the cause of death.

(7) "Limited dissection" means the incision into or dissection of a dead body for diagnosis or evidence collection and the term includes without being limited to an external examination but does not include an individual examination of the:

(A) Brain;

(B) Neck organs;

(C) Thoracic organs; and

(D) Abdominal organs

but may include an examination of any but not all of the categories of organs specified in subparagraphs (A) through (D) of this paragraph.

(8) "Local medical examiner" means a person meeting the requirements and authorized to perform the duties specified in subsection (b) of Code Section 45–16–23.

(9) "Medical examiner" means:

(A) The chief medical examiner;

(B) A regional medical examiner;

(C) A county medical examiner;

(D) A local medical examiner; or

(E) Any person who is employed by the state and appointed as a medical examiner as of December 1, 1989, who continues to perform the duties and exercise the powers of a medical examiner under this article when such performance and exercise are within the scope of such employment.

(10) "Medical examiner's inquiry" means an inquiry made by a medical examiner into the circumstances surrounding a death which is required to be reported under the provisions of Code Section 45–16–24, which inquiry may include, but is not required to include, a scene investigation, an external examination, a limited dissection, an autopsy, or any combination thereof.

(11) "Medical examiner's investigator" means a person meeting the requirements and authorized to perform the duties specified in subsection (d) of Code Section 45–16–23.

(12) "Peace officer in charge" means any peace officer of the Georgia State Patrol or agent of the Georgia Bureau of Investigation, sheriff or sheriff's deputy, peace officer assigned to the coroner's office, county policeman, city policeman, or city detective who may be in charge of the investigation of any case involving a death covered by Code Sections 45–16–27 and 45–16–32.

(13) "Regional medical examiner" means a medical examiner who is employed by the Georgia Bureau of Investigation and who is a pathologist appointed by the chief medical examiner pursuant to Code Section 35–3–153.

(14) "Scene investigation" means an examination by the medical examiner or medical examiner's investigator of the area surrounding a dead body or area where a death or agonal event occurred.

(15) "Unattended death," "died unattended," or "died unattended by a physician" means a death where a person dies of apparently natural causes and has no physician who can certify the death as being due to natural causes. If the suspected cause of death directly involves any trauma or complication of such trauma, the death must be reported to the coroner or county medical examiner. An unattended death also occurs when a person is admitted in an unresponsive state to a hospital and dies within 24 hours of admission.

Laws 1953, Jan.-Feb. Sess., p. 602, § 2; Laws 1960, p. 1009, § 1; Laws 1988, p. 1631, § 1; Laws 1990, p. 8, § 45; Laws 1990, p. 1735, § 3; Laws 1992, p. 6, § 45; Laws 1992, p. 1436, § 3; Laws 1997, p. 1421, § 4; Laws 1998, p. 128, § 45; Laws 2003, Act 203, § 1, eff. May 31, 2003.

§ 45–16–22. Duties of director of division

(a) The director of the division is authorized and directed to cooperate with and assist the peace officers in charge, medical examiners, and coroners of the state in making the facilities of the division available for the performing of medical examiners' inquiries on dead bodies as required by this article.

(b) The county governing authority shall after consulting with the coroner, if any, be authorized to appoint one or more local medical examiners who shall be licensed physicians or pathologists. The chief medical examiner may, at the request of a county governing authority, authorize one or more licensed physicians or pathologists at convenient locations throughout the state to act as local medical examiners in performing medical examiners' inquiries as required by this article. The chief medical examiner shall confer with local county officials in making appointments of regional and local medical examiners. Any regional or local medical examiner appointed by the chief medical examiner shall have such jurisdiction within this state as designated by the chief medical examiner.

(c) Except as otherwise provided in this article, it shall be in the sole discretion of the medical examiner to determine whether or not an autopsy or limited dissection is required; provided, however, that the medical examiner shall give due consideration to the opinions of the coroner and the peace officer in charge regarding the requirements of accepted investigation techniques and the rules of evidence applicable thereto.

(d) In the event that any local medical examiner or regional medical examiner is unable or unwilling to serve in any case, the coroner or the peace officer in charge may call upon the chief medical examiner, who shall perform a medical examiner's inquiry or direct another medical examiner to perform such inquiry.

(e) For each external examination so performed, in cases where limited dissection or autopsy of the body is not required, the medical examiner shall receive the fee set in accordance with the provisions of Code Section 35–3–151. The fee in each case is to be paid from funds of the county in which the act was committed; or, if the county in which the act was committed is unknown, the fee shall be paid from funds of the county in which the body was found. In the event the place in which the act was committed is not known but is later established, the county in which the act was committed shall be responsible for payment of fees incurred by the medical examiner. Subject to funds being appropriated or otherwise available for such purpose, the chief medical examiner shall provide transportation of the deceased person to the site of the autopsy, if such autopsy is to be performed by a state or regional medical examiner employed by the state, and to return the body to the county where the death occurred.

(f) When death occurs in a hospital as a direct result and consequence of acts or events taking place in a county other than the one in which such death occurs, the body shall be returned to the county in which such acts or events took place. When a dead body is found in a county in which the acts or events leading to death did not occur, it shall be returned to the county in which the acts or events did occur, if known. The coroner or local medical examiner of the county in which such acts or events took place shall assume jurisdiction and the medical examiner's inquiry, if any performed, shall be paid for from funds of the county in which such acts or events took place.

(f.1) When death occurs in a hospital as a direct result and consequence of acts or events taking place in a county other than the one in which such death occurs, the hospital shall immediately notify the coroner or the county medical examiner of the county in which the acts or events resulting in the death occurred.

(g) In the event that a medical examiner's inquiry is performed by the chief medical examiner or an employee thereof, no fee therefor shall be imposed pursuant to this Code section. In the event that a medical examiner's inquiry is performed by a medical examiner regularly employed at a fixed compensation by any county or group of counties, no fee shall be imposed upon any county or group of counties employing that medical examiner at a fixed compensation.

(h) Any person holding office as a medical examiner pursuant to an appointment of the state medical examiner on May 1, 1997, shall continue in the exercise of his or her functions and duties until such person's successor has been duly appointed.

Laws 1953, Jan.-Feb. Sess., p. 602, § 3; Laws 1960, p. 1009, § 2; Laws 1969, p. 38, § 1; Laws 1974, p. 503, § 1; Laws 1979, p. 1321, § 1; Laws 1984, p. 812, § 1; Laws 1985, p. 843, § 4; Laws 1989, p. 417, § 1; Laws 1990, p. 8, § 45; Laws 1990, p. 1735, § 3; Laws 1997, p. 1421, § 5; Laws 1998, p. 128, § 45; Laws 2009, Act 29, § 1A, eff. July 1, 2009.

§ 45–16–23. Delegation of powers to local medical examiners, forensic consultants, and medical examiner's investigators

(a) Notwithstanding any other provision of this chapter, any coroner or county medical examiner may delegate to a local medical examiner, forensic consultant, or medical examiner's investigator the power to perform those duties of such coroner or medical examiner specified in this Code section if the person to whom such power is thus delegated meets the applicable requirements of this Code section for the performance of such duties, but the performance of those delegated duties shall not in any manner infringe upon or diminish the authority of the peace officer in charge at the scene of the crime.

(b) A local medical examiner shall be a licensed physician appointed by the state medical examiner to perform scene investigations, external examinations, limited dissections, autopsies, or any combination of such duties.

(c) A forensic consultant shall be an expert in a field of forensic science, including but not limited to odontology or anthropology, appointed and authorized by the state medical examiner to examine human remains and evidence under the medical examiner's jurisdiction.

(d) A medical examiner's investigator shall be a person employed by a medical examiner to perform duties of such medical examiner with the same authority as the medical examiner while at the scene of death and during subsequent investigation, except that no medical examiner's investigator is authorized to make any arrest or perform official external examinations, limited dissections, or autopsies.

Laws 1953, Jan.-Feb. Sess., p. 602, § 24; Laws 1990, p. 1735, § 3.

§ 45–16–24. Notices of death to coroners or county medical examiners; orders to conduct medical examiner's inquiries

(a) When any person dies in any county in this state:

(1) As a result of violence;

(2) By suicide or casualty;

(3) Suddenly when in apparent good health;

(4) When unattended by a physician;

(5) In any suspicious or unusual manner, with particular attention to those persons 16 years of age and under;

(6) After birth but before seven years of age if the death is unexpected or unexplained;

(7) As a result of an execution carried out pursuant to the imposition of the death penalty under Article 2 of Chapter 10 of Title 17;

(8) When an inmate of a state hospital or a state, county, or city penal institution; or

(9) After having been admitted to a hospital in an unconscious state and without regaining consciousness within 24 hours of admission,

it shall be the duty of any law enforcement officer or other person having knowledge of such death to notify immediately the coroner or county medical examiner of the county in which the acts or events resulting in the death occurred or the body is found. For the purposes of this Code section, no person shall be deemed to have died unattended when the death occurred while the person was a patient of a hospice licensed under Article 9 of Chapter 7 of Title 31.

(b) A coroner or county medical examiner who is notified of a death pursuant to subsection (a) of this Code section shall order a medical examiner's inquiry of that death.

(c) Whenever an affidavit is made and filed with a court having criminal jurisdiction attesting that a person came to his death by foul play, that court may interrogate and examine witnesses, if any exist, as to the necessity of a medical examiner's inquiry. Should the court decide that a medical examiner's inquiry is essential to the ends of justice, such inquiry shall be ordered by that court.

(d) A medical examiner's inquiry required under this Code section shall be reduced to writing and filed as provided in Code Section 45-16-32. At the time of such filing, a copy of the medical examiner's inquiry into a death reported to a coroner or county medical examiner pursuant to paragraph (6) of subsection (a) of this Code section shall also be transmitted to the department of family and children services of the county in which the child resided at the time of death.

Laws 1953, Jan.-Feb. Sess., p. 602, § 8; Laws 1984, p. 812, § 2; Laws 1985, p. 1073, § 1; Laws 1990, p. 1735, § 3; Laws 1994, p. 391, § 1; Laws 2009, Act 29, § 1B, eff. July 1, 2009.

§ 45-16-25. Duties of coroner or county medical examiner upon receipt of notice

(a)(1) Upon receipt of the notice required by Code Section 45-16-24, the coroner or county medical examiner shall immediately take charge of the body. If a registered professional nurse authorized to make a pronouncement of death under Code Section 31-10-16 or a qualified physician is not available, a coroner, deputy coroner, or medical examiner's investigator may make a pronouncement of death at the investigation scene if, and only if, one or more of the following conditions is met:

(A) The body is in a state of rigor mortis with lividity present;

(B) The body is in a state of decomposition evidenced by a component of putrefaction;

(C) The body is skeletonized; or

(D) Death has been established by qualified emergency medical services personnel.

(2) It shall be the duty of a coroner notified as required by Code Section 45-16-24 to summon a medical examiner and proper peace officer. It shall be the duty of a county medical examiner so notified to summon a proper peace officer. When present at the scene of death, the peace officer shall have jurisdiction over the scene of death. The medical examiner or coroner and the peace officer shall together make inquiries regarding the cause, manner, and circumstances of death. If either the peace officer or medical examiner is not present at the scene of death, then whichever of the two officers is present shall have jurisdiction over the scene of death. If neither the peace officer nor the medical examiner is present at the scene of death in any county in which the office of coroner has not been replaced by a county medical examiner, the coroner shall assume the responsibility of such officers at the scene of death and shall have the body transported to a local medical examiner who shall conduct a medical examiner's inquiry. The medical examiner, at any time, to facilitate examination, when he or she deems it necessary, may have the body embalmed or retain it for refrigeration for preservation or to avoid the threat of infectious disease prior to release of the body to the next of kin. Such expense of embalming shall be paid by the county of the coroner's or medical examiner's jurisdiction.

(b) When positive identification of dead bodies has not been established conclusively through personal visual examination of the remains by persons well acquainted with the decedent in life or by comparison of fingerprints or footprints or by identification of unique physical characteristics, such as prosthetic appliances, or by comparison of skeletal X-rays, including previous fractures, or by amputations, the medical examiner must either chart or X-ray the decedent's dentition or call upon a licensed dentist of the medical examiner's choosing to carry out a dental examination of the body. This may be accomplished either by examination in situ or by removal of the jaws with teeth to the dentist's office. The dentist shall chart the deceased's dentition and make two copies, one of which shall be filed with the medical examiner's inquiry report to the division and the other with the Georgia Crime Information Center of the Georgia Bureau of Investigation. The dentist may, at his or her discretion, make such X-rays of the mouth as he or she deems necessary. The dentist shall be paid a fee as determined in accordance with Code Section 35-3-151. These fees shall be paid by the county of the coroner's or local medical examiner's jurisdiction.

(c) The coroner or county medical examiner shall, in the absence of the next of kin of the deceased person, take possession of all property of value found on such person, make an exact inventory thereof on his or her report, and surrender the same to the person entitled to its custody or possession. The coroner, medical examiner, or peace officer shall take possession of any objects, anatomical specimens, or articles which, in his or her opinion, may be helpful in establishing the cause of death, manner of death, or identification of the deceased; and in cooperation with a forensic laboratory he or she may make such tests and examinations of said objects, specimens, or articles as may be necessary or useful in determining the cause of death, manner of death, or the identity of the deceased. At his or her discretion, the medical examiner or coroner may dispose of such objects, specimens, or articles when the medical examiner's or coroner's need for their retention has ended. In the event that a criminal prosecution arises, all such objects and articles together with reports of any examinations made upon them shall be retained in the custody of the investigating agency or the forensic laboratory which conducted the examination until their production as evidence is required by the prosecuting officer or upon written order of the peace officer in charge or court having proper jurisdiction.

(d) The Georgia Bureau of Investigation is authorized to perform a post mortem examination and autopsy on a person whose death occurs within a state owned or leased building or on the curtilage of such building. The Georgia Bureau of Investigation shall have jurisdiction relating to the investigation of such a death, and this authority and jurisdiction shall supersede any other authority or jurisdiction provided for by this article relating to a post mortem examination or autopsy.

Laws 1953, Jan.-Feb. Sess., p. 602, § 9; Laws 1960, p. 1009, § 6; Laws 1985, p. 843, § 5; Laws 1989, p. 829, § 1; Laws 1990, p. 8, § 45; Laws 1990, p. 1735, § 3; Laws 1990, p. 1968, § 1; Laws 1996, p. 364, § 1; Laws 1997, p. 1421, § 6; Laws 2000, p. 1585, §§ 1, 2; Laws 2009, Act 103, § 1, eff. July 1, 2009; Laws 2010, Act 503, § 1, eff. July 1, 2010.

§ 45-16-25.1. Release of dead bodies

A dead body, other than skeletal remains, taken into custody under this article shall be released to the next of kin of the deceased, or to the agent of the next of kin, no later than 24 hours after the demand for release by that next of kin, or agent thereof, unless by that time the peace officer, medical examiner, or coroner has made a written finding that foul play may have been involved in the death of the deceased.

Laws 1983, p. 728, § 1; Laws 1990, p. 1735, § 3.

§ 45-16-26. When medical examiner may assume duties of coroner

When there is no coroner or deputy coroner in a county in which the office of coroner has not been replaced by a county medical examiner or when both are absent from the county when needed or will not or cannot perform the duties required under this article, the medical examiner shall assume the duties and responsibilities of the coroner. When the medical examiner is performing the duties of the coroner in such cases, such medical examiner may sign the death certificate except when an inquest is held.

Laws 1953, Jan.-Feb. Sess., p. 602, § 22; Laws 1984, p. 812, § 3; Laws 1985, p. 843, § 6; Laws 1990, p. 1735, § 3.

Formerly Code 1863, § 573; Code 1868, § 637; Code 1873, § 596; Code 1882, § 596; Civil Code 1895, § 4074; Penal Code 1895, § 1268; Civil Code 1910, § 4671; Penal Code 1910, § 1350; Code 1933, § 21–204.

§ 45–16–27. When inquests required; investigation fees and costs; photographs and video recordings not subject to disclosure

(a) Coroners shall require an inquest to be conducted in their respective counties as follows:

(1) When any person dies under any circumstances specified in paragraphs (1) through (8) of subsection (a) of Code Section 45–16–24; provided, however, that an inquest is not required to be held, although the coroner is authorized to hold an inquest, under the following circumstances:

(A) When upon the completion of the medical examiner's inquiry the peace officer in charge and the medical examiner are satisfied that, even though death resulted from violence, no foul play was involved. In this event, the peace officer in charge and the medical examiner shall make a written report of their investigation and findings to the division as set forth in Code Section 45–16–32 and upon their recommendation, the coroner shall make and file a proper death certificate;

(B) When there is sufficient evidence to establish the cause and manner of death, even though the medical examiner's inquiry revealed that death resulted from foul play;

(C) When no demand for an inquest is made within 30 days after the filing of the death certificate. However, if such demand is made by the party or parties affected by the death, the coroner is authorized to hold the inquest;

(D) When upon the completion of the medical examiner's inquiry the medical examiner and peace officer in charge are sufficiently satisfied that death resulted from natural causes, and that medical examiner or coroner is willing to and does sign and file a proper death certificate, and no demand for an inquest is made within 30 days thereafter;

(D.1) In cases of deaths resulting from an accident involving any civil aircraft, it shall be the responsibility of the peace officer in charge to notify the National Transportation Safety Board or the Federal Aviation Administration of such accident, to proceed to the scene and guard the area in such manner that no bodies, wreckage, cargo, or mail shall be moved or disturbed until authorized by a representative of the National Transportation Safety Board or the Federal Aviation Administration except to the extent necessary to remove persons injured or trapped, to protect the wreckage from further damage, or to protect the public from injury. Where it is necessary to move aircraft wreckage, mail, or cargo, sketches, descriptive notes, and photographs shall be made, if possible, of the original positions and condition of the wreckage and any significant impact marks. The coroner or medical examiner shall assist investigators from the National Transportation Safety Board or the Federal Aviation Administration as authorized by federal law;

(E) When after full and complete investigation no evidence of foul play is found in cases of hidden cause of death which fall under the jurisdiction of the coroner. The coroner shall be authorized to sign the death certificate on the basis of the information given to him in the reports of the peace officer in charge and the medical examiner, provided that, in such hidden causes of death, after a complete investigation, if sufficient medical history is obtained by the coroner, the peace officer in charge, or the medical examiner to disclose the cause of death and if the attending physician will sign the death certificate, such cases shall not come under the jurisdiction of the coroner; provided, further, that, if there are sufficient competent eyewitnesses to an act in the opinion of the peace officer in charge, such cases shall not come under the jurisdiction of the coroner; or

(F) In cases of deaths of personnel in the armed forces of the United States government resulting from airplane disasters involving airplanes of the armed forces, including crashes or explosions, which deaths shall not come under the jurisdiction of the coroner. It shall be the responsibility of the peace officer in charge to notify the proper armed forces of the United States government immediately of such airplane crashes or explosions in order that they may send their trained forces to the scene for investigation. It shall be the duty of the peace officer in charge, when notified of such crashes or explosions, to proceed to the scene and guard the area in such manner that no bodies or parts of said airplanes shall be moved or disturbed until the arrival of proper investigating officers from the armed forces of the United States government;

(2) When an inmate of a state hospital or a state, county, or city penal institution dies unexpectedly without an attending physician or as a result of violence. The chief medical examiner or his or her designee, regional medical examiner, or local medical examiner shall perform all medical examiners' inquiries. The coroner, in those counties in which such office has not been replaced by a local medical examiner, shall hold an inquest after receiving the written reports as set forth in Code Section 45–16–32;

(3) When ordered by a court in connection with a medical examiner's inquiry ordered by that court pursuant to subsection (c) of Code Section 45–16–24; or

(4) Notwithstanding any other provisions of this subsection, no person shall be deemed to have died unattended by a physician when the death occurred while the person was a patient of a hospice licensed under Article 9 of Chapter 7 of Title 31.

(b) On and after January 1, 2007, coroners shall be entitled to an investigation fee of $175.00 where no jury is impaneled or a fee of $250.00 where a jury is impaneled and shall be paid upon receipt of a monthly statement to the county treasury. A deputy coroner shall receive the same fee as the coroner for the performance of services in place of the coroner and shall be paid upon receipt of a monthly statement to the county treasury. Such fee shall be paid within ten days after receipt of the coroner's monthly statement by the county where the investigation or inquest is held except in counties where the coroner receives an annual salary, in which case no fee shall be imposed upon the county by such salaried coroner or deputy coroner.

(b.1) Any local Acts providing for the compensation of the various coroners shall remain in full force and effect, except in those instances where such local Acts provide for a salary in an amount which is less than the amount of compensation such coroner would be entitled to pursuant to subsection (b) of this Code section in which case the coroner may select on an annual basis beginning January 1, 2007, to be compensated pursuant to subsection (b) of this Code section or by the salary provided for by local Act.

(c) When a coroner or a medical examiner or a medical examiner from the office of chief medical examiner, as established in Code Section 35–3–153, conducts an investigation into the death of an individual, the coroner, medical examiner, or medical examiner from the office of chief medical examiner shall be authorized to issue subpoenas to compel the production of any books, records, including but not limited to medical records from hospitals, medical clinics, psychiatric hospitals, physicians' offices, chiropractors' offices, and any other health care delivery facility, or papers relevant to the cause of death including without limitation AIDS confidential information as defined by Code Section 31–22–9.1. Any books, records, or papers received by the coroner, medical examiner, or medical examiner from the office of chief medical examiner pursuant to the subpoena must be regarded as confidential information and privileged and not subject to disclosure under Article 4 of Chapter 18 of Title 50. The actual costs of copying any books, records, or papers for the purposes of responding to a subpoena under this subsection shall be paid out of county funds to the person or entity required to respond to that subpoena, and the governing authority of the county of which that coroner or county medical examiner is a public officer shall pay those costs within 30 days after a bill therefor is submitted to the county. A medical examiner from the office of chief medical examiner shall pay the costs of copying from state funds within 30 days after a bill therefor is submitted to the state.

(d) Autopsy photographs shall not be subject to disclosure pursuant to Article 4 of Chapter 18 of Title 50; provided, however, that this subsection shall have no application to the disclosure of such photographs to law enforcement agencies and prosecutors for law enforcement purposes or, in closed criminal investigations, to medical schools, medical facilities, and physicians for medical purposes; to individuals who have secured a written release from the deceased's next of kin; or to the next of kin. It shall be the responsibility of the next of kin to show proof of the familial relationship. For purposes of securing a written release or when access to the photographs is requested by the next of kin, the deceased's next of kin shall be:

(1) The spouse of the deceased if living;

(2) If there is no living spouse of the deceased, an adult child of the deceased;

(3) If there is no living spouse or adult child, a parent of the deceased;

(4) If there is no living spouse, adult child, or parent, a sibling of the deceased;

(5) If there is no living spouse, adult child, parent, or sibling of the deceased, a grandparent of the deceased;

(6) If none of the above are living, an uncle of the deceased;

(7) If none of the above are living, an aunt of the deceased; or

(8) If none of the above are living, a first cousin of the deceased.

A superior court may, in closed criminal investigations, order the disclosure of such photographs upon findings in writing that disclosure is in the public interest and that it outweighs any privacy interest that may be asserted by the deceased's next of kin. In any such action, the court shall review the photographs in question in camera and may condition any disclosure on such measurers as the court may deem necessary to accommodate the interests of the parties before it.

(e)(1) Crime scene photographs and video recordings, including photographs and video recordings created or produced by a state or local agency or by a perpetrator or suspect at a crime scene, which depict or describe a deceased person in a state of dismemberment, decapitation, or similar mutilation including, without limitation, where the deceased person's genitalia are exposed, shall not be subject to disclosure pursuant to Article 4 of Chapter 18 of Title 50; provided, however, that this subsection shall not prohibit disclosure of such material to the deceased's next of kin or to an individual who has secured a written release from the next of kin. It shall be the responsibility of the next of kin to show proof of the familial relationship. For purposes of such access, the deceased's next of kin shall be:

(A) The spouse of the deceased if living;

(B) If there is no living spouse of the deceased, an adult child of the deceased; or

(C) If there is no living spouse or adult child, a parent of the deceased.

(2) Subject to the provisions of paragraph (3) of this subsection, in the case of closed criminal investigations a superior court may order the disclosure of such photographs or video recordings upon findings in writing that disclosure is in the public interest and outweighs any privacy interest that may be asserted by the deceased person's next of kin. In making such determination, the court shall consider whether such disclosure is necessary for public evaluation of governmental performance, the seriousness of the intrusion into the family's right to privacy, and whether such disclosure is the least intrusive means available considering the availability of similar information in other public records. In any such action, the court shall review the photographs in question in camera with the custodian of crime scene materials present and may condition any disclosure on such condition as the court may deem necessary to accommodate the interests of the parties.

(3) Prior to releasing any crime scene material described in paragraph (1) of this subsection, the custodian of such material shall give the deceased person's next of kin at least two weeks' notice. No court shall order a disclosure pursuant to paragraph (2) of this subsection which would disregard or shorten the duration of such notice requirement.

(4) The provisions of this subsection shall apply to all undisclosed material which is in the custody of a state or local agency on the effective date of this subsection and to any such material which comes into the custody of a state or local agency after such date.

(5) This subsection shall not apply to disclosure of crime scene material to counsel representing a convicted defendant in a habeas corpus action pursuant to Chapter 14 of Title 9, on an extraordinary motion for new trial under Code Section 5–5–40 or 5–5–41, or in a federal habeas corpus action under Section 2254 or 2255 of Title 28 of the United States Code for the purpose of preparing to file or litigating such proceedings. Counsel may disclose such materials to his or her client and any expert or investigator assisting counsel but shall not otherwise disseminate such materials, except to the extent they may be necessary exhibits in court proceedings. A request pursuant to this paragraph shall clearly state that such request is being made for the purpose of preparing to file and litigate proceedings enumerated in this paragraph.

(6) The director of the Georgia Bureau of Investigation and the Board of Public Safety shall promulgate rules and regulations governing the viewing of materials described in paragraph (1) of this subsection by bona fide credentialed members of the press.

Laws 1823, Cobb's 1851 Digest, p. 537; Laws 1893, p. 116, § 1; Laws 1901, p. 44, § 1; Laws 1953, Jan.-Feb. Sess., p. 602, § 5; Laws 1960, p. 1009, § 4; Laws 1961, p. 437, § 1; Laws 1980, p. 543, § 5; Laws 1981, p. 611, § 2; Laws 1984, p. 812, § 4; Laws 1985, p. 1073, § 2; Laws 1986, p. 10, § 45; Laws 1986, p. 1594, § 2; Laws 1988, p. 722, § 1; Laws 1990, p. 1735, § 3; Laws 1995, p. 350, § 1; Laws 1997, p. 1421, §§ 7, 8; Laws 1999, p. 869, § 3; Laws 2002, p. 667, § 1; Laws 2006, Act 649, § 12, eff. July 1, 2006; Laws 2010, Act 414, § 3, eff. May 20, 2010.

Formerly Code 1863, § 566; Code 1868, § 630; Code 1873, § 589; Code 1882, § 589; Penal Code 1895, § 1255; Penal Code 1910, § 1337; Code 1933, § 21–202.

Historical and Statutory Notes

Laws 2010, Act 414, § 2, provides:

"The General Assembly finds that photographs or video recordings of certain crime scene photos depict the deceased in graphic and often disturbing fashion. Such photographs or video may depict or describe the deceased nude, grossly dismembered, or decapitated. As such photographs or video recordings are highly sensitive depictions of the deceased which, if viewed, copied, or publicized, could result in trauma, sorrow, humiliation, or emotional injury to the immediate family of the deceased, as well as injury to the memory of the deceased. The legislature finds that the existence of certain publications and the Internet and the proliferation of personal computers throughout the world encourages and promotes the wide dissemination of photographs and video recordings 24 hours a day and that widespread unauthorized dissemination of such images would subject the immediate family of the deceased to continuous injury."

§ 45–16–27.1. When autopsies required

(a) Where a coroner or county medical examiner has been notified pursuant to paragraph (6) of subsection (a) of Code Section 45–16–24 of the death of any person after birth but before seven years of age whose death is unexpected or unexplained, the medical examiner's inquiry required by Code Section 45–16–25 shall include an autopsy unless that inquiry shows that such death was expected or explainable with a reasonable degree of medical certainty.

(b) The provisions of this Code section shall apply notwithstanding subsection (b) of Code Section 45–16–22 or any other provision of this article.

Laws 1990, p. 1735, § 3; Laws 2002, p. 415, § 45.

§ 45–16–28. Authority to perform autopsy

In the case of death of any person under such circumstances as would not require a medical examiner's inquiry under Code Section 45–16–24, any physician who is duly licensed under the laws of this state or any other state having licensing requirements equal to or greater than those imposed by this state shall be deemed to have been legally authorized to perform an autopsy upon the body of a deceased person when such autopsy has been consented to by the person assuming custody of the body for the purposes of burial, such as the husband, wife, father, mother, child, guardian, next of kin, or, in the absence of any of the foregoing, a friend of such deceased person charged by law with the responsibility of burial. If two or more of such persons assume custody of the body, the consent of one of them shall be deemed sufficient legal authorization for the performance of the autopsy.

Laws 1953, Jan.-Feb. Sess., p. 602, § 6; Laws 1990, p. 1735, § 3.

§ 45–16–29. Removal of body prior to investigation prohibited

No person shall move or authorize the removal of any body from the place where the same is found until the investigation is completed and such removal is authorized by the coroner or medical examiner present at such investigation; or, if no such coroner or medical examiner is present, the peace officer shall authorize such removal; provided, however, that this Code section shall not apply to the removal of a body where the death occurred while the person was a patient of a hospice licensed under Article 9 of Chapter 7 of Title 31. If the death resulted from an accident involving the operation of civil aircraft, no body shall be removed until authorized by the representative of the National Transportation Safety Board or the Federal Aviation Administration.

Laws 1960, p. 1009, § 9; Laws 1985, p. 843, § 7; Laws 1985, p. 1073, § 3; Laws 1990, p. 1735, § 3; Laws 1997, p. 1421, § 9.

§ 45–16–30. Removal of body across state line prior to investigation prohibited

No person shall move or transport a body across a Georgia state line until the investigation of the case and the medical examiner's inquiry are complete and until the removal of the body is authorized by the coroner or medical examiner. Except when the conduct is a violation of Code Section 16–10–94, any person who violates this Code section shall be guilty of a misdemeanor and, upon conviction thereof, shall be punished by a fine of not less than $ 500.00 or more than $ 1,000.00 or 60 days in jail, or both.

Laws 1960, p. 1009, § 9; Laws 1985, p. 843, § 8; Laws 1990, p. 1735, § 3; Laws 1997, p. 1421, § 9.

§ 45–16–31. Removal of body for purpose of medical examiner's inquiry; photographs and investigation of premises where found

When the deceased body lies in a place inconvenient for holding a medical examiner's inquiry, the medical examiner or coroner shall be allowed to remove the body to the autopsy room of the nearest public hospital or morgue. If neither the coroner nor the medical examiner is immediately available, the peace officer may assume the authority to have the body moved to such facility. When such facility is not reasonably available, the body may be removed to such other suitable place as may be designated by the coroner or the medical examiner or by the peace officer in charge in the absence of the coroner or medical examiner. If the peace officer in charge is present, no such body shall be removed until photographs of the body and surrounding premises have been made and a thorough investigation of the premises has been made by the proper investigating authorities.

Laws 1850, Cobb's 1851 Digest, p. 540; Laws 1862–63, p. 166, § 2; Laws 1953, Jan.-Feb. Sess., p. 602, § 7; Laws 1960, p. 1009, § 5; Laws 1985, p. 843, § 9; Laws 1990, p. 1735, § 3.

Formerly Code 1868, § 4039; Code 1873, § 4110; Code 1882, § 4110; Penal Code 1895, § 1269; Penal Code 1910, § 1351; Code 1933, § 21–206.

§ 45–16–32. Report of medical examiner's inquiry and coroner's investigation; procedure where foul play indicated

The medical examiner and coroner shall complete a report of each medical examiner's inquiry and coroner's investigation and shall maintain permanent records of such reports. The coroner or county medical examiner may file all original reports with the clerk of the superior court of the county. In cases where such report indicates a suspicion of foul play, the medical examiner and peace officer in charge shall transmit any specimens, samples, or other evidence to a forensic laboratory for analysis. In cases where reports indicating foul play are verified by the forensic laboratory, the laboratory shall provide a completed lab report to the appropriate prosecuting attorney where the acts or events leading to the death occurred.

Laws 1953, Jan.-Feb. Sess., p. 602, § 4; Laws 1960, p. 1009, § 3; Laws 1984, p. 812, § 5; Laws 1985, p. 843, § 10; Laws 1989, p. 417, § 2; Laws 1990, p. 1735, § 3; Laws 1999, p. 869, § 4; Laws 2010, Act 503, § 2, eff. July 1, 2010.

§ 45–16–33. Inquest

Upon the completion of the medical examiner's inquiry by the medical examiner, as provided in Code Section 45–16–24, and after verification by the division when such verification is required, the coroner shall then make an inquest into the death of such deceased person as provided in Code Section 45–16–27.

Laws 1953, Jan.-Feb. Sess., p. 602, § 10; Laws 1960, p. 1009, § 7; Laws 1990, p. 1735, § 3.

§ 45–16–34. Attendance and oath of witnesses; subpoenas for production of books, records, or papers

(a) The coroner shall issue subpoenas to or otherwise compel the attendance of witnesses; and he shall administer to such witnesses the following oath:

"The evidence that you shall give this inquest on behalf of the state concerning the death of ____ (or a person unknown, as the case may be) shall be the truth, the whole truth, and nothing but the truth, so help you God."

(b) When a coroner conducts an inquest into the death of an individual, he shall be authorized to issue subpoenas to compel production of any books, records, or papers relevant to the cause of death. Any books, records, or papers received by the coroner pursuant to the subpoena must be regarded as confidential information and privileged and not subject to disclosure under Article 4 of Chapter 18 of Title 50. The actual costs of copying any books, records, or papers for the purpose of responding to a coroner's subpoena under this subsection shall be paid out of county funds to the person or entity required to respond to that subpoena, and the governing authority of the county of which that coroner is a public officer shall pay those costs within 30 days after a bill therefor is submitted to the county; provided, however, that the county shall not be responsible for duplication costs under $ 25.00.

Laws 1823, Cobb's 1851 Digest, p. 539; Laws 1953, Jan.-Feb. Sess., p. 602, § 11; Laws 1986, p. 1594, § 3; Laws 1988, p. 13, § 45; Laws 1990, p. 1735, § 3.

Formerly Code 1863, § 4007; Code 1868, § 4035; Code 1873, § 4106; Code 1882, § 4106; Penal Code 1895, § 1263; Penal Code 1910, § 1345; Code 1933, § 21-207.

§ 45-16-35. Recognizances of witnesses to appear in court; warrant for arrest of suspected person

If the inquest discloses facts which lead or may lead to the prosecution of any person for the homicide of the person for whom the inquest is held, the coroner shall require all witnesses who testify to facts material to the issues involved in such prosecution to enter into a recognizance to appear in the superior court of the county in which the inquest is held and to give evidence against the defendant in such prosecution; and he shall also petition for the issuance of a warrant for the arrest of the person suspected of the homicide, which warrant shall be returnable as other warrants.

Laws 1823, Cobb's 1851 Digest, p. 539; Laws 1953, Jan.-Feb. Sess., p. 602, § 12; Laws 1990, p. 1735, § 3.

Formerly Code 1863, § 4008; Code 1868, § 4036; Code 1873, § 4107; Code 1882, § 4107; Penal Code 1895, § 1264; Penal Code 1910, § 1346; Code 1933, § 21-208.

§ 45-16-36. Jury; fees

The coroner shall summon and impanel five jurors and one alternate juror to hold an inquest, which jurors shall decide the verdict by a majority vote. The first grand jury impaneled at the fall term of the superior courts of the several counties shall fix the compensation of said jurors for the next succeeding year but such compensation shall not be less than $ 5.00 nor more than $ 25.00 per diem. It shall be the duty of the coroner or other person discharging the duties of the coroner to give a certificate of the fact of such service to each juror. Upon presentation of such certificate to the proper fiscal authority of the county in which the inquest is held, such fiscal authority shall pay the juror for his services.

Laws 1823, Cobb's 1851 Digest, p. 538; Laws 1884-85, p. 92, § 1; Laws 1893, p. 116, § 3; Laws 1953, Jan.-Feb. Sess., p. 204, § 1; Laws 1953, Jan.-Feb. Sess., p. 602, § 13; Laws 1969, p. 761, § 1; Laws 1982, p. 718, §§ 1, 2; Laws 1990, p. 1735, § 3.

Formerly Penal Code 1895, § 1257; Penal Code 1910, § 1339; Code 1933, § 21-209.

§ 45-16-37. No coroner's jury impaneled until investigation complete; jury not required to view body

No coroner's jury shall be impaneled until the investigation is completed and copies of the reports of the medical examiner and the peace officer in charge are received by the coroner. The jury is not required to view the body.

Laws 1960, p. 1009, § 9; Laws 1990, p. 1735, § 3.

§ 45-16-38. Summoning jury; form of precept; duty of sheriff

Whenever a coroner receives notice of the death of any person within the limits of the county of which he is coroner, which death occurred under circumstances which make it his duty, under the law, to hold an inquest, he shall make out a precept directed to the sheriff or any constable of the county having jurisdiction requiring him to summon a jury of inquest selected from the grand jury or traverse jury lists of the last excused term of the superior court of such county to appear before the coroner at the time and place mentioned in the precept, which precept may be in the following form:

State of Georgia
_____ County
To the sheriff or any lawful constable of said county,
Greeting:

You are required immediately to summon six persons of said county, chosen from the lists of grand jurors and traverse jurors of the last excused term of the superior court of said county, to be and appear before me, the undersigned, coroner of the county aforesaid, at _____, in said county, on the _____ day of _____ at _____ :_____ _____. M. of that same day, then and there to inquire of, do, and execute all such things as in behalf of the state shall be given them in charge concerning the death of _____ (or a person unknown, as the case may be), and be you then and there with this precept to certify what you have done in the premises and further to do whatsoever else may in behalf of the state be enjoined upon you.

Given under my hand and seal, this the _____ day of _____, in the year of our Lord _____.

_______________ Coroner (L.S.)

Such precept shall be immediately executed by the sheriff or constable in whose hands it may be placed; and, if the services of the sheriff or a constable cannot be conveniently obtained, the coroner may summon the jury himself.

Laws 1823, Cobb's 1851 Digest, p. 537; Laws 1953, Jan.-Feb. Sess., p. 602, § 14; Laws 1960, p. 1009, § 8; Laws 1990, p. 1735, § 3; Laws 2002, p. 415, § 45.

Formerly Code 1863, § 4002; Code 1868, § 4030; Code 1873, § 4101; Code 1882, § 4101; Penal Code 1895, § 1259; Penal Code 1910, § 1341; Code 1933, § 21-210.

§ 45-16-39. Oath of foreman and other jurors

(a) The following oath shall be administered to the foreman of the jury by the coroner:

> "You, as foreman of the inquest, shall diligently inquire and true presentment make, on behalf of the State of Georgia, how and in what manner _____ (or a person deceased, unknown, as the case may be) came to his death and of such other matters relating to the same as shall be lawfully required of you, according to evidence, so help you God."

(b) The remainder of the jury shall be sworn by the coroner as follows:

"The same oath which the foreman of this inquest has taken on his part each of you shall observe and keep upon your part, so help you God."

Laws 1823, Cobb's 1851 Digest, p. 538; Laws 1953, Jan.-Feb. Sess., p. 602, § 16; Laws 1990, p. 1735, § 3.

Formerly Code 1863, § 4005; Code 1868, § 4033; Code 1873, § 4104; Code 1882, § 4104; Penal Code 1895, § 1261; Penal Code 1910, § 1343; Code 1933, § 21–212.

§ 45–16–40. Charge to jury as to findings; authority of jury in absence of charge

(a) The coroner shall charge the jurors to declare, and they shall so declare, whether the person for whom the inquest is held died by:

(1) Homicide;

(2) Suicide;

(3) Accident;

(4) Natural causes; or

(5) Undetermined causes

and all of the circumstances relating to the death.

(b) The jury shall have full and unrestricted power to inquire and pass upon all the matters and things thus given them in charge and they shall have this power even if the whole or a part of the charge is omitted.

Laws 1823, Cobb's 1851 Digest, p. 538; Laws 1953, Jan.-Feb. Sess., p. 602, § 17; Laws 1990, p. 1735, § 3.

Formerly Code 1863, § 4006; Code 1868, § 4034; Code 1873, § 4105; Code 1882, § 4105; Penal Code 1895, § 1262; Penal Code 1910, § 1344; Code 1933, § 21–213.

§ 45–16–41. Penalty for juror failing to attend inquest

Any juror failing to attend and serve on a coroner's inquest after being duly summoned may be fined by the coroner in a sum not exceeding $ 100.00 to be levied and collected by execution issued by the coroner unless such defaulting juror shall file in the office of the judge of the probate court a good and sufficient excuse for the default to be judged by the next probate court held thereafter.

Laws 1823, Cobb's 1851 Digest, p. 538; Laws 1953, Jan.-Feb. Sess., p. 602, § 15; Laws 1984, p. 812, § 6; Laws 1990, p. 1735, § 3.

Formerly Code 1863, § 4003; Code 1868, § 4031; Code 1873, § 4102; Code 1882, § 4102; Penal Code 1895, § 1260; Penal Code 1910, § 1342; Code 1933, § 21–211.

§ 45–16–42. Results of medical examiner's inquiry as evidence

In all inquests the results of the medical examiner's inquiry performed shall be offered in evidence either by oral testimony of the medical examiner or by introduction of a copy of the report filed with the director of the division, as verified in the cases requiring verification. The jury shall be free to reach a verdict in accord or discord with such evidence but in all cases such evidence must be presented to them for their consideration.

Laws 1953, Jan.-Feb. Sess., p. 602, § 18; Laws 1990, p. 1735, § 3.

§ 45–16–43. Reports of medical examiners' inquiries as evidence in courts or other proceedings

Reports of medical examiners' inquiries performed as provided in this article and copies of records, photographs, laboratory findings, and reports in the office of the director of the division, when duly attested by said director, shall be received as evidence in any court or other proceeding for any purpose for which the original could be received without any proof of the official character of the person whose name is signed thereto.

Laws 1953, Jan.-Feb. Sess., p. 602, § 19; Laws 1990, p. 1735, § 3.

§ 45–16–44. Disposition of body after medical examiner's inquiry and inquest

After the medical examiner's inquiry and inquest have been completed, the dead body shall be delivered to the person legally entitled thereto for burial. If no person claims the body, it shall be turned over to the coroner of the county where death occurred for disposition as provided by law. If the deceased has an estate out of which burial expenses can be paid, either in whole or in part, such estate shall be taken for such purpose before any expense under this Code section is imposed upon any county.

Laws 1953, Jan.-Feb. Sess., p. 602, § 20; Laws 1990, p. 1735, § 3.

§ 45–16–45. Disinterment of bodies

In order to implement this article, coroners are authorized to disinter any body already buried and, like a sheriff, to command the power of the county for that purpose. Medical examiners, other than local medical examiners, may likewise exercise such authority in any case wherein such authority is granted by an order of the judge of the superior court of the county. Such orders may be granted by judges of the superior courts, in their discretion, upon petition of any medical examiner other than a local medical examiner.

Laws 1953, Jan.-Feb. Sess., p. 602, § 21; Laws 1990, p. 1735, § 3.

Formerly Code 1863, § 567; Code 1868, § 631; Code 1873, § 590; Code 1882, § 590; Penal Code 1895, § 1258; Penal Code 1910, § 1340; Code 1933, § 21–205.

§ 45–16–46. Blood specimens from persons unable to give consent; fee of medical examiner

When any person has been admitted to a hospital or morgue as a result of any casualty and for any reason whatsoever is unable to give his or her consent to the taking of a sample of blood for analytical purposes, the coroner or peace officer in charge of the investigation of the circumstances surrounding the casualty may notify a medical examiner for the purpose of obtaining a blood sample to test for the presence of intoxicating substances or in the case of a dead body and where appropriate for the presence of infectious agents. The blood may be drawn by the medical examiner or at the medical examiner's direction. The medical examiner or his or her designee shall be entitled to a fee set in accordance with Code Section 35–3–151 for performing these services, which fee shall be paid in the same manner as set out in Code Section 45–16–22. The peace officer may also request any licensed physician, nurse, emergency medical technician, medical or laboratory technician, or other qualified person to withdraw blood for purposes of this Code section, in which event such person shall incur no civil or criminal liability. The medical examiner or the peace officer in charge shall submit the blood specimens to the division for analysis; and a report shall be submitted by the division to the submitting officer.

Laws 1961, p. 437, § 2; Laws 1974, p. 561, § 1; Laws 1982, p. 959, §§ 1, 2; Laws 1984, p. 812, § 7; Laws 1989, p. 829, § 2; Laws 1990, p. 1735, § 3; Laws 1997, p. 1421, § 10.

§ 45–16–47. Violations relating to Georgia Death Investigation Act

Except as provided in Code Section 45–16–30, any person who violates this article shall be guilty of a misdemeanor.

Laws 1960, p. 1009, § 9; Laws 1990, p. 1735, § 3.

§ 45–16–48. Employment of court reporter by coroner

A coroner may be authorized to employ, at his discretion, a court reporter who is certified under Article 2 of Chapter 14 of Title 15, "The Georgia Court Reporting Act," to record the proceedings of any inquest. The cost of acquiring the services of a certified court reporter shall be paid from the funds of the county where the inquest is held.

Laws 1984, p. 812, § 8; Laws 1990, p. 1735, § 3.

§ 45–16–49. Continuation of fees at specified rate

The fees heretofore authorized to be paid in cases arising under this article prior to May 1, 1997, shall continue to be paid at the rate specified therein until such time as the Board of Public Safety promulgates rules prescribing such fees as provided by paragraph (5) of Code Section 35–3–151.

Laws 1998, p. 128, § 45.

§ 45–16–50. Biological substances used for canine service training

A medical examiner within the state of Georgia is authorized to provide to an approved canine instructor or school certain biological substances such as human blood or bodily fluids for the sole purpose of utilizing such substances for the training and handling of police canines in body recovery of human remains or rescue of persons. Such biological substances shall be contained and transported in accordance with appropriate health and safety standards.

Laws 2009, Act 103, § 2, eff. July 1, 2009.

Article 3

Georgia Coroner's Training Council

§ 45–16–60. Short title

This article shall be known as "The Georgia Coroner's Training Council Act."

Laws 1985, p. 797, § 1.

§ 45–16–61. Definitions

As used in this article, the term:

(1) "Certified coroner" means a coroner who has the appropriate required certificate of training issued by the council on file with the Board of Public Safety.

(2) "Coroner" means any person appointed or elected in a county to serve as coroner or deputy coroner.

(3) "Council" means the Georgia Coroner's Training Council.

(4) "School" means any school, college, university, academy, or training program approved by the council and the Board of Public Safety which offers basic, in-service, advanced, specialized, or continuing training, or a combination thereof, and includes within its meaning a combination of course curriculum, instructors, and facilities which meets the standards required by the council.

Laws 1985, p. 797, § 1; Laws 1990, p. 8, § 45.

§ 45–16–62. Establishment; membership; duties

(a) There is established a council which shall be known and designated as the "Georgia Coroner's Training Council" which shall be composed of the superintendent of the Georgia Police Academy or his designee, which member shall not be a voting member; five coroners appointed by the Board of Public Safety, three of whom will be selected from a list of five persons recommended by the Georgia Coroner's Association; and one physician trained in forensic pathology and appointed by the Board of Public Safety, which physician member shall not be a voting member of the council but shall advise the council regarding the training course curriculum for coroners. The term of office of the physician member appointed in 1990 shall begin September 1, 1990, and that and all subsequent terms for that office shall be for four years and until the appointment and qualification of a successor. The five coroners appointed shall serve for terms of four years. The term of office of the member initially appointed in 1987 shall begin September 1, 1987. Upon the expiration of a member's term of office, such member shall continue to serve on the council until his successor is appointed and qualified. Any person, other than the physician member, appointed to the council who ceases to serve as a coroner shall be ineligible to continue service on the council. The Georgia Police Academy shall establish a curriculum advisory committee to provide information beneficial to the development of courses at the Georgia Police Academy. Members of the committee will be selected by the superintendent of the Georgia Police Academy.

(b) Membership on the council does not constitute public office, and no member shall be disqualified from holding office by reason of his membership.

(c) Vacancies on the council shall be filled as provided in subsection (a) of this Code section for the remainder of the unexpired term.

Laws 1985, p. 797, § 1; Laws 1987, p. 340, § 1; Laws 1990, p. 333, § 2; Laws 1990, p. 1735, § 4.

§ 45–16–63. Oath of office; certificate of appointment

Immediately and before entering upon the duties of office, the members of the council shall take the oath of office and shall file the same with the Board of Public Safety, which, upon receiving the oath of office, shall issue to each member a certificate of appointment.

Laws 1985, p. 797, § 1; Laws 1986, p. 10, § 45.

§ 45–16–64. Officers; quorum; records; reports

(a) The council at its initial meeting, which shall be held promptly after the appointment of its members, shall elect from among its members a chairman and a vice-chairman who shall serve until the first meeting in the succeeding year. Thereafter, the chairman and the vice-chairman shall be elected at the first meeting of each calendar year.

(b) The superintendent of the Georgia Police Academy or his designee shall serve as secretary to the council.

(c) A simple majority of the councilmembers shall constitute a quorum for the transaction of business.

(d) The council shall maintain minutes of its meetings and such other records as it deems necessary.

(e) The council shall report at least annually to the Board of Public Safety and to the General Assembly as to its activities.

Laws 1985, p. 797, § 1; Laws 1987, p. 340, § 2; Laws 1990, p. 1967, § 1; Laws 2002, p. 415, § 45.

§ 45–16–65. Functions, powers, and responsibilities

The council is vested with the following functions, powers, and responsibilities:

(1) To make all the necessary rules and regulations to carry out this article;

(2) To cooperate with and secure the cooperation of every department, agency, or instrumentality of the state government or its political subdivisions in furtherance of the purposes of this article;

(3) To approve schools and to prescribe minimum qualifications for instructors at approved schools;

(4) To issue a certificate of certification to any coroner satisfactorily complying with an approved training program;

(5) To withdraw or suspend the certification of any coroner who has performed or is performing the duties of a coroner in violation of this chapter;

(6) To do any and all things necessary or convenient to enable it wholly and adequately to perform its duties and to exercise the power granted to it; and

(7) To prescribe, by rules and regulations, the minimum requirements for curricula and standards composing the initial in-service, advanced, specialized, and continuing training courses for certification.

Laws 1985, p. 797, § 1; Laws 1986, p. 10, § 45; Laws 1990, p. 333, § 3.

§ 45–16–66. Training to maintain status of certified coroner

(a) In order to maintain the status of a certified coroner, each person certified as such shall complete such additional training per annum during each year in which he or she serves as coroner as provided by the Georgia Coroner's Training Council in its rules and regulations, but such training course shall not be less than 16 hours per year. Each coroner and deputy coroner shall file a certificate of additional training with such council.

(b) No person serving as a coroner shall charge or collect any fee, charge, or cost of any kind for his services, including those fees specified in this article, unless such person is a certified coroner.

Laws 1985, p. 797, § 1; Laws 1989, p. 14, § 45; Laws 1990, p. 333, § 4; Laws 1990, p. 1735, § 5; Laws 1994, p. 356, § 2.

§ 45–16–67. Injunctions and restraining orders

On its own initiative or on the verified complaint of any person that a person has performed or is performing the duties of coroner in violation of this article, the council may file an action seeking equitable relief in its own name in the superior court of any county in this state having jurisdiction of such person. Such action shall allege the facts and pray for a temporary restraining order and temporary injunction against such person restraining him from violating this article. Upon proof thereof, the court shall issue a restraining order, temporary injunction, or permanent injunction without requiring allegation or proof that the plaintiff has no adequate remedy at law. The right of injunction provided for in this Code section shall be in addition to any other remedy which the council has.

Laws 1985, p. 797, § 1.

Article 4

Office of Medical Examiner

§ 45–16–80. Abolition of office of coroner and establishment of office of medical examiner

(a) In any county of this state the General Assembly by local law is authorized to abolish the office of coroner and establish in lieu thereof the office of medical examiner, which medical examiner shall have the qualifications, powers, and duties provided in this Code section, and who shall be appointed and compensated and have the expenses of office paid as provided in this Code section. The local law abolishing the office of coroner shall specify the effective date of such abolition, which date shall be the date the office of medical examiner is established for the county to which that local law is applicable.

(b) A local law abolishing the office of coroner pursuant to this Code section shall comply with the provisions of Code Section 1–3–11, requiring approval in referendums to abolish certain offices.

(c) To be eligible for the office of medical examiner, as established pursuant to this Code section, a person shall:

(1) Have a doctor of medicine degree and be licensed to practice medicine under the provisions of Chapter 34 of Title 43;

(2) Be eligible for certification by the American Board of Pathology; and

(3) Have at least one year of medico-legal training or one year of active experience in a scientific field in which legal or judicial procedures are involved at the county, state, or federal level.

(d) The requirements for medical examiners established pursuant to paragraphs (2) and (3) of subsection (c) of this Code section may be waived by the governing authority of any county in which the office of medical examiner is established pursuant to this Code section but may not be waived for any person for a longer period than one year.

(e) The medical examiner for any county in which the office of medical examiner is established pursuant to this Code section shall be appointed by the governing authority of that county, shall serve at the pleasure of that governing authority, shall be compensated in an amount determined by that governing authority, and all expenses of the office of such medical examiner shall, subject to county budgetary limitations, be paid from the general funds of that county.

(f) All of the functions, powers, rights, and duties of and heretofore exercised by the coroner of a county for which is established the office of medical examiner pursuant to this Code section with reference to post-mortem examinations and autopsies shall be performed and exercised by the medical examiner of that county, except that medical examiner shall have no authority to summon and impanel a jury to hold inquests.

(g) A medical examiner whose office is established for a county pursuant to this Code section shall be authorized to perform all of the functions prescribed for a coroner under the provisions of Article 2 of this chapter, the "Georgia Death Investigation Act," except that medical examiner shall have no authority to summon and impanel a jury to hold inquests.

(h) The provisions of Article 2 of this chapter, the "Georgia Death Investigation Act," including but not limited to the penalty provisions, shall apply in all cases regarding a medical examiner whose office is established pursuant to this Code section, except the provisions relating to the holding of inquests shall not apply.

(i) A medical examiner whose office is established for a county pursuant to this Code section shall not be required to meet any county residency requirements established by Code Section 45–2–1.

(j) Nothing in this Code section shall be construed to affect any medical examiner whose office was established or authorized by any amendment to the Constitution continued pursuant to Article XI, Section I, Paragraph IV of the Constitution.

Laws 1988, p. 722, § 2; Laws 1992, p. 6, § 45; Laws 1993, p. 91, § 45.

TITLE 46

PUBLIC UTILITIES AND PUBLIC TRANSPORTATION

CHAPTER 2

PUBLIC SERVICE COMMISSION

Article 5

Article 5

Miscellaneous Offenses and Penalties

§ 46–2–90. Liability for unlawful acts

If any company under the jurisdiction of the commission does, causes to be done, or permits to be done any act which is prohibited, forbidden, or declared to be unlawful, or fails to do any act which is required either by a law of this state or by an order of the commission, such company shall be liable to the persons affected thereby for all loss, damage, or injury caused thereby or resulting therefrom. An action to recover for such loss, damage, or injury may be brought in any court of competent jurisdiction by any such person. In case of recovery, if the jury finds that such act or failure to act was willful, it may fix a reasonable attorney's fee, which shall be taxed and collected as part of the costs of the case.

Laws 1907, p. 72, § 9.

Formerly Civil Code 1910, § 2666; Code 1933, § 93–415.

§ 46–2–91. Civil penalty for violation of laws or regulations

(a) Any person, firm, or corporation (referred to in this Code section as a "utility") subject to the jurisdiction of the commission, which utility willfully violates any law administered by the commission or any duly promulgated regulation issued thereunder or which fails, neglects, or refuses to comply with any order after notice thereof, shall be liable to a penalty not to exceed $ 15,000.00 for such violation and an additional penalty not to exceed $ 10,000.00 for each day during which such violation continues.

(b)(1) The commission, after a hearing conducted after not less than 30 days' notice, shall determine whether any utility has willfully violated any law administered by the commission or any duly promulgated regulation issued thereunder, or has failed, neglected, or refused to comply with any order of the commission. Upon an appropriate finding of a violation, the commission may impose by order such civil penalties as are provided by subsection (a) of this Code section. In each such proceeding, the commission shall maintain a record as provided in paragraph (8) of subsection (a) of Code Section 50–13–13 including all pleadings, a transcript of proceedings, a statement of each matter of which the commission takes official notice, and all staff memoranda or data submitted to the commission in connection with its consideration of the case. All penalties and interest thereon (at the rate of 10 percent per annum) recovered by the commission shall be paid into the general fund of the state treasury.

(2) Any party aggrieved by a decision of the commission may seek judicial review as provided in subsection (c) of this Code section.

(c)(1) Any party who has exhausted all administrative remedies available before the commission and who is aggrieved by a final decision of the commission in a proceeding described in subsection (b) of this Code section may seek judicial review of the final order of the commission in the Superior Court of Fulton County.

(2) Proceedings for review shall be instituted by filing a petition within 30 days after the service of the final decision of the commission or, if a rehearing is requested, within 30 days after the decision thereon. A motion for rehearing or reconsideration after a final decision by the commission shall not be a prerequisite to the filing of a petition for review. Copies of the petition shall be served upon the commission and all parties of record before the commission.

(3) The petition shall state the nature of the petitioner's interest, the facts showing that the petitioner is aggrieved by the decision, and the ground, as specified in paragraph (6) of this subsection, upon which the petitioner contends that the decision should be reversed. The petition may be amended by leave of court.

(4) Within 30 days after service of the petition, or within such further time as is stipulated by the parties or as is allowed by the court, the agency shall transmit to the reviewing court the original or a certified copy of the entire record of the proceedings under review. By stipulation of all parties to the review proceedings, the record may be shortened. A party unreasonably refusing to stipulate that the record be limited may be taxed for the additional costs. The court may require or permit subsequent corrections or additions to the record.

(5) If, before the date set for hearing, application is made to the court for leave to present additional evidence, and it is shown to the satisfaction of the court that the additional evidence is material and there were good reasons for failure to present it in the proceedings before the agency, the court may order that the additional evidence be taken before the commission upon such procedure as is determined by the court. The commission may modify its findings and decision by reason of the additional evidence and shall file that evidence and any modifications, new findings, or decisions with the reviewing court.

(6) The review shall be conducted by the court without a jury and shall be confined to the record. The court shall not substitute its judgment for that of the commission as to the weight of the evidence on questions of fact. The court may affirm the decision of the commission or remand the case for further proceedings. The court may reverse the decision of the commission if substantial rights of the petitioner have been prejudiced because the commission's findings, inferences, conclusions, or decisions are:

(A) In violation of constitutional or statutory provisions;

(B) In excess of the statutory authority of the commission;

(C) Made upon unlawful procedure;

(D) Clearly not supported by any reliable, probative, and substantial evidence on the record as a whole; or

(E) Arbitrary or capricious.

(7) A party aggrieved by an order of the court in a proceeding authorized under subsection (b) of this Code section may appeal to the Supreme Court of Georgia or to the Court of Appeals of Georgia in accordance with Article 2 of Chapter 6 of Title 5, the "Appellate Practice Act."

(d) The commission may file in the superior court in the county in which the person under order resides or in the county in which the violation occurred or, if the person is a corporation, in the county in which the corporation maintains its principal place of business a certified copy of a final order of the commission unappealed or of a final order of the commission affirmed upon appeal, whereupon the court shall render judgment in accordance therewith and notify the parties. The judgment shall have the same effect, and all proceedings in relation thereto shall thereafter be the same, as though the judgment had been rendered in an action duly heard and determined by the court.

Laws 1973, p. 677, § 2; Laws 1992, p. 1640, § 1; Laws 1997, p. 708, § 1; Laws 2004, Act 479, § 1, eff. July 1, 2004; Laws 2006, Act 737, § 1, eff. July 1, 2006.

Formerly Code 1933, § 93–309.2.

Historical and Statutory Notes

The 2006 amendment by Act 737 added subsec. (d).

§ 46–2–92. Penalties; proceedings to recover

(a) Every company under the jurisdiction of the commission, and all officers, agents, and employees of every such company, shall obey, observe, and comply with every order made by the commission under authority of law. Any company under the jurisdiction of the commission, or any officer, agent, or employee thereof, who or which violates any provision of this Code section, or who or which fails, omits, or neglects to obey, observe, and comply with any rule, regulation, order, direction, or requirement of the commission, shall forfeit to the state a sum of not more than $5,000.00 for each offense, the amount to be fixed by the presiding judge. Every violation of this Code section or any other Code section, or of any rule, regulation, order, direction, or requirement of the commission shall be a separate and distinct offense; in case of a continued violation, every day a violation thereof takes place shall be deemed a separate and distinct offense.

(b) An action for the recovery of the penalty provided in subsection (a) of this Code section may be brought in the county of the principal office in this state of such company, or in the county of the state where such violation occurs and such wrong is perpetrated, or in any county in this state through which the company operates. Where the violation consists of an excessive charge for the carriage of freight or passengers or for any other service rendered, as such violation is described in Code Section 46–9–250, an action may be brought in any county in which the charges are made, or through which counties it was intended that such passengers or freight should have been carried, or through which counties such company operates. Any action pursuant to this Code section shall be brought in the name of the state by direction of the Governor.

(c) Any proceeding to enforce the penalty provided in subsection (a) of this Code section may be tried at the first term of the court to which it is brought and shall be given precedence over other business by the presiding judge. The court shall not be adjourned until such proceeding is legally continued or disposed of. The decision in such case may be taken to the Court of Appeals as in other cases.

Laws 1907, p. 72, § 12; Laws 1946, p. 726, § 1.

Formerly Civil Code 1910, § 2667; Code 1933, § 93–416.

§ 46–2–93. Penalties for aiding and abetting in violations of rules; venue; evidence

Every officer, agent, or employee of any company under the jurisdiction of the commission who violates or procures, aids, or abets any violation by any such company of any provision of this title; or who fails to obey, observe, or comply with any order of the commission; or who aids or abets any such company in its failure to obey, observe, and comply with any such order, direction, or provision, shall be guilty of a misdemeanor. Such officer, agent, or employee shall be subject to prosecution in any county in which the company or the officer, agent, or employee violates any provision of this title or any provision of any order of the commission, or in any county through which the company operates. Such officer, agent, or employee shall also be subject to prosecution under this title in any county in which a subordinate agent or employee of the company violates any provision of this title, by the approval or direction, or in consequence of the approval or direction, of such officer, agent, or employee; and the agent or employee who locally in any county violates the rules or directions of said commission pursuant to the direction or authority of a superior officer may be called as a witness and be compelled to testify as to the authority by which he acted. Such testimony shall not be used against such subordinate employee or agent, nor shall he thereafter be subject to prosecution for said offense.

Laws 1907, p. 72, § 13; Laws 1982, p. 3, § 46.

Formerly Civil Code 1910, § 2668; Penal Code 1910, § 527; Code 1933, § 93–9901.

§ 46–2–94. Repealed by Laws 2004, Act 479, § 2, eff. July 1, 2004

Historical and Statutory Notes

The repealed section, relating to operation as a household goods carrier for hire without having a valid certificate of public convenience and necessity; and providing penalties, was derived from Laws 1992, p. 1640, § 2.

§ 46–2–95. Actions to enjoin violations

The commission may bring a civil action to enjoin the violation of any law administered by the commission or any rule, order, or regulation established by the commission. It shall not be necessary to allege or prove that there is no adequate remedy at law to obtain an injunction under this Code section.

Laws 2002, p. 475, § 5.

CHAPTER 5

TELEPHONE AND TELEGRAPH SERVICE

Article 1

Article 1

General Provisions

§ 46–5–1. Power of eminent domain; occupation of land and railroad rights-of-way regulated; powers of county or municipal authorities; construction of telegraph or telephone lines

(a)(1) Any telegraph or telephone company chartered by the laws of this or any other state shall have the right to construct, maintain, and operate its lines and facilities upon, under, along, and over the public roads and highways and rights of way of this state with the approval of the county or municipal authorities in charge of such roads, highways, and rights of way. The approval of such municipal authorities shall be limited to the process set forth in paragraph (3) of subsection (b) of this Code section, and the approval of the county shall be limited to the permitting process set forth in subsection (c) of this Code section. Upon making due compensation, as defined for municipal authorities in paragraph (9) of subsection (b) of this Code section and as provided for counties in subsection (c) of this Code section, a telegraph or telephone company shall have the right to construct, maintain, and operate its lines through or over any lands of this state; on, along, and upon the right of way and structures of any railroads; and, where necessary, under or over any private lands; and, to that end, a telegraph or telephone company may have and exercise the right of eminent domain.

(2) Notwithstanding any other law, a municipal authority or county shall not:

(A) Require any telegraph or telephone company to apply for or enter into an individual license, franchise, or other agreement with such municipal authority or county; or

(B) Impose any occupational license tax or fee as a condition of placing or maintaining lines and facilities in its public roads and highways or rights of way, except as specifically set forth in this Code section.

(3) A county or municipal authority shall not impose any occupational license, tax, fee, regulation, obligation, or requirement upon the provision of the services described in paragraphs (1) and (2) of Code Section 46–5–221, including any occupational license, tax, fee, regulation, obligation, or requirement specifically set forth in any part of this chapter other than Part 4.

(4) Whenever a telegraph or telephone company exercises its powers under paragraph (1) of this subsection, the posts, arms, insulators, and other fixtures of its lines shall be erected, placed, and maintained so as not to obstruct or interfere with the ordinary use of such railroads or public roads and highways, or with the convenience of any landowners, more than may be unavoidable. Any lines constructed by a telegraph or telephone company on the right of way of any railroad company shall be subject to relocation so as to conform to any uses and needs of such railroad company for railroad purposes. Such fixtures, posts, and wires shall be erected at such distances from the tracks of said railroads as will prevent any and all damage to said railroad companies by the falling of said fixtures, posts, or wires upon said railroad tracks; and such telegraph or telephone companies shall be liable to said railroad companies for all damages resulting from a failure to comply with this Code section.

(5) No county or municipal authority shall impose upon a telegraph or telephone company any build-out requirements on network construction or service deployment, and, to the extent that a telegraph or telephone company has elected alternative regulation pursuant to Code Section 46–5–165, such company may satisfy its obligations pursuant to paragraph (2) of Code Section 46–5–169 by providing communications service, at the company's option, through any affiliated companies and through the use of any technology or service arrangement; provided, however, that such company shall remain subject to its obligations as set forth in paragraphs (4) and (5) of Code Section 46–5–169.

(b)(1) Except as set forth in paragraph (6) of this subsection, any telegraph or telephone company that places or seeks to place lines and facilities in the public roads and highways or rights of way of a municipal authority shall provide to such municipal authority the following information:

(A) The name, address, and telephone number of a principal office and local agent of such telegraph or telephone company;

(B) Proof of certification from the Georgia Public Service Commission of such telegraph or telephone company to provide telecommunications services in this state;

(C) Proof of insurance or self-insurance of such telegraph or telephone company adequate to defend and cover claims of third parties and of municipal authorities;

(D) A description of the telegraph or telephone company's service area, which description shall be sufficiently detailed so as to allow a municipal authority to respond to subscriber inquiries. For the purposes of this paragraph, a telegraph or telephone company may, in lieu of or as supplement to a written description, provide a map on 8 ½ by 11 inch paper that is clear and legible and that fairly depicts the service area within the boundaries of the municipal authority. If such service area is less than the boundaries of an entire municipal authority, the map shall describe the boundaries of the geographic area to be served in clear and concise terms;

(E) A description of the services to be provided;

(F) An affirmative declaration that the telegraph or telephone company shall comply with all applicable federal, state, and local laws and regulations, including municipal ordinances and regulations, regarding the placement and maintenance of facilities in the public rights of way that are reasonable, nondiscriminatory, and applicable to all users of the public rights of way, including the requirements of Chapter 9 of Title 25, the "Georgia Utility Facility Protection Act"; and

(G) A statement in bold type at the top of the application as follows: "Pursuant to paragraph (2) of subsection (b) of Code Section 46–5–1 of the Official Code of Georgia Annotated, the municipal authority shall notify the applicant of any deficiencies in this application within 15 business days of receipt of this application."

(2) If an application is incomplete, the municipal authority shall notify the telegraph or telephone company within 15 business days of the receipt of such application; such notice shall specifically identify all application deficiencies. If no such notification is given within 15 business days of the receipt of an application, such application shall be deemed complete.

(3) Within 60 calendar days of the receipt of a completed application, the municipal authority may adopt such application by adoption of a resolution or ordinance or by notification to the telegraph or telephone company. The failure of a municipal authority to adopt an application within 60 calendar days of the receipt of a completed application shall constitute final adoption of such application.

(4) If it modifies its service area or provisioned services identified in the original application, the telegraph or telephone company shall notify the municipal authority of changes to the service area or the services provided. Such notice shall be given at least 20 days prior to the effective date of such change. Such notification shall contain a geographic description of the new service area or areas and new services to be provided within the jurisdiction of the affected municipal authority, if any. The municipal authority shall provide to all telegraph and telephone companies located in its rights of way written notice of annexations and changes in municipal corporate boundaries which, for the purposes of this Code section, shall become effective 30 days following receipt.

(5) An application adopted pursuant to this Code section may be terminated by a telegraph or telephone company by submitting a notice of termination to the affected municipal authority. For purposes of this Code section, such notice shall identify the telegraph or telephone company, the affected service area, and the effective date of such termination, which shall not be less than 60 calendar days from the date of filing the notice of termination.

(6) Any telegraph or telephone company that has previously obtained permits for the placement of its facilities, has specified the name of such telegraph or telephone company in such permit application, has previously placed its facilities in any public right of way, and has paid and continues to pay any applicable municipal authority's occupational license taxes, permit fees, franchise fees, except as set forth in paragraph (8) of this subsection, or, if applicable, county permit fees shall be deemed to have complied with this Code section without any further action on the part of such telegraph or telephone company except as set forth in paragraphs (8), (9), (11), and (17) of this subsection.

(7) Any telegraph or telephone company that has placed lines and facilities in the public roads and highways or rights of way of a municipal authority without first obtaining permits or otherwise notifying the appropriate municipal authority of its presence in the public roads and highways or rights of way shall provide the information required by paragraph (1) of this subsection, if applicable, to such municipal authority on or before October 1, 2008. As of October 1, 2008, if any telegraph or telephone company, other than those who meet the requirements of paragraph (6) of this subsection, has failed or fails to provide the information required by paragraph (1) of this subsection to the municipal authority in which its lines or facilities are located, such municipal authority shall provide written notice to such telegraph or telephone company giving that company 15 calendar days from the date of receipt of such notice to comply with subsection (b) of this Code section. In the event the 15 calendar day cure period expires without compliance, such municipal authority may petition the Georgia Public Service Commission which shall, after an opportunity for a hearing, order the appropriate relief.

(8)(A) In the event any telegraph or telephone company has an existing, valid municipal franchise agreement as of January 1, 2008, the terms and conditions of such existing franchise agreement shall only remain effective and enforceable until the expiration of the existing agreement or December 31, 2012, whichever shall first occur.

(B) In the event any telegraph or telephone company is paying an existing occupational license tax or fee, based on actual recurring local services revenues, as of January 1, 2008, such payment shall be considered the payment of due compensation without further action on the part of the municipal authority. In the event that the rate of such existing tax or fee exceeds 3 percent of actual recurring local service revenues, that rate shall remain effective until December 31, 2012; thereafter, the payment by such telegraph or telephone company at the rate of 3 percent shall be considered the payment of due compensation without further action on the part of the municipal authority.

(9) As used in this Code section, "due compensation" for a municipal authority means an amount equal to no more than 3 percent of actual recurring local service revenues received by such company from its retail, end user customers located within the boundaries of such municipal authority. "Actual recurring local service revenues" means those revenues customarily included in the Uniform System of Accounts as prescribed by the Federal Communications Commission for Class "A" and "B" companies; provided, however, that only the local service portion of the following accounts shall be included:

(A) Basic local service revenue, as defined in 47 C.F.R. 32.5000;

(B) Basic area revenue, as defined in 47 C.F.R. 32.5001;

(C) Optional extended area revenue, as defined in 47 C.F.R. 32.5002;

(D) Public telephone revenue, as defined in 47 C.F.R. 32.5010;

(E) Local private line revenue, as defined in 47 C.F.R. 35.5040; provided, however, that the portion of such accounts attributable to audio and video program transmission service where both terminals of the private line are within the corporate limits of the municipal authority shall not be included;

(F) Other local exchange revenue, as defined in 47 C.F.R. 32.5060;

(G) Local exchange service, as defined in 47 C.F.R. 32.5069;

(H) Network access revenue, as defined in 47 C.F.R. 32.5080;

(I) Directory revenue, as defined in 47 C.F.R. 32.5320; provided, however, that the portion of such accounts attributable to revenue derived from listings in portion of directories not considered white pages shall not be included;

(J) Nonregulated operating revenue, as defined in 47 C.F.R. 32.5280; provided, however, that the portion of such accounts attributable to revenues derived from private lines shall not be included; and

(K) Uncollectible revenue, as defined in 47 C.F.R. 32.5300.

Any charge imposed by a municipal authority shall be assessed in a nondiscriminatory and competitively neutral manner.

(10) Any due compensation paid to municipal authorities pursuant to paragraph (9) of this subsection shall be in lieu of any other permit fee, encroachment fee, degradation fee, disruption fee, business license tax, occupational license tax, occupational license fee, or other fee otherwise permitted pursuant

to the provisions of subparagraph (A) of paragraph (7) of Code Section 36–34–2 or Code Section 32–4–92 et seq. or any other provision of law regardless of nomenclature.

(11) A telegraph or telephone company with facilities in the public rights of way of a municipal authority shall begin assessing due compensation, as defined in subsection (a) of this Code section, on subscribers on the date that service commences unless such company is currently paying a municipal authority's occupational license tax. Such due compensation shall be paid directly to each affected municipal authority within 30 calendar days after the last day of each calendar quarter. In the event that due compensation is not paid on or before 30 calendar days after the last day of each calendar quarter, the affected municipal authority shall provide written notice to such telegraph or telephone company, giving such company 15 calendar days from the date such company receives such notice to cure any such nonpayment. In the event the due compensation remitted to the affected municipal authority is not postmarked on or before the expiration of the 15 day cure period, such company shall pay interest thereon at a rate of 1 percent per month to the affected municipal authority. If the 15 day cure period expires on a Saturday, a Sunday, or a state legal holiday, the due date shall be the next business day. A telegraph or telephone company shall not be assessed any interest on late payments if due compensation was submitted in error to a neighboring municipal authority.

(12) Each municipal authority may, no more than once annually, audit the business records of a telegraph or telephone company to the extent necessary to ensure payment in accordance with this Code section. As used in this Code section, "audit" means a comprehensive review of the records of a company which is reasonably related to the calculation and payment of due compensation. Once any audited period of a company has been the subject of a requested audit, such audited period of such company shall not again be the subject of any audit. In the event of a dispute concerning the amount of due compensation due to an affected municipal authority under this Code section, an action may be brought in a court of competent jurisdiction by an affected municipal authority seeking to recover an additional amount alleged to be due or by a company seeking a refund of an alleged overpayment; provided, however, that any such action shall be brought within three years following the end of the quarter to which the disputed amount relates, although such time period may be extended by written agreement between the company and such affected municipal authority. Each party shall bear the party's own costs incurred in connection with any dispute. The auditing municipal authority shall bear the cost of the audit; provided, however, that if an affected municipal authority files an action to recover alleged underpayments of due compensation and a court of competent jurisdiction determines the company has underpaid due compensation due for any 12 month period by 10 percent or more, such company shall be required to pay such municipal authority's reasonable costs associated with such audit along with any due compensation underpayments; provided, further, that late payments shall not apply. All undisputed amounts due to a municipal authority resulting from an audit shall be paid to the municipal authority within 45 days, or interest shall accrue.

(13) The information provided pursuant to paragraph (1) of this subsection and any records or information furnished or disclosed by a telegraph or telephone company to an affected municipal authority pursuant to paragraph (12) of this subsection shall be exempt from public inspection under Code Section 50–18–70. It shall be the duty of such telegraph or telephone company to mark all such documents as exempt from Code Section 50–18–70, et seq., and the telegraph or telephone company shall defend, indemnify, and hold harmless any municipal authority and any municipal officer or employee in any request for, or in any action seeking, access to such records.

(14) No acceptance of any payment shall be construed as a release or as an accord and satisfaction of any claim an affected municipal authority may have for further or additional sums payable as due compensation.

(15) Any amounts overpaid by a company as due compensation shall be deducted from future due compensation owed.

(16) A telegraph or telephone company paying due compensation pursuant to this Code section may designate that portion of a subscriber's bill attributable to such charge as a separate line item of the bill and recover such amount from the subscriber.

(17) Nothing in this Code section shall affect the authority of a municipal authority to require telegraph or telephone companies accessing the public roads and highways and rights of way of a municipal authority to obtain permits and otherwise comply with the reasonable regulations established pursuant to paragraph (10) of subsection (a) of Code Section 32–4–92.

(18) If a telegraph or telephone company does not have retail, end user customers located within the boundaries of a municipal authority, then the payment by such company at the same rates that such payments were being made as of January 1, 2008, to a municipal authority for the use of its rights of way shall be considered the payment of due compensation; provided, however, that at the expiration date of any existing agreement for use of such municipal rights of way or December 31, 2012, whichever is earlier, the payment at rates in accordance with the rates set by regulations promulgated by the Department of Transportation shall be considered the payment of due compensation. Provided, further, that if a telegraph or telephone company begins providing service after January 1, 2008, and such telegraph or telephone company does not have retail, end user customers located within the boundaries of a municipal authority, the payment by such company at rates in accordance with the rates set by regulations promulgated by the Department of Transportation to a municipal authority for the use of its rights of way shall be considered the payment of due compensation.

(19) Nothing in this Code section shall be construed to affect any franchise fee payments which were in dispute on or before January 1, 2008.

(c) If a telegraph or telephone company accesses the public roads and highways and rights of way of a county and such county requires such telegraph or telephone company to pay due compensation, such due compensation shall be limited to an administrative cost recoupment fee which shall not exceed such county's direct, actual costs incurred in its permitting process, including issuing and processing permits, plan reviews, physical inspection and direct administrative costs; and such costs shall be demonstrable and shall be equitable among applicable users of such county's roads and highways or rights of way. Permit fees shall not include the costs of highway or rights of way acquisition or any general administrative, management, or maintenance costs of the roads and highways or rights of way and shall not be imposed for any activity that does not require the physical disturbance of such public roads and highways or rights of way or does not impair access to or full use of such public roads and highways or rights of way. Nothing in this Code section shall affect the authority of a county to require a telegraph or telephone company to comply with reasonable regulations for construction of telephone lines and facilities in public highways or rights of way pursuant to the provisions of paragraph (6) of Code Section 32–4–42.

Laws 1873, p. 69, § 2; Laws 1889, p. 141, §§ 1, 2; Laws 1905, p. 79, § 1; Laws 2008, Act 533, § 1, eff. July 1, 2008.

Formerly Code 1873, § 3023; Code 1882, § 3023; Civil Code 1895, §§ 2346, 2347; Civil Code 1910, §§ 2810, 2811; Code 1933, §§ 104–204, 104–205.

Historical and Statutory Notes

In 2008, the Code Commission, in subpar. (a)(2)(B), substituted "Code section" for "Code Section"; and in par. (b)(11), substituted "subsection

(a) of this Code section" for "paragraph (a) of this subsection" in the first sentence. See § 28–9–5.

§ 46–5–2. Avoiding or attempting to avoid payment for telecommunication services

(a) It shall be unlawful for any person to avoid or attempt to avoid or to cause another to avoid the lawful charges, in whole or in part, for any telecommunication service as defined in subsection (a) of Code Section 46–5–3 or for the transmission of a message, signal, or other communication by telephone or telegraph or over telecommunication or telegraph facilities by the use of any fraudulent scheme, means, or method, or by the use of any unlawful telecommunication device as defined in subsection (a) of Code Section 46–5–3 or other mechanical, electric, or electronic device; provided, however, that this Code section and Code Sections 46–5–3 and 46–5–4 shall not apply to amateur radio repeater operation involving a dial interconnect.

(b)(1) Except as otherwise provided in paragraph (2) of this subsection, any person who violates this Code section shall be guilty of a misdemeanor; provided, however, that upon conviction of a second or subsequent such offense under this Code section, the defendant commits a felony and shall be punished by a fine of not more than $ 5,000.00 or imprisoned for not less than one nor more than five years, or both.

(2) Any person who violates this Code section by avoiding or causing another to avoid lawful charges for any telecommunication service which lawful charges are in an amount in excess of $ 10,000.00 commits a felony and shall be punished by a fine of not more than $ 5,000.00 or imprisoned for not less than one nor more than five years, or both.

(3) The court may, in addition to any other sentence authorized by law, order a person convicted under this Code section to make restitution for the offense.

(4) Any person, corporation, or other entity aggrieved by a violation of this Code section may, in a civil action in any court of competent jurisdiction, obtain appropriate relief, including preliminary and other equitable or declaratory relief, compensatory and punitive damages, reasonable investigation expenses, cost of suit, and reasonable attorney's fees.

(5) Compensatory damages awarded by a court in a civil action under this Code section shall be computed as one of the following:

(A) At any time prior to the entering of a final judgment, the complaining party may elect to recover the actual damages suffered by the complaining party as a result of the violation of this Code section;

(B) In any case where a violator commits more than one violation of this Code section, the complaining party, at any time before final judgment is entered, may elect to recover, in lieu of actual damages, an award of statutory damages for all violations involved in the action in a sum not less than $ 250.00 nor more than $ 10,000.00 per violation. The amount of statutory damages shall be determined by the court as the court considers just;

(C) In any case where the court finds that any of the violations of this Code section were committed willfully and for the purposes of commercial advantage or financial gain, the court in its discretion may increase the award of damages, whether actual or statutory, by an amount of not more than $ 50,000.00; or

(D) Nothing in this paragraph shall prohibit the recovery of other types of damages otherwise authorized under paragraph (4) of this subsection.

Laws 1975, p. 1534, §§ 1, 3; Laws 1976, p. 1179, §§ 1, 3; Laws 1977, p. 1170, § 1; Laws 1984, p. 22, § 46; Laws 1996, p. 1085, § 1; Laws 2001, p. 848, § 1.

Historical and Statutory Notes

In 2001, the Code Commission, in subpar. (b)(5)(D), substituted "this paragraph" for "paragraph (5) of this subsection". See § 28–9–5.

§ 46–5–3. Making, possessing, or transferring of unlawful telecommunication device, or plans for making same; concealment of existence, origin or destination of any telecommunication

(a) As used in this Code section, the term:

(1) "Telecommunication service" means any service provided for a charge or compensation to facilitate the origination, transmission, emission, or reception of signs, signals, data, writings, images, sounds, or intelligence of any nature by telephone or telephone service, including public pay telephones, or cable television service (CATV), including cellular or other wireless telephones, wire, radio, electromagnetic, photoelectronic, or photo-optical system.

(2) "Telecommunication service provider" means a person, corporation, or other entity which provides telecommunication service, including public pay telephones and including a cellular, paging, or other wireless communications company or other person, corporation, or entity which, for a fee, supplies the facility, cell site, mobile telephone switching office, or other equipment or telecommunication service.

(3) "Unlawful telecommunication device" means any telecommunications device that is capable, or has been illegally altered, modified, or programmed or reprogrammed alone or in conjunction with another access device or other equipment so as to be capable, of acquiring or facilitating the acquisition of any electronic serial number, mobile identification number, personal identification number, or any telecommunication service without the consent of the telecommunication service provider or without the consent of the legally authorized user of the telecommunication device. The term includes telecommunications devices altered to obtain service without the consent of the telecommunication service provider, tumbler phones, counterfeit or clone microchips, scanning receivers of wireless telecommunication service of a telecommunication service provider, and other instruments capable of disguising their identity or location or of gaining access to a communications system operated by a telecommunication service provider. Such term shall not apply to any device operated by a law enforcement agency or telecommunication service provider in the normal course of its activities.

(b) It shall be unlawful for any person knowingly to:

(1) Make or possess any unlawful telecommunication device designed, adapted, or used:

(A) For commission of a theft of telecommunication service in violation of Code Section 46–5–2 or to acquire or facilitate the acquisition of telecommunications service without the consent of the telecommunication service provider; or

(B) To conceal, or to assist another to conceal, from any supplier of telecommunication service or from any lawful authority the existence or place of origin or of destination of any telecommunication;

(2) Sell, give, transport, or otherwise transfer to another, or offer or advertise for sale, any unlawful telecommunication device, or plans or instructions for making or assembling the same, under circumstances evincing an intent to use or employ such unlawful telecommunication device; or to allow such unlawful telecommunication device to be used or employed for a purpose described in paragraph (1) of this subsection or knowing or having reason to believe that the same is intended to be so used or that the aforesaid plans or instructions are intended to be used for making or assembling such unlawful telecommunication device; or

(3) Publish plans or instructions for making or assembling or using any unlawful telecommunication device.

(c)(1) Any person who violates this Code section shall be guilty of a felony and, upon conviction thereof, shall be punished by a fine of not more than $ 1,000.00 or by imprisonment in the penitentiary for not less than one nor more than five years, or both; provided, however, that upon conviction of a second or subsequent such offense under this Code section, the defendant shall be punished by a fine of not more than $ 5,000.00 or imprisoned for not less than three nor more than ten years, or both.

(2) The court may, in addition to any other sentence authorized by law, order a person convicted under this Code section to make restitution for the offense.

(3) Any person, corporation, or other entity aggrieved by a violation of this Code section may, in a civil action in any court of competent jurisdiction, obtain appropriate relief, including preliminary and other equitable or declaratory relief, compensatory and punitive damages, reasonable investigation expenses, cost of suit, and reasonable attorney's fees.

(4) Compensatory damages awarded by a court in a civil action under this Code section shall be computed as one of the following:

(A) At any time prior to the entering of a final judgment, the complaining party may elect to recover the actual damages suffered by the complaining party as a result of the violation of this Code section;

(B) In any case where a violator commits more than one violation of this Code section, the complaining party, at any time before final judgment is entered, may elect to recover, in lieu of actual damages, an award of statutory damages of not less than $ 250.00 nor more than $ 10,000.00 for each unlawful telecommunications device involved in the action. The amount of statutory damages shall be determined by the court as the court considers just;

(C) In any case where the court finds that any of the violations of this Code section were committed willfully and for the purposes of commercial advantage or financial gain, the court in its discretion may increase the award of statutory damages by an amount of not more than $ 50,000.00 for each unlawful telecommunication device involved in the action; or

(D) Nothing in this paragraph shall prohibit the recovery of other types of damages otherwise authorized under paragraph (3) of this subsection.

Laws 1975, p. 1534, §§ 2, 3; Laws 1976, p. 1179, §§ 2, 3; Laws 1982, p. 3, § 46; Laws 1996, p. 1085, § 2; Laws 2001, p. 848, § 2.

Historical and Statutory Notes

In 2001, the Code Commission, in subsec. (a), inserted a comma following "Code section"; in subpar. (c)(4)(D), substituted "this paragraph" for "paragraph (4) of this subsection". See § 28–9–5.

§ 46–5–4. Seizure and disposal of devices or plans therefor used for theft of telecommunication services

Any unlawful telecommunication device as defined in subsection (a) of Code Section 46–5–3 or other instrument, apparatus, equipment, or device, or any plan or instruction therefor, referred to in Code Section 46–5–3 may be seized by court order, or under a search warrant issued by a judge or a magistrate, or incident to a lawful arrest. Upon the conviction of any person for a violation of any provisions of Code Section 46–5–2 or 46–5–3, such instrument, apparatus, equipment, device, plan, or instruction shall be either destroyed as contraband by the sheriff of the county in which such person was convicted or turned over to the telephone company or telecommunication service provider in whose territory such instrument, apparatus, equipment, device, plan, or instruction was seized.

Laws 1976, p. 1179, § 2; Laws 1996, p. 1085, § 3.

§ 46–5–5. Inclusion of local exchanges 495 and 567 in current 404 area code or newly designated area code

Local exchanges 495 and 567 shall be included in the current 404 area code on or before July 1, 1996, and removed from the 706 area code; provided, however, that if a geographic area of the 404 area code is designated as a different area code and such geographic area is contiguous to a part of the geographic area where local exchange 495 or 567 is operational, then nothing in this Code section shall prohibit local exchange 495 or 567 from being included in the newly designated area code.

Laws 1995, p. 886, § 1.

§ 46–5–6. Rules and regulations relating to public pay telephones

The Public Service Commission shall have the exclusive power and authority to prescribe rules and regulations for the operation, maintenance, location, and deployment of public pay telephones within this state.

Laws 2001, p. 848, § 3.

§ 46–5–7. Telephone directory information; confidentiality of address and location of family violence shelters

(a) Prior to January 1, 2005, each person, corporation, or other entity that provides telephone service in this state and each person, corporation, or other entity that publishes, disseminates, or otherwise provides telephone directory information or listings of telephone subscribers in this state shall file a plan with the commission setting forth in detail how such person, corporation, or other entity will protect the confidentiality of the address or location of family violence shelters, as defined in Code Section 19–13–20, in this state. Such plan shall describe the manner in which the person, corporation, or other entity will identify all such shelters and the manner in which the person, corporation, or other entity will keep the location and address of such shelters confidential.

(b) Such persons, corporations, and other entities shall update such plans at least every 24 months.

(c) Such original and updated plans shall be approved by the commission within a reasonable time upon a determination that the plans are reasonably effective in identifying the family violence shelters in the state and in maintaining the confidentiality of the location and address of such family violence shelters. If the commission determines that a plan is inadequate, it shall state the basis on which the plan was determined to be inadequate and shall allow the person, corporation, or other entity filing such plan a period of not more than 30 days to file a revised plan that is acceptable to the commission.

(d) Such plans shall not be open to examination by the public and shall be exempt from disclosure under the provisions of Article 4 of Chapter 18 of Title 50.

(e) Within three days of filing original plans or updates with the commission, each person, corporation, or other entity subject to this Code section shall submit a copy of all original plans, updated plans, and revised plans to the State Commission on Family Violence, which is authorized to provide comments concerning such plans to the commission in order to aid in review and approval of such plans.

(f) The filing or approval of such plans shall not in any manner be a defense to any action or prosecution.

Laws 2004, Act 589, § 2, eff. May 14, 2004.

Historical and Statutory Notes

Laws 2004, Act 589, § 1, provides:

"This Act shall be known as and may be cited as the 'Family Violence Shelter Confidentiality Act of 2004.' "

§ 46–5–8. Termination of wireless communications service contracts; active duty service members

(a) As used in this Code section, the term "service member" means an active duty member of the regular or reserve component of the United States armed forces, the United States Coast Guard, the Georgia National Guard, or the Georgia Air National Guard on ordered federal duty for a period of 90 days or longer.

(b) Any service member may terminate his or her wireless telecommunications service contract by providing the wireless telecommunications provider with a written notice of termination, effective on the date specified in the notice, which date shall be at least 30 days after receipt of the notice by the wireless telecommunications provider, if any of the following criteria are met:

(1) The service member is required, pursuant to a permanent change of station orders, to move outside the area served by the wireless telecommunications provider or to an area where the type of wireless telecommunications service being provided to the service member is not available from the wireless telecommunications provider;

(2) The service member is discharged or released from active duty or state active duty and will return from such duty to an area not served by the wireless telecommunications provider or where the type of telecommunications service contracted for is not available from the wireless telecommunications provider;

(3) The service member is released from active duty after having entered into a contract for wireless telecommunications service while on active duty status and the wireless telecommunications provider does not provide telecommunications service or the same type of wireless telecommunications service contracted for in the region of the service member's home of record prior to entering active duty;

(4) The service member receives military orders requiring him or her to move outside the continental United States; or

(5) The service member receives temporary duty orders, temporary change of station orders, or active duty or state active duty orders to an area not served by the wireless telecommunications provider or where the type of wireless telecommunications service contracted for is not available from the wireless telecommunications provider, provided such orders are for a period exceeding 60 days.

(c) The written notice to the wireless telecommunications provider must be accompanied by either a copy of the official military orders or a written verification signed by the service member's commanding officer.

(d) Upon termination of a contract under this Code section, the service member is liable for the amount due under the contract prorated to the effective date of the termination payable at such time as would have otherwise been required by the terms of the contract. The service member is not liable for any other fees due to the early termination of the contract as provided for in this Code section.

(e) The provisions of this Code section shall apply to any contract for wireless telecommunications service entered into on or after July 1, 2005, and to any renewals, modifications, or extensions of any such contract in effect on such date and may not be waived or modified by the agreement of the parties under any circumstances.

Laws 2005, Act 48, § 8, eff. July 1, 2005.

Article 2

Telephone Service

Part 1

General Provisions

§ 46–5–20. Removal of telephone used for illegal purposes; procedure; exemption of telephone company from liability

(a) When any municipal, county, state, or federal law enforcement officer acting within his apparent jurisdiction has reason to believe that certain telephone facilities or any part thereof are being used or have been used in violation of any federal law, the laws of the State of Georgia, or the ordinances of any municipality therein, that officer may make oath or affidavit stating his belief to the district attorney of the judicial circuit in which the telephone facilities are located. Thereupon, the district attorney shall petition the judge of the superior court of that circuit to issue a rule nisi which shall be promptly served upon the person in whose name the telephone facilities are listed, requiring the party, within a reasonable time to be fixed by the judge, which shall not be less than 48 hours from time of service of the petition on said party, to show cause before the judge why the telephone facilities should not be promptly removed. At the hearing on the rule nisi the burden of proof shall be upon the petitioner.

(b) Upon a finding by the court that the telephone facilities are being or have been used in violation of the laws described in subsection (a) of this Code section, the court shall issue an order requiring the telephone company which is rendering service over the facilities to disconnect and remove such facilities. Upon receipt of such order, which shall be served upon an officer of the telephone company by the sheriff of the county in which the telephone facilities are installed or by his duly authorized deputies, the telephone company shall proceed within a reasonable time to disconnect and remove such facilities and discontinue all telephone service rendered over the facilities until further order of the court.

(c) The law enforcement officer who applies to the district attorney for the removal of such facilities shall, in his official capacity, be a necessary party to any proceeding or action arising out of or under this Code section.

(d) No telephone company shall be liable for any damages, penalty, or forfeiture, whether civil or criminal, for any act performed in compliance with any order issued by the judge of the superior court under this Code section.

Laws 1962, p. 149, §§ 1–3; Laws 1982, p. 3, § 46.

§ 46–5–21. Penalty for making obscene or harassing telephone calls

(a) It shall be a misdemeanor for any person, by means of telephone communication in this state, to:

(1) Make any comment, request, suggestion, or proposal which is obscene, lewd, lascivious, filthy, or indecent;

(2) Make a telephone call, whether or not conversation ensues, without disclosing his identity and with intent to annoy, abuse, threaten, or harass any person at the called number;

(3) Make or cause the telephone of another repeatedly or continuously to ring, with intent to harass any person at the called number; or

(4) Make repeated telephone calls, during which conversation ensues, solely to harass any person at the called number.

(b) Any person who knowingly permits any telephone under his control to be used for any purpose prohibited by this Code section shall be guilty of a misdemeanor.

Laws 1968, p. 9, § 1.

Validity

This section was held unconstitutional in the case of McKenzie v. State, 2005, 279 Ga. 265, 626 S.E.2d 77.

§ 46–5–22. Obscene, lewd, lascivious, etc. comments prohibited

(a) It shall be unlawful for any person, by means of a telephone communication for commercial purposes, to make directly or by means of an electronic recording device, any comment, request, suggestion, or proposal which is obscene, lewd, lascivious, filthy, or indecent. Any person who makes any such comment, request, suggestion, or proposal may be subject to prosecution under this Code section regardless of whether such person placed or initiated the telephone call.

(b) It shall be unlawful for any person to permit knowingly any telephone or telephone facility connected to a local exchange telephone under such person's control to be used for any purpose prohibited by this Code section.

(c) Any person who violates any provision of this Code section shall be guilty of a misdemeanor. For purposes of this subsection, each day of a violation shall constitute a separate offense.

(d) A court may grant a preliminary injunction under this Code section after due notice to the party to be enjoined and upon a sufficient showing of the likelihood of ultimate success in a prosecution under this Code section and showing that such injunction would be in the public interest. Such injunction shall be dissolved by the court if a full trial on the merits is not scheduled within such period as may be specified by the court not to exceed 30 days.

(e) In the event that a person applies to a local exchange telephone company for use of the local exchange telephone company's facilities for the purpose of transmitting a recorded commercial message, the local exchange telephone company shall have the authority to review the message and deny the applicant's request for facilities if the message appears to violate the provisions of this Code section.

Laws 1985, p. 1310, § 1.

§ 46–5–23. Regulation of use of automatic telephone dialing and announcing equipment

(a)(1) As used in this Code section, the term "ADAD equipment" means any device or system of devices which is used, whether alone or in conjunction with other equipment, for the purpose of automatically selecting or dialing telephone numbers and disseminating prerecorded messages to the numbers so selected or dialed.

(2) It shall be unlawful for any person to use, to employ or direct another person to use, or to contract for the use of ADAD equipment for the purpose of advertising or offering for sale, lease, rental, or as a gift any goods, services, or property, either real or personal, primarily for personal, family, or household use or for the purpose of conducting polls or soliciting information where:

(A) Consent is not received prior to the initiation of the calls as specified in paragraph (3) of this subsection;

(B) Such use is other than between the hours of 8:00 A.M. and 9:00 P.M.;

(C) The ADAD equipment will operate unattended or is not so designed and equipped with an automatic clock and calendar device that it will not operate unattended, even in the event of power failures;

(D) Such use involves either the random or sequential dialing of telephone numbers;

(E) The telephone number required to be stated in subparagraph (G) of this paragraph is not one which during normal business hours is promptly answered in person by a person who is an agent of the person on whose behalf the automatic calls are made and who is willing and able to provide information concerning the automatic calls;

(F) The automatic dialing and recorded message player does not automatically and immediately terminate its connection with any telephone call within ten seconds after the person called fails to give consent for the playing of a recorded message or hangs up his or her telephone;

(G) The recorded message fails to state clearly the name and telephone number of the person or organization initiating the call within the first 25 seconds of the call and at the conclusion of the call; or

(H) Such use involves calls to telephone numbers which at the request of the customer have been omitted from the telephone directory published by the local exchange company serving the customer or involves calls to hospitals, nursing homes, fire protection agencies, or law enforcement agencies;

(3)(A) A person may give consent to a call made with ADAD equipment when a line operator introduces the call and states an intent to play a recorded message. Any such consent shall apply only to one particular call and shall not constitute prior consent to receive further calls through the use of such ADAD equipment.

(B) Any person wishing to receive telephone calls through the use of ADAD equipment shall give his or her written consent to the person using, employing or directing another person to use, or contracting for the use of such ADAD equipment. Any forms used for such written consent by any person using, employing or directing another person to use, or contracting for the use of such ADAD equipment shall clearly and conspicuously state its purpose and effect and clearly and conspicuously give notice of how the consent may be withdrawn. A record of such written consent shall be maintained by the person to whom consent is given and shall be made available to the commission or its authorized representative, without further action, during normal business hours and following reasonable notice. Such consent shall, unless withdrawn, be valid for a period of two years from the date on which it is executed; and such record of written consent shall be maintained by the person to whom consent is given for at least the same period of time. Any consent to receive telephone calls through the use of ADAD equipment shall be void and withdrawn on the fifteenth day following the receipt of a letter withdrawing such consent. It shall be unlawful for any person to whom written consent is given to fail to maintain the record of such written consent for the time period required by this paragraph or to prevent or hinder the commission or its authorized representative from inspecting any such record of written consent.

(b) It shall not be unlawful for any person to use, to employ or direct another person to use, or to contract for the use of ADAD equipment in any manner covered by the provisions of subparagraphs (a)(2)(B) through (a)(2)(G) of this Code section when:

(1) Calls are made with ADAD equipment by a nonprofit organization, or by an individual using such calls other than for commercial profit-making purposes, and the calls do not involve the advertisement or offering for sale, lease, or rental of goods, services, or property;

(2) Calls made with ADAD equipment relate to payment for, service of, or warranty coverage of previously ordered or purchased goods or services; or

(3) Calls made with ADAD equipment relate to collection of lawful debts.

(c) It shall be unlawful for any person to connect any ADAD equipment to any telephone line in this state for the purpose of making telephone calls to persons in this state through the use of ADAD equipment unless a permit has been issued for such ADAD equipment by the commission. Any person desiring to use ADAD equipment in this state shall make application for a permit to the commission on forms prescribed by the commission and shall pay a fee as prescribed by the commission for such permit. Permits shall be renewed biennially as prescribed by the commission and upon payment of a renewal fee. The fees charged shall cover the administrative cost for the issuance of such permits. Permits shall be subject to suspension or revocation for any violation of this Code section.

(d) The provisions of this Code section shall supersede any prior rule, regulation, or order of the commission governing the use of ADAD equipment but shall not prohibit or supersede any future rule, regulation, or order of the commission governing the use of ADAD equipment except to the extent that any such rule, regulation, or order directly conflicts with this subsection. Except for criminal sanctions, the commission is charged with the responsibility of enforcing this Code section; and the commission shall require local exchange companies to file with the commission appropriate tariff revisions to implement this subsection. Any person who operates or utilizes ADAD equipment in violation of the provisions of this Code section shall be subject to disconnection of telephone service if the violation does not cease within ten days from the date of notification to such person by the local exchange company; and the tariff revisions filed by local exchange companies shall provide for the giving of such notification by local exchange companies and for such disconnection of service.

(e) Any person who violates any provision of this Code section shall be guilty of a misdemeanor.

Laws 1987, p. 1159, § 1; Laws 1990, p. 8, § 46.

§ 46–5–24. Unlawful to use automated dialing equipment or United States mail to solicit calls to 976 number

(a) As used in this Code section, the term:

(1) "ADAD equipment" means any device or system of devices which is used, whether alone or in conjunction with other equipment, for the purpose of automatically selecting or dialing telephone numbers and disseminating prerecorded messages to the numbers so selected or dialed.

(2) "976 number" means any seven-digit telephone number the first three digits of which are 976 or any other combination of numbers and for which a per-call fee is charged for calling such telephone number.

(b)(1) It shall be unlawful for any person making use of a 976 number for the receipt of incoming calls to use, to employ or direct another person to use, or to contract for the use of ADAD equipment for the purpose of soliciting any person to call such 976 number.

(2) It shall be unlawful for any person making use of a 976 number for the receipt of incoming calls to use, to employ or direct another person to use, or to contract for the use of the United States mail for the purpose of soliciting any person to call such 976 number.

(c) No telephone exchange company shall provide access to a 976 number or numbers to any person who solicits calls to such number or numbers through the use of ADAD equipment or through the use of the United States mail. The telephone exchange companies shall, upon the order of the commission, withdraw access to a 976 number or numbers from any person if calls to such number or numbers are solicited by ADAD equipment or are solicited through the use of the United States mail.

(d) The provisions of this Code section shall supersede any rule, regulation, or order governing the use of 976 numbers if such is in conflict with this Code section. Except for criminal sanctions, the commission is charged with the responsibility of enforcing this Code section. Any person who violates any provision of this Code section shall be subject to disconnection of 976 number telephone service if the commission determines that any violation has occurred and upon the commission's, thereafter, issuing an order directing such disconnection.

(e) Any person who violates any provision of subsection (b) of this Code section shall be guilty of a misdemeanor.

Laws 1988, p. 1246, § 1.

§ 46–5–25. Telephonic transmission of unsolicited commercial facsimile messages prohibited

(a) As used in this Code section, the term "telefacsimile" shall refer to any process by which electronic signals are transmitted by any telephone system for conversion into written text.

(b) It shall be unlawful for any person to initiate the transmission of, employ or direct another person to initiate the transmission of, or contract for the initiation of the transmission of an unsolicited facsimile message for the commercial purpose of advertising or offering the sale, lease, rental, or gift of any goods, services, or real or personal property.

(c)(1) Subsection (b) of this Code section shall not apply where the recipient has consented to the receipt of one or more telefacsimile messages or where there exists a prior contractual or business relationship between the recipient and the initiator or the initiator's principal.

(2) The exception provided for in paragraph (1) of this subsection shall not apply where the recipient has notified the initiator or the initiator's principal that the recipient does not wish to receive further telefacsimile messages from the initiator or the initiator's principal.

(d) Any person who violates this Code section shall be guilty of a misdemeanor and upon conviction shall be punished by a fine not to exceed $1,000.00. Each transmission of a facsimile message in violation of this Code section shall constitute a separate offense.

(e) The commission is charged with the responsibility of civil enforcement of this Code section and the commission shall require local exchange companies to file with the commission appropriate tariff revisions to implement this subsection. Any person who violates the provisions of this Code section shall be subject to disconnection of telephone service if the violation does not cease within ten days from the date of notification to such person by the local exchange company; and the tariff revisions filed by local exchange companies shall provide for the giving of such notification by local exchange companies and for such disconnection of service.

Laws 1990, p. 252, § 1.

§ 46–5–26. Telephone utilities or companies to provide access to live telephone operator

(a) Each telecommunications utility and telecommunications company that provides operator service shall ensure that a caller may obtain access to a live operator through a method designed to be easily and clearly understandable and accessible to the caller. A telecommunications utility or telecommunications company shall submit to the Public Service Commission the method by which the telecommunications utility or telecommunications company shall provide access to a live operator for review, except for a telecommunications utility or telecommunications company whose operator services are under the jurisdiction, regulation, and rules of the Public Service Commission. This Code section applies regardless of the method by which the telecommunications utility or telecommunications company provides the operator service. The requirements of this Code section shall not apply to telephones located in prisons or jail facilities or to wireless telecommunication services. For the purpose of this Code section, "operator services" means services that are provided when a caller dials "0".

(b) The failure of a telecommunications utility or telecommunications company to provide access to a live operator as required in subsection (a) of this Code section shall not serve as the basis for a cause of action for personal injuries or damage to property.

Laws 1994, p. 520, § 1.

§ 46–5–27. Regulation of telephone solicitations; violations

(a) The General Assembly finds that:

(1) The use of the telephone to market goods and services is pervasive now due to the increased use of cost-effective telemarketing techniques;

(2) Over 30,000 businesses actively telemarket goods and services to business and residential customers;

(3) Every day, over 300,000 solicitors place calls to more than 18 million Americans, including citizens of this state;

(4) Telemarketing, however, can be an intrusive and relentless invasion of the privacy and peacefulness of individuals;

(5) Many citizens of this state are outraged over the proliferation of nuisance calls from telemarketers;

(6) Individuals' privacy rights and commercial freedom of speech can be balanced in a way that accommodates both the privacy of individuals and legitimate telemarketing practices; and

(7) It is in the public interest to establish a mechanism under which the individual citizens of this state can decide whether or not to receive telemarketing calls.

(b) As used in this Code section, the term:

(1) "Caller identification service" means a type of telephone service which permits telephone subscribers to see the telephone number of incoming telephone calls.

(2) "Residential, mobile, or wireless subscriber" means a person who has subscribed to telephone service from a local exchange company or mobile or wireless telephone service provider or other persons living or residing with such person.

(3) "Telephone solicitation" means any voice communication over a telephone line for the purpose of encouraging the purchase or rental of, or investment in, property, goods, or services, but does not include communications:

(A) To any residential, mobile, or wireless subscriber with that subscriber's prior express invitation or permission;

(B) By or on behalf of any person or entity with whom a residential, mobile, or wireless subscriber has a prior or current business or personal relationship; or

(C) By or on behalf of a charitable organization which has filed a registration statement pursuant to Code Section 43–17–5, is exempt from such registration under paragraphs (1) through (6) of subsection (a) of Code Section 43–17–9, or is exempt from such registration as a religious organization or agency referred to in paragraph (2) of Code Section 43–17–2.

Such communication may be from a live operator, through the use of ADAD equipment as defined in Code Section 46–5–23, or by other means.

(c) No person or entity shall make or cause to be made any telephone solicitation to the telephone line of any residential, mobile, or wireless subscriber in this state who has given notice to the commission, in accordance with regulations promulgated under subsection (d) of this Code section, of such subscriber's objection to receiving telephone solicitations.

(d)(1) The commission shall establish and provide for the operation of a data base to compile a list of telephone numbers of residential, mobile, and wireless subscribers who object to receiving telephone solicitations. It shall be the duty of the commission to have such data base in operation no later than January 1, 1999.

(2) Such data base may be operated by the commission or by another entity selected by and awarded a contract by the commission.

(3) No later than January 1, 1999, the commission shall promulgate regulations which:

(A) Require each local exchange company to inform its residential, mobile, or wireless subscribers of the opportunity to provide notification to the commission or its contractor that such subscriber objects to receiving telephone solicitations;

(B) Specify the methods by which each residential, mobile, or wireless subscriber may give notice to the commission or its contractor of his or her objection to receiving such solicitations and methods for revocation of such notice;

(C) Specify the length of time for which a notice of objection shall be effective and the effect of a change of telephone number on such notice;

(D) Specify the methods by which such objections and revocations shall be collected and added to the data base;

(E) Specify the methods by which any person or entity desiring to make telephone solicitations will obtain access to the data base as required to avoid calling the telephone numbers of residential, mobile, or wireless subscribers included in the data base; and

(F) Specify such other matters relating to the data base that the commission deems desirable.

(4) If, pursuant to 47 U.S.C. Section 227(c)(3), the Federal Communications Commission establishes a single national data base of telephone numbers of subscribers who object to receiving telephone solicitations, the commission shall include the part of such single national data base that relates to Georgia in the data base established under this Code section.

(e) The commission may provide by rule or regulation for administrative fees to be imposed upon:

(1) A residential, mobile, or wireless subscriber for each notice of inclusion in the data base established under this Code section; provided, however, that the commission shall not set this fee in an amount greater than $5.00; and

(2) A person or entity desiring to make telephone solicitations for access to or for electronic copies of the data base established under this Code section.

(f)(1) Information contained in the data base established under this Code section shall be used only for the purpose of compliance with this Code section or in a proceeding or action under subsection (h) or (i) of this Code section. Such information shall not be subject to public inspection or disclosure under Article 4 of Chapter 18 of Title 50.

(2) No person shall knowingly compile or disseminate or compile and disseminate information obtained from the data base for any reason other than those legitimate purposes established by law. Any person found guilty of violating this subsection shall be guilty of a misdemeanor and upon conviction shall be punished by a fine not to exceed $1,000.00. Each instance of an unauthorized disclosure of information from the data base shall constitute a separate offense.

(g)(1) Any person or entity who makes a telephone solicitation to the telephone line of any residential, mobile, or wireless subscriber in this state shall, at the beginning of such call, state clearly the identity of the person or entity initiating the call.

(2) No person or entity who makes a telephone solicitation to the telephone line of a residential, mobile, or wireless subscriber in this state shall knowingly utilize any method to block or otherwise circumvent such subscriber's use of a caller identification service.

(h) The administrator appointed pursuant to subsection (g) of Code Section 10–1–395 shall have authority to initiate proceedings, pursuant to Code Section 10–1–397, relating to a knowing violation or threatened knowing violation of subsection (c) or (g) of this Code section. Such proceedings include without limitation proceedings to issue a cease and desist order, to issue an order imposing a civil penalty up to a maximum of $ 2,000.00 for each knowing violation, and to seek additional relief in any superior court of competent jurisdiction. Such actions shall be brought in the name of the state. The provisions of Code Sections 10–1–398, 10–1–398.1, and 10–1–405 shall apply to proceedings initiated by the administrator under this subsection. The administrator is authorized to issue investigative demands, issue subpoenas, administer oaths, and conduct hearings in the course of investigating a violation of subsection (c) or (g) of this Code section, in accordance with the provisions of Code Sections 10–1–403 and 10–1–404.

(i) Any person who has received more than one telephone solicitation within any 12 month period by or on behalf of the same person or entity in violation of subsection (c) or (g) of this Code section may either bring an action to enjoin such violation; bring an action to recover for actual monetary loss from such knowing violation or to receive up to $ 2,000.00 in damages for each such knowing violation, whichever is greater; or bring both such actions.

(j) It shall be a defense in any action or proceeding brought under subsection (h) or (i) of this Code section that the defendant has established and implemented, with due care, reasonable practices and procedures to effectively prevent telephone solicitations in violation of this Code section.

(k) No action or proceeding may be brought under subsection (h) or (i) of this Code section:

(1) More than two years after the person bringing the action knew or should have known of the occurrence of the alleged violation; or

(2) More than two years after the termination of any proceeding or action by the State of Georgia, whichever is later.

(*l*) A court of this state may exercise personal jurisdiction over any nonresident or his or her executor or administrator as to an action or proceeding authorized by this Code section in accordance with the provisions of Code Section 9–10–91.

(m) The remedies, duties, prohibitions, and penalties of this Code section are not exclusive and are in addition to all other causes of action, remedies, and penalties provided by law.

(n) No provider of telephone caller identification service shall be held liable for violations of this Code section committed by other persons or entities.

Laws 1998, p. 505, § 1; Laws 2003, Act 211, § 1, eff. July 1, 2003; Laws 2004, Act 564, § 46, eff. May 13, 2004.

Historical and Statutory Notes

The 2003 amendment by Act 211, in subsec. (a), deleted "to the home" following "services" in par. (1), substituted "individuals" for "of home" in par. (4), deleted "to their homes" following "nuisance calls" in par. (5), and deleted "in their homes" following "telemarketing calls" in par. (7); in subsec. (b), deleted "residential" following "subscribed to" and "the" preceding "other persons living", and inserted ", mobile or wireless" and "or mobile or wireless telephone service provider," in par. (2), and inserted ", mobile, or wireless" in pars. (3)(A) and (3)(B); in subsec. (c), inserted ", mobile, or wireless", in subsec. (d), inserted ", mobile, and wireless" in par. (1), substituted "selected by and awarded a contract by" for "under contract with" in par. (2), inserted ", mobile, or wireless" in pars. (3)(A), (3)(B), and (3)(E), and substituted "and methods for" for "or" in par. (3)(B); rewrote subsecs. (e) and (f); and, in subsec. (g), inserted ", mobile, or wireless" in pars. (1) and (2). Prior to amendment, subsecs. (e) and (f) had read:

"(e) A residential subscriber shall be charged a fee of $ 5.00, payable to the commission, for each notice for inclusion in the data base established under this Code section. A person or entity desiring to make telephone solicitations shall be charged a fee of $ 10.00 per year payable to the commission for access to or for paper or electronic copies of the data base established under this Code section.

"(f) Information contained in the data base established under this Code section shall be used only for the purpose of compliance with this Code section or in a proceeding or action under subsection (h) or (i) of this Code section. Such information shall not be subject to public inspection or disclosure under Article 4 of Chapter 18 of Title 50."

The 2004 amendment by Act 564 was a provision contained in a correction bill.

§ 46–5–28. Consent of wireless service subscriber required for inclusion in telephone data base

(a) As used in this Code section, the term:

(1) "Service supplier" means a person or entity who provides wireless service to a telephone subscriber.

(2) "Traditional telephone directory" means a telephone directory, in any format, containing a majority of the landline telephone numbers for the given geographic coverage area for that directory.

(3) "Wireless service" means "commercial mobile service" as defined under Section 332(D) of the Federal Telecommunications Act of 1996 (47 U.S.C. Section 157, et seq.), regulations of the Federal Communications Commission, and the Omnibus Budget Reconciliation Act of 1993 (P.L. 103–66) and includes real-time, two-way interconnected voice service which is provided over networks which utilize intelligent switching capability and offer seamless handoff to customers. The term does not include one-way signaling service, data transmission service, nonlocal radio access line service, or a private telecommunications service.

(4) "Wireless telephone data base" means any collection of telephone numbers that identifies the names and telephone numbers of multiple subscribers of one or more service suppliers.

(b) A service supplier or any direct or indirect affiliate or agent of a service supplier providing the name and dialing number of a subscriber for inclusion in any wireless telephone data base which is or will be made publicly available shall not include the dialing number of any wireless service subscriber without first obtaining the express consent of that subscriber. The subscriber's consent shall meet all of the following requirements:

(1) It shall be recorded in oral, electronic, or written form;

(2) It shall be:

(A) A separate document that is not attached to any other document or if it is within another document shall be in a separate section of the document that includes the disclosure;

(B) A separate screen or if it is within another screen shall be in a separate section of the screen that includes the disclosure; or

(C) A sound recording of a discrete verbal confirmation;

(3) It shall be unambiguous and conspicuously disclose that the subscriber is consenting to have the subscriber's dialing number sold or licensed as part of a publicly accessible wireless telephone data base; and

(4) The service supplier must disclose in an unambiguous and conspicuous manner to the wireless customer that upon consent: (A) the customer is agreeing to have his or her wireless number accessed by anyone who utilizes the wireless telephone data base; and (B) if the customer has a rate plan that charges the customer for usage, that calls received as a result, unsolicited or otherwise, will be applied against the subscriber's planned minutes.

(c) A subscriber who provides express consent pursuant to subsection (b) of this Code section may revoke that consent at any time. A service supplier shall comply with the subscriber's request to opt out within a reasonable period of time, not to exceed 60 days.

(d) A subscriber shall not be charged for making the choice to not be listed in a publicly accessible wireless telephone data base.

(e) This Code section does not apply to the provision of telephone numbers to the following parties for the purposes indicated; provided, however, that such parties shall use such telephone numbers solely for the purposes indicated and shall not transfer such telephone numbers to any third party:

(1) Any law enforcement agency, fire protection agency, public health agency, public environmental health agency, city or county emergency services planning agency, or private for-profit agency operating under contract with, and at the direction of, one or more of these agencies, for the exclusive purpose of responding to a 9–1–1 call or communicating an imminent threat to life or property. This information or these records shall not be open to examination for any purpose not directly connected with the administration of the services specified in this paragraph;

(2) A lawful process issued under state or federal law;

(3) A service supplier providing service between service areas for the provision to the subscriber of telephone service between service areas, or third parties for the limited purpose of providing collection and billing services for the service supplier;

(4) A service supplier to effectuate a subscriber's request to transfer the subscriber's assigned telephone number from the subscriber's existing service supplier to a new service supplier;

(5) The commission; or

(6) A traditional telephone directory publisher, for the purposes of publishing a directory in any format, so long as the information was published before July 1, 2005.

(f) Subsequent to July 1, 2005, a traditional telephone directory publisher must obtain the wireless subscriber's recorded oral, electronic, or written consent for the wireless subscriber's name and wireless dialing number to be published in a traditional telephone directory.

(g) No service supplier shall sell or otherwise provide a list of wireless numbers to any telemarketer except that such numbers may be provided to a telemarketer affiliated with the service supplier for the sole purpose of facilitating communication by or on behalf of the service supplier as permitted under subparagraph (b)(3)(B) of Code Section 46–5–27.

(h) Every deliberate violation of this Code section is grounds for a civil suit by the aggrieved subscriber against the service supplier responsible for the violation.

(i) No service supplier shall be subject to criminal or civil liability for the release of customer information as authorized by this Code section.

Laws 2005, Act 370, § 1, eff. July 1, 2005; Laws 2006, Act 453, § 46, eff. April 14, 2006.

CHAPTER 7

MOTOR CARRIERS

Article 1

Article 2

Article 3

Article 1

Motor Common or Contract Carriers.

§ 46–7–1. Definitions

As used in this chapter, the term "commission" means the Public Service Commission.

Laws 2000, p. 951, § 9–4; Laws 2005, Act 68, § 28–2, eff. July 1, 2005.

§ 46–7–2. Regulation of motor common or contract carriers of persons or property

Unless expressly prohibited by federal law, the commission is vested with power to regulate the business of any person engaged in the transportation as a common or contract carrier of persons or property, either or both, for hire by motor vehicle on any public highway of this state.

Laws 1931, p. 199, § 3; Laws 1996, p. 950, § 3; Laws 2000, p. 951, § 9–4; Laws 2005, Act 68, § 28–2, eff. July 1, 2005.

Formerly Code 1933, § 68–603.

§ 46–7–3. Requirement of certificate of public convenience and necessity; proof of insurance; valid certification number

(a) No motor common or contract carrier of passengers or household goods shall, except as otherwise provided in this article, operate without first obtaining from the commission a certificate.

(b) Before a motor common or contract carrier may enter into any contract for the transportation of passengers, the carrier shall provide to all parties to the agreement a copy of the carrier's proof of legally required minimum insurance coverage and a valid certification number demonstrating that the carrier is currently certified by the commission, the Federal Motor Carrier Safety Administration, or any other similarly required certifying agency. Any contract entered into in violation of this Code section shall be void and unenforceable.

Laws 1931, p. 199, § 4; Laws 1996, p. 950, § 3; Laws 2000, p. 951, § 9–4; Laws 2004, Act 479, § 3, eff. July 1, 2004; Laws 2005, Act 68, § 28–2, eff. July 1, 2005; Laws 2010, Act 447, § 2, eff. July 1, 2010.

Formerly Code 1933, § 68–604.

Historical and Statutory Notes

Laws 2010, Act 447, § 3, provides:

"This Act shall become effective on July 1, 2010, and shall apply to agreements entered into on or after such date."

§ 46–7–4. Issuance, terms, and conditions of certificate

The commission may issue the certificate applied for or issue it for the partial exercise of the privilege sought and may attach to the exercise of the rights granted by such certificate such terms and conditions as, in its judgment, may be required.

Laws 1931, p. 199, § 4; Laws 1996, p. 950, § 3; Laws 2000, p. 951, § 9–4; Laws 2004, Act 479, § 4, eff. July 1, 2004; Laws 2005, Act 68, § 28–2, eff. July 1, 2005.

Formerly Code 1933, § 68–605.

Historical and Statutory Notes

In 2004, the Code Commission deleted the comma following "sought" and substituted "may be required" for "may require". See § 28–9–5.

§ 46–7–5. Revocation, suspension, or change of certificate

The commission may, at any time after notice and opportunity to be heard and for reasonable cause, suspend, revoke, alter, or amend any certificate issued under this article, under the "Motor Carrier Act of 1929," under the "Motor Carrier Act of 1931," or under prior law, if it shall be made to appear that the holder of the certificate has willfully violated or refused to observe any of the lawful and reasonable orders, rules, or regulations prescribed by the commission or any of the provisions of this article or any other law of this state regulating or taxing motor vehicles, or both, or if in the opinion of the commission the holder of the certificate is not furnishing adequate service.

Laws 1931, p. 199, § 4; Laws 1996, p. 950, § 3; Laws 2000, p. 951, § 9–4; Laws 2004, Act 479, § 5, eff. July 1, 2004; Laws 2005, Act 68, § 28–2, eff. July 1, 2005.

Formerly Code 1933, § 68–607.

Historical and Statutory Notes

Laws 2004, Act 479, rewrote the section, which had read:

"(a) The commissioner may, at any time after notice and opportunity to be heard and for reasonable cause, suspend, revoke, alter, or amend any certificate issued under this article, under the 'Motor Carrier Act of 1929,' under the 'Motor Carrier Act of 1931,' or under prior law, if it shall be made to appear that the holder of the certificate has willfully violated or refused to observe any of the lawful and reasonable orders, rules, or regulations prescribed by the commissioner or any of the provisions of this article or any other law of this state regulating or taxing motor vehicles, or both, or if in the opinion of the commissioner the holder of the certificate is not furnishing adequate service, or if the continuance of said certificate in its original form is incompatible with the public interest.

"(b) If and when the commissioner shall undertake to revoke or modify any certificate on account of the public interest on the ground that the traffic conditions are such as not to justify the number of motor carriers which have been granted certificates over the route or routes in question, the preference shall be given to certificates in order of the time of their issuance, so that those which have been issued later in time shall, other things being equal, be canceled rather than those issued earlier in time."

The 2005 amendment by Act 68 substituted "commission" for "commissioner" each place it appeared.

§ 46–7–6. Transfer of certificate

Any certificate issued pursuant to this article may be transferred or hypothecated upon application to and approval by the commission, and not otherwise.

Laws 1931, p. 199, § 4; Laws 1996, p. 950, § 3; Laws 2000, p. 951, § 9–4; Laws 2005, Act 68, § 28–2, eff. July 1, 2005.

Formerly Code 1933, § 68–608.

§ 46–7–7. Considerations determining granting of certificate

(a) The commission shall issue a certificate to a person authorizing transportation as a motor common or contract carrier of passengers or household goods subject to the jurisdiction of the commission if it finds that the person is fit, willing, and able to provide the transportation to be authorized by the certificate and to comply with regulations of the commission. Fitness encompasses three factors:

(1) The applicant's financial ability to perform the service it seeks to provide;

(2) The applicant's capability and willingness to perform properly and safely the proposed service; and

(3) The applicant's willingness to comply with the laws of Georgia and the rules and regulations of the commission.

(b) The initial burden of making out a prima-facie case that an applicant is fit to provide such service rests with the applicant.

(c) Upon an applicant making out a prima-facie case as to the carrier's ability to provide the service, the burden shifts to protestant to show that the authority sought should not be granted.

(d) A protest of a motor carrier of passengers or of household goods to an application will not be considered unless the protesting carrier:

(1) Possesses authority from the commission to handle, in whole or in part, the authority which is being applied for and is willing and able to provide service and has performed service during the previous 12 month period or has actively in good faith solicited service during such period;

(2) Has pending before the commission an application previously filed with the commission for substantially the same authority; or

(3) Is granted by the commission leave to intervene upon a showing of other interests which in the discretion of the commission would warrant such a grant.

(e) The commission may issue a certificate without a hearing if the application is unprotested or unopposed.

Laws 1931, p. 199, § 4; Laws 1950, p. 186, § 1; Laws 1986, p. 1283, § 3; Laws 1996, p. 950, § 3; Laws 2000, p. 951, § 9–4; Laws 2004, Act 479, § 6, eff. July 1, 2004; Laws 2005, Act 68, § 28–2, eff. July 1, 2005.

Formerly Code 1933, § 68–609.

§ 46–7–8. Rules as to application for certificate

The commission shall adopt rules prescribing the manner and form in which motor carriers of passengers or household goods shall apply for certificates required by this article. Such rules shall require that the application be in writing, under oath, and that the application:

(1) Contain full information concerning the applicant's financial condition, the equipment proposed to be used, including the size, weight, and capacity of each vehicle to be used, and other physical property of the applicant;

(2) State the complete route or routes over which the applicant desires to operate and the proposed time schedule of the operation; and

(3) Contain any such other or additional information as the commission may order or require.

Laws 1931, p. 199, § 5; Laws 1996, p. 950, § 3; Laws 2000, p. 951, § 9–4; Laws 2004, Act 479, § 7, eff. July 1, 2004; Laws 2005, Act 68, § 28–2, eff. July 1, 2005.

Formerly Code 1933, § 68–610.

§ 46–7–9. Fees for issuance of, amendment to, or transfer of certificate

The commission shall collect the following fees pursuant to this article:

(1) A fee of $ 75.00 to accompany each application for a certificate, or amendment to an existing certificate, where the applicant owns or operates fewer than six motor vehicles;

(2) A fee of $ 150.00 to accompany each application for a certificate, or amendment to an existing certificate, where the applicant owns or operates six to 15 motor vehicles;

(3) A fee of $ 200.00 to accompany each application for a certificate, or amendment to an existing certificate, where the applicant owns or operates more than 15 motor vehicles;

(4) A fee of $ 75.00 to accompany each application for transfer of a certificate;

(5) A fee of $ 50.00 to accompany each application for intrastate temporary emergency authority under Code Section 46–7–13; and

(6) A fee of $ 50.00 to accompany each application for a motor carrier of property permit.

Laws 1931, p. 199, § 17; Laws 1980, p. 618, § 2; Laws 1996, p. 950, § 3; Laws 2000, p. 951, § 9–4; Laws 2004, Act 479, § 8, eff. July 1, 2004; Laws 2005, Act 68, § 28–2, eff. July 1, 2005.

Formerly Code 1933, § 68–622.

§ 46–7–10. Hearing on application; notice

The commission, upon the filing of a petition for a certificate, shall fix a time and place for hearing thereon and shall, at least ten days before the hearing, give notice thereof by advertising the same at the expense of the applicant in a newspaper in Atlanta, in which sheriffs' notices are published. If no protest is filed with the commission or if the protest is subsequently withdrawn, the commission may issue the certificate without a hearing.

Laws 1931, p. 199, § 6; Laws 1996, p. 950, § 3; Laws 2000, p. 951, § 9–4; Laws 2004, Act 479, § 9, eff. July 1, 2004; Laws 2005, Act 68, § 28–2, eff. July 1, 2005.

Formerly Code 1933, § 68–611.

§ 46–7–11. Certificate refused or revoked; new application

When a petition for a certificate under this article has been in whole or in part denied by the commission, or has been granted by the commission, and the order of the commission granting same has been quashed or set aside by a court of competent jurisdiction, a new application by the same petitioner or applicant therefor shall not be again considered by the commission within three months from the date of the order denying the same or the judgment of the court quashing or setting aside the order.

Laws 1931, p. 199, § 27; Laws 1996, p. 950, § 3; Laws 2000, p. 951, § 9-4; Laws 2004, Act 479, § 10, eff. July 1, 2004; Laws 2005, Act 68, § 28-2, eff. July 1, 2005.

Formerly Code 1933, § 68-630.

§ 46-7-12. Certificate of indemnity insurance; self insurance

(a) No motor carrier of household goods or passengers shall be issued a certificate unless there is filed with the commission a certificate of insurance for such applicant or holder on forms prescribed by the commission evidencing a policy of indemnity insurance by an insurance company licensed to do business in this state, which policy must provide for the protection, in case of passenger vehicles, of passengers and the public against injury proximately caused by the negligence of such motor carrier, its servants, or its agents; and, in the case of vehicles transporting household goods, to secure the owner or person entitled to recover against loss or damage to such household goods for which the motor carrier may be legally liable . The commission shall determine and fix the amounts of such indemnity insurance and shall prescribe the provisions and limitations thereof. The insurer shall file such certificate. The failure to file any form required by the commission shall not diminish the rights of any person to pursue an action directly against a motor carrier's insurer.

(b) The commission shall have power to permit self-insurance, in lieu of a policy of indemnity insurance, whenever in its opinion the financial ability of the motor carrier so warrants.

(c) It shall be permissible under this article for any person having a cause of action arising under this article to join in the same action the motor carrier and the insurance carrier, whether arising in tort or contract.

Laws 1931, p. 199, § 7; Laws 1937, p. 730, § 2; Laws 1996, p. 950, § 3; Laws 2000, p. 951, § 9-4; Laws 2000, p. 1583, § 1; Laws 2002, p. 1378, § 9; Laws 2005, Act 68, § 28-2.1, eff. July 1, 2005.

Formerly Code 1933, § 68-612.

Historical and Statutory Notes

In 2000, the Code Commission, in the last sentence of subsec. (c), substituted "commissioner" for "commission". See § 28-9-5.

§ 46-7-12.1. Motor carrier transportation contract; indemnity clause

(a) As used in this Code section, the term:

(1) "Motor carrier transportation contract" means a contract, agreement, or understanding covering:

(A) The transportation of property for compensation or hire by the motor carrier;

(B) Entrance on property by the motor carrier for the purpose of loading, unloading, or transporting property for compensation or hire; or

(C) A service incidental to activity described in subparagraph (A) or (B) of this paragraph, including, but not limited to, storage of property.

Motor carrier transportation contract shall not include the Uniform Intermodal Interchange and Facilities Access Agreement administered by the Intermodal Association of North America or other agreements providing for the interchange, use, or possession of intermodal chassis, containers, or other intermodal equipment.

(2) "Promisee" means the promisee and any agents, employees, servants, or independent contractors who are directly responsible to the promisee except for motor carriers party to a motor carrier transportation contract with a promisee and such motor carrier's agents, employees, servants, or independent contractors directly responsible to such motor carrier.

(b) Notwithstanding any provision of law to the contrary, a provision, clause, covenant, or agreement contained in, collateral to, or affecting a motor carrier transportation contract that purports to indemnify, defend, or hold harmless, or has the effect of indemnifying, defending, or holding harmless, the promisee from or against any liability for loss or damage resulting from the negligence or intentional acts or omissions of the promisee is against the public policy of this state and is void and unenforceable.

Laws 2005, Act 68, § 28-2.1, eff. July 1, 2005; Laws 2009, Act 114, § 3, eff. July 1, 2009.

Historical and Statutory Notes

The 2009 amendment by Act 114 rewrote the section which had read:

"(a) No motor common carrier or motor contract carrier shall be issued a permit unless there is filed with the state revenue commissioner a certificate of insurance for such applicant or holder on forms prescribed by the commissioner evidencing a policy of indemnity insurance by an insurance company licensed to do business in this state, which policy must provide for the protection of passengers in the case of passenger vehicles and for protection of the public against injury proximately caused by the negligence of such motor common or motor contract carrier, its servants, or its agents. The state revenue commissioner shall determine and fix the amounts of such indemnity insurance and shall prescribe the provisions and limitations thereof. The insurer shall file such certificate. The failure to file any form required by the state revenue commissioner shall not diminish the rights of any person to pursue an action directly against a motor common or motor contract carrier's insurer.

"(b) The state revenue commissioner shall have power to permit self-insurance, in lieu of a policy of indemnity insurance, whenever in his or her opinion the financial ability of the motor common or motor contract carrier so warrants.

"(c) It shall be permissible under this article for any person having a cause of action arising under this article to join in the same action the motor common or motor contract carrier and the insurance carrier, whether arising in tort or contract."

Laws 2009, Act 114, § 10(a), provides:

"(a) Section 3 of this Act shall become effective on July 1, 2009, and shall apply to contracts entered into on or after such date."

§ 46-7-13. Temporary emergency authority

Notwithstanding any other provision of law to the contrary, in order to authorize the provision of passenger or household goods service for which there is an immediate and urgent need to a point or points, or within a territory, with respect to which there is no motor common or contract carrier service capable of meeting such need, upon receipt of an application for temporary emergency authority and upon payment of the appropriate fee as fixed by statute, the commission, under the authority of this Code section, may, in its discretion and without a hearing or other prior proceeding, grant to any person temporary motor carrier authority for such service. The order granting such authority shall contain the commission's findings supporting its determination under the authority of this Code section that there is an unmet immediate and urgent need for such service and shall contain such conditions as the commission finds necessary with respect to such authority. Unless otherwise provided in this Code section, such emergency temporary motor carrier authority, unless suspended or revoked for good cause within such period, shall be valid for such time as the commission shall specify but not for more than an aggregate of 30 days. Such authority shall in no case be renewed and shall create no presumption that corresponding permanent authority will be granted thereafter, except that, where a motor carrier granted temporary emergency motor carrier authority under the provisions of this Code section makes application during the period of said temporary emergency authority for permanent motor common or contract carrier authority corresponding to that authorized in its temporary emergency authority, the temporary emergency motor carrier authority will be extended to the finalization of the permanent authority application unless sooner suspended or revoked for good cause within the extended period.

Laws 1973, p. 641, § 1; Laws 1980, p. 475, § 1; Laws 1983, p. 462, § 1; Laws 1996, p. 950, § 3; Laws 2000, p. 951, § 9–4; Laws 2005, Act 68, § 28–2, eff. July 1, 2005.

Formerly Code 1933, § 68–611.1.

§ 46–7–14. Discontinuance of service after giving notice

A motor common or contract carrier of passengers may discontinue its entire service on any route upon 30 days' published notice to be prescribed by the commission, and thereupon its certificate therefor shall be canceled. A motor common or contract carrier of passengers may discontinue any part of its service on any route upon 30 days' published notice, subject, however, to the right of the commission to withdraw its certificate for such route if, in the opinion of the commission, such diminished service is not adequate or is no longer compatible with the public interest.

Laws 1931, p. 199, § 14; Laws 1996, p. 950, § 3; Laws 2000, p. 951, § 9–4; Laws 2005, Act 68, § 28–2, eff. July 1, 2005.

Formerly Code 1933, § 68–619.

§ 46–7–15. Carriers engaged in exempt passenger intrastate commerce; registration permit

No subdivision of this state, including cities, townships, or counties, shall levy any excise, license, or occupation tax of any nature on a motor carrier, or on the equipment of a motor carrier, or on the right of a motor carrier to operate such equipment, or on any incidents of the business of a motor carrier.

Laws 1931, p. 199, § 18; Laws 1937, p. 469, § 1; Laws 1943, p. 351, § 1; Laws 1973, p. 643, § 3; Laws 1980, p. 475, § 2; Laws 1986, p. 1283, § 4; Laws 1988, p. 1607, § 1; Laws 1996, p. 950, § 3; Laws 2000, p. 951, § 9–4; Laws 2005, Act 68, § 28–3, eff. July 1, 2005; Laws 2009, Act 114, § 4, eff. Oct. 1, 2009; Laws 2010, Act 624, § 46, eff. June 3, 2010.

Formerly Code 1933, § 68–623.

Historical and Statutory Notes

Laws 2009, Act 114, § 10(b) and (c), provides:

"(b) Sections 4 and 5 of this Act shall become effective October 1, 2009, for the purpose of adopting rules and regulations to implement the federal Unified Carrier Registration Act of 2005.

(c) "The remaining sections of this Act shall become effective upon its approval by the Governor or upon its becoming law without such approval."

§ 46–7–15.1. Repealed by Laws 2009, Act 114, § 5, eff. October 1, 2009

Historical and Statutory Notes

The repealed section, relating to motor carrier of property permits, was derived from Laws 1996, p. 950, § 3; Laws 2000, p. 951, § 9–4; Laws 2004, Act 479, § 11; Laws 2005, Act 68, § 28–3

§ 46–7–16. Repealed by Laws 2009, Act 114, § 6, eff. May 4, 2009

Historical and Statutory Notes

The repealed section, relating to motor carriers engaged solely in interstate commerce and registration, was derived from Laws 1931, p. 199, § 30; Laws 1968, p. 392, § 1; Laws 1973, p. 643, § 4; Laws 1980, p. 475, § 3; Laws 1986, p. 1283, § 5; Laws 1988, p. 1607, § 2; Laws 1989, p. 14, § 46; Laws 1996, p. 950, § 3; Laws 2000, p. 951, § 9-4; Laws 2002, p. 415, § 46; Laws 2004, Act 479, § 12; Laws 2005, Act 68, § 28-3; Code 1933, 68-633.

§ 46–7–17. Agents for service on nonresident motor carriers; service of process; venue; enforcement

(a) Each nonresident motor carrier shall, before any permit is issued to it under this article or at the time of registering as required by Code Section 46–7–16, designate and maintain in this state an agent or agents upon whom may be served all summonses or other lawful processes in any action or proceeding against such motor carrier growing out of its carrier operations; and service of process upon or acceptance or acknowledgment of such service by any such agent shall have the same legal force and validity as if duly served upon such nonresident carrier personally. Such designation shall be in writing, shall give the name and address of such agent or agents, and shall be filed in the office of the state revenue commissioner. Upon failure of any nonresident motor carrier to file such designation with the state revenue commissioner or to maintain such an agent in this state at the address given, such nonresident carrier shall be conclusively deemed to have designated the Secretary of State and his or her successors in office as such agent; and service of process upon or acceptance or acknowledgment of such service by the Secretary of State shall have the same legal force and validity as if duly served upon such nonresident carrier personally, provided that notice of such service and a copy of the process are immediately sent by registered or certified mail or statutory overnight delivery by the Secretary of State or his or her successor in office to such nonresident carrier, if its address be known. Service of such process upon the Secretary of State shall be made by delivering to his or her office two copies of such process with a fee of $10.00.

(b) Except in those cases where the Constitution of Georgia requires otherwise, any action against any resident or nonresident motor common or contract carrier for damages by reason of any breach of duty, whether contractual or otherwise, or for any violation of this article or of any order, decision, rule, regulation, direction, demand, or other requirement established by the state revenue commissioner, may be brought in the county where the cause of action or some part thereof arose; and if the motor common or contract carrier or its agent shall not be found for service in the county where the action is instituted, a second original may issue and service be made in any other county where the service can be made upon the motor common or contract carrier or its agent. The venue prescribed by this Code section shall be cumulative of any other venue provided by law.

Laws 1931, p. 199, § 13; Laws 1963, p. 376, § 1; Laws 1965, p. 418, § 1; Laws 1983, p. 1474, § 5; Laws 1996, p. 950, § 3; Laws 2000, p. 951, § 9–4; Laws 2000, p. 1589, § 3; Laws 2005, Act 68, § 28–3, eff. July 1, 2005.

Formerly Code 1933, § 68–618.

§ 46–7–18. Powers over rates

The commission shall prescribe just and reasonable rates, fares, and charges for transportation by motor common and contract carriers of passengers and household goods and for all services rendered by motor common and contract carriers in connection therewith. The tariffs therefor shall be in such form and shall be filed and published in such manner and on such notice as the commission may prescribe. Such tariffs shall also be subject to change on such notice and in such manner as the commission may prescribe. In order to carry out the purposes of this Code section, including the publication and maintenance of just, reasonable, and nondiscriminatory rates and charges, the commission shall establish a collective rate–making procedure for all carriers of passengers and household goods. Failure on the part of any motor common or contract carrier to comply with this Code section or the rules and regulations promulgated under this Code section may result in suspension or cancellation of said carrier's operating authority by the commission.

Laws 1931, p. 199, § 8; Laws 1980, p. 1119, § 2; Laws 1983, p. 529, § 1; Laws 1996, p. 950, § 3; Laws 2000, p. 951, § 9–4; Laws 2005, Act 68, § 28–2, eff. July 1, 2005.

Formerly Code 1933, § 68–613.

§ 46–7–19. No discrimination in rates, service, etc.

No motor common or contract carrier of passengers or household goods shall charge, demand, collect, or receive a greater or lesser or different compensation for the transportation of passengers and property or for any service rendered in connection therewith than the rates, fares, and charges prescribed or approved by order of the commission; nor shall any such motor carrier unjustly discriminate against any person in its rates, fares, or charges for service. The commission may prescribe, by general order, to what persons motor common and contract carriers of passengers or household goods may issue passes or free transportation; may prescribe reduced rates for special occasions; and may fix and prescribe rates and schedules.

Laws 1931, p. 199, § 9; Laws 1996, p. 950, § 3; Laws 2000, p. 951, § 9–4; Laws 2005, Act 68, § 28–2, eff. July 1, 2005.

Formerly Code 1933, § 68–614.

§ 46–7–20. Carriage of baggage and liability therefor

Motor common or contract carriers of passengers shall not be compelled to carry baggage of passengers, except hand baggage, the character, amount, and size of which the motor carrier may limit by its rules and regulations, subject to the approval of the commission; and the commission may by rule or regulation limit the amount of the liability of the motor carrier therefor. If a motor carrier shall elect to carry the personal baggage of passengers (other than hand baggage), the commission shall prescribe just and reasonable rates therefor and such other rules and regulations with respect thereto as may be reasonable and just, and may by rule or regulation limit the amount of the liability of the motor carrier therefor.

Laws 1931, p. 199, § 12; Laws 1996, p. 950, § 3; Laws 2000, p. 951, § 9–4; Laws 2005, Act 68, § 28–2, eff. July 1, 2005.

Formerly Code 1933, § 68–617.

§ 46–7–21. Repealed by Laws 1996, p. 950, § 3, eff. April 15, 1996

§ 46–7–22. Repealed by Laws 1986, p. 1283, § 6, eff. April 9, 1986

§ 46–7–23. Books and accounts; examination

The commission shall prescribe the books and the forms of accounts to be kept by the holders of certificates under this article, which books and accounts shall be preserved for such reasonable time as may be prescribed by the commission. The books and records of every certificate holder shall be at all times open to the inspection of any agent of the commission for such purpose. The commission shall have the power to examine the books and records of all motor carriers to whom it has granted certificates or permits to operate under this article and to examine under oath the officers and agents of any motor carrier with respect thereto.

Laws 1931, p. 199, § 19; Laws 1996, p. 950, § 3; Laws 2000, p. 951, § 9–4; Laws 2005, Act 68, § 28–4, eff. July 1, 2005.

Formerly Code 1933, § 68–625.

§ 46–7–24. Size, weight, speed of common carrier's vehicles; schedules

Motor carriers shall observe the laws of this state in respect to size, weight, and speed of their vehicles. Intrastate motor carriers of passengers shall, and interstate motor carriers of passengers may, file with the commission the schedules upon which they propose to operate their vehicles, which schedules shall be such that the net running time of vehicles between terminal points shall not exceed the lawful speed limit; and any motor carrier of passengers filing such a schedule shall be allowed to operate his or her vehicles on the highway at a rate of speed not exceeding the lawful speed limit in order to maintain a schedule so filed.

Laws 1931, p. 199, § 32; Laws 1996, p. 950, § 3; Laws 2000, p. 951, § 9–4; Laws 2005, Act 68, § 28–2, eff. July 1, 2005.

Formerly Code 1933, § 68–634.

§ 46–7–25. Repealed by Laws 1996, p. 950, § 3, eff. April 15, 1996

§ 46–7–26. Authority to make rules for safety

(a) The commissioner of public safety shall have the authority to promulgate rules and regulations for the safe operation of motor vehicles and drivers and the safe transportation of hazardous materials. Any such rules and regulations promulgated or deemed necessary by the commissioner of public safety shall include the following:

(1) Every motor vehicle and all parts thereof shall be maintained in a safe condition at all times; and the lights, brakes, and equipment shall meet such safety requirements as the commissioner of public safety shall from time to time promulgate;

(2) Every driver employed to operate a motor vehicle for a motor carrier shall be at least 18 years of age, of temperate habits and good moral character, possess a valid driver's license, not use or possess prohibited drugs or alcohol while on duty, and shall be fully competent to operate the motor vehicle under his or her charge;

(3) Accidents arising from or in connection with the operation of motor common or contract carriers shall be reported to the commissioner of transportation in such detail and in such manner as the commissioner of transportation may require; and

(4) The commissioner of public safety shall require every motor common, contract, exempt, and private carrier's vehicles to have attached to each unit or vehicle such distinctive markings as shall be adopted by the commissioner of public safety. Such identification requirements shall comply with the applicable provisions of the federal Unified Carrier Registration Act of 2005.

(b) Regulations governing the safe operation of motor vehicles and drivers and the safe transportation of hazardous materials may be adopted by administrative order, including, but not limited to, referencing compatible federal regulations or standards without compliance with the procedural requirements of Chapter 13 of Title 50, provided that such compatible federal regulations or standards shall be maintained on file by the Department of Public Safety and made available for inspection and copying by the public, by means including, but not limited to, posting on the department's computer Internet site. The commissioner of public safety may comply with the filing requirements of Chapter 13 of Title 50 by filing with the office of the Secretary of State merely the name and designation of such rules, regulations, standards, and orders. The courts shall take judicial notice of rules, regulations, standards, or orders so adopted or published.

(c) The commissioner of public safety may, pursuant to rule or regulation, specify and impose civil monetary penalties for violations of laws, rules, and regulations relating to driver and motor carrier safety and transportation of hazardous materials. Except as may be hereafter authorized by law, the maximum amount of any such monetary penalty shall not exceed the maximum penalty authorized by law or rule or regulation for the same violation immediately prior to July 1, 2005.

Laws 1931, p. 199, § 24; Laws 1972, p. 1015, § 1604; Laws 1981, p. 409, §§ 1, 2; Laws 1996, p. 950, § 3; Laws 2000, p. 809, § 2; Laws 2000, p. 951, § 9–4; Laws 2002, p. 415, § 46; Laws 2005, Act 68, § 28–5, eff. July 1, 2005; Laws 2009, Act 114, § 7, eff. May 4, 2009; Laws 2010, Act 624, § 46, eff. June 3, 2010.

Formerly Code 1933, § 68–627.

Historical and Statutory Notes

The 2005 amendment by Act 68 rewrote the section which had read:

"The commissioner shall have the authority to promulgate rules and regulations for the safe operation of motor vehicles and drivers and the safe transportation of hazardous materials. Any such rules and regulations promulgated or deemed necessary by the commissioner shall include the following:

"(1) Every motor vehicle and all parts thereof shall be maintained in a safe condition at all times; and the lights, brakes, and equipment shall meet such safety requirements as the commissioner shall from time to time promulgate. Specifically but without limitation, the commissioner shall promulgate rules or regulations for the safe operation of trailers or semitrailers effective on and after July 1, 2000, consistent with the applicable provisions of Code Section 40–8–50;

"(2) Every driver employed to operate a motor vehicle for a motor common or contract carrier shall be at least 18 years of age, of temperate habits and good moral character, possess a valid driver's license, not use or possess prohibited drugs or alcohol while on duty, and shall be fully competent to operate the motor vehicle under his or her charge;

"(3) Accidents arising from or in connection with the operation of motor common or contract carriers shall be reported to the commissioner in such detail and in such manner as the commissioner may require; and

"(4) The commissioner shall require every motor common and contract carrier to have attached to each unit or vehicle such distinctive markings or tags as shall be adopted by the commissioner."

The 2010 amendment by Act 624 was a provision in a corrections bill.

§ 46–7–27. Rules and orders

The Public Service Commission, Department of Public Safety, and Department of Revenue are authorized to adopt such rules and orders as they may deem necessary in the enforcement of this chapter. Such rules and orders shall have the same dignity and standing as if such rules and orders were specifically provided in this chapter.

Laws 1931, p. 199, § 26; Laws 1996, p. 950, § 3; Laws 2000, p. 951, § 9–4; Laws 2004, Act 564, § 46, eff. May 13, 2004; Laws 2005, Act 68, § 28–5.1, eff. July 1, 2005.

Formerly Code 1933, § 68–629.

§§ 46–7–28, 46–7–29. Repealed by Laws 2000, p. 951, § 9–4, eff. July 1, 2001

§ 46–7–30. Enforcement

The commission is authorized to enforce this article by instituting actions for injunction, mandamus, or other appropriate relief.

Laws 1931, p. 199, § 13; Laws 1963, p. 376, § 1; Laws 1996, p. 950, § 3; Laws 2000, p. 951, § 9–4; Laws 2005, Act 68, § 28–2, eff. July 1, 2005.

Formerly Code 1933, § 68–618.

§ 46–7–31. Injunction against motor carrier

Any motor carrier which operates on the public highways of this state without the required certificate or permit, or after such certificate or permit has been canceled, or without having registered its vehicle or vehicles as provided for in this article, or which operates otherwise than is permitted by the terms of such certificate or permit or the laws of this state may be enjoined from operating on the public highways of this state upon the bringing of a civil action by the commission, by a competing motor carrier or rail carrier, or by any individual.

Laws 1931, p. 199, § 29; Laws 1996, p. 950, § 3; Laws 2000, p. 951, § 9–4; Laws 2004, Act 479, § 13, eff. July 1, 2004; Laws 2005, Act 68, § 28–2, eff. July 1, 2005.

Formerly Code 1933, § 68–632.

§ 46–7–32. No vested right or perpetual franchise

Nothing in this article or any other law shall be construed to vest in the owner, holder, or assignee of any certificate or permit issued under this article any vested right to use the public highways of this state and shall not be construed to give to any motor carrier any perpetual franchise over such public highways.

Laws 1931, p. 199, § 28; Laws 1996, p. 950, § 3; Laws 2000, p. 951, § 9–4; Laws 2004, Act 479, § 14, eff. July 1, 2004.

Formerly Code 1933, § 68–631.

§ 46–7–33. Complaints; review of orders

In all respects in which the commission has power and authority under this article, proceedings may be instituted, complaints made and filed with it, process issued, hearings held, and opinions, orders, and decisions made and filed. Any final order of the commission may be reviewed by any court of competent jurisdiction under the conditions and subject to the limitations prescribed by law which relate to the commission.

Laws 1931, p. 199, § 16; Laws 1996, p. 950, § 3; Laws 2000, p. 951, § 9–4; Laws 2004, Act 564, § 46, eff. May 13, 2004; Laws 2005, Act 68, § 28–2, eff. July 1, 2005.

Formerly Code 1933, § 68–621.

§ 46–7–34. Certificates granted under prior laws

(a) All certificates of public convenience and necessity to operate as a motor common or contract carrier of passengers or household goods issued prior to January 1, 1995, shall continue in full force and effect until revoked by the commission or surrendered by the holders thereof.

(b) All certificates of public convenience and necessity authorizing transportation of property and all registration permits for intrastate exempt commodity transportation that were in effect on December 31, 1994, shall be deemed null and void as of midnight December 31, 1994, and revoked by operation of law effective January 1, 1995. All persons holding certificates of public convenience and necessity authorizing transportation of property and all persons holding registration permits for intrastate exempt commodity transportation issued prior to January 1, 1995, who received a motor carrier of property permit from the Public Service Commission pursuant to its emergency rules shall be deemed to hold a motor carrier of property permit issued under Code Section 46–7–15.1.

(c) Any person holding a certificate of public convenience and necessity authorizing transportation of property issued prior to January 1, 1995, and any person holding a registration permit for intrastate exempt commodity transportation issued prior to January 1, 1995, who did not apply for a motor carrier of property permit pursuant to the Public Service Commission's rules on or before July 15, 1995, shall be deemed to have surrendered all rights to operate as a motor carrier for hire in Georgia and may not operate any motor carrier on or over any public highway of this state without first securing a motor carrier of property permit from the commission, upon application and payment of the required application fee.

Laws 1931, p. 199, § 4; Laws 1996, p. 950, § 3; Laws 2000, p. 951, § 9–4; Laws 2005, Act 68, § 28–2, eff. July 1, 2005.

Formerly Code 1933, § 68–606.

§ 46–7–35. Repealed by Laws 1986, p. 1283, § 7, eff. April 9, 1986

§ 46–7–36. Motor carriers engaged in both intrastate and interstate commerce

In circumstances where a motor common or contract carrier is engaged in both interstate and intrastate commerce, it shall nevertheless be subject to all the provisions of this article so far as it separately relates to commerce carried on exclusively in this state. It is not intended that the commission shall have the power of regulating the interstate commerce of such motor carrier, except to the extent expressly authorized by this article as to such commerce. Code Sections 46–7–14 and 46–7–18 through 46–7–20 and 46–7–23 do not apply to purely interstate commerce nor to carriers exclusively engaged in interstate commerce. When a motor common or contract carrier is engaged in both intrastate and interstate commerce, it shall be subject to all the provisions of this article so far as they separately relate to commerce carried on in this state.

Laws 1931, p. 199, § 30; Laws 1973, p. 643, § 4; Laws 1987, p. 3, § 46; Laws 1996, p. 950, § 3; Laws 2000, p. 951, § 9–4; Laws 2005, Act 68, § 28–2, eff. July 1, 2005.

Formerly Code 1933, § 68–633.

§ 46–7–37. Private carriers

(a) Except as otherwise provided in this Code section, this article shall not apply to private carriers engaged exclusively in the transportation of goods belonging to the individual, firm, partnership, corporation, or association owning, controlling, operating, or managing the motor vehicle in private transportation over any public highway in this state.

(b) Private carriers shall be subject to the requirements of Code Sections 46–7–26 and 46–7–27, as well as the jurisdiction of the commissioner of public safety, pursuant to Article 5 of Chapter 2 of Title 35.

(c) Private carriers are not required to hold certificates or permits issued by the commission.

Laws 1996, p. 950, § 3; Laws 2000, p. 951, § 9–4; Laws 2004, Act 479, § 15, eff. July 1, 2004; Laws 2005, Act 68, § 28–2, eff. July 1, 2005; Laws 2009, Act 114, § 8, eff. May 4, 2009.

§ 46–7–38. Motor carriers prohibited from accepting rebates or drawbacks or from issuing transportation passes

(a) Any officer, agent, or employee of any corporation, and any other person, who knowingly accepts or receives any rebate or drawback from the rates, fares, or charges established or approved by the commission for motor common or contract carriers of passengers or household goods, or who procures, aids, or abets therein, or who uses or accepts from such motor carrier any free pass or free transportation not authorized or permitted by law or by the orders, rules, or regulations of the commission, or who procures, aids, or abets therein, shall be guilty of a misdemeanor.

(b) The possession of goods, wares, or merchandise loaded on a motor vehicle consigned to any person, firm, or corporation, being transported or having been transported over the public highways in this state, without the authority of a permit or certificate for so transporting having been issued by the commission under this article, shall be prima–facie evidence that such transportation of such goods, wares, or merchandise was an intentional violation of the law regulating the transportation of persons and property over the public highways in this state.

(c) Any person claiming the benefit of any exception made in this article shall have the burden of proving that he or she falls within the exception.

Laws 1931, p. 199, § 20; Laws 1996, p. 950, § 3; Laws 2000, p. 951, § 9–4; Laws 2005, Act 68, § 28–2, eff. July 1, 2005.

Formerly Code 1933, § 68–9911.

§ 46–7–39. Violations

(a) Every officer, agent, or employee of any corporation and every person who violates or fails to comply with this chapter relating to the regulation of motor carriers or any order, rule, or regulation of the Public Service Commission, Department of Public Safety, or Department of Revenue, or who procures, aids, or abets therein, shall be guilty of a misdemeanor.

(b) No person shall drive or operate, or cause the operation of, a motor vehicle in violation of an out-of-service order. As used in this subsection, the term "out-of-service order" means a temporary prohibition against operating as a carrier or driving or moving a motor vehicle, freight container or any cargo thereon, or any package containing a hazardous material.

(c) Misdemeanor violations of this chapter may be prosecuted, handled, and disposed of in the manner provided for by Chapter 13 of Title 40.

Laws 1996, p. 950, § 3; Laws 2000, p. 951, § 9–4; Laws 2005, Act 68, § 28–2, eff. July 1, 2005; Laws 2005, Act 68, § 28–5.2, eff. July 1, 2005; Laws 2009, Act 114, § 9, eff. May 4, 2009.

Historical and Statutory Notes

The 2005 amendment by Act 68 substituted "chapter" for "article" following "fails to comply with this" and substituted "Public Service Commission, Department of Public Safety, or Department of Revenue" for "commissioner" following "or regulation of the".

The 2009 amendment by Act 114, designated existing section as subsec. (a), and added subsecs. (b) and (c).

Article 2

Motor Contract Carriers

§§ 46–7–50 to 46–7–79. Repealed by Laws 1996, p. 950, § 4, eff. April 15, 1996

Article 3

Limousine Carriers

§ 46–7–85.1. Definitions

As used in this article, the term:

(1) "Certificate" means a certificate issued by the commission.

(2) "Chauffeur" means any person with a Georgia state driver's license who meets the qualifications as prescribed in Code Section 46–7–85.10 and who is authorized by the commissioner of driver services to drive a limousine under this article.

(3) "Commission" means the Public Service Commission.

(4) "Limousine" means any motor vehicle that meets the manufacturer's specifications for a luxury limousine with a designed seating capacity for no more than ten passengers and with a minimum of five seats located behind the operator of the vehicle, and which does not have a door at the rear of the vehicle designed to allow passenger entry or exit; further, no vehicle shall be permitted to be operated both as a taxicab and a limousine.

(5) "Limousine carrier" means any person operating a prearranged service regularly rendered to the public by furnishing transportation as a motor common carrier for hire, not over fixed routes, by means of one or more unmetered:

(A) Limousines;

(B) Extended limousines;

(C) Sedans;

(D) Extended sedans;

(E) Sport utility vehicles;

(F) Extended sport utility vehicles;

(G) Other vehicles with a capacity for transporting no more than 10 persons for hire; or

(H) Any combination of subparagraphs (A) through (G) of this paragraph on the basis of telephone contract or written contract. A limousine carrier shall not use per capita rates or charges.

(6) "Person" means any individual, firm, partnership, corporation, company, association, or joint–stock association, and includes any trustee, receiver, assignee, or personal representative thereof.

(7) "Public highway" means every public street, road, or highway in this state.

Laws 1994, p. 1238, § 2; Laws 2000, p. 951, § 9–4; Laws 2004, Act 479, § 16, eff. July 1, 2004; Laws 2005, Act 68, § 28–6, eff. July 1, 2005; Laws 2007, Act 357, § 2, eff. July 1, 2007.

§ 46–7–85.2. Operation in accordance with law

No limousine carrier shall operate any limousine for the transportation of passengers for compensation on any public highway in this state except in accordance with the provisions of this article.

Laws 1994, p. 1238, § 2; Laws 2000, p. 951, § 9–4; Laws 2005, Act 68, § 28–6, eff. July 1, 2005.

§ 46–7–85.3. Certificate of public convenience and necessity required

No person may engage in the business of a limousine carrier over any public highway in this state without first having obtained from the commission a certificate to do so.

Laws 1994, p. 1238, § 2; Laws 2000, p. 951, § 9–4; Laws 2004, Act 479, § 17, eff. July 1, 2004; Laws 2005, Act 68, § 28–6, eff. July 1, 2005.

§ 46–7–85.4. Application and requirements for certificate

(a) The commission shall prescribe the form of the application for the certificate and shall prescribe such reasonable requirements as to notice, publication, proof of service, maintenance of adequate liability insurance coverage, and information as may, in its judgment, be necessary and may establish fees as part of such certificate process.

(b) A certificate shall be issued to any qualified applicant, provided that such applicant is a limousine carrier business domiciled in this state, authorizing the operations covered by the application if it is found that the applicant is fit, willing, and able to perform properly the service and conform to the provisions of this article and the rules and regulations of the commission and has not been convicted of any felony as such violation or violations are related to the operation of a motor vehicle.

Laws 1994, p. 1238, § 2; Laws 2000, p. 951, § 9–4; Laws 2005, Act 68, § 28–6, eff. July 1, 2005.

§ 46–7–85.5. Regulation with respect to safety of equipment; inspections

(a) It shall be the duty of the commission to regulate limousine carriers with respect to the safety of equipment.

(b) The commission shall require safety and mechanical inspections at least on an annual basis for each vehicle owned and operated by a limousine carrier. The commission shall provide, by rule or regulation, for the scope of such inspections, the qualifications of persons who may conduct such inspections, and the manner by which the results of such inspections shall be reported to the commission.

Laws 1994, p. 1238, § 2; Laws 2000, p. 951, § 9–4; Laws 2003, Act 180, § 1, eff. Oct. 1, 2003; Laws 2004, Act 564, § 46, eff. May 13, 2004; Laws 2005, Act 68, § 28–6, eff. July 1, 2005.

§ 46–7–85.6. Certificates nontransferrable

No certificate issued under this article may be leased, assigned, or otherwise transferred or encumbered unless authorized by the commission.

Laws 1994, p. 1238, § 2; Laws 2000, p. 951, § 9–4; Laws 2005, Act 68, § 28–6, eff. July 1, 2005.

§ 46–7–85.7. Cancellation, revocation, or suspension of certificate

The commission may cancel, revoke, or suspend any certificate issued under this article on any of the following grounds:

(1) The violation of any of the provisions of this article;

(2) The violation of an order, decision, rule, regulation, or requirement established by the commission pursuant to this article;

(3) Failure of a limousine carrier to pay a fee imposed on the carrier within the time required by law or by the commission;

(4) Failure of a limousine carrier to maintain required insurance in full force and effect; and

(5) Failure of a limousine carrier to operate and perform reasonable services.

Laws 1994, p. 1238, § 2; Laws 2000, p. 951, § 9–4; Laws 2005, Act 68, § 28–6, eff. July 1, 2005.

Historical and Statutory Notes

The 2005 amendment by Act 68 substituted "commission" for "commissioner" throughout the section.

§ 46–7–85.8. Operation after cancellation, revocation, or suspension of permit

After the cancellation or revocation of a certificate or during the period of its suspension, it is unlawful for a limousine carrier to conduct any operations as such a carrier.

Laws 1994, p. 1238, § 2; Laws 2000, p. 951, § 9–4; Laws 2004, Act 479, § 18, eff. July 1, 2004; Laws 2005, Act 68, § 28–6, eff. July 1, 2005.

Historical and Statutory Notes

The 2005 revision of Article 3 by Act 68 amended the section without amendment.

§ 46–7–85.9. Chauffeur's permit required

Pursuant to rules and regulations prescribed by the commissioner of driver services, each chauffeur employed by a limousine carrier shall secure from the Department of Driver Services a permit as a limousine chauffeur. A chauffeur's permit issued under this Code section shall be upon a form prescribed by the commissioner of driver services and shall bear thereon a distinguishing number assigned to the permittee, the full name and a photograph of the permittee, and such other information or identification as is required by the commissioner of driver services. Every chauffeur employed by a limousine carrier shall have his or her chauffeur's permit in his or her immediate possession at all times while operating a limousine. All applications for a chauffeur's permit shall be accompanied by such fee as the commissioner of driver services shall prescribe. The chauffeur's permit shall be valid for four calendar years. The Department of Driver Services may issue a chauffeur's permit by mail.

Laws 1994, p. 1238, § 2; Laws 2000, p. 951, § 9–4; Laws 2004, Act 479, § 19, eff. July 1, 2004; Laws 2005, Act 68, § 28–6, eff. July 1, 2005.

Historical and Statutory Notes

The 2005 amendment rewrote the section which had read:

"Pursuant to rules and regulations prescribed by the commissioner, each chauffeur employed by a limousine carrier shall register with the commissioner and secure a permit as a limousine chauffeur. A chauffeur's permit issued under this subsection shall be upon a form prescribed by the commissioner and shall bear thereon a distinguishing number assigned to the permittee, the full name and a photograph of the permittee, and such other information or identification as is required by the commissioner. Every chauffeur employed by a limousine carrier shall have his or her chauffeur's permit in his or her immediate possession at all times while operating a limousine. All applications for a chauffeur's permit shall be accompanied by such fee as the commissioner shall prescribe. The chauffeur's permit shall be valid for four calendar years. The commissioner may issue a chauffeur's permit by mail."

§ 46–7–85.10. Qualifications of applicants for chauffeur's permit

In order to secure a chauffeur's permit, an applicant must provide the following information on a form provided by the commissioner of driver services. The applicant must:

(1) Be at least 18 years of age;

(2) Possess a valid Georgia driver's license which is not limited as defined in Code Section 40–5–64;

(3) Not have been convicted, been on probation or parole, or served time on a sentence for a period of ten years previous to the date of application for any felony or any other crime of moral turpitude or a pattern of misdemeanors that evidences a disregard for the law unless he or she has received a pardon and can produce evidence of same. For the purposes of this paragraph, a plea of nolo contendere shall be considered to be a conviction, and a conviction for which a person has been free from custody and free from supervision for at least ten years shall not be considered a conviction unless the conviction is for a dangerous sexual offense which is contained in Code Section 42–1–12 or the criminal offense was committed against a victim who was a minor at the time of the offense;

(4) Submit at least one set of classifiable electronically recorded fingerprints to the department in accordance with the fingerprint system of identification established by the director of the Federal Bureau of Investigation. The department shall transmit the fingerprints to the Georgia Crime Information Center, which shall submit the fingerprints to the Federal Bureau of Investigation for a search of bureau records and an appropriate report and promptly conduct a search of state records based upon the fingerprints. After receiving the report from the Georgia Crime Information Center and the Federal Bureau of Investigation, the department shall determine whether the applicant may be certified; and

(5) Be a United States citizen, or if not a citizen, present federal documentation verified by the United States Department of Homeland Security to be valid documentary evidence of lawful presence in the United States under federal immigration law.

Laws 1994, p. 1238, § 2; Laws 2000, p. 951, § 9–4; Laws 2002, p. 1378, § 10; Laws 2005, Act 68, § 28–6, eff. July 1, 2005; Laws 2010, Act 633, § 31, eff. July 1, 2010.

Historical and Statutory Notes

In 2002, the Code Commission, in subdiv. (3)(B) and subdiv. (3)(C), substituted "described" for "prescribed". See § 28–9–5.

The 2005 amendment by Act 68 substituted "commissioner of driver services" for "commissioner" in the first sentence of the introductory paragraph.

§ 46–7–85.11. General law preempts regulation by political subdivisions; exceptions

The State of Georgia fully occupies and preempts the entire field of regulation over limousine carriers as regulated by this article; provided, however, that the governing authority of any county or municipal airport shall be authorized to permit any limousine carrier doing business at any such airport and may establish fees as part of such permitting process; provided, further, that such fees shall not exceed the airport's approximate cost of permitting and regulating limousine carriers; and provided, further, that such governing authorities of such airports shall accept a chauffeur's permit issued by the Department of Driver Services to the driver and evidence of a certificate issued to the limousine carrier by the Public Service Commission as adequate evidence of sufficient criminal background investigations and shall not require any fee for any further criminal background investigation. The list of licensed limousine carriers on the website of the Public Service Commission shall be sufficient evidence that a limousine carrier has a certificate issued by the Public Service Commission.

Laws 1994, p. 1238, § 2; Laws 2000, p. 951, § 9–4; Laws 2005, Act 68, § 28–6, eff. July 1, 2005; Laws 2008, Act 532, § 1, eff. July 1, 2008.

§ 46–7–85.12. Commission's authorization to set or modify rates and charges limited

(a) Notwithstanding the powers granted to the commission regarding tariffs of other common carriers or contract carriers, the commission is not authorized to set, adjust, or change rates or charges for transportation of passengers, property, or passengers and property by a vehicle of a type listed in paragraph (5) of Code Section 46–7–85.1 that is managed, operated, owned, leased, rented, or controlled by a limousine carrier.

(b) Any tariff issued by the commission that exists as of June 30, 2007, that regulates the rates or charges for transportation of passengers, property, or passengers and property by a vehicle of a type listed in paragraph (5) of Code Section 46–7–85.1 that is managed, operated, owned, leased, rented, or controlled by a limousine carrier shall be void.

Laws 1994, p. 1238, § 2; Laws 2000, p. 951, § 9–4; Laws 2005, Act 68, § 28–6, eff. July 1, 2005; Laws 2007, Act 357, § 3, eff. July 1, 2007.

§ 46–7–85.13. Notice to carrier of order, regulation, or requirement to be directed against carrier

Before the commission shall enter any order, regulation, or requirement directed against any limousine carrier, such carrier shall first be given reasonable notice and an opportunity to be heard on the matter.

Laws 1994, p. 1238, § 2; Laws 2000, p. 951, § 9–4; Laws 2005, Act 68, § 28–6, eff. July 1, 2005.

§ 46–7–85.14. Repealed by Laws 2005, Act 68, § 28–6, eff. July 1, 2005

Historical and Statutory Notes

Repealed § 46–7–85.14, relating to temporary permits, was derived from Laws 1994, p. 1238, § 2; Laws 2000, p. 951, § 9-4. The repealing law also reserved the section designation.

§ 46–7–85.15. License plates

Each limousine carrier which registers any vehicle under this article shall, for each such certificated vehicle, affix to the center of the front bumper of each such certificated vehicle a standard size license plate bearing the following information: (1) limousine company name, (2) city and state of principal domicile, (3) company telephone number, and (4) the vehicle classification, IE–1. The cost for such license plate shall be the sole responsibility of the limousine carrier and must be placed on each certificated vehicle prior to said vehicle being placed in service.

Laws 1994, p. 1238, § 2; Laws 2000, p. 951, § 9–4; Laws 2005, Act 68, § 28–6, eff. July 1, 2005.

§ 46–7–85.16. Repealed by Laws 2000, p. 951, § 9–4, eff. July 1, 2001

Historical and Statutory Notes

The section designation was reserved by Laws 2005, Act 68, § 28–6, eff. July 1, 2005

§ 46–7–85.17. Rules and regulations

The commission shall promulgate such rules and regulations as are necessary to effectuate and administer the provisions of this article.

Laws 1994, p. 1238, § 2; Laws 2000, p. 951, § 9–4; Laws 2005, Act 68, § 28–6, eff. July 1, 2005.

§ 46–7–85.18. Motor carrier authorization number required in advertisements

In any advertisement for a limousine carrier, whether by print, radio, television, other broadcast, or electronic media including but not limited to Internet advertising and any listing or sites on the World Wide Web, the limousine carrier shall include the motor carrier authorization number issued to it by the Public Service Commission.

Laws 2007, Act 357, § 4, eff. July 1, 2007.

§ 46–7–85.19. Commercial indemnity and liability insurance required

Each limousine carrier shall obtain and maintain commercial indemnity and liability insurance with an insurance company authorized to do business in this state which policy shall provide for the protection of passengers and property carried and of the public against injury proximately caused by the negligence of the limousine carrier, its servants, and its agents. The commission shall determine and fix the amounts of such insurance and shall prescribe the provisions and limitations of such insurance.

Laws 2007, Act 357, § 4, eff. July 1, 2007.

§ 46–7–85.20. Enforcement by commission; violations

The commission is authorized to enforce Code Sections 46–7–85.18 and 46–7–85.19 in accordance with the provisions of Code Section 46–7–90 and Article 5 of Chapter 2 of this title. Additionally, the commission may hear a petition by a third party asserting that a limousine carrier has violated Code Section 46–17–85.18 or 46–7–85.19 and may impose the penalties and seek the remedies set out in Code Section 46–7–90 and Article 5 of Chapter 2 of this title if the commission finds such a violation.

Laws 2007, Act 357, § 4, eff. July 1, 2007.

§ 46–7–85.21. Application of article

The provisions of this article and the powers granted to the commission by this article to regulate limousines and limousine carriers shall apply to every vehicle of a type listed in paragraph (5) of Code Section 46–7–85.1 that is managed, operated, owned, leased, rented, or controlled by a limousine carrier.

Laws 2007, Act 357, § 4, eff. July 1, 2007.

Article 4

Reciprocal Agreements

§ 46–7–90. Penalties; hearings; judicial review

(a) Any motor or common contract carrier subject to the jurisdiction of the commission, which carrier willfully violates any law administered by the commission or any duly promulgated regulation issued thereunder or which fails, neglects, or refuses to comply with any order after notice thereof, shall be liable to a penalty not to exceed $15,000.00 for such violation and an additional penalty not to exceed $10,000.00 for each day during which such violation continues.

(b)(1) The commission, after a hearing conducted after not less than 30 days' notice, shall determine whether any carrier has willfully violated any law administered by the commission or any duly promulgated regulation issued thereunder, or has failed, neglected, or refused to comply with any order of the commission. Upon an appropriate finding of a violation, the commission may impose by order such civil penalties as are provided by subsection (a) of this Code section or by subsection (a) of Code Section 46–7–91. In each such proceeding, the commission shall maintain a record as provided in paragraph (8) of subsection (a) of Code Section 50–13–13 including all pleadings, a transcript of proceedings, a statement of each matter of which the commission takes official notice, and all staff memoranda or data submitted to the commission in connection with its consideration of the case. All penalties and interest thereon (at the rate of 10 percent per annum) recovered by the commission shall be paid into the general fund of the state treasury.

(2) Any party aggrieved by a decision of the commission may seek judicial review as provided in subsection (c) of this Code section.

(c)(1) Any party who has exhausted all administrative remedies available before the commission and who is aggrieved by a final decision of the commission in a proceeding described in subsection (b) of this Code section may seek judicial review of the final order of the commission in the Superior Court of Fulton County.

(2) Proceedings for review shall be instituted by filing a petition within 30 days after the service of the final decision of the commission or, if a rehearing is requested, within 30 days after the decision thereon. A motion for rehearing or reconsideration after a final decision by the commission shall not be a prerequisite to the filing of a petition for review. Copies of the petition shall be served upon the commission and all parties of record before the commission.

(3) The petition shall state the nature of the petitioner's interest, the facts showing that the petitioner is aggrieved by the decision, and the ground, as specified in paragraph (6) of this subsection, upon which the petitioner contends that the decision should be reversed. The petition may be amended by leave of court.

(4) Within 30 days after service of the petition, or within such further time as is stipulated by the parties or as is allowed by the court, the agency shall transmit to the reviewing court the original or a certified copy of the entire record of the proceedings under review. By stipulation of all parties to the review proceedings, the record may be shortened. A party unreasonably refusing to stipulate that the record be limited may be taxed for the additional costs. The court may require or permit subsequent corrections or additions to the record.

(5) If, before the date set for hearing, application is made to the court for leave to present additional evidence, and it is shown to the satisfaction of the court that the additional evidence is material and there were good reasons for failure to present it in the proceedings before the agency, the court may order that the additional evidence be taken before the commission upon such procedure as is determined by the court. The commission may modify its findings and decision by reason of the additional evidence and shall file that evidence and any modifications, new findings, or decisions with the reviewing court.

(6) The review shall be conducted by the court without a jury and shall be confined to the record. The court shall not substitute its judgment for that of the commission as to the weight of the evidence on questions of fact. The court may affirm the decision of the commission or remand the case for further proceedings. The court may reverse the decision of the commission if substantial rights of the petitioner have been prejudiced because the commission's findings, inferences, conclusions, or decisions are:

(A) In violation of constitutional or statutory provisions;

(B) In excess of the statutory authority of the commission;

(C) Made upon unlawful procedure;

(D) Clearly not supported by any reliable, probative, and substantial evidence on the record as a whole; or

(E) Arbitrary or capricious.

(7) A party aggrieved by an order of the court in a proceeding authorized under subsection (b) of this Code section may appeal to the Supreme Court of Georgia or to the Court of Appeals of Georgia in accordance with Article 2 of Chapter 6 of Title 5, the "Appellate Practice Act."

Laws 2004, Act 479, § 20, eff. July 1, 2004; Laws 2005, Act 68, § 28–2, eff. July 1, 2005.

Historical and Statutory Notes

Former § 46–7–90 was repealed by Laws 2000, p. 951, § 9-4, eff. July 1, 2001

§ 46–7–91. Fines; costs; interest; not bar to criminal prosecution

(a) Whenever the commission, after a hearing conducted in accordance with the provisions of subsection (b) of Code Section 46–7–90, finds that any person, firm, or corporation is operating as a household goods carrier for hire without a valid certificate issued by the commission or is holding itself out as such a carrier without such a certificate in violation of subsection (b) of this Code section, the commission may impose a fine of not more than $5,000.00 for each violation. The commission may assess the person, firm, or corporation an amount sufficient to cover the reasonable expense of investigation incurred by the commission. The commission may also assess interest at the rate specified in paragraph (1) of subsection (b) of Code Section 46–7–90 on any fine or assessment imposed, to commence on the day the fine or assessment becomes delinquent. All fines, assessments, and interest collected by the commission shall be paid into the general fund of the state treasury. Any party aggrieved by a decision of the commission under this subsection may seek judicial review as provided in subsection (c) of Code Section 46–7–90.

(b) Any person, firm, or corporation who knowingly and willfully issues, publishes, or affixes or causes or permits the issuance, publishing, or affixing of any oral or written advertisement, broadcast, or other holding out to the public, or any portion thereof, that the person, firm, or corporation is in operation as a household goods carrier for hire without having a valid certificate issued by the commission is guilty of a misdemeanor. Any fine or assessment imposed by the commission pursuant to the provisions of subsection (a) of this Code section shall not bar criminal prosecution pursuant to the provisions of this subsection.

Laws 2004, Act 479, § 21, eff. July 1, 2004; Laws 2005, Act 68, § 28–2, eff. July 1, 2005.

Historical and Statutory Notes

Former § 46–7–91 was repealed by Laws 2000, p. 951, § 9-4, eff. July 1, 2001

§ 46–7–92. Prohibition on alcohol consumption by persons under the age of 21 while being transported

Any carrier subject to the jurisdiction of the commission that transports passengers shall comply with the provisions of paragraph (1) of subsection (a) of Code Section 3–3–23, concerning consumption of alcoholic beverages by persons under the age of 21. The commission shall provide to all such carriers, at the time of registration or renewal of a certificate, an informational packet emphasizing the prohibition on alcohol consumption by persons under the age of 21 while being transported by the carrier.

Laws 2010, Act 633, § 32, eff. July 1, 2010.

Article 5

Motor Vehicle Safety Inspections

§§ 46–7–100, 46–7–101. Repealed by Laws 2000, p. 951, § 9–4, eff. July 1, 2001

TITLE 48

REVENUE AND TAXATION

CHAPTER 9

MOTOR FUEL AND ROAD TAXES

Article 2

Article 2

Road Tax on Motor Carriers

§ 48–9–30. Definitions

As used in this article, the term:

(1) "Motor carrier" means any person who operates or causes to be operated any motor vehicle, as defined in this Code section, on any highway in this state.

(2) "Motor fuel" means any liquid, regardless of its composition or properties, used to propel a motor vehicle.

(3) "Motor vehicle" means any passenger vehicle that has seats for more than 20 passengers in addition to the driver and any vehicle or combination of vehicles used, designed, or maintained for transportation of property and having two axles and a gross vehicle weight exceeding 26,000 pounds or having three or more axles regardless of weight. The term "motor vehicle" does not mean:

(A) School buses;

(B) Vehicles operated by the state, any political subdivision of the state, or the United States; or

(C) Transit buses operated exclusively within this state.

(4) "Operations" means operation of any motor vehicle, whether loaded or empty, whether or not for compensation, and whether owned by or leased to the motor carrier who operates it or causes it to be operated.

Laws 1968, p. 360, § 1; Laws 1978, p. 309, § 2; Laws 1979, p. 5, § 103; Laws 1981, p. 1857, § 43; Laws 1992, p. 2095, § 2.

Formerly Code 1933, § 91A–5101.

§ 48–9–31. Levy of road tax

A road tax for the privilege of using the streets and highways of this state is imposed upon every motor carrier. The tax shall be equivalent to the taxes imposed by Article 1 of this chapter and shall be calculated on the amount of motor fuel used by the motor carrier in its operations within this state. Except as credit for certain taxes as provided in this article, the tax imposed on motor carriers by this Code section is in addition to taxes imposed on motor carriers by any other law.

Laws 1968, p. 360, § 2; Laws 1978, p. 309, § 2; Laws 1980, p. 10, § 36.

Formerly Code 1933, § 91A–5102.

§ 48–9–32. Payment of road tax and calculation of amount of motor fuel used in State

For the purposes of making payment of taxes and filing reports pursuant to this article, the year is divided into four quarters of three consecutive months each. The first quarter of the year shall consist of the months of January, February, and March. The road tax shall be paid by each motor carrier to the commissioner on or before the last day of the month immediately following the quarter with respect to which tax liability under this article accrues and shall be calculated upon the amount of motor fuel used by the motor carrier in its operations within this state during the quarter ending on the last day of the preceding month. The amount of motor fuel used in the operations of any motor carrier within this state shall be the proportion of the total amount of motor fuel used in its entire operations within and outside this state which the total number of miles traveled within this state bears to the total number of miles traveled within and outside this state.

Laws 1968, p. 360, § 3; Laws 1978, p. 309, § 2.

Formerly Code 1933, § 91A–5103.

§ 48–9–33. Reports of motor carriers

Every motor carrier subject to the road tax imposed by this article shall make to the commissioner on or before the last day of April, July, October, and January such reports of its operations during the quarter of the year ending on the last day of the preceding month as the commissioner requires. The commissioner may by regulation permit motor carriers having an annual road tax not in excess of an amount set by the commissioner to file annual reports. The commissioner by regulation may exempt from the reporting requirements of this Code section motor carriers all of whose operations are within this state.

Laws 1968, p. 360, § 6; Laws 1978, p. 309, § 2; Laws 1990, p. 799, § 6.

Formerly Code 1933, § 91A–5106.

§ 48–9–34. Joint reports by motor carriers

(a) Two or more motor carriers regularly engaged in the transportation of passengers on through buses and on through tickets in pool service, at their option and with the consent of the commissioner, may make joint reports of their entire operations in this state. The road taxes imposed by this article shall be calculated on the basis of the joint reports as though the motor carriers were a single motor carrier. The motor carriers making the reports shall be jointly and severally liable for the taxes.

(b) Joint reports authorized by this Code section shall show the total number of miles traveled in this state and the total number of gallons of motor fuel purchased in this state by the reporting motor carriers. Credits or refunds to which the motor carriers are entitled shall not be allowed as credits or refunds to any other motor carrier. Motor carriers filing joint reports, however, shall permit all motor carriers engaged in this state in pool operations with them to join in filing joint reports.

Laws 1968, p. 360, § 8; Laws 1978, p. 309, § 2.

Formerly Code 1933, § 91A–5108.

§ 48–9–35. Credit for payment of motor fuel tax

Every motor carrier subject to the road tax shall be entitled to a credit on the tax equivalent to the amount of motor fuel tax imposed by Article 1 of this chapter on all motor fuel purchased by the motor carrier during the quarter within this state for use in operations either within or outside this state when the motor fuel tax imposed by this state has been paid by the motor carrier. Evidence of the payments of the motor fuel tax in the form required by the commissioner shall be furnished by each motor carrier claiming the credit allowed. When the amount of the credit to which any motor carrier is entitled for any quarter exceeds the amount of the road tax for which the carrier is liable for same quarter, the excess may be allowed pursuant to regulations promulgated by the commissioner as a credit on the road tax for which the motor carrier would be otherwise liable for the subsequent quarter or quarters. Allowed credits may be carried forward and utilized no later than the succeeding two calendar years.

Laws 1968, p. 360, § 4; Laws 1978, p. 309, § 2.

Formerly Code 1933, § 91A–5104.

§ 48–9–36. Refunds to motor carriers

(a) Any motor carrier which accrues credits in excess of 2,000 gallons in any quarter under Code Section 48–9–35 shall be entitled to a refund of the credits subject to the conditions set forth in this Code section.

(b) All applications for refunds must be filed with the commissioner within 180 days from the end of any quarter in which credits are accumulated. Applications shall be in the form prescribed by the commissioner, shall be sworn to, and shall be supported by evidence satisfactory to the commissioner.

(c) Any motor carrier entitled to a refund may give a bond in an amount of not less than $ 1,000.00 payable to the state and conditioned that the motor carrier will pay all road taxes due and to become due under this article. As long as the bond remains in force, the commissioner may issue refunds to the motor carrier in the amounts appearing to be due on applications without first auditing the records of the motor carrier. The bond shall be in the form and with such surety as required by the commissioner.

(d) The commissioner shall not issue refunds in excess of the amount of the bond or bonds except after audit of the applicant's records. Except as otherwise provided by the commissioner, sufficient records must be produced in this state for audit.

(e) To enable the commissioner to make the refunds authorized by this Code section, the Office of the State Treasurer, under warrants drawn by the Governor, shall remit to the commissioner, from funds appropriated by law for that purpose, an amount equivalent to the refunds. Before the Governor issues a warrant for this purpose, he shall require that the commissioner certify the name of each applicant and the amount to which he is entitled. The refunds provided by this Code section shall be nonassignable.

(f) Refunds claimed and paid pursuant to this Code section shall bear no interest.

Laws 1968, p. 360, § 5; Laws 1971, p. 684, § 1; Laws 1978, p. 309, § 2; Laws 1979, p. 5, § 104; Laws 1982, p. 3, § 48; Laws 1993, p. 1402, § 18; Laws 2010, Act 621, § 2, eff. July 1, 2010.

Formerly Code 1933, § 91A–5105.

§ 48–9–37. Leased motor vehicles

(a) The lessee of a motor vehicle, but not the lessor of a motor vehicle, shall be deemed a motor carrier for the purposes of this article unless otherwise specifically provided in this Code section.

(b) A lessor of motor vehicles may be deemed a motor carrier with respect to motor vehicles leased to others by him and with respect to motor fuel consumed by the motor vehicles when the lessor supplies or pays for the motor fuel consumed by the motor vehicles or makes rental or other charges calculated to include the cost of the motor fuel. The commissioner shall provide by rules and regulations for the presentation to other motor carriers and to the general public of satisfactory evidence and identification of the motor carrier status. Any lessee motor carrier may exclude from his reports pursuant to this article motor vehicles of which he is the lessee when the motor vehicles have been leased from a lessor who is a motor carrier pursuant to this Code section.

(c) Subsections (a) and (b) of this Code section shall govern primary liability of lessors and lessees of motor vehicles pursuant to this article. If a lessor or lessee who is primarily liable fails in whole or in part to discharge this liability, the failing party or other lessor or lessee party to the transaction shall be jointly and severally responsible and liable for compliance with this article and for the payment of any tax due pursuant to this article. The aggregate amount of any taxes collected by the state pursuant to this article, however, shall not exceed the total amount of tax due on the account of the transaction in question together with any costs and penalties imposed.

Laws 1968, p. 360, § 7; Laws 1978, p. 309, § 2.

Formerly Code 1933, § 91A–5107.

§ 48–9–38. Registration card, vehicle identification marker, fees, temporary permits and temporary authorizations

(a) Unless otherwise excluded from the scope of this article, no motor carrier shall operate or cause to be operated in this state any motor vehicle unless and until he has:

(1) Registered with the commissioner and secured a motor carrier registration card. A duplicate of the registration card shall be carried in each motor vehicle at all times in this state; and

(2) Secured from the commissioner an identification marker for each motor vehicle. The identification marker shall be attached or affixed to the motor vehicle in the place and manner prescribed by the commissioner so that the marker is clearly displayed at all times.

(b) Registration cards and identification markers shall be issued on an annual basis as of January 1 of each year and shall be valid until the next succeeding December 31. The commissioner, in his discretion, may authorize renewal of registration cards and identification markers without the necessity of issuing new cards and markers. All registration cards and identification markers issued by the commissioner shall remain the property of the state and may be recalled for any violation of this article or of the regulations promulgated under this article. The commissioner shall not issue a registration card or an identification marker to any motor carrier who has outstanding motor carrier, motor fuel, sales, or income tax liabilities or other penalties or fees owed to the Department of Transportation of this state unless the liabilities are being appealed as provided by law.

(c) Prior to the issuance of each identification marker, a fee of $ 3.00 shall be paid to the commissioner. Upon application for identification markers by a motor carrier, the applicant shall declare the type of fuel used in vehicles for which identification markers are to be issued and any other information that the commissioner may require for the effective administration of this article.

(d) The commissioner may authorize a motor vehicle to be operated in an emergency without a registration card and identification marker for a period not in excess of 30 days. The authorization shall be granted by letter or facsimile message.

(e) A motor carrier may obtain a temporary permit which shall be good for one motor vehicle for a period of ten consecutive days beginning and ending on the dates specified on the face of the permit. Temporary permits are to be obtained by motor carriers having only infrequent trips into and through this state. The fee for the permit shall be $ 16.00 and no reports shall be required from such motor carriers. Temporary permits shall be issued in lieu of annual registration required under this article. A temporary permit shall be carried in the vehicle for which it was issued at all times when the vehicle is in this state. The commissioner may issue a temporary permit by facsimile message or letter.

Laws 1968, p. 360, § 9; Laws 1978, p. 309, § 2; Laws 1978, p. 1609, § 1; Laws 1979, p. 5, § 105; Laws 1981, p. 1857, § 44; Laws 1992, p. 2095, § 3.

Formerly Code 1933, § 91A–5109.

§ 48–9–39. Failure to carry identification card or display identification marker

(a) It shall be unlawful for any person to operate or cause to be operated on any highway in this state any motor vehicle that does not carry the registration card required by Code Section 48–9–38 or any motor vehicle that does not display in the manner prescribed by the commissioner the identification marker that Code Section 48–9–38 requires to be displayed.

(b) Any person who violates subsection (a) of this Code section shall be guilty of a misdemeanor and, upon conviction thereof, shall be punished by a fine of not less than $ 50.00 nor more than $ 200.00. Each day's operation in violation of this Code section shall constitute a separate offense.

Laws 1968, p. 360, § 18; Laws 1978, p. 309, § 2.

Formerly Code 1933, § 91A–9920.

§ 48–9–40. Keeping and preservation of records; estimate of amount of road tax due

(a) Every motor carrier shall keep such records as may be necessary for the effective administration of this article and for the reporting and justification of the amount of tax liability pursuant to this article. All such records shall be kept in the form required by the commissioner and shall be safely preserved for a period of three years in such a manner as to ensure their security and availability for inspection by the commissioner or his authorized agents. Upon application in writing after an audit of the motor carrier's records has been made, the commissioner may consent to the destruction of the records within the three-year period.

(b) The commissioner and his authorized agents and representatives may inspect during regular business hours the books and records of any motor carrier subject to the road tax imposed by this article.

(c) Whenever any motor carrier neglects or refuses to file any report or neglects or refuses to keep records as prescribed by this article, the commissioner, using the best information available, shall estimate, determine, and fix the amount of taxes and penalties payable by the motor carrier under this article. In any action or proceeding under this Code section, any assessment by the commissioner shall constitute prima-facie evidence of the claim of the state. The burden of proof shall be upon the motor carrier to show that the assessment was incorrect or contrary to law.

(d) The commissioner may enter into agreements with the appropriate authorities of other jurisdictions having statutes similar to this article for the cooperative audit of motor carriers' reports and returns. In performing any such audit or part of an audit, the officers and employees of the other jurisdiction or jurisdictions shall be deemed authorized agents of this state for such purpose.

Laws 1968, p. 360, § 10; Laws 1978, p. 309, § 2.

Formerly Code 1933, § 91A–5110.

§ 48–9–41. Assessment and collection of deficiencies

(a)(1) When any motor carrier is in default in the payment of any road taxes due under this article, the commissioner shall assess the road taxes due in the manner provided by law. Except as otherwise provided in paragraph (2) of this subsection, any assessment for road taxes due under this article shall be made within the time limits specified in Code Section 48–2–49.

(2) When the motor carrier has filed a report under this article which contains fraudulent statements or omissions of material facts, the effect of which is to make the taxpayer's report a fraudulent representation, the commissioner may reopen the tax period and make any additional assessment of taxes due at any time within seven years from the last date on which the report could have been timely filed by the taxpayer.

(b) The commissioner shall collect any deficiencies and road taxes due under this article by levy, garnishment, attachment, or action or by any other provision of law for collection of delinquent state taxes.

Laws 1968, p. 360, § 11; Laws 1972, p. 834, § 1; Laws 1978, p. 309, § 2; Laws 1985, p. 1350, § 5.

Formerly Code 1933, § 91A–5111.

§ 48–9–42. Secretary of State as process agent of nonresident motor carriers

The acceptance by a nonresident motor carrier of the rights and privileges conferred by law permitting the operation of motor vehicles on the public highways of this state, as evidenced by the operation of a motor vehicle by the nonresident either personally or through an agent or employee on the public highways of this state, or by the operation by the nonresident either personally or through an agent or employee of a motor vehicle on the public highways of this state other than as so permitted or regulated, shall be deemed equivalent to the appointment by the nonresident motor carrier of the Secretary of State or his successor in office as his agent for service of process or notice in any action, assessment proceedings, or other proceeding against him or his personal representative arising out of or by reason of any provision of this article relating to the motor vehicle or relating to the liability for road tax with respect to operation of the motor vehicle on the highways of this state. The acceptance or operation shall be an acknowledgment by the nonresident motor carrier of his agreement that any such process against or notice to him or his personal representative shall be of the same legal force and validity as if the process or notice were served on him personally or on his personal representative.

Laws 1968, p. 360, § 13; Laws 1978, p. 309, § 2; Laws 1982, p. 3, § 48.

Formerly Code 1933, § 91A–5113.

§ 48–9–43. Department of Public Safety to aid in enforcement

The commissioner of public safety shall utilize the personnel of the Department of Public Safety as necessary to assist in enforcing this article. The officers of the Department of Public Safety shall have the powers of peace officers including, but not limited to, the powers of making arrests, serving process, and appearing in court in all matters relating to the administration and enforcement of this article.

Laws 1968, p. 360, § 14; Laws 1978, p. 309, § 2.

Formerly Code 1933, § 91A–5114.

§ 48–9–44. Enforcement powers of revenue agents

Each person appointed by the commissioner as a special agent or enforcement officer of the department shall have all the powers of a police officer of this state when engaged in the enforcement of this article.

Laws 1972, p. 381, § 1; Laws 1978, p. 309, § 2.

Formerly Code 1933, § 91A–5115.

§ 48–9–45. Penalties

(a) Whenever any motor carrier operates a motor vehicle in violation of the registration provisions of this article, the motor carrier shall be subject to a penalty of $ 25.00 for each motor vehicle in violation.

(b) Whenever any motor carrier required to file a report as provided by this article fails to file the report within the time prescribed, he shall be subject to a penalty of $ 25.00 for each failure to file.

(c) Whenever any motor carrier fails to pay the road taxes or any part of the road taxes due pursuant to this article, the motor carrier shall be subject to a penalty of $ 10.00 or 10 percent of the amount of the unpaid tax due, whichever is greater, and to interest on the unpaid tax at the rate specified in Code Section 48–2–40 from the time the road tax became due until the tax is paid.

(d) Any penalties and interest imposed by this Code section shall be assessed and collected by the commissioner in the manner provided by law. In addition to imposing penalties and interest, the commissioner may suspend or revoke any certificate, permit, or other evidence of right issued by the commissioner and held by the motor carrier found to be in default.

Laws 1968, p. 360, § 12; Laws 1978, p. 309, § 2; Laws 1980, p. 1759, § 3.

Formerly Code 1933, § 91A–5112.

§ 48–9–46. Road tax on motor carriers; penalty for false statements

(a) It shall be unlawful for any person willfully and knowingly to make a false statement orally or in writing or in the form of a receipt for the sale of motor fuel for the purpose of obtaining or attempting to obtain or assisting any other person to obtain or attempt to obtain a credit, refund, or reduction of liability for taxes under this article.

(b) It shall be unlawful for any person required by this article to make a report willfully to fail to make such report at the time required by law.

(c) Any person who violates subsection (a) or subsection (b) of this Code section shall be guilty of a misdemeanor.

Laws 1968, p. 360, § 17; Laws 1978, p. 309, § 2; Laws 1983, p. 1834, § 12.

Formerly Code 1933, § 91A–9919.

TITLE 49

SOCIAL SERVICES

CHAPTER 4

PUBLIC ASSISTANCE

Article 1

General Provisions

§ 49–4–15. Fraud in obtaining public assistance; repayment

(a) Any person who by means of a false statement, failure to disclose information, or impersonation, or by other fraudulent device, obtains or attempts to obtain, or any person who knowingly or intentionally aids or abets such person in the obtaining or attempting to obtain:

(1) Any grant or payment of public assistance, food stamps, or medical assistance (Medicaid) to which he is not entitled;

(2) A larger amount of public assistance, food stamp allotment, or medical assistance (Medicaid) than that to which he is entitled; or

(3) Payment of any forfeited grant of public assistance;

or any person who, with intent to defraud the department, aids or abets in the buying or in any way disposing of the real property of a recipient of public assistance shall be guilty of a misdemeanor unless the total amount of the value of public assistance, food stamps, and medical assistance (Medicaid) so obtained exceeds $ 500.00, in which event such person shall be guilty of a felony and, upon conviction thereof, shall be punished by imprisonment for not less than one nor more than five years. In determining the amount of value of public assistance, food stamps, and medical assistance obtained by false statement, failure to disclose information, or impersonation, or other fraudulent device, the total amount obtained during any uninterrupted period of time shall be treated as one continuing offense.

(b) It shall be a fraudulent device within the meaning of subsection (a) of this Code section, and punishable as therein provided, for any person:

(1) Knowingly to use, alter, or transfer food stamp coupons or authorizations to purchase food stamp coupons in any manner not authorized by law;

(2) Knowingly to possess food stamp coupons or authorizations to purchase food stamp coupons when he or she is not authorized by law to possess them;

(3) Knowingly to possess or redeem food stamp coupons or benefits when he or she is not authorized by law to possess or redeem them; or

(4) Knowingly to use or redeem food stamp coupons or benefits in any manner or for purposes not authorized by law.

(c) (1) Any person who obtains any payment of public assistance to which he is not entitled or in excess of that to which he is entitled shall be liable to the state for the amount of such overpayment.

(2) Any person who intentionally, with knowledge of the fraud, aids or abets any recipient of public assistance in obtaining or attempting to obtain any payment of public assistance to which the recipient is not entitled or a payment in excess of that to which he is entitled shall also be liable to the state for the amount of such payment.

(3) Any person who receives any payment of public assistance to which he is not entitled or in excess of that to which he is entitled shall be liable to the state for the amount of such overpayment.

(4) Subject to the limitations provided in this paragraph, the amount of such overpayment may be recovered by civil action and, if the person receiving such overpayment continues on assistance, by proportionate reduction of future public assistance grants, in accordance with regulations of the board which shall conform to the federal Social Security Act [1] and federal regulations promulgated pursuant thereto, until the excess amount has been paid. In any case in which, under this subsection, a person is liable to repay any sum, such sum may be collected without interest by civil action brought in the name of the department. Any repayment required by this subsection may be waived by the department, and the method of repayment, if any, including recoupments from current assistance grants, shall be determined by the department. Recoupment may be initiated without regard to whether the department has obtained a judgment in a civil action but shall not be initiated prior to notice and an opportunity for a hearing in accordance with this article. The department shall make such waivers and determinations of repayment and the manner of repayment in accordance with regulations of the board which shall conform to the federal Social Security Act and the federal regulations promulgated pursuant thereto.

(d) Any felony offense under this Code section may be prosecuted by accusation as provided in Code Section 17–7–70.1.

(e) (1) Prior to the filing of an accusation or the return of an indictment, a prosecuting attorney may defer further prosecution of such accusation or indictment and shall have the authority to enter into a consent agreement with the individual in which such individual admits to any overpayment, consents to disqualification for such period of time as is or may hereafter be provided by law, and agrees to repay, as restitution, such overpayment. Such agreement may provide for a lump sum repayment, installment payments, formula reduction of benefits, or any combination thereof. Such agreement shall toll the running of the statute of limitations for such offense for the period of the agreement. A consent agreement entered into in accordance with this subsection shall not constitute a criminal charge.

(2) Any such agreement shall be filed in the criminal docket of the court having jurisdiction over the violation of this Code section without the necessity of the state filing an accusation or an indictment being returned by a grand jury. The clerk shall enter upon the docket "CONSENT AGREEMENT NOT A CRIMINAL CHARGE."

(3) Upon successful completion of the terms and conditions of the consent agreement, criminal prosecution of the individual for such offense shall be barred; provided, however, that nothing in this paragraph shall prohibit the state from introducing evidence of such offense as a similar transaction in any

subsequent prosecution or for the purpose of impeachment. The successful completion of the terms and conditions of the agreement shall not be considered a criminal conviction.

(4) If the individual fails to comply with the terms of such consent agreement, the state may proceed with a criminal prosecution.

(f) Any person convicted of an offense stated in this Code section shall, upon the first such conviction, be ineligible to receive any form of public assistance or food stamps for a period of one year. For a second such conviction, such person shall be barred from receiving any form of public assistance or food stamps in this state for life; provided, however, that nothing in this subsection shall be construed so as to preempt any other law or regulation which would require an earlier denial of such benefits.

Laws 1965, p. 385, § 13; Laws 1973, p. 183, § 1; Laws 1975, p. 477, § 1; Laws 1976, p. 1490, § 1; Laws 1978, p. 994, § 1; Laws 1978, p. 1964, § 1; Laws 1989, p. 466, § 1; Laws 1996, p. 1517, §§ 1, 1.2; Laws 1997, p. 1021, § 3.

1 42 U.S.C.A. § 301 et seq.

Historical and Statutory Notes

Laws 1996, p. 1517, § 3, provides:

"No later than July 1, 1996, the Department of Human Resources shall request from the appropriate federal agencies any waivers necessary to implement any part of this Act. Each portion of this Act for which such waiver is required shall become effective only if the waiver is obtained, and in that event shall become effective upon the ninetieth day following the receipt of such waiver. The remainder of this Act shall become effective July 1, 1996."

The waivers referred to in Laws 1996, p. 1517, § 3, were applied for with regard to the public assistance provisions of subsec. (f) of this section. Subsequently, passage of the federal "Personal Responsibility and Work Opportunity Reconciliation Act of 1996" eliminated the need for the waivers, and the public assistance provisions of subsec. (f) therefore did not take effect.

Article 7

Medical Assistance Generally

§ 49–4–146.1. Unlawful to obtain benefits and payments under certain circumstances; penalties; procedures

(a) As used in this Code section, the term:

(1) "Agent" means any person who has been delegated the authority to obligate or act on behalf of a provider.

(2) "Convicted" means that a judgment of conviction has been entered by any federal, state, or other court, regardless of whether an appeal from that judgment is pending.

(3) "Indirect ownership interest" means any ownership interest in an entity that has an ownership interest in the provider entity. The term includes an ownership interest in any entity that has an indirect ownership interest in the provider entity.

(4) "Managing employee" means a general manager, business manager, administrator, director, or other individual who exercises operational or managerial control over, or who directly or indirectly conducts, the day-to-day operation of the institution, organization, or agency.

(5) "Payment" includes a payment or approval for payment, any portion of which is paid by the Georgia Medicaid program, or by a contractor, subcontractor, or agent for the Georgia Medicaid program pursuant to a managed care program operated, funded, or reimbursed by the Georgia Medicaid program.

(6) "Person" means any person, firm, corporation, partnership, or other entity.

(7) "Person with an ownership or control interest" means a person who:

(A) Has ownership interest totaling 5 percent or more in a provider;

(B) Has an indirect ownership interest equal to 5 percent or more in a provider;

(C) Has a combination of direct and indirect ownership interests equal to 5 percent or more in a provider;

(D) Owns an interest of 5 percent or more in any mortgage, deed of trust, note, or other obligation secured by the provider entity if that interest equals at least 5 percent of the value of the property or assets of the provider;

(E) Is an officer or director of a provider that is organized as a corporation; or

(F) Is a partner in a provider entity that is organized as a partnership.

(8) "Provider" means an actual or prospective provider of medical assistance under this chapter. The term "provider" shall also include any managed care organization providing services pursuant to a managed care program operated, funded, or reimbursed by the Georgia Medicaid program.

(b) It shall be unlawful:

(1) For any person or provider to obtain, attempt to obtain, or retain for himself, herself, or any other person any medical assistance or other benefits or payments under this article, or under a managed care program operated, funded, or reimbursed by the Georgia Medicaid program, to which the person or provider is not entitled, or in an amount greater than that to which the person or provider is entitled, when the assistance, benefit, or payment is obtained, attempted to be obtained, or retained, by:

(A) Knowingly and willfully making a false statement or false representation;

(B) Deliberate concealment of any material fact; or

(C) Any fraudulent scheme or device; or

(2) For any person or provider knowingly and willfully to accept medical assistance payments to which he or she is not entitled or in an amount greater than that to which he or she is entitled or knowingly and willfully to falsify any report or document required under this article.

(c) Any person violating paragraph (1) or (2) of subsection (b) of this Code section shall be guilty of a felony and, upon conviction thereof, shall be punished for each offense by a fine of not more than $ 10,000.00, or by imprisonment for not less than one year nor more than ten years, or by both such fine and imprisonment. In any prosecution under this Code section, the state has the burden of proving beyond a reasonable doubt that the defendant intentionally committed the acts for which he or she is charged.

(c.1)(1) Any person committing abuse shall be liable for a civil monetary penalty equal to two times the amount of any excess benefit or payment. This penalty shall be collected on the same terms as a penalty imposed pursuant to subsection (d) of this Code section, except as to the amount specified in items (1) and (2) of that subsection, but shall not be imposed cumulatively with a penalty under such subsection.

(2) Abuse is defined as a provider knowingly obtaining or attempting to obtain medical assistance or other benefits or payments under this article to which the provider knows he or she is not entitled when the assistance, benefits, or payments are greater than an amount which would be paid in accordance with those provisions of the department's policies and procedures manual which are adopted pursuant to public notice, and the assistance, benefits, or payments directly or indirectly result in unnecessary costs to the medical assistance program. Isolated instances of unintentional errors in billing, coding, and costs reports shall not constitute abuse. Miscoding shall not constitute abuse if there is a good faith basis that the codes used were appropriate under the department's policies and proce-

dures manual and there was no deceptive intent on the part of the provider.

(d) In addition to any other penalties provided by law, each person violating subsection (b) of this Code section shall be liable to a civil penalty equal to the greater of (1) three times the amount of any such excess benefit or payment or (2) $ 1,000.00 for each excessive claim for assistance, benefit, or payment. Additionally, interest on the penalty shall be paid at the rate of 12 percent per annum from the date of payment of any such excessive amount, or from the date of receipt of any claim for an excessive amount when no payment has been made, until the date of payment of such penalty to the department.

(e)(1) Whenever the commissioner proposes to recover an amount provided for in subsection (d) of this Code section, he shall give 30 days' written notice of his intended actions. The notice shall inform the person in violation of subsection (b) of this Code section of his right to a hearing, the method by which he may obtain a hearing, and that he may be represented by an authorized representative, such as legal counsel, relative, friend, or other spokesman, or that he may represent himself.

(2) All hearings held by virtue of this subsection shall be conducted in the same manner as any other contested case within the department and shall be subject to the rules and regulations regarding hearings within the department. As in all contested cases within the department, the person against whom the commissioner is proceeding under this subsection shall have the right to appeal any adverse administrative decision to the superior court of the county of his residence or to the Superior Court of Fulton County once he exhausts all administrative remedies within the department.

(3) If the person against whom the commissioner is proceeding under this subsection fails to request a hearing or fails to exhaust all administrative remedies within the department, then his case shall be treated as an unappealed administrative decision. In any unappealed administrative decision where the aggrieved party fails to request a hearing or fails to exhaust all administrative remedies, the commissioner shall issue an order to the person against whom the commissioner is proceeding, directing payment of any amount found to be due pursuant to subsection (d) of this Code section within ten days after service of the order. Upon failure to comply with the commissioner's order, the commissioner may issue a certificate to the clerk of the superior court of the county of residence of the person who is the subject of the order. A copy of such certificate shall be served upon the person against whom the order was entered. Thereupon, the clerk shall immediately enter upon his record of docketed judgments the name of the person so indebted, that the debt is owed to the state, a designation of the statute under which such amount is found to be due, the amount due, and the date of the certification. Such entry shall have the same force and effect as the entry of a docketed judgment in the superior court. Such entry on the docket by the commissioner shall be without prejudice to the right of the aggrieved party to contest such entry by affidavit of illegality or as otherwise provided by law.

(f) The department may refuse to accept a statement of participation, deny a request for reinstatement, refuse to exercise its option to renew a statement of participation, suspend or withhold those payments arising from fraud or willful misrepresentation under the Medicaid program, or terminate the participation of any provider other than a natural person if that provider or any person with an ownership or control interest or any agent or managing employee of such provider has been:

(1) Convicted of violating paragraph (1) or (2) of subsection (b) of this Code section;

(2) Convicted of committing any other criminal offense related to any program administered under Title XVIII, XIX, or XX of the Social Security Act of 1935,[1] as amended; or

(3) Excluded or suspended from participation in the medicare program for fraud or abuse.

In making a decision pursuant to this subsection, the department shall consider the facts and circumstances of the specific case, including but not limited to the nature and severity of the crime or violation and the extent to which it adversely affected medical assistance recipients and the program.

(g) The department shall refuse to accept a statement of participation, deny a request for reinstatement, refuse to exercise its option to renew a statement of participation, or terminate the participation of any provider who is a natural person if that provider or any agent or managing employee of such provider has been convicted of:

(1) Violating subsection (b) of this Code section; or

(2) Committing any other criminal offense related to any program administered under Title XVIII, XIX, or XX of the Social Security Act of 1935, as amended.

(h) The department shall reinstate a provider whose participation in the medical assistance program was terminated pursuant to subsection (f) or (g) of this Code section if the conviction upon which the termination was based is reversed or vacated or if the decision of the administrative law judge is reversed in accordance with the department's rules and regulations.

(i) It shall be the duty of the department to identify and investigate violations of this article and to turn over to the prosecuting attorney, for prosecution, any information concerning any recipient of medical assistance who violates this article.

Subsec. (j) effective January 1, 2010.

(j) As necessary to enforce the provisions of this article, the department or its duly authorized agents may submit to the state revenue commissioner the names of applicants for medical assistance or other benefits or payments provided under this article, as well as the relevant income threshold specified therein. If the department elects to contract with the state revenue commissioner for such purposes, the state revenue commissioner and his or her agents or employees shall notify the department whether or not each submitted applicant's income exceeds the relevant income threshold provided. The department shall pay the state revenue commissioner for all costs incurred by the Department of Revenue pursuant to this subsection. No information shall be provided by the Department of Revenue to the department without an executed cooperative agreement between the two departments. Any tax information secured from the federal government by the Department of Revenue pursuant to express provisions of Section 6103 of the Internal Revenue Code may not be disclosed by the Department of Revenue pursuant to this subsection. Any person receiving any tax information under the authority of this subsection is subject to the provisions of Code Section 48–7–60 and to all penalties provided under Code Section 48–7–61 for unlawful divulging of confidential tax information.

Laws 1981, p. 962, § 1; Laws 1985, p. 1395, §§ 1, 2; Laws 1994, p. 97, § 49; Laws 1997, p. 679, § 1; Laws 1997, p. 1596, § 1; Laws 1998, p. 128, § 49; Laws 1998, p. 664, § 1; Laws 2006, Act 760, § 2, eff. May 3, 2006; Laws 2007, Act 18, § 49, eff. May 11, 2007; Laws 2009, Act 20, § 1, eff. Jan. 1, 2010.

[1] 42 U.S.C.A. § 1395 et seq., § 1396 et seq., or § 1397 et seq.

Historical and Statutory Notes

The 2007 amendment by Act 18 was a provision contained in a correction bill.

CHAPTER 4A

DEPARTMENT OF JUVENILE JUSTICE

§ 49–4A–9. Children who have previously been adjudged to have committed act which is a felony

(a) Any child who has previously been adjudged to have committed an act which is a felony if tried in a superior court and who, on a second or subsequent occasion, is convicted of a felony in a superior court may, in the discretion of the court, be sentenced into the custody of the department as otherwise provided by law or be committed as a youthful offender as authorized in Chapter 7 of Title 42; provided, further, that any child convicted of a felony punishable by death or by confinement for life shall only be sentenced into the custody of the Department of Corrections.

(b) Any final order of judgment by the court in the case of any such child shall be subject to such modification from time to time as the court may consider to be for the welfare of such child. No commitment of any child to any institution or other custodial agency shall deprive the court of jurisdiction to change the form of the commitment or transfer the custody of the child to some other institution or agency on such conditions as the court may see fit to impose, the duty being constant upon the court to give to all children subject to its jurisdiction such oversight and control in the premises as will be conducive to the welfare of the child and the best interests of the state; provided, however, that the release or parole of any child committed to the department for detention in any of its institutions under the terms of this chapter during the period of one year from the date of commitment shall be had only with the concurrence and recommendation of the commissioner or the commissioner's designated representative; provided, further, that upon releasing or paroling any child adjudicated delinquent for the commission of a designated felony act as defined in Code Section 15–11–63 and committed to the department for detention in any of its institutions under the terms of this chapter, the department shall provide notice to any person who was the victim of the child's delinquent acts that the child is being released or paroled. As long as a good faith attempt to comply with the notice requirement of this subsection has been made, the department and employees of the department shall not be liable for damages incurred by reason of the department's failure to provide the notice required by this subsection.

(c) After the expiration of one year from the date of commitment, the committing court shall review the case and make such order with respect to the continued confinement or release of the child back to the committing court for further disposition as the court deems proper.

(d) In the event adequate facilities are not available, the department shall have the right to transfer youths committed to the department under this Code section to the Department of Corrections for incarceration in an appropriate facility designated by the Department of Corrections.

(e) Any child under 17 years of age who is sentenced in the superior court and committed to the department may be eligible to participate in all youth development center programs and services including community work programs, sheltered workshops, special state sponsored programs for evaluation and services under the Division of Rehabilitation Services of the Department of Labor and the Department of Behavioral Health and Developmental Disabilities, and under the general supervision of youth development center staff at special planned activities outside of the youth development center. When such a child sentenced in the superior court is approaching his or her seventeenth birthday, the department shall notify the court that a further disposition of the child is necessary. The department shall provide the court with information concerning the participation and progress of the child in programs described in this subsection. The court shall review the case and determine if the child, upon becoming 17 years of age, should be placed on probation, have his or her sentence reduced, be transferred to the Department of Corrections for the remainder of the original sentence, or be subject to any other determination authorized by law.

Laws 1992, p. 1983, § 24; Laws 1995, p. 619, § 9; Laws 2000, p. 20, § 27; Laws 2000, p. 1137, § 2; Laws 2002, p. 1324, § 1–22; Laws 2009, Act 102, § 3–4, eff. July 1, 2009.

Part IV

GLOSSARY

The definitions of the words appearing in this Glossary are taken from ***Black's Law Dictionary****, Eighth Edition, 2004, by Bryan A. Garner, Editor in Chief, published by West, a Thomson business. In some instances the definitions included are not the total definitions as they appear in* ***Black's Law Dictionary*** *but rather are a selection of the portion of the definition deemed pertinent to the subject matter of this manual. The object of this Glossary is to supply the "plain language" definitions to assist peace officers in the performance of their duties. Therefore, in some instances, it has been necessary to paraphrase the definition as it appears in* ***Black's*** *to simplify language.*

The Westlaw database ***BLACKS*** *contains the entire contents of the* ***Black's Law Dictionary*** *(8th Edition, 2004), the classic legal resource published by West, a Thomson business revised and edited by Bryan A. Garner, Editor in Chief.*

Parenthetical references refer to page numbers of ***Black's Law Dictionary, Eighth Edition.***

Abandonment Giving up property or rights with no intention to reclaim and no person designated to claim; includes both intention and act of abandonment. (p. 2)

Abatable Nuisance "A nuisance so easily removable that the aggrieved party may lawfully cure the problem without notice to the liable party, such as overhanging tree branches." (see p. 1097 of Nuisance)

Ability Capacity to perform an act. (p. 4)

Abjudicate [From the Latin "abjudicatio"] To deny or take away right by an adverse decision of the court. (p. 5)

Accusation "A formal charge of criminal wrongdoing .. usually presented to a court or magistrate having jurisdiction to inquire into the alleged crime.; An informal statement that a person has engaged in an illegal or immoral act." (p. 23)

Acquit "To clear (a person) of a criminal charge; To pay or discharge (a debt or claim)." (p. 25)

Adult One who has reached legal age, generally 18 years; typically 17 years in criminal cases. (p. 56)

Affiant A person who makes an affidavit. (p. 62)

Affidavit A written or printed statement of facts, made voluntarily, and (confirmed by oath or affirmation), taken before a person with authority to administer such oath or affirmation (like a notary public). (p. 62)

Affirm To confirm or ratify, as when a court affirms a lower court ruling; opposite of reverse. (p. 64)

Affray "Fighting, by mutual consent, of two or more persons in some public place, to the terror of onlookers, . . . if one person unlawfully attacks another who resorts to self-defense, the first is guilty of assault and battery, but there is no affray." (p. 65)

Appellate Court A court with authority (jurisdiction) to review the decision of a lower court. (see p. 378 of Court)

Arraignment "The initial step in a criminal prosecution whereby the defendant is brought before the court to hear the charges and to enter a plea." (p. 116)

Bench Warrant A warrant issued by the court either in case of contempt or indictment, or for a witness who does not appear when subpoenaed. (p. 164)

Bound "A limitation or restriction on action . . . constrained by a contractual or other obligation." (p. 198)

Brief A written statement prepared by an attorney summarizing the facts of a case, pertinent laws, and how these laws are applied to the facts in support of the attorney's case. (p. 204)

Burden of Proof The necessity of proving a fact or facts disputed in a lawsuit. In a criminal case, burden of proof "beyond a reasonable doubt" lies with prosecutor. (p. 209)

Carnal Knowledge "Sexual intercourse, especially with an underage female." (p. 226)

Case Law The law of a particular subject based on previous cases on that subject, as opposed to based on statutes. (p. 229)

Citation A writ issued by a court commanding the person named to appear on a certain day and do a certain thing or show reasons why he should not; also, an order issued by police to appear before a court at a later date. (p. 260)

Commitment The act of directing that a person be taken to a jail or mental health facility; also, the proceedings directing confinement for treatment of a mentally ill or incompetent person. (p. 288)

Common Law "The body of law derived from judicial decisions, rather than from statutes or constitutions." (p. 293)

Competency (to stand trial) "Mental ability to understand problems and make decisions. A criminal defendant's ability to stand trial, measured by the capacity to understand the proceedings, to consult meaningfully with counsel, and to assist in the defense." (p. 302)

Concurrent Sentences Two or more jail sentences, all or part of which are served at the same time. (see p. 1393 of Sentence)

Consecutive Sentences One jail sentence is served immediately after another. (see p. 1393 of Sentence)

Consent "Agreement, approval, or permission as to some act or purpose, especially given voluntarily by a competent person." (p. 323)

Corpus Delicti "The material substance on which a crime has been committed; the physical evidence of a crime, such as the corpse of a murdered person." (p. 369)

Criminal Intent "An intent to commit an actus reus without any justification, excuse, or other defense." (p. 402)

Decree "A judicial decision in a court of equity, admiralty, divorce, or probate—similar to a judgment of a court of law." (p. 440)

Default Judgment A judgment awarded to a plaintiff because the defendant failed to plead or offer a defense. (p. 449)

Demeanor "Outward appearance or behavior, such as facial expressions, tone of voice, gestures, and the hesitation or readiness to answer questions. In evaluating a witness's credibility, the jury may consider the witness's demeanor." (p. 463)

Deponent One who testifies under oath; one who gives or swears to a written testimony. (p. 471)

Deposition The written responses of a witness to a series of questions posed outside of court (usually in a lawyer's office), sworn to for use in a trial. (p. 472)

Disavow "To disown; to disclaim knowledge of; to repudiate" (p. 495)

Ex Facto [Latin "from a fact"] "From or in consequence of a fact or action" (p. 613)

Ex Parte [Latin "from the part"] "On or from one party only, usually without notice to or argument from the adverse party . . . done or made at the instance and for the benefit of one party only, and without notice to, or argument by, any person adversely interested." (p. 616)

Ex Post Facto [Latin "from a thing done afterward"] "After the fact; retroactivity." (p. 620)

Exclusionary Rule A rule which prohibits evidence obtained in violation of the U. S. Constitution from being used as evidence in court. (p. 606)

Expunge "To erase or destroy." (p. 621)

Expungement of Record "The removal of a conviction (especially for a first offense) from a person's criminal record." (p. 621)

Fruits of Crime "The proceeds acquired through criminal acts." (p. 694)

Grand Jury A group of citizens sworn and instructed by the court to hear and collect information concerning criminal accusations in their area and return indictments, if they are satisfied that enough evidence exists to warrant a trial; grand juries are composed of not less than six and not more than twenty-three persons. (p. 719)

Gross Negligence Intentional failure to perform duty in "reckless disregard of a legal duty and of the consequences to another party, who may typically recover exemplary damages." (p. 1062 of Negligence)

Impediment "A hindrance or obstruction." (p. 768)

Incompetent "(Of a witness) unqualified to testify; (Of evidence) inadmissible." (p. 780)

Indictment An accusation in writing, brought by a grand jury, charging the person named with a crime which must be proved at trial. (p. 788)

Indigent One who lacks sufficient means to support himself; poor or needy. (p. 788)

Inquest An investigation by coroner or medial examiner, sometimes with aid of jury, into the circumstances of a sudden, violent or suspicious death; a judicial inquiry. (p. 808)

Intent "The state of mind accompanying an act; Intent is the mental resolution or determination to do it." (p. 825)

Intrinsic Value "The inherent value of a thing, without any special features that might alter its market value." (see p. 1587 of Value)

Jurisdiction The authority by which courts and judicial officers exercise their duty; also, the geographic area and/or type of case over which a court has authority. (p. 867)

Just Cause A cause based on legal and reasonable grounds. "Often the burden placed on a litigant (usually by court rule or order) to show why a request should be granted or an action excused." (see Good Cause on p. 235 of Cause)

Lien A charge of claim against another's property. (p. 941)

Litigation A lawsuit, including all proceedings. (p. 952)

Magistrate "A judicial officer with strictly limited jurisdiction and authority, often on the local level and often restricted to criminal cases." For example, a justice of the peace. (p. 970)

Malfeasance "A wrongful or unlawful act; especially wrongdoing or misconduct by a public official." (p. 976)

Malice The intentional doing of a wrongful act without just cause with the intent to inflict injuriy or break the law. (see p. 943 of Lien)

Mechanics' Lien A claim against a structure or the land it is built on which secures priority of payment for work performed and materials used in the construction or repair of the structure. (p. 1002)

Misdemeanor A lesser offense than a felony, usually punishable by fine or imprisonment other than in the penitentiary. (p. 1020)

Modus Operandi [From the Latin "a manner of operating"] "A method of operating or a manner of procedure; especially a pattern of criminal behavior so distinctive that investigators attribute it to the work of the same person." (M. O.) (p. 1026)

Motion An application made to a court or a judge for a ruling or order in favor of the applicant. (p. 1036)

Nisi [From the Latin, meaning "unless" (E Meaning such is the case unless the defendant can show cause against it. (p. 1072)

No Bill In the opinion of the grand jury, not enough evidence exists to warrant a charge. (p. 1073)

"Nol Pros" [From the Latin nolle prosequi (E To abandon; meaning the prosecuting attorney will not further prosecute the case. (p. 1074)

Nolo Contendere [Latin "I do not wish to contend"] "NO CONTEST; A criminal defendant's plea that, while not admitting guilt, the defendant will not dispute the charge; often preferable to a guilty plea, which can be used against the defendant in a later civil lawsuit." (p. 1074)

Notice to Produce A document directing a party to produce certain materials in court. (see p. 1331 of Request for Production)

Order Nisi A conditional order allowing a specific amount of time to complete a required act, failure of which makes the order absolute. (see Decree Nisi on p. 441 of Decree)

Perjury Wilful false testimony under oath during a judicial proceeding. (p. 1175)

Petit Jury "A jury (usually consisting of 12 persons) summoned and empaneled in the trial of a specific case." (see p. 874 of Jury)

Post Facto "After the fact." (p. 1205) See **Ex Post Facto.** (p. 620)

Presentment A written accusation of a crime made by the grand jury based on their own initiation. (p. 1222)

Punitive Damages "Damages awarded in addition to actual damages when the defendant acted with recklessness, malice, or decit." (see p. 418 of Damages)

Quash To annul or make void; for example, a court may quash an indictment. (p. 1278)

Quasi [From the Latin, "as if" (E; indicates a certain resemblance may exist between two subjects which are essentially or materially different. (p. 1278)

Reasonable Doubt "Beyond a reasonable doubt" is the standard used by a jury to determine whether a criminal defendant is guilty. In deciding whether guilt has been proved beyond a reasonable doubt, the jury must begin with the presumption that the defendant is innocent. (p. 1293)

Rigor Mortis A temporary stiffening of the muscles and joints of the body after death. (p. 1352)

Search Warrant "A judge's written order authorizing the law-enforcement officer to conduct a search of a specified place and to seize evidence." (p. 1379)

Statutory Law created by an enactment of the legislature; relating to or existing as a result of such a law. (p. 1451)

Subpoena "A writ commanding a person to appear before a court or other tribunal, subject to a penalty for failing to comply." (p. 1467)

Subpoena Duces Tecum "A subpoena ordering the witness to appear and to bring specified documents or records." (p. 1467)

Suppress To stop something that exists or to prevent something from occurring. (p. 1481)

Venue The geographical location in which a case may be tried. (p. 1591)

Verdict "A jury's finding or decision on the factual issues of a case. In a nonjury trial, a judge's resolution of the issues of a case." (p. 1592)

Warrant "A writ directing or authorizing someone to do an act, especially one directing a law enforcer to make an arrest, a search, or a seizure." (p. 1616)

Writ "A court's written order, in the name of a state or other competent legal authority, commanding the addressee to do or refrain from doing some specified act." (p. 1640)

Writ of Habeas Corpus "A writ employed to bring a person before a court, most frequently to ensure that the party's imprisonment or detention is not illegal." (see p. 728 of Habeas Corpus)

Index to Part I

Index to Part III

CHILDREN AND MINORS—Cont'd

WORDS AND PHRASES—Cont'd

WORDS AND PHRASES—Cont'd

WORDS AND PHRASES—Cont'd

WORDS AND PHRASES—Cont'd